C000177951

NORTH
LINCOLNSHIRE
COUNCIL

NORTH LINCOLNSHIRE
LIBRARIES
SCUNTHORPE
REFERENCE LIBRARY

International WHO'S WHO of Authors AND Writers

2005

International WHO'S WHO of Authors AND Writers 2005

20th Edition

Europa Publications
Taylor & Francis Group
LONDON AND NEW YORK

First published 1934

Haines House, 21 John Street, London, WC1N 2BP, United Kingdom
(A member of the Taylor & Francis Group)

ISBN: 1 85743 264 9
ISSN: 1740-018X

Typeset and printed by Unwin Brothers Limited,
The Gresham Press, Old Woking, Surrey

FOREWORD

The 20th Edition of the INTERNATIONAL WHO'S WHO OF AUTHORS AND WRITERS provides biographical information on writers, novelists, journalists, essayists, dramatists, poets and editors. The biographies include, where available, personal and contact details, information on career and honours, as well as publications and contributions to books and periodicals.

For each edition existing entrants are given the opportunity to make necessary amendments and additions to their biographies. Supplementary research is done by the Europa Publications editorial department in order to ensure that the book is as up to date as possible on publication.

In addition to the biographical information, the directory section provides details of literary awards and prizes, organizations and literary agents. The introduction contains a list of abbreviations and international telephone codes. The names of entrants whose death has been reported over the past year are included in the obituary.

Readers are referred to the book's companion title, the INTERNATIONAL WHO'S WHO IN POETRY 2005, for a comprehensive collection of information on the most prominent international poets.

The assistance of the individuals and organizations included in this publication in providing up-to-date material is invaluable, and the editors would like to take this opportunity to express their appreciation.

September 2004

ALPHABETIZATION KEY

The list of names is alphabetical, with the entrants listed under surnames. If part of an entrant's name is in parentheses, indicating that this name is not usually used, this will be ignored for the purposes of the alphabetical listing.

All names beginning Mc or Mac are treated as Mac, e.g. McDevitt before MacDonald.

Names with Arabic prefixes are normally listed after the prefix, except when requested otherwise by the entrant.

In the case of surnames beginning with De, Des, Du, van or von the entries are normally found under the prefix.

Names beginning St are listed as if they began Saint, e.g. St Germain before Salamun.

In the case of an entrant whose name is spelt in a variety of ways, a cross reference is provided. An entrant who is known by a pseudonym or best known by another name, is usually listed under this name, or a cross reference is provided.

CONTENTS

ABBREVIATIONS

AA Associate in Arts
AB Alberta; Bachelor of Arts
ABC Australian Broadcasting Corporation; Australian Broadcasting Commission
AC Companion of the Order of Australia
ACA American Composers' Alliance
Acad. Academy
ACLS American Council of Learned Societies
ACT Australian Capital Territory
Admin. Administrator, Administrative
AFofM American Federation of Musicians
AFTRA American Federation of Television and Radio Artists
AG Aktiengesellschaft (Joint Stock Company)
AGMA American Guild of Musical Artists
AIDS acquired immunodeficiency syndrome
AK Alaska
aka also known as
AL Alabama
ALCS Authors' Lending and Copyright Society
AM Member of the Order of Australia; Master of Arts; amplitude modulation
AO Officer of the Order of Australia
Apdo Apartado (Post Box)
approx. approximately
APRA Australian Performing Rights Society
Apt Apartment
apto apartamento
A & R Artists and Repertoire
AR Arkansas
ARCA Associate of the Royal College of Art
ARCM Associate of the Royal College of Music
ARCO Associate of the Royal College of Organists
ARCS Associate of the Royal College of Science
ASCAP American Society of Composers, Authors and Publishers
Asscn Association
Assoc. Associate
Asst Assistant
ATD Art Teacher's Diploma
Aug. August
autobiog. autobiography
Avda Avenida (Avenue)
AZ Arizona

b. born
BA Bachelor of Arts
BAC&S British Academy of Composers and Songwriters
BAFTA British Academy of Film and Television Arts
BArch Bachelor of Architecture
BASCA British Association of Songwriters, Composers and Authors (now BAC&S)
BBC British Broadcasting Corporation
BC British Columbia
BCL Bachelor of Civil Law
BD Bachelor of Divinity
Bd Board
Bdwy Broadway
BE Bachelor of Engineering; Bachelor of Education
BEd Bachelor of Education
BEng Bachelor of Engineering
BFA Bachelor in Fine Arts
BFI British Film Institute
biog. biography
BJ Bachelor of Journalism
Bldg Building
BLitt Bachelor of Letters
BLS Bachelor in Library Science
Blvd Boulevard
BM Bachelor of Music; Bachelor of Medicine
BME Bachelor of Music Education
BMEd Bachelor of Music Education
BMI Broadcast Music Inc
BMus Bachelor of Music
BP Boîte postale (Post Box)
BPhil Bachelor of Philosophy
bros brothers
BS Bachelor of Science; Bachelor of Surgery
BSc Bachelor of Science
BSE Bachelor of Science in Engineering (USA)
BSFA British Science Fiction Association
BTh Bachelor of Theology
BTI British Theatre Institute

c. circa; child, children
CA California
CAMI Columbia Artists Management International
CBC Canadian Broadcasting Corporation
CBE Commander of (the Order of) the British Empire
CBS Columbia Broadcasting System
CBSO City of Birmingham Symphony Orchestra
CCMA Canadian Country Music Association
CD compact disc
CD-ROM compact disc read-only memory
CEO Chief Executive Officer
Chair. Chairman, Chairwoman, Chairperson
Cia Companhia
Cía Compañía
Cie Compagnie
circ. circulation
CMA Country Music Association
CMG Companion of (the Order of) St Michael and St George
CNRS Centre National de la Recherche Scientifique
c/o care of
Co. Company; County
CO Colorado; Chamber Orchestra
Col. Colonia, Colima (hill)
Coll. College
Comm. Commission
Commdr Commandeur
COO Chief Operating Officer
Corpn Corporation
CP Case Postale; Caixa Postal; Casella Postale (Post Box)
Cres. Crescent
Ct Court
CT Connecticut
Cttee Committee
CUNY City University of New York
CVO Commander of the Royal Victorian Order
CWA (British) Crime Writers' Association

d. daughter(s)
DBE Dame Commander of (the Order of) the British Empire
DC District of Columbia; Distrito Central
DD Doctor of Divinity
Dd'ES Diplôme d'études supérieures
DE Delaware
Dec. December
DEd Doctor of Education
Dept Department
D. ès L. Docteur ès Lettres
D. ès Sc. Docteur ès Sciences
devt development
DF Distrito Federal
DFA Doctor of Fine Arts; Diploma of Fine Arts
DHL Doctor of Hebrew Literature
DipEd Diploma in Education

ABBREVIATIONS

DipTh	Diploma in Theology
Dir	Director
DJ	disc jockey
DJur	Doctor of Law
DLitt	Doctor of Letters
DM	Doctor of Music
DMA	Doctor of Musical Arts
DME	Doctor of Musical Education
DMEd	Doctor of Musical Education
DMus	Doctor of Music
DMusEd	Doctor of Music Education
DN	Distrito Nacional
DPhil	Doctor of Philosophy
dpto	departamento
Dr(a)	Doctor(a)
DSc	Doctor of Science
DSocSci	Doctor of Social Science
DTh	Doctor of Theology
DVD	digital versatile disc
E	East(ern)
EC	European Community
Ed.	Editor
Edif.	Edificio (Building)
edn	edition
e.g.	exempli gratia (for example)
EMI	Electrical and Musical Industries
ENO	English National Opera
EP	extended-play (record)
esq.	esquina (corner)
etc.	et cetera
EU	European Union
eV	eingetragener Verein
Exec.	Executive
f.	founded
Feb.	February
FL	Florida
FLS	Fellow of the Linnaean Society
FM	frequency modulation
FMA	Florida Music Association
fmr(ly)	former(ly)
FRAM	Fellow of the Royal Academy of Music
FRCM	Fellow of the Royal College of Music
FRCO	Fellow of the Royal College of Organists
FRGS	Fellow of the Royal Geographical Society
FRHistS	Fellow of the Royal Historical Society
FRS	Fellow of the Royal Society
FRSA	Fellow of the Royal Society of Arts
FRSL	Fellow of the Royal Society of Literature
GA	Georgia
Gen.	General
GmbH	Gesellschaft mit beschränkter Haftung (Limited Liability Company)
GMT	Greenwich Mean Time
Gov.	Governor
GP	General Practitioner
GPO	General Post Office
GRSM	Graduate of the Royal School of Music
GSMD	Guildhall School of Music and Drama, London (formerly GSM)
hc	honoris causa
HHD	Doctor of Humanities
HI	Hawaii
HIV	human immunodeficiency virus
HM	His (or Her) Majesty
HMV	His Master's Voice
Hon.	Honorary; Honourable
Hons	Honours
HRH	His (or Her) Royal Highness
HS	Heraldry Society
IA	Iowa
IBA	Independent Broadcasting Authority
ID	Idaho
i.e.	id est (that is to say)
IL	Illinois
IMC	International Music Council
IN	Indiana
Inc.	Incorporated
incl.	including
Inst.	Institute
int.	international
IPC	Institute of Professional Critics
ISM	Incorporated Society of Musicians
IRCAM	Institut de Recherche et Coordination Acoustique/Musique
ISCM	International Society for Contemporary Music
ISM	Incorporated Society of Musicians
ITA	Independent Television Authority
ITN	Independent Television News
ITV	Independent Television
Jan.	January
JD	Doctor of Jurisprudence
JP	Justice of the Peace
Jr	Junior
jt	joint
KBE	Knight Commander, Order of the British Empire
KCVO	Knight Commander of the Royal Victorian Order
km	kilometre(s)
KS	Kansas
KY	Kentucky
LA	Louisiana
LAMDA	London Academy of Music and Dramatic Art
LEA	Local Education Authority
L. ès L.	Licencié ès Lettres
L. ès Sc.	Licencié ès Sciences
LHD	Doctor of Humane Letters
Lic. en Let.	Licenciado en Letras
LLB	Bachelor of Laws
LLD	Doctor of Laws
LL.L	Licentiate of Laws
LLM	Master of Laws
LP	long-playing (record)
LPO	London Philharmonic Orchestra
LRCP	Licenciate, Royal College of Physicians, London
LRSM	Licenciate, Royal Schools of Music
LSE	London School of Economics and Political Science
LSO	London Symphony Orchestra
Lt	Lieutenant
LTCL	Licenciate of Trinity College of Music, London
Ltd	Limited
LW	long wave
LWT	London Weekend Television
m.	married
MA	Massachusetts; Master of Arts
Man.	Manager; Managing
MAT	Master of Arts and Teaching
MB	Manitoba
MBA	Master of Business Administration
MBE	Member of (the Order of) the British Empire
MC	master of ceremonies
MD	Maryland; Music Director
MDiv	Master in Divinity
ME	Maine
MEd	Master in Education
mem.	member
MEngSc	Master of Engineering
Met	Metropolitan Opera House, New York
MFA	Master of Fine Arts
MHRA	Modern Humanities Research Association
MHz	megahertz (megacycles)
MI	Michigan
MIDI	Musical Instrument Digital Interface
mil.	military
MIT	Massachusetts Institute of Technology
MLA	Modern Language Association

MLitt	Master of Letters; Master of Literature
MLS	Master in Library Science
MM	Master of Music
MME	Master of Music Education
MMEd	Master of Music Education
MMus	Master of Music
MN	Minnesota
MO	Missouri
MOBO	Music of Black Origin
MP	Member of Parliament
MPh	Master of Philosophy (USA)
MPhil	Master of Philosophy
MRCS	Member, Royal College of Surgeons of England
MS	Mississippi; Master of Science; manuscript
MSA	Memphis Songwriters' Association
MSc	Master of Science
MSO	Melbourne Symphony Orchestra
MT	Montana
Mt	Mount
MTh	Master of Theology
MTV	Music Television
MusB	Bachelor of Music
MusD	Doctor of Music
MusDoc	Doctor of Music
MusM	Master of Music
MVO	Member of the Royal Victorian Order
MW	medium wave
MWA	Mystery Writers of America
N	North(ern)
NABOB	National Association of Black Owned Broadcasters
NARAS	National Academy of Recording Arts & Sciences
NAS	National Academy of Songwriters
nat.	national
NB	New Brunswick
NBC	National Broadcasting Company
NC	North Carolina
ND	North Dakota
NDD	National Diploma in Design
NE	Nebraska; North-east(ern)
NEA	National Endowment for the Arts
NEH	National Endowment for the Humanities
NF	Newfoundland
NFSPS	National Federation of State Poetry Societies
NH	New Hampshire
NHK	Nippon Hôsô Kyôkai (Japanese broadcasting system)
NJ	New Jersey
NM	New Mexico
NME	New Musical Express
no.	number
Nov.	November
nr	near
NRK	Norsk Rikskringkasting (Norwegian broadcasting system)
NS	Nova Scotia
NSAI	Nashville Songwriters' Association International
NSW	New South Wales
NT	Northwest Territories; Northern Territory
NU	Nunavut Territory
NUJ	National Union of Journalists
NV	Nevada
NW	North-west(ern)
NY	New York (State)
NYPO	New York Philharmonic Orchestra
NYSO	New York Symphony Orchestra
NZSA	New Zealand Society of Authors
OBE	Officer of (the Order of) the British Empire
Oct.	October
Of.	Oficina (Office)
OH	Ohio
OK	Oklahoma
ON	Ontario
ONZ	Order of New Zealand
ONZM	Officer, New Zealand Order of Merit
OR	Oregon
org.	organization
ORTF	Office de Radiodiffusion-Télévision Française
OST	original soundtrack
OUP	Oxford University Press
p.	page
PA	Pennsylvania
PBS	Public Broadcasting Service
PE	Prince Edward Island
PEN	Poets, Playwrights, Essayists, Editors and Novelists (Club)
PETA	People for the Ethical Treatment of Animals
PF	Postfach (Post Box)
PGCE	Post Graduate Certificate of Education
PhB	Bachelor of Philosophy
PhD	Doctor of Philosophy
PhL	Licenciate of Philosophy
Pl.	Place
PLC	Public Limited Company
PMB	Private Mail Bag
pnr	partner
PO	Philharmonic Orchestra
PO Box	Post Office Box
Pres.	President
PR(O)	Public Relations (Officer)
Prod.	Producer
Prof.	Professor
promo	promotional
PRS	Performing Right Society
pt.	part
Pty	Proprietary
Publ.(s)	Publication(s)
QC	Québec
QEH	Queen Elizabeth Hall, London
Qld	Queensland
QSO	Queen's Service Order; Queensland Symphony Orchestra
q.v.	quod vide (to which refer)
RADA	Royal Academy of Dramatic Art
RAH	Royal Albert Hall, London
RAI	Radio Audizioni Italiane
RAM	Royal Academy of Music
R&B	Rhythm and Blues
RCM	Royal College of Music
RCO	Royal College of Organists
Rep.	Republic
retd	retired
rev. edn	revised edition
RFH	Royal Festival Hall, London
RGS	Royal Geographical Society
RI	Rhode Island
RIAS	Radio im Amerikanischen Sektor
RLPO	Royal Liverpool Philharmonic Orchestra
RMA	Royal Musical Association
RMCM	Royal Manchester College of Music
RNCM	Royal Northern College of Music, Manchester
RNLI	Royal National Life-boat Institution
RO	Radio Orchestra
ROC	Rock Out Censorship
ROH	Royal Opera House, Covent Garden
rpm	revolutions per minute
RPO	Royal Philharmonic Orchestra
RSA	Royal Society of Arts
RSAMD	Royal Scottish Academy of Music and Drama
RSC	Royal Shakespeare Company
RSL	Royal Society of Literature
RSNO	Royal Scottish National Orchestra (formerly SNO)
RSO	Radio Symphony Orchestra
RSPB	Royal Society for Protection of Birds
RTÉ	Radio Telefís Éireann
RTF	Radiodiffusion-Télévision Française
RTS	Royal Television Society

S	South(ern); San
s.	son(s)
SA	Société Anonyme, Sociedad Anónima (Limited Company); South Australia
SACEM	Société d'Auteurs, Compositeurs et Editeurs de Musique
SAG	Screen Actors' Guild
SC	South Carolina
SD	South Dakota
SE	South-east(ern)
Sec.	Secretary
Sept.	September
SFWA	Science Fiction and Fantasy Writers of America
SGA	Songwriters' Guild of America
SK	Saskatchewan
SL	Sociedad Limitada
SO	Symphony Orchestra
SOAS	School of Oriental and African Studies
SOCAN	Society of Composers, Authors and Music Publishers of Canada
SOSA	State Opera of South Australia
SPNM	Society for the Promotion of New Music
Sr	Senior
St	Saint
Sta	Santa
STB	Bachelor of Sacred Theology
STD	Doctor of Sacred Theology
Ste	Sainte
STL	Reader or Professor of Sacred Theology
STM	Master of Sacred Theology
str	strasse
SUNY	State University of New York
SVSA	South West Virginia Songwriters' Association
SW	South-west(ern); short wave
TCL	Trinity College of Music, London
TLS	Times Literary Supplement
TN	Tennessee
trans.	translated; translation; translator
Treas.	Treasurer
TV	television
TX	Texas
u.	utca (street)
UCLA	University of California at Los Angeles
UHF	ultra-high frequency
UK	United Kingdom (of Great Britain and Northern Ireland)
ul.	ulitsa (street)
UN	United Nations
UNESCO	United Nations Educational, Scientific and Cultural Organization
UNICEF	United Nations Children's Fund
Univ.	University
Urb.	Urbanización (urban district)
US(A)	United States (of America)
USSR	Union of Soviet Socialist Republics
UT	Utah
VA	Virginia
VC	Victoria Cross
VHF	very high frequency
VI	(US) Virgin Islands
Vic.	Victoria
Vol.(s)	Volume(s)
VSO	Victoria State Opera
VT	Vermont
W	West(ern)
WA	Western Australia; Washington (State)
WI	Wisconsin
WNO	Welsh National Opera
WV	West Virginia
WY	Wyoming
YT	Yukon Territory

INTERNATIONAL TELEPHONE CODES

To make international calls to telephone and fax numbers listed in the book, dial the international code of the country from which you are calling, followed by the appropriate code for the country you wish to call (listed below), followed by the area code (if applicable) and telephone or fax number listed in the entry.

	Country code	+or −GMT*
Afghanistan	93	+4½
Albania	355	+1
Algeria	213	+1
Andorra	376	+1
Angola	244	+1
Antigua and Barbuda	1 268	−4
Argentina	54	−3
Armenia	374	+4
Australia	61	+8 to +10
Australian External Territories:		
Australian Antarctic Territory	672	+3 to +10
Christmas Island	61	+7
Cocos (Keeling) Islands	61	+6½
Norfolk Island	672	+11½
Austria	43	+1
Azerbaijan	994	+5
The Bahamas	1 242	−5
Bahrain	973	+3
Bangladesh	880	+6
Barbados	1 246	−4
Belarus	375	+2
Belgium	32	+1
Belize	501	−6
Benin	229	+1
Bhutan	975	+6
Bolivia	591	−4
Bosnia and Herzegovina	387	+1
Botswana	267	+2
Brazil	55	−3 to −4
Brunei	673	+8
Bulgaria	359	+2
Burkina Faso	226	0
Burundi	257	+2
Cambodia	855	+7
Cameroon	237	+1
Canada	1	−3 to −8
Cape Verde	238	−1
The Central African Republic	236	+1
Chad	235	+1
Chile	56	−4
China, People's Republic	86	+8
Special Administrative Regions:		
Hong Kong	852	+8
Macao	853	+8
China (Taiwan)	886	+8
Colombia	57	−5
The Comoros	269	+3
Congo, Democratic Republic	243	+1
Congo, Republic	242	+1
Costa Rica	506	−6
Côte d'Ivoire	225	0
Croatia	385	+1
Cuba	53	−5
Cyprus	357	+2
'Turkish Republic of Northern Cyprus'	90 392	+2
Czech Republic	420	+1
Denmark	45	+1
Danish External Territories:		
Faroe Islands	298	0
Greenland	299	−1 to −4
Djibouti	253	+3
Dominica	1 767	−4
Dominican Republic	1 809	−4
Ecuador	593	−5
Egypt	20	+2
El Salvador	503	−6
Equatorial Guinea	240	+1
Eritrea	291	+3
Estonia	372	+2
Ethiopia	251	+3
Fiji	679	+12
Finland	358	+2
Finnish External Territory:		
Åland Islands	358	+2
France	33	+1
French Overseas Departments:		
French Guiana	594	−3
Guadeloupe	590	−4
Martinique	596	−4
Réunion	262	+4
French Overseas Collectivité Départementale:		
Mayotte	269	+3
Overseas Collectivité Territoriale:		
Saint Pierre and Miquelon	508	−3
French Overseas Territories:		
French Polynesia	689	−9 to −10
Wallis and Futuna Islands	681	+12
French Overseas Country:		
New Caledonia	687	+11
Gabon	241	+1
Gambia	220	0
Georgia	995	+4
Germany	49	+1
Ghana	233	0
Greece	30	+2
Grenada	1 473	−4
Guatemala	502	−6
Guinea	224	0
Guinea-Bissau	245	0
Guyana	592	−4
Haiti	509	−5
Honduras	504	−6
Hungary	36	+1
Iceland	354	0
India	91	+5½
Indonesia	62	+7 to +9
Iran	98	+3½
Iraq	964	+3
Ireland	353	0
Israel	972	+2
Italy	39	+1
Jamaica	1 876	−5
Japan	81	+9
Jordan	962	+2
Kazakhstan	7	+6
Kenya	254	+3
Kiribati	686	+12 to +13
Korea, Democratic People's Republic (North Korea)	850	+9

	Country code	+or –GMT*
Korea, Republic (South Korea)	82	+9
Kuwait	965	+3
Kyrgyzstan	996	+5
Laos	856	+7
Latvia	371	+2
Lebanon	961	+2
Lesotho	266	+2
Liberia	231	0
Libya	218	+1
Liechtenstein	423	+1
Lithuania	370	+2
Luxembourg	352	+1
Macedonia, former Yugoslav republic	389	+1
Madagascar	261	+3
Malawi	265	+2
Malaysia	60	+8
Maldives	960	+5
Mali	223	0
Malta	356	+1
Marshall Islands	692	+12
Mauritania	222	0
Mauritius	230	+4
Mexico	52	–6 to –7
Micronesia, Federated States	691	+10 to +11
Moldova	373	+2
Monaco	377	+1
Mongolia	976	+7 to +9
Morocco	212	0
Mozambique	258	+2
Myanmar	95	+6½
Namibia	264	+2
Nauru	674	+12
Nepal	977	+5¾
Netherlands	31	+1
Netherlands Dependencies:		
Aruba	297	–4
Netherlands Antilles	599	–4
New Zealand	64	+12
New Zealand's Dependent and Associated Territories:		
Tokelau	690	–10
Cook Islands	682	–10
Niue	683	–11
Nicaragua	505	–6
Niger	227	+1
Nigeria	234	+1
Norway	47	+1
Norwegian External Territory:		
Svalbard	47	+1
Oman	968	+4
Pakistan	92	+5
Palau	680	+9
Palestinian Autonomous Areas	970	+2
Panama	507	–5
Papua New Guinea	675	+10
Paraguay	595	–4
Peru	51	–5
The Philippines	63	+8
Poland	48	+1
Portugal	351	0
Qatar	974	+3
Romania	40	+2
Russian Federation	7	+2 to +12
Rwanda	250	+2
Saint Christopher and Nevis	1 869	–4
Saint Lucia	1 758	–4
Saint Vincent and the Grenadines	1 784	–4
Samoa	685	–11
San Marino	378	+1
São Tomé and Príncipe	239	0
Saudi Arabia	966	+3

	Country code	+or –GMT*
Senegal	221	0
Serbia and Montenegro	381	+1
Seychelles	248	+4
Sierra Leone	232	0
Singapore	65	+8
Slovakia	421	+1
Slovenia	386	+1
Solomon Islands	677	+11
Somalia	252	+3
South Africa	27	+2
Spain	34	+1
Sri Lanka	94	+6
Sudan	249	+2
Suriname	597	–3
Swaziland	268	+2
Sweden	46	+1
Switzerland	41	+1
Syria	963	+2
Tajikistan	992	+5
Tanzania	255	+3
Thailand	66	+7
Timor-Leste	670	+9
Togo	228	0
Tonga	676	+13
Trinidad and Tobago	1 868	–4
Tunisia	216	+1
Turkey	90	+2
Turkmenistan	993	+5
Tuvalu	688	+12
Uganda	256	+3
Ukraine	380	+2
United Arab Emirates	971	+4
United Kingdom	44	0
United Kingdom Crown Dependencies	44	0
United Kingdom Overseas Territories:		
Anguilla	1 264	–4
Ascension Island	247	0
Bermuda	1 441	–4
British Virgin Islands	1 284	–4
Cayman Islands	1 345	–5
Diego Garcia (British Indian Ocean Territory)	246	+5
Falkland Islands	500	–4
Gibraltar	350	+1
Montserrat	1 664	–4
Pitcairn Islands	872	–8
Saint Helena	290	0
Tristan da Cunha	2 897	0
Turks and Caicos Islands	1 649	–5
United States of America	1	–5 to –10
United States Commonwealth Territories:		
Northern Mariana Islands	1 670	+10
Puerto Rico	1 787	–4
United States External Territories:		
American Samoa	1 684	–11
Guam	1 671	+10
United States Virgin Islands	1 340	–4
Uruguay	598	–3
Uzbekistan	998	+5
Vanuatu	678	+11
Vatican City	39	+1
Venezuela	58	–4
Viet Nam	84	+7
Yemen	967	+3
Zambia	260	+2
Zimbabwe	263	+2

* The times listed compare the standard (winter) times in the various countries. Some countries adopt Summer (Daylight Saving) Time—i.e. +1 hour—for part of the year.

OBITUARY

AIKEN, Joan	4 January 2004
ALCOCK, Vivien	11 October 2004
ARDLEY, Neil Richard	23 February 2004
BABINGTON, Anthony Patrick	10 May 2004
BARNES, Peter	1 July 2004
BARTLEY, Robert LeRoy	10 December 2004
BENSON, Mary	20 June 2000
BOORSTIN, Daniel Joseph	28 February 2004
BOOTH, Martin	12 February 2004
BULLOCK, Alan Louis Charles (Lord Bullock of Leafield)	2 February 2004
CADY, Jack Andrew	14 January 2004
CAGE, Hugh Barnett	27 June 2004
CARLING, Finn	12 March 2004
CAUSLEY, Charles Stanley	4 November 2003
COOKE, Alfred Alistair	30 March 2004
CORMAN, Cid	12 March 2004
DRUCKER, Henry Matthew	30 October 2002
DYMOKE, Juliet	–
EWBANK, Inga-Stina	7 June 2004
EZEKIEL, Nissim	9 January 2004
FEINBERG, Joel	29 March 2004
FOOT, Paul	18 July 2004
FRAME, Janet Paterson	29 January 2004
GORDON, Giles	14 November 2003
GUNN, Thomson (Thom) William	25 April 2004
HAMPSHIRE, Sir Stuart Newton	13 June 2004
HEILBRUN, Carolyn Gold	9 October 2003
HENRY, Carl F. H.	7 December 2003
HOLLINGDALE, Reginald John	28 September 2001
HUGHES, Monica Mary	7 March 2003
ISAACS, Alan	5 April 2004
JORDAN, June M.	14 June 2002
KAYE, Mary Margaret	29 January 2004
KENNER, (William) Hugh	24 November 2003
KING, Michael	30 March 2004

LAWRENCE, Jerome	29 February 2004
LEVENDOSKY, Charles Leonard	14 March 2004
LIVERSIDGE, (Henry) Douglas	–
LUARD, Nicholas	25 May 2004
MCWHIRTER, Norris Dewar	19 April 2004
MANCHESTER, William	1 June 2004
MODIGLIANI, Franco	25 September 2003
MORAES, Dominic	2 June 2004
MORGAN, (George) Frederick	20 February 2004
MOWAT, David	29 February 2004
NICOL, Donald MacGillivray	25 September 2003
NUTTALL, Jeffrey	4 January 2004
PIMLOTT, Benjamin John	10 April 2004
RHODES, Philip	–
RICHARDS, Alun	2 June 2004
RIDLEY, Jasper Godwin	1 July 2004
RIPLEY, Alexandra Braid	10 January 2004
ROBINSON, Ian Norman Baker	20 April 2004
ROSENTHAL, Jack Morris	29 May 2004
SAUNDERS, James Arthur	29 January 2004
SEGÀL, Judah Benzion	23 October 2003
SELBY, Hubert, Jr	26 April 2004
STEVEN, Stewart Gustav	19 January 2004
TALBOT, Norman Clare	8 January 2004
TERRAINE, John Alfred	28 December 2003
THISTLETHWAITE, Frank	17 February 2003
TURNBULL, Gael Lundin	2 July 2004
USTINOV, Peter Alexander	28 March 2004
VAN STAAVEREN, Jacob	4 July 1999
VLADIMOV, Georgij Nikolayevich	19 October 2003
WALKER, Ted	19 March 2004
WELCH, James P., Jr	4 August 2003
WICKHAM, Glynne William Gladstone	27 January 2004
WILLIAMS, David	26 September 2003
WOLLHEIM, Richard Arthur	4 November 2003

INTERNATIONAL WHO'S WHO OF AUTHORS AND WRITERS

A

AARON, Hugh, (Max Barnet), BA; American writer; b. 30 Nov. 1924, Worcester, MA; m. Ann Stein 1989; one s. two d. *Education:* Univ. of Chicago. *Publications:* Business Not as Usual 1993, When Wars Were Won 1995, It's All Chaos 1996, Letters from the Good War 1997, Films in Review 1998, Suzy, Fair Suzy 1998; as Max Barnet: Driven 1995, Go West Old Man 1996; contrib. to Sail Magazine, Wall Street Journal. *Address:* c/o Stones Point Press, 6 Henderson Lane, Cushing, ME 04563, USA (Office). *E-mail:* books@stonespoint.com (Office); haaron@adelphia.net (Home). *Website:* www.stonespoint.com (Office); www.hughaaron.com.

ABBENSETTS, Michael; British writer; b. 8 June 1938, British Guiana. *Education:* Queen's Coll., Guyana, Stanstead Coll., QC, Sir George Williams Univ., Montréal. *Career:* security attendant, Tower of London 1963–67; staff mem., Sir John Soane's Museum, London 1968–71; resident playwright, Royal Court Theatre, London 1974; Visiting Prof. of Drama, Carnegie Mellon Univ., Pittsburgh 1981; writer for radio and television. *Plays:* Sweet Talk (London 1973, New York 1974), Alterations (London and New York 1978, revised prod. London 1985), Samba (London 1980), In the Mood (London 1981), Outlaw (Leicester and London 1983), El Dorado (London 1984). *Publications:* Empire Road (novel, from TV series) 1979. *Honours:* George Devine Award 1973, Arts Council Bursary 1977, Afro-Caribbean Award 1979. *Literary Agent:* Sheil Associates, 43 Doughty Street, London, WC1N 2LF, England.

ABBS, Peter Francis, BA, DPhil; writer, poet and editor; *Professor of Creative Writing, University of Sussex*; b. 22 Feb. 1942, Cromer, Norfolk, England; m. Barbara Beazeley 1963 (divorced 2002); one s. two d. *Education:* Univ. of Bristol, Univ. of Sussex. *Career:* Lecturer in Education 1976–85, Reader 1985–99, Prof. of Creative Writing 1999–, Univ. of Sussex; founding mem. New Metaphysical Art. *Publications:* English for Diversity: A Polemic 1969, The Forms of Narrative: A Practical Guide (with John Richardson) 1970, Autobiography in Education 1974, The Black Rainbow: Essays on the Present Breakdown of Culture (ed.) 1975, Root and Blossom: Essays on the Philosophy, Practice and Politics of English Teaching 1976, Proposal for a New College (with Graham Carey) 1977, For Man and Islands (poems) 1978, Reclamations: Essays on Culture, Mass-Culture and the Curriculum 1979, Songs of a New Taliesin (poems) 1979, English Within the Arts: A Radical Alternative 1982, Living Powers: The Arts in Education (ed.) 1987, A is for Aesthetic: Essays on Creative and Aesthetic Education 1988, The Symbolic Order: A Contemporary Reader on the Arts Debate (ed.) 1989, The Forms of Poetry: A Practical Guide (with John Richardson) 1991, Icons of Time: An Experiment in Autobiography 1991, The Educational Imperative 1994, The Polemics of Imagination: Essays on Art, Culture and Society 1996, Love After Sappho (poems) 1999, Selected Poems 2001, Against the Flow: Education, the Arts and Postmodern Culture 2003; contrib. to scholarly and literary periodicals. *Address:* c/o Graduate Research Centre in the Humanities, Arts Bldg B, University of Sussex, Falmer, Brighton BN1 9QN, England.

ABEL, Sam, BA, MA, PhD; writer, editor and educator; b. 5 Oct. 1957, Norwood, MA, USA; pnr Craig B. Palmer 1994. *Education:* Dartmouth College, Indiana Univ. *Career:* Assoc. Instructor, Indiana Univ., Bloomington 1981–82; Instructor, Moorhead State Univ., Moorhead, MN 1983–84, Asst Prof., DePauw Univ., Greencastle, IN 1985–90, Dartmouth Coll., Hanover, NH 1990–; book review ed., reader 1990–93, Co-Ed. 1993–, New England Theatre Journal; Consulting Ed., Theatre History Studies 1996–; consultant for OUP, Univ. of Michigan Press, Indiana Univ., Warner Bentley Theatre; dir various stage productions; mem. Asscn for Theatre in Higher Education, MLA, American Soc. for Theatre Research, Popular Culture Asscn. *Publications:* Opera in the Flesh: Sexuality in Operatic Performance 1996, Irrational Entertainment: Reflections on Opera for the Twenty-First Century 1998; contrib. articles and reviews to periodicals, journals and anthologies, including Journal of Dramatic Theory and Criticism, Journal of Popular Culture, Memory, Practice, Desire: Gay Performances, New England Theatre Journal, A Night at the Opera, Media Representation of Opera, Notable Gays and Lesbians in American Theatre History, Opera News, Terrance McNally: A Casebook, Theatre Annual: A Journal of Performance Studies, Theatre History Studies, Theatre Journal, Theatre Survey, Theatre Topics, Western European Studies. *Honours:* Dartmouth Coll. Marcus Heiman Award for the Creative and Performing Arts 1979, Burke Research Grant 1990–93, Indiana Univ. Graduate Fellow 1979–80, American Coll. Theatre Festival Regional Award for Dramatic Criticism 1980, American Coll. Theatre Festival Regional Award for Playwriting 1981, DePauw Univ. Creative Project Grant 1988, DePauw Univ. Course Development Grant 1989. *Address:* c/o New England Theatre Journal, PMB 502, 198 Tremont Street, Boston, MA 02116-4750, USA.

ABELSON, Philip Hauge; American physicist, editor and writer; b. 27 April 1913, Tacoma, WA; m. Neva Martin 1936; one d. *Education:* Washington State Coll., Univ. of California at Berkeley. *Career:* Asst Physicist, Dept of Terrestrial Magnetism, Carnegie Inst. of Washington 1939–41, staff mem. of Dept 1946–53, Dir Geophysical Lab. 1953–71; Pres., Carnegie Inst. of Washington 1971–78, trustee 1978–; Principal Physicist and Civilian-in-Charge, Naval Research Lab. Branch, Navy Yard, Philadelphia 1941–46; Co-Ed., Journal of Geophysical Research 1959–65; Ed. Science 1962–85; Resident Fellow, Resources for the Future Inc 1985–88; mem. Nat. Insts of Health Biophysics and Biophysical Chem. Study Section 1956–59; mem. Gen. Advisory Cttee to Atomic Energy Comm. 1960–63; mem. Cttee on Science and Public Policy of Nat. Acad. of Sciences 1962–63; mem. numerous other bodies; Consultant to NASA 1960–63; work includes identification of uranium fission products 1939–40, co-discovery of neptunium 1940, separation of uranium isotopes 1943, biosynthesis in micro-organisms 1953, amino acids in fossils 1955, fatty acids in rocks 1956; mem. NAS, AAAS (scientific adviser 1985–, Exec. Dir (acting) 1989), American Philosophical Soc., American Geophysical Union (pres. 1972–74), Int. Union of Geological Sciences (pres. 1972–76). *Publications:* Studies in Biochemistry in Escherichia coli (co-author) 1955, Research in Geochemistry Vols 1 and 2 (ed.) 1959, Energy: Use, Conservation and Supply (ed.) 1974, Energy for Tomorrow 1975, Food: Politics, Economics, Nutrition and Research (ed.) 1975, Materials: Renewable and Nonrenewable (ed.) 1976, Electronics: The Continuing Revolution (ed.) 1977, Enough of Pessimism 1985. *Honours:* Distinguished Alumnus Award, Washington State Univ. 1962, Hon. DSc (Yale) 1964, (Southern Methodist Univ.) 1969, (Tufts Univ.) 1976, Hon. DHL (Univ. of Puget Sound) 1968; Physical Sciences Award, Washington Acad. of Sciences 1950, Hillebrand Award, Chemical Soc. of Washington 1962; Modern Medicine Award 1967, Joseph Priestley Award 1973, Kalinga Prize for Popularization of Science 1973, American Medical Asscn Scientific Achievement Award 1974, Nat. Medal of Science 1989; US Navy Distinguished Civilian Service Medal 1945. *Address:* c/o AAAS, 1200 New York Avenue NW, Suite 100, Washington, DC 20005-3941, USA.

ABISH, Walter; Writer; b. 24 Dec. 1931, Vienna, Austria; m. Cecile Abish. *Career:* mem. PEN, American Centre, Exec. Board, 1982–88; New York Foundation for the Arts, Board of Govs, 1990–93; Fellow, American Acad. of Arts and Sciences, 1998–. *Publications:* Duel Site, 1970; Alphabetical Africa, 1974; Minds Meet, 1975; In the Future Perfect, 1977; How German Is It, 1980; 99: The New Meaning, 1990; Eclipse Fever, 1993. Contributions: Antaeus; Conjunctions; Granta; Manuskripte; New Directions Annual; Paris Review; Partisan Review; Tri-Quarterly; Salmagundi. *Honours:* Ingram Merrill Foundation Grant, 1977; National Endowment for the Arts Fellowships, 1979, 1985; PEN-Faulkner Award, 1981; Guggenheim Fellowship, 1981; Deutscher Akademischer Austauschdienst Residency, Berlin, 1987; John D. and Catherine T. MacArthur Foundation Fellowship, 1987–92; Medal of Merit, American Acad. of Arts and Letters, 1991; Lila Wallace-Reader's Digest Fellowship, 1992–95; Hon. DLitt, SUNY at Oneonta, 1996. *Address:* PO Box 485, Cooper Station, NY 10276, USA.

ABLEMAN, Paul; writer; b. 13 June 1927, Leeds, Yorkshire, England; m.; two s. *Education:* King's Coll., London. *Publications:* Even His Enemy (with Gertrude Macauley) 1948, I Hear Voices 1958, As Near As I Can Get 1962, Green Julia (play) 1966, Tests (playlets) 1966, Vac 1968, Blue Comedy: Madly in Love, Hawk's Night 1968, The Twilight of the Vilp 1969, Bits: Some Prose Poems 1969, Tornado Pratt 1977, Shoestring (novelization of television play) 1979, Porridge (novelization of screenplay) 1979, Shoestring's Finest House 1980, County Hall (novelization of television series) 1981, The Anatomy of Nakedness 1982, The Doomed Rebellion 1983, The Secret of Consciousness: How the Brain Tells the 'Story of Me' 1999. *Address:* Flat 36, Duncan House, Fellows Road, London, NW3, England.

ABOULELA, Leila; Writer; b. 1964, Sudan; m.; three c. *Education:* Economics, Univ. of Khartoum, 1985; MSc, Statistics, LSE. *Career:* co-writer of a play broadcast on BBC Radio Four; Lecturer and research asst; resides in Scotland. *Publications:* The Translator (novel), 1999; Coloured Lights (short stories), 2001. Contributions: The Museum, short story in Opening Spaces collection, 2000. *Honours:* Caine Prize for African Writing (for short story The Museum) 2000. *Address:* c/o African Writers Series, Heinemann Educational Publishers, Halley Ct, Jordan Hill, Oxford OX2 8EJ, England.

ABRAHAM, Henry Julian, BA, MA, PhD; political scientist; b. 25 Aug. 1921, Offenbach am Main, Germany; m. Mildred Kosches 1954; two s. *Education:* Kenyon Coll., Columbia Univ., Univ. of Pennsylvania. *Career:* instructor, 1949–53, Asst Prof., 1953–57, Assoc. Prof., 1957–62, Prof. of Political

Science, 1962–72, Univ. of Pennsylvania; Henry L. and Grace Doherty Memorial Foundation Prof. in Government and Foreign Affairs, 1972–78, James Hart Prof. in Government and Foreign Affairs, 1978–, Univ. of Virginia; Visiting Lecturer and Visiting Prof. at many universities and colleges in the USA and abroad; mem. American Judicature Society; American Political Science Asscn, vice-pres., 1980–82; American Society for Legal History; English-Speaking Union; International Political Science Asscn; National Asscn of Scholars; Southern Political Science Asscn. *Publications:* Elements of Democratic Government (with J. A. Corry), fourth edn, 1964; The Judicial Process: An Introductory Analysis of the Courts of the United States, England, and France, 1962; The Judiciary: The Supreme Court in the Governmental Process, 1965; Essentials of American National Government (with J. C. Phillips), third edn, 1971; Freedom and the Court: Civil Rights and Liberties in the United States, 1967; Justices and Presidents: A Political History of Appointments to the Supreme Court, 1974; American Democracy, 1983; Justices, President and Senators: A History of Supreme Court Appointments from Jay to Clinton, 1999. Contributions: numerous chapters in books, articles, monographs and essays. *Honours:* Fulbright Lecturer, 1959–60; American Philosophical Society Fellow, 1960–61, 1970–71, 1979; Rockefeller Foundation Resident Scholar, Bellagio, Italy, 1978; Thomas Jefferson Award, Univ. of Virginia, 1983; Hon. degrees, 1972, 1982, 1982, 1987, 1996; First Lifetime Achievement Award, Organized Section on Law and Courts, American Political Science Asscn, 1996. *Address:* 906 Fendall Terrace, Charlottesville, VA 22903, USA.

ABRAHAMS, Peter Henry; novelist; b. 19 March 1919, Vrededorp, Johannesburg, South Africa; m. Daphne Elizabeth Miller; three c. *Education:* Church of England mission schools and colleges. *Career:* Controller, West Indian News, Jamaica 1955–64; Chair., Radio Jamaica, Kingston 1977–80. *Publications:* Song of the City, 1945; Mine Boy, 1946; The Path of Thunder, 1948; Wild Conquest, 1950; Tell Freedom, 1954; A Wreath for Udomo, 1956; A Night of Their Own, 1965; This Island Now, 1966; The View from Coyaba, 1985; The Coyoba Chronicles: Reflections on the Black Experience in the Twentieth Century, 2000. Short Story Collections: Dark Testament, 1942. Poetry: A Black Man Speaks of Freedom, 1938. *Address:* Red Hills, PO Box 20, St Andrew, Jamaica.

ABRAHAMS, Roger (David); Prof. of Folklore and Folklife and Writer; b. 12 June 1933, Philadelphia, PA, USA. *Education:* BA, Swarthmore College, 1955; MA, Columbia Univ., 1958; PhD, Univ. of Pennsylvania, 1961. *Career:* Instructor, 1960–63, Asst Prof., 1963–66, Assoc. Prof., 1966–69, Prof. of English and Anthropology, 1969–79, Chair., English Dept, 1974–79, Univ. of Texas at Austin; Alexander H. Kenan Prof. of Humanities and Anthropology, Pitzer College and Scripps College, Claremont, CA, 1979–85; Prof. of Folklore and Folklife, Univ. of Pennsylvania, 1985–; various visiting professorships; mem. American Folklore Society, pres., 1978–79; International Society for Folk Narrative Research. *Publications:* Deep Down in the Jungle: Negro Narrative Folklore from the Streets of Philadelphia, 1964; Anglo-American Folksong Style (with George W. Foss Jr), 1968; Positively Black, 1970; Deep the Water, Shallow the Shore: Three Essays on Shantying in the West Indies, 1974; Talking Black, 1976; Afro-American Folk Culture: An Annotated Bibliography, 1977; Between the Living and the Dead: Riddles Which Tell Stories, 1980; The Man-of-Words in the West Indies, 1983; Singing the Master: The Emergence of African-American Culture in the Plantation South, 1992. *Honours:* Guggenheim Fellowship, 1965–66; American Folklore Society Fellow, 1970; National Humanities Institute Fellow, 1976–77; Lifetime Achievement Award, American Folklore Society, 1989.

ABRAMS, Meyer Howard, BA, MA, PhD; writer and academic; b. 23 July 1912, Long Branch, NJ, USA; m. Ruth Gaynes 1937; two d. *Education:* Harvard Univ., Univ. of Cambridge. *Career:* Instructor in English, 1938–42, Research Assoc., Psycho-Acoustic Laboratory, 1942–45, Harvard Univ.; Asst Prof., 1945–47, Assoc. Prof., 1947–53, Prof. of English, 1953–61, Frederic J. Whiton Prof., 1961–73, Class of 1916 Prof., 1973–83, Prof. Emeritus, 1983–, Cornell Univ.; Visiting Lecturer at several institutions of higher learning; mem. American Acad. of Arts and Sciences; American Acad. of Arts and Letters; American Asscn of Univ. Profs; American Philosophical Society; British Acad., corresponding fellow; MLA of America; Founders' Group, National Humanities Center. *Publications:* The Milk of Paradise: The Effects of Opium Visions on the Works of De Quincey, Crabbe, Francis Thompson and Coleridge, 1934; The Mirror and the Lamp: Romantic Theory and the Critical Tradition, 1953; A Glossary of Literary Terms, 1957; Natural Supernaturalism: Tradition and Revolution in Romantic Literature, 1971; The Correspondent Breeze: Essays in English Romanticism, 1984; Doing Things With Texts: Essays in Criticism and Critical Theory, 1989. Editor: The Poetry of Pope, 1954; Literature and Belief, 1958; English Romantic Poets: Modern Essays in Criticism, 1960; The Norton Anthology of English Literature, 1962; Wordsworth: A Collection of Critical Essays, 1972; William Wordsworth: Prelude, 1979. Contributions: several vols. *Honours:* Rockefeller Foundation Fellowship, 1946–47; Ford Foundation Fellowship, 1953; Fulbright Scholarship, 1954; Guggenheim Fellowships, 1958, 1960; Fellow, Center for Advanced Study in the Behavioral Sciences, 1967; Christian Gauss Prize, 1954; James Russell Lowell Prize, MLA of America, 1971; Visiting Fellow, All Soul's College, Oxford, 1977; Award in Humanistic Studies, American Acad. of Arts and Sciences, 1984; Distinguished Scholar Award, Keats-Shelley Asscn, 1987; American Acad. and Institute of Arts and Letters Award, 1990. *Address:* 378 Savage Farm Drive, Ithaca, NY 14850, USA.

ABRAMSON, Jill, BA; American newspaper editor; *Managing Editor, New York Times*; b. 1954; m. Henry Griggs; two c. *Education:* Harvard Univ. *Career:* Ed. in Chief, Legal Times, Washington, DC 1986–88; Deputy Bureau Chief and investigative reporter, Wall Street Journal 1988–97; joined New York Times 1997, Enterprise Ed., Washington Bureau 1997–99, Washington Ed. 1999–2000, Washington Bureau Chief 2000–03, Man. Ed. 2003–. *Publications include:* Where They Are Now 1986, Strange Justice (with Jane Mayer) 1994. *Honours:* Nat. Press Club Award 1992. *Address:* The New York Times, 229 West 43rd Street, New York, NY 10036, USA (Office). *Telephone:* (212) 556-8000 (Office).

ABSE, Dannie, DLitt, LRCP, MRCS, FRSL; British author, poet and physician; b. 22 Sept. 1923, Cardiff, Wales; m. Joan Mercer 1951; one s. two d. *Education:* St Illtyd's Coll. Cardiff, Univ. Coll. Cardiff, King's Coll. London and Westminster Hosp., London. *Career:* first book of poems published while still a medical student 1948; qualified as doctor 1950; Squadron-Leader RAF 1951–55; doctor in charge of chest clinic at Cen. Medical Establishment, Cleveland Street, London 1954–89; Writer-in-Residence, Princeton Univ., NJ, USA 1973–74; Pres. Poetry Soc. 1979–92, Welsh Acad. 1996 (Fellow 1993); mem. Council, Royal Soc. of Literature. *Publications:* poetry: Funland and Other Poems 1973, Way Out in the Centre 1981, White Coat, Purple Coat: Collected Poems 1948–1988 1989, Remembrance of Crimes Past 1990, On the Evening Road 1994, Arcadia, One Mile 1998; editor: Voices in the Gallery 1986, The Music Lover's Literary Companion (with Joan Abse) 1989, The Hutchinson Book of Post-War British Poets 1989, Twentieth-Century Anglo-Welsh Poetry 1997, New and Collected Poems 2002; fiction: Pythagoras (a play), Ash on a Young Man's Sleeve 1954, Some Corner of a English Field 1956, O Jones, O Jones 1970, Ask the Bloody Horse 1986, There was a Young Man from Cardiff 2001, The Strange Case of Dr Simmonds and Dr Glas 2002; other: Journals from the Ant Heap 1986, Intermittent Journals 1994, A Welsh Retrospective 1997, Goodbye, Twentieth Century 2001; contributions: BBC and various publs in the UK and USA. *Honours:* Hon. Fellow, Univ. of Wales Coll. of Medicine 1999; Hon. DLitt (Univ. of Wales) 1989, (Glamorgan) 1997; Welsh Arts Council Literature Prize 1971, 1987, Henry Foyle Award 1960, 1964, Jewish Chronicle Award, Cholmondeley Award 1983, 1985. *Literary Agent:* PFD, Drury House, 34–43 Russell Street, London, WC2B 5HA. *Address:* 85 Hodford Road, London, NW11 8NH, England.

ACCAD, Evelyne, MA, PhD; professor and writer; b. 6 Oct. 1943, Beirut, Lebanon. *Education:* Beirut Coll. for Women, Anderson Coll., Ball State Univ., Indiana Univ. *Career:* Prof., Univ. of Illinois at Urbana-Champaign, mem. core faculty African Center, Women's Studies Center, Middle East Studies Program, Campus Honors Faculty 1974–; teacher, Beirut Univ. Coll. 1978–84, Northwestern Univ. 1991; mem. of jury, Int. Neustadt Prize for Literature. *Publications:* Veil of Shame: The Role of Women in the Modern Fiction of North Africa and the Arab World 1978, Montjoie Palestine! or Last Year in Jerusalem 1980, L'Excisée 1982, Coquelicot du Massacre 1988, Sexuality and War: Literary Masks of the Middle East 1990, Des femmes, des hommes et la guerre: Fiction et Réalité au Proche-Orient (France-Lebanon Literary Award ADELF) 1993, Blessures des Mots 1993, Wounding Words: A Woman's Journal in Tunisia 1996, Voyages en Cancer (trans. as The Wounded Breast: Intimate Journeys Through Cancer) (Prix Phénix 2001) 2000; other: four ed vols, 14 book chapters and 73 articles. *Honours:* Florence Howard Award (hon. mention) 1975, special recognition Illinois Arts Council Creative Writing Fellowship 1979, Fulbright Awards 1983–85, 2002, Studies of Cultural Values and Ethics Program Award 1992, 1996–97. *Address:* Department of French, 2090 Foreign Languages Bldg, University of Illinois, Urbana, IL (Office); 306 W Michigan, Urbana, IL 61801, USA.

ACHEBE, (Albert) Chinualumogu (Chinua); writer, poet and academic; b. 16 Nov. 1930, Ogidi, Nigeria; m. Christie Chinwe Okoli 1961; two s. two d. *Education:* University College, Ibadan, 1948–53; BA, Univ. of London, 1953; Received training in broadcasting, BBC, London, 1956. *Career:* Producer, 1954–58, Controller, Eastern Region, Enugu, Nigeria, 1958–61, Founder-Dir, Voice of Nigeria, 1961–66, Nigerian Broadcasting Corpn, Lagos; Senior Research Fellow, 1967–72, Prof. of English, 1976–81, Prof. Emeritus, 1985–, University of Nigeria, Nsukka; Ed., Okike: A Nigerian Journal of New Writing, 1971–; Prof. of English, University of Massachusetts, 1972–75; Dir, Okike Arts Centre, Nsukka, 1984–; Founder-Publisher, Uwa Ndi Igbo: A Bilingual Journal of Igbo Life and Arts, 1984–; Pro-Chancellor and Chair. of the Council, Anambra State University of Technology, Enugu, 1986–88; Charles P. Stevenson Prof., Bard College, New York, 1990–; Visiting Prof. and Lecturer at universities in Canada and the USA; mem. American Acad. of Arts and Letters, foreign hon. mem., 1982; Asscn of Nigerian Authors, founder and pres., 1981–86; Vice-pres., Royal African Society, London, 1998; Commonwealth Arts Organization; MLA of America, hon. fellow; FRSL, 1981; Writers and Scholars International, London; Nigerian Acad. of Letters, 1999; American Acad. of Arts and Sciences, foreign hon. mem., 2002. *Publications:* Fiction: Things Fall Apart, 1958; No Longer at Ease, 1960; Arrow of God, 1964; A Man of the People, 1966; Anthills of the Savannah, 1987. Short Stories: The Sacrificial Egg and Other Stories, 1962; Girls at War, 1973. Children's Fiction: Chike and the

River, 1966; How the Leopard Got His Claws (with John Iroaganachi), 1972; The Flute, 1978; The Drum, 1978. Poetry: Beware, Soul-Brother and Other Poems, 1971; Christmas in Biafra and Other Poems, 1973. Essays: Morning Yet on Creation Day, 1975; The Trouble With Nigeria, 1983; Hopes and Impediments, 1988; Home and Exile, 2000. Editor: Don't Let Him Die: An Anthology of Memorial Poems for Christopher Okigbo (with Dubem Okafor), 1978; Aka Weta: An Anthology of Igbo Poetry (with Obiora Udechukwu), 1982; African Short Stories (with C. L. Innes), 1984; The Heinemann Book of Contemporary African Short Stories (with C. L. Innes), 1992; Essay and Poems: Another Africa (with Robert Lyons), 1998. Contributions: New York Review of Books; Transition; Callaloo. *Honours:* Margaret Wrong Memorial Prize, 1959; Nigerian National Trophy, 1961; Jock Campbell/New Statesman Award, 1965; Commonwealth Poetry Prize, 1972; Neil Gunn International Fellow, Scottish Arts Council, 1975; Lotus Award for Afro-Asian Writers, 1975; Nigerian National Order of Merit 1979; Order of the Federal Republic of Nigeria, 1979; Commonwealth Foundation Senior Visiting Practitioner Award, 1984; Campion Medal, New York, 1996; National Creativity Award, Nigeria, 1999; 36 hon. doctorates, 1972–2002. *Literary Agent:* David Higham Associates, 5–8 Lower John Street, Golden Square, London W1F 9HA, England. *Address:* Bard College, Annandale on Hudson, NY 12504, USA.

ACKERMAN, Diane; Poet, Writer and University Teacher; b. 7 Oct. 1948, Waukegan, IL, USA. *Education:* Boston University, 1966–67; BA, English, Pennsylvania State University, 1970; MFA, Creative Writing, 1973, MA, English, 1976, PhD, English, 1978, Cornell University. *Career:* Teaching Asst, 1971–78, Lecturer, 1978, Visiting Writer, 1987, Visiting Prof., 1998–2000, Cornell University; Asst Prof., University of Pittsburgh, 1980–83; Writer-in-Residence, College of William and Mary, 1982–83, Ohio University, 1983, New York University, 1986, Columbia University, 1986–87; Writer-in-Residence, 1983–86, Dir, Writers' Program, 1984–86, Washington University; Staff Writer, New Yorker magazine, 1988–94; Visiting Prof., Society for the Humanities, Cornell University, 1998–2000; National Endowment, Humanities Distinguished Prof. of English, University of Richmond, 2001. *Publications:* The Planets: A Cosmic Pastoral, 1976; Wife of Light, 1978; Twilight of the Tenderfoot, 1980; Lady Faustus, 1983; On Extended Wings, 1985; Reverse Thunder, 1988; A Natural History of the Senses, 1990; Jaguar of Sweet Laughter: New and Selected Poems, 1991; The Moon by Whale Light and Other Adventures Among Bats, Crocodilians, Penguins and Whales, 1991; A Natural History of Love, 1994; The Rarest of the Rare, 1995; Monk Seal Hideaway, 1995; A Slender Thread, 1997; Bats: Shadows in the Night, 1997; I Praise My Destroyer, 1998; The Norton Book of Love (ed. with Jeanne Mackin), 1998; Deep Play, 1999; Cultivating Delight: A Natural History of My Garden, 2001. Contributions: numerous anthologies, books, newspapers, journals and magazines. *Honours:* Abbie Copps Poetry Prize, 1974; National Endowment for the Arts Creative Writing Fellowships, 1976, 1986; Black Warrior Review Poetry Prize, 1981; Pushcart Prize, 1984; Peter I. B. Lavan Award, Acad. of American Poets, 1985; Lowell Thomas Award, 1990; New York Times Book Review Notable Books of the Year, 1991, 1992, and New and Noteworthy Books of the Year, 1993, 1997; Wordsmith Award, 1992; Literary Lion, New York Public Library, 1994; John Burroughs Nature Award, 1997; Art of Fact Award, 2000; Best American Essays Citation, 2001; Molecule named in her honour, Dianeackerone; Guggenheim Fellowship, 2003. *Literary Agent:* William Morris Agency, 1325 Avenue of the Americas, New York, NY 10019, USA. *E-mail:* da31@cornell.edu.

ACKERMAN, Susan Yoder; Teacher and Writer; b. 2 Nov. 1945, Newport News, VA, USA; m. Robert W. Ackerman II 12 July 1969; one s. two d. *Education:* Eastern Mennonite College, 1962–64; BA, College of William and Mary, 1968; Graduate studies, Univ. of Virginia, Longwood College and Hampton Univ. *Career:* Elementary School Teacher, Newport News, VA, 1966–67, 1972; Teacher of English as a Foreign Language, Lubumbashi, Zaire, 1969–70, Kongolo, Zaire, 1979–80; Middle and High School French Teacher, Newport News, 1984–86, 1989–96; Day Care Dir, Newport News, 1989–90; Elementary School Principal, 2000–; Writer-in-Residence, Island Institute, Sitka, AK, 2000; Speaker on African experiences and on writing; Leader, workshops on writing children's fiction; mem. Society of Children's Book Writers and Illustrators. *Publications:* Copper Moons, 1990; The Flying Pie and Other Stories, 1996. Contributions: Educational testing material; Stories and articles to periodicals incl.: Cricket; On the Line; With; Instructor; Story Friends; Christian Living; Purpose; Together; Live; Mothering Click; Cicada. *Address:* 524 Marlin Dr., Newport News, VA 23602, USA. *E-mail:* susan@ackerman.net.

ACKLIN, Jürg; Psychoanalyst and Writer; b. 20 Feb. 1945, Zürich, Switzerland; m. Claudia Acklin-Gaiser, 1984, two d. *Education:* Social Sciences, Universities of Zürich and Bremen; Doctoral Thesis, 1974. *Career:* Leader, Literturclub, Swiss Television. *Publications:* Fiction: Michael Häuptli, 1969; Alias, 1971; Das Uberhandnehmen, 1973; Der Aufstieg des Fesselballons, 1980; Der Känguruhmann, 1992; Das Tangopaat, 1994; Froschgesang, 1996; Der Vater, 1998. *Honours:* C. F. Meyer Prize, 1971; Bremer Literature Prize, 1972; Zürcher Buch Prize, 1997. *Address:* Flühgasse 1g, 8008 Zürich, Switzerland.

ACKROYD, Peter, CBE, MA, FRSL; British writer; b. 5 Oct. 1949, London. *Education:* St Benedict's School, Ealing, Clare Coll., Cambridge and Yale Univ. *Career:* Literary Ed. The Spectator 1973–77, Jt Man. Ed. 1978–82; Chief Book Reviewer The Times 1986–; Mellon Fellow Yale Univ. *Play:* The Mystery of Charles Dickens 2000. *Television:* Charles Dickens (BBC 2), Peter Ackroyd's London (BBC 2) 2004. *Publications:* novels: The Great Fire of London 1982, The Last Testament of Oscar Wilde 1983 (Somerset Maugham Prize 1984), Hawksmoor 1985 (Whitbread Award, Guardian Fiction Prize), Chatterton 1987, First Light 1989, English Music 1992, The House of Doctor Dee 1993, Dan Leno and the Limehouse Golem 1994, Milton in America 1996, The Plato Papers 1999, The Clerkenwell Tales (short stories) 2003; non-fiction: Notes for a New Culture 1976, Dressing Up: Transvestism and Drag: The History of an Obsession 1979, Ezra Pound and his World 1980, T. S. Eliot 1984 (Whitbread Award, Heinemann Award), Dickens 1990, Introduction to Dickens 1991, Blake 1995, The Life of Thomas More 1998, London: the Biography 2000, Dickens: Public Life and Private Passion 2002, The Collection 2002, Albion: The Origins of the English Imagination 2002, Illustrated London 2003, The Beginning: Voyages Through Time (juvenile) 2003; poetry: London Lickpenny 1973, Country Life 1978, The Diversions of Purley 1987. *Honours:* Hon. DLitt (Exeter Univ.), (London Guildhall), (City Univ.), (Univ. Coll., London); Somerset Maugham Award 1984, W. H. Heinemann Award RSL 1985, Whitbread Book of the Year Award for Biography 1985, and for Fiction 1986, Guardian Ficiton Award 1986. *Literary Agent:* Anthony Sheil Associates Ltd, 43 Doughty Street, London, WC1N 2LF, England. *Telephone:* (20) 7405-9351.

ACLAND, Alice (see Wignall, Anne).

ACOSTA, Devashish Donald; Writer; b. 9 Nov. 1956, New York, NY, USA. *Education:* MFA, Fiction, San Diego State University. *Publications:* Felicitavia: A Spiritual Journey, 1997; When the Time Comes, 1998; Sadvipra, 2000. *Address:* c/o Innerworld Publications, PO Box 1613, San German, Puerto Rico 00683, USA.

ADAIR, Gilbert; British writer and film critic; b. 29 Dec. 1944, Edinburgh, Scotland. *Publications:* novels: Alice Through the Needle's Eye 1984, Peter Pan and the Only Children 1987, The Holy Innocents: A Romance 1988 (Author's Club First Novel Award 1989), Love and Death on Long Island 1990, The Death of the Author 1992, Jizzrim 1993, Jizzrim 2 1994, Jizzrim 3 1995, Jizzrim 4 1996, The Key to the Tower: A Novel 1997, A Closed Book 1999, The Dreamers 2003, Buenas Noches Buenos Aires 2003, The Act of Roger Murgatroyd 2005; poem: The Rape of the Cock 1991; non-fiction: Hollywood's Vietnam: From the Green Berets to Apocalypse Now (aka Vietnam on Film: From the Green Berets to Apocalypse Now) 1981 (revised and enlarged 1989), Signs of Life: Book 1, a Documentary 1982, A Night at the Pictures: Ten Decades of British Film (with Nick Roddick) 1985, Myths and Memories 1986, The Postmodernist Always Rings Twice: Reflections on Culture in the 90s 1992, Flickers: An Illustrated Celebration of 100 Years of Cinema 1995, Surfing the Zeitgeist 1997, The Real Tadzio: Thomas Mann's 'Death in Venice' and the boy who inspired it 2001; adaptation: Alice and Her Friends from Wonderland 1986; editor: Movies 1999; translations: Kubrick (by Michel Ciment) 1983, John Boorman (by Michel Ciment) 1986, Letters/François Truffaut (aka François Truffaut: Correspondence 1945–1984) 1989, A Void (by Georges Perec) (Scott Moncrieff Translation Prize); contrib. to Wonder Tales: Six French Stories of Enchantment 1996. *Literary Agent:* Blake Friedmann Literary, Film & TV Agency, 122 Arlington Road, London, NW1 7HP, England. *Telephone:* (20) 7284-0408. *Fax:* (20) 7284-0442. *Website:* www.blakefriedmann.co.uk. *Address:* c/o Faber and Faber Ltd, 3 Queen Square, London, WC1N 3AU, England. *Telephone:* (20) 7465-0045. *Fax:* (20) 7465-0034.

ADAIR, James Radford; writer and editor; b. 2 Feb. 1923, Asheville, NC, USA. *Career:* Ed., Power for Living, Free Way, Teen Power, and Counselor weekly churchpapers 1949–77; Sr Ed., Victor Books Division, Scripture Press Publications Inc, Wheaton, IL 1970–96. *Publications:* Saints Alive 1951, God's Power Within (ed.) 1961, We Found Our Way Out (ed. with Ted Miller) 1965, The Old Lighthouse 1966, The Man from Steamtown 1967, Tom Skinner: Top Man of the Lords and Other Stories (ed.) 1967, M. R. DeHaan: The Man and his Ministry 1969, Hooked on Jesus (ed.) 1971, A Greater Strength (with Jerry Jenkins) 1975, Surgeon on Safari 1976, Escape from Darkness (ed. with Ted Miller) 1982, 101 Days in the Gospels with Oswald Chambers (ed. with Harry Verploegh) 1992, 101 Days in the the Epistles with Oswald Chambers (ed. with Harry Verploegh) 1994, A New Testament Walk with Oswald Chambers (with Harry Verploegh) 1998, The Story of Scripture Press: The Whole Word for the Whole World 1998, Through the Year (with Warren W. Wiersbe) 1999, Be Quoted: From A to Z (with Warren W. Wiersbe) 2000. *Address:* 703 Webster Avenue, Wheaton, IL 60187, USA.

ADAM SMITH, Patricia (Patsy) Jean, OBE; writer; b. 31 May 1926, Gippsland, Vic., Australia. *Career:* Adult Education Officer, Hobart, Tasmania, 1960–66; Manuscripts Field Officer, State Library of Victoria, 1970–82; Pres., Federal Fellowship of Australian Writers, 1973–75. *Publications:* Hear the Train Blow, 1963; Moon Bird People, 1964; There Was a Ship, 1965; Tiger Country, 1966; The Rails Go Westward, 1967; Folklore of Australian Railmen, 1969; No Tribesmen, 1970; Tasmania Sketchbook, 1972; Launceston Sketchbook, 1972; Port Arthur Sketchbook, 1973; Carcoo Salute, 1973; The Desert Railway, 1974; Romance of Australian Railways, 1974; The Anzacs, 1978; Outback Heroes, 1981; The Shearers, 1982;

Australian Women at War, 1984; Heart of Exile, 1986; Prisoner of War from Gallipoli to Korea, 1992; Goodbye Girlie, 1994. *Honours:* Triennial Award; AM. *Address:* 47 Hawksburn Road, South Yarra, Vic. 3141, Australia.

ADAMS, Chuck (see Tubb, Edwin Charles).

ADAMS, Daniel (see Nicole, Christopher (Robin)).

ADAMS, Deborah; Writer and Poet; b. 22 Jan. 1956, Tennessee, USA; m.; three c. *Education:* University of Tennessee at Martin; Austin Peay University. *Career:* Adjunct Faculty, Nashville State Technical Institute; mem. Appalachian Writers' Asscn; MWA; Sisters in Crime. *Publications:* Fiction: All the Great Pretenders, 1992; All the Crazy Winters, 1992; All the Dark Disguises, 1993; All the Hungry Mothers, 1994; All the Deadly Beloved, 1995; All the Blood Relatives, 1997. Poetry: Propriety, 1976; Looking for Heroes, 1984. *Address:* Route 4, PO Box 664, Waverly, TN 37185, USA.

ADAMS, Glenda; Writer, Playwright and Screenwriter; b. 30 Dec. 1939, Sydney, NSW, Australia. *Education:* BA, University of Sydney, 1962; MS, Columbia University, 1965. *Career:* mem. Australian Society of Authors; Australian Writers' Guild; PEN American Center. *Publications:* Lies and Stories, 1976; The Hottest Night of the Century (short stories), 1979; Games of the Strong (novel), 1982; Dancing on Coral (novel), 1987; Longleg (novel), 1990; The Tempest of Clemenza (novel), 1996. Productions: Pride and Wrath (TV plays, ABC), 1993; The Monkey Trap (play, Griffin Theatre Co, Sydney), 1998. Contributions: periodicals. *Honours:* Fellow, New York State Creative Artist Programme Service, 1975–76; Senior Fellow, Australia Council, 1979; Fiction Fellow, National Endowment for the Arts, 1980; Miles Franklin Literary Award, 1987; Age Fiction Book of the Year, 1990; Australian National Book Council Award for Fiction, 1991. *Literary Agent:* Australian Literary Management, 2A Booth St, Balmain, NSW 2041, Australia. *Address:* c/o Goodman Assocs, 500 West End Ave, New York, NY 10025, USA.

ADAMS, Harold; Writer; b. 20 Feb. 1923, Clark, SD, USA; m. Betty E. Skogsberg 17 Sept. 1959 (divorced April 1965); one d. *Education:* BA, University of Minnesota, 1950. *Career:* mem. Authors' Guild; MWA. *Publications:* Murder, 1981; Paint the Town Red, 1982; The Missing Moon, 1983; The Naked Liar, 1985; The Fourth Widow, 1986; When Rich Men Die, 1987; The Barbed Wire Noose, 1987; The Man Who Met the Train, 1988; The Man Who Missed the Party, 1989; The Man Who Was Taller Than God, 1992; A Perfectly Proper Murder, 1993; A Way with Widows, 1994; The Ditched Blonde, 1995; The Hatchet Job, 1996; The Ice Pick Artist, 1997; No Badge, No Gun, 1998; Lead, So I Can Follow, 2000. *Honours:* Shamus Award, Best Private Eye Novel, 1992; Minnesota Book Award, Mystery and Detective, 1993. *Literary Agent:* Ivy Fischer Stone. *Address:* 12916 Greenwood Rd, Minnetonka, MN 55343, USA.

ADAMS, Hazard (Simeon); Prof. of Humanities Emeritus, Writer, Poet and Ed.; b. 15 Feb. 1926, Cleveland, OH, USA; m. Diana White, 17 Sept. 1949, two s. *Education:* BA, Princeton University, 1948; MA, 1949, PhD, 1953, University of Washington. *Career:* Instructor, Cornell University, 1952–56; Asst Prof., University of Texas, 1956–59; Assoc. Prof. to Prof., Michigan State University, 1959–64; Fulbright Lecturer, Trinity College, Dublin, 1961–62; Prof., University of California at Irvine, 1964–77, 1990–94; Byron W. and Alice L. Lockwood Prof. of Humanities, 1977–97, Prof. Emeritus, 1997–, University of Washington. *Publications:* Blake and Yeats: The Contrary Vision, 1955; William Blake: A Reading of the Shorter Poems, 1963; The Contexts of Poetry, 1963; The Horses of Instruction: A Novel, 1968; The Interests of Criticism, 1969; The Truth About Dragons: An Anti-Romance, 1971; Lady Gregory, 1973; The Academic Tribes, 1976; Philosophy of the Literary Symbolic, 1983; Joyce Cary's Trilogies: Pursuit of the Particular Real, 1983; Antithetical Essays in Literary Criticism and Liberal Education, 1990; The Book of Yeats's Poems, 1990; The Book of Yeats's Vision, 1995; The Farm at Richwood and Other Poems, 1997; Many Pretty Toys: A Novel, 1999; Home: A Novel, 2001. Editor: Poems by Robert Simeon Adams, 1952; Poetry: An Introductory Anthology, 1968; Fiction as Process (with Carl Hartman), 1968; William Blake: Jerusalem, Selected Poems and Prose, 1970; Critical Theory Since Plato, 1971; Critical Theory Since 1965 (with Leroy Searle), 1986; Critical Essays on William Blake, 1991. Contributions: numerous poetry, scholarly and critical journals. *Honours:* Guggenheim Fellowship, 1974. *Address:* 3930 NE 157th Pl., Seattle, WA 98155, USA.

ADAMS, James MacGregor David; Journalist and Author; b. 22 April 1951, Newcastle upon Tyne, England; m. Rene Thatcher Riley, 1 July 1990, one d. *Education:* Harrow, 1964–69; Neuchâtel University, 1979–71. *Publications:* The Unnatural Alliance, 1984; The Financing of Terror, 1986; Secret Armies, 1988; Ambush (the War Between the SAS and the IRA) with Robin, Morgan and Anthony Bambridge, 1988; Merchants of Death, 1990; The Final Terror, 1991; Bull's Eye, 1992; Taking the Tunnel, 1993. Contributions: Sunday Times; Washington Post; Los Angeles Times; Atlantic. *Literary Agent:* Janklow & Nesbit Associates, 445 Park Ave, New York, NY 10022, USA. *Address:* c/o The Sunday Times, 1 Pennington St, London E1 9XW, England.

ADAMS, Joanna Z. (see Koch, Joanne Barbara).

ADAMS, Perseus; Writer, Journalist, Poet and Teacher (retd); b. 11 March 1933, Cape Town, South Africa; m. 1958. *Education:* BA, University of Cape Town, 1952; Certificate of Education, 1961. *Career:* Journalist; English Teacher. *Publications:* The Land at My Door, 1965; Grass for the Unicorn, 1975; Cries and Silences: Selected Poems, 1996. Contributions: numerous, mostly to Contrast, Cape Town. *Honours:* South Africa State Poetry Prize, 1963; Festival of Rhodesia Prize, 1970; Keats Memorial International Prize, 1971; Bridport Arts Festival Prize, 1984; Co-winner, Writing Section, Bard of the Year, 1993. *Address:* 21 Mapesbury Rd, Kilburn, London NW2, England.

ADAMS, Richard George, MA, FRSL; author and poet; b. 9 May 1920, Newbury, Berkshire, England; m. Barbara Elizabeth Acland 26 Sept. 1949; two d. *Education:* Worcester College, Oxford. *Career:* Civil Servant, 1948–74; mem. John Clare Society; Walter de la Mare Society. *Publications:* Watership Down, 1972; Shardik, 1974; Nature Through the Seasons (with Max Hooper), 1975; The Tyger Voyage, 1976; The Plague Dogs, 1977; The Ship's Cat, 1977; Nature Day and Night, 1978; The Iron Wolf, 1980; The Girl in a Swing, 1980; Voyage Through the Antarctic (with Ronald Lockley), 1982; Maia, 1984; The Bureaucats, 1985; A Nature Diary, 1985; Occasional Poets (anthology), 1986; The Legend of Te Tuna, 1986; Traveller, 1988; The Day Gone By (autobiog.), 1990; Tales from Watership Down, 1996; The Outlandish Knight, 2000. Contributions: numerous journals and magazines. *Honours:* Carnegie Medal, 1972; Guardian Award for Children's Literature, 1972; Medal, CA Young Readers' Asscn, 1977. *Address:* 26 Church Street, Whitchurch, Hampshire RG28 7AR, England.

ADAMSON, Donald; Critic, Biographer and Historian; b. 30 March 1939, Culcheth, Cheshire, England; m. Helen Freda Griffiths, 24 Sept. 1966, two s. *Education:* Magdalen College, Oxford, 1956–59; University of Paris, France, 1960–61; MA, MLitt, DPhil (Oxon). *Career:* Visiting Fellow, Wolfson College, Cambridge; mem. Fellow, Society of Antiquaries; FRSL; Fellow, Institute of Linguists. *Publications:* T. S. Eliot: A Memoir, 1971; The House of Nell Gwyn (co-author), 1974; Les Romantiques Français devant la Peinture espagnole, 1989; Blaise Pascal: Mathematician, Physicist, And Thinker About God, 1995; Rides Round Britain, The Travel Journals of John Byng, 5th Viscount Torrington, 1996; The Curriers' Company: A Modern History, 2000. Other: various trans of Balzac and Maupassant. *Honours:* JP, Cornwall, England, 1993; Knight of St John, 1998; Chevalier, Ordre des Palmes Académiques, France, 1986. *Address:* Dodmore House, The Street, Meopham, Kent DA13 0AJ, England. *Telephone:* (7747) 733931. *E-mail:* aimsworthy@aol.com. *Website:* www.dodmore.co.uk.

ADAMSON, Robert Harry; Australian poet, writer and publisher; b. 17 May 1943, Sydney, NSW; m. 1st Cheryl Adamson 1973; m. 2nd Juno Adamson 1989; one s. *Career:* Assoc. Ed. 1968–70, Ed. 1970–75, Asst Ed. 1975–77, New Poetry magazine, Sydney; Ed. and Dir, Prism Books, Sydney 1970–77; Founding Ed. and Dir (with Dorothy Hewett), Big Smoke Books, Sydney 1979–; Founder (with Michael Wilding), Paper Bark Press 1988–; mem. Australian Soc. of Authors, Poetry Soc. of Australia (pres. 1970–80). *Publications:* poetry: Canticles on the Skin 1970, The Rumour 1971, Swamp Riddles 1974, Theatre I–XIX 1976, Cross the Border 1977, Selected Poems 1977, Where I Come From 1979, The Law at Heart's Desire 1982, The Clean Dark 1989, Robert Adamson Selected Poems 1970–1989 1990, Waving to Hart Crane 1994, Mulberry Leaves: New and Selected Poems 1970–2001 2002, Reading the River: Selected Poems 2004; fiction: Zimmer's Essay (with Bruce Hanford) 1974, Wards of the State: An Autobiographical Novella 1992; editor: Australian Writing Now (with Manfred Jurgensen) 1988; contrib. to periodicals. *Honours:* Australia Council Fellowships 1976, 1977, Grace Leven Prize for Poetry 1977, Kenneth Slessor Award 1990, Turnbull-Fox Philips Poetry Prize 1990, C. J. Dennis Prize for Poetry 1990. *Address:* PO Box 59, Brooklyn, NSW 2083, Australia.

ADCOCK, Fleur, OBE, MA, FRSL; British writer; b. 10 Feb. 1934, Papakura, New Zealand; m. 1st Alistair Teariki Campbell 1952 (divorced 1958); two s.; m. 2nd Barry Crump 1962 (divorced 1966). *Education:* Victoria Univ. Wellington. *Career:* Asst Lecturer Univ. of Otago 1958, Asst Librarian 1959–61; with Alexander Turnbull Library 1962; with FCO 1963–79; freelance writer 1979–; Northern Arts Fellowship in Literature, Univs of Newcastle-upon-Tyne and Durham 1979–81; Eastern Arts Fellowship, Univ. of E Anglia 1984; Writer-in-Residence, Univ. of Adelaide 1986; mem. Poetry Soc., Vice-Pres. *Publications:* The Eye of the Hurricane 1964, Tigers 1967, High Tide in the Garden 1971, The Scenic Route 1974, The Inner Harbour 1979, Below Loughrigg 1979, The Oxford Book of Contemporary New Zealand Poetry (ed.) 1982, Selected Poems 1983, The Virgin and the Nightingale: Medieval Latin Poems 1983, Hotspur: A Ballad for Music 1986, The Incident Book 1986, The Faber Book of 20th Century Women's Poetry 1987, Orient Express: Poems by Grete Tartler (trans.) 1989, Time Zones 1991, Letters from Darkness: Poems by Daniela Crasnaru (trans.) 1991, High Primas and the Archpoet (ed. and trans.) 1994, The Oxford Book of Creatures (ed. with Jacqueline Simms) 1995, Looking Back 1997, Poems 1960–2000 2000. *Honours:* Buckland Award 1967, 1979, Jessie MacKay Award 1968, 1972, Cholmondeley Award 1976, NZ Book Award 1984. *Address:* 14 Lincoln Road, London, N2 9DL, England. *Telephone:* (20) 8444-7881.

ADDINGTON, Larry Holbrook, BA, MA, PhD; academic and writer; *Professor of History Emeritus, The Citadel*; b. 16 Nov. 1932, Charlotte, NC,

USA. *Education:* University of North Carolina at Chapel Hill, Duke University. *Career:* Asst Prof., San Jose State College, 1962–64; Asst Prof., 1964–66, Assoc. Prof., 1966–70, Prof., 1970–94, Prof. Emeritus, 1994–, of History, The Citadel; Visiting Prof., Duke University, 1976–77; mem. American Historical Asscn; Society for Military History; National Honor Society; Charter Mem., The Citadel Chapter, 1974. *Publications:* From Moltke to Hitler: The Evolution of German Military Doctrine, 1865–1939, 1966; Firepower and Maneuver: The European Inheritance in the Two World Wars, 1967; Firepower and Maneuver: Historical Case Studies, 1969; The Blitzkrieg Era and the German General Staff, 1865–1941, 1971; The Patterns of War Since the Eighteenth Century, 1984; The Patterns of War Through the Eighteenth Century, 1990; America's War in Vietnam: A Short Narrative History, 2000. Contributions: Encyclopedias, books and scholarly journals. *Honours:* AMI Award for Best Seminal Work, 1984. *Address:* 1341 New Castle Street, Charleston, SC 29407, USA.

ADEBAYO, Diran; Nigerian novelist, critic and journalist; b. 1968, London. *Education:* Malvern Public School, Univ. of Oxford. *Career:* broadcaster for LWT. *Publications:* novels: Some Kind of Black 1996, My Once Upon a Time 2000; contrib. to The Guardian, Daily Mail, Daily Express, The Voice. *Honours:* Saga Prize 1996. *Literary Agent:* c/o Abacus, Little, Brown & Co. (UK), Brettenham House, Lancaster Place, London, WC2E 7EN, England. *Telephone:* (20) 7911-8000. *Fax:* (20) 7911-8100. *Website:* www.timewarnerbooks.co.uk.

ADELBERG, Doris (see Orgel, Doris).

ADHIKARI, Santosh Kumar; College Administrator (retd), Writer and Poet; b. 24 Nov. 1923, West Bengal, India; m. March 1948, one s. two d. *Education:* University of Calcutta, 1943; Diploma, Industrial Finance, Indian Institute of Bankers, Mumbai; Diploma in Management, Indian Institute of Management. *Career:* Principal, Staff College, United Bank of India, Kolkata, retd 1983; Vidyasagar Lecturer, University of Calcutta, 1979; Speaker, Bengal Studies Conference, University of Chicago, 1990; Editor, Spark, 1975–96; mem. Asiatic Society; Akhil Bharat, Bhasa Sahitya Sammelan; Founder, first Sec., Vidyasagar Research Centre; Former Sec., PEN, West Bengal Branch. *Publications:* Vidyasagar: Educator, Reformer and Humanist; Paari (Bengali poetry); Novels, short stories, biographies, poetry collections and anthologies, 1948–2002. Contributions: All India Radio and major journals. *Honours:* Prasad Puraskar for Poetry, 1986; Hon. title of Bharat Bhasa Bhusan, 1991. *Address:* c/o Vidyasagar Research Centre, 81 Raja Basanta Roy Rd, Kolkata, 700029, India.

ADICHIE, Chimamanda Ngozi; Nigerian poet, writer and playwright. *Publications:* novel: Purple Hibiscus 2004; short stories: Lye, The American Embassy, My Mother The Crazy African, You in America 2001; poetry: Decisions 1997; play: For Love of Biafra 1998; contrib. to Prism International, Poetry Magazine, Posse Review, Zoetrope All-Story, Allegheny Review of Undergraduate Literature, Iowa Review. *Honours:* Caine Prize for African Writing 2002. *Address:* c/o Spectrum Books, African Books Collective, The Jam Factory, 27 Park End Street, Oxford, OX1 1HU, England. *E-mail:* RAdichie@aol.com.

ADICKES, Sandra, BA, MA, PhD; academic and writer; *Professor Emerita, Winona State University*; b. 14 July 1933, New York, NY, USA; three d. *Education:* Douglass Coll., Hunter Coll., CUNY, New York Univ. *Career:* Prof. of English 1988–98, Prof. Emerita 1998–, Winona State Univ. *Publications:* The Social Quest 1991, Legends of Good Women (novel) 1992, To Be Young Was Very Heaven: Women in New York Before the First World War 1997; contrib. to reference books and journals. *Address:* 19 David Court, Dayton, NJ 08810, USA. *E-mail:* s.adickes@att.net.

ADLER, Carole Schwerdtfeger, BA, MS; writer; b. 23 Feb. 1932, Long Island, NY, USA; m. Arnold R. Adler 1952; three s. *Education:* Hunter College, CUNY, Russell Sage Coll. *Career:* mem. Soc. of Children's Book Writers, Authors' Guild. *Publications:* The Magic of the Glits, 1979; The Silver Coach, 1979; In Our House Scott is My Brother, 1980; The Cat That Was Left Behind, 1981; Down By the River, 1981; Shelter on Blue Barns Road, 1981; Footsteps on the Stairs, 1982; The Evidence That Wasn't There, 1982; The Once in a While Hero, 1982; Some Other Summer, 1982; The Shell Lady's Daughter, 1983; Get Lost Little Brother, 1983; Roadside Valentine, 1983; Shadows on Little Reef Bay, 1984; Fly Free, 1984; Binding Ties, 1985; With Westie and the Tin Man, 1985; Good-Bye Pink Pig, 1985; Split Sisters, 1986; Kiss the Clown, 1986; Carly's Buck, 1987; Always and Forever Friends, 1988; If You Need Me, 1988; Eddie's Blue Winged Dragon, 1988; One Sister Too Many, 1989; The Lump in the Middle, 1989; Help Pink Pig!, 1990; Ghost Brother, 1990; Mismatched Summer, 1991; A Tribe for Lexi, 1991; Tuna Fish Thanksgiving, 1992; Daddy's Climbing Tree, 1993; Willie, the Frog Prince, 1994; That Horse Whiskey, 1994; Youn Hee and Me, 1995; Court Yard Cat, 1995; What's to be Scared of, Suki?, 1996; More Than a Horse, 1997; Her Blue Straw Hat, 1997; Not Just A Summer Crush, 1998; Winning, 1999; One Unhappy Horse, 2001. *Honours:* William Allen White Award, 1980; Golden Kite Award, 1980; American Library Asscn Best Young Adult Book, 1984; Children's Book Award, Child Study Committee, 1986; IRA Children's Selections, 1987, 1991; ASPCA Henry Berg Award, 2001. *Address:* 7041 N Cathedral Rock Place, Tucson, AZ 85718, USA.

ADLER, Margot Susanna; Journalist, Radio Producer and Talk Show Host; b. 16 April 1946, Little Rock, AR, USA. *Education:* BA, University of California, Berkeley, 1968; MS, Columbia School of Journalism, 1970; Nieman Fellow, Harvard University, 1982. *Career:* mem. Authors' Guild; American Federation of Radio and Television Artists. *Publications:* Drawing Down the Moon: Witches, Druids, Goddess-Worshippers and Other Pagans in America Today, 1979; Heretic's Heart: A Journey Through Spirit and Revolution, 1997. *Literary Agent:* Jane Rotrosen. *Address:* 333 Central Park W, New York, NY 10025, USA.

ADLER, Renata; Writer; b. 19 Oct. 1938, Milan, Italy. *Education:* BA, Bryn Mawr College, 1959; Dd'ES, Sorbonne University, Paris, 1961; MA, Harvard University, 1962; Law Degree, Yale University. *Career:* Writer-Reporter, New Yorker magazine, 1962–68, 1970–82; Fellow, Trubull College, Yale University, 1969–72; Assoc. Prof. of Theatre and Cinema, Hunter College, CUNY, 1972–73; mem. American Acad. and Institute of Arts and Letters; PEN. *Publications:* Toward a Radical Middle: Fourteen Pieces of Reporting and Criticism, 1969; A Year in the Dark: Journal of a Film Critic, 1968–69, 1970; Speedboat (novel), 1976; Pitch Dark (novel), 1983; Reckless Disregard: Westmoreland v. CBS et al: Sharon v. Time, 1986; Politics and Media: Essays, 1988; Gone: The Last Days of the New Yorker, 1999; Private Capacity, 2000. Contributions: many periodicals. *Honours:* Guggenheim Fellowship, 1973–74; First Prize, O. Henry Short Story Awards, 1974; American Acad. and Institute of Arts and Letters Award, 1976; Ernest Hemingway Prize, 1976.

ADLER, Warren; Author; b. 16 Dec. 1927, New York, NY, USA; m. Sonia Kline, 6 May 1951, three s. *Education:* BA, New York University, 1947; New School University, New York. *Career:* Ed., Queens Post, Forest Hills, NY; Pres., advertising and public relations agency, Washington, DC, 1959–78; mem. Century Asscn; Lotos Club; PEN; Authors' Guild. *Publications:* Undertow, 1974; Options, 1974; Banquet Before Dawn, 1976; The Henderson Equation, 1976; Trans-Siberian Express, 1977; The Sunset Gang, 1978; The Casanova Embrace, 1978; Blood Ties, 1979; Natural Enemies, 1980; The War of the Roses, 1981; American Quartet, 1982; American Sextet, 1983; Random Hearts, 1984; Twilight Child, 1989; Immaculate Deception, 1991; Senator Love, 1991; Private Lies, 1992; The Witch of Watergate, 1992; The Ties That Bind, 1994; Never Too Late for Love, 1996; Jackson Hole, Uneasy Eden, 1997; Mourning Glory, 1997; Cult: A Novel of Brainwashing and Death, 2002. *Address:* 45 Huckleberry Dr., Jackson, WY 83001; 300 E 56th St, New York, NY 10022, USA.

ADNAN, Etel; Poet, Writer, Painter and Tapestry Designer; b. 24 Feb. 1925, Beirut, Lebanon. *Education:* Sorbonne, University of Paris; University of California, Berkeley; Harvard University. *Career:* Teacher, Philosophy of Art and Humanities, Dominican College, San Rafael, CA, 1958–72; Cultural Ed., Al-Safa, Lebanon, 1972–79, L'Orient-Le Jour, Lebanon, 1974–79; Paintings exhibited around the world; mem. Poetry Center, San Francisco. *Publications:* Poetry: Moonshots, 1966; Five Senses for One Death, 1971; From A to Z, 1982; The Indian Never Had a Horse and Other Poems, 1985; The Arab Apocalypse, 1989; The Spring Flowers Own and the Manifestations of the Voyage, 1990. Novel: Sitt Marie-Rose, 1982. Other: Journey to Mount Tamalpais, 1986; Of Cities and Women, 1993; Paris, When It's Naked, 1993; There, 1995. Contributions: poems and short stories in many publications. *Honours:* France-Pays-Arabes Prize, 1978. *Address:* 35 Marie St, Sausalito, CA 94965, USA.

ADOFF, Arnold; Poet, Writer and Literary Agent; b. 16 July 1935, New York, NY, USA; m. Virginia Hamilton, 19 March 1960, two c. *Education:* BA, City College, CUNY, 1956; Columbia University, 1956–58; New School for Social Research Poetry Workshops, New York, 1965–67. *Career:* Teacher, New York City Public Schools, 1957–69; Literary Agent, Yellow Springs, OH, 1977–; Distinguished Visiting Prof., Queens College, CUNY, 1986–87; Guest Lecturer in many US venues. *Publications:* Poetry: Black Is Brown Is Tan, 1973; Make a Circle Keep Us In: Poems for a Good Day, 1975; Big Sister Tells Me That I'm Black, 1976; Tornado!: Poems, 1977; Under the Early Morning Trees, 1978; Where Wild Willie, 1978; Eats: Poems, 1979; I Am the Running Girl, 1979; Friend Dog, 1980; OUTside INside Poems, 1981; Today We Are Brother and Sister, 1981; Birds, 1982; All the Colors of the Race, 1982; The Cabbages Are Chasing the Rabbits, 1985; Sports Pages, 1986; Flamboyan, 1988; Greens, 1988; Chocolate Dreams, 1989; Hard to Be Six, 1990; In for Winter, Out for Spring, 1991. Other: Malcolm X (biog.), 1970; MA nDA LA (picture book), 1971. Editor: I Am the Darker Brother: An Anthology of Modern Poems by Negro Americans, 1968; Black on Black: Commentaries by Negro Americans, 1968; City in All Directions: An Anthology of Modern Poems by Black Americans, 1970; Brothers and Sisters: Modern Stories by Black Americans, 1970; It Is the Poem Singing into Your Eyes: An Anthology of New Young Poets, 1971; The Poetry of Black America: An Anthology of the 20th Century, 1973; My Black Me: A Beginning Book of Black Poetry, 1974; Celebrations: A New Anthology of Black American Poetry, 1978. Contributions: articles and reviews in periodicals. *Honours:* Children's Book of the Year Citations, Child Study Asscn of America, 1968, 1969, 1986; American Library Asscn Notable Book Awards, 1968, 1970, 1971, 1972, 1979; Best Children's Book Citations, School Library Journal, 1971, 1973; Notable Children's Trade Book Citation, Children's Book Council-National Council for Social Studies, 1974; Jane Addams Peace Asscn Special Certificate, 1983; Children's Choice Citation, International Reading Asscn-

Children's Book Council, 1985; National Council of Teachers of English Poetry Award, 1988. *Address:* Arnold Adoff Agency, PO Box 293, Yellow Springs, OH 45387, USA.

ADRIAN, Frances (see Polland, Madelaine Angela).

AFRICANO, Lillian, (Nora Ashby, Lila Cook, Jessica March); Author and Columnist; b. 7 June 1935, Paterson, NJ, USA; m. (divorced); two s. one d. *Education:* BA, summa cum laude, Barnard College, 1957; Columbia University Graduate School, 1958. *Career:* Arts Ed., The Villager, 1971; News Ed., Penthouse/Forum, 1973; Columnist, New York Times Syndicate, 1977, Woman's World, 1980; mem. Drama Desk, vice-pres., sec.; Outer Critics' Circle; American Society of Journalists and Authors; Authors' Guild. *Publications:* Businessman's Guide to the Middle East, 1977; Doctor's Walking Book (co-author), 1980; Something Old, Something New, 1983; Passions, 1985; Gone From Breezy Hill (as Nora Ashby), 1985; Illusions (as Jessica March), 1988; Consenting Adults (as Lila Cook), 1988; Temptations (as Jessica March), 1989; Obsessions, 1990. Contributions: New York Times; New York News; Reader's Digest; Harper's Bazaar; Woman's Day; Woman's World; National Review; Nation.

AGARD, John; Guyanan poet, children's writer and editor; b. 21 June 1949; pnr Grace Nichols. *Career:* sub-ed. and feature writer, Guyana Sunday Chronicle newspaper; moved to England 1977; touring lecturer with Commonwealth Inst.; writer-in-residence, South Bank Centre London 1993; poet-in-residence, BBC Educ. Dept 1997–98. *Publications include:* Shoot Me with Flowers 1974, Letters for Lettie and Other Stories 1979, Dig Away Two-Hole Tim 1981, Man to Pan (Casa de las Américas Prize, Cuba) 1982, I Din Do Nuttin and Other Poems 1983, Limbo Dancer in Dark Glasses 1983, Livingroom 1983, Mangoes and Bullets: Selected and New Poems 1972-84 1985, Say it Again, Granny! 1986, Lend Me Your Wings 1987, Life Doesn't Frighten Me At All (ed.) 1989, Go Noah Go! 1990, Laughter is an Egg 1990, The Calypso Alphabet 1990, No Hickory, No Dockory, No Dock (with Grace Nichols) 1991, The Emperor's Dan-dan 1992, A Stone's Throw from Embankment: The South Bank Collection 1993, The Great Snakeskin (play for children) 1993, Grandfather's Old Bruk-a-Down Car 1994, Oriki and the Monster Who Hated Balloons 1994, The Monster Who Loved Cameras 1994, The Monster Who Loved Telephones 1994, The Monster Who Loved Toothbrushes 1994, A Caribbean Dozen (co-ed.) 1994, Poems in My Earphone (ed.) 1995, Eat a Poem, Wear a Poem 1995, Get Back, Pimple! 1996, Why is the Sky? (ed.) 1996, We Animals Would Like a Word With You (Bronze Award, Nestle Smarties Book Prize) 1996, From the Devil's Pulpit 1997, Brer Rabbit: The Great Tug-o-War 1998, Points of View with Professor Peekabo 2000, Weblines 2000, A Child's Year of Stories and Poems (with Michael Rosen and Robert Frost) 2000, Hello New: New Poems for a New Century (ed.) 2000, Come Back to Me My Boomerang (with Lydia Monks) 2001, Number Parade: Number Poems from 0–100 (with Jackie Kay, Grace Nichols, Nick Toczek and Michael Rosen) 2002, Under The Moon and Over the Sea (co-ed.) 2002, Einstein, The Girl Who Hated Maths 2002, Hello H2O 2003; contrib. to Caribbean Poetry Now 1984, The Penguin Book of Caribbean Verse (ed.) 1986, Border Country: Poems in Progress 1991, Grandchildren of Albion 1992, The Heinemann Book of Caribbean Poetry 1992, Another Day on your Foot and I Would Have Died 1996. *Honours:* Arts Council Bursary 1989, Paul Hamlyn Award for Poetry 1997, Cholmondley Award 2004. *Address:* c/o Bloodaxe Books Ltd, Highgreen, Tarset, Northumberland NE48 1RP, England. *Website:* www.bloodaxebooks.com.

AGBOLUAJE, Oladipo (Dipo), PhD; Nigerian playwright; b. UK. *Education:* Open Univ. *Career:* involved in Eclipse Writers' Lab. *Plays:* Early Morning 2003, Royal Phone 2004, Mother Courage and her Children (adaptation) 2004. *Address:* c/o Oval House Theatre, 52–54 Kennington Oval, London, SE11 5SW, England. *Website:* www.ovalhouse.com.

AGEE, Jonis; writer, poet and academic; b. 31 May 1943, Omaha, NE, USA; m. Paul McDonough; one d. *Education:* BA, University of Iowa, 1966; MA, 1969, PhD, 1976, SUNY at Binghamton. *Career:* Teacher, College of St Catherine, St Paul, Minnesota, 1975–95; Literary Consultant, Walker Arts Center, Minneapolis, 1978–84; Adjunct Teacher, Macalester College, St Paul, Minnesota, 1980–88; Teacher and Ed., Literary Post Program for Senior Citizen Writers, 1986–89; Prof., University of Michigan, 1995–; many poetry readings; mem. Literary Guild. *Publications:* Houses (poem), 1976; Mercury (poems), 1981; Two Poems, 1982; Border Crossings (ed.), 1984; Stiller's Pond (ed.), 1988; Bend This Heart (short stories), 1989; Pretend We've Never Met (short stories), 1989; Sweet Eyes (novel), 1991; Strange Angels (novel), 1993; A .38 Special and a Broken Heart (short stories), 1995; South of Resurrection (novel), 1997; Acts of Love on Indigo Road: New and Selected Stories, 2003. Contributions: anthologies and periodicals. *Honours:* Minnesota State Arts Board Award, 1977; National Endowment for the Arts Fellowship, 1978; Loft-McKnight Awards, 1987, 1991. *Address:* 503 S First Street, Ann Arbor, MI 48103, USA.

AGUALUSA, José Eduardo; novelist and poet; b. 13 Dec. 1960, Huambo, Angola. *Education:* Instituto Superior de Agronomia, Lisbon, Portugal. *Career:* newspaper and radio journalist, journal Público; mem. União dos Escritores Angolanos. *Television:* A Hora das Cigarras (series, Antena 1, RDP Africa). *Publications:* A Conjura 1989, D. Nicolau Água-Rosada e outras estorias verdadeiras e inverosimeis (short stories) 1991; Coração dos Bosques (poems) 1991, A Feira dos Assombrados 1992, Lisboa Africana (non-fiction, with others) 1993, Estação das Chuvas 1996, Nação Crioula (trans. as Creole) 1997; contrib. Pais e Filhos magazine. *Honours:* Grand Prize for Literature, Portugal 1997. *Address:* c/o Arcadia Books Ltd, 15–16 Nassau Street, London, W1N 7RF, England. *E-mail:* agualusa@hotlink.com.br. *Website:* www.agualusa.com.

AGUIRRE, Eugenio; Writer; b. 31 July 1944, México, DF, Mexico; m. 6 Aug. 1971; one s. one d. *Education:* BA, Law, MA, Literature, Universidad Nacional Autónoma de México. *Career:* Lecturer, University of Lawrence, KS, USA; Wabash College, USA; Writers' Asscn of Panama; several bank and government offices, Mexico; mem. Past pres., Asociación de Escritores de México; Board, Sociedad General de Escritores de México; International PEN Club. *Publications:* Fiction: Jesucristo Perez, 1973; Pajar de Imaginación, 1975; El caballero de las espadas, 1978; Gonzalo Guerrero, 1980; El testamento del diablo, 1981; En el campo, 1982; Cadaver exquisito, 1984; El rumor que llego del mar, 1985; Pájaros de fuego, 1986; Un mundo de niño lleno de mar, 1986; Pasos de sangre, 1988; Amor de mis amores, 1988; De cuerpo entero, 1991; El guerrero del sur, 1991; Cosas de ángeles y otros cuentos, 1992; Los niños de colores, 1993; Elena o el laberinto de la lujuria, 1994; El demonio me visita, 1994; La fascinación de la bestia, 1994; Desierto ardiente, 1995; Ruiz Massieu: el mejor enemigo, 1995. Contributions: Mexican and foreign publications. *Honours:* Great Silver Medal, International Acad. of Lutece, Paris, 1981. *Address:* Buhos no. 32, Fracc Loma de Guadalupe, México, DF, 01720, Mexico.

AHERN, Cecelia; Irish novelist; b. 1981. *Education:* Griffith Coll. Dublin. *Career:* mem. of pop group Shimma 1999–2000. *Publications:* novel: P.S. I Love You 2004. *Literary Agent:* c/o HarperCollins Publishers Ltd, 77–85 Fulham Palace Road, London, W6 8JB, England. *Telephone:* (20) 8741-7070. *Fax:* (20) 8307-4440. *Website:* www.harpercollins.co.uk.

AHLMARK, Per, BA; Swedish politician, journalist, novelist and poet; *Adviser, Elie Wiesel Foundation for Humanity*; b. 15 Jan. 1939, Stockholm; m. 1st (divorced); one s. one d.; m. 2nd Bibi Andersson 1978 (divorced); m. 3rd Lilian Edström; one s. *Career:* Leader of Young Liberals 1960–62; columnist for Expressen 1961–95, for Dagens Nyheter 1997–; mem. Parl. 1967–78; Deputy Chair. Swedish-Israeli Friendship Org. 1970–97; mem. Council of Europe 1971–76; mem. Royal Comms. on Literature, Human Rights, etc. in the 1970s; Leader, Folkpartiet (Liberal Party) 1975–78; Deputy Prime Minister and Minister of Labour 1976–78; Deputy Chair. Martin Luther King Fund 1968–73; Chair. Swedish Film Inst. 1978–81; Founder and Deputy Chair. Swedish Comm. Against Antisemitism 1983–95; Adviser to Elie Wiesel Foundation for Humanity, New York 1987–; mem. UN Watch, Geneva 1993–; mem. Acad. Universelle des Cultures, Paris; Fellow Wissenschaftskolleg zu Berlin 1998–99. *Publications:* An Open Sore, Tyranny and the Left, many political books, essays and numerous articles, three books of poetry, one novel. *Honours:* Hon. Fellow, Hebrew Univ., Jerusalem 1992; Defender of Jerusalem Award, New York 1986. *Address:* Folkungag 61, 11622 Stockholm, Sweden.

AHLSEN, Leopold; Author; b. 12 Jan. 1927, Munich, Germany; m. Ruth Gehwald, 1964, one s. one d. *Publications:* 13 plays, 23 radio plays, 42 television plays, five novels. *Honours:* Gerhart Hauptmann Prize; Schiller-Forderungspreis; Golden Bildschirm; Horspielpreis der Kriegsblinden; Silver Nymph of Monaco. *Address:* Waldschulstr 58, 81827 Munich, Germany.

AHMAD, Datuk Shahnon; Author; b. 1933, Sik, Kedah, Malaysia. *Education:* BA, Australia, 1971; MA, Univ. of Science, Penang, 1975. *Career:* Head, Islamic Centre, Univ. of Science, Penang, –1996; taught literature, Dean, School of Humanities, Univ. of Science, Penang, –1999. *Publications:* Anjing-anjing, 1964; Debu merah, 1965; Terdedah, 1965; Rentong (Rope of Ash), 1965; Ranjau Sepanjang Jalan (No Harvest but a Thorn), 1966; Protes, 1967; Menteri, 1967; Perdana, 1969; Srengenge, 1973; Sampah, 1974; Kemelut, 1977; Selasai sudah, 1977; Seluang menolak Baung, 1978; Penglibatan dalam puisi, 1978; Gubahan novel, 1979; The Third Notch and Other Stories, 1980; Kesusasteraan dan etika Islam, 1981; Al-syiqaq, 1985; Tok Guru, 1988; Ummi dan Abang Syeikhul, 1992; Pongang sastera: gema karya kreatif dan kesannya terhadap khalayak, 1995; Shit, 1999. *Honours:* National Literary Award, 1982; Malaysian National Laureate, 1984. *Address:* c/o School of Humanities, Universiti Sains Malaysia, Minden, 11800 Penang, Malaysia.

AHRENS, Bridget, BA, MPh, MFA; writer; b. 9 Jan. 1958, Buffalo, NY, USA; m. 1981; one s. one d. *Education:* SUNY, University of California, Vermont College. *Career:* Instructor, Fiction and Non-Fiction Writing, Lebanon College, 1990–; Assoc. Ed., AIDS and Society: An International Research and Policy Bulletin; mem. Poets and Writers. *Publications:* Our Lady of the Keyboard, 1989; The Problems and Pitfalls of Writing about Sex, 1989; A Woman's Place is Intuition, 1990; The Art of Baking, The Politics of Love, 1991; The Eye of the Needle, 1991; Atlas's Revenge, 1992. *Honours:* Fellowship, Vermont Council on the Arts, 1992.

AICHINGER, Ilse; Novelist and Playwright; b. 1 Nov. 1921, Vienna, Austria. *Education:* University of Vienna, 1945–48. *Career:* Mem. of Grupe 47, 1951–. *Publications:* Die Grössere Hoffnung, 1948; Rede Unter dem Galgen, 1953; Eliza, Eliza, 1965; Selected Short Stories and Dialogue, 1966; Nachricht und Tag: Erzählungen, 1970; Schlechte Worter, 1976; Meine Sprache und Ich Erzählungen, 1978; Spiegelesichte: Erzählungen und

Dialoge, 1979. Plays, Zu Keiner Stunde, 1957, 1980; Besuch im Pfarrhaus, 1961; Auckland: 4 Horspiele, 1969; Knopfe, 1978; Weisse Chrysanthemum, 1979; Radio Plays, Selected Poetry and Prose of Ilse Aichinger, 1983; Collected Works, eight vols, 1991. *Honours:* Belgian Europe Festival Prize, 1987; Town of Solothurn Prize, 1991. *Address:* c/o Fischer Verlag, PO Box 700480, 60008 Frankfurt, Germany.

AIDOO, (Christina) Ama Ata; writer, poet and playwright; b. 1942, Abeadzi Kyiakor, Gold Coast, Ghana; one d. *Education:* Univ. of Ghana. *Career:* Lecturer, Cape Coast Univ., 1970–73; Consultant Prof., Phelps-Stokes Fund Ethnic Studies Program, Washington, 1974–75; Consultant at universities, academies and research institutes in Africa, Europe and the USA; Minister of Education, 1982–83; Chair., African Regional Panel of the Commonwealth Writers' Prize, 1990, 1991; mem. Fellow, Institute for African Studies. *Publications:* Fiction: No Sweetness Here (short stories), 1970; Our Sister Killjoy or Reflections from a Black-Eyed Squint, 1977; The Eagle and the Chicken and Other Stories (children's), 1987; Changes: A Love Story, 1991; The Girl Who Can and Other Stories, 1999. Poetry: Someone Talking to Sometime, 1985; Birds and Other Poems, 1987. Plays: The Dilemma of a Ghost, 1965; Anowa, 1970. Contributions: numerous magazines and journals. *Honours:* Commonwealth Writers Prize, for the Africa region, 1993. *Address:* PO Box 4930, Harare, Zimbabwe. *Telephone:* (4) 731901.

AIRA, César; Argentine novelist, essayist and dramatist; b. 23 Feb. 1949, Coronel Pringles; m.; two c. *Career:* fmr lecturer, Universidad de Buenos Aires, Universidad de Rosario. *Plays:* El mensajero 1996, Madre e hijo 1993. *Publications:* novels: Moreira 1975, Ema, la cautiva 1981, La luz argentina 1983, Las ovejas 1984, Canto Castrato 1984, Una novela china 1987, Los fantasmas 1990, El bautismo 1991, La liebre 1991, Embalse 1992, La guerra de los gimnasios 1992, La prueba 1992, El llanto 1992, El volante 1992, Cómo me hice monja 1993, El infinito 1994, La costurera y el viento 1994, Los misterios de Rosario 1994, La fuente 1995, Los dos payasos 1995, Dante y Reina, Abeja 1996, La serpiente 1997, El Mago, Cumpleaños, La villa, La pastilla de hormona, El juego de los mundos, El Sueño 1998, Las curas milagrosas del Dr Aira 1998, La mendiga 1998, El congreso de literatura 1999, Un episodio en la vida del pintor viajero 2000, Fragmento de un diario en los Alpes 2002, El tilo 2003; short stories: El vestido rosa 1984, Cecil Taylor, La trompeta de mimbre 1998; essays: Copi 1991, Nouvelles impressions du Petit Maroc 1991, Taxol: precedido de Duchamp en México y La broma 1997, Alejandra Pizarnik 1998, Las tres fechas 2001, Edward Lear 2004; non-fiction: Diccionario de autores latinoamericanos; contrib. to numerous periodicals and books world-wide. *Address:* c/o Beatriz Viterbo Editora, España 1150 (2000), Rosario, Argentina. *E-mail:* info@beatrizviterbo.com.ar. *Website:* www.beatrizviterbo.com.ar.

AKAEKE ONWUEME, Tess (see Onwueme, Osonye Tess).

AKAVIA, Miriam; writer and translator; b. 20 Nov. 1927, Kraków, Poland; m. 1946; two d. *Publications:* Adolescence of Autumn, 1975; Ha mechir, 1978; Galia & Miklosh, 1982; Karmi Sheli, 1984; Adventure on a Bus, 1986; Ma Vigne A Moi, 1992; The Other Way: The Story of a Group (in Hebrew), 1992; An End To Childhood (in English), 1995, (in Polish), 1996; Jurek and Ania, 2000; Lomhullas, 2000; Short Stories, 2000. Contributions: various literary magazines. *Honours:* Gold Medal, Poland, 1991; Prime Minister's Prize, Israel, 1993; Wizo Prize, Tel-Aviv, 1998. *Address:* PO Box 53050, 61530 Tel-Aviv, Israel.

AKENSON, Donald Harman; Prof. of History, Writer and Ed.; b. 22 May 1941, Minneapolis, MN, USA. *Education:* BA, Yale College, 1962; MEd, 1963, PhD, 1967, Harvard University. *Career:* Allston Burr Senior Tutor, Dunster House, Harvard College, 1966–67; Asst Prof. of History, Yale College, 1967–70; Assoc. Prof. of History, 1970–74, Prof. of History, 1974–, Queen's University, Kingston, ON; Senior Ed., McGill-Queen's University Press, 1982–; Beamish Research Prof., Institute of Irish Studies, University of Liverpool, 1998–; various visiting professorships and lectureships. *Publications:* The Irish Education Experiment: The National System of Education in the Nineteenth Century, 1969; The Changing Uses of the Liberal Arts College: An Essay in Recent Educational History (with L. F. Stevens), 1969; The Church of Ireland: Ecclesiastical Reform and Revolution, 1800–1885, 1971; Education and Enmity: The Control of Schooling in Northern Ireland, 1920–50, 1973; The United States and Ireland, 1973; A Mirror to Kathleen's Face: Education in Independent Ireland, 1922–60, 1975; Local Poets and Social History: James Orr, Bard of Ballycarry (with W. H. Crawford), 1977; Between Two Revolutions: Islandmagee, Co Antrim, 1798–1920, 1979; A Protestant in Purgatory: Richard Whately, Archbishop of Dublin, 1981; The Irish in Ontario: A Study in Rural History, 1984; Being Had: Historians, Evidence and the Irish in North America, 1985; Small Differences: Irish Catholics and Irish Protestants, 1815–1921, An International Perspective, 1988; Half the World From Home: Perspectives on the Irish in New Zealand, 1990; Occasional Papers on the Irish in South Africa, 1991; God's Peoples: Covenant and Land in South Africa, Israel and Ulster, 1992; Colonies: Canada to 1867 (with others), 1992; The Irish Diaspora: A Primer, 1993; Conor: A Biography of Conor Cruise O'Brien (two vols), 1994; If the Irish Ran the World: Montserrat, 1630–1730, 1997; Surpassing Wonder: The Invention of the Bible and the Talmuds, 1998; Saint Saul: A Skeleton Key to the Historical Jesus, 2000. Fiction: The Lazar House Notebooks, 1981: Brotherhood Week in Belfast, 1984; The Orangeman: The Life and Times of Igle Gowan, 1986; The Edgerston Audit, 1987; At Face Value: The Life and Times of Eliza McCormack/John White, 1990. Contributions: learned books and journals. *Honours:* Fellow, Royal Society of Canada, 1976; Guggenheim Fellowship, 1984–85; Chalmers Prize, 1985; Landon Prize, 1987; FRHistS, 1988; Grawemeyer Award for Ideas Improving World Order, 1993; Trillium Prize, 1995; Hon. doctorates, McMaster University, 1995, Lethbridge University, 1996, University of Guelph, 2000; Molson Prize Laureate, 1996. *Address:* c/o Dept of History, Queen's University, Kingston, ON K7L 3N6, Canada.

AKERS, Alan Burt (see Bulmer, Henry Kenneth).

AKMAKJIAN, Alan Paul; University Teacher, Poet and Writer; b. 18 July 1948, Highland Park, MI, USA. *Education:* BA, 1973, MA, 1974, Eastern Michigan University; PhD, University of Texas at Dallas, St John's University, New York, Wayne State University, Detroit, 1979; MA, California State University, San Francisco, 1991. *Career:* Teacher, California State University, San Francisco, 1985, St John's University, New York City, 1994–95, University of Texas at Dallas, 1995–; Instructor, Poets in the Schools, CA, 1986–91; mem. Acad. of American Poets; Associated Writing Programs; MLA; PEN; Poetry Society of America. *Publications:* Treading Pages of Water, 1992; Let the Sun Go, 1992; California Picnic, 1992; Grounded Angels, 1993; Breaking the Silence, 1994; California Picnic and Other Poems, 1997. Contributions: anthologies, journals, reviews and magazines. *Honours:* National Endowment for the Arts Grant, 1984; California Arts Council Grant, 1984; St John's University Fellowship, 1994–95; University of Texas Fellowships, 1994–95, 1995–96, 1996–97; Texas Public Educational Grant, 1996–97. *Address:* 2200 Waterview Pkwy, Apt 2134, Richardson, TX 75080, USA.

AKSYONOV, Vasily Pavlovich; Author; b. 20 Aug. 1932, Kazan, Russia; m. 1st Kira Mendeleva, 1957; m. 2nd Maya Karmen, 1979, one s. *Education:* Graduated, Leningrad Medical Institute, 1956. *Career:* Founding Co-Ed., Metropol journal, 1979; Exiled to USA, 1980; Writer-in-Residence, University of Michigan, University of Southern California, George Washington University; returned to Russia, 1992; Lecturer, George Mason University, 1995–; mem. Union of Russian Writers. *Publications:* Colleagues, 1960; Starry Ticket, 1961; Oranges from Morocco, 1963; Catapult, 1964; Time, My Friend, Time, 1964; Always on Sale, 1965; The Empty Barrels, 1968; Love of Electricity, 1971; My Grandpa is a Monument, 1972; Samson and Samsoness, 1972; Around the Clock Non-Stop, 1976; Your Murderer, 1977; The Steel Bird and Other Stories, 1979; The Four Temperaments, 1979; Our Golden Ironware, 1980; The Burn, 1980; The Island of Crimea, 1981; An Aristopheana, 1981; Paper Landscape, 1983; The Right to the Island, 1983; The Heron, 1984; Say 'Cheese', 1985; In Search of a Genre, 1986; The Blues with a Russian Accent (screenplay), 1987; In Search of Melancholy Baby, 1987; Our Garden Fronburg, 1989; The Day of the First Snowfall, 1990; Capital Displacement, 1990; The Yolk of an Egg, 1990; Rendezvous, 1991; The Moscow Saga, 1993; The Negative of a Positive Hero, 1996; New Sweet Style, 1998. *Address:* c/o Random House Inc, 201 E 50th St, New York, NY 10022, USA.

AKUNIN, Boris; Russian (b. Georgian) writer; b. (Grigory Shalvovich Chkhartishvili), 1956, Georgia. *Education:* Moscow State Univ. *Career:* Deputy Ed.-in-Chief Inostrannaya Literatura (magazine) –2000; Ed.-in-Chief Anthology of Japanese Literature (20 vols); Chair. Exec. Bd Pushkin Library (Soros Foundation). *Publications:* Azazel, Leviafan, The Turkish Gambit, Death of Achilles, Special Errands, Counsellor of State, Coronation or the Last of the Novels 1998–2000, Pelageya and the White Bulldog 2000, Lovers of Death (two vols) 2000, Tales for Idiots (essays), The Writer and Suicide (non-fiction) 1999, The Winter Queen 2003, Murder on the Leviathan 2004, contrib. to numerous reviews and criticisms, numerous translations of Japanese, American and English literature. *Address:* Poema Press Publications, Zvezdny blvd 23, 129075 Moscow, Russia (Office). *Telephone:* (095) 925-42-05 (Home). *E-mail:* erikavoronova@mtu-net.ru (Office). *Website:* www.akunin.ru (Office).

ALBAHARI, David; Serbian writer; b. 1948, Pec, Yugoslavia. *Career:* emigrated to Canada 1994; Markin-Flanagan distinguished writer-in-residence, Univ. of Calgary 1995–96; mem. Federation of Jewish Communities of Yugoslavia (pres. 1991). *Publications:* novels: Sudija Dimitrijevic 1978, Cink 1988 (trans. as Tsing 1997), Kratka knjiga 1993, Snezni covek 1995, Mamac 1996 (NIN Prize; trans. as Bait 2001), Mrak 1997, Gec i Majer 1998 (trans. as Götz and Meyer 2004); other: Porodicno vreme 1978, Obicne price 1978, Opis smrti 1982 (Ivo Andric Prize), Fras u supi 1984, Jednostavnost 1988, Pelerina 1993 (Stanislav Winaver Prize), Izabrane price 1994, Words are Something Else (trans.) 1996, Neobicne price 1999. *Address:* c/o Northwestern University Press, 629 Noyes Street, Evanston, IL 60208-4210, USA.

ALBANY, James (see Rae, Hugh Crauford).

ALBEE, Edward Franklin, III; American playwright; b. 12 March 1928, Virginia. *Education:* Lawrenceville and Choate Schools, Washington, Valley Forge Military Acad., Paand Trinity Coll., Hartford. *Career:* Comm. Chair. Brandeis Univ. Creative Arts Awards 1983, 1984; Pres. The Edward F. Albee Foundation Inc.; Distinguished Prof., Univ. of Houston 1988–; mem. Dramatists Guild Council, PEN America, The American Acad., Nat. Inst. of Arts and Letters. *Plays include:* The Zoo Story (Vernon Rice Award

1960) 1958, The Death of Bessie Smith 1959, The Sandbox 1959, Fam and Yam 1959, The American Dream (Foreign Press Asscn Award 1961) 1960, Who's Afraid of Virginia Woolf? (Drama Critics' Circle Award for Best Play) 1961–62, stage adaptation of The Ballad of the Sad Café (Carson McCuller) 1963, Tiny Alice 1964, Malcolm (from novel by James Purdy) 1965, A Delicate Balance (Pulitzer Prize 1966) 1966, Everything in the Garden (after a play by Giles Cooper) 1967, Box 1968, Quotations from Chairman Mao Tse-tung 1968, All Over 1971, Seascape (Pulitzer Prize 1975) 1974, Listening 1975, Counting the Ways 1976, The Lady from Dubuque 1977–79, Lolita (adapted from Vladimir Nabokov) 1979, The Man Who Had Three Arms 1981, Finding the Sun 1982, Marriage Play 1986–87, Three Tall Women (Pulitzer Prize 1994) 1990–91, Fragments 1993, The Play About the Baby 1996, The Goat, or, Who is Sylvia? 2000, Occupant 2001. *Honours:* Tony Awards 1963, 1996, Gold Medal, American Acad. and Inst. of Arts and Letters 1980; inducted, Theater Hall of Fame 1985, Kennedy Center Award 1996, Nat. Medal of Arts 1996. *Address:* 14 Harrison Street, New York, NY 10013; 320 Old Montauk Highway, Montauk, NY 11954, USA.

ALBERT, Bill; Writer and Economist; b. 16 Dec. 1942, New York, NY, USA; m. 1st Ada Rapoport (divorced 1990); m. 2nd Gillian Ann Albert 15 Sept. 1990; one s. two d. *Education:* BA, University of California, Berkeley, 1964; PhD, LSE, 1968. *Career:* Reader in Economic History, University of East Anglia, Norwich, England, 1968–93. *Publications:* Fiction: Et Rodriguez alors?, 1990; Desert Blues, 1994; Castle Garden, 1996. *Literary Agent:* Lora Fountain, Agence Littéraire Lora Fountain, 7 rue de Belfort, 75011 Paris, France.

ALBERT, Gábor; Writer and Ed.; b. 30 Oct. 1929, Hungary; m. Zsuzsanna Marek, 30 Oct. 1954, one s. one d. *Education:* Eötvös Lorand University, 1955. *Career:* Librarian, Széchényi National Library, 1955–64; Institute of Musicology, 1964–95; Ed.-in-Chief, Új Magyarország, 1991–92, Magyarok Világlapja, 1992–96; mem. Asscn of Hungarian Writers. *Publications:* Dragon and Octahedron (short stories); After Scattering (essays); Where Are Those Columns (novel); In a Shell (novel); Book of Kings (novel); Heroes of the Failures (essays); Atheist (short stories); Final Settlement of a Wedding (short stories); Stephen King's Tart Wine (essays), 1993; ...We Have Survived Him (novel), 1996; The Stone Don't Feel It (essays), 1998; I am Reading the Letters of B. Szemere (essay), 1999; The Old Dog Is About To Cast His Coat (essays), 2001; Vaults, Gargoyles, Rosettes (memoirs), 2002. Contributions: periodicals. *Address:* Erdő u 150, 2092 Budakeszi, Hungary.

ALBERT, Neil; Attorney; b. 12 May 1950, Los Angeles, CA, USA; m. Linda Kling, 28 May 1979. *Education:* BS, Philosophy, Psychology, 1972, MA, Counselling, 1973, University of Oregon; JD, Villanova Law School, 1976. *Career:* Attorney, Lancaster, PA, 1976–; mem. MWA. *Publications:* The January Corpse, 1991; The February Trouble, 1992; Burning March, 1993; Cruel April, 1994; Appointment in May, 1996; Tangled June, 1997. *Literary Agent:* Blanche Schlessinger. *Address:* 2226 Main St, Narvon, PA 17602, USA. *E-mail:* nalbert@epix.net.

ALBERT, Susan Wittig, (Robin Paige); Writer; b. 2 Jan. 1940, Maywood, IL, USA; m. 1st (divorced); three c.; m. 2nd William Albert 1986. *Education:* BA, University of Illinois, 1967; PhD, University of California at Berkeley, 1972. *Career:* Instructor, University of San Francisco, 1969–71; Asst Prof., 1972–77, Assoc. Prof., 1977–79, Assoc. Dean, Graduate School, 1977–79, University of Texas at Austin; Dean, Sophie Newcomb College, 1979–81; Graduate Dean, 1981–82, Prof. of English, 1981–87, Vice-Pres. for Academic Affairs, 1982–86, Southwest Texas State University; mem. Garden Writers of America; Herb Society of America; MWA; Sisters in Crime; Story Circle Network, pres. and journal ed., 1997–. *Publications:* Fiction: Thyme of Death, 1992; Witches' Bane, 1993; Hangman's Root, 1994; Rosemary Remembered, 1995; Rueful Death, 1996; Love Lies Bleeding, 1997; Chile Death, 1998; Lavender Lies, 1999; Mistletoe Man, 2000; Bloodroot, 2001. Co-Author as Robin Paige: Death at Bishop's Keep, 1994; Death at Gallow's Green, 1995; Death at Daisy's Folly, 1997; Death at Devil's Bridge, 1998; Death at Rottingdean, 1999; Death at Whitechapel, 2000; Death at Epsom Downs, 2001; Death at Dartmoor, 2002. Children's Books: Author or co-author of about 60 books. Non-Fiction: Stylistic and Narrative Structures in the Middle English Verse Romances, 1977; The Participating Reader (co-author), 1979; Work of Her Own: How Women Create Success and Fulfillment off the Traditonal Career Track, 1992; Writing from Life: Telling Your Soul's Story, 1997. *Address:* PO Box 1616, Bertram, TX 78605, USA.

ALBEVERIO MANZONI, Solvejg; Painter, Writer and Poet; b. 6 Nov. 1939, Arogno, Switzerland; m. Sergio Albeverio, 7 Feb. 1970, one d. *Education:* Textile Designer, Diploma, Como, Italy, 1960; Art Courses, Zürich, 1969; Drawing and Etching Studies, Oslo, 1974–77. *Career:* Exhibitions in many countries; mem. Associazione Scrittori della Svizzera Italiana; PEN; Sculptors and Architects; Swiss Society of Painters; Swiss Society of Writers. *Publications:* Da stanze chiuse; Il pensatore con il mantello come meteora; Il fiore, il frutto, triandro donna; Frange di solitudine; Spiagge confinanti; La carcassa color del cielo; La ronda. Contributions: Literary journals and reviews. *Honours:* Premio Ascona, 1987; Pro Helvetia Prize, 1995. *Address:* Liebfrauenweg 5B, 53125 Bonn, Germany.

ALBRIGHT, Daniel; Prof. of English and Writer; b. 29 Oct. 1945, Chicago, IL, USA; m. Karin Larson, 18 June 1977, one d. *Education:* BA, Rice University, 1967; MPhil, 1969, PhD, 1970, Yale University. *Career:* Asst Prof., 1970–75, Assoc. Prof., 1975–81, Prof., 1981–87, University of Virginia; Visiting Prof., University of Munich, 1986–87; Prof., 1987–, Richard L. Turner Prof. in the Humanities, 1995–, University of Rochester. *Publications:* The Myth against Myth: A Study of Yeats' Imagination in Old Age, 1972; Personality and Impersonality: Lawrence, Woolf, Mann, 1978; Representation and the Imagination: Beckett, Kafka, Nabokov and Schoenberg, 1981; Lyricality in English Literature, 1985; Tennyson: The Muses' Tug-of-War, 1986; Stravinsky: The Music-Box and the Nightingale, 1989; W. B. Yeats: The Poems (ed.), 1990; Quantum Poetics: Yeats, Pound, Eliot, and the Science of Modernism, 1997; Untwisting the Serpent: Modernism in Music, Literature, and the Visual Arts, 2000; Berlioz's Semi-Operas: Roméo et Juliette and La damnation de Faust, 2001. Contributions: various periodicals. *Honours:* National Endowment for the Arts Fellowship, 1973–74; Guggenheim Fellowship, 1976–77. *Address:* 121 Van Voorhis Rd, Pittsford, NY 14534, USA.

ALCALÁ, Kathleen; Writer and Ed.; b. 29 Aug. 1954, Compton, CA, USA; m. Wayne C. Roth, 21 July 1979, one s. *Education:* BA, Stanford University, 1976; MA, University of Washington, 1985. *Career:* Grantwriter, Administrator, public broadcasting, other non-profit groups, 1976–89; Board Mem., Seattle Review, 1986–; Contributing Ed., Raven Chronicles; mem. PEN West; Authors' Guild; Artist Trust; Clarion West. *Publications:* Mrs Vargas and the Dead Naturalist, 1992; Spirits of the Ordinary (novel, produced as play), 1997; The Flower in the Skull, 1998; Treasures in Heaven, 2000. Contributions: journals and periodicals, including: Americas Review; American Voice; Calyx; Seattle Review; Before Columbus Review; Black Ice; Chiricu; Seattle Times; Ploughshares; The Colorado Review; Hopscotch; Anthologies, including: Women and Aging; Dreams in a Minor Key: Magic Realism by Women; Mirrors Beneath the Earth; Dreamers and Desperadoes; A Writer's Journal; Cracking the Earth; Fantasmas; Norton's Anthology of Latino Literature. *Honours:* Milliman Scholar of Creative Writing, University of Washington, 1984; Artist Trust GAP Grants, 1989, 1991; Invitational Residency at Cottages at Hedgebrook; King County Fiction Publication Project, 1990; Authors' Award, Brandeis University Women's Committee, 1994; Washington State-Artist Trust Fellowship, 1996; Pacific NW Booksellers Asscn Award, 1998; Western States Book Award and Gov.'s Writng Award, 1999; Washington State Book Award, 2000. *Literary Agent:* Kim Witherspoon and Assocs, New York, USA. *Address:* c/o Kim Witherspoon and Assocs, 235 E 31st St, New York, NY 10016, USA. *Website:* www.kathleenalcala.com.

ALDERSEY-WILLIAMS, Hugh Arthur; Journalist and Author; b. 17 June 1959, London, England; m. Moira Morrissey, 2 Sept. 1989. *Education:* BA, 1980, MA, 1984, St John's College, Cambridge. *Career:* mem. Society of Authors; RSA. *Publications:* New American Design, 1988; World Design: Nationalism and Globalism in Design, 1992; The Most Beautiful Molecule: The Discovery of the Buckyball, 1995. Other: Monographs on leading designers and various book chapters. Contributions: The Independent; Independent on Sunday. *Address:* c/o The Caroline Davidson Literary Agency, 5 Queen Anne's Gdns, London W4 1TU, England.

ALDING, Peter (see Jeffries, Roderic (Graeme)).

ALDISS, Brian Wilson, DLitt, FRSL; British writer, critic and actor; b. 18 Aug. 1925, Norfolk; m. 2nd Margaret Manson 1965 (died 1997); two s. two d. *Education:* Framlingham Coll. and West Buckland School. *Career:* fmr soldier, draughtsman, bookseller and film critic; Literary Ed. Oxford Mail 1957–69; Pres. British Science Fiction Asscn 1960–65; Jt-Pres. European Science Fiction Cttees 1976–80; Chair. John W. Campbell Memorial Award 1976–77; Chair. Cttee of Man. Soc. of Authors 1977–78; mem. Literature Advisory Panel, Arts Council 1978–80; Chair. Cultural Exchanges Cttee of Authors 1978; Judge, Booker McConnell Prize 1981; Pres. World SF 1982–84; Ed. S.F. Horizons 1964–; Vice-Pres. H. G. Wells Soc., W. Buckland School 1997–. *Opera:* Oedipus on Mars. *Plays (author):* SF Blues, Kindred Blood in Kensington Gore, Monsters of Every Day (Oxford Literary Festival) 2000, Drinks with The Spider King (Florida) 2000; acted in own productions 1985–2002. *Publications:* The Brightfount Diaries 1955, Space, Time & Nathaniel 1957, Non-Stop (Jules Verne Award 1977) 1958, The Male Response 1959, Hothouse (Hugo Award 1962) 1962, The Airs of Earth 1963, The Dark Light Years 1964, Greybeard 1964, Earthworks 1965, Best Science Fiction Stories of Brian W. Aldiss 1965, The Saliva Tree (Nebula Award) 1965, Cities and Stones: A Traveller's Jugoslavia 1966, Report on Probability A 1968, Barefoot in the Head 1969, Intangibles Inc., 1969, A Brian Aldiss Omnibus 1969, The Hand-Reared Boy 1970, The Shape of Further Things 1970, A Soldier Erect 1971, The Moment of Eclipse (British Science Fiction Asscn Award 1972) 1971, Brian Aldiss Omnibus 2 1971, Penguin Science Fiction Omnibus (ed.) 1973, Comic Inferno 1973, Billion Year Spree (III Merit Award 1976) 1973, Frankenstein Unbound (made into film directed by Roger Corman) 1973, The Eighty-Minute Hour 1974, Hell's Cartographers (ed.) 1975, Space Odysseys, Evil Earths, Science Fiction Art 1975, The Malacia Tapestry, Galactic Empires (two vols) 1976, Last Orders, Brothers of the Head 1977, Perilous Planets 1977, A Rude Awakening 1978, Enemies of the System 1978, This World and Nearer Ones 1979, Pile 1979, New Arrivals, Old Encounters 1979, Moreau's Other Island 1980, Life in the West 1980, An Island called Moreau 1981, Foreign Bodies 1981, Helliconia Spring 1982, Science Fiction Quiz 1983, Helliconia Summer 1983, Seasons in Flight 1984, Helliconia Winter 1985, The Pale Shadow of Science 1985, ... And the Lurid Glare of the Comet 1986, Trillion

Year Spree (Hugo Award 1987) 1986, Ruins 1987, Forgotten Life 1988, Science Fiction Blues 1988, Best SF Stories of Brian W. Aldiss 1988, Cracken at Critical 1989, A Romance of the Equator 1990, Bury My Heart at W. H. Smith's 1990, Dracula Unbound 1991, Remembrance Day 1993, A Tupolev Too Far 1993, Somewhere East of Life 1994, The Detached Retina 1995, At the Caligula Hotel (poems) 1995, The Secret of this Book 1995, Songs from the Steppes of Central Asia 1996, The Twinkling of an Eye 1998, The Squire Quartet (four vols) 1998, When the Feast is Finished 1999, White Mars 1999, Supertoys Last All Summer Long (made into Kubrick–Spielberg film A.I. 2001) 2001, The Cretan Teat 2001, Super-State 2002, Researches and Churches in Serbia 2002, The Dark Sun Rises (poems) 2002, Affairs in Hampden Ferrers 2004, Jocasta 2005, Sanity and the Lady 2005; contributions: TLS, Nature. *Honours:* Hon. DLitt 2000; Ditmar Award for World's Best Contemporary Science Fiction Writer 1969, first James Blish Award for Excellence in Criticism 1977, Pilgrim Award 1978, John W. Campbell Award 1983, Kurt Lasswitz Award 1984, IAFA Distinguished Scholarship Award 1986, J. Lloyd Eaton Award 1988, Prix Utopie (France) 1999, Grand Master of Science Fiction 2000. *Address:* Hambleden, 39 St Andrew's Road, Old Headington, Oxford, OX3 9DL, England. *Telephone:* (1865) 762464. *Fax:* (1865) 744435. *E-mail:* aldiss@dial.pipex.com (Office). *Website:* www.brianwaldiss.com (Office).

ALDRIDGE, (Harold Edward) James; British author and journalist; b. 10 July 1918, White Hills, Vic., Australia; m. Dina Mitchnik 1942; two s. *Career:* with Herald and Sun, Melbourne, Australia 1937–38, Daily Sketch and Sunday Dispatch, London 1939; with Australian Newspaper Service and North American Newspaper Alliance (as war corresp.), Finland, Norway, Middle East, Greece, USSR 1939–45; corresp. for Time and Life, Tehran 1944. *Plays:* 49th State 1947, One Last Glimpse 1981. *Publications:* Signed with Their Honour 1942, The Sea Eagle 1944, Of Many Men 1946, The Diplomat 1950, The Hunter 1951, Heroes of the Empty View 1954, Underwater Hunting for Inexperienced Englishmen 1955, I Wish He Would Not Die 1958, Gold and Sand (short stories) 1960, The Last Exile 1961, A Captive in the Land 1962, The Statesman's Game 1966, My Brother Tom 1966, The Flying 19 1966, Living Egypt (with Paul Strand) 1969, Cairo: Biography of a City 1970, A Sporting Proposition 1973, The Marvellous Mongolian 1974, Mockery in Arms 1974, The Untouchable Juli 1975, One Last Glimpse 1977, Goodbye Un-America 1979, The Broken Saddle 1982, The True Story of Lilli Stubek (Australian Children's Book of the Year 1985) 1984, The True Story of Spit Mac Phee (Guardian Children's Fiction Prize) 1985, The True Story of Lola MacKellar 1993, The Girl From the Sea 2003. *Honours:* Rhys Memorial Award 1945, New South Wales Premier's Literary Award 1986; Lenin Peace Prize 1972. *Literary Agent:* Curtis Brown Ltd, Haymarket House, 28–29 Haymarket, London, SW1Y 4SP, England. *Telephone:* (20) 7393-4400. *Fax:* (20) 7393-4401. *E-mail:* info@curtisbrown.co.uk. *Website:* www.curtisbrown.co.uk.

ALDRIDGE, John Watson; Critic and Writer; b. 26 Sept. 1922, Sioux City, IA, USA; m. 1st, five s.; m. 2nd Patricia McGuire Eby, 16 July 1983. *Education:* BA, University of California at Berkeley, 1947. *Career:* Lecturer, Princeton University, 1953–54, Bread Loaf Writers' Conference, 1966–69; Special Adviser on American Studies, American Embassy, Bonn, 1972–73; Book Critic, MacNeil/Lehrer Report, PBS TV, 1983–84. *Publications:* After the Lost Generation, 1951; In Search of Heresy, 1956; The Party at Cranton, 1960; Time to Murder and Create, 1966; In the Country of the Young, 1970; The Devil in the Fire, 1972; The American Novel and the Way We Live Now, 1983; Talents and Technicians, 1992; Classics and Contemporaries, 1992. *Honours:* Rockefeller Foundation Fellowship, 1976. *Address:* 381 N Main St, Madison, GA 30650, USA.

ALDRIDGE, Sarah (see Marchant, Anyda).

ALDUY, Dominique, MA; French newspaper executive and economist; b. 23 Feb. 1944, Paris; m. Jean-Paul Alduy 1969; one s. two d. *Education:* Univ. of Paris, Inst. d'Etudes Politiques de Paris and Pennsylvania State Univ., USA. *Career:* in charge of local community financial studies, Ministry of Equipment 1972–76; Rep. to Secr.-Gen. for New Towns 1976–78; in charge of Habitat and Environment Comm., Comm. Gen. du Plan 1979–81; Social Policies Rep. to Cabinet of the Prime Minister 1981–83; Dir of Programmes, Caisse des Dépôts et Consignations 1983–86, Dir Devt of Deposits-Devt 1986, Pres., Dir-Gen. of Communication Devt 1986–89; Dir-Gen. Société Nat de Programmes—France Régions 3 (FR3) 1989–93, apptd Dir-Gen. Film 3 production 1989; Dir-Gen. Centre Nat d'Art et de Culture Georges Pompidou 1993–94; Dir-Gen. Le Monde newspaper 1994–, mem. Bd of Dirs Le Monde and Le Monde SA 1995–; Co-Man. Cahiers du Cinéma; Pres. L'Asscn Européenne des éditeurs de journaux (ENPA) 2000–. *Honours:* Chevalier de la Légion d'Honneur. *Address:* Le Monde, 21 bis rue Claude Bernard, 75242 Paris Cedex 05 (Office); 74A rue Lecourbe, 75015 Paris, France (Home).

ALEGRIA, Claribel; Writer and Poet; b. 12 May 1924, Esteli, Nicaragua; m. Darwin J. Flakoll 29 Dec. 1947 (died 1995); one s. three d. *Education:* BA, George Washington University, Washington, DC, USA. *Publications:* Anillo de silencio, 1948; Suite, 1950; Vigilias, 1953; Acuario, 1955; Huésped de mi tiempo, 1961; Via única, 1965; Aprendizenje, 1972; Pagar a cobrar y otros poemas, 1973; Sobevivo, 1978; Suma y sigue, 1981; Y este poema río, 1989; Luisa en el país de la realidad, 1989; Fugues, 1993; Thresholds, 1996; Sorrow, 1999. Contributions: many periodicals. *Honours:* Premio Casa de las Americas, Havana, Cuba, 1978; Dr hc, University of Eastern Connecticut, 1998. *Address:* Apdo A-36, Managua, Nicaragua.

ALEX, Peter (see Haining, Peter (Alexander)).

ALEXANDER, Brooke, BA; American art dealer and publisher; b. 26 April 1937, Los Angeles; m. Carolyn Rankin 1967; two d. *Education:* Yale Univ. *Career:* f. Brooke Alexander Inc. to publish and distribute graphic art 1968, expanded co. 1975; f. Brooke Alexander Editions, opened separate gallery for graphics 1989; partner in Madrid gallery, Galería Weber, Alexander y Cobo 1991–; mem. Governing Bd Yale Univ. Art Gallery 1988–. *Address:* 59 Wooster Street, New York, NY 10012-4349, USA. *Telephone:* (212) 925-4338.

ALEXANDER, Caroline Elizabeth, BA, PhD; writer; b. 13 March 1956, Florida, USA. *Education:* Florida State University, University of Oxford, Columbia University. *Career:* mem. American Philological Society, RGS. *Publications:* One Dry Season: In the Footsteps of Mary Kingsley, 1990; The Way to Xanadu, 1994; Battle's End; Mrs Chippy's Last Expedition, 1997; The Endurance, 1998; The Bounty: The True Story of the Mutiny on the Bounty, 2003. Contributions: New Yorker; Smithsonian; Independent; Sunday Telegraph Weekend Magazine; Others. *Honours:* Mellon Fellowship, Rhodes Scholarship. *Literary Agent:* Gillon Aitken Associates Ltd, 18–21 Cavaye Place, London, SW10 9PT, England. *Telephone:* (20) 7373-8672. *Fax:* (20) 7373-6002.

ALEXANDER, Christine Anne; academic and writer; b. 9 July 1949, Hastings, New Zealand; m. Peter Fraser Alexander 1977; one s. one d. *Education:* BA, 1970, MA, 1971, University of Canterbury; PhD, University of Cambridge, 1978. *Career:* Asst Lectureship, University of Canterbury, 1972; Tutor, 1978–83, Lecturer, 1986–88, Senior Lecturer, 1988–92, Assoc. Prof., 1993–, University of New South Wales, Australia; mem. Brontë Society; Australasian Language and Literature Asscn; Australian Victorian Studies Asscn; Australian and South Pacific Asscn for Comparative Literary Studies; Cambridge Society; Jane Austen Society; Asscn for the Study of Australian Literature; Bibliographical Society of Australia and New Zealand; Society for Textual Scholarship; Society for the History of Authorship, Reading and Publishing. *Publications:* Bibliography of the Manuscripts of Charlotte Brontë, 1982; The Early Writings of Charlotte Brontë, 1983; An Edition of the Early Writings of Charlotte Brontë, three vols, 1987–; The Art of the Brontës, 1994. Contributions: Books and journals. *Honours:* New Zealand Postgraduate Scholarships; New Zealand University Women's Fellowship; Travel Grants; Special Research Grants; British Acad. Rose Mary Crawshay Prize, 1984; Australian Research Council Senior Research Fellowship; Fellow, Australian Acad. of the Humanities, 1995. *Address:* School of English, University of New South Wales, Sydney, NSW 2052, Australia.

ALEXANDER, Clare; British literary agent. *Career:* Ed. with Penguin Books 1981–97, later Publishing Dir Viking; Ed.-in-Chief, Macmillan 1997–98; Literary Agent, later Dir, Gillon Aitken Assocs 1998–. *Literary Agent:* Gillon Aitken Associates Ltd, 18–21 Cavaye Place, London, SW10 9PT, England. *Telephone:* (20) 7373-8672. *Fax:* (20) 7373-6002. *E-mail:* clare@gillonaitken.co.uk.

ALEXANDER, Doris Muriel, BA, MA, PhD; Prof. and writer; b. 14 Dec. 1922, Newark, NJ, USA. *Education:* University of Missouri, University of Pennsylvania, New York University. *Career:* Instructor, Rutgers University 1950–56; Assoc. Prof., then Dept Chair, CUNY 1956–62; mem. Asscn of Literary Scholars and Critics, Eugene O'Neill Society. *Publications:* The Tempering of Eugene O'Neill 1962, Creating Characters with Charles Dickens 1991, Eugene O'Neill's Creative Struggle 1992, Creating Literature Out of Life 1996, Eugene O'Neill's Last Plays: Separating Art from Autobiography 2004; contrib. to many journals. *Honours:* Penfield Fellowship, New York University, 1946; Fulbright Prof., University of Athens, 1966–67. *E-mail:* dalex1@tin.it.

ALEXANDER, Elisabeth; German poet and writer; b. 21 Aug. 1922, Linz/Rhein. *Career:* freelance writer 1970–; contributor to Feuilleton des Heidelberger Tageblatts magazine 1975–82; publs in newspapers and magazines and for radio and TV, including Frankfurter Rundschau, Basler Zeitung, Frankfurter Hefte, Badische Neueste Nachrichten, Die Zeit, Passagen, Mannheimer Morgen; Visiting Writer, Texas Tech. Univ., USA 1986; lecture tours of USA, Guest Lecturer Goethe Inst. Amsterdam, Paris, Brussels, Montréal etc.; works translated into English, French and Chinese. *Publications include:* poetry: Bums 1971, Ich bin kein Pferd 1976, Brotkrumen 1977, Ich hänge mich ans schwarze Brette 1979, Wo bist du Trost 1980, Glückspfennig – Gedichte für das ganze Jahr 1984, Zeitflusen 1986, Die Uhr läuft rückwärts wenn der Schnee fällt 1994; novels and short stories: Die Frau, die lachte 1975, Fritte Pomm (for children) 1976, Die törichte Jungfrau 1978, Sie hätte ihre Kinder töten sollen 1982, Damengeschichte 1983, Lisas Liebe 1994, Domizil Heidelberg 1995, Bauchschuß, Am Fußende des Bettes (co-author) 2000, Werksausgabe 1. Die sieben Häute der Hanna Winter 2002; co-writer and ed. of many other works, works feature in anthologies. *Honours:* First Prize, Poetensitz 1996. *Address:* Erwin-Rohde-Str. 22, 69120 Heidelberg, Germany.

ALEXANDER, Gary Roy; writer; b. 18 Jan. 1941, Bremerton, WA, USA; m. Shari 1969; three d. *Education:* Olympic Community Coll., Univ. of Washington. *Career:* mem. MWA. *Publications:* Pigeon Blood 1988, Unfunny Money 1989, Kiet and the Golden Peacock 1989, Kiet and the Opium War 1990, Deadly Drought 1991, Dead Dinosaurs 1994, Kiet Goes West 1992, Blood Sacrifice 1993; contrib. many stories and travel articles in magazines. *Address:* 6709 S 238th Place, H-102, Kent, WA 98032, USA. *E-mail:* alexagr61@hotmail.com.

ALEXANDER, Helen Anne, CBE, MA, MBA; British publishing executive; *Chief Executive Officer, The Economist Group*; b. 10 Feb. 1957; m. Tim Suter 1985; two s. one d. *Education:* Hertford Coll. Oxford, Institut Européen d'Admin des Affaires (INSEAD), France. *Career:* mem. staff Gerald Duckworth 1978–79, Faber & Faber 1979–83; joined The Economist Group 1984, Man. Dir Economist Intelligence Unit 1993–96, Group CEO 1997–; Dir (non-exec.) Northern Foods PLC 1994–, British Telecom PLC 1998–2002, Centrica PLC; Dir Writers and Scholars (publs include The Index on Censorship); Trustee Tate Gallery; mem. Ethics Cttee, London Univ. Coll. Hosp. *Honours:* Hon. Fellow Hertford Coll., Oxford. *Address:* The Economist Group, 25 St James's Street, London, SW1A 1HG, England (Office). *Telephone:* (20) 7830-7000 (Office). *Website:* www.economistgroup.com (Office).

ALEXANDER, Lloyd (Chudley); Writer; b. 30 Jan. 1924, Philadelphia, PA, USA; m. Janine Denni, 8 Jan. 1946, one d. *Education:* West Chester State Teachers College, 1942; Lafayette College, 1943; Sorbonne, University of Paris, 1946. *Career:* Author-in-Residence, Temple University, 1970–74; mem. Amnesty International; Authors' Guild; Authors' League of America; PEN. *Publications:* And Let the Credit Go, 1955; My Five Tigers, 1956; Janine is French, 1958; My Love Affair with Music, 1960; Park Avenue Vet (with Louis Camuti), 1962; Fifty Years in the Doghouse, 1963; My Cats and Me: The Story of an Understanding, 1989. Children's Fiction: Border Hawk: August Bondi, 1959; Aaron Lopez and the Flagship Hope, 1960; Time Cat: The Remarkable Journeys of Jason and Gareth, 1963; Coll and His White Pig, 1965; The Truthful Harp, 1967; The Marvelous Misadventures of Sebastian, 1970; The King's Fountain, 1971; The Four Donkeys, 1972; The Foundling and Other Tales of Prydain, 1973; The Cat Who Wished to Be a Man, 1973; The Wizard in the Tree, 1975; The Town Cats and Other Tales, 1977; The First Two Lives of Lukas-Kasha, 1978; The Remarkable Journey of Prince Jen, 1991; The Fortune-Tellers, 1992; The House Gobbaleen, 1995; The Arkadians, 1995; The Iron Ring, 1997; Gypsy Rizka, 1999; How the Cat Swallowed Thunder, 2000; The Gawgon and the Boy, 2001; The Rope Trick, 2002. *Honours:* Newbery Honor Book, 1965; Newbery Medal, 1969; National Book Award, 1971; Drexel Awards, 1972, 1976; American Book Award, 1982; Austrian Children's Book Award, 1984; Regina Medal, Catholic Library Asscn, 1986; Church and Synagogue Library Asscn Award, 1987; Lifetime Achievement Award, Pennsylvania Center for the Book in Philadelphia, 1991; Horn Book Award, 1993. *Address:* 1005 Drexel Ave, Drexel Hill, PA 19026, USA.

ALEXANDER, Meena; academic, poet and writer; b. 17 Feb. 1951, Allahabad, India; m. David Lelyveld, 1 May 1979, one s. one d. *Education:* BA, University of Khartoum, 1969; PhD, University of Nottingham, 1973. *Career:* Lecturer, 1977–79, Reader, 1979, University of Hyderabad; Asst Prof., Fordham University, 1980–87; Asst Prof., 1987–89, Assoc. Prof., 1989–92, Prof. of English, 1992–99, Distinguished Prof. of English and Women's Studies, 1999–, Hunter College and the Graduate School and University Center, CUNY; mem. MLA; PEN American Center. *Publications:* The Poetic Self: Towards a Phenomenology of Romanticism, 1979; Stone Roots (poems), 1980; House of a Thousand Doors (poems and prose), 1988; Women in Romanticism: Mary Wollstonecraft, Dorothy Wordsworth and Mary Shelley, 1989; The Storm: A Poem in Five Parts, 1989; Nampally Road (novel), 1991; Night-Scene: The Garden (poem), 1992; Fault Lines (memoir), 1993; River and Bridge (poems), 1995; The Shock of Arrival: Reflections on Postcolonial Experience (poems and prose), 1996; Manhattan Music (novel), 1997; Illiterate Heart (poems), 2002; Raw Silk (poems), 2004. Contributions: Books, anthologies and periodicals. *Honours:* Altrusa International Award, 1973; MacDowell Colony Fellow, 1993, 1998; International Writer-in-Residence, Arts Council of England, 1995; Lila Wallace Writer-in-Residence, Asian American Renaissance, Minneapolis, 1995; New York State Foundation for the Arts, Poetry Award, 1999; Poet-in-Residence, National University of Singapore, 1999; Fondation Ledig-Rowohlt Residency, Château de Lavigny, 2001; Commission for Poetry International, Royal Festival Hall, London, 2002; Fulbright Scholar Award, India, 2002; PEN Open Book Award, 2002. *Address:* c/o Graduate School and University Center, City University of New York, 365 Fifth Avenue, New York, NY 10016, USA. *E-mail:* malexander@gc.cuny.edu.

ALEXANDER, Sue; Writer; b. 20 Aug. 1933, Tucson, AZ, USA; m., two s. one d. *Education:* Drake University, 1950–52; Northwestern University, 1952–53. *Career:* mem. The Society of Children's Book Writers and Illustrators, Chair., Board of Dirs; The Children's Literature Council of Southern California, Mem. of Board; Friends of Children and Libraries; California Readers' Asscn. *Publications:* Small Plays for You and a Friend, 1973; Nadir of the Streets, 1975; Peacocks Are Very Special, 1976; Witch, Goblin and Sometimes Ghost, 1976; Small Plays for Special Days, 1977; Marc the Magnificent, 1978; More Witch, Goblin and Ghost Stories, 1978; Seymour the Prince, 1979; Finding Your First Job, 1980; Whatever Happened to Uncle Albert? and Other Puzzling Plays, 1980; Witch, Goblin and Ghost in the Haunted Woods, 1981; Witch, Goblin and Ghost's Book of Things to Do, 1982; Nadia the Willful, 1983; Dear Phoebe, 1984; World Famous Muriel, 1984; Witch, Goblin and Ghost Are Back, 1985; World Famous Muriel and the Scary Dragon, 1985; America's Own Holidays, 1986; Lila on the Landing, 1987; There's More – Much More, 1987; World Famous Muriel and the Magic Mystery, 1990; Who Goes Out on Halloween?, 1990; Sara's City, 1995; What's Wrong Now, Millicent?, 1996; One more Time, Mama, 1999; Behold the Trees, 2001. Contributions: Short stories to Los Angeles Times. *Honours:* Dorothy C. McKenzie Award for distinguished contribution to the field of children's literature, 1980. *Literary Agent:* Curtis Brown Ltd, 10 Astor Pl., New York, NY 10003, USA. *Address:* 6846 McLaren, Canoga Park, CA 91307, USA.

ALEXIE, Sherman, BA; poet and novelist; b. 7 Oct. 1966, Spokane, WA, USA; m. Diane 1994; two s. *Education:* Washington State Univ., Pullman. *Career:* Spokane/Coeur d'Alene Indian; stand-up comedian, poet, songwriter, writer. *Publications:* The Business of Fancydancing (short stories and poems, also screenplay), 1991; The Lone Ranger and Tonto Fist Fight in Heaven (short stories), 1993; Old Shirts and New Skins (poems), 1993; I Would Steal Horses (poems), 1993; First Indian on the Moon (poems), 1993; Reservation Blues (novel), 1995; Water Flowing Home (poems), 1995; The Summer of Black Widows (poems), 1996; Indian Killer (novel), 1996; Smoke Signals (screenplay), 1998; The Man Who Loves Salmon (poems), 1998; The Toughest Indian in the World (short stories), 2000; One Stick Song (poems), 2000; Ten Little Indians (short stories), 2003. Contributions: The Stranger; Indiana Review; New Yorker. *Honours:* PEN/Hemingway Best First Book award, 1993; Malamud short story award (with Richard Ford), 2001. *Address:* FallsApart Productions Inc, PMB 2294, 10002 Aurora Avenue N, Suite 36, Seattle, WA 98133-9334, USA. *E-mail:* fallsapart_fans@hotmail.com. *Website:* www.fallsapart.com.

ALEXIEVITCH, Svetlana; Belarusian writer; b. 1948, Ukraine. *Publications:* U voiny ne zhenskoe litso, 1985; Aposhniya svedki. kniga nedzitsyachyh raskaza?, 1985; Tsynkavyya hlopchyki, 1991; U vainy ne zhanochae ablichcha, 1991; Zacharavanyya smertsu, 1993; Charnobyl'skaya malitva (English trans. as Voices from Chernobyl: Chronicle of the Future), 1999. *Address:* c/o Chatto & Windus, Random House, 20 Vauxhall Bridge Road, London SW1V 2SA, England. *E-mail:* svett_al@hotmail.com.

ALI, Monica; Bangladeshi/British novelist; b. 1967, Dhaka, E Pakistan (now Bangladesh); m. Simon Torrance; one s. one d. *Education:* Wadham Coll., Oxford. *Publications:* Brick Lane (WHSmith People's Choice best debut novel award) 2003, Knife (short story in The Weekenders: Adventures in Calcutta) 2004. *Honours:* Granta's Best of Young British Novelists list 2003, British Book Awards Newcomer of the Year 2004. *Literary Agent:* The Marsh Agency, 11 Dover Street, London, W1S 4LJ, England. *Telephone:* (20) 7399-2800. *Fax:* (20) 7399-2801. *Website:* www.marsh-agency.co.uk.

ALI, Tariq; Political Activist and Writer; b. 21 Oct. 1943, Lahore, India. *Education:* BA, Punjab University, 1963; University of Oxford. *Career:* mem. Fourth International. *Publications:* Fiction: Redemption, 1990; Shadows of the Pomegranate Tree, 1992; Fear of Mirrors, 1998; The Book of Saladin, 1999; The Stone Woman, 2000. Non-Fiction: The Thoughts of Chairman Harold (compiler), 1967; The New Revolutionaries: A Handbook of the International Radical Left (ed.), 1969; Pakistan: Military Rule or People's Power?, 1970; The Coming British Revolution, 1972; Chile: Lessons of the Coup: Which Way to Workers' Power? (with Gerry Hedley), 1974; 1968 and After: Inside the Revolution, 1978; Trotsky for Beginners, 1980; Can Pakistan Survive?, 1983; What Is Stalinism? (ed.), 1984; The Stalinist Legacy: Its Impact on Twentieth-Century World Politics (ed.), 1984; An Indian Dynasty: The Story of the Nehru-Gandhi Family, 1985; Street Fighting Years: An Autobiography of the Sixties, 1987; Revolution from Above: Where is the Soviet Union Going?, 1988; Moscow Gold (with Howard Brenton), 1990; 1968: Marching in the Streets (with Susan Watkins), 1998; Ugly Rumours (with Howard Brenton), 1998; Masters of the Universe?: NATO's Balkan Crusade (ed.), 2000; The Clash of Fundamentalisms: Crusades, Jihads and Modernity, 2002; The Clash of Fundamentalisms: Bush in Babylon—Recolonising Iraq, 2003. Contributions: periodicals, incl. London Review of Books. *Address:* 27 Drylands Rd, London N8 9HN, England.

ALIOTH, Gabrielle; Swiss novelist; b. 21 April 1955, Basel; m. Martin Alioth. *Career:* writer-in-residence, Univ. of Southern California, California State Univ.; mem. of Irish delegation 1996, Swiss delegation 1998 at the Frankfurt Book Fair; mem. PEN. *Publications:* novels: Der Narr (trans. as The Fool) 1990, Wie ein kostbarer Stein (trans. as Like a Precious Stone) 1994, Die Arche der Frauen (trans. as Women's Arch) 1996, Die Stumme Reiterin (trans. as The Silent Rider) 1998. *Honours:* Hamburg Literary Award for Best First Novel. *Literary Agent:* Verlag Nagel & Kimche AG, V-Nr. 1320 506, Nordstr. 9, 8035, Zürich, Switzerland. *Telephone:* (41) 1 366 66 80. *Fax:* (41) 1 366 66 88. *E-mail:* info@nagel-kimche.ch. *Website:* www.nagel-kimche.ch.

ALKHATIB, Burhan, BEng, MA; writer and translator; b. 10 Oct. 1944, Mosaib, Babel, Iraq; m. 1st 1978 (divorced 1982); m. 2nd 1988 (divorced 1994); two s. one d. *Education:* Univ. of Baghdad, Gorky Literary Inst. Moscow. *Career:* mem. Writers' Union of Sweden. *Publications:* Khutwat ila Alufq Albaid (Steps Toward a Distant Horizon) 1967, Dabab fi Addahira (Mist at Midday) 1968, Shiqqatun fi Shari' Abi Nuwas (An Apartment on Abi Nuwas Street) 1972, Ajusur Azujajiyya (Bridges of Glass) 1975, Ashari 'aljadid (A New Street) 1980, Nujum Oldhuhr (Under the Heat of Midday) 1986, Suqut Sparta (The Fall of Sparta) 1992, Layla Baghdadia (A Baghdad Night) 1993, Babel alfaiha (The Aromatic Babylon) 1995, Thalik assaif fi Iskendria (That Summer in Alexandria) 1998, Aljanain Almuglaqa (The Closed Gardens) 2000; other: translations of 13 books; contrib. to Arab magazines and journals. *Address:* Berg V 22 tr 3, 19631 Kungsangen, Sweden.

ALLABY, John Michael; Author and Ed.; b. 18 Sept. 1933, Belper, Derbyshire, England; m. Ailsa Marthe McGregor 3 Jan. 1957; one s. one d. *Career:* mem. Asscn of British Science Writers; New York Acad. of Sciences; Society of Authors. *Publications:* Inventing Tomorrow, 1976; Dictionary of the Environment, 1977; The Oxford Dictionary of Natural History, 1980; A Year in the Life of a Field, 1981; Animal Artisans, 1982; The Greening of Mars, 1984; The Concise Oxford Dictionary of Earth Sciences, 1986; All the National Trails in England and Wales, 1987; Conservation at Home, 1988; Guide to Gaia, 1989; Concise Oxford Dictionary of Zoology, 1991; Concise Oxford Dictionary of Botany, 1992; Elements: Air, 1992; Elements: Water, 1992; Elements: Fire, 1993; Elements: Earth, 1993; The Concise Oxford Dictionary of Ecology, 1994; Facing the Future, 1995; How the Weather Works, 1995; Basic Environmental Science, 1996; Dangerous Weather, six vols, 1998; Temperate Forests, 1998; Biomes, nine vols, 1999; DK Guide to Weather, 2000; Encyclopedia of Weather and Climate, 2001; Deserts, 2001; Facts on File: Weather and Climate Handbook, 2002. Contributions: newspapers and magazines. *Honours:* Junior Prize, Aventis Prize for Science Books, 2001. *Address:* Braehead Cottage, Tighnabruaich, Argyll PA21 2ED, Scotland. *E-mail:* mike_allaby@compuserve.com. *Website:* www.michaelallaby.com.

ALLAN, Keith; Reader in Linguistics, Writer and Ed.; b. 27 March 1943, London, England; m. Wendy F. Allan, 1 Jan. 1993, two d. *Education:* BA, University of Leeds, 1964; MLitt, Linguistics, 1970, PhD, Linguistics, 1977, University of Edinburgh. *Career:* Research Assoc., Nuffield Language Development Research Project, Dept of Child Life and Health, University of Edinburgh, 1967–70; Lecturer in English Language, Ahmadu Bello University, Zaria, Nigeria, 1970–73; Lecturer in Linguistics, University of Essex, 1973–74, University of Nairobi, 1975–77; Guest Prof. in Linguistics, Gesamthochschule, Paderborn, Germany, 1975; Senior Tutor in Linguistics, 1978–81, Lecturer in Linguistics, 1982–87, Senior Lecturer in Linguistics, 1988–91, Acting Prof. and Head, Dept of Linguistics, 1992–93, Reader in Linguistics, 1992–, Monash University; Visiting Prof. in Linguistics, University of Arizona, 1990; Visiting Fellow, Clare College, Cambridge, 2000–. *Publications:* Linguistic Meaning (two vols), 1986; Oxford International Encyclopedia of Linguistics (semantics ed.), 1991; Euphemism and Dysphemism: Language Used as Shield and Weapon (with Kate Burridge), 1991; Natural Language Semantics, 2001. Contributions: Reference works, scholarly books and professional journals. *Honours:* Fellow, Australian Acad. of Humanities, 1994–, Chair., linguistics and philology section, 1997–2000. *Address:* c/o Language and Society Centre, Monash University, PO Box 11A, Menzies Bldg, Vic. 3800, Australia.

ALLASON, Rupert William Simon; Writer and Ed.; b. 8 Nov. 1951, London, England; m. Nicole Van Moppes 15 June 1979 (divorced 1996); one s. one d. *Education:* University of Grenoble; University of London. *Career:* Ed., World Intelligence Review, 1985–; MP for Torbay, Conservative Party, 1987–97; mem. Special Forces Club. *Publications:* SPY! (with Richard Deacon), 1980; British Security Service Operations 1909–45, 1981; A Matter of Trust: MI5 1945–72, 1982; MI6: British Secret Intelligence Service Operations 1909–45, 1983; The Branch: A History of the Metropolitan Police Special Branch, 1983; Unreliable Witness: Espionage Myths of the Second World War, 1984; GARBO (with Juan Pjujol), 1985; GCHQ: The Secret Wireless War, 1986; Molehunt, 1987; The Friends: Britain's Postwar Secret Intelligence Operations, 1988; Games of Intelligence, 1989; Seven Spies Who Changed the World, 1991; Secret War: The Story of SOE, 1992; The Faber Book of Espionage, 1993; The Illegals, 1993; The Faber Book of Treachery, 1995; The Secret War for the Falklands, 1997; Counterfeit Spies, 1998; Crown Jewels, 1998; Venona, 1999; The Third Secret, 2000. *Address:* 6 Burton Mews, London SW1W 9EP, England. *E-mail:* westintel@compuserve.com.

ALLBEURY, Theodore Edward le Bouthillier, (Ted Allbeury, Richard Butler, Patrick Kelly); writer; b. 20 Oct. 1917. *Career:* mem. Soc. of Authors. *Publications:* A Choice of Enemies 1973, Snowball 1974, The Special Collection 1975, Palomino Blonde 1975, The Only Good German 1976, Moscow Quadrille 1976, The Man with the President's Mind 1977, The Lantern Network 1978, Consequence of Fear 1979, The Alpha List 1979, The Twentieth Day of January 1980, The Reaper 1980, The Other Side of Silence 1981, The Secret Whispers 1981, All Our Tomorrows 1982, Shadow of Shadows 1982, Pay Any Price 1983, The Judas Factor 1984, No Place To Hide 1984, The Girl from Addis 1984, Children of Tender Years 1985, The Choice 1986, The Seeds of Treason 1986, The Crossing 1987, A Wilderness of Mirrors 1988, Deep Purple 1989, A Time Without Shadows 1990, Other Kinds of Treason 1990, Dangerous Edge 1991, Show Me a Hero 1992, The Line Crosser 1993, As Time Goes By 1994, Beyond the Silence 1995, The Long Run 1996, Aid and Comfort 1997, Shadow of a Doubt 1998; as Patrick Kelly: Codeword Cromwell 1980, The Lonely Margins 1981; as Richard Butler: Where All the Girls are Sweeter 1975, Italian Assets 1976. *Literary Agent:* Blake Friedmann Literary Agency, 122 Arlington Road, London, NW1 7HP, England. *Telephone:* (20) 7284-0408. *Fax:* (20) 7284-0442. *Website:* www.blakefriedmann.co.uk.

ALLDRITT, Keith; Prof. of English and Writer; b. 10 Dec. 1935, Wolverhampton, England; m. Joan Hardwick, 10 April 1980, one s. one d. *Education:* BA, MA, St Catharine's College, Cambridge. *Career:* mem. Arnold Bennett Society; Society of Authors; D. H. Lawrence Society; International Churchill Society; MLA. *Publications:* The Making of George Orwell, 1969; The Visual Imagination of D. H. Lawrence, 1970; The Good Pit Man, 1975; The Lover Next Door, 1977; Elgar on the Journey to Hanley, 1978; Poetry as Chamber Music, 1978; Modernism in the Second World War, 1989; Churchill the Writer: His Life as a Man of Letters, 1992; The Greatest of Friends: Franklin Roosevelt and Winston Churchill 1939–45, 1995. *Honours:* FRSL. *Literary Agent:* Murray Pollinger Agency. *Address:* 48 Church St, Lichfield, Staffordshire WS13 6ED, England.

ALLEN, Blair H.; Writer, Poet, Ed. and Artist; b. 2 July 1933, Los Angeles, CA, USA; m. Juanita Aguilar Raya, 27 Jan. 1968, one s. one d. *Education:* AA, San Diego City College, 1964; University of Washington, 1965–66; BA, San Diego State University, 1970. *Career:* Book Reviewer, Los Angeles Times, 1977–78; Special Feature Ed., Cerulean Press and Kent Publications, 1982–; mem. Asscn for Applied Poetry; Beyond Baroque Foundation; California State Poetry Society; Medina Foundation. *Publications:* Televisual Poems for Bloodshot Eyeballs, 1973; Malice in Blunderland, 1974; N/Z, 1979; The Atlantis Trilogy, 1982; Dreamwish of the Magician, 1983; Right Through the Silver Lined 1984 Looking Glass, 1984; The Magical World of David Cole (ed.), 1984; Snow Summits in the Sun (ed.), 1988; Trapped in a Cold War Travelogue, 1991; May Burning into August, 1992; The Subway Poems, 1993; Bonfire on the Beach, by John Brander (ed.), 1993; The Cerulean Anthology of Sci-Fi/Outer Space/Fantasy/Poetry and Prose Poems (ed.), 1995; When the Ghost of Cassandra Whispers in My Ears, 1996; Ashes Ashes All Fall Down, 1997; Around the World in 56 Days, 1998; Thunderclouds from the Door, 1999; Jabberbunglemerkeltoy, 1999; The Athens Café, 2000; The Day of the Jamberee Call, 2001; Assembled I Stand, 2002; Wine of Starlight, 2002. Contributions: numerous periodicals and anthologies. *Honours:* First Prize for Poetry, Pacificus Foundation Competition, 1992; various other hons and awards. *Address:* PO Box 162, Colton, CA 92324-0162, USA.

ALLEN, Diogenes; Prof. of Philosophy and Writer; b. 17 Oct. 1932, Lexington, KY, USA; m. Jane Mary Billing, 8 Sept. 1958, three s., one d. *Education:* BA, University of Kentucky, 1954; Princeton University, 1954–55; BA, 1957, MA, 1961, University of Oxford; BD, 1959, MA, 1962, PhD, 1965, Yale University. *Career:* Ordained, Presbyterian Church, 1959; Pastor, Windham Presbyterian Church, NH, 1958–61; Asst Prof., 1964–66, Assoc. Prof., 1966–67, York University, Toronto; Assoc. Prof., 1967–74, Prof. of Philosophy, 1974–81, Chair., Dept of Theology, 1977–79, 1988–91, Stuart Prof. of Philosophy, 1981–2002, Princeton Theological Seminary; mem. American Philosophical Asscn; American Theological Society; American Weil Society, co-founder and exec. board mem.; Asscn étude pensées S. Weil; Canadian Philosophical Asscn; Leibniz Gesellschaft; Society of Christian Philosophers; American Acad. of Religion. *Publications:* Leibniz' Theodicy (ed.), 1966; The Reasonableness of Faith, 1968; Finding Our Father, 1974, second edn as The Path of Perfect Love, 1992; Between Two Worlds, 1977, second edn as Temptation, 1986; Traces of God in a Frequently Hostile World, 1981; Three Outsiders: Pascal, Kierkegaard and Simone Weil, 1983; Mechanical Explanations and the Ultimate Origin of the Universe According to Leibniz, 1983; Philosophy for Understanding Theology, 1985; Love: Christian Romance, Marriage and Friendship, 1987; Christian Relief in a Postmodern World: The Full Wealth of Conviction, 1989; Quest: The Search for Meaning Through Christ, 1990; Primary Reading in Philosophy for Understanding Theology (ed. with Eric Springsted), 1992; Nature, Spirit, and Community: Issues in the Thought of Yesterday for Help Today (with Eric Springsted), 1997; Spiritual Theology, 1997; Steps Along the Way, 2002. Contributions: scholarly books and journals. *Honours:* Rhodes Scholar, 1955–57, 1963–64; Rockefeller Doctoral Fellow, 1962–64; Research Fellowships, Asscn of Theological Schools, 1975–76, Center of Theological Inquiry, 1985–86, 1994–95; Pew Evangelical Scholarship, 1991–92; John Templeton Awards in Science and Theology, 1992, 1993, and Prize for Best Courses in Science and Religion, 1995; Fellow, St Deiniol's Library, Hawarden, N Wales, 2003. *Address:* 70 Lillie St, Princeton Jct., NJ 08550, USA.

ALLEN, Edward (Hathaway); Writer and Poet; b. 20 Oct. 1948, New Haven, CT, USA. *Education:* Iowa Writers' Workshop on Poetry, 1975; MA, 1986, PhD, English, Ohio University. *Career:* Asst Prof., Rhodes College, Memphis, TN, 1989–91; mem. Acad. of American Poets; Associated Writing Programs; MLA; Poets and Writers; Writers' Guild of America. *Publications:* Fiction: Straight Through the Night, 1989; Mustang Sally, 1992. Contributions: newspapers and periodicals.

ALLEN, John (see Perry, Ritchie).

ALLEN, John B. (see Westlake, Donald Edwin).

ALLEN, Paula Gunn; Writer, Poet and University Lecturer; b. 1939, Cubero, NM, USA. *Education:* BA; MFA; PhD. *Career:* Lecturer, San Francisco State University, University of New Mexico, Fort Lewis College,

University of California at Berkeley. *Publications:* The Blind Lion, 1974; Sipapu: A Cultural Perspective, 1975; Coyote's Daylight Trip, 1978; A Cannon Between My Knees, 1981; From the Center: A Folio of Native American Art and Poetry (ed.), 1981; Shadow Country, 1982; Studies of American Indian Literature: Critical Essays and Course Designs (ed.), 1983; The Woman Who Owned the Shadows, 1983; The Sacred Hoop: Recovering the Feminine in American Indian Traditions (essays), 1986; Skins and Bones, 1988; Spider Woman's Granddaughters: Traditional Tales and Contemporary Writing by Native American Women (ed.), 1989; Grandmothers of the Light: A Medicine Woman's Sourcebook, 1991; Columbus and Beyond, 1992; Voice of the Turtle, 1994. *Honours:* American Book Award, 1990; Ford Foundation Grant; National Endowment for the Arts Award. *Address:* c/o Diane Cleaver Inc, 55 Fifth Ave, 15th Floor, New York, NY 10003, USA.

ALLEN, Roberta; Writer; b. 6 Oct. 1945, New York, NY, USA. *Career:* Creative Writing Instructor, Parsons School of Design, 1986; Guest Lecturer, Murdoch University, Perth, Australia, 1989; Instructor, The Writer's Voice, 1992–97, The New School, 1993–2002, New York University, 1993–2001; Adjunct Asst Prof., School of the Arts, Columbia University, 1998–99; mem. PEN. *Publications:* The Traveling Woman, 1986; The Daughter, 1992; Amazon Dream, 1993; Certain People, 1997; Fast Fiction, 1997; The Dreaming Girl, 2000; The Playful Way to Serious Writing, 2002. Contributions: various anthologies, journals and periodicals. *Honours:* LINE grant, 1985; Yaddo Fellowships, 1987, 1993; VCCA, 1994; Tennessee Williams Fellow, 1998. *Literary Agent:* DeAnna Heindel, 136 E 57th St, New York, NY 10022, USA.

ALLEN, William L.; American editor and executive; b. 28 Dec. 1940, Tyler, TX. *Education:* Georgia Tech., Louisiana State Univ. *Career:* served in US army as lieutenant late 1960s, ran several military newspapers; became freelance photographer; joined Nat. Geographic magazine 1969, Illustrations Ed. 1985–92, Sr Asst Ed., then Assoc. Ed. 1992–95; Ed.-in-Chief, Nat. Geographic Soc. 1995– (also bd mem.); bd mem. Nat. Geographic Editiorial Foundation, Nat. Space Biomedical Research Inst., Inst. of Nautical Archaeology, Teton Science School, Nat. Council of the World Wildlife Fund, Council on Foreign Relations; mem. Cosmos Club. *Honours:* Nat. Magazine Award 2000. *Literary Agent:* National Geographic, 1145 17th Street NW, Washington, DC 20036-4688, USA. *Website:* www.nationalgeographic.com.

ALLENDE, Isabel; Chilean (b. Peruvian) writer; b. 8 Aug. 1942, Lima; m. 1st Miguel Frias 1962; one s. one d.; m. 2nd William Gordon 1988. *Career:* journalist, Paula magazine 1967–74, Mampato magazine 1969–74; Channel 13 World Hunger Campaign 1964; Channel 7, various humorous programmes 1970–74; Maga-Cine-Ellas 1973; Admin. Marroco School, Caracas 1978–82; freelance journalist, El Nacional newspaper, Caracas 1976–83; Visiting Teacher, Montclair State Coll., NJ 1985, Univ. of Virginia, Charlottesville 1988, Univ. of Calif., Berkeley 1989; writer 1981–; Pres. Chamber of Deputies, Chile 2003–. *Plays:* Paula, Stories of Eva Luna, The House of the Spirits, Eva Luna. *Publications:* novels: The House of the Spirits 1982, Of Love and Shadows 1984, Eva Luna 1986, Aphrodite 1998, Daughter of Fortune 1999, Portrait in Sepia 2000, The Kingdom of the Golden Dragon 2003; short stories: Tales of Eva Luna 1990, The Infinite Plan 1992; memoirs: Paula 1995, Aphrodite 1997, My Invented Country: A Nostalgic Journey Through Chile 2003; children's story: La Gorda de Porcelana 1984, The City of the Beasts 2002. *Honours:* Hon. Prof. (Chile) 1991; Hon. mem. Acad. of Devt and Peace, Austria 2000; Hon. DLitt (New York State) 1991; Novel of the Year, Panorama Literario (Chile) 1983, Point de Mire (Belgium) 1985, Author of the Year and Book of the Year (Germany) 1984, Grand Prix d'Evasion (France) 1984, Colima for Best Novel (Mexico) 1985, Author of the Year (Germany) 1986, Mulheres Best Novel (Portugal) 1987, Dorothy and Lillian Gish Prize 1998, Sara Lee Frontrunner Award 1998, GEMS Women of the Year Award 1999, Donna Dell'Anno Award (Italy) 1999, WILLA Literary Award (USA) 2000. *Literary Agent:* Carmen Balcells, Diagonal 580, Barcelona 21, Spain. *Address:* 116 Caledonia Street, Sausalito, CA 94965, USA.

ALLISON, Dorothy; Writer and Poet; b. 11 April 1949, Greenville, SC, USA. *Education:* BA, Florida Presbyterian College, 1971; MA, New School for Social Research. *Career:* mem. Authors' Guild; PEN; Writers' Union. *Publications:* Fiction: Trash, 1988; Bastard Out of Carolina, 1992; Cavedweller, 1998. Poetry: The Women Who Hate Me, 1983. Non-Fiction: Skin: Talking About Sex, Class and Literature, 1994; Two or Three Things I Know for Sure, 1995. *Honours:* Lambda Literary Awards for Best Small Press Book and Best Lesbian Book, 1989. *Address:* PO Box 136, Guerneville, CA 95446, USA.

ALLISON, John; British editor and critic. *Career:* former organist at Cape Town Cathedral, S Africa; music critic for The Times; Ed., Opera magazine. *Publications:* Edward Elgar: Sacred Music 1994, Mitchell Beazley Pocket Guide to Opera 1998; contrib. to Opera News, BBC Music Magazine, Classic FM Magazine, Financial Times, London Evening Standard, The Observer, The Australian. *Address:* Opera Magazine, 36 Black Lion Lane, London, W6 9BE, England. *E-mail:* editor@operamag.clara.co.uk. *Website:* www.opera.co.uk.

ALLOTT, Miriam; Prof. of English Emeritus and Writer; b. 16 June 1920, London, England; m. Kenneth Allott 2 June 1951 (died 1973). *Education:* MA, 1946, PhD, 1949, University of Liverpool. *Career:* Lecturer to Reader in English Literature, 1948–73, Andrew Cecil Bradley Prof. of Modern English Literature, 1973–81, University of Liverpool; Prof. of English, 1981–85, Prof. Emeritus, 1985–, Birkbeck College, University of London; mem. English Asscn, exec. committee. *Publications:* The Art of Graham Greene (with Kenneth Allott), 1951; Novelists on the Novel, 1959; The Complete Poems of Matthew Arnold (ed. with Kenneth Allott), 1965; The Complete Poems of John Keats (ed.), 1970; Matthew Arnold (with R. H. Super), 1986. Contributions: scholarly books and journals. *Honours:* William Noble Fellowship in English Literature, 1946–48; Hon. Senior Fellow, University of Liverpool. *Address:* 21 Mersey Ave, Liverpool L19 3QU, England.

ALLOUACHE, Merzak; Algerian film director and writer; b. 6 Oct. 1944, Algiers; m. Lazib Anissa 1962; one d. *Career:* worked in Nat. Inst. of Cinema, Algiers, later in Inst. of Film, Paris; after return to Algeria worked as Adviser, Ministry of Culture. *Films include:* Our Agrarian Revolution (documentary) 1973, Omar Gatlato, Les aventures d'un héros, L'homme qui regardait les fenêtres 1982, Bab El-Oued City 1994, Lumiére et Compagnie 1995, Salut Cousin! 1996, Dans la décapotable 1996, Alger–Beyrouth: Pour Mémoire 1998, Pepe Carvalho: La Solitude du Manager (TV) 1999, À bicyclette (TV) 2001, L'Autre Monde 2001, Chouchou 2003. *Publications:* Bab El-Oued (novel) 1994. *Honours:* Silver Prize, Moscow Festival; Tanit D'Or Prize, Carthage 1979. *Address:* Cité des Asphodèles, Bt D15, 183 Ben Aknoun, Algiers, Algeria. *Telephone:* 79 33 60.

ALMODÓVAR, Pedro; Spanish film director and screenplay writer; b. 25 Sept. 1951, Calzada de Calatrava, Ciudad Real, Castilla La Mancha. *Career:* fronted a rock band; worked at Telefónica for ten years; started career with full-length super-8 films; made 16mm short films 1974–83. *Films as writer and director:* Film político 1974, Dos putas, o historia de amor que termina en boda 1974, El Sueño, o la estrella 1975, Homenaje 1975, La caída de Sódoma 1975, Blancor 1975, Sea caritativo 1976, Muerte en la carretera 1976, Sexo va, sexo viene 1977, Salomé 1978, ¡Folle... folle... fólleme Tim! 1978, Pepe, Luci, Bom y otras chicas del montón 1980, Laberinto de pasiones 1982, Entre tinieblas 1983, ¿Qué he hecho yo para merecer esto? 1985, Matador 1986, La ley del deseo 1987, Mujeres al borde de un ataque de nervios (Felix Award) 1988, ¡Atame! 1990, Tacones lejanos 1991, Kika 1993, La flor de mi secreto 1995, Carne trémula 1997, Todo sobre mi madre (Acad. Award for Best Foreign Language Film) 1999, Hable con ella (BAFTA Award for Best Film not in the English language 2003, Acad. Award for Best Original Screenplay 2003) 2002, La mala educación 2004. *Films as producer:* Laberinto de pasiones 1982, Mujeres al borde de un ataque de nervios 1988, Acción mutante 1993, Mi nombre es sombra (assoc. producer) 1996, Cuernos de espuma 1996, El Espinazo del diablo 2001, Mi vida sin mí (exec. producer) 2003, La Mala educación 2004. *Publications:* Fuego en las entrañas 1982, The Patty Diphusa Stories and Other Writings 1992. *Address:* c/o El Deseo SA, Ruiz Perelló 15, Madrid 28028, Spain; Miramax Films, 18 E 48th Street, New York, NY 10017, USA.

ALMOND, Brenda Margaret; Prof. of Moral and Social Philosophy and Writer; b. 19 Sept. 1937, Liverpool, England; m. Charles Desmond Cohen, 9 Jan. 1960, one s., three d. *Education:* BA, 1959; MPhil, 1976, University of London. *Career:* Lecturer in Philosophy, Universities of Ghana, 1959–60, Keele, 1960–62, Brighton, 1967–74, Surrey, 1974–86; Prof. of Moral and Social Philosophy, University of Hull, 1986–2001; mem. Austrian Acad. of Sciences, elected corresponding mem., 1999. *Publications:* Education and the Individual, 1981; Moral Concerns, 1987; AIDS: A Moral Issue (ed.), 1990; The Philosophical Quest, 1990; Exploring Philosophy, 1995; Exploring Ethics: Traveller's Tale, 1998. *Honours:* Hon. Doctorate, University of Utrecht, Netherlands, 1998. *Address:* c/o Philosophy, Humanities, University of Hull, Hull HU6 7RX, England.

ALMOND, David, BA; British writer; b. 15 May 1951, Newcastle upon Tyne, England. *Education:* Univ. of East Anglia. *Career:* fmr teacher; Ed., Panurge magazine 1987–93. *Plays:* Wild Girl Wild Boy 2001. *Publications:* short story collections: Sleepless Nights 1985, A Kind of Heaven 1997, Country Stars 2000; juvenile fiction: Skellig 1998, Kit's Wilderness 1999, Heaven Eyes 2000, Secret Heart 2002, The Fire-Eaters 2003. *Honours:* Whitbread Children's Book of the Year 1998, 2003, Carnegie Medal, Smarties Prize, Smarties Prize Silver Medal, Nestlé Smarties Prize Gold Award. *Address:* c/o Hodder Children's Books, Publicity Department, 338 Euston Road, London, NW1 3BH, England. *Website:* www.davidalmond.com.

ALONZO, Anne-Marie; Author, Poet, Dramatist, Journalist and Publisher; b. 13 Dec. 1951, Alexandria, Egypt. *Education:* BA, 1976, MA, 1978, PhD, 1986, University of Montréal. *Career:* Co-founder and Vice-Pres., Auto/Graphe theatre and production co, 1981–87; Co-founder, Les Editions Trois, 1985; Co-founder and Dir, Trois review, 1985–99; Founder and Co-ordinator, Festival de Trois, 1989–; mem. Amnesty International; Artistes pour la paix; PEN International; Société littéraire de Laval; Society of Composers, Authors and Music Publishers of Canada; Union de écrivaines et écrivains québécois; CEAD. *Publications:* Une lettre rouge orange et ocre, 1984; Bleus de mine, 1985; Ecoute, Sultane, 1987; Seul le désir, 1987; Esmai, 1987; Le livre des ruptures, 1988; Lead Blues, 1990; L'Immobile, 1990; Linked Alive (co-author), 1990; Galia qu'elle nommait amour, 1992; Margie Gillis, la danse des marches, 1993; Lettres a Cassandre (with Denise

Desautels), 1994; Tout au loin la lumière, 1994; La nuit, 2001. Contributions: various publications. *Honours:* Prix Emile-Nelligan, 1985; Grand Prix d'excellence artistique en creation littéraire, 1992; Mem. of the Order of Canada, 1997. *Address:* 2033 Jessop, Laval, QC H7S 1X3, Canada.

ALPERT, Cathryn; Writer; b. 4 Jan. 1952, Santa Monica, CA, USA; m. Marco Alpert, 8 Feb. 1982, two s. three d. *Education:* BA, 1973, MA, 1974, PhD, 1979, University of California at Los Angeles. *Career:* Asst Prof., Centre College, 1980–84; Writer, 1984–; mem. San Francisco Literary Society, board dir. *Publications:* Rocket City – MacMurray and Beck, 1995; Rocket City – Vintage Contemporaries, 1996. Contributions: Puerto Del Sol; Thema; Wittenberg Review. *Honours:* Second Place, O. Henry Festival Short Story Contest, 1989; Hon. Mention, Raymond Carver Short Story Contest, 1989; First Place, Amaranth Review Short Fiction Contest, 1991; Third Place, CPU Short Story Contest, 1991. *Literary Agent:* Felicia Eth. *Address:* 555 Bryant St, Suite 350, Palo Alto, CA 94301, USA.

ALPHONSO-KARKALA, John B.; Writer, Poet and Prof. of Literature; b. 30 May 1923, South Kanara, Mysore State, India; m. Leena Anneli Hakalehto, 20 Dec. 1964, three c. *Education:* BA, 1950, MA, 1953, Mumbai University; University of London, 1954–55; PhD, Columbia University, 1964. *Career:* Visiting Lecturer, City College, CUNY, 1963; Asst Prof., 1964–65, Assoc. Prof., 1965–68, Prof. of Literature, 1969–, SUNY at New Paltz; Visiting Prof., Columbia University, 1969–70; mem. American Oriental Society; Asscn for Asian Studies; International Congress of Comparative Literature; International Congress of Orientalists; MLA of America. *Publications:* Indo-English Literature in the Nineteenth Century, 1970; Anthology of Indian Literature (ed.), 1971, revised edn as Ages of Rishis, Buddha, Acharyas, Bhaktas and Mahatma, 1987; Bibliography of Indo-English Literature, 1800–1966 (ed. with Leena Karkala), 1974; Comparative World Literature: Seven Essays, 1974; Passions of the Nightless Night (novel), 1974; Jawaharlal Nehru: A Literary Portrait, 1975; When Night Falls (poems), 1980; Vedic Vision (ed.), 1980; Joys of Jayanagara (novel), 1981; Indo-English Literature: Essays (with Leena Karkala), 1994. *Address:* 20 Millrock Rd, New Paltz, NY 12561, USA.

ALSTON, William (Payne); Prof. of Philosophy and Writer; b. 29 Nov. 1921, Shreveport, LA, USA; m. 1st Mary Frances Collins 15 Aug. 1943 (divorced); one d.; m. 2nd Valerie Tibbetts Barnes 3 July 1963. *Education:* BM, Centenary College, 1942; PhD, University of Chicago, 1951. *Career:* Instructor, 1949–52, Asst Prof., 1952–56, Assoc. Prof., 1956–61, Prof., 1961–71, Acting Chair., 1961–64, Dir of Graduate Studies, 1966–71, Dept of Philosophy, University of Michigan; Visiting Lecturer, Harvard University, 1955–56; Fellow, Centre for Advanced Studies in Behavioural Sciences, 1965–66; Prof. of Philosophy, Douglass College, Rutgers University, 1971–76, University of Illinois at Urbana-Champaign, 1976–80, Syracuse University, 1980–; Austin Fagothey Visiting Prof. of Philosophy, Santa Clara University, 1991; mem. American Acad. of Arts and Sciences; Society for Philosophy and Psychology, pres., 1976–77; American Philosophical Asscn, pres. of Central Division, 1978–79; Society of Christian Philosophers, pres., 1978–81; American Theological Society; Society for Philosophy of Religion. *Publications:* Religious Belief and Philosophical Thought, 1963; Readings in Twentieth Century Philosophy (with G. Nakhnikian), 1963; The Philosophy of Language, 1964; The Problems of Philosophy: Introductory Readings (with R. B. Brandt), 1967; Divine Nature and Human Language, 1989; Epistemic Justification, 1989; Perceiving God, 1991; The Reliability of Sense Perception, 1993; A Realist Conception of Truth, 1996; Illocutionary Acts and Sentence Meaning, 2000. Editor: Philosophical Research Archives, 1974–77; Faith and Philosophy, 1982–90; Cornell Studies in the Philosophy of Religion, 1987–. Contributions: scholarly books and journals. *Honours:* DLitt Hum. hc, Church Divinity School of the Pacific, 1988; Chancellor's Exceptional Academic Achievement Award, Syracuse University, 1990. *Address:* c/o Dept of Philosophy, Syracuse University, Syracuse, NY 13244, USA.

ALTER, Robert Bernard, BA, MA, PhD; academic and literary critic; b. 2 April 1935, New York, NY, USA; m. Carol Cosman 1974; three s. one d. *Education:* Columbia College, Harvard University. *Career:* Instructor, Asst Prof. of English, Columbia University, 1962–66; Assoc. Prof. of Hebrew and Comparative Literature, 1967–69, Prof. of Hebrew and Comparative Literature, 1969–89, Class of 1937 Prof., 1989–, University of California, Berkeley; mem. American Comparative Literature Asscn; Asscn of Literary Scholars and Critics; Council of Scholars of the Library of Congress; American Acad. of Arts and Sciences. *Publications:* Partial Magic, 1975; Defenses of the Imagination, 1978; Stendhal: A Biography, 1979; The Art of Biblical Narrative, 1981; Motives for Fiction, 1984; The Art of Biblical Poetry, 1985; The Pleasures of Reading in an Ideological Age, 1989; Necessary Angels, 1991; The World of Biblical Literature, 1992; Hebrew and Modernity, 1994; Genesis: Translation and Commentary, 1996; Canon and Creativity: Modern Writing and the Authority of Scripture, 2000. Contributions: Commentary; New Republic; New York Times Book Review; London Review of Books; TLS. *Honours:* English Institute Essay Prize, 1965; National Jewish Book Award for Jewish Thought, 1982; Present Tense Award for Religious Thought, 1986; Award for Scholarship, National Foundation for Jewish Culture, 1995. *Address:* 1475 Le Roy Avenue, Berkeley, CA 94708, USA.

ALTHER, Lisa, BA; American writer and university professor; *Professor and Basler Chair, East Tennessee State University*; b. 23 July 1944, Kingsport, Tenn.; m. Richard Alther 1966 (divorced); one d. *Education:* Wellesley Coll., Radcliffe Coll. *Career:* editorial asst, Atheneum Publrs, New York 1967–68; freelance writer 1968–; Lecturer, St Michael's Coll., Winooski, Vt 1980–81; Prof. and Basler Chair, East Tenn. State Univ. 1999–. *Publications:* Kinflicks 1975, Original Sins 1980, Other Women 1984, Bedrock 1990, Birdman and the Dancer 1993, Five Minutes in Heaven 1995; contributions: periodicals. *Address:* 1086 Silver Street, Hinesburg, VT 05461, USA. *Telephone:* (802) 482-3141. *Fax:* (802) 482-3141. *E-mail:* lalther@aol.com.

ALTICK, Richard Daniel; academic and writer; b. 19 Sept. 1915, Lancaster, PA, USA; m. Helen W. Keller 1942; two d. *Education:* BA, Franklin and Marshall College, 1936; PhD, University of Pennsylvania, 1941. *Career:* Faculty, 1945, Regent's Prof. of English, 1968–82, Regent's Prof. Emeritus of English, 1982–, Ohio State University, Columbus. *Publications:* Preface to Critical Reading, 1946; The Cowden Clarkes, 1948; The Scholar Adventurers, 1950; The English Common Reader: A Social History of the Mass Reading Public, 1800–1900, 1957; The Art of Literary Research, 1963; Lives and Letters: A History of Literary Biography in England and America, 1965; Carlyle: Past and Present (ed.), 1965; Browning's Roman Murder Story (with J. F. Loucks), 1968; To Be in England, 1969; Victorian Studies in Scarlet, 1970; Browning: The Ring and the Book (ed.), 1971; Victorian People and Ideas: A Companion for the Modern Reader of Victorian Literature, 1973; The Shows of London, 1978; Paintings from Books: Art and Literature in Britain 1760–1900, 1985; Deadly Encounters: Two Victorian Sensations (in the UK as Evil Encounters), 1986; Writers, Readers and Occasions, 1989; The Presence of the Present: Topics of the Day in the Victorian Novel, 1991; Punch: The Lively Youth of a British Institution 1841–51, 1997. *Honours:* Guggenheim Fellowship, 1975. *Address:* 276 W Southington Avenue, Worthington, OH 43085, USA.

ALVAREZ, Alfred, BA, MA; poet and author; b. 5 Aug. 1929, London, England; m. 1966, two s. one d. *Education:* Corpus Christi Coll., Oxford. *Career:* poetry critic and Ed., Observer 1956–66; Advisory Ed., Penguin Modern European Poets 1964–76. *Publications:* The Shaping Spirit, 1958; The School of Donne, 1961; The New Poetry, 1962; Under Pressure, 1965; Beyond All the Fiddle, 1968; Penguin Modern Poets No. 18, 1970; Apparition, 1971; The Savage God, 1971; Beckett, 1973; Hers, 1974; Autumn to Autumn and Selected Poems, 1978; Hunt, 1978; Life After Marriage, 1982; The Biggest Game in Town, 1983; Offshore, 1986; Feeding the Rat, 1988; Rain Forest, 1988; Day of Atonement, 1991; Faber Book of Modern European Poetry, 1992; Night, 1995; Where Did It All Go Right?, 1999; Poker Bets, Bluffs and Bad Beats, 2001; New and Selected Poems, 2002. Contributions: numerous magazines and journals. *Honours:* Vachel Lindsay Prize for Poetry 1961, Hon. DLitt (University of East London) 1998, Hon. Fellow, Corpus Christi Coll., Oxford 2001. *Literary Agent:* Gillon Aitken Associates Ltd, 18–21 Cavaye Place, London, SW10 9PT, England. *Telephone:* (20) 7373-8672. *Fax:* (20) 7373-6002.

AMABILE, George; Prof. of English, Poet and Writer; b. 29 May 1936, Jersey City, NJ, USA. *Education:* BA, Amherst College, 1957; MA, University of Minnesota, 1961; PhD, University of Connecticut, 1969. *Career:* Lecturer, 1963, Asst Prof., 1966–68, 1969–71, Assoc. Prof., 1972–86, Prof. of English, 1987–, University of Manitoba; Visiting Writer-in-Residence, University of British Columbia, 1968–69; various readings, Manitoba Theatre Centre, radio, and television; mem. League of Canadian Poets; Western Canadian Publishers' Asscn. *Publications:* Blood Ties, 1972; Open Country, 1976; Flower and Song, 1977; Ideas of Shelter, 1981; The Presence of Fire, 1982; Four of a Kind, 1994; Rumours of Paradise/Rumours of War, 1995. Contributions: many anthologies, journals, and periodicals. *Honours:* Canada Council Grants, 1968, 1969, 1981, 1982, 1995, 1996; Canadian Authors' Asscn National Prize for Poetry, 1983; Third Prize, CBC National Literary Competition, 1992. *Address:* c/o Dept of English, University of Manitoba, Winnipeg, MB R3T 2N2, Canada.

AMADI, Elechi; Writer and Educator; b. 12 May 1934, Aluu, Nigeria; m. 1st Dorah Nwonne Ohale, 1957; m. 2nd Priye Iyalla, 1991, four s., eight d. *Education:* Government College, Umuaphia; University College, Ibadan; Brookings Institution, Washington, DC. *Career:* Army Officer, 1963–66, 1968–69; Principal, Asa Grammar School, 1967; Permanent Sec., 1973–83, Commissioner of Education, 1987–89, and of Lands and Housing, 1989–90, Rivers State Government; Writer-in-Residence and Lecturer, 1984–85, Dean of Arts, 1985–86, Head of Dept of Literature, 1991–93, Rivers State College of Education; Founder-Dir, Elechi Amadi School of Creative Writing, 1997–. *Publications:* The Concubine, 1966; The Great Ponds, 1969; Sunset in Biafra, 1973; The Slave, 1978; Ethics in Nigerian Culture, 1982; Estrangement, 1986. Plays: Isiburu, 1969; Peppersoup, and The Road to Ibadan, 1977; Dancer of Johannesburg, 1979. Other: Hymn and Prayer books. *Address:* PO Box 331, Port Harcourt, Nigeria.

AMAL, Nukila; Indonesian novelist; b. 1971, Ternate. *Education:* Bandung Tourism Acad. *Publications:* novel: Cala Ibi 2003; contrib. to Kalam. *Literary Agent:* c/o Pena Gaia Klasik, Jakarta, Indonesia Indonesia.

AMANN, Jürg; writer and dramatist; b. 2 July 1947, Winterthur, Switzerland. *Education:* PhD, Univ. of Zürich. *Career:* mem. Authors of Switzerland AdS; PEN. *Publications:* Das Symbol Kafka, 1974; Hardenberg, 1978; Verirren oder das plötzliche Schweigen des Robert Walser, 1978; Die Kunst des wirkungsvollen Abgangs, 1979; Die Baumschule, 1982; Franz Kafka, 1983; Nachgerufen, 1983; Ach, diese Wege sind sehr dunkel, 1985; Patagonien, 1985; Robert Walser, 1985; Fort, 1987; Aus dem Hohen Lied, 1987; Nach dem Fest, 1988; Tod Weidigs, 1989; Der Rücktritt, 1989; Der Vater der Mutter und der Vater des Vaters, 1990; Der Anfang der Angst, 1991; Der Lauf der Zeit, 1993; Zwei oder drei Dinge, 1993; Über die Jahre, 1994; Und über die Liebe wäre wieder zu sprechen, 1994; Robert Walser, 1995; Rondo, 1996; Schöne Aussicht, 1997; Iphigenie oder Operation Meereswind, 1998; Ikarus, 1998; Golomir, 1999; Kafka, 2000; Am Ufer des Flusses, 2001; Kein Weg nach Rom, 2001; Mutter töten, 2003; Sternendrift, 2003. *Honours:* Ingeborg Bachmann Prize, 1982; Conrad Ferdinand Meyer Prize, 1983; Schiller Foundation Award, 1989; Art Prize of Winterthur, 1989; International Awards for Radio Plays, 1998, 1999, 2000; Schiller Prize, 2001. *Literary Agent:* Piper Verlag, Arche Verlag, Haymon Verlag, Eremiten-Presse, Sessler Verlag. *Address:* Haus Zum Spiegel, Napfgasse, 3, 8001 Zürich, Switzerland.

AMANSHAUSER, Gerhard; Writer; b. 2 Jan. 1928, Salzburg, Austria. *Education:* Technical University of Graz; Universities of Vienna, Austria and Marburg. *Publications:* Aus der Leben der Quaden, 1968; Der Deserteur, 1970; Ärgernisse eines Zauberers, 1973; Schloss mit späten Gäten, 1975; Grenzen, 1977; Aufzeichnungen einer Sonde, 1979; List der Illusionen, 1985; Gedichte, 1986; Fahrt zur verbotenen Stadt, 1987; Der Ohne Namen See, 1988; Moloch Horridus, 1989; Lektüre, 1991; Gegensätze, 1993; Das Erschlagen von Stechmücken, 1993; Tische, Stühle und Bierseidel, 1997; Mansardenbuch, 1999; Terrassenbuch, 1999; Der Sprung ins dritte Jahrtausend (von Gerhard und Martin Amanshauser), Erzn, 1999; Als Barbar im Prater: Autobiographie einer Jugend, 2001; Ohren-Wurst aus Österreich: Satiren, 2002; Der Rote Mann wird eingeschneit (children's book), 2002; Entlarvung der Flüchtig Skizzierten Herren (with CD), 2003. Contributions: Literatur und Kritik; Neues Forum; Protokolle; Neue Rundschau. *Honours:* Georg Trakl Promotion Prize, 1952; Theodor Körner Prize, 1970; Rauriser Literaturpreis, 1973; Förderungspreis der Stadt Salzburg, 1975; Preis der Salzburger Wirtschaft, 1985; Alma Johanna Koenig Preis, 1987; Dr hc, 1993; Würdigungspreis für Literatur, Bundesministeriums für Unterricht und Kunst, 1994. *Address:* Brunnhausgasse 10, 5020 Salzburg, Austria.

AMB, Daniel (see Andersen, Baltser).

AMBERT, Alba; Writer and Poet; b. 10 Oct. 1946, San Juan, Puerto Rico; m. Walter McCann, 11 Feb. 1984, one d. *Education:* BA, University of Puerto Rico, 1974; MEd, 1975, DEd, 1980, Harvard University. *Career:* Bilingual Teacher, Boston Public Schools, 1975–80; Asst Prof. and Dir, Bilingual Special Education Teacher Training Program, University of Hartford, 1980–84; Visiting Scientist, MIT, 1984–85; Senior Research Scholar, Athens College, Greece, 1985–93; Writer-in-Residence, Richmond University, 1993–; mem. Authors' Guild; Writer's Union. *Publications:* Fiction: Porque hay silencio, 1989; A Perfect Silence, 1995; The Eighth Continent and Other Stories, 1997; An Inclination of Mirrors, 1997. Poetry: Gotas sobre el columpio, 1980; The Fifth Sun, 1989; Habito tu nombre, 1994; At Dawn We Start Again, 1997. Children's Books: Thunder from the Earth, 1997; Why the Wild Winds Blow, 1997; Face to Sky, 1998. *Honours:* Ford Foundation Fellowship, 1984; Institute of Puerto Rican Literature Award, 1989; Carey McWilliams Award, 1996; Pres.'s Award, Massachusetts Asscn for Bilingual Education, 1997. *Address:* c/o Richmond University, Queens Rd, Richmond, Surrey TW10 6JP, England.

AMBROSE, David (Edwin); Playwright, Screenwriter and Novelist; b. 21 Feb. 1943, Chorley, Lancashire, England; m. Laurence Huguette Hammerli, 13 Sept. 1979. *Education:* LLB, Merton College, Oxford, 1965. *Career:* mem. Dramatists' Club, London. *Publications:* Fiction: The Man Who Turned Into Himself, 1993; Mother of God, 1995; Hollywood Lies; Superstition, 1997; Coincidence, 2002; A Memory of Demons, 2003. Other: many television plays and screenplays world-wide; also Seige, Cambridge Theatre, London, 1972. *Honours:* First Prize Screenplay, Sitges Film Festival, 1980. *Literary Agent:* William Morris Agency (UK) Ltd, 52–53 Poland St, London W1F 7LX, England.

AMERY, Carl; Writer; b. 9 April 1922, Munich, Germany; m. Marijane Gerth, 10 April 1950, three s., two d. *Education:* Humanistisches Gymnasium, 1940; Literary and Language Studies, Munich and Washington, DC, 1946–50. *Career:* Ed., Bavarian Radio, 1950, 1962; Dir, Munich Library System, 1967–71; mem. German Writers' Asscn; PEN Centre, Germany. *Publications:* Die Grosse Deutsche Tour, 1959; Die Kapitulation (essays), 1963; Das Ende der Vorsehung (essays), 1972; Das Koenigsprojekt, 1974; Natur als Politik, 1976; Bileams Esel, 1981; Die Wallfahrer, 1986; Das Geheimnis der Krypta, 1990; Die Botschaft des Jahrtausends, 1994; Hitler als Vorlaeufer, 1998; Global Exit, 2002. *Honours:* Cross of Merit, Germany, 1988. *Address:* Draechslstr 7, 81541 Munich, Germany.

AMES, Jonathan, ; American writer. *Publications:* I Pass Like Night 1989, The Extra Man 1998, What's Not to Love?: The Adventures of a Mildly Perverted Young Writer 2000, My Less Than Secret Life 2002, Wake Up, Sir! 2004; contrib. to McSweeny's, boldtype. *Address:* c/o Scribner Book Company, Simon & Schuster, 1230 Avenue of the Americas, New York, NY 10020, USA. *E-mail:* jonathanames2@aol.com. *Website:* www.jonathanames.com.

AMETTE, Jacques-Pierre, (Paul Clément); French novelist and playwright; b. 18 May 1943, Normandy. *Career:* French correspondent, New York Times, numerous French newspapers. *Plays:* Les sables mouvants 1974, Le maître-nageur 1989, Les environs de Heilbronn 1989, La Waldstein 1991, Après nous 1991, Singe 1992, Le mal du pays 1992, Passions secrètes, crimes d'avril 1993, Appassionata 1993, La clarière 1997. *Publications include:* novels: La congé 1965, Élisabeth Skerla 1966, La vie comme ca 1974, Bermuda 1977, La nuit tombante 1978, Jeunesse dans une ville normande 1981, Enquête d'hiver 1985, L'après-midi 1987, La peau du monde 1992, Province 1995, L'Homme du silence 1999, Ma vie, son oeuvre 2001, La maîtresse de Brecht 2003; other: Un voyage en province 1970, Les lumières de l'Antarctique 1973, Confessions d'un enfant gâté 1986, L'adieu à la raison 1993, Stendhal: 3 juin 1819 1994; as Paul Clément: Exit 1981, Je tue à la campagne 1982. *Honours:* Prix Roger Nimier 1986, Prix CIC du Théâtre 1992, Prix Contre-point 1997, Prix Goncourt 2003. *Address:* c/o Editions Albin Michel, 22 rue Huyghens, 75014 Paris, France. *Website:* www.albin-michel.fr.

AMICOLA, José; Prof. and Writer; b. 15 Feb. 1942, Buenos Aires, Argentina. *Education:* Lic. en Let, Universidad de Buenos Aires, Argentina; PhD, Universität Göttingen, Germany, 1982. *Career:* mem. Instituto Intern Literatura Iberoamericana, Pittsburgh. *Publications:* Sobre Cortázar, 1969; Astrología y fascismo en la obra de Arlt, 1984; Manuel Puig y la tela que atrapa al lector, 1992; Dostoievski, 1994; De la forma a la información, 1997; Camp y postvanguardia, 2000; Batalla de los géneros: Novela gótica versus novela de educación, 2003. *Honours:* Premio Banco Mercantil, 1992. *Address:* Las Heras, 3794-11A, 1425 Buenos Aires, Argentina. *E-mail:* vesuvienne99@hotmail.com.

AMIREDJIBI, Chabua; Writer, Editor and Politician; b. (Mzechabuk I. Amiredjibi), 18 Nov. 1921, Tbilisi, Georgia; m. Tamar Djavakhishvili 1966; four s. (one deceased) two d. *Education:* Tbilisi State Univ.; A. Pushkin Tbilisi Pedagogical Inst. *Career:* as student of Tbilisi State Univ. was arrested for political activities 1944, sentenced to 25 years' imprisonment in Gulag, released 1959; Dir Advertising-Information Bureau Goskinoprokat 1965–70; Chief Ed. Kino anthology 1970–83; Dir Mematiane documentary film studio 1983–89; MP 1992–96; Chair. Defence Fund of Georgia 1992–96; f. PEN Centre of Georgia, Pres. 1994–97, Hon. Chair. 1998–; Publr and Ed.-in-Chief Ganakhlebuli Iveria newspaper 1999–; mem. editorial boards of several journals and newspapers; mem. Writers' Union of Georgia, 1964–. *Publications:* Road (short stories), 1964; Tales for Children, 1966; Data Tutashkhia (novel), 1973, (film screenplay), 1979; Gora Mborgali (novel), 1994. *Honours:* USSR State Prize, 1979; Honoured Art Worker of Georgia, 1987; Order of Honour, 1994; Sh. Rustaveli Prize, 1994; Order of King Vakhtang Gorgasili (First Class), 2001. *Address:* 8/45 Tamarashvili St, 380062 Tbilisi, Georgia.

AMIS, Martin Louis, BA; British writer; b. 25 Aug. 1949, Oxford; m. 1st Antonia Phillips 1984 (divorced 1996); two s.; m. 2nd Isabel Fonseca 1998; two d. *Education:* Exeter Coll., Oxford. *Career:* Asst Ed., TLS 1971, Fiction and Poetry Ed. TLS 1974–75; Asst Literary Ed., New Statesman 1975–77, Literary Ed. 1977–79; special writer for The Observer newspaper 1980–. *Publications:* fiction: The Rachel Papers (Somerset Maugham Award 1974) 1973, Dead Babies 1975, new edn as Dark Secrets 1977, Success 1978, Other People: A Mystery Story 1981, Money: A Suicide Note 1984, Einstein's Monsters (short stories) 1987, London Fields 1989, Time's Arrow, or, the Nature of the Offence 1991, God's Dice 1995, The Information 1995, Night Train 1997, Heavy Water and Other Stories 1999, Yellow Dog 2003; non-fiction: My Oxford (with others) 1977, Invasion of the Space Invaders 1982, The Moronic Inferno and Other Visits to America 1986, Visiting Mrs Nabokov and Other Excursions 1993, Experience: A Memoir (James Tait Black Memorial Prize for Biography 2001) 2000, The War Against Cliché (essays and reviews 1971–2000) 2001, Koba the Dread: Laughter and Twenty Million 2002; contrib. to many publications. *Literary Agent:* Wylie Agency (UK) Ltd, 4–8 Rodney Street, London, N1 9JH, England. *Telephone:* (20) 7843-2150. *Fax:* (20) 7843-2151.

AMMANITI, Niccolò; Author; b. 1966, Rome, Italy. *Publications:* Branchie (novel), 1994; Nel nome del figlio (essays, with Massimo Ammaniti), 1995; Fango (short stories), 1996; Ti prendo e ti porto via, 1999; Io non ho paura (I'm Not Scared), 2001. Contributions: short stories in anthologies: Gioventù cannibale, 1966; Tutti i denti del mostro sono perfetti, 1997. *Honours:* Viareggio-Repaci prize. *Address:* c/o Einaudi, via Biancamano 2, 10121 Torino, Italy.

AMOR, Anne Clark, (Anne Clark); Writer; b. 4 Feb. 1933, London, England; m. 23 Feb. 1982, one s. one d. *Education:* BA, English, Birkbeck College, University of London. *Career:* mem. Lewis Carroll Society, founder mem., pres., trustee, 1969–; Oscar Wilde Society, committee mem., 1993–. *Publications:* Beasts and Bawdy, 1975; Lewis Carroll: A Biography, 1979; The Real Alice, 1981; Mrs Oscar Wilde: A Woman of Some Importance, 1983; William Holman Hunt: The True Pre-Raphaelite, 1989; Lewis Carroll: Child of the North, 1995; Wonderland Come True to Alice in Lyndhurst, 1996; Charles Dodgson and Alice Liddell Go to Paris, 1997. Editor: Letters to Skeffington Dodgson from His Father; The Carrollian. Contributions: Books; Periodicals, including: Washington Post; Los Angeles Times; The Lady; Literary Review; Books and Bookmen; The Wildean. *Address:* 16 Parkfields Ave, Kingsbury, London NW9 7PE, England.

ANAND, Mulk Raj; Writer and Critic; b. 12 Dec. 1905, Peshawar, India; m. 1st Kathleen van Gelder 1939 (divorced 1948); m. 2nd Shirin Vajifdar 1950; one d. *Education:* Khalsa College, Amritsar; Punjab Univ., 1924; PhD, Cambridge and London Universities, 1929. *Career:* active in Nationalist and Gandhi movements; lecturer, London County Council, Workes Educational Assoc., London, League of Nations School of Intellectual Co-operation, Geneva, various Indian universities, 1948–66; BBC broadcaster, film scriptwriter, British Ministry of Information; f. and fmr Ed., Marg magazine, India, 1946; Dir, Kutub Publishers; Tagore Prof. of Literature and Fine Art, Punjab Univ., Chandigarh, 1960s; Visiting Prof., Institute of Advanced Studies, Simla, 1967–68; Pres., Lokayata Trust, 1970; mem. Indian National Academy of Letters; Fellow, Indian National Academy of Arts (Fine Art Chair., 1965–70); Indian National Book Trust. *Publications:* Fiction: The Lost Child and Other Stories, 1934; Untouchable, 1935; Coolie, 1936; Two Leaves and a Bud, 1937; The Village, 1939; Across the Black Waters, 1940; The Sword and the Sickle, 1942; India Speaks (play), 1943; The Barbers' Trade Union and Other Stories, 1944; The Big Heart, 1945; The Tractor and the Corn Goddess and Other Stories, 1947; Private Life of an Indian Prince, 1953; Reflections on the Golden Bd and Other Stories, 1954; Selected Stories, 1954; The Power of Darkness and Other Stories, 1959; The Old Woman and the Cow, 1960; The Story of Chacha Nehru, 1965; Lajwanti and Other Stories, 1966; Selected Short Stories, 1977. Non-fiction: Persian Painting, 1930; Curries and Other Indian Dishes, 1932; The Hindu View of Art, 1933; The Golden Breath, 1933; Lament on the Death of a Master of the Arts, 1938; Marx and Engels on India, 1939; Letters on India, 1942; Apology for Heroism, 1946; Homageto Tagore, 1946; The Bride's Book of Beauty (with K. Hutheesing), 1947; On Education, 1947; The King-Emperor's English, 1948; The Story of India, 1948; Letters Written to Indian Air, 1949; The Indian Theatre, 1950; The Story of Man, 1952; The Dancing Foot, 1957; India in Colour, 1958; Kama Kala, 1958; Homage to Khajuraho, 1960; The Road, 1961; Is There a Contemporary Indian Civilization?, 1963; Death of a Hero, 1963; The Third Eye, 1963; Bombay, 1965; The Volcano, 1967; The Humanism of M. K. Gandhi, 1967; Delhi, Agra, Sikri, 1968; Konorak (with others), 1968; Indian Ivories, 1970; Ajanta, 1970; Roots and Flowers, 1972; Author to Critic: The Letters of Mulk Raj Anand to Saros Cowasjee, 1973; Between Tears and Laughter, 1973; Album of Indian Paintings, 1973; Tantra Magic (with A. Mookerjee), 1978; The Humanism of Jawaharlal Nehru, 1978; Seven Little Known Birds of the Inner Eye, 1978; Only Connect: Letters to Indian Friends–E. M. Forster, a Profile, 1979; The Humanism of Rabindranath Tagore, 1979; Maya of Mohenjo-Daro, 1980; Conversations in Bloomsbury, 1981; Ellora, 1984; Madhubani Painting, 1984; Pilpali Sahib: The Story of a Childhood Under the Raj, 1985; Poet-Painter: Paintings by Rabindranath Tagore, 1985; Three Eminent Personalities on the Ram Janambhoomi, 1989; Amrita Sher-Gil, 1989; Pilpali Sahib: The Story of a Big Ego in a Small Boy, 1990; Old Myth and New Myth: Letters from Mulk Raj Anand to K. V. S. Murti Anand, 1991; Little Plays of Mahatma Gandhi, 1991; Caliban and Gandhi: Letters to 'Bapu' from Bombay, 1991. Autobiography: Seven Ages of Man: Seven Summers, 1951, Morning Face, 1968, Confessions of a Lover, 1976, The Bubble, 1984. Contributions: Criterion; Ed. of numerous vols. *Honours:* Hon. DLitt, Univs of Delhi, Benares, Andhra, Patiala, Shantiniketan; Laureate of International Peace Prize; Leverhulme Fellow for Research in Hindustani literature. *Address:* Jassim House, 25 Cuffe Parade, Colaba, Mumbai 400005, India.

ANAYA, Rudolfo; writer, dramatist, poet, editor and academic; b. 30 Oct. 1937, Pastura, NM, USA; m. Patricia Lawless 1966. *Education:* Browning Business School, 1956–58; BEd, 1963, MA, English Literature, 1969, MA, Guidance and Counselling, 1972, University of Mexico. *Career:* Teacher, Public Schools, Albuquerque, 1963–70; Dir, Counselling Center, 1971–73, Prof., Dept of Language and Literature, 1974–93, Prof. Emeritus, 1993–, University of New Mexico; Lecturer, Universidad Anahuas, México, DF, 1974; Founder-Ed., Blue Mesa Review, 1989–93; Martin Luther King Jr/César Chávez/Rosa Parks Visiting Prof., University of Michigan at Ann Arbor, 1996; Guest Prof., University of Oklahoma, 1997; Assoc. Ed., American Book Review. *Publications:* Fiction: Bless Me, Ultima, 1972; Heart of Aztlan, 1976; Tortuga, 1979; The Legend of La Llorona, 1984; Lord of the Dawn: The Legend of Quetzalcoatl, 1987; Albuquerque, 1992; Zia Summer, 1995; Rio Grande Fall, 1996; Jalamanta: A Message From the Desert, 1996; Isis in the Heart, 1998; Shaman Winter, 1999. Short Stories: The Silence of the Llano, 1982; The Anaya Reader (anthology), 1995. Children's Fiction: The Farolitos of Christmas (picture book), 1995; Maya's Children (picture book), 1997; Farolitos for Abuelo (picture book), 1999; My Land Sings: Stories From the Rio Grande, 1999; Roadrunner's Dance, 2000; Elegy of the Death of César Chávez, 2000. Editor: Voices from the Rio Grande (co-ed.), 1976; Cuentos Chicanos: A Short Story Anthology (co-ed.), 1984; Voces: An Anthology of Nuevo Mexicano Writers, 1987; Atzlan: Essays on the Chicano Homeland (co-ed.), 1989; Tierra: Contemporary Short Fiction of New Mexico, 1989. Other: Cuentos: Tales from the Hispanic Southwest (trans.), 1980; The Adventures of Juan Chicaspatas (epic poem), 1985; A Chicano in China (travel journal), 1986; Descansos: An Interrupted Journey (with Estevan Arellano and Denise Chávez), 1997; several plays. Contributions: anthologies, textbooks and literary magazines. *Honours:* several hon. doctorates; Premio Quinto Sol, 1971; American Book Award, Before Columbus Foundation, 1979; National Endowment for the Arts Fellowship, 1980; New Mexico Governor's Award for Excellence and Achievement in Literature, 1980; W. K. Kellogg Foundation Fellowship, 1983–86; New Mexico Eminent Scholar Award, 1989; Rockefeller Foundation Residency, Bellagio, Italy, 1991; PEN West Award for Fiction, 1993; Excellence in the Humanities Award, New Mexico Endowment for the Humanities, 1995; Tomás Rivera Mexican American Children's Book Awards, 1995, 2000; Distinguished Achievement Award, Western Literature Asscn, 1997; Arizona Adult Authors Award, Arizona Library Asscn, 2000; Wallace Stegner Award, Center of the American West, 2001; National Asscn of Chicano/Chicana Studies Scholar, 2002. *Address:* 5324 Cañada Vista NW, Albuquerque, NM 87120, USA.

ANDAHAZI, Federico; Argentine writer; b. 1963, Buenos Aires. *Publications:* Las piadosas (short story) 1995, Por encargo (short story) 1995, La trilliza (short story) (first prize Concurso de Cuento Buenos Artes Joven II) 1996, El anatomista (novel) 1997, Las piadosas (collection of short stories) 1998. *Address:* c/o Random House, 1745 Broadway, Third Floor, New York, NY 10019, USA (Office).

ANDELSON, Robert V.; Prof. of Philosophy Emeritus, Writer and Ed.; b. 19 Feb. 1931, Los Angeles, CA, USA; m. Bonny Orange Johnson, 7 June 1964. *Education:* BA equivalent, University of Chicago, 1952; MA, 1954, PhD, 1960, University of Southern California. *Career:* Asst Prof. to Prof. of Philosophy Emeritus, Auburn University, 1965–92; Editorial Board, American Journal of Economics and Sociology, 1969–; Distinguished Research Fellow, American Institute for Economic Research, 1993–; corpn mem. and dir, 1999–; mem. International Union for Land-Value Taxation and Free Trade, pres., 1997–2001; Robert Schalkenbach Foundation, vice-pres., 1998–2001. *Publications:* Imputed Rights: An Essay in Christian Social Theory, 1971; Critics of Henry George (ed. and co-author), 1979; Commons Without Tragedy (ed. and co-author), 1991; From Wasteland to Promised Land (with J. M. Dawsey), 1992; Land-Value Taxation Around the World (ed. and co-author), third edn, 2000. Contributions: scholarly journals. *Honours:* Foundation for Social Research Award, 1959; Relm Foundation Award, 1967; George Washington Honor Medals, Freedoms Foundation, 1970, 1972. *Address:* 534 Cary Drive, Auburn, AL 36830, USA.

ANDERSEN, Baltser, (Daniel Amb); Schoolteacher, Author and Poet; b. 3 Jan. 1956, Ribe, Denmark; m. Magdaline Mattak, 26 Dec. 1984, two d. *Education:* Tonder, 1975; Århus, 1976, 1986–88. *Career:* Teacher, Tonder, 1981, Greenland, 1982–87; Leader, Greenlandic Peace Movement, Sorsunnata, 1984–87; mem. Norse Mythological Circle, Alfheim; Danish Writers' Union; Red-Green Alliance, 1993–. *Publications:* Poetry: Interlocking Hands, 1973; To Be Awake, 1974; Grey Asphalt, 1979; Travelling Spaceship, 1992; Angantyr and the Black Sword, 1993. Essay: In the Name of Democracy. Contributions: many Danish newspapers.

ANDERSEN, Benny Allan; Author; b. 7 Nov. 1929, Copenhagen, Denmark; m. Cynthia La Touche Andersen, 28 Dec. 1981. *Publications:* Den Musikalske al, 1960; Den Indre Bowlerhat, 1964; Portraetgaller, 1966; Tykke Olsen M. Fl, 1968; Her i Reservatet, 1971; Himmelspraet, 1979; Tiden og Storken, 1985; Chagall & Skorpiondans, 1991; Denne Kommen og Gaen, 1993. Contributions: anthologies; Poetry Now; Prism International; West Coast Review; Literary Review; Scandinavian Review; Liberte; Svetova Literature.

ANDERSON, Barbara, BSc, BA; New Zealand writer and dramatist; b. 14 April 1926; m. Neil Anderson; two s. *Education:* Univ. of Otago, Victoria Univ., Wellington. *Career:* mem. PEN New Zealand (cttee mem. 1992–94). *Publications:* Uncollected Short Stories 1985, I Think We Should Go into the Jungle (short stories) 1989, Girls High 1990, We Could Celebrate 1991, Portrait of the Artist's Wife 1992, All the Nice Girls 1993, The House Guest 1995, Proud Garments 1996, The Peacocks and Other Stories (aka Glorious Things) 1997, Beginnings (essay) 1998, Long Hot Summer 1999, The Swing Around 2002, Change of Heart 2003; several radio plays, short stories. *Honours:* John Cowie Reid Memorial Award (play) 1986, Ansett/Sunday Star Short Story Award 1988, Timaru Herald/Aoraki Short Story Award 1990, Victoria Univ. Fellowship 1991, Goodman Fielder Wattie Award 1992, Scholarship of Letters 1994. *Literary Agent:* PFD, Drury House, 34–43 Russell Street, London, WC2B 5HA, England. *Website:* www.pfd.co.uk. *Address:* Victoria University Press, Victoria University, PO Box 600, Wellington, New Zealand.

ANDERSON, David Daniel, BS, MA, PhD; academic and writer; b. 8 June 1924, Lorain, OH, USA; m. Patricia Ann Rittenhour 1953. *Education:* Bowling Green State University, Michigan State University. *Career:* Distinguished University Prof., Dept of American Thought and Language, Michigan State University, East Lansing, 1957–; Ed., Midwestern Miscellany Annual; Exec. Sec., Society for the Study of Midwestern Literature, 1971–73. *Publications:* Louis Bromfield, 1964; Critical Studies in American Literature, 1964; Sherwood Anderson, 1967; Sherwood Anderson's Winesburg, Ohio, 1967; Brand Whitlock, 1968; The Black Experience (ed.-in-chief), 1969; Abraham Lincoln, 1970; The Literary Works of Abraham Lincoln, 1970; The Dark and Tangled Path (with R. Wright), 1971; Sunshine and Smoke, 1971; Robert Ingersoll, 1972; Mid-America I–XIV, 1974–87; Sherwood Anderson: Dimensions of His Literary Art (essays), 1976; Woodrow Wilson, 1978; Sherwood Anderson: The Writer at his Craft, 1979; Ignatius Donnelly, 1980; William Jennings Bryan, 1981; Critical

Essays on Sherwood Anderson, 1981; Michigan: A State Anthology, 1982; Route Two, Titus, Ohio, 1993. *Address:* Department of American Thought and Language, Michigan State University, East Lansing, MI 48821, USA.

ANDERSON, Kevin James, BS; writer and editor; b. 27 March 1962, Racine, WI, USA; m. 1st Mary Franco Nojhuis 1983 (divorced 1987); m. 2nd Rebecca Moesta 1991; one step-s. *Education:* Univ. of Wisconsin-Madison. *Career:* Technical Writer-Ed., Lawrence Livermore National Laboratory 1983–; columnist, Materials Research Soc. 1988–; copy ed., Int. Soc. for Respiratory Protection 1989–; mem. SFWA, Horror Writers of America. *Publications:* Novels (author or co-author): Lifeline, 1991; The Trinity Paradox, 1991; Afterimage, 1992; Assemblers of Infinity, 1993; Ill Wind, 1995; Virtual Destruction, 1996; Ignition, 1997; Fallout, 1997; Hidden Empire, 2002. X-Files series: Ground Zero, 1995; Ruins, 1996. Other Science Fiction: Resurrection Inc, 1988; Climbing Olympus, 1994; Blindfold, 1995; Born of Elven Blood, 1995; Bounty Hunters, 1996; War of the Worlds: Global Dispatches (anthology, ed.), 1996. Gamearth series: Gamearth, 1989; Gameplay, 1989; Game's End, 1990. Star Wars series: Darksaber, 1995; Dark Lords, 1997; Delusions of Grandeur, 1997; Diversity Alliance, 1997; Jedi Bounty, 1997. Star Wars: Jedi Academy trilogy: Jedi Search, 1994; Dark Apprentice, 1994; Champions of the Force, 1994. Star Wars: Young Jedi Knights series: The Lost Ones, 1995; Shadow Academy, 1995; Heirs of the Force, 1995; Darkest Knight, 1996; Lightsabers, 1996; Jedi under Siege, 1996; Shards of Alderaan, 1997. Star Wars anthologies (ed.): Star Wars: Tales from the Mos Eisley Cantina, 1995; Star Wars: Tales from Jabba's Palace, 1995; Star Wars: Tales of the Bounty Hunters 1996. Star Wars: Tales of the Jedi series: Dark Lords of the Sith, 1996; Golden Age of Sith, 1997. Non-Fiction: The Illustrated Star Wars University, 1995; Star Wars: The Mos Eisley Cantina Pop-Up Book, 1995. Contributions: anthologies and periodicals. *Honours:* Bram Stoker Award 1988. *Literary Agent:* John Silbensack, Trident Media Group LLC, 41 Madison Avenue, New York, NY 10010, USA.

ANDERSON, Matthew Smith; historian and academic; b. 23 May 1922, Perth, Scotland; m. Olive Ruth Gee 1954; two d. *Education:* MA, 1947, PhD, 1952, Univ. of Edinburgh. *Career:* Asst Lecturer in History, Univ. of Edinburgh, 1947–49; Asst Lecturer, 1949–53, Lecturer, 1953–61, Reader, 1961–72, Prof. of International History, (retd), LSE; mem. Royal Historical Society; Past and Present Society. *Publications:* Britain's Discovery of Russia, 1553–1815, 1958; Europe in the Eighteenth Century, 1713–1783, 1961; The Eastern Question, 1966; Eighteenth Century Europe, 1966; The Great Powers and the Near East, 1774–1923, 1970; The Ascendancy of Europe, 1815–1914, 1972; British Parliamentary Papers Relating to Russia, 1800–1900: A Critical Commentary, 1973; Peter the Great, 1978; Historians and Eighteenth-Century Europe, 1979; War and Society in Europe of the Old Regime, 1618–1789, 1988; The Rise of Modern Diplomacy, 1450–1919, 1993; The War of the Austrian Succession, 1740–1748, 1995; The Origins of the Modern European State System 1494–1618, 1998. Contributions: numerous historical periodicals. *Address:* 45 Cholmeley Crescent, Highgate, London N6 5EX, England.

ANDERSON, Michael Falconer; Author and Journalist; b. 16 Jan. 1947, Aberdeen, Scotland; m. Hildegarde Becze, 16 April 1970, two s. *Career:* Newspaper and Magazine Ed.; Chief Sub-Ed. of a national weekly; Sub-Ed. of a daily newspaper; Showbusiness Writer; Reporter; Correspondent in newspapers, television and radio; mem. Society of Authors; National Union of Journalists. *Publications:* The Woodsmen, 1986; The Unholy, 1987; God of a Thousand Faces, 1987; The Covenant, 1988; Black Trinity, 1989; The Clan of Golgotha Scalp, 1990; numerous short stories and plays for radio and television. Contributions: Feature articles on subjects including travel, history, the environment and books, in newspapers and magazines worldwide.

ANDERSON, Quentin; writer and academic; b. 21 July 1912, Minnewaukan, ND, USA. *Education:* BA, 1937, PhD, 1953, Columbia University; MA, Harvard University, 1945. *Career:* Columbia University, 1939–82; University of Sussex, 1966–67; University of Barcelona, 1985. *Publications:* Selected Short Stories by Henry James, 1950; The American Henry James, 1957; The Proper Study: Essays on Western Classics (with Joseph A. Mazzeo), 1962; The Imperial Self: An Essay in American Literary and Cultural History, 1971; Art, Politics and Will: Essays in Honor of Lionel Trilling (with others), 1977; Making Americans: An Essay on Individualism and Money, 1992. *Honours:* National Endowment for the Humanities, Senior Fellow, 1973; Fellow, National Humanities Center, 1979–80, New York Institute for the Humanities, 1981–2001; Paley Lecturer, Hebrew University of Jerusalem, 1982. *Address:* 29 Claremont Avenue, New York, NY 10027, USA.

ANDERSON, Rachel; Writer and Dramatist; b. 18 March 1943, Hampton Court, Surrey, England; m. David Bradby, four c. *Publications:* Pineapple, 1965; The Purple Heart Throbs: A Survey of Popular Romantic Fiction, 1850–1972, 1974; Dream Lovers, 1978; For the Love of Sang, 1990. Young Children's Fiction: Tim Walks, 1985; The Cat's Tale, 1985; Wild Goose Chase, 1986; Jessy Runs Away, 1988; Best Friends, 1991; Jessy and the Long-Short Dress, 1992; Tough as Old Boots, 1991; Little Lost Fox, 1992. Older Children's Fiction: Moffatt's Road, 1978; The Poacher's Son, 1982; The War Orphan, 1984; Little Angel Comes to Stay, 1985; Renard the Fox (with David Bradby), 1986; Little Angel, Bonjour, 1988; French Lessons, 1988; The Boy Who Laughed, 1989; The Bus People, 1989; Paper Faces, 1991; When Mum Went to Work, 1992; The Working Class, 1993; Blackwater, 1994; The Scavenger's Tale, 1998; Warlands, 2000; Moving Times Trilogy, 1999–2000. *Honours:* Medical Journalists' Asscn Award, 1990; 25th Anniversary Guardian Children's Fiction Award, 1992. *Address:* c/o Oxford University Press, Great Clarendon St, Oxford OX2 6DP, England.

ANDERSON, Robert David, MA, FSA; lecturer and writer; b. 20 Aug. 1927, Shillong, Assam, India. *Education:* Gonville and Caius Colls, Cambridge. *Career:* Dir of Music, Gordonstoun School 1958–62; Extra-Mural Lecturer, Univ. of London 1966–77; Assoc. Ed., The Musical Times 1967–85; Visiting Lecturer, City Univ. 1983–92; mem. Egypt Exploration Soc. (hon. sec. 1971–82). *Publications:* Egyptian Antiquities in the British Museum III: Musical Instruments 1976, Wagner 1980, Egypt in 1800 (jt ed.) 1988, Elgar in Manuscript 1990, Elgar 1993, Elgar and Chivalry 2002; contrib. to The Musical Times. *Honours:* Hon. DMus (City Univ.) 1985, Hon. DHist (Russian State Univ. for Humanities, Moscow) 2000; Hon. Prof. in History, State Univ. of Rostov-on-Don 2002. *Address:* 54 Hornton Street, London, W8 4NT, England.

ANDERSON, Robert Woodruff; Playwright, Screenwriter and Novelist; b. 28 April 1917, New York, NY, USA. *Education:* BA, Magna Cum Laude, 1939, MA, 1940, Harvard University. *Career:* mem. Dramatists' Guild, pres., 1971–73; Authors' League Council; Writers' Guild of America West; American Playwrights' Theatre, board of trustees; Theatre Hall of Fame, 1981; PEN. *Publications:* Plays: Tea and Sympathy, 1953; All Summer Long, 1954; Silent Night Lonely Night, 1959; The Days Between, 1965; You Know I Can't Hear When the Water's Running, 1967; I Never Sang for My Father, 1968; Solitaire/Double Solitaire, 1971; Free and Clear, 1983. Co-Author: Elements of Literature, 1988. Fiction: After, 1973; Getting Up and Going Home, 1978. Screenplays: Tea and Sympathy, 1956; Until They Sail, 1957; The Nun's Story, 1959; The Sand Pebbles, 1966; I Never Sang For My Father, 1970; The Last Act is a Solo, 1991; Absolute Strangers, 1991. *Honours:* Writers' Guild Award, 1970; Ace Award, 1991. *Address:* 14 Sutton Pl. S, New York, NY 10022, USA.

ANDERSON-DARGATZ, Gail; Writer; b. 14 Nov. 1963, Kamloops, BC, Canada; m. Floyd Dargatz, 28 April 1990. *Education:* BA, Creative Writing, University of Victoria. *Career:* mem. Canadian Writers' Union. *Publications:* The Miss Hereford Stories, 1994; The Cure for Death by Lightning, 1996; The Glass Room, 1998. Contributions: periodicals. *Honours:* First Prize for Fiction, Federation of British Columbia Writers, 1988; Okanagan Short Story Award, Canadian Author and Bookman, 1992; First Prize for Fiction, CBC Radio Literary Awards, 1995; Giller Prize, 1996. *Address:* c/o Denise Bukowski, 125B Dupont St, Toronto, ON M5R 1VR, Canada.

ANDRÉE, Alice (see Cluysenaar, Anne).

ANDRESKI, Stanislav Leonard, MSc, PhD; writer and academic; b. 18 May 1919, Czestochowa, Poland; two s. two d. *Education:* Univ. of Poznań, London School of Economics. *Career:* military service in Polish Army 1937–38, 1939–42, 1943–47; Lecturer in Sociology Rhodes Univ. 1947–53; Sr Research Fellow in Anthropology Manchester Univ. 1954–56; Lecturer in Econs Acton Tech. Coll., London 1956–57; Lecturer in Man. Studies Brunel Coll. of Tech., London 1957–60; Prof. of Social Sciences, Santiago, Chile 1960–61; Sr Research Fellow Nigerian Inst. of Social and Economic Research, Ibadan, Nigeria 1962–64; Prof. of Sociology Univ. of Reading 1964–84, Head of Dept 1964–82, Prof. Emer. 1984–; part-time Prof. Polish Univ. in London 1969–99, Duxx School of Business, Monterey, Mexico 1995–98, Wyższa Szkoła Języków Obcych i Ekonomii, Czestochowa, Poland 1998–2002; Visiting Prof. City Univ. of NY 1968–69, Simon Frazer Univ., Vancouver, Canada 1976–77; mem. Editorial Bd Journal of Strategic Studies; mem. Writers' Guild, Inst. of Patentees and Inventors. *Publications:* Military Organisation and Society 1954, Elements of Comparative Sociology 1964, Parasitism and Subversion: The Case of Latin America 1966, The African Predicament: A Study in Pathology of Modernisation 1968, Social Sciences as Sorcery 1972, The Prospects of a Revolution in the USA 1973, Max Weber's Insights and Errors 1984, Syphilis, Puritanism and Witch Hunts: Historical Explanations in the Light of Medicine and Psychoanalysis with a Forecast About Aids 1989, Wars, Revolutions, Dictatorships 1992; Ed.: Herbert Spencer: Principles of Sociology 1968, Herbert Spencer: Structure, Function and Evolution 1971, The Essential Comte 1974, Reflections on Inequality 1975, Max Weber on Capitalism, Bureaucracy and Religion 1984; contribs: approximately 90 articles in learned journals including British Journal of Sociology, Japanese Journal of Sociology, Science Journal, European Journal of Sociology, Encounter. *Address:* Farriers, Village Green, Upper Basildon, Berkshire RG8 8LS, England. *Telephone:* (1491) 671318.

ANDREW, Prudence (Hastings); Author; b. 23 May 1924, London, England. *Education:* BA, history, St Anne's College, Oxford, 1946. *Publications:* The Hooded Falcon, 1960; Ordeal by Silence, 1961; Ginger Over the Wall, 1962; A Question of Choice, 1963; Ginger and Batty Billy, 1963; The Earthworms, 1964; Ginger and No. 10, 1964; The Constant Star, 1964; A Sparkle from the Coal, 1964; Christmas Card, 1966; Mr Morgan's Marrow, 1967; Mister O'Brien, 1972; Rodge, Sylvie and Munch, 1973; Una and Grubstreet, 1973; Goodbye to the Rat, 1974; The Heroic Deeds of Jason Jones, 1975; Where Are You Going To, My Pretty Maid?, 1977; Robinson

Daniel Crusoe, 1978 (in USA as Close Within My Own Circle, 1980); The Other Side of the Park, 1984. *Address:* c/o W. Heinemann Ltd, 10 Upper Grosvenor St, London W1X 9PA, England.

ANDREWS, Graham, BA; writer; b. 3 Feb. 1948, Belfast, Northern Ireland; m. Agnes Helena Ferguson 1982. *Education:* Open University, Milton Keynes, England. *Career:* Assoc. Ed., Extro Science Fiction Magazine, 1980–81; Staff Writer, World Asscn for Orphans and Abandoned Children, 1990–91; mem. Society of Authors; RSL; BSFA. *Publications:* The Fragile Future 1990, The WAO Vocational Training Programme 1990, Darkness Audible (science fiction novel) 1991, St James Guide to Fantasy Writers (contributor) 1996, Dr Kilcasey in Space: A Bio-Bibliography of James White 2000, Gideon's Day/Gideon of Scotland Yard 2003, The Man Who Met His Maker (play) 2004, Two Just Men: Richard S. Prather and Shell Scott; contrib. to Belfast Telegraph, Brussels Bulletin, The Guardian, F & SF, Interzone, Million, Vector, Foundation, Locus, Book and Magazine Collector. *Honours:* Aisling Gheal (Bright Vision) Award, Irish Science Fiction Asscn, 1980; First Prize in playwriting, American Theatre Co of Brussels, 2001. *Address:* Avenue du Merle 37, 1640 Rhode-Saint-Genese, Belgium.

ANDRUKHOVYCH, Yuriy; Ukrainian novelist and poet; b. 13 March 1960, Ivano-Frankivsk. *Education:* Ukrainian Institute of Polygraphy 1982, Maxim Gorky Literary Inst., Moscow 1989–91. *Career:* Military service 1983–84; Co-Founder, literary performance group, 'Bu-Ba-Bu' (Burlesque-Bluster-Buffoonery) 1985; Literary readings in American universities including Harvard, Yale, Columbia, Pennsylvania State University and La Salle University 1998; Fulbright Scholar in Residence Dept of Germanic and Slavic Languages, Penn State Univ.; works translated into German, Finnish, Russian, English and French. *Publications:* poetry: The Sky and Squares 1985, Downtown 1989, Exotic Birds and Plants 1991; fiction: Army Stories (short stories) 1989, Rekreatsii 1992, Moscoviada 1993, Perverziia 1996; other: A Military March for an Angel (screenplay) 1989; essays; contribs in trans. to Agni, Salt Hill, Exquisite Corpse. *Honours:* Blahovist, 1993; Helen Shcherban-Lapika Foundation Award, 1996; Novel of the Year Prize, Suchasnist, 1997; Lesia & Petro Kovalev Award, 1998.

ANGEL, Leonard Jay, BA, MA, PhD; writer, dramatist and lecturer; b. 20 Sept. 1945; m. Susan; one s. one d. one step-d. *Education:* McGill University, University of British Columbia. *Career:* Dept of Creative Writing, University of British Columbia 1981–82, University of Victoria 1984–86; mem. Playwrights Canada, 1976–88; Guild of Canadian Playwrights, chair., British Columbia region, 1978–79; Regional Representative, 1980–81; Writers' Guild of Canada, 1993. *Publications:* Antietam, 1975; Isadora and G. B., 1976; The Unveiling, 1981; The Silence of the Mystic, 1983; Eleanor Marx, 1985; How to Build a Conscious Machine, 1989; Englightenment East and West, 1994; The Book of Miriam, 1997. Contributions: Dialogue and Dialectic, Dialogue, 1991; Six of One: Capilano Review, 1985. *Honours:* First Prize, Short Fiction, McGill Daily, 1963; First Prize (joint), Playhouse Theatre Award, 1971; Canada Council Artist Grants, 1979, 1982. *Address:* 865 Durward Avenue, Vancouver, BC V5V 2Z1, Canada.

ANGELOU, Maya; poet, writer and academic; b. (Marguerite Johnson), 4 April 1928, St Louis, MO, USA; m. 1st Tosh Angelou (divorced); m. 2nd Paul Du Feu 1973 (divorced); one s. *Education:* Studied music; Received training in modern dance from Martha Graham, Pearl Primus, and Ann Halprin, in drama from Frank Silvera and Gene Frankel. *Career:* Taught modern dance, Rome Opera and Hambina Theater, Tel-Aviv, 1955; Appeared in Off-Broadway plays; Northern Co-ordinator, Southern Christian Leadership Conference, 1959–60; Asst Admin., School of Music and Drama, Institute of African Studies, University of Ghana, 1963–66; Lecturer, University of California at Los Angeles, 1966; Writer-in-Residence, University of Kansas, 1970; Distinguished Visiting Prof., Wake Forest University, 1974, Wichita State University, 1974, California State University at Sacramento, 1974; First Reynolds Prof. of American Studies, Wake Forest University (lifetime appointment), 1981–; many TV appearances in various capacities; Recording, as Miss Calypso: Rev-Ola (album), 1957; mem. Dirs' Guild; Harlem Writers' Guild; Women's Prison Asscn, advisory board. *Publications:* Poetry: Just Give Me a Cool Drink of Water 'fore I Die, 1971; Oh Pray My Wings Are Gonna Fit Me Well, 1975; And Still I Rise, 1978; Shaker, Why Don't You Sing?, 1983; Poems: Maya Angelou, 1986; Now Sheba Sings the Song, 1987; I Shall Not Be Moved, 1990; On the Pulse of Morning, for the inauguration of President Bill Clinton, 1993; The Complete Collected Poems of Maya Angelou, 1994; Phenomenal Woman: Four Poems Celebrating Women, 1994; A Brave and Startling Truth, 1995. Fiction: Mrs Flowers: A Moment of Friendship, 1986. Non-Fiction: I Know Why the Caged Bird Sings, 1970; Gather Together in My Name, 1974; Singin' and Swingin' and Gettin' Merry Like Christmas, 1976; The Heart of a Woman, 1981; All God's Children Need Traveling Shoes, 1986; Even the Stars Look Lonesome (essays), 1997; A Song Flung Up to Heaven, 2002. Other: The Least of These (play), 1966; Georgia Georgia (screenplay), 1972; My Painted House, My Friendly Chicken, and Me (children's book), 1994. *Honours:* Yale University Fellowship, 1970; Rockefeller Foundation Scholarship, Italy, 1975; Mem., American Revolution Bicentennial Commission, 1975–76; Woman of the Year in Communications, 1976; Golden Eagle Award for documentary, 1977; Matrix Award, 1983; North Carolina Award in Literature, 1987; Distinguished Woman of North Carolina, 1992; Horatio Alger Award, 1992; Spingarn Medal, 1993; Grammy Award for Best Spoken Word or Non-Traditional Album, 1994; National Women's Hall of Fame, 1998; National Medal of Arts, 2000; Order of Kilimanjaro Award, National Asscn for the Advancement of Colored People, 2001; numerous hon. degrees. *Literary Agent:* Dave La Camera, Lordly and Dame Inc, 51 Church Street, Boston, MA 02116, USA.

ANGHELAKI-ROOKE, Katerina; poet and translator; b. 22 Feb. 1939, Athens, Greece. *Education:* Univs of Nice, Athens and Geneva. *Career:* freelance translator 1962–; Visiting Prof. (Fulbright), Harvard Univ. 1980; Visiting Fellow, Princeton Univ. 1987. *Publications:* Wolves and Clouds 1963, Poems 1963–69 1971, The Body is the Victory and the Defeat of Dreams (in English) 1975, The Scattered Papers of Penelope 1977, The Triumph of Constant Loss 1978, Counter Love 1982, The Suitors 1984, Beings and Things on Their Own (in English) 1986, When the Body 1988, Wind Epilogue 1990, Empty Nature 1993, Tristiu 1995, The Flesh is a Beautiful Desert 1996, From Purple into Night (in English) 1997, Matter Alone 2001, La Chair beau désert (in French and Greek) 2001, Translating into Love Life's End 2003; trans of works by Shakespeare, Albee, Dylan Thomas, Beckett, and from Russian of Pushkin, Mayiakorski, Lermontov. *Honours:* Greek National Poetry Prize 1985, Greek Acad. Ouranis Prize 2000. *Address:* Synesiou Kyrenes 4, 114 71 Athens, Greece.

ANGLUND, Joan Walsh; Children's Writer; b. 3 Jan. 1926, Hinsdale, IL, USA. *Education:* Chicago Art Institute, 1944. *Publications:* A Friend is Someone Who Likes You, 1958; Look Out the Window, 1959; The Brave Cowboy, 1959; Love is a Special Way of Feeling, 1960; In a Pumpkin Shell: A Mother Goose ABC, 1960; Christmas Is a Time of Giving, 1961; Cowboy and His Friend, 1961; Nibble Nible Mousekin: A Tale of Hansel and Gretel, 1962; Cowboy's Secret Life, 1963; Spring is a New Beginning, 1963; Childhood Is a Time of Innocence, 1964; A Pocketful of Proverbs (verse), 1964; A Book of Good Tidings from the Bible, 1965; What Color is Love?, 1966; A Year is Round, 1966; A Cup of Sun: A Book of Poems, 1967; A Is for Always: An ABC Book, 1968; Morning Is a Little Child (verse), 1969; A Slice of Snow: A Book of Poems, 1970; Do You Love Someone?, 1971; The Cowboy's Christmas, 1972; A Child's Book of Old Nursery Rhymes, 1973; Goodbye, Yesterday: A Book of Poems, 1974; Storybook, 1978; Emily and Adam, 1979; Almost a Rainbow, 1980; A Gift of Love, five vols, 1980; A Christmas Cookie Book, 1982; Rainbow Love, 1982; Christmas Candy Book, 1983; A Christmas Book, 1983; See the Year, 1984; Coloring Book, 1984; Memories of the Heart, 1984; Teddy Bear Tales, 1985; Baby Brother, 1985; All About Me!, 1986; Christmas is Here!, 1986; Tubtime for Thaddeus, 1986; A Mother Goose Book, 1991; A Child's Year, 1992; Love is a Baby, 1992; The Way of Love, 1992; Bedtime Book, 1993; The Friend We Have Not Met, 1993; Peace is a Circle of Love, 1993. *Address:* c/o Random House, 201 E 50th St, New York, NY 10022, USA.

ANGREMY, Jean-Pierre, (Pierre-Jean Rémy); Diplomat and Author; b. 21 March 1937, Angouleme, France; m. 1st Odile Cail 1963 (divorced 1979); one s. one d.; m. 2nd Sophie Schmit 1986; one s. *Education:* Institut d'Études Politiques, 1955–60; Brandeis University, 1958–59; École Nationale d'Administration, 1960–63. *Career:* Diplomatic Service, Hong Kong, 1963; Second Sec., Beijing, 1964, London, 1966; First Sec., London, 1968; Counsellor, Ministry of Foreign Affairs, 1971; Dir and Programme Co-ordinator, ORTF, 1972; Cultural Counsellor, French Embassy, London, 1975–79, French Ministry of Culture, 1979–81; Consul General de France, Florence, 1985–87; Dir-Gen., Cultural Exchanges, Ministry of Foreign Affairs, 1987–90; French Ambassador to UNESCO, 1990–93; Dir, French Acad., Rome, 1994–97; Pres., Bibliothèque Nationale de France, Paris, 1997–; mem. Académie Française, 1987. *Publications:* Et Gulliver mourut de sommeil, 1961; Midi ou l'attentat, 1962; Gaugins a gogo, 1971; La sac du palais d'été, 1971; Urbanisme, 1972; Une mort sale, 1973; La vie d'Adrian Putney, 1973; Ava, la mort de Floria Tosca, memoires secrets pour servir a l'histoire de ce siècle, 1974; Rever la vie, 1975; La figure dans la pierre, 1976; Chine: Un itineraire, 1977; Les enfans du parc, 1977; Si j'etais romancier, 1977; Callas: Une vie, 1978; Les nouvelles aventures du Chevalier de la Barre, 1978; Orient Express, 1979; Cordelia ou l'Angleterre, 1979; Don Giovanni, 1979; Pandora, 1980; Slaue pour moir le monde, 1980; Un voyage d'hiver, 1981; Don Juan, 1982; Le dernier été, 1983; Mata Hari, 1983; La vie d'un hero, 1985; Une ville immortelle, 1986; Des Chatevoux Allamagne, 1987; Toscanes, 1989; Algerie bords-de-Seine, 1990; Un cimitière rouge en Nouvelle Angleterre, 1991; Desir d'Europe, 1995; Le Rose et le Blanc, 1997; La nuit de Ferraro, 1999. *Honours:* Officier, Légion d'honneur; Officier, Ordre nat. du Mérite; Commdr, Ordre des Arts et des Lettres. *Address:* Bibliothèque Nationale de France, 58 rue de Richelieu, 75002 Paris, France.

ANGUS, Ian (see Mackay, James Alexander).

ANGUS, Tom (see Powell, Geoffrey Stewart).

ANHAVA, Tuomas; Poet and Trans; b. 5 June 1927, Helsinki, Finland. *Publications:* several vols of poems, including: Runoja, 1953; 36 runoja, 1958; Runoja 1961, 1961; Kuudes kirja, 1966; Runot 1951–1966, 1967; Valitut runot, 1976. Contributions: periodicals.

ANMAR, Frank (see Nolan, William Francis).

ANNWN, David, (David James Jones); Poet, Critic and Lecturer; b. 9 May 1953, Congleton, Cheshire, England; m. 26 April 1994. *Education:* Wigan Technical College, 1970–72; BA, English, 1975, PhD, Modern Poetry, 1978, University College of Wales, Aberystwyth; PGCE, Bath University, 1979.

Career: Postgraduate Tutor, Aberystwyth University, 1975–78; Lecturer, 1981–88, Head of English Degree Work, 1988–95, Wakefield College; Lecturer, Tutor, and Examiner, Open University, 1995–96; Lecturer in Creative Writing, Leeds University, 1996; mem. Humanities and Arts Higher Education Network; Northern Asscn of Writers in Education; Welsh Acad. *Publications:* Poetry: Foster the Ghost, 1984; King Saturn's Book, 1986; The Other, 1988; Primavera Violin, 1990; The Spirit/That Kiss, 1993; Dantean Designs, 1995; Danse Macabre, Death and the Printers (with Kelvin Corcoran, Alan Halsey, and Gavin Selerie), 1997. Other: Inhabited Voices: Myth and History in the Poetry of Seamus Heaney, Geoffrey Hill and George Mackay Brown, 1984; Catgut and Blossom: Jonathon Williams in England (ed.), 1989; A Different Can of Words (ed.), 1992; Presence, Spacing Sign: The Graphic Art of Peterjon Skelt, 1993; Hear the Voice of the Bard!: The Early Bards, William Blake and Robert Duncan, 1995; Poetry in the British Isles: Non-Metropolitan Perspectives, 1995; Inner Celtia (with Alan Richardson), 1996; A Breton Herbal: Translations of Poems by Eugene Guillevic, 1998. Contributions: anthologies: Anglo-Welsh Review; Poetry Wales; Ambit; Iron; Scintilla; David Jones Society Journal. *Honours:* Winner, International Collegiate Eisteddfod, 1975; Prize, Ilkley Arts Festival, 1982; Bursary Award, Yorkshire Arts, 1985; First Prize, Cardiff International Poetry Competition, 1996. *Address:* 3 Westfield Park, College Grove, Wakefield, West Yorkshire WF1 3RP, England.

ANTHONY, Evelyn; Writer; b. 3 July 1928, England; m. Michael Ward-Thomas, 1955. *Education:* Convent of Sacred Heart, Roehampton. *Publications:* Imperial Highness, 1953; Curse Not the King, 1954; Far Flies the Eagle, 1955; Anne Boleyn, 1957; Victoria and Albert, 1958; Elizabeth, 1960; Charles the King, 1961; The Heiress, 1964; The Rendezvous, 1967; Anne of Austria, 1968; The Legend, 1969; The Assassin, 1970; The Tamarind Seed, 1971; The Occupying Power, 1973; The Malaspiga Exit, 1974; The Persian Ransom, 1975; The Silver Falcon, 1977; The Return, 1978; The Grave of Truth, 1979; The Defector, 1980; The Avenue of the Dead, 1981; Albatross, 1982; The Company of Saints, 1983; Voices on the Wind, 1985; No Enemy but Time, 1987; The House of Vandekar, 1988; The Scarlet Thread, 1989; The Relic, 1991; The Doll's House, 1992; Exposure, 1993; Bloodstones, 1994; The Legacy, 1996. *Honours:* US Literary Guild Award, 1958; Yorkshire Post Fiction Prize, 1974; High Sheriff of Essex, 1994; Deputy Lieutenant of Essex, 1995. *Literary Agent:* AP Watt Ltd, 20 John St, London WC1N 2DR, England. *Address:* Horham Hall, Thaxted, Essex, England.

ANTHONY, Michael; Writer; b. 10 Feb. 1930, Mayaro, Trinidad and Tobago; m. Yvette Francesca, 8 Feb. 1958, two s. two d. *Education:* Junior Technical College, San Fernando, Trinidad. *Career:* Sub-Ed., Reuters News Agency, London, 1964–68; Asst Ed., Texas Star, Texaco Trinidad, Pointe-a-Pierre, Trinidad and Tobago, 1972–88; Teacher of Creative Writing, University of Richmond, VA, USA, 1992. *Publications:* Fiction: The Games Were Coming, 1963; The Year in San Fernando, 1965; Green Days by the River, 1967; Streets of Conflict, 1976; All That Glitters, 1981; Bright Road to Eldorado, 1982. Short Stories: Cricket in the Road and Other Stories, 1973; Sandra Street and Other Stories, 1973; Folk Tales and Fantasies, 1976; The Chieftain's Carnival and Other Stories, 1993. Other: Glimpses of Trinidad and Tobago, with a Glance at the West Indies, 1974; King of the Masquerade, 1974; Profile Trinidad: A Historical Survey from the Discovery to 1900, 1975; The Making of Port-of-Spain, 1757–1939, 1978; Port-of-Spain in a World War, 1939–1945, 1984; First in Trinidad, 1985; Heroes of the People of Trinidad and Tobago, 1986; A Brighter and Better Day, 1987; Towns and Villages of Trinidad and Tobago, 1988; Parade of the Carnivals of Trinidad, 1839–1989, 1989; The Golden Quest: The Four Voyages of Christopher Columbus, 1992; In the Heat of the Day, 1996; Historical Dictionary of Trinidad and Tobago, 1997; The High Tide of Intrigue, 2001; Butler, Till the Final Bell, 2002. Editor: The History of Aviation in Trinidad and Tobago, 1913–1962, 1987. Contributions: various periodicals. *Address:* 99 Long Circular Rd, St James, Port-of-Spain, Trinidad and Tobago.

ANTHONY, Patricia; Writer and Educator; b. 29 March 1947, San Antonio, TX, USA; m. Dennis John Hunt April 1967 (divorced 1974); one s. one d. *Education:* BA, English, Univ. of Texas, Austin; MA, Universidade Federal de Santa Catarina, Florianopolis, Brazil. *Career:* Visiting Prof. of English Literature, Univ. of Lisbon, Portugal; Assoc. Prof. of English, Universidade Federal de Santa Catarina, Florianopolis, Brazil; Adjunct Prof. of Creative Writing, Southern Methodist Univ., USA. *Publications:* Fiction: Cold Allies, 1993; Brother Termite, 1993; Conscience of the Beagle, 1993; Happy Policeman, 1994; Cradle of Splendor, 1996; God's Fires, 1997; Flanders, 1998. Short stories: Eating Memories, 1997. Contributions: Short stories to magazines incl. Aboriginal SF. *Honours:* Best First Novel Award, for Cold Allies, Locus, 1993. *Literary Agent:* Meredith Bernstein Literary Agency, 2112 Broadway, Suite 503A, New York, NY 10023, USA. *Address:* 9712 Amberton Pkwy, Dallas, TX 75243, USA. *E-mail:* patanthony@mindspring.com.

ANTHONY, Piers, BA; American writer; b. (Piers Anthony Dillingham Jacob), 6 Aug. 1934, Oxford, England; m. Carol Marble 1956; two d. *Education:* Goddard College, University of South Florida. *Publications:* Chthon, 1967; Omnivore, 1968; Sos the Rope, 1968; The Ring (with Robert E. Margroff), 1968; Macroscope, 1969; The E.S.P. Worm (with Robert E. Margroff), 1970; Orn, 1971; Prostho Plus, 1971; Var the Stick, 1972; Kiai!, 1974; Mistress of Death, 1974; Rings of Ice, 1974; Triple Détente, 1974; The Bamboo Bloodbath, 1975; Neq the Sword, 1975; Ninja's Revenge, 1975; Phthor, 1975; Amazon Slaughter, 1976; Ox, 1976; But What of Earth? (with Robert Coulson), 1976; Steppe, 1976; Cluster, 1977; Hasan, 1977; A Spell for Chameleon, 1977; Chaining the Lady, 1978; Kirlian Quest, 1978; The Source of Magic, 1979; Castle Roogna, 1979; God of Tarot, 1979; The Pretender (with Frances Hall), 1979; Split Infinity, 1980; Vision of Tarot, 1980; Faith of Tarot, 1980; Thousandstar, 1980; Blue Adept, 1981; Centaur Aisle, 1981; Mute, 1981; Juxtaposition, 1982; Ogre, Ogre, 1982; Viscous Circle, 1982; Night Mare, 1983; Dragon on a Pedestal, 1983; On a Pale Horse, 1983; Refugee, 1983; Mercenary, 1984; Bearing an Hourglass, 1984; Anthonology, 1985; Crewel Lye: A Caustic Yarn, 1985; With a Tangled Skein, 1985; Politician, 1985; Executive, 1985; Ghost, 1986; Golem in the Gears, 1986; Shade of the Tree, 1986; Statesman, 1986; Out of Phaze, 1987; Vale of the Vole, 1987; Wielding a Red Sword, 1987; Being a Green Mother, 1987; Dragon's Gold (with Robert E. Margroff), 1987; Bio of an Ogre, 1988; For Love of Evil, 1988; Heaven Cent, 1988; Robot Adept, 1988; Serpent's Silver (with Robert E. Margroff), 1988; Pornucopia, 1988; Dead Morn, 1988; Total Recall, 1989; Unicorn Point, 1989; And Eternity, 1990; Isle of View, 1990; Firefly, 1990; Hard Sell, 1990; Phaze Doubt, 1990; Through the Ice (with Robert Kornwise), 1990; Orc's Opal (with Robert E. Margroff), 1990; Chimaera's Copper (with Robert E. Margroff), 1990; Tatham Mound, 1991; Virtual Mode, 1991; MerCycle, 1991; Question Quest, 1991; Alien Plot, 1992; The Color of Her Panties, 1992; Fractal Mode, 1992; The Caterpillar's Question (with Jose Farmer), 1992; If I Pay Thee Not in Gold, 1993; Killobyte, 1993; Letters to Jenny, 1993; Demons Don't Dream, 1993; Chaos Mode, 1993; Isle of Woman, 1993; Mouvar's Magic (with Robert E. Margroff), 1993; Harpy Thyme, 1994; Shame of Man, 1994; Tales from the Great Turtle, 1994; Geis of the Gargoyle, 1995; Roc and a Hard Place, 1995; Yon Ill Wind, 1996; The Willing Spirit (with Alfred Tells), 1996; The Continuing Xanth Saga, 1997; Hope of Earth, 1997; Faun and Games, 1997; Quest for the Fallen Star (with James Richey and Alan Riggs), 1998. *Honours:* Science Fiction Award, Pyramid Books/Magazine of Fantasy and Science Fiction/Kent Productions, 1967; British Fantasy Award, 1977. *Address:* c/o Ace Books, 375 Hudson Street, New York, NY 10014, USA.

ANTIN, David; Prof. of Visual Arts and Poet; b. 1 Feb. 1932, New York, NY, USA; m. Eleanor Fineman, 1960, one s. *Education:* BA, City College, CUNY, 1955; MA in Linguistics, New York University, 1966. *Career:* Chief Ed. and Scientific Dir, Research Information Service, 1958–60; Curator, Institute of Contemporary Art, Boston, 1967; Dir, University Art Gallery, 1968–72, Asst Prof., 1968–72, Prof. of Visual Arts, 1972–, University of California at San Diego. *Publications:* Definitions, 1967; Autobiography, 1967; Code of Flag Behavior, 1968; Meditiations, 1971; Talking, 1972; After the War, 1973; Talking at the Boundaries, 1976; Who's Listening Out There?, 1980; Tuning, 1984; Poèmes Parlés, 1984; Selected Poems 1963–73, 1991; What it Means to be Avant Garde, 1993; A Conversation with David Antin (with Charles Bernstein), 2002. Contributions: periodicals. *Honours:* Longview Award, 1960; University of California Creative Arts Award, 1972; Guggenheim Fellowship, 1976; National Endowment for the Humanities Fellowship, 1983; PEN Award for Poetry, 1984; Getty Research Fellow, 2002. *Address:* PO Box 1147, Del Mar, CA 92014, USA.

ANTOINE, Yves; Prof., Writer and Poet; b. 12 Dec. 1941, Port-au-Prince, Haiti; one d. *Education:* MEd, 1972, DLitt, 1988, University of Ottawa. *Career:* mem. Union of Writers, QC; Ligue des Droits et Liberté; Asscn des auteurs de l'Outaouais québécois. *Publications:* La Veillée, 1964; Témoin Oculaire, 1970; Au gré des heures, 1972; Les sabots de la nuit, 1974; Alliage, 1979; Libations pour le soleil, 1985; Sémiologie et personnage romanesque chez Jacques S. Alexis, 1993; Polyphonie (poems and prose), 1996; La mémoire à fleur de peau, 2002. Contributions: Une affligeante réalité, Le Droit, Ottawa, 1987; L'indélébile, Symbiosis, Ottawa, 1992; Inventeurs et savants noirs, 1998. *Honours:* Guest, Harambee Foundation Society, 1988; Carter G. Woodward Award, International Council of Outaouais (Québec, Canada), 1999. *Address:* 200 blvd Cité des Jeunes, apt 403, Hull, QC J8Y 6M1, Canada.

ANTOKOLETZ, Elliott Maxim, BA, MA, PhD; American musicologist and writer; *Professor of Musicology, University of Texas at Austin*; b. 3 Aug. 1942, Jersey City, NJ; m. Juana Canabal 1972; one s. *Education:* Juilliard School of Music, Hunter Coll., Graduate School and Univ. Center CUNY. *Career:* Lecturer and mem. of faculty string quartet, Queens Coll., CUNY 1973–76; Prof. of Musicology 1976–, Head Musicology Division 1992–94, Univ. of Texas at Austin; co-ed., Int. Journal of Musicology 1992–; mem. American Musicological Soc. *Publications:* The Music of Béla Bartók: A Study of Tonality and Progression in Twentieth-Century Music 1984, Béla Bartók: A Guide to Research 1988, Twentieth Century Music 1992, Bartók Perspectives (ed. with V. Fischer and B. Suchoff) 2000, Musical Symbolism in the Operas of Debussy and Bartók 2004; contrib. three chapters to The Bartók Companion, one chapter to Sibelius Studies; contrib. to scholarly books and professional journals. *Address:* c/o School of Music, University of Texas at Austin, Austin, TX 78712, USA.

ANTÓNIO, Mário, (Mário António Fernandes de Oliveiro); Poet, Writer and Trans; b. 5 April 1934, Maquela do Zombo, Angola. *Publications:* many vols of poems, essays, short stories and trans. Contributions: numerous magazines and journals.

ANTROBUS, John; Dramatist, Author and Screenwriter; b. 2 July 1933, London, England; m. Margaret McCormick 1958 (divorced 1980); two s. one

d. *Education:* King Edward VII Nautical College; Royal Military Acad., Sandhurst. *Career:* mem. Writers' Guild of America West; Writers' Guild of Great Britain. *Publications:* Plays: The Bed-Sitting Room (with Spike Milligan), 1963; Captain Oate's Left Sock, 1969; Walton on Thames, 1970, revised edn as The Bed-Sitting Room 2, 1983; Crete and Sergeant Pepper, 1972; Jonah, 1979; Hitler in Liverpool, 1980; One Orange for the Baby, 1980; Up in the Hide, 1980; When Did You Last See Your Trousers? (with Ray Galton), 1986. Screenplays: Carry on Sergeant (with Norman Hudis), 1958; Idol on Parade, 1959; The Wrong Arm of the Law (with others), 1962; The Big Job (with Talbot Rothwell), 1965; The Bed-Sitting Room (with Charles Wood), 1969. Children's Books: The Boy with Illuminating Measles, 1978; Help! I'm a Prisoner in a Toothpaste Factory, 1978; Ronnie and the Haunted Rolls Royce, 1982; Ronnie and the Great Knitted Robbery, 1982; Ronnie and the High Rise, 1992; Ronnie and the Flying Carpet, 1992. Contributions: Radio and television. *Honours:* George Devine Award, 1970; Writers' Guild Award, 1971; Arts Council Bursaries, 1973, 1976, 1980, 1982; Banff Television Festival Award for Best Comedy, 1987. *Address:* 20 Powis Mews, London W11 1JN, England.

ANTUNES, Xana; British newspaper editor; b. 1965. *Career:* began career in journalism with The Independent business section 1988; TV journalist on Business Daily (Channel 4); Business News Ed., Evening Standard 1992–93; Deputy Business Ed., then Business Ed. New York Post 1993–2000, Ed. New York Post 2000–01; host of feature writing seminars 2002–03. *Address:* c/o New York Post, 1211 Avenue of the Americas New York, NY 10036, USA.

ANVIL, Christopher (see Crosby, Harry Clifton).

APPELFELD, Aharon; Israeli novelist; b. 1932, Czernowitz, Poland. *Education:* Hebrew Univ., Jerusalem. *Career:* emigrated to Palestine 1946; Lecturer, Be'er Shev'a University 1984. *Publications:* In the Wilderness 1965, Frost in the Land 1965, At Ground Level 1968, Five Stories 1970, The Skin and the Gown 1971, My Master the River 1971, Like the Pupil of an Eye 1972, Years and Hours 1975, Lika a Hundred Witnesses: A Selection 1975, The Age of Wonders 1978, Essays in the First Person 1979, Badenheim 1939 1980, Tzili: The Story of a Life 1983, The Shirt and the Stripes 1983, The Retreat 1985, At One and the Same Time 1985, To the Land of the Cattails 1986, The Immortal Bartfuss 1988, Tongues of Fire 1988, Writing and the Holocaust 1988, For Every Sin 1989, The Railway 1991, Katerina 1992. *Honours:* H. H. Wingate Literary Award 1989. *Address:* c/o Keter Publishing House, PO Box 7145, Jerusalem 91071, Israel.

APPELGREN, Anne Marie; Author and Trans; b. 12 March 1956, Ekenaes, Finland; m.; two c. *Publications:* Novels: Salto Mortal, 1990; Skuggan av Saturnus, 1992. Non-Fiction: Astrologi i dag. Självkännedom genom symboler, 1994. Other: Trans of various books into Swedish. *Address:* PO Box 297, Straengnaes, Sweden. *E-mail:* charmiene@telia.com. *Website:* www.charmiene.com.

APPIAH, Kwame Anthony; American academic and writer; b. 8 May 1954, London, England. *Education:* Kwame Nkrumah Univ. of Science and Tech., Ghana; PhD, Univ. of Cambridge, England. *Career:* raised in Ghana; taught at Univ. of Ghana; has held position of Prof. of Philosophy and Prof. of African Studies and African-American Studies at Univ. of Cambridge, England, Yale Univ., New Haven, CT, Cornell Univ., Ithaca, NY, Duke Univ., Durham, NC and Harvard Univ., Cambridge, MA 1991–2002; Prof. of Philosophy and African-American Studies, Princeton Univ., Princeton, NJ 2002–. *Publications:* Assertion and Conditionals 1985, For Truth in Semantics 1986, Necessary Questions: An Introduction to Philosophy 1989, Avenging Angel (novel) 1991, In My Father's House: Africa in the Philosophy of Culture (essays—Annisfield-Wolf Book Award 1993, African Studies Asscn Herskovits Award 1993) 1992, Nobody Likes Letitia (novel) 1994, Another Death in Venice (novel) 1995, Color Consciousness: The Political Morality of Race (with Amy Gutman) (North American Soc. for Social Philosophy Annual Book Award) 1996, The Dictionary of Global Culture (with Henry Louis Gates, Jr) 1996, Africana: The Encyclopedia of African and African American Experience 1999; Ed.: Early African-American Classics 1990; Co-Ed.: Critical Perspectives Past and Present (series) 1993, Identities (essays) 1995. *Address:* c/o Barker Center, Harvard University, 12 Quincy Street, Cambridge, MA 02138, USA.

APPLE, Max (Isaac); Prof. of English and Writer; b. 22 Oct. 1941, Grand Rapids, MI, USA; one s. one d. *Education:* BA, 1963, PhD, 1970, University of Michigan; Graduate Studies, Stanford University, 1964. *Career:* Asst Prof., Reed College, Portland, OR, 1970–71; Asst Prof., 1972–76, Assoc. Prof., 1976–80, Prof. of English, 1980–, Rice University; mem. MLA; PEN; Texas Institute of Letters. *Publications:* Studies in English (with others), 1975; The Oranging of America and Other Stories, 1976; Zip: A Novel of the Left and the Right, 1978; Southwest Fiction (ed.), 1980; Three Stories, 1983; Free Agents, 1984; The Propheteers: A Novel, 1987; Roomates: My Grandfather's Story (memoir), 1994. Contributions: many publications. *Honours:* National Endowment for the Humanities Fellowship, 1971; Jesse Jones Awards, Texas Institute of Letters, 1976, 1985; Ribalous Award, Hadassah Magazine, 1985. *Address:* c/o Dept of English, Rice University, Houston, TX 77001, USA.

APPLEBAUM, Anne; American writer and journalist; b. 25 July 1964, Washington, DC; m. Radek Sikorski; two c. *Education:* Univ. of Yale, LSE, Univ. of Oxford. *Career:* Warsaw correspondent for The Economist 1988; journalist, numerous journals in Central and Eastern Europe 1988–92; Foreign Ed. and Deputy Ed. The Spectator, London; columnist, The Daily Telegraph, The Sunday Telegraph, Evening Standard; Political Ed., Evening Standard 1997; currently columnist and editiorial bd mem., The Washington Post; broadcasting work includes Newsnight (BBC2), Today (BBC Radio 4), Week in Westminster (BBC Radio 4), CNN, MSNBC, CBS, Sky News. *Publications:* non-fiction: Between East and West: Across the Borderlands of Europe 1995, Gulag: A History 2003; contrib. to Wall Street Journal, Int. Herald Tribune, Foreign Affairs, Boston Globe, Independent, Guardian, Commentaire, Suddeutsche Zeitung, Newsweek, New Criterion, Weekly Standard, New Republic, New York Review of Books, Nat. Review, New Statesman, TLS, Literary Review. *Honours:* Charles Douglas-Home Memorial Trust Award for Journalism 1992, Adolph Bentnick Prize for European non-fiction 1996. *Address:* The Washington Post, 1150 15th Street NW, Washington, DC 20071, USA. *E-mail:* applebaumanne@washpost.com. *Website:* www.washingtonpost.com; www.anneapplebaum.com.

APPLEMAN, Marjorie Haberkorn, BA, MA; dramatist and poet; b. Fort Wayne, IN, USA; m. Philip Appleman. *Education:* Northwestern University, Indiana University, Sorbonne, University of Paris. *Career:* Prof. of English and Playwriting, New York University, Columbia University; International Honors Program, Indiana University; mem. Authors' League of America; Circle East Theater Co; Dramatists' Guild; League of Professional Theatre Women; PEN American Center; Poets and Writers; Acad. of American Poets. *Publications:* Plays: Seduction Duet, 1982; The Commuter, 1985. Other: Over 60 plays given in full productions or staged readings, 1971–2002. Poetry: Against Time, 1994. Opera libretto: Let's Not Talk About Lenny Anymore, 1989. Contributions: numerous anthologies and journals. *Honours:* several playwriting awards. *Address:* PO Box 5058, East Hampton, NY 11937, USA. *E-mail:* applemanmh@yahoo.com.

APPLEMAN, Philip Dean; writer, poet and academic; b. 8 Feb. 1926, Kendallville, IN, USA; m. Marjorie Ann Haberkorn 1950. *Education:* BS, 1950, PhD, 1955, Northwestern University; MA, University of Michigan, 1951. *Career:* Fulbright Scholar, University of Lyon, 1951–52; Instructor to Prof., 1955–67, Prof., 1967–84, Distinguished Prof. of English, 1984–86, Distinguished Prof. Emeritus, 1986–, Indiana University; Dir and Instructor, International School of America, 1960–61, 1962–63; Visiting Prof., SUNY at Purchase, 1973, Columbia University, 1974; Visiting Scholar, New York University, University of Southern California at Los Angeles; John Steinbeck Visiting Writer, Long Island University at Southampton, 1992; mem. Acad. of American Poets; American Asscn of University Profs; Authors' Guild of America; MLA; National Council of Teachers of English; PEN American Center; Poetry Society of America; Poets and Writers. *Publications:* Fiction: In the Twelfth Year of the War, 1970; Shame the Devil, 1981; Apes and Angels, 1989. Poetry: Kites on a Windy Day, 1967; Summer Love and Surf, 1968; Open Doorways, 1976; Darwin's Ark, 1984; Darwin's Bestiary, 1986; Let There Be Light, 1991; New and Selected Poems, 1956–1996, 1996. Non-Fiction: The Silent Explosion, 1965. Editor: 1859: Entering an Age of Crisis, 1959; Darwin, 1970; The Origin of Species, 1975; An Essay on the Principle of Population, 1976. Contributions: numerous publications. *Honours:* Ferguson Memorial Award, Friends of Literature Society, 1969; Christopher Morley Awards, Poetry Society of America, 1970, 1975; Castanola Award, Poetry Society of America, 1975; National Endowment for the Arts Fellowship, 1975; Pushcart Prize, 1985; Humanist Arts Award, American Humanist Asscn, 1994; Friends of Darwin Award, National Center for Science Education, 2002. *Address:* PO Box 5058, East Hampton, NY 11937, USA. *E-mail:* applemanmp@yahoo.com.

APT, Bryan Andrew, BLS, MS; writer; b. 30 May 1965, Fort Collins, CO, USA. *Education:* Princeton University, Iowa State University, Indiana University. *Publications:* Case of the Missing Detective: Mystery Down Under, 1995; Search for Freedom – Distinctions between Illusory and Actual Human Freedom: Dickens and Engels, 1999; Tragic Time and Comic Time in Shakespeare's Plays, 1999; Under the Apple Tree: Musings and Poetry, 2001; Images of Light and Darkness in Heart of Darkness: Undermining Nineteenth-Century Idealism, 2003. *Honours:* National Merit Scholar; US Tennis Asscn ranked player. *Address:* c/o Harper Benton Press, 1017 Burnett Avenue, Ames, IA 50010, USA.

ARCHER, Geoffrey Wilson; author; b. 21 May 1944, London, England; m. Eva Janson; one s. one d. *Career:* Researcher, Southern TV, 1964; Reporter, Anglia TV, Norwich, 1965–69, Tyne-Tees TV, Newcastle, 1969, ITN, 1969–95; Defence Correspondent, 1980–95; mem. Society of Authors; CWA. *Publications:* Fiction: Skydancer, 1987; Shadow Hunter, 1989; Eagle Trap, 1992; Scorpion Trail, 1995; Java Spider, 1997; Fire Hawk, 1998; The Lucifer Network, 2001; The Burma Legacy, 2002; Dark Angel 2004. *Address:* c/o Century/Arrow Books, 20 Vauxhall Bridge Road, London SW1V 2SA, England. *E-mail:* ga@geoffreyarcher.co.uk. *Website:* www.geoffreyarcher.co.uk.

ARCHER OF WESTON-SUPER-MARE, Baron (Life Peer), cr. 1992, of Mark in the County of Somerset; **Jeffrey Howard Archer;** British author and fmr politician; b. 15 April 1940; m. Mary Archer 1966; two s. *Education:* Wellington School and Brasenose Coll., Oxford. *Career:* mem. GLC for

Havering 1966–70; MP for Louth (Conservative) 1969–74; Deputy Chair. Conservative Party 1985–86; sentenced to four years' imprisonment for perjury and perverting the course of justice July 2001, released July 2003. *Play:* The Accused (writer and actor) 2000. *Publications:* Not a Penny More, Not a Penny Less 1975, Shall We Tell the President? 1977, Kane and Abel 1979, A Quiver Full of Arrows 1980, The First Miracle (with Craigie Aitchison) 1980, The Prodigal Daughter 1982, First Among Equals 1984, A Matter of Honour 1985, Beyond Reasonable Doubt (play) 1987, A Twist in the Tale (short stories) 1988, Exclusive (play) 1989, As the Crow Flies 1991, Honour Among Thieves 1993, Twelve Red Herrings (short stories) 1994, The Fourth Estate 1996, The Collected Short Stories 1997, The Eleventh Commandment 1998, To Cut a Long Story Short (short stories) 2000, A Prison Diary Vols I and II 2002, Sons of Fortune 2003, In the Lap of the Gods 2004. *Address:* Peninsula Heights, 93 Albert Embankment, London, SE1 7TY; The Old Vicarage, Grantchester, Cambridge, CB3 9ND, England.

ARCHIBALD, Rupert Douglas; Author and Playwright; b. 25 April 1919, Port of Spain, Trinidad. *Education:* BA, McGill University, 1946. *Career:* Ed., Progress Magazine, 1952; Mem., Editorial Board, Clarion Newspaper, 1954–56. *Publications:* Junction Village, 1954; Anne Marie, 1958; The Bamboo Clump, 1962; The Rose Slip, 1962; Old Maid's Tale, 1965; Island Tide, 1972; Defeat with Honour, 1973; Isidore and the Turtle (novel), 1973.

ARDAI, Charles; Author and Ed.; b. 25 Oct. 1969, New York, NY, USA. *Education:* BA, English, summa cum laude, Columbia University, 1991. *Career:* Contributing Ed., Computer Entertainment and K-Power, 1985; Ed., Davis Publications, 1990–91; mem. MWA. *Publications:* Great Tales of Madness and the Macabre, 1990; Kingpins, 1992; Futurecrime, 1992. Contributions: Alfred Hitchcock's Mystery Magazine; Ellery Queen's Mystery Magazine; Twilight Zone; The Year's Best Horror Stories; Computer Gaming World; and others. *Honours:* Pearlman Prize for Fiction, Columbia University, 1991. *Address:* 350 E 52nd St, New York, NY 10022, USA.

ARDEN, John; British dramatist and writer; b. 26 Oct. 1930, Barnsley, Yorkshire, England; m. Margaretta Ruth D'Arcy 1957; five s. (one deceased). *Education:* King's College, Cambridge; Edinburgh College of Art. *Career:* Fellow in Playwriting, University of Bristol, 1959–60; Visiting Lecturer, New York University, 1967; Regent's Lecturer, University of California at Davis, 1973; Writer-in-Residence, University of New England, Australia, 1975. *Publications:* Fiction: Silence Among the Weapons, 1982; Books of Bale, 1988; Cogs Tyrannic, 1991; Jack Juggler and the Emperor's Whore, 1995; The Stealing Steps, 2003. Essays: To Present the Pretence, 1977; Awkward Corners (with Margaretta D'Arcy), 1988. Plays: All Fall Down, 1955; The Waters of Babylon, 1957; Live Like Pigs, 1958; Sergeant Musgrave's Dance, 1959; The Happy Haven (with Margaretta D'Arcy), 1960; The Business of Good Government (with Margaretta D'Arcy), 1960; Wet Fish, 1962; The Workhouse Donkey, 1963; Ironhand, 1963; Ars Longa Vita Brevis (with Margaretta D'Arcy), 1964; Armstrong's Last Goodnight, 1964; Left-Handed Liberty, 1965; Friday's Hiding (with Margaretta D'Arcy), 1966; The Royal Pardon (with Margaretta D'Arcy), 1966; Muggins is a Martyr (with Margaretta D'Arcy and C.A.S.T.), 1968; The Hero Rises Up (musical with Margaretta D'Arcy), 1968; Two Autobiographical Plays, 1972; The Ballygombeen Bequest (with Margaretta D'Arcy), 1972; The Island of the Mighty (with Margaretta D'Arcy), 1972; The Non-Stop Connolly Show (with Margaretta D'Arcy), 1975; Vandaleur's Folly (with Margaretta D'Arcy), 1978; The Little Gray Home in the West (with Margaretta D'Arcy), 1978; The Making of Muswell Hill (with Margaretta D'Arcy), 1979. Radio Plays: The Life of Man, 1956; The Bagman, 1969; Keep Those People Moving (with Margaretta D'Arcy), 1972; Pearl, 1977; Don Quixote (adaptation after Cervantes), 1980; Garland for a Hoar Head, 1982; The Old Man Sleeps Alone, 1982; The Manchester Enthusiasts (with Margaretta D'Arcy), 1984; Whose is the Kingdom? (with Margaretta D'Arcy), 1988; A Suburban Suicide (with Margaretta D'Arcy), 1994; Six Little Novels of Wilkie Collins (adaptation), 1997; Woe Alas, the Fatal Cashbox!, 1999; Wild Ride to Dublin, 2003. Television Plays: Soldier Soldier, 1960; Wet Fish, 1962. *Honours:* Evening Standard Drama Award, 1960; Arts Council Playwriting Award, 1972; PEN Short Story Prize, 1992; V. S. Pritchett Short Story Prize, 1999. *Literary Agent:* Casarotto Ramsay Ltd, National House, 60–66 Wardour Street, London W1V 3HP, England.

ARDEN, William (see Lynds, Dennis).

ARENDT, Erica Elisabeth (see Harvor, Elisabeth).

ARGUELLES, Ivan Wallace; Poet, Publisher and Librarian; b. 24 Jan. 1939, Rochester, MN, USA; m. 1st Claire Birnbaum Aug. 1958 (divorced 1960); m. 2nd Marilla Calhourn Elder 27 Oct. 1962; two s. *Education:* University of Minnesota; BA, Classics, University of Chicago, 1961; Graduate Studies, Classics, New York University; MLS, Vanderbilt University, 1968. *Career:* Guest Lecturer, Rampo College, NJ, 1978; Co-Founder, Rock Steady Press, San Francisco, 1988, Pantograph Press, Berkeley, 1992. *Publications:* Instamatic Reconditioning, 1978; The Invention of Spain, 1978; Captive of the Vision of Paradise, 1983; The Tattoed Heart of the Drunken Sailor, 1983; Manicomio, 1984; Nailed to the Coffin of Life, 1985; What Are They Doing to My Animal?, 1986; The Structure of Hell, 1986; Pieces of the Bone-Text Still There, 1987; Baudelaire's Brain, 1988; Looking for Mary Lou: Illegal Syntax, 1989; 'THAT' Goddess, 1992; Hapax Legomenon, 1993; The Tragedy of Momus, 1993; Enigma and Variations: Paradise is Persian for Park, 1996; Madonna Septet, two vols, 2000; Chac Prostibulario (with John M. Bennett), 2002; Triloka, 2003. Contributions: anthologies and magazines. *Address:* 1740 Walnut Street, No. 4 Berkeley, CA 94709, USA. *E-mail:* iarguell@hotmail.com.

ARGUETA, Manilo; Poet and Novelist; b. 24 Nov. 1935, San Miguel, El Salvador. *Education:* Universidad Nacional, San Salvador. *Publications:* Fiction: El valle des hamacas, 1970; Caperucita en la zona rosa, 1977; One Day of Life, 1980; Cuzcatalan, Where the Southern Sea Beats, 1987. Poetry: Poemas, 1967; En el costado de la luz, 1979; El Salvador, 1990. Editor: Poesia de El Salvador, 1983. *Honours:* University of Central America Prize, 1980. *Address:* c/o Chatto and Windus, 20 Vauxhall Bridge Rd, London SW1N 2SA, England.

ARIAS, Arturo, PhD; Guatemalan novelist and literary critic; b. 1950. *Education:* Univ. of Paris. *Career:* Pres., Latin American Studies Asscn 2001–03; currently Dir of Latin American Studies, Univ. of Redlands. *Film screenplays include:* El Norte 1984. *Publications:* novels: Despues de las bombas (trans. as After the Bombs) 1979, Itzam Na 1981, Jaguar en Llamas 1989, Los caminos de Paxil 1990, Cascabel 1998, Sopa de caracól 2003; criticism: La identidad de la palabra (trans. as The Identity of the Word) 1998, Gestos ceremoniales (trans. as Ceremonial Gestures) 1998, Miguel Angel Asturias's Mulata 2001, The Rigoberta Menchu Controversy 2001; contrib. to Rattlesnake 2003. *Honours:* Casa de las Americas Prize, Anna Seghers Scholarship (twice). *Literary Agent:* c/o Curbstone Press, 321 Jackson Street, Willimantic, CT 06226-1738, USA. *E-mail:* info@curbstone.org. *Website:* www.curbstone.org.

ARIDJIS, Homero; Mexican author, poet and diplomatist; *President Emeritus, International PEN*; b. 6 April 1940, Contepec, Michoacán; m. Betty Ferber 1965, two d. *Education:* Autonomous Univ. of Mexico 1961. *Career:* lecturer in Mexican literature at univs in USA; Cultural Attaché, Embassy in Netherlands 1972, later Amb. to Switzerland and the Netherlands; Man. Cultural Inst., Michoacán, Dir Festival Int. de Poesia 1981, 1982, 1987; f. Review Correspondencias; Chief Ed. Dialogos; Visiting Prof., Univ. of Indiana and New York Univ.; Poet-in-Residence, Columbia Univ. Translation Center, New York; co-f. Pres. Grupo de los Cien 1985 (100 internationally renowned artists and intellectuals active in environmental affairs); Nichols Chair in the Humanities and the Public Sphere, Univ. of Calif. at Irvine; Pres. International PEN 1997–2003, Pres. Emer. 2003–. *Publications include:* poetry: Los ojos desdoblados 1960, Antes del reino 1963, Ajedrez-Navegaciones 1969, Los espacios azules 1969 (Blue Spaces 1974), Quemar las naves 1975, Vivir para ver 1977, Construir la muerte 1982, Obra poética 1960–86 1987, Imágenes para el fin del milenio 1990, Nueva expulsión del paraíso 1990, El poeta en peligro de extinción 1992, Tiempo de ángeles 1994, Ojos de otro mirar 1998 (Eyes to See Otherwise: Selected Poems of Homero Aridjis 2002), El ojo de la ballena 2001; prose: La tumba de Filidor 1961, Mirándola dormir 1964, Perséfone 1967 (Persephone 1986), El poeta niño 1971, Noche de independencia 1978, Espectáculo del año dos mil 1981, Playa nudista y otros relatos 1982, 1492 vida y tiempos de Juan Cabezón de Castilla 1985, El último Adán 1986, Memorias del nuevo mundo 1988, Gran teatro del fin del mundo 1989, La leyenda de los soles 1993, El Señor de los últimos días: Visiones del año dos mil 1994, ¿En quién piensas cuando haces el amor? 1996, Apocalipsis con figuras 1997, La montaña de las mariposas 2000, El silencio de Orlando 2000, La zona del silencio 2002. *Honours:* Guggenheim Fellow 1966–67, 1979–80; Hon. DHumLitt (Indiana) 1993; Global 500 Award 1987, Novedades Novela Prize 1988, Grinzane Cavour Prize for Best Foreign Fiction 1992, Prix Roger Caillois, France 1997, Presea Generalisimo José María Morelos, City of Morelia 1998, Environmentalist of the Year Award, Latin Trade Magazine 1999, John Hay Award, Orion Soc. 2000, Forces for Nature Award, National Resources Defense Council 2001, Green Cross Millennium Award for Int. Environmental Leadership, Global Green, USA 2002. *Address:* International PEN, 9–10 Charterhouse Buildings, Goswell Road, London, EC1M 7AT, England. *Telephone:* (20) 7253-4308. *Fax:* (20) 7253-5711. *E-mail:* intpen@dircon.co.uk. *Website:* www.internatpen.org.

ARJOUNI, Jakob; German novelist and playwright; b. 8 Oct. 1964, Frankfurt am Main. *Plays:* The Garage 1988, Nobleman Daughter 1996. *Publications:* novels: Happy Birthday Turk 1987, More Beer 1987, One Man One Murder 1991, And Still Drink More! 1994, Magic Hoffman 1996, One Death to Die 1997; short story collections: A Friend 1998, Kismet 2001. *Address:* c/o No Exit Press, Oldcastle Books, PO Box 394, Harpenden, Hertfordshire AL5 1XJ, England. *E-mail:* info@noexit.co.uk. *Website:* www.noexit.co.uk.

ARKOUN, Mohammed; Prof. of Islamic Studies Emeritus and Writer; b. 1 Feb. 1932, Algeria; one s. one d. *Education:* PhD, Sorbonne, University of Paris, 1969. *Career:* Prof. of Islamic Studies, Sorbonne, University of Paris, 1961–93; Visiting Prof., Europe, USA, Indonesia and Arab world. *Publications:* L'Humanismé arabe au 4e/10e Siècle, 1982; Rethinking Islam, 1995; The Unthought in Contemporary Islamic Thought, 2001; Penser l'islam aujourd hui, 2001. Contributions: Books and journals. *Honours:* Officier, Légion d'honneur. *Address:* PO Box 12565, Aiin-Diab, Casablanca, Morocco.

ARLEN, Leslie (see Nicole, Christopher (Robin)).

ARLEN, Michael (John); Author; b. 9 Dec. 1930, London, England; m. Alice Albright, 1972, four d. *Education:* BA, Harvard University, 1952. *Career:*

mem. Authors' Guild; PEN. *Publications:* Living-Room War, 1969; Exiles, 1970; An American Verdist, 1972; Passage to Ararat, 1974; The View From Highway One, 1975; Thirty Seconds, 1980; The Camera Age, 1982; Say Goodbye to Sam, 1984. Contributions: New Yorker magazine. *Honours:* National Book Award, 1975; Le Prix Bremond, 1976; Hon. DLitt, 1984. *Address:* 1120 Fifth Ave, New York, NY 10128, USA.

ARMAH, Ayi Kwei; Novelist and Poet; b. 1939, Sekondi Takoradi, Ghana. *Education:* Sociology, Harvard Univ.; MFA, Creative Writing, Columbia Univ. *Career:* Fmr trans, Révolution Africaine magazine; Scriptwriter, Ghana TV, 1964; Ed., Jeune Afrique magazine, Paris, 1967–68; Teacher, College of National Education, Chamg'omge, Tanzania, National Univ. of Lesotho, various other institutes. *Publications:* Novels: The Beautyful Ones Are Not Yet Born, 1968; Fragments, 1970; Why Are We So Blest?, 1972; Two Thousand Seasons, 1973; The Healers, 1978; Osiris Rising, 1995. Contributions: Short stories and articles in Présense Africaine, Okyeame, Harper's, The Atlantic Monthly, New African, West Africa. *Address:* c/o African Writers Series, Heinemann Educational Publishers, Halley Ct, Jordan Hill, Oxford OX2 8EJ, England.

ARMEL, Aliette; French historian. *Career:* critic for Magazine littéraire 1984–. *Publications:* non-fiction: Marguerita Duras 1990, Michel Leiris 1997; novels: Antigone 1999, Le voyage de Bilqîs 2002. *Address:* Magazine littéraire, 4 rue du Texel, 75014 Paris, France. *Telephone:* 1 40 47 44 90. *Fax:* 1 40 47 44 98. *Website:* www.magazine-litteraire.com.

ARMES, Roy (Philip); Author and Lecturer; b. 16 March 1937, Norwich, England; m. Margaret Anne Johnson, 12 Aug. 1960, one s. two d. *Education:* BA, University of Bristol, 1959; Teacher's Certificate, University of Exeter, 1960; PhD, University of London, 1978. *Career:* Teacher, Royal Liberty School, Romford, 1960–69; Assoc. Lecturer in Film, University of Surrey, 1969–72; Research Fellow, 1969–72, Lecturer, 1972–73, Hornsey College of Art; Senior Lecturer, 1973–78, Reader in Film and Television, 1978–, Middlesex Polytechnic; Visiting Lecturer at many colleges and universities. *Publications:* French Cinema Since 1946, two vols, 1966; The Cinema of Alain Resnais, 1968; French Film, 1970; Patterns of Realism, 1972; Film and Reality: An Historical Survey, 1974; The Ambiguous Image, 1976; A Critical History of British Cinema, 1978; The Films of Alain Robbe-Grillet, 1981; French Cinema, 1984; Third World Film Making and the West, 1987; Action and Image: Dramatic Structure in Cinema, 1994. Contributions: many books and periodicals. *Address:* 19 New End, Hampstead, London NW3, England.

ARMITAGE, Gary Edric, (Robert Edric), BA, PhD; writer; b. 14 April 1956, Sheffield, England; m. Sara Jones 1978. *Education:* Hull Univ. *Publications:* Winter Garden 1985, A Season of Peace 1985, A New Ice Age 1986, Across the Autumn Grass 1986; as Robert Edric: A Lunar Eclipse 1989, In the Days of the American Museum 1990, The Broken Lands 1992, Hallowed Ground 1993, The Earth Made of Glass 1994, Elysium 1995, In Desolate Heaven 1997, The Sword Cabinet 1999, The Book of the Heathen 2000, Peacetime 2002, Cradle Song 2003, Siren Song 2004; contrib. to various periodicals. *Honours:* James Tait Black Memorial Prize 1985, Trask Award 1985, Soc. of Authors Award 1994, Arts Council Bursary 1995. *Address:* Glenfinnan, Springbank Avenue, Hornsea, East Yorkshire HU18 1ED, England.

ARMITAGE, Ronda (Jacqueline); Author, Teacher and Family Therapist; b. 11 March 1943, Kaikoura, New Zealand; m. David Armitage, 1966, two c. *Education:* Teacher's Certificate, 1962, Teacher's Diploma, 1969, Hamilton Teacher's College. *Career:* Schoolteacher, Duvauchelle, New Zealand, 1964–66, London, England, 1966, Auckland, New Zealand, 1968–69; Adviser on Children's Books, Dorothy Butler Ltd, Auckland, 1970–71; Asst Librarian, Lewes Priory Comprehensive School, Sussex, England, 1976–77; Teacher, East Sussex County Council, England, 1978–; Family Therapist; mem. Society of Authors. *Publications:* Let's Talk About Drinking, 1982; New Zealand, 1983. Children's Fiction: The Lighthouse Keeper's Lunch, 1977; The Trouble With Mr Harris, 1978; Don't Forget, Matilda!, 1978; The Bossing of Josie, 1980, in the USA as The Birthday Spell, 1981; Ice Creams for Rosie, 1981; One Moonlit Night, 1983; Grandma Goes Shopping, 1984; The Lighthouse Keeper's Catastrophe, 1986; The Lighthouse Keeper's Rescue, 1989; When Dad Did the Washing, 1990; Watch the Baby, Daisy, 1991; Looking After Chocolates, 1992; A Quarrel of Koalas, 1992; The Lighthouse Keeper's Picnic, 1993; The Lighthouse Keeper's Cat, 1996; Flora and the Strawberry Red Birthday Party, 1997; Queen of the Night, 1999; Family Violence, 1999. Contributions: Features in children's magazine, Aquila, 1998, 1999, 2000. *Honours:* Esther Glen Award, New Zealand Library Asscn, 1978. *Address:* Old Tiles Cottage, Church Lane, Hellingly, East Sussex BN27 4HA, England.

ARMITAGE, Simon Robert, BA, MA; British poet and writer; b. 26 May 1963, Huddersfield, West Yorkshire, England; m. Alison Tootell 1991. *Education:* Portsmouth Polytechnic, Manchester Univ. *Career:* Probation Officer, Greater Manchester Probation Service 1988–93; Poetry Ed., Chatto and Windus 1993–95. *Publications:* Zoom! 1989, Xanadu 1992, Kid 1992, Book of Matches 1993, The Dead Sea Poems 1995, Travelling Songs 2001, Little Green Man 2001, The Universal Home Doctor 2002, The White Stuff 2004; contrib. to Sunday Times, TLS, Guardian, Observer, Independent. *Honours:* Eric Gregory Award 1988, Sunday Times Young Writer of the Year 1993, Forward Poetry Prize 1993, Lannan Award 1994. *Address:* 3 Netherley, Marsden, Huddersfield HD7 6XN, England.

ARMSTRONG, David Malet, AO, BPhil, PhD, FBA; Australian academic and writer; *Professor Emeritus of Philosophy, University of Sydney*; b. 8 July 1926, Melbourne; m. Jennifer Mary de Bohun Clark 1982. *Education:* Dragon School, Oxford, UK, Geelong Grammar School, Sydney Univ., Exeter Coll. Oxford, Univ. of Melbourne. *Career:* Asst Lecturer in Philosophy, Birkbeck Coll., London, UK 1954–55; Lecturer, Sr Lecturer in Philosophy, Univ. of Melbourne 1956–63; Challis Prof. of Philosophy, Univ. of Sydney 1964–91, Prof. Emer. 1992–; Fellow Australian Acad. of Humanities, British Acad. *Publications:* Berkeley's Theory of Vision 1961, Perception and the Physical World 1961, Bodily Sensations 1962, A Materialist Theory of the Mind 1968, Belief, Truth and Knowledge 1973, Universals and Scientific Realism 1978, The Nature of the Mind and Other Essays 1983, What is a Law of Nature? 1983, Consciousness and Causality (with Norman Malcolm) 1984, A Combinatorial Theory of Possibility 1989, Universals: An Opinionated Instruction 1989, Dispositions: A Debate (with C. B. Martin and U. T. Place) 1996, A World of States of Affairs 1997, The Mind-Body Problem: An Opinionated Introduction 1999; contributions: scholarly books and journals. *Address:* Department of Philosophy, University of Sydney, Sydney, NSW 2006; 206 Glebe Point Road, Glebe, NSW 2037, Australia. *Telephone:* (2) 9351-2466 (Office); (2) 9660-1435 (Home). *Fax:* (2) 9660-8846. *E-mail:* david.armstrong@philosophy.usyd.edu.au (Office).

ARMSTRONG, Jeannette Christine, DFA, BFA; Okanagan, mem. of Penticton Indian Band writer, poet and educator; b. 5 Feb. 1948, Canada; one s. one d. *Education:* Okanagan Coll., Univ. of Victoria, BC. *Career:* Adjunct Prof., En'owkin School of Writing, University of Victoria, BC, 1989–; mem. PEN International; Writers' Union of Canada. *Publications:* Enwhisteetkwa, 1982; Neekna and Chemai, 1984; Slash, 1985; Native Creative Process, 1991; Breath Tracks, 1991; Looking at the Words of Our People, 1993; Whispering in Shadows, 2000; Native Poetry in Canada: A Contemporary Anthology. *Honours:* Children's Book Centre Choice Award, 1983. *Address:* c/o Theytus Books, Green Mountain Road, Lot 45, RR No. 2, Site 50, Comp. 8, Penticton, BC V2A 6J7, Canada.

ARMSTRONG, John Alexander; academic and writer; b. 4 May 1922, Saint Augustine, FL, USA; m. Annette Taylor 1952; three d. *Education:* PhB, 1948, MA, 1949, University of Chicago; University of Frankfurt am Main, 1949–50; PhD, Public Law and Government, 1953, Certificate of Russian Institute, 1954, Columbia University. *Career:* Research Analyst, War Documentation Project, Alexandria, Virginia, 1951, 1953–54; Asst Prof., University of Denver, 1952; Visiting Asst Prof., Russian Institute, Columbia University, 1957; Asst Prof. to Philippe de Commynes Prof. of Political Science (presently Emeritus), University of Wisconsin, Madison, 1954–86; mem. American Political Science Asscn; American Historical Asscn; American Asscn for Advancement of Slavic Studies, pres. 1965–67; Council on Foreign Relations. *Publications:* Ukrainian Nationalism, 1955; The Soviet Bureaucratic Elite, 1959; The Politics of Totalitarianism, 1961; Ideology, Politics and Government in the Soviet Union, 1962; Soviet Partisans in World War II (ed.), 1964; The European Administrative Elite, 1973; Nations Before Nationalism, 1982. Contributions: numerous political and historical journals. *Honours:* Guggenheim Fellowships, 1967, 1975; Ralph J. Bunche Award, American Political Science Asscn, 1983; American Asscn for Advancement of Slavic Studies Award, 1997. *Address:* 40 Water Street, Saint Augustine, FL 32084, USA.

ARMSTRONG, Karen Andersen, MA, MLitt; British writer; b. 14 Nov. 1944, Stourbridge, England. *Education:* St Anne's College, Oxford. *Career:* Jr Research Fellow, Bedford Coll., London 1973–76; Head of English, James Allen's Girls' School, Dulwich 1976–82; Lecturer, Leo Baeck Coll. 1993–. *Publications:* Through the Narrow Gate 1981, The Gospel According to Women 1986, Holy War 1988, Muhammaed, A Biography of the Prophet 1991, A History of God 1993, A History of Jerusalem 1996, In the Beginning, A New Reading of Genesis 1996, The Battle for God 2000, Islam: A Short History 2000, The Spiral Staircase: A Memoir 2004; contrib. to The Times, The Sunday Times, London Illustrated News, The Economist, The Independent, The Guardian, The Daily Telegraph, European Judaism, The Tablet. *Honours:* Muslim Public Affairs Council Media Award 1999. *Literary Agent:* Felicity Bryan, 2A N Parade, Banbury Road, Oxford OX2 6PE, England.

ARMSTRONG, Patrick Hamilton; University Lecturer and Writer; b. 10 Oct. 1941, Leeds, Yorkshire, England; m. Moyra E. J. Irvine 8 Aug. 1964; two s. *Education:* BSc, 1963, DipEd, 1964, MA, 1966, University of Durham; PhD, 1970. *Career:* Faculty, School of Earth and Geographical Sciences, University of Western Australia; Chief Examiner, International Baccalaureate Organization; Ed., Geographers-Biobibligraphic Studies. *Publications:* Discovering Ecology, 1973; Discovering Geology, 1974; The Changing Landscape, 1975; Series of children's books for Ladybird Books, 1976–79; Ecology, 1977; Reading and Interpretation of Australian and New Zealand Maps, 1981; Living in the Environment, 1982; The Earth: Home of Humanity, 1984; Charles Darwin in Western Australia, 1985; A Sketch Map Geography of Australia, 1988; A Sketch Map Physical Geography for Australia, 1989; Darwin's Desolate Islands, 1992; The English Parson-

Naturalist: A Companionship between Science and Religion, 2000. Contributions: New Scientist; Geographical Magazine; East Anglian Magazine; Geography; Cambridgeshire Life; Eastern Daily Press; Work and Travel Abroad; West Australian Newspaper; Weekly Telegraph; numerous scholarly and scientific journals. *Literary Agent:* Curtis Brown Pty, PO Box 19, Paddington, NSW 2021, Australia. *Address:* School of Earth and Geographical Sciences, University of Western Australia, Nedlands, WA 6907, Australia.

ARMSTRONG OF ILMINSTER, Baron (Life Peer), cr. 1988, of Ashill in the County of Somerset; **Robert Temple Armstrong,** GCB, KCB, CVO, MA; British fmr civil servant; b. 30 March 1927, Oxford; m. 1st Serena Mary Benedicta Chance 1953 (divorced 1985); two d.; m. 2nd (Mary) Patricia Carlow 1985. *Education:* Eton Coll. and Christ Church, Oxford. *Career:* Asst Prin. Treasury 1950–55, Pvt. Sec. to Economic Sec. 1953–54; Pvt. Sec. to Chancellor of the Exchequer (Rt Hon. R. A. Butler) 1954–55; Prin. Treasury 1955–64; Asst Sec. Cabinet Office 1964–66; Asst Sec. Treasury 1966–68; Prin. Pvt. Sec. to Chancellor of the Exchequer (Rt Hon. Roy Jenkins) 1968; Under-Sec. Treasury 1968–70; Prin. Pvt. Sec. to the Prime Minister 1970–75; Deputy Under-Sec. of State, Home Office 1975–77, Perm. Under-Sec. of State 1977–79; Sec. of the Cabinet 1979–87; Perm. Sec. Man. and Personnel Office 1981–87; Head, Home Civil Service 1981–87; Chair. Biotechnology Investments Ltd 1989–2000; Chair. Forensic Investigative Assocs PLC 1997–2003; Chair. Hestercombe Gardens Trust 1995–, Bd of Govs Royal Northern Coll. of Music 2000–; Sec. Radcliffe Cttee on Monetary System 1957–59; Sec. to the Dirs, Royal Opera House, Covent Garden 1968–87, Dir 1988–93; Dir Bristol and West Bldg Soc. 1988–97 (Chair. 1993–97), Bank of Ireland and other cos; Chair. Bd of Trustees, Victoria and Albert Museum 1988–98; mem. Rhodes Trust 1975–97; Fellow, Eton Coll. 1979–94; Chancellor, Univ. of Hull 1994–; Trustee Leeds Castle Foundation 1987– (Chair. 2001–); Pres. The Literary Soc. 2004–. *Honours:* Hon. Student, Christ Church 1985; Hon. Bencher, Inner Temple 1986; Hon. LLD. *Address:* House of Lords, Westminster, London, SW1A 0PW, England. *Telephone:* (20) 7219-4983. *Fax:* (20) 7219-1259.

ARNOLD, Emily (see Mccully, Emily Arnold).

ARNOLD, Heinz Ludwig; writer, critic and editor; b. 29 March 1940, Essen, Ruhr, Germany. *Education:* University of Göttingen. *Career:* Ed., Text und Kritik, 1963, Kritisches Lexikon zur Deutschsprachigen Gegenwartsliteratur, 1978, Kritisches Lexikon zur Fremdsprachigen Gegenwartsliteratur, 1983; mem. Asscn of German Writers; PEN; Deutsche Akademie für Sprache und Dichtung, Darmstadt; OH Tulip Order. *Publications:* Brauchen wir noch die Literatur?, 1972; Gespräche mit Schriftstellern, 1975; Gespräch mit F. Dürrenmatt, 1976; Handbuch der Deutschen Arbeiterliteratur, 1977; Als Schriftsteller leben, 1979; Vom Verlust der Scham und dem allmaehlichen Verschwinden der Demokratie, 1988; Krieger Waldgaenger, Anarch. Versuch über E. Jünger, 1990; Querfahrt mit Dürrenmatt, 1990–96; Die Drei Sprünge der Westdeutschen Gegenwartsliteratur, 1993; Die Deutsche Literatur 1945–1960, 11 vols, 1995–2000; Grundzüge der Literaturwissenschaft, 1996; F. Dürrenmatt, Gespräche, 1996; Einigkeit und aus Ruinen, 1999; Arthur Schnitzler: Ausgewählte Werke, eight vols, 1999–2002; Da schwimmen manchmal ein paar Sätze vorbei..., 2001; 'Was bin ich?' Über Max Frisch, 2002; Arbeiterlyrik 1842–1932 2003. Contributions: Die Zeit; Frankfurter Rund-schau; Frankfurter Allgemeine Zeitung; various radio stations. *Honours:* Hon. Prof., University of Göttingen. *Address:* Tuckermannweg 10, 37085 Göttingen, Germany.

ARNOLD, Margot (see Cook, Petronelle Marguerite Mary).

ARNOULT, Erik (see Orsenna, Erik).

ARRABAL, Fernando; Author, Poet, Dramatist and Artist; b. 11 Aug. 1932, Melilla, Morocco; m. Luce Moreau 1958; one s. one d. *Education:* University of Madrid. *Career:* Political prisoner in Spain, 1967; Co-Founder, Panique Movement. *Publications:* Fiction: Baal Babylone, 1959; L'enterrement de la sardine, 1961; Arrabal celebrando la ceremonia de la confusión, 1966; La torre herida por el rayo, 1983; La piedra de la locura, 1984; La Reverdie, 1985; La piedra iluminada, 1985; La virgen roja, 1987; La hija de King Kong, 1988; La extravagante cruzada de un castrado enamorado, 1990; La tueuse du jardin d'hiver, 1994; El Mono, 1994; La dudosa luz del día, 1994; Le funambule de Dieu, 1998; Ceremonia por un teniente abandonado, 1998; Porté disparu, 2000; Levitación, 2000. Plays: Ceremonia por un negro asesinado, 1966; La marcha real, 1975; La torre de Babel, 1976; En la cuerda floja (Balada del tren fantasma), 1977; Pic-nic, El triciclo, El laberinto, 1977; Inquisición, 1982; El rey de Sodoma, 1983; ...Y pondrán esposas a las flores, 1984; El cementerio de automóviles, El Arquitecto y el Emperador de Asiria, 1984; Las delicias de la carne, 1985; Fando y Lis, Guernica, La bicicleta del condenado, 1986; Teatro Bufo, 1986; Teatro pánico, 1986; Una cabra sobre una nube, 1975; La primera comunión, 1967; La travesía del imperio, 1988; Como lirio entre espinas, 1992; Bestialidad erótica, 1997; Teatro completo, 1997; Carta de amor, 1999. Poetry: La pierre de la folie, 1963; Cent sonnets, 1965; Humbles paradis, 1985; Liberté couleur de femme ou Adieu Bebylone, 1993; Arrabalesques, 1993; Diez poemas pánicos y un cuento, 1997. Essays: Carta al General Franco, 1972; Carta a los militantes comunistas españoles, 1978; Carta a los comunistas españoles y otras cartas, 1981; Carta a Fidel Castro, 1983; Carta a Jose María Aznar, 1993; Carta al Rey de España, 1995; Cartas a Baltazar. *Honours:* Premio Nacional de Superdotado, 1942; Recipient Award, Ford Foundation, New York, USA, 1959; Prix Lugné-Poe du Théâtre, 1965; Société des Auteurs Prize, 1966; Grand Prix du Théâtre, 1967; Grand Prix de l'Humour Noir, 1968; Obie Award, 1976; Premio Nadal, 1984; Worlds Theatre Prize, 1984; Medalla de Oro de Bellas Artes, 1986; Prix du Théâtre, Académie Française, 1993; Premio Internacional de Novela Vladimir Nabokov, 1994; Premio Espasa de Ensayo, 1994; Médaille d'Or du Ministère de la Culture, Egypt, 1994; Prix Théâtre au pluriel, 1994; Officier, Ordre des Arts et des Lettres, 1995; Premier Prix Théâtre de la Roseraie, 1995; Medalla de Oro del Círculo de Bellas Artes de Madrid, 1995; Medalla de Oro de la Ciudad de Melilla, 1995; Grand Prix, Société des Gens de Lettres, 1996; Prix du Centre National du Livre, 1996; Grand Prix de la Ville d'Antibes, 1997; Center of Civilization and Culture Medal, New York Univ., 1997; Order of Marko Marulic, Croatia, 1997; Prix de la Société des Auteurs, 1998; Premio Mariano de Cavia, 1998; Premio Alessandro Manzoni di Poesia, Italy, 1999; Satrape du Collège de Pataphysique, 2000; Premio Cine y Literatura Eninci, 2000; Premio Nacional de las Letras Teresa de Ávila, 2000; Premio Ercilla al mejor espectáculo del año, 2001; Premio Nacional de Teatro, 2001. *Address:* 22 rue Jouffroy d'Abbans, 75017 Paris, France. *Website:* www.arrabal.org.

ARRIAGA JORDÁN, Guillermo; Mexican scriptwriter; b. 1958, Mexico City. *Career:* Prof. of Film, Instituto Tecnológico de Estudios Superiores de Monterrey. *Screenplays:* Amores Perros 2000, Powder Keg 2001, Escuádron guillotina 2001, 21 Grams (with Alejandro González Iñárritu; Satellite Award for Best Original Screenplay) 2003. *Publications:* novels: Escuádron guillotina 1991, Un Dulce olor a muerte (trans. as A Sweet Scent of Death) 1994, El Búfalo en la noche 2000. *Address:* c/o Faber and Faber Ltd, 3 Queen Square, London, WC1N 3AU, England.

ARROW, Kenneth (Joseph); Prof. of Economics Emeritus and Writer; b. 23 Aug. 1921, New York, NY, USA; m. Selma Schweitzer, 31 Aug. 1947, two s. *Education:* BS, Social Sciences, City College, CUNY, 1940; MA, 1941, PhD, 1951, Columbia University. *Career:* Asst Prof., University of Chicago, 1948–49; Acting Asst Prof., 1949–50, Assoc. Prof., 1950–53, Prof. of Economics, Statistics and Operations Research, 1953–68, Joan Kenney Prof. of Economics, Prof. of Operations Research, 1979–91, Prof. Emeritus, 1991–, Stanford University; Prof. of Economics, 1968–74, James Bryant Conant University Prof., 1974–79, Harvard University; mem. American Acad. of Arts and Sciences, vice-pres., 1979–81, 1991–93; American Economic Asscn, pres., 1973; American Philosophical Society; British Acad., corresponding mem.; International Economic Asscn, pres., 1983–86; National Acad. of Sciences; Pontifical Acad. of Social Sciences; Finnish Acad. of Arts and Sciences. *Publications:* Social Choice and Individual Values, 1951; Mathematical Studies in Inventory and Production (co-author), 1958; Studies in Linear and Nonlinear Programming (co-author), 1958; Time Series Analysis of Inter-industry Demands (co-author), 1959; Essays in the Theory of Risk Bearing, 1971; Public Investment, the Rate of Return and Optimal Fiscal Policy (co-author), 1971; General Competitive Analysis (co-author), 1971; The Limits of Organization, 1974; Studies in Resource Allocation Processes (co-author), 1977; Collected Papers, six vols, 1983–85; Social Choice and Multicriterion Decision Making (co-author), 1985. Contributions: Professional journals. *Honours:* John Bates Clark Medal, American Economic Asscn, 1957; Nobel Memorial Prize in Economic Science, 1972; Guggenheim Fellowship, 1972–73; Von Neumann Prize; 21 hon. doctorates. *Address:* c/o Dept of Economics, Stanford University, Stanford, CA 94305-6072, USA.

ARSAND, Daniel; French novelist and publisher; b. 9 July 1950, Avignon. *Career:* bookseller, publisher; established Les Editions de la Sphere 1979–. *Publications:* novels: La Province des ténèbres (trans. as The Land of Darkness) (Prix Fémina) 1998, En silence 2000. *Literary Agent:* c/o Dedalus Ltd, Langford Lodge, St Judith's Lane, Sawtry, Cambridgeshire PE28 5XE, England. *E-mail:* info@dedalusbooks.com. *Website:* wwww.dedalusbooks .com.

ARTEAGA, Alfred, BA, MA, MFA, PhD; writer, poet and university educator; b. 2 May 1950, Los Angeles, CA, USA; m. Dec. 1972 (divorced 1995); three d. *Education:* University of California, Santa Cruz, Columbia University. *Career:* Instructor in Mexican-American Studies, San Jose City College, CA, 1977–87; Asst Prof. of English, University of Houston, 1987–90; Asst Prof. of English, University of California, Berkeley, 1990–98. *Publications:* Cantos (poems), 1991; An Other Tongue: Nation and Ethnicity in the Linguistic Borderlands (ed.), 1994; First Words: Origins of the European Nation, 1994; House with the Blue Bed (essays), 1997; Chicano Poetics: Heterotexts and Hybridities, 1997; Love in the Time of Aftershocks (poems), 1998. Contributions: anthologies including Spivak Reader; Essays and poems to journals including: Stanford Humanities Review; Critical Studies; Baldus; River Styx; Electronic journals. *Honours:* Rockefeller Foundation Fellow, 1993–94; Poetry Fellow, National Endowment for the Arts, 1995. *E-mail:* bluebed@hotmail.com.

ARTHUR, Elizabeth Ann; writer; b. 15 Nov. 1953, New York, NY, USA; m. Steven Bauer 1982. *Education:* BA, English, University of Victoria, 1978; Diploma, Education, 1979. *Career:* Visiting Instructor, Creative Writing, University of Cincinnati, 1983–84; Visiting Asst Prof., English, Miami University, 1984–85; Asst Prof., English, 1985–92, Assoc. Prof., 1992–96, Indiana University-Purdue University at Indianapolis; Visiting Assoc. Prof., English, Miami University, 1996; mem. Poets and Writers. *Pub-*

lications: Island Sojourn (memoir), 1980; Beyond the Mountain (novel), 1983; Bad Guys (novel), 1986; Binding Spell (novel), 1988; Looking for the Klondike Stone (memoir), 1993; Antarctic Navigation, (novel), 1995; Bring Deeps (novel), 2003. Contributions: New York Times; Outside; Backpacker; Ski-XC; Shenandoah. *Honours:* William Sloane Fellowship, Bread Loaf Writers' Conference, 1980; Writing Fellowship, Ossabaw Island Project, 1981; Grant in Aid, Vermont Council on the Arts, 1982; Fellowship in Prose, National Endowment for the Arts, 1982–83; Master Artist Fellowship, Indiana Arts Commission, Indianapolis, 1988; Fellowship in Fiction, National Endowment for the Arts, 1989–90; Antarctic Artists' and Writers' Grant, National Science Foundation, 1990; Critics' Choice Award for Antarctic Navigation, 1995; Notable Book, New York Times Book Review, 1995. *Address:* c/o Bloomsbury Publishing PLC, 38 Soho Square, London W1D 3HB, England. *E-mail:* eaa@elizabetharthur.org.

ARTHUR, Rasjid Arthur James, MA; journalist; b. 7 June 1928, Stirling, Scotland. *Education:* Edinburgh Univ. *Career:* National Service, RAF 1950–52; local reporter, Stirling 1952–54; Sub-Ed. 1954–55, leader writer 1955–64, The Scotsman; Features Ed., News Ed. and writer, Central Office of Information, London 1965–78; freelance writer on environment, development and related topics 1978–; mem. Chartered Inst. of Journalists. *Publications:* contrib. to many articles on environmental subjects for British and int. magazines of the water industry and for the London Press Service of the Press Asscn. *Address:* 32 Midway, Middleton Cheney, Banbury, OX17 2QW, England. *E-mail:* raj@rasjid.fsnet.co.uk.

ARZILLE, Juliette d'; writer; b. 23 Nov. 1932, La Neuveille, Switzerland; m. Walter Friedemann 1955; one s. one d. *Education:* music and autodidactical literary education. *Career:* mem., Literature Committee, Canton of Neuchâtel, 1993–; mem. PEN International; Swiss Society of Writers; AENJ. *Publications:* Le deuxieme soleil, 1973; Identite suivi de les embellies, 1976; Une innocence verte, 1982; Nocturne, 1984; Esquisses et propos, 1986; D'ici et d'ailleurs, 1989; Hommage pluriel, 1998; Alentour, 1998; Acqua serena, 1998. Contributions: newspapers and magazines. *Honours:* French Literature Award, Canton of Bern, 1982. *Address:* En Arzille, 1788 Praz, Switzerland.

ASANTE, Molefi Kete; Prof. and Poet; b. 14 Aug. 1942, Vaidosta, CA, USA; m. Kariamu Welsh, 1981, two s. one d. *Education:* BA, Oklahoma Christian University, 1964; MA, Pepperdine University, 1965; PhD, University of California at Los Angeles, 1968. *Career:* Prof., University of California at Los Angeles, 1969–73, SUNY at Buffalo, 1973–84, Temple University, 1984–; mem. African Writers' Union, vice-pres., 1994–. *Publications:* Break of Dawn, 1964; Epic in Search of African Kings, 1979; Afrocentricity, 1980; The Afrocentric Idea, 1987; Kemet, Afrocentricity and Knowledge, 1992; Classical Africa, 1992; African American History, 1995; African Intellectual Heritage, 1996; Love Dance, 1997; African American Atlas, 1998. Contributions: journals. *Honours:* Hon. degrees, citations and awards. *Literary Agent:* Marie Brown Assocs, New York, USA. *Address:* Temple University, Philadelphia, PA 19122, USA.

ASARE, Meshack; Ghanian children's writer; b. 1945. *Education:* Univ. of Science and Technology, Kumasi, Univ. of Wisconsin at Madison, USA. *Publications include:* Tawia Goes to Sea 1970, I am Kofi 1972, Mansa Helps at Home 1973, The Brassman's Secret 1981, The Canoe's Story 1982, Chipo and the Bird on the Hill 1984, Cat: In Search of a Friend 1986, Seeing the World 1989, Bury my Bones but Keep my Words: African Tales for Retelling 1991, Halima's Dilemma 1992, The Frightened Thief 1993, Sosu's Call 1998. *Address:* c/o African Books Collective, The Jam Factory, 27 Park End Street, Oxford, OX1 1HU, England. *E-mail:* abc@africanbookscollective .com. *Website:* www.africanbookscollective.com.

ASARO, Catherine (Ann); Astrophysicist and Writer; b. 6 Nov. 1955, Oakland, CA, USA; m. John Kendall Cannizzo, 9 Aug. 1986, one d. *Education:* BS, University of California, Los Angeles, 1978; MA, 1983, PhD, 1985, Harvard University; Postdoctoral study, University of Toronto, 1985–87. *Career:* Consultant to Lawrence Livermore Laboratory, 1978–83, Biodesign, 1987, Harvard-Smithsonian Center for Astrophysics, 1991; Asst Prof. of Physics, 1987–90, Affiliated Scholar, 1990–91, Kenyon College, Gambier, Ohio; Pres., Molecudyne Research, Laurel, MD, 1990–; Visiting Scientist, Max Planck Institute for Astrophysics, 1991–92; Ed., Publisher, Mindsparks: The Magazine of Science and Science Fiction, 1993–; Columnist, Tangent periodical; mem. SFWA; American Asscn of Physics Teachers; American Physicists Society. *Publications:* Science Fiction: Primary Inversion, 1995; Catch the Lightning, 1996; The Last Hawk, 1997; The Radiant Seas, 1998; The Veiled Web, 1999; The Quantum Rose, 2000; The Phoenix Code, 2000; Ascendant Sun, 2000; Spherical Harmonic, 2001. Contributions: anthologies including: Christmas Forever; Analog; Periodicals and scholarly journals including: Analog; Journal of Chemical Physics; New York Review of Science Fiction; American Journal of Physics; International Journal of Quantitative Chemistry; SFWA Bulletin; Science Fiction Age; Pirate Writings; Physical Review Letters. *Honours:* AnLab Analog Readers Poll; Homer Award; Sapphire Award; National Readers Choice Award, Prism Award, UTC Award. *Address:* c/o Molecudyne Research, PO Box 1302, Laurel, MD 20725, USA. *E-mail:* asaro@sff.net.

ASCHERSON, (Charles) Neal; journalist, editor and writer; b. 5 Oct. 1932, Edinburgh, Scotland; m. 1st Corinna Adam 1958 (divorced 1984); two d.; m. 2nd Isabel Hilton 1984; one s. one d. *Education:* Eton College; MA, King's College, Cambridge, 1955. *Career:* Reporter and Leader Writer, Manchester Guardian, 1956–58; Commonwealth Correspondent, 1959–60; Reporter, 1960–63, Central Europe Correspondent, 1963–68, Eastern Europe Correspondent, 1968–75, Scottish Politics Correspondent, 1975–79, The Scotsman; Foreign Writer, 1979–85, Assoc. Ed., 1985–89, Columnist, 1985–90, The Observer; Columnist, The Independent on Sunday, 1990–98; Ed., Public Archaeology, 1998–. *Publications:* The King Incorporated, 1963; The Polish August: The Self-Limiting Revolution, 1981; The Struggles for Poland, 1987; Games with Shadows, 1988; Black Sea, 1995; Stone Voices, 2002. *Honours:* Hon. doctorates, universities of Strathclyde, Edinburgh, St Andrews, Open University, Paisley; Reporter of the Year, 1982, Journalist of the Year, 1987, Granada Awards; James Cameron Award, 1989; David Watt Memorial Prize, 1991; Golden Insignia, Order of Merit, Poland, 1992; Hon. Fellow, King's College, Cambridge, 1993; George Orwell Award, Political Quarterly, 1993; Saltire Award for Literature, 1995; 50th Anniversary Award of the Political Studies Asscn, 2000. *Address:* 27 Corsica Street, London N5 1JT, England.

ASH, John; Writer, Poet and Teacher; b. 29 June 1948, Manchester, England. *Education:* BA, University of Birmingham, 1969. *Publications:* The Golden Hordes: International Tourism and the Pleasure Periphery (with Louis Turner), 1975; Casino: A Poem in Three Parts, 1978; The Bed and Other Poems, 1981; The Goodbyes, 1982; The Branching Stairs, 1984; Disbelief, 1987; The Burnt Pages, 1991. Contributions: periodicals. *Honours:* Ingram Merrill Foundation Grant, 1985; Writing Foundation Award, 1986.

ASHANTI, Baron James; poet, writer, editor, critic and lecturer; b. 5 Sept. 1950, New York, NY, USA; m. Brenda Cummings, 11 Sept. 1979, one s. one d. *Career:* Literary Ed., Impressions Magazine, 1972–75; City and Third World Ed., Liberation News Service, 1974–79; Contributing Ed., The Paper, 1978; Lecturer; Dir, Arts-in-Education Program, Frederick Douglass Creative Arts Center, New York, 1988–. *Publications:* Nubiana, 1977; Nova, 1990. Contributions: many periodicals. *Honours:* Killen Prize for Poetry, St Peter's College, 1982; PEN Fellowships, 1985, 1987. *Address:* 274 W 140th Street, Apt No. 45, New York, NY 10030, USA.

ASHBERY, John Lawrence, MA; American poet, author and critic; b. 28 July 1927, Rochester, NY. *Education:* Deerfield Acad., Mass, Harvard, Columbia and New York Univs. *Career:* asst, Literature Dept, Brooklyn (NY) Public Library 1949; copywriter, Oxford Univ. Press, New York 1951–54, McGraw-Hill Book Co. 1954–55; went to France as a Fulbright Scholar 1955–56, 1956–57, lived there 1958–65; Art Critic, Int. edn New York Herald-Tribune, Paris 1960–65; Co-Ed. Locus Solus, Lans-en-Vercors, France 1960–62, Art and Literature, Paris 1964–67; Art Critic, Art International, Lugano 1961–63, New York Magazine 1978–80, Newsweek 1980–85; Paris corresp. Art News, New York 1964–65, Exec. Ed. 1965–72; Prof. of English and Co-Dir MFA Program in Creative Writing, Brooklyn Coll., NY (CUNY) 1974–90, Distinguished Prof. 1980–90, Distinguished Prof. Emer. 1990–; Poetry Ed. Partisan Review, New York 1976–80; Charles Eliot Norton Prof. of Poetry, Harvard Univ. 1989–90; Charles P. Stevenson, Jr Prof. of Languages and Literature, Bard Coll., Annandale-on-Hudson, NY 1990–; Chancellor Acad. of American Poets 1988–99; Leader, Fondation d'Art de La Napoule 1989; mem. American Acad. of Arts and Letters 1980–, American Acad. of Arts and Sciences 1983–; works translated into more than 20 languages. *Plays:* The Heroes 1952, The Compromise 1956, The Philosopher 1963, Three Plays 1978. *Publications include:* poetry: Turandot and Other Poems 1953, Some Trees 1956, The Tennis Court Oath 1962, Rivers and Mountains 1966, The Double Dream of Spring 1970, Three Poems 1972, The Vermont Notebook 1975, Self-Portrait in a Convex Mirror (Pulitzer Prize 1975, Nat. Book Award 1975, Nat. Book Critics' Circle Award 1975) 1975, Houseboat Days 1979, As We Know 1979, Shadow Train 1981, A Wave 1984, Selected Poems 1985, April Galleons 1987, Flow Chart 1991, Hotel Lautréamont 1992, And the Stars Were Shining 1994, Can You Hear, Bird 1995, Wakefulness 1998, Girls on the Run 1999, Your Name Here 2000, As Umbrellas Follow Rain 2001, Chinese Whispers 2002; novel: A Nest of Ninnies (with J. Schuyler) 1969; essays and criticism: Fairfield Porter 1983, R. B. Kitaj (with others) 1983, Reported Sightings: Art Chronicles 1957–1987 1989, Other Traditions (The Charles Eliot Norton Lectures at Harvard) 2000; numerous translations from French including works by Raymond Roussel, Max Jacob, Alfred Jarry, Antonin Artaud and Pierre Martory, including Every Question but One 1990, The Landscape is behind the Door 1994. *Honours:* Chevalier des Arts et Lettres 1993; Officier, Légion d'honneur 2002; Hon. DLitt (Southampton Coll. of Long Island Univ.) 1979, (Univ. of Rochester, NY) 1994, (Harvard Univ.) 2001; recipient of numerous awards, grants and honours, including two Guggenheim Fellowships 1967, 1973, MacArthur Fellow 1985–90, Horst Bienek Prize for Poetry (Bavarian Acad. of Fine Arts) 1991, Ruth Lilly Prize for Poetry 1992, Antonio Fraternelli Int. Prize for Poetry (Accad. Nazionale dei Lincei, Rome) 1992, Robert Frost Medal (Poetry Soc. of America) 1995, Grand Prix de Biennales Internationales de Poésie (Brussels) 1996, Gold Medal for Poetry (American Acad. of Arts and Letters) 1997, Bingham Poetry Prize 1998, Walt Whitman Citation of Merit (State of New York and New York State Writers' Inst.) 2000, Signet Soc. Medal for Achievement in the Arts 2001, Wallace Stevens Award (Acad. of American Poets) 2001. *Address:* c/o

George Borchardt Inc., 136 East 57th Street, New York, NY 10022-2707; Bard College, Department of Languages and Literature, PO Box 5000, Annandale-on-Hudson, NY 12504-5000, USA.

ASHBY, Nora (see Africano, Lillian).

ASHE, Geoffrey Thomas, BA, FRSL; writer and lecturer; b. 29 March 1923, London, England; m. 1st Dorothy Irene Train 1946 (deceased); four s. one d.; m. 2nd Maxine Lefever 1992 (divorced); m. 3rd Patricia Chandler 1998. *Education:* Univ. of British Columbia, Canada, Trinity College, Cambridge. *Career:* Assoc. Ed., Arthurian Encyclopaedia, 1986; mem. Medieval Acad. of America; Camelot Research Committee, sec. *Publications:* King Arthur's Avalon, 1957; From Caesar to Arthur, 1960; Land to the West, 1962; The Land and the Book, 1965; Gandhi, 1968; The Quest for Arthur's Britain, 1968; Camelot and the Vision of Albion, 1971; The Art of Writing Made Simple, 1972; The Finger and the Moon, 1973; The Virgin, 1976; The Ancient Wisdom, 1977; Miracles, 1978; Guidebook to Arthurian Britain, 1980; Kings and Queens of Early Britain, 1982; Avalonian Quest, 1982; The Discovery of King Arthur, 1985; Landscape of King Arthur, 1987; Mythology of the British Isles, 1990; King Arthur: The Dream of a Golden Age, 1990; Dawn Behind the Dawn, 1992; Atlantis, 1992; The Traveller's Guide to Arthurian Britain, 1997; The Book of Prophecy, 1999; The Hell-Fire Clubs, 2000; Merlin, 2001; Laybrinths and Mazes, 2003. Contributions: numerous magazines and journals. *Literary Agent:* Rogers, Coleridge and White Ltd, 20 Powis Mews, London W11 1JN, England. *Address:* Chalice Orchard, Well House Lane, Glastonbury, Somerset BA6 8BJ, England.

ASHER, Neal Lewis; Writer; b. 4 Feb. 1961, Billericay, Essex, England. *Education:* Mechanical and Production Engineering ONC. *Publications:* Another England, 1989; Out of the Leaflight, 1991; Mason's Rats, 1992; The Thrake, 1993; Woodsmith, 1993; Dragon in the Flower, 1993; Blue Holes and Bloody Waters, 1994; Mason's Rats II, 1994; Stinging Things, 1994; Adaptogenic, 1994; The Flame, 1994; Great African Vampire, 1994; Stones of Straw, 1994; Oceana Foods, 1994; Jable Sharks, 1994; Cavefish, 1995; Spatterjay, 1995; Jack O'Gravestones, 1995; Snairls, 1995; The Bacon, 1996; Page Dow, 1996; The Devil You Know, 1996; The Berserker Captain, 1996; Alternative Hospital, 1996; Floundering, 1996; Plastipak, 1996; The Gurnard, 1997; Snow in the Desert, 1997; Conversations, 1998; Cowl, 2004. *Address:* 22 Snoreham Gdns, Latchingdon, Chelmsford, Essex CM3 6UN, England.

ASHFORD, Jeffrey (see Jeffries, Roderic (Graeme)).

ASHLEY, Bernard; Writer; b. 2 April 1935, London, England. *Education:* Teachers Certificate; Advanced Diploma, Cambridge Institute of Education. *Career:* mem. Writers' Guild; BAFTA; Greenwich Theatre, board of govs. *Publications:* The Trouble with Donovan Croft, 1974; Terry on the Fence, 1975; All My Men, 1977; A Kind of Wild Justice, 1978; Break in the Sun, 1980; Dinner Ladies Don't Count, 1981; Dodgem, 1982; High Pavement Blues, 1983; Janey, 1985; Running Scared, 1986; Bad Blood, 1988; The Country Boy, 1989; The Secret of Theodore Brown, 1989; Clipper Street, 1990; Seeing off Uncle Jack, 1992; Cleversticks, 1993; Three Seven Eleven, 1993; Johnnie's Blitz, 1995; I Forgot, Said Troy, 1996; A Present for Paul, 1996; City Limits, 1997; Tiger Without Teeth, 1998; Growing Good, 1999; Little Soldier, 1999; Revenge House, 2002; Double the Love, 2002; The Bush, 2003; Freedom Flight, 2003. Contributions: Books for Your Children; Junior Education; Books for Keeps; Times Educational Supplement; School Librarian. *Honours:* The Other Award, 1976; RTS Best Children's Entertainment Programme, 1993; Hon. Doctorate in Education, Univ. of Greenwich, 2002. *Address:* 128 Heathwood Gdns, London SE7 8ER, England.

ASHTON, Dore, BA, MA; writer; *Professor of Art History, Yale University*; b. 21 May 1928, Newark, NJ, USA; m. 1st Adja Yunkers 1952 (died 1983); two d.; m. 2nd Matti Megged (died 2003). *Education:* University of Wisconsin, Harvard University. *Career:* Assoc. Ed., Art Digest, 1951–54; Art Critic, New York Times, 1955–60; Lecturer, Pratt Institute, 1962–63; Head, Dept of Humanities, School of Visual Arts, 1965–68; Prof. of Art History, Cooper Union, 1969–; Adjunct Prof. of Art History, CUNY, 1973, Columbia University, 1975, New School for Social Research, 1986, Yale Univ. 1995–; Assoc. Ed., Arts, 1974–92; mem. International Asscn of Art Critics. *Publications:* Abstract Art Before Columbus, 1957; Poets and the Past, 1959; Philip Guston, 1960; Redon, Moreau, Bresden (co-author), 1961; The Unknown Shore, 1962; Rauschenberg's Dante, 1964; Richard Lindner, 1969; Pol Bury, 1971; Picasso on Art, 1972; Cultural Guide New York, 1972; The New York School: A Cultural Reckoning, 1973; A Joseph Cornell Album, 1974; Yes, But: A Critical Biography of Philip Guston, 1976; A Fable of Modern Art, 1980; Rosa Bonheur: A Life and Legend (with Denise Browne Hare), 1981; American Art Since 1945, 1982; About Rothko, 1983; 20th Century Artists on Art, 1985; Out of the Whirlwind, 1987; Fragonard in the Universe of Painting, 1988; Noguchi East and West, 1992; The Delicate Thread: Hiroshi Teshigahara, 1997; William Tucker, 2001; The Walls of the Heart: Life and Work of David Rankin, 2002; The Black Rainbow: Fernando de Szyszlo, 2003. Contributions: journals and magazines. *Honours:* Ford Foundation Fellow, 1960; Graham Fellow, 1963; Mather Award for Art Criticism, College Art Asscn, 1963; Guggenheim Fellowship, 1964; National Endowment for the Humanities Grant, 1980; Art Criticism Prize, St Louis Art Museum, 1988. *Address:* 217 E 11th Street, New York, NY 10003, USA.

ASHTON, Robert; academic; b. 21 July 1924, Chester, England; m. Margaret Alice Sedgwick 1946; two d. *Education:* Magdalen College School, Oxford, 1938–40; University College, Southampton, 1946–49; BA, London, 1949; PhD, LSE, 1953. *Career:* Asst Lecturer, Lecturer, Senior Lecturer, Nottingham University, 1952–63; Visiting Assoc. Prof., University of California, Berkeley, 1962–63; Prof., 1963–89, Emeritus Prof., 1989–, University of East Anglia; Visiting Fellow, All Souls College, Oxford, 1974–75, 1987; mem. FRHistS, 1961–, vice-pres., 1983–84. *Publications:* The English Civil War: Conservatism and Revolution 1603–49, 1978; The Crown and the Money Market 1603–40, 1960; James I by his Contemporaries, 1969; The City and the Court 1603–1643, 1979; Reformation and Revolution, 1558–1660, 1984; Counter Revolution: The Second Civil War and its Origins 1646–1648, 1994. Contributions: Economic History Review; Bulletin of Institute of Historical Research; Past and Present; Historical journals. *Address:* The Manor House, Brundall, Norwich NR13 5JY, England.

ASIMOV, Janet O. Jeppson; Physician and Writer; b. 6 Aug. 1926, Ashland, PA, USA; m. Isaac Asimov 30 Nov. 1973 (died 1992). *Education:* BA, Stanford University, 1948; MD, New York University College of Medicine, 1952; Diploma, Psychoanalysis, William Alanson White Institute, 1960. *Career:* mem. SFWA; William Alanson White Society; American Acad. of Psychoanalysis; American Psychiatric Asscn. *Publications:* The Second Experiment, 1974; The Last Immortal, 1980; The Mysterious Cure, 1985; The Package in Hyperspace, 1988; Mind Transfer, 1988; Murder at the Galactic Writers' Society, 1995; Norby and the Terrified Taxi, 1997; It's Been a Good Life, by Isaac Asimov (ed.), 2002. with Isaac Asimov: Laughing Space, 1982; Norby, the Mixed-Up Robot, 1983; Norby's Other Secret, 1984; Norby and the Lost Princess, 1985; Norby and the Invaders, 1985; Norby and the Queen's Necklace, 1986; Norby Finds a Villain, 1987; Norby and Yobo's Great Adventure, 1989; Norby and the Oldest Dragon, 1990; Norby Down to Earth, 1991; Norby and the Court Jester, 1991. Contributions: several journals; Science column in various newspapers. *Address:* 10 W 66th St, New York, NY 10023, USA.

ASMUNDSDOTTIR, Steinunn; Environmental Educator, Writer, Editor and Poet; b. 1 March 1966, Reykjavík, Iceland. *Career:* Ed., Andblaer (Breeze) magazine, 1995–; mem. Icelandic Writers' Union. *Publications:* Solo on the Rainbow, 1989; Words of the Muses, 1993; A House on the Moor, 1996. Contributions: various publications. *Address:* Egilsstadir IV, 700 Egilsstadir, Iceland.

ASPLER, Tony; Writer; b. 12 May 1939, London, England; one s. one d. *Education:* BA, McGill University, Canada, 1959. *Career:* mem. Crime Writers of Canada, founding chair., 1982–84. *Publications:* Streets of Askelon, 1972; One of My Marionettes, 1973; Chain Reaction (with Gordon Pape), 1978; The Scorpion Sanction (with Gordon Pape), 1980; Vintage Canada, 1983; The Music Wars (with Gordon Pape), 1983; Titanic (novel), 1989; Blood is Thicker than Beaujolais (novel), 1993; Cellar and Silver (with Rose Murray), 1993; Aligoté to Zinfandel, 1994; The Beast of Barbaresco (novel), 1996; Death on the Douro (novel), 1997; Travels With My Corkscrew (non-fiction), 1998; The Wine Lover Cooks (with Kathleen Sloan), 1999; Canadian Wine for Dummies, 2000. Contributions: periodicals. *Literary Agent:* Livingston Cooke. *Address:* 53 Craighurst Ave, Toronto, ON M4R 1J9, Canada.

ASSAD, Rifat al-, PhD; Syrian politician, newspaper publisher and fmr army officer; b. 22 Aug. 1937, Kerdaha; m. Lyn Al-Khayer 1973; eight s. eight d. *Career:* officer in Syrian Army 1963–94, Founder and Commdr of Defence Regts 1965–84, mem. Regional Command of Syria 1975; Prof., Coll. of Law, Damascus Univ. 1976; Vice-Pres. of Syria 1984; Founder and Publr Al-Forsan magazine, Damascus 1966–84, Paris and London 1984–92, Al-Shah daily newspaper, Paris 1988, Shaza magazine, Paris 1986 and Memo magazine, Cyprus 1986; Founder and Pres. League of Higher Studies, Grads. and Research 1974. *Publications:* many econ. and political articles in Arabic newspapers and magazines. *Honours:* many Syrian decorations; Légion d'honneur, Hon. Decoration of Morocco. *Address:* c/o Mezzeh, Jabal, Damascus, Syria. *Telephone:* 6621623. *Fax:* 682080393.

ASSELINEAU, Roger Maurice, (Maurice Herra), LèsL, DèsL; academic, poet and writer; b. 24 March 1915, Orléans, France. *Education:* Sorbonne, Paris. *Career:* mem. Former pres., French Asscn for American Studies; MLA of America, hon. mem.; Hemingway Society; International Asscn of University Profs of English; Société des Gens de Lettres. *Publications:* L'Evolution de Walt Whitman, 1954; The Literary Reputation of Mark Twain, 1954; Poésies incomplètes, 1959; E. A. Poe, 1970; Transcendentalist Constant in American Literature, 1980; St John de Crevecoeur: The Life of an American Farmer (with Gay Wilson Allen), 1987; Poésies incomplètes (II), 1989; Poètes anglais de la Grande Guerre, 1991; Poèmes de Guerre 1939–1944, 1991; The Evolution of Walt Whitman, 1999; Miracles et Miettes, 2002. Contributions: Etudes Anglaises; Revue de Littérature Comparée; Forum; Dialogue; Calamus; Walt Whitman Quarterly Review; Diadème; Flammes Vives; Le Bayou; Cahiers du Nouvel Humanisme; Les Hommes Sans Epaule; Iô; Calamus, Oc. *Honours:* Walt Whitman Prize, Poetry Society of America; Hon. Doctorate, University of Poznań. *Address:* 114 avenue Leon Blum, 92160 Antony, France.

ASSOULINE, Pierre; Writer and Ed.; b. 1953, Casablanca, Morocco. *Career:* Ed., Lire magazine, France. *Publications:* Gaston Gallimard: Un demi-siècle d'edition française, 1984, English trans. as Gaston Gallimard: A Half-Century of French Publishing, 1988; Une éminence grise: Jean Jardin (1904–1976), 1986; L'homme de l'art: D. H. Kahnweiler, 1884–1979, 1988, English trans. as An Artful Life: A Biography of D. H. Kahnweiler, 1884–1979, 1990; Albert Londres: Vie et mort d'un grand reporter, 1884–1932, 1989; Monsieur Dassault, 1993; Trois hommes d'influence, 1994; Hergé: Biographie, 1996; Simenon: Biographie, 1992, English trans. as Simenon: A Biography, 1997. Other: De nos envoyés spéciaux: les coulisses du reportage (co-author), 1977; Lourdes: Histoires d'eau, 1980; Les nouveaux convertis: Enquête sur les chrétiens, des juifs et des musulmans pas comme les autres, 1982; L'épuration des intellectuels, 1944–1945, 1985; Le fleuve combelle, 1997. *Address:* 72 Blvd Flandrin, 75016 Paris, France.

ASTLEY, Neil; editor, poet and writer; b. England. *Career:* f., Ed., Bloodaxe Books 1978–. *Publications:* Poetry: Darwin Survivor, 1988; Biting My Tongue, 1995. Editor, anthologies: Pleased to See Me: 69 Very Sexy Poems; Ten North-East Poets, 1980; Bossy Parrot: Best Children's Poems, 1987; Poetry with an Edge, 1988; Tony Harrison, 1991; New Blood, 1999; Staying Alive: Real Poems for Unreal Times, 2002; The Heavy Bear Who Goes with Me (with Brendan Kennelly), 2002. Novels: The End of My Tether, 2002. *Honours:* Eric Gregory Award; Hon. DLitt, Newcastle Univ. *Literary Agent:* AP Watt Ltd, 20 John Street, London, WC1N 2DR, England. *Address:* Bloodaxe Books Ltd, Highgreen, Tarset, Northumberland NE48 1RP, England. *Telephone:* (1434) 240500. *Fax:* (1434) 240505. *E-mail:* editor@bloodaxebooks.demon.co.uk. *Website:* www.bloodaxebooks.com.

ASTLEY, Thea, (Beatrice May); Novelist; b. 25 Aug. 1925, Brisbane, Qld, Australia; m. Edmund John Gregson, 1948, one s. *Education:* BA, University of Brisbane, 1947. *Career:* Senior Tutor, then Fellow in English, Macquarie University, Sydney, NSW, 1968–85. *Publications:* Girl With a Monkey, 1958; A Descant for Gossips, 1960; The Well-Dressed Explorer, 1962; The Slow Natives, 1965; A Boat Load of Home Folk, 1968; The Acolyte, 1972; A Kindness Cup, 1974; Hunting the Wild Pineapple, 1979; An Item from the Late News, 1982; Beachmasters, 1985; It's Raining in Mango, 1987; Reach Tin River, 1990; Vanishing Points, 1992; Coda, 1994; Drylands, 1999. *Honours:* Miles Franklin Awards, 1962, 1965, 1972, 2000; Age Book of the Year Awards, 1975, 1996; Patrick White Award, 1989. *Address:* c/o Elise Goodman, Goodman Assocs, 500 West End Ave, New York, NY 10024, USA.

ASTOR, Gerald (Morton); Writer; b. 3 Aug. 1926, New Haven, CT, USA; m. Sonia Sacoder, 23 Nov. 1949, three s. *Education:* BA, Princeton University, 1949; Columbia University, 1949–51. *Career:* mem. Authors' Guild; Authors' League of America. *Publications:* The New York Cops: An Informed History, 1971; '...And a Credit to His Race': The Hard Life and Times of Joseph Louis Barrow aka Joe Louis, 1974; The Charge is Rape, 1974; A Question of Rape, 1974; Hot Paper, 1975; Photographing Sports: John Zimmerman, Mark Kauffman and Neil Leifer (with Sean Callahan), 1975; Brick Agent: Inside the Mafia for the FBI (with Anthony Villano), 1977; The Disease Detectives: Deadly Medical Mysteries and the People Who Solved Them, 1983; The 'Last' Nazi: The Life and Times of Dr. Joseph Mengele, 1985; The Baseball Hall of Fame Anniversary Book, 1988; The PGA World Golf Hall of Fame Book, 1991; Hostage: My Nightmare in Beirut (with David Jacobsen), 1991; A Blood-Dimmed Tide: The Battle of the Bulge by the Men Who Fought It, 1992; Battling Buzzards: The Odyssey of the 517th Regimental Parachute Combat Team, 1943–1945, 1993; June 6, 1944: The Voices of D-Day, 1994; Operation Iceberg: The Invasion and Conquest of Okinawa in World War II: An Oral History, 1995; Crisis in the Pacific: The Battles for the Philippines, 1996; The Mighty Eighth: The Air War in Europe by the Men Who Flew It, 1997; The Bloody Forest: Battle for the Huertgen: September 1944–January 1945, 2000. Contributions: periodicals. *Address:* 50 Sprain Valley Rd, Scarsdale, NY 10583, USA.

ATIYAH, Sir Michael Francis, Kt, OM, MA, PhD, ScD, FRS, FRSE; British mathematician; *Honorary Professor, University of Edinburgh*; b. 22 April 1929, London; m. Lily Brown 1955; three s. *Education:* Victoria Coll., Egypt, Manchester Grammar School and Trinity Coll. Cambridge. *Career:* Research Fellow, Trinity Coll., Cambridge 1954–58, Hon. Fellow 1976, Master 1990–97, Fellow 1997–; Fellow, Pembroke Coll., Cambridge 1958–61 (Hon. Fellow 1983), Univ. Lecturer 1957–61; Reader, Oxford Univ. and Fellow St Catherine's Coll., Oxford 1961–63, Hon. Fellow 1991; Savilian Prof. of Geometry, Univ. of Oxford and Fellow of New Coll., Oxford 1963–69, Hon. Fellow 1999; Prof. of Mathematics, Inst. for Advanced Study, Princeton, NJ 1969–72; Royal Soc. Research Prof., Oxford Univ. 1973–90, Fellow St Catherine's Coll., Oxford 1973–90; Dir Isaac Newton Inst. of Math. Sciences, Cambridge 1990–96; Chancellor Univ. of Leicester 1995–; Pres. London Mathematical Soc. 1974–76, Pres. Mathematical Assn 1981; mem. Science and Eng Research Council 1984–89; Pres. Pugwash Confs 1997–2002; mem. Council Royal Soc. 1984–85, Pres. 1990–95; Foreign mem. American Acad. of Arts and Sciences, Swedish Acad. of Sciences, Leopoldina Acad. (Germany), NAS, Acad. des Sciences (France), Royal Irish Acad., Third World Acad. of Science, Indian Nat. Science Acad., Australian Acad. of Sciences, Chinese Acad. of Sciences, American Philosophical Soc., Ukrainian Acad. of Sciences, Russian Acad. of Sciences, Georgian Acad. of Sciences, Venezuelan Acad. of Sciences, Accad. Nazionale dei Lincei, Royal Spanish Acad. of Sciences, Norwegian Acad. of Science and Letters. *Publications:* K-Theory 1966, Commutative Algebra 1969, Geometry and Dynamics of Magnetic Monopoles 1988, Collected Works (five vols) 1988, The Geometry and Physics of Knots 1990. *Honours:* Hon. Prof. Univ. of Edinburgh 1997–; Hon. Fellow Darwin Coll., Cambridge 1992, FREng 1993, Faculty of Actuaries 1999, Univ. of Wales Swansea 1999; Commdr Order of the Cedars; Order of Andreas Bello (Venezuela); Hon. DSc (Bonn, Warwick, Durham, St Andrew's, Dublin, Chicago, Edinburgh, Cambridge, Essex, London, Sussex, Ghent, Reading, Helsinki, Leicester, Rutgers, Salamanca, Montreal, Waterloo, Wales, Queen's-Kingston, Keele, Birmingham, Lebanon, Open, Brown, Oxford, Prague, Chinese, Hong Kong, Heriot-Watt Univs); Dr hc (UMIST) 1996; Fields Medal, Int. Congress of Mathematicians, Moscow 1966, Royal Medal of Royal Soc. (UK) 1968, De Morgan Medal, London Math. Soc. 1980, Copley Medal of Royal Soc. (UK) 1988, Feltrinelli Prize, Accad. Nazionale dei Lincei 1981, King Faisal Int. Prize for Science 1987, Benjamin Franklin Medal (American Philosophical Soc.), Nehru Medal (Indian Nat. Science Acad.), Abel Prize (jtly with Isadore Singer) 2004. *Address:* University of Edinburgh, School of Mathematics, Mayfield Road, Edinburgh, EH9 3JZ (Office); 3/8 West Grange Gardens, Edinburgh, EH9 2RA, Scotland. *Telephone:* (131) 650-5086 (Office); (131) 667-0898 (Home). *E-mail:* M.atiyah@ed.ac.uk (Home).

ATKINSON, Kate, BA; British writer and playwright; b. 1951, York, England; m. (divorced); two d. *Education:* Univ. of Dundee. *Career:* fmrly home help, teacher and short story writer for women's magazines; writer 1988–. *Plays include:* Nice 1996, Abandonment 2000. *Publications:* Behind the Scences at the Museum (novel) (Whitbread First Novel award and Book of the Year 1996, Boeker Prize, SA, Livre Book of the Year, France) 1995, Human Croquet (novel) 1997, Emotionally Weird (novel) 2001, Not the End of the World (short stories) 2002, Case Histories (novel) 2004; contrib. short stories to Daily Telegraph, BBC2, BBC Radio 4, Daily Express, Daily Mail, Scotsman. *Honours:* Ian St James Award 1993. *Address:* c/o Transworld Publishers Ltd, 61–63 Uxbridge Road, London, W5 5SA, England.

ATLAN, Liliane; Writer, Poet and Dramatist; b. 14 Jan. 1932, Montpellier, France; m. June 1952 (divorced 1976); one s. one d. *Education:* Diploma, Philosophy, Sorbonne, University of Paris, 1953; Studies in Modern Literature, CAPES, 1960. *Publications:* Poetry: Lapsus, 1971; Bonheur mais sur quel ton le dire, 1996; Peuples d'argile, forêts d'etoiles, 2000; Little Bibles for Bad Times, 2003. Plays: Monsieur Fugue ou le mal de terre, 1967; The Messiahs, 1969; The Little Car of Flames and Voices, 1971; The Musicians, the Migrants, 1976; Lessons in Happiness, 1982; An Opera for Terezin, 1997; The Red Seas, 1998; My Name is No, 1998; Monsieur Fugue, 2000. Other: videotext. *Honours:* Chevalier, Ordre des Arts et des Lettres, 1984; Prix Villa Medicis, 1992; Prize, Radio SACD, 1999; Prix Mémoire de la Shoah, 1999. *Address:* 70 rue du javelot, 75645 Paris cédex 13, France.

ATLAS, Ronald M., BS, MS, PhD; American academic and writer; b. 1946, New York, NY. *Education:* New York State Univ., Rutgers Univ. *Career:* Nat. Research Council Research Assoc., Jet Propulsion Laboratory 1972–73; faculty mem. Univ. of Louisville 1973–, currently Prof. of Biology; Pres., American Soc. for Microbiology; Ed., CRC Critical Reviews in Microbiology. *Publications:* Handbook of Media for Environmental Microbiology 1993, Handbook of Media for Clinical Microbiology (co-author) 1995, Handbook of Microbiological Media (second edn) 1996. *Address:* American Society for Microbiology, 1752 N Street NW, Washington, DC 20036-2904; c/o University of Louisville Graduate School, Houchens Building, Room 105, Louisville, KY 40292, USA. *Telephone:* (502) 852-3957. *Fax:* (502) 852-2365. *E-mail:* r.atlas@louisville.edu. *Website:* www.louisville.edu; www.asm.org.

ATTALI, Jacques; French international bank official and writer; *President, Attali et Associés*; b. 1 Nov. 1943, Algiers; twin brother of Bernard Attali; m. Elisabeth Allain 1981; one s. one d. *Education:* Ecole Polytechnique, Inst. d'Etudes Politiques de Paris, Ecoles des Mines de Paris, Ecole Nat. d'Admin. *Career:* started career as mining engineer, then Lecturer in Econs, Ecole Polytechnique; Auditeur, Council of State; Adviser to the Pres. 1981–91; State Councillor 1989–91; Pres. EBRD, London 1991–93; Pres. Attali et Associés (ACA) 1994–; mem. Council of State 1981–90, 1993–; Admin. KeeBoo 2000–. *Publications:* Analyse économique de la vie politique 1972, Modèles politiques 1973, Anti-économique (with Marc Guillaume) 1974, La parole et l'outil 1975, Bruits, Essai sur l'économie politique de la musique 1976, La nouvelle économie française 1977, L'ordre cannibale 1979, Les trois mondes 1981, Histoires du temps 1982, La figure de Fraser 1984, Un homme d'influence 1985, Au propre et au Figuré 1988, La vie éternelle (novel) 1989, Millennium: Winners and Losers in the Coming World Order 1991, 1492 1991, Verbatim (Tome I) 1993, Europe(s) 1994, Verbatim (Tome II) 1995, Economie de l'Apocalypse 1995, Tome III 1996, Chemins de Sagesse 1996, Au delà de nulle part 1997, Dictionnaire du XXIe siècle 1998, Les portes du ciel 1999, La femme du menteur 1999, Fraternités 1999, Blaise Pascal ou le génie français 2000, Bruits 2001, L'homme nomade 2003. *Honours:* Dr hc (Univ. of Kent, Univ. of Haifa). *Address:* ACA, 28 rue Bayard, 75008 Paris, France.

ATTALLAH, Naim Ibrahim, FRSA; British publisher and financial adviser; *Chairman, Namara Group*; b. 1 May 1931, Haifa, Palestine; m. Maria Nykolyn 1957; one s. *Education:* Coll. des Frères, Haifa and Battersea Polytechnic, London. *Career:* Propr Quartet Books 1976–, Women's Press 1977–, Robin Clark 1980–, Pipeline Books 1978–2000, The Literary Review 1981–2001, The Wire 1984–2000, Acad. Club 1989–96, The Oldie

1991–2001; Group Chief Exec. Asprey PLC 1992–96, Deputy Chair. Asprey (Bond Street) 1992–98; Man. Dir Mappin and Webb 1990–95; Exec. Dir Garrard 1990–95; Chair. Namara Group of cos 1973–, launched Parfums Namara 1985, Avant L'Amour and Après L'Amour 1985, Naïdor 1987, L'Amour de Namara 1990. *Films produced:* The Slipper and the Rose (with David Frost 1975, Brimstone and Treacle (Exec. Producer) 1982 and several TV documentaries. *Theatre:* Happy End (Co-Presenter) 1975, The Beastly Beatitudes of Balthazar B. (Presenter and Producer) 1981, Trafford Tanzi (Co-Producer) 1982. *Publications:* Women 1987, Singular Encounters 1990, Of a Certain Age 1992, More of a Certain Age 1993, Speaking for the Oldie 1994, A Timeless Passion 1995, Tara and Claire (novel) 1996, Asking Questions 1996, A Woman a Week 1998, In Conversation with Naim Attalah 1998, Insights 1999, Dialogues 2001. *Honours:* Hon. MA (Surrey) 1993; Retail Personality of the Year, UK Jewellery Awards 1993. *Address:* 25 Shepherd Market, London, W1J 7PP, England. *Telephone:* (20) 7499-2901. *Fax:* (20) 7499-2914. *E-mail:* nattallah@aol.com (Office).

ATTENBOROUGH, Sir David Frederick, Kt, CH, CVO, CBE, MA, FRS; British broadcaster, naturalist and writer; b. 8 May 1926, London; brother of Lord Attenborough; m. Jane Elizabeth Ebsworth Oriel 1950 (died 1997); one s. one d. *Education:* Wyggeston Grammar School, Leicester and Clare Coll., Cambridge. *Career:* Royal Navy 1947–49; Editorial Asst in publishing house 1949–52; with BBC Television 1952–73, Producer of zoological, archaeological, travel, political and other programmes 1952–64, Controller BBC 2 1964–68, Dir of Programmes, TV 1969–73; writer, presenter BBC series: Tribal Eye 1976, Wildlife on One, annually 1977–2004, Life on Earth 1979, The Living Planet 1984, The First Eden 1987, Lost World, Vanished Lives 1989, The Trials of Life 1990, Life in the Freezer 1993, The Private Life of Plants 1995, The Life of Birds 1998, State of the Planet 2000, The Blue Planet (narrator) 2001, The Life of Mammals 2002; Huw Wheldon Memorial Lecturer, RTS 1987; Pres. BAAS 1990–91, Royal Soc. for Nature Conservation 1991–96; mem. Nature Conservancy Council 1975–82; Fellow, Soc. of Film and Television Arts 1980; Int. Trustee, World Wild Life Fund 1979–86; Trustee, British Museum 1980–2000, Science Museum 1984–87, Royal Botanical Gardens, Kew 1986–92. *Publications:* Zoo Quest to Guiana 1956, Zoo Quest for a Dragon 1957, Zoo Quest in Paraguay 1959, Quest in Paradise 1960, Zoo Quest to Madagascar 1961, Quest under Capricorn 1963, The Tribal Eye 1976, Life on Earth 1979, The Zoo Quest Expeditions 1982; The Living Planet 1984, The First Eden, The Mediterranean World and Man 1987, The Trials of Life 1990, The Private Life of Plants 1994, The Life of Birds 1998 (BP Natural World Book Prize), The Life of Mammals 2002, Life on Air (memoirs) 2002. *Honours:* Hon. Fellow, Clare Coll., Cambridge 1980, UMIST 1980, Inst. of Biology; Hon. DLitt (Leicester, London, Birmingham, City); Hon. DSc (Liverpool, Ulster, Sussex, Bath, Durham, Keele, Heriot-Watt, Bradford, Nottingham); Hon. LLD (Bristol, Glasgow) 1977; Hon. DUniv (Open Univ.) 1980, (Essex) 1987, Antwerp 1993; Dr hc (Edin.) 1994; Special Award, Guild of TV Producers 1961, Silver Medal, Royal TV Soc. 1966, Silver Medal, Zoological Soc. of London 1966, Desmond Davis Award, Soc. of Film and TV Arts 1970, UNESCO Kalinga Prize 1982, Medallist, Acad. of Natural Sciences, Philadelphia 1982, Founders Gold Medal, Royal Geographical Soc. 1985, Int. Emmy Award 1985, Encyclopedia Britannica Award 1987, Kew Award 1996, Edin. Medal, Edin. Science Festival 1998, BP Natural World Book Prize 1998, Faraday Prize, Royal Soc. 2003, Int. Documentary Asscn Career Achievement Award 2003, Raffles Medal, Zoological Soc. of London 2004, Caird Medal, Nat. Maritime Museum 2004, British Book Awards Lifetime Achievement Award 2004. *Address:* 5 Park Road, Richmond, Surrey, TW10 6NS, England.

ATTENBOROUGH, Philip John, CBE; British book publisher; b. 3 June 1936; m. Rosemary Littler 1963; one s. one d. *Education:* Rugby School, Trinity Coll., Oxford. *Career:* joined Hodder & Stoughton 1957, Dir 1963, Sales Dir 1969; Chair. Hodder & Stoughton Ltd and Hodder & Stoughton Holdings Ltd 1975–93, Deputy Chair. Hodder Headline PLC 1993–96; Chair. The Lancet Ltd 1977–91; Dir Book Tokens Ltd 1985–96; mem. Council, Publishers' Asscn 1976–92, Pres. 1983–85; UK Rep. Fédération des Editeurs Européens 1986–93; mem. Exec. Cttee, Int. Publishers' Asscn 1988–96, Vice-Pres. 1992–96; Chair., British Council Publishers' Advisory Cttee 1989–93; Adviser, UNESCO Publishing 1992–95; mem. Governing Body, SPCK 1999–. *Publication:* The Rebirth of European Publishing: An Anglo-European Perspective of '1992' (essay) 1991. *Address:* Coldhanger, Seal Chart, Sevenoaks, Kent, TN15 0EJ, England. *Telephone:* (1732) 761516. *Fax:* (1732) 763258.

ATWOOD, Margaret Eleanor, CC, BA, AM, MA, FRSC; Canadian poet, writer and critic; b. 18 Nov. 1939, Ottawa, ON; m. Graeme Gibson; one d. *Education:* Victoria Coll., Univ. of Toronto, Radcliffe Coll., Cambridge, Harvard Univ. *Career:* Lecturer in English, Univ. of British Columbia 1964–65; Instructor in English, Sir George Williams Univ., Montréal 1967–68, Univ. of Alberta 1969–70; Asst Prof. of English, York Univ., Toronto 1971–72; writer-in-residence, Univ. of Toronto 1972–73; MFA Hon. Chair, Univ. of Alabama, Tuscaloosa 1985; Berg Chair, New York Univ. 1986; writer-in-residence, Macquarie Univ., Australia 1987, Trinity Univ., San Antonio, TX 1989; mem. Writers' Union of Canada (pres. 1981–82), Int. PEN (pres. of Canadian Centre (English Speaking) 1984–86). *Radio script:* The Trumpets of Summer 1964. *Television screenplays:* The Servant Girl 1974, Snowbird 1981, Heaven on Earth (with Peter Pearson) 1986. *Publications:* poetry: Double Persephone 1961, The Circle Game 1964, Kaleidoscopes Baroque 1965, Talismans for Children 1965, Speeches for Doctor Frankenstein 1966, The Animals in That Country 1968, The Journals of Susanna Moodie 1970, Procedures for Underground 1970, Power Politics 1971, You Are Happy 1974, Selected Poems 1976, Marsh, Hawk 1977, Two-Headed Poems 1978, True Stories 1981, Notes Towards a Poem That Can Never Be Written 1981, Snake Poems 1983, Interlunar 1984, Selected Poems II: Poems Selected and New 1976–1986 1986, Selected Poems 1966–1984 1990, Margaret Atwood Poems 1965–1975 1991, Morning in the Burned House 1995; fiction: The Edible Woman 1969, Surfacing 1972, Lady Oracle 1976, Dancing Girls 1977, Life Before Man 1979, Bodily Harm 1981, Encounters with the Element Man 1982, Murder in the Dark 1983, Bluebeard's Egg 1983, Unearthing Suite 1983, The Handmaid's Tale 1985, Cat's Eye 1988, Wilderness Tips 1991, Good Bones 1992, The Robber Bride 1993, Alias Grace 1996, The Blind Assassin 2000, Oryx and Crake 2003; juvenile: Up in the Tree 1978, Anna's Pet 1980, For the Birds 1990, Princess Prunella and the Purple Peanut 1995, Rude Ramsay and the Roaring Radishes 2003; non-fiction: Survival: A Thematic Guide to Canadian Literature 1972, Days of the Rebels 1815–1840 1977, Second Words: Selected Critical Prose 1982, Strange Things: The Malevolent North in Canadian Literature 1995, Negotiating with the Dead: A Writer on Writing 2002; editor: The New Oxford Book of Canadian Verse in English (ed.) 1982, The Oxford Book of Canadian Short Stories in English (with Robert Weaver) 1986, The Canlit Foodbook 1987, The Best American Short Stories (ed. with Shannon Ravenel) 1989, The New Oxford Book of Canadian Short Stories in English (with Robert Weaver) 1995; contrib. to Canadian Literature, Maclean's, Saturday Night, This Magazine, New York Times Book Review, The Globe and Mail, The Nation, Books in Canada, The Washington Post, Harvard Educational Review, many others. *Honours:* Gov.-Gen.'s Awards 1966, 1986, Guggenheim Fellowship 1981, Arthur C. Clarke Award for Best Science Fiction 1987, Commonwealth Literary Prizes regional winner 1987, 1994, Foreign Hon. Mem., American Acad. of Arts and Sciences 1988, Order of Ontario 1990, Centennial Medal, Harvard Univ. 1990, Commemorative Medal, 125th Anniversary of Canadian Confederation 1992, Chevalier, Ordre des Arts et des Lettres 1994, Giller Prize 1996, Premio Mondello 1997, Booker Prize 2000, Int. Crime Writers' Asscn Dashiell Hammett Award 2001, Radcliffe Medal 2003, Harold Washington Literary Award 2003, numerous other awards, hon. degrees. *Literary Agent:* McClelland & Stewart, 481 University Avenue, Suite 900, Toronto, ON M5G 2E9, Canada. *Website:* www.owtoad.com.

AUBERT, Alvin (Bernard); Prof. of English Emeritus and Poet; b. 12 March 1930, Lutcher, LA, USA; m. 1st Olga Alexis 1948 (divorced); one d.; m. 2nd Bernardine Tenant 1960; two d. *Education:* BA, Southern University, Baton Rouge, 1959; MA, University of Michigan, 1960; University of Illinois at Urbana-Champaign, 1963–64, 1966–67. *Career:* Instructor, 1960–62, Asst Prof., 1962–65, Assoc. Prof. of English, 1965–70, Southern University; Visiting Prof. of English, University of Oregon at Eugene, 1970; Assoc. Prof., 1970–74, Prof. of English, 1974–79, SUNY at Fredonia; Founder-Ed., Obsidian magazine, 1975–85; Prof. of English, 1980–92, Prof. Emeritus, 1992–, Wayne State University, Detroit. *Publications:* Against the Blues, 1972; Feeling Through, 1975; South Louisiana: New and Selected Poems, 1985; If Winter Come: Collected Poems, 1994; Harlem Wrestler, 1995. *Honours:* Bread Loaf Writers Conference Scholarship, 1968; National Endowment for the Arts Grants, 1973, 1981; Co-ordinating Council of Literary Magazines Grant, 1979; Annual Callaloo Award, 1989. *Address:* 18234 Parkside Ave, Detroit, MI 48221, USA.

AUBRY, Cécile; Author, Scriptwriter and Film Dir; b. 3 Aug. 1928, Paris, France; m. Prince Brahim el Glaoui 1951 (divorced); one s. *Education:* Lycée Victor Duruy, Paris. *Career:* appeared in prin. role in Clouzot's film Manon 1948; subsequent roles in films The Black Rose 1950, Barbe Bleue 1951 and in Italian and French films 1951; author and director of numerous television scripts and series 1961–72, including Poly, Belle et Sébastien, Sébastien Parmi les Hommes, Sébastien et la Mary Morgane, Le Jeune Fabre. *Publications:* three novels 1974–85, several children's books. *Honours:* Officier, Ordre des Arts et des Lettres. *Address:* Le Moulin Bleu, 6 chemin du Moulin Bleu, 91410 St-Cyr-sous-Dourdan, France.

AUCHINCLOSS, Kenneth; Editor; b. 3 July 1937, New York, NY, USA; m. Eleanor Johnson 1971; one s. one d. *Education:* Harvard Coll.; Balliol Coll., Oxford. *Career:* Asst to Deputy Sec. US Dept of Commerce 1961; Exec. Asst to US Special Trade Rep. 1963; mem. staff, Inst. for Advanced Study 1965; Assoc. Ed. Newsweek 1966–68, Gen. Ed. 1968–72, Sr Ed. 1972, Exec. Ed. 1972–76, Man. Ed. 1976–95, Ed. Int. Edn 1986–95, Ed.-at-Large 1996–2002. *Address:* 40 E 62nd St, New York, NY 10021-8018, USA.

AUCHINCLOSS, Louis Stanton, LLB, DLitt; American author and lawyer; b. 27 Sept. 1917; m. Adele Lawrence 1957; three s. *Education:* Groton School, Yale Univ. and Univ. of Virginia. *Career:* admitted to New York Bar 1941, Assoc. Sullivan and Cromwell 1941–51, Hawkins, Delafield and Wood, New York 1954–58, Partner 1958–86; Lt, USN 1941–45; Pres. American Acad. of Arts and Letters 1997–2000; Pres. Museum of the City of New York; mem. Nat. Inst. of Arts and Letters. *Publications:* The Indifferent Children 1947, The Injustice Collectors 1950, Sybil 1952, A Law for the Lion 1953, The Romantic Egoists 1954, The Great World and Timothy Colt 1956, Venus in Sparta 1958, Pursuit of the Prodigal 1959, House of Five Talents 1960, Reflections of a Jacobite 1961, Portrait in

Brownstone 1962, Powers of Attorney 1963, The Rector of Justin 1964, Pioneers and Caretakers 1965, The Embezzler 1966, Tales of Manhattan 1967, A World of Profit 1969, Motiveless Malignity 1969, Edith Wharton: A Woman in Her Time 1971, I Come as a Thief 1972, Richelieu 1972, The Partners 1974, A Winter's Capital 1974, Reading Henry James 1975, The Winthrop Covenant 1976, The Dark Lady 1977, The Country Cousin 1978, Persons of Consequence 1979, Life, Law and Letters 1979, The House of the Prophet 1980, The Cat and the King 1981, Watchfires 1982, Exit Lady Masham 1983, The Book Class 1984, Honorable Men 1985, Diary of a Yuppie 1986, Skinny Island 1987, The Golden Calves 1988, Fellow Passengers 1989, The Vanderbilt Era 1989, J. P. Morgan 1990, The Lady of Situations 1991, False Gods 1992, Three Lives 1993, Tales of Yesteryear 1994, Collected Stories 1994, The Style's the Man 1994, The Education of Oscar Fairfax 1995, The Man Behind the Book 1996, La Gloire 1996, The Atonement 1997, Woodrow Wilson 2000, The Scarlet Letters 2003; contributions: New York Review of Books, New Criterion. *Address:* 1111 Park Avenue, New York, NY 10028, USA (Home).

AUEL, Jean Marie; Writer; b. 18 Feb. 1936, Chicago, IL, USA; m. Ray Bernard Auel 19 March 1954; two s. three d. *Education:* MBA, Univ. of Portland, 1976. *Career:* mem. Authors' Guild; International Women's Forum, board of dirs, 1985–93; Mensa, hon. vice-pres., 1990–; Oregon Museum of Science and Industry, board of dirs, 1993–96; Oregon Writers' Colony; PEN. *Publications:* Clan of the Cave Bear, 1980; The Valley of Horses, 1982; The Mammoth Hunters, 1985; The Plains of Passage, 1990; The Shelters of Stone, 2002. *Honours:* Excellence in Writing Award, Pacific North West Booksellers Asscn, 1980; Vicki Penziner Matson Memorial Award, Friends of Literature, Chicago, IL, 1980; DLitt, University of Portland, 1984; Golden Plate Award, Notable Author, American Acad. of Achievement, 1986; HHD, Univ. of Maine, 1986; LHD, Mount Vernon Coll., 1986; Centennial Medal, Smithsonian Institution, 1990; HHD, Pacific Univ., 1995. *Literary Agent:* Jean V. Naggar Literary Agency, 216 E 75th St, New York, NY 10021, USA.

AUERBACH, Nina Joan, BA, MA, PhD; American academic and writer; b. 24 May 1943, New York, NY. *Education:* Univ. of Wisconsin at Madison, Columbia Univ. *Career:* Adjunct Prof., Hunter College, CUNY, 1969–70; Asst Prof. of English, California State University at Los Angeles, 1970–72; Asst Prof., 1972–77, Assoc. Prof., 1977–83, Prof., 1983–, of English, University of Pennsylvania; mem. MLA of America, Victorian Soc. of America. *Publications:* Communities of Women: An Idea in Fiction, 1978; Woman and the Demon: The Life of a Victorian Myth, 1982; Romantic Imprisonment: Women and Other Glorified Outcasts, 1985; Ellen Terry: Player in Her Time, 1987; Private Theatrical: The Lives of the Victorians, 1990; Forbidden Journeys: Fairy Tales and Fantasies by Victorian Women Writers (ed. with U. C. Knoepflmacher), 1992; Our Vampires, Ourselves, 1995; Daphne Du Maurier: Haunted Heiress, 2000. Contributions: books and periodicals, incl. London Review of Books. *Honours:* Ford Foundation Fellowship, 1975–76; Radcliffe Institute Fellowship, 1975–76; Guggenheim Fellowship, 1979–80. *Address:* Department of English, University of Pennsylvania, Philadelphia, PA 19104, USA.

AUMBRY, Alan (see Bayley, Barrington (John)).

AUSTER, Paul, BA, MA; American writer and poet; b. 3 Feb. 1947, Newark, NJ; m. 1st Lydia Davis 1974 (divorced 1982); one s.; m. 2nd Siri Hustvedt 1982; one d. *Education:* Columbia High School, NJ, Columbia Coll., New York, Columbia Univ., New York. *Career:* worked as census taker; oil tank utility man. on the Esso Florence; moved to Paris, France 1970, returned to USA 1974; worked as translator; Tutor in Storywriting and Trans., Princeton Univ. 1986–90; juror, Cannes Film Festival 1997; mem. PEN. *Screenplays:* Smoke 1995, Blue in the Face 1995, Lulu on the Bridge 1998. *Publications:* fiction: City of Glass 1985, Ghosts 1986, The Locked Room 1986, In the Country of Last Things 1987, Moon Palace 1989, The Music of Chance 1990, Leviathan 1992, Mr Vertigo 1994, Timbuktu 1999, The Book of Illusions 2002, True Tales of American Life 2001, Oracle Night 2003; non-fiction: White Spaces 1980, The Invention of Solitude 1982, The Art of Hunger 1982, Hand to Mouth (memoir) 1989, The Red Notebook 1995, Why Write? 1996, Translations 1996, Collected Prose 2003; poetry: Unearth 1974, Wall Writing 1976, Fragments From Cold 1977, Facing the Music 1980, The Random House Book of Twentieth-Century French Poetry (ed.) 1982, Disappearances: Selected Poems 1988, I Thought My Father Was God 2001. *Honours:* Nat. Endowment for the Arts fellowships 1979, 1985; Prix Médicis Étranger 1993; Chevalier, Ordre des Arts et des Lettres. *Literary Agent:* Carol Mann Agency, 55 Fifth Avenue, New York, NY 10003, USA. *Address:* c/o Faber and Faber Ltd, 3 Queen Square, London, WC1N 3AU, England (Office). *Website:* www.paulauster.co.uk.

AUSTIN, Brett (see Floren, Lee).

AVERY, Gillian Elise; writer and editor; b. 30 Sept. 1926, England; m. Anthony Oliver Lockshut 1952; one d. *Career:* Junior Reporter, Surrey Mirror, Redhill, Surrey, 1944–47; Staff, Chambers's Encyclopaedia, London, 1947–50; Asst Illustrations Ed., Clarendon Press, Oxford, 1950–54. *Publications:* Children's books: The Warden's Niece, 1957; Trespassers at Charlcote, 1958; James Without Thomas, 1959; The Elephant War, 1960; To Tame a Sister, 1961; The Greatest Gresham, 1962; The Peacock House, 1963; The Italian Spring, 1964; The Call of theValley, 1966; A Likely Lad, 1971; Huck and Her Time Machine, 1977; Adult fiction: The Lost Railway, 1980; Onlookers, 1983; Non-fiction: Nineteenth-Century Children: Heroes and Heroines in English Children's Stories (with Angela Bull), 1965; Victorian People in Life and Literature, 1970; The Echoing Green: Memories of Regency and Victorian Youth, 1974; Childhood's Pattern, 1975; Children and Their Books: a Celebration of the Work of Iona and Peter Opie (ed. with Julia Briggs), 1989; The Best Type of Girl: a History of Girls' Independent Schools, 1991; Behold the Child: American Children and Their Books, 1621-1922, 1994; Representations of Childhood Death (ed. with Kimberley Reynolds, 1999; Cheltenham Ladies: A History of the Cheltenham Ladies' College, 2003. Editor: many books. *Honours:* Guardian Award, 1972. *Address:* 32 Charlbury Road, Oxford OX2 6UU, England.

AVI (see Wortis, Avi).

AVICE, Claude (Pierre Marie), (Pierre Barbet, David Maine, Oliver Sprigel); Writer; b. 16 May 1925, Le Mans, France; m. Marianne Brunswick, 23 July 1952, two s. one d. *Education:* Diplomas in Bacteriology, Serology and Parasitology, 1954, PhD, Summa cum laude, in Pharmacy, 1955, Institut Pasteur, University of Paris. *Career:* Pharmacist, Paris, 1952–81; Science Fiction Writer, 1962–. *Publications:* Les Grognards d'Eridan, 1970, English trans. as The Napoleons of Eridanus, 1976; A quoi songent les psyborgs?, 1971, English trans. as Games Psyborgs Play, 1973; L'Empire du Baphomet, 1972, English trans. as Baphomet's Meteor, 1972; La Planete enchantée, 1973, English trans. as Enchanted Planet, 1975; Liane de Noldaz, 1973, English trans. as The Joan-of-Arc Replay, 1978; L'Empereur d'Eridan, 1982, English trans. as The Emperor of Eridanus, 1983. Contributions: many publications both fiction and non-fiction. *Honours:* Gold Medal, International Institute of Science Fiction, Poznań, Poland. *Address:* 4 Sq. de l'ave du Bois, 75116 Paris, France.

AVISON, Margaret (Kirkland); Poet and Writer; b. 23 April 1918, Galt, ON, Canada. *Education:* BA, English, Victoria College, University of Toronto, 1940; Indiana University; University of Chicago; Graduate Studies, University of Toronto, 1963–66. *Career:* Teacher, Scarborough College, University of Toronto, 1966–68; Writer-in-Residence, University of Western Ontario, 1972–73. *Publications:* Poetry: Winter Sun, 1960; The Dumbfounding, 1966; Sunblue, 1978; No Time, 1989; Margaret Avison: Selected Poems, 1991. Other: A Kind of Perseverance (lectures), 1993. *Honours:* Guggenheim Fellowship, 1956; Gov.-Gen.'s Awards for Poetry, 1960, 1990. *Address:* c/o Oxford University Press Canada, 70 Wynford Dr., Don Mills, Toronto, ON M3C 1J9, Canada.

AWOONOR, Kofi; Educator, Diplomat, Poet and Writer; b. 13 March 1935, Wheta, Ghana; four s., one d. *Education:* BA, University of Ghana, 1960; MA, University of London, 1968; PhD in Comparative Literature, SUNY at Stony Brook, 1973. *Career:* Research Fellow, Institute of American Studies, 1960–64; Dir, Ghana Ministry of Information Film Corpn, 1964–67; Poet-in-Residence, 1968, Asst Prof., 1968–72, Assoc. Prof., 1973–74, Chair, Dept of Comparative Literature, 1974–75, SUNY; Senior Lecturer, Prof. of Literature, and Dean of the Faculty of Arts, University of Cape Coast, 1977–82; Ghana Ambassador to Brazil, 1984–88, Cuba, 1988–90, United Nations, 1990–. *Publications:* Rediscovery and Other Poems, 1964; Night of My Blood, 1971; This Earth, My Brother, 1972; Ride Me, Memory, 1973; Guardian of the Sacred Word, 1974; Breast of the Earth (essays), 1974; The House by the Sea, 1978; Until the Morning After: Collected Poems 1963–1985, 1987; Ghana: A Political History, 1990; Comes the Voyage at Last, 1992; Latin American and Caribbean Notebook, 1993. *Honours:* Trans. Award, Columbia University, 1972; Ghana Book Award, 1978; Commonwealth Poetry Prize, 1989; Distinguished Authors Award, Ghana Asscn of Writers, 1992. *Address:* c/o Permanent Mission of Ghana to the United Nations, 19 E 47th St, New York, NY 10017, USA.

AXTON, David (see Koontz, Dean Ray).

AYCKBOURN, Sir Alan; Theatre Dir, Playwright and Artistic Dir; b. 12 April 1939, London, England; m. 1st Christine Roland 1959 (divorced 1997); two s.; m. 2nd Heather Stoney 1997. *Career:* Founder mem., Victoria Theatre Co, Stoke on Trent, 1962–64; Drama Producer, BBC Radio, 1964–70; Artistic Dir, Stephen Joseph Theatre, Scarborough, 1971–; Cameron Mackintosh Prof. of Contemporary Theatre, Oxford, 1992; mem. Garrick Club; FRSA. *Publications:* Mr Whatnot, 1963; Relatively Speaking, 1965; How the Other Half Loves, 1969; Family Circles, 1970; Time and Time Again, 1971; Absurd Person Singular, 1972; The Norman Conquests, 1973; Absent Friends, 1974; Confusions, 1974; Bedroom Farce, 1975; Just Between Ourselves, 1976; Ten Times Table, 1977; Joking Apart, 1978; Sisterly Feelings, 1979; Taking Steps, 1979; Season's Greetings, 1980; Suburban Strains (music by Paul Todd), 1980; Way Upstream, 1981; Intimate Exchanges, 1982; It Could Be Any One Of Us, 1983; A Chorus of Disapproval, 1984; Woman in Mind, 1985; A Small Family Business, 1987; Henceforward…, 1987; Man of the Moment, 1988; Mr A's Amazing Maze Plays, 1988; The Revengers' Comedies, 1989; Invisible Friends, 1989; Body Language, 1990; This Is Where We Came In, 1990; Wildest Dreams, 1991; My Very Own Story, 1991; Time of My Life, 1992; Communicating Doors, 1994; The Musical Jigsaw Play (music by John Pattison), 1994; A Word From Our Sponsor (music from John Pattison), 1995; By Jeeves (music by Andrew Lloyd Webber), 1996; The Champion of Paribanou, 1996; Things We Do For Love, 1997; Comic Potential, 1998; The Boy Who Fell Into A Book, 1998; House & Garden, 1999; Callisto 5, 1999; Whenever (music by

Denis King), 2000; Damsels in Distress Trilogy: GamePlan, 2001, FlatSpin, 2001, RolePlay, 2001; Snake in the Grass, 2002; The Jollies, 2002; The Crafty Art of Playmaking, 2002; Orvin: Champion of Champions, 2003. *Honours:* Hon. degrees, Univs of Hull, 1981, Bretton, 1982, Keele, 1987, Leeds, 1987, York, 1992, Bradford, 1994, Wales, Cardiff, 1995, Open Univ., 1998, Univ. of Manchester, 2003; CBE, 1987; Knighted, 1997. *Address:* c/o Casarotto Ramsay and Assocs Ltd, National House, 60–66 Wardour St, London W1V 4ND, England. *Website:* www.alanayckbourn.net.

AYRES, Pamela (Pam), MBE; British writer, poet and broadcaster; b. 19 March 1947; m. Dudley Russell 1982; two s. *Education:* Faringdon Secondary Modern School, Berks. *Career:* served in Women's RAF 1965–69; writer and performer. *TV includes:* Opportunity Knocks 1975, The World of Pam Ayres 1977, numerous specials in UK, Hong Kong and Canada. *Radio includes:* Pam Ayres Radio Show 1995, Pam Ayres on Sunday 1996–99. *Publications include:* Some of Me Poetry 1976, Some More of Me Poetry 1976, Thoughts of a Late-Night Knitter 1978, All Pam's Poems 1978, Bertha and the Racing Pigeon 1979, The Ballad of Bill Spinks' Bedstead and Other Poems 1981, Dear Mum 1985, Guess Who? 1987, Guess What? 1987, When Dad Fills in the Garden Pond 1988, When Dad Cuts Down the Chestnut Tree 1988, Piggo and the Nosebag 1990, Piggo Has a Train Ride 1990, The Bear Who Was Left Behind 1991, Pam Ayres: The Works 1992, Guess Why? 1994, With These Hands: a Collection of Work 1997, The Nubbler 1997. *Address:* PO Box 64 Cirencester, GL7 5YD, England (Office). *Telephone:* (1285) 644622 (Office). *Fax:* (1285) 642291 (Office). *E-mail:* acornents@btconnect.com (Office). *Website:* www.pamayres.com (Office).

AYRES, Philip James, BA, PhD, FRHistS; writer and academic; b. 28 July 1944, SA, Australia; m. 1st Maruta Sudrabs 1965 (divorced 1981); m. 2nd Patricia San Martin 1981; one s. *Education:* University of Adelaide. *Career:* Lecturer, 1972–79, Senior Lecturer, 1979–93, Assoc. Prof., 1993–, Monash University; Visiting Prof., Vassar College, New York, 1993; Visiting Fellow, Boston University, 2001; mem. Australian Council, literature board, deputy chair., 2000–02. *Publications:* The Revenger's Tragedy, 1977; The English Roman Life, 1980; Malcolm Fraser: A Biography, 1987; Classical Culture and the Idea of Rome in Eighteenth Century England, 1997; Douglas Mawson, 1999; Owen Dixon, 2002. Editor: Ben Jonson: Sejanus His Fall, 1990; 3rd Earl of Shaftesbury, Characteristics, 1999. Contributions: English Literary Renaissance; Modern Philology; Studies in Bibliography; Studies in English Literature; Studies in Philology. *Honours:* Fellow, Australian Acad. of the Humanities. *Address:* 13 Harris Avenue, Glen Iris, Vic. 3146, Australia.

AZZOPARDI, Trezza, MA; British writer; b. 1961, Cardiff, Wales. *Education:* Univ. of East Anglia. *Career:* examiner for Norwich School of Art. *Publications:* The Hiding Place (Geoffrey Faber Memorial Prize) 2000, Remember Me 2004; contrib. to Neon Lit 1, Take Twenty, New Writing 9. *Address:* c/o Picador, 25 Eccleston Place, London, SW1W 9NF, England. *Telephone:* (20) 7881-8000. *Fax:* (20) 7881-8001.

B

BA JIN; Chinese writer and journalist; b. (LI YAOTANG), 25 Nov. 1904, Chengdu, Sichuan Prov.; m. Xiao Shan 1944 (died 1972); one s. one d. *Education:* Foreign Language School, Chengdu. *Career:* studied in France and adopted name Ba Jin (taken from first syllable of Bakunin and the last of Kropotkin) 1926; Ed. fortnightly prov. Ban Yue 1928; writer and translator, Shanghai 1929; visited Japan 1934; Chief Ed. Shanghai Cultural Life Publishing House 1935; joined Lu Xun's China Literary Work Soc. 1936; Co-Ed. (with Mao Dun) Shouting Weekly and Bonfire Weekly 1937; Vice-Chair. Union of Chinese Writers 1953 (now Chair.); Deputy to NPC 1954; Chief. Ed. People's Literature 1957–58; Vice-Chair. China Fed. of Literary and Art Circles 1960; Chief Ed. Shanghai Literature 1961; in disgrace 1968–77; Vice-Chair. 5th Municipal CPPCC Cttee, Shanghai 1977–83; mem. Presidium 6th Nat. CPPCC Cttee 1983–88; Vice-Chair. 7th Nat. Cttee CPPCC 1988–93, 8th Nat. Cttee 1993–98, 9th Nat. Cttee 1998–; Exec. Council, China Welfare Inst. 1978–; Vice-Chair. China Fed. of Literary and Art Circles 1978–; Pres. China PEN Centre 1980–, Chinese Writers' Asscn 1981– (Chair. 2001), China Literature Foundation 1986–; Hon. Pres. Fiction Soc. 1984–; Hon. Chair. China Shakespeare Research Foundation 1984–; Hon. mem. AAAS 1985. *Publications include:* Extinction 1928, The Family 1931, Trilogy of Love 1932–33, The History of the Nihilist Movement 1936, Spring 1937, Autumn 1940, Festival Day of Warsaw 1950, Living Among Heroes 1953, Three Comrades 1962, Random Thoughts (5 vols) 1979–86, Essays by the Sickbed 1984. *Honours:* Medal of Int. Friendship, USSR 1990. *Address:* c/o China PEN, Shatan Beijie 2, Beijing, People's Republic of China. *Website:* www.bajin.com (Office).

BABADJHAN, Ramz; Uzbekistan poet and playwright; b. 2 Aug. 1921, Uzbekistan; m. 1947; one s. two d. *Education:* Pedagogical Inst., Tashkent. *Career:* Deputy Chair. Uzbek Writers' Union; mem. CPSU 1951–91; Chair. Uzbek Republican Cttee on Relations with African and Asian Writers; Pres. Soc. on Cultural Relations with Compatriots Living Abroad 'Vatan' 1990–94; first works published 1935. *Publications include:* Dear Friends, Thank You, My Dear, The Heart Never Sleeps, Selected Poetry, A Poet Lives Twice, Living Water, Yusuf and Zuleyha, 1001 Crane, Sides, Uncle and Nephew, You Cannot Deceive a Gipsy. *Honours:* USSR State Prize 1972. *Address:* Beshchinar str. 34, 700070 Tashkent, Uzbekistan. *Telephone:* (371) 55-61-06.

BABINEAU, Jean Joseph; Teacher and Writer; b. 10 Aug. 1952, Moncton, NB, Canada; m. Gisèle Ouellette, 27 Aug. 1993, one s. *Education:* BA, 1977; BA, French, 1981; BEd, 1985. *Career:* mem. AAAPNB. *Publications:* Bloupe, 1993; Gîte, 1998. Contributions: Éloizes; Mœbius; Mots en Volet; Littéréalité; Satellite; Nouvelles d'Amérique; Virages; Le Front. *Honours:* Canada Council Exploration Grant, 1989; New Brunswick Arts Branch Creation Grant, 1998. *Address:* Gîte, Grand-Barachois, NB, Canada.

BACHMAN, Richard (see King, Stephen Edwin).

BACKSCHEIDER, Paula; Prof. of English, Writer and Ed.; b. 31 March 1943, Brownsville, TN, USA; m. Nickolas Andrew Backscheider, 18 Jan. 1964, one s. one d. *Education:* BA, 1964, PhD, 1972, Purdue University; MS, Southern Connecticut State College, 1967. *Career:* Asst Prof., Rollins College, Winter Park, FL, 1973–75; Asst Prof., 1975–78, Assoc. Prof., 1978–87, Prof. of English, 1987–, University of Rochester; Stevens-Philpott Eminent Scholar, Auburn University, 1992–; mem. American Society for Eighteenth-Century Studies, pres., 1992; MLA. *Publications:* An Annotated Bibliography of Twentieth-Century Studies of Women and Literature, 1660–1800 (with Felicity Nussbaum and Philip Anderson), 1977; Probability, Time, and Space in Eighteenth-Century Literature (ed.), 1979; Eighteenth-Century Drama (ed.), 69 vols, 1979–83; A Being More Intense: The Prose Works of Bunyan, Swift, and Defoe, 1984; Daniel Defoe: Ambition and Innovation, 1986; Daniel Defoe: His Life, 1989; Spectacular Politics: Theatrical Power and Mass Culture in Early Modern England (ed. with Timothy Dykstal), 1996; Popular Fiction by Women, 1660–1730: An Anthology (ed. with John J. Richetti), 1996; Reflections on Biography, 1999; Revising Women: Eighteenth-Century 'Women's Fiction' and Social Engagement (ed.), 2000. Contributions: Reference works, scholarly books and professional journals. *Honours:* American Philosophical Society Grants, 1975, 1980, 1986; National Endowment for the Humanities Fellowship, 1983; American Antiquarian Society Fellowship, 1987; British Council Prize for Best Humanities Book, 1990; Guggenheim Fellowship, 1991. *Address:* c/o Dept of English, Auburn University, Auburn, AL 36849, USA.

BADAWI, Mohamed Mustafa; Lecturer and Writer; b. 10 June 1925, Alexandria, Egypt. *Education:* BA, Alexandria University, 1946; BA, 1950, PhD, 1954, University of London. *Career:* Research Fellow, 1947–54, Lecturer, 1954–60, Asst Prof., 1960–64, Alexandria University, Egypt; Lecturer, University of Oxford, and Brasenose College, 1964–92; Fellow, St Antony's College, Oxford, 1967–; Ed., Journal of Arabic Literature, Leiden, 1970; Advisory Board Mem., Cambridge History of Arabic Literature. *Publications:* An Anthology of Modern Arabic Verse, 1970; Coleridge as Critic of Shakespeare, 1973; A Critical Introduction to Modern Arabic Poetry, 1975; Background to Shakespeare, 1981; Modern Arabic Literature and the West, 1985; Modern Arabic Drama in Egypt, 1987; Early Arabic Drama, 1988; Modern Arabic Literature: Cambridge History of Arabic Literature (ed.), 1992; A Short History of Modern Arabic Literature, 1993; several books and vols of verse in Arabic. *Honours:* King Faisal International Prize for Arabic Literature. *Address:* St Antony's College, Oxford OX2 6JF, England.

BADCOCK, Gary David; academic, writer and editor; b. 13 Jan. 1961, Bay Roberts, Canada; m. Susan Dorothy Greig 1988; two d. *Education:* BA, 1981, MA, 1984, Memorial University of Newfoundland; BD, 1987, PhD, 1991, University of Edinburgh, Scotland. *Career:* Teaching Fellow, University of Aberdeen, 1991–92; Meldrum Lecturer in Dogmatic Theology, University of Edinburgh, 1993–99; Asst Prof., Huron College, London, Ontario, 1999–2002, Assoc. Prof., 2002–. *Publications:* Disruption to Diversity: Edinburgh Divinity, 1846–1996 (ed. with D. F. Wright), 1996; Theology After the Storm, by John McIntyre (ed.), 1995; Light of Truth and Fire of Love, 1997; The Way of Life, 1998. Contributions: Co-author, books and scholarly journals. *Honours:* Leslie Tarr Award, 1998. *Address:* Faculty of Theology, Huron University College, London, ON, Canada, N6G 1H3. *E-mail:* gbadcock@uwo.ca.

BAERWALD, Hans Herman, BA, MA, PhD; academic and writer; b. 18 June 1927, Tokyo, Japan. *Education:* University of California at Berkeley. *Career:* Asst Prof., 1956–61, Assoc. Prof., 1961–62, of Government, Miami University, Oxford, Ohio; Lecturer, 1962–65, Assoc. Prof., 1965–69, Prof., 1969–91, of Political Science, University of California at Los Angeles. *Publications:* The Purge of Japanese Leaders Under the Occupation, 1959; American Government: Structure, Problems, Policies (with Peter H. Odegard), 1962; Chinese Communism: Selected Documents (with Dan N. Jacobs), 1963: The American Republic, Its Government and Politics (with Peter H. Odegard), 1964; Japan's Parliament: An Introduction, 1974; Party Politics in Japan, 1986. Contributions: Asian Survey. *Honours:* Order of the Sacred Treasure with Gold and Silver Star, Japan, 1989. *Address:* 2221 Barnett Road, St Helens, CA 94574, USA.

BAGDIKIAN, Ben Haig; Prof. and Writer; b. 30 Jan. 1920, Marash, Turkey; m. Marlene Griffith Bagdikian, 4 Nov. 1983, two s. *Education:* AB, Clark University. *Career:* Asst Managing Ed., National News, The Washington Post; Prof., Dean, Graduate School of Journalism, University of California, Berkeley, CA. *Publications:* In the Midst of Plenty: The Poor in America, 1964; The Information Machines, 1973; The Effete Conspiracy and Other Crimes of the Press, 1973; Caged: Eight Prisoners and Their Keepers, 1976; The Media Monopoly, 1983, 7th edn as The New Media Monopoly; Double Vision: Reflections on My Heritage, Life and Profession, 1995. Contributions: More than 200 to national magazines and journals. *Honours:* Peabody Award, 1951; Sidney Hillman Award, 1955; John Simon Guggenheim Fellow, 1962; LHD, Brown University 1961; LittD, Clark University, 1963; Berkeley Citation, 1990; LHD, University of Rhode Island, 1992; James Madison Award, American Library Asscn, 1998. *Address:* 25 Stonewall Road, Berkeley, CA 94705, USA.

BAHN, Paul Gerard; Archaeologist and Writer; b. 29 July 1953, Hull, England. *Education:* BA, 1974, MA, 1978, PhD, 1979, University of Cambridge. *Career:* Research Fellow, University of Liverpool, 1979–82; Senior Research Fellow, University of London, 1982–83; J. Paul Getty Postdoctoral Fellow, 1985–86. *Publications:* Easter Island, Earth Island, 1992; The Story of Archaeology, 1995; Archaeology: A Very Short Introduction, 1996; The Cambridge Illustrated History of Archaeology, 1996; Tombs, Graves and Mummies, 1996; Journey Through the Ice Age, 1997; Lost Cities, 1997; The Cambridge Illustrated History of Prehistoric Art, 1998; Disgraceful Archaeology, 1999; Wonderful Things, 1999; Archaeology: Theories, Methods and Practice, revised third edn, 2000; Atlas of World Archaeology, 2000; Mammoths, second edn, 2000; The Archaeology Detectives, 2001; The Penguin Guide to Archaeology, 2001; Archaeology: The Definitive Guide, 2002; Written in Bones, 2003; The Enigmas of Easter Island, 2003. Contributions: periodicals. *Literary Agent:* Watson, Little Ltd, Capo di Monte, Windmill Hill, London NW3 6RJ, England.

BAIGELL, Matthew; Prof. of Art History and Writer; b. 27 April 1933, New York, NY, USA; m. Renee Moses, 1 Feb. 1959, two d. *Education:* BA, University of Vermont, 1954; MA, Columbia University, 1955; PhD, University of Pennsylvania, 1965. *Career:* Instructor, 1961–65, Asst Prof., 1965–67, Assoc. Prof. of Art, 1967–68, Ohio State University; Assoc. Prof., 1968–72, Prof., 1972–78, Prof. II, 1978–, Rutgers, the State University of New Jersey at New Brunswick. *Publications:* A History of American Painting, 1971; A Thomas Hart Benton Miscellany (ed.), 1971; The American Scene: American Painting in the 1930s, 1974; Thomas Hart Benton, 1974; Charles Burchfield, 1976; The Western Art of Frederic Remington, 1976; Dictionary of American Art, 1979; Albert Bierstadt, 1981; Thomas Cole, 1981; A Concise History of American Painting and Sculpture, 1984; The Papers of the American Artists' Congress (1936), 1985; Artists Against War and Fascism (ed. with J. Williams), 1986; Soviet Dissident Artists: Interviews After Perestroika (with Renee Baigell), 1995; Jewish-American Artists and the Holocaust, 1997; Artist and Identity in Twentieth-Century America, 2001. *Address:* c/o Dept of Art History, Rutgers, the State

University of New Jersey at New Brunswick, New Brunswick, NJ 08903, USA.

BAIGENT, Beryl; Teacher, Writer and Poet; b. 16 Dec. 1937, Llay, Wrexham, North Wales; m. Alan H. Baigent, 19 Jan. 1963, three d. *Education:* BA in Physical Education, MA in English Literature, University of Western Ontario, London, Canada. *Career:* mem. Celtic Arts Asscn; Canadian Poetry Asscn; League of Canadian Poets, Ontario Representative, 1994–96. *Publications:* The Quiet Village, 1972; Pause, 1974; In Counterpoint, 1976; Ancestral Dreams, 1981; The Sacred Beech, 1985; Mystic Animals, 1988; Absorbing the Dark, 1990; Hiraeth: In Search of Celtic Origins, 1994; Triptych: Virgins, Victims, Votives, 1996; The Celtic Tree Calendar, 1999; The Mary Poems, 2000. Contributions: various anthologies and periodicals including Poetry and Spiritual Practice 2002. *Honours:* Ontario Weekly Newspaper Award, 1979; Fritch Memorial, Canadian Authors Asscn, 1982; Ontario Arts Council Awards, 1983, 1985, 1987; Kent Writers Award, 1986; Black Mountain Award, 1986; Canada Council Touring Awards, 1990, 1992, 1993, 1994, 1998; Forest City Poetry Award, 1991; International Affairs Touring Award, 1991; Welsh Arts Council Awards, 1993, 1994, 1996, 1998, 1999; Muse Journal Award, 1994. *Address:* 137 Byron Avenue, Thamesford, ON N0M 2M0, Canada.

BAIL, Murray; Author; b. 22 Sept. 1941, Adelaide, SA, Australia; m. Margaret Wordsworth 1965. *Education:* Norwood Technical High School, Adelaide. *Publications:* Contemporary Portraits and Other Stories, 1975; Homesickness, 1980; Holden's Performance, 1987; The Faber Book of Contemporary Australian Short Stories (ed.), 1988; Longhand: A Writer's Notebook, 1989; Eucalyptus, 1998; Camouflage (short stories), 2001. *Honours:* Age Book of the Year Award, 1980; National Book Council Award, 1980; Victorian Premier's Award, 1988; Commonwealth Writers Prize, 1999; Miles Franklin Award, 1999.

BAILEY, Anthony (Cowper); Author and Journalist; b. 5 Jan. 1933, Portsmouth, England. *Education:* BA, 1955, MA, 1956, Merton College, Oxford. *Career:* Staff Writer, New Yorker magazine, 1956–92; mem. Authors' Guild; International PEN; Society of Authors. *Publications:* Making Progress, 1959; The Mother Tongue, 1961; The Inside Passage, 1965; Through the Great City, 1967; The Thousand Dollar Yacht, 1968; The Light in Holland, 1970; In the Village, 1971; A Concise History of the Low Countries, 1972; Rembrandt's House, 1978; Acts of Union: Reports on Ireland, 1973–79, 1980; America, Lost and Found, 1981; Along the Edge of the Forest: An Iron Curtain Journey, 1983; England, First and Last, 1985; Spring Jaunts: Some Walks, Excursions, and Personal Explorations of City, Country and Seashore, 1986; Major André, 1987; The Outer Banks, 1989; A Walk Through Wales, 1992; Responses to Rembrandt, 1994; A Coast of Summer: Sailing New England Waters from Shelter Island to Cape Cod, 1994. *Honours:* Overeas Press Club Award, 1974. *Address:* c/o Donadio and Ashworth Inc, 231 W 22nd St, New York, NY 10011, USA.

BAILEY, David Roy Shackleton; academic, writer, editor and translator; b. 10 Dec. 1917, Lancaster, England; m. 1st Hilary Ann Bardwell 1967 (divorced 1974); m. 2nd Kristine Zvirbulis 1994. *Education:* BA, 1939, MA, 1943, LittD, 1957, University of Cambridge. *Career:* Fellow, 1944–55, Praelector, 1954–55, Fellow and Deputy Bursar, 1964, Senior Bursar, 1965–68, Gonville and Caius College, Cambridge; University Lecturer in Tibetan, University of Cambridge, 1948–68; Fellow and Dir of Studies in Classics, Jesus College, Cambridge, 1955–64; Visiting Lecturer in Classics, Harvard College, 1963; Prof. of Latin, 1968–74, Adjunct Prof., 1989–, University of Michigan; Andrew V. Raymond Visiting Prof., SUNY at Buffalo, 1973–74; Prof. of Greek and Latin, 1975–82, Pope Prof. of Latin Language and Literature, 1982–88, Prof. Emeritus, 1988–, Harvard University; Ed., Harvard Studies in Classical Philology, 1978–84; Visiting Prof., Peterhouse, Cambridge, 1980–81; mem. American Acad. of Arts and Science, fellow, 1979–; American Philosophical Society; British Acad., fellow. *Publications:* The Sátapañcasátka of Matrceta, 1951; Propertiana, 1956; Towards a Text of Cicero ad Atticum, 1960; Ciceronis Epistulae ad Atticum IX–XVI, 1961; Cicero's Letters to Atticus, vols I and II, 1965, vol. V, 1966, vol. VI, 1967, vols III and IV, 1968, vol. VII, 1970; Cicero, 1971; Two Studies in Roman Nomenclature, 1976; Cicero: Epistulae ad Familiares, 2 vols, 1977; Cicero's Letters to Atticus, 1978; Cicero's Letters to His Friends, 2 vols, 1978; Towards a Text of Anthologia Latina, 1979; Selected Letters of Cicero, 1980; Cicero: Epistulae ad Q Fratrem et M Brutum, 1981; Profile of Horace, 1982; Anthologia Latina I.l, 1982; Horatius, 1985; Cicero: Philippics, 1986; Ciceronis Epistulae, 4 vols, 1987–88; Lucanus, 1988; Onomasticon to Cicero's Speeches, 1988; Quintilianus: Declamationes minores, 1989; Martialis, 1990; Back from Exile, 1991; Martial, 3 vols, 1993; Homoeoteleuton in Latin Dactylic Verse, 1994; Onomasticon to Cicero's Letters, 1995; Onomasticon to Cicero's Treatises, 1996; Selected Classical Papers, 1997; Valerius Maximus, two vols, 2000; Statius: Silvae, 2003; Statius: Thebaid, two vols, 2004. Contributions: scholarly periodicals. *Honours:* Charles Goodwin Prize, American Philological Asscn, 1978; National Endowment for the Humanities Fellowship, 1980–81; Hon. DLitt, University of Dublin, 1984; Kenyon Medal, British Acad., 1985; Hon. Mem., Society for Roman Studies, 1999; Hon. Fellow, Gonville and Caius College, 2000. *Address:* 303 North Division, Ann Arbor, MI 48104, USA.

BAILEY, Martin; Journalist; b. 26 Oct. 1947, London, England. *Education:* PhD, LSE, 1974. *Career:* The Observer, 1983–. *Publications:* Freedom Railway, 1976; Oilgate: The Sanctions Scandal, 1979; A Green Part of the World, 1984; Young Vincent: Van Gogh's Years in England, 1990; Van Gogh: Letters from Provence, 1990; Van Gogh in England: Portrait of the Artist as a Young Man, 1992. *Honours:* Journalist of the Year, 1979. *Literary Agent:* PFD, Drury House, 34–43 Russell St, London WC2B 5HA, England. *Address:* The Observer, Chelsea Bridge House, Queenstown Rd, London SW8 4NN, England.

BAILEY, Paul; Writer; b. 16 Feb. 1937, London, England. *Education:* Central School of Speech and Drama, 1953–56. *Career:* Literary Fellow, Universities of Newcastle upon Tyne and Durham, 1972–74; Bicentennial Fellowship, USA, 1976; Visiting Lecturer in English, North Dakota State University, 1977–79. *Publications:* At the Jerusalem, 1967; Trespasses, 1970; A Distant Likeness, 1973; Peter Smart's Confessions, 1977; Old Soldiers, 1980; An English Madam, 1982; Gabriel's Lament, 1986; An Immaculate Mistake (memoir), 1989; Hearth and Home, 1990; Sugar Cane, 1993; The Oxford Book of London (ed.), 1995; Kitty and Virgil, 1998; Three Queer Lives, 2002; Uncle Rudolph, 2002; A Dog's Life (memoir), 2003. Contributions: many newspapers. *Honours:* Somerset Maugham Award, 1968; Arts Council Award, 1968; E. M. Forster Award, 1978; George Orwell Memorial Prize, 1978; FRSL, 1982. *Address:* 79 Davisville Rd, London W12 9SH, England.

BAILEY, Sly; British publishing and media executive; *Chief Executive, Trinity Mirror PLC*; b. (Sylvia Grice), 24 Jan. 1962, London; m. Peter Bailey 1998. *Education:* St Saviours and St Olaves Grammar School for Girls. *Career:* telephone sales exec. at The Guardian 1984; joined The Independent 1987; moved to IPC Magazines 1989, Advertizing Sales Exec. 1994, mem. Bd of Dirs 1994–2003, Man. Dir TX 1997, Chief Exec. 1999–2003; Chief Exec. Trinity Mirror PLC 2003–; Dir (non-exec.) Littlewoods PLC April–Sept. 2002. *Honours:* Periodical Publrs Asscn Marcus Morris Award for Outstanding Contrib. to Publishing Industry 2002. *Address:* Trinity Mirror PLC, 1 Canada Square, Canary Wharf, London, E14 5AP, England (Office). *Telephone:* (20) 7293-2203 (Office). *Fax:* (20) 7293-3225 (Office). *Website:* www.trinity.plc.uk (Office).

BAILYN, Bernard; professor and writer; b. 10 Sept. 1922, Hartford, CT, USA; m. Lotte Lazarsfeld, 18 June 1952, two s. *Education:* AB, Williams College, 1945; MA, 1947, PhD, 1953, Harvard University. *Career:* Instructor, 1953–54, Asst Prof., 1954–58, Assoc. Prof., 1958–61, Prof. of History, 1961–66, Winthrop Prof. of History, 1966–81, Adams University Prof., 1981–93, Dir, Charles Warren Center for Studies in American History, 1983–94, James Duncan Phillips Prof. of Early American History, 1991–93, Prof. Emeritus, 1993–, Harvard University; Trevelyan Lecturer, 1971, Pitt Prof. of American History, 1986–87, University of Cambridge; Fellow, British Acad., and Christ's College, Cambridge, 1991; Jefferson Lecturer Nat. Endowment for the Humanities 1998, First Millennium Lecturer The White House 1998mem. American Acad. of Arts and Sciences; American Historical Asscn, pres., 1981; American Philosophical Society; National Acad. of Education; Royal Historical Society, Academia Europaea, Russian Acad. of Sciences, Mexican Acad. of History and Geography. *Publications:* The New England Merchants in the Seventeenth Century, 1955; Massachusetts Shipping, 1697–1714: A Statistical Study (with Lotte Bailyn), 1959; Education in the Forming of American Society: Needs and Opportunities for Study, 1960; Pamphlets of the American Revolution, 1750–1776, Vol. 1 (ed.), 1965; The Apologia of Robert Keayne: The Self-Portrait of a Puritan Merchant (ed.), 1965; The Ideological Origins of the American Revolution, 1967; The Origins of American Politics, 1968; The Intellectual Migration: Europe and America, 1930–1960 (ed. with Donald Fleming), 1969; Religion and Revolution: Three Biographical Studies, 1970; Law in American History (ed. with Donald Fleming), 1972; The Ordeal of Thomas Hutchinson, 1974; The Great Republic: A History of the American People (with others), 1977; The Press and the American Revolution (ed. with John B. Hench), 1980; The Peopling of British North America: An Introduction, 1986; Voyagers to the West: A Passage in the Peopling of America on the Eve of the Revolution, 1986; Faces of Revolution: Personalities and Themes in the Struggle for American Independence, 1990; Strangers within the Realm: Cultural Margins of the First British Empire (ed. with Philip B. Morgan), 1991; The Debate on the Constitution: Federalist and Antifederalist Speeches, Articles and Letters during the Struggle over Ratification, 2 vols, 1993; On the Teaching and Writing of History, 1994, To Begin the World Anew 2003. Contributions: scholarly journals. *Honours:* Bancroft Prize, 1968; Pulitzer Prizes in History, 1968, 1987; National Book Award in History, 1975; Catton Prize for lifetime achievement in writing history Soc. for American Historians 2000, Thomas Jefferson Medal American Philosophical Soc., 1993; Hon. doctorates. *Address:* 170 Clifton St, Belmont, MA 02478, USA.

BAINBRIDGE, Dame Beryl Margaret, CBE, FRSL; British writer; b. 21 Nov. 1934, Liverpool, England; three c. *Career:* actress, Repertory Theatres in the UK 1949–60; clerk, Gerald Duckworth & Co Ltd, London 1971–73. *Publications:* A Weekend with Claude, 1967; Another Part of the Wood, 1968; Harriet Said, 1972; The Dressmaker, 1973; The Bottle Factory Outing, 1974; Sweet William, 1975; A Quiet Life, 1976; Injury Time, 1977; Young Adolf, 1978; Winter Garden, 1980; English Journey or the Road to Milton Keynes, 1984; Watson's Apology, 1984; Mum & Mr Armitage, 1985; Forever England, 1986; Filthy Lucre, 1986; An Awfully Big Adventure, 1989; The Birthday Boys, 1991; Every Man For Himself, 1996; Master

Georgie, 1998; According to Queeney, 2001. *Honours:* Guardian Fiction Award, 1974; Whitbread Awards, 1977, 1997; Hon. DLitt, University of Liverpool, 1986; James Tate Black Memorial Award, 1998; WHSmith Fiction Award, 1998; David Cohen British Literature Prize, 2003; Heywood Hill Literary Prize 2004. *Address:* 42 Albert Street, London NW1 7NU, England.

BAINBRIDGE, Cyril; Author and Journalist; b. 15 Nov. 1928, Bradford, West Yorkshire, England; m. Barbara Hannah Crook, 20 Jan. 1953, one s. two d. *Education:* Negus College, Bradford. *Career:* Reporter, Bingley Guardian, 1944–45, Yorkshire Observer & Bradford Telegraph, 1945–54, Press Asscn, 1954–63; Asst News Ed., 1963–67, Deputy News Ed., 1967–69, Regional News Ed., 1969–77, Managing News Ed., 1977–82, Asst Managing Ed., 1982–88, The Times; mem. Brontë Society; Chartered Institute of Journalists; Society of Authors. *Publications:* Pavilions on the Sea; Brass Triumphant; The Brontës and Their Country; North Yorkshire and North Humberside; One Hundred Years of Journalism; The News of the World Story, 1993. Contributions: newspapers, magazines and periodicals. *Literary Agent:* Laurence Pollinger. *Address:* 6 Lea Rd, Hemingford Grey, Huntingdon, Cambs PE28 9ED, England.

BAINES, John, (Dario Salas Sommer); Writer, Lecturer and Philosopher; b. 4 March 1935, Santiago, Chile. *Education:* Dario Salas College, Santiago de Chile, 1954–59; BA, Humanities and Arts, University of Santiago, 1959. *Career:* mem. Authors' Guild of America, 1988–. *Publications:* In Spanish: Hypsoconciencia, 1965; Los Brujos Hablan, 1968; El Hombre Estelar, 1979; La Ciencia del Amor, 1982; Existe la Mujer?, 1983; El Desarrollo del Mundo Interno, 1984; Moral para el Siglo XXI, 1998; In English: The Secret Science, 1980; The Stellar Man, 1985; The Science of Love, 1993; Hypsoconsciousness, 1995; Some titles published in German, Russian, Bulgarian, Italian, Portuguese and Latvian. *Address:* PO Box 8556, FDR Station, New York, NY 10150, USA.

BAITZ, Jon Robin; Playwright; b. 1961, Los Angeles, CA, USA; Plays: The Film Society, 1987; Dutch Landscape, 1989; The Substance of Fire, 1991; Three Hotels, 1993; The End of the Day, 1993. Contributions: anthologies. *Honours:* Fellow, American Acad. and Institute of Arts and Letters, 1994. *Literary Agent:* William Morris Agency, 1325 Avenue of the Americas, New York, NY 10019, USA.

BAJWA, Rupa; Indian novelist; b. 1976, Amritsar. *Publications:* The Sari Shop 2004. *Address:* c/o Penguin Books Ltd, 80 Strand, London, WC2R 0RL, England. *Website:* www.penguin.co.uk.

BAKER, Alison; Writer; b. 7 Aug. 1953, Lancaster, Pennsylvania, USA. *Education:* BA, Reed College, 1975; MLS, Indiana University, 1977. *Publications:* How I Came West, and Why I Stayed, 1993; Thousands Live!, 1996. Contributions: anthologies and periodicals. *Honours:* George Garrett Fiction Award, 1992; First Prize, O. Henry Collection, 1994. *Literary Agent:* Brandt & Hochman Literary Agents Inc, 1501 Broadway, New York, NY 10036, USA.

BAKER, David (Anthony); Prof. of English, Poet and Ed.; b. 27 Dec. 1954, Bangor, Maine, USA; m. Ann Townsend, 19 July 1987. *Education:* BSE, 1976, MA, 1977, Central Missouri State University; PhD, University of Utah, 1983. *Career:* Poetry Ed., 1980–81, Ed.-in-Chief, 1981–83, Quarterly West; Visiting Asst Prof., Kenyon College, 1983–84; Asst Ed., 1983–89, Poetry Ed./Consulting Poetry Ed., 1989–94, Poetry Ed., 1994–, Kenyon Review; Asst Prof. of English, 1984–90, Assoc. Prof. of English, 1990–97, Prof. of English, 1997–, Denison University; Visiting Telluride Prof., Cornell University, 1985; Contributing Ed., The Pushcart Prize, 1992–; Visiting Assoc. Prof., University of Michigan, 1996; many poetry readings; mem. Associated Writing Programs; MLA; National Book Critics Circle; Poetry Society of America; Poets and Writers. *Publications:* Poetry: Looking Ahead, 1975; Rivers in the Sea, 1977; Laws of the Land, 1981; Summer Sleep, 1984; Haunts, 1985; Sweet Home, Saturday Night, 1991; Echo for an Anniversary, 1992; After the Reunion, 1994; Holding Katherine, 1997; Heresy and the Ideal: On Contemporary Poetry, 2000; Changeable Thunder, 2001. Editor: The Soil is Suited to the Seed: A Miscellany in Honor of Paul Bennett, 1986; Meter in English: A Critical Engagement, 1996. Contributions: anthologies and periodicals. *Honours:* Margaret Bridgman Scholar of Poetry, Bread Loaf, 1982; Outstanding Writer, Pushcart Press, 1982, 1984, 1985, 1986, 1990, 1991, 1994, 1995; James Wright Prize for Poetry, Mid-American Review, 1983; National Endowment for the Arts Fellowship, 1985–86; Bread Loaf Poetry Fellow, 1989; Pushcart Prize, 1992; Mary Carolyn Davies Award, Poetry Society of America, 1995; Thomas B. Fordham Endowed Chair in Creative Writing, Denison University, 1996; Ohio Arts Council Fellowship, 2000; Guggenheim Fellowship, 2000–01. *Address:* 135 Granview Rd, Granville, OH 43023, USA.

BAKER, Houston Alfred, Jr; Prof. of English and of Human Relations, Writer, Ed. and Poet; b. 22 March 1943, Louisville, KY, USA; m. Charlotte Pierce-Baker, 10 Sept. 1966, one s. *Education:* BA, magna cum laude, Howard University, 1965; MA, 1966, PhD, 1968, University of California at Los Angeles; PhD Studies, University of Edinburgh, 1967–68. *Career:* Instructor, Howard University, 1966; Instructor, 1968–69, Asst Prof. of English, 1969–70, Yale University; Assoc. Prof. and Mem., Center for Advanced Studies, 1970–73, Prof. of English, 1973–74, University of Virginia; Prof. of English, 1974–, Dir, Afro-American Studies Program, 1974–77, Albert M. Greenfield Prof. of Human Relations, 1982–, Dir, Center for the Study of Black Literature and Culture, 1987–, University of Pennsylvania; Fellow, Center for Advanced Study in the Behavioral Sciences, 1977–78, National Humanities Center, 1982–83; Bucknell Distinguished Scholar, University of Vermont, 1992; Berg Visiting Prof. of English, New York University, 1994; Fulbright 50th Anniversary Distinguished Fellow, Brazil, 1996; Senior Fellow, School of Criticism and Theory, Cornell University, 1996–2002; mem. College Language Asscn; English Institute, board of supervisors, 1989–91; MLA, pres., 1992. *Publications:* A Many-Colored Coat of Dreams: The Poetry of Countee Cullen, 1974; The Journey Back: Issues in Black Literature and Criticism, 1980; Blues, Ideology, and Afro-American Literature: A Vernacular Theory, 1984; Modernism and Harlem Renaissance, 1987; Afro-American Poetics: Revisions of Harlem and the Black Aesthetic, 1988; Workings of the Spirit: A Poetics of Afro-American Women's Writing, 1991; Black Studies, Rap, and the Academy, 1993. Poetry: No Matter Where You Travel, You Still Be Black, 1979; Spirit Run, 1982; Blues Journeys Home, 1985. Editor: various books. Contributions: scholarly books and journals. *Honours:* Alumni Award for Distinguished Achievement in Literature and the Humanities, Howard University, 1985; Distinguished Writer of the Year Award, Middle Atlantic Writers Asscn, 1986; Creative Scholarship Award, College Language Asscn of America, 1988; Pennsylvania Governor's Award for Excellence in the Humanities, 1990; several hon. doctorates. *Address:* c/o Center for the Study of Black Literature and Culture, University of Pennsylvania, Philadelphia, PA 19104, USA.

BAKER, Kenneth (Wilfred), (Lord Baker of Dorking); Politician and Writer; b. 3 Nov. 1934, Newport, Wales; m. Mary Elizabeth Gray-Muir, 1963, one s. two d. *Education:* Magdalen College, Oxford. *Career:* MP, Conservative Party, Acton, 1968–70, St Marylebone, 1970–83, Mole Valley, 1983–97; Minister of State and Minister for Information Technology, 1981–84; Secretary of State for the Environment, 1985–86, and for Education and Science, 1986–89; Chancellor, Duchy of Lancaster, and Chair., Conservative Party, 1989–90; Sec. of State for the Home Dept, 1990–92. *Publications:* I Have No Gun But I Can Spit, 1980; London Lines (ed.), 1982; The Faber Book of English Parodies (ed.), 1990; The Faber Book of Conservatism (ed.), 1993; The Turbulent Years: My Life in Politics, 1993; The Prime Ministers: An Irreverent Political History in Cartoons, 1995; The Kings and Queens: An Irreverent History of the British Monarchy, 1995; The Faber Book of War Poetry (ed.), 1996; Children's English History in Verse (ed.), 2000; The Faber Book of Landscape Poetry (ed.), 2000. *Honours:* Companion of Honour, 1992; Life Peer, 1997. *Address:* c/o House of Lords, Westminster, London SW1A 0PW, England. *Telephone:* (20) 7219-3000.

BAKER, Margaret Joyce; writer; b. 21 May 1918, Reading, Berkshire, England. *Education:* King's College, London. *Publications:* The Fighting Cocks, 1949; Four Farthings and a Thimble, 1950; A Castle and Sixpence, 1951; The Family That Grew and Grew, 1952; Lions in the Potting Shed, 1954; The Wonderful Wellington Boots, 1955; Anna Sewell and Black Beauty, 1956; The Birds of Thimblepins, 1960; Homer in Orbit, 1961; The Cats of Honeytown, 1962; Castaway Christmas, 1963; Cut off from Crumpets, 1964; The Shoe Shop Bears, 1964; Home from the Hill, 1968; Snail's Place, 1970; The Last Straw, 1971; Boots and the Ginger Bears, 1972; The Sand Bird, 1973; Lock, Stock and Barrel, 1974; Sand in Our Shoes, 1976; The Gift Horse, 1982; Catch as Catch Can, 1983; Beware of the Gnomes, 1985; The Waiting Room Doll, 1986; Fresh Fields for Daisy, 1987. *Address:* Prickets, Old Cleeve, Nr Minehead, Somerset TA24 6HW, England.

BAKER, Maureen; Prof. of Sociology and Writer; b. 9 March 1948, Toronto, ON, Canada; m. David J. Tippin, 22 July 1983. *Education:* BA, Psychology and Sociology, 1970, MA, Sociology, 1972, University of Toronto; PhD, Sociology, University of Alberta, 1975. *Career:* Asst Prof., Dept of Sociology and Postdoctoral Fellow, Faculty of Social Work, University of Toronto, 1978–83; Consultant, Canadian Advisory Council on the Status of Women, Ottawa, 1983–84; Senior Research Officer, Political and Social Affairs Division, Parliament of Canada, 1984–90; Prof. in Social Work, McGill University, Montréal, Canada, 1990–97; Visiting Scholar, University of New South Wales, 1997; Visiting Fellow, Australian Institute for Family Studies, Melbourne, 1997, University of Bristol, School for Policy Studies, 1998, Univ. of Bath, School for Social and Policy Studies, 2002; Prof., Sociology Dept, 1998–, Head of Dept, 1998–2001, 2003–, University of Auckland, New Zealand; mem. Australian Sociology Asscn; Canadian Sociology and Anthropology Asscn; Sociological Asscn for Aotearoa/New Zealand. *Publications:* Families: Changing Trends in Canada, 1984; What will Tomorrow Bring?, 1985; Aging in Canadian Society, 1988; Families in Canadian Society, 1989; Canada's Changing Families: Challenges to Public Policy, 1994; Canadian Family Policies: Cross-National Comparisons, 1995; Poverty, Social Assistance and the Employability of Mothers: Restructuring Welfare States (with D. Tippin), 1999; Families, Labour and Love, 2001. Contributions: scholarly books and journals. *Honours:* numerous research grants. *Address:* Dept of Sociology, University of Auckland, Auckland, New Zealand. *E-mail:* ma.baker@auckland.ac.nz.

BAKER, Nicholson; American writer; b. 7 Jan. 1957, Rochester, NY; m. Margaret Brentano 1985; two c. *Education:* The School Without Walls, Rochester, Eastman Music School, Rochester, Haverford Coll., Pennsylvania. *Publications:* fiction: The Mezzanine 1990, Room Temperature 1991, Vox 1993, The Fermata 1995, The Everlasting Story of Nory 1999, A Box of Matches 2003, Checkpoint 2004; non-fiction: 'Weeds: A Talk at the Library', in Reclaiming San Francisco: history, politics, culture (anthology) 1998, U and I 1992, The Size of Thoughts 1997, Double Fold 2002; contrib. essays and short stories to periodicals, including New Yorker, Atlantic Monthly, New York Review of Books, Esquire, American Scholar, New York Times, London Review of Books, Literary Outtakes, Little Magazine, StoryQuarterly. *Address:* c/o Alfred Knopf, 1745 Broadway, New York, NY 10019, USA.

BAKER, Paul Raymond; academic; b. 28 Sept. 1927, Everett, Washington, USA; m. Elizabeth Kemp; one c. *Education:* AB, Stanford University, 1949; MA, Columbia University, 1951; PhD, Harvard University, 1960. *Career:* Prof. of History, 1965–, Dir of American Civilization Program, 1972–92, New York University. *Publications:* Views of Society and Manners in America, by Frances Wright D'Arusmont, 1963; The Fortunate Pilgrims: Americans in Italy 1800–1860, 1964; The Atomic Bomb: The Great Decision, 1968; The American Experience, 5 vols, 1976–79; Richard Morris Hunt, 1980; Stanny: The Gilded Life of Stanford White, 1989. Contributions: Around the Square, 1982; Master Builders, 1985; The Architecture of Richard Morris Hunt, 1986. *Honours:* The Turpie Award in American Studies, 1994. *Address:* c/o Dept of History, New York University, 53 Washington Square S, New York, NY 10012 USA.

BAKER, Peter Gorton; writer; b. 28 March 1924, Eastbourne, Sussex, England. *Career:* reporter, Sussex Daily News 1944–45; chief reporter, Kinematograph Weekly 1945–53; Ed., films and filming magazine; British representative on film festival juries at Cannes, Venice, Moscow, Berlin 1953–70. *Television plays:* The Offence, Little Girl Blue, contrib. to many TV drama series. *Publications:* fiction: To Win a Prize on Sunday, Casino, Cruise, Clinic, The Bedroom Sailors, Babel Beach, Jesus. *Address:* Calle Don Juan de Málaga 6, Málaga 29015, Spain.

BAKER, Russell (Wayne); Columnist and Writer; b. 14 Aug. 1925, Loudoun County, Virginia, USA; m. Miriam Emily Nash, 11 March 1950, two s. one d. *Education:* BA, Johns Hopkins University, 1947. *Career:* Staff, Baltimore Sun, 1947–54; Washington Bureau, 1954–62; Columnist, Editorial Page, 1962–, New York Times; mem. American Acad. and Institute of Arts and Letters; American Acad. of Arts and Sciences, fellow. *Publications:* City on the Potomac, 1958; American in Washington, 1961; No Cause for Panic, 1964; All Things Considered, 1965; Our Next President, 1968; Poor Russell's Almanac, 1972; The Upside Down Man, 1977; Home Again, Home Again (with others), 1979; So This is Depravity, 1980; Growing Up, 1982; The Rescue of Miss Yaskell and Other Pipe Dreams, 1983; The Norton Book of Light Verse (ed.), 1986; The Good Times, 1989; There's a Country in My Cellar: The Best of Russell Baker, 1990; Russell Baker's Book of American Humor, 1993. *Honours:* Frank Sullivan Memorial Award, 1976; George Polk Award for Commentary, 1979; Pulitzer Prizes for Distinguished Commentary, 1979, and for Biography, 1983; Elmer Holmes Bobst Prize for Non-Fiction, 1983; Howland Memorial Prize, Yale University, 1989; Fourth Estate Award, National Press Club, 1989; various hon. doctorates. *Address:* c/o New York Times, 229 W 43rd St, New York, NY 10036, USA.

BAKER, William; Prof. and Writer; b. 6 July 1944, Shipston, Warwicks, England; m. 16 Nov. 1969, two d. *Education:* BA, Sussex University, 1963–66; MPhil, University of London, 1966–69; PhD, 1974; MLS, Loughborough, 1986. *Career:* Lecturer; Thurrock Technical College, 1969–71; Ben-Gurion University, 1971–77; University of Kent, 1977–78; West Midlands College, 1978–85; Prof., Pitzer College, Claremont, CA, 1981–82; Housemaster, Clifton College, 1986–89; Prof., 1989–2003, Presidential Research Prof., 2003–, Northern Illinois University; Ed., The Year's Work in English Studies, 2000–; mem. Bibliographical Society of America; American Library Asscn; MLA. *Publications:* Harold Pinter, 1973; George Eliot and Judaism, 1975; The Early History of the London Library, 1992; Literary Theories: A Case Study in Critical Performance, 1996; Nineteenth Century British Book Collectors and Bibliographers, 1997; Twentieth Century British Book Collectors and Bibliographers, 1999; Pre-Nineteenth Century British Book Collectors and Bibliographers, 1999; The Letters of Wilkie Collins, 1999; Twentieth Century Bibliography and Textual Criticism, 2000; A Companion to the Victorian Novel, 2002; Wilkie Collins's Library: A Reconstruction, 2002; George Eliot: A Bibliographical History, 2002. Other: Edns of letters by George Henry Lewes, George Eliot and Wilkie Collins. *Honours:* Ball Brothers Foundation Fellowship, Lilly Library, Indiana University, 1993; Bibliographical Society of America Fellowship, 1994–95; American Philosophical Society Grant, 1997; Outstanding Academic Book of the Year Award, 2000; National Endowment of the Humanities Senior Fellowship, 2002–03; Bibliographical Society of America, council. *Address:* Dept of English, Northern Illinois University, DeKalb, IL, USA.

BAKEWELL, Joan Dawson, CBE, BA; British broadcaster and writer; b. 16 April 1933, Stockport; m. 1st Michael Bakewell 1955 (divorced 1972); one s. one d.; m. 2nd Jack Emery 1975 (divorced 2001). *Education:* Stockport High School for Girls and Newnham Coll., Cambridge. *Career:* TV critic The Times 1978–81, columnist Sunday Times 1988–90; Assoc. Newnham Coll., Cambridge 1980–91, Assoc. Fellow 1984–87; Gov. BFI 1994–99, Chair. 1999–2003. *TV includes:* Sunday Break 1962, Home at 4.30 (writer and producer) 1964, Meeting Point, The Second Sex 1964, Late Night Line Up 1965–72, The Youthful Eye 1968, Moviemakers at the National Film Theatre 1971, Film 72, Film 73, Holiday 74, 75, 76, 77, 78 (series), Reports Action (series) 1976–78, Arts UK: OK? 1980, Heart of the Matter 1988–2000, My Generation 2000, One Foot in the Past 2000, Taboo (series) 2001. *Radio includes:* Artist of the Week 1998–99, The Brains Trust 1999–, Belief 2000. *Publications:* The New Priesthood: British Television Today (jtly) 1970, A Fine and Private Place (jtly) 1977, The Complete Traveller 1977, The Heart of the Heart of the Matter 1996, The Centre of the Bed: An Autobiography 2003; contribs to journals. *Honours:* Dimbleby Award, BAFTA 1995. *Literary Agent:* Knight Ayton Management, 10 Argyll Street, London, W1V 1AB, England.

BAKR, Salwa, BA; novelist; b. June 1949, Cairo, Egypt. *Education:* Ayn Shams Univ., Cairo. *Career:* film and theatre critic for Arabian language publs; concentrated on creative writing 1985–; founder, Hagar journal 1993. *Publications:* Zinat at the President's Funeral 1986, Atiyyah's Shrine 1987, About the Soul that was Spirited Away 1989, The Golden Chariot Does Not Ascend to Heaven 1991, The Wiles of Men and Other Stories (trans. by Denys Johnson Davies) 1992, Monkey Business 1992, Depicting the Nightingale 1993, Rabbits 1994, Inverse Rhythms 1996, Night and Day 1997, El-Bashmouri Vol. 1 1998, Vol. 2 2000, Dream of Years (play) 2002, Streams of Time 2003. *Address:* c/o Atelier of Writers, Karim al-Dawla Street, Talat Harb Square, Cairo, Egypt.

BALABAN, John; Prof. of English, Writer, Poet and Trans; b. 2 Dec. 1943, Philadelphia, Pennsylvania, USA; m. 28 Nov. 1970, one d. *Education:* BA, Pennsylvania State University, 1966; AM, Harvard University, 1967. *Career:* Instructor in Linguistics, University of Can Tho, South Viet Nam, 1967–68; Instructor, 1970–73, Asst Prof., 1973–76, Assoc. Prof., 1976–82, Prof., 1982–92, of English, Pennsylvania State University; Prof. of English, Dir of Creative Writing, University of Miami, 1992–2000; Prof. of English and Poet-in-Residence, North Carolina State University, Raleigh, 2000–; mem. American Literary Trans Asscn, pres., 1994–97; National Endowment for the Arts Trans. Panel, chair, 1993–94. *Publications:* Vietnam Poems, 1970; Vietnamese Folk Poetry (ed. and trans.), 1974; After Our War (poems), 1974; Letters From Across the Sea (poems), 1978; Ca Dao Vietnam: A Bilingual Anthology of Vietnamese Folk Poetry (ed. and trans.), 1980; Blue Mountain (poems), 1982; Coming Down Again (novel), 1985; The Hawk's Tale (children's fiction), 1988; Three Poems, 1989; Vietnam: The Land We Never Knew, 1989; Words for My Daughter (poems), 1991; Remembering Heaven's Face (memoir), 1991; Vietnam: A Traveler's Literary Companion (ed. with Nguyen Qui Duc), 1996; Locusts at the Edge of Summer: New and Selected Poems and Translations, 1997; Spring Essence: The Poetry of Ho Xuan Huong (trans. and ed.), 2000. Contributions: anthologies, books, scholarly journals and periodicals. *Honours:* National Endowment for the Humanities Younger Humanist Fellow, 1971–72; Lamont Selection, Acad. of American Poets, 1974; Fulbright-Hays Senior Lectureship in Romania, 1976–77; Steaua Prize, Romanian Writers Union, 1978; National Endowment for the Arts Fellowships, 1978, 1985; Fulbright Distinguished Visiting Lectureship in Romania, 1979; Vaptsarov Medal, Union of Bulgarian Writers, 1980; National Poetry Series Book Selection, 1990; Pushcart Prize XV, 1990; William Carlos Williams Award, 1997. *Address:* Dept of English, Box 8105, North Carolina State University, Raleigh, NC 27695, USA.

BALABANOV, Alexei O.; Russian film director, producer and scriptwriter; b. 25 Feb. 1959, Sverdlovsk. *Education:* Gorky State Pedagogical Inst. *Career:* asst dir Sverdlovsk Film Studio 1983–87, freelance 1987–. *Films:* Yegor and Nastya (dir) 1989, From the History of Aerostatics in Russia (dir) 1990, Happy Days (dir and scriptwriter) 1991, The Castle (dir and scriptwriter) 1994, Secrets Shared with a Stranger (producer) 1994, The Arrival of a Train (dir and scriptwriter) 1995, Sergey Eisenstein (producer) 1995, The Brother (dir and scriptwriter) 1997, Of Freaks and Men (dir and scriptwriter) 1998, The Brother 2 (dir and scriptwriter) 2000, War (dir and scriptwriter) 2002. *Honours:* Youth Film Festival prize, Kiev 1991, Moscow Film Festival Debut jury prize 1992, Kinotaur Film Festival, Sochi, jury prize 1994 and best movie prize 1997.

BALCOMB, Mary Nelson; Painter-Etcher and Writer; b. 29 April 1928, Ontonagon, Michigan, USA; m. Robert S. Balcomb, 3 July 1948, one s. one d. *Education:* AA, American Acad. of Art, 1948; BFA cum laude, University of New Mexico, 1967; MFA, University of Washington, 1971. *Career:* mem. Authors' Guild. *Publications:* Nicolai Fechin: Russian and American Artist, 1975; Les Perhacs Sculptor, 1978; William F. Reese: American Artist, 1984; Robin-Robin: A Journal, 1995; Sergei-Bongart: Russian American Artist, 2002. Contributions: periodicals. *Address:* PO Box 1922, Silverdale, WA 98383, USA.

BALDACCI, David; Writer; b. 1960, Richmond, VA, USA; m. Michelle Baldacci, two c. *Education:* BA, Virginia Commonwealth University; JD, University of Virginia. *Publications:* Absolute Power, 1996; Total Control, 1997; The Winner, 1997; The Simple Truth, 1998; Saving Faith, 1999; Wish You Well, 2000; Last Man Standing, 2001; Split Second, 2003. Contributions: periodicals. *Honours:* WHSmith Thumping Good Read Award for Fiction, 1997. *Address:* c/o Aaron Priest Literary Agency, 708 Third Ave, New York, NY 10017, USA.

BALL, Brian Neville, BA, MA; writer; b. 19 June 1932, Cheshire, England. *Education:* University of London, University of Sheffield. *Career:* Staff Mem. to Senior Lecturer in English, Doncaster College of Education,

1965–81. *Publications:* over 50 books, including: Basic Linguistics for Secondary Schools, 3 vols, 1966–67; Lay Down Your Wife for Another, 1971; Night of the Robots (in the USA as The Regiments of Night), 1972; The Venomous Serpent (in the USA as The Night Creature), 1974; Witchfinder: The Mark of the Beast, 1976; Witchfinder: The Evil at Monteine, 1977; The Witch in Our Attic, 1979; The Baker Street Boys, 1983; Frog Island Summer, 1987; Magic on the Tide, 1995. Contributions: anthologies, newspapers, radio, and television. *Address:* c/o Hamish Hamilton Ltd, 27 Wrights Lane, London W8 5TZ, England.

BALLANTYNE, Sheila; Writer and Teacher; b. 26 July 1936, Seattle, Washington, USA; m. Philip Speilman, 22 Dec. 1963, one s. one d. *Education:* BA, Mills College. *Career:* Dominican College, 1983; Mills College, 1984–97; Bay Area Writers Workshop, 1988, 1989; mem. Authors' Guild; National Writers Union; PEN. *Publications:* Norma Jean the Termite Queen, 1975; Imaginary Crimes, 1982; Life on Earth, 1988. Contributions: New Yorker; American Review; Prize Stories: O. Henry Awards; Short Story International; Aphra. *Honours:* O. Henry Award; MacDowell Colony Fellowship; Guggenheim Fellowship; National Women's Political Caucus Distinguished Achievement Award. *Address:* 2 Encina Pl., Berkeley, CA 94705, USA.

BALLARD, James Graham; British novelist and writer; b. 15 Nov. 1930, Shanghai, China; m. Helen Mary Mathews 1954 (died 1964); one s. two d. *Education:* King's College, Cambridge. *Publications:* The Drowned World, 1963; The Terminal Beach, 1964; The Drought, 1965; The Crystal World, 1966; The Disaster Area, 1967; Crash, 1973; Vermilion Sands, 1973; Four-Dimensional Nightmare, 1974; Concrete Island, 1974; High Rise, 1975; Low Flying Aircraft, 1976; The Unlimited Dream Company, 1979; Myths of the Near Future, 1982; Empire of the Sun, 1984; The Voices of Time, 1985; The Venus Hunters, 1986; The Day of Forever, 1986; The Day of Creation, 1987; Running Wild, 1988; War Forever, 1990; The Kindness of Women, 1991; Rushing to Paradise, 1994; Cocaine Nights, 1996; Super-Cannes, 2000; The Atrocity Exhibition, 2000; The Complete Short Stories, 2001; Millennium People, 2003. *Honours:* Guardian Fiction Prize, 1984; James Tait Black Memorial Prize, 1984. *Address:* 36 Old Charlton Road, Shepperton, Middlesex, England.

BALLEM, John Bishop; Lawyer, Novelist and Poet; b. 2 Feb. 1925, New Glasgow, NS, Canada; m. Grace Louise Flavelle 31 Aug. 1951; two s. one d. *Education:* BA, 1946, MA, 1948, LLB, 1949, Dalhousie Univ.; LLM, Harvard Univ., 1950. *Career:* of counsel: Gowling Lafleur Henderson LLP; mem. Crime Writers of Canada; International Bar Asscn; Law Society of Alberta; Writers' Guild of Alberta; Writers' Union of Canada; Canadian Bar Asscn. *Publications:* Fiction: The Devil's Lighter, 1973; The Dirty Scenario, 1974; The Judas Conspiracy, 1976, new edn as Alberta Alone, 1981; The Moon Pool, 1978; Sacrifice Play, 1981; The Marigot Run, 1983; The Oilpatch Empire, 1985; Death Spiral, 1989; The Barons, 1991; Manchineel, 2000; Murder as a Fine Art, 2001; Sonata, 2004. Poetry: Lovers and Friends, 2000. Non-Fiction: The Oil and Gas Lease in Canada, 1973. Contributions: numerous short stories; legal articles in various learned journals. *Honours:* Queen's Counsel, 1966; Hon. Doctor of Laws, Univ. of Calgary, 1993. *Address:* 700 Second Street SW, Suite 1400, Calgary, AB T2P 4V5, Canada.

BALLENTINE, Lee (Kenney); Poet, Writer, Publisher and Ed.; b. 4 Sept. 1954, Teaneck, NJ, USA; m. Jennifer Moore, 20 Aug. 1983, one s. *Education:* Harvey Mudd College, 1972–73; University of California at San Diego, 1973; New Mexico State University, 1974; University of Colorado, 1974–75; BSc, SUNY at Albany, 1976; Postgraduate Studies, University of Colorado, 1976–77, University of California at Berkeley, 1977–78. *Career:* Publisher, Ocean View Press, 1981–89, Ocean View Books, 1989–; Co-founder and Pres., Ocean View Technical Publications, 1989–91, Professional Book Center, 1991–; mem. American Book Producers Asscn; Bookbuilders West; PEN West; Rocky Mountain Book Publishers Asscn; Science Fiction Poetry Asscn; SFWA; United States Chess Federation. *Publications:* Directorial Information, 1981; Basements in the Music Box (poems), 1986; Poly: New Speculative Writing (ed.), 1989; Dream Protocois (poems), 1992; Phase Language (poems), 1995. Contributions: anthologies and periodicals. *Honours:* Readercon Small Press Book Award, 1989; Best Scholarly-Limited Book, 1989, Certificate of Merit, 1995, Bookbuilders West; Anatomy of Wonder Best Book, 1995. *Address:* Professional Book Center, PO Box 9249, Denver, CO 80209, USA. *E-mail:* lee@probook.net.

BALMER, Josephine; British poet and translator. *Publications:* Sappho: Poems and Fragments 1992, Classical Women Poets 1995, Catallus: Poems of Love and Hate 2004, Chasing Catullus 2004; contrib. to Spare Rib, Women's Review, The Guardian, Independent on Sunday, The Observer. *Literary Agent:* c/o Bloodaxe Books Ltd, Highgreen, Tarset, Northumberland NE48 1RP, England. *Telephone:* (1434) 240500. *Fax:* (1434) 240505. *Website:* www.bloodaxebooks.com.

BALOGH, Mary; Writer and Teacher; b. 24 March 1944, Swansea, Wales; m. Robert Balogh, 1969, one s. two d. *Education:* BA, University of Wales, 1965. *Career:* English Teacher, Kipling High School, Saskatchewan, Canada, 1967–82; Principal, English Teacher, Windthorst High School, Saskatchewan, 1982–88; mem. Saskatchewan Writers' Guild. *Publications:* Fiction: A Masked Deception, 1985; The Double Wager, 1985; Red Rose, 1985; A Chance Encounter, 1986; The Trysting Place, 1986; The First Snowdrop, 1987; The Wood Nymph, 1987; The Constant Heart, 1987; Gentle Conquest, 1987; Secrets of the Heart, 1988; The Ungrateful Governess, 1988; An Unacceptable Offer, 1988; Daring Masquerade, 1989; A Gift of Daisies, 1989; The Obedient Bride, 1989; Lady with a Black Umbrella, 1989; The Gilded Web, 1989; A Promise of Spring, 1990; Web of Love, 1990; The Incurable Matchmakers, 1990; Devil's Web, 1990; An Unlikely Duchess, 1990; A Certain Magic, 1991; Snow Angel, 1991; The Secret Pearl, 1991; The Ideal Wife, 1991; Christmas Beau, 1991; The Counterfeit Betrothal, 1992; The Notorious Rake, 1992; A Christmas Promise, 1992; Beyond the Sunrise, 1992; A Precious Jewel, 1993; Deceived, 1993; Courting Julia, 1993; Dancing with Clara, 1994; Tangled, 1994; Tempting Harriet, 1994; Dark Angel, 1994; A Christmas Belle, 1994; Longing, 1994; Lord Carew's Bride, 1995; Heartless, 1995; The Famous Heroine, 1996; Truly, 1996; The Plumed Bonnet, 1996; Indiscreet, 1997; Temporary Wife, 1997; Silent Melody, 1997; A Christmas Bride, 1997; Unforgiven, 1998; Thief of Dreams, 1998; Irresistible, 1998; The Last Waltz, 1998; One Night for Love, 1999; More than a Mistress, 2000; No Man's Mistress, 2001. Novellas in collections including A Regency Christmas series; Short stories: Full Moon Magic, 1992; Tokens of Love, 1993; Rakes and Rogues, 1993; Moonlight Lovers, 1993. *Honours:* Best New Regency Author Award, 1985; Best Regency Author Award, 1988; Career Achievement Award, 1989, Best Regency Novel Award, 1991, Best Regency Romance Award, 1992, Career Achievement for Short Stories Award, 1993, Romantic Times; Northern Lights Best Historical Novella Award, 1996. *Literary Agent:* Maria Carvainis, 1350 Avenue of the Americas, New York, NY 10019, USA. *Address:* Box 571, Kipling, Saskatchewan, Canada S0G 2S0.

BAMBÁSEK, Ladislav (see Vladislav, Jan).

BAMBER, Juliette Madelaine; Poet, Writer, Occupational Therapist and Counsellor; b. 21 Aug. 1930, Tidworth, England; m. Donald Liddle 1957 (divorced 1995); two s. *Education:* Graduated, Psychology, Birkbeck College, 1960. *Publications:* Breathing Space, 1991; On the Edge, 1993; Altered States, 1996; Touch Paper, 1996; The Ring of Words, 1996; The Wasting Game, 1997; The Long Pale Corridor, 1998; Flying Bird, 2000. *Honours:* Blue Nose Poet of the Year, 1998; Houseman Prize, 2000. *Address:* 9 Western Rd, East Finchley, London N2 9JB, England.

BANCROFT, Anne; Author; b. 17 April 1923, London, England; two s. two d. *Education:* Sidney Webb Teacher's Training College, 1961–63. *Career:* mem. Society of Authors; Society of Women Writers and Journalists. *Publications:* Religions of the East, 1974; Twentieth Century Mystics and Sages, 1976, republished 1989; Zen: Direct Pointing to Reality, 1980; The Luminous Vision, 1980, republished 1989; Six Medieval Mystics, 1981; Chinese New Year, 1984; Festivals of the Buddha, 1984; The Buddhist World, 1984; The New Religious World, 1985; Origins of the Sacred: The Spiritual Way in Western Tradition, 1987; Weavers of Wisdom, 1989. *Address:* 1 Grange Villas, The Street, Charmouth, Bridport, Dorset DT6 6QQ, England.

BANDELE, Biyi; Playwright and Novelist; b. 13 Oct. 1967, Kafanchan, Nigeria. *Education:* Dramatic Arts, Obafemi Awolowo University, Ile-Ife, 1990. *Career:* Assoc. Writer, Royal Court Theatre, London, 1992–; Writer-in-Residence, Talawa Theatre Company, 1994–95; Resident Dramatist, Royal National Theatre Studio, 1996; mem. Society of Authors; Writers Guild; PEN. *Publications:* Fiction: The Man Who Came in from the Back of Beyond, 1991; The Sympathetic Undertaker and Other Dreams, 1991. Plays: Rain, produced, 1991; Marching for Fausa, produced, 1993; Two Horsemen, produced, 1994; Resurrections, produced, 1994; Death Catches the Hunter, produced, 1995; Things Fall Apart, produced, 1997; Thieves Like Us, produced, 1998. Screenplays: Not Even God Is Wise Enough, 1993; Bad Boy Blues, 1996. *Honours:* Award, International Student Playscript Competition; Arts Council Writers Bursary; Award, London New Play Festival, 1994. *Literary Agent:* The Agency, 24 Pottery Lane, Holland Park, London W11 4LZ, England.

BANFIELD, Stephen David; professor of music and writer; b. 15 July 1951, Dulwich, London, England. *Education:* BA, Clare College, Cambridge, 1972; Harvard Univ., 1975–76; DPhil, St John's College, Oxford, 1980. *Career:* Lecturer, 1978–88, Senior Lecturer, 1988–92, Univ. of Keele; Elgar Prof. of Music, 1992–2003, Head, School of Performance Studies, 1992–97, and Dept of Music, 1996–98, Univ. of Birmingham; Visiting Prof. of Musicology, Univ. of Minnesota, 1998; Stanley Hugh Badock Prof. of Music, Univ. of Bristol, 2003–; mem. American Musicological Society; Royal Musical Asscn; FRSA; Society for American Music; Kurt Weill Foundation; Royal College of Organists, fellow. *Publications:* Sensibility and English Song, 1985; Sondheim's Broadway Musicals, 1993; The Blackwell History of Music in Britain, Vol. VI: The Twentieth Century (ed.), 1995; Gerald Finzi, 1997. Contributions: scholarly books and journals. *Honours:* First Kurt Weill Prize, USA; Irving Lowens Award, USA, 1995. *Address:* Dept of Music, Victoria Rooms, Queens Road, Bristol BS8 1SA, England.

BANKS, Brian Robert; Teacher, Writer and Poet; b. 4 Oct. 1956, Carshalton, Surrey, England; one s. two d. *Education:* Westminster College; Middlesex Polytechnic. *Career:* mem. Société de J-K Huysmans, Paris; 1890s Society. *Publications:* The Image of J-K Huysmans, 1990; Phantoms of the Belle Epoque, 1993; Atmosphere and Attitudes, 1993; Life and Work of Bruno Schulz, 2000. Contributions: Books and journals. *Address:* c/o 4 Meretune Court, Martin Way, Morden, Surrey SM4 4AN, England.

BANKS, Iain Menzies, BA; British writer; b. 16 Feb. 1954, Fife, Scotland. *Education:* Univ. of Stirling. *Career:* worked as technician, British Steel 1976, IBM, Greenock 1978; writes fiction as Iain Banks and science fiction as Iain M. Banks. *Publications:* as Iain Banks: The Wasp Factory 1984, Walking on Glass 1985, The Bridge 1986, Espedair Street 1987, Canal Dreams 1989, The Crow Road 1992, Complicity 1993, Whit 1995, A Song of Stone 1997, The Business 1999, Look to Windward 2000, Dead Air 2002, Raw Spirit: In Search of the Perfect Dram (non-fiction) 2003; as Iain M. Banks: Consider Phlebas 1987, The Player of Games 1988, The State of the Art 1989, Use of Weapons 1990, Against a Dark Background 1993, Feersum Endjinn 1994, Excession 1996, Inversions 1998, The Algebraist 2004. *Honours:* BSFA Best Novel 1997. *Address:* c/o Publicity Department, Time Warner Books UK, Brettenham House, Lancaster Place, London, WC2E 7EN, England. *Telephone:* (20) 7911-8000. *Fax:* (20) 7911-8100. *E-mail:* mail@iainbanks.net. *Website:* www.iainbanks.net.

BANKS, Lynne Reid; Writer, Journalist and Playwright; b. 31 July 1929, London, England; m. Chaim Stephenson, 1965, three s. *Education:* Italia Conti Stage School, 1946; RADA, 1947–49. *Career:* Actress, 1949–54; Reporter and Scriptwriter, Independent Television News, London, 1955–62; English Teacher, Western Galilee, Israel, 1963–71; Writer, Lecturer, Journalist, 1971–; mem. Society of Authors; PEN. *Publications:* The L-Shaped Room, 1960; An End to Running, 1962; Children at the Gate, 1968; The Backward Shadow, 1970; Two is Lonely, 1974; Dark Quartet: The Story of the Brontës, 1976; Path to the Silent Country: Charlotte Brontë's Years of Fame, 1977; Defy the Wilderness, 1981; Torn Country: An Oral History of the Israeli War of Independence, 1982; The Warning Bell, 1984; Casualities, 1986; Fair Exchange, 1998. Children's Fiction: One More River, 1973; Sarah and After: The Matriarchs, 1975; The Adventures of King Midas, 1976; The Farthest-Away Mountain, 1977; My Darling Villain, 1977; I, Houdini: The Autobiography of a Self-Educated Hamster, 1978; Letters to My Israeli Sons: The Story of Jewish Survival, 1979; The Indian in the Cupboard, 1980; The Writing on the Wall, 1981; Maura's Angel, 1984; The Fairy Rebel, 1985; Return of the Indian, 1985; Melusine: A Mystery, 1988; The Secret of the Indian, 1988; The Magic Hare, 1992; The Mystery of the Cupboard, 1993; Broken Bridge, 1994; Harry the Poisonous Centipede, 1996; Angela and Diabola; Moses in Egypt, 1998; The Key to the Indian, 1999; Alice-by-Accident, 2000; Harry the Poisonous Centipede's Big Adventure, 2000; The Dungeon, 2002. Plays: It Never Rains, 1954; All in a Row, 1956; The Killer Dies Twice, 1956; Already, It's Tomorrow, 1962; The Wednesday Caller (television), 1963; The Last Word on Julie (television), 1964; The Gift, 1965; The Stowaway (radio), 1967; The Eye of the Beholder (television), 1977; The Real Thing, 1977; Lame Duck (radio), 1978; Purely from Principal (radio), 1985; The Travels of Yoshi and the Tea-Kettle (children), 1993. Anthologies: Is Anyone There?, 1978; Women Writing 3, 1980; A Treasury of Jewish Stories, 1996; Ballet Stories; Rolf Harris's Favourite Animal Stories, 2000. *Honours:* Best Books for Young Adults Award, American Library Asscn, 1977; Outstanding Books of the Year Award, 1981, Notable Books Award, 1986, New York Times; Children's Books of the Year Award, 1987; Rebecca Caudill Young Reader's Books Award, Illinois Asscn for Media in Education, 1988; Smarties Silver Medal 1998. *Address:* c/o Sheila Watson, Capo di Monte, Windmill Hill, London NW3 6RJ, England.

BANKS, Russell, BA; novelist; b. 28 March 1940, Newton, Massachusetts, USA; four d. *Education:* University of North Carolina. *Career:* mem. American Acad. of Arts and Letters; PEN American Centre; Co-ordinating Council of Literary Magazines. *Publications:* Searching for Survivors, 1975; Family Life, 1975; Hamilton Stark, 1978; The New World, 1978; The Book of Jamaica, 1980; Trailerpark, 1982; The Relation of My Imprisonment, 1984; Continental Drift, 1985; Success Stories, 1986; Affliction, 1989; Sweet Hereafter, 1992; Rule of the Bone, 1995; Cloudsplitter, 1998; The Angel on the Roof, 2000. Contributions: New York Times Book Review; Washington Post; American Review; Vanity Fair; Antaeus; Partisan Review; New England Review; Fiction International; Boston Globe Magazine. *Honours:* Best American Short Stories, 1971, 1985; Fels Award, fiction, 1974; Prize story, O. Henry Awards, 1975; St Lawrence Award, fiction, 1976; Guggenheim Fellowship, 1976; National Endowment for the Arts Fellowships, 1977, 1983; John dos Passos Award, 1986; Award, American Acad. of Arts and Letters, 1986. *Literary Agent:* Steven Barclay Agency, 12 Western Avenue, Petaluma, CA 94952, USA. *Telephone:* (707) 773-0654. *Fax:* (707) 778-1868. *Website:* www.barclayagency.com.

BANNERMAN, Mark (see Lewing, Anthony Charles).

BANNISTER, Jo; Writer; b. 31 July 1951, Rochdale, England. *Education:* Birmingham; Nottingham; Bangor, Northern Ireland. *Career:* mem. Society of Authors; CWA. *Publications:* The Matrix, 1981; The Winter Plain, 1982; A Cactus Garden, 1983; Striving With Gods, 1984; Mosaic, 1987; The Mason Codex, 1988; Gilgamesh, 1989; The Going Down of the Sun, 1989; Shards, 1990, revised edn as Critical Angle, 1999; Death and Other Lovers, 1991; A Bleeding of Innocents, 1993; Sins of the Heart (US edn as Charisma), 1994; A Taste for Burning, 1995; The Lazarus Hotel, 1996; No Birds Sing, 1996; The Primrose Convention, 1997; Broken Lines, 1999; The Hireling's Tale, 1999; Changelings, 2000; The Primrose Switchback, 2000; Echoes of Lies, 2001; True Witness, 2002; Reflections, 2003. *Honours:* Catherine Pakenham Award, 1972; British Press Award, 1976; Northern Ireland Press Award, 1982. *Address:* 12 Ballybuttle Cottages, Abbey Rd, Millisle, Co Down BT22 2EQ, Northern Ireland. *Telephone:* (2891) 861247.

BANTOCK, Gavin Marcus August; Poet and Writer; b. 4 July 1939, Barnt Green, Worcestershire, England. *Education:* BA, 1963, Diploma of Education, 1964, MA, 1968, University of Oxford. *Career:* Educator in British schools, 1964–69; Faculty, Dept of English, Reitaku University, Chiba-ken, Japan, 1969–94. *Publications:* Christ: A Poem in Twenty-Six Parts, 1965; Juggernaut: Selected Poems, 1968; A New Thing Breathing, 1969; Anhaga, 1970; Gleeman, 1972; Eirenikon, 1973; Isles, 1974; Dragons, 1979; Just Think of It, 2002; Floating World, 2002; SeaManShip, 2003. Other: essay collections. Contributions: anthologies and numerous magazines. *Honours:* Richard Hillary Memorial Prize, 1964; Alice-Hunt-Bartlett Prize, 1966; Eric Gregory Award, 1969; Arvon Foundation Prize, 1998; Cardiff International Poetry Prize, 1999. *Address:* c/o Peter Jay, Anvil Press Poetry, 69 King George Street, London, SE10 8PX, England. *E-mail:* gb@gol.com. *Website:* homepage.mac.com/gavinbantock.

BANVILLE, John; Irish author; b. 8 Dec. 1945, Wexford; m. Janet Dunham; two s. *Education:* St Peter's Coll., Wexford. *Career:* fmrly night copy ed. The Irish Times, Literary Ed. 1988–99, Chief Literary Critic and Assoc. Literary Ed. 1999–2002. *Film script:* The Last September 1998. *Plays:* The Broken Jug (after Kleist) 1994, God's Gift (after Kleist's "Amphitryon") 2000. *Publications:* 13 novels including: Nightspawn 1971, Birchwood 1973, Dr Copernicus 1976, Kepler 1983, The Newton Letter 1985, Mefisto 1987, The Book of Evidence (Guinness Peat Aviation Prize 1989) 1989, Ghosts 1993, Athena 1995, The Untouchable 1996, Eclipse 2000, Shroud 2003; non-fiction: Prague Pictures: Portraits of a City 2003; contributions: New York Review of Books, Irish Times, New Republic. *Honours:* Lannan Foundation Award 1998. *Literary Agent:* Gillon Aitken Associates Ltd, 18–21 Cavaye Place, London, SW10 9PT, England. *Telephone:* (20) 7373-8672. *Fax:* (20) 7373-6002.

BAPTISTE, Eric; French radio executive. *Education:* École nationale d'administration. *Career:* Gen. Man. of Radio France Int. 1990–95; Vice-Pres. Radio Néo; Sec.-Gen. of Int. Confederation of Societies of Authors and Composers (CISAC) 1999–; chair. of govt think tank on digital convergence. *Publications:* Rapport sur les relations entre les diffuseurs télévisuels et les producteurs cinématographiques et audiovisuals 1989, L'infosphère: stratégies des medias et role de l'État 2000. *Address:* c/o CISAC, 20–26 blvd du Parc, 92200, Neuilly-sur-Seine, France. *Telephone:* 1-55-62-08-50. *Fax:* 1-55-62-08-60. *E-mail:* cisac@cisac.org. *Website:* www.cisac.org.

BARAKA, Amiri (see Jones, (Everett) Leroi).

BARAŃCZAK, Stanisław, PhD; Polish poet and literary critic; b. 13 Nov. 1946, Poznań; m.; one s. one d. *Education:* Adam Mickiewicz Univ., Poznań. *Career:* Asst Lecturer Prof. Adam Mickiewicz Univ. 1969–80; in the USA 1981–; Prof. of Slavic Languages and Literatures Harvard Univ., 1981–84, Alfred Jurzykowski Prof. 1984–; Co-Ed. Zeszyty Literackie 1982–; Assoc. Ed. The Polish Review 1986–87, Ed.-in-Chief 1987–90; mem. American Asscn for Polish-Jewish Studies, American Asscn for Advancement of Slavic Studies, PEN Polish Center, Polish Inst. of Arts and Sciences in America, Polish Writers' Asscn, Union of Polish Authors, Union of Polish Writers Abroad. *Publications:* poetry collections: Korekta twarzy (Face Correction) 1968, Jednym tchem (In One breath) 1970, Dziennik poranny (Morning Diary) 1972, Sztuczne oddychanie (Breathing Underwater) 1974, Ja wiem, że to niesłuszne (I know That It's Wrong) 1977, Atlantyda (Atlantis) 1986, Widokówka z tego świata (A Postcard from This World) 1988, The Weight of the Body 1989, Podróż zimowa (Winter Journey) 1994, Chirurgiczna precyzja (Surgical Precision) 1999; criticism includes: Ironia i Harmonia (Irony and Harmony) 1973, Etyka i poetyka (Ethics and Poetry) 1979; Przed i po (Before and After) 1988, Tablica z Macondo (Board from Macondo) 1990, Ocalone w tłumaczeniu (Saved in Translation 1992), Fioletowa krowa (Violet Cow) 1993; essays: Breathing Under Water and Other East European Essays 1990, Poezja i duch uogólnienia (Poetry and the Spirit of Generalization); numerous trans of English, American and Russian poetry and of William Shakespeare. *Honours:* Chivalric Cross of the Order of Polonia Restituta 1991; Alfred Jurzykowski Foundation Literary Award 1980, Guggenheim Fellowship 1989, Terrence Des Pres Poetry Prize 1989, Special Diploma for Lifetime Achievement in Promoting Polish Culture Abroad, Polish Minister of Foreign Affairs 1993, Co-Winner PEN Best Trans. Award 1996. *Address:* 8 Broad Dale, Newton Wille, MA 02160, USA.

BARANSKAIA, Natalia Vladimirovna; Russian writer; b. 31 Dec. 1908; m. (died 1943); two d. *Education:* Moscow State Univ. *Career:* publishing and museum work, Pushkin museum –1966; contrib. to Novyi mir (New World) 1968–. *Publications include:* novels: Den' pominoveniia (trans. as Day of Remembrance) 1989, Stranstvie bezdomnykh: Zhizneopisanie 1999; short story collections: Otritsatel'naia Zhizel (trans. as A Negative Gazelle) 1977, Zhenshchina s zontikom (trans. as Woman with an Umbrella) 1981, Portret podarennyi drugu (trans. as Portrait Presented to a Friend) 1982, A Week Like Any Other (in trans.) 1989. *Address:* c/o Seal Press, 300 Queen Anne Avenue N, #375, Seattle, WA 98109, USA. *Website:* www.sealpress.com.

BARBALET, Margaret, MA; writer; b. Adelaide, SA, Australia; m. Jack Barbalet 1970 (divorced 1989); three s. *Education:* Adelaide University.

Career: Historian, Adelaide Children's Hospital, 1973–74; Research Officer, Adelaide City Council, 1973–75; Research Consultant, Commonwealth Schools Commission, 1984–88; Staff, Dept of Foreign Affairs and Trade, Australia, 1990–; mem. Australian Society of Authors. *Publications:* Far From a Low Gutter Girl: The Forgotten World of State Wards, 1983; Blood in the Rain (novel), 1986; Steel Beach (novel), 1988; The Wolf (children's book), 1991; Lady, Baby, Gypsy, Queen (novel), 1992; The Presence of Angels (novel), 2001; Reggie, Queen of the Street (children's book), 2003. *Honours:* Literature Grant, 1985; New Writers Fellowship, 1986; H. C. Coombs Creative Arts Fellow, ANU, 1998; ACT Literature Fellowship, 1999; Harold White Fellow, National Library of Australia, 2001; Writing Fellow, 2001; Literature Grant, 2002. *Address:* c/o Penguin Books, PO Box 701, Hawthorn, Vic. 3122, Australia.

BARBER, Elizabeth Jane; Prof. of Linguistics and Archaeology and Writer; b. 2 Dec. 1940, Pasadena, CA, USA; m. Paul Thomas Barber, 14 June 1965. *Education:* BA, Bryn Mawr College, 1962; PhD, Yale University, 1968. *Career:* Research Assoc., Princeton University, 1968–69; Asst Prof., Assoc. Prof., Full Prof. of Linguistics and Archaeology, Occidental College, 1970–. *Publications:* Archaeological Decipherment, 1974; Prehistoric Textiles, 1991; Women's Work: The First 20,000 Years, 1994; The Mummies of Ürümchi, 1998. Contributions: scholarly books and journals. *Honours:* Costume Society of America's Davenport Book Prize; American Historical Asscn, Breasted Prize in Ancient History. *Address:* Language Dept, Occidental College, Los Angeles, CA 90041, USA.

BARBER, Richard William; publisher and author; b. 30 Oct. 1941, Dunmow, Essex, England; m. Helen Tolson 1970; one s. one d. *Education:* BA, MA, 1967, PhD, 1982, Corpus Christi College, Cambridge. *Career:* mem. RSL; Royal Historical Society; Society of Antiquaries. *Publications:* Arthur of Albion, 1961; The Knight and Chivalry, 1972; Edward Prince of Wales and Aquitaine, 1976; Companion Guide to South West France, 1977; Tournaments, 1978; The Arthurian Legends, 1979; The Penguin Guide to Medieval Europe, 1984; Fuller's Worthies, 1987; The Worlds of John Aubrey, 1988; Pilgrimages, 1991; Myths and Legends of the British Isles, 1998; Legends of Arthur, 2000; The Holy Grail, 2004. Contributions: Arthurian Literature. *Honours:* Somerset Maugham Award, 1972; Times Higher Educational Supplement Book Award, 1978. *Address:* Stangrove Hall, Alderton, Nr Woodbridge, Suffolk IP12 3BL, England.

BARBET, Pierre (see Avice, Claude Pierre Marie).

BARBOSA, Miguel; Writer, Dramatist, Poet and Painter; b. 22 Nov. 1925, Lisbon, Portugal. *Education:* University of Lisbon. *Career:* mem. Accademia Internazionale Greci-Marino di Lettere, Arti e Scienze; Society of Portuguese Authors. *Publications:* Fiction: Trineu do Morro, 1972; Mulher Mancumba, 1973; A Pileca no Poleiro, 1976; As Confissoes de Um Cacador de Dinossauros, 1981; Esta Louca Profissao de Escritor, 1983; Cartas a Um Fogo-Fatuo, 1985. Poetry: Dans un Cri de Couleurs, 1991; Um Gesto no Rosto da Utopia, 1994; Prima del Verbo, 1995; Mare di Illusioni Naufragate, 1995; Preludio Poético de um Vagabundo da Madrugada, 1996; Mouthfuls of Red Confetti and the Hunt for God's Skull, 1996; O Teu Corpo na Minha Alma, 1996. Other: Plays and short stories. Contributions: various publications. *Honours:* several for art. *Address:* Ave João Crisostomo 91–92, Lisbon 1050, Portugal.

BARBOUR, Douglas (Fleming); Prof. of English, Poet and Writer; b. 21 March 1940, Winnipeg, Manitoba, Canada; m. M. Sharon Nicoll, 21 May 1966. *Education:* BA, Acadia University, 1962; MA, Dalhousie University, 1964; PhD, Queen's University, Kingston, Ontario, 1976. *Career:* Teacher, Alderwood Collegiate Institute, 1968–69; Asst Prof., 1969–77, Assoc. Prof., 1977–82, Prof. of English, 1982–, University of Alberta; mem. Asscn of Canadian University Teachers; League of Canadian Poets, co-chair., 1972–74. *Publications:* Poetry: Land Fall, 1971; A Poem as Long as the Highway, 1971; White, 1972; Song Book, 1973; He and She and, 1974; Visions of My Grandfather, 1977; Shore Lines, 1979; Vision/Sounding, 1980; The Pirates of Pen's Chance (with Stephen Scobie), 1981; The Harbingers, 1984; Visible Visions: Selected Poems, 1984; Canadian Poetry Chronicle, 1985. Other: Worlds Out of Words: The Science Fiction Novels of Samuel R. Delany, 1978; The Maple Laugh Forever: An Anthology of Canadian Comic Poetry (ed. with Stephen Scobie), 1981; Writing Right: New Poetry by Canadian Women (ed. with Marni Stanley), 1982; Tesseracts 2 (ed. with Phyllis Gollieb), 1987; B. P. Nichol and His Works, 1992; Daphne Marlatt and Her Works, 1992; John Newlove and His Works, 1992; Michael Ondaatje, 1993. *Address:* c/o Dept of English, University of Alberta, Edmonton, AB T6G 2E5, Canada.

BARBOUR, Ian Graeme, BD, PhD; American physicist and theologian; b. 5 Oct. 1923, Peking (now Beijing), (People's Republic of) China. *Education:* Swarthmore Coll., Duke Univ., Univ. of Chicago, Yale Univ. *Career:* Asst Prof., Assoc. Prof. of Physics, Kalamazoo Coll. 1949–53; Asst Prof. of Physics, Assoc. Prof. of Religion Carleton Coll., Northfield, Minn.1955–73, Prof. of Religion 1974–86, Winifred and Atherton Bean Prof. of Science, Tech. and Soc. 1981–86, Carleton Prof. Emer. Dept of Religion 1986–; Lilly Visiting Prof. of Science, Theology and Human Values Purdue Univ. 1973–74; Gifford Lecturer Univ. of Aberdeen, Scotland 1989–91; mem. American Acad. of Religion, Soc.for Values in Higher Educ. *Publications:* Christianity and the Scientist 1960, Issues in Science and Religion 1966, Science and Religion: New Perspectives on the Dialogue (ed) 1968, Science and Secularity: The Ethics of Technology 1970, Earth Might Be Fair (ed) 1971, Western Man and Environmental Ethics (ed) 1972, Myths, Models and Paradigms 1974, Finite Resources and the Human Future (ed) 1976, Technology, Environment and Human Values 1980, Energy and American Values (co-author) 1982, Religion in an Age of Science (Gifford Lectures) 1990, Ethics in an Age of Technology 1993, Religion and Science: Historical and Contemporary Issues 1997, When Science Meets Religion 2000, Nature, Human Nature and God 2002; contributions: scientific and religious journals. *Honours:* Ford Faculty Fellowship 1953–54, Harbison Award for Distinguished Teaching, Danforth Foundation 1963–64, Guggenheim Fellowship 1967–68, Fulbright Fellowship 1967–68, ACLS Fellowship 1976–77, Nat. Endowment for the Humanities Fellowship 1976–77, Nat. Humanities Center Fellow 1980–81, American Acad. of Religion Book Award 1993, Templeton Prize for Progress in Religion 1999. *Address:* Carleton College, Northfield, MN 55057, USA. *E-mail:* ibarbour@carleton.edu.

BARER, Burl; Writer; b. 8 Aug. 1947, Walla Walla, WA, USA; m. Britt Johnsen, 2 March 1974, one s. one d. *Education:* University of Washington. *Career:* mem. MWA. *Publications:* Selections from the Holy Quran, 1987; The Saint: A Complete History in Print, Radio, Film and Television, 1993; Man Overboard: The Counterfeit Resurrection of Phil Champagne, 1994; The Saint, 1997; Capture the Saint, 1998. Contributions: Books and periodicals. *Honours:* Edgar Award, 1994.

BARFOOT, Joan, BA; Canadian novelist and journalist; b. 17 May 1946, Owen Sound, Ont. *Education:* University of Western Ont. *Career:* reporter, Religion Ed. Windsor Star 1967–69; feature and news writer Mirror Publications, Toronto 1969–73, Toronto Sunday Sun 1973–75; with London Free Press 1976–79, 1980–94; has taught journalism and creative writing at School of Journalism, Univ. of Western Ont.; Canadian Del. First Int. Feminist Book Fair and Festival, UK 1983; Juror Books in Canada First Novel Award 1987, Gov.-Gen.'s Award for English Language Canadian Fiction 1995, Trillium Literary Award 1996, 1999; mem. Writers' Union of Canada, PEN Canada. *Publications:* Abra 1978, Dancing in the Dark 1982, Duet for Three 1985, Family News 1989, Plain Jane 1992, Charlotte and Claudia Keeping in Touch 1994, Some Things About Flying 1997, Getting Over Edgar 1999, Critical Injuries 2001. *Honours:* Books in Canada First Novel Award 1978, Marian Engel Award 1992. *Address:* 286 Cheapside Street, London, Ont. N6A 2A2, Canada. *E-mail:* jbarfoot@sympatico.ca (Office). *Website:* www3.sympatico.ca/jbarfoot (Office).

BARICCO, Alessandro; Italian writer and playwright; b. 1958, Turin. *Career:* music critic, La Repubblica; cultural correspondent, La Stampa; collaboration with French band, Air, to produce backing music for City 2003. *Plays:* Novecento 1994, Davila Roa 1996, Partita Spagnola 2003. *Publications:* novels: Castelli di rabbia (trans. as Lands of Glass) (Premio Selezione Campiello, Prix Médicis étranger) 1991, Oceano Mare (trans. as Ocean Sea) (Premio Viareggio) 1993, Seta (trans. as Silk) 1996, City 1999, Senza sangue (trans. as Without Blood) 2002; non-fiction: Il Genio in fuga 1988, L'anima di Hegel e le mucche del Wisconsin 1992, Barnum (collection of articles) 1995, Barnum 2 (collection of articles) 1998, Next 2002; contrib. to Il Corriere. *Honours:* several literary prizes. *Address:* c/o Alfred A. Knopf Inc, 299 Park Avenue, New York, NY 10171, USA.

BARICH, Bill; Writer; b. 23 Aug. 1943, Winona, MN, USA. *Education:* BA, Colgate University, 1965. *Career:* Staff Writer, The New Yorker, 1981–94; Adjunct Prof., University of California at Berkeley, 1988–89, 1999–; mem. PEN. *Publications:* Laughing in the Hills, 1980; Travelling Light, 1984; Hard to Be Good, 1987; Big Dreams, 1994; Carson Valley, 1997; Crazy for Rivers, 1999; The Sporting Life, 1999. Contributions: periodicals. *Honours:* Guggenheim Fellowship, 1985; Marin County Arts Council Fellow, 1995; San Francisco Public Library Literary Laureate, 1998. *Address:* c/o International Creative Management, 40 W 57th St, New York, NY 10019, USA.

BARKER, Clive; writer, dramatist and artist; b. 1952, Liverpool, England. *Education:* University of Liverpool. *Publications:* Fiction: The Damnation Game, 1985; The Inhuman Condition, 1985; Weaveworld, 1987; Cabal, 1988; The Great and Secret Show, 1989; Imajica, 1991; The Hellbound Heart, 1991; The Thief of Always, 1992; Emerville, 1994; Sacrament, 1996; Galilee, 1998; The Essential Clive Barker, 1999; Coldheart Canyon: A Hollywood Ghost Story, 2001; Abarat, 2002; Abarat II: Days of Magic, Nights of War 2004. Plays: Forms of Heaven: Three Plays, 1996; Incarnations: Three Plays, 1998; screenplays. *Address:* c/o HarperCollins, 10 E 53rd Street, New York, NY 10022, USA. *Website:* www.clivebarker.com.

BARKER, Dennis Malcolm; journalist and writer; b. 21 June 1929, Lowestoft, England; m. Sarah Katherine Alwyn; one d. *Education:* Nat. Diploma in Journalism 1959. *Career:* reporter and Sub-Ed., Suffolk Chronicle & Mercury, Ipswich 1947–48; reporter, feature writer, theatre and film critic, East Anglian Daily Times 1948–58; Ed. and Editorial Dir, East Anglian Architecture & Building Review 1956–58; Estates and Property Ed. and theatre critic, Express & Star, Wolverhampton 1958–63; Midlands correspondent, The Guardian 1963–67, reporter, feature writer, columnist 1967–91; mem. NUJ, Newspaper Press Fund, Writers' Guild of Great Britain, Broadcasting Press Guild, Soc. of Authors. *Publications:* fiction: Candidate of Promise 1969, The Scandalisers 1974, Winston Three Three Three 1987; non-fiction: Soldiering On (The People of the Forces Trilogy, vol. I) 1981, One Man's Estate 1983, Parian Ware 1985, Ruling the

Waves (The People of the Forces Trilogy, vol. II) 1986, Guarding the Skies (The People of the Forces Trilogy, vol. III) 1989, Fresh Start 1990, The Craft of the Media Interview 1998, How to Deal with the Media 2000, Seize the Day (contributor) 2001; contrib. to BBC, Punch, The Guardian 1991–. *Address:* 67 Speldhurst Road, London, W4 1BY, England.

BARKER, Elspeth; Writer; b. 16 Nov. 1940, Edinburgh, Scotland; m. George Granville Barker 29 July 1989; three s. two d. *Education:* St Leonards School, Scotland, 1953–57; Univ. of Oxford, 1958–61. *Publications:* O Caledonia, 1991; Anthology of Loss, 1997. Contributions: Independent on Sunday; Guardian; Harpers & Queen; TLS; Vogue; Big Issue; Sunday Times; Observer; Daily Mail. *Honours:* David Higham Award, Scottish Arts Council; Angel Literary Award; RSL Winifred Holtby Award. *Address:* Bintry House, Itteringham, Aylsham, Norfolk NR11 7AT, England.

BARKER, Howard, MA; dramatist and poet; b. 28 June 1946, London, England. *Education:* University of Sussex. *Career:* resident dramatist, Open Space Theatre, London 1975–75. *Publications:* over 30 plays, including Collected Plays, Vol. I, 1990; poetry.

BARKER, Nicola; writer; b. 30 March 1966, Ely, Cambridgeshire, England. *Education:* Univ. of Cambridge. *Publications:* Love Your Enemies (short stories) 1992, Reversed Forecast (novel) 1994, Small Holdings (novel) 1995, Heading Inland (short stories) 1996, Wide Open (novel) 1998, Five Miles From Outer Hope (novel) 2000, Behindlings (novel) 2002, The Three Button Trick (short stories) 2003, Clear (novel) 2004; contrib. to Time Out Book of London Short Stories, Food With Feeling (story adapted for BBC Radio 4). *Honours:* David Higham Prize for Fiction, jt winner, Macmillan Silver PEN Award for Fiction, Mail on Sunday/John Llewellyn Rhys Award 1997, IMPAC Dublin Literary Award 2000, one of Granta's Best of Young British Novelists 2003. *Literary Agent:* Rogers, Coleridge & White Ltd, 20 Powis Mews, London, W11 1JN, England.

BARKER, Patricia (Pat) Margaret, CBE, BSc(Econ), FRSL; British author; b. 8 May 1943, Thornaby-on-Tees; m. David Barker 1978; one s., one d. *Education:* London School of Econs. *Career:* taught in colls of further educ. 1965–70; Patron New Writing North; mem. Soc. of Authors, PEN. *Publications:* novels: Union Street 1982, Blow Your House Down 1984, The Century's Daughter 1986 (retitled Liza's England 1996), The Man Who Wasn't There 1989; trilogy of First World War novels: Regeneration 1991, The Eye in the Door 1993, The Ghost Road (Booker Prize 1995) 1995; Another World 1998, Border Crossing 2001, Double Vision 2003. *Honours:* Hon. Fellow LSE 1998; Hon. MLitt (Teesside) 1993; Hon. DLitt (Napier) 1996, (Durham) 1998, (Hertfordshire) 1998, (London) 2002; Dr hc (Open Univ.) 1997; Fawcett Prize 1983, Guardian Prize for Fiction 1993, Northern Electric Special Arts Award 1994. *Literary Agent:* Gillon Aitken Associates, 18–21 Cavaye Place, London, SW10 9PT, England. *Telephone:* (20) 7373-8672. *Fax:* (20) 7373-6002.

BARKER, Paul; journalist, editor, writer and broadcaster; b. 24 Aug. 1935, Mytholmroyd, Yorkshire, England; m. Sally Huddleston; three s. one d. *Education:* MA, Univ. of Oxford. *Career:* Ed., New Society, 1968–86; Dir, Advisory Ed., Fiction Magazine, 1982–87; Social Policy Ed., Sunday Telegraph, 1986–88; Visiting Fellow, Univ. of Bath, 1986–2000; Columnist, 1987–92, Social Policy Commentator, 1992–, London Evening Standard; Assoc. Ed., The Independent Magazine, 1988–90; Reviewer, TLS, 1991–; Editorial Board and Essayist, Prospect, 1995–; Columnist, New Statesman, 1996–99; mem. Institute of Community Studies, sr research fellow; FRSA. *Publications:* A Sociological Portrait, 1972; One for Sorrow, Two for Joy, 1972; The Social Sciences Today, 1975; Arts in Society, 1977; The Other Britain, 1982; Founders of the Welfare State, 1985; Britain in the Eighties, 1989; Towards a New Landscape, 1993; Young at Eighty, 1995; Gulliver and Beyond, 1996; Living as Equals, 1996; A Critic Writes, 1997; Town and Country, 1998; Non-Plan, 2000. *Honours:* Leverhulme Research Fellow, 1993–95; Fellowship in Built Environment, 2000–02. *Address:* 15 Dartmouth Park Avenue, London NW5 1JL, England.

BARKER, Ralph Hammond; Author; b. 21 Oct. 1917, Feltham, Middlesex, England; m. 1st Joan Muriel Harris 17 May 1948 (died 13 May 1993); one d.; m. 2nd Diana Darvey 30 June 1995 (died 11 April 2000). *Education:* Hounslow College, 1926–34. *Career:* RAF, 1940–46, 1949–61; Retd as Flight Lieutenant. *Publications:* Down in the Drink, 1955; The Ship-Busters, 1957; The Last Blue Mountain, 1959; Ten Great Innings, 1964; The Thousand Plan, 1965; Ten Great Bowlers, 1967; Great Mysteries of the Air, 1967; Verdict on a Lost Flyer, 1969; Aviator Extraordinary, 1969; Test Cricket: England v Australia (with Irving Rosenwater), 1969; The Schneider Trophy Races, 1971; One Man's Jungle, 1975; The Blockade Busters, 1976; The Cricketing Family Edrich, 1976; The Hurricats, 1978; Not Here, But in Another Place, 1980; The RAF at War, 1981; Innings of a Lifetime, 1982; Good-Night, Sorry for Sinking You, 1984; Children of the Benares, 1987; Purple Patches, 1987; That Eternal Summer, 1990; The Royal Flying Corps in France, two vols, 1994–95, combined edn, 2002. Contributions: Sunday Express; The Cricketer. *Honours:* Buchpreis des Deutschen Alpenvereins, 1982. *Address:* Old Timbers, 16 Aldercombe Lane, Caterham, Surrey CR3 6ED, England.

BARKER, Rodney; Writer; b. 9 Feb. 1946, Lewisburg, Pennsylvania, USA; m. Star York. *Education:* BA, Knox College, 1968; Graduate study, San Francisco State University. *Career:* mem. International PEN. *Publications:* The Hiroshima Maidens, 1985; The Broken Circle, 1992; Dancing with the Devil, 1996; And the Waters Turned to Blood, 1997. *Literary Agent:* Janklow & Nesbit Associates, 445 Park Ave, New York, NY 10022, USA. *E-mail:* rbarker@cybermesa.com.

BARKLEM, Jill; British children's writer and illustrator; b. Epping; m. 1977. *Education:* studied art in London. *Publications:* Spring Story 1980, Summer Story 1980, Autumn Story 1980, Winter Story 1980, The Secret Staircase 1983, The High Hills 1986, Sea Story 1990, Poppy's Babies 1994, Wilfred's Birthday 1995, Nice for Mice 1999, Wilfred to the Rescue 2005. *Address:* Brambly Hedge, The Barn, 41 Church Hill, Epping, Essex CM16 4RA, England (Office). *Telephone:* (1992) 573052. *Fax:* (1992) 575483. *E-mail:* info@bramblyhedge.co.uk. *Website:* www.bramblyhedge.co.uk.

BARLOW, Frank, CBE, BA, BLitt, MA, DPhil; historian and academic; b. 19 April 1911, Wolstanton, England; m. Moira Stella Brigid Garvey 1936; two s. *Education:* St John's Coll., Oxford. *Career:* Asst Lecturer, University College London, 1936–40; War Service, India, Ceylon, Singapore, 1941–46 (Intelligence Corps, 1942–46), final rank, major; Lecturer, 1946–49, Reader, 1949–53, Prof. of History and Head of the Dept of History, 1953–76, Emeritus Prof., 1976–, Deputy Vice-Chancellor, 1961–63, Public Orator, 1974–76, University of Exeter; mem. British Acad., fellow; FRSL. *Publications:* The Letters of Arnulf of Lisieux, 1939; Durham Annals and Documents of the Thirteenth Century, 1945; Durham Jurisdictional Peculiars, 1950; The Feudal Kingdom of England, 1955; The Life of King Edward the Confessor (ed. and trans.), 1962; The English Church, 1000–1066, 1963; William I and the Norman Conquest, 1965; Edward the Confessor, 1970; Winchester in the Early Middle Ages (with Martin Biddle, Olof von Feilitzen and D. J. Keene), 1976; the English Church, 1066–1154, 1979; The Norman Conquest and Beyond, 1983; William Rufus, 1983; Thomas Beckett, 1986; Introduction to Devonshire Domesday Book, 1991; English Episcopal Acta, XI–XII (Exeter 1046–1257), 1995; The Carmen de Hastingae Proelio of Guy, Bishop of Amiens (ed. and trans.), 1999; The Godwins, 2002. Contributions: various professional journals. *Honours:* Fereday Fellow, St John's College, Oxford, 1935–38; Hon. DLitt, Exon, 1981; Hon. Fellow, St John's College, Oxford, 2001. *Address:* Middle Court Hall, Kenton, Exeter, EX6 8NA, England.

BARLTROP, Robert (Arthur Horace); Journalist and Writer; b. 6 Nov. 1922, Walthamstow, England; m. Mary Gleeson, 18 July 1947, three s. *Education:* Teacher's Certificate, Forest Training College, 1950. *Career:* Ed., Socialist Standard, 1972–78, Cockney Ancestor, 1983–86; Columnist and feature-writer, Recorder Newspapers, 1985–; mem. Institute of Journalists. *Publications:* The Monument, 1974; Jack London: The Man, the Writer, the Rebel, 1977; The Bar Tree, 1979; The Muvver Tongue, 1980; Revolution: Stories and Essays by Jack London (ed.), 1981; My Mother's Calling Me, 1984; A Funny Age, 1985; Bright Summer, Dark Autumn, 1986. Contributions: Magazines and newspapers. *Address:* 77 Idmiston Rd, London E15 1RG, England.

BARNABY, Charles Frank, MSc, PhD; British physicist; *Chairman, World Disarmament Campaign (UK)*; b. 27 Sept. 1927, Andover, Hants.; m. Wendy Elizabeth Field 1972; one s. one d. *Education:* Andover Grammar School and Univ. of London. *Career:* Physicist, UK Atomic Energy Authority 1950–57; mem. Sr Scientific Staff, Medical Research Council, Univ. Coll. Medical School 1957–68; Exec. Sec. Pugwash Confs on Science and World Affairs 1968–70; Dir Stockholm Int. Peace Research Inst. (SIPRI) 1971–81; Prof. of Peace Studies, Free Univ., Amsterdam 1981–85; Dir World Disarmament Campaign (UK) 1982–; Chair. Just Defence 1982–; Consultant Oxford Research Group 1998–; Ed. Int. Journal of Human Rights. *Publications:* Man and the Atom 1971, Ed. Preventing the Spread of Nuclear Weapons 1971, Co-ed. Anti-ballistic Missile Systems 1971, Disarmament and Arms Control 1973, Nuclear Energy 1975, The Nuclear Age 1976, Prospects for Peace 1980, Future Warfare (ed. and co-author) 1983, Space Weapons 1984, Star Wars Brought Down to Earth 1986, The Automated Battlefield 1986, The Invisible Bomb 1989, The Gaia Peace Atlas 1989, The Role and Control of Weapons in the 1990s 1992, How Nuclear Weapons Spread 1993, Instruments of Terror 1997, How to Build a Nuclear Bomb and Other Weapons of Mass Destruction 2003; articles in scientific journals. *Honours:* Hon. DSc (Frei Univ., Amsterdam) 1982, (Southampton) 1996. *Address:* Brandreth, Chilbolton, Stockbridge, Hants., SO20 6HW, England. *Telephone:* (1264) 860423 (Home). *Fax:* (1264) 860868. *E-mail:* frank@barnabyc.fsnet.co.uk.

BARNARD, Robert, (Bernard Bastable); Crime Writer; b. 23 Nov. 1936, Burnham on Crouch, Essex, England; m. Mary Louise Tabor 7 Feb. 1963. *Education:* BA, Balliol Coll., Oxford, 1959; Dr Phil, Univ. of Bergen, Norway, 1972. *Career:* Lecturer in English, Univ. of New England, Armidale, NSW, 1961–66; Lecturer, then Sr Lecturer in English, Univ. of Bergen, 1966–76; Prof. of English, Univ. of Tromsø, Norway, 1976–84; mem. CWA; Brontë Society, Chair., 1996–99, 2002–; Society of Authors. *Publications:* Death of an Old Goat, 1974; A Little Local Murder, 1976; Death on the High C's, 1977; Blood Brotherhood, 1977; Unruly Son (aka Death of a Mystery Writer), 1978; Posthumous Papers (aka Death of a Literary Widow), 1979; Death in a Cold Climate, 1980; Mother's Boys (aka Death of a Perfect Mother), 1981; Sheer Torture (aka Death by Sheer Torture), 1981; Death and the Princess, 1982; The Missing Brontë (aka The Case of the Missing Brontë), 1983; Little Victims (aka School for Murder),

1983; A Corpse in a Gilded Cage, 1984; Out of the Blackout, 1985; The Disposal of the Living (aka Fête Fatale), 1985; Political Suicide, 1986; Bodies, 1986; Death in Purple Prose (aka The Cherry Blossom Corpse), 1987; The Skeleton in the Grass, 1987; At Death's Door, 1988; Death and the Chaste Apprentice, 1989; A City of Strangers, 1990; A Scandal in Belgravia, 1991; A Fatal Attachment, 1992; A Hovering of Vultures, 1993; The Masters of the House, 1994; The Bad Samaritan, 1995; The Corpse at the Haworth Tandoori, 1999; The Mistress of Alderley, 2002; The Bones in the Attic, 2002; A Cry from the Dark, 2003. As Bernard Bastable: To Die Like a Gentleman, 1993; Dead, Mr Mozart, 1995; Too Many Notes, Mr Mozart, 1995. Contributions: short stories and essays. *Honours:* CWA Cartier Diamond Dagger, 2003. *Literary Agent:* Gregory & Co. *Address:* Hazeldene, Houghley Lane, Leeds LS13 2DT, England.

BARNES, Christopher John, BA, MA, PhD; academic and writer; *Professor of Slavic Languages and Literatures, University of Toronto*; b. 10 March 1942, Sheffield, England; m. Svetlana Tzapina 1994; two d. *Education:* Corpus Christi College, Cambridge. *Career:* Lecturer in Russian Language and Literature, University of St Andrews, Scotland, 1967–89; Prof. and Chair. of the Dept of Slavic Languages and Literatures, University of Toronto, 1989–; mem. American Asscn for the Advancement of Slavic Studies; American Asscn of Teachers of Slavic and East European Languages; British Royal Musical Asscn; British Universities Asscn of Slavists; Canadian Asscn of Slavists; MLA of America. *Publications:* Studies in Twentieth-Century Russian Literature (ed.), 1976; Boris Pasternak: Collected Short Prose (ed. and trans.), 1977; Boris Pasternak: The Voice of Prose (ed. and trans.) 2 vols, 1986, 1990; Boris Pasternak: A Literary Biography, Vol. 1, 1890–1928, 1989, Vol. 2, 1928–1960, 1998; Boris Pasternak and European Literature (ed.), 1990. Contributions: scholarly journals. *Address:* c/o Department of Slavic Languages and Literatures, University of Toronto, Toronto, Ontario M5S 1A1, Canada.

BARNES, Clive (Alexander); Journalist and Dance and Theatre Critic; b. 13 May 1927, London, England; m. 2nd Patricia Amy Evelyn Winckley 26 June 1958; one s. one d. *Education:* King's College, London; BA, St Catherine's College, Oxford, 1951. *Career:* Co-Ed., Arabesque, 1950; Asst Ed., 1950–58, Assoc. Ed., 1958–61, Exec. Ed., 1961–65, Dance and Dancers; Administrative Officer in Town Planning, London County Council, 1952–61; Chief Dance Critic, 1961–65, New York Correspondent, 1970–, The Times, London; Dance Critic, 1965–78, Drama Critic, 1967–78, New York Times; Assoc. Ed. and Chief Dance and Drama Critic, New York Post, 1978–. *Publications:* Ballet in Britain Since the War, 1953; Frederick Ashton and His Ballets, 1961; Ballet Here and Now (with A. V. Coton and Frank Jackson), 1961; Ballett, 1965: Chronik und Bilanz des Ballettjahres (ed. with Horst Koegler), 1965; Ballett 1966: Chronik und Bilanz des Ballettjahres (ed. with Horst Koegler), 1966; Fifty Best Plays of the American Theatre from 1787 to the Present (ed.), 4 vols, 1969; Best American Plays: Sixth Series, 1963–1967 (ed. with John Gassner), 1971; Best American Plays: Seventh Series (ed.), 1975; Inside American Ballet Theatre, 1977; Nureyev, 1982; Best American Plays: Eighth Series, 1974–1982 (ed.), 1983; Best American Plays: Ninth Series, 1983–1992 (ed.), 1993. Contributions: many periodicals. *Honours:* Knight of the Order of Dannebrog, Denmark, 1972; CBE, 1975. *Address:* 241 W 23rd St, Apt 4A, New York, NY 10011, USA.

BARNES, Dick, (Richard Gordon Barnes); Prof. of English Emeritus, Poet, Writer, Dramatist and Rubboardist; b. 5 Nov. 1932, San Bernardino, CA, USA; m. Patricia Casey, 30 July 1982, five s., four d. *Education:* BA, Pomona College, 1954; AM, Harvard University, 1955; PhD, Claremont Graduate School, 1959. *Career:* Part-Time Instructor, 1956–58, Instructor, 1961–62, Asst Prof., 1962–67, Assoc. Prof., 1967–72, Prof., 1972–98, Prof. Emeritus, 1998–, Pomona College; numerous poetry readings. *Publications:* Poetry: A Lake on the Earth, 1982; The Real Time Jazz Band Song Book, 1990; Few and Far Between, 1994. Chapbooks: The Complete Poems of R. G. Barnes, 1972; Thirty-One Views of San Bernardino, 1975; Hungry Again the Next Day, 1978; Lyrical Ballads, 1979; All Kinds of Tremendous Things Can Happen, 1982; A Pentecostal, 1985. Plays: Nacho, 1964; A Lulu for the Lively Arts, 1965; San Antonio Noh, 1966; The Cucamonga Wrapdown, 1967; The Eighth Avatar, 1970; The Death of Buster Quinine, 1972; Purple, 1973; The Detestable Life of Alfred Furkeisar, 1975; The Bradford and Barnes Poverty Circus, 1977; Tenebrae, 1979; Come Sunday, 1982; A New Death of Buster Quinine, 1994; The Sand Mirror, 1998. Other: Trans, films and recordings. Contributions: many anthologies and magazines. *Address:* 434 W Seventh St, Claremont, CA 91711, USA.

BARNES, Jim Weaver; Writer, Poet and Teacher; b. 22 Dec. 1933, Summerfield, OK, USA; m. Carolyn 23 Nov. 1973; two s. *Education:* BA, Southeastern Oklahoma State University, 1964; MA, 1966, PhD, 1972, University of Arkansas. *Career:* mem. PEN Center West; Assoc. Writing Programs. *Publications:* Fish on Poteau Mountain, 1980; American Book of the Dead, 1982; Season of Loss, 1985; La Plata Canata, 1989; Sawdust War, 1992; Paris, 1997; On Native Ground, 1997; Numbered Days, 1999; On a Wing of the Sun, 2001. Contributions: Poetry Chicago; Nation; American Scholar; Georgia Review; Poetry Northwest; Quarterly West; Prairie Schooner; Mississippi Review; Plus 400. *Honours:* National Endowment for the Arts Fellowship, 1978; Oklahoma Book Award, 1993; Camargo Foundation Fellowships, 1996, 2001; American Book Award, 1998. *Address:* 914 Pine St, Macon, MO 63525, USA.

BARNES, Jonathan, FBA; British professor of philosophy; *Professor of Ancient Philosophy, University of Paris IV–Sorbonne*; b. 26 Dec. 1942, Much Wenlock; m. Jennifer Mary Postgate 1964; two d. *Education:* City of London School and Balliol Coll., Oxford. *Career:* Lecturer in Philosophy Exeter Coll. Oxford 1967–68, Fellow Oriel Coll. 1968–78, Balliol Coll. 1978–94; Prof. of Ancient Philosophy, Univ. of Oxford 1989–94, Univ. of Geneva 1994–2002, Univ. of Paris IV–Sorbonne 2003–; visiting posts at Univ. of Chicago 1966–67, Inst. for Advanced Study, Princeton 1972, Univ. of Massachusetts 1973,Univ. of Texas 1981, Wissenschaftskolleg zu Berlin 1985, Univ. of Alberta 1986, Univ. of Zurich 1987, Istituto Italiano per la Storia della Filosofia 1989, 1994, 1999, Ecole Normale Supérieure, Paris 1996, Scuola Normale di Pisa 2002; mem. L'Acad. scientifique, Geneva, Aristotelian Soc., Mind Asscn. *Publications:* The Ontological Argument 1972, Aristotle's Posterior Analytics 1975, The Presocratic Philosophers 1979, Doubt and Dogmatism (with M. F. Burnyeat and M. Schofield) 1980, Aristotle 1982, Science and Speculation (with J. Brunschwig and M. F. Burnyeat) 1982, The Complete Works of Aristotle 1984, The Modes of Scepticism (with J. Annas) 1985, Early Greek Philosophy 1987, Matter and Metaphysics (with M. Mignucci 1988, Philosophia Togata (with M. Griffin) Vol. I 1989, Vol. II 1997, The Toils of Scepticism 1991, Sextus Empiricus: Outlines of Scepticisim (with J. Annas) 1994, The Cambridge Companion to Aristotle 1995, Logic and the Imperial Stoa 1997, The Cambridge History of Hellenistic Philosophy (with K. Algra, J. Mansfield and M. Schofield) 1999, Porphyry: Introduction 2003. *Honours:* Hon. Fellow American Acad. of Arts and Sciences 1999; Condorcet Medal 1996, John Locke Lecturer, Univ. of Oxford 2004. *Address:* Les Charmilles, 36200 Ceaulmont; 12 blvd Arago, 75013 Paris, France. *E-mail:* jonathanbarnes@wanadoo.fr.

BARNES, Julian Patrick, (Dan Kavanagh, Basil Seal), BA; British writer; b. 19 Jan. 1946, Leicester, England; m. Pat Kavanagh. *Education:* City of London School, Magdalen Coll. Oxford. *Career:* lexicographer, Oxford English Dictionary Supplement 1969–72; Asst Literary Ed. New Statesman 1977–79, reviewer 1977–81, TV critic 1979–82; Contributing Ed. New Review, London 1977–78; Deputy Literary Ed. Sunday Times, London 1979–81; TV Critic The Observer 1982–86; Hon. Fellow Magdalen Coll., Oxford 1996–. *Publications:* Metroland 1980, Before She Met Me 1982, Flaubert's Parrot (Geoffrey Faber Memorial Prize, Prix Médicis 1986) 1984, Staring at the Sun 1986, A History of the World in 10½ Chapters 1989, Talking it Over (Prix Femina Etranger 1992) 1991, The Porcupine 1992, Letters From London 1990–95 (articles) 1995, Cross Channel (short stories) 1996, England, England 1998, Love, etc 2000, Something to Declare (essays) 2002, In the Land of Pain, by Alphonse Daudet (ed. and trans.) 2002, The Lemon Table (short stories) 2004, The Pedant in the Kitchen 2004; as Dan Kavanagh: Duffy 1980, Fiddle City 1981, Putting the Boot In 1985, Going to the Dogs 1987. *Honours:* Somerset Maugham Award 1981, Geoffrey Faber Memorial Prize 1985, E. M. Forster Award, US Acad. of Arts and Letters 1986, Gutenberg Prize 1987, Grinzane Cavour Prize, Italy 1988, Shakespeare Prize, Germany 1993; Officier, Ordre des Arts et des Lettres 1995. *Literary Agent:* PFD, Drury House, 34–43 Russell Street, London, WC2B 5HA, England. *Website:* www.julianbarnes.com.

BARNES, Richard John Black, FRGS; editor and writer; b. 13 Aug. 1950, Nyasaland, Malawi; m. Lucette Aylmer 1975; one s. one d. *Education:* Stonyhurst College, Royal College of Agriculture, Polytechnic of Central London. *Career:* mem. Public Monuments and Sculpture Asscn. *Publications:* The Sun in the East, 1983; Eye on the Hill: Horse Travels in Britain, 1987; John Bell, Sculptor, 1999; The Year of Public Sculpture–Norfolk, 2001. *Address:* c/o Frontier Publishing, Windetts Farm, Long Lane, Kirstead, Norwich NR15 1EG, England.

BARNET, Max (see Aaron, Hugh).

BARNET, Miguel; Cuban writer; b. 28 Nov. 1950, Havana. *Career:* Pres. of Fernando Ortiz Foundation; mem. of Honor Council, Extraordinary Staff of Nuestra América of Anthropological Sciences Faculty, Autonomous Univ., Yucatan, Mexico. *Publications:* Cimarron 1966, Biography of a Runaway Slave 1970, Cancion de Rachel (trans. as Rachel's Song) 1979, Gallego 1981, La fuente viva 1983, Autógrafos cubanos 1989, Mapa del tiempo 1989, La vida real 1989, Oficio de ángel 1989, Con pies de gato 1993, Los orejas del conejo 1995, Reyes y sin coronas (trans. as Kings Without Crowns) 2001, Afro-Cuban Religions 2001. *Honours:* Medal of Colony City, Germany ; Distinction for Nat. Culture, La Giraldillo de la Habana, Garcia Lorca Prize (Spain), Nat. Prize for Literature 1994, Int. Book Fair Honour 2002. *Literary Agent:* c/o Curbstone Press, 321 Jackson Street, Willimantic, CT 06226-1738, USA. *E-mail:* info@curbstone.org. *Website:* www.curbstone .org.

BARNETT, Anthony Peter John, MA; writer, poet and publisher; b. 10 Sept. 1941, London, England. *Education:* Univ. of Essex. *Career:* Editorial Dir, Allardyce, Barnett, Publishers; Ed., Fable Bulletin: Violin Improvisation Studies, 1993–2000, online 2000–. *Publications:* Poetry: Blood Flow, 1975; Fear and Misadventure, 1977; The Resting Bell: Collected Poems, 1987. Prose and Poetry: Carp and Rubato, 1995; Anti-Beauty, 1999. Prose: Lisa Lisa, 2000. Other: Desert Sands: The Recordings and Performances of Stuff Smith, 1995; Black Gypsy: The Recordings of Eddie South, 1999. Contributions: New Grove Dictionary of Music and Musicians; New Grove

Dictionary of Jazz; anthologies, journals and periodicals. *Address:* c/o Allardyce, Barnett, Publishers, 14 Mount Street, Lewes, East Sussex BN7 1HL, England. *Website:* www.abar.net.

BARNETT, Correlli (Douglas); Author; b. 28 June 1927, Norbury, Surrey, England; m. Ruth Murby 28 Dec. 1950; two d. *Education:* BA, 1951, MA, 1955, Exeter College, Oxford. *Career:* Keeper of the Churchill Archives Centre, 1977–95; Fellow, Churchill College, Cambridge, 1977–,; Defence Lecturer, Univ. of Cambridge, 1980–84. *Publications:* The Hump Organisation, 1957; The Channel Tunnel (co-author), 1958; The Desert Generals, 1960; The Swordbearers, 1963; Britain and Her Army, 1970; The Collapse of British Power, 1972; Marlborough, 1974; Strategy and Society, 1975; Bonaparte, 1978; The Great War, 1979; The Audit of War, 1986; Engage the Enemy More Closely: The Royal Navy in the Second World War, 1991; The Lost Victory: British Dreams, British Realities 1945–1950, 1995; The Verdict of Peace: Britain Between Her Yesterday and the Future, 2001. *Honours:* Best Television Documentary Script Award, Screenwriter's Guild, 1964; RSL Award, 1970; Chesney Gold Medal, Royal United Services Institute for Defence Studies, 1991; Yorkshire Post Book of the Year Award, 1991; DSc hc, Cranfield Univ., 1993; CBE, 1997; Hon. FCGI, 2003. *Literary Agent:* David Higham Associates, 5–8 Lower John St, Golden Sq., London W1F 9HA, England. *Address:* Catbridge House, East Carleton, Norwich NR14 8JX, England.

BARNETT, Paul le Page, (Dennis Brezhnev, Eve Devereux, Freddie Duff-Ware, John Grant, Armytage Ware); writer and editor; b. 22 Nov. 1949, Aberdeen, Scotland; m. Catherine Stewart 1974; two d. *Career:* mem. West Country Writers' Asscn. *Publications:* As John Grant: Book of Time (with Colin Wilson), 1979; A Book of Numbers, 1982; The Depths of Cricket, 1986; Earthdoom (with David Langford), 1987; The Advanced Trivia Quizbook, 1987; Great Mysteries, 1988; Great Unsolved Mysteries of Science, 1989; Albion, 1991; Unexplained Mysteries of the World, 1991; The World, 1992; Monsters, 1992; The Hundredfold Problem, 1994; Encyclopedia of Fantasy Art Techniques (with Ron Tiner), 1996; Encyclopedia of Fantasy (ed. with John Clute), 1997. As Paul Barnett: Planet Earth: An Encyclopedia of Geology (ed. with A. Hallam and Peter Hutchinson); Phaidon Concise Encyclopedia of Science and Technology (contributing ed.), 1978; Strider's Galaxy, 1997. As Eve Devereux: Book of World Flags, 1992; Ultimate Card Trick Book, 1994. As Armytage Ware (joint pseudonym with Ron Tiner): Parlour Games, 1992; Conjuring Tricks, 1992; Juggling and Feats of Dexterity, 1992; Card Games, 1992. As Freddie Duff-Ware (joint pseudonym with Ron Tiner): Practical Jokes, 1993. *Address:* 17 Polsloe Road, Exeter, Devon EX1 2HL, England.

BARNHARDT, Wilton; Writer; b. 25 July 1960, Winston-Salem, NC, USA. *Education:* BA, Michigan State University, 1982; MPhil, University of Oxford, 1989. *Publications:* Emma Who Saved My Life, 1989; Gospel, 1993; Show World, 1998. Contributions: magazines.

BARNSLEY, Victoria; British publisher; *CEO, HarperCollins UK*; b. 4 March 1954; m. Nicholas Howard 1992; one d. one step-s. *Education:* Loughborough High School, Beech Lawn Tutorial Coll., Edinburgh Univ., Univ. Coll. London, York Univ. *Career:* with Junction Books 1980–83; founder, Chair. and CEO Fourth Estate 1984–2000; CEO HarperCollins UK 2000–; Trustee Tate Gallery 1998–; Dir Tate Enterprises Ltd 1998–; council mem. Publishers Asscn 2001–. *Address:* HarperCollins, Ophelia House, 77–85 Fulham Palace Road, London, W6 8JB, England (Office). *Telephone:* (20) 8741-7070 (Office). *Fax:* (20) 8307-4440 (Office). *E-mail:* contact@harpercollins.co.uk (Office). *Website:* www.harpercollins.co.uk (Office).

BARNSTONE, Willis; Scholar, Poet, Novelist and Prof. of Comparative Literature; b. 13 Nov. 1927, Lewiston, ME, USA; two s. one d. *Education:* BA, cum laude, French and Philosophy, Bowdoin College, 1948; MA, English and Comparative Literature, Columbia University, 1956; PhD, Comparative Literature, Yale University, 1960. *Career:* Asst Prof. of Romance Languages, Wesleyan University, 1959–62; Prof. of Comparative Literature, Spanish and Portuguese, Indiana University, 1966–; Visiting Prof., various universities, 1967–73; Senior Fulbright Prof., English Literature, Instituto Superior del Profesorado, Profesorado de Lenguas Vivas, Buenos Aires, 1975–76; Senior Fulbright Prof., English and American Literature, Peking Foreign Studies University, 1984–85; mem. PEN; Poetry Society of America. *Publications:* From This White Island, 1959; A Sky of Days, 1967; A Day in the Country, 1971; China Poems, 1976; Stickball on 88th Street, 1978; Overheard, 1979; Ten Gospels and a Nightingale, 1981; The Alphabet of Night, 1984; Five AM in Beijing, 1987; With Borges on an Ordinary Evening in Buenos Aires, 1992; ABC of Translating Poetry (illustrated), 1993; The Poetics of Translation, 1993; Funny Ways of Staying Alive: Poems and Ink Drawings, 1993; Sunday Morning in Fascist Spain: A European Memoir (1948–1953), 1995; The Secret Reader: 501 Sonnets, 1996; The Poems of Sappho: A New Translation, 1997; The Literatures of Asia, Africa and Latin America (co-ed. with Tony Barnstone), 1998; To Touch the Sky: Spiritual, Mystical and Philosophical Poems in Translation, 1999; Algebra of Night: New and Selected Poems, 1948–1998, 1998; The Apocalypse (Revelation): A New Translation with Introduction, 2000; The New Covenant: The Four Gospels and Apocalypse. Newly Translated from the Greek and Informed by Semitic Sources, 2002; Literatures of the Middle East (ed. with Tony Barnstone), 2002; Literatures of Latin America (ed.), 2002. *Honours:* Cecil Hemley Memorial Award, 1968, Lucille Medwick Memorial Awards, 1978, 1982, Gustav Davidson Memorial Awards, 1980, 1988, Emily Dickinson Award, 1985, Poetry Society of America; W. H. Auden Award, New York State Arts Council, 1986; National Poetry Competition Award, Chester H. Jones Foundation, 1988. *Address:* Dept of Comparative Literature, Indiana University, Bloomington, IN 47405, USA.

BARON, Carolyn, BA; American publishing executive, editor and author; *Senior President and Publisher, Dell Publishing Company*; b. 25 Jan. 1940, Detroit; m. Richard W. Baron 1975. *Education:* Univ. of Mich. *Career:* Ed., Editorial Production Dir Holt, Rinehart & Winston, New York 1965–71; Man. Ed. E. P. Dutton Co. Inc., New York 1971–74, Exec. Ed. 1974–75; Admin. Ed. Pocket Books, Simon & Schuster, New York 1975–78, Vice-Pres., Ed.-in-Chief 1978–79; Vice-Pres., Ed.-in-Chief Crown Publs, New York 1979–81; Vice-Pres. Dell Publishing Co., New York 1981–86, Sr Pres., Publr 1986–; Sr Vice-Pres. Bantam, Doubleday, Dell 1989–. *Publications:* The History of Labor Unions in the US 1971, Re-entry Game 1974, Board Sailboats: A Buying Guide 1977; articles in magazines. *Address:* Dell Publishing Co. Inc., 1540 Broadway, New York, NY 10036, USA.

BARON, Martin, BA, MBA; American journalist; *Editor, The Boston Globe*; b. Tampa, FL. *Education:* Lehigh Univ. *Career:* state reporter, business writer The Miami Herald 1976–79; joined Los Angeles Times 1979, apptd Business Ed. 1983, Asst. Man. Ed. for 'Column One' 1991, Ed. Orange Co. Edn 1993; joined The New York Times 1996, Assoc. Man. Ed. responsible for night-time news operations 1997–99; Exec. Ed. The Miami Herald 1999–2002; Ed. The Boston Globe 2002–. *Honours:* ; Pulitzer Prize 2001, Ed. of the Year, Editor & Publisher Magazine 2002. *Address:* The Boston Globe, 135 Morrissey Boulevard, POB 2378, Boston, MA 02107-2378, USA (Office). *Telephone:* (617) 929-2000 (Office). *Fax:* (617) 929-3192 (Office). *E-mail:* news@globe.com (Office). *Website:* www.boston.com (Office).

BARR, James; professor, Biblical scholar and writer; b. 20 March 1924, Glasgow, Scotland; Emeritus. m. Jane J. S. Hepburn, 1950, two s. one d. *Education:* Daniel Stewart's College, Edinburgh; MA, 1948, BD, 1951, University of Edinburgh; MA, 1976, BD, DD, 1981, Oxon. *Career:* Minister, Church of Scotland, Tiberias, Israel, 1951–53; Prof. of New Testament Literature and Exegesis, Presbyterian College, Montréal, 1953–55; Prof. of Old Testament Literature and Theology, University of Edinburgh, 1955–61, Princeton Theological Seminary, NJ, 1961–65; Prof. of Semitic Languages and Literatures, University of Manchester, 1965–76; Ed., Journal of Semitic Studies, 1965–76; Oriel Prof. of the Interpretation of Holy Scripture and Fellow, Oriel College, Oxford, 1976–78; Regius Prof. of Hebrew 1978–89, University of Oxford, Prof. Emeritus, 1989; Prof. of Hebrew Bible, 1989–98, Distinguished Prof., 1994–98, Prof. Emeritus, 1998–, Vanderbilt University; many visiting professorships and lectureships; Mem., Institute for Advanced Study, Princeton, NJ, 1985; mem. American Philosophical Society, Göttingen Acad. of Sciences, Germany; corresponding mem. Norwegian Acad., Royal Swedish Acad. of Science. *Publications:* The Semantics of Biblical Language, 1961; Biblical Words for Time, 1962; Old and New in Interpretation, 1966; Comparative Philology and the Text of the Old Testament, 1968; The Bible in the Modern World, 1973; Fundamentalism, 1977; The Typology of Literalism, 1979; Explorations in Theology 7: The Scope and Authority of the Bible, 1980; Holy Scripture: Canon, Authority, Criticism, 1983; Escaping from Fundamentalism, 1984; The Variable Spellings of the Hebrew Bible, 1988; The Garden of Eden and the Hope of Immortality, 1992; Biblical Faith and Natural Theology, 1993; The Concept of Biblical Theology, 1999; History and Ideology in the Old Testament, 2000. Contributions: scholarly books and journals. *Honours:* many hon. doctorates; Hon. mem. Society of Biblical Literature, USA, Guggenheim Fellowship, 1965, Fellow, British Acad., 1969, Hon. Fellow, Oriel College, Oxford, 1980; Fellow, American Acad. of Arts and Sciences, 1993. *Address:* 1432 Sitka Ct, Claremont, CA 91711, USA. *E-mail:* jmsbarr@aol.com.

BARR, Patricia Miriam; writer; b. 25 April 1934, Norwich, Norfolk, England. *Education:* BA, University of Birmingham; MA, University College London. *Career:* mem. Society of Authors. *Publications:* The Coming of the Barbarians, 1967; The Deer Cry Pavilion, 1968; A Curious Life for a Lady, 1970; To China with Love, 1972; The Memsahibs, 1976; Taming the Jungle, 1978; Chinese Alice, 1981; Uncut Jade, 1983; Kenjiro, 1985; Coromandel, 1988; The Dust in the Balance, 1989. *Honours:* Winston Churchill Fellowship for Historical Biography, 1972. *Address:* 6 Mount Pleasant, Norwich NR2 2DG, England.

BARRETT, Andrea; Writer; b. 16 Nov. 1954, Boston, Massachusetts, USA. *Education:* BS in Biology, Union College, Schenectady, New York, 1974. *Publications:* Lucid Stars, 1988; Secret Harmonies, 1989; The Middle Kingdom, 1991; The Forms of Water, 1993; Ship Fever & Other Stories, 1996; The Voyage of the Narwhal, 1998; Servants of the Map, 2001. Contributions: anthologies and magazines. *Honours:* National Endowment for the Arts Fellowship in Fiction, 1992; Peden Prize, Missouri Review, 1995; Hon. Doctor of Letters, Union College, 1996; Southern Review Fiction Prize, 1996; National Book Award in Fiction, 1996; Pushcart Prize, 1997; Guggenheim Fellowship, 1997. *Address:* c/o Wendy Weil Literary Agency, 232 Madison Ave, Suite 1300, New York, NY 10016, USA.

BARRETT, Charles Kingsley; academic and writer; b. 4 May 1917, Salford, England; m. Margaret E. Heap 1944; one s. one d. *Education:* BA, 1938, MA, 1942, BD, 1948, DD, 1956, Univ. of Cambridge. *Career:* Lecturer, 1945–58, Prof., 1958–82, Univ. of Durham; mem. Studiorum Novi Testamenti Societas, pres., 1973–74; Society for Old Testament Study; Royal Norwegian Society of Sciences and Letters, 1991; Hon. Mem., Society of Biblical Literature (USA). *Publications:* The Holy Spirit and the Gospel Tradition, 1947; The Epistle to the Romans, 1957; From First Adam to Last, 1962; The First Epistle to the Corinthians, 1968; The Signs of an Apostle, 1970; The Second Epistle to the Corinthians, 1973; The Gospel According to St John, 1955; Freedom and Obligation, 1985; Paul: An Introduction to His Thought, 1994; The Acts of the Apostles, two vols, 1994, 1998; Jesus and the Word, 1996; Jesus, Paul and John, 1999; Acts: A Shorter Commentary, 2002; On Paul: Essays on his Life, Work and Influence in the Early Church, 2003. Contributions: many learned journals. *Honours:* Fellow, British Acad., 1961; Burkitt Medal for Biblical Studies, 1966; Hon. DD, Hull Univ., 1970; Aberdeen Univ., 1972; DTh, Hamburg Univ., 1981; Hon. Fellow, Pembroke College, Cambridge, 1995. *Address:* 22 Rosemount, Pity Me, Durham DH1 5GA, England. *Telephone:* (191) 3861340.

BARRETT, Susan (Mary); Writer; b. 24 June 1938, Plymouth, England; m. Peter Barrett, 18 June 1960, one s. one d. *Publications:* Louisa, 1969; Moses, 1970; The Circle Sarah Drew (with Peter Barrett), 1970; The Square Ben Drew (with Peter Barrett), 1970; Noah's Ark, 1971; Private View, 1972; Rubbish, 1974; The Beacon, 1981; Travels with a Wildlife Artist: Greek Landscape and Wildlife (with Peter Barrett), 1986; Stephen and Violet, 1988; A Day in the Life of a Baby Deer: The Fawn's First Snowfall (with Peter Barrett), 1996. *Address:* c/o Toby Eady Assocs Ltd, Orme Ct, Third Floor, London W2 4RL, England. *E-mail:* susie.barrett@btopenworld.com.

BARRINGTON, Judith Mary, BA, MA; poet, memoirist and critic; b. 7 July 1944, Brighton, England. *Career:* West Coast Ed., Motheroot Journal, 1985–93; Poet-in-the-Schools, Oregon, and Washington, 1986–2000; Dir, The Flight of the Mind Writing Workshops, 1984–2000; Pres., Soapstone Inc, a writing retreat; mem. National Writers Union; Poetry Society of America. *Publications:* Deviation, 1975; Why Children (co-author), 1980; Trying to Be an Honest Woman, 1985; History and Geography, 1989; An Intimate Wilderness (ed.), 1991; Writing the Memoir: From Truth to Art, 1997; Lifesaving: A Memoir, 2000; Horses and the Human Soul 2004. Contributions: anthologies, journals, and magazines. *Honours:* Fairlie Place Essay Prize, 1963; Jeanette Rankin Award for Feminist Journalism, 1983; Oregon Institute of Literary Arts Fellowships, 1989, 1992, 1999; Andres Berger Award in Creative Non-Fiction, 1996; Dulwich Festival Poetry Prize, 1996; Stuart H. Holbrook Award, Literary Arts Inc, 1997; Lambda Literary Award, 2001. *Address:* 622 SE 29th Avenue, Portland, OR 97214, USA. *Website:* www.judithbarrington.com.

BARROW, Jedediah (see Benson, Gerard John).

BARROW, Robin St Clair; Prof. of Education and Author; b. 18 Nov. 1944, Oxford, England. *Education:* BA, MA, 1967, University of Oxford; Postgraduate Certificate in Education, Institute of Education, London, 1968; PhD, University of London, 1972. *Career:* Lecturer in Philosophy of Education, 1972–80, Personal Readership in Education, 1980–82, University of Leicester; Visiting Prof. of Philosophy of Education, University of Western Ontario, 1977–78; Prof. of Education, 1982–, Dean of Education, 1992–, Simon Fraser University, Burnaby, BC; mem. Philosophy of Education Society of Great Britain, vice-chair., 1980–83; Northwestern Philosophy of Education Society of North America, pres., 1984–85; Canadian Philosophy of Education Society, pres., 1990–91; Royal Society of Canada, fellow, 1996–. *Publications:* Athenian Democracy, 1973; An Introduction to the Philosophy of Education, 1974; Sparta, 1975; Plato, Utilitarianism and Education, 1975; Moral Philosophy for Education, 1975; Greek and Roman Education, 1976; Plato and Education, 1976; Common Sense and the Curriculum, 1976; Plato's Apology, 1978; The Canadian Curriculum: A Personal View, 1978; Radical Education, 1978; Happiness, 1979; The Philosophy of Schooling, 1981; Injustice, Inequality and Ethics, 1982; Language and Thought: Rethinking Language Across the Curriculum, 1982; Giving Teaching Back to Teachers: A Critical Introduction to Curriculum Theory, 1984; A Critical Dictionary of Educational Concepts: An Appraisal of Selected Ideas and Issues in Educational Theory and Practice, 1986; Understanding Skills: Thinking, Feeling and Caring, 1990; Utilitarianism: A Contemporary Statement, 1991; Beyond Liberal Education (ed. with Patricia White), 1993; Language, Intelligence and Thought, 1993. Contributions: Books and scholarly journals. *Address:* Faculty of Education, Simon Fraser University, Burnaby, BC V5A 1S6, Canada.

BARRY, Edward William, BA; American publishing executive; b. 24 Nov. 1937, Stamford, Conn.; m. Barbara H. Walker 1963; one s. one d. *Education:* Univ. of Conn. *Career:* Pres. The Free Press, New York 1972–82, Oxford Univ. Press Inc., New York 1982–2000; Sr Vice-Pres. Macmillan Publishing Co., New York 1973–82; mem. Exec. Council Professional and Scholarly Publications 1993, Advisory Bd Pace Univ. Grad. Program in Publishing 1990–, Bd Dirs Asscn of American Publrs 1995; Trustee Columbia Univ. Press 2000–. *Honours:* Hon. LittD (Univ. of Oxford) 2000. *Address:* 266 Old Poverty Road, Southbury, CT 06488-1769, USA (Home). *Telephone:* (212) 251-0416 (Office). *E-mail:* edwardbarry@cs.com (Office).

BARRY, James P.; Writer and Ed.; b. 23 Oct. 1918, Alton, IL, USA; m. Anne Elizabeth Jackson, 16 April 1966. *Education:* BA cum laude, Ohio State University. *Career:* Dir, Ohioana Library Asscn, 1977–88; Ed., Ohioana Quarterly, 1977–88; mem. Ohioana Library Asscn. *Publications:* Georgian Bay: The Sixth Great Lake, 1968; The Battle of Lake Erie, 1970; Bloody Kansas, 1972; The Noble Experiment, 1972; The Fate of the Lakes, 1972; The Louisiana Purchase, 1973; Ships of the Great Lakes: 300 Years of Navigation, 1973; Wrecks and Rescues of the Great Lakes, 1981; Georgian Bay: An Illustrated History, 1992; Old Forts of the Great Lakes, 1994; Hackercraft, 2002; American Powerboats, 2003. *Honours:* American Society of State and Local History Award, 1974; Great Lakes Historian of the Year, Marine History Society of Detroit, 1995. *Address:* 353 Fairway Blvd, Columbus, OH 43213, USA.

BARRY, Mike (see Malzberg, Barry).

BARRY, Sebastian; Writer, Dramatist and Poet; b. 5 July 1955, Dublin, Ireland. *Education:* BA, Trinity College, Dublin, 1977. *Career:* Writer-in-Asscn and Dir of the Board, Abbey Theatre, Dublin, 1989–90; mem. Aosdana; Irish Writers' Union. *Publications:* Inherited Boundaries, 1984; The Engine of Owl-Light, 1987; Boss Grady's Boys, play, 1989; Fanny Hawke Goes to the Mainland Forever (verse), 1989; The Steward of Christendom, 1997; Prayers of Sherkin, 1997; White Woman Street, 1997; The Only True History of Lizzie Finn, 1997; Our Lady of Sligo, 1998; The Whereabouts of Eneas McNulty, 1998; The Water Colourist, 1998; The Rhetorical Town: Poems, 1999; Annie Dunne, 2002. Contributions: periodicals. *Honours:* Arts Council Bursary, 1982; Iowa International Writing Fellowship, 1984; Hawthornden International Fellowships, 1985, 1988; BBC/Stewart Parker Award, 1989. *Literary Agent:* AP Watt Ltd, 20 John St, London WC1N 2DR, England.

BARSKY, Robert F.; researcher, academic and writer; b. 18 May 1961, Montréal, QC, Canada; two s. *Education:* Vanier Coll., 1978–80; BA, Brandeis Univ., 1984; MA, 1987, PhD, 1992, McGill Univ.; postdoctoral study, Free Univ., Brussels, Belgium. *Career:* Content Analysis Researcher, Trans-Canada Social Policy Research Centre, Montréal, 1985–91; Ethnic Studies and Refugee Studies Researcher, Institut Québecois de Recherche sur la Culture, Montréal, 1991–93; Refugee Studies Researcher, Institut National de la Recherche Scientifique, Montréal, 1993–95; Assoc. Prof. of English, Univ. of Western Ontario, London, ON, 1995–; Visiting Fellow, 2000, Canadian Bicentennial Prof., 2002, Yale Univ.; Founder, Past Co-Ed., Discours social/Social Discourse: Discourse Analysis and Text Sociocriticism; Founder, Past Ed., 415 South Street; Assoc. Ed., SubStance; Prof., Dept of French and Italian, Vanderbilt Univ., USA; mem. Scarlet Key. *Publications:* Bakhtin and Otherness, 1991; Constructing a Productive Other: Discourse Theory and the Convention Refugee Hearing, 1994; Introduction à la théorie littéraire, 1997; Noam Chomsky: A Life of Dissent, 1997; Arguing and Justifying, 2000; Philosophy and the Passions (trans.), 2000; French Theory Today (ed. with Eric Méchoulan), 2002; Workers' Councils, by Anton Pannekoek (ed.), 2003. Contributions: periodicals. *Address:* c/o Dept of French and Italian, Program in Comparative Literature, Furman Hall, Vanderbilt University, PO Box 6312 Station B, Nashville, TN 37235, USA. *E-mail:* robert.barsky@vanderbilt.edu. *Website:* pantheon.yale.edu/~rfb5.

BARSTOW, Stanley (Stan), FRSL; writer, playwright and scriptwriter; b. 28 June 1928, Horbury, Yorkshire, England; m. Constance Mary Kershaw 1951; one s. one d. *Publications:* Fiction: A Kind of Loving, 1960; Ask Me Tomorrow, 1962; Joby, 1964; The Watchers on the Shore, 1966; A Raging Calm, 1968; The Right True End, 1976; A Brother's Tale, 1980; Just You Wait and See, 1986; B-Movie, 1987; Give Us This Day, 1989; Next of Kin, 1991. Short Stories: The Desperados, 1961; A Season with Eros, 1971; The Glad Eye and Other Stories, 1984. Plays: Listen for the Trains, Love, 1970; Stringer's Last Stand (with Alfred Bradley), 1971. Non-Fiction: In My Own Time (autobiog.), 2001. Other: Television plays and scripts. *Honours:* Best British Dramatization Award, Writers Guild of Great Britain, 1974; Best Drama Series Award, British Broadcasting Press Guild, 1974; Writer's Award, RTS, 1975; Hon. MA, Open University, 1982; Hon. Fellow, Bretton College, 1985. *Literary Agent:* The Agency, 24 Pottery Lane, Holland Park, London W11 4LZ, England.

BARTH, John Robert, AB, PhL, MA, STB, STL, PhD; academic and writer; b. 23 Feb. 1931, Buffalo, NY, USA. *Education:* Bellarmine College, Fordham University, Woodstock College, Harvard University. *Career:* Society of Jesus; Asst Prof. of English, Canisius College, Buffalo, 1967–70; Asst Prof. of English, Harvard University, 1970–74; Assoc. Prof. of English, 1974–77, Prof. of English, 1977–88, Chair., Dept of English, 1980–83, University of Missouri-Columbia; Thomas I Gasson Prof. of English, 1985–86, Dean, College of Arts and Sciences, 1988–99, James P. McIntyre Prof. of English, 1999–, Boston College; mem. American Asscn of University Profs; Conference on Christianity and Literature; Friends of Coleridge; Keats-Shelley Asscn; MLA; Wordsworth-Coleridge Asscn, pres., 1979. *Publications:* Coleridge and Christian Doctrine, 1969; Religious Perspectives in Faulkner's Fiction: Yoknapatawpha and Beyond (ed.), 1972; The Symbolic Imagination: Coleridge and the Romantic Tradition, 1977; Marginalia: The Collected Works of Samuel Taylor Coleridge (ed. with George Whalley), 1984–; Coleridge and the Power of Love, 1988; Coleridge, Keats and the Imagination: Romanticism and Adam's Dream-Essays in Honor of Walter

Jackson Bate (ed. with John L. Mahoney), 1990; The Fountain Light: Studies in Romanticism and Religion (ed.), 2002; Romanticism and Transcendence: Wordsworth, Coleridge, and the Religious Imagination, 2003. Contributions: books and journals. *Honours:* Book of the Year Award, Conference on Christianity and Literature, 1977; Curators' Annual Book Award, University of Missouri, 1988. *Address:* c/o Department of English, 24 Quincy Road, Boston College, Chestnut Hill MA 02467, USA.

BARTH, John Simmons; academic and writer; b. 27 May 1930, Cambridge, MD, USA; m. 1st Harriette Anne Strickland 1950 (divorced 1969); two s. one d.; m. 2nd Shelly Rosenberg 1970. *Education:* Juilliard School of Music; AB, 1951, MA, 1952, Johns Hopkins University. *Career:* Instructor, 1953–56, Asst Prof., 1957–60, Assoc. Prof., 1960–65, of English, Pennsylvania State University; Prof. of English, 1965–71, Edward H. Butler Prof. of English, 1971–73, SUNY at Buffalo; Alumni Centennial Prof. of English and Creative Writing, 1973–90, Prof. Emeritus, 1990–, Johns Hopkins University; mem. American Acad. and Institute of Arts and Letters; American Acad. of Arts and Sciences. *Publications:* Fiction: The Floating Opera, 1956; The End of the Road, 1958; The Sot-Weed Factor, 1960; Giles, Goat-Boy: or, the Revised New Syllabus, 1966; Lost in the Funhouse: Fiction for Print, Tape, Live Voice, 1964; Chimera, 1972; LETTERS, 1979; Sabbatical: A Romance, 1982; Tidewater Tales: A Novel, 1987; The Last Voyage of Somebody the Sailor, 1991; Once Upon a Time: A Floating Opera, 1994; On with the Story (short stories), 1996; Coming Soon!!!, 2001. Non-Fiction: The Literature of Exhaustion, and the Literature of Replenishment, 1982; The Friday Book: Essays and Other Nonfiction, 1984; Don't Count on It: A Note on the Number of 1001 Nights, 1984; Further Fridays: Essays, Lectures, and Other Nonfiction, 1984–1994, 1995; Coming Soon!!!, 2001. Contributions: Books and many periodicals. *Honours:* Brandeis University Creative Arts Award, 1965; Rockefeller Foundation Grant, 1965–66; National Institute of Arts and Letters Grant, 1966; National Book Award, 1973; F. Scott Fitzgerald Award, 1997; Lannan Foundation Award, 1998; PEN/Malamud Award, 1998; Lifetime Achievement in Letters Award, Enoch Pratt Free Library, 1999. *Address:* Writing Seminars, John Hopkins University, Baltimore, MD 21218, USA.

BARTLETT, Christopher John; Writer; b. 12 Oct. 1931, Bournemouth, England; m. Shirley Maureen Briggs, 7 Aug. 1958, three s. *Education:* BA, History, University College, Exeter, 1953; PhD, International History, LSE, 1956. *Career:* Asst Lecturer, University of Edinburgh, 1957–59; Lecturer in Modern History, University of the West Indies, Jamaica, 1959–62, Queen's College, Dundee, 1962–68; Reader in International History, 1968–78, Prof. of International History, 1978–96, Head, Dept of History, 1983–88, Emeritus and Hon. Prof. of International History, 1996–2002, University of Dundee. *Publications:* Great Britain and Sea Power, 1815–53, 1963; Castlereagh, 1966; Britain Pre-eminent: Studies of British World Influence in the Nineteenth Century (ed.), 1969; The Long Retreat: A Short History of British Defence Policy, 1945–70, 1972; The Rise and Fall of the Pax Americana: American Foreign Policy in the Twentieth Century, 1974; A History of Postwar Britain, 1945–74, 1977; The Global Conflict, 1880–1990: The International Rivalry of the Great Powers, 1984; British Foreign Policy in the Twentieth Century, 1989; 'The Special Relationship': A Political History or Anglo-American Relations Since 1945, 1992; Defence and Diplomacy: Britain and the Great Powers, 1815–1914, 1993; Peace, War and the European Great Powers, 1814–1914, 1996. Contributions: UK Chapters, Annual Register, 1987–97; Scholarly books and journals. *Honours:* FRHistS; Royal Society of Edinburgh, fellow.

BARTLETT, Robert John, BA, MA, DPhil, FRHistS, FBA, FRSE, FSA; academic, writer and editor; *Bishop Wardlaw Professor, University of St Andrews*; b. 27 Nov. 1950, London, England; m. Honora Elaine Hickey 1979; one s. one d. *Education:* Peterhouse, Cambridge, St John's College, Oxford. *Career:* Lecturer in History, University of Edinburgh, 1980–86; Mem., Institute for Advanced Study, Princeton, NJ, and Visiting Fellow, Davis Center, Dept of History, Princeton University, 1983–84; Prof. of Medieval History, University of Chicago, 1986–92; Prof. of Mediaeval History, 1992–, Bishop Wardlaw Prof., 1997–, University of St Andrews; Assoc. Ed., New Dictionary of National Biography, 1994–; British Acad. Reader, 1995–97; Sackler Scholar, Mortimer and Raymond Sackler Institute of Advanced Studies, University of Tel-Aviv, 2001. *Publications:* Gerald of Wales, 1146–1223, 1982; Trial by Fire and Water; The Medieval Judicial Ordeal, 1986; Medieval Frontier Societies (ed. with Angus MacKay), 1989; The Making of Europe: Conquest, Colonization and Cultural Change 950–1350, 1993; England Under the Norman and Angevin Kings 1075–1225, 2000; Medieval Panorama (ed.), 2001; Life and Miracles of St Modwenna, by Geoffrey of Burton (ed. and trans.), 2002; The Hanged Man 2004; contrib. to scholarly books and journals. *Honours:* Jr Fellow, University of Michigan Society of Fellows, 1979–80; Alexander von Humboldt Fellow, University of Göttingen, 1988–89; Wolfson Literary Prize for History, 1993. *Address:* c/o Department of Mediaeval History, University of St Andrews, St Andrews KY16 9AL, Scotland.

BARTON, John; Theologian, Prof. and Writer; b. 17 June 1948, London, England; m. Mary Burn 16 July 1973; one d. *Education:* BA, MA, Keble College, 1973, DPhil, Merton College, 1974, DLitt, St Cross College, 1988, Oxford. *Career:* Jr Research Fellow, Merton College, Oxford, 1973–74; Univ. Lecturer in Theology, 1974–89, Reader in Biblical Studies, 1989–91, Univ. of Oxford; Fellow, St Cross College, Oxford, 1974–91; Oriel and Laing Prof. of the Interpretation of Holy Scripture and Fellow, Oriel College, Oxford, 1991–; Canon Theologian, Winchester Cathedral, 1991–. *Publications:* Amos's Oracles Against the Nations, 1980; Reading the Old Testament, 1984; Oracles of God, 1986; People of the Book?, 1988; Love Unknown, 1990; What is the Bible?, 1991; Isaiah 1–39, 1995; The Spirit and the Letter, 1997; Making the Christian Bible, 1997; Ethics and the Old Testament, 1998; The Cambridge Companion to Biblical Interpretation, 1998; The Oxford Bible Commentary, 2001; Joel and Obadiah, 2002; The Biblical World, 2002. *Honours:* Hon. DTh, Univ. of Bonn, 1998. *Address:* c/o Oriel College, University of Oxford, Oxford OX1 4EW, England.

BARTY-KING, Mark Baxter, MC, FRSA; British publishing executive; *Chairman, Wade & Doherty Literary Agency*; b. 3 March 1938, London; m. 1st Margild Bolten 1963 (divorced 1975); two s.; m. 2nd Marilyn Barrett 1976; two s. *Education:* Winchester Coll. *Career:* nat. service, 13th/18th Royal Hussars, Aden, Oman, Malaya 1957–61; with Abelard Schuman, NY 1962–63, John Howell Books, San Francisco 1964–65, Heinemann Group 1966–74 (Dir Peter Davies Ltd 1969, William Heinemann Ltd 1971); Editorial Dir Granada Publishing 1974–81, Man. Dir Hardback Div. 1981–83; joined Transworld Publishers Ltd 1984, Deputy Man. Dir Publishing 1992, Man. Dir and CEO 1995–2000, Chair. 2001–03; f. Bantam Press 1985; Chair. (non-exec.) Wade & Doherty Literary Agency 2004–; mem. Council Publishers Asscn 1995–99, Gen. Books Council 1999–2002, Court, Worshipful Co. of Merchant Taylors 1992–, Chair. Govs St John's School, Northwood 1997–. *Address:* 46 Elms Road, London, SW4 9EX (Home); Wade & Doherty Literary Agency, 33 Cormorant Lodge, Thomas More Street, London, E1W 1AU, England (Office). *Telephone:* (20) 7622-7641 (Home); (20) 7622-1544 (Home). *Fax:* (20) 7622-1544 (Home). *E-mail:* MarkBartyKing@aol.com (Home).

BARZUN, Jacques Martin, AB, PhD, FRSA, FRSL; American writer and academic; *Professor Emeritus, Columbia University*; b. 30 Nov. 1907, Créteil, France; m. 1st Mariana Lowell 1936 (died 1979); two s. one d.; m. 2nd Marguerite Lee Davenport 1980. *Education:* Lycée Janson de Sailly and Columbia Univ. *Career:* Instructor in History, Columbia Univ. 1929, Asst Prof. 1938, Assoc. Prof. 1942, Prof. 1945, Dean of Graduate Faculties 1955–58, Dean of Faculties and Provost 1958–67, Seth Low Prof. 1960–67, Univ. Prof. 1967–75; Prof. Emer. 1975–; Literary Adviser, Scribner's 1975–93; fmr Dir Council for Basic Educ., New York Soc. Library, Open Court Publications Inc., Peabody Inst.; mem. Advisory Council, Univ. Coll. at Buckingham, Editorial Bd Encyclopedia Britannica 1979–; mem. Acad. Delphinale (Grenoble), American Acad. and Inst. of Arts and Letters (Pres. 1972–75, 1977–78), American Historical Asscn, Royal Soc. of Arts, American Arbitration Asscn, American Philosophical Soc., Royal Soc. of Literature, American Acad. of Arts and Sciences; Extraordinary Fellow, Churchill Coll., Cambridge 1961. *Publications:* The French Race: Theories of its Origins and their Social and Political Implications Prior to the Revolution 1932, Race: A Study in Modern Superstition 1937, Of Human Freedom 1939, Darwin, Marx, Wagner: Critique of a Heritage 1941, Romanticism and the Modern Ego (revised edn as Classic, Romantic, and Modern) 1943, Introduction to Naval History (with Paul H. Beik, George Crothers and E. O. Golob) 1944, Teacher in America 1945, Berlioz and the Romantic Century 1950, God's Country and Mine: A Declaration of Love Spiced with a Few Harsh Words 1954, Music in American Life 1956, The Energies of Art: Studies of Authors, Classic and Modern 1956, The Modern Researcher (with Henry F. Graff) 1957, Lincoln the Literary Genius 1959, The House of Intellect 1959, Science, the Glorious Entertainment 1964, The American University: How it Runs, Where it is Going 1968, On Writing, Editing and Publishing: Essays Explicative and Horatory 1971, A Catalogue of Crime (with Wendell Hertig Taylor) 1971, The Use and Abuse of Art 1974, Clio and the Doctors: Psycho-History, Quanto-History and History 1974, Simple and Direct: A Rhetoric for Writers 1975, Critical Questions 1982, A Stroll with William James 1983, A Word or Two Before You Go 1986, The Culture We Deserve 1989, Begin Here: On Teaching and Learning 1990, An Essay on French Verse for Readers of English Poetry 1991, From Dawn to Decadence: 500 Years of Western Cultural Life 2000, A Jacques Barzun Reader 2001; editor: Pleasures of Music 1950, The Selected Letters of Lord Byron 1953, New Letters of Berlioz (also trans.) 1954, The Selected Writings of John Jay Chapman 1957, Modern American Usage; translator: Diderot: Rameau's Nephew 1952, Flaubert's Dictionary of Accepted Ideas 1954, Evenings with the Orchestra 1956, Courteline: A Rule is a Rule 1960, Beaumarchais: The Marriage of Figaro 1961; contrib. articles to various scholarly and non-scholarly periodicals and journals. *Honours:* Chevalier Légion d'honneur, Presidential Medal of Freedom, USA; George Polk Memorial Award 1967. *Address:* 18 Wolfeton Way, San Antonio, TX 78218, USA.

BASINGER, Jeanine (Deyling); Prof. of Film Studies, Curator and Writer; b. 3 Feb. 1936, Ravenden, AR, USA; m. John Peter Basinger, 22 Sept. 1967, one d. *Education:* BS, 1957, MS, 1959, South Dakota State University. *Career:* Instructor, South Dakota State University, 1958–59; Teaching Assoc., 1971–72, Adjunct Lecturer, 1972–76, Adjunct Assoc. Prof., 1976–80, Assoc. Prof., 1980–84, Prof., 1984–88, Corwin-Fuller Prof. of Film Studies, 1988–, Wesleyan University; Founder-Curator, Wesleyan Cinema Archives, 1985–; mem. American Film Institute, trustee. *Publications:* Working with Kazan (ed. with John Frazer and Joseph W. Reed), 1973; Shirley Temple, 1975; Gene Kelly, 1976; Lana Turner, 1977; Anthony

Mann: A Critical Analysis, 1979; Anatomy of a Genre: World War II Combat Films, 1986; The It's A Wonderful Life Book, 1986; A Woman's View: How Hollywood Saw Women, 1930–1960, 1993; American Cinema: 100 Years of Filmmaking, 1994; Silent Stars, 1999. Contributions: Books and periodicals. *Honours:* Distinguished Alumni Award, 1994 and Hon. PhD, 1996, South Dakota State University; Outstanding Teaching Award, Wesleyan University, 1996; William K. Everson Award, Best Film Book of the Year. *Address:* 133 Lincoln St, Middletown, CT 06457, USA.

BASS, Cynthia; Writer; b. 17 Oct. 1949, Washington, DC, USA; m. Steven Seltzer. *Education:* BA, MA, Doctoral Studies, University of California at Berkeley. *Publications:* Sherman's March, 1994; Maiden Voyage, 1996. Contributions: periodicals. *Address:* 1926 Contra Costa Blvd, No. 217, Pleasant Hill, CA 94523, USA.

BASS, Rick; Writer; b. 7 March 1958, Fort Worth, Texas, USA. *Education:* BS, Utah State University, 1979. *Publications:* The Deer Pasture, 1985; Wild to the Heart, 1987; Oil Notes, 1989; The Watch: Stories, 1989; Platte River, 1994; The Lost Grizzlies, 1995; In the Loyal Mountains: Stories, 1995; The Book of YAAK, 1996; Where the Sea Used to Be, 1998; Fiber, 1998; The New Wolves, 1998; Brown Dog of the YAAK, 1999; Colter, 2000; The Hermit's Story (short stories), 2002. Contributions: anthologies and periodicals. *Honours:* Pushcart Prize; O. Henry Award; PEN-Nelson Award, 1988. *Literary Agent:* Bob Dattila, Livingston, Montana. *Address:* Rt 1, Troy, MT 59935, USA.

BASS, Thomas (Alden); Writer; b. 9 March 1951, Chagrin Falls, Ohio, USA. *Education:* AB, University of Chicago, 1973; PhD, University of California, 1980. *Career:* mem. Authors' Guild; PEN. *Publications:* The Eudaemonic Pie (The Newtonian Casino), 1985; Camping with the Prince and Other Tales of Science in Africa, 1990; Reinventing the Future: Conversations with the World's Leading Scientists, 1993; Vietnamerica: The War Comes Home, 1996; The Predictors, 1999. Contributions: Audubon; New York Times; New Yorker; Smithsonian; Wired. *Address:* 31 Rue Saint Placide, Paris 75006, France. *E-mail:* tbass@hamilton.edu.

BASTABLE, Bernard (see Barnard, Robert).

BATCHELOR, John Barham; Prof. of English Literature, Writer and Ed.; b. 15 March 1942, Farnborough, England; m. Henrietta Jane Letts 14 Sept. 1968; two s. one d. *Education:* MA, 1964, PhD, 1969, Magdalene College, Cambridge; MA, Univ. of New Brunswick, 1965. *Career:* Lecturer in English, Birmingham Univ., 1968–76; Fellow and Tutor, New College, Oxford, 1976–90; Joseph Cowen Prof. of English Literature, Univ. of Newcastle upon Tyne, 1990; Adjunct Prof. (in asscn with Ruskin Programme), Univ. of Lancaster, 2002–; mem. International Asscn of Profs of English; Founding Fellow, English Asscn (UK); Chair., Higher Education Cttee of the English Asscn. *Publications:* Mervyn Peake, 1974; Breathless Hush (novel), 1974; The Edwardian Novelists, 1982; H. G. Wells, 1985; Virginia Woolf, 1991; The Life of Joseph Conrad: A Critical Biography, 1994; The Art of Literary Biography (ed.), 1995; Shakespearean Continuities (joint ed.), 1997; John Ruskin: No Wealth But Life, 2000. Contributions: TLS; Observer; Daily Telegraph; Economist; Articles in English; Yearbook of English Studies; Review of English Studies; Dictionary of National Biography. *Literary Agent:* Felicity Bryan, 2a N Parade, Oxford, England. *Address:* Dept of English, University of Newcastle, Newcastle upon Tyne NE1 7RU, England.

BATE, (Andrew) Jonathan, PhD, FBA; British professor of English literature; *Professor of Shakespeare and Renaissance Literature, University of Warwick*; b. 26 June 1958, Sevenoaks, Kent, England; m. 1st Hilary Gaskin 1984 (divorced 1995); m. 2nd Paula Jayne Byrne 1996; one s. one d. *Education:* St. Catherine's Coll., Cambridge. *Career:* Harkness Fellow, Harvard Univ. 1980–81; Research Fellow, St Catherine's Coll., Cambridge 1983–85, Hon. Fellow 2000–; Fellow Trinity Hall, Cambridge, lecturer 1985–90; King Alfred Prof. of English Literature, Univ. of Liverpool 1991–2003; Prof. of Shakespeare and Renaissance Literature, Univ. of Warwick 2003–; Research Reader, British Acad. 1994–96; Leverhulme Personal Research Prof. 1999–2004; Ed. Arden Shakespeare series. *Radio:* features for BBC Radio 3, reviews for BBC Radio 4. *Publications:* Shakespeare and the English Romantic Imagination 1986, Charles Lamb: Essays of Elia (ed.) 1987, Shakespearean Constitutions: Politics, Theatre, Criticism 1730–1830 1989, Romantic Ecology: Wordsworth and the Environmental Tradition 1991, The Romantics on Shakespeare (ed.) 1992, Shakespeare and Ovid 1993, The Arden Shakespeare: Titus Andronicus (ed.) 1995, Shakespeare: An Illustrated Stage History (ed.) 1996, The Genius of Shakespeare 1997, The Cure for Love (novel) 1998, The Song of the Earth 2000, John Clare: A Biography 2003, I Am: The Selected Poetry of John Clare (ed.) 2003. *Honours:* Calvin & Rose Hoffman Prize 1996. *Literary Agent:* Wylie Agency Ltd, 17 Bedford Square, London, WC1B 3JA. *Address:* Department of English, University of Warwick, Coventry, CV4 7AL, England (Office).

BATES, Harry (see Home, Stewart Ramsay).

BATES, Milton James, BA, MA, PhD; academic and writer; *Professor of English, Marquette University*; b. 4 June 1945, Warrensburg, MO, USA; m. 1972; one s. one d. *Education:* St Louis University, University of California at Berkeley. *Career:* Asst Prof. of English, Williams College, 1975–81; Asst Prof., 1981–86, Assoc. Prof., 1986–91, Prof., 1991–, of English, Marquette University; Fulbright Distinguished Lecturer, Beijing Foreign Studies University, 2000; mem. Wallace Stevens Society, secretary, 1990–. *Publications:* Wallace Stevens: A Mythology of Self, 1985; Sur Plusieurs Beaux Sujects: Wallace Stevens' Commonplace Book, 1989; Wallace Stevens: Opus Posthumous, revised edn, 1989; The Wars We Took to Vietnam: Cultural Conflict and Storytelling, 1996. Contributions: articles and book reviews in journals and periodicals. *Honours:* Notable Book of the Year, New York Times Book Review, 1985; Outstanding Achievement in Literature, Wisconsin Library Asscn, 1985; Guggenheim Fellowship, 1989–90; National Jesuit Book Award, 1999; Council for Wisconsin Writers Scholarly Book Award, 1996. *Address:* Department of English, Marquette University, PO Box 1881, Milwaukee, WI 53201, USA.

BATTESTIN, Martin Carey, BA, PhD; academic and writer; *Professor of English Emeritus, University of Virginia*; b. 25 March 1930, New York, NY, USA; m. Ruthe Rootes 1963; one s. (died 1999) one d. *Education:* Princeton Univ. *Career:* Instructor 1956–58, Asst Prof. 1958–61, Wesleyan Univ.; Asst Prof. 1961–63, Assoc. Prof. 1963–67, Prof. 1967–75, William R. Kenan Jr Prof. of English 1975–98, Chair Dept of English 1983–86, Prof. of English Emeritus 1998–, Univ. of Virginia; Visiting Prof., Rice Univ. 1967–68; Assoc., Clare Hall, Cambridge 1972; mem. Asscn of Literary Scholars and Critics, American Soc. for 18th Century Studies, Int. Asscn of Univ. Profs of English, The Johnsonians, MLA. *Publications:* The Moral Basis of Fielding's Art: A Study of 'Joseph Andrews' 1959, The Providence of Wit: Aspects of Form in Augustan Literature and the Arts 1974, New Essays by Henry Fielding: His Contributions to 'The Craftsman' (1734–39) and Other Early Journalism 1989, Henry Fielding: A Life (with Ruthe R. Battestin) 1993, A Henry Fielding Companion 2000; editor: Henry Fielding: 'Joseph Andrews' and 'Shamela' 1961, Henry Fielding: The History of the Adventures of Joseph Andrews 1967, Tom Jones: A Collection of Critical Essays 1968, Henry Fielding: The History of Tom Jones, a Foundling (with Fredson Bowers) (two vols) 1974, Henry Fielding: Amelia 1983, British Novelists, 1660–1800 1985, The Works of Tobias Smollett (mem. editorial bd, Georgia edn) 1987–, The Correspondence of Henry and Sarah Fielding (with Clive T. Probyn) 1993, Smollett's translation of Cervantes' Don Quixote (ed. with O. M. Brack) 2003; contrib. to books and scholarly journals. *Honours:* ACLS Fellowships 1960–61, 1972, Guggenheim Fellowship 1964–65, Council of the Humanities Sr Fellow, Princeton Univ. 1971–, Center for Advanced Studies, Univ. of Virginia 1974–75, Nat. Endowment for the Humanities Bicentennial Research Fellow 1975–76, Festschrift 1997, Visiting Fellow, Lincoln Coll., Oxford 1999. *Address:* 1832 Westview Road, Charlottesville, VA 22903, USA.

BATTIN, B. W., (S. W. Bradford, Alexander Brinton, Warner Lee, Casey McAllister); Writer; b. 15 Nov. 1941, Ridgewood, NJ, USA; m. Sandra McCraw, 14 Feb. 1976. *Education:* BA, University of New Mexico, 1969. *Publications:* As B. W. Battin: Angel of the Night, 1983; The Boogeyman, 1984; Satan's Servant, 1984; Mary, Mary, 1985; Programmed for Terror, 1985; The Attraction, 1985; The Creep, 1987; Smithereens, 1987; Demented 1988; As Warner Lee: Into the Pit, 1989; It's Loose, 1990; Night Sounds, 1992; As S. W. Bradford: Tender Prey, 1990; Fair Game, 1992; As Alexander Brinton: Serial Blood, 1992; As Casey McAllister: Catch Me if You Can, 1993. *Literary Agent:* Dominick Abel, New York. *Address:* 711 N Mesa Rd, Belen, NM 87002, USA.

BATTISCOMBE, (Esther) Georgina Harwood; biographer; b. 21 Nov. 1905, London, England; m. Lt Col C. F. Battiscombe 1932; one d. *Education:* St Michael's School, Oxford; BA, History, Lady Margaret Hall, Oxford. *Career:* mem. FRSL; Society of Authors. *Publications:* Charlotte Mary Yonge, 1943; Mrs Gladstone, 1956; John Keble, 1963; Queen Alexandra, 1970; Lord Shaftesbury, 1974; Reluctant Pioneer, Life of Elizabeth Wordsworth, 1978; Christina Rossetti, 1981; The Spencers of Althorp, 1984; Winter Song, 1992. Contributions: Times; Sunday Telegraph; TLS; Spectator; Country Life; Books & Bookmen; History Today. *Honours:* James Tait Black Memorial Prize, 1963. *Literary Agent:* A. M. Heath & Co Ltd, 79 St Martin's Lane, London WC2N 4RE, England. *Address:* Thamesfield, Wargrave Road, Henley-on-Thames RG9 2LX, England.

BATTLES, Roxy (Edith Baker); Writer, Poet, Children's Author and Teacher; b. 29 March 1921, Spokane, Washington, USA; m. Willis Ralph Battles, 2 May 1941, one s. two d. *Education:* AA, Bakersfield Junior College, 1940; BA, California State University, 1959; MA, Pepperdine University, 1976. *Career:* Elementary Teacher, Torrance Unified Schools, 1959–85; Instructor, Torrance Adult School, 1968–88, Pepperdine University, 1976–79; Instructor, Creative Writing, Los Angeles Harbor College, 1995; mem. Southwest Manuscripters. *Publications:* Over the Rickety Fence, 1967; The Terrible Trick or Treat, 1970; 501 Balloons Sail East, 1971; The Terrible Terrier, 1972; One to Teeter Totter, 1973; Eddie Couldn't Find the Elephants, 1974; What Does the Rooster Say, Yoshio?, 1978; The Secret of Castle Drai, 1980; The Witch in Room 6, 1987; The Chemistry of Whispering Caves, 1989; The Lavender Castle (stage play), 1996. Contributions: numerous periodicals. *Honours:* National Science Award, 1971; United Nations Award, 1978; Author-in-Residence, American School of Madrid, Spain, 1991. *Address:* 560 S Helberta Avenue, Redondo Beach, CA 90277, USA.

BAUER, Caroline Feller; Author and Lecturer; b. 12 May 1935, Washington, DC, USA; m. 21 Dec. 1969, one d. *Education:* BA, Sarah Lawrence

College, 1956; MLS, Columbia University, 1958; PhD, University of Oregon, 1971. *Career:* mem. American Library Assen; Society of Children's Book Writers. *Publications:* My Mom Travels a Lot, 1981; This Way to Books, 1983; Too Many Books, 1984; Celebrations, 1985; Rainy Day, 1986; Snowy Day, 1986; Midnight Snowman, 1987; Presenting Reader's Theater, 1987; Windy Day, 1988; Halloween, 1989; Read for the Fun of It, 1992; New Handbook for Storytellers, 1993; Putting on a Play, 1993; Valentine's Day, 1993; Thanksgiving Day, 1994; The Poetry Break, 1995; Leading Kids to Books Through Magic, 1996. *Honours:* ERSTED Award for Distinguished Teaching; Christopher Award; Dorothy McKenzie Award for Distinguished Contribution to Children's Literature.

BAUER, Douglas; Writer; b. 17 Aug. 1945, Cheyenne, WY, USA. *Publications:* Prairie City, IA: Three Seasons at Home, 1979; Dexterity, 1989; The Very Air, 1993; The Book of Famous Iowans, 1997; The Stuff of Fiction: Advice on Craft. *Honours:* National Endowment for the Arts Fellowship; Massachusetts Artists Foundation Fellowship; Boston Public Library Literary Light. *Literary Agent:* Elyse Cheney, Sanford J. Greenburger Associates Inc, 55 Fifth Ave, New York, NY 10003, USA.

BAUER, Steven (Albert); Prof. of English, Writer and Poet; b. 10 Sept. 1948, Newark, NJ, USA; m. Elizabeth Arthur, 19 June 1982. *Education:* BA, Trinity College, Hartford, CT, 1970; MFA, University of Massachusetts, Amherst, 1975. *Career:* Instructor, 1979–81, Asst Prof., 1981–82, Colby College, Waterville, Maine; Asst Prof., 1982–86, Assoc. Prof., 1986–96, Prof., 1996–, of English, Dir of Creative Writing, 1986–96, Internal Dir of Creative Writing, 1996–2001, Miami University, Oxford, Ohio. *Publications:* Satyrday (novel), 1980; The River (novel), 1985; Steven Spielberg's Amazing Stories, 2 vols, 1986; Daylight Savings (poems), 1989; The Strange and Wonderful Tale of Robert McDoodle (The Boy Who Wanted to be a Dog), children's book, 1999; A Cat of a Different Color (novel for children), 2000. Contributions: Essays, stories and poems in many periodicals. *Honours:* Strousse Award for Poetry, Prairie Schooner, 1982; Master Artist Fellowship Award, Indiana Arts Council, 1988; Peregrine Smith Poetry Prize, 1989; Parents' Choice Recommended Writer, 2000. *Address:* 14100 Harmony Rd, Bath, IN 47010, USA. *E-mail:* banersa@muohio.edu.

BAUER, Yehuda; historian and academic; b. 6 April 1926, Prague, Czechoslovakia; two d. *Education:* BA, 1949, MA, 1950, Univ. of Wales; PhD, Hebrew Univ., Jerusalem, 1960. *Career:* Served in Palmach Forces of the Haganah (Jewish Underground), 1944–45, and in Israel's War of Independence, 1948–49; Lecturer, 1961–73, Head of Division of Holocaust Studies, 1968–95, Assoc. Prof., 1973–77, Head, 1973–75, 1977–79, Prof., 1977–95, Institute of Contemporary Jewry, Hebrew Univ.; Founder-Chair., Vidal Sassoon International Center for the Study of Antisemitism, Hebrew Univ., 1982–95; Ed., Journal of Holocaust and Genocide Studies, 1986–95; Visiting Prof., Univ. of Honolulu at Manoa, 1992, Yale Univ., 1993; Distinguished Visiting Prof., Ida E. King Chair of Holocaust Studies, Richard Stockton College, NJ, 1995–96, 2002; Dir, International Center for Holocaust Studies, Yad Vashem, Jerusalem, 1996–2001. *Publications:* (in English): From Diplomacy to Resistance: A History of Jewish Palestine, 1939–1945, 1970; My Brother's Keeper, 1974; Flight and Rescue, 1975; The Holocaust in Historical Perspective, 1978; The Jewish Emergence From Powerlessness, 1979; The Holocaust as Historical Experience (ed.), 1981; American Jewry and the Holocaust, 1982; History of the Holocaust, 1984; Jewish Reactions to the Holocaust, 1988; Out of the Ashes, 1989; Jews for Sale?: Nazi–Jewish Negotiations, 1939–1945, 1994; Rethinking the Holocaust, 2001. Contributions: scholarly books, yearbooks and journals. *Address:* c/o International Center for Holocaust Studies, Yad Vashem, PO Box 3477, Jerusalem 91034, Israel.

BAUMAN, Janina; Writer; b. 18 Aug. 1926, Warsaw, Poland; m. Zygmunt Bauman 18 Aug. 1948; three d. *Education:* Acad. of Social Sciences, 1951; Univ. of Warsaw, 1959. *Career:* Script Ed., Polish Film, 1948–68. *Publications:* Winter in the Morning, 1986: A Dream of Belonging, 1988; various other books and short stories published in Poland, 1990–. Contributions: Jewish Quarterly; Oral History; Polin; British Journal of Holocaust Education; Thesis Eleven. *Honours:* Award by Polityka Weekly, Poland, 1991. *Address:* 1 Lawnswood Gdns, Leeds, Yorkshire LS16 6HF, England. *E-mail:* janinabauman@aol.com.

BAUMAN, Zygmunt; Prof. of Sociology Emeritus and Writer; b. 19 Nov. 1925, Poznań, Poland; m. Janina (née Lewinson) Bauman, 18 Aug. 1948, three d. *Education:* MA, 1954, PhD, 1956, University of Warsaw. *Career:* Chair., Dept of Sociology, University of Warsaw, 1964–68; Prof. of Sociology, University of Tel-Aviv, 1968–71, University of Leeds, 1971–91; mem. British Sociological Assen; Polish Sociological Assen. *Publications:* Culture as Praxis, 1972; Hermeneutics and Social Science, 1977; Memories of Class, 1982; Legislators and Interpreters, 1987; Modernity and the Holocaust, 1989; Modernity and Ambivalence, 1990; Intimations of Postmodernity, 1991; Thinking Sociologically, 1991; Mortality, Immortality and Other Life Strategies, 1992; Postmodern Ethics, 1993; Life in Fragments, 1995; Postmodernity and Its Discontents, 1996; Globalization: The Human Consequences, 1998; Work, Consumerism and the New Poor, 1998; In Search of Politics, 1999; Liquid Modernity, 2000; Individualized Society, 2001; Community: Seeking Safety in an Uncertain World, 2001; Society Under Siege, 2002. Contributions: scholarly journals and general periodicals. *Honours:* Amalfi Prize for Sociology and Social Sciences, 1989; Hon. Doctorates, Universities of Oslo, 1997, Lapland, 1999, Uppsala, 2000; Theodore W. Adorno Prize, 1998. *Address:* 1 Lawnswood Gdns, Leeds LS16 6HF, England.

BAUMBACH, Jonathan; writer and academic; b. 5 July 1933, New York, USA; three s. one d. *Education:* AB, Brooklyn College, CUNY, 1955; MFA, Columbia University, 1956; PhD, Stanford University, 1961. *Career:* Instructor, Stanford University, 1958–60; Asst Prof., Ohio State University, 1961–64; Dir of Writing, New York University, 1964–66; Prof., English, Brooklyn College, CUNY, 1966–; Visiting professorships, Tufts University, 1970, University of Washington, 1978, 1983; mem. Teachers and Writers Collaborative, board of dirs; National Society of Film Critics, chair., 1982–84. *Publications:* The Landscape of Nightmare, 1965; A Man to Conjure With, 1965; What Comes Next, 1968; Reruns, 1974; Babble, 1976; Chez, Charlotte and Emily, 1979; Return of Service, 1979; My Father More or Less, 1984; The Life and Times of Major Fiction, 1987; Separate Hours, 1990; Seven Wives, 1994. Contributions: Movie Critic, Partisan Review, 1973–82; Articles, Fiction in Esquire; New American Review; Tri Quarterly; Iowa Review; North American Review; Fiction. *Honours:* National Endowment for the Arts Fellowship, 1978; Guggenheim Fellowship, 1980; O. Henry Prize Stories, 1980, 1984, 1988. *Address:* 320 Stratford Road, New York, NY 11218, USA.

BAUSCH, Richard (Carl); Author and Prof. of English; b. 18 April 1945, Fort Benning, GA, USA; m. Karen Miller, 3 May 1969, two s. one d. *Education:* BA, George Mason University, 1974; MFA, University of Iowa, 1975. *Career:* Prof. of English, George Mason University, 1980–; mem. Associated Writing Programs. *Publications:* Real Presence, 1980; Take Me Back, 1981; The Last Good Time, 1984; Spirits and Other Stories, 1987; Mr Field's Daughter, 1989; The Fireman's Wife and Other Stories, 1990; Violence, 1992; Rebel Powers, 1993; Rare and Endangered Species: A Novella and Stories, 1994; The Selected Stories of Richard Bausch, 1996; Good Evening Mr and Mrs America, and All the Ships at Sea, 1996; In the Night Season, 1998; Someone to Watch Over Me, 1999. *Honours:* Guggenheim Fellowship, 1984. *Address:* Dept of English, George Mason University, 4400 University Dr., Fairfax, VA 22030, USA.

BAUSCH, Robert (Charles); Writer and College Instructor; b. 18 April 1945, Fort Benning, GA, USA; m. 1st Geri Marrese, 21 March 1970, divorced 1982, three d.; m. 2nd Denise Natt, 14 Aug. 1982, one s. *Education:* University of Illinois, 1967–68; Northern Virginia College, 1970–72; BA, 1974, MA, 1975, MFA, 2001, George Mason University. *Career:* Instructor in Creative Writing, Northern Virginia Community College, 1975–. *Publications:* On the Way Home, 1982; The Lives of Riley Chance, 1984; Almighty Me, 1991; The White Rooster and Other Stories, 1995; A Hole in the Earth, 2000; The Gypsy Man, 2002. Contributions: periodicals. *Address:* c/o Northern Virginia Community College, 15200 Neabsco Mills Rd, Woodbridge, VA 22191, USA.

BAWDEN, Nina Mary, CBE, MA, JP, FRSL; English novelist; b. 19 Jan. 1925, Ilford, Essex; m. 1st H. W. Bawden 1947; two s. (one deceased); m. 2nd Austen S. Kark 1954 (died 2002); one d. two step-d. *Education:* Ilford Co. High School, Somerville Coll., Oxford. *Career:* Asst, Town and Country Planning Assen 1946–47; JP, Surrey 1968; Pres. Soc. of Women Writers and Journalists 1981–; Hon. Fellow, Somerville Coll., Oxford; mem. PEN; council mem. Soc. of Authors. *Publications:* Who Calls the Tune 1953, The Odd Flamingo 1954, The Solitary Child 1956, Devil by the Sea 1958, Just Like a Lady 1960, In Honour Bound 1961, Tortoise by Candlelight 1963, A Little Love, A Little Learning 1965, A Woman of My Age 1967, The Grain of Truth 1969, The Birds on the Trees 1970, Anna Apparent 1972, George Beneath a Paper Moon 1974, Afternoon of a Good Woman 1976, Familiar Passions 1979, Walking Naked 1981, The Ice House 1983, Circles of Deceit (also adapted for TV) 1987, Family Money (also adapted for TV) 1991, In My Own Time (autobiog.) 1994, A Nice Change 1997; for children: The Secret Passage 1963, The Runaway Summer 1969, Carrie's War 1973 (Phoenix Award 1993) (also adapted for BBC TV 2003), The Peppermint Pig 1975 (Guardian Prize for Children's Literature 1975), The Finding 1985, Princess Alice 1985, Keeping Henry 1988, The Outside Child 1989, Humbug 1992, The Real Plato Jones 1993, Granny the Pig 1995, Off the Road 1998, Ruffian on the Stair 2001. *Honours:* Yorkshire Post Novel of the Year Award 1976. *Literary Agent:* Curtis Brown Ltd, Haymarket House, 28–29 Haymarket, London, SW1Y 4SP. *Telephone:* (20) 7393-4400. *Fax:* (20) 7393-4401. *E-mail:* info@curtisbrown.co.uk. *Website:* www.curtisbrown.co.uk. *Address:* 22 Noel Road, London, N1 8HA, England; 19 Kapodistriou, Nauplion 21100, Greece. *Telephone:* (20) 7226-2839 (Office). *Fax:* (20) 7359-7103.

BAXT, George; Writer; b. 11 June 1923, New York, NY, USA. *Education:* City and Brooklyn Colleges, CUNY. *Publications:* A Queer Kind of Death, 1966; A Parade of Cockeyed Creatures, 1967; I! Said the Demon, 1968; Burning Sappho, 1972; The Dorothy Parker Murder Case, 1984; The Alfred Hitchcock Murder Case: An Unauthorized Novel, 1986; The Tallulah Bankhead Murder Case, 1987; The Talking Picture Murder Case, 1990; The Mae West Murder Case, 1993; The Marlene Dietrich Murder Case, 1993; The Bette Davis Murder Case, 1994; The Clark Gable and Carole Lombard Murder Case, 1997. Contributions: Ellery Queen Mystery Magazine. *Address:* c/o St Martin's Press, 175 Fifth Ave, New York, NY 10010, USA.

BAXTER, Charles; Prof. of English, Author and Poet; b. 13 May 1947, Minneapolis, Minnesota, USA; m. Martha Hauser, one s. *Education:* BA, Macalester College, 1969; PhD, SUNY at Buffalo, 1974. *Career:* Asst Prof., 1974–79, Assoc. Prof., 1979–85, Prof. of English, 1985–89, Wayne State University; Faculty, Warren Wilson College, 1986; Visiting Faculty, 1987, Prof. of English, 1989–, University of Michigan. *Publications:* Fiction: Harmony of the World, 1984; Through the Safety Net, 1985; First Light, 1987; A Relative Stranger, 1990; Shadow Play, 1993; Believers, 1997; The Feast of Love, 2000. Non-Fiction: Burning Down the House, 1997. Poetry: Chameleon, 1970; The South Dakota Guidebook, 1974; Imaginary Paintings and Other Poems, 1990. Contributions: numerous anthologies, journals, reviews, and newspapers. *Honours:* National Endowment for the Arts Grant, 1983; Guggenheim Fellowship, 1985–86; Arts Foundation of Michigan Award, 1991; Lila Wallace-Reader's Digest Foundation Fellowship, 1992–95; Michigan Author of the Year Award, 1993; American Acad. of Arts and Letters Award in Literature, 1997. *Address:* 1585 Woodland Dr., Ann Arbor, MN 48103, USA.

BAXTER, Craig, BA, AM, PhD; academic, writer and consultant; b. 16 Feb. 1929, Elizabeth, NJ, USA; m. Barbara T. Stevens 1984 (died 2003); one s. one d. *Education:* Univ. of Pennsylvania. *Career:* US Foreign Service, Vice-Consul, Mumbai 1958–60, Political Officer, New Delhi 1961–64, Deputy Principal Officer and Political Officer, Lahore 1965–68, Analyst for India 1968–69, Sr Political Officer for Pakistan and Afghanistan 1969–71, Visiting Assoc. Prof. in Social Sciences, United State Military Acad. 1971–74, Political Counselor, Accra 1974–76, and Dhaka 1976–78, Officer-in-Charge, Int. Scientific Relations for the Near East, South Asia, and Africa 1978–80; Lecturer, Mount Vernon College, Washington, DC, 1981; Visiting Prof. of Political Science and Diplomat-in-Residence 1981–82, Prof. of Politics and History 1982–99, Chair of Dept of Political Science 1991–94, Juniata Coll., Huntingdon, Pennsylvania; consultant to various organizations; mem. American Foreign Service Asscn, Asscn for Asian Studies, American Inst. of Pakistan Studies (pres. 1993–99), American Inst. of Bangladesh Studies (pres. 1989–98). *Publications:* The Jana Sangh: A Biography of an Indian Political Party 1969, Bangladesh: A New Nation in an Old Setting 1984, Zia's Pakistan: Politics and Stability in a Frontline State (ed. and contributor) 1985, Government and Politics in South Asia (with Yogendra K. Malik, Charles H. Kennedy and Robert C. Oberst) 1987, Historical Dictionary of Bangladesh (with Syedur Rahman) 1989, Pakistan Under the Military: Eleven Years of Zia ul-Haq (with Shahid Javed Burki) 1990, Bangladesh: From a Nation to a State 1996, Pakistan 1997 (with Charles H. Kennedy) 1998, Pakistan 2000 (with Charles H. Kennedy) 2000, Pakistan on the Brink 2003; contrib. to books, encyclopedias and scholarly journals. *Honours:* Outstanding Academic Book, American Library Asscn 1996, Distinguished Asianist Mid-Atlantic Region Asscn for Asian Studies 2002. *Address:* RR No. 4, Box 103, Huntingdon, PA 16652, USA. *E-mail:* cbaxter@pennswoods.net.

BAXTER, John; Writer; b. 14 Dec. 1939, Sydney, NSW, Australia. *Education:* Waverly College, Sydney, 1944–54. *Career:* Dir of Publicity, Australian Commonwealth Film Unit, Sydney, 1968–70; Lecturer in Film and Theatre, Hollins College, 1974–78; Freelance TV Producer and Screenwriter, 1978–87; Visiting Lecturer, Mitchell College, 1987. *Publications:* The Off Worlders, 1966, in Australia as The God Killers: Hollywood in the Thirties, 1968; The Pacific Book of Australian Science Fiction, 1970; The Australian Cinema, 1970; Science Fiction in the Cinema, 1970; The Gangster Film, 1970; The Cinema of Josef von Sternburg, 1971; The Cinema of John Ford, 1971; The Second Pacific Book of Australian Science Fiction, 1971; Hollywood in the Sixties, 1972; Sixty Years of Hollywood, 1973; An Appalling Talent: Kent Russell, 1973; Stunt: The Story of the Great Movie Stunt Men, 1974; The Hollywood Exiles, 1976; The Fire Came By (with Thomas R. Atkins), 1976; King Vidor, 1976; The Hermes Fall, 1978; The Bidders (in UK as Bidding), 1979; The Kid, 1981; The Video Handbook (with Brian Norris), 1982; The Black Yacht, 1982; Who Burned Australia? The Ash Wednesday Fires, 1984; Filmstruck, 1987; Bondi Blues, 1993; Fellini, 1993; Buñuel, 1994; Steven Spielberg: The Unauthorised Biography, 1996; Woody Allen: A Biography, 1999; Stanley Kubrick, 1999; George Lucas: Mythmaker, 2000; The Making of Dungeons and Dragons: The Movie; A Pound of Paper: Confessions of a Book Addict, 2002. Screenplays: The Time Guardian, 1988. TV Series: The Cutting Room, 1986; First Take, 1986; Filmstruck, 1986. *Literary Agent:* Curtis Brown Ltd, Haymarket House, 28–29 Haymarket, London, SW1Y 4SP, England. *Telephone:* (20) 7393-4400. *Fax:* (20) 7393-4401. *E-mail:* info@curtisbrown.co.uk. *Website:* www.curtisbrown.co.uk.

BAXTER, Stephen, MA, PhD; British writer; b. 1957, Liverpool, England. *Education:* Univ. of Cambridge, Univ. of Southampton. *Publications:* Fiction: Raft, 1991; Timelike Infinity, 1992; Anti-Ice, 1993; Flux, 1993; Ring, 1994; The Time Ships, 1995; Voyage, 1996; Titan, 1997; Vacuum Diagrams (short stories), 1997; Gulliverzone, 1997; Traces (short stories), 1998; Moonseed, 1998; Webcrash, 1998; Manifold 1: Time, 1999; Silverhair, 1999; Longtusk, 2000; Manifold 2: Space, 2000; The Light of Other Days (with Arthur C. Clarke), 2000; Icebones, 2001; Manifold 3: Origin, 2001; Evolution, 2002; Phase Space (short stories), 2002; Destiny's Children 1: Coalescent, 2003; Exultant 2004. Non-Fiction: Angular Distribution Analysis in Acoustics, 1986; Reengineering Information Technology (with David Lisburn), 1994; The Role of the IT/IS Manager, 1996; Deep Future, 2001; Omegatropic, 2001; Revolutions in the Earth: James Hutton and the True Age of the Earth, 2003. Other: Irina (online publ.), 1996; numerous short stories; ed. of anthologies; articles and talks. Contributions: anthologies, science and computing journals, science fiction magazines; radio and television. *Honours:* John W. Campbell Award for Best Novel, 1996; BSFA Award for Best Novel, 1996, for Best Short Story, 1998, for Best Non-Fiction, 2001; Philip K. Dick Awards for Best Novel, 1997, 1999. *Literary Agent:* PFD, Drury House, 34–43 Russell Street, London, WC2B 5HA, England.

BAYBARS, Taner, (Timothy Bayliss); British writer and painter; b. 18 June 1936, Cyprus; one d. *Education:* Turkish Lycée. *Career:* mem. Club de Vin d'Angoulême; Poetry Society of London; Arts Septemaniens of Narbonne. *Publications:* To Catch a Falling Man, 1963; A Trap for the Burglar, 1965; Selected Poems of Nazim Hikmet, 1967; The Moscow Symphony (Hikmet), 1970; Plucked in a Far-Off Land, 1970, (translated into Turkish as Uzak Ulke, 1997); The Day Before Tomorrow (Hikmet), 1972; Susila in the Autumn Woods, 1974; Narcissus in a Dry Pool, 1978; Pregnant Shadows, 1981; A Sad State of Freedom, 1990; Selected Poems (in Turkish trans.), 1997; Don't Go Back to Kyrenia (trans. of Mehmet Yashin's poems), 2001. Contributions: Critical Quarterly, Ambit; Orte; Détours d'Ecritures; Hudson Review; Dalhousie Review; M25; Europe; Kitap-Lik. *Literary Agent:* MBA Literary Agents Ltd, 62 Grafton Way, London W1T 5DW, England. *Address:* 2 rue de L'Evêque, 34360 Saint-Chinian, France. *E-mail:* tbaybars@wanadoo.fr.

BAYLEY, Barrington (John), (Alan Aumbry, P. F. Woods); Author; b. 9 April 1937, Birmingham, England; m. Joan Lucy Clarke 31 Oct. 1969; one s. one d. *Publications:* Star Virus, 1970; Annihilation Factor, 1972; Empire of Two Worlds, 1972; Collision with Chronos, 1973; The Fall of Chronopolis, 1974; The Soul of the Robot, 1974; The Garments of Caean, 1976; The Grand Wheel, 1977; The Knights of the Limits, 1978; Star Winds, 1978; The Seed of Evil, 1979; The Pillars of Eternity, 1982; The Zen Gun, 1984; The Forest of Peldain, 1985; The Rod of Light, 1985; Eye of Terror, 1999; The Sinners of Erspia, 2002; The Great Hydration, 2002. *Honours:* Seiun Award for Best Foreign Science Fiction Novel Published in Japan, 1984–85; BSFA Award for Best Short Fiction, 1996. *Address:* 48 Turreff Ave, Donnington, Telford, Shropshire TF2 8HE, England.

BAYLEY, John (Oliver); Prof. of English Literature (retd) and Writer; b. 27 March 1925, Lahore, India; m. 1st Iris Murdoch 1956 (died 1999); m. 2nd Audhild Villers 2000. *Education:* Eton College, 1938–43; BA, English, New College, Oxford, 1950. *Career:* Mem., St Antony's College and Magdalen College, Oxford, 1951–55; Fellow and Tutor in English, New College, Oxford, 1955–74; Warton Prof. of English Literature and Fellow, St Catherine's College, Oxford, 1974–92; mem. British Acad., fellow. *Publications:* In Another Country (novel), 1954; The Romantic Survival: A Study in Poetic Evolution, 1956; The Characters of Love, 1961; Tolstoy and the Novel, 1966; Pushkin: A Comparative Commentary, 1971; The Uses of Division: Unity and Disharmony in Literature, 1976; An Essay on Hardy, 1978; Shakespeare and Tragedy, 1981; The Order of Battle at Trafalgar, 1987; The Short Story: Henry James and Elizabeth Bowen, 1988; Housman's Poems, 1992; Alice (novel), 1994; The Queer Captain (novel), 1995; George's Liar (novel), 1996; The Red Hat (novel), 1997; Iris: A Memoir of Iris Murdoch, 1998; Iris and the Friends: A Year of Memories, 1999; The Widower's House, 2001. *Honours:* CBE. *Address:* c/o St Catherine's College, Oxford OX1 3UJ, England.

BAYLEY, Peter Charles, MA; academic and writer; b. 25 Jan. 1921, Gloucester, England. *Education:* University of Oxford. *Career:* Fellow, University College, 1947–72; Praelector in English, 1949–72, University Lecturer, 1952–72, University of Oxford; Master, Collingwood College, University of Durham, 1972–78; Berry Prof. and Head of English Dept, 1978–85, Berry Prof. Emeritus, 1985–, University of St Andrews, Fife. *Publications:* Edmund Spenser, Prince of Poets, 1971; Poems of Milton, 1982; An ABC of Shakespeare, 1985; Editor: The Faerie Queene, by Spenser, Book II, 1965, Book 1, 1966, 1970; Loves and Deaths, 1972; A Casebook on Spenser's Faerie Queene, 1977. Contributions: Patterns of Love and Courtesy, 1966; Oxford Bibliographical Guides, 1971; C. S. Lewis at the Breakfast Table, 1979; The Encyclopedia of Oxford, 1988; Sir William Jones 1746–94, 1998. *Address:* 63 Oxford Street, Woodstock, Oxford OX20 1TJ, England.

BAYLISS, Timothy (see Baybars, Taner).

BEACH, Eric; Poet and Writer; b. 1947, New Zealand. *Publications:* St Kilda Meets Hugo Ball, 1974; In Occupied Territory, 1977; A Photo of Some People in a Football Stadium, 1978; Weeping for Lost Babylon, 1996. Contributions: anthologies. *Address:* c/o HarperCollins, 10 E 53rd St, New York, NY 10022, USA.

BEAGLE, Peter Soyer, BA; writer, musician, singer and songwriter; b. 20 April 1939, New York, NY, USA; m. 1st Enid Nordeen 1964 (divorced 1980); one s. two d.; m. 2nd Padma Hejmadi 1988. *Education:* University of Pittsburgh. *Career:* many readings, lectures, and concerts; Visiting Asst Prof., University of Washington, 1988. *Publications:* Fiction: A Fine and Private Place, 1960; The Last Unicorn, 1968; The Folk of the Air, 1986; The Innkeeper's Song, 1993; The Unicorn Sonata, 1996. Fiction Collections: The Fantasy Worlds of Peter S. Beagle, 1978; Giant Bones, 1997; The Rhinoceros Who Quoted Nietzsche, and Other Odd Acquaintances, 1997. Editor:

Peter Beagle's Immortal Unicorn (with Janet Berliner), 1995. Opera Libretto: The Midnight Angel, 1993. Non-Fiction: I See By My Outfit, 1965; The California Feeling, 1969; American Denim: A New Folk Art, 1975; The Lady and Her Tiger (with Pat Derby), 1976; The Garden of Earthly Delights, 1982; In the Presence of Elephants (with Pat Derby), 1995. Contributions: anthologies, periodicals, films, and television. *Address:* 373 63rd Street, Oakland, CA 94618-1257, USA.

BEALES, Derek (Edward Dawson); Prof. of Modern History Emeritus and Writer; b. 12 June 1931, Felixstowe, England. *Education:* BA, 1953, MA, PhD, 1957, Univ. of Cambridge. *Career:* Research Fellow, 1955–58, Fellow, 1958–, Tutor, 1961–70, Vice-Master, 1973–75, Sidney Sussex College; Asst Lecturer, 1962–65, Lecturer, 1965–80, Chair., Faculty Board of History, 1979–81, Prof. of Modern History, 1980–97, Emeritus Prof., 1997–, Univ. of Cambridge; Ed., Historical Journal, 1971–75; Mem. of Council, Royal Historical Society, 1984–87; British Acad. Representative, Standing Cttee for Humanities, European Science Foundation, 1993–99; Recurring Visiting Prof., Central European Univ., Budapest, 1995–; mem. Athenaeum. *Publications:* England and Italy 1859–60, 1961; From Castlereagh to Gladstone, 1969; The Risorgimento and the Unification of Italy, 1971, revised edn (with E. F. Biagini), 2002; History and Biography, 1981; History, Society and the Churches (ed. with G. F. A. Best), 1985; Joseph II: In the Shadow of Maria Theresa 1741–80, 1987; Mozart and the Habsburgs, 1993; Sidney Sussex College Quatercentenary Essays (ed. with H. B. Nisbet), 1996; Prosperity and Plunder: European Catholic Monasteries in the Age of Revolution, 1650–1815, 2003. *Honours:* Doctor of Letters, 1988; Fellow, British Acad., 1989; Stenton Lecturer, Univ. of Reading, 1992; Birkbeck Lecturer, Trinity College, Cambridge, 1993; Leverhulme 2000 Emeritus Fellowship, 2001–03. *Address:* Sidney Sussex College, Cambridge CB2 3HU, England. *E-mail:* deb1000@cam.ac.uk.

BEAR, Carolyn Ann, (Chlöe Rayban); writer; b. 10 April 1944, Exeter, England; m. Peter Julian Bear; two d. *Education:* University of Western Australia; MA, Philosophy, University of Newcastle upon Tyne. *Publications:* Under Different Stars, 1988; Wild Child, 1991; Virtual Sexual Reality, 1994; Love in Cyberia, 1996; Screen Kiss, 1997; Clash on the Catwalk, 1997; Havana to Hollywood, 1997; Street to Stardom, 1997; Models Move On, 1998; Terminal Chic, 2000. *Literary Agent:* Laura Cecil Literary Agency, 17 Alwyne Villas, London, N1 2HG, England.

BEAR, Gregory Dale, AB; writer; b. 20 Aug. 1951, San Diego, CA, USA; m. 1st Christina Nielsen 1975 (divorced 1981); m. 2nd Astrid Anderson 1983; one s. one d. *Education:* San Diego State College. *Career:* mem. SFWA (pres. 1988–90). *Publications:* Hegira, 1979; Psychlone, 1979; Beyond Heaven's River, 1980; Strength of Stones, 1981; The Wind From a Burning Woman, 1983; Corona, 1984; The Infinity Concerto, 1984; Eon, 1985; Blood Music, 1985; The Serpent Mage, 1986; The Forge of God, 1987; Sleepside Story, 1987; Eternity, 1988; Hardfought, 1988; Early Harvest, 1988; Tangents, 1989; Queen of Angels, 1990; Heads, 1990; Anvil of Stars, 1992; Moving Mars, 1993; Legacy, 1995; Dinosaur Summer, 1998; Darwin's Radio, 1999; Vitals, 2002; Darwin's Children, 2003. *Honours:* awards from SFWA. *Address:* 506 Lakeview Road, Alderwood Manor, WA 98036, USA.

BEARDSLEY, John Douglas; writer, poet, editor, reviewer and teacher; b. 27 April 1941, Montréal, QC, Canada. *Education:* BA, University of Victoria, BC, 1976; MA, York University, Toronto, Ontario, 1978. *Career:* Chief Ed., Gregson Graham Ltd, 1980–82; Senior Instructor, Dept of English, University of Victoria, 1981–; Writer, Ed. and Graphic Designer, 1982–85, Writer, Ed. and Proofreader, 1985–, Beardsley and Assocs, Victoria. *Publications:* Going Down into History, 1976; The Only Country in the World Called Canada, 1976; Six Saanich Poems, 1977; Play on the Water: The Paul Klee Poems, 1978; Premonitions and Gifts (with Theresa Kishkan), 1979; Poems (with Charles Lillard), 1979; Pacific Sands, 1980; Kissing the Body of My Lord: The Marie Poems, 1982; Country on Ice, 1987; A Dancing Star, 1988; The Rocket, the Flower, the Hammer and Me (ed.), 1988; Free to Talk, 1992; Inside Passage, 1994; Wrestling with Angels (Selected Poems, 1960–1995), 1996; My Friends the Strangers, 1996; Our Game (ed.), 1998; No One Else is Lawrence! (with Al Purdy), 1998; The Man Who Outlived Himself (with Al Purdy), 2000. Contributions: anthologies, newspapers, magazines and periodicals. *Honours:* Canada Council Arts Award, 1978; British Columbia Millennium Book Award, 2000. *Address:* 1074 Lodge Avenue, Victoria, BC V8X 3A8, Canada.

BEASLEY, John David, (David Sellers); writer and social worker; b. 26 Oct. 1944, Hornsea, Yorkshire, England; m. Marian Ruth Orford 1969; one s. two d. *Education:* Univ. of London, Polytechnic of North London. *Career:* United Kingdom Band of Hope Union 1960–70; social worker, London Borough of Tower Hamlets 1970–94; mem. Soc. of Authors. *Publications:* Who Was Who in Peckham 1985, The Bitter Cry Heard and Heeded 1989, 500 Quotes and Anecdotes 1992, Origin of Names in Peckham and Nunhead 1993, Peckham and Nunhead Churches 1995, Peckham Rye Park Centenary 1995, Peckham and Nunhead 1995, Another 500 Quotes and Anecdotes 1996, Transport in Peckham and Nunhead 1997, East Dulwich 1998, The Story of Peckham and Nunhead 1999, Peckham and Nunhead Remembered 2000, Southwark Remembered 2001, East Dulwich Remembered 2002; contrib. to Challenge, South London Memories in South London Press. *Honours:* Southwark Civic Award 1997. *Address:* South Riding, 6 Everthorpe Road, London, SE15 4DA, England.

BEASLEY, William Gerald, BA, PhD; academic and writer; *Professor Emeritus, School of Oriental and African Studies*; b. 22 Dec. 1919, England. *Education:* Univ. of London. *Career:* Prof. of History of the Far East, School of Oriental and African Studies, London 1954–83, Prof. Emeritus 1983–. *Publications:* Great Britain and the Opening of Japan 1833–1858 1951, Select Documents on Japanese Foreign Policy 1853–1868 (ed. and trans.) 1955, Historians of China and Japan (ed. with E. G. Pulleyblank) 1961, The Modern History of Japan 1963, The Meiji Restoration 1972, Modern Japan: Aspects of History, Literature and Society (ed.) 1975, Japanese Imperialism 1894–1945 1987, The Rise of Modern Japan 1990, Japan Encounters the Barbarian: Japanese Travellers in America and Europe 1995, The Japanese Experience: A Short History of Japan 1999. *Address:* 172 Hampton Road, Twickenham, TW2 5NJ, England.

BEASLEY-MURRAY, George Raymond, BD, MTh, MA, DD, PhD; academic and writer; b. 10 Oct. 1916, London, England; m. Ruth Weston 1942; three s. one d. *Education:* King's College, University of London, University of Cambridge. *Career:* Lecturer, 1950–56, Principal, 1958–73, Spurgeon's College, London; Prof. of Greek New Testament, Ruschlikon, Zürich, 1956–58; Prof., 1973–80, Senior Prof., 1980–92, Southern Baptist Seminary, Louisville, KY; mem. Catholic Biblical Asscn of America; Society of Biblical Literature; Studiorum Novi Testamenti Societas; Tyndale Fellowship for Biblical and Theological Research. *Publications:* Jesus and the Future, 1954; A Commentary on Mark Thirteen, 1957; Baptism in the New Testament, 1962; Baptism Today and Tomorrow, 1966; Commentary on Gospel of John, Word Biblical Commentary, 1987; Gospel of Life: Theology in the Fourth Gospel, 1991; Jesus and the Last Days, 1993; Preaching the Gospel from the Gospels, 1996. Contributions: books and scholarly journals.

BEATTIE, Ann; Short Story Writer and Poet; b. 7 Sept. 1947, Washington, DC, USA. *Education:* BA, American University, Washington, DC, 1969; MA, University of Connecticut, 1970. *Publications:* Secrets and Surprises, 1978; Where You'll Find the Other Stories, 1986; What Was Mine and Other Stories, 1991; With This Ring, 1997; My Life, Starring Dara Falcon, 1998; Park City: New and Selected Stories, 1998; New and Selected Poems, 1999; Perfect Recall (short stories), 2001; The Doctor's House, 2002. Contributions: various publications. *Literary Agent:* Janklow & Nesbit Associates, 445 Park Ave, New York, NY 10022, USA.

BEATY, (Arthur) David, MBE; writer; b. 28 March 1919, Hatton, Ceylon; m. Betty Joan Campbell Smith 1948; three d. *Education:* MA, History, Merton College, Oxford, 1940; MPhil, Psychology, University College, 1965; Airline Transport Pilot's Licence; Navigation and Radio Licences. *Career:* RAF, 1940–46; Squadron Leader, British Overseas Airways Corporation, Senior Captain, Principal Atlantic Routes, 1946–53; Foreign Office, 1966–74; mem. Royal Aeronautical Society. *Publications:* The Take Off, 1948; The Heart of the Storm, 1954; The Proving Flight, 1956; Cone of Silence, 1958; Call Me Captain, 1959; Village of Stars, 1960; The Wind off the Sea, 1962; The Siren Song, 1964; Milk and Honey, 1964; Sword of Honour, 1965; The Human Factor in Aircraft Accidents, 1969; The Temple Tree, 1971; Electric Train, 1974; The Water Jumper: History of North Atlantic Flight, 1976; Excellency, 1977; The Complete Sky Traveller, 1978; The White Sea Bird, 1979; Wings of the Morning, with Betty Beaty, 1982; Strange Encounters, 1982; The Stick, 1984; The Blood Brothers, 1987; Eagles, 1990; The Naked Pilot, 1991; Light Perpetual, Airmen's Memorial Windows, 1995; The Ghosts of the Eighth Attack, 1998. *Address:* Manchester House, Church Hill, Slindon, Near Arundel, West Sussex BN18 0RD, England.

BEAUCHEMIN, Yves; Author; b. 26 June 1941, Noranda, QC, Canada; m. Viviane St Onge, 26 May 1973, two c. *Education:* BA, Collège de Joliette, 1962; Licence ès lettres, University of Montréal, 1965. *Career:* mem. Amnesty International; International PEN; Union des écrivaines et des écrivains québécois, pres., 1986–87. *Publications:* L'enfirouapé, 1974; Le matou, 1981, English trans. as The Alley Cat, 1986; Du sommet d'un arbre, 1986; Juliette Pomerleau, 1989; Finalement... les enfants, 1991; Une histoire a faire japper, 1991; Antoine et Alfred, 1992; Le second violon, 1996. Contributions: newspapers, magazines, and radio. *Honours:* Prix France-Quèbec, 1975; Prix de la communauté urbaine, Montréal, 1982; Prix des jeunes romanciers, Journal de Montréal, 1982; Prix du roman de l'ete, Cannes, France, 1982. *Address:* 247 Saint-Jacques St, Longueil, QC J4H 3B8, Canada.

BEAULIEU, Victor-Lévy; Author and Dramatist; b. 2 Sept. 1945, Saint-Paul-de-la-Croix, QC, Canada; m. Francine Cantin, two d. *Education:* University of Rallonge. *Publications:* Jos Connaissant, 1970, English trans., 1982; Pour saluer Victor Hugo, 1971; Les Grands-Pères, 1972, English trans. as The Grandfathers: A Novel, 1975; Jack Kerouac: Essai-poulet, 1972, English trans. as Don Quixote in Nighttown, 1978; Manuel de la petite littérature de Québec, 1974; Blanche forcée, 1975; Ma Corriveau, suivi de La sorcellerie en finale sexuée, 1976; N'évoque plus que le désenchantement de ta ténèbre, mon si pauvre Abel, 1976; Sagamo Job J, 1977; Monsieur Melville, 3 vols, 1978, English trans., 1984; Una, 1980; Satan Belhumeur, 1981, English trans., 1983; Moi Pierre Leroy, prophète, martyr et un peu felé du chaudron, 1982; Entre la sainteté et le terrorisme, 1984; Docteur Ferron, 1991. Other: Television Series: Race de Monde, 1978–81; L'héritage, 1987–89; Montréal PQ, 1991–94; Bouscotte, 1997–2001. Contributions: various publications. *Honours:* Grand Prix de la Ville de Montréal, 1972; Governor-General's Award for Fiction, 1974;

Beraud-Molson Prize, 1981; Prix Canada-Belgique, 1981. *Address:* c/o Union des écrivaines et des écrivains québécois, La Maison des écrivains, 3492 Ave Laval, Montréal, QC H2X 3C8, Canada.

BEAUMAN, Sally (Vanessa); Writer and Journalist; b. 25 July 1944, Torquay, Devon, England; one s. *Education:* MA, English Literature, Girton College, Cambridge, 1963–66. *Career:* Assoc. Ed., New York magazine, 1968–72; Features Ed., Harper's Bazaar, 1969–71; Contributing and Arts Ed., Telegraph magazine, 1971–79; mem. Society of Authors. *Publications:* The Royal Shakespeare Company's Centenary Production of Henry V (ed. and introduction), 1976; The Royal Shakespeare Company: A History of Ten Decades, 1983; Destiny, 1987; Dark Angel, 1990; Secret Lives, 1994; Lovers and Liars, 1994; Danger Zones, 1996; Deception and Desire, 1998; Sextet, 1998; Rebecca's Tale, 2001. Other: Also writes as Vanessa James. Contributions: newspapers and periodicals. *Literary Agent:* PFD, Drury House, 34–43 Russell St, London WC2B 5HA, England.

BEAUMONT, Roger Alban, BS, MS, PhD; academic and writer; b. 2 Oct. 1935, Milwaukee, Wisconsin, USA; m. Jean Beaumont 1974; one s. two d. *Education:* University of Wisconsin, Madison, Kansas State University. *Career:* Part-Time Lecturer, 1965–67, 1969–73, Assoc. Dir, Center for Advanced Study in Organization Science, 1970–73, Assoc. Prof. of Organization Science, 1972–74, University of Wisconsin, Milwaukee; Instructor, University of Wisconsin, Oshkosh, 1968–69; Fellow, Inter-University Seminar on the Armed Forces and Society, 1969–; Part-time Lecturer, Marquette University, 1970–73; Assoc. Prof., 1974–79, Prof. of History, 1979–2003, Texas A & M University; Co-Founder and North American Ed., Defense Analysis, 1983–90; mem. American Military Institute, trustee, 1978–81, chair., editorial advisory board, 1984–85; Dept of the Army Historical Advisory Committee, 1983–87; International Institute for Strategic Studies, 1974–92. *Publications:* War in the Next Decade (ed. with Martin Edmonds), 1974; Military Elites: Special Fighting Units in the Modern World, 1974; Sword of the Raj: The British Army in India, 1747–1947, 1977; Special Operations and Elite Units, 1939–1988: A Reference Guide, 1988; Joint Military Operations: A Short History, 1993; War, Chaos and History, 1994; The Nazis' March to Chaos, 2000; Right Backed by Might: The International Air Force Concept, 2001. Other: 5 monographs; 19 book chapters. Contributions: Reference works and many scholarly journals. *Honours:* Dept of the Army Patriotic Civilian Service Award, 1987; Secretary of the Navy Fellow, History Dept, US Naval Acad., 1989–90; Faculty Teaching Award, Delta Delta Delta Sorority, 1994; Research Award, College of Liberal Arts, 1997. *Address:* 308 E Brookside Drive, Bryan, TX 77801, USA.

BEAUSOLEIL, Claude; poet, writer, translator, editor and academic; b. 1948, Montréal, QC, Canada. *Education:* BA, Collège Sainte-Marie, University of Montréal; Bac Specialisé, MA, Université du Québec a Montréal; PhD, Sherbrooke University. *Career:* Prof. of Québec Literature, Collège Edouard-Montpetit, Longueuil, 1973–; Ed., Livrès urbaines. *Publications:* Intrusion ralentie, 1972; Journal mobile, 1974; Promenade modern style, 1975; Sens interdit, 1976; La surface du paysage, 1979; Au milieu du corps l'attraction s'insinue, 1980; Dans la matière revant comme une émeute, 1982; Le livre du voyage, 1983; Concrete City: Selected Poems 1972–82, 1983; Une certaine fin de siècle, two vols, 1983, 1991; Les livres parlent, 1984; Il y a des nuits que nous habitons tous, 1986; Extase et déchirure, 1987; Grand hotel des étrangers, 1988; Fureur de Mexico, 1992; Montréal est une vill de poèmes vous savez, 1992; L'Usage du temps, 1994. *Honours:* Prix Emile-Nelligan, 1980; Ordre des francophones d'Amérique, 1989. *Address:* c/o Union des écrivaines et des écrivains québécois, La Maison des Écrivains, 3492 Avenue Laval, Montréal H2X 3C8, Canada.

BEAVER, Bruce (Victor); Journalist, Writer and Poet; b. 14 Feb. 1928, Sydney, NSW, Australia; m. Brenda Bellam, 30 Sept. 1963. *Career:* mem. Australian Society of Authors. *Publications:* Under the Bridge, 1961; Seawall and Shoreline, 1964; The Hot Spring, 1965; You Can't Come Back, 1966; Open at Random, 1967; Letters to Live Poets, 1969; Lauds and Plaints, 1968–72, 1974; Odes and Days, 1975; Death's Directives, 1978; As It Was: Selected Poems, 1979; Prose Sketches, 1986; Charmed Lives, 1988; New and Selected Poems, 1960–90, 1991. Contributions: periodicals. *Honours:* Poetry Society of Australia Awards, 1983; Christopher Brennan Award, Fellowship of Australian Writers, 1983; New South Wales State Literary Awards Special Citation, 1990; AM Award, 1991. *Address:* 14 Malvern Ave, Manly, NSW 2095, Australia.

BEAVER, Paul Eli; journalist, writer and broadcaster; b. 3 April 1953, Winchester, England; m. Ann Middleton 1978 (divorced 1993); one s. *Education:* Sheffield City Polytechnic; Henley Management College. *Career:* Ed., IPMS Magazine, 1976–80, Helicopter World, 1981–86, Defence Helicopter World, 1982–86, Jane's Videotape, 1986–87; Asst Compiler, Jane's Fighting Ships, 1987–88; Managing Ed., Jane's Defence Yearbooks, 1988–89; Publisher, Jane's Defence Weekly, 1989–93; Defence Commentator, Sky News, 1990–2001; Senior Publisher, Jane's SENTINEL, 1993–94; Group Spokesman for Jane's, 1994–; Defence and Aerospace Correspondent, CNBC Europe, 1994–97; Research Fellow, Centre for Defence and International Security Studies, Lancaster Univ., 1997–; Defence Commentator, BBC, 2001–. *Publications:* Ark Royal: A Pictorial History, 1979; U-Boats in the Atlantic, 1979; German Capital Ships, 1980; German Destroyers and Escorts, 1981; Fleet Command, 1984; Invincible Class, 1984; Encyclopaedia of Aviation, 1986; Encyclopaedia of the Fleet Air Arm Since 1945, 1987; The Gulf States Regional Security Assessment, 1993; The Balkans Regional Security Assessment, 1994; D-DAY: Private Lines, 1994; The South China Sea Regional Security Assessment, 1994; The CIS Regional Security Assessment, 1994; The North Africa Regional Security Assessment, 1994; The China and North East Asia Regional Security Assessment, 1995; Baltics and Central Europe Regional Security Assessment, 1996; The Modern Royal Navy, 1996. Contributions: many journals. *Address:* 36 Great Smith Street, London SW1P 3BU, England.

BEBB, Prudence; Writer; b. 20 March 1939, Catterick, North Yorkshire, England. *Education:* BA, 1960, Diploma in Education, 1961, Sheffield University. *Career:* Teacher, Snaith School, 1961–63; History Teacher, Howden School, 1963–90; mem. PEN. *Publications:* The Eleventh Emerald, 1981; The Ridgeway Ruby, 1983; The White Swan, 1984; The Nabob's Nephew, 1985; Life in Regency York, 1992; Butcher, Baker, Candlestick Maker, 1994; Georgian Poppleton, 1994; Life in Regency Harrogate, 1994; Life in Regency Scarborough, 1997; Life in Regency Whitby, 2000. Contributions: Impressions, the Journal of the Northern Branch of the Jane Austen Society. *Address:* 12 Bracken Hills, Upper Poppleton, York YO26 6DH, England.

BECHMANN, Roland (Philippe); Architect, Historian and Writer; b. 1 April 1919, Paris, France; m. Martine Cohen, 18 July 1942, six d. *Education:* Licencié és Lettres, 1938; Government Architect Diploma, 1944; Doctor (3C) in Geography, 1978. *Career:* Architect; Chief Ed., Amenagement et Nature, 1966–; mem. Asscn des Journalistes de l'Environnement; Société des Gens de Lettres; AVISTA (USA). *Publications:* Les Racines des Cathedrales, L'architecture gothique, expression des conditions du milieu, 1981; Des Arbres et des Hommes: La foret au Moyen Age, 1984, English trans. as Trees and Man: The Forest in the Middle Ages, 1990; Carnet de Villard de Honnecourt XIII e siècle (joint author), 1986; Villard de Honnecourt Disegni (joint author), 1987; Villard de Honnecourt: La pensée technique au XIIIe siècle et sa communication, 1991; L'Arbre du Ciel (novel), 1997. Other: Villard de Honnecourt's Portfolio (CD-ROM), 2000. Contributions: journals. *Honours:* Chevalier, Légion d'honneur, 1952; Croix de guerre, 1994. *Address:* 7 Villa de Buzenval, 92100 Boulogne-Billancourt, France.

BECK, Albert, BA, MFA; American artist, poet, writer and educator; b. 4 April 1931, Scranton, PA; m. Carmen Federowich, two s. one d. *Education:* Northwestern Univ., US Army Administrative School, Sorbonne, Univ. of Paris, Clayton Univ., St Louis. *Career:* Dean of Students, Kansas City Art Inst., MO 1967–68; Assoc. Prof. of Art and Head of Art Dept 1968–96, artist-in-residence 1996–97, Culver-Stockton Coll.; Dir, Pyrapod Gallery 1996–; mem. Missouri Arts Council, Missouri Writers' Guild, Hannibal Arts Council. *Publications:* Gnomes and Poems 1992, Sight Lines 1996, Songs from the Rainbow Worm 1997, Beaucoup Haiku 1999, God is in the Glove Compartment 2000, Survival Weapons 2001, Warm Verse, Cold Turkey 2002, Rapping Paper, Mythic Thundermugs 2002, Conversations with Lizard Bones and Wizard Stones 2003; contribs to professional journals. *Honours:* various painting, pottery and poetry awards. *Address:* 5987 County Road 231, Monroe City, MO 63456, USA. *E-mail:* abeck@marktwain.net.

BECK, James (Henry); Prof. of Art History and Writer; b. 14 May 1930, New York, NY, USA; m. Darma Tercinod, 9 April 1956, one s. one d. *Education:* BA, Oberlin College, 1952; MA, New York University, 1954; PhD, Columbia University, 1963. *Career:* Asst Prof., University of Alabama, 1958–59, Arizona State University, 1959–61; Faculty, 1961–72, Prof. of Art History, 1972–, Chair., Dept of Art History, 1984–90, Columbia University; Herodotus Fellow, Institute for Advanced Study, Princeton, NJ, 1967; Fellow, Center for Italian Renaissance Studies, 1967–68, 1972, Visiting Scholar, 1983, Harvard University; Founder-Pres., ArtWatch Inc, 1992–. *Publications:* Marioano di Jacopo detto il Taccola: 'Liber Tertius', 1969; Jacopo della Quercia e San Petronio, 1970; Michelangelo: A Lesson in Anatomy, 1975; Raphael, 1976; Masaccio: The Documents, 1978; Leonardo's Rules of Painting: An Unconventional Approach to Modern Art, 1979; Italian Renaissance Painting, 1981; The Doors of the Florentine Bapistry, 1985; The Sepulchral Monument for Ilaria del Caretto by Jacopo della Quercia, 1988; Jacopo della Quercia, 1991; The Tyranny of the Detail, 1992; The Culture, the Business and the Scandal, 1993; Raphael, the Camera della Segnatura, 1993; The Three Worlds of Michelangelo, 1999. Contributions: scholarly books and professional journals. *Honours:* Guggenheim Fellowship, 1973–74.

BECKER, Gary Stanley; Prof. of Economics and Sociology; b. 2 Dec. 1930, Pottsville, Pennsylvania, USA; m. 1st Doria Slote 19 Sept. 1954 (deceased); two d.; m. 2nd Guity Nashat 31 Oct. 1979; two s. *Education:* AB, Princeton University, 1951; AM, 1953, PhD, 1955, University of Chicago. *Career:* Asst and Assoc. Prof. of Economics, 1957–60; Prof. of Economics, Columbia University; Prof. of Economics, 1969–83; University Prof. of Economics and Sociology, 1983–, University of Chicago; Columnist, Business Week, 1985–; mem. Economic History Asscn; National Acad. of Sciences; American Economic Asscn; American Statistical Asscn; Econometric Society; American Acad. of Arts and Sciences; National Asscn of Business Economists; American Philosophical Society; Pontifical Acad. of Sciences; International Union for the Scientific Study of Population; National Acad. of Education. *Publications:* The Economics of Discrimination, 1957; Human Capital,

1964; Human Capital and the Personal Distribution of Income: An Analytical Approach, 1967; Economic Theory, 1971; Essays in the Economics of Crime and Punishment (ed. with William M. Landes), 1974; The Allocation of Time and Goods Over the Life Cycle (with Gilbert Ghez), 1975; Essays in Labor Economics in Honor of H. Gregg Lewis (ed.), 1976; The Economic Approach to Human Behavior, 1976; A Treatise on the Family, 1981; Accounting for Tastes, 1996; The Economics of Life (with Guity Nashat Becker), 1996. Contributions: Books and journals. *Honours:* Nobel Prize for Economic Science, 1992; 13 hon. doctorates. *Address:* Dept of Economics, University of Chicago, 1126 E 59th St, Chicago, IL 60637, USA.

BECKER, Jürgen; Poet, Writer and Dramatist; b. 10 July 1932, Cologne, Germany; m. 1st Marie 1954 (divorced 1965); one s.; m. 2nd Rango Bohne 1965; one step-s. one step-d. *Education:* University of Cologne, 1953–54. *Career:* Writer, Westdeutscher Rundfunk, Cologne, 1959–64; Reader, Rowohlt Verlag, 1964–66; Reader, Suhrkamp Verlag, 1973–74; Head, Dept of Drama, Deutschlandfunk, Cologne, 1974–93; mem. Akademie der Künste, Berlin-Brandenburg; Deutsche Akademie für Sprache und Dichtung eV, Darmstadt; PEN Centre, Federal Republic of Germany. *Publications:* Felder, 1964; Ränder, 1968; Umgebungen, 1970; Schnee, 1971; Das Ende der Landschaftsmalerei, 1974; Erzahl mir nichts vom Krieg, 1977; In der verbleibenden Zeit, 1979; Erzählen bis Ostende, 1981; Gedichte 1965–1980, 1981; Odenthals Küste, 1986; Das Gedicht von der wiedervereinigten Landschaft, 1988; Das englische Fenster, 1990; Foxtrott im Erfurter Stadion, 1993; Korrespondenzen mit Landschaft (with Rango Bohne), 1996; Der fehlende Rest, 1997; Aus der Geschichte der Trennungen, 1999. Other: various radio plays. *Honours:* Literature Prize, Cologne, 1968; Literature Prize, Bavarian Acad. of Fine Arts, Munich, 1980; Critics' Prize, 1981; Literature Prize, Bremen, 1986; Peter Huchel Prize, 1994; Literature Prize, Berlin, 1994; Heinrich Böll Prize, 1995. *Address:* Am Klausenberg 84, 51109 Cologne, Germany.

BECKER, Lucille Frackman, BA, MA, PhD; academic and writer; b. 4 Feb. 1929, USA. *Education:* University of Mexico, Barnard College, Teachers College Columbia University, Université d'Aix-Marseille, Columbia University. *Career:* Part Time Instructor, Columbia University, 1954–58, University College, Rutgers University, 1958–68; Assoc. Prof. of French, 1968–77, Chair, Dept of French, 1976–81, Prof. of French, 1977–93, Prof. of French Emerita, 1993–, Drew University; mem. American Asscn of Teachers of French; American Asscn of University Profs; French Institute/Alliance Française; MLA; South Atlantic MLA. *Publications:* Le Maître de Santiago, by Henry de Montherlant (co-ed.), 1965; Henry de Montherlant, 1970; Louis Aragon, 1971; Georges Simenon, 1977; Françoise Mallet-Joris, 1985; Twentieth-Century French Women Novelists, 1989; Pierre Boulle, 1996; Georges Simenon Revisited, 1999. Contributions: scholarly books and journals. *Address:* 82 Harding Drive, South Orange, NJ 07079, USA.

BECKET, Henry S. A. (see Goulden, Joseph C.).

BECKETT, Wendy, (Sister Wendy), MA; British art historian and nun; b. 25 Feb. 1930, Johannesburg, South Africa. *Education:* Oxford Univ. *Career:* Carmelite nun. *Television:* several series for BBC and Public Broadcasting Service (US) including Sister Wendy's Grand Tour, Sister Wendy's Story of Painting. *Publications:* A Thousand Masterpieces, The Story of Painting, Meditations, My Favourite Things, Sister Wendy's American Collection 2000. *Literary Agent:* Toby Eady Associates Ltd, Third Floor, 9 Orme Court, London, W2 4RL, England. *Telephone:* (20) 7792-0092. *Fax:* (20) 7792-0879. *E-mail:* toby@tobyeady.demon.co.uk. *Website:* www.tobyeadyassociates.co.uk.

BECKLES WILLSON, Robina Elizabeth; Writer; b. 26 Sept. 1930, London, England; m. Anthony Beckles Willson, one s. one d. *Education:* BA, 1948, MA, 1952, University of Liverpool. *Career:* Teacher, Liverpool School of Art, 1952–56, Ballet Rambert Educational School, London, 1956–58. *Publications:* Leopards on the Loire, 1961; A Time to Dance, 1962; Musical Instruments, 1964; A Reflection of Rachel, 1967; The Leader of the Band, 1967; Roundabout Ride, 1968; Dancing Day, 1971; The Last Harper, 1972; The Shell on Your Back, 1972; What a Noise, 1974; The Voice of Music, 1975; Musical Merry-go-Round, 1977; The Beaver Book of Ballet, 1979; Eyes Wide Open, 1981; Anna Pavlova: A Legend Among Dancers, 1981; Pocket Book of Ballet, 1982; Secret Witch, 1982; Square Bear, 1983; Merry Christmas, 1983; Holiday Witch, 1983; Sophie and Nicky series, 2 vols, Hungry Witch, 1984; Music Maker, 1986; Sporty Witch, 1986; The Haunting Music, 1987; Mozart's Story, 1991; Just Imagine, 1993; Harry Stories in Animal World, 1996; Ambulance!, 1996; Very Best Friend, 1998. *Literary Agent:* A. M. Heath & Co Ltd, 79 St Martin's Lane, London WC2N 4RE, England. *Address:* 44 Popes Ave, Twickenham, Middlesex TW2 4RE, England.

BECKWITH, Lillian; Author; b. 25 April 1916, Ellesmere Port, England; m. Edward Thornthwaite Comber, 3 June 1937, one s. one d. *Education:* Ornum College, Birkenhead. *Career:* mem. Society of Authors; Mark Twain Society; Women of the Year Asscn, Consultative Committee. *Publications:* The Hebridean Stories: The Hill is Lonely, 1959; The Sea for Breakfast, 1961; The Loud Halo, 1964; Green Hand, 1967; A Rope in Case, 1968; About My Father's Business, 1971; Lightly Poached, 1973; The Spuddy, 1974; Beautiful Just, 1975; The Lillian Beckwith Hebridean Cookbook, 1976; Bruach Blend, 1978; A Shine of Rainbows, 1984; A Proper Woman, 1986; The Bay of Strangers, 1989; The Small Party, 1989; An Island Apart, 1992. Contributions: Countryman; Woman's Own and various other magazines for women. *Literary Agent:* Curtis Brown Ltd, Haymarket House, 28–29 Haymarket, London, SW1Y 4SP, England. *Telephone:* (20) 7393-4400. *Fax:* (20) 7393-4401. *E-mail:* info@curtisbrown.co.uk. *Website:* www.curtisbrown.co.uk.

BEDAU, Hugo Adam; Prof. of Philosophy Emeritus and Author; b. 23 Sept. 1926, Portland, Oregon, USA; m. 1st Jan Mastin, 1952, divorced 1988, three s., one d.; m. 2nd Constance Putnam, 1990. *Education:* BA, University of Redlands, 1949; MA, Boston University, 1951; MA, 1953, PhD, 1961, Harvard University. *Career:* Instructor, Dartmouth College, 1953–54; Lecturer, Princeton University, 1954–57, 1958–61; Assoc. Prof., Reed College, 1962–66; Prof. of Philosophy, Tufts University, 1966–99; mem. American Asscn of University Profs; American Philosophical Asscn; American Society for Political and Legal Philosophy. *Publications:* Victimless Crimes: Two Views (with Edwin M. Schur), 1974; The Courts, the Constitution, and Capital Punishment, 1977; Current Issues and Enduring Questions (with Sylvan Barnet), 1987; Death is Different: Studies in the Morality, Law, and Politics of Capital Punishment, 1987; In Spite of Innocence (with Michael Radelet and Constance Putnam), 1992; Critical Thinking, Reading, and Writing (with Sylvan Barnet), 1993; Thinking and Writing About Philiosophy, 1996; Making Mortal Choices, 1996. Editor: The Death Penalty in America, 1964; Civil Disobedience: Theory and Practice, 1969; Justice and Equality, 1971; Capital Punishment in the United States (with Chester M. Pierce), 1976; Civil Disobedience in Focus, 1991. Contributions: many books, journals, and magazines. *Honours:* Visiting Life Fellow, Clare Hall, Cambridge, 1980, 1988, Max Planck Institutes, Heidelberg and Freiburg im Breisgau, 1988, Wolfson College, Oxford, 1989; Romanell-Phi Beta Kappa Prof. of Philosophy, 1995; August Vollmer Award, American Society of Criminology, 1997; Roger Baldwin Award, Civil Liberties Union of Massachusetts, 2002. *Address:* Dept of Philosophy, Tufts University, Medford, MA 02155, USA.

BEDFORD, Martyn Corby, MA; writer; b. 10 Oct. 1959, Croydon, Surrey, England; m. Damaris Croxall 1994. *Education:* Univ. of East Anglia. *Career:* Lecturer in Creative Writing Univ. of Manchester 2001–. *Publications:* Acts of Revision (Yorkshire Post Best First Work Award) 1996, Exit, Orange & Red 1997, The Houdini Girl 1999, Black Cat 2000. *Literary Agent:* Curtis Brown Ltd, Haymarket House, 28–29 Haymarket, London, SW1Y 4SP, England. *Telephone:* (20) 7393-4400. *Fax:* (20) 7393-4401. *E-mail:* info@curtisbrown.co.uk. *Website:* www.curtisbrown.co.uk.

BEDFORD, Sybille, OBE, CLit, FRSL; British author; b. 16 March 1911, Berlin; m. Walter Bedford 1935. *Education:* pvt. schools in Italy, France and England. *Career:* literary journalist 1930s–; Vice-Pres. English PEN 1979. *Publications:* A Visit to Don Otavio 1953, A Legacy 1956, The Trial of Doctor Adams 1958, The Best We Can Do 1958, The Faces of Justice 1961, A Favourite of the Gods 1968, A Compass Error 1968, Aldous Huxley: A Biography (Vol. I) 1973, (Vol. II) 1974, Jigsaw: An Unsentimental Education 1989, As It Was 1990, Pleasures and Landscapes 2003. *Address:* c/o Lutyens & Rubinstein, 231 Westbourne Park Road, London, W11 1EB, England. *Telephone:* (20) 7792-4855.

BEECHING, Jack; Writer and Poet; b. 8 May 1922, Hastings, Sussex, England. *Publications:* Fiction: Let Me See Your Face, 1958; The Dakota Project, 1967; Death of a Terrorist, 1982; Tides of Fortune, 1988. Non-Fiction: The Chinese Opium Wars, 1975; An Open Path: Christian Missionaries 1515–1914, 1979; The Galleys at Lepanto, 1982. Poetry: Aspects of Love, 1950; The Polythene Maidenhead, in Penguin Modern Poets, 1969; Twenty-Five Short Poems, 1982; The View From the Balloon, 1990; The Invention of Love, 1996; Poems 1940–2000, 2000. *Address:* c/o Tessa Sayle Agency, 11 Jubilee Pl., London SW3 3CE, England.

BEER, Dame Gillian Patricia Kempster, DBE, LittD, FBA; British professor of English literature and college president; b. 27 Jan. 1935; m. John Bernard Beer 1962; three s. *Education:* St Anne's Coll., Oxford. *Career:* Asst Lecturer, Bedford Coll., London 1959–62; part-time Lecturer, Univ. of Liverpool 1962–64; Asst Lecturer, Univ. of Cambridge 1966–71, Lecturer, then Reader in Literature and Narrative 1971–89, Prof. of English 1989–94, King Edward VII Prof. of English Literature 1994–2002, Pres. Clare Hall 1994–2001; Fellow Girton Coll. 1965–94; Vice-Pres. British Acad. 1994–96; Trustee British Museum 1992–2002; Chair. Poetry Book Soc. 1992–96; Pres. History of Science Section, BAAS; Chair. Judges, Booker Prize 1997. *Publications:* Meredith: a change of masks 1970, The Romance 1970, Darwin's Plots 1983, George Eliot 1986, Arguing with the Past 1989, Open Fields 1996, Virginia Woolf: The Common Ground 1996. *Honours:* Hon. mem. American Acad. of Arts and Sciences; Hon. Fellow Univ. of Wales (Cardiff) 1996, St Anne's Coll., Oxford; Hon. DLitt (Liverpool) 1995; Dr hc (Leicester), (APU), (Sorbonne, Paris); Medals from MIT and Nat. Autonomous Univ., Mexico. *Address:* Clare Hall, Herschel Road, Cambridge, CB3 9AL (Office); 6 Belvoir Terrace, Cambridge, CB2 2AA, England (Home). *Telephone:* (1223) 332360 (Office); (1223) 356384 (Home). *Fax:* (1223) 332333 (Office). *E-mail:* gpb1000@cam.ac.uk (Office).

BEERS, Burton Floyd, AB, MA, PhD; academic and writer; b. 13 Sept. 1927, Chemung, New York, USA; m. Pauline Cone Beers 1952; one s. one d. *Education:* Hobart College, Duke University. *Career:* Instructor, 1955–57, Asst Prof., 1957–61, Assoc. Prof., 1961–66, Prof., 1966–96, North Carolina State University; mem. American Historical Asscn; Asscn for Asian Studies; Asscn of Historians in North Carolina; Historical Society of North

Carolina; North Carolina Literary and Historical Society; Society for Historians of American Foreign Relations; Southern Historical Asscn. *Publications:* Vain Endeavor: Robert Lansing's Attempts to End the American-Japanese Rivalry, 1962; The Far East: A History of Western Impacts and Eastern Responses, 1830–1875 (with Paul H. Clyde), sixth edn, 1975; China in Old Photographs, 1981; North Carolina's China Connection 1840–1949 (with Lawrence Kessler and Charles LaMonica), 1981; North Carolina State University: A Pictorial History (with Murray S. Downs), 1986; The Vietnam War: An Historical Case Study (with Rose Ann Mulford), 1997; Living in our World (chief exec. ed.), 1998. Contributions: Textbooks, books, scholarly journals, and periodicals. *Honours:* Alexander Quarles Holladay Medal for Excellence, North Carolina State University Board of Trustees, 1992; Medal for Excellence, Hobart and William Smith Colleges, 1994; Watauga Medal, North Carolina State University, 1998.

BEEVOR, Antony, FRSL; British historian and novelist; b. 14 Dec. 1946, London, England; m. Artemis Cooper 1986; one s. one d. *Education:* Winchester Coll., Grenoble Univ., Royal Military Acad., Sandhurst. *Career:* Exec. Council French Theatre Season 1997; mem., Management Cttee of the Soc. of Authors 2001–; Lees-Knowles Lecturer, Univ. of Cambridge 2002; Visiting Prof., Birkbeck Coll., London 2002–; mem. Soc. of Authors, RGS, Anglo Hellenic League, Friends of the British Libraries, London Library (mem. of cttee). *Publications:* The Spanish Civil War 1982, The Enchantment of Christina Von Retzen (novel) 1988, Inside the British Army 1990, Crete: The Battle and the Resistance 1991, Paris After the Liberation 1944–49 1994, Stalingrad 1998, Berlin: The Downfall 1945 2002, The Mystery of Olga Chekhova 2004; contrib. to TLS, Times, Telegraph, Independent, Spectator. *Honours:* Runciman Award 1992, Chevalier, Ordre des Arts et des Lettres 1997, Samuel Johnson Prize for Non-Fiction 1999, Wolfson Prize for History 1999, Hawthornden Prize 1999. *Address:* 54 Saint Maur Road, London, SW6 4DP, England.

BEGLEY, Louis; Lawyer and Writer; b. 6 Oct. 1933, Stryj, Poland; m. 1st Sally Higginson 11 Feb. 1956 (divorced May 1970); two s. one d.; m. 2nd Anka Muhlstein 30 March 1974. *Education:* AB, 1954, LLB, 1959, Harvard University. *Career:* Specialist in international corporate law; writer; lecturer; mem. Bar Asscn of the City of New York; Council on Foreign Relations; American Philosophical Society. *Publications:* Fiction: Wartime Lies, 1991; The Man Who Was Late, 1993; As Max Saw It, 1994; About Schmidt, 1996; Mistler's Exit, 1998; Schmidt Delivered, 2000; Shipwreck, 2003. Non-Fiction: Das Gelobte Land, 2002; Venedig Unter Vier Augen (with Anka Muhlstein), 2003. Contributions: periodicals. *Honours:* Irish Times-Aer Lingus International Fiction Prize, 1991; PEN/Ernest Hemingway First Fiction Award, 1992; Prix Médicis Étranger, 1992; Jeanette-Schocken Preis, Bremerhaven Bürgerpreis für Literatur, 1995; American Acad. of Arts and Letters Award in Literature, 1995; Konrad-Adenauer Stiftung Literaturpreis, 1999. *Literary Agent:* Georges Borchardt, 136 E 57th St, New York, NY 10022, USA.

BÉGUIN, Louis-Paul; Writer and Poet; b. 31 March 1923, Amiens, France. *Education:* BA, Sorbonne, University of Paris. *Career:* mem. PEN, Québec; Québec Writers Union. *Publications:* Miroir de Janus, 1966; Impromptu de Québec, 1974; Un homme et son langage, 1977; Problèmes de langage, 1978; Idoles et Paraboles, 1982; Yourcenar, 1982; Poèmes et pastiches, 1985; Parcours paralleles, 1988; Ange Pleureur, 1991; Poèmes depuis la tendre enfance, 1995; The Weeping Angel, 1996; Écrits des trois pignans, 1998. Contributions: newspapers and magazines. *Honours:* Poetry Award, 1967; Prix Montcalm, 1974.

BEHAR, Ruth; Prof. of Anthropology, Poet and Writer; b. 12 Nov. 1956, Havana, Cuba; m. David Frye, 6 June 1982, one s. *Education:* BA, Wesleyan University, 1977; MA, 1981, PhD, 1983, Princeton University. *Career:* Asst Prof., 1986–89, Assoc. Prof., 1989–94, Prof. of Anthropology, 1994–, University of Michigan at Ann Arbor. *Publications:* Santa Maria del Monte: The Presence of the Past in a Spanish Village, 1986, revised edn as The Presence of the Past in a Spanish Village: Santa Maria del Monte, 1991; Translated Woman: Crossing the Border with Esperanza's Story, 1993; Bridges to Cuba (Puentes a Cuba) (ed.), 1995; Las Visiones de una Bruja Guachichil en 1599: Hacia una Perspectiva Indígena Sobre la Conquista de San Luis Potosal, 1995; Women Writing Culture (co-ed.), 1995; The Vulnerable Observer: Anthropology That Breaks Your Heart, 1996. Contributions: anthologies, scholarly journals and literary periodicals. *Honours:* John D. and Catherine T. MacArthur Foundation Fellowship, 1988–93; Guggenheim Fellowship, 1995–96. *Address:* c/o Dept of Anthropology, University of Michigan, 1020 LSA Bldg, Ann Arbor, MI 48109, USA.

BEHR, Edward (Samuel); Journalist, Ed. and Writer; b. 7 May 1926, Paris, France; m. Christiane Wagrez, 1 April 1967. *Education:* BA, 1951, MA, 1953, Magdalene College, Cambridge. *Career:* Correspondent, Reuters, 1950–54, Time Inc, 1957–63; Contributing Ed., Saturday Evening Post, 1963–65; Reporter-Dir, Cinq Colonnes a la Une TV Programme, 1963–65; Paris Correspondent, 1965–66, Hong Kong Bureau Chief, 1966–68, Paris Bureau Chief, 1968–72, European Ed., Paris, 1973–83, Cultural Ed., 1984–87, Contributing Ed., 1987–, Newsweek Magazine. *Publications:* The Algerian Problem, 1961; Lai Ying: The Thirty-Sixth Way: A Personal Account of Imprisonment and Escape from Red Chine (trans. and ed. with Sydney Liu), 1969; Bearings: A Foreign Correspondent's Life Behind the Lines, 1978, UK edn as Anyone Here Been Raped and Speaks English?, 1981; Getting Even (novel), 1980; The Last Emperor (novel based on the film), 1987; Hirohito: Behind the Myth, 1989; The Complete Book of Les Misérables, 1990; Indonesia: A Voyage Through the Archipelago, 1990; The Story of Miss Saigon (with Mark Steyn), 1991; Kiss the Hand You Cannot Bite: The Rise and Fall of the Ceausescus, 1991; The Good Frenchman: The True Story of the Life and Times of Maurice Chevalier, 1993; Une Amérique qui fait peur, 1995. *Honours:* Gutenberg Prize, 1988. *Address:* c/o Newsweek, 162 Faubour St Honore, Paris 75008, France.

BEIGBEDER, Frédéric; Novelist; b. 21 Sept. 1965, Neuilly-sur-Seine, France. *Publications:* Mémoire d'un jeune homme dérangé, 1990; Vacances dans le coma, 1994; L'Amour dure trois ans, 1997; Nouvelles sous ecstasy, 1999; Barbie (Barbie (Universe of Fashion)), 1998; 99 francs (£9.99, aka £6.99), 2000; Dernier inventaire avant liquidation, 2001. *Address:* c/o Éditions Grasset, 61 rue des Saints-Pères, 75006 Paris, France.

BEILHARZ, Manfred; German director and producer; b. 13 July 1938, Böblingen. *Education:* Universität Tübingen, Universität München, Paris, London. *Career:* founded Studiobühne at München; Asst Dir Münchner Kammerspiele; Dir and head of literary dept, Westfälisches Landestheater 1968; Artistic Dir, Tübingen Landestheater 1970–75, City Theatre of Freiburg 1976–-83, City Theatre of Kassel 1983–91, Schauspiel, Bonn 1991–92; Genralintendant, Municipal Theatre of Bonn 1997–2002; Dir Hessisches Staatstheater Wiesbaden; mem. Acad. of Performing Arts, Frankfurt, European Theatre Convention, Brussels and Paris; Vice-Pres. Hessischen Theaterakademie, Frankfurt; Pres. Int. Theatre Inst.; Chair. Dramaturgische Gesellschaft, Berlin. *Plays and opera directed:* Marat Sade, The Mother, Threepenny Opera, Mahagonny, A Romantic Woman, A Midsummer Night's Dream, Fidelio, The Hot Oven, L'enfant et les sortilèges, Love of Three Oranges, Falstaff, Spring Awakening, Schauspiel Bonn 1997, Wozzeck, Opera Bonn, Der Zerbrochne Krug. *Address:* c/o ITI, 1 rue Miollis, 75732 Paris, France. *Telephone:* 1-45-68-48-80. *Fax:* 1-45-66-48-80. *E-mail:* iti@unesco.org.

BEISSEL, Henry (Eric); Poet, Dramatist, Writer, Trans., Ed. and Teacher; b. 12 April 1929, Cologne, Germany; m. 1st Ruth Heydasch, two d.; m. 2nd Arlette Francière, 3 April 1981, one d. *Education:* University of London, 1949; BA, 1958, MA, 1960, University of Toronto. *Career:* Teacher, University of Edmonton, 1962–64, University of Trinidad, 1964–66; Faculty, 1966–96, Prof. of English Emeritus, 1997–, Distinguished Emeritus Prof., 2000–, Concordia University, Montréal; Founder-Ed., Edge Journal, 1963–69; mem. League of Canadian Poets, pres., 1980–81; PEN; Playwrights Canada; Writers Union of Canada. *Publications:* Poetry: Witness the Heart, 1963; New Wings for Icarus, 1966; The World is a Rainbow, 1968; Face on the Dark, 1970; The Salt I Taste, 1975; Cantos North, 1980; Season of Blood, 1984; Poems New and Selected, 1987; Ammonite, 1987; Dying I Was Born, 1992; Stones to Harvest, 1993; The Dragon and the Pearl, 2002. Plays: Inook and the Sun, 1974; Goya, 1978; Under Coyote's Eye, 1980; The Noose, 1989; Improvisations for Mr X, 1989; Inuk, 2000. Other: Kanada: Romantik und Wirklichkeit, 1981; Raging Like a Fire: A Celebration of Irving Layton (ed. with Joy Bennett), 1993; Trans of poetry and plays. Contributions: journals. *Honours:* Epstein Award, 1958; Davidson Award, 1959; Deutscher Akademischer Austauschdienst Fellowship, 1977; Walter-Bauer Literaturpreis, Germany, 1994. *Address:* Box 339, Alexandria, Ontario K0C 1A0, Canada. *E-mail:* beifran@glen-net.ca.

BÉKÉS, Pál; Hungarian author, playwright and translator. *Career:* Iowa Int. Writing Program, USA 1997; Artistic Dir, Magyar Magic festival, UK 2003. *Publications:* 16 publications include Darvak 1979, Szerelmem útközben 1983, Lakótelepi mítoszok 1984, Törzsi viszonyok 1990, A noi partorség szeme láttara 1992. *Honours:* Fulbright Scholarship, USA 1992–93. *Address:* c/o Hungarian Cultural Centre, 10 Maiden Lane, Covent Garden, London, WC2E 7NA, England.

BEKRI, Tahar, PhD; Tunisian writer, literary critic, essayist and poet; b. 7 July 1951, Gabès; m. Annick Le Thoër 1987. *Education:* Univ. of Tunisia, Sorbonne, Univ. of Paris. *Career:* maître de conférences, Univ. of Paris X, Nanterre. *Publications:* Poèmes bilingues 1978, Exils 1979, Le Laboureur du soleil 1983, Les Lignes sont des arbres 1984, Le Chant du roi errant 1985, Malek Haddad 1986, Le Coeur rompu aux océans 1988, Les Chapelets d'attache 1994, Littératures de Tunisie et du Maghreb 1994, Poèmes à Selma 1996, Les Songes impatients 1997, Journal de neige et de feu 1997, Le pêcheur de lunes 1998, Inconnues Saisons (trans. as Unknown Seasons) 1999, De la littérature tunisienne et maghrébine 1999, Marcher sur l'oubli 2000; contrib. to various publications. *Honours:* Officier, Mérite Culturel, Tunisia 1993. *Address:* 32 rue Pierre Nicole, 75005 Paris, France.

BELITT, Ben; Prof. of Literature and Languages, Poet and Writer; b. 2 May 1911, New York, NY, USA. *Education:* BA, 1932, MA, 1934, Postgraduate Studies, 1934–36, University of Virginia. *Career:* Asst Literary Ed., The Nation, 1936–37; Faculty Mem. to Prof. of Literature and Languages, Bennington College, Vermont, 1938–; mem. Authors' Guild; PEN; Vermont Acad. of Arts and Sciences, fellow. *Publications:* Poetry: Wilderness Stair, 1955; The Enemy Joy: New and Selected Poems, 1964; Nowhere But Light: Poems, 1964–1969, 1970; The Double Witness: Poems, 1970–1976, 1977; Possessions: New and Selected Poems, 1938–1985, 1986; Graffiti, 1990. Other: School of the Soldier, 1949; Adam's Dream: A Preface to Translation, 1978; The Forged Feature: Toward a Poetics of Uncertainty, 1994; Ed. and trans. of several vols. Contributions: Books. *Honours:* Shelley Memorial

Award in Poetry, 1936; Guggenheim Fellowship, 1947; Brandeis University Creative Arts Award, 1962; National Institute of Arts and Letters Award, 1965; National Endowment for the Arts Grant, 1967–68; Ben Belitt Lectureship Endowment, Bennington College, 1977; Russell Loines Award for Poetry, American Acad. and Institute of Arts and Letters, 1981; Rockefeller Foundation Residency, Bellagio, Italy, 1984; Williams/Derwood Award for Poetry, 1986. *Address:* PO Box 88, North Bennington, VT 05257, USA.

BELL, Antonia (see Rae-Ellis, Vivienne).

BELL, Edward; British publisher; b. 2 Aug. 1949; m. Junette Bannatyne 1969; one s. two d. *Education:* Airdrie High School. *Career:* with Hodder & Stoughton 1970–85; Man. Dir Collins Gen. Div. 1985–89; launched Harper Paperbacks in USA 1989; Deputy Chief Exec., HarperCollins UK 1990–91, Chief Exec. 1991–92, Chair. 1992–2000; Chair. HarperCollins India 1994–2000; Dir (non-exec.) Haynes Publishing 2001, Be Cogent Ltd, Management Diagnostics Ltd; Chair. (non-exec.) OAG Worldwide Ltd 2001; Chair. Those Who Can Ltd 2001; Partner, Bell Lomax Literary and Sport Agency 2002; Gov. Kent Inst. of Art and Design 2002. *Address:* The Bell Lomax Agency, James House, 1 Babmaes Street, London, SW1Y 6HF, England (Office). *Telephone:* (20) 7930-4447 (Office). *Fax:* (20) 7925-0118 (Office). *E-mail:* eddie@bell-lomax.co.uk.

BELL, Hilary; Australian playwright; b. 1966; m. Phillip Johnston. *Education:* Australia's Nat. Inst. of Drama (NIDA) Playwright Studio, Australia Film Television & Radio School (AFTRS), Juilliard School, New York, USA. *Plays:* Fortune 1995, Wolf Lullaby 1997, The Falls 2001. *Literary Agent:* RGM Associates, PO Box 128, Surry Hills, NSW 2010, Australia. *Telephone:* 61 2 9281 3911. *Fax:* 61 2 9281 4705. *E-mail:* info@rgm.com.au. *Website:* www.rgm.com.au.

BELL, Madison Smartt; Author and College Teacher; b. 1 Aug. 1957, Nashville, Tennessee, USA; m. Elizabeth Spires, 15 June 1985. *Education:* AB, Princeton University, 1979; MA, Hollins College, 1981. *Career:* Lecturer, Poetry Center of the 92nd Street YMHA, New York City, 1984–86; Writer-in-Residence, Dir of the Creative Writing Program, Goucher College, 1984–86, 1988–; Visiting Lecturer, University of Iowa, 1987–88; Visiting Assoc. Prof., Johns Hopkins University, 1989–95. *Publications:* Fiction: The Washington Square Ensemble, 1983; Waiting for the End of the World, 1985; Straight Cut, 1986; Zero db, 1987; The Year of Silence, 1987; Soldier's Joy, 1989; Barking Man, 1990; Doctor Sleep, 1991; Save Me, Joe Louis, 1993; All Souls' Rising, 1995; Ten Indians, 1996. Non-Fiction: Readers' guides on various authors, 1979–83; The History of the Owen Graduate School of Management, 1988. Contributions: Fiction in many anthologies and periodicals; Essays, book reviews, etc. *Honours:* Lillian Smith Award, 1989; Guggenheim Fellowship, 1991; George A and Eliza Gardner Howard Foundation Award, 1991–92; National Endowment for the Arts Fellowship, 1992. *Address:* 6208 Pinehurst Rd, Baltimore, MD 21212, USA.

BELL, Marvin Hartley, BA, MA, MFA; American academic, poet and writer; *Flannery O'Connor Professor of Letters, University of Iowa*; b. 3 Aug. 1937, New York, NY; m. Dorothy Murphy; two s. *Education:* Alfred Univ., Univ. of Chicago, Univ. of Iowa. *Career:* Faculty, Writers Workshop 1965–, Flannery O'Connor Prof. of Letters 1986–, Univ. of Iowa; Distinguished Visiting Prof., Univ. of Hawaii 1981; Visiting Lecturer, Goddard Coll. 1970; Visiting Prof., Univ. of Washington 1982; Distinguished Poet-in-Residence, Wichita State Univ. 2004; Lila Wallace-Reader's Digest Writing Fellow, Univ. of Redlands 1991–93; Woodrow Wilson Visiting Fellow, Saint Mary's Coll. of California 1994–95, Pacific Univ. 1996–97, Nebraska-Wesleyan Univ. 1996–97, Hampden-Sydney Coll. 1998–99, West Virginia Wesleyan Coll. 2000–01, Birmingham Southern Coll. 2000–01, Illinois Coll. 2002–03, Bethany Coll. 2003–04; Series Poetry Ed., Pushcart Prize 1997–; First Poet Laureate of the State of Iowa 2000–; Prague Seminars 2002, 2004. *Publications:* poetry: Things We Dreamt We Died For 1966, A Probable Volume of Dreams 1969, The Escape Into You 1971, Residue of Song 1974, Stars Which See, Stars Which Do Not See 1977, These Green-Going-to-Yellow 1981, Segues: A Correspondence in Poetry (with William Stafford) 1983, Drawn by Stones, by Earth, by Things That Have Been in the Fire 1984, New and Selected Poems 1987, Iris of Creation 1990, The Book of the Dead Man 1994, Ardor: The Book of the Dead Man, Vol. 2 1997, Poetry for a Midsummer's Night 1998, Wednesday: Selected Poems 1966–1997 1998, Nightworks: Poems 1962–2000 2000, Rampant 2004; other: Old Snow Just Melting: Essays and Interviews 1983, A Marvin Bell Reader: Selected Prose and Poetry 1994; contrib. to many anthologies and periodicals. *Honours:* Lamont Award, Acad. of American Poets 1969, Guggenheim Fellowship 1977, Nat. Endowment for the Arts Fellowships 1978, 1984, American Poetry Review Prize 1982, Sr Fulbright Scholar 1983, 1986, Hon. Doctorate of Letters (Alfred Univ.) 1986, American Acad. of Arts and Letters Award in Literature 1994, American Poetry Review Shestack Prize 2003. *Address:* 1416 E College Street, Iowa City, IA 52245, USA.

BELL, Robin; Writer, Poet and Broadcaster; b. 4 Jan. 1945, Dundee, Scotland; two d. *Education:* MA, St Andrews University, Scotland; MS, Columbia University, New York, USA. *Publications:* Sawing Logs, 1980; Strathinver: A Portrait Album, 1984; Radio Poems, 1989; Scanning the Forth Bridge, 1994; Le Château des Enfants, 2000; Chapeau!, 2002; Civil Warrior, 2002. Editor: The Best of Scottish Poetry, 1989; Collected Poems of the Marquis of Montrose, 1990; Bittersweet Within My Heart, The Collected Poems of Mary, Queen of Scots, 1992. *Honours:* Best Documentary Television and Radio Industries of Scotland Award, 1984; Sony Award for Best British Radio Feature, 1985. *Address:* The Orchard Muirton, Auchterarder, Perthshire PH3 1ND, Scotland.

BELL BURNELL, S. Jocelyn, CBE, PhD, FRS; British astrophysicist and university administrator; b. 15 July 1943; m. (divorced); one s. *Career:* Lecturer, Univ. of Southampton 1968–73; part-time with Mullard Space Lab., Univ. Coll. London 1974–82; part-time with Royal Observatory, Edin. 1982–91; Chair. Physics Dept Open Univ. 1991–99; Dean of Science, Univ. of Bath 2001–04; Visiting Prof. for Distinguished Teaching, Princeton Univ. 1999–2000; Visiting Prof., Univ. of Oxford 2004–; Pres. Royal Astronomical Soc. 2002–04; discovered the first four pulsars; frequent radio and TV broadcaster on science, on being a woman in science and on science and religion. *Publications:* two books, approximately 70 scientific papers and 35 Quaker publs. *Honours:* Hon. Fellow New Hall, Cambridge 1996; 15 hon. doctorates, including Univs of Cambridge and London ; Joseph Black Medal and Cowie Book Prize, Glasgow Univ. 1962, Michelson Medal, Franklin Inst., USA 1973, J. Robert Oppenheimer Memorial Prize, Center for Theoretical Studies, Fla 1978, Beatrice M. Tinsley Prize, American Astronomical Soc. (first recipient) 1987, Herschel Medal, Royal Astronomical Soc., London 1989, Edinburgh Medal 1999, Magellanic Premium, American Philosophical Soc. 2000, Joseph Priestly Award, Dickinson Coll., Pa 2002. *Address:* Faculty of Science, University of Bath, Bath, BA2 7AY, England (Office). *Telephone:* (1225) 383965 (Office). *Fax:* (1225) 383353 (Office). *E-mail:* s.j.b.burnell@bath.ac.uk (Office).

BELLAMY, David (James), OBE; Botanist, Writer and Broadcaster; b. 18 Jan. 1933, England; m. Rosemary Froy, 1959, two s. three d. *Education:* BSc, Chelsea College of Science and Technology and PhD, Bedford College, London. *Career:* Lecturer, then Senior Lecturer, Dept of Botany, 1960–80, Hon. Prof. of Adult and Continuing Education, 1980–82, University of Durham; Pres., WATCH, 1982, Population Concern, 1988–, National Asscn of Environmental Education, 1989–, Wildlife Trust Partnership, 1996–; Special Prof., University of Nottingham, 1987–; Visiting Prof. of Natural Heritage Studies, Massey University, New Zealand, 1988–89; Dir, David Bellamy Assocs environmental consultants, 1988–97, Bellamy & Nevard The Conservation Consultants 2003–; Scriptwriter and Presenter, many radio and television programmes; mem. Fellow, Institute of Biologists. *Publications:* Peatlands, 1974; Bellamy on Botany, 1974; Bellamy's Britain, 1975; Bellamy's Europe, 1977; Life Giving Sea, 1977; Botanic Man, 1978; Half of Paradise, 1979; The Great Seasons, 1981; Backyard Safari, 1981; Discovering the Countryside with David Bellamy, 4 vols, 1982–83; The Mouse Book, 1983; Bellamy's New World, 1983; The Queen's Hidden Garden, 1984; Turning the Tide, 1986; The Vanishing Bogs of Ireland, 1986; Bellamy's Changing Countryside, 4 vols, 1989; England's Last Wilderness (with Brendan Quayle), 1989; England's Lost Wilderness, 1990; Wilderness in Britain (with Jane Gifford), 1991; How Green are You?, 1991; Tomorrow's Earth, 1991; World Medicine (with Andrea Pfister), 1992; Blooming Bellamy, 1993; Poo You and the Potoroo's Loo, 1997; Jolly Green Giant (autobiog.) 2002, The Bellamy Herbal 2003, A Natural Life 2003. *Honours:* Hon. Fellow, Linnaean Soc. 1997, Chartered Inst. of Water and Environmental Man.Order of the Golden Ark, the Netherlands 1989Hon. Prof. Univ. of Central Queensland 1998United Nations Environmental Program Global 500 Award 1990, Duke of Edinburgh's Award for Underwater Research, BAFTA Richard Dimbleby Award, RGS Busk Medal 2002. *Address:* Mill House, Bedburn, Bishop Auckland, County Durham DL13 3NW, England.

BELLAMY, Joe David; Prof. of English, Writer and Poet; b. 29 Dec. 1941, Cincinnati, Ohio, USA; m. Connie Sue Arendsee, 16 Sept. 1964, one s. one d. *Education:* Duke University, 1959–61; BA, Literature, Antioch College, 1964; MFA, English and Creative Writing, University of Iowa, 1969. *Career:* Instructor, 1969–70, Asst Prof., 1970–72, Mansfield State College, Pennsylvania; Publisher and Ed., Fiction International magazine and press, 1972–84; Asst Prof., 1972–74, Assoc. Prof., 1974–80, Prof. of English, 1980–, St Lawrence University, Canton, New York; Program Consultant in American Literature, Divisions of Public Programs and Research Programs, National Endowment for the Humanities, 1976–90; Pres. and Chair, Board of Dirs, Co-ordinating Council of Literary Magazines, 1979–81, and Associated Writing Programs, 1990; Distinguished Visiting Prof., George Mason University, 1987–88; Dir, Literature Program, National Endowment for the Arts, 1990–92; Whichard Distinguished Prof. in the Humanities, East Carolina University, 1994–96; mem. National Book Critics Circle. *Publications:* Apocalypse: Dominant Contemporary Forms, 1972; The New Fiction: Interviews with Innovative Writers, 1974; Superfiction, or the American Story Transformed, 1975; Olympic Gold Medallist (poems), 1978; Moral Fiction: An Anthology, 1980; New Writers for the Eighties: An Anthology, 1981; Love Stories/Love Poems: An Anthology (with Roger Weingarten), 1982; American Poetry Observed: Poets on Their Work, 1984; The Frozen Sea (poems), 1988; Suzi Sinzinnati (novel), 1989; Atomic Love (short stories), 1993; Literary Luxuries: American Writing at the End of the Millennium, 1995. Contributions: Books, anthologies, journals and magazines. *Honours:* Bread Loaf Scholar-Bridgman Award, 1973; National Endowment for the Humanities Fellowship, 1974; Fels Award, 1976; Co-ordinating Council of Literary Magazine Award for Fiction, 1977; Kansas Quarterly-Kansas Arts Commission Fiction Prize, 1982; New York State

Council on the Arts Grant in Fiction, 1984; National Endowment for the Arts Fellowship for Creative Writers, 1985; Eds' Book Award, 1989. *Address:* 1145 Lawson Cove, Virginia Beach, VA 23455, USA.

BELLE, Pamela Dorothy Alice; Author; b. 16 June 1952, Ipswich, England; m. Steve Thomas, 6 Aug. 1990, two s. *Education:* BA, History, University of Sussex, England, 1972–75; Postgraduate Teaching Certificate, Coventry College of Education, 1975–76. *Career:* mem. Society of Authors; Historical Novel Society. *Publications:* The Moon in the Water, 1983; The Chains of Fate, 1984; Alathea, 1985; The Lodestar, 1987; Wintercombe, 1988; Herald of Joy, 1989; A Falling Star, 1990; Treason's Gift, 1992; The Silver City, 1994; The Wolf Within, 1995; Blood Imperial, 1996; Mermaid's Ground, 1998; No Love Lost, 1999. Contributions: periodicals. *Address:* 61 New Rd, Bromham, Chippenham, Wilts SN15 2JB, England.

BELLI, Gioconda; Poet and Author; b. 9 Dec. 1949, Managua, Nicaragua; m. 2nd Charles Castaldi 10 April 1987; four c. *Education:* Advertising and Journalism, Charles Morris Price School, Philadelphia; Advertising Management, INCAE (Harvard University School of Business Administration in Central America); Philosophy and Literature, Georgetown University, Washington, DC. *Career:* Mem., Political-Diplomatic Commission, 1978–79, International Press Liaison, 1982–83, Exec. Secretary and Spokesperson for the Electoral Campaign, 1983–84, Sandinista National Liberation Front; Dir of Communications and Public Relations, Ministry of Economic Planning, 1979–82; Foreign Affairs Secretary, Nicaragua Writer's Union, 1983–88; Managing Dir, Sistema Nacional de Publicidad, 1984–86. *Publications:* Poetry: Sobre la Grama, 1972, English trans. as On the Grass; Línea de Fuego, 1978, English trans. as Line of Fire; Truenos y Arco Iris, 1982; Amor Insurrecto (anthology), 1985; De la Costilla de Eva, 1987, English trans. as From Eve's Rib; El Ojo de la Mujer, 1991; Sortilegio contral el Frío (erotic collection), 1992; Apogeo, 1997. Fiction: La mujer Habitada, 1988, English trans. as The Inhabited Woman, 1994; Sofía de los Presagios, 1990; Waslala, 1996. Other: The Workshop of the Butterflies (children's story), 1994. Contributions: anthologies and periodicals. *Honours:* National University Poetry Prize, Nicaragua, 1972; Casa de las Americas Poetry Prize, Cuba, 1978; Friedrich Ebhert Foundation Booksellers, Eds and Publishers Literary Prize, Germany, 1989; Anna Seghers Literary Fellowship, Germany, 1989. *Address:* 1842 Union St, San Francisco, CA 94123, USA.

BELLOW, Saul; Writer; b. 10 June 1915, Lachine, QC, Canada; m. 1st Anita Goshkin, divorced, one s.; m. 2nd Alexandra Tschacbasov, 1956, divorced, one s.; m. 3rd Susan Glassman, 1961, divorced, one s.; m. 4th Alexandra Ionesco Tuleca, 1974, divorced; m. 5th Janis Freedman, 1989. *Education:* University of Chicago, 1933–35; BS, Northwestern University, 1937. *Career:* Instructor, Pestalozzi-Froebel Teachers College, Chicago, 1938–42; Editorial Dept, Great Books of the Western World, Encyclopaedia Britannica, Chicago, 1943–46; Instructor, 1946, Asst Prof., 1948–49, Assoc. Prof., 1954–59, University of Minnesota; Visiting Lecturer, New York University, 1950–52; Creative Writing Fellow, Princeton University, 1952–53; Teacher, Bard College, 1953–54; Grunier Distinguished Services Prof., University of Chicago, 1962–; Lecturer, University of Oxford, 1990; Prof., Boston University, 1993–; mem. American Acad. of Arts and Letters. *Publications:* Fiction: Dangling Man, 1944; The Victim, 1947; The Adventures of Augie March, 1953; Seize the Day, 1956; Henderson the Rain King, 1959; Herzog, 1964; Mr Sammler's Planet, 1970; Humboldt's Gift, 1975; The Dean's December, 1982; More Die of Heartbreak, 1986; A Theft, 1989; The Bellarosa Connection, 1989; The Actual, 1997; Ravelstein, 2000. Stories: Mosby's Memoirs and Other Stories, 1968; Him With His Foot in His Mouth and Other Stories, 1984; Something to Remember Me By: Three Tales, 1991; Occasional Pieces, 1993; Collected Stories, 2001. Plays: The Wrecker, 1954; The Last Analysis, 1964; Under the Weather, 1966. Non-Fiction: To Jerusalem and Back: A Personal Account, 1976; It All Adds Up: From the Dim Past to the Uncertain Future, 1994. Contributions: many periodicals. *Honours:* Guggenheim Fellowship, 1948; National Book Awards, 1954, 1964, 1970; Nobel Prize for Literature, 1976; Pulitzer Prize in Fiction, 1976; American Acad. of Arts and Letters Gold Medal, 1977; Brandeis University Creative Arts Award, 1978; Commdr., Légion d'honneur, 1983, Order of Arts and Letters, 1985, France; National Medal of Arts, 1988; National Book Award Lifetime Achievement Award, 1990. *Address:* Boston University, 745 Commonwealth Ave, Boston, MA 02215, USA.

BELSHAW, Cyril Shirley, PhD, FRSC; Canadian anthropologist, writer and publisher; b. 3 Dec. 1921, Waddington, NZ; m. Betty J. Sweetman 1943 (deceased); one s. one d. *Education:* Auckland Univ. Coll. and Victoria Coll., Wellington (Univ. of New Zealand), London School of Econs. *Career:* Dist Officer and Deputy Commr for Western Pacific, British Solomon Islands 1943–46; Sr Research Fellow, Australian Nat. Univ. 1950–53; Prof. Univ. of British Columbia 1953–86, Prof. Emer. 1986–; Dir Regional Training Centre for UN Fellows, Van. 1961–62; Ed. Current Anthropology 1974–84; mem. numerous UNESCO comms, working parties and consultancy groups; Pres. Int. Union of Anthropological and Ethnological Sciences 1978–83, XIth Int. Congress of Anthropological and Ethnological Sciences 1983; Exec. American Anthropological Assoc. 1969–70; Chair. Standing Cttee Social Sciences and Humanities Pacific Science Asscn 1968–76; Hon. Life mem. Royal Anthropological Inst. 1978, Pacific Science Asscn 1981; Ed. The Anthroglobe Journal 1998–2000; Propr Webzines of Vancouver; Man. Ed. EVE-Enjoy Vancouver Electronically 1997–, www.anthropologising.ca 2001–. *Publications:* Island Administration in the South West Pacific 1950, Changing Melanesia 1954, In Search of Wealth 1955, The Great Village 1957, The Indians of British Columbia (with others) 1958, Under the Ivi Tree 1964, Anatomy of a University 1964, Traditional Exchange and Modern Markets (edns in 5 languages) 1965, The Conditions of Social Performance 1970, Towers Besieged 1974, The Sorcerer's Apprentice 1976, The Complete Good Dining Guide to Restaurants in Greater Vancouver 1984, Where is Utopia – Controlling Social Evolution (online) 2000. *Honours:* Hon. Life Fellow Royal Anthropoligcal Inst., Pacific Science Asscn, Asscn for the Social Anthropology of Oceania. *Address:* Suite 2901, 969 Richards Street, Vancouver, BC, V6B 1A8, Canada. *Telephone:* (604) 739-8130. *E-mail:* cbelshaw@telus.net (Home). *Website:* www.evevancouver.ca; www.anthropologising.ca.

BELTING, Hans; Prof. of Art History and New Media and Writer; b. 7 July 1935, Andernach, Germany. *Education:* Art History, Archaeology, University of Mainz, University of Rome; PhD, Art History; Visiting Fellow, Harvard University; Studies with Ernst Kitzinger, Dumbarton Oaks, Washington, DC. *Career:* Asst Prof. of Art History, University of Hamburg, 1966; Prof. of Art History, University of Heidelberg, 1970–80, University of Munich, 1980–93; Visiting Prof., Harvard University, 1984; Meyer Shapiro Visiting Prof., Columbia University, 1989, 1990; Prof. of Art History and New Media, 1993–, Chair., Anthropology Programme, 2000–02, School for New Media, Karlsruhe; mem. Wissenschaftkolleg, Berlin; American Acad. of Arts and Sciences; Medieval Acad. of America. *Publications:* Die Basilica de SS Martiti in Cimitile und ihr frühmittelalterlicher Freskenzyklus, 1962; Die Euphemia-Kirche am Hippodrom in Istabul und ihre Fresken (with Rudolf Naumann), 1966; Studien zur beneventanischen Malerei, 1968; Das illuminierte Buch in der spätbyzantinischen Gesellschaft, 1970; Die Oberkirche von San Francesco in Assisi: Ihre Dekoration als Aufgabe und die Genese einer neuen Wandmalerei, 1977; The Mosaics and Frescoes of St Mary Pammakaritos (with Cyril Mango and Doula Mouriki), 1978; Patronage in 13th Century Constantinople: An Atelier of Later Byzantine Book Illumination and Calligraphy (with Hugo Buchthal), 1978; Die Bibel des Niketas: Ein Werk der höfischen Buchkunst in Byanz und sein antikes Vorbild (with Guglielmo Cavallo), 1979; Das bild und sein Publikum in Mittelalter: Form und Funktion früher Bildtafeln der Passion, 1981, English trans. as The Image and Its Public in the Middle Ages, 1990; Jan van Ecyk als Erzählet (with Dagmar Eichberger), 1983; Das Ende der Kunstgeschichte?: Überlegungen zur heutigen Kunsterfahrung und historischen Kunstforschung, 1983, English trans. as The End of the History of Art?, 1987; Max Beckmann: Die Tradition als Problem in der Kunst der Moderne, 1984, English trans., 1989; Giovanni Bellini Pictà: Ikone und Bilderzählung in der venezianischen Malerei, 1985; Alex Katz: Bilder und Zeichnungen, 1989; Bild und Kult: Eine Geschichte des Bildes vor dem Zeitalter der Kunst, 1990, English trans. as Likeness and Presence: A History of the Image Before the Era of Art, 1993; Die Deutschen und ihre Kunst: Ein schwieriges Erbe, 1992, English trans. as The Germans and Their Art, 1998; Thomas Struth: Museums Photographs, 1993, English trans., 1998; Der Ort der Bilder (with Boris Groys), 1993; Die Erfindung des Gemäldes: Das erste Jahrhundert der neiderländischen Malerei (with Christiane Kruse), 1994; Das unsichtbare Meisterwerk: Die modernen Mythen der Kunst, 1998, English trans. as The Invisible Masterpiece, 2001; Identität im Zweifel: Ansichten der deutschen Kunst, 1999; Theatres: Interiors of Cinema Spaces (with Hiroshi Sugimoto), 2000; Bild-Anthropologie: Entwürfe für eine Bildwissenschaft, 2001; Hieronymous Bosch: Der Garten der Lüste, 2002, English trans. as Hieronymus Bosch: Gardens of Earthly Delights, 2002. Contributions: scholarly books and journals. *Honours:* Orden pour le mérite für Wissenschaften und Künste; Hon. Chair, University of Heidelberg; European Chair, Collège de France. *Address:* c/o Institut für Kunstwissenschaft, Staatliche Hochschule für Gestaltung, Lorenzstrasse 16, 76135 Karlsruhe, Germany. *E-mail:* hans.belting@hfg-karlsruhe.de.

BEN JELLOUN, Tahar; Moroccan writer and poet; b. 1 Dec. 1944, Fès; m. Aicha Ben Jelloun 1986; two s. two d. *Education:* Lycée Regnault de Tanger, Faculté de Lettres de Rabat and Univ. of Paris. *Career:* columnist Le Monde 1973–, La Repubblica (Italy) and La Vanguardia (Spain); mem. Haut Conseil de la francophonie, Conseil supérieur de la langue française; UN Goodwill Amb. for Human Rights. *Publications:* fiction: Harrouda 1973, La Réclusion solitaire 1976 (trans. as Solitaire 1988), Moha le fou, Moha le sage 1978, La Prière de l'absent 1980, Muha al-ma'twah, Muha al-hakim 1982, L'Écrivain public 1983, L'Enfant de sable 1985 (trans. as The Sand Child 1987), La Nuit sacrée 1987 (trans. as The Sacred Night 1989), Jour de silence à Tanger 1990 (trans. as Silent Day in Tangier 1991), Les Yeux baissés 1991, L'Ange aveugle 1992, L'Homme rompu 1994, Corruption 1995, Le Premier amour est toujours le dernier 1995, Les Raisins de la galère 1995, La Soudure fraternelle 1995, La Nuit de l'erreur 1997, L'Auberge des pauvres 1999, Labyrinthe des Sentiments 1999, Cette aveuglante absence de lumière (trans. as The Blinding Absence of Light) (Impac Dublin Literary Award 2004) 2001, Amours sorcières 2003; poems: Hommes sous linceul de silence 1970, Cicatrice du soleil 1972, Le Discours du chameau 1974, La Mémoire future: Anthologie de la nouvelle poésie du Maroc 1976, Les Amandiers sont morts de leurs blessures 1976, A l'insu du souvenir 1980, Sahara 1987, La Remontée des cendres 1991, Poésie Complète (1966–95) 1995; plays: Chronique d'une solitude 1976, Entretien avec Monsieur Said Hammadi, ouvrier algérien 1982, La Fiancée de l'eau 1984; non-fiction: La Plus haute des solitudes: Misère sexuelle d'émigrés nord-africains 1977, Haut Atlas: L'Exil de pierres 1982, Hospitalité française: Racisme et immigration maghrebine 1984, Marseille, comme un matin d'insomnie 1986, Giacometti 1991, Le Racisme expliqué à ma fille 1998, L'islam expliqué aux enfants 2002. *Honours:* Chevalier des Arts et des Lettres, Légion d'honneur; Prix de l'Amitié Franco-Arabe 1976, Médaille du Mérite Nat. (Morocco), Prix Goncourt 1987, Prix des Hemisphere 1991, UN Global Tolerance Award 1998. *Address:* Editions du Seuil, BP 80, 27 rue Jacob, 75261 Paris cedex 06, France (Office). *Website:* www.taharbenjelloun .org (Office).

BEN-RAFAEL, Eliezer; Prof. of Sociology and Writer; b. 3 Oct. 1938, Brussels, Belgium; m. Miriam Neufeld, 3 Aug. 1960, two d. *Education:* BA, 1966, MA, 1970, PhD, 1973, Hebrew University, Jerusalem. *Career:* Research Fellow, Harvard University, 1974–75; Prof. of Sociology, 1980–, Jima and Zalman Weinberg Chair of Political Sociology, 1997–, University of Tel-Aviv; Directeur d'Études Associé, École des Hautes Études en Sciences Sociales, 1984–85; Visiting Scholar, Oxford Centre for Postgraduate Hebrew Studies, 1989–90; Co-Ed., Israel Social Sciences Review, 1992–; mem. Israel Society of Sociology, pres., 1994–; International Institute of Sociology, vice-pres. *Publications:* The Emergence of Ethnicity: Cultural Groups and Social Conflict in Israel, 1982; Le kibboutz, 1983; Status, Power and Conflict in the Kibbutz, 1988; Ethnicity, Religion and Class in Israeli Society, 1991; Language, Identity and Social Division: The Case of Israel, 1994; Crisis and Transformation: The Kibbutz at Century's End, 1997; Language and Communication in Israel, 2000; Identités Juives, 50 sages repondent à Ben-Gourion, 2001; Identity, Culture and Globalization, 2001. Contributions: Professional journals. *Address:* Dept of Sociology, University of Tel-Aviv, Tel-Aviv 69978, Israel.

BENACQUISTA, Tonino; novelist; b. 1 Sept. 1961, Choisy-le-Roi, Paris, France. *Career:* fmr museum nightwatchman and train guard. *Publications include:* novels: Trois carrées sur frond rouge 1990, La commedia des ratés 1991, Morsures de l'aube 1993, Saga 2001, Quelqu'un d'autre 2002, Holy Smoke 2004. *Honours:* Trophee 813, Grand Prix des lectrices de Elle, Prix Mystére de la Critique. *Address:* c/o Bitter Lemon Press, 37 Arundel Gardens, London, W11 2LW, England. *E-mail:* books@bitterlemonpress .com. *Website:* www.bitterlemonpress.com.

BENCE-JONES, Mark; Writer; b. 29 May 1930, London, England; m. Gillian Pretyman, 2 Feb. 1965, one s. two d. *Education:* BA, 1952, MA, 1958, Pembroke College, Cambridge; MRAC, Royal Agricultural College, Cirencester, 1954. *Publications:* All a Nonsense, 1957; Paradise Escaped, 1958; Nothing in the City, 1965; The Remarkable Irish, 1966; Palaces of the Raj, 1973; Clive of India, 1974; The Cavaliers, 1976; Burke's Guide to Irish Country Houses, 1978; The British Aristocracy (co-author), 1979; The Viceroys of India, 1982; Ancestral Houses, 1984; Twilight of the Ascendancy, 1987; A Guide to Irish Country Houses, 1989; The Catholic Families, 1992; Life in an Irish Country House, 1996. Contributions: Books and periodicals. *Address:* Glenville Park, Glenville, County Cork, Ireland.

BENCHLEY, Peter (Bradford); Writer; b. 8 May 1940, New York, NY, USA; m. Winifred B. Wesson, 19 Sept. 1964, two s. one d. *Education:* BA, Harvard University, 1961. *Career:* Reporter, Washington Post, 1963; Assoc. Ed., Newsweek magazine, New York City, 1963–67; Staff Asst, Office of the Pres. of the US, Washington, DC, 1967–69; Writer, Narrator, and Host, The American Sportsman television programme, 1974–83, Galapagos television special, 1987; Host and Narrator, Sharks television special, 1989, Expedition Earth television series, 1990–96; Co-Creator, Dolphin Cove television series, 1989; Exec. Producer, Beast television miniseries, 1996. *Publications:* Time and a Ticket, 1964; Jaws, 1974; The Deep, 1976; The Island, 1978; The Girl of the Sea of Cortez, 1982; Q Clearance, 1986; Rummies, 1989; Beast, 1991; White Shark, 1994. Other: various screenplays. Contributions: newspapers and magazines. *Address:* c/o International Creative Management, 40 W 57th St, New York, NY 10019, USA.

BENEDETTI, Mario; Uruguayan writer and poet; b. 14 Sept. 1920, Paso de los Toros, Tacuarembo; m. Luz López. *Education:* Colegio Alemán. *Career:* journalist on Marcha (weekly) and literary, film and theatre critic on El Diario, Tribuna Popular and La Mañana. *Publications:* fiction: Esta mañana 1949, El último viaje y otros cuentos 1951, Quién de nosotros 1953, Montevideanos 1959, La Tregua 1963, Gracias por el Fuego 1965, La muerte y otras sorpresas 1968, Con o sin nostalgia 1977, Viento del exilio 1981, El amor, las mujeres y la vida 1995; plays: Ustedes por ejemplo 1953, El Reportaje 1958, Ida y vuelta 1958; poetry: La víspera indeleble 1945, Sólo mientras tanto 1950, Poemas de la oficina 1956, Poemas del hoyporhoy 1965, Inventario 1965, Contra los puentes levadizos 1966, A ras de sueño 1967; essays: Peripecia y novela 1948, Marcel Proust y otros ensayos 1951, Literatura uruguaya siglo XX 1963, Letras del continente mestizo 1967, Sobre artes y oficios 1968. *Address:* c/o Curbstone Press, 321 Jackson Street, Willimantic, CT 06226-1738, USA.

BENEDICTUS, David (Henry); Writer, Dramatist, Reviewer and Dir; b. 16 Sept. 1938, London, England; m. Yvonne Daphne Antrobus 1971; one s. one d. *Education:* BA, English, Balliol College, Oxford, 1959. *Career:* BBC News and Current Affairs, 1961, Ed., Readings, 1989–91, and Radio 3 Drama, 1992, Sr Prod., Serial Readings, 1992–95, BBC Radio; Drama Dir, 1962, Story Ed., 1965, BBC TV; Asst Dir, RSC, 1970; Writer-in-Residence, Sutton Library, Surrey, 1975, Kibbutz Gezer, Israel, 1978, Bitterne Library, Southampton, 1983–84; Antiques Correspondent, Evening Standard, 1977–80; Judith E. Wilson Visiting Fellow, Cambridge, and Fellow Commoner, Churchill College, Cambridge, 1981–82; Commissioning Ed., Drama Series, Channel 4 TV, 1984–86. *Publications:* The Fourth of June, 1962; You're a Big Boy Now, 1963; This Animal is Mischievous, 1965; Hump, or Bone by Bone Alive, 1967; The Guru and the Golf Club, 1969; A World of Windows, 1971; The Rabbi's Wife, 1976; Junk: How and Where to Buy Beautiful Things at Next to Nothing Prices, 1976; A Twentieth Century Man, 1978; The Antique Collector's Guide, 1980; Lloyd George (after Elaine Morgan's screenplay), 1981; Whose Life is it Anyway? (after Brian Clarke's screenplay), 1981; Who Killed the Prince Consort?, 1982; Local Hero (after Bill Forsyth's screenplay), 1983; The Essential London Guide, 1984; Floating Down to Camelot, 1985; The Streets of London, 1986; The Absolutely Essential London Guide, 1986; Little Sir Nicholas, 1990; Odyssey of a Scientist (with Hans Kalmus), 1991; Sunny Intervals and Showers, 1992; The Stamp Collector, 1994; How to Cope When the Money Runs Out, 1998. Plays: Betjemania, 1976; The Golden Key, 1982; What a Way to Run a Revolution!, 1985; You Say Potato, 1992. Contributions: newspapers and magazines. *Address:* c/o Weidenfeld and Nicholson, 5 Upper St Martin's Lane, London WC2H 9EA, England.

BENEDIKT, Michael; Writer, Poet, Critic and Ed.; b. 26 May 1935, New York, NY, USA. *Education:* BA, New York University, 1956; MA, Columbia University, 1961. *Career:* Professorships in Literature and Poetry, Bennington College, 1968–69, Sarah Lawrence College, 1969–73, Hampshire College, 1973–75, Vassar College, 1976–77, Boston University, 1977–79; Contributing Ed., American Poetry Review, 1973–; Poetry Ed., Paris Review, 1974–78; mem. PEN Club of America; Poetry Society of America. *Publications:* The Body (verse), 1968; Sky (verse), 1970; Mole Notes (prose poems), 1971; Night Cries (prose poems), 1976; The Badminton at Great Barrington or Gustav Mahler and the Chattanooga Choo-Choo (poems), 1980. Anthologies: Modern French Theatre: The Avant-Garde, Dada and Surrealism (with George E. Wellwarth), 1964, in the UK as Modern French Plays: An Anthology from Jarry to Ionesco, 1965; Post-War German Theatre (with George E. Wellwarth), 1967; Modern Spanish Theatre (with George E. Wellwarth), 1968; Theatre Experiment, 1968; The Poetry of Surrealism, 1975; The Prose Poem: An International Anthology, 1976. Contributions: Agni Review; Ambit; Art International; Art News; London Magazine; Massachusetts Review; New York Quarterly; Paris Review; Partisan Review; Poetry. *Honours:* Guggenheim Fellowship, 1968–69; Bess Hokin Prize, 1969; National Endowment for the Arts Prize, 1970; Benedikt: A Profile (critical monograph/Festschrift), 1978; National Endowment for the Arts Fellowship, 1979–80; Retrospective, Library of Congress, videotape, 1986.

BENFIELD, Derek; playwright and actor; b. Bradford, Yorkshire, England; m. Susan Elspeth Lyall Grant 1953; one s. one d. *Education:* Bingley Grammar School, RADA. *Career:* mem. Society of Authors. *Publications:* Plays: Wild Goose Chase, 1956; Running Riot, 1958; Post Horn Gallop, 1965; Murder for the Asking, 1967; Off the Hook, 1970; Bird in the Hand, 1973; Panic Stations, 1975; Caught on the Hop, 1979; Beyond a Joke, 1980; In for the Kill, 1981; Look Who's Talking, 1984; Touch & Go, 1985; Fish Out of Water, 1986; Flying Feathers, 1987; Bedside Manners, 1988; A Toe in the Water, 1991; Don't Lose the Place, 1992; Anyone for Breakfast?, 1994; Up and Running, 1995; A Fly in the Ointment, 1996; Two and Two Together, 1998; Second Time Around, 2000; In at the Deep End, 2003. *Address:* c/o Lemon Unna & Durbridge Ltd, 24 Pottery Lane, Holland Park, London W11 4LZ, England.

BENFORD, Gregory Albert, BA, MS, PhD; American physicist and science fiction author; b. 30 Jan. 1941, Mobile, AL; m. Joan Abbe 1967; one s. one d. *Education:* University of Oklahoma, University of California at San Diego. *Career:* Fellow, 1967–69, Research Physicist, 1969–71, Lawrence Radiation Laboratory, Livermore, California; Asst Prof., 1971–73, Assoc. Prof., 1973–79, Prof. of Physics, 1979–, University of California at Irvine; mem. American Physical Society, Royal Astronomical Society, SFWA, Social Science Exploration. *Publications:* Deeper Than the Darkness, 1970, revised edn as The Stars in the Shroud, 1979; If the Stars Are Gods (with Gordon Eklund), 1977; In the Ocean of Night, 1977; Find the Changeling (with Gordon Eklund), 1980; Shiva Descending (with William Rotsler), 1980; Timescape, 1980; Against Infinity, 1983; Across the Sea of Suns, 1984; Artifact, 1985; Of Space-Time and the River, 1985; In Alien Flesh, 1986; Heart of the Comet (with David Brin), 1986; Great Sky River, 1987; Under the Wheel (with others), 1987; Hitler Victorious: Eleven Stories of the German Victory in World War II (ed. with Martin H. Greenberg), 1987; We Could Do Worse, 1988; Tides of Light, 1989; Beyond the Fall of Night (with Arthur C. Clarke), 1990; Centigrade 233, 1990; Matter's End (ed.), 1991; Chiller, 1993; Furious Gulf, 1994; Far Futures, 1995; Sailing Bright Eternity, 1995; Foundation's Fear, 1997; Immersion and Other Short Novels 2002, Beyond Infinity 2004. *Honours:* Woodrow Wilson Fellowship, 1963–64; Nebula Awards, SFWA, 1975, 1981; BSFA Award, 1981; John W. Campbell Award, World Science Fiction Convention, 1981; Ditmar Award, Australia, 1981; various grants. *Address:* c/o Orbit, Brettenham House, Lancaster Place, London, WC2E 7EN, England.

BENÍTEZ, Sandra; Writer; b. 26 March 1941, Washington, DC, USA; m. James F. Kondrick, 25 May 1980, two s. *Education:* BS in Education, 1963,

MA in Comparative Literature, 1974, Northeast Missouri State University. *Career:* Distinguished Edelstein-Keller Writer-in-Residence, University of Minnesota, 1997; mem. Authors' Guild; Poets and Writers. *Publications:* A Place Where the Sea Remembers, 1993; Bitter Grounds, 1997; The Weight of All Things, 2000. *Honours:* Minnesota Book Award for Fiction, 1993; Barnes and Noble Fiction Award, 1994. *Address:* c/o Ellen Levine Literary Agency, 15 E 26th St, No. 1801, New York, NY 10010, USA.

BENJAMIN, David (see Slavitt, David Rytman).

BENN, Anthony (Tony) Neil Wedgwood, MA; writer; b. 3 April 1925, London, England; m. Caroline Middleton De Camp 1949 (deceased); three s. one d. *Education:* New College, Oxford. *Career:* MP, Bristol South East, 1950–60, 1963–83, Chesterfield, 1984–2001, Mem., 1959–60, 1962–93, Chair., 1971–72, National Exec. Committee, Labour Party; Postmaster-General, 1964–66; Privy Counsellor, 1964–; Minister of Technology, 1966–70; Secretary of State for Industry and Minister for Posts and Telecommunications, 1974–75; Secretary of State fof Energy, 1975–79; Pres., European Economic Community Council of Energy Ministers, 1977, Socialist Campaign Group of Labour MPs, 1987–; Visiting Prof., LSE; mem. National Union of Journalists. *Publications:* The Privy Council as a Second Chamber, 1957; The Regeneration of Britain, 1964; The New Politics, 1970; Speeches, 1974; Arguments for Socialism, 1979; Arguments for Democracy, 1981; Parliament, People and Power, 1982; Writings on the Wall: A Radical and Socialist Anthology 1215–1984 (ed.), 1984; Out of the Wilderness: Diaries 1963–1967, 1987; Office Without Power: Diaries 1968–1972, 1988; Fighting Back: Speaking Out for Socialism in the Eighties, 1988; Against the Tide: Diaries 1973–1976, 1989; Conflicts of Interest: Diaries 1977–1980, 1990; A Future for Socialism, 1991; The End of an Era: Diaries 1980–1990, 1992; Common Sense: A New Constitution for Britain (co-author), 1993; Years of Hope: Diaries, Letters and Papers 1940–1962, 1994; The Benn Diaries 1940–1990, 1995; Free at Last: Diaries 1990–2001, 2002; Free Radical: New Century Essays, 2003; Dare to be a Daniel (autobiog.) 2004. Contributions: various journals in the United Kingdom and abroad; Broadcaster: various current affairs programmes. *Address:* 12 Holland Park Avenue, London W11 3QU, England.

BENNACK, Frank Anthony, Jr; American publishing executive; b. 12 Feb. 1933, San Antonio; m. Luella Smith 1951; five d. *Education:* Univ. of Maryland and St Mary's Univ. *Career:* advertising account exec. San Antonio Light 1950–53, 1956–58, Advertising Man. 1961–65, Asst Publr 1965–67, Publr 1967–74; Gen. Man. (newspapers), Hearst Corpn New York 1974–76, Exec. Vice-Pres. and COO 1975–78, Pres. and CEO 1978–2002, Vice-Chair. Bd, Chair. Exec. Cttee 2002–; Chair. Museum of TV and Radio, NY City 1991–; Pres. Tex. Daily Newspaper Asscn 1973–; Dir J.P. Morgan Chase & Co., Wyeth, Polo Ralph Lauren Corpn, Metropolitan Opera of New York; Dir, Vice-Chair. Lincoln Center for the Performing Arts; Dir Newspaper Asscn of American (fmrly American Newspaper Publrs Asscn), Chair. 1992–93; Gov., Vice-Chair. New York Presbyterian Hosp.; mem. Bd of Dirs Mfrs Hanover Trust Co., New York. *Address:* Hearst Corporation, 959 8th Avenue, New York, NY 10019, USA.

BENNASSAR, Bartolomé; Prof. of History, Historian and Novelist; b. 8 April 1929, Nîmes, France; m. 20 April 1954, one s. two d. *Education:* University of Montpellier; University of Toulouse. *Career:* Prof. of History, High Schools of Rodez, Agen and Marseille; Asst Prof., Prof., then Pres., University of Toulouse Le Mirail. *Publications:* Valladolid au siècle d'or, 1967; Recherches sur les grandes épidémies dans le Nord de l'Espagne, 1969; L'Homme espagnol, 1975, US trans. as The Spanish Character; L'Inquisition espagnole XV-XIX, 1979; Un siècle d'or espagnol, 1982; Histoire d'Espagnols, 1985; Les Chrétiens d'Allah, 1989; 1492: Un monde nouveau?, 1991; Histoire de la tauromachie, 1993; Franco, 1995; Le Voyage en Espagne, 1998. Fiction: Le baptême du Mort, 1962; Picture: le dernier saut, 1970; Les tribulations de Mustafa des Six-Fours, 1995. Other: numerous Italian and Spanish trans. Contributions: Annales ESC; L'Histoire; Historia. *Honours:* Bronze Medal, Centre National de la Recherche Scientifique; Dr hc, University of Valladolid, Spain. *Address:* 11 allée de Val d'Aran, 31240 Saint-Jean, France.

BENNETT, Alan, BA; British playwright and actor; b. 9 May 1934, Leeds. *Education:* Leeds Modern School, Exeter Coll., Oxford. *Career:* Jr Lecturer, Modern History, Magdalen Coll., Oxford 1960–62; co-author and actor Beyond the Fringe, Edin. 1960, London 1961, New York 1962; Trustee Nat. Gallery 1993–98. *Plays:* On the Margin (TV series, author and actor) 1966, Forty Years On (author and actor) 1968, Getting On 1971, Habeas Corpus 1973, The Old Country 1977, Enjoy 1980, Kafka's Dick 1986, Single Spies 1988, The Wind in the Willows (adapted for Nat. Theatre) 1990, The Madness of George III 1991 (film 1995), The Lady in the Van 1999, The History Boys (Royal Nat. Theatre, London) 2004. *Radio:* The Last of the Sun 2004. *Television scripts:* A Day Out (film) 1972, Sunset Across the Bay (TV film) 1975, A Little Outing, A Visit from Miss Prothero (plays) 1977, Doris and Doreen, The Old Crowd, Me! I'm Afraid of Virginia Woolf, All Day on the Sands, Afternoon Off, One Fine Day 1978–79, Intensive Care, Our Winnie, A Woman of No Importance, Rolling Home, Marks, Say Something Happened, An Englishman Abroad 1982, The Insurance Man 1986, Talking Heads (Olivier Award) 1992, 102 Boulevard Haussmann 1991, A Question of Attribution 1991, Talking Heads 2 1998. *Films:* A Private Function 1984, Prick Up Your Ears 1987, The Madness of King George 1994. *Television documentaries:* Dinner at Noon 1988, Poetry in Motion 1990, Portrait or Bust 1994, The Abbey 1995, Telling Tales 1999. *Publications:* Beyond the Fringe (with Peter Cook, Jonathan Miller and Dudley Moore) 1962, Forty Years On 1969, Getting On 1972, Habeas Corpus 1973, The Old Country 1978, Enjoy 1980, Office Suite 1981, Objects of Affection 1982, The Writer in Disguise 1985, Two Kafka Plays 1987, Talking Heads 1988, Single Spies 1989, Poetry in Motion 1990, The Lady in the Van 1991, The Wind in the Willows (adaptation) 1991, The Madness of George III 1992, Writing Home (autobiog.) 1994, Diaries 1997, The Clothes They Stood Up In 1998, Talking Heads 2 1998, The Complete Talking Heads 1998, A Box of Alan Bennett 2000, Father, Father! Burning Bright 2000, The Laying on of Hands 2001; regular contrib. to London Review of Books. *Honours:* Hon. Fellow Royal Acad. 2000; Hon. Fellow Exeter Coll., Oxford; Hon. DLitt (Leeds); Evening Standard Award 1961, 1969, Hawthornden Prize 1988, two Oliver Awards 1993, Evening Standard Film Award 1996, Lifetime Achievement Award, British Book Awards 2003. *Literary Agent:* PFD, Drury House, 34–43 Russell Street, London, WC2B 5HA, England. *Telephone:* (20) 7376-7676.

BENNETT, Bruce (Harry); Prof. of English, Ed. and Writer; b. 23 March 1941, Perth, WA, Australia; m. Patricia Ann Bennett 8 July 1967; one s. one d. *Education:* BA, DipEd, Univ. of Western Australia, 1963; BA, 1967, MA, 1972, Univ. of Oxford; MA, Ed, Univ. of London, 1974. *Career:* Lecturer, 1968–75, Senior Lecturer, 1975–85, Assoc. Prof., 1985–92, Univ. of Western Australia; Co-Ed., Westerly: A Quarterly Review, 1975–92; Prof. of English, School of Humanities, Univ. of New South Wales, Australian Defence Force Acad.; mem. Asscn for the Study of Australian Literature, pres., 1983–85; Australian Society of Authors; Asscn of Commonwealth Literature and Language Studies, vice-chair; MLA of America; PEN International, Australia-India Council, 2002–. *Publications:* Place, Region and Community, 1985; An Australian Compass: Essays on Place and Direction in Australian Literature, 1991; Spirit in Exile: Peter Porter and his Poetry, 1991; Oxford Literary History of Australia (co-ed.), 1998; Australian Short Fiction: A History, 2002. Other: ed., co-ed. of various vols, incl.: Resistance and Reconciliation: Writing in the Commonwealth, 2003. Contributions: many books and journals. *Honours:* Rhodes Scholar, Pembroke College, Oxford, 1964–67; WA Premier's Award, Historical and Critical Studies, 1992; AO, 1993. *Address:* c/o School of Humanities, University of New South Wales, Australian Defence Force Acad., Canberra, ACT 2600, Australia.

BENNETT, John J.; Writer; b. 8 Aug. 1938, New York, NY, USA. *Education:* George Washington University; University of Munich. *Publications:* Tripping in America, 1984; Crime of the Century, 1986; The New World Order, 1991; Bodo (novel), 1995; Karmic Four-Star Buckaroo, 1997. Contributions: Chicago Review; Exquisite Corpse; Northwest Review; Transatlantic Review; New York Quarterly; Seattle Weekly. *Honours:* First Prize for Fiction, Iron Country, 1978; William Wantling Award, 1987; Darrell Bob Houston Award, 1988. *Address:* PO Box 1634, Ellensburg, WA 98926, USA.

BENNETT, Louise (Simone); Lecturer and Poet; b. 7 Sept. 1919, Kingston, Jamaica; m. Eric Coverley. *Education:* RADA, London. *Career:* Resident Artist, BBC (West Indies section) 1945–46, 1950–53; Residencies in Coventry, Huddersfield and Amersham, United Kingdom; Drama Specialist, Jamaica Social Welfare Commission, 1955–60; Lecturer, Drama and Jamaican Folklore, University of the West Indies, Kingston, 1959–61; Lecturer, television and radio commentator in Jamaica. *Publications:* Dialect Verses, 1940; Jamaican Dialect Verses, 1942; Jamaican Humour in Dialect, 1943; Miss Lulu Sez, 1948; Anancy Stories and Dialect Verses, 1950; Laugh with Louise, 1960; Jamaica Labrish, 1966; Anancy and Miss Lou, 1979; Selected Poems, 1982; Aunt Roachy Seh, 1993. Other: various recordings of Jamaican songs and poems. *Honours:* Order of Jamaica; MBE; Silver Musgrave Medal, Institute of Jamaica; Norman Manly Award of Excellence, University of the West Indies, 1982. *Address:* Enfield House, Gordon Town, St Andrew, Jamaica.

BENNETT, Paul (Lewis); Prof. of English (retd), Poet, Writer, Gardener and Orchardist; b. 10 Jan. 1921, Gnadenhutten, Ohio, USA; m. Martha Jeanne Leonhart 31 Dec. 1941 (died 1995); two s. *Education:* BA, Ohio University, 1942; AM, Harvard University, 1947. *Career:* Instructor, Samuel Adams School of Social Studies, Boston, 1945–46; Teaching Asst, Harvard University, 1945–46; Instructor in English, University of Maine, Orono, 1946–47; Instructor to Prof. of English, 1947–86, Poet-in-Residence, 1986–, Denison University; Gardener and Orchardist, 1948–; Consultant, Aerospace Laboratories, Owens-Corning Fiberglass Corp, 1964–67, Ohio Arts Council, 1978–81, Ohio Board of Regents, 1985–86. *Publications:* Poetry: A Strange Affinity, 1975; The Eye of Reason, 1976; Building a House, 1986; The Sun and What It Says Endlessly, 1995; Appalachian Mettle, 1997. Fiction: Robbery on the Highway, 1961; The Living Things, 1975; Follow the River, 1987; Fact Book: Max: The Tail of a Waggish Dog, 1999. Contributions: many periodicals. *Honours:* National Endowment for the Arts Fellowship, 1973–74; Significant Achievement Award, Ohio University, 1992.

BENNETT, William John, BA, PhD, JD; lawyer, educator and writer; b. 31 July 1943, New York, NY, USA; m. Mary Elaine Glover 1982; two s. *Education:* Williams College, University of Texas, Harvard University Law School. *Career:* Asst Prof., University of Southern Mississippi, 1967–68, University of Texas, 1970, University of Wisconsin, 1973; Resident Adviser and Tutor, Harvard University, 1969–71; Asst Prof. and Asst to the Pres.,

Boston University, 1971–76; Exec. Dir, 1976–79, Pres. and Dir, 1979–81, National Humanities Center, Triangle Park, NC; Adjunct Assoc. Prof., University of North Carolina and North Carolina State University, 1979–81; Chair., National Endowment for the Humanities, Washington, DC, 1981–85; Secretary of Education, US Dept of Education, Washington, DC, 1985–88; Partner, Dunnels, Duvall, Bennett and Porter, Washington, DC, 1988–; Dir, National Drug Policy, Exec. Office of the Pres. of the US, Washington, DC, 1989–90; Co-Dir, Empower America, Washington, DC, 1993; mem. American Society for Political and Legal Philosophy; National Acad. of Education; National Humanities Faculty; Society for Values in Higher Education; Southern Education Communications Asscn. *Publications:* Counting by Race: Equality from the Founding Fathers to Bakke and Weber (with Terry Eastland), 1979; Our Children and Our Country: Improving America's Schools and Affirming the Common Culture, 1988; The De-Valuing of America: The Fight for Our Culture and Our Children, 1992; The Book of Virtues: A Treasury of Great Moral Stories, 1993; The Index of Leading Cultural Indicators: Facts and Figures of the State of American Society, 1994; The Moral Compass: Stories for a Life's Journey, 1995; Our Sacred Honor, 1997; The Death of Outrage: Bill Clinton and the Assault on American Ideals, 1998. Contributions: various publications. *Honours:* many hon. doctorates. *Address:* 862 Venable Place NW, Washington, DC 20012, USA.

BENOIST, Alain de; Journalist, Essayist and Lecturer; b. 11 Dec. 1943, Saint-Symphorien, France; m. Doris M. Christians, 21 June 1972, two s. *Education:* Diploma, Lycées Montaigne et Louis-le-Grand, Paris. *Career:* Ed.-in-Chief, L'Observateur européen, 1964–68, Nouvelle Ecole, 1969–, Midi-France, 1970–71; Journalist, L'Echo de la presse et de la publicité, 1968, Courrier de Paul Dehème, 1969–76; Critic, Valeurs actuelles and Spectacle du monde, 1970–82, Figaro-Magazine, 1977–92; Dir, Krisis, 1988–; mem. several societies, research groups, etc. *Publications:* Les Indo-Européens, 1966; L'Empirisme logique et la Philosophie du Cercle de Vienne, 1970; Avec ou sans Dieu, 1970; Morale et Politique de Nietzsche, 1974; Vu de droite: Anthologie critique des idées contemporaines, 1977; Les Idées a l'endroit, 1979; Guide pratique des prénoms, 1980; Comment peut-on etre paien?, 1981; Feter Noël, 1982; Orientations pour des années décisives, 1982; Traditions d'Europe, 1983; Démocratie: Le problème, 1985; Europe, Tiers monde, même combat, 1986; Le Grain de sable, 1994; La Ligne de mire, 1995; L'Empire intérieur, 1995; Céline et l'Allemagne, 1996; Famille et société, 1996; Ernst Jünger, 1997; L'écume et les galets, 2000; Dernière année, 2002, Critiques-Théoriques 2003. Contributions: various publications. *Honours:* Grand prix de l'essai de l'Académie française, 1978. *Address:* 5 rue Carrière-Mainguet, 75011Paris, France. *E-mail:* alain.de .benoist@noos.fr.

BENSLEY, Connie; Poet and Writer; b. 28 July 1929, London, England; m. J. A. Bensley, 2 Aug. 1952, two s. *Education:* Diploma, Social Sciences, University of London, 1962. *Career:* Poetry Ed., PEN Magazine, 1984–85; mem. Poetry Society. *Publications:* Progress Report, 1981; Moving In, 1984; Central Reservations, 1990; Choosing to be a Swan, 1994; The Back and the Front of It, 2000. Contributions: Observer; Poetry Review; Spectator; TLS. *Honours:* First Place, TLS Poetry Competition, 1986; Second Place, Leek Poetry Competition, 1988; Prizewinner, Arvon/Observer Poetry Competition, 1994; Second Place, Tate Gallery Poetry Competition, 1995. *Address:* 49 Westfields Ave, Barnes, London SW13 0AT, England.

BENSON, Eugene; academic and writer; b. 6 July 1928, Larne, Northern Ireland; m. Renate Niklaus 1968; two s. *Education:* BA, National University of Ireland, 1950; MA, University of Western Ontario, 1958; PhD, University of Toronto, 1966. *Career:* Lecturer, Royal Military College, Kingston, Ontario, 1960–61; Asst Prof. of English, Laurentian University, 1961–64; Asst Prof., 1965–67, Assoc. Prof., 1967–71, Prof. of English, 1971–93, University Prof. Emeritus, 1994–, University of Guelph; mem. Asscn of Canadian Theatre Historians; Canadian Asscn of Irish Studies; Writers' Union of Canada, chair., 1983–84, elected life mem., 2001; PEN Canada, co-pres. 1984–85. *Publications:* Encounter: Canadian Drama in Four Media, anthology (ed.), 1973; The Bulls of Ronda (novel), 1976; Power Game, or the Making of a Prime Minister (novel), 1980; J. M. Synge, 1982; English-Canadian Theatre (co-author), 1987; Oxford Companion to Canadian Theatre (co-ed.), 1989; Encyclopedia of Post-Colonial Literatures in English (co-ed.), 1994; The Oxford Companion to Canadian Literature (co-ed.), 1997. *Address:* 55 Palmer Street, Guelph, ON N1E 2P9, Canada.

BENSON, Gerard John, (Jedediah Barrow); poet, writer and editor; b. 9 April 1931, London, England; m. 2nd; one s. one d. *Education:* Rendcomb College; Exeter University; Diplomas, Drama and Education, Central School of Speech and Drama, University of London; IPA. *Career:* Resident Tutor, Arvon Foundation and Taliesen Trust; Senior Lecturer, Central School of Speech and Drama; Co-originator and Administrator of Poems on the Underground, 1986–; Arts Council Poet-in-Residence, Dove Cottage, Wordsworth Trust, 1994–; British Council Poet-in-Residence, Cairo and Alexandria, 1997; British Council Writer-in-Residence, Stavanger and Kristiansand, 1998; Poetry in Practice, Poet-in-Residence, Ashwell Medical Centre, Bradford, 2000–01; mem. Barrow Poets; Quaker Arts Network; Poems on the Underground; Poetry Society, education advisory panel; National Asscn of Writers in Education, chair., 1992; Society of Authors. *Publications:* Name Game, 1971; Gorgon, 1983; This Poem Doesn't Rhyme (ed.), 1990; Tower Block Poet: Sequence of 15 poems commissioned by BBC Radio, 1990; Co-ed. of the ten Poems on the Underground anthologies, 1991–2001; The Magnificent Callisto, 1993; Does W Trouble You? (ed.), 1994; Evidence of Elephants, 1995; In Wordsworth's Chair, 1995; Love Poems on the Underground, 1996; Bradford and Beyond, 1997; Hlep! (15 poems with woodcuts by Ros Cuthbert), 2001; The Poetry Business, 2002; To Catch an Elephant (poems for children), 2002. Contributions: newspapers, journals, reviews, and the Internet. *Honours:* Signal Award for Poetry, 1991. *Address:* 46 Ashwell Road, Manningham, Bradford, West Yorkshire BD8 9DU, England.

BENTLEY, Eric, BA, BLitt, PhD; American dramatist; b. 14 Sept. 1916, Bolton, Lancashire, England; m. 1st Maja Tschernjakow (divorced); m. 2nd Joanne Davis 1953; two s. *Education:* Univ. of Oxford, Yale Univ. *Career:* Drama Critic, New Republic, 1952–56; Charles Eliot Norton Prof. of Poetry, Harvard University, 1960–61; Katharine Cornell Prof. of Theatre, SUNY at Buffalo, 1975–82; Fulbright Prof., Belgrade, 1980; Prof. of Comparative Literature, University of Maryland, College Park, 1982–89; mem. American Acad. of Arts and Sciences, 1969–; American Acad. of Arts and Letters, 1990–. *Publications:* Larry Park's Day in Court, 1979; Lord Alfred's Lover, 1979; The Kleist Variations, 1982; Monstrous Martyrdoms, 1985; The Pirandello Commentaries, 1985; The Brecht Memoir, 1986; German Requiem, 1990; Round 2, 1991; Bentley on Brecht, 1999. *Honours:* Festschrift: The Critic and the Play, 1986; Florida Theatre Festival named in his honour, 1992; Hon. Doctorate, New School for Social Research, 1992; Robert Lewis Award for Life Achievement in the Theatre, 1992; Inducted into Theater Hall of Fame, New York, 1998. *Address:* 194 Riverside Dr., New York, NY 10025, USA.

BERENBAUM, Michael; Prof. of Theology, Museum and Foundation Exec. and Writer; b. 31 July 1945, Newark, NJ, USA; m. Melissa Patack, 25 June 1995, one s. one d. *Education:* AB, Philosophy, Queens College, CUNY, 1967; Jewish Theological Seminary, 1963–67; Hebrew University, 1965–66; Boston University, 1967–69; PhD, Florida State University, 1975. *Career:* Hymen Goldman Prof. of Theology, Georgetown University, 1983–97; Senior Scholar, Religious Action Center, 1986–89; Adjunct Prof. of Judaic Studies, American University, 1987; Project Dir, United States Holocaust Memorial Museum, 1988–93; Dir, United States Holocaust Research Institute, 1993–97; Pres. and CEO, Survivors of Shoah Visual History Foundation, 1997–; Prof. of Theology, University of Judaism, 1998–. *Publications:* The World Must Know: A History of the Holocaust, 1993; Anatomy of the Auschwitz Death Camp (ed. with Israel Gutman), 1994; What Kind of God? (ed. with Betty Rogers Rubenstein), 1995; Witness to the Holocaust: An Illustrated Documentary History of the Holocaust in the Words of Its Victims, Perpetrators and Bystanders, 1997; The Holocaust and History: The Known, the Unknown, the Disputed and the Reexamined, 1998. *Honours:* Silver Angel Award, 1981; Simon Rockower Memorial Award, 1986, 1987. *Address:* 2101 Hillsboro Ave, Los Angeles, CA 90035, USA.

BERENDT, John (Lawrence); Journalist and Writer; b. 5 Dec. 1939, Syracuse, NY, USA. *Education:* BA, Harvard University, 1961. *Career:* Assoc. Ed., 1961–69, Columnist, 1982–94, Esquire; Ed., New York magazine, 1977–82; mem. PEN. *Publications:* Midnight in the Garden of Good and Evil, 1994. Contributions: periodicals. *Address:* c/o Random House, 299 Park Ave, New York, NY 10171, USA.

BERESFORD, Anne (see Hamburger, Anne (Ellen)).

BERESFORD, Elisabeth, MBE; writer; b. Paris, France; one s. one d. *Career:* Founder, Alderney Youth Trust. *Publications:* children's fiction: The Television Mystery 1957, Trouble at Tullington Castle 1958, Gappy Goes West 1959, Two Gold Dolphins 1961, Game, Set and Match 1965, The Hidden Mill 1965, The Black Mountain Mystery 1967, Sea-Green Magic 1968, Stephen and the Shaggy Dog 1970, The Wandering Wombles 1970, Dangerous Magic 1972, The Secret Railway 1973, The Wombles at Work 1973, The Wombles Annual 1975–78, Snuffle to the Rescue 1975, Orinoco Runs Away 1975, Bungo Knows Best 1976, Tobermory's Big Surprise 1976, Wombling Free 1978, The Happy Ghost 1979, Curious Magic 1980, The Four of Us 1982, The Animals Nobody Wanted 1982, The Tovers 1982, The Adventures of Poon 1984, One of the Family 1985, The Ghosts of Lupus Street School 1986, The Secret Room 1987, Emily and the Haunted Castle 1987, The Oscar Puffin Book 1987, Once Upon a Time Stories 1988, The Island Railway Armada Adventure 1989, Rose 1992, Charlie's Ark 1992, The Wooden Gun 1992, Tim the Trumpet 1992, Jamie and the Rola Polar Bear 1993, Lizzy's War 1993, Rola Polar Bear and the Heatwave 1995, Lizzy's War, Part II 1996, The Smallest Whale 1996, Chris the Climber 1997, Island Treasure 1998, Shansi's Surprise 1998, Ghost of Wimbledon Common 1998, Orinoco the Magnificent 1998, Tomsk to the Rescue 1998, Beautiful Boating Weather 1998, Camping and Cloudberries 1998, Six Womble Picture Books 1998, Seven Womble Picture Books 1999, Pirate Gold 2000, Tommy in Trouble 2000, Tessa on TV 2000, The Sleep Wombler 2001; adult fiction: Paradise Island 1963, Escape to Happiness 1964, Roses Round the Door 1965, Island of Shadows 1966, Veronica 1967, A Tropical Affair 1968, Saturday's Child 1969, Love Remembered 1970, Love and the SS Beatrice 1972, Pandora 1974, The Steadfast Lover 1980, The Silver Chain 1980. *Literary Agent:* Juvenilia, Avington, Winchester, Hampshire SO21 1DB, England; The Agency, 24 Pottery Lane, Holland Park, London, W11 4LZ, England. *Address:* Little Street, Alderney GY9 3TT, Channel Islands (Home).

BERESFORD-HOWE, Constance; Prof. of English and Novelist; b. 10 Nov. 1922, Montréal, QC, Canada; m. 31 Dec. 1960, one s. *Education:* BA, 1945, MA, 1946, McGill University; PhD, Brown University, 1950. *Career:* mem. International PEN; International PEN, Writers in Prison Committee. *Publications:* The Book of Eve, 1973; A Population of One, 1976; The Marriage Bed, 1980; Night Studies, 1984; Prospero's Daughter, 1989; A Serious Widow, 1990. *Honours:* Dodd Mead Intercollegiate Literary Fellowship, 1948; Canadian Booksellers Award, 1974. *Address:* c/o McClelland and Stewart, 481 University Ave, Toronto, Ontario M4V 1E2, Canada.

BERG, Elizabeth; Writer; b. 2 Dec. 1948, USA; m. Howard Berg 30 March 1974 (divorced); two d. *Education:* University of Minnesota; St Mary's College. *Publications:* Family Traditions: Celebrations for Holidays and Everyday, 1992; Durable Goods, 1993; Talk Before Sleep, 1994; Range of Motion, 1995; The Pull of the Moon, 1996; Joy School, 1997; What We Keep, 1998; Until the Real Thing Comes Along, 1999; Escaping Into the Open: The Art of Writing True, 1999; Open House, 2000; Never Change, 2001; Ordinary Life, 2002. Contributions: periodicals. *Honours:* New England Book Award for Fiction, 1997. *Address:* c/o International Creative Management, 40 W 57th St, New York, NY 10019, USA.

BERG, Stephen Walter, BA; American poet and writer; *Joint Editor, American Poetry Review*; b. 2 Aug. 1934, Philadelphia, PA; m. Millie Lane 1959; two d. *Education:* Univ. of Pennsylvania, Boston Univ., Univ. of Iowa, Indiana Univ. *Career:* teacher, Temple Univ., Philadelphia, Princeton Univ., Haverford Coll., Pennsylvania; Prof., Philadelphia Coll. of Art; Poetry Ed., Saturday Evening Post 1961–62; Founding Ed. (with Stephen Parker and Rhoda Schwartz), American Poetry Review 1972–. *Publications:* poetry: Berg Goodman Mezey 1957, Bearing Weapons 1963, The Queen's Triangle: A Romance 1970, The Daughters 1971, Nothing in the Word: Versions of Aztec Poetry 1972, Grief: Poems and Versions of Poems 1975, With Akmatova at the Black Gates: Variations 1981, In It 1986, First Song, Bankei, 1653 1989, Homage to the Afterlife 1991, New and Selected Poems 1992, Oblivion: Poems 1995; editor: Naked Poetry: Recent American Poetry in Open Forms (with Robert Mezey) 1969, Between People (with S. J. Marks) 1972, About Women (with S. J. Marks) 1973, The New Naked Poetry (with Robert Mezey) 1976, In Praise of What Persists 1983, Singular Voices: American Poetry Today 1985, The Body Electric: America's Best Poetry from The American Poetry Review (co-ed.) 2001; other: Sea Ice: Versions of Eskimo Songs 1988; contrib. to periodicals. *Honours:* Rockefeller-Centro Mexicano de Escritores Grant, 1959–61; National Trans. Center Grant, 1969; Frank O'Hara Prize, Poetry magazine, 1970; Guggenheim Fellowship, 1974; National Endowment for the Arts Grant, 1976; Columbia University Trans. Center Award, 1976. *Address:* 2005 Mount Vernon Street, Philadelphia, PA 19130, USA. *Address:* The American Poetry Review, 117 S 17th Street, Suite 910, Philadelphia, PA 19103, USA (Office). *Telephone:* (215) 496-0439. *Fax:* (215) 569-0808. *E-mail:* sberg@aprweb.org. *Website:* www.aprweb.org.

BERG, Y. L. (see Elberg, Yehuda).

BERGÉ, Carol; Writer, Poet, Ed., Publisher and Antiques Dealer; b. 4 Oct. 1928, New York, NY, USA; m. Jack Henry Berge, June 1955, one s. *Education:* New York University; New School for Social Research, New York City. *Career:* Ed., 1970–84, Publisher, 1991–93, CENTER Magazine and Press; Distinguished Prof. of Literature, Thomas Jefferson College, Allendale, Michigan, 1975–76; Instructor, Goddard College, 1976; Teacher, University of California Extension Program, Berkeley, 1976–77; Assoc. Prof., University of Southern Mississippi, 1977–78; Ed., Mississippi Review, 1977–78; Visiting Prof., University of New Mexico, 1978–79, 1987; Visiting Lecturer, Wright State University, Dayton, Ohio, 1979, SUNY at Albany 1980–81; Proprietor, Blue Gate Gallery of Art and Antiques, 1988–; mem. Authors League; MacDowell Fellows Asscn; National Press Women; Poets & Writers. *Publications:* Fiction: The Unfolding, 1969; A Couple Called Moebius, 1972; Acts of Love: An American Novel, 1973; Timepieces, 1977; The Doppler Effect, 1979; Fierce Metronome, 1981; Secrets, Gossip and Slander, 1984; Zebras, or, Contour Lines, 1991. Poetry: The Vulnerable Island, 1964; Lumina, 1965; Poems Made of Skin, 1968; The Chambers, 1969; Circles, as in the Eye, 1969; An American Romance, 1969; From a Soft Angle: Poems About Women, 1972; The Unexpected, 1976; Rituals and Gargoyles, 1976; A Song, A Chant, 1978; Alba Genesis, 1979; Alba Nemesis, 1979. Editor: Light Years: The New York City Coffeehouse Poets of the 1960s, 2004. Reportage: The Vancouver Report, 1965. Contributions: anthologies and periodicals. *Honours:* New York State Council on the Arts CAPS Award, 1974; National Endowment for the Arts Fellowship, 1979–80. *Address:* 2070 Calle Contento, Santa Fe, NM 87505, USA. *Telephone:* (505) 438-3979. *E-mail:* carolberge@earthlink.net.

BERGEL, Hans; Author; b. 26 July 1925, Kronstadt, Romania. *Education:* History of Arts, University of Cluj-Napoca. *Career:* mem. Die Künstlergilde, Esslingen; PEN International; Institut für deutsche Kultur und Geschichte Südosteuropas, Munich. *Publications:* Rumanien, Portrait einer Nation, 1969; Ten Southern European Short Stories, 1972; Die Sachsen in Siebenburgen nach dreissig Jahren Kommunismus, 1976; Der Tanz in Ketten, 1977; Siebenburgen, 1980; Gestalten und Gewalten, 1982; Hermann Oberth oder Der mythische Traum vom Fliegen, 1984; Der Tod des Hirten, 1985; Literaturgeschichte der Deutschen in Siebenburgen, 1987; Das Venusherz (short novel), 1987; Weihnacht ist uberall (eleven short stories), 1988. Contributions: periodicals. *Honours:* Short Story Prize, Bucharest, 1957, Bonn, 1972; Georg Dehio Prize, Esslingen, 1972; Goethe Foundation Prize, Basel, 1972; Medien Prizes, Bavarian Broadcasting Company, 1983, 1989; Bundesverdienstkreuz, 1987; Saxon of Transylvania Culture Prize, 1988; Geyphius-Prize, 1990. *Address:* Rabensteinstrasse 28, 8000 Munich 60, Germany.

BERGER, François; Barrister, Poet and Writer; b. 16 May 1950, Neuchâtel, Switzerland. *Education:* Licence Degree in Law, Neuchâtel University, 1977; Barrister, Neuchâtel. *Career:* mem. Asscn des écrivains de langue française; Asscn des écrivains neuchâtelois et jurassiens; Canton of Neuchâtel, literature committee pres.; Société suisse des écrivains. *Publications:* Poetry: Mémoire d'anges, 1981; Gestes du veilleur, 1984; Le Pré, 1986, Italian trans., 1996; Les Indiennes, 1988; Le Repos d'Ariane, 1990. Fiction: Le jour avant, 1995; Le voyage de l'Ange, 1999. Contributions: L'Express Feuille d'Avis de Neuchâtel. *Honours:* Louise Labé Prize, Paris, 1982; Citation of Distinction, Schiller Foundation, Zürich, 1985; Auguste Bachelin Prize, Neuchâtel, 1988. *Address:* 28, Rebatte, CH-2068 Hauterive (Neuchâtel), Switzerland.

BERGER, John (Peter); Author, Dramatist, Poet and Art Critic; b. 5 Nov. 1926, London, England; m. twice, three c. *Education:* Central School of Art, London; Chelsea School of Art, London. *Career:* Painting exhibitions, Wildenstein, Refern and Leicester Galleries, London; Art Critic, Tribune, New Statesman; many television appearances; Visiting Fellow, BFI, 1990–. *Publications:* A Painter in Our Time, 1958; Marcel Frishman, 1958; Permanent Red, 1960; The Foot of Clive, 1962; Corker's Freedom, 1964; The Success and Failure of Picasso, 1965; A Fortunate Man: The Story of a Country Doctor (with J. Mohr), 1967; G, 1972; The Seventh Man, 1975; About Looking, 1980; Another Way of Telling (with J. Mohr), 1982; Question of Geography (with Nella Bielski), 1984; The White Bird, 1985; Francisco Goya's Last Portrait (with Nella Bielski), 1989; Once in Europa, 1989; Lilac and Flag, 1991; Keeping a Rendezvous, 1992; To the Wedding, 1995; Photocopies, 1996; Pages of the Wound: Poems, Drawings, Photographs, 1956–96, 1996; King: A Street Story, 1999. *Honours:* Booker Prize, 1972; James Tait Black Memorial Prize, 1972; Guardian Fiction Prize, 1973; New York Critics' Prize, 1976; George Orwell Memorial Prize, 1977; Barcelona Film Festival Europa Award, 1989. *Address:* Quincy, Mieussy, 74440 Taninges, France.

BERGER, Thomas Louis, BA; American writer; b. 20 July 1924, Cincinnati, OH; m. Jeanne Redpath 1950. *Education:* Univ. of Cincinnati and Columbia Univ. Grad. School. *Career:* mil. service 1943–46; Assoc. Ed., Popular Science Monthly 1952–53; Distinguished Visiting Prof. Southampton Univ. 1975–76; Visiting Lecturer, Yale Univ. 1981, 1982; Regents Lecturer, Univ. of Calif. at Davis 1982; Dial Fellow 1962. *Play:* Other People 1970. *Publications:* Crazy in Berlin 1958, Reinhart in Love 1962, Little Big Man 1964, Killing Time 1967, Vital Parts 1970, Regiment of Women 1973, Sneaky People 1975, Who is Teddy Villanova? 1977, Arthur Rex 1978, Neighbors 1980, Reinhart's Women 1981, The Feud 1983, Nowhere 1985, Being Invisible 1987, The Houseguest 1988, Changing the Past 1989, Orrie's Story 1990, Meeting Evil 1992, Robert Crews 1994, Suspects 1996, The Return of Little Big Man 1999, Best Friends 2003, Adventures of the Artificial Woman 2004. *Honours:* Hon. LittD (Long Island) 1986; Rosenthal Award, Nat. Inst. of Arts and Letters 1965, Western Heritage Award 1965, Ohiona Book Award 1982. *Literary Agent:* Don Congdon Associates, 156 Fifth Avenue, Suite 625, New York, NY 10010-7002. *Telephone:* (212) 645-1229. *Fax:* (212) 727-2688. *E-mail:* doncongdon@aol.com. *Address:* PO Box 11, Palisades, NY 10964, USA.

BERGMAN, Ingmar; playwright, screenwriter, film director and theatre producer; b. 14 July 1918, Uppsala, Sweden; m. Ingrid Karlebovon Rosen 1971 (died 1995); eight c. (from previous marriages). *Education:* Stockholm Univ. *Career:* Prod., Royal Theatre, Stockholm, 1940–42; scriptwriter and prod., Svensk Filmindustri, 1940–44; theatre man., Hälsingborg City Theatre, 1944–46; Dir, Gothenburg City Theatre, 1946–49, Malmö City Theatre, 1953–60, Dramaten, Stockholm, 1960–66, Mme de Sade Theatre, 1989; Chair., European Cinema Society, 1989–; Dir, numerous theatre productions and films; mem. Swedish Acad. of Letters. *Publications:* Plays: Kaspers död, 1942; Jack Hos Skådespelarna, 1946; Mig Till Skräck.., 1947; Kamma Noll, 1948; Moraliteter, 1948; Staden, 1950–51; Mordet i Barjärna, 1952; Trämålning, 1954; En Passion, 1972; Ur Marioneternas Liv, 1980. Screenplays: Hets (Frenzy), 1944; Eva (with others), 1948; Frånskild (Divorced, with others), 1951; Sista Paret Ut (The Last Couple Out, with others), 1956; Det Sjunde Inseglet (The Seventh Seal), 1957; Smultronstället (Wild Strawberries), 1957; Nära Livet (So Close to Life, with Ulla Isaksson), 1958; The Magician, 1960; Lustgarden (Pleasure Garden, with others), 1961; Fanny och Alexander (Fanny and Alexander), 1983; Bilder (Images: My Life in Film), 1990; Trolösan (Faithless), 2000. Other: Bergman on Bergman (essays), 1970; Four Stories, 1977; Laterna Magica (The Magic Lantern, autobiog.), 1987; Den Goda Viljan (novel and screenplay, The Best Intentions), 1992; Söndagsbarn (Sunday's Child), 1994; Bergman's List, 1995; Enskilda Samtal (Private Conversations), 1996; Persona and Shame (trans.), 2001. *Honours:* Erasmus Prize, 1965; Award for Best Dir, National Society of Film Critics, 1970; Order of the Yugoslav Flag, 1971; Luigi Pirandello International Theatre Prize, 1971; Goethe Award (Frankfurt), 1976; Gold Medal of Swedish Acad., 1977; Acad. Award, Best Foreign Film, 1983; Commander, Légion d'honneur, 1985; European

Film Award, 1988; Dr hc, Univ. of Rome, 1988; Prix Sonning, 1989; Praemium Imperiale Prize (Japan), 1991; Dorothy and Lilian Gish Prize, 1995. *Address:* c/o Marion Boyars Publishers, 24 Lacy Road, London SW15 1NL, England.

BERGON, Frank; novelist and academic; b. 24 Feb. 1943, Ely, Nevada, USA; m. Holly St John Bergon 1979. *Education:* BA, English, summa cum laude, Boston College, 1965; Postgraduate Studies, Stanford University, 1965–66; PhD, English, Harvard University, 1973. *Career:* Teaching Fellow, Harvard University, 1968–70; Lecturer, Newton College, 1971–72; Prof. of English, 1972–, Dir, American Culture Program, 1982–85, Vassar College; Visiting Assoc. Prof., University of Washington, 1980–81; mem. MLA; Western Literature Asscn; Asscn of the Study of Literature and the Environment. *Publications:* Stephen Crane's Artistry, 1975; Looking Far West: The Search for the American West in History, Myth and Literature (co-ed.), 1978; The Western Writings of Stephen Crane (ed.), 1979; The Wilderness Reader (ed.), 1980; Shoshone Mike (novel), 1987; A Sharp Lookout: Selected Nature Essays of John Burroughs (ed.), 1987; The Journals of Lewis & Clark (ed.), 1989; The Temptations of St Ed & Brother S (novel), 1993; Wild Game (novel), 1995. Contributions: American Literary History; Terra Nova; Journal of Nature and Culture. *Honours:* Wallace Stegner Fellowship, 1965–66; Nevada Writers Hall of Fame, 1998. *Address:* 136 Chapel Hill Road, Highland, NY 12528, USA. *E-mail:* bergon@vassar.edu.

BERGONZI, Bernard; writer, poet and academic; b. 13 April 1929, London, England. *Education:* BLitt, 1961, MA, 1962, Wadham College, Oxford. *Career:* Senior Lecturer, 1966–71, Prof. of English, 1971–92, Prof. Emeritus, 1992–, University of Warwick, Coventry. *Publications:* The Early H. G. Wells, 1961; Heroes' Twilight, 1965; Innovations: Essays on Art and Ideas, 1968; T. S. Eliot: Four Quartets: A Casebook, 1969; The Situation of the Novel, 1970; T. S. Eliot, 1972; The Turn of a Century, 1973; H. G. Wells: A Collection of Critical Essays, 1975; Gerard Manley Hopkins, 1977; Reading the Thirties, 1978; Years: Sixteen Poems, 1979; Poetry 1870–1914, 1980; The Roman Persuasion (novel), 1981; The Myth of Modernism and Twentieth Century Literature, 1986; Exploding English, 1990; Wartime and Aftermath, 1993; David Lodge, 1995; War Poets and Other Subjects, 1999; A Victorian Wanderer, 2003. *Address:* 19 St Mary's Crescent, Leamington Spa CV31 1JL, England.

BERGSON, Leo (see Stebel, Sidney Leo).

BERKELEY, Humphry John; Writer, Author and Former MP; b. 1 Feb. 1926, Marlow, England. *Education:* BA, 1947, MA, 1963, Pembroke College, Cambridge. *Career:* MP, Conservative Party, Lancaster, 1959–66, joined Labour Party, 1970; Chair., United Nations Asscn of Great Britain and Northern Ireland, 1966–70; mem. Savile Club. *Publications:* The Power of the Prime Minister, 1968; Crossing the Floor, 1972; The Life and Death of Rochester Sneath, 1974; The Odyssey of Enoch: A Political Memoir, 1977; The Myth That Will Not Die: The Formation of the National Government, 1978; Faces of the Eighties (with Jeffrey Archer), 1987. Contributions: Times; Sunday Times; Daily Telegraph; Financial Times; Spectator; New Statesman. *Literary Agent:* Mark Hamilton, A. M. Heath & Co Ltd, 79 St Martin's Lane, London WC2N 4RE, England. *Address:* 3 Pages Yard, Church St, Chiswick, London W4 2PA, England.

BERKOFF, Steven; Actor, Dir and Writer; b. 3 Aug. 1937, London, England; m. 1st Alison Minto, 1970, divorced; m. 2nd Shelley Lee, 1976, divorced. *Education:* Webber-Douglas Acad. of Dramatic Art, London, 1958–59; École Jacques Lecoq, Paris, 1965. *Career:* Actor in many plays, films and television; Dir of plays. *Publications:* Gross Intrusion and Other Stories, 1979; Steven Berkoff's America, 1988; I am Hamlet, 1989; A Prisoner in Rio, 1989; The Theatre of Steven Berkoff, 1992; Coriolanus in Deutschland, 1992; Overview, 1994; Free Asscn (autobiog.), 1996; Graft: Tales of an Author, 1998. *Address:* c/o Joanna Marston, 1 Clareville Grove Mews, London SW7 5AH, England.

BERKSON, Bill, (William Craig Berkson); poet, critic, editor and academic; b. 30 Aug. 1939, New York, NY, USA; m. 1st Lynn O'Hare 1975 (divorced); one s. one d.; m. 2nd Constance Lewallen 1998. *Education:* Brown Univ., 1957–59; Columbia Univ., 1959–60; New School for Social Research, New York, 1959–61; New York Univ. Institute of Fine Arts, 1960–61. *Career:* Instructor, New School for Social Research, 1964–69; Visiting Fellow, Yale Univ., 1969–70; Ed. and Publisher, Big Sky magazine and books, 1971–78; Adjunct Prof., Southampton Coll., Long Island Univ., 1980; Marin Community Coll., 1983–84; Assoc. Prof., California Coll. of Arts and Crafts, 1983–84; Prof. and Co-ordinator of Public Lectures Programme, 1984–, Dir, Letters and Science, 1994–99, San Francisco Art Institute; Visiting Artist/Scholar, American Acad. in Rome, 1991. *Publications:* Saturday Night: Poems, 1960–1961, 1961; Shining Leaves, 1969; Two Serious Poems and One Other (with Larry Fagin), 1972; Recent Visitors, 1973; Hymns of St Bridget (with Frank O'Hara), 1975; Enigma Variations, 1975; Ants, 1975; 100 Women, 1975; The World of Leon (with Ron Padgett, Larry Fagin and Michael Brownstein), 1976; Blue is the Hero: Poems, 1960–1975, 1976; Red Devil, 1983; Lush Life, 1983; Start Over, 1984; Serenade, 2000; Fugue State, 2001; Hymns of St Bridget and Other Writings (with Frank O'Hara), 2002; 25 Grand View, 2002; The Sweet Singer of Modernism and Other Art Writings, 2003. Other: ed. or co-ed. of several books. Contributions: anthologies, periodicals, quarterlies and journals. *Honours:* Dylan Thomas Memorial Award, 1959; Poets Foundation Grant, 1968; Yaddo Fellowship, 1968; National Endowment for the Arts Fellowship, 1980; Briarcombe Fellowship, 1983; Artspace Award, 1990; Fund for Poetry Awards, 1995, 2001. *Address:* 25 Grand View Avenue, San Francisco, CA 94114, USA. *E-mail:* berkson@pacbell.net.

BERMAN, David; academic and writer; b. 20 Nov. 1942, New York, NY, USA; m. Aileen Jill Mitchell 1970 (divorced 2001); two s. two d. *Education:* BA, New School for Social Research, New York, 1965; MA, Univ. of Denver, 1966; PhD, Trinity College, Dublin, 1972; Diploma in Psychoanalytic Psychotherapy, St Vincent's Hospital, Dublin, 1992. *Career:* Senior Lecturer in Philosophy, 1981–94, Fellow, 1984, Assoc. Prof. of Philosophy, 1994–, Head of Philosophy Dept, 1997–2002, Trinity College, Dublin. *Publications:* A History of Atheism in Britain: From Hobbes to Russell, 1988; George Berkeley: Eighteenth Century Responses (ed.), two vols, 1989; George Berkeley's Alciphron or the Minute Philosopher in Focus (ed.), 1993; George Berkeley: Idealism and the Man, 1994; Arthur Schopenauer's World as Will and Idea (ed.), 1995; Berkeley: Experimental Philosophy, 1997. Contributions: reference works, books, scholarly journals. *Address:* c/o Department of Philosophy, Trinity College, University of Dublin, Dublin 2, Ireland.

BERNARD, David Kane; Pastor, Author and Ed.; b. 20 Nov. 1956, Baton Rouge, USA; m. Connie Sharpe Bernard, 6 June 1981, two s. one d. *Education:* BA, Rice University; Greek, Wesley Biblical Seminary; JD, University of Texas. *Career:* Instructor, Administrator, Jackson College of Ministries, 1981–86; Assoc. Ed., United Pentecostal Church International, 1986–; Pastor, New Life United Pentecostal Church, Austin, Texas, 1992–; mem. Society for Pentecostal Studies. *Publications:* In Search of Holiness, 1981; The Oneness of God, 1983; The New Birth, 1984; Practical Holiness, 1985; A History of Christian Doctrine, 3 vols, 1995–99; Spiritual Gifts, 1997. Contributions: Pentecostal Herald; Forward. *Honours:* Word Aflame Press Writer of the Year, 1987.

BERNARD, Oliver Owen; poet and translator; b. 6 Dec. 1925, Chalfont St Peter, Buckinghamshire, England; two s. two d. *Education:* BA, Goldsmiths College, 1953; ACSD, Central School of Speech and Drama, 1971. *Career:* Teacher of English, Suffolk and Norfolk, 1964–74; Advisory Teacher of Drama, Norfolk Education Committee, 1974–81; mem. British Actors' Equity Asscn; Speak-a-Poem, committee mem.; William Morris Society. *Publications:* Country Matters, 1960; Rimbaud: Collected Poems (translating ed.), 1961; Apollinaire: Selected Poems (trans.), 1965; Moons and Tides, 1978; Poems, 1983; Five Peace Poems, 1985; The Finger Points at the Moon (trans.), 1989; Salvador Espriu: Forms and Words, 1990; Getting Over It (autobiog.), 1992; Quia Amore Langueo (trans.), 1995; Verse Etc, 2001. Contributions: various publications. *Honours:* Gold Medal for Verse Speaking, Poetry Society, 1982. *Address:* 1 East Church Street, Kenninghall, Norwich NR16 2EP, England.

BERNARD, Robert (see Martin, Robert Bernard).

BERNAYS, Anne Fleischman; Writer and Teacher; b. 14 Sept. 1930, New York, NY, USA; m. Justin Kaplan, 29 July 1954, three d. *Education:* BA, Barnard College, 1952. *Career:* mem. PEN New England. *Publications:* Growing Up Rich (novel); Professor Romeo (novel); What If? (non-fiction, with Pamela Painter); Back Then (non-fiction, with Justin Kaplan); The Language of Names (with Justin Kaplan). Contributions: New York Times Book Review; Nation; Sports Illustrated; Travel and Leisure; Sophisticated Traveller. *Honours:* Edward Lewis Wallant Award; Bellagio Study and Conference Centre Residency. *Literary Agent:* Sterling Lord Literistic Inc, 65 Bleecker St, New York, NY 10012, USA.

BERNE, Stanley, BS, MA; research professor and writer; b. 8 June 1923, Port Richmond, Staten Island, NY, USA; m. Arlene Zekowski 1952. *Education:* Rutgers Univ., New York Univ., Louisiana State Univ., Baton Rouge. *Career:* Assoc. Prof. of English, Eastern New Mexico Univ. at Portales 1960–80, Research Prof. of English 1980–; Chair. American-Canadian Publrs Inc. 1980–97; mem. PEN, New England Small Press Asscn, Rio Grande Writers' Asscn, Santa Fe Writers. *Television:* host, co-producer Future Writing Today (series on KENW-TV, PBS) 1984–85. *Publications:* A First Book of the Neo-Narrative 1954, Cardinals and Saints: On the aims and purposes of the arts in our time 1958, The Dialogues 1962, The Multiple Modern Gods and Other Stories 1969, The New Rubaiyat of Stanley Berne (poems) 1973, Future Language 1976, The Great American Empire 1981, Every Person's Little Book of P-L-U-T-O-N-I-U-M (with Arlene Zekowski) 1992, Alphabet Soup: A Dictionary of Ideas 1993, To Hell with Optimism 1996, Dictionary of the Avant-Gardes 1998, Gravity Drag 1998, The Living Underground 1999, Swimming to Significance 1999, Extremely Urgent Messages 2000, Empire Sweets, or How I Learned to Live and Love in the Greatest Empire on Earth 2003, Legal Tender, or It's All About Money! 2003, You and Me, or How to Survive in the Greatest Empire on Earth! 2003; contrib. to anthologies and other publications. *Honours:* Literary research awards, Eastern New Mexico Univ. 1966–76. *Literary Agent:* Pamela Tree, Rising Tide Press, PO Box 6136, Santa Fe, NM, USA. *Address:* Box 4595, Santa Fe, NM 87502, USA.

BERNSTEIN, Carl; Journalist and Writer; b. 14 Feb. 1944, Washington, DC, USA; m. Nora Ephron, 14 April 1976, divorced, two s. *Education:* University of Maryland, 1961–64. *Career:* Copyboy to Reporter, Washington Star, 1960–65; Reporter, Elizabeth Journal, NJ, 1965–66, Washington Post,

1966–76; Washington Bureau Chief, 1979–81, Correspondent, 1981–84, ABC-TV; Correspondent, Contributor, Time magazine, 1990–91; Visiting Prof., New York University, 1992–; Contributing Ed., Vanity Fair, 1997–. *Publications:* All the President's Men (with Bob Woodward), 1973; The Final Days (with Bob Woodward), 1976; Loyalties: A Son's Memoir, 1989; His Holiness (with Marco Politi), 1996. *Honours:* Drew Pearson Prize for Investigative Reporting, 1972; Pulitzer Prize Citation, 1972; Hon. LLD, Boston University, 1975. *Literary Agent:* Janklow & Nesbit Associates, 445 Park Ave, New York, NY 10022, USA.

BERNSTEIN, Charles, AB; professor of poetry and poetics, poet, writer and editor; b. 4 April 1950, New York, NY, USA; m. Susan Bee Laufer 1977; one s. one d. *Education:* Harvard College. *Career:* Freelance writer in the medical field, 1976–89; Visiting Lecturer in Literature, Univ. of California at San Diego, 1987; Lecturer in Creative Writing, Princeton Univ., 1989, 1990; David Gray Prof. of Poetry and Letters, State Univ. of New York at Buffalo, 1990–2003; Prof. of English, Univ. of Pennsylvania, 2003–. *Publications:* Poetry: Asylums, 1975; Parsing, 1976; Shade, 1978; Poetic Justice, 1979; Senses of Responsibility, 1979; Legend (with others), 1980; Controlling Interests, 1980; Disfrutes, 1981; The Occurrence of Tune, 1981; Stigma, 1981; Islets/Irritations, 1983; Resistance, 1983; Veil, 1987; The Sophist, 1987; Four Poems, 1988; The Nude Formalism, 1989; The Absent Father in Dumbo, 1990; Fool's Gold (with Susan Bee), 1991; Rough Trades, 1991; Dark City, 1994; The Subject, 1995; Republics of Reality: Poems 1975–1995, 2000; With Strings, 2001. Essays: Content's Dream: Essays 1975–1984, 1986; A Poetics, 1992; My Way: Speeches and Poems, 1999. Editor: L=A=N=G=U=A=G=E Book (with Bruce Andrews), four vols, 1978–84; The Politics of Poetic Form: Poetry and Public Policy, 1990; Close Listening: Poetry and the Performed Word, 1998. Contributions: numerous anthologies, collections, and periodicals. *Honours:* William Lyon Mackenzie King Fellow, Simon Fraser University, 1973; National Endowment for the Arts Fellowship, 1980; Guggenheim Fellowship, 1985; University of Auckland Foundation Fellowship, 1986; New York Foundation for the Arts Fellowships, 1990, 1995; American Society of Composers, Authors and Publishers Standard Award, 1993; Roy Harvey Pearce/Archive for New Poetry Prize, 2000. *Address:* 119 Bennet Hall, University of Pennsylvania, Philadelphia, PA 19104-6273, USA.

BERNSTEIN, Marcelle; Writer and Journalist; b. 14 June 1945, Manchester, England; m. Eric Clark 12 April 1972; one s. two d. *Career:* Staff, The Guardian, Daily Mirror, Observer; mem. Society of Authors. *Publications:* Nuns, 1976; Sadie, 1983; Salka, 1986; Lili, 1988; Body and Soul (dramatised as a prizewinning six-part TV series), 1991; Sacred and Profane (filmed as La Pacte du Silence), 1995; Saints and Sinners, 1998. Contributions: numerous US and British magazines. *Honours:* Arts Council Award, 1986; Helene Heroys Award, 1988. *Literary Agent:* Carole Blake, Blake Friedmann Agency, 122 Arlington Road, London NW1 7HP, England.

BERNSTEIN, Robert Louis; American publisher; b. 5 Jan. 1923, New York, NY; m. Helen Walter 1950; three s. *Education:* Harvard Univ. *Career:* US Army Air Force 1943–46; with Simon & Schuster (book publrs) 1946–57, Gen. Sales Man. 1950–57; Random House Inc. 1958–61, Vice-Pres. (Sales) 1961–63, First Vice-Pres. 1963–65, Pres. and CEO 1966–89, Chair. 1975–89; Publr at Large, Adviser John Wiley & Sons Inc. 1991–98; Vice-Chair. Asscn of American Publrs 1970–72, Chair. 1972–73; Chair. Asscn of American Publrs Cttee on Soviet-American Publishing Relations 1973–74, on Int. Freedom to Publish 1975; Chair. US Helsinki Watch Cttee, New York, 1979–92, Founding Chair. 1992; Chair. Fund for Free Expression 1975–90, Founding Chair. 1990; Founding Chair. Human Rights Watch 1975–; Co-Chair. Human Rights in China 1999–; fmr mem. Council on Foreign Relations, Nat. Advisory Cttee Amnesty Int.; mem. Americas Watch, Asia Watch, Middle East Watch, Africa Watch, Advisory Cttee Carter-Menil Human Rights Foundation, Advisory Bd Robert F. Kennedy Foundation Human Rights Award, Int. Liberal Education Bd Bard Coll.; Vice-Pres. Bd of Dirs Aaron Diamond Foundation, The Century Asscn. *Honours:* Hon. LLD (New School for Social Research) 1991, (Hofstra) 1998; Human Rights Award (Lawyers' Cttee for Human Rights) 1987, Spirit of Liberty Award for the American Way 1989, Barnard Medal of Distinction, Barnard Coll. 1990, Liberty Award, Brandeis Univ. 1994, Eleanor Roosevelt Human Rights Award 1998 and other awards. *Address:* 277 Park Avenue, 49th Floor, New York, NY 10172-0003, USA (Office). *E-mail:* r.l.bernstein@att.net.

BERRIDGE, Elizabeth; Author and Critic; b. 3 Dec. 1919, London, England; m. Reginald Moore, 1940, one s. one d. *Career:* Critic, BBC, Spectator, Books and Bookmen, Tribune, Country Life, 1952–74; Fiction Reviewer, Daily Telegraph, 1967–88; Evening Standard; Judge, David Higham First Novel Award, 1989–97; mem. Chase Charity, Trustee; Fellow, PEN; FRSL, 1998. *Publications:* House of Defence, 1945; Story of Stanley Brent, 1945; Be Clean, Be Tidy, 1949; Upon Several Occasions, 1953; Across the Common, 1964; Rose Under Glass, 1967; Sing Me Who You Are, 1972; That Surprising Summer, 1973; The Barretts at Hope End (ed.), 1974; Run for Home, 1981; Family Matters, 1981; People at Play, 1982; Touch and Go, 1995; Tell It to a Stranger (short stories), 2000; Flying Solo (short stories), 2003. Contributions: periodicals. *Literary Agent:* David Higham Associates, 5–8 Lower John St, Golden Sq., London W1F 9HA, England.

BERRY, Adrian Michael, FRGS, FRAS; writer and journalist; b. 15 June 1937, London, England. *Education:* Christ Church, Oxford. *Career:* Correspondent, Time Magazine, New York, 1965–67; Science Correspondent, Daily Telegraph, London, 1977–96; Fellow, British Interplanetary Society 1986–. *Publications:* The Next Ten Thousand Years: A Vision of Man's Future in the Universe, 1974; The Iron Sun: Crossing the Universe Through Black Holes, 1977; From Apes to Astronauts, 1981; The Super Intelligent Machine, 1983; High Skies and Yellow Rain, 1983; Koyama's Diamond (fiction), 1984; Labyrinth of Lies (fiction), 1985; Ice With Your Evolution, 1986; Computer Software: The Kings and Queens of England, 1985; Harrap's Book of Scientific Anecdotes, 1989; The Next 500 Years, 1995; Galileo and the Dolphins, 1996; The Giant Leap, 1999. *Address:* 11 Cottesmore Gardens, Kensington, London W8, England.

BERRY, Francis; poet, writer and academic; b. 23 March 1915, Ipoh, Malaysia; m. 1st Nancy Melloney Graham 1947; one s. one d.; m. 2nd Eileen Marjorie Lear 1970. *Education:* University College of the South West, 1937–39, 1946–47; BA, University of London, 1947; MA, University of Exeter, 1949. *Career:* Prof. of English Literature, University of Sheffield, 1967–70; Prof. of English, Royal Holloway, University of London, 1970–80; mem. FRSL. *Publications:* Gospel of Fire, 1933; Snake in the Moon, 1936; The Iron Christ, 1938; Fall of a Tower, 1943; The Galloping Centaur, 1952; Murdock and Other Poems, 1955; Poets' Grammar, 1958; Morant Bay and Other Poems, 1961; Poetry and the Physical Voice, 1962; Ghosts of Greenland, 1966; The Shakespeare Inset, 1966; I Tell of Greenland, 1977; From the Red Fort, 1984; Collected Poems, 1994. Contributions: periodicals; BBC. *Address:* 4 Eastgate Street, Winchester, Hampshire SO23 8EB, England.

BERRY, Ila; Poet and Writer; b. 9 June 1922, USA. *Education:* AA, Fullerton College, CA; BA, John F. Kennedy University, Orinda, CA; MA, English and Creative Writing, San Francisco State University, 1985. *Career:* mem. California Federation of Chaparral Poets, Robert Frost Chapter; California State Poetry Society; California Writers Club; Ina Coolbrith Circle, pres., 1977–79; National League of American Pen Women. *Publications:* Poetry: Come Walk With Me, 1979; Rearranging the Landscape, 1986; Rowing in Eden, 1987; Behold the Bright Demons, 1993. Contributions: periodicals. *Honours:* Jessamyn West Creative Award, 1969; Woman of Distinction, Fullerton College, 1969. *Address:* 761 Sequoia Woods Pl., Concord, CA 94518, USA.

BERRY, James; Poet, Writer and Ed.; b. 1925, Fair Prospect, Jamaica. *Publications:* Bluefoot Traveller: An Anthology of West Indian Poets in Britain (ed.), 1976; Fractured Circles, 1979; News for Babylon: The Chatto Book of West Indian-British Poetry (ed.), 1984; Chain of Days, 1985; The Girls and Yanga Marshall (short stories), 1987; A Thief in the Village and Other Stories, 1988; Don't Leave an Elephant to Go and Chase a Bird, 1990; When I Dance (poems), 1991; Ajeema and His Son, 1992. *Honours:* C. Day-Lewis Fellowship; Poetry Society Prize, 1981; Boston Globe/Horn Book Award, 1993. *Address:* c/o Hamish Hamilton Ltd, 27 Wrights Lane, London W8 5TZ, England.

BERRY, Paul; Writer and Lecturer; b. 25 Dec. 1919, Weston-by-Welland, England. *Publications:* Daughters of Cain (with Renee Huggett), 1956; By Royal Appointment: A Biography of Mary Ann Clarke, Mistress of the Duke of York 1803–07, 1970; The Selected Journalism of Winifred Holtby and Vera Brittain (joint ed.), 1985; Vera Brittain: A Life (with Mark Bostridge), 1995; Winifred Holtby: Selected Short Stories (ed. with Marion Shaw), 1997. *Address:* 1 Bridgefoot Cottages, Stedham, Midhurst, Sussex, England.

BERRY, Wendell Erdman; writer, poet and academic; b. 5 Aug. 1934, Henry County, KY, USA; m. Tanya Amyx Berry 1957; one s. one d. *Education:* BA, 1956, MA, 1957, University of Kentucky. *Career:* Instructor, Georgetown College, 1957–58; E. H. Jones Lecturer in Creative Writing, 1959–60, Visiting Prof. of Creative Writing, 1968–69, Stanford University; Asst Prof., New York University, 1962–64; Faculty Mem., 1964–77, Prof., 1987–93, University of Kentucky; Elliston Poet, University of Cincinnati, 1974; Writer-in-Residence, Centre College, 1977, Bucknell University, 1987. *Publications:* Fiction: Nathan Coulter, 1960; A Place on North, 1967; The Memory of Old Jack, 1974; The Wild Birds, 1986; Remembering, 1988; The Discovery of Kentucky, 1991; Fidelity, 1992; A Consent, 1993; Watch With Me, 1994; A World Lost, 1996. Poetry: The Broken Ground, 1964; Openings, 1968; Findings, 1969; Farming: A Handbook, 1970; The Country of Marriage, 1973; Sayings and Doings, 1975; Clearing, 1977; A Part, 1980; The Wheel, 1982; Collected Poems, 1985; Sabbaths, 1987; Sayings and Doings and an Eastward Look, 1990; Entries, 1994; The Farm, 1995. Non-Fiction: The Long-Legged House, 1969; The Hidden Wound, 1970; The Unforeseen Wilderness, 1971; A Continuous Harmony, 1972; The Unsettling of America, 1977; Recollected Essays 1965–1980, 1981; The Gift of Good Land, 1981; Standing by Words, 1983; Home Economics, 1987; What Are People For?, 1990; Harlan Hubbard: Life and Work, 1990; Standing on Earth, 1991; Sex, Economy, Freedom and Community, 1993; Another Turn of the Crank, 1995; Life is a Miracle: An Essay Against Modern Superstition, 2000. *Honours:* Guggenheim Fellowship, 1962; Rockefeller Fellowship, 1965; National Institute of Arts and Letters Award, 1971; Jean Stein Award, American Acad. of Arts and Letters, 1987; Lannan Foundation Award for Non-Fiction, 1989; T. S. Eliot Award, Ingersoll Foundation, 1994; Award for

Excellence in Poetry, The Christian Century, 1994; Harry M. Caudill Conservationist Award, Cumberland Chapter, Sierra Club, 1996. *Address:* Lanes Landing Farm, Port Royal, KY 40058, USA.

BERTOLINO, James; Poet, Writer and University Teacher; b. 4 Oct. 1942, Hurley, Wisconsin, USA; m. Lois Behling, 29 Nov. 1966. *Education:* BS, University of Wisconsin, 1970; MFA, Cornell University, 1973. *Career:* Teacher, Washington State University, 1970–71, Cornell University, 1971–74, University of Cincinnati, 1974–84, Washington Community Colleges, 1984–91, Chapman University, 1989–96, Western Washington University, 1991–96. *Publications:* Poetry: Employed, 1972; Soft Rock, 1973; The Gestures, 1975; Making Space for Our Living, 1975; The Alleged Conception, 1976; New & Selected Poems, 1978; Precint Kali, 1982; First Credo, 1986; Snail River, 1995. Chapbooks: Drool, 1968; Day of Change, 1968; Stone Marrow, 1969; Becoming Human, 1970; Edging Through, 1972; Terminal Placebos, 1975; Are You Tough Enough for the Eighties?, 1979; Like a Planet, 1993. Contributions: Poetry in 27 anthologies; Prose in 3 anthologies; Poetry, stories, essays, and reviews in periodicals. *Honours:* Hart Crane Poetry Award, 1969; Discovery Award, 1972; National Endowment for the Arts Fellowship, 1974; Quarterly Review of Literature International Book Awards, 1986, 1995; Djerassi Foundation Residency, 1987; Bumbershoot Big Book Award, 1994.

BESS, Clayton (see Locke, Robert Howard).

BESSON, Philippe; French writer and lawyer; b. 29 Jan. 1967, Barbezieux, Charente. *Education:* Lycée Montaigne de Bordeaux, École Supérieure de Commerce de Rouen. *Career:* lawyer and teacher of social law, Paris 1989. *Publications:* En l'absence des hommes (trans. as In the Absence of Men) (Prix Emmanuel-Roblès) 2001, Son frère 2001, L'arrière-saison (Grand Prix TRL-Lire 2003) 2002, Un garcon d'Italie 2003. *E-mail:* phillipebesson@free.fr. *Website:* www.phillipebesson.free.fr.

BETTARINI, Mariella; Writer, Poet and Teacher; b. 31 Jan. 1942, Florence, Italy. *Education:* Teacher's Diploma, 1964. *Career:* Elementary School Teacher; Co-Founder, Ed. and Publisher, Salvo Imprevisti, 1973. *Publications:* Il pudore e l'effondersi, 1966; Il leccio, 1968; La rivoluzione copernicana, 1970; Terra di tutti e altre poesie, 1972; Dal vero, 1974; In bocca alla balena, 1977; Storie d'Ortensia: Romanza, 1978; Felice di essare: Scritti sulla condizione della donna e sulla sessualità, 1978; Diario fiorentino, 1979; Chi è il poeta? (co-ed.), 1980; Ossessi oggetti-Spiritate materie, 1981; Il viaggio-Il corpo, 1982; La nostra gioventù: 18 gennaio 1976, 1982; Poesie vegetali, 1982; Psicografia, 1982; Vegetali figure: 1978–82, 1983; I Guerrieri di Riace di Mario Grasso, 1984; Tre lustri ed oltre: Antologia poetica 1963–1981, 1986; Amorosa persona, 1989. *Address:* c/o Salvatore Sciascia Editori, Corso Umberto 1111, 93100 Caltanissetta, Italy.

BETTS, Raymond Frederick, BA, MA, PhD; academic and writer; b. 23 Dec. 1925, Bloomfield, NJ, USA; m. Irene Donahue 1956; two s. one d. *Education:* Rutgers University, Columbia University; Doctorat d'Université, University of Grenoble; Certificat d'Études africaines, Institut d'Études Politiques, University of Paris. *Career:* Instructor to Asst Prof., Bryn Mawr College, 1956–61; Asst Prof. to Prof., Grinnell College, 1961–71; Prof. of History, 1971–98, Dir, Gaines Center for the Humanities, 1983–98, University of Kentucky; Contributing Ed., Britannia Com, 1999–; mem. African Studies Asscn; American Historical Asscn; French Colonial Historical Society; Society for French Historical Studies. *Publications:* Assimilation and Asscn in French Colonial Theory, 1890–1914, 1961; The Scramble for Africa (ed.), 1966; Europe Overseas: Phases of Imperialism, 1968; The Ideology of Blackness (ed.), 1971; The False Dawn: European Imperialism in the Nineteenth Century, 1975; Tricouleur: A Brief History of Modern French Colonial Empire, 1978; Europe in Retrospect: A Brief History of the Last Two Hundred Years, 1979; Uncertain Dimensions: Western Overseas Empires in the Twentieth Century, 1985; France and Decolonisation, 1991; Decolonization, 1998. Contributions: Books and scholarly journals. *Honours:* Hallam Book Awards, University of Kentucky, 1976, 1986; Great Teacher Award, University of Kentucky, 1979, 1998; Outstanding Kentucky Humanist Award, Kentucky Humanities Council, 1989. *Address:* 311 Mariemont Drive, Lexington, KY 40505, USA.

BEVERLEY, Jo; Writer; b. 22 Sept. 1947, Morecambe, Lancashire, England; m. Kenneth Beverley, 1971, two s. *Education:* University of Keele, 1970. *Career:* mem. Canadian Romance Authors Network; Romance Writers of America; SF Canada; Writers' Union of Canada. *Publications:* Lord Wraybourne's Betrothed, 1988; The Stanforth Secrets, 1989; The Stolen Bride, 1990; If Fancy Be the Food of Love, 1991; Emily and the Dark Angel, 1991; The Fortune Hunter, 1991; An Arranged Marriage, 1991; The Christmas Angel, 1992; An Unwilling Bride, 1992; Lord of My Heart, 1992; Dark Champion, 1993; My Lady Notorious, 1993; Forbidden, 1994; Dangerous Joy, 1995; Tempting Fortune, 1995; The Shattered Rose, 1996; Something Wicked, 1997; Forbidden Magic, 1998; Lord of Midnight, 1998. Contributions: anthologies. *Honours:* Career Achievement for Regency Romance, 1992, and for Regency Historical, 1997, Romantic Times; Inducted, Romance Writers of America Hall of Fame, 1993. *Address:* c/o Alice Orr Agency, 305 Madison Ave, Suite 1166, New York, NY 10165, USA. *E-mail:* jobeverley@poboxes.com.

BEWES, Richard Thomas; Anglican Rector and Writer; b. 1 Dec. 1934, Nairobi, Kenya; m. Elisabeth Ingrid Jaques, 18 April 1964, two s. one d. *Education:* Marlborough School, 1948–53; MA, Emmanuel College, Cambridge, 1954–57; Ridley Hall Theological College, Cambridge, 1957–59. *Career:* mem. Guild of British Songwriters. *Publications:* Talking About Prayer, 1979; The Pocket Handbook of Christian Truth, 1981; The Church Reaches Out, 1981; John Wesley's England, 1981; The Church Overcomes, 1983; On the Way, 1984; Quest for Life, 1985; The Church Marches On, 1986; When God Surprises, 1986; A New Beginning, 1989; The Resurrection, 1989; Does God Reign?, 1995; Speaking in Public–Effectively, 1998; Open Home, Open Bible, 2000; The Lamb Wins, 2000; The Stone That Became a Mountain, 2001; Ten Steps in Prayer, 2001; Words That Circled the World, 2001; The Top 100 Questions, 2002; Wesley Country, 2003. *Address:* 2 All Souls Pl., London W1B 3DA, England.

BHARTIA, Shobhana; Indian newspaper executive; b. 4 Jan. 1957, Calcutta (now Kolkata); m. Shyam Sunder Bhartia 1974; two s. *Education:* Loreto House, Calcutta. *Career:* Exec. Dir The Hindustani Times Ltd 1986–, Vice-Chair. and Editorial Dir; Dir Press Trust of India Ltd 1987, Indian Airlines, New Delhi 1988–90, Air Travel Bureau Pvt. Ltd 1989; Chair. and Treas. Bd of Govs, Delhi Coll. of Arts and Commerce 1988–90; Chair. HT Vision Ltd 1990–; Chair. Bd of Govs Shyama Prasad Mukherjee Coll. (for Women) 1992; mem. Sri Mata Vaishnu Devi Shrine Bd, Katra 1991; Pres. FICCI (women's org.), Leader dels to Australia, NZ, the Philippines and to World Congress of Women Conf. (Moscow, fmr USSR) 1987–88. *Honours:* Int. Cultural Devt Org. Award 1989, Mahila Shiromani Award 1990, Lok Shri Award, Inst. of Econ. Studies 1990, Vijaya Shri Award, Int. Friendship Soc. of India 1991, Delhi Chamber of Commerce Outstanding Businesswoman Award 2001. *Address:* Hindustani Times House, 18–20 Kasturba Gandhi Marg, New Delhi, 110 065, India. *Telephone:* (11) 3317955 (Office); (11) 6830260 (Home). *Fax:* (11) 3319021 (Office).

BHATTACHARYA, Nalinaksha; civil servant and writer; b. 2 April 1949, Kolkata, India; m. Manju Bhattacharya 1982. *Education:* BSc, University of Calcutta; Short Story Writing Correspondence Course, London School of Journalism, 1986–87. *Publications:* Hem and Football, novel, 1992; Hem and Maxine, novel, 1995; A Fistful of Desire, novel, 1997; Short stories. Contributions: BBC World Service; London Magazine; New Writing 5. *Honours:* First Prize in Short Story Writing, American University Centre, Kolkata, 1977. *Literary Agent:* Lavinia Trevor, 7 The Glasshouse, 49A Goldhawk Road, London W12 8QP, England. *Address:* Sector 8/121, R. K. Puram, New Delhi 110022, India.

BIBBY, Peter Leonard, BA, DipEd; poet, writer, dramatist and screenwriter; b. 21 Dec. 1940, London, England; m. 1967; two s. two d. *Education:* University of Western Australia, Murdoch University. *Career:* fmr Ed., Fellowship of Australian Writers, Bagabala Books; mem. Australian Film Institute, Australian Writers' Guild, Computer Graphics Asscn, Fellowship of Australian Writers. *Publications:* Island Weekend 1960; contrib. to various anthologies and journals. *Honours:* Tom Collins Literary Awards, 1978, 1982; Lyndall Hadow National Short Story Award, 1983; Donald Stuart National Short Story Award, 1985.

BIBERGER, Erich Ludwig; Poet, Writer and Ed.; b. 20 July 1927, Passau, Germany. *Education:* Passau. *Career:* Founder-Dir, Internationale Regensbürger Literaturtage, 1967–94, Internationale Jungautoren-Wettbewerbe, 1972–94; Founder-Ed., RSG Studio International, 1973–, RSG Forum 15/25, 1977–; mem. Regensburg Asscn of Authors, chair., 1960–, hon. pres., 1995–; Humboldt-Gesellschaft für Wissenschaft und Kunst, 1993–; Bayerischer Kulturrat, 1998–. *Publications:* Dreiklang der Stille (poems), 1955; Rundgang über dem Nordlicht (prose), 1958; Die Traumwelle (novel), 1962; Denn im Allsein der Welt (poems), 1966; Gar mancher (satirical verses), 1967; Anthology Quer, 1974; Anthology 3, 1979; Andere Wege bis Zitterluft (poems), 1982; Nichts als das Meer (poems), 1984; Zwei Pfund Morgenduft (feuilletons), 1987; Drei Millimeter Erd-Kugel, Trei Milimetristerapamanteasca (poems), 1997; Fantasieschutzgebeit, Imagainationis hortulus (haiku), 1998. *Honours:* several, including establishment of the Erich-und-Maria-Biberger Preises für Verdienste um die Literature, 1995. *Address:* Altmühlstrasse 12, 93059 Regensburg, Germany.

BICHSEL, Peter; Author; b. 24 March 1935, Lucerne, Switzerland; m. Therese Spörri, 1956, one s. one d. *Education:* Graduate, Teacher's College, Solothurn, 1955. *Career:* Writer-in-Residence, Oberlin College, Ohio, 1971–72; Visiting Lecturer, Univ. of Essen, 1980, Univ. of Frankfurt am Main, 1982, Dartmouth College, Hanover, NH, 1987, Middlebury College, Vermont, 1989, CUNY, 1992; mem. Akademie der Künste; American Asscn of Teachers of German, hon. mem.; Deutsche Akademie für Sprache und Dichtung, Darmstadt, corresponding mem. *Publications:* Eigentlich möchte Frau Blum den Milchmann kennenlernen, 1964; Das Gästehaus, 1965; Die Jahreszeiten, 1967; Kindergeschichten, 1969; Des Schweizers Schweiz, 1969; Geschichten zur falschen Zeit, 1979; Der Leser: Das Erzählen, 1982; Der Busant: Von Trinkern, Polizisten und der schönen Magelone, 1985; Schulmeistereien, 1985; Irgendwo anderswo, 1986; Im Gegenteil, 1990; Zur Stadt Paris, 1993; Die Totaldemokraten, 1998; Cherubin Hammer und Cherubin Hammer, 1999. *Honours:* Gruppe 47 Prize, 1965; Lessing Prize, Hamburg, 1965; Arts Prize, Solothurn, 1979; Literature Prize, Bern, 1979; Johann Peter Hebel Prize, 1986; Culture Prize, Lucerne, 1989. *Address:* Nelkenweg 24, 4512 Bellach, Switzerland.

BIDDISS, Michael Denis; academic and writer; b. 15 April 1942, Farnborough, Kent, England; m. Ruth Margaret Cartwright 1967; four d. *Education:* MA, PhD, Queens' College, Cambridge, 1961–66; Centre des Hautes Études Européennes, University of Strasbourg, 1965–66. *Career:* Fellow in History, Downing College, Cambridge, 1966–73; Lecturer/Reader in History, University of Leicester, 1973–79; Prof. of History, University of Reading, 1979–; mem. Historical Asscn, pres., 1991–94; Faculty, History and Philosophy of Medicine, Society of Apothecaries, London, pres., 1994–98; Royal Historical Society, joint vice-pres., 1995–99. *Publications:* Father of Racist Ideology, 1970; Gobineau: Selected Political Writings (ed.), 1970; Disease and History (co-author), 1972; The Age of the Masses, 1977; Images of Race (ed.), 1979; Thatcherism: Personality and Politics (co-ed.), 1987; The Nuremberg Trial and the Third Reich, 1992; The Uses and Abuses of Antiquity (co-ed.), 1999; The Humanities in the New Millennium (co-ed.), 2000. *Address:* School of History, University of Reading, Whiteknights, Reading RG6 6AA, England.

BIEBER, Konrad, LèsL, PhD; American writer and translator; *Professor of French and Comparative Literature Emeritus, SUNY*; b. 24 March 1916, Berlin, Germany; m. Tamara Siew 1939 (died 1995); one s. *Education:* Sorbonne, University of Paris, Yale University. *Career:* Instructor in French, Yale University, 1948–53; Instructor, Middlebury French Summer School, 1949–51, 1956; Visiting Lecturer in French and Comparative Literature, University of Colorado at Boulder, 1952; Asst Prof., 1953–57, Assoc. Prof., 1957–60, Prof. of French and Chair., Dept of French, 1959–68, Connecticut College, New London; Prof. of French and Comparative Literature, 1968–86, Prof. Emeritus, 1986–, SUNY. *Publications:* L'Allemagne vue par les Écrivains de la Résistance Française (preface by Albert Camus), 1954; Simone de Beauvoir, 1979; Outwitting the Gestapo (trans. of Lucie Aubrac's Ils partiront dans l'Ivresse), 1993. Contributions: Encyclopedias, dictionaries, books and journals. *Honours:* Guggenheim Fellowship, 1957–58; Chevalier, Ordre des Palmes Académiques, 1970; Book-of-the-Month and History Club selections, 1993. *Address:* 1211 Foulkeways, Gwynedd, PA 19436, USA.

BIELSKI, Alison Joy Prosser; poet, writer and lecturer; b. 24 Nov. 1925, Newport, Gwent, Wales; m. 1st Dennis Ford Treverton Jones 1948; m. 2nd Anthony Edward Bielski 1955; one s. one d. *Career:* Lecturer, Writers on Tour, Welsh Arts Council; mem. Gwent Poetry Society; Society of Women Writers and Journalists; Welsh Acad.; Welsh Union of Writers. *Publications:* The Story of the Welsh Dragon, 1969; Across the Burning Sand, 1970; Eve, 1973; Flower Legends of the Wye Valley, 1974; Shapes and Colours, 1974; The Lovetree, 1974; Mermaid Poems, 1974; Seth, 1980; Night Sequence, 1981; Eagles, 1983; The Story of St Mellons, 1985; That Crimson Flame, 1996; The Green-Eyed Pool, 1997. Contributions: anthologies and journals. *Honours:* Premium Prize, Poetry Society, 1964; Anglo-Welsh Review Poetry Prize, 1970; Arnold Vincent Bowen Poetry Prize, 1971; Third Place, Alice Gregory Memorial Competition, 1979; Orbis Poetry Prize, 1984; Second Prize, Julia Cairns Trophy, Society of Women Writers and Journalists, 1984, 1992. *Address:* 64 Glendower Court, Velindre Road, Whitchurch, Cardiff CF14 2TJ, Wales.

BIERMANN, Wolf; Poet, Songwriter and Musician; b. 15 Nov. 1936, Hamburg, Germany; m. Christine Bark, two s. *Education:* Humboldt University, Berlin, 1959–63. *Career:* Asst Dir, Berliner Ensemble, 1957–59; Song and guitar performances throughout Germany. *Publications:* Die Drahtharfe: Balladen, Gedichte, Lieder, 1965; Mit Marx-und Engelszungen, 1968; Der Dra-Dra (play), 1970; Für meine Genossen, 1972; Deutschland: Ein Wintermärchen, 1972; Nachlass I, 1977; Wolf Biermann; Poems and Ballads, 1977; Preussicher Ikarus, 1978; Verdrehte welt das seh'ich gerne, 1982; Und als ich von Deutschland nach Deutschland: Three Contemporary German Poets, 1985; Affenels und Barrikade, 1986; Alle Lieder, 1991; Ich hatte viele Bekümmernis: Meditation on Cantata No. 21 by J. S. Bach, 1991; Vier Neue Lieder, 1992. *Honours:* Büchner Prize, 1991; Möricke Prize, 1991; Heine Prize, 1993. *Address:* c/o Verlag Kiepenheuer und Witsch, Rondorferstrasse 5, 5000 Colonge-Marienurg, Germany.

BIGSBY, Christopher William Edgar; Prof. of American Literature, Broadcaster and Novelist; b. 27 June 1941, Dundee, Scotland. *Education:* BA, MA, Sheffield University; PhD, Nottingham University. *Career:* Lecturer in American Literature, University College of Wales, 1966–69; Lecturer, 1969–73, Senior Lecturer, 1973–85, Prof. of American Literature, 1985–, University of East Anglia. *Publications:* Confrontation and Commitment: A Study of Contemporary American Drama, 1967; Edward Albee, 1969; The Black American Writer (ed.), 1969; Three Negro Plays, 1969; Dada and Surrealism, 1972; Approaches to Popular Culture, 1975; Tom Stoppard, 1976; Superculture, 1976; Edward Albee, 1976; The Second Black Renaissance, 1980; Contemporary English Drama, 1981; Joe Orton, 1982; A Critical Introduction to 20th Century American Drama, 3 vols, 1982, 1984, 1985; The Radical Imagination and the Liberal Tradition, 1982; David Mamet, 1985; Cultural Change in the United States since World War II, 1986; Plays by Susan Glaspell, 1987; File on Miller, 1988; Modern American Drama: 1945–1990, 1992, revised edn as Modern American Drama: 1945–2000, 2000; Hester (novel), 1994; Pearl (novel), 1995; 19th Century American Short Stories (ed.), 1995; Portable Arthur Miller (ed.), 1995; Still Lives (novel), 1996; Cambridge Companion to Arthur Miller (ed.), 1998; Cambridge History of American Theatre (joint ed.), three vols, 1998, 1999, 2000; Contemporary American Playwrights, 1999; Writers in Conversation (ed.), 2000. Contributions: Radio; Television; TLS; Times Higher Education Supplement; Sunday Independent; American Quarterly; Modern Drama; Theatre Quarterly; Guardian; Sunday Telegraph. *Honours:* FRSL, 2000. *Literary Agent:* Shiel Land Assocs. *Address:* 3 Church Farm, Colney, Norwich, England.

BILGRAMI, Akeel; academic; b. 28 Feb. 1950, Hyderabad, India; m. Carol Rovane 1990; one d. *Education:* BA, Mumbai University, 1970; BA, University of Oxford, 1974; PhD, University of Chicago, 1983. *Career:* Prof. of Philosophy, Chair. of Philosophy Dept, Columbia University; mem. American Philosophical Society. *Publications:* Belief and Meaning, 1992; Self-Knowledge and Intentionality, 1996; Internal Dialectics: The Moral Psychology of Identity. Contributions: Journal of Philosophy; Philosophical Quarterly; Philosophical Topics. *Honours:* Rhodes Scholarship, 1971; Whitney Humanities Fellow, 1992. *Address:* 110 Morningside Drive, No. 58, New York, NY 10027, USA.

BILLING, Graham John; Author; b. 12 Jan. 1936, Dunedin, New Zealand; Dramatist; Poet. m. Rowan Innes Cunningham, 29 Aug. 1978, one s. one d. by previous marriage. *Education:* Otago University, 1955–58. *Career:* Staff, Dunedin Evening Star, 1958–62; Antarctic Division, DSIR, 1962–64; New Zealand Broadcasting Corporation News Service and TV Service, 1964–67; Staff, Dominion Sunday Times, 1967–69; Lecturer, writing, Mitchell College Advanced Education, Bathurst, Australia, 1974–75. *Publications:* Forbush and the Penguins, 1965; The Alpha Trip, 1969; Statues, 1971; The Slipway, 1973; The Primal Therapy of Tom Purslane, 1980; Changing Countries (poems), 1980. Non-Fiction: South: Man and Nature in Antarctica, 1965; New Zealand, the Sunlit Land, 1966; The New Zealanders, 1974. Radio Plays: Forbush and the Penguins, 1965; Mervyn Gridfern versus the Babsons, 1965; The Slipway, 1976; The Prince of Therapy of Tom Purslane, 1980. *Address:* 89 Mersey St, St Albans, Christchurch 1, New Zealand.

BILLINGTON, James (Hadley); Historian and Librarian; b. 1 June 1929, Bryn Mawr, PA, USA; m. Marjorie Anne Brennan, 22 June 1957, two s. two d. *Education:* BA, Princeton University, 1950; DPhil, Balliol College, Oxford, 1953. *Career:* Lecturer in History, 1957–58, Fellow, Russian Research Center, 1958–59, Asst Prof. of History, 1958–61, Harvard University; Visiting Research Prof., University of Helsinki, 1960–61, Institute of History, Acad. of Sciences of the USSR, Moscow, 1966–67, École des Hautes Études en Sciences Sociales, Paris, 1985, 1988; Assoc. Prof. of History, 1962–64, Prof. of History, 1964–73, Princeton University; Dir, American Asscn for Slavic Studies, 1968–71, Woodrow Wilson International Center for Scholars, Washington, DC, 1973–87; Chair., Board of Foreign Scholarships, 1971–73; Librarian of Congress, Washington, DC, 1987–; mem. American Acad. of Arts and Sciences; American Philosophical Society. *Publications:* Mikhailovsky and Russian Populism, 1958; The Icon and the Axe: An Interpretive History of Russian Culture, 1966; The Arts of Russia, 1970; Fire in the Minds of Men: Origins of the Revolutionary Faith, 1980; Russia Transformed: Breakthrough to Hope, Moscow, August 1991, 1992; The Face of Russia, 1998. Contributions: scholarly journals. *Honours:* numerous hon. doctorates; Rhodes Scholar, 1950–53; Guggenheim Fellowship, 1960–61; Commdr, Ordre des Arts et des Lettres, 1991; Gwangha Medal, Republic of Korea, 1991; Woodrow Wilson Award, Princeton University, 1992; Knight Commander's Cross, Order of Merit, Germany, 1996. *Address:* c/o Office of the Librarian, Library of Congress, 101 Independent Ave, Washington, DC 20540, USA.

BILLINGTON, Michael (Keith); Drama Critic and Writer; b. 16 Nov. 1939, Leamington Spa, England; m. Jeanine Bradlaugh 1977; one d. *Education:* BA, St Catherine's College, Oxford. *Career:* Writer, The Times, 1965–71; Film Critic, Birmingham Post, 1968–78, Illustrated London News, 1968–81; Drama Critic, The Guardian, 1971–, Country Life, 1988–; Visiting Prof., Dept of English, King's College, London, 2002–. *Publications:* The Modern Actor, 1974; How Tickled I Am, 1977; The Performing Arts (ed.), 1980; The Guinness Book of Theatre Facts and Feats, 1982; Alan Ayckbourn, 1983; Tom Stoppard, 1987; Peggy Ashcroft, 1988; Twelfth Night (ed.), 1990; One Night Stands, 1993; The Life and Work of Harold Pinter, 1996; Stage and Screen Lives (ed.), 2001. Contributions: radio and television. *Honours:* IPC Critic of the Year, 1974; IPC Theatre Critic of the Year, 1993, 1995, 1997. *Address:* 15 Hearne Rd, London W4 3NJ, England.

BILLINGTON, Rachel (Mary); Writer; b. 11 May 1942, Oxford, England; m. 16 Dec. 1967, two s. two d. *Education:* BA, English, University of London. *Career:* mem. Society of Authors; PEN, vice-pres. *Publications:* Over 20 books, including: Loving Attitudes, 1988; Theo and Matilda, 1990; The First Miracles, 1990; Bodily Harm, 1992; The Family Year, 1992; The Great Umbilical, 1994; Magic and Fate, 1996; The Life of Jesus (for children), 1996; Perfect Happiness, 1996; Tiger Sky, 1998; The Life of St. Francis (for children), 1999; A Woman's Life; Far Out! (for children), 2002. Contributions: various publications, radio and television. *Address:* The Court House, Poyntington, Near Sherborne, Dorset DT9 4LF, England.

BINCHY, Maeve, BA; Irish writer; b. 28 May 1940, Dalkey, Co Dublin; m. Gordon Thomas Snell 1977. *Education:* Univ. Coll. Dublin. *Career:* teacher of history and French, Pembroke School, Dublin 1961–68; columnist, Irish Times 1968–2000. *Publications:* short story collections: Central Line 1978, Victoria Line 1980, Dublin Four 1982, Victoria Line/Central Line (revised edn of two earlier titles, aka London Transports) 1983, This Year it Will be Different 1996, Return Journey 1998; novels: Silver Wedding 1979, Light a Penny Candle 1982, The Lilac Bus 1984, Echoes 1985, Firefly Summer 1987, Circle of Friends 1990, The Copper Beech 1992, The Glass Lake 1994, Evening Class 1996, Tara Road 1999, Scarlet Feather 2000, Quentins 2002, Nights of Rain and Stars 2004; non-fiction: Aches and Pains 2000; other: several plays. *Honours:* Hon. DLit (Nat. Univ. of Ireland) 1990, (Queen's Belfast) 1998; Int. Television Festival Golden Prague Award, Czech TV 1979, Jacobs Award 1979, WHSmith Fiction Award 2001. *Literary Agent:* Christine Green, 6 Whitehorse Mews, Westminster Bridge Road, London, SE1 7QD, England. *E-mail:* info@christinegreen.co.uk. *Website:* www .christinegreen.co.uk. *Address:* PO Box 6737, Dun Laoghaire, Co Dublin, Ireland. *Website:* www.maevebinchy.com.

BINDING, Tim; British author and scriptwriter; b. 1947, Germany. *Career:* Ed., Penguin Books, Commissioning Ed., Simon & Schuster. *Publications:* novels: In the Kingdom of Air 1993, A Perfect Execution 1996, Island Madness (aka Lying with the Enemy) 1998, Anthem 2003; co-author: The Last Salute (with Simon Nye); non-fiction: Firebrand: Writing Today (ed.) 1983, On Ilkley Moor: The Story of an English Town 2001; contrib. to Granta 56. *Honours:* Soc. of Authors Travelling Scholarship 2004. *Address:* c/o Picador, 20 New Wharf Road, London, N1 9RR, England. *Telephone:* (20) 7014-6000. *Fax:* (20) 7014-6001. *Website:* www.panmacmillan.com.

BINEBINE, Mahi; Moroccan novelist and artist; b. 1959, Marrakesh. *Career:* teacher of mathematics, painter. *Publications:* novels: Le Sommeil de l'esclave 1992, Les Funérailles du lait 1994, L'Ombre du Poete 1997, Cannibales (trans. as Welcome to Paradise) 1999, Pollens 2001; illustrator: L'Ecriture au tournant by Abdellatif Laâbi 2000. *Literary Agent:* c/o Granta Books, 2–3 Hanover Yard, Noel Road, London, N1 8BE, England. *Telephone:* (20) 7704-9976. *Fax:* (20) 7354-3469. *Website:* www.granta.co.uk.

BINGHAM, Charlotte Marie-Thérèse; Writer and Dramatist; b. 29 June 1942, Sussex, England; m. Terence Brady, 15 Jan 1964, one s. one d. *Education:* The Priory, Haywards Heath; Sorbonne, University of Paris. *Publications:* Coronet Among the Weeds, 1963; Lucinda, 1965; Coronet Among the Grass, 1972; Victoria (with Terence Brady), 1972; Rose's Story (with Terence Brady), 1973; Victoria and Company (with Terence Brady), 1974; Yes—Honestly (with Terence Brady), 1977; Belgravia, 1983; Country Life, 1984; At Home, 1986; To Hear a Nightingale, 1988; The Business, 1989; In Sunshine or in Shadow, 1991; Stardust, 1992; By Invitation Only, 1993; Nanny, 1993; Change of Heart, 1994; Debutantes, 1995; The Nightingale Sings, 1996; Grand Affair, 1997; Love Song, 1998; The Kissing Garden, 1999; The Love Knot, 2000; The Blue Note, 2000; Distant Music, 2001; The Moon at Midnight, 2002; Daughters of Eden, 2004. Other: TV series and films; stage works. *Honours:* Romantic Novelists Best Novel Award, Romantic Novelists Asscn, 1995. *Address:* c/o United Authors, Garden Studios, 11–15 Betterton St, London WC2H 9BP, England.

BINGHAM, Kate; British poet and novelist. *Education:* Univ. of Oxford. *Publications:* novels: Mummy's Legs 1998, Slipstream 2000; poetry: Cohabitation 1998, Eighteenth 2003. *Honours:* Eric Gregory Award from the Soc. of Authors 1996. *Literary Agent:* c/o Seren Books, First & Second Floors, 38–40 Nolton Street, Bridgend, Glamorgan CF31 3BN, Wales.

BINYON, Timothy John, MA, DPhil; British author and academic; b. 1940. *Education:* Univ. of Oxford. *Career:* Lecturer, Leeds Univ.; Lecturer in Russian Literature, Univ. of Oxford; senior research fellow, Wadham Coll., Oxford. *Publications:* fiction: Swan Song 1982, Greek Gifts 1989; non-fiction: Russian: A Beginner's Course (co-author) 1962, A Soviet Verse Reader (ed.) 1964, Murder Will Out: The Detective in Fiction from Poe to the Present 1989, Pushkin: a Biography (BBC4 Samuel Johnson Prize) 2003; contrib. to The Telegraph. *Address:* c/o Wadham College, University of Oxford, Oxford, OX1 3PN, England. *Website:* www.wadham.ox.ac.uk.

BIRCH, Carol; Novelist; b. 3 Jan. 1951, Manchester, England; m. Martin Lucas Butler, 26 Oct. 1990, two s. *Education:* University of Keele, 1968–72. *Career:* mem. Society of Authors. *Publications:* Life in the Palace, 1988; The Fog Line, 1989; The Unmaking, 1992; Songs of the West, 1994; Little Sister, 1998; Come Back, Paddy Riley, 2000; Turn Again Home, 2003; In a Certain Light, 2004. Contributions: TLS; Independent; New Statesman. *Honours:* David Higham Prize; Geoffrey Faber Memorial Award. *Literary Agent:* Mic Cheetham Agency. *Address:* c/o Mic Cheetham Agency, 11–12 Dover St, London W1X 3PH, England.

BIRD, Charles (see Wittich, John Charles Bird).

BIRD, Kai; Writer; b. 2 Sept. 1951, Eugene, OR, USA; m. Susan Gloria Goldmark, 7 June 1975, one s. *Education:* BA, History, Carleton College, 1973; MSc, Journalism, Northwestern University, 1975. *Publications:* The Chairman: John J. McCloy, The Making of the American Establishment, 1992; Hiroshima's Shadow: Writings on the Denial of History and the Smithsonian Controversy (ed. with Lawrence Lifshultz), 1998; The Color of Truth: McGeorge Bundy and William Bundy, Brothers in Arms: A Biography, 1998. Contributions: periodicals and journals. *Honours:* John D. and Catherine T. MacArthur Foundation Writing Fellowship; German Marshall Fund Fellow; Alicia Patterson Journalism Fellowship; Guggenheim Fellowship. *Address:* 1914 Biltmore St NW, Washington, DC 20009, USA.

BIRDSELL, Sandra (Louise); Writer; b. 22 April 1942, Hamiota, Manitoba, Canada; m. Stanley Vivian Birdsell, 1 July 1959, one s. two d. *Career:* several writer-in-residencies; Instructor in English, Capilano College, North Vancouver; mem. Manitoba Writers Guild; PEN International; Writers Guild of Canada; Writers Union of Canada. *Publications:* Night Travellers, 1982; Ladies of the House, 1984; The Missing Child, 1989; The Chrome Suite, 1992; The Two-Headed Calf, 1997; The Town That Floated Away, 1997; The Russlander, 2001. Contributions: various publications. *Honours:* Gerald Lampert Memorial Award, 1982; WHSmith/Books in Canada First Novel Award, 1989; McNally Robinson Award for Manitoba Book of the Year, 1992. *Address:* 755 Westminster Ave, Winnipeg, Manitoba R3G 1A5, Canada.

BIRLEY, Julia (Davies); Writer; b. 13 May 1928, London, England; m. 12 Sept. 1954, one s., three d. *Education:* BA, Classics, Oxon. *Career:* mem. PEN; Charlotte Yonge Society. *Publications:* Fiction: The Children on the Shore; The Time of the Cuckoo; When You Were There; A Serpent's Egg; Dr Spicer. Other: short stories and plays. Contributions: Guardian. *Address:* Upper Bryn, Longtown, Hereford HR2 0NA, England.

BIRMINGHAM, Stephen; Writer; b. 28 May 1931, Hartford, CT, USA; m. Janet Tillson, 5 Jan. 1951, divorced, one s. two d. *Education:* BA, Williams College, 1950; Postgraduate Studies, University of Oxford, 1951. *Career:* Advertising Copywriter, Needham, Harper & Steers Inc, 1953–67; mem. New England Society of the City of New York. *Publications:* Young Mr Keefe, 1958; Baraba Greer, 1959; The Towers of Love, 1961; Those Harper Women, 1963; Fast Start, Fast Finish, 1966; Our Crowd: The Great Jewish Families of New York, 1967; The Right People, 1968; Heart Troubles, 1968; The Grandees, 1971; The Late John Marquand, 1972; The Right Places, 1973; Real Lace, 1973; Certain People: America's Black Elite, 1977; The Golden Dream: Suburbia in the 1970s, 1978; Jacqueline Bouvier Kennedy Onassis, 1978; Life at the Dakota, 1979; California Rich, 1980; Duchess, 1981; The Grandes Dames, 1982; The Auerbach Will, 1983; The Rest of Us, 1984; The LeBaron Secret, 1986; America's Secret Aristocracy, 1987; Shades of Fortune, 1989; The Rothman Scandal, 1991; Carriage Trade, 1993. Contributions: periodicals. *Address:* 1247 Ida St, Cincinnati, OH 45202, USA.

BISCHOFF, David Frederick; writer; b. 15 Dec. 1951, Washington, DC, USA. *Career:* staff mem., NBC-TV, Washington, DC, 1974–; Assoc. Ed., Amazing Magazine. *Publications:* The Seeker (with Christopher Lampton), 1976; Quest (children's), 1977; Strange Encounters (children's), 1977; The Phantom of the Opera (children's), 1977; The Woodman (with Dennis R. Bailey), 1979; Nightworld, 1979; Star Fall, 1980; The Vampires of the Nightworld, 1981; Tin Woodman (with Dennis Bailey), 1982; Star Spring, 1982; War Games, 1983; Mandala, 1983; Day of the Dragonstar (with Thomas F. Monteleone), 1983; The Crunch Bunch, 1985; Destiny Dice, 1985; Galactic Warriors, 1985; The Infinite Battle, 1985; The Macrocosmic Conflict, 1986; Manhattan Project, 1986; The Unicorn Gambit, 1986; Abduction: The UFO Conspiracy, 1990; Revelation: The UFO Conspiracy, 1991; Deception: The UFO Conspiracy, 1991; Aliens Versus Predator: Hunter's Planet, 1994.

BISHOP, James Drew; Journalist; b. 18 June 1929, London, England; m. 5 June 1959; two s. *Education:* BA, History, Corpus Christi College, Cambridge, 1953. *Career:* Foreign Correspondent, 1957–64, Foreign News Ed., 1964–66, Features Ed., 1966–70, The Times; Ed., 1971–87, Ed.-in-Chief, 1987–94, The Illustrated London News; mem. Asscn of British Eds, chair., 1987–96. *Publications:* Social History of Edwardian Britain, 1977; Social History of the First World War, 1982; The Story of The Times (with Oliver Woods), 1983; Illustrated Counties of England (ed.), 1985; The Sedgwick Story, 1998. Contributions: books, newspapers, magazines. *Address:* 67 Parliament Hill, London NW3 2TB, England. *E-mail:* jamesbishop3@compuserve.com.

BISHOP, Jan (see Mcconchie, Lyn).

BISHOP, Michael (Lawson); Writer, Poet and Ed.; b. 12 Nov. 1945, Lincoln, NE, USA; m. Jeri Whitaker, 7 June 1969, one s. one d. *Education:* BA, 1967, MA, 1968, University of Georgia. *Career:* Writer-in-Residence, LaGrange College, 1997–; mem. SFWA; Science Fiction Poetry Asscn. *Publications:* Fiction: A Funeral for the Eyes of Fire, 1975, revised edn as Eyes of Fire, 1980; And Strange at Ecbatan the Trees, 1976; Stolen Faces, 1977; A Little Knowledge, 1977; Transfigurations, 1979; Under Heaven's Bridge (with Ian Watson), 1981; No Enemy but Time, 1982; Who Made Steve Cry?, 1984; Ancient of Days, 1985; The Secret Ascension, or, Philip K. Dick Is Dead, Alas, 1987; Unicorn Mountain, 1988; Apartheid, Superstrings and Mordecai Thubana, 1989; Count Geiger's Blues, 1992; Brittle Innings, 1994; Would It Kill You to Smile? (with Paul Di Filippo), 1998; Muskrat Courage (with Paul di Filippo), 2000. Short Stories: Catacomb Years, 1979; Blooded on Arachne, 1982; One Winter in Eden, 1984; Close Encounters with the Deity, 1986; Emphatically Not SF, Almost, 1990; At the City Limits of Fate, 1996; Brighten to Incandescence, 2003. Poetry: Windows and Mirrors, 1977; Time Pieces, 1999; Novella Collection: Blue Kansas Sky, 2000. Editor: Changes (anthology with Ian Watson), 1982; Light Years and Dark (anthology), 1984; Nebula Awards: SFWA's Choices for the Best Science Fiction and Fantasy, vols 23–25, 1989–91. Contributions: anthologies and periodicals. *Honours:* Phoenix Award, 1977; Clark Ashton Smith Award, 1978; Rhysling Award, Science Fiction Poetry Asscn, 1979; Nebula Awards, SFWA, 1981, 1982; Mythopoetic Fantasy Award, 1988; Locus Award for Best Fantasy Novel, 1994; Hon. LHD, LaGrange College, 2001. *Address:* Box 646, Pine Mountain, GA 31822, USA.

BISHOP, Pike (see Obstfeld, Raymond).

BISHOP, Wendy; Prof. of English, Writer and Poet; b. 13 Jan. 1953, Japan; m. 1st Marvin E. Pollard Jr, one s. one d.; m. 2nd Conrad Dean Newman. *Education:* BA, English, 1975, BA, Studio Art, 1975, MA, English, Creative Writing, 1976; MA, English, Teaching Writing, 1979, University of California at Davis; PhD, English, Rhetoric and Linguistics, Indiana University of Pennsylvania, 1988. *Career:* Bayero University, Kano, Nigeria, 1980–81; Northern Arizona University, 1981–82; Chair, Communications, Humanities, and Fine Arts, Navajo Community College, Tsaile, AZ, 1984–85; Asst Prof. of English, University of Alaska, Fairbanks, 1985–89; Prof. of English, Florida State University, Tallahassee, 1989–; Chair, Conference on College Composition and Communication, 2001; mem. Associated Writing Programs; MLA; National Council of Teachers of English; National Writing Centres Asscn; Poetry Society of America. *Publications:* Released into Language: Options for Teaching Creative Writing, 1990; Something Old, Something New: College Writing Teachers and Classroom Change, 1990; Working Words: The Process of Creative Writing, 1992; The Subject in Writing: Essays by Teachers and Students in Writing, 1993; Colors of a Different Horse (ed. with Hans Ostrom), 1994; Water's Night (poems with Hans Ostrom), 1994; Genres of Writing: Mapping the Territories of Discourse (ed. with Hans Ostrom), 1997; Mid-Passage (poems), 1997; Teaching Lives: Essays and Stories, 1997; Touching Liliana (poems), 1998; Ethnographic Writing Research-Writing it Down, Writing It Up and Reading It, 1999; When We Say We're Home: A Quartet of Place and Memory (co-author), 1999; Metro: Journeys in Writing Creatively (co-author), 2000; In Praise of Pedagogy: Poetry, Flash Fiction and Essays on Composing (co-ed.), 2000; The Subject is Reading: Essays by Teachers and Students (ed.), 2000; Thirteen Ways of Looking for a Poem: A Guide to Writing Poetry, 2000. Contributions: poems, fiction, and essays in various reviews and journals. *Honours:* Joseph Henry Jackson Award, 1980; several fellowships; many literary awards. *Address:* c/o Dept of English, Florida State University, Tallahassee, FL 32306, USA.

BISSETT, Bill; Poet and Artist; b. 23 Nov. 1939, Halifax, NS, Canada. *Education:* Dalhousie University, 1956–57; University of British Columbia, 1963–65. *Career:* Ed., Printer, Blewointmentpress, Vancouver, 1962–83. *Publications:* The Jinx Ship and other Trips: Poems-drawings-collage, 1966; We Sleep Inside Each Other All, 1966; Fires in the Temple, 1967; Where Is Miss Florence Riddle, 1967; What Poetiks, 1967; Gossamer Bed Pan, 1967; Lebanon Voices, 1967; Of the Land/Divine Service Poems, 1968; Awake in the Red Desert, 1968; Killer Whale, 1969; Sunday Work?, 1969; Liberating Skies, 1969; The Lost Angel Mining Company, 1969; The Outlaw, 1970; Blew Trewz, 1970; Nobody Owns the Earth, 1971; Air 6, 1971; Dragon Fly, 1971; Four Parts Sand: Concrete Poems, 1972; The Ice Bag, 1972; Poems for Yoshi, 1972; Drifting into War, 1972; Air 10-11-12, 1973; Pass the Food, Release the Spirit Book, 1973; The First Sufi Line, 1973; Vancouver Mainland Ice and Cold Storage, 1973; Living with the Vishyan, 1974; What, 1974; Drawings, 1974; Medicine My Mouths on Fire, 1974; Space Travel, 1974; You Can Eat it at the Opening, 1974; The Fifth Sun, 1975; The Wind up Tongue, 1975; Stardust, 1975; An Allusyun to Macbeth, 1976; Plutonium Missing, 1976; Sailor, 1978; Beyond Even Faithful Legends, 1979; Soul Arrow, 1980; Northern Birds in Color, 1981; Parlant, 1982; Seagull on Yonge Street, 1983; Canada Geese Mate for Life, 1985; Animal Uproar, 1987; What we Have, 1989; Hard 2 Beleev, 1990; Incorrect Thoughts, 1992; Vocalist with the Luddites, Dreaming of the Night, 1992; The Last Photo of the Human Soul, 1993; th Influenza uv Logik, 1995; loving without being vulnrabul, 1997; Offthroad (cassette), 1998; Skars on the Seehors, 1999; b leev abul char ak trs, 2000; Offthroad (with CD), 2000; rainbow mewsick (ed.), 2002; peter among th towring boxes, 2002; unmatching phenomena I (with CD), 2002. *Address:* Box 272, Str F, Toronto, Ontario M4Y 2L7, Canada.

BISSON, Thomas Noel; Prof. of Medieval History and Writer; b. 30 March 1931, New York, NY, USA; m. Margaretta C. Webb, 18 Aug. 1962, two d. *Education:* BA, Haverford College, 1953; MA, 1955, PhD, 1958, Princeton University. *Career:* Instructor in History, Amherst College, 1957–60; Asst Prof., Brown University, 1960–65; Assoc. Prof., Swarthmore College, 1965–67; Assoc. Prof., 1967–69, Prof., 1969–87, University of California at Berkeley; Prof., 1986–88, Henry Charles Lea Prof. of Medieval History, 1988–, Chair., Dept of History, 1991–95, Harvard University; mem. American Philosophical Society; Fellow, British Acad.; Fellow, Medieval Acad. of America, pres., 1994–95; FRHistS. *Publications:* Assemblies and Representation in Languedoc in the Thirteenth Century, 1964; Medieval Representative Institutions: Their Origins and Nature, 1973; Conservation of Coinage: Monetary Exploitation and its Restraint in France, Catalonia and Aragon (c. AD 1000–c. AD 1225), 1979; Fiscal Accounts of Catalonia Under the Early Court-Kings, 1151–1213, two vols, 1985; The Medieval Crown of Aragon: A Short History, 1986; Medieval France and Her Pyrenean Neighbors, 1989; Tormented Voices: Power, Crisis, and Humanity in Rural Catalonia, 1140–1200, 1998. Contributions: scholarly books and professional journals. *Honours:* Guggenheim Fellowship, 1964–65; Hon. Doctorate, University of Barcelona, 1991. *Address:* c/o Dept of History, Robinson Hall, Harvard University, Cambridge, MA 02138, USA.

BISSOONDATH, Neil (Devindra); Author; b. 19 April 1955, Arima, Trinidad. *Education:* BA, French, York University, Toronto, 1977. *Publications:* Digging Up the Mountains (short stories), 1985; A Casual Brutality (novel), 1988; On the Eve of Uncertain Tomorrows (short stories), 1990; The Innocence of Age (novel), 1992; In Selling Illusions: The Cult of Multiculturalism in Canada, 1994; Doing the Heart Good, 2001. Contributions: periodicals. *Honours:* Canadian Authors Asscn Literary Award, 1993. *Address:* c/o Random House Inc, 201 E 50th St, New York, NY 10022, USA.

BISWAS, Brian; Writer; b. 7 March 1957, Columbus, OH, USA; m. Elizabeth Phelan, 21 Jan. 1977, one s. one d. *Education:* BA, Antioch College, 1980; MS, University of Illinois, 1986. *Publications:* Short Stories: The Bridge, 1991; Solitary Confinement, 1992; The Museum of North African Treasures, 1992; A Sea Voyage, 1992; The Nature of Love, 1993; Fare-Thee-Well, 1993; Others, 1993; The Vulture, 1997; A Betrayal, 1999; Apologia Du Amore, 2000; The Crystal, 2000; A Soldier's Lament, 2003. Contributions: various literary journals. *Address:* 412 Holly Lane, Chapel Hill, NC 27517, USA. *E-mail:* bbiswas@email.unc.edu.

BJØRNVIG, Thorkild Strange, DPhil; Danish poet and writer; b. 2 Feb. 1918; m. 1st Grete Damgaard Pedersen 1946; m. 2nd Birgit Hornum 1970; two s. one d. *Education:* Cathedral School, Århus and Univ. of Århus. *Career:* mem. Danish Acad. 1960. *Publications:* poetry: Stjaernen bag Gavlen 1947, Anubis 1955, Figur og Ild 1959, Vibrationer 1966, Ravnen 1968, Udvalgte digte 1970, Morgenmørke 1977, Den dobbelte Lykke 1982, Gennem Regnbuen 1987, Siv Vand og Måne 1993; essays: Rilke og tysk Tradition 1959, Begyndelsen 1960, Kains Alter 1964, Oprør mod Neonguden 1970, Virkeligheden er til 1973, Pagten, mit Venskab med Karen Blixen 1974, Delfinen 1975, Stoffets Krystalhav 1975, Det religiøse menneskes ansigter 1975, Også for naturens skyld 1978, Barnet og dyret i industrisamfundet, Abeguder, Miljødigte 1975–80 1981, Den følende planet 1988, Epidlmeteus Miljødigte 1980–90 1991, Digtere 1991, Siv vand og måna 1993, Udsat på hjertets bjerge (trans. of poems by Rainer Maria Rilke) 1995, Samlede Digte 1947–93 1998. *Honours:* several prizes including Arisseian Prize for trans. (EU) 1996 and Rungsted Lund Prize 1998. *Address:* Issehoved 41, 8305 Samsø, Denmark.

BLACK, David; Writer; b. 21 April 1945, Boston, MA, USA; m. Deborah Hughes Keehn, 22 June 1968, one s. one d. *Education:* BA, Amherst College, 1967; MFA, Columbia University, 1971. *Career:* Writer-in-Residence, Mt Holyoke College, 1982–86; Contributing Ed., Rolling Stone, 1986–89; mem. International Asscn of Crime Writers; MWA; PEN; Writers' Guild-East. *Publications:* Mirrors, 1968; Ekstasy, 1975; Like Father, 1978; The King of Fifth Avenue, 1981; Minds, 1982; Murder at the Met, 1984; Medicine Man, 1985; Peep Show, 1986; The Plague Years, 1986. Other: various television scripts. Contributions: numerous national and international magazines. *Honours:* Gold Medal for Excellence in Writing, Writers' Foundation of America, 1992. *Address:* c/o Mystery Writers of America, 17 E 47th St, New York, NY 10017, USA.

BLACK, David Macleod, MA; British poet and translator; b. 8 Nov. 1941, Cape Town, South Africa. *Education:* University of Edinburgh, University of Lancaster. *Career:* teacher, Chelsea Art School, London, 1966–70; Lecturer and supervisor, Westminster Pastoral Foundation, London, 1972–2000. *Publications:* Rocklestrakes, 1960; From the Mountain, 1963; Theory of Diet, 1966; With Decorum, 1967; A Dozen Short Poems, 1968; Penguin Modern Poets 11, 1968; The Educators, 1969; The Old Hag, 1972; The Happy Crow, 1974; Gravitations, 1979; Collected Poems 1964–1987, 1991; A Place for Exploration, 1991. Contributions: Modern Poetry in Translation, 1998, 2000; Poetry London; Other periodicals and journals; Anthologies. *Honours:* Arts Council of Great Britain Bursary, 1968; Scottish Arts Council Prize, 1968, and Publication Award, 1991. *Address:* 30 Cholmley Gardens, Aldred Road, London NW6 1AG, England. *Website:* www.dmblack.co.uk.

BLACK, Jim (see Haining, Peter (Alexander)).

BLACK OF CROSSHARBOUR, Baron (Life Peer), cr. 2001, of Crossharbour in the London Borough of Tower Hamlets; **Conrad M. Black,** Kt, PC, OC, LittD, LLD; British (b. Canadian) publisher and business executive; b. 25 Aug. 1944, Montreal, Québec; m. 1st Joanna Catherine Louise Black 1978 (divorced 1991); two s. one d.; m. 2nd Barbara Amiel 1992. *Education:* Carleton, Laval, McGill Univs. *Career:* Chair. and CEO Ravelston Corpn Ltd; acquired Daily Telegraph newspaper group 1985; Chair. The Telegraph PLC 1987; Chair. Telegraph Group –2004; Chair. Saturday Night Magazine Inc.; Chair. Hollinger Int. Inc. 1985–2004, CEO 1985–2003, Chair. Chair.'s Exec. Cttee; Chair. Bd and Exec. Cttee Argus Corpn Ltd; Deputy Chair. American Publishing Co. (now Hollinger Int.), John Fairfax (Australia); Dir Canadian Imperial Bank of Commerce; Dir Brascan Ltd, The Spectator (1828) Ltd, UniMédia Inc., Eaton's of Canada Ltd, Financial Post Co. Ltd, Key Publishers Co. Ltd, Southam Inc. (Chair., CEO 1996–), Sotheby's 1997–; Patron The Malcolm Muggeridge Foundation; mem. Advisory Bd, The Nat. Interest, Washington, DC, Steering Cttee and Advisory Group, Bilderberg Meetings, Chair.'s Council, Americas Soc., Int. Inst. for Strategic Studies, Gulfstream Aerospace Corpn. *Publications:* Duplessis 1977, A Life in Progress (autobiog.) 1994. *Honours:* Hon. LLD (St Francis Xavier) 1979, (McMaster) 1979, (Carleton) 1989, Hon. LittD (Windsor) 1979. *Address:* c/o The Telegraph PLC, 1 Canada Square, Canary Wharf, London, E14 5DT, England.

BLACKBOURN, David Gordon; Prof. of History and Writer; b. 1 Nov. 1949, Spilsby, Lincolnshire, England; m. Deborah Frances Langton, 13 April 1985, one s. one d. *Education:* BA, History, 1970, MA, 1974, PhD, 1976, University of Cambridge. *Career:* Research Fellow, Jesus College, Cambridge, 1973–76; Research Fellow, Institute of European History, Mainz, 1974–75, Alexander von Humboldt Foundation, Bonn-Bad Godesberg, 1984–85; Lecturer in History, Queen Mary College, 1976–79, Lecturer, 1979–85, Reader, 1985–89, Prof. of Modern European History, 1989–92, Birkbeck College, University of London; Visiting Kratter Prof. of European History, Stanford University, 1989–90; Prof. of History, 1992–97, Coolidge Prof. of History, 1997–, Harvard University; Annual Lecture, German Historical Institute, London, 1998; mem. Advisory Bd Institute for European History, Mainz, editorial bd Past and Present, Cttee on Hon. Foreign mems, AHA. *Publications:* Class, Religion and Local Politics in Wilhelmine Germany, 1980; Mythen Deutscher Geschichtsschreibung (with Geoff Eley), 1980; The Peculiarities of German History (with Geoff Eley), 1984; Populists and Patricians: Essays in Modern German History, 1987; Volksfrömmigkeit und Fortschrittsglaube im Kulturkampf, 1988; The German Bourgeoisie (ed. with Richard J. Evans), 1991; Marpingen: Apparitions of the Virgin Mary in Bismarckian Germany, 1993; The Fontana History of Germany: The Long Nineteenth Century, 1780–1918, 1997. Contributions to scholarly books, professional journals, weeklies and newspapers. *Honours:* FRHistS, 1987; American Historical Asscn Best Book in German History, 1993; Guggenheim Fellowship, 1994–95. *Address:* Minda de Gunzburg Center for European Studies, Harvard University, 27 Kirkland St, Cambridge, MA 02138, USA. *E-mail:* dgblack6@fas.harvard.edu.

BLACKBURN, Alexander Lambert; Prof. of English Emeritus, Writer and Ed.; b. 6 Sept. 1929, Durham, NC, USA; m. Inés Dölz, 14 Oct. 1975, two s. one d. *Education:* BA, Yale University, 1951; MA, English, University of North Carolina, 1955; PhD, English, University of Cambridge, 1963. *Career:* Instructor, Hampden-Sydney College, 1960–61, University of Pennsylvania, 1963–65; Lecturer, University of Maryland European Division, 1967–72; Prof. of English, 1973–95, Prof. Emeritus, 1996–, University of Colorado Springs; mem. Authors' Guild; PEN West; Colorado Authors League; Asscn of Literary Scholars and Critics; Western American Literary Asscn. *Publications:* The Myth of the Picaro, 1979; The Cold War of Kitty Pentecost, novel, 1979; Ed., The Interior Country: Stories of the Modern West, 1987; A Sunrise Brighter Still: The Visionary Novels of Frank Waters, 1991; Ed., Higher Elevations: Stories from the West, 1993; Suddenly a Mortal Splendor, novel, 1995; Creative Spirit: Towards a Better World, 2001. Contributions: Founder and Ed.-in-Chief; Writers Forum, 1974–95. *Honours:* Faculty Book Award, Colorado University, 1993; Runner-up, Colorado Book Award, 1996. *Address:* 6030 Twin Rock Ct, Colorado Springs, CO 80918, USA. *Telephone:* (719) 599-4023.

BLACKBURN, Julia Karen Eugenie, BA, FRSL; writer; b. 12 Aug. 1948, London, England; m. 1st 1978 (divorced 1995); one s. one d.; m. 2nd 1999. *Education:* York University. *Career:* mem. Society of Authors, PEN. *Publications:* The White Men, 1978; Charles Waterton, 1989; The Emperor's Last Island, 1991; Daisy Bates in the Desert, 1994; The Book of Colour, 1995; The Leper's Companions, 1999; For a Child: A Selection of the Poems of Thomas Blackburn, 1999; Old Man Goya, 2002. *Literary Agent:* Toby Eady Associates Ltd, Third Floor, 9 Orme Court, London, W2 4RL, England. *Telephone:* (20) 7792-0092. *Fax:* (20) 7792-0879. *E-mail:* toby@tobyeady.demon.co.uk. *Website:* www.tobyeadyassociates.co.uk.

BLACKBURN, Simon W., PhD, DPhil, FBA; British professor of philosophy; b. 12 July 1944, Bristol; m. Angela Bowles 1968; one s. one d. *Education:* Clifton Coll. Bristol and Trinity Coll., Cambridge. *Career:* Research Fellow, Churchill Coll. Cambridge 1967–69; Fellow and Tutor in Philosophy, Pembroke Coll. Oxford 1969–90; Ed. Mind 1984–90; Edna J. Koury Distinguished Prof. of Philosophy, Univ. of NC 1990–2000; Adjunct Prof., ANU 1993–; Prof. of Philosophy, Univ. of Cambridge 2001–. *Publications:* Reason and Prediction 1970, Spreading the Word 1984, Essays in Quasi-Realism 1993, Oxford Dictionary of Philosophy 1994, Ruling Passions 1998, Think 1999, Being Good 2001, Lust 2004. *Honours:* Hon. LLD (Sunderland). *Address:* Faculty of Philosophy, University of Cambridge, Sidgwick Avenue, Cambridge, CB3 0NE (Office); 141 Thornton Road, Cambridge, CB3 9DA, England (Home). *Telephone:* (1223) 528278 (Office). *E-mail:* swb24@cam.ac.uk (Office). *Website:* www.phil.cam.ac.uk/~swb24/ (Office).

BLACKMAN, Malorie; British writer; b. 1962, London; one d. *Education:* Honor Oak Grammar School, Thames Polytechnic. *Career:* database man. for Reuters; full-time writer 1990–. *Publications include:* juvenile: Not So Stupid! 1990, Elaine You're a Brat 1991, Girl Wonder and the Terrific Twins 1991, That New Dress 1991, A New Dress for Maya 1992, Hacker 1992, Girl Wonder's Winter Adventures 1992, Trust Me 1992, Betsey Biggalow the Detective 1992, Betsey Biggalow is Here! 1993, Operation Gadgetman! 1993, Hurricane Betsey 1993, Crazy Crocs 1994, Rachel and the Difference Thief 1994, Magic Betsey 1994, My Friend's a Gris-Quok! 1994, All Aboard 1995, Deadly Dare 1995, Truth! 1995, Jack Sweettooth the 73rd 1995, Whizziwig 1995, Mrs Spoon's Family 1995, A.N.T.I.D.O.T.E. 1996, Betsey's Birthday Surprise 1996, Grandma's Haunted Handbag 1996, Peril on Planet Pelia 1997, The Mellion Moon Mystery 1997, The Computer Ghost 1997, The Secret of the Terrible Hand 1997, Space Race 1997, Pig Heart Boy 1997, Quasar Quartz Quest 1997, Lie Detectives 1998, Aesop's Fables 1998, Words Last Forever 1998, Fangs 1998, Tell Me No Lies 1999, Dangerous Reality 1999, Forbidden Game 1999, Dizzy's Walk 1999, Whizziwig Returns 1999, Hostage 1999, Marty Monster 1999, Noughts and Crosses 2001, Snow Dog 2001, The Monster Crisp-Guzzler 2002, Dead Gorgeous 2002, I Want A Cuddle 2002, Jessica Strange 2002, The Amazing Adventures of Girl Wonder 2003, An Eye for an Eye 2003, Sinclair the Wonder Bear 2003, Cloud Busting 2004, Knife Edge 2004, Ellie and the Cat 2004; contrib. to A Christmas Tree of Stories 1999, Animal Avengers 1999. *Honours:* Young Telegraph's Fully Booked Award, WHSmith Mind Boggling Book Award 1994, Children's Book Award 2001. *Literary Agent:* c/o Random House UK Ltd, 20 Vauxhall Bridge Road, London, SW1V 2SA, England. *Telephone:* (20) 7840-8400. *Fax:* (20) 7233-6117. *Website:* www.randomhouse.co.uk.

BLACKWELL, Julian Toby; British bookseller; b. 10 Jan. 1929; m. Jennifer Jocelyn Darley Wykeham 1953; two s. one d. *Education:* Winchester Coll. and Trinity Coll., Oxford. *Career:* served 5th Royal Tank Regt 1947–49; 21st SAS (TA) 1950–59; Dir and Chair. various Blackwell cos 1956–; Chair. The Blackwell Group Ltd 1980–94; Pres. Blackwell Ltd 1995–, Chair. 1996–99; Chair. Council, ASLIB 1966–68; Pres. Booksellers' Asscn 1980–82; Chair. Thames Business Advice Centre 1986–97, Heart of England TEC 1989–94, Fox FM 1989–98, Cottontail Ltd 1990–; Chair. Son White Memorial Trust 1991–; DL (Oxfordshire) 1988. *Honours:* Hon. DLitt (Robert Gordon) 1997, DUniv (Sheffield Hallam) 1998. *Address:* c/o Blackwell, 50 Broad Street, Oxford, OX1 3BQ, England. *Telephone:* (1865) 792111. *Website:* www.blackwell.com.

BLAINEY, Geoffrey Norman; historian and writer; b. 11 March 1930, Melbourne, Vic., Australia; m. Ann Heriot 1957; one d. *Education:* Wesley College, Melbourne; Queen's College, University of Melbourne. *Career:* Reader in Economic History, 1963–68, Prof., 1968–76, Ernest Scott Prof., 1977–88, Dean, Faculty of Arts, 1982–87, University of Melbourne; Prof. of Australian Studies, Harvard University, 1982–83; Inaugural Chancellor, University of Ballarat, 1994–98; mem. Australia Council, chair., 1977–81; Commonwealth Literary Fund, chair., 1971–73; National Council for Centenary of Federation, chair., 2001. *Publications:* The Peaks of Lyell, 1954; A Centenary History of the University of Melbourne, 1957; Gold and Paper, 1958; Mines in the Spinifex, 1960; The Rush That Never Ended, 1963; A History of Camberwell, 1965; If I Remember Rightly: The Memoirs of W. S. Robinson, 1966; Wesley College: The First Hundred Years (co-author and ed.), 1967; The Tyranny of Distance, 1966; Across a Red World, 1968; The Rise of Broken Hill, 1968; The Steel Master, 1971; The Causes of War, 1973; Triumph of the Nomads, 1975; A Land Half Won, 1980; The Blainey View, 1982; Our Side of the Country, 1984; All for Australia, 1984; The Great Seesaw, 1988; A Game of our Own: The Origins of Australian Football, 1990; Odd Fellows, 1991; Eye on Australia, 1991; Jumping Over the Wheel, 1993; The Golden Mile, 1993; A Shorter History of Australia, 1994; White Gold, 1997; A History of the AMP, 1999; In Our Time, 1999; A Short History of the World, 2000; This Land is All Horizons, 2001. *Honours:* Gold Medal, Australian Literature Society, 1963; Encyclopaedia Britannica Gold Award, New York, 1988. *Address:* PO Box 257, East Melbourne, Vic. 3002, Australia.

BLAIR, Claude, OBE, BA, MA; antiquary and art historian; b. 30 Nov. 1922, Manchester, England. *Education:* University of Manchester. *Career:* Asst, Tower of London Armouries, 1951–56; Hon. Ed., Journal of Arms and Armour Society, 1953–77; Asst Keeper, 1956–72, Deputy Keeper, 1966–72, Keeper, 1972–82, Metalwork, Victoria and Albert Museum, London; Consultant, Christie's, London, 1982–. *Publications:* European Armour, 1958; European and American Arms, 1962; Pistols of the World, 1968; Three Presentation Swords in the Victoria and Albert Museum, 1972; The James A de Rothschild Collection at Waddesdon Manor: Arms, Armour and Base-Metalwork, 1974; Pollard's History of Firearms, 1983; A History of Silver, 1987; The Crown Jewels (gen. ed.), 1998. *Honours:* Fellow, 1956, Gold Medal, 1998, Society of Antiquaries. *Literary Agent:* MBA Literary Agents Ltd, 62 Grafton Way, London W1T 5DW, England. *Address:* 90 Links Road, Ashtead, Surrey KT21 2HW, England.

BLAIR, David Chalmers Leslie, Jr; Writer and Composer; b. 8 April 1951, Long Beach, CA, USA. *Education:* BA, California State University at Long Beach, 1979; Postgraduate Studies, University of Aix-en-Provence, 1979–80. *Publications:* Death of an Artist, 1982; Vive la France, 1993; Death of America, 1994; Mother, 1998; Evening in Wisconsin, 2001; The Girls (& Women) I Have Known, 2001; A Small Snack Shop in Stockholm, 2002. *Address:* 19331 105th Ave, Cadott, WI 54727, USA. *Telephone:* (715) 382-4925. *Website:* www.motorcoat.com/davidblair.

BLAIR, Iain John, (Emma Blair); Novelist; b. 12 Aug. 1942, Glasgow, Scotland; m. 26 April 1975, two s. *Education:* Royal Scottish Acad. of Music and Dramatic Art. *Career:* mem. Romantic Novelists Asscn; British Actors Equity. *Publications:* Where No Man Cries, 1982; Nellie Wildchild, 1983; Hester Dark, 1984; This Side of Heaven, 1985; Jessie Gray, 1985; The Princess of Poor Street, 1986; Street Song, 1986; When Dreams Come True, 1987; A Most Determined Woman, 1988; The Blackbird's Tale, 1989; Maggie Jordan, 1990; Scarlet Ribbons, 1991; The Water Meadows, 1992. *Literary Agent:* Rogers, Coleridge & White Ltd, 20 Powis Mews, London W11 1JN, England. *Address:* The Old Vicarage, Stoke Canon, Near Exeter, Devon EX5 4AS, England.

BLAIR, Jessica (see Spence, William (John Duncan)).

BLAIS, Marie-Claire; Writer, Dramatist and Poet; b. 5 Oct. 1939, Québec, QC, Canada. *Education:* Literature and Philosophy, Laval University. *Career:* mem. Académie Royale de langue et de littérature françaises de Belgique, Brussels. *Publications:* Fiction: La Belle Bete (English trans. as Mad Shadows), 1959; Tete blanche, 1960; Le Jour est noir (English trans. as The Day is Dark), 1962; Une saison dans la vie d'Emmanuel (English trans. as A Season in the Life of Emmanuel), 1965; L'imsoumise (English trans. as The Fugitive), 1966; David Sterne, 1967; Manuscrits de Pauline Archange (English trans. as Manuscripts of Pauline Archange), 1968; Vivre! Vivre!, 1969; Les Apparences (English trans. as Durer's Angel), 1971; Le Loup (English trans. as The Wolf), 1972; Un Joualonais, sa Joualonie (English trans. as St Lawrence Blues), 1973; Fièvre et autres textes dramatiques, 1974; Une liaison parisienne (English trans. as A Literary Affair), 1975; L'Océan suivi de Murmures, 1977; La Nef des sorcières, 1977; Les Nuits de l'Underground (English trans. as Nights in the Underground), 1978; Le Sourd dans la ville (English trans. as Deaf to the City), 1980; Visions d'Anna (English trans. as Anna's World), 1982; Pierre ou La Guerre du printemps 81, 1984; Sommeil d'hiver, 1986; L'Ile, 1988; L'Ange de la solitude (English trans. as Angel of Solitude), 1989; Pierre, 1991; Soifs (English trans. as These Festive Nights), 1995; Dans la foudre et la lumière, 2002. Poetry: Pays voiles, 1964; Existences, 1964. Autobiography: Parcours d'un écrivain notes américaines, 1993. *Honours:* Prix de la Langue française, 1961; Guggenheim Fellowship, 1963; Prix France-Québec, Paris, 1966; Prix Médicis Étranger, 1966; Gov.-Gen. of Canada Prizes, 1969, 1979, 1996; Order of Canada, 1975; Prix Belgique-Canada, Brussels, 1976; Prix Athanase-David, Québec, 1982; Prix de l'Académie Française, Paris, 1983; Commemorative Medal for the 125th Anniversary of the Confederation of Canada, 1982; Ordre nat. du Québec, 1995; W. O. Mitchell Prize, Toronto, 2000; Prix de la Fondation Prince Pierre de Monaco, 2002. *Address:* 4411 Rue St Denis, Apt 401, Montréal, QC H2J 2L2, Canada.

BLAISE, Clark (Lee); Writer and Teacher; b. 10 April 1940, Fargo, ND, USA; m. Bharati Mukherjee, 19 Sept. 1963, two s. *Education:* AB, Denison University, 1961; MFA, University of Iowa, 1964. *Career:* Prof., Concordia University, 1966–78, York University, 1978–80, Skidmore College, 1980–81, 1982–83; Visiting Prof., 1981–82, Dir, International Writing Program, 1990–, University of Iowa; Writer-in-Residence, David Thompson University Center, 1983, Emory University, 1985; Adjunct Prof., Columbia University, 1986; Visiting Profesor, University of California, Berkeley, 1998–2000; mem. PEN. *Publications:* A North American Education, 1973; Tribal Justice, 1974; Days and Nights in Calcutta (with B. Mukherjee), 1977; Here and Now (co-ed.), 1977; Lunar Attractions, 1978; Lusts, 1983; Resident Alien, 1986; The Sorrow and the Terror: The Haunting Legacy of the Air India Tragedy, 1987; Man and His World, 1992; I Had a Father: A Post-Modern Autobiography, 1993; If I Were Me (novel), 1997; New and Selected Stories, 2000; Time Lord: Sir Sandford Fleming and the Creation of Standard Time, 2000. Contributions: various publications. *Honours:* Guggenheim Fellowship; Canada Council Grants; Hon. PhD, Denison University, 1979. *Literary Agent:* Janklow & Nesbit Associates, 445 Park Ave, New York, NY 10022, USA.

BLAKE, James Carlos; Writer; b. May 1948, Tampico, Mexico. *Career:* mem. Texas Institute of Letters. *Publications:* The Pistoleer, 1995; The Friends of Pancho Villa, 1996; In the Rogue Blood, 1997; Red Grass River: A Legend, 1998; Borderlands: Short Fiction, 1999; Wildwood Boys: A Novel, 2000. *Honours:* First Prize, Quarterly West Novella Competition, 1991; Los Angeles Times Book Prize, 1997; Chautauqua South Fiction Award, Library Foundation, Martin County, FL, 1999; Southwest Book Award, Border Regional Library Asscn, 1999. *Address:* c/o William Morrow & Co, 10 E 53rd St, New York, NY 10022, USA.

BLAKE, Jennifer (see Maxwell, Patricia Anne).

BLAKE, Norman (Francis); Prof., Writer, Ed. and Trans; b. 19 April 1934, Ceara, Brazil. *Education:* BA, 1956, BLitt, 1959, MA, 1960, University of Oxford. *Career:* Lecturer, 1959–68, Senior Lecturer, 1968–73, Prof., 1973–, University of Sheffield. *Publications:* The Saga of the Jomsvikings, 1962; The Phoenix, 1964; Caxton and His World, 1969; William Caxton's Reynard the Fox, 1970; Middle English Religious Prose, 1972; Selections from William Caxton, 1973; Caxton's Quattuor Sermiones, 1973; Caxton's Own Prose, 1975; Caxton: England's First Publisher, 1976; The English Language in Medieval Literature, 1977; Non-Standard Language in English Literature, 1981; Shakespeare's Language, 1983; Textual Tradition of the Canterbury Tales, 1985; William Caxton: A Bibliographical Guide, 1985; Traditional English Grammar and Beyond, 1988; Index of Printed Middle English Prose, 1985; The Language of Shakespeare (with R. E. Lewis and A. S. G. Edwards), 1989; An Introduction to the Languages of Literature, 1990; William Caxton and English Literary Culture, 1991; The Cambridge History of the English Language, Vol. II: 1066–1476, 1992; Introduction to English Language (with J. Moorhead), 1993; William Caxton, 1996; Essays in Shakespeare's Language, 1996; History of the English Language, 1996. *Address:* Dept of English Language and Linguistics, University of Sheffield, Sheffield S10 2TN, England.

BLAKE, Quentin Saxby; Illustrator, Author and Teacher; b. 16 Dec. 1932, Sidcup, Kent, England. *Education:* Downing College, Cambridge; London Inst. of Educ.; Chelsea School of Art. *Career:* freelance illustrator, 1957–; Tutor, Royal College of Art, 1965–86, Head of Illustration Dept, 1978–86, Visiting Prof., 1989–; first Children's Laureate, 1999–2001. *Publications:* illustrations for over 250 works for children and adults, including collaborations with Roald Dahl, Russell Hoban, Joan Aiken, Michael Rosen, John Yeoman. Author: Patrick 1968; Mister Magnolia 1980; Quentin Blake's Nursery Rhyme Book 1983; Mrs Armitage on Wheels 1987; Mrs Armitage Queen of the Road; Mrs Armitage and the Big Wave; The Story of the Dancing Frog; Quentin Blake's ABC 1989; Angelo, 1990; All Join In 1992; Cockatoos 1992; Simpkin 1993; La Vie de la Page, 1995; The Puffin Book of Nonsense Verse, 1996; The Green Ship 1998; Clown, 1998; Drawing for the Artistically Undiscovered (with John Cassidy), 1999; Fantastic Daisy Artichoke 1999; Words and Pictures, 2000; The Laureate's Party, 2000; Zagazoo, 2000; Tell Me a Picture, 2001; Loveykins, 2002; A Sailing Boat in the Sky, 2002; Laureate's Progress, 2002. *Honours:* Senior Fellow, Royal College of Art, 1988; Hon. Fellow, Brighton Univ., 1996, Downing College, Cambridge, 2000; Hon. RA; Chevalier des Arts et des Lettres, 2002; Dr hc, London Inst., 2000, Northumbria, 2001, RCA, 2001; OBE. *Literary Agent:* AP Watt Ltd, 20 John St, London WC1N 2DR, England. *Address:* Flat 8, 30 Bramham Gardens, London SW5 0HF, England. *Website:* www.quentinblake.com.

BLAMIRES, Harry; Lecturer in Higher Education and Author; b. 6 Nov. 1916, Bradford, England; m. Nancy Bowles, 26 Dec. 1940, five s. *Education:* BA, 1938, MA, 1945, University College, Oxford. *Career:* Head, English Dept, 1948–72, Dean, Arts and Sciences, 1972–76, King Alfred's College, Winchester; Clyde Kilby Visiting Prof. of English, Wheaton College, Wheaton, IL, 1987; mem. Society of Authors. *Publications:* Repair the Ruins, 1950; The Devil's Hunting Grounds, 1954; Cold War in Hell, 1955, Blessing Unbounded, 1955; The Faith and Modern Error, 1956; The Will and the Way, 1957; The Kirkbride Conversations, 1958; The Offering of Man, 1959; The Christian Mind, 1963; A Defence of Dogmatism, 1965; The Bloomsday Book: Guide to Joyce's Ulysses, 1966; Word Unheard: Guide Through Eliot's Four Quartets, 1969; Milton's Creation, 1971; A Short History of English Literature, 1974; Where Do We Stand?, 1980; Twentieth-Century English Literature, 1982; Guide to 20th Century Literature in English, 1983; On Christian Truth, 1983; Words Made Flesh, 1985, UK edn as The Marks of the Maker, 1987; The Victorian Age of Literature, 1988; Meat Not Milk, 1988; The Age of Romantic Literature, 1989; A History of Literary Criticism, 1991; The Queen's English, 1994; The Cassell Guide to Common Errors in English, 1997; The Penguin Guide to Plain English, 2000; The Post-Christian Mind, 2001; Compose Yourself—and Write Good English, 2003. *Honours:* Hon. DLitt, Southampton University, 1993. *Address:* Pinfold, 3 Glebe Close, Keswick, Cumbria CA12 5QQ, England.

BLANCHARD, Stephen (Thomas); Writer; b. 8 Dec. 1950, Hull, Yorkshire, England; m. Sarah Rookledge, two s. one d. *Education:* University of Liverpool, 1968–70. *Career:* mem. Society of Authors. *Publications:* Fiction: Gagarin and I, 1995; Wilson's Island, 1997. Contributions: Stories and articles to magazines. *Honours:* McKitterick Prize, Society of Authors, 1996; First Novel Award, Yorkshire Post, 1996. *Literary Agent:* Rachel Calder, Tessa Sayle Agency, 11 Jubilee Pl., London SW3 3TE, England. *Address:* 74 Rectory Grove, London SW4 0ED, England.

BLAND, Peter; Poet, Reviewer, Actor and Dramatist; b. 12 May 1934, Scarborough, Yorkshire, England; m. Beryl Matilda Connolly, 27 April 1956, one s. two d. *Education:* English, Victoria University of Wellington, New Zealand. *Career:* Journalist and Talks Producer, New Zealand Broadcasting Corp, 1960–64; Co-Founder, Dir, Actor and Dramatist, Downstage Theatre, Wellington, 1964–68; Actor, West End plays and numerous television productions, London; Leading role, Came a Hot Friday (New Zealand film), 1985. *Publications:* Poetry: My Side of the Story, 1964; The Man with the Carpet Bag, 1972; Mr Maui, 1976; Stone Tents, 1981; The Crusoe Factor, 1985; Selected Poems, 1987; Paper Boats, 1991; Selected Poems, 1998; Ports of Call, 2003. Plays: Father's Day, 1967; George the Mad Ad Man, 1967. Contributions: anthologies and periodicals. *Honours:* Macmillan-Brown Prize for Creative Writing, Victoria University of Wellington, 1958; Melbourne Arts Festival Literary Award, 1960; Queen Elizabeth II Arts Council Drama Fellowship, 1968; Cholmondeley Award for Poetry, 1977; Best Film Actor Award, Guild of Film and Television Arts, New Zealand, 1985; Poetry Book Society Recommendation, 1987; Observer/Arvon Foundation International Poetry Prize, 1990. *Address:* c/o Carcanet Press, Fourth Floor, Alliance House, Cross Street, Manchester M2 7AP, England.

BLANDIANA, Ana, BA; Romanian writer and poet; b. 25 March 1942, Timişoara; m. Romulus Rusan 1960. *Education:* Univ. of Cluj. *Career:* columnist Romania literary magazine 1974–88; has given numerous lectures on cultural and civic issues in the UK, France, Netherlands, Norway, Austria and Germany; has participated in int. seminars on human rights and multiculturalism in Canada, France, Greece, Germany, USA, Norway and Russian Fed., confs at Univ. of Rome 1991, The German Rectors' Conf., Bonn 1992, Free Univ. of Berlin 1992, Univ. of Paris, Sorbonne 1993, Univ. of Vienna 1994, Univ. of Prague 1994, Univ. of Heidelberg, Austria 1995, INALCO, Paris 1996, and poetry festivals in Finland, Paris, Romania, USA, Italy, UK, France, Austria and Norway; Pres. Academia Civica Foundation, Romanian PEN Centre (has participated in several int. confs). *Publications include:* Poetry: First Person in the Plural 1964, The Vulnerable Heel 1966, The Third Sacrament 1960, 50 Poems 1970, October, November, December 1982, Poems 1974, The Sleep in the Sleep 1977, Events in my Garden 1980,

The Eye of the Cricket 1981, The Sand Hour 1984, The Prey Star 1986, Other Events in my Garden 1987, Events on my Street 1988, Poems 1988, The Architecture of the Waves 1990, 100 Poems 1991; Essays: The Witness Quality 1970, I Write, You Write, He/She Writes 1975, The Most Beautiful of the Possible Worlds 1978, Passage of Mirrors 1983, Self-portrait with Palimpsest 1985, City of Syllables 1987; Short Stories: Four Seasons 1977, Projects of the Past 1982, Imitation of a Nightmare 1995; Novel: The Drawer with Applause 1992, The Sun After the Death 2002. *Honours:* Poetry Prize, Romanian Writers' Union 1969, 2000, Poetry Prize, Romanian Acad. 1970, Poetry Prize, Asscn of Writers in Bucharest 1980, Int. Herder Prize, Austria 1982, Opera Omnia Prize 2002, Int. Vilenica Prize, Slovenia 2002. *Address:* Academia Civica, Piata Amzei 13 et 2, CP 22-216, Bucharest (Office); Str. Transilvaniei 56, 70778 Bucharest, Romania (Home). *Telephone:* (21) 3129852 (Office). *Fax:* (21) 3125854 (Office); (21) 3111112 (Home). *E-mail:* acivica@fx.ro (Office). *Website:* www.memorialsighet.ro (Office).

BLANNING, Timothy Charles William; academic, writer and editor; b. 21 April 1942, Wells, Somerset, England; m. Nicky Jones 1988; one c. *Education:* BA, 1963, MA, 1967, PhD, 1967, LittD, 1998, University of Cambridge. *Career:* Research Fellow, 1965–68, Fellow, 1968–, Sidney Sussex College, Cambridge; Asst Lecturer in History, 1972–76, Lecturer in History, 1976–87, Reader in Modern European History, 1987–92, Prof. of Modern European History, 1992–, University of Cambridge; mem. Fellow, British Acad., 1990–; FRHistS. *Publications:* Joseph II and Enlightened Despotism, 1970; Reform and Revolution in Mainz 1743–1803, 1974; The French Revolution in Germany, 1983; The Origins of the French Revolutionary Wars, 1986; The French Revolution: Aristocrats versus Bourgeois?, 1987, revised second edn as The French Revolution: Class War or Culture Clash?, 1997; Joseph II, 1994; The French Revolutionary Wars 1787–1802, 1996; The Oxford Illustrated History of Modern Europe (ed.), 1996; The Rise and Fall of the French Revolution (ed.), 1996; History and Biography: Essays in Honour of Derek Beales (ed. with David Cannadine), 1996; Reform in Great Britain and Germany 1750–1850 (ed. with Peter Wende), 1999; The Short Oxford History of Europe: Vol. 8, The Eighteenth Century (ed.), 2000, Vol. 9, The Nineteenth Century (ed.), 2000; The Oxford History of Modern Europe (ed.), 2000; The Culture of Power and the Power of Culture: Old Regime Europe 1660–1789, 2002. Contributions: scholarly books and journals. *Honours:* Pilkington Teaching Prize, University of Cambridge, 2000. *Address:* c/o Faculty of History, University of Cambridge, West Road, Cambridge CB3 9EF, England.

BLASER, Robin (Francis); Prof. of English and Poet; b. 18 May 1925, Denver, CO, USA. *Education:* MA, 1954, MLS, 1955, University of California at Berkeley. *Career:* Prof. of English, Centre for the Arts, Simon Fraser University, Burnaby, BC, Canada, 1972–86. *Publications:* The Moth Poem, 1964; Les Chimères, 1965; Cups, 1968; The Holy Forest Section, 1970; Image-nations 1-12 and The Stadium of the Mirror, 1974; Image-nations 13–14, 1975; Suddenly, 1976; Syntax, 1983; The Faerie Queene and the Park, 1987; Pell Mell, 1988; The Holy Forest, 1993. *Honours:* Poetry Society Award, 1965; Canada Council Grant, 1989–90; Fund for Poetry Award, New York, 1995. *Address:* 1636 Trafalgar St, Vancouver, BC V6K 3R7, Canada.

BLASHFORD-SNELL, John Nicholas; writer, explorer and soldier; b. 22 Oct. 1936, Hereford, England. *Education:* Victoria College, Jersey, Channel Islands; Royal Military Acad., Sandhurst. *Publications:* A Taste for Adventure, 1978; Operation Drake, 1981; In the Wake of Drake (with M. Cable), 1982; Mysteries: Encounters with the Unexplained, 1983; Operation Raleigh: The Start of an Adventure, 1985; Operation Raleigh: Adventure Challenge (with Ann Tweedy), 1988; Operation Raleigh: Adventure Unlimited (with Ann Tweedy), 1990; Something Lost Behind the Ranges, 1994; Mammoth Hunt (with Rula Lenska), 1996; Kota Mama: Retracing the Lost Trade Routes of Ancient South American Peoples (with Richard Snailham), 2000; East to the Amazon (with Richard Snailham, 2002). Contributions: periodicals. *Address:* c/o Scientific Exploration Society, Expedition Base, Motcombe, Dorset SP7 9PB, England.

BLATTY, William Peter, MA, DHumLitt; American writer and screenwriter; b. 7 Jan. 1928, New York, NY; m. Julie Alicia Witbrodt 1983; three s. three d. *Education:* Georgetown Univ., George Washington Univ. and Seattle Univ. *Career:* served in USAF 1951–54; ed. with US Information Agency 1955–57; Publicity Dir Univ. Southern Calif. 1957–58; Public Relations Dir Loyola Univ., Los Angeles 1959–60. *Screenplays:* The Man from the Diner's Club 1961, Promise Her Anything 1962, John Goldfarb, Please Come Home 1963, A Shot in the Dark 1964, The Great Bank Robbery 1967, What Did You Do in the War, Daddy? 1965, Gunn 1967, Darling Lili 1968, Twinkle, Twinkle, 'Killer' Kane (Golden Globe for Best Movie Screenplay) 1973, Mastermind 1976, The Ninth Configuration (also dir) 1978, The Exorcist (Golden Globe for Best Movie Screenplay 1980) 1973, The Exorcist III 1990. *Writing for television:* Watts Made Out of Thread (series episode) (American Film Festival Blue Ribbon and Gabriel Award). *Publications:* Which Way to Mecca, Jack? 1959, John Goldfarb, Please Come Home 1963, I, Billy Shakespeare 1965, Twinkle, Twinkle, 'Killer' Kane 1966, The Exorcist 1970, I'll Tell Them I Remember You (autobiog.) 1973, The Exorcist: From Novel to Film 1974, The Ninth Configuration 1978, Legion 1983, Demons Five, Exorcists Nothing 1996, Elsewhere 1999. *Honours:* Acad. Award of Acad. Motion Picture, Arts and Sciences 1973, Acad. of Fantasy, Science Fiction and Horror award 1980, Stoker Award for Lifetime Achievement 1998.

BLAYNE, Diana (see Kyle, Susan (Eloise Spaeth)).

BLEAKLEY, David (Wylie); Educator, Public Servant and Writer; b. 11 Jan. 1925, Belfast, Northern Ireland; m. Winifred Wason, 5 Aug. 1949, three s. *Education:* Diploma in Economics and Political Science, Ruskin College, Oxford, 1949; BA, 1951, MA, 1955, Queen's University, Belfast. *Career:* Principal, Belfast Further Education Centre, 1955–58; MP, Labour Party, Victoria, Parliament of Northern Ireland, Belfast, 1958–65; Lecturer in Industrial Relations, Kivukoni College, Dar-es-Salaam, 1967–69; Head, Dept of Economics and Political Studies, Methodist College, Belfast, 1969–79; Minister of Community Relations, Government of Northern Ireland, 1971; Mem., Northern Ireland Labour Party, East Belfast, Northern Ireland Assembly, 1973–75; Visiting Senior Lecturer in Peace Studies, University of Bradford, 1974–; Chief Exec., Irish Council of Churches, 1980–92; Pres., Church Mission Society, 1983–97. *Publications:* Ulster Since 1800: Regional History Symposium, 1958; Young Ulster and Religion in the Sixties, 1964; Peace in Ulster, 1972; Faulkner: A Biography, 1974; Saidie Patterson: Irish Peacemaker, 1980; In Place of Work, 1981; The Shadow and Substance, 1983; Beyond Work: Free to Be, 1985; Will the Future Work?, 1986; Europe: A Christian Vision, 1992; Ageing and Ageism in a Technological Society, 1994; Peace in Ireland: Two States, One People, 1995; C. S. Lewis: At Home in Ireland, 1998. Contributions: BBC and periodicals. *Honours:* Appointed Privy Councillor, 1971; Hon. MA, Open University, 1975; CBE, 1984. *Address:* 8 Thornhill, Bangor, County Down BT19 1RD, Northern Ireland.

BLEASDALE, Alan; playwright and novelist; b. 23 March 1946; m. Julia Moses 1970; two s. one d. *Education:* Padgate Teachers Training College. *Career:* Teacher 1967–75. *Publications:* Scully, 1975; Who's Been Sleeping in My Bed, 1977; No More Sitting on the Old School Bench, 1979; Boys From the Blackstuff, 1982; Are You Lonesome Tonight?, 1985; No Surrender, 1986; Having a Ball, 1986; It's a Madhouse, 1986; The Monocled Mutineer, 1986; GBH (television series), 1991; On the Ledge, 1993; Jake's Progress (television series), 1995; Oliver Twist, 1999. *Honours:* BAFTA Writer's Award, 1982; RTS Writer's Award, 1982; Broadcasting Press Guild TV Award for Best Series, 1982; Best Musical, London Evening Standard Drama Awards, 1985; Hon. DLitt (Liverpool Polytechnic), 1991; Best Writer, Monte Carlo International TV Festival, 1996. *Address:* c/o Harvey Unna and Stephen Durbridge Ltd, 24 Pottery Lane, Holland Park, London W11 4LZ, England.

BLEDSOE, Lucy Jane; Writer and Ed.; b. 1 Feb. 1957, Portland, Oregon, USA; Companion: Patricia E. Mullan. *Education:* Williams College, 1975–77; BA, University of California at Berkeley, 1979. *Career:* Instructor, University of California Graduate Program of Creative Writing; Instructor, Creative Writing workshops in adult literacy programmes; mem. Media Alliance; National Writers Union; PEN. *Publications:* Sweat: Stories and a Novella, 1995; The Big Bike Race, 1995; Working Parts, 1997; Tracks in the Snow, 1997. Editor: Gay Travels, 1998; Lesbian Travels, 1998. Contributions: Books and magazines. *Honours:* PEN Syndicated Fiction Award, 1985; Creative Writing Fellowship, Money for Women/Barbara Deming Memorial Fund, 1989; Gay/Lesbian/Bisexual Award for Literature, 1998. *Address:* 1226 Cedar St, Berkeley, CA 94702, USA.

BLICKER, Seymour; Writer; b. 12 Feb. 1940, Montréal, QC, Canada; m. Susan Wanda Colman, 13 June 1963, three s., one d. *Education:* BA, Loyola College, 1962. *Career:* Special Lecturer, Creative Writing, Concordia University, 1978–90; mem. Writers Guild of Canada; Playwrights Union of Canada; Acad. of Canadian Cinema and Television; Writers Guild of America West. *Publications:* Fiction: Blues Chased a Rabbit, 1969; Shmucks, 1972; The Last Collection, 1976. Stage Plays: Up Your Alley, 1987; Never Judge a Book By Its Cover, 1987; Pals, 1995; Home Free, 1998; Pipe Dreams, 1999; Found Money, 2003. *Honours:* Canada Council Senior Arts Fellowship, 1974; British Council International New Playwriting Award for the Americas Region, 1997. *Address:* 7460 Kingsley Rd, No. 804, Montréal, QC H4W 1P3, Canada. *E-mail:* seymour.blicker@sympatico.ca.

BLOCH, Chana; Prof. of English, Poet, Trans., Critic and Essayist; b. 15 March 1940, New York, NY, USA; m. Ariel Bloch 26 Oct. 1969 (divorced); two s. *Education:* BA, Cornell Univ., 1961; MA, 1963, MA, 1965, Brandeis Univ.; PhD, Univ. of California at Berkeley, 1975. *Career:* Instructor of English, Hebrew Univ., Jerusalem, 1964–67; Assoc. in Near Eastern Studies, Univ. of California at Berkeley, 1967–69; Instructor, 1973–75, Asst Prof., 1975–81, Assoc. Prof., 1981–87, Chair., Dept of English, 1986–89, Prof. of English, 1987–2003, Dir, Creative Writing Program, 1993–2001, Prof. Emerita, 2003–, Mills College, Oakland, CA; mem. PEN; Poetry Society of America; MLA. *Publications:* Poetry: The Secrets of the Tribe, 1981; The Past Keeps Changing, 1992; Mrs Dumpty, 1998. Literary Criticism: Spelling the Word: George Herbert and the Bible, 1985. Translator: Dahlia Ravikovitch: A Dress of Fire, 1978; Yehuda Amichai: The Selected Poetry (with Stephen Mitchell), 1986; Dahlia Ravikovitch: The Window: New and Selected Poems (with Ariel Bloch), 1989; The Song of Songs: A New Translation, Introduction and Commentary (with Ariel Bloch), 1995; Open Closed Open, by Yehuda Amichai (with Chana Kronfeld), 2000. Contributions: poetry, trans, criticism and essays in various anthologies and periodicals. *Honours:* Discovery Award, Poetry Centre, New York, 1974; Trans. Award, Columbia University, 1978; National Endowment for the Humanities Fellowship, 1980; Book of the Year Award, Conference on Christianity and Literature, 1986; Writers Exchange Award, Poets and Writers, 1988; Yaddo Residencies, 1988, 1990, 1993, 1994, 1995, 1996, 1997, 1999, 2001; MacDowell Colony Residencies, 1988, 1992, 1993, 2000; Djerassi Foundation Residencies, 1989, 1991; National Endowment for the Arts Fellowships, 1989–90, 1999; Felix Pollak Prize, 1998; California Book Award Silver Medal in Poetry, 1999; PEN Award for Poetry in Trans., 2001. *Address:* c/o Dept of English, Mills College, Oakland, CA 94613, USA. *E-mail:* chana@mills.edu.

BLOCK, Lawrence; American novelist; m. Lynne. *Career:* mem. MWA (past pres.), Private Eye Writers of America (past pres.). *Publications:* You Could Call it Murder 1961, Mona 1961, Cinderella Sims 1961, Coward's Kiss 1961, The Girl With the Long Green Heart 1965, Deadly Honeymoon 1967, After the First Death 1969, The Specialists 1969, Such Men are Dangerous 1969, The Triumph of Evil 1971, Ronald Rabbit is a Dirty Old Man 1971, Not Comin' Home to You 1974, Ariel 1980, Random Walk 1988, Small Town 2003; Evan Tanner series: The Thief who Couldn't Sleep 1966, The Canceled Czech 1966, Tanner's Twelve Swingers 1967, Two for Tanner (aka The Scoreless Thai) 1968, Tanner's Tiger 1968, Here Comes a Hero 1968, Me Tanner, You Jane 1970, Tanner on Ice 1998; Matthew Scudder series: The Sins of the Fathers 1976, In the Midst of Death 1976, Time to Murder and Create 1977, A Stab in the Dark 1981, Eight Million Ways to Die 1982, When the Sacred Ginmill Closes 1986, Out on the Cutting Edge 1989, A Ticket to the Boneyard 1990, A Dance at the Slaughterhouse 1991, A Walk Among the Tombstones 1992, The Devil Knows You're Dead 1993, A Long Line of Dead Men 1994, Even the Wicked 1996, Everybody Dies 1998, Hope to Die 2001; Bernie Rhodenbarr series: Burglars Can't be Choosers 1977, The Burglar in the Closet 1978, The Burglar Who Liked to Quote Kipling 1979, The Burglar Who Studied Spinoza 1980, The Burglar Who Painted Like Mondrian 1983, The Burglar Who Traded Ted Williams 1994, The Burglar Who Thought he was Bogart 1995, The Burglar in the Library 1997, The Burglar in the Rye 1999, The Burglar on the Prowl 2004; Chip Harrison series: No Score 1970, Chip Harrison Scores Again 1971, Make Out With Murder (aka The Five Little Rich Girls) 1974, The Topless Tulip Caper 1975; Keller series: Hit Man 1998, Hit List 2000; contrib. anthologies; articles and short stories in American Heritage, Redbook, Playboy, Cosmopolitan, GQ, New York Times. *Honours:* Nero Wolfe Award 1979, four Shamus Awards, Japanese Maltese Falcon awards 1986, 1989, four Edgar Awards, Philip Marlowe Award, Life Achievement award, Private Eye Writers of America, MWA Grand Master, two Société 813 trophies, presented with the key to the city of Muncie, IN. *Address:* 299 W 12th Street, Suite 12-D, New York, NY 10014, USA. *E-mail:* LawBloc@aol.com. *Website:* www.lawrenceblock.com.

BLOND, Anthony, MA; author; b. 20 March 1928, Sale, England; m. Laura Hesketh 1981, one s. *Education:* New Coll., Oxford. *Career:* Active with Anthony Blond Ltd 1957–71; Dir, Blond and Brigg Ltd publishers, London 1971–90. *Publications:* The Publishing Game 1971, Family Business 1978, The Lord My Light 1982, A Book on Books 1983, Blond's Roman Emperors 1994, Carnets d'un Promeneur Anglais en France 1997; contrib. to Literary Review, Spectator. *Literary Agent:* Gillon Aitken Associates Ltd, 18–21 Cavaye Place, London, SW10 9PT, England. *Telephone:* (20) 7373-8672. *Fax:* (20) 7373-6002. *Address:* 9 rue Thiers, 87300 Bellac, France.

BLONDEL, Jean Fernand Pierre; Political Scientist and Writer; b. 26 Oct. 1929, Toulon, France; m. 1st Michele Hadet, 1954, divorced; m. 2nd Teresa Ashton, 1982, two d. *Education:* Diploma, Institut d'etudes politiques, Paris, 1953; Law, University of Paris; BLitt, St Antony's College, Oxford, 1955; Graduate Studies, University of Manchester. *Career:* Lecturer in Political Institutions, University of Keele, 1958–63; Fellow, American Council of Learned Societies, 1963–64; Founding Prof., Dept of Government, University of Essex, 1964–83; Co-Founder and Dir, European Consortium of Political Research, 1970–78; Scholar, Russell Sage Foundation, 1984–85; Prof. of Political Science, 1985–94, Prof. Fellow, 1994–, European University Institute, Florence; Visiting Prof., Univ. of Siena, 1995–; mem. American Political Science Asscn; Asscn Française de Science Politique; British Political Studies Asscn; Royal Swedish Acad. of Sciences. *Publications:* Voters, Parties and Leaders, 1963; An Introduction to Conservative Government, 1969; Comparative Legislatures, 1973; Political Parties, 1978; World Leaders, 1980; The Discipline of Politics, 1982; The Organisation of Governments, 1982; Government Ministers in the Contemporary World, 1985; Political Leadership, 1993; Governing Together (ed. with F. Muller-Rommel), 1993; Comparative Government, second edn, 1995; Party and Government (ed. with M. Cotta), 1996; People and Parliament in the European Union (with R. Sinnott and P. Svensson), 1998; Democracy, Governance and Economic Performance (ed. with I. Marsh and T. Inoguchi), 1999; The Nature of Party Government (ed. with M. Cotta), 2000; Cabinets in Eastern Europe (with F. Muller-Rommel), 2001. Contributions: Professional journals. *Honours:* Hon. Doctorates, University of Salford, 1990, University of Essex, 1992, Catholic University of Louvain, 1992, University of Turku, 1995. *Address:* c/o European University Institute, Via dei Roccettini 9, 50016 San Domenico di Fiesole, Italy. *E-mail:* jean .blondel@iue.it.

BLOOM, Harold, PhD; American professor of humanities; *Sterling Professor of Humanities, Yale University*; b. 11 July 1930, New York; m. Jeanne Gould 1958; two s. *Education:* Cornell and Yale Univs. *Career:* mem. Faculty, Yale Univ. 1955–, Prof. of English 1965–77, DeVane Prof. of Humanities 1974–77, Prof. of Humanities 1977–, Sterling Prof. of Humanities 1983–; Visiting Prof. Hebrew Univ. Jerusalem 1959, Breadloaf Summer School 1965–66, Soc. for Humanities, Cornell Univ. 1968–69; Visiting Univ. Prof. New School of Social Research, New York 1982–84; Charles Eliot Norton Prof. of Poetry, Harvard Univ. 1987–88; Berg Visiting Prof. of English, New York Univ. 1988–94; mem. American Acad. and Inst. of Arts and Letters, American Philosophical Soc.; Guggenheim Fellow 1962; Fulbright Fellow 1955. *Publications:* Shelley's Mythmaking 1959, The Visionary Company 1961, Blake's Apocalypse 1963, Commentary to Blake 1965, Yeats 1970, The Ringers in the Tower 1971, The Anxiety of Influence 1973, Wallace Stevens: The Poems of Our Climate 1977, A Map of Misreading 1975, Kabbalah and Criticism 1975, Poetry and Repression 1976, Figures of Capable Imagination 1976, The Flight to Lucifer: A Gnostic Fantasy 1979, Agon: Towards a Theory of Revisionism 1981, The Breaking of the Vessels 1981, The Strong Light of the Canonical 1987, Freud: Transference and Authority 1988, Poetics of Influence: New and Selected Criticism 1988, Ruin the Sacred Truths 1989, The Book of J 1990, The American Religion 1991, The Western Canon 1994, Omens of Millennium 1996, Shakespeare: The Invention of the Human 1998, How to Read and Why 2000, Stories and Poems for Extremely Intelligent Children of All Ages 2000, Genius: A Mosaic of One Hundred Exemplary Creative Minds 2002, Hamlet: Poem Unlimited 2003, Best Poems of the English Language: Chaucer to Hart Crane 2003, Where Shall Wisdom be Found? 2004. *Honours:* Hon. Dr St Michael's Coll., Univ. of Rome, Univ. of Bologna, Univ. of Coimbra, Boston Coll., Yeshiva Univ., Univ. of Mass. at Dartmouth, Univ. of Córdoba; Newton Arvin Award 1967; Melville Cane Award, Poetry Soc. of America 1970; Zabel Prize, American Inst. of Arts and Letters 1982; MacArthur Foundation Fellowship 1985; Christian Gauss Prize 1989, Gold Medal for Criticism, American Acad. of Arts and Letters 1999, Int. Prize of Catalonia 2002, Alfonso Reyes Prize (Mexico) 2003. *Address:* 179 Linden Street, New Haven, CT 06511, USA.

BLOUNT, Roy Alton, Jr, (Noah Sanders, C. R. Ways); Writer, Poet and Screenwriter; b. 4 Oct. 1941, Indianapolis, IN, USA; m. 1st Ellen Pearson, 6 Sept. 1964, divorced March 1973, one s. one d.; m. 2nd Joan Ackermann, 1976, divorced 1990. *Education:* BA, magna cum laude, Vanderbilt University, 1963; MA, Harvard University, 1964. *Career:* Staff., Decatur-DeKalb News, GA, 1958–59, Morning Telegraph, New York City, 1961, New Orleans Times-Picayune, 1963; Reporter, Editorial Writer, Columnist, Atlanta Journal, 1966–68; Staff Writer, 1968–74, Assoc. Ed., 1974–75, Sports Illustrated; Contributing Ed., Atlantic Monthly, 1983–. *Publications:* About Three Bricks Shy of a Load, 1974, revised edn as About Three Bricks Shy–and the Load Filled Up: The Story of the Greatest Football Team Ever, 1989; Crackers: This Whole Many-Sided Thing of Jimmy, More Carters, Ominous Little Animals, Sad-Singing Women, My Daddy and Me, 1980; One Fell Soup, or, I'm Just a Bug on the Windshield of Life, 1982; What Men Don't Tell Women, 1984; Not Exactly What I Had in Mind, 1985; It Grows on You: A Hair-Raising Survey of Human Plumage, 1986; Soupsongs/Webster's Ark, 1987; Now, Where Were We?, 1989; First Hubby, 1990; Camels Are Easy, Comedy's Hard, 1991; Roy Blount's Book of Southern Humor, 1994; Be Sweet: A Conditional Love Story, 1998; If Only You Knew How Much I Smell You, 1998; I Am Puppy, Hear Me Yap, 2000; Am I Pig Enough For You Yet?, 2001. Contributions: many anthologies and periodicals. *Address:* c/o Atlantic Monthly, 77 N Washington St, Suite 5, Boston, MA 02114, USA.

BLUME, Judy; Author; b. 12 Feb. 1938, Elizabeth, NJ, USA; m. George Cooper; three c. *Education:* BS, Education, New York Univ., 1961. *Career:* f. and trustee, The Kids Fund; board mem., Authors' Guild, Society of Children's Book Writers and Illustrators, National Coalition Against Censorship. *Publications:* Children's Fiction: The One in the Middle is the Green Kangaroo; The Pain and the Great One; Freckle Juice; Iggie's House; Blubber; Are You There God? It's Me, Margaret; Then Again, Maybe I Won't; It's Not the End of the World; Starring Sally J. Freedman As Herself; Deenie; Just As Long As We're Together; Here's to You, Rachel Robinson; Tales of a Fourth Grade Nothing; Superfudge; Fudge-a-mania; Otherwise Known as Sheila the Great; Tiger Eyes; Forever; Double Fudge, 2002. Non-fiction: Letters to Judy: What Kids Wish They Could Tell You; Places I Never Meant To Be, Original Stories by Censored Writers (ed.). Adult Fiction: Wifey; Smart Women; Summer Sisters. *Honours:* Distinguished Alumna, New York Univ., 1996; American Library Asscn Margaret A. Edwards Award for Lifetime Achievement, 1996; numerous other awards. *Address:* c/o Pan MacMillan Ltd, 20 New Wharf Rd, London N1 9RR, England. *Website:* www.judyblume.com.

BLUMENTHAL, Michael Charles; writer, poet and academic; b. 8 March 1949, Vineland, NJ, USA; one s. *Education:* BA, Philosophy, SUNY at Binghamton, 1969; JD, Cornell University, 1974. *Career:* Bingham Distinguished Poet-in-Residence, University of Louisville, 1982; Briggs-Copeland Lecturer, Asst Prof. of Poetry, 1983–88, Assoc. Prof. of English, Dir of Creative Writing, 1988–93, Harvard University; Senior Fulbright Lecturer in American Literature, Eötvös Lorand University, Budapest, 1992–95; Distinguished Visiting Writer-in-Residence, Boise State University, 1996;

Assoc. Prof. of English, University of Haifa, 1996; Visiting Writer, Southwest Texas State University, 1997–98; Distinguished Visiting Poet-in-Residence, Wichita State University, 1999; Distinguished Writer-in-Residence, Santa Clara University, CA, 2001; Lecturer in Creative Non-Fiction, American University of Paris, 2001–02; Distinguished Visiting Prof. of American Literature, Université Jean Monnet, Saint-Etienne, France, 2001–; mem. Associated Writing Programs; PEN American Center; Poetry Society of America; Poets and Writers. *Publications:* Sympathetic Magic, 1980; Days We Would Rather Know, 1984; Laps, 1984; Against Romance, 1987; The Wages of Goodness, 1992; To Wed & To Woo: Poets on Marriage (ed.), 1992; Weinstock Among the Dying, 1993; When History Enters the House: Central European Essays, 1998; Dusty Angel, 1999; All My Mothers and Fathers, 2002. Contributions: Reviews, quarterlies and journals. *Honours:* First Book Prize, Water Mark Poets of North America, 1980; Juniper Prize, University of Massachusetts, 1984; Lavan Younger Poets Prize, Acad. of American Poets, 1986; Guggenheim Fellowship, 1989; Harold U. Ribelow Prize for Jewish Fiction, Hadassah magazine, 1994. *Address:* 28 rue Thubaneau, 13001, Marseille, France. *E-mail:* mcblume@attglobal.net.

BLUNDELL, Sue; Lecturer and Writer; b. 4 Aug. 1947, Manchester, England. *Education:* BA, 1968, PhD, 1975, Westfield College, Univ. of London; Dip Cont Ed, Goldsmiths College, London, 1989. *Career:* Part-time Lecturer, Birkbeck College, London, 1979–; Asst Lecturer of Classical Civilization, Open Univ., 1986–2002; academic tutor, Architectural Asscn, London, 1994–. *Publications:* The Origins of Civilisation in Greek and Roman Thought, 1986; Women in Ancient Greece, 1995; The Sacred and the Feminine in Ancient Greece (ed. with Margaret Williamson), 1998; Women in Classical Athens, 1998. *Address:* 59b Goodge St, London W1T 1TJ, England.

BLY, Robert Elwood, MA; American writer and poet; b. 23 Dec. 1926, Madison, Minn.; m. 1st Carolyn McLean 1955 (divorced 1979); m. 2nd Ruth Counsell 1980; five c. *Education:* Harvard Univ. and Univ. of Iowa. *Career:* served US Navy 1944–46; f. and Ed. The Fifties 1958–, later The Sixties and Seventies Press; f. American Writers Against the Vietnam War 1966. *Publications include:* (poems) Silence in the Snowy Fields 1962, The Light Around the Body 1967, Chrysanthemums 1967, Ducks 1968, The Morning Glory: Another Thing That Will Never Be My Friend 1969, The Teeth Mother Naked at Last 1971, Poems for Tennessee (with William Stafford and William Matthews) 1971, Christmas Eve Service at Midnight at St Michael's 1972, Water Under the Earth 1972, The Dead Seal Near McClure's Beach 1973, Sleepers Joining Hands 1973, Jumping out of Bed 1973, The Hockey Poem 1974, Point Reyes Poems 1974, Old Man Rubbing his Eyes 1975, The Loon 1977, Visiting Emily Dickinson's Grave and Other Poems 1979, This Tree Will Be Here for a Thousand Years 1979, Finding An Old Ant Mansion 1981, The Man in the Black Coat Turns 1982, Four Ramages 1983, The Whole Moisty Night 1983, Out of the Rollling Ocean 1984, Mirabai Versions 1984, In the Month of May 1985, A Love of Minute Particulars 1985, Loving a Woman in Two Worlds 1985, Selected Poems (Ed.) 1986, The Moon on the Fencepost 1988, The Apple Found in the Plowing 1989, What Have I Ever Lost By Dying?: Collected Prose Poems 1993, Gratitude to Old Teachers 1993, Meditations on the Insatiable Soul 1994, Morning Poems 1997, Eating the Honey of Words: New and Selected Poems 1999, The Best American Poetry (Ed.) 1999, The Night Abraham Called to the Stars 2001; (prose poems) The Morning Glory 1973, This Body is Made of Eating the Honey of Words: New and Selected Poems 1999, The Best American Poetry (Ed.) 1999, This Body is Made of Camphor and Gopherwood 1977; (criticism) Leaping Poetry 1975; Forty Poems Touching on Recent American History (Ed.) 1967, A Poetry Reading Against the Vietnam War 1966, The Sea and the Honeycomb 1966, The Soul is Here for its Own Joy 1995; trans. of vols of poetry from Swedish, Norwegian, German, Spanish and Hindi. *Honours:* Fulbright Award 1956–57, Amy Lowell Fellow 1964–65, Guggenheim Fellow 1965–66, Rockefeller Foundation Fellow 1967, Nat. Book Award in Poetry 1968. *Address:* 1904 Girard Avenue South, Minneapolis, MN 55403, USA.

BLYTH, Alan; Music Critic and Ed.; b. 27 July 1929, London, England; m. Ursula Zumloh. *Education:* MA, University of Oxford. *Career:* Contributor as Critic, The Times, 1963–76; Assoc. Ed., Opera, 1967–84; Music Ed., Encyclopaedia Britannica, 1971–76; Critic, Daily Telegraph, 1976–89; mem. Critics' Circle; Garrick Club. *Publications:* The Enjoyment of Opera, 1969; Colin Davis, A Short Biography, 1972; Opera on Record (ed.), 1979; Remembering Britten, 1980; Wagner's Ring: An Introduction, 1980; Opera on Record 2 (ed.), 1983; Opera on Record 3 (ed.), 1984; Song on Record (ed.), two vols, 1986, 1988; Choral Music on Record, 1990; Opera on CD, 1992; Opera on Video, 1995. Contributions: Gramophone; BBC. *Address:* 22 Shilling St, Lavenham, Suffolk CO10 9RH, England.

BLYTHE, Julia (see Bogle, Joanna Margaret).

BLYTHE, Ronald George; Author; b. 6 Nov. 1922, Acton, Suffolk, England. *Career:* Lay Canon, St Edmundsbury Cathedral, 2003; mem. FRSL; Society of Authors; John Clare Society, pres.; Fabian Society. *Publications:* A Treasonable Growth, 1960; Immediate Possession, 1961; The Age of Illusion, 1963; Akenfield, 1969; William Hazlett: Selected Writings (ed.), 1970; The View in Winter, 1979; From the Headlands, 1982; The Stories of Ronald Blythe, 1985; Divine Landscapes, 1986; Each Returning Day, 1989; Private Words, 1991; Word from Wormingford, 1997; First Friends, 1998; Going to Meet George, 1998; Talking About John Clare, 1999; Out of the Valley, 2000; The Circling Year, 2001; Talking to the Neighbours, 2002. Other: Critical Studies of Jane Austen, Thomas Hardy, Leo Tolstoy, Henry James, Literature of the Second World War; Ed. of various authors' works. Contributions: Observer; Sunday Times; New York Times; Listener; Atlantic Monthly; London Magazine; Tablet; New Statesman; Bottegue Oscure; Guardian. *Honours:* Heinemann Award, 1969; Society of Authors Travel Scholarship, 1970; Angel Prize for Literature, 1986; Hon. MA, Univ. of East Anglia, 1991; Hon. MLitt, Lambeth, 2001; Hon. DLitt, Univ. of East Anglia, 2001, Essex Univ., 2002. *Address:* Bottengoms Farm, Wormingford, Colchester, Essex, England.

BOARDMAN, Sir John, BA, MA; academic; b. 20 Aug. 1927, Ilford, Essex, England. *Education:* Magdalene College, Cambridge. *Career:* Asst Keeper, Ashmolean Museum, 1955–59; Reader in Classical Archaeology, 1959–78, Lincoln Prof. of Classical Art and Archaeology, 1978–94, University of Oxford; Ed., Journal of Hellenic Studies, 1958–65; Co-Ed., Oxford Monographs in Classical Archaeology; Delegate, OUP, 1979–89; mem. British Acad., fellow, 1969–. *Publications:* S. Marinatos and M. Hirmer: Crete and Mycenae (trans.), 1960; The Cretan Collection in Oxford, 1961; Island Gems, 1963; The Date of the Knossos Tablets, 1963; The Greek Overseas, 1964; Greek Art, 1964; Excavations at Tocra (with J. Dorig, W. Fuchs and M. Hirmer), 1966; Architecture of Ancient Greece (with J. Dorig); Greek Emporio, 1967; Pre-Classical Style and Civilisation, 1967; Engraved Gems: The Ionides Collection, 1968; Archaic Greek Gems, 1968; Eros in Greece (with E. la Rocca), 1978; Greek Sculpture: Archaic Period, 1978; Catalogue of Gems and Finger Rings (with M. L. Vollenweider), Vol. I, 1978; Castle Ashby Corpus Vasorum (with M. Robertson), 1979; Greek Sculpture: Classical Period, 1985; The Parthenon and its Sculptures, 1985; Athenian Red Figure Vases: Classical Period, 1989; The Diffusion of Classical Art in Antiquity, 1994; Greek Sculpture: The Late Classical Period, 1995; Early Greek Vase Painting, 1997; The Great God Pan, 1998; Persia and the West, 2000; The History of Greek Vases, 2001; The Archaeology of Nostalgia, 2002. *Honours:* Knighted, 1989; Prof. of Ancient History, Royal Acad., 1989–; Hon. doctorates, University of Athens, 1990, University of Paris, 1994. *Address:* 11 Park Street, Woodstock, Oxford OX20 1SJ, England.

BOAST, Philip (James); Writer; b. 30 April 1952, London, England; m. Rosalind Thorpe, 20 June 1981, two s. one d. *Education:* Mill Hill School, 1965–69. *Publications:* The Assassinators, 1976; London's Child, 1987; The Millionaire, 1989; Watersmeet, 1990; Pride, 1991; The Londons of London, 1992; Gloria, 1993; London's Daughter, 1994; City, 1994; The Foundling, 1995; Resurrection, 1996; Deus, 1997; Sion, 1998; Era, 2000. Contributions: Science Fiction Monthly. *Literary Agent:* Dorian Literary Agency. *Address:* Upper Thornehill, 27 Church Rd, St Marychurch, Torquay, Devon TQ1 4QY, England. *E-mail:* philipboast@beeb.net.

BOCEK, Alois (see Vanicek, Zdenek).

BOCOCK, Robert James; Sociologist, Writer and Lecturer; b. 29 Sept. 1940, Lincoln, Lincolnshire, England. *Education:* Diploma, University of London, 1963; PhD, Brunel University, 1973. *Career:* Lecturer in Sociology, Brunel University, 1966–79, Open University, Buckinghamshire, 1979–; mem. Asscn of University Teachers; British Sociological Asscn. *Publications:* Ritual in Industrial Society, 1974; Freud and Modern Society, 1976; An Introduction to Sociology, 1980; Sigmund Freud, 1983; Religion and Ideology (ed.), 1985; Hegemony, 1986; Consumption, 1993. Contributions: journals.

BODEN, Anthony Norman; Writer; b. 21 April 1938, Altrincham, Cheshire, England; m. Elizabeth Anne Miles, one s. one d. *Education:* BA, Open University, 1994. *Career:* Royal Air Force, retiring in the rank of Group Captain, 1957–89; Festival Administrator, Three Choirs Festival, Gloucester, 1989–99; mem. Ivor Gurney Society, chair., 1995–2002; Ivor Gurney Estate, trustee; Edward Thomas Fellowship; Friends of the Dymock Poets. *Publications:* Stars in a Dark Night: The Letters of Ivor Gurney to the Chapman Family, 1986; F. W. Harvey: Soldier Poet, 1988; Three Choirs: A History of the Festival, 1992; The Parrys of the Golden Vale, 1998. *Honours:* Officer (Brother) of the Order of St John, 1987. *Address:* Chosen Hay, The Green, Churchdown, Gloucester GL3 2LF, England.

BODEN, Margaret Ann, MA, DSc, PhD, FBA, FRSA; British academic and writer; *Research Professor of Cognitive Science, University of Sussex*; b. 26 Nov. 1936, London, England; m. John Raymond Spiers 1967 (divorced 1981); one s. one d. *Education:* Newnham Coll., Cambridge, Harvard Graduate School. *Career:* Asst Lecturer, Lecturer in Philosophy, Univ. of Birmingham 1959–65; Lecturer 1965–72, Reader 1972–80, Prof. of Philosophy and Psychology 1980–2002, Founder-Dean, School of Cognitive Sciences, later Centre for Cognitive Science 1987, Research Prof. of Cognitive Science 2002–, Univ. of Sussex; co-founder and Dir, Harvester Press 1968–85; mem. 1992–95, Vice-Pres. and Chair. of Council 1993–95, Royal Institution of Great Britain; mem., Bd of Curators, School of Advanced Study, Univ. of London 1995–; Fellow, American Asscn for Artificial Intelligence 1993–, European Co-ordinating Cttee for Artificial Intelligence 1999–, Royal Inst. of Philosophy (council 1987–), British Acad. (council mem. 1988–91, vice-pres. 1989–91); mem. Academia Europea 1993–. *Publications:* Purposive Explanation in Psychology 1972, Artificial Intelligence and Natural Man 1977, Piaget 1977, Minds and Mechanisms 1981, Computer Models of Minds 1988, Artificial Intelligence in Psychology 1989, The Philosophy of Artificial Intelligence (ed.) 1990, The Creative Mind: Myths and Mechanisms 1990, Dimensions of Creativity (ed.) 1994, Artificial Intelligence and the Mind (co-ed.) 1994, The Philosophy of Artificial Life (ed.) 1996, Artificial Intelligence (ed.) 1996; contrib. to scholarly books and journals. *Address:* c/o Centre for Cognitive Science, University of Sussex, Brighton, BN1 9QH, England.

BOGAARDS, Carla; Dutch novelist and poet; b. 12 July 1947, Voorburg. *Publications:* Ik kom op niets 1982, Lena en de mannen 1985, De reigers van Amsterdam 1987, De bruinvisvrouw 1989, Lillian sugar baby 1990, Meisjesgenade 1992, Eigen vlees en bloed 1995, God bewogen 1997, Het gezichtsbedrog 2000. *Literary Agent:* c/o J.M. Meulenhoff BV, PO Box 100, 1000 Amsterdam AC, Netherlands.

BOGDANOR, Vernon (Bernard); Prof. of Government and Writer; b. 16 July 1943, London, England; m. Judith Evelyn Beckett, 1972, divorced 2000, two s. *Education:* BA, PPE, 1964, MA, 1968, Queen's College, Oxford. *Career:* Fellow, 1966–, Senior Tutor, 1979–85, 1996–97, Vice-Principal, 1998–2000, Brasenose College, Oxford; Mem., Council, Hansard Society for Parliamentary Government, 1981–97; Special Adviser, House of Lords Select Committee on European Communities, 1982–83, House of Commons Public Service Committee, 1996; Reader in Government, 1990–96, Prof. of Government, 1996–, University of Oxford; Mem., UK Delegation, Conference on Security and Co-operation in Europe, Oslo, 1991. *Publications:* Devolution, 1979; The People and the Party System, 1981; Multi-Party Politics and the Constitution, 1983; Democracy and Elections (ed.), 1984; The Blackwell Encyclopaedia of Political Institutions (ed.), 1987; Constitutions in Democratics Politics (ed.), 1988; The Blackwell Encyclopaedia of Political Science (ed.), 1992; Comparing Constitutions (co-author), 1995; The Monarchy and the Constitution, 1995; Politics and the Constitution: Essays on British Government, 1996; Power and the People: A Guide to Constitutional Reform, 1997; Devolution in the United Kingdom, 1999; The British Constitution in the Twentieth Century (ed.), 2003. Contributions: scholarly books and journals. *Honours:* FRSA, 1992; Fellow, British Acad., 1997; Hon. Fellow, Society for Advanced Legal Studies, 1997; CBE, 1998. *Literary Agent:* AP Watt Ltd, 20 John St, London WC1N 2DR, England. *Address:* Brasenose College, Oxford OX1 4AJ, England.

BOGLE, Joanna Margaret, (Julia Blythe); Author and Journalist; b. 7 Sept. 1952, Carshalton, Surrey, England; m. James Stewart Lockhart Bogle, 20 Sept. 1980. *Career:* Local Borough Councillor, London Borough of Sutton, 1974–81; Governor, London Oratory School, 1976–86; mem. Vice-Chair., Catholic Writers Guild, 1992–. *Publications:* A Book of Feasts and Seasons, 1986; When the Summer Ended (with Cecylia Wolkowinska), 1991; A Heart for Europe (with James Bogle), 1992; Caroline Chisholm, 1993; Come On In–It's Awful! (ed.), 1994; We Didn't Mean to Start a School, 1998. Contributions: local newspapers, 1970–74; South London News, 1984–86; Catholic Times, 1994–; various national newspapers, 1980–. *Address:* c/o 58 Hanover Gardens, London SE11 5TN, England.

BOHJALIAN, Chris; Novelist and Journalist; b. 12 Aug. 1960, White Plains, New York, USA; m. Victoria Blewer, 13 Oct. 1984. *Career:* mem. PEN. *Publications:* A Killing in the Real World, 1988; Hangman, 1990; Past the Bleachers, 1992; Water Witches, 1995; Midwives, 1997; The Law of Similars, 1999; Trans-Sister Radio, 2000; The Buffalo Soldier, 2002; Idyll Banter, 2003. *Honours:* New England Booksellers Asscn, Discovery Prize; New England Book Award, 2002. *Address:* c/o Ellen Levine Literary Agency, 15 E 26th St, Suite 1801, New York, NY 10010, USA.

BOISVERT, France, (Marguerite de Nevers); French Teacher, Writer and Poet; b. 10 June 1959, Sherbrooke, QC, Canada; one s. *Education:* MLitt, 1986; PhD, French Literature, 2001. *Career:* mem. Union des écrivaines et des écrivains québécois; Asscn internationale des Études québécoises; Élue au Conseil d'administration de l'UNEQ (1992–93, 1995). *Publications:* Les Samourailles (fiction), 1987; Li Tsing-tao ou Le grand avoir (fiction), 1989; Massawippi (poem), 1992; Comme un vol de gerfauts (poem), 1993; Les Vents de l'Aube (prose), 1997; Le Voyageur aux yeux d'onyx (prose), 2002. Contributions: Liberté; La Presse; Le Devoir. *Honours:* Bursaries, Minister of Culture, Québec, 1989, 1990, 1991. *Address:* A/S UNEQ Maison des Écrivains, 3492 Ave Laval, Montréal, QC H2X 3C8, Canada. *E-mail:* france59boisvert@yahoo.ca.

BOK, Derek, MA, JD; American university administrator and academic; *300th Anniversary University President Professor, Harvard University*; b. 22 March 1930, Bryn Mawr, Pa; m. Sissela Ann Myrdal (d. of Karl Gunnar and Alva Myrdal) 1955; one s. two d. *Education:* Univs of Stanford, Harvard, George Washington and Inst. of Political Science, Paris Univ. *Career:* served US Army 1956–58; Asst Prof. of Law, Harvard Univ. 1958–61, Prof. 1961–, Dean 1968–71; Dean, 300th Anniversary Univ. Prof. 1991–; Harvard Law School 1968–71; Pres. Harvard Univ. 1971–91; Dir, Nat. Chair. Common Cause 1999–; Chair. Spencer Foundation 2002–; Facility Chair. Haupen Center for Non-Profit Orgs 2002–. *Publications include:* The First Three Years of the Schuman Plan, Cases and Materials on Labor Law (with Archibald Cox), Labor and the American Community (with John Dunlop), The Federal Government and the University, Beyond the Ivory Tower: Social Responsibilities of the Modern University 1982, Higher Learning 1986, Universities and the Future of America 1990, The Cost of Talent 1993, The State of the Nation 1997, The Shape of the River (jtly) 1998, The Trouble with Government 2001, Universities in the Marketplace: the commercialization of higher education 2004. *Address:* Harvard University, J.F.K. School of Government, Cambridge, MA 02138, USA. *Telephone:* (617) 495-1502.

BOK, Sissela (Ann); Philosopher, Distinguished Fellow and Writer; b. 2 Dec. 1934, Stockholm, Sweden; m. Derek Bok, 7 May 1955, one s. two d. *Education:* BA, 1957, MA, 1958, George Washington University; PhD, Harvard University, 1970. *Career:* Lecturer, Simmons College, Boston, 1971–72, Harvard-MIT Division of Health Sciences and Technology, Cambridge, 1975–82, Harvard University, 1982–84; Assoc. Prof., 1985–89, Prof. of Philosophy, 1989–92, Brandeis University; Fellow, Center for Advanced Study, Stanford, CA, 1991–92; Distinguished Fellow, Harvard Center for Population and Development Studies, 1993–; mem. American Philosophical Asscn; Hasting Center, fellow, 1972–2002, dir, 1976–84, 1994–97; Pulitzer Prize Board, 1988–97, chair., 1996–97. *Publications:* Lying: Moral Choice in Public and Private Life, 1978; Secrets: On the Ethics of Concealment and Revelation, 1982; Alva: Ett kvinnoliv, 1987; A Strategy for Peace, 1989; Alva Myrdal: A Daughter's Memoir, 1991; Common Values, 1996; Mayhem: Violence as Public Entertainment, 1998. Contributions: scholarly publications. *Honours:* George Orwell Award, 1978; Melcher Awards, 1978, 1991; Abram L. Sacher Silver Medallion, Brandeis University, 1985; St Botolph Foundation Award, 2002; Hon. doctorates, Mt Holyoke College, 1985, George Washington University, 1986, Clark University, 1988, University of Massachusetts, 1991, Georgetown University, 1992; Radcliffe College Graduate Society Medal, 1993; Barnard College Medal of Distinction, 1995. *Address:* c/o Harvard Center for Population and Development Studies, Bow St, Cambridge, MA 02138, USA.

BOLAM, Robyn, (Marion Lomax); Prof. of Literature, Poet and Ed.; b. 20 Oct. 1953, Newcastle upon Tyne, England; m. Michael Lomax, 29 Aug. 1974, divorced 1999. *Education:* BA, Librarianship, 1974, BA, English and American Studies, 1979, University of Kent; DPhil, University of York, 1983. *Career:* Part-time Lecturer, King Alfred's College, 1983–86; Creative Writing Fellow, University of Reading, 1987–88; Lecturer, Senior Lecturer in English, 1988–95, Prof. of Literature, 1995–98, St Mary's College, Strawberry Hill, Middlesex; Writer-in-Residence, University of Stockholm, 1998–; mem. National Asscn for Writers in Education; Poetry Society; Society of Authors. *Publications:* Poetry: The Peepshow Girl, 1989; Raiding the Borders, 1996. Non-Fiction: Stage Images and Traditions: Shakespeare to Ford, 1987. Editor: Time Present and Time Past: Poets at the University of Kent 1965–1985, 1985; Four Plays by John Ford, 1995; The Rover, by Alpha Behn, 1995; Out of the Blue (with Steven Harman), 1998. Contributions: Collections of essays, anthologies and periodicals. *Honours:* E. C. Gregory Award, Society of Authors, 1981; First Prize, Cheltenham Festival Poetry Competition, 1981; Hawthornden Fellowship, 1993. *Address:* c/o Bloodaxe Books Ltd, Highgreen, Tarset, Northumberland NE48 1RP, England.

BOLAND, Michael (John); Poet and Civil Servant; b. 14 Nov. 1950, Kingston, Surrey, England. *Career:* Ed., The Arcadian, poetry magazine; mem. PEN; Society of Civil Service Authors; Keats-Shelley Memorial Asscn; Wordsworth Trust; Friends of Coleridge; MIAP. *Publications:* The Midnight Circus; The Trout… Minus One (co-author), 1993. Contributions: Envoi; Purple Patch; Weyfarers; Firing Squad; various anthologies. *Honours:* Patricia Chown Sonnet Award. *Address:* 11 Boxtree Lane, Harrow Weald, Middlesex HA3 6JU, England.

BOLGER, Dermot; Novelist, Dramatist, Poet and Ed.; b. 6 Feb. 1959, Finglas, Ireland; m. Bernadette Bolger, 1988, two c. *Education:* Beneavin College Secondary School. *Career:* Founder-Ed., Raven Arts Press, 1979–92; Exec. Ed., New Island Books, 1992–. *Publications:* Fiction: Night Shift, 1985; The Woman's Daughter, 1987; The Journey Home, 1990; Emily's Shoes, 1992; A Second Life, 1994; Father's Music, 1997; Finbar's Hotel (collaborative novel), 1997; Ladies Night at Finbar's Hotel (collaborative novel), 1999; Temptation, 2000; The Valparaiso Voyage, 2001. Plays: The Lament for Arthur Cleary, 1989; Blinded by the Light, 1990; In High Germany, 1990; The Holy Ground, 1990; One Last White Horse, 1991; The Dublin Bloom, 1994; April Bright, 1995; The Passion of Jerome, 1999; Consenting Adults, 2000. Poetry: The Habit of Flesh, 1979; Finglas Lilies, 1980; No Waiting America, 1981; Internal Exiles, 1986; Leinster Street Ghosts, 1989; Taking My Letters Back: New and Selected Poems, 1998. Editor: The Dolmen Book of Irish Christmas Stories, 1986; The Bright Wave: Poetry in Irish Now, 1986; 16 on 16: Irish Writers on the Easter Rising, 1988; Invisible Cities: The New Dubliners: A Journey through Unofficial Dublin, 1988; Invisible Dublin: A Journey through Its Writers, 1992; The Picador Book of Contemporary Irish Fiction, 1993; 12 Bar Blues (with Aidan Murphy), 1993; The New Picador Book of Contemporary Irish Fiction, 2000; Druids, Dudes and Beauty Queens: The Changing Face of Irish Theatre, 2001. Contributions: anthologies. *Honours:* A. E. Memorial Prize, 1986; Macauley Fellowship, 1987; A. Z. Whitehead Prize, 1987; Samuel Beckett Award, 1991; Edinburgh Fringe First Awards, 1991, 1995; Stewart Parker BBC Award, 1991; Playwright in Asscn, Abbey Theatre, Dublin, 1998. *Literary Agent:* AP Watt Ltd, 20 John St, London WC1N 2DR, England.

BONANNO, David; American; *Joint Editor, American Poetry Review*. *Career:* joint Ed., American Poetry Review 1973–; teaches workshops on poetry and literary publishing; co-ordinator, poetry-in-the-high-schools programme in Philadelphia; mem. Literary Advisory panel, Pennsylvania Council on the Arts. *Publications:* The Body Electric: America's Best Poetry from The American Poetry Review (co-ed.) 2001. *Address:* The American Poetry Review, 117 S 17th Street, Suite 910, Philadelphia, PA 19103, USA (Office). *Telephone:* (215) 496-0439. *Fax:* (215) 569-0808. *E-mail:* dbonanno@aprweb.org. *Website:* www.aprweb.org.

BOND, Edward; British playwright, director and poet; b. 18 July 1934, London; m. Elisabeth Pablé 1971. *Career:* Northern Arts Literary Fellowship 1977–79; resident theatre writer, Univ. of Essex 1982–83. *Publications:* plays: The Pope's Wedding 1962, Saved 1965, Narrow Road to the Deep North 1968, Early Morning 1968, Passion 1971, Black Mass 1971, Lear 1972, The Sea 1973, Bingo 1974, The Fool 1976, A-A-America! (Grandma Faust and The Swing) 1976, Stone 1976, The Bundle 1978, The Woman 1979, The Worlds 1980, The Activist Papers 1980, Restoration 1981, Summer: A Play for Europe 1982, Derek 1983, Human Cannon 1985, The War Plays (Red Black and Ignorant, The Tin Can People, Great Peace) 1985, Jackets 1989, In the Company of Men 1990, September 1990, Olly's Prison 1993, Tuesday 1993, Coffee: A Tragedy 1994, At the Inland Sea (A Play for Young People) 1996, Eleven Vests (A Play for Young People) 1997, The Crime of the Twenty-first Century 1999, The Children (A Play for Two Adults and Sixteen Children) 2000, Chair 2000, Have I None 2000, Existence 2002, Born 2004, The Balancing Act 2004, The Short Electra 2004, Collected Plays (seven vols) 1977–2003 2004; short stories: Fables 1982; opera librettos of music by Hans Werner Henze: We Come to the River 1977, The English Cat 1983; ballet libretto of music by Henze: Orpheus 1982; translations: Chekhov's The Three Sisters 1967, Wedekind's Spring Awakening 1974, Wedekind's Lulu: A Monster Tragedy (with Elisabeth Bond-Pablé) 1992; other: Theatre Poems and Songs 1978, Collected Poems 1978–1985 1987, Notes on Post-Modernism 1990, Letters (five vols) 1994–2001, Notes on Imagination 1995, Selected Notebooks Vol. 1 2000, Vol. 2 2001, The Hidden Plot: Notes on Theatre and the State 2000. *Honours:* Hon. DLitt (Yale) 1977; George Devine Award 1968, John Whiting Award 1968. *Address:* c/o Casarotto Ramsay, National House, 60–66 Wardour Street, London, W1V 3HP, England (Office). *Telephone:* (20) 7287-4450. *Fax:* (20) 7287-9128.

BOND, (Thomas) Michael, OBE; author; b. 13 Jan. 1926, Newbury, Berkshire, England; m. 1st Brenda Mary Johnson 1950 (divorced 1981); one d. one s.; m. 2nd Susan Marfrey Rogers 1981. *Education:* Presentation College. *Publications:* Children's Books: A Bear Called Paddington, 1958; More About Paddington, 1959; Paddington Helps Out, 1960; Paddington Abroad, 1961; Paddington at Large, 1962; Paddington Marches On, 1964; Paddington at Work, 1966; Here Comes Thursday, 1966; Thursday Rides Again, 1968; Paddington Goes to Town, 1968; Thursday Ahoy, 1969; Parsley's Tail, 1969; Parsley's Good Deed, 1969; Parsley's Problem Present, 1970; Parsley's Last Stand, 1970; Paddington Takes the Air, 1970; Thursday in Paris, 1971; Michael Bond's Book of Bears, 1971; Michael Bond's Book of Mice, 1971; The Day the Animals Went on Strike, 1972; Paddington Bear, 1972; Paddington's Garden, 1972; Parsley Parade, 1972; The Tales of Olga de Polga, 1971; Olga Meets Her Match, 1973; Paddington's Blue Peter Story Book, 1973; Paddington at the Circus, 1973; Paddington Goes Shopping, 1973; Paddington at the Seaside, 1974; Paddington at the Tower, 1974; Paddington on Top, 1974; Windmill, 1975; How to Make Flying Things, 1975; Eight Olga Readers, 1975; Olga Carries On, 1976; Paddington Takes the Test, 1979; Paddington's Cartoon Book, 1979; J. D. Polson and the Liberty Head Dime, 1980; J. D. Polson and the Dillogate Affair, 1981; Paddington on Screen, 1981; Olga Takes Charge, 1982; The Caravan Puppets, 1983; Paddington at the Zoo, 1984; Paddington's Painting Exhibition, 1985; Oliver the Greedy Elephant, 1985; Paddington Minds the House, 1986; Paddington at the Palace, 1986; Paddington's Busy Day, 1987; Paddington and the Magical Maze, 1987; Paddington: A Classic Collection, 1997; Paddington and the Christmas Surprise, 1997; Paddington at the Carnival, 1998; Paddington and the Tutti Frutti Rainbow, 1998; Paddington – My Scrapbook, 1999; Paddington's Party Tricks, 2000; Paddington in Hot Water, 2000; Paddington Goes to Hospital, 2001; Paddington Treasury, 2001; Olga Moves House, 2001; Olga Follows Her Nose, 2002; Paddington and the Grand Tour, 2003. Adult Books: Monsieur Pamplemousse, 1983; Monsieur Pamplemousse and the Secret Mission, 1984; Monsieur Pamplemousse on the Spot, 1986; Monsieur Pamplemousse Takes the Cure, 1987; The Pleasures of Paris, Guide Book, 1987; Monsieur Pamplemousse Aloft, 1989; Monsieur Pamplemousse Investigates, 1990; Monsieur Pamplemousse Rests His Case, 1991; Monsieur Pamplemousse Stands Firm, 1992; Monsieur Pamplemousse on Location, 1992; Monsieur Pamplemousse Takes the Train, 1993; Bears and Forebears (autobiog.), 1996; Monsieur Pamplemousse Afloat, 1998; Monsieur Pamplemousse on Probation, 2000; Monsieur Pamplemousse on Vacation, 2002; Monsieur Pamplemousse Hits the Headlines, 2003. *Literary Agent:* The Agency, 24 Pottery Lane, Holland Park, London W11 4LZ, England.

BOND, Nancy Barbara, BA, DipLib; librarian and writer; b. 8 Jan. 1945, Bethesda, MD, USA. *Education:* Mount Holyoke Coll., Coll. of Librarianship, Wales. *Career:* Instructor, part-time, Simmons College, Centre for the Study of Children's Literature, 1979–2001. *Publications:* A String in the Harp, 1976; The Best of Enemies, 1978; Country of Broken Stone, 1980; The Voyage Begun, 1981; A Place to Come Back To, 1984; Another Shore, 1988; Truth to Tell, 1994; The Love of Friends, 1997. *Honours:* International Reading Asscn Award, 1976; Newbery Honour, 1976; Welsh Arts Council Tir na n'Og Award, 1976. *Address:* 109 The Valley Road, Concord, MA 01742, USA.

BONDER, Nilton; Writer and Rabbi; b. 27 Dec. 1957, Porte Alegre, Brazil; m. Esther Bonder, 15 Oct. 1991, one s. one d. *Education:* BS, Catholic University of Rio de Janeiro, 1980; BA, 1982, MA, 1984, Rabbi, 1985, Jewish Theological Seminary, New York City. *Publications:* A Tractade on Impunity, 1993; The Art of Saving Yourself, 1994; The Jewish Way of Problem Solving, 1995; Secret Portals, 1996; The Kabbalah of Money, 1996; The Kabbalah of Envy, 1997; The Kabbalah of Food, 1998. *Literary Agent:* Karen Schindler, PO Box 19051, 04599-970 São Paulo, SP, Brazil. *E-mail:* iibonder@ax.apc.org.br.

BONHAM-CARTER, Victor; Author; b. 13 Dec. 1913, Bearsted, Kent, England; m. 1st Audrey Stogdon 22 July 1938; two s.; m. 2nd Cynthia Clare Sanford 9 Feb. 1979. *Education:* MA, Magdalene College, Cambridge, 1935. *Career:* Historian, Records Officer, Dartington Hall Estate, 1951–65; Sec., Royal Literary Fund, 1966–82; Joint Sec., Society of Authors, London, 1966–82; mem. FRSL; Exmoor Society, pres., 1975–. *Publications:* The English Village, 1952; Dartington Hall (with W. B. Curry), 1958; Exploring Parish Churches, 1959; Farming the Land, 1959; In a Liberal Tradition, 1960; Soldier True (US edn as The Strategy of Victory), 1965; Surgeon in the Crimea (ed.), 1968; The Survival of the English Countryside (US edn as Land and Environment), 1971; Authors by Profession, two vols, 1978, 1984; The Essence of Exmoor, 1991; What Countryman, Sir? (autobiog.), 1996; A Filthy Barren Ground (ed.), 1998. *Address:* The Mount, Milverton House, Taunton, Somerset TA4 1QZ, England.

BONNEFOY, Yves Jean; French poet, writer, translator and academic; b. 24 June 1923, Tours; m. Lucy Vines 1968; one d. *Education:* Philosophy degree, University of Paris. *Career:* Assoc. Prof., University of Nice, 1973–76, University of Aix-en-Provence, 1979–81; Prof., Collège de France, Paris, 1981–93. *Publications:* Poetry: Du mouvement et de l'immobilité de Douve, 1953, English trans. as On the Motion and Immobility of Douve, 1968; Peintures murales de la France gothique, 1954; Hier régnant désert, 1958; L'Improbable, 1959; La Seconde Simplicité, 1961; Rimbaud par lui-même, 1961, English trans. as Rimbaud, 1973; Anti-Plato, 1962; Mirò, 1964, English trans., 1967; Pierre écrite, 1965, English trans. as Words in Stone, 1976; Un rêve fait à Mantoue, 1967; La Poésie française et le principe d'identité, 1967; Selected Poems, 1968; Rome 1630: L'horizon du premier baroque, 1970; L'Arrière-pays, 1972; L'Ordalie, 1975; Dans le leurre du seuil, 1975; Terre seconde, 1976; Rue Traversière, 1977; Le Nuage rouge, 1977; Poèmes, 1978, English trans. as Poems, 1959–1975, 1985; The Origin of Language, 1980; Entretiens sur la poésie, 1980; La Présence et l'Image, 1983; Things Dying, Things Newborn, 1986; La Vérité de Parole, 1988; The Act and the Place of Poetry: Selected Essays, 1989; In the Shadow's Light, 1990; Early Poems, 1947–1959, 1991; Alberto Giacometti: A Biography of His Work, 1991; Mythologies, 2 vols, 1991; Roman and European Mythologies, 1992; Greek and Egyptian Mythologies, 1992; Asian Mythologies, 1993; American, African and European Mythologies, 1993; New and Selected Poems, 1995; Dessin, couleur, et lumière, 1995; La Vie errante, 1995; The Lure and the Truth of Painting: Selected Essays on Art, 1995; Shakespeare et Yeats, 1998; Lieux et destins de l'image: un cours de poétique au Collège de France, 1981–93; La Communauté des traducteurs, 2000; Les planches courbes, 2001; Le Théâtre des enfants, 2001; L'enseignement et l'exemple de Léopardi, 2001; Breton en avant de Joi, 2001; Sous l'horizon du langage, 2002; Remarques sur le regard, 2002; Giacometti (trans.), 2002; Le poète et 'le flot mouvant des multitudes' 2003; La hantise du Ptyx 2003; Shakespeare and the French Poet 2004. Contributions: many reviews and journals. *Honours:* Prix de l'Express, 1958; Cecil Hamly Award, 1967; Prix des Critiques, 1971; Prix Montaigne, 1978; Grand Prix de Poésie, Académie Française, 1981; Grand Prix, Société des gens de Lettres, 1987; Bennet Award, Hudson Review, 1988; Bourse Goncourt, 1991; Prix Balzan, 1995; Prix national de Poésie, 1996; Mutsuoko Shiki Prize, 2000; many hon. doctorates. *Address:* 63 rue Lepic, 75018 Paris, France.

BONNER, Gerald, BA, MA, FSA; academic and writer; *University Reader Emeritus, University of Durham*; b. 18 June 1926, London, England; m. Priscilla J. Hodgson 1967; one s. one d. *Education:* Wadham Coll., Oxford. *Career:* Asst Keeper, Dept of Manuscripts, British Museum 1953–64; Lecturer in Theology 1964–69, Personal Readership 1969–89, Reader Emeritus 1989–, Univ. of Durham; Distinguished Prof. of Early Christian Studies, Catholic Univ. of America, Washington, DC 1991–94; Visiting Prof. in Augustinian Studies, Villanova Univ., Pennsylvania 1999; mem. North American Patristic Soc., Société Internationale d'Études Patristiques. *Publications:* The Warfare of Christ 1962, St Augustine of Hippo: Life and Controversies 1963, Famulus Christi: Essays in Commemoration of the Thirteenth Centenary of the Venerable Bede (ed.) 1976, God's Decree and Man's Destiny: Studies on the Thought of St Augustine of Hippo 1987, St Cuthbert, His Cult and His Community to AD 1200 (ed. with David Rollason and Clare Stancliffe) 1989, Church and Faith in the Patristic Tradition: Augustine, Pelagianism, and Early Christian Northumbria 1996, Augustine of Hippo: The Monastic Rules 2004; contrib. to scholarly journals. *Honours:* Johannes Quasten Award for Excellence and Leadership, School of Religious Studies, Catholic Univ. of America, Washington, DC 1994. *Address:* 7 Victoria Terrace, Durham, DH1 4RW, England.

BONNER, Terry Nelson (see Krauzer, Steven Mark).

BONTLY, Thomas John, BA, PhD; academic and writer; b. 25 Aug. 1939, Madison, Wisconsin, USA; m. Marilyn R. Mackie 1962; one s. *Education:* University of Wisconsin at Madison, Corpus Christi College, Cambridge, Stanford University. *Career:* Asst Prof., 1966–71, Assoc. Prof., 1971–76, Co-ordinator of Creative Writing, 1975–77, 1987–90, 1995–97, and Chair., 1979–82, Dept of English, Prof., 1976–, University of Wisconsin-Milwaukee; Fulbright Senior Lectureship, West Germany, 1984; mem. Council for Wisconsin Writers, board of dirs, 1991–. *Publications:* Fiction: The Competitor, 1966; The Adventures of a Young Outlaw, 1974; Celestial Chess, 1979; The Giant's Shadow, 1989. Other: Short stories in anthologies and many periodicals; Essays and reviews. *Honours:* Wallace Stegner Creative Writing Fellowship, 1965–66; Maxwell Perkins Commemorative Award, 1966; First Prizes for Short Fiction, Council for Wisconsin Writers, 1975, 1989, 1997; Wisconsin Arts Board New Work Award, 1990. *Literary Agent:* Curtis Brown Ltd, 10 Astor Place, New York, NY 10003, USA. *Address:* Department of English, University of Wisconsin-Milwaukee, Milwaukee, WI 53201, USA.

BOOKER, Christopher (John Penrice); Journalist and Writer; b. 7 Oct. 1937, Eastbourne, Sussex, England; m. Valerie Booker, 1979, two s. *Education:* Corpus Christi College, Cambridge. *Career:* Contributor, 1959–97, Way of the World column, 1987–90, Daily Telegraph; Liberal News, 1960; Jazz Critic, 1961, Columnist, 1990–, Sunday Telegraph; Ed., 1961–63, Regular Contributor, 1965–, Private Eye; Resident Scriptwriter, That Was the Week That Was, 1962–63; Contributor, Spectator, 1962–87; Ed., Global Britain, 1998–. *Publications:* The Neophiliacs: A Study of the Revolution in English Life in the 50s and 60s, 1969; Goodbye London (with Candida Lycett-Green), 1973; The Booker Quiz, 1976; The Seventies, 1980; The Games War: A Moscow Journal, 1981; The Repatriations from Austria in 1945, 1990; The Mad Officials: How the Bureaucrats Are Strangling Britain (with Richard North), 1994; The Castle of Lies: Why Britain Must Get Out of Europe (with Richard North), 1996; A Looking Glass Tragedy: The Controversy Over the Repatriations from Austria in 1945, 1997; Scared to Death: An Anatomy of Food Scare Phenomenon (with Richard North), 1999. *Honours:* Co-Winner, Campaigning Journalist of the Year, 1973; Aims of Industry Free Enterprise Award, 1992. *Address:* The Old Rectory, Litton, Bath BA3 4PW, England.

BOOTH, Geoffrey Thornton, (Edward Booth O. P.), BA, MA, PhD; writer, teacher and Roman Catholic Dominican Priest; b. 16 Aug. 1928, Evesham, Worcestershire, England. *Education:* Univ. of Cambridge. *Career:* Entered English province, Order of Dominicans, 1952; Ordained, Roman Catholic Priest, 1958; Lecturer, Pontifical Beda College, 1978–80, Pontifical University of St Thomas, 1980–88, Rome. *Publications:* Aristotelian Aporetic Ontology in Islamic and Christian Thinkers, 1983; Saint Augustine and the Western Tradition of Self Knowing: The Saint Augustine Lecture 1986, 1989. Contributions: The New Grove Dictionary of Music and Musicians, 1980; La Production du livre universitaire au moyen age: Exemplar et Pecia, 1988; Kategorie und Kategorialität, Historisch-Systematische Untersuchungen zum Begriff der Kategorie im philosophischen Denken, Festschrift für Klaus Hartmann, 1990; Gott und sein Bild–Augustins De Trinitate im Spiegel der neueren Forschung, 2000; Also many articles and book reviews in journals.

BOOTH, Philip; Prof. of English (retd) and Poet; b. 8 Oct. 1925, Hanover, NH, USA; m. Margaret Tillman, 1946, three d. *Education:* AB, Dartmouth College, 1948; MA, Columbia University, 1949. *Career:* Asst Prof., Wellesley College, 1954–61; Assoc. Prof., 1961–65, Prof. of English and Poet-in-Residence, 1965–85, Syracuse University. *Publications:* Letter from a Distant Land, 1957; The Islanders, 1961; North by East, 1966; Weathers and Edges, 1966; Margins: A Sequence of New and Selected Poems, 1970; Available Light, 1976; Before Sleep, 1980; Relations: Selected Poems, 1950–85, 1986; Selves, 1990; Pairs: New Poems, 1994; Trying to Say It: Outlooks and Insights on How Poems Happen, 1996; Lifelines: New and Selected Poems 1950–1999, 1999. *Honours:* Guggenheim Fellowships, 1958, 1965; Theodore Roethke Prize, 1970; National Endowment for the Arts Fellowship, 1980; Acad. of American Poets Fellowship, 1983; Rockefeller Fellowship, 1986; Maurice English Poetry Award, 1987. *Address:* PO Box 330, Castine, ME 04421, USA.

BOOTH, Rosemary, (Frances Murray); History Teacher and Author; b. 10 Feb. 1928, Glasgow, Scotland; m. Robert Edward Booth, 28 Aug. 1950, three d. *Education:* University of Glasgow, 1945–47; MA, 1965, Ed Diploma, 1966, University of St Andrews; Teacher's Certificate, Dundee College of Education, 1966. *Career:* History Teacher; Author. *Publications:* Ponies on the Heather, 1966; The Dear Colleague, 1972; The Burning Lamp, 1973; The Heroine's Sister, 1975; Ponies and Parachutes, 1975; Red Rowan Berry, 1976; Castaway, 1978; White Hope, 1978; Payment for the Piper, 1983, US edn as Brave Kingdom; The Belchamber Scandal, 1985; Shadow Over the Islands, 1986. *Literary Agent:* David Higham Associates, 5–8 Lower John St, Golden Sq., London W1F 9HA, England.

BOOTH, Stephen, BA; British journalist and novelist; b. 1952, Burnley, Lancashire, England; m. *Education:* Birmingham Polytechnic. *Career:* fmrly sports reporter and journalist on local newspapers, night shift sub-ed. on Scottish Daily Express, production ed. on Farming Guardian. *Publications:* novels: Black Dog 2000, Dancing with the Virgins 2001, Blood on the Tongue 2002, Blind to the Bones 2003, One Last Breath 2004. *Honours:* Lichfield Prize at the Lichfield Int. Arts Festival 1999, Barry Award for Best British Crime Novel 2000, 2001, CWA Dagger in the Library 2003. *Address:* c/o HarperCollins Publishers Ltd, 77–85 Fulham Palace Road, London, W6 8JB, England. *Website:* www.stephen-booth.com.

BORDEN, Louise Walker, BA; writer; b. 30 Oct. 1949, Cincinnati, OH, USA; m. Peter A. Borden 1971; one s. two d. *Education:* Denison University. *Career:* mem. Society of Children's Book Writers; Authors' Guild. *Publications:* Caps, Hats, Socks and Mittens 1989, The Neighborhood Trucker 1990, The Watching Game 1991, Albie the Lifeguard 1993, Just in Time for Christmas 1994, Paperboy 1996, The Little Ships 1997, Thanksgiving Is... 1997, Good-bye, Charles Lindbergh 1998, Good Luck, Mrs K! 1999, A. Lincoln and Me 1999, Sleds on Boston Common 2000, Fly High 2001, America Is... 2002, Touching the Sky – Flying Adventures of Wilbur and Orville Wright 2003, Sea Clocks – The Story of Longitude 2004, The A+ Custodian 2004, The Greatest Skating Race – A WW2 Story from the Netherlands 2004. *Honours:* Parents' Choice Award 1997; Silver Gertie Award 1998; Christopher Award 1999; Goodall Award 2000, Ohioana Children's Literature Award 2002, Denison Univ. Alumni Citation Award 2002. *Address:* 628 Myrtle Avenue, Terrace Park, OH 45174, USA. *Fax:* (513) 831-9032. *Website:* www.louiseborden.com.

BORDEN, William Vickers, AB, MA; writer, poet, dramatist and editor; *Professor Emeritus, University of North Dakota*; b. 27 Jan. 1938, Indianapolis, IN, USA; m. Nancy Lee Johnson 1960; one s. two d. *Education:* Columbia Univ., Univ. of California at Berkeley. *Career:* instructor 1962–64, Asst Prof. 1966–70, Assoc. Prof. 1970–82, Prof. of English 1982–90, Chester Fritz Distinguished Prof. of English 1990–97, Prof. Emeritus 1998–, Univ. of North Dakota; Fiction Ed., North Dakota Quarterly 1986–2002; mem. American Soc. of Composers, Authors and Publishers, Authors' League of America, Dramatists' Guild, PEN. *Plays include:* The Last Prostitute 1980, Tap Dancing Across the Universe 1981, Loon Dance 1982, The Only Woman Awake is the Woman Who Has Heard the Flute 1983, Makin' It 1984, The Consolation of Philosophy 1986, Sakakawea (musical drama) 1987, When the Meadowlark Sings 1988, Meet Again 1990, Turtle Island Blues 1991, Don't Dance Me Outside 1993, Gourmet Love 1996, Bluest Reason 2001. *Publications:* fiction: Superstore (novel) 1967, many short stories; poetry: Slow Step and Dance (chapbook) 1991, Eurydice's Song 1999; other: numerous plays, screenplays, radio plays and video scripts; contrib. to many anthologies and periodicals. *Honours:* North Dakota Centennial Drama Prize 1989, American Soc. of Composers, Authors and Publishers Awards 1990, 1991, 1992, Burlington Northern Award, Univ. of North Dakota 1990, Minnesota Distinguished Artist Award 1992, Minnesota State Arts Board Career Opportunity Grant 1996. *Address:* 7996 S FM 548, Royse City, TX 75189, USA. *E-mail:* wborden@paulbunyan.net. *Website:* www.intraart.com/williamborden.

BORDIER, Roger; Author, Dramatist and Poet; b. 5 March 1923, Blois, France; m. Jacqueline Bouchaud. *Publications:* Fiction: La cinquième saison, 1959; Les blés, 1961; Le mime, 1963; L'Entracte, 1965; Un âge d'or, 1967; Le tour de ville, 1969; Les éventails, 1971; L'océan, 1974; Demain l'éte, 1977; La grande vie, 1981; Les temps heureux, 1983; La longue file, 1984; 36 La fête, 1985; La belle de mai, 1986; Les saltimvanques de la révolution, 1989; Vel d'hib, 1989; Les fusils du ler Mai, 1991; Chroniques de la cité joyeuse, 1995; L'interrogatoire, 1998. Poetry: Les épicentres, 1951. Other: several plays. Contributions: journals, radio and television. *Honours:* Prix Renaudot, 1961; Officier, Ordre des Arts et des Lettres. *Address:* 8 rue Geoffroy St Hilaire, 75005 Paris, France.

BORDO, Susan (Rebecca); Prof. of Philosophy and Writer; b. 24 Jan. 1947, Newark, NJ, USA; m. 1968, divorced 1971. *Education:* BA, Carleton University, 1972; PhD, SUNY at Stony Brook, 1982. *Career:* Assoc. Prof. of Philosophy, 1987–93, Joseph C. Georg Prof., 1991–94, Le Moyne College, Syracuse, New York; Visiting Assoc. Prof., Duke University, 1989; Prof. of Philosophy, Otis A Singletary Chair in the Humanities, University of Kentucky, Lexington, 1994–; mem. American Philosophical Asscn; Society for Phenomenology and Existential Philosophy; Society for Women in Philosophy; American Studies Asscn. *Publications:* The Flight to Objectivity: Essays on Cartesianism and Culture, 1987; Gender-Body-Knowledge: Feminist Reconstructions of Being and Knowing (co-ed.), 1989; Unbearable Weight: Feminism, Western Culture, and the Body, 1993; Twilight Zones: The Hidden Life of Cultural Images from Plato to O. J., 1997; Feminist Interpretation of Descartes (ed.), 1999; The Male Body: A New Look at Men in Public and in Private, 1999. *Honours:* Visiting Scholar in Women's Studies, Douglass College, Rutgers University, 1985; ACLS-Ford Foundation Fellowship, 1988; Rockefeller Humanist-in-Residence, Duke University and University of North Carolina Center for Research on Women, 1987–88; Scholar of the Year Award, Le Moyne College, 1990; Notable Book of the Year, New York Times, 1993; Distinguished Publication Award, Asscn for Women in Psychology, 1994. *Literary Agent:* Sanford J. Greenburger Associates Inc, 55 Fifth Ave, New York, NY 10003, USA. *Address:* Dept of English, University of Kentucky, 1215 Paterson Office Tower, Lexington, KY 40506, USA.

BORGE MARTÍNEZ, Tomás; Nicaraguan politician, writer, poet and journalist; b. 13 Aug. 1930, Matagalpa; m. 1st Yelba Mayorga (assassinated by Nat. Guard 1979); m. 2nd Josefina Cerda; eight d. *Education:* Nat. Univ.

León and Granada. *Career:* first took part in activities against Somoza 1943, sentenced to eight years in prison 1956, escaped 1958, founder Frente Sandinista de Liberación Nacional (FSLN) 1961, guerrilla leader in Río Coco-Bocay, Pancasán and in clandestine struggle in the cities, captured by Somoza's agents 1976 and sentenced to 180 years of imprisonment, suffered torture and thirty months isolation, liberated in 1978 after attack on Nat. Palace; mem. Nat. Directorate FSLN 1978–; Minister of the Interior 1979–90, Adjoint Commdr Armed Forces, First Vice-Pres. Perm. Conference of Political Parties in Latin America (COPPPAL); founder Espartaco (magazine) 1946 and El Universitario (newspaper) 1950; jury mem. Festival of New Latin American Film 1990, House of Americas Award 1991. *Publications:* Carlos, el Amanecer ya no es una Tentación 1979, Los Primeros Pasos 1981, Estamos Creando una Nueva Sociedad 1981, La Mujer en la Revolución 1983, La Revolución Combate Contra la Teología de la Muerte 1983, El Axioma de la Esperanza 1984, Nicaragua: Justicia y Revolución 1986, Cristianismo y Revolución 1987, Una Relación Mágica 1989, La Paciente Impaciencia (House of America Award) 1989, La Ceremonia Esperada 1990. *Honours:* Dr hc Autonomous Univ. of Puebla, Mexico 1981. *Address:* Apartado 1229, Managua, Nicaragua. *Telephone:* 43853-52.

BORIS, Martin; Writer; b. 7 Aug. 1930, New York, NY, USA; m. Gloria Shanf, 13 June 1952, one s. two d. *Education:* BA, New York University, University Heights, 1951; MA, New York University, Washington Square, 1953; BA, Long Island University, Brooklyn College of Pharmacy, 1957. *Publications:* Two and Two, 1979; Woodridge 1946, 1980; Brief Candle, 1990. *Address:* 1019 Northfield Rd, Woodmere, NY 11598, USA.

BORN, Anne; Poet, Reviewer and Trans; b. 9 July 1930, Cooden Beach, Sussex, England; m. Povl Born, 1 June 1950, three s., one d. *Education:* MA, University of Copenhagen, 1955; MLitt, University of Oxford, 1978. *Career:* Writer-in-Residence, Barnstaple, 1983–85, Kingsbridge, 1985–87, Buckinghamshire, 1996; mem. Society of Authors; Trans' Asscn, chair., 1987, 1993–95; University Women's Club; Fellow of Hawthornden Castle. *Publications:* 12 poetry collections, four history books, 35 translated books. Contributions: TLS; Ambit; Rialto; Green Book; Scratch; Cimarron Review; Tears in the Fence; The Frogmore Papers; Other Poetry; Salzbury Poetry Review; Troubleshare; Oasis; Links; Seam; Odyssey. *Honours:* some 20 prizes and commendations. *Address:* Oversteps, Froude Rd, Salcombe, South Devon TQ8 8LH, England. *Fax:* (1548) 844384. *E-mail:* overstep@globalnet.co.uk.

BORSON, Roo, (Ruth Elizabeth Borson); Poet and Writer; b. 20 Jan. 1952, Berkeley, CA, USA. *Education:* University of California at Santa Barbara, 1969–71; BA, Goddard College, 1973; MFA, University of British Columbia, 1977. *Career:* Writer-in-Residence, University of Western Ontario, 1987–88, Concordia University, 1993, Green College, University of British Columbia, 2000; mem. International PEN; Pain Not Bread; Writer's Union of Canada. *Publications:* Landfall, 1977; Rain, 1980; In the Smoky Light of the Fields, 1980; A Sad Device, 1982; The Whole Night, Coming Home, 1984; The Transparence of November/Snow (with Kim Maltman), 1985; Intent, or the Weight of the World, 1989; Night Walk: Selected Poems, 1994; Water Memory, 1996; Introduction to the Introduction to Wang Wei (with Kim Maltman and Andy Patten), 2000. Contributions: many anthologies and periodicals. *Honours:* MacMillan Prize for Poetry, University of British Columbia, 1977; First Prize, 1982, Third Prize, 1989, for Poetry, and Third Prize for Personal Essay, 1990, CBC.

BOSLEY, Keith Anthony; Poet and Trans; b. 16 Sept. 1937, Bourne End, Buckinghamshire, England; m. Satu Salo, 27 Aug. 1982, three s. *Education:* Universities of Reading, Paris, and Caen, 1956–60; BA, French. *Career:* Staff, BBC, 1961–93; Visiting Lecturer, BBC and British Council, Middle East, 1981; mem. Finnish Literature Society, Helsinki, corresponding mem. *Publications:* The Possibility of Angels, 1969; And I Dance, 1972; Dark Summer, 1976; Mallarmé: The Poems (trans.), 1977; Eino Leino: Whitsongs (trans.), 1978; Stations, 1979; The Elek Book of Oriental Verse, 1979; From the Theorems of Master Jean de La Ceppède (trans.), 1983; A Chiltern Hundred, 1987; The Kalevala (trans.), 1989; I Will Sing of What I Know (trans.), 1990; Luis de Camões: Epic and Lyric (trans.), 1990; The Kanteletar (trans.), 1992; The Great Bear (trans.), 1993; Aleksis Kivi: Odes (trans.), 1994; André Frénaud: Rome the Sorceress (trans.), 1996; Eve Blossom has Wheels: German Love Poetry, 1997; Skating on the Sea: Poetry from Finland, 1997; An Upton Hymnal, 1999. Contributions: many newspapers, reviews, magazines and journals. *Honours:* Finnish State Prize for Trans, 1978; First Prize, British Comparative Literature Asscn Trans. Competition, 1980; First Prize, Goethe Society Trans. Competition, 1982; Knight, First Class, Order of the White Rose of Finland, 1991; Pension, Royal Literary Fund, 2001. *Address:* 108 Upton Rd, Upton-cum-Chalvey, Slough SL1 2AW, England.

BOTSFORD, Keith, (I. I. Magdalen); Italian/American journalist and novelist; b. 29 March 1928, Brussels, Belgium. *Career:* Prof. of Journalism, History and Int. Relations, Boston, USA; journalist, sports writer, food writer and US correspondent for journals, incl. The Sunday Times, The Independent, La Stampa. *Publications:* as Keith Botsford: fiction: Master Race 1955, The Eighth Best-Dressed Man in the World 1958, Benvenuto 1961, The March-man 1965, Dominguin 1972, The Mothers 2001; non-fiction: Driving Ambition (with Alan Jones) 1981, Keke (with Keke Rosberg) 1985, The Champion of Formula 1 1988, The Republic of Letters (with Saul Bellow) 1999, Editors (with Saul Bellow) 2001; as I. I. Magdalen: fiction: The Search for Anderson 1982, Ana P. 1983, Lennie and Vance and Benji 2002, Emma H. 2003. *Address:* c/o The Toby Press, PO Box 8531, New Milford, CT 06776-8531, USA. *Website:* www.tobypress.com.

BOTTING, Douglas Scott, MA, FRGS; writer; b. 22 Feb. 1934, London, England; m. 1964; two d. *Education:* St Edmund Hall, Oxford. *Career:* exploration film-maker, BBC TV; Special Correspondent, BBC, Geographical Magazine, Time-Life and other periodicals; mem. Royal Inst. of Int. Affairs, Soc. of Authors, Biographers' Club, NCICA. *Publications:* Island of the Dragon's Blood 1958, The Knights of Bornu 1961, One Chilly Siberian Morning 1965, Humboldt and the Cosmos 1973, Wilderness Europe 1976, Rio de Janeiro 1977, The Pirates 1978, The Second Front 1978, The U-Boats 1979, The Giant Airships 1980, The Aftermath in Europe 1945, Nazi Gold 1984, In the Ruins of the Reich 1985, Wild Britain 1988, Hitler's Last General: The Case Against Wilhelm Mohnke 1989, America's Secret Army 1989, Gavin Maxwell: A Life 1993, Sex Appeal: The Art and Science of Sexual Attraction (with Kate Botting) 1995, Gerald Durrell: The Authorised Biography 1999, The Saga of Ring of Bright Water 2000, Dr Eckener's Dream Machine: The Historic Saga of the Round-the-World Zeppelin 2001, Hitler and Women – the Love Life of Adolf Hitler 2004; contrib. to Oxford Dictionary of National Biography, BBC TV and radio, various periodicals. *Literary Agent:* Johnson & Alcock Ltd, Clerkenwell House, 45–47 Clerkenwell Green, London, EC1R 0HT, England. *Address:* 2 The Old School House, 1 Dinton Road, Kingston upon Thames, Surrey KT2 5JT, England. *E-mail:* douglasbotting@compuserve.com.

BOUCHÈNE, Abderrahmane; Algerian publisher; b. 1941, Algiers; m.; four c. *Education:* Algeria and Lausanne Univs. *Career:* worked in family clothing shop; admin. posts at Société nat. d'édition et de diffusion, Entreprise nat. du livre and Ministry of Culture; f. Editions Bouchène publishing house, Kouba, in late 1980s; by 1990 owner of two bookshops in Algiers, one in Riad-El-Feth; forced to flee Algeria and close business 1994; exile in Tunisia 1994–96; moved to Paris and set up new co. specializing in Algerian historical texts and historical anthropology of Maghreb socs. *Address:* Editions Bouchène, 113–115 rue Danielle-Casanova, 93200 Saint-Denis, Paris, France (Office). *Telephone:* 1-48-20-93-75 (Office). *E-mail:* edbouchene@aol.com (Office).

BOUCHER, David (Ewart George); Prof. of European Studies, Writer and Ed.; b. 15 Oct. 1951, Ebbw Vale, Monmouthshire, Wales; m. Clare Mary French Mullen, 8 Sept. 1979, two d. *Education:* University College, Swansea, 1973–76; BA, LSE, 1976; MSc, 1977, PhD, 1983, University of Liverpool. *Career:* Tutorial Fellow, 1980–83; Temporary Lecturer in Politics, 1983–84, University College, Cardiff; Lecturer, 1985–88, Senior Lecturer in Politics, 1988–89, La Trobe University, Melbourne, Australia; Research Fellow, 1989–90, Lecturer, 1990, Senior Lecturer in Politics, 1991, Australian National University, Canberra; Reader, 1995–98, Prof. of Political Theory and Government, 1998–2000, University of Wales, Swansea; Professorial Fellow, Cardiff University, 2000–; mem. Political Studies Asscn. *Publications:* Texts in Context: Revisionist Methods for Studying the History of Ideas, 1985; The Social and Political Thought of R. G. Collingwood, 1989; A Radical Hegelian: The Political Thought of Henry Jones (with Andrew Vincent), 1994; Political Theories of International Relations: From Thucydides to the Present, 1998; Steel Skill and Survival, 2000; British Idealism and Political Theory (with Andrew Vincent), 2000; Politics, Poetry and Protest: Bob Dylan and Leonard Cohen, 2003. Editor: Essays in Political Philosophy, by R. G. Collingwood, 1989; The New Leviathan, revised edn, by R. G. Collingwood, 1992; The Social Contract from Hobbes to Rawls (with Paul Kelly), 1994; Philosophy, Politics and Civilization (with T. Modood and J. Connelly), 1995; The British Idealists, 1997; Social Justice: From Hume to Walzer (with Paul Kelly), 1998; Political Thinkers (with Paul Kelly), 2003. Contributions: scholarly journals. *Honours:* FRHistS. *Address:* School of European Studies, University of Wales, Cardiff, Cardiff CF10, Wales. *E-mail:* boucherde@cardiff.ac.uk.

BOULANGER, Daniel; Author, Poet and Dramatist; b. 24 Jan. 1922, Compiègne, Oise, France; m. 2nd Clémence Dufour; four s. three d. *Education:* Petit Séminaire Saint-Charles, Chauny. *Career:* mem. Académie Goncourt, 1983–. *Publications:* Fiction: Les noces du merle, 1963; Retouches, 1969; Vessies et lanternes, 1971; Fouette cocher, 1974; La confession d'Omer, 1991; Un eté à la diable, 1992; Ursacq, 1993; A la courte paille, 1993; Le retable wasserfall et etiquettes, 1994; Caporal supérieur, 1994; Le miroitier, 1995; Taciturnes, 1995; Tombeau d'héraldine, 1997; Talbard, 1998; Le ciel de bargetal, 1999. Other: numerous plays and screenplays; several poetry collections. *Honours:* Prix de la Nouvelle, 1963; Prix Max Jacob, 1970; Prix de l'Académie française, 1971; Prix Goncourt, 1974; Prix Pierre de Monaco, 1979; Prix Kléber Haedens, 1983; Officier, Légion d'honneur; Officier, Ordre nat. du Mérite; Commdr, Ordre des Arts et des Lettres. *Address:* 22 rue du Heaume, 60300 Senlis, France.

BOULTON, James Thompson; Prof. of English Studies Emeritus and Writer; b. 17 Feb. 1924, Pickering, Yorkshire, England; m. Margaret Helen Leary, 6 Aug. 1949, one s. one d. *Education:* BA, University College, University of Durham, 1948; BLitt, Lincoln College, University of Oxford, 1952; PhD, University of Nottingham, 1960. *Career:* Pilot, RAF, 1943–46; Lecturer, Senior Lecturer, Reader in English Literature, 1951–63, Prof., 1964–75, Dean, Faculty of Arts, 1970–73, University of Nottingham; Prof.

of English Studies and Head of Dept, 1975–88, Dean of Faculty of Arts, 1981–84, Public Orator, 1984–88, Dir, 1987–99, Deputy Dir, 1999–, Institute for Advanced Research in Arts and Social Sciences, Prof. Emeritus, 1989–, University of Birmingham. *Publications:* Edmund Burke: Sublime and Beautiful (ed.), 1958; The Language of Politics in the Age of Wilkes and Burke, 1963; Samuel Johnson: The Critical Heritage, 1971; Defoe: Memoirs of a Cavalier (ed.), 1972; The Letters of D. H. Lawrence (ed.) (eight vols), 1979–2000; Selected Letters of D. H. Lawrence (ed.), 1997; The Writings and Speeches of Edmund Burke, Vol. One (co-ed.), 1997. *Honours:* FRSL, 1968; Hon. DLitt, University of Durham, 1991, University of Nottingham, 1993; Fellow, British Acad., 1994. *Address:* c/o Institute for Advanced Research in Arts and Social Sciences, University of Birmingham, Edgbaston, Birmingham B15 2TT, England.

BOURAOUI, Nina; French writer; b. 31 July 1967, Rennes. *Education:* Lycée Français (Algiers, Algeria) and Zurich (Switzerland), Inst. Catholique (Paris) and Univ. of Paris II (Panthéon-Assas). *Publication:* La Voyeuse interdite (Prix Livre Inter) 1991, Poing mort 1992, Le bal des murènes 1996, L'âge blessé 1998, Garçon manqué 2000, Le Jour du séisme 2001, La Vie heureuse 2002, Poupée Bella 2004. *Address:* 47 rue Claude Bernard, 75005 Paris, France. *Telephone:* (1) 43-37-54-31.

BOURJAILY, Vance Nye, AB; writer and academic; b. 17 Sept. 1922, Cleveland, OH, USA; m. 1st Bettina Yensen 1946; two c.; m. 2nd Yasmin Mobul 1985; one c. *Education:* Bowdoin College. *Career:* Co-Founder, Ed., Discovery, 1951–53; Faculty, University of Iowa Writers Workshops, 1958–80; Distinguished Visiting Prof., Oregon State University, 1968; Visiting Prof., University of Arizona, 1977–78; Boyd Prof., Louisiana State University, 1985–. *Publications:* The End of My Life, 1947; The Hound of the Earth, 1953; The Violated, 1958; Confessions of a Spent Youth, 1960; The Unnatural Enemy, 1963; The Man Who Knew Kennedy, 1967; Brill Among the Ruins, 1970; Country Matters, 1973; Now Playing at Canterbury, 1976; A Game Men Play, 1980; The Great Fake Book, 1987; Old Soldier, 1990; Fishing By Mail: The Outdoor Life of a Father and Son, 1993. *Honours:* American Acad. of Arts and Letters Award, 1993. *Address:* c/o Dept of English, Louisiana State University, Baton Rouge, LA 70803, USA.

BOURNE, Stephen, MA, FCA; British publisher; *CEO, Cambridge University Press.* *Career:* trained as a chartered accountant; Development Dir and Chair. of the Printing Division, Cambridge Univ. Press 1997–2002; CEO, Cambridge Univ. Press 2002–; bd mem., Britten Sinfonia. *Address:* Cambridge University Press, The Edinburgh Building, Shaftesbury Road, Cambridge, CB2 2RU, England. *Website:* www.cup.cam.ac.uk.

BOUZFOUR, Ahmed; Moroccan author. *Publications:* Nanna (short story), Qounqous (short story collection) 2003; contrib. to Aljamía, Banipal. *Address:* c/o Union des écrivains du Maroc, Rabat, Morocco.

BOVA, Benjamin (Ben) William, BA, MA; writer, editor and lecturer; b. 8 Nov. 1932, Philadelphia, Pennsylvania, USA. *Education:* Temple University, SUNY at Albany. *Career:* Editorial Dir, Omni Magazine; Ed., Analog Magazine; Lecturer; mem. British Interplanetary Society, fellow; National Space Society, pres. emeritus; PEN; SFWA. *Publications:* Gremlins, Go Home!, 1974; Notes to a Science Fiction Writer, 1975; Science: Who Needs It?, 1975; Viewpoint, 1977; The Exiles Trilogy, 1980; Vision of Tomorrow, 1982; The Astral Mirror, 1985; Voyager Two: The Alien Within, 1986; As on a Darkling Plain, 1991; Empire Builders, 1993; Orion and the Conqueror, 1994; Orion Among the Stars, 1995; Moonwar, 1998. Contributions: numerous books and periodicals. *Honours:* Distinguished Alumnus, 1981, Alumni Fellow, 1982, Temple University. *Address:* 32 Gramercy Park S, New York, NY 10003, USA.

BOWDEN, Jim (see Spence, William (John Duncan)).

BOWDEN, Roland Heywood; Poet and Dramatist; b. 19 Dec. 1916, Lincoln, England; m. 2 Jan. 1946, one s. one d. *Education:* School of Architecture, Liverpool University, 1934–39. *Career:* mem. National Poetry Secretariat. *Publications:* Poems From Italy, 1970; Every Season is Another, 1986. Plays: Death of Paolini, 1980; After Neruda, 1984; The Fence, 1985. Contributions: Arts Review: London Magazine; Panurge; Words International. *Honours:* Arts Council Drama Bursary, 1978; Cheltenham Festival Poetry Prize, 1982; First Prize, All-Sussex Poets, 1983. *Address:* 2 Roughmere Cottage, Lavant, Chichester, West Sussex PO18 0BG, England.

BOWEN, Kevin; American poet and translator; m.; two c. *Career:* served with the US Army in Viet Nam 1968–69; currently Dir William Joiner Centre for the Study of War and its Social Consequences, Univ. of Massachusetts in Boston. *Publications:* poetry: Playing Basketball with the Viet-Cong 1994; editor: Mountain Poetry: Vietnamese Poetry from the Wars 1948–93 1998, 6 Vietnamese Poets 2002; contrib. to Distant Road 1999. *Address:* c/o Curbstone Press, 321 Jackson Street, Willimantic, CT 06226-1738, USA. *E-mail:* info@curbstone.org. *Website:* www.curbstone.org.

BOWEN, Lynne; Author; b. 22 Aug. 1940, Indian Head, Saskatchewan, Canada. *Education:* BSc, University of Alberta, 1963; MA, University of Victoria, 1980. *Career:* Rogers Communications Co-Chair of Creative Non-Fiction Writing, 1992–, Co-Chair, Creative Writing Program, 2000–02, University of British Columbia; mem. Writers' Union of Canada; PEN International. *Publications:* Boss Whistle: The Coal Miners of Vancouver Island Remember, 1982; Three Dollar Dreams, 1987; Muddling Through: The Remarkable Story of the Barr Colonists, 1992; Those Lake People: Stories of Cowichan Lake, 1995; Robert Dunsmuir, Laird of the Mines, 1999. *Honours:* Canadian Historical Asscn Regional Certificates of Merit, 1984, 1993; Lieutenant Governor's Medal, 1987; Hubert Evans Non-Fiction Prize, 1993. *Address:* 4982 Fillinger Crescent, Nanaimo, BC V9V 1J1, Canada. *E-mail:* lynne@island.net.

BOWERING, George Henry, OC, MA; Canadian writer, poet and lecturer; *Parliamentary Poet Laureate;* b. 1 Dec. 1936, Penticton, BC; m. Angela Luoma 1962 (died 1999); one d. *Education:* Victoria Coll., Univ. of British Columbia, Univ. of Western Ontario. *Career:* served as Royal Canadian Air Force photographer 1954–57; lecturer Univ. of Calgary 1963–66; writer-in-residence Sir George Williams Univ., Montreal 1967–68, lecturer 1968–71; lecturer Simon Fraser Univ., Burnaby, BC 1972–2001; Parl. Poet Laureate of Canada 2002–04. *Play:* The Home for Heroes 1962. *Radio plays:* George Vancouver CBC) 1972, Sitting in Mexico (CBC) 1973, Music in the Park (CBC) 1986, The Great Grandchildren of Bill Bissett's Mice (CBC) 1989. *Television play:* What Does Eddie Williams Want? (CBC) 1966. *Publications:* poetry collections: Sticks & Stones 1963, Points on the Grid 1964, The Man in Yellow Boots/El hombre de las botas amarillas 1965, The Silver Wire 1966, Rocky Mountain Foot 1969, The Gangs of Kosmos 1969, Touch: Selected Poems 1960–1969 1971, In the Flesh 1974, The Catch 1976, Poem & Other Baseballs 1976, The Concrete Island 1977, Another Mouth 1979, Particular Accidents: Selected Poems 1981, West Window: Selected Poetry 1982, Smoking Poetry 1982, Smoking Mirrow 1982, Seventy-One Poems for People 1985, Delayed Mercy & Other Poems 1986, Urban Snow 1992, George Bowering Selected: Poems 1961–1992 1993; chapbooks: How I Hear Howl 1967, Two Police Poems 1969, The Sensible 1972, Layers 1–13 1973, In Answer 1977, Uncle Louis 1980, Spencer & Groulx 1985, Quarters 1991, Do Sink 1992, Sweetly 1992, Blondes on Bikes 1997, A, You're Adorable 1998, 6 Little Poems in Alphabetical Order 2000, Some Writers 2001, Joining the Lost Generation 2002; long poems: Sitting in Mexico 1965, George,Vancouver 1970, Geneve 1971, Autobiology 1972, Curious 1973, At War With the U.S. 1974, Allophanes 1976, Ear Reach 1982, Kerrisdale Elegies 1984, His Life: A Poem 2000, Baseball: A poem in the magic number 9 2003; novels: Mirror on the Floor 1967, A Short Sad Book 1977, Burning Water 1980, En eaux troubles 1982, Caprice 1987, Harry's Fragments 1990, Shoot! 1994, Parents from Space 1994, Piccolo Mondo 1998, Diamondback Dog 1998; short story collections: Flycatcher & Other Stories 1974, Concentric Circles 1977, Protective Footwear 1978, A Place to Die 1983, The Rain Barrel 1994, Standing on Richards 2004; non-fiction: Al Purdy 1970, Three Vancouver Writers 1979, A Way with Words 1982, The Mask in Place 1983, Craft Slices 1985, Errata 1988, Imaginary Hand 1988, The Moustache: Memories of Greg Curnoe (memoir) 1993, Bowering's B.C. 1996, Egotists and Autocrats – the Prime Ministers of Canada 1999, A Magpie Life (memoir) 2001, Cars (memoir) 2002, Stone Country 2003. *Honours:* Hon. DLit (British Columbia) 1997, (Western Ontario) 2003; Gov.-Gen.'s Award for poetry 1967, for fiction 1980, bp Nichol Chapbook Awards for Poetry 1991, 1992, Canadian Authors' Asscn Award for Poetry 1993. *Address:* 303 Fielden Avenue, Port Colborne, ON L3K 4T5, Canada (Home). *Telephone:* (905) 834-0642 (Home). *E-mail:* bowering@sfu.ca (Home).

BOWERING, Marilyn (Ruthe); Poet and Writer; b. 13 April 1949, Winnipeg, Ontario, Canada; m. Michael S. Elcock, 3 Sept. 1982, one d. *Education:* University of British Columbia, 1968–69; BA, 1971, MA, 1973, University of Victoria; University of New Brunswick, 1975–78. *Career:* Writer-in-Residence, Aegean School of Fine Arts, Paris, 1973–74; Visiting Lecturer, 1978–82, Lecturer in Creative Writing, 1982–86, 1989, Visiting Assoc. Prof. of Creative Writing, 1993–96, University of Victoria, BC; Faculty, 1992, Writer-in-Residence, 1993–94, Banff Centre, Alberta, Memorial University of Newfoundland, 1995; mem. League of Canadian Poets; Writers Union of Canada. *Publications:* Poetry: The Liberation of Newfoundland, 1973; One Who Became Lost, 1976; The Killing Room, 1977; Third/Child Zian, 1978; The Book of Glass, 1978; Sleeping with Lambs, 1980; Giving Back Diamonds, 1982; The Sunday Before Winter, 1984; Anyone Can See I Love You, 1987; Grandfather was a Soldier, 1987; Calling All the World, 1989; Love As It Is, 1993; Human Bodies: New and Collected Poems, 1987–99, 1999. Fiction: The Visitors Have All Returned, 1979; To All Appearances a Lady, 1990. Editor: Many Voices: An Anthology of Contemporary Canadian Indian Poetry (with David A Day), 1977; Guide to the Labor Code of British Columbia, 1980. Contributions: anthologies and journals. *Honours:* many Canada Council Awards for Poetry; Du Maurier Award for Poetry, 1978; National Magazine Award for Poetry, 1989; Long Poem Prize, Malahat Review, 1994. *Address:* c/o League of Canadian Poets, 54 Wolseley St, Third Floor, Toronto, ON M5T 1AS, Canada.

BOWKER, Gordon; Writer and Journalist; b. 19 March 1934, Birmingham, England. *Education:* BA, University of Nottingham, 1960; MA, 1966, PhD, 1993, University of London. *Career:* Teacher, Goldsmiths College, University of London, 1966–91; mem. PEN; Society of Authors; Writers Guild. *Publications:* Under Twenty (ed.), 1966; Freedom: Reason or Revolution (ed.), 1970; Malcolm Lowry Remembered (ed.), 1985; Malcolm Lowry: Under the Volcano (ed.), 1988; Apparently Incongruous Parts: The Worlds of Malcolm Lowry (co-ed.), 1990; Pursued by Furies: A Life of Malcolm Lowry, 1993; Through the Dark Labyrinth, 1996; George Orwell, 2003. *Literary Agent:* David Higham Associates, 5–8 Lower John St, Golden Sq., London W1F 9HA, England.

BOWKER, John Westerdale; Prof. and Writer; b. 30 July 1935, London, England. *Education:* BA, Oxford, 1958. *Career:* Fellow, Corpus Christi College, Cambridge, 1962–74; Lecturer, University of Cambridge, 1965–74; Prof. of Religious Studies, University of Lancaster, 1974–85; Fellow, Dean, Trinity College, Cambridge, 1984–93; Hon. Cannon, Canterbury Cathedral, 1985–; Gresham Prof., 1992–97, Fellow, 1997–, Gresham College, London. *Publications:* The Targums and Rabbinic Literature, 1969; Problems of Suffering in Religions of the World, 1970; Jesus and the Pharisees, 1973; The Sense of God: Sociological, Anthropological and Psychological Approaches to the Origin of the Sense of God, 1973; Uncle Bolpenny Tries Things Out, 1973; The Religious Imagination and the Sense of God, 1978; Worlds of Faith, 1983; Violence and Aggression (ed.), 1984; Licensed Insanities, 1987; The Meanings of Death, 1991; A Year to Live, 1991; Hallowed Ground, 1993; Is God a Virus? Genes, Culture and Religion, 1995; The Oxford Dictionary of World Religions, 1997; World Religions, 1997; The Complete Bible Handbook, 1998; What Muslims Believe, 1998; God: A Brief History, 2002. *Honours:* Harper Collins Biennial Prize, 1993; Benjamin Franklin Award, 1999. *Address:* 14 Bowers Croft, Cambridge CB1 8RP, England.

BOWLER, Peter John, BA, MSc, PhD; academic and writer; *Professor of History of Science, Queen's University*; b. 8 Oct. 1944, Leicester, England; m. Sheila Mary Holt 1966; one s. one d. *Education:* Univ. of Cambridge, Univ. of Sussex, Univ. of Toronto. *Career:* Asst Prof., Univ. of Toronto, 1971–72; Lecturer, Science Univ. of Malaysia, Penang, 1972–75; Asst Prof., Univ. of Winnipeg, 1975–79; Lecturer, 1979–87, Reader, 1987–92, Prof. of History of Science, 1992–, Queen's Univ., Belfast; mem. Royal Irish Acad.; British Society for the History of Science; History of Science Society. *Publications:* Fossils and Progress: Paleontology and the Idea of Progressive Evolution in the Nineteenth Century, 1976; The Eclipse of Darwinism: Anti-Darwinian Evolution Theories in the Decades Around 1900, 1983; Evolution: The History of an Idea, 1984; Theories of Human Evolution: A Century of Debate, 1844–1944, 1986; The Non-Darwinian Revolution: Reinterpreting a Historical Myth, 1988; The Mendelian Revolution: The Emergence of Hereditarian Concepts in Modern Science and Society, 1989; The Invention of Progress: The Victorians and the Past, 1990; Darwin: L'origine delle specie, 1990; Charles Darwin: The Man and his Influence, 1990; The Fontana History of the Environmental Sciences, 1992, US edn as The Norton History of the Environmental Sciences, 1993; Biology and Social Thought, 1850–1914, 5 lectures, 1993; Darwinism, 1993; E. Ray Lankester and the Making of Modern British Biology (ed. and co-author with J. Lester), 1995; Life's Splendid Drama: Evolutionary Biology and the Reconstruction of Life's Ancestry, 1860–1940, 1996; Reconciling Science and Religion: The Debate in Early Twentieth-Century Britain, 2001. Contributions: journals. *Address:* c/o School of Anthropological Studies, Queen's University of Belfast, Belfast BT7 1NN, Northern Ireland.

BOWLING, Harry; Writer; b. 30 Sept. 1931, Bermondsey, London, England; m. Shirley Burgess, 27 July 1957, one s. two d. *Publications:* Conner Street's War, 1988; Tuppence to Tooley Street, 1989; Ironmonger's Daughter, 1989; Paragon Place, 1990; Gaslight in Page Street, 1991; The Girl From Cotton Lane, 1992; Backstreet Girl, 1993. *Address:* Headline Book Publishing plc, Headline House, 79 Great Tichfield St, London W1P 7FN, England.

BOWLT, John Ellis, BA, MA, PhD; American academic and writer; b. 6 Dec. 1943, London, England; m. Nicoletta Misler 1981. *Education:* University of Birmingham, University of St Andrews, Scotland. *Career:* Lecturer, University of St Andrews, 1968–79, University of Birmingham, 1970; Asst Prof., University of Kansas at Lawrence, 1970–71; Asst to Assoc. Prof., 1971–81, Assoc. Prof. to Prof., 1981–88, University of Texas, Austin; Visiting Prof., University of Otago, New Zealand, 1982, Hebrew University, Jerusalem, 1985; Prof., University of Southern California, Los Angeles, 1988–; mem. American Asscn for the Advancement of Slavic Studies; College Art Asscn, New York. *Publications:* Russian Formalism (ed. with Stephen Bann), 1973; The Russian Avant-Garde: Theory and Criticism 1902–1934, 1976; The Silver Age: Russian Art of the Early Twentieth Century, 1979; The Life of Vasilii Kandinsky in Russian Art (with Rose Carol Washton-Long), 1980; Pavel Filonov: A Hero and His Fate (with Nicoletta Misler), 1984; Mikalojus Konstantinas Ciurlionis: Music of the Spheres (with Alfred Senn and Danute Staskevicius), 1986; Russian Samizdat Art (co-author), 1986; Gustav Kluzis, 1988; Aus Vollem Halse: Russische Buchillustration und Typographie 1900–1930 (with B. Hernad), 1993; Russian and East European Paintings in the Thyssen-Bornemisza Collection (with Nicoletta Misler), 1993; The Salon Album of Vera Sudeikin-Stravinsky, 1995. Contributions: Books, scholarly journals, periodicals and exhibition catalogues. *Honours:* British Council Scholarship, 1966–68; Woodrow Wilson National Fellowship, 1971; National Humanities Institute Fellow, Yale University, 1977–78; Fulbright-Hays Award, Paris, 1981; ACLS Award, Italy, 1984; Senior Fellow, Wolfsonian Foundation, Miami, 1995. *Address:* c/o Dept of Slavic Languages and Literatures, University of Southern California at Los Angeles, Los Angeles, CA 90089, USA.

BOX, Edgar (see Vidal, Gore).

BOYCOTT, Rosie; British journalist and author; b. 13 May 1951; m. 1st David Leitch (divorced); one d.; m. 2nd Charles Howard 1999. *Education:* Cheltenham Ladies Coll., Kent Univ. *Career:* f. Spare Rib 1972; est. Virago Books 1973; worked on Village Voice (magazine), New York; subsequently edited Arabic women's magazine in Kuwait; Features Ed. Honey; Deputy Ed. Daily Mail's Male and Femail pages; Ed. Discount Traveller; Commissioning Ed. The Sunday Telegraph; Deputy Ed. Harpers & Queen 1989; Deputy Ed. and Features Ed. (British) Esquire 1991, Ed. 1992–96, of Ind. on Sunday 1996–98, of the Ind. 1998, of the Express 1998–2001, of the Express on Sunday 1998–2001; Chair., Panel of Judges, Orange Prize for Fiction 2001; mem. Exec. Cttee English PEN. *Publications:* A Nice Girl Like Me (autobiog.) 1983, All For Love 1985. *Address:* c/o English Centre of International PEN, 33 Islington High Street, London, N1 9LH, England.

BOYD, William Andrew Murray, MA, FRSL; British author; b. 7 March 1952, Ghana; m. Susan Anne (née Wilson) Boyd 1975. *Education:* Gordonstoun School, Glasgow Univ., Jesus Coll., Oxford. *Career:* lecturer in English, St Hilda's Coll., Oxford 1980–83; TV critic, New Statesman 1981–83. *Publications include:* A Good Man in Africa (Whitbread Prize 1981, Somerset Maugham Award 1982) 1981 (screenplay 1994), On the Yankee Station 1981, An Ice-Cream War (John Llewellyn Rhys Prize) 1982, Stars and Bars 1984 (screenplay 1988), School Ties 1985, The New Confessions 1987, Scoop (screenplay) 1987, Brazzaville Beach (McVities Prize and James Tait Black Memorial Prize) 1990, Aunt Julia and the Scriptwriter (screenplay) 1990, Mr Johnson (screenplay) 1990, Chaplin (screenplay) 1992, The Blue Afternoon (novel) 1993, A Good Man in Africa (screenplay) 1994, The Destiny of Nathalie 'X' 1995, Armadillo 1998 (screenplay 2001), Nat Tate: An American Artist 1998, The Trench (screenplay, also dir) 1999, Sword of Honour (screenplay) 2001, Any Human Heart 2002, Fascination 2004. *Honours:* Hon. DLitt (St Andrews), (Glasgow), (Stirling); Chevalier des Arts et des Lettres. *Literary Agent:* The Agency, 24 Pottery Lane, Holland Park, London, W11 4LZ, England.

BOYLAN, Clare Catherine; Novelist and Writer; b. 21 April 1948, Dublin, Ireland; m. Alan Wilkes 18 Sept. 1970. *Career:* Ed., Young Woman Magazine, 1968; Feature Writer, Evening Press, 1972; Ed., Image Magazine, 1980–83; mem. Irish PEN; Aosdána. *Publications:* Fiction: Holy Pictures, 1983; Last Resorts, 1984; Black Baby, 1988; Home Rule, 1992; Room for a Single Lady, 1997; Beloved Stranger, 1999; Emma Brown, 2003. Short Stories: A Nail on the Head, 1983; Concerning Virgins, 1989; That Bad Woman, 1996; Another Family Christmas, 1997; The Collected Short Stories, 2000. Non Fiction: The Literary Companion to Cats, 1994. Contributions: New York Times; Sunday Times; Irish Times; Guardian; Independent; Telegraph. *Honours:* Journalist of the Year, 1974; Spirit of Life Arts Award, 1997. *Literary Agent:* Rogers, Coleridge & White Ltd, 20 Powis Mews, London W11 1JN, England.

BOYLE, Thomas Coraghessan, BA, MFA, PhD; American academic and writer; b. 2 Dec. 1948, Peekskill, NY, USA; m. Karen Kvashay 1974; two s. one d. *Education:* SUNY at Potsdam, University of Iowa. *Career:* Founder-Dir, Creative Writing Program, 1978–86, Asst Prof., 1978–82, Assoc. Prof., 1982–86, Prof., 1986–, of English, University of Southern California at Los Angeles; mem. National Endowment of the Arts Literature Panel, 1986–87. *Publications:* Descent of Man, 1979; Water Music, 1982; Budding Prospects, 1984; Greasy Lake, 1985; World's End, 1987; If the River Was Whiskey, 1989; East is East, 1990; The Road to Wellville, 1993; Without a Hero, 1994; The Tortilla Curtain, 1995; Riven Rock, 1998; T.C. Boyle Stories, 1998; A Friend of the Earth, 2000; After the Plague, 2001; Drop City, 2003. Contributions: numerous anthologies and periodicals. *Honours:* National Endowment for the Arts Grants, 1977, 1983; Guggenheim Fellowship, 1988; PEN/Faulkner Award, 1988; Commonwealth Club of California Gold Medal for Literature, 1988; O. Henry Short Story Awards, 1988, 1989; Prix Passion Publishers' Prize, France, 1989; Eds' Choice, New York Times Book Review, 1989; Hon. Doctor of Humane Letters, SUNY, 1991; Harold D. Vursell Memorial Award, American Acad. of Arts and Letters, 1993; Prix Médicis Étranger, 1997. *Address:* c/o Department of English, University of Southern California, Los Angeles, CA 90089, USA. *Website:* www.tcboyle.com.

BRACKENBURY, Alison, BA; poet and writer; b. 20 May 1953, Gainsborough, Lincolnshire, England. *Education:* St Hugh's College, Oxford. *Radio play:* The Country of Afternoon 1985. *Publications:* Journey to a Cornish Wedding 1977, Two Poems 1979, Dreams of Power and Other Poems 1981, Breaking Ground and Other Poems 1984, Christmas Roses and Other Poems 1988, Selected Poems 1991, 1829 1994, After Beethoven 1999, The Story of Sigurd 2002; contrib. to journals, including PN Review. *Honours:* Eric Gregory Award 1982, Cholmondeley Award 1997. *Address:* c/o Carcanet Press, Fourth Floor, Alliance House, Cross Street, Manchester M2 7AP, England. *Website:* www.alisonbrackenbury.co.uk.

BRADBURY, Edward P. (see Moorcock, Michael John).

BRADBURY, Ray (Douglas); Writer, Poet and Dramatist; b. 22 Aug. 1920, Waukegan, IL, USA; m. Marguerite Susan McClure, 27 Sept. 1947, four d. *Education:* Public Schools. *Career:* mem. SFWA; Screen Writers Guild of America; Writers Guild of America. *Publications:* Fiction: The Martian Chronicles, 1950; Dandelion Wine, 1957; Something Wicked This Way Comes, 1962; Death is a Lonely Business, 1985; A Graveyard for Lunatics, 1990; Green Shadows, White Whale, 1992. Short Story Collections: Dark Carnival, 1947; The Illustrated Man, 1951; The Golden Apples of the Sun, 1953; Fahrenheit 451, 1953; The October Country, 1955; A Medicine for Melancholy, 1959; The Ghoul Keepers, 1961; The Small Assassin, 1962; The Machineries of Joy, 1964; The Vintage Bradbury, 1965; The Autumn

People, 1965; Tomorrow Midnight, 1966; Twice Twenty-Two, 1966; I Sing the Body Electric!, 1969; Bloch and Bradbury: Ten Masterpieces of Science Fiction (with Robert Bloch), 1969; Whispers From Beyond (with Robert Bloch), 1972; Harrap, 1975; Long After Midnight, 1976; To Sing Strange Songs, 1979; Dinosaur Tales, 1983; A Memory of Murder, 1984; The Toynbee Convector, 1988; Kaleidoscope, 1994; Quicker Than the Eye, 1996; Driving Blind, 1997. Poetry: Old Ahab's Friend, and Friend to Noah, Speaks His Piece: A Celebration, 1971; When Elephants Last in the Dooryard Bloomed: Celebrations for Almost Any Day in the Year, 1973; That Son of Richard III: A Birth Announcement, 1974; Where Robot Mice and Robot Men Run Round in Robot Towns, 1977; Twin Hieroglyphs That Swim the River Dust, 1978; The Bike Repairman, 1978; The Author Considers His Resources, 1979; The Aqueduct, 1979; The Attic Where the Meadow Greens, 1979; The Last Circus, 1980; The Ghosts of Forever, 1980; The Haunted Computer and the Android Pope, 1981; The Complete Poems of Ray Bradbury, 1982; The Love Affair, 1983; Forever and the Earth, 1984; Death Has Lost Its Charm for Me, 1987. Plays: The Meadow, 1960; Way in the Middle of the Air, 1962; The Anthem Sprinters and Other Antics, 1963; The World of Ray Bradbury, 1964; Leviathan 99, 1966; The Day it Rained Forever, 1966; The Pedestrian, 1966; Dandelion Wine, 1967; Christus Apollo, 1969; The Wonderful Ice-Cream Suit and Other Plays, 1972; Madrigals for the Space Age, 1972; Pillars of Fire and Other Plays for Today, Tomorrow, and Beyond Tomorrow, 1975; That Ghost, That Bride of Time: Excerpts from a Play-in-Progress, 1976; The Martian Chronicles, 1977; Farenheit 451, 1979; A Device Out of Time, 1986; Falling Upward, 1988. Non-Fiction: Teacher's Guide: Science Fiction, 1968; Zen and the Art of Writing, 1973; Mars and the Mind of Man, 1973; The Mummies of Guanajuato, 1978; Beyond, 1984: Remembrance of Things Future, 1979; Los Angeles, 1984; Orange County, 1985; The Art of Playboy, 1985; Yestermorrow: Obvious Answers to Impossible Futures, 1991; Ray Bradbury on Stage: A Chrestomathy of His Plays, 1991; Journey to Far Metaphor: Further Essays on Creativity, Writing, Literature, and the Arts, 1994; The First Book of Dichotomy, The Second Book of Symbiosis, 1995. Other: TV and film scripts, incl.: Moby Dick (screenplay), 1956; Alfred Hitchcock Show; Twilight Zone. *Honours:* O. Henry Prizes, 1947, 1948; National Institute of Arts and Letters Award, 1954; Writers Club Award, 1974; Balrog Award for Best Poet, 1979; PEN Body of Work Award, 1985; Hon. Medal, National Book Foundation, 2000. *Address:* 10265 Cheviot Dr., Los Angeles, CA 90064, USA.

BRADFORD, Barbara Taylor; British journalist and writer; b. 10 May 1933, Leeds, Yorkshire, England; m. Robert Bradford 1963. *Career:* ed., columnist, British and US periodicals. *Publications:* Complete Encyclopedia of Homemaking Ideas 1968, How to Be the Perfect Wife 1969, Easy Steps to Successful Decorating 1971, Making Space Grow 1979, A Woman of Substance 1979, Voice of the Heart 1983, Hold the Dream 1985, Act of Will 1986, To Be the Best 1988, The Women in his Life 1990, Remember 1991, Angel 1993, Everything to Gain 1994, Dangerous to Know 1995, Love in Another Town 1995, Her Own Rules 1996, A Secret Affair 1996, Power of a Woman 1997, A Sudden Change of Heart 1999, Where You Belong 2000, The Triumph of Katie Byrne 2001, Three Weeks in Paris 2002, Emma's Secret 2003, Unexpected Blessings 2004. *Address:* c/o Bradford Enterprises, 450 Park Avenue, Suite 1903, New York, NY 10022, USA. *Website:* www.barbarataylorbradford.com.

BRADFORD, Karleen; Writer; b. 16 Dec. 1936, Toronto, Ontario, Canada; m. James Creighton Bradford, 22 Aug. 1959, two s. one d. *Education:* BA, University of Toronto, 1959. *Career:* Chair, Public Lending Right Commission of Canada, 1998–2000; mem. PEN; IBBY; Writers' Union of Canada. *Publications:* A Year for Growing, 1977; The Other Elizabeth, 1982; Wrong Again, Robbie, 1983; I Wish There Were Unicorns, 1983; The Stone in the Meadow, 1984; The Haunting at Cliff House, 1985; The Nine Days Queen, 1986; Write Now!, 1988; Windward Island, 1989; There Will be Wolves, 1992; Thirteenth Child, 1994; Animal Heroes, 1995; Shadows on a Sword, 1996; More Animal Heroes, 1996; Dragonfire, 1997; A Different Kind of Champion, 1998; Lionhearts Scribe, 1999, Canadian Library Assсn Young Adult Novel Award, 1993. *Address:* RR No. 2, Owen Sound, ON N4K 5N4, Canada.

BRADFORD, S. W. (see Battin, B. W.).

BRADFORD, Sarah Mary Malet (Viscountess Bangor); British writer; b. 3 Sept. 1938, Bournemouth; m. 1st Anthony John Bradford 1959; one s. one d.; m. 2nd Viscount Bangor 1976. *Education:* St Mary's Convent, Shaftesbury and Lady Margaret Hall, Oxford. *Career:* manuscript expert at Christie's 1975–78. *Publications:* Portugal and Madeira 1969, Portugal 1973, Cesare Borgia 1976, The Englishman's Wine 1969, re-published as The Story of Port 1978, Disraeli 1982, Princess Grace 1984, King George VI 1989, Sacheverell Sitwell 1993, Elizabeth, A Biography of Her Majesty The Queen 1996, America's Queen: The Life of Jacqueline Kennedy Onassis 2000, Lucrezia Borgia: Life, Love and Death in Renaissance Italy 2004; contrib. to periodicals. *Literary Agent:* Gillon Aitken Associates Ltd, 18–21 Cavaye Place, London, SW10 9PT, England. *Telephone:* (20) 7373-8672. *Fax:* (20) 7373-6002. *E-mail:* reception@aitkenassoc.demon.co.uk.

BRADHURST, Jane, BA, MSc, DipEd, ; Australian writer, dramatist and poet; b. 28 Oct. 1926, Sydney, NSW; m. Colin Russell-Jones (deceased); two s. one d. *Education:* University of Sydney, University of Canberra, Goulburn CAE. *Career:* mem. Australian Capital Territory Writers' Centre, Australian Writers' Guild. *Publications:* The Flowers of the Snowy Mountains 1977, Document of Our Day: Women of the Pre-Pill Generation 1986, Three One Act Plays 1987, Duet String Trio Quartet 1987, Animalia in Australia 1992, 100 Poems 1993, The BD II 1995, Love in a Hot Climate 1996, Three Festival Plays 1998, Summertime (musical) 1998, There is no Mystery (anthology) 1999, Mystery in Manhattan 2000, Always on Call: Tales of an Outback Doctor 2002, Outback Lives and Border Fence Brides – more tales of an outback doctor 2004. *Honours:* several drama awards. *Address:* PO Box 9009, Deakin, ACT 2600, Australia.

BRADLEE, Benjamin Crowninshield; Newspaper Editor; b. 26 Aug. 1921, Boston, MA, USA; m. 1st Jean Saltonstall 1942; one s.; m. 2nd Antoinette Pinchot 1956; one s. one d.; m. 3rd Sally Quinn 1978; one s. *Education:* AB, Harvard Univ. *Career:* reporter, NH Sunday News, Manchester 1946–48, Washington Post 1948–51; Press Attaché, US Embassy, Paris 1951–53; European corresp. Newsweek, Paris 1953–57; reporter, Washington Bureau, Newsweek 1957–61, Sr Ed. and Chief of Bureau 1961–65; Man. Ed. Washington Post 1965–68, Vice-Pres. and Exec. Ed. 1968–91, Vice- Pres. at Large 1991–; Chair. History of St Mary's City Comm. 1992–. *Publications:* That Special Grace, 1964; Conversations with Kennedy, 1975; A Good Life: Newspapering and Other Adventures (autobiog.), 1995. *Honours:* Burton Benjamin Award, 1995. *Address:* c/o Washington Post, 1150 15th St NW, Washington, DC 20071-0001, USA.

BRADLEY, Clive, CBE, MA; British publishing and media executive and barrister; *Convenor, Confederation of Information Communication Industries*; b. 25 July 1934, London. *Education:* Felsted School, Essex, Clare Coll., Cambridge and Yale Univ., USA. *Career:* barrister (Middle Temple); with BBC 1961–63; Broadcasting Officer, Labour Party 1963–65; Political Ed., The Statist 1965–67; Group Labour Adviser, Int. Publishing Corpn and Deputy Gen. Man. Mirror Group Newspapers 1967–73; Dir The Observer 1973–75; Chief Exec. The Publishers Asscn 1976–97; Dir Confed. of Information Communication Industries 1984–; Deputy Chair. Central London Valuation Tribunal; Chair. Age Concern, Richmond 2001–03, Richmond upon Thames Arts Council 2003–; Gov. Felsted School. *Publications:* many articles and broadcasts on politics, econs, industrial relations, industry media and current affairs. *Address:* 8 Northumberland Place, Richmond-upon-Thames, Surrey, TW10 6TS, England (Home). *Telephone:* (20) 8940-7172 (Home). *Fax:* (20) 8940-7603 (Home). *E-mail:* bradley_clive@btopenworld.com (Home).

BRADLEY, George; Writer and Poet; b. 22 Jan. 1953, Roslyn, New York, USA; m. Spencer Boyd, 8 Sept. 1984. *Education:* BA, Yale University, 1975; University of Virginia, 1977–78. *Publications:* Terms to Be Met, 1986; Of the Knowledge of Good and Evil, 1991; The Fire Fetched Down, 1996; The Yale Younger Poets Anthology (ed.), 1998; Some Assembly Required, 2001. Contributions: periodicals. *Honours:* Acad. of American Poets Prize, 1978; Yale Younger Poets Prize, 1985; Lavan Younger Poets Award, 1990; Witter Bynner Prize, 1992. *Address:* 82 W Main St, Chester, CT 06412, USA.

BRADLEY, John; Teacher, Writer and Poet; b. 26 Sept. 1950, New York, NY, USA; m. Jana Brubaker, 27 May 1988, one s. *Education:* BA, History, 1973, BA, English, 1977, University of Minnesota; MA, English, Colorado State University, 1981; MFA, Bowling Green State University, 1989. *Career:* Instructor in English, Bowling Green State University, 1989–91, Northern Illinois University, 1992–. *Publications:* Love in Idleness: The Poetry of Roberto Zingarello, 1989; Atomic Ghost: Poets Respond to the Nuclear Age, 1995; Learning to Glow: A Nuclear Reader, 2000. Contributions: Ironwood; Rolling Stone; Poetry East. *Honours:* National Endowment for the Arts Fellowship.

BRADLEY, John Edmund, Jr; Writer; b. 12 Aug. 1958, Opelousas, LA, USA. *Education:* BA, Louisiana State University, 1980. *Publications:* Tupelo Nights, 1988; The Best There Ever Was, 1990; Love & Obits, 1992; Smoke, 1994; My Juliet, 2000. Contributions: Esquire, Sports Illustrated and other periodicals. *Address:* 2035 Delmar St, Opelousas, LA 70570, USA.

BRADWELL, James (see Kent, Arthur (William Charles)).

BRADY, James Winston; Writer and Broadcaster; b. 15 Nov. 1928, New York, NY, USA; m. Florence Kelly, 12 April 1958, two d. *Education:* AB, Manhattan College, 1950; New York University. *Publications:* Fiction: Paris One, 1977; Nielsen's Children, 1979; Press Lord, 1981; Holy Wars, 1983; Designs, 1986. Non-Fiction: The Coldest War, 1990; Fashion Show, 1992. Contributions: Parade; Esquire; Advertising Age; TV Guide; People; Harper's Bazaar. *Honours:* Emmy Award, 1973–74. *Address:* PO Box 1584, East Hampton, NY 11937, USA.

BRADY, Joan, BS; American writer; b. 4 Dec. 1939, San Francisco, CA; m. Dexter Masters 1963, one s. *Education:* Columbia Univ., Open Univ. *Publications:* The Imposter (novel) 1979, The Unmaking of a Dancer (autobiog.) 1982, Theory of War (novel) (Whitbread Novel of the Year and Book of the Year 1993, Prix du Meilleur Livre Étranger 1995) 1992, Prologue (autobiog.) 1994, Death Comes for Peter Pan (novel) 1996, The Emigré (novel) 1999, Bleedout (novel) 2004; contrib. to Harpers, London Times, Sunday Times, Telegraph, Independent. *Honours:* National Endowment for the Arts Grant 1986. *Literary Agent:* Curtis Brown Ltd, Haymarket House, 28–29 Haymarket, London, SW1Y 4SP, England. *Telephone:* (20) 7393-4400. *Fax:* (20) 7393-4401. *E-mail:* info@curtisbrown.co

.uk. *Website:* www.curtisbrown.co.uk. *Address:* Fiona Spencer Thomas, 709 Beatty House, Dolphin Square, London, SW1V 3PN, England. *E-mail:* jbrady@btinternet.com.

BRADY, Nicholas (see Levinson, Leonard).

BRADY, Terence Joseph; Dramatist, Writer and Actor; b. 13 March 1939, London, England; m. Charlotte Mary Therese Bingham, one s. one d. *Education:* BA Moderatorship, History and Political Science, Trinity College, Dublin, 1961. *Career:* Actor in films, radio and television; mem. Point-to-Point Owners Asscn; Society of Authors. *Publications:* Rehearsal, 1972; Victoria (with Charlotte Bingham), 1972; Rose's Story (with Charlotte Bingham), 1973; Victoria and Company (with Charlotte Bingham), 1974; The Fight Against Slavery, 1976; Yes--Honestly, 1977; Point-to-Point (with Michael Felton), 1990. Other: Television Films: Losing Control, 1987; The Seventh Raven, 1987; This Magic Moment, 1988; Riders, 1990; Polo, 1993. Contributions: Stage, radio, television series and periodicals. *Honours:* BBC Radio Writers' Guild Award, 1972. *Address:* United Authors Ltd, Garden Studios, 11–15 Betterton St, London WC2 9BP, England.

BRAGG, Baron (Life Peer), cr. 1998, of Wigton in the County of Cumbria; **Melvyn Bragg,** MA, FRSL, FRTS; British author and television presenter; *Controller of Arts and Features, London Weekend TV*; b. 6 Oct. 1939, Carlisle; m. 1st Marie-Elisabeth Roche 1961 (deceased); one d.; m. 2nd Catherine M. Haste 1973; one s. one d. *Education:* Nelson-Thomlinson Grammar School, Wigton and Wadham Coll., Oxford. *Career:* BBC Radio and TV Producer 1961–67; TV Presenter and Ed. The South Bank Show for ITV 1978–; Head of Arts, London Weekend TV 1982–90, Controller of Arts and Features 1990–; Deputy Chair. Border TV 1985–90, Chair. 1990–96; novelist 1965–; writer and broadcaster 1967–, writer and presenter of BBC Radio Four's Start the Week 1988–98, In Our Time 1998–, Routes of English 1999–, The Adventure of English 2001; mem. Arts Council and Chair. Literature Panel of Arts Council 1977–80; Pres. Cumbrians for Peace 1982–, Northern Arts 1983–87, Nat. Campaign for the Arts 1986–; Gov. LSE 1997–; Chancellor Leeds Univ. 1999–; mem. Bd Really Useful Co. 1989–90; Pres. Nat. Acad. of Writing; Pres. MIND; Appeal Chair. Royal Nat. Inst. for the Blind Talking Books Appeal. *Plays:* Mardi Gras 1976, Orion 1977, The Hired Man 1985, King Lear in New York 1992. *Screenplays:* Isadora, The Music Lovers, Jesus Christ Superstar, A Time to Dance. *Novels:* For Want of a Nail 1965, The Second Inheritance 1966, Without a City Wall 1968, The Hired Man 1969, A Place in England 1970, The Nerve 1971, The Hunt 1972, Josh Lawton 1972, The Silken Net 1974, A Christmas Child 1976, Autumn Manoeuvres 1978, Kingdom Come 1980, Love and Glory 1983, The Cumbrian Trilogy 1984, The Maid of Buttermere 1987, A Time to Dance (televised 1992) 1990, Crystal Rooms 1992, Credo 1996, The Sword and the Miracle 1997, The Soldier's Return 1999, A Son of War 2001. *Other publications:* Speak for England 1976, Land of the Lakes 1983, Laurence Olivier 1984, Rich, The Life of Richard Burton 1988, The Seventh Seal: A Study on Ingmar Bergman 1993, On Giants' Shoulders 1998 Crossing the Lines 2003, The Adventure of English 2003. *Honours:* Hon. Fellow Lancashire Polytechnic 1987, The Library Asscn 1994, Wadham Coll. Oxford 1995, Univ. of Wales, Cardiff 1996; Domus Fellow St Catherine's Coll. Oxford 1990; Hon. DLitt (Liverpool) 1986, (Council for Nat. Academic Awards) 1990, (Lancaster) 1990, (South Bank) 1997, (Leeds) 2000, (Bradford) 2000; Hon. DUniv (Open Univ.) 1988; Hon. DCL (Northumbria) 1994; Hon. DSc (UMIST) 1998, (Brunel) 2000; Dr hc (St. Andrews) 1993, (Sunderland) 2001John Llewellyn-Rhys Memorial Award 1968, PEN Award for Fiction 1970, Richard Dimbleby Award for Outstanding Contribution to Television 1987, Ivor Novello Award for Best Musical 1985, VLV Award 2000, WHSmith Literary Award 2000, four Prix Italia awards, various BAFTAs. *Address:* 12 Hampstead Hill Gardens, London, NW3 2PL, England.

BRAINE, David; University Lecturer and Research Fellow and Writer; b. 2 Sept. 1940, Devonshire, England. *Education:* BA, History, 1962, BPhil, 1965, Magdalen College, Oxford. *Career:* Lecturer, 1965–89, Hon. Lecturer, 1989–, University of Aberdeen; mem. American Catholic Philosophical Asscn; Aristotelian Society. *Publications:* Medical Ethics and Human Life, 1982; The Reality of Time and the Existence of God, 1988; Ethics, Technology and Medicine (ed. and contributor with Harry Lesser), 1992. Contributions: scholarly books and professional journals. *Honours:* Demyship, Magdalen College, Oxford; Gifford Fellow, University of Aberdeen, 1981–87. *Address:* 104–106 High St, Old Aberdeen AB2 3HE, Scotland.

BRAMPTON, Sally; Editor and Novelist; one d. *Career:* fmr Ed., British Elle magazine, Red magazine; prof., Central Saint Martins College of Art and Design. *Publications:* Good Grief, 1992; Lovesick, 1995; Concerning Lily, 1998; Love, Always, 2000. *Address:* c/o Central Saint Martins College of Art & Design, Southampton Row, London WC1B 4AP, England. *E-mail:* sallybrampton@hotmail.com.

BRANCH, Edgar Marquess; University Prof., Educator, Ed. and Author; b. 21 March 1913, Chicago, IL, USA; m. Mary Josephine Emerson, 29 April 1939, one s. two d. *Education:* University College, University of London, England, 1932–33; BA, Beloit College, 1934; Brown University, 1934–35; MA, University of Chicago, 1938; PhD, University of Iowa, 1941. *Career:* Instructor, 1941–43, Asst Prof., 1943–49, Assoc. Prof., 1949–57, Prof., 1957–64, Chair., Dept of English, 1959–64, Research Prof., 1964–78, Miami University, Oxford, Ohio; mem. MLA of America; National Council of Teachers of English; James T. Farrell Society. *Publications:* The Literary Apprenticeship of Mark Twain, 1950; James T. Farrell, 1963; Clemens of the Call, 1969; James T. Farrell, 1971; Men Call Me Lucky, 1985; Mark Twain and the Starchy Boys, 1992; Studs Lonigan's Neighborhood and the Making of James T. Farrell, 1996; A Paris Year: Dorothy and James T. Farrell in Paris 1931–32, 1998. Contributions: anthologies, magazines, and journals. *Honours:* National Endowment for the Humanities Fellowships, 1971–72, 1976–77; Benjamin Harrison Medallion, Miami University, 1978; Guggenheim Fellowship, 1978–79; Distinguished Service Citation, Beloit College, 1979; Mark Twain Circle of America, Lifetime Achievement Award, 1992; Mid American Award for Distinguished Contributions to the Study of Midwestern Literature, Society for the Study of Midwestern Literature, 1994; First MLA Prize for Distinguished Scholarly Edition, 1995; Pegasus Award, Ohioana Library Asscn, 1996. *Address:* 4810 Bonham Rd, Oxford, OH 45056, USA.

BRANCH, Taylor; Writer; b. 14 Jan. 1947, Atlanta, GA, USA; m. Christina Macy, one s. one d. *Education:* AB, University of North Carolina, 1968; Postgraduate Studies, Princeton University, 1968–70. *Career:* Staff, Washington (DC) Monthly magazine, 1970–73, Harper's magazine, New York City, 1973–75, Esquire magazine, New York City, 1975–76. *Publications:* Blowing the Whistle: Dissent in the Public Interest (with Charles Peters), 1972; Second Wind: The Memoirs of an Opinionated Man (with Bill Russell), 1979; The Empire Blues, 1981; Labyrinth (with Eugene M. Propper), 1982; Parting the Waters: America in the King Years, 1954–63, 1988; Pillar of Fire: America in the King Years, 1963–65, 1998. *Honours:* Christopher Award, 1988; Pulitzer Prize in History, 1989; National Humanities Medal, 1999. *Address:* 116 E De La Guerra St, No. 7, Santa Barbara, CA 93101, USA.

BRAND, Alice Glarden; Poet, Writer and Prof. of English; b. 8 Sept. 1938, New York, NY, USA; m. Ira Brand, 10 April 1960, three c. *Education:* University of Rochester, 1956–58; BA, City College, CUNY, 1960; MEd, 1973, DEd, 1979, Rutgers University. *Career:* Asst Prof., 1980–86, Assoc. Prof. of English, 1987, University of Missouri at St Louis; Visiting Scholar, University of California at Berkeley, 1982–83; Assoc. Prof. of English and Dir of Writing, Clarion University of Pennsylvania, 1987–89; Assoc. Prof., 1989–91, Dir of Composition, 1989–93, Prof. of English, 1992–99, SUNY at Brockport; many workshops, lectures and readings; mem. Acad. of American Poets; MLA; National Council of Teachers of English; Poetry Society of America; Poets and Writers. *Publications:* Poetry: As it Happens, 1983; Studies on Zone, 1989. Other: Therapy in Writing: A Psycho-Educational Enterprise, 1980; The Psychology of Writing: The Affective Experience, 1989; Presence of Mind: Writing and the Domain Beyond the Cognitive (ed. with Richard L. Graves), 1994; Court of Common Pleas, 1996; Writing in the Majors: A Guide to Disciplinary Faculty, 1998. Contributions: numerous anthologies and periodicals. *Honours:* New Jersey State Council on the Arts Fellowship in Poetry, 1981; Residencies, Yaddo Artist's Colony, 1986, 1987, 1991; Wildwood Poetry Prize, 1988; Hon. Mention, National Writers' Union National Poetry Competition, 1993. *Address:* 1235 N Astor St, No. 2, Chicago, IL 60610, USA.

BRAND, Dionne, BA, MA; Canadian poet, novelist, essayist and film-maker; b. 1953, Guayguayare, Trinidad. *Education:* Univ. of Toronto, Ontario Inst. for Studies in Education. *Career:* f. mem., ed., Our Lives newspaper; extensive community work; f. mem., fmr Chair., Women's Issues Committee of the Ontario Coalition of Black Trade Unionists; fmr writer-in-residence, Halifax City Regional Library; fmr teacher of poetry, West Coast Women and Words Society Summer School and Retreat; Writer-in-residence, Univ. of Toronto, 1990–91; Teacher, creative writing, Univ. of Guelph, 1991–92; Documentary films: Older, Stronger, Wiser (assoc. dir), 1989, Sisters in the Struggle (co-dir), 1991, Long Time Comin' (co-dir), 1993. *Publications:* Poetry: 'Fore Day Morning: Poems, 1978; Earth Magic: Poetry for Young People, 1978; Primitive Offensive, 1982; Winter Epigrams and Epigrams to Ernesto Cardenal in Defense of Claudia, 1983; Chronicles of the Hostile Sun, 1984; No Language is Neutral, 1990; Land to Light On, 1997; At the Full and Change of the Moon, 1999; Thirsty, 2001. Other: Rivers Have Sources, Trees Have Roots: Speaking of Racism (with Krisantha Sri Bhaggiydatta), 1986; Sight Specific: Lesbians and Representation, 1988; Sans Souci (short stories), 1988; No Burden to Carry: Narratives of Black Working Women in Ontario 1920s to 1950s (with Lois de Shield), 1991; Bread out of Stone (essays), 1994; In Another Place, Not Here (novel), 1996. Contributions: journals incl.: Spear, Fuse Magazine, Network, the Harriet Tubman Review, Fireweed, Poetry Canada Review, Canadian Women Studies, Resources for Feminist Research, Canadian Women Poets; Anthologies: Grammar of Dissent: Poetry and Prose by Claire Harris, M. Nourbese Philip and Dionne Brand, 1994; Other Voices; The Penguin Book of Caribbean Verse; Poetry by Canadian Women; Stories by Canadian Women; Her True-True Name: An Anthology of Women's Writing from the Caribbean; Other Solitudes: Canadian Multicultural Fictions; Eyeing the North Star: Directions in African-Canadian Literature. *Honours:* Gov.-Gen.'s Literary Award, 1997. *Address:* c/o Northwest Passages, 628 Penzer Street, Kamloops, BC V2C 3G5, Canada.

BRAND, Stewart, BS; American editor, writer and publisher; *President, The Long Now Foundation*; b. 14 Dec. 1938, Rockford, Ill.; m. 1st Lois Jennings 1966 (divorced 1972); m. 2nd Ryan Phelan 1983; one s. from a previous relationship. *Education:* Phillips Exeter Acad., Stanford Univ. *Career:*

served US Army 1960–62; fmrly with Merry Pranksters; consultant to Gov. of Calif. 1976–78; research scientist Media Lab., MIT 1986; Visiting Scholar Royal Dutch/Shell 1986; f. America Needs Indians, The Well (Internet bulletin Bd) 1984–; co-f. Global Business Network consultancy 1988–, The Long Now Foundation 1996– (also Pres.), All Species project 2000–; Trustee Santa Fe Inst. 1989–. *Television:* How Buildings Learn (writer and presenter) 1997. *Publications:* Two Cybernetic Frontiers 1974, The Media Lab 1987, How Buildings Learn 1994, The Clock of the Long Now 1999; editor, publr: The Last Whole Earth Catalog 1968–71 (Nat. Book Award), Whole Earth Epilog 1974, The Co-Evolution Quarterly 1974–85, The Next Whole Earth Catalog 1980–81, Whole Earth Software Catalog (ed.-in-chief) 1983–85. *Address:* The Long Now Foundation, POB 29462, Presidio of San Francisco, CA 94129-0462, USA (Office). *Telephone:* (415) 561-6582 (Office). *Fax:* (415) 561-6297 (Office). *E-mail:* services@longnow.org (Home). *Website:* www.longnow.org (Office).

BRANDON, Sheila (see Rayner, Claire Berenice).

BRANDT, Diana (Di) Ruth, BTh, BA, MA, PhD; poet and writer; b. 31 Jan. 1952, Winkler, Manitoba, Canada; m. Les Brandt 1971 (divorced 1990); two d. *Education:* Canadian Mennonite Bible College, University of Manitoba, University of Toronto. *Career:* Faculty, University of Winnipeg, 1986–95; Writer-in-Residence, University of Alberta, 1995–96; Research Fellow, University of Alberta, 1996–97; Assoc. Prof. of English and Creative Writing, University of Windsor, 1997–; mem. Canadian PEN; League of Canadian Poets; Manitoba Writers' Guild; Writers' Union of Canada. *Publications:* Poetry: questions i asked my mother, 1987; Agnes in the sky, 1990; mother, not mother, 1992; Jerusalem, beloved, 1995. Other: Wild Mother Dancing: Maternal Narrative in Canadian Literature, 1993; Dancing Naked: Narrative Strategies for Writing Across Centuries, 1996. Contributions: various publications. *Honours:* Gerald Lampert Award for Best First Book of Poetry in Canada, 1987; McNally Robinson Award for Manitoba Book of the Year, 1990; Silver National Magazine Award, 1995; Canadian Authors' Asscn National Poetry Award, 1996.

BRANDT, Jorgen Gustava; Danish poet, novelist and essayist; b. 1929. *Career:* worked for the Cultural Dept, Danish Radio. *Publications:* Her omkring 1974, Jatháram 1976, Ophold 1977, Lyset i stenene 1977, Almanak 1977, Köbenhavnerluft 1977, Idiotes: Med blade af livet i klostret 20 1980, Hop: Nye digte 1982, By: Byen i digte 1983, Selected Longer Poems 1983, Harlekinade 1985, Scala suite 1986. *Address:* c/o Curbstone Press, 321 Jackson Street, Willimantic, CT 06226-1738, USA. *E-mail:* info@curbstone.org. *Website:* www.curbstone.org.

BRANFIELD, John Charles; Writer and Teacher; b. 19 Jan. 1931, Burrow Bridge, Somerset, England; m. Kathleen Elizabeth Peplow, two s. two d. *Education:* MA, Queens' College, Cambridge; MEd, University of Exeter. *Publications:* A Flag in the Map, 1960; Look the Other Way, 1963; In the Country, 1966; Nancekuke, 1972; Sugar Mouse, 1973; The Fox in Winter, 1980; Thin Ice, 1983; The Falklands Summer, 1987; The Day I Shot My Dad, 1989; Lanhydrock Days, 1991; A Breath of Fresh Air, 2001; Ella and Charles Naper, Art and Life at Lamorna, 2003. *Literary Agent:* AP Watt Ltd, 20 John St, London WC1N 2DR, England. *Address:* Mingoose Villa, Mingoose, Mount Hawke, Truro, Cornwall TR4 8BX, England.

BRANIGAN, Keith; Prof. of Prehistory and Archaeology and Writer; b. 15 April 1940, Buckinghamshire, England; m. Kuabrat Sivadith, 20 June 1965, one s. two d. *Education:* BA, 1963, PhD, 1966, University of Birmingham. *Career:* Research Fellow, University of Birmingham, 1965–66; Lecturer, University of Bristol, 1966–67; Prof. of Prehistory and Archaeology, University of Sheffield, 1976–; mem. Prehistory Society, vice-pres., 1984–86; Dir, Sheffield Centre for Aegean Archaeology, 1997–. *Publications:* Copper and Bronzeworking in Early Bronze Age Crete, 1968; The Foundations of Palatial Crete: A Survey of Crete in the Early Bronze Age, 1970; The Tombs of Mesara: A Study of Funerary Architecture and Ritual in Southern Crete, 2800–1700 B.C., 1970; Latimer: Belgic, Roman, Dark Age, and Early Modern Farm, 1971; Town and Country: The Archaeology of Verulamium and the Roman Chilterns, 1973; Reconstructing the Past: A Basic Introduction to Archaeology, 1974; Aegean Metalwork of the Early and Middle Bronze Ages, 1974; Atlas of Ancient Civilizations, 1976; Prehistoric Britain: An Illustrated Survey, 1976; The Roman West Country: Classical Culture and Celtic Society (ed. with P. J. Fowler), 1976; The Roman Villa in South-West England, 1977; Gatcombe: The Excavation and Study of a Romano-British Villa Estate, 1967–1976, 1978; Rome and the Brigantes: The Impact of Rome on Northern England (ed.), 1980; Roman Britain: Life in an Imperial Province, 1980; Hellas: The Civilizations of Ancient Greece (with Michael Vickers), 1980; Atlas of Archaeology, 1982; Prehistory, 1984; The Catuvellauni, 1986; Archaeology Explained, 1988; Romano-British Cavemen (with M. J. Dearne), 1992; Dancing with Death: Life and Death in Southern Crete c.3000–2000 B.C., 1993; Lexicon of the Greek and Roman Cities and Place Names in Antiquity, c.1500 B.C.-A.D. 500 (ed. with others), 1993; The Archaeology of the Chilterns (ed.), 1994; Barra: Archaeological Research on Ben Tangaval (with P. Foster), 1995; Cemetery and Society in the Aegean Bronze Age (ed.), 1998; From Barra to Berneray (with P. Foster), 2000; Barra and the Bishop's Isles (with P. Foster), 2002; Urbanism in the Aegean Bronze Age (ed.), 2002. Contributions: Professional journals. *Honours:* Society of Antiquaries, fellow, 1970–. *Address:* c/o Dept of Prehistory and Archaeology, University of Sheffield, Sheffield S10 2TN, England.

BRANTLINGER, Patrick Morgan; Prof. of English and Writer; b. 20 March 1941, Indianapolis, IN, USA; m. Ellen Anderson, 21 June 1963, two s. one d. *Education:* BA, Antioch College, 1964; MA, 1965, PhD, 1968, Harvard University. *Career:* Asst Prof., 1968–74, Assoc. Prof., 1974–79, Prof., 1979–, of English, Chair, Dept of English, 1990–94, Indiana University; Ed., Victorian Studies, 1980–90; mem. Midwest Victorian Studies Asscn; MLA. *Publications:* The Spirit of Reform: British Literature and Politics, 1832–1867, 1977; Bread and Circuses: Theories of Mass Culture and Social Decay, 1983; Rule of Darkness: British Literature of Imperialism, 1830–1914, 1986; Crusoe's Footprints: Cultural Studies in Britain and America, 1990; Fictions of State: Culture and Credit in Britain, 1694–1994, 1996; The Reading Lesson: Mass Literacy as Threat in Nineteenth Century British Fiction, 1998; Who Killed Shakespeare? What's Happened to English Since the Radical Sixties, 2001. Contributions: scholarly books and journals. *Honours:* Guggenheim Fellowship, 1978; National Endowment for the Humanities Fellowship, 1983. *Address:* c/o Dept of English, Indiana University, Bloomington, IN 47405, USA.

BRATA, Sasthi, (Sasthibrata Chakravarti); Writer and Poet; b. 16 July 1939, Kolkata, India; m. Pamela Joyce Radcliffe, divorced. *Education:* University of Calcutta. *Career:* London Columnist, Statesman, 1977–80. *Publications:* Eleven Poems, 1960; Confessions of an Indian Woman Eater, 1971; She and He, 1973; Encounter (short stories), 1978; The Sensorous Guru: The Making of a Mystic President, 1980. *Address:* 33 Savernake Rd, London NW3 2JU, England.

BRATHWAITE, (Edward) Kamau; academic, poet, writer and editor; b. 11 May 1930, Bridgetown, Barbados; m. Doris Monica Welcome 1960; one s. *Education:* Harrison College, Barbados; BA, History, 1953, CertEd, 1954, Pembroke College, Cambridge; DPhil, University of Sussex, 1968. *Career:* Education Officer, Ministry of Education, Ghana, 1955–62; Tutor, Extra-mural Dept, University of the West Indies, St Lucia, 1962–63; Lecturer, 1963–76, Reader, 1976–82, Prof. of Social and Cultural History, 1982–, University of the West Indies, Kingston; Founding Secretary, Caribbean Artists Movement, 1966; Ed., Savacou magazine, 1970–; Visiting Fellow, Harvard University, 1987; several visiting professorships. *Publications:* Poetry: Rights of Passage, 1967; Masks, 1968; Islands, 1969; Penguin Modern Poets 15 (with Alan Bold and Edwin Morgan), 1969; Panda No. 349, 1969; The Arrivants: A New World Trilogy, 1973; Days and Nights, 1975; Other Exiles, 1975; Poetry '75 International, 1975; Black + Blues, 1976; Mother Poem, 1977; Soweto, 1979; Word Making Man: A Poem for Nicolas Guillen, 1979; Sun Poem, 1982; Third World Poems, 1983; X-Self, 1987; Sappho Sakyi's Meditations, 1989; Shar, 1990. Other: Folk Culture of the Slaves in Jamaica, 1970; The Development of Creole Society in Jamaica, 1770–1820, 1971; Caribbean Man in Space and Time, 1974; Contradictory Omens: Cultural Diversity and Integration in the Caribbean, 1974; Our Ancestral Heritage: A Bibliography of the Roots of Culture in the English-Speaking Caribbean, 1976; Wars of Respect: Nanny, Sam Sharpe, and the Struggle for People's Liberation, 1977; Jamaica Poetry: A Checklist 1686–1978, 1979; Barbados Poetry: A Checklist, Slavery to the Present, 1979; Kumina, 1982; Gods of the Middle East, 1982; National Language Poetry, 1982; The Colonial Encounter: Language, 1984; History of the Voice: The Development of a National Language in Anglophone Caribbean Poetry, 1984; Jah Music, 1986; Roots, 1986. Editor: Iouanaloa: Recent Writing from St Lucia, 1963; New Poets from Jamaica, 1979; Dream Rock, 1987. *Honours:* Arts Council of Great Britain Bursary, 1967; Camden Arts Festival Prize, 1967; Cholmondeley Award, 1970; Guggenheim Fellowship, 1972; Bussa Award, 1973; Casa de las Américas Prize, 1976; Fulbright Fellowships, 1982–83, 1987–88; Musgrave Medal, Institute of Jamaica, 1983. *Address:* c/o Department of History, University of the West Indies, Mona, Kingston 7, Jamaica.

BRAUN, Volker; German poet and playwright; b. 7 May 1939, Dresden. *Education:* Univ. of Leipzig. *Career:* Asst Dir Deutsches Theater, Berlin 1972–77, Berlin Ensemble 1979–90; mem. Akad. der Künste, Berlin. *Plays:* Grosser Frieden 1979, Dmitri 1982, Die Ubergangsgesellschaft 1987, Lenins Tod 1988, Transit Europa: Der Ausflug der Toten 1988, Böhmen am Meer 1992. *Publications:* poetry: Gegen die symmetrische Welt 1974, Training des aufrechten Gangs 1979, Langsamer knirschender Morgen 1987, Der Stoff zum Leben 1990, Lustgarten Preussen 1996; prose: Unvollendete Geschichte 1977, Hinze-Kunze-Roman 1985, Bodenloser Satz 1990, Der Wendehals: Eine Enterhaltung 1995, Das Wirklichgewollte 2000; essays: Verheerende Folgen magnelnden Anscheins innerbetrieblicher Demokratie 1988. *Honours:* Heinrich Mann Prize 1980, Bremen Literature Prize 1986, Nat. Prize, First Class 1988, Berlin Prize 1989, Schiller Commemorative Prize 1992, Büchner Prize 2000. *Address:* Wolfshagenerstrasse 68, 13187 Berlin, Germany (Home).

BRAVERMAN, Melanie; Writer; b. 9 Oct. 1960, Iowa City, IA, USA; Companion of Sally Randolph. *Education:* Evergreen State College. *Publications:* East Justice, novel, 1996. *Honours:* Fellow in Poetry and Fiction, Massachusetts Cultural Council, 1996. *Literary Agent:* Edite Kroll Literary Agency, 12 Grayhurst Park, Portland, ME 04102, USA. *E-mail:* mrb@well.com.

BRAY, John Jefferson, LLB, LLD; barrister, retd chief justice and poet; b. 16 Sept. 1912, Adelaide, SA, Australia. *Education:* University of Adelaide. *Career:* admitted to South Australian Bar, 1933; Chief Justice of South Australia, 1967–78; Chancellor, University of Adelaide, 1968–83; mem. Australian Society of Authors; Friendly Street Poets, Adelaide. *Publications:* Poems, 1962; Poems 1961–71, 1972; Poems 1972–79, 1979; The Bay of Salamis and Other Poems, 1986; Satura: Selected Poetry and Prose, 1988; The Emperor's Doorkeeper (occasional addresses), 1988; Seventy Seven (poems), 1990. Contributions: periodicals. *Honours:* South Australian Non-Fiction Award, Adelaide Festival of the Arts, 1990. *Address:* 39 Hurtle Square, Adelaide, SA 5000, Australia.

BRAYBROOKE, Neville (Patrick Bellairs); Writer, Poet and Dramatist; b. 30 May 1923, London, England. *Publications:* London Green: The Story of Kensington Gardens, Hyde Park, Green Park and St James' Park, 1959; The Idler (novel), 1960; The Delicate Investigation (play), 1969; Four Poems for Christmas, 1986; Dialogue With Judas (poem), 1989; Two Birthdays (poem), 1996; Life of Olivia Manning (with Isobel English), 2001. Contributions: periodicals. *Address:* 29 Castle Rd, Cowes PO31 7QZ, Isle of Wight.

BRAYFIELD, Celia Frances; British author and journalist; b. 21 Aug. 1945, Wembley Park; one d. *Education:* St. Paul's Girls' School, Universitaire de Grenoble. *Career:* feature writer, Daily Mail 1969–71, TV critic, Evening Standard 1974–82, The Times 1983–88; columnist, Sunday Telegraph 1989–90, The Times 1998–; contrib. to numerous other media; Dir Nat. Acad. of Writing 1999–2003; Trustee One Parent Families 1988–; mem. Soc. of Authors. *Publications:* The Body Show Book 1981, Glitter: The Truth About Fame 1985, Pearls 1987, The Prince 1990, White Ice 1993, Harvest 1995, Bestseller 1996, Getting Home 1998, Sunset 1999, Heartswap 2000, Mr Fabulous and Friends 2003, Wild Weekend 2004, Deep France 2004; contrib. various journals, magazines and newspapers. *Literary Agent:* Curtis Brown Ltd, Haymarket House, 28–29 Haymarket, London, SW1Y 4SP, England. *Telephone:* (20) 7393-4400. *Fax:* (20) 7393-4401. *E-mail:* info@curtisbrown.co.uk. *Website:* www.curtisbrown.co.uk. *Website:* www.celiabrayfield.com.

BRECHER, Michael; Political Science Educator; b. 14 March 1925, Montréal, QC, Canada; m. Eva Danon, 7 Dec. 1950, three c. *Education:* BA, McGill University, 1946; MA, 1948, PhD, 1953, Yale University. *Career:* Faculty, 1952–63, Prof., 1963–93, R. B. Angus Prof., 1993–, McGill University; Visiting Prof., University of Chicago, Hebrew University of Jerusalem, University of California at Berkeley, Stanford University; mem. Shastri Indo-Canadian Institute, founder, 1968, pres., 1969–1971; International Studies Asscn, pres., 1999–2000. *Publications:* The Struggle for Kashmir, 1953; Nehru: A Political Biography, 1959; The New States of Asia, 1963; Succession in India, 1966; India and World Politics, 1968; Political Leadership in India, 1969; The Foreign Policy System of Israel, 1972; Israel, The Korean War and China, 1974; Decisions in Israel's Foreign Policy, 1975; Studies in Crisis Behavior, 1979; Decisions in Crisis, 1980; Crisis and Change in World Politics, 1986; Crises in the Twentieth Century, 2 vols, 1988; Crisis, Conflict and Instability, 1989; Crises in World Politics, 1993; A Study of Crisis, 1997; Millennial Reflections on International Studies, five vols (ed.), 2002. Contributions: 85 articles in professional journals. *Honours:* Canada Council and Social Sciences and Humanities Research Council of Canada, Frequent Research Grantee; Killam Awards; Watamull Prize, American Historical Asscn; Woodrow Wilson Foundation Award, American Political Science Asscn; Fieldhouse Teaching Award, McGill University; Distinguished Scholar Award, International Studies Asscn.; Léon-Gérin Prix du Québec, 2000; McGill University Award for High Distinction in Research, 2000. *Address:* McGill University, 855 Sherbrooke St W, Montréal, QC H3A 2T7, Canada.

BREE, Marlin; Author and Publisher; b. 16 May 1933, Norfolk, NE, USA; m. Loris Gutzmer 5 Oct. 1963; one s. *Education:* BA and Certificate in Journalism, University of Nebraska, Lincoln, 1955. *Career:* Ed.'s Reporter, Stars and Stripes Newspaper, 1956; Ed., Sunday Magazine, Minneapolis Star-Tribune, 1968–72; Columnist, Corporate Report Magazine, 1973–77; Editorial Dir, Marlor Press, 1983–; mem. Minnesota Press Club, pres., 1963; Midwest Book Awards, chair, 1992. *Publications:* Alone Against the Atlantic (co-author), 1981; In the Teeth of the Northeaster, 1988; Call of the North Wind, 1996; Kid's Travel Fun Book (co-author and illustrator), 2000; Wake of the Green Storm: A Survivor's Tale, 2001. *Address:* 4304 Brigadoon Dr., St Paul, MN 55126, USA. *Website:* www.marlinbree.com.

BREILLAT, Catherine; Film Dir, Screenwriter and Novelist; b. 1948, Bressuire, France. *Career:* Prof. of Auteur Cinema, European Grad. School, Switzerland. Films roles: Last Tango in Paris 1972, Dracula Père et Fils 1977. Films directed: Une vraie jeune fille (A Real Young Girl) 1975 (released 2000), Tapage nocturne (Nocturnal Uproar) 1979, 36 Fillette (Virgin) 1988, Sale comme un ange (Dirty Like an Angel) 1990, Parfait Amour (Perfect Love, jtly) 1996, Romance 1999, À ma soeur! (Fat Girl) 2001, Brève traversée (TV) 2001, Scènes intimes 2002, Sex is Comedy. *Publications:* L'homme facile (novel), Tapage nocturne 1979, Romance 1999, Le livre du plaisir 1999, Une vraie jeune fille 2000, À ma soeur! 2001, Pornocratie 2001, Ein Mädchen 2001. Screenplays: Catherine et Cie. (Catherine & Co., jtly) 1975, Bilitis 1977, La peau (The Skin) 1981, Et la nave va (And the Ship Sails On) 1983, L'araignée de satin (The Satin Spider) 1984, Police 1985, Milan noir (Black Milan, jtly) 1987, Zanzibar (jtly) 1988, La nuit de l'océan (The Night of the Ocean, jtly) 1988, Aventure de Catherine C. (The Adventure of Catherine C., jtly) 1990, Le diable au corps 1990, La Thune (Money, jtly) 1991, Couples et amants (Couples and Lovers, jtly) 1994, Viens jouer dans la cour des grands (TV) 1997, Selon Matthieu 2000. *Address:* c/o European Graduate School, Ringacker, 3953 Leuk-Stadt, Switzerland.

BRENDEL, Alfred; Austrian pianist and writer; b. 5 Jan. 1931, Wiesenberg; m. 1st Iris Heymann-Gonzala 1960 (divorced 1972); one d.; m. 2nd Irene Semler 1975; one s. two d. *Career:* studied piano under Sofija Deželić (Zagreb), Ludovika v. Kaan (Graz), Edwin Fischer (Lucerne), Paul Baumgartner (Basel), Edward Steuermann (Salzburg); studied composition under A. Michl (Graz) and harmony under Franjo Dugan (Zagreb); first piano recital 1948; concert tours through Europe, Latin America, North America 1963–; Australia 1963, 1966, 1969, 1976; has appeared at many music festivals, including Salzburg 1960–, Vienna, Edinburgh, Aldeburgh, Athens, Granada, Puerto Rico and has performed with most of the major orchestras of Europe and USA, etc.; numerous recordings, including complete piano works of Beethoven, Schubert's piano works 1822–28; mem. Acad. of Arts and Sciences (USA). *Publications:* essays on music and musicians in Phono, Fono Forum, Österreichische Musikzeitschrift, Music and Musicians, Hi-Fi Stereophonie, New York Review of Books, Die Zeit, Frankfurter Allgemeine Zeitung, Musical Thoughts and Afterthoughts 1976, Music Sounded Out (essays) 1990, Fingerzeig 1996, Störendes Lachen während des Jaworts 1997, One Finger Too Many 1998, Kleine Teufel 1999, Collected Essays on Music 2000, Augerechnet Ich 2001 (English edn The Veil of Order: In Conversation with Martin Meyer 2002), Spiegelbild und Schwarzer Spuk (poems) 2003, Cursing Bagels (poems) 2004. *Honours:* Hon. RAM; Hon. RCM; Hon. Fellow, Exeter Coll. Oxford 1987; Commdr des Arts et des Lettres 1985, Hon. KBE 1989, Ordre pour le Mérite (Germany) 1991; Hon. DMus (London) 1978, (Oxford) 1983, (Exeter) 1998, (Southampton) 2002; Hon. DLitt (Sussex) 1981; Dr hc (Warwick) 1991, (Yale) 1992, (Cologne) 1995; Premio Città de Bolzano, Concorso Busoni 1949, Grand Prix du Disque 1965, Edison Prize (five times 1973–87), Grand Prix des Disquaires de France 1975, Deutscher Schallplattenpreis (four times 1976–84, 1992), Wiener Flötenuhr (six times 1976–87), Gramophone Award (six times 1977–83), Japanese Record Acad. Award (five times 1977–84, with Scottish Symphony Orchestra/Sir Charles Mackerras 2002), Japanese Grand Prix 1978, Franz Liszt Prize (four times 1979–83), Frankfurt Music Prize 1984, Diapason D'Or Award 1992, Heidsieck Award for Writing on Music 1990, Hans von Bülow-Medaille, Kameradschaft der Berliner Philharmoniker e. V., 1992, Ehrenmitgliedschaft der Wiener Philharmoniker 1998, Léonie Sonnings Musikpris, Denmark 2002, Ernst von Siemens Musikpreis 2004. *Address:* 7 St George's Court, 131 Putney Bridge Road, London, SW15 2PA, England. *Telephone:* (20) 8874-3222. *Fax:* (20) 8877-3113.

BRENDON, Piers George Rundle, MA, PhD; writer; b. 21 Dec. 1940, Stratton, Cornwall, England; m. Vyvyen Davis 1968; two s. *Education:* Magdalene Coll., Cambridge. *Career:* Lecturer in History 1966–79, Head, Dept of History 1977–79, Cambridgeshire Coll. of Arts and Technology; Keeper of the Archives Center and Fellow, Churchill Coll., Cambridge 1995–2001; broadcaster. *Publications:* Reading They've Liked (ed. with William Shaw), 1967; Reading Matters (ed. with William Shaw), 1969; By What Authority? (ed. with William Shaw), 1972; Hurrell Froude and the Oxford Movement, 1974; Hawker of Morwenstow: Portrait of a Victorian Eccentric, 1975; Eminent Edwardians, 1979; The Life and Death of the Press Barons, 1982; Winston Churchill: A Brief Life, 1984; Ike: The Life and Times of Dwight D. Eisenhower, 1986; Our Own Dear Queen, 1986; Thomas Cook: 150 Years of Popular Tourism, 1991; The Windsors: A Dynasty Revealed, 1995; The Motoring Century: The Story of the Royal Automobile Club, 1997; The Dark Valley: A Panorama of the 1930s, 2000; contrib. to periodicals, including The Guardian. *Address:* 4B Millington Road, Cambridge CB3 9HP, England.

BRENT, Madeleine (see O'Donnell, Peter).

BRENTON, Howard; Playwright and Poet; b. 13 Dec. 1942, Portsmouth, England. *Education:* BA, St Catharine's College, Cambridge, 1965. *Career:* Resident Dramatist, Royal Court Theatre, London, 1972–73; Resident Writer, University of Warwick, 1978–79; Granada Artist-in-Residence, University of California, Davis, 1997; Arts and Humanities Research Board Fellow, Birmingham University, 2000–03. *Publications:* Notes from a Psychotic Journal and Other Poems, 1969; Revenge, 1969; Scott of the Antarctic (or what God didn't see), 1970; Christie in Love and Other Plays, 1970; Lay By (co-author), 1972; Plays for Public Places, 1972; Hitler Diaries, 1972; Brassneck (with David Hare), 1973; Magnificence, 1973; Weapons of Happiness, 1976; The Paradise Run (television play), 1976; Epsom Downs, 1977; Sore Throats, with Sonnets of Love and Opposition, 1979; The Life of Galileo (adaptor), 1980; The Romans in Britain, 1980; Plays for the Poor Theatre, 1980; Thirteenth Night and A Short Sharp Shock, 1981; Danton's Death (adaptor), 1982; The Genius, 1983; Desert of Lies (television play), 1983; Sleeping Policemen (with Tunde Ikoli), 1984; Bloody Poetry, 1984; Pravda (with David Hare), 1985; Dead Head (television series), 1987; Greenland, 1988; H.I.D. (Hess is Dead), 1989; Iranian Night (with Tariq Ali), 1989; Diving for Pearls (novel), 1989; Moscow Gold (with Tariq Ali), 1990; Berlin Bertie, 1992; Playing Away (opera libretto), 1994; Hot Irons (essays and diaries), 1995; Adaptation of Goethe's Faust, 1996; Plays I, 1996; Plays II, 1996; In Extremis, 1997; Ugly Rumours (with Tariq Ali), 1998; Collateral Damage (with Tariq Ali and Andy de la Tour), 1999; Snogging Ken (with Tariq Ali and Andy de la Tour), 2000; Kit's Play, 2000; Democratic Demons, 2000; Spooks (TV series, BBC1, seven episodes), 2002–03. *Honours:* Hon. doctorate, Univ. of North London, 1996, Univ. of Westminster, 1999. *Address:* c/o Casarotto Ramsay Ltd, National House, 60–66 Wardour St, London W1V 3HP, England.

BRETT, Simon Anthony Lee; Writer; b. 28 Oct. 1945, Surrey, England; m. Lucy Victoria McLaren, 27 Nov. 1971, two s. one d. *Education:* BA, English, Wadham College, Oxford, 1967. *Career:* mem. CWA, chair., 1986–87; Detection Club; PEN; Society of Authors, chair., 1995–97. *Publications:* 17 Charles Paris crime novels, 1975–97; A Shock to the System, 1984; Dead Romantic, 1985; six Mrs Pargeter crime novels, 1986–99; The Booker Book, 1989; How to be a Little Sod, 1992; Singled Out, 1995; The Body on the Beach, 2000; The Hanging in the Hotel, 2003. Editor: several Faber books. Other: After Henry (radio and television series), 1985–92. *Honours:* Best Radio Feature, Writers' Guild, 1973; Outstanding Radio Programme, Broadcasting Press Guild, 1987. *Literary Agent:* Michael Motley. *Address:* Frith House, Burpham, Arundel, West Sussex BN18 9RR, England.

BRETTON, Barbara; Writer; b. 25 June 1950, New York, NY, USA; m. Roy Bretton, 8 Sept. 1968. *Education:* Queens College, CUNY. *Career:* mem. Romance Writers of America. *Publications:* Love Changes, 1983; The Sweetest of Debts, 1984; No Safe Place, 1985; Starfire, 1985; The Edge of Forever, 1986; Promises in the Night, 1986; Shooting Star, 1986; Somewhere in Time, 1992; One and Only, 1994; The Invisible Groom, 1994; Tomorrow and Always, 1994; Destiny's Child, 1995; Maybe This Time, 1996; Guilty Pleasure, 1996; Operation: Baby, 1997; Sleeping Alone, 1997; The Perfect Wife, 1997; Always, 1998; Operation: Family, 1998. Contributions: anthologies and periodicals.

BREW, (Osborne Henry) Kwesi, BA; fmr ambassador and poet; b. 27 May 1928, Cape Coast, Ghana. *Education:* University College of the Gold Coast, Legon. *Career:* fmr Ghanian Ambassador to Britain, India, France, USSR, Germany and Mexico. *Publications:* The Shadows of Laughter, 1968; African Panorama and Other Poems, 1981. Contributions: anthologies and periodicals. *Honours:* British Council Prize. *Address:* c/o Greenfield Review Press, PO Box 80, Greenfield Center, NY 12833, USA.

BREWER, Derek Stanley; Prof. of English Emeritus, Writer, Poet and Ed.; b. 13 July 1923, Cardiff, Wales; m. Lucie Elisabeth Hoole 17 Aug. 1951; three s. two d. *Education:* BA, 1941–42, MA, 1945–48, Magdalen College, Oxford; PhD, Univ. of Birmingham, 1956; LittD, Univ. of Cambridge, 1980. *Career:* Asst Lecturer, then Lecturer, 1949–56, Sr Lecturer, 1958–64, Univ. of Birmingham; Prof., International Christian Univ., Tokyo, 1956–58; Lecturer, 1965–76, Reader, 1976–83, Prof., 1983–90, Prof. Emeritus, 1990–, Univ. of Cambridge; Fellow, 1965–77, Master, 1977–90, Life Fellow, 1990–, Emmanuel College, Cambridge; Ed., The Cambridge Review, 1984–90. *Publications:* Chaucer, 1953; Proteus, 1958; Chaucer and His World, 1978; Symbolic Stories, 1980; English Gothic Literature, 1983; Medieval Comic Tales (ed.), 1996; A Critical Companion to the Gawain-poet (ed.), 1996; A New Introduction to Chaucer, 1998; Seatonian Exercises and Other Verses, 2000; The World of Chaucer, 2000. Contributions: scholarly books and journals. *Honours:* several hon. doctorates; Seatonian Prizes for Poetry, 1969, 1972, 1979, 1980, 1983, 1986, 1988, 1992, 1994, 1999; Hon. Mem., 1981, Medal, 1997, Japan Acad.; Corresponding Fellow, Medieval Society of America, 1987; Hon. Fellow, The English Asscn, 2001. *Address:* c/o Emmanuel College, Cambridge CB2 3AP, England.

BREWSTER, Elizabeth Winifred; academic, poet and novelist; b. 26 Aug. 1922, Chipman, NB, Canada. *Education:* BA, University of New Brunswick, 1946; MA, Radcliffe College, Cambridge, Massachusetts, 1947; BLS, University of Toronto, 1953; PhD, Indiana University, 1962. *Career:* Faculty, Dept of English, University of Victoria, 1960–61; Reference Librarian, Mt Allison University, 1961–65; Visiting Asst Prof. of English, University of Alberta, 1970–71; Asst Prof., 1972–75, Assoc. Prof., 1975–80, Prof., 1980–90, Prof. Emeritus, 1990–, of English, University of Saskatchewan; mem. League of Canadian Poets; Writers' Union of Canada; Saskatchewan Writers' Guild; PEN. *Publications:* East Coast, 1951; Lillooet, 1954; Roads, 1957; Passage of Summer: Selected Poems, 1969; Sunrise North, 1972; In Search of Eros, 1974; The Sisters, 1974; It's Easy to Fall on the Ice, 1977; Sometimes I Think of Moving, 1977; Digging In, 1982; Junction, 1982; The Way Home, 1982; A House Full of Women, 1983; Selected Poems of Elizabeth Brewster, 1944–1984, 1985; Entertaining Angels, 1988; Spring Again, 1990; The Invention of Truth, 1991; Wheel of Change, 1993; Footnotes to the Book of Job, 1995; Away from Home (autobiog.), 1995; Garden of Sculpture, 1998; Burning Bush, 2000; Jacob's Dream, 2002. *Honours:* E. J. Pratt Award for Poetry, University of Toronto, 1953; Pres.'s Medal for Poetry, University of Western Ontario, 1980; Hon. LittD, University of New Brunswick, 1982; Canada Council Award, 1985; Lifetime Award for Excellence in the Arts, Saskatchewan Arts Board, 1995; Mem., Order of Canada, 2001. *Address:* 206, 910 Ninth Street E, Saskatoon, SK S7H 0N1, Canada.

BREYTENBACH, Breyten; South African poet and writer; b. 16 Sept. 1939, Bonnievale. *Education:* Univ. of Cape Town. *Publications:* And Death White as Words: Anthology 1978, In Africa Even the Flies Are Happy: Selected Poems 1964–77 1978, Mouroir: Mirrornotes of a Novel 1984, End Papers 1986, All One Horse 1990, The Memory of Birds in Times of Revolution (essays) 1996. *Honours:* Rapport Prize 1986. *Address:* c/o Faber and Faber Ltd, 3 Queen Square, London, WC1N 3AU, England.

BREZHNEV, Dennis (see Barnett, Paul (Le Page)).

BRICKNER, Richard Pilpel, BA; writer and teacher; b. 14 May 1933, New York, NY, USA. *Education:* Middlebury College, Columbia College. *Career:* Adjunct in Writing, City College, CUNY, 1967–70; Faculty, Writing Program, New School for Social Research, New York City, 1970–. *Publications:* Fiction: The Broken Year, 1962; Bringing Down the House, 1972; Tickets, 1981; After She Left, 1988. Non-Fiction: My Second Twenty Years, 1976. Contributions: American Review; Life; New Leader; New York Times Book Review; Time. *Honours:* National Endowment for the Arts Grant, 1974; Guggenheim Fellowship, 1983. *Address:* 245 E 72nd Street, New York, NY 10021, USA.

BRIEN, Alan; Novelist and Journalist; b. 12 March 1925, Sunderland, England; m. 1st Pamela Mary Jones, 1947, three d.; m. 2ndNancy Newbold Ryan, one s. one d., 1961; m. 3rd Jill Sheila Tweedie, 1973. *Education:* BA, English Literature, Jesus College, Oxford. *Career:* Assoc. Ed., Mini-Cinema, 1950–52, Courier, 1952–53; Film Critic, Columnist, Truth, 1953–54; TV Critic, Observer, 1954–55; Film Critic, 1954–56, New York Correspondent, 1956–58, Evening Standard; Drama Critic, Features Ed., 1958–61, Columnist, 1963–65, Spectator; Columnist, Sunday Daily Mail, 1958–62, Sunday Dispatch, 1962–63; Political Columnist, Sunday Pictorial, 1963–64; Drama Critic, Sunday Telegraph, 1964–67; Columnist New Statesman, 1966–72, Punch, 1972–84; Diarist, 1967–75, Film Critic, 1976–84, Sunday Times. *Publications:* Domes of Fortune, 1979; Lenin: The Novel, 1986; Heaven's Will (novel), 1989; And When Rome Falls (novel), 1991. Contributions: various professional journals. *Address:* 14 Falkland Rd, London NW5, England.

BRIERLEY, David; Author; b. 30 July 1936, Durban, South Africa; m. (separated); one d. *Education:* BA, Oxon. *Publications:* Cold War, 1979; Blood Group O, 1980; Big Bear, Little Bear, 1981; Shooting Star, 1983; Czechmate, 1984; Skorpion's Death, 1985; Snowline, 1986; One Lives, One Dies, 1987; On Leaving a Prague Window, 1995; The Horizontal Woman, 1996; The Cloak-and-Dagger Girl, 1998; Death & Co, 1999. *Literary Agent:* James Hale. *Address:* La Cave, Les Trémoulèdes, 34390 St Vincent d'Olargues, France.

BRIGGS, Asa, (Lord Briggs of Lewes); Historian and Writer; b. 7 May 1921, Keighley, Yorkshire, England; m. Susan Anne Banwell, 1955, two s. two d. *Education:* History Tripos, Sidney Sussex College, Cambridge, 1941; BSc, Economics, London, 1941. *Career:* Fellow, 1945–55, Provost, 1976–91, Worcester College, Oxford; Reader in Recent Social and Economic History, University of Oxford, 1950–55; Prof. of Modern History, University of Leeds, 1955–61; Prof. of History, 1961–76, Dean of Social Studies, 1961–65, Provisional Vice-Chancellor, 1961–67, Vice-Chancellor, 1967–76, University of Sussex; Governor, BFI, 1970–76; Chair., European Institute of Education, 1974–84; Chancellor, Open University, 1979–94; mem. British Acad., fellow; Ephemera Society, pres., 1984–; Historical Asscn, vice-pres., 1986; Social History Society, pres., 1976–; Victorian Society, pres., 1983–. *Publications:* Patterns of Peacemaking (with D. Thomson and E. Meyer), 1945; History of Birmingham, 1865–1938, 1952; Victorian People, 1954; Friends of the People, 1956; The Age of Improvement, 1959; Chartist Studies (ed.), 1959; History of Broadcasting (ed.) (five vols), 1961–95; Victorian Cities, 1963; The Nineteenth Century (ed.), 1970; Cap and Bell (with Susan Briggs), 1972; Essays in the History of Publishing (ed.), 1974; Essays in Labour History, 1918–1939, 1977; Governing the BBC, 1979; From Coalbrookdale to the Crystal Palace, 1980; The Power of Steam, 1982; Marx in London, 1982; A Social History of England, 1983; The BBC: The First Fifty Years, 1985; The Franchise Affair (with Joanna Spicer), 1986; Victorian Things, 1988; The Channel Islands: Occupation and Liberation, 1949–45, 1995; Fins de Siècle (co-ed.), 1996; Modern Europe, 1789–1989 (co-author), 1997; The History of Bethlem (co-author), 1997; Chartism, 1998; Go to It!: War and Work, 1939–1945, 1999; A Social History of the Media (with Peter Burke), 2002. *Honours:* numerous hon. doctorates; Hon. Mem., American Acad. of Arts and Sciences, 1970; Marconi Medal, 1975; Life Peer, 1976; Medal, l'Académie d'Architecture, France, 1982; Wolfson Prize for History, 2000. *Address:* The Caprons, Keere St, Lewes, Sussex BN7 1TY, England.

BRIGGS, Raymond Redvers, NDD, DFA, FSIAD; British writer, illustrator and cartoonist; b. 18 Jan. 1934, Wimbledon; m. Jean T. Clark 1963 (died 1973). *Education:* Rutlish School, Merton, Wimbledon School of Art and Slade School of Fine Art, London. *Career:* freelance illustrator 1957–; children's author 1961–;mem. RSL, Soc. of Authors. *Publications:* The Strange House 1961, Midnight Adventure 1961, Ring-a-Ring o' Roses 1962, Sledges to the Rescue 1963, The White Land 1963, Fee Fi Fo Fum 1964, The Mother Goose Treasury 1966, Jim and the Beanstalk 1970, The Fairy Tale Treasury 1972, Father Christmas 1973 (also film version), Father Christmas Goes on Holiday 1975, Fungus the Bogeyman 1977, The Snowman 1978 (also film version), Gentleman Jim 1980 (also stage version), When the Wind Blows 1982 (stage and radio versions 1983, animated film version 1987), The Tinpot Foreign General and the Old Iron Woman 1984, The Snowman Pop-Up 1986, Unlucky Wally 1987, Unlucky Wally

Twenty Years On 1989, The Man 1992, The Bear 1994 (also film version), Ethel and Ernest 1998, UG 2001, Blooming Books (autobiog. with Nicolette Jones) 2003, The Puddleman 2004. *Honours:* awards include Kate Greenaway Medal 1966, 1973, BAFTA Award, Francis Williams Illustration Award (Victoria & Albert Museum) 1982, Broadcasting Press Guild Radio Award 1983, Children's Author of the Year 1992, Kurt Maschler Award 1992, Illustrated Book of the Year Award 1998, Smarties Silver Award 2001. *Address:* Weston, Underhill Lane, Westmeston, nr Hassocks, Sussex, BN6 8XG, England.

BRINDLEY, Lynne Janie, MA, FLA, FRSA, CCMI; British librarian; *Chief Executive, The British Library*; b. 2 July 1950, London; m. Timothy Stuart Brindley 1972. *Education:* Truro High School, Univ. of Reading, Univ. Coll. London. *Career:* Head of Marketing and of Chief Exec.'s Office, British Library 1979–85, Chief Exec. British Library 2000–; Dir of Library and Information Services, also Pro-Vice Chancellor, Aston Univ. 1985–90; Prin. Consultant, KPMG 1990–92; Librarian and Dir of Information Services, LSE 1992–97; Librarian and Pro-Vice Chancellor, Univ. of Leeds 1997–2000, Visiting Prof. of Knowledge Man., 2000–; Visiting Prof. of Information Man., Leeds Metropolitan Univ. 2000–03; mem. Int. Cttee on Social Science Information, UNESCO 1992–97, Lord Chancellor's Advisory Cttee on Public Records 1992–98, Stanford Univ. Advisory Council for Libraries and Information Resources 1999–, Resource Bd 2002–, EPSRC User Panel 2002–04, Ithaka Bd; Trustee Thackray Medical Museum, Leeds 1999–2001; Fellow Univ. Coll. London 2002. *Publications:* numerous articles on electronic libraries and information man. *Honours:* Freeman, City of London 1989; Liveryman, Goldsmiths' Co. 1993; Hon. DLitt (Nottingham Trent) 2001, (Oxford) 2002, (Leicester) 2002, (Sheffield) 2004, (Reading) 2004; Hon. DPhil (London Guildhall) 2002. *Address:* The British Library, 96 Euston Road, London, NW1 2DB (Office); 85 New River Head, 173 Rosebery Avenue, London, EC1R 4UP, England (Home). *Telephone:* (20) 7412-7273 (Office). *Fax:* (20) 7412-7268 (Office). *E-mail:* chief-executive@bl.uk (Office). *Website:* www.bl.uk (Office).

BRINGHURST, Robert, BA, MFA; American poet and writer; b. 16 Oct. 1946, Los Angeles, Calif.; one d. *Education:* MIT, Univ. of Utah, Defense Language Institute, Indiana Univ., Univ. of British Columbia. *Career:* General Ed. Kanchenjunga Poetry Series 1973–79; Reviews Ed. Canadian Fiction Magazine 1974–75; Visiting Lecturer Univ. of British Columbia 1975–77, Lecturer 1979–80; Poet-in-Residence Banff School of Fine Arts 1983, Ojibway and Cree Cultural Centre Writers' Workshops 1985–86, Univ. of Western Ontario 1998–99; Adjunct Lecturer Frost Centre for Native Studies and Canadian Studies 1983–84, Adjunct Prof. 1998–, and Centre for Studies in Publishing 2000–, Simon Fraser Univ.; Lecturer Trent Univ. 1984, Ashley Fellow 1994; Contributing Ed. Fine Print: A Review for the Arts of the Book 1985–90; Writer-in-Residence Univ. of Edinburgh 1989–90. *Publications:* The Shipwright's Log 1972, Cadastre 1973, Bergschrund 1975, The Stonecutter's Horses 1979, Tzuhalem's Mountain 1982, The Beauty of the Weapons: Selected Poems 1972–82 1982, Visions: Contemporary Art in Canada 1983, The Raven Steals the Light 1984, Ocean, Paper, Stone 1984, Tending the Fire 1985, The Blue Roofs of Japan 1986, Pieces of Map, Pieces of Music 1986, Conversations with Toad 1987, The Black Canoe 1991, The Elements of Typrographic Style 1992, The Calling: Selected Poems 1970–95 1995, Elements 1995, Native American Oral Literatures and the Unity of the Humanities 1998, A Story as Sharp as a Knife: The Classical Haida Mythtellers and Their World 1999, A Short History of the Printed Word 1999, The Book of Silences 2001, Ursa Major 2003, The Old in Their Knowing 2003, Prosodies of Meaning 2003; trans: Nine Visits to the Mythworld (by Ghandl of the Qayahl Llaanas) 2000, Being in Being: The Collected Works of Skaay of the Qquuna Qiighawaay 2001, The Fragments of Parmenides 2003; contribs: many anthologies. *Honours:* Macmillan Prize 1975, Alcuin Society Design Awards 1984, 1985, Canadian Broadcasting Corporation Poetry Prize 1985, Guggenheim Fellowship 1987–88. *Address:* POB 51, Heriot Bay, BC V0P 1H0, Canada.

BRINK, André Philippus; South African academic, writer and dramatist; b. 29 May 1935, Vrede; m.; three s. one d. *Education:* Potchefstroom University, Sorbonne, University of Paris. *Career:* Prof. of Afrikaans and Dutch Literature, Rhodes University, 1980–89; Prof. of English, University of Cape Town, 1990–2000. *Publications:* File on a Diplomat, 1966; Looking on Darkness, 1974; An Instant in the Wind, 1976; Rumours of Rain, 1978; A Dry White Season, 1979; A Chain of Voices, 1982; Mapmakers (essays), 1983; The Wall of the Plague, 1984; The Ambassador, 1985; States of Emergency, 1988; An Act of Terror, 1991; The First Life of Adamastor, 1993; On the Contrary, 1993; Imaginings of Sand, 1996; Reinventing a Continent (essays), 1996; Devil's Valley, 1998; The Novel: Language and Narrative from Cervantes to Calvino, 1998; The Rights of Desire, 2000; The Other Side of Silence, 2002; Before I Forget 2004; several plays; contrib. to periodicals. *Honours:* Reina Prinsen Geerlings Prize, 1964; CNA Awards for Literature, 1965, 1978, 1982; Martin Luther King Memorial Prize, 1979; Prix Médicis Étranger, 1979; Chevalier, Légion d'honneur, 1983; Commdr, Ordre des Arts et des Lettres, 1992; Hon. doctorates, Univ. of the Witwatersrand, 1992, Univ. of the Free State, 1997, Université de Montpellier, 1997, Rhodes Univ., 2001, Univ. of Pretoria, 2003; Premio Mondello, Italy, 1997; Commonwealth Writers Prize, 2003. *Address:* c/o Department of English, University of Cape Town, Rondebosch 7701, South Africa.

BRINKLEY, Alan; historian and academic; *Allan Nevins Professor of History, Columbia University*; b. 2 June 1949, Washington, DC, USA; m. Evangeline Morphos 1989. *Education:* AB, Public and International Affairs, Princeton University, 1971; AM, 1975, PhD, 1979, History, Harvard University. *Career:* Asst Prof. of History, MIT 1978–82; visiting position 1980, Dunwalke Assoc. Prof. of American History 1982–88, Harvard Univ.; Prof. of History, Graduate School and Univ. Center, CUNY 1988–91; visiting positions, Princeton Univ. 1991, Univ. of Turin 1992, New York Univ. 1993, École des Hautes Études en Sciences Sociales, Paris 1996; Prof. of History 1991–98, Allan Nevins Prof. of History 1998–, Provost 2003–, Columbia Univ.; Harmsworth Prof. of American History, Univ. of Oxford 1998–99; Fellow, Society of American Historians 1984– (exec. board mem. 1989–); mem. American Historical Asscn, Organization of American Historians (exec. board mem. 1990–93), Century Foundation (trustee 1995–, chair. 1999–), Nat. Humanities Center (trustee 2004–), American Acad. of Arts and Sciences. *Publications:* Voices of Protest: Huey Long, Father Coughlin, and the Great Depression, 1982; American History: A Survey 1983; The Unfinished Nation: A Concise History of the American People, 1993; The End of Reform: New Deal Liberalism in Recession and War, 1995; Eyes of the Nation: A Visual History of the United States (with others), 1997; New Federalist Papers (with Kathleen Sullivan and Nelson Polsby), 1997; Liberalism and Its Discontents, 1998; The Chicago Handbook for Teachers (co-ed.), 1999; The Reader's Companion to the American Presidency (co-ed.), 2000. Contributions: scholarly books and journals. *Honours:* National Endowment for the Humanities Fellowship, 1972–73; ACLS Fellowship, 1981; Robert L. Brown Prize, Louisiana Historical Asscn, 1982; National Book Award for History, 1983; Guggenheim Fellowship, 1984–85; Woodrow Wilson Center for International Scholars Fellowship, 1985; Joseph R. Levenson Memorial Teaching Prize, Harvard University, 1987; National Humanities Center Fellowship, 1988–89; Media Studies Center Fellowship, 1993–94; Russell Sage Foundation Fellowship, 1996–97. *Address:* c/o Department of History, Columbia University, New York, NY 10027, USA.

BRINKLEY, Douglas (Gregg); Prof. of History and Author; b. 14 Dec. 1960, Atlanta, GA, USA. *Education:* BA, Ohio State University, 1982; MA, 1983, PhD, 1989, Georgetown University. *Career:* Instructor, US Naval Acad., 1987; Visiting Research Fellow, Woodrow Wilson School of Public Policy and International Affairs, 1987–88; Lecturer, Princeton University, 1988; Asst Prof. of History, Hofstra University, 1989–93; Visiting Assoc. Dir, 1993–94, Dir, 1994–, Eisenhower Center for American Studies, Assoc. Prof. of History 1993–96; Ambrose Prof. of American History, Univ. of New Orleans, 1997–; Contributing Ed., L.A. Times, American History; mem. Council on Foreign Relations, Theodore Roosevelt Asscn, Franklin and Eleanor Roosevelt Inst., Century Asscn, National D-Day Museum. *Publications:* Jean Monnet: The Path of European Unity (ed. with Clifford Hackett), 1991; The Atlantic Charter (ed. with D. Facey-Crowther), 1992; Dean Acheson: The Cold War Years, 1953–1971, 1992; Driven Patriot: The Life and Times of James Forrestal (with Townsend Hoopes), 1992; Dean Acheson and the Making of US Foreign Policy (ed.), 1993; Theodore Roosevelt: The Many-Sided American (ed. with Gable and Naylor), 1993; The Majic Bus: An American Odyssey, 1993; Franklin Roosevelt and the Creation of the United Nations (with Townsend Hoopes), 1997; John F. Kennedy and Europe (ed.), 1997; Hunter S. Thompson: The Proud Highway Saga of a Desperate Southern Gentleman 1955–1967 (ed.), 1997; American Heritage: History of the United States, 1998; The Unfinished Presidency: Jimmy Carter's Journey Beyond The White House, 1998; Rosa Parks: A Biography, 2000; Hunter S. Thompson: Fear and Loathing in America (ed.), 2001. Contributions: Books, popular magazines and scholarly journals. *Honours:* New York Times Notable Book of the Year Citations, 1993, 1998; Stessin Award for Distinguished Scholarship, Hofstra University, 1993; Theodore and Franklin Roosevelt Naval History Prize, 1993; Bernath Lecture Prize, 1996; Hon. Doctorate in Humanities, Trinity College, CT, 1997. *Address:* c/o Eisenhower Center, University of New Orleans, 923 Magazine St, New Orleans, LA 70130, USA.

BRINTON, Alexander (see Battin, B. W.).

BRISCO, Patty A. (see Matthews, Patricia Anne).

BRISTOW, Robert O'Neil; Author; b. 17 Nov. 1926, St Louis, MO, USA; m. 1st Gaylon Walker 23 Dec. 1950 (divorced); two s. two d; m. 2nd Gail Hamiter Rosen 25 August 2003. *Education:* BA, 1951, MA, 1965, University of Oklahoma. *Career:* Writer-in-Residence, Winthrop College, South Carolina, 1961–87. *Publications:* Time for Glory, 1968; Night Season, 1970; A Faraway Drummer, 1973; Laughter in Darkness, 1974. Contributions: Approximately 200 Short Stories to magazines and journals. *Honours:* Award for Literary Excellence, 1969; Friends of American Writer's Award, 1974. *Address:* 613 1/2 Charlotte Ave, Rock Hill, SC 29730, USA. *E-mail:* rbristow@cetlink.net.

BRITTAN, Sir Samuel; Journalist and Writer; b. 29 Dec. 1933, London, England. *Education:* Degree, Economics, Jesus College, Cambridge, 1955; MA, Cantab. *Career:* various posts, 1955–61, Principal Economic Commentator, 1966–, Asst Ed., 1978–95, Financial Times; Economics Ed., Observer, 1961–64; Fellow, 1973–74, Visiting Fellow, 1974–82, Nuffield College, Oxford; Visiting Prof. of Economics, Chicago Law School, 1978; Hon. Prof. of Politics, Warwick University, 1987–92. *Publications:* The

Treasury Under the Tories, 1964, revised edn as Steering the Economy, 1969; Left or Right: The Bogus Dilemma, 1968; The Price of Economic Freedom: A Guide to Flexible Rates, 1970; Capitalism and the Permissive Society, 1973, revised edn as A Restatement of Economic Liberalism, 1988; Is There an Economic Consensus?, 1973; The Delusion of Incomes Policy (with P. Lilley), 1977; The Economic Consequences of Democracy, 1977; How to End the 'Monetarist' Controversy, 1981; The Role and Limits of Government: Essays in Political Economy, 1983; Capitalism with a Human Face, 1995; Essays: Moral, Political and Economic, 1998. Contributions: many journals. *Honours:* Financial Journalist of the Year Award, 1971; George Orwell Prize for Political Journalism, 1980; Hon. doctorates, Heriot-Watt University, 1985, University of Essex, 1994; Ludwig Erhard Prize, 1988; Hon. Fellow, Jesus College, Cambridge, 1988; Chevalier, Légion d'honneur, 1993; Knighted, 1993. *Address:* c/o Financial Times, Number One Southwark Bridge, London SE1 9HL, England.

BROBST, Richard Alan; Teacher, Poet, Writer and Ed.; b. 13 May 1958, Sarasota, FL, USA; m. Pamela Millace, 27 Dec. 1986, two s. one d. *Education:* BA, University of Florida, 1988. *Career:* Co-founder and Ed., Albatross Poetry Journal, 1986–99; Resident Poet, Charlotte County Schools, 1989–. *Publications:* Inherited Roles, 1997; Dancing With Archetypes, 1998; Songs From the Lost Oaks, 1999; The Cody Star, 2000. Contributions: anthologies and periodicals. *Honours:* Winner, Duanne Locke Chapbook Series, 1997. *Address:* 17145 Urban Ave, Port Charlotte, FL 33954, USA. *E-mail:* aliasd13@aol.com.

BROCK, James; Educator, Poet and Writer; b. 2 Dec. 1958, Boise, ID, USA; m. Annette Sisson, 13 Oct. 1984, divorced March 1993, one s. *Education:* BA, College of Idaho, 1981; MFA, 1984, PhD, 1992, Indiana University. *Career:* Assoc. Instructor, Indiana University, 1982–83; Ed., Indiana Review, 1985–87; Asst Prof., Belmont University, 1988–93; Visiting Asst Prof., Idaho State University, Pocatello, 1993–96; Instuctor, East Stroudsburg University, 1996–97; mem. Associated Writing Programs; Popular Culture Asscn. *Publications:* The Sunshine Mine Disaster (poems), 1995. Contributions: anthologies, quarterlies, reviews and journals. *Honours:* Acad. of American Poets Award, 1985; National Endowment for the Arts Creative Writing Fellowship, 1990; Alex Haley Fellow, Tennessee Arts Commission, 1991; Poetry Fellow, Idaho Commission for the Arts, 1996. *Address:* PO Box 419, Analomink, PA 18320, USA.

BROCK, Rose (see Hansen, Joseph).

BROCK, William Ranulf; Prof. of Modern History (retd) and Writer; b. 16 May 1916, Farnham, Surrey, England; m. Constance Helen Brown, 8 July 1950, one s. one d. *Education:* BA, 1937, MA, 1945, PhD, 1941, Trinity College, Cambridge. *Career:* Fellow, Selwyn College, Cambridge; Prof. of Modern History, University of Glasgow, 1967–81; mem. British Acad., fellow; British Asscn of American Studies, founding mem.; FRHistS. *Publications:* Lord Liverpool and Liberal Toryism, 1941; Character of American History, 1960; An American Crisis, 1963; Conflict and Transformation: USA 1944–77, 1973; USA 1739–1870 (Sources of History), 1975; Parties and Political Conscience (USA 1840–52), 1979; Evolution of American Democracy, 1979; Welfare, Democracy and the New Deal, 1988; Selwyn College: A History (with P. H. M. Cooper), 1994. *Honours:* Hon. DLitt, University of Cambridge, 1998. *Address:* 49 Barton Rd, Cambridge CB3 9LG, England.

BRODER, David Salzer; journalist, editor and writer; b. 11 Sept. 1929, Chicago Heights, IL, USA; m. Ann Creighton Collar 1951; four s. *Education:* BA, 1947, MA, 1951, University of Chicago. *Career:* Reporter, Pantagraph, Bloomington, IL, 1953–55, Congressional Quarterly, Washington, DC, 1955–60, Washington Star, 1960–65, New York Times, 1965–66; Reporter, 1966–75, Assoc. Ed., 1975–, Washington Post; Syndicated Columnist; mem. American Acad. of Arts and Sciences, fellow; American Political Science Asscn; American Society of Public Administration; Gridiron Club; National Press Club. *Publications:* The Republican Establishment (with Stephen Hess), 1967; The Party's Over: The Failure of Politics in America, 1972; Changing of the Guard: Power and Leadership in America, 1980; Behind the Front Page: A Candid Look at How the News is Made, 1987; The Man Who Would be President: Dan Quayle (with Bob Woodward), 1992; Democracy Derailed: Initiative Campaigns and the Power of Money, 2000. Contributions: Books, newspapers and magazines. *Honours:* Fellow, John F. Kennedy School of Government, Harvard University, 1969–70; Pulitzer Prize in Journalism, 1973; Poynter Fellow, Yale University and Indiana University, 1973; Carey McWilliams Award, 1983; Fourth Estate Award, National Press Club, 1988; Elijah Parrish Lovejoy Award, 1990. *Address:* c/o Washington Post, 1150 15th Street NW, Washington, DC 20071, USA.

BRODERICK, Damien Francis; writer; b. 22 April 1944, Melbourne, Vic., Australia. *Education:* BA, Monash University, 1966; PhD, Deakin University, 1990. *Career:* Writer-in-Residence, Deakin University, 1986; Senior Fellow, University of Melbourne. *Publications:* A Man Returned (short stories), 1965; The Zeitgeist Machine (ed.), 1977; The Dreaming Dragons, 1980; The Judas Mandala, 1982; Valencies (with Rory Barnes), 1983; Transmitters, 1984; Strange Attractors (ed.), 1985; The Black Grail, 1986; Striped Holes, 1988; Matilda at the Speed of Light (ed.), 1988; The Dark Between the Stars (short stories), 1991; The Lotto Effect, 1992; The Sea's Furthest End, 1993; The Architecture of Babel: Discourses of Literature and Science, 1994; Reading by Starlight: Postmodern Science Fiction, 1995; The White Abacus, 1997; Zones (with Rory Barnes), 1997; Theory and its Discontents, 1997; The Spike, 1997; Not the Only Planet (ed.), 1998; Centaurus (co-ed. with David G. Hartwell), 1999; The Last Mortal Generation, 1999; Stuck in Fast Forward (with Rory Barnes), 1999; The Book of Revelation (with Rory Barnes), 1999; Transrealist Fiction, 2000; The Game of Stars and Souls, 2000; Earth is But a Star (ed.), 2001; Transcension, 2002; Jack and the Aliens, 2002. Contributions: periodicals. *Honours:* Australian Science Fiction Achievement Awards, 1981, 1985, 1989; Aurealis Award, 1998; Ditmar Award, 1998. *Literary Agent:* Richard Curtis Associates Inc., 171 E 74th Street, Second Floor, New York, NY 10021, USA. *Website:* www.curtisagency.com. *Website:* www.thespike.us.

BRODEUR, Hélène, BA; writer; b. 13 July 1923, Val Racine, QC, Canada; m. Robert L. Nantais 1947; three s. two d. *Education:* Teacher's Certificate, Ottawa University Normal School; Ottawa University, Canadian Government College. *Career:* Writer-in-Residence, Visiting Prof., French Creative Writing, Ottawa University; mem. Ontario Authors Asscn; Union des écrivains; PEN International; Press Club. *Publications:* Chroniques du Nouvel-Ontario, Vol. 1, La quête d'Alexandre, 1981, Vol. 2, Entre l'aube et le jour, 1983, Vol. 3, Les routes incertaines, 1986, Vol. 4 L'Ermitage, 1996; Alexander, 1983; Rose-Delima, 1987; The Honourable Donald, 1990. Mini-series for Television: Les Ontariens, 1983. Contributions: Extension Magazine, 1968; A serial, Murder in the Monastery. *Honours:* Champlain Award, 1981; Le Droit Award, 1983; Prix du Nouvel-Ontario, 1984.

BRODEUR, Paul Adrian, Jr; Writer; b. 16 May 1931, Boston, Massachusetts, USA; (Divorced); one s. one d. *Education:* BA, Harvard College, 1953. *Career:* Staff Writer, The New Yorker magazine, 1958–96; Lecturer, Columbia University Graduate School of Journalism, 1969–80, Boston University School of Public Communications, 1978–79, University of California at San Diego, 1989. *Publications:* The Sick Fox, 1963; The Stunt Man, 1970; Downstream, 1972; Expendable Americans, 1974; The Zapping of America, 1977; Outrageous Misconduct, 1985; Restitution, 1985; Currents of Death, 1989; The Great Power-Line Coverup, 1993; Secrets, 1997. Contributions: The New Yorker magazine. *Honours:* Sidney Hillman Prize, 1973; Columbia University National Magazine Award, 1973; American Asscn for the Advancement of Science Award, 1976; Guggenheim Fellowship, 1976–77; Alicia Patterson Foundation Fellowship, 1978; American Bar Asscn Certificate of Merit, 1983; United Nations Environment Program Global 500 Honor Roll, 1989; Public Service Award, American Society of Professional Journalists, 1990. *Address:* c/o The New Yorker, 4 Times Sq., New York, NY 10036-6592, USA.

BRØGGER, Suzanne; Danish writer, poet and dramatist; b. 18 Nov. 1944, Copenhagen; m. Keld Zeruneith 1991. *Education:* Univ. of Copenhagen. *Career:* mem. Danish Acad. *Publications include:* Fri os fra kærlighed (Deliver Us From Love) 1973, Kærlighedens veje og vildveje (Love's Paths and Pitfalls) 1975, Creme Fraiche (Crème Fraîche) 1978, Ja (Yes) 1984, Efter Orgiet (play, After the Orgy) 1991, Transparence (Transparency) 1993, Mørk (play, Dark) 1994, En gris der har været oppe at slås kan man ikke stege (A Fighting Pig is Too Tough to Eat) 1979, Tone (epic poem) 1981, Vølvens spådom (Völuspā, adaptation) 1994, The Jade Cat (novel, in trans.) 1997. *Honours:* Gabor Prize 1987. *Address:* Knudstrup Gl Skole, 4270 Hong, Denmark; c/o Gyldendal, Klareboderne 3, 1001 Copenhagen K, Denmark. *Website:* www.gyldendal.dk.

BROKS, Paul, DPhil; British neuropsychologist. *Education:* Univs of Sheffield and Oxford. *Career:* practising neuropsychologist, Leeds and Sheffield; academic posts at Birmingham and Sheffield; Sr Clinical Lecturer, Univ. of Plymouth 2000; columnist Prospect Magazine. *Publications:* Into the Silent Land: Travels in Neuropsychology 2003; contrib. to Schitzotypy: Implications for Illness and Health 1997, numerous journals. *Address:* Department of Psychology, University of Plymouth, Portland Square, Plymouth, England. *Telephone:* (1752) 233826. *E-mail:* p.broks@plymouth.ac.uk.

BROMBERT, Victor Henri, BA, MA, PhD; American writer and academic; *Emeritus Professor of Romance and Comparative Literatures, Princeton University*; b. 11 Nov. 1923, Germany; m. Beth Anne Archer 1950; one s. one d. *Education:* Yale University, University of Rome. *Career:* Faculty 1951–58, Assoc. Prof. 1958–61, Prof. 1961–75, Benjamin F. Barge Prof. of Romance Literatures 1969–75, Yale Univ.; Henry Putnam Univ. Prof. of Romance and Comparative Literatures 1975–99, Emeritus Prof. of Romance and Comparative Literatures 1999–, Princeton Univ.; many visiting lectureships and professorships; mem. American Acad. of Arts and Sciences (fellow), American Comparative Literature Asscn, American Asscn of Teachers of French, American Philosophical Soc., MLA (pres. 1989), Société des Études Françaises, Société des Études Romantiques. *Publications:* The Criticism of T. S. Eliot, 1949; Stendhal et la Voie Oblique, 1954; The Intellectual Hero, 1961; Stendhal: A Collection of Critical Essays (ed.), 1962; The Novels of Flaubert, 1966; Stendhal: Fiction and the Themes of Freedom, 1968; Flaubert par lui-même, 1971; La Prison romantique, 1976; The Romantic Prison: The French Tradition, 1978; Victor Hugo and the Visionary Novel, 1984; The Hidden Reader, 1988; In Praise of Antiheroes, 1999; Trains of Thought, 2002. Contributions: many books, journals and periodicals. *Honours:* Fulbright Fellowship 1950–51, Guggenheim Fellowships 1954–55, 1970, National Endowment for the Humanities Senior Fellow 1973–74, Hon. degrees, (Univ> of Chicago) 1981, (Univ. of Toronto) 1997, Rockefeller Foundation Resident Fellow, Bellagio, Italy

1975, 1990, Médaille Vermeil de la Ville de Paris 1985, Officier, Ordre des Palmes Académiques. *Address:* 49 Constitution Hill W, Princeton, NJ 08540, USA.

BROME, Vincent; Author; b. 14 July 1910, London, England. *Publications:* Clement Attlee, 1949; H. G. Wells, 1951; The Way Back: The Story of Lieutenant Commander Pat O'Leary, 1953; Aneurin Bevan: A Biography, 1953; Acquaintance with Grief, 1954; The Last Surrender, 1954; Six Studies in Quarrelling, 1958; Sometimes at Night, 1959; Frank Harris, 1959, revised edn as Frank Harris: The Life and Loves of a Scoundrel, 1960; We Have Come a Long Way, 1962; The Problem of Progress, 1963; Love in Our Time, 1964; Four Realist Novelists: Arthur Morrison, Edwin Pugh, Richard Whiting, and William Pett Ridge, 1965; The International Brigades: Spain, 1936–39, 1965; The World of Luke Simpson, 1966; The Embassy, 1967, revised edn as The Ambassador and the Spy, 1973; Freud and His Early Circle: The Struggle of Psychoanalysis, 1967, revised edn as Freud and His Disciples, 1984; The Surgeon, 1967, revised edn as The Operating Theatre, 1968; The Imaginary Crime, 1969; The Revolution, 1969; Confessions of a Writer, 1970; The Brain Operators, 1971; Reverse Your Verdict: A Collection of Private Prosecutions, 1971; London Consequences, 1972; The Day of Destruction, 1974; The Happy Hostage, 1976; Diary of a Revolution, 1978; Jung: Man and Myth, 1978; Havelock Ellis: Philosopher of Sex, 1979; Ernest Jones: Freud's Alter Ego, 1982, revised edn as Ernest Jones: A Biography, 1983; The Day of the Fifth Moon, 1984; J. B. Priestley, 1988; The Other Pepys, 1992. Other: Six plays produced, one at Edinburgh. Contributions: Times; Sunday Times; New York Times; Observer; New Statesman; Others. *Address:* 45 Great Ormond St, London WC1, England.

BROMIGE, David Mansfield; Canadian poet, writer and professor of English; b. 22 Oct. 1933, London, England; m., one s. one d. *Education:* BA, University of British Columbia, 1962; MA, 1964, ABD, 1969, University of California at Berkeley. *Career:* Poetry Ed., Northwest Review, 1962–64; Instructor, University of California at Berkeley, 1965–69; Lecturer, California College of Arts and Crafts, 1969, University of San Francisco, 2000–; Prof. of English, Sonoma State University, CA, 1970–93; Contributing ed., Avec, Penngrove, 1986–, Kaimana, Honolulu, 1989–. *Publications:* The Gathering, 1965; Please, Like Me, 1968; The Ends of the Earth, 1968; The Quivering Roadway, 1969; Threads, 1970; Ten Years in the Making, 1973; Three Stories, 1973; Birds of the West, 1974; Out of My Hands, 1974; Spells and Blessings, 1974; Tight Corners and What's Around Them, 1974; Credences of Winter, 1976; Living in Advance, 1976; My Poetry, 1980; P-E-A-C-E, 1981; In the Uneven Steps of Hung Chow, 1982; It's the Same Only Different, 1984; The Melancholy Owed Categories, 1984; You See, 1985; Red Hats, 1986; Desire, 1988; Men, Women and Vehicles, 1990; Tiny Courts in a World Without Scales, 1991; They Ate, 1992; The Harbormaster of Hong Kong, 1993; A Cast of Tens, 1994; Romantic Traceries, 1994; From the First Century, 1995; Piccolomondo, 1998; Establishing, 1999; Authenticizing, 2000. Contributions: anthologies and periodicals. *Honours:* Macmillan Poetry Prize, 1957–59; Poet Laureate, University of California (all campuses), 1965; Discovery Award, 1969, Poetry Fellowship, 1980, National Endowment for the Arts; Canada Council Grant in Poetry, 1976–77; Pushcart Prize in Poetry, 1980; Western States Arts Federation Prize in Poetry, 1988; Gertrude Stein Award in Innovative Writing, 1994; Living Treasure Award, Sonoma County, 1994; Award, Fund for Poetry, 1998.

BRONNER, Leila Leah, BA, MA, LittD; Prof. and writer; b. 22 April 1930, Czechoslovakia; m. Joseph Bronner 1950; three c. *Education:* Beth Jacob Teachers Seminary of America, Hebrew University, Jerusalem, University of the Witwatersand, University of Pretoria. *Career:* Assoc. Prof., University of the Witwatersrand, 1960–84; Senior Lecturer, Hebrew Teachers College, 1966–78; Visiting Fellow, Harvard University, 1984; Visiting Prof., Yeshiva University, 1985–87; Visiting Scholar, University of Southern California at Los Angeles, 1986–87; Adjunct Assoc. Prof., University of Judaism, 1987–90; Prof., Institute of Bible and Jewish Studies, 1991–; mem. American Society for Religion; Asscn of Jewish Studies; National Asscn of Profs of Hebrew; Ou Testamentiese Werkgemeenskap in Suid Africa; Society for Biblical Literature; World Union of Jewish Studies, Jerusalem. *Publications:* Sects and Separatism During the Second Jewish Commonwealth, 1967; The Stories of Elijah and Elisha, 1968; Biblical Personalities and Archaeology, 1974; From Eve to Esther: The Rabbinic Reconstruction of Biblical Woman, 1994; Stories of Biblical Mothers: Maternal Power in the Hebrew Bible. Contributions: numerous books and journals. *Honours:* Leila Bronner School, Johannesburg, named after her. *Address:* 180 N Las Palmas Avenue, Los Angeles, CA 90004, USA.

BROOKE, Christopher Nugent Lawrence; Prof. of Ecclesiastical History Emeritus, Writer and Ed.; b. 23 June 1927, Cambridge, England; m. Rosalind Beckford Clark 18 Aug. 1951; three s. (one deceased). *Education:* Winchester College, 1940–45; BA, 1948, MA, 1952, DLitt, 1973, Gonville and Caius College, Cambridge. *Career:* Fellow, Gonville and Caius College, Cambridge, 1949–56, 1977–; Asst Lecturer, 1963–54, Lecturer, 1954–56, Dixie Prof. of Ecclesiastical History, 1977–94, Prof. Emeritus, 1994–, University of Cambridge; Prof. of Medieval History, University of Liverpool, 1956–67; Gen. Ed., Nelson's, later Oxford Medieval Texts, 1959–87; Prof. of History, Westfield College, University of London, 1967–77; Mem., Royal Commission on Historical Monuments, 1977–83; mem. Bavarian Acad. of Sciences, corresponding mem.; FRHistS, Hon. Vice-Pres.; Fellow, Society of Arts; Medieval Acad. of America, corresponding fellow; Monumenta Germaniae Historica, corresponding mem.; Society of Antiquaries, pres., 1981–84. *Publications:* The Letters of John of Salisbury (ed.), two vols, 1955, 1979; The Dullness of the Past, 1957; Carte Nativorum (ed.), 1960; From Alfred to Henry III, 1961; The Saxon and Norman Kings, 1963; Europe in the Central Middle Ages, 1964; Gilbert Foliot and His Letters (ed. with A. Morey), 1965; The Letters and Charters of Gilbert Foliot (ed. with others), 1967; Time the Archsatirist, 1968; The Twelfth Century Renaissance, 1970; Structure of Medieval Society, 1971; Medieval Church and Society, 1971; Heads of Religious Houses, England and Wales, 940–1216 (ed. with D. Knowles and V. London), 1972; The Monastic World (with W. Swaan), 1974; London, 800–1216 (with G. Keir), 1975; Marriage in Christian History, 1977; Councils and Synods (ed. with D. Whitelock and M. Brett), Vol. I, 1981; Popular Religion in the Middle Ages, 1000–1300 (with R. B. Brooke), 1984; A History of Gonville and Caius College, 1985; The Church and the Welsh Border, 1986; Oxford and Cambridge (with J. R. L. Highfield and W. Swaan, 1988; The Medieval Idea of Marriage, 1989; David Knowles Remembered (with others), 1991; A History of the University of Cambridge, Vol. IV, 1870–1990, 1993; Jane Austen: Illusion and Reality, 1999; Churches and Churchmen in Medieval Europe (with R. B. Brooke), 1999; A History of Emmanuel College, Cambridge (with others), 1999. Contributions: learned books and journals. *Honours:* Fellow, British Acad., 1970; Lord Mayor's Midsummer Prize, City of London, 1981; Hon. Doctorate, University of York, 1984; Life Fellow, Gonville and Caius College, Cambridge, 1994; CBE, 1995. *Address:* Gonville and Caius College, Cambridge CB2 1TA, England.

BROOKE, Robert Taliaferro (Tal), BA, MDiv; American author and lecturer; b. 21 Jan. 1945, Washington, DC. *Education:* Univ. of Virginia, Princeton Univ. *Career:* Vice-Pres. of Public Relations, Telecom Inc 1982–83; Pres. and Chair., Spiritual Counterfeits Project Inc, Conservative think-tank, Berkeley, CA 1989–; founder End Run Publ. 1999–; lecturer on Eastern thought and the occult at colls, univs, conventions and seminars in the USA and abroad; many radio and television appearances; mem. Int. Platform Asscn, Authors' Guild, Soc. of the Cincinnati. *Publications:* Lord of the Air 1976, 1990, The Other Side of Death 1979, Riders of the Cosmic Circuit 1986, Millennium Edition 2002, Avatar of Night 1987, Harvest (with Chuck Smith) 1988, When the World Will Be As One 1989, Virtual Gods 1997, Conspiracy to Silence the Son 1998, One World 2000, The Mystery of Death 2001. *Honours:* Spring Arbor National Bestseller 1989, first place Critical Review Category, National EPA Awards 1991. *Address:* SCP Inc, PO Box 4308, Berkeley, CA 94704, USA. *Website:* www.endrunpublishing.com.

BROOKE-ROSE, Christine, PhD; British professor of English, writer and critic; b. 1923, Geneva, Switzerland. *Education:* Univs of London and Oxford. *Career:* researcher and critic 1955–; reviewer Times Literary Supplement, The Times, Observer, The Sunday Times, The Listener, The Spectator, The London Magazine 1956–68; Lecturer, Univ. of Paris 1969–75, Prof. of English Language and Literature 1975–88. *Publications:* novels: The Languages of Love 1957, The Sycamore Tree 1958, The Dear Deceit 1960, The Middlemen 1961, Out (Soc. of Authors Travelling Prize 1965) 1964, Such 1965, Between 1968, Thru 1975, Amalgamemnon 1984, Xorandor 1986, Verbivore 1990, Textermination 1991, Remake 1996, Next 1998, Subscript 1999; criticism: A Grammar of Metaphor 1958, A ZBC of Ezra Pound 1971, A Rhetoric of the Unreal 1981, Stories, Theories and Things 1991, Invisible Author 2002; short stories: Go When You See the Green Man Walking 1969. *Honours:* Hon. Fellow Somerville Coll. Oxford 1996; Hon. DLitt (East Anglia) 1988; James Tait Black Memorial Prize 1966, Arts Council Translation Prize 1969. *Address:* c/o Cambridge University Press, POB 110, Cambridge, CB2 3RL, England.

BROOKENS, Diane, BEd, MA; British/American teacher, poet and writer; b. 29 May 1952, Raleigh, NC. *Education:* Univ. of London, Hertfordshire Univ. *Career:* Founder-Dir, Naturama School of Drama 1985; appearances on radio and TV, incl. poetry readings on BBC Radio Lancashire 1992–2004; mem. Asscn of Lamda Teachers, Poetry Soc., Writers' Guild of Great Britain. *Publications:* The Artistic Value of the American Musical 1977, Timothy Earle and Other Poems for Children 1986, Poems from a Chrysalis 1997, A Linguistic Analysis of Past Life Regression 1998, Across the Atlantic: Memories of America 2000, Back to Blackpool: The Lancashire Poems 2001; contrib. to poetry magazines and reviews. *Honours:* first prize for self-publishing poetry, David Thomas Charitable Trust, Writers News and Writing Magazine 1998. *Address:* 42 Pinner Court, Pinner Road, Pinner, Middlesex HA5 5RJ, England.

BROOKNER, Anita, CBE, BA, PhD, FRSL; British teacher, writer and art historian; b. 16 July 1928, London. *Education:* James Allen's Girls' School, King's Coll., London, Courtauld Inst. and Paris. *Career:* Visiting Lecturer in Art History, Univ. of Reading 1959–64; Lecturer, Courtauld Inst. of Art 1964–77, Reader in Art History 1977–87; Slade Prof., Univ. of Cambridge 1967–68; Fellow New Hall Cambridge, King's Coll. London. *Publications:* fiction: A Start in Life 1981, Providence 1982, Look at Me 1983, Hôtel du Lac (Booker Prize) 1984, Family and Friends 1985, A Misalliance 1986, A Friend from England 1987, Latecomers 1988, Lewis Percy 1989, Brief Lives 1990, A Closed Eye 1991, Fraud 1992, A Family Romance 1993, A Private View 1994, Incidents in the rue Laugier 1995, Altered States 1996, Soundings 1997, Visitors 1997, Falling Slowly 1998, Undue Influence 1999,

The Bay of Angels 2000, The Next Big Thing 2002, The Rules of Engagement 2003; non-fiction: An Iconography of Cecil Rhodes 1956, J. A. Dominique Ingres 1965, Watteau 1968, The Genius of the Future: Studies in French Art Criticism 1971, Greuze: The Rise and Fall of an Eighteenth-Century Phenomenon 1972, Jacques-Louis David, a Personal Interpretation: Lecture on Aspects of Art 1974, Jacques-Louis David 1980; editor: The Stories of Edith Wharton (two vols) 1988, 1988; contrib. to books and periodicals, including Burlington Magazine. *Honours:* Hon. DLitt (Loughborough Univ. of Tech.) 1990; Dr hc (Smith Coll., USA); Commdr, Ordre des Arts et des Lettres 2002. *Address:* 68 Elm Park Gardens, London, SW10 9PB, England. *Telephone:* (20) 7352-6894.

BROOKS, George Edward, AB, MA, PhD; academic, historian and writer; b. 20 April 1933, Lynn, Massachusetts, USA; m. 1st Mary C. Crowley 1957; two s.; m. 2nd Elaine Claire Rivron 1985; two d. *Education:* Dartmouth College, Boston University. *Career:* Instructor, Boston University, 1960, 1962; Asst Prof., 1962–68, Assoc. Prof., 1968–75, Prof., 1975–, Indiana University; Visiting Assoc. Prof., Tufts University, 1969; Visiting Fulbright Prof., University of Zimbabwe, 1984; Visiting Prof., Shandong University, People's Republic of China, 1985; mem. African Studies Asscn, fellow; Liberian Studies Asscn; MANSA/Mande Studies Asscn; World History Asscn, exec. council, 1990–93. *Publications:* New England Merchants in Africa: A History Through Documents, 1802–1865 (ed. with Norman R. Bennett), 1965; Yankee Traders, Old Coasters and African Middlemen: A History of American Legitimate Trade with West Africa in the Nineteenth Century, 1970; The Kru Mariner in the Nineteenth Century: An Historical Compendium, 1972; Themes in African and World History, 1973; Perspectives on Luso-African Commerce and Settlement in The Gambia and Guinea-Bissau Region, 16th–19th Centuries, 1980; Kola Trade and State-Building: Upper Guinea Coast and Senegambia, 15th–17th Centuries, 1980; Western Africa to c.1860 A.D.: A Provisional Historical Scheme Based on Climate Periods, 1985; Landlords and Strangers: Ecology, Society, and Trade in Western Africa, 1000–1630, 1993; The Aspen World History Handbook: An Organizational Framework, Lessons, and Book Reviews for Non-Centric World History (ed. with Dik A Daso, Marilynn Hitchens, and Heidi Roupp), 1994; Getting Along Together: World History Perspectives for the 21st Century, 1999; Eurafricans in Western Africa, 2003. Contributions: many scholarly books and journals. *Honours:* Ford Foundation Training Fellowship, 1960–62; Social Science Research Council Grant, 1971–72; National Endowment for the Humanities Grant, 1976–77; Indiana University Pres.'s Council on International Programs Award, 1978; ACLS Grant, 1990; Visiting Fellowship, Africa, Precolonial Achievement Conference, Humanities Research Centre, Australian National University, 1995. *Address:* 1615 E University Street, Bloomington, IN 47401-5201, USA. *Website:* www.indiana.edu.

BROOKS, Melvin (Mel) Kaminsky; American actor, writer, producer and director; b. 28 June 1926, Brooklyn, New York, NY; m. 1st Florence Baum; two s. one d.; m. 2nd Anne Bancroft 1964; one s. *Career:* script writer for TV series Your Show of Shows 1950–54, Caesar's Hour 1954–57, Get Smart 1965; set up feature film production co. Brooksfilms. *Television:* Mad About You (Emmy Award for Outstanding Guest Actor in a Comedy Series 1997, 1998, 1999). *Films include:* The Critic (writer, cartoon) (Academy Award 1964) 1963, The Producers (writer, dir) (Acad. Award for Best Screenplay) 1968, The Twelve Chairs (writer, dir, actor) 1970, Shinbone Alley (writer) 1971, Blazing Saddles (writer, dir, actor) 1974, Young Frankenstein (writer, dir) 1974, Silent Movie (writer, dir, actor) 1976, High Anxiety (writer, dir, actor, producer) 1977, The Muppet Movie (actor) 1979, The Elephant Man (exec. producer) 1980, History of the World Part I (writer, dir, actor, producer) 1981, My Favourite Year 1982, To Be or Not to Be (actor, producer) 1983, The Doctor and the Devils (exec. producer) 1985, Solarbabies (exec. producer) 1986, Fly I 1986, Spaceballs (writer, dir, actor, producer) 1987, 84 Charing Cross Road (exec. producer) 1987, Fly II 1989, Life Stinks (writer, dir, actor, producer) 1991, The Vagrant (exec. producer) 1992, Robin Hood: Men in Tights (writer, dir, actor, producer) 1993, The Little Rascals (actor) 1994, Dracula: Dead and Loving It (writer, dir, actor, producer) 1995, Svitati (actor) 1999. *Musical:* The Producers: The New Mel Brooks Musical (producer, co-writer, composer) (Tony Awards for Best Book, Best Score, Best Musical) 2001. *Address:* c/o The Culver Studios, 9336 W Washington Boulevard, Culver City, CA 90232, USA.

BROSMAN, Catharine Savage, BA, MA, PhD; academic, poet and writer; *Professor of French Emerita, Tulane University*; b. 7 June 1934, Denver, CO, USA; m. Paul W. Brosman Jr 1970 (divorced 1993); one d. *Career:* Instructor, Rice Univ. 1960–62; Asst Prof. of French, Sweet Briar Coll. 1962–63, Univ. of Florida 1963–66; Assoc. Prof. of French, Mary Baldwin Coll. 1966–68; Assoc. Prof. of French 1968–72, Prof. of French 1972–92, Kathryn B. Gore Prof. of French 1992–96, Prof. Emerita 1997–, Tulane Univ.; De Velling and Willis Visiting Prof., Univ. of Sheffield 1996. *Publications:* poetry (with prose): Watering 1972, Abiding Winter 1983, Journeying from Canyon de Chelly 1990, The Shimmering Maya and Other Essays 1994, Passages 1996, The Swimmer and Other Poems 2000, Places in Mind 2000, Finding Higher Ground: A Life of Travels 2003, Petroglyphs: Poems and Prose 2003, The Muscled Truce 2003; non-fiction: André Gide: l'évolution de sa pensée religieuse 1962, Malraux, Sartre, and Aragon as Political Novelists 1964, Roger Martin du Gard 1968, Jean-Paul Sartre 1983, Jules Roy 1988, Art as Testimony: The Work of Jules Roy 1989, An Annotated Bibliography of Criticism on André Gide, 1973–1988 1990, Simone de Beauvoir Revisited 1991, Visions of War in France: Fiction, Art, Ideology 1999, Existential Fiction 2000, Albert Camus 2000; editor: French Novelists, 1900–1930 1988, French Novelists, 1930–1960 1988, French Novelists since 1960 1989, Nineteenth-Century French Fiction Writers, 1800–1860: Romantics and Realists 1992, Nineteenth-Century French Fiction Writers, 1860–1900: Naturalists and Beyond 1992, Twentieth-Century French Culture, 1900–1975 1995, Retour aux 'Nourritures terrestres': Le Centenaire d'un bréviaire (with David H. Walker) 1997; contrib. to Southern Review, Sewanee Review, Southwest Review, New England Review, Georgia Review, Shenandoah, Critical Quarterly, Interim, American Scholar. *Honours:* Third Place Award, Best Poems of 1973. *Address:* 1550 Second Street, Suite 7-I, New Orleans, LA 70130, USA. *E-mail:* cbrosman@tulane.edu.

BROSSARD, Nicole; Poet and Novelist; b. 27 Nov. 1943, Montréal, QC, Canada. *Education:* Licence ès Lettres, 1968, Scolarité de maîtrise en lettres, 1972, Université de Montréal; Bacc. spécialisé en pédagogie, Université du Québec à Montréal, 1971. *Career:* mem. l'Académie des Lettres du Québec, 1993–; Académie mondiale de la poésie, 2001. *Publications:* Poetry: Mécanique jongleuse (trans. as Daydream Mechanics), 1973; Le centre blanc, 1978; The Story So Far 6 (ed.), 1978; Amantes (trans. as Lovhers), 1980; Double Impression, 1984; Mauve, 1984; Character/Jeu de lettres, 1986; Sous la langue/Under Tongue (bilingual edn), 1987; A tout regard, 1989; Installations, 1989; Langues obscures, 1991; Anthologie de la poésie des femmes au Québec (ed.), 1991; La Nuit verte du parc labyrinthe (trilingual edn), 1992; Vertige de l'avant-scène, 1997; Musée de l'os et de l'eau, 1999; Musée de l'os et de l'eau (trans. as Museum of Bone and Water), 1999; Au présent des veines, 1999; Poèmes à dire la francophonie, 2002; Cahier de roses et de civilisation, 2003; Je m'en vais à Trieste, 2003. Fiction: Un livre (trans. as A Book), 1970; Sold-Out, 1973; French Kiss, 1974; L'amèr (trans. as These Our Mothers, or, The Disintegrating Chapter), 1977; Le Sens apparent (trans. as Surfaces of Sense), 1980; Picture Theory, 1982; Le Désert mauve (trans. as Mauve Desert), 1987; Baroque d'aube (trans. as Baroque at Dawn), 1995; Hier, 2001; Journal intime. Essays: La Lettre aérienne (trans. as The Aerial Letter), 1985. Contributions: numerous anthologies. *Honours:* Gov.-Gen. Prizes, 1974, 1984; Chapbook Award, Therafields Foundation, 1986; Grand Prix de Poésie, Foundation Les Forges, 1989, 1999; Prix Athanase-David, 1991; Hon. doctorates, Universities of Western Ontario, 1991, Sherbrooke, 1997. *Address:* 34 Ave Robert, Outrement, QC H3S 2P2, Canada.

BROUMAS, Olga; Poet and Trans; b. 6 May 1949, Hermoupolis, Greece; m. Stephen Edward Bangs, 1973, divorced 1979. *Education:* BA, University of Pennsylvania, 1970; MFA, University of Oregon at Eugene, 1973. *Career:* Instructor, University of Oregon, 1972–76; Visiting Assoc. Prof., University of Idaho, 1978; Poet-in-Residence, Goddard College, Plainfield, Vermont, 1979–81, Women Writers Center, Cazenovia, New York, 1981–82; Founder-Assoc. Faculty, Freehand Women Writers and Photographers Community, Provincetown, Massachusetts, 1982–87; Visiting Assoc. Prof., Boston University, 1988–90; Fanny Hurst Poet-in-Residence, 1990, Dir Creative Writing, 1995–, Brandeis University. *Publications:* Restlessness, 1967; Caritas, 1976; Beginning with O, 1977; Soie Sauvage, 1980; Pastoral Jazz, 1983; Black Holes, Black Stockings, 1985; Perpetua, 1989; Sappho's Gymnasium, 1994; Eros, Eros, Eros (trans.), 1998; Rave: Poems 1975–1999, 1999. *Honours:* Yale Younger Poets Award, 1977; National Endowment for the Arts Grant, 1978; Guggenheim Fellowship, 1981–82. *Address:* 162 Mill Pond Dr., Brewster, MA 02631, USA.

BROWN, Andrew; British writer. *Career:* Scandinavian correspondent and reporter, The Spectator 1980s; Religious Affairs correspondent, writer, Independent 1986–96; currently writes for the Guardian, writes and presents analysis programmes for BBC Radio 4. *Publications:* Watching the Detectives 1988, The Darwin Wars: The Scientific Battle for the Soul of Man 2002, In the Beginning was the Worm: Finding the Secrets of Life in a Tiny Hermaphrodite 2003; contrib. to News of the World, Vogue, New York Review of Books, Guardian, Times, Sunday Telegraph, Daily Mail, Daily Express, Church Times, New Statesman, Salon, Waterlog. *Honours:* Templeton Prize 1995. *Address:* c/o Simon & Schuster, HarperCollins Publishers Ltd, Customer Services, Westerhill Road, Bishopbriggs, Glasgow G64 2QT, Scotland. *E-mail:* readers_editor@darwinwars.com. *Website:* www.darwinwars.com; www.thewormbook.com.

BROWN, Archibald Haworth; Prof. of Politics and Writer; b. 10 May 1938, Annan, Scotland; m. Patricia Susan Cornwell, 23 March 1963, one s. one d. *Education:* BSc, Economics, LSE, 1962; MA, University of Oxford, 1972. *Career:* Lecturer in Politics, Glasgow University, 1964–71; British Council Exchange Scholar, Moscow University, 1967–68; Lecturer in Soviet Institutions, 1971–89, Prof. of Politics, 1989–, University of Oxford; Visiting Prof. and Henry L. Stimson Lecturer, Yale University, 1980; Visiting Prof., University of Connecticut, 1980, Columbia University, 1985, University of Texas at Austin, 1990–91; Distinguished Visiting Fellow, Kellogg Institute for International Studies, University of Notre Dame, 1998; mem. American Asscn for the Advancement of Slavic Studies; American Political Science Asscn; British Acad., fellow; Foreign Hon. Mem., American Acad. of Arts and Sciences; British National Asscn for Slavonic and East European Studies; International Political Science Asscn; Political Studies Asscn of the United Kingdom; Acad. of Learned Societies for the Social Sciences.

Publications: Soviet Politics and Political Science, 1974; The Soviet Union Since the Fall of Khrushchev (ed. with Michael Kaser), 1975; Political Culture and Political Change in Communist States (ed. with Jack Gray), 1977; Authority, Power, and Policy in the USSR: Essays Dedicated to Leonard Schapiro (ed. with T. H. Rigby and Peter Reddaway), 1980; The Cambridge Encyclopedia of Russia and the Soviet Union (ed. with John Fennell, Michael Kaser, and Harry T. Willetts), 1982; Soviet Policy for the 1980s (ed.), 1982; Political Culture and Communist Studies (ed.), 1984; Political Leadership in the Soviet Union (ed.), 1989; The Soviet Union: A Biographical Dictionary (ed.), 1990; New Thinking in Soviet Politics (ed.), 1992; The Cambridge Encyclopedia of Russia and the Former Soviet Union (ed. with Michael Kaser and Gerald S. Smith), 1994; The Gorbachev Factor, 1996; The British Study of Politics in the Twentieth Century (ed. with Jack Hayward and Brian Barry), 1999; Contemporary Russian Politics: A Reader, 2001; Gorbachev, Yeltsin and Putin: Political Leadership in Russia's Transition (ed. with Lilia Shevtsova), 2001. Contributions: scholarly journals and symposia. *Address:* St Antony's College, University of Oxford, Oxford OX2 6JF, England.

BROWN, Craig (Edward Moncrieff); Journalist and Author; b. 23 May 1967, England; m. Frances Welch, 1987, one s. one d. *Education:* University of Bristol. *Career:* Columnist (as Wallace Arnold), The Spectator, 1987–, The Times, 1988, Private Eye, 1989–, Independent on Sunday, 1991, The Evening Standard, 1993–, The Guardian (as Bel Littlejohn), 1995–; Restaurant Columnist, Sunday Times, 1988–93. *Publications:* The Marsh Marlowe Letters, 1983; A Year Inside, 1988; The Agreeable World of Wallace Arnold, 1990; Rear Columns, 1992; Welcome to My Worlds, 1993; Craig Brown's Greatest Hits, 1993; The Hounding of John Thenos, 1994; The Private Eye Book of Craig Brown Parodies, 1995; This is Craig Brown, 2003. *Address:* c/o The Evening Standard, Northcliffe House, 2 Derry St, London, W8 5EE, England.

BROWN, Dan; American writer; b. Exeter, NH; m. Blythe Brown. *Education:* Phillips Exeter Acad., Amherst Coll. *Career:* English teacher. *Publications:* Digital Fortress 1998, Angels and Demons 2001, Deception Point 2002, The Da Vinci Code 2003. *Literary Agent:* Heide Lange, Sandford J. Greenburger Associates Inc., 55 Fifth Avenue, New York, NY 10003, USA. *Telephone:* (212) 206-5600. *Fax:* (212) 463-8718. *Website:* www.danbrown.com.

BROWN, Diana; Research Librarian and Author; b. 8 Aug. 1928, Twickenham, England; m. Ralph Herman Brown 31 Dec. 1964 (deceased); two d. *Education:* AA, San Jose City College, 1974; BA, 1975, MLS, 1976, MA, 1977, San Jose State University. *Career:* Librarian, Signetics Corp, Sunnyvale, CA, 1978–79, NASA/Ames Research Center, Moffett Field, 1979–80; Academic Information Specialist, University of Phoenix, San Jose Division, 1984–86; Research Librarian, San Jose Public Library, 1988–; mem. Authors' Guild; Jane Austen Society; Special Libraries Asscn. *Publications:* The Emerald Necklace, 1980; Come Be My Love, 1981; A Debt of Honour, 1981; St Martin's Summer, 1981; The Sandalwood Fan, 1983; The Hand of a Woman, 1984; The Blue Dragon, 1988. *Honours:* American Library Asscn Booklist Outstanding Adult Novel, 1984. *Address:* Gate Tree Cottage, PO Box 2846, Carmel by the Sea, CA 93921, USA.

BROWN, Eleanor; British poet and writer; b. 1969. *Education:* Univ. of York. *Career:* Writing Fellow, Univ. of Strathclyde. *Plays:* Philocteles by Sophocles (adaptation) 1997. *Publications:* poetry: Maiden Speech 1996. *Address:* c/o Bloodaxe Books Ltd, Highgreen, Tarset, Northumberland NE48 1RP, England. *Telephone:* (1434) 240500. *Fax:* (1434) 240505. *Website:* www.bloodaxebooks.com.

BROWN, Ian James Morris, MA, DipEd, MLitt, PhD, FRSA; academic and playwright; b. 28 Feb. 1945, Barnet, England; m. 1st Judith Sidaway 1969 (divorced 1997); m. 2nd Nicola Axford 1997; one s. one d. *Education:* University of Edinburgh, Crewe and Alsager College. *Career:* Lecturer in Drama, Dunfermline College, Edinburgh, 1971–76; Senior Principal Lecturer, Crewe and Alsager College, 1978–86; Drama Dir, Arts Council of Great Britain, 1986–94; Reader in Drama, 1994–95, Head of Drama, 1995–99, Prof. of Drama, 1999–2002, Dean of Arts, 1999–2002, Queen Margaret University College, Edinburgh; Dir, Scottish Centre for Cultural Management and Policy, 1996–2002; mem. Scottish Society of Playwrights, chair., 1973–75, 1984–87, 1997–99; BTI, chair., 1985–87. *Publications:* Plays: Mother Earth, 1970; The Bacchae, 1972; Carnegie, 1973; The Knife, 1973; Rabelais, 1973; The Fork, 1976; New Reekie, 1977; Mary, 1977; Runners, 1978; Mary Queen and the Lock Tower, 1979; Pottersville, 1982; Joker in the Pack, 1983; Beatrice, 1989; First Strike, 1990; The Scotch Play, 1991; Wasting Reality, 1992; Margaret, 2000; A Great Reckoning, 2000. Poetry: Poems for Joan, 2001.

BROWN, James Willie, Jr (see Komunyakaa, Yusef).

BROWN, John Russell; Prof. of Theatre, Theatre Dir and Writer; b. 15 Sept. 1923, Bristol, England; m. Hilary Sue Baker, 5 April 1961, one s. two d. *Education:* BA, 1949, BLitt, 1951, University of Oxford; PhD, University of Birmingham, 1960. *Career:* Fellow, Shakespeare Institute, Stratford-upon-Avon, 1951–53; Faculty, 1955–63, Head, Dept of Drama and Theatre Arts, 1964–71, University of Birmingham; Prof. of English, Sussex University, 1971–82; Assoc. Dir and Head of Script Dept, National Theatre, London, 1973–88; Prof. of Theatre Arts, SUNY at Stony Brook, 1982–85; Artistic Dir, Project Theatre, 1985–89, Prof. of Theatre, 1985–97, University of Michigan; Consultant, 1994–2000, Hon. Visiting Prof., 2000–, Middlesex University; Dir of various theatre productions in Europe and North America; Visiting Lecturer or Prof. in Europe, North America and New Zealand; mem. Advisory Council, Theatre Museum, 1974–83, chair., 1979–83; Arts Council of Great Britain, drama panel chair., 1980–83. *Publications:* Shakespeare and his Comedies, 1957; Shakespeare: The Tragedy of Macbeth, 1963; Shakespeare's Plays in Performance, 1966; Effective Theatre, 1969; Shakespeare's The Tempest, 1969; Shakespeare's Dramatic Style, 1970; Theatre Language, 1972; Free Shakespeare, 1974; Discovering Shakespeare, 1981; Shakespeare and His Theatre, 1982; A Short Guide to Modern British Drama, 1983; Shakescenes, 1993; William Shakespeare: Writing for Performance, 1996; What is Theatre?: An Introduction and Exploration, 1997; New Sites for Shakespeare, 1999; William Shakespeare: The Tragedies, 2001; Shakespeare and the Theatrical Event, 2002. Contributions: General Ed., Stratford-upon-Avon Studies, 1960–67; Stratford-upon-Avon Library, 1964–69; Theatre Production Studies, 1981–2002; Theatre Concepts, 1992–2001; Theatres of the World, 2001; Oxford Illustrated History of Theatre, 1995. Editor: various plays of Shakespeare. Contributions: scholarly journals. *Address:* 318 The Circle, Queen Elizabeth St, London SE1, England.

BROWN, Malcolm Carey; Historian; b. 7 May 1930, Bradford, West Yorkshire, England; m. Beatrice Elsie Rose Light, 19 Dec. 1953, two s. one d. *Education:* BA, English, 1952, MA, 1957, St John's College, Oxford. *Career:* General Trainee, BBC, 1955; Production Asst, BBC TV, 1958–60; Television Documentary Producer, BBC, 1960–86; Freelance Historian, Imperial War Museum, 1989–; Hon. Research Fellow, Centre for First World War Studies, University of Birmingham, 2002. *Publications:* Scapa Flow (co-author), 1968; Tommy Goes to War, 1978; Christmas Truce (co-author), 1984; A Touch of Genius (co-author), 1988; The Letters of T. E. Lawrence (ed.), 1988; The Imperial War Museum Book of the First World War, 1991; The Imperial War Museum Book of the Western Front, 1993; The Imperial War Museum Book of the Somme, 1996; The Imperial War Museum Book of 1918: Year of Victory, 1998; Verdun 1916, 1999; Spitfire Summer, 2000. *Address:* 4 Northbury Ave, Ruscombe, Reading RG10 9LG, England.

BROWN, Patricia Ann Fortini; University Prof. and Art Historian; b. 16 Nov. 1936, Oakland, CA, USA; m. 1st Peter Claus Meyer, May 1957, divorced 1978, two s.; m. 2nd Peter Robert Lamont Brown, Aug. 1980, divorced 1989. *Education:* AB, 1959, MA, 1978, PhD, 1983, University of California at Berkeley. *Career:* Asst Prof., 1983–89, Assoc. Prof., 1989–91, Andrew W. Mellon Prof., 1991–95, Prof., 1997–, Chair, Dept of Art and Archaeology, 1999–, Princeton University; Slade Prof. of Fine Arts, University of Cambridge, 2001; mem. Renaissance Society of America; American Acad. in Rome; College Art Asscn. *Publications:* Venetian Narrative Painting in the Age of Carpaccio, 1988; Venice and Antiquity: The Venetian Sense of the Past, 1996; The Renaissance in Venice: A World Apart, 1997. Contributions: Art History; Christian Science Monitor; Monitor Book Review; Burlington Magazine; Renaissance Quarterly; Biography; Journal of the Society of Architectural Historians. *Honours:* Premio Salotto Veneto, Italy; Phyllis Goodhart Gordan Book Prize, 1998. *Address:* Dept of Art and Archaeology, Princeton University, Princeton, NJ 08544, USA.

BROWN, Paul, BSc, MScSoc, PhD; Australian playwright and lecturer. *Education:* Univ. of New South Wales. *Career:* fmrly documentary maker for television, Campaign Man. for Greenpeace Australia; founder, Death Defying Theatre (now Urban Theatre Projects) 1981; Lecturer in History and Philosophy of Science. *Plays:* Aftershcoks 1993, Room 207 Nikola Tesla 2003. *Literary Agent:* RGM Associates, PO Box 128, Surry Hills, NSW 2010, Australia. *Telephone:* (2) 9281-3911. *Fax:* (2) 9281-4705. *E-mail:* info@rgm.com.au. *Website:* www.rgm.com.au.

BROWN, Peter Robert Lamont; Prof. of History and Writer; b. 26 July 1935, Dublin, Ireland; m. 1st Friedl Esther, 1959, two d.; m. 2nd Patricia Ann Fortini, 1980; m. 3rd Elizabeth Gilliam, 1989. *Education:* MA, New College, Oxford. *Career:* Harmsworth Senior Scholar, 1956, Lecturer in Medieval History, 1970–75, Merton College, Oxford; Fellow, All Souls College, Oxford, 1956–75; Special Lecturer in Late Roman and Early Byzantine History, 1970–73, Reader, 1973–75, University of Oxford; Prof. of History, Royal Holloway College, London, 1975–78; Prof. of History and Classics, University of California at Berkeley, 1978–86; Visiting Prof., 1983–86, Rollins Prof. of History, 1986–, Princeton University. *Publications:* Augustine of Hippo: A Biography, 1967; The World of Late Antiquity, 1971; Religion and Society in the Age of St Augustine, 1971; The Making of Late Antiquity, 1978; The Cult of the Saints: Its Rise and Function in Latin Christianity, 1980; Society and the Holy in Late Antiquity, 1982; The Body and Society: Men, Women and Sexual Renunciation in Early Christianity, 1989; Power and Persuasion in Late Antiquity: Towards a Christian Empire, 1992; Authority and the Sacred: Aspects of the Christianization of the Roman World, 1995; The Rise of Western Christendom: Triumph and Diversity, AD 200–1000, 1996. Contributions: scholarly journals. *Honours:* Fellow, American Acad. of Arts and Sciences, 1978; several hon. doctorates. *Address:* c/o Dept of History, Princeton University, Princeton, NJ 08544, USA.

BROWN, Rebecca; American writer, journalist and teacher; b. 1956. *Publications:* Evolution of Darkness and Other Stories 1984, The Haunted

House 1986, The Children's Crusade 1989, The Terrible Girls 1990, Annie Oakley's Girl 1993, The Gifts of the Body 1994, What Keeps Me Here: A Book of Stories 1996, Dogs: A Modern Bestiary 1997, The End of Youth 2003, Excerpts from a Family Medical Dictionary 2003. *Honours:* Lambda Literary Award, Boston Book Review Award, Washington State Governor's Award, Pacific Northwest Bookseller's Award. *Address:* c/o Granta, 1755 Broadway, New York, NY 10019, USA. *Telephone:* (212) 246-1313. *Fax:* (212) 586-8003. *Website:* www.granta.com.

BROWN, Rita Mae; Writer and Poet; b. 28 Nov. 1944, Hanover, PA, USA. *Education:* University of Florida; AA, Broward Junior College, 1965; BA, New York University, 1968; Cinematography Certificate, New York School of the Visual Arts, 1968; PhD, Institute for Policy Studies, Washington, DC, 1973. *Career:* Writer-in-Residence, Cazenovia College, New York, 1977–78; Pres., American Artists Inc, 1980–; Visiting Instructor, University of Virginia, 1992; mem. International Acad. of Poets; PEN International; Poets and Writers. *Publications:* The Hand that Cradles the Rock (poems), 1971; Babyfruit Jungle, 1973; Songs to a Handsome Woman (poems), 1973; In Her Day, 1976; A Plain Brown Rapper (essays), 1976; Six of One, 1978; Southern Discomfort, 1982; Sudden Death, 1983; High Hearts, 1986; The Poems of Rita Mae Brown, 1987; Starting from Scratch: A Different Kind of Writer's Manual, 1988; Bingo, 1988; Wish You Were Here, 1990; Rest in Pieces, 1992; Venus Envy, 1993; Dolley: A Novel of Dolley Madison in Love and War, 1994; Murder at Monticello, or, Old Sins, 1994; Pay Dirt, or, Adventures at Ash Lawn, 1995; Murder, She Meowed, 1996; Riding Shotgun, 1996; Rita Will: Memoir of a Literary Rabble-Rouser, 1997; Murder on the Prowl, 1998; Cat on the Scent, 1998; Loose Lips, 1999; Sneaky Pie's Cookbook for Mystery Lovers, 1999; Outfoxed, 2000; Pawing Through the Past, 2000. Other: Screenplays; teleplays. Contributions: anthologies. *Honours:* National Endowment for the Arts Grant, 1978; Co-Winner, Writers Guild of America Award, 1983; New York Public Library Literary Lion, 1987; Hon. Doctorate, Wilson College, 1992. *Address:* c/o American Artists Inc, PO Box 4671, Charlottesville, VA 22905, USA.

BROWN, Rosellen; writer, poet and academic; b. 12 May 1939, Philadelphia, PA, USA; m. Marvin Hoffman, 16 March 1963, two d. *Education:* BA, Barnard College, 1960; MA, Brandeis University, 1962. *Career:* Instructor, Tougaloo College, Mississippi, 1965–67; Staff, Bread Loaf Writer's Conference, Middlebury, Vermont, 1974, 1991, 1992; Instructor, Goddard College, Plainfield, Vermont, 1976; Visiting Prof. of Creative Writing, Boston University, 1977–78; Assoc. Prof. in Creative Writing, University of Houston, 1982–85, 1989–. *Publications:* Some Deaths in the Delta and Other Poems, 1970; The Whole World Catalog: Creative Writing Ideas for Elementary and Secondary Schools (with others), 1972; Street Games: A Neighborhood (short stories), 1974; The Autobiography of My Mother (novel), 1976; Cora Fry (poems), 1977; Banquet: Five Short Stories, 1978; Tender Mercies (novel), 1978; Civil Wars: A Novel, 1984; A Rosellen Brown Reader: Selected Poetry and Prose, 1992; Before and After (novel), 1992; Cora Fry's Pillow Book (poems), 1994; Half a Heart, 2000. Contributions: Books, anthologies and periodicals. *Honours:* Woodrow Wilson Fellow, 1960; Howard Foundation Grant, 1971–72; National Endowment for the Humanities Grants, 1973–74, 1981–82; Radcliffe Institute Fellow, 1973–75; Great Lakes Colleges New Writers Award, 1976; Guggenheim Fellowship, 1976–77; American Acad. and Institute of Arts and Letters Award, 1988; Ingram Merrill Grant, 1989–90. *Address:* c/o Creative Writing Program, University of Houston, Houston, TX 77204, USA.

BROWN, Stewart; academic, writer, poet and editor; b. 14 March 1951, Lymington, Hampshire, England; m. Priscilla Margaret Brant 1976; one s. one d. *Education:* BA, Falmouth School of Art, 1978; MA, University of Sussex, 1979; PhD, University of Wales, 1987. *Career:* Lecturer in English, Bayero University, Kano, Nigeria, 1980–83; Reader in African and Caribbean Literature, University of Birmingham, 1988–; mem. Welsh Acad. *Publications:* Mekin Foolishness (poems), 1981; Caribbean Poetry Now, 1984; Zinder (poems), 1986; Lugard's Bridge (poems), 1989; Voiceprint: An Anthology of Oral and Related Poetry from the Caribbean (ed. with Mervyn Morris and Gordon Rohler), 1989; Writers from Africa: A Readers' Guide, 1989; New Wave: The Contemporary Caribbean Short Story, 1990; The Art of Derek Walcott: A Collection of Critical Essays, 1991; The Heinemann Book of Caribbean Poetry (with Ian McDonald), 1992; The Art of Kamau Brathwaite: A Collection of Critical Essays, 1995; The Pressures of the Text: Orality, Texts and the Telling of Tales, 1995; Caribbean New Voices I, 1996; The Oxford Book of Caribbean Short Stories (with John Wickham), 1998; African New Voices, 1999; Elsewhere: New and Selected Poems, 1999; All are Involved: The Art of Martin Carter, 2000; Kiss and Quarrel: Youba/English, Strategies of Mediation, 2000. Contributions: anthologies and periodicals. *Honours:* Eric Gregory Award, 1976; Southwest Arts Literature Award, 1978; Hon. Fellow, Centre for Caribbean Studies, University of Warwick, 1990. *Address:* Centre of West African Studies, University of Birmingham, Edgbaston, Birmingham B15 2TT, England. *E-mail:* s.brown@bham.ac.uk.

BROWN, Terence; Prof. of Anglo-Irish Literature, Writer and Ed.; b. 17 Jan. 1944, Loping, China; m. Suzanne Marie Krochalis, 1969, one s. one d. *Education:* BA, 1966, PhD, 1970, Trinity College, Dublin. *Career:* Lecturer, 1968–82, Dir of Modern English, 1976–83, Fellow, 1976–86, Registrar, 1980–81, Assoc. Prof. of English, 1982–93, Prof. of Anglo-Irish Literature, 1993–, Trinity College, Dublin; mem. International Asscn for the Study of Irish Literatures; Royal Irish Acad.; European Society for the Study of English, board mem.; Academia Europaea; International Asscn of Profs of English. *Publications:* Time Was Away: The World of Louis MacNeice (ed. with Alec Reid), 1974; Louis MacNeice: Sceptical Vision, 1975; Northern Voices: Poets from Northern Ulster, 1975; The Irish Short Story (ed. with Patrick Rafroidi), 1979; Ireland: A Social and Cultural History, 1922–1979, 1981, revised edn as Ireland: A Social and Cultural History, 1922 to the Present, 1985; The Whole Protestant Community: The Making of a Historical Myth, 1985; Hermathena (ed. with N. Grene), 1986; Samuel Ferguson: A Centenary Tribute (ed. with B. Hayley), 1987; Ireland's Literature: Selected Essays, 1988; Traditions and Influence in Anglo-Irish Literature (ed. with N. Grene), 1989; The Field Day Anthology of Irish Writing (contributing ed.), 1991; James Joyce: Dubliners (ed.), 1992; Celticism (ed.), 1996; Journalism: Derek Mahon, Selected Prose (ed.), 1996; The Life of W. B. Yeats: A Critical Biography, 1999, 2001. Hon. Companion of St Michael and St George, 2002. *Address:* Dept of English, Trinity College, Dublin 2, Ireland. *E-mail:* tbrown@tcd.ie.

BROWN, Christina (Tina) Hambley, MA, CBE; British writer and magazine editor; b. 21 Nov. 1953, Maidenhead; m. Harold Matthew Evans 1981; one s. one d. *Education:* Univ. of Oxford. *Career:* columnist, Punch magazine 1978; Ed.-in-Chief Tatler Magazine 1979–83, of Vanity Fair Magazine, New York 1984–92, London 1991–92; Ed. The New Yorker 1992–98, Talk magazine 1999–2002; Partner and Chair. Talk Media 1998–, Talk Miramax Books 1998–; columnist, Washington Post 2003–. *Publications:* Under the Bamboo Tree (play) (Sunday Times Drama Award) 1973, Happy Yellow (play) 1977, Loose Talk 1979, Life as a Party 1983, The Icarus Complex 2005. *Honours:* Most Promising Female Journalist, Katherine Pakenham Prize Sunday Times 1973, Young Journalist of the Year 1978, Univ. Southern Calif. (USC) Distinguished Achievement in Journalism Award 1994. *Literary Agent:* Ed Victor Ltd, 6 Bayley Street, Bedford Square, London, WC1B 3HE, England. *Address:* c/o Miramax, 375 Greenwich Street, New York, NY 10013, USA (Office). *Fax:* (212) 830-5838.

BROWN TOBIN, Meryl (see Tobin, Meryl Elaine).

BROWNE, Michael Dennis; American academic, writer and poet; b. 28 May 1940, Walton-on-Thames, England; m. Lisa Furlong McLean 1981; one s. two d. *Education:* BA, Hull University, 1962; University of Oxford, 1962–63; Ministry of Education Teacher's Certificate, 1963; MA, University of Iowa, 1967. *Career:* Visiting Lecturer, University of Iowa, 1967–68; Instructor, 1967, 1968, Visiting Adjunct Asst Prof., 1968, Columbia University; Faculty, Bennington College, Vermont, 1969–71; Visiting Asst Prof., 1971–72, Asst Prof., 1972–75, Assoc. Prof., 1975–83, Prof., 1983–, University of Minnesota; mem. The Loft; Poetry Society of America. *Publications:* The Wife of Winter, 1970; Sun Exercises, 1976; The Sun Fetcher, 1978; Smoke From the Fires, 1985; You Won't Remember This, 1992; Selected Poems 1965–1995, 1997. Contributions: numerous anthologies and journals. Other: Texts for various musical compositions. *Honours:* Fulbright Scholarship, 1965–67; Borestone Poetry Prize, 1974; National Endowment for the Arts Fellowships, 1977, 1978; Bush Fellowship, 1981; Loft-McKnight Writers' Award, 1986; Minnesota Book Award for Poetry, 1993, 1998. *Address:* 2111 E 22nd Street, Minneapolis, MN 55404, USA.

BROWNJOHN, Alan (Charles); Poet, Novelist and Critic; b. 28 July 1931, London, England. *Education:* BA, 1953, MA, 1961, Merton College, Oxford. *Career:* Lecturer, Battersea College of Education, 1965–76, Polytechnic of the South Bank, 1976–79; Visiting Lecturer, London Metropolitan Univ., 2001–; Poetry Critic, New Statesman, 1968–76, Encounter, 1978–82, Sunday Times, 1990–; mem. FRSL; Arts Council of Great Britain Literature Panel, 1968–72; Poetry Society, chair., 1982–88; Writers' Guild of Great Britain; Society of Authors. *Publications:* Poetry: Travellers Alone, 1954; The Railings, 1961; The Lions' Mouths, 1967; Sandgrains on a Tray, 1969; Penguin Modern Poets 14, 1969; First I Say This: A Selection of Poems for Reading Aloud, 1969; Brownjohn's Beasts, 1970; Warrior's Career, 1972; A Song of Good Life, 1975; A Night in the Gazebo, 1980; Collected Poems, 1982; The Old Flea-Pit, 1987; The Observation Car, 1990; In the Cruel Arcade, 1994; The Cat Without E-Mail, 2001. Fiction: To Clear the River, 1964; The Way You Tell Them, 1990; The Long Shadows, 1997; A Funny Old Year, 2001. Other: Philip Larkin, 1975; Meet and Write, 1985–87; The Gregory Anthology, 1990. Translations: Torquato Tasso (play), Goethe, 1985; Horace (play), Corneille, 1996. *Address:* 2 Belsize Park, London NW3, England.

BROWNLOW, Kevin; Author, Film Dir and Former Film Ed.; b. 2 June 1938, Crowborough, Sussex, England. *Publications:* The Parade's Gone By, 1968; How It Happened Here, 1968; Adventures with D. W. Griffith, (ed.), 1973; Hollywood: The Pioneers, 1979; The War, the West, and the Wilderness, 1979; Napoleon: Abel Gance's Classic Film, 1983; Behind the Mask of Innocence, 1990; David Lean: A Biography, 1996; Mary Pickford Rediscovered, 1999. *Address:* c/o Photoplay, 21 Princess Rd, London NW1 8JR, England.

BROXHOLME, John Franklin, (Duncan Kyle, James Meldrum); Former Journalist and Author; b. 11 June 1930, Bradford, England; m. Alison Millar Hair, 22 Sept. 1956, three c. *Education:* Bradford, England. *Publications:* As Duncan Kyle: A Cage of Ice, 1970; Flight into Fear, 1972; A Raft of Swords, 1973; The Suvarov Adventure, 1974; Terror's Cradle, 1975; White-Out, 1976; In Deep, 1976; Black Camelot, 1978; Green River High,

1979; Stalking Point, 1981; The King's Commissar, 1984; The Dancing Men, 1985; The Honey Ant, 1988. As James Meldrum: The Semonov Impulse, 1975.

BRUCE, (William) Harry; journalist, editor and writer; b. 8 July 1934, Toronto, ON, Canada; m. Penny Meadows 1955; two s. one d. *Education:* BA, Mount Allison University, 1955; LSE, 1956–57; Massey College, University of Toronto, 1969–70. *Career:* Reporter, Ottawa Journal, 1955–59, Globe and Mail, 1959–61; Asst Ed., 1961–64, Columnist, 1970–71, Maclean's; Managing Ed., Saturday Night, 1964–65, Canadian Magazine, 1965–66; Assoc. Ed. and Columnist, Star Weekly, 1967–68; Columnist, Toronto Daily Star, 1968–69; Talk-show Host, CBC-TV, Halifax, NS, 1972; Ed., 1979–80, Exec. Ed., 1981, Atlantic Insight; Ed., Atlantic Salmon Journal, 1991–. *Publications:* The Short Happy Walks of Max MacPherson, 1968; Nova Scotia, 1975; Lifeline, 1977; R.A.: The Story of R. A. Jodrey, Entrepreneur, 1979; A Basket of Apples: Recollections of Historic Nova Scotia, 1982; The Gulf of St Lawrence, 1984; Each Moment as it Flies, 1984; Movin' East: The Further Writings of Harry Bruce, 1985; The Man and the Empire: Frank Sobey, 1985; Down Home: Notes of a Maritime Son, 1988; Maud: The Life of L. M. Montgomery, 1992; Corporate Navigator, 1995. Contributions: various anthologies and periodicals. *Honours:* Evelyn Richardson Memorial Literary Award, 1978; Brascan Award for Culture, National Magazine Awards, 1981; Top Prize for Magazine Writing, Atlantic Journalism Awards, 1983, 1984, 1986, 1993; City of Dartmouth Book Award, 1989; Booksellers' Choice Award, Atlantic Provinces Booksellers' Asscn, 1989.

BRUCE, Robert Vance; historian and academic; b. 19 Dec. 1923, Malden, Massachusetts, USA. *Education:* MIT, 1941–43; BS, University of New Hampshire, 1945; AM, 1947, PhD, 1953, Boston University. *Career:* Instructor, University of Bridgeport, 1947–48; History Master, Lawrence Acad., Groton, Massachusetts, 1948–51; Research Asst to Benjamin P. Thomas, 1953–54; Instructor to Prof. of History, 1955–84, Prof. Emeritus, 1984–, Boston University; Visiting Prof., University of Wisconsin at Madison, 1962–63; mem. Fellow, American Asscn for the Advancement of Science; Society of American Historians, fellow. *Publications:* Lincoln and the Tools of War, 1956; 1877: Year of Violence, 1959; Bell: Alexander Graham Bell and the Conquest of Solitude, 1973; The Launching of Modern American Science, 1846–1876, 1987. Contributions: various publications. *Honours:* Guggenheim Fellowship, 1957–58; Huntington Library Fellow, 1966; Pulitzer Prize in History, 1988; Distinguished Alumni Award, Boston University, 1991. *Address:* 3923 Westpark Court NW, Olympia, WA 98502, USA.

BRUCE-LOCKHART, Robin; Author; b. 13 April 1920, London, England; m. 1st Margaret Crookdake, 14 Dec. 1941, divorced 1953, one d.; m. 2nd Eila McLean, 1987. *Education:* Royal Naval College, Dartmouth; Economics, University of Cambridge. *Career:* Foreign Man., Financial Times, 1946–53; General Man., Beaverbrook Newspapers, Daily Express, Sunday Express, Evening Standard, 1953–60; Mem., London Stock Exchange, 1960; mem. Chair., Sussex Author Asscn, 1970–78. *Publications:* Half Way to Heaven: The Secret Life of the Carthusians, 1965; Reilly: Ace of Spies, 1967; Reilly: The First Man, 1987; Listening to Silence, 1997. Contributions: various, in various countries. *Address:* c/o Campbell, Thomson & McLaughlan Ltd, 1 Kings Mews, London WC1N 2JA, England.

BRUCHAC, Joseph; Author, Poet, Storyteller, Publisher and Ed.; b. 16 Oct. 1942, Saratoga Springs, New York, USA; m. Carol Worthen, 12 June 1964, two s. *Education:* AB, Cornell University, 1965; MA, Syracuse University, 1966; Graduate Studies, SUNY at Albany, 1971–73; PhD, Union Institute, Ohio, 1975. *Career:* Co-Founder, Dir, Greenfield Review Press, 1969–; Ed., Greenfield Review literary magazine, 1971–90; Visiting Scholar and Writer-in-Residence at various institutions; Mem., Dawnland Singers, 1993–; mem. National Asscn for the Preservation and Perpetuation of Storytelling; PEN; Poetry Society of America. *Publications:* Fiction and Poetry: Indian Mountain and Other Poems, 1971; Turkey Brother and Other Iroquois Folk Tales, 1976; The Dreams of Jesse Brown (novel), 1977; Stone Giants and Flying Heads: More Iroquois Folk Tales, 1978; The Wind Eagle and Other Abenaki Stories, 1984; Iroquois Stories, 1985; Walking With My Sons and Other Poems, 1986; Near the Mountains: New and Selected Poems, 1987; Keepers of the Earth (short stories), 1988; The Faithful Hunter: Abenaki Stories, 1988; Long Memory and Other Poems, 1989; Return of the Sun: Native American Tales from the Northeast Woodlands, 1989; Hoop Snakes, Hide-Behinds and Side-Hill Winders: Tall Tales from the Adirondacks, 1991; Keepers of the Animals (with Michael Caduto) (short stories), 1991; Thirteen Moons on Turtle's Back (with Jonathan London) (poems and stories), 1992; Dawn Land (novel), 1993; The First Strawberries, 1993; Flying With the Eagle, Racing the Great Bear (short stories), 1993; The Girl Who Married the Moon (with Gayle Ross) (short stories), 1994; A Boy Called Slow, 1995; The Boy Who Lived With Bears (short stories), 1995; Dog People (short stories), 1995; Long River (novel), 1995; The Story of the Milky Way (with Gayle Ross), 1995; Beneath Earth and Sky, 1996; Children of the Long House (novel), 1996; Four Ancestors: Stories, Songs and Poems from Native North America, 1996. Other: Survival This Way: Interviews with Native American Poets, 1987; The Native American Sweat Lodge: History and Legends, 1993; Roots of Survival: Native American Storytelling and the Sacred, 1996. Editor: Over 15 books. Contributions: many anthologies, books and periodicals. *Honours:* National Endowment for the Arts Fellowship, 1974; Rockefeller Foundation Humanities Fellowship, 1982–83; American Book Award, 1985; Notable Children's Book in the Language Arts Award, 1993; Scientific American Young Readers Book Award, 1995; Parents Choice Award, 1995; American Library Asscn Notable Book Award, 1996; Knickerbocker Award for Juvenile Literature, New York Library Asscn, 1996. *Address:* PO Box 308, Greenfield Center, NY 12833, USA.

BRUCKNER, Pascal; Author and Lecturer; b. 15 Dec. 1948, Paris, France; m. Violaine Barret 1970 (divorced 1973); one s.; pnr Caroline Thompson; one d. *Education:* Sorbonne, Univ. of Paris I; Jussieu, Univ. of Paris II. *Career:* Lecturer, Institut d'Études Politiques, Paris, 1990–; visiting professorships, USA. *Publications:* Le nouveau désordre amoureux, 1977; Le divin enfant, 1992; La tentation de l'innocence, 1995; Les voleurs de beauté, 1997; Les ogres anonymes, 1998; l'euphorie perpétuelle: Essai sur le devóir de bonheur, 2000. *Honours:* Chevalier, Ordre des Arts et des Lettres; Prix Médicis Étranger, 1995; Prix Renaudot, 1995. *Address:* 8 rue Marie Stuart, 75002 Paris, France.

BRULOTTE, Gaëtan; Prof. and Writer; b. April 1945, Lévis, QC, Canada. *Education:* BA, 1966, 1969, MA, 1972, Laval University; PhD, École des Hautes Études en Sciences Sociales, Paris, 1977. *Career:* Instructor, Laval University, 1969; Prof. of French, Trois-Rivières College, 1970–83; Visiting Prof., Université du Québec á Trois-Rivières, 1973, 1980, 1981, 1989, 1990, University of New Mexico, 1981, 1982, 1983, 1984, 1993–94, University of California at Santa Barbara, 1982, Brevard Community College, 1983–84, Université Stendahl, 1993, Sorbonne, Paris, 1994; Distinguished Visiting Prof., New Mexico State University, 1988; Visiting Prof., 1984–88, Prof., 1988–, University of South Florida; mem. International Comparative Literature Asscn; International Council on Francophone Studies; MLA. *Publications:* L'Imaginaire et l'écriture: Ghelderode, 1972; Aspects du texte érotique, 1977, revised edn as Oeuvres de chair: Figures du discours érotique, 1998; L'Emprise (novel), 1979, English trans. as Double Exposure, 1988; Écrivains de la Mauricie (ed.), 1981; Le Surveillant (short stories), 1982, English trans. as The Secret Voice, 1990; Ce qui nous tient, 1988; L'Univers du peintre Jean Paul Lemieux (critical essay), 1996; Les cahiers de Limentinus: Lectures fin de Siècle (essays) 1998, Epreuves (short stories) 1999, Le Client (play) 2001, La Vie de Biais (short stories) 2002. Contributions: Books, anthologies, textbooks, scholarly journals and periodicals. *Honours:* Adrienne-Choquette Award, 1981; France-Québec Award, 1983; First Prize, XI CBC Radio Drama Contest, 1983; Literary Grand Prize, Trois-Rivières, 1989; John-Glassco Trans. Award, 1990; Theodore and Venette Ashkounes-Ashford Distinguished Scholar Award, 1999. *Address:* c/o World Language Education, University of South Florida, Tampa, FL 33620, USA. *E-mail:* brulotte@chumal.cas.usf.edu.

BRUMMER, Alexander, BSc, MBA; journalist; b. 25 May 1949, Hove, England; m. Tricia Brummer; two s. *Education:* University of Southampton, University of Bradford Management Center. *Career:* fmr Financial Ed., The Guardian. *Publications:* American Destiny 1986, Hanson: A Biography 1994, Weinstock: A Biography 1998.

BRUNNER, Eva; Writer, Playwright and Trans; b. 26 Nov. 1952, Lucerne, Switzerland. *Education:* Communications, American College of Rome, c/o University of Charleston, West Virginia, 1979–82. *Career:* mem. Swiss Writers' Asscn. *Publications:* Plays: Kalt, 1984; Granit, 1985; Alles Wird Gut, 1994; Frieda Flachmann, 1997; Sutters Salut, 1998. Radio: Geist trug die Steine, 1988; Herrscher und Herrscherin, 1989; Der Schweiz den Rückenkehren, 1991. *Honours:* various scholarships. *Address:* Kuglerstrasse 22, 10439 Berlin, Germany. *E-mail:* evabrunner@aol.com.

BRUNSKILL, Ronald William; Architect (retd), Prof. and Writer; b. 3 Jan. 1929, Lowton, England; m. Miriam Allsopp, 1960, two d. *Education:* BA, 1951, MA, 1952, PhD, 1963, University of Manchester. *Career:* Commonwealth Fund Fellow in Architecture and Town Planning, MIT, 1956–57; Architect, Williams Deacon's Bank, 1957–60; Lecturer, 1960–73, Senior Lecturer, 1973–84, Reader in Architecture, 1984–89, Hon. Fellow, School of Architecture, 1989–95, University of Manchester; Partner, 1966–69, Consultant, 1969–73, Carter, Brunskill & Assocs, architects; Visiting Prof., University of Florida at Gainesville, 1969–70; Pres., Vernacular Architect Group, 1974–77; Hon. Visiting Prof., 1994–95, Prof., School of the Built Environment, 1995–2001, De Montfort University; mem. Cumberland and Westmorland Antiquarian and Archaeological Society, vice-pres., 1975–90, pres., 1990–93; Historic Buildings Council for England, 1978–84; Cathedrals Advisory Committee for England, 1981–91; Cathedrals Fabric Commission, 1991–96; Ancient Monuments Society, hon. architect, 1983–88, vice-chair., 1988–90, chair., 1990–2000; Royal Commission on the Ancient and Historical Monuments for Wales, 1983–97, vice-chair. 1993–97; British Historic Buildings Trust, trustee, 1985–92; Historic Buildings and Monuments Commission, 1989–95; Friends of Friendless Churches, chair., 1990–98, pres., 1999–. *Publications:* Illustrated Handbook of Vernacular Architecture, 1971; Vernacular Architecture of the Lake Counties, 1974; English Brickwork (with Alec Clifton-Taylor), 1977; Traditional Buildings of Britain, 1981; Traditional Farm Buildings of Britain, 1982; Timber Building in Britain, 1985; Brick Building in Britain, 1990; Houses and Cottages of Britain, 1997; Traditional Farm Building of Britain and Their Conservation, 1999; Vernacular Architecture: An Illustrated Handbook, 2000; Traditional Buildings of Cumbria, 2002. Contributions: scholarly journals. *Honours:* Fellow, Society of Antiquaries, 1975–; Pres.'s Award, Manchester Society of Architects, 1977; OBE, 1990; Hon. Doctor of Art, De Montfort University. *Address:* 8 Overhill Rd, Wilmslow SK9 2BE, England.

BRUSSIG, Thomas; Writer, Poet and Playwright; b. 1965, Berlin, Germany. *Publications:* Wasserfarben (poems), 1991; Helden wie wir (trans. as Heroes Like Us), 1995; Am kürzeren Ende der Sonnenallee, 1999; Heimsuchung (play), 2000. Contributions: Die Welt; Die Welt am Sonntag; FAZ; Tageszeitung; Süddeutsche Zeitung; Max; Wir sind nostalgisch, weil wir Menschen sind (essay in Sehnsucht nach dem Kommunismus), 2001. *Honours:* Drehbuchpreis der Bundesregierung (with Leander Haußmann), 1999; Hans-Fallada-Preis der Stadt Neumünster, 2000. *Address:* c/o The Harvill Press, Random House, 20 Vauxhall Bridge Rd, London SW1V 2SA, England. *Website:* www.thomasbrussig.de.

BRUTON, Eric, (Eric Moore); Author and Company Dir; b. 1915, London, England. *Career:* Managing Dir, NAG Press Ltd, Colchester, 1963–93, Diamond Boutique Ltd, 1965–80; Chair., Things & Ideas Ltd, 1970–78; mem. British Horological Institute, 1955–62; CWA, 1959–62; Gemmological Asscn of Great Britain, council mem., 1972–91, pres., 1994–95; National Asscn of Goldsmiths, pres., 1983–85. *Publications:* True Book about Clocks, 1957; Death in Ten Point Bold, 1957; Die Darling Die, 1959; Violent Brothers, 1960; True Book about Diamonds, 1961; The Hold Out, 1961; King Diamond, 1961; The Devil's Pawn, 1962; Automation, 1962; Dictionary of Clocks and Watches, 1962; The Laughing Policeman, 1963; The Longcase Clock, 1964; The Finsbury Mob, 1964; The Smithfield Slayer, 1964; The Wicked Saint, 1965; The Fire Bug, 1967; Clocks and Watches 1400–1900, 1967; Clocks and Watches, 1968; Diamonds, 1970; Antique Clocks and Clock Collecting, 1974; The History of Clocks, 1978; The Wetherby Collection of Clocks, 1980; Legendary Gems, 1984; Collector's Dictionary of Clocks and Watches, 1999. *Honours:* Eric Bruton Medal created for awarding to outstanding student in annual international diamond exams, 1996.

BRUYN, Günter de; Author; b. 1 Nov. 1926, Berlin, Germany; one s. *Education:* Library Science, Berlin. *Career:* mem. Akademie der Künste, Berlin; Deutsche Akademie für Sprache und Dichtung e. v., Darmstadt. *Publications:* Der Hohlweg, 1963; Buridans Esel, 1968; Preisverleihung, 1972; Das Leben des Jean Paul Richter, 1975; Tristan und Isolde, 1975; Märkische Forschungen: Erzahlung für Freunde der Literaturgeschichte, 1978; Im Querschnitt, 1979; Babylon, 1980; Neue Herlichkeit, 1984; Rahels erste Liebe: Rahel Levin und Karl Graf von Finckenstein in ihren Briefen, 1985; Frauendienst, 1986; Lesefreuden: Uber Bücher und Menschen, 1986; Jubelschreie, Trauergesänge: Deutsche Befindlichkeiten, 1991; Zwischenbilanz: Eine Jugen in Berlin, 1992; Vierzig Jahre: Ein Lebensbericht, 1996. *Honours:* Heinrich Mann Prize, 1965; Lion Feuchtwanger Prize, 1980; Thomas Mann Prize, 1990; Heinrich Böll Prize, 1990; Grant Cross of Merit, Federal Republic of Germany, 1994; Konrad Adenauer Foundation Prize for Literature, 1996. *Address:* Blabber 1, 1548 Görsdorf Bei Beeskow, Germany.

BRYAN, Lynne; Writer; b. 10 May 1961, Leicester, England. *Education:* BA, Humanities, Wolverhampton Polytechnic, 1980–83; MA, Creative Writing, University of East Anglia, 1984–85. *Publications:* Envy at the Cheese Handout, 1995; Gorgeous, 1999; Like Rabbits, 2002. Contributions: anthologies and magazines. *Honours:* Eastern Arts Grants, 1996, 1999, 2003; BBC Arts Council Award, 1996; Authors Foundation Award, 2003. *Literary Agent:* Greene & Heaton Ltd, 37 Goldhawk Rd, London W12 8QQ, England. *Website:* www.lynnebryan.co.uk.

BRYANS, Robin (see Harbinson-Bryans, Robert).

BRYANT, Dorothy (Mae); Writer, Dramatist, Teacher and Publisher; b. 8 Feb. 1930, San Francisco, CA, USA; m. 1st 1949 (divorced 1964); one s. one d.; m. 2nd Robert Bryant 18 Oct. 1968; one step-s. one step-d. *Education:* BA, 1950, MA, 1964, San Francisco State University. *Career:* Teacher, High School, 1953–64, San Francisco State University, San Francisco Mission Adult School, Golden Gate College, 1961–64, Contra Costa College, 1964–76; Publisher, Ata Books, 1978–. *Publications:* Fiction: Ella Price's Journal, 1972; The Kin of Ata Are Waiting for You, 1976; Miss Giardino, 1978; The Garden of Eros, 1979; Prisoners, 1980; Killing Wonder, 1981; A Day in San Francisco, 1983; Confessions of Madame Psyche, 1986; The Test, 1991; Anita, Anita, 1993. Plays: Dear Master, 1991; Tea With Mrs Hardy, 1992; The Panel, 1996; The Trial of Cornelia Connelly, 1996; Posing for Gauguin, 1998. Non-Fiction: Writing a Novel, 1979; Myths to Lie By: Essays and Stories, 1984, Literary Lynching 2002. *Honours:* American Book Award 1987. *E-mail:* dorbob@CWnet.com.

BRYANT, Joseph Allen, Jr; academic and writer; b. 26 Nov. 1919, Glasgow, KY, USA; m. 1st Mary Virginia Woodruff 1946; two s.; m. 2nd Sara C. Bryant 1993. *Education:* AB, Western Kentucky University, 1940; MA, Vanderbilt University, 1941; PhD, Yale University, 1948. *Career:* Instructor to Assoc. Prof., Vanderbilt University, 1945–56; Assoc. Prof., University of the South at Sewanee, 1956–59, Duke University, 1959–61; Prof., University of North Carolina, Greensboro, 1961–68, Syracuse University, 1968–71, University of Kentucky, 1973–90; mem. MLA. *Publications:* Hippolyta's View: Some Christian Aspects of Shakespeare's Plays, 1961; The Compassionate Satirist: Ben Jonson and His Imperfect World, 1972; Understanding Randall Jarrell, 1986; Shakespeare and the Uses of Comedy, 1986; Twentieth Century Southern Literature, 1997. *Honours:* Hon. DLitt, University of the South, 1993.

BRYCE ECHENIQUE, Alfredo; Peruvian writer; b. 19 Feb. 1939, Lima. *Publications:* Huerto cerrado (short stories) 1968, Un mundo para Julius (novel) 1970, La felicidad ja ja (short stories) 1974, Tantas veces Pedro (novel) 1977, A vuelo de buen cubero y otras crónicas (non-fiction) 1977, La vida exagerada de Martín Romaña (novel) 1981, El hombre que hablaba de Octavia de Cádiz 1984, Magdalena peruana y otros cuentos (short stories) 1986, Crónicas personales 1986, La última mudanza de Felipe Carrillo (novel) 1988, Dos señoras conversan (novella) 1990, Permiso para vivir (Antimemorias) (memoir) 1993, No me esperen en abril (novel) 1995, A trancas y barrancas (articles) 1997, Reo de nocturnidad (novel) 1997, Guía triste de París (short stories) 1999, La amigdalitis de Tarzán (novel) 1999, El huerto de mi amada 2002. *Honours:* Premio Nacional de Literatura de Perú 1972, Premio Passion, France 1983, Encomienda de Isabel la Católica, Spain 1993, Premio Nacional de Narrativa, Spain 1998, Commdr., Ordre des Arts et des Lettres 2000, Encomienda de Alfonso X El Sabio, Spain 2000, Premio Grinzane Cavour, Piemonte, Italy 2002, Premio Planeta, Spain 2002. *Address:* c/o Alfaguara, Avenida San Felipe 731, Jesús María, Lima, Peru.

BRYSON, Bill; American author; b. 1951, Des Moines, IA; m.; four c. *Education:* Drake Univ. *Career:* author of travel books and books on linguistics; travelled to England and worked as orderly in mental hosp. 1973; worked as journalist for The Times and the Independent; returned with his family to USA 1993; apptd to selection panel, Book of the Month Club 2001; Commissioner for English Heritage. *Publications:* Penguin Dictionary of Troublesome Words (re-printed as Bryson's Dictionary of Troublesome Words) 1985, The Lost Continent 1987, The Mother Tongue: English and How It Got That Way, Made in America 1994, Neither Here Nor There: Travels in Europe 1995, Notes From a Small Island 1995, A Walk in the Woods 1998, I'm a Stranger Here Myself (essays, aka Notes From a Big Country) 1999, In a Sunburned Country (aka Down Under) 2000, The Best American Travel Writing (ed.), African Diary 2002, A Short History of Nearly Everything (Aventis Prize 2004) 2003. *Literary Agent:* The Marsh Agency, 11 Dover Street, London, W1S 4LJ, England. *Telephone:* (20) 7399-2800. *Fax:* (20) 7399-2801. *Website:* www.marsh-agency.co.uk. *Address:* c/o Publicity Department, Transworld Publishers, 61–63 Uxbridge Road, London, W5 5SA, England.

BRZEZINSKI, Zbigniew Kazimierz, PhD; American (naturalized 1958) professor of government and fmr government official; *Counsellor, Center for Strategic and International Studies;* b. 28 March 1928, Warsaw, Poland; m. Emilie Anna (Muska) Benes 1955; two s. one d. *Education:* McGill and Harvard Univs. *Career:* settled in N America 1938; Instructor in Govt and Research Fellow, Russian Research Center, Harvard Univ. 1953–56; Asst Prof. of Govt, Research Assoc. of Russian Research Center and of Center for Int. Affairs, Harvard Univ. 1956–60; Assoc. Prof. of Public Law and Govt, Columbia Univ. 1960–62, Prof. 1962–89 (on leave 1966–68, 1977–81) and Dir Research Inst. on Communist Affairs 1961–77 (on leave 1966–68); mem. Policy Planning Council, Dept of State 1966–68; mem. Hon. Steering Cttee, Young Citizens for Johnson 1964; Dir Foreign Policy Task Force for Vice-Pres. Humphrey 1968; Asst to the Pres. for Nat. Security Affairs 1977–81; mem. Nat. Security Council 1977–81; Counsellor, Center for Strategic and Int. Studies, Washington, DC 1981–; Robert E. Osgood Prof. of American Foreign Policy, Paul Nitze School of Advanced Int. Studies, Johns Hopkins Univ. 1989–; Fellow, American Acad. of Arts and Sciences 1969–; mem. Council on Foreign Relations, New York, Bd of Trustees, Freedom House; Guggenheim Fellowship 1960, Ford Fellowship 1970. *Publications include:* Political Controls in the Soviet Army 1954, The Permanent Purge–Politics in Soviet Totalitarianism 1956, Totalitarian Dictatorship and Autocracy (with Carl Joachim Friedrich) 1957, The Soviet Bloc–Unity and Conflict 1960, Ideology and Power in Soviet Politics 1962, Africa and the Communist World (ed. and contrib.) 1963, Political Power: USA/USSR (with Samuel P. Huntington) 1964, Alternative to Partition: For a Broader Conception of America's Role in Europe 1965, Dilemmas of Change in Soviet Politics (ed. and contrib.) 1969, Between Two Ages: America's Role in the Technetronic Era 1970, The Fragile Blossom: Crisis and Change in Japan 1972, The Relevance of Liberalism 1977, Power and Principle: Memoirs of the National Security Adviser 1977–1981 1983, Game Plan: A Geostrategic Framework for the Conduct of the US-Soviet Contest 1986, In Quest of National Security 1988, The Grand Failure: The Birth and Death of Communism in the 20th Century 1989, Out of Control: Global Turmoil on the Eve of the Twenty-First Century 1993, The Grand Chessboard: American Primacy and its Geostrategic Imperatives 1996; contrib. to many publications, journals and periodicals. *Honours:* Dr hc (Alliance Coll.) 1966, (Coll. of the Holy Cross) 1971, (Fordham Univ.) 1979, (Williams Coll.) 1986, (Georgetown Univ.) 1987, (Catholic Univ. of Lublin) 1990, (Warsaw Univ.) 1991; Presidential Medal of Freedom 1981, Order of White Eagle (Poland) 1995, Order of Merit (Ukraine) 1996, Masaryk Order 1998, Gedymim Order 1998. *Address:* Center for Strategic and International Studies, 1800 K Street NW, Washington, DC 20006, USA (Office). *Telephone:* (202) 833-2408 (Office). *Fax:* (202) 833-2409 (Office). *E-mail:* zb@csis.org (Office). *Website:* www.csis.org (Office).

BUCHANAN, Mark; Writer. *Publications:* Ubiquity: The Science of History, or Why the World is Simpler Than We Think, 2000; Nexus: Small Worlds and the Groundbreaking Science of Networks, 2002; Small World: Uncovering Nature's Hidden Networks, 2002. *Address:* c/o Weidenfeld & Nicolson, Orion House, 5 Upper St Martin's Lane, London WC2H 9EA, England.

BUCHER, Werner; Poet, Writer, Journalist and Ed.; b. 19 Aug. 1938, Zürich, Switzerland; m. Josiane Fidanza, 2 May 1968. *Career:* mem. Swiss Writers' Union. *Publications:* Nicht Solche Aengste, du... (poems), 1974; Zeitzünder 3: Dank an den Engel, 1987; Was ist mit Lazarus?, 1989; Einst & Jetzt & Morgen (poems), 1989; Ein anderes Leben: Versuch, sich einem Unbekannten anzunahern; De Wand: Roman; Eigentlich wunderbar, das Leben...: Tagtag-Gedichte und Nachtnacht-Nachrichten; Das bessere Ende: Gedichte; Mouchette (poem), 1995; Wegschleudern die Brillen, die Lügen (poems), 1995; Unruhen, 1997; Wenn der zechpreller gewinnt (poems), 1997; Urwaldhus, Tierhag, Ochsenhutte & Co, Die Schonsten Ostschweizer Beizen, 1997; Im Schatten des Campanile, 2000; Weitere Stürme sind angesagt (poems), 2002. Contributions: Entwürfe; Tobel und Hoger; Listerarisches aus dem Appenzellerland, 2001. *Address:* Rest, Kreuz, 9427 Zelg-Wolfhalden, Switzerland. *Website:* www.wernerbucher.ch.

BUCHHEIM, Lothar-Günther; German author and publisher; b. 6 Feb. 1918, Weimar, Thüringen; m. Diethild Wickboldt 1955; one s. one d. *Education:* Dresden Acad., Art Acad., Munich. *Career:* served in German navy; f. Kunstbuchverlag, Feldafing and started collection, "the most important private collection", of the work of German Expressionists; owner and Publr Buchheim Verlag, Feldafing. *Publications:* Tage und Nächte steigen aus dem Strom 1941, Die Künstlergemeinschaft "Brücke" 1956, Der Blaue Reiter und die Neue Künstlervereinigung Munich 1958, Graphik des deutschen Expressionismus 1959, Max Beckmann 1959, Otto Mueller 1963, Das Boot 1973, U-Boot-Krieg 1976, Staatsgala 1977, Mein Paris 1977, Die Tropen von Feldafing 1978, Staatszirkus 1978, Der Luxusliner 1980, U 96 1981, Der Film-Das Boot 1981, Das Segelschiff 1982, Die U-Boot-Fahrer 1985, Das Museum in den Wolken 1986, Zu Tode gesiegt–Der Untergang der U-Boote 1988, Malerbuch 1988, Die Festung 1995, Jäger im Weltmeer 1996, Der Abschied 2000. *Honours:* Dr hc (Duisburg) 1985; Ernst-Hoferichter Prize, Munich 1993; Bundesverdienstkreuz, Grosses Verdienstkreuz des Verdienstordens, Bayerischer Verdienstorden, Ehrenbürger von Chemnitz, Grosses Verdienstkreuz mit Stern des Verdienstordens, Bayerischer Maximiliansorden 1998; Max-Pechstein-Ehrenpreis der Stadt Zwickau 1999, Ehrenpreis des Landkreises Weilheim-Schongau 2002. *Address:* Biersackstr. 23, 82340 Feldafing, Germany. *Telephone:* (8157) 1221. *Fax:* (8157) 3143. *Website:* www.buchheimmuseum.de.

BUCHOLZ, Arden; Historian; b. 14 May 1936, Chicago, IL, USA; m. Sue Tally, 7 July 1962, two c. *Education:* BA, Dartmouth College, 1958; Diploma, University of Vienna, 1960; MA, 1965, PhD, 1972, University of Chicago. *Career:* Teacher of English, Amerikan Orta Okulu, Talas-Kayseri, Turkey, 1958–60; Served to Lieutenant, US Army, including Counterintelligence, Germany, 1961–64; Teacher of History, Latin School of Chicago, 1965–70; Distinguished Teaching Prof. of History, SUNY at Brockport, 1970–; Programme Co-Dir, Brunel University, Uxbridge, England, 1987–88. *Publications:* Hans Delbruck and the German Military Establishment, 1985; Moltke, Schlieffen, and Prussian War Planning, 1991; Delbruck's Modern Military History, 1997; Moltke and The German Wars, 1864–1871, 2001. *Honours:* Outstanding Book in Military History Citation, International Commission on Military History, 1991. *Address:* 13510 Roosevelt Highway, Waterport, NY 14571, USA.

BUCHWALD, Art; Columnist and Author; b. 20 Oct. 1925, Mt Vernon, New York, USA; m. Ann McGarry, 11 Oct. 1952, one s. two d. *Education:* University of Southern California, Los Angeles, 1945–48. *Career:* Syndicated columnist for newspapers around the world; mem. American Acad. of Arts and Sciences; American Acad. of Humor Columnists. *Publications:* Paris After Dark, 1950; Art Buchwald's Paris, 1954; The Brave Coward, 1957; More Caviar, 1958; Un Cadeau Pour le Patron, 1958; A Gift From the Boys, 1959; Don't Forget to Write, 1960; How Much is That in Dollars?, 1961; Is it Safe to Drink the Water?, 1962; Art Buchwald's Secret List to Paris, 1963; I Chose Capitol Punishment, 1963; And Then I Told the President, 1965; Son of the Great Society, 1966; Have I Ever Lied to You?, 1968; The Establishment is Alive and Well in Washington, 1969; Counting Sheep, 1970; Getting High in Government Circles, 1971; I Never Danced at the White House, 1973; The Bollo Caper, 1974; I Am Not a Crook, 1974; Irving's Delight, 1975; Washington is Leaking, 1976; Down the Seine and Up the Potomac, 1977; The Buchwald Stops Here, 1978; Laid Back in Washington, 1981; While Reagan Slept, 1983; You CAN Fool All of the People All of the Time, 1985; I Think I Don't Remember, 1987; Whose Rose Garden is it Anyway?, 1989; Lighten Up, George, 1991; Leaving Home: A Memoir, 1994; I'll Always Have Paris, 1996. *Honours:* Priz de la Bonne Humeur, 1958; Pulitzer Prize in Commentary, 1982. *Address:* 2000 Pennsylvania Ave NW, Washington DC 20006, USA.

BUCHWALD, Christoph; German publishing executive. *Career:* fmrly Ed. Hanser, Munich; fmrly Publr Luchterhand Literaturverlag; now with Suhrkamp Verlag KG, Frankfurt 1998–. *Address:* Suhrkamp Verlag KG, Frankfurt a.M., Postfach 101945, Germany (Office). *Telephone:* (69) 756010 (Office). *Fax:* (69) 75601522 (Office). *Website:* www.suhrkamp.de (Office).

BUCKLEY, William Frank, Jr, BA; American editor and writer; b. 24 Nov. 1925, New York, NY; m. Patricia Taylor 1950; one s. *Education:* Univ. of Mexico, Yale Univ. *Career:* Assoc. Ed., American Mercury magazine 1952; Founder-Ed. 1955–88, Ed.-in-Chief 1988–90, Ed.-at-Large 1991–2004, National Review magazine; host, Firing Line TV programme 1966–99; Lecturer, New School for Social Research 1967–68; Froman Distinguished Prof., Russell Sage Coll. 1973; US Delegate, 28th General Assembly, United Nations 1973; mem. Council on Foreign Relations. *Publications:* God and Man at Yale, 1951; McCarthy and His Enemies (with L. Brent Bozell), 1954; Up from Liberalism, 1959; Rumbles Left and Right, 1963; The Unmaking of a Mayor, 1966; The Jeweler's Eye, 1968; The Governor Listeth, 1970; Cruising Speed, 1971; Inveighing We Will Go, 1972; Four Reforms, 1973; United Nations Journal, 1974; Execution Eve, 1975; Saving the Queen, 1976; Airborne, 1976; Stained Glass, 1978; A Hymnal, 1978; Who's On First, 1980; Marco Polo, If You Can, 1982; Atlantic High, 1982; Overdrive, 1983; The Story of Henri Tod, 1984; The Temptation of Wilfred Malachey, 1985; See You Later Alligator, 1985; Right Reason, 1985; High Jinx, 1986; Racing Through Paradise, 1987; Mongoose, R.I.P., 1988; On the Firing Line, 1989; Gratitude, 1990; Tucker's Last Stand, 1991; Windfall, 1992; In Search of Anti-Semitism, 1992; Happy Days Were Here Again: Reflections of a Libertarian Journalist, 1993; A Very Private Plot, 1994; The Blackford Oakes Reader, 1995; Brothers No More, 1995; Buckley: The Right Word, 1996; Nearer My God: An Autobiography of Faith, 1997; The Lexicon, 1998; The Redhunter, 1999; Spytime: The Undoing of James Jesus Angleton, 2000; Nuremberg: The Reckoning, 2002. Editor: The Committee and Its Critics, 1962; Odyssey of a Friend: Whittaker Chamber's Letters to William F. Buckley Jr., 1954–61, 1970; American Conservative Thought in the Twentieth Century, 1970; Keeping the Tablets (with Charles Kesler), 1988. Contributions: Books and periodicals. *Honours:* Best Columnist of the Year Award, 1967; Distinguished Achievement Award in Journalism, 1968, Julius Award for Outstanding Public Service, 1990, University of Southern California; Emmy Award for Outstanding Program Achievement, National Acad. of Television Arts and Sciences, 1969; Bellarime Medal, 1977; Shelby Cullom Davis Award, 1986; Presidential Medal of Freedom, 1991; Gold Medal, National Institute of Social Sciences, 1992. *Address:* c/o National Review, 215 Lexington Avenue, New York, NY 10016, USA.

BUCKLEY, William K.; Prof., Writer and Poet; b. 14 Nov. 1946, San Diego, CA, USA; m. Mary Patricia, 25 Nov. 1969, one s. *Education:* BA, University of San Diego, 1969; MA, 1972, MA, 1975, California State University at San Diego; PhD, Miami University, Oxford, Ohio, 1980. *Career:* Instructor, San Diego Community Colleges, 1972–90; Co-Founder and Co-Ed., Recovering Literature, 1972–; Dir, Learning Skills Center, California State University at San Diego, 1974–75; Teaching Fellow, Miami University, Oxford, Ohio, 1975–79; Visiting Asst Prof., Hanover College, 1979–82; Visiting Asst Prof., 1982–84, Prof., 1985–, Indiana University Northwest, Gary, IN; mem. Acad. of American Poets. *Publications:* A Half-Century of Céline, co-author, 1983; Critical Essays on Louis-Ferdinand Céline, ed., 1989; Senses' Tender: Recovering the Novel for the Reader, 1989; New Perspectives on the Closing of the American Mind, co-ed., 1992; Lady Chatterley's Lover: Loss and Hope, 1993. Poetry: Meditation on the Grid, 1995; By the Horses Before the Rains, 1996; Heart Maps, 1997; Images Entitled to Their Recoil From Utopia, 1998; 81 Mygrations, 1998; Athena in Steeltown, 1999; Sylvia's Bells, 2002. *Honours:* Best Chapbook of the Year, Modern Poetry, 1997. *Address:* c/o Dept of English, Indiana University Northwest, 3400 Broadway, Gary, IN 46408, USA.

BUDBILL, David; Writer, Poet and Dramatist; b. 13 June 1940, Cleveland, OH, USA. *Education:* BA, Philosophy, minor Art History, Muskingum College, New Concord, Ohio, 1962; Philosophy, Columbia University, 1961; MDiv, Theology, Literature, Union Theological Seminary, New York, 1967. *Career:* Poet-in-Residence, Niagara Erie Writers, Buffalo, NY, 1984, Jamestown Community College, Jamestown, New York, 1986, 1987; mem. PEN; Dramatists' Guild. *Publications:* Barking Dog, 1968; The Chain Saw Dance, 1977; Pulp Cutters' Nativity, 1981; From Down to the Village, 1981; Why I Came to Judevine, 1987; Judevine: The Complete Poems, 1991; Danvis Tales: Selected Stories by Rowland Robinson (ed.), 1995; Little Acts of Kindness, 1995; Moment to Moment, 1999. Play: Two for Christmas, 1996. Contributions: many anthologies and periodicals. *Honours:* Williamstown Repertory Theatre Playwright's Fellowship, 1965; Publication Grant, American Studies Institute, 1967; Poetry Fellowships, Vermont Council on the Arts, 1973, 1977, 1979; Kirkus Reviews Best Books, 1974, 1976; Guggenheim Fellowship, 1982–83; Playwriting Fellowship, National Endowment for the Arts, 1991; San Francisco Bay Area Critics' Circle Award, 1991. *Address:* 4592 E Hill Rd, Wolcott, VT 05680, USA.

BUDD, Holly (see Judd, Alan).

BUDDEE, Paul (Edgar); Author and Poet; b. 12 March 1913, Western Australia, Australia; m. Elizabeth Vere Bremner, 1944, one s. one d. *Education:* Claremont Teachers College. *Career:* mem. Australian Society of Authors; Fellowship of Writers; PEN International. *Publications:* Stand To and Other War Poems, 1943; The Oscar and Olga Trilogy, 1943–47; The Unwilling Adventurers, 1967; The Mystery of Moma Island, 1969; The Air Patrol Series, 1972; The Ann Rankin Series, 1972; The Escape of the Fenians, 1972; The Peter Devlin Series, 1972; The Escape of John O'Reilly, 1973; The Call of the Sky, 1978; The Fate of the Artful Dodger, 1984; Poems of the Second World War, 1986. Contributions: many periodicals. *Honours:* Australia Commonwealth Literary Board Grants, 1977, 1978, 1984; OAM, 1989. *Address:* 2 Butson Rd, Leeming, WA 6149, Australia.

BUDDEN, Julian Medforth, OBE, BA, BMus, MA, FBA; musicologist and writer; b. 9 April 1924, Hoylake, Cheshire, England. *Education:* Queen's Coll., Oxford, Royal Coll. of Music, London. *Career:* music library clerk, BBC radio 1951, Music Presentation Asst 1955, Prod. for Music Programmes 1955–70, Chief Prod. for Opera 1970–76, Music Organizer for External Services 1976–83; editorial cttee mem. Critical Edition of the Works of G. Verdi; Pres., Centro Studi Giacomo Puccini, Lucca. *Publications:* The Operas of Verdi (three vols) 1973, 1978, 1981, Verdi 1985, Puccini 2002; contrib. to professional journals, including Music and Letters, Musical Times, The Listener. *Honours:* Yorkshire Post Award for Best Book on Music 1979, Derek Allen Prize, British Acad. 1980, Premio Diego Fabbri 1989. *Address:* 94 Station Road, Finchley, London, N3 2SG, England; via Fratelli Bandiera 9, 50137 Florence, Italy.

BUDRYS, Algirdas Jonas; Lithuanian/American writer, editor and publisher; b. 9 Jan. 1931, Königsberg, Germany; m. Edna F. Duna 1954; four s. *Education:* University of Miami, Columbia University. *Career:* Ed.-in-Chief, Regency Books, 1962–63, Playboy Press, 1963–65; Operations Man., Woodall Publishing Co, 1974–75; Pres., Unifont Co, 1975–; Ed. and Publisher, Tomorrow Speculative Fiction magazine, 1992–; mem. Science Fiction Hall of Fame. *Publications:* Fiction: False Night, 1954, revised edn as Some Will Not Die, 1962; Man of Earth, 1955; Who?, 1958; The Falling Torch, 1959; Rogue Moon, 1960; The Iron Thorn, 1967; Michaelmas, 1977; Hard Landing, 1993. Collections: The Unexpected Dimension, 1960; The Furious Future, 1963; Blood and Burning, 1979. Non-Fiction: Truman and the Pendergasts, 1963; Bicycles: How They Work and How to Fix Them, 1976; Writing to the Point, 1994. Contributions: numerous magazines. *Address:* 824 Seward Street, Evanston, IL 60202, USA.

BUECHNER, (Carl) Frederick; writer and minister; b. 11 July 1926, New York, NY, USA; m. Judith Friedrike Merck 1956; three c. *Education:* AB, Princeton University, 1947; BD, Union Theological Seminary, 1958. *Career:* Teacher of Creative Writing, New York University, summers, 1954, 1955; Ordained Minister, United Presbyterian Church, 1958; Chair., Dept of Religion, 1958–67, Minister, 1960–67, Phillips Exeter Acad.; William Belden Noble Lecturer, Harvard University, 1969; Russell Lecturer, Tufts University, 1971; Lyman Beecher Lecturer, Yale University, 1977; Harris Lector, Bangor Seminary, 1979; Smyth Lecturer, Columbia Seminary, 1981; Lecturer, Trinity Institute, 1990; mem. Council on Religion in Independent Schools, regional chair., 1958–63; National Council of Churches, committee on literature, 1954–57; Presbytery of Northern New England. *Publications:* A Long Day's Dying, 1950; The Season's Difference, 1952; The Return of Ansel Gibbs, 1958; The Final Beast, 1965; The Magnificent Defeat, 1966; The Hungering Dark, 1969; The Alphabet of Grace, 1970; The Entrance to Porlock, 1970; Lion Country, 1971; Open Heart, 1972; Wishful Thinking, 1973; The Faces of Jesus, 1974; Love Feast, 1974; Telling the Truth, 1977; Treasure Hunt, 1977; The Book of Bebb, 1979; Peculiar Treasures, 1979; Godric, 1980; The Sacred Journey, 1982; Now and Then, 1983; A Room Called Remember, 1984; Brendan, 1987; Whistling in the Dark, 1988; The Wizard's Tide, 1990; Telling Secrets, 1991; The Clown in the Belfry, 1992; Listening to Your Life, 1992; The Son of Laughter, 1993; The Longing for Home, 1996; On the Road with the Archangel, 1997; The Storm, 1998; The Eyes of the Heart, 1999; Speak What We Feel, 2001. *Honours:* O'Henry Prize, 1955; Richard and Hinda Rosenthal Award, 1958. *Address:* RR1, Box 1145, Pawlet, VT 05761, USA.

BUIDA, Yuri; Russian author; b. 1954, USSR. *Publications:* Don Domino (novel), Yermo (novel), Boris and Gleb (novel), The Prussian Bride (short stories) 1998, Zero Train (novel) 2001; contrib. to Glas, Novy Mir, Znamya, Oktyabr, Volga. *Address:* c/o Dedalus Ltd, Langford Lodge, St Judith's Lane, Sawtry, Cambridgeshire PE28 5XE, England. *E-mail:* info@dedalusbooks.com. *Website:* www.dedalusbooks.com.

BUISSERET, David Joseph, PhD, FRHistS; writer, historian and academic; b. 18 Dec. 1934, Totland Bay, Isle of Wight, England; m. Patricia Connolly 1961; three s. two d. *Education:* Corpus Christi College, Cambridge. *Career:* Research Fellow, Corpus Christi College, Cambridge, 1961–64; Lecturer to Senior Lecturer, 1964–72, Reader, 1972–75, Prof. of History, 1975–80, University of the West Indies; Ed., The Jamaican Historical Review, 1968–80, Terrae Incognitae, 1982–; Dir, Hermon Dunlap Smith Center for the History of Cartography, Newberry Library, Chicago, 1980–95; Jenkins and Virginia Garrett Prof. in Southwestern Studies and the History of Cartography, University of Texas at Arlington, 1995–. *Publications:* Sully and the Growth of Centralized Government in France, 1598–1610, 1969; The Wars of Religion, Vol. 10 of the Hamlyn History of the World, 1969; Historic Jamaica from the Air (with J. S. Tyndale-Biscoe), 1969; Les Oeconomies Royales de Sully (ed. with Bernard Barbiche), Vol. I, 1970, Vol. II, 1988; The Fortifications of Kingston, 1660–1900, 1971; Huguenots and Papists, 1972; A Popular History of the Port of Kingston, 1973; Port Royal, Jamaica (with Michael Pawson), 1975; Historic Architecture of the Caribbean, 1980; Henry IV, 1984; Histoire de l'Architecture dans la Caraibe, 1984; Skokie: A Community History using Old Maps (with Gerald Danzer), 1985; From Sea Charts to Satellite Images: Interpreting North American History through Maps (ed.), 1990; Historic Illinois from the Air, 1990; A Guidebook to Resources for Teachers of the Columbian Encounter (ed. with Tina Reithmaier), 1992; Monarchs, Ministers and Maps: The Emergence of Cartography as a Tool of Government in Early Modern Europe (ed.), 1992; Elk Grove: A Community History in Maps (with James Issel), 1996; Rural Images: The Estate Map in the Old and New Worlds (ed.), 1996; Envisioning the City, 1998; France in America (ed.), 1998; Creolization in the Americas (with Steven Reinhardt) 2000, Ingénieurs et Fortifications avant Vauban: l'Organisation d'un service royal aux XVIe-XVIIe Siècles 2001, The Mapmaker's Quest: Depicting New Worlds in Renaissance Europe 2003. Contributions: scholarly books and journals. *Honours:* Centennial Medal, Institute of Jamaica, 1979; Chevalier, Ordre des Palmes Académiques, France, 1993; various grants. *Address:* 2901 Norwood Lane, Arlington, TX 76013, USA.

BULARD, Martine, LèsL; French newspaper editor; b. 12 June 1952. *Career:* Chief Econ. Columnist on L'Humanité newspaper (organ of the French Communist Party) 1980–, Ed-in-Chief L'Humanité Dimanche; columnist for Le Monde Diplomatique. *Address:* L'Humanité-Dimanche, rue Jean Jaurès, 93528 Saint Denis Cedex, France. *Telephone:* (1) 49-22-72-72. *Fax:* (1) 49-22-73-00.

BULLOCK, Michael; dramatist, writer and poet; *Professor Emeritus, University of British Columbia*; b. 19 April 1918, London, England. *Education:* Hornsey College of Art. *Career:* Commonwealth Fellow, 1968, Prof. of Creative Writing, 1969–83, Prof. Emeritus, 1983–, University of British Columbia, Vancouver, Canada; McGuffey Visiting Prof. of English, Ohio University, Athens, Ohio, 1969; New Asia Ming Yu Visiting Scholar, 1989, Writer-in-Residence, 1996, New Asia College, Chinese University of Hong Kong; Adviser, New Poetry Society of China, 1995–. *Publications:* Poetry: Transmutations, 1938; Sunday is a Day of Incest, 1961; World Without Beginning Amen, 1963; Two Voices in My Mouth/Zwei Stimmen in meinem Mund, 1967; A Savage Darkness, 1969; Black Wings White Dead, 1978; Lines in the Dark Wood, 1981; Quadriga for Judy, 1982; Prisoner of the Rain, 1983; Brambled Heart, 1985; Dark Water, 1987; Poems on Green Paper, 1988; The Secret Garden, 1990; Avatars of the Moon, 1990; Labyrinths, 1992; The Walled Garden, 1992; The Sorcerer with Deadly Nightshade Eyes, 1993; The Inflowing River, 1993; Moons and Mirrors, 1994; Dark Roses, 1994; Stone and Shadow, 1996; Der Grüne Mond, 1997; Sonnet in Black and Other Poems, 1998; Erupting in Flowers, 1999; Nocturnes: Poems of Night, 2000; Wings of the Black Swan: Poems of Love and Loss, 2001; Colours, 2003. Fiction: Sixteen Stories as They Happened, 1969; Green Beginning Black Ending, 1971; Randolph Cranstone and the Pursuing River, 1975; Randolph Cranstone and the Glass Thimble, 1977; The Man with Flowers Through His Hands, 1985; The Double Ego, 1985; Randolph Cranstone and the Veil of Maya, 1986; The Story of Noire, 1987; Randolph Cranstone Takes the Inward Path, 1988; The Burning Chapel, 1991; The Invulnerable Ovoid Aura, Stories and Poems, 1995. Other: Selected Works, 1936–1996 (co-eds Peter Loeffler and Jack Stewart), 1998. Contributions: many anthologies. *Honours:* Schlegel-Tieck German Trans. Prize, 1966; British New Fiction Society Book of the Month, 1977; Canada Council French Trans. Award, 1979; San Francisco Review of Books Best Book List, 1982; San Jose Mercury News Best Booklist, 1984; Okanagan Short Fiction Award, 1986. *Address:* Suite 103, 3626 W 28th Avenue, Vancouver, BC V6S 1S4, Canada. *E-mail:* michaelhbullock@hotmail.com. *Website:* www.m_bullock.tripod.com.

BULMER, Henry Kenneth, (Alan Burt Akers, Ken Blake, Ernest Corley, Arthur Frazier, Adam Hardy, Kenneth Johns, Philip Kent, Bruno Krauss, Neil Langholm, Karl Maras, Charles R. Pike, Andrew Quiller, Richard Silver, Tully Zetford); Author; b. 14 Jan. 1921, London, England; m. Pamela Buckmaster, 7 March 1953, one s. two d. *Publications:* City Under the Sea, 1957; The Ulcer Culture, 1969; Dray Prescot Saga, 1972; Roller Coaster World, 1972; Fox Series, 1972–77; Sea Wolf Series, 1978–82; Strike Force Falklands, 1984–86; Fox and Falklands. Contributions: periodicals. *Address:* 5 Holly Mansions, 20 Frant Rd, Tunbridge Wells, Kent TN2 5SN, England.

BUNCH, Richard Alan; College Instructor, Poet and Writer; b. 1 June 1945, Honolulu, HI, USA; m. Rita Anne Glazar 11 Aug. 1990; one s. one d. *Education:* AA, Liberal Arts, Napa Valley College, 1965; BA, Communication, Stanford University, 1967; MA, History, University of Arizona, 1969; MDiv, 1970, DD, 1971, Graduate Studies, Philosophy, 1972–75, Vanderbilt University; Graduate Studies, Asian Religions, Temple University, 1975–76; JD, University of Memphis, 1980; Teaching Credential, Sonoma State University, 1988. *Career:* Instructor in Philosophy, Belmont University, 1973–74, Chapman University, 1986–87; Instructor in Law, University of Memphis, 1982–83; Instructor in Humanities, Napa Valley College, 1985–, Diablo Valley College, 1991–94, 1997; Instructor in Law, 1986–87, and in Philosophy, 1990–91, Sonoma State University; mem. Acad. of American Poets; Ina Coolbirth Poetry Circle. *Publications:* Poetry: Summer Hawk, 1991; Wading the Russian River, 1993; A Foggy Morning, 1996; Santa Rosa Plums, 1996; South by Southwest, 1997; Rivers of the Sea, 1998; Sacred Space, 1998; Greatest Hits: 1970–2000, 2001. Prose: Night Blooms, 1992. Play: The Russian River Returns, 1999. Contributions: many reviews. *Honours:* Grand Prize, Ina Coolbirth National Poetry Day Contest, 1989; Jessamyn West Prize, 1990. *Address:* 248 Sandpiper Dr., Davis, CA 965616, USA.

BURCH, Claire; Writer, Poet and Film-maker; b. 19 Feb. 1925, New York, NY, USA; m. Bradley Bunch 14 April 1944 (deceased); one s. (deceased) two d. *Education:* BA, Washington Square College, 1947. *Career:* mem. Writer's Guild. *Publications:* Stranger in the Family, 1972; Notes of a Survivor, 1972; Shredded Millions, 1980; Goodbye My Coney Island Baby, 1989; Homeless in the Eighties, 1989; Solid Gold Illusion, 1991; You Be the Mother Follies, 1994; Homeless in the Nineties, 1994; Stranger on the Planet: The Small Book of Laurie, 1996. Contributions: periodicals. *Honours:* Carnegie Awards, 1978, 1979; California Arts Council Grants, 1991, 1992, 1993, 1994; Seva Foundation Award, 1996. *Address:* c/o Regent Press, 6020A Adeline, Oakland, CA 94808, USA.

BURCHILL, Julie; British journalist and writer; b. 3 July 1959, Bristol; m. 1st Tony Parsons (divorced); m. 2nd Cosmo Landesman (divorced). *Career:* journalist NME (New Music Express) 1976–79, The Face, 1979–84, Mail on Sunday, 1984–93, Sunday Times, 1993–94, Guardian, 1998–; freelance journalist Sunday Express; founder Modern Review. *TV includes:* Prince (film), several plays. *Publications:* The Boy Looked at Johnny 1979, Love It or Shove It 1983, Girls on Film 1986, Damaged Goods 1987, Ambition 1989, Sex and Sensibility 1992, No Exit 1993, I Knew I Was Right (autobiog.) 1998, Diana 1998, Married Alive 1998, On Beckham 2002, Sugar Rush 2004. *Literary Agent:* Simpson Fox, 52 Shaftesbury Avenue, London, W1V 7OE, England.

BURDA, Hubert, DPhil; German publisher and author; b. 9 Feb. 1940, Heidelberg. *Education:* Univ. of Munich. *Career:* Man. Bild & Funk 1966–74; partner, Burda GmbH 1974, now Chair. Burda Group; Co-Publr Elle-Verlag GmbH, Munich; co-f. Europe Online SA, Luxembourg; Publr Anna, Bunte, Burda Moden, Das Haus, Elle, Elle Bistro, Elle Deco, Elle TopModel, Focus, Focus Online, Focus TV, Freundin, Freizeit Revue, Futurekids, Glücks Revue, Haus + Garten, Lisa, Lisa Kochen & Backen, Lisa Wohnen & Dekorieren, Mein schöner Garten, Meine Familie & ich, Norddeutsche Neueste Nachrichten, Schweriner Volkszeitung, Starwatch Navigation, Super Illu, Super TV, TraXXX, Verena; mem. Bd German School of Journalism, Munich; f. Petrarca Prize (for poetry), Bambi (Media-Prize), Corp. Art Prize 1997. *Address:* Arabellastrasse 23, 81925 Munich, Germany.

BURENGA, Kenneth L.; American publishing executive; b. 30 May 1944, Somerville, NJ; m. Jean Case 1964; one s. one d. *Education:* Rider Coll. *Career:* budget accountant, Dow Jones & Co., S Brunswick, NJ 1966–67, Asst Man. data processing control 1968–69, staff asst for systems devt 1970–71, Man. systems devt and control 1972–76, circulation marketing Man. 1977–78, circulation sales dir 1979–80, Vice-Pres. circulation and circulation dir 1980–86; Chief Financial Officer and Admin. Officer, Dow Jones & Co., New York 1986–88, Exec. Vice-Pres., Gen. Man. 1989–91; fmrPres. COO Dow Jones & Co. Inc. 1991 and Gen. Man. Wall Street Journal 1989; mem. Bd of Dirs Dow Jones Courier.

BURGESS, Michael Roy, (Robert Reginald), AB, MLS; librarian, publisher, writer and editor; b. 11 Feb. 1948, Fukuoka, Japan; m. Mary Alice Wickizer Rogers 1976; one step-s. one step-d. *Education:* Gonzaga University, University of Southern California at Los Angeles. *Career:* periodicals librarian 1970–75, Asst Librarian 1975–78, Sr Asst Librarian 1978–81, Assoc. Librarian 1981–84, Librarian with rank of Prof. 1984–, California State Univ. at San Bernardino; Ed., Newcastle Publishing Co Inc, North Hollywood, CA 1971–92; co-founder, Publisher, Ed., Borgo Press, San Bernardino, CA 1975–99; owner Millefleurs 1999–; mem. American Asscn of University Profs, American Civil Liberties Union, American Library Asscn, Horror Writers of America, Int. PEN, SFWA, MWA, Science Fiction Research Asscn, World Science Fiction Soc. *Publications:* author of some 95 titles, numerous others as ed.; contrib. numerous articles and short works. *Honours:* Pilgrim Award 1993. *Address:* c/o California State University at San Bernardino, 5500 University Parkway, San Bernardino, CA 92407, USA. *E-mail:* mburgess@csusb.edu. *Website:* www.millefleurs.tv.

BURGIN, Richard Weston, BA, MA, MPhil; academic, writer and editor; *Professor of Communication and English, St Louis University*; b. 30 June 1947, Boston, MA, USA; m. Linda K. Harris 1991; one s. one step-d. *Education:* Brandeis Univ., Columbia Univ. *Career:* instructor, Tufts Univ. 1970–74; Critic-at-Large, Boston Globe Magazine 1973–74; Founding Ed. and Dir, New York Arts Journal 1976–83; Visiting Lecturer, Univ. of California at Santa Barbara 1981–84; Assoc. Prof. of Humanities, Drexel Univ. 1984–96; Founder-Ed., Boulevard literary journal 1985–; Prof. of Communication and English, St Louis Univ. 1996–; mem. Nat. Book Critics Circle 1988–. *Publications:* Conversations with Jorge Luis Borges 1969, The Man with Missing Parts (novella) 1974, Conversations with Isaac Bashevis Singer 1985, Man Without Memory (short stories) 1989, Private Fame (short stories) 1991, Fear of Blue Skies (short stories) 1998, Jorge Luis Borges: Conversations (ed.) 1998, Ghost Quartet (novel) 1999, The Spirit Returns (short stories) 2001, Stories and Dreamboxes (short stories, with illustrations by Gloria Vanderbilt) 2002; contrib. to many anthologies and periodicals. *Honours:* Pushcart Prizes 1983, 1986, 1999, 2002, various hon. mentions and listings. *Address:* 7545 Cromwell Drive, Apt 2N, St Louis, MO 63105, USA. *Telephone:* (314) 862-2643. *Website:* www.richardburgin.com.

BURKE, Gregory; British playwright; b. 1969, Dunfermline, Scotland. *Career:* writer-in-residence at the Nat. Theatre Studio. *Plays:* Gagarin Way 2001, The Straits 2003. *Honours:* Pearson Television Bursary 2002. *Address:* c/o Faber & Faber Ltd, 3 Queen Square, London, WC1N 3AU, England. *Telephone:* (20) 7465-0045. *Fax:* (20) 7465-0034. *Website:* www.faber.co.uk.

BURKE, James Lee; Author; b. 5 Dec. 1936, Houston, Texas, USA; m. Pearl Pai, 22 Jan. 1960, one s., three d. *Education:* University of Southwest Louisiana, 1955–57; BA, 1959, MA, 1960, University of Missouri. *Career:* mem. Amnesty International. *Publications:* Half of Paradise, 1965; To the Bright and Shining Sun, 1970; Lay Down My Sword and Shield, 1971; Two for Texas, 1983; The Convict and Other Stories, 1985; The Lost Get-Back Boogie, 1986; The Neon Rain, 1987; Heaven's Prisoners, 1988; Black Cherry Blues, 1989; A Morning for Flamingos, 1990; A Stained White Radiance, 1992; Texas City, Nineteen Forty-Seven, 1992; In the Electric Mist with Confederate Dead, 1993; Dixie City Jam, 1994; Burning Angel, 1995; Heartwood, 1999; Purple Cane Road, 2000; Bitterroot, 2001; Jolie Blon's Bounce, 2002; White Doves at Morning, 2002; Last Car to Elysian Fields, 2003. Contributions: periodicals. *Honours:* Bread Loaf Fellow, 1970; Southern Federation of State Arts Agencies Grant, 1977; Guggenheim Fellowship, 1989; Edgar Allan Poe Awards, MWA, 1989, 1998. *Address:* c/o Orion Publishing Group Ltd, Orion House, 5 Upper St Martin's Lane, London WC2H 9EA, England.

BURKE, John Frederick, (Owen Burke, Harriet Esmond, Jonathan George, Joanna Jones, Robert Miall, Sara Morris, Martin Sands); Author; b. 8 March 1922, Rye, England; m. 1st Joan Morris 13 Sept. 1940; five d.; m. 2nd Jean Williams 29 June 1963; two s. *Career:* Production Man., Museum Press; Editorial Man., Paul Hamlyn Books for Pleasure Group: European Story Ed., 20th Century Fox Productions; mem. Society of Authors; Danish Club. *Publications:* Swift Summer, 1949; An Illustrated History of England, 1974; Dr Caspian Trilogy, 1976–78; Musical Landscapes, 1983; Illustrated Dictionary of Music, 1988; A Traveller's History of Scotland, 1990; Bareback, 1998; Death by Marzipan, 1999; We've Been Waiting for You, 2000; Stalking Widow, 2000; The Second Strain, 2002. Other: film and TV novelizations. Contributions: The Bookseller; Country Life; Denmark. *Honours:* Atlantic Award in Literature, 1948–49. *Literary Agent:* David Higham Associates, 5–8 Lower John St, Golden Sq., London W1F 9HA, England. *Address:* 5 Castle Gardens, Kirkcudbright, Dumfries & Galloway DG6 4JE, Scotland.

BURKE, (Ulick) Peter; academic and writer; b. 16 Aug. 1937, Stanmore, England; m. 1st Susan Patricia Dell 1972 (divorced 1983); m. 2nd Maria Lúcia García Pallares 1989. *Education:* St John's College, Oxford, 1957–60; BA, 1960, MA, 1964, St Antony's College, Oxford. *Career:* Asst Lecturer to Reader in Intellectual History, Univ. of Sussex, 1962–78; Fellow, Emmanuel College, Cambridge, 1979–; Visiting Prof., Univ. of São Paulo, 1986, 1987, Nijmegen Univ., 1992–93, Groningen Univ., 1998–99, Heidelberg Univ., 2002; Reader in Cultural History, 1988–96, Prof. of Cultural History, 1996–, Univ. of Cambridge; Fellow, Wissenschaftskolleg, Berlin, 1989–90. *Publications:* The Renaissance Sense of the Past, 1969; Culture and Society in Renaissance Italy, 1972; Venice and Amsterdam: A Study of Seventeenth Century Elites, 1974; Popular Culture in Early Modern Europe, 1978; Sociology and History, 1980; Montaigne, 1981; Vico, 1985; Historical Anthropology in Early Modern Italy: Essays on Perception and Communication, 1987; The Renaissance, 1987; The French Historical Revolution: The Annales School 1929–1989, 1990; The Fabrication of Louis XIV, 1992; History and Social Theory, 1992; Antwerp: A Metropolis in Europe, 1993; The Art of Conversation, 1993; The Fortunes of the Courtier, 1995; Varieties of Cultural History, 1997; The European Renaissance, 1998; A Social History of Knowledge, 2001. Contributions: learned books and journals. *Honours:* Fellow, British Acad., 1994; Erasmus Prize, 1999. *Address:* 14 Warkworth Street, Cambridge CB1 1EG, England.

BURKHOLZ, Herbert Laurence; Author; b. 9 Dec. 1932, New York, NY, USA; m. Susan Blaine, 1 Nov. 1961, two s. *Education:* BA, New York University, 1951. *Career:* Writer-in-Residence, College of William and Mary, 1975. *Publications:* Sister Bear, 1969; Spy, 1969; The Spanish Soldier, 1973; Mulligan's Seed, 1975; The Death Freak, 1978; The Sleeping Spy, 1983; The Snow Gods, 1985; The Sensitives, 1987; Strange Bedfellows, 1988; Brain Damage, 1992; Writer-in-Residence, 1992; The FDA Follies, 1994. Contributions: New York Times; Town & Country; Playboy; Penthouse; Longevity. *Honours:* Distinguished Scholar, 1976. *Address:* c/o Georges Borchardt Inc, 136 E 57th St, New York, NY 10022, USA.

BURLEIGH, Michael (Christopher Bennet); Prof. of History and Writer; b. 3 April 1955, London, England; m. Linden Mary Brownbridge, 1990. *Education:* BA, University College London, 1977; PhD, Bedford College, London, 1982. *Career:* Weston Junior Research Fellow, New College, Oxford, 1984–87; British Acad. Postdoctoral Fellow, Queen Mary College, 1987–88; Lecturer, 1988–93, Reader in International History, 1993–95, LSE; Distinguished Research Prof. in Modern European History, Cardiff University, 1995–2000; Raoul Wallenburg Visiting Prof. of Human Rights, Rutgers University, 1999–2000; William R. Kenan Prof. of History, Washington and Lee University, 2000–. *Publications:* Prussian Society and the German Order, 1984; Germany Turns Eastwards: A Study of 'Ostforschung' in the Third Reich, 1988; The Racial State: Germany 1933–1945, 1991; Death and Deliverance: 'Euthanasia' in Germany, 1994; Confronting the Nazi Past: New Debates on Modern German History (ed.), 1996; Ethics and

Extermination: Reflections on Nazi Genocide, 1997; The Third Reich: A New History, 2000. *Honours:* FRHistS, 1988. *Address:* c/o Dept of History, Washington and Lee University, Lexington, VA 24450, USA.

BURLEY, William John; Writer; b. 1 Aug. 1914, Falmouth, Cornwall, England; m. Muriel Wolsey, 10 April 1938, two s. *Education:* Balliol College, Oxford, 1950–53. *Career:* mem. Authors Copyright and Lending Society; CWA; South West Writers. *Publications:* A Taste of Power, 1966; Three Toed Pussey, 1968; Death in Willow Pattem, 1969; Guilt Edged, 1971; Death in a Salubrious Place, 1973; Wycliffe and the Schoolgirls, 1976; The Schoolmaster, 1977; Charles and Elizabeth, 1979; Wycliffe and the Beales, 1983; Wycliffe and the Four Jacks, 1985; Wycliffe and the Quiet Virgin, 1986; Wycliffe and the Windsor Blue, 1987; Wycliffe and the Tangled Web, 1988; Wycliffe and the Cycle of Death, 1989; Wycliffe and a Dead Flautist, 1991; Wycliffe and the Last Rites, 1992; Wycliffe and the Dunes Mystery, 1993; Wycliffe and the House of Fear, 1995; Wycliffe and the Redhead, 1997; Wycliffe and the Guild of Nine, 2000. Novels successfully adapted for television, fourth series. *Address:* St Patricks, Holywell, Newquay, Cornwall TR8 5PT, England.

BURN, Gordon, BA; British writer; b. 16 Jan. 1948, Newcastle upon Tyne, England. *Education:* University of London. *Publications:* Somebody's Husband, Somebody's Son: The Story of Peter Sutcliffe, 1984; Pocket Money, 1986; Alma Cogan: A Novel, 1991; Fullalove (novel), 1995; Happy Like Murderers, 1998; On the Way to Work (with Damien Hirst), 2001; The North of England Home Service, 2003. Contributions: Sunday Times Magazine; Telegraph; Face; Independent; Guardian; TLS. *Honours:* Whitbread First Novel Award 1991, Hon. DLitt (University of Plymouth) 1992. *Literary Agent:* Gillon Aitken Associates Ltd, 18–21 Cavaye Place, London, SW10 9PT, England. *Telephone:* (20) 7373-8672. *Fax:* (20) 7373-6002.

BURN, Michael Clive; Writer and Poet; b. 11 Dec. 1912, London, England; m. Mary Walter 1947. *Education:* Winchester and New Coll., Oxford. *Career:* POW, Colditz 1944; staff The Times 1938–39; correspondent, Vienna, Budapest, Belgrade 1947–49; mem. Soc. of Authors. *Publications:* Yes Farewell, 1946; The Modern Everyman, 1947; Childhood at Oriol, 1951; The Midnight Diary, 1952; The Flying Castle, 1954; Mr Lyward's Answer, 1956; The Trouble with Jake, 1967; The Debatable Land, 1970; Out on a Limb, 1973; Open Day and Night, 1978; Mary and Richard, 1988; Turned Towards the Sun: An Autobiography, 2003. Contributions: articles and poems to Encounter, Guardian, TLS. *Honours:* Keats Poetry First Prize 1973. *Address:* Beudy Gwyn, Minffordd, Gwynedd, North Wales.

BURNET, Sir James (William Alexander), (Alastair Burnet); Journalist; b. 12 July 1928, Sheffield, Yorkshire, England; m. Maureen Campbell Sinclair, 1958. *Education:* Worcester College, Oxford. *Career:* Sub-Ed., Leader Writer, Glasgow Herald, 1951–58; Leader Writer, 1958–62, Ed., 1965–74, The Economist; Political Ed., 1963–64, Broadcaster, 1976–91, Assoc. Ed., 1982–91, Independent Television News; Ed., Daily Express, 1974–76; Dir, Times Newspapers Holdings Ltd, 1982–, United Racecourses Holdings Ltd, 1985–94; mem. Institute of Journalists, hon. vice-pres., 1990–. *Publications:* The Time of Our Lives (with Willie Landels), 1981; The Queen Mother, 1985. Contributions: Television programmes. *Honours:* Richard Dimbleby Awards, BAFTA, 1966, 1970, 1979; Judges' Award, RTS, 1981; Knighted, 1984.

BURNETT, John; Prof. of Social History Emeritus and Author; b. 20 Dec. 1925, Nottingham, England; m. Denise Brayshaw 2 Aug. 1951; one s. *Education:* BA, 1946, MA, 1950, LLB, 1951, Univ. of Cambridge; PhD, Univ. of London, 1958. *Career:* Lecturer, Guildford Technical College, London, 1948–59; Head, Liberal Studies, South Bank Polytechnic, London, 1959–63, General Studies, Brunel College of Technology, 1963–66; Reader, 1966–73, Prof., 1973–90, in Social History, Pro-Vice-Chancellor, 1980–85, Prof. Emeritus, 1990–, Brunel Univ.; mem. Social History Society of the UK, chair., 1985–90. *Publications:* Plenty and Want: A Social History of Food in England, 1966; A History of the Cost of Living, 1969; Useful Toil, 1974; A Social History of Housing, 1978; Destiny Obscure, 1982; The Autobiography of the Working Class (ed. with David Vincent and David Mayall), three vols, 1984–89; Idle Hands, 1994; The Origins and Development of Food Policies in Europe (ed. with D. J. Oddy), 1994; Liquid Pleasures: A Social History of Drinks in Modern Britain, 1999. Contributions: scholarly journals. *Honours:* André Simon Award, 2000. *Address:* Castle Dene, Burgess Wood Rd, Beaconsfield, Buckinghamshire HP9 1EQ, England.

BURNHAM, Sophy; Writer and Dramatist; b. 12 Dec. 1936, Baltimore, MD, USA; m. David Bright Burnham, 12 March 1960, divorced 1984, two d. *Education:* BA, cum laude, Smith College, 1958. *Career:* Acquisitions Ed., David McKay Inc, 1971–73; Contributing Ed., Town & Country, 1975–80, New Art Examiner, 1985–86; Independent Consultant to various organizations, 1975–88; Adjunct Lecturer, George Mason University, 1982–83; Staff Writer, New Woman magazine, 1984–92; Staff Writer and Columnist, Museum & Arts/Washington, 1987–96; Exec. Dir, Fund for New American Plays, John F. Kennedy Center for the Performing Arts, Washington, DC, 1992–96; mem. Authors' Guild; Authors League of America; Cosmos Club. *Publications:* The Exhibits Speak, 1964; The Art Crowd, 1973; The Threat to Licensed Nuclear Facilities (ed.), 1975; Buccaneer (novel), 1977; The Landed Gentry, 1978; The Dogwalker (novel), 1979; A Book of Angels, 1990; Angel Letters, 1991; Revelations (novel), 1992; The President's Angel (novel), 1993; For Writers Only, 1994; The Ecstatic Journey: Walking the Mystical Path in Everyday Life, 1997; The Treasure of Montségur (novel), 2002; The Path of Prayer, 2002. Plays: Penelope, 1976; The Witch's Tale, 1978; The Study, 1979, revised edn as Snowstorms, 1993; Beauty and the Beast, 1979; The Nightingale, 1980; The Meaning of Life, 2001; Prometheus, 2002. Contributions: essays and articles in many periodicals; seminars, talks, workshops. *Honours:* Daughter of Mark Twain, Mark Twain Society, 1974; First Prize, Women's Theatre Award, Seattle, 1981; Helene Wurlitzer Foundation Grants, 1981, 1983, 1991; Virginia Duvall Mann Award, 1993. *Literary Agent:* anne@aeliterary.com. *Address:* 1405 31st St NW, Washington, DC 20007, USA. *Telephone:* (202) 333-9215. *Website:* www.sophyburnham.com.

BURNS, Alan; writer, dramatist and academic; b. 29 Dec. 1929, London, England; m. 1st Carol Lynn 1954; m. 2nd Jean Illien 1980; one s. two d. *Education:* Merchant Taylors' School, London. *Career:* C. Day-Lewis Writing Fellow, Woodberry Down School, 1973; Prof. of English, University of Minnesota, 1977–90; Writer-in-Residence, Associated Colleges of the Twin Cities, Minneapolis-St Paul, 1980; Writing Fellow, Bush Foundation of Minnesota, 1984–85; Lecturer, Lancaster University, 1993–96. *Publications:* Buster, 1961; Europe After the Rain, 1965; Celebrations, 1967; Babel, 1969; Dreamerika, 1972; The Angry Brigade, 1973; The Day Daddy Died, 1981; Revolutions of the Night, 1986; Art by Accident, 1997. Plays: Palach, 1970; To Deprave and Corrupt, 1972; The Imagination on Trial, 1981. Contributions: journals and periodicals. *Honours:* Arts Council Maintenance Grant, 1967, and Bursaries, 1969, 1973. *Address:* Creative Writing Dept, Lancaster University, Lancaster LA1 4YN, England.

BURNS, James MacGregor; political scientist, historian, academic and writer; b. 3 Aug. 1918, Melrose, Massachusetts, USA; m. 1st Janet Rose Dismorr Thompson 1942 (divorced 1968); two s. two d.; m. 2nd Joan Simpson Meyers 1969 (divorced 1991). *Education:* BA, Williams College, 1939; Postgraduate Studies, National Institute of Public Affairs, 1939–40; MA, 1947, PhD, 1947, Harvard University; Postdoctoral Studies, LSE, 1949. *Career:* Faculty, 1941–47, Asst Prof., 1947–50, Assoc. Prof., 1950–53, Prof. of Political Science, 1953–88, Prof. Emeritus, 1988–, Williams College; Senior Scholar, Jepson School of Leadership, University of Richmond, 1990–93; Scholar-in-Residence, Center for Political Leadership and Participation, University of Maryland at College Park, 1993–; mem. American Civil Liberties Union; American Historical Asscn; American Legion; American Philosophical Asscn; American Political Science Asscn, pres., 1975–76; International Society of Political Psychology, pres., 1982–83; New England Political Science Asscn, pres., 1960–61. *Publications:* Okinawa: The Last Battle (co-author), 1947; Congress on Trial: The Legislative Process and the Administrative State, 1949; Government by the People: The Dynamics of American National Government and Local Government (with Jack Walter Peltason and Thomas E. Cronin), 1952; Roosevelt: The Lion and the Fox, 1956; Functions and Policies of American Government (with Jack Walter Peltason), 1958; John Kennedy: A Political Profile, 1960; The Deadlock of Democracy: Four-Party Politics in America, 1963; Presidential Government: The Crucible of Leadership, 1966; Roosevelt: The Soldier of Freedom, 1970; Uncommon Sense, 1972; Edward Kennedy and the Camelot Legacy, 1976; State and Local Politics: Government by the People, 1976; Leadership, 1978; The American Experiment: Vol. I, The Vineyard of Liberty, 1982, Vol. II, The Workshop of Democracy, 1985, Vol. III, The Crosswinds of Freedom, 1989; The Power to Lead: The Crisis of the American Presidency, 1984; Cobblestone Leadership: Majority Rule, Minority Power (with L. Marvin Overby), 1990; A People's Charter: The Pursuit of Rights in America (with Stewart Burns), 1991; Dead Centre: Clinton-Gore Leadership and the Perils of Moderation (with Georgia Sorenson), 2000; The 3 Roosevelt's: Patrician Leaders Who Transformed America, 2001. *Honours:* Tamiment Institute Award for Best Biography, 1956; Woodrow Wilson Prize, 1957; Pulitzer Prize in History, 1971; National Book Award, 1971; Francis Parkman Prize, Society of American Historians, 1971; Sarah Josepha Hale Award, 1979; Christopher Awards, 1983, 1990; Harold D. Lassell Award, 1984; Robert F. Kennedy Book Award, 1990; Rollo May Award in Humanistic Services, 1994. *Address:* Highgate Barn, High Mowing, Bee Hill Road, Williamstown, MA 01267, USA.

BURNS, Jim; Writer and Poet; b. 19 Feb. 1936, Preston, Lancashire, England. *Education:* BA, Bolton Institute of Technology, 1980. *Career:* Ed., Move, 1964–68, Palantir, 1976–83; Jazz Ed., Beat Scene, 1990–. *Publications:* A Single Flower, 1972; The Goldfish Speaks from Beyond the Grave, 1976; Fred Engels in Woolworth's, 1977; Internal Memorandum, 1982; Out of the Past: Selected Poems 1961–1986, 1987; Confessions of an Old Believer, 1996; The Five Senses, 1999; As Good a Reason As Any, 1999; Beats, Bohemians and Intellectuals, 2000; Take It Easy, 2003. Contributions: London Magazine; Stand; Ambit; Jazz Journal; Critical Survey; The Guardian; New Statesman; Tribune; New Society; Penniless Press; Prop; Verse; others. *Address:* 11 Gatley Green, Gatley, Cheadle, Cheshire SK8 4NF, England.

BURNS, Ralph, MFA; poet, editor and academic; b. 8 June 1949, Norman, OK, USA; m. Candace Wilson Calhoun 1974; one s. *Education:* University of Montana. *Career:* Prof., University of Arkansas at Little Rock, 1985–; Ed., Crazyhorse magazine. *Publications:* Us, 1983; Any Given Day, 1985; Mozart's Starling, 1991; Swamp Candles, 1996. *Honours:* Two National Endowment for the Arts Fellowships; Iowa Poetry Prize, 1996. *Address:* 315 Linwood Court, Little Rock, AR 72205, USA.

BURNS, Rex Sehler; Emeritus Professor of English and Writer; b. 13 June 1935, San Diego, CA, USA; m. Terry Fostvedt, 1987, divorced, 1996, three s., one d. *Education:* AB, Stanford University, 1958; MA, 1963, PhD, 1965, University of Minnesota. *Career:* Asst Prof., Central Missouri State College, 1965–68; Assoc. Prof., 1968–75, Prof. of English, 1975–2000, Chair., Dept of English, 1996–99, University of Colorado at Denver; Fulbright Lecturer, Aristotle University, Thessaloniki, 1969–70, Universidad Catolico, Buenos Aires, 1974; Book Reviewer, Rocky Mountain News, 1982–92; Senior Lecturer, University of Kent, Canterbury, 1992–93; mem. International Asscn of Crime Writers; MWA. *Publications:* Fiction: The Alvarez Journal, 1975; The Farnsworth Score, 1977; Speak for the Dead, 1978; Angle of Attack, 1979; The Avenging Angel, 1983; Strip Search, 1984; Ground Money, 1986; Suicide Season, 1987; The Killing Zone, 1988; Parts Unknown, 1990; When Reason Sleeps, 1991; Body Guard, 1991; Endangered Species, 1993; Blood Line, 1995; The Leaning Land, 1997. Editor: Crime Classics: The Mystery Story from Poe to the Present (with Mary Rose Sullivan), 1990. Non-Fiction: Success in America: The Yeoman Dream and the Industrial Revolution, 1976. Contributions: periodicals and anthologies; Starz Encore Mystery Channel. *Honours:* Edgar Allan Poe Award, MWA, 1976; Colorado Authors League Awards, 1978, 1979, 1980; Pres.'s Teaching Scholar (Lifetime Title), University of Colorado System, 1990; University Service Award.

BURNSHAW, Stanley; Publisher, Poet and Writer; b. 20 June 1906, New York, NY, USA; m. Lydia Powsner 2 Sept. 1942 (deceased); one d. *Education:* BA, University of Pittsburgh, 1925; University of Poitiers, France, 1927; University of Paris, 1927; MA, Cornell University, 1933. *Career:* Pres. and Ed.-in-Chief, The Dryden Press, 1937–58; Program Dir, Graduate Institute of Book Publishing, New York University, 1958–62; Vice-Pres., Holt, Rinehart and Winston, publishers, 1958–67; Regents Visiting Lecturer, University of California, 1980; Visiting Distinguished Prof., Miami University, 1989. *Publications:* Poems, 1927; The Great Dark Love, 1932; Andre Spire and His Poetry, 1933; The Iron Land, 1936; The Bridge, 1945; The Revolt of the Cats in Paradise, 1945; Early and Late Testament, 1952; Caged in an Animal's Mind, 1963; The Hero of Silence, 1965; In the Terrified Radiance, 1972; Mirages: Travel Notes in the Promised Land, 1977; Robert Frost Himself, 1986; A Stanley Burnshaw Reader, 1990; The Seamless Web, 1991. Contributions: many periodicals. *Honours:* National Institute of Arts and Letters Award, 1971; Hon. Doctorate of Humane Letters, Hebrew Union College, 1983; Hon. DLitt, CUNY, 1996.

BURRINGTON, Ernest; British newspaper executive; b. 13 Dec. 1926; m. Nancy Crossley 1950; one s. one d. *Career:* reporter, Oldham Chronicle 1941–44, reporter and sub-ed. 1947–49; mil. service 1945–47; sub-ed. Bristol Evening World 1950; sub-ed. Daily Herald, Manchester 1950, night ed. 1955, London night 1957; night ed. IPC Sun 1964, Asst ed. 1965; Asst ed. and night News Int. Sun 1969; deputy night ed. Daily Mirror 1970; Deputy Ed. Sunday People 1971, Assoc. Ed. 1972; Ed. The People 1985–88, 1989–90; Dir Mirror Group Newspapers 1985–92, Deputy Chair. and Asst Publr 1988–91, Man. Dir 1989–91, Chair. 1991–92; Chair. Syndication Int. 1989–92; Deputy Chair. Mirror Publishing Co. 1989–91; Dir Mirror Group Magazine and Newsday Ltd 1989–92, Legionstyle Ltd 1991–92, Mirror Colour Print Ltd 1991–92; Dir (non-exec.) Sunday Correspondent 1990, The European 1990–91, IQ Newsgraphics 1990–92, Sygma Picture Agency, Paris 1990–91; Deputy Publr Globe Communications, Montreal, Canada 1993–95, Exec. Vice-Pres. and Assoc. Publr 1995–96; Pres. Atlantic Media 1996–98; Consultant Head of Marketing Harveys PLC, UK 1998–2000; mem. Council Nat. Press Asscn 1988–92, Int. Press Inst. British Exec. 1988–92, Foreign Press Asscn; Trustee Int. Centre for Child Studies 1986–90; Life mem. NUJ 1960–. *Honours:* Hon. Life mem. NUJ 1996; Hon. Red Devil (Manchester United Football Club) 1985. *Address:* 17499 Tiffany Trace Drive, Boca Raton, FL 33487, USA; South Hall, Dene Park, Shipbourne Road, Tonbridge, TN11 9NS, England. *Telephone:* (561) 995-9897 (USA); (1732) 368517 (England). *Fax:* (561) 995-9897 (USA); (1732) 368517 (England). *E-mail:* burringtone@aol.com (Home).

BURROW, John Anthony; Prof. and Writer; b. 1932, Loughton, England. *Education:* BA, 1953, MA, 1955, Christ Church, Oxford. *Career:* Fellow, Jesus College, Oxford, 1961–75; Winterstoke Prof., Univ. of Bristol, 1976–98. *Publications:* A Reading of Sir Gawain and the Green Knight, 1965; Geoffrey Chaucer: A Critical Anthology, 1969; Ricardian Poetry: Chaucer, Gower Langland and the Gawain Poet, 1971; Sir Gawain and the Green Knight, 1972; English Verse 1300–1500, 1977; Medieval Writers and Their Work, 1982; Essays on Medieval Literature, 1984; The Ages of Man, 1986; A Book of Middle English, 1992; Langlands Fictions, 1993; Thomas Hoccleve, 1994; Thomas Hoccleve's Complaint and Dialogue, 1999; The Gawain-Poet, 2001; Gestures and Looks in Medieval Narrative, 2002. *Address:* 9 The Polygon, Clifton, Bristol, England.

BURROW, John Wyon, MA, PhD, FBA, FRHistS; British professor of history; *Emeritus Fellow, Balliol College Oxford*; b. 4 June 1935, Southsea; m. Diane Dunnington 1958; one s. one d. *Education:* Exeter School and Christ's Coll., Cambridge. *Career:* Research Fellow, Christ's Coll. Cambridge 1959–62; Fellow and Dir of Studies in History, Downing Coll. Cambridge 1962–65; Reader, School of European Studies, Univ. of E Anglia 1965–69; Reader in History, Univ. of Sussex 1969–82, Prof. of Intellectual History 1982–95; Visiting Fellow All Souls Coll. Oxford Univ. 1994–95, Prof. of European Thought and Fellow of Balliol Coll. 1995–2000, Emer. Fellow 2001–; Research Prof. of History, Univ. of Sussex 2000–; Visiting Prof. Univ. of Calif. Berkeley 1981; Visiting Fellow, History of Ideas Unit, ANU 1983; Carlyle Lecturer, Univ. of Oxford 1985; Ed. History of European Ideas 1996–; Distinguished Visiting Prof., Ben Gurion Univ. of the Negev 1988; delivered Gauss Seminars, Princeton Univ. 1988. *Publications:* Evolution and Society 1966, A Liberal Descent 1981, That Noble Science of Politics (with S. Collini and D. Winch) 1983, Gibbon 1985, Whigs and Liberals 1988, The Crisis of Reason 2000. *Honours:* Hon. Dr Political Sciences (Bologna) 1988; Wolfson Prize for History 1981. *Address:* Balliol College, Oxford, OX1 3BJ; 22 Bridge Street, Witney, Oxon. OX18 2HY, England (Home). *Telephone:* (1993) 201396.

BURROWAY, Janet (Gay); Prof., Writer and Poet; b. 21 Sept. 1936, Tucson, AZ, USA; m. 1st Walter Eysselinck 1961 (divorced 1973); two s.; m. 2nd William Dean Humphries 1978 (divorced 1981); m. 3rd Peter Ruppert 1993; one step-d. *Education:* University of Arizona, 1954–55; AB, Barnard College, 1958; BA, 1960, MA, 1965, University of Cambridge; Yale School of Drama, 1960–61. *Career:* Instructor, Harpur College, Binghamton, New York, 1961–62; Lecturer, University of Sussex, 1965–70; Assoc. Prof., 1972–77, Prof., 1977–, MacKenzie Prof. of English, 1989–95, Robert O. Lawson Distinguished Prof., 1995–2002, Emerita, 2002–, Florida State University; Fiction Reviewer, Philadelphia Enquirer, 1986–90; Reviewer, New York Times Book Review, 1991–; Essay-Columnist, New Letters: A Magazine of Writing and Art, 1994–; mem. Associated Writing Programs; Authors' Guild. *Publications:* Fiction: Descend Again, 1960; The Dancer From the Dance, 1965; Eyes, 1966; The Buzzards, 1969; The Truck on the Track, 1970; The Giant Jam Sandwich, 1972; Raw Silk, 1977; Opening Nights, 1985; Cutting Stone, 1992. Poetry: But to the Season, 1961; Material Goods, 1980. Other: Writing Fiction: A Guide to Narrative Craft, 1982; Embalming Mom (essays), 2002; Imaginative Writing: The Elements of Craft, 2002. Contributions: numerous journals and periodicals. *Honours:* National Endowment for the Arts Fellowship, 1976; Yaddo Residency Fellowships, 1985, 1987; Lila Wallace-Reader's Digest Fellow, 1993–94; Carolyn Benton Cockefaire Distinguished Writer-in-Residence, University of Missouri, 1995; Woodrow Wilson Visiting Fellow, Furman University, Greenville, South Carolina, 1995; Visiting Writer, Erskine College, Due West, South Carolina, 1997, Drury College, Springfield, IL, 1999. *Literary Agent:* Brandt & Hochman Literary Agents Inc, 1501 Broadway, New York, NY 10036, USA. *Address:* 240 De Soto St, Tallahassee, FL 32303, USA; 59 Carlton Mansions, Randolph Ave, London W9 1NR, England. *E-mail:* jburroway@english.fsu.edu.

BURTON, Anthony George Graham; Writer and Broadcaster; b. 24 Dec. 1934, Thornaby, England; m. 28 March 1959, two s. one d. *Career:* mem. Outdoor Writers Guild. *Publications:* A Programmed Guide to Office Warfare, 1969; The Jones Report, 1970; The Canal Builders, 1972; The Reluctant Musketeer, 1973; Canals in Colour, 1974; Remains of a Revolution, 1975; The Master Idol, 1975; The Miners, 1976; The Navigators, 1976; Josiah Wedgwood, 1976; Canal, 1976; Back Door Britain, 1977; A Place to Stand, 1977; Industrial Archaeological Sites of Britain, 1977; The Green Bag Travellers, 1978; The Past At Work, 1980; The Rainhill Story, 1980; The Past Afloat, 1982; The Changing River, 1982; The Shell Book of Curious Britain, 1982; The National Trust Guide to Our Industrial Past, 1983; The Waterways of Britain, 1983; The Rise and Fall of King Cotton, 1984; Walking the Line, 1985; Wilderness Britain, 1985; Britain's Light Railways, 1985; The Shell Book of Undiscovered Britain and Ireland, 1986; Britain Revisited, 1986; Landscape Detective, 1986; Opening Time, 1987; Steaming Through Britain, 1987; Walk the South Downs, 1988; Walking Through History, 1988; The Great Days of the Canals, 1989; Cityscapes, 1990; Astonishing Britain, 1990; Slow Roads, 1991; The Railway Builders, 1992; Canal Mania, 1993; The Grand Union Canal Walk, 1993; The Railway Empire, 1994; The Rise and Fall of British Shipbuilding, 1994; The Cotswold Way, 1995; The Dales Way, 1995; The West Highland Way, 1996; The Southern Upland Way, 1997; William Cobbett: Englishman, 1997; The Wye Valley Walk, 1998; The Caledonian Canal, 1998; Best Foot Forward, 1998; The Cumbria Way, 1999; The Wessex Ridgeway, 1999; Thomas Telford, 1999; Weekend Walks: Dartmoor and Exmoor, 2000; Weekend Walks: The Yorkshire Dales, 2000; Traction Engines, 2000; Richard Trevithick, 2000; The Orient Express, 2001; Weekend Walks: The Peak District, 2001; The Anatomy of Canals: The Early Years, 2001; The Daily Telegraph Guide to Britain's Working Past, 2002, The Anatomy of Canals: The Mania Years 2002, Daily Telegraph Guide to Britain's Maritime Past 2003, Hadrian's Wall Path 2003, The Anatomy of Canals: Decline & Renewal 2003. *Literary Agent:* Sara Menguc, 4 Hatch Pl., Kingston upon Thames KT2 5NB, England. *Address:* 31 Lansdown, Stroud, Gloucestershire, GL5 1BG, England.

BURTON, Gabrielle; Writer and Poet; b. 21 Feb. 1939, Lansing, MI, USA; m. Roger V. Burton, 18 Aug. 1962, five d. *Education:* BA, Marygrove College, Michigan, 1960; MFA, American Film Institute, Los Angeles, 1997. *Career:* Teacher, Fiction in the Schools, Writers in Education Project, New York, 1985; various prose readings and workships. *Publications:* I'm Running Away From Home But I'm Not Allowed to Cross the Street, 1972; Heartbreak Hotel, 1986; Manna From Heaven (screenplay, filmed), 2000. Contributions: numerous publications. *Honours:* MacDowell Colony Fellowships, 1982, 1987, 1989; Yaddo Fellowship, 1983; Maxwell Perkins Prize, 1986; Great Lakes Colleges Asscn Award, 1987; Bernard De Voto

Fellow in Non-Fiction, Bread Loaf Writer's Conference, 1994; Mary Pickford Foundation Award for First Year Screenwriter, 1996; First Prize, Austin Film Festival Screenwriting Contest, 1999; Nicholl Fellow, 2000. *Address:* 211 LeBrun Rd, Eggetsville, NY 14226, USA.

BURTON, Tim; American film director and screenwriter; b. 25 Aug. 1958, Burbank, Calif.; pnr Helena Bonham Carter; one s. *Education:* Calif. Arts Inst. *Career:* began career as animator, Walt Disney Studios (projects included The Fox and the Hound and The Black Cauldron). *Films directed:* Vincent (also animator) 1982, Luau 1982, Hansel and Gretel (TV) 1982, Frankenweenie (short, for Disney) 1984, Pee-Wee's Big Adventure 1985, Alfred Hitchcock Presents (TV episode, The Jar) 1985, Beetlejuice 1988, Batman 1989, Edward Scissorhands (also producer) 1991, Batman Returns (also producer) 1992, Ed Wood (also producer) 1994, Mars Attacks! (also producer) 1996, Sleepy Hollow 1999, Planet of the Apes 2001, Big Fish 2003; producer:Beetlejuice (TV series) 1993, Family Dog (TV series) 1993, The Nightmare Before Christmas 1993, Cabin Boy 1994, Batman Forever 1996, James and the Giant Peach 1996, Lost in Oz (TV series) 2000. *Publications:* My Art and Films 1993, The Melancholy Death of Oyster Boy and Other Stories 1997, Burton on Burton 2000; various film tie-in books; screenplays: The Island of Doctor Agor 1971, Stalk of the Celery 1979, Vincent 1982, Luau 1982, Beetlejuice (story) 1988, (TV series creator) 1989, Edward Scissorhands (story) 1990, The Nightmare Before Christmas (story) 1993, Lost in Oz (TV pilot episode story) 2000, Point Blank (TV series) 2002. *Honours:* short-length film awards include two from Chicago Film Festival. *Literary Agent:* Chapman, Bird & Grey, 1990 South Bundy Drive, Suite 200, Los Angeles, CA 90025, USA. *Website:* www.timburton.com.

BUSBY, F. M., BSc, BScEE; writer; b. 11 March 1921, Indianapolis, IN, USA; m. Elinor Doub 1954; one d. *Education:* Washington State Univ. *Career:* mem. SFWA (vice-pres. 1974–76), Spectator Amateur Press Soc. *Publications:* Cage a Man 1974, The Proud Enemy 1975, Rissa Kerguelen 1976, The Long View 1976, All These Earths 1978, Zelde M'tana 1980, The Demu Trilogy 1980, Star Rebel 1984, The Alien Debt 1984, Rebel's Quest 1985, Rebels' Seed 1986, Getting Home 1987, The Breeds of Man 1988, Slow Freight 1991, The Singularity Project 1993, Islands of Tomorrow 1994, Arrow from Earth 1995, The Triad Worlds 1996; contrib. approximately 45 shorter works in anthologies and magazines. *Address:* 2852 14th Avenue W, Seattle, WA 98119, USA. *E-mail:* fmbusby001@aol.com.

BUSBY, Roger Charles; writer and public relations officer; b. 24 July 1941, Leicester, England. *Education:* Certificate in Journalism, University of Aston, Birmingham. *Career:* Journalist, Caters News Agency, Birmingham, 1959–66; Journalist, Birmingham Evening Mail, 1966–73; Head of Public Relations, Devon & Cornwall Police, 1973–; mem. CWA; Institute of Public Relations; National Union of Journalists. *Publications:* Main Line Kill, 1968; Robbery Blue, 1969; The Frighteners, 1970; Deadlock, 1971; A Reasonable Man, 1972; Pattern of Violence, 1973; New Face in Hell, 1976; Garvey's Code, 1978; Fading Blue, 1984; The Hunter, 1986; Snow Man, 1987; Crackhot, 1990; High Jump, 1992. *Address:* Sunnymoor, Bridford, Nr Exeter, Devon, England.

BUSCH, Frederick (Matthew); Prof. of Literature and Writer; b. 1 Aug. 1941, New York, NY, USA; m. Judith Burroughs, 29 Nov. 1963, two s. *Education:* BA, Muhlenberg College, 1962; MA, Columbia University, 1967. *Career:* Magazine Writer; Instructor to Prof., 1966–87, Fairchild Prof. of Literature, 1987–2003, Writer-in-Residence, 2003–, Colgate University; Acting Dir, Program in Creative Writing, University of Iowa, 1978–79; Visiting Lecturer, Creative Writing Program, Columbia University, 1979; mem. Authors' Guild of America; PEN; Writers Guild of America. *Publications:* I Wanted a Year Without Fall, 1971; Breathing Trouble, 1973; Hawkes, 1973; Manual Labor, 1974; Domestic Particulars, 1976; The Mutual Friend, 1978; Hardwater Country, 1979; A Dangerous Profession, 1980; Invisible Mending, 1984; Sometimes I Live in the Country, 1986; Absent Friends, 1989; Harry and Catherine, 1990; Closing Arguments, 1991; Long Way From Home, 1993; The Children in the Woods: New and Selected Stories, 1994; Girls, 1997; A Dangerous Profession (essays), 1998; The Night Inspector, 1999; Don't Tell Anyone, 2000; A Memory of War, 2003. Contributions: various periodicals. *Honours:* National Endowment for the Arts Fellowship, 1976; Guggenheim Fellowship, 1981–82; Ingram Merrill Foundation Fellowship, 1981–82; National Jewish Book Award for Fiction, Jewish Book Council, 1985; PEN/Malamud Award, 1991; Award of Merit for Short Fiction, American Acad. of Arts and Letters, 2001; American Acad. of Arts and Sciences. *Literary Agent:* Elaine Markson, USA; Rachel Calder, UK. *Address:* 839 Turnpike Rd, Sherburne, NY 13460, USA.

BUSH, Duncan (Eric); Poet, Writer and Teacher; b. 6 April 1946, Cardiff, Wales; m. Annette Jane Weaver, 4 June 1981, two s. *Education:* BA, in English and European Literature, Warwick University, 1978; Exchange Scholarship, Duke University, USA, 1976–77; DPhil, Research in English Literature, Wadham College, Oxford, 1978–81. *Career:* European ed., The Kansas Quarterly and Arkansas Review; Writing Tutor with various institutions; mem. Welsh Acad.; Society of Authors. *Publications:* Aquarium, 1983; Salt, 1985; Black Faces, Red Mouths, 1986; The Genre of Silence, 1987; Glass Shot, 1991; Masks, 1994; The Hook, 1997; Midway, 1998. Editor: On Censorship, 1985. Contributions: BBC and periodicals. *Honours:* Eric Gregory Award for Poetry, 1978; Barbara Campion Memorial Award for Poetry, 1982; Welsh Arts Council Prizes for Poetry; Arts Council of Wales Book of the Year, 1995. *Literary Agent:* PFD, Drury House, 34–43 Russell St, London WC2B 5HA, England. *Address:* Godre Waun Oleu, Brecon Rd, Ynyswen, Penycae, Powys SA9 1YY, Wales.

BUSH, Ronald; Prof. of American Literature and Writer; b. 16 June 1946, Philadelphia, Pennsylvania, USA; m. Marilyn Wolin, 14 Dec. 1969, one s. *Education:* BA, University of Pennsylvania, 1968; BA, University of Cambridge, 1970; PhD, Princeton University, 1974. *Career:* Asst to Assoc. Prof., Harvard University, 1974–82; Assoc. Prof., 1982–85, Prof., 1985–97, California Institute of Technology; Visiting Fellow, Exeter College, Oxford, 1994–95; Drue Heinz Prof. of American Literature, University of Oxford, 1997–. *Publications:* The Genesis of Ezra Pound's Cantos, 1976; T. S. Eliot: A Study in Character and Style, 1983; T. S. Eliot: The Modernist in History (ed.), 1991; Prehistories of the Future: The Primitivist Project and the Culture of Modernism (ed. with Elazar Barkan), 1995; Claiming the Stones/Naming the Bones: Cultural Property and the Negotiation of National and Ethnic Identity (ed. with Elazar Barken), 2003. Contributions: scholarly books and journals. *Honours:* National Endowment for the Humanities fellowships, 1977–78, 1992–93. *Address:* St John's College, Oxford OX1 3JP, England. *E-mail:* ron.bush@english.ox.ac.uk.

BUSHNELL, Candace; American writer; b. 1959, Glastonbury, CT; m. Charles Askegard 2002. *Education:* Rice Univ., TX, New York Univ. *Career:* wrote 'Sex and the City' column, New York Observer 1994–96; host, TV programme Sex, Lives and Video Clips (VH-1) 1997. *Publications:* Sex and the City 1997, Four Blondes 2000, Trading Up 2003. *Address:* c/o Little, Brown and Co, Brettenham House, Lancaster Place, London, WC2E 7EN, England.

BUTALA, Sharon Annette; Writer; b. 24 Aug. 1940, Nipawin, Saskatchewan, Canada; m. Peter Butala, 21 May 1976, one s. *Education:* BEd, 1962, BA, 1963, Postgraduate Diploma in Special Education, 1973, University of Saskatchewan. *Career:* mem. PEN Canada; Saskatchewan Writers' Guild; Writer's Union of Canada. *Publications:* Fiction: Country of the Heart, 1984; Queen of the Headaches, 1985; The Gates of the Sun, 1986; Luna, 1988; Fever, 1990; Upstream, 1991; The Fourth Archangel, 1992; The Garden of Eden, 1998; Real Life, 2002. Non-Fiction: Harvest, 1992; The Perfection of the Morning, 1994; Coyote's Morning Cry, 1995; Wild Stone Heart, 2000; Old Man on His Back, 2002. Contributions: periodicals. *Honours:* Saskatchewan Book Award for Non-Fiction, 1994; Marian Engel Award, 1998; Hon. LLD, University of Regina, 2000; Officer to the Order of Canada, 2002. *Address:* 94 Harbord St, Toronto, Ontario M5S 1G6, Canada.

BUTLER, Gwendoline (Williams), (Jennie Melville); Author; b. 19 Aug. 1922, London, England; m. Lionel Butler, 16 Oct. 1949 (deceased), one d. *Education:* MA, Lady Margaret Hall, Oxford, 1948. *Career:* Historical Crime Critic, Crime Time Magazine, 1999–2002; mem. CWA, panel; Reform Club; Detection Club, hon. sec., 1992–95; MWA. *Publications:* Receipt for Murder, 1956; Dead in a Row, 1957; The Dull Dead, 1958; The Murdering Kind, 1958; The Interloper, 1959; Death Lives Next Door, US edn as Dine and Be Dead, 1960; Make Me a Murderer, 1961; Coffin on the Water, 1962; Coffin in Oxford, 1962; Coffin for Baby, 1963; Coffin Waiting, 1963; Coffin in Malta, 1964; A Nameless Coffin, 1966; Coffin Following, 1968; Coffin's Dark Number, 1969; A Coffin form the Past, 1970; A Coffin for Pandora, 1973, US edn as Olivia, 1974; A Coffin for the Canary, US edn as Sarsen Place, 1974; The Vesey Inheritance, 1975; Brides of Friedberg, US edn as Meadowsweet, 1977; The Red Staircase, 1979; Albion Walk, 1982; Coffin on the Water, 1986; Coffin in Fashion, 1987; Coffin Underground, 1988; Coffin in the Black Museum, 1989; Coffin and the Paper Man, 1990; Coffin the Museum of Crime, 1990; Coffin on Murder Street, 1992; Cracking Open a Coffin, 1992; A Coffin for Charley, 1993; The Coffin Tree, 1994; A Dark Coffin, 1995; A Double Coffin, 1996; Butterfly, 1996; Let There Be Love, 1997; Coffin's Game, 1997; A Grave Coffin, 1998; Coffin's Ghost, 1999; The King Cried Murder, 2000; A Cold Coffin, 2000; Coffin Knows the Answer. As Jennie Melville: Come Home and Be Killed, 1962; Burning Is a Substitute for Loving, 1963; Murderers' Houses, 1964; There Lies Your Love, 1965; Nell Alone, 1966; A Different Kind of Summer, 1967; The Hunter in the Shadows, 1969; A New Kind of Killer, An Old Kind of Death, 1970, US edn as A New Kind of Killer, 1971; Ironwood, 1972; Nun's Castle, 1973; Raven's Forge, 1975; Dragon's Eye, 1976; Axwater, US edn as Tarot's Tower, 1978; Murder Has a Pretty Face, 1981; The Painted Castle, 1982; The Hand of Glass, 1983; Listen to the Children, 1986; Death in the Garden, 1987; Windsor Red, 1988; A Cure for Dying, 1989; Witching Murder, 1990; Footsteps in the Blood, 1990; Dead Set, 1992; Whoever Has the Heart, 1993; Baby Drop, 1994; The Morbid Kitchen, 1995; The Woman Who Was Not There, 1996; Revengeful Death, 1997; Stone Dead, 1998; Dead Again, 1999. *Honours:* Silver Dagger, CWA, 1973; Silver Rose Bowl, Romantic Novelists Asscn, 1981; Ellery Queen Short Story Award; Judge Ellis Peters Memorial Historical Crime Fiction Contest, 2000; FRSA. *Address:* 32 Harvest Rd, Englefield Green, Egham, Surrey TW20 0QS, England.

BUTLER, Leo; British playwright; b. 1975, S Yorkshire, England. *Plays:* Made of Stone 2000, Redundant 2001, Devotion 2002, Lucky Dog 2004. *Honours:* George Devine Award 2001. *Address:* c/o Methuen Publishing Ltd, 215 Vauxhall Bridge Road, London, SW1V 1EL, England. *Telephone:* (20) 7828-2838. *Fax:* (20) 7233-9827. *Website:* www.methuen.co.uk.

BUTLER, Marilyn (Speers); Rector, Prof. and Author; b. 11 Feb. 1937, Kingston on Thames, England. *Education:* BA, 1958, PhD, 1966, University of Oxford. *Career:* Current Affairs Producer, BBC, 1960–63; Research Fellow, St Hilda's College, Oxford, 1970–73; Fellow, Tutor, St Hugh's College, Lecturer, University of Oxford, 1973–86; King Edward VII Prof., University of Cambridge, 1986–93; Professorial Fellow, King's College, Cambridge, 1988–93; Rector, Exeter College, Oxford, 1993–. *Publications:* Maria Edgeworth: A Literary Biography, 1972; Jane Austen and the War of Ideas, 1975; Peacock Displayed: A Satirist in His Context, 1979; Romantics, Rebels and Reactionaries, 1760–1830, 1981; Burke, Paine, Godwin and the Revolution Controversy, 1984; Collected Works of Mary Wollstonecraft, 1989; Maria Edgeworth, Castle Rackrent and Ennui (ed.), 1992; Frankenstein, the 1818 Edition (ed.), 1993; Northanger Abbey (ed.), 1995. *Address:* Exeter College, Oxford OX1 3DP, England.

BUTLER, Richard (see Allbeury, Theodore Edward Le Bouthillier).

BUTLER, Robert Olen; Author, Screenwriter and Prof. of Creative Writing; b. 20 Jan. 1945, Granite City, IL, USA; m. 1st Carol Supplee, 10 Aug. 1968, divorced Jan. 1972; m. 2nd Marylin Geller, 1 July 1972, divorced July 1987, two s.; m. 3rd Maureen Donlan, 21 July 1987, divorced March 1995; m. 4th Elizabeth Dewberry, 23 April 1995. *Education:* BS, Northwestern University, 1967; MA, University of Iowa, 1969; Postgraduate Studies, New School for Social Research, New York City, 1979–81. *Career:* Ed.-in-Chief, Energy User News, 1975–85; Prof., Master of Fine Arts in Creative Writing Program, McNeese State University, 1985–; Faculty, various summer writing conferences; mem. Writers Guild of America West. *Publications:* The Alleys of Eden, 1981; Sun Dogs, 1982; Countrymen of Bones, 1983; On Distant Ground, 1985; Wabash, 1987; The Deuce, 1989; A Good Scent from a Strange Mountain, 1992; They Whisper, 1994; Coffee, Cigarettes, and a Run in the Park, 1996; Tabloid Dreams, 1996; The Deep Green Sea, 1998. Other: several screenplays. Contributions: anthologies, newspapers, and journals. *Honours:* Charter Recipient, Tu Do Chinh Kien Award, Vietnam Veterans of America, 1987; Emily Clark Balch Award, Virginia Quarterly Review, 1991; Southern Review/Louisiana State University Prize for Short Fiction, 1992; Hon. Doctor of Humane Letters, McNeese State University, 1993; Notable Book Citation, American Library Asscn, 1993; Richard and Hinda Rosenthal Foundation Award, American Acad. of Arts and Letters, 1993; Guggenheim Fellowship, 1993; Pulitzer Prize for Fiction, 1993; National Endowment for the Arts Fellowship, 1994; Lotos Club Award of Merit, 1996; William Peden Prize, Missouri Review, 1997; Author of the Year Award, Illinois Asscn of Teachers of English, 1997. *Address:* 665 Sixth St, Lake Charles, LA 70601, USA.

BUTLIN, Martin (Richard Fletcher); Art Consultant and Writer; b. 7 June 1929, Birmingham, England; m. Frances Caroline Chodzko, 1969. *Education:* BA, 1952, MA, 1957, Trinity College, Cambridge; BA, Courtauld Institute of Art, 1955, DLit, 1984. *Career:* Asst Keeper, 1955–67, Keeper of Historic British Collection, 1967–89, Tate Gallery, London; Art Consultant, Christie's, London, 1989–; mem. British Acad., fellow, 1984–. *Publications:* A Catalogue of the Works of William Blake in the Tate Gallery, 1957; Samuel Palmer's Sketchbook of 1824, 1962; Turner Watercolours, 1962; Turner (with Sir John Rothenstein), 1964; Tate Gallery Catalogues: The Modern British Paintings, Drawings and Sculpture (with Mary Chamot and Dennis Farr), 1964; The Later Works of J. M. W. Turner, 1965; William Blake, 1966; The Blake-Varley Sketchbook of 1819, 1969; The Paintings of J. M. W. Turner (with E. Joll), 1977; The Paintings and Drawings of William Blake, 1981; Aspects of British Painting 1550–1800, from the Collection of the Sarah Campbell Blaffer Foundation, 1988; Turner at Petworth (with Mollie Luther and Ian Warrell), 1989; William Blake in the Collection of the National Gallery of Victoria (with Ted Gott and Irena Zdanowicz), 1989; The Oxford Companion to J. M. W. Turner (ed. with Evelyn Joll and Like Herrmann), 2001. Contributions: periodicals. *Honours:* Mitchell Prize for the History of Art, 1978; CBE, 1990. *Address:* 74c Eccleston Sq., London SW1V 1PJ, England.

BUTLIN, Ron; Poet and Writer; b. 17 Nov. 1949, Edinburgh, Scotland; m. Regula Staub, 18 June 1993. *Education:* MA, DipCDAE, University of Edinburgh. *Career:* Writer-in-Residence, University of Edinburgh, 1983, 1985, Midlothian Region, 1990–91, Craigmillar Literary Trust, 1997–98, University of St Andrews, 1998–; Writer-in-Residence, 1993, Examiner in Creative Writing, 1997–, Stirling University; mem. Scottish Arts Council, literature committee, 1995–96. *Publications:* Creature Tamed by Cruelty, 1979; The Exquisite Instrument, 1982; The Tilting Room, 1984; Ragtime in Unfamiliar Bars, 1985; The Sound of My Voice, 1987; Faber Book of Twentieth Century Scottish Poetry, 1992; Histories of Desire, 1995; Night Visits, 1997; When We Jump We Jump High! (ed.), 1998; Our Piece of Good Fortune, 2002; Panther Book of Scottish Short Stories, 2002; No More Angels, 2002; Vivaldi, The Jumping Cardinal, God and the Number Three, 2003. Contributions: reviews, periodicals and journals. *Honours:* Writing Bursaries, 1977, 1987, 1990, 1994, 2002; Scottish Arts Council Book Awards, 1982, 1984, 1985; Scottish-Canadian Writing Fellow, 1984; Poetry Book Society Recommendation, 1985. *Address:* 7W Newington Pl., Edinburgh EH9 1QT, Scotland.

BUTOR, Michel Marie François; writer, poet and academic; b. 14 Sept. 1926, Mons-en-Baroeul, Nord, France; m. Marie-Josephe Mas 1958; four d. *Education:* Licence en philosophie, 1946, Diplôme d'études supérieures de philosophie, 1947, Sorbonne, University of Paris; Docteur es Lettres, Université of Tours, 1972. *Career:* Assoc. Prof., University of Vincennes, 1969, University of Nice, 1970–73; Prof. of Modern French Language and Literature, University of Geneva, 1973–91; Visiting Professorships in the USA. *Publications:* Passage de Milan, 1954; L'Emploi du temps, 1956, English trans. as Passing Time, 1960; La Modification, 1957, English trans. as Change of Heart, 1959; La Génie du lieu, 5 vols, 1958, 1971, 1978, 1988, 1995; Degrés, 1960, English trans. as Degrees, 1961; Répertoire, 5 vols, 1960, 1964, 1968, 1974, 1982; Histoire extraordinaire: Essai sur un rêve de Baudelaire, 1961, English trans. as Histoire extraordinaire: Essay on a Dream of Baudelaire's, 1969; Mobile: Étude pour une representation des Etats-Unis, 1962, English trans. as Mobile: Study for a Representation of the United States, 1963; Description de San Marco, 1963, English trans. as Description of San Marco, 1983; Illustrations, 4 vols, 1964, 1969, 1973, 1976; 6,810,00 litres d'eau par seconde: Étude stéréophonique, 1965, English trans. as Niagara, 1969; Essai sur 'Les Essais', 1968; La Rose des vents: 32 rhumbs pour Charles Fourier, 1970; Matière de rêves, 5 vols, 1975, 1976, 1977, 1981, 1985; Improvisations sur Flaubert, 1984; Improvisations sur Henri Michaux, 1985; Improvisations sur Rimbaud, 1989; Improvisations sur Michel Butor, 1994; L'Útilité Poétique, 1995; Gyroscope, 1996; Ici et là, 1997; Improvisations sur Balzac, 1998; Entretiens, 1999; many other vols of fiction, poetry and essays. *Honours:* Chevalier, Ordre nat. du Mérite; Chevalier, Ordre des Arts et des Lettres; several literary prizes. *Address:* à l'Ecart, 216 pl. de l'église, 74380 Lucinges, France.

BUTTER, Peter Herbert; University Prof., Writer and Ed.; b. 7 April 1921, Coldstream, Scotland; m. Bridget Younger, 30 Aug. 1958, one s. two d. *Education:* MA, Balliol College, Oxford 1948. *Career:* mem. International Asscn of University Profs of English. *Publications:* Shelley's Idols of the Cave, 1954; Francis Thompson, 1961; Edwin Muir, 1962; Edwin Muir: Man & Poet, 1966; Shelley's Alastor, Prometheus Unbound and Other Poems (ed.), 1971; Selected Letters of Edwin Muir (ed.), 1974; Selected Poems of William Blake (ed.), 1982; The Truth of Imagination: Some Uncollected Essays and Reviews of Edwin Muir (ed.), 1988; Complete Poems of Edwin Muir (ed.), 1992; William Blake (ed.), 1996. Contributions: Akros; Lines Review; Modern Language Review; North Wind; Review of English Literature; Review of English Studies; Scottish Literary Journal. *Address:* Ashfield, Prieston Rd, Bridge of Weir, Renfrewshire PA11 3AW, Scotland.

BUTTERS, Dorothy Gilman (see Gilman, Dorothy).

BUTTERWORTH, Jeremy (Jez); British writer, playwright and film director; b. 4 March 1969, London; m. Gilly Richardson. *Education:* Verulam School, St Albans, Univ. of Cambridge. *Films as director:* Mojo 1997, Birthday Girl 2001. *Plays:* Mojo 1995, Birthday Girl (with Tom Butterworth) 2001, The Night Heron 2002. *Honours:* George Dence Award for Most Promising Playwright 1995, Writers' Guild New Writer of the Year Award 1995, Evening Standard Award for Most Promising Playwright 1995, Olivier Award for Britain's Best Comedy 1995. *Literary Agent:* Curtis Brown Ltd, Haymarket House, 28–29 Haymarket, London, SW1Y 4SP, England. *Telephone:* (20) 7393-4400. *Fax:* (20) 7393-4401. *E-mail:* info@curtisbrown.co.uk. *Website:* www.curtisbrown.co.uk.

BUTTERWORTH, (David) Neil; composer, conductor, writer and broadcaster; b. 4 Sept. 1934, London, England; m. Anne Mary Barnes 1960; three d. *Education:* BA, English, 1957, BA, Music, 1958, University of London; Guildhall School of Music and Drama, London, 1960–62; MA, Nottingham University, 1965. *Career:* Lecturer, Kingston College of Technology, 1960–68; Conductor, Edinburgh Schools Choir, 1968–72, Glasgow Orchestral Society, 1975–83, 1989–, Edinburgh Chamber Orchestra, 1983–85; Head of Music Dept, Napier College, Edinburgh, 1968–87; mem. Incorporated Society of Musicians; Performing Rights Society; Scottish Society of Composers. *Publications:* 400 Aural Training Exercises, 1970; A Musical Quiz Book, 1974; Haydn, 1976; Dvořák, 1980; A Dictionary of American Composers, 1983; Aaron Copland, 1984; Sight-singing Exercises from the Masters, 1984; 20th Century Sight-singing Exercises, 1984; Vaughan Williams, 1989; Neglected Music, 1991; The American Symphony, 1998. Contributions: periodicals. *Honours:* Conducting Prize; Fellow, London College of Music; Winston Churchill Travelling Fellowship. *Address:* The Lodge, E High Street, Greenlaw, Berwickshire TD10 6UF, Scotland.

BUTTS, Anthony, BA, MA, MFA; American writer and poet; b. 28 July 1969, Detroit, MI. *Education:* Wayne State University, Western Michigan University, University of Missouri at Columbia. *Career:* co-host, Different Voices interview show (KOPN-FM Radio); mem. Conference on Christianity and Literature; assoc. mem. Acad. of American Poets. *Publications:* Fifth Season 1997, Evolution 1998.

BUZAN, Barry; Prof. of International Relations, Writer and Ed.; b. 28 April 1946, London, England; m. Deborah Skinner, 10 March 1973. *Education:* BA, University of British Columbia, 1968; PhD, LSE, 1973. *Career:* Research Fellow, Institute of International Relations, University of British Columbia, 1973–75; Lecturer, 1976–83, Senior Lecturer, 1983–88, Reader, 1988–89, Dept of International Studies, Prof., 1990–95, Dept of Politics and International Studies, University of Warwick; Dir, Project on European Security, Copenhagen Peace Research Institute, 1988–; Co-Ed., The New International Relations series, 1991–; Visiting Prof., Graduate School of International Relations, International University of Japan, 1993; Research Prof. of International Studies, University of Westminster, 1995–2002; Olof

Palme Visiting Prof., Sweden, 1997–98; Prof. of International Relations, LSE, 2002'. *Publications:* Seabed Politics, 1976; Change and the Study of International Relations: The Evaded Dimension (ed. with R. J. Barry Jones), 1981; People, States, and Fear: The National Security Problem in International Relations, 1983, second edn as An Agenda for International Security Studies in the Post-Cold War Era, 1991; South Asian Insecurity and the Great Powers (co-author), 1986; An Introduction to Strategic Studies: Military Technology and International Relations, 1987; The International Politics of Deterrence (ed.), 1987; The European Security Order Recast: Scenarios for the Post-Cold War Era (co-author), 1990; The Logic of Anarchy: Neorealism to Structural Realism (co-author), 1993; Identity, Migration and the New Security Agenda in Europe (co-author), 1993; The Mind Map Book (with T. Buzan), 1993; Security: A New Framework for Analysis (co-author), 1998; Anticipating the Future: Twenty Millennia of Human Progress (with G. Segal), 1998; The Arms Dynamic in World Politics (with E. Herring), 1998; International Systems in World History: Remaking the Study of International Relations (with R. Little), 2000; Regions and Powers: The Structure of International Security (with O. Waever), 2003. Contributions: many scholarly publications. *Honours:* Francis Deak Prize, American Journal of International Law, 1982; Fellow, British Acad., 1998; Academician, Asscn of Learned Societies in the Social Sciences, 2001. *Address:* Garden Flat, 17 Lambolle Rd, London NW3 4HS, England.

BUZO, Alexander John; Playwright; b. 23 July 1944, Sydney, NSW, Australia; Author. m. Merelyn Johnson, 21 Dec. 1968. *Education:* BA, University of NSW, 1966. *Career:* Resident Dramatist, Melbourne Theatre Co, 1972–73; Writer-in-Residence, James Cook Univ., 1985, Univ. of Wollongong, 1989, Central Queensland Univ., 1991, Univ. of Indonesia, 1995, Brisbane Grammar School, 2000; mem. Centre for Australian Language and Literature Studies. *Publications:* Tautology, 1980; Meet the New Class, 1981; The Search for Harry Allway, 1985; Glancing Blows, 1987; The Young Person's Guide to the Theatre, 1988; The Longest Game, 1990; Prue Flies North, 1991; Kiwese, 1994; A Dictionary of the Almost Obvious, 1998, A Dictionary of the Almost Obvious 1998. Plays: Norm and Ahmed, 1967; Rooted, 1968; The Front Room Boys, 1969; Macquarie, 1971; Coralie Lansdowne Says No, 1974; Martello Towers, 1976; Makassar Reef, 1978; Big River, 1980; The Marginal Farm, 1983; Pacific Union, 1995, Normie and Tuan 1999. Contributions: Sydney Morning Herald; The Australian; Quadrant; Overland; Show Cause; Jakarta Post; Pacific Islands Monthly; New Straits Times; Wisden Australia. *Honours:* Gold Medal, Australian Literature Society, 1973; Alumni Award, Univ. of NSW, 1998, Alumni Award Univ. of NSW 1998. *Address:* 14 Rawson Ave, Queens Park, Sydney, NSW 2022, Australia. *E-mail:* ajbu@ozemail.com.au.

BYAM SHAW, Nicholas Glencairn; British publisher; b. 28 March 1934, London; m. 1st Joan Elliott 1956 (divorced 1973); two s. one d.; m. 2nd Suzanne Filer (née Rastello) 1974; m. 3rd Constance Mary Wilson (née Clarke) 1987. *Education:* Royal Naval Coll., Dartmouth. *Career:* served RN, retiring with rank of Lt 1951–56; on staff of Collins (printers and publrs), Sales Man. 1956–64; joined Macmillan Publrs Ltd as Sales Man. 1964, Deputy Man. Dir 1968, Man. Dir 1970–90, Chair. 1990–97, Deputy Chair. 1998–99; Dir St Martin's Press 1980–99 (Deputy Chair. 1997–99), Pan Books Ltd 1983–99 (Chair. 1986–99), Gruppe Georg von Hotzbrinck, Stuttgart, Germany 1996–99; mem. British Council Publrs' Advisory Cttee, Byam Shaw School Council. *Address:* 9 Kensington Park Gardens, London, W11 3HB, England. *Telephone:* (20) 7221-4547.

BYATT, Dame Antonia Susan, (Dame Antonia Duffy), BA, FRSL; writer and editor; b. 24 Aug. 1936, Sheffield, Yorkshire, England; m. 1st Ian Charles Rayner Byatt 1959 (divorced 1969); one s. (deceased) one d.; m. 2nd Peter John Duffy 1969; two d. *Education:* Newnham Coll., Cambridge, Bryn Mawr Coll., Somerville Coll., Oxford. *Career:* Extra-Mural Lecturer, Univ. of London, 1962–71; Lecturer in Literature, Central School of Art and Design, 1965–69; Lecturer in English, 1972–81, Senior Lecturer, 1981–83, Univ. Coll. London; Assoc., Newnham Coll., Cambridge, 1977–82; Mem., Social Effects of Television Advisory Group, BBC, 1974–77; Mem., Board of Communications and Cultural Studies, 1978–84, Board of Creative and Performing Arts, 1985–87, CNAA; Mem., Kingman Cttee on English Language, 1987–88; Board mem., British Council, 1993–98; Broadcaster; Reviewer; mem. PEN; Society of Authors, chair., 1986–88. *Publications:* Fiction: Shadow of the Sun, 1964; The Game, 1967; The Virgin in the Garden, 1978; Still Life, 1985; Sugar and Other Stories, 1987; Possession: A Romance, 1990; Angels and Insects (novellas), 1992; The Matisse Stories, 1993; The Djinn in the Nightingale's Eye: Five Fairy Tales, 1994; Babel Tower, 1996; Elementals, Stories of Fire and Ice, 1998; The Biographer's Tale, 2000; A Whistling Woman, 2002; Little Black Book of Stories, 2003. Other: Degrees of Freedom, 1965, revised edn as Degrees of Freedom: The Early Novels of Iris Murdoch, 1994; Wordsworth and Coleridge in Their Time, 1970, revised edn as Unruly Times: Wordsworth and Coleridge in Their Time, 1989; Iris Murdoch, 1976; The Mill on the Floss, by George Eliot (ed.), 1979; Selected Essays, Poems and Other Writings, by George Eliot (ed.), 1989; Dramatic Monologues, by Robert Browning (ed.), 1990; Passions of the Mind, 1991; New Writing 4 (ed. with Alan Hollinghurst), 1995; Imagining Characters: Conversations About Women Writers: Jane Austen, Charlotte Brontë, George Eliot, Willa Cather, Iris Murdoch, and Toni Morrison (with Ignes Sodre), 1995; New Writing 6 (ed. with others), 1997; The Oxford Book of English Short Stories (ed.), 1998; On Histories and Stories, 2000; Portraits in Fiction, 2001; The Bird Hand Book (co-author), 2001. Contributions: Body Art, short story in The Phantom Museum and Henry Wellcome's Collection of Medical Curiosities, 2003. *Honours:* PEN/Macmillan Silver Pen of Fiction, 1986; Hon. doctorates, Universities of Bradford, 1987, Durham, 1991, York, 1991, Nottingham, 1992, Liverpool, 1993, Portsmouth, 1994, London, 1995, Cambridge, 1999, Sheffield, 2000; Booker Prize, 1990; Irish Times/Aer Lingus International Fiction Prize, 1990; Best Book in the Commonwealth Prize, Eurasian Section, 1991; Premio Malaparte, Italy, 1995; Mythopoeic Fantasy Award for Adult Literature, 1998; Hon. Fellow, Newnham College, Cambridge, 1999, London Institute, 2000; Shakespeare Prize for contributions to British culture, Toepfer Foundation, 2002. *Literary Agent:* Steven Barclay Agency, 12 Western Avenue, Petaluma, CA 94952, USA. *Telephone:* (707) 773-0654. *Fax:* (707) 778-1868. *Website:* www.barclayagency.com. *Address:* 37 Rusholme Road, London, SW15 3LF, England. *Website:* www.asbyatt.com.

BYNG, Jamie, BA; British publishing director; *Director, Canongate Books*; b. 1969, Winchester; m. (separated); two s. *Education:* Edinburgh Univ. *Career:* joined Canongate Books as unpaid worker 1994, bought the co. 1994, Dir 1994–. *Address:* Canongate Books, 14 High Street, Edinburgh EH1 1TE, Scotland (Office). *Telephone:* (131) 557-5111 (Office). *Fax:* (131) 557-5211 (Office). *E-mail:* info@canongate.co.uk (Office). *Website:* www.canongate.co.uk (Office).

BYRD, Harry Flood, Jr; American newspaperman and politician; b. 20 Dec. 1914; m. Gretchen B. Thomson 1941 (died 1989); two s. one d. *Education:* John Marshall High School, Richmond, Virginia Military Inst. and Univ. of Virginia. *Career:* ed. and writer Winchester Evening Star 1935, Ed. and Publr 1935–81, Ed. and Publr Harrisonburg Daily News-Record 1937–2000; also active in firm of H. F. Byrd, Inc., apple growers; mem. Virginia State Senate 1947–65; mem. Democratic State Cen. Cttee 1940–70; served USNR 1941–46; Dir Associated Press 1950–66; US Senator from Virginia (succeeding his father, Harry Flood Byrd) 1965–83; Independent. *Address:* Rockingham Publishing Co. Inc., 2 North Kent Street, Winchester, Virginia, VA 22601 (Office); 411 Tennyson Avenue, Winchester, Virginia, VA 22601, USA (Home). *Telephone:* (540) 662-7745 (Office). *Fax:* (540) 667-6729 (Office).

BYRNE, John Keyes (see Leonard, Hugh).

C

CABOT, Meggin (Meg) Patricia, (Patricia Cabot, Jenny Carroll), BFA; American writer; b. Bloomington, IN; m. *Education:* Indiana Univ. *Career:* frmly illustrator, asst man. of undergraduate dormitory, New York Univ. *Publications:* as Patricia Cabot, adult fiction: Where Roses Grow Wild 1998, Portrait of my Heart 1999, An Improper Proposal 1999, A Little Scandal 2000, Lady of Skye 2000, Educating Caroline 2001, Kiss the Bride 2002, contrib. novella to anthology A Season in the Highlands 2000; as Meg Cabot, juvenile fiction: The Princess Diaries 2000, The Princess Diaries, Vol. II: Princess in the Spotlight 2001, The Princess Diaries, Vol. III: Princess in Love 2002, Nicola and the Viscount 2002, All-American Girl 2002, The Boy Next Door 2002, She Went All the Way 2002, Victoria and the Rogue 2003, The Princess Diaries, Vol. IV: Princess in Waiting 2003, Princess Lessons: A Princess Diaries Book 2003, The Princess Diaries, Vol. IV and a Half: Project Princess 2003, Boy Meets Girl 2004, The Princess Diaries, Vol. V: Princess in Pink 2004, Perfect Princess: A Princess Diaries Book 2004, Teen Idol 2004; as Jenny Carroll, juvenile fiction: The Mediator: Shadowland 2000, 1-800-WHERE-R-YOU: When Lightning Strikes 2001, The Mediator: Ninth Key 2001, The Mediator: Reunion 2001, 1-800-WHERE-R-YOU: Code Name Cassandra 2001, The Mediator: Darkest Hour 2001, 1-800-WHERE-R-YOU: Safe House 2002, 1-800-WHERE-R-YOU: Sanctuary 2002, Haunted: A Tale of the Mediator 2003. *Literary Agent:* The Marsh Agency, 11 Dover Street, London, W1S 4LJ, England. *Telephone:* (20) 7399-2800. *Fax:* (20) 7399-2801. *Website:* www.marsh-agency.co.uk. *Website:* www.megcabot.com.

CABRERA INFANTE, Guillermo; British writer; b. 22 April 1929, Gibara, Cuba; m. 1st Marta Calvo 1953 (divorced 1961); m. 2nd Míriam Gómez 1961; two d. *Education:* School of Journalism, Univ. of Havana. *Career:* wrote first short story 1947; film critic, Carteles Magazine 1954–60, Man. Ed. 1957–60; f. Cinemateca de Cuba 1950; Ed. Lunes 1959–61; diplomatist in Belgium 1962–65; film writer 1966–; feature writer for English, Spanish and S American magazines and newspapers; Lecturer in USA, Spain and England 1978–; Guest Dir Telluride Film Festival 1992, Miami Film Festival 1993; mem. jury Cannes Film Festival 1994. *Screenplays:* Wonderwall 1967, Vanishing Point 1970, Under the Volcano 1972, Holy Smoke 1985, The Lost City 1990, A Twentieth-Century Job 1991. *Publications:* Así en la paz como en la guerra (short stories) 1960, Un oficio del siglo XX (film criticism) 1963, Tres tristres tigres (novel) 1965, Vista del amanecer en el trópico, O, Exorcismos de estilo 1974, Arcadia todas las noches 1978, La Habana para un infante difunto (novel) 1979, Holy Smoke: Smoking and the Cinema 1985, A Twentieth Century Job 1991, Mea Cuba 1992, Writes of Passage 1993, Delito por bailar el chachachá (short stories) 1995, Ella cantaba boleros (novellas) 1995, Cine o sardina (essays) 1997, Vidas para leerlas (biog.) 1998, Todo está hecho con espejos (complete short stories) 1999, Libro de las ciudades (travel) 1999, Infantería (anthology) 2000. *Honours:* Dr hc (Fla Int. Univ.) 1993; Biblioteca Breve Prize, Barcelona 1964, Guggenheim Fellowship 1970, Prix du Meilleur Livre Etranger, Paris 1971, Writer of the Year at Puterbaugh Conf., Univ. of Okla 1987, Sancho IV Medal (Universidad Complutense, Madrid) 1993, Premio Letterario Illa (Italy) 1994, Premio Cervantes (Spain) 1997. *Address:* 53 Gloucester Road, London, SW7, England. *Telephone:* (20) 7589-4254. *Fax:* (20) 7584-7370.

CADE, Robin (see Nicole, Christopher (Robin)).

CAFFREY, Idris; Writer; b. 16 Nov. 1949, Rhayader, Powys, Wales. *Education:* Swansea College of Education, 1968–71. *Publications:* Pacing Backwards, 1996; Pathways, 1997; Other Places, 1998; Warm Rain, 2000; Touch the Earth, 2001; Departures and Returns, 2002. *Address:* 5 Lyndale, Wilnecote, Tamworth B77 5DX, England.

CAHILL, Mike (see Nolan, William Francis).

CAIPÍN, Áine an (see Wilton-Jones, Anni).

CAIRNCROSS, Frances Anne, BA, MA; British journalist; *Chairwoman, Economic and Social Research Council*; b. 30 Aug. 1944, Otley, Yorkshire, England; m. Hamish McRae 1971, two d. *Education:* St Anne's Coll., Oxford and Brown Univ., Providence, RI, USA. *Career:* staff mem. The Times 1967–69, The Banker 1969, The Observer 1969–71; economics correspondent, The Guardian 1973–81, Women's Ed. 1981–84; Britain Ed., The Economist 1984–89, Public Policy Ed. 1997–2000, Management Ed. 2000–; Chair., Economic and Social Research Council 2001–; High Sheriff of London 2004–; elected to the Rectorship of Exeter Coll., Oxford 2004–; Dir (non-exec.) Alliance & Leicester PLC; Sr Fellow at School of Public Policy, UCLA. *Publications:* Capital City (with Hamish McRae) 1971, The Second Great Crash 1973, The Guardian Guide to the Economy 1981, Changing Perceptions of Economic Policy 1981, Second Guardian Guide to the Economy 1983, Guide to the Economy 1987, Costing the Earth 1991, Green, Inc. 1995, The Death of Distance 1997, The Company of the Future 2002. *Honours:* hon. fellowship St Anne's Coll., Oxford, visiting fellowship Nuffield Coll.; Dr hc Univs of Glasgow, Birmingham, City and Loughborough. *Address:* c/o Exeter College, University of Oxford, Oxford, OX1 3DP, England.

CAIRNS, David (Adam); Music Critic and Writer; b. 8 June 1926, Loughton, Essex, England; m. Rosemary Goodwin, 19 Dec. 1959, three s. *Education:* Trinity College, Oxford. *Career:* Music Critic, Evening Standard, and Spectator, 1958–62, Financial Times, 1963–67, New Statesman, 1967–70, Sunday Times, 1983–92; Classical Programme Co-ordinator, Philips Records, 1967–73; Distinguished Visiting Scholar, Getty Center for the History of Art and Humanities, 1992; Visiting Resident Fellow, Merton College, Oxford, 1993. *Publications:* The Memoirs of Hector Berlioz (ed. and trans.), 1969; Responses: Musical Essays and Reviews, 1973; The Magic Flute, 1980; Falstaff, 1982; Berlioz, 2 vols, 1989, 2000. *Honours:* Officier, Ordre des Arts des Lettres, 1991; Derek Allen Memorial Prize, British Acad., 1990; Royal Philharmonic Society Award, 1990; Yorkshire Post Prize, 1990; CBE, 1997; Whitbread Biography Prize, 1999; Royal Philharmonic Society Award, 1999; Samuel Johnson Non-Fiction Prize, 2000. *Address:* 49 Amerland Rd, London SW18 1QA, England.

CALCAGNO, Anne; academic, writer and poet; b. 14 Nov. 1957, San Diego, CA, USA; m. Leo 1986, one s. one d. *Education:* BA, English, Williams College, 1979; MFA, Fiction and Poetry, University of Montana, 1984. *Career:* Part-time Lecturer, North Park College and American Conservatory of Music, Chicago, 1989–91; Teacher, School of the Art Institute of Chicago, 1990–93; Artist-in-Education, Illinois Arts Council, 1992–93; Lecturer, 1992–93, Assoc. Prof. of English, 1993–, DePaul University; mem. Associated Writing Programs; Authors' Guild; Poets and Writers. *Publications:* Pray for Yourself (short stories), 1993; Travelers Tales, Italy (ed.), 1998. Contributions: anthologies and periodicals. *Honours:* National Endowment for the Arts Creative Writing Fellowship, 1989; Illinois Arts Council Artists Fellowship, 1993; James D. Phelan Literary Award, San Francisco Foundation, 1993; Silver Medal, ForeWord Travel Book of the Year, 1999; Ed.'s Choice Award, Journey Woman, 1999; Illinois Arts Council Literary Award, 2003. *Address:* c/o Department of English, DePaul University, 802 W Belden Ave, Chicago, IL 60614-3214, USA.

CALDECOTT, Moyra, BA, MA; British author; b. 1 June 1927, Pretoria, South Africa; m. Oliver Zerffi Stratford Caldecott 1951; two s. one d. *Education:* University of Natal. *Publications:* The Weapons of the Wolfhound, 1976; The Sacred Stones, Vol. I, The Tall Stones, 1977, Vol. II, The Temple of the Sun, 1977, Vol. III, Shadow on the Stones, 1978; Adventures by Leaf Light, 1978; The Lily and the Bull, 1979; Child of the Dark Star, 1980; The King of Shadows: A Glastonbury Story, 1981; The Twins of the Tylwyth Teg, 1983; Taliesin and Avagddu, 1983; Bran, Son of Llyr, 1985; The Tower and the Emerald, 1985; Guardians of the Tall Stones, 1986; The Son of the Sun, 1986; The Silver Vortex, 1987; Etheldreda, 1987; Women in Celtic Myth, 1988; Daughter of Amun, 1989; The Green Lady and the King of Shadows, 1989; The Daughter of Ra, 1990; The Crystal Legends, 1990; Myths of the Sacred Tree, 1993; The Winged Man, 1994; Mythical Journeys: Legendary Quests, 1996; The Waters of Sul, 1998; contrib. to anthologies and periodicals. *Electronic publications:* Hatshepsut: Daughter of Amun 2000, Akhenaten: Son of the Sun 2000, Tutankhamun and the Daughter of Ra 2000, The Ghost of Akhenaten, The Eye of Callanish.

CALDER, Angus Lindsay Ritchie; Writer and Poet; b. 5 Feb. 1942, Sutton, Surrey, England; m. 1st Jenni Daiches; m. 2nd Kate Kyle; two s. two d. *Education:* MA, King's College, Cambridge, 1960–63; DPhil, University of Sussex, 1963–68. *Career:* Lecturer in Literature, University of Nairobi, 1968–71; Staff Tutor in Arts, Open University in Scotland, 1979–93; Visiting Prof. of English, University of Zimbabwe, 1992; Ed., Journal of Commonwealth Literature; mem. Scottish PEN. *Publications:* The People's War: Britain, 1939–1945, 1969; Russia Discovered: Nineteenth Century Fiction, 1976; Revolutionary Empire: The Rise of the English-Speaking Empires, 1981; The Myth of the Blitz, 1991; Revolving Culture: Notes From the Scottish Republic, 1994; Waking in Waikato (poems), 1997; Horace in Tollcross (poems), 2000; Scotlands of the Mind, 2002; Colours of Grief (poems), 2002; Gods, Mongrels and Demons: 101 Brief but Essential Lives, 2003; Disasters and Heroes: War, Memory and Representation, 2003; Dipa's Bowl (poems), 2003. Contributions: Cencrastus; Chapman; Herald; London Review of Books; New Statesman; Scotland on Sunday. *Honours:* Eric Gregory Award, 1967; John Llewellyn Rhys Memorial Prize, 1970; Scottish Arts Council Book Awards, 1981, 1994; Scottish Arts Council Writer's Bursary, 2002. *Address:* 15 Spittal St, Edinburgh EH3 9DY, Scotland.

CALDER, Elisabeth Nicole, BA; British publisher; b. 20 Jan. 1938, New Zealand; m. 1st Richard Henry Calder 1958 (divorced 1972); one s. one d.; m. 2nd Louis Baum. *Education:* Palmerston North Girls' High School, Univ. of Canterbury, New Zealand. *Career:* reader, Metro-Goldwyn-Mayer Story Dept, 1969–70; Publicity Man., Victor Gollancz, 1971–74, Editorial Dir, 1975–78; Editorial Dir, Jonathan Cape, 1978–86; f. (with Nigel Newton), Publishing Dir, Bloomsbury Publishing, 1986–; co-f., Groucho media club; f., Parati International Literary Festival, Brazil, 2003–; Chair., Royal Court Theatre 2001–. *Address:* Bloomsbury Publishing, 38 Soho Square, London W1V 5DF, England.

CALDER, John Mackenzie; British publisher, critic and playwright; *Managing Director, Calder Publishers Ltd*; b. 25 Jan. 1927; m. 1st Mary A. Simmonds 1949; one d.; m. 2nd Bettina Jonic 1960 (dissolved 1975); one d.

Education: Gilling Castle, Yorks., Bishops Coll. School, Canada, McGill Univ., Montreal, Sir George Williams Coll. and Univ. of Zürich, Switzerland. *Career:* f. and Man. Dir John Calder (Publishers) Ltd 1950–91, Calder Publs Ltd 1991–, Calder and Boyars Ltd 1964–75, f. Calder Bookshop; expanded to Edin. 1971; organized literature confs., Edin. Festival 1962, 1963, Harrogate Festival 1969; f. Ledlanet Nights (music and opera festival) Kinross-shire 1963–74; Pres. Riverrun Press Inc., New York 1978–; Prof. of Literature and Philosophy, Ecole Active Bilingue, Paris 1994–96; lecturer in History, Univ. of Paris-Nanterre 1995; acquired bookselling business of Better Books, London 1969; Chair. North American Book Clubs 1982–89, Fed. of Scottish Theatres 1972–74; Co-founder, Defence of Literature and the Arts Soc.; Dir of other cos assoc. with opera, publishing etc.; f. Samuel Beckett Theatre, Waterloo, London. *Plays include:* Lorca, The Voice, The Trust. *Publications:* A Samuel Beckett Reader, The Burroughs Reader 1981, New Beckett Reader 1983, Henry Miller Reader 1985, Nouveau Roman Reader 1986, The Defence of Literature 1991, The Garden of Eros 1992, The Philosophy of Samuel Beckett 1998, What's Wrong, What's Right (poetry) 1999, Pursuit (autobiog.) 2001. *Honours:* Chevalier des Arts et des Lettres, Officier et Chevalier Ordre nat. du Mérite. *Address:* Calder Publications Ltd, 51 The Cut, London, SE1 8LF, England (Office); Riverrun Press Inc., 100 Newfield Avenue, Edison, NJ 08837, USA (Office); 9 rue de Ramainville, 93100 Montreuil, France. *Telephone:* (20) 7633-0599 (UK) (Home); (212) 889-6850 (USA) (Office); 1-49-88-75-12 (France). *Fax:* 1-48-59-66-68 (France). *E-mail:* info@calderpublications.com (Office). *Website:* www.calderpublications.com (Office).

CALDER, Nigel David Ritchie, BA, MA; British writer; b. 2 Dec. 1931, London, England; m. Elisabeth Palmer 1954; two s. three d. *Education:* Sidney Sussex Coll., Cambridge. *Career:* research physicist, Mullard Research Laboratories, Redhill, Surrey 1954–56; staff writer 1956–60, Science Ed. 1960–62, Ed. 1962–66, New Scientist; Science Correspondent, New Statesman 1959–62, 1966–71; mem. Asscn of British Science Writers, Cruising Asscn, Royal Astronomical Soc., RGS; hon. fellow American Asscn for the Advancement of Science 1986. *Publications:* The Environment Game (aka Eden Was No Garden: an Inquiry into the Environment of Man) 1967, Technopolis: Social Control of the Uses of Science 1969, Violent Universe: An Eyewitness Account of the New Astronomy 1970, The Mind of Man: An Investigation into Current Research on the Brain and Human Nature 1970, Restless Earth: A Report on the New Geology 1972, The Life Game: Evolution and the New Biology 1974, The Weather Machine: How Our Weather Works and Why it is Changing 1975, The Human Conspiracy 1976, The Key to the Universe: A Report on the New Physics 1977, Spaceships of the Mind 1978, Einstein's Universe 1979, Nuclear Nightmares: An Investigation into Possible Wars 1980, The Comet is Coming!: The Feverish Legacy of Mr Halley 1981, Timescale: An Atlas of the Fourth Dimension 1984, 1984 and Beyond: Nigel Calder Talks to his Computer About the Future 1984, The English Channel 1986, The Green Machines 1986, Future Earth: Exploring the Frontiers of Science (ed. with John Newell) 1989, Scientific Europe 1990, Spaceship Earth 1991, Giotto to the Comets 1992, Beyond This World 1995, The Manic Sun 1997, Magic Universe: The Oxford Guide to Modern Science 2003; contrib. to TV documentaries, numerous periodicals. *Honours:* UNESCO Kalinga Prize 1972. *Address:* 26 Boundary Road, Northgate, Crawley, West Sussex RH10 8BT, England. *E-mail:* nc@windstream.demon.co.uk.

CALDERWOOD, James Lee; academic and writer; b. 7 April 1930, Corvallis, OR, USA; m. Cleo Xeniades Calderwood 1955; two s. *Education:* BA, University of Oregon, 1953; PhD, University of Washington, 1963. *Career:* Instructor, Michigan State University, 1961–63; Asst Prof., University of California at Irvine, 1963–66; Asst Prof., 1966–68, Assoc. Prof., 1968–71, Prof., 1971–94, Assoc. Dean of Humanities, 1974–94, Prof. Emeritus, 1994–, University of California at Irvine. *Publications:* Shakespearean Metadrama, 1971; Metadrama in Shakespeare's Henriad, 1979; To Be and Not to Be: Negation and Metadrama in Hamlet, 1983; If It Were Done: Tragic Action in Macbeth, 1986; Shakespeare and the Denial of Death, 1987; The Properties of Othello, 1989; A Midsummer Night's Dream, 1992. Editor: Forms of Poetry (with H. E. Toliver), 1968; Perspectives on Drama (with H. E. Toliver), 1968; Perspectives on Poetry (with H. E. Toliver), 1968; Perspectives on Fiction (with H. E. Toliver), 1968; Forms of Drama (with H. E. Toliver), 1969; Essays in Shakespearean Criticism (with H. E. Toliver), 1969; Shakespeare's Love's Labour's Lost, 1970; Forms of Prose Fiction (with H. E. Toliver), 1972; Forms of Tragedy (with H. E. Toliver), 1972. Contributions: scholarly journals. *Honours:* Alumni Achievement Award, University of Oregon, 1991. *Address:* 1323 Terrace Way, Laguna Beach, CA 92651, USA.

CALDWELL, Grant; writer, poet and teacher; b. 6 March 1947, Melbourne, Vic., Australia. *Career:* Ed.-Publisher, MEUSE art and literature magazine, 1980–82; Teacher, Victoria College of the Arts, University of Melbourne, 1995–2000. *Publications:* Poetry: The Screaming Frog That Ralph Ate, 1979; The Bells of Mr Whippy, 1982; The Nun Wore Sunglasses, 1984; The Life of a Pet Dog, 1993; You Know What I Mean, 1996. Other: The Revolt of the Coats (short stories), 1988; Malabata (autobiog.), 1991. Contributions: anthologies, newspapers and magazines. *Address:* c/o Hale and Iremonger, 19 Eve Street, Erskineville, NSW 22043, Australia.

CALHOUN, Craig Jackson; Prof. of Sociology, Writer and Ed.; b. 16 June 1952, Watseka, IL, USA; m. Pamela F. DeLargy, two c. *Education:* BA, Anthropology, University of Southern California, 1972; MA, Anthropology, Columbia University, 1974; MA, Social Anthropology, Manchester University, 1975; PhD, Sociology and History, St Antony's College, Oxford, 1980. *Career:* Instructor, 1977–80, Asst Prof., 1980–85, Assoc. Prof., 1985–89, Prof. of Sociology and History, 1989–96, Dir, University Center for International Studies, 1993–96, University of North Carolina at Chapel Hill; Ed., Comparative Social Research, 1988–93, Sociological Theory, 1994–; Visiting Lecturer, 1991, Prof., part-time, 1993–, University of Oslo; Prof. of Sociology, Chair, Dept of Sociology, New York University, 1996–; mem. American Anthropological Asscn; American Historical Asscn; American Sociological Asscn; International Sociological Asscn; International Studies Asscn; Royal Anthropological Institute; Social Science History Asscn; Society for the Study of Social Problems; Sociological Research Asscn. *Publications:* The Anthropological Study of Education (ed. with F. A. J. Ianni), 1976; The Question of Class Struggle: Social Foundations of Popular Radicalism During the Industrial Revolution, 1982; Sociology (with Donald Light and Suzanne Keller), 1989; Structures of Power and Constraint: Essays in Honor of Peter M. Blau (ed. with W. R. Scott and M. Meyer), 1990; Habermas and the Public Sphere (ed.), 1992; Bourdieu: Critical Perspectives (ed. with E. LiPuma and M. Postone), 1993; Social Theory and the Politics of Identity (ed.), 1994; Neither Gods Nor Emperors: Students and the Struggle for Democracy in China, 1995; Critical Social Theory: Culture, History and the Challenge of Difference, 1995. Contributions: numerous books and scholarly journals. *Honours:* W. K. Kellogg National Fellowship, 1982–85; Distinguished Contribution to Scholarship Award, Section on Political Sociology, American Sociological Asscn, 1995. *Address:* Dept of Sociology, New York University, 269 Mercer St, New York, NY 10003, USA.

CALISHER, Hortense, (Jack Fenno); Writer; b. 20 Dec. 1911, New York, NY, USA; m. 1st two s.; m. 2nd Curtis Harnack, 23 March 1959. *Education:* AB, Barnard College, 1932. *Career:* Adjunct Prof., Barnard College, 1956–57, Columbia University, 1968–70, City College, CUNY, 1969; various visiting professorships and lectureships; mem. American Acad. of Arts and Letters, pres., 1987–90; PEN, pres., 1986–87. *Publications:* Fiction: False Entry, 1961; Textures of Life, 1962; Journal from Ellipsis, 1965; The New Yorkers, 1969; Queenie, 1971; Standard Dreaming, 1972; Eagle Eye, 1973; On Keeping Women, 1977; Mysteries of Motion, 1984; The Bobby-Soxer, 1986; Age, 1987; The Small Bang, 1992; In the Palace of the Movie King, 1994. Other: Collected Stories, 1975; The Novellas of Hortense Calisher, 1998. Non-Fiction: Herself (autobiog.), 1972; Kissing Cousins (memoir), 1988. Contributions: periodicals. *Honours:* Guggenheim Fellowships, 1952, 1955; American Acad. of Arts and Letters Award, 1967; Kafka Prize, University of Rochester, 1987; National Endowment for the Arts Lifetime Achievement Award, 1989. *Address:* c/o Donadio & Assocs, 121 W 27th St, Suite 704, New York, NY 10001, USA.

CALLAGHAN, Barry; Writer, Poet, Ed., Publisher, Trans. and Prof.; b. 5 July 1937, Toronto, ON, Canada; Emeritus. one s. *Education:* BA, 1960, MA, 1962, St Michael's College, University of Toronto. *Career:* Teacher, Atkinson College, York University, Toronto, 1965–2003; Literary Ed., Telegram, Toronto, 1966–71; Host and Documentary Producer, Weekend, CBC-TV, 1969–72; Founder-Publisher, Exile, 1972–, Exile Editions, 1976–; Writer-in-Residence, University of Rome, 1987. *Publications:* Poetry: The Hogg Poems and Drawings, 1978; As Close As We Came, 1982; Stone Blind Love, 1987; Hogg: The Poems and Drawings, 1997; Hogg, Seven Last Words, 2001. Fiction: The Black Queen Stories, 1982; The Way the Angel Spreads Her Wings, 1989; When Things Get Worst, 1993; A Kiss is Still a Kiss, 1995. Non-Fiction: Barrelhouse Kings, 1998. Editor: various anthologies and books. *Honours:* many National Magazine Awards; Gold Medal, University of Western Ontario, 1979; Co-Winner, International Authors Festival Award, Harbourfront, Toronto, 1986; Toronto Arts Award, 1993; Hon. Doctor of Letters, SUNY, 1999; Hon. Doctor of Laws, Guelph Univ., ON, 2001. *Address:* 20 Dale Ave, Toronto, Ontario M4W 1K4, Canada.

CALLICOTT, John Baird; academic and writer; b. 9 May 1941, Memphis, TN, USA; m. 1st Ann Nelson Archer 1963 (divorced 1985); one s.; m. 2nd Frances Moore Lappe 1985 (divorced 1990). *Education:* BA, Rhodes College, 1963; MA, 1966, PhD, 1972, Syracuse University. *Career:* Lecturer, Syracuse University, 1965–66; Instructor, University of Memphis, 1966–69; Asst Prof., 1969–74, Assoc. Prof., 1974–82, Prof. of Philosophy, 1982–95, Prof. of Natural Resources, 1984–95, University of Wisconsin at Stevens Point; Prof. of Philosophy, University of North Texas, 1995–; mem. American Philosophical Asscn; American Society for Environmental History; International Society for Ecosystem Health; International Society for Environmental Ethics, pres., 1997–2000; Society for Asian and Comparative Philosophy; Society for Conservation Biology. *Publications:* Plato's Aesthetics: An Introduction to the Theory of Forms, 1972; Clothed-in-Fur and Other Tales: An Introduction to An Ojibwa World View, 1982; In Defense of the Land Ethic: Essays in Environmental Philosophy, 1989; Earth's Insights: A Survey of Ecological Ethics from the Mediterranean Basin to the Australian Outback, 1994; Beyond the Land Ethic: More Essays in Environmental Philosophy, 1999. Editor: several books. Contributions: many books and numerous journals. *Honours:* Woodrow Wilson Fellow, 1963–64; University Scholar Award, University of Wisconsin at Stevens Point, 1995. *Address:* c/o Department of Philosophy and Religion, University of North Texas, PO Box 310920, Denton, TX 76203-0920, USA.

CALLIL, Carmen Thérèse, BA, FRSA; Australian publisher; b. 15 July 1938, Melbourne. *Education:* Star of the Sea Convent, Loreto Convent, Melbourne and Melbourne Univ. *Career:* settled in England 1963; Buyer's Asst, Marks and Spencer 1963–65; Editorial Asst, Hutchinson Publishing Co. 1965–66, B. T. Batsford 1966–67, Publicity Man., Granada Publishing 1967–70, André Deutsch 1971–72; f. Carmen Callil Ltd, Book Publicity Co. and Virago Press 1972; Chair. and Man. Dir Virago Press 1972–82, Chair. 1982–95, Man. Dir Chatto and Windus, The Hogarth Press 1983–93; Publr-at-Large Random House, UK 1993–94; Ed.-at-Large Knopf, New York 1993–94; mem. Bd Channel 4 1985–91, Random Century Bd 1989–94; Gov. Museum of London 1992–; Chair. Booker Prize for Fiction 1996. *Publications:* The Modern Library: The 200 Best Novels in England Since 1950 (jtly) 1999, Darquier's Nebula 2005. *Honours:* Hon. DLitt (Sheffield) 1994, (Oxford Brookes Univ.) 1995; Hon. DUniv (York) 1995, (Open) 1997; Int. Women's Writing Guild Distinguished Service Award. *Literary Agent:* Rogers, Coleridge & White, 20 Powis Mews, London, W11 1JN, England. *Address:* 30 Bedford Square, London, WC1B 3EG, England.

CALLISON, Brian (Richard); Writer; b. 13 July 1934, Manchester, England; m. Phyllis Joyce Jobson, 12 May 1958, two s. *Education:* Dundee College of Art, 1954–56. *Career:* mem. Royal Institute of Nagivation; Society of Authors. *Publications:* A Flock of Ships, 1970; A Plague of Sailors, 1971; Dawn Attack, 1972; A Web of Salvage, 1973; Trapp's War, 1974; A Ship is Dying, 1976; A Frenzy of Merchantmen, 1977; The Judas Ship, 1978; Trapp's Peace, 1979; The Auriga Madness, 1980; The Sextant, 1981; Spearfish, 1982; Bone Collectors, 1984; Thunder of Crude, 1986; Trapp and World War Three, 1988; The Trojan Hearse, 1990; Crocodile Trapp, 1993; Ferry Down, 1998; The Stollenberg Legacy, 2000. *Address:* c/o Harper Collins Publishers, 77–85 Fulham Palace Rd, Hammersmith, London W6 8JB, England.

CALLOW, Philip Kenneth; Writer and Poet; b. 26 Oct. 1924, Birmingham, England. *Education:* St Luke's College, Exeter 1968–70. *Career:* Open Univ. *Publications:* The Hosanna Man, 1956; Common People, 1958; Native Ground, 1959; Pledge for the Earth, 1960; The Honeymooners, 1960; Turning Point, 1961; Clipped Wings, 1963; The Real Life, 1964; In My Own Land, 1965; Going to the Moon, 1968; The Bliss Body, 1969; Flesh of Morning, 1971; The Lamb, 1971; Bare Wires, 1972; Yours, 1972; Son and Lover: The Young D. H. Lawrence, 1975; The Story of My Desire, 1976; Janine, 1977; The Subway to New York, 1979; Cave Light, 1981; Woman with a Poet, 1983; New York Insomnia, 1984; Poetry: Icons, 1987; Soliloquires of an Eye, 1990; Some Love, 1991. *Address:* Little Thatch, Haselbury, Nr Crewkerne, Somerset, England.

CALLOW, Simon Philip Hugh, CBE; British actor, director and writer; b. 15 June 1949. *Education:* London Oratory Grammar School, Queen's Univ., Belfast, Drama Centre. *Career:* debut Edinburgh Festival 1973; repertory seasons, Lincoln and Traverse Theatre, Edin.; work at the fringe theatre, the Bush, London; joined Joint Stock Theatre Group 1977, Nat. Theatre 1979. *Stage appearances include:* Passing By 1975, Plumbers Progress 1975, Arturo Ui 1978, Titus Andronicus 1978, Mary Barnes 1978, As You Like It 1979, Amadeus 1979, Sisterly Feeling 1979, Total Eclipse 1982, Restoration 1982, The Beastly Beatitudes of Balthazar B 1982, The Relapse 1983, On The Spot 1984, Melancholy Jacques 1984, Kiss of the Spider Woman 1985, Faust 1988, Single Spies 1988, 1989, The Destiny of Me 1993, The Alchemist 1996, The Importance of Being Oscar 1997, Chimes at Midnight 1997, The Mystery of Charles Dickens 2000–02, Through the Leaves 2003, The Holy Terror 2004. *Films include:* Amadeus 1983, A Room With A View 1984, The Good Father 1985, Maurice 1986, Manifesto 1987, Mr and Mrs Bridge 1991, Postcards from the Edge 1991, Soft Top Hard Shoulder 1992, Four Weddings and A Funeral 1994, Jefferson in Paris 1994, Victory 1994, Le Passager Clandestin 1995, England, My England 1995, Ace Ventura: When Nature Calls 1995, James and the Giant Peach (voice) 1996, The Scarlet Tunic 1996, Woman In White 1997, Bedrooms and Hallways 1997, Shakespeare in Love 1997, No Man's Land 2000, Thunder pants 2001, A Christmas Carol 2001, George and the Dragon 2002, Phantom of the Opera 2004. *TV appearances:* Wings of Song 1977, Instant Enlightenment inc. VAT 1979, La Ronde 1980, Man of Destiny 1982, Chance in a Million 1982–84, Deadhead 1984, Handel 1985, David Copperfield 1986, Cariani and the Courtesan 1987, Old Flames 1989, Patriot Witness 1989, Trial of Oz 1991, Bye Bye Columbus 1992, Femme Fatale 1993, Little Napoleons 1994, An Audience with Charles Dickens 1996, A Christmas Dickens 1997, The Woman in White 1998, Trial-Retribution 1999, 2000, Galileo's Daughter, The Mystery of Charles Dickens 2002, Angels in America 2003. *Directed:* Loving Reno 1983, Passport 1985, Nicolson Fights Croydon 1986, Amadeus 1986, The Infernal Machine 1986, Così Fan Tutte 1987, Jacques and His Master 1987, Shirley Valentine (theatre production) 1988/89, Die Fledermaus 1989/90, Facades 1988, Single Spies 1988/89, Stevie Wants to Play the Blues 1990, The Ballad of the Sad Café (film) 1991, Carmen Jones 1991, My Fair Lady 1992, Shades 1992, The Destiny of Me 1993, Carmen Jones 1994, Il Trittico 1995, Les Enfants du Paradis (RSC) 1996, Stephen Oliver Trilogy 1996, La Calisto 1996, Il Turco in Italia 1997, HRH 1997, The Pajama Game 1999, The Consul 1999, Tomorrow Week (play for radio) 1999, Le Roi Malgré Lui 2003, Jus' Like That 2003, Le Roi malgré lui 2003. *Publications:* Being An Actor 1984, A Difficult Actor: Charles Laughton 1987, Shooting the Actor, or the Choreography of Confusion (with Dusan Makevejev) 1990, Acting in Restoration Comedy 1991, Orson Welles: The Road to Xanadu 1995, Les Enfants du Paradis 1996, Snowdon – On Stage 1996, The National 1997, Love is Where it Falls 1999, Shakespeare on Love 2000, Charles Laughton's the Night of the Hunter 2000, Oscar Wilde and His Circle 2000, The Nights of the Hunter 2001, Henry IV Part 1 2002, Henry IV Part 2 2003, Dicken's Christmas 2003; translations of works of Cocteau, Kundera, Prévert, Chabrier; weekly column in Sunday Express, Independent, Country Life; contrib. to The Times, The Sunday Times, The Guardian, The Observer, Evening Standard, etc. *Honours:* Hon. DLitt (Queen's Univ., Belfast) 1999, (Birmingham) 2000; Evening Standard Patricia Rothermere Award 1999. *Address:* c/o BAT, 180 Wardour Street, London, W1V 3AA, England.

CALLWOOD, June; Writer; b. 2 June 1924, Chatham, Ontario, Canada; m. Trent Frayne 13 May 1944; two s. (one deceased) two d. *Career:* Reporter, Brantford Expositor, 1941, Toronto Globe and Mail, 1942; Freelance Journalist, 1945–; Columnist, Globe and Mail, 1983–89; mem. Writers Union of Canada; Canadian Centre PEN; Toronto Arts Council; Founder and pres., Casey House Hospice, 1988; Co-Chair., Campaign Against Child Poverty, 1998. *Publications:* Emma, 1984; Twelve Weeks in Spring, 1986; Emotions, 1986; Jim: A Life with AIDS, 1988; The Sleepwalker, 1990; Trial Without End, 1995; The Man Who Lost Himself, 2000. *Honours:* City of Toronto Award of Merit, 1974; Mem., Order of Canada, 1978, Officer, 1986, Companion, 2001; Canadian News Hall of Fame, 1984; Windsor Press Club Quill Award, 1987; Order of Ontario, 1988; Udo Award, 1989; Lifetime Achievement Award, 1991; Margaret Lawrence Lecture, 1993; 17 hon. degrees. *Address:* 21 Hillcroft Dr., Toronto, Ontario M9B 4X4, Canada.

CALVERT, Peter Anthony Richard, FRHistS; Prof. of Politics and Writer; b. 19 Nov. 1936, Islandmagee, County Antrim, Northern Ireland; m. Susan Ann Milbank, 1987. *Education:* Campbell College, Belfast; Queens' College, Cambridge; University of Michigan. *Career:* Lecturer 1964–71, Univ. of Southampton, Senior Lecturer 1971–74, Reader 1974–83, Prof. of Politics 1984–2002, Prof. Emeritus 2002–; mem. Royal Historical Soc., Royal Institute of International Affairs. *Publications:* The Mexican Revolution 1910–1914, 1968; A Study of Revolution, 1970; The Falklands Crisis, 1982; Guatemala, 1985; The Foreign Policy of New States, 1986; Argentina: Political Culture and Instability (with Susan Calvert) 1989; Revolution and Counter Revolution, 1990; Latin America in the 20th Century (with Susan Calvert), 1990, 1993; An Introduction to Comparative Politics, 1993; International Politics of Latin America, 1994; Politics and Society in the Third World (with Susan Calvert), 1995, 2001; Revolution and International Politics, 1996; The South, the North and the Environment (with Susan Calvert), 1999; Comparative Politics: An Introduction, 2002. Editor: The Process of Political Succession, 1987; The Central American Security System, 1988; Political and Economic Encyclopedia of South America and the Caribbean, 1991; The Resilience of Democracy (with Peter Burnell), 1999, Civil Society in Democratization (Ed., with Peter Burnell) 2003, Border and Territorial Disputes, 4th Edn 2003. Contributions: International Affairs; Political Studies; World Today. *Address:* School of Social Sciences, University of Southampton, Southampton SO17 1BJ, England.

CALVOCORESSI, Peter John Ambrose; British writer, book publisher and university lecturer; b. 17 Nov. 1912, Karachi, Pakistan; m. Barbara Dorothy Eden 1938; two s. *Education:* Eton Coll. and Balliol Coll., Oxford. *Career:* called to Bar 1935; RAF Intelligence 1940–45; assisted Trial of Major War Criminals, Nuremberg 1945–46; on staff, Royal Inst. of Int. Affairs 1949–54; partner Chatto & Windus, publishers 1955–65; Reader in Int. Relations, Sussex Univ. 1965–71; Ed. Dir Penguin Books 1972, Publr and Chief Exec. 1973–76; Chair. Open Univ. Educational Enterprises Ltd 1979–88; mem. UN sub-comm. on the Prevention of Discrimination 1961–71; Chair. The London Library 1970–73. *Publications:* Nuremberg: The Facts, the Law and the Consequences 1947, Survey of International Affairs: Vols for 1947–48, 1949–50, 1951, 1952 and 1953, Middle East Crisis (with Guy Wint) 1957, South Africa and World Opinion 1961, World Order and New States 1962, Total War (with Guy Wint) 1972, The British Experience: 1945–75, Top Secret Ultra 1980, A Time for Peace 1987, Who's Who in the Bible 1987, Resilient Europe 1991, Threading My Way 1994, Fall Out: World War II and the Shaping of Postwar Europe 1997, World Politics 1945–2000 2001. *Honours:* Hon. DUniv (Open Univ.) 1989. *Address:* 1 Queens Parade, Bath, BA1 2NJ, England. *Telephone:* (1225) 333903.

CAMERON, Averil Millicent; academic, writer and editor; b. 8 Feb. 1940, Leek, Staffordshire, England; m. Alan Douglas Edward Cameron 1962 (divorced 1980); one s. one d. *Education:* MA, Somerville College, Oxford; PhD, University College London, 1966. *Career:* Asst Lecturer in Classics, 1965, Lecturer in Classics, 1968, Reader in Ancient History, 1970, Prof. of Ancient History, 1978–89, Head, Dept of Classics, 1985–89, Prof. of Late Antique and Byzantine Studies and Dir of the Centre for Hellenic Studies, 1989–94, Visiting Prof., 1995–98, King's College, London; Visiting Asst Prof., Columbia University, 1967–68; Visiting Mem., 1977–78, Distinguished Visitor, 1992, Institute for Advanced Study, Princeton; Ed., Journal of Roman Studies, 1985–90; Sather Prof. of Classical Literature, University of California at Berkeley, 1986; Visiting Prof., Collège de France, Paris, 1987; Wolfson Research Reader in History, British Acad., 1990–92; Lansdowne Lecturer, University of Victoria, 1992; Warden, Keble College, Oxford, 1994–; Prof. of Late Antique and Byzantine History, 1998–, Pro-Vice-Chancellor, 2001–, University of Oxford; mem. Academia Europaea; British National Byzantine Committee, chair., 1983–89; Cathedrals Fabric

Commission for England, chair., 1999–; Institute of Classical Studies, chair., advisory council, 2001–; Society for the Promotion of Roman Studies, vice-pres., 1983–95, 1999–, pres., 1995–98. *Publications:* Procopius, 1967; Agathias, 1970; Corippus: In laudem Iustini minoris, 1976; Change and Continuity in Sixth-Century Byzantium, 1981; Images of Women in Antiquity (co-ed.), 1983; Constantinople in the Early Eighth Century: The Parastaseis Syntomai Chronikai (co-ed.), 1984; Procopius and the Sixth Century, 1985; History as Text: The Writing of Ancient History (ed.), 1989; The Greek Renaissance in the Roman Empire (ed.), 1990; Christianity and the Rhetoric of Empire, 1991; The Byzantine and Early Islamic Near East (co-ed.), Vol. I, Problems in the Literary Source Material, 1992, Vol. II, Land Use and Settlement Patterns, 1994, Vol. III, States, Resources and Armies, 1995; The Later Roman Empire, 1993; The Mediterranean World in Late Antiquity, AD 395–600, 1993; Changing Cultures in Early Byzantium (ed.), 1996; The Cambridge Ancient History, Vol. XIII, The Late Empire (ed.), 1998, Vol. XIV, Late Antiquity: Empire and Successors (ed.), 2001; Eusebius: Life of Constantine (ed. with S. G. Hall), 1999; Fifty Years of Prosopography: Rome, Byzantium and Beyond (ed.), 2003. Contributions: scholarly journals. *Honours:* Fellow, British Acad., 1981, Society of Antiquaries, 1982, King's College, London, 1987, Ecclesiastical History Society, 2000; Hon. DLitt, University of Warwick, 1996, University of St Andrews, 1998, Queen's University, Belfast, 2000, Aberdeen Univ., 2003; CBE, 1999; Hon. DTh, University of Lund, 2001. *Address:* c/o Keble College, Oxford OX1 3PG, England.

CAMERON, Charla (see Skinner, Gloria Dale).

CAMERON, Donald (Allan), (Silver Donald Cameron); Author; b. 21 June 1937, Toronto, Ontario, Canada; m. 1st Catherine Ann Cahoon 21 Aug. 1959; three s. one d.; m. 2nd Lulu Terrio 17 May 1980 (died 6 April 1996); one s.; m. 3rd Marjorie L. Simmins 14 March 1998. *Education:* BA, University of British Columbia, 1959; MA, University of California, 1962; PhD, University of London, 1967. *Career:* Assoc. Prof. of English, University of New Brunswick, 1968–71; Writer-in-Residence, 1978–80, Dean, School of Community Studies, 1994–96, Special Asst to the Pres., 1997–99, University College of Cape Breton, NS; Writer-in-Residence, University of Prince Edward Island, 1985–86, Nova Scotia College of Art and Design, 1987–88; mem. Writers Federation, NS. *Publications:* Faces of Leacock, 1967; Conversations with Canadian Novelists, 1973; The Education of Everett Richardson, 1977; Seasons in the Rain (essays), 1978; Dragon Lady, 1980; The Baitchopper (children's novel), 1982; Schooner: Bluenose and Bluenose II, 1984; Outhouses of the West, 1988; Wind, Whales and Whisky: A Cape Breton Voyage, 1991; Lifetime: A Treasury of Uncommon Wisdoms (co-author), 1992; Once Upon a Schooner: An Offshore Voyage In Bluenose II, 1992; Iceboats to Superferries: An Illustrated History of Marine Atlantic (co-author); Sniffing the Coast: An Acadian Voyage, 1993; Sterling Silver: Rants, Raves and Revelations, 1994; The Living Beach, 1998. Other: numerous articles, radio dramas, short stories, television scripts and stage plays. *Honours:* 4 National Magazine Awards; Best Short Film, Canadian Film Celebration; City of Dartmouth Book Award, 1992; Atlantic Provinces Booksellers Choice Award, 1992. *Address:* PO Box 555, D'Escoussse, NS B0E 1K0, Canada.

CAMERON, Matt; Australian playwright and screenwriter. *Plays:* Tear From a Glass Eye 1996, Man the Balloon 2001, Ruby Moon 2003, Mister Melancholy (aka The Hermits), Footprints on Water, The Eskimo Calling, Whispering Death. *Television writing:* Sea Change 1998, Small Tales and True 1998, Introducing Gary Petty (also co-creator and dir) 2000, The Third Eleven. *Honours:* ANPC New Dramatists' Award, Wal Cherry Play of the Year Award, British Council Int. New Playwriting Award. *Literary Agent:* RGM Associates, PO Box 128, Surry Hills, NSW 2010, Australia. *Telephone:* (2) 9281-3911. *Fax:* (2) 9281-4705. *E-mail:* info@rgm.com.au. *Website:* www.rgm.com.au.

CAMERON WATT, Donald; academic, writer and historian; b. 17 May 1928, Rugby, England; m. 1st Marianne R. Grau 1951 (died 1962); m. 2nd Felicia Cobb Stanley 1962 (died 1997); one s. one step-d. *Education:* BA, 1951, MA, 1954, Oriel College, Oxford. *Career:* Asst Lecturer, 1954–56, Lecturer, 1956–61, Senior Lecturer, 1962–66, Reader, 1966–72, Titular Prof., 1971–82, Stevenson Prof. of International History, 1982–93, Prof. Emeritus, 1993–, LSE, University of London; Ed., Survey of International Affairs, 1962–71; Chair., Greenwich Forum, 1974–84; Official Historian, Cabinet Office Historical Section, 1976–95. *Publications:* Britain and the Suez Canal, 1956; Documents on the Suez Crisis, 1957; Britain Looks to Germany, 1965; Personalities and Policies: Studies in the Formulation of British Foreign Policy in the 10th Century, 1965; A History of the World in the 20th Century, 1967; Contemporary History in Europe, 1969; Hitler's Mein Kampf, 1969; Current British Foreign Policy, 1970–72; Documents on British Foreign Affairs, 1867–1939, 1985–97; Succeeeding John Bull, America in Britain's Place 1900–1975, 1983; How War Came, 1989; Argentina Between the Great Powers, 1990. *Honours:* Fellow, British Acad.; DLitt, Oxon; Polish Acad. of Arts and Sciences, fellow; Wolfson Prize, 1990; Hon. Fellow, Oriel College, Oxford, 1998. *Literary Agent:* PFD, Drury House, 34–43 Russell Street, London WC2B 5HA, England. *Address:* c/o London School of Economics and Political Science, Houghton Street, London WC2A 2AE, England.

CAMPBELL, Alistair Te Ariki; Writer, Poet and Dramatist; b. 25 June 1925, Rarotonga, New Zealand; m. 1st Fleur Adcock, 1952; m. 2nd Meg Andersen, 1958, three s., two d. *Education:* BA, Victoria University of Wellington, 1953; Diploma of Teaching, Wellington Teachers' College, 1954. *Career:* Senior Ed., New Zealand Council for Educational Research, 1972–87; Writer's Fellow, Victoria University of Wellington, 1992; mem. PEN International, New Zealand Centre. *Publications:* Poetry: Mine Eyes Dazzle, 1950; Sanctuary of Spirits, 1963; Wild Honey, 1964; Blue Rain, 1967; Kapiti: Selected Poems, 1972; Dreams, Yellow Lions, 1975; The Dark Lord of Savaiki, 1980; Collected Poems, 1981; Soul Traps, 1985; Stone Rain: The Polynesian Strain, 1992; Death and the Tagua, 1995; Pocket Collected Poems, 1996; Gallipoli and Other Poems, 1999; Maori Battalion, 2001; Poets in Our Youth: Four Letters in Verse, 2002. Fiction: The Frigate Bird, 1989; Sidewinder, 1991; Tia, 1993; Fantasy with Witches, 1998. Autobiography: Island to Island, 1984. Plays: The Suicide, 1965; When the Bough Breaks, 1970. Contributions: Landfall; New Zealand Listener; Poetry New Zealand; New Zealand Poetry Yearbook; Comment; Poetry Australia. *Honours:* Gold Medal for TV documentary, La Spezia International Film Festival, 1974; New Zealand Book Award for Poetry, 1982; Pacific Islands Artists Award, 1998; Hon. D.Litt, 1999. *Address:* 4B Rawhiti Rd, Pukerua Bay, Wellington, New Zealand.

CAMPBELL, Donald; poet and dramatist; b. 25 Feb. 1940, Caithness, Scotland; m. Jean Fairgrieve 1966; one s. *Career:* writer-in-residence, Edinburgh Education Dept 1974–77, Royal Lyceum Theatre 1981–82; Fellow in Creative Writing, Univ. of Dundee 1987–89; William Soutar Fellow, Perth Libraries 1991–93; Royal Literary Fund Fellow, Napier Univ. 2000–02. *Publications:* poetry: Poems 1971, Rhymes 'n' Reasons 1972, Murals: Poems in Scots 1975, Blether: A Collection of Poems 1979, A Brighter Sunshine 1983, Selected Poems 1870–90 1990, Playing for Scotland 1996, Edinburgh: A cultural and literary history 2003; plays for stage, radio and television. *Address:* 85 Spottiswoode Street, Edinburgh, EH9 1BZ, Scotland.

CAMPBELL, Ewing; writer and academic; b. 26 Dec. 1940, Alice, TX, USA. *Education:* BBA, North Texas State University, 1968; MA, University of Southern Mississippi, 1972; PhD, Oklahoma State University, 1980. *Career:* Lecturer, University of Texas at Austin, 1981–82, Oklahoma State University, 1982–83, Wharton Community College, 1983–84; Asst Prof., 1984–90, Assoc. Prof., 1990–, Full Prof., 1999–, Texas A & M University; mem. Texas Institute of Letters. *Publications:* Fiction: Weave It Like Nightfall, 1977; The Way of Sequestered Places, 1982; The Rincón Triptych, 1984; The Tex-Mex Express, 1993; Madonna, Maleva, 1995. Short Fiction: Piranesi's Dream, 1986. Criticism: Raymond Carver: A Study of the Short Fiction, 1992. Contributions: Stories and articles to many periodicals. *Honours:* Fulbright Scholar, Argentina, 1989, Spain, 1997; National Endowments for the Arts Fellowship, 1990; Dobie-Paisano Ralph A. Johnston Award, 1992; Chris O'Malley Fiction Prize, 1998; American Literary Fiction Prize, 2002. *Address:* English Department, Texas A & M University, College Station, TX 77843-4227, USA.

CAMPBELL, Ian; academic and writer; b. 25 Aug. 1942, Lausanne, Switzerland. *Education:* MA, Univ. of Aberdeen, 1964; PhD, Univ. of Edinburgh, 1970. *Career:* Reader in English, 1967–92, Prof. of Scottish and Victorian Literature, 1992–, Univ. of Edinburgh; British Council Appointments, France, Germany; mem. Carlyle Society, pres.; Scottish Asscn for the Speaking of Verse; Asscn for Scottish Literary Studies, council mem. *Publications:* Thomas Carlyle Letters, 30 vols, 1970–2002; Carlyle, 1974; Nineteenth Century Scottish Fiction: Critical Essays, 1978; Thomas and Jane, 1980; Kailyard, 1981; Lewis Grassic Gibbon, 1986; Spartacus, 1987. Contributions: numerous papers to learned journals. *Honours:* British Acad. Research Fellowship, 1980. *Address:* Dept of English, University of Edinburgh, David Hume Tower, George Square, Edinburgh EH8 9JX, Scotland. *E-mail:* Ian.Campbell@ed.ac.uk.

CAMPBELL, John Malcolm, MA, PhD; writer; b. 2 Sept. 1947, London, England; m. Alison McCracken 1972; one s. one d. *Education:* Charterhouse, University of Edinburgh. *Career:* mem. Society of Authors; Royal Historical Society. *Publications:* Lloyd George: The Goat in the Wilderness 1977, F. E. Smith, First Earl of Birkenhead 1983, Roy Jenkins: A Biography 1983, Nye Bevan and the Mirage of British Socialism 1987, The Experience of World War II (ed.) 1989, Makers of the Twentieth Century (ed.) 1990–92, Edward Heath 1993, Margaret Thatcher: Vol. I: The Grocer's Daughter 2000, Vol. II: The Iron Lady 2003, Reference and Consciousness 2003; contrib. regular book reviews to The Times, TLS, The Independent, Sunday Telegraph. *Honours:* Yorkshire Post, Best First Book Award; NCR Book Award for Non-Fiction, 1994. *Address:* 2 Lansdowne Crescent, London W11 2NH, England.

CAMPBELL, Judith (see Pares, Marion).

CAMPBELL, Philip Henry Montgomery, PhD, FInstP, FRAS; British journalist and academic; *Editor-in-Chief, Nature*; b. 19 April 1951; m. Judie Yelton 1980 (died 1992); two s. *Education:* Shrewsbury School, Univ. of Bristol, Queen Mary Coll., London, Univ. of Leicester. *Career:* postdoctoral research asst, Dept of Physics, Univ. of Leicester 1977–79; Asst Ed. Nature journal 1979–82, Physical Sciences Ed. 1982–88; founding Ed., Physics World magazine 1988–95; Ed., Nature journal and Ed.-in-Chief, Nature journal and Nature publications 1995–, Dir, Nature Publishing Group

1997–; Trustee Cancer Research UK. *Radio:* broadcasts on BBC World Service. *Publications:* numerous papers and articles in journals, magazines and newspapers. *Honours:* Hon. DSc (Leicester) 1999. *Address:* c/o Nature Publishing Group, The Macmillan Building, 4 Crinan Street, London, N1 9XW, England. *Telephone:* (20) 7833-4000. *Fax:* (20) 7843-4596. *E-mail:* exec@nature.com. *Website:* www.nature.com.

CAMPBELL, Ramsey; Writer and Film Reviewer; b. 4 Jan. 1946, Liverpool, England; m. Jenny Chandler, 1 Jan. 1971, one s. one d. *Career:* Film Reviewer, BBC Radio Merseyside, 1969–; Full-time Writer, 1973–; mem. British Fantasy Society, pres.; Society of Fantastic Films. *Publications:* Fiction: The Doll Who Ate His Mother, 1976; The Face That Must Die, 1979; The Parasite, 1980; The Nameless, 1981; Incarnate, 1983; The Claw, 1983, US edn as Night of the Claw; Obsession, 1985; The Hungry Moon, 1986; The Influence, 1988; Ancient Images, 1989; Midnight Sun, 1990; The Count of Eleven, 1991; The Long Lost, 1993; The One Safe Place, 1995; The House on Nazareth Hill, 1996; The Last Voice They Hear, 1998; Silent Children, 2000; The Darkest Part of the Woods, 2002; The Overnight, 2003. Short Stories: The Inhabitant of the Lake and Less Welcome Tenants, 1964; Demons by Daylight, 1973; The Height of the Scream, 1976; Dark Companions, 1982; Cold Print, 1985; Black Wine (with Charles L. Grant), 1986; Night Visions 3 (with Clive Barker and Lisa Tuttle), 1986; Scared Stiff, 1987; Dark Feasts: The World of Ramsey Campbell, 1987; Waking Nightmares, 1991; Alone With the Horrors, 1993; Strange Things and Stranger Places, 1993; Ghosts and Grisly Things, 1998; Told by the Dead, 2003. Novella: Needing Ghosts, 1990. Other: Ramsey Campbell, Probably (collected non-fiction), 2002. *Honours:* Liverpool Daily Post and Echo Award for Literature, 1993; World Fantasy Award, Bram Stoker Award, Best Collection, 1994; Best Novel, International Horror Guild, 1998; Grand Master, World Horror Convention, 1999; Lifetime Achievement Award, Horror Writers' Asscn, 1999. *Literary Agent:* Pimlico Agency, USA; Ralph Vicinanza, foreign; Caren Bohrman, film and TV. *Address:* 31 Penkett Rd, Wallasey CH45 7QF, Merseyside, England. *Website:* www.ramseycampbell.com.

CAMPION, Daniel Ray, AB, MA, PhD; editor, poet and literary critic; b. 23 Aug. 1949, Oak Park, IL, USA; pnr JoAnn E. Castagna. *Education:* University of Chicago, University of Illinois, Chicago, University of Iowa. *Career:* Production Ed., Encyclopaedia Britannica Inc, Chicago, IL, 1972–74; Children's Book Ed., Follett Publishing Company, Chicago, 1977–78; Teaching and Research Asst, University of Iowa, Iowa City, 1978–84; Test Specialist, Senior Ed., ACT Inc, Iowa City, 1984–; mem. Authors' Guild; MLA; Midwest MLA; National Council of Teachers of English; Society for the Study of Midwestern Literature. *Publications:* Walt Whitman: The Measure of his Song (co-ed.), 1981; Calypso (poems), 1981; Peter De Vries and Surrealism, 1995. Contributions: Poetry and articles to periodicals, including College English; Literary Magazine Review; The Writer's Chronicle; Hispanic Journal; Rolling Stone; Chicago Tribune; Chicago Reader; Ascent; Poet Lore; English Journal; Poetry. *Honours:* Festival of the Arts Poetry Award, University of Chicago, 1967; All-Nations Poetry Contest Award, Triton College, River Grove, IL, 1975; Poetry Award, Illinois Arts Council, 1979. *Address:* 1700 E Rochester Avenue, Iowa City, IA 52245, USA.

CAMPTON, David; Playwright and Children's Fiction Writer; b. 5 June 1924, Leicester, England. *Career:* mem. Writers Guild of Great Britain. *Publications:* On Stage: Containing 17 Sketches and 1 Monologue, 1964; Resting Place, 1964; The Manipulator, 1964; Split Down the Middle, 1965; Little Brother, Little Sister and Out of the Flying Pan, 1966; Two Leaves and a Stalk, 1967; Angel Unwilling, 1967; Ladies Night: 4 Plays for Women, 1967; More Sketches, 1967; Laughter and Fear, 9 One-Act Plays, 1969; The Right Place, 1969; On Stage Again: Containing 14 Sketches and 2 Monologues, 1969; Now and Then, 1970; The Life and Death of Almost Everybody, 1970; Timesneeze, 1970; Gulliver in Lilliput (reader), 1970; Gulliver in The Land of Giants (reader), 1970; The Wooden Horse of Troy (reader), 1970; Jonah, 1971; The Cagebirds, 1971; Us and Them, 1972; Carmilla, 1972; In Committee, 1972; Come Back Tomorrow, 1972; Three Gothic Plays, 1973; Modern Aesop (reader), 1976; One Possessed, 1977; What Are You Doing Here?, 1978; The Do-It-Yourself Frankenstein Outfit, 1978; Zodiac, 1978; After Midnight: Before Dawn, 1978; Pieces of Campton, 1979; Parcel, 1979; Everybody's Friend, 1979; Who Calls?, 1980; Attitudes, 1980; Freedom Log, 1980; Dark Wings, 1981; Look-Sea, 1981; Great Whales, 1981; Who's a Hero, Then?, 1981; Dead and Alive, 1983; But Not Here, 1984; Singing in the Wilderness, 1986; Mrs Meadowsweet, 1986; The Vampyre (children's book), 1986; Our Branch in Brussels, 1986; Cards, Cups and Crystal Ball, 1986; Can You Hear the Music?, 1988; The Winter of 1917, 1989; Smile, 1990; Becoming a Playwright, 1992; The Evergreens, 1994; Permission to Cry, 1996. Contributions: Amateur Stage; Writers News; Drama; Whispers. *Address:* 35 Liberty Rd, Glenfield, Leicester LE3 8JF, England.

CANIN, Ethan; Writer; b. 19 July 1960, Ann Arbor, MI, USA. *Education:* BA, Stanford University, 1982; MFA, University of Iowa, 1984; MD, Harvard University, 1992. *Publications:* Emperor of the Air, 1988; Blue River, 1991; The Palace Thief, 1994; For Kings and Planets, 1998; Carry Me Across the Water, 2001. Contributions: anthologies and periodicals. *Address:* c/o Maxine Groffsky Literary Agency, 2 Fifth Ave, New York, NY 10011, USA.

CANNADINE, David Nicholas; Prof. of History, Writer and Ed.; b. 7 Sept. 1950, Birmingham, England; m. Linda Jane Colley 1982; one d. (deceased). *Education:* BA, 1972, MA, 1975, DLitt, 1993, Clare College, Cambridge; Princeton University; DPhil, St John's College, Oxford, 1975. *Career:* Resident Fellow, 1975–77, Asst Lecturer, 1976–80, Lecturer, 1980–88, in History, St John's College, Cambridge; Dir of Studies in History, 1977–83, Fellow, 1977–78, Tutor, 1979–81, Christ's College, Cambridge; Gen. Ed., Studies in Modern History, 1979–, Penguin History of Britain, 1989–, Penguin History of Europe, 1991–, Historical Research, 1998–; Visiting Mem., Institute for Advanced Study, Princeton, NJ, 1980–81; Fellow, Berkeley College, Yale University, 1985–, ACLS, 1990–91, J. P. Morgan Library, New York, 1992–98; Prof. of History, 1988–92, Moore Collegiate Prof. of History, 1992–98, Columbia University; Visiting Prof., Birkbeck College, University of London, 1995–97; Visiting Fellow, Whitney Humanities Center, Yale University, 1995–98; Visiting Scholar, Pembroke College, Cambridge, 1997; Dir, Institute of Historical Research, London, 1998–; Prof. of History, University of London, 1998–; mem. Fellow, British Acad., 1999; FRHistS, 1981; FRSA, 1998; FRSL, 1999. *Publications:* Lords and Landlords: The Aristocracy and the Towns, 1774–1967, 1980; Patricians, Power and Politics in Nineteenth-Century Towns (ed. and contributor), 1982; H. J. Dyos: Exploring the Urban Past (co-ed. and contributor), 1982; Rituals of Royalty: Power and Ceremonial in Traditional Societies (co-ed. and contributor), 1987; The Pleasures of the Past, 1989; Winston Churchill's Famous Speeches (ed. and contributor), 1989; The First Modern Society: Essays in English History in Honour of Lawrence Stone (co-ed. and contributor), 1989; The Decline and Fall of the British Aristocracy, 1990; G. M. Trevelyan: A Life in History, 1992; Aspects of Aristocracy: Grandeur and Decline in Modern Britain, 1994; History and Biography: Essays in Honour of Derek Beales (co-ed. and contributor), 1996; Class in Britain, 1998; History in Our Time, 1998; Making History Now, 1999; Ornamentalism: How the British Saw Their Empire, 2001; In Churchill's Shadow: Confronting the Past in Modern Britain, 2002. Contributions: scholarly books and journals. *Honours:* T. S. Ashton Prize, Economic History Society, 1977; Silver Jubilee Prize, Agricultural History Society, 1977; Lionel Trilling Prize, 1990; Dean's Distinguished Award in the Humanities, Columbia University, 1996. *Address:* c/o Institute of Historical Research, Senate House, Malet St, London WC1E 7HU, England.

CANNON, Curt (see Hunter, Evan).

CANNON, Frank (see Mayhar, Ardath).

CANNON, Geoffrey John; Writer; b. 12 April 1940, Witham, Essex, England; m. 2nd; two s. one d. *Education:* MA, Balliol College, Oxford, 1961. *Career:* mem. Vice-Pres., Sustain, 1999–; Co-Founder, Caroline Walker Trust; Founder, Serpentine Running Club, 1982-; Co-founder and mem. exec. committee, World Health Policy Forum, 2000–. *Publications:* Dieting Makes You Fat (co-author), 1983; The Food Scandal (with Caroline Walker), 1984; Fat To Fit, 1986; The Politics of Food, 1987; Food and Health: The Experts Agree, 1992; Superbug, 1995; Food, Nutrition and Cancer: A Global Perspective (ed.), 1997. *Honours:* Visiting Prof., University of Brasilia, 2000–. *Literary Agent:* Deborah Rogers. *Address:* c/o World Cancer Research Fund, 19 Harley St, London W1N 1DA, England.

CANNON, Steve; Writer, Dramatist, Educator and Publisher; b. 10 April 1935, New Orleans, LA, USA; one s. (deceased). *Education:* BA, History, University of Nebraska, 1954. *Career:* Prof. of Humanities, Medgar Evers College, CUNY, 1971–92; mem. PEN, New York Chapter. *Publications:* Groove, Bang and Jive Around, 1969; Introduction to Rouzing the Rubble, 1991; Reminicin' in C, 1995. Plays: The Set Up, 1991; Chump Change, 1992; Nothing to Lose, 1993; Now What, What Now?, 1994; En Vogue, 1994; Top of the World, 1995; Marvellous, 1996. *Address:* 285 E Third St, New York, NY 10009, USA.

CANTALUPO, Charles; Prof. of English, Poet and Writer; b. 17 Oct. 1951, Orange, NJ, USA; m. 1st Catherine Musello 21 Aug. 1976 (died 1983); one s. (deceased); m. 2nd Barbara Dorosh 29 Oct. 1988; one s. three d. *Education:* Univ. of Kent at Canterbury, 1972; BA, Washington Univ., St Louis, 1973; MA, 1978, PhD, 1980, Rutgers Univ. *Career:* Teaching Asst, 1973–76, Instructor, 1977–79, Rutgers Univ.; Instructor, 1980–81, Asst Prof., 1981–89, Assoc. Prof., 1989–96, Prof. of English, 1996–99, Prof. of English and Comparative Literature, 1999–2001, Prof. of English, Comparative Literature and African Studies, 2002–, Pennsylvania State Univ., Schuylkill Haven. *Publications:* The Art of Hope (poems), 1983; A Literary Leviathan: Thomas Hobbe's Masterpiece of Language, 1991; The World of Ngugi wa Thiong'o (ed.), 1995; Poetry, Mysticism, and Feminism: From th' Nave to the Chops, 1995; Ngugi wa Thiong'o: Text and Contexts (ed.), 1995; Anima/l Wo/man and Other Spirits (poems), 1996; We Have Our Voice: Selected Poems of Reesom Haile (trans.), 2000; We Invented the Wheel: Poems by Reesom Haile (trans.), 2002; Light the Lights (poems), 2004. Contributions: books, anthologies, scholarly journals, periodicals, newspapers and websites. *Honours:* American Acad. of Poets Prize, 1976. *Address:* c/o Dept of English, Pennsylvania State University, 200 University Dr., Schuylkill Haven, PA 17972, USA.

CANTOR, Norman Frank; American writer; b. 19 Nov. 1929, Winnipeg, Manitoba, Canada; m. Mindy M. Cantor; one s. one d. *Education:* BA, University of Manitoba, 1951; MA, 1953, PhD, 1957, Princeton University; Rhodes Scholar, University of Oxford, 1954–55. *Career:* Instructor to Asst

Prof. of History, Princeton University, 1955–60; Visiting Prof., Johns Hopkins University, 1960, Yeshiva University, 1960–61, 1963–64, Brooklyn College, CUNY, 1972–74; Assoc. Prof. to Prof., Columbia University, 1960–66; Prof., Brandeis University, 1966–70; Distinguished Prof. of History, SUNY at Binghamton, 1970–76; Prof. of History, University of Illinois at Chicago Circle, 1976–78; Prof. of History, 1978–80, Prof. of History and Sociology, 1980–85, Affiliated Prof. of Legal History, 1982–88, Prof. of History, Sociology, and Comparative Literature, 1983–2000, Prof. Emeritus of History, 2000–, New York University; Fulbright Visiting Prof., University of Tel-Aviv, 1987–88; University Distinguished Visiting Scholar, Adelphi University, 1988–89; Lecturer in Jewish History, Institute of Secular Jewish Humanism, Detroit, 1996–; mem. FRHistS. *Publications:* Church, Kingship and Lay Investiture, 1958; Medieval History: The Life and Death of a Civilization, 1963, revised edn as The Civilization of the Middle Ages, 1993; How to Study History (with R. Schneider), 1967; The English, 1968; The Age of Protest, 1969; Western Civilization, 2 vols, 1969–70; Perspectives on the European Past, 1971; The Meaning of the Middle Ages, 1973; Twentieth Century Culture, 1988; Inventing the Middle Ages, 1991; The Civilization of the Middle Ages, 1993; Medieval Lives, 1994; The Medieval Reader, 1994; The Sacred Chain, 1994; The Jewish Experience, 1996; The American Century, 1997; Imagining the Law, 1997; Encyclopedia of the Middle Ages, 1999; In the Wake of the Plague: The Black Death and the World it Made, 2001. Contributions: Books and scholarly journals. *Honours:* National Book Critics Circle Award, 1991; New York Public Library Award, 1998. *Address:* 3901 S Ocean Drive, Apt 11E, Hollywood, FL 33019, USA.

CANTSIN, Monty (see Home, Stewart Ramsay).

CAPIE, Forrest Hunter, BA, MSc, PhD, FRSA; academic; *Professor of Economic History, City University, London*; b. 1 Dec. 1940, Glasgow, Scotland; m. Dianna Dix 1967. *Education:* Univ. of Auckland, New Zealand, Univ. of London. *Career:* Lecturer, Univ. of Warwick, 1972–74, Univ. of Leeds, 1974–79; Visiting Lecturer, 1978–79, Lecturer, 1979–82, Senior Lecturer, 1982–83, Reader, 1983–86, Prof. of Economic History, 1986–, City Univ., London; various guest lectureships; Ed., Economic History Review, 1993–; mem. Asscn of Business Historians; Cliometrics Society; Economic History Asscn; Economic History Society; Royal Economic Society; Western Economics Asscn. *Publications:* The British Economy Between the Wars (with M. Collins), 1983; Depression and Protectionism: Britain Between the Wars, 1983; A Monetary History of the United Kingdom, 1870–1982: Data Sources and Methods (with A. Webber), 1985; Financial Crises and the World Banking System (ed. with G. E. Wood), 1986; Monetary Economics in the 1980s: Some Themes from Henry Thornton (ed. with G. E. Wood), 1989; A Directory of Economic Institutions (ed.), 1990; Unregulated Banking: Chaos or Order? (ed. with G. E. Wood), 1991; Major Inflations in History (ed.), 1991; Protectionism in the World Economy (ed.), 1992; Did the Banks Fail British Industry? (with M. Collins), 1992; Monetary Regimes in Transition (ed. with M. Bordo), 1993; A History of Banking (ed.), 10 vols, 1993; Tariffs and Growth, 1994; The Future of Central Banking (with Charles Goodhart, Stanley Fischer and Norbert Schnadt), 1994; Monetary Economics in the 1990s (ed. with G. E. Wood), 1996; Asset Prices and the Real Economy (ed. with G. E. Wood), 1997; Policy Makers on Policy (ed. with G. E. Wood), 2001; World Economic Liberalization in Historical Perspective, 2001; Capital Controls: A Cure Worse Than the Disease, 2002. Contributions: scholarly books and journals. *Honours:* several grants and fellowships. *Address:* 2 Fitzroy Road, Primrose Hill, London NW1 8TX, England.

CAPUTO, Philip (Joseph); Author and Screenwriter; b. 10 June 1941, Chicago, IL, USA; m. 1st Jill Esther Ongemach, 21 June 1969, divorced 1982, two s.; m. 2nd Marcelle Lynn Besse, 30 Oct. 1982, divorced 1985; m. 3rd Leslie Blanchard Ware, 4 June 1988. *Education:* Purdue University; BA, Loyola University, 1964. *Career:* Staff, 1969–72, Foreign Correspondent, 1972–77, Chicago Tribune; Freelance Writer, 1977–; Screenwriter, Mercury-Douglas Productions, Paramount Pictures, 1987–; mem. Authors' Guild. *Publications:* A Rumor of War (memoir), 1977; Horn of Africa (novel), 1980; Del Corso's Gallery (novel), 1983; Indian Country: A Novel, 1987; Means of Escape (memoir), 1991; Equation for Evil (novel), 1996; Exiles (3 novellas), 1997; The Voyage (novel), 1999. Contributions: various periodicals. *Honours:* Pulitzer Prize for Reporting (with George Bliss), 1973; George Polk Award, 1973; Overseas Press Club Award; Sidney Hillman Award. *Address:* c/o Aaron Priest Literary Agency, 708 Third Ave, New York, NY 10017, USA.

CARD, Orson Scott, (Brian Green, Byron Walley); Writer; b. 24 Aug. 1951, Richland, WA, USA; m. Kristine Allen, 17 May 1977, two s. three d. *Education:* BA, Theatre, Brigham Young University, 1975; MA, English, University of Utah, 1981. *Career:* mem. Authors' Guild; SFWA. *Publications:* Capitol, 1978; Hot Sleep: The Worthing Chronicle, 1978; A Planet Called Treason, 1979, revised edn as Treason, 1988; Songmaster, 1980; Unaccompanied Sonata and Other Stories, 1980; Saintspeak: The Mormon Dictionary, 1981; Ainge, 1982; Hart's Hope, 1983; A Woman of Destiny, 1983, revised edn as Saints, 1988; The Worthing Chronicle, 1983; Ender's Game, 1985; Speaker for the Dead, 1986; Cardography, 1987; Free Lancers (with others), 1987; Seventh Son, 1987; Wyrms, 1987; Characters and Viewpoint, 1988; Red Prophet, 1988; Folk of the Fringe, 1989; The Abyss, 1989; Prentice Alvin, 1989; How to Write Science Fiction and Fantasy, 1990; Eye for Eye–The Tunesmith (with Lloyd Biggle), 1990; Maps in a Mirror: The Short Fiction of Orson Scott Card, 1990; Worthing Saga, 1990; Xenocide, 1991; The Changed Man, 1992; Cruel Miracles, 1992; Flux, 1992; The Memory of Earth, 1992; Lost Boys, 1992; The Call of the Earth, 1993; Monkey Sonatas, 1993; The Ships of Earth, 1993; Lovelock (with Kathryn H. Kidd), 1994; Earthfall, 1994; Turning Hearts: Short Stories on Family Life (ed. with David C. Dollahite), 1994; Alvin Journeyman, 1995; Earthborn, 1995; Children of the Mind, 1996; Pastwatch: The Redemption of Christopher Columbus, 1996; Treasure Box, 1996; Stone Tables, 1997; Heartfire, 1998; Homebody, 1998; Enchantment, 1999; Ender's Shadow, 1999; Magic Mirror 1999, Sarah 2000, Shadow of the Hegemon 2001, Rebekah, 2001, Shadow of the Hegemon, 2001, Shadow Puppets 2002, The Crystal City 2003. Contributions: periodicals. *Honours:* John W. Campbell Award, World Science Fiction Convention, 1978; Utah State Institute of Fine Arts Prize, 1980; Hamilton-Brackett Awards, 1981, 1986; Nebula Awards, 1985, 1986; Hugo Awards, 1986, 1987; Locus Awards, 1987, 1988, 1989; Mythopoeic Fantasy Award, Mythopoeic Society, 1988. *Address:* c/o Barbara Bova, 3951 Gulf Shore Blvd, PH1B, Naples, FL 34103, USA.

CARDENAL, Ernesto; Nicaraguan Roman Catholic priest and poet; b. 20 Jan. 1925, Granada. *Education:* University of Mexico, Columbia University, New York. *Career:* Roman Catholic priest 1965–; Minister of Culture 1979–90. *Publications:* Proclama del conquistador, 1947; Gethsemani, Ky., 1960; La hora O, 1960; Epigramas: Poemas, 1961; Oracion por Marilyn Monroe and Other Poems, 1965; El estrecho dudoso, 1966; Poemas, 1967; Psalms of Struggle and Liberation, 1967; Mayapan, 1968; Poemas reunidos 1949–69, 1969; Homage to the American Indians, 1969; Zero Hour and Other Documentary Poems, 1971; Poemas, 1971; Canto nacional, 1973; Oraculo sobre Managua, 1973; Poesia escogida, 1975; Apocalypse and Other Poems, 1977; Canto a un pais que nace, 1978; Nueva antologia poetica, 1979; Waslala, 1983; Poesia dela nueva Nicaragua, 1983; Flights of Victory, 1984; With Walker in Nicaragua and Other Early Poems 1949–54, 1985; From Nicaragua with Love: Poems 1976–1986, 1986; Golden UFOS: The Indian Poems, 1992; Cosmic Canticle, 1993. *Honours:* Premio de la Paz Grant 1980. *Address:* Apdo A-252, Managua, Nicaragua. *Address:* c/o Curbstone Press, 321 Jackson Street, Willimantic, CT 06226-1738, USA.

CARDOSO PIRES, José (Augusto Neves); Novelist and Dramatist; b. 2 Oct. 1925, Peso, Castelo, Branco, Portugal. *Education:* University of Lisbon. *Career:* Literary Dir of various publishing houses in Lisbon. *Publications:* Historuas de amor, 1952; Estrada 43, 1955; A ancorado, 1958; Jogos de azar, 1963; O hospede de Job, 1963; O delfin, 1968; Dinossauro excelentissimo, 1972; O burro-em-pe, 1978; Ballad of Dogs' Beach: Dossier of a Crime, 1982; Alexandra Alpha, 1987; A Republica dos Corvos, 1988. Plays: O render dos herois, 1960; Corpo-delito na sala de espelhos, 1980. *Honours:* Grande Premio do Romance e da Novela, 1983. *Address:* Rua São Joao de Brito 7-1, 1700 Lisbon, Portugal.

CAREW, Jan Rynveld; academic, writer and poet; b. 24 Sept. 1925, Agricola, Guyana. *Career:* Lecturer in Race Relations, University of London Extra-Mural Dept, 1953–57; Writer and Ed., BBC Overseas Service, London, 1954–65; Ed., African Review, Ghana, 1965–66; CBC Broadcaster, Toronto, 1966–69; Senior Fellow, Council of Humanities and Lecturer, Dept of Afro-American Studies, Princeton University, 1969–72; Prof., Dept of African-American Studies, Northwestern University, 1972–87; Visiting Clarence J. Robinson Prof. of Caribbean Literature and History, George Mason University, 1989–91; Visiting Prof. of International Studies, Illinois Wesleyan University, 1992–93. *Publications:* Streets of Eternity, 1952; Black Midas, 1958, US edn as A Touch of Midas; 1958; The Last Barbarian, 1961; Green Winter, 1964; University of Hunger, 1966; The Third Gift, 1975; The Origins of Racism and Resistance in the Americas, 1976; Rape of the Sun-people, 1976; Children of the Sun, 1980; Sea Drums in My Blood, 1981; Grenada: The Hour Will Strike Again, 1985; Fulcrums of Change, 1987. *Address:* Dept of African-American Studies, Northwestern University, Evanston, IL 60208, USA.

CAREY, John, BA, DPhil, FBA, FRSL; British academic, literary critic, writer and editor; *Emeritus Professor of English Literature, University of Oxford*; b. 5 April 1934, London, England; m. Gillian Booth 1960; two s. *Education:* St John's College, Oxford. *Career:* Harmsworth Senior Scholar, Merton College, 1957–58; Lecturer, Christ Church, Oxford, 1958–59; Andrew Bradley Jr Research Fellow, Balliol College, Oxford, 1959–60; Tutorial Fellow, Keble College, Oxford, 1960–64, St John's College, Oxford, 1964–75; Merton Prof. of English Literature, 1976–2001, Emeritus Prof., 2001–, University of Oxford; T. S. Eliot Memorial Lecturer, University of Kent, 1989. *Publications:* The Poems of John Milton (ed. with Alastair Fowler), 1968; Milton, 1969; The Violent Effigy: A Study of Dickens' Imagination, 1973; Thackeray, Prodigal Genius, 1977; John Donne: Life, Mind and Art, 1981; William Golding: The Man and His Books (ed.), 1986; Original Copy: Selected Reviews and Journalism, 1987; The Faber Book of Reportage (ed.), 1987; John Donne (ed.), 1990; The Intellectuals and the Masses, 1992; The Faber Book of Science (ed.), 1995; The Faber Book of Utopias (ed.), 1999; Pure Pleasure, 2000. Contributions: Principal Book Reviewer, Sunday Times. *Honours:* Hon. Fellow, St John's College, 1991, Balliol College, Oxford, 1992. *Literary Agent:* Toby Eady Associates Ltd, Third Floor, 9 Orme Court, London, W2 4RL, England. *Telephone:* (20) 7792-0092. *Fax:*

(20) 7792-0879. *E-mail:* toby@tobyeady.demon.co.uk. *Website:* www.tobyeadyassociates.co.uk. *Address:* Merton College, Oxford OX1 4SD, England.

CAREY, Peter Philip, FRSL; Australian author; b. 7 May 1943, Bacchus Marsh, Vic.; m. 2nd Alison Summers 1985; two s. *Education:* Geelong Grammar School and Monash Univ. *Career:* fmr partner McSpedden Carey Advertising Consultants, Sydney; Writer-in-Residence New York Univ. 1990; now teacher Columbia Univ. and Princeton Univ. *Screenplays:* (jtly): Bliss, Until the End of the World, Oscar and Lucinda 1998. *Publications:* The Fat Man in History (short stories) 1974 (in UK as Exotic Pleasures 1981), War Crimes (short stories) 1979 (NSW Premier's Award), Bliss (novel) 1981 (Miles Franklin Award, Nat. Book Council Award, NSW Premier's Award), Illywhacker (novel) 1985 (Age Book of the Year Award, Nat. Book Council Award, Victorian Premier's Award), Oscar and Lucinda 1988 (Booker Prize for Fiction 1988, Miles Franklin Award, Nat. Book Council Award, Adelaide Festival Award, Foundation for Australian Literary Studies Award), Until the End of the World 1990, The Tax Inspector (novel) 1991, The Unusual Life of Tristan Smith (novel) 1994 (Age Book of the Year Award), Collected Stories 1995, The Big Bazoohley (children's novel) 1995, Jack Maggs 1997, The True History of the Kelly Gang (Booker Prize 2001) 2000, 30 Days in Sydney: A Wildly Distorted Account 2001, My Life as a Fake 2003. *Honours:* Hon. LittD (Queensland). *Address:* c/o Amanda Urban, ICM, 40 West 57th Street, New York, NY 10019, USA.

CARFAX, Catherine (see Fairburn, Eleanor M.).

CARKEET, David (Corydon); Prof. and Author; b. 15 Nov. 1946, Sonora, CA, USA; m. Barbara Lubin, 16 Aug. 1975, three d. *Education:* AB, University of California at Davis, 1968; MA, University of Wisconsin, 1970; PhD, Indiana University, 1973. *Career:* Asst Prof., 1973–79, Assoc. Prof., 1979–87, Prof., 1987–, University of Missouri. *Publications:* Fiction: Double Negative, 1980; The Greatest Slump of All Time, 1984; I Been There Before, 1985; The Full Catastrophe, 1990; The Error of Our Ways, 1997. Young Adult Fiction: The Silent Treatment, 1988; Quiver River, 1991. Contributions: scholarly journals; Short stories and popular essays in periodicals. *Honours:* James D. Phelan Award in Literature, San Francisco Foundation, 1976; Notable Books of the Year, New York Times Book Review, 1981, 1990, 1997; O. Henry Award, 1982; National Endowment for the Arts Fellowship, 1983. *Address:* 9307 Old Bonhomme Rd, St Louis, MO 63132, USA. *E-mail:* carkeet@umsl.edu.

CARLILE, Henry (David); Prof. of English, Poet and Writer; b. 6 May 1934, San Francisco, CA, USA; one d. *Education:* AA, Grays Harbor College, 1958; BA, 1962, MA, 1967, University of Washington. *Career:* Instructor, 1967–69, Asst Prof., 1969–72, Assoc. Prof., 1972–78, Prof. of English, 1980–, Portland State University; Visiting Lecturer, Writers Workshop, University of Iowa, 1978–80. *Publications:* The Rough-Hewn Table, 1971; Running Lights, 1981; Rain, 1994. Contributions: many anthologies, reviews, and journals. *Honours:* National Endowment for the Arts Discovery Grant, 1970, and Fellowship in Poetry, 1976; Devins Award, 1971; PEN Syndicated Fiction Awards, 1983, 1986; Ingram Merrill Poetry Fellowship, 1985; Helen Foundation Award, 1986; Pushcart Prizes, 1986, 1992; Poetry Award, Crazyhorse, 1988; Oregon Arts Commission Literary Fellowship, 1994. *Address:* c/o Dept of English, Portland State University, PO Box 751, Portland, OR 97207, USA.

CARMI, T. (see Charny, Carmi).

CARMICHAEL, Jack Blake, BA, PhD; writer, poet and editor; b. 31 Jan. 1938, Ravenswood, West Virginia, USA; m. Julie Ann Carmichael 1981; four d. *Education:* Ohio Wesleyan University, Michigan State University, University of Oregon. *Career:* Ed. and Publisher, Dynamics Press 1990–; mem. Acad. of American Poets. *Publications:* Fiction: A New Slain Knight, 1991; Black Knight, 1991; Tales of the Cousin, 1992; Memoirs of the Great Gorgeous, 1992; The Humpty Boys in Michigan, 1996; Here Me America, with other poems and short stories, 1999. Contributions: poems in anthologies and journals. *Honours:* Hon. Co-Chair. Business Advisory Council; Outstanding Achievement Award, American Poetry Asscn 1990, Poet of the Year, Materials Dynamics 2003, Nat. Republican Congressional Cttee Leadership Award 2004. *Address:* c/o Dynamics Press, 519 S Rogers Street, Mason, MI 48854, USA.

CARMICHAEL, Joel; Author, Ed. and Trans; b. 31 Dec. 1915, New York, NY, USA. *Education:* BA, MA, University of Oxford, 1940; Sorbonne, University of Paris; École Nationale des Langues Orientales Vivantes. *Career:* European Correspondent, The Nation magazine, 1946–47; Ed., Midstream magazine, 1975–87, 1990–2000. *Publications:* An Illustrated History of Russia, 1960; The Death of Jesus, 1962; A Short History of the Russian Revolution, 1964; The Shaping of the Arabs: A Study in Ethnic Identity, 1967; Karl Marx: The Passionate Logician, 1967; An Open Letter to Moses and Muhammed, 1968; A Cultural History of Russia, 1968; Arabs and Jews, 1969; Trotsky: An Appreciation of His Life, 1976; Stalin's Masterpiece, 1977; Arabs Today, 1977; St Paul and the Jews, 1980; The Birth of Christianity: Reality and Myth, 1989; The Satanizing of the Jews: Origin and Development of Mystical Anti-Semitism, 1992; The Unriddling of Christian Origins: A Secular Account, 1995. Translations: (from Russian) The Russian Revolution 1917, N. N. Sukhanov, 1955; Anna Karenina, Leo Tolstoy, 1975. Contributions: journals and periodicals. *Honours:* Fulbright Fellowship, 1949–51. *Address:* 302 W 86th St, New York, NY 10024, USA.

CARON, Louis; Author, Poet and Dramatist; b. 1942, Sorel, QC, Canada. *Career:* mem. Académie des lettres de Québec, 1995–. *Publications:* L'illusionniste suivi de Le guetteur, 1973; L'emmitouflé, 1977, English trans. as The Draft-Dodger, 1980; Bonhomme sept-heures, 1978; Le canard de bois, 1981; La corne de brume, 1982; Le coup de poing, 1990; La tuque et le béret, 1992; Le bouleau et l'epinette, 1993. Other: many radio and television plays. *Honours:* Prix Hermes, France, 1977; Prix France-Canada, 1977; Prix Ludger-Duvernay, Société Saint-Jean-Baptiste, Montréal, 1984. *Address:* c/o Union des écrivaines et des écrivains québécois, La Maison des écrivains, 3492 Ave Laval, Montréal, QC H2X 3C8, Canada.

CARPENTER, Bogdana Maria Magdalene; American academic, writer and translator; *Professor of Slavic Languages and Literatures, University of Michigan at Ann Arbor*; b. 2 June 1941, Czestochowa, Poland; m. John Randell Carpenter 1963; one s. one d. *Education:* MA, University of Warsaw, 1963; PhD, University of California at Berkeley, 1974. *Career:* Acting Asst Prof., 1971–73, Lecturer, 1973–74, University of California at Berkeley; Asst Prof., University of Washington, Seattle, 1974–83; Staff Reviewer, World Literature Today, 1977–; Asst Prof., 1983–85, Assoc. Prof., 1985–91, Prof. of Slavic Languages and Literatures, 1991–, Chair, Dept of Slavic Languages and Literatures, 1991–95, University of Michigan, Ann Arbor; mem. The Polish Review, advisory board, 1993–. *Publications:* The Poetic Avant-Garde in Poland, 1918–1939, 1983; Cross Currents: A Yearbook of Central European Culture (assoc. ed.), 1987–93; Monumenta Polonica: The First Four Centuries of Polish Poetry, 1989. Translator: Works by Zbigniew Herbert (with John Carpenter): Selected Poems of Zbigniew Herbert, 1977; Report from the Besieged City and Other Poems, 1987; Still Life with a Bridle, 1991; Mr Cogito, 1993; Elegy for Departure and Other Poems, 1999; The King of Ants, 1999. Contributions: Books, scholarly journals, and general periodicals. *Honours:* Witter Bynner Poetry Trans. Prize, Poetry Society of America, 1979; National Endowment for the Humanities Trans. Grant, 1987–88; ACLS Fellowship, 1990–91; First Prize, American Council for Polish Culture Clubs, 1991; Columbia University Trans. Center Merit Award, 1992. *Address:* 1606 Granger, Ann Arbor, MI 48104, USA.

CARPENTER, Humphrey (William Bouverie); Writer, Dramatist, Broadcaster and Musician; b. 29 April 1946, Oxford, England; m. Mari Christina Prichard 1973; two d. *Education:* Marlborough Coll.; MA, DipEd, Keble Coll., Oxford. *Career:* Staff Producer, BBC Radio, Oxford, 1970–74; freelance writer and broadcaster, 1975–; Founder, Vile Bodies band, 1983, Mushy Pea Theatre Co for children, 1984; Programme Dir, Cheltenham Festival of Literature, 1994–96; mem. FRSL, 1983–. *Publications:* A Thames Companion (with Mari Prichard), 1975; J. R. R. Tolkien: A Biography, 1977; The Inklings, 1978; Jesus, 1980; The Letters of J. R. R. Tolkien (ed. with Christopher Tolkien), 1981; W. H. Auden: A Biography, 1981; The Oxford Companion to Children's Literature (ed. with Mari Prichard), 1984; OUDS: A Centenary History of the Oxford University Dramatic Society, 1985; Secret Gardens: The Golden Age of Children's Literature, 1985; Geniuses Together: American Writers in Paris, 1987; A Serious Character: The Life of Ezra Pound, 1988; The Brideshead Generation: Evelyn Waugh and his Friends, 1989; Benjamin Britten: A Biography, 1992; The Envy of the World: Fifty Years of the BBC Third Programme and Radio 3, 1996; Dennis Potter, 1998; That Was Satire That Was, 2000; Spike Milligan (biog.), 2003. Children's Books: The Joshers, 1977; The Captain Hook Affair, 1979; Mr Majeika, 1984; Mr Majeika and the Music Teacher, 1986; Mr Majeika and the Haunted Hotel, 1987; The Television Adventures of Mr Majeika, 1987; More Television Adventures of Mr Majeika, 1990; Mr Majeika and the School Play, 1991; Mr Majeika and the School Book Week, 1992; Wellington and Boot (with Jenny McDade), 1991; What Did You Do At School Today?, 1992; Charlie Crazee's Teevee, 1993; Mr Majeika and the School Inspector, 1993; Mr Majeika and the Ghost Train, 1994; Shakespeare Without the Boring Bits, 1994; Mr Majeika and the School Caretaker, 1996; The Puffin Book of Classic Children's Stories (ed.), 1996. Other: several plays for stage and radio. *Honours:* Somerset Maugham Award, 1978; E. M. Forster Award, American Acad. of Arts and Letters, 1984; Duff Cooper Memorial Prize, 1988; Royal Philharmonic Society Award, 1992. *Address:* 6 Farndon Rd, Oxford OX2 6RS, England.

CARPENTER, Lucas; Prof. of English, Writer, Poet and Ed.; b. 23 April 1947, Elberton, GA, USA; m. Judith Leidner, 2 Sept. 1972, one d. *Education:* BS, College of Charleston, 1968; MA, University of North Carolina at Chapel Hill, 1973; PhD, SUNY at Stony Brook, 1982. *Career:* Instructor, SUNY at Stony Brook, 1973–78; Instructor, 1978–80, Assoc. Prof. of English, 1980–85, Suffolk Community College; Editorial Consultant, Prentice-Hall Inc, 1981–; Assoc. Prof. of English, 1985–94, Prof. of English, 1994–, Charles Howard Candler Prof. of English, 2000, Oxford College of Emory University; mem. National Council of Teachers of English; Poetry Atlanta; Poetry Society of America; Southeast MLA. *Publications:* A Year for the Spider (poems), 1972; The Selected Poems of John Gould Fletcher (ed. with E. Leighton Rudolph), 1988; The Selected Essays of John Gould Fletcher (ed.), 1989; John Gould Fletcher and Southern Modernism, 1990; The Selected Correspondence of John Gould Fletcher (ed. with E. Leighton

Rudolph), 1996; Perils of the Affect (poems), 2002. Contributions: anthologies, scholarly journals, and periodicals. *Honours:* Resident Fellow in Poetry and Fiction Writing, Hambidge Center for the Creative Arts, 1991; Oxford College Prof. of the Year Awards, 1994, 1996; Fulbright Distinguished Scholar, Belgium, 1999. *Address:* c/o Dept of English, Oxford College of Emory University, Oxford, GA 30267, USA.

CARR, Caleb; Author and Historian; b. 2 Aug. 1955, New York, NY, USA. *Education:* Kenyon College, 1973–75; BA, New York University, 1977. *Publications:* Casing the Promised Land, 1980; America Invulnerable: The Quest for Absolute Security, from 1812 to Star Wars (with James Chace), 1988; The Devil Soldier: The Story of Frederick Townsend Ward, 1991; The Alienist, 1994; The Angel of Darkness, 1997; Killing Time, 2000. Contributions: Professional journals, newspapers and periodicals. *Address:* c/o International Creative Management, 40 W 57th St, New York, NY 10019, USA.

CARR, Glyn (see Styles, (Frank) Showell).

CARR, Margaret, (Martin Carroll, Carole Kerr); Writer; b. 25 Nov. 1935, Salford, England. *Publications:* Begotten Murder, 1967; Spring into Love, 1967; Blood Vengeance, 1968; Goodbye is Forever, 1968; Too Beautiful to Die, 1969; Hear No Evil, 1971; Tread Warily at Midnight, 1971; Sitting Duck, 1972; Who's the Target?, 1974; Not for Sale, 1975; Shadow of the Hunter, 1975; A Time to Surrender, 1975; Out of the Past, 1976; Twin Tragedy, 1977; Lamb to the Slaughter, 1978; The Witch of Wykham, 1978; Daggers Drawn, 1980; Stolen Heart, 1981; Deadly Pursuit, 1991; Dark Intruder, 1991. *Address:* Waverly, Wavering Lane, Gillingham, Dorset SP8 4NR, England.

CARR, Pat Moore, BA, MA, PhD; writer and university teacher; b. 13 March 1932, Grass Creek, WY, USA; m. 1st Jack Esslinger 1955 (divorced 1970); m. 2nd Duane Carr 1971; one s. three d. *Education:* Rice Univ., Tulane Univ. *Career:* teacher, Texas Southern Univ. 1956–58, Univ. of New Orleans 1961, 1965–69, 1987–88, Univ. of Texas at El Paso 1969–79, Univ. of Arkansas at Little Rock 1983, 1986–87, Western Kentucky Univ. 1988–96; mem. Int. Women's Writing Guild (bd mem. 1996–), Texas Inst. of Letters, PEN, Dairy Hollow Writers' Colony (bd mem.). *Publications:* fiction: The Grass Creek Chronicle 1976, Bluebirds 1993, Beneath the Hill 1999, If We Must Die 2002; short story collections: The Women in the Mirror 1977, Night of the Luminarias 1986, Sonahchi 1988, Our Brothers' War 1993; criticism: Bernard Shaw 1976, Mimbres Mythology 1979, In Fine Spirits 1986; contrib. articles and short stories in numerous publications, including The Southern Review, Best American Short Stories. *Honours:* South and West Fiction Award 1969, Library of Congress Marc IV Award for Short Fiction 1970, Nat. Endowment for the Humanities Award 1973, Iowa Fiction Award 1977, Texas Inst. of Letters Short Story Award 1978, Arkansas Endowment for the Humanities Award 1985, Green Mountain Short Fiction Award 1986, First Stage Drama Award 1990, Al Smith Fellowship in Fiction 1995, Chateau de Lavigny Writing Fellowship 1999, Texas Council of the Arts Literary Award 2000. *Address:* 10695 Venice Road, Elkins, AR 72727, USA.

CARR, Sir (Albert) Raymond Maillard; historian, writer and editor; b. 11 April 1919, Bath, England; m. Sara Ann Mary Strickland 1950; three s. one d. *Education:* BA, Christ Church, Oxford, 1941. *Career:* Gladstone Research Exhibitioner, Christ Church, Oxford, 1941; Lecturer, University College London, 1945–46; Fellow, All Souls College, Oxford, 1946–53, New College, Oxford, 1953–64; Fellow, 1964–, Sub-Warden, 1966–68, Warden, 1968–87, St Antony's College, Oxford; Prof. of the History of Latin America, University of Oxford, 1967–68; Distinguished Prof., Boston University, 1980; King Juan Carlos Prof. of Spanish History, New York University, 1992; mem. FRSL; Royal Acad. of History, Madrid, corresponding mem. *Publications:* Spain, 1808–1939, 1966; Latin America, 1969; The Republic and the Civil War in Spain (ed.), 1971; English Fox Hunting, 1976; The Spanish Tragedy: The Civil War in Perspective, 1977; Spain: Dictatorship to Democracy (co-author), 1979; Modern Spain, 1980; Fox-Hunting (with Sara Carr), 1982; Puerto Rico: A Colonial Experiment, 1984; The Spanish Civil War (ed.), 1986; The Chances of Death: A Diary of the Spanish Civil War (ed.), 1995; Visiones de fin de siglo, 1999; Spain: A History (ed.), 2001. Contributions: scholarly books and journals. *Honours:* Grand Cross of the Order of Alfonso el Sabio, 1983; Knighted, 1987; Hon. Fellow, University of Exeter, 1987, St Antony's College, Oxford, 1988; Order of Infante Dom Henrique, Portugal, 1989; Premio Príncipe de Asturias, 1999. *Address:* Burch, North Molton, South Molton EX36 3JU, England.

CARR, Roberta (see Roberts, Irene).

CARR, Terry (Gene), (Norman Edwards); Writer, Ed. and Lecturer; b. 19 Feb. 1937, Grants Pass, Oregon, USA. *Education:* AA, City College of San Francisco, 1957; University of California at Berkeley, 1957–59. *Career:* Ed., Ace Books, 1964–71, SFWA Bulletin, 1967–68; Founder, SFWA Forum, 1967–68. *Publications:* Warlord of Kor (with Ted White), 1963; World's Best Science Fiction (ed.), 7 vols, 1965–71; Universe (ed.), 13 vols, 1971–83; The Best Science Fiction of the Year (ed.), 13 vols, 1972–84; The Light at the End of the Universe (short stories), 1976; Cirque, 1977; Classic Science Fiction: The First Golden Age (ed.), 1978; The Year's Finest Fantasy (ed.), 1978–84; Between Two Worlds, 1986; Spill! The Story of the Exxon Valdez, 1991.

CARRIER, Roch; Author, Dramatist and Poet; b. 13 May 1937, Sainte-Justine-de-Dorchester, QC, Canada; m. Diane Gosselin, 1959, two d. *Education:* Collège Saint-Louis; BA, MA, University of Montréal; Doctoral Studies, Sorbonne, University of Paris. *Career:* Secretary-General, Théatre du Nouveau Monde, Montréal; Teacher, Collège Militaire, St-Jean; Dir, Canada Council, until 1997. *Publications:* Fiction: Jolis deuils, 1964; La guerre, yes sir!, 1968, English trans., 1970; Floralie, ou es-tu?, 1969, English trans. as Floralie, Where Are You?, 1971; Il est par la le soleil, 1970, English trans. as Is it the Sun, Philibert?, 1972; Le deux-millième é'tage, 1973, English trans. as They Won't Demolish Me!, 1974; Le jardin des délices, 1975, English trans. as The Garden of Delights, 1978; Les enfants du bonhomme dans la lune, 1979, English trans. as The Hockey Sweater and Other Stories, 1979; Il n'y a pas de pays sans grand-père, 1979, English trans. as No Country Without Grandfathers, 1981; Les fleurs vivent-elles ailleurs que sur la terre, 1980; La dame qui avait des chaines aux cheville, 1981; De l'amour dans la feraille, 1984, English trans. as Heartbreaks Along the Road, 1987; La fleur et autres personnages, 1985; Prières d'un enfant très très sage, 1988; L'homme dans le placard, 1991; Fin, 1992; The Longest Home Run, 1993; Petit homme tornade, 1996. Plays: La celeste bicyclette, 1980, English trans. as The Celestial Bycycle, 1982; Le cirque noir, 1982; L'ours et le kangourou, 1986. Other: various poems. *Honours:* Prix Littéraire de la Province de Québec, 1965; Grand Prix Littéraire de la Ville de Montréal, 1980; Québec Writer of the Year, 1981. *Address:* c/o Canada Council, 350 Albert St, PO Box 1047, Ottawa, ON K1P 5V8, Canada.

CARRIER, Warren (Pendleton); University Chancellor (retd), Writer and Poet; b. 3 July 1918, Cheviot, Ohio, USA; m. 1st Marjorie Jane Regan 3 April 1947 (deceased); one s.; m. 2nd Judy Lynn Hall 14 June 1973; one s. *Education:* Wabash College, 1938–40; AB, Miami University, Oxford, Ohio, 1942; MA, Harvard University, 1948; PhD, Occidental College, 1962. *Career:* Founder-Ed., Quarterly Review of Literature, 1943–44; Assoc. Ed., Western Review, 1949–51; Asst Prof., University of Iowa, 1949–52; Assoc. Prof., Bard College, 1953–57; Faculty, Bennington College, 1955–58; Visiting Prof., Sweet Briar College, 1958–60; Prof., Deep Springs College, CA, 1960–62, Portland State University, Oregon, 1962–64; Prof., Chair., Dept of English, University of Montana, 1964–68; Assoc. Dean, Prof. of English and Comparative Literature, Chair., Dept of Comparative Literature, Livingston College, Rutgers University, 1968–69; Dean, College of Arts and Letters, San Diego State University, 1969–72; Vice-Pres., Academic Affairs, University of Bridgeport, CT, 1972–75; Chancellor, University of Wisconsin at Platteville, 1975–82. *Publications:* City Stopped in Time, 1949; The Hunt, 1952; The Cost of Love, 1953; Reading Modern Poetry (co-ed.), 1955; Bay of the Damned, 1957; Toward Montebello, 1966; Leave Your Sugar for the Cold Morning, 1977; Guide to World Literature (ed.), 1980; Literature from the World (co-ed.), 1981; The Diver, 1986; Death of a Chancellor, 1986; An Honorable Spy, 1992; Murder at the Strawberry Festival, 1993; An Ordinary Man, 1997; Death of a Poet, 1999; Risking the Wind, 2000; Justice at Christmas, 2000. Contributions: periodicals. *Honours:* Award for Poetry, National Foundation for the Arts, 1971; Collady Prize for Poetry, 1986. *Address:* 69 Colony Park Circle, Galveston, TX 77551, USA.

CARRIÈRE, Jean Paul Jacques; Writer; b. 6 Aug. 1928, Nîmes, France; m. 1st Michèle Bollé, two s.; m. 2nd Françoise Battistini, 1978, one s. *Education:* Collège Saint Stanislas; Collège de l'Assomption; Lycée Aphonse Daudet, Nîmes. *Career:* mem. PEN Club. *Publications:* Les forêts du nouveau monde, 1956; Retour à Uzes, 1968; L'epervier de maheux, 1972; Jean Giono, 1973; L'univers de Jean Carrière, 1975; La caverne des pestiférés, two vols, 1978–79; Les années sauvages, 1986; Le prix du Goncourt, 1986; Le dernier été d'occident, 1987; Voyage d'hiver en Provence, 1987; Cévennes, 1988; Jean Fusaro, ou la peinture réhabilitée, 1988; Un grain de beauté sur la lune, 1990; Droits, devoirs et crocodile: Essai politique (co-author), 1992; L'indifférence des etoiles, 1994; Achigen, 1995; L'etoffe des rêves, 1996; L'empire des songes, 1998; Un jardin pour l'éternel, 1999; Le fer dans la plaie, 2000. *Honours:* Prix de l'Académie Française, 1968; Prix Goncourt, 1972; Prix du Roman de l'Été, 1999; Prix du Sud, 2000. *Address:* Les Broussanes, Domessargues, 30350 Ledignan, France.

CARRINGTON, Ruth (see James, Michael Leonard).

CARROLL, Jenny (see Cabot, Meggin (Meg) Patricia).

CARROLL, Martin (see Carr, Margaret).

CARROLL, Paul (Donnelly Michael); Prof. of English, Poet and Writer; b. 15 July 1927, Chicago, IL, USA; m. Maryrose Carroll, June 1979, one s. *Education:* MA, University of Chicago, 1952. *Career:* Poetry Ed., Chicago Review, 1957–59; Ed., Big Table Magazine, 1959–61, Big Table Books, Follett Publishing Company, 1966–71; Visiting Poet and Prof., University of Iowa, 1966–67; Prof. of English, University of Illinois, 1968–. *Publications:* Edward Dahlberg Reader (ed.), 1966; The Young American Poets, 1968; The Luke Poets, 1971; New and Selected Poems, 1978; The Garden of Earthly Delights, 1986; Poems, 1950–1990, 1990. Contributions: periodicals. *Address:* 1682 N Ada St, Chicago, IL 60622, USA.

CARRUTH, Hayden; poet, writer and academic; b. 3 Aug. 1921, Waterbury, CT, USA; m. 1st Sara Anderson 1943; one d.; m. 2nd Eleanor Ray 1952; m. 3rd Rose Marie Dorn 1961; one s.; m. 4th Joe-Anne McLaughlin 1989. *Education:* AB, University of North Carolina, 1943; MA, University of

Chicago, 1948. *Career:* Ed.-in-Chief, Poetry magazine, 1949–50; Assoc. Ed., University of Chicago Press, 1950–51; Project Administrator, Intercultural Publications Inc, New York City, 1952–53; Poet-in-Residence, Johnson State College, Vermont, 1972–74; Adjunct Prof., University of Vermont, 1975–78; Poetry Ed., Harper's magazine, 1977–83; Prof., 1979–85, 1986–91, Prof. Emeritus, 1991–, Syracuse University; Prof., Bucknell University, 1985–86. *Publications:* Poetry: The Crow and the Heart, 1946–1959, 1959; In Memoriam: G.V.C., 1960; Journey to a Known Place, 1961; The Norfolk Poems: 1 June to 1 September 1961, 1962; North Winter, 1964; Nothing for Tigers: Poems, 1959–1964, 1965; Contra Mortem, 1967; For You, 1970; The Clay Hill Anthology, 1970; From Snow and Rock, From Chaos: Poems, 1965–1972, 1973; Dark World, 1974; The Bloomingdale Papers, 1975; Loneliness: An Outburst of Hexasyllables, 1976; Aura, 1977; Brothers, I Loved You All, 1978; Almanach du Printemps Vivarois, 1979; The Mythology of Dark and Light, 1982; The Sleeping Beauty, 1983; If You Call This Cry a Song, 1983; Asphalt Georgics, 1985; Lighter Than Air Craft, 1985; The Oldest Killed Lake in North America, 1985; Mother, 1985; The Selected Poetry of Hayden Carruth, 1986; Sonnets, 1989; Tell Me Again How the White Heron Rises and Flies Across the Nacreous River at Twilight Toward the Distant Islands, 1989; Collected Shorter Poems, 1946–1991, 1992; Collected Longer Poems, 1994; Scrambled Eggs and Whiskey: Poems, 1991–1995, 1995; Dr Jazz, 2001. Other: Appendix A (novel), 1963; After 'The Stranger': Imaginary Dialogues with Camus, 1964; Working Papers: Selected Essays and Reviews, 1981; Effluences from the Sacred Caves: More Selected Essays and Reviews, 1984; Sitting In: Selected Writings on Jazz, Blues, and Related Topics, 1986; Beside the Shadblow Tree (memoir), 2000. Editor: A New Directions Reader (with James Laughlin), 1964; The Voice That is Great Within Us: American Poetry of the Twentieth Century, 1970; The Bird/Poem Book: Poems on the Wild Birds of North America, 1970. Contributions: various periodicals. *Honours:* Bess Hokin Prize, 1954; Vachel Lindsay Prize, 1956; Levinson Prize, 1958; Harriet Monroe Poetry Prize, 1960; Bollingen Foundation Fellowship, 1962; Helen Bullis Award, 1962; Carl Sandburg Award, 1963; Emily Clark Balch Prize, 1964; Eunice Tietjens Memorial Prize, 1964; Guggenheim Fellowships, 1965, 1979; Morton Dauwen Zabel Prize, 1967; National Endowment for the Humanities Fellowship, 1967; Governor's Medal, Vermont, 1974; Sheele Memorial Award, 1978; Lenore Marshall Poetry Prize, 1978; Whiting Writers Award, 1986; National Endowment for the Arts Senior Fellowship, 1988; Ruth Lilly Poetry Prize, 1990; National Book Critics Circle Award in Poetry, 1993; National Book Award for Poetry, 1996. *Address:* RR 1, PO Box 128, Munnsville, NY 13409, USA.

CARRUTHERS, Peter (Michael); Philosopher, Prof. and Writer; b. 16 June 1952, Manila, Philippines; m. Susan Levi, 21 Oct. 1978, two s. *Education:* University of Leeds, 1971–77; Balliol College, Oxford, 1977–79. *Career:* Lecturer, University of St Andrews, 1979–81, Queens University of Belfast, 1981–83, University of Essex, 1985–91; Visiting Prof., University of Michigan, 1989–90; Senior Lecturer, 1991–92, Prof., 1992–, University of Sheffield; mem. Aristotelian Society. *Publications:* The Metaphysics of the Tractatus, 1990; Introducing Persons: Theories and Arguments in the Philosophy of Mind, 1991; Human Knowledge and Human Nature: A New Introduction to the Ancient Debate, 1992; The Animals Issue: Moral Theory in Practice, 1992. Contributions: journals. *Address:* Dept of Philosophy, University of Sheffield, Sheffield S10 2TN, England.

CARSON, Anne, MA, PhD; Canadian professor of classics, poet and writer; *John MacNaughton Professor of Classics, McGill University*; b. 21 June 1950, Toronto, ON. *Education:* Univ. of Toronto. *Career:* Prof. of Classics, Univ. of Calgary 1979–80, Princeton Univ. 1980–87, Emory Univ. 1987–88; John MacNaughton Prof. of Classics, McGill Univ. 1988–, Dir of Grad. Studies, Classics; Guggenheim Fellowship 1999; John D. and Catherine T. MacArthur Foundation Fellowship 2001. *Publications:* Eros the Bittersweet: An Essay 1986, Short Talks 1992, Plainwater 1995, Glass, Irony and God 1995, Autobiography of Red 1998, Economy of the Unlost 1999, Men in the Off Hours (Griffin Poetry Prize 2001) 2000, The Beauty of the Husband (Poetry Book Soc. T. S. Eliot Prize 2001) 2001, Sophocles' Electra 2001, If Not, Winter: Fragments of Sappho (trans.) 2002; contribs to anthologies and journals. *Honours:* Lannan Literary Award 1996, Pushcart Prize for Poetry 1997. *Address:* Department of Classics, Room 823, Stephen Leacock Building, 855 Sherbrooke Street West, Montréal, QC H3A 2T7 (Office); 5900 Esplanade Avenue, Montréal, QC H2T 3A3, Canada (Home). *E-mail:* decreation@hotmail.com (Office).

CARSON, Paul; Northern Irish doctor and novelist; b. 1950, Belfast, Co. Down. *Education:* Garron Tower school. *Publications:* novels: Scalpel 1997, Cold Steel 1999, Final Duty 2000, Ambush 2004; poetry: Size of Happiness 2003, Zero Meridian 2004. *Address:* c/o William Heinemann, Random House UK Ltd, 20 Vauxhall Bridge Road, London, SW1V 2SA, England. *Website:* www.randomhouse.co.uk.

CARTANO, Tony; Author and Ed.; b. 27 July 1944, Bayonne, France; m. Françoise Perrin, 10 Nov. 1966, one s. one d. *Education:* Licence es Lettres, 1964, Diploma d'Études Supérieures, 1965, University of Paris. *Career:* Dir, Foreign Dept, Editions Albin Michel, Paris. *Publications:* Le Single Hurteur, 1978; Malcolm Lowry (essay), 1979; Blackbird, 1980; La Sourde Oreille, 1982; Schmutz, 1987; Le Bel Arturo, 1989; Le soufflé de Satan, 1991; American Boulevard (travel book), 1992. *Honours:* Chevalier, Ordre des Arts et des Lettres.

CARTER, (Edward) Graydon; American magazine editor; b. 14 July 1949; m. Cynthia Williamson 1982; three s. one d. *Education:* Carleton Univ.; Univ. of Ottawa. *Career:* Ed. The Canadian Review 1973–77; writer Time 1978–83, Life 1983–86; f., Ed. Spy 1986–91; Ed. New York Observer 1991–92; Ed.-in-Chief Vanity Fair 1992–; Hon. Ed. Harvard Lampoon 1989. *Address:* Vanity Fair, Condé Nast Bldg, 4 Times Square, New York, NY 10036-6522, USA.

CARTER, Nick (see Lynds, Dennis).

CARTER, Robert Ayres, AB; writer and lecturer; b. 16 Sept. 1923, Omaha, NE, USA; m. 1983; two s. *Education:* New School for Social Research, New York. *Career:* mem. Poets and Writers; MWA; International Asscn of Crime Writers; The Players, life mem. *Publications:* Manhattan Primitive, 1972; Written in Blood, 1992, US edn as Casual Slaughters; Final Edit, 1994; Three Textbooks. Contributions: Publishers Weekly; International Journal of Book Publishing. *Honours:* Fulbright Scholar 1949. *Address:* 510 N Meadow Street, Richmond, VA 23220, USA.

CARTER, Stephen Lisle, BA, JD; American author and professor of law; *William Nelson Cromwell Professor of Law, Yale University*; b. 1954, Washington, DC; m.; c. *Education:* Stanford and Yale Univs. *Career:* fmr Note Ed. Yale Law Journal; admitted to Bar, Washington, DC 1981; law clerk, Judge Spottswood W. Robinson III, US Court of Appeal, Washington, DC 1979–80; law clerk, Justice Thurgood Marshall, US Supreme Court 1980–81; Assoc. Shea & Gardner, Washington, DC 1981–82; Asst Prof. of Law, Yale Univ. 1982–84, Assoc. Prof. 1984–85, Prof. 1986–91, William Nelson Cromwell Prof. of Law 1991–; Official Adviser to US Pres. Bill Clinton 1993. *Publications include:* Reflections of an Affirmative Action Baby 1991, The Culture of Disbelief 1993, The Confirmation Mess 1994, Integrity 1996, The Dissent of the Governed 1998, Civility 1998, God's Name in Vain 2000, The Emperor of Ocean Park 2002. *Honours:* Hon. LLD (Univ. of Notre Dame) 1996. *Address:* Yale Law School, POB 208215, New Haven, CT 06520 (Office); c/o Knopf Publishing (Author Mail), 1745 Broadway, New York, NY 10019, USA (Office). *E-mail:* stephen.carter@yale.edu (Office). *Website:* www.yale.edu (Office).

CARTWRIGHT, Justin, (Suzy Crispin, Penny Sutton); Writer; b. 1933, South Africa. *Education:* University of Oxford. *Publications:* Fighting Men, 1977; The Revenge, 1978; The Horse of Darius, 1980; Freedom for the Wolves, 1983; Interior, 1988; Look at It This Way, 1990; Masai Dreaming, 1993; In Every Face I Meet, 1995; Not Yet Home, 1996; Leading the Cheers, 1999; Half in Love, 2002; White Lightning, 2002. *Literary Agent:* PFD, Drury House, 34–43 Russell St, London WC2B 5HA, England.

CARWARDINE, Richard John; academic and writer; b. 12 Jan. 1947, Cardiff, Wales; m. Linda Margaret Kirk 1975. *Education:* BA, Univ. of Oxford, 1968; MA, 1972; DPhil, 1975. *Career:* Lecturer, Senior Lecturer, Reader, Prof., Univ. of Sheffield, 1971–2002; Visiting Prof., Syracuse Univ., New York, 1974–75; Visiting Fellow, Univ. of North Carolina, Chapel Hill, 1989; Rhodes Prof. of American History, Univ. of Oxford, 2002–. *Publications:* Transatlantic Revivalism: Popular Evangelicalism in Britain and America 1790–1865, 1978; Evangelicals and Politics in Antebellum America, 1993; Lincoln, 2003. *Address:* St Catherine's College, University of Oxford, Oxford OX1 3UJ, England.

CARY, Jud (see Tubb, Edwin Charles).

CARY, Lorene (Emily); Writer; b. 29 Nov. 1956, Philadelphia, Pennsylvania, USA; m. R. C. Smith 27 Aug. 1983; two d. one step-s. *Education:* BA, MA, 1978, University of Pennsylvania; MA, University of Sussex, 1979. *Career:* Assoc. Ed., TV Guide, 1980–82; Contributing Ed., Newsweek Magazine, 1991; Lecturer, University of Pennsylvania, 1995–; mem. PEN; Authors' Guild. *Publications:* Black Ice, 1991; The Price of a Child, 1995; Pride, 1998. *Honours:* Hon. Doctorate of Letters. *Address:* Dept of English, University of Pennsylvania, 34th and Walnut Sts, Philadelphia, PA 19104, USA.

CASEY, John Dudley; writer and academic; b. 18 Jan. 1939, Worcester, Massachusetts, USA; m. Rosamond Pinchot Pittman 1982; four d. *Education:* BA, Harvard College, 1962; LLB, Harvard Law School, 1965; MFA, University of Iowa, 1967. *Career:* Prof., University of Virginia, 1972–92, 1999–; mem. PEN. *Publications:* An American Romance, 1977; Testimony and Demeanor, 1979; Spartina, 1989; Supper at the Black Pearl, 1996; The Half-Life of Happiness, 1998. Contributions: Stories, articles and reviews in newspapers and magazines. *Honours:* Guggenheim Fellowship, 1979–80; Friends of American Writers Award, 1980; National Endowment for the Arts Fellowship, 1983; National Book Award, 1989; O. Henry Award, 1989; Ingram Merril Fellowship, 1990; Residency, American Acad. in Rome, 1990–91. *Address:* c/o Michael Carlisle, 24 E 64th Street, New York, NY 10021, USA.

CASS, Sir Geoffrey Arthur, Kt, MA, CCMI; British publishing executive and arts and lawn tennis administrator; b. 11 Aug. 1932, Bishop Auckland; m. Olwen Mary Richards, JP, DL 1957; four d. *Education:* Queen Elizabeth Grammar School, Darlington and Jesus Coll., Oxford. *Career:* Nuffield Coll., Oxford 1957–58; RAF 1958–60; ed. Automation 1960–61; Consultant, PA Man. Consultants Ltd 1960–65; Pvt. Man. Consultant, British Communications Corpn and Controls and Communications Ltd 1965; Dir Controls and Communications Ltd 1966–69; Dir George Allen & Unwin 1965–67,

Man. Dir 1967–71; Dir Weidenfeld Publrs. 1972–74, Univ. of Chicago Press, UK 1971–86; Chief Exec. Cambridge Univ. Press 1972–92, Consultant 1992–; Sec. Press Syndicate, Univ. of Cambridge 1974–92; Univ. Printer 1982–83, 1991–92; Fellow, Clare Hall, Cambridge 1979–; Trustee Shakespeare Birthplace Trust 1982–94 (Life Trustee 1994–); Chair. Royal Shakespeare Co. 1985–2000 (Deputy Pres. 2000–), Royal Shakespeare Theatre Trust 1983–, British Int. Tennis and Nat. Training 1985–90, Nat. Ranking Cttee; mem. Bd of Man., Lawn Tennis Asscn of GB 1985–90, 1993–2000, Deputy Pres. 1994–96, Pres. 1997–99, Chair. British Tennis Foundation 2003–; mem. Cttee of Man., Wimbledon Championships 1990–2002; Pres., Chair. or mem. numerous other trusts, bds, cttees, charitable appeals and advisory bodies particularly in connection with theatre, sport and medicine; Oxford tennis Blue and badminton; played in Wimbledon Tennis Championships 1954, 1955, 1956, 1959; British Veterans Singles Champion, Wimbledon 1978. *Publications:* articles in professional journals. *Honours:* Hon. Fellow, Jesus Coll., Oxford 1998; Chevalier, Ordre des Arts et Lettres. *Address:* Middlefield, Huntingdon Road, Cambridge, CB3 0LH, England.

CASS, Zoe (see Low, Lois Dorothea).

CASSELLS, Cyrus Curtis; Poet, Teacher and Trans; b. 16 May 1957, Dover, DE, USA. *Education:* BA, Stanford University, 1979. *Career:* mem. PEN; Poetry Society of America. *Publications:* The Mud Actor, 1982; Soul Make a Path Through Shouting, 1994; Beautiful Signor, 1997. Contributions: Southern Review; Callaloo; Translation; Seneca Review; Quilt; Sequoia. *Honours:* Acad. of American Poets Prize, 1979; National Poetry Series Winner, 1982; Callaloo Creative Writing Award, 1983; Massachusetts Artists Foundation Fellowship, 1985; National Endowment for the Arts Fellowship, 1986; Lavan Younger Poets Award, 1992; Lannan Award, 1993; William Carlos Williams Award, 1994. *Address:* c/o Mary Cassells, 2190 Belden Pl., Escondido, CA 92029, USA.

CASTANEDA, Omar; Prof. and Writer; b. 6 Sept. 1954, Guatemala City, Guatemala; m. 1st 11 Aug. 1984; m. 2nd 26 Feb. 1992, one s. one d. *Education:* BA, 1980, MFA, 1983, Indiana University. *Career:* Prof., University of Washington; mem. MLA; PEN. *Publications:* Remembering to Say Mouth or Face, 1993; Imagining Isabel, 1994. Contributions: many periodicals. *Honours:* various awards. *Address:* Dept of English, Western Washington University, Bellingham, WA 98225, USA.

CASTEL, Albert Edward; historian and academic; b. 11 Nov. 1928, Wichita, KS, USA; m. GeorgeAnn Bennett 1959; one s. one d. *Education:* BA, 1950, MA, 1951, Wichita State University; PhD, University of Chicago, 1955. *Career:* Instructor, University of California at Los Angeles, 1957–58; Asst Prof., Waynesburg College, Pennsylvania, 1958–60; Asst Prof., 1960–63, Assoc. Prof., 1963–67, Prof., 1967–91, Western Michigan University. *Publications:* A Frontier State of War, 1958; William Clarke Quantrill, 1962; Sterling Price and the Civil War in the West, 1968; The Guerrilla War, 1974; The Yeas and Nays: Key Congressional Votes (co-author), 1975; Fort Sumter: 1861, 1976; The Presidency of Andrew Johnson, 1979; Decision in the West: The Atlanta Campaign of 1864, 1992; Winning and Losing in the Civil War: Essays and Stories, 1996; Bloody Bill Anderson (co-author), 1998; Tom Taylor's Civil War, 2000; Articles of War, 2001. Contributions: many scholarly journals. *Honours:* Albert J. Beveridge Award, American Historical Asscn, 1957; Best Author Award, Civil War Times Illustrated, 1979; Peterson Award, Eastern National Park and Monument Asscn, 1989; Harwell Award, Atlanta Civil War Round Table, 1993; Lincoln Prize, Gettysburg College, 1993; Truman Award, Civil War Round Table of Kansas City, 1994. *Address:* 166 Westwood Drive, Hillsdale, MI 49242, USA.

CASTEL-BLOOM, Orley; Israeli novelist; b. 1960, Tel-Aviv. *Education:* Tel-Aviv Univ. *Publications:* novels: Heichan Ani Nimtzet (trans. as Where Am I?) 1990, Dolly City 1992, Ha-Mina Lisa (trans. as The Mina Lisa) 1995, Taking the Trend 1998, Human Parts 2002; short story collections: Not Far from the Centre of Town 1987, Hostile Surroundings 1989, Unbidden Stories 1993, Free Radicals 2000, Selected Stories 1987–2004 2004; juvenile: Let's Behave Ourselves 1997. *Honours:* Tel-Aviv Prize for Literature 1990, Newman Prize 2003. *Address:* c/o Jewish Book Council, PO Box 38247, London, NW3 5YQ, England.

CASTELL, Megan (see Williams, Jeanne R.).

CASTILLO, Michel Xavier Janicot del; Author; b. 2 Aug. 1933, Madrid, Spain. *Education:* Jesuit College, Ubeba, Spain; Lycée Janson-de-Sailly, Paris. *Career:* mem. PEN; Société des Gens de Lettres. *Publications:* Tanguy, 1957; La guitare, 1958; Le colleur d'affiches, 1959; Le manège espagnol, 1960; Tara, 1962; Gerardo Laïn, 1969; Le vent de la nuit, 1973; Le silence des pierres, 1975; Le sortilège espagnol, 1977; Les Cyprés meurent en Italie, 1979; Les louves de l'escurial, 1980; La nuit du décret, 1981; La gloire de Dina, 1984; Nos Andalousies, 1985; Le démon de l'oubli, 1987; Mort d'un poète, 1989; Une femme en soi, 1991; Le crime des pères, 1993; Rue des archives, 1994; Mon frère l'idiot, 1995; La tunique d'infamie, 1997; De père français, 1998; Colette, une certaine France, 1999; L'adieu au siècle, 2000. *Honours:* Prix des Neufs, 1957; Prix des Magots, 1973; Grand Prix des Libraires, 1973; Prix Chateaubriand, 1975; Prix Renaudot, 1981; Prix Maurice Genevoix, 1994; Prix Femina, 1999; Chevalier, Légion d'honneur; Commdr, Ordre des Arts et des Lettres.

CASTLEDEN, Rodney; Geomorphologist, Writer, Archaeologist and Composer; b. 23 March 1945, Worthing, Sussex, England; m. Sarah Dee, 29 July 1987. *Education:* BA, Geography, Hertford College, 1967, Dip Ed, 1968, MA, 1972, MSc, Geomorphology, 1980, University of Oxford. *Career:* mem. Geological Society, fellow; FRGS; Society of Authors. *Publications:* Classic Landforms of the Sussex Coast, 1982; The Wilmington Giant: The Quest for a Lost Myth, 1983; Classic Landforms Series (ed.), 1983–99; The Stonehenge People: An Exploration of Life in Neolithic Britain, 1987; The Knossos Labyrinth, 1989; Minoans: Life in Bronze Age Crete, 1990; Book of British Dates, 1991; Neolithic Britain, 1992; The Making of Stonehenge, 1993; World History: A Chronological Dictionary of Dates, 1994; British History: A Chronological Dictionary of Dates, 1994; The Cerne Giant, 1996; Knossos, Temple of the Goddess, 1996; Atlantis Destroyed, 1998; Out in the Cold, 1998; The English Lake District, 1998; The Search for King Arthur, 1999; Ancient British Hill Figures, 2000; Winfrith (opera), 2000; The Concise Encyclopedia of World History, 2003; The Concise Encyclopedia of British History, 2003; History of World Events, 2003; Britain 3000 BC, 2003. Contributions: 90 articles published in various journals and magazines. *Address:* 15 Knepp Close, Brighton, Sussex, BN2 4LD, England. *E-mail:* rodney@castledean.fsnet.co.uk.

CASTRO, Brian (Albert); Writer and Teacher; b. 16 Jan. 1950, Kowloon, Hong Kong; m. Josephine Mary Gardiner, 10 Aug. 1976. *Education:* MA, University of Sydney, 1976. *Career:* Journalist, Asiaweek, Hong Kong, 1983–87, All-Asia Review of Books, Hong Kong, 1989–; Writer-in-Residence, Mitchell College, NSW, 1985; Visiting Fellow, Nepean College, Kingswood, NSW, 1988; Tutor in Literary Studies, University of Western Australia, 1989–. *Publications:* Birds of Passage, 1982; Pomeroy, 1991; Double-Wolf, 1991; After China, 1992; Drift, 1994; Stepper, 1998. Contributions: anthologies and periodicals. *Honours:* several, including Book of the Year Award, 1992. *Address:* c/o Allen and Unwin Ltd, 8 Napier St, North Sydney, NSW 2059, Australia.

CAULDWELL, Frank (see King, Francis Henry).

CAUTE, (John) David, DPhil, FRSL; writer; b. 16 Dec. 1936, Alexandria, Egypt. *Education:* Wadham College, Oxford. *Career:* Fellow, All Soul's College, Oxford, 1959–65; Visiting Prof., New York and Columbia Univs, 1966–67; Reader in Social and Political Theory, Brunel Univ., 1967–70; Regent's Lecturer, Univ. of California, 1974; Literary and Arts Ed., New Statesman, London, 1979–80; Co-Chair., Writers Guild of Great Britain, 1981–82. *Publications:* At Fever Pitch, 1959; Comrade Jacob, 1961; Communism and the French Intellectuals 1914–1960, 1964; The Decline of the West, 1966; The Left in Europe Since 1789, 1966; Essential Writings of Karl Marx (ed.), 1967; The Fanon, 1970; Demonstration, 1971; The Occupation, 1971; The Illusion, 1971; The Fellow-Travellers, 1973; Collisions: Essays and Reviews, 1974; Cuba Yes?, 1974; The Great Fear: The Anti-Communist Purge Under Truman and Eisenhower, 1978; The K-Factor, 1983; Under the Skin: The Death of White Rhodesia, 1983; The Espionage of The Saints, 1986; News From Nowhere, 1986; Sixty-Eight: The Year of the Barricades, 1988; Veronica of the Two Nations, 1989; The Women's Hour, 1991; Joseph Losey: A Revenge on Life, 1994; Orwell and Mr Blair, 1994; Fatima's Scarf, 1998; The Dancer Defects: The Struggle for Cultural Supremacy During the Cold War, 2003. Radio Plays: The Demonstration, 1971; Fallout, 1972; The Zimbabwe Tapes, 1983; Henry and the Dogs, 1986; Sanctions, 1988; Animal Fun Park, 1995. *Address:* 41 Westcroft Square, London W6 0TA, England.

CEDERING, Siv; Writer, Poet and Artist; b. 5 Feb. 1939, Sweden; one s. two d. *Career:* mem. Co-ordinating Council of Literary Magazines; PEN; Poetry Society of America; Poets and Writers. *Publications:* Mother Is, 1975; The Juggler, 1977; The Blue Horse, 1979; Oxen, 1981; Letters from the Floating Worlds, 1984. Contributions: Harper's; Ms; New Republic; Paris Review; Partisan Review; New York Times; Georgia Review; Fiction Interntional Shenandoah; Confrontation; Over 80 anthologies and textbooks. *Honours:* New York Foundation Fellowships, 1985, 1992. *Address:* PO Box 800, Amagansett, NY 11930, USA.

CELATI, Gianni; Novelist; b. 1937, Sondrio, Ferrara, Italy. *Career:* Lecturer in Anglo-American Literature, University of Bologna. *Publications:* Comiche, 1971; Le avventure di Guizzardi, 1971; Il chiodo in testa, 1975; Finzioni occidentali, 1975; La banda dei sospiri, 1976; La bottega dei mimi, 1977; Lunario del paradiso, 1978; Narratori delle pianure, 1985; Quattro novelle sulle apparenze, 1987; Verso la foce, 1989; Parlamenti buffi, 1989; Profili delle nuvole, 1989. Other: Ed. and trans. *Honours:* Mondello Prize, 1990. *Address:* c/o Feltrinelli, Via Andegari 6, 20121 Milan, Italy.

CERCAS, Javier; Spanish novelist; b. 1962. *Career:* teacher, Univ. of Illinois –1989; Lecturer in Spanish Literature, Univ. of Gerona 1989–. *Publications:* El móvil (trans. as The Motive) 1987, El inquilino (trans. as The Tenant) 1989, La obra literaria de Gonzalo Suárez 1993, El vientre de la balleria (trans. as The Belly of the Whale) 1997, Relatos reales (trans. as True Tales) 2000, Soldados de Salamina (trans. as Soldiers of Salamis) (Independent Foreign Fiction Prize 2004) 2001; contrib. to El País (Catalan edn). *Honours:* Premi Libreter, Premi Ciutat de Barcelona, Premio de la Crítica de Chile, Premio Salambó, Premio Qué Leer, Premio Extremadura, Premio Grinzane-Cavour. *Address:* c/o Bloomsbury Publishing PLC, 38 Soho Square, London, W1V 5DF, England. *Website:* www.bloomsbury.com.

CERONETTI, Guido; Italian writer, philosopher, poet and translator; b. 1927, Turin. *Publications:* La carta è stanca 1976, La musa ulcerosa: Scritti vari e inediti 1978, Un viaggio in Italia 1981-83 1983, Albergo Italia 1985, Briciole di colonna 1987, Aquilegia: Favola sommersa 1988, Amor di busta 1991, Silence of the Body: Materials for the Study of Medicine (co-author) 1993, N.U.E.D.D. (Nuovi ultimi esasperati deliri disarmati) 2001. *Address:* c/o Einaudi Editore, Via Biancamo 2, 10121 Turin, Italy.

CÉSAIRE, Aimé Fernand, LèsL; French politician, poet and dramatist; b. 25 June 1913, Basse-Pointe, Martinique; m. Suzanne Roussi 1937; four s. two d. *Education:* Fort-de-France, Martinique and Lycée Louis-le-Grand, Paris, Ecole Normale Supérieure and the Sorbonne. *Career:* teaching career 1940–45; mem. Constituent Assemblies 1945 and 1946; Deputy for Martinique 1946–93; Pres. Parti Progressiste Martiniquais; Mayor of Fort-de-France 1945–2001; Pres. Conseil régional, Martinique 1983–86; Pres. Soc. of African Culture, Paris. *Publications:* verse: Les armes miraculeuses 1946, Cahier d'un retour au pays natal 1947, Soleil cou coupé 1948, Corps perdu 1960, Ferrements 1960, Cadastre 1961, L'Etat de l'union 1966, Moi, laminaire 1982; poetry: Aimé Césaire: The Collected Poetry 1983, Oeuvres complètes et inédites 1994; essays: Discours sur le colonialisme; plays: Et les chiens se taisaient 1956, La tragédie du roi Christophe 1964, Une saison au Congo 1966, Une tempête (adaptation of Shakespeare) 1969; other: Toussaint L'ouverture: La révolution française et le problème colonial 1960. *Honours:* Grand Prize for Verse 1982. *Address:* c/o La Mairie, boulevard de général de Gaulle, 97200 Fort-de-France, Martinique, West Indies.

CHABON, Michael, MFA; American writer; b. 1964, Columbia, Md; m.; one s. one d. *Education:* Univ. of Pittsburgh, Univ. of Calif., Irvine. *Publications:* The Mysteries of Pittsburgh 1988, A Model World (short stories) 1991, Wonder Boys 1995 (film 2000), Werewolves in Their Youth (short stories) 1995, The Amazing Adventures of Kavalier & Clay 2000 (Pulitzer Prize for fiction 2001); short stories published in several magazines. *Honours:* Publishers Weekly Best Book 1995, New York Times Notable Book 1995, O. Henry Award 1999. *Literary Agent:* Steven Barclay Agency, 12 Western Avenue, Petaluma, CA 94952, USA. *Telephone:* (707) 773-0654. *Fax:* (707) 778-1868. *Website:* www.barclayagency.com.

CHADWICK, Cydney; Writer and Ed.; b. 12 July 1959, Oakland, CA, USA. *Education:* Sonoma State University; Kootenay School of Writing, 1996. *Career:* Regional Sales Man., Chadwick Marketing, Penngrove, CA, 1984–92; Exec. Dir, Syntax Projects for the Arts; Freelance Typesetter, Designer, Ed. and Manuscript Consultant; mem. PEN West. *Publications:* Enemy Clothing, stories; 1993; Dracontic Nodes (chapbook), 1993; Persistent Disturbances, stories, chapbook, 1994; Oeuvres, story, chapbook, 1994; The Gift Horse's Mouth, story, chapbook, 1995; Interims, stories, chapbook, 1997; Inside the Hours, fiction, 1998; Benched, novella, 2000; Flesh and Bone, 2001. *Honours:* Gertrude Stein Award in Innovative Writing, 1995; Fellow, California Arts Council, 1997; New American Writing Award in Fiction, 1998; Creative Writing Fellowship, National Endowment for the Arts, 2001; Independent Book Publishers' Award, 2002. *Address:* PO Box 1059, Penngrove, CA 94951, USA. *E-mail:* aveclivres@yahoo.com.

CHADWICK, Geoffrey (see Wall, Geoffrey).

CHADWICK, Sir Henry; Prof. of Divinity Emeritus and Writer; b. 23 June 1920, Bromley, Kent, England; m. Margaret Elizabeth Brownrigg, 1945, three d. *Education:* BA and BMus, Magdalene College, Cambridge, 1941. *Career:* Asst Master, Wellington College, 1945; Fellow, 1946–58, Junior Proctor, 1948–49, Queens' College, Cambridge; Ed., Journal of Theological Studies, 1954–85; Regius Prof. of Divinity and Canon, 1959–69, Dean, 1969–79, Christ Church, Oxford; Delegate, OUP, 1960–79; Gifford Lecturer, University of St Andrews, 1962–64; Birkbeck Lecturer, 1965, Regius Prof. of Divinity, 1979–83, Prof. Emeritus, 1983–, University of Cambridge; Pro-Vice-Chancellor, 1974–75, Sarum Lecturer, 1982–83, University of Oxford; Fellow, Eton, 1976–79, Magdalene College, Cambridge, 1979–87; Master, Peterhouse, Cambridge, 1987–93; mem. American Acad. of Arts and Sciences, foreign hon. mem.; American Philosophical Society; Correspondant de l'Académie des Inscriptions et des Belles Lettres, Institut de France. *Publications:* Contra Celsum, by Origen (trans.), 1953; Alexandrian Christianity (with J. E. L. Oulton), 1954; Lessing's Theological Writings, 1956; The Sentences of Sextus, 1959; Early Christian Thought and the Classical Tradition, 1966; The Early Church, 1967; The Treatise on the Apostolic Tradition of St Hippolytus of Rome, ed. by G. Dix, revised edn, 1968; Some Reflections on Conscience, 1969; Enigma of Saint Paul, 1969; Priscillian of Avila, 1976; Boethius, 1981; History and Thought of the Early Church, 1982; Augustine, 1986; Atlas of the Christian Church (ed.), 1987; Originality of Early Christian Ethics, 1990; History of Christianity 1: The Early Church, 1990; Saint Augustine: Confessions (trans.), 1991; Heresy and Orthodoxy in the Early Church, 1991; The Penguin History of the Church Vol. 1: The Story of Emergent Christianity from the Apostolic Age to the Dividing of the Ways Between the Greek East and the Latin West, 1993; Tradition and Exploration, 1994; Not Angels but Anglicans, 1999; Augustine: A Very Short Introduction, 2000; The Church in Ancient Society: From Galilee to Gregory the Great, 2001. Contributions: The Oxford History of the Classical World, 1986; The Oxford Illustrated History of Christianity, 1990; The Cambridge Ancient History, Vol. XIII, 1997. *Honours:* Hon. Fellow, Queens' College, Cambridge, 1958, Magdalene College, Cambridge, 1962, St Anne's College, Oxford, 1979, Trinity College, Cambridge, 1987, Peterhouse, Cambridge, 1993; Fellow, British Acad., 1960; Humboldt Prize, 1983; KBE, 1989; Lucas Prize, Tübingen, 1991; Orden pour le mérite für Wissenschaften und Künste, Germany, 1993. *Address:* 46 St John St, Oxford OX1 2LH, England.

CHADWICK, (William) Owen; historian; b. 20 May 1916, Bromley, Kent, England; m. Ruth Hallward 1949; two s. two d. *Education:* BA, 1939, St John's College, Cambridge. *Career:* Dean, Trinity Hall, 1949–56, Master, Selwyn College, 1956–83, Dixie Prof. of Ecclesiastical History, 1958–68, Regius Prof. of Modern History, 1968–83, Vice-Chancellor, 1969–71, University of Cambridge; Chancellor, University of East Anglia, 1985–94; mem. Fellow, British Acad.; FRHistS. *Publications:* John Cassian, 1950; The Founding of Cuddesdon, 1954; From Bossuet to Newman, 1957; Western Asceticism, 1958; Creighton on Luther, 1959; Mackenzie's Grave, 1959; Victorian Miniature, 1960; The Mind of the Oxford Movement, 1960; From Uniformity to Unity 1662–1962 (with G. Nuttall), 1962; Westcott and the University, 1962; The Reformation, 1964; The Victorian Church, Vol. 1, 1966, Vol. II, 1970; Acton and Gladstone, 1976; The Oxford History of the Christian Church (ed. with Henry Chadwick), 1976–; The Secularization of the European Mind, 1977; Catholicism and History, 1978; The Popes and European Revolution, 1981; Newman, 1983; Hensley Henson: A Study in the Friction Between Church and State, 1983; Britain and the Vatican in the Second World War, 1986; Michael Ramsey, 1990; The Spirit of the Oxford Movement: Tractarian Essays, 1990; The Christian Church in the Cold War, 1992; A History of Christianity, 1995; A History of the Popes 1830–1914, 1998; Acton and History, 1998; The Early Reformation on the Continent, 2001. Contributions: Times (London); New Statesman; Spectator; Guardian; Sunday Times; Observer; History journals. *Honours:* Wolfson Prize for History, 1981; Knighted, 1982; Order of Merit, 1983. *Address:* 67 Grantchester Street, Cambridge CB3 9HZ, England.

CHADWICK, Whitney; Prof. of Art and Writer; b. 28 July 1943, Niagara Falls, New York, USA; m. Robert A Bechtle, 6 Nov. 1982. *Education:* BA, Middlebury College, 1965; MA, 1968, PhD, 1975, Pennsylvania State University. *Career:* Lecturer, 1972, Asst Prof., 1973–77, Assoc. Prof., 1978, MIT; Visiting Asst Prof. of Art History, University of California at Berkeley, 1977; Assoc. Prof., 1978–82, Prof. of Art, 1982–, San Francisco State University; Eleanor Tufts Distinguished Visiting Lecturer, Southern Methodist University, 1995; Visiting Prof., Massachusetts College of Art, 1996; Visiting Scholar, Institute for Research on Women and Gender, Stanford University, 1997–98. *Publications:* Myth and Surrealist Painting, 1929–1939, 1980; Women Artists and the Surrealist Movement, 1985; Women, Art, and Society, 1990; Significant Others: Creativity and Intimate Partnership, 1993; Leonora Carrington: La Realidad de la Imaginacion, 1995; Framed, 1998; Mirror Images: Women, Surrealism and Self-Represéntaion (ed.), 1998. Contributions: Books, scholarly journals, and exhibition catalogues; Oxford Art Journal. *Honours:* National Endowment for the Humanities Fellowship, 1981–82; British Council Travel Grant, 1994. *Address:* 871 De Haro St, San Francisco, CA 94107, USA.

CHAGALL, David; Author and Journalist; b. 22 Nov. 1930, Philadelphia, Pennsylvania, USA; m. Juneau Joan Alsin, 15 Nov. 1957. *Education:* Swarthmore College, 1948–49; BA, Pennsylvania State University, 1952; Sorbonne, University of Paris. *Career:* Assoc. Ed., IEE, 1960–61; Investigative Reporter, Nation Magazine, 1975–; Ed., Publisher, Inside Campaigning, 1984; Contributing Ed., Los Angeles Magazine, 1986–89; Host, TV Series, The Last Hour, 1994–; Chair., Selective Service Board, 1999; mem. Authors' Guild; American Acad. of Political Science. *Publications:* The Century God Slept, 1963; Diary of a Deaf Mute, 1971; The Spieler for the Holy Spirit, 1972; The New Kingmakers, 1981; Television Today, 1981; The Sunshine Road, 1988; The World's Greatest Comebacks, 1989; Surviving the Media Jungle, 1996; Media and Morality, 1999; Target: Special Victims of the Holocaust, 2000. Contributions: periodicals. *Honours:* Carnegie Award, 1964; National Book Award, 1972; Health Journalism Award, 1980; Presidential Achievement Award, 1982. *Address:* PO Box 85, Agoura Hills, CA 91376, USA. *E-mail:* dchagall@aol.com.

CHAKRAVARTI, Sasthibrata (see Brata, Sasthi).

CHALFONT, Baron (Life Peer), cr. 1964; **(Arthur) Alun Gwynne Jones,** PC, OBE, MC, FRSA; British politician and writer; b. 5 Dec. 1919, Lantarnam, Wales; m. Dr Mona Mitchell 1948; one d. (deceased). *Education:* West Monmouth School. *Career:* commissioned into S. Wales Borderers (24th Foot) 1940; served in Burma 1941–44, Malaya 1955–57, Cyprus 1958–59; resgnd comm. 1961; Defence Corresp. The Times, London 1961–64; Consultant on foreign affairs to BBC TV, London 1961–64; Minister of State for Foreign Affairs 1964–70, Minister for Disarmament 1964–67, 1969–70, in charge of day-to-day negotiations for Britain's entry into Common Market 1967–69; Perm. Rep. to Western European Union 1969–70; Foreign Ed. New Statesman 1970–71; Chair. All-Party Defence Group House of Lords 1980–96, Pres. 1996–; Chair. Industrial Cleaning Papers 1979–86, Peter Hamilton Security Consultants Ltd 1984–86, UK Cttee for Free World 1981–89, European Atlantic Group 1983–, VSEL Consortium PLC 1987–93, Marlborough Stirling Group 1994–99; Deputy Chair. IBA 1989–90; Chair. Radio Authority 1991–94; Pres. Hispanic and Luso Brazilian Council 1975–80, Royal Nat. Inst. for Deaf 1980–87, Llangollen Int. Music Festival 1979–90; Chair. Abington Corpn (Consultants) Ltd 1981–, Nottingham Building Soc. 1983–90, Southern Mining Corpn 1997–99; Dir

W S. Atkins Int. 1979–83, IBM UK Ltd 1973–90 (mem. IBM Europe Advisory Council 1973–90), Lazard Brothers and Co. Ltd 1983–90, Shandwick PLC 1985–95, Triangle Holdings 1986–90, TV Corpn PLC 1996–2001; Pres. Freedom in Sport Int.; mem. Int. Inst. of Strategic Studies, Royal Inst.; Hon. Fellow Univ. Coll. Wales, Aberystwyth 1974. *Publications:* The Sword and the Spirit 1963, The Great Commanders (ed.) 1973, Montgomery of Alamein 1976, Waterloo: Battle of Three Armies (ed.) 1979, Star Wars: Suicide or Survival 1985, Defence of the Realm 1987, By God's Will: A Portrait of the Sultan of Brunei 1989, The Shadow of My Hand (autobiog.) 2000; contrib. to The Times and nat. and professional journals. *Address:* House of Lords, London, SW1A 0PW, England.

CHALIDZE, Valeriy Nikolayevich; Russian writer, physicist and publisher; b. 1938, Moscow; m. *Education:* Moscow Univ., then Faculty of Physics, Tbilisi Univ. 1965. *Career:* head of research unit in Plastics Research Inst., Moscow 1965–70; removed from post 1970; mem. of USSR Human Rights Cttee; dissident activity 1969–, when started samizdat journal Obshchestvennyye problemy (Problems of Society), trip to USA to lecture on human rights in USSR, subsequently deprived of Soviet citizenship 1972; currently living in New York. *Publications include:* numerous samizdat articles and books and Ugolovnaya Rossiya (Capital Punishment in Russia) 1977, USSR – The Workers' Movement 1978. A Foreigner in the Soviet Union. A Juridical Memoir 1980, Communism Vanquished (Stalin) 1981, The Responsibility of a Generation 1982, National Problems and Perestroika 1988, The Dawn of the Legal Reform 1990, Responsibility of the Generation 1991, A Hierarchical Man 1991.

CHALKER, Jack Laurence, BA, MLA; writer; b. 17 Dec. 1944, Norfolk, VA, USA; m. Eva C. Whitley 1978. *Education:* Towson State College, Johns Hopkins University. *Career:* Founder-Ed., 1960–72, Editorial and Marketing Dir, 1961–, Mirage Press Ltd, Baltimore; mem. SFWA; World Science Fiction Society. *Publications:* Fiction: A Jungle of Stars, 1976; Midnight at the Well of Souls, 1977; Dancers in the Afterglow, 1978; Exiles at the Well of Souls, 1978; Quest for the Well of Souls, 1978; The Web of the Chosen, 1978; A War of Shadows, 1979; And the Devil Will Drag You Under, 1979; The Return of Nathan Brazil, 1979; Twilight at the Well of Souls: The Legacy of Nathan Brazil, 1980; The Devil's Voyage, 1981; Lilith: A Snake in the Grass, 1981; Cerebrus: A Wolf in the Fold, 1982; Charon: A Dragon at the Gate, 1982; The Identity Matrix, 1982; Medusa: A Tiger by the Tail, 1983; Spirits of Flux and Anchor, 1984; Empires of Flux and Anchor, 1984; The River of Dancing Gods, 1984; Demons of the Dancing Gods, 1984; The Messiah Choice, 1985; Downtiming the Night Side, 1985; Masters of Flux and Anchor, 1985; The Birth of Flux and Anchor, 1985; The Armlet of the Gods, 1986; Children of Flux and Anchor, 1986; Lords of the Middle Dark, 1986; The Labyrinth of Dreams, 1987; Pirates of the Thunder, 1987; When the Changewinds Blow, 1987; Dance Band on the Titanic, 1988; Masks of the Martyrs, 1988; Riders of the Wind, 1988; War of the Maelstrom, 1988; Warriors of the Storm, 1988; The Demons at Rainbow Bridge, 1989; Songs of the Dancing Gods, 1990; The Red Tape War (with Mike Resnick and George Alec Effinger), 1991; The Run to Chaos Keep, 1992; The Ninety Trillion Fausts, 1992; The Shadow Dancers, 1992; The Maze in the Mirror, 1992; Echoes of the Well of Souls, 1993; Gods of the Well of Souls, 1994; Shadow of the Well of Souls, 1994; The Cybernetic Walrus, 1995; Horrors of the Dancing Gods, 1995; The Marching Hare Network, 1996; The Hot-Wired Dodo, 1997; Priam's Lens, 1999; The Sea is Full of Stars, 1999; Belshazzar's Serpent, 2000; Ghost of the Well of Souls, 2000; The Morceau Factor, 2000; Melchior's Fire, 2001; Kaspar's Box, 2001. Non-Fiction: Jack Chalker (autobiog.), 1985. *Address:* c/o Mirage Press Ltd, PO Box 28, Manchester, MD 21102, USA.

CHAMBERLAIN, Lesley, BA, MLitt; British writer; b. 26 Sept. 1951, Rochford, Essex; one d.; m. Pavel Seifter 1999. *Education:* Univ. of Exeter and Wolfson Coll., Oxford. *Career:* Lecturer, Portsmouth Polytechnic 1977–86; corresp. and Sr Sub-Ed. Reuters, Moscow 1978–79; freelance writer and teacher 1986–, regular contrib. to The TLS, Los Angeles Times Book Review, The Independent and other nat. publs. *Publications include:* The Food and Cooking of Russia 1982, The Food and Cooking of Eastern Europe 1989, In the Communist Mirror 1990, Volga, Volga A Journey Down the Great River 1994, Nietzsche in Turin 1996, In a Place Like That 1998, The Secret Artist – A Close Reading of Sigmund Freud 2000, The Good Man in Russia 2002, Girl in a Garden (novel) 2003, Motherland: a Philosophical History of Russia 2004. *Address:* c/o Atlantic Books, Ormond House, 26–27 Boswell Street, London, WC1N 3JZ, England (Office).

CHAMBERLAIN, Velma (see Richeson, Cena Golder).

CHAMBERLIN, Ann; Writer and Dramatist; b. 28 March 1954, Salt Lake City, UT; m. Curt F. Setzer, 14 Sept. 1978, two s. *Education:* Brigham Young University; University of Utah; University of Tel-Aviv. *Publications:* The Virgin and the Tower, 1979; Tamar, 1994; Sofia, 1996; The Sultan's Daughter, 1997; The Reign of the Favored Women, 1999; Leaving Eden, The Merlin of St Gilles' Well, 1999; The Merlin of the Oak Wood, 2001. *Honours:* several book and drama awards. *Address:* PO Box 71114, Salt Lake City, UT 84171, USA. *E-mail:* setzers@msn.com. *Website:* www.annchamberlin.com.

CHAMBERS, Aidan; Author and Publisher; b. 27 Dec. 1934, Chester-le-Street, County Durham, England; m. Nancy Harris Lockwood, 30 March 1968. *Education:* Borough Road College, Isleworth, University of London. *Career:* mem. Society of Authors; Fellow, English Asscn; School Library Asscn, pres., 2003–. *Publications:* The Reluctant Reader, 1969; Introducing Books to Children, 1973; Breaktime, 1978; Seal Secret, 1980; The Dream Cage, 1981; Dance on My Grave, 1982; The Present Takers, 1983; Booktalk, 1985; Now I Know, 1987; The Reading Environment, 1991; The Toll Bridge, 1992; Tell Me: Children, Reading and Talk, 1993; Only Once, 1998; Postcards From No Man's Land, 1999; Reading Talk, 2001. Contributions: numerous magazines and journals. *Honours:* Children's Literature Award for Outstanding Criticism, 1978; Eleanor Farjeon Award, 1982; Silver Pencil Awards, 1985, 1986, 1994; Carnegie Medal, 1999; Stockport School Book Award KS4, 2000; Hans Christian Andersen Award, 2002; Michael L. Printz Award, 2003; J. Hunt Award, 2003; Dr hc, Umea Univ. Sweden, 2003. *Address:* Lockwood, Station Rd, Woodchester, Stroud, Gloucs GL5 5EQ, England. *Website:* www.aidanchambers.co.uk.

CHAMOISEAU, Patrick; Writer; b. 12 March 1953, Fort de France, Martinique; m. Ghislaine Chamoiseau, 19 Dec. 1975, one c. *Education:* Licencié en Droit Privé, University of Sceaux, France. *Publications:* Manman Dlo contre la fée Carabosse; Chronique des sept misères, 1986; Solibo Magnifique, 1988, English trans. as Solibo Magnificent, 1998; Martinique, 1988; Eloge de la créolité (co-author), 1989; Lettres créoles: Traces antillaises et continentales de la littérature (co-author), 1991; Texaco, 1992; Antan d'enfance, 1993; Au temps de l'antan, 1994, English trans. as Creole Folktales, 1994; Guyane: Traces-mémoires du bagne, 1994; Chemin-d'école, 1994, English trans. as School Days, 1997; Biblique des derniers gestes, 2001. *Honours:* Prix Goncourt, 1992; Prix Garbet de la Caraibe, 1993. *Address:* 31 Favorite, 97232 Larentin, Martinique.

CHAMPION, Larry Stephen; academic and writer; b. 27 April 1932, Shelby, NC, USA; m. Nancy Ann Blanchard 1956; one s. two d. *Education:* BA, Davidson College, 1954; MA, University of Virginia, 1955; PhD, University of North Carolina, 1961. *Career:* Instructor, Davidson College, 1955–56, University of North Carolina, Chapel Hill, 1959–60; Instructor, 1960–61, Asst Prof., 1961–65, Assoc. Prof., 1965–68, Prof. of English, 1968–94, North Carolina State University; mem. MLA; National Council of Teachers of English; Renaissance English Text Society; Renaissance Society of America; International Shakespeare Society; Shakespeare Asscn of America. *Publications:* Ben Jonson's 'Dotages': A Reconsideration of the Late Plays, 1967; The Evolution of Shakespeare's Comedy: A Study in Dramatic Perspective, 1970; Quick Springs of Sense: Studies in the Eighteenth Century (ed.), 1974; Shakespeare's Tragic Perspective: The Development of His Dramatic Technique, 1976; Tragic Patterns in Jacobean and Caroline Drama: A Study in Perspective, 1977; Perspective in Shakespeare's English Histories, 1980; King Lear: An Annotated Bibliography Since 1940, 2 vols, 1981; Thomas Dekker and the Traditions of English Drama, 1985; The Essential Shakespeare: An Annotated Bibliography of Major Modern Studies, 1986; The Noise of Threatening Drum: Dramatic Strategy and Political Ideology in Shakespeare and the English Chronicle Plays, 1990. Contributions: Books and scholarly journals. *Honours:* Acad. of Outstanding Teachers Award, 1966; Alumni Distinguished Prof., 1987. *Address:* 5320 Sendero Drive, Raleigh, NC 27612, USA.

CHAN, Stephen; academic, writer and poet; b. 11 May 1949, Auckland, New Zealand. *Education:* BA, 1972, MA, 1975, University of Auckland; MA, King's College, London, 1977; PhD, University of Kent, Canterbury, 1992. *Career:* International Civil Servant, Commonwealth Secretariat, 1977–83; Lecturer in International Relations, University of Zambia, 1983–85; Faculty, University of Kent, 1987–96; Prof. in International Relations and Ethics, Head of International Studies, Dean of Humanities, Nottingham Trent University, 1996–. *Publications:* The Commonwealth Observer Group in Zimbabwe: A Personal Memoir, 1985; Issues in International Relations: A View from Africa, 1987; The Commonwealth in World Politics: A Study of International Action, 1965–85, 1988; Exporting Apartheid: Foreign Policies in Southern Africa, 1978–1988, 1990; Social Development in Africa Today: Some Radical Proposals, 1991; Kaunda and Southern Africa: Image and Reality in Foreign Policy, 1991; Twelve Years of Commonwealth Diplomatic History: Commonwealth Summit Meetings, 1979–1991, 1992; Mediation in South Africa (ed. with Vivienne Jabri), 1993; Renegade States: The Foreign Policies of Revolutionary States (ed. with Andrew Williams), 1994; Towards a Multicultural Roshamon Paradigm in International Relations, 1996; Portuguese Foreign Policy in Southern Africa (with M. Venancio), 1996; Theorists and Theorising in International Relations (ed. with Jarrold Wiener), 1997; War and Peace in Mozambique (with M. Vanancio), 1998; Giving Thought: Currents in International Relations (ed. with Jarrold Wiener), 1998; Twentieth Century International History (ed. with Jarrold Wiener), 1998; Zambia and the Decline of Kaunda 1984–1998, 2000; Security and Development in Southern Africa, 2001. Poetry: Postcards from Paradise (with Rupert Glover and Merlene Young), 1971; Arden's Summer, 1975; Songs of the Maori King, 1986; Crimson Rain, 1991. *Honours:* Visiting fellowships; Hon. LittD, WAAC, Istanbul; Hon. Prof., University of Zambia, 1993–95. *Address:* c/o Dept of International Studies, Nottingham Trent University, Clifton Lane, Nottingham NG11 8NS, England.

CHANCE, Jane; Prof. of English, Writer, Poet and Ed.; b. 26 Oct. 1945, Neosho, MO, USA; m. 1st Dennis Carl Nitzsche, June 1966, divorced 1967, one d.; m. 2nd Paolo Passaro 30 April 1981 (divorced 2002); two s. *Education:* BA, English, Purdue University, 1967; AM, English, 1968, PhD,

English, 1971, University of Illinois. *Career:* Lecturer, 1971–72, Asst Prof. of English, 1972–73, University of Saskatchewan; Asst Prof., 1973–77, Assoc. Prof., 1977–80, Prof. of English, 1980–, Rice University; Hon. Research Fellow, University College London, 1977–78; Mem., Institute for Advanced Study, Princeton, NJ, 1988–89; General Ed., Library of Medieval Women, 1988–; Visiting Research Fellow, Institute for Advanced Studies in the Humanities, University of Edinburgh, 1994; Eccles Research Fellow, University of Utah, Humanities Centre, 1994–95; various guest and plenary lectures; mem. American Asscn of University Profs; Authors' Guild; Christine de Pizan Society; International Asscn of Neo-Latin Studies; International Society in Classical Studies; Medieval Acad. of America; MLA; South Central MLA. *Publications:* The Genius Figure in Antiquity and the Middle Ages, 1975; Tolkien's Art: A 'Mythology for England', 1979; Woman as Hero in Old English Literature, 1986; Tolkien's Lord of the Rings: The Mythology of Power, 1992; Medieval Mythography, two vols, 1994, 2000; The Mythographic Chaucer: The Fabulation of Sexual Politics, 1995. Editor: various books. Contributions: scholarly books and journals. *Honours:* Hon. Research Fellow, University College London, 1977–78; National Endowment for the Humanities Fellowship, 1977–78; Guggenheim Fellowship, 1980–81; Rockefeller Foundation Residency, Bellagio, Italy, 1988; South Central MLA Best Book Award, 1994. *Address:* Dept of English MS-30, Rice University, PO Box 1892, Houston TX 77251-1892, USA. *Telephone:* (713) 348-2625 (Office). *Fax:* (713) 348-5991. *E-mail:* jchance@rice.edu. *Website:* www.ruf.rice.edu/~jchance.

CHANCE, Megan; Writer; b. 31 Dec. 1959, Columbus, OH, USA; m. Kany Levine, 1995; two d. *Education:* BA, Western Washington University, 1983. *Career:* mem. Romance Writers of America. *Publications:* A Candle in the Dark, 1993; After the Frost, 1994; The Portrait, 1995; A Heart Divided, 1996; Fall from Grace, 1977; The Way Home, 1997; The Gentleman Caller, 1998; A Season in Eden, 1999; Susannah Morrow, 2002. *Honours:* Reviewer's Choice Award for Best First Historical Novel, Romantic Times, 1993; RITA Award for Excellence in Romantic Fiction, 1994; Emerald City Keeper Award for Best Historical Romance, 1997.

CHANDLER, David (Geoffrey); Military Historian; b. 15 Jan. 1934, England. *Education:* DLitt, Oxford, 1991. *Career:* British Army Officer, 1957–60; Lecturer, 1960–64, Senior Lecturer, 1964–69, Deputy Head, 1969–80, Head, 1980–94, Royal Military Acad., Sandhurst; Pres., 1967–86, Pres. Emeritus, 1986–, British Military History Commission; Vice-Pres., International Commission of Military History, 1975–94; Ed., David Chandler's Newsletter on the Age of Napoleon, 1987–89; Military Affairs Visiting Prof., Quantico, 1991; Trustee, Royal Armouries, Tower of London, later Leeds, 6 years; mem. European Union of Re-enactment Societies; Napoleonic Society of Great Britain; FRHistS. *Publications:* A Traveller's Guide to Battlefields of Europe, 1965; The Campaigns of Napoleon, 1966; Marlborough as Military Commander, 1973; The Art of Warfare on Land, 1975; The Art of Warfare in the Age of Marlborough, 1976; Atlas of Military Strategy, 1980; A Journal of Marlborough's Wars, 1984; Napoleon's Military Maxims, 1987; On the Napoleonic Wars, 1994; The Oxford Illustrated History of the British Army, 1994. Contributions: History Today. *Honours:* Literary Award, Napoleonic Society of America, 1994; Literary Award, International Napoleonic Society of Canada, 1995. *Address:* Hindford, Monteagle Lane, Yateley, Hampshire, England.

CHANDLER, Frank (see Harknett, Terry).

CHANDLER, Otis; American newspaper executive; b. 23 Nov. 1927, Los Angeles; m. 1st Marilyn Chandler 1951 (divorced 1981); m. 2nd Bettina Whitaker 1981; three s. two d. *Education:* Andover Acad., Mass. and Stanford Univ. *Career:* trainee, Times Mirror Co. 1953, Asst to Pres. (assigned to Mirror-News) 1957, Marketing Man., Los Angeles Times 1958–60, Publr, Los Angeles Times 1960–80, Publr and CEO 1978–80; Vice-Pres. Times Mirror Co. 1961, Dir 1962, Sr Vice-Pres. 1966–80; Vice-Chair. Bd Times Mirror Co. 1968–80, Chair. and Ed.-in-Chief 1981–85, Chair. of Exec. Cttee 1986. *Address:* c/o Times Mirror Square, Los Angeles, CA 90053, USA (Office).

CHANDRA, Ramesh, BSc; Indian newspaper executive; b. 15 Aug. 1925, Najibabad, Uttar Pradesh; m. Chandrakanta Jain 1948; two s. *Education:* Banaras Hindu Univ. *Career:* fmr Sr Vice-Chair. Municipal Bd Najibabad; joined Times of India 1959; Exec. Dir Bennett, Coleman & Co. Ltd (The Times of India Group of Publs); fmr Chair. Press Trust of India; fmr Pres. Indian Newspaper Soc.; Pres. Chrysanthemum Soc. of India, All India Digambar Jain Parishad; Man. Trustee, Bharatiya Jnanpith; Thomson Foundation Fellow, UK 1968. *Publications:* articles on newspaper management in various journals. *Address:* Bharatiya Jananpith, 18 Institutional Area, Lodi Road, New Delhi 110003 (Office); C-48 Gulmohar Park, New Delhi 110049, India (Home). *Telephone:* (11) 331-8191 (Office); (11) 685-2909 (Home). *Fax:* (11) 465-4197 (Office); (11) 696-9523 (Home). *E-mail:* jnanpith@satyam.net.in (Office).

CHANDRA, Vikram; writer and academic; b. 23 July 1961, New Delhi, India. *Education:* St Xavier's College, Mumbai, 1978–81; BA, Pomona College, 1984; MA, Johns Hopkins University, 1987; MFA, University of Houston, 1992. *Career:* Adjunct Prof., University of Houston, 1987–93; Visiting Writer, 1994–95, Asst Prof., 1995–, George Washington University. *Publications:* Red Earth and Pouring Rain, 1995; Love and Longing in Bombay, 1997. Contributions: periodicals. *Honours:* Discovery Prize, Paris Review, 1994; David Higham Prize, Book Trust, London, 1995; Commonwealth Writers Prize for Best First Published Book, 1996, and for Best Book, Eurasia region, 1998. *Address:* c/o Dept of English, George Washington University, Washington, DC 20052, USA.

CHANEY, Edward Paul de Gruyter, BA, MPhil, PhD, FSA, FRSA; academic and writer; b. 11 April 1951, Hayes, Middlesex, England; m. Lisa Maria Jacka 1973 (divorced); two d. *Education:* Univ. of Reading, Warburg Inst., London, European Univ. Inst., Florence. *Career:* Lecturer, Univ. of Pisa 1979–85; Adjunct Asst Prof., Charles A. Strong Center, Georgetown Univ. Florence Program, Villa Le Balze, Florence 1982, 1983; Assoc., Harvard Univ. Center for Italian Renaissance Studies, Villa I Tatti, Florence 1984–85; Shuffrey Research Fellow in Architectural History, Lincoln Coll., Oxford 1985–90; part-time History of Art Lecturer, Oxford Polytechnic 1991, Oxford Brookes Univ. 1993–; historian, London Division, English Heritage 1991–93; Prof. of Fine and Decorative Arts and Chair of History of Collecting Research Centre, Southampton Inst.; mem. of exec. cttee or editorial bd, Wyndham Lewis Soc., Walpole Soc., Catholic Record Soc., British Art Journal, British-Italian Soc. *Publications:* Oxford, China and Italy: Writings in Honour of Sir Harold Acton on his Eightieth Birthday (ed. with N. Ritchie) 1984, The Grand Tour and the Great Rebellion: Richard Lassels and 'The Voyage of Italy' in the Seventeenth Century 1985, Florence: A Travellers' Companion (with Harold Acton) 1986, England and the Continental Renaissance: Essays in Honour of J. B. Trapp (ed. with Peter Mack) 1990, English Architecture: Public and Private: Essays for Kerry Downes (ed. with John Bold) 1993, The Evolution of the Grand Tour: Anglo-Italian cultural relations since the Renaissance 1998, The Evolution of English Collecting: Receptions of Italian Art in the Tudor and Stuart Periods 2003; contrib. to reference works, books, scholarly journals, periodicals, etc. *Honours:* Laurea di Dottore in Lingue e Letterature Straniere, Univ. of Pisa 1983; hon. life mem. British Inst. of Florence 1984, hon. assoc. Soc. of Fine Art Auctioneers; Commendatore of the Italian Republic 2003. *Address:* Southampton Institute, E Park Terrace, Southampton SO14 0RF, England.

CHANG, Iris Shun-Ru, BS, MA; American journalist and writer; b. 28 March 1968, Princeton, NJ; m. Bretton Lee Douglas 1991. *Education:* Univ. of Illinois, John Hopkins Univ. *Publications:* non-fiction: Thread of the Silkworm 1995, The Rape of Nanking: The Forgotten Holocaust of World War II 1997, The Chinese in America: A Narrative History 2003; contrib. to Chicago Tribune, Associated Press, New York Times. *Honours:* MacArthur Foundation Peace and Int. Co-operative Award 1992, Origin Chinese American Women Nat. Woman of the Year Award 1998. *Address:* PO Box 641104, San Jose, CA 95164, USA. *E-mail:* irischang@aol.com.

CHANG, Jung, PhD; British writer; b. 25 March 1952, Yibin, People's Republic of China; m. Jon Halliday 1991. *Education:* Univ. of York. *Publications:* Madame Sun Yet-sen (with Jon Halliday) 1986, Wild Swans: Three Daughters of China 1991. *Honours:* NCR Book Award, 1992; Writers' Guild Best Non-Fiction Book, 1992; Fawcett Society Book Award, 1992; Book of the Year, UK, 1993; hon. doctorates, Univ. of Buckingham, 1996, Univ. of Warwick, 1997, Univ. of York, 1997, Open Univ., 1998. *Literary Agent:* Gillon Aitken Associates Ltd, 18–21 Cavaye Place, London, SW10 9PT, England. *Telephone:* (20) 7373-8672. *Fax:* (20) 7373-6002.

CHANNER, Colin; Jamaican novelist; b. 1963, Kingston. *Career:* teacher of fiction writing in London and New York; bass player for reggae band Pipecock Jaxxon; founder and artistic dir of Calabash Int. Literary Festival. *Publications:* novels: Waiting in Vain 1998, I'm Still Waiting (novella, featured in anthology Got to be Real) 2001, Satisfy My Soul 2002, Passing Through 2004. *Address:* c/o Ballentine/One World, 1745 Broadway, New York, NY 10019, USA. *Telephone:* (212) 782-9000. *Website:* www.randomhouse.com. *E-mail:* colin@colinchanner.com. *Website:* www.colinchanner.com.

CHAO, Patricia; Writer and Poet; b. 9 July 1955, Carmel-by-the-Sea, CA, USA. *Education:* BA, Creative Writing, Brown University, 1979; MA, English, New York University, 1992. *Career:* Creative Writing Teacher, Sarah Lawrence College, Bronxville, NY; Ed., Global City Review special issue, 1996. *Publications:* Fiction: Monkey King, 1997. Children's Fiction: On the Silk Road; Mimi and the Tea Ceremony; The Lost and Found Twins. Contributions: periodicals and books. *Honours:* Rose Low Memorial Poetry Prize, Brown University, 1978; Fellowship, New York University Master's Programme in Creative Writing, 1990–92; Dean's Fiction Prize, New York University, 1992; New Voice Award for Poetry, The Writer's Voice, 1996; several residencies.

CHAPLIN, Jenny, (Tracie Telfer, Wendy Wentworth); editor, publisher, writer and poet; b. 22 Dec. 1928, Glasgow, Scotland; m. J. McDonald Chaplin 1951; one d. *Education:* Jordanhill College of Education. *Career:* Founder, Ed., Publisher, International: The Writers Rostrum, 1984–93. *Publications:* Tales of a Glasgow Childhood, 1994; Alone in a Garden, 1994; Happy Days in Rothesay, 1995; From Scotland's Past, 1996; Childhood Days in Glasgow, 1996; Thoughts on Writing (with Fay Goldie and V. Cuthbert), 1996; An Emigrant's Farewell, in A Scottish Childhood, Vol. II, anthology of memoirs from famous Scottish people, 1998; We Belonged to Glasgow, 2001. Contributions: The Scots Magazine; The Highlander Magazine; Scottish Memories; The Scottish Banner; Anthologies. *Honours:*

Proclaimed Champion Poet of Largs, Ayrshire, 2000; Fellow, Society of Antiquaries, Scotland, 2000. *Address:* Tigh na Mara Cottage, 14 Ardbeg Road, Rothesay, Bute PA20 0NJ, Scotland.

CHAPLINA, Natalya; Russian newspaper editor; b. 15 Feb. 1957, Leningrad (now St Petersburg); m 2nd Viktor Cherkesov 1996; two d. *Education:* St Petersburg State Univ. *Career:* journalist 1975–; Founder and Editor-in-Chief Chas Pik (first independent newspaper in Russian Fed) 1990–, Chair. Bd of Dirs; project leader, Rosbalt agency; has written five books. *Honours:* USSR Journalists' Union award 1991, Russian Journalists' Union award 1994. *Address:* Chas Pik, Nevsky pr 81, 191040 St Petersburg, Russia. *Telephone:* (812) 279-25-65. *Fax:* (812) 279-22-70. *E-mail:* news@chaspik.spb.su.

CHAPMAN, (F.) Ian, CBE, CBIM, FRSA, FFCS; British publisher; *Vice-President, National Academy of Writing*; b. 26 Oct. 1925, St Fergus, Aberdeenshire, Scotland; m. Marjory Stewart Swinton, MA 1953; one s. one d. *Education:* Shawlands Acad., Ommer School of Music, Glasgow. *Career:* served in RAF 1943–44; miner (nat. service) 1945–47; with William Collins Sons & Co. Ltd (fmrly W.M. Collins Holdings PLC, now Harper Collins) 1947, Man. Trainee New York br. 1950–51, Sales Man. London br. 1955; mem. main operating Bd, Group Sales Dir 1959, Jt Man. Dir 1967–76, Deputy Chair. 1976–81, Chair. CEO 1981–89; Deputy Chair. Orion Publishing Group 1993–94, Dir William Collins overseas cos. 1968–89: Canada 1968–89, USA 1974–89, S. Africa 1978–89, NZ 1978–89, William Collins Int. Ltd 1975–89; Chair. Scottish Radio Holdings PLC (fmrly Radio Clyde) 1972–96 (Hon. Pres. 1996–2000), Harvill Press 1976–89, Hatchards Ltd 1976–89, William Collins Publrs Ltd 1979–81, The Listener Publs PLC 1988–93, RadioTrust PLC 1997–2001, Guinness Publrs Ltd 1991–98; Dir Pan Books Ltd 1962–84 (Chair. 1973–76), Book Tokens Ltd 1981–94, Ind. Radio News 1984–85, Stanley Botes Ltd 1986–89, Guinness PLC (non-exec.) 1986–91; Pres.-Dir Gen. Guinness Media SAS, Paris 1996–99; f. Chapmans Publrs. Chair. and Man. Dir 1989–94; Trustee Book Trade Benevolent Soc. 1982–2003; Trustee The Publrs Asscn 1989–97; mem. Gov. Council SCOTBIC; mem. Council Publishers Asscn 1962–77, Vice-Pres. 1978, Pres. 1979–81; Chair. Nat. Acad. of Writing 2000–03, Vice-Pres. 2003–; mem. Bd Book Devt Council 1967, Ancient House Bookshop 1972–89, Scottish Opera, Theatre Royal Ltd 1974–79, IRN Ltd 1983–85; Chair. Advisory Bd Strathclyde Univ. Business School 1985–88. *Honours:* Hon. DLitt (Strathclyde Univ.) 1990; Scottish Free Enterprise Award 1985. *Address:* Kenmore, 46 The Avenue, Cheam, Surrey, SM2 7QE, England (Home). *Telephone:* (20) 8642-1820 (Home). *Fax:* (20) 8642-7439. *E-mail:* fic@onetel.net.uk.

CHAPMAN, Jean; Writer; b. 30 Oct. 1939, England; m. Lionel Alan Chapman, 24 March 1951, one s. two d. *Education:* BA, Open University, 1989. *Career:* Creative Writing Tutor, East Midlands Arts and Community Colleges; mem. Society of Authors; Chair., Romantic Novelists Asscn. *Publications:* The Unreasoning Earth, 1981; Tangled Dynasty, 1984; Forbidden Path, 1986; Savage Legacy, 1987; The Bellmakers, 1990; Fortune's Woman, 1992; A World Apart, 1993; The Red Pavilion, 1995; The Soldier's Girl, 1997; This Time Last Year, 1999; A New Beginning, 2001; And a Golden Pear, 2002. Other: many short stories. *Literary Agent:* Jane Judd. *Address:* 3 Arnesby Lane, Peatling Magna, Leicester LE8 5UN, England.

CHAPMAN, Stanley David, BSc, MA, PhD; academic and writer; b. 31 Jan. 1935, Nottingham, England; m.; two s. *Education:* LSE, Univ. of Nottingham, Univ. of London. *Career:* Lecturer, 1968–73, Pasold Reader in Business History, 1973–, Prof., 1993–, Univ. of Nottingham; Ed., Textile History Bi Annual, 1984–2002. *Publications:* The Early Factory Masters, 1967; The Beginnings of Industrial Britain, 1970; The History of Working Class Housing, 1971; The Cotton Industry in the Industrial Revolution, 1972; Jesse Boot of Boots the Chemists, 1974; The Devon Cloth Industry in the 18th Century, 1978; Stanton and Staveley, 1981; The Rise of Merchant Banking, 1984; Merchant Enterprise in Britain from the Industrial Revolution to World War I, 1992; Hosiery and Knitwear: Four Centuries of Small-Scale Industry in Britain, 1589–2000, 2002. *Address:* Rochester House, Halam Road, Southwell, Nottinghamshire NG25 0AD, England.

CHAPPELL, Fred (Davis); University Teacher, Poet and Writer; b. 28 May 1936, Canton, NC, USA; m. Susan Nicholls, 2 Aug. 1959, one s. *Education:* BA, 1961, MA, 1964, Duke University. *Career:* Teacher, University of North Carolina at Greensboro, 1964–; Poet Laureate, North Carolina, 1997–2003. *Publications:* Poetry: The World Between the Eyes, 1971; River, 1975; The Man Twiced Married to Fire, 1977; Bloodfire, 1978; Awakening to Music, 1979; Wind Mountain, 1979; Earthsleep, 1980; Driftlake: A Lieder Cycle, 1981; Midquest, 1981; Castle Tzingal, 1984; Source, 1985; First and Last Words, 1989; C: 100 Poems, 1993; Spring Garden: New and Selected Poems, 1995; Poetry Collection: Family Gathering, 2000. Fiction: It is Time, Lord, 1963; The Inkling, 1965; Dagon, 1968; The Gaudy Place, 1972; I Am One of You Forever, 1985; Brighten the Corner Where You Are, 1989; Farewell, I'm Bound to Leave You, 1996; Look Back All the Green Valley, 1999. Short Fiction: Moments of Light, 1980; More Shapes Than One, 1991. Collection: The Fred Chappell Reader, 1987. Other: Plow Naked: Selected Writings on Poetry, 1993; A Way of Happening: Observations of Contemporary Poetry, 1998. *Honours:* Rockefeller Grant, 1967–68; National Institute of Arts and Letters Award, 1968; Prix de Meilleur des Livres Étrangers, Académie Française, 1972; Sir Walter Raleigh Prize, 1972; Roanoke-Chowan Poetry Prizes, 1972, 1975, 1979, 1980, 1985, 1989; North Carolina Award in Literature, 1980; Bollingen Prize in Poetry, 1985; World Fantasy Awards, 1992, 1994; T. S. Eliot Prize, Ingersoll Foundation, 1993; Aiken Taylor Award in Poetry, 1996. *Address:* 305 Kensington Rd, Greensboro, NC 27403, USA.

CHAPPLE, John Alfred Victor; academic and writer; b. 25 April 1928, Barnstaple, Devonshire, England. *Education:* BA, 1953, MA, 1955, University College London. *Career:* Asst, University College, 1953–55; Research Asst, Yale University, 1955–58; Asst Lecturer, Aberdeen University, 1958–59; Asst Lecturer, 1959–61, Lecturer, 1961–67, Senior Lecturer, 1967–71, Manchester University; Prof., 1971–92, Prof. Emeritus, 1992–, Hull University; Visiting Fellow, Corpus Christi College, Cambridge, 1991–92; mem. Gaskell Society, pres., 1992–; International Asscn of University Profs of English; Larkin Society; Johnson Society; Friends of Erasmus Darwin House. *Publications:* The Letters of Mrs Gaskell, 1966; Documentary and Imaginative Literature 1880–1920, 1970; Elizabeth Gaskell: A Portrait in Letters, 1980; Science and Literature in the 19th Century, 1986; Private Voices: The Diaries of Elizabeth Gaskell and Sophia Holland, 1996; Elizabeth Gaskell: The Early Years, 1998; Further Letters of Mrs Gaskell, 2000. *Address:* 8 Lomax Close, Lichfield WS13 7EY, England.

CHARBONNEAU, Eileen; Writer; b. 11 April 1951, Long Island, NY, USA; m. Edward Gullo 19 Aug. 1972; two d. one s. *Education:* BA, SUNY at Fredonia; River Arts Film School, Woodstock, New York. *Publications:* The Ghosts of Stony Clove, 1988; In the Time of the Wolves., 1994; The Mound Builders' Secret, 1994; Disappearance at Harmony Festival, 1994; Honor to the Hills, 1996; Waltzing in Ragtime, 1996; The Randolph Legacy, 1997; Rachel LeMoyne, 1998; The Connor Emerald, 2000. Contributions: periodicals. *Honours:* Golden Medallion Award, Romance Writers of America, 1989; Best Books Citations, American Library Asscn, 1994, Council of Books for Children, 1996; Washington Post Book World, 1998; Christopher Columbus Screenwriting Award, 1999. *Address:* PO Box 20, Cold Spring, NY 10516, USA. *E-mail:* eileencharbonneau@hotmail.com.

CHARKIN, Richard Denis Paul, MA; British publishing executive; *CEO, Macmillan Ltd*; b. 17 June 1949, London; m. Susan Mary Poole 1972; one s. two d. *Education:* Haileybury, Imperial Service Coll., Cambridge Univ. and Harvard Business School. *Career:* Science Ed. Harrap & Co. 1972; Sr Publishing Man. Pergamon Press 1973; Medical Ed. Oxford Univ. Press 1974, Head of Science and Medicine 1976, Head of Reference 1980; Man. Dir Academic and Gen. 1984; joined Octopus Publishing Group (Reed Int. Books) 1988; Chief Exec. Reed Consumer Books 1989–94, Exec. Dir Reed Books Int. 1988–96, Chief Exec. 1994–96; CEO Current Science Group 1996–97; CEO Macmillan Ltd 1998–; Visiting Fellow Green Coll. Oxford 1987; Chair. Common Purpose 1998–; Dir (non-exec.) Scoot.com PLC 2000–, X-Refer Ltd 2000–; mem. man. cttee John Wisden; mem. Publishers Asscn (vice-pres. 2004–(05, pres. 2005–06)). *Address:* Macmillan Ltd, The Macmillan Building, 4 Crinan Street, London, N1 9XW (Office); 3 Redcliffe Place, London, SW10 9DB, England (Home). *Telephone:* (20) 7843-3600 (Office). *Fax:* (20) 7843-3648 (Office). *Website:* www.macmillan.co.uk.

CHARLES, Nicholas J. (see Kuskin, Karla Seidman).

CHARNAS, Suzy McKee; Writer; b. 22 Oct. 1939, New York, NY, USA; m. Stephen Charnas 4 Oct. 1968; one step-s. one step-d. *Education:* BA, Barnard College, 1961; MA, New York University, 1965. *Career:* mem. Authors' Guild; SFWA; Dramatists Guild. *Publications:* Walk to the End of the World, 1974; Motherlines, 1979; The Vampire Tapestry, 1980; The Bronze King, 1985; Dorothea Dreams, 1986; The Silver Glove, 1988; The Golden Thread, 1989; The Kingdom of Kevin Malone, 1993; Vampire Dreams (play), 1990; The Furies, 1994; The Ruby Tear, 1997; The Conqueror's Child, 1999. Contributions: Womens Review of Books. *Honours:* Nebula Award, 1980; Hugo Award, 1989; Tiptree Award, 1999. *Address:* 212 High St NE, Albuquerque, NM 87102, USA.

CHARNY, Carmi, (T. Carmi); Israeli poet, editor and teacher; b. 31 Dec. 1925, New York, NY, USA; m. Lilach Peled, three s. *Education:* BA, Yeshiva University, 1946; Graduate Studies, Columbia University, 1946, Sorbonne, University of Paris, 1946–47, Hebrew University, 1947, 1949–51. *Career:* Ziskind Visiting Prof. of Humanities, Brandeis University, 1969–70; Adjunct Assoc. Prof., University of Tel-Aviv, 1971–73; Visiting Fellow, Oxford Centre for Postgraduate Hebrew Studies, 1974–76; Visiting Prof., Hebrew Union College, Jerusalem, 1978–, Stanford University, 1979, Yale University, 1986, New York University, 1986, University of Texas at Austin, 1987; mem. Acad. for the Hebrew Language; Writers Asscn of Israel. *Publications:* poetry: as T. Carmi: Mum Vahalom, 1951; Eyn Prahim Shehorim, 1953; Sheleg Birushalayim, 1955; Hayam Ha'aharon, 1958; Nehash Hanehoshet, 1961, English trans. as The Brass Serpent, 1964; Ha'unicorn Mistakel Bamar'ah, 1967; Tevi'ah, 1967; Davar Aher/Selected Poems, 1951–1969, 1970; Somebody Likes You, 1971; Hitnatslut Hamehaber, 1974; T. Carmi and Dan Pagis: Selected Poems (with Dan Pagis), 1976; El Erets Aheret, 1977; Leyad Even Hato'im, 1981, English trans. as At the Stone of Losses, 1983; Hatsi Ta'avati, 1984; Ahat Hi Li, 1985; Shirim Min Ha'azuva, 1989; Emet Vehova, 1993. Editor: as T. Carmi: The Modern Hebrew Poem Itself (with Stanley Burnshaw and Ezra Spicehandler), 1965; The Penguin Book of Hebrew Verse, 1981. Other: Trans of plays into Hebrew. Contributions: periodicals. *Honours:* Brenner Prize for Literature,

1972; Prime Minister's Awards for Creative Writing, 1973, 1994; Guggenheim Fellowship, 1987–88; Bialik Prize, 1990; Hon. Doctor of Humane Letters, Hebrew Union College, Jewish Institute of Religion, 1993. *Address:* Hebrew Union College, Jewish Institute of Religion, 13 King David Street, Jerusalem 94101, Israel.

CHARRY, Brinda S., PhD; writer and broadcaster; b. Bangalore, India. *Education:* Syracuse Univ., NY, USA. *Career:* teaches at Syracuse Univ., NY, USA. *Publications:* The Hottest Day of the Year (novel), 2001; Shadow (short story), 2003. Contributions: Indian periodicals. *Honours:* Katha Awards, 1998, 2003; winner, Asian Age Short Story Competition; winner, Hindu-Picador Short Story Competition. *Address:* c/o Penguin Books India Pvt Ltd, #11 Community Centre, Panchsheel Park, New Delhi, India.

CHARYN, Jerome; Author and Educator; b. 13 May 1937, New York, NY, USA. *Education:* BA, Columbia College, 1959. *Career:* English Teacher, High School of Music and Art, School of Performing Arts, New York City, 1962–64; Asst Prof., Stanford University, 1965–68; Prof., Lehman College, CUNY, 1968–80; Founding Ed., The Dutton Review, 1970; Lecturer, Princeton University, 1980–86; Prof. of Film Studies, American University of Paris, 1995–; mem. PEN; Authors' Guild; Writers Guild of America; International Asscn of Crime Writers. *Publications:* Once Upon a Droshky, 1964; On the Darkening Green, 1965; Going to Jerusalem, 1967; American Scrapbook, 1969; The Single Voice: An Anthology of Contemporary Fiction, 1969; The Troubled Vision, 1970; The Tar Baby, 1973; Blue Eyes, 1975; Marilyn the Wild, 1976; The Franklin Scare, 1977; Secret Isaac, 1978; The Seventh Babe, 1979; Darlin' Bill, 1980; Panna Maria, 1982; Pinocchio's Nose, 1983; The Isaac Quartet, 1984; Metropolis, 1986; Paradise Man, 1987; Movieland, 1989; The Good Policeman, 1990; Maria's Girls, 1992; Montezuma's Man, 1993; Little Angel Street, 1994; El Bronx, 1997; The Dark Lady from Belorusse, 1997; Death of a Tango King, 1998; Citizen Sidel, 1999; Captain Kidd, 1999; The Black Swan, 2000; Hurricane Lady, 2001; Sizzling Chops and Devilish Spins, 2001; The Isaac Quartet, 2002; Bronx Boy, 2002; Gangsters and Gold Diggers, 2003. *Honours:* Commdr, Ordre des Arts et des Lettres, 2002. *Literary Agent:* Georges Borchardt. *Address:* 302 W 12th St, Apt 10c, New York, NY 10014, USA. *E-mail:* jeromecharyn@aol.com. *Website:* www.jeromecharyn.com.

CHASE, Elaine Raco; Author; b. 31 Aug. 1949, Schenectady, New York, USA; m. Gary Dale Chase, 26 Oct. 1969, one s. one d. *Education:* AA, Albany Business College, 1968; Union College, 1968; SUNY, 1977. *Career:* mem. Romance Writers of America; Sisters in Crime, national pres., 1995–96. *Publications:* Rules of the Game, 1980; Tender Yearnings, 1981; A Dream Come True, 1982; Double Occupancy, 1982; Designing Woman, 1982; No Easy Way Out, 1983; Video Vixen, 1983; Best Laid Plans, 1983; Special Delivery, 1984; Lady Be Bad, 1984; Dare the Devil, 1987; Dark Corners, 1988; Partners in Crime, 1994; Amateur Detective (non-fiction), 1996. Contributions: several publications. *Honours:* Walden Book Award, 1985; Top Romantic Supsense Series Award, 1987–88. *Address:* 4333 Majestic Lane, Fairfax, VA 22033, USA.

CHASE, Isobel (see De Guise, Elizabeth (Mary Teresa)).

CHATTERJEE, Debjani; writer, poet, editor, storyteller and translator; b. 21 Nov. 1952, Delhi, India; m. Brian D'Arcy 1983. *Education:* BA, American University in Cairo, 1972; MA, University of Kent, Canterbury, 1973; PhD, University of Lancaster, 1977; PGCE, Sheffield City Polytechnic, 1981. *Career:* Chair. National Asscn of Writers in Education; Vice-Chair. Bengali Women's Support Group and Book Project 1985–; mem. Poetry Society, India, UK, Arts Council of England, Literature Advisory Group 1996–99, Mini Mushaira 1996–. *Publications:* Peaces; Poems for Peace, 1987; Whistling Still: Bloody Lyres, 1989; I Was That Woman, 1989; Northern Poetry, Vol. II, 1991; The Sun Rises in the North, 1993; A Little Bridge, 1997; Albino Gecko, 1998; Songs in Exile (trans.), 1999; Cette-Femme La…, 2000; The Redbeck Anthology of British South Asian Poetry, 2000; Animal Antics, 2000; My Birth Was Not in Vain: Selected Poems by Seven Bengali Women, 2001, Jade Horse Torso: Poems and Translations 2003, Rainbow World: Poems from Many Cultures 2003, Generations of Ghazals: Ghazals by Nasir Kazmi & Basir Sultan Kazmi 2003, Daughters of a Riverine Land 2003. Other: The Role of Religion in A Passage to India, 1984; The Elephant-Headed God and Other Hindu Tales, 1989; Barbed Lines, 1990; Sweet and Sour, 1993; The Parrot's Training (trans.), 1993; The Monkey God and Other Hindu Tales, 1993; Sufi Stories from Around the World, 1994; Nyamia and the Bag of Gold, 1994; Home to Home, 1995; The Most Beautiful Child, 1996; Album (trans.), 1997; The Message of Thunder and Other Plays, 1999; The Snake Prize and Other Folk Tales from Bengal, 1999, Who Cares? Reminiscences of Yemeni Carers in Sheffield 2001. *Honours:* Shankars International Children's Competition Poetry Prize; Lancaster LitFest Poems Competition Winner; Peterloo Poets Open Poetry Competition Afro-Caribbean/Asian Prize; Southport Writers' Circle Poetry Competition, second prize; Artrage Annual Literature Award; Raymond Williams Community Publishing Prize, 1990; Yorkshire and Humberside Arts Writer's Award, 1995. *Address:* 11 Donnington Road, Sheffield S2 2RF, England. *Website:* mysite.freeserve.com/DebjaniChatterjee.

CHATTERTON-NEWMAN, Roger; Author; b. 17 March 1949, Haslemere, Surrey, England. *Career:* Editorial Staff, Haymarket Publishing, 1970–89; Deputy Ed., PQ International. *Publications:* A Hampshire Parish, 1976; Brian Boru, King of Ireland, 1983; Murtagh and the Vikings, 1986; Betwixt Petersfield and Midhurst, 1991; Edward Bruce: A Medieval Tragedy, 1992; Polo at Cowdray, 1992; Murtagh the Warrior, 1996. Contributions: Hampshire Magazine; Horse and Hound; Polo Quarterly International; West Sussex History; Downs Country; International Polo Review; The Ring Fort Annual. *Honours:* Commendation, Reading Asscn of Ireland Awards, 1987. *Address:* Rose Cottage, Rake, West Sussex GU33 7JA, England.

CHAUDHURI, Amit, BA, DPhil; writer; b. 15 May 1962, Kolkata, India; m. Rinka Khastgir 1991. *Education:* Univ. of London, Balliol Coll., Oxford. *Career:* Creative Arts Fellow, Wolfson Coll., Oxford 1992–95; Leverhulme Fellow in English, Univ. of Cambridge 1997–99. *Publications:* A Strange and Sublime Address 1991, Afternoon Raag 1993, Freedom Song 1998, A New World 2000, Real Time: Stories and a Reminiscence 2002, D. H. Lawrence and 'Difference': Postcoloniality and the Poetry of the Present 2003; contrib. to anthologies and periodicals, including London Review of Books. *Honours:* Betty Trask Award 1991, Commonwealth Writers' Prize for Best First Book 1992, K. Blundell Trust Award 1993, Southern Arts Literature Prize 1993, Arts Council of Great Britain Writers' Award 1993–94, Soc. of Authors Encore Prize 1994, Los Angeles Times Book Award for Fiction 2000. *Literary Agent:* AP Watt Ltd, 20 John Street, London, WC1N 2DR, England. *Address:* 6 Sunny Park, Flat 10, Eighth Floor, Kolkata 700019, India.

CHEDID, Andrée; Author, Poet and Dramatist; b. 20 March 1920, Cairo, Egypt; m. Louis A. Chedid, 23 Aug. 1942, one s. one d. *Education:* BA, American University, Cairo, 1942. *Publications:* Fiction: Le Sommeil délivré, 1952, English trans. as From Sleep Unbound, 1983; Jonathan, 1955; Le Sixième Jour, 1960, English trans. as The Sixth Day, 1988; Le Survivant, 1963; L'Autre, 1969; La Cité fertile, 1972; Nefertiti et le rêve d'Akhnaton, 1974; Les Marches de sable, 1981; La Maison sans racines, 1985, English trans. as The Return to Beirut, 1989; L'Enfant multiple, 1989, English trans. as The Multiple Child, 1995; Lucy: La femme verticale, 1998; Le Message, 2000. Poetry: numerous books, including: Textes pour un poème, 1949–1970, 1987; Poèmes pour un texte, 1970–1991, 1991; Selected Poems of Andrée Chedid, 1995; Fugitive Suns: Selected Poetry, 1999; Rythmes (poems), 2002. Other: short story collections, plays, essays and children's books. *Honours:* Prix Louise Labe, 1966; L'aigle d'or de la poésie, 1972; Bourse Goncourt de la Nouvelle, 1974; Grand Prix des Lettres Françaises, l'Académie Royale de Belgique, 1975; Prix de l'Afrique Méditerranéenne, 1975; Prix de l'Académie Mallarmé, 1976; Prix de Poésie, Société des Gens de Lettres, 1991; Prix de PEN Club International, 1992; Prix Paul Morand, l'Académie Française, 1994; Prix Albert Camus, 1995; Bourse Goncourt de la Poésie, 2002. *Address:* c/o Flammarion, 26 rue Racine, 75006 Paris, France.

CHEETHAM, Anthony John Valerian, BA; British publisher; b. 12 April 1943; m. 1st Julia Rollason 1969 (divorced); two s. one d.; m. 2nd Rosemary de Courcy 1979 (divorced); two d.; m. 3rd Georgina Capel 1997. *Education:* Eton Coll., Balliol Coll., Oxford. *Career:* Editorial Dir Sphere Books 1968; Man. Dir Futura Publs 1973, Macdonald Futura 1979; Chair. Century Publishing 1982–85; Man. Dir Century Hutchinson 1985; Chair. and CEO Random Century Group 1989–91; Founder and CEO Orion Publishing Group (fmrly Orion Books) 1991–. *Publication:* Richard III 1972. *Address:* Orion Publishing Group Ltd, Orion House, 5 Upper St Martins Lane, London, WC2H 9EA (Office); 20 Grove Park, London, SE5 8LH, England. *Telephone:* (20) 7240-3444 (Office); (20) 7733-8204. *Fax:* (20) 7240-4822 (Office). *E-mail:* info@orionbooks.co.uk. *Website:* www.orionbooks.co.uk.

CHELES, Luciano; Prof. of Italian Studies and Writer; b. 7 Sept. 1948, Cairo, Egypt. *Education:* BA, Italian and French Studies, Reading University, 1973; PGCE, University College, Cardiff, 1974; MPhil, History of Art, Essex University, 1980; PhD, Lancaster University, 1992. *Career:* Senior Lecturer in Italian Studies, Lancaster University, 1994–2000; Visiting Lecturer, University of Lyons II, 1994–95, 1996; University of Poitiers, France, 2000–; mem. Asscn for the Study of Modern Italy; Istituto di Studi Rinascimentali; Society for Renaissance Studies. *Publications:* The Studiolo di Urbino: An Iconographic Investigation, 1986, revised Italian edn as Lo Studiolo di Urbino: Iconografia di un microcosmo principesco, 1991; Neo-Fascism in Europe (ed. with R. G. Ferguson and M. Vaughan), 1991, revised edn as The Far Right in Western and Eastern Europe, 1995; Grafica Utile: L'affiche d'utilité publique en Italie, 1975–1995, 1995; The Art of Persuasion: Political Communication in Italy, from 1945 to the 1990s (ed. with L. Sponza), 2001. Contributions: scholarly books and journals. *Honours:* Frontino-Montefeltro Prize, 1992. *Address:* Département d'Études Italiennes, Université de Poitiers, 86000 Poitiers, France.

CHEN JIANGONG; Chinese writer; b. Nov. 1949, Beihai, Guangxi Prov. *Education:* Peking Univ. *Career:* joined Beijing Writers' Asscn 1981; Sec. of Secr., Chinese Writers' Asscn 1995–2001, Vice-Chair. 2001–. *Publications:* A Girl with the Eyes of a Red Phoenix, Selected Novels by Chen Jiangong, No. 9 Huluba Alley, Letting Go, Curly Hair, Previous Offence. *Address:* Beijing Writers' Association, Beijing, People's Republic of China.

CHEN JO-HSI, BA, MA; novelist; b. 15 Nov. 1938, Taiwan. *Education:* Taiwan National University, Johns Hopkins University. *Career:* Lecturer, University of California at Berkeley 1983. *Publications:* Fiction: Mayor Yin, 1976; Selected Works by Jo-Hsi Chen, 1976; The Old Man, 1978; Repatriation, 1978; The Execution of Mayor Yin, and Other Stories from the Great Proletarian Cultural Revolution, 1978; Inside and Outside the Wall,

1981; Tu Wei, 1983; Selected Short Stories by Jo-Hsi Chen, 1983; Foresight, 1984; The Two Hus, 1985; Paper Marriage, 1986; The Old Man and Other Stories, 1986; Woman from Guizhou, 1989; Wangzhou's Sorrows, 1995; Home of Daughters, 1998; Create a Paradise, 1998. Other: Reminiscences of the Cultural Revolution, 1979; Random Notes, 1981; Democracy Wall and the Unofficial Journals, 1982; Read to Kill Time, 1983; Flower Grown Naturally, 1987; Trip to Tibet, 1988; Trip to Inner Mongolia, 1988. *Honours:* Wu Zhuoliu Prize 1978. *Address:* 428 Boynton Avenue, Berkeley, CA 94707, USA.

CHERKOVSKI, Neeli, (Neeli Cherry); Writer, Poet and Ed.; b. 1945, Los Angeles, CA, USA; Partner, Jesse Guinto Cabrera, 1983. *Education:* San Bernardino Community College; BA, California State University, 1967; Hebrew Union College, Jewish Institute of Religion. *Publications:* Poetry: Anthology of Los Angeles Poets (co-ed.), 1972; Don't Make a Move, 1973; Public Notice, 1975; The Waters Reborn, 1975; Love Proof, 1981; Clear Wind, 1983; Ways in the Wood, 1993; Animal, 1996; Elegy for Bob Kaufman, 1996. Other: Ferlinghetti: A Life, 1979; Whitman's Wild Children, 1988; Hank: The Life of Charles Bukowski, 1991.

CHERNOW, Ron; Author; b. 3 March 1949, New York, NY, USA; m. Valerie Stearn, 22 Oct. 1979. *Education:* BA, Yale College, 1970; MA, Pembroke College, Cambridge, 1972. *Career:* mem. Authors' Guild. *Publications:* The House of Morgan: An American Banking Dynasty and the Rise of Modern Finance, 1990; The Warburgs: The Twentieth-Century Odyssey of a Remarkable Jewish Family, 1993; Titan: The Life of John D. Rockefeller Sr, 1998. Contributions: various periodicals. *Honours:* Jack London Award, United Steelworkers of America, 1980; National Book Award, 1990; Ambassador Book Award, English-Speaking Union of the United States, 1990. *Address:* c/o Melanie Jackson, 250 W 57th St, Suite 1119, New York, NY 10107, USA.

CHERRY, Carolyn Janice, (C. J. Cherryh); Writer; b. 1 Sept. 1942, St Louis, MO, USA. *Education:* BA, University of Oklahoma, 1964; MA, Johns Hopkins University, 1965. *Career:* mem. National Space Society; SFWA. *Publications:* The Faded Sun, 1978; Downbelow Station, 1981; The Pride of Chanur, 1982; Chanur's Venture, 1984; Forty Thousand in Gehenna, 1984; Cuckoo's Egg, 1985; Chanur's Homecoming, 1986; Visible Light, 1986; Angel with the Sword, 1987; The Paladin, 1988; Rusalka, 1989; Rimrunners, 1990; Chernevog, 1991; Heavy Time, 1991; Chanur's Legacy, 1992; The Goblin Mirror, 1993; Hellburner, 1993; Faery in Shadow, 1994; Tripoint, 1994; Fortress in the Eye of Time, 1995; Invader, 1995; Rider at the Gate, 1995; Cloud's Rider, 1996; Lois and Clark, 1996; Inheritor, 1996; Fortress of Owls, 1998. *Honours:* John Campbell Award, 1977; Hugo Awards, 1979, 1982, 1989. *Address:* c/o Warner Books Inc, 1271 Avenue of the Americas, New York, NY 10020, USA.

CHERRY, Neeli (see Cherkovski, Neeli).

CHERRYH, C. J. (see Cherry, Carolyn Janice).

CHESSEX, Jacques; novelist and poet; b. 1 March 1934, Payerne, Switzerland. *Education:* University of Lausanne. *Publications:* La Tête ouverte, 1962; La Confession du pasteur Burg, 1967; A Father's Love, 1973; L'Ardent Royaume, 1975; Le Séjour des morts, 1977; Les Yeux jaunes, 1979; Où vont mourir les oiseaux, 1980; Judas le transparent, 1983; Jonas, 1987; Morgane Madrigal, 1990; Sosie d'un saint, 2000; Monsieur, 2001. Poetry: Le Jour proche, 1954; Chant du printemps, 1955; Une Voix la nuit, 1957; Batailles dans l'air, 1959; Le Jeûne de huit nuits, 1966; L'Ouvert obscur, 1967; Elégie, soleil du regret, 1976; La Calviniste, 1983; Feux d'orée, 1984; Comme l'os, 1988. Non-Fiction: Maupassant et les autres, 1981; Mort d'un cimetière, 1989; Flaubert, ou le désert en abîme, 1991; Notes sur Saura, 2001. *Honours:* Prix Goncourt, 1973; Commdr, Ordre des Arts et des Lettres, 1984; Chevalier, Légion d'honneur, 2002. *Address:* Editions Grasset, 61 rue des Sts-Pères, 75006 Paris, France.

CHEUSE, Alan; Author, Critic and University Teacher; b. 23 Jan. 1940, Perth Amboy, NJ, USA; m. 1st Mary Agan, 7 Oct. 1964, divorced 1974, one s.; m. 2nd Kristin M. O'Shee, 17 Aug. 1991, two d. *Education:* Lafayette College, 1957–58; BA, English Literature, 1961, PhD, Comparative Literature, 1974, Rutgers University. *Career:* Faculty, Bennington College, 1970–78, George Mason University, 1987–; Co-Dir, 1978–85, Acting Dir, 1986–87, Bennington Summer Writing Workshops; Visiting Lecturer, University of Tennessee, 1980–83, University of Virginia, 1987; Book Commentator, All Things Considered, National Public Radio, 1983–; Visiting Fellow, University of the South, 1984; Writing Program, University of Michigan, 1984–86; Producer-Host, The Sound of Writing, Center for the Book/National Public Radio, 1988–99; Visiting Writer, University of Houston, 1991–92; mem. National Book Critics Circle; PEN. *Publications:* Fiction: Candace & Other Stories, 1980; The Bohemians, 1982; The Grandmothers' Club, 1986; The Tennessee Waltz and Other Stories, 1990; The Light Possessed, 1990; Lost and Old Rivers, 1999. Other: Fall Out of Heaven, 1987; The Sound of Writing: Stories from the Radio (ed. with Caroline Marshall), 1991; Listening to Ourselves: More Stories from the Sound of Writing (ed. with Caroline Marshall), 1994; Talking Horse: Bernard Malamud on Life and Work (ed. with Nicholas Delbanco), 1996; Listening to the Page: Adventures in Reading and Writing, 2001. Contributions: anthologies, reference books, reviews, journals and newspapers. *Honours:* National Endowment for the Arts Creative Writing Fellowship, 1979–80; New York Time Notable Book of the Year Citation, 1982; Antioch Review Prize for Distinguished Non-Fiction, 2001. *Address:* 3611 35th St NW, Washington, DC 20016, USA.

CHEVALIER, Tracy, MA; American writer; b. Oct. 1962, Washington, DC; m.; one s. *Education:* Oberlin Coll., OH, USA, Univ. of East Anglia, England. *Career:* fmr reference book ed. –1993; moved to London, England 1984. *Publications:* The Virgin Blue 1997, Girl with a Pearl Earring 1999, Falling Angels 2001, The Lady and the Unicorn 2003. *Literary Agent:* Jonny Geller, Curtis Brown, Haymarket House, 28–29 Haymarket, London, SW1Y 4SP, England. *Telephone:* (20) 7393-4400. *E-mail:* tracy@tchevalier.com. *Website:* www.tchevalier.com.

CHICHETTO, James William; Writer, Poet, Prof. and Priest; b. 5 June 1941, Boston, MA, USA. *Education:* BA, Stonehill College, 1964; MA, Holy Cross College, 1968; MA, Wesleyan University, 1978. *Career:* Ordained Priest, Congregation of Holy Cross, 1968; Educator, Missionary, Peru, 1968–72; Assoc. Ed., Gargoyle Magazine, 1974–80; Ed., 1982–87, Artist, 1990–, The Connecticut Poetry Review; Prof. of Writing, Stonehill College, North Easton, MA, 1982–; mem. Connecticut Literary Forum, 1985–; National Asscn of Scholars, 2000–. *Publications:* Poems, 1975; Dialogue: Emily Dickinson and Christopher Cauldwell, 1978; Stones: A Litany, 1980; Gilgamesh and Other Poems, 1983; Victims, 1987; Homage to Father Edward Sorin, 1992; Dream of Norumbega, 2000; Reckoning Genocide, 2002. Contributions: Boston Phoenix; Colorado Review; Boston Globe; The Manhattan Review; The Patterson Review; The Connecticut Poetry Review; America; Perversions of Justice; Indigenous Peoples of Angloamerican Law; others. *Honours:* Book Grants, National Endowment for the Arts, 1980, 1983; Sri Chinmoy Poetry Award, 1984. *Address:* c/o Stonehill College, North Easton, MA 02357, USA. *E-mail:* jchichetto@stonehill.edu.

CHILDISH, Billy; Painter, Poet and Songwriter; b. 1959, Chatham, Kent, England; m. Julie Childish; one c. *Publications:* Poems from the Barrier Block, 1984; Monks Without God, 1986; Companions in a Death Boat, 1987; To the Quick, 1988; Girl in the Tree, 1988; Maverick Verse, 1988; Admissions to Strangers, 1989; Death of a Wood, 1989; The Silence of Words (short stories), 1989; The Deathly Flight of Angels, 1990; Like a God I Love All Things, 1990; Child's Death Letter, 1990; The Hart Rises, 1991; Poems of Laughter and Violence: Selected Poetry 1981–86, 1992; Poems to Break the Harts of Impossible Princesses, 1994; Days With a Hart Like a Dog, 1994; Big Hart and Balls, 1995; Messerschmitt Pilot's Severed Hand, 1996; My Fault (novel), 1996; Billy Childish and His Famous Headcoat, 1997; Notebooks of a Naked Youth (novel), 1997; I'd Rather You Lied: Selected Poems 1980–1998, 1999; Chatham Town Welcomes Desperate Men, 2001. *Address:* c/o Hangman Books, 11 Boundary Rd, Chatham, Kent ME4 6TS, England. *Website:* www.billychildish.com.

CHILTON, Bruce; Prof. of Religion and Writer; b. 27 Sept. 1949, Roslyn, New York, USA; m. Odile Sevault, 3 July 1982, two s. *Education:* AB, Bard College, 1971; MDiv, General Theological Seminary, 1974; PhD, St John's College, Cambridge, 1976. *Career:* Lecturer in Biblical Studies, Sheffield University, England, 1976–85; Lillian Claus Prof. of the New Testament, Yale University, 1985–87; Bernard Iddings Prof. of Religion, Bard College, Annandale, New York, 1987–; Rector, Church of St John the Evangelist, 1987–; mem. Studiorum Novi Testamenti Societas; Society of Biblical Literature. *Publications:* The Glory of Israel: The Theology and Provinence of the Isaiah Targum, 1983; The Kingdom of God in the Teaching of Jesus (ed.), 1984; A Galilean Rabbi and his Bible: Jesus' Own Interpretation of Isaiah, 1984; Targumic Approaches to the Gospels: Essays in the Mutual Definition of Judaism and Christianity, 1986; The Isaiah Targum, trans., 1987; Beginning New Testament Study, 1986, 1987; Jesus and the Ethics of the Kingdom (co-author), 1988; Profiles of a Rabbi: Synoptic Opportunities in Reading about Jesus, 1989; The Temple of Jesus: His Sacrificial Program within a Cultural History of Sacrifice, 1992; A Feast of Meanings: Eucharistic Theologies from Jesus through Johannine Circles, 1994; Studying the Historical Jesus: Evaluations of the State of Current Research (co-ed.), 1994; Judaic Approaches to the Gospel, 1994; Judaism in the New Testament: Practices and Beliefs (co-author), 1995; Revelation: The Torah and the Bible (co-author), 1995; Pure Kingdom: Jesus' Vision of God, 1996; The Body of Faith: Israel and the Church (co-author), 1996; Trading Places: The Intersecting Histories of Judaism and Christianity (co-author), 1996; The Intellectual Foundations of Christian and Jewish Discourse: The Philosophy of Religious Argument (co-author), 1997; Jesus' Prayer and Jesus' Eucharist: His Personal Practice of Spirituality, 1997; Trading Places Sourcebook: Readings in the Intersecting Histories of Judaism and Christianity, 1997. *Honours:* Heinrich Hertz Scholar, Germany; Asher Edelman Fellow, Bard College; Bishop Henry Martin Memorial Lecturer, University College of Emmanuel and St Chad; Evangelical Fellow, Pew Charitable Trust. *Address:* Bard College, Annandale, NY 12504, USA.

CHINODYA, Shimmer, (B. Chirasha); Novelist; b. 1957, Gweru, Zimbabwe; m. *Education:* Literature and Education, Univ. of Zimbabwe; MA, Creative Writing, Univ. of Iowa, USA, 1985. *Career:* curriculum developer, materials designer, ed. and screenwriter; Distinguished Visiting Prof. in creative writing, St Lawrence Univ., New York, 1995–97. *Publications:* Dew in the Morning, 1982; Farai's Girls, 1984; Child of War (as B. Chirasha), 1985; Harvest of Thorns, 1990; Can We Talk and Other Stories, 1998; several children's books as B. Chirasha. *Honours:* Commonwealth Writers Prize for

African Literature, 1990; numerous fellowships. *Address:* c/o African Writers Series, Heinemann Educational Publishers, Halley Ct, Jordan Hill, Oxford OX2 8EJ, England.

CHIRASHA, B. (see Chinodya, Shimmer).

CHISHOLM, Anne, FRSL; British biographer and reviewer; m. Michael Davie. *Career:* mem. RSL (mem. of council). *Publications:* non-fiction: Philosophers of the Earth 1972, Nancy Cunard: A Biography 1979, Faces of Hiroshima: A Report 1985, Beaverbrook: A Life (with Michael Davie) 1992, Rumer Godden: A Storyteller's Life 1998. *Honours:* Silver PEN Award 1979. *Address:* c/o Pan Macmillan Ltd, 20 New Wharf Road, London, N1 9RR, England. *Website:* www.macmillan.co.uk.

CHISSELL, Joan Olive; Musicologist; b. 22 May 1919, Cromer, Norfolk, England. *Education:* Assoc., Royal College of Music, Graduate, Royal School of Music, Royal College of Music, 1937–42. *Career:* Piano teacher, Royal College of Music Jr Dept, 1942–53; Lecturer, Extra-Mural Dept, Oxford and London Univs, 1942–48; Broadcaster, BBC, 1943–; Asst Music Critic, The Times, 1948–79; Reviewer, The Gramophone, 1968–2003; mem. Critics Circle; Royal College of Music Society; Royal Life Boat Society. *Publications:* Robert Schumann, 1948; Chopin, 1965; Schumann's Piano Music, 1972; Brahms, 1977; Clara Schumann: A Dedicated Spirit, 1983. Contributions: A Companion to the Concerto, 1988; numerous journals and magazines. *Honours:* City of Zwickau Robert Schumann Prize, 1991. *Address:* Flat D, 7 Abbey Rd, St Johns Wood, London NW8 9AA, England.

CHITHAM, Edward Harry Gordon; Education Consultant and Writer; b. 16 May 1932, Harborne, Birmingham, England; m. Mary Patricia Tilley, 29 Dec. 1962, one s. two d. *Education:* BA, MA (Classics), Jesus College, Cambridge, 1952–55; PGCE, University of Birmingham, 1955–56; MA, English, University of Warwick, 1973–77; PhD, University of Sheffield, 1983. *Career:* mem. FRSA, 1997; Asscn of Classics Teachers; Gaskell Society; Brontë Society. *Publications:* The Black Country, 1972; Ghost in the Water, 1973; The Poems of Anne Brontë, 1979; Brontë Facts and Brontë Problems (with T. J. Winnifrith), 1983; Selected Brontë Poems (with T. J. Winnifrith), 1985; The Brontës' Irish Background, 1986; A Life of Emily Brontë, 1987; Charlotte and Emily Brontë (with T. J. Winnifrith), 1989; A Life of Anne Brontë, 1991; A Bright Start, 1995; The Poems of Emily Brontë (with Derek Roper), 1996; The Birth of Wuthering Heights: Emily Brontë at Work, 1998. Contributions: Byron Journal; Gaskell Society Journal; ISIS Magazine; Brontë Society Transactions. *Address:* 25 Fugelmere Close, Harborne, Birmingham B17 8SE, England.

CHITTICK, William C., BA, PhD; American writer and academic; b. Milford, CT. *Education:* Univ. of Tehran, Iran. *Career:* Prof. of Comparative Studies, Inter-departmental Doctoral Program in Anthropological Sciences, State Univ. of New York at Stony Brook. *Publications include:* The Sufi Path of Knowledge 1989, Adornment of Hearts 1991, Imaginal Worlds 1994, The Vision of Islam (co-author) 1996, The Self-Disclosure of God 1997, Sufism: A Short Introduction 2000; The Heart of Islamic Philosophy 2001, American Foreign Policy: History, Substance and Progress 2001. *Address:* Department of Anthropology, State University of New York, Stony Brook, NY 11794-8081, USA. *E-mail:* wchittick@notes.cc.sunysb.edu.

CHITTY, Susan Elspeth, (Lady Chitty); British writer, journalist and lecturer; b. 18 Aug. 1929, London, England; m. Sir Thomas Willes Chitty 1951, one s. three d. *Education:* Somerville Coll., Oxford. *Publications:* fiction: The Diary of a Fashion Model 1958, White Huntress 1963, My Life and Horses 1966; non-fiction: The Woman Who Wrote Black Beauty 1972, The Beast and the Monk 1975, Charles Kingsley and North Devon 1976, On Next to Nothing (with Thomas Willes Chitty) 1976, The Great Donkey Walk (with Thomas Willes Chitty) 1977, The Young Rider 1979, Gwen John 1876–1939 1981, Now to My Mother 1985, That Singular Person Called Lear 1988; editor: The Intelligent Woman's Guide to Good Taste 1958, The Puffin Book of Horses 1975, Antonia White: Diaries 1926–1957 two vols 1991–92, Playing the Game: Biography of Henry Newbolt 1997. *Literary Agent:* Curtis Brown Ltd, Haymarket House, 28–29 Haymarket, London, SW1Y 4SP, England. *Telephone:* (20) 7393-4400. *Fax:* (20) 7393-4401. *E-mail:* info@curtisbrown.co.uk. *Website:* www.curtisbrown.co.uk. *Address:* Bow Cottage, West Hoathly, Sussex RH19 4QF, England.

CHITTY, Sir Thomas Willes, (Thomas Hinde), Bt; British author; b. 2 March 1926, Felixstowe; m. Susan Elspeth Chitty (née Hopkinson) 1951; one s. three d. *Education:* Winchester Coll. and Univ. Coll., Oxford. *Career:* served in Royal Navy 1944–47; with Shell group 1953–60; Granada Arts Fellow, Univ. of York 1964–65; Visiting lecturer, Univ. of Illinois 1965–67; Visiting Prof. Boston Univ. 1969–70; now freelance writer. *Achievements:* expedition on foot and donkey with wife and two young daughters, Santiago to Salonika 1975–76. *Publications include:* fiction: Mr Nicholas 1952, Happy As Larry 1957, For the Good of the Company 1961, A Place Like Home 1962, The Cage 1962, Ninety Double Martinis 1963, The Day the Call Came 1964, Games of Chance 1965, The Village 1966, High 1968, Bird 1970, Generally a Virgin 1972, Agent 1974, Our Father 1975, Daymare 1980; non-fiction: Spain 1963, On Next to Nothing (with Susan Elspeth Chitty) 1976, The Great Donkey Walk (with Susan Elspeth Chitty) 1977, The Cottage Book 1979, Sir Henry and Sons (autobiog.) 1980, Stately Gardens of Britain 1983, A Field Guide to the English Country Parson 1983, Forests of Britain 1984, The Domesday Book: England's Heritage, Then and Now 1986, Courtiers: 900 Years of Court Life 1986, Tales from the Pump Room: An Informal History of Bath 1988, Capability Brown 1986, Imps of Promise: A History of the King's School Canterbury 1990, Looking-Glass Letters (ed.) (letters of Lewis Carroll) 1991, Paths of Progress, A History of Marlborough College 1992, A History of Highgate School 1993, A History of King's College School 1994, Carpenter's Children: A History of the City of London School 1995, An Illustrated History of the University of Greenwich 1996, The Martlet and the Griffen: A History of Abingdon School 1997. *Address:* c/o Andrew Hewson, John Johnson, 45–47 Clerkenwell Green, London, EC1R 0HT (Office); Bow Cottage, West Hoathly, Sussex, RH19 4QF, England. *Telephone:* (20) 7251-0125 (Office); (1342) 810269. *E-mail:* thomas.chitty@ukgateway.net (Home).

CHOMSKY, (Avram) Noam, MA, PhD; American theoretical linguist and writer; *Professor Emeritus, Department of Linguistics, Massachusetts Institute of Technology*; b. 7 Dec. 1928, Philadelphia, PA; m. Carol Schatz 1949; one s. two d. *Education:* Univ. of Pennsylvania. *Career:* Asst Prof., MIT 1955–58, Assoc. Prof. 1958–61, Prof. of Modern Languages 1961–66, Ferrari P. Ward Prof. of Modern Languages and Linguistics 1966–76, Institute Prof. 1976–; Visiting Prof., Columbia Univ. 1957–58; Nat. Science Foundation Fellow, Princeton Inst. for Advanced Study 1958–59; American Council of Learned Socs Fellow, Center for Cognitive Studies, Harvard Univ. 1964–65; Linguistics Soc. of America Prof., Univ. of California at Los Angeles 1966; Beckman Prof., Univ. of California at Berkeley 1966–67; John Locke Lecturer, Univ. of Oxford 1969; Shearman Lecturer, Univ. Coll. London 1969; Bertrand Russell Memorial Lecturer, Univ. of Cambridge 1971; Nehru Memorial Lecturer, Univ. of New Delhi 1972; Whidden Lecturer, McMaster Univ. 1975; Huizinga Memorial Lecturer, Univ. of Leiden 1977; Woodbridge Lecturer, Columbia Univ. 1978; Kant Lecturer, Stanford Univ. 1979; Jeanette K. Watson Distinguished Visiting Prof., Syracuse Univ. 1982; Pauling Memorial Lecturer, Oregon State Univ. 1995; mem. American Acad. of Arts and Sciences, Linguistic Soc. of America, American Philosophical Asscn, American Acad. of Political and Social Science, NAS, Bertrand Russell Peace Foundation, Deutsche Akademie der Naturforscher Leopoldina, Nat. Acad. of Sciences, Royal Anthropological Inst., Utrecht Soc. of Arts and Sciences; Fellow, American Asscn for the Advancement of Science; corresp. Fellow, British Acad. *Publications include:* Syntactic Structures 1957, Current Issues in Linguistic Theory 1964, Aspects of the Theory of Syntax 1965, Cartesian Linguistics 1966, Topics in the Theory of Generative Grammar 1966, Language and Mind 1968, The Sound Pattern of English (with Morris Halle) 1968, American Power and the New Mandarins 1969, At War with Asia 1970, Problems of Knowledge and Freedom 1971, Studies on Semantics in Generative Grammar 1972, For Reasons of State 1973, The Backroom Boys 1973, Counter-revolutionary Violence (with Edward Herman) 1973, Peace in the Middle East? 1974, Reflections on Language 1975, The Logical Structure of Linguistic Theory 1975, Essays on Form and Interpretation 1977, Human Rights and American Foreign Policy 1978, Language and Responsibility 1979, The Political Economy of Human Rights (two vols, with Edward Herman) 1979, Rules and Representations 1980, Lectures on Government and Binding 1981, Radical Priorities 1981, Towards a New Cold War 1982, Concepts and Consequences of the Theory of Government and Binding 1982, Fateful Triangle: The United States, Israel and the Palestinians 1983, Modular Approaches to the Study of the Mind 1984, Turning the Tide 1985, Knowledge of Language: Its Nature, Origins and Use 1986, Barriers 1986, Pirates and Emperors 1986, Generative Grammar: Its Basis, Development and Prospects 1987, On Power and Ideology 1987, Language and Problems of Knowledge 1987, Language in a Psychological Setting 1987, The Chomsky Reader 1987, The Culture of Terrorism 1988, Manufacturing Consent (with Edward Herman) 1988, Language and Politics 1988, Necessary Illusions 1989, Deterring Democracy 1991, What Uncle Sam Really Wants 1992, Chronicles of Dissent 1992, Year 501: The Conquest Continues 1993, Rethinking Camelot: JFK, the Vietnam War and US Political Culture 1993, Letters from Lexington: Reflections on Propaganda 1993, The Prosperous Few and the Restless Many 1993, Language and Thought 1994, World Orders, Old and New 1994, The Minimalist Program 1995, Powers and Prospects 1996, Class Warfare 1996, The Common Good 1998, Profit over People 1998, The New Military Humanism 1999, New Horizons in the Study of Language and Mind 2000, Rogue States: The Rule of Force in World Affairs 2000, A New Generation Draws the Line 2000, Architecture of Language 2000, Propaganda and the Public Mind 2001, 9-11 2001, Understanding Power 2002, On Nature and Language 2002, Middle East Illusions 2003, Hegemony or Survival: America's Quest for Global Dominance 2003; numerous lectures, contribs. to scholarly journals. *Honours:* Hon. Fellow, British Psychological Soc. 1985, Royal Anthropological Inst.; Hon. DHL (Chicago) 1967, (Loyola Univ., Swarthmore Coll.) 1970, (Bard Coll.) 1971, (Mass.) 1973, (Maine, Gettysburg Coll.) 1992, (Amherst Coll.) 1995, (Buenos Aires) 1996; Hon. DLitt (London) 1967, (Delhi) 1972, Visva-Bharati (West Bengal) 1980, (Pa) 1984, (Cambridge) 1995; hon. degrees (Tarragona) 1998, (Guelph) 1999, (Columbia) 1999, (Connecticut) 1999, (Pisa) 1999, (Harvard) 2000, (Toronto) 2000, (Western Ontario) 2000, Kolkata (2001); George Orwell Award, Nat. Council of Teachers of English 1987, Kyoto Prize in Basic Sciences 1988, James Killian Award (MIT) 1992; Helmholtz Medal, Berlin Brandenburgische Akad. Wissenschaften 1996, Benjamin Franklin Medal, Franklin Inst., Philadelphia 1999, Rabindranath Tagore Centenary Award,

Asiatic Soc. 2000, Peace Award, Turkish Publrs Asscn 2002. *Address:* Department of Linguistics and Philosophy, Massachusetts Institute of Technology, 77 Massachusetts Avenue, Cambridge, MA 02139 (Office); 15 Suzanne Road, Lexington, MA 02420, USA (Home). *Telephone:* (617) 253-7819 (Office); (781) 862-6160 (Home). *Fax:* (617) 253-9425 (Office). *E-mail:* chomsky@mit.edu (Office).

CHORLTON, David; writer, poet and artist; b. 15 Feb. 1948, Spittal-an-der-Drau, Austria; m. Roberta Elliott 1976. *Education:* Stockport Coll. *Publications:* Without Shoes 1987, The Village Painters 1990, Measuring Time 1990, Forget the Country You Came From 1992, Outposts 1994, Assimilation 2000, Common Sightings 2001, A Normal Day Amazes Us 2003, Return to Waking Life 2004; contrib. to many reviews and journals. *Address:* 118 W Palm Lane, Phoenix, AZ 85003, USA.

CHOYCE, Lesley; Canadian academic, writer, poet and editor; b. 21 March 1951, Riverside, NJ, USA; m. Terry Paul 1974; two d. *Education:* BA, Rutgers University, 1972; MA, Montclair State College, 1974; MA, CUNY, 1983. *Career:* Ed., Pottersfield Press, 1979–; Prof., Dalhousie University, 1986–. *Recordings:* Long Lost Planet 1996, Sea Level 1998. *Publications:* Adult Fiction: Eastern Sure, 1981; Billy Botzweiler's Last Dance, 1984; Downwind, 1984; Conventional Emotions, 1985; The Dream Auditor, 1986; Coming Up for Air, 1988; The Second Season of Jonas MacPherson, 1989; Magnificent Obsessions, 1991; Ecstasy Conspiracy, 1992; Margin of Error, 1992; The Republic of Nothing, 1994; The Trap Door to Heaven, 1996; Beautiful Sadness, 1997; Dance the Rocks Ashore, 1997; World Enough, 1998, The Summer of Apartment X 1999, Cold Clear Morning 2001. Young Adult Fiction: Skateboard Shakedown, 1989; Hungry Lizards, 1990; Wavewatch, 1990; Some Kind of Hero, 1991; Wrong Time, Wrong Place, 1991; Clearcut Danger, 1992; Full Tilt, 1993; Good Idea Gone Bad, 1993; Dark End of Dream Street, 1994; Big Burn, 1995; Falling Through the Cracks, 1996, Couleurs Troubles 1997, Roid Rage 1999, Refuge Cove 2002, Shoulder the Sky 2002. Poetry: Re-Inventing the Wheel, 1980; Fast Living, 1982; The End of Ice, 1985; The Top of the Heart, 1986; The Man Who Borrowed the Bay of Fundy, 1988; The Coastline of Forgetting, 1995; Beautiful Sadness, 1998, Caution to the Wind 2000. Non-Fiction: An Avalanche of Ocean, 1987; December Six: The Halifax Solution, 1988; Transcendental Anarchy (autobiog.), 1993; Nova Scotia: Shaped by the Sea, 1996. Editor: Chezzetcook, 1977; The Pottersfield Portfolio, 7 vols, 1979–85; Visions from the Edge (with John Bell), 1981; The Cape Breton Collection, 1984; Ark of Ice: Canadian Futurefiction, 1992. *Honours:* Event Magazine's Creative Non-fiction Competition Winner, 1990; Dartmouth Book Awards, 1990, 1995; Ann Connor Brimer Award for Children's Literature, 1994; Authors Award, Foundation for the Advancement of Canadian Letters 1995, Landmar East Literacy Award 2000, Poet Laureate Peter Gzowski Invitational Golf Tournament 2000. *Address:* 83 Leslie Road, East Lawrencetown, NS B2Z 1P8, Canada.

CHRAIBI, Driss; Novelist and Dramatist; b. 15 July 1926, El Jadida, Morocco; m. Sheena McCallion, 1978. *Education:* Studied in Casablanca and Paris. *Career:* Prof., University of Laval, Québec, 1969–70. *Publications:* The Simple Past, 1954; The Butts, 1955; L'Ane, 1956; De Tous les Horizons, 1958; La Foule, 1961; Heirs to the Past, 1962; Un ami viendra vous voir, 1966; La Mother Comes of Age, 1982; Mort au Canada, 1974; Une Enquête au Pays, 1981; Mother Spring, 1982; Birth at Dawn, 1986; L'Homme du livre, 1994. Other: Radio plays. *Honours:* Société des Auteurs Prize, 1990. *Address:* 15 rue Paul Pons, 26400 Crest, France.

CHRISTENSEN, Inger; Danish poet, playwright and essayist; b. 16 Jan. 1935. *Plays:* Intriganterne 1972, En vinteraften i Ufa og andre spil 1987. *Publications include:* poetry: Lys 1962, Graes 1963, Det 1969, Brev i april 1970, Alfabet 1981, Sommerfugledalen - et requiem 1991, Samlede digte 1998; novels: Evighedsmaskinen 1964, Det malede vaerelse 1976; juvenile fiction: Den store ukendte rejse 1982; essays: Del af labyrinten 1982, Hemmelighedstilstanden 2000. *Address:* c/o Bloodaxe Books Ltd, Highgreen, Tarset, Northumberland NE48 1RP, England. *Website:* www.bloodaxebooks.com.

CHRISTENSEN, Lars Saabye; Norwegian poet, author and playwright; b. 21 Sept. 1953, Oslo. *Career:* Ed., Signaler 1986–90. *Plays:* Columbus' ankomst (Hørespillprisen 1981–82) 1981, Mekka 1994. *Publications:* poetry: Historien om Gly (Tarjei Vesaas' Debutantpris) 1976, Ordbok 1977, Kamelen i mitt hertje 1978, Jaktmarker 1979, Paraply 1982, Åsteder 1986, Stempler 1989, Versterålen: Lyset, livet, landskapet 1989, Hvor er det blitt av alle gutta 1991, Den akustiske skyggen 1993, Nordmarka 1993, Den andre siden av blått 1996, Falleferdig himmel 1998, Pasninger 1998, Under en sort paraply (with Niels Fredriok Dahl) 1998, Pinnsvinsol 2000, Mann for sin katt 2000, Sanger & steiner 2003; novels: Amatøren 1977, Billettene 1980, Jokeren 1981, Beatles 1984, Blodets bånd 1985, Sneglene 1987, Herman (trans. as Herman) 1988, Bly (Bokhandlerprisen) 1990, Gutten som ville være en av gutta 1992, Jubel 1995, Halvbroren (trans. as The Half Brother) (Bokhandlerprisen) 2001, Maskeblomstfamilien 2003; other fiction: Ingens 1992, Den Misunnnelige frisøren 1997, Noen som elsker hverandre 1999, Kongen som ville ha mer enn en krone (with Randall Meyers and Anita Killi) 1999; contrib. to Alexandrias aske 1993. *Honours:* Cappelenprisen 1984, Rivertonprisen 1987, Kritikerpris 1988, Amandaprisen 1991, Doblougprisen 1993, Riksmålprisen 1997, Sargsborgrisen 1999, Aamoudt-statuetten 2001, Brageprisen 2001, Den norske leserprisen 2001, Natt & Dags bokpris 2001, Nordisk Råds Litteratuur Pris 2002. *Literary Agent:* J. W. Cappelens Forslag AS, PB 350, 0101, Oslo, Norway. *Telephone:* 22365000. *Fax:* 22365040. *Website:* www.cappelen.no. *Address:* c/o Arcadia Books, Turnaround Publishers Services, Unit 3, Olympia Trading Estate, Coburg Road, London, N22 6TZ, England.

CHRISTIAN, Beatrix; Australian playwright and screenwriter. *Education:* Nat. Inst. of Drama. *Career:* affiliate writer and writer-in-residence, Sydney Theatre Co 1993–94; writer-in-residence, Sydney Theatre Co 2002. *Plays:* Inside Dry Water 1993, Blue Murder 1994, The Governor's Family 1997, Faust's House, Fred, Old Masters, The Promised Land, Spumante Romantica, Ten Things Not to Do on a First Date, Then the Mountain Comes; adaptations: A Doll's House (Ibsen), Life is a Dream (Calderón de la Barca); adaptations with Benedict Andrews: Three Sisters (Chekhov). *Television writing:* White Colour Blue. *Film screenplay:* Jindabyne 2005. *Honours:* Sydney Critics' Circle Award for Best Australian Play, New York New Dramatists' Award 1997, Queensland Premier's Literary Award. *Literary Agent:* RGM Associates, PO Box 128, Surry Hills, NSW 2010, Australia. *Telephone:* (2) 9281-3911. *Fax:* (2) 9281-4705. *E-mail:* info@rgm.com.au. *Website:* www.rgm.com.au.

CHRISTIAN, John (see Dixon, Roger).

CHRISTOPHER, Nicholas; Poet and Writer; b. 28 Feb. 1951, New York, NY, USA; m. Constance Barbara Davidson, 20 Nov. 1980. *Education:* AB, Harvard College, 1973. *Career:* Adjunct Prof. of English, New York University; Lecturer, Columbia University. *Publications:* On Tour with Rita (poems), 1982; A Short History of the Island of Butterflies (poems), 1986; The Soloist (novel), 1986; Desperate Characters (poems), 1988; Under 35: The New Generation of American Poets (ed.), 1989; In the Year of the Comet (poems), 1992; 5 Degrees and Other Poems, 1994; Walk and Other Poems, 1995; Veronica (novel), 1996; Somewhere in the Night: Film Noir and the American City, 1997. Contributions: anthologies and periodicals. *Honours:* New York Foundation for the Arts Fellowship, 1986; National Endowment for the Arts Fellowship, 1987; Peter I B. Lavan Award, Acad. of American Poets, 1991; Guggenheim Fellowship, 1993; Melville Cane Award, 1994. *Literary Agent:* Janklow & Nesbit Associates, 445 Park Ave, New York, NY 10022, USA.

CHURCH, Robert; Author; b. 20 July 1932, London, England; m. Dorothy June Bourton, 15 April 1953, two d. *Education:* Beaufoy College, London, 1946–48. *Career:* Metropolitan Police, 1952–78; Probation Service, 1978–88. *Publications:* Murder in East Anglia, 1987; Accidents of Murder, 1989; More Murder in East Anglia, 1990; Anglian Blood (co-ed.), 1995; Well Done Boys, 1996. Contributions: miscellaneous journals. *Honours:* Winner, Salaman Prize for Non-Fiction, 1997. *Address:* Woodside, 7 Crome Walk, Gunton Park, Lowestoft, Suffolk NR32 4NF, England.

CHURCHILL, Caryl; Dramatist; b. 3 Sept. 1938, London, England; m. David Harter, 1961, three s. *Education:* BA, Lady Margaret Hall, Oxford, 1960. *Publications:* Owners, 1973; Light Shining in Buckinghamshire, 1976; Traps, 1977; Vinegar Tom, 1978; Cloud Nine, 1979; Top Girls, 1982; Fen, 1983; Collected Plays, 2 vols, 1985, 1988; A Mouthful of Birds (with D. Lan), 1986; Serious Money, 1987; Ice Cream, 1989; Hot Fudge, 1990; Mad Forest, 1990; Lives of the Great Poisoners (with I. Spink and O. Gough), 1991; The Skriker, 1994; This is a Chair, 1997; Blue Heart, 1997; Far Away, 2000; A Number, 2002. Other: various radio and television plays. *Address:* c/o Casarotto Ramsay Ltd, National House, 60–66 Wardour St, London W1V 3HP, England.

CIFERRI, Elvio, DLitt; Italian writer, historian and professor; b. 1 April 1965, Città di Castello. *Education:* Perugia Univ. *Career:* Prof. of History and Italian Literature, Perugia Univ. 1992, Prof. Leopoldo and Alice Franchetti Inst., Castello 1999. *Publications:* non-fiction: Editti e notificazioni di mons. Giovanni Muzi vescovo di Città di Castello 1989, Luigi Piccardini e il suo tempo 1993, Tifernati illustri, 3 vols 2000–03; contrib. to numerous journals, Biblioteca Sanctorum, Encyclopedia of the Romantic Era 2004. *Honours:* Gold Medal Atheste Prize for historical research 2002. *Address:* Via Toscana 51, 06010 Lerchi, Italy. *Telephone:* (75) 8554902. *E-mail:* elcif@tiscalinet.it (Home). *Website:* www.elviociferri.it.

CIRESI, Rita; writer and academic; b. 29 Sept. 1960, New Haven, CT, USA. *Education:* BA, New College, 1981; MA, University of Iowa, 1983; MFA, Pennsylvania State University, 1988. *Career:* Asst Prof. of English, Hollins College, 1992–95; Asst Prof., 1995, Assoc. Prof., 1995–, University of South Florida; mem. American Italian Historical Asscn; Associated Writing Programs; Italian American Writers' Asscn. *Publications:* Mother Rocket, 1993; Blue Italian, 1996; Pink Slip, 1999; Sometimes I Dream in Italian, 2000. Contributions: anthologies, reviews and quarterlies. *Honours:* Master Fellowship, Pennsylvania Council on the Arts, 1989; Flannery O'Connor Award, 1991; Teaching Fellow, Wesleyan Writers Conference, 1995; William Faulkner Prize, 1997. *Address:* c/o Department of English, University of South Florida, Tampa, FL 33634, USA.

CISNEROS, Sandra, BA; American writer and poet; b. 20 Dec. 1954, Chicago, IL. *Education:* Loyola Univ. *Publications:* Bad Boys 1980, The House on Mango Street 1983, The Rodrigo Poems 1985, My Wicked, Wicked Ways 1987, Woman Hollering Creek and Other Stories 1991, Hairs-Pelitos 1994, Loose Women 1994, Caramelo 2002; contrib. to periodicals. *Honours:* National Endowment for the Arts Fellowships 1982, 1987, American Book

Award 1985, Lannan Foundation Award 1991, John D. and Catherine T. MacArthur Foundation Fellowship 1995. *Literary Agent:* Susan Bergholz Literary Services, 17 W 10th Street, Suite 5, New York, NY 10011, USA.

CIXOUS, Hélène; Prof. of Comparative Literature, Author and Dramatist; b. 5 June 1937, Oran, Algeria; one d. one s. *Education:* Agrégation, English Literature, 1959, Doctorat d'etat ès Lettres, 1968, Lycée d'Alger, Lycée de Sceaux, Sorbonne. *Career:* settled in France, 1955; Staff, University of Bordeaux, 1962–65; Asst Lecturer, Sorbonne, 1965–67; Lecturer, University of Paris X, Nanterre, 1967–68; Co-founder, Chair., Prof. of Literature, 1968–, Founder-Dir, Centre d'Etudes Féminines, 1974–, University of Paris VIII, Vincennes; Distinguished Visiting Prof., Northwestern Univ., Chicago, 1995–; visiting prof. and lecturer at numerous conferences and symposia, notably in Europe, N America, Japan and India; mem. Conseil Scientifique, Fondation de France. *Publications:* Fiction: Le Prénom de Dieu, 1967; Dedans, 1969; Le Troisième corps, 1970; Les Commencements, 1970; Un vrai jardin, 1971; Neutre, 1972; Tombe, 1973; Portrait du soleil, 1973; Révolutions pour plus d'un Faust, 1975; Souffles, 1975; La, 1976; Partie, 1976; Angst, 1977; Préparatifs de noces au-delà de l'abîme, 1978; Vivre l'orange, 1979; Anankè, 1979; Illa, 1980; With ou l'art de l'innocence, 1981; Limonade tout était si infini, 1982; Le Livre de Promethea, 1983; La bataille d'Arcachon, 1986; Manne, 1988; Jours de l'An, 1990; L'Ange au secret, 1991; Déluge, 1992; Beethoven à jamais, 1993; La fiancée juive, 1995; Messie, 1996; Or, les lettres de mon père, 1997; Osnabrück, 1999; Le Jour où je n'étais pas là, 2000; Les Rêveries de la femme sauvage, 2000; Benjamin à Montaigne, il ne faut pas le dire, 2001; Manhattan, lettres de la préhistoire, 2002. Plays: La Pupille, 1971; Portrait de Dora, 1976; Le nom d'Oedipe, 1978; La prise de l'école de Madhubaï, 1986; L'histoire terrible mais inachevée de Norodom Sihanouk, roi du Cambodge, 1985; L'Indiade ou l'Inde de leurs rêves, 1987; On ne part pas on ne revient pas, 1991; Voile noire voile blanche, 1994; L'histoire (qu'on ne connaîtra jamais), 1994; La Ville Parjure ou le Réveil des Erinyes, 1994; Tambours sur la Digue, 1999; Rouen, la trentième nuit de mai 31, 2001. Essays: L'exil de James Joyce, 1969; Prénoms de personne, 1974; La jeune née, 1975; La venue à l'écriture, 1977; Entre l'écriture, 1986; L'heure de Clarice Lispector, 1989; Readings: The Poetics of Blanchot, Joyce, Kafka, Lispector, Tsvetaeva, 1992; Three Steps on the Ladder of Writing, 1993; Photos de racines, 1994; Stigmata: Escaping Texts, 1998; Portait de Jacques Derrida en jeune saint juif, 2001. *Honours:* Prix Médicis Étranger, 1969; Southern Cross of Brazil, 1989; Chevalier, Légion d'honneur, 1994; Prix des critiques, 1994, 2000; Ambassador of Star Awards, Pakistan, 1997; Officier, Ordre nat. du Mérite, 1998; Molière Award, 2000; numerous hon. doctorates. *Literary Agent:* Myriam Diocaretz, Worldwide Rights and Publishing Consultants. *Address:* Centre d'Études Féminines, Université de Paris VIII, 2 rue de la Liberté, 93526 Saint Denis Cedex 02, France; c/o Éditions Galilée, 5 rue Linné, 75005 Paris, France. *E-mail:* m.diocaretz@inter.nl.net.

CLANCY, Joseph Patrick Thomas; College Teacher, Writer and Poet; b. 8 March 1928, New York, NY, USA; m. Gertrude Wiegand, 31 July 1948, four s., four d. *Education:* BA, 1947, MA, 1949, PhD, 1957, Fordham University. *Career:* Faculty, 1948, Prof., 1962, Marymount Manhattan College; mem. American Literary Trans' Asscn; Dramatists' Guild; Yr Academi Gymreig; Eastern States Celtic Asscn; St Davids Society of New York. *Publications:* The Odes and Epodes of Horace, 1960; Medieval Welsh Lyrics, 1965; The Earliest Welsh Poems, 1970; 20th Century Welsh Poems, 1982; Gwyn Thomas: Living a Life, 1982; The Significance of Flesh: Poems, 1950–83, 1984; Bobi Jones: Selected Poems, 1987. Contributions: Poetry Wales; Planet; Anglo Welsh Review; Book News from Wales; Epoch; College English; America. *Honours:* American Philosophical Society Fellowships, 1963, 1968; National Trans. Centre Fellowship, 1968; Welsh Arts Council, Literature Award, 1971, Major Bursary, 1972; National Endowment for the Arts Trans. Fellowship, 1983; St Davids Society of New York Annual Award, 1986. *Address:* 1549 Benson St, New York, NY 10461, USA.

CLANCY, Laurence James; academic and writer; b. 2 Dec. 1942, Melbourne, Vic., Australia; m. (divorced); two s. *Education:* BA, Melbourne University, 1964; MA, La Trobe University, 1973. *Career:* mem. PEN International. *Publications:* A Collapsible Man, 1975; The Wife Specialist, 1978; Xavier Herber, 1981; Perfect Love, 1983; The Novels of Vladimir Nabokov, 1984; City to City, 1989; A Reader's Guide to Australian Fiction, 1992; The Wild Life Reserve, 1994. Contributions: newspapers and journals. *Honours:* Co-Winner, National Book Council Award, 1975; Australian Natives Asscn Award, 1983. *Address:* 227 Westgarth Street, Northcote, Vic. 3070, Australia.

CLANCY, Thomas (Tom) L., Jr, BA; American writer; b. 12 March 1947, Baltimore, MD; m. Wanda Thomas 1969; one s. three d. *Education:* Loyola Coll. *Publications:* The Hunt for Red October 1984, Red Storm Rising 1986, Patriot Games 1987, Cardinal of the Kremlin 1988, Clear and Present Danger 1989, The Sum of all Fears 1991, Without Remorse 1992, Submarine 1993, Debt of Honour 1994, Tom Clancy's Op Centre (with Steve Pieczenik) 1994, Reality Check 1995, Games of Statel (with Steve Pieczenik) 1996, Tom Clancy's Op Centre II (with Steve Pieczenik) 1996, Executive Orders 1996, Into the Storm (with Fred Franks Jr) 1997, Rainbow Six 1998, Carrier 1999, The Bear and the Dragon 2000, Red Rabbit 2002, The Teeth of the Tiger 2003. *Address:* Red Storm Entertainment Inc., 3200 Gateway Center Boulevard, Morrisville, NC 27560, USA. *Website:* www.redstorm.com.

CLARE, Ellen (see Sinclair, Olga Ellen).

CLARK, Anne (see Amor, Anne Clark).

CLARK, Brian Robert; Dramatist; b. 3 June 1932, Bournemouth, England; m. 1st Margaret Paling 1961; two s.; m. 2nd Anita Modak 1983; one step-s. one step-d.; m. 3rd Cherry Potter 1990. *Education:* Redland College of Education, Bristol; Central School of Speech and Drama, London; BA, English, Nottingham University. *Career:* Staff Tutor in Drama, University of Hull, 1966–70; Founder, Amber Lane Press, 1978. *Publications:* Group Theatre, 1971; Whose Life is it Anyway?, 1978; Can You Hear Me at the Back?, 1979; Post Mortem, 1979; The Petition, 1986; In Pursuit of Eve–A dramatic sonnet sequence, 2001. Other: Over 30 television plays, 1971–; several stage plays. *Honours:* Society of West Theatre Award for Best Play, 1977; FRSL, 1985. *Address:* c/o Judy Daish Assocs, 83 Eastbourne Mews, London W2 6LQ, England.

CLARK, Curt (see Westlake, Donald Edwin).

CLARK, David Ridgley; academic and writer; b. 17 Sept. 1920, Seymour, CT, USA; m. Mary Adele Matthieu 1948; two s. two d. *Education:* BA, Wesleyan University, 1947; MA, 1950, PhD, 1955, Yale University. *Career:* Instructor, 1951–57, Asst Prof., 1957–58, Assoc. Prof., 1958–65, Prof., 1965–85, University of Massachusetts; Visiting Prof., St Mary's College, Notre Dame, IN, 1985–87; Visiting Prof., Williams College, Williamstown, Massachusetts, 1989–91; mem. American Conference for Irish Studies; International Asscn for the Support of Anglo-Irish Literature; MLA of America. *Publications:* A Curious Quire, 1962; W. B. Yeats and the Theatre of Desolate Reality, 1965; Irish Renaissance, 1965; Dry Tree, 1966; Riders to the Sea, 1970; A Tower of Polished Black Stones: Early Versions of the Shadowy Waters, 1971; Twentieth Century Interpretations of Murder in the Cathedral, 1971; Druid Craft, 1971; That Black Day: The Manuscripts of Crazy Jane on the Day of Judgement, 1980; W. B. Yeats: The Writing of Sophocles' King Oedipus (with James McGuire), 1989; W. B. Yeats: The Winding Stair (1929): Manuscript Materials, 1995; W. B. Yeats: Words for Music Perhaps and Other Poems (1932): Manuscript Materials, 1999; The Collected Works of W. B. Yeats, Vol. II, The Plays, 2001; Parnell's Funeral and Other Poems, from A Full Moon in March: Manuscript Materials, 2003. *Address:* 481 Holgerson Road, Sequim, WA 98382, USA.

CLARK, Eric; Author and Journalist; b. 29 July 1937, Birmingham, England; m. Marcelle Bernstein, 12 April 1972, one s. two d. *Career:* Staff of various newspapers including, Daily Mail, The Guardian, The Observer until 1972; Full-time Author, 1972–; mem. Society of Authors; Authors' Guild; PEN International UK Centre, fellow; CWA; MWA. *Publications:* Len Deighton's London Dossier (part-author), 1967; Everybody's Guide to Survival, 1969; Corps Diplomatique, 1973, US edn as Diplomat, 1973; Black Gambit, 1978; The Sleeper, 1979; Send in the Lions, 1981; Chinese Burn, 1984, US edn as China Run, 1984; The Want Makers (Inside the Hidden World of Advertising), 1988; Hide and Seek, 1994. Contributions: Observer; Sunday Times; Daily Mail; Daily Telegraph; Washington Post; Los Angeles Times; Melbourne Age. *Address:* c/o Child and Company, 1 Fieet St, London EC4Y 1BD, England.

CLARK, Johnson (John) Pepper, BA; Nigerian poet, dramatist and professor of English; b. 3 April 1935, Kiagbodo; m. Ebunoluwa Bolajoko Odutola; one s. three d. *Education:* Govt Coll. Ughelli, Univ. Coll. Ibadan, Princeton Univ. *Career:* Ed. The Horn (Ibadan) 1958; head of features, editorial writer Express Group of Newspapers, Lagos 1961–62; Research Fellow Inst. of African Studies, Univ. of Lagos 1963–64, Lecturer, Dept of English 1965–69, Sr Lecturer 1969–72, Prof. of English 1972–80; consultant UNESCO 1965–67; Ed. Black Orpheus (journal) 1965–78; Visiting Distinguished Fellow, Center for Humanities, Wesleyan Univ., Conn. 1975–76; Visiting Research Prof., Inst. of African Studies, Univ. of Ibadan 1979–80; Distinguished Visiting Prof. of English, Writer in Residence, Lincoln Univ., Pa 1989; Visiting Prof. of English, Yale Univ., Conn. 1990; Trustee, mem. Petroleum (Special) Trust Fund and Man. Bd, Abuja 1995–; mem. Nat. Council of Laureates (Nigeria) 1992. *Drama includes:* Song of a Goat 1961, Three Plays 1964, Ozidi 1968, The Bikoroa Plays 1985, The Wives' Revolt. *Poetry published includes:* Poems 1962, A Reed in the Tide 1965, Casualties 1970, A Decade of Tongues 1981, State of the Union 1985, Mandela and Other Poems 1988, A Lot From Paradise 1997. *Other publications:* America, Their America 1964, The Example of Shakespeare 1970, Transcription and Translation from the Oral Tradition of the Izon of the Niger Delta; The Ozidi Saga (trans.) 1977, The Hero as a Villain 1978. *Honours:* Nigerian Nat. Merit Award, Nigerian Nat. Order of Merit; Foundation Fellow Nigerian Acad. of Letters 1996. *Address:* GPO Box 1668, Marina, Lagos; 23 Oduduwa Crescent, GRA, Ikeja, Lagos; Okemeji Place, Funama, Kiagbodo, Burutu Local Government Area, Delta State, Nigeria. *Telephone:* (1) 497-8436 (Lagos). *Fax:* (1) 497-8463 (Lagos).

CLARK, Jonathan Charles Douglas; Distinguished Prof. of British History and Writer; b. 28 Feb. 1951, London, England; m. Katherine Redwood Penovich 1996. *Education:* BA, 1972, PhD, 1981, University of Cambridge. *Career:* Research Fellow, Peterhouse, Cambridge, 1977–81; Fellow, 1986–95, Senior Research Fellow, 1995, All Souls College, Oxford; Visiting Prof., Committee on Social Thought, University of Chicago, 1993; Joyce and Elizabeth Hall Distinguished Prof. of British History, University of Kansas, 1995–; Distinguished Visiting Lecturer, University of Manitoba, 1999;

Visiting Prof., Forschungszentrum Europäische Aufklärung, Potsdam, 2000; Visiting Prof., University of Northumbria, 2001–; mem. FRHistS; Ecclesiastical History Society; Church of England Record Society; North American Conference on British Studies; British Society for Eighteenth Century Studies. *Publications:* The Dynamics of Change, 1982; English Society 1688–1832, 1985, second edn as English Society 1660–1832, 2000; Revolution and Rebellion, 1986; The Memoirs and Speeches of James, 2nd Earl Waldegrave (ed.), 1988; Ideas and Politics in Modern Britain (ed.), 1990; The Language of Liberty, 1993; Samuel Johnson, 1994; Reflections on the French Revolution, by Edmund Burke (ed.), 2001; Samuel Johnson in Historical Context (co-ed.), 2002; Our Shadowed Present: Modernism, Postmodernism and History, 2003. Contributions: scholarly books and journals, and to periodicals. *Address:* University of Kansas, Dept of History, 3001 Wescoe Hall, 1445 Jayhawk Blvd, Lawrence, KS 66045–7590, USA.

CLARK, LaVerne Harrell; Writer, Photographer and Lecturer; b. 6 June 1929, Smithville, Texas, USA; m. L. D. Clark, 15 Sept. 1951. *Education:* BA, Texas Woman's University, 1950; Columbia University, 1951–54; MA, 1962, MFA, 1992, University of Arizona. *Career:* Reporter, Librarian, Fort Worth Press, 1950–51; Sales and Advertising Dept, Columbia University Press, 1951–53; Asst, Promotion News Dept, Episcopal Diocese, New York, 1958–59; Founding Dir, 1962–66, Photographer, 1966–99, Poetry Centre, University of Arizona; mem. Texas Institute of Letters; PEN; National League of American PEN Women; Western Writers of America; Society of Southwestern Authors; Mari Sandoz Heritage Society, hon. board mem.; Westerners International; Women in Communications. *Publications:* They Sang for Horses, 1966; The Face of Poetry, 1976; Focus 101, 1979; Revisiting the Plains Indians Country of Mari Sandoz, 1979; The Deadly Swarm and Other Stories, 1985; Keepers of the Earth, 1997; Mari Sandoz's Native Nebraska, 2000. Contributions: periodicals. *Honours:* American Philosophical Society Grant, 1967–69; University of Chicago Folklore Prize, 1967; Non-Fiction Award, Biennial Letters Contest, 1968; Distinguished Alumna Award, 1973; Julian Ocean Literary Prize, 1984; Philip A Danielson Award, Westerners International, 1992; Best First Novel, Western Writers of America, 1998. *Address:* 604 Main St, Smithville, TX 78957, USA. *E-mail:* lhldclark@aol.com.

CLARK, Mary Higgins, BA; American author and business executive; b. 24 Dec. 1931, New York; m. Warren Clark 1949 (died 1964); two s. three d. *Education:* Fordham Univ. *Career:* advertising Asst Remington Rand 1946; stewardess, Pan Am 1949–50; radio scriptwriter, producer Robert G. Jennings 1965–70; Vice-Pres., partner, Creative Dir, Producer Radio Programming, Aerial Communications, New York 1970–80; Chair. Bd, Creative Dir D.J. Clark Enterprises, New York 1980–; mem. American Acad. of Arts and Sciences, Mystery Writers of America, Authors League. *Publications:* Aspire to the Heavens, A Biography of George Washington 1969, Where Are the Children? 1976, A Stranger is Watching 1978, The Cradle Will Fall 1980, A Cry in the Night 1982, Stillwatch 1984, Weep No More, My Lady 1987, While My Pretty One Sleeps 1989, The Anastasia Syndrome 1989, Loves Music, Loves to Dance 1991, All Around the Town 1992, I'll Be Seeing You 1993, Remember Me 1994, The Lottery Winner 1994, Bad Behavior 1995, Let Me Call You Sweetheart 1995, Silent Night 1996, Moonlight Becomes You 1996, My Gal Sunday 1996, Pretend You Don't See Her 1997, The Plot Thickens 1997, You Belong to Me 1998, All Through the Night 1998, We'll Meet Again 1999, Before I Say Good-Bye 2000, Deck the Halls (with Carol Higgins Clark) 2000, Daddy's Little Girl 2002, On the Street Where You Live 2002, Mount Vernon Love Story: A Novel of George and Martha Washington 2002, The Second Time Around 2003, Nighttime is My Time 2004. *Honours:* several hon. degrees; Grand Prix de Littérature Policière, France 1980. *Address:* 210 Central Park S, New York, NY 10019, USA.

CLARK, Patricia Denise, (Claire Lorrimer, Patricia Robins, Susan Patrick); Writer and Poet; b. 1 Feb. 1921, Hove, Sussex, England. *Career:* mem. Society of Authors; Romantic Novelists' Asscn. *Publications:* As Claire Lorrimer: A Voice in the Dark, 1967; The Shadow Falls, 1974; Relentless Storm, 1975; The Secret of Quarry House, 1976; Mavreen, 1976; Tamarisk, 1978; Chantal, 1980; The Garden (a cameo), 1980; The Chatelaine, 1981; The Wilderling, 1982; Last Year's Nightingale, 1984; Frost in the Sun, 1986; House of Tomorrow (biog.), 1987; Ortolans, 1990; The Spinning Wheel, 1991; Variations (short stories), 1991; The Silver Link, 1993; Fool's Curtain, 1994; Beneath the Sun, 1996; Connie's Daughter, 1997; The Reunion, 1997; The Woven Thread, 1998; The Reckoning, 1998; Second Chance, 1998; An Open Door, 1999; Never Say Goodbye, 2000; Search for Love, 2000; For Always, 2001; The Faithful Heart, 2002. As Patricia Robins: To the Stars, 1944; See No Evil, 1945; Three Loves, 1949; Awake My Heart, 1950; Beneath the Moon, 1951; Leave My Heart Alone, 1951; The Fair Deal, 1952; Heart's Desire, 1953; So This is Love, 1953; Heaven in Our Hearts, 1954; One Who Cares, 1954; Love Cannot Die, 1955; The Foolish Heart, 1956; Give All to Love, 1956; Where Duty Lies, 1957; He Is Mine, 1957; Love Must Wait, 1958; Lonely Quest, 1959; Lady Chatterley's Daughter, 1961; The Last Chance, 1961; The Long Wait, 1962; The Runaways, 1962; Seven Loves, 1962; With All My Love, 1963; The Constant Heart, 1964; Second Love, 1964; The Night is Thine, 1964; There Is But One, 1965; No More Loving, 1965; Topaz Island, 1965; Love Me Tomorrow, 1966; The Uncertain Joy, 1966; The Man Behind the Mask, 1967; Forbidden, 1967; Sapphire in the Sand, 1968; Return to Love, 1968; Laugh on Friday, 1969; No Stone Unturned, 1969; Cinnabar House, 1970; Under the Sky, 1970; The Crimson Tapestry, 1972; Play Fair with Love, 1972; None But He, 1973; Fulfilment, 1993; Forsaken, 1993; Forever, 1993; The Legend, 1997. *Address:* Chiswell Barn, Marsh Green, Edenbridge, Kent TN8 5PR, England.

CLARKE, Anna; Author; b. 28 April 1919, Cape Town, South Africa. *Education:* BSc, Economics, University of London, 1945; BA, Open University, 1975; MA, University of Sussex, 1975. *Career:* Private Secretary, Victor Gollancz Publishers, 1947–50, Eyre and Spottiswoode, Publishers, 1951–53; Administrative Secretary, British Asscn for American Studies, London, 1956–63. *Publications:* The Poisoned Web, 1979; Poison Parsley, 1979; Last Voyage, 1980; Game, Set and Danger, 1981; Desire to Kill, 1982; We the Bereaved, 1982; Soon She Must Die, 1983; Last Judgement, 1985; Cabin 3033, 1986; The Mystery Lady, 1986; Last Seen in London, 1987; Murder in Writing, 1988; The Whitelands Affair, 1989; The Case of the Paranoid Patient, 1993; The Case of the Ludicrous Letters, 1994. Contributions: Short stories in Ellery Queen Mystery Magazine, New York. *Address:* c/o Wendy Lipkind, 165 E 66th St, New York, NY 10021, USA.

CLARKE, Sir Arthur Charles, CBE, BSc; writer; b. 16 Dec. 1917, Minehead, Somerset, England; m. Marilyn Mayfield 1953 (divorced 1964). *Education:* King's College, London. *Career:* mem. American Astronomical Asscn, hon. fellow; Asscn for the Advancement of Science; Asscn of British Science Writers, hon. life mem.; British Interplanetary Society, hon. fellow; Franklin Institute, fellow; International Acad. of Astronautics, hon. fellow; International Writers' Asscn, fellow; King's College, London, fellow; Royal Astronomical Society, fellow; Society of Authors; UN Asscn of Sri Lanka, hon. life pres.; Patron, trustee and board mem. of many other asscns and societies. *Publications:* Non-Fiction: Voices from the Sky, 1945; Interplanetary Flight, 1950; The Making of a Moon, 1951; The Exploration of Space, 1951; The Exploration of the Moon, 1954; The Young Traveller in Space, 1954; The Coast of Coral, 1956; The Reefs of Taprobane, 1957; Voice Across the Sea, 1958; The Challenge of the Sea, 1960; The Challenge of the Spaceship, 1960; The First Five Fathoms (with Mike Wilson), 1960; Indian Ocean Adventure (with Mike Wilson), 1961; Profiles of the Future, 1962; Indian Ocean Treasure (with Mike Wilson), 1964; The Treasure of the Great Reef (with Mike Wilson), 1964; The Promise of Space, 1968; Report on Planet Three, 1972; The View from Serendip, 1977; 1984: Spring: A Choice of Futures, 1984; The Odyssey File (with Peter Hyams), 1985; Astounding Days, 1989; How the World Was One, 1992; The Snows of Olympus, 1994; Greetings, Carbon-Based Bipeds!, 1999; Boy Beneath the Sea (with Mike Wilson), 1958; Man and Space (with others), 1964; First on the Moon (with others), 1970; Into Space (with Robert Silverberg), 1971; Beyond Jupiter (with Chesley Bonestell), 1972; Ascent to Orbit: A Scientific Autobiography, 1984; By Space Posessed, 1993. Fiction: Prelude to Space, 1951; The Sands of Mars, 1951; Islands in the Sky, 1952; Against the Fall of Night, 1953; Childhood's End, 1953; Expedition to Earth, 1953; Earthlight, 1955; The City and the Stars, 1956; Reach for Tomorrow, 1956; The Deep Range, 1957; Tales from the White Hart (short stories), 1957; The Other Side of the Sky, 1958; Across the Sea of Stars, 1959; A Fall of Moondust, 1961; From the Oceans, From the Stars, 1962; Tales of Ten Worlds (short stories), 1962; Glide Path, 1963; Dolphin Island, 1963; Prelude to Mars, 1965; The Nine Billion Names of God (short stories), 1967; The Lion of Comarre, 1968; 2001: A Space Odyssey, 1968; The Wind from the Sun, 1972; Of Time and Stars, 1972; The Lost Worlds of 2001, 1972; The Best of Arthur C. Clarke, 1973; Rendezvous with Rama, 1973; Imperial Earth, 1975; The Fountains of Paradise, 1979; 2010: Odyssey Two, 1982; The Sentinel (short stories), 1983; The Songs of Distant Earth, 1986; 2061: Odyssey Three, 1987; Cradle (with Gentry Lee), 1988; A Meeting with Medusa (short stories), 1989; Rama II (with Gentry Lee), 1989; Ghost from the Grand Banks, 1990; Tales from Planet Earth (short stories), 1990; The Garden of Rama (with Gentry Lee), 1991; More than One Universe (short stories), 1991; Rama Revealed (with Gentry Lee), 1993; The Hammer of God, 1993; Richter 10 (with Mike McQuay), 1996; 3001: The Final Odyssey, 1998; Trigger (with Mike Kube-McDowell), 1999; The Light of Other Days (with Stephen Baxter), 2000; The Other Side of the Sky (short stories), 2003. Other: edited various books. Contributions: journals and periodicals. *Honours:* UNESCO Kalinga Prize, 1961; Stuart Ballantine Gold Medal, Franklin Institute, 1963; Nebula Awards, SFWA, 1973, 1974, 1979; John W. Campbell Award, 1974; Vidya Jyothi Medal, 1986; Grand Master, SFWA, 1986; Charles A. Lindbergh Award, 1987; NASA Distinguished Public Service Medal, 1995; Pres. of Italy Medal, 2001; Isaac Asimov Memorial Award, 2001; many hon. doctorates and other awards and prizes. *Address:* 25 Barnes Place, Colombo 7, Sri Lanka.

CLARKE, Austin; Canadian writer; b. 1934, Barbados. *Education:* Univ. of Toronto. *Career:* fmrly journalist and broadcaster, teacher of creative writing and cultural attaché to the Barbados Embassy in the USA. *Publications:* novels: Survivors of the Crossing 1964, The Meeting Place 1967, Storm of Fortune 1971, The Bigger Light 1975, The Prime Minister 1977, Proud Empires 1988, The Origin of Waves 1997, The Question 1999, The Polished Hoe 2004; short story collections: Among Thistles and Thorns 1965, When He Was Free and Young and He Used to Wear Silks 1971, When Women Rule 1985, Nine Men Who Laughed 1986, In This City 1992, There are No Elders 1993; memoir: Growing Up Stupid Under the Union Jack 1980. *Honours:* Commonwealth Writers' Prize (UK), W. O. Mitchell Prize

(Canada), Giller Prize (Canada). *Literary Agent:* The Bukowski Agency, 14 Prince Arthur Avenue, Suite 202, Toronto, ON M5R 1A9, Canada. *Website:* www.thebukowskiagency.com.

CLARKE, Brenda (Margaret Lilian), (Brenda Honeyman, Kate Sedley); Author; b. 30 July 1926, Bristol, England; m. Ronald John Clarke 5 March 1955; one s. one d. *Publications:* The Glass Island, 1978; The Lofty Banners, 1980; The Far Morning, 1982; All Through the Day, 1983; A Rose in May, 1984; Three Women, 1985; Winter Landscape, 1986; Under Heaven, 1988; An Equal Chance (US edn as Riches of the Heart), 1989; Sisters and Lovers, 1990; Beyond the World, 1991; A Durable Fire, 1993; Sweet Auburn, 1995. As Brenda Honeyman: Richard by Grace of God, 1968; The Kingmaker, 1969; Richmond and Elizabeth, 1970; Harry the King, 1971; Brother Bedford, 1972; Good Duke Humphrey, 1973; The King's Minions, 1974; The Queen and Mortimer, 1974; Edward the Warrior, 1975; All the King's Sons, 1976; The Golden Griffin, 1976; At the King's Court, 1977; A King's Tale, 1977; Macbeth, King of Scots, 1977; Emma, the Queen, 1978; Harold of the English, 1979. As Kate Sedley: Death and the Chapman, 1991; The Plymouth Cloak, 1992; The Hanged Man, 1993; The Holy Innocents, 1994; The Eve of St Hyacinth, 1995; The Wicked Winter, 1996; The Brothers of Glastonbury, 1997; The Weaver's Inheritance, 1998; The Saint John's Fern, 1999; The Goldsmith's Daughter, 2001; The Lammas Feast, 2002; Nine Men Dancing, 2003. *Literary Agent:* David Grossman Literary Agency Ltd, 118b Holland Park Ave, London W11 4UA, England. *Address:* 25 Torridge Rd, Keynsham, Bristol BS31 1QQ, England.

CLARKE, Gillian, BA; poet, editor, translator and tutor of creative writing; b. 8 June 1937, Cardiff, Glamorgan, Wales. *Education:* University College, Cardiff. *Career:* Lecturer, Gwent College of Art and Design, Newport 1975–82; Ed., Anglo-Welsh Review 1976–84; Pres., Ty Newydd (Welsh creative writers' house), Gwynedd 1993–; mem. Welsh Acad. (chair. 1988–93). *Publications:* Poetry: Snow on the Mountain, 1971; The Sundial, 1978; Letter From a Far Country, 1982; Selected Poems, 1985; Letting in the Rumour, 1989; The King of Britain's Daughter, 1993; Collected Poems, 1997; Five Fields, 1998; The Animal Wall, 1999; Nine Green Gardens, 2000; Making the Beds for the Dead 2004. Editor: The Poetry Book Society Anthology, 1987–88, 1987; The Whispering Room, 1996; I Can Move the Sea (anthology), 1996; translations. *Honours:* Fellow, University of Wales, Cardiff, 1984; Hon. Fellow, University of Wales, Aberystwyth, 1995–, University of Wales, Swansea, 1996; Cholmondeley Award for Poetry, 1997; Owain Glyndwr Award for Outstanding Contribution to Arts in Wales, 1999. *Address:* Blaen Cwrt, Talgarreg, Llandysul, Ceredigion SA44 4EU, Wales.

CLARKE, (Victor) Lindsay, BA; British writer; b. 14 Aug. 1939, Halifax, West Yorkshire, England; m. Phoebe Clare Mackmin 1980; one d. *Education:* King's Coll., Cambridge. *Career:* Co-ordinator of Liberal Studies, Norwich City Coll.; Co-Dir, European Centre, Friends World Coll.; writer-in-residence and Assoc. Lecturer in Creative Writing, Univ. of Wales, Cardiff. *Publications:* Sunday Whiteman 1987, The Chymical Wedding 1989, Alice's Masque 1994, Essential Celtic Mythology 1997, Parzival and the Stone from Heaven 2001, The War at Troy 2004. *Honours:* Whitbread Award for the Novel 1989. *Literary Agent:* PFD, Drury House, 34–43 Russell Street, London, WC2B 5HA, England.

CLARKE, Mary; editor and writer; b. 23 Aug. 1923, London, England. *Career:* London Correspondent, Dance Magazine, New York, 1943–55; Asst Ed. and Contributor, Ballet Annual, 1952–63; Asst Ed., 1954–63, Ed., 1963–, Dancing Times; London Ed., Dance News, New York, 1955–70; Dance Critic, The Guardian, 1977–94. *Publications:* The Sadler's Wells Ballet: A History and Appreciation, 1955; Six Great Dancers, 1957; Dancers of Mercury: The Story of Ballet Rambert, 1962; Ballet: An Illustrated History (with Clement Crisp), 1973; Making a Ballet (with Clement Crisp), 1974; Introducing Ballet (with Clement Crisp), 1976; Encyclopedia of Dance and Ballet (ed., with David Vaughan), 1977; Design for Ballet (with Clement Crisp), 1978; Ballet in Art (with Clement Crisp), 1978; The History of Dance (with Clement Crisp), 1981; Dancer: Men in Dance (with Clement Crisp), 1984; Ballerina (with Clement Crisp), 1987. Contributions: Encyclopaedia Britannica, New Dictionary of National Biography, newspapers, magazines. *Honours:* Second Prize, Cafe Royal Literary for Best Book on the Theatre, 1955; Queen Elizabeth II Coronation Award, Royal Acad. of Dancing, 1990; Knight, Order of Dannebrog, Denmark, 1992; Nijinsky Medal, Polish Ministry of Culture, 1995. *Address:* 54 Ripplevale Grove, London N1 1HT, England.

CLARKSON, Ewan; England; b. 23 Jan. 1929, ,. *Education:* MA, University of Exeter, 1984. *Publications:* Break for Freedom, 1967; Halic: The Story of a Grey Seal, 1970; The Running of the Deer, 1972; In the Shadow of the Falcon, 1973; Wolf Country: A Wilderness Pilgrimage, 1975; The Badger of Summercombe, 1977; The Many Forked Branch, 1980; Wolves, 1980; Reindeer, 1981; Eagles, 1981; Beavers, 1981; In the Wake of the Storm, 1984; Ice Trek, 1986; King of the Wild, 1990; The Flight of the Osprey, 1995. *Address:* Moss Rose Cottage, Preston, Newton Abbot, Devon TQ12 3PP, England.

CLARKSON, J. F. (see Tubb, Edwin Charles).

CLARKSON, Stephen; Prof. of Political Economy and Writer; b. 21 Oct. 1937, London, England; m. Christina McCall, 1 Sept. 1978, three d. *Education:* Upper Canada College, 1955; BA, Sorbonne, University of Paris, 1964. *Career:* Lecturer, 1964–65, Asst Prof., 1965–67, Assoc. Prof., 1967–80, Prof. of Political Economy, 1980–, University of Toronto; Senior Fellow, Columbia University, 1967–68; Policy Chair., Liberal Party, Ontario, 1969–73; Dir, Maison Française de Toronto, 1972; Jean Monnet Fellow, European University Institute, 1995–96; mem. Canadian Institute of International Affairs; Canadian Political Science Asscn; International Political Science Asscn; University League for Social Reform, pres. *Publications:* An Independent Foreign Policy for Canada? (ed.), 1968; L'Analyse Soviétique des problèmes indiens de sous-développement, 1970; Visions 2020: Fifty Canadians in Search of a Future (ed.), 1970; City Lib: Parties and Reform in Toronto, 1972; The Soviet Theory of Development: India and the Third World in Marxist-Leninist Scholarship, 1978; Canada and the Reagan Challenge: Crisis in the Canadian-American Relationship, 1982; Trudeau and Our Times (co-author), Vol. 1, The Magnificent Obsession, 1990, vol. 2, The Heroic Delusion, 1994. Contributions: scholarly books and professional journals. *Honours:* Rhodes Scholar, 1959; Woodrow Wilson Fellow, 1961; John Porter Prize, 1984; Governor-General's Award for Non-Fiction, 1990. *Address:* c/o University College, King's College Circle, Toronto, Ontario M5S, Canada.

CLAUS, Hugo; Writer, Poet, Screenwriter and Trans; b. 5 April 1929, Bruges, Belgium; m. 1st Elly Overzier 1955 (divorced); m. 2nd Sylvia Kristel (divorced); m. 3rd Veerle Claus-De Wit. *Career:* Stage and film dir., screenplay writer, incl.: De Vijanden (dir), 1967; Vrijdag (dir), 1980; Het Sacrament (dir), 1989. *Publications:* Kleine reeks, 1947; Registreren (poems), 1948; De blijde en onvoorziene week (with Karel Appel), 1950; De metsiers (novel, The Duck Hunt), 1950; Zonder vorm van proces, 1950; Tancredo Infrasonic, 1950; Over het werk van Corneille, 1951; De hondsdagen, 1952; Een huis dat tussen nacht en morgen staat, 1953; Natuurgetrouw, 1954; De Oostakkerse gedichten (poems), 1955; Paal en Perk (with Corneille), 1955; Een bruid in de morgen (A Bride in the Morning), 1955; De Koele Minnaar, 1956; Het lied van de moordenaar, 1957; Suiker (play), 1958; De zwarte keizer, 1958; Mama, kijk, zonder handen!, 1959; Een geverfde ruiter, 1961; De dans van de reiger, 1962; Omtrent Deedee, 1963; Love Song (with Karel Appel), 1963; De verwondering (novel), 1963; Karel Appel, schilder (Karel Appel, painter), 1963; De man van Tollund, 1963; Het teken van de Hamster, 1964; Louis Paul Boon, 1964; Oog om oog (with van Sanne Sannes), 1964; Gedichten 1948–1963, 1965; Het landschap, 1965; Die schilderijen van Roger Raveel, 1965; Acht toneelstukken, 1966; Relikwie, 1967; De vijanden, 1967; De avonturen van Belgman, 1967; Morituri, 1968; Masscheroen, 1968; Reconstructie (libretto, with others), 1969; Motet, 1969; Genesis (with Roger Raveel), 1969; Natuurgetrouwer, 1969; Vrijdag (play, Friday), 1969; Tand om tand, 1970; Het leven en de werken van Leopold II (play, The Life and Works of Leopold II), 1970; Heer Everzwijn, 1970; Van horen zeggen, 1970; Dag, jij, 1971; Schola Nostra, 1971; Schola Nostra door Dorothea van Male, 1971; Interieur, 1971; Gebed om geweld, 1972; Het Jaar van de kreeft (novel), 1972; De vossejacht, toonelstuk naar Ben Jonson, 1972; Schaamte (novel), 1972; Figuratief, 1973; In het Wilde Westen, De groene ridder, deel 1, 1973; De paladijnen, De groene ridder, deel 2, 1973; Aan de evenaar, De groene ridder, deel 7, 1973; Pas de deux, 1973; Gekke Gerrit, 1973; Wangebeden, 1973; De groene ridder, 1973; Thuis (Back Home), 1975; Het graf van Pernath, 1976; Het Jansenisme, 1977; Jessica!, 1977; De vluchtende Atalanta, 1977; Het huis van Labdakos (play), 1977; De Wangebeden, 1978; Zwart, 1978; Het verlangen (novel, Desire), 1978; Claustrum, 1979; Fuga, 1979; Gedichten 1969–1978, 1979; Het Teken van de Hamster, 1979; Dertien manieren om een fragment van Alechinsky te zien, 1980; De verzoeking, 1980; Ontmoetingen met Corneille en Karel Appel, 1980; Phaedra, 1980; Een Hooglied, 1981; Jan de Lichte, 1981; Almanak, 1982; Mexico vandaag (with Freddy de Vree), 1982; Het haar van de hond (The Hair of the Dog), 1982; Het verdriet van België (novel, The Sorrow of Belgium), 1983; Serenade, 1984; Blindeman, 1985; Georg Faust (libretto), 1985; Alibi, 1985; De mensen Hiernaast, 1985; Een weerzinwekkend bezoek, 1985; Gevulde contouren, 1985; Wyckaert (with Freddy de Vree), 1986; Bewegen, 1986; Evergreens, 1986; Gedichten van Hugo Claus, 1986; Het verschijnsel, 1986; Sonnetten, 1986; Hugo Claus: Selected Poems, 1986; Bewegen (with van Willy Legendre), 1986; In Kolonos, 1986; Sporen, 1987; Hymen, 1987; Voor Pierre, 1987; Sonnetten, 1987; Mej honderd gedichten, 1987; Chateau Migraine, 1987; Beelden, 1987; Een zachte vernieling, 1988; Het schommelpaard, 1988; Toneel I, 1988; Gilles en de nacht, 1989; Toneel II, 1989; De zwaardvis (novella, The Swordfish), 1989; Kort dagboek, 1989; Perte Totale, 1989; Four Works for the Theatre, 1990; Toneel III, 1991; De Sporen, 1993; Onder de torens, 1993; Toneel IV, 1993; Belladonna (novel), 1994; Gedichten 1948–1993, 1994; De eieren van de kaaiman, 1995; De verlossing, 1996; Visite: Winteravond, 1996; De Geruchten (novel), 1996; Onvoltooid verleden, 1997; Zoek de zeven, 1997; De Komedianten (Pas de deux II), 1997; Oktober '43, 1998; Voor de reiziger, 1998; De aap in Efese, 1998; Het laatste bed, 1998; Verhalen, 1999; Het huis van de liefde, 1999; Wreed geluk, 1999. *Honours:* State Prize for Dutch Letters; Herman Gorter Prize.

CLAVEL, Bernard; Author, Dramatist and Painter; b. 29 May 1923, Lons-le-Saunier, France; m. 1st, three s.; m. 2nd Josette Pratte, 1982. *Publications:* L'ouvrier de la nuit, 1956; Qui m'emporte, 1958; L'espagnol, 1959; Malataverne, 1960; La maison des autres, 1962; Celui qui voulait voir la mer, 1963; Le coeur des vivants, 1964; La voyage de père, 1965; L'Hercule sur la place, 1966; Victoire au mans, 1968; L'espion aux yeux verts, 1969;

Le massacre des innocents, 1970; Le seigneur du fleuve, 1972; Le silence des armes, 1974; La boule de neige, 1975; La saison des loups, 1976; Ecrit sur la neige, 1977; La femme de guerre, 1978; L'Iroquoise, 1979; La bourrelle, 1980; Odile et le vent du large, 1981; L'homme du labrador, 1982; Harricana, 1983; Le roi des poissons, 1984; Misere, 1985; Amarot, 1986; L'Angélus du soir, 1988; Retour au pays, 1990; Meutre sur le grandvaux, 1991; La révolte à deux sous, 1992; Cargo pour l'enfer, 1993; Les roses de Verdun, 1994; Le carcajou, 1995; Jésus le fils du charpentier, 1996; Contes et légendes du Bordelais, 1997; Achille le singe, 1998; Le commencement du monde, 1999; La louve du noirmont, 2000. Other: many additional books, essays, short stories, radio and television plays, children's books, etc. Contributions: periodicals. *Honours:* various literary prizes. *Address:* Albin Michel, 22 rue Huyghens, 75014 Paris, France.

CLAYTON, John Jacob, AB, MA, PhD; academic and writer; *Professor of English, University of Massachusetts at Amherst*; b. 5 Jan. 1935, New York, NY, USA; m. 1st Marilyn Hirsch 1956 (divorced 1974); one s. one d.; m. 2nd Marlynn Krebs (divorced 1983); one s.; m. 3rd Sharon Dunn 1984; one s. *Education:* Columbia University, New York University, Indiana University. *Career:* Instructor, University of Victoria, BC, 1962–63; Lecturer, Overseas Division, University of Maryland, 1963–64; Asst Prof. of Humanities, Boston University, 1964–69; Assoc. Prof., 1969–75, Prof. of English, 1975–, University of Massachusetts at Amherst. *Publications:* Saul Bellow: In Defense of Man, 1968; What Are Friends For? (novel), 1979; Bodies of the Rich (short stories), 1984; Gestures of Healing: Anxiety and the Modern Novel, 1991; Radiance (collection of stories), 1998; The Man I Never Wanted To Be (novel), 1998. Editor: The D. C. Heath Introduction to Fiction. Contributions: anthologies and periodicals. *Honours:* Second Prize, O. Henry Prize Stories, 1995; Ohio State University Award in short fiction, 1998; Pushcart Prize, 1998. *Address:* 12 Lawton Road, RFD 3, Amherst, MA 01002, USA.

CLAYTON, Martin David; Art Historian and Writer; b. 30 Dec. 1967, Harrogate, England. *Education:* BA, History of Art, 1986–90, MA, 1993, Christ's College, Cambridge. *Career:* Asst Curator, Royal Library, Windsor Castle. *Publications:* Leonardo da Vinci: The Anatomy of Man, 1992; Poussin: Works on Paper, 1995; Leonardo da Vinci: A Curious Vision, 1996. *Literary Agent:* John Johnstone Ltd. *Address:* Royal Library, Windsor Castle, Berkshire, England.

CLEARY, Jon (Stephen); Writer; b. 22 Nov. 1917, Sydney, NSW, Australia; m. Constantine Lucas 1946; two d. (one deceased). *Education:* Marist Brothers School, NSW. *Publications:* The Small Glories, 1945; You Can't See Round Corners, 1947; The Long Shadow, 1949; Just Let Me Be, 1950; The Sundowners, 1952; The Climate of Courage, 1954; Justin Bayard, 1955; The Green Helmet, 1957; Back of Sunset, 1959; The Siege of Pinchgut, 1959; North from Thursday, 1960; The Country of Marriage, 1961; Forest of the Night, 1962; Pillar of Salt, 1963; A Flight of Chariots, 1964; The Fall of an Eagle, 1965; The Pulse of Danger, 1966; The High Commissioner, 1967; The Long Pursuit, 1968; Season of Doubt, 1969; Remember Jack Hoxie, 1970; Helga's Webb, 1971; The Liberators, 1971; The Ninth Marquess, 1972; Ransom, 1973; Peter's Pence, 1974; The Safe House, 1975; A Sound of Lightning, 1976; High Road to China, 1977; Vortex, 1977; The Beaufort Sisters, 1979; A Very Pirate War, 1980; The Golden Sabre, 1981; The Faraway Drums, 1981; Spearfield's Daughter, 1982; The Phoenix Tree, 1984; The City of Fading Light, 1985; Dragons at the Party, 1987; Now and Then, Amen, 1988; Babylon South, 1989; Murder Song, 1990; Pride's Harvest, 1991; Dark Summer, 1992; Bleak Spring, 1993; Autumn Maze, 1994; Winter Chill, 1995; Endpeace, 1996; A Different Turf, 1997; Five-Ring Circus, 1998; Dilemma, 1999; Bear Pit, 2000; Yesterday's Shadow, 2001. *Honours:* Winner, ABC National Play Competition, 1945; Crouch Literary Prize, 1951; Edgar Award for Best Crime Novel, 1974; First Lifetime Award, Australian Crime Writers' Society, 1998. *Address:* c/o HarperCollins, 23 Ryde Rd, Pymble, NSW 2073, Australia.

CLEMENS, Kate (see Mackey, Mary).

CLÉMENT, Paul (see Amette, Jacques-Pierre).

CLIFTON, (Thelma) Lucille; poet, writer and academic; b. 27 June 1936, Depew, NY, USA; m. Fred James Clifton 1958 (died 1984); two s. four d. *Education:* Howard Univ. 1953–55; Fredonia State Teachers Coll. 1955. *Career:* Poet-in-Residence Coppin State Coll. 1974–79; Poet Laureate of Maryland 1974–85; Prof. of Literature and Creative Writing Univ. of Calif. at Santa Cruz 1985–89; Distinguished Prof. of Literature St Mary's Coll. of Maryland 1989–91, Distinguished Prof. of Humanities 1991–, Hilda C. Landers Endowed Chair in the Liberal Arts 2000–; Blackburn Prof. of Creative Writing, Duke Univ. 1998–; mem. Acad. of American Poets, chancellor 1999–, Authors' Guild, Authors' League of America, Int. PEN, Poetry Soc. of America. *Publications:* Poetry: Good Times 1969, Good News about the Earth: New Poems 1972, An Ordinary Woman 1974, Two-Headed Woman 1980, Good Woman: Poems and a Memoir 1969–1980, 1987, Next: New Poems 1987, Ten Oxherding Pictures 1988, Quilting: Poems 1987–1990, 1991, The Book of Light 1993, The Terrible Stories 1998, Blessing the Boats: New and Selected Poems 1988–2000, 2000; other: Generations of Americans: A Memoir 1976, over 20 books for children 1970–2001; contribs to anthologies and periodicals. *Honours:* Nat. Endowment for the Arts Awards 1969, 1970, 1972, Juniper Prize, Univ. of Massachusetts 1980, Coretta Scott King Award, American Library Asscn 1984, Andrew White Medal, Loyola Coll. in Maryland 1993, named Maryland Living Treasure 1993, Lannan Literary Award for Poetry 1997, inducted Nat. Literature Hall of Fame for African-American Writers 1998, Lenore Marshall Poetry Prize 1998, Los Angeles Times Poetry Prize 1998, Lila Wallace/Reader's Digest Award 1999, Nat. Book Award for Poetry 2001, Pushcart Prize 2001, Emmy Award. *Address:* c/o Marc Apter, Public and Media Relations, St Mary's College of Maryland, 107 Calvert Hall, St Mary's City, MD 20686, USA.

CLOUDSLEY, Timothy; University Lecturer, Poet and Writer; b. 18 Sept. 1948, Cambridge, England; m. Rhona Cleugh, 18 July 1987, two s. *Education:* BA, Cantab, 1971; MA, 1974; Postgraduate Research, Durham University, 1972–74. *Career:* Lecturer, Sociology, Newcastle University, 1972–74, Napier University, Edinburgh, 1974–76, Heriot-Watt University, Edinburgh, 1976–77, Glasgow Caledonian University, 1977–; mem. Open Circle (Arts and Literature Organization), Glasgow, literary secretary, 1990–96. *Publications:* Poems to Light (Through Love and Blood), 1980; Mair Licht (anthology), 1988; The Construction of Nature (social philosophy), 1994; Coincidence (anthology), 1995; Incantations From Streams of Fire, 1997; Poems, 1998. Contributions: Northlight Poetry Review; Understanding Magazine; Interactions; Romantic Heir; The People's Poetry; Cadmium Blue Literary Journal; Le Journal des Poètes. *Address:* 31 Hamilton Dr., Glasgow G12 8DN, Scotland.

CLOUGH, Brenda Wang, BA; writer; b. 13 Nov. 1955, Washington, DC, USA; m. Lawrence A. Clough 1977; one d. *Education:* Carnegie Mellon University. *Publications:* The Crystal Crown, 1984; The Dragon of Mishbil, 1985; The Realm Beneath, 1986; The Name of the Sun, 1988; An Impossible Summer, 1992; How Like a God, 1997; Doors of Death and Life, 2000. Contributions: Short stories in anthologies and periodicals. *Address:* 1941 Barton Hill Road, Reston, VA 20191, USA. *Website:* www.sff.net/people/Brenda.

CLOUTIER, Cécile; poet, writer and academic; b. 13 June 1930, Québec, QC, Canada; m. Jerzy Wojciechowski 1966; two d. *Education:* BA, Collège de Sillery, 1951; Licence-ès-Lettres, 1953, Diplôme d'Etudes Supérieures, 1954, Université Laval; Doctorat en Esthétique, Université de Paris, 1962; MA, McMaster University, 1978; MA, University of Toronto, 1981; Doctorat en Psychologie, Université de Tours, 1983. *Career:* Prof. of French and Québec Literature, University of Ottawa, 1958–64; Prof. of Aesthetics and French and Québec Literature, 1964–95, Prof. Emerita, 1995–, University of Toronto; mem. Asscn des Ecrivains de Langue Française; PEN Club de France; Société des Ecrivains; Société des Gens de Lettres de Paris; Union des écrivaines et des écrivains québécois. *Publications:* Mains de sable, 1960; Cuivre et soies, 1964; Cannelles et craies, 1969; Paupières, 1970; Câblogrammes, 1972; Chaleuils, 1979; Springtime of Spoken Words, 1979; Près, 1983; Opuscula Aesthetica Nostra: Essais sur L'Esthétique, 1984; La Girafe, 1984; L'Echangeur, 1985; L'Ecouté, 1986; Solitude Rompue, 1986; Lampées, 1990; Périhélie, 1990; La poésie de l'Hexagone, 1990; Ancres d'Encre, 1993; Ostraka. Contributions: various publications. *Honours:* Medal, Société des Ecrivains de France, 1960; Centennial Medal, Canada, 1967; Governor-General's Award for Poetry, 1986; Medal Société des Poètes Français, 1994. *Address:* 44 Farm Greenway, Don Mills, ON M3A 3M2, Canada.

CLUYSENAAR, Anne, (Alice Andrée), BA; Irish academic, poet, songwriter, librettist and painter; b. 15 March 1936, Brussels, Belgium; m. Walter Freeman Jackson 1976. *Education:* Trinity Coll., Dublin, University of Edinburgh. *Career:* Asst Lecturer, University of Manchester, 1957–58; Reader to (blind) critic and novelist, Percy Lubbock, 1959; Librarian, Chester Beatty Library of Oriental Manuscripts, Dublin; Lecturer, King's College, Aberdeen, 1963–65, University of Lancaster, 1965–71, Huddersfield Polytechnic, 1972, University of Birmingham, 1973–76, Sheffield City Polytechnic, 1976–89; Part-time Lecturer, University of Wales, Cardiff, 1990–2002; mem. Co-founder and Secretary, Usk Valley Vaughan Asscn, 1995–; Founding General Ed., now Poetry Ed., U.V.V.A. journal, Scintilla; Fellow, Welsh Acad., 2001–; Verbal Arts Asscn, chair, 1983–86. *Publications:* A Fan of Shadows, 1967; Nodes, 1971; Introduction to Literary Stylistics, 1976; Selected Poems of James Burns Singers (ed.), 1977; Poetry Introduction 4, 1978; Double Helix, 1982; Timeslips: New and Selected Poems, 1997. Contributions: various publications. *Address:* Little Wentwood Farm, Llantrisant, Usk, Gwent NP15 1ND, Wales. *E-mail:* anne.cluysenaar@virgin.net.

COASE, Ronald Harry, BCom, DScEcon; British writer; *Professor Emeritus and Senior Fellow in Law and Economics, University of Chicago*; b. 29 Dec. 1910, London, England; m. Marian Ruth Hartung 1937. *Education:* LSE. *Career:* Asst Lecturer, Dundee School of Economics, 1932–34, University of Liverpool, 1934–35; Asst Lecturer to Reader, LSE, 1935–40, 1946–51; Head, Statistical Division, Forestry Commission, 1940–41; Statistician, later Chief Statistician, Central Statistical Office, Offices of War Cabinet, 1941–46; Prof., University of Buffalo, 1951–58, University of Virginia, 1958–64; Ed., Journal of Law and Economics, 1964–92; Clifford R. Musser Prof., 1964–82, Prof. Emeritus and Senior Fellow in Law and Economics, 1982–, University of Chicago; mem. American Acad. of Arts and Sciences, fellow; American Economic Asscn, distinguished fellow; British Acad., corresponding fellow; European Acad.; LSE, hon. fellow; Royal Economic Society. *Publications:* British Broadcasting: A Study in Monopoly, 1950;

The Firm, the Market and the Law, 1988; Essays on Economics and Economists, 1994. *Honours:* Rockefeller Fellow, 1948; Senior Research Fellow, Hoover Institution, Stanford University, 1977; Nobel Prize for Economic Science, 1991; Hon. doctorates. *Address:* The Hallmark, 2960 N Lake Shore Drive, Chicago, IL 60657, USA.

COATES, Kenneth Sidney; academic and writer; b. 16 Sept. 1930, Leek, Staffordshire, England; m. Tamara Tura 1969; three s. three d. (one deceased). *Education:* Mature State Scholar, 1956, BA, 1959, Nottingham University. *Career:* Asst Tutor to Senior Tutor, 1960–80, Reader, 1980–89, Special Prof. in Adult Education, 1990–, Nottingham University; MEP (Labour Party, then Independent Labour), 1989–99; Ed., The Spokesman; mem. Bertrand Russell Peace Foundation. *Publications:* Industrial Democracy in Great Britain (with A. J. Topham), 1967; Poverty: The Forgotten Englishman (with R. L. Silburn), 1970; The New Unionism (with A. J. Topham), 1972; Trade Unions in Britain (with A. J. Topham), 1980; Heresies: The Most Dangerous Decade, 1984; Trade Unions and Politics (with A. J. Topham), 1986; Think Globally, Act Locally, 1988; The Making of the Transport and General Workers' Union (with A. J. Topham), 1991; A European Recovery Programme, 1993; Full Employment for Europe (with Stuart Holland), 1995; Common Ownership: Clause Four and the Labour Party, 1995; The Right to Work: The Loss of Our First Freedom, 1995; Dear Commissioner (ed.), 1996; The Blair Revelation (co-author), 1996; Community Under Attack: The Struggle for Survival in the Coalfield Communities of Britain (co-author), 1997; Straw Wars, 2001. *Address:* Russell House, Bulwell Lane, Nottingham NG6 0BT, England.

COBEN, Harlan, BA; American writer; b. 4 Jan. 1962, Newark, NJ; m. Anne Armstrong 1988; two s. two d. *Education:* Amherst Coll. *Career:* mem. MWA, Sisters in Crime. *Publications:* novels: Play Dead 1990, Miracle Cure 1991, Deal Breaker (World Mystery Conference Anthony Award for Best Paperback Original Novel 1996) 1995, Drop Shot 1996, Fade Away (MWA Edgar Award for Best Paperback Original Mystery Novel, Shamus Award for Best Paperback Original Novel, Private Eye Writers of America 1997) 1996, Back Spin 1997, One False Move (WHSmith Fresh Talent award) 1997, The Final Detail 1999, Darkest Fear 2000, Tell No One 2001, Gone For Good (WHSmith Thumping Good Read award) 2002, No Second Chance 2003, Just One Look 2004; short stories: A Simple Philosophy 1999, The Key to my Father 2003. *Literary Agent:* Aaron Priest Literary Agency, 708 Third Avenue, New York, NY 10017, USA. *E-mail:* me@harlancoben.com. *Website:* www.harlancoben.com.

COBURN, Andrew; writer; b. 1 May 1932, Exeter, NH, USA. *Education:* Suffolk University, Boston. *Publications:* Fiction: The Trespassers, 1974; The Babysitter, 1979; Off Duty, 1980; Company Secrets, 1982; Widow's Walk, 1984; Sweetheart, 1985; Love Nest, 1987; Goldilocks, 1989; No Way Home, 1992; Voices in the Dark, 1994; Birthright, 1997. Contributions: Transatlantic Magazine. *Honours:* Hon. DLitt, Merrimack College, USA, 1986. *Address:* 303 Walnut Street, Westfield, NJ 07090, USA.

COBURN, Donald Lee; dramatist; b. 4 Aug. 1938, Baltimore, MD, USA; m. 1st Nazlee Joyce French 1964 (divorced 1971); one s. one d.; m. 2nd Marsha Woodruff Maher 1975. *Education:* public schools in Baltimore. *Career:* mem. Authors League of America; Dramatists Guild of America; Société des Auteurs et Compositeurs Dramatiques; Texas Institute of Letters; Writers Guild of America. *Publications:* Plays: The Gin Game, 1977; Bluewater Cottage, 1979; The Corporation Man, 1981; Currents Turned Awry, 1982; Guy, 1983; Noble Adjustment, 1986; Anna-Weston, 1988; Return to Blue Fin, 1991. Screenplays: Flights of Angels, 1987; A Virgin Year, 1992. *Honours:* Pulitzer Prize in Drama, 1978; Golden Apple, 1978. *Address:* c/o Writers' Guild of America, 555 W 57th Street, New York, NY 10019, USA.

CODINA, Pedro Jeta Ramirez; Spanish journalist and newspaper executive; *Director, El Mundo*; b. 26 March 1952, Logroño; m. 1st Rocío Fernández Iglesias; m. 2nd Agatha Ruíz de la Prada; one s. one d. *Education:* Univ. of Navarre. *Career:* Prof. of Contemporary Spanish Literature, Lebanon Valley Coll., PA, U.S.A. 1973–74; with La Actualidad Económica 1974–76; wrote a weekly column for ABC; corresp. for El Noticiero Universal, Madrid; Dir. of Diario 16 1980; currently Dir. El Mundo. *Address:* El Mundo, Pradillo 42, 28002 Madrid, Spain (Office). *Telephone:* (91) 5864800 (Office). *Fax:* (91) 5864848 (Office). *Website:* www.elmundo.es (Office).

CODRESCU, Andrei, BA; American professor of English, writer, poet, editor and radio and television commentator; b. 20 Dec. 1946, Sibiu, Romania; m. Alice Henderson 1969 (divorced 1998); two s. *Education:* University of Bucharest. *Career:* Prof. of English, Louisiana State University, 1966–; Commentator, All Things Considered, National Public Radio; Ed., Exquisite Corpse, literary journal. *Publications:* Fiction: The Repentence of Lorraine, 1994; The Blood Countess, 1995; Messiah, 1999–. Poetry: Comrade Past and Mister Present, 1991; Belligerence, 1993; Alien Candor: Selected Poems, 1970–1995, 1996. Essays: Raised by Puppets Only to be Killed by Research, 1987; Craving for Swan, 1988; The Disappearance of the Outside: A Manifesto for Escape, 1990; The Hole in the Flag: A Romanian Exile's Story of Return and Revolution, 1991; Road Scholar: Coast to Coast Late in the Century, 1993; The Muse is Always Half-Dressed in New Orleans, 1995; Zombification: Essays from NPR, 1995; The Dog With the Chip in His Neck: Essays from NPR & Elsewhere, 1996; Ay, Cuba! A Socio-Erotic Journey, 1999. Editor: American Poetry Since 1970: Up Late, 1988; The Stiffest of the Corpse: An Exquisite Corpse Reader, 1983–1990, 1990; American Poets Say Goodbye to the 20th Century, 1996. Film: Road Scholar, Public Broadcasting Service, 1994. *Honours:* George Foster Peabody Award, 1995; Freedom of Speech Award, American Civil Liberties Union, 1995; Literature Prize, Romanian Cultural Foundation, 1996. *Address:* 1114 Peniston, New Orleans, LA 70115, USA.

CODY, James (see Rohrbach, Peter Thomas).

COE, Jonathan, BA, MA, PhD; British writer; b. 19 Aug. 1961, Birmingham, England; m. Janine McKeown 1989. *Education:* Trinity Coll., Cambridge, Warwick Univ. *Publications:* The Accidental Woman 1987, A Touch of Love 1989, The Dwarves of Death 1990, Humphrey Bogart: Take It and Like It 1991, James Stewart: Leading Man 1994, What A Carve Up! 1994, The House of Sleep 1997, The Rotters' Club 2001, The Closed Circle 2004, Like a Fiery Elephant: the Story of B. S. Johnson 2004; contrib. to periodicals. *Honours:* John Llewellyn Rhys Prize 1995, Prix du Meilleur Livre Étranger 1996, Writers' Guild Award 1997, Prix Médicis Étranger 1998, Bollinger Everyman Wodehouse Prize 2001. *Literary Agent:* Peake Associates, 14 Grafton Crescent, London, NW1 8SL, England.

COE, Tucker (see Westlake, Donald Edwin).

COELHO, Paulo; Author; b. Aug. 1947, Rio de Janeiro, Brazil. *Education:* Attended law school. *Publications:* Arquivos do inferno, 1982; O diário de um mago (trans. as The Pilgrimage, aka The Diary of a Magus: The Road to Santiago), 1987; O alquimista (trans. as The Alchemist), 1988; Brida, 1990; O Dom Supremo (trans. as The Gift), 1991; As valkírias (trans. as The Valkyries), 1992; Maktub, 1994; Na margem do rio Piedra eu sentei e chorei (trans. as By the River Piedra I Sat Down and Wept), 1994; Frases, 1995; O Monte Cinco (trans. as The Fifth Mountain), 1996; O manual do guerreiro da luz (trans. as Manual of the Warrior of Light), 1997; Love Letters from a Prophet (in trans.), 1997; Veronika decide morrer (trans. as Veronika Decides to Die), 1998; Paulo Coelho: The Confessions of a Pilgrim (in trans.), 1999; O demônio e a Srta Prym (trans. as The Devil and Miss Prym), 2000; Fathers, Sons and Grandsons (in trans.), 2001; Onze minutos (trans. as Eleven Minutes), 2003. *Honours:* Prix Lectrices d'Elle, France, 1995; Golden Book Awards, Yugoslavia, 1995, 1996, 1997, 1998, 1999, 2000; Chevalier, Ordre des Arts et des Lettres, 1996; Flaiano International Award, Italy, 1996; Super Grinzane Cavour Book Award, Italy, 1996; Comendador de Ordem do Rio Branco, Brazil, 1998; Golden Medal of Galicia, Spain, 1999; Chevalier, Légion d'honneur, 2000; Crystal Mirror Award, Poland, 2000; XXIII Premio Internazionale Fregene, Italy, 2001; Bambi Award, Germany, 2001; Elected mem., Brazilian Acad. of Arts, 2002. *Literary Agent:* Sant Jordi Asociados Agencia Literaria SL, Arquitecte Sert no. 31, 5° 1a, 08005 Barcelona, Spain. *Website:* www.paulocoelho.com.

COETZEE, John Maxwell, MA, PhD; South African writer and academic; b. 9 Feb. 1940, Cape Town; one s. one d. *Education:* Univ. of Cape Town, Univ. of Texas. *Career:* Asst Prof. of English, State Univ. of NY Buffalo 1968–71; Lecturer, Univ. of Cape Town 1972–76, Sr Lecturer 1977–80, Assoc. Prof. 1981–83, Prof. of Gen. Literature 1984–2001, attached to Univ. of Adelaide, Australia 2002–; Prof. of Social Thought, Univ. of Chicago, USA 2001–, Distinguished Service Prof. *Publications:* Dusklands 1974, In the Heart of the Country 1977, Waiting for the Barbarians 1980, Life and Times of Michael K (Booker-McConnell Prize 1983, Prix Femina Etranger 1985) 1983, Foe 1986, White Writing 1988, Age of Iron (Sunday Express Book of the Year Prize 1990) 1990, Doubling the Point: Essays and Interviews (ed. by David Atwell) 1992, The Master of Petersburg (Premio Mondello 1994, Irish Times Int. Fiction Prize 1995) 1994, Giving Offence: Essays on Censorship 1996, Boyhood 1997, The Lives of Animals (lecture) 1999, Disgrace (Booker Prize 1999, Commonwealth Writers Prize 2000) 1999, The Humanities in Africa 2001, Stranger Shores: Essays 1986–1999 2001, Youth 2002, Elizabeth Costello: Eight Lessons 2003. *Honours:* Dr hc (Strathclyde) 1985, (State Univ. of New York) 1989, (Cape Town) 1995, (Oxford) 2002; CNA Literary Award 1977, 1980, 1983, Geoffrey Faber Prize 1980, James Tait Black Memorial Prize 1980, Jerusalem Prize 1987, Prix Meilleur Livre 2002, Premio Grinzane 2003, Nobel Prize for Literature 2003. *Address:* PO Box 3090, Newton, S Australia 5074, Australia. *E-mail:* john.coetzee@adelaide.edu.au (Home).

COFFEY, Brian (see Koontz, Dean Ray).

COFFEY, Marilyn June; writer, poet and academic; b. 22 July 1937, Alma, NE, USA; m. 1961 (divorced); one s. *Education:* BA, University of Nebraska, 1959; MFA, Brooklyn College, CUNY, 1981. *Career:* Faculty, Pratt Institute, New York, 1966–69, 1973–90; Adjunct Communication Instructor, St Mary's College, Lincoln, NE, 1990–92; Assoc. Prof. of Creative Writing, Ft Hays State University, 1992–; mem. E. A. Burnett Society, charter mem.; Poets and Writers. *Publications:* Marcella (novel), 1973; Great Plains Patchwork (non-fiction), 1989; A Cretan Cycle: Fragments Unearthed From Knossos (poems), 1991; Creating the Classic Short Story: A Workbook, 1995; Delicate Footsteps: Poems About Real Women, 1995. Contributions: anthologies, journals, reviews, and newspapers. *Honours:* Pushcart Prize, 1976; Master Alumnus, University of Nebraska, 1977; Winner, Newark Public Library Competitions, NJ, 1985, 1987–88; several grants. *Address:* c/o Department of English, Fort Hays State University, Hays, KS 67601, USA.

COFFMAN, Virginia (Edith), (Victor Cross, Virginia Du Vaul, Jeanne Duval, Anne Stanfield); Author; b. 30 July 1914, San Francisco, CA, USA. *Education:* AB, University of California at Berkeley, 1938. *Publications:* Survivor of Darkness, 1973; The Ice Forest, 1976; Looking Glass, 1979; The Lombard Cavalcade, 1982; Dark Winds, 1985; The Royles, 3 vols, 1991, 1992, 1994. *Address:* c/o Severn House Publishers Ltd, 41 E 57th St, 15th Floor, New York, NY 10022, USA.

COGSWELL, Frederick William; academic, author, poet, editor and translator; b. 8 Nov. 1917, East Centreville, NB, Canada; m. 1st Margaret Hynes 3 July 1944 (died 2 May 1985); two d.; m. 2nd Gail Fox 8 Nov. 1985. *Education:* BA, 1949, MA, 1950, University of New Brunswick; PhD, University of Edinburgh, 1952. *Career:* Asst Prof., 1952–57, Assoc. Prof., 1957–61, Prof., 1961–83, Prof. Emeritus, 1983–, University of New Brunswick; Ed., Fiddlehead Magazine, 1952–66, Humanities Asscn Bulletin, 1967–72; mem. League of Canadian Poets; PEN; Writers Federation of New Brunswick. *Publications:* The Stunted Strong, 1955; The Haloed Tree, 1956; Testament of Cresseid, 1957; Descent from Eden, 1959; Lost Dimensions, 1960; A Canadian Anthology, 1960; Five New Brunswick Poets, 1962; The Arts in New Brunswick, 1966; Star People, 1968; Immortal Plowman, 1969; In Praise of Chastity, 1970; One Hundred Poems of Modern Québec, 1971; The Chains of Liliput, 1971; The House Without a Door, 1973; Against Perspective, 1979; A Long Apprenticeship: Collected Poems, 1980; Pearls, 1983; The Edge to Life, 1987; The Best Notes Merge, 1988; Black and White Tapestry, 1989; Unfinished Dreams: Contemporary Poetry of Acadie, 1990; Watching an Eagle, 1991; When the Right Light Shines, 1992; In Praise of Old Music, 1992; In My Own Growing, 1993; As I See It, 1994; In Trouble With Light, 1996. *Honours:* Order of Canada.

COHAN, Tony, (Anthony Robert Cohan); Writer; b. 28 Dec. 1939, New York, NY, USA; m. 1 June 1974; one d. *Education:* BA, University of California, 1961. *Career:* mem. Authors' Guild; PEN. *Publications:* Nine Ships, 1975; Canary, 1981; The Flame, 1983; Opium, 1984; Agents of Desire, 1997; Mexicolor, 1997; On Mexican Time, 2000; Native State, 2003. *Honours:* Notable Book of the Year, 1981. *Address:* PO Box 1170, Venice, CA 90294, USA.

COHEN, Daniel; Author; b. 12 March 1936, Chicago, IL, USA; m. Susan Handler 2 Feb. 1958; one d. (deceased). *Education:* Journalism degree, University of Illinois, 1959. *Career:* Asst Ed., 1960–65, Managing Ed., 1965–69, Science Digest; mem. Authors' Guild. *Publications:* About 100 books of young adult non-fiction; 10 children's books; 20 other books; Over 25 books in collaboration with wife.

COHEN, Leonard, OC, BA; Canadian singer and songwriter; b. 21 Sept. 1934, Montreal; two c. *Education:* McGill Univ. *Career:* f. country-and-western band, The Buckskin Boys 1951; initially wrote poetry, winning McGill Literary Award for first collection; moved to New York in early 1960s. *Compositions include:* Suzanne, Priests, Sisters of Mercy, Hey, That's No Way to Say Goodbye, Story of Isaac, Bird On A Wire. *Recordings include:* The Songs of Leonard Cohen 1968, Songs From A Room 1969, Songs of Love and Hate 1971, Live Songs 1973, New Skin For the Old Ceremony 1974, Greatest Hits 1975, The Best of Leonard Cohen 1976, Death of a Ladies' Man 1977, Recent Songs 1979, Various Positions 1985, I'm Your Man 1988, The Future 1992, Cohen Live 1994, More Best Of 1997, Live Songs 1998, Ten New Songs 2001. *Publications:* Let Us Compare Mythologies 1956 (McGill Literary Award), The Spice-Box of Earth 1961, The Favourite Game 1963, Flowers for Hitler 1964, Beautiful Losers 1966, Parasites of Heaven 1966, Selected Poems 1956–1968 1968, The Energy of Slaves 1972, Death of a Ladies' Man 1978, Book of Mercy 1984, Stranger Music: Selected Poems and Songs 1993. *Honours:* William Harold Moon Award (Recording Rights Organization of Canada) 1984, Juno Hall of Fame 1991. *Literary Agent:* Kelley Lynch, Stranger Management Inc., 419 North Larchmont Boulevard, Suite 91, Los Angeles, CA 90004, USA.

COHEN, Marcel; Author; b. 9 Oct. 1937, Asnières, France. *Education:* École Supérieure de Journalisme, Paris; École du Louvre, Paris. *Publications:* Galpa, 1969; Malestroit: Chroniques du Silence, 1973; Voyage à Waizata, 1976; Murs, 1979; Du désert au livre: Entretiens avec Edmond Jabès, 1981, English trans. as From the Desert to the Book, 1990; Miroirs, 1981, English trans. as Mirrors, 1998; Je ne sais pas le nom, 1986; Le grand paon-de-nuit, 1990, English trans. as The Peacock Emperor Moth, 1995; Lettre à Antonio Saura, 1997; Assassinat d'un garde, 1998; Faits, 2002. Contributions: anthologies, journals and magazines. *Address:* 197 rue de Grenelle, 75007 Paris, France.

COHEN, Michael Joseph; Prof. of History and Writer; b. 29 April 1940, London, England. *Education:* BA, University of London, 1969; PhD, LSE, 1971. *Career:* Lecturer, 1972–77, Senior Lecturer, 1977–81, Assoc. Prof., 1981–86, Prof., 1986–, Lazarus Philips Chair of History, 1990–, Bar Ilan University; Visiting Prof., Stanford University, 1977, 1981, Hebrew University, Jerusalem, 1978–80, 1981–83, Duke University and University of North Carolina, Chapel Hill, 1980–81, University of British Columbia, 1985–86; Bernard and Audre Rapaport Fellow, American Jewish Archives, Cincinnati, 1988–89; Meyerhoff Visiting Prof. of Israel Studies, University of Maryland, College Park, 1992–98; Mem., Institute of Advanced Studies, Princeton, 1998; Visiting Prof., San Diego State University, 1999, Centre for International Studies, LSE, 2002–03. *Publications:* Palestine: Retreat From the Mandate, 1936–45, 1978; Palestine and the Great Powers 1945–48, 1982; Churchill and the Jews, 1985; The Origins of the Arab-Zionist Conflict, 1914–1948, 1987; Palestine to Israel: From Mandate to Independence, 1988; Truman and Israel, 1990; Fighting World War Three from the Middle East: Allied Contingency Plans, 1945–1954, 1997. Editor: The Weizmann Letters, Vols XX, XXI, 1936–1945, 1979; The History of the Founding of Israel, Part III, The Struggle for the State of Israel, 1939–1948, 10 vols, 1988; Bar-Ilan Studies in Modern History, 1991; British Security Problems in the Middle East During the 1930s: The Conquest of Abyssinia to World War Two (with Martin Kolinsky), 1992; The Demise of Empire: Britain's Responses to Nationalist Movements in the Middle East, 1943–1955 (with Martin Kolinsky), 1998. Contributions: scholarly journals. *Address:* c/o General History Dept, Bar-Ilan University, 52900 Ramat-Gan, Israel.

COHEN, Morton Norton, (John Moreton); academic and writer; b. 27 Feb. 1921, Calgary, AB, Canada. *Education:* AB, Tufts University, 1949; MA, 1950, PhD, 1958, Columbia University. *Career:* Tutor to Prof., City College, CUNY, 1952–81, Mem., Doctoral Faculty, 1964–81, Deputy Exec. Officer, PhD Programme in English, 1976–78, 1979–80, Prof. Emeritus, 1981–, CUNY; FRSL, 1996–; mem. Lewis Carroll Society; Lewis Carroll Society of North America; Lewis Carroll Society of Japan; Century Asscn, New York. *Publications:* Rider Haggard: His Life and Works, 1960; A Brief Guide to Better Writing (co-author), 1960; Rudyard Kipling to Rider Haggard: The Record of a Friendship, 1965; Lewis Carroll's Photographs of Nude Children, 1978, republished as Lewis Carroll, Photographer of Children: Four Nude Studies, 1979; The Russian Journal II, 1979; The Letters of Lewis Carroll (ed.), 2 vols, 1979; Lewis Carroll and the Kitchins, 1980; Lewis Carroll and Alice 1832–1882, 1982; The Selected Letters of Lewis Carroll, 1982; Lewis Carroll and the House of Macmillan (co-ed.), 1987; Lewis Carroll: A Biography, 1995; Reflections in a Looking Glass (A Celebration of Lewis Carroll's Photographs), 1998; Lewis Carroll and His Illustrators, 2003. Contributions: many magazines, journals, papers and books. *Honours:* Fulbright Fellow, 1954–55, 1974–75; Guggenheim Fellowship, 1966–67; Research Grant, National Endowment for the Humanities, 1974–75; Publication Grant, Guggenheim Foundation, 1979. *Literary Agent:* AP Watt Ltd, 20 John Street, London WC1N 2DR, England. *Address:* 55 E Ninth Street, Apt 10-D, New York, NY 10003, USA.

COHEN, Stephen Frand, BA, MA, PhD; academic and writer; *Professor of Russian Studies and History, New York University*; b. 25 Nov. 1938, Indianapolis, IN, USA; m. 1st Lynn Blair 1962 (divorced); one s. one d.; m. 2nd Katrina vanden Heuvel 1988; one d. *Education:* Indiana University, Russian Institute Certificate, Columbia University. *Career:* Instructor, Columbia College, 1965–68; Junior Fellow, 1965–68, Senior Fellow, 1971–73, 1976–77, 1985, Assoc., 1972–85, Visiting Prof., 1973–84, Visiting Scholar, 1980–81, Columbia University; Asst Prof., 1968–73, Assoc. Prof., 1973–80, Prof., 1980–98, Prof. Emeritus, 1998–, Princeton University; Prof. of Russian Studies and History, New York University, 1998–; mem. American Asscn for the Advancement of Slavic Studies; American Historical Asscn; American Political Science Asscn; Council on Foreign Relations. *Publications:* The Great Purge Trial (co-ed.), 1965; Bukharin and the Bolshevik Revolution: A Political Biography, 1888–1938, 1973; The Soviet Union Since Stalin (co-ed.), 1980; An End to Silence: Uncensored Opinion in the Soviet Union (ed.), 1982; Rethinking the Soviet Experience: Politics and History Since 1917, 1985; Sovieticus: American Perceptions and the Soviet Realities, 1985; Voices of Glasnost: Interviews with Gorbachev's Reformers (co-author and co-ed.), 1989; Failed Crusade: America and the Tragedy of Post Communist Russia, 2000. Contributions: books, scholarly journals and periodicals; Contributing Ed., The Nation. *Honours:* Guggenheim Fellowships, 1976–77, 1989; Rockefeller Foundation Humanities Fellowship, 1980–81; National Endowment for the Humanities Fellowship, 1984–85; Page One Award for Column Writing, 1985; Fulbright-Hays Faculty Research Abroad Fellowship, 1988–89; Indiana University Distinguished Alumni Award, 1998; New York University Award for Excellence in Teaching, 2001; Columbia University Harriman (Russian) Institute Alumnus of the Year, 2002. *Address:* Department of Russian Studies, New York University, 19 University Place, New York, NY 10003-4556, USA.

COHEN, Susan; Author; b. 27 March 1938, Chicago, IL, USA; m. Daniel Cohen 2 Feb. 1958; one d. (deceased). *Education:* University of Illinois, 1957–59; BA, New School for Social Research, 1960; MSW, Adelphi University, 1962. *Publications:* 25 books in collaboration with husband; 8 Gothic books; 4 mystery books. *Address:* 24 Elizabeth St, Port Jervis, NY 12771, USA.

COHN, Samuel Kline, Jr; Prof. of Medieval History and Writer; b. 13 April 1949, Birmingham, AL, USA; m. Genevieve A Warwick, 15 July 1994, two s. *Education:* BA, Union College, 1971; MA, University of Wisconsin at Madison, 1973; Dip di Statistica, Università degli Studi di Firenze, 1976–77; PhD, Harvard University, 1978. *Career:* Asst Prof., Wesleyan University, 1978–79; Asst Prof., 1979–85, Assoc. Prof., 1986–89, Prof. of History, 1989–95, Brandeis University; Visiting Prof., Brown University, 1990–91; Prof. of Medieval History, University of Glasgow, 1995–; mem. American Historical Asscn; Society for Italian Historical Studies; FRHistS. *Publications:* The Laboring Classes in Renaissance Florence, 1980; Death and Property in Siena 1205–1800: Strategies for the Afterlife, 1988; The Cult of Remembrance and the Black Death: Six Renaissance Cities in

Central Italy, 1992; Portraits of Medieval and Renaissance Living: Essays in Memory of David Herlihy (ed.), 1996; Women in the Streets: Essays on Sex and Power in the Italian Renaissance, 1996; The Black Death and the Transformation of the West (with David Herlihy), 1996; Creating the Florentine State: Peasants and Rebellion 1348–1434, 1999. Contributions: scholarly books and journals. *Honours:* Hon. Krupp Foundation Fellowship, 1976; Fulbright-Hays Fellowship, Italy, 1977; Fellow, Center for European Studies, Harvard University, 1977–; National Endowment for the Humanities Research Fellowship, 1982–83; Guest Fellow, Villa I Tatti, Settignano, Italy, 1988–89; Howard R. Marraro Prize, American Catholic Historical Asscn, 1989; Outstanding Academic Book Selection, Choice magazine, 1993; Villa I Tatti Fellowship, 1993–94; Guggenheim Fellowship, 1994–95.

COLE, Barry; Writer and Poet; b. 13 Nov. 1936, Woking, Surrey, England; m. Rita Linihan, 1959, three d. *Career:* Northern Arts Fellow in Literature, Universities of Durham and Newcastle upon Tyne, 1970–72. *Publications:* Blood Ties, 1967; Ulysses in the Town of Coloured Glass, 1968; A Run Across the Island, 1968; Moonsearch, 1968; Joseph Winter's Patronage, 1969; The Search for Rita, 1970; The Visitors, 1970; The Giver, 1971; Vanessa in the City, 1971; Pathetic Fallacies, 1973; Dedications, 1977; The Edge of the Common, 1989; Inside Outside: New and Selected Poems, 1997; Lola and the Train, 1999; Ghosts Are People Too, 2003. Contributions: The Oxford Book of Twentieth Century Verse, British Poetry Since 1945 (anthology). *Address:* 68 Myddelton Sq., London EC1R 1XP, England.

COLE, John Morrison; journalist, broadcaster and writer; b. 23 Nov. 1927, Belfast, Northern Ireland; m. Margaret Isobel Williamson 1956; four s. *Education:* University of London. *Career:* mem. Athenaeum Club. *Publications:* The Poor of the Earth, 1976; The Thatcher Years, 1987; As It Seemed to Me: Political Memoirs, 1995. Contributions: Guardian; New Statesman. *Honours:* Granada Television Newspaper Award, 1960; RTS Broadcast Journalist of the Year Award, 1990; BAFTA Richard Dimbleby Award, 1992; Hon. Doctorates, Open University, 1992, Queen's University, Belfast, 1992, University of Ulster, 1992, University of St Andrews, 1993.

COLE, Peter; American poet and translator; b. 1957, Paterson, NJ. *Career:* Visiting Prof., Wesleyan Univ., Middlebury Coll.; editorial bd mem., Ibis Editions. *Publications:* poetry: Rift 1990, Hymns and Qualms 1998; nine books of translations from Hebrew and Arabic poetry and prose. *Honours:* National Endowment for the Humanities Fellowship, National Endowment for the Arts Fellowship, John Simon Guggenheim Foundation Fellowship ; MLA Scaglione Translation Prize, TLS Porjes Hebrew Translation Prize. *Address:* c/o Ibis Editions, PO Box 8074, German Colony, Jerusalem, Israel. *E-mail:* ibis@netvision.net.il. *Website:* www.ibiseditions.com.

COLEGATE, Isabel (Diana); Novelist; b. 10 Sept. 1931, London, England; m. Michael Briggs 12 Sept. 1953; two s. one d. *Career:* mem. Author's Society. *Publications:* The Blackmailer, 1958; A Man of Power, 1960; The Great Occasion, 1962; Statues in a Garden, 1964; Orlando King, 1968; Orlando at the Brazen Threshold, 1971; Agatha, 1973; News from the City of the Sun, 1979; The Shooting Party, 1980 (filmed 1985); A Glimpse of Sion's Glory, 1985; Deceits of Time, 1988; The Summer of the Royal Visit, 1991; Winter Journey, 1995; A Pelican in the Wilderness: Hermits, Solitaries and Recluses, 2002. *Honours:* FRSL, 1981; WHSmith Literary Award, 1981; Hon. MA, Univ. of Bath, 1988. *Address:* Midford Castle, Bath BA1 7BU, England.

COLEMAN, Jane Candia; Writer and Poet; b. 1 Jan. 1939, Pittsburgh, PA, USA; m. Bernard Coleman, 27 March 1965, divorced 1989, two s. *Education:* BA, Creative Writing, University of Pittsburgh. *Career:* mem. Authors' Guild; Women Writing the West. *Publications:* No Roof But Sky (poems), 1990; Stories From Mesa Country, 1991; Discovering Eve (short stories), 1993; Shadows in My Hands (memoir), 1993; The Red Drum (poems), 1994; Doc Holliday's Woman (novel), 1995; Moving On (short stories), 1997; I, Pearl Hart (novel), 1998; The O'Keefe Empire (novel), 1999; Doc Holliday's Gone (novel), 1999; Borderlands (short stories), 2000; Desperate Acts (novel), 2001; The Italian Quartet (novel), 2001; Mountain Time (memoir), 2001; Country Music (short stories), 2002; Wives and Lovers (short stories), 2002. Contributions: periodicals. *Honours:* Western Heritage Awards, 1991, 1992, 1994, Spur Awards for short fiction Western Writers of America 1993, 1995, Arizona Comm. on the Arts Poetry Grant 1993. *Address:* 1702 E Lind Rd, Tucson, AZ 85719, USA.

COLEMAN, Terry, (Terence Francis Frank); journalist and writer; b. 13 Feb. 1931, Bournemouth, England; m. 1st Lesley Fox-Strangeways Vane 1954 (divorced); two d.; m. 2nd Vivien Rosemary Lumsdaine Wallace 1981; one s. one d. *Education:* LLB, University of London, 1958. *Career:* Ed., Savoir Faire; Sub-Ed., Sunday Mercury, and Birmingham Post; Reporter, then Arts Correspondent, 1961–70, Chief Feature Writer, 1970–74, 1976–79, New York Correspondent, 1980–81, Special Correspondent, 1982–89, Guardian; Special Writer, Daily Mail, 1974–76; Assoc. Ed., The Independent, 1989–91; Columnist, Guardian and Mail on Sunday, 1992–; mem. Society of Authors; FRSA. *Publications:* The Railway Navvies, 1965; A Girl for the Afternoons, 1965; Providence and Mr Hardy (with Lois Deacon), 1966; The Only True History: Collected Journalism, 1969; Passage to America, 1971; The Liners, 1976; The Scented Brawl: Collected Journalism, 1978; Southern Cross, 1979; Thanksgiving, 1981; Movers and Shakers: Collected Interviews, 1987; Thatcher's Britain, 1987; Empire, 1993; W. G. Grace: A Biography, 1997; Nelson: The Man and the Legend, 2001; Olivier: The Authorised Biography, 2004. Contributions: various publications. *Honours:* Yorkshire Post Prize for Best First Book of the Year, 1965; Feature Writer of the Year, British Press Awards, 1982; Journalist of the Year, Granada Awards, 1987. *Address:* 18 North Side, London SW4 0RQ, England.

COLEMAN, Wanda; Poet and Writer; b. 13 Nov. 1946, Los Angeles, CA, USA. *Publications:* Mad Dog Black Lady, 1979; Imagoes, 1983; Heavy Daughter Blues: Poems and Stories, 1968–1986, 1987; A War of Eyes and Other Stories, 1988; Women for All Seasons: Poetry and Prose About the Transitions in Women's Lives (ed. with Joanne Leedom-Ackerman), 1988; Dicksboro Hotel and Other Travels, 1989; African Sleeping Sickness: Stories and Poems, 1990; Hand Dance, 1993; Native in a Strange Land: Trials & Tremors, 1996; Bathwater Wine, 1998; Mambo Hips & Make Believe: A Novel, 1999. Contributions: anthologies and periodicals. *Honours:* Fellowships; Lenore Marshall Poetry Prize, Acad. of American Poets, 1999.

COLERIDGE, Geraldine Margaret (Gill); British literary agent; b. 26 May 1948; m. David Roger Leeming 1974; two s. *Education:* Queen Anne's School, Caversham and Marlborough Secretarial Coll., Oxford. *Career:* Mem. staff BPC Partworks, Sidgwick & Jackson, Bedford Square Book Bang until 1971; Publicity Man. Chatto & Windus 1971–72; Dir and Literary Agent, Anthony Sheil Assocs 1973–88; Partner Rogers, Coleridge & White, Literary Agents 1988–; Pres. Assoc. of Authors' Agents 1988–91. *Address:* Rogers, Coleridge & White, 20 Powis Mews, London, W11 1JN, England. *Telephone:* (20) 7221-3717. *Fax:* (20) 7229-9084.

COLERIDGE, Nicholas David; Journalist and Author; b. 4 March 1957, London, England; m. Georgia Elizabeth Metcalfe, 22 July 1989, three s., one d. *Education:* Trinity College, Cambridge. *Career:* Ed., Harpers & Queen Magazine, 1986–89; Editorial Dir, 1989–91, Managing Dir, 1992–, Condé Nast Publishers; Vice-Pres., Condé Nast International, 1999–. *Publications:* Tunnel Vision, 1981; Around the World in 78 Days, 1984; Shooting Stars, 1984; The Fashion Conspiracy, 1988; How I Met My Wife and Other Stories, 1991; Paper Tigers, 1993; With Friends Like These, 1997; Streetsmart, 1999; Godchildren, 2002. Contributions: Harpers & Queen; Spectator; Daily Telegraph; Sunday Telegraph; Tatler; Evening Standard; GQ; Vanity Fair. *Honours:* Young Journalist of the Year, 1983; Mark Boxer Award for Editorial Excellence, BSME, 2001. *Address:* 38 Princedale Rd, London W11, England.

COLES, Donald Langdon; Prof. and Poet; b. 12 April 1928, Woodstock, Ontario, Canada; m. 28 Dec. 1958, one s. one d. *Education:* BA, Victoria College; MA, University of Toronto; MA (Cantab), 1954. *Career:* Fiction Ed., The Canadian Forum, 1975–76; Dir, Creative Writing Programme, York University, 1979–85; Poetry Ed., May Studio, Banff Centre for the Fine Arts, 1984–93; mem. PEN International. *Publications:* Sometimes All Over, 1975; Anniversaries, 1979; The Prinzhorn Collection, 1982; Landslides, 1986; K in Love, 1987; Little Bird, 1991; Forests of the Medieval World, 1993; Someone Has Stayed in Stockholm: Selected and New Poems, 1994; Kurgan, 2000. Contributions: Saturday Night; Canadian Forum; London Review of Books; Poetry (Chicago); Globe and Mail; Arc; Ariel. *Honours:* CBC Literary Competition, 1980; Gold Medal for Poetry, National Magazine Awards, 1986; Gov.-Gen.'s Award for Poetry, Canada, 1993; Trillium Prize, Ontario, 2000. *Address:* 122 Glenview Ave, Toronto, Ontario M4R 1P8, Canada.

COLES, Robert Martin, AB, MD, ; American physician, writer and poet; *Professor of Psychiatry and Medical Humanities, Harvard University*; b. 12 Oct. 1929, Boston, Massachusetts, USA; m. Jane Hallowell; three s. *Education:* Harvard Coll., Columbia Univ. of Physicians and Surgeons; internship, Univ. of Chicago Clinics; psychiatric residencies Massachusetts General Hospital, McLean Hospital. *Career:* Research Psychiatrist, Health Services 1963–, Lecturer on General Education 1966–, Prof. of Psychiatry and Medical Humanities 1977–, Harvard Univ.; Contributing Ed., New Republic 1966–, American Poetry Review 1972–, Aperture 1974–, Literature and Medicine 1981–, New Oxford Review 1981–; Visiting Prof. of Public Policy, Duke Univ. 1973–; Ed., Children and Youth Services Review 1978–; Visiting Prof. of Psychiatry, Dartmouth Coll. 1989; Fellow, American Acad. of Arts and Sciences, American Psychiatric Asscn, Inst. of Society, Ethics, and Life Sciences; mem. American Orthopsychiatric Asscn. *Publications:* Children of Crisis (five vols) 1967–78, The Middle Americans 1970, The Geography of Faith 1971, The Old Ones of New Mexico 1973, William Carlos Williams 1975, Walker Percy 1978, Flannery O'Connor's South 1980, The Moral Life of Children 1986, The Political Life of Children 1986, Simone Weil 1987, Dorothy Day 1987, The Call of Stories: Teaching and the Moral Imagination 1989, Rumors of Another World 1989, The Spiritual Life of Children 1990, Anna Freud: The Dream of Psychoanalysis 1992, Collected Essays: Omnibus 1993, The Call of Service: A Witness to Idealism 1993, The Story of Ruby Bridges 1995, The Moral Intelligence of Children 1997, Old and On Their Own 1998; contrib. to numerous books, journals, reviews, magazines and periodicals. *Honours:* McAlpin Medal, Nat. Asscn of Mental Health 1972, Pulitzer Prize in General Non-Fiction 1973, Weatherford Prize, Berea Coll. and Council of Southern Mountains 1973, Lillian Smith Award, Southern Regional Council 1973, MacArthur Prize Fellow 1981, Sarah Josepha Hale Award 1986, Christopher Medals

1989, 1991, Gold Medal, Coll. of Physicians and Surgeons, Columbia Univ. 1991, US Presidential Medal of Freedom 1998; numerous hon. doctorates. *Address:* 81 Carr Road, Concord, MA 01742, USA.

COLFER, Eoin; Irish children's writer; b. 14 May 1965, Wexford; m. Jackie; two s. *Career:* fmr teacher. *Publications:* juvenile: Benny and Omar 1998, Benny and Babe 1999, The Wish List 2000, Artemis Fowl 2001, Artemis Fowl: The Arctic Incident 2002, Artemis Fowl: The Eternity Code 2003, The Seventh Dwarf (novella) 2004, The Supernaturalist 2004, The Artemis Fowl Files 2004; for younger children: Going Potty 1999, Ed's Funny Feet 2000, Ed's Bed 2001, The Legend of Spud Murphy 2004; other: plays. *Honours:* British Book Awards WHSmith Children's Book of the Year 2001, WHSmith Book Award 2002, German Children's Book Award 2004. *Address:* c/o Ed Victor Ltd, 6 Bayley Street, Bedford Square, London, WC1B 3HE, England. *Website:* www.eoincolfer.com.

COLLEY, Linda; Historian and Author; b. 1949, UK. *Career:* fmrly at Univ. of Cambridge, Yale Univ.; currently School Prof. of History and Leverhulme Research Prof., European Institute, LSE; mem. Fellow, British Acad. *Publications:* In Defiance of Oligarchy: The Tory Party 1714–1760, 1982; Namier, 1989; Britons: Forging the Nation 1707–1837, 1992; Captives: Britain, Empire and the World 1600–1850, 2002. *Address:* c/o Jonathan Cape, Random House, 20 Vauxhall Bridge Rd, London SW1V 2SA, England. *E-mail:* l.colley@lse.ac.uk.

COLLIER, Catrin (see Watkins, Karen Christna).

COLLIER, Michael (Robert); Prof. of English, Poet, Writer and Ed.; b. 25 May 1953, Phoenix, AZ, USA; m. Katherine A. Branch, 2 May 1981, two s. *Education:* BA, Interdisciplinary Studies, Connecticut College, 1976; MFA, Creative Writing, University of Arizona, 1979. *Career:* Lecturer in English, George Mason University, 1982, Trinity College, Washington, DC, 1982–83; Writing Staff, The Writer's Center, Bethesda, MD, 1982–85; Visiting Lecturer, 1984–85, Adjunct Instructor, 1985–86, Asst Prof. of English, 1986–90, Prof. of English, 1995–, University of Maryland at College Park; Visiting Lecturer, Johns Hopkins University, 1986–89, Yale University, 1990, 1992; Teacher, Warren Wilson College, 1991–93, 1996; Assoc. Staff, 1992–94, Dir, 1994–, Bread Loaf Writers' Conference, Middlebury College; mem. Acad. of American Poets; Poetry Society of America. *Publications:* Poetry: The Clasp and Other Poems, 1986; The Folded Heart, 1989; The Neighbor, 1995; The Ledge, 2000. Editor: The Wesleyan Tradition: Four Decades of American Poetry, 1993; The New Bread Loaf Anthology of Contemporary American Poetry (with Stanley Plumly), 1999; The New American Poets: A Bread Load Anthology, 2000. Contributions: anthologies, journals and magazines. *Honours:* Writing Fellow, Fine Arts Work Center, Provincetown, 1979–80; 'Discovery' The Nation Award, 1981; Margaret Bridgeman Scholar in Poetry, 1981, Theodore Morrison Fellow in Poetry, 1986, Bread Loaf Writers' Conference; National Endowment for the Arts Creative Writing Fellowships, 1984, 1994; Alice Faye di Castagnola Award, Poetry Society of America, 1988; Fellow, Timothy Dwight College, Yale University, 1992–96; Guggenheim Fellowship, 1995–96; Maryland Arts Council Grant, 2000; Poet Laureate of Maryland, 2001. *Address:* 111 Smithwood Ave, Catonsville, MD 21228, USA.

COLLINS, Billy, PhD; American poet and professor of English; *Distinguished Professor, Lehman College, City University of New York*; b. 22 March 1941, New York; m. Diane Collins 1979. *Education:* Holy Cross Coll., Univ. of California at Riverside. *Career:* Prof. of English Lehman Coll., City Univ. of New York 1969–2001, Distinguished Prof. 2001–; Visiting Writer Poets House, N Ireland 1993–96, Lenoir-Rhyne Coll. 1994, Ohio State Univ. 1998; Resident Poet Burren Coll. of Art, Ireland 1996, Sarah Lawrence Coll. 1998–2000; Adjunct Prof. Columbia Univ. 2000–01; conducts summer poetry workshops at Univ. Coll. Galway, Ireland; Library of Congress's Poet Laureate Consultant in Poetry 2001, US Poet Laureate 2001–03; Fellow, New York Foundation for the Arts, Nat. Endowment for the Arts, Guggenheim Foundation; NEA Fellowship 1993; Guggenheim Fellowship 1995. *Publications include:* Pokerface 1977, Video Poems 1980, The Apple that Astonished Paris 1988, Questions About Angels 1991, The Art of Drowning 1995, Picnic, Lightning 1998, Taking Off Emily Dickinson's Clothes 2000, Sailing Alone Around the Room: New and Selected Poems 2001, Nine Horses 2002; poems in many anthologies, including The Best American Poetry 1992, 1993, 1997 and periodicals, including Poetry, American Poetry, Review, American Scholar, Harper's, Paris Review and The New Yorker. *Honours:* New York Foundation for the Arts Poetry Fellowship 1986, Nat. Endowment for the Arts Creative Writing Fellowship 1988, Nat. Poetry Series Competition Winner 1990, Bess Hokin Prize 1991,Literary Lion, New York Public Library 1992, Frederick Bock Prize 1992, Guggenheim Fellowship 1993, Levinson Prize 1995, Paterson Poetry Prize 1999, J. Howard and Barbara M. J. Wood Prize 1999, Pushcart Prize 2002. *Address:* c/o Lehman College, 250 Bedford Park Boulevard West, Business Office, Shuster Hall Building, Bronx, New York, NY 10468, USA (Office); 185 Route 202, Somers, NY 10589 (Home). *Website:* www.lehman.cuny.edu (Office); www.bigsnap.com (Home). *Literary Agent:* Steven Barclay Agency, 12 Western Avenue, Petaluma, CA 94952, USA. *Telephone:* (707) 773-0654. *Fax:* (707) 778-1868. *Website:* www.barclayagency.com.

COLLINS, Gail, BA, MA; American writer, editor and columnist; b. 25 Nov. 1945, Cincinnati, OH; m. Dan Collins. *Education:* Marquette Univ., Univ. of Massachusetts at Amherst, Columbia Univ. *Career:* columnist, United Press Int., New York Daily News 1985–91, New York Newsday 1991–; Editorial Board, New York Times 1995–. *Publications include:* non-fiction: The Millennium Book (with Dan Collins), Scorpion Tongues: The Irresistible History of Gossip in American Politics 1998, America's Women: Four Hundred Years of Dolls, Drudges, Helpmates and Heroines 2003. *Address:* The New York Times, 500 Seventh Avenue, Eighth Floor, New York, NY 10018, USA. *Website:* www.nytimes.com.

COLLINS, Hunt (see Hunter, Evan).

COLLINS, Jackie; writer; b. England; m. Oscar Lerman. *Publications:* The World is Full of Married Men, 1968; The Stud, 1969; Sunday Simmons and Charlie Brick, 1971; Lovehead, 1974; The World is Full of Divorced Women, 1975; The Love Killers, 1977; Lovers and Gamblers, 1977; The Bitch, 1979; Chances, 1981; Sinners, 1981; Hollywood Wives, 1983; Lucky, 1985; Hollywood Husbands, 1986; Rock Star, 1988; Lady Boss, 1990; American Star, 1993; Hollywood Kids, 1994; Vendetta: Lucky's Revenge, 1997; Thrill, 1998; L.A. Connections, 1998; Dangerous Kiss, 1999; Lethal Seduction, 2000; Hollywood Wives: The New Generation, 2001; Deadly Embrace, 2002; Hollywood Divorces, 2003. *Address:* c/o Simon and Schuster, 1230 Avenue of the Americas, New York, NY 10020, USA.

COLLINS, Jim, (James Lee Collins); Author and Ed.; b. 30 Dec. 1945, Beloit, Wisconsin, USA; m. Joan Hertel, 27 Dec. 1974, two s. *Career:* mem. Colorado Authors League; National Writers Club; Western Writers of America. *Publications:* Comanche Trail, 1984; Gone to Texas, 1984; War Clouds, 1984; Campaigning, 1985; Orphans Preferred, 1985; Riding Shotgun, 1985; Mister Henry, 1986; The Brass Boy, 1987; Spencer's Revenge, 1987; Western Writers Handbook, 1987; Settling the American West, 1993. Contributions: The Blue and the Gray; Writers Digest Magazine.

COLLINS, Joan Henrietta, OBE; actress and writer; b. 23 May 1933, London, England; m. 1st Maxwell Reed, 1954, divorced 1957; m. 2nd George Anthony Newley, 1963, divorced 1970, one s. one d.; m. 3rd Ronald S. Kass, 1972, divorced 1983; m. 4th Peter Holm, 1985, divorced 1987; m. 5th Percy Gibson, 2002. *Education:* RADA. *Career:* Actress in numerous stage, film, and television productions. *Publications:* Past Imperfect, 1978; The Joan Collins Beauty Book, 1980; Katy: A Fight for Life, 1982; Prime Time, 1988; Love and Desire and Hate, 1990; My Secrets, 1994; Too Damn Famous, 1995; Second Act, 1997; My Friends' Secrets, 1998; Joan's Way, 2002; Star Quality, 2002; Misfortune's Daughters 2004. *Honours:* Best Television Actress, Golden Globe, 1982; Favourite Television Performer, People's Choice, 1985. *Address:* c/o Paul Keylock, 16 Bulbecks Walk, South Woodham Ferrers, Essex CM3 5ZN, England.

COLLINS, Larry, (John Laurence Collins Jr.); Author; b. 14 Sept. 1929, Hartford, CT, USA. *Education:* BA, Yale University, 1951. *Career:* Correspondent, United Press International, Paris, Rome and Beirut, 1957–59; Correspondent, Beirut, 1959–61, Bureau Chief, Paris, 1961–65, Newsweek magazine. *Publications:* Is Paris Burning? (with Dominique Lapierre), 1965; Or I'll Dress You in Mourning, 1968; O Jerusalem, 1972; Freedom at Midnight, 1975; The Fifth Horseman, 1980; Fall from Grace, 1985; Maze, 1989; Black Eagles, 1993; Le Jour du Miracle: D-Day Paris, 1994; Tomorrow Belongs to Us, 1998. *Honours:* Deauville Film Festival Literary Award, 1985; Mannesman Talley Literary Prize, 1989. *Address:* La Biche Niche, 83350 Ramatuelle, France.

COLLINS, Michael (see Lynds, Dennis).

COLLINS, Philip (Arthur William); Prof. of English (retd) and Author; b. 28 May 1923, London, England. *Education:* MA, Emmanuel College, Cambridge, 1947. *Career:* Warden, Vaughan College, 1954–62; Senior Lecturer, 1962–64, Prof. of English, 1964–82, University of Leicester; Mem., Board of Dirs, The National Theatre, 1976–82. *Publications:* James Boswell, 1956; English Christmas (ed.), 1956; Dickens and Crime, 1962; Dickens and Education, 1963; The Impress of the Moving Age, 1965; Thomas Cooper the Chartist: Byron and the Poets of the Poor, 1969; A Dickens Bibliography, 1970; Dickens: A Christmas Carol: The Public Reading Version, 1971; Bleak House: A Commentary, 1971; Dickens: The Critical Heritage (ed.), 1971; Reading Aloud: A Victorian Metier, 1972; Charles Dickens: The Public Readings (ed.), 1975; Charles Dickens: David Copperfield, 1977; Charles Dickens: Hard Times (ed.), 1978; Dickens: Interviews and Recollections (ed.), 1981; Thackeray: Interviews and Recollections (ed.), 1982; Tennyson, Poet of Lincolnshire, 1985; The Annotated Dickens (ed. with Edward Giuliano), 1986; Tennyson: Seven Essays (ed.), 1992. Contributions: Encyclopaedia Britannica; Listener; TLS. *Address:* 26 Knighton Dr., Leicester LE2 3HB, England.

COLLINSON, Patrick; Prof. of Modern History Emeritus and Writer; b. 10 Aug. 1929, Ipswich, England; m. Elizabeth Albinia Susan Selwyn, 1960, two s. two d. *Education:* BA, Pembroke College, Cambridge, 1952; PhD, University of London, 1957. *Career:* Research Fellow, Institute of Historical Research, 1954–55, Research Asst, 1955–56, University College London; Lecturer in History, University of Khartoum, 1956–61; Asst Lecturer in Ecclesiastical History, 1961–62, Lecturer, 1962–69, Fellow, 1976, King's College, London; Prof. of History, University of Sydney, 1969–75, University of Kent at Canterbury, 1976–84; Visiting Fellow, All Souls College, Oxford, 1981; Chair., Advisory Editorial Board, Journal of Ecclesiastical History, 1982–93; Prof. of Modern History, University of Sheffield,

1984–88; Regius Prof. of Modern History, 1988–96, Prof. Emeritus, 1996–, University of Cambridge; Fellow, Trinity College, Cambridge, 1988–; various visiting lectureships; mem. Academia Europaea; Church of England Record Society, pres., 1991–; Ecclesiastical History Society, pres., 1985–86. *Publications:* The Elizabethan Puritan Movement, 1967; Archbishop Grindal, 1519–1583: The Struggle for a Reformed Church, 1979; The Religion of Protestants: The Church in English Society, 1559–1625, 1982; Godly People: Essays on English Protestantism and Puritanism, 1983; English Puritanism, 1983; The Birthpangs of Protestant England: Religious and Cultural Change in the 16th and 17th Centuries, 1988; Elizabethan Essays, 1994; A History of Canterbury Cathedral (co-author), 1995; The Reformation in English Towns, 1500–1640 (co-ed.), 1998; A History of Emmanuel College, Cambridge (co-author), 1999; Short Oxford History of the British Isles: The Sixteenth Century (ed.), 2002; Elizabethans, 2003; The Reformation, 2003; Conferences and Combination Lectures in the Elizabethan Church (co-ed.), 2003. Contributions: scholarly books and journals. *Honours:* several hon. doctorates; FRHistS, 1967, council mem., 1977–81, vice-pres., 1983–87, 1994–98, hon. vice-pres., 2002–; Fellow, British Acad., 1982, council mem., 1986–89; CBE, 1993; Medlicott Medal, 1998. *Address:* The Winnats, Cannonfields, Hathersage, Hope Valley S32 1AG, England.

COLLIS, Louise Edith; Writer; b. 29 Jan. 1925, Arakan, Burma. *Education:* BA, History, Reading University, England, 1945. *Career:* mem. Society of Authors; International Asscn of Art Critics. *Publications:* Without a Voice, 1951; A Year Passed, 1952; After the Holiday, 1954; The Angel's Name, 1955; Seven in the Tower, 1958; The Apprentice Saint, 1964; Solider in Paradise, 1965; The Great Flood, 1966; A Private View of Stanley Spencer, 1972; Maurice Collis Diaries (ed.), 1976; Impetuous Heart: The Story of Ethel Smyth, 1984. Contributions: Books and Bookmen; Connoisseur; Art and Artists; Arts Review; Collectors Guide; Art and Antiques. *Address:* 65 Cornwall Gardens, London SW7 4BD, England.

COLOMBO, John (Robert); Writer, Poet, Ed., Trans. and Consultant; b. 24 March 1936, Kitchener, ON, Canada; m. Ruth Florence Brown, 11 May 1959, two s. one d. *Education:* Waterloo College, 1956–57; BA, 1959, Graduate Studies, 1959–60, University of Toronto. *Career:* Asst Ed., Ryerson Press, 1960–63; Consulting Ed., McClelland & Stewart, 1963–70; Gen. Ed., The Canadian Global Almanac, 1992–2000. *Publications:* Author, ed. or trans. of over 153 titles, including collections of quotations, anthologies, poetry, mysteries, folklore. Contributions: periodicals; Radio and TV programmes. *Honours:* Centennial Medal, 1967; First Writer-in-Residence, Mohawk College, 1979–80; Hon. DLitt, York University, 1998; various prizes and awards including: Harbourfront Literary Award. *Address:* 42 Dell Park Ave, Toronto, ON M6B 2T6, Canada. *E-mail:* jrc@inforamp.net. *Website:* www.colombo.ca.

COLQUHOUN, Keith; Journalist and Novelist; b. 5 Aug. 1937, London, England; three s., three d. *Career:* Chief Sub-Ed., London Daily Herald, Sun, 1959–70; Managing Ed., Observer, 1970–77; News Ed., Far Eastern Economic Review, Hong Kong, 1977–80; Asian Affairs Writer, The Economist, 1980–. *Publications:* The Money Tree, 1958; Point of Stress, 1960; The Sugar Coating, 1973; St Petersburg Rainbow, 1975; Goebbels and Gladys, 1981; Filthy Rich, 1982; Kiss of Life, 1983; Foreign Wars, 1985; Mad Dog, 1992; Killing Stalin, 2002. *Address:* The Old Rectory, East Mersea, Essex, England.

COLTON, James (see Hansen, Joseph).

COLVIN, Sir Howard (Montagu); Historian and Writer; b. 15 Oct. 1919, Sidcup, Kent, England; m. Christina Edgeworth Butler, 16 Aug. 1943, two s. *Education:* BA, University College London; MA, University of Oxford, 1948. *Career:* Asst Lecturer, University College London, 1946–48; Tutor in History, 1948–78, Fellow, 1948–87, Emeritus Fellow, 1987–, Librarian, 1950–84, St John's College, Oxford; Reader in Architectural History, University of Oxford, 1965–87; Mem., several royal commissions; mem. Fellow, British Acad.; FRHistS; Fellow, Society of Antiquaries; Society of Architectural Historians of Great Britain, pres., 1979–81. *Publications:* The White Canons in England, 1951; A Biographical Dictionary of English Architects, 1660–1840, 1954, second edn as A Biographical Dictionary of British Architects, 1600–1840, 1978; The History of the King's Works (gen. ed. and part author), six vols, 1963–82; A History of Deddington, 1963; Catalogue of Architectural Drawings in Worcester College Library, 1964; Architectural Drawings in the Library of Elton Hall (with Maurice Craig), 1964; The Country Seat (ed. with John Harris), 1970; Building Accounts of King Henry III, 1971; Unbuilt Oxford, 1983; Calke Abbey, Derbyshire, 1985; The Canterbury Quadrangle: St John's College, Oxford, 1988; All Souls: An Oxford College and its Buildings (with J. S. G. Simmons), 1989; Architecture and the After-Life, 1991; Essays in English Architectural History, 1999. Contributions: Professional journals. *Honours:* CBE, 1964; Wolfson Prize for History, 1978; CVO, 1983; Knighted, 1995. *Address:* 50 Plantation Rd, Oxford OX2 6JE, England.

COMAROFF, John Lionel; American writer; *Harold H. Swift Distinguished Service Professor of Anthropology and Social Sciences, University of Chicago*; b. 1 Jan. 1945, Cape Town, South Africa; m. Jean Rakoff 1967; one s. one d. *Education:* BA, University of Cape Town, 1966; PhD, University of London, 1973. *Career:* Lecturer in Social Anthropology, University College of Swansea, 1971–72, University of Manchester, 1972–78; Visiting Asst Prof. of Anthropology, 1978, Assoc. Prof. of Anthropology and Sociology, 1981–87, Prof. of Anthropology and Social Sciences, 1987–96, Harold H. Swift Distinguished Service Prof. of Anthropology and Social Sciences, 1996–, University of Chicago; Directeur d'Études, 1988, Directeur d'Études Associé, 1995, École des Hautes Études en Sciences Sociales, Paris; mem. Royal Anthropological Institute, fellow; African Studies Asscn; International African Institute, fellow; Asscn of Social Anthroplogists; American Anthropological Asscn, fellow; Asscn of Political and Legal Anthropology, pres., 1995–96. *Publications:* The Structure of Agricultural Transformation in Barolong, 1977; Rules and Processes: The Cultural Logic of Dispute in an African Context (with S. A. Roberts), 1981; Of Revelation and Revolution: Christianity and Colonialism in South Africa (with Jean Comaroff), 1991; Ethnography and the Historical Imagination (with Jean Comaroff), 1992; Modernity and its Malcontents: Ritual and Power in Africa (ed. with Jean Comaroff), 1993; Perspectives on Nationalism and War (ed. with Paul C. Stern), 1993. Contributions: scholarly books and journals. *Honours:* National Endowment for the Humanities Grants, 1984–85, 1986–87; National Science Foundation Grants, 1986–87, 1993; Spencer Foundation Grant, 1991; Laing Prize, University of Chicago, 1993; American Acad. of Arts and Sciences, 1995; Spencer Foundation Mentor Award, 1996. *Address:* c/o Dept of Anthropology, University of Chicago, 1126 E 59th Street, Chicago, IL 60637, USA.

COMDEN, Betty; American playwright and screenwriter; b. (Basya Cohen), 3 May 1919, New York, NY. *Career:* writer and performer, the Revuers; mem. Dramatists' Guild (council mem.). *Plays:* with Adolph Green: On the Town, Adelphi Theatre 1944 (Screen Writers' Guild Award), Billion Dollar Baby, Alvin Theatre 1945, Two on the Aisle, Mark Hellinger Theatre 1951, Wonderful Town, Winter Garden Theatre 1953 (Tony Award), Peter Pan, Winter Garden 1954, Bells are Ringing, Shubert Theatre 1956, Say, Darling, ANTA Playhouse 1958, A Party with Betty Comden and Adolph Green, John Golden Theatre 1958 (Obie Award), Do Re Mi, St James Theatre 1960, Subways are for Sleeping, St James 1961, Fade Out - Fade In, Mark Hellinger 1964, Hallelujah, Baby!, Martin Beck Theatre 1967 (Tony Award 1968), Applause, Palace Theatre 1970 (Tony Award), Lorelei, Palace Theatre 1974, On the Twentieth Century, St James 1978 (Tony Award), A Doll's Life, Mark Hellinger 1982, Singin' in the Rain, George Gershwin Theatre 1985, The Will Rogers Follies, Palace Theatre 1991. *Film screenplays:* Good News 1947, Auntie Mame 1958, What a Way to Go! 1964; with Adolph Green: The Barkleys of Broadway 1949, Singin' in the Rain 1952, The Band Wagon (Screen Writers' Guild Award) 1953, It's Always Fair Weather (Screen Writers' Guild Award) 1955, Bells are Ringing 1960, Applause 1973. *Publications:* non-fiction: Off Stage (autobiog.) 1995. *Honours:* Mayor of New York Certificate of Excellence; Hon. DMus (Univ. of Indiana) ; Theatre World Award 1945, Governor Cuomo Award 1994, Screen Laurel Award 2001, The Dramatists' Guild Lifetime Achievement Award 2002, Creative Arts Award, Kaufman Centre, New York 2003.

COMINI, Alessandra; Prof. of Art History and Author; b. 24 Nov. 1934, Winona, Minnesota, USA. *Education:* BA, Barnard College, 1956; MA, University of California, Berkeley, 1964; PhD, Columbia University, 1969. *Career:* Instructor, 1968–69, Asst Prof., 1969–74, Columbia University; Visiting Asst Prof., 1970, 1973, Assoc. Prof., 1974–75, Prof., 1976–, University Distinguished Prof. of Art History, 1983–, Southern Methodist University; Alfred Hodder Fellow, Princeton University, 1972–73; Visiting Asst Prof., Yale University, 1973; Assoc. Ed., Arts Magazine, 1977–88; Lansdown Prof., University of Victoria, BC, 1981; Visiting Distinguished Prof., California State University, Chico, 1990; Distinguished Visiting Fellow, European Humanities Research Centre, University of Oxford, 1996; mem. College Art Asscn of America; Texas Institute of Letters; Women's Caucus for Art. *Publications:* Schiele in Prison, 1973; Egon Schiele's Portraits, 1974; Gustav Klimt, 1975; Egon Schiele, 1976; The Fantastic Art of Vienna, 1978; The Changing Image of Beethoven: A Study in Mythmaking, 1987; Egon Schiele's Nudes, 1994. Contributions: Books, journals, magazines, and exhibition catalogues. *Honours:* Charles Rufus Morey Book Award, College Art Asscn of America, 1976; Grand Decoration of Honour for Services to the Austrian Republic, 1990; Lifetime Achievement Award, Women's Caucus for Art, 1995. *Address:* 2900 McFarlin, Dallas, TX 75205, USA.

COMPTON, David Guy, (Guy Compton, Frances Lynch); writer; b. 19 Aug. 1930, London, England. *Education:* Cheltenham College, Gloucester. *Career:* Ed., Reader's Digest Condensed Books, London, 1969–81. *Publications:* Too Many Murderers, 1962; Medium for Murder, 1963; Dead on Cue, 1964; Disguise for a Dead Gentleman, 1964; High Tide for Hanging, 1965; The Quality of Mercy, 1965; Farewell Earth's Bliss, 1966; The Silent Multitude, 1966; And Murder Came Too, 1966; Synthajoy, 1968; The Palace, 1969; The Electric Crocodile, 1970; Hot Wireless Sets, Aspirin Tablets, the Sandpaper Sides of Used Matchboxes and Something that Might Have Been Castor Oil, 1971; The Missionaries, 1972; The Continuous Katherine Mortenhoe, 1974; Twice Ten Thousand Miles, 1974; The Fine and Handsome Captain, 1975; Stranger at the Wedding, 1977; A Dangerous Magic, 1978; A Usual Lunacy, 1978; Windows, 1979; In the House of Dark Music, 1979; Ascendancies, 1980; Scudder's Game, 1985; Ragnarok (with John Gribbin), 1991; Normansland, 1992; Stammering, 1993; Justice City, 1994; Back of Town Blues, 1996. *Literary Agent:* David Higham Associates, 5–8 Lower John Street, Golden Square, London W1F 9HA, England.

CONDÉ, Maryse; Author, Dramatist and Prof. of French; b. 11 Feb. 1937, Pointe-à-Pitre, Guadeloupe; m. 1st Mamadou Condé, 1958, divorced 1981, three c.; m. 2nd Richard Philcox, 1982, one c. *Education:* PhD, Sorbonne, University of Paris, 1976. *Career:* Programme Prod., French Services, BBC, London, 1968–70, France Culture, Radio France Internationale, Paris 1980–85; Asst, Jussieu, 1970–72, Lecturer, Nanterre, 1973–80, Chargé de cours, Sorbonne, 1980–85, University of Paris; Prof. of French, University of California at Berkeley, 1989–92, University of Maryland at College Park, 1992–95, Columbia University, 1995–; Visiting Prof., California Institute of Technology, 1989, University of Virginia, 1993–95, Harvard University, 1995; many visiting lectureships. *Publications:* Fiction: Heremakhonon, 1976, English trans., 1982; Une Saison à Rihata, 1981, English trans. as A Season in Rihata, 1988; Ségou: Les murailles de terre, 1984, English trans. as Segu, 1987; Ségou II: La terre en miettes, 1985, English trans. as The Children of Segu, 1989; Pays Melé, suivi de, Nanna-ya, 1985, English trans. as Land of Many Colors, and Nanny-ya, 1999; Moi, Tituba, sorcière noire, 1986, English trans. as I, Tituba, Black Witch of Salem, 1992; La Vie scelerate, 1987, English trans. as Tree of Life: A Novel of the Caribbean, 1992; Antan Révolysion, 1989; Traversée de la mangrove, 1990, English trans. as Crossing the Mangrove, 1995; Les derniers rois mages, 1992, English trans. as The Last of the African Kings, 1997; La colonie du nouveau monde, 1993; La migration des coeurs, 1995, English trans. as Windward Heights, 1998; Desirada, 1997, English trans., 2000; La Belle Créole, 2001. Plays: Dieu nous l'a donne, 1972; Mort d'Oluwemi d'Ajumako, 1973; Le Morne de Massabielle, 1974, English trans. as The Hills of Massabielle, 1991; Pension les Alizes, 1988, English trans. as The Tropical Breeze Hotel, 1994; Comédie d'amour, 1993. Other: Anthologie de la littérature africaine d'expression française (ed.), 1966; La Poesie antillaise (ed.), 1977; Le Roman antillais (ed.), 1977; La Civilisation du bossale, 1978; Le profil d'une oeuvre: Cahier d'un retour au pays natal, 1978; La Parole des femmes: Essai sur des romancieres des Antilles de langue française, 1979; Bouquet de voix pour Guy Tirolien (ed.), 1990; Hugo le terrible, 1991; L'heritage de Caliban (ed. with others), 1992; Penser la creolite (with Madelaine Cottenet-Hage), 1995; Conversations with Maryse Condé (with Françoise Pfaff), 1996; Nouvelles d'Amérique (ed. with Lise Gauvin), 1998; Le Coeur à Rire et à Pleurer: Contes vrais de mon enfance, 1998, English trans. as Tales from the Heart, 2000; Celanire cou-coupé: Roman fantastique, 2000; La belle Créole, 2001; Oratorio Créole, 2001. Contributions: anthologies and journals. *Honours:* Fulbright Scholar, 1985–86; Prix littéraire de la Femme, 1986; Prix Alain Boucheron, 1986; Hon. doctorates, Occidental College, 1986, Lehman College, CUNY, 1994; Guggenheim Fellowship, 1987–88; Académie Française Prize, 1988; Prix Carbet de la Caraibe, 1997; Marguerite Yourcenar Prize, 1999; Lifetime Achievement Award, New York University, 1999; Commdr, Ordre des Arts et des Lettres, 2001. *Address:* c/o Dept of French and Romance Philology, Columbia University, New York, NY 10027, USA.

CONEY, Michael (Greatrex); Writer; b. 28 Sept. 1932, Birmingham, England; m. Daphne Coney, 14 May 1957, one s. one d. *Publications:* King of the Scepter'd Isle, 1969; A Judge of Men, 1969; Whatever Became of the McGowans?, 1971; The Snow Princess, 1971; Susanna! Susanna!, 1971; Mirror Image, 1972; The Bridge on the Scraw, 1973; Syzygy, 1973; Friends Come in Boxes, 1973; The Hero of Downways, 1973; The Hook, the Eye and the Whip, 1974; Winter's Children, 1974; Monitor Found in Orbit, 1974; The Jaws That Bite, The Claws That Catch, 1975; Charisma, 1975; The Hollow Where, 1975; Trading Post, 1976; Hello Summer, Goodbye, 1976; Brontomek!, 1976; Just an Old-Fashioned War Story, 1977; Penny on a Skyhorse, 1979; The Ultimate Jungle, 1979; Neptune's Children, 1981; Cat Karina, 1982; The Celestial Steam Locomotive, 1983; The Byrds, 1983; Gods of the Greataway, 1984; Fang, the Gnome, 1988; No Place for a Sealion, 1993; A Tomcat Called Sabrina, 1993; Sophie's Spyglass, 1993; Die Lorelie, 1993; The Small Penance of Lady Disdain, 1993; Tea and Hamsters, 1994. *Honours:* Best British Novel Award, BSFA, 1976. *Address:* 2082 Neptune Rd, Sidney, BC V8L 5J5, Canada.

CONKIN, Paul Keith, BA, MA, PhD; historian and writer; *Distinguished Research Professor, Vanderbilt University*; b. 25 Oct. 1929, Chuckey, TN, USA; m. Dorothy L. Tharp 1954; one s. two d. *Education:* Milligan College, Vanderbilt University. *Career:* Asst Prof. of Philosophy and History, University of Southwestern Louisiana, 1957–59; Asst Prof., 1959–61, Assoc. Prof., 1961–66, Prof. of History, 1966–67, University of Maryland at College Park; Prof. of History, 1967–76, Merle Curti Prof. of History, 1976–79, University of Wisconsin at Madison; Distinguished Prof. of History, 1979–2000, Distinguished Research Prof., 2000–, Vanderbilt University; mem. American Historical Asscn; Organization of American Historians; Southern Historical Asscn, pres., 1996–97. *Publications:* Tomorrow a New World: The New Deal Community Program, 1959; Two Paths to Utopia: The Hutterites and the Llano Colony, 1964; F. D. R. and the Origins of the Welfare State, 1967, also published as The New Deal, 1967; Puritans and Pragmatists: Eight Eminent American Thinkers, 1968; The Heritage and Challenge of History (with Roland N. Stromberg), 1971; Self-evident Truths, 1974; A History of Recent America (with David Burner), 1974; New Directions in American Intellectual History (ed. with John Higham), 1979; Prophets of Prosperity: America's First Political Economists, 1980; TVA: Fifty Years of Grass-Roots Bureaucracy (ed. with Erwin C. Hargrove), 1983; Gone with the Ivy: A Biography of Vanderbilt University (with Henry Lee Swint and Patricia S. Miletich), 1985; Big Daddy from the Padernales: Lyndon Baines Johnson, 1986; The Southern Agrarians, 1988; Heritage and Challenge: The History and Theory of History (with Roland N. Stromberg), 1989; Cane Ridge, America's Pentecost, 1990; The Four Foundations of American Government: Consent, Limits, Balance, and Participation, 1994; The Uneasy Center: Reformed Christianity in Antebellum America, 1995; American Originals: Homemade Varieties of Christianity, 1997; When All Gods Trembled: Darwinism, Scopes, and American Intellectuals, 1998; A Requiem for the American Village, 2000. Contributions: scholarly books and journals. *Honours:* Albert J. Beveridge Award in American History, 1958; Guggenheim Fellowship, 1966–67; National Endowment for the Humanities Senior Fellowship, 1972–73, University Fellowship, 1990. *Address:* 1003 Tyne Blvd, Nashville, TN 37220, USA.

CONLEY, Robert Jackson, BA, MA; writer and poet; b. 29 Dec. 1940, Cushing, OK, USA; m. Evelyn Snell 1978. *Education:* Midwestern State University. *Career:* Instructor in English, Northern Illinois University, 1968–71, Southwest Missouri State University, 1971–74; Co-ordinator of Indian Culture, Eastern Montana College, 1975–77; Dir of Indian Studies, 1979–86, Assoc. Prof. of English, 1986–90, Morningside College; mem. International Poetry Society; Western Writers of America. *Publications:* Twenty-One Poems, 1975; Adawosgi: Swimmer Wesley Snell, A Cherokee Memorial, 1980; Echoes of Our Being (ed.), 1982; The Rattlesnake Band and Other Poems, 1984; Back to Malachi, 1986; The Actor, 1987; Killing Time, 1988; Wilder and Wilder, 1988; The Witch of Goingsnake and Other Stories, 1988; Colfax, 1989; The Saga of Henry Starr, 1989; Quitting Time, 1989; Go-ahead Rider, 1990; Ned Christie's War, 1990; Strange Company, 1991; Mountain Windsong: A Novel of the Trail of Tears, 1992; The Way of the Priests, 1992; Nickajack, 1992; Border Line, 1993; The Dark Way, 1993; The Long Trail North, 1993; The White Path, 1993; The Long Way Home, 1994; Geronimo: An American Legend (with John Milius and Larry Gross), 1994; To Make a Killing, 1994; Crazy Snake, 1994; The Way South, 1994; Zeke Proctor: Cherokee Outlaw, 1994; The Dark Island, 1995; Captain Dutch, 1995; Outside the Law, 1995; The War Trail North, 1995; War Woman: A Novel of the Real People, 1997; The Meade Solution, 1998; The Peace Chief: A Novel of the Real People, 1998; Incident at Buffalo Crossing, 1998; Brass, 1999; Cherokee Dragon: A Novel of the Real People, 2000; Barjack, 2000; Fugitive's Trail, 2000; Broke Loose, 2000; The Gunfighter, 2001; A Cold Hard Trail, 2001; Spanish Jack: A Novel of the Real People, 2001. Contributions: anthologies and periodicals. *Honours:* Spur Awards, Western Writers of America, 1992, 1995; Inducted, Oklahoma Professional Writers Hall of Fame, 1996; Oklahoma Writer of the Year, University of Oklahoma Professional Writing Program, 1999; Cherokee Medal of Honor, Cherokee Honor Society, 2000. *Address:* PO Box 1871, Tahlequah, OK 74464, USA.

CONLEY, Tom Clark; Prof. of French and Writer; b. 7 Dec. 1943, New Haven, CT, USA; m. Verena Conley; one s. one d. *Education:* BA, Lawrence Univ. of Wisconsin, 1965; MA, Columbia Univ., 1966; Sorbonne, Univ. of Paris, 1968; PhD, Univ. of Wisconsin, Madison, 1971. *Career:* Asst Prof., Assoc. Prof., Prof. of French, 1971–95, Head, Dept of French and Italian, 1983–88, Univ. of Minnesota, Twin Cities; Prof. of French, Harvard Univ., 1995–; several visiting positions; mem. International Asscn of Philosophy and Literature; MLA of America; Midwest MLA; Société française des seiziémistes. *Publications:* Su realismo: Lectura de Buñuel, 1988; Film Hieroglyphics: Ruptures in Classical Cinema, 1991; The Graphic Unconscious in Early Modern French Writing, 1992; The Self-Made Map: Cartographic Writing in Early Modern France, 1996; L'Inconscient graphique, 2000; Cartographies of Cinema, 2004. Other: trans. of seven vols. Contributions: books; numerous articles and reviews to periodicals. *Honours:* Woodrow Wilson Fellow, 1965–66; Fulbright Fellow, 1968–69; ACLS Fellow, 1975–76; Grants, 1975, Summer Fellow, 1988, National Endowment for the Humanities; Quintennial Fellow, 1988–89, Hermon Dunlap Smith Fellow, 1992, Newberry Library; Medal of Honour, Ville de Tours, 1990; Fellow, Institute for Research in the Humanities, University of Wisconsin, Madison, 1990–91; Guggenheim Fellow, 2003–04. *Address:* 85 Dunster St, Cambridge, MA 02138, USA. *E-mail:* tconley@fas.harvard.edu. *Website:* www.fas.harvard.edu/~rll.

CONLON, Kathleen (see Lloyd, Kathleen Annie).

CONN, Stewart; Poet and Playwright; b. 5 Nov. 1936, Glasgow, Scotland. *Career:* Radio Producer, Glasgow, 1962–77, Head of Radio Drama, Edinburgh, 1977–92, BBC; Literary Adviser, Royal Lyceum Theatre, Edinburgh, 1972–75; appointed to Edinburgh's poet laureateship, the Edinburgh Makar, 2002–; mem. Knight of Mark Twain; Royal Scottish Acad. of Music and Drama, fellow; Pres., Shore Poets; Scottish Society of Playwrights. *Publications:* Poetry: Thunder in the Air, 1967; The Chinese Tower, 1967; Stoats in the Sunlight (US edn as Ambush and Other Poems), 1968; An Ear to the Ground, 1972; PEN New Poems, 1973–74 (ed.), 1974; Under the Ice, 1978; In the Kibble Palace: New and Selected Poems, 1987; The Luncheon of the Boating Party, 1992; In the Blood, 1995; At the Aviary, 1995; The Ice Horses (ed.), 1996; Stolen Light: Selected Poems, 1999. Plays: The Aquarium and Other Plays, 1976; Thistlewood, 1979; The Burning in Scots Plays of the 70s, 2000. Prose and Poetry: Distances, 2001. Contributions: anthologies, journals, radio. *Honours:* E. C. Gregory Award, 1964; Scottish Arts Council Awards and Poetry Prize, 1968, 1978, 1992; English-Speaking Union Travel Scholarship, 1984; Scottish Arts Council Playwrights Bursary, 1995; Society of Authors Travel Bursary, 1996.

Literary Agent: Lemon Unna & Durbridge Ltd, 24 Pottery Lane, Holland Park, London W11 4LZ, England. *Address:* 1 Fettes Row, Edinburgh EH3 6SF, Scotland. *E-mail:* stewart@jsconn.freeserve.co.uk.

CONNELL, Evan Shelby, Jr; Author and Poet; b. 17 Aug. 1924, Kansas City, MO, USA. *Education:* Dartmouth College, 1941–43; BA, University of Kansas, 1947; Graduate Studies, Stanford University, 1947–48, Columbia University, 1948–49, San Francisco State College. *Career:* Ed., Contact magazine, 1960–65; mem. American Acad. of Arts and Letters. *Publications:* Fiction: The Anatomy Lesson and Other Stories, 1957; Mrs Bridge, 1959; The Patriot, 1960; At the Crossroads: Stories, 1965; The Diary of a Rapist, 1966; Mr Bridge, 1969; The Connoisseur, 1974; Double Honeymoon, 1976; St Augustine's Pigeon, 1980; The Alchymist's Journal, 1991; The Collected Stories of Evan S. Connell, 1995; Deus Lo Volt!: Chronicle of the Crusades, 2000. Poetry: Notes From a Bottle Found on the Beach at Carmel, 1963; Points for a Compass Rose, 1973. Non-Fiction: A Long Desire, 1979; The White Lantern, 1980; Son of the Morning Star: Custer and the Little Bighorn, 1984; Mesa Verde, 1992; The Aztec Treasure House, 2001. Contributions: periodicals. *Honours:* Eugene F. Saxton Fellow, 1953; Guggenheim Fellowship, 1963; Rockefeller Foundation Grant, 1967; California Literature Silver Medal, 1974; Los Angeles Times Book Award, 1985; American Acad. of Arts and Letters Award, 1987; Lannan Foundation Lifetime Achievement Award, 2000. *Address:* c/o Fort Marcy 13, 320 Artist Rd, Sante Fe, NM 87501, USA.

CONNELLY, Mark; Writer and College Instructor; b. 8 July 1951, Philadelphia, PA, USA. *Education:* BA, English, Carroll College, 1973; MA, Creative Writing, 1974, PhD, English, 1984, University of Wisconsin, Milwaukee. *Career:* Instructor, Milwaukee Area Technical College, 1986–; mem. Irish Cultural and Heritage Center of Wisconsin, vice-pres.; MLA. *Publications:* The Diminished Self: Orwell and the Loss of Freedom, 1987; The Sundance Reader, 1997; Orwell and Gissing, 1997; The Sundance Writer, 2000; Deadly Closets: The Fiction of Charles Jackson, 2001. Contributions: Short stories in Milwaukee Magazine; Wisconsin Review; Indiana Review. *Honours:* Fiction Award, Milwaukee Magazine, 1982. *Address:* 700 W State St, Milwaukee, WI 53233, USA.

CONNELLY, Michael; American novelist; b. 1956, Philadelphia, PA. *Education:* Univ. of Florida. *Career:* crime reporter for newspapers based in Daytona Beach and Fort Lauderdale, Florida and for the Los Angeles Times. *Television writing:* Level 9 (co-creator, writer and producer) 2000. *Publications:* novels: The Black Echo 1992, The Black Ice 1992, The Concrete Blonde 1994, The Last Coyote 1995, The Poet 1996, Trunk Music 1997, Angels Flight 1998, Blood Work 1998, Void Moon 1999, A Darkness More Than Night 2001, City of Bones 2002, Chasing the Dime 2002, Lost Light 2003, The Narrows 2004; editor: The Best American Mystery Stories 2003. *Honours:* Anthony Award, Macavity Award, Nero Award, Barry Award, Ridley Award, Maltese Falcon Award (Japan), .38 Caliber Award (France), Grand Prix (France), Premio Bancarella Award (Italy), Edgar Award for Best First Novel. *Address:* c/o Orion Publishing Group Ltd, 5 Upper St Martin's Lane, London, WC2H 9EA, England. *Website:* www.michaelconnelly.com.

CONNOLLY, Ray; Writer; b. 4 Dec. 1940, St Helens, Lancashire, England. *Education:* BSc, LSE, 1963. *Career:* Columnist, London Evening Standard, 1967–73, 1983–84, The Times, 1989–90. Publications and Screenplays: A Girl Who Came to Stay, 1973; That'll Be the Day, 1973; Stardust, 1974; Trick or Treat?, 1975; James Dean: The First American Teenager, 1975; Newsdeath, 1978; A Sunday Kind of Woman, 1980; Honky Tonk Heroes, 1980; John Lennon 1940–1980, 1981; The Sun Place, 1981; An Easy Game to Play, 1982; Stardust Memories, 1983; Forever Young, 1984; Lytton's Diary, 1985; Defrosting the Fridge, 1988; Perfect Scoundrels, 1989; Sunday Morning, 1992; Shadows on a Wall, 1994; In the Sixties (anthology), 1995; Lost Fortnight, 1996; The Rhythm of Life, 1997. *Honours:* Stardust, Best Original British Screenplay, Writers Guild of Great Britain, 1974. *Literary Agent:* Rogers, Coleridge & White Ltd, 20 Powis Mews, London W11 1JN, England.

CONNOR, Joan; Writer, Poet and Educator; b. 21 Jan. 1954, Holyoke, MA, USA; m. Nils Wessell, separated, one s. *Education:* BA cum laude, Mount Holyoke College, 1976; MA, Middlebury College, 1984; MFA, Vermont College, 1995. *Career:* Assoc. Fiction Ed., Chelsea, 1994–96; Visiting Prof., 1995–96, Asst Prof. of English, 1996–, Ohio University, Athens; mem. Associated Writing Programs; Young Writers' Institute. *Publications:* Here on Old Route 7, 1997; We Who Live Apart, 2000. Contributions: anthologies and periodicals. *Honours:* Fellow, Vermont Studio Colony, 1990, MacDowell Colony, 1992, Virginia Center for the Creative Arts, 1993, Yaddo Colony, 1993. *Address:* 328 Carroll Rd, Athens, OH 45701, USA. *E-mail:* connor@oak.cats.ohiou.edu.

CONNORS, Bruton (see Rohen, Edward).

CONQUEST, (George) Robert Acworth; historian, writer and poet; b. 15 July 1917, Malvern, Worcestershire, England; m. 1st Joan Watkins 1942 (divorced 1948); two s.; m. 2nd Tatiana Mihailova 1948 (divorced 1962); m. 3rd Caroleen Macfarlene 1964 (divorced 1978); m. 4th Elizabeth Neece 1 Dec. 1979. *Education:* University of Grenoble, France, 1935–36; Magdalen College, Oxford, 1936–39. *Career:* Mem., Foreign Service, 1946–56; Fellow, LSE, 1956–58, Columbia University, 1964–65, Woodrow Wilson International Center, 1976–77, Hoover Institution, 1977–79, 1981–; Visiting Poet, University of Buffalo, 1959–60; Literary Ed., The Spectator, 1962–63; Distinguished Visiting Scholar, Heritage Foundation, 1980–81; Research Assoc., Harvard University, 1982–83; Adjunct Fellow, Center for Strategic and International Studies, 1983–; Jefferson Lecturer in Humanities, 1993; mem. British Acad., corresponding fellow, 1994; FRSL, 1972. *Publications:* Poems, 1955; A World of Difference, 1955; New Lines (ed.), 1956; Common Sense About Russia, 1960; Power and Policy in the USSR, 1961; Courage of Genius, 1962; Between Mars and Venus, 1962; New Lines II (ed.), 1963; The Egyptologists (with Kingsley Amis), 1965; Russia After Khrushchev, 1965; The Great Terror, 1968; Arias from a Love Opera, 1969; The Nation Killers, 1970; Lenin, 1972; Kolyma, 1978; The Abomination of Moab, 1979; Present Danger, 1979; Forays, 1979; We and They, 1980; What to Do When the Russians Come, 1984; Inside Stalin's Secret Police, 1985; The Harvest of Sorrow, 1986; New and Collected Poems, 1988; Tyrants and Typewriters, 1989; Stalin and the Kirov Murder, 1989; The Great Terror Reassessed, 1990; Stalin: Breaker of Nations, 1991; Reflections on a Ravaged Century, 1999; Demons Don't, 1999. Contributions: various publications. *Honours:* OBE, 1955; MA, 1972, DLitt, 1975, Oxon; Companion of the Order of St Michael and St George, 1996. *Address:* 52 Peter Coutts Circle, Stanford, CA 94305, USA.

CONRAN, Shirley (Ida); Writer; b. 21 Sept. 1932, London, England; m. Terence Conran, 1955, divorced 1962, two s. *Education:* Southern College of Art, Portsmouth, England. *Career:* Founder, Co-Owner, Conran Fabrics Ltd, 1957–62; Design Consultant and Design Writer for various periodicals. *Publications:* Superwoman: Everywoman's Book of Household Management, 2 vols, 1975, 1977; Superwoman Yearbook, 1976; Superwoman Yearbook, 1977; Superwoman Two, 1977; Future: How to Survive Life After Thirty, 1979, revised edn as Futurewoman: How to Survive Life, 1981; Lace: A Novel, 1982; The Magic Garden, 1983; Lace II, 1985; The Legend, 1985; Savages, 1987; Down with Superwoman, 1990; The Amazing Umbrella Shop, 1990; Crimson, 1992; Tiger Eyes, 1994; The Revenge of Mimi Quinn, 1998.

CONRAN, Tony, (Anthony Conran); Poet, Dramatist, Trans. and Critic; b. 7 April 1931, Kharghpur, India. *Education:* BA, 1953, MA, 1956, University of Wales. *Career:* Research Asst, 1957–66, Research Fellow and Tutor in English, 1966–80, University of Wales, Bangor; mem. Welsh Acad., 1970; British Pteridological Society; English Folk Dance and Song Society; SIEF Ballad commission; Welsh Union of Writers; Asscn for the Study of Welsh Writers in English. *Publications:* Formal Poems, 1960; Metamorphoses, 1961 Stalae, 1966; Poems 1951–67, 4 vols, 1965–67, combined edn, 1974; The Penguin Book of Welsh Verse, 1967; Claim, Claim, Claim, 1969; Spirit Level, 1974; Life Fund, 1979; The Cost of Strangeness: Essays on the English Poets of Wales, 1982; Welsh Verse, 1987; Bloddeuwedd and Other Poems, 1989; Castles, 1993; The Angry Summer by Idris Davies (ed.), 1993; All Hallows: A Symphony in Three Movements, 1995; Visions and Praying Mantids: The Angelogical Notebooks, 1997; The Peacemakers, by Waldo Williams (trans.), 1997; Frontiers in Anglo Welsh Poetry, 1997; A Theatre of Flowers: Collected Pastorals, 1998; Eros Proposes a Toast, 1998; A Gwynedd Symphony, 1999; Ragbag for Folkies: Poems and Songs, 2001; Branwen and Other Dance Dramas and Plays, 2003. Contributions: numerous magazines and journals. *Honours:* Welsh Arts Council Prize, 1960, 1989; Second Prize, BBC Wales Writer of the Year Award, 1993; Welsh Union of Writers, Tony Conran Festival, Bangor, 1995; Hon. Fellow, Welsh Acad., 1995; Hon. DLitt, University of Wales, 1997. *Address:* Min Menai, Siliwen Rd, Bangor, Gwynedd LL57 2BS, Wales.

CONROY, (Donald) Patrick, BA; writer; b. 26 Oct. 1945, Atlanta, GA, USA; m. 1st Barbara Bolling 1969 (divorced 1977); three d.; m. 2nd Lenore Guerewitz 1981 (divorced 1995); one s. two d. *Education:* The Citadel. *Career:* mem. Authors' Guild of America; PEN; Writers Guild. *Publications:* The Boo, 1970; The Water is Wide, 1972; The Great Santini, 1976; The Lords of Discipline, 1980; The Prince of Tides, 1986; Beach Music, 1995. *Honours:* Ford Foundation Leadership Development Grant, 1971; Anisfield-Wolf Award, Cleveland Foundation, 1972; National Endowment for the Arts Award for Achievement in Education, 1974; Governor's Award for the Arts, GA, 1978; Lillian Smith Award for Fiction, Southern Regional Council, 1981. *Address:* c/o Houghton Mifflin Co, 222 Berkeley Street, Boston, MA 02116, USA.

CONSTANT, Paule; writer and academic; b. 25 Jan. 1944, Gan, France; m. Auguste Bourgeade 1968; one s. one d. *Education:* University of Bordeaux; Sorbonne, University of Paris. *Career:* Asst Lecturer in French Literature, University of Abijan, 1968–75; Maître-asst, then Maître de Conférences in French Literature and Civilization, 1975–90, Institute of French Studies for Foreign Students, 1986–95, Prof., 1995–, University of Aix-Marseille III. *Publications:* Ouregano, 1980; Propriété privée, 1981; Balta, 1983; White Spirit, 1989; Le grand châpal, 1991; Le fille du gobernator, 1994; Confidence pour confidence, 1998. Contributions: periodicals. *Honours:* Grand Prix de l'Essai, 1987, Grand Prix de Roman, 1990, Académie Française; Prix François Mauriac, 1990; Prix Goncourt, 1998; Chevalier, Légion d'honneur. *Address:* 29 rue Cardinale, 13100 Aix-en-Provence, France.

CONSTANTINE, David John, BA, PhD; British poet, writer and translator; *Co-Editor, Modern Poetry in Translation*; b. 4 March 1944, Salford, Lancashire, England; m. Helen Frances Best 1966; one s. one d. *Education:*

Wadham Coll., Oxford. *Career:* Lecturer to Senior Lecturer in German, Univ. of Durham 1969–81; Fellow in German, Queen's Coll., Oxford 1981–2000; Co-Ed. (with Helen Constantine), Modern Poetry in Translation magazine 2004–; mem. Poetry Soc., Soc. of Authors. *Publications:* poetry: A Brightness to Cast Shadows 1980, Watching for Dolphins 1983, Mappi Mundi 1984, Madder 1987, Selected Poems 1991, Caspar Hauser 1994, Sleeper 1995, The Pelt of Wasps 1998, Something for the Ghosts 2002; fiction: Davies 1985, Back at the Spike 1994; non-fiction: The Significance of Locality in the Poetry of Friedrich Hölderlin 1979, Early Greek Travellers and the Hellenic Ideal 1984, Hölderlin 1988, Friedrich Hölderlin 1992, Fields of Fire: A Life of Sir William Hamilton 2001; translator: Hölderlin: Selected Poems 1996, Henri Michaux: Spaced, Displaced (with Helen Constantine) 1992, Philippe Jaccottet: Under Clouded Skies/Beauregard (with Mark Treharne) 1994, Goethe: Elective Affinities 1994, Kleist: Selected Writings 1998, Hölderlin's Sophocles 2001, Hans Magnus Enzensberger: Lighter Than Air 2002; editor: German Short Stories 2 1972. *Honours:* Alice Hunt Bartlett Prize 1984, Runciman Prize 1985, Southern Arts Literature Prize 1987, European Poetry Trans. Prize 1998. *Address:* Modern Poetry in Translation, The Queen's College, Oxford, OX1 4AW, England (Office). *E-mail:* david.constantine@queens.ox.ac.uk. *Website:* www.kcl.ac.uk/mpt.

CONSTANTINE, Helen Frances; British translator; *Co-Editor, Modern Poetry in Translation*; b. (Helen Frances Best); m. David Constantine 1966; one s. one d. *Career:* Co-Ed. (with David Constantine), Modern Poetry in Translation magazine 2004–. *Publications:* translator: Henri Michaux: Spaced, Displaced (with David Constantine) 1992, Paris Tales: A Literary Tour of the City 2004. *Address:* Modern Poetry in Translation, The Queen's College, Oxford, OX1 4AW, England (Office). *Website:* www.kcl.ac.uk/mpt.

CONSTANTINE, Storm; Writer; b. 12 Oct. 1956, England. *Publications:* The Enchantments of Flesh and Spirit, 1987; The Bewitchments of Love and Hate, 1988; The Fulfillments of Fate and Desire, 1989; The Monstrous Regiment, 1989; Hermetech, 1991; Aleph, 1991; Burying the Shadow, 1992; Sign for the Sacred, 1993; Calenture, 1994; Stalking Tender Prey, 1995; Scenting Hallowed Blood, 1996. *Address:* 35 Ingestre Rd, Stafford ST17 4DJ, England.

COOK, Christopher Piers; Writer and Historian; b. 20 June 1945, Leicester, England. *Education:* BA, History, 1967, MA, 1970, University of Cambridge; DPhil, Modern History, University of Oxford, 1974. *Career:* Ed., Pears Cyclopedia, 1976–. *Publications:* Sources in British Political History, 6 vols, 1975–84; The Slump (with John Stevenson), 1976; Dictionary of Historical Terms, second edn, 1989; World Political Almanac, 1989; Longman Handbook of World History Since 1914, 1991; Britain Since 1945 (with John Stevenson), 1995; What Happened Where (with Diccon Bewes), 1996; Longman Handbook of Modern American History 1763–1996 (with David Waller), 1997; Longman Handbook of Modern European History 1763–1997, 1998; Longman Handbook of the Modern World (with John Stevenson), 1998; European Political Facts of the Twentieth Century (with John Paxton), fifth edn, 2001; A Short History of the Liberal Party 1900–2001, 2002; Longman Handbook of Modern British History 1714–2001, 2002; Longman Handbook of Twentieth Century Europe (with John Stevenson), 2003. Contributions: Guardian; TLS; THES. *Honours:* FRHistS, 1977. *Address:* c/o Pears Cyclopedia, Penguin Books, 80 Strand, London WC2R 0RL, England.

COOK, David; Actor and Writer; b. 21 Sept. 1940, Preston, Lancashire, England. *Education:* Royal College of Dramatic Art, 1959–61. *Career:* Professional Actor, 1961–; Writer-in-Residence, St Martin's College, Lancaster, England, 1982–83; mem. Society of Authors. *Publications:* Albert's Memorial, 1972; Happy Endings, 1974; Walter, 1978; Winter Doves, 1979; Sunrising, 1983; Missing Persons, 1986; Crying Out Loud, 1988; Walter and June, 1989; Second Best, 1991. *Honours:* E. M. Forster Award, 1977; Hawthornden Prize, 1978; Southern Arts Fiction Prize, 1984; Arthur Welton Scholarship, 1991; Oddfellows Social Concern Award, 1992. *Literary Agent:* Deborah Rogers, 20 Powis Mews, London W11 1JN, England. *Address:* 7 Sydney Pl., London SW7 3NL, England.

COOK, Glen (Charles); Writer; b. 9 July 1944, New York, NY, USA; m. Carol Ann Fritz, 14 June 1971, three s. *Education:* University of Missouri, 1962–65. *Publications:* The Heirs of Babylon, 1972; Shadow of All Night Falling, 1979; October's Baby, 1980; All Darkness Met, 1980; Shadowline, 1982; Starfishers, 1982; Stars' End, 1982; The Swordbearer, 1982; The Black Company, 1984; The Fire in His Hands, 1984; Shadows Linger, 1984; Doomstalker, 1985; A Matter of Time, 1985; Passage at Arms, 1985; Warlock, 1985; The White Rose, 1985; With Mercy Toward None, 1985; Ceremony, 1986; Reap the East Wind, 1987; Sweet Silver Blues, 1987; All Ill Fate Marshalling, 1988; Bitter Gold Hearts, 1988; Cold Copper Tears, 1988; The Dragon Never Sleeps, 1988; Old Tin Sorrows, 1989; Shadow Games, 1989; The Silver Spike, 1989; The Tower of Fear, 1989; Dread Brass Shadows, 1990; Dreams of Steel, 1990; Sung in Blood, 1990; Red Iron Nights, 1991; Deadly Quicksilver Lies, 1993; Bleak Seasons, 1996; Petty Pewter Gods, 1996; She is the Darkness, 1997; Water Sleeps, 1999; Faded Steel Heat, 2000; Soldiers Live, 2000; Angry Lead Skies, 2002. Contributions: anthologies and periodicals. *Address:* 4106 Flora Pl., St Louis, MO 63110, USA.

COOK, Lila (see Africano, Lillian).

COOK, Paul, BA, MA, PhD; University Lecturer and Writer; b. 12 Nov. 1950, Tucson, AZ, USA. *Education:* Northern Arizona Univ., Arizona State Univ., Univ. of Utah. *Career:* Senior Lecturer in English, Arizona State University, Tempe 1987–. *Publications:* Duende Meadow, 1985; Halo, 1986; On the Rim of the Mandala, 1987; Fortress on the Sun, 1997. *Literary Agent:* Richard Curtis Associates Inc., 171 E 74th Street, Second Floor, New York, NY 10021, USA. *Website:* www.curtisagency.com. *Address:* 1108 W Cornel, Tempe, AZ 85283, USA. *E-mail:* pcook@dancris.com.

COOK, Petronelle Marguerite Mary, (Margot Arnold); Writer and Teacher; b. 16 May 1925, Plymouth, Devon, England; m. Philip R. Cook, 20 July 1949, two s. one d. *Education:* BA, 1946, Diploma in Prehistoric Archaeology and Anthropology, 1947, MA, 1950, University of Oxford. *Career:* mem. New England Historic and Genealogical Society; Cornwall Family History Society. *Publications:* The Officers' Woman, 1972; The Villa on the Palatine, 1975; Marie, 1979; Exit Actors, Dying, 1980; The Cape Cod Caper, 1980; Death of a Voodoo Doll, 1981; Zadok's Treasurer, 1981; Affairs of State, 1981; Love Among the Allies, 1982; Lament for a Lady Laird, 1982; Death on the Dragon's Tongue, 1982; Desperate Measures, 1983; Sinister Purposes, 1985; The Menehune Murders, 1989; Toby's Folly, 1990; The Catacomb Conspiracy, 1991; The Cape Cod Conundrum, 1992; Dirge for a Dorset Druid, 1994; The Midas Murders, 1995; Survivors and Non-Survivors, 2002. As Petronelle Cook: The Queen Consorts of England, 1993. Contributions: numerous short stories to magazines. *Honours:* University of Oxford Archaeological Society, pres., 1945; Fiction Prize, National Writers Club, 1983. *Address:* 11 High School Rd, Hyannis, MA 02601, USA.

COOK, Robin; Physician and Writer; b. 4 May 1940, New York, NY, USA; m. Barbara Ellen Mougin, 18 July 1979. *Education:* BA, Wesleyan University, 1962; MD, Columbia University, 1966; Postgraduate Studies, Harvard University. *Career:* Resident in General Surgery, Queen's Hospital, Honolulu, 1966–68; Resident in Ophthalmology, 1971–75, Staff, 1975–, Massachusetts Eye and Ear Infirmary, Boston. *Publications:* Fiction: The Year of the Intern, 1972; Coma, 1977; Sphinx, 1979; Brain, 1981; Fever, 1982; Godplayer, 1983; Mindbend, 1985; Outbreak, 1987; Mortal Fear, 1988; Mutation, 1989; Harmful Intent, 1990; Vital Signs, 1990; Blindsight, 1991; Terminal, 1992; Fatal Cure, 1994; Acceptable Risk, 1995; Contagion, 1996; Invasion, 1997; Chromosone 6, 1997; Toxin, 1998.

COOK, Stanley; Lecturer (retd) and Poet; b. 12 April 1922, Austerfield, Yorkshire, England; m. Kathleen Mary Daly, one s. two d. *Education:* BA, Christ Church, Oxford, 1943. *Career:* Lecturer, Huddersfield Polytechnic, 1969–81; Ed., Poetry Nottingham, 1981–85. *Publications:* Form Photograph, 1971; Sign of Life, 1972; Staff Photograph, 1976; Alphabet, 1976; Woods Beyond a Cornfield, 1981; Concrete Poems, 1984; Barnsdale, 1986; Selected Poems, 1972–86, 1986; The Northern Seasons, 1988. Other: Children's poems. *Honours:* Cheltenham Festival Competition Prize, 1972. *Address:* 600 Barnsley Rd, Sheffield, South Yorkshire S5 6UA, England.

COOK, Stanton R., BS; American newspaper publisher; b. 3 July 1925, Chicago, Ill.; m. Barbara Wilson 1950 (died 1994). *Education:* Northwestern Univ. *Career:* Dist sales rep. Shell Oil Co. 1949–51; Production Eng Chicago Tribune Co. 1951–60, Asst Production Man. 1960–65, Production Man. 1965–67, Production Dir 1967–70, Dir Operations 1970, Gen. Man. 1970–72, Publr 1973–90, Pres. 1972–74, Chief Officer 1974–76, Chair. 1974–81; Dir Tribune Co. Chicago 1972–96, Pres. and CEO 1974–88, Chair. 1989–91; Chair. Chicago Nat. League Ball Club (Chicago Cubs) 1990–94; Dir A.P. 1975–84; Deputy Chair. and Dir Fed. Reserve Bank of Chicago 1980–83, Chair. 1984–85; mem. Bd of Dirs. Robert R. McCormick Tribune Foundation 1990–; numerous trusteeships. *Address:* 224 Raleigh Road, Kenilworth, IL 60043-1209, USA.

COOK, Thomas H.; writer; b. 19 Sept. 1947, Fort Payne, Alabama, USA; m. Susan Terner 1978; one d. *Education:* BA, Georgia State College, 1969; MA, Hunter College, CUNY, 1972; MPhil, Columbia University, 1976. *Career:* Teacher of English and History, Dekalb Community College, Clarkston, GA, 1978–81; Contributing Ed. and Book Review Ed., Atlanta magazine, 1978–82; mem. Authors' Guild; Authors' League. *Publications:* Fiction: Blood Innocents, 1980; The Orchids, 1982; Tabernacle, 1983; Elena, 1986; Sacrificial Ground, 1988; Flesh and Blood, 1989; Streets of Fire, 1989; Night Secrets, 1990; The City When It Rains, 1991; Evidence of Blood, 1991; Mortal Memory, 1993; Breakheart Hill, 1995; The Chatham School Affair, 1996; Instruments of Night, 1998; Places in the Dark, 2000; The Interrogation, 2002. Non-Fiction: Early Graves: The Shocking True-Crime Story of the Youngest Woman Ever Sentenced to Death Row, 1990; Blood Echoes: The True Story of an Infamous Mass Murder and Its Aftermath, 1992. Contributions: Atlanta Magazine. *Honours:* Edgar Allan Poe Awards, 1981, 1988; Hammett Prize, International Asscn of Crime Writers, 1995; Award, MWA, 1996. *Address:* c/o Russell & Volkening, 50 W 29th Street, New York, NY 10017, USA.

COOKE, John Peyton; editor and writer; b. 7 March 1967, Amarillo, TX, USA. *Education:* University of Wisconsin at Madison. *Career:* Assoc. Ed., Scientific American Medicine periodical, New York, 1994–; mem. MWA. *Publications:* The Lake, 1989; Out for Blood, 1991; Torsos, 1993; The Chimney Sweeper, 1994; Haven, 1996; The Rape of Ganymede, 1998. Contributions: anthologies and periodicals. *Honours:* First Place, Wyoming Young Author, 1982. *Address:* c/o Mysterious Press/Warner Books, 1271 Avenue of the Americas, New York, NY 10020, USA.

COONEY, Raymond George Alfred; actor, dramatist and director; b. 30 May 1932, London, England; m. Linda Dixon 1962; two s. *Career:* mem. Dramatists Club. *Publications:* Plays, both solo and in collaboration with others: One for the Pot, 1961; Chase Me, Comrade, 1964; Charlie Girl, 1965; Bang Bang Beirut, 1966; Not Now, Darling, 1967; My Giddy Aunt, 1968; Move Over Mrs Markham, 1969; Why Not Stay for Breakfast?, 1970; There Goes the Bride, 1974; Run For Your Wife, 1984; Two Into One, 1985; Wife Begins at Forty, 1986; It Runs in the Family, 1987; Out of Order, 1990; Funny Money, 1994; Caught in the Net, 2000. *Address:* Hollowfield Cottage, Littleton, Surrey GU3 1HN, England.

COOPER, Jilly, OBE; British writer; b. 21 Feb. 1937, Hornchurch, Essex; m. Leo Cooper 1961; one s. one d. *Education:* Godolphin School, Salisbury. *Career:* reporter, Middx Ind. 1957–59; account exec.; copy writer; publr's reader; receptionist; model; switchboard operator; temp. typist 1959–69; columnist The Sunday Times 1969–82, Mail on Sunday 1982–87. *Publications:* How to Stay Married 1969, How Survive from Nine to Five 1970, Jolly Super 1971, Men and Super Men 1972, Jolly Super Too 1973, Women and Super Women 1974, Jolly Superlative 1975, Emily 1975, Super Men and Super Women 1976, Bella 1976, Harriet 1976, Octavia 1977, Work and Wedlock 1977, Superjilly 1977, Imogen 1978, Prudence 1978, Class 1979, Intelligent and Loyal 1980, Supercooper 1980, Violets and Vinegar (ed with Tom Hartman) 1980, The British in Love (ed) 1980, Love and Other Heartaches 1981, Jolly Marsupial 1982, Animals in War 1983, Leo and Jilly Cooper on Rugby 1984, The Common Years 1984, Riders 1985, Hotfoot to Zabriskie Point 1985, How to Survive Christmas 1986, 1996, Turn Right at the Spotted Dog 1987, Rivals 1988, Angels Rush In 1990, Polo 1991, The Man Who Made Husbands Jealous 1993, Araminta's Wedding 1993, Apassionata 1996, Score! 1999, Pandora 2002. *Honours:* Lifetime Achievement Award, British Book Awards 1998. *Literary Agent:* Vivienne Schuster, Curtis Brown Ltd, Fourth Floor, Haymarket House, 28–29 Haymarket, London, SW1Y 4SP, England. *Telephone:* (20) 7393-4400. *Fax:* (20) 7393-4401. *E-mail:* cb@curtisbrown.co.uk. *Website:* www.curtisbrown.co.uk.

COOPER, Richard Newell, AB, MSc, PhD; academic and writer; *Maurits C. Boas Professor of International Economics, Harvard University*; b. 14 June 1934, Seattle, WA, USA; m. 1st Carolyn Cahalan 1956; one s. one d.; m. 2nd Jin Chen 2000; one s. *Education:* Oberlin College, LSE, Harvard University. *Career:* Senior Staff Economist, Council of Economic Advisers to the Pres. of the USA, 1961–63; Asst Prof., 1963–65, Frank Altschul Prof. of International Economics, 1966–77, Provost, 1972–74, Yale University; Deputy Asst Secretary of State for International Affairs, 1965–66, Under-Secretary of State for Economic Affairs, 1977–81, US Dept of State; Maurits C. Boas Prof. of International Economics, Harvard University, 1981–; Chair., Federal Reserve Bank, Boston, 1990–92, National Intelligence Council, 1995–97; mem. American Acad. of Arts and Sciences, fellow; Aspen Strategy Group; Council on Foreign Relations; Trilateral Commission. *Publications:* The Economics of Interdependence, 1968; A Re-ordered World (ed. and contributor), 1973; Economic Policy in an Interdependent World, 1986; The International Monetary System, 1987; Can Nations Agree? (co-author), 1989; Economic Stabilization and Debt in Developing Countries, 1992; Boom, Crisis and Adjustment: The Macroeconomic Experience of Developing Countries (co-author), 1993; Environment and Resource Policies for the World Economy, 1994; Macroeconomic Policy and Adjustment in Korea, 1970–1990 (ed. and contributor), 1994; Trade Growth in Transition Economies (co-ed. and contributor), 1997; What the Future Holds (co-ed.), 2002. Contributions: Professional journals. *Honours:* Marshall Scholarship, UK, 1956–58; Brookings Fellow, 1960–61; Ford Foundation Faculty Fellowship, 1970–71; Fellow, Center for the Study of Behavioral Sciences, 1975–76; Hon. LLD, Oberlin College, 1978; Foreign Affairs Award, US Dept of State, 1981; National Intelligence Distinguished Service Medal, 1996; Dr hc, University of Paris, 2001. *Address:* c/o Weatherhead Center for International Affairs, Harvard University, 1737 Cambridge Street, Cambridge, MA 02138, USA.

COOPER, Susan Mary, MA; writer; b. 23 May 1935, Burnham, Buckinghamshire, England; m. 1st Nicholas J. Grant 1963 (divorced 1982); one s. one d.; m. 2nd Hume Cronyn 1996 (died 2003). *Education:* Somerville College, Oxford. *Career:* mem. Authors' Guild, Society of Authors, Writers' Guild of America. *Publications:* Mandrake 1964, Behind the Golden Curtain: A View of the USA 1965, Essays of Five Decades by J. B. Priestley (ed.) 1968, J. B. Priestley: Portrait of an Author 1970, Foxfire (play with Hume Cronyn) 1982, Dreams and Wishes: Essays on Writing for Children 1996; children's fiction: Over Sea, Under Stone 1965, Dawn of Fear 1970, The Dark is Rising 1973, Greenwitch 1973, The Grey King 1975, Silver on the Tree 1975, Jethro and the Jumbie 1979, Seaward 1983, The Selkie Girl 1986, The Silver Cow: A Welsh Tale 1983, Matthew's Dragon 1991, Tam Lin 1991, Danny and the Kings 1993, The Boggart 1993, The Boggart and the Monster 1997, King of Shadows 1999, Frog 2002, Green Boy 2002, The Magician's Boy 2005; television screenplays; contrib. to periodicals and anthologies. *Honours:* Horn Book Fanfares, 1967, 1971, 1974, 1976, 1987, 1994, 2000; Boston Globe-Horn Book Awards, 1974, 1999; Newbery Honor Book, 1974; Newbery Medal, 1976; Tir na n-Og Awards, Welsh Arts Council, 1976, 1977; Silver Hugo Award, 1984; Writers' Guild of America Awards, 1984, 1985; Christopher Award, 1985; Judy Lopez Memorial Award for Children's Literature, 1993; Children's Book Award, Scottish Arts Council, 1999; Five ALA Notable Children's Books; Two Carnegie Medal Honor Books; Humanitas Prize. *Address:* c/o Margaret K. McElderry Books, Simon & Schuster, 1230 Sixth Avenue, New York, NY 10020, USA. *Website:* www.thelostland.com.

COOVER, Robert (Lowell), MA; Writer, Dramatist, Poet and University Teacher; b. 4 Feb. 1932, Charles City, IA, USA; m. Maria del Pilar Sans-Mallagre, 3 June 1959, one s. two d. *Education:* Southern Illinois University, Indiana University, University of Chicago. *Career:* Teacher, Bard College, 1966–67, University of Iowa, 1967–69, Princeton University, 1972–73, Brown University, 1980–; various guest lectureships and professorships; mem. American Acad. and Institute of Arts and Letters, American Acad. of Arts & Sciences, PEN International, Bd of Dirs The Electronic Literature Org., numerous adv. bds. *Publications:* The Origin of the Brunists, 1966; The Universal Baseball Asscn, J. Henry Waugh, Prop., 1968; Pricksongs & Descants (short fictions), 1969; A Theological Position (plays), 1972; The Public Burning, 1977; A Political Fable (The Cat in the Hat for President), 1980; Spanking the Maid, 1982; In Bed One Night & Other Brief Encounters (short fictions) 1983, Gerald's Party, 1986; A Night at the Movies, 1987; Whatever Happened to Gloomy Gus of the Chicago Bears?, 1987; Pinocchio in Venice, 1991; John's Wife, 1996; Briar Rose, 1997, Ghost Town 1998, The Grand Hotels (of Joseph Cornell) 2002, The Adventures of Lucky Pierre, 2002. Contributions: Plays, poems, fiction, trans, essays and criticism in numerous publications and anthologies. *Honours:* William Faulkner Award for Best First Novel 1966, Rockefeller Foundation Grant 1969, Guggenheim Fellowships 1971, 1974, Obie Awards 1972–73, American Acad. of Arts and Letters Award 1976, National Endowment of the Humanities Grant 1985, Rhode Island Gov.'s Arts Award 1988, Deutscher Akademischer Austauschdienst Fellowship, Berlin 1990, Rhode Island Pell Award 1999, Lannan Foundation Fellowship 2000. *Address:* c/o Dept of English, Brown University, Providence, RI 02912, USA. *Telephone:* (401) 863-1152.

COPE, Robert Knox, (Jack Cope); Writer, Poet and Ed.; b. 3 June 1913, Mooi River, Natal, South Africa; m. Lesley de Villiers, 4 June 1942, two s. *Career:* Co-Founder and Ed., Contrast, South African, literary magazine, 1960–80. *Publications:* Lyrics and Diabtribes, 1948; Selected Poems of Ingrid Jonker (co-trans.), 1968; The Rain Maker, 1971; The Student of Zend, 1972; My Son Max, 1977. Editor: Penguin Book of South African Verse. Other: Stage, radio and television adaptations. Contributions: School textbooks and magazines. *Honours:* British Council Award, 1960; Carnegie Fellowship, 1966; CNA Prize, Argus Prize, and Gold Medallist for Literature, Veld Trust Prize, 1971; Hon. DLitt, Rhodes University.

COPE, Wendy Mary, MA, FRSL; British writer and poet; b. 21 July 1945, Erith, Kent. *Education:* Farringtons School, St Hilda's Coll., Oxford, Westminster Coll. of Educ., Oxford. *Career:* primary school teacher, London 1967–86; freelance writer 1986–; mem. Soc. of Authors (man. cttee 1992–95). *Publications include:* Across the City 1980, Hope and the 42 1984, Making Cocoa for Kingsley Amis 1986, Poem from a Colour Chart of House Paints 1986, Men and Their Boring Arguments 1988, Does She Like Wordgames? 1988, Twiddling Your Thumbs 1988, The River Girl 1990, Serious Concerns 1992, If I Don't Know 2001; editor: Is That the New Moon? – Poems by Women Poets 1989, The Orchard Book of Funny Poems 1993, The Funny Side 1998, The Faber Book of Bedtime Stories 2000, Heaven on Earth – 101 Happy Poems 2001, George Herbert: Verse and Prose (a selection) 2002; contribs to newspapers and reviews. *Honours:* Hon. DLitt (Southampton), (Oxford Brookes) 2003; Cholmondeley Award for Poetry 1987, Michael Braude Award for Light Verse, American Acad. of Arts and Letters 1995. *Literary Agent:* PFD, Drury House, 34–43 Russell Street, London, WC2B 5HA, England.

COPELAND, Ann (see Furtwängler, Virginia Walsh).

COPLEY, Paul; Actor and Writer; b. 25 Nov. 1944, Denby Dale, Yorkshire, England; m. Natasha Pyne, 7 July 1972. *Education:* Teachers Certificate, Northern Counties College of Education. *Career:* Freelance Actor/Writer; mem. Writers Guild. *Publications:* Staged: Pillion, Bush Theatre, London, 1977; Viaduct, Bush Theatre, London, 1979; Tapster, Stephen Joseph Theatre, Scarborough, 1981; Fire-Eaters, Tricycle Theatre, London, 1984; Calling, Stephen Joseph Theatre, Scarborough, 1986; Broadcast: On May-Day, BBC Radio 4 Sunday Play, 1986, repeated World Service, 1987, Radio 4, 1996; Tipperary Smith, BBC Radio 4, 1994; Words Alive, BBC Education Radio, 1996–98; episodes of King Street Junior, Radio 4, 1995–98. *Address:* Casarotto Ramsay Ltd, 60 Wardour St, London W1V 4ND, England.

CORBEN, Beverly Balkum; Educator (retd), Poet, Writer and Artist; b. 6 Aug. 1926, USA; m. Herbert Charles Corben 25 Oct. 1957; one step-s. two step-d. *Education:* AA, Santa Monica College, 1950; BA, University of California, Los Angeles, 1960; MA, Case Western Reserve University, 1972. *Career:* Teaching Asst, 1972–73, Dir of Writing Laboratory, 1973–78, 1980–82, Scarborough College, University of Toronto, Canada; Visiting Scholar, 1978–80, Scholar-in-Residence, 1982–88, Harvey Mudd College; mem. Mississippi Poetry Society; Gulf Coast Writers Asscn; Writers Unlimited, pres., 1991, 1992; Acad. of American Poets. *Publications:* On Death and Other Reasons for Living (poems), 1972. Contributions: Poetic Justice; Texas Review; Voices International; Prophetic Voices; Modern Haiku; Old Hickory Review. *Honours:* Cleveland State University Hon. Alumna, 1971; More than 60 awards for poetry and fiction nationwide, 1989–.

CORBIN, Alain; Prof. of History and Writer; b. 12 Jan. 1936, Courtomer, France; m. Annie Lagorce, 9 Sept. 1963, two s. *Education:* BA, MA, 1959, PhD, 1968, PhD, 1973, University of Caen. *Career:* Asst Lecturer, University of Limoges, 1968–69; Senior Lecturer, 1969–72, Asst Prof., 1973–85, Prof. of History, 1985–86, University of Tours; Prof. of History, University of Paris, 1987–. *Publications:* (in English trans.) The Foul and the Fragrant: Odor and the French Social Imagination, 1986; A History of Private Life, Vol. 4, From the Fires of Revolution to the Great War (with Michelle Perrot), 1990; The Village of Cannibals: Rage and Murder in France, 1870, 1991; Women for Hire: Prostitution and Sexuality in France After 1850, 1992; The Lure of the Sea, 1994; Time, Desire, and Horror, 1996; Village Bells: Sound and Meaning in the Nineteenth-Century Countryside, 1998. Contributions: scholarly books and journals. *Address:* c/o University of Paris I, Panthéon-Sorbonne, 17 rue de la Sorbonne, 75005 Paris, France.

COREN, Alan; Writer and Broadcaster; b. 27 June 1938, London, England; m. Anne Kasriel, 14 Oct. 1963, one s. one d. *Education:* BA, 1960, MA, 1980, Wadham College, Oxford; University of Minnesota, 1961; Yale University, 1962; University of California at Berkeley, 1962–63. *Career:* Asst Ed., 1963–66, Literary Ed., 1966–69, Deputy Ed., 1969–77, Ed., 1978–87, Punch; Television Critic, 1971–78, Columnist, 1988–, The Times; Columnist, Daily Mail, 1972–76, Mail on Sunday, 1984–92, Sunday Express, 1992–96; Rector, University of St Andrews, 1973–76; Ed., The Listener, 1988–89. *Publications:* The Dog It Was That Died, 1965; All Except the Bastard, 1969; The Sanity Inspector, 1974; The Bulletins of Idi Amin, 1974; Golfing for Cats, 1975; The Further Bulletins of Idi Amin, 1975; The Arthur Books (children's fiction), 1976–83; The Lady From Stalingrad Mansions, 1977; The Peanut Papers, 1977; The Rhinestone as Big as the Ritz, 1979; The Punch Book of Short Stories (ed.), three vols, 1979, 1980, 1981; The Pick of Punch (ed.), 1979–87; Tissues for Men, 1980; The Best of Alan Coren, 1980; The Cricklewood Diet, 1982; Present Laughter, 1982; The Penguin Book of Modern Humour (ed.), 1983; Bumf, 1984; Something for the Weekend, 1986; Bin Ends, 1987; Seems Like Old Times, 1989; More Like Old Times, 1990; A Year in Cricklewood, 1991; Toujours Cricklewood?, 1993; Sunday Best, 1993; Animal Passions (ed.), 1994; A Bit on the Side, 1995; The Alan Coren Omnibus, 1996; The Cricklewood Dome, 1998. Contributions: newspapers, magazines, journals, radio and television. *Honours:* Commonwealth Fellowship, 1961–63; Ed. of the Year, British Society of Magazine Eds, 1986; Hon. DLitt, University of Nottingham, 1993. *Address:* c/o Robson Books, Bolsover House, Clipstone St, London W1P 7EB, England.

CORK, Richard Graham; Art Critic and Writer; b. 25 March 1947, Eastbourne, England; m. Vena Jackson March 1970; two s. two d. *Education:* MA, PhD, Trinity Hall, Cambridge. *Career:* Art Critic, Evening Standard, 1969–77, 1980–83, The Listener, 1984–90; Ed., Studio International, 1975–79; Durning-Lawrence Lecturer, University College London, 1987; Slade Prof. of Fine Art, Cambridge, 1989–90; Chief Art Critic, The Times, 1991–2002; Henry Moore Foundation Senior Fellow, Courtauld Institute of Art, London, 1992–95; mem. Arts Council Visual Arts Panel, chair.; British Council Visual Arts Advisory Cttee; Contemporary Art Society; South Bank Board Visual Art Advisory Panel; Syndics of Fitzwilliam Museum, Cambridge; Paul Mellon Centre Advisory Council. *Publications:* Vorticism and Abstract Art in the First Machine Age, two vols, 1975–76; The Social Role of Art, 1979; Art Beyond the Gallery in Early Twentieth Century England, 1985; David Bomberg, 1987; Architect's Choice, 1992; A Bitter Truth: Avant-Garde Art and the Great War, 1994; Bottle of Notes: Claes Oldenburg and Coosje van Bruggen, 1997; Jacob Epstein, 1999; Everything Seemed Possible: Art in the 1970s, 2003; New Spirit, New Sculpture, New Money: Art in the 1980s, 2003; Breaking Down the Barriers: Art in the 1990s, 2003; Annus Mirabilis? Art in the Year 2000, 2003. Contributions: catalogues and periodicals. *Honours:* John Llewelyn Rhys Memorial Prize, 1976; Sir Banister Fletcher Award, 1986; National Art Collections Fund Award, 1995. *Address:* 24 Milman Rd, London NW6 6EG, England.

CORKHILL, Annette Robyn, (Annette Robyn Vernon); Writer, Poet and Trans; b. 10 Sept. 1955, Brisbane, Australia; m. Alan Corkhill, 18 March 1977, two s. one d. *Education:* BA, 1977; DipEd, 1978; MA, 1985; PhD, 1993. *Publications:* The Jogger: Anthology of Australian Poetry, 1987; Destination, Outrider, 1987; Mangoes Encounter – Queensland Summer, 1987; Age 1, LINQ, 1987; Two Soldiers of Tiananmen, Earth Against Heaven, 1990; Australian Writing: Ethnic Writers 1945–1991, 1994; The Immigrant Experience in Australian Literature, 1995. Contributions: Outrider; Australian Literary Studies. *Honours:* Hon. Mention, The Creativity Centre, Harold Kesteven Poetry Prize, 1987. *Address:* 5 Wattletree Pl., The Gap, Qld 4061, Australia. *E-mail:* translation@uq.net.au.

CORLEY, Ernest (see Bulmer, Henry Kenneth).

CORMAN, Avery; Novelist; b. 28 Nov. 1935, New York, NY, USA; m. Judith Lishinsky, 5 Nov. 1967, two s. *Education:* BS, New York University, 1952. *Career:* mem. PEN American Center; Writers Guild of America. *Publications:* Oh God!, 1971; Kramer Vs Kramer, 1977; The Bust-Out King, 1977; The Old Neighborhood, 1980; Fifty, 1987; Prized Possessions, 1991; The Big Hype, 1992. *Literary Agent:* Janklow & Nesbit Associates, 445 Park Ave, New York, NY 10022, USA.

CORN, Alfred; Poet, Writer, Critic and Trans; b. 14 Aug. 1943, Bainbridge, GA, USA; m. Ann Jones, 1967, divorced 1971. *Education:* BA, Emory University, 1965; MA, Columbia University, 1967. *Career:* Poet-in-Residence, George Mason University, 1980, Blaffer Foundation, New Harmony, IN, 1989, James Thurber House, 1990; Humanities Lecturer, New School for Social Research, New York City, 1988; Ellison Chair in Poetry, University of Cincinnati, 1989; Bell Distinguished Visiting Prof., University of Tulsa, 1992; Hurst Residency in Poetry, Washington University, St Louis, 1994; numerous college and university seminars and workshops; many poetry readings; mem. National Book Critics Circle; PEN; Poetry Society of America. *Publications:* Poetry: All Roads at Once, 1976; A Call in the Midst of the Crowd, 1978; The Various Light, 1980; Tongues on Trees, 1980; The New Life, 1983; Notes from a Child of Paradise, 1984; An Xmas Murder, 1987; The West Door, 1988; Autobiographies, 1992; Present, 1997. Novel: Part of His Story, 1997. Criticism: The Metamorphoses of Metaphor, 1987; Incarnation: Contemporary Writers on the New Testament (ed.), 1990; The Pith Helmet, 1992; A Manual of Prosody, 1997. Contributions: Books, anthologies, scholarly journals, and periodicals. *Honours:* Woodrow Wilson Fellow, 1965–66; Fulbright Fellow, Paris, 1967–68; Ingram Merrill Fellowships, 1974, 1981; National Endowment for the Arts Fellowships for Poetry, 1980, 1991; Gustav Davidson Prize, Poetry Society of America, 1983; American Acad. and Institute of Arts and Letters Award, 1983; New York Foundation for the Arts Fellowships, 1986, 1995; Guggenheim Fellowship, 1986–87; Acad. of American Poets Prize, 1987; Yaddo Corporation Fellowship in Poetry, 1989; Djerassi Foundation Fellowship in Poetry, 1990; Rockefeller Foundation Fellowship in Poetry, Bellagio, Italy, 1992; MacDowell Colony Fellowships in Poetry, 1994, 1996.

CORNWELL, Bernard, (Susannah Kells), BA; writer; b. 23 Feb. 1944, London, England; m. Judy Acker 1980. *Education:* Univ. of London. *Publications:* Redcoat 1987, Wildtrack 1988, Sea Lord (aka Killer's Wake) 1989, Crackdown (aka Murder Cay) 1990, Stormchild 1991, Scoundrel 1992, Stonehenge 2000 BC 1999, The Archer's Tale 2001, Gallows Thief 2001, The Last Kingdom 2004; Starbuck Chronicles series: Rebel 1993, Copperhead 1994, Battle Flag 1995, The Bloody Ground 1996; Arthur series: The Winter King 1995, Enemy of God 1996, Excalibur 1997; Sharpe series: Sharpe's Eagle 1981, Sharpe's Gold 1981, Sharpe's Company 1982, Sharpe's Sword 1983, Sharpe's Enemy 1984, Sharpe's Honour 1985, Sharpe's Regiment 1986, Sharpe's Siege 1987, Sharpe's Rifles 1988, Sharpe's Revenge 1989, Sharpe's Waterloo 1990, Sharpe's Devil 1992, Sharpe's Battle 1995, Sharpe's Tiger 1997, Sharpe's Triumph 1998, Sharpe's Fortress 1999, Sharpe's Trafalgar 2000, Sharpe's Prey 2001, Sharpe's Skirmish (short story) 2002, Sharpe's Havoc 2003, Sharpe's Escape 2004; Grail Quest series: Harlequin 2000, Vagabond 2002, Heretic 2003; as Susannah Kells: A Crowning Mercy 1983, The Fallen Angels 1984, Coat of Arms 1986, The Aristocrats 1987. *Literary Agent:* Toby Eady Associates Ltd, Third Floor, 9 Orme Court, London, W2 4RL, England. *Telephone:* (20) 7792-0092. *Fax:* (20) 7792-0879. *E-mail:* toby@tobyeady.demon.co.uk. *Website:* www.tobyeadyassociates.co.uk; www.bernardcornwell.net.

CORNWELL, David John Moore, (John le Carré); Writer; b. 19 Oct. 1931, Poole, Dorset, England; m. 1st Alison Ann Veronica Sharp 1954 (divorced 1971); three s.; m. 2nd Valerie Jane Eustace 1972; one s. *Education:* Univ. of Bern, 1948–49; BA, Lincoln Coll., Oxford, 1956. *Career:* Teacher, Eton Coll., 1956–58; Foreign Service, 1959–64. *Publications:* Call for the Dead, 1961; Murder of Quality, 1962; The Spy Who Came in From the Cold, 1963; The Looking Glass War, 1965; A Small Town in Germany, 1968; The Naive and Sentimental Lover, 1971; Tinker Tailor Soldier Spy, 1974; The Honourable Schoolboy, 1977; Smiley's People, 1979; The Quest for Karla (collected edn of previous three titles), 1982; The Little Drummer Girl, 1983; A Perfect Spy, 1986; The Russia House, 1989; The Secret Pilgrim, 1991; The Night Manager, 1993; Our Game, 1995; The Tailor of Panama, 1997; Single and Single, 1999; The Constant Gardener, 2000; Absolute Friends, 2004. *Honours:* Somerset Maugham Award, 1963; Edgar Allan Poe Award, 1965, Grand Master Award, 1986, MWA; James Tait Black Memorial Prize, 1977; Gold Dagger Award, 1978, Diamond Dagger Award, 1988, CWA; Hon. Fellow, Lincoln Coll., Oxford, 1984; Premio Malaparte, 1987; Nikos Kazantzakis Prize, 1991; Hon. doctorates, St Andrew's Univ., Exeter Univ., Southampton Univ., Bath Univ. *Literary Agent:* David Higham Associates, 5–8 Lower John St, Golden Sq., London W1F 9HA, England.

CORNWELL, Patricia Daniels, BA; American writer; b. 9 June 1957, Miami, FL. *Education:* Davidson Coll. (NC). *Career:* police reporter Charlotte Observer, NC 1979–81; computer analyst Office of the Chief Medical Examiner Richmond, VA 1985–91; mem. Authors' Guild, Int. Asscn of Identification, Int. Crime Writers Asscn, Nat. Asscn of Medical Examiners. *Publications include:* non-fiction: A Time of Remembering: The Story of Ruth Bell Graham 1983 (re-issued as Ruth: a Portrait 1997); fiction: Postmortem (John Creasey Award, British Crime Writers' Asscn 1991, Anthony Award, Boucheron Award, World Mystery Convention, MacAvity Award, Mystery Readers Int) 1990, Body of Evidence 1991, All That Remains 1992, Cruel and Unusual 1993, The Body Farm 1994, From Potter's Field 1995, Cause of Death 1996, Hornet's Nest 1996, Unnatural Exposure 1997, Point of Origin 1998, Southern Cross 1999, Black Notice 1999, The Last Precinct 2001, Isle of Dogs 2001, Portrait of a Killer: Jack the Ripper 2002, Blow Fly 2003, Trace 2004. *Honours:* Investigative Reporting Award, N Carolina Press Asscn 1980, Gold Medallion Book Award, Evangelical Christian Publishers Asscn 1985, Edgar Award 1990,

Prix du Roman d'Aventure 1991, Gold Dagger Award 1993, Sherlock Holmes Award 1999. *Address:* c/o Little, Brown & Co., Brettenham House, Lancaster Place, London WC2E 7EN, England; c/o Don Congdon Associates Inc., 156 5th Ave, Suite 625, New York, NY 10010–7002, USA.

COSGRAVE, Patrick; Writer; b. 28 Sept. 1941, Dublin, Ireland; m. 1st Ruth Dudley Edwards, 1965, divorced; m. 2nd Norma Alice Green, 1974, divorced, one d.; m. 3rd Shirley Ward, 1981. *Education:* BA, 1964, MA, 1965, University College, Dublin; PhD, Peterhouse, Cambridge, 1968. *Career:* London Ed., Radio Telefis Eireann, 1968–69; Conservative Research Department, 1969–71; Political Ed., The Spectator, 1971–75; Features Ed., Telegraph Magazine, 1974–76; Special Adviser to Rt Hon. Mrs Margaret Thatcher, 1975–79; Managing Ed., Quartet Crime (Quartet Books), 1979–81. *Publications:* The Public Poetry of Robert Lowell, 1969; Churchill at War: Alone, 1974; Cheyney's Law (novel), 1976; Margaret Thatcher: A Tory and Her Party, 1978, second edn as Margaret Thatcher: Prime Minister, 1979; The Three Colonels (novel), 1979; R. A. Butler: An English Life, 1981; Adventure of State (novel), 1984; Thatcher: The First Term, 1985; Carrington: A Life and a Policy, 1985; The Lives of Enoch Powell, 1989; The Strange Death of Socialist Britain, 1992. Contributions: various journals and magazines.

ĆOSIĆ, Dobrica; Writer and Politician; b. 29 Dec. 1921, Velika Drenova, Yugoslavia. *Education:* University of Belgrade. *Career:* Journalist, then freelance writer; Founder, Committee for Defence of Freedom of Thought and Speech; Pres., Federal Republic of Yugoslavia, 1992–93; mem. Serbian Acad. of Arts and Sciences. *Publications:* Far Away is the Sun, 1951; Roots, 1954; Seven Days in Budapest, 1957; Divisions, 1961; Responsibilities, 1964; A Fairy Tale, 1966; Power and Anxieties, 1971; This Land, This Time, 4 vols, 1972–79; The Real and the Possible, 1982; Sinner, 1985; Renegade, 1986; Serbian Question: Democratic Question, 1987; Believer, 1990; Changes, 1992; A Time of Power, 1996. *Address:* c/o Serbian Acad. of Arts and Sciences, Belgrade, Serbia and Montenegro.

COSSERY, Albert; French writer and poet; b. 1913, Cairo, Egypt. *Career:* fmrly in Egyptian merchant navy; emigrated to Paris 1945. *Publications:* poetry: Les Morsures 1931; fiction: Les hommes oubliés de Dieu (trans. as Men God Forgot) 1942, La maison de la mort certaine (trans. as The House of Certain Death) 1942, Les fainéants dans la vallée fertile (trans. as The Lazy Ones) 1947, Mendiants et orgueilleux (trans. as If All Men were Beggars, aka A Room in Cairo, Proud Beggars) 1945, La violence et la derision 1964, Un complot de saltimbanques 1973, Une ambition dans le désert 1984, Les couleurs d'infamie 1999. *Address:* c/o Hotel La Louisiane, 60 rue de Seine, 75006 Paris,France.

COSTANZA, Mary Scarpone, BFA, BS; artist, writer, poet and lecturer; b. 14 May 1927, Berwyn, PA, USA; m. John Costanza 1951; one s. one d. *Education:* Tyler School of Fine Arts, Temple University. *Career:* Dir, Costanza Art Gallery; Painting exhibitions; mem. American-Italian Historical Asscn; Authors' Guild; Holocaust Memorial Museum. *Publications:* Kaddish/Six Million, 1978; The Living Witness: Art in the Concentration Camps and Ghettos, 1982; Shoah (poems), 1997; Country Cousins (short stories), 1999. *Honours:* grants and awards. *Address:* 737 Polo Road, Bryn Mawr, PA 19010, USA.

COTTERILL, Kenneth Matthew; Playwright; b. 17 Sept. 1950, Sheffield, England; m. Marilyn Bokiagon, 6 Oct. 1984, one s. *Education:* BA, University of Queensland, 1980; Queensland University of Technology, 1981. *Career:* mem. Australian Writers Guild; Playlab. *Publications:* Re-Electing Roger; Richard the Third's Revenge; Perfect Murder; Rhinoceros Hides. Contributions: periodicals. *Honours:* Australia Bicentennial Award; Australia Day Award for Culture, 1994. *Address:* 44 Martin Ave, Mareeba, Qld, Australia.

COULOMBE, Charles Aquila; Writer; b. 8 Nov. 1960, New York, NY, USA. *Education:* New Mexico Military Institute, Roswell, 1978–80. *Career:* mem. Authors' Guild; Catholic Writer's Guild of Great Britain. *Publications:* Everyman Today Call Rome, 1987; The White Cockade, 1990; Puritan's Progress, 1996; A Guide to Royal America, 2000. Contributions: periodicals. *Honours:* Christ the King Award, Christian Law Institute, 1992. *Address:* PO Box 660771, Arcadia, CA 91066, USA.

COULTER, Harris Livermore; Writer, Trans. and Interpreter; b. 8 Oct. 1932, Baltimore, MD, USA; m. Catherine Nebolsine, 10 Jan. 1960, two s. two d. *Education:* BA, Yale University, 1954; PhD, Columbia University, 1969. *Career:* mem. American Institute of Homeopathy. *Publications:* Divided Legacy: A History of the Schism in Medical Thought, Vol. I: The Patterns Emerge, 1975, Vol. II: The Origins of Modern Western Medicine, 1977, Vol. III: Homeopathy and the American Medical Asscn, 1981, Vol. IV: Twentieth-Century Medicine: The Bacteriological Era, 1994; Homeopathic Science and Modern Medicine, 1981; DPT: A Shot in the Dark (with Barbara Fisher), 1985; Vaccination, Social Violence, and Criminality, 1990; The Controlled Clinical Trial: An Analysis, 1991; Aids and Syphilis: The Hidden Link. *Honours:* Hahnemann Prize, Société Royale Belge d'Homéopathie, 1985; La Medalla d'Or del Centenari, Academia Medico-Homepatica de Barcelona, 1990. *Address:* Center for Empirical Medicine, 4221 45th St NW, Washington, DC 20016, USA.

COULTON, James (see Hansen, Joseph).

COUPLAND, Douglas Campbell; Canadian writer and artist; b. 30 Dec. 1961, Baden-Solingen, Germany. *Education:* Emily Carr Inst. for Art and Design, Vancouver, also studied in Japan and Italy. *Publications:* Generation X: Tales for an Accelerated Culture 1991, Shampoo Planet 1992, Life After God 1994, Microserfs 1995, Polaroids from the Dead (non-fiction) 1996, Girlfriend in a Coma 1997, Miss Wyoming 1999, City of Glass (non-fiction) 2000, God Hates Japan 2001, All Families are Psychotic 2001, Souvenir of Canada (non-fiction) 2002, School Spirit (non-fiction) 2002, Hey Nostradamus! 2003, September 10 (play) 2004, Souvenir of Canada 2 (non-fiction) 2004, Eleanor Rigby 2004; contrib. to Art Forum, New Republic, New York Times, Wired. *Address:* c/o Fiona McMorrough, Flamingo, HarperCollinsPublishers, 77–85 Fulham Palace Road, Hammersmith, London, W6 8JB, England. *E-mail:* fionam@fmcm.co.uk. *Address:* c/o Writer's Union of Canada, 40 Wellington Street E, Third Floor, Toronto, ON M5E 1C7, Canada. *Website:* www.coupland.com.

COURTER, Gay; Writer and Film-maker; b. 1 Oct. 1944, Pittsburgh, Pennsylvania, USA; m. Philip Courter, 18 Aug. 1968, two s. *Education:* AB, Drama, Film, Antioch College, Ohio, 1966. *Career:* mem. Authors' Guild; Writers Guild of America East; Guardian Ad Litem; International Childbirth Asscn. *Publications:* The Bean Sprout Book, 1974; The Midwife, 1981; River of Dreams, 1984; Code Ezra, 1986; Flowers in the Blood, 1990; The Midwife's Advice, 1992; I Speak for This Child, 1995. Contributions: Parents; Women's Day; Publishers Weekly; Others. *Address:* 121 NW Crystal St, Crystal River, FL 34428, USA.

COURTNEY, Dayle (see Goldsmith, Howard).

COURTNEY, Nicholas Piers; Author; b. 20 Dec. 1944, Berkshire, England; m. Vanessa Hardwicke 30 Oct. 1980. *Education:* Nautical College, Berkshire, 1966; Royal Agricultural College, Cirencester; MRICS, MRAC. *Career:* mem. Brook's. *Publications:* Shopping and Cooking in Europe, 1980; The Tiger: Symbol of Freedom, 1981; Diana: Princess of Wales, 1982; Royal Children, 1982; Prince Andrew, 1983; Sporting Royals, 1983; Diana, Princess of Fashion, 1984; Queen Elizabeth, The Queen Mother, 1984; The Very Best of British, 1985; In Society: The Brideshead Years, 1986; Princess Anne, 1986; Luxury Shopping in London, 1987; Sisters in Law, 1988; A Stratford Kinshall, 1989; The Mall, 1990; Windsor Castle, 1991; A Little History of Antiques, 1995; Gale Force 10: The Life and Legacy of Admiral Beaufort, 2002. Contributions: Times; Redbook; Spectator; Independent; House and Garden. *Address:* 9 Kempson Rd, London SW6 4PX, England.

COUSINEAU, Philip Robert; Writer; b. 26 Nov. 1952, Columbia, South Carolina, USA. *Education:* BA, cum laude, Journalism, University of Detroit, 1974. *Publications:* The Hero's Journey: Joseph Campbell on His Life and Work, 1990; The Soul of the World, 1991; Deadlines: A Rhapsody on a Theme of Famous Last Words, 1991; Soul: An Archaeology: Readings from Socrates to Ray Charles, 1994; Prayers at 3am, 1995; Design Outlaws (with Christopher Zelov), 1996. Contributions: Parabola Magazine; Paris Magazine. *Address:* c/o Harper San Francisco, 1160 Battery St, San Francisco, CA 94111, USA.

COUTO, Mia; Mozambican writer and journalist; b. 1955, Beira. *Career:* fmr Dir Mozambique Information Agency; columnist Notícias daily newspaper, Tempo magazine. *Publications:* Raiz d'orvalho (poems) 1983, Vozes Anoitecidas (trans. as Voices Made Night) 1986, Cada homem e uma raca 1991 (trans. as Every Man is a Race 1994), Terra Sonambula 1992, Under the Frangipani, The Last Flight of the Flamingo, and collections of short stories. *Address:* c/o Notícias, Rua Joaquim Lapa 55, CP 327, Maputo, Mozambique (Office); c/o African Writers Series, Heinemann Educational Publishers, Halley Ct, Jordan Hill, Oxford, OX2 8EJ, England.

COUZYN, Jeni, BA; Canadian poet, psychotherapist, lecturer and broadcaster; b. 26 July 1942, South Africa. *Education:* University of Natal. *Career:* Writer-in-Residence, University of Victoria, BC 1976; founder and Dir, Bethesda Arts Centre, Nieu Bethesda, South Africa 1999–; mem. Guild of Psychotherapists, Poetry Soc. (general council 1968–75). *Publications:* Flying, 1970; Monkeys' Wedding, 1972; Christmas in Africa, 1975; House of Changes, 1978; The Happiness Bird, 1978; Life by Drowning, 1983; In the Skin House, 1993; Homecoming, 1998; A Time to Be Born, 1999; Selected Poems, 2000. Editor: Bloodaxe Book of Contemporary Women Poets, 1985; Singing Down the Bones, 1989. Other: Children's books and edns of poetry. *Honours:* Arts Council of Great Britain grants 1971, 1974, Canada Council grants 1977, 1983. *Literary Agent:* Andrew Mann, 1 Old Compton Street, London W1V 5PH, England. *Address:* c/o Bloodaxe Books Ltd, Highgreen, Tarset, Northumberland NE48 1RP, England.

COVARRUBIAS ORTIZ, Miguel; writer, poet and academic; b. 27 Feb. 1940, Monterrey, Mexico; m. Silvia Mijares 1967; two d. *Education:* Licenciado en letras, 1973, Maestria en letras espagnolas (pasantia), 1987, Universidad Autónoma de Nuevo León, Monterrey. *Career:* Dir, Centre for Literary and Linguistic Research, 1976–79, and Institute of Fine Arts, 1976–79, Co-ordinator, Creative Writing Workshop, 1981–, Universidad Autónoma de Nuevo León, Monterrey; mem. Deslinde (culture review), dir, 1985–; Sociedad General de Escritores de Mexico. *Publications:* Fiction: La raiz ausente, 1962; Custodia de silencios, 1965; Minusculario, 1966. Poetry: El poeta, 1969; El segundo poeta, 1977; Pandora, 1987. Essays: Papeleria, 1970; Olavide o Sade, 1975; Nueva papeleria, 1978; Papeleria en tramite, 1997. Editor: Antologia de autores contemporáneos, 1972, 1974, 1975, 1979,

1980; Desde el Cerro de la Silla, 1992; Traduction: El traidor, 1993; Conversations: Junto a una taza de café, 1994. Contributions: various publications. *Honours:* Second Place, Story, Xalapa Arts Festival, 1962; Arts Prize, Literature, Universidad Autónoma de Nuevo León, Monterrey, 1989; Medal of Civic Merit in Literature and Arts, Gobierno del Estado du Nuevo León, 1993; Poetry Trans. Prize, National Institute of Fine Arts, Mexico, 1993. *Address:* Kant 2801, Contry-La Silla, Guadalupe, NL, México, DF, 67170, Mexico.

COVINGTON, Vicki; Writer; b. 22 Oct. 1952, Birmingham, AL, USA; m. Dennis Covington, 24 Dec. 1977, two d. *Education:* BA, 1974, MSW, 1976, University of Alabama. *Publications:* Gathering Home, 1988; Bird of Paradise, 1990; Night Ride Home, 1992; The Last Hotel for Women, 1996. *Honours:* National Endowment for the Arts Fellowship, 1988. *Address:* c/o International Creative Management, 40 W 57th St, New York, NY 10019, USA.

COWASJEE, Saros; academic, writer and editor; b. 12 July 1931, Secundrabad, India. *Education:* BA, St John's College, Agra, 1951; MA, Agra University, 1955; PhD, University of Leeds, 1960. *Career:* Asst Ed., Times of India Press, Mumbai, 1961–63; Teacher, 1963–71, Prof. of English, 1971–95, Prof. Emeritus, 1995–, University of Regina, Canada; General Ed., Literature of the Raj series, Arnold Publishers, New Delhi, 1984–; mem. Cambridge Society; Writers Union of Canada; Asscn of Commonwealth Literature and Language Studies. *Publications:* Sean O'Casey: The Man Behind the Plays, 1963; Sean O'Casey, 1966; Stories and Sketches, 1970; Goodbye to Elsa (novel), 1974; Coolie: An Assessment (criticism), 1976; So Many Freedoms: A Study of the Major Fiction of Mulk Raj Anand, 1977; Nude Therapy (short stories), 1978; The Last of the Maharajas (screenplay), 1980; Studies in Indian and Anglo-Indian Fiction, 1993; The Assistant Professor (novel), 1996. Editor: Stories from the Raj, 1982; More Stories from the Raj and After, 1986; Women Writers of the Raj, 1990; The Best Short Stories of Flora Annie Steel, 1995; Orphans of the Storm: Stories on the Partition of India, 1995; The Oxford Anthology of Raj Stories, 1998; Four Raj Novels, 2004. Contributions: reviews and journals. *Address:* Suite 308, 3520 Hillside Street, Regina, SK S4S 5Z5, Canada. *E-mail:* saros .cowasjee@uregina.ca.

COWDREY, Herbert Edward John; Historian and Writer; b. 29 Nov. 1926, Basingstoke, Hants, England; m. Judith Watson Davis 14 July 1959; one s. two d. *Education:* BA, 1949, MA, 1951, DD, 2000, Univ. of Oxford. *Career:* Deacon, 1952; Priest, 1953; Tutor and Chaplain, St Stephen's House, Oxford, 1952–56; Fellow and Tutor in Modern History, 1956–87, Senior Research Fellow in Modern History, 1987–94, Emeritus Fellow, 1994–, St Edmund Hall, Oxford; Leverhulme Emeritus Fellow, 1996–98. *Publications:* The Cluniacs and the Gregorian Reform, 1970; The Epistolae Vagantes of Pope Gregory VII, 1972; Two Studies in Cluniac History, 1978; The Age of Abbot Desiderius, 1983; Popes, Monks and Crusaders, 1984; Pope Gregory VII, 1998; The Crusades and Latin Monasticism, 1999; Popes and Church Reform in the 11th Century, 2000; The Register of Pope Gregory VII: An English Translation, 2002; Lanfranc: Scholar, Monk and Archbishop, 2003. Contributions: scholarly journals. *Address:* 30 Oxford Rd, Old Marston, Oxford OX3 0PQ, England.

COWELL, Stephanie; Writer; b. 25 July 1943, New York, NY, USA; m. Russell O'Neal Clay, 2 Dec. 1995, two s. *Education:* Self-educated. *Career:* mem. Authors' Guild. *Publications:* Nicholas Cooke (actor, soldier, physician, priest), 1993; The Physician of London, 1995; The Players: Shakespeare, 1997. *Honours:* American Book Award, 1996. *Address:* 585 West End Ave, New York, NY 10024, USA.

COX, (Charles) Brian, CBE, BA, MA, MLitt, FRSL; academic, writer, poet and editor; b. 5 Sept. 1928, Grimsby, Lincolnshire, England. *Education:* Pembroke Coll., Cambridge. *Career:* Lecturer, Senior Lecturer, University of Hull, 1954–66; Co-Ed., Critical Quarterly, 1959–; Prof. of English Literature, 1966–93, Prof. Emeritus, 1993–, Pro-Vice-Chancellor, 1987–91, University of Manchester; Visiting Prof., King's College, London, 1994; Hon. Fellow, Westminster College, Oxford, 1994; Mem., Arts Council, 1996–98; mem. Chair, North West Arts Board, 1994–2000. *Publications:* The Free Spirit, 1963; Modern Poetry (with A. E. Dyson), 1963; Conrad's Nostromo, 1964; The Practical Criticism of Poetry (with A. E. Dyson), 1965; Poems of This Century (ed. with A. E. Dyson), 1968; Word in the Desert (ed. with A. E. Dyson), 1968; The Waste Land: A Casebook (ed. with A. P. Hinchliffe), 1968; The Black Papers on Education (ed. with A. E. Dyson), 1971; The Twentieth Century Mind (ed. with A. E. Dyson), 3 vols, 1972; Conrad: Youth, Heart of Darkness and The End of the Tether (ed.), 1974; Joseph Conrad: The Modern Imagination, 1974; Black Paper 1975 (ed. with R. Boyson), 1975; Black Paper 1977 (ed. with R. Boyson), 1977; Conrad, 1977; Every Common Sight (verse), 1981; Two Headed Monster (verse), 1985; Cox on Cox: An English Curriculum for the 1990s, 1991; The Great Betrayal: Autobiography, 1992; Collected Poems, 1993; The Battle for the English Curriculum, 1995; African Writers (ed.), 1997; Literacy is Not Enough (ed.), 1998; Emeritus (poems), 2001. *Honours:* Hon. DLitt, De Montfort University, 1999. *Address:* 20 Park Gates Drive, Cheadle Hulme, Stockport SK8 7DF, England.

COX, Richard; Writer; b. 8 March 1931, Winchester, Hampshire, England; m. 1963, two s. one d. *Education:* MA, English, St Catherine's College, Oxford, 1955. *Career:* Staff Correspondent, Daily Telegraph, 1966–72; Mem., States of Alderney, 2003–. *Publications:* Operation Sealion, 1974; Sam, 1976; Auction, 1978; KGB Directive, 1981; Ground Zero, 1985; An Agent of Influence, 1988; Park Plaza, 1991; Eclipse, 1996; Murder at Wittenham Park, 1998. Contributions: periodicals. *Address:* 18 Hauteville, Alderney GY9 3UA, Channel Islands.

COX-JOHNSON, Ann (see Saunders, Ann Loreille).

COYLE, Harold; Writer; b. 6 Feb. 1952, New Brunswick, NJ, USA; m. Patricia A. Bannon, 5 Oct. 1974, two s. one d. *Education:* BA, History, Virginia Military Institute, 1974. *Career:* Commissioned Officer, US Army, 1974–91; mem. Asscn of Civil War Sites; Reserve Officers Asscn. *Publications:* Team Yankee, 1987; Sword Point, 1988; Bright Star, 1991; Trial by Fire, 1992; The Ten Thousand, 1993; Code of Honor, 1994. *Literary Agent:* William Morris Agency, 1325 Avenue of the Americas, New York, NY 10019, USA.

COZ, Steve; American editor and publishing executive; b. 26 March 1957, Grafton, Mass.; m. Valerie Virga 1987. *Education:* Harvard Univ. *Career:* freelance writer various US publs 1979–82; reporter Nat. Enquirer, Fla 1982–95, Ed.-in-Chief 1995–; American celebrity analyst BBC Radio 1995–96. *Honours:* Edgar Hoover Memorial Award for Distinguished Public Service 1996; Haven House Award of Excellence for Outstanding Reporting on Domestic Violence Issues 1996. *Address:* American Media Inc., 5401 NW Broken Sound Boulevard, Boca Raton, FL 33487, USA.

COZZARELLI, Nicholas R.; American editor and academic; *Editor-in-Chief, Proceedings of the National Academy of Sciences. Career:* elected Ed.-in-Chief, Proceedings of the National Academy of Sciences 1989–; Prof. of Biochemistry and Molecular Biology, Univ. of California at Berkeley. *Publications:* editor: Mechanisms of Deoxyribonucleic Acid Replication and Recombination 1984, DNA Topology and its Biological Effects: Monograph 20 (with others) 1990; numerous research papers. *Address:* National Academy of Sciences, 500 Fifth Street NW, Washington, DC 20001, USA. *Website:* www.pnas.edu. *Address:* University of California, Berkeley Department of Molecular & Cell Biology, 61A Koshland Hall, Berkeley, CA 94720-3204, USA (Office). *Telephone:* (510) 642-5266 (Office). *Fax:* (510) 643-1079 (Office). *E-mail:* ncozzare@socrates.berkeley.edu (Office). *Website:* mcb.berkeley.edu/labs/cozzarelli (Office).

CRACE, Jim, BA; British writer and dramatist; b. 1 March 1946, Brocket Hall, Lemsford, Hertfordshire, England; m. Pamela Ann Turton 1975; one s. one d. *Education:* Birmingham Coll. of Commerce, Univ. of London. *Publications:* Continent 1986, The Gift of Stones 1988, Arcadia 1992, Signals of Distress 1994, The Slow Digestions of the Night 1995, Quarantine 1997, Being Dead 1999, The Devil's Larder 2001, Genes 2001, Six 2003, Genesis 2003; short stories: Refugees 1977, Annie, California Plates 1977, Helter Skelter, Hang Sorrow, Care'll Kill a Cat 1977, Seven Ages 1980; other: radio plays. *Honours:* Dr hc (Univ. of Central England) 2000; David Higham Award 1986, Guardian Prize for Fiction 1986, Whitbread Awards 1986, 1997, Antico Fattore Prize, Italy 1988, GAP Int. Prize for Literature 1989, Soc. of Authors Travel Award 1992, RSL Winifred Holtby Memorial Prize 1995, E. M. Forster Award 1996, Nat. Critics' Circle Award, USA 2001. *Literary Agent:* David Godwin Associates, 55 Monmouth Street, London, WC2H 9DG, England.

CRAFT, Robert (Lawson); Conductor and Writer; b. 20 Oct. 1923, Kingston, NY, USA. *Education:* BA, Juilliard School of Music, New York, 1946; Berkshire Music Center, Tanglewood; Studied conducting with Pierre Monteux. *Career:* Conductor, Evenings-on-the-Roof and Monday Evening Concerts, Los Angeles, 1950–68; Asst to, later closest assoc. of Igor Stravinsky, 1948–71; numerous collaborations with Stravinsky; Conducted first performances of various later works by Stravinsky; Conducted works ranging from Monteverdi to Boulez; US premiere of Berg's Lulu (two-act version) Santa Fe, 1963; many recordings incl. works of Stravinsky, Webern, Schoenberg; Schoenberg series for Koch International, 1998. *Publications:* with Stravinsky: Conversations with Igor Stravinsky, 1959; Memories and Commentaries, 1960; Expositions and Developments, 1962; Dialogues and a Diary, 1963; Themes and Episodes, 1967; Retrospections and Conclusions, 1969; Chronicle of a Friendship, 1972; Prejudices in Disguise, 1974; with Vera Stravinsky: Stravinsky in Photographs and Documents, 1976; Current Convictions: Views and Reviews, 1977; Present Perspectives, 1984; Stravinsky's Selected Correspondence (trans. and ed., two vols), 1982, 1984; Stravinsky: Glimpses of a Life, 1992; The Moment of Existence: Music, Literature and the Arts, 1996; An Improbable Life, 2003. Contributions: articles in various journals and other publications. *Address:* 1390 South Ocean Blvd, Pompano Beach, FL 33062, USA.

CRAGGS, Stewart Roger; Academic Librarian and Writer; b. 27 July 1943, Ilkley, West Yorkshire, England; m. Valerie J. Gibson 28 Sept. 1968; one s. one d. *Education:* MCLIP, Leeds Polytechnic, 1968; FCLIP, 1974; MA, 1978, PhD, 1982, Univ. of Strathclyde. *Career:* Teesside Polytechnic, 1968–69; JA Jobling, 1970–72; Sunderland Polytechnic, later Univ., 1973–95; Consultant, William Walton Edition, OUP, 1995–. *Publications:* William Walton: A Thematic Catalogue, 1977; Arthur Bliss: A Bio-Bibliography, 1988; Richard Rodney Bennett: A Bio-Bibliography, 1990; John McCabe: A Bio-Bibliography, 1991; William Walton: A Source Book, 1993; John Ireland: A Catalogue, Discography and Bibliography, 1993; Alun Hoddinott: A Bio-Bibliography, 1993; Edward Elgar: A Source Book, 1995; William

Mathias: A Bio-Bibliography, 1995; Arthur Bliss: A Source Book, 1996; Soundtracks: An International Dictionary of Composers for Films, 1998; Malcolm Arnold: A Bio-Bibliography, 1998; William Walton: Music and Literature, 1999; Lennox Berkeley: A Source Book, 2000; Benjamin Britten: A Bio-Bibliography, 2001; Arthur Bliss: Music and Literature, 2002; Peter Maxwell Davies: A Source Book, 2002. *Honours:* McColvin Medal for Best Reference Book, Library Asscn, 1990; Prof. of Music Bibliography, Univ. of Sunderland, 1993. *Address:* 106 Mount Rd, High Barnes, Sunderland SR4 7NN, England. *E-mail:* stewcraggs@aol.com.

CRAIG, Alisa (see Macleod, Charlotte).

CRAIG, Amanda Pauline; Novelist and Journalist; b. 22 Sept. 1959, South Africa; m. Robin John Cohen, 27 July 1988, one s. one d. *Education:* Clare College, Cambridge, 1979–81. *Career:* mem. Society of Authors, Management Committee, 2000. *Publications:* Foreign Bodies, 1990; A Private Place, 1991; A Vicious Circle, 1996; In a Dark Wood, 2000; Love in Idleness, 2003. Contributions: periodicals. *Honours:* Young Journalist of the Year, 1996; Catherine Pakenham Award, 1998. *Literary Agent:* Curtis Brown Ltd, Haymarket House, 28–29 Haymarket, London, SW1Y 4SP, England. *Telephone:* (20) 7393-4400. *Fax:* (20) 7393-4401. *E-mail:* info@curtisbrown.co .uk. *Website:* www.curtisbrown.co.uk. *Website:* www.amandacraig.com.

CRAIG, George; American publishing executive. *Career:* Dir Production, Honeywell Computers Scotland 1965–74; Vice-Chair. and Group Man. Dir William Collins, UK 1974–87; Pres. and CEO Harper & Row Publrs Inc. (now HarperCollins Publrs), New York 1987–96; mem. Bd of Dirs The News Corpn Ltd; mem. Editorial Advisory Bd Publrs Weekly Int. *Address:* c/o HarperCollins Publishers, 10 East 53rd Street, New York, NY 10022, USA. *Telephone:* (212) 207-7000. *Fax:* (212) 207-7759.

CRAIG, Gordon Alexander, AB, BLitt, MA, PhD; retd academic and writer; b. 26 Nov. 1913, Glasgow, Scotland; m. Phyllis Halcomb 1939; one s. three d. *Education:* Princeton University, Balliol College, Oxford. *Career:* Instructor, Yale University, 1939–41; Instructor to Prof., Princeton University, 1941–61; Mem., Institute for Advanced Study, Princeton, NJ, 1951; Fellow, Center for Advanced Study in the Behavioral Sciences, 1956–57; Shaw Lecturer, Johns Hopkins University, 1958; Haynes Lecturer, University of California at Riverside, 1961; Prof. of History, 1961–85, J. E. Wallace Sterling Prof. of Humanities, 1969–85, Stanford University; Curti Lecturer, University of Wisconsin, 1982; mem. American Acad. of Arts and Sciences; American Historical Asscn, pres., 1982; American Philosophical Society; British Acad., fellow; Comité International des Sciences Historiques. *Publications:* The Politics of the Prussian Army, 1640–1945, 1955; From Bismarck to Adenauer: Aspects of German Statecraft, 1958; Europe Since 1815, 1961; The Battle of Königgrätz, 1964; War, Politics and Diplomacy: Selected Essays, 1966; Germany, 1866–1945, 1978; The Germans, 1982; Force and Statecraft: Diplomatic Problems of Our Time (with Alexander L. George), 1983; The End of Prussia, 1984; Geld und Geist: Zürich im Zeitalter des Liberalismus, 1830–1869, 1988, English trans. as The Triumph of Liberalism: Zürich in the Golden Age, 1830–1869, 1989; Die Politik der Unpolitischen: Deutsche Schriftsteller und die Macht, 1770–1871, 1993, English trans. as The Politics of the Unpolitical: German Writers and the Problem of Power, 1770–1871, 1995; Geneva, Zürich, Basel: History, Culture, National Identity (with Nicolas Bouvier and Lionel Grossman), 1994. Editor: Makers of Modern Strategy: Military Thought from Machiavelli to Hitler (with Edward Mead Earle and Felix Gilbert), 1943; The Diplomats, 1919–1939 (with Felix Gilbert), 1953; Treitschke's History of Modern Germany, 1975; Economic Interest, Militarism and Foreign Policy: Essays of Eckart Kehr, 1977; Makers of Modern Strategy: From Machiavelli to the Nuclear Age (with Peter Paret and Felix Gilbert), 1986; The Diplomats, 1939–1979 (with Francis L. Loewenheim), 1994; Über Fontane, 1997. *Honours:* Hon. Prof., Free University of Berlin, 1962–; Guggenheim Fellowships, 1969–70, 1982–83; Commander's Cross of the Legion of Merit, Federal Republic of Germany, 1984; Goethe Medaille, Goethe Gesellschaft, 1987; Hon. Fellow, Balliol College, Oxford, 1989–; Mem., Orden Pour le Merité für Wissenschaften und Künste, 1990–. *Address:* 451 Oak Grove Avenue, Menlo Park, CA 94025, USA.

CRAIG, Jasmine (see Cresswell, Jasmine (Rosemary)).

CRAIK, Elizabeth Mary, MA, MLitt; academic, writer and editor; *Professor of Classics, Kyoto University*; b. 25 Jan. 1939, Portmoak, Scotland; m. Alexander Craik 1964; one s. one d. *Education:* University of St Andrews, Girton College, Cambridge. *Career:* Research Fellow in Greek, University of Birmingham, 1963–64; Asst Lecturer to Senior Lecturer in Greek, University of St Andrews, 1964–97; Prof. of Classics, Kyoto University, Japan, 1997–; mem. Classical Society of Japan; Cambridge Philological Society; Hellenic Society. *Publications:* The Dorian Aegean, 1980; Marriage and Property (ed.), 1984; Euripides: Phoenician Women, 1988; Owls to Athens (ed.), 1990; Hippocrates: Places in Man, 1998; Stobaeus: The Seven Deadly Sins, 1998. Contributions: scholarly journals. *Honours:* British Acad. Awards, 1981, 1986; Carnegie Trust Award, 1986; Hon. DLitt, University of St Andrews, 2000. *Address:* Department of Classics, Faculty of Letters, Kyoto University, Kyoto 606, Japan.

CRAIK, Thomas Wallace; Prof. of English Emeritus, Writer and Ed.; b. 17 April 1927, Warrington, England; m. Wendy Ann Sowter, 25 Aug. 1955, divorced 1975, one s. *Education:* BA, English Tripos, Part 1, 1947, Part 2, 1948, MA, 1952, PhD, 1952, Christ's College, Cambridge. *Career:* Asst Lecturer, 1953, Lecturer, 1954–65, University of Leicester; Lecturer, 1965–67, Senior Lecturer, 1967–73, University of Aberdeen; Prof. of English, University of Dundee, 1973–77; Prof. of English, 1977–89, Prof. of English Emeritus, 1989–, University of Durham; mem. International Shakespeare Asscn. *Publications:* The Tudor Interlude, 1958; The Comic Tales of Chaucer, 1964. Editor: Marlowe: The Jew of Malta, 1966; Shakespeare: Twelfth Night, 1975; Beaumont and Fletcher: The Maid's Tragedy, 1988; Shakespeare: The Merry Wives of Windsor, 1989; Shakespeare: King Henry V, 1995. Contributions: scholarly journals; British Acad. Shakespeare Lecture, 1979. *Address:* 8 Little Dene, Lodore Rd, Newcastle upon Tyne NE2 3NZ, England.

CRAMER, Richard Ben, BA, MS; journalist and writer; b. 12 June 1950, Rochester, NY, USA. *Education:* Johns Hopkins Univ., Columbia Univ. *Publications:* Ted Williams: The Season of the Kid 1991, What It Takes: The Way to the White House 1992, How Israel Lost: The Four Questions 2004; contrib. to periodicals. *Honours:* journalism awards. *Literary Agent:* Sterling Lord Literistic Inc, 65 Bleecker Street, New York, NY 10012, USA.

CRANE, Hamilton (see Mason, Sarah J.).

CRANE, Richard Arthur; Writer; b. 4 Dec. 1944, York, England; m. Faynia Williams 5 Sept. 1975; two s. two step-d. *Education:* BA (Hons), Classics and English, 1966, MA, 1971, Jesus College, Cambridge. *Career:* Fellow in Theatre, University of Bradford, 1972–74; Resident Dramatist, National Theatre, 1974–75; Fellow in Creative Writing, University of Leicester, 1976; Literary Man., Royal Court Theatre, 1978–79; Assoc. Dir, Brighton Theatre, 1980–85; Dramaturg, Tron Theatre, Glasgow, 1983–84; Visiting Writers Fellowship, University of East Anglia, 1988; Writer-in-Residence, Birmingham Polytechnic, 1990–91, HM Prison Bedford, 1993; Lecturer in Creative Writing, University of Sussex, 1994–. *Publications:* Thunder, 1976; Gunslinger, 1979; Crippen, 1993; Under the Stars, 1994. Stage Plays: The Tenant, 1971; Crippen, 1971; Decent Things, 1972; Secrets, 1973; The Quest, 1974; Clownmaker, 1975; Venus and Superkid, 1975; Bloody Neighbours, 1975; Satan's Ball, 1977; Gogol, 1979; Vanity, 1980; Brothers Karamazov, 1981; The Possessed, 1985; Mutiny! (with David Essex), 1985; Soldier Soldier (with Tony Parker) 1986; Envy (with Donald Swann), 1986; Pushkin, 1987; Red Magic, 1988; Rolling the Stone, 1989; Phaedra (with Michael Glenny), 1990; Baggage and Bombshells, 1991; Under the Stars, 1993. Editor: Poems from the Waiting Room, 1993; The Last Minute Book, 1995; Pandora's Books, 1997. Television Plays: Rottingdean, 1980; The Possessed, 1985. Radio Plays: Gogol, 1980; Decent Things, 1984; Optimistic Tragedy, 1986; Anna and Marina, 1991; Understudies, 1992; Vlad the Impaler, 1992; The Sea The Sea (classic serial), 1993; Plutopia (with Donald Swann), 1994; Eugene Onegin, 1999. Contributions: Edinburgh Fringe; Guardian; Index on Censorship, TLS. *Honours:* Edinburgh Fringe First Awards, 1973, 1974, 1975, 1977, 1980, 1986, 1987, 1988, 1989. *Address:* c/o Casarotto-Ramsay Ltd, National House, 60–66 Wardour St, London W1V 3HP, England.

CRASTA, Richard, (Avatar Prabhu); Author; b. 12 May 1952, Bangalore, India; m Jovita Crasta, 10 Dec. 1978, divorced 2000, three s. *Education:* BA, University of Mysore; MA, Literature and Journalism, American University; MFA, Columbia University. *Career:* mem. PEN. *Publications:* The Revised Kama Sutra: A Novel of Colonialism and Desire, 1993; Beauty Queens, Children and the Death of Sex (essays), 1997; Eaten by the Japanese (ed. and contributor), 1998; Impressing the Whites, 2000. Contributions: periodicals.

CRAWFORD, John William, AA, BA, BSE, MSE, DEd; poet, writer and academic; *Professor of English Emeritus, Henderson State University*; b. 2 Sept. 1936, Ashdown, AR, USA; m. Kathryn Bizzell 1962; one s. one d. *Education:* Texarkana College, Ouachita Baptist College, Drake University, Oklahoma State University. *Career:* Instructor in English, Clinton Community College, 1962–66; Asst Prof., 1967–68, Assoc. Prof., 1968–73, Prof. of English, 1973–97, Chair., Dept of English, 1977–86, Prof. Emeritus, 1997–, Henderson State University; mem. Arkansas Philological Asscn; College English Asscn; Poets' Roundtable of Arkansas; South Central MLA. *Publications:* Poetry: Making The Connection, 1989; I Have Become Acquainted With the Rain, 1997. Non-Fiction: Shakespeare's Comedies: A Guide, 1968; Shakespeare's Tragedies: A Guide, 1968; Steps to Success: A Study Skills Handbook, 1976; Discourse: Essays on English and American Literature, 1978; Romantic Criticism of Shakespearean Drama, 1978; Early Shakespearian Actresses, 1984; The Learning, Wit and Wisdom of Shakespeare's Renaissance Women, 1997. Contributions: anthologies, reviews, quarterlies, journals, etc. *Honours:* Sybil Nash Abrams Prizes, 1982, 1995; Merit Award, Poets' Roundtable of Arkansas, 1988; Arkansas Haiku Society Award, 1998. *Address:* PO Box 1813 Walnut, Arkadelphia, AR 71923, USA.

CRAWFORD, Robert; University Prof. of English, Writer and Poet; b. 23 Feb. 1959, Bellshill, Scotland; m. Alice Wales, 2 Sept. 1988. *Education:* MA, 1981; DPhil, 1985. *Career:* Elizabeth Wordsworth Junior Research Fellow, Oxford, 1984–87; British Acad. Postdoctoral Fellow, Glasgow University, 1987–89; Lecturer, 1989–95, Prof. of English, 1995–, Modern Scottish Literature, University of St Andrews; mem. English Asscn; Royal Society of Edinburgh. *Publications:* Poetry: A Scottish Assembly, 1990; Sharawaggi (with W. N. Herbert), 1990; Talkies, 1992; Masculinity, 1996; Spirit

Machines, 1999; The Tip of My Tongue, 2003. Prose: The Savage and the City in the Work of T. S. Eliot, 1987; Devolving English Literature, 1992; Identifying Poets: Self and Territory in Twentieth Century Poetry, 1993; The Modern Poet, 2001. Contributions: anthologies, including: Other Tongues, 1990; The Penguin Book of Poetry from Britain and Ireland since 1945 (ed. with Simon Armitage), 1998; The New Penguin Book of Scottish Verse (with Mick Imlah), 2000; Scottish Religious Poetry (ed. with Meg Bateman and James McGonigal), 2000. *Honours:* Gregory Award; Poetry Book Society Recommendations; Selected for Arts Council of Great Britain's New Generation Poets, 1994; Scottish Arts Council Book Award. *Literary Agent:* David Godwin Associates, 55 Monmouth St, London WC2H 9DG, England. *Address:* School of English, University of St Andrews, Fife KY16 9AL, Scotland.

CRAWFORD, Robert (see Rae, Hugh Crauford).

CRAWFORD, Thomas; Hon; b. 6 July 1920, Dundee, Scotland; Reader in English; Author. m. Jean Rennie McBride, 19 Aug. 1946, one s. one d. *Education:* MA, University of Edinburgh, 1944; MA, University of Auckland, 1953. *Career:* Lecturer, 1953–60, Senior Lecturer, 1961–62, Assoc. Prof. of English, 1962–65, University of Auckland; Lecturer in English, University of Edinburgh, 1965; Commonwealth Research Fellow, McMaster University, Hamilton, Ontario, Canada, 1966–67; Reader in English, 1967–85, Hon. Reader in English, 1985–, University of Aberdeen; Ed., Scottish Literary Journal, 1974–84; mem. Asscn for Scottish Literary Studies, pres., 1984–88; Saltire Society; Scots Language Society; Scottish Text Society. *Publications:* Burns: A Study of the Poems, 1960; Scott, 1965; Sir Walter Scott: Selected Poems (ed.), 1972; Love, Labour, and Liberty, 1976; Society and the Lyric, 1979; Longer Scottish Poems 1650–1830, 1987; Boswell, Burns and the French Revolution, 1989; The Correspondence of James Boswell and William Johnson Temple 1756–1795: Vol. I, 1756–1777 (ed.), 1997. Contributions: scholarly journals. *Address:* 34 Summerhill Terrace, Aberdeen AB15 6HE, Scotland.

CRAY, Robert (see Emerson, Ru).

CREASEY, Jeanne (see Williams, Jeanne R.).

CRECY, Jeanne (see Williams, Jeanne R.).

CREECH, Sharon, BA, MA; American children's writer; b. 29 July 1945, Cleveland, OH; m.; one s. one d. *Education:* Hiram Coll., George Mason Univ. *Career:* fmr teacher, editorial asst, indexer, researcher. *Publications:* Absolutely Normal Chaos 1990, Walk Two Moons 1994, Pleasing the Ghost 1995, The Ghost of Uncle Arvie 1996, Chasing Redbird 1997, Bloomability 1998, The Wanderer 2000, Fishing in the Air 2000, A Fine Fine School 2001, Love That Dog 2001, Granny Torrelli Makes Soup 2003, Ruby Holler 2002, Heartbeat 2004. *Honours:* US Newbery Medal 1995, 2001, Claudia Lewis Poetry Award 2002, Christopher Award 2002, Mitten Award 2002, Carnegie Award. *Address:* c/o Bloomsbury Publishing PLC, 38 Soho Square, London, W1V 5DF, England. *Telephone:* (20) 7494-2111. *Fax:* (20) 7434-0151. *Website:* www.bloomsbury.com.

CREELEY, Robert White, MA; writer, poet and academic; b. 21 May 1926, Arlington, Massachusetts, USA; m. 1st Ann McKinnon 1946 (divorced 1955); two s. one d.; m. 2nd Bobbie Louise Hall 1957 (divorced 1976); four d.; m. 3rd Penelope Highton 1977; one s. one d. *Education:* Harvard Univ., Black Mountain Coll., Univ. of New Mexico. *Career:* teacher, Black Mountain Coll. 1954–55; Lecturer, Univ. of British Columbia 1962–63; Visiting Lecturer, Univ. of New Mexico 1961–62, Lecturer 1963–66, Visiting Prof. 1968–69, 1979, 1980, 1981; Visiting Prof. SUNY at Buffalo 1966–67, Prof. 1967–78, David Gray Prof. of Poetry and Letters 1978–89, Samuel P. Capen Prof. of Poetry and Humanities 1989–2004, Dir Poetics Programme 1990–99; Visiting Prof., San Francisco State Coll. 1970–71, Univ. of Maine at Orono 2000–02; Advisory Ed., American Book Review 1983–, Sagetrieb 1983–, New York Quarterly 1984–; Chancellor, Acad. of American Poets 1999–2002; lectures and readings at univs and community centres, tours world-wide; mem. American Acad. of Arts and Letters, American Acad. of Arts and Sciences, PEN American Center. *Publications:* poetry: For Love, Poems 1950–60 1962, Words 1967, Pieces 1969, A Day Book 1972, Selected Poems 1976, Hello 1978, Later 1979, Mirrors 1983, Collected Poems 1945–75 1983, Memory Gardens 1986, Windows 1990, Echoes 1994, Life and Death 1998, So There, Poems 1976–1983 1998, Just in Time, Poems 1984–1994 2001, If I Were Writing This 2003; prose: The Island 1963, The Gold Diggers 1965, Mabel: A Story 1976, The Collected Prose 1984, Tales Out of School 1993; criticism: A Quick Graph 1970, Was That a Real Poem and Other Essays 1976, Collected Essays 1989, 2003, Day Book of a Virtual Poet 1998, Autobiography 1990; editor: Selected Writings of Charles Olson 1967, Whitman, Selected Poems 1973, The Essential Burns 1989, Charles Olson, Selected Poems 1993, George Oppen Selected Poems 2003. *Honours:* Bicentennial Chair of American Studies, Univ. of Helsinki 1988, Distinguished Prof., SUNY 1989, Hon. DLitt (New Mexico) 1993; Guggenheim Fellowships 1964, 1967, Rockefeller Grantee 1965, Shelley Memorial Award 1981, Frost Medal, 1987, Poetry Soc. of America, Nat. Endowment for the Arts grant 1982, Berlin Artists Programme grants 1983, 1987, Leone d'Oro Premio Speziale 1984, Distinguished Fulbright Award, Walt Whitman Citation State Poet of New York 1989–91, Horst Bienek Preis für Lyrik Munich 1993, Fulbright Award Univ. of Auckland 1995, America Award in Poetry 1995, Lila Wallace-Reader's Digest Writer's Award 1996, Bollingen Prize 1999, American Book Award Before Columbus Foundation 2000, Golden Rose Award New England Poetry Club 2001, Lifetime Achievement Award Lannan Foundation 2001, Bogliasco Foundation Fellowship 2002. *Literary Agent:* Steven Barclay Agency, 12 Western Avenue, Petaluma, CA 94952, USA. *Telephone:* (707) 773-0654. *Fax:* (707) 778-1868. *Website:* www.barclayagency.com. *Address:* Brown University, PO Box 1852, Providence, RI 02912, USA.

CREGIER, Don Mesick, BA, MA, PhD; historian and writer; b. 28 March 1930, Schenectady, NY, USA; m. Sharon Kathleen Ellis 1965. *Education:* Union College, New York, University of Michigan, Columbia Pacific University. *Career:* Asst Instructor, Clark University, Worcester, Massachusetts, 1952–54; Instructor, University of Tennessee at Martin, 1956–57; Asst Prof., Baker University, Baldwin, KS, 1958–61; Asst Prof., Keuka College, Keuka Park, New York, 1962–64; Visiting Asst Prof., St John's University, Collegeville, Minnesota, 1964–65; Senior Fellow and Tutor, Mark Hopkins College, Brattleboro, Vermont, 1965–66; Assoc. Prof., St Dunstan's University, Charlottetown, PE, 1966–69; Assoc. Prof., 1969–85, Prof. of History, 1985–96, Adjunct Prof., 1996–2002, University of Prince Edward Island; Abstractor, ABC/Clio Information Services, 1978–; Foreign Book Review Ed., Canadian Review of Studies in Nationalism, 1996–98; mem. Historical Society; American Historical Asscn; Society for Academic Freedom and Scholarship; Canadian Asscn of University Teachers; Mark Twain Society; North American Conference on British Studies. *Publications:* Bounder from Wales: Lloyd George's Career Before the First World War, 1976; Novel Exposures: Victorian Studies Featuring Contemporary Novels, 1979; Chiefs Without Indians: Asquith, Lloyd George, and the Liberal Remnant, 1916–1935, 1982; The Decline of the British Liberal Party: Why and How?, 1985; Freedom and Order: The Growth of British Liberalism Before 1868, 1988; The Rise of the Global Village (co-author), 1988. Contributions: Reference works and professional journals. *Honours:* Mark Hopkins Fellow, 1965; Canada Council Fellow, 1972, Research Grant, Social Sciences and Humanities Research Council of Canada, 1984–86. *Address:* PO Box 1100, Montague, PE COA 1RO, Canada. *E-mail:* dcregier@upei.ca.

CREMONA, John Joseph; fmr chief justice, academic, historian and poet; b. 6 Jan. 1918, Gozo, Malta; m. Marchioness Beatrice Barbaro of St George 1949; one s. two d. *Education:* BA, 1939, LLD, cum laude, 1942, University of Malta; DLitt, University of Rome, 1939; BA, 1946, PhD, Law, 1951, University of London. *Career:* Crown Counsel, 1947; Lecturer in Constitutional Law, Royal University of Malta, 1947–65; Attorney General, 1957–64; Prof. of Criminal Law, 1959–65, Prof. Emeritus, 1965–, Pro-Chancellor, 1971–74, University of Malta; Crown Advocate-General, 1964–65; Vice-Pres., Constitutional Court and Court of Appeal, 1965–71; Judge, 1965–92, Vice-Pres., 1986–92, European Court of Human Rights; Chief Justice and Pres., Constitutional Court, Court of Appeal, and Court of Criminal Appeal, 1971–81; Judge, 1986–92, Vice-Pres., 1986–92, European Tribunal in Matters of State Immunity; mem. FRHistS; Human rights and environmental organizations. *Publications:* Non-Fiction: The Treatment of Young Offenders in Malta, 1956; The Malta Constitution of 1835, 1959; The Legal Consequences of a Conviction in the Criminal Law of Malta, 1962; The Constitutional Development of Malta, 1963; From the Declaration of Rights to Independence, 1965; Human Rights Documentation in Malta, 1966; Selected Papers, 1946–89, 1990; The Maltese Constitution and Constitutional History, 1994; Malta and Britain: The Early Constitutions, 1996. Poetry: Eliotropi, 1937; Songbook of the South, 1940; Limestone 84 (with others), 1978; Malta Malta, 1992. Contributions: Law reviews. *Honours:* Knight of Magisterial Grace, Sovereign Military Order of Malta; Companion of the National Order of Merit of Malta; Chevalier, Légion d'honneur; Knight of the Grand Cross, Order of Merit, Italy; Hon. Fellow, LSE. *Address:* Villa Barbaro, Main Street, Attard, Malta.

CRESSWELL, Helen; Author; b. 11 July 1934, Nottinghamshire, England; m. Brian Rowe, 14 Aug. 1962, divorced 1995, two d. *Education:* BA, English, King's College, London. *Publications:* Sonya-by-the-Shire, 1961; Jumbo Spencer, 1963; The White Sea Horse, 1964; Pietro and the Mule, 1965; Jumbo Back to Nature, 1965; Where the Wind Blows, 1966; Jumbo Afloat, 1966; The Piemakers, 1967; A Tide for the Captain, 1967; The Signposters, 1968; The Sea Piper, 1968; The Barge Children, 1968; The Nightwatchman, 1969; A Game of Catch, 1969; A Gift from Winklesea, 1969; The Outlanders, 1970; The Wilkses, 1970; The Bird Fancier, 1971; At the Stroke of Midnight, 1971; The Beachcombers, 1972; Lizzie Dripping, 1972; Thee Bongleweed, 1972; Lizzie Dripping Again, 1974; Butterfly Chase, 1975; The Winter of the Birds, 1975; The Bagthorpe Saga, 7 parts, 1977–88; My Aunt Polly, 1979; My Aunt Polly By the Sea, 1980; Dear Shrink, 1982; The Secret World of Polly Flint, 1982; Ellie and the Hagwitch, 1984; Time Out, 1987; Whodunnit, 1987; Moondial, 1987; Two Hoots, 1988; The Story of Grace Darling, 1988; Dragon Ride, 1988; Trouble, 1988; Rosie and the Boredom Eater, 1989; Whatever Happened in Winklesea?, 1989; Meet Posy Bates, 1990; Hokey Pokey Did It!, 1990; Posy Bates Again, 1991; Lizzie Dripping and the Witch, 1991; Posy Bates and the Bag Lady, 1992; The Watchers, 1993; Classic Fairy Tales Retold, 1993; The Little Sea More, 1995; Stonestruck, 1995; Mystery at Winklesea, 1995; Polly Thumb, 1995; Giant, 1996. *Address:* Old Church Farm, Eakring, Newark, Notts NG22 0DA, England.

CRESSWELL, Jasmine Rosemary, (Jasmine Craig), BA, MA; American writer; b. 14 Jan. 1941, Dolgelly, Wales; m. Malcolm Candlish 1963; one s.

three d. *Education:* University of Melbourne, Macquarie University, Case Western Reserve University. *Career:* mem. Authors' Guild, Colorado Authors' League, Novelists Inc (founder and past pres.), Rocky Mountain Fiction Writers. *Publications include:* Nowhere to Hide, 1992; Keeping Secrets, 1993; Eternity, 1994; Desires and Deceptions, 1995; No Sin Too Great, 1996; Secret Sins, 1997; The Daughter, 1998; The Disappearance, 1999; The Conspiracy, 2001; The Third Wife, 2002. *Honours:* Colorado Romance Writer of the Year Awards 1986, 1987. *Literary Agent:* Dominick Abel Literary Agency Inc, 146 W 82nd Street, No. 1B, New York, NY 10024, USA.

CREWE, Quentin Hugh; Author and Journalist; b. 14 Nov. 1926, London, England; two s. three d. *Education:* Eton College, 1940–45; Trinity College, Cambridge, 1945–46. *Career:* mem. FRSL. *Publications:* A Curse of Blossom, 1960; The Frontiers of Privilege, 1961; Great Chefs of France, 1978; International Pocket Book of Food, 1980; In Search of the Sahara, 1983; The Last Maharaja, 1985; Touch the Happy Isles, 1987; In the Realms of Gold, 1989–; Well I Forget the Rest (autobiog.), 1991; Foods from France, 1993; Crewe House, 1995; Letters from India, 1998. Contributions: Queen; Vogue; Spectator; Daily Mail; Times; Evening Standard. *Address:* 9 Bliss Mill, Chipping Norton, Oxfordshire OX7 5JR, England.

CREWS, Frederick Campbell; academic and writer; b. 20 Feb. 1933, Philadelphia, PA, USA; m. Elizabeth Peterson 1959; two d. *Education:* BA, Yale University, 1955; PhD, Princeton University, 1958. *Career:* Instructor, 1958–60, Asst Prof., 1960–62, Assoc. Prof., 1962–66, Prof. of English, 1966–94, Prof. Emeritus, 1994–, University of California at Berkeley; Ward-Phillips Lecturer, University of Notre Dame, 1974–75; Dorothy T. Burstein Lecturer, University of California at Los Angeles, 1984; Frederick Ives Carpenter Visiting Prof., University of Chicago, 1985; Nina Mae Kellogg Lecturer, Portland State University, Oregon, 1989; David L. Kubal Memorial Lecturer, California State University, Los Angeles, 1994; mem. American Acad. of Arts and Sciences, fellow; Committee for the Scientific Investigation of Claims of the Paranormal, advisory board. *Publications:* The Tragedy of Manners, 1957; E. M. Forster: The Perils of Humanism, 1962; The Pooh Perplex, 1963; The Sins of the Fathers, 1966; Starting Over (ed.), 1970; Psychoanalysis and Literary Process (ed.), 1970; The Random House Handbook, 1974; The Random House Reader (ed.), 1981; Out of My System, 1975; The Borzoi Handbook for Writers (co-author), 1985; Skeptical Engagements, 1986; The Critics Bear It Away, 1992; The Memory Wars (co-author), 1995; Unauthorized Freud (ed.), 1998; Postmodern Pooh, 2001. Contributions: scholarly journals and to magazines. *Honours:* Fulbright Lecturer, Turin, 1961–62; ACLS Fellow, 1965–66; Center for Advanced Study in the Behavioral Sciences Fellow, 1965–66; Guggenheim Fellowship, 1970–71; Distinguished Teaching Award, University of California at Berkeley, 1985; Spielvogel Diamonstein PEN Prize, 1992. *Address:* 636 Vincente Avenue, Berkeley, CA 94707, USA.

CREWS, Harry (Eugene); Prof. of English and Writer; b. 6 June 1935, Alma, GA, USA; m. Sally Thornton Ellis, 24 Jan. 1960, divorced, two s. *Education:* BA, 1960, MSEd, 1962, University of Florida. *Career:* Teacher of English, Broward Junior College, Fort Lauderdale, 1962–68; Assoc. Prof., 1968–74, Prof. of English, 1974–, University of Florida, Gainesville. *Publications:* The Gospel Singer, 1968; Naked in Garden Hills, 1969; This Thing Don't Lead to Heaven, 1970; Karate is a Thing of the Spirit, 1971; Car, 1972; The Hawk is Dying, 1973; The Gypsy's Curse, 1974; A Feast of Snakes, 1976; A Childhood: The Biography of a Place, 1978; Blood and Grits, 1979; The Enthusiast, 1981; Florida Frenzy, 1982; A Grit's Triumph, 1983; Two, 1984; All We Need of Hell, 1987; The Knockout Artist, 1988; Body, 1990; Scar Lover, 1992; Celebrations, 1998.

CRICHTON, (John) Michael, (Michael Douglas, Jeffrey Hudson, John Lange), AB, MD; American film director and writer; b. 23 Oct. 1942, Chicago, IL; m. Anne-Marie Martin Crichton (divorced); one d. *Education:* Harvard Univ., Salk Inst. for Biological Sciences, CA. *Career:* Henry Russell Shaw Travelling Fellow 1964–65; Visiting Lecturer in Anthropology, Univ. of Cambridge 1965; visiting writer, MIT 1988; mem. Authors' Guild (council 1995–), Writers' Guild of America, Dirs' Guild of America, Acad. of Motion Picture Arts and Sciences, PEN American Center, Acad. of Television Arts and Sciences. *Film screenplays:* The Andromeda Strain 1971, Westworld (also dir) 1973, Terminal Man 1974, Coma (also dir) 1977, The Great Train Robbery (also dir) 1978, Looker (also dir) 1981, Runaway (also dir) 1984, Rising Sun (co-writer) 1993, Jurassic Park (co-writer) 1993, Disclosure 1995, Congo 1995, Twister (co-writer) 1996, The Lost World 1997, Sphere 1997, Thirteenth Warrior 1999. *Television:* creator and exec. prod. ER 1994–. *Publications:* fiction: The Andromeda Strain 1969, The Terminal Man 1972, The Great Train Robbery 1975, Eaters of the Dead 1976, Congo 1980, Sphere 1987, Jurassic Park 1990, Rising Sun 1992, Disclosure 1993, The Lost World 1995, Airframe 1996, Timeline 1999, Prey 2002; as Michael Douglas: Dealing, or Berkeley-to-Boston Forty-Brick Lost-Bag Blues 1971; as Jeffery Hudson: A Case of Need 1968; as John Lange: Odds On 1966, Scratch One 1967, Easy Go 1968, The Venom Business 1969, Zero Cool 1969, Grave Descend 1970, Drug of Choice 1970, Binary 1972; non-fiction: Five Patients 1970, Jasper Johns 1977, Electronic Life 1983, Travels 1988. *Honours:* MWA Edgar Allan Poe Awards 1968, 1980, Asscn of American Medical Writers Award 1970, Acad. of Motion Picture Arts and Sciences Technical Achievement Award 1995, George Foster Peabody Award, Writer's Guild of America Award for best long form television script 1995, Emmy Award for Best Dramatic Series 1996, Ankylosaur named Bienosaurus crichtoni 2000. *Literary Agent:* International Creative Management, 40 W 57th Street, New York, NY 10025, USA. *E-mail:* info@crichton-official.com. *Website:* www.crichton-official.com.

CRICK, Bernard; Emeritus Prof. and Writer; b. 16 Dec. 1929, England. *Education:* University College London. *Career:* Political writer, biographer and journalist; Literary Ed., Political Quarterly; Prof. of Politics, Birkbeck College, London, 1971–84; Emeritus Prof., University of London, 1993–. *Publications:* The American Science of Politics, 1958; In Defence of Politics, 1962; The Reform of Parliament, 1964; Theory and Practice: Essays in Politics, 1972; Basic Forms of Government, 1973; Crime, Rape and Gin: Reflections on Contemporary Attitudes to Violence, Pornography and Addiction, 1977; Political Education and Political Literacy, 1978; George Orwell: A Life, 1980; Orwell Remembered (co-ed.), 1984; Socialism, 1987; Politics and Literature, 1987; Political Thoughts and Polemics, 1990; National Identities (ed.), 1991. *Honours:* Hon. Fellow, Birkbeck College; Hon. doctorates, Queens University, Belfast, Universities of Sheffield, East London, Kingston. *Address:* 8A Bellevue Terrace, Edinburgh EH7 4DT, Scotland.

CRICK, Donald Herbert; Writer; b. 16 July 1916, Sydney, NSW, Australia; m. 24 Dec. 1943, one d. *Career:* mem. Australian Society of Authors, board of management. *Publications:* Fiction: Bikini Girl, 1963; Martin Place, 1964; Period of Adjustment, 1966; A Different Drummer, 1972; The Moon to Play With, 1981. Screenplays: The Veronica, 1983; A Different Drummer, 1985; The Moon to Play With, 1987. Contributions: Sydney Morning Herald; The Australian; Overland; The Australian Author. *Honours:* Mary Gilmore Centenary Award, Novel, 1966; Rigby Anniversary Award, Novel, 1980; Awgie Screenplay Award, 1983–85. *Address:* 1/1 Elamang Ave, Kirribilli, NSW 2061, Australia.

CRISCUOLO, Anthony Thomas, (Tony Crisp); Writer; b. 10 May 1937, Amersham, Buckinghamshire, England; four s. one d. *Publications:* Yoga and Relaxation, 1970; Do You Dream?, 1971; Yield, 1974; Yoga and Childbirth, 1975; The Instant Dream Book, 1984; Mind and Movement, 1987; Dream Dictionary, 1990; Liberating the Body, 1992; The Hand Book, 1994; Superminds, 1998; Dreams and Dreaming, 1999; Coincidences, 2000; Dream Power, 2003. Contributions: newspapers, journals, radio and television. *Address:* 1 Troedyrhiw, Caerlan, Abercrave, Swansea SA9 1SX, Wales. *Telephone:* (1639) 731091. *E-mail:* tony@dreamhawk.com. *Website:* www.dreamhawk.com.

CRISP, Tony (see Criscuolo, Anthony Thomas).

CRISPIN, Suzy (see Cartwright, Justin).

CRITCHLEY, Sir Julian (Michael Gordon); Writer, Broadcaster and Journalist; b. 8 Dec. 1930, Chelsea, London, England; m. 1st Paula Joan Baron, 1955, divorced 1965, two d.; m. 2nd Heather Goodrick, 1965, one s. one d. *Education:* Sorbonne, University of Paris; MA, Pembroke College, Oxford. *Career:* MP, Conservative Party, Rochester and Chatham, 1959–64, Aldershot and North Hants, 1970–74, Aldershot, 1974–97; Chair., Western European Union Defence Committee, 1975–79, Conservative Party Media Committee, 1976–81; Steward, British Boxing Board of Control, 1987–91; Judge, Whitbread Book of the Year Competition, 1996; mem. various professional organizations. *Publications:* Collective Security (with O. Pick), 1974; Warning and Response, 1978; The North Atlantic Alliance and the Soviet Union in the 1980s, 1982; Nuclear Weapons in Europe (co-author), 1984; Westminster Blues, 1985; Britain: A View from Westminster (ed.), 1986; Heseltine: The Unauthorized Biography, 1987; Palace of Varieties: An Insider's View of Westminster, 1989; Hung Parliament, 1991; Floating Voter, 1992; A Bag of Boiled Sweets (autobiog.), 1995–96; Borderlands, 1996; Collapse of Start Party (with Morrison Halnow), 1997. Contributions: Books and periodicals. *Honours:* Political Journalist of the Year, 1985; Knighted, 1995. *Address:* 19 Broad St, Ludlow SY8 1NG, England.

CRITCHLOW, Donald T.; Historian, Writer and Ed.; b. 18 May 1948, Pasadena, CA, USA; m. Patricia Critchlow, 1978, two d. *Education:* BA, San Francisco State University, 1970; MA, History, 1972, PhD, History, 1978, University of California at Berkeley. *Career:* Teaching Asst, 1974, Research Asst, Institute of Industrial Relations, 1975, Acting Instructor in Environmental Studies, 1977, University of California at Berkeley; Acting Instructor in History, San Francisco State University, 1976; Asst Prof. of History, North Central College, Napierville, IL, 1978–81, University of Dayton, 1981–83; Asst Prof., then Assoc. Prof. of History, University of Notre Dame, 1983–91; Ed., Journal of Policy History; Series Ed., Critical Issues in European and American History. *Publications:* The Brookings Institution, 1916–1952: Expertise and the Public Interest in a Democratic Society, 1985; Socialism in the Heartland: The Midwestern Experience, 1890–1920 (ed.), 1986; Federal Social Policy: The Historical Dimension (co-ed.), 1989; Poverty and Public Policy in Modern America (co-ed.), 1989; America! A Concise History (co-author), 1995; Studebaker: The Life and Death of an American Corporation, 1996; The Politics of Abortion and Birth Control in Historical Perspective (ed.), 1996; The Serpentine Way: Family Planning Policy in Postwar America: Elites, Agendas, and Political Mobilization, 1997. *Address:* 2623 Colston, Chevy Chase, MD 20815, USA.

CROFT, Andy; Poet and Writer; b. 13 June 1956, Handforth, Cheshire, England; m. Nikki Wray, four s., two d. *Education:* BA, 1978, PhD, 1986,

University of Nottingham. *Career:* Full-time Lecturer, University of Leeds, 1983–96; Writer-in-Residence, Great North Run, 2000, HMP Holme House, 2000–; mem. Chair., Artistic Dir, Write Around Festival, 1989–99. *Publications:* Red Letter Days, 1990; Out of the Old Earth, 1994; The Big Meeting, 1994; Nowhere Special, 1996; Gaps Between Hills, 1996; A Weapon in the Struggle, 1998; Selected Poems of Randall Swingler, 2000; Just as Blue, 2001; Great North, 2001; Headland, 2001. Contributions: The Guardian; The Independent; London Magazine; Marxism Today; Labour History Review; The Listener; The New Statesman. *Address:* c/o Cleveland Arts, Gurney House, Gurney St, Middlesbrough TS1 1JL, England.

CROFT, Julian (Charles Basset); Prof. and Writer; b. 31 May 1941, Newcastle, NSW, Australia; m. 1st Loretta De Plevitz, 23 Oct. 1967, one s.; m. 2nd Caroline Ruming, 12 Dec. 1987, one s. *Education:* BA, University of New South Wales, 1961; MA, University of Newcastle, NSW, 1966. *Career:* Lecturer, University of Sierra Leone, 1968–70; Assoc. Prof., 1970–94, Prof., 1994–, University of New England, Armidale, Australia; mem. Asscn for the Study of Australian Literature. *Publications:* T. J. Jones, 1975; The Collected Poems of T. Harri James (ed. with Don Dale-Jones), 1976; Breakfasts in Shanghai (poems), 1984; Their Solitary Way (novel), 1985; The Portable Robert D. FitzGerald (ed.), 1987; Confessions of a Corinthian, 1991; The Life and Opinions of Tom Collins, 1991; After a War (Any War), 2002. *Address:* Dept of English, University of New England, Armidale 2351, Australia.

CRONIN, Anthony; Author and Poet; b. 23 Dec. 1928, Enniscorthy, County Wexford, Ireland; m. Thérèse Campbell, 1955, two d. *Education:* BA, University College, Dublin, 1948. *Career:* Visiting Lecturer, University of Montana, 1966–68; Poet-in-Residence, Drake University, 1968–70; Columnist, Irish Times, 1973–86; Cultural Adviser, Irish Prime Minister, 1980–83, 1987–92. *Publications:* Poems, 1957; Collected Poems, 1950–73, 1973; Reductionist Poem, 1980; RMS Titanic, 1981; 41 Sonnet Poems, 1982; New & Selected Poems, 1982; Letter to an Englishman, 1985; The End of the Modern World, 1989. Fiction: The Life of Riley, 1964; Identity Papers, 1979. Biography: No Laughing Matter: The Life and Times of Flann O'Brian, 1989. Memoir: Dead as Doornails, 1976. Essays: Heritage Now, 1983; An Irish Eye, 1985; Samuel Beckett: The Last Modernist, 1996. *Honours:* Marten Toonder Award, 1983. *Address:* 9 Rainsford Ave, Dublin 8, Ireland.

CRONIN, Vincent Archibald Patrick; Author; b. 24 May 1924, Tredegar, Wales; m. Chantal De Rolland, 25 Aug. 1949, two s. three d. *Education:* Harvard University, 1941–43; BA, Trinity College, Oxford, 1947. *Publications:* The Golden Honeycomb, 1954; The Wise Man from the West, 1955; The Last Migration, 1957; A Pear to India, 1959; The Letter after Z, 1960; Louis XIV, 1964; Four Women in Pursuit of an Ideal, 1965; The Florentine Renaissance, 1967; The Flowering of the Renaissance, 1970; Napoleon, 1971; Louis and Antoinette, 1974; Catherine, Empress of all the Russias, 1978; The View from Planet Earth, 1981; Paris on the Eve, 1989; Paris: City of Light 1919–1939, 1995. *Address:* Manor de Brion, Dragey Par, 50530 Sartilly, France.

CRONON, William John; academic and writer; b. 11 Sept. 1954, New Haven, CT, USA; m. Nancy Elizabeth Fey 1977; one s. one d. *Education:* BA, University of Wisconsin at Madison, 1976; MA, 1979, MPhil, 1980, PhD, 1990, Yale University; DPhil, University of Oxford, 1981. *Career:* Asst Prof., 1981–86, Assoc. Prof., 1986–91, Prof. of History, 1991–92, Yale University; Frederick Jackson Turner Prof. of History, Geography, and Environmental Studies, University of Wisconsin at Madison, 1992–; mem. Agricultural History Society; American Anthropological Asscn; American Antiquarian Society; American Historical Asscn; American Society for Environmental History; American Society for Ethnohistory; American Studies Asscn; Asscn of American Geographers; Ecological Society of America; Economic History Asscn; Forest History Society; Organization of American Historians; Society of American Historians; Urban History Asscn. *Publications:* Changes in the Land: Indians, Colonists, and the Ecology of New England, 1983; Nature's Metropolis: Chicago and the Great West, 1991; Under an Open Sky: Rethinking America's Western Past (co-ed. with George Miles and Jay Gitlin), 1992; Uncommon Ground: Toward Reinventing Nature (ed.), 1995. Contributions: Books and scholarly journals. *Honours:* Rhodes Scholarship, 1976–78; Francis Parkman Prize, 1984; Bancroft Prize, 1992; George Perkins Marsh Prize, American Society for Environmental History, 1992; Charles A Weyerhaeuser Award, Forest History Society, 1993; Guggenheim Fellowship, 1995. *Address:* c/o Dept of History, 3211 Humanities Building, 455 N Park Street, University of Wisconsin at Madison, Madison, WI 53706, USA.

CROOK, Joseph Mordaunt, CBE, BA, MA, DPhil, FBA; academic and writer; *Emeritus Professor of Architectural History, Royal Holloway and Bedford New College*; b. 27 Feb. 1937, London, England; m. 1st Margaret Mullholland 1964; m. 2nd Susan Mayor 1975. *Education:* Wimbledon College, Univ. of Oxford. *Career:* Asst Lecturer, Univ. of Leicester, 1963–65; Lecturer, 1965–75, Reader in Architectural History, 1975–81, Bedford College, London; Ed., Architectural History, 1967–75; Slade Prof. of Fine Art, Univ. of Oxford, 1979–80; Visiting Fellow, Brasenose College, Oxford, 1979–80, Humanities Research Centre, Australian National Univ., Canberra, 1985, Gonville and Caius College, Cambridge, 1986; Prof. of Architectural History, 1981–99, Emeritus Prof., 1999–, Dir, Victorian Studies Centre, 1990–99, Royal Holloway and Bedford New College; Waynflete Lecturer and Visiting Fellow, Magdalen College, Oxford, 1984–85; Public Orator, Univ. of London, 1988–90; Humanities Fellow, Princeton Univ., 1990; Supernumerary Fellow, Brasenose College, Oxford, 2002–; mem. council, British Acad. 1989–92; mem. Historic Buildings Council for England, 1974–80; Society of Architectural Historians of Great Britain, exec. committee, 1964–77, pres., 1980–84; Victorian Society, exec. committee, 1970–77, council, 1978–88. *Publications:* The Greek Revival, 1968; Victorian Architecture: A Visual Anthology, 1971; The British Museum, 1972; The Greek Revival: Neo-Classical Attitudes in British Architecture 1760–1870, 1973; The Reform Club, 1973; The History of the King' Works (co-author), Vol. VI, 1973, Vol. V, 1976; William Burges and the High Victorian Dream, 1981; Axel Haig and the Victorian Vision of the Middle Ages (co-author), 1984; The Dilemma of Style: Architectural Ideas from the Picturesque to the Post-Modern, 1987; John Carter and the Mind of the Gothic Revival, 1995; The Rise of the Nouveaux Riches: Style and Status in Victorian and Edwardian Architecture, 1999; The Architects' Secret: Victorian Critics and the Image of Gravity, 2003. Editor: Eastlake: A History of the Gothic Revival, 1970; Kerr: The Gentleman's House, 1972; The Strange Genius of William Burges, 1981; Clark: The Gothic Revival, 1995. Contributions: books and scholarly journals. *Honours:* Hitchcock Medallion, 1974; Freeman, 1979, Liveryman, 1984, Worshipful Company of Goldsmiths. *Address:* 55 Gloucester Avenue, London NW1 7BA, England.

CROOKER, Barbara Poti; College Instructor, Writer and Poet; b. 21 Nov. 1945, Cold Spring, NY, USA; m. Richard McMaster Crooker, 26 July 1975, one s., three d. *Education:* BA, Douglass College, Rutgers University, 1967; MS Education, Elmira College, 1975. *Career:* Instructor, County College of Morris, 1978–79, Women's Center, Cedar Crest College, 1982–85, Lehigh Community College, 1993, Cedar Crest College, 1999–; Asst Prof., Northampton County Area Community College, 1980–82; Artist-in-Education (poet in the schools), 1989–93; mem. Poetry Society of America; Acad. of American Poets. *Publications:* Writing Home, 1983; Starting from Zero, 1987; Looking for the Comet Halley, 1987; The Lost Children, 1989; Obbligato, 1992; Moving Poems; In the Late Summer Garden, 1998; Ordinary Life, 2001; The White Poems, 2001; Paris, 2002; Greatest Hits, 2003. Contributions: anthologies, reviews, quarterlies, journals and magazines. *Honours:* Pennsylvania Council on the Arts Fellowships, 1985, 1989, 1993; Winner, Passages North and National Endowment for the Arts Emerging Writers Competition, 1987; Phillips Award, Stone Country, 1988; Virginia Center for the Creative Arts Fellowships, 1990, 1992, 1994, 1995, 1997, 1998, 2000, 2001, 2003; First Prize, Karamu Poetry Contest, 1997; Hon. Mention and Special Mention, Comstock Prize, 1998; First Place, Y2K Writing Prize, New Millennium Writings, 2000; Grand Prize Winner, Dancing Poetry Contest, 2000; Winner, Byline Chapbook Competition, 2001; winner, April is the Cruelest Month competition, 2003; Thomas Merton Poetry of the Sacred Prize, 2003. *Address:* 7928 Woodsbluff Run, Fogelsville, PA 18051, USA. *E-mail:* bcrooker@ix.netcom.com.

CROSBY, Harry Clifton, (Christopher Anvil); Writer; b. 1925, USA; m. Joy Dolores Douglas, 5 June 1949, one s. one d. *Education:* Williams College; Juniata College. *Publications:* Mind Partner, 1960; The Day the Machines Stopped, 1964; Strangers in Paradise, 1969; Pandora's Planet, 1972; Warlord's World, 1975; The Steel, the Mist, and the Blazing Sun, 1980; Pandora's Legions, 2002; Interstellar Patrol, 2003. Contributions: Magazines and journals. *Address:* 300 Crosby Rd, Cayuta, NY 14824, USA.

CROSLAND, Margaret (McQueen); Writer and Trans; b. 17 June 1920, Bridgnorth, Shropshire, England; m. Max Denis, 1950, divorced 1959, one s. *Education:* BA, University of London, 1941. *Career:* mem. Society of Authors. *Publications:* Strange Tempe (poems), 1946; Madame Colette: A Provincial in Paris, 1953; Jean Cocteau, 1955; Ballet Carnival: A Companion to Ballet, 1955; Home Book of Opera, 1957; Ballet Lover's Dictionary, 1962; Louise of Stolberg, Countess of Albany, 1962; The Young Ballet Lover's Companion, 1962; Colette-The Difficulty of Loving: A Biography, 1973; Raymond Radiguet: A Biographical Study with Selections from His Work, 1976; Women of Iron and Velvet: French Women Writers after George Sand, 1976; Beyond the Lighthouse: English Women Novelists in the Twentieth Century, 1981; Piaf, 1985, revised edn as A Cry from the Heart, 2002; The Passionate Philosopher: A de Sade Reader, 1991, revised edn as The Marquis de Sade Reader, 2000; Simone de Beauvoir: The Woman and Her Work, 1992; Sade's Wife, 1995; The Enigma of Giorgio de Chirico, 1999; Madame de Pompadour: Sex, Culture and the Power Game, 2000. Editor: Marquis de Sade: Selected Letters, 1965; Jean Cocteau: My Contemporaries, 1967; Cocteau's World: An Anthology of Major Writings by Jean Cocteau, 1972. Translator: Over 30 books. *Honours:* Prix de Bourgogne, France, 1973–74; Enid McLeod Prize, Franco-British Society, 1992–93. *Literary Agent:* Jeffrey Simmons. *Address:* 25 Thornton Meadow, Wisborough Green, Billingshurst RH 14 0BW, England. *E-mail:* crosden@aol.com.

CROSS, Anthony Glenn; Prof. of Slavonic Studies, Writer and Ed.; b. 21 Oct. 1936, Nottingham, England; m. Margaret Elson, 11 Aug. 1960, two d. *Education:* BA, 1960, MA, 1964, PhD, 1966, Trinity Hall, Cambridge; AM, Harvard University, 1961; LittD, University of East Anglia, 1981; LittD, Fitzwilliam College, Cambridge, 1998. *Career:* Lecturer, 1964–69, Senior Lecturer, 1969–72, Reader in Russian, 1972–81, University of East Anglia; Visiting Fellow, University of Illinois, 1969–70, All Souls College, Oxford,

1977–78; Reviews Ed., Journal of European Studies, 1971–; Ed., Study Group on Eighteenth-Century Russia Newsletter, 1973–; Roberts Prof. of Russian, University of Leeds, 1981–85; Chair., British Academic Committee for Liaison with Soviet Archives, 1983–95; Prof. of Slavonic Studies, 1985–, Fellow, Fitzwilliam College, 1986–, University of Cambridge; mem. British Universities Asscn of Slavists, pres., 1982–84. *Publications:* N. M. Karamzin, 1971; Russia Under Western Eyes 1517–1825, 1971; Russian Literature in the Age of Catherine the Great (ed.), 1976; Anglo-Russian Relations in the Eighteenth Century, 1977; Great Britain and Russia in the Eighteenth Century (ed.), 1979; By the Banks of the Thames, 1980; Russia and the West in the Eighteenth Century (ed.), 1981; The Tale of the Russian Daughter and her Suffocated Lover, 1982; Eighteenth Century Russian Literature, Culture and Thought: A Bibliography (joint ed.), 1984; The Russian Theme in English Literature, 1985; Russia and the World of the Eighteenth Century (joint ed.), 1988; An English Lady at the Court of Catherine the Great (ed.), 1989; Anglophilia on the Throne: The British and the Russians in the Age of Catherine II, 1992; Engraved in the Memory: James Walker, Engraver to Catherine the Great and his Russian Anecdotes (ed.), 1993; Anglo-Russica: Aspects of Anglo-Russian Cultural Relations in the Eighteenth and Early Nineteenth Centuries, 1993; Literature, Lives and Legality in Catherine's Russia (joint ed.), 1994; By the Banks of the Neva: Chapters From the Lives of the British in Eighteenth-Century Russia, 1996; Russia in the Reign of Peter the Great: Old and New Perspectives (ed.), 1998; Britain and Russia in the Age of Peter the Great: Historical Documents (joint ed.), 1998; Peter the Great through British Eyes: Perceptions and Representations of the Tsar since 1698, 2000; Catherine the Great and the British: A Pot-Pourri of Essays, 2001; St Petersburg 1703–1825 (ed.), 2003. Contributions: scholarly journals. *Honours:* Frank Knox Fellow, Harvard Univ., 1960–61; British Acad., fellow, 1989; Academician, Russian Acad. of the Humanities, 1995; Antsiferov Prize, St Petersburg, 1998; Nove Prize, 1998; Dashkova Medal, Moscow, 2003. *Address:* c/o Dept of Slavonic Studies, University of Cambridge, Sidgwick Ave, Cambridge CB3 9DA, England.

CROSS, Gillian, MA, DPhil; British children's writer; b. 24 Dec. 1945, London; m. Martin Cross 1967; two s. two d. *Education:* Univ. of Oxford, Univ. of Sussex. *Publications:* The Runaway 1979, The Iron Way 1979, Revolt at Ratcliff's Rags 1980, Save Our School 1981, A Whisper of Lace 1981, The Dark Behind the Curtain 1982, The Demon Headmaster 1982, The Mintyglo Kid 1983, Born of the Sun 1983, On the Edge 1984, The Prime Minister's Brain 1985, Swimathon! 1986, Chartbreak 1986, Roscoe's Leap 1987, A Map of Nowhere 1988, Rescuing Gloria 1989, Twin and Super-Twin 1990, Wolf 1990, The Monster from Underground 1990, Gobbo the Great 1991, Rent-A-Genius 1991, New World 1992, The Great Elephant Chase (aka The Great American Elephant Chase) 1992, Beware Olga 1993, The Tree House 1993, The Furry Maccaloo 1993, The Revenge of the Demon Headmaster 1994, What Will Emily Do? 1994, The Crazy Shoe Shuffle 1995, Posh Watson 1995, The Roman Beanfeast 1996, Pictures in the Dark 1996, The Demon Headmaster Strikes Again 1996, The Demon Headmaster Takes Over 1997, The Goose Girl 1998, Tightrope 1999, Down With the Dirty Danes 2000, Calling a Dead Man (aka Phoning a Dead Man) 2001, The Treasure in the Mud 2001, Facing the Demon Headmaster 2002, Beware of the Demon Headmaster 2002. *Honours:* Library Asscn Carnegie Medal 1990, Whitbread Children's Novel Award 1992, Smarties Prize 1992. *Address:* c/o Oxford Children's Books, Oxford University Press, Great Clarendon Street, Oxford, OX2 6DP, England. *E-mail:* gillian@gilliancross.co.uk. *Website:* www.gillian-cross.co.uk.

CROSS, Victor (see Coffman, Virginia (Edith)).

CROSSAN, John Dominic; theologian, writer and academic; b. 17 Feb. 1934, Nenagh, County Tipperary, Ireland. *Education:* Philosophy and Theology, Stonebridge Priory, Lake Bluff, IL, 1951–57; DD, Maynooth College, Kildare, Ireland, 1959; Diploma, Sacred Scripturre Licentiate, Pontifical Biblical Institute, Rome, 1961; Diploma, Ecole Biblique, Jerusalem, 1966. *Career:* Mem., Servites religious order, 1950–69; Ordained Roman Catholic Priest, 1957–69; Asst Prof. of Biblical Studies, Stonebridge Priory, Lake Bluff, IL, 1961–65; Asst Prof. of Biblical Studies, Stonebridge Priory, Lake Bluff, IL, 1961–65; Asst Prof. of Biblical Studies, Mundelein Seminary, IL, 1967–68, Catholic Theological Union, Chicago, 1968–69; Assoc. Prof., 1969–73, Prof. of Religious Studies, 1973–95, Prof. Emeritus, 1995–, DePaul University, Chicago; Chair, Parables Seminar, 1972–75; Ed., Semeia: An Experimental Journal for Biblical Criticism, 1980–86; Co-Chair, Jesus Seminar, 1985–96; Croghan Bicentennial Visiting Prof. of Religion, Williams College, Williamstown, Massachusetts, 1996; mem. American Acad. of Religion; Catholic Biblical Asscn; Chicago Society of Biblical Research, pres., 1978–79; Society of Biblical Literature; Studiorum Novi Testamenti Societas. *Publications:* Scanning the Sunday Gospel, 1966; The Gospel of Eternal Life, 1967; In Parables: The Challenge of the Historical Jesus, 1973; The Dark Interval: Towards a Theology of Story, 1975; Raid on the Articulate: Comic Eschatology in Jesus and Borges, 1976; Finding Is the First Act: Trove Folktales and Jesus' Treasure Parable, 1979; Cliffs of Fall: Paradox and Polyvalence in the Parables of Jesus, 1980; A Fragile Craft: The Work of Amos Niven Wilder, 1981; In Fragments: The Aphorisms of Jesus, 1983; Four Other Gospels: Shadows on the Contours of Canon, 1985; Sayings Parallels: A Workbook for the Jesus Tradition, 1986; The Cross that Spoke: The Origins of the Passion Narrative, 1988; The Historical Jesus: The Life of a Mediterranean Jewish Peasant, 1991; Jesus: A Revolutionary Biography, 1994; The Essential Jesus: Original Sayings and Earliest Images, 1994; Who Killed Jesus?: Exposing the Roots of Anti-Semitism in the Gospel Story of the Death of Jesus, 1995; Who is Jesus?: Answers to Your Questions about the Historical Jesus, 1996; The Birth of Christianity, 1998. Contributions: many scholarly books and journals. *Honours:* American Acad. of Religion Award for Excellence in Religious Studies, 1989; Via Sapientiae Award, DePaul University, 1995. *Address:* 608 S Main Avenue, No. 31, Clermont, FL 34711, USA.

CROSSLEY-HOLLAND, Kevin (John William); Prof., Poet, Writer, Ed. and Trans; b. 7 Feb. 1941, Mursley, Buckinghamshire, England; m. 1st Caroline Fendall Thompson, 1963, two s.; m. 2nd Ruth Marris, 1972; m. 3rd Gillian Paula Cook, 1982, two d.; m. 4th Linda Marie Waslien, 1999. *Education:* MA, St Edmund Hall, Oxford. *Career:* Fiction and Poetry Ed., Macmillan & Co, 1962–69; Lecturer in English, Tufts-in-London Programme, 1967–78; Gregory Fellow in Poetry, University of Leeds, 1969–71; Talks Producer, BBC, 1972; Editorial Dir, Victor Gollancz, 1972–77; Lecturer in English Language and Literature, University of Regensburg, 1979–80; Editorial Consultant, Boydell and Brewer, 1983–89; Arts Council Fellow in Writing, Winchester School of Art, 1983, 1984; Visiting Prof. of English and Fulbright Scholar-in-Residence, St Olaf College, MN, 1987–89; Endowed Chair in Humanities and Fine Arts, University of St Thomas, St Paul, MN, 1991–95; mem. Dir, Minnesota Composers Forum, 1993–97; Steering Committee, King's Lynn Festival, 1997; Co-founder and Chair., Poetry-next-to-the-Sea, 1997–; Patron, Thomas Lovell Beddoes Society, 2000, Society of Storytelling, 2003. *Publications:* Poetry: The Rain-Giver, 1972; The Dream-House, 1976; Between My Father and My Son, 1982; Time's Oriel, 1983; Waterslain, 1986; The Painting-Room, 1988; East Anglian Poems, 1989; New and Selected Poems, 1991; The Language of Yes, 1996; Poems from East Anglia, 1997; Selected Poems, 2001. Children's Fiction: Havelok the Dane, 1964; King Horn, 1965; The Green Children, 1966; The Callow Pit Coffer, 1968; Wordhoard (with Jill Paton Walsh), 1969; The Pedlar of Swaffham, 1971; The Sea Stranger, 1973; Green Blades Rising, 1974; The Fire-Brother, 1974; The Earth-Father, 1976; The Wildman, 1976; The Dead Moon, 1982; Beowulf, 1982; The Mabinogion (with Gwyn Thomas), 1984; Axe-Age, Wolf-Age, 1985; Storm, 1985; The Fox and the Cat: Animal Tales from Grimm (with Susanne Lugert), 1985; British Folk Tales, 1987; The Quest for the Olwen (with Gwyn Thomas), 1988; Boo!: Ghosts and Graveyards, 1988; Dathera Dad: Fairy Tales, 1988; Small Tooth Dog: Wonder Tales, 1988; Piper and Pooka: Boggarts and Bogles, 1988; Wulf, 1988; Under the Sun and Over the Moon, 1989; Sleeping Nanna, 1989; Sea Tongue, 1991; Tales from Europe, 1991; Long Tom and the Dead Hand, 1992; The Tale of Taliesin (with Gwyn Thomas), 1992; The Labours of Herakles, 1993; The Old Stories: Tales From East Anglia and the Fen Country, 1997; Short!, 1998; The King Who Was and Will Be, 1998; Arthur: The Seeing Stone, 2000; Enchantment, 2000; The Ugly Duckling, 2001; Arthur: At the Crossing Places, 2001; Viking!, 2002; Arthur: King of the Middle March, 2003. Non-Fiction: Pieces of Land: A Journey to Eight Islands, 1972; The Norse Myths, 1980; The Stones Remain (with Andrew Rafferty), 1989. Editor: Running to Paradise, 1967; Winter's Tales for Children 3, 1967; Winter's Tales 14, 1968; New Poetry 2 (with Patricia Beer), 1976; The Faber Book of Northern Legends, 1977; The Faber Book of Northern Folk-Tales, 1980; The Riddle Book, 1982; Folk-Tales of the British Isles, 1985; The Oxford Book of Travel Verse, 1986; Northern Lights, 1987; Medieval Lovers, 1988; Medieval Gardens, 1990; Peter Grimes by George Crabbe, 1990; The Young Oxford Book of Folk-Tales, 1998; The New Exeter Book of Riddles, 1999. Drama: The Wuffings (with Ivan Cutting), 1997. Other: Individual poems; Trans from Old English; Opera Libretti; Programmes for television and radio. Contributions: numerous journals and magazines. *Honours:* Arts Council Awards, Best Book for Young Children, 1966–68; Poetry Book Society Choice, 1976, and Recommendation, 1986; Carnegie Medal, 1986; FRSL, 1998; Bronze Medal, Nestlé Smarties Prize, 2000; Guardian Children's Fiction Award, 2001; Tir na n-Og Award, 2001; Silver Medal, Spoken Awards, 2001; Hon. Fellow, St Edmund Hall, Oxford, 2001. *Literary Agent:* Rogers, Coleridge & White Ltd, 20 Powis Mews, London W11 1JN, England. *Address:* Clare Cottage, Burnham Market, Norfolk PE31 8HE, England. *E-mail:* kevin@crossley-holland.com.

CROWE, John (see Lynds, Dennis).

CROWE, Thomas Rain; Writer, Poet, Ed., Publisher and Trans; b. 23 Aug. 1949, Chicago, IL, USA; Partner, Nan Watkins, one s. *Education:* BA, Furman University, 1972. *Career:* Ed., Beatitude Press, San Francisco, CA, 1974–78; Founder-Dir, San Francisco International Poetry Festival, 1976; Founder-Ed., Katuah Journal, Asheville, NC, 1983–87; Publisher, New Native Press, Cullowhee, NC, 1988–; Master Class Instructor, South Carolina Gov.'s School for the Arts, 1989, 1990; Ed.-at-Large, Asheville Poetry Review, 1994–2001; Founder-Prod., Fern Hill Records, 1994–; Founder-Performer, The Boatrockers, 1996; mem. Amnesty International; Foundation for Global Sustainability. *Publications:* Learning to Dance (poems), 1985; Poems of Che Guevara's Dream, 1991; The Sound of Light (poems and music), 1991; Night Sun (poems), three vols, 1993; The Laugharne Poems, 1997; Writing the Wind: A Celtic Resurgence (co-ed. and trans.), 1997; In Wineseller's Street: Poems of Hafiz (trans.), 1998; Drunk on the Wine of the Beloved: 100 Poems of Hafiz (trans.), 2001. Other: several translations, 1991–2001. *Honours:* Thomas E. McDill Poetry Prize, 1980; International Merit Award, Atlanta Review, 1996; Publishers' Book of the Year Award, Appalachian Writers Asscn, 1997. *Address:* 407 Canada Rd, Tuskaseegee, NC 28783, USA. *E-mail:* newnativepress@hotmail.com.

CROWLEY, John; Writer; b. 1 Dec. 1942, Presque Isle, Maine, USA. *Education:* BA, Indiana University, 1964. *Publications:* The Deep, 1975; Beasts, 1976; Engine Summer, 1979; Little Big, 1981; Ægypt, 1987; Novelty (short stories), 1989; Great Work of Time, 1991; Antiquities: Seven Stories, 1993; Love & Sleep, 1994; Dæmonomania, 2000; The Translator, 2002. Other: Film Scripts; Television scripts, including America Lost and Found, The World of Tomorrow, and No Place to Hide. Contributions: periodicals. *Honours:* World Fantasy Award, 1982; American Film Festival Award, 1982; American Acad. and Institute of Arts and Letters Award in Literature, 1992. *Address:* Box 395, Conway, MA 01341, USA.

CROZIER, Andrew; Poet and Senior Lecturer in English; b. 1943, England. *Education:* MA, University of Cambridge; PhD, University of Essex. *Career:* Senior Lecturer in English, University of Sussex. *Publications:* Poetry: Love Litter of Time Spent, 1967; Train Rides: Poems from '63 and '64, 1968; Walking on Grass, 1969; In One Side and Out the Other (with John James and Tom Phillips), 1970; Neglected Information, 1973; The Veil Poem, 1974; Printed Circuit, 1974; Seven Contemporary Sun Dials (with Ian Potts), 1975; Pleats, 1975; Duets, 1976; Residing, 1976; High Zero, 1978; Were There, 1978; Utamaro Variations, 1982; All Where Each Is, 1985; Ghosts in the Corridor (with Donald Davie and C. H. Sisson), 1992. Other: A Various Art (ed. with Tim Longville), 1987. *Address:* c/o University of Sussex, Falmer, Brighton, Sussex BN1 9RH, England.

CROZIER, Brian Rossiter, (John Rossiter); British writer and journalist; b. 4 Aug. 1918, Kuridala, Queensland, Australia; m. 1st Mary Lillian Samuel 1940 (died 1993); one s. three d.; m. 2nd Jacqueline Marie Mitchell 1999. *Education:* Lycée, Montpellier, Peterborough Coll., Harrow, Trinity Coll. of Music, London. *Career:* music and art critic, London 1936–39; reporter and sub-ed., Stoke On Trent, Stockport, London 1940–41; aeronautical inspection 1941–43; sub-ed., Reuters 1943–44, News Chronicle 1944–48, sub-ed. and writer Sydney Morning Herald, Australia 1948–51; corresp., Reuters-AAP 1951–52; features ed., Straits Times, Singapore 1952–53; leader writer and corresp., The Economist 1954–64; BBC commentator, English, French and Spanish overseas services 1954–66, Chair. Forum World Features 1965–74; Ed., Conflict Studies 1970–75; Co-founder and Dir Inst. for the Study of Conflict 1970–79, Consultant 1979–; Columnist, Now!, London 1980–81, Nat. Review, New York 1978–90 (contributing ed. 1982–), The Times 1982–84, The Free Nation, London 1982–89; Adjunct Scholar, The Heritage Foundation 1983–95; Distinguished Visiting Fellow, Hoover Inst., Stanford, Calif., USA 1996–2001. *Art Exhibitions:* London 1948, Sydney 1949–50. *Publications:* The Rebels 1960, The Morning After 1963, Neo-Colonialism 1964, South-East Asia in Turmoil 1965, The Struggle for the Third World 1966, Franco 1967, The Masters of Power 1969, The Future of Communist Power (in USA: Since Stalin) 1970, De Gaulle (vol. I) 1973, (vol. II) 1974, A Theory of Conflict 1974, The Man Who Lost China (Chiang Kai-shek) 1977, Strategy of Survival 1978, The Minimum State 1979, Franco: Crepúsculo de un hombre 1980, The Price of Peace 1980, Socialism Explained (co-author) 1984, This War Called Peace (co-author) 1984, The Andropov Deception (novel) (under pseudonym John Rossiter) 1984, The Grenada Documents (ed.) 1987, Socialism: Dream and Reality 1987, The Gorbachev Phenomenon 1990, Communism: Why Prolong its Death Throes? 1990, Free Agent: The Unseen War 1993, The KGB Lawsuits 1995, Le Phénix rouge (co-author) 1995, The Rise and Fall of the Soviet Empire 1999 and contribs to journals in numerous countries. *Address:* 18 Wickliffe Avenue, Finchley, London, N3 3EJ, England (Home). *Telephone:* (20) 8346-8124 (Home). *Fax:* (20) 8346-4599.

CRUMEY, Andrew David William Bernard, BSc, PhD; writer; b. 12 Oct. 1961, Glasgow, Scotland. *Education:* Imperial College, London. *Career:* care worker, 1987–88; Research Assoc., Imperial College and Leeds University, 1989–92; school teacher, Newcastle upon Tyne, 1992–96; writer, 1996–. *Publications:* Music in a Foreign Language (novel), 1994; Pfitz (novel), 1995; D'Alembert's Principle (novel), 1996; Mr Mee, 2000; Mobius Dick 2004. *Honours:* Saltire Society Award for Best First Book, 1994; Arts Council Writer's Award. *Literary Agent:* A. M. Heath & Co Ltd, 79 St Martin's Lane, London WC2N 4RE, England.

CRYSTAL, David, OBE, BA, PhD, FCST, FBA; writer and editor; b. 6 July 1941, Lisburn, County Antrim, Northern Ireland; m. 1st Molly Stack 1964 (died 1976); two s. two d.; m. 2nd Hilary Norman 1976; one s. *Education:* Univ. Coll. London. *Career:* Asst Lecturer, University College of North Wales, 1963–65; Lecturer and Reader, 1965–76, Prof. of Linguistic Science, 1976–85, University of Reading; Hon. Prof., University of Wales, Bangor, 1985–; Ed., Child Language Teaching and Therapy, 1985–96, Linguistics Abstracts, 1985–96; Consultant Ed., English Today, 1986–94. *Publications:* Linguistics, Language and Religion 1965, What Is Linguistics? (third edn) 1974, The English Tone of Voice 1975, Child Language, Learning and Linguistics 1976, Working with LARSP 1979, Eric Partridge: In His Own Words 1980, A Dictionary of Linguistics and Phonetics 1980, Introduction to Language Pathology 1980, Clinical Linguistics 1981, Directions in Applied Linguistics 1981, Linguistic Controversies 1981, Profiling Linguistic Disability 1982, Linguistic Encounters with Language Handicap 1984, Language Handicap in Children 1984, Who Cares About English Usage? 1984, Listen to Your Child 1986, The English Language 1988, Cambridge Encyclopedia of Language 1987, Rediscover Grammar 1988, The Cambridge Encyclopedia 1990, Language A–Z 1991, Nineties Knowledge 1992, An Encyclopedic Dictionary of Language and Languages 1992, The Cambridge Factfinder 1993, The Cambridge Biographical Encyclopaedia 1994, The Cambridge Encyclopedia of the English Language 1995, Discover Grammar 1996, English as a Global Language 1997, Language Play 1998, Words on Words 2000, Language Death 2000, John Bradburne's Mutemwa 2000, Language and the Internet 2001, Shakespeare's Words 2002, The New Penguin Encyclopedia 2002, The New Penguin Factfinder 2003, The Penguin Concise Encyclopedia 2003, The Stories of English 2004, The Language Revolution 2004; other: children's non-fiction books. *Honours:* Wheatley Medal 2001. *Address:* Akaroa, Gors Avenue, Holyhead, Anglesey LL65 1PB, Wales. *E-mail:* crystal@dial.pipex.com. *Website:* www.crystalreference.com.

CSOÓRI, Sándor; Hungarian poet and writer; b. 3 Feb. 1930, Zámoly, Co. Fejér. *Education:* Lenin Inst., Budapest. *Career:* contrib. to Irodalmi Újság (monthly) 1954–55, Új hang (monthly) 1955–56; drama critic Mafilm Studio 1968; joined opposition movt 1980; participated in political discussions of Monor 1985 and Lakitelek 1987; Founding mem. Hungarian Democratic Forum 1987, presidium mem. 1988–92; Chair. Illyés Gyula Foundation 1990–94; Pres. World Fed. of Hungarians 1991–. *Publications:* selected poems: Fölröppen a madár (Up Flies the Bird) 1954, Ördögpille (Demon Butterfly) 1957, Elmaradt lázálom (Postponed Nightmare) 1980, Knives and Nails 1981, Hóemléke (Memory of Snow) 1983, Várakozás a tavaszban (Waiting in the Spring) 1983, Menekülés a magányból (Escape from Loneliness) 1962, Hattyúkkal ágyútűzben (In Cannon Fire with Swans) 1995, Ha volna életem (If I Had a Life) 1996; sociographies: Tudósítás a toronyból (Report From the Tower) 1963, Kubai utinapló (Cuban Travel Diary) 1965; essay volumes: Faltól falig (From Wall to Wall) 1968, Nomád napló (Nomadic Diary) 1979, Félig bevallott élet (Half Confessed Life) 1984, Készülődés a számadásra (Preparation for Final Reckoning) 1987, Nappali hold (Daytime Moon) 1991, Tenger és diólevél I. II. (The Sea and Nut Leaves) 1994, Száll a alá poklokra (Descent into Hell) 1997; film scripts: Tízezer nap (Ten thousand days), Földobott kő (The thrown-up stone), 80 huszár (Eighty Hussars), Tüske a köröm alatt (A Thorn under the Fingernail), Hószakadás (Snow-Storm), Nincs idö (No Time Left). *Honours:* Attila József Prize 1954, Cannes Film Festival Prize 1964, 1968, Herder Prize 1981, Kossuth Prize 1990, Eeva Joenpelto Prize 1995. *Address:* 1068 Budapest, Benczúr u. 15, Hungary.

CULP, Marguerite (see Kearns, Marguerite).

CULVER, Timothy J. (see Westlake, Donald Edwin).

CUMMING, Peter E.; Writer, Dramatist and Teacher; b. 23 March 1951, Brampton, Ontario, Canada; m. Mary Shelleen Nelson, 14 Oct. 1970. *Education:* BA, English Literature, 1972; Diploma in Education, 1976; MA, English Literature, 1992. *Career:* Resident Artist in Drama, Wilfrid Laurier University, 1972–73; Exec. Dir, Atlantic Publishers Asscn, 1984–85; mem. Playwrights Union of Canada; Writers Union of Canada; Canadian Society of Children's Authors, Illustrators, and Performers; Asscn of Canadian College and University Teachers of English. *Publications:* Snowdreams, 1982; Ti-Jean, 1983; A Horse Called Farmer, 1984; Mogul and Me, 1989; Out on the Ice in the Middle of the Bay, 1993. Contributions: Contributing ed., Quill and Quire, 1982–84. *Honours:* First Prize, Children's Prose, 1980, First Prize, Adult Fiction, 1981, Writers Federation of Nova Scotia; Toronto Board of Education Canada Day Playwriting Competition, 1981; Our Choice, Children's Book Centre, 1984, 1989, 1993; Hilroy Award for Innovative Teaching, 1990; George Wicken Prize in Canadian Literature, 1994; Tiny Torgi Award, 1995. *Address:* 201 Front St, Stratford, Ontario N5A 4H8, Canada.

CUMMINS, Walter (Merrill); Prof. of English, Writer and Editor; b. 6 Feb. 1936, Long Branch, NJ, USA; m. 1st Judith Gruenberg 14 June 1957 (divorced 1981); m. 2nd Alison Cunningham 14 Feb. 1981; two d. *Education:* BA, Rutgers Univ., 1957; MA, 1962, MFA, 1962, PhD, 1965, Univ. of Iowa. *Career:* Instructor, Univ. of Iowa, 1962–65; Asst Prof., 1965–69, Assoc. Prof., 1969–74, Prof. of English, 1974–2002, Prof. Emeritus, 2002–, Fairleigh Dickinson Univ.; Assoc. Ed., 1978–83, Ed.-in-Chief, 1983–2002, Ed. Emeritus, 2002–, The Literary Review. *Publications:* A Stranger to the Deed (novel), 1968; Into Temptation (novel), 1968; The Other Sides of Reality: Myths, Visions and Fantasies (co-ed.), 1972; Student Writing Guide (co-ed.), 1973; Witness (short stories), 1975; Managing Management Climate (with George G. Gordon), 1979; Where We Live (short stories), 1983; Shifting Borders: East European Poetry of the Eighties (ed.), 1993. Contributions: Stories, articles and reviews in many publs. *Honours:* New Jersey State Council on the Arts Fellowship, 1982–83; National Endowment for the Arts Grants, 1987–88, 1990–91; Distinguished Retiring Editor, Council of Editors of Learned Journals, 2002. *Address:* 6 Hanover Rd, Florham Park, NJ 07932, USA. *E-mail:* wcummins@att.net.

CUMPER, Pat; British playwright; b. 1955, Jamaica. *Education:* Univ. of Cambridge. *Radio contributions:* Another Country (BBC Radio 3), A Caribbean Blue (BBC Radio 4), Home Truths (BBC Radio 4), Something Understood (BBC Radio 4). *Television plays:* Doctors (BBC1). *Plays:* Fallen Angel and the Devil Concubine 1989, The Key Game 2002; musicals: Fabula

Urbis (with Simon Deacon) 2002, Elysium. *Literary Agent:* Bill McLean Personal Management Ltd, 23B Deodar Road, London, SW15 2NP, England. *Telephone:* (20) 8789-8191.

CUNLIFFE, Barrington (Windsor), (Barry Cunliffe); Archaeologist, Prof. and Writer; b. 10 Dec. 1939, Portsmouth, Hampshire, England; m. Margaret Herdman, 5 Jan. 1979, one s. one d. *Education:* BA, 1961, MA, 1963, PhD, 1966, LittD, 1976, St John's College, Cambridge. *Career:* Lecturer in Classics, University of Bristol, 1963–66; Prof. of Archaeology, University of Southampton, 1966–72; Prof. of European Archaeology and Fellow, Keble College, Oxford, 1972–; Commissioner, Historic Buildings and Monuments Commission for England, 1987–92; Governor, Museum of London, 1995–97; Trustee, British Museum, 2000–; mem. British Acad., Fellow; Medieval Society; Prehistoric Society; Royal Archaeological Institute; Society of Antiquaries, fellow, vice-pres., 1982–86, pres., 1994–95. *Publications:* Excavations at Richborough, Vol. 5, 1968; Roman Bath (ed.), 1969; Excavations at Fishbourne, 1961–69, 2 vols, 1971; Fishbourne: A Roman Palace and its Gardens, 1971; Roman Baths Discovered, 1971; Guide to the Roman Remains of Bath, 1971; The Cradle of England, 1972; The Making of the English, 1973; The Regni, 1974; Iron Age Communities in Britain: An Account of England, Scotland, and Wales from the Seventh Century BC until the Roman Conquest, 1974; Excavations at Porchester Castle, Hants, 5 vols, 1975, 1976, 1977, 1985, 1994; Rome and the Barbarians, 1975; Oppida: The Beginnings of Urbanisation in Barbarian Europe (with Trevor Rowley), 1976; Hengistbury Head, 1978; Rome and Her Empire, 1978; The Celtic World, 1979; Excavating Bath, 1950–75 (ed.), 1979; Coinage and Society in Britain and Gaul: Some Current Problems (ed.), 1981; Antiquity and Man (ed.), 1982; Danebury: Anatomy of an Iron Age Hillfort, 1983; Aspects of the Iron Age in Central Southern Britain (ed. with David Miles), 1984; Danebury: An Iron Age Hillfort in Hampshire, Vols 1 and 2, 1984, Vols 4 and 5, 1991, Vol. 6, 1995; Heywood Sumner's Wessex, 1985; Temple of Sulis Minerva at Bath (with Peter Davenport), Vol. I, 1985; The City of Bath, 1986; Hengistbury Head, Darcet, Vol. I, 1987; Origins: The Roots of European Civilisation (ed.), 1987; Mount Batten, Plymouth: A Prehistoric and Roman Port, 1988; Greeks, Romans & Barbarians: Spheres of Interaction, 1988; Wessex to AD 1000, 1993; The Oxford Illustrated Prehistory of Europe (ed.), 1994; Social Complexity and the Development of Towns in Iberia (ed. with S. Keay), 1995; The Ancient Celts, 1997; Science and Stonehenge (ed. with C. Renfrew), 1997; The Guaddajoz Project, Andalucia in the First Millennium BC (with M-C Fernandez Castro), 1999; The Daneburg Environs Programme, Vols 1 and 2, 2000; Facing the Ocean, 2001; The Extraordinary Voyage of Pytheas the Greek, 2001. Contributions: periodicals and archaeological journals. *Honours:* CBE, 1994; Hon. doctorates, University of Sussex, University of Bath and Open University; American Historical Asscn James Henry Breasted Prize, 2001. *Address:* Institute of Archaeology, University of Oxford, 36 Beaumont St, Oxford OX1 2PG, England.

CUNNINGHAM, Michael, MA, MFA; American novelist; b. 6 Nov. 1952, Cincinnati, OH. *Education:* Stanford Univ., Univ. of Iowa. *Career:* fmr bartender; joined Univ. of Ia Writers' Workshop 1978; writer for Carnegie Corpn; now Adjunct Asst Prof., Columbia Univ.; Guggenheim Fellowship 1993. *Publications:* Golden States 1984, A Home at the End of the World 1990, Flesh and Blood 1995, The Hours (Pulitzer Prize, PEN/Faulkner Award for Fiction 1999) 1998. *Honours:* Lambda Literary Award for Gay Men's Fiction 1995. *Literary Agent:* Steven Barclay Agency, 12 Western Avenue, Petaluma, CA 94952, USA. *Telephone:* (707) 773-0654. *Fax:* (707) 778-1868. *Website:* www.barclayagency.com. *Address:* Columbia University, Creative Writing Center, Room 415, 2970 Broadway, New York, NY 10027-6939, USA (Office).

CUPITT, Don, BA, MA; ecclesiastic and writer; b. 22 May 1934, Oldham, England; m. Susan Marianne Day 28 Dec. 1963; one s. two d. *Education:* Trinity Hall, Cambridge, Westcott House, Cambridge. *Career:* ordained 1959; Curate, St Philip's Church, Salford 1959–62; Vice-Principal, Westcott House, Cambridge 1962–65; Fellow 1965–96, Dean 1966–91, Life Fellow 1996–, Emmanuel Coll., Cambridge; Cambridge Univ. Asst Lecturer in Divinity 1968–73, Lecturer in Divinity 1973–96. *Publications:* Christ and the Hiddenness of God 1971, Crisis of Moral Authority 1972, The Leap of Reason 1976, The Worlds of Science and Religion 1976, Who Was Jesus? (with Peter Armstrong) 1977, Jesus and the Gospel of God 1979, The Nature of Man 1979, The Debate About Christ 1979, Explorations in Theology 1979, Taking Leave of God 1980, The World to Come 1982, The Sea of Faith 1984, Only Human 1985, Life Lines 1986, The Long-Legged Fly 1987, The New Christian Ethics 1988, Radicals and the Future of the Church 1989, Creation Out of Nothing 1990, What is a Story? 1991, The Time Being 1992, After All 1994, The Last Philosophy 1995, Solar Ethics 1995, After God: The Future of Religion 1997, Mysticism After Modernity 1998, The Religion of Being 1998, The Revelation of Being 1998, The New Religion of Life in Everyday Speech 1999, The Meaning of It All in Everyday Speech 1999, Kingdom Come in Everyday Speech 2000, Philosophy's Own Religion 2000, Reforming Christianity 2001, Emptiness and Brightness 2001, Is Nothing Sacred? 2002, Life, Life 2003, The Way to Happiness: A Theory of Religion 2004. *Honours:* Hon. DLitt (Univ. of Bristol) 1985, Fellow, Jesus Seminar, Westar Inst., CA 2001. *Address:* c/o Emmanuel College, Cambridge, CB2 3AP, England.

CURREY, Richard; Writer; b. 19 Oct. 1949, West Virginia, USA. *Education:* West Virginia University, 1972–74; Howard University, 1976–79. *Career:* Writer, 1972–; Visiting Prof., University of New Mexico, 1993; Distinguished Writer-in-Residence, Wichita State University, 1993; Mem., Writers Film Project, Chesterfield Film Company, 1996–97; Gives readings from his works. *Publications:* Fatal Light, 1988; The Wars of Heaven, 1990; Crossing Over: The Vietnam Stories, 1993; Lost Highway, 1997. *Honours:* D. H. Lawrence Fellow in Literature, 1981; Fellow, National Endowment for the Arts, 1982, 1987; Short Fiction Prize, Associated Writing Programs, 1984; O. Henry Award, 1988; Special Citation, Hemingway Foundation, 1989; Excellence in the Arts Award, Vietnam Veterans of America, 1989; Pushcart Prize, 1990; Fellow, Western States Arts Federation, 1993; Writer-in-Residence, State of West Virginia, 1994; Daugherty Award in the Humanities, 1997. *Address:* 160 Washington NE, No. 185, Albuquerque, NM 87108, USA.

CURRIE JONES, Edwina, MA, MSc; British politician, writer and broadcaster; b. 13 Oct. 1946, Liverpool; m. 1st Raymond F. Currie 1972 (divorced 2001); two d.; m. 2nd John Jones 2001. *Education:* Liverpool Inst. for Girls, St Anne's Coll., Oxford, London School of Econs. *Career:* teacher and lecturer in econs, econ. history and business studies 1972–81; mem. Birmingham City Council 1975–86; Conservative MP for Derbyshire S 1983–97; Parl. Pvt. Sec. to Sec. of State for Educ. and Science 1985–86; Parl. Under-Sec. of State for Health 1986–88; mem. Parl. Select Cttee on Social Services 1983–86; Jt Chair. Conservative Group for Europe 1995–97; Vice-Chair. European Movt 1995–99; Jt Chair. Future of Europe Trust 1995–97. *Radio presenter:* Late Night Currie, BBC 1998–2003. *Publications:* Life Lines 1989, What Women Want 1990, Three Line Quips 1992, A Parliamentary Affair (novel) 1994, A Woman's Place (novel) 1996, She's Leaving Home (novel) 1997, The Ambassador (novel) 1998, Chasing Men (novel) 2000, This Honourable House (novel) 2001, Diaries (1987–92) 2002. *Honours:* Speaker of the Year, Asscn of Speakers' Clubs 1990, 1994 Campaigner of the Year, The Spectator/Highland Park Parliamentarian of the Year Awards. *Address:* c/o Curtis Brown, Haymarket, London, SW1Y 4SP, England (Office); c/o Little, Brown (UK) Ltd, Brettenham House, Lancaster Place, London, WC2E 7EN, England. *Telephone:* (20) 7396-6600 (Office).

CURTEIS, Ian (Bayley); Dramatist; b. 1 May 1935, London, England; m. 1st Dorothy Joan Armstrong 1964 (divorced); two s.; m. 2nd Joanna Trollope 12 April 1985 (divorced); two step-d.; m. 3rd Lady Deidre Grantley; two step-s. *Education:* University of London. *Career:* mem. Writers Guild of Great Britain, pres., 1998-2001. *Publications:* Long Voyage Out of War, 1971; Churchill and the Generals, 1980; Suez 1956, 1980; The Falklands Play, 1987. Other: numerous television plays and series, radio plays, screenplays, stage plays and adaptations. *Honours:* Grand Prize for Best Program, New York International Film and TV Festival, 1981. *Address:* 2 Warwick Sq., London SW1V 2AA, England; Markenfield Hall, Ripon, North Yorkshire, HG4 3AD, England. *Telephone:* (20) 7821-8606; (1765) 603411.

CURTIS, Anthony Samuel; Journalist, Ed. and Writer; b. 12 March 1926, London, England; m. Sarah Curtis 3 Oct. 1960; three s. *Education:* BA (Inter MA), English, Merton College, Oxford, 1950. *Career:* Deputy Ed., TLS, 1959–60; Literary Ed., Sunday Telegraph, 1960–70, Financial Times, 1970–90; mem. Royal Literary Fund, treasurer, 1975–98; FRSA; Society of Authors, pension fund trustee; London Library Committee Mem.; Literary Society. *Publications:* The Pattern of Maugham, 1974; Somerset Maugham: The Critical Heritage (with John Whitehead), 1987; Lit Ed: On Reviews and Reviewing, 1998; Before Bloomsbury: The 1890s Diaries of Three Kensington Ladies, 2002. Contributions: periodicals and radio. *Honours:* Harkness Fellowship in Journalism, USA, 1958–59. *Address:* 9 Essex Villas, London W8 7BP, England. *E-mail:* anticurtis@aol.com.

CURTIS, Tony; Prof. of Poetry and Poet; b. 26 Dec. 1946, Carmathen, Wales; m. Margaret Blundell, 1970, one s. one d. *Education:* BA, University College of Swansea, 1968; MFA, Goddard College, Vermont, 1980. *Career:* Prof. of Poetry, University of Glamorgan. *Publications:* Poetry: Walk Down a Welsh Wind, 1972; Home Movies, 1973; Album, 1974; The Deerslayers, 1978; Carnival, 1978; Preparations: Poems, 1974–79, 1980; Letting Go, 1983; Selected Poems, 1970–85, 1986; The Last Candles, 1989; Taken for Pearls, 1993. Other: Islands (radio play), 1975; Out of the Dark Wood: Prose Poems, Stories, 1977; Dannie Abse, 1985; The Art of Seamus Heaney (ed.), 1986; How to Study Modern Poetry, 1990; How Poets Work (ed.), 1996. *Honours:* National Poetry Competition Winner, 1984; Dylan Thomas Prize, 1993; Cholmondeley Award, 1997. *Address:* Pentwyn, 55 Colcot Rd, Barry, South Glamorgan CF6 8BQ, Wales.

CURTIS, Wade (see Pournelle, Jerry Eugene).

CUSK, Rachel, BA; British writer; b. 8 Feb. 1967, Canada; m. Adrian Clarke; two d. *Education:* St Mary's Convent, Cambridge and New Coll., Oxford. *Career:* writer 1992–. *Publications:* novels: Saving Agnes (Whitbread First Novel Award 1993) 1992, The Temporary 1995, The Country Life (Somerset Maugham Award) 1997, The Lucky Ones 2003; non-fiction: A Life's Work 2001. *Address:* The Dower House, Nettlecombe, Williton, Somerset, TA4 4HS, England.

CUSSLER, Clive Eric; writer and advertising executive; b. 15 July 1931, Aurora, IL, USA; m. Barbara Knight 1955; three c. *Education:* Pasadena City College, Orange Coast College, California State University. *Career:*

advertising directorships; Fellow, Explorers Club; mem. RGS. *Publications:* The Mediterranean Caper, 1973; Iceberg, 1975; Raise the Titanic, 1976; Vixen O-Three, 1978; Night Probe, 1981; Pacific Vortex, 1982; Deep Six, 1984; Cyclops, 1986; Treasure, 1988; Dragon, 1990; Sahara, 1992; Inca Gold, 1994; Shock Wave, 1996; Flood Tide, 1997; Serpent, 1999; Atlantis Found, 1999; Blue Gold, 2000; Valhalla Rising, 2001; Fire Ice (with Paul Kemprecos), 2002; Sea Hunters II, 2002; The Golden Buddha, 2003; White Death 2003. *Honours:* numerous advertising awards. *Address:* c/o Penguin Putnam, 375 Hudson Street, New York, NY 10014, USA.

CUTTS, Simon; British artist, poet and publisher; b. 30 Dec. 1944, Derby; m. 1st Annira Uusi-Illikainen (divorced 1973); one s.; m. 2nd Margot Hapgood (died 1985). *Education:* Herbert Strutt Grammar School, Belper, Derbyshire, Nottingham Coll. of Art, Trent Polytechnic. *Career:* travel and miscellaneous employment including The Trent Bookshop, Nottingham 1962–69; Jt Ed. Tarasque Press 1964–72; publishing, lecturing and writing 1972–74; Dir and Co-Partner Coracle Press Books (now Coracle Production and Distribution) 1975–87; Dir, Coracle Press Gallery 1983–86; Dir Victoria Miro Gallery 1985–; org. of exhbns in Europe and New York. *Publications:* numerous publs, including Quelques Pianos 1976, Pianostool Footnotes 1983, Petits-Airs for Margot 1986, Seepages 1988. *Address:* Victoria Miro, 21 Cork Street, London, W1 (Office); 4/16 Courtfield Gardens, London, SW5, England (Home). *Telephone:* (20) 7734-5082 (Office); (20) 7370-4301 (Home).

CZERNEDA, Julie Elizabeth, BSc; writer and editor; b. 11 April 1955, Exeter, ON, Canada; m. Roger Henry Czerneda 1976; one s. one d. *Education:* University of Waterloo, University of Saskatchewan, Queen's University, Kingston, ON. *Career:* Pres., Czerneda Publishing Inc 1991–98. *Publications:* Fiction: A Thousand Words for Stranger, 1997; Beholder's Eye, 1998; Ties of Power, 1999; Changing Vision, 2000. Other: many non-fiction books, 1986–99. Contributions: anthologies. *E-mail:* julie.czerneda@sff.net.

D

DABYDEEN, Cyril, BA, MA, MPA; poet and writer; b. 15 Oct. 1945, Guyana. *Education:* Lakehead Univ., Thunder Bay, Queen's Univ., Kingston. *Career:* juror, Neustadt Int. Prize for Literature 2000, Gov.-Gen.'s Award for Literature 2000; speaker, reader across Canada, USA, UK, Europe, India, Cuba, Caribbean and South America; currently Lecturer in English, Univ. of Ottawa; mem. US Asscn of Commonwealth Language and Literature Studies, Int. PEN. *Publications:* poetry: Distances 1977, Goatsong 1977, Heart's Frame 1979, This Planet Earth 1980, Islands Lovelier Than a Vision 1988, Coastland: New and Selected Poems 1989, Dark Swirl 1989, Stoning the Wind 1994, Born in Amazonia 1996, Discussing Columbus 1997, Hemisphere of Love 2003, Imaginary Origins: Selected Poems 2004; fiction: Still Close to the Island 1980, To Monkey Jungle 1986, The Wizard Swami 1989, Dark Swirl 1989, Jogging in Havana 1992, Sometimes Hard 1994, Berbice Crossing (short stories) 1996, Black Jesus and Other Stories 1997, My Brahmin Days and Other Stories 2000, North of the Equator (short stories) 2001, Play a Song, Somebody (short stories) 2004; editor: A Shapely Fire: Changing the Literary Landscape 1987, Another Way to Dance: Contemporary Asian Poetry from Canada and the US 1996; contrib. to Canadian Forum, Canadian Fiction Magazine, Fiddlehead, Dalhousie Review, Antigonish Review, World Literature Today, Atlanta Review, The Critical Quarterly, Wascana Review, Literary Review, Globe and Mail, Caribbean Quarterly, Kunapipi. *Honours:* Sandbach Parker Gold Medal, A. J. Seymour Lyric Poetry Prize, Poet Laureate of Ottawa, Okanagan Fiction Award, recipient Canada Council, Ontario Arts Council, Ottawa-Carleton Region Literary Awards, Certificate of Merit for the Arts, honoured for work in race relations City of Ottawa and the Federation of Canadian Municipalities. *Address:* 106 Blackburn, Ottawa, ON K1N BA7, Canada. *E-mail:* cdabydeen@ncf.ca.

DABYDEEN, David, BA, PhD, FRSL; poet, writer and academic; *Professor of Literature, Warwick University*; b. 9 Dec. 1955, Guyana. *Education:* University of Cambridge, University of London. *Career:* Junior Research Fellow, University of Oxford, 1983–87; Prof. of Literature, Warwick University, 1987–; mem. Arts Council of Great Britain, literature panel, 1985–89; Guyana's Ambassador to UNESCO, 1997. *Publications:* Slave Song, 1984; Coolie Odyssey, 1988; The Intended, 1991; Disappearance, 1993; Turner, 1994; The Counting House, 1996; Across the Dark Waters: Indian Identity in the Caribbean, 1996; A Harlot's Progress, 1999; Our Lady of Demerara 2004. Contributions: various periodicals. *Honours:* Commonwealth Poetry Prize, 1984; Guyana Literature Prize, 1992. *Address:* c/o Warwick University, Coventry CV4 7AL, England.

DACEY, Philip; Poet and Teacher; b. 9 May 1939, St Louis, MO, USA; m. Florence Chard, 1963, divorced 1986, two s. one d. *Education:* BA, St Louis University, 1961; MA, Stanford University, 1967; MFA, University of Iowa, 1970. *Career:* Instructor in English, University of Missouri at St Louis, 1967–68; Faculty, Dept of English, Southwest State University, Marshall, Minnesota, 1970–; Distinguished Writer-in-Residence, Wichita State University, 1985. *Publications:* Poetry: The Beast with Two Backs, 1969; Fist, Sweet Giraffe, The Lion, Snake, and Owl, 1970; Four Nudes, 1971; How I Escaped from the Labyrinth and Other Poems, 1977; The Boy Under the Bed, 1979; The Condom Poems, 1979; Gerard Manley Hopkins Meets Walt Whitman in Heaven and Other Poems, 1982; Fives, 1984; The Man with Red Suspenders, 1986; The Condom Poems II, 1989; Night Shift at the Crucifix Factory, 1991. Editor: I Love You All Day: It is That Simple (with Gerald M. Knoll), 1970; Strong Measures: Contemporary American Poetry in Traditional Forms (with David Jaus), 1986. *Honours:* Woodrow Wilson Fellowship, 1961; New York YM-YWHA Discovery Award, 1974; National Endowment for the Arts Fellowships, 1975, 1980; Minnesota State Arts Board Fellowships, 1975, 1983; Bush Foundation Fellowship, 1977; Loft-McKnight Fellowship, 1984; Fulbright Lecturer, 1988. *Address:* Route 1, Box 89, Lynd, MN 56157, USA.

DACRE, Paul Michael; Newspaper Editor; b. 14 Nov. 1948, London, England; m. Kathleen Thomson 1973; two s. *Education:* Univ. Coll. School, London; Leeds Univ. *Career:* reporter, feature writer, Assoc. Features Ed., Daily Express 1970–76, Washington and New York Corresp. 1976–79; New York Bureau Chief, Daily Mail 1980, News Ed., London 1981–85, Asst Ed. (News and Foreign) 1986, Asst Ed. (Features) 1987, Exec. Ed. 1988, Assoc. Ed. 1989–91, Ed. 1992–, Ed.-in-Chief Assoc. Newspapers 1998–; Ed. Evening Standard 1991–92; Dir Associated Newspaper Holdings 1991–, Daily Mail & General Trust PLC 1998–, Teletext Holdings Ltd 2000–; mem. Press Complaints Comm. 1998–. *Address:* c/o Daily Mail, Northcliffe House, 2 Derry St, London W8 5TT, England.

D'AGUIAR, Fred, BA, RMN; poet, novelist, dramatist, essayist and professor of English; b. 2 Feb. 1960, London, England. *Education:* Maudsley Hosp., University of Kent. *Career:* Writer-in-Residence, London Borough of Lewisham, 1986–87, Birmingham Polytechnic, 1988–89; Instructor in Writing, Arvon Foundation, 1986–; Judith Wilson Visiting Fellow, University of Cambridge 1989–90; Northern Arts Literary Fellow, Newcastle and Durham universities 1990–92; Visiting Writer, Amherst College, Massachusetts 1992–94; Asst Prof. of English, Bates College, Lewiston, Maine, 1994–95; Prof. of English, University of Miami 1995–2003; Prof., Dir Creative Writing Virginia Polytechnic Inst. and State Univ. 2003–. *Television:* Sweet Thames 1992, Rwanda Stories 1995, The Longest Memory 1998. *Play:* A Jamaican Airman Foresees His Death 1995. *Publications:* Poetry: Mama Dot 1985, Airy Hall 1989, British Subjects 1993, Bill of Rights 1998, Bloodlines, verse novel 2000, An English Sampler, New and Selected Poems 2001. Fiction: The Longest Memory 1994; Dear Future 1996; Feeding the Ghosts 1998; Bethany Bettany 2003. Co-Editor: The New British Poetry 1989. Selected essays in: The Age of Anxiety 1996, Black British Culture and Society 1999, Best American Essays 2000. *Honours:* Guyana Poetry Award 1987BBC Race in the Media Award 1992; Most Innovative Film Award, British Film Institute 1993; Whitbread First Novel Award 1995; David Higham First Novel Award 1995; Guyana Fiction Award 1996. *Literary Agent:* David Higham Associates, 5 Lower John Street, London W1, England. *Telephone:* (20) 7393-4400. *Fax:* (20) 7393-4401. *E-mail:* fredd@vt.edu. *Website:* Fred D'Aguiar.com.

DAHLEN, Beverly Jean; Poet and Teacher; b. 7 Nov. 1934, Portland, Oregon, USA; m. Richard Pervier, 1957, divorced 1966. *Education:* BA, Language Arts, California State University, Humboldt, 1956; Postgraduate studies in Education and Creative Writing, California State University at San Francisco, 1966–69. *Career:* Asst Secretary, Poetry Center, California State University, San Francisco, 1967–73; Creative Writing Teacher, California Poetry-in-the-Schools Project, 1970–74; Creative Writing Teacher, East Bay Community Arts Project, 1974–80; Adult Learning Center, City College of San Francisco, 1980–; Creative Writing Teacher, College of Marin, San Francisco State University; Teacher, summer writing workshops, Foothill College, Los Altos, CA, Lake Placid Art Center, Lake Place, New York, Naropa Institute, Boulder, CO; Founder, HOWever. *Publications:* Poetry: Out of the Third, 1974; A Letter at Easter: To George Stanley, 1976; The Egyptian Poems, 1983; A Reading, 1–7, 1985; A Reading, 11–17, 1989; A Reading, 9–10, 1992. Contributions: periodicals including: Shocks Magazine; Room; Bed; Isthmus; Transfer; Feminist Studies; Ironwood; Poetics Journal; Sagetrieb; Conjunctions; Acts; Hambone; HOW(ever). *Honours:* Residency, Briarcombe, Bolinas, CA, 1983; Residency, Djerrasi Foundation, Woodside, CA, 1984. *Address:* c/o Chax Press, 101 W Sixth Street, Tucson, AZ 85701, USA.

DAICHES, David, CBE, MA, DPhil, FRSL; academic and writer; b. 2 Sept. 1912, Sunderland, England; m. Isobel Janet Mackay 1937; one s. two d. *Education:* Edinburgh University, University of Oxford. *Career:* Fellow, Balliol College, Oxford, 1936–37; Asst Prof., University of Chicago, 1939–43; Prof., Cornell University, 1946–51, Sussex University, 1961–77; University Lecturer, 1951–61, Fellow, Jesus College, 1957–62, Cambridge; Dir, Institute for Advanced Studies, Edinburgh University, 1980–86; mem. Asscn for Scottish Literary Studies, hon. pres.; MLA of America, hon. mem.; Saltire Society, hon. pres. *Publications:* 45 books including: The Novel and the Modern World, 1939; Robert Burns, 1950; Two Worlds, 1956; A Critical History of English Literature, 1960; The Paradox of Scottish Culture, 1964; God and the Poets, 1984; Edinburgh: A Traveller's Companion, 1986; A Weekly Scotsman and Other Poems, 1994. *Honours:* Scottish Arts Council Book Award 1973, Scottish Book of the Year Award 1984, various hon. doctorates. *Address:* 22 Belgrave Crescent, Edinburgh, EH4 3AL, Scotland.

DALAI LAMA, The, temporal and spiritual head of Tibet; Fourteenth Incarnation, (Tenzin Gyatso); Tibetan; b. 6 July 1935, Taktser, Amdo Prov., NE Tibet. *Career:* born of Tibetan peasant family in Amdo Prov.; enthroned at Lhasa 1940; rights exercised by regency 1934–50; assumed political power 1950; fled to Chumbi in S Tibet after abortive resistance to Chinese State 1950; negotiated agreement with China 1951; Vice-Chair. Standing Cttee CPPCC, mem. Nat. Cttee 1951–59; Hon. Chair. Chinese Buddhist Asscn 1953–59; Del. to Nat. People's Congress 1954–59; Chair. Preparatory Cttee for the 'Autonomous Region of Tibet' 1955–59; fled Tibet to India after suppression of Tibetan national uprising 1959; Dr of Buddhist Philosophy (Monasteries of Sera, Drepung and Gaden, Lhasa) 1959; Supreme Head of all Buddhist sects in Tibet (Xizang). *Publications:* My Land and People 1962, The Opening of the Wisdom Eye 1963, The Buddhism of Tibet and the Key to the Middle Way 1975, Kindness, Clarity and Insight 1984, A Human Approach to World Peace 1984, Freedom in Exile (autobiog.) 1990, My Tibet 1990, The Way to Freedom 1995, The Good Heart 1996, Beyond Dogma 1996, Ethics for the New Millennium 1998, Violence and Compassion 1998, Art of Happiness (co-author) 1999, Ancient Wisdom, Modern World 1999, The Path to Tranquility: Daily Wisdom 1999, Transforming the Mind: Eight Verses on Generating Compassion and Transforming Your Life 2000, A Simple Path: Basic Buddhist Teachings by His Holiness the Dalai Lama 2000, The Art of Living: A Guide to Contentment, Joy and Fulfillment 2001, Stages of Meditation: Training the Mind for Wisdom 2001, Compassionate Life 2001, His Holiness the Dalai Lama: In My Own Words 2001, Essence of the Heart Sutra 2002, How to Practice 2002, The Spirit of Peace 2002. *Honours:* Memory Prize 1989, Congressional Human Rights Award 1989, Nobel Peace Prize 1989, Freedom Award (USA) 1991. *Address:* Thekchen Choeling, McLeod Ganj 176219, Dharamsala, Himachal Pradesh, India.

DALE, Peter John; Poet, Writer and Trans; b. 21 Aug. 1938, Addlestone, Surrey, England; m. Pauline Strouvelle, 29 June 1963, one s. one d.

Education: BA, English, St Peter's College, Oxford, 1963. *Career:* Teacher of Secondary Schools, 1963–93; Co-Ed., Agenda, 1972–96; Editorial Dir, Between the Lines, 1997–; Poetry Ed., Oxford Today, 1999–; mem. Society of Authors; Trans Assen. *Publications:* Poetry: Walk from the House, 1962; The Storms, 1968; Mortal Fire, 1976; One Another (sonnet sequence), 1978; Too Much of Water, 1983; A Set of Darts (epigrams with W. S. Milne and Robert Richardson), 1990; Earth Light: New Poems, 1991; Edge to Edge: Selected Poems, 1996; Da Capo (poem sequence), 1997; Under the Breath, 2002. Prose: Michael Hamburger in Conversation with Peter Dale, 1998; An Introduction to Rhyme, 1998; Anthony Thwaite in Conversation with Peter Dale and Ian Hamilton, 1999; Richard Wilbur in Conversation with Peter Dale, 2000; Peter Dale in Conversation with Cynthia Haven, 2003. Translator: Selected Poems of François Villon, 1978; Poems of Jules Laforgue, 1986; The Divine Comedy, terza rima version, 1996; Poems of Jules Laforgue, 2001; Poems of François Villon, 2001. Contributions: journals and periodicals. *Honours:* Arts Council Bursary, 1970. *Address:* 10 Selwood Rd, Sutton, Surrey SM3 9JU, England.

DALESKI, Hillel Matthew; academic and writer; b. 19 July 1926, Johannesburg, South Africa; m. 1st Aviva Prop 1950 (divorced); four c.; m. 2nd Shirley Kaufman 1974. *Education:* BA, 1947, BA, 1949, MA, 1952, University of the Witwatersrand; PhD, Hebrew University, Jerusalem, 1963. *Career:* Asst Lecturer to Assoc. Prof., 1958–76, Prof. of English 1976–, Chair., Dept of English, 1968–70, 1984–85, Provost, School of Overseas Students, 1973–76, Hebrew University, Jerusalem; mem. Dickens Society, pres., 1985. *Publications:* The Forked Flame: A Study of D. H. Lawrence, 1965; Dickens and the Art of Analogy, 1970; Joseph Conrad: The Way of Dispossession, 1977; The Divided Heroine: A Recurrent Pattern in Six English Novels, 1984; Unities: Studies in the English Novel, 1985; Thomas Hardy and Paradoxes of Love, 1997. *Honours:* Israel Acad. of Sciences and Humanities, 1993; Hon. Foreign Mem., American Acad. of Arts and Sciences, 1999; Israel Prize Laureate, 2000. *Address:* Dept of English, Hebrew University, Jerusalem, Israel.

DALLEK, Robert; Prof. of History, Author and Biographer; b. 16 May 1934, New York, NY, USA; m. 1st Ilse F. Shatzkin 20 Nov. 1959 (died Oct. 1962); m. 2nd Geraldine R. Kronmal 22 Aug. 1965; one s. one d. *Education:* BA, History, Univ. of Illinois, 1955; MA, History, 1957, PhD, History, 1964, Columbia Univ. *Career:* Instructor in History, Columbia Univ., 1960–64; Asst Prof. to Prof. of History, Univ. of California at Los Angeles, 1964–94; Research Assoc., Southern California Psychoanalytic Institute, 1981–85; Commonwealth Fund Lecturer, Univ. Coll. London, 1984; Thompson Lecturer, Univ. of Wyoming, 1986; Charles Griffin Lecturer, Vassar Coll., 1987; Visiting Prof., California Institute of Technology, 1993, LBJ School of Public Affairs, Univ. of Texas, 1996; Harmsworth Visiting Prof., Univ. of Oxford, 1994–95; Prof. of History, Boston Univ., 1996; Marjorie Harris Weiss Lecturer, Brown Univ., 1998; Herbert Marcuse Lecturer, Brandeis Univ., 1999; Harry Seigle Lecturer, Washington Univ., St Louis, 2001; Charles Grant Lecturer, Middlebury Coll., 2001; George Bancroft Lecturer, US Naval Acad., 2001; mem. American Acad. of Arts and Sciences, fellow; American Psychoanalytic Assen; Society of American Historians, fellow; Society of Historians of American Foreign Relations, pres., 1995. *Publications:* Democrat and Diplomat: The Life of William E. Dodd, 1968; Western Europe (ed.), Vol. I of The Dynamics of World Power: A Documentary History of United States Foreign Policy, 1945–1973, 1973; Franklin D. Roosevelt and American Foreign Policy, 1932–1945, 1979; The American Style of Foreign Policy: Cultural Politics and Foreign Affairs, 1983; Ronald Reagan: The Politics of Symbolism, 1984; The Great Republic: A History of the American People (with others), third edn, 1985; Lone Star Rising: Lyndon Johnson and His Times, 1908–1960, 1991; The Encyclopedia of 20th-Century American History (assoc. ed. with others), four vols, 1995; Hail to the Chief: The Making and Unmaking of American Presidents, 1996; Flawed Giant: Lyndon Johnson and His Times, 1961–1973, 1998; John F. Kennedy: An Unfinished Life, 1917–1963, 2003. Contributions: scholarly books and journals. *Honours:* Guggenheim Fellowship, 1973–74; Senior Fellow, National Endowment for the Humanities, 1976–77; Bancroft Prize, 1980; Humanities Fellow, Rockefeller Foundation, 1981–82; Notable Book Citations, New York Times Book Review, 1983, 1991, 1998; Fellow, ACLS, 1984–85; Research Grants, Lyndon B. Johnson Foundation, 1984–85, 1988–89. *Address:* 2138 Cathedral Ave NW, Washington, DC 20008, USA. *E-mail:* rdallek@aol.com.

DALMAS, John; Author; b. 3 Sept. 1926, Chicago, IL, USA; m. Gail Hill, 15 Sept. 1954, one s. one d. *Education:* BSc, Michigan State College, 1954; Master of Forestry, University of Minnesota, 1955; PhD, Colorado State University, 1967. *Career:* mem. SFWA; Vasa Order of America. *Publications:* The Yngling, 1969; The Varkaus Conspiracy, 1983; Touch the Stars: Emergence (with Carl Martin), 1983; Homecoming, 1984; The Scroll of Man, 1985; Fanglith, 1985; Aspen: Its Ecology and Management in the Western United States (sr author), 1985; The Reality Matrix 1986; The Walkaway Clause, 1986; The Regiment, 1987; The Playmasters (with Rodney Martin), 1987; Return to Fanglith, 1987; The Lantern of God, 1987; The General's President, 1988; The Lizard War, 1989; The White Regiment, 1990; The Kalif's War, 1991; The Yngling and the Circle of Power, 1992; The Orc Wars (collection), 1992; The Regiment's War, 1993; The Yngling in Yamato, 1994; The Lion of Farside, 1995; The Bavarian Gate, 1997; The Three Cornered War, 1999; The Lion Returns, 1999; Soldiers, 2001; The Puppet Master, 2001; Otherwhens, Otherwheres, 2003. Contributions: professional journals, fiction magazines and themed anthologies. *Address:* 1425 W Glass Ave, Spokane, WA 99206, USA. *E-mail:* dalmas@earthlink.net. *Website:* www.sfwa.org/members/dalmas.

DALRYMPLE, Theodore; British physician, psychiatrist and essayist; b. (Anthony Daniels), 1949, London. *Career:* works in a British prison; Contributing Ed., City Journal, New York; columnist, The Spectator, London. *Publications:* Life at the Bottom: The Worldview that Makes the Underclass 2003; contrib. to The Spectator, The Times, The Daily Telegraph, New Statesman, New Criterion, National Review, Wall Street Journal. *Address:* City Journal, Manhattan Institute for Policy Research, 52 Vanderbilt Avenue, New York, NY 10017, USA. *E-mail:* cj@city-journal.org. *Website:* www.city-journal.org.

DALRYMPLE, William Benedict, MA, FRSL, FRGS; writer; b. 20 March 1965, Edinburgh, Scotland; m. Olivia Fraser; two s. one d. *Education:* Trinity Coll., Cambridge. *Career:* mem. PEN. *Publications:* In Xanadu 1989, City of Djinns 1993, From the Holy Mountain 1997, The Age of Kali 1998, White Mughals: Love and Betrayal in Eighteenth-Century India 2002; contrib. to TLS, Spectator, Sunday Times, Guardian, New York Times. *Honours:* Yorkshire Post Best First Work Award 1990, Scottish Arts Council award 1990, Thomas Cook Travel Book Award 1994, Sunday Times Young British Writer of the Year 1994, Scottish Arts Council Autumn Book Award 1997, BAFTA Grierson Award for best documentary 2002, Royal Scottish Geographical Society Mungo Park Medal 2002, Wolfson History Prize 2003, Scottish Book of the Year 2003. *Literary Agent:* David Godwin Associates, 55 Monmouth Street, London, WC2H 9DG, England. *Address:* 1 Pages' Yard, Church Street, London, W4 2PA, England. *E-mail:* pagesyard@aol.com. *Website:* www.williamdalrymple.com.

DALTON, Amanda; British writer; b. 1957, Coventry, Warwickshire. *Career:* teacher; organiser of writing courses at The Arvon Foundation in Lumb Bank; Education Officer for Royal Exchange Theatre, Manchester. *Publications:* The Dad Baby 1994, Room of Leaves (adapted for BBC Radio 4 1998) 1996, How to Disappear 1999; contrib. to Comma: Anthology of Short Stories 2002. *Address:* c/o Bloodaxe Books Ltd, Highgreen, Tarset, Northumberland NE48 1RP, England. *Website:* www.bloodaxebooks.com.

DANA, Robert (Patrick); Emeritus Prof. of English and Poet; b. 2 June 1929, Allston, Massachusetts, USA; m. 1st Mary Kowalke, 2 June 1951, divorced 1973, three c.; m. 2nd Margaret Sellen, 14 Sept. 1974. *Education:* AB, Drake University, 1951; MA, University of Iowa, 1954. *Career:* Asst Prof., Assoc. Prof., Prof. of English, Cornell College, Mount Vernon, IA, 1953–94; Distinguished Visiting Poet, University of Florida, 1975–76, Wayne State University, 1978–79, University of Idaho, 1980, Wichita State University, 1982, Stockholm University, 1996; Ed., Hillside Press, Mount Vernon, 1957–67; Ed., 1964–68, Contributing Ed., 1991–, North American Review; Contributing Ed., American Poetry Review, 1973–88, New Letters, 1980–83; mem. Acad. of American Poets; PEN; Associated Writing Programs; Poetry Society of America. *Publications:* My Glass Brother and Other Poems, 1957; The Dark Flags of Waking, 1964; Journeys from the Skin: A Poem in Two Parts, 1966; Some Versions of Silence: Poems, 1967; The Power of the Visible, 1971; In a Fugitive Season, 1980; What the Stones Know, 1984; Blood Harvest, 1986; Against the Grain: Interviews with Maverick American Publishers, 1986; Starting Out for the Difficult World, 1987; What I Think I Know: New and Selected Poems, 1990; Wildebeest, 1993; Yes, Everything, 1994; Hello, Stranger: Beach Poems, 1996; A Community of Writers: Paul Engle and The Iowa Writers' Workshop, 1999; Summer, 2000; The Morning of the Red Admirals, 2004. Contributions: New Yorker; New York Times; Poetry; Georgia Review; Manoa. *Honours:* Rainer Maria Rilke Prize, 1984; National Endowment for the Arts Fellowships, 1985, 1993; Delmore Schwartz Memorial Poetry Award, 1989; Carl Sandburg Medal for Poetry, 1994; Pushcart Prize, 1996. *Address:* 1466 Westview Dr., Coralville, IA 52241, USA.

DANGAREMBGA, Tsitsi; Zimbabwean novelist, playwright and filmmaker; b. 1959, Mutoko, Southern Rhodesia. *Education:* Univ. of Cambridge, Univ. of Zimbabwe, Deutsche Film and Fernseh Akademie, Berlin. *Publications:* The Letter (short story), 1985; Nervous Conditions (novel), 1988. Other: The Lost of the Soil (play), 1983; She No Longer Weeps (play), 1987; Neria (film), 1992; Everyone's Child (film), 1996. *Honours:* Commonwealth Writers' Prize 1989. *Address:* c/o The Women's Press, 34 Great Sutton Street, London EC1V 0DX, England.

DANGOR, Achmat; South African poet and novelist; b. 1948, Newclare, Johannesburg. *Career:* mem., Black Thoughts 1970s, Congress of South African Writers (COSAW) 1980s. *Play:* Majiet 1986. *Publications:* poetry: Bulldozer 1983, Private Voices 1992; novels: The Z Town Trilogy 1989, Bitter Fruit 2003; short story collections: Waiting for Leila 1978, Kafka's Cure: A Novella and Three Other Stories 1997; co-editor: Voices from Within: Black Poetry from South Africa 1986; contrib. to The Return of the Amasi Bird 1982, Modern South African Poetry 1984, New Nation, Staffrider. *Honours:* Mofolo-Plomer Prize, BBC Prize for African Poetry. *Address:* c/o Random House UK Ltd, 20 Vauxhall Bridge Road, London, SW1V 2SA, England. *Website:* www.randomhouse.co.uk.

DANIEL, Colin (see Windsor, Patricia).

DANIEL, Wayne Wendell; academic and writer; b. 14 Feb. 1929, Tallapoosa, GA, USA; m. Mary Yarbrough 1956; one s. two d. *Education:* BSEd, University of Georgia, 1951; MPH, University of North Carolina, 1959; PhD, University of Oklahoma, 1965. *Career:* Statistical Research Asst, 1957–58, Research Statistician, 1959–60, Biostatistical Analyst, 1960–63, Chief, Mental Health Statistics Section, Biostatistics Service, 1965–67, Dir, Biostatistics Service, 1967–68, Chief Statistician, 1968, Georgia Dept of Public Health; Asst Prof. to Prof. of Decision Sciences, 1968–91, Prof. Emeritus, 1991–, Georgia State University; mem. American Public Health Asscn, fellow. *Publications:* Biostatistics: A Foundation for Analysis in the Health Sciences, 1974; Business Statistics for Management and Economics (with James C. Terrell), 1975; Introductory Statistics with Applications, 1977; Applied Nonparametric Statistics, 1978; Essentials of Business Statistics, 1984; Pickin' on Peachtree: A History of Country Music in Atlanta, 1990. Contributions: numerous journals and periodicals. *Address:* 2943 Appling Drive, Chamblee, GA 30341-5113, USA.

DANIELS, Dorothy, (Danielle Dorsett, Angela Gray, Cynthia Kavanaugh, Helaine Ross, Suzanne Somers, Geraldine Thayer, Helen Gray Weston); Writer; b. 1 July 1915, Waterbury, CT, USA; m. 7 Oct. 1937. *Education:* Normal School, New Brittain, CT. *Career:* mem. Authors' Guild; National League of American Pen Women, hon. mem.; Ventura County Writers. *Publications:* The Magic Ring, 1978; Purple and the Gold, 1978; Yesterday's Evil, 1980; Veil of Treachery, 1980; Legend of Death, 1980; Valley of Shadows, 1980; Monte Carlo, 1981; Saratoga, 1981; Sisters of Valcour, 1981; For Love and Valcour, 1983; Crisis at Valcour, 1985; Illusion of Haven's Edge, 1990. *Address:* 6107 Village 6, Camarillo, CA 93010, USA.

DANIELS, Max (see Gellis, Roberta Leah).

DANIELS, Olga (see Sinclair, Olga Ellen).

DANN, Colin Michael; Author; b. 10 March 1943, Richmond, Surrey, England; m. Janet Elizabeth Stratton, 4 June 1977. *Career:* mem. Society of Authors. *Publications:* The Animals of Farthing Wood, 1979; In the Grip of Winter, 1981; Fox's Feud, 1982; The Fox Cub Bold, 1983; The Siege of White Deer Park, 1985; The Ram of Sweetriver, 1986; King of the Vagabonds, 1987; The Beach Dogs, 1988; The Flight from Farthing Wood, 1988; Just Nuffin, 1989; In the Path of the Storm, 1989; A Great Escape, 1990; A Legacy of Ghosts, 1991; The City Cats, 1991; Battle for the Park, 1992; The Adventure Begins, 1994; Copycat, 1998; Nobody's Dog, 1999; Journey to Freedom, 1999; Lion Country, 2000; Pride of the Plains, 2002. *Honours:* Arts Council National Award for Children's Literature, 1980. *Address:* Castle Oast, Ewhurst Green, East Sussex, England.

DANN, Jack; Author, Writer, Lecturer and Ed.; b. 15 Feb. 1945, Johnson City, NY, USA; m. 1st Jeanne Van Buren 1 Jan. 1983 (divorced Aug. 1994); one step-s. one d.; m. 2nd Janeen Suzanne Webb 17 June 1995. *Education:* BA, 1968, Graduate Studies, 1971, SUNY at Binghamton; St John's Law School, 1969–70. *Career:* Man. Ed., SFWA Bulletin, 1970–75; Instructor, Writing, Science Fiction, Broome Community College, Binghamton, NY, 1972, 1990, 1991; Asst Prof., Cornell University, Ithaca, NY, 1973; Mem., Board of Dirs, National Home Life Assurance Company, New York; Principal Partner, Aultman Robertson and Assocs advertising and public relations firm; mem. SFWA; Authors' Guild; World Future Society. *Publications:* Faster Than Light: An Anthology of Stories about Interstellar Travel (ed. with George Zenrowski), 1976; Starhiker: A Novel, 1977; Christs and Other Poems, 1978; Timetipping (short stories), 1980; Junction, 1981; The Man Who Melted, 1984; Slow Dancing In Time (short stories with Gardner Dozois, Michael Swanwick, Susan Casper, Jack L. Haldeman II), 1990; Echoes of Thunder (short novel, with Jack L. Haldeman II), 1991; High Steel (with Jack C. Haldeman II), 1993; The Memory Cathedral: A Secret History of Leonardo da Vinci, 1995; The Silent, 1998; BAD Medicine, 2000; Jubilee: The Essential Jack Dann, 2001; Da Vinci Rising, 2001; Counting Coup, 2001. Ed. or joint Ed.: Wandering Stars: An Anthology of Jewish Fantasy and Science Fiction, 1974; Immortal, 1977; Future Power, 1976; Aliens!, 1980; Unicorns!, 1982; Magicats!, 1984; Bestiary!, 1985; Mermaids!, 1985; Sorcerers!, 1986; Bestiary, 1986; In the Field of Fire, 1987; Demons!, 1987; Dogtails!, Seaserpents!, 1989; Dinosaurs!, 1990; Little People, 1991; Magicats II, 1991; Unicorns II, 1992; Dragons, 1993; Invaders, 1993; Horses!, 1994; Angels, 1995; Dinosaurs II, 1995; Hackers, 1996; Timegates, 1997; Clones, 1998; Nanotech, 1998; Future War, 1999; Armageddons, 1999; Aliens Among Us, 2000; Space Soldiers, 2001; Genometry, 2001; Dreaming Down Under, 2001; Future Sports, 2002. Contributions: New Dimensions; Orbit; New Worlds; Asimov's Science Fiction Magazines; Fiction Writers' Handbook. *Honours:* Esteemed Knight, Mark Twain Society, 1975–; Co-Winner, Gilgamesh Award, 1986; Nebula Award for Best Novella, 1996, and for Best Science Fiction Story, 1997, SFWA; Ditmar Award for Best Anthology, 1999; World Fantasy Award for Best Anthology, 1999. *Address:* 825 Front St, Binghamton, NY 13905, USA; PO Box 6231, St Kilda Rd Central, Melbourne, Vic. 3004, Australia.

DANTICAT, Edwidge, BA, MFA; American writer; b. 19 Jan. 1969, Port-au-Prince, Haiti. *Education:* Barnard Coll., Brown Univ. *Publications:* fiction: Breath, Eyes, Memory 1994, Krik? Krak! 1995, The Farming of Bones 1998, The Dew Breaker 2004; non-fiction: Odillon Pierre, Artist of Haiti (with Jonathan Demme) 1999; editor: The Beacon Best of 2000: Great Writing by Women and Men of All Colors and Cultures 2000, The Butterfly's Way: Voices from the Haitian Dyaspora in the United States 2001. *Honours:* Granta's Best of American Novelists Citation 1996, American Book Award, Before Columbus Foundation 1998. *Address:* c/o Soho Press, 853 Broadway, No. 1903, New York, NY 10003, USA.

DANTO, Arthur Coleman; academic, writer and editor; b. 1 Jan. 1924, Ann Arbor, MI, USA; m. 1st Shirley Rovetch 1946 (died 1978); two d.; m. 2nd Barbara Westman 1980. *Education:* BA, Wayne State Univ., 1948; MA, 1949, PhD, 1952, Columbia Univ.; Postgraduate Studies, Univ. of Paris, 1949–50. *Career:* Teacher, 1952–72, Johnsonian Prof. of Philosophy, 1972–92, Chair., Philosophy Dept, 1979–87, Prof. Emeritus, 1992–, Columbia Univ.; Ed., Journal of Philosophy, 1975–; Art Critic, The Nation, 1984–. *Publications:* Analytical Philosophy of History, 1965; Nietzsche as Philosopher, 1965; Analytical Philosophy of Knowledge, 1968; What Philosophy Is, 1968; Mysticism and Morality, 1972; Analytical Philosophy of Action, 1973; Jean-Paul Sartre, 1975; The Transfiguration of the Commonplace, 1981; Narration and Knowledge, 1985; The Philosophical Disenfranchisement of Art, 1986; The State of the Art, 1987; Connections to the World, 1989; Encounters and Reflections, 1990; Beyond the Brillo Box, 1992; Embodied Meaning, 1994; Playing with the Edge, 1995; After the End of Art, 1996; The Madonna of the Future, 2000; The Abuse of Beauty, 2003. Contributions: articles and reviews in many publications. *Honours:* Fulbright Scholarship, 1949–50; Guggenheim Fellowships, 1969, 1982; Distinguished Fulbright Prof. to Yugoslavia, 1976; Lionel Trilling Book Prize, 1982; George S. Polk Award for Criticism, 1985; National Book Critics Circle Award in Criticism, 1990; New York Public Library Literary Lion, 1993; Frank Jewett Mather Prize in Criticism, College Art Asscn, 1996. *Address:* 420 Riverside Drive, New York, NY 10025, USA. *E-mail:* acd1@columbia.edu.

DAOUST, Jean-Paul; Writer, Poet, Teacher and Ed.; b. 30 Jan. 1946, Valleyfield, QC, Canada. *Education:* MA, University of Montréal, 1976. *Career:* Prof., Cegep Edouard-Montpetit, Québec; Mem., Editorial Board, magazine Estuaire; mem. Union des écrivaines et des écrivains québécois. *Publications:* Poetry: Oui, cher: Récit, 1976; Chaises longues, 1977; Portrait d'intérieur, 1981; Poèmes de Babylone, 1982; Taxi, 1984; Dimanche après-midi, 1985; La peau du coeur et son opéra, 1985; Les garçons magiques, 1986; Suite contemporaine, 1987; Les Cendres bleues, 1990; Rituels d'Amérique, 1990; Les Poses de la lumière, 1991; Du Dandysme, 1991; L'Amérique, 1993; Poèmes faxés (co-author), 1994; 111, Wooster Street, 1996; Taxi pour Babylone, 1996; Les Chambres de la Mer, 1991; Les Saisons de L'Ange, Tome I, 1997, Tome II, 1999; Blue Ashes, 1999; Les versets amoureux, 2001; Lèvres ouvertes, 2001; Roses labyrinthes, 2002. Other: Soleils d'acajou (novel), 1983; Le Désert Rose (novel), 2000. *Honours:* Gov.-Gen.'s Literary Award in Poetry, 1990. *Address:* 151 chemin Champoux, Ste Mélanie, QC J0K 3A0, Canada.

DARBY, John; Prof. of Ethnic Studies and Writer; b. 18 Nov. 1940, Belfast, Northern Ireland; m. Marie Darby, 13 April 1966, two s. *Education:* BA, Modern History, 1962, Diploma, Education, 1970, Queen's University, Belfast; Certificate, Education, St Joseph's College of Education, Belfast, 1963; DPhil, University of Ulster, 1985. *Career:* Teacher of History, St Malachy's College, Belfast, 1963–71; Research and Publications Officer, Northern Ireland Community Relations Commission, Belfast, 1971–74; Lecturer in Social Administration, New University of Ulster, 1974–85; Assoc. in Education, Graduate School of Education, Harvard University, 1980; Dir, Centre for the Study of Conflict, 1985–91, Prof. of Ethnic Studies, 1985–98, University of Ulster; Visiting Prof., Center for International Studies, Duke University, 1988; Dir, Ethnic Studies Network, 1991–, INCORE (Initiative on Conflict Resolution and Ethnicity), University of Ulster and United Nations University, Japan, 1992–97; Prof. of Comparative Ethnic Studies, University of Notre Dame, IN, 2000–. *Publications:* Conflict in Northern Ireland, 1976; Northern Ireland: Background to the Conflict (ed.), 1983; Dressed to Kill: Cartoonists and the Northern Irish Conflict, 1983; Intimidation and the Control of Conflict in Northern Ireland, 1986; Political Violence (ed. with N. Dodge and A. C. Hepburn), 1990; Scorpions in a Bottle, 1997; The Management of Peace Processes (ed. with R. MacGinty), 2000; The Effects of Violence on Peace Processes, 2001; Guns and Government: The Management of the Northern Ireland Peace Process, 2002; Contemporary Peacekeeping (ed. with Roger MacGinty), 2003. Contributions: many books and journals. *Honours:* Outstanding Academic Book Citation, Choice, 1977; Visiting Scholar, Rockefeller Centre, Bellagio, Italy, 1990; Guest Fellow, Woodrow Wilson Center, Washington, DC, 1992; OBE, 1997; Hon. Prof., University of Sunderland, 1997; Jennings Randolph Senior Fellow, US Institute of Peace, Washington, DC, 1998; Visiting Prof., University of Notre Dame, IN, 1999–2001; Fellow, Fulbright New Century Scholars Program, 2003. *Address:* 61 Strand Rd, Portstewart BT55 7LU, Northern Ireland.

D'ARGY SMITH, Marcelle; British magazine editor; b. 1947. *Career:* fmr Ed. Cosmopolitan magazine until 1995; freelance journalist and broadcaster 1995–97; Ed. Woman's Journal 1997–99; stood as Pro Euro Conservative cand., European elections 1999. *Publication:* The Lovers' Guide: What Women Really Want 2002. *Honours:* Women's Magazine Ed. of the Year 1991. *Address:* c/o Woman's Journal, Kings Reach Tower, Stamford Street, London, SE1, England.

DARKE, Marjorie Sheila; Children's Author; b. 25 Jan. 1929, Birmingham, England; m. 1952; two s. one d. *Education:* Leicester College of Art,

1947–50; Central School of Art, London, 1950–51. *Career:* mem. Society of Authors; International PEN. *Publications:* for young adults: Ride the Iron Horse, 1973; The Star Trap, 1974; A Question of Courage, 1975; The First of Midnight, 1977; A Long Way to Go, 1978; Comeback, 1981; Tom Post's Private Eye, 1982; Messages and Other Shivery Tales, 1984; A Rose From Blighty, 1990. for beginner readers: Mike's Bike, 1974; What Can I Do?, 1975; The Big Brass Band, 1976; My Uncle Charlie, 1977; Carnival Day, 1979. Children's: Kipper's Turn, 1976; Kipper Skips, 1979; Imp, 1985; The Rainbow Sandwich, 1989; Night Windows, 1990; Emma's Monster, 1992; Just Bear and Friends, 1996. *Literary Agent:* Rogers, Coleridge & White, 20 Powis Mews, London W11 1JN, England.

DARKO, Amma; Novelist; b. 1956, Tamale, Ghana; m.; three c. *Education:* Univ. of Science and Technology, Kumasi, 1980. *Career:* Tax inspector; mem. Fellow, Cambridge Seminar. *Publications:* Beyond the Horizon, 1991; The Housemaid, 1998. *Address:* c/o African Writers Series, Heinemann Educational Publishers, Halley Ct, Jordan Hill, Oxford OX2 8EJ, England.

DARLING, Julia, MA; British poet, playwright and writer. *Education:* Newcastle Univ. *Career:* fmrly worked with group, The Poetry Virgins; fmr Associate Royal Literary Fellow, Newcastle Univ.; currently on Project Fellowship, Newcastle Univ.; Writer-in-Residence, Live Theatre, Newcastle; various contributions to art exhibitions and projects. *Publications:* Small Beauties (poems), 1988; Unbound (poems, ed.), 1993; Bloodlines (short stories), 1995; Crocodile Soup (novel), 1998; Tangles and Starbursts: Living with Dementia (non-fiction), 2001; The Taxi Driver's Daughter (novel), 2003; Sudden Collapses In Public Places (poems), 2003. Plays: Attachments; Doughnuts Like Fanny's; Personal Belongings; The Last Post; Posties; Eating the Elephant; Venetia Love Goes Netting; Personal Belongings; Sea-life. Contributions: short story anthologies: Biting Back; Snap Shots; Gas and Air; England Calling; New Writing Ten; Book of the North (CD-ROM). *Honours:* Royal Literary Fund Fellow, Newcastle University; Northern Rock Foundation Writer's Award, 2003. *Literary Agent:* Curtis Brown Ltd, Haymarket House, 28–29 Haymarket, London, SW1Y 4SP, England. *Telephone:* (20) 7393-4400. *Fax:* (20) 7393-4401. *E-mail:* info@curtisbrown.co.uk. *Website:* www.curtisbrown.co.uk. *E-mail:* julia@juliadarling.co.uk. *Website:* www.juliadarling.co.uk.

DARNTON, Robert (Choate); Prof. of European History and Writer; b. 10 May 1939, New York, NY, USA; m. Susan Lee Glover, 29 June 1963, one s. two d. *Education:* BA Magna cum Laude, Harvard College, 1960; Bachelor of Philosophy in History, 1962, Doctorate of Philosophy in History, 1964, University of Oxford. *Career:* Asst Prof., 1968–71, Assoc. Prof., 1971–72, Prof., 1972–, Shelby Cullom Davis Prof. of European History, 1985–, Dir, Program in European Cultural Studies, 1987–95, Princeton University; Dir d'Études, École des Hautes Études en Sciences Sociales, Paris, 1971, 1981, 1985; Fellow, Center for Advanced Study in the Behavioral Sciences, Stanford, 1973–74, Netherlands Institute for Advanced Study, 1976–77, Institute for Advanced Study, Berlin, 1989–90, 1993–94; Mem., Institute for Advanced Study, Princeton, NJ, 1977–81, All Souls College, Oxford, 1996–; George Eastman Visiting Prof., University of Oxford, 1986–87; Lecturer, Collège de France, 1987; Hon. Prof., University of Warwick, 1996–; mem. Academia Europaea; Académie Royale de Langue et de Littérature Françaises, Belgium; American Acad. of Arts and Sciences, fellow; American Antiquarian Society; American Philosophical Society; American Society for Eighteenth-Century Studies; International Society for Eighteenth-Century Studies, pres., 1987–91; American Historical Asscn, pres., 1999. *Publications:* Mesmerism and the End of the Enlightenment, 1968; The Business of Enlightenment: A Publishing History of the Encyclopédie, 1979; The Literary Underground of the Old Regime, 1982; The Great Cat Massacre and Other Episodes in French Cultural History, 1984; Revolution in Print: The Press in France 1775–1800 (ed. with Daniel Roche), 1989; The Kiss of Lamourette: Reflections in Cultural History, 1989; Edition et sédition: L'univers de la littérature clandestine au XVIIIe siècle, 1991; Berlin Journal, 1989–1990, 1991; Gens de Lettres, Gens du Livre, 1992; The Forbidden Best-Sellers of Prerevolutionary France, 1995; The Corpus of Clandestine Literature in France, 1769–1789, 1995; Démocratie (ed. with Olivier Duhamel), 1998; George Washington's False Teeth: An Unconventional Guide to the Eighteenth Century, 2003. *Honours:* John D. and Catherine T. MacArthur Foundation Fellowship, 1982–87; Los Angeles Times Book Prize, 1984; Officer, Ordre des Arts et des Lettres, 1993; Prix Médicis Étranger, 1991; Prix Chateaubriand, 1991; National Book Critics Circle Award, 1996; Chevalier, Légion d'honneur, 1999. *Address:* c/o Dept of History, Princeton University, 129 Dickinson Hall, Princeton, NJ 08544, USA.

DARRIEUSSECQ, Marie; Novelist; b. 3 Jan. 1969, Bayonne, France. *Education:* École Normale Superieure, Paris. *Publications:* Truismes (trans. as Pig Tales), 1996; Naissance des fantômes (trans. as My Phantom Husband), 1998; Le Mal de mer (trans. as Undercurrents, aka Breathing Underwater), 1999; Précisions sur les vagues, 1999; Bref séjour chez les vivants (trans. as A Brief Stay With the Living), 2001; Le Bébé, 2002; White, 2003. *Address:* c/o Faber and Faber Ltd, 3 Queen Sq., London WC1N 3AU, England.

DARUWALLA, Keki Nasserwanji, MA; poet and writer; b. 24 Jan. 1937, Lahore, India; m. Khorshed Keki Daruwalla 1965. *Education:* Punjab University, Chandigarh. *Career:* Visiting Fellow, Queen Elizabeth House, Oxford, 1980–81; mem. Sahitya Akademi, advisory board for English, 1983–87. *Publications:* Poetry: Under Oion, 1970; Apparition in April, 1971; Crossing of Rivers, 1976; Winter Poems, 1980; The Keeper of the Dead, 1982; Landscapes, 1987; A Summer of Tigers, 1995. Fiction: Sword and Abyss, 1979. Editor: Two Decades of Indian Poetry, 1960–80, 1981; The Minister for Permanent Unrest, 1996. Contributions: anthologies, journals, and periodicals. *Honours:* Sahitya Akademi Award, 1984; Commonwealth Poetry Award, Asia Region, 1987. *Address:* 79 Mount Kailash, Pocket-A, SFS Apartments, New Delhi 110065, India.

DARVILL, Timothy (Charles); Prof. of Archaeology; b. 22 Dec. 1957, Cheltenham, England. *Education:* BA, Archaeology, 1979, PhD, 1983, University of Southampton. *Career:* Dir, Timothy Darvill Archaeological Consultants, 1985–91; Prof. of Archaeology, Bournemouth University, 1991–; mem. Cotswold Archaeological Trust, Chair., 1992–; Council for British Archaeology; Institute of Field Archaeologists, Chair., 1989–91; Council of the National Trust, 1988–97; Neolithic Studies Group, Coordinator, 1983–; Subject Committee for Archeaology, chair., 2000–; Society of Antiquaries of London, Fellow; Society of Antiquaries of Scotland, Fellow. *Publications:* Megalithic Chambered Tombs of the Cotswold-Severn Region, 1982; The Archaeology of the Uplands, 1986; Prehistoric Britain, 1987; Ancient Monuments in the Countryside, 1987; Prehistoric Gloucestershire, 1987; Neolithic Houses in Northwest Europe and Beyond (ed. with Julian Thomas), 1996; Prehistoric Britain from the Air, 1996; The Concise Oxford Dictionary of Archaeology, 2002. Contributions: scholarly books and journals. *Address:* c/o School of Conservation Sciences, Bournemouth University, Poole House, Talbot Campus, Fern Barrow Poole, Dorset BH12 5BB, England.

D'ARZILLE, Juliette (see Arzille, Juliette d').

DAS, Kamala; Poetry Ed., Poet and Writer; b. 31 March 1934, Malabar, South India; m. K. Madhava Das, 1949, three s. *Education:* Private. *Career:* Poetry Ed., Illustrated Weekly of India, Mumbai, 1971–79. *Publications:* Poetry: Summer in Calcutta: Fifty Poems, 1965; The Descendants, 1967; The Old Playhouse and Other Poems, 1973; Tonight This Savage Rite: The Love Poetry of Kamala Das and Pritish Nandy, 1979; Collected Poems, 1987. Fiction: Alphabet of Lust, 1977; Manomi, 1987; The Sandalwood Tree, 1988. *Honours:* Kerala Sahitya Acad. Award for Fiction, 1969; Asian World Prize for Literature, 1985. *Address:* Sthanuvilas Bungalow, Sastgamangalam, Trivndrum 10, Kerala, India.

DASSANOWSKY, Robert von; Writer, Poet, Ed., University Prof. and Film Producer; b. 28 Jan. 1960, New York, NY, USA. *Education:* Graduate, American Acad. of Dramatic Arts, Pasadena, CA, 1977–78; American Film Institute Conservatory Program, Los Angeles, 1979–81; BA, 1985, MA, 1988, PhD, 1992, University of California at Los Angeles. *Career:* Founding Ed., Rohwedder: International Magazine of Literature and Art, 1986–93; Corresponding Ed., Rampike, 1991–; Editorial Board, Osiris, 1991–; Visiting Asst Prof. of German, University of California, 1992–93; Asst Prof. of German, 1993–99, Assoc. Prof. of German and Film, 1999–, Chair, Dept of Languages and Cultures, 2001–, Interim Chair, Dept of Visual and Performing Arts, 2001–02, University of Colorado at Colorado Springs; Editorial Board, Modern Austrian Literature, 1997–2000, Poetry Salzbury Review, 2002–; Co-Head, Bevedere Film, 1999–; Board mem., LA Flickapalooza film festival, 2001–, TIE The Int. Experimental Cinema Exposition 2002–, Denver British Film Festival 2003–; German Ed. The Adirondack Review 2002–; Columnist Celluloid: The Austrian Film Magazine 2002–mem. MLA; PEN/USA West; Austrian PEN; Poet and Writers; American Federation of Film Producers; Society for Cinema Studies; Screen Actors Guild; Founder and Vice-Pres., International Alexander Lernet-Holenia Society 1997–; Founder and Vice-Pres., Austrian American Film Asscn. 1998–; PEN Colorado, founding-pres., 1994–99, 2001–02. *Films:* Exec. producer: Semmelweis, 2001, Epicure 2001, The Nightmare Stumbles Past 2002, Believe 2002, Wilson Chance 2003. *Publications:* Phantom Empires: The Novels of Alexander Lernet-Holenia and the Question of Postimperial Austrian Identity, 1996; Hans Raimund: Verses of a Marriage (trans.), 1996; Telegrams from the Metropole: Selected Poetry, 1999; Alexander Lernet-Holenia: Mars in Aries (trans.) 2003. Other: several plays and television scripts. Contributions: Contributing Ed., Gale Encyclopedia of Multicultural America, 1999; Editorial Board and Contributor, International Dictionary of Films and Film-makers, 2000; Poetry and articles in periodicals and anthologies. *Honours:* Academico hc, Academia Culturale d'Europa, Italy, 1989; University of Colorado Pres.'s Fund for the Humanities Grants, 1996, 2001; Outstanding Teaching Award, University of Colorado, 2001; Elected Mem., European Acad. of Arts and Sciences, 2001. *Address:* c/o Dept of Languages and Cultures, University of Colorado, Colorado Springs, CO 80933, USA.

DATHORNE, Oscar Ronald; Professor of English, Writer and Poet; b. 19 Nov. 1934, Georgetown, Guyana. *Education:* BA, 1958, MA, 1960, PhD, 1966, University of Sheffield; Graduate Certificate in Education, 1959, Diploma in Education, 1967, University of London; MBA, MPA, 1984, University of Miami. *Career:* Assoc. Prof., Ahmadu Bello University, Zaria, 1959–63, University of Ibadan, 1963–66; UNESCO Consultant to the Government of Sierra Leone, 1967–68; Prof. of English, Njala University College, University of Sierra Leone, 1968–69; Prof. of African Literature, Howard University, 1970; Prof. of Afro-American Literature, University of

Wisconsin, Madison, 1970–71; Prof. of English and Black Literature, Ohio State University, 1975–77; Prof. of English, University of Miami, Coral Gables, FL, 1977–. *Publications:* Dumplings in the Soup (novel), 1963; The Scholar Man (novel), 1964; Carribean Narrative (ed.), 1965; Carribean Verse (ed.), 1967; Africa in Prose, 1969; The Black Mind, 1975; African Literature in the Twentieth Century, 1976; Dark Ancestor, 1981; Dele's Child, 1985; Imagining the World: Typical Belief vs Reality in Global Encounters, 1994. *Address:* Dept of English, University of Miami, Coral Gables, FL 33124, USA.

DAUGHARTY, Janice; Writer; b. 24 Oct. 1944, Valdosta, GA, USA; m. Seward Daugharty, 25 Dec. 1963, one s. two d. *Education:* Valdosta State University. *Publications:* Dark of the Moon, 1994; Going through the Change, 1994; Necessary Lies, 1995; Pawpaw Patch, 1996; Earl in the Yellow Shirt, 1997; Whistle, 1998; Like a Sister, 1999. *Address:* c/o Virginai Barber, The Writers Shop, 101 Fifth Ave, New York, NY, USA.

DAUNTON, Martin James; academic; b. 7 Feb. 1949, Cardiff, Wales; m. Claire Gobbi 1984. *Education:* BA, Univ. of Nottingham, 1970; PhD, Univ. of Kent, 1974. *Career:* Lecturer, Univ. of Durham, 1973–79; Lecturer, 1979–85, Reader, 1985–89, Prof. of History, 1989–97, University College London; Convenor, Studies in History series, Royal Historical Society, 1995–2000; Prof. Economic History, 1997–, Chair., Faculty of History, 2001–03, Chair., School of Humanities and Social Sciences, 2003–, Univ. of Cambridge; Trustee, National Maritime Museum, 2002–; mem. Royal Historical Society, pres., 2004–. *Publications:* Coal Metropolis: Cardiff; House and Home in the Victorian City, 1850–1914; Royal Mail: The Post Office Since 1840; A Property Owning Democracy?; Progress and Poverty; Trusting Leviathan; Just Taxes, 2003. Contributions: Economic History Review; Past & Present; Business History; Historical Research; Journal of Urban History; Charity, Self-Interest and Welfare in the English Past, 1996; English Historical Review; Twentieth Century British History; Empire and Others, 1999. *Honours:* Fellow of the British Acad., 1997. *Address:* Churchill College, Cambridge CB3 0DS, England. *E-mail:* mjd42@cam.ac.uk.

DAVERIO, John; musicologist, writer and academic; b. 19 Oct. 1954, Sharon, Pennsylvania, USA. *Education:* Fellow, Tanglewood Music Center, 1971–73; BM, 1975, MM, 1977, PhD, 1983, Boston University. *Career:* Lecturer, Longy School of Music, 1981–83; Asst Prof., 1983–89, Chair, Dept of Musicology, 1987–, Assoc. Prof., 1989–98, Prof. of Music, 1998–, Boston University; mem. Board of Dirs, American Musicological Society, 2000–02. *Publications:* Nineteenth-Century Music and the German Romantic Ideology, 1993; Robert Schumann: Herald of a 'New Poetic Age', 1997. Contributions: Journal of the American Musicological Society; 19th Century Music; Acta Musicologica; Journal of Musicology; Musical Quarterly; Music and Letters; Journal of Musicological Research; Il Saggiatore Musicale; The New Grove Dictionary of Music and Musicians, revised edn, 2001. *Honours:* Alfred Einstein Prize, 1988; Outstanding Academic Book Citation, Choice, 1997. *Address:* c/o Boston University College of Fine Arts, School of Music, 855 Commonwealth Avenue, Boston, MA 02215, USA. *E-mail:* daverio@bu.edu.

DAVEY, Frankland Wilmot, BA, MA, PhD; writer, poet and editor; *Carl F. Klinck Professor of Canadian Literature, University of Western Ontario*; b. 19 April 1940, Vancouver, BC, Canada; m. 1st Helen Simmons 1962 (divorced 1969); m. 2nd Linda McCartney 1969; one s. one d. *Education:* University of British Columbia, Vancouver, University of Southern California at Los Angeles. *Career:* Lecturer, 1963–67, Asst Prof., 1967–69, Royal Roads Military College, Victoria, BC; Writer-in-Residence, Sir George Williams University, Montréal, 1969–70; Asst Prof., 1970–72, Assoc. Prof., 1972–80, Prof. of English, 1980–90, Chair, Dept of English, 1985–88, 1989–90, York University, Toronto; Carl F. Klinck Prof. of Canadian Literature, University of Western Ontario, London, 1990–; mem. Assen of Canadian College and University Teachers of English, pres., 1994–96. *Publications:* Poetry: D-Day and After, 1962; City of the Gulls and Sea, 1964; Bridge Force, 1965; The Scarred Hill, 1966; Four Myths for Sam Perry, 1970; Weeds, 1970; Griffon, 1972; King of Swords, 1972; L'An Trentiesme: Selected Poems 1961–70, 1972; Arcana, 1973; The Clallam, 1973; War Poems, 1979; The Arches: Selected Poems, 1981; Capitalistic Affection!, 1982; Edward and Patricia, 1984; The Louis Riel Organ and Piano Company, 1985; The Abbotsford Guide to India, 1986; Postcard Translations, 1988; Popular Narratives, 1991; Cultural Mischief: A Practical Guide to Multiculturalism, 1996. Criticism: Five Readings of Olson's 'Maximus', 1970; Earle Birney, 1971; From There to Here: A Guide to English-Canadian Literature Since 1960, 1974; Louis Dudek and Raymond Souster, 1981; The Contemporary Canadian Long Poem, 1983; Surviving the Paraphrase: 11 Essays on Canadian Literature, 1983; Margaret Atwood: A Feminist Poetics, 1984; Reading Canadian Reading, 1988; Post-National Arguments: The Politics of the Anglophone-Canadian Novel Since 1967, 1993; Reading 'KIM' Right, 1993; Canadian Literary Power: Essays on Anglophone-Canadian Literary Conflict, 1994; Karla's Web: A Cultural Examination of the Mahaffy-French Murders, 1994. Contributions: Books and journals. *Honours:* Macmillan Prize, 1962; Dept of Defence Arts Research Grants, 1965, 1966, 1968; Canada Council Fellowships, 1966, 1974; Humanities Research Council of Canada Grants, 1974, 1981; Canadian Federation for the Humanities Grants, 1979, 1992; Social Sciences and Humanities Research Council Fellowship, 1981. *Address:* 499 Dufferin Avenue, London, Ontario N6B 2A1, Canada.

DAVEY, William; Poet and Writer; b. 20 March 1913, New York, NY, USA; m. 7th Susan Steenrod 19 Nov. 1965. *Education:* Princeton University; University of California at Berkeley; New York University; Sorbonne, University of Paris. *Career:* Commando, First Special Service Force, Canadian-American Elite Unit, World War II; Contributing and Foreign Language Ed., The Long Story magazine, 1991–2003; mem. Poetry Society of America; Poetry Society of Virginia; World Congress of Poets. *Publications:* Dawn Breaks the Heart (novel), 1932; Arms, Angels, Epitaphs (poems); The Angry Dust (novel), 1995; Trial of Pythagoras and Other Poems, 1996; Lost Adulteries and Other Stories, 1998; Bitter Rainbow and Other Stories, 1999. Contributions: anthologies, periodicals and magazines. *Address:* Lions Watch Farm, PO Box 129, Keene, VA 22946, USA.

DAVIDSON, Basil Risbridger; Writer; b. 9 Nov. 1914, Bristol, England; m. Marion Young, 7 July 1943, three s. *Publications:* Old Africa Rediscovered, 1959; The African Slave Trade, 1961; The Africans, 1969; Africa in Modern History, 1978; Special Operations Europe, 1980; The Fortunate Isles, 1989; African Civilisation Revisited, 1991; The Black Man's Burden: Africa and the Curse of the Nation-State, 1992; The Search for Africa, 1994. *Honours:* Military Cross, British Army; Bronze Star, US Army; Anisfield-Wolf Award, 1959; Agnelli Visiting Prof., University of Turin, 1990; several hon. doctorates.

DAVIDSON, Lionel, (David Line); Author; b. 31 March 1922, Hull, Yorkshire, England; m. 1st Fay Jacobs 1949 (died 1988); two s.; m. 2nd Frances Ullman 1989. *Publications:* The Night of Wenceslas, 1960; The Rose of Tibet, 1962; A Long Way to Shiloh, 1966; Run for Your Life, 1966; Making Good Again, 1968; Smith's Gazelle, 1971; Mike and Me, 1974; The Sun Chemist, 1976; The Chelsea Murders, 1978; Under Plum Lake, 1980; Screaming High, 1985; Kolymsky Heights, 1994. *Honours:* Silver Quill Award, Authors Club, 1961; Gold Dagger Awards, CWA, 1961, 1967, 1979; Cartier Diamond Dagger Award for Lifetime Achievement, CWA, 2001. *Literary Agent:* Curtis Brown Ltd, Haymarket House, 28–29 Haymarket, London, SW1Y 4SP, England. *Telephone:* (20) 7393-4400. *Fax:* (20) 7393-4401. *E-mail:* info@curtisbrown.co.uk. *Website:* www.curtisbrown.co.uk.

DAVIDSON, Michael; Prof. of Literature, Poet and Writer; b. 18 Dec. 1944, Oakland, CA, USA; m. 1st Carol Wikarska, 1970, divorced 1974; m. 2nd Lois Chamberlain, 1988, two c. *Education:* BA, San Francisco State University, 1967; PhD, SUNY at Buffalo, 1971; Post-doctoral Fellow, University of California at Berkeley, 1974–75. *Career:* Visiting Lecturer, San Diego State University, 1973–76; Curator, Archive for New Poetry, 1975–85, Prof. of Literature, 1977–, University of California at San Diego. *Publications:* Poetry: Exchanges, 1972; Two Views of Pears, 1973; The Mutabilities, and the Foul Papers, 1976; Summer Letters, 1976; Grillwork, 1980; Discovering Motion, 1980; The Prose of Fact, 1981; The Landing of Rochambeau, 1985; Analogy of the Ion, 1988; Post Hoc, 1990. Other: The San Francisco Renaissance: Poetics and Community at Mid-Century, 1989. Contributions: periodicals. *Honours:* National Endowment for the Arts Grant, 1976. *Address:* c/o Dept of Literature, University of California at San Diego, La Jolla, CA 92093, USA.

DAVIES, (Edward) Hunter; writer; b. 7 Jan. 1936, Renfrew, Scotland; m. Margaret Forster 1960; one s. two d. *Education:* BA, DipEd, University College, Durham, England. *Publications:* 40 books including: Here We Go Round the Mulberry Bush, 1965; The Beatles, 1968; The Glory Game, 1972; A Walk Along the Wall, 1974; A Walk Around the Lakes, 1979; In Search of Columbus, 1991; Wainwright: The Biography, 1998; The Eddie Stobart Story, 2001. Contributions: Sunday Times, 1960–84; Punch, 1979–89; Independent, London, 1990–2000; New Statesman, 1998–. *Address:* 11 Boscastle Road, London NW5, England.

DAVIES, (Ivor) Norman Richard, MA, PhD, FBA, FRHistS; British academic and writer; b. 8 June 1939, Bolton, England; m. 1st Maria Zielińska 1966; one s.; m. 2nd Maria Korzeniewicz 1984; one s. *Education:* Univ. of Grenoble, Magdalen Coll., Oxford, Univ. of Sussex, Jagiellonian Univ. *Career:* Alistair Horne Research Fellow, St Antony's Coll., Oxford 1969–71; Lecturer 1971–84, Reader 1984–85, Prof. of Polish History 1985–96, Prof. Emeritus 1996–, Univ. of London; Visiting Prof., Columbia Univ. 1974, McGill Univ. 1977–78, Hokkaido Univ. 1982–83, Stanford Univ. 1985–86, Harvard Univ. 1991; Sr Research Assoc., Univ. of Oxford 1997–. *Publications:* White Eagle, Red Star: The Polish–Soviet War of 1919–1920 1972, God's Playground: A History of Poland (two vols) 1981, Heart of Europe: A Short History of Poland 1984, Europe: A History 1996, The Isles: A History 1999, Microcosm: Portrait of a Central European City (with Roger Moorehouse) 2002, Rising '44: The Battle for Warsaw 2004; contrib. to scholarly books and journals. *Honours:* Knight Cross, Order of Polonia Restituta, Poland 1984, Commander Cross, Order of Merit, Poland 1992. *Address:* c/o Wolfson College, Oxford, OX2 6UD, England.

DAVIES, Pauline (see Fisk, Pauline).

DAVIES, Peter Ho; Writer; b. 1966, Coventry, England; m. *Education:* BS, Physics, Manchester Univ.; BA, English, Univ. of Cambridge; MA, Creative Writing, Boston Univ. *Career:* Business man., Varsity magazine; dir, creative writing programme, Univ. of Michigan. *Publications:* The Ugliest

House in the World (short stories), 1998; Equal Love (short stories), 2000; The Bad Shepherd (novel), 2004. Contributions: short stories in: Atlantic; Granta; Best American Short Stories, 1995, 1996, 2001. *Honours:* H. L. Davis Oregon Book Award, 1997; John Llewellyn Rhys Prize, 1998; O. Henry Award, 1998; PEN Macmillan Prize, 1999; New York Times Notable Book of the Year, 2000. *Address:* c/o Granta, PO Box 23152, Jackson, MS 39225, USA.

DAVIES, Peter Joseph; physician and writer; b. 15 May 1937, Terang, Vic., Australia; m. Clare Loughnan 1960; one d. *Education:* MB, 1961; MRACP, 1968; FRACP, 1974; MRCP, 1970; MD, 1991. *Career:* mem. Royal Australian College of Physicians; Gastro-Enterological Society of Australia; Royal Musical Asscn; American Musicological Society; Friends of Mozart, New York; Friends International Stiftung Mozareum, Salzburg. *Publications:* Mozart in Person: His Character and Health, 1989; Mozart's Health, Illnesses and Death, 1993; The Cause of Beethoven's Deafness, 1996; Beethoven in Person: His Deafness, Illnesses and Death, 2001; The Character of a Genius: Beethoven in Perspective, 2002. Contributions: Journal of Medical Biography, 1995. *Address:* 14 Hamilton Street, East Kew, Vic. 3102, Australia.

DAVIES, Piers Anthony David, LLB; barrister, solicitor, screenwriter and poet; b. 15 June 1941, Sydney, NSW, Australia; m. Margaret Elaine Haswell 1973; one d. *Education:* Univ. of Auckland, City of London Coll. *Career:* Barrister and Solicitor, Wackrow, Williams and Davies, Auckland, New Zealand; Chair., Short Film Fund, New Zealand Film Commission 1987–91; mem. Int. Law Asscn (Cultural Heritage Law Cttee 1997–). *Writing for film:* screenplays: The Life and Flight of Rev Buck Shotte (with Peter Weir) 1969, Homesdale (with Peter Weir) 1971, The Cars That Ate Paris (with Peter Weir) 1973, Skin Deep 1978, The Lamb of God 1985, A Fair Hearing 1995; documentary: R. V. Huckleberry Finn 1979, Olaf's Coast 1982. *Publications:* East and Other Gong Songs 1967, Day Trip from Mount Meru 1969, Diaspora 1974, Bourgeois Homage to Dada 1974, Central Almanac (ed.) 1974, Jetsam 1984; contrib. to anthologies and periodicals, chapters in Law Stories 2003, Encyclopaedia of New Zealand Forms and Precedents (ongoing). *Honours:* Officer of New Zealand, Order of Merit. *Address:* 16 Crocus Place, Remuera, Auckland 5, New Zealand.

DAVIES, Stephanie (Stevie), BA, MA, PhD, FRSL; Welsh writer and lecturer; b. 2 Dec. 1946, Swansea; four c. *Education:* Univ. of Manchester. *Career:* Lecturer in English Literature, Victoria Univ. of Manchester 1971–84, Salford Univ. 1989–90; Sr Research Fellow in English Literature, Univ. of Surrey 1994–2001; Royal Literary Fund Writing Fellow, Univ. of Wales Swansea 2001–03; Fellow Welsh Acad. *Publications:* Fiction: Boy Blue, 1987; Primavera, 1990; Arms and the Girl, 1992; Closing the Book, 1994; Four Dreamers and Emily, 1996; The Web of Belonging, 1997; Impassioned Clay, 1999; The Element of Water, 2001; Kith and Kin 2003. Other: Renaissance Views of Man, 1978; Images of Kingship in 'Paradise Lost': Milton's Politics and Christian Liberty, 1983; Emily Brontë: The Artist as a Free Woman, 1983; The Idea of Woman in Renaissance Literature: The Feminine Reclaimed, 1987; Emily Brontë, 1988; Virginia Woolf's 'To the Lighthouse', 1989; John Milton, 1991; Shakespeare's 'Twelfth Night', 1993; Emily Brontë: Heretic, 1994; John Donne, 1994; Henry Vaughan, 1995; Shakespeare's 'The Taming of the Shrew', 1995; Emily Brontë, 1998; Unbridled Spirits: Women of the English Revolution, 1640–1660, 1998. Contributions: Reference books, anthologies, quarterlies, reviews and journals. *Honours:* Fawcett Society Book Prize 1989, Book of the Year, Arts Council of Wales 1998, Society of Authors travel grant 1999. *Address:* 9 Oystermouth Court, Castle Road, Mumbles, Swansea SA3 5TD, Wales. *E-mail:* steviedavies@spirit.plus.com.

DAVIES, William Thomas Pennar; Author and Poet; b. 12 Nov. 1911, Aberpennar, Glamorgan, Wales; m. Rosemarie Wolff, 26 June 1943, four s., one d. *Education:* BA, University of Wales, 1932; BLitt, University of Oxford, 1938; PhD, Yale University, 1943. *Publications:* Fiction: Anadl o'r Uchelder, 1958; Caregel Nwyf, 1966; Meibion Darogan, 1968; Llais y Durtur, 1985. Poetry: Cinio'r Cythraul, 1946; Naw Wftt, 1957; Yr Efrydd o lyn Cynon, 1961; Y Tlws yn y Lotws, 1971; Llef, 1987. Non-Fiction: Cudd fy Meiau, 1957; Rhwng Chwedl a Chredo, 1966. Contributions: Reviews and periodicals. *Honours:* Commonwealth Fund Fellow, 1936–38; Fellow, 1938–40, Fellow hc, 1986, Hon. DD, 1987, University of Wales; Hon. Fellow, Welsh Acad., 1989. *Address:* 10 Heol Grosvenor, Sgeti, Abertawe, Swansea SA2 0SP, Wales.

DAVIS, Albert Joseph, Jr, (Albert Belisle Davis); Alcee Fortier Distinguished Prof., Author and Poet; b. 23 June 1947, Houma, LA, USA; m. 1st Carol Anne Campbell 24 Feb. 1968 (divorced 1992); one s.; m. 2nd Mary Archer Freet 31 Dec. 1994; one d. *Education:* BA, English and History, Nicholls State Univ., 1969; MA, Creative Writing, Colorado State Univ., 1974; PhD, English, Univ. of Louisiana at Lafayette, 2002. *Career:* Novelist-in-Residence, 1991–, Distinguished Service Prof. of Languages and Literature, 1994–, Assoc. Dean, College of Arts and Sciences, 1999–2001, Alcee Fortier Distinguished Prof., 2003–, Nicholls State Univ.; mem. Acad. of American Poets; Associated Writing Programs; Louisiana Asscn of Educators; Louisiana Division of the Arts, literary panel, 1995–97; National Education Asscn; PEN American Center. *Publications:* What They Wrote on the Bathhouse Walls (poems), 1989; Leechtime (novel), 1989; Marquis at Bay (novel), 1992; Virginia Patout's Parish (poems), 1999. Contributions: anthologies and literary journals. *Honours:* Ione Burden Award for the Novel, 1983; John Z. Bennet Award for Poetry, 1984; Louisiana Division of the Arts Creative Writing Fellowship, 1989. *Address:* c/o Dept of General Studies, Nicholls State University, PO Box 2106, Thibodaux, LA 70310, USA.

DAVIS, Burke; Historian and Biographer; b. 24 July 1913, Durham, NC, USA; m. 1st Evangeline McLennan, 11 Aug. 1940, divorced 1980, one s. one d.; m. 2nd Juliet H. Burnett, 6 Feb. 1982. *Education:* Duke University, 1931–32, 1933–34; Guilford College, 1935–36; AB, University of North Carolina, 1937. *Career:* Ed., Feature Writer and Sports Ed., Charlotte News, NC, 1937–47; Reporter, Baltimore Evening Sun, MD, 1947–52, Greensboro News, NC, 1951–60; Writer and Historian, Colonial Williamsburg, Virginia, 1960–78; Biography Juror, Pulitzer Prizes, 1980s. *Publications:* Whisper My Name, 1949; The Ragged Ones, 1951; Yorktown, 1952; They Called Him Stonewall, 1954; Gray Fox: Robert E. Lee and the Civil War, 1956; Jeb Stuart, The Last Cavalier, 1957; To Appomattox, 1959; Our Incredible Civil War, 1960; Marine! The Life of Chesty Puller; The Cowpens-Guilford Courthouse Campaign, 1962; America's First Army, 1962; Appomattox: Closing Struggle of the Civil War, 1963; The Summer Land, 1965; A Rebel Raider (co-author), 1966; The Billy Mitchell Affair, 1967; A Williamsburg Galaxy, 1967; The World of Currier & Ives (co-author), 1968; Get Yamamoto, 1969; Yorktown: The Campaign that won America, 1969; Billy Mitchell Story, 1969; Black Heroes of the American Revolution, 1971; Jamestown, 1971; Thomas Jefferson's Virginia, 1971; Amelia Earhart, 1972; Biography of a Leaf, 1972; Three for Revolution, 1975; Biography of a Kingsnake, 1975; George Washington and the American Revolution, 1975; Newer and Better Organic Gardening, 1976; Biography of a Fish Hawk, 1976; Old Hickory: A Life of Andrew Jackson, 1977; Mr Lincoln's Whiskers, 1978; Sherman's March, 1980; The Long Surrender, 1985; The Southern Railway, 1985; War Bird: The Life and Times of Elliott White Springs, 1986; Civil War: Strange and Fascinating Facts, 1989. *Address:* 4100 Well Spring, Greensboro, NC 27410, USA.

DAVIS, David Brion; Prof. of History and Writer; b. 16 Feb. 1927, Denver, CO, USA; m. 1st; one s. two d.; m. 2nd Toni Hahn Davis 9 Sept. 1971; two s. *Education:* AB, Dartmouth College, 1950; AM, 1953, PhD, 1956, Harvard University; Litt D, Dartmouth College, 1977; Litt D, University of New Haven, 1986; Litt D, Columbia University, 1999. *Career:* Instructor, Dartmouth College, 1953–54; Asst Prof., 1955–58, Assoc. Prof., 1958–63, Prof. and Ernest I White Prof. of History, 1963–69, Cornell University; Fulbright Senior Lecturer, American Studies Research Centre, Hyderabad, India, 1967; Harmsworth Prof., University of Oxford, 1969–70; Prof. and Farnam Prof. of History, 1969–78, Sterling Prof. of History, 1978–2001, Emeritus Prof., 2001–, Yale University; Fellow, Center for Advanced Study in the Behavioral Sciences, Stanford, 1972–73; Fulbright Lecturer, Universities of Guyana and the West Indies, 1974; French-American Foundation Chair in American Civilization, École des Hautes Études en Sciences Sociales, Paris, 1980–81; Gilder-Lehrman Inaugural Fellow, 1996–97; Dir, The Gilder-Lehrman Center at Yale for the Study of Slavery, Resistance and Abolition, 1998–2004; mem. American Acad. of Arts and Sciences; American Antiquarian Society; American Philosophical Society; British Acad., corresponding fellow; Institute of Early American History and Culture; Organization of American Historians. *Publications:* Homicide in American Fiction, 1798–1860: A Study in Social Values, 1957; The Problem of Slavery in Western Culture, 1966; Ante-Bellum Reform (ed.), 1967; The Slave Power Conspiracy and the Paranoid Style, 1969; Was Thomas Jefferson an Authentic Enemy of Slavery?, 1970; The Fear of Conspiracy: Images of un-American Subversion from the Revolution to the Present (ed.), 1971; The Problem of Slavery in the Age of Revolution, 1770–1823, 1975; The Great Republic (with others), 1977; Antebellum American Culture: An Interpretive Anthology, 1979; The Emancipation Moment, 1984; Slavery and Human Progress, 1984; Slavery in the Colonial Chesapeake, 1986; From Homicide to Slavery: Studies in American Culture, 1986; Revolutions: Reflections on American Equality and Foreign Liberations, 1990; The Antislavery Debate: Capitalism and Abolitionism as a Problem in Historical Interpretation (with Thomas Bender), 1992; Challenging the Boundaries of Slavery, 1993; The Boisterous Sea of Liberty: A Documentary History of America from Discovery Through the Civil War (with Steven Mintz), 1998; In the Image of God: Religion, Moral Values, and Our Heritage of Slavery, 2001. Contributions: scholarly journals. *Honours:* Guggenheim Fellowship, 1958–59; Pulitzer Prize in General Non-Fiction, 1967; Anisfield-Wolf Award, 1967; Albert J. Beveridge Award, American Historical Asscn, 1975; National Book Award, 1976; Bancroft Prize, Columbia University, 1976; Organization of American Historians, pres., 1988–89; Presidential Medal for Outstanding Leadership and Achievement, Dartmouth College, 1991. *Address:* c/o Dept of History, PO Box 208324, Yale University, New Haven, CT 06520, USA. *E-mail:* david.b.davis@yale.edu.

DAVIS, Richard (Dick), BA, MA, PhD, FRSL; British academic and poet; *Professor of Persian, Ohio State University*; b. 18 April 1945, Portsmouth, Hampshire, England; m. Afkham Darbandi 1974; two d. *Education:* King's Coll., Cambridge, Univ. of Manchester. *Career:* fmrly teacher in Greece, Italy and Iran; teacher, Univs of Tehran, Iran 1970–78, Durham, Newcastle, California at Santa Barbara, USA; freelance writer, translator and reviewer 1978–84; poetry critic, The Listener 1980–86; Contributing Ed., PN Review 1983–89; Asst Prof., Dept of Near Eastern Languages and

Cultures, Ohio State Univ. 1988–93, Assoc. Prof. of Persian 1993, currently Prof. of Persian and Chair. *Publications:* Shade Mariners (poems, chapbook) 1970, In the Distance (poems) 1975, Seeing the World (poems) (Heinemann Award 1981) 1980, Selected Writings of Thomas Traherne (ed.) 1980, Visitations (poems, chapbook) 1983, Wisdom and Wilderness: The Achievement of Yvor Winters (criticism) 1983, What the Mind Wants (poems, chapbook) 1984, The Conference of the Birds (trans. from the Persian of Attar, with Afkham Darbandi) (American Institute of Iranian Studies Translation Prize 2001) 1984, The Covenant (poems) 1984, The Little Virtues (trans. of Le Piccole Virtu by Natalia Ginzburg) 1985, The City and The House (trans. of La Citta e la Casa by Natalia Ginzburg) 1986, Lares (poems, chapbook) 1986, The Rubaiyat of Omar Khayyam, trans. by Edward Fitzgerald (ed.) 1989, Devices and Desires: New and Selected Poems (The Times and The Daily Telegraph Book of the Year) 1989, A Kind of Love: New & Selected Poems (Ingram Merrill Award 1993) 1991, The Legend of Seyavash (trans. of part of The Shahnameh by Ferdowsi) 1992, Epic and Sedition: the Case of Ferdowsi's Shahnameh (Persian Heritage Foundation Award) 1993, My Unce Napoleon (trans. of Dai Jan Napoleon by Iraj Pezeshkzad) (American Institute of Iranian Studies Translation Prize 2000) 1996, Touchwood: Poems 1991–1995 1996, Medieval Persian Epigrams (trans.) (Poetry Soc. of Great Britain recommendation) 1996, The Lion and the Throne: Stories from the Shahnameh of Ferdowsi (vol. one) 1998, Fathers and Sons: Stories from the Shahnameh of Ferdowsi (vol. two) 2000, Belonging (poems) (Economist Book of the Year) 2002, Panthea's Children: Hellenistic Novels and Medieval Persian Romances 2002; contrib. poems to numerous magazines and journals, including TLS, The Listener, The Spectator, Critical Quarterly, Poetry Review, Poetry Nation Review, Paris Review, Southern Review, Sequoia, Spectrum, The Hudson Review, Drastic Measures, Numbers, Helix, Other Poetry, Rialto, Agenda, Poetry Durham, TriQuarterly, Cambridge Review, Sewanee Review, Threepenny Review, Yale Review, New Criterion, Hellas, The Epigrammatist, la fontana, Dark Horse; contrib. articles and reviews to TLS, Journal of American Oriental Studies, International Journal of Middle Eastern Studies, Iranian Studies, Encyclopaedia Iranica, Encyclopaedia of Islam, Threepenny Review, New York Review of Books. *Honours:* Arts Council of Great Britain Writers' Award 1979, British Inst. of Persian Studies Award 1981, Fulbright Travel Award 1987, Guggenheim Fellow 1999–2000, Nat. Endowment for the Humanities Fellow 2001, Encyclopaedia Iranica Ferdowsi Award for Services to Persian Poetry 2001, Ohio State Univ. Distinguished Scholar Award 2002. *Address:* Department of Near Eastern Languages and Cultures, Ohio State University, 207E Jennings Hall, 1735 Neil Avenue, Columbus, OH 43210, USA (Office). *Telephone:* (614) 292-5643 (Office). *Fax:* (614) 292-1262 (Office). *E-mail:* davis.77@osu.edu (Office). *Website:* nelc.ohio-state.edu/people/person.cfm?ID=190.

DAVIS, Dorothy Salisbury; Writer; b. 26 April 1916, Chicago, IL, USA; m. Harry Davis, 25 April 1946. *Education:* AB, Barat College, Lake Forest, IL, 1938. *Career:* mem. MWA; CWA; Authors' Guild. *Publications:* A Gentle Murderer, 1951; Men of No Property, 1956; The Evening of the Good Samaritan, 1961; Enemy and Brother, 1967; Where the Dark Streets Go, 1969; The Little Brothers, 1974; A Death in the Life, 1976; Scarlet Night, 1980; Lullaby of Murder, 1984; Tales for a Stormy Night, 1985; The Habit of Fear, 1987; A Gentleman Called, 1989; Old Sinners Never Die, 1991; Black Sheep, White Lambs, 1993. Contributions: New Republic. *Honours:* Grand Master's Award, MWA, 1985; Lifetime Achievement Award, Bouchereon XX, 1989. *Address:* Palisades, New York, NY 10964, USA.

DAVIS, Jack Leonard; poet, dramatist and writer; b. 11 March 1917, Perth, WA, Australia; m. Madelon Jantine Wilkens 1987; one d. *Career:* writer-in-residence, Murdoch Univ. 1982; mem. Aboriginal Writers Oral Literature and Dramatists Asscn; Australian Writers Guild; PEN International. *Publications:* The First Born and Other Poems, 1968; Jagardoo Poems from Aboriginal Australia, 1978; The Dreamers (play), 1983; Kullark (play), 1983; John Pat and Other Poems, 1988; Burungin (Smell the Wind) (play), 1989; Plays From Black Australia, 1989. Contributions: Identity. *Honours:* Human Rights Award, 1987; BHP Award, 1988; Australian Artists Creative Fellowship, 1989; Hon. doctorates. *Address:* 3 Little Howard Street, Fremantle, WA, Australia.

DAVIS, James Madison, Jr; Writer and Professor; b. 10 Feb. 1951, Charlottesville, VA, USA; m. 1st Simonne Evelyn Eck, 21 May 1977, divorced, two s.; m. 2nd Melissa Anne Haymes, 20 Dec. 1997, one s. *Education:* George Washington University, 1968; Franklin and Marshall College, 1969–70; BA, Anthropology, University of Maryland at College Park, 1973; MA, Johns Hopkins University, 1975; PhD, English, University of Southern Mississippi, 1979. *Career:* Instructor of English and Journalism, Allegany Community College, Cumberland, MD, 1975–77; Instructor, Part-time Instructor and Teaching Asst, University of Southern Mississippi, 1977–79; Asst Prof. of English Composition, 1979–84, Assoc. Prof. of English, 1984–90, Prof. of English, 1990–91, Pennsylvania State University at Erie; Writer-in-Residence, Mercyhurst College, 1989, 1990; Prof., Professional Writing Program, University of Oklahoma at Norman, 1991–; mem. International Asscn of Crime Writers, North America branch, pres., 1993–97, sec., 1997–2001. *Publications:* Fiction: The Murder of Frau Schütz, 1988; White Rook, 1990; Bloody Marko, 1991; Red Knight, 1992; And the Angels Sing, 1996. Other: Intro 14 (co-ed.), 1984; Critical Essays on Edward Albee (with Philip C. Kolin), 1986; Dick Francis, 1989; Conversations with Robertson Davies, 1989; Stanislaw Lem, 1990; The Shakespeare Name Dictionary (with A. Daniel Frankforter), 1995, UK edn as The Shakespeare Name and Place Dictionary, 1995; Murderous Schemes (contributing ed. with Donald Westlake), 1996; The Novelist's Essential Guide to Creating Plot, 2000; Alfred Hitchcock in the Vertigo Murders, 2000. Contributions: Books, newspapers, reviews, quarterlies and journals. *Honours:* Resident Fellow in Prose, 1974, Resident Fellow in Fiction, 1981, Fellowship, 1988, Virginia Center for the Creative Arts; Best Fiction Prize, Contemporary, 1978; Resident Fellow in Fiction, Ragdale Foundation, 1982, Hambridge Center for Creative Arts and Sciences, 1982; Pennsylvania Council of the Arts Fellowship in Fiction, 1984; Edgar Allan Poe Scroll Award, MWA, 1988. *Address:* 1713 Asbury Ct, Norman, OK 73071, USA. *Telephone:* (405) 321-5033. *E-mail:* jmadisondavis@ou.edu.

DAVIS, Jon Edward, BA, MFA; poet, writer and academic; *Professor of Creative Writing and Literature, Institute of American Indian Arts*; b. 28 Oct. 1952, New Haven, CT, USA; m. Terry Lynne Layton 1978; one d. *Education:* University of Bridgeport, University of Montana. *Career:* Ed., CutBank 1982–85; Managing Ed., Shankpainter 1986–87; Fellow 1986–87, Co-ordinator, Writing Program 1987–88, Fine Arts Work Center, Provincetown, MA; Visiting Asst Prof., Salisbury State University, MD 1988–90; Prof. of Creative Writing and Literature, Inst. of American Indian Arts, Santa Fe, NM 1990–; Co-Ed., Countermeasures 1993–. *Publications:* poetry: West of New England 1983, Dangerous Amusements 1987, The Hawk, The Road, The Sunlight After Clouds 1995, Local Color 1995, Scrimmage of Appetite 1995; contrib. to anthologies, reviews, quarterlies and journals. *Honours:* Connecticut Poetry Circuit Competition winner 1980, Acad. of American Poets Prize 1985, INTRO Award for Fiction 1985, Nat. Endowment for the Arts Fellowship 1986, Richard Hugo Memorial Award, CutBank 1988, Maryland Arts Council Fellowship 1990, Owl Creek Press Chapbook Contest winner 1994, Palanquin Press Chapbook Contest winner 1995. *Address:* Faculty in Creative Writing, Institute of American Indian Arts, 83 A Van Nu Po Road, Santa Fe, NM, USA. *E-mail:* jdavis@iaia.edu.

DAVIS, Margaret (Thomson); Writer; b. 24 May 1926, Bathgate, West Lothian, Scotland; (Divorced); one s. *Education:* Albert Secondary Modern School, Glasgow. *Career:* mem. PEN; Scottish Labour History Society; Society of Authors. *Publications:* The Breadmakers, 1972; A Baby Might Be Crying, 1973; A Sort of Peace, 1973; The Prisoner, 1974; The Prince and the Tobacco Lords, 1976; Roots of Bondage, 1977; Scorpion in the Fire, 1977; The Dark Side of Pleasure, 1981; The Making of a Novelist, 1982; A Very Civilized Man, 1982; Light and Dark, 1984; Rag Woman, Rich Woman, 1987; Mothers and Daughters, 1988; Wounds of War, 1989; A Woman of Property, 1991; A Sense of Belonging, 1993; Hold Me Forever, 1994; Kiss Me No More, 1995; A Kind of Immortality, 1996; Burning Ambition, 1997; Gallaghers, 1998; The Glasgow Belle, 1998; A Tangled Web, 1999; The Clydesiders, 2000; The Gourlay Girls, 2001; Strangers in a Strange Land, 2001; The Clydesiders at War, 2002. Contributions: 200 short stories in various periodicals. *Address:* c/o Heather Jeeves Literary Agency, 9 Kingsfield Crescent, Witney, Oxon OX28 2JB, England.

DAVIS, William Virgil, AB, MA, MDiv, PhD; academic, writer and poet; *Professor of English, Baylor University*; b. 26 May 1940, Canton, OH, USA; m. Carol Demske 1971; one s. *Education:* Ohio University, Pittsburgh Theological Seminary. *Career:* Teaching Fellow, 1965–67, Asst Prof. of English, 1967–68, Consultant, Creative Writing Program, 1992–98, Ohio University; Asst Prof. of English, Central Connecticut State University, 1968–72, University of Illinois, Chicago, 1972–77; Assoc. Prof. of English, 1977–79, Prof. of English and Writer-in-Residence, 1979–, Centennial Prof., 2002–03, Baylor University; Guest Prof., University of Vienna, 1979–80, 1989–90, 1997, University of Copenhagen, 1984; Visiting Scholar-Guest Prof., University of Wales, Swansea, 1983; Writer-in-Residence, University of Montana, 1983; Adjunct MFA Faculty, Southwest Texas State University, 1990–98; Adjunct Mem., Graduate Faculty, Texas Christian University, 1992–96; mem. Acad. of American Poets; International Asscn of University Profs of English; MLA; PAMLA; SCMLA; Poetry Society of America; Poets and Writers; Texas Asscn of Creative Writing Teachers; Texas Institute of Letters, councillor, 1993–97. *Publications:* George Whitefield's Journals, 1737–1741 (ed.), 1969; Theodore Roethke: A Bibliography (contributing ed.), 1973; One Way to Reconstruct the Scene, 1980; The Dark Hours, 1984; Understanding Robert Bly, 1988; Winter Light, 1990; Critical Essays on Robert Bly (ed.), 1992; Miraculous Simplicity: Essays on R. S. Thomas (ed.), 1993; Robert Bly: The Poet and His Critics, 1994. Contributions: articles in scholarly journals and poems in numerous anthologies and other publications. *Honours:* Scholar in Poetry, 1970, John Atherton Fellow in Poetry, 1980, Bread Loaf Writers' Conference; Ordained Minister, Presbyterian Church in the USA, 1971; Yale Series of Younger Poets Award, 1979; Lilly Foundation Grant, 1979–80; Calliope Press Chapbook Prize, 1984; Outstanding Faculty Mem., Baylor University, 1989; James Sims Prize in American Literature, 2002; Fellowship in Creative Writing, Poetry, Writers' League of Texas, 2002. *Address:* 2633 Lake Oaks Road, Waco, TX 76710, USA. *E-mail:* william_davis@baylor.edu.

DAVIS-GARDNER, Angela; writer and academic; b. 21 April 1942, Charlotte, NC, USA; one s. *Education:* BA, Duke University, 1963; MFA, University of North Carolina at Greensboro, 1965. *Career:* mem. Authors' Guild; Poets and Writers. *Publications:* Felice, 1982; Forms of Shelter,

1991. Contributions: Short stories in: Kansas Quarterly, Carolina Quarterly; Crescent Review; Greensboro Review; other literary quarterlies. *Honours:* Artists Fellowship, North Carolina Arts Council, 1981–82; Sir Walter Raleigh Award, 1991; Best Novel by North Carolinian. *Address:* Dept of English, North Carolina State University, Box 8105, Raleigh, NC 27695, USA.

DAVIS-GOFF, Annabel Claire; Writer; b. 19 Feb. 1942, Ireland; m. Mike Nichols, 1976, divorced 1987, one s. one d. *Publications:* Night Tennis, 1978; Tail Spin, 1980; Walled Gardens, 1989; The Literary Companions to Gambling, 1996; The Dower House, 1998; This Cold Country, 2002. *Literary Agent:* Sterling Lord Literistic Inc, 65 Bleecker St, New York, NY 10012, USA.

DAVISON, Geoffrey Joseph; Writer; b. 10 Aug. 1927, Newcastle upon Tyne, England; m. Marlene Margaret Wilson, 15 Sept. 1956, two s. *Education:* TD; FRICS. *Career:* mem. Pen and Palette Club. *Publications:* The Spy Who Swapped Shoes, 1967; Nest of Spies, 1968; The Chessboard Spies, 1969; The Fallen Eagles, 1970; The Honorable Assassins, 1971; Spy Puppets, 1973; The Berlin Spy Trap, 1974; No Names on Their Graves, 1978; The Bloody Legionnaires, 1981; The Last Waltz (Vienna May 1945), 2001; The Colombian Contract, 2001; The Dead Island, 2001. *Address:* 95 Cheviot View, Ponteland, Newcastle upon Tyne NE20 9BH, England. *E-mail:* daviponte@onetel.net.uk.

DAVISON, Liam; writer and educator; b. 29 July 1957, Melbourne, Vic., Australia; m. Francesca White 1983; one s. one d. *Education:* BA, Melbourne State College, 1970. *Career:* Instructor in Creative Writing, Peninsular College of Technical and Further Education; freelance writer 1988–. *Publications:* The Velodrome, novel, 1988; The Shipwreck Party, short stories, 1989; Soundings, novel, 1993; The White Woman, novel, 1994. *Honours:* Australia Council-Literature Board Fellowships, 1989, 1991; Marten Bequest Travelling Scholarship for Prose, 1992; National Book Council Banjo Award for Fiction, 1993.

DAVISON, Peter (Hubert); Poet, Writer and Ed.; b. 27 June 1928, New York, NY, USA; m. 1st Jane Truslow 7 March 1959 (died 1981); one s. one d.; m. 2nd Joan Edelman Goody 11 Aug. 1984. *Education:* AB, Harvard College, 1949; Fulbright Scholar, St John's College, Cambridge, 1949–50. *Career:* Asst Ed., Harcourt, Brace and Co, 1950–51, 1953–55; Asst to Dir, Harvard University Press, 1955–56; Assoc. Ed., 1956–59, Exec. Ed., 1959–64, Dir, 1964–79, Senior Ed., 1979–85, Atlantic Monthly Press; Poetry Ed., The Atlantic Monthly, 1972–; Ed., Peter Davison imprint, Houghton Mifflin Co, 1985–98. *Publications:* Poetry: The Breaking of the Day, 1964; The City and the Island, 1966; Pretending to Be Asleep, 1970; Walking the Boundaries, 1974; A Voice in the Mountain, 1977; Barn Fever, 1981; Praying Wrong: New and Selected Poems, 1959–84, 1984; The Great Ledge: New Poems, 1989; The Poems of Peter Davison, 1957–95, 1995; Breathing Room, 2000. Prose: Half Remembered: A Personal History, 1973; One of the Dangerous Trades: Essays on the Work and Workings of Poetry, 1991; The Fading Smile: Poets in Boston 1955–60, 1994. Contributions: many journals, reviews and periodicals. *Honours:* Yale Series of Younger Poets Award, 1963; American Acad. of Arts and Letters Award, 1972; James Michener Prizes, 1981, 1985; New England Booksellers Award for Literary Excellence, 1995; Massachusetts Book Award, 2001. *Address:* 70 River St, No. 2, Boston, MA 02108, USA.

DAWE, (Donald) Bruce, BA, AM, MLitt, PhD; academic, poet and writer; b. 15 Feb. 1930, Fitzroy, Vic., Australia; m. 1st Gloria Desley Blain 1964 (died 1997); two s. two d.; m. 2nd Ann Elizabeth Qualtrough 1999. *Education:* University of Queensland. *Career:* Lecturer, 1971–78, Senior Lecturer, 1978–83, DDIAE; Writer-in-Residence, University of Queensland, 1984; Senior Lecturer, 1985–90, Assoc. Prof., 1990–93, School of Arts, Darling Heights, Toowoomba; mem. Australian Asscn for Teaching English, hon. life mem.; Centre for Australian Studies in Literature; Victorian Asscn for Teaching of English, hon. life mem. *Publications:* No Fixed Address, 1962; A Need of Similar Name, 1964; Beyond the Subdivisions, 1968; An Eye for a Tooth, 1969; Heat-Wave, 1970; Condolences of the Season: Selected Poems, 1971; Just a Dugong at Twilight, 1974; Sometimes Gladness: Collected Poems 1954–97 (5th Edn); Over Here Harv! and Other Stories, 1983; Towards Sunrise, 1986; This Side of Silence, 1990; Bruce Dawe: Essays and Opinions, 1990; Mortal Instruments: Poems 1990–1995, 1995; A Poets' People, 1999, No Cat – and That's That!, The Chewing-gum Kid 2002, Show and Tell 2003, The Headlong Traffic: poems and prose monologues 2003, Bruce Dawe, Hier und Anderswo/Here and Elsewhere (poems selected and trans. by Manfred Jurgensen). Contributions: various periodicals. *Honours:* Hon. DLitt (S Queensland 1995, NSW 1997Myer Poetry Prizes 1966, 1969; Ampol Arts Award for Creative Literature 1967; Dame Mary Gilmore Medal Australian Literary Society 1973; Braille Book of the Year 1978; Grace Leven Prize for Poetry 1978; Patrick White Literary Award 1980; Christopher Brennan Award 1984; Distinguished Alumni Award UNE 1996, Philip Hodgson Medal for Literary Excellence 1997, Australian Arts Council Emeritus Writers Award 2000, Centenary Medal 2003. *Address:* c/o Pearson Education, 95 Coventry Street, South Melbourne 32059, Australia.

DAWE, Gerald Chartres, BA, MA; poet and college lecturer; b. 22 April 1952, Belfast, Northern Ireland; m. Dorothea Melvin 1979; one s. one d. *Education:* Univ. of Ulster, Univ. Coll., Galway. *Career:* Tutor in English, Asst Lecturer, Univ. Coll., Galway 1978–87; Lecturer 1987–, Dir, MPhil in Creative Writing 1997–, Lecturer in English and Dir of the Oscar Wilde Centre for Irish Writing 1999–, Trinity Coll., Dublin; Burns Visiting Prof., Boston Coll. 2005; mem. Int. Asscn for the Study of Irish Literature, Irish Writers' Union, Poetry Ireland. *Publications:* Poetry: Sheltering Places, 1978; The Lundys Letter, 1985; Sunday School, 1991; Heart of Hearts, 1995; The Morning Train, 1999; Lake Geneva, 2003. Criticism: Across a Roaring Hill: The Protestant Imagination in Modern Ireland, with Edna Longley, 1985; How's the Poetry Going?: Literary Politics and Ireland Today, 1991; The Poet's Place, with John Wilson Foster, 1991; Against Piety: Essays in Irish Poetry, 1995; The Rest is History, 1998; Stray Dogs and Dark Horses (selected essays), 2000. Editor: The Younger Irish Poets, 1982; Krino (anthology with Jonathan Williams), 1986–96; The Younger Irish Poets 1982, 1991; The Ogham Stone (anthology with Michael Mulreany), 2001. Contributions: newspapers, reviews and journals. *Honours:* Macaulay Fellowship in Literature 1984, Hawthornden Int. Writers Fellowship 1988, Ledwig-Rowholt Fellowship 1999, Fellow, English Asscn 2003, Fellow, Trinity Coll., Dublin 2004; Major State Award 1974–77, Arts Council Bursary for Poetry 1980, Ulster Titanic Soc. Lifetime Achievement Award 2002. *Address:* c/o Oscar Wilde Centre, School of English, Trinity College, Dublin 2, Ireland. *E-mail:* gdawe@tcd.ie.

DAWES, Kwame Senu Neville; poet, playwright and critic; b. 28 July 1962, Accra, Ghana; m. Lorna Marie; three c. *Education:* BA, English, Univ. of the West Indies, 1983; Graduate research in English, Univ. of the West Indies, 1984; PhD, English, Univ. of New Brunswick, 1992. *Career:* moved to Jamaica, 1971; Chair. of the Division of Arts and Letters, 1993–96; Asst Prof. in English, Univ. of South Carolina at Sumter, 1992–96; Guest Lecturer, Univ. of South Carolina, Columbia, 1994; Assoc. Prof. of English, Univ. of South Carolina, 1996–, Dir of MFA/Creative Writing programme, 2001–; Series Ed., Caribbean Play Series, Peepal Tree Books, UK, 1999–; Criticism Ed., Obsidian II literary journal, Raleigh, NC, 2000–; Programmer, annual Calabash International Literary Festival, Jamaica, 2000–; Dir, USC English Dept Spring Writers Festival, 2002–; mem. National Book Critics' Circle; Board mem., South Carolina Humanities Council; Mem., Advisory Board, South Carolina Book Festival. *Publications:* Poetry: Progeny of Air, 1994; Resisting the Anomie, 1995; Prophets, 1995; Jacko Jacobus, 1996; Requiem, 1996; Shook Foil, 1998; Wheel and Come Again: Reggae Anthology (ed.), 1998; Mapmaker (chapbook), 2000; Midland, 2001; Selected Poems, 2002. Fiction: A Place to Hide (short stories), 2002; Bivouac (novel), 2003. Plays: In the Warmth of the Cold; And the Gods Fell; In Chains of Freedom; The System; The Martyr; It Burns and it Stings; Charity's Come; Even Unto Death; Friends and Almost Lovers; Dear Pastor; Confessions; Brown Leaf; Coming in from the Cold; Song of an Injured Stone (musical); In My Garden; Charades; Passages; Salut Haiti (radio poem/drama); Samaritans (radio play); New World A-Comin' (radio play); A Celebration of Struggle; Stump of the Terebinth; Valley Prince; One Love, 2001. Non-Fiction: Natural Mysticism: Towards a New Reggae Aesthetic (literary criticism), 1998; Talk Yuh Talk: Interviews with Caribbean Poets, 2000; Bob Marley: Lyrical Genius, 2002. Contributions: Beat Magazine, Black Issues, Black Warrior Review, Bristol Evening Post, Calabash, Caribbean Writer, Dagens Nyheter (Sweden), Globe and Mail, Impact, Library Journal, Lines, Morning Star, Poetry London Newsletter, Poetry Review, Publishers Weekly, The Atlanta Journal/Constitution, The Brunswickan, The Courier, The Daily Gleaner, The Daily News, The English Review, The Guardian, The Herald, The London Times, The Observer, The State, The Sumter Item, The Telegraph Journal, The Voice, Time Out London, Venue, Wasafiri, Western Daily Press, World Literature Today, World Literature Written in English. *Honours:* Hon. Fellow, Univ. of Iowa International Writing Program, 1986; Forward Poetry Prize for Best First Collection, 1994; Individual Artist Fellowship, South Carolina Arts Commission, 1996; Assoc. Fellow, Univ. of Warwick, 1996; Poetry Business Chapbook Competition, 2000; Hollis Summers Poetry Prize, Ohio Univ. Press, 2000; Pushcart Prize, 2001. *Address:* c/o English Department, University of South Carolina, Columbia, SC 29208, USA (Office); 4 Doral Court, Columbia, SC 29229, USA (Home). *E-mail:* dawesk@gwm.sc.edu.

DAWKINS, (Clinton) Richard, MA, DPhil, FRS, FRSL; British biologist and author; *Charles Simonyi Professor of the Public Understanding of Science, University of Oxford*; b. 26 March 1941, Nairobi, Kenya; m. 1st Marian Stamp 1967 (divorced 1984); m. 2nd Eve Barham 1984; one d.; m. 3rd Hon. Lalla Ward 1992. *Education:* Balliol Coll., Oxford. *Career:* Asst Prof. of Zoology, Univ. of Calif., Berkeley, USA 1967–69; Lecturer, Univ. of Oxford 1970–89, Reader in Zoology 1989–96, Charles Simonyi Reader in the Public Understanding of Science 1995–96, Charles Simonyi Prof.1996–; Ed. Animal Behaviour 1974–78, Oxford Surveys in Evolutionary Biology 1983–86; Fellow New College, Oxford 1970–; Gifford Lecturer Univ. of Glasgow 1988, Sidgwick Memorial Lecturer Newnham Coll., Cambridge 1988; Kovler Visiting Fellow Univ. of Chicago 1990; Nelson Lecturer Univ. of Calif. at Davis 1990. *Television includes:* Nice Guys Finish First, BBC 1985, The Blind Watchmaker, BBC 1986, Break the Science Barrier, Channel 4 1994, Royal Institution Christmas Lectures, BBC 1992, Big Ideas in Science, Channel 5 2004. *Publications include:* The Selfish Gene 1976, The Extended Phenotype 1982, The Blind Watchmaker (RSL Prize 1987, LA Times Literature Prize 1987) 1986, River Out of Eden 1995, Climbing Mount Improbable 1996, Unweaving the Rainbow: Science, Delusion and the Appetite for Wonder 1998, A Devil's Chaplain (essays)

2003. *Honours:* Hon. Fellow Regent's Coll., London 1988; Hon. DLitt (St Andrews) 1995, (ANU Canberra) 1996; Hon. DSc (Westminster) 1997, (Hull) 2001; Hon. DUniv (Open Univ.) 2003; numerous awards including Silver Medal, Zoological Soc. 1989, Michael Faraday Award, Royal Soc. 1990, Nakayama Prize 1994, Int. Cosmos Prize 1997, Kistler Prize 2001. *Address:* Oxford University Museum, Parks Road, Oxford, OX1 3PW, England (Office). *E-mail:* simonyi.professor@oum.ox.ac.uk (Office).

DAWNAY, Caroline Margaret; British literary agent; b. 22 Jan. 1950, Reading; one s. *Education:* St Mary's School, Wantage, Oxon., Univ. per Stranieri, Florence, Italy and Alliance Française, Paris. *Career:* Noel Gay Artists 1968–70, Michael Joseph publishers, London 1971–77; Dir A. D. Peters & Co. Ltd 1977–88, Peters Fraser & Dunlop Group Ltd 1988–; Dir June Hall Literary Agency; Treas. Asscn of Authors' Agents 1991–94, Pres. 1994–97. *Address:* PFD, Drury House, 34–43 Russell Street, London, WC2B 3HA, England. *Telephone:* (20) 7344-1000.

DAWSON, Clay (see Levinson, Leonard).

DAWSON, Janet, BS, MA; writer and fmr journalist; b. 31 Oct. 1949, Purcell, Oklahoma, USA. *Education:* University of Colorado at Boulder, California State University at Hayward. *Career:* mem. MWA; Sisters in Crime; Private Eye Writers of America; American Crime Writers League; Authors' Guild; Mystery Readers International. *Publications:* Kindred Crimes, 1990; Till the Old Men Die, 1993; Take a Number, 1993; Don't Turn Your Back on the Ocean, 1994; Nobody's Child, 1995; A Credible Threat, 1996; Witness to Evil, 1997; Where the Bodies are Buried, 1998. Short Stories: By the Book; Little Red Corvette; Invisible Time; Witchcraft; Mrs Lincoln's Dilemma; What the Cat Dragged In. *Honours:* Award for Best First Private Eye Novel, St Martin's Press-Private Eye Writers Asscn, 1990. *Literary Agent:* Charlotte Sheedy Literary Agency, 65 Bleecker Street, 12th Floor, New York, NY 10012, USA.

DAWSON, Jill Dianne, BA, MA; British writer, poet, editor and teacher; b. 1962, Durham, England; pnr Meredith Bowles; two s. *Education:* Univ. of Nottingham, Sheffield Hallam Univ. *Career:* mem. Nat. Asscn of Writers in Education, Soc. of Authors. *Publications:* School Tales (ed.) 1990, How Do I Look? (non-fiction) 1991, Virago Book of Wicked Verse (ed.) 1992, Virago Book of Love Letters (ed.) 1994, Wild Ways (ed. with Margo Daly), White Fish with Painted Nails (poems) 1994, Trick of the Light (novel) 1996, Magpie (novel) 1998, Fred and Edie (novel) 2001, Gas & Air (ed. with Margo Daly), Wild Boy (novel) 2003; contrib. to anthologies and periodicals. *Honours:* Eric Gregory Award 1992, second prize, London Writers Short Story Competition 1994, Blue Nose Poet of the Year 1995, London Arts Board New Writers 1998. *Literary Agent:* PFD, Drury House 34–43 Russell Street, London, WC2B 5HA, England. *Telephone:* (20) 7836-9539. *E-mail:* aelam@pfd.co.uk. *Website:* www.jilldawson.co.uk.

DE ARAUGO, Sarah Therese (Tess); writer; b. 26 May 1930, Lismore, Vic., Australia; m. Maurice De Araugo 1950; two s. two d. *Education:* Notre Dame de Sion College, Warragal, Vic. *Career:* mem. Australian Society of Authors; Fellowship of Australian Writers; Royal Historical Society of Victoria; Women Writers of Australia; Nepean Historical Society. *Publications:* You Are What You Make Yourself To Be, 1980; The Kurnai of Gippsland, 1985; Boonorong on the Mornington Peninsula, 1993. Contributions: Encyclopaedias and periodicals. *Honours:* New South Wales Premier's Award for Australian Literature, 1985; Banjo Award, Australian Literature, National Book Council, 1985; Fellowship, 1987, Writer's Grant, 1989, Australian Literature Board; Short Story Award, PEN International, Australia, 1991. *Address:* 19 Grenville Grove, Rosebud West, Vic. 3940, Australia.

DE BERNIÈRES, Louis, MA; British writer; b. (Louis Henry Piers de Bernière-Smart), 8 Dec. 1954, London. *Education:* Bradfield Coll., Berkshire, Univ. of Manchester, Leicester Polytechnic, Inst. of Educ., Univ. of London. *Career:* landscape gardener 1972–73; teacher and rancher, Colombia 1974; philosophy tutor 1977–79; car mechanic 1980; English teacher 1981–84; bookshop asst 1985–86; supply teacher 1986–93; mem. PEN. *Publications:* The War of Don Emmanuel's Nether Parts 1990, Señor Vivo and the Coca Lord 1991, The Troublesome Offspring of Cardinal Guzman 1992, Captain Corelli's Mandolin 1994, Labels 1997, The Book of Job 1999, Gunter Weber's Confession 2001, Sunday Morning at the Centre of the World 2001, Red Dog 2001, Birds Without Wings 2004; contrib. to Second Thoughts, Granta. *Literary Agent:* Lavinia Trevor Agency, 7 The Glasshouse, 49A Goldhawk Road, London, W12 8QP, England. *Telephone:* (1986) 788665.

DE BOISSIÈRE, Ralph Anthony Charles; Australian writer; b. 6 Oct. 1907, Port-of-Spain, Trinidad; m. Ivy Alcantara 1935; two d. *Publications:* Crown Jewel (novel) 1952, Calypso Isle (play) 1955, Rum and Coca-Cola (novel) 1956, No Saddles for Kangaroos (novel) 1964, Autobiography 1996, The Call of the Rainbow 2000, Homeless in Paradise 2003. *Address:* 10 Vega Street, North Balwyn, Vic. 3104, Australia.

DE BONO, Edward Francis Charles Publius; Author and Academic; b. 19 May 1933, UK; m. Josephine Hall-White 1971; two s. *Education:* St Edward's Coll., Malta; Royal Univ. of Malta; Christ Church, Oxford. *Career:* Research Asst, Univ. of Oxford 1958–60, Jr Lecturer in Medicine 1960–61; Asst Dir of Research, Dept of Investigative Medicine, Cambridge Univ. 1963–76, Lecturer in Medicine 1976–83; Dir Cognitive Research Trust, Cambridge 1971–; Sec.- Gen. Supranational Independent Thinking Org. (SITO) 1983–; f. Edward de Bono Nonprofit Foundation; Hon. Registrar St Thomas' Hosp. Medical School, Harvard Medical School; Hon. Consultant Boston City Hosp. 1965–66; Chair. Council, Young Enterprise Europe 1998–; creator of two TV series: The Greatest Thinkers 1981, de Bono's Thinking Course 1982; planet DE73 named edebono after him. *Publications:* The Use of Lateral Thinking, 1967; The Five-Day Course in Thinking, 1968; The Mechanism of Mind, 1969; Lateral Thinking: a textbook of creativity, 1970; The Dog Exercising Machine, 1970; Technology Today, 1971; Practical Thinking, 1971; Lateral Thinking for Management, 1971; Children Solve Problems, 1972; Po: Beyond Yes and No, 1972; Think Tank, 1973; Eureka: a history of inventions, 1974; Teaching Thinking, 1976; The Greatest Thinkers, 1976; Wordpower, 1977; The Happiness Purpose, 1977; The Case of the Disappearing Elephant, 1977; Opportunities: a handbook of Business Opportunity Search, 1978; Future Positive, 1979; Atlas of Management Thinking, 1981; de Bono's Thinking Course, 1982; Conflicts: a better way to resolve them, 1985; Six Thinking Hats, 1985; Letter to Thinkers, 1987; I am Right You are Wrong, 1990; Positive Revolution for Brazil, 1990; Six Action Shoes, 1991; Serious Creativity, 1992; Teach Your Child to Think, 1992; Water Logic, 1993; Parallel Thinking, 1994; Teach Yourself to Think, 1995; Mind Pack, 1995; Edward de Bono's Textbook of Wisdom, 1996; How to be More Interesting, 1997; Simplicity, 1998; New Thinking for the New Millennium, 1999; Why I Want to be King of Australia, 1999; The Book of Wisdom, 2000; The de Bono Code, 2000. Contributions: numerous publs in Nature, Lancet, Clinical Science, American Journal of Physiology. *Address:* Cranmer Hall, Fakenham, Norfolk NR21 9HX, England; L2 Albany, Piccadilly, London W1V 9RR, England. *Website:* www.edwarddebono.com.

DE BOTTON, Alain; Swiss writer; b. 20 Dec. 1969, Zürich. *Education:* Gonville and Caius Coll., Cambridge. *Publications:* Essays in Love (aka On Love) 1993, The Romantic Movement: Sex, Shopping, and the Novel 1994, Kiss and Tell 1995, How Proust Can Change Your Life: Not a Novel 1997, The Consolations of Philosophy 2000, The Art of Travel (Charles Veillon European Essay Prize, Switzerland 2003) 2002, Status Anxiety 2004; contrib. articles, book and television reviews to various periodicals. *Honours:* Chevalier, Ordre des Arts et des Lettres 2003. *Literary Agent:* PFD, Drury House, 34–43 Russell Street, London, WC2B 5HA, England. *Telephone:* (20) 7344-1000. *Fax:* (20) 7352-7356. *E-mail:* cdawnay@pfd.co.uk. *Website:* www.pfd.co.uk. *Address:* 73 Sterndale Road, London, W14 OHU, England. *E-mail:* adb@netcomuk.co.uk. *Website:* www.alaindebotton.com.

DE CRESPIGNY, (Richard) Rafe Champion; historian and writer; b. 16 March 1936, Adelaide, SA, Australia; m. Christa Charlotte Boltz; one s. one d. *Education:* BA, 1957, MA, 1961, University of Cambridge; BA, University of Melbourne, 1961; BA, 1962, MA, 1964, PhD, 1968, Australian National University. *Career:* Lecturer, 1964–70, Senior Lecturer, 1970–73, Reader in Chinese, 1973–, Australian National University, Canberra; Master, University House, 1991–2001; Adjunct Prof. of Asian Studies, 1999–; mem. Australian Acad. of the Humanities, fellow; Chinese Studies Asscn of Australia, pres., 1999–2001. *Publications:* The Biography of Sun Chien, 1966; Official Titles of the Former Han Dynasty (with H. H. Dubs), 1967; The Last of the Han, 1969; The Records of the Three Kingdoms, 1970; China: The Land and Its People, 1971; China This Century: A History of Modern China, 1975; Portents of Protest, 1976; Northern Frontier, 1984; Emperor Huan and Emperor Ling, 1989; Generals of the South, 1990; To Establish Peace, 1996. *Address:* c/o Faculty of Asian Studies, Australian National University, Canberra, ACT 0200, Australia.

DE GRASSE TYSON, Neil, BA, PhD; American astrophysicist and writer; b. New York, NY; m.; two c. *Education:* Bronx High School of Science, Univ. of Harvard, Columbia Univ. *Career:* full-time research scientist at Princeton Univ., NJ; essayist for Natural History magazine 1995–; part of cttee studying the future of the US Aerospace Industry 2001, and the Implementation of the US Space Exploration Policy 2004; currently Dir of Hayden Planetarium, NY; astrophysicist at American Museum of Natural History. *Publications include:* non-fiction: Merlin's Tour of the Universe 1989, Universe Down to Earth 1994, Just Visiting This Planet 1998, The Sky is Not the Limit: Adventures of an Urban Astrophysicist 2000, One Universe: at Home in the Cosmos 2000, Cosmic Horizons: Astronomy at the Cutting Edge (ed.) 2001. *Address:* Department of Astrophysics, American Museum of Natural History, Central Park West at 79th Street, New York, NY 10024, USA. *Telephone:* (212) 769-5912. *Fax:* (212) 769-5934. *E-mail:* tyson@amnh.org. *Website:* research.amnh.org/~tyson.

DE GROEN, Alma; New Zealand playwright and screenwriter; b. 1941. *Career:* moved to Australia 1964; became playwright 1970; writer-in-residence, West Australia Inst. of Technology 1986; dramaturg, Griffin Theatre Co 1987. *Plays include:* The Joss Adams Show 1970, Perfectly All Right (aka Sweatproof Boy) 1972, The After-Life of Arthur Cravan 1973, Chidley 1977, Going Home 1978, Vocations (also screenplay) 1981, The Rivers of China 1986, The Girl Who Saw Everything 1991, Wicked Sisters 2003. *Television writing:* Man of Letters (ABC) 1985, Singles, After Marcuse (ABC), Rafferty's Rules: The Women (Channel 7) 1988. *Radio writing:* Available Light (ABC) 1991, Stories in the Dark (with Ian D. MacKenzie). *Honours:* Premier's Literary Award for Drama in New South Wales and

Victoria. *Literary Agent:* RGM Associates, PO Box 128, Surry Hills, NSW 2010, Australia. *Telephone:* (2) 9281-3911. *Fax:* (2) 9281-4705. *E-mail:* info@rgm.com.au. *Website:* www.rgm.com.au.

DE GRUCHY, John W(esley); Prof. of Christian Studies, Writer and Ed.; b. 18 March 1939, Pretoria, South Africa; m. Isobel Dunstan, two s. one d. *Education:* BA, 1958, BD, 1960, Rhodes University; MTh, Chicago Theological Seminary, 1964; DTh, University of South Africa, 1971; DSocSci, University of Cape Town, 1996; DLitt hc, Chicago Theological Seminary, 2002. *Career:* Ordained Minister, United Congregational Church, 1961; Pastor, Durban, 1961–68, Johannesburg, 1968–73; Dir, South African Council of Churches, 1968–73; Lecturer, 1973–75, Senior Lecturer, 1975–80, Assoc. Prof., 1980–86, Robert Selby Taylor Prof. of Christian Studies, 1986–, Dir, Graduate School in Humanities, 2000–03, Sr Research Scholar, 2003–, University of Cape Town; Founder-Ed., Journal of Theology for Southern Africa, 1973–; Pres., United Congregational Church, 1980–81. *Publications:* The Church Struggle in South Africa, 1979; Apartheid is a Heresy (ed. with Charles Villa-Vicencio), 1983; Bonhoeffer and South Africa, 1985; Resistance and Hope: South African Essays in Honour of Beyers Naude (ed. with Charles Villa-Vicencio), 1985; Cry Justice! Prayers, Meditations, and Readings from South Africa, 1986; Theology and Ministry in Context and Crisis: A South African Perspective, 1987; Dietrich Bonhoeffer: Witness to Jesus Christ, 1987; Reinhold Niebuhr (ed. with Larry Rasmussen), 1988; Karl Barth: Theologian of Freedom (ed. with Clifford Green), 1989; Karl Rahner: Theologian of the Graced Search for Meaning (ed. with Geoffrey Kelly), 1989; Adolf von Harnack: Liberal Theology at Its Height (ed. with H. Martin Rumscheidt), 1989; A Southern African Guide to World Religions (ed. with Martin Prozesky), 1991; In Word and in Deed: Towards a Practical Theology of Social Transformation: A Framework for Reflection and Training (with Jim Cochrane and Robin Petersen), 1991; Liberating Reformed Theology: A South African Contribution to an Ecumenical Debate, 1991; Doing Ethics in Context: South African Perspectives (ed. with Charles Villa-Vicencio), 1994; Religion and the Reconstuction of Civil Society (ed. with Stephen Martin), 1995; Living Faiths in South Africa (ed. with Martin Prozesky), 1995; Christianity and Democracy, 1995; Bonhoeffer for a New Day: Theology in a Time of Transition (ed.), 1997; The Cambridge Companion to Dietrich Bonhoeffer, 1999; Facing the Truth: South African Faith Communities and the Truth and Reconciliation Commission (ed. with Jim Cochrane and Stephen Martin), 1999; The London Missionary Society in Southern Africa: Historical Essays in Celebration of the Bicentenary of the LMS in Southern Africa, 1799–1999 (ed.), 2000; Christianity, Art, and Transformation, 2001. Contributions: scholarly journals. *Address:* c/o Graduate School of Humanities, University of Cape Town, Post Bag Rondebosch 7701, Cape Town, South Africa.

DE GUISE, Elizabeth (Mary Teresa), (Isobel Chase, Elizabeth Hunter); Writer; b. 1934, Nairobi, Kenya. *Education:* Open University. *Career:* mem. Campaign for Nuclear Disarmament; Pax Christi; Romantic Novelists Asscn. *Publications:* Romance Novels as Elizabeth Hunter: Fountains of Paradise, 1983; London Pride, 1983; Shared Destiny, 1983; A Silver Nutmeg, 1983; Kiss of the Rising Sun, 1984; Rain on the Wind, 1984; Song of Surrender, 1984; A Tower of Strength, 1984; A Time to Wed, 1984; Loving Relations, 1984; Eye of the Wind, 1985; Legend of the Sun, 1985; The Painted Veil, 1986; The Tides of Love, 1988. Romance Novels as Isobel Chase: The House of Scissors, 1972; The Dragon's Cave, 1972; The Edge of Beyond, 1973; A Man of Kent, 1973; The Elban Adventure, 1974; The Cornish Hearth, 1975; A Canopy of Rose Leaves, 1976; The Clouded Veil, 1976; The Desert Castle, 1976; Singing in the Wilderness, 1976; The Whistling Thorn, 1977; The Mouth of Truth, 1977; Second Best Wife, 1978; Undesirable Wife, 1978. Historical Novels as Elizabeth De Guise: Dance of the Peacocks, 1988; Flight of the Dragonfly, 1990; Came Forth the Sun, 1991; Bridge of Sighs, 1992. Contributions: Women & Home; Woman's Weekly. *Address:* 113 Nun St, St Davids, Haverfordwest, Dyfed SA62 6BP, Wales.

DE KRETSER, Michelle, MA; Australian writer; b. Colombo, Sri Lanka. *Education:* Melbourne Univ., Univ. of the Sorbonne, Paris. *Career:* moved to Australia aged 14; fmrly teacher in Montpellier, ed. for Lonely Planet, freelance ed. *Publications:* fiction: The Rose Grower 1999, The Hamilton Case (Commonwealth Writers Prize, SE Asia and South Pacific Region 2004) 2003; editor: Brief Encounters: Stories of Love, Sex and Travel 1998. *Address:* c/o Random House Australia, 20 Alfred Street, Milson's Point, NSW 2061, Australia.

de la BILLIÈRE, Gen. Sir Peter (Edgar de la Cour), Kt, KCB, KBE, DSO, MC, DL; British army officer (retd) and banker (retd); b. 29 April 1934, Plymouth; m. Bridget Constance Muriel Goode 1965; one s. two d. *Education:* Harrow School, Staff Coll., Royal Coll. of Defence Studies. *Career:* joined King's Shropshire Light Infantry 1952; commissioned, Durham Light Infantry; served Japan, Korea, Malaya (despatches 1959), Jordan, Borneo, Egypt, Aden, Gulf States, Sudan, Oman, Falkland Islands; Commdg Officer, 22 Special Air Service (SAS) Regt 1972–74; Gen. Staff Officer 1 (Directing Staff), Staff Coll. 1974–77; Commdr British Army Training Team, Sudan 1977–78; Dir SAS and Commdr SAS Group 1978–83; Commdr British Forces, Falkland Islands and Mil. Commr 1984–85; Gen. Officer Commdg Wales 1985–87; Col Comdt. Light Div. 1986–90; Lt-Gen. Officer commanding SE Dist 1987–90; Commdr British Forces in Middle East Oct. 1990–91; rank of Gen. 1991 after Gulf War, Ministry of Defence Adviser on Middle East 1991–92; retd from army June 1992; Pres. SAS Asscn 1991–96, Army Cadet Force 1992–99; mem. Council Royal United Services Inst. 1975–77; Chair. Jt Services Hang Gliding 1986–88; Cdre Army Sailing Asscn 1989–90; Commr Duke of York's School 1988–90; Freeman City of London 1991; Hon. Freeman Fishmongers' Co. 1991; Pres. Harrow School Asscn 2002–; Trustee Imperial War Museum 1992–99; Dir (non-exec.), Middle East and Defence Adviser, Robert Fleming Holdings 1992–99; Chair. Meadowland Meats 1994–2002; Jt Chair. Dirs FARM Africa 1995–2001 (mem. Bd 1992–2001); DL Hereford and Worcester 1993; Trustee Naval and Mil. Club 1999–2003, mem. Bd 1999–2003; Pres. Friends of Imperial War Museum 2003; Pres. Harrow Asscn 2002–. *Television:* Discovery: Clash of the Generals 2004. *Publications:* Storm Command: a personal story of the Gulf War 1992, Looking for Trouble (autobiog.) 1994, Supreme Courage: Heroic Stories from 150 Years of the Victoria Cross 2004. *Honours:* Hon. DSc (Cranfield) 1992; Hon. DCL (Durham) 1993; Legion of Merit Chief Commdr (USA), Order of Abdul Aziz 2nd Class (Saudi Arabia), Meritorious Service Cross (Canada), Kuwait Decoration of the First Class, Order of Qatar Sash of Merit.

DE LA MARTINIÈRE, Hervé; French publisher. *Career:* sales, Hachette; Ed., Hachette Littérature, Hachette-Réalités, Nathan; f. Editions la Martinière 1992, Pres. Groupe La Martinière. *Address:* 2 rue Christine, 75006, Paris, France. *Telephone:* 1-40-51-52-00. *Fax:* 1-40-51-52-05. *Website:* www.lamartiniere.fr.

DE LANGE, Nicholas (Robert Michael); Scholar and Trans; b. 7 Aug. 1944, Nottingham, England. *Education:* MA, 1969, DPhil, 1970, Christ Church, Oxford; PhD, 1971, DD, 2001, Univ. of Cambridge. *Career:* mem. British Asscn of Jewish Studies; Society of Authors; Trans Asscn; Fellow, Wolfson College, Cambridge. *Publications:* Apocrypha, 1978; Atlas of the Jewish World, 1984; Judaism, 1986; Illustrated History of the Jewish People, 1997; An Introduction to Judaism, 2000; Ignaz Maybaum: A Reader, 2001. Other: many trans. Contributions: Tel-Aviv Review; Jerusalem Review. *Honours:* George Webber Prize for Trans., 1990; TLS/Porjes Prize for Trans., 2001. *Address:* Faculty of Divinity, West Rd, Cambridge CB3 9BS, England. *E-mail:* nrml1@cam.ac.uk.

DE LINT, Charles Henri Diederick Hoefsmit; Canadian editor, writer, poet and musician; b. 22 Dec. 1951, Bussum, Netherlands; m. MaryAnn Harris 1980. *Career:* owner-Ed., Triskell Press; writer-in-residence, Ottawa and Gloucester Public Libraries, 1995; mem. SFWA, Science Fiction Writers of Canada. *Publications:* Drink Down the Moon: A Novel of Urban Faerie, 1990; Death Leaves an Echo, 1991; Dreaming Place, 1992; From a Whisper to a Scream, 1992; Dreams Underfoot: The Newford Collection, 1993; Memory and Dream, 1994; The Ivory and the Horn, 1995; Trader, 1997; Someplace to be Flying, 1998; Moonlight and Vines, 1999; Forests of the Heart, 2000. Contributions: anthologies and periodicals. *Address:* PO Box 9480, Ottawa, ON K1G 3V2, Canada.

DE PALCHI, Alfredo; Poet and Editor; b. 13 Dec. 1926, Verona, Italy; m. 1st Sonia Raiziss 1952 (deceased); one d.; m. 2nd Rita Di Pace 23 June 1988. *Education:* Sorbonne, University of Paris. *Career:* Ed., Chelsea Publications Inc. *Publications:* Modern European Poetry, Italian section (co-ed.), 1966; Sessioni con l'analista (poems), 1967, in English as Sessions with My Analyst, 1970; Mutazioni (poems), 1988; The Scorpion's Dark Dance (poems), 1993; Costellazione Anonima (poems), 1998, in English as Anonymous Constellation, 1997; The Metaphysical Streetcar Conductor: Sixty Poems by Luciano Erba, 1998; Addictive Aversions (poems), 1999; Paradigma (poems), 2001. Contributions: Reviews, quarterlies and journals including: American Poetry Review; The Nation; Chicago Review; New Letters; Poetry TriQuarterly. *Honours:* Premio Nazionale di Poesia, Città di S. Vito al Tagliamento. *Address:* 33 Union Square W, New York, NY 10003, USA.

DE ROO, Anne (Louise); Writer; b. 1931, Gore, New Zealand. *Education:* BA, University of Canterbury, Christchurch, 1952. *Publications:* Children's Fiction: The Gold Dog, 1969; Moa Valley, 1969; Boy and the Sea Beast, 1971; Cinnamon and Nutmeg, 1972; Mick's Country Cousins, 1974; Scrub Fire, 1977; Traveller, 1979; Because of Rosie, 1980; Jacky Nobody, 1983; The Bat's Nest, 1986; Friend Troll, Friend Taniwha, 1986; Mouse Talk, 1990; The Good Cat, 1990; Hepzibah Mouse's ABC, 1991; Sergeant Sal, 1991; Hepzibah's Book of Famous Mice, 1993. Fiction: Hope Our Daughter, 1990; Becoming Fully Human, 1991; And We Beheld His Glory, 1994. Plays: The Dragon Master, 1978; The Silver Blunderbuss, 1984. *Honours:* ICI Bursary, 1981. *Address:* 38 Joseph St, Palmerston North, New Zealand.

DE SOUZA, Eunice; Reader in English, Poet and Writer; b. 1 Aug. 1940, Poona, India. *Education:* BA, 1960, PhD, 1988, University of Mumbai. *Career:* Reader in English, 1969–, Head, Dept of English, 1990–, St Xavier's College, Mumbai. *Publications:* Folk Tales from Gujarat, 1975; Himalayan Tales, 1978; Fix, 1979; Women in Dutch Painting, 1988; Ways of Belonging: Selected Poems, 1990; Selected and New Poems, 1994; Nine Indian Women Poets (ed.), 1997; Talking Poems, 1999. Other: several children's books. *Honours:* Poetry Book Society Recommendation, 1990. *Address:* c/o Dept of English, St Xavier's College, Mumbai 400 001, India.

DE WEESE, Thomas Eugene (Gene), (Jean DeWeese, Thomas Stratton, Victoria Thomas); writer; b. 31 Jan. 1934, Rochester, IN, USA; m. Beverly Amers 1955. *Education:* Valparaiso Technical Institute, IN, Indiana University, Kokomo, University of Wisconsin, Milwaukee, Marquette University, Milwaukee. *Publications:* Fiction: Jeremy Case, 1976; The Wanting Factor, 1980; A Different Darkness, 1982; Something Answered, 1983; Chain of Attack, 1987; The Peacekeepers, 1988; The Final Nexus, 1988; Renegade, 1991; Into the Nebula, 1995; King of the Dead, 1996; Lord of the Necropolis, 1997. (Wth Robert Coulson): The Invisibility Affair, 1967; The Mind-Twisters Affair, 1967; Gates of the Universe, 1975; Now You See It/Him/Them…, 1976; Charles Fort Never Mentioned Wombats, 1977; Nightmare Universe, 1985.(As Jean DeWeese): The Reimann Curse, 1975; The Moonstone Spirit, 1975; The Carnelian Cat, 1975; Cave of the Moaning Wind, 1976; Web of Guilt, 1976; The Doll With Opal Eyes, 1976; Nightmare in Pewter, 1978; Hour of the Cat, 1980; The Backhoe Gothic, 1981. (As Victoria Thomas): Ginger's Wish (with Connie Kugi), 1987. Other: Black Suits From Outer Space; several other science fiction novels for children. Non-Fiction: Fundamentals of Space Navigation, 1968; Fundamentals of Digital Computers, 1972; Fundamentals of Integrated Circuits, 1972; Making American Folk Art Dolls (with Gini Rogowski), 1975; Computers in Entertainment and the Arts, 1984. Contributions: anthologies and magazines. *Honours:* Best Novel Awards, 1976, 1982, Best Juvenile Book Award, 1979, Council for Wisconsin Writers; Notable Science Book of the Year, NSTA, 1984. *Address:* 2718 N Prospect, Milwaukee, WI 53211, USA.

DEAMBROSIS, Mercedes; Spanish/Greek novelist; b. 1 Oct. 1955, Madrid, Spain. *Publications include:* Milagrosa (novel) 2002. *Address:* c/o Dedalus Ltd, Langford Lodge, St Judith's Lane, Sawtry, Cambridgeshire PE28 5XE, England. *E-mail:* info@dedalusbooks.com. *Website:* www.dedalusbooks.com.

DEANE, John F.; Irish poet, writer and translator; b. 1943, Achill Island, Co. Mayo. *Education:* Mungret and Univ. Coll. Dublin. *Career:* teacher; re-founded Poetry Ireland and Poetry Ireland Review 1979; Ed., The Dedalus Press. *Publications:* poetry: Stalking After Time 1977, High Sacrifice 1981, Winter in Meath 1984, Road with Cypress and Star 1988, The Stylized City: Selected and New Poems 1991, Walking on Water 1994, Toccata and Fugue 2001, Manhandling the Deity 2003; novels: One Man's Place 1994, Flightlines 1996, Undertow 2002; short story collections: Free Range 1994, The Coffin Master and Other Stories 2000; translator of works by Marin Sorescu, Tomas Tranströmer and Jacques Rancourt. *Honours:* Robert Penn Warren Prize 2000, Howard Nemerov Sonnet Award 2001, Firman Houghton Award 2002, Robert Frost Award 2002, New Criterion Poetry Prize 2004. *Address:* The Dedalus Press, 24 The Heath, Cypress Downs, Dublin, 6W, Ireland. *Fax:* (353) 1 490 2582. *E-mail:* deanejohn@hotmail.com. *Website:* homepage.tinet.ie/~johndeane/.

DEANE, Seamus (Francis); Prof. of Irish Studies, Writer and Poet; b. 9 Feb. 1940, Derry City, Northern Ireland; m. Marion Treacy, 19 Aug. 1963, separated, three s., two d. *Education:* BA, 1961, MA, 1963, Queen's University, Belfast; PhD, University of Cambridge, 1966. *Career:* Visiting Fulbright and Woodrow Wilson Scholar, Reed College, Oregon, 1966–67; Visiting Lecturer, 1967–68, Visiting Prof., 1978, University of California at Berkeley; Prof. of Modern English and American Literature, University College, Dublin, 1980–93; Walker Ames Prof., University of Washington, Seattle, 1987; Julius Benedict Distinguished Visiting Prof., Carleton College, Minnesota, 1988; Keough Prof. of Irish Studies, University of Notre Dame, IN, 1993–; mem. Aosdána (Irish Artists' Council); Field Day Theatre and Publishing Company, dir; Royal Irish Acad. *Publications:* Fiction: Reading in the Dark, 1996. Poetry: Gradual Wars, 1972; Rumours, 1977; History Lessons, 1983; Selected, 1988. Non-Fiction: Celtic Revivals: Essays in Modern Irish Literature, 1880–1980, 1985; A Short History of Irish Literature, 1986, reissued, 1994; The French Revolution and Enlightenment in England, 1789–1832, 1988; Strange Country: Ireland, Modernity and Nationhood, 1790–1970, 1997. Editor: The Adventures of Hugh Trevor by Thomas Holcroft, 1972; The Sale Catalogues of the Libraries of Eminent Persons, Vol. IX, 1973; Nationalism, Colonialism and Literature, 1990; The Field Day Anthology of Irish Writing, 3 vols, 1991; Penguin Twentieth Century Classics: James Joyce, five vols, 1993; Future Crossings (with K. Ziarek), 2000. *Honours:* AE Memorial for Literature, 1973; American-Irish Fund, Literature, 1989; Guardian Fiction Prize, 1997; Irish Times International Fiction Award, 1997; Irish Times Fiction Award, 1997; LWT South Bank Award for Literature, 1997; Ruffino Antico-Fattore International Literature Award, Florence, 1998. *Address:* c/o Sonya Land, Sheil Land Assocs Ltd, 43 Doughty St, London WC1N 2LF, England.

DEAR, Nick; Playwright; b. 11 June 1955, Portsmouth, England; Partner: Penny Downie, two s. *Education:* BA, European Literature, University of Essex, 1977. *Career:* Playwright-in-Residence, Essex University, 1985, Royal Exchange Theatre, 1987–88; mem. Writer's Guild of Great Britain. *Publications:* Temptation, 1984; The Art of Success, 1986; Food of Love, 1988; A Family Affair (after Ostrovsky), 1988; In the Ruins, 1989; The Last Days of Don Juan (after Tirso), 1990; Le Bourgeois Gentilhomme (after Molière), 1992; Pure Science, 1994; Zenobia, 1995; Summerfolk (after Gorky), 1999; The Villains' Opera, 2000; The Promise (after Arbuzov), 2002; Power, 2003. Other: several radio plays. Films: The Monkey Parade, 1983; The Ranter, 1988; Persuasion, 1995; The Gambler, 1997; The Turn of the Screw, 1999; Cinderella, 2000; Byron, 2003; Eroica, 2003. Opera Libretti: A Family Affair, 1993; Siren Song, 1994; The Palace in the Sky, 2000. *Honours:* John Whiting Award, 1987; BAFTA Award, 1996; Broadcasting Press Guild Award, 1996; South Bank Show Theatre Award, 1999. *Address:* c/o Rosica Colin Ltd, 1 Clareville Grove Mews, London SW7 5AH, England.

DEARDEN, James Shackley; Writer and Ed.; b. 9 Aug. 1931, Barrow-in-Furness, England. *Career:* Curator, Ruskin Galleries, Bembridge School, Isle of Wight and Brantwood Coniston, 1957–96; mem. Ruskin Society; Ruskin Asscn, secretary and treasurer; Turner Society; Companion of the Guild of St George, Dir for Ruskin Affairs; Old Bembridgians Asscn, past pres.; Isle of Wight Foot Beagles, fmr master; Friends of Ruskin's Brantwood, hon. life mem. and vice-pres. *Publications:* The Professor: Arthur Severn's Memoir of Ruskin, 1967; A Short History of Brantwood, 1967; Iteriad by John Ruskin (ed.), 1969; Facets of Ruskin, 1970; Ruskin and Coniston (with K. G. Thorne), 1971; John Ruskin, 1973; Turner's Isle of Wight Sketch Book, 1979; John Ruskin e Les Alpi, 1989; John Ruskin's Camberwell, 1990; A Tour to the Lakes in Cumberland: John Ruskin's Diary for 1830 (ed.), 1990; John Ruskin and Victorian Art, 1993; Ruskin, Bembridge and Brantwood, 1994; Hare Hunting on the Isle of Wight, 1996; John Ruskin, A Life in Pictures, 1999; King of the Golden River by John Ruskin (ed.), 1999. Contributions: Book Collector; Connoisseur; Apollo; Burlington; Bulletin of John Rylands Library; Country Life; Ruskin Newsletter (ed.); Ruskin Research Series (gen. ed.); Journal of Pre-Raphaelite Studies (editorial advisory board); Whitehouse Edition of Ruskin's Works (jt gen. ed.). *Honours:* Hon. DLitt, Univ. of Lancaster, 1998. *Address:* 4 Woodlands, Foreland Rd, Bembridge, Isle of Wight, England.

DE'ATH, Richard (see Haining, Peter (Alexander)).

DEAVER, Jeffery Wilds, DJur; American novelist; b. 6 May 1950, Chicago. *Education:* Univ. of Missouri, Fordham Law School. *Career:* magazine journalist, lawyer, full-time writer 1990–. *Publications:* fiction: Voodoo 1987, Manhattan is My Beat 1988, Death of a Blue Movie Star 1990, Hard News 1991, Shallow Graves 1992, Mistress of Justice 1992, Bloody River Blues 1993, The Lesson of her Death 1993, Praying for Sleep 1994, A Maiden's Grave 1995, The Bone Collector 1997, The Coffin Dancer 1998, The Devil's Teardrop 1999, The Empty Chair (WHSmith Thumping Good Read Award 2001) 2000, Speaking in Tongues 2000, Hell's Kitchen 2001, The Blue Nowhere 2001, The Stone Monkey 2002, The Vanished Man 2003, Twisted 2004, Garden of Beasts 2004; editor: A Century of Great Suspense Stories 2001, A Hot and Sultry Night for Crime 2003; non-fiction: The Complete Law School Companion 1992; contrib. to Crimes of the Heart 1995, The Best of the Best 1997, Irreconcilable Differences 1999, The World's Finest Mystery and Crime Stories vols 1, 3 and 4 (2000–03), A Confederacy of Crime 2000, Opening Shots 2 2001, Much Ado About Murder 2002, Men from Boys 2003. *Address:* c/o Hodder & Stoughton, 338 Euston Road, London, NW1 3BH, England. *E-mail:* info@jefferydeaver.com. *Website:* www.jefferydeaver.com.

DEBRAY, (Jules) Régis; French author and government official; b. 2 Sept. 1940, Paris; m. Elisabeth Burgos 1968; one d. *Education:* Ecole normale supérieure de la rue d'Ulm. *Career:* colleague of Che Guevara, imprisoned in Bolivia 1967–70; Co-Ed., Comité d'études sur les libertés 1975; adviser on foreign affairs to François Mitterrand; responsible for Third World Affairs, Secr.-Gen. of Presidency of Repub. 1981–84; Office of Pres. of Repub. 1984–85, 1987–88; Maître des requêtes, Conseil d'Etat 1985–93; Sec.-Gen. Conseil du Pacifique Sud 1986–. *Publications:* La Critique des armes 1973, La Guerilla du Che 1974, Entretiens avec Allende 1971, Les Epreuves du fer 1974, L'Indésirable 1975, La Neige brûle 1977, Lettre aux communistes français et á quelques autres 1978, Le Pouvoir intellectuel en France 1979, Le Scribe 1980, Critique de la raison politique 1981, La Puissance et les rêves 1984, Les Empires contre l'Europe 1985, Comète, ma comète 1986, Eloges 1986, Les Masques 1987, Que vive la République 1988, A demain de Gaulle 1990, Cours de médiologie générale 1991, Christophe Colomb, le visiteur de l'aube: les traités de Tordesillas 1992, Vie et mort de l'image: une histoire du regard en Occident 1992, Contretemps: Eloge des idéaux perdus 1992, Ledannois 1992, L'Etat séducteur 1993, L'Oeil naïf 1994, Manifestes médiologiques 1994, Par amour de l'art 1998, L'Abus monumental 1999, Croire, voir, faire 1999, L'Emprise 2000, i.f. suite et fin 2000, Introduction à la médiologie 2000, Loués soient les seigneurs 2000, L'Enseignement du fait religieux dans l'école laïque 2002, L'Edit de Caracalla ou plaidoyer pour les Etats-Unis d'occident 2002, L'Ancien Testament à travers 100 chefs-d'œuvre de la peinture 2003, Le Nouveau Testament à travers 100 chefs-d'œuvre de la peinture 2003, Dieu, un itinéraire 2003, Haïti et la France: Rapport à Dominique de Villepin, ministre des Affaires étrangères 2004, Le siecle et la règle 2004, Ce que nous voile le voile 2004, La Mythologie gréco-latine à travers 100 chefs-d'oeuvres de la peinture 2004, L'Histoire ancienne à travers 100 chefs-d'oeuvres de la peinture 2004, Chroniques de l'idiotie triomphante 2004. *Honours:* Prix Fémina 1977. *Address:* Editions Gallimard, 5 rue Sébastien Bottin, 75007 Paris, France.

DECLEMENTS, Barthe; Writer; b. 8 Oct. 1920, Seattle, Washington, USA; m. 1st Don Macri, divorced; m. 2nd Gordon Greimes, divorced, four c. *Education:* Western Washington College, 1940–42; BA, 1944, MEd, 1970, University of Washington, Seattle. *Career:* Schoolteacher, 1944–46, 1961–78; High School Counselor, 1978–83. *Publications:* Nothing's Fair in Fifth Grade, 1981; How Do You Lose Those Ninth Grade Blues?, 1983; Seventeen and In-Between, 1984; Sixth Grade Can Really Kill You, 1985;

I Never Asked You to Understand Me, 1986; Double Trouble (with Christopher Greimes), 1987; No Place For Me, 1987; The Fourth Grade Wizards, 1988; Five-Finger Discount, 1989; Monkey See, Monkey Do, 1990; Wake Me at Midnight, 1991; Breaking Out, 1991; The Bite of the Gold Bug, 1992; The Pickle Song, 1993; Tough Loser, 1994; Spoiled Rotten, 1996; Liar, Liar, 1998. Contributions: periodicals. *Honours:* Over 25 awards. *Address:* c/o Viking Penguin, 375 Hudson St, New York, NY 10014, USA.

DEEDES, Baron (Life Peer), cr. 1986, of Aldington in the County of Kent; **William Francis Deedes,** KBE, PC, MC, DL; British politician and newspaper editor; b. 1 June 1913, Aldington, Kent; m. Evelyn Hilary Branfoot 1942 (died 2004); two s. (one deceased) three d. *Education:* Harrow School. *Career:* journalist with Morning Post 1931–37; war corresp. on Abyssinia 1935; served in war of 1939–45, Queen's Westminsters (12 King's Royal Rifle Corps); MP (Conservative) for Ashford Div. of Kent 1950–74; Parl. Sec., Ministry of Housing and Local Govt 1954–55; Parl. Under-Sec. Home Dept 1955–57; DL, Kent 1962; Minister without Portfolio (Information) 1962–64; mem. Advisory Cttee on Drug Dependence 1967–74; Chair. Select Cttee on Immigration and Race Relations 1970–74; Ed. Daily Telegraph 1974–86, mem. editorial staff 1986–. *Publications:* Dear Bill: W. F. Deedes Reports (autobiog.) 1997, At War with Waugh 2003, Brief Lives 2004. *Honours:* Hon. DCL (Kent) 1988; Special Award, British Press Awards 1992. *Address:* New Hayters, Aldington, Kent, TN25 7DT, England. *Telephone:* (1233) 720269.

DEFORD, Frank; Writer and Ed.; b. 16 Dec. 1938, Baltimore, MD, USA; m. Carol Penner, 28 Aug. 1965, one s. two d. *Education:* BA, Princeton University, 1962. *Career:* Contributing Ed., Sports Illustrated, 1962–69, 1998–, Vanity Fair, 1993–96; Writer, Commentator, Cable News Network, 1980–86, National Public Radio, 1980–89, 1991–, NBC, 1986–89, ESPN, 1992–96, HBO, 1996–; Ed.-in-Chief, The National, 1989–91; Writer, Newsweek Magazine, 1991–93, 1996–98. *Publications:* Five Strides on the Banked Track, 1969; Cut'N'Run, 1971; There She Is, 1972; The Owner, 1974; Big Bill Tilden: The Triumphs and the Tragedy, 1977; Everybody's All-American, 1981; Alex: The Life of a Child, 1982; Spy in the Deuce Court, 1987; World's Tallest Midget, 1988; Casey on the Loose, 1989; Love and Infamy, 1993; The Other Adonis, 2001; An American Summer, 2002. Contributions: numerous magazines. *Honours:* Sportswriter of the Year, National Asscn of Sportswriters and Sportscasters, 1982–88; Emmy, 1988; Cable Ace, 1996; National Asscn of Sportwriters and Sportscasters, Hall of Fame, 1998. *Literary Agent:* Sterling Lord Literistic Inc, 65 Bleecker St, New York, NY 10012, USA. *Address:* Box 1109, Greens Farms, CT 06436, USA.

DEGHETT, Stephanie Coyne; Creative Writing Professor, Poet and Ed.; b. 31 Aug. 1951, Saranac Lake, NY, USA; m. Victor J. DeGhett 1980; one d. *Education:* BA, English, State University College, Potsdam, 1976; MA, English, University of Vermont, Burlington, 1982. *Career:* Graduate Teaching Fellow, University of Vermont; Instructor, English Dept, SUNY at Canton; Instructor, Creative Writing Program, State University College at Potsdam; Poetry Ed., Blueline magazine, 1988–; mem. SUNY Writers Council, Poets and Writers. *Publications:* The Physics of Sensation, 1996; Best of Blueline Anthology (poetry ed.), 2002. Contributions: River of Dreams: American Poems from the St Lawrence Valley (anthology), 1990; Fringillirosadae (poem in New England Review), 1994; Some Old Extravagance of Being (poem in American Poets), 1999; With Child (poem in Potpourri), 2000; The Solace of Apparent Danger (short story in Clackamas Review), 2002; Clemency (short story in New Orphic Review), 2003; Augury, and Diptych (poems in Fiddlehead), 2003; Field Notes; North Country; Old Roses; Wordsmith; Airfoil. *Address:* English Dept, State University College, Potsdam, NY 13676, USA. *E-mail:* deghetsc@potsdam .edu.

DEGUY, Michel; Poet, Writer and Ed.; b. 23 May 1930, Paris, France. *Education:* Philosophy Studies, Paris. *Career:* Ed., Poésie, 1972–; University Prof., Paris. *Publications:* Les Meurtrières, 1959; Fragments du cadastre, 1960; Poèmes de la presqu'île, 1961; Approche de Hölderlin, 1962; Le Monde de Thomas Mann, 1963; Biefs, 1964; Actes, 1966; Oui-dire, 1966; Histoire des rechutes, 1968; Figurations, 1969; Tombeau de Du Bellay, 1973; Poèmes 1960–1970, 1973; Reliefs, 1975; Jumelages suivi de Made in U.S.A., 1978; Donnant, donnant, 1981; La Machine matriomoniale ou Marivaux, 1982; René Girard et le problème du mal (with J-P Dupuy), 1982; Gisants, 1985; Poèmes II; 1970–1980, 1986; Brevets, 1986; Choses de la poésie et affaire culturelle, 1986; Le Comité: Confessions d'un lecteur de grande maison, 1988; La Poésie n'est pas seule: Court traité de Poétique, 1988; Arrets fréquents, 1990; Aux heures d'affluence, 1993; A ce qui n'en finit pas, 1995; L'Energie du Desespoir, 1998; La Raison Poétique, 2000; L'Impair, 2000; Spleen de Paris, 2001; Poèmes en pensée, 2001. *Honours:* Grand Prix national de Poésie, 1989. *Address:* 26 rue Las-Cases, Paris 75007, France.

DEIGHTON, Len, (Leonard Cyril Deighton); Writer; b. 18 Feb. 1929, London, England. *Education:* Royal College of Art, 1952–55. *Publications:* The Ipcress File, 1962; Horse Under Water, 1963; Funeral in Berlin, 1964; Action Cook Book: Len Deighton's Guide To Eating, 1965, US edn as Cookstrip Cook Book; Ou est le Garlic: Len Deighton's French Cook Book, 1965, revised edn as Basic French Cooking, 1978; The Billion Dollar Brain, 1966; An Expensive Place to Die, 1967; London Dossier (ed.), 1967; The Assassination of President Kennedy (co-author), 1967; Only When I Larf, 1968; Len Deighton's Continental Dossier: A Collection of Cultural Culinary, Historical, Spooky, Grim and Preposterous Facts, 1968; Bomber, 1970; Declarations of War (short stories), 1971; Close-Up, 1972; Spy Story, 1974; Yesterday's Spy, 1975; Twinkle, Twinkle, Little Spy, 1976; Fighter: The True Story of the Battle of Britain, 1977; SS-GB, 1978; Airshipwreck (with Arnold Schwartsman), 1978; Blitzkrieg: From the Rise of Hitler to the Fall of Dunkirk, 1979; Battle of Britain, 1980; XPD 1981; Goodbye Mickey Mouse, 1982; Berlin Game, 1983; Mexico Set, 1984; London Match, 1985; Spy Hook, 1988; Spy Line, 1989; ABC of French Food, 1989; Spy Sinker, 1990; Basic French Cookery Course, 1990; MAMista, 1991; City of Gold, 1992; Violent Ward, 1993; Blood, Tears and Folly, 1993; Faith, 1994; Hope, 1995; Charity, 1996. *Address:* c/o Jonathon Clowes Ltd, 10 Iron Bridge House, Bridge Approach, London NW1 8BD, England.

DEKKER, Carl (see Lynds, Dennis).

DELANEY, Francis (Frank) James Joseph; Irish broadcaster and writer; b. 24 Oct. 1942, Tipperary. *Career:* television and radio broadcaster, journalist, RTE News Dublin, BBC Northern Ireland, BBC TV and BBC Radio 4; mem. Athenaeum, Chelsea Arts. *Publications:* James Joyce's Odyssey 1981, Betjeman Country 1983, The Celts 1986, A Walk in the Dark Ages 1988, My Dark Rosaleen (novella) 1989, Legends of the Celts 1989, The Sins of the Mothers 1992, A Walk to the Western Isles 1993, Telling the Pictures 1993, A Stranger in Their Midst 1995, The Amethysts 1997, Desire and Pursuit 1998, Pearl 1999, At Ruby's 2001, Jim Hawkins and the Curse of Treasure Island (as Francis Bryan) 2001, Ireland: A Novel 2004. *Address:* c/o HarperCollins Publishers, 77–85 Fulham Palace Road, Hammersmith, London, W6 8JB, England. *E-mail:* authors@harpercollins.co.uk. *Website:* www.harpercollins.co.uk.

DELANEY, Lawrence (Larry); Canadian newspaper editor and publisher; b. 30 Aug. 1942, Eastview, ON; m. Joanne Bonell 1964; one s. one d. *Career:* co-founder, Ed. and publisher, Country Music News, Canada's national music newspaper 1980–, providing international exposure and profile for Canadian country music artists and industry; mem. Canadian Country Music Asscn, CMA, CPPA. *Honours:* received CCMA Country Music Person of the Year citation 11 times; inducted into Canadian Country Music Hall of Fame 1989, Ottawa Valley Country Music Hall of Fame 1993, CCMA Hall of Honour 1996. *Address:* Country Music News, PO Box 7323 Vanier Terminal, Ottawa, ON K1L 8E4, Canada (Office). *E-mail:* Larry@CountryMusicNews.ca. *Website:* www.countrymusicnews.ca.

DELANEY, Shelagh; Playwright; b. 25 Nov. 1939, Salford, Lancashire, England; one d. *Education:* Broughton Secondary School. *Publications:* Plays: A Taste of Honey, 1958; The Lion in Love, 1960. Films: A Taste of Honey; The White Bus, 1966; Charlie Bubbles, 1968; Dance with a Stranger, 1985. Television Plays: St Martin's Summer, 1974; Find Me First, 1979. Television Series: The House That Jack Built, 1977 (stage adaptation, New York, 1979). Radio Plays: So Does The Nightingale, 1980; Don't Worry About Matilda, 1983. *Honours:* Charles Henry Foyle New Play Award; Arts Council Bursary, 1961; New York Drama Critics Award, 1961; British Film Acad. Award, Robert Flaherty Award, 1961; Prix Film Jeunesse Étranger, Cannes, 1985. *Address:* c/o Sayle Screen, 11 Jubilee Pl., London SW3 3TD, England.

DELANY, Samuel R(ay); Writer and Prof. of Comparative Literature; b. 1 April 1942, New York, NY, USA; m. 24 Aug. 1961, divorced 1980, one s. one d. *Education:* City College, CUNY, 1960, 1962–63. *Career:* Ed., Wuark, 1970–71; Senior Fellow, Center for 20th Century Studies, University of Wisconsin, Milwaukee, 1977; Society for the Humanities, Cornell University, 1987; Prof. of Comparative Literature, University of Massachusetts, Amherst, 1988–. *Publications:* The Jewels of Aptor, 1962; The Fall of the Towers, Vol. 1, Captives of the Flames, 1963, as Out of the Dead City, 1968, Vol. 2, The Towers of Toron, 1964, Vol. 3, City of a Thousand Suns, 1965; The Ballad of Beta-2, 1965; Empire Star, 1966; Babel-17, 1966; The Einstein Intersection, 1967; Nova, 1968; Driftglass: Ten Tales of Speculative Fiction, 1971; Dhalgren, 1975; Triton, 1976; The Jewel-Hinged Jaw: Notes on the Language of Science Fiction, 1977; The American Shore, 1978; Empire, 1978; Nebula Award Winners 13 (ed.), 1979; Distant Stars, 1981; Stars in My Pocket Like Grains of Sand, 1984; Starboard Wine: More Notes on the Language of Science Fiction, 1984; The Splendour and Misery of Bodies, 1985; Flight from Neveryon, 1985; They Fly at Ciron, 1992; Neveryon, 1993; Tales of Neveryon, 1993; The Mad Man, 1994; Aye, and Gomorrah, 2003. *Literary Agent:* Henry Morrison, Box 234, Bedford Hills, NY 10507, USA. *Address:* c/o Bantam Books, 666 Fifth Ave, New York, NY 10019, USA.

DELBANCO, Andrew Henry, AB, AM, PhD; academic and writer; b. 20 Feb. 1952, White Plains, NY, USA; m. Dawn Ho Delbanco 1973; one s. one d. *Education:* Harvard University. *Career:* Asst Prof., Harvard University, 1981–85; Assoc. Prof., 1985–87, Prof., 1987–, Julian Clarence Levi Prof. in the Humanities, 1995–, Columbia University; Adjunct Prof., Yale University, 1989; mem. Society of American Historians. *Publications:* William Ellery Channing: An Essay on the Liberal Spirit in America, 1981; The Puritan Ordeal, 1989; The Death of Satan: How Americans Have Lost the Sense of Evil, 1995; Required Reading: Why Our American Classics Matter Now, 1997. Editor: The Puritans in America: A Narrative Anthology (with Alan Heimert), 1985; The Sermons of Ralph Waldo Emerson, Vol. II (with

Teresa Toulouse), 1990; The Portable Abraham Lincoln, 1992. Contributions: Professional journals and to general periodicals. *Honours:* Guggenheim Fellowship; ACLS Fellowship; National Endowment for the Humanities Fellowship; National Humanities Center Fellowship. *Address:* c/o Dept of English and Comparative Literature, Columbia University, 1150 Amsterdam Avenue, New York, NY 10027, USA.

DELBANCO, Nicholas Franklin; American writer and academic; b. 27 Aug. 1942, London, England; m. Elena Carter Greenhouse 1970; two d. *Education:* BA, History and Literature, Harvard University, 1963; MA, English and Comparative Literature, Columbia University, 1966. *Career:* Faculty, Language and Literature Division, Bennington College, 1966–85; Founder-Dir, Bennington College Writing Workshops, 1977–85; Visiting Lecturer, Iowa Writers Program, University of Iowa, 1979; Adjunct Prof., School of the Arts, Columbia University, 1979, 1996, 1997; Visiting Writer-in-Residence, Trinity College, 1980; M. Scott Bundy Visiting Prof. of English, Williams College, 1982, 1985; Staff, Bread Loaf Writers' Conference, 1984–94; Prof. of English, Skidmore College, 1984–85; Prof., University of Michigan at Ann Arbor, 1985–; mem. Associated Writing Programs; Authors' League; Authors' Guild; Signet Society; New York State Writers Institute; PEN. *Publications:* The Martlet's Tale (novel), 1966; Grasse 3/23/66 (novel), 1968; Consider Sappho Burning (novel), 1969; News (novel), 1970; In the Middle Distance (novel), 1971; Fathering (novel), 1973; Small Rain (novel), 1975; Possession (novel), 1977; Sherbrookes (novel), 1978; Stillness (novel), 1980; Group Portrait: Conrad, Crane, Ford, James, and Wells, 1982; About My Table and Other Stories, 1983; The Beaux Arts Trio: A Portrait, 1985; Running in Place: Scenes from the South of France, 1989; The Writers' Trade, and Other Stories, 1990; Speaking of Writing: Selected Hopwood Lectures (ed.), 1990; Writers and Their Craft: Short Stories and Essays on the Narrative (ed. with Laurence Goldstein), 1991; In the Name of Mercy (novel), 1995; Talking Horse: Bernard Malamud on Life and Art (ed. with Alan Cheuse), 1996; Old Scores (novel), 1997; The Lost Suitcase: Reflections on the Literary Life, 2000; What Remains (novel), 2000; The Writing Life: Further Hopwood Lectures (ed.), 2000; The Countess of Stanlein Restored: A History of the Paganini Stradivarius Violoncello of 1707, 2002. Contributions: periodicals, anthologies, quarterlies, reviews and journals. *Honours:* National Endowment for the Arts Creative Writing Fellowships, 1973, 1982; Guggenheim Fellowship, 1980; National Endowment for the Arts/PEN Syndicated Fiction Awards, 1983, 1985, 1989; MacDowell Colony Fellowship, 1985; Yaddo Fellowships, 1987, 1989, 1994; Robert Frost Collegiate Professorship, University of Michigan, 1998; Michigan Author of the Year, 2002. *Literary Agent:* Brandt & Hochman Literary Agents Inc, 1501 Broadway, New York, NY 10036, USA. *Address:* c/o The Hopwood Room, 1186 Angell Hall, University of Michigan at Ann Arbor, Ann Arbor, MI 48109, USA.

DELEHANTY, Randolph; Writer, Lecturer and Museum and Parks Consultant; b. 5 July 1944, Memphis, Tennessee, USA. *Education:* BA, Georgetown University, 1966; MA, University of Chicago, 1968; MA, 1969, PhD, 1992, Harvard University. *Career:* Historian, Presidio Trust, Golden Gate National Recreation Area; Book Reviewer, Minneapolis Star-Tribune. *Publications:* San Francisco: Walks and Tours in the Golden Gate City, 1980; California: A Guidebook, 1984; Preserving the West, 1985; In the Victorian Style, 1991; New Orleans: Elegance and Decadence, 1993; San Francisco: The Ultimate Guide, 1995; Classic Natchez, 1996; Art in the American South, 1996; Randolph Delehanty's Ultimate Guide to New Orleans, 1998; San Francisco Victorians, 2000; A Guide to San Francisco Recreation and Parks, 2000; Treasure Houses: Louisiana Museums for a New Millennium, 2000. Contributions: The Companion to Southern Literature, 2002. *Address:* 2004 Gough St, San Francisco, CA 94109-3418, USA. *E-mail:* randolph_delehanty@post.harvard.edu.

DeLILLO, Don, BA; American writer; b. 20 Nov. 1936, New York City; m. Barbara Bennett 1975. *Education:* Cardinal Hayes High School, Fordham Coll., New York. *Career:* fmr advertising copywriter Ogilvy, Benson & Mather. *Plays:* The Day Room 1987, The Rapture of the Athlete Assumed into Heaven 1990, Valparaiso 1999, The Mystery at the Middle of Ordinary Life 2000. *Publications:* Americana 1971, End Zone 1972, Great Jones Street 1973, Ratner's Star 1976, Players 1977, Running Dog 1978, Amazons 1980, The Names 1982, White Noise 1985 (Nat. Book Award 1985), Libra 1988 (Irish Times/Aer Lingus Int. Fiction Prize 1989), Mao II 1991 (PEN/Faulkner Award 1992), Underworld 1997, The Body Artist 2000, Cosmopolis 2003. *Honours:* Award in Literature, American Acad. and Inst. of Arts and Letters 1984, Jerusalem Prize for the Freedom of the Individual in Soc. 1999, William Dean Howells Medal 2000. *Address:* c/o Wallace Literary Agency, 177 E 70th Street, New York, NY 10021, USA.

DELORIA, Victor (Vine), Jr; Prof. and Writer; b. 26 March 1933, Martin, SD, USA. *Education:* BS, Iowa State University, 1958; MST, Lutheran School of Theology, Chicago, 1963; JurD, University of Colorado School of Law, Boulder, 1970. *Career:* Exec. Dir, National Congress of American Indians, Washington, DC, 1964–67; Prof. of Law and Political Science, University of Arizona at Tucson, 1978–80; Prof. of American Indian Studies, Prof. of History, and Adjunct Prof. of Law, Religious Studies, and Political Science, University of Colorado at Boulder, 1990–2000; mem. numerous professional organizations and editorial boards. *Publications:* Custer Died For Your Sins: An Indian Manifesto, 1969; We Talk, You Listen: New Tribes, New Turf, 1970; Of Utmost Good Faith, 1971; God is Red: A Native View of Religion, 1973; Behind the Trail of Broken Treaties: An Indian Declaration of Independence, 1974; The Indian Affair, 1974; Indians of the Pacific Northwest: From the Coming of the White Man to the Present Day, 1977; The Metaphysics of Modern Existence, 1979; American Indians, American Justice (with Clifford Lytle), 1983; The Nations Within: The Past and Future of American Indian Sovereignty (with Clifford Lytle), 1984; Frank Waters: Man and Mystic, 1993; Red Earth, White Lies, 1995; Spirit and Reason, 1999; Singing for a Spirit, 1999; Documents of American Indian Diplomacy (with Raymond DeMallie), 1999; Tribes, Treaties and Constitutional Tribulations (with David Wilkins), 2000; Power and Place: Essays in American Indian Education (with Daniel Wildcat), 2001. Contributions: many books, journals, and periodicals. *Honours:* Anisfield-Wolf Award, 1970; Distinguished Alumni Award, Iowa State University, 1977; Distinguished Alumni in the Field of Legal Education, University of Colorado School of Law, 1985; Lifetime Achievement Award, Mountains and Plains Booksellers Asscn, 1996; Non-Fiction Book of the Year Award, Colorado Center for the Book, 1996; Lifetime Achievement Award, Native Writers of America, 1996. *Address:* 3170 Howell Rd, Golden, CO 80401, USA.

DEMARIA, Robert; Prof. of English Emeritus, Author and Poet; b. 28 Sept. 1928, New York, NY, USA; m. 1st Maddalena Buzeo; m. 2nd Ellen Hope Meyer, three s., one d. *Education:* BA, 1948, MA, 1949, PhD, 1959, Columbia University. *Career:* Instructor, University of Oregon, 1949–52; Asst Prof., Hofstra University, 1952–61; Assoc. Dean, New School for Social Research, New York City, 1961–64; Prof. of English, 1965–97, Prof. Emeritus, 1997–, Dowling College; Ed. and Publisher, The Mediterranean Review, 1969–73. *Publications:* Fiction: Carnival of Angels, 1961; Clodia, 1965; Don Juan in Lourdes, 1966; The Satyr, 1972; The Decline and Fall of America, 1973; To Be a King, 1976; Outbreak, 1978; Blowout, 1979; The Empress, 1980; Secret Places, 1981; A Passion for Power, 1983; Sons and Brothers, 2 vols, 1985; Stone of Destiny, 1986; That Kennedy Girl, 1999; The White Road, 2000. Textbooks: The College Handbook of Creative Writing, 1991; A Contemporary Reader for Creative Writing, 1995. Contributions: Fiction, poetry, and articles in numerous publications. *Address:* 106 Vineyard Pl., Port Jefferson, NY 11777, USA.

DEMARIS, Ovid (see Desmarais, Ovide E.).

DEMETILLO, Ricaredo; Prof. of Humanities (retd), Poet and Writer; b. 2 June 1920, Dumangas, Philippines. *Education:* AB, Silliman University, 1947; MFA, University of Iowa, 1952. *Career:* Asst Prof., 1959–70, Chair., Dept of Humanities, 1961–62, Assoc. Prof., 1970–75, Prof. of Humanities, 1975–86, University of the Philippines. *Publications:* Poetry: No Certain Weather, 1956; La Via: A Spiritual Journey, 1958; Daedalus and Other Poems, 1961; Barter in Panay, 1961; Masks and Signature, 1968; The Scare-Crow Christ, 1973; The City and the Thread of Light, 1974; Lazarus, Troubadour, 1974; Sun, Silhouttes and Shadow, 1975; First and Last Fruits, 1989. Novel: The Genesis of a Troubled Vision, 1976. Play: The Heart of Emptiness is Black, 1973. Non-Fiction: The Authentic Voice of Poetry, 1962; Major and Minor Keys, 1986. *Address:* 38 Balacan St, West Ave, Quezon City, Philippines.

DEMOS, John Putnam; Prof. of History and Writer; b. 2 May 1937, Cambridge, Massachusetts, USA; m. Elaine Virginia Damis, 27 July 1963, two c. *Education:* BA, 1959, Postgraduate Studies, 1963–68, Harvard University; Postgraduate Studies, University of Oxford, 1959–60; MA, University of California at Berkeley, 1961. *Career:* Teaching Fellow, Harvard University, 1966–68; Asst Prof., 1968–72, Prof. of History, 1972–86, Brandeis University; Prof. of History, Yale University, 1986–; mem. American Historical Asscn. *Publications:* A Little Commonwealth: Family Life in Plymouth Colony, 1970; Remarkable Providences, 1600–1760 (ed.), 1972; Turning Points: Historical and Sociological Essays on the Family (ed. with Sarane Boocock), 1978; Entertaining Satan: Witchcraft and the Culture of Early New England, 1982; Past, Present, and Personal, 1986; The Unredeemed Captive, 1994. Contributions: scholarly journals and other publications. *Honours:* Bancroft Prize in American History, Columbia University, 1983; Francis Parkman Prize, 1995; Ray Allen Billington Prize, 1995. *Address:* c/o Dept of History, Yale University, PO Box 208324, New Haven, CT 06520, USA.

DEMPSTER, Nigel Richard Patton; editor and writer; b. 1 Nov. 1941, England; m. 1st Emma de Bendern 1971 (divorced 1974); m. 2nd Lady Camilla Godolphin Osborne 1977; one d. *Career:* Journalist, Daily Express, 1963–71; London Correspondent, Status magazine, USA, 1965–66; Columnist ('Grovel'), Private Eye magazine, 1969–85, Daily Mail, 1971–; Ed., Mail Diary, 1973–, Mail on Sunday Diary, 1986–; Editorial Exec., Mail Newspapers Plc, 1973–; Broadcaster, ABC, USA, CBC, Canada, 1976–; TV-am, 1983–92; Resident Panelist, Headliners, Thames TV, 1987–89. *Publications:* HRH The Princess Margaret: A Life Unfulfilled, 1981; Heiress: The Story of Christina Onassis, 1989; Nigel Dempster's Address Book, 1990; Behind Palace Doors (with Peter Evans), 1993; Dempster's People, 1998. *Address:* c/o Daily Mail, Northcliffe House, Derry Street, London W8 5TT, England.

DENGLER, Sandy; Writer; b. 8 June 1939, Newark, Ohio, USA; m. William F. Dengler, 11 Jan. 1963, two d. *Education:* BS, Bowling Green State University, Ohio, 1961; MS, Arizona State University, 1967. *Career:* mem. MWA; Society of Vertebrate Palaeontologists; Writers' Guild. *Publications:*

Non-Fiction: Fanny Crosby, 1985; John Bunyan, 1986; D. L. Moody, 1987; Susanna Wesley, 1987; Florence Nightingale, 1988. Fiction: Barn Social, 1978; Yosemite's Marvellous Creatures, 1979; Summer of the Wild Pig, 1979; Melon Hound, 1980; The Horse Who Loved Picnics, 1980; Mystery at McGehan Ranch, 1982; Chain Five Mystery, 1984; Summer Snow, 1984; Winterspring, 1985; This Rolling Land, 1986; Jungle Gold, 1987; Code of Honor, 1988; Power of Pinjarra, 1989; Taste of Victory, 1989; East of Outback, 1990; Death Valley, 1993; Cat Killer, 1993; Dublin Crossing, 1993; Mouse Trapped, 1993; Gila Monster, 1994; Last Dinosaur, 1994; Murder on the Mount, 1994; Shamrock Shore, 1994; Emerald Sea, 1994; The Quick and the Dead, 1995; King of the Stars, 1995; Hyaenas, 1998; African Adventure, 2003. Contributions: journals and magazines. *Honours:* Writer of the Year, Warm Beach, 1986; Golden Medallion, Romance Writers of America, 1987. *Address:* 2623 Cypress Ave, Norman, OK 73072, USA.

DENKER, Henry; Writer and Playwright; b. 25 Nov. 1912, New York, NY, USA. *Education:* LLB, New York University, 1934. *Career:* mem. Dramatists Guild, council, 1970–73; Authors' Guild; Authors League, council; Writers Guild of America East. *Publications:* I'll Be Right Home, Ma, 1947; My Son, the Lawyer, 1949; Salome: Princess of Galilee, 1951; The First Easter, 1951; The Child is Mine, 1955; The Director, 1970; The Kingmaker, 1972; A Place for the Mighty, 1974; The Physicians, 1975; The Experiment, 1976; The Starmaker, 1977; The Scofield Diagnosis, 1977; The Actress, 1978; Error of Judgement, 1979; Horowitz and Mrs Washington, 1979, as play, 1980; The Warfield Syndrome, 1981; Outrage, 1982, as play, 1983, as film, 1985; The Healers, 1983; Kincaid, 1984; Robert, My Son, 1985; Judge Spence Dissents, 1986; The Choice, 1987; The Retreat, 1988; A Gift of Life, 1989; Payment in Full, 1990; Doctor on Trial, 1991; Mrs Washington and Horowitz, too, 1992; Labyrinth, 1994; This Child is Mine, 1995; To Marcy, With Love, 1996; Benjie, 1999; Class Action, 2002. Plays: Time Limit, 1957; A Far Country, 1961; A Case of Libel, 1963; What Did We Do Wrong?, 1967; The Headhunters, 1976; The Second Time Around, 1977; Outrage, 1987; Tea With Madam Bernhardt, 1991; Curtain Call, 1999. *Literary Agent:* Mitch Douglas, International Creative Management, 40 W 57th St, New York, NY 10019. USA. *Address:* 241 Central Park W, New York, NY 10024, USA.

DENNETT, Daniel Clement, DPhil; American philosopher, university professor and author; *University Professor and Director, Center for Cognitive Studies, Tufts University*; b. 28 March 1942, Beirut; m. Susan Bell 1962; one s. one d. *Education:* Phillips Exeter High School, Wesleyan Univ., Harvard Univ., Oxford Univ. *Career:* Asst Prof. of Philosophy, Univ. of Calif., Irvine 1965–70, Assoc. Prof. 1971; Assoc. Prof., Tufts Univ. 1971–75, Prof. 1975–85, Distinguished Arts and Sciences Prof. 1985–2000, Dir Center for Cognitive Studies, Tufts 1985–, Univ. Prof. 2000–; Visiting Prof., Harvard 1973–74, Pittsburgh 1975, Oxford 1979, Ecole Normale Supérieure, Paris 1985; Visiting Fellow, All Souls Coll. Oxford 1979; John Locke Lecturer, Oxford 1983, Gavin David Young Lecturer, Adelaide, Australia 1984; Woodrow Wilson Fellow 1963, Guggenheim Fellow 1973, 1986, Fulbright Fellow 1978; Fellow Center for Advanced Study in Behavioral Sciences 1979, American Acad. of Arts and Sciences 1987. *Publications:* Content and Consciousness 1969, Brainstorms 1978, The Mind's I (with Douglas Hofstadter) 1981, Elbow Room 1984, The Intentional Stance 1987, Consciousness Explained 1991, Darwin's Dangerous Idea 1995, Kinds of Minds 1996, Brainchildren 1998, Freedom Evolves 2003; numerous articles in professional journals. *Address:* Center for Cognitive Studies, Tufts University, Medford, MA 02155, USA (Office). *Telephone:* (617) 627-3297 (Office). *Fax:* (617) 627-3952 (Office).

DENNIS, Carl; Poet, Writer and Prof. of English; b. 17 Sept. 1939, St Louis, MO, USA. *Education:* Oberlin College, 1957–58; University of Chicago, 1958–59; BA, University of Minnesota, 1961; PhD, University of California at Berkeley, 1966. *Career:* Prof. of English, SUNY at Buffalo, 1966–; Sometime faculty mem., Writing Program, Warren Wilson College; mem. PEN. *Publications:* Poetry: A House of My Own, 1974; Climbing Down, 1976; Signs and Wonders, 1979; The Near World, 1985; The Outskirts of Troy, 1988; Meetings with Time, 1992; Ranking the Wishes, 1997; Practical Gods, 2001. Other: Poetry as Persuasion, 2001. Contributions: many anthologies, quarterlies, reviews and journals. *Honours:* Guggenheim Fellowship; National Endowment for the Arts Fellowship; Fellow, Rockefeller Study Center, Bellagio, Italy; Ruth Lilly Prize, 2000; Pulitzer Prize in Poetry, 2002. *Address:* 49 Ashland Ave, Buffalo, NY 14222, USA.

DENNIS, Everette Eugene, Jr; Foundation Exec., Educator and Author; b. 15 Aug. 1942, Seattle, Washington, USA; m. Emily J. Smith, 15 June 1988. *Education:* BS, University of Oregon, 1964; MA, Syracuse University, 1966; PhD, University of Minnesota, 1974. *Career:* Asst Prof., Journalism, Mass Communication, Kansas State University, Manhattan, 1968–72; Instructor, Asst Prof., Assoc. Prof., School of Journalism and Mass Communication, University of Minnesota, 1972–81; Visiting Prof., Medill School of Journalism, Northwestern University, 1976–77; Dean, Prof., School of Journalism, University of Oregon, 1981–84; Exec. Dir, The Freedom Forum Media Studies Center, Columbia University; Senior Vice-Pres., The Freedom Forum, Arlington, Virginia; Ed.-in-Chief, Media Studies Journal; mem. International Communication Asscn; Eastman House International Museum of Photographs; American Antiquarian Society; Asscn for Education in Journalism and Mass Communication; International Press Institute; Society of Professional Journalists. *Publications:* Other Voices: The New Journalism in America, 1973; The Media Society, 1978; The Economics of Libel, 1986; Understanding Mass Communication (ed.), 1988; Demystifying Media Technology, 1993; America's Schools and the Mass Media, 1993; The Culture of Crime, 1995; Radio, The Forgotten Medium, 1995; American Communication Research, 1996. Contributions: Hundreds of articles to popular, professional and scholarly periodicals. *Honours:* Harvard University Fellowships, 1978–79, 1980, 1981; Other fellowships; various writing prizes and awards.

DENNISTON, Rev. Robin Alastair, MA, MSc, PhD; British publisher and ecclesiastic; b. 25 Dec. 1926, London; m. 1st Anne Alice Kyffin Evans 1950 (died 1985); one s. two d.; m. 2nd Dr Rosa Susan Penelope Beddington 1987 (died 2001). *Education:* Westminster School and Christ Church, Oxford. *Career:* Ed. Collins 1950–59; Man. Dir Faith Press 1959–60; Ed. Prism 1959–61; Promotion Man. Hodder & Stoughton Ltd 1960–64, Editorial Dir 1966, Man. Dir 1968–72, also Dir Mathew Hodder Ltd and subsidiary cos; Deputy Chair. George Weidenfeld & Nicolson (and subsidiary cos) 1973; Chair. (non-exec.) A. R. Mowbray & Co. 1974–88; Chair. Sphere Books 1975–76, Thomas Nelson & Sons (and subsidiary cos) 1975, Michael Joseph Ltd 1975, George Rainbird Ltd 1975; Dir Thomson Publs Ltd 1975, Hamish Hamilton Ltd 1975, (non-exec.) W. W. Norton 1989–; Academic Publr Oxford Univ. Press 1978, Sr Deputy Sec. to the Dels. 1984–88, Oxford Publr 1984–88; Student of Christ Church 1978; ordained Deacon 1978, Priest 1979; Hon. Curate Parish of Clifton-on-Teme 1978, New with S Hinksey 1985; Non-Stipendiary Minister, Great with Little Tew 1987–90, Burntisland and St Columba's Aberdour, Fife 1990–93; Priest-in-charge Great with Little Tew and Over Worton with Nether Worton 1995–2002. *Publications:* The Young Musicians 1956, Partly Living 1967, Part Time Priests? (ed.) 1960, (co-ed.) Anatomy of Scotland 1992, Churchill's Secret War: Diplomatic Decrypts, the Foreign Office and Turkey 1942–4 1997, Trevor Huddleston: A Life 1999. *Address:* 25 Pyndar Court, Newland, Malvern, Worcs.,WR13 5AX , England (Home). *Telephone:* (1684) 573141 (Home).

DEPESTRE, René; French poet and writer; b. 29 Aug. 1926, Jacmel, Haiti; m. Nelly Campano 1962. *Education:* Sorbonne, University of Paris. *Career:* Attaché, Office of Culture, UNESCO, Paris, 1982–86. *Publications:* Poetry: Etincelles, 1945; Gerbe de sang, 1946; Minerai noir, 1956; Un arc-en-ciel pour l'occident chrétien, 1967; Journal d'un animal marin (selected poems, 1956–90), 1990; Au matin de la négritude, 1990; Anthologie personnelle, 1993. Fiction: Alléluia pour une femme jardin, 1973; Le Mat de cocagne, 1979; Hadriana dans tous mes reves, 1988; Eros dans un train chinois: Neuf histories d'amour et un conte sorcier, 1990. Non-Fiction: Pour la révolution, pour la poésie, 1969; Bonjour et adieu a la négritude, 1980. *Honours:* Prix Goncourt, 1982; Prix Renaudot, 1988. *Address:* 31 bis, Route de Roubia, 11200 Lezignan-Corbières, France.

DERFLER, (Arnold) Leslie; academic and writer; b. 11 Jan. 1933, New York, NY, USA; m. Gunilla Derfler 1962; four d. *Education:* BA, City College, CUNY, 1954; University of Chicago, 1956; University of Paris, 1960; MA, 1957, PhD, 1962, Columbia University. *Career:* Faculty, City College, CUNY, 1959–62, Carnegie Mellon University, 1962–68, University of Massachusetts, Amherst, 1968–69; Prof. of History, Florida Atlantic University, 1969–; Visiting Prof., London Center, Florida State University, 1985. *Publications:* The Dreyfus Affair: Tragedy of Errors, 1963; The Third French Republic, 1870–1940, 1966; Socialism Since Marx, 1973; Alexandre Millerand: The Socialist Years, 1977; President and Parliament: A Short History of the French Presidency, 1984; An Age of Conflict: Readings in 20th Century European History, 1990; Paul Lafargue and the Founding of French Marxism, 1842–1882, 1991; Paul Lafargue and the Flowering of French Socialism, 1882–1911, 1998. *Honours:* American Philosophical Society Grants, 1967, 1976, 1981, 1991; Distinguished Scholar Award, Florida Atlantic University, 1982; National Endowment for the Humanities Fellowship, 1984–85. *Address:* c/o Department of History, Florida Atlantic University, Boca Raton, FL 33431, USA.

DERIEX, Suzanne, (Suzanne Piguet-Cuendet); Novelist; b. 16 April 1926, Yverdon, Switzerland; m. Jean-François Piguet, 7 May 1949, three s. *Education:* Lic Math Sc; Semi-lic Theol, University of Lausanne, Switzerland. *Publications:* Corinne, 1961; San Domenico, 1964; L'enfant et la mort, 1968; Pour dormir sans rêves, 1980; L'homme n'est jamais seul, 1983; Les sept vies de Louise Croisier née Moraz, 1996; Un arbre de vie, 1995; Exils, 1999; La Tourmente, 2001. *Honours:* Prize of Jubilé de Lyceum Club de Suisse, 1963; Prix Veillon, 1968; Prix Pro Helvetia, 1983; Prix Alpes-Jura and Prix des Murailles, 1988; Prix du Livre vaudois, 1990. *Address:* Rte de Lausanne 11, 1096 Cully, Switzerland.

DERR, Mark (Burgess); Writer; b. 20 Jan. 1950, Baltimore, MD, USA; m. Gina L. Maranto, 11 Sept. 1982. *Education:* AB, 1972, MA, 1973, Johns Hopkins University. *Publications:* Some Kind of Paradise: A Chronicle of Man and the Land in Florida, 1989; Over Florida, 1992; The Frontiersman: The Real Life and the Many Legends of Davy Crockett, 1993; Dog's Best Friend: Annals of the Dog-Human Relationship, 1997. Contributions: The Atlantic; Audubon Society; Natural History; New York Times. *Address:* 4245 Sheridan Ave, Miami Beach, FL 33140, USA.

DERRICOTTE, Toi; Prof. of English, Poet and Author; b. 11 April 1941, Hamtramck, Michigan, USA; m. C. Bruce Derricotte, 30 Dec. 1967, one s. *Education:* BA, Special Education, Wayne State University, 1965; MA, English Literature and Creative Writing, New York University, 1984.

Career: Master Teacher and Poet in the Schools, New Jersey State Council on the Arts and Maryland State Council on the Arts, 1973–88; Assoc. Prof. of English Literature, Old Dominion University, 1988–90; Commonwealth Prof., George Mason University, 1990–91; Assoc. Prof., 1991–97, Prof. of English, 1998–, University of Pittsburgh; Visiting Prof., New York University, 1992; many poetry readings around the world; mem. Acad. of American Poets; Associated Writing Programs; MLA; PEN; Poetry Society of America. *Publications:* The Empress of the Death House, 1978; Natural Birth, 1983; Creative Writing: A Manual for Teachers (with Madeline Bass), 1985; Captivity, 1989; Tender, 1997; The Black Notebooks, 1997. Contributions: numerous anthologies and journals. *Honours:* MacDowell Colony Fellowship, 1982; New Jersey State Council on the Arts Poetry Fellowship, 1983; Lucille Medwick Memorial Award, Poetry Society of America, 1985; National Endowment for the Arts Creative Writing Fellowships, 1985, 1990; Pushcart Prizes, 1989, 1998; Poetry Committee Book Award, Folger Shakespeare Library, Washington, DC, 1990; Yaddo Residency, 1997; Anisfield-Wolf Book Award for Non-Fiction, 1998; Award in Non-Fiction, Black Caucus, American Library Asscn, 1998; Paterson Poetry Prize, 1998. *Address:* c/o Dept of English, University of Pittsburgh, Pittsburgh, PA 15260, USA.

DERRIDA, Jacques; Philosopher and Writer; b. 15 July 1930, El Biar, Algeria; m. Marguérite Aucouturier, 1957, two s. *Education:* École Normale Supérieure, Paris, 1952–56; Licence es Lettres, 1953, Licence de Philosophie, 1953, Diplome d'Études Supérieures, 1954, Sorbonne, University of Paris; Certificat d'Ethnologie, 1954, Agregation de Philosophie, 1956, Doctorat en Philosophie, 1967, Doctorat d'Etat es Lettres, 1980; Graduate Studies, Harvard University, 1956–57. *Career:* Prof. de lettres supérieures, Lycée du Mans, 1959–60; Prof. of Philosophy, Sorbonne, University of Paris, 1960–64, École Normale Supérieure, Paris, 1964–84; Dir, École des Hautes Études en Sciences Sociales, Paris, 1984–; many visiting lectureships and professorships. *Publications:* La voix et le phénomène: Introduction au probleme du signe dans la phénomènologie de Husserl, 1967, English trans. as Speech and Phenomena and Other Essays on Husserl's Theory of Signs, 1973; De la grammatologie, 1967, English trans. as Of Grammatology, 1976; L'écriture et la difference, 1967, English trans. as Writing and Difference, 1978; La dissémination, 1972, English trans., 1981; Marges de la philosophie, 1972, English trans. as Margins of Philosophy, 1982; Glas, 1974, English trans., 1986; L'archeologie du frivole, 1976, English trans. as The Archeology of the Frivolous: Reading Condillac, 1980; Eperons: Les styles de Nietzsche, 1976, English trans. as Spurs: Nietzsche's Styles, 1979; Limited Inc: abc, 1977; La vérité en peinture, 1978; La carte postale: De Socrate à Freud et au-dela, 1980, English trans. as The Post Card: From Socrates to Freud and Beyond, 1987; L'oreille de l'autre: Otobiographies, transferts, traductions: Textes et debats avec Jacques Derrida, 1982, English trans. as The Ear of the Other: Otobiography, Transference, Translation, 1985; Signeponge/Signsponge (French and English text), 1984; Mémoires: Lectures for Paul de Man, 1986; De l'esprit: Heidegger et la question, 1987, English trans. as Of Spirit: Heidegger and the Question, 1989; Mémoires d'aveugle, L'autoportrait et autres ruins, 1990, English trans. as Memoirs of the Blind, the Self-Portrait and Other Ruins, 1993; Donner le temps, 1, Fausse monnai, 1991, English trans. as Given Time, 1: Counterfeit Money, 1992; L'autre cap: Suivre de la democratie ajournaee, 1991, English trans. as The Other Heading: Reflections of Today's Europe, 1992; A Derrida Reader: Between the Blinds, 1991; Donner la mort, 1992, English trans. as The Gift of Death, 1995; Apories: Mourir-s' attendre aux 'limites de la vérite', 1993, English trans. as Aporias: Dying-Awaiting (One Another at) the 'Limits of Truth', 1993; Spectres de Marx: L'état de la dette, le travail du deuil et la nouvelle internationale, 1993, English trans. as Spectres of Marx, State of the Debt, the Work of Mourning, and the New Internationale, 1994; Politiques de l'amitié, 1994, English trans. as The Politics of Friendship, 1997; Mal d'archive, une impression freudienne, 1995, English trans. as Archive Fever: A Freudian Impression, 1996; Résistances, de la psychanalyse, 1996, English trans. as Resistance of Psychoanalysis, 1998; La monolinguisme de l'autre, ou la prothèse d'origine, 1996, English trans. as Monolingualism of the Other, or, The Prosthesis of Origin, 1998; Adieu à Emmanuel Levines, 1997, English trans. as Adieu to Emmanuel Levinas, 1999; De l'hospitalité: Anne Dufourmantelle invite Jacques Derrida à repondre, 1997, English trans. as Of Hospitality: Anne Dufourmantelle Invites Jacques Derrida to Respond, 2000; Tourner les mots: Au bord d'un film (with Saffa Fathy), 2000. *Honours:* Liste d'aptitude a l'enseignement Supérieur, 1968; Officier, Ordre des Palmes Academiques, 1980; Hon. doctorates, Columbia University, 1980, University of Louvain, 1983, University of Essex, 1987, University of Cambridge, 1992; Commdr, Ordre des Arts et des Lettres, 1983; Prix Nietzsche, Asscn Internationale de Philosophie, 1988. *Address:* c/o École des Hautes Études en Sciences Sociales, 54 Bouelvard Raspail, 75006 Paris, France.

DERSHOWITZ, Alan Morton, LLB; American lawyer and academic; *Professor of Law, Harvard University*; b. 1 Sept. 1938, New York, NY; m. Carolyn Cohen; two s. one d. *Education:* Brooklyn Coll. and Yale Univ. *Career:* admitted to DC Bar 1963, Mass. Bar 1968, US Supreme Court 1968; Law clerk to Chief Judge David Bazelon, US Court of Appeal 1962–63, to Justice Arthur Goldberg, US Supreme Court 1963–64; mem. Faculty, Harvard Coll. 1964–, Prof. of Law 1967–; Fellow, Center for Advanced Study of Behavioral Sciences 1971–72; consultant to Dir Nat. Inst. for Mental Health (NIMH) 1967–69, (Pres.'s Comm. on Civil Disorders) 1967, (Pres.'s Comm. on Causes of Violence) 1968, (Nat. Asscn for Advancement of Colored People Legal Defense Fund) 1967–68, Pres.'s Comm. on Marijuana and Drug Abuse 1972–73, (Ford Foundation Study on Law and Justice) 1973–76; rapporteur, Twentieth Century Fund Study on Sentencing 1975–76; Guggenheim Fellow 1978–79; mem. Comm. on Law and Social Action, American Jewish Congress 1978; Dir American Civil Liberties Union 1968–71, 1972–75, Asscn of Behavioral and Social Sciences, NAS 1973–76; Chair. Civil Rights Comm. New England Region, Anti-Defamation League, B'nai B'rith 1980. *Publications:* Psychoanalysis, Psychiatry and the Law (with others) 1967, Criminal Law: Theory and Process 1974, The Best Defense 1982, Reversal of Fortune: Inside the von Bülow Case 1986, Taking Liberties: A Decade of Hard Cases, Bad Laws and Bum Raps 1988, Chutzpah 1991, Contrary to Popular Opinion 1992, The Abuse Excuse 1994, The Advocate's Devil 1994, Reasonable Doubt 1996, The Vanishing American Jew 1997, Sexual McCarthyism 1998, Just Revenge 1999, The Genesis of Justice 2000, Supreme Injustice: How the High Court Hijacked Election 2000 2001, Letters to a Young Lawyer 2001, Shouting Fire: Civil Liberties in a Turbulent Age 2002, Why Terrorism Works 2002, America Declares Independence 2003, The Case for Israel 2003, America on Trial 2004; contrib. articles to legal journals. *Honours:* Hon. MA (Harvard Coll.) 1967; Hon. LLD (Yeshiva) 1989. *Address:* Harvard University Law School, 1575 Massachusetts Avenue, Cambridge, MA 02138-2801, USA.

DESAI, Anita, BA, FRSL; Indian writer and academic; *Professor of Writing, Massachusetts Institute of Technology*; b. 24 June 1937, Mussoorie; m. Ashvin Desai 1958; two s. two d. *Education:* Miranda House, University of Delhi. *Career:* Helen Cam Visiting Fellow, 1986–87, Hon. Fellow, 1988, Girton College, Cambridge; Elizabeth Drew Prof., Smith College, Northampton, Massachusetts, 1987–88; Purington Prof. of English, Mount Holyoke College, South Hadley, Massachusetts, 1988–92; Ashby Fellow, 1989, Hon. Fellow, 1991, Clare Hall, Cambridge; Prof. of Writing, MIT, 1993–; mem. American Acad. of Arts and Letters, hon. mem.; PEN; Sahitya Akademi, India. *Publications:* Cry, the Peacock, 1963; Voices in the City, 1965; Bye-Bye Blackbird, 1971; Where Shall We Go This Summer?, 1973; Fire on the Mountain, 1978; Games at Twilight, 1979; Clear Light of Day, 1980; The Village by the Sea, 1983; In Custody, 1984; Baumgartner's Bombay, 1988; Journey to Ithaca, 1995; Fasting, Feasting, 1999; Diamond Dust and Other Stories, 2000; The Zigzag Way 2004; contrib. to periodicals. *Honours:* Winifred Holtby Award, RSL, 1978; Sahitya Akademi Award, 1978; Federation of Indian Publishers Award, 1978; Guardian Prize for Children's Fiction, 1983; Hadassah Prize, Hadassah Magazine, New York, 1989; Padma Sri, India, 1990; Literary Lion, New York Public Library, 1993; Neil Gunn International Writers Fellowship, Scotland, 1994; Moravia Prize, Rome, 1999. *Literary Agent:* Rogers, Coleridge & White Ltd, 20 Powis Mews, London W11 1JN, England.

DESHPANDE, Shashi, BA, MA, BL; Indian writer; b. 19 Aug. 1938, Dharwad; m. D. H. Deshpande 1962; two s. *Education:* Univs of Bombay and Mysore. *Career:* fmrly worked for a law journal and magazine; full-time writer 1970–; mem. Sahitya Akademi Bd for English 1989–94. *Film script:* Drishti 1990. *Publications:* Forgive Us Our Sins (play, trans. from Kannada), The Legacy and Other Stories 1978, The Dark Holds no Terrors 1980, If I Die Today 1982, Come Up and Be Dead 1982, Roots and Shadows 1983, It Was Dark (short stories) 1986, The Miracle and Other Stories 1986, It Was the Nightingale (short stories) 1986, That Long Silence 1988, The Binding Vine 1993, The Intrusion and Other Stories 1994, A Matter of Time 1996, Small Remedies 2000, The Stone Women (short stories) 2000, Writing from the Margin and other essays 2003, Collected Stories, Vol. I 2003. *Honours:* Thirumathi Rangammal Prize 1984, Sahitya Akademi Award for a Novel 1990, Nanjangud Thirumalamba Award 1991. *Literary Agent:* Alison M. Bond Agency, 155 W 72nd Street, New York, NY 10023, USA. *Address:* 409 41st Cross, Jayanagar V Block, Bangalore 560041, India. *Telephone:* (80) 26636228. *Fax:* (80) 26641137. *E-mail:* shashid@vsnl.com (Home).

DESMARAIS, Ovide E., (Ovid Demaris); Writer and Newspaper Reporter; b. 6 Sept. 1919, Biddeford, Maine, USA; m. Inez E. Frakes, 15 May 1942, two d. *Education:* AB, College of Idaho, 1948; Law, Syracuse University; MS, Boston University, 1950. *Publications:* Mystery novels: Ride the Gold Mare, 1956; The Hoods Take Over, 1957; The Long Night, 1957; The Lusting Drive, 1958; The Slasher, 1959; The Enforcer, 1960; The Extortioners, 1960; The Gold-Plated Sewer, 1960; Candyleg, 1961 (as Machine Gun McCanin, 1970); The Parasite, 1963; The Organization, 1965 (as The Contract, 1970); The Overlord, 1972. Other: Lucky Luciano, 1960; The Lindbergh Kidnapping Case, 1961; The Dillinger Story, 1961; The Green Felt Jungle (with Edward Reid), 1963; Jack Ruby (with Gary Wills), 1968; Captive City: Chicago in Chains, 1969; America the Violent, 1970; Poso del Mundo: Inside the Mexican-American Border, 1970; Dirty Business: The Corporate-Political Money-Power Game, 1974; The Director: An Oral Biography of J. Edgar Hoover, 1975; Brothers in Blood: The International Terrorist Network, 1977; The Last Mafioso: The Treacherous World of Jimmy Fratianno, 1981; The Vegas Legacy, 1983; The Boardwalk Jungle, 1987; J. Edgar Hoover: As They Knew Him, 1994. Contributions: Professional journals and periodicals.

DESMÉE, Gilbert Georges; Writer, Ed. and Educator; b. 29 Jan. 1951, Suresnes, France; m. Maria Desmée, 1 Oct. 1952. *Education:* Diploma, University of Cachan, 1973; Diploma, University of Versailles, 1981.

Career: Dir, Sapriphage literary review, 1988–2001; mem. ELVIR. *Publications:* Le Schiste Métamorphique, 1990; L'Infini pour respirer in Histoire de livres d'artistes, 1991; Un Magdalénien Contemporain in Robert Pérot, 1994; En écho des corps d'écriture, 1995; Je m'en dit tu, 1996; Seul le geste serait fécond, 1997. Contributions: anthologies, including: Le Bel Aujourd'hui; Boris Lejeune; journals, including: Encres Vives; Sapriphage; Agone; Contre-Vox; L'Estracelle; Textuerre; Présage; L'Arbre à Paroles; Le Cri d'Os. *Address:* 118 Ave Pablo Picasso, 92000 Nanterre, France.

DESMOND, Richard Clive; British publishing and media executive; *Chairman, Northern & Shell PLC;* b. 8 Dec. 1951; m. Janet Robertson 1983; one s. *Career:* Advertisement Exec. Thomson Newspapers 1967–68; Group Advertisement Man. Beat Publs Ltd 1968–74; f. Northern & Shell Network 1974 (later Northern & Shell PLC) Chair. 1974–; launched Int. Musician (magazine) 1974; Demonde Advertising 1976–89; Publr Next, Fitness, Cook's Weekly, Venture, Penthouse, Bicycle, Stamps, Electric Blue, Rock CD, Guitar, For Woman, Attitude, Arsenal, Liverpool; f. Fantasy Channel 1995, OK! Magazine 1993–, OK! TV 1999–; owner Express Newspapers 2000–. *Address:* Northern & Shell PLC, Ludgate House, 245 Blackfriars Road, London, SE1 9UX, England (Office). *Telephone:* (20) 7928-8000 (Office). *Fax:* (20) 7922-7789 (Office). *E-mail:* ed98@cityscape.co.uk (Office).

DETHERIDGE, Andrew John; Writer, Poet and Lecturer; b. 11 April 1969, Stourport, Worcestershire, England; m. Alexandra Jayne Cope. *Education:* BA, Ancient History and History, University of Nottingham, 1990; PGCE (FAHE), MA, English Studies, 2000, University of Wolverhampton. *Career:* English/History Teacher, St Peter's School, 1994–95; English Teacher, George Dixon School, 1995–96, Castle High School, 1996–99; Lecturer and Poet-in-Residence, Sandwell College, West Midlands, 1999–; mem. Mem. of numerous magazines; Equity. *Publications:* Naked, 1999; In The Light of Dreams, 2000; Ocean's Spray, 2001; In Character, 2001; The City of the Dead, 2002; The World Spins Darkly, 2002; Vast Skies, 2002. Contributions: Poetry, short stories, haiku, senryu in numerous magazines and anthologies. *Honours:* One of the Top 100 Poets of the Year, Forward Press, 1999; Winner, Partners in Poetry Open Competition, 1999; Second Prize, Partners in Poetry Open Competition, 2000; Joint First Prize, East Barnet Festival Competition, 2001. *Address:* 8 High Haden Road, Haden Hill, Cradley Heath, West Midlands B64 7PG, England.

DEVANE, Terry (see Healy, Jeremiah).

DEVEREAUX, Emily (see Lewis-Smith, Anne Elizabeth).

DEVERELL, Rex Johnson; Playwright; b. 17 July 1941, Toronto, Ontario, Canada; m. Rita Joyce Shelton, 24 May 1967, one s. *Education:* BA, 1963, BD, 1966, McMaster University; STM, Union Theological Seminary, 1967. *Career:* Resident Playwright, Globe Theatre, Regina, 1975–91; Pres., Playwrights Union of Canada, 1991–93; mem. Saskatchewan Writers Guild; Playwrights Union of Canada; Saskatchewan Playwrights Centre; Amnesty International. *Publications:* Boiler Room Suite, 1978; Superwheel, 1979; Drift, 1981; Black Powder, 1981. Other: Deverell of the Globe (anthology), television and radio scripts, opera libretti and children's plays. Contributions: Canadian Theatre Review; Canadian Children's Literature; Canadian Drama; Prairie Fire; Grain. *Honours:* McMaster University Honour Society, 1963; Ohio State Award, 1974; Canadian Authors Asscn Medal, 1978; Major Armstrong Award, 1986. *Address:* 36 Oneida Ave, RR 4, Coldwater, Ontario L0K 1E0, Canada.

DEVERELL, William H(erbert); Author; b. 4 March 1937, Regina, Saskatchewan, Canada; m. Tekla Melnyk, one s. one d. *Education:* BA, LLB, University of Saskatchewan, 1962. *Career:* Staff, Saskatoon Star-Phoenix, 1956–60, Canadian Press, Montréal, 1960–62, Vancouver Sun, 1963; Partner in law firm, Vancouver, 1964–79; Writer, 1979–; mem. British Columbia Bar Asscn; British Columbia Civil Liberties Asscn; CWA; Crime Writers of Canada; Writers Union of Canada, chair., 1994–95. *Publications:* Fiction: Needles, 1979; High Crimes, 1979; Mecca, 1983; Dance of Shiva, 1984; Platinum Blues, 1988; Mindfield, 1989; Kill All the Lawyers, 1994. Non-Fiction: Fatal Cruise: The Trial of Robert Frisbee, 1991; Street Legal – The Betrayal, 1995; Trial of Passion, 1997. *Honours:* McClelland and Stewart/Seal First Novel Award, 1979; Book of the Year Award, Periodical Distributors Asscn of Canada, 1980; Arthur Ellis Canadian Crime Writer Award, 1998; Dashiel Hammett International Asscn of Crime Writers Award, 1998. *Address:* Box 14, Rural Route 1, North Pender Island, BC V0N 2M0, Canada.

DEVEREUX, Eve (see Barnett, Paul (Le Page)).

DEW, Robb (Reavill) Forman; Writer; b. 26 Oct. 1946, Mount Vernon, Ohio, USA; m. Charles Burgess Dew, 26 Jan. 1968, two s. *Education:* Louisiana State University. *Publications:* Dale Loves Sophie to Death, 1982; The Time of Her Life, 1984; Fortunate Lives, 1991; A Southern Thanksgiving: Recipes and Musings for a Manageable Feast, 1992; The Family Heart: A Memoir of When Our Son Came Out, 1994. *Honours:* American Book Award First Novel, 1982. *Address:* c/o Russell and Volkening, 50 W 29th St, Apt 7E, New York, NY 10001, USA.

DEWDNEY, Christopher; Poet and Writer; b. 9 May 1951, London, Ontario, Canada; m. 1st Suzanne Dennison, 1971, divorced 1975, one d.; m. 2nd Lise Downe, 1977, divorced 1990, one s.; m. 3rd Barbara Gowdy. *Education:* South and Westminster Collegiate Institutes, London, Ontario; H. B. Beal Art Annex, London, Ontario. *Career:* Assoc. Fellow, Winters College, York University, Toronto, 1984; Poetry Ed., Coach House Publishing, Toronto, 1988; Academic Adviser, Columet College, York University, 1997–. *Publications:* Poetry: Golders Green, 1972; A Paleozoic Geology of London, Ontario, 1973; Fovea Centralis, 1975; Spring Trances in the Control Emerald Night, 1978; Alter Sublime, 1980; The Cenozoic Asylum, 1983; Predators of the Adoration: Selected Poems 1972–1982, 1983; Permugenesis, 1987; The Radiant Inventory, 1988; Demon Pond, 1994. Other: The Immaculate Perception, 1986; Recent Artifacts from the Institute of Applied Fiction, 1990; Concordant Proviso Ascendant: A Natural History of Southwestern Ontario, Book III, 1991; The Secular Grail, 1993; Demon Pond, 1994; Last Flesh, 1998; Signal Fires, 2000; The Natural History, 2002. Contributions: periodicals. *Honours:* Design Canada Award, 1974; CBC Prize, 1986; Fellow, Columet College, York University; Fellow, McLuhen Program in Culture and Technology. *Address:* c/o McClelland and Stewart Inc, 481 University Ave, Suite 900, Toronto, Ontario M5G 2E9, Canada.

DEWEESE, Jean (see De Weese, Thomas Eugene (Gene)).

DEWHIRST, Ian; Librarian (retd), Writer and Poet; b. 17 Oct. 1936, Keighley, Yorkshire, England. *Education:* BA, Victoria University of Manchester, 1958. *Career:* Staff, Keighley Public Library, 1960–91; mem. Yorkshire Dialect Society; Brontë Society; Edward Thomas Fellowship; Assoc. of the Library Asscn; FRSA, 2000. *Publications:* The Handloom Weaver and Other Poems, 1965; Scar Top and Other Poems, 1968; Gleanings From Victorian Yorkshire, 1972; A History of Keighley, 1974; Yorkshire Through the Years, 1975; Gleanings from Edwardian Yorkshire, 1975; The Story of a Nobody, 1980; You Don't Remember Bananas, 1985; Keighley in Old Picture Postcards, 1987; In the Reign of the Peacemaker, 1993; Down Memory Lane, 1993; Images of Keighley, 1996; A Century of Yorkshire Dialect (co-ed.), 1997. Contributions: Yorkshire Ridings Magazine; Lancashire Magazine; Dalesman; Cumbria; Pennine Magazine; Transactions of the Yorkshire Dialect Society; Yorkshire Journal. *Honours:* Hon. Doctor of Letters, University of Bradford, 1996; MBE, 1999. *Address:* 14 Raglan Ave, Fell Lane, Keighley, West Yorkshire BD22 6BJ, England.

DEWHURST, Eileen Mary; Author; b. 27 May 1929, Liverpool, England; Divorced. *Education:* MA, English Language and Literature, St Anne's College, Oxford, 1956. *Career:* mem. CWA; Society of Authors. *Publications:* Crime novels: Death Came Smiling, 1975; After the Ball, 1976; Curtain Fall, 1977; Drink This, 1980; Trio in Three Flats, 1981; Whoever I Am, 1982; The House That Jack Built, 1983; There Was a Little Girl, 1984; Playing Safe, 1985; A Private Prosecution, 1986; A Nice Little Business, 1987; The Sleeper, 1988; Dear Mr Right, 1990; The Innocence of Guilt, 1991; Death in Candie Gardens, 1992; Now You See Her, 1995; The Verdict on Winter; 1996; Alias the Enemy, 1997; Roundabout, 1998; Death of a Stranger, 1999; Double Act, 2000; Closing Stages, 2001; No Love Lost, 2001; Easeful Death, 2003. Contributions: Ellery Queen's Mystery Magazine; CWA Annual Anthologies. *Address:* c/o Gregory and Co, 3 Barb Mews, London W6 7PA, England.

DEWHURST, Keith; Writer; b. 24 Dec. 1931, Oldham, England; m. 1st Eve Pearce 14 July 1958 (divorced 1980); one s. two d.; m. 2nd Alexandra Cann 4 Nov. 1980. *Education:* BA, Peterhouse, Cambridge, 1953. *Career:* Sports Writer, Evening Chronicle, Manchester, 1955–59; Presenter, Granada TV, 1968–69, BBC2 TV, London, 1972; Arts Columnist, The Guardian, London, 1969–72; Writer-in-Residence, Western Australia APA, Perth, 1984. *Publications:* Lark Rise to Candleford (two plays), 1980; Captain of the Sands (novel), 1981; Don Quixote (play), 1982; McSullivan's Beach (novel), 1986; Black Snow (play), 1992; War Plays (plays), 1997; Philoctetes (trans. play), 2000. *Literary Agent:* Alexandra Cann Representation. *Address:* 12 Abingdon Rd, London W8 6AF, England.

DEXTER, (Norman) Colin, OBE, BA, MA; writer; b. 29 Sept. 1930, Stamford, Lincolnshire, England; m. Dorothy Cooper 1956; one s. one d. *Education:* Christ's College, Cambridge, University of Oxford. *Career:* mem. CWA, Detection Club. *Publications:* Last Bus to Woodstock, 1975; Last Seen Wearing, 1976; The Silent World of Nicholas Quinn, 1977; Service of All the Dead, 1979; The Dead of Jericho, 1981; The Riddle of the Third Mile, 1983; The Secret of Annexe 3, 1986; The Wench is Dead, 1989; The Jewel That Was Ours, 1991; The Way Through the Woods, 1992; Morse's Greatest Mystery, 1993; The Daughters of Cain, 1994; Death is Now My Neighbour, 1996; The Remorseful Day, 1999. Contributions: anthologies. *Honours:* Silver Dagger Awards, 1979, 1981, Gold Dagger Awards, 1989, 1992, Cartier Diamond Dagger Award, 1997, CWA; Macavity Award, Best Short Story, 1995; Lotos Club Medal of Merit, New York, 1996; Sherlock Holmes Award, 1999; Hon. MA, Univ. of Leicester, 1996; Hon. DLitt, Oxford Brookes Univ., 1998; Freedom of the City of Oxford, 2001. *Address:* 456 Banbury Road, Oxford OX2 7RG, England.

DEXTER, Pete(r Whittemore); Columnist and Author; b. 22 July 1943, Pontiac, Michigan, USA; m. Dian McDonough; one c. *Education:* BA, University of South Dakota, 1969. *Career:* Columnist, Philadelphia Daily News, 1976–86, Esquire magazine, 1985–86, Sacramento Bee, 1986–. *Publications:* God's Pocket, 1983; Dead Wood, 1986; Paris Trout, 1988; Brotherly Love, 1991; The Paperboy, 1994; Train, 2003. *Honours:* Mark Twain Award, Associated Press, California-Nevada, 1987; National Book

Award, 1988; Penn West Award, Los Angeles, 1988; Bay Area Book Reviewers Award, 1988. *Address:* c/o Sacramento Bee, 21st and Q Streets, Sacramento, CA 95852, USA.

DI BLASI, Debra; Educator and Writer; b. 27 May 1957, Kirksville, MO, USA; m. Carlos Roberto Di Blasi, 1984, divorced 1989. *Education:* University of Missouri, Columbia, 1975–78; BFA, Kansas City Art Institute, 1985; San Francisco State University, 1989. *Career:* Advertising Man., Robert Half of Northern California, San Francisco, 1986–89; Advertising Production Man., MacWeek, San Francisco, 1989; Asst to the Exec. Dir, Accessible Arts Inc, Kansas City, MO, 1990–92; Senior Secretary, International Network Design and Engineering Dept, Spring Communications, Kansas City, MO, 1992–95; Writing Tutor, 1994, Learning Specialist, 1995–, Kansas City Art Institute, Kansas City, MO; Judge, River of Words National Poetry Competition, 1997; Assoc. Guest Ed., SOMA; Lectures, readings from her works; mem. National Geographic Society; Writers Place; Kansas City Art Institute Alumni Circle. *Publications:* The Season's Condition (screenplay), 1993; Drought (screenplay), 1997; Drought and Say What You Like (novellas), 1997; Prayers of an Accidental Nature (novellas), 1999. Contributions: short stories in anthologies, incl.: Lovers: Writings by Women, 1992; Exposures: Essays by Missouri Women, 1997; short stories in periodicals, incl.: Moondance; Cottonwood; Potpourri; New Letters; Sou'wester; New Delta Review; AENE; Colorado-North Review; Transfer; Essays, articles and reviews to periodicals, incl.: SOMA; New Art Examiner. *Honours:* Eyster Prize for Fiction, for short story An Interview with My Husband, New Delta Review, 1991. *Address:* c/o Kansas City Art Institute, 4415 Warwick Blvd, Kansas City, MO 64111, USA.

DI CICCO, Pier Giorgio; Roman Catholic Priest and Poet; b. 5 July 1949, Arezzo, Italy. *Education:* BA, 1972, BEd, 1973, Master of Divinity, 1990, University of Toronto; Bachelor of Sacred Theology, St Paul's University, 1990. *Career:* Founder-Poetry Ed., Poetry Toronto Newsletter, 1976–77; Assoc. Ed., Books in Canada, 1976–79; Co-Ed., 1976–79, Poetry Ed., 1980–82, Waves; Ordained Roman Catholic Priest and Assoc. Pastor, St Anne's Church, Brampton, Ontario, 1993–. *Publications:* We Are the Light Turning, 1975; The Sad Facts, 1977; The Circular Dark, 1977; Dancing in the House of Cards, 1977; A Burning Patience, 1978; Roman Candles: An Anthology of 17 Italo-Canadian Poets (ed.), 1978; Dolce-Amaro, 1979; The Tough Romance, 1979; A Straw Hat for Everything, 1981; Flying Deeper into the Century, 1982; Dark to Light: Reasons for Humanness: Poems 1976–1979, 1983; Women We Never See Again, 1984; Twenty Poems, 1984; Post-Sixties Nocturne, 1985; Virgin Science: Hunting Holistic Paradigms, 1986; The City of Hurried Dreams, 1993. *Honours:* Canada Council Awards, 1974, 1976, 1980; Carleton University Italo-Canadian Literature Award, 1979. *Address:* PO Box 344, King City, Ontario L0G 1K0, Canada.

DI MICHELE, Mary; Canadian poet, writer and academic; b. 6 Aug. 1949, Lanciano, Italy; m. (divorced); one d. *Education:* BA, University of Toronto, 1972; MA, University of Windsor, 1974. *Career:* Poetry Ed., Toronto Life, 1980–81, Poetry Toronto, 1982–84; Writer-in-Residence, University of Toronto, 1985–86, Metro Reference Library, Toronto, 1986, Regina Public Library, 1987–88; Writer-in-Residence, 1990, then Assoc. Prof., Creative Writing Programme, Concordia University; mem. Italian-Canadian Writers Asscn; Writers Union. *Publications:* Poetry: Tree of August, 1978; Bread and Chocolate, 1980; Mimosa and Other Poems, 1981; Necessary Sugar, 1984; Immune to Gravity, 1986; Luminous Emergencies, 1990; Stranger in You: Selected Poems & New, 1995; Debriefing the Rose, 1998. Novel: Under My Skin, 1994. Editor: Anything is Possible, 1984. Contributions: anthologies and periodicals. *Honours:* First Prize for Poetry, CBC Literary Competition, 1980; Silver Medal, DuMaurier Poetry Award, 1982; Air Canada Writing Award, 1983. *Address:* c/o Dept of English, Concordia University, 1455 de Maisonneuve Blvd W, Montréal, QC H3G 1M8, Canada.

DI PRIMA, Diane; Poet, Writer, Dramatist, Trans., Publisher and Artist; b. 6 Aug. 1934, New York, NY, USA; m. 1st Alan S. Marlowe, 1962, divorced 1969; m. 2nd Grant Fisher 1972 (divorced 1975); two s. three d. *Education:* Swarthmore College, 1951–53. *Career:* Co-Founder, New York Poets Theater, 1961–65; Co-Ed. (with LeRoi Jones), 1961–63, Ed., 1963–69, Floating Bear magazine; Publisher, Poets Press, 1964–69, Eidolon Editions, 1974–; Faculty, Naropa Institute, 1974–97, New College of California, San Francisco, 1980–87; Co-Founder, San Francisco Institute of Magical and Healing Arts, 1983–91; Senior Lecturer, California College of Arts and Crafts, Oakland, 1990–92; Visiting Faculty, San Francisco Art Institute, 1992; Adjunct Faculty, California Institute of Integral Studies, 1994–95; Master Poet-in-Residence Columbia College Chicago 2000. *Publications:* This Kind of Bird Flies Backward, 1958; Ed., Various Fables from Various Places, 1960; Dinners and Nightmares, 1961, 1998; The New Handbook of Heaven, 1962; Translator, The Man Condemned to Death, 1963; Poets Vaudeville, 1964; Seven Love Poems from the Middle Latin, 1965; Haiku, 1966; New Mexico Poem, 1967; Earthsong, 1968; Hotel Albert, 1968; Ed., War Poems, 1968; Memoirs of a Beatnik, 1969, 1988; LA Odyssey, 1969; The Book of Hours, 1970; Kerhonkson Journal 1966, 1971; Revolutionary Letters, 1971; The Calculus of Variation, 1972; Loba, Part 1, 1973; Ed., The Floating Bear: a Newsletter, 1973; Freddie Poems, 1974; Brass Furnace Going Out, 1975; Selected Poems 1956–1975, 1975; Loba, Part 2, 1976; Loba as Eve, 1977; Loba, Parts 1–8, 1978; Wyoming Series, 1988; The Mysteries of Vision, 1988; Pieces of a Song: Selected Poems, 1990; Seminary Poems, 1991; The Mask is the Path of the Star, 1993; Loba, Parts 9–16, 1998; Recollections of My Life as a Woman, 2001, Fun with Forms 2001, Towers Down (with Clive Matson) 2002, The Ones I Used to Laugh With 2003; work trans. into over 20 languages. Contributions: Over 300 literary and popular magazines and newspapers; Work appeared in over 100 anthologies. *Honours:* National Endowment for the Arts Grants, 1966, 1973; Co-ordinating Council of Little Magazines Grants, 1967, 1970; Lapis Foundation Awards, 1978, 1979; Institute for Aesthetic Development Award, 1986; Lifetime Service Award, National Poetry Asscn, 1993; Hon. DLitt, St Lawrence University, Canton, New York, 1999. *Literary Agent:* Sandra Dijkstra, PO Box 4500, Del Mar, CA 92014, USA. *Address:* 78 Niagara Ave, San Francisco, CA 94112, USA.

DIAMOND, Jared (Mason); Physiologist, Ecologist and Author; b. 10 Sept. 1937, Boston, Massachusetts, USA; m. Marie M. Cohen, 1982, two c. *Education:* BA, Harvard University, 1958; PhD, Physiology, University of Cambridge, 1961. *Career:* Fellow in Physiology, Trinity College, Cambridge, 1961–65; Junior Fellow, Harvard University Society of Fellows, 1962–65; Assoc. in Biophysics, Harvard Medical School, Cambridge, Massachusetts, 1965–66; Assoc. Prof. of Physiology, 1966–68, Prof., 1968–, University of California Medical School, Los Angeles; Research Assoc., Dept of Ornithology, American Museum of Natural History, 1973–, Los Angeles County Museum of Natural History, 1985–; mem. National Science Acad.; Fellow, American Acad. of Arts and Sciences; Fellow, American Ornithologists Union; American Physiological Society; Biophysics Society; American Society of Naturalists; American Philosophical Society. *Publications:* Avifauna of the Eastern Highlands of New Guinea, 1972; Ecology and Evolution of Communities (co-ed.), 1975; Birds of Karkar and Bagabag Islands, New Guinea (co-author), 1979; Community Ecology (co-author), 1986; The Third Chimpanzee: The Evolution and Future of the Human Animal, 1992, UK edn as The Rise and Fall of the Third Chimpanzee, 1992; Guns, Germs, and Steel: The Fates of Human Societies, 1997. Other: Over 500 research papers on physiology, ecology and ornithology. Contributions: Discover; Natural History; Nature. *Honours:* National Science Foundation Fellow, 1958–61, 1961–62; Bowditch Prize, American Physiological Society, 1976; Kroc Foundation Lecturer, Western Asscn of Physicians, 1978; Burr Award, National Geographic Society, 1979; MacArthur Foundation Fellowship, 1985; Los Angeles Times Book Prize, 1992; Science Book Prize, New Scientist, London, 1992; Pulitzer Prize, 1998; National Medal of Science, 1999; Tyler Prize, 2001. *Address:* Dept of Physiology, School of Medicine, University of California, Los Angeles, CA 90024, USA.

DIAZ, Junot, BA, MFA; American writer; b. 1968, Santo Domingo, Dominican Republic. *Education:* Rutgers University, Cornell University. *Publications:* Drown 1996, Negocios 1997; contrib. to New Yorker, Paris Review, African Verse, anthologies. *Address:* c/o Riverhead Books, 375 Hudson Street, New York, NY 10014, USA.

DIB, Mohammed; Algerian novelist and poet; b. 1920, Tlemcen. *Publications:* Algérie trilogy (La grande maison 1952, L'incendie 1954, Le métier à tisser 1957), Au café 1957, Baba fekran 1959, Un éte africain 1959, Ombre gardiénne (poems) 1961, Qui se souvient de la mer 1962, Cours sur la rive sauvage 1964, Le talisman 1966, La danse du roi 1968, Formulaires (poems) 1970, Dieu en Barbarie 1970, Le maitre de chasse 1973, L'histoire du chat qui boude 1974, Omneros (poems) 1975, Habel 1977, Feu beau feu (poems) 1979, Mille hourras pour une guerre 1980, Les terrasses d'Orsol 1985, O vive (poems) 1987, Le sommeil d'Eve 1989, Neiges de marbre 1990, Le désert sans détour 1992, L'infante Maure 1994, L'arbre à dires 1998, L'Enfant-Jazz (poems) 1998, Le cœur insulaire 2000, LA Trip 2003. *Honours:* Grand Prix de la Francophonie 1994, Prix Mallarmé 1998. *Address:* c/o Éditions du Seuil, 27 rue Jacob, 75261 Paris, Cedex 06, France.

DIBDIN, Michael John; writer and artist; b. 21 March 1947, Wolverhampton, England; m. 1st Benita Mitbrodt, 1971, divorced 1986; m. 2nd Sybil Sheringham, 1987, divorced 1995; m. 3rd Kathrine Beck, 1997, two d. *Education:* University of Sussex; University of Alberta. *Publications:* The Last Sherlock Holmes Story, 1978; A Rich Full Death, 1986; Ratking, 1988; The Tryst, 1989; Vendetta, 1990; Dirty Tricks, 1991; Cabal, 1992; The Dying of the Light, 1993; Dead Lagoon, 1994; Dark Spectre, 1995; Così fan tutte, 1996; A Long Finish, 1998; Blood Rain, 1999, Thanksgiving 2000, And Then You Die 2002, Medusa 2003. *Honours:* Golden Dagger Award CWA 1988, Grand Prix des Romans Policiers 1994. *Literary Agent:* PFD, Drury House, 34–43 Russell St, London WC2B 5HA, England.

DICKEY, Christopher; Journalist and Writer; b. 31 Aug. 1951, Nashville, Tennessee, USA; m. 1st Susan Tuckerman, 29 Nov. 1969, divorced Dec. 1979; m. 2nd Carol Salvatore, 22 March 1980, one s. *Education:* BA, University of Virginia, 1972; MS, Boston University, 1974. *Career:* Staff, Washington Post, 1974–86; Cairo Bureau Chief, 1986–88, Paris Bureau Chief, 1988–93, 1995–, Middle East Regional Ed., 1993–95, Newsweek; mem. Council on Foreign Relations. *Publications:* With the Contras: A Reporter in the Wilds of Nicaragua, 1986; Expats: Travels in Arabia, from Tripoli to Teheran, 1990; Innocent Blood (novel), 1997; Summer of Deliverance: A Memoir of Father and Son, 1999. Contributions: periodicals. *Honours:* Interamerican Press Asscn Award, 1980; Mary Hemingway Award, Overseas Press Club, 1983; Edward Weintal Award for Diplomatic Reporting, Georgetown University. *Address:* c/o Newsweek, 251 W 57th St, New York, NY 10019, USA.

DICKIE, Margaret; Prof. of English and Writer; b. 13 Sept. 1935, Bennington, Vermont, USA; m. Benjamin Uroff, 1961, divorced 1978, two d. *Education:* AB, Middlebury College, 1956; PhD, Brown University, 1965. *Career:* Asst Prof., then Prof. of English, 1967–87, Dept Head, 1983–87, University of Illinois at Urbana-Champaign; Helen S. Lancer Distinguished Prof., University of Georgia, Athens, 1987–; Mem., Board of Trustees, University of Georgia Foundation; mem. MLA of America; American Studies Asscn. *Publications:* Hart Crane: The Patterns of His Poetry, 1975; Sylvia Plath and Ted Hughes, 1979; On the Modernist Long Poem, 1986; Lyric Contingencies: Emily Dickinson and Wallace Stevens, 1991; Gendered Modernisms: Women Poets and Their Readers (co-ed.), 1996; Stern, Bishop, and Rich: Lyrics of Love, War, and Place, 1997. *Honours:* Distinguished Alumni Award, Middlebury College. *E-mail:* mmdickie@parallel.park.uga.edu.

DICKINSON, Donald Percy; Writer and Teacher; b. 28 Dec. 1947, Prince Albert, Saskatachewan, Canada; m. Chellie Eaton, 1 May 1970, two s. one d. *Education:* BA, University of Saskatchewan, 1973; MFA, University of British Columbia, 1979. *Career:* Fiction Ed., Prism International, 1977–79; Teacher of English, Lillooet Secondary School, 1981–2003; mem. Oldtimers' Hockey Asscn; Writers' Union of Canada. *Publications:* Novel: The Crew, 1993; Robbiestime, 2000. Short Stories: Third Impressions, 1982; Fighting the Upstream, 1987; Blue Husbands, 1991. Contributions: Best Canadian Short Fiction, 1984; Words We Call Home, 1990; The New Writers, 1992; The Porcupine Quill Reader, 1996. *Honours:* Bankson Award, 1979; Ethel Wilson Fiction Prize, 1991. *Address:* 554 Victoria St, Box 341, Lillooet, BC V0K 1V0, Canada.

DICKINSON, Margaret (see Muggeson, Margaret Elizabeth).

DICKINSON, Peter; Composer, Pianist and Writer; b. 15 Nov. 1934, Lytham, Lancashire, England; m. Bridget Jane Tomkinson; two s. *Education:* LRAM; ARCM, Piano Performance; Organ Scholar Queens' College, Cambridge; MA Music; ARCO Sawyer Prize; FRCO; Stewart of Rannoch Scholar; Juilliard School of Music, New York, USA; DMus (London). *Career:* various teaching posts in New York, London and Birmingham; First Prof. of Music, 1974–84, Emeritus, 1984–, Keele Univ.; Prof., 1991–97, Emeritus Prof., 1997–, Goldsmiths' College, Univ. of London; Head of Music, Institute of United States Studies, Univ. of London; Performances and radio and television recordings as pianist, mostly with sister, Meriel Dickinson; compositions include: Orchestral works (Merseyside Echoes, 1985), concertos (Piano, 1984, Violin, 1986), chamber music, choral works, songs, keyboard music, church music; recordings include: Piano Concerto; Outcry; Organ Concerto; Song Cycles (Auden, Dylan Thomas, Cummings, Heath-Stubbs, Lord Berners); Rags, Blues and Parodies (Burns, Corso, Lord Byron, Stevie Smith, Satie etc); American Trio; organ and piano works. *Publications:* Editor: 20 British Composers, 1975; The Complete Songs and Piano Music of Lord Berners, 1982; The Music of Lennox Berkeley, 1989; Marigold: The Music of Billy Mayerl, 1999; Copland Connotations: Studies and Interviews, 2002. Contributions: various books and journals, incl. book chapters and dictionaries. *Honours:* Hon. DMus, Keele Univ., 1999. *Address:* c/o Novello & Co, 8–9 Frith St, London W1V 5TZ, England.

DICKSON, Mora Agnes; Author and Artist; b. 20 April 1918, Glasgow, Scotland. *Education:* Diploma of Art, Edinburgh College of Art, 1941; Certificate, Byam Shaw School of Drawing and Painting, London, 1950. *Publications:* New Nigerians, 1960; Baghdad and Beyond, 1961; A Season in Sarawak, 1962; A World Elsewhere, 1964; Israeli Interlude, 1966; Count Us In, 1968; Longhouse in Sarawak, 1971; Beloved Partner, 1974; A Chance to Serve (ed.), 1977; The Inseparable Grief, 1977; Assignment in Asia, 1979; The Powerful Bond, 1980; Nannie, 1988. *Address:* 19 Blenheim Rd, London W4, England.

DIDION, Joan, BA; American writer; b. 5 Dec. 1934, Sacramento; m. John Gregory Dunne 1964 (died 2003); one d. *Education:* Univ. of California, Berkeley. *Career:* Assoc. Features Ed. Vogue magazine 1956–63; fmr columnist Esquire, Life, Saturday Evening Post, fmr contributor Nat. Review; now freelance writer; mem. American Acad. of Arts and Letters, American Acad. of Arts and Sciences, Council on Foreign Relations. *Screenplays:* The Panic in Needle Park 1971, A Star is Born 1976, True Confessions 1981, Hills Like White Elephants 1991, Broken Trust 1995, Up Close and Personal 1996. *Publications include:* novels: Run River 1963, Play It as It Lays 1970, A Book of Common Prayer 1977, Telling Stories 1978, Democracy 1984, The Last Thing He Wanted 1996; essays: Slouching Towards Bethlehem 1969, The White Album 1978, After Henry 1992; non-fiction: Salvador 1983, Miami 1987, After Henry 1992, Political Fictions 2001, Where I Was From: A Memoir 2003. *Honours:* First Prize Vogue's Prix de Paris 1956, Morton Dauwen Zabel Prize (American Acad. of Arts and Letters) 1978, Edward McDowell Medal 1996, George Polk Award 2001. *Literary Agent:* Janklow & Nesbit, 445 Park Avenue, New York, NY 10022-2606, USA.

DIEKMANN, Kai; German newspaper executive; *Editor-in-Chief, Bild;* b. 1965. *Career:* corresp. Bild and Bild am Sonntag, Bonn 1987; chief reporter Illustrierten Bunte, Munich 1989–91; Chief Ed. Bild-Zeitung, Berlin 1991–92, Chief Ed. and Chief Political Corresp. Bild-Zeitung, Hamburg 1992–97, Chief Corresp. Bild and Bild am Sonntag, Bonn 1987; Chief Reporter Illustrierten Bunte, Munich 1989–91; Chief Ed. Welt am Sonntag 1998–2000, Ed.-in-Chief Bild and Publr Bild and Bild am Sonntag 2001–. *Publications include:* (co-author) Rita Süssmuth im Gespräch 1994, Die neue Bundespräsident im Gespräch 1994, Helmut Kohl: Ich wollte Deutschlands Einheit 1996. *Address:* Bild, Axel-Springer-Platz 1, 20355 Hamburg, Germany (Office). *Telephone:* (40) 34700 (Office). *Fax:* (40) 345811 (Office). *Website:* www.bild.de (Office).

DIEZ, Rolo; Argentine novelist, screenwriter and journalist; b. 1940, Buenos Aires. *Publications:* Los compañeros 1987, Una baldosa en el valle de la muerte 1992, La Vida que me doy (Flauta Magica) 2001, Papel Picado 2003, Tequila Blue 2004. *Address:* c/o Bitter Lemon Press, 37 Arundel Gardens, London, W11 2LW, England. *E-mail:* books@bitterlemonpress.com. *Website:* www.bitterlemonpress.com.

DIFORIO, Robert G., BA; American publishing executive; b. 19 March 1940, Mamaroneck, NY; m. Birgit Rasmussen 1983; one s. one d. *Education:* Williams Coll., Mass. and Harvard Business School's Advanced Man. Programme. *Career:* Vice-Pres. Kable News Co. 1970; Vice-Pres. and Sales Man. New American Library (NAL) 1972, Sr Vice-Pres. and Marketing Dir 1976, Pres. and Publisher 1980–81, CEO and Chair. Bd NAL/E. P. Dutton 1983–89; Prin. D4EO Literary Agency 1991–. *Address:* 7 Indian Valley Road, Weston, CT 06883, USA (Office). *Telephone:* (203) 544-7180 (Office); (203) 544-7182 (Home). *Fax:* (203) 544-7160 (Office). *E-mail:* d4eo@optonline.net (Office). *Website:* www.publishersmarketplace.com/members/d4eo (Office).

DIGBY, John (Michael); Emigrated, USA, 1978; b. 18 Jan. 1938, London, England; Poet; Collagist. m. 1st Erica Susan Christine Berwick-Stephens, 1963, divorced, one s.; m. 2nd Joan Hildreth Weiss, 3 March 1979. *Publications:* The Structure of Biofocal Distance, 1974; Sailing Away From Night, 1978; To Amuse a Shrinking Sun, poems, 1985; The Collage Handbook (with Joan Digby), 1985; Miss Liberty, 1986; Incantation, 1987; Inspired by Drink (ed. with Joan Digby), 1988; The Wood Engravings of John de Pol (ed. with Joan Digby), 1988; A Parliament of Owls, 1989. *Address:* 30 Kellogg St, Oyster Bay, NY 11771, USA.

DIGGINS, John P(atrick); Distinguished Prof. of History and Writer; b. 1 April 1935, San Francisco, CA, USA; m. Jacy Battles, 17 Feb. 1960, divorced April 1977, one s. one d. *Education:* BA, University of California at Berkeley, 1957; MA, San Francisco State College, 1959; PhD, University of Southern California at Los Angeles, 1964. *Career:* Assoc. Prof., later Prof. of History, University of California at Irvine; Distinguished Prof. of History, CUNY; mem. ACLS; American Historical Asscn; American Philosophical Society; American Studies Asscn. *Publications:* Mussolini and Fascism: The View from America, 1972; The American Left in the Twentieth Century, 1973; Up from Communism: Conservative Odysseys in American History, 1975; The Bard of Savagery: Thornstein Veblen and Modern Social Theory, 1978; The Problem with Authority in America (ed. with Mark E. Kahn), 1981; The Lost Soul of American Politics: Virtue, Self-Interest, and the Foundations of Liberalism, 1984; The Proud Decades: America in War and Peace, 1941–1960, 1988; The Rise and Fall of the American Left, 1992; The Promise of Pragmatism: Modernism and the Crisis of Knowledge and Authority, 1994; Max Weber: Politics and the Spirit of Tragedy, 1996; The Liberal Persuasion: Arthur Schlesinger Jr and the Challenge of the American Past, 1997; On Hallowed Ground: Abraham Lincoln and the Foundations of American History, 2000. Contributions: scholarly books and journals. *Honours:* National Endowment for the Humanities Fellowship, 1972–73; John H. Dunning Award, American Historical Asscn, 1973; Guggenheim Fellowship, 1975–76. *Address:* c/o Graduate School and University Center, City University of New York, 365 Fifth Ave, New York, NY 10016, USA. *E-mail:* jdiggins@gc.cuny.edu.

DILKS, David Neville; Historian and Writer; b. 17 March 1938, Coventry, England; m. Jill Medlicott, 1963, one s. *Education:* BA, Modern History, Hertford College, Oxford, 1959; St Antony's College, Oxford. *Career:* Asst Lecturer, then Lecturer in International History, LSE, 1962–70; Prof. of International History, 1970–91, Chair., School of History, 1974–79, Dean, Faculty of Arts, 1975–77, University of Leeds; Visiting Fellow, All Souls College, Oxford, 1973; Vice-Chancellor, University of Hull, 1991–99; mem. British National Committee for the History of the Second World War, 1983–, pres., international committee, 1992–2000; Politeia, advisory council, 1995–. *Publications:* Curzon in India, two vols, 1969–70; The Diaries of Sir Alexander Cadogan (ed.), 1971; Retreat from Power (ed.), two vols, 1981; The Missing Dimensions: Governments and Intelligence Communities in the Twentieth Century (ed.), 1984; Neville Chamberlain, Vol. I, Pioneering and Reform, 1869–1929, 1984; Grossbritannien und der deutsche Widerstand (co-ed.), 1994; Barbarossa: The Axis and the Allies (co-ed.), 1994. Contributions: scholarly journals. *Honours:* Curzon Prize, University of Oxford, 1960; Freeman, 1979, Liveryman, 1984–, Goldsmiths' Co; FRSL, 1986; Médaille de Vermeil, Académie Française, 1994; Hon. Doctor of History, Russian Acad. of Sciences, 1996; Fellow, City and Guilds of London Institute, 1999. *Address:* Wits End, Long Causeway, Leeds LS16 8EX, England.

DILLARD, Annie; Author, Adjunct Prof. and Writer-in-Residence; b. 30 April 1945, Pittsburgh, Pennsylvania, USA; m. 1st Richard Dillard, 4 June 1964; m. 2nd Gary Clevidence, 12 April 1980; m. 3rd Robert D. Richardson Jr, 1988. *Education:* BA, 1967, MA, 1968, Hollins College. *Career:* Scholar-in-Residence, Western Washington University, 1975–79; Visiting Prof., 1979–81, Adjunct Prof., 1983–, Writer-in-Residence, 1987–, Wesleyan

University; mem. PEN International; Poetry Society of America; Western Writers of America; Century Assn; National Assn for the Advancement of Colored People; Society of American Historians; American Acad. of Arts and Letters. *Publications:* Pilgrim at Tinker Creek, 1974; Holy the Firm, 1977; Teaching a Stone to Talk, 1983; Encounters with Chinese Writers, 1984; An American Childhood, 1987; The Writing Life, 1989; The Living, 1992; The Annie Dillard Reader, 1994; Tickets for a Prayer Wheel, 1994; Mornings Like This, 1995; For the Time Being, 1999. *Honours:* Pulitzer Prize, 1975; New York Press Club Award, 1975; Washington Governor's Award, 1977; National Endowment for the Arts Grant, 1985; Guggenheim Fellowship, 1986; Appalachian Gold Medallion, 1989; Ambassador Book Award, 1990; Campion Award, 1994; Milton Prize, 1994. *Address:* c/o Tim Seldes, Russel & Volkening, 50 W 29th St, New York 10001, USA.

DILLARD, Richard Henry Wilde; academic, writer, poet and editor; b. 11 Oct. 1937, Roanoke, Virginia, USA; m. 1st Annie Doak 1965 (divorced 1972); m. 2nd Cathy Hankla 1979. *Education:* BA, Roanoke College, Salem, Virginia, 1958; MA, 1959, PhD, 1965, University of Virginia. *Career:* Instructor, Roanoke College, 1961, University of Virginia, 1961–64; Asst Prof., 1964–68, Assoc. Prof., 1968–74, Prof. of English, 1974–, Hollins College, Virginia; Contributing Ed., Hollins Critic, 1966–77; Ed.-in-Chief, Children's Literature, 1992–. *Publications:* Fiction: The Book of Changes, 1974; The First Man on the Sun, 1983; Omniphobia, 1995. Poetry: The Day I Stopped Dreaming About Barbara Steele and Other Poems, 1966; News of the Nile, 1971; After Borges, 1972; The Greeting: New and Selected Poems, 1981; Just Here, Just Now, 1994. Non-Fiction: Horror Films, 1976; Understanding George Garrett, 1988. Editor: The Experience of America: A Book of Readings (with Louis D. Rubin Jr), 1969; The Sounder Few: Essays from 'The Hollins Critic' (with George Garrett and John Rees Moore), 1971. Contributions: periodicals. *Honours:* Acad. of American Poets Prize, 1961; Ford Foundation Grant, 1972; O. B. Hardison Jr Poetry Award, Folger Shakespeare Library, Washington, DC, 1994. *Address:* PO Box 9671, Hollins College, CA 24020, USA.

DILLINGHAM, William Byron; of American Literature and Writer; b. 7 March 1930, Atlanta, GA, USA; Emeritus Prof; m. Elizabeth Joiner, 3 July 1952, one s. two d. *Education:* BA, 1955, MA, 1956, Emory University; PhD, University of Pennsylvania, 1961. *Career:* Instructor, 1956–58, Asst Prof., Assoc. Prof., Prof., Charles Howard Candler Prof. of American Literature, 1959–96, Emeritus Prof. 1996–; Emory University; Advisory Boards, Nineteenth-Century Literature, South Atlantic Bulletin. *Publications:* Humor of the Old Southwest, 1965; Frank Norris: Instinct and Art, 1969; An Artist in the Rigging: The Early Work of Herman Melville, 1972; Melville's Short Fiction, 1853–1856, 1977; Melville's Later Novels, 1986; Practical English Handbook, ninth edn, 1992, 10th edn, 1996; Melville and His Circle: The Last Years, 1996. Contributions: many articles and reviews to scholarly journals. *Address:* 1416 Vistaleaf Dr., Decatur, GA 30033, USA.

DILLON, Millicent Gerson, BA, MA; writer; b. 24 May 1925, New York, NY, USA; m. 1st Murray Lesser 1948 (divorced 1959); two d. *Education:* Hunter College, CUNY, San Francisco State University. *Career:* mem. PEN, Authors' Guild. *Publications:* Baby Perpetua and Other Stories, 1971; The One in the Back is Medea (novel), 1973; A Little Original Sin: The Life and Work of Jane Bowles, 1981; After Egypt, 1990; The Dance of the Mothers (novel), 1991; You Are Not I: A Portrait of Paul Bowles, 1998; Harry Gold: A Novel, 2000. Contributions: Southwest Review; Witness; Threepenny Review; The New Yorker; Raritan. *Honours:* Five O. Henry Short Story Awards; Best American Short Stories, 1992; Guggenheim Fellowship; National Endowment for the Humanities Fellowship. *Literary Agent:* Ira Silverberg, Donadio and Olson, 121 W 27th Street, New York, NY 10001, USA. *Address:* 83 Sixth Avenue, San Francisco, CA 94118, USA.

DILSAVER, Paul; Poet, Writer and Ed.; b. 8 Dec. 1949, Colorado, USA. *Education:* BA, Philosophy, University of Southern Colorado, 1972; MA, English, 1973, Additional Graduate Studies, 1974, 1975, Colorado State University; MFA, Creative Writing, Bowling Green State University, Ohio, 1979; BS, Accounting, SUNY, 1996. *Career:* Instructor, Laramie County Community College, Cheyenne, WY, 1973–74, Casper College, WY, 1974–77, Western Illinois University, Macomb, 1979–81; Poetry Ed., Rocky Mountain Creative Arts Journal and Chapbook Series, 1974–78; Poet-in-Residence, Wyoming Arts Council, 1977–78; Ed., Blue Light Books, 1979–, Blue Light Review, 1983–91; Asst Prof. of English, Carroll College, Helena, Montana, 1981–84; Lecturer in English, University of Southern Colorado, 1986–91; Visiting Instructor of English, Anoka-Ramsey College, Coon Rapids, Minnesota, 1991–92. *Publications:* Malignant Blues (poems), 1976; Words Wyoming (anthology), 1976; A Brutal Blacksmith: An Anvil of Bruised Tissue (poems), 1979; Encounters with the Antichrist (prose poems), 1982; Character Scatology (poems), 1984; Stories of the Strange (fiction), 1985; Nurtz! Nurtz! (novel), 1989; A Cure for Optimism (poems), 1993; The Toilet Papers (anthology), 1994; Medi-Phoria, 1999; Hardcore Haiku, 2000. Contributions: various anthologies and periodicals. *Address:* PO Box 1621, Pueblo, CO 81002, USA.

DIMARCO, Cris, BA, MAT; editor and writer; b. (Cris Newport), 14 July 1960, Melrose Park, IL, USA; m.; two c. *Education:* Univ. of Massachusetts at Boston, Tufts Univ. *Career:* Asst Prof. of English 1991, Assoc. Prof. of English 1994, New Hampshire Technical Inst.; Sr Ed., Windstorm Creative 1997–. *Publications:* Sparks Might Fly 1994, The White Bones of Truth 1994, Queen's Champion: The Legend of Lancelot Retold 1997, 1001 Nights: Exotica 1 1999, Exotica 2 2002, Kresh: The Golton Box 2004; contrib. to periodicals. *Address:* PO Box 28, Port Orchard, WA 98366, USA. *E-mail:* crisdimarco@windstormcreative.com.

DIMBLEBY, David, MA; British broadcaster and journalist; b. 28 Oct. 1938, London; m. 1st Josceline Gaskell 1967 (dissolved 2000); one s. two d.; m. 2nd Belinda Giles 2000; one s. *Education:* Charterhouse, Christ Church, Oxford, Univs of Paris and Perugia. *Career:* presenter and interviewer BBC Bristol 1960–61; Chair. Dimbleby and Sons Ltd 1986–2001, fmrly Man. Dir 1967. *Broadcasts include:* Quest (religious programme), What's New? (children's science), People and Power 1982–83; General Election Results Programmes 1979, 1983, 1987, 2001, various programmes for the Budget, by-elections, local elections etc.; presenter Question Time BBC 1993–. *Documentary films include:* Ku-Klux-Klan, The Forgotten Million, Cyprus: The Thin Blue Line 1964–65, South Africa: The White Tribe 1979 (Royal TV Soc. Supreme Documentary Award), The Struggle for South Africa 1990 (US Emmy Award, Monte Carlo Golden Nymph), US–UK Relations: An Ocean Apart 1988, David Dimbleby's India 1997; live commentary on many public occasions including: State Opening of Parliament, Trooping the Colour, Wedding of HRH Prince Andrew and Sarah Ferguson, HM The Queen Mother's 90th Birthday Parade (Royal TV Soc. Outstanding Documentary Award), Funeral of Diana, Princess of Wales 1997, Memorial services including Lord Olivier (Royal TV Soc. Outstanding Documentary Award). *Publication:* An Ocean Apart (with David Reynolds) 1988. *Honours:* Richard Dimbleby Award BAFTA 1998. *Address:* 14 King Street, Richmond, Surrey, TW9 1NF, England.

DIMBLEBY, Jonathan, BA; British broadcaster, journalist, writer and farmer; b. 31 July 1944, Aylesbury, Buckinghamshire, England; m. Bel Mooney 1968; one s. one d. *Education:* Univ. Coll. London. *Career:* reporter, BBC Bristol 1969–70, BBC Radio, World at One 1970–71; reporter, This Week, Thames TV 1972–78, 1986–88, TV Eye 1979; reporter, Yorkshire TV, Jonathan Dimbleby in Evidence: The Police (series), The Bomb 1980, The Eagle and the Bear 1981, The Cold War Game 1982, The American Dream 1984, Four Years On – The Bomb 1984; Assoc. Ed./Presenter, First Tuesday 1982–86; Presenter/Ed. Jonathan Dimbleby on Sunday, TV-am 1985–86, On the Record, BBC TV 1988–93, Charles: the Private Man, the Public Role, Central TV 1994, Jonathan Dimbleby, London Weekend Television (LWT) 1995–; Presenter, Any Questions?, BBC Radio 4 1987–, Any Answers? 1989–, main presenter of Gen. Election coverage, ITV 1997; writer/presenter The Last Governor, BBC 1997; An Ethiopian Journey, LWT 1998, A Kosovo Journey, LWT 2000, Michael Heseltine – A Life in the Political Jungle, LWT 2000; Pres. Voluntary Service Overseas 1999–, Soil Assn 1997–, Royal Soc. for the Protection of Birds 2001–, Bath Festivals Trust 2003; Vice-Pres. Council for Protection of Rural England 1997–; Trustee Richard Dimbleby Cancer Fund, One World Broadcasting Trust, Forum for the Future. *Publications:* Richard Dimbleby 1975, The Palestinians 1979, The Prince of Wales: A Biography 1994, The Last Governor 1997. *Honours:* Richard Dimbleby Award 1974. *Literary Agent:* David Higham Associates, Ltd, 5 Lower John Street, Golden Square, London, W1R 4HA, England. *Telephone:* (20) 7437-7888.

DINNERSTEIN, Leonard; Prof. of History and Writer; b. 5 May 1934, New York, NY, USA; m. Myra Anne Rosenberg, 20 Aug. 1961, one s. one d. *Education:* BA, City College, CUNY, 1955; MA, 1960, PhD, 1966, Columbia University. *Career:* Instructor, New York Institute of Technology, 1960–65; Asst Prof., Fairleigh Dickinson University, 1967–70; Assoc. Prof., 1970–72, Prof. of American History, 1972–, University of Arizona, Tucson. *Publications:* The Leo Frank Case, 1968; The Aliens (with F. C. Jaher), 1970, as Uncertain Americans, 1977; American Vistas (with K. T. Jackson), 1971; Antisemitism in the United States, 1971; Jews in the South (with M. D. Palsson), 1973; Decisions and Revisions (with J. Christie), 1975; Ethnic Americans: A History of Immigration and Assimilation (with D. M. Reimers), 1975; Natives and Strangers (with R. L. Nichols and D. M. Reimers), 1979; America and the Survivors of the Holocaust, 1982; Uneasy at Home, 1987; Antisemitism in America, 1994. *Address:* 1981 Miraval Cuarto, Tucson, AZ 85718, USA.

DIRIE, Waris; Somalian writer and model; b. 1964. *Career:* emigrated to London 1978; maid to Somalian ambassador, janitor McDonald's, model; f. Desert Dawn; hon. mem. Club of Budapest; UNFPA special ambassador for women's rights in Africa 1997–. *Publications:* Desert Flower 1998, Desert Dawn 2002. *Address:* c/o Virago Press, Brettenham House, Lancaster Place, London, WC2E 7EN, England. *Telephone:* (20) 7911-8000. *Fax:* (20) 7911-8100.

DISCH, Thomas M(ichael), (Leonie Hargrave, Dobbin Thorpe); Writer, Poet, Dramatist, Librettist and Lecturer; b. 2 Feb. 1940, Des Moines, IA, USA. *Education:* Cooper Union, New York; New York University. *Career:* Lecturer at colleges and universities; Artist-in-Residence, College of William and Mary, 1996; mem. National Book Critics Circle; PEN; Writers Guild. *Publications:* Fiction: The Genocides, 1965; Mankind Under the Leash, 1966; The House That Fear Built (with John Sladek), 1966; Echo Round His Bones, 1967; Black Alice (with John Sladek), 1968; Camp Concentration, 1968; The Prisoner, 1969; 334, 1974; Clara Reeve, 1975; On Wings of Song, 1979; Triplicity, 1980; Neighboring Lives (with Charles Naylor), 1981; The Businessman: A Tale of Terror, 1984; Amnesia 1985; The

M.D.: A Horror Story, 1991; The Priest: A Gothic Romance, 1995. Poetry: The Right Way to Figure Plumbing, 1972; ABCDEFG HIJKLM NOPQRST UVWXYZ, 1981; Orders of the Retina, 1982; Burn This, 1982; Here I Am, There You Are, Where Were We, 1984; Yes, Let's: New and Selected Poetry, 1989; Dark Verses and Light, 1991; The Dark Old House, 1995. Criticism: The Castle of Indolence, 1995; The Dreams Our Stuff is Made of: How Science Fiction Conquered the World, 1998. Other: Short story collections; plays; opera libretti; Children's books. Contributions: many anthologies and periodicals. *Honours:* O. Henry Prizes, 1975, 1979; John W. Campbell Memorial Award, 1980; BSFA Award, 1981. *Address:* Box 226, Barryville, NY 12719, USA.

DISIPIO, Rocco Thomas; Writer; b. 17 Dec. 1949, Philadelphia, Pennsylvania, USA; m. Jane Heeres Newell, 1974, divorced. *Education:* BSc, Police Administration, Michigan State University, 1971. *Publications:* Arcadia Ego, 1995; Darkness Paradise, 1998. Contributions: Exile; Canadian Literary Journal. *Honours:* USA Today Award, 1998.

DISKI, Jenny; British writer; b. 1947, London. *Education:* Univ. Coll. London. *Career:* teacher 1970s–early 1980s; contrib. to The Observer, London Review of Books. *Television writing:* A Fair and Easy Passage, The Ultimate Object of Desire. *Publications:* novels: Nothing Natural 1986, Rainforest 1987, Then Again 1990, Happily Ever After 1991, Monkey's Uncle 1994, The Dream Mistress 1996, Only Human: A Comedy 2000, After These Things 2004; short stories: The Vanishing Princess 1995; essay collections: Don't 1998, A View from the Bed 2001; travel writing: Stranger on a Train: Daydreaming and Smoking Around America with Interruptions 2002; autobiography: Skating to Antarctica 1997. *Honours:* Thomas Cook Travel Book Award 2003. *Address:* c/o Little, Brown & Co., Time Warner Book Group, Brettenham House, Lancaster Place, London, WC2E 7EN, England.

DIVINE, Robert Alexander, BA, MA, PhD; academic and writer; *Professor of American History Emeritus, University of Texas at Austin*; b. 10 May 1929, New York, NY, USA; m. 1st Barbara Christine Renick 1955; three s. one d. (died 1993); m. 2nd Darlene S. Harris 1996 (died 2003). *Education:* Yale Univ. *Career:* Instructor 1954–57, Asst Prof. 1957–61, Assoc. Prof. 1961–63, Prof. 1963–80, George W. Littlefield Prof. of American History 1981–96, Prof. Emeritus 1996–, Univ. of Texas at Austin; Fellow, Center for Advanced Study in the Behavioural Sciences, Stanford 1962–63; Albert Shaw Lecturer, Johns Hopkins Univ. 1968; mem. Soc. for Historians of American Foreign Relations. *Publications:* American Immigration Policy 1924–1952 1957, The Illusion of Neutrality 1962, The Reluctant Belligerent: American Entry into World War II 1965, Second Chance: The Triumph of Internationalism in America During World War II 1967, Roosevelt and World War II 1969, Foreign Policy and US Presidential Elections 1940–1960 (two vols) 1974, Since 1945: Politics and Diplomacy in Recent American History 1975, Blowing on the Wind 1978, Eisenhower and the Cold War 1981, America: Past and Present (with T. H. Breen, George Fredrickson and R. Hal Williams) 1984, America Past and Present (co-author) 1984, The Sputnik Challenge 1993, Perpetual War for Perpetual Peace 2000; editor: American Foreign Policy 1960, The Age of Insecurity: America 1920–1945 1968, Twentieth-Century America: Contemporary Documents and Opinions (with John A. Garraty) 1968, American Foreign Policy Since 1945 1969, Causes and Consequences of World War II 1969, The Cuban Missile Crisis 1971, Exploring the Johnson Years 1981, The Johnson Years: Vol. Two, Vietnam, the Environment and Science 1987, The Johnson Years: Vol. Three, LBJ at Home and Abroad 1994; contrib. to scholarly books and journals. *Honours:* Rockefeller Humanities Fellowship 1976–77, Graduate Teaching Award, Univ. of Texas 1986, Eugene E. Emme Astronautical Literature Award 1993. *Address:* 10617 Sans Souci Place, Austin, TX 78759, USA. *E-mail:* rdivine@austin.rr.com.

DIXON, Roger, (John Christian, Charles Lewis); Author and Playwright; b. 6 Jan. 1930, Portsmouth, England; m. Carolyn Anne Shepheard, 28 June 1966, two s. four d. *Publications:* Noah II, 1970; Christ on Trial, 1973; The Messiah, 1974; Five Gates to Armageddon (as John Christian), 1975; The Cain Factor (as Charles Lewis), 1975; Going to Jerusalem, 1977; Georgiana, 1984; Return to Nebo, 1991. Musical: The Commander of New York (with Phil Medley and Basil Bova), 1987. Other: Over 50 radio plays and series. *Address:* Badgers, Warren Lane, Cross-in-Hand, Heathfield, Sussex, England.

DIXON, Stephen; Writer and University Teacher; b. 6 June 1936, New York, NY, USA; m. Anne Frydman, 17 Jan. 1982, two d. *Education:* BA, City College, CUNY, 1958. *Publications:* No Relief, 1976; Work, 1977; Too Late, 1978; Quite Contrary, 1979; 14 Stories, 1980; Movies, 1983; Time to Go, 1984; Fall and Rise, 1985; Garbage, 1988; Love and Will, 1989; The Play and Other Stories, 1989; All Gone, 1990; Friends, 1990; Frog, 1991; Long Made Short, 1993; The Stories of Stephen Dixon, 1994; Interstate, 1995; Man on Stage, 1996; Gould, 1997; Sleep, 1999; 30, 1999; Tisch, 2000; I., 2002. Contributions: anthologies and periodicals. *Honours:* Stegner Fiction Fellowship, Stanford University, 1964–65; National Endowment of the Arts Grants, 1974–75, 1990–91; American Acad. and Institute of Arts and Letters Award, 1983; John Train Prize, Paris Review, 1984; Guggenheim Fellowship, 1985–86. *Address:* 1315 Boyce Ave, Baltimore, MD 21204, USA.

DJEBAR, Assia, (Fatima-Zohra Imalayen); Algerian novelist, poet, dramatist, film-maker and professor; b. 4 Aug. 1936, Cherchell; m. 1st Ahmed Ould-Rouïs 1958 (divorced); m. 2nd Malek Alloula 1980. *Education:* Lycée Fénélon, Paris 1954, École Normale Supérieure de Sèvres, France 1955–56. *Career:* taught history at University of Algiers; Prof. and Dir Center for French and Francophone Studies, Louisiana State University 1997–. *Publications:* La soif 1957 (English trans. as The Mischief 1958), Les impatients 1958, Women of Islam 1961, Les enfants du nouveau monde 1962, Les alouettes naïves 1967, Poèmes pour l'Algérie heureuse 1969, Rouge l'aube (with Walid Garn) 1969, La nouba des femmes du Mont Chenoua 1969, Les femmes d'Alger dans leur appartement 1980 (English trans. as Women of Algiers in Their Apartment 1992), L'amour la fantasia 1985 (English trans. as Fantasia: An Algerian Cavalcade 1993), Ombre sultane 1987 (English trans. as A Sister to Scheherazade 1987), Loin de Médine 1991 (English trans. as Far from Medina 1994), Chronique d'un été algérien 1993, Le blanc de l'Algérie 1995 (English trans. as Algerian White 2001), Vaste est la prison 1995 (English trans. as So Vast the Prison 1999), Oran, langue morte 1997, Les nuits de Strasbourg 1997, Ces voix qui m'assiègent 1999; other: films: La nouba des femmes du Mont Chenoua 1979, La zerda ou les chants d'oubli 1982. *Honours:* International Critics' Prize, Venice Film Festival 1979, Prix Maurice Maeterlinck 1995, Neustadt International Prize for Literature 1996, Yourcenar Prize 1997, Friedenspreis des Deutschen Buchhandels 2000. *Address:* c/o Center for French and Francophone Studies, Louisiana State University, Baton Rouge, LA 70803, USA.

DJERASSI, Carl; Prof. of Chemistry, Author and Playwright; b. 29 Oct. 1923, Vienna, Austria; m. Diane Wood Middlebrook, 20 June 1985, one s. *Education:* AB summa cum laude, Kenyon College, 1942; PhD, University of Wisconsin, 1945. *Career:* Assoc. Prof., 1952–53, Prof. of Chemistry, 1953–59, Wayne State University; Prof. of Chemistry, Stanford University, 1959–; mem. National Acad. of Sciences; American Acad. of Arts and Sciences; Swedish, German, Brazilian and Mexican Academies of Science; Royal Society of Chemistry. *Publications:* Optical Rotatory Dispersion, 1959; Steroid Reactions, 1963; Mass Spectrometry of Organic Compounds (with H. Budzikiewicz and D. H. Williams), 1967; The Politics of Contraception, 1979; The Futurist and Other Stories, 1988; Cantor's Dilemma (novel), 1989; Steroids Made It Possible, 1990; The Clock Runs Backward (poems), 1991; The Pill, Pygmy Chimps, and Degas' Horse (autobiog.), 1992; The Bourbaki Gambit (novel), 1994; From the Lab into the World (collected essays), 1994; Marx, Deceased (novel), 1996; Menachem's Seed (novel), 1997; NO (novel), 1998; This Man's Pill (memoir), 2001. Plays: An Immaculate Misconception, 1998; Oxygen (with Roald Hoffmann), 2000; ICSI: A Pedagogic Wordplay for Two Voices, 2002; Calculus (Newton's Whores), 2002; NO: A Pedagogic Wordplay for Three Voices (with Pierre Laszlo), 2003. Unpublished Play: Ego, 2003. Contributions: Kenyon Review; Southern Review; Grand Street; New Letters; Exquisite Corpse; Michigan Quarterly Review; South Dakota Review; Frank; Midwest Quarterly. *Honours:* National Medal of Science, 1973; National Medal of Technology, 1991. *Address:* Dept of Chemistry, Stanford University, Stanford, CA 94305-5080, USA. *E-mail:* djerassi@stanford.edu. *Website:* www.djerassi.com.

DOBAI, Péter, DipEd; writer, poet and screenwriter; b. 12 Aug. 1944, Budapest, Hungary; m. 1st Donatella Failioni 1972; m. 2nd Maria Mate 1992. *Education:* University of Budapest. *Career:* mem. Hungarian Acad. of Artists; Hungarian Writers' Assn, Exec. Board; PEN Club, Hungary. *Publications:* fiction: Csontmolnárok 1974, Tartozó élet 1975, Lavina 1980, Vadon 1982, Háromszögtan 1983, A birodalom ezredese 1985, Iv 1988, Lendkerék 1989; short story collections: Játék a szobákkal 1976, Sakktábla két figurával 1978; poetry: Kilovaglás egy öszi erödböl 1973, Egy arc módosulásai 1976, Hanyatt 1978, Az éden vermei 1985, Válogatott versek 1989, Vitorlák emléke 1994, Önmúltszázad 1996, Versek egyelnémult klavírra 2002, Ma könnyebb. Holnap messzebb 2004; essays: Augyali agresszió 2002; 15 screenplays 1971–95. *Honours:* József Attila Prize, 1976; several awards, Hungarian Literary Foundation and Minister of Culture; various screenplay awards. *Address:* Közraktár u 12/B, 1093 Budapest, Hungary.

DOBBS, Michael John; Author; b. 14 Nov. 1948, England. *Education:* MA, University of Oxford, 1968–71; MALD, PhD, Fletcher School of Law and Diplomacy, USA, 1971–75. *Career:* Deputy Chair., Saatchi and Saatchi, 1983–91, Conservative Party, 1994–95. *Publications:* House of Cards, 1989; Wall Games, 1990; Last Man to Die, 1991; To Play the King, 1992; The Touch of Innocents, 1994; The Final Cut, 1995; Goodfellowe M.P., 1997; The Buddha of Brewer Street, 1998; Winston's War, 2002; Never Surrender, 2003. Contributions: Mail on Sunday. *Address:* c/o HarperCollins Publishers, 77–85 Fulham Palace Rd, Hammersmith, London W6 8JB, England.

DOBSON, Andrew (Nicholas Howard); Prof. of Politics and Writer; b. 15 April 1957, Doncaster, England. *Education:* BA, Politics, Reading University, 1979; DPhil, Politics, University of Oxford, 1983. *Career:* Editorial Board, Environmental Values, 1991–, Environmental Politics, 1991–, Anarchist Studies, 1991–; Lecturer in Politics, 1983–93, Chair of Politics, Keele University, 1993–2001; Chair of Politics, Open Univ., 2001–; Chair, Editorial Board, Environmental Politics. *Publications:* An Introduction to the Politics and Philosophy of José Ortega y Gasset, 1989; Green Political Thought, 1990; The Green Reader: Essays Toward a Sustainable Society (ed.), 1991; The Politics of Nature: Explorations in Green Political Theory (ed. with Paul Lucardie), 1993; Jean-Paul Sartre and the Politics of Reason: A Theory of History, 1993; Justice and the Environment: Conceptions of Environmental Sustainability and Theories of Distributive Justice, 1998; Fairness and Futurity: Essays on Environmental Sustainability and Social Justice, 1999; Citizenship and the Environment, 2003. Contributions: numerous articles and book reviews to magazines and journals. *Honours:* Spanish Government Scholar, 1983–84; Postdoctoral Fellow, Economic and Social Science Research Council, 1984–87. *Address:* Open University, Walton Hall, Milton Keynes MK7 6AA, England.

DOBSON, Joanne; writer and academic; b. 27 March 1942, New York, NY, USA; m. David Eugene Dobson 1963; one s. two d. *Education:* BA, King's College, Briarcliff Manor, New York, 1963; MA, SUNY at Albany, 1977; PhD, University of Massachusetts at Amherst, 1985. *Career:* Founding Mem., 1983–93, Mem., Editorial Board, 1993–96, Legacy: Journal of American Women Writers; General Co-ed., American Women Writers reprint series, Rutgers University Press, 1984–92; Visiting Prof. of English and American Studies, Amherst College, Amherst, Massachusetts, 1985–86; Visiting Asst Prof. of English, Tufts University, Medford, Massachusetts, 1986–87; Asst Prof., 1987–92, Assoc. Prof. of English, 1992–, Fordham University, Bronx, New York; Mem., Editorial Board, American Literature, 1995–97; mem. Founding Mem., Emily Dickinson International Society, Mem., Board of Dirs, 1988–91. *Publications:* The Hidden Hand (ed.), 1988; Dickinson and the Strategies of Reticence: The Woman Writer in Nineteenth-Century America, 1989; Quieter than Sleep (novel), 1997; The Northbury Papers (novel), 1998; The Raven and the Nightingale (novel), 1999; Cold and Pure and Very Dead (novel), 2000. Contributions: periodicals including American Quarterly. *Literary Agent:* Deborah Schneider, Gelfman Schneider, 250 W 57th Street, New York, NY 10107, USA. *Address:* Department of English, Fordham University, Bronx, NY 10458, USA. *E-mail:* dedcons@aol.com.

DOBSON, Rosemary de Brissac, AO; Australian writer, poet and editor; b. 18 June 1920, Sydney, NSW; m. Alexander Thorley Bolton 1951; two s. one d. *Education:* Frensham School (Mittagong, NSW) and Univ. of Sydney. *Career:* teacher of Art; mem. Editorial Dept Angus and Robertson Publrs, Sydney; freelance writer 1951–. *Publications:* In a Convex Mirror 1944, The Ship of Ice and Other Poems 1948, Child with a Cockatoo and Other Poems 1955, Australian Poets: Rosemary Dobson 1963, Cock Crow 1965, Songs for all Seasons 1968, Focus on Ray Crooke (prose) 1971, Selected Poems 1973, Moscow Trefoil (jtly) 1975, Greek Coins: A Sequence of Poems 1977, Australian Voices (ed.) 1978, Over the Frontier 1978, Seven Russian Poets (jtly) 1979, Selected Poems 1980, The Three Fates and Other Poems 1984, Summer Press 1987, Collected Poems 1991, Untold Lives: A Sequence of Poems 1992, Untold Lives and Later Poems 2000. *Honours:* Hon. DLitt (Sydney) 1996; Officer Order of Australia for Services to Literature 1987; Robert Frost Prize 1979, Sr Literary Fellowship Australia Council 1980, Patrick White Award for Literature 1984, Grace Leven Prize for Poetry 1984, Victoria Premier's Literary Awards for Poetry (jtly) 1985, Australia Council Emer. Award 1996, Age Book of the Year Award 2000. *Literary Agent:* Curtis Brown Pty Ltd, POB 19, Paddington, NSW 2021, Australia. *Address:* 61 Stonehaven Crescent, Deakin, ACT 2600, Australia (Home). *Telephone:* (6) 281 1436 (Home). *Fax:* (6) 281 5842 (Home).

DOBYNS, Stephen; Professor of Creative Writing, Poet and Writer; b. 19 Feb. 1941, Orange, NJ, USA; m., three c. *Education:* Shimer College, Mount Carroll, IL, 1959–60; BA, Wayne State University, 1964; MFA, University of Iowa, 1967. *Career:* Instructor, SUNY at Brockport, 1968–69; Reporter, Detroit News, 1969–71; Visiting Writer, University of New Hampshire, 1973–75, University of Iowa, 1977–79, Boston University, 1978–79, 1980–81, Syracuse University, 1986; Faculty, Goddard College, Plainfield, Vermont, 1978–80, Warren Wilson College, Swannanoa, NC, 1982–87; Prof. of Creative Writing, Syracuse University, New York, 1987–. *Publications:* Poetry: Concurring Beasts, 1972; Griffon, 1976; Heat Death, 1980; The Balthus Poems, 1982; Black Dog, Red Dog, 1984; Cemetery Nights, 1987; Body Traffic, 1991; Velocities: New and Selected Poems, 1966–1992, 1994; Common Carnage, 1996; Pallbearers Envying the One Who Rides, 1999. Fiction: A Man of Little Evils, 1973; Saratoga Longshot, 1976; Saratoga Swimmer, 1981; Dancer with One Leg, 1983; Saratoga Headhunter, 1985; Cold Dog Soup, 1985; Saratoga Snapper, 1986; A Boat Off the Coast, 1987; The Two Deaths of Señora Puccini, 1988; Saratoga Bestiary, 1988; The House of Alexandrine, 1989; Saratoga Hexameter, 1990; After Shocks/Near Escapes, 1991; Saratoga Haunting, 1993; The Wrestler's Cruel Study, 1993; Saratoga Backtalk, 1994; Saratoga Fleshpot, 1995; Saratoga Trifecta, 1995; The Church of Dead Girls, 1997; Saratoga Strongbox, 1998; Boy in the Water, 1999; Eating Naked, 2000. *Honours:* Lamont Poetry Selection Award, 1971; MacDowell Colony Fellowships, 1972, 1976; Yaddo Fellowships, 1972, 1973, 1977, 1981, 1982; National Endowment for the Arts Grants, 1974, 1981; Guggenheim Fellowship, 1983; National Poetry Series Prize, 1984. *Address:* c/o Bloodaxe Books Ltd, Highgreen, Tarset, Northumberland NE48 1RP, England.

DOCHERTY, John (see Sills-Docherty, Jonathan John).

DOCTOROW, Edgar Lawrence, AB; American novelist and dramatist; b. 6 Jan. 1931, New York; m. Helen Esther Setzer 1954; one s. two d. *Education:* Kenyon Coll., Gambier, Ohio, Columbia Univ. *Career:* served with US army 1953–55; Script Reader Columbia Pictures 1959; Ed. New American Library, New York 1960–64; Ed.-in-Chief Dial Press., New York 1964–69, Publr 1969; writer-in-residence Univ. of Calif., Irvine 1969–70; mem. faculty Sarah Lawrence Coll., Bronxville, NY 1971–78; Creative Writing Fellow Yale School of Drama 1974–75; Creative Artists Program Service Fellow 1973–74; Visiting Sr Fellow Council on Humanities, Princeton Univ. 1980–81, Prof. of English 1982–87; Gluckman Prof. of American and English Letters, New York Univ. 1987–; mem. Authors Guild (dir), American PEN (dir), Writers Guild of America East, Century Asscn; Guggenheim Fellow 1973. *Publications:* Welcome to Hard Times 1960, Big as Life 1966, The Book of Daniel 1971, Ragtime 1975, Drinks before Dinner (play) 1975, Loon Lake 1980, Lives of the Poets: Six Stories and a Novella 1984, World's Fair 1985, Billy Bathgate 1988, Jack London, Hemingway and the Constitution: Selected Essays 1977–92 1993, The Waterworks 1994, Poets and Presidents: Selected Essays 1994, The Best American Short Stories (ed. with Katrina Kenison) 2000, City of God 2000, Sweet Land Stories 2004, Reporting the Universe 2004. *Honours:* Hon. LHD (Kenyon Coll.) 1976, (Hobart Coll.) 1979; Arts and Letters Award (American Acad. and Nat. Inst. Art) 1976, Nat. Book Critics Circle Award 1976, 1982, 1990, Guggenheim Fellow 1973, American Book Award 1986, William Dean Howells Medal, American Acad. of Arts and Letters 1990, PEN/Faulkner Prize 1990, Nat. Humanities Medal 1998, Commonwealth Award 2000. *Literary Agent:* International Creative Management, 40 W 57th Street, New York, NY 10022. *Address:* English Department, New York University, 19 University Place, Second Floor, New York, NY 10003; c/o Random House Publishers, 210 E 50th Street, New York, NY 10022, USA (Office).

DODD, Wayne Donald, BA, MA, PhD; poet, writer, editor and academic; b. 23 Sept. 1930, Clarita, OK, USA; m. 1st Betty Coshow 1958 (divorced 1980); m. 2nd Joyce Barlow 1981; two c. *Education:* University of Oklahoma. *Career:* Instructor, 1960–64, Asst Prof. of English, 1964–68, University of Colorado at Boulder; Fellow, Center for Advanced Studies, Wesleyan University, 1964; Assoc. Prof., 1968–73, Prof. of English, 1973–94, Edwin and Ruth Kennedy Distinguished Prof. of Poetry, 1994–2001, Prof. Emeritus, 2001–, Ohio University; Ed., Ohio Review, 1971–2001; mem. Associated Writing Programs. *Publications:* poetry: We Will Wear White Roses, 1974; Made in America, 1975; The Names You Gave It, 1980; The General Mule Poems, 1981; Sometimes Music Rises, 1986; Echoes of the Unspoken, 1990; Of Desire and Disorder, 1994; The Blue Salvages, 1998; Is 2003. Fiction: A Time of Hunting, 1975. Other: Poets on the Line (ed.), 1987; Toward the End of the Century: Essays into Poetry, 1992; Art and Nature: Essays by Contemporary Writers (ed.), 1993; Mentors (ed.), 1994. Contributions: anthologies, reviews, quarterlies and journals. *Honours:* ACLS Fellowship, 1964–65; Ohio Arts Council Fellowships, 1980, 1989, 1998; National Endowment for the Arts Fellowship in Poetry, 1982; Krout Award for Lifetime Achievement in Poetry, Ohioana Library Foundation, 1991; Rockefeller Foundation Fellowship, 1995; Ohio Gov.'s Award for the Arts, 2001. *Address:* 11292 Peach Ridge Road, Athens, OH 45701, USA.

DOHERTY, Berlie; Writer, Dramatist and Poet; b. 6 Nov. 1943, Liverpool, England; m. Gerard Doherty, 17 Dec. 1966, divorced 1996, one s. two d. *Education:* BA, English, Durham University, 1964; Postgraduate Certificate, Social Studies, Liverpool University, 1965; Postgraduate Certificate, Education, Sheffield University, 1976. *Career:* mem. Arvon Foundation, Lumb Bank, chair., 1988–93. *Publications:* Fiction: Requiem, 1991; The Vinegar Jar, 1994. Children's Books: How Green You Are, 1982; The Making of Fingers Finnigan, 1983; White Peak Farm, 1984; Children of Winter, 1985; Granny Was a Buffer Girl, 1986; Tilly Mint Tales, 1986; Tilly Mint and the Dodo, 1988; Paddiwak and Cosy, 1988; Tough Luck, 1988; Spellhorn, 1989; Dear Nobody, 1990; Snowy, 1992; Big, Bulgy, Fat Black Slug, 1993; Old Father Christmas, 1993; Street Child, 1993; Walking on Air (poems), 1993; Willa and Old Miss Annie, 1994; The Snake-Stone, 1995; The Golden Bird, 1995; Dear Nobody (play), 1995; The Magical Bicycle, 1995; Our Field, 1996; Morgan's Field (play), 1996; Daughter of the Sea, 1996. Contributions: periodicals. *Honours:* Boston Globe-Horn Book Award, 1987; Burnley Children's Book of the Year Award, 1987; Carnegie Medals, 1987, 1991; Writer's Guild of Great Britain Children's Play Award, 1994.

DOLIS, John, BA, MA, PhD; academic, writer and poet; *Associate Professor of English, Pennsylvania State University;* b. 25 April 1945, St Louis, MO, USA. *Education:* St Louis Univ., Loyola Univ., Chicago. *Career:* Teaching Asst 1967–69, 1970–73, Lecturer 1974–75, 1978–80, Loyola Univ., Chicago; Instructor, Columbia Coll. 1970–71, Northeastern Illinois Univ. 1978–80, Univ. of Kansas 1981–85; Fulbright Lecturer, Univ. of Turin 1980–81; Asst Prof. 1985–92, Assoc. Prof. 1992–, Pennsylvania State Univ., Scranton; Sr Fulbright Lecturer, Univ. of Bucharest 1989–90; Visiting Prof. of American Culture and Literature, Bilkent Univ., Ankara 1995–96; mem. editorial bd, Antemnae, Arizona Quarterly, Nathaniel Hawthorne Review; mem. American Culture Asscn, American Literature Asscn, American Philosophical Asscn, Asscn for Applied Psychoanalysis, Int. Asscn for Philosophy and Literature, Int. Husserl and Phenomenological Research Soc., Int. Soc. for Phenomenology and the Human Sciences, Int. Soc. for Phemomenology and Literature, MLA, Nathaniel Hawthorne Soc., Nat. Social Science Asscn, Soc. for the Advancement of American Philosophy, Soc. for Phenomenology and Existential Philosophy, Soc. for Philosophy and Psychiatry, Soc. for Romanian Studies, Thoreau Soc., World Phenomenology Inst. *Publications:* The Style of Hawthorne's Gaze: Regarding Subjectivity 1993, Bl( )nk Space 1993, Time Flies: Butterflies 1999, Tracking Thoreau: Double-Crossing

Nature and Technology 2005; contrib. articles in scholarly journals, poems in anthologies and magazines. *Honours:* Nat. Endowment for the Humanities Fellowships 1979, 1988, Pharmakon Research Int. Award for Excellence in Scholarly Activities, Pennsylvania State Univ. 1991, various grants. *Address:* 711 Summit Pointe, Scranton, PA 18508, USA. *E-mail:* jjd3@psu.edu.

DOLL, Mary Aswell; Prof. of English; b. 4 June 1940, New York, NY, USA; m. William Elder Doll Jr, 25 June 1966, divorced 1994, one s. *Education:* BA, Connecticut College, New London, 1962; MA, Johns Hopkins University, 1970; PhD, Syracuse University, 1980. *Career:* Asst Prof., SUNY at Oswego, 1978–84; Lecturer, University of Redlands, CA, 1985–88; Asst Prof., Loyola University, 1988; Visiting Asst Prof., Tulane University, 1988; Assoc. Prof., 1989–93, Prof., 1993–, Our Lady of Holy Cross College; Prof., Savannah College of Art and Design; mem. MLA; Pres., Thomas Wolfe Society; American Acad. of Religion. *Publications:* Rites of Story: The Old Man at Play, 1987; Beckett and Myth: An Archetypal Approach, 1988; In the Shadow of the Giant: Thomas Wolfe, 1988; Walking and Rocking, 1989; Joseph Campbell and the Power of the Wilderness, 1992; Stoppard's Theatre of Unknowing, 1993; To the Lighthouse and Back, 1996; Like Letters in Running Water: A Mythopoetics of Curriculum, 2000. Contributions: periodicals. *Honours:* Outstanding Book Citation Choice, 1989; Sears-Roebuck Teaching Excellence Award. *Address:* 527 E 56th St, Savannah, GA 31405, USA.

DOLLIMORE, Jonathan; Prof. of English and Writer; b. 31 July 1948, Leighton Buzzard, England. *Education:* BA, University of Keele, 1974; PhD, University of London, 1984. *Career:* Lecturer, 1976–89, Senior Lecturer, 1989–90, Reader, 1990–93, Prof. of English, 1993–95, School of English and American Studies, Prof., Graduate Research Centre for the Humanities, 1995–99, University of Sussex; Visiting Fellow, Humanities Research Centre, Canberra, 1988, Human Sciences Research Council of South Africa, 1996; Mellon Fellow, National Humanities Center, NC, 1988–89; Scholar-in-Residence, Centre for Renaissance and Baroque Studies, University of Maryland, 1991–92; Cecil and Ida Green Visiting Prof., University of British Columbia, 1997; Prof. of English, University of York, 1999–; Visiting Prof., LeHigh University, University of Oregon and University of Tel-Aviv, 2002. *Publications:* The Selected Plays of John Webster (ed. with Alan Sinfield), 1983; Radical Tragedy: Religion, Ideology and Power in the Drama of Shakespeare and his Contemporaries, 1984; Political Shakespeare: New Essays in Cultural Materialism (ed. with Alan Sinfield), 1985; Sexual Dissidence: Augustine to Wilde, Freud to Foucault, 1991; Death, Desire and Loss in Western Culture, 1998; Sex, Literature and Censorship, 2001. Contributions: many scholarly books and journals. *Address:* c/o Dept of English and Related Literature, University of York, Heslington, York YO10 5DD, England.

DOMMISSE, Ebbe; Newspaper Editor; b. 14 July 1940, Riversdale, South Africa; m. Daléne Laubscher 1963; two s. one d. *Education:* Paarl Boys High School; BA, Univ. of Stellenbosch; MSc, Graduate School of Journalism, Columbia Univ. *Career:* reporter, Die Burger, Cape Town 1961, Chief sub-ed. 1968, News Ed. 1971; Asst Ed. and political commentator, Beeld, Johannesburg (founder mem. of new Johannesburg daily) 1974; Asst Ed. Die Burger 1979, Sr Asst Ed. 1984, Ed. 1990–; mem. Exec. mem., Nasionale Koerante; Trustee, Helpmekaarfonds; Akad. vir Wetenskap en Kuns. *Publications:* Broedertwis (with Alf Ries), 1982; Leierstryd (with Alf Ries), 1990. *Honours:* Nieman Travel Fellowship, 1987. *Address:* Die Burger, 40 Heerengracht, PO Box 692, Cape Town 8000, South Africa.

DONALD, David Herbert; Prof. of History Emeritus and Author; b. 1 Oct. 1920, Goodman, Mississippi, USA; m. Aida DiPace, 1955, one s. *Education:* AB, Millsaps College, Jackson, Mississippi, 1941; Graduate Study in History, University of North Carolina, 1942; MA, 1942, PhD, 1945, in History, University of Illinois. *Career:* Instructor, 1947–49, Asst Prof., 1951–52, Assoc. Prof., 1952–57, Prof. of History, 1957–59, Columbia University; Assoc. Prof. of History, Smith College, 1949–51; Visiting Assoc. Prof., Amherst College, 1950; Fulbright Lecturer in American History, University College of North Wales, 1953–54; Mem., Institute for Advanced Study, 1957–58; Harmsworth Prof. of American History, University of Oxford, 1959–60; Prof. of History, Princeton University, 1959–62; Harry C. Black Prof. of American History and Dir of the Institute of Southern History, Johns Hopkins University, 1962–73; Charles Warren Prof. of American History and Prof. of American Civilization, 1973–91, Prof. Emeritus, 1991–, Harvard University; mem. American Acad. of Arts and Sciences, fellow; American Antiquarian Society; American Historical Asscn; Massachusetts Historical Asscn; Organization of American Historians; Southern Historical Asscn, pres., 1969; Hon. doctorates. *Publications:* Lincoln's Herndon, 1948; Divided We Fought: A Pictorial History of the War, 1861–1865, 1952; Inside Lincoln's Cabinet: The Civil War Diaries of Salmon P. Chase, 1954; Lincoln Reconsidered: Essays on the Civil War Era, 1956; Charles Sumner and the Coming of the Civil War, 1960; Why the North Won the Civil War, 1960; The Civil War and Reconstruction (with J. G. Randall), second edn, 1961; The Divided Union, 1961; The Politics of Reconstruction, 1863–1867, 1965; The Nation in Crisis, 1861–1877, 1969; Charles Sumner and the Rights of Man, 1970; The South Since the War (with Sidney Andrews), 1970; Gone for a Soldier: The Civil War Memoirs of Private Alfred Bellard, 1975; The Great Republic: A History of the American People (with others), 1977; Liberty and Union: The Crisis of Popular Government, 1830–1890, 1978; Look Homeward: A Life of Thomas Wolfe, 1987; Lincoln, 1995. Contributions: scholarly journals. *Honours:* Pulitzer Prizes in Biography, 1960, 1988; Guggenheim Fellowships, 1964–65, 1985–86; C. Hugh Holman Prize, MLA, 1988; Distinguished Alumnus Award, University of Illinois, 1988; Benjamin L. C. Wailes Award, Mississippi Historical Society, 1994; Lincoln Prize, 1996; Christopher Award, 1996; Distinguished Non-Fiction Award, American Library Asscn, 1996. *Address:* 41 Lincoln Rd, PO Box 6158, Lincoln, MA 01773, USA.

DONALDSON, (Charles) Ian Edward; academic and writer; b. 6 May 1935, Melbourne, Vic., Australia; m. 1st Tasmin Jane Procter 1962 (divorced 1990); one s. one d.; m. 2nd Grazia Maria Therese Gunn 1991. *Education:* BA, University of Melbourne, 1958; BA, 1960, MA, 1964, Magdalen College, Oxford. *Career:* Senior Tutor in English, 1958, Visiting appointment, 1991, University of Melbourne; Harmsworth Senior Scholar, Merton College, Oxford, 1960–62; Fellow and Lecturer in English, Wadham College, Oxford, 1962–69; CUF Lecturer in English, University of Oxford, 1963–69; Visiting appointments, University of California at Santa Barbara, 1967–68, Gonville and Caius College, Cambridge, 1985, Cornell University, 1988, Folger Shakespeare Library, Washington, DC, 1988; Prof. of English, 1969–91, Foundation Dir, Humanities Research Centre, 1974–90, Australian National University, Canberra, Interim Dir 2004–; Regius Prof. of Rhetoric and English Literature, University of Edinburgh, 1991–95; Grace I Prof. of English King's College Cambridge 1995–2002, Dir Centre for Research in the Arts, Social Sciences and Humanities 2001–03, Fellow 1995–2004. *Publications:* The World Upside Down: Comedy From Jonson to Fielding, 1970; Ben Jonson: Poems (ed.), 1975; The Rapes of Lucretia: A Myth and its Transformations, 1982; Jonson and Shakespeare (ed.), 1983; Transformations in Modern European Drama (ed.), 1983; Seeing the First Australians (ed. with Tasmin Donaldson), 1985; Ben Jonson, 1985; Shaping Lives: Reflections on Biography (co-ed.), 1992; Jonson's Walk to Scotland, 1993; The Death of the Author and the Life of the Poet, 1995; Ben Jonson: Selected Poems (ed.), 1995; Jonson's Magic Houses, 1997. Contributions: scholarly journals. *Honours:* Fellow Australian Acad. of the Humanities 1975; Fellow British Acad. 1993 (Corresponding Fellow 1987); Fellow Royal Society of Edinburgh 1993. *Address:* 11 Grange Road, Cambridge CB3 9AS, England.

DONALDSON, Julia; British children's writer and teacher; b. 1948, London. *Education:* Univ. of Bristol. *Career:* children's songwriter for BBC TV and radio. *Plays:* All Aboard 1995, Problem Page 2000, High Impact 2000, Bombs and Blackberries 2003. *Publications:* juvenile fiction: A Squash and a Squeeze 1993, The Magic Twig 1995, Mr Snow 1996, Spacegirl Sue 1996, Storyworlds 1997, Books and Crooks 1998, Waiter! Waiter! 1998, The Brownie King 1998, The Gruffalo 1999, Rabbit's Nap 2000, Hide and Seek Pig 2000, Fox's Socks 2000, Monkey Puzzle 2000, Postman Bear 2000, Blue Banana 2002, Night Monkey Day Monkey 2002, Room on the Broom 2002, Spinderella 2002, The Dinosaur's Diary 2002, Princess Mirror-Belle 2003, The Smartest Giant in Town 2003, The Spiffiest Giant in Town 2003, Chameleons: Brick-a-Breck 2003, Conjuror Cow 2003, The Magic Paintbrush 2003, The Snail and the Whale 2003, The Wrong Kind of Bark 2004, One Ted Falls Out of Bed 2004, Crazy Mayonnaisy Mum 2004, Sharing a Shell 2004, The Gruffalo's Child 2004, Wriggle and Roar!: Rhymes to Join in With 2004, Rose's Hat 2005, Princess Mirror-Belle 2 2005, Chocolate Mousse for Greedy Goose 2005, Hippo Has a Hat 2005. *Address:* Macmillan Children's Books, 25 Eccleston Place, London, SW1W 9NF, England. *Website:* www.macmillan.co.uk.

DONALDSON, Stephen Reeder, (Reed Stephens), BA, MA; American writer; b. 13 May 1947, Cleveland, OH; m. 1st (divorced); m. 2nd Stephanie 1980; one s. one d. *Education:* Coll. of Wooster, Kent State Univ. *Career:* Assoc. Instructor, Ghost Ranch Writers' Workshops 1973–77; Contributing Ed., Journal of the Fantastic in the Arts; mem. Int. Asscn for the Fantastic in the Arts. *Publications:* Thomas Covenant series: The Chronicles of Thomas Covenant the Unbeliever, Vol. I Lord Foul's Bane 1977, Vol. 2 The Illearth War 1977, Vol. 3 The Power that Preserves 1977; The Second Chronicles of Thomas Covenant, Vol. 1 The Wounded Land 1980, Vol. 2 The One Tree 1982, Vol. 3 White Gold Wielder 1983; The Last Chronicles of Thomas Covenant, Vol. I The Runes of the Earth 2004; Mordant's Need, Vol. 1 The Mirror of Her Dreams 1986, Vol. 2 A Man Rides Through 1987; the Gap sequence: The Gap Into Conflict: The Real Story 1991, The Gap Into Vision: Forbidden Knowledge 1991, The Gap Into Power: A Dark and Hungry God Arises 1992, The Gap Into Madness: Chaos and Order 1994, The Gap Into Ruin: This Day All Gods Die 1996; other novels: Gilden-Fire 1982, Daughter of Regals and Other Tales 1984, Reave the Just and Other Tales 1999, The Man Who Fought Alone 2001; as Reed Stephens: The Man Who Killed His Brother 1980, The Man Who Risked His Partner 1984, The Man Who Tried to Get Away 1990; editor: Strange Dreams: Unforgettable Fantasy Stories 1993; contrib. to magazines. *Honours:* Hon. DLitt (Coll. of Wooster) 1993; British Fantasy Soc. Best Novel Award 1978, World Science Fiction Convention John W. Campbell Award 1979, Balrog Awards 1981, 1983, 1985, Saturn Award 1983. *Literary Agent:* Howard Morhaim Literary Agency, 841 Broadway, Suite 604, New York, NY 10003, USA. *Website:* www.stephendonaldson.com.

DONALDSON, William, MA, PhD; teacher and writer; b. 19 July 1944, Ellon; two s. one d. *Education:* Aberdeen University. *Career:* Registrar of the North East Survey; Teacher of English; Assoc. Lecturer, Open University.

Publications: Popular Literature in Victorian Scotland 1986, The Jacobite Song 1988, The Language of the People 1989, The Highland Pipe and Scottish Society 2000, Pipers: A Guide to the Players and Music of the Highland Bagpipe 2003. *Honours:* Blackwell Prize 1988, Scottish Arts Council Book Award 1989, Piper & Drummer Online Award 2000. *Address:* c/o Tuckwell Press, The Mill House, Phantassie, East Linton EH40 3DG, Scotland.

DONGLI JIEFU (see Zhang Changxin).

DONLEAVY, James Patrick; Irish writer and dramatist; b. 23 April 1926, New York, NY, USA; m. 1st Valerie Heron (divorced); one s. one d.; m. 2nd Mary Wilson Price (divorced); one s. one d. *Education:* Trinity College, Dublin. *Publications:* fiction: The Ginger Man 1955, A Singular Man 1963, Meet My Maker the Mad Molecule (short stories) 1964, The Saddest Summer of Samuel S 1966, The Beastly Beatitudes of Balthazar B 1968, The Onion Eaters 1971, A Fairy Tale of New York 1973, The Destinies of Darcy Dancer, Gentleman 1977, Schultz 1979, Leila: Further in the Destinies of Darcy Dancer, Gentleman 1983, Are You Listening Rabbi Löw? 1987, That Darcy, That Dancer, That Gentleman 1990, The Lady Who Liked Clean Rest Rooms 1996; plays: The Ginger Man 1961, Fairy Tales of New York 1961, A Singular Man 1964, The Plays of J. P. Donleavy 1973, The Beastly Beatitudes of Balthazar B 1981; other: What They Did In Dublin with The Ginger Man 1961, Meet My Maker the Mad Molecule (short stories) 1964, The Unexpurgated Code: A Complete Manual of Survival and Manners 1975, De Alfonce Tennis: The Superlative Game of Eccentric Champions, Its History, Accoutrements, Rules, Conduct, and Regimes 1984, J. P. Donleavy's Ireland: In All Her Sins and in Some of Her Graces 1986, A Singular Country 1989, The History of the Ginger Man 1994, The Wrong Information is Being Given Out at Princeton 1998, Prince Charming (memoirs) 1999. Contributions: periodicals. *Honours:* Most Promising Playwright Award, Evening Standard, 1960; Brandeis University Creative Arts Award, 1961–62; American Acad. of Arts and Letters Grant, 1975; Worldfest Houston Gold Award, 1992; Cine Golden Eagle Award, 1993. *Address:* Levington Park, Mullingar, County Westmeath, Ireland.

DONNELLY, Jennifer; American writer; b. Portchester, NY; m.; one d. *Education:* Univ. of Rochester. *Career:* fmr antiques dealer, reporter, copywriter. *Publications:* fiction: The Tea Rose 2002; juvenile: Humble Pie 2002, A Gathering Light (aka A Northern Light) (Carnegie Medal 2004) 2003. *Honours:* Printz Honor Award, Borders Original Voices Young Adult Prize. *Address:* c/o Bloomsbury Publishing PLC, 38 Soho Square, London, W1D 3HB, England. *E-mail:* jen@jenniferdonnelly.com. *Website:* www.jenniferdonnelly.com.

DONNER, Jörn Johan; Writer, Film Dir, Politician and Diplomat; b. 5 Feb. 1933, Helsinki, Finland; m. 1st Inga-Britt Wik 1954 (divorced 1962); m. 2nd Jeanette Bonnier 1974 (divorced 1988); m. 3rd Bitte Westerlund 1995; five s. one d. *Education:* BA, Helsinki Univ., 1959. *Career:* worked as writer and film dir, Finland and Sweden, writing own film scripts; Dir of many films and some television series; Co-Ed., Arena, 1951–54; Co-f., Finnish Film Archive, 1957; film critic, Swedish newspaper Dagens Nyheter, 1961; CEO, Jörn Donner Productions, 1966–; Dir, Swedish Film Institute, Stockholm, 1972–75, Exec. Prod., 1975–78, Man. Dir, 1978–82; Host of TV talk show (Sweden and Finland), 1974–95; Chair. Bd, Finnish Film Foundation, 1981–83, 1986–89, 1992–95; mem. Bd, Marimekko Textiles and other cos; mem., Helsinki City Council, 1969–1972, 1984–92; MP, 1987–95; Vice-Chair., Foreign Affairs Cttee, 1991–95; Chair., Finnish EFTA Parliamentarians, 1991–95; Consul-Gen. of Finland, Los Angeles, 1995–96; mem., European Parliament, 1996–99. *Publications:* Välsignade Liv, 1951; Slå Dig Inte Till Ro, 1952; Brev, 1954; Jag, Erik Anders, 1955; Bordet, 1957; Rapport Från Berlin (Report From Berlin), 1958; På Ett Sjukhus, 1960; Helsingfors Finlands Ansikte, 1961; Djävulens Ansikte. Ingmar Bergmans Filmer, 1962; Rapport Från Donau (Report From The Danube), 1962; Nya Boken om Vårt Land, 1967; Världsboken, 1968; Tapaus Naisenkuvia, 1970; Sommar av Kärkek Och Sorg, 1971; Marina Maria, 1972; Sverigeboken, 1973; Nu Måste Du, 1974; Angelas Krig, 1976; Sagt och Gjort, 1976; Jakob och Friheten, 1978; Ihmisen Ääni, 1980; Jag, Jörn Johan Donner, Född den 5 Februari 1933 i Helsingfors, 1980; Angela och Kärleken, 1981; Gabriels Dag, 1982; Dagbok Från Filminstitutet, 1982; Far och Son, 1984; Viettelysten Aika, 1985; Hemåt i Höstregn, 1985; Motströms, 1986; Presidenten, 1986; Kaupungin Sydämessä, 1987; Frihetens Fångar, 1989; Houkutusten Aamu on se Aamu, Jolloin Kuvaukset Alkavat (with Risto Hannula), 1990; Rapport Från Europa, 1990; Fazer 100, 1991; Huset Där Jag Bor, 1992; Tillfälligheters Spel, 1993; Husrum, 1993; En Kärleks Historia, 1994; Varför Finns Jag Till, 1998; Den Finlandsvenska Dikten, 2001; Hjärtat är en Svekfull Vän, 2001; Kärlekens Ingenmansland, 2002; Elämme, Siis Kuolemme (With John Vikström), 2002. Contributions: Vapaa Sana; Hufvudstadsbladet; Helsingin Sanomat; Aamulehti; Suomen Kuvalehti; various Scandinavian and international journals. *Honours:* Opera Prima Award, Venice Film Festival, 1963; Vittorio de Sica Prize, Sorrento, 1978; Acad. Award for Producer of Best Foreign Language Picture, (Fanny and Alexander), 1984; Finlandia Award for Literature, 1985. *Address:* Pohjoisranta 12, 00170 Helsinki, Finland (office); Pargasövägen 208, 10600 Ekenäs, Finland (home). *E-mail:* j.donner@surfnet.fi (home).

DONOGHUE, Denis; Prof., Literary Critic and Writer; b. 1 Dec. 1928, Tullow, Co Carlow, Ireland. *Education:* BA, Latin and English, 1949, MA, English, 1952, PhD, English, 1957, University College, Dublin; Royal Irish Acad. of Music, Dublin. *Career:* Asst Lecturer, 1954–57, College Lecturer in English, 1957–62, 1963–64, Prof. of Modern English and American Literature, 1965–79, University College, Dublin; University Lecturer in English, University of Cambridge, Fellow, King's College, Cambridge, 1964–65; Henry James Chair of English and American Letters and University Prof., New York University, 1979–; several visiting professorships and lectureships. *Publications:* The Third Voice: Modern British and American Verse Drama, 1959; Connoisseurs of Chaos: Ideas of Order in Modern American Poetry, 1965; An Honoured Guest: New Essays on W. B. Yeats (ed. with J. R. Mulryne), 1965; The Ordinary Universe; Soundings in Modern Literature, 1968; Jonathan Swift: A Critical Introduction, 1969; Emily Dickinson, 1969; Jonathan Swift: A Critical Anthology (ed.), 1971; Thieves of Fire, 1974; Seven American Poets (ed.), 1975; The Sovereign Ghost: Studies in Imagination, 1976; Poems of R. P. Blackmur (ed.), 1978; Ferocious Alphabets, 1981; The Arts Without Mystery, 1983; We Irish: Essays on Irish Literature and Society, 1986; Selected Essays of R. P. Blackmur (ed.), 1986; Reading America, 1987; England, Their England: Commentaries on English Language and Literature, 1988; America in Theory (ed. with Louis Menand and Leslie Berlowitz), 1988; Warrenpoint, 1990; Being Modern Together, 1991; The Pure Good of Theory, 1992; The Old Moderns: Essays on Literature and Theory, 1994; Walter Pater: Lover of Strange Souls, 1995; The Practice of Reading, 1998: Words Alone: The Poet T. S. Eliot, 2000; Adam's Curse: Reflections on Literature and Religion, 2001; Speaking of Beauty, 2003. Contributions: scholarly books and journals. *Honours:* Hon. DLitt, National Univ. of Ireland, Queen's Univ., Belfast; various fellowships. *Address:* 37 Washington Sq. W, Apt 17C, New York, NY 10011, USA. *E-mail:* ddl@nyu.edu.

DONOGHUE, Emma, BA, PhD; writer and dramatist; b. 24 Oct. 1969, Dublin, Ireland. *Education:* University College, Dublin, University of Cambridge. *Career:* mem. Authors' Society; Writers' Union of Canada; Playwrights' Guild of Canada. *Publications:* Passions Between Women, 1993; Stir-Fry (novel), 1994; Hood (novel), 1995; Kissing the Witch (short stories), 1997; What Sappho Would Have Said, US edn as Poems Between Women (anthology), 1997; We Are Michael Field (biog.), 1998; Ladies and Gentlemen (play), 1998; The Mammoth Book of Lesbian Short Stories (anthology), 1999; Slammerkin (novel), 2000; The Woman Who Gave Birth to Rabbits (short stories), 2002; Life Mask (novel) 2004. *Honours:* American Library Asscn Gay, Lesbian and Bisexual Book Award, 1997; Ferro-Grumley Fiction Award, 2002. *Literary Agent:* Caroline Davidson, 5 Queen Anne's Gardens, London, W4 1TU, England. *E-mail:* emma@emmadonoghue.com. *Website:* www.emmadonoghue.com.

DONOVAN, Anne; British writer and teacher; b. 1956, Coatbridge, North Lanarkshire, Scotland; m.; one s. *Education:* Univ. of Glasgow. *Publications:* Hieroglyphics and Other Stories 2001, Buddha Da (novel) 2003. *Honours:* Canongate Prize. *Address:* c/o Canongate Books, 14 High Street, Edinburgh, EH1 1TE, Scotland. *E-mail:* info@canongate.co.uk. *Website:* www.canongate.co.uk.

DONOVAN, Gerard; poet and novelist; b. Wexford, Ireland. *Education:* Johns Hopkins Univ. *Career:* frmly taught at Johns Hopkins Univ., Univ. of Arkansas; currently Adjunct Assoc. Prof. of English, Southampton Coll., New York, USA. *Publications:* Columbus Rides Again (poems), 1992; Kings and Bicycles (poems), 1995; The Lighthouse (poems), 2000; Schopenhauer's Telescope (novel), 2003. Other: short stories. Contributions: The Sewanee Review; New Statesman; Stand; Irish Times; Poetry Ireland Review; The Salmon; Writing in the West; Paris Review. *Address:* c/o Salmon Publishing, Knockeven, Cliffs of Moher, County Clare, Ireland.

DONOVAN, Paul James Kingsley; Author and Journalist; b. 8 April 1949, Sheffield, Yorkshire, England; m. Hazel Case, 27 Oct. 1979, one s. two d. *Education:* MA, Oriel College, Oxford. *Career:* Reporter and TV Critic, Daily Mail, 1978–85; Showbusiness Ed. and Critic, Today, 1986–88; Radio Columnist, Sunday Times, 1988–. *Publications:* Roger Moore, 1983; Dudley, 1988; The Radio Companion, 1991; All Our Todays, 1997. Contributions: newspapers including The Times, Sunday Times, Observer, Guardian; New Dictionary of National Biography. *Address:* 11 Stile Hall Gardens, London W4 3BS, England. *E-mail:* pauldon@scribbler.freeserve.co.uk.

DOODY, Margaret Anne, DPhil; Canadian academic; *John and Barbara Glynn Family Professor of Literature, University of Notre Dame*; b. 21 Sept. 1939, St John, NB. *Education:* Centreville Regional High School, NB, Dalhousie Univ., Halifax, Lady Margaret Hall, Oxford. *Career:* Instructor in English 1962–64; Asst Prof., English Dept Vic. Univ. 1968–69; lecturer, Univ. Coll. of Swansea, Wales 1969–77; Visiting Assoc. Prof. of English, Univ. of Calif. at Berkeley 1976–77, Assoc. Prof. 1977–80; Prof. of English, Princeton Univ. 1980–89; Andrew W. Mellon Prof. of Humanities and Prof. of English, Vanderbilt Univ., Nashville 1989–99, Dir Comparative Literature 1992–99; John and Barbara Glynn Family Prof. of Literature, Univ. of Notre Dame 2000–; Commonwealth Fellowship 1960–62; Canada Council Fellowship 1964–65; Imperial Oil Fellowship 1965–68; Guggenheim Foundation Fellowship 1978. *Play:* Clarissa (co-writer), New York 1984. *Publications:* A Natural Passion: A Study of the Novels of Samuel

Richardson 1974, Aristotle Detective 1978, The Alchemists 1980, The Daring Muse 1985, Frances Burney: The Life in the Works 1988, Samuel Richardson: Tercentenary Essays (ed. with Peter Sabor) 1989, The True Story of the Novel 1996, Anne of Green Gables (ed. with Wendy Barry and Mary Doody Jones) 1997, Aristotle e la giustizia poetica 2000, Poison in Athens (fiction) 2004. *Honours:* Hon. LLD (Dalhousie) 1985; Rose Mary Crawshay Prize 1986. *Address:* English Department, University of Notre Dame, Notre Dame, IN 46556 (Office); 435 Edgewater Drive, Mishawaka, IN 46545, USA (Home). *Telephone:* (219) 631-9723 (Office); (219) 257-7927 (Home). *E-mail:* Doody.y@md.edu (Home); margaret.doody.1@nd.edu.

DÖPFNER, Mathias, MA; German publishing executive; *CEO and Head of Newspapers Division, Axel Springer AG*; b. 15 Jan. 1963, Bonn; m. *Career:* journalist, Frankfurter Allgemeine Zeitung 1982; dir public relations agency 1988–90; fmr Asst to CEO, Gruner & Jahr, Hamburg; Ed.-in-Chief Wochenpost, Berlin 1994–96, Hamburger Morgenpost 1996–98; joined Axel Springer AG 1998, fmr Ed.-in-Chief Die Welt, mem. Man. Bd, Multimedia Div. 2000–, Head of Newspapers Div. 2000–, CEO 2002–. *Address:* Axel Springer Verlag AG, Axel-Springer-Platz 1, 20350 Hamburg, Germany (Office). *Telephone:* (40) 34722370 (Office). *Fax:* (40) 34729037 (Office). *Website:* www.asv.de (Office).

DOR, Moshe; Poet, Journalist and Ed.; b. 9 Dec. 1932, Tel-Aviv, Palestine; m. Ziona Dor, 29 March 1955, two s. *Education:* Hebrew University of Jerusalem, 1949–52; BA, Political Science, University of Tel-Aviv, 1956. *Career:* Counsellor for Cultural Affairs, Embassy of Israel, London, England, 1975–77; Distinguished Writer-In-Residence, American University, Washington, DC, 1987; mem. Asscn of Hebrew Writers, Israel; National Federation of Israel Journalists; Israel Pen Centre, pres., 1988–90. *Publications:* From the Outset, 1984; On Top of the Cliff (in Hebrew), 1986; Crossing the River, 1989; From the Outset (selected poems in Dutch trans.), 1989; Crossing the River (selected poems in English trans.), 1989; Love and Other Calamities (poems in Hebrew), 1993; Khamsin (memoirs and poetry in English trans.), 1994; The Silence of the Builder (poems in Hebrew), 1996; Co-ed., English anthologies of Israeli Hebrew poetry: The Burning Bush, 1977; The Stones Remember, 1991; After the First Rain, 1997. Other books of poetry, children's verse, literary essays, interviews with writers, trans of poetry and literature from English into Hebrew. *Honours:* Honourable Citation, International Hans Christian Andersen Prize for Children's Literature, 1975; Holon Prize for Literature, 1981; Prime Minister's Award for Creative Writing, 1986; Bialik Prize for Literature, 1987. *Address:* 6623 Fairfax Rd, Chevy Chase, MD 20815, USA.

DORESKI, William; Prof. of English, Writer and Poet; b. 10 Jan. 1946, Stafford, CT, USA; m. Carole Doreski, 17 June 1981. *Education:* BA, 1975, MA, 1977, Goddard College; PhD, Boston University, 1983; Postdoctoral Studies, Princeton University, 1987, Dartmouth College, 1994. *Career:* Writer-in-Residence, Emerson College, 1973–75; Instructor in Humanities, Goddard College, 1975–80; Asst Prof., 1982–87, Assoc. Prof., 1988–91, Prof. of English, 1992–, Keene State College, NH; mem. American Studies Asscn; Associated Writing Programs; Asscn of Scholars and Critics; MLA; New Hampshire Writers' Project; Robert Frost Society; Wallace Stevens Society. *Publications:* The Testament of Israel Potter, 1976; Half of the Map, 1980; Earth That Sings: The Poetry of Andrew Glaze, 1985; How to Read and Interpret Poetry, 1988; The Years of Our Friendship: Robert Lowell and Allen Tate, 1990; Ghost Train, 1991; The Modern Voice in American Poetry, 1995; Sublime of the North and Other Poems, 1997; Pianos in the Woods, 1998; Shifting Colors: The Public and the Private in the Poetry of Robert Lowell, 1999. Contributions: Books, journals, reviews, quarterlies, and magazines. *Honours:* Poet Lore Trans. Prize, 1975; Black Warrior Prize, 1979; National Endowment for the Humanities Grants, 1987, 1995; Whiting Foundation Fellowship, 1988; Clay Potato Fiction Prize, 1997; Frith Press Poetry Award, 1997. *Address:* c/o Dept of English, Keene State College, Keene, NH 03435, USA.

DORET, Michel, BA, BS, MA, MPhil, PhD; architect, artist, writer and poet; b. 5 Jan. 1938, Petion-Ville, Haiti; m. Liselotte Bencze 1970. *Education:* Pace Univ., New York Univ., SUNY, George Washington Univ. *Career:* founder and Dir, Les Editions Amon Ra 1982–97; founder-producer Michel's Video Studios New York 2000–; three art collections displayed in over 30 group and solo exhibitions in Europe, the USA and on the intenet; festivals; mem. several literary organizations. *Videos as producer:* 150 films in three series, 30 shown on Channel 20 Public Access Long Island Broadcasting Station. *Publications:* Isolement 1979, La Poésie francophone (eight vols) 1980, Panorama de la poésie feminine Suisse Romande 1982, Panorama de la poésie feminine francophone 1984, La negritude dans la poésie haitienne 1985, Poétesses Genevoises francophones 1985, Haiti en Poésie 1990, Les Mamelles de Lutèce 1991, Lyrisme du Moi 1992, The History of the Architecture of Ayiti (two vols) 1995; contrib. to numerous books, journals, reviews and other publications. *Honours:* various medals, diplomas, and hon. mentions. *Address:* 26 Mellow Lane, Westbury, NY 11590, USA. *E-mail:* mdor26@aol.com. *Website:* www.micheldoret.com.

DORFMAN, Vladimiro Ariel; Chilean writer, dramatist and poet; *Walter Hines Page Research Professor of Literature and Latin, Duke University*; b. 6 May 1942, Buenos Aires, Argentina; m. Angélica 1966; two s. *Education:* Univ. of Chile, Santiago. *Career:* Walter Hines Page Research Prof. of Literature and Latin, Center for International Studies, Duke University, Durham, NC, 1984–. *Publications:* Fiction: Hard Rain, 1973; My House is On Fire, 1979; Widows, 1983; Dorando la pildora, 1985; Travesia, 1986; The Last Song of Manuel Sendero, 1986; Mascara, 1988; Konfidenz, 1995; Blake's Therapy, 2001; The Rabbit's Rebellion, 2001; The Burning City (with Joaquin Dorfman), 2003. Poetry: Missing, 1982; Last Waltz in Santiago and Other Poems of Exile and Disappearance, 1988; In Case of Fire in a Foreign Land, 2002. Plays: Widows, 1988; Death and the Maiden, 1991; Reader, 1992; Who's Who (with Rodrigo Dorfman), 1997; Speak Truth to Power: Voices from Beyond the Dark, 2000; Purgatorio, 2003; The Other Side, 2003; Picasso Lost and Found, 2003. Films: Death and the Maiden, 1994; Prisoners in Time, 1995; My House is on Fire, 1997; In Case of Fire in a Foreign Land, 2002. Non-Fiction: How to Read Donald Duck (with Armand Mattelart), 1971; The Empire's Old Clothes, 1983; Some Write to the Future, 1991; Heading South, Looking North: A Bilingual Journey, 1998; Exorcising Terror: The Incredible Ongoing Trial of General Augusto Pinochet, 2002. *Honours:* Olivier Award, London 1991; Time Out Award, 1991; Literary Lion, New York Public Library, 1992; Dora Award, 1994; Charity Randall Citation, International Poetry Forum, 1994; Best Film for Television, Writers Guild of Great Britain, 1996; Fellow, American Acad. of Arts and Sciences, 2001; ALDA Prize, Denmark, 2002. *Address:* c/o Center for International Studies, Duke University, PO Box 90404, Durham, NC 27708, USA.

DORMER, Richard; Irish actor and playwright. *Career:* co-founder and writer-in-residence, Ransom Productions 2002–. *Films:* Billy Budd, Beautiful Thing, Una Pooka, In the Heart of America, Observe the Sons of Ulster, A Further Gesture. *Television:* Casualty, Soldier Soldier, Holy Cross. *Plays:* Hurricane 2002. *Honours:* The Stage Best Actor Award, BBC Stewart Parker Award. *Address:* Ransom Productions, 15 Church Street, Belfast, BT1 1PG, Northern Ireland. *Telephone:* (28) 9096-4320. *E-mail:* info@ransomproductions.co.uk. *Website:* www.ransomproductions.co.uk.

DORN, Ed(ward Merton); Poet, Writer, Trans., Anthropologist, Ethnologist and Prof.; b. 2 April 1929, Villa Grove, IL, USA; m. Jennifer Dunbar, 1969. *Education:* University of Illinois at Urbana-Champaign, 1949–50; BA, Black Mountain College, 1954. *Career:* Lecturer, Idaho State University, Pocatello, 1961–65; Co-Ed., Wild Dog, Pocatello, 1964–65; Visiting Prof., University of Kansas, Lawrence, 1968–69; Fulbright Lecturer in American Literature, Mem., English Dept, 1969–70, 1974–75, University of Essex, Colchester, England; Regent's Lecturer, University of California at Riverside, 1973–74; Writer-in-Residence, University of California at San Diego, La Jolla, 1976; Prof., University of Colorado at Boulder, 1977–. *Publications:* Poetry: The Newly Fallen, 1961; Hands Up!, 1964; From Gloucester Out, 1964; Idaho Out, 1965; Geography, 1965; The North Atlantic Turbine, 1967; Gunslinger I, 1968, II, 1969; The Midwest Is That Space Between the Buffalo Statler and the Lawrence Eldridge, 1969; The Cosmology of Finding Your Spot, 1969; Twenty-Four Love Songs, 1969; Songs: Set Two, A Short Count, 1970; Spectrum Breakdown: A Microbook, 1971; By the Sound, 1971; The Cycle, 1971; A Poem Called Alexander Hamilton, 1971; The Hamadyas Baboon at the Lincoln Park Zoo, 1972; Gunslinger, Book III: The Winterbook, Prologue to the Great Book IV Kornerstone, 1972; Recollections of Gran Apacheria, 1974; Manchester Square (with Jennifer Dunbar), 1975; Collected Poems: 1956–1974, 1975; Hello, La Jolla, 1978; Selected Poems, 1978; Abhorrences, 1989. Fiction: Some Business Recently Transacted in the White World (short stories), 1971. Non-Fiction: What I See in the Maximum Poems, 1960; Prose 1 (with Michail Rumaker and Warren Tallamn), 1964; The Rites of Passage: A Brief History, 1965; The Shoshoneans: The People of the Basin-Plateau, 1966; Way West: Essays and Verse Accounts 1963–1993, 1993. Translations: Our Word: Guerrilla Poems From Latin America (with Gordon Brotherston), 1968; Tree Between Two Walls (with Gordon Brotherston), 1969; Selected Poems of Cesar Vallejo, 1976. *Honours:* D. H. Lawrence Fellow, 1969.

DORNER, Majorie; Prof. of English Literature and Writer; b. 21 Jan. 1942, Luxembourg, Wisconsin, USA; two d. *Education:* BA, English, St Norbert College, 1964; MA, English, Marquette University, 1965; PhD, English, Purdue University, 1971. *Career:* Prof. of English Literature, Winona State University, Minnesota, 1971–. *Publications:* Nightmare, 1987; Family Closets, 1989; Freeze Frame, 1990; Winter Roads, Summer Fields, 1992; Blood Kin, 1992. Contributions: various publications. *Honours:* Minnesota Book Awards, 1991, 1993. *Address:* 777 W Broadway, Winona, MN 55987, USA.

DORR, James Suhrer, BS, MA; writer and poet; b. 12 Aug. 1941, Pensacola, FL, USA; m. Ruth Michelle Clark 1975 (divorced 1982). *Education:* MIT, Indiana University. *Career:* technical writer, Ed., Wrubel Computing Center, Bloomington, IN, 1969–81; writer, Marketing Consultant, The Stackworks, 1982; Assoc. Ed., Bloomington Area Magazine, 1983–86; freelance writer, 1982–; mem. SFWA; Horror Writers Asscn; Science Fiction Poetry Asscn; Short Mystery Fiction society. *Publications:* Towers of Darkness (poems), 1990; Strange Mistresses (short fiction), 2001. Contributions: Borderlands II, 1991; Grails, 1992; Dark Destiny I and II, 1994–95; Dante's Disciples, 1996; Darkside: Horror for the Next Millennium, 1996; Dark Tyrants, 1997; Gothic Ghosts, 1997; Asylums and Labyrinths, 1997; The Best of Cemetery Dance, 1998; New Mythos Legends, 1999; Children of Cthulhu, 2002; The Darker Side: Generations of Horror, 2002; other anthologies, periodicals, journals, reviews, magazines, quarterlies, and newspapers. *Honours:* Rhysling Hon. Mention, 1993, 1995, 1996, 1997, 2001. *Address:* 1404 E Atwater, Bloomington, IN 47401, USA.

DORSETT, Danielle (see Daniels, Dorothy).

DORSEY, Candas Jane; Writer, Poet and Editor; b. 16 Nov. 1952, Edmonton, AB, Canada. *Education:* BA, University of Alberta, 1975; BSW, University of Calgary, 1979. *Career:* Freelance Writer and Ed., Edmonton Bullet, Edmonton, AB, 1980; Has also worked in theatre and as Social Worker. *Publications:* This Is for You (poems), 1973; Orion Rising (poems), 1974; Results of the Ring Toss (poems), 1976; Hardwired Angel (novel, co-author), 1987; Machine Sex and Other Stories, 1988; Tesseracts Three: Canadian Science Fiction (co-ed.), 1990; Leaving Marks (poems), 1992; Dark Earth Dreams (novel, co-author), 1995; Black Wine, 1997. Contributions: Short fiction to books including: Getting Here; Tesseracts. *Honours:* First Prize, shared with co-author, for Hardwired Angel, Ninth Annual Pulp Press International 3-Day Novel Competition, 1987. *Address:* c/o Porcepic Books, 4252 Commerce Circle, Victoria, BC V8Z 4M2, Canada.

DOTY, Mark, BA, MFA; American writer, poet and professor; b. 10 Aug. 1953, Maryville, TN. *Education:* Drake Univ., Goddard Coll. *Career:* Faculty, MFA Writing Program, Vermont College, 1981–94, Writing and Literature, Goddard College, 1985–90; Guest Faculty, Sarah Lawrence College, 1990–94, 1996; Fannie Hurst Visiting Prof., Brandeis University, 1994; Visiting Faculty, University of Iowa, 1995, 1996, Columbia University, 1996; Prof., Creative Writing Program, University of Utah, 1997–. *Publications:* Turtle, Swan, 1987; Bethlehem in Broad Daylight, 1991; My Alexandria, 1993; Atlantis, 1995; Heaven's Coast (memoir), 1996; Firebird (memoir), 1999; Source, 2001. Contributions: many anthologies and journals. *Honours:* Theodore Roethke Prize, 1986; National Endowment for the Arts Fellowships in Poetry, 1987, 1995; Pushcart Prizes, 1987, 1989; Los Angeles Times Book Prize, 1993; Ingram Merrill Foundation Award, 1994; National Book Critics Circle Award, 1994; Guggenheim Fellowship, 1994; Whiting Writers Award, 1994; Rockefeller Foundation Fellowship, Bellagio, Italy, 1995; New York Times Notable Book of the Year, citations, 1995, 1996; American Library Asscn Notable Book of the Year, 1995; T. S. Eliot Prize, 1996; Bingham Poetry Prize, 1996; Ambassador Book Award, 1996; Lambda Literary Award, 1996. *Address:* c/o Creative Writing Program, University of Utah, Salt Lake City, UT 84112, USA.

DOUGHTY, Louise; Novelist and Playwright; b. 4 Sept. 1963, Melton Mowbray, England. *Education:* BA, English Literature, Leeds Univ., 1981–84; MA, Creative Writing, Univ. of East Anglia, 1987. *Career:* mem. Society of Authors, 1998–. *Publications:* Fiction: Crazy Paving, 1995; Dance With Me, 1996; Honey-Dew, 1998; Fires in the Dark, 2003. Radio Plays: Maybe, 1991; The Koala Bear Joke, 1994; Nightworkers, 1999. *Honours:* Radio Times Drama Award, 1991; Ian St James Award, 1991. *Address:* c/o Antony Harwood Ltd, Office 109, Riverbank House, 1 Putney Bridge Approach, London SW6 3JD, England.

DOUGLAS, Garry (see Kilworth, Garry Douglas).

DOUGLAS, Michael (see Crichton, (John) Michael).

DOVE, Rita Frances, BA, MFA; American writer, poet and academic; *Commonwealth Professor, University of Virginia*; b. 28 Aug. 1952, Akron, OH; m. Fred Viebahn 1979; one d. *Education:* Miami Univ., OH, Univ. of Tübingen, Germany and Univ. of Iowa. *Career:* Asst Prof. Ariz. State Univ., Tempe 1981–84, Assoc. Prof. 1984–87, Prof. of English 1987–89; Assoc. Ed., Callaloo 1986–; adviser and Contributing Ed., Gettysburg Review 1987–, TriQuarterly 1988–, Georgia Review 1994, Bellingham Review 1996–; Prof. Univ. of Va, Charlottesville 1989–93, Commonwealth Prof. of English 1993–; Poet Laureate of the USA 1993–95; Consultant in Poetry, Library of Congress 1993–95; writer-in-residence, Tuskegee Inst. Ala 1982; poetry panellist, Nat. Endowment for Arts, Washington, DC 1984–86 (chair. 1985); judge Pulitzer Prize in Poetry 1991 (chair. of jury 1997), Nat. Book Award in Poetry 1991 and other awards; mem. Acad. of American Poets, Associated Writing Programs, Poetry Soc. of America, Poets and Writers. *Publications:* poetry: Ten Poems 1977, The Only Dark Spot in the Sky 1980, The Yellow House on the Corner 1980, Mandolin 1982, Museum 1983, Thomas and Beulah (Pulitzer Prize in Poetry 1987) 1986, The Other Side of the House 1988, Grace Notes 1989, Selected Poems 1993, Lady Freedom Among Us 1994, Mother Love 1995, Evening Primrose 1998, On the Bus with Rosa Parks 1999, Best American Poetry (ed.) 2000, American Smooth 2004; other: Fifth Sunday (short stories) 1985, Through the Ivory Gate (novel) 1992, The Darker Face of Earth (verse play) 1994, The Poet's World (essays) 1995. *Honours:* numerous hon. degrees; Fulbright Fellow 1974–75, Nat. Endowment for the Arts grants 1978, 1989, Portia Pittman Fellow, Tuskegee Inst. 1982, Guggenheim Fellowship 1984, Rockefeller Foundation Residency in Bellagio, Italy 1988, Mellon Fellow, Nat. Humanities Center 1989, Fellow, Center for Advanced Studies, Univ. of Virginia 1989–92; Acad. of American Poets Peter I. B. Lavan Younger Poets Award 1986, General Electric Foundation Award for Younger Writers 1987, Ohio Governor's Award 1988, NAACP Great American Artist Award 1993, American Acad. of Achievement Golden Plate Award 1993, Folger Shakespeare Library Renaissance Forum Award 1994, Charles Frankel Prize/Nat. Humanities Medal 1996, Heinz Award in the Arts and Humanities 1996, Sara Lee Frontrunner Award 1997, Barnes and Noble Writers Award 1997, Levinson Prize 1998, Ohioana Library Book Award 2000, New York Public Library Literary Lion 2000, Duke Ellington Lifetime Achievement Award in the Literary Arts, Ellington Fund in Washington, DC 2001. *Address:* Department of English, University of Virginia, Charlottesville, VA 22903, USA. *Telephone:* (804) 924-6618 (Office).

DOVRING, Karin Elsa Ingeborg, MA, PhD, PhilLic; American writer, poet and dramatist; b. 5 Dec. 1919, Stenstorp, Sweden; m. Folke Dovring 1943. *Education:* College of Commerce, Göteborg, Lund University, Göteborg University. *Career:* journalist 1940–60; Research Assoc., Harold D. Lasswell, Yale University 1953–78, University of Illinois at Urbana-Champaign 1968–69; Visiting Lecturer, many universities and colleges; Research Prof. of Communications and Media Studies, Univ. of Illinois 2002; mem. International Society of Poets, USA; Acad. of American Poets, elected mem., 2002. *Publications:* Songs of Zion, 1951; Road of Propaganda, 1959; Land Reform as a Propaganda Theme, third edn, 1965; Optional Society, 1972; Frontiers of Communication, 1975; No Parking This Side of Heaven (short stories), 1982; Harold D. Lasswell: His Communication with a Future, 1987; Heart in Escrow (novel), 1990; Faces in a Mirror (poems), 1995; Shadows on a Screen (poems), 1996; Whispers on a Stage (poems), 1996; English as Lingua Franca, 1997; In the Service of Persuasion: English as Lingua Franca across the Globe, 2001; Propaganda is the Poetry of Politics, 2002; Changing Scenery (poems), 2003. Other: film and television plays; contrib. to anthologies, including 'Life Expectancy' poem in Our 100 Most Famous Poets – The Brief Chroniclers of Our Time 2004; contrib. to professional journals. *Honours:* International Poetry Hall of Fame, 1996; Hon. Lifetime Mem., Société Jean Jacques Rousseau, Geneva, 1947. *Address:* 613 W Vermont Avenue, Urbana, IL 61801, USA.

DOWNES, David Anthony; Prof. of English Emeritus and Writer; b. 17 Aug. 1927, Victor, CO, USA; m. Audrey Romaine Ernst, 7 Sep 1949, one s., three d. *Education:* BA, cum laude, Regis University, 1949; MA, Marquette University, 1950; PhD, University of Washington, 1956. *Career:* Asst Prof., Prof., Chair. of Dept, University of Seattle, 1953–68; Prof. of English, Dean of Humanities and Fine Arts, 1968–72, Dir of Educational Development Projects, 1972–73, Dir of Humanities Programme, 1973–74, Dir of Graduate English Studies, 1975–78, Chair. of Dept, 1978–84, Prof. Emeritus, 1991, California State University, Chico; Consultant, Cowles Rare Book Library, Gonzaga University, 1997. *Publications:* Gerard Manley Hopkins: A Study of His Ignatian Spirit, 1959; Victorian Portraits: Hopkins and Pater, 1965; Pater, Kingsley and Newman, 1972; The Great Sacrifice: Studies in Hopkins, 1983; Ruskin's Landscape of Beatitude, 1984; Hopkins' Sanctifying Imagination, 1985; The Ignatian Personality of Gerard Manley Hopkins, 1990; Hopkins' Achieved Self, 1996. Contributions: scholarly books and journals. *Honours:* Exceptional Merit Awards for Scholarship, 1984, 1988, 1990, 1992; Hon. Doctor of Law, Gonzaga University, 1997. *Address:* 1076 San Ramon Dr., Chico, CA 95973, USA.

DOWNIE, Leonard, Jr; Newspaper Editor; b. 1 May 1942, Cleveland, OH, USA; m. 1st Barbara Lindsey 1960 (divorced 1971); two s.; m. 2nd Geraldine Rebach 1971 (divorced 1997); one s. one d.; m. 3rd Janice Galin 1997. *Education:* MA, Ohio State Univ. *Career:* joined The Washington Post 1964, became investigative reporter in Washington, specializing in crime, housing and urban affairs; helped to supervise coverage of Watergate affair; Asst Man. Ed. Metropolitan News 1974–79; London Corresp. Washington Post 1979–82, Nat. Ed. 1982–84, Man. Ed. 1984–91; Exec. Ed. 1991–; Dir LA Times–Washington Post News Service 1991–, Int. Herald Tribune 1996–2002. *Publications:* Justice Denied, 1971; Mortgage on America, 1974; The New Muckrakers, 1976; The News About the News (with Robert G. Kaiser), 1993. *Honours:* Hon. LLD, Ohio State Univ.; two Washington-Baltimore Newspaper Guild Front Page Awards; American Bar Asscn Gavel Award for legal reporting; John Hancock Award for business and financial writing; Alicia Patterson Foundation Fellow, 1971–72. *Address:* c/o The Washington Post, 1150 15th Street NW, Washington, DC 20071, USA.

DOWNIE, Mary Alice Dawe, BA; Canadian writer; b. (Mary Alice Dawe Hunter), 12 Feb. 1934, Alton, IL, USA; m. John Downie 1959; three d. *Education:* Trinity Coll., Univ. of Toronto. *Career:* Book Review Ed., Kingston Whig-Standard, 1973–78; mem. Writers' Union of Canada; PEN. *Publications:* The Wind Has Wings: Poems from Canada (with Barbara Robertson), 1968; Honor Bound (with John Downie), 1971; Scared Sarah, 1974; Dragon on Parade, 1974; The Last Ship, 1980; Jenny Greenteeth, 1981; A Proper Acadian (with George Rawlyk), 1982; The Wicked Fairy-Wife, 1983; Alison's Ghost (with John Downie), 1984; Stones and Cones (with Jillian Gilliland), 1984; The New Wind Has Wings: Poems from Canada (with Barbara Robertson), 1984; The Window of Dreams: New Canadian Writing for Children, 1986; The Well-Filled Cupboard (with Barbara Robertson), 1987; How the Devil Got His Cat, 1988; The Buffalo Boy and the Weaver Girl (with Mann Hwa Huang-Hsu), 1989; Doctor Dwarf and Other Poems for Children, by A. M. Klein (with Barbara Robertson), 1990; Cathal the Giant-Killer and the Dun Shaggy Filly, 1991; Written in Stone: A Kingston Reader (with M. A. Thompson), 1993; The Cat Park, 1993; Snow Paws, 1996; Bright Paddles, 1999; Danger in Disguise (with John Downie), 2000. Contributions: Hornbook Magazine; Pittsburgh Press; Kingston Whig-Standard; Ottawa Citizen; Globe and Mail; Montreal Gazette; OWL Magazine; Chickadee; Crackers. *Address:* 190 Union Street, Kingston, ON K7L 2P6, Canada. *Telephone:* (613) 5423-3464. *Fax:* (613) 5423-3464. *E-mail:* downiej@post.queensu.ca.

DOWNING, Michael Bernard; Assistant Professor of Humanities, Writer, Poet and Ed.; b. 8 May 1958, Pittsfield, Massachusetts, USA. *Education:* AB magna cum laude, Harvard University, 1980. *Career:* Senior Ed., Oceanus periodical, Woods Hole, Massachusetts, 1983–84, FMR periodical, Milan, Italy, 1984–86; Instructor in English, Bentley College, Waltham, Massachusetts, 1987–88; Instructor, 1988–91, Asst Prof. of Humanities, Dir of Writing Programme, 1992–, Wheelock College, Boston, Massachusetts; mem. PEN; Authors' Guild; Authors League of America; Share Our Strength, writers committee. *Publications:* A Narrow Time (novel), 1987; Mother of God (novel), 1990; The Last Shaker (play, produced 1995); Perfect Agreement (novel), 1997. Contributions: anthologies including Louder than Words; Stories, poems, essays and reviews to periodicals including: America; Commonweal; Harvard; Salopian. *Honours:* Harvard-Shrewsbury Fellow, Shropshire, England, 1980–81; Best Book Citation, Newsday, 1997. *E-mail:* downing 58@aol.com.

DOYLE, Charles Desmond, (Mike Doyle); academic, writer and poet; b. 18 Oct. 1928, Birmingham, England; m. 1st Helen Merlyn Lopdell 1952 (deceased); m. 2nd Doran Ross Smithells 1959 (divorced); m. 3rd Rita Jean Brown 1992; three s. one d. *Education:* Diploma of Teaching, 1956, BA, 1957, MA, 1959, University of New Zealand; PhD, University of Auckland, 1968. *Career:* Assoc. Prof., 1968–76, Prof. of English, 1976–93, Prof. Emeritus, 1993–, University of Victoria, BC, Canada; mem. New Canterbury Literary Society; Writers Union of Canada; PEN Canada. *Publications:* A Splinter of Glass, 1956; The Night Shift: Poems on Aspects of Love (with others), 1957; Distances, 1963; Messages for Herod, 1965; A Sense of Place, 1965; Quorum-Noah, 1970; Abandoned Sofa, 1971; Earth Meditations, 1971; Earthshot, 1972; Preparing for the Ark, 1973; Pines (with P. K. Irwin), 1975; Stonedancer, 1976; A Month Away from Home, 1980; A Steady Hand, 1982; The Urge to Raise Hats, 1989; Separate Fidelities, 1991; Intimate Absences: Selected Poems 1954–1992, 1993; Trout Spawning at the Lardeau River, 1997. Non-Fiction: R. A. K. Mason, 1970; James K. Baxter, 1976; William Carlos Williams and the American Poem, 1982; William Carlos Williams: The Critical Heritage (ed.), 1982; The New Reality (co-ed.), 1984; Wallace Stevens: The Critical Heritage (ed.), 1985; After Bennett (co-ed.) 1986; Richard Aldington: A Biography, 1989; Richard Aldington: Reappraisals (ed.), 1990. Contributions: journals, reviews, and periodicals. *Honours:* UNESCO Creative Arts Fellowship, 1958–59; ACLS Fellowship, 1967–68. *Address:* 641 Oliver Street, Victoria, BC V8S 4W2, Canada.

DOYLE, Roddy; Irish writer and playwright; b. 1958, Dublin; m. Belinda Doyle; two s. *Career:* lecturer at universities. *Play:* Brown Bread 1992, USA 1992. *Publications:* The Commitments 1987, screenplay (with Dick Clement and Ian La Frenais) 1991, The Snapper 1990, screenplay 1992, The Van 1991, Paddy Clarke Ha Ha Ha (Booker Prize) 1993, The Woman Who Walked into Doors 1996, A Star Called Henry 1999, The Giggler Treatment 2000, Rory and Ita 2002, Oh, Play That Thing 2004. *Address:* c/o Patti Kelly, Viking Books, 375 Hudson Street, New York, NY 10014, USA (Office).

DRABBLE, Margaret, CBE, BA; British author; b. 5 June 1939, Sheffield; A. S. Byattsister of ; m. 1st Clive Swift 1960 (divorced 1975); two s. one d.; m. 2nd Michael Holroyd 1982. *Education:* Newnham Coll., Cambridge. *Career:* Chair., Nat. Book League 1980–82; Ed. The Oxford Companion to English Literature 1979–2000; Vice-Patron, Child Psychotherapy Trust 1987–; Hon. mem. American Acad. of Arts and Letters 2002; Hon. Fellow, Sheffield City Polytechnic 1989. *Publications:* fiction: A Summer Bird-Cage 1963, The Garrick Year 1964, The Millstone 1965 (John Llewelyn Rhys Memorial Prize 1966), Jerusalem the Golden 1967, The Waterfall 1969, The Needle's Eye 1972, The Realms of Gold 1975, The Ice Age 1977, The Middle Ground 1980, The Radiant Way 1987, A Natural Curiosity 1989, Safe as Houses 1990, The Gates of Ivory 1991, The Witch of Exmoor 1996, The Peppered Moth 2001, The Seven Sisters 2002; plays: Laura 1964, Isadora 1968, Thank You All Very Much 1969, Bird of Paradise 1969; non-fiction: Wordsworth 1966, Arnold Bennett: A Biography 1974, The Genius of Thomas Hardy (ed.) 1976, For Queen and Country: Britain in the Victorian Age 1978, A Writer's Britain 1979, The Oxford Companion to English Literature (ed.) 1985, 2000, The Concise Oxford Companion to English Literature (ed. with Jenny Stringer) 1987, Angus Wilson: A Biography 1995. *Honours:* Hon. DLitt (Sheffield) 1976, (Bradford) 1988, (Hull) 1992, Hon. doctorates (Manchester) 1987, (Keele) 1988, (East Anglia) 1994, (York) 1995; James Tait Black Memorial Prize 1968, Book of the Year Award, Yorkshire Post 1972, E. M. Forster Award, American Acad. of Arts and Letters 1973. *Literary Agent:* PFD, Drury House, 34–43 Russell Street, London, WC2B 5HA, England. *Telephone:* (20) 7344-1000.

DRACKETT, Phil(ip Arthur), (Paul King); Writer and Broadcaster; b. 25 Dec. 1922, Finchley, Middlesex, England; m. Joan Isobel Davies, 19 June 1948. *Education:* Woodhouse School, 1934–39; Junior County Award, University of Cambridge; General Schools, University of London. *Career:* mem. Sports Writers Asscn; Guild of Motoring Writers; British Ice Hockey Writers Asscn; Friends of Mundesley Library. *Publications:* Fighting Days 1942, Come Out Fighting (with Matt Wells) 1944, Speedway 1951, Motor Racing 1952, Motoring 1955, You and Your Car (with Leslie Webb) 1958, Great Moments in Motoring 1958, You and Your Motor Cycle (with Aubrey Thompson) 1959, Automobiles Work Like This 1960, Veteran Cars 1961, Motor Rallying 1963, Passing the Test 1964, Young Car Drivers Companion (as Paul King) 1964, Taking Your Car Abroad 1965, Let's Look at Cars 1966, Slot Car Racing 1968, International Motor Racing (4 Vols, Ed.) 1969–72, Like Father Like Son 1969, Rally of the Forests, 1970; Car Care Tips 1973, Motor Racing Champions (2 Vols, Ed.) 1973–74, Book of the Veteran Car 1973, Purnell Book of Great Disasters 1978, Purnell Book of Dangermen 1979, Encyclopaedia of the Motor Car (Ed.) 1979, Wonderful World of Cars 1979, Inns and Harbours of North Norfolk 1980, The Car Makers 1980, The Story of the RAC International Rally 1980, Vintage Cars 1981, The Classic Mercedes-Benz 1983, Brabham, Story of a Racing Team 1985, Flashing Blades, The Story of British Ice Hockey 1987, They Call it Courage: The Story of the Segrave Trophy 1990; Benetton–Ford: A Racing Partnership 1990, revised 1992, Vendetta on Ice 1993, Just Another Incident (with Jack Kemsley) 1994, Ice Hockey Films 1995, Total Ice Hockey Encyclopedia (contributor) 1998, Champions on Ice (with Dennis Fill) 2000. Contributions: newspapers and magazines. *Honours:* First Hon. Life Mem., British Ice Hockey Writers Asscn. *Address:* 9 Victoria Rd, Mundesley, Norfolk NR11 8RG, England.

DRAKE, Barbara (Ann); Prof. of English, Poet and Writer; b. 13 April 1939, Abilene, KS, USA; m. 1st Albert Drake, 28 Dec. 1960, divorced 1985, one s. two d.; m. 2nd William Beckman, 1986. *Education:* BA, 1961, MFA, 1966, University of Oregon. *Career:* Instructor, Michigan State University, 1974–83; Prof. of English, Linfield College, 1983–. *Publications:* Poetry: Narcissa Notebook, 1973; Field Poems, 1975; Love at the Egyptian Theatre, 1978; Life in a Gothic Novel, 1981; What We Say to Strangers, 1986; Bees in Wet Weather, 1992; Space before A, 1996. Other: Peace at Heart: An Oregon Country Life (memoir), 1998. Contributions: many books, anthologies, reviews, quarterlies and journals. *Honours:* Northwest Arts Foundation Grant, 1985; National Endowment for the Arts Fellowship, 1986; Edith Green Distinguished Prof. Award, Linfield College, 1993. *Address:* c/o Linfield College, 900 SE Baker St, McMinnville, OR 97128, USA.

DRAKE, Nick; British poet and translator; b. 1961. *Publications:* poetry: Chocolate and Salt (pamphlet) 1990, The Man in the White Suit 1999; non-fiction: The Poetry of W. B. Yeats 1991; translator: Peribañez and Comendador of Ocaña, by Lope de Vega 1998. *Honours:* Eric Gregory Award 1990, Forward Prize for Best First Collection. *Literary Agent:* c/o Bloodaxe Books Ltd, Highgreen, Tarset, Northumberland NE48 1RP, England. *Telephone:* (1434) 240500. *Fax:* (1434) 240505. *Website:* www.bloodaxebooks.com.

DRAPER, Alfred Ernest; Author; b. 26 Oct. 1924, London, England; m. Barbara Pilcher, 31 March 1951, two s. *Education:* North West London Polytechnic. *Career:* mem. National Union of Journalists, life mem. *Publications:* Swansong for a Rare Bird, 1969; The Death Penalty, 1972 (made into a French Film); Smoke Without Fire, 1974; The Prince of Wales, 1975; The Story of the Goons, 1976; Operation Fish, 1978; Amritsar, 1979; Grey Seal, 1981; Grey Seal: The Restless Waves, 1983; The Raging of the Deep, 1985; Storm over Singapore, 1986; The Con Man, 1987; Dawns Like Thunder, 1987; The Great Avenging Day, 1989; A Crimson Splendour, 1991; Operation Midas, 1993. Contributions: numerous periodicals. *Address:* 31 Oakridge Ave, Radlett, Herts WD7 8EW, England.

DRAPER, Hastings (see Jeffries, Roderic (Graeme)).

DRAPER, Ronald Philip; academic and writer; b. 3 Oct. 1928, Nottingham, England; m. Irene Margaret Aldridge 1950; three d. *Education:* BA, 1950, PhD, 1953, University of Nottingham. *Career:* Lecturer in English, University of Adelaide, 1955–56; Lecturer, 1957–68, Senior Lecturer, 1968–73, University of Leicester; Prof., 1973–86, Regius Chalmers Prof. of English, 1986–94, Prof. Emeritus, 1994–, University of Aberdeen. *Publications:* D. H. Lawrence, 1964. D. H. Lawrence: The Critical Heritage (ed.), 1970; Hardy: The Tragic Novels (ed.), 1975; George Eliot, The Mill on the Floss and Silas Marner, 1977; Tragedy, Developments in Criticism (ed.), 1980; Lyric Tragedy, 1985; The Winter's Tale: Text and Performance, 1985; Hardy: Three Pastoral Novels, 1987; The Literature of Region and Nation, 1989; An Annotated Critical Bibliography of Thomas Hardy (with Martin Ray), 1989; The Epic: Developments in Criticism (ed.), 1990; A Spacious Vision: Essays on Hardy (co-ed.), 1994; An Introduction to Twentieth-Century Poetry in England, 1999; Shakespeare: The Comedies, 2000. Contributions: Books and scholarly journals. *Address:* Maynestay, Chipping Campden, Gloucestershire GL55 6DJ, England.

DRAZEN, Jeffrey M., BS, MD; American writer; *Editor-in-Chief, New England Journal of Medicine*; b. 19 May 1946, St Louis, MO. *Career:* Prof. in the Dept of Environmental Health, Harvard School of Public Health; Parker B. Francis Prof. of Medicine, Dept of Medicine, Brigham and Women's Hospital; Ed.-in-Chief, New England Journal of Medicine. *Publications:* Five Lipoxygenase Products in Asthma (ed.) 1998; contrib. to Genomic Medicine: Articles from the New England Journal of Medicine 2001. *Address:* New England Journal of Medicine, 10 Shattuck Street, Boston, MA 02115-6094, USA. *Telephone:* (617) 734-9800. *Fax:* (617) 739-9864. *E-mail:* jmdrazen@nejm.org. *Website:* www.nejm.org.

DREW, Bettina; Writer, Poet and Teacher; b. 23 April 1956, New York, NY, USA. *Education:* BA, Philosophy, University of California, Berkeley, 1977; MA, Creative Writing, City College, CUNY, 1983; MA, American Studies,

Yale University, 1995. *Career:* Lecturer in English, College of New York; Lecturer in Humanities, New York University, 1990–93; Part-time Acting Instructor, Yale University, 1995–97; mem. PEN American Center; Biography Seminar, New York University. *Publications:* Nelson Algren: A Life on the Wild Side, 1989; The Texas Stories of Nelson Algren (ed.), 1995; Crossing the Expendable Landscape, 1997. Contributions: Boulevard; The Writer; Chicago Tribune; Threepenny Review; Washington Post Book World; Chicago Tribune Book World; Ms; Black American Literature Forum; Michigan Quarterly Review; Poems to various magazines. *Literary Agent:* Theresa Park, Sanford J. Greenburger Associates Inc, 55 Fifth Ave, New York, NY 10003, USA.

DREWE, Robert Duncan; writer and dramatist; b. 9 Jan. 1943, Melbourne, Vic., Australia; m. 3rd Candida Baker; four s. two d. *Education:* Hale School, Perth, WA. *Career:* Literary Ed., The Australian, 1972–75; Writer-in-Residence, University of Western Australia, Nedlands, 1979, La Trobe University, Bundoora, Victoria, 1986; Columnist, Mode, Sydney, and Sydney City Monthly, 1981–83; mem. Australian Society of Authors. *Publications:* The Savage Crows, 1976; A Cry in the Jungle Bar, 1979; Fortune, 1986; Our Sunshine, 1991; The Picador Book of the Beach (ed.), 1993; The Drowner (novel), 1996; The Penguin Book of the City (ed.), 1997; Walking Ella (non-fiction), 1998; The Shark Net: Memories and Murder, 2000. Short Stories: The Bodysurfers, 1983; The Bay of Contented Men, 1989. Plays: The Bodysurfers, 1989; South American Barbecue, 1991. Contributions: The Bulletin; The Australian; TLS; Granta. *Honours:* National Book Council Award, 1987; Commonwealth Writers' Prize, 1990; Australian Creative Artists' Fellowship, 1993–96; Hon. DLitt, University of Queensland, 1997; New South Wales, Victorian, West Australian and South Australian premiers' literary prizes, 1997; Book of the Year, 1997; Adelaide Festival Prize for Literature, 1998. *Literary Agent:* Hickson Associates, 128 Queen Street, Woolahra, NSW 2025, Australia.

DRISCOLL, Peter (John); Writer and Journalist; b. 4 Feb. 1942, London, England; m. Angela Hennessy, 14 Jan. 1967, one s. one d. *Education:* BA, University of the Witwatersrand, 1967. *Career:* Reporter, Rand Daily Mail, Johannesburg, South Africa, 1959–67; Sub-ed., Scriptwriter, ITV News, London, 1969–73. *Publications:* The White Lie Assignment, 1971; The Wilby Conspiracy, 1972; In Connection with Kilshaw, 1974; The Barboza Credentials, 1976; Pangolin, 1979; Heritage, 1982; Spearhead, 1987; Secrets of State, 1991. *Literary Agent:* David Higham Associates, 5–8 Lower John St, Golden Sq., London W1F 9HA, England.

DRIVER, Charles Jonathan, (Jonty); Writer, Poet and Schools Consultant; b. 19 Aug. 1939, Cape Town, South Africa; m. Ann Elizabeth Hoogewerf, 1967, two s. one d. *Education:* BA, BEd, University of Cape Town, 1958–62; MPhil, Trinity College, Oxford, 1967. *Career:* The Master, Wellington College, Crowthorne, Berkshire, 1989–2000; Ed., Conference and Common Room, 1993–2000. *Publications:* Elegy for a Revolutionary, 1968; Send War in Our Time, O Lord, 1970; Death of Fathers, 1972; A Messiah of the Last Days, 1974; I Live Here Now (poems), 1979; Occasional Light (poems, with Jack Cope), 1979; Patrick Duncan (biog.), 1980, paperback, 2000; Hong Kong Portraits (poems), 1985; In the Water-Margins (poems), 1994; Holiday Haiku (poems), 1996; Requiem (poems), 1998. Contributions: numerous magazines and journals. *Honours:* FRSA. *Address:* Apple Yard Cottage, Mill Lane, Northiam, nr Rye, Sussex, TN31 6JU, England. *E-mail:* jontydriver@hotmail.com.

DRIVER, Paul William; Music Critic and Writer; b. 14 Aug. 1954, Manchester, England. *Education:* MA, Univ. of Oxford, 1979. *Career:* Music Critic, The Boston Globe, 1983–84, Sunday Times, 1985–; Mem., Editorial Board, Contemporary Music Review; Patron, Manchester Musical Heritage Trust; mem. Critics Circle. *Publications:* A Diversity of Creatures (ed.), 1987; Music and Text (ed.), 1989; Manchester Pieces, 1996; Penguin English Verse, vols 1–6 (ed.), 1995; Penguin Popular Poetry, vols 1–6 (ed.), 1996. Contributions: Sunday Times; Financial Times; Tempo; London Review of Books; Opera; New York Times; numerous others. *Literary Agent:* Rogers, Coleridge & White Ltd, 20 Powis Mews, London W11 1JN, England. *Address:* 15 Victoria Rd, London NW6 6SX, England. *E-mail:* paul@pauldriver4044.freeserve.co.uk.

DRUCKER, Peter (Ferdinand); writer, consultant and fmr teacher; b. 19 Nov. 1909, Vienna, Austria; m. Doris Schmitz, 1937, one s., three d. *Education:* Austria, Germany and England. *Career:* Investment Banker, London, 1933–36; Prof. of Philosophy and Politics, Bennington College, Vermont, 1942–49; International Management Consultant to businesses and governments, 1943–; Prof. of Management, New York University, 1950–72; Clarke Prof. of Social Science, Claremont Graduate University, CA, 1971–; Professorial Lecturer in Oriental Art, Claremont Colleges, CA, 1980–86; mem. American Acad. of Management, Fellow; Fellow International Acad. of Management. *Publications:* on society, economics and politics: The End of Economic Man 1938, 1995, The Future of Industrial Man 1942, 1995, The New Society 1949, 1993, America's Next Twenty Years (essays) 1957, The Landmarks of Tomorrow 1959, 1996, The Age of Discontinuity 1969, 1996, Men, Ideas & Politics (essays) 1971, The Unseen Revolution 1976 (republ. as The Pension Fund Revolution 1996), Toward the Next Economics (essays) 1981, The New Realities 1989, 2003, The Ecological Vision (essays) 1982, Post-Capitalist Society 1993, Drucker on Asia 1996, Managing in the Next Society 2002; on management: Concept of the Corporation 1946, 1993, The Practice of Management 1954, 1993, Managing for Results 1964, 1993, The Effective Executive 1966, 1993, Technology, Management and Society (essays) 1972, Management: Tasks, Responsibilities, Practices 1974, 1993, Managing in Turbulent Times 1980, 1993, The Changing World of the Executive 1982, Innovation and Entrepreneurship 1985, 1993, The Frontiers of Management (essays) 1986, 1997, Managing the Non-Profit Organization 1990, 1992, Managing for the Future (essays) 1992, Managing in a Time of Great Change (essays) 1995, Peter Drucker on the Profession of Management (essays) 1998, Management Challenges for the 21st Century 1999; anthologies: The Essential Drucker on Management 2001, A Functioning Society 2002; novels: The Last of All Possible Worlds 1982; The Temptation To Do Good 1984; autobiography: Adventures of a Bystander 1979 1991, 1998. Contributions: Magazines; Columnist, Wall Street Journal, 1975–95. *Honours:* Order of the Sacred Treasure of Japan; Grand Cross of Austria; Presidential Medal of Freedom; 25 hon. doctorates. *Address:* Claremont Graduate University, Claremont, CA 91711, USA.

DRUMMOND, June; Author; b. 15 Nov. 1923, Durban, South Africa. *Education:* BA, English, University of Cape Town. *Career:* mem. Soroptimist International; Writers Circle of South Africa. *Publications:* Slowly the Poison, 1975; The Patriots, 1979; The Trojan Mule, 1982; The Bluestocking, 1985; Junta, 1989; The Unsuitable Miss Pelham, 1990. *Address:* 24 Miller Grove, Durban 4001, South Africa.

DRYSDALE, Helena (Claire); Writer; b. 6 May 1960, London, England; m. Richard Pomeroy, 21 May 1987, two d. *Education:* Trinity College, Cambridge, 1978–82; BA, History, Art History, Cambridge. *Career:* mem. RGS; Society of Authors. *Publications:* Alone Through China and Tibet, 1986; Dancing With the Dead, 1991; Looking for Gheorghe: Love and Death in Romania (aka Looking for George), 1995; Mother Tongues: Travels Through Tribal Europe, 2002. Contributions: Vogue; Marie Claire; Independent; Independent on Sunday; Sunday Times; Daily Telegraph; Harpers and Queen; Cosmopolitan; World. *Honours:* Exhibitioner, Trinity College; PEN/J. R. Ackerley Award for Autobiography, 1995. *Literary Agent:* AP Watt Ltd, 20 John St, London WC1N 2DR, England. *Address:* 22 Stockwell Park Rd, London SW9 OAJ, England. *Website:* www.helenadrysdale.com.

DU VAUL, Virginia (see Coffman, Virginia (Edith)).

DUBE, Marcel; Dramatist, Author, Poet and Trans; b. 3 Jan. 1930, Montréal, QC, Canada; m. Nicole Fontaine, April 1956. *Education:* BA, Collège Sainte-Marie, 1951; University of Montréal; Theatre schools, Paris, 1953–54. *Career:* mem. Académie canadienne-française, fellow; Federation of Canadian Authors and Artists, pres., 1959; Royal Society of Canada, fellow. *Publications:* Over 30 plays, including: Zone, 1955, English trans., 1982; Un simple soldat, 1958; Le temps des lilas, 1958, English trans. as Time of the Lilacs, 1990; Florence, 1958; Bilan, 1968; Les beaux dimanches, 1968; Au retour des oies blanches, 1969, English trans. as The White Geese, 1972; Hold-up! (with Louis-George Carrier), 1969; Un matin commes les autres, 1971; Le neufrage, 1971; De l'autre coté du mur, 1973; L'impromptu de Québec, ou Le testament, 1974; L'été s'appelle Julie, 1975; Le réformiste, ou L'honneur des hommes, 1977; Le trou, 1986; L'Amérique a sec, 1986. Other: Television series. Poetry: Poèmes de sable, 1974. Non-Fiction: Textes et documents, 1968; La tragédie est un acte de foi, 1973; Jean-Paul Lemieux et le livre, 1988; Andrée Lachapelle: Entre ciel et terre, 1995. *Honours:* Prix Victor-Morin, Saint-Jean-Baptiste Society, 1966; Prix David, Québec, 1973; Molson Prize, Canada Council, 1984; Académie canadienne-française Medal, 1987. *Address:* c/o Société professionalle des auteurs et des compositeurs du Québec, 759 Sq. Victoria, No. 420, Montréal, QC H2Y 2J7, Canada.

DUBERMAN, Martin (Bauml); Prof. of History and Writer; b. 6 Aug. 1930, New York, NY, USA. *Education:* BA, Yale University, 1952; MA, 1953, PhD, 1957, Harvard University. *Career:* Teaching Fellow, Harvard University, 1955–57; Instructor, 1957–61, Morse Fellow, 1961–62, Yale University; Bicentennial Preceptor and Asst Prof., 1962–65, Assoc. Prof., 1965–67, Prof., 1967–71, Princeton University; Distinguished Prof. of History, Lehman College and Graduate School and University Center, CUNY, 1972–; Founder-Dir, Center for Lesbian and Gay Studies, Graduate School and Univ. Center, CUNY, 1991–; Visiting Randolph Distinguished Prof., Vassar College, 1992; Assoc. Ed., Journal of the History of Sexuality, 1993–, Masculinities: Interdisciplinary Studies on Gender, 1993–; Journal of Gay and Lesbian Psychotherapy, 2000–. *Publications:* Charles Francis Adams, 1807–1886, 1960; In White America, 1964; The Antislavery Vanguard: New Essays on the Abolitionists (ed.), 1965; James Russell Lowell, 1966; The Uncompleted Past, 1969; The Memory Bank, 1970; Black Mountain: An Exploration in Community, 1972; Male Armor: Selected Plays, 1968–1974, 1975; Visions of Kerouac, 1977; About Time: Exloring the Gay Past, 1986; Hidden from History: Reclaiming the Gay and Lesbian Past (co-ed.), 1989; Paul Robeson, 1989; Cures: A Gay Man's Odyssey, 1991; Mother Earth: An Epic Play on the Life of Emma Goldman, 1991; Stonewall, 1993; Midlife Queer, 1996; A Queer World: The Center for Lesbian and Gay Studies Reader (ed.), 1997; Queer Representations: Reading Lives, Reading Cultures (ed.), 1997; Left Out: The Politics of Exclusion (essays), 1999. Contributions: journals and newspapers. *Honours:* Bancroft Prize, 1961; Vernon Rice/Drama Desk Award, 1965; Pres.'s Gold Medal in Literature, Borough of Manhattan, 1988; 2 Lambda Book Awards, 1990; Distinguished

Service Award, Asscn of Gay and Lesbian Psychiatrists, 1996; Key to the City of Cambridge, MA, 1994; Legal Public Service Award, 1995; NOMAS Men's Studies Award, 1998; GALA Award, 1998. *Address:* c/o Graduate School and University Center, City University of New York, 33 W 42nd St, Room 404N, New York, NY 10036, USA.

DUBERSTEIN, Larry; Writer and Cabinetmaker; b. 18 May 1944, New York, NY, USA; three d. *Education:* BA, Wesleyan University, 1966; MA, Harvard University, 1971. *Publications:* Nobody's Jaw, 1979; The Marriage Hearse, 1983; Carnovsky's Retreat, 1988; Postcards From Pinsk, 1991; Eccentric Circles, 1992; The Alibi Breakfast, 1995; The Handsome Sailor, 1998; The Mt Monadnock Blues, 2003. Contributions: articles, essays, reviews in Saturday Review, Boston Review, The National, The Phoenix, New York Times Book Review, Boston Globe. *Honours:* New American Writing Awards, 1987, 1991; New York Times Notable Book, 1998. *Address:* Box 609, Cambridge, MA 02139, USA.

DUBIE, Norman Evans, Jr; Professor of English, Writer and Poet; b. 10 April 1945, Barre, Vermont, USA. *Education:* BA, Goddard College, 1969; MFA, University of Iowa, 1971. *Career:* Teaching Asst, Goddard College, 1967–69; Teaching Asst, 1969–70, Writing Fellow, 1970–71, Distinguished Lecturer and Mem. of the Graduate Faculty, 1971–74, University of Iowa; Poetry Ed., Iowa Review, 1971–72, Now Magazine, 1973–74; Asst Prof., Ohio University, 1974–75; Lecturer, 1975–76, Dir, Creative Writing, 1976–77, Assoc. Prof., 1978–81, Prof. of English, 1982–, Arizona State University. *Publications:* The Horsehair Sofa, 1969; Alehouse Sonnets, 1971; Indian Summer, 1973; The Prayers of the North American Martyrs, 1975; Popham of the New Song, 1975; In the Dead of Night, 1975; The Illustrations, 1977; A Thousand Little Things, 1977; Odalisque in White, 1978; The City of the Olesha Fruit, 1979; Comes Winter, the Sea Hunting, 1979; The Everlastings, 1980; The Window in the Field, 1982; Selected and New Poems, 1983; The Springhouse, 1986; Groom Falconer, 1989; Radio Sky, 1991; The Clouds of Magellan, 1991; The Choirs of June and January, 1993. Contributions: anthologies and periodicals. *Honours:* Bess Hokin Prize, 1976; Guggenheim Fellowship, 1977–78; Pushcart Prize, 1978–79; National Endowment for the Arts Grant, 1986; Ingram Merrill Grant, 1987. *Address:* c/o Dept of English, Arizona State University, Tempe, AZ 85281, USA.

DUBOIS, M. (see Kent, Arthur William Charles).

DUCHARME, Réjean; Novelist, Dramatist, Screenwriter, Sculptor and Painter; b. 12 Aug. 1941, Saint-Félix-de-Valois, QC, Caanda. *Education:* École Polytechnique, Montréal. *Publications:* Fiction: L'avalée des avalés, 1966; English trans. as The Swallower Swallowed, 1968; Le nez qui voque, 1967; L'océantume, 1968; La fille de Christophe Colomb, 1969; L'huver de force, 1973; Les enfantomes, 1976; Dévadé, 1990; Va savoir, 1994. Plays: Le Cid maghané, 1968; Le marquis qui perdit, 1970; Inès Pérée et Inat Tendu, 1976; HA! ha!..., 1982. Screenplays: Les bons débarras (with Francis Manckiewicz), 1979; Les beaux souvenirs (with Francis Manckiewicz), 1981. *Honours:* Governor-General's Awards for Fiction, 1966, and Drama, 1982.

DUCKWORTH, Marilyn; Writer; b. 10 Nov. 1935, Auckland, New Zealand; m. 1st Harry Duckworth, 28 May 1955; m. 2nd Ian Macfarlane, 2 Oct. 1964; m. 3rd Dan Donovan, 9 Dec. 1974; m. 4th John Batstone, 8 June 1985, four d. *Career:* mem. NZSA PEN, New Zealand. *Publications:* A Gap in the Spectrum, 1959; The Matchbox House, 1960; A Barbarous Tongue, 1963; Over the Fence is Out, 1969; Disorderly Conduct, 1984; Married Alive, 1985; Rest for the Wicked, 1986; Pulling Faces, 1987; A Message From Harpo, 1989; Explosions on the Sun, 1989; Unlawful Entry, 1992; Seeing Red, 1993; Leather Wings, 1995; Cherries on a Plate (ed.), 1996; Studmuffin, 1997; Camping on the Faultline, 2000; Swallowing Diamonds, 2003. Contributions: Landfall; New Zealand Listener; Critical Quarterly; Islands; others. *Honours:* New Zealand Literary Fund Scholarship in Letters, 1961, 1994; Katherine Mansfield Fellowship, 1980; New Zealand Book Award for Fiction, 1985; OBE, 1987; Fulbright Visiting Writers Fellowship, 1987; Australia-New Zealand Writers Exchange Fellowship, 1989; Victoria University of Wellington Writers Fellowship, 1990; Auckland University Literary Fellowship, 1996. *Literary Agent:* Curtis Brown Pty, PO Box 19, Paddington, NSW 2021, Australia. *Address:* 41 Queen St, Wellington, New Zealand. *E-mail:* marilynduckworth@hotmail.com.

DUCORNET, Erica Lynn, (Rikki Ducornet); Writer, Artist and Teacher; b. 19 April 1943, New York, NY, USA; one s. *Education:* Bard College, 1964. *Career:* Novelist-in-Residence, University of Denver, 1988–; Visiting Prof., University of Trento, Italy, 1994; mem. PEN. *Publications:* The Stain, 1984; Entering Fire, 1986; The Fountains of Neptune, 1989; Eben Demarst, 1990; The Jade Cabinet, 1993; The Butcher's Tales, 1994; Phosphor in Dreamland, 1995; The Word 'Desire', 1997; The Fan-Maker's Inquisition, 1999. Contributions: periodicals. *Honours:* Critics Choice Award, 1995; Charles Flint Kellogg Award in Arts and Letters, 1998. *Address:* c/o Dept of English, University of Denver, Denver, CO 80208, USA.

DUDLEY, Helen (see Hope-Simpson, Jacynth (Ann)).

DUEMER, Joseph; academic, poet and writer; b. 31 May 1951, San Diego, CA, USA; m. Carole A. Mathery 1987. *Education:* BA, University of Washington, 1978; MFA, University of Iowa, 1980. *Career:* Lecturer, Western Washington University, 1981–83, San Diego State University, 1983–87; Assoc. Prof. of Humanities, Clarkson University, 1987–; Poet-in-Residence, St Lawrence University, 1990; mem. Associated Writing Programs, board of dirs, 1998–2002. *Publications:* Poetry: Fool's Paradise, 1980; The Light of Common Day, 1985; Customs, 1987; Static, 1996; Primitive Alphabets, 1998. Editor: Dog Music (with Jan Simmerman), 1996. Contributions: Reference books, anthologies, reviews, journals, magazines and radio. *Honours:* National Endowment for the Arts Creative Writing Fellowships, 1984, 1992, and National Endowment for the Humanities Grants, 1985, 1995. *Address:* c/o Clarkson University, Potsdam, NY 13699, USA.

DUFF, Alan; Columnist and Writer; b. 26 Oct. 1950, Rotorua, New Zealand; m. Joanna Robin Harper, Sept. 1990. *Career:* Syndicated newspaper columnist, 1971–. *Publications:* Once Were Warriors, 1994; One Night Out Stealing, 1995. *Address:* 51 Busby Hill, Havelock North, New Zealand.

DUFF-WARE, Freddie (see Barnett, Paul (Le Page)).

DUFFY, Carol Ann, CBE, BA, FRSL; British poet and dramatist; b. 23 Dec. 1955, Glasgow, Scotland; one d. *Education:* St Joseph's Convent, Stafford and Univ. of Liverpool. *Career:* Poetry Ed. of AMBIT 1983–; Lecturer in Creative Writing, Manchester Metropolitan Univ. 1996–; mem. Poetry Soc. (vice-pres.). *Plays:* Take My Husband 1984, Cavern Dreams 1986, Grimm Tales 1994, More Grimm Tales 1997. *Publications:* poetry: Fleshweathercock 1973, Standing Female Nude (Scottish Arts Council Award) 1985, Selling Manhattan (Scottish Arts Council Award, Somerset Maugham Award 1988) 1987, Home and Away 1988, The Other Country (Dylan Thomas Award) 1990, Mean Time (Whitbread Poetry Award, Forward Poetry Prize, Scottish Arts Council Book Award) 1993, Selected Poems 1994, The Pamphlet 1998, The World's Wife 1999, Time's Tidings 1999, Feminine Gospels 2001, Underwater Farmyard 2002. *Honours:* C. Day-Lewis Fellowships 1982–84, Eric Gregory Award 1985, Cholmondeley Award 1992, Lannan Award (USA) 1995, Signal Poetry Award 1997. *Address:* c/o Anvil Press, 69 King George Street, London, SE10 8PX, England. *Telephone:* (20) 8858-2946.

DUFFY, Eamon; Writer; b. 1947, Dundalk, Ireland. *Education:* Hull Univ.; PhD, Selwyn College, Cambridge. *Publications:* Challoner and His Church: Catholic Bishop in Georgian England, 1981; What Catholics Believe About Mary, 1989; The Stripping of the Altars: Traditional Religion in England 1400–1580, 1992; The Creed in the Catechism: The Life of God for Us, 1996; Saints and Sinners: A History of the Popes, 1997; The Voices of Morebath: Reformation and Rebellion in an English Village, 2001. Contributions: New York Review of Books. *Honours:* Longman's History Today prize, 1994; Hawthornden Prize, 2002. *Address:* c/o Yale University Press London, 47 Bedford Sq., London WC1B 3DP, England.

DUFFY, Maureen Patricia, BA, FRSL; British writer and poet; b. 21 Oct. 1933, Worthing, Sussex, England. *Education:* Trowbridge High School for Girls, Sarah Bonnell High School for Girls, King's Coll., London. *Career:* staged pop art exhbn with Brigid Brophy 1969; Chair. Greater London Arts Literature Panel 1979–81, Authors Lending and Copyright Soc. 1982–94, Copyright Licensing Agency 1996–99 (Vice-Chair. 1994–96); Pres. Writers' Guild of GB 1985–88 (Jt Chair. 1977–78); co-founder Writers' Action Group 1972–79; Vice-Pres. European Writers Congress 1992–2003 (Pres. 2003–), Beauty without Cruelty 1975–, British Copyright Council 1998–2003 (Vice-Chair. 1981–86, Chair. 1989–98, Hon. Pres. 2003); Fellow, King's Coll. London 2002. *Radio:* The Passionate Shepherdess, Only Goodnight. *Television:* Upstairs Downstairs (Episode 11). *Plays:* Pearson (London Playwrights' Award), Rites (Nat. Theatre) 1969, A Nightingale in Bloomsbury Square (Hampstead Theatre) 1974, The Masque of Henry Purcell (Southwark Theatre). *Publications:* That's How It Was 1962, The Single Eye 1964, The Microcosm 1966, The Paradox Players 1967, Lyrics for the Dog Hour (poems) 1968, Wounds 1969, Love Child 1971, The Venus Touch 1971, The Erotic World of Faery 1972, I Want to Go to Moscow 1973, Capital 1975, Evesong (poems) 1975, The Passionate Shepherdess 1977, Housespy 1978, Memorials of the Quick and the Dead (poems) 1979, Inherit the Earth 1980, Gorsaga 1981, Londoners: An Elegy 1983, Men and Beasts 1984, Collected Poems 1949–84 1985, Change 1987, A Thousand Capricious Chances: Methuen 1889–1989 1989, Illuminations 1991, Occam's Razor 1992, Henry Purcell (biog.) 1994, Restitution 1998, England: The Making of a Myth from Stonehenge to Albert Square 2001, Alchemy 2004. *Honours:* Hon. Pres. Authors Lending and Copyright Soc. 2002; Fellow King's College 2002; CISAC Gold Medal for Literature 2002. *Address:* 18 Fabian Road, London, SW6 7TZ, England. *Telephone:* (20) 7385-3598. *Fax:* (20) 7385-2468.

DUFFY, Stella; British writer and actress; b. 1963, London. *Education:* Victoria Univ. *Career:* raised in New Zealand, returned to England 1987. *Plays:* The Hand, Jackson's Lane Theatre 1995, Close to You, Hen and Chickens Theatre 1996, Crocodiles and Bears, BAC 1999, The Tedious Predictability of Falling in Love, Immaculate Conceit, Lyric Hammersmith 2003. *Publications:* novels: Calendar Girl 1994, Wavewalker 1996, Beneath the Blonde 1997, Singling Out the Couples 1998, Fresh Flesh 1999, Eating Cake 1999, Immaculate Conceit 2000, State of Happiness 2004; editor: Tart Noir (with Lauren Henderson) 2002. *Address:* c/o Virago Press, Brettenham House, Lancaster Place, London, WC2E 7EN, England. *Telephone:* (20) 7911-8000.

DUGGAN, Christopher; University Lecturer and Writer; b. 11 April 1957, London, England; m. Jennifer Virginia Mundy, 2 June 1987. *Education:* BA, Merton College, Oxford, 1979. *Career:* Junior Research Fellow, Wolfson College, Oxford, 1983–85; Fellow, All Soul's College, Oxford, 1985; Lecturer in Italian History, Dir of Centre for the Advanced Study of Italian Society, University of Reading, 1987–. *Publications:* A History of Sicily (co-author), 1986; Fascism and the Mafia, 1989; A Concise History of Italy, 1994; Francisco Crispi, 2003. Contributions: articles and reviews to various journals and newspapers. *Address:* 10 Hamilton Rd, London NW10 1NY, England.

DUKE, Elizabeth (see Wallington, Vivienne Elizabeth).

DUKORE, Bernard Frank; academic and writer; b. 11 July 1931, New York, NY, USA; one s. two d. *Education:* BA, Brooklyn College, CUNY, 1952; MA, Ohio State University, 1953; PhD, University of Illinois, 1957. *Career:* Instructor, Hunter College, CUNY, 1957–60; Asst Prof., University of Southern California, Los Angeles, 1960–62; Asst to Assoc. Prof., California State University, Los Angeles, 1962–66; Assoc. Prof. to Prof. of Theatre, CUNY, 1966–72; Prof. of Drama and Theatre, University of Hawaii, 1972–86; University Distinguished Prof. of Theatre Arts and Humanities, 1986–97, Prof. Emeritus, 1997–, Virginia Polytechnic Institute and State University, Blacksburg; mem. American Theatre Asscn, fellow; Pinter Society. *Publications:* Bernard Shaw, Dir, 1971; Bernard Shaw, Playwright, 1973; Dramatic Theory and Criticism, 1974; Where Laughter Stops: Pinter's Tragicomedy, 1976; Collected Screenplays of Bernard Shaw, 1980; Money and Politics in Ibsen, Shaw and Brecht, 1980; The Theatre of Peter Barnes, 1981; Harold Pinter, 1982; Alan Ayckbourn: A Casebook, 1991; The Drama Observed (ed. and annotator), 4 vols, 1992–93; Shaw and the Last Hundred Years (ed.), 1994; Barnestorm: The Plays of Peter Barnes, 1995; Bernard Shaw and Gabriel Pascal, 1996; Not Bloody Likely: The Columbia Book of Bernard Shaw Quotations, 1997; Shaw on Cinema (ed. and annotator), 1997; Sam Peckinpah's Feature Films, 1999; Shaw's Theatre, 2000. *Honours:* Guggenheim Fellowship, 1969–70; National Endowment for the Humanities Fellowships, 1976–77, 1984–85, 1990; Fulbright Research Scholarship, England and Ireland, 1991–92. *Address:* c/o School of the Arts, Virginia Polytechnic Institute & State University, Blacksburg, VA 24061-0141, USA. *E-mail:* bdukore@rt .edn.

DUMAS, Claudine (see Malzberg, Barry).

DUMMETT, Sir Michael (Anthony Eardley); Prof. of Logic Emeritus and Writer; b. 27 June 1925, London, England; m. Ann Chesney, 1951, three s., two d. *Education:* Winchester College; Christ Church, Oxford. *Career:* Fellow, 1950–79, Emeritus Fellow, 1979–, Senior Research Fellow, 1974–79, All Souls College, Oxford; Commonwealth Fund Fellow, University of California, Berkeley, 1955–56; Reader in the Philosophy of Mathematics, 1962–74, Wykeham Prof. of Logic, 1979–92, Prof. of Logic Emeritus, 1992–, University of Oxford; Fellow, 1979–92, Fellow Emeritus, 1992–98; Hon. Fellow, 1998–; New College, Oxford; various visiting lectureships and professorships; mem. American Acad. of Arts and Sciences, hon. mem.; British Acad., fellow; Academia Europaea. *Publications:* Frege: Philosophy of Language, 1973; The Justification of Deduction, 1973; Elements of Intuitionism, 1977; Truth and Other Enigmas, 1978; Immigration: Where the Debate Goes Wrong, 1978; Catholicism and the World Order, 1979; The Game of Tarot, 1980; Twelve Tarot Games, 1980; The Interpretation of Frege's Philosophy, 1981; Voting Procedures, 1984; The Visconti-Sforza Tarot Cards, 1986; Ursprünge der analytischen Philosophie, 1988, revised edn as Origins of Analytical Philosophy, 1993; Frege and Other Philosophers, 1991; The Logical Basis of Metaphysics, 1991; Frege: Philosophy of Mathematics, 1991; Grammar and Style for Examination Candidates and Others, 1993; The Seas of Language, 1993; Il Mondo e l'Angelo, 1993; I Tarocchi siciliani, 1995; A Wicked Pack of Cards (with R. Decker and T. Depaulis), 1996; Principles of Electoral Reform, 1997; On Immigration and Refugees, 2001; La natura e il futuro della filosofia, 2001; History of the Occult Tarot (with R. Decker), 2002. Contributions: various books and scholarly journals. *Honours:* Hon. doctorates, Universities of Nijmegen, 1982, Oxford, 1989, Caen, 1991, Aberdeen, 1991; Lakatos Award in the Philosophy of Science, 1994; Rolf Schock Prize for Philosophy and Logic, 1995; Knighted, 1999. *Address:* 54 Park Town, Oxford OX2 6SJ, England.

DUMONT, André; Writer; b. 12 April 1929, Campbellton, NB, Canada; m. Germaine Richard, 1958, two s. two d. *Education:* BA, 1961; BEd, 1964. *Publications:* Français Renouvele I, 1964, II, 1966; Le Parti Acadien (co-author), 1972; Jeunesse Mouvementée, 1979; Quand Je Serai Grand, 1989; Pour un Français Moderne, 1990; Avancez en Arrière, 1996. Contributions: Over 100 articles on different topics, mostly political. *Address:* 505-830 Ave Ernest-Gagnon, Québec, QC G1S 3R3, Canada.

DUNANT, Peter (see Dunant, Sarah).

DUNANT, Sarah, (Peter Dunant), BA; British writer and broadcaster; b. 8 Aug. 1950, London, England; pnr Ian David Willox; two d. *Education:* Newnham Coll., Cambridge. *Publications:* as Sarah Dunant: Snow Falls in a Hot Climate 1988, Birth Marks 1991, Fatlands 1993, The War of the Words: Essays on Political Correctness (ed.) 1994, Under My Skin 1995, The Age of Anxiety (ed.) 1996, Transgressions 1997, Mapping the Edge 1999, The Birth of Venus 2003; as Peter Dunant: Exterminating Angels (co-author) 1983, Intensive Care (co-author) 1986; contrib. to various London magazines, Listener, Guardian. *Honours:* CWA Silver Dagger Award 1993. *Literary Agent:* Gillon Aitken Associates Ltd, 18–21 Cavaye Place, London, SW10 9PT, England. *Telephone:* (20) 7373-8672. *Fax:* (20) 7373-6002.

DUNCAN, Lois; Writer; b. 28 April 1934, Philadelphia, Pennsylvania, USA; m. Donald W. Arquette, 15 July 1965, two s. three d. *Education:* Duke University, 1952–53; BA, University of New Mexico, 1977. *Publications:* Ransom, 1966; A Gift of Magic, 1971; I Know What You Did Last Summer, 1973; Down a Dark Hall, 1974; Summer of Fear, 1976; Killing Mr Griffin, 1978; Daughters of Eve, 1979; Stranger With My Face, 1981; My Growth as a Writer, 1982; The Third Eye, 1984; Locked in Time, 1985; Horses of Dreamland, 1986; The Twisted Window, 1987; Songs From Dreamland, 1989; The Birthday Moon, 1989; Don't Look Behind You, 1989; Who Killed My Daughter?, 1992; The Circus Comes Home, 1993; Psychic Connections: A Journey into the Mysterious World of Psi (co-author William Roll), 1995; The Magic of Spider Woman, 1996; Gallows Hill, 1997; Night Terrors (edited anthology), 1997; Trapped (edited anthology), 1998. *Address:* c/o Dell Publishing, 1540 Broadway, New York, NY 10036, USA.

DUNCAN-JONES, Katherine Dorothea, BLitt, MA; British academic and editor; *Professor Emerita, University of Oxford*; b. 13 May 1941; m. Andrew N. Wilson 1971 (divorced 1990); two d. *Education:* King Edward VI High School for Girls, Birmingham and St Hilda's Coll., Oxford. *Career:* Fellow and Tutor in English Literature, Somerville Coll., Oxford 1966–; Prof. of English Literature, Univ. of Oxford 1998–2001, Prof. Emerita 2001–; mem. RSL. *Publications include:* biography: Sir Philip Sidney: Courtier Poet 1991, Ungentle Shakespeare 2001; editor: Miscellaneous Prose of Sir Philip Sidney 1977, Sir Philip Sidney 1989, Shakespeare's Sonnets 1997; contrib. to Review of English Studies, TLS and other journals. *Honours:* Mary Ewart Research Fellow, Somerville Coll. 1963–65, Fellow, New Hall, Cambridge 1965–66, Hon. Research Fellow, Univ. Coll. London 2000; Ben Jonson Discoveries Prize 1996. *Address:* c/o Somerville College, Oxford, OX2 6HD, England.

DUNCKER, Patricia, MA, DPhil; writer; *Professor of Creative Writing, University of East Anglia*; b. 29 June 1951, Kingston, Jamaica. *Education:* Univ. of Cambridge, Univ. of Oxford. *Career:* Lecturer, Roehampton Inst. 1978–80, Oxford Polytechnic 1980–86, Univ. of Poitiers, France 1987–91, Univ. of Wales, Aberystwyth 1991–2002; Prof. of Creative Writing, Univ. of East Anglia 2002–; mem. Soc. of Authors, Yr Academi Gymreig (The Welsh Acad.), PEN, RSA. *Publications:* Sisters and Strangers: An Introduction to Contemporary Feminist Fiction 1992, Hallucinating Foucault 1996, Cancer Through the Eyes of Ten Women 1996, Monsieur Shoushana's Lemon Trees 1997, James Miranda Barry (aka The Doctor) 1999, The Deadly Space Between 2002, Writing on the Wall 2002, Seven Tales of Sex and Death 2003; contrib. to Critical Quarterly, Stand Magazine, Women: A Cultural Review. *Honours:* Dillons First Fiction Award, McKitterick Prize. *Literary Agent:* Victoria Hobbs, A. M. Heath & Co Ltd, 79 St Martin's Lane, London, WC2N 4RE, England. *Address:* School of English and American Studies, University of East Anglia, Norwich, Norfolk NR4 7TJ, England. *E-mail:* p .duncker@uea.ac.uk.

DUNHAM, William Wade; Prof. of Mathematics and Writer; b. 8 Dec. 1947, Pittsburgh, Pennsylvania, USA; m. Penelope Higgins, 26 Sept. 1970, two s. *Education:* BS, University of Pittsburgh, 1969; MS, 1970, PhD, 1974, Ohio State University. *Career:* Truman Koehler Prof. of Mathematics, Muhlenberg College, 1992–; mem. Mathematical Asscn of America; National Council of Teachers of Mathematics. *Publications:* Journey Through Genius: The Great Theorems of Mathematics, 1990; The Mathematical Universe, 1994; Euler: The Master of Us All, 1999. Contributions: American Mathematical Monthly; Mathematics Magazine; College Mathematics Journal; Mathematics Teacher. *Honours:* M. M. Culver Award, University of Pittsburgh, 1969; Master Teacher Award, Hanover College, 1981; National Endowment for the Humanities Summer Seminars on Great Theorems, 1988–96; Humanities Achievement Award for Scholarship, Indiana Humanities Council, 1991; George Pólya Award, Mathematical Asscn of America, 1993; Trevor Evans Award, Mathematical Asscn of America, 1997; Lindback Teaching Award, Muhlenberg College, 2001. *Address:* Dept of Mathematics, Muhlenberg College, Allentown, PA 18104, USA.

DUNKERLEY, James; Reader in Politics and Writer; b. 15 Aug. 1953, Wokingham, England. *Education:* BA, University of York, 1974; BPhil, Hertford College, Oxford, 1977; PhD, Nuffield College, Oxford, 1979. *Career:* Researcher, Latin America Bureau, London, 1979–80, 1983–84; Research Fellow, Institute for Latin American Studies, University of London, 1981–82, Centre for Latin American Studies, University of Liverpool, 1982–83; Fellow, Kellogg Institute, University of Notre Dame, IN, 1985; Reader in Politics, Queen Mary and Westfield College, University of London, 1986–, Prof. 1990–; Dir Inst. ofLatin American Studies London 1998–. *Publications:* Unity is Strength: Trade Unions in Latin America (with C. Whitehouse), 1980; Bolivia: Coup d'Etat, 1980; The Long War: Dictatorship and Revolution in El Salvador, 1982; Rebellion in the Veins: Political Struggle in Bolivia, 1952–1982, 1984; Granada: Whose Freedom? (with F. Amburseley), 1984; Origenes del poder militar en Bolivia 1879–1935, 1987; Power in the Isthmus: A Political History of Central

America, 1988; Political Suicide in Latin America and Other Essays, 1992; The Pacification of Central America, 1994, Warriors and Scribes 2000; Americana, The Americas in the World, around 1850 2000. Contributions: scholarly journals, newspapers, and magazines. *Address:* c/o Institute of Latin American Studies, 31 Tavistock Square, London WC1H 9HA, England.

DUNLAP, Susan; Writer; b. 20 June 1943, Kew Gardens, New York, USA; m. Newell Dunlap, 1970. *Education:* BA, English, Bucknell University, 1965; MAT, English, University of North Carolina, 1966. *Career:* mem. Founding Mem., Sisters in Crime, pres., 1990–91. *Publications:* An Equal Opportunity Death, 1984; Karma, 1984; As a Favor, 1984; Not Exactly a Brahmin, 1985; The Bohermian Connection, 1986; The Last Annual Slugfest, 1986; Too Close to the Edge, 1987; A Dinner to Die For, 1987; Pious Deception, 1989; Diamond in the Buff, 1990; Rogue Wave, 1991; Death and Taxes, 1993; Time Expired, 1993; High Fall, 1994; Sudden Exposure, 1995; Cop Out, 1997. Other: Deadly Allies II: Private Eye Writers of America and Sisters in Crime Collaborative Anthology (co-ed.), 1994. Contributions: numerous short stories to periodicals including: Ellery Queen's Mystery Magazine; Alfred Hitchcock's Mystery Magazine. *Address:* c/o Dominick Abel, 146 W 82nd St, New York, NY 10024, USA.

DUNMORE, Helen, BA, FRSL; British poet and novelist; b. 1952, Yorkshire; m.; one s. one d. one step-s. *Education:* York Univ. *Publications include:* poetry: The Apple Fall 1983, The Sea Skater 1986 (Poetry Soc. Alice Hunt Bartlett Award), The Raw Garden 1988 (Poetry Book Soc. Choice), Short Days, Long Nights: New & Selected Poems 1991, Secrets 1994 (Signal Poetry Award 1995), Recovering a Body 1994, Bestiary 1997, Out of the Blue: New and Selected Poems 2001; fiction: Going to Egypt 1992, Zennor in Darkness 1993 (McKitterick Prize1994), In the Money 1993, Burning Bright 1994, A Spell of Winter 1995 (Orange Prize for Women Writers of Fiction 1996), Talking to the Dead 1996, Your Blue-Eyed Boy 1998, With Your Crooked Heart 1999, The Siege 2001, The Silver Bead 2003; short stories: Love of Fat Men 1997, Ice Cream 2000, Mourning Ruby 2003. *Honours:* Hon. Fellow Royal Soc. of Literature. *Literary Agent:* Caradoc King, A. P. Watt Ltd, 20 John Street, London, WC1N 2DR, England. *Telephone:* (20) 7405-6774. *Fax:* (20) 7831-2154.

DUNMORE, John; University Prof. and Writer; b. 6 Aug. 1923, Trouville, France; m. Joyce Megan Langley, 22 April 1946, one s. one d. *Education:* BA, University of London, 1950; PhD, University of New Zealand, 1962. *Career:* mem. Australasian Language and Literature Asscn, pres., 1980–82. *Publications:* French Explorers in the Pacific, 1966–69; The Fateful Voyage of the St Jean Baptiste, 1969; Norman Kirk: A Portrait, 1972; Pacific Explorer, 1985; New Zealand and the French, 1990; The French and the Maoris, 1992; Who's Who in Pacific Navigation, 1992; The Journal of La Perouse, 1994–95; I Remember Tomorrow, 1998; Monsieur Baret: First Woman Around the World, 2002; The Pacific Journal of Bougainville, 2003. Contributions: numerous learned journals and periodicals. *Honours:* New Zealand Book of the Year, 1970; Legion of Honour, 1976; Academic Palms, 1986; New Zealand Commemoration Medal, 1990; Massey Medal, 1993; Companion New Zealand Order of Merit, 2001. *Address:* 9B Pounamu Ave, Greenhithe, Auckland, New Zealand.

DUNN, Douglas Eaglesham, OBE, BA, FRSL; British poet; *Professor of Creative Writing, University of St Andrews;* b. 23 Oct. 1942, Inchinnan, Scotland; m. 1st Lesley B. Wallace 1964 (died 1981); m. 2nd Lesley Jane Bathgate 1985; one s. one d. *Education:* Univ. of Hull. *Career:* full-time writer 1971–91; Writer-in-residence Duncan of Jordanstone Coll. of Art and Dundee Dist Libraries 1986–88; Fellow in Creative Writing, Univ. of St Andrews 1989–91, Prof. 1991–, Head School of English 1994–99; Dir St Andrews Scottish Studies Inst. 1992–; Hon. Visiting Prof. Dundee Univ. 1987–89; mem. Scottish PEN. *Publications:* Terry Street 1969 (Somerset Maugham Award 1972), The Happier Life 1972, New Poems 1972–73 (ed.) 1973, Love or Nothing 1974 (Faber Memorial Prize 1976), A Choice of Byron's Verse (ed.) 1974, Two Decades of Irish Writing (criticism) 1975, The Poetry of Scotland (ed.) 1979, Barbarians 1979, St Kilda's Parliament 1981 (Hawthornden Prize 1982), Europa's Lover 1982, A Rumoured City: New Poets from Hull (ed.) 1982, To Build a Bridge: A Celebration of Humberside in Verse (ed.) 1982, Elegies 1985 (Whitbread Poetry Award and Whitbread Book of the Year 1986), Secret Villages (short stories) 1985, Selected Poems 1986, Northlight 1988, New and Selected Poems 1989, Poll Tax: The Fiscal Fake 1990, Andromache 1990, The Essential Browning (ed.) 1990, Scotland. An Anthology (ed.) 1991, Faber Book of Twentieth Century Scottish Poetry (ed.) 1992, Dante's Drum-Kit 1993, Boyfriends and Girlfriends (short stories) 1995, Oxford Book of Scottish Short Stories (ed.) 1995, The Donkey's Ears, The Year's Afternoon 2000, 20th Century Scottish Poems (ed.) 2000. *Honours:* Hon. Fellow, Humberside Coll. 1987; Hon. LLD (Dundee) 1987; Hon. DLitt (Hull) 1995; Cholmondeley Award 1989. *Address:* School of English, The University, St Andrews, Fife, KY16 9AL, Scotland (Office). *Telephone:* (1334) 462666 (Office). *Fax:* (1334) 462655 (Office). *E-mail:* ded@st-andrews.ac.uk (Office).

DUNN, John Montfort, BA, FBA, FRSA; academic and writer; *Professor of Political Theory, University of Cambridge;* b. 9 Sept. 1940, Fulmer, England; m. 1st Susan Deborah Fyvel 1965 (divorced 1971); m. 2nd Judith Frances Bernal 1973 (divorced 1987); two s. (one deceased); m. 3rd Ruth Ginette Scurr 1997; two d. *Education:* King's College, Cambridge. *Career:* Harkness Fellow, Harvard Univ., 1964–65; Official Fellow in History, Jesus College, Cambridge, 1965–66; Dir of Studies in History, 1966–72, Lecturer in Political Science, 1972–77, Reader in Politics, 1977–87, Prof. of Political Theory, 1987–, Univ. of Cambridge; Fellow, King's College, Cambridge, 1966–; Visiting Lecturer, Univ. of Ghana, 1968–69; Visiting Prof., Univ. of Mumbai, 1979–80, Tokyo Metropolitan Univ., 1983–84; Distinguished Visiting Prof., Tulane Univ., New Orleans, 1986; Benjamin Evans Lippincott Distinguished Prof., Univ. of Minnesota, 1990; Olmsted Visiting Prof., Yale Univ., 1991. *Publications:* The Political Thought of John Locke, 1969; Modern Revolutions, 1972; Dependency and Opportunity: Political Change in Ahafo (with A. F. Robertson), 1973; West African States: Failure and Promise (ed.), 1978; Western Political Theory in the Face of the Future, 1979; Political Obligation in its Historical Context, 1980; Locke, 1984; The Politics of Socialism, 1984; Rethinking Modern Political Theory, 1985; The Economic Limits to Modern Politics (ed.), 1989; Contemporary West African States (ed.), 1989; Interpreting Political Responsibility, 1990; Democracy: The Unfinished Journey (ed.), 1992; Contemporary Crisis of the Nation State? (ed.), 1994; The History of Political Theory, 1995; Great Political Thinkers (ed. with Ian Harris), 21 vols, 1997; The Cunning of Unreason: Making Sense of Politics, 2000; Pensare la Politica, 2002; Locke: A Very Short Introduction, 2003. Contributions: scholarly journals. *Honours:* foreign hon. mem., American Acad. of Arts and Sciences. *Address:* The Merchant's House, 31 Station Road, Swavesey, Cambridge CB4 5QJ, England.

DUNN, Stephen; Poet and Writer; b. 24 June 1939, New York, NY, USA; m. 1st Lois Kelly 1964 (divorced) two d.; m. 2nd Barbara Hurd 15 Feb. 2003. *Education:* BA, History, Hofstra Univ., 1962; New School for Social Research, New York City, 1964–66; MA, Creative Writing, Syracuse Univ., 1970. *Career:* Asst Prof., Southwest Minnesota State College, Marshall, 1970–73; Visiting Poet, Syracuse Univ., 1973–74, Univ. of Washington at Seattle, 1980; Assoc. Prof. to Prof., 1974–90, Distinguished Prof., Richard Stockton College of NJ; Adjunct Prof. of Poetry, Columbia Univ., 1983–87. *Publications:* Poetry: Five Impersonations, 1971; Looking for Holes in the Ceiling, 1974; Full of Lust and Good Usage, 1976; A Circus of Needs, 1978; Work and Love, 1981; Not Dancing, 1984; Local Time, 1986; Between Angels, 1989; Landscape at the End of the Century, 1991; New and Selected Poems, 1974–1994, 1994; Loosestrife, 1996; Riffs and Reciprocities, 1998; Different Hours, 2000; Local Visitations, 2003. Other: Walking Light: Essays and Memoirs, 1993. Contributions: periodicals. *Honours:* Acad. of American Poets Prize, 1970; National Endowment for the Arts Fellowships, 1973, 1982, 1989; Bread Loaf Writers Conference Robert Frost Fellowship, 1975; Theodore Roethke Prize, 1977; New Jersey Arts Council Fellowships, 1979, 1983; Helen Bullis Prize, 1982; Guggenheim Fellowship, 1984; Levinson Prize, 1988; Oscar Blumenthal Prize, 1991; James Wright Prize, 1993; American Acad. of Arts and Letters Award, 1995; Pulitzer Prize in Poetry, 2001. *Address:* 790 Piney Run Rd, Frostburg, MD 21532, USA.

DUNNE, Dominick; Novelist and Essayist; b. 29 Oct. 1925, Hartford, CT, USA; m. Ellen Griffin 24 April 1952 (divorced); two s. one d. (deceased). *Education:* BA, Williams College, 1949. *Career:* Television and film producer; Co-Founder, Dunne-Didion-Dunne film production company. *Publications:* The Winners: Part II of Joyce Haber's 'The Users', 1982; The Two Mrs Grenvilles, 1985; Fatal Charms, and Other Tales of Today, 1986; People Like Us, 1988; An Inconvenient Woman, 1990; The Mansions of Limbo, 1991; A Season in Purgatory, 1993; Another City, Not My Own: A Novel in the Form of a Memoir, 1997; The Way We Lived Then: Recollections of a Well-Known Name Dropper, 1999; Justice: Crimes, Trials and Punishments, 2001. *Address:* c/o Crown Publishing, 299 Park Ave, New York, NY 10171, USA.

DuNOUR, Shlomo; Israeli writer and teacher; b. 1921, Łodz, Poland; m. Mirian DuNour. *Career:* moved to Palestine 1938; leader of the Aliyat Ha Noar Movement; teacher, Dept of History, Hebrew Univ., Univ. of Haifa. *Publications include:* novels: Yet Another 1978, Adiel 2001. *Honours:* Newman Prize 1978, Jerusalem Prize for Literature 1999. *Address:* c/o The Toby Press, PO Box 8531, New Milford, CT 06776-8531, USA. *Website:* www.tobypress.com.

DUONG THU HUONG; Vietnamese writer and screenwriter; b. 3 Jan. 1947, Thai Binh province; m. 1968 (divorced 1981); one s. one d. *Education:* Ecole de Théorie Professionnelle (Ministry of Culture) and Ecole de Formation Littéraire Nguyen Du. *Career:* volunteer, Cultural Activities, Binh Tri Thien 1968–77; film studio work North Viet Nam from 1977; mem. Exec. Cttee Asscn des Cinéastes 1989. *Publications in translation:* Paradise of the Blind 1994, Novel Without a Name 1995, Memories of a Pure Spring 2000; four scripts, one children's novel, ten collections of stories. *Honours:* First Prize, Concours de récit 1979, Gold Medal, two Silver Medals Vietnamese Film Festivals for feature films scripted. *Address:* Association des Cinéastes Vietnamiens, 51 rue de Tran hung Dao, Hanoi, Viet Nam; c/o Editions des Femmes, 6 rue de Mézières, 75006 Paris, France.

DURAND, Claude; French publisher; b. 9 Nov. 1938, Livry-Gargan (Seine-et-Oise); m. Carmen Perea 1965; two s. *Education:* Ecole normale d'instituteurs de Versailles. *Career:* fmr schoolteacher; Literary Dir Editions du Seuil 1965–78; Gen. Man. Editions Grasset 1978–80; Chair. and CEO Librairie Arthème Fayard 1980–, Librairie Stock 1991–98; Chair. Bd of Dirs Inst. Mémoire de l'édition contemporaine 1990–93, Deputy Chair.

1993–. *Publication:* La Nuit zoologique (novel, Prix Médicis) 1979. *Honours:* Chevalier, Légion d'honneur, Chevalier, Ordre nat. du Mérite, Commdr des Arts et des Lettres. *Address:* Librairie Fayard, 75 rue des Saints-Pères, 75006 Paris (Office); 46 rue de Naples, 75008 Paris, France (Home).

DURBAN, (Rosa) Pam; academic and writer; b. 4 March 1947, Aiken, SC, USA; m. Frank H. Hunter 1983. *Education:* BA, University of North Carolina at Greensboro, 1969; MFA, University of Iowa, 1979. *Career:* Ed., Atlanta Gazette, 1974–75; Visiting Asst Prof. of Creative Writing, SUNY at Geneseo, 1979–80; Asst Prof. of Creative Writing, Murray State University, 1980–81; Assoc. Prof. of Creative Writing, Ohio University, 1981–86; Prof. of English and Creative Writing, Georgia State University, 1986–. *Publications:* All Set about with Fever Trees and Other Stories, 1985; The Laughing Place, 1993; So Far Back, 2000. Contributions: anthologies and periodicals. *Honours:* James A. Michener Fellowship, University of Iowa, 1982–83; Rinehart Award in Fiction, Rinehart Foundation, 1984; Ohio Arts Council Fellowships, 1983–84, 1986–87; Whiting Writer's Award, 1987; National Endowment for the Arts Creative Writing Fellowship, 1998. *Address:* c/o Department of English, Georgia State University, Atlanta, GA 30303, USA.

DURKIN, Barbara (Rae Wernecke); Writer; b. 13 Jan. 1944, Baltimore, MD, USA; m. William J. Durkin, 20 May 1973, two s. *Education:* AA, Essex Community College, 1964; BS, Towson State College, 1966; Graduate Studies, Morgan State College, 1968, John Hopkins University, 1968–70. *Career:* mem. American PEN Women; International Women's Writing Guild. *Publications:* Oh, You Dundalk Girls, Can't You Dance the Polka?, 1984; Visions and Viewpoints (ed.), 1993. *Honours:* Best of 1984 List, American Library Asscn, 1984. *Address:* 531 Phillips Rd, Webster, NY 14580, USA.

DÜRRSON, Werner, PhD; poet, writer, dramatist and translator; b. 12 Sept. 1932, Schwenningen am Neckar, Germany. *Education:* Trossingen, Tübingen, Munich. *Career:* mem. Asscn Internationale des Critiques littéraires, Paris, Asscn of German Writers, PEN. *Publications:* Schubart (play) 1980, Stehend bewegt (poem) 1980, Der Luftkünstler (prose) 1983, Wie ich lese? (essay) 1986, Ausleben (selection of poems) 1988, Abbreviaturen (aphorisms) 1989, Werke (poetry and prose, four vols) 1992, Ausgewählte Gedichte (poems) 1995, The Kattenhorn Silence (trans. by Michael Hamburger) 1995, Stimmen aus der Gutenberg-Galaxis (literary essays) 1997, Der verkaufte Schatten 1997, Wasserspiele (poems) 1999, Pariser Spitzen (poems) 2001; other: several works in co-operation with painters, including Klaus Staeck, Erich Heckel, HAP Grieshaber, Jonny Friedlaender, and musicians, including Klaus Fessmann; trans of authors, including Guillaume d'Aquitaine, Marguerite de Navarre, Stéphane Mallarmé, Arthur Rimbaud, Yvan Goll, René Char and Henri Michaux; contrib. to anthologies and radio. *Honours:* Lyric Poetry Prize, South West German Press, 1953; German Awards for Short Stories, 1973, 1983; Literary Prize, Stuttgart, 1978; Literary Prize, Überlingen, 1985; Bundesverdienstkreuz, 1993; Prize of the Schiller Foundation, Weimar, 1997; Eichendorff Literary Prize, 2001. *Address:* Schloss Neufra, 88499 Riedlingen, Germany.

DURST, Paul; Writer; b. 23 April 1921, Archbald, Pennsylvania, USA. *Education:* Colorado State College, 1938–40; Northwest Missouri State College, 1940–41. *Publications:* Die! Damn You, 1952; Bloody River, 1953; Trail Herd North, 1953; Guns of Circle 8 (as Jeff Cochran), 1954; Along the Yermo Rim (as John Shane), 1954; My Deadly Angel (as John Chelton), 1955; Showdown, 1955; Justice, 1956; Kid From Canadian, 1956; Prairie Reckoning, 1956; Sundown in Sundance (as John Shane), 1956; Six-Gun Thursday (as John Shane), 1956; Gunsmoke Dawn (as John Shane), 1957; John Law, Keep Out, 1957; Ambush at North Platte, 1957; The River Flows West, 1957; If They Want Me Dead (as Peter Bannon), 1958; If I Should Die (as Peter Bannon), 1958; Kansas Guns, 1958; Dead Man's Range, 1958; The Gun Doctor, 1959; Johnny Nation, 1960; Whisper Murder Softly (as Peter Bannon), 1963; Backlash, 1967; Badge of Infamy, 1968; Intended Treason: What Really Happened to the Gunpowder Plot, 1970; A Roomful of Shadows (autobiog.), 1975; The Florentine Table, 1980; Paradiso Country, 1985. *Address:* The Keep, West Wall, Presteigne, Powys LD8 2BY, Wales.

DUVAL, Jeanne (see Coffman, Virginia (Edith)).

DWORKIN, Andrea; Writer and Lecturer; b. 26 Sept. 1946, Camden, NJ, USA. *Education:* BA, Bennington College, 1968. *Career:* mem. Amnesty International; Authors' Guild; Authors' League of America; National Abortion Rights Action League; National Organization for Women; National Women's Political Caucus; PEN; Planned Parenthood; Women's Institute for Freedom of the Press. *Publications:* Woman Hating, 1974; Our Blood: Prophecies and Discourses on Sexual Politics, 1976; Marx and Gandhi Were Liberals: Feminism and the 'Radical' Left, 1977; Why So-called Radical Men Love and Need Pornography, 1978; The New Woman's Broken Heart (short stories), 1980; Pornography: Men Possessing Women, 1981; Right-Wing Women; The Politics of Domesticated Females, 1983; Ice and Fire (fiction), 1986; Intercourse, 1987, 10th edn, 1997; Pornography and Civil Rights: A New Day for Women's Equality (with Catharine A. MacKinnon), 1988; Letters From a War Zone: Writings, 1976–1989, 1989; Mercy (fiction), 1990; Life and Death: Unapologetic Writings on the Continuing War Against Women, 1997; In Harm's Way: The Pornography Civil Rights Hearings (ed. with Catherine A. MacKinnon), 1998; Scapegoat: The Jews, Israel, and Women's Liberation, 2000. Contributions: anthologies and periodicals. *Address:* c/o Elaine Markson, 44 Greenwich Ave, New York, NY 10011, USA.

DWORKIN, Ronald (Myles); Prof. of Jurisprudence and Writer; b. 11 Dec. 1931, Worcester, Massachusetts, USA; m. Betsy Ross (deceased); one s. one d. *Education:* BA, 1953, LLB, 1957, Harvard University; BA, University of Oxford, 1955. *Career:* Admitted to the Bar, New York, 1959; Faculty, 1962–69, Hohfeld Prof. of Jurisprudence, 1968–69, Yale Law School; Visiting Prof. of Philosophy, 1963, 1974–75, Gauss Seminarian, 1966, Princeton University; Master, Trumbull College, 1966–69; Frank H. Sommer Visiting Prof. of Law, Stanford University, 1967; Prof. of Jurisprudence, University of Oxford, 1969–98; Prof. of Law, New York University, 1975–; Academic Freedom Lecturer, University of the Witwatersrand, 1976; Prof.-at-Large, Cornell University, 1976–; Visiting Prof. of Law and Philosophy, 1977, Visiting Prof. of Philosophy, 1979, Harvard University; Quain Prof. of Jurisprudence, University College London, 1998–; mem. American Acad. of Arts and Sciences; British Acad., fellow. *Publications:* Taking Rights Seriously, 1977; Philosophy of Law (ed.), 1977; A Matter of Principle, 1985; Law's Empire, 1986; A Bill of Rights for Britain, 1990; Life's Dominion, 1993; Freedom's Law, 1996; Sovereign Virtue, 2000. Contributions: Professional journals. *Address:* c/o School of Law, New York University, 40 Washington Sq. S, New York, NY 10012, USA.

DWYER, Deanna (see Koontz, Dean Ray).

DWYER, K. R. (see Koontz, Dean Ray).

DYBEK, Stuart; Poet, Writer and Prof. of English; b. 10 April 1942, Chicago, IL, USA; m. Caren Bassett, 1966, one s. one d. *Education:* BS, 1964, MA, 1967, Loyola University; MFA, University of Iowa, 1973. *Career:* Teaching Asst, 1970–72, Teaching and Writing Fellow, 1972–73, University of Iowa; Prof. of English, Western Michigan University, 1973–; Guest Writer and Teacher, Michigan Council for the Arts' Writer in the Schools Program, 1973–92; Faculty, Warren Wilson MFA Program in Creative Writing, 1985–89; Visiting Prof. of Creative Writing, Princeton University, 1990, University of California, Irvine, 1995; University of Iowa Writers' Workshop, 1998; Writer-in-Residence, Northwestern Univ., 2001–02; numerous readings, lectures and workshops. *Publications:* Brass Knuckles (poems), 1979; Childhood and Other Neighbourhoods (short stories), 1980; The Coast of Chicago (short stories), 1990; The Story of Mist (short stories and prose poems), 1994; I Sailed with Magellan (novel), 2003. Contributions: many anthologies and magazines. *Honours:* Award in Fiction, Society of Midwest Authors, 1981; Cliffdwellers Award for Fiction, Friends of American Literature, 1981; Special Citation, PEN/Hemingway Prize Committee, 1981; Michigan Council for the Arts Grants, 1981, 1992; Guggenheim Fellowship, 1982; National Endowment for the Arts Fellowships, 1982, 1994; Pushcart Prize, 1985; First Prize, O. Henry Award, 1985; Nelson Algren Prize, 1985; Whiting Writers Award, 1985; Michigan Arts Award, Arts Foundation of Michigan, 1986; American Acad. of Arts and Letters Award for Fiction, 1994; PEN/Malamud Award, 1995; Rockefeller Residency, Bellagio, Italy, 1996; Lannan Writers Award, 1998. *Address:* 320 Monroe, Kalamazoo, MI 49006, USA. *E-mail:* sdybek@earthlink.net.

DYER, Charles; Playwright; b. 17 July 1928, Shrewsbury, England; m. Fiona 20 Feb. 1960; three s. *Publications:* Turtle in the Soup, 1948; Who On Earth, 1950; Poison in Jest, 1952; Jovial Parasite, 1955; Red Cabbage and Kings, 1958; Rattle of a Simple Man (novel, play, film), 1962; Staircase (novel, play, film), 1966; Mother Adam, 1970; Lovers Dancing, 1982. Other: various screenplays. *Address:* Old Wob, Gerrards Cross, Buckinghamshire SL9 8SF, England.

DYER, Geoff; Writer; b. 5 June 1958, Cheltenham, England. *Education:* Corpus Christi College, Oxford, 1980. *Publications:* Ways of Telling (criticism), 1986; The Colour of Memory (novel), 1989; But Beautiful (novel), 1991; The Search (novel), 1993; The Missing of the Somme (non-fiction), 1994; Out of Sheer Rage (literary essay), 1997; Paris Trance (novel), 1998; Anglo-English Attitudes (essays), 1999; Yoga for People Who Can't be Bothered to Do It (essays), 2003. Contributions: Granta, LA Weekly, Nerve, The Observer. *Honours:* Somerset Maugham Prize, 1992. *Address:* c/o Abacus Books, Brettenham House, Lancaster Place, London WC2E 7EN, England.

DYER, James Frederick; Archaeological Writer; b. 23 Feb. 1934, Luton, England. *Education:* MA, Leicester University, 1964. *Career:* Ed., Shire Archaeology, 1974–; mem. Society of Authors; Royal Archaeological Institute; Society of Antiquaries. *Publications:* Southern England: An Archaeological Guide, 1973; Penguin Guide to Prehistoric England and Wales, 1981; Discovering Archaeology in England and Wales, 1985; Discovering Prehistoric England, 1993; Ancient Britain, 1995; The Stopsley Book, 1998. Contributions: Bedfordshire Magazine; Illustrated London News; Archaeological Journal. *Honours:* Hon. Doctor of Arts, University of Luton, 1999. *Address:* 6 Rogate Rd, Luton, Bedfordshire LU2 8HR, England. *Telephone:* (1582) 724808.

DYSON, Anthony Edward, MA, MLitt; writer; b. 28 Nov. 1928, London, England. *Education:* Pembroke College, Cambridge. *Career:* Lecturer, University College of Wales, Bangor 1955–63. Co-Founder, Dir, Critical Quarterly Society, 1960–84; Visiting Prof., Concordia University, Montréal, Canada, 1967, 1969, University of Connecticut, USA, 1976; General

Ed., Macmillan Casebooks, England, 1968–; Dir, Norwich Tapes Ltd, England, 1979–; Hon. Fellow, former Reader in English, University of East Anglia, Norwich, 1963–1982. *Publications:* Modern Poetry (with C. B. Cox), 1963; The Crazy Fabric: Essays in Irony, 1965; The Practical Criticism of Poetry (with C. B. Cox), 1965; Modern Judgements on Dickens, 1968; Word in the Desert (with C. B. Cox), 1968; Casebook on Bleak House, 1969; Black Papers on Education, 3 vols, 1969–70; The Inimitable Dickens, 1970; Between Two Worlds: Aspects of Literary Form, 1972; Twentieth Century Mind (with C. B. Cox), 3 vols, 1972; English Poetry: Select Bibliographical Guides, 1973; English Novel: Select Bibliographical Guides, 1974; Casebook on Paradise Lost (with Julian Lovelock), 1974; Education and Democracy (with Julian Lovelock), 1975; Yeats, Eliot and R. S. Thomas: Riding the Echo, 1981; Poetry Criticism and Practice, 1986; Thom Gunn, Ted Hughes and R. S. Thomas, 1990; The Fifth Dimension, 1996. Contributions: numerous journals. *Address:* c/o Macmillan Publishers, Hampshire RG21 2XS, England.

DYSON, Freeman John; American academic and writer; b. 15 Dec. 1923, Crowthorne, England; m. 1st Verena Haefeli-Huber 1950 (divorced 1958); one s. one d.; m. 2nd Imme Jung 1958; four d. *Education:* BA, Univ. of Cambridge, 1945; Graduate Studies, Cornell Univ., 1947–48, Institute for Advanced Study, Princeton, NJ, 1948–49. *Career:* Research Fellow, Trinity College, Cambridge, 1946–49; Warren Research Fellow, Univ. of Birmingham, England, 1949–51; Prof. of Physics, Cornell Univ., 1951–53; Prof. of Physics, 1953–94, Prof. Emeritus, 1994–, Institute for Advanced Study; mem. American Physical Society; National Acad. of Sciences; Royal Society, fellow. *Publications:* Symmetry Groups in Nuclear and Particle Physics, 1966; Neutron Stars and Pulsars, 1971; Disturbing the Universe, 1979; Values at War, 1983; Weapons and Hope, 1984; Origins of Life, 1986; Infinite in All Directions, 1988; From Eros to Gaia, 1992; Imagined Worlds, 1997; The Sun, the Genome and the Internet, 1999. *Honours:* Heineman Prize, American Institute of Physics, 1966; Lorentz Medal, Royal Netherlands Acad. of Sciences, 1966; Hughes Medal, Royal Society, 1968; Max Planck Medal, German Physical Society, 1969; J. Robert Oppenheimer Memorial Prize, Center for Theoretical Studies, 1970; Harvey Prize, Israel Institute of Technology, 1977; Wolf Prize, Wolf Foundation, 1981; National Book Critics Circle Award, 1984; Templeton Prize for Progress in Religion, 2000; Hon. doctorates. *Address:* 105 Battle Road Circle, Princeton, NJ 08540, USA. *E-mail:* dyson@ias.edu.

E

EADY, F. R. (see Kerner, Fred).

EAGLETON, Terence (Terry) Francis, MA, PhD; academic and writer; *Professor of Cultural Theory, University of Manchester*; b. 22 Feb. 1943, Salford, England; m. 1st Elizabeth Rosemary Galpin 1966; three s.; m. 2nd Willa Murphy 1996. *Education:* Trinity Coll., Cambridge, Jesus Coll., Cambridge. *Career:* Fellow in English, Jesus Coll., Cambridge, 1964–69; Tutorial Fellow, Wadham Coll., 1969–89, Lecturer in Critical Theory, 1989–92, Fellow, Linacre Coll., 1989–92, Thomas Warton Prof. of Literature and Fellow of St Catherine's Coll. Oxford 1992–; Prof. of Cultural Theory and John Rylands Fellow Univ. of Manchester 2000–; Fellow British Acad. *Publications:* Criticism and Ideology, 1976; Marxism and Literary Criticism, 1976; Walter Benjamin, 1981; Literary Theory: An Introduction, 1983; The Function of Criticism, 1984; The Rape of Clarissa, 1985; Against the Grain, 1986; William Shakespeare, 1986; The Ideology of the Aesthetic, 1990; Ideology: An Introduction, 1993; Heathcliff and the Great Hunger: Studies in Irish Culture, 1995; The Illusions of Postmodernism, 1996; Crazy John and the Bishop and Other Essays on Irish Culture, 1998; Scholars and Rebels in Ireland, 1999; The Idea of Culture, 2000; The Gatekeeper: A Memoir, 2002, Sweet Violence: A Study of the Tragic 2002, Figures of Dissent (essays) 2003, After Theory 2003. Contributions: periodicals incl. London Review of Books. *Honours:* Irish Sunday Tribune Arts Award, 1990; hon. doctorates. *Address:* Department of English, University of Manchester, Oxford Road, Manchester M13 9PL, England.

EARLEY, Tony; Writer; b. 1961, San Antonio, TX, USA; m. Sarah Earley. *Education:* BA, Warren Wilson College, 1983; MFA, University of Alabama at Tuscaloosa. *Career:* Instructor, Carnegie-Mellon University, University of Alabama; Prof. of Creative Writing, Vanderbilt University. *Publications:* Here We Are in Paradise, 1994; Jim the Boy: A Novel, 2000; Somehow Form a Family: Stories That Are Mostly True, 2001. Contributions: anthologies and periodicals. *Honours:* PEN Syndicated Fiction Award, 1993; Best of Young American Novelists Citation, Granta, 1996. *Address:* c/o Gordon Kato, 133 W 75th St, Suite 1A, New York, NY 10023, USA.

EARLS, Nick; Writer, Ed. and Physician; b. 8 Oct. 1963, Newtownards, Northern Ireland; m. Sarah Garvey, 13 April 1991. *Education:* MBBS, University of Queensland. *Career:* Medical Practitioner, Brisbane, Qld, Australia, 1987–94; Freelance Writer, 1988–; Continuing Medical Education Ed., Medical Observer, Qld, 1994–. *Publications:* Passion (short stories), 1992; After January (young adult novel), 1996; Zigzag Street (novel), 1996. Contributions: Short fiction to anthologies including Nightmares in Paradise. *Honours:* 3M Talking Book of the Year Award, Young People's Category, 1996; Notable Book, CBE-International Youth Library, Munich, 1997, both for After January. *Literary Agent:* Curtis Brown Pty, PO Box 19, Paddington, NSW 2021, Australia. *E-mail:* nickearls@peg.apc.org.

EARLY, Gerald; academic, writer and poet; b. 21 April 1952, Philadelphia, PA, USA; m. Ida Haynes 1977; two d. *Education:* BA cum laude, English, University of Pennsylvania, 1974; MA, English, 1980, PhD, English, 1982, Cornell University. *Publications:* Tuxedo Junction: Essays on American Culture, 1990; My Soul's High Song, 1991; Lure and Loathing, 1993; Daughters: One Family and Fatherhood, 1994; Culture of Bruising, 1994; How the War in the Streets is Won, 1995. Contributions: Essays, reviews and poetry to many journals including: American Poetry Review; Northwest Review; Tar River Poetry; Raccoon; Seneca Review; Obsidian ll; Black American Literature Forum. *Honours:* Whiting Foundation Writers' Award, 1988; CCLM-General Electric Foundation Award for Younger Writers, 1988; several Fellowships. *Address:* Washington University, Campus Box 1109, One Brookings Drive, St Louis, MO 63130, USA.

EASTAUGH, Kenneth; Critic and Writer; b. 30 Jan. 1929, Preston, England. *Career:* Television Critic, 1965–67, Show Business Writer, 1967–70, Daily Mirror, London; Chief Show Business Writer, The Sun, London, 1970–73; TV Columnist, The Times, London, 1977; Film Critic, Prima Magazine, 1976–; Music Critic, Classical Music Weekly, 1976–; Chief Show Business Exec., Daily Star, London, 1978–83. *Publications:* The Event (television play), 1968; Better Than a Man (televsion play), 1970; Dapple Downs (radio serial), 1973–74; Awkward Cuss (play), 1976; Havergal Brian: The Making of a Composer (biog.), 1976; Coronation Street (television series), 1977–78; The Carry On Book (cinema), 1978; Havergal Who? (television documentary), 1980; Mr Love (novel, screenplay), 1986; Dallas (television serial), 1989; Embers (play), 1998; The New Carry On Book, 1998. *Literary Agent:* Curtis Brown Ltd, Haymarket House, 28–29 Haymarket, London, SW1Y 4SP, England. *Telephone:* (20) 7393-4400. *Fax:* (20) 7393-4401. *E-mail:* info@curtisbrown.co.uk. *Website:* www.curtisbrown.co .uk.

EASTHOPE, Antony Kelynge Revington; Prof. and Writer; b. 14 April 1939, Portsmouth, England; m. Diane Garside, 1 Feb. 1972, one s. two d. *Education:* BA, 1961, MA, 1965, MLitt, 1967, Christ's College, Cambridge. *Career:* Brown University, RI, USA, 1964–66; Warwick University, England, 1967–68; Manchester Metropolitan University, 1969–. *Publications:* Poetry as Discourse, 1983; What a Man's Gotta Do, 1986; British Post-Structuralism, 1988; Poetry and Phantasy, 1989; Literary into Cultural Studies, 1991; Wordsworth, Now and Then, 1993; Englishness and National Culture, 1999. Contributions: numerous magazines and journals. *Honours:* Charter Fellow, Wolfson College, Oxford, 1985–86; Visiting Fellow, University of Virginia, 1990. *Address:* 27 Victoria Ave, Didsbury, Manchester M20 8QX, England.

EASTON, Robert Olney; Writer; b. 4 July 1915, San Francisco, CA, USA; m. Jane Faust, 24 Sept. 1940, four d. *Education:* Stanford University, 1933–34; BS, Harvard University, 1938; MA, University of California, 1960. *Publications:* The Happy Man, 1943; Lord of Beasts (co-author), 1961; The Book of the American West (co-author), 1963; The Hearing, 1964; Californian Condor (co-author), 1964; Max Brand, 1970; Black Tide, 1972; This Promised Land, 1982; China Caravans, 1982; Life and Work (co-author), 1988; Power and Glory, 1989; Love and War (co-author), 1991. Contributions: Magazines.

EATON, Charles Edward; Poet and Writer; b. 25 June 1916, Winston-Salem, NC, USA; m. Isabel Patterson, 1950. *Education:* Duke University, 1932–33; BA, University of North Carolina at Chapel Hill, 1936; Princeton University, 1936–37; MA in English, Harvard University, 1940. *Career:* Instructor in Creative Writing, University of Missouri, 1940–42; Vice-Consul, American Embassy, Rio de Janeiro, 1942–46; Prof. of Creative Writing, University of North Carolina, 1946–52; mem. American Acad. of Poets. *Publications:* Poetry: The Bright Plain, 1942; The Shadow of the Swimmer, 1951; The Greenhouse in the Garden, 1956; Countermoves, 1963; On the Edge of the Knife, 1970; The Man in the Green Chair, 1977; Colophon of the Rover, 1980; The Thing King, 1983; The Work of the Wrench, 1985; New and Selected Poems 1942–1987, 1987; A Guest on Mild Evenings, 1991; The Country of the Blue, 1994; The Fox and I, 1996; The Scout in Summer, 1999; The Jogger by the Sea, 2000; Between the Devil and the Deep Blue Sea, 2003. Fiction: A Lady of Pleasure, 1993. Short Stories: Write Me From Rio, 1959; The Girl From Ipanema, 1972; The Case of the Missing Photographs, 1978; New and Selected Stories 1959–1989, 1989. Other: The Man From Buena Vista, New and Selected Non-Fiction, 2001. Contributions: Magazines and journals. *Honours:* Bread Loaf Writers' Conference Robert Frost Fellowship, 1941; Ridgely Torrence Memorial Award, 1951; Gertrude Boatwright Harris Award, 1955; Arizona Quarterly Awards, 1956, 1975, 1977, 1979, 1982; Roanoke-Chowan Awards, 1970, 1987, 1991; Oscar Arnold Young Award, 1971; O. Henry Award, 1972; Alice Faye di Castagnola Award, 1974; Arvon Foundation Award, 1980; Hollins Critic Award, 1984; Brockman Awards, 1984, 1986; Kansas Quarterly Awards, 1987; North Carolina Literature Award, 1988; Fortner Award, 1993; Hon. DLitt, St Andrews College, NC, 1998. *Address:* 808 Greenwood Rd, Chapel Hill, NC 27514, USA.

EATWELL, Baron (Life Peer), cr. 1992, of Stratton St Margaret in the County of Wiltshire; **John Leonard Eatwell,** PhD; British academic; *Professor of Financial Policy, University of Cambridge*; b. 2 Feb. 1945; m. Hélène Seppain 1970 (divorced); two s. one d. *Education:* Headlands Grammar School, Swindon, Queens' Coll. Cambridge, Harvard Univ., USA. *Career:* Teaching Fellow Grad. School of Arts and Sciences, Harvard Univ. 1968–69; Research Fellow Queens' Coll. Cambridge 1969–70; Fellow Trinity Coll. Cambridge 1970–96, Asst Lecturer Faculty of Econs and Politics, Cambridge Univ. 1975–77, Lecturer 1977–, Pres. Queens' Coll. 1997–; Visiting Prof. of Econs New School for Social Research, New York 1982–96; Econ. Adviser to Neil Kinnock, Leader of Labour Party 1985–92; Opposition Spokesman on Treasury Affairs and on Trade and Industry, House of Lords 1992–93, Prin. Opposition spokesman on Treasury and Econ. Affairs 1993–97; Trustee Inst. for Public Policy Research 1988–95, Sec. 1988–97, Chair. 1997–; Dir (non-exec.) Anglia TV Group 1994–2001, Cambridge Econometrics Ltd 1996–; Chair. Extemporary Dance Theatre 1990, Crusaid 1993–98, British Screen Finance Ltd 1997–2000 and assoc. cos; Gov. Contemporary Dance Trust 1991–95; Dir Arts Theatre Trust, Cambridge 1991–98, Bd, Securities and Futures Authority 1997–; mem. Bd Royal Opera House 1998–2002; Chair. Royal Ballet 1998–2001, Commercial Radio Cos Asscn 2000–, British Library Bd 2001–; mem. Regulatory Decisions Cttee, FSA 2001–; Dir Cambridge Endowment for Research in Finance 2002–. *Publications:* An Introduction to Modern Economics (with Joan Robinson) 1973, Whatever Happened to Britain? 1982, Keynes's Economics and the Theory of Value and Distribution (ed. with Murray Milgate) 1983, The New Palgrave: A Dictionary of Economics, 4 Vols 1987, The New Palgrave Dictionary of Money and Finance, 3 Vols 1992 (both with Murray Milgate and Peter Newman), Transformation and Integration: Shaping the Future of Central and Eastern Europe (jtly) 1995, Global Unemployment: Loss of Jobs in the '90s (ed.) 1996, Not "Just Another Accession": The Political Economy of EU Enlargement to the East (jtly) 1997, Global Finance at Risk: the Case for International Regulation (with L. Taylor) 2000, Hard Budgets, Soft States 2000, Social Policy Choices in Central and Eastern Europe 2002, International Capital Markets (with L. Taylor) 2002; articles in scientific journals. *Address:* The President's Lodge, Queens' College, Cambridge, CB3 9ET, England. *Telephone:* (1223) 335556. *Fax:* (1223) 335555. *E-mail:* president@quns.cam.ac.uk (Office).

EBERHART, Richard Ghormley, BA, MA; academic, poet and writer; *Professor of English Emeritus, Dartmouth College*; b. 5 April 1904, Austin,

MN, USA; m. Helen Elizabeth Butcher 1941; one s. one d. *Education:* Dartmouth College, St John's College, Cambridge, Harvard University. *Career:* Founder-Pres., Poets' Theater, Cambridge, MA, 1951; Visiting Prof. of English and Poet-in-Residence, University of Washington, 1952–53, Wheaton College, Norton, MA, 1954–55; Prof. of English, University of Connecticut, 1953–54; Resident Fellow in Creative Writing and Christian Gauss Lecturer, Princeton University, 1955–56; Prof. of English, 1956–70, Poet-in-Residence, 1956–, Prof. Emeritus, 1970–, Dartmouth College; Consultant in Poetry, Library of Congress, Washington, DC, 1959–61; Distinguished Visiting Prof., 1974–75, Visiting Prof., 1975–86, University of Florida at Gainesville; Adjunct Prof., Columbia University, 1975; Regents' Prof., University of California at Davis, 1975; mem. Acad. of American Poets, fellow; American Acad. of Arts and Letters; American Acad. of Arts and Sciences. *Publications:* A Bravery of Earth, 1930; Reading the Spirit, 1937; Song and Idea, 1942; Poems New and Selected, 1944; Burr Oaks, 1947; Brotherhood of Men, 1949; An Herb Basket, 1950; Selected Poems, 1951; Undercliff, 1953; Great Praises, 1957; Collected Poems, 1930–1960, 1960; Collected Verse Plays, 1962; The Quarry, 1964; Selected Poems, 1930–1965, 1965; New Directions, 1965; Thirty-One Sonnets, 1967; Shifts of Being, 1968; Fields of Grace, 1972; Collected Poems, 1930–1976, 1976; Poems to Poets, 1976; Survivors, 1979; Of Poetry and Poets, 1979; Ways of Light, 1980; New Hampshire: Nine Poems, 1980; Four Poems, 1980; A Celebration, 1980; Chocorua, 1981; Florida Poems, 1981; The Long Reach, 1984; Collected Poems, 1930–1986, 1986; Negative Capability, 1986; Maine Poems, 1988; New and Collected Poems, 1990. Contributions: Books and periodicals. *Honours:* Hon. doctorates; Harriet Monroe Memorial Prize, 1950; Shelley Memorial Prize, 1951; Bollingen Prize, 1962; Pulitzer Prize in Poetry, 1966; National Book Award, 1977; Poet Laureate of New Hampshire, 1979; Sarah Josepha Hale Award, 1982; Robert Frost Medal, Poetry Society of America, 1986. *Address:* 80 Lyme Road, Apt 161, Hanover, NH 03755, USA.

EBERT, Alan; Author; b. 14 Sept. 1935, New York, NY, USA. *Education:* BA, Brooklyn College, CUNY, 1957; MA, Fordham University, 1975. *Career:* mem. American Society of Journalists and Authors. *Publications:* The Homosexuals, 1977; Every Body is Beautiful (with Ron Fletcher), 1978; Intimacies, 1979; Traditions (novel), 1981; The Long Way Home (novel), 1984; Marriages (novel), 1987. Contributions: Family Circle; Essence; Look; Us; Good Housekeeping. *Address:* 353 W 56th St, New York, NY 10019, USA.

EBERT, Roger (Joseph); Film Critic, Writer and Lecturer; b. 18 June 1942, Urbana, IL, USA; m. Chaz Hammelsmith, 18 July 1992. *Education:* BS, University of Illinois, 1964; University of Cape Town, 1965; University of Chicago, 1966–67. *Career:* Reporter, News Gazette, Champaign-Urbana, IL, 1958–66; Instructor, Chicago City College, 1967–68; Film Critic, Chicago Sun-Times, 1967–, US Magazine, 1978–79, WMAQ-TV, Chicago, 1980–83, WLS-TV, Chicago, 1984–, New York Post, 1986–88, New York Daily News, 1988–92, Compu Serve, 1991–, Microsoft Cinemania, 1994–97; Lecturer, University of Chicago, 1969–; Co-Host, Sneak Previews, WTTW-TV, Chicago, 1977–82; At the Movies, syndicated television programme, 1982–86; Siskel and Ebert, syndicated television programme, 1986–99; Ebert and Roeper and the Movies, syndicated television programme, 1999–; mem. Acad. of London; American Newspaper Guild; National Society of Film Critics; Writers' Guild of America. *Publications:* An Illini Century, 1967; A Kiss is Still a Kiss, 1984; Roger Ebert's Movie Home Companion (annual vols), 1986–93, subsequently Roger Ebert's Video Companion, 1994–98; The Perfect London Walk (with Daniel Curley), 1986; Two Weeks in the Midday Sun: A Cannes Notebook, 1987; The Future of the Movies: Interviews with Martin Scorsese, Steven Spielberg, and George Lucas (with Gene Siskel), 1991; Behind the Phantom's Mask, 1993; Ebert's Little Movie Glossary, 1994; The Future of the Movies: The Computer Insectiary (co-author), 1994; Roger Ebert's Book of Film, 1996; Questions for the Movie Answer Man, 1997; Roger Ebert's Movie Yearbook, 1998–; Ebert's Bigger Little Movie Glossary, 1999; I Hated, Hated, Hated This Movie, 2000. Contributions: newspapers and magazines. *Honours:* Overseas Press Club Award, 1963; Rotary Fellow, 1965; Pulitzer Prize for Criticism, 1975; Chicago Emmy Award, 1979; Hon. Doctorate, University of Colorado, 1993; Kluge Fellow in Film Studies, University of Virginia, 1995–96. *Address:* c/o Chicago Sun-Times, 401 N Wabash, Chicago, IL 60611, USA.

EBERT, Tibor, BA; writer, poet and dramatist; b. 14 Oct. 1926, Bratislava, Czechoslovakia; m. Eva Gati 1968; one d. *Education:* Ferenc Liszt Acad. of Music, Eötvös Lórand University, Budapest. *Career:* Dramaturg, József Attila Theatre, Budapest, 1984–85; Ed.-in-Chief, Agora Publishers, Budapest, 1989–92; Ed., Hirvivo Literary Magazine, 1990–92; mem. PEN Club; Asscn of Hungarian Writers; Literary Asscn Berzsenyi. *Publications:* Mikrodrámák, 1971; Rosarium, 1987; Kobayashi, 1989; Legenda egy fúvószenekarról, 1990; Jób könyve, 1991; Fagyott Orpheusz (poems), 1993; Esö, 1996; Egy város glóriája, 1997; Bartók, 1997; Eredök, 1998; Éltem, 1998; Drámák, 2000; Bolyongás, 2001; Vecseruye, 2001; Kaleidoszkóp, 2002; Álmomban, 2002. Other: several plays performed on stage including: Les Escaliers; Musique de Chambre; Demosthenes; Esterházy. Contributions: numerous short stories, poems, dramas and essays to several leading Hungarian literary journals and magazines. *Honours:* Hon. mem., Franco-Hungarian Society, 1980–; Bartók Prize, 1987; Commemorative Medal, City of Pozsony-Pressburg-Bratislava, 1991; Esterházy Prize, 1993; Order of Hungarian Republic, 1996. *Address:* Csévi u 15c, 1025 Budapest, Hungary.

ECHENOZ, Jean Maurice Emmanuel; writer; b. 26 Dec. 1947, Orange, France; one s. *Education:* University of Aix-en-Provence, Sorbonne, University of Paris. *Publications:* Le Méridien de Greenwich, 1979; Cherokee, 1983; L'équipée malaise (trans. as Double Jeopardy), 1986; L'occupation des sols, 1988; Lac, 1989; Nous trois, 1992; Les grandes blondes (trans. as Big Blondes), 1995; Un an, 1997; Je m'en vais (trans. as I'm Gone), 1999; Au Piano, 2003. Contributions: newspapers and journals. *Honours:* Prix Fénélon, 1980; Prix Georges Sadoul, 1980; Prix Médicis Étranger, 1983; Grand Prix, Société des gens de lettres, 1990; European Literature Prize, Glasgow, 1990; Prix Novembre, 1995; Grand Prix, City of Paris, 1997; Prix Goncourt, 1999. *Address:* c/o Editions de Minuit, 7 rue Bernard-Palissy, 75006 Paris, France.

ECO, Umberto, PhD; Italian academic and writer; b. 5 Jan. 1932, Alessandria; m. Renate Ramge 1962; one s. one d. *Education:* Univ. of Turin. *Career:* Asst Lecturer, 1956–63, Lecturer 1963–64, Univ. of Turin; Lecturer, Univ. of Milan, 1964–65; Prof., Univ. of Florence, 1966–69; Visiting Prof., New York Univ., 1969–70, 1976, Northwestern Univ., 1972, Yale Univ., 1977, 1980, 1981, Columbia Univ., 1978, 1984; Prof. of Semiotics, Milan Polytechnic, 1970–71, Univ. of Bologna, 1971–; mem. International Asscn for Semiotic Studies. *Publications:* Il Problema Estetico in San Tommaso (trans. as The Aethetics of Thomas Aquinas), 1956; Sviluppo dell'Estetica Medioevale (trans. as Art and Beauty in the Middle Ages), 1959; Diario Minimo, 1963; La Struttura Assente, 1968; Il Costume di Casa, 1973; Trattato di Semiotica Generale, 1976; Il Nome della Rosa (novel, trans. as The Name of the Rose), 1981; Sette anni di desiderio 1977–83, 1984; Il Pendolo di Foucault, 1988; L'isola del giorno prima (novel, trans. as The Island of the Day Before), 1995; Serendipities, 1997; Kant and the Platypus, 1999; Baudolino, 2002; Mouse or Rat?: Translation as Negotiation, 2003. Contributions: various publications. *Honours:* Medici Prize, 1982; McLuhan Teleglobe Prize, 1985; Hon. DLitt, Univ. of Glasgow, 1990, Univ. of Kent, 1992. *Address:* Piazza Castello 13, 20121 Milan, Italy.

EDDINGS, David; Writer; b. 7 July 1931, Spokane, WA, USA; m. Judith Leigh Schall, 27 Oct. 1962. *Education:* BA, Reed College, 1954; MA, University of Washington, Seattle, 1961. *Publications:* High Hunt, 1973; Pawn of Prophecy, 1982; Queen of Sorcery, 1982; Magician's Gambit, 1983; Castle of Wizardry, 1984; Guardians of the West, 1987; King of the Margos, 1988; Demon Lord of Karanda, 1988; The Diamond Throne, 1989; The Sorceress of Darshiva, 1989; The Ruby Knight, 1990; The Seeress of Kell, 1991; The Losers, 1992; The Sapphire Rose, 1992; Domes of Fire, 1993; The Hidden City, 1994; The Shining Ones, 1994; Belgorath the Sorcerer, 1995; Polgara the Sorceress, 1997; The Riven Codex, 1998; The Redemption of Althalus, 2000. *Address:* c/o Ballantine Books Inc, 201 E 50th St, New York, NY 10022, USA.

EDGAR, David Burman, BA; British writer; b. 26 Feb. 1948, Birmingham; m. Eve Brook 1979 (died 1998); two step-s.; pnr Stephanie Dale. *Education:* Oundle School, Manchester Univ. *Career:* Fellow in Creative Writing, Leeds Polytechnic 1972–74; Resident Playwright, Birmingham Repertory Theatre 1974–75, Bd mem. 1985–; Lecturer in Playwriting, Univ. of Birmingham 1975–78, Dir of Playwriting Studies 1989–, Prof. 1995–99; Founder Writers' Union 1970s; UK/US Bicentennial Arts Fellow resident in USA 1978–79; Literary Consultant, RSC 1984–88; Fellow Birmingham Polytechnic 1991, Judith E. Wilson Fellow, Clare Hall, Cambridge 1996. *Plays:* Two Kinds of Angel 1970, Rent or Caught in the Act 1972, State of Emergency 1972, The Dunkirk Spirit 1974, Dick Deterred 1974, O Fair Jerusalem 1975, Saigon Rose 1976, Blood Sports 1976, Destiny (for RSC) 1976, Wreckers 1977, The Jail Diary of Albie Sachs (for RSC) 1978, Mary Barnes 1978–79, Teendreams 1979, The Adventures of Nicholas Nickleby (adaptation for RSC) 1980, Maydays (for RSC) 1983, Entertaining Strangers 1985, That Summer 1987, The Shape of the Table 1990, Dr Jekyll and Mr Hyde (adaptation for RSC) 1991, Pentecost 1994, Other Place 1994, Young Vic 1995, Albert Speer (adaptation for Nat. Theatre) 2000, The Prisoner's Dilemma 2001, Continental Divide 2003. *TV Plays:* I Know What I Meant 1974, Baby Love 1974, Vote for Them 1989, Buying a Landslide 1992, Citizen Locke 1994. *Radio:* Ecclesiastes 1977, A Movie Starring Me 1991. *Film:* Lady Jane 1986. *Publications:* Destiny 1976, Wreckers 1977, Teendreams 1979, Maydays 1983, Plays One 1987, The Second Time as Farce 1988, Heartlanders 1989, Plays Two 1990, Plays Three 1991, Pentecost 1995, State of Play (ed.) 1999, Albert Speer 2000, The Prisoner's Dilemma 2001. *Honours:* Hon. Sr Research Fellow, Univ. of Birmingham 1988–92, Hon. Prof. 1992–; Hon. MA (Bradford) 1986; DUniv (Surrey) 1993, (Birmingham) 2002; Soc. of West End Theatres Best Play Award 1980, Tony Award for Best Play 1981, Plays and Players Award for Best Play 1983, Evening Standard Award for Best Play 1985. *Literary Agent:* Alan Brodie Representation, 211 Piccadilly, London, W1V 9LD. *Telephone:* (20) 7917-2871. *Fax:* (20) 7917-2872.

EDGECOMBE, Jean Marjorie, BA; author; b. 28 Feb. 1914, Bathurst, NSW, Australia; m. Gordon Henry Edgecombe, 2 Feb. 1945, two d., two s. *Education:* Sydney University. *Career:* mem. Australian Conservation Foundation, The Australian Museum Soc., Australian Society of Authors, Hornsby Shire Historical Society, Nat. Trust of Australia (NSW), State

Library of NSW Foundation, Wildlife Preservation Soc. Queensland, The Coast and Mountain Walkers of NSW. *Publications:* Discovering Lord Howe Island (with Isobel Bennett), 1978; Discovering Norfolk Island (with Isobel Bennett), 1983; Flinders Island, the Furneaux Group, 1985; Flinders Island and Eastern Bass Strait 1986; Lord Howe Island, World Heritage Area, 1987; Phillip Island and Western Port, 1989; Norfolk Island, South Pacific: Island of History and Many Delights 1991; Discovering Flinders Island 1992; Discovering King Island, Western Bass Strait, 1993. Contributions: articles and poems to various publications. *Honours:* Medal of the Order of Australia 1995. *Address:* 7 Oakleigh Avenue, Thornleigh, 2120 NSW, Australia.

EDRIC, Robert (see Armitage, Gary Edric).

EDSON, Russell; Poet and Writer; b. 9 April 1935, USA; m. Frances Edson. *Education:* Art Students' League, New York; New School for Social Research, New York; Columbia University; Black Mountain College, NC. *Publications:* Poetry: Appearances: Fables and Drawings, 1961; A Stone is Nobody's: Fables and Drawings, 1964; The Boundary, 1964; The Very Thing That Happens: Fables and Drawings, 1964; The Brain Kitchen: Writings and Woodcuts, 1965; What a Man Can See, 1969; The Childhood of an Equestrian, 1973; The Calm Theatre, 1973; A Roof with Some Clouds Behind It, 1975; The Intuitive Journey and Other Works, 1976; The Reason Why the Closet-Man is Never Sad, 1977; Edson's Mentality, 1977; The Traffic, 1978; The Wounded Breakfast: Ten Poems, 1978; With Sincerest Regrets, 1981; Wuck Wuck Wuck!, 1984; The Wounded Breakfast, 1985; Tick Tock, 1992; The Tunnel: Selected Poems, 1994. Fiction: Gulping's Recital, 1984; The Song of Percival Peacock, 1992. *Honours:* Guggenheim Fellowship, 1974; National Endowment for the Arts Grant, 1976, and Fellowship, 1982; Whiting Foundation Award, 1989. *Address:* 29 Ridgeley St, Darien, CT 06820, USA.

EDWARDS, Anne; Writer; b. 20 Aug. 1927, Porchester, NY, USA. *Education:* University of California at Los Angeles, 1943–46; Southern Methodist University, 1947–48. *Publications:* A Child's Bible (adaptation) 1967; The Survivors, 1968; Miklos Alexandrovitch is Missing, 1969; Shadow of a Lion, 1970; The Hesitant Heart, 1974; Judy Garland: A Biography, 1974; Haunted Summer, 1974; The Inn and Us (with Stephen Citron), 1975; Child of Night, 1975; P. T. Barnum, 1976; The Great Houdini, 1977; Vivien Leigh: A Biography, 1977; Sonya: The Life of the Countess Tolstoy, 1981; The Road to Tara: The Life of Margaret Mitchell, 1983; Matriarch: Queen Mary and the House of Windsor, 1984; A Remarkable Woman: Katherine Hepburn, 1985; Early Reagan: The Rise to Power, 1986; The Demilles: An American Dynasty, 1987; American Princess: A Biography of Shirley Temple, 1988; Royal Sisters: Queen Elizabeth and Princess Margaret, 1990; Wallis: The Novel, 1991; The Grimaldis of Monaco: Centuries of Scandals, Years of Grace, 1992; La Divina, 1994; Throne of Gold: The Lives of the Aga Khans, 1995; Streisand: It Only Happens Once, 1996. *Address:* c/o International Creative Management Inc, 40 W 57th St, New York, NY 10019, USA.

EDWARDS, F. E. (see Nolan, William Francis).

EDWARDS, Jorge; Author; b. 29 July 1931, Santiago, Chile. *Education:* Law and philosophy, University of Chile; Political science, Princeton University. *Career:* various diplomatic positions, 1957–73. *Publications:* El patio, 1952; Gente de la ciudad, 1962; El peso de la noche, 1965; Las máscaras, 1967; Temas y variaciones, 1969; Persona non grata, 1973; Los convidados de piedra, 1978; El museo de cera, 1981; La mujer imaginaria, 1985; El anfitrión, 1988; Adiós, poeta…, 1990; Fantasmas de carne y hueso, 1992; El origen del mundo, 1996. *Honours:* Literary Prizes, City of Santiago, 1961, 1991; Essay Prize, City of Santiago, 1991; Premio Cervantes, Spain, 2000.

EDWARDS, Josh (see Levinson, Leonard).

EDWARDS, Norman (see Carr, Terry (Gene)).

EDWARDS, Philip Walter, BA, MA, PhD, FBA; academic, writer and editor; b. 7 Feb. 1923, Barrow-in-Furness, England; m. 1st Hazel Valentine 1947 (died 1950); m. 2nd Sheila Mary Wilkes 1952; three s. one d. *Education:* Univ. of Birmingham. *Career:* Lecturer in English, Univ. of Birmingham, 1946–60; Prof. of English Literature, Trinity College, Dublin, 1960–66; Visiting Prof., Univ. of Michigan, 1964–65, Williams College, Williamstown, MA, 1969, Univ. of Otago, 1980, International Christian Univ., Tokyo, 1989; Prof. of Literature, Univ. of Essex, 1966–74; Visiting Fellow, All Souls College, Oxford, 1970–71; King Alfred Prof. of English Literature, Univ. of Liverpool, 1974–90. *Publications:* Sir Walter Ralegh, 1953; The Spanish Tragedy (ed.), 1959; Shakespeare and the Confines of Art, 1968; Massinger: Plays and Poems (ed. with C. Gibson), 1976; Pericles, Prince of Tyre (ed.), 1976; Threshold of a Nation, 1979; Hamlet, Prince of Denmark (ed.), 1985; Shakespeare: A Writer's Progress, 1986; Last Voyages, 1988; The Story of the Voyage, 1994; Sea-Mark: The Metaphorical Voyage, Spenser to Milton, 1997; The Journals of Captain Cook (ed.), 1999. Contributions: scholarly books and journals. *Address:* High Gillinggrove, Gillinggate, Kendal, Cumbria LA9 4JB, England.

EDWARDS, Rebecca Jane; Writer, Poet and Artist; b. 4 April 1969, Batlow, NSW, Australia; one d. *Education:* BA, Japanese Language and Culture, University of Queensland, 1992. *Career:* Writer-in-Residence, James Cook University, Townsville, Qld, 1996; mem. Fellowship of Australian Writers; New South Wales Poets' Union; Queensland Artworkers' Alliance; Queensland Writers' Centre. *Publications:* Eating the Experience, 1994; Eat the Ocean (contributor), 1996. Contributions: anthologies and journals. *Honours:* Red Earth Award, Northern Territories Section, 1989; Ford Memorial Medals, University of Queensland, 1991, 1992; Fifth Regional Illustrated Poetry Competition, 1995.

EGAN, Gregory Mark; Writer; b. 20 Aug. 1961, Perth, WA, Australia. *Education:* BSc, University of Western Australia, 1981. *Publications:* Fiction: An Unusual Angle, 1983; Quarantine, 1992; Permutation City, 1994; Distress, 1995; Diaspora, 1997; Teranesia, 1999. Short Stories: Axiomatic, 1995; Luminous, 1998. Contributions: Interzone Magazine; Asimov's Science Fiction Magazine. *Honours:* John W. Campbell Memorial Award, 1995; Hugo Award, 1999. *Literary Agent:* Curtis Brown Ltd, Haymarket House, 28–29 Haymarket, London, SW1Y 4SP, England. *Telephone:* (20) 7393-4400. *Fax:* (20) 7393-4401. *E-mail:* info@curtisbrown.co.uk. *Website:* www.curtisbrown.co.uk.

EGGERS, Dave; American writer; m. Vendela Vida 2003. *Career:* Ed., Might magazine 1994–97, Timothy McSweeney's Quarterly Concern, or 'McSweeney's', journal and publishers 1998–. *Publications:* A Heartbreaking Work of Staggering Genius (autobiog.) 2000, You Shall Know Our Velocity (novel) 2003; contrib. to The Guardian. *Address:* McSweeney's, 826 Valencia Street, San Francisco, CA 94110, USA. *E-mail:* letters@mcsweeneys.net. *Website:* store.mcsweeneys.net.

EGLETON, Clive Frederick William; writer, retd army officer and retd civil servant; b. 25 Nov. 1927; m. Joan Evelyn Lane 1949 (died 1996); two s. *Education:* Staff College, Camberley. *Career:* mem. CWA, Society of Authors. *Publications:* A Piece of Resistance, 1970; Last Post for a Partisan, 1971; The Judas Mandate, 1972; Seven Days to a Killing, 1973; The October Plot, 1974; Skirmish, 1975; State Visit, 1976; The Mills Bomb, 1978; Backfire, 1979; The Winter Touch, 1981; A Falcon for the Hawks, 1982; The Russian Enigma, 1982; A Conflict of Interests, 1983; Troika, 1984; A Different Drummer, 1985; Picture of the Year, 1987; Gone Missing, 1988; Death of a Sahib, 1989; In the Red, 1990; Last Act, 1991; A Double Deception, 1992; Hostile Intent, 1993; A Killing in Moscow, 1994; Death Throes, 1994; A Lethal Involvement, 1995; Warning Shot, 1996; Blood Money, 1997; Dead Reckoning, 1999; The Honey Trap, 2000; One Man Running, 2001; Cry Havoc, 2002. *Address:* Dolphin House, Beach House Lane, Bembridge PO35 5TA, Isle of Wight.

EGNER, Eugen; German writer and draughtsman; b. 10 Oct. 1951, Ingelfingen. *Career:* contributed cartoons to Titanic and Die Rabe, short stories to Die Rabe, Frankfurter Rundschau. *Publications include:* novels: Tagebuch eines Trinkers (trans. as From the Diary of an Alcoholic) 1991, Der künstliche Mann (trans. as The Artificial Man) 1992, Die Tagebücher des W. A. Mozart (trans. as The Diaries of W. A. Mozart) 1998, Androiden auf Milchbasis (trans. as Androids from Milk) 2002. *Address:* c/o Dedalus Ltd, Langford Lodge, St Judith's Lane, Sawtry, Cambridgeshire PE28 5XE, England. *E-mail:* info@dedalusbooks.com. *Website:* www.dedalusbooks.com.

EHLE, John Marsden, Jr; Writer; b. 13 Dec. 1925, Asheville, NC, USA; m. 1st Gail Oliver, 30 Aug. 1952, divorced April 1967; m. 2nd Rosemary Harris, 22 Oct. 1967, one d. *Education:* BA, University of North Carolina at Chapel Hill, 1949. *Career:* Faculty, University of North Carolina at Chapel Hill, 1951–63; Special asst to Gov. Terry Sanford, NC, 1963–64; Programme Officer, Ford Foundation, New York, 1964–65; Mem., White House Group for Domestic Affairs, 1964–66; Special Consultant, Duke University, 1976–80; mem. Authors' League; PEN; State of North Carolina Awards Commission, 1982–93. *Publications:* Fiction: Move Over, Mountain, 1957; Kingstree Island, 1959; Lion on the Hearth, 1961; The Land Breakers, 1964; The Road, 1967; Time of Drums, 1970; The Journey of August King, 1971; The Changing of the Guard, 1975; The Winter People, 1981; Last One Home, 1983; The Widows Trial, 1989. Non-Fiction: The Free Men, 1965; The Survivor, 1968; Trail of Tears: The Rise and Fall of the Cherokee Nation, 1988; Dr Frank: Living with Frank Porter Graham, 1993. Screenplay: The Journey of August King, 1995. *Honours:* Walter Raleigh Prizes for Fiction, North Carolina Dept of Cultural Affairs, 1964, 1967, 1970, 1975, 1984; Mayflower Society Cup, 1965; State of North Carolina Award for Literature, 1972; Gov.'s Award for Distinguished Meritorious Service, NC, 1978; Lillian Smith Prize, Southern Regional Council, 1982; Distinguished Alumnus Award, University of North Carolina at Chapel Hill, 1984; Thomas Wolfe Memorial Award, Western North Carolina Historical Asscn, 1984; W. D. Weatherford Award, Berea College, 1985; Caldwell Award, North Carolina Humanities Council, 1995. *Address:* 125 Westview Drive NW, Winston-Salem, NC 27104, USA.

EHRET, Terry; Poet and University Lecturer; b. 12 Nov. 1955, San Francisco, CA, USA; m. Donald Nicholas Moe, 7 April 1979, three c. *Education:* BA, Stanford University, 1977; Chapman College, 1979–81; MA, San Francisco State University, 1984. *Career:* Instructor in English, Santa Rosa Junior College, 1991–; Lecturer in Poetry, Sonoma State University, 1994–, San Francisco State University, 1995–99; founding Ed., Sixteen Rivers Press, 1999–; many poetry readings and lectures; mem. Acad. of American Poets; Associated Writing Programs; California Poets in the Schools; Poets and Writers. *Publications:* Suspensions (with Steve Gilmartin and Susan Herron Sibbet), 1990; Lost Body, 1993; Travel/How We Go on Living, 1995; Translations from the Human Language, 2001. Contributions: Reviews and journals. *Honours:* National Poetry Series Award, 1992; California Commonwealth Club Book Award for Poetry, 1994; Pablo Neruda Poetry Prize, Nimrod magazine, 1995. *Address:* 924 Sunnyslope Rd, Petaluma, CA 94952, USA.

EHRLICH, Eugene; Lexicographer and Writer; b. 21 May 1922, New York, NY, USA. *Education:* BS, City College, CUNY, 1942; MA, Columbia University, 1948. *Career:* Asst Prof., Fairleigh Dickinson University, 1946–48; Assoc. in English, Columbia University, 1949–87. *Publications:* How to Study Better, 1960; The Art of Technical Writing (with D. Murphy), 1962; Researching and Writing Term Papers and Reports (with D. Murphy), 1964; College Developmental Reading (with D. Murphy and D. Pace), 1966; Basic Grammar for Writing (with D. Murphy), 1970; Concise Index to English (with D. Murphy), 1974; Basic Vocabulary Builder, 1975; English Grammar, 1976; Punctuation, Capitalization and Spelling, 1977; Oxford American Dictionary (with others), 1980; The Oxford Illustrated Literary Guide to the United States (with Gorton Carruth), 1982; Speak for Success, 1984; Amo, Amas, Amat and More, 1985; The Bantam Concise Handbook of English, 1986; Harper's Dictionary of Foreign Terms, no. three, 1990; Collins Gem Dictionary, 1990; Collins Gem Thesaurus, 1990; Choose the Right Word (with S. I. Hayakawa), 1994; Veni, Vidi, Vici, 1995; The Highly Selective Dictionary for the Extraordinarily Literate, 1997; Les Bons Mots, 1997. *Address:* c/o HarperCollins, 10 E 53rd St, New York, NY 10022, USA.

EHRLICH, Paul Ralph, BA, MA, PhD; American biologist, academic and writer; b. 29 May 1932, Philadelphia, PA; m. Anne Fitzhugh Howland 1954; one d. *Education:* University of Pennsylvania, University of Kansas. *Career:* Research Assoc., University of Kansas, 1958–59; Asst Prof., 1959–62, Assoc. Prof., 1962–66, Prof., 1966–, Bing Prof. of Population Studies, 1976–, Stanford University; Pres., Center for Conservation Biology, 1988–; Correspondent, NBC News, 1989–92; mem. American Acad. of Arts and Sciences, fellow; American Philosophical Society, fellow; American Society of Naturalists; Entomological Society of America; Lepidopterists Society; National Acad. of Sciences; Society for the Study of Evoloution; Society of Systematic Zoology. *Publications:* How to Know the Butterflies, 1961; Process of Evolution, 1963; Principles of Modern Biology, 1968; Population Bomb, 1968; Population, Resources, Environment: Issues in Human Ecology, 1970; How to be a Survivor, 1971; Global Ecology: Readings Toward a Rational Strategy for Man, 1971; Man and the Ecosphere, 1971; Introductory Biology, 1973; Human Ecology: Problems and Solutions, 1973; Ark II: Social Response to Environmental Imperatives, 1974; The End of Affluence: A Blueprint for the Future, 1974; Biology and Society, 1976; Race Bomb, 1977; Ecoscience: Population, Resources, Environment, 1977; Insect Biology, 1978; The Golden Door: International Migration, Mexico, and the US, 1979; Extinction: The Causes and Consequences of the Disappearance of Species, 1981; The Machinery of Nature, 1986; Earth, 1987; The Science of Ecology, 1987; The Birder's Handbook, 1988; New World/New Mind, 1989; The Population Explosion, 1990; Healing the Planet, 1991; Birds in Jeopardy, 1992; The Birdwatchers Handbook, 1994; The Stork and the Plow, 1995; Betrayal of Science and Reason, 1996; A World of Wounds, 1997; Human Natures, 2000; Wild Solutions, 2001; One With Nineveh 2004. Contributions: scholarly journals. *Honours:* World Wildlife Federation Medal, 1987; Co-Winner, Crafoord Prize in Population Biology and Conservation Biology Diversity, 1990; John D. and Catherine T. MacArthur Foundation Fellowship, 1990–95; Volvo Environmental Prize, 1993; United Nations Sasakawa Environmental Prize, 1994; Heinz Prize for the Environment, 1995; Tyler Prize for Environmental Achievement, 1998; Heineken Prize for Environmental Sciences, 1998; National Audubon Society, One Hundred Champions of Conservation, 1998; Blue Planet Prize of the Asahi Glass Foundation, Japan, 1999; Distinguished Scientist Award, AIBS, 2001; Eminent Ecologist Award, Ecological Society of America, 2001; National Outdoor Book Award, Nature and Envitonment Category, 2001. *Address:* c/o Department of Biological Sciences, Stanford University, Stanford, CA 94305, USA.

EISELE, Robert; Playwright; b. 9 June 1948, Altadena, CA, USA. *Education:* BA, 1971, MFA, 1974, University of California at Los Angeles. *Career:* Playwrighting Fellow and Actor, American Conservatory Theatre, 1975–76; Assoc. Prof. of Theatre Arts, Rio Hondo College, CA, 1976–87; mem. Acad. of Television Arts and Sciences; Actors' Equity Asscn; Dramatists' Guild; Screen Actors' Guild; Writers' Guild of America. *Publications:* Plays; Television scripts. *Honours:* Samuel Goldwyn Writing Award, 1973; Oscar Hammerstein Playwrighting Fellowship, 1973–74; Donald Davis Dramatic Writing Award, 1974; American Conservatory Theatre Playwrighting Fellowship, 1975–76; First Prize, Theatre Arts Corpn Contest, 1979; Humanitas Award, 1986. *Address:* c/o Ken Shearman & Assocs, 99507 Santa Monica Blvd, No. 212, Beverly Hills, CA 90210, USA.

EISENBERG, Deborah; Writer; b. 20 Nov. 1945, Chicago, IL, USA. *Education:* Marlboro College, Vermont; BA, New School College, New School for Social Research, 1968. *Career:* Teacher, MFA Creative Writing Program, University of Virginia. *Publications:* Pastorale (play, produced 1982); Transactions in a Foreign Currency (short stories), 1986; Under the 82nd Airborne (short stories), 1992; Air, 24 Hours: Jennifer Bartlett (monograph), 1994; The Stories (So Far) of Deborah Eisenberg, 1996; All Around Atlantis, 1997. *Honours:* O. Henry Awards, 1986, 1995, 1997, 2002; Whiting Writer's Award, 1987; Guggenheim Fellowship, 1987; Deutscher Akademischer Austauschdienst Fellowship, Berlin, 1991; Friends of American Writers Award, 1993; Ingram Merrill Foundation Award, 1993; Award for Literature, American Acad. of Arts and Letters, 1993; Smart Foundation Prize for Best Story in Yale Review, 1996; The Rae Award for the Short Story, 2000; Lannon Foundation Fellowship, 2003. *Literary Agent:* Janklow & Nesbit Associates, 445 Park Ave, New York, NY 10022, USA.

EKINS, Paul Whitfield, BSc, MSc, MPhil, PhD; British economist and writer; b. 24 July 1950, Jakarta, Indonesia; m. Susan Anne Lofthouse 1979; one s. *Education:* Imperial Coll., London, Birkbeck Coll., London, Univ. of Bradford. *Career:* Research Fellow, School of Peace Studies, Univ. of Bradford 1987–90; Research Assoc., Dept of Applied Economics, Univ. of Cambridge 1991–98; Senior Lecturer 1996–98, Reader 1998–2000, Prof. 2000–02, School of Politics, Int. Relations and the Environment, Keele Univ.; Head Environment Group, Policy Studies Inst. 2002–; Prof., Univ. of Westminster 2002–; mem. Global 500 Forum, Int. Soc. for Ecological Economics, Royal Comm. on Environmental Pollution 2002–. *Publications:* The Living Economy: A New Economics in the Making (ed.) 1986, A New World Order: Grassroots Movements for Global Change 1992, Wealth Beyond Measure: An Atlas of New Economics (with Mayer Hillman and Robert Hutchison) 1992, Real Wealth: Green Economics in the Classroom (with Ken Webster) 1994, Global Warming and Energy Demand (ed. with Terry Barker and Nick Johnstone) 1995, Economic Growth and Environmental Sustainability 2000; contrib. to books, journals, reviews and newspapers. *Honours:* Hon. Fellow, Centre for Social and Environmental Accounting Research, Univ. of Dundee 1992–, Global 500 Award for Environmental Achievement, UNEP 1994. *Address:* c/o Policy Studies Institute, 100 Park Village East, London, NW1 3SR, England.

EKLUND, Gordon (Stewart); Writer; b. 24 July 1945, Seattle, WA, USA; one d. *Education:* Contra Costra College, 1973–75. *Career:* mem. SFWA. *Publications:* The Eclipse of Dawn, 1971; A Trace of Dreams, 1972; Beyond the Resurrection, 1973; All Times Possible, 1974; Serving in Time, 1975; Falling Toward Forever, 1975; If the Stars are Gods, 1976; The Dance of the Apocalypse, 1976; The Grayspace Beast, 1976; Find the Changeling, 1980; The Garden of Winter, 1980; Thunder on Neptune, 1989. Contributions: Analog; Galaxy; If Science Fiction; Fantasy and Science Fiction; Universe; New Dimensions; Amazing Stories; Fantastic. *Honours:* Nebula Award, 1975.

EKWENSI, Cyprian; Author and Pharmacist; b. 26 Sept. 1921, Minna, Northern Nigeria. *Education:* Govt College, Ibadan; Achimota College, Ghana; School of Forestry, Ibadan; Higher College, Yaba; Chelsea School of Pharmacy, Univ. of London; Iowa Univ. *Career:* Lecturer in Biology, Chem. and English, Igbobi College, Lagos, 1947–49; Lecturer, School of Pharmacy, Lagos, 1949–56; Pharmacist, Nigerian Medical Service, 1956; Head of Features, Nigerian Broadcasting Corpn, 1956–61; Dir of Information, Fed. Ministry of Information, Lagos, 1961–66; Dir of Information Services, Enugu, 1966; Chair., East Cen. State Library Board, Enugu, 1971–75; Man. Dir, Star Printing and Publishing Co. Ltd, 1975–79, Niger Eagle Press, 1981–; Visiting Lecturer, Iowa Univ.; mem. Pharmaceutical Societies of Great Britain and Nigeria; Nigerian Arts Council; Society of Nigerian Authors; Inst. Public Relations Nigeria and UK. *Publications:* When Love Whispers; Ikolo the Wrestler, 1947; The Leopard's Claw, 1950; People of the City, 1954; Passport of Mallam Ilia; The Drummer Boy, 1960; Jagua Nana, 1961; Burning Grass; An African Night's Entertainment; Yaba Roundabout Murder, 1962; Beautiful Feathers, 1963; Great Elephant Bird; Rainmaker, 1965; Lokotown; Juju Rock; Trouble in Form VI; Iska; Boa Suitor, 1966; Coal Camp Boy, 1973; Samankwe in the Strange Forest, 1974; Samankwe and the Highway Robbers; Restless City; Christmas Gold, 1975; Survive the Peace, 1976; Divided We Stand, 1980; Motherless Baby, 1980; Jaguanana's Daughter, 1986; For a Roll of Parchment, 1986; Beneath the Convent Wall, 1987; Restless City and Xmas Gold; Behind the Convent Wall, 1988; Death at Mile Two, 1988; Lagos Love Deal, 1988; Masquerade Time, 1991; King Forever, 1992. *Honours:* Dag Hammarskjöld Int. Award for Literary Merit, 1968. *Address:* Hillview Cres., Independence Layout, PO Box 317, Enugu, Nigeria.

ELBERG, Yehuda, (Y. L. Berg, Y. Renas); Novelist; b. 15 May 1912, Poland; two s. one d. *Education:* Rabbinnical Ordination, 1929; Textile Engineering, 1932. *Career:* Author-in-Residence, Bar-Ilan University Israel, 1988; Lecturer in Hebrew Studies, University of Oxford, 1990, 1994; mem. PEN International. *Publications:* Under Copper Skies, 1951; On the Tip of a Mast, 1974; Scattered Stalks, 1976; Tales, 1980; The Empire of Kalman the Cripple, 1983; In Clay Houses, I and II, 1983; A Man Is But a Man, 1983; Between Morning and Evening, 1983; The Fifteen Powers, 1989; Ship of the Hunted (novel), 1988; The Empire of Kalman the Cripple (novel), 1988. *Honours:* Feffer Prize, Congress for Jewish Culture, São Paulo, Brazil, 1951; J. I. Segal Awards, Montréal, 1975, 1988; Wasjslic-Cymerman Award, Sydney, Australia, 1975; Gonopolsky Prize, Paris, 1977; Manger Prize, Yiddish Literature, Government of Israel, City of Tel-Aviv and Manger Prize Foundation, 1977; Prime Minister's Award, Yiddish Literature, Israel, 1984; I. M. Wisenberg Prize, Congress for Jewish Culture, New York, 1984. *Address:* 1745 Cedar Ave, Montréal, QC H3G 1A7, Canada.

ELDER, Karl, BS, MS, MFA; poet, writer, editor and academic; *Jacob and Lucile Fessler Professor of Creative Writing, Lakeland College*; b. 7 July 1948, Beloit, WI, USA; m. Brenda Kay Olson 1969; two s. *Education:* Northern Illinois Univ., Wichita State Univ. *Career:* instructor, Southwest

Missouri State Univ. 1977–79; Faculty, 1979–89, Jacob and Lucile Fessler Prof. of Creative Writing and poet-in-residence, Lakeland Coll. 1990–. *Publications:* poetry: Can't Dance an' It's Too Wet to Plow 1975, The Celibate 1982, Phobophobia 1987, What Is the Future of Poetry? (ed.) 1991, A Man in Pieces 1994, The Geocryptogrammatist's Pocket Compendium of the United States 2001, Mead: Twenty-six Abecedariums 2005; contrib. to many anthologies, reviews, quarterlies and journals. *Honours:* Lucien Stryk Award for Poetry 1974, Illinois Arts Council Award 1975, and Grant 1977, Outstanding Teacher Award, Lakeland Coll. 1987, Robert Schuricht Endowment 1993, Pushcart Prize 2000, Mikrokosmos Prize for Poetry 2002. *Address:* c/o Creative Arts Division, Lakeland College, PO Box 359, Sheboygan, WI 53082, USA. *Telephone:* (920) 565-1276. *E-mail:* kelder@excel.net. *Website:* www.greatlakeswritersfestival.org; www1.lakeland.edu/seems/.

ELDERKIN, Susan; Novelist and Journalist; b. 1968. *Education:* Univ. of Cambridge; MA, Creative Writing, Univ. of East Anglia. *Publications:* Sunset Over Chocolate Mountains, 2000; The Voices, 2003. *Honours:* Amazon.co.uk Award; Betty Trask Award. *Address:* c/o Fourth Estate, 77–85 Fulham Palace Rd, London W6 8JB, England.

ELDRED-GRIGG, Stevan (Treleaven); Writer and Historian; b. 5 Oct. 1952, Grey Valley, New Zealand; m. Lauree Arlene Hunter, 13 Nov. 1976, divorced 1994, three s. *Education:* MA, University of Canterbury, 1975; PhD, Australian National University, 1978. *Career:* Postdoctoral Fellow, University of Canterbury, Christchurch, 1981; Judge, New Zealand Book Awards, 1984; Writing Fellow, 1986, Scholar-in-Letters, 1991, Victoria University; New Zealand Writing Fellow, Iowa University, Iowa City, USA; mem. PEN New Zealand Centre, Canterbury Provincial Committee. *Publications:* Fiction: Oracles and Miracles, 1987, adapted as radio play, 1989; The Siren Celia, 1989; The Shining City, 1991; Gardens of Fire, 1993; Mum, 1995. Non-Fiction: A Southern Gentry: New Zealanders Who Inherited the Earth, 1980; A New History of Canterbury, 1982; New Zealand Working People, 1890–1990, 1990; My History, I Think, 1994. Contributions: Short stories to periodicals including: Island; Landfall; New Zealand Listener; Historical essays to periodicals including: New Zealand Journal of History; Journal of the Royal Australian Historical Society. *Honours:* A. V. Reed Memorial Book Award, 1984; Second Prize, Goodman Fielder Wattie Award, Book Publishers' Asscn of New Zealand, 1988; Commonwealth Writers Prize, 1988. *Literary Agent:* Curtis Brown Pty, PO Box 19, Paddington, NSW 2021, Australia. *Address:* 377 River Rd, Christchurch, New Zealand.

ELDRIDGE, Colin Clifford; university professor and writer; *Professor of History, University of Wales*; b. 16 May 1942, Walthamstow, England; m. Ruth Margaret Evans, 3 Aug. 1970, one d. *Education:* BA, 1963, PhD, 1966, Nottingham University. *Career:* Lecturer, 1968–75, Senior Lecturer in History, 1975–92, Reader, 1992–98, Prof. 1998–, University of Wales, Lampeter; mem. Historical Asscn; Asscn of History Teachers in Wales; British Asscn of Canadian Studies; British Australian Studies Asscn. *Publications:* England's Mission: The Imperial Idea in the Age of Gladstone and Disraeli, 1973; Victorian Imperialism, 1978; Essays in Honour of C. D. Chandaman, 1980; British Imperialism in the 19th Century, 1984; Empire, Politics and Popular Culture, 1989; From Rebellion to Patriation: Canada and Britain in the Nineteenth and Twentieth Centuries, 1989; Disraeli and the Rise of a New Imperialism, 1996; The Imperial Experience: From Carlyle to Forster, 1996; The Zulu War, 1879, 1996; Kith and Kin: Canada, Britain and the United States form the Revolution to the Cold War, 1997. Contributions: various learned journals. *Honours:* FRHistS. *Address:* Tanerdy, Cilau Aeron, Lampeter, Dyfed SA48 8DL, Wales.

ELDRIDGE, David; British playwright; b. 1974. *Education:* Univ. of Exeter. *Plays:* Serving it Up 1996, Under the Blue Sky 2001, Festen 2004, M.A.D. 2004. *Address:* c/o Methuen Publishing Ltd, 215 Vauxhall Bridge Road, London, SW1V 1EJ, England. *Telephone:* (20) 7828-2838. *Fax:* (20) 7233-9827. *Website:* www.methuen.co.uk.

ELEGANT, Robert Sampson; British author and journalist; b. 7 March 1928, New York, NY, USA; m. 1st Moira Clarissa Brady, 16 April 1956 (died 20 January 1999), one s. one d.; m. 2nd Ursula Rosemary Righter née Douglas, 10 May 2003. *Education:* BA, University of Pennsylvania, 1946; US Army Language School, 1947–48; Yale University, 1948; MA, 1950, MS, 1951, Columbia University. *Career:* War, Southeast Asia Correspondent, various agencies, 1951–61; Central European Bureau, Newsweek, 1962–64; Los Angeles Times, Washington Post, 1965–70; Foreign Affairs Columnist, 1970–76; Visiting Prof. Univ. of S Carolina 1979, Boston Univ. 1994–95; mem. Authors' League of America; Hong Kong Foreign Correspondents' Club. *Publications:* China's Red Masters, 1951; The Dragon's Seed, 1959; The Centre of the World, 1961; Mao v Chiang: The Battle for China, 1972; The Great Cities, Hong Kong, 1977; Pacific Destiny, 1990. Fiction: A Kind of Treason, 1966; The Seeking, 1969; Dynasty, 1977; Manchu, 1980; Mandarin, 1983; White Sun, Red Star, 1987; Bianca, 1992; The Everlasting Sorrow, 1994; Last Year in Hong Kong, 1997; The Big Brown Bears, 1998; Bianca, 2000. Contributions: newspapers and periodicals. *Honours:* Pulitzer Fellow, 1951–52; Ford Foundation Fellowship, 1954–55; Overseas Press Club Awards, 1963, 1966, 1967, 1972; Edgar Allan Poe Award, 1967, Sigma Delta Chi Award 1996; Fellow, American Enterprise Institute for Public Policy Research, Washington, DC, 1976–78; Senior Fellow, Institute for Advanced Study, Berlin, 1993–94. *Literary Agent:* Christopher Sinclair-Stevenson, 3 South Terrace, London SW7, England. *Address:* 10 Quick St, London N1 8HL, England. *Telephone:* (20) 7837-1009. *Fax:* (20) 7837-1009.

ELIOT, Karen (see Home, Stewart Ramsay).

ELISHA, Ron; Medical Practitioner and Playwright; b. 19 Dec. 1951, Jerusalem, Israel; m. Bertha Rita Rubin, 6 Dec. 1981, one s. one d. *Education:* BM, BS, Melbourne University, 1975. *Career:* mem. Australian Writers' Guild; International PEN; Fellowship of Australian Writers. *Publications:* In Duty Bound, 1983; Two, 1985; Einstein, 1986; The Levine Comedy, 1987; Pax Americana, 1988; Safe House, 1989; Esterhaz, 1990; Impropriety, 1993; Choice, 1994; Pigtales, 1994; Unknown Soldier, 1996; Too Big, 1997; The Goldberg Variations, 2000. Contributions: Business Review Weekly; The Age; Vogue Australia; Generation Magazine; Australian Book Review; Centre Stage Magazine; Melbourne Jewish Chronicle; The Westerly Medical Observer. *Honours:* Best Stage Play, 1982, 1984; Major Award, 1982; Gold Award, Best Screenplay, Houston International Film Festival, 1990; Best TV Feature, Australian Writers' Guild Award, 1992. *Address:* 2 Malonga Ct, North Caulfield, Vic. 3161, Australia. *E-mail:* relisha@bigpond.net.au.

ELKINS, Aaron; Writer; b. 24 July 1935, New York, NY, USA; m. 1st Toby Siev, 1959, divorced 1972, two s.; m. 2nd Charlotte Trangmar, 1972. *Education:* BA, Hunter College, CUNY, 1956; Graduate Studies, University of Wisconsin at Madison, 1957–59; MA, University of Arizona, 1960; MA, California State University at Los Angeles, 1962; DEd, University of California at Berkeley, 1976. *Career:* Dir, Management Development, Contra Costa County Government, 1971–76, 1980–83; Lecturer, University of Maryland at College Park, European Division, 1976–78, 1984–85; Management Analyst, US Office of Personnel Management, San Francisco, 1979–80; Mem., Clallam County Civil Service Commission, 1987–. *Publications:* Fellowship of Fear, 1982; The Dark Place, 1983; Murder in the Queen's Armes, 1985; A Deceptive Clarity, 1987; Old Bones, 1987; Dead Men's Hearts, 1994; Loot, 1999. *Honours:* Edgar Allan Poe Award, MWA, 1988. *Address:* c/o Karpfinger Agency, 500 Fifth Ave, Suite 2800, New York, NY 10110, USA.

ELLIOT, Alistair; Poet, Trans., Ed. and Librarian (retd); b. 13 Oct. 1932, Liverpool, Lancashire, England; m. 1956, two s. *Education:* Fettes College, Edinburgh; BA, MA, Christ Church, Oxford. *Career:* Librarian, Kensington Public Library, London, 1959–61, Keele University, 1961–65, Pahlavi University, Iran, 1965–67, Newcastle University, 1967–82. *Publications:* Air in the Wrong Place, 1968; Contentions, 1977; Kisses, 1978; Talking to Bede, 1982; Talking Back, 1982; On the Appian Way, 1984; My Country: Collected Poems, 1989; Turning the Stones, 1993; Facing Things, 1997. Editor: Poems by James I and Others, 1970; Virgil, The Georgics with John Dryden's Translation, 1981. Editor and Translator: French Love Poems (bilingual), 1991; Italian Landscape Poems (bilingual), 1993; Roman Food Poems, 2003. Translator: Alcestis, by Euripides, 1965; Peace, by Aristophanes, 1965; Femmes Hombres, by Paul Verlaine, 1979; The Lazarus Poems, by Heinrich Heine, 1979; Medea, by Euripides, 1993; La Jeune Parque, by Paul Valéry, 1997. Contributions: many journals, reviews and magazines. *Honours:* Arts Council of Great Britain Grant, 1979; Ingram Merrill Foundation Fellowships, 1983, 1989; Prudence Farmer Awards, New Statesman, 1983, 1991; Djerassi Foundation Fellowship, 1984; Cholmondeley Award, Society of Authors, 2000. *Literary Agent:* PFD, Drury House, 34–43 Russell St, London WC2B 5HA, England. *Address:* 27 Hawthorn Rd, Newcastle upon Tyne NE3 4DE, England.

ELLIOT, Bruce (see Field, Edward).

ELLIOTT, Sir John (Huxtable); Prof. of Modern History (retd) and Writer; b. 23 June 1930, Reading, Berkshire, England; m. Oonah Sophia Butler 22 March 1958. *Education:* BA, 1952, PhD, 1955, Trinity College, Cambridge. *Career:* Fellow, Trinity College, Cambridge, 1954–67; Asst Lecturer in History, 1957–62, Lecturer in History, 1962–67, Univ. of Cambridge; Prof. of History, 1968–73, Fellow, 1998, King's College, London; Prof., Institute for Advanced Study, Princeton, NJ, 1973–90; King Juan Carlos Visiting Prof., New York Univ., 1988; Regius Prof. of Modern History and Fellow, Oriel College, Oxford, 1990–97; mem. American Acad. of Arts and Sciences, fellow, 1977; American Philosophical Society; Hispanic Society of America, corresponding mem., 1975, hon. fellow, 1997; Real Academia de la Historia, Madrid, corresponding fellow, 1965; Royal Acad. of Letters, Barcelona, 1992. *Publications:* The Revolt of the Catalans, 1963; Imperial Spain, 1469–1716, 1963; Europe Divided, 1559–1598, 1968; The Old World and the New, 1492–1650, 1970; The Diversity of History (ed. with H. G. Koenigsberger), 1970; Memoriales y cartas del Conde Duque de Olivares (with J. F. de la Peña), two vols, 1978, 1980; A Palace for a King (with Jonathan Brown), 1980; Richelieu and Olivares, 1984; The Count-Duke of Olivares, 1986; Spain and its World, 1500–1700, 1989; The Hispanic World (ed.), 1991; The World of the Favourite (ed. with Laurence Brockliss), 1999; The Sale of the Century (ed. with Jonathan Brown). Contributions: scholarly journals. *Honours:* several hon. doctorates; Fellow, British Acad., 1972; Commander, 1984, Grand Cross, 1988, Order of Alfonso X el Sabio; Leo Gershoy Award, American Historical Asscn, 1985; Wolfson Literary Prize for History, 1987; Commander, 1987, Grand Cross, 1996, Order of Isabel la Católica; Medalla de Oro al Mérito en las Bellas Artes, Spain, 1990; Hon.

Fellow, Trinity College, Cambridge, 1991, Oriel College, Oxford, 1997; Knighted, 1994; Premio Príncipe de Asturias, 1996; Gold Medal, Spanish Institute, New York, 1997; Balzan Prize for History 1500–1800, International Balzan Foundation, 1999; Cross of St George, Catalonia, 1999. *Address:* 122 Church Way, Iffley, Oxford OX4 4EG, England.

ELLIOTT, Sir Roger James, Kt, MA, DPhil, FRS; British physicist and publisher; b. 8 Dec. 1928, Chesterfield; m. Olga Lucy Atkinson 1952; one s. two d. *Education:* Swanwick Hall School, Derbyshire and New Coll., Oxford. *Career:* Research Assoc. Univ. of Calif., Berkeley 1952–53; Research Fellow, Atomic Energy Research Est., Harwell 1953–55; Lecturer, Univ. of Reading 1955–57; Lecturer, Oxford Univ. 1957–65, Reader 1965–74, Fellow, St John's Coll. 1957–74 (now Hon. Fellow), New Coll. 1974–96 (now Hon. Fellow), Wykeham Prof. of Physics 1974–89, Prof. of Physics 1989–96, now Emer. Prof.; Del. Oxford Univ. Press 1971–88, Chair. Computer Bd 1983–87, Sec. to Dels and Chief Exec. 1988–93; mem. Bd Blackwell Ltd 1996–, Chair. 1999–2002; Visiting Prof. Univ. of Calif., Berkeley 1960–61; Miller Visiting Prof. Univ. of Ill., Urbana 1966; Visiting Distinguished Prof. Fla State Univ. 1981, Mich. State Univ. 1997–2000; Physical Sec. and Vice-Pres. Royal Soc. (London) 1984–88; Treas. Publrs Asscn 1990–92, Pres. 1992–93; Chair. ICSU Press 1997–2002, Disability Information Trust 1998–2001; mem. Bd (part-time) UKAEA 1988–94, British Council 1990–98; Treas. ICSU Press 2002. *Publications:* Magnetic Properties of Rare Earth Metals 1972, Solid State Physics and its Applications 1973; articles in learned journals. *Honours:* Hon. DSc (Paris) 1983, (Bath) 1991, (Essex) 1993; Maxwell Medal (Physical Soc.) 1968, Guthrie Medal 1989. *Address:* 11 Crick Road, Oxford, OX2 6QL, England (Home). *Telephone:* (1865) 273997. *Fax:* (1865) 273947.

ELLIS, Alice Thomas (see Haycraft, Anna (Margaret)).

ELLIS, Bret Easton, BA; American writer; b. 7 March 1964, Los Angeles, CA. *Education:* Bennington Coll. *Career:* mem. Authors' Guild. *Publications:* Less Than Zero 1985, The Rules of Attraction 1987, American Psycho 1989, The Informers 1994, Glamorama 1998; contrib. to Rolling Stone, Vanity Fair, Elle, Wall Street Journal, Bennington Review. *Literary Agent:* Amanda Urban, International Creative Management, 40 W 57th Street, New York, NY 10019, USA.

ELLIS, Charles Richard, MA; American publishing executive; b. 20 July 1935, New York; m. 1st Nathalie Likwas 1957 (divorced 1963); one s.; m. 2nd Jeanne Laurent 1963; four step-s. *Education:* Princeton and Columbia Univs. *Career:* teacher, Barnard School, New York 1958–63; Man. Scientific Research Assocs Chicago 1963–68; Exec. Ed. DC Heath, Boston 1968–70; Chair. and Man. Dir DC Heath Ltd, UK 1970–75; Co-Man. Dir Pergamon Press, UK 1975–78; Marketing Dir Elsevier Publishing, Amsterdam 1978–81; Pres. Elsevier Scientific Publishing Co. New York 1981–88; Exec. Vice-Pres. John Wiley & Sons, New York 1988–90, Pres., CEO 1990–97, Sr Adviser 1998–; Pres. Bd of Trustees, Princeton Univ. Press. 1987–; Chair. Asscn of American Publrs 1992–94; Vice-Chair. Int. Publrs Asscn 1996–. *Honours:* Chevalier des Arts et des Lettres. *Address:* John Wiley & Sons, 605 Third Avenue, New York, NY 10158 (Office); 300 East 54th Street, New York, NY 10022, USA (Home). *Telephone:* (212) 850-6000 (Office). *Fax:* (212) 850-6088 (Office).

ELLIS, David George; Prof., Writer and Trans; b. 23 June 1939, Swinton, Lancashire, England; m. 24 Sept. 1966, two d. *Education:* MA, 1964, PhD, 1970, University of Cambridge. *Career:* Lecturer, La Trobe University, Melbourne, Vic., Australia, 1968–72; Lecturer, Senior Lecturer, Prof., University of Kent at Canterbury, England, 1972–. *Publications:* Stendhal, Memoirs of an Egotist (trans.), 1975; Wordsworth, Freud and the Spots of Time: Interpretation in 'The Prelude', 1985; D. H. Lawrence's Non-Fiction: Art, Thought and Genre (with Howard Mills), 1988; Imitating Art: Essays in Biography (ed.), 1993; Dying Game, vol. three, New Cambridge Biography of D. H. Lawrence, 1998; Literary Lives: Biography and the Search for Understanding, 2000. *Address:* English School, University of Kent at Canterbury, Canterbury CT2 7NX, England.

ELLIS, John Martin, BA, PhD; American academic, writer and editor; b. 31 May 1936, London, England; m. Barbara Stephanie Rhoades 1978; two s. two d. one step-d. *Education:* University of London. *Career:* Tutorial Asst in German, University College of Wales, Aberystwyth, 1959–60; Asst Lecturer in German, University of Leicester, 1960–63; Asst Prof. of German, University of Alberta, Edmonton, 1963–66; Assoc. Prof. of German Literature, 1966–70, Prof. of German Literature, 1970–94, Dean, Graduate Division, 1977–86, Prof. Emeritus, 1994–, University of California at Santa Cruz; Visiting Prof., University of Kent at Canterbury, 1970–71; Literary Ed., Heterodoxy, 1992–; mem. Asscn of Literary Scholars and Critics, sec.-treasurer, 1994–2000; National Asscn of Scholars. *Publications:* Schiller's Kalliasbriefe and the Study of His Aesthetic Theory, 1969; Kleist's Prinz Friedrich von Homburg: A Critical Study, 1970; Narration in the German Novelle, 1974; The Theory of Literary Criticism: A Logical Analysis, 1974; Heinrich von Kleist: Studies in the Character and Meaning of His Writings, 1979; One Fairy Story Too Many: The Brothers Grimm and Their Tales, 1983; Against Deconstruction, 1989; Language, Thought and Logic, 1993; Literature Lost: Social Agendas and the Corruption of the Humanities, 1997. Contributions: scholarly journals. *Honours:* Guggenheim Fellowship, 1970–71; National Endowment for the Humanities Fellowships, 1975–76, 1992; Peter Shaw Memorial Award, National Asscn of Scholars, 1998. *Address:* 144 Bay Heights, Soquel, CA 95073, USA. *E-mail:* john.ellis@earthlink.net.

ELLIS, Peter Berresford, (Peter MacAlan, Peter Tremayne); Writer; b. 10 March 1943, Coventry, Warwickshire, England; m. Dorothea Cheesmur, Sept. 1966. *Education:* Brighton College of Art, University of East London. *Career:* mem. Celtic League, international chair., 1988–90; CWA; Irish Literary Society; London Asscn for Celtic Education, chair., 1989–90, vice-pres., 1990–96; FRHistS; Royal Society of Antiquaries of Ireland, fellow; Society of Authors. *Publications:* Wales – A Nation Again!: The Nationalist Struggle for Freedom, 1968; The Creed of the Celtic Revolution, 1969; The Scottish Insurrection of 1820 (with Seumas Mac a'Ghobhainn), 1970; The Problem of Language Revival (with Seumas Mac a'Ghobhainn), 1971; A History of the Irish Working Class, 1972; The Cornish Language and Its Literature, 1974; Hell or Connaught!: The Cromwellian Colonisation of Ireland, 1652–1660, 1975; The Boyne Water: The Battle of the Boyne, 1690, 1976; The Great Fire of London: An Illustrated Account, 1976; Caesar's Invasion of Britain, 1978; A Voice From the Infinite: The Life of Sir Henry Rider Haggard, 1856–1925, 1978; MacBeth: High King of Scotland, 1040–57 AD, 1979; By Jove, Biggles!: The Life of Captain W. E. Johns (with Piers Williams), 1981; The Liberty Tree, 1982; The Last Adventurer: The Life of Talbot Mundy, 1879–1940, 1984; Celtic Inheritance, 1985; The Celtic Revolution: A Study in Anti-Imperialism, 1985; The Rising of the Moon: A Novel of the Fenian Invasion of Canada, 1987; A Dictionary of Irish Mythology, 1987; The Celtic Empire: The First Millennium of Celtic History, c. 1000 BC–51 AD, 1990; A Guide to Early Celtic Remains in Britain, 1991; A Dictionary of Celtic Mythology, 1992; Celt and Saxon: The Struggle for Britain AD 410–937, 1993; The Celtic Dawn: A History of Pan Celticism, 1993; The Book of Deer, 1994; The Druids, 1994; Celtic Women: Women in Celtic Society and Literature, 1996; Celt and Greek: Celts in the Hellenic World, 1997; Celt and Roman: The Celts of Italy, 1998; The Chronicles of the Celts: New Tellings of Their Myths and Legends, 1999; Erin's Blood Royal: The Gaelic Noble Dynasties of Ireland, 2001. As Peter MacAlan: The Judas Battalion, 1983; Airship, 1984; The Confession, 1985; Kitchener's Gold, 1986; The Valkyrie Directive, 1987; The Doomsday Decree, 1988; Fireball, 1991; The Windsor Protocol, 1993. As Peter Tremayne: The Hound of Frankenstein, 1977; Dracula Unborn, 1977; The Vengeance of She, 1978; The Revenge of Dracula, 1978; The Ants, 1979; The Curse of Loch Ness, 1979; The Fires of Lan-Kern, 1978; Dracula, My Love, 1980; Zombie!, 1981; The Return of Raffles, 1981; The Morgow Rises!, 1982; The Destroyers of Lan-Kern, 1982; The Buccaneers of Lan-Kern, 1983; Snowbeast!, 1983; Raven of Destiny, 1984; Kiss of the Cobra, 1984; Swamp!, 1985; Angelus!, 1985; My Lady of Hy-Brasil and Other Stories, 1987; Nicor!, 1987; Trollnight!, 1987; Ravenmoon, 1988; Island of Shadows, 1991; Aisling and Other Irish Tales of Terror, 1992; Murder by Absolution, 1994; Shroud for the Archbishop, 1995; Suffer Little Children, 1995; The Subtle Serpent, 1996; The Spider's Web, 1997; The Un-Dead: The Legend of Bram Stoker and Dracula (with Peter Haining), 1997; Valley of the Shadow, 1998; The Monk Who Vanished, 1999; Act of Mercy, 1999; Hemlock at Vespers, 2000; Our Lady of Darkness, 2000. Contributions: anthologies, newspapers and magazines. *Honours:* Bard of the Cornish Gorsedd, 1987; Irish Post Award, 1988. *Literary Agent:* A. M. Heath & Co Ltd, 79 St Martin's Lane, London WC2N 4RE, England.

ELLIS, Richard J.; Prof. of Politics and Writer; b. 27 Nov. 1960, Leicester, England; m. Juli Takenaka, 18 July 1987. *Education:* BA, University of California, Santa Cruz, 1982; MA, Political Science, 1984, PhD, Political Science, 1989, University of California, Berkeley. *Career:* Asst Prof., 1990–95, Assoc. Prof., 1995–99, Mark O. Hatfield Prof. of Politics, 1999–, Willamette University, Salem, OR; mem. American Political Science Asscn; Organization of American Historians. *Publications:* Dilemmas of Presidential Leadership (co-author), 1989; Cultural Theory (co-author), 1990; American Political Cultures, 1993; Presidential Lightning Rods: The Politics of Blame Avoidance, 1994; Politics, Policy and Culture (co-ed.), 1994; Culture Matters: Essays in Honor of Aaron Wildavsky (co-ed.), 1997; The Dark Side of the Left: Illiberal Egalitarianism in America, 1997; Speaking to the People: The Rhetorical Presidency in Historical Perspective, 1998; The Founding of the American Presidency, 1999; Democratic Delusions; The Initiative Process in America, 2002. Contributions: Comparative Studies in Society and History; Journal of Behavioural Economics; Presidential Studies Quarterly; Journal of Theoretical Politics: Studies in American Political Development; Review of Politics; Polity; Western Political Quarterly; Critical Review; American Political Science Review. *Honours:* Regents Fellowship, University of California, 1983–85; I. G. S. Harris Fellowship, 1986–88; Summer Stipend, National Endowment for the Humanities, 1991; Fellowship, George and Eliza Howard Foundation, 1993–94; Arnold L. and Lois S. Graves Award in the Humanities, 1998. *Address:* Willamette University, Salem, OR 97301, USA.

ELLIS, (Christopher) Royston George, (Richard Tresillian); writer, lecturer and poet; b. 10 Feb. 1941, Pinner, Middlesex, England; one s. *Career:* Asst Ed., Jersey News and Features Agency, 1961–63; Assoc. Ed., Canary Islands Sun, Las Palmas, 1963–66; Ed., The Educator, Dir, Dominica Broadcasting Services and Reuters, Cana Correspondent, 1974–76; Man. Ed., Wordsman Features Agency, 1977–86; Editorial Consultant, Explore Sri Lanka, 1990–; Travel and Colonial Property Correspondent, Sunday

Times, Colombo, 1991–; Man. Dir, Wordsman Ltd, 1997; mem. Institute of Rail Transport, India; Royal Commonwealth Society. *Publications:* Jiving to Gyp, 1959; Rave, 1960; The Big Beat Scene, 1961; The Rainbow Walking Stick, 1961; Rebel, 1962; Burn Up, 1963; The Mattress Flowers, 1963; The Flesh Merchants, 1966; The Rush at the End, 1967; The Bondmaster Series (seven books), 1977–83; The Fleshtrader Series (three books), 1984–85; The Bloodheart Series (three books), 1985–87; Giselle, 1987; Guide to Mauritius, 1988–98; India By Rail, 1989–97; Sri Lanka By Rail, 1994; A Maldives Celebration (with Gemunu Amarasinghe), 1997; A Man For All Islands, 1998; Festivals of the World: Madagascar, Trinidad 1999; A Hero In Time, 2001; Sri Lanka, 2002. Contributions: newspapers and magazines. *Honours:* Dominica National Poetry Awards, 1967, 1971. *Address:* Horizon Cottage, Kaikawala-Induruwa, Sri Lanka. *Website:* www.roystonellis.com.

ELLISON, Harlan Jay; Author; b. 27 May 1934, Cleveland, OH, USA; m. 1st Charlotte Stein, 1956, divorced 1959; m. 2nd Billie Joyce Sanders, 1961, divorced 1962; m. 3rd Lory Patrick, 1965, divorced 1965; m. 4th Lori Horwitz, 1976, divorced 1977; m. 5th Susan Toth, 1986. *Education:* Ohio State University, 1953–55. *Career:* Instructor, Clarion Writer's Workshop, Michigan State University, 1969–77, 1984; Book Critic, Los Angeles Times, 1969–82; Editorial Commentator, CBC, 1972–78, Sci-Fi Channel, USA, 1993–; Pres., Kilimanjaro Corpn, 1979–; Host, 2000X, radio series; mem. SFWA, vice-pres., 1965–66; Writers' Guild of America. *Publications:* Harlan Ellison's Dream Corridor (comic book), 1995; The City on the Edge of Forever, 1995; Slippage, 1997; Edgeworks Vols I–V, 1996–98; The Essential Ellison: A 50-Year Retrospective, 2001. Contributions: newspapers. Film and Television: Over 60 screenplays and teleplays. *Honours:* Nebula Awards, 1965, 1969, 1977; various Hugo Awards, 1966–86; Edgar Allan Poe Awards, 1974, 1988; British Fantasy Award, 1978; American Mystery Award, 1987; Bram Stoker Awards, 1987, 1989, 1994, 1995, 2000; Life Achievement Award, World Fantasy Convention, 1993; Four-times winner, Writers' Guild Award; Brandeis University (National Women's Committee): Words, Wit and Wisdom Award, 1998. *Address:* PO Box 55548, Sherman Oaks, CA 91413, USA.

ELLMANN, Lucy; American writer and critic; b. IL; one d. *Education:* Univ. of Essex, UK and Courtauld Inst., London. *Career:* has lived in Oxford since the age of 13; mem. judging panel Irish Times–Aer Lingus Int. Fiction Prize 1992. *Publications:* novels: Just Desserts (Guardian Fiction Prize) 1988, Varying Degrees of Hopelessness 1991, Man or Mango 1998, Dot in the Universe 2003; contrib. to various periodicals and newspapers, including TLS, Guardian, Sunday Telegraph and Observer. *Address:* c/o Bloomsbury Publishing, 37 Soho Square, London, W1D 3HB, England.

ELLROY, James, (Lee Earle Ellroy); writer; b. 4 March 1948, Los Angeles, CA, USA; m. 1st Mary Doherty; m. 2nd Helen Knode. *Publications:* Brown's Requiem, 1981; Clandestine, 1982; Blood on the Moon, 1984; Because the Night, 1984; Killer on the Road, 1986; Suicide Hill, 1986; Silent Terror, 1986; The Black Dahlia, 1987; The Big Nowhere, 1988; L.A. Confidential, 1990; White Jazz, 1992; Hollywood Nocturnes, 1994; American Tabloid, 1995; My Dark Places: An L.A. Crime Memoir, 1996; L.A. Noir, 1998; Crimewave: Reportage and Fiction from the Underside of L.A., 1999; The Cold Six Thousand, 2001; Destination: Morgue (collection of writings), 2003. *Address:* c/o Sobel Weber Assocs Inc, 146 E 19th Street, New York, NY 10003, USA.

ELMSLIE, Kenward Gray; Poet and Librettist; b. 27 April 1929, New York, NY, USA. *Education:* BA, Harvard University, 1950. *Career:* mem. American Society of Composers, Authors and Publishers. *Publications:* Poetry: The Champ, 1968; Album, 1969; Circus Nerves, 1971; Motor Disturbance, 1971; The Orchid Stories, 1972; Tropicalism, 1976; The Alphabet Work, 1977; Communications Equipment, 1979; Moving Right Along, 1980; Bimbo Dirt, 1981; 26 Bars, 1986; Sung Sex, 1989; Pay Dirt (with Joe Brainard), 1992; Champ Dust, 1994; Bare Bones, 1995; Routine Disruptions: Selected Poems and Lyrics, 1998; Cyberspace (with Trevor Winkfield), 2000; Blast from the Past, 2000; Nite Soil, 2000; Snippets, 2002; Opera Libretti: Lizzie Borden, 1966; Miss Julie, 1966; The Sweet Bye and Bye, 1973; The Seagull, 1974; Washington Square, 1976; Three Sisters, 1986. Play: City Junket, 1987. Musical Plays: The Grass Harp, 1971; Lola, 1982; Postcards on Parade, 1993. Contributions: many anthologies, reviews and journals. *Honours:* Frank O'Hara Poetry Award, 1971. *Address:* PO Box 38, Calais, VT 05648, USA. *Website:* www.kenwardelmslie.com.

ELSOM, John Edward; Author, Dramatist, Journalist, Broadcaster and Lecturer; b. 31 Oct. 1934, Leigh on Sea, Essex, England; m. Sally Mays, 3 Dec. 1956, two s. *Education:* BA, 1956; PhD, City University, London, 1991. *Career:* Script Adviser, Paramount Pictures, 1960–68; Theatre Critic, London Magazine, 1963–68, The Listener, 1972–82; Correspondent, Contemporary Review, 1978–88; Lecturer, Course Leader, Arts Criticism, City University, London, 1986–96; Consultant, South Bank University, 1996–97, School for Oriental and African Studies, University of London, 1997; Dir, Arts Interlink, arts management consultancy; mem. Liberal Party of Great Britain, Art and Broadcasting Committee; International Asscn of Theatre Critics, hon. pres.; Liberal Party's Arts and Broadcasting Committee, Chair. and Convenor, 1978–88. *Publications:* Theatre Outside London, 1969; Erotic Theatre, 1972; Post-War British Theatre, 1976; The History of the National Theatre, 1978; Change and Choice, 1978; Post-War British Theatre Criticism (ed.), 1981; Is Shakespeare Still Our Contemporary? (ed.), 1989; Cold War Theatre, 1992; Missing the Point, 1998. Other: plays published and produced. Contributions: Observer; Mail on Sunday; Encounter; TLS; The World and I; Sunday Telegraph; Plays International; Plays & Players; San Diego Union; numerous others. *Literary Agent:* John McLaughlin. *Address:* 14 Homersham Rd, Kingston-upon-Thames, Surrey KT1 3PN, England.

ELTIS, Walter Alfred; British economist and writer; b. 23 May 1933, Warnsdorf, Czechoslovakia; m. Shelagh Mary Owen 1959; one s. two d. *Education:* Wycliffe College; Emmanuel College, Cambridge; BA, University of Cambridge; MA, Nuffield College, Oxford, 1960; DLitt, University of Oxford, 1990. *Career:* Research Fellow in Economics, 1958–60, Fellow and Tutor in Economics, 1963–88, Emeritus Fellow, 1988–, Exeter College, Oxford; Lecturer in Economics, University of Oxford, 1961–88; Visiting Reader in Economics, University of Western Australia, 1970–71; Visiting Prof., University of Toronto, 1976–77, European University, Florence, 1979, University of Reading, 1992–; Economic Dir, 1986–92, Dir-Gen., 1988–92, National Economic Development Office, London; Chief Economic Adviser to the Pres. of the Board of Trade, 1992–95; Gresham Prof. of Commerce, Gresham College, London, 1993–96; mem. Reform Club, chair., 1994–95; Political Economy Club; European Society for the History of Economic Thought, vice-pres., 2000–04. *Publications:* Growth and Distribution, 1973; Britain's Economic Problem: Too Few Producers (with Robert Bacon), 1976; The Classical Theory of Economic Growth, 1984; Keynes and Economic Policy (with Peter Sinclair), 1988; Classical Economics, Public Expenditure and Growth, 1993; Britain's Economic Problem Revisited, 1996; Condillac, Commerce and Government (ed. with Shelagh M. Eltis), 1998; Britain, Europe and EMU, 2000. Contributions: Economic journals and bank reviews. *Address:* Danesway, Jarn Way, Boars Hill, Oxford OX1 5JF, England.

ELTON, Benjamin (Ben) Charles, BA; British writer and performer; b. 3 May 1959; m. Sophie Gare 1994. *Education:* Godalming Grammar School, South Warwickshire Coll. of Further Educ., Manchester Univ. *Career:* first professional appearance Comic Strip Club 1981; numerous tours as stand-up comic 1986–. *Film:* Maybe Baby (writer and dir) 2000, Much Ado About Nothing (actor) 1993. *Television:* writer: Alfresco 1982–83, The Young Ones (jtly) 1982–84, Happy Families 1985, Filthy Rich and Catflap 1986, Blackadder II (jtly) 1987, Blackadder the Third (jtly) 1988, Blackadder Goes Forth (jtly) 1989, The Thin Blue Line (jtly) 1995–96; writer and performer: South of Watford (jtly, documentary series) 1984–85, Friday Live 1987–88, Saturday Live 1985–87, Ben Elton Live 1989, 1993, 1997, The Man from Auntie 1990, 1994, Stark 1993, The Ben Elton Show (jtly) 1998. *Theatre:* Gasping 1990, Silly Cow 1991, Popcorn 1996, Blast from the Past 1998, The Beautiful Game (musical, book and lyrics) 2000, We Will Rock You (story to musical) 2002, Tonight's the Night (story to musical) 2003. *Albums:* Motormouth 1987, Motorvation 1989. *Publications:* novels: Bachelor Boys 1984, Stark 1989, Gridlock 1992, This Other Eden 1993, Popcorn 1996, Blast from the Past 1998, Inconceivable 1999, Dead Famous 2001, High Society 2002. *Honours:* British Acad. Best Comedy Show Awards 1984, 1987, Best New Comedy Laurence Olivier Award 1998. *Literary Agent:* Phil McIntyre, Second Floor, 35 Soho Square, London, W1D 3QX, England.

EMECHETA, (Florence Onye) Buchi, BSc; British writer and lecturer; b. 21 July 1944, Lagos, Nigeria; m. Sylvester Onwordi 1960; three d. two s. *Education:* Methodist Girls' High School, Lagos and Univ. of London. *Career:* fmr librarian and community worker; Sr Research Fellow, Visiting Prof. of English, Univ. of Calabar 1980–81; Lecturer, Yale Univ., USA 1982, Univ. of London 1982; numerous visiting professorships at univs in USA; Propr Ogwugwn Afo Publishing Co.; mem. Home Sec.'s Advisory Council on Race 1979, Arts Council 1982–83, PEN Int. *Publications:* In the Ditch 1972, Second Class Citizen 1975, The Bride Price 1976, The Slave Girl 1977, The Joys of Motherhood 1979, Naura Power 1981, Destination Biafra 1982, Double Yoke 1982, A Land of Marriage 1983, The Rape of Shavi 1983, Head Above Water (autobiog.) 1984, Gwendolen 1989, Kehinde 1994; children's books: Titch the Cat 1979, Nowhere to Play 1980, The Moonlight Bride 1981, The Wrestling Match 1981; contrib. to newspapers and periodicals, including New Statesman, New Society, New International Sunday Times Magazine. *Honours:* Jack Campbell Award, New Statesman 1979, one of Best Young British Writers 1983.

EMERSON, Ru, (Robert Cray), LLB; writer; b. 15 Dec. 1944, Monterey, CA, USA. *Education:* University of Montana, LA Co. Bar Asscn. *Career:* mem. SFWA. *Publications:* Princess of Flames, 1986; To the Haunted Mountains, 1987; In the Caves of Exile, 1988; On the Seas of Destiny, 1989; SpellBound, 1990, Beauty and the Beast 1990; Trilogy: Night Threads (The Calling of the Three 1990, The Two in Hiding 1991, One Land, One Duke 1993); The Bard's Tale: Fortress of Frost and Fire (with Mercedes Lackey), 1993; The Sword and the Lion, 1993, Trilogy: Night Threads (The Craft of Light 1993, The Art of the Sword 1994, The Science of Power 1995), Xena: Warrior Princess, The Empty Throne 1996, Xena: Warrior Princess, The Huntress and the Sphynx 1997; Xena: Warrior Princess, The Thief of Hermes 1997, Voices of Chaos (with A. C. Crispin) 1998, Against the Giants 1999, Trilogy: Xena: Warrior Princess, (Go Quest, Young Man 1999, Questward Ho! 2000, How the Quest Was Won 2000), Keep on the Borderland 2001. Contributions: anthologies and magazines. *Address:* 2600 Reuben Boise Road, Dallas, OR 97338, USA. *E-mail:* ruemerson@aol.com.

EMMETT, Nicholas; Writer and Trans; b. 22 July 1935, Dublin, Ireland; m. Anne Brit Emmett, 20 May 1965. *Education:* Philosophy, University of Oslo; Literature, University of Galway. *Career:* Taxi-Owner and Driver, six years; Interpreter-Trans., Indian Embassy, Oslo, Norway, 1973; Founding Co-Ed., Ragtime, English cultural magazine, Norway; mem. The Irish Writers' Union; Society of Authors. *Publications:* The Cave (novel), 1987; The Red Mist and Other Stories, 1988; Brains on the Dump (short story), 1991. Contributions: 87 short stories and articles in newspapers, anthologies and magazines, England, USA, Ireland, Norway; 23 stories broadcast on BBC and Irish National Radio. *Honours:* Writing Grant, Irish Arts Council. *Address:* Rathcoffey N, Donadea, Co Kildare, Ireland.

ENAHORO, Chief Anthony, C.FR.; Nigerian politician, journalist, newspaper publisher and company director; b. 22 July 1923, Uromi Ishan, Bendel State; m. Helen Ediae 1954; four s. one d. *Education:* Govt Schools Uromi and Owo, King's Coll. Lagos. *Career:* journalist 1942–52; Ed. Southern Nigerian Defender 1944–45, Daily Comet 1945–49; Assoc. Ed. West African Pilot; Ed.-in-Chief Nigerian Star 1950–52; foundation mem. Action Group Party, later Acting Gen. Sec. and Fed. Vice-Pres.; Chair. Uromi Dist Council and Ishan Div. Council; mem. Western House of Assembly and Fed. House of Reps and Party Chief Whip 1951–54; Dir Nat. Coal Bd 1953–56; Minister of Home Affairs, Transport, Information and Midwest Affairs and Leader of the House (Western Region) 1954–59; Fed. MP and Opposition Spokesman on Foreign Affairs, Internal Affairs and Legislature Affairs 1959–63; moved motion for self-govt and attended all constitutional talks preceding independence in 1960; detained during Emergency period Western Region 1962, fled to Britain, extradited and imprisoned in Nigeria for treasonable felony; released by mil. govt 1966; Leader, Midwest State del. to Constitutional Conf. and mem. Constitutional Cttee 1966; Fed. Commr for Information, Culture, Youth, Sports, Co-operatives and Labour 1967–75; mem. Nat. Democratic Coalition (NADECO); Fed. Commr for Special Duties 1975; Pres. World Black and African Festival of Arts and Culture 1972–75; State Chair. Nat. Party of Nigeria 1978–80; Chair. Cttees Edo State Movt 1981–, Nigerian Shippers Council 1982; detained Aug.–Dec. 1994. *Publication:* Fugitive Offender (autobiog.). *Honours:* Hon. DSc (Benin) 1972. *Address:* Rainbow House, 144 Upper Mission Road, P.M.B. 1425, Benin City, Nigeria. *Telephone:* 200803 (Office); 243770 (Home).

ENG, Stephen Richard; Biographer, Poet, Literary Journalist and Scholar; b. 31 Oct. 1940, San Diego, CA, USA; m. Anne Jeanne Kangas, 15 May 1969, two s. two d. *Education:* BA, English Literature, George Washington University, Washington, DC, 1963; MS, Education (Counselling), Portland State University, Oregon, 1973. *Career:* Poetry Ed., The Diversifier, 1977–78; Assoc. Ed., Triads, 1985; Dir and Ed., Nashville House, 1991–; Staff Book Reviewer, Nashville Banner, 1993–98; mem. Broadcast Music Inc, 1972–; Syndic, F. Marion Crawford Memorial Society, 1978–; Country Music Asscn, 1990–; Science-Fiction Poetry Asscn, 1990–. *Publications:* Elusive Butterfly and Other Lyrics (ed.), 1971; The Face of Fear and Other Poems (ed.), 1984; The Hunter of Time: Gnomic Verses (ed.), 1984; Toreros: Poems (ed.), 1990; Poets of the Fantastic (co-ed.), 1992; A Satisfied Mind: The Country Music Life of Porter Wagoner, 1992; Jimmy Buffett: The Man From Margaritaville Revealed, 1996; Yellow Rider and Other Lyrics, 2000. Contributions: Lyric; Night Cry; Journal of Country Music; Tennessee Historical Quarterly; Bookpage; Nashville Banner; Music City Blues; Space & Time. *Honours:* American Poets' Fellowship Society Certificate of Merit, 1973; Co-Winner, Rhysling Award, Science Fiction Poetry Asscn, 1979; Best Writer, 1979, 1983, Special Achievement, 1985, Small Press Writers and Artists Organization. *Address:* PO Box 111864, Nashville, TN 37222, USA.

ENGEL, Howard; Writer; b. 2 April 1931, Toronto, ON, Canada; m. 1st Marian Ruth Passmore, 1962, one s. one d.; m. 2nd Janet Evelyn Hamilton, 1978, one s. *Education:* St Catharine's Collegiate Institute; BA, McMaster University, 1955; Ontario College of Education, 1956. *Career:* Writer-in-Residence, Hamilton Public Library, 1989; Barker Fairley Distinguished Visitor in Canadian Culture, University College, University of Toronto, 1995–96; mem. Crime Writers of Canada, chair., 1986–87; International Asscn of Crime Writers; MWA; Writers' Guild of Canada. *Publications:* The Suicide Murders, 1980; The Ransom Game, 1981; Murder on Location, 1982; Murder Sees the Light, 1984; A City Called July, 1986; A Victim Must Be Found, 1988; Dead and Buried, 1990; Murder in Montparnasse, 1992; Criminal Shorts: Mysteries by Canadian Crime Writers (ed. with Eric Wright), 1992; There Was an Old Woman, 1993; Getting Away With Murder, 1995; Lord High Executioner: An Unashamed Look at Hangmen, Headsmen, and Their Kind, 1996; Mr Doyle and Dr Bell, 1997; A Child's Christmas in Scarborough, 1997; The Cooperman Variations, 2001. Contributions: Radio and television. *Honours:* Arthur Ellis Award for Crime Fiction, 1984; Harbourfront Festival Prize, 1990; Hon. LLD, Brock University, 1994. *Literary Agent:* Beverley Slopen, Toronto. *Address:* 281 Major St, Toronto, ON M5S 2L5, Canada.

ENGEL, Johannes K.; Journalist and Editor; b. 29 April 1927, Berlin, Germany; m. Ruth Moter 1951; one s. one d. *Career:* journalist Int. News Service and Der Spiegel magazine 1946–, Office Man., Frankfurt am Main 1948, Dept Head 1951, Ed.-in-Chief, Hamburg 1961. *Address:* Kirchenredder 7, 22339 Hamburg, Germany.

ENGELL, Hans; Politician and Newspaper Editor; b. 8 Oct. 1948, Copenhagen, Denmark. *Education:* Coll. of Journalism. *Career:* journalist for Berlingske newspaper consortium 1968–78; Head of Press Service of Conservative People's Party 1978–82; MP 1984–, Minister for Defence 1982–87, of Justice 1989–93; Chair. Conservative Parl. Group 1987–89; Leader Conservative People's Party 1995–97; Ed.-in-Chief Ekstra Bladet 2000–. *Address:* c/o Ekstra Bladet, Rådhuspladsen, 1785 Copenhagen, Denmark. *E-mail:* hans.engell@eb.dk.

ENGELS, John (David); Prof. of English, Poet and Writer; b. 19 Jan. 1931, South Bend, IN, USA; m. Gail Jochimsen, 1957, four s., two d. *Education:* BA, University of Notre Dame, 1952; University College, Dublin, 1955; MFA, University of Iowa, 1957. *Career:* Instructor, Norbert College, West De Pere, Wisconsin, 1957–62; Asst Prof., 1962–70, Prof. of English, 1970–, St Michael's College, Winooski Park, Vermont; Visiting Lecturer, University of Vermont, 1974, 1975, 1976; Slaughter Lecturer, Sweet Briar College, 1976; Writer-in-Residence, Randolph Macon Women's College, 1992. *Publications:* Poetry: The Homer Mitchell Place, 1968; Signals from the Safety Coffin, 1975; Blood Mountain, 1977; Vivaldi in Early Fall, 1981; The Seasons in Vermont, 1982; Weather-Fear: New and Selected Poems 1958–1982, 1983; Cardinals in the Ice Age, 1987; Walking to Cootehill: New and Selected Poems 1958–1992, 1993; Big Water, 1995. Other: Writing Techniques (with Norbert Engels), 1962; Experience and Imagination (with Norbert Engels), 1965; The Merrill Checklist of William Carlos Williams (ed.), 1969; The Merrill Studies in Paterson (ed.), 1971. *Honours:* Bread Loaf Writers' Conference Scholarship, 1960, and Robert Frost Fellowship, 1976; Guggenheim Fellowship, 1979. *Address:* c/o Dept of English, St Michael's College, Winooski Park, VT 05404, USA.

ENGLADE, Ken(neth Francis); Former Journalist and Writer; b. 7 Oct. 1938, Memphis, TN, USA; m. 1st Sharon Flynn, 27 Nov. 1960, divorced, two s. one d.; m. 2nd Sara Elizabeth Crewe, 29 Feb. 1980, divorced 1991; m. 3rd Heidi Hizel, 3 Jan. 1997. *Education:* BA, Louisiana State University, 1960. *Career:* mem. American Society of Journalists and Authors; Authors' Guild; Southwest Writers. *Publications:* Non-Fiction: Cellar of Horror, 1989; Murder in Boston, 1990; Beyond Reason: The True Story of a Shocking Double Murder, a Brilliant and Beautiful Virginia Socialite, and a Deadly Psychotic Obsession, 1990; Deadly Lessons, 1991; A Family Business, 1992; To Hatred Turned: A True Story of Love and Death in Texas, 1992; Blood Sister, 1994; Hot Blood: The Millionairess, the Money, and the Horse Murders, 1996. Fiction: People of the Plains, 1996; The Tribes, 1996; The Soldiers, 1996; Battle Cry, 1996. *Address:* c/o St Martin's Press, 175 Fifth Ave, New York, NY 10010, USA.

ENGLE, Margarita; Novelist and Poet; b. 2 Sept. 1951, Pasadena, CA, USA; m. Curtis Engle, 18 April 1978, one s. one d. *Education:* BS, Agronomy, California Polytechnic University, Pomona, 1974; MS, Botany, Iowa State University, Ames, 1977. *Career:* mem. PEN USA West. *Publications:* Singing to Cuba, 1993; Skywriting, 1995. *Honours:* Cintas Fellowship, San Diego Book Award. *Literary Agent:* Julie Castiglia, 1155 Camino Del Mar, Suite 510, Del Mar, CA 92014, USA.

ENQUIST, Anna; Dutch writer, poet, psychoanalyst and musician; b. 19 July 1945, Amsterdam; m. B. E. Widlund. *Education:* Univ. of Leiden, The Hague Conservatory. *Career:* pianist, psychology teacher, school psychologist; staff, Netherlands Psychoanalytical Institute 1987–2000. *Publications:* Soldatenliederen 1991, Jachtscènes 1993, The Masterpiece 1994, The Secret 1997, The Injury 1999, The Fire Was Here 2003, The Ice Carriers 2003. *Honours:* Debuut Prize 1994, Trouw Publiekprize 1997. *Literary Agent:* The Susijn Agency, Third Floor, 64 Great Titchfield Street, London, W1W 7QH, England. *Telephone:* (20) 7580-6341. *Fax:* (20) 7580-8626. *E-mail:* info@thesusijnagency.com. *Website:* www.thesusijnagency.com.

ENQUIST, Lynn W.; American editor and writer. *Career:* Ed.-in-Chief, Journal of Virology, American Soc. for Microbiology. *Publications:* contrib. to Experiments with Gene Fusions 1984, Principles of Virology: Molecular Biology, Pathogenesis and Control 1999. *Address:* Journal of Virology, American Society for Microbiology, 1752 North Street NW, Washington, DC 20036-2904, USA. *Website:* www.jvi.asm.org.

ENQUIST, Per Olov; Novelist, Playwright, Journalist and Poet; b. 1934, Hjoggböle, Sweden; m. 2nd Lone Bastholm. *Education:* MA, Univ. of Uppsala, 1964. *Career:* Visiting Prof., UCLA, 1973. *Publications:* Kristallögat, 1961; Färdvägen, 1963; Magnetisörens Femte Vinter, 1964; Bröderna Casey, 1964; Hess, 1966; Sextiotalskritik, 1966; Legionärerna, 1968; Sekonden, 1971; Katedralen i München, 1972; Berättelser Från de Inställda Upprorens Tid (short stories), 1974; Tribadernas Natt, 1975; Chez Nous (with Anders Ehnmark), 1976; Musikanternas Uttåg, 1978; Mannen På Trottoaren, 1979; Till Fedra, 1980; Från Regnormarnas Liv, 1981; En Triptyk, 1981; Doktor Mabuses Nya Testamente (with Anders Ehnmark), 1982; Strindberg Ett Liv, 1984; Nedstörtad Ängel, 1985; Två Reportage om Idrott, 1986; I Lodjurets Timma, 1988; Kapten Nemos Bibliotek, 1991; Hamsun (screenplay), 1996; Bildmakarna (play), 1998; Livläkarens Besök, 1999; Systrarna (play), 2000; Lewis Resa, 2001. Contributions: literary criticism in newspapers, incl.: Uppsala Nya Tidning, Svenska Dagbladet, Expressen. *Honours:* Nordic Council literary prize, 1968; August Award, 1999; Independent Foreign Fiction Prize, 2003. *Address:* c/o Vintage, Random House, 20 Vauxhall Bridge Rd, London SW1V 2SA, England.

ENSLIN, Theodore (Vernon); Poet and Writer; b. 25 March 1925, Chester, PA, USA; m. 1st Mildred Marie Stout, 1945, divorced 1961, one s. one d.; m. 2nd Alison Jane Jose, 1969, one s. *Education:* Studied composition with Nadia Boulanger. *Career:* Columnist, The Cape Codder, Orleans, MA, 1949–56. *Publications:* Poetry: The Work Proposed, 1958; New Sharon's Prospect, 1962; The Place Where I Am Standing, 1964; To Come to Have Become, 1966; The Diabelli Variations and Other Poems, 1967; 2/30–6/31: Poems 1967, 1967; The Poems, 1970; Forms, five vols, 1970–74; The Median Flow: Poems 1943–73, 1974; Ranger, Ranger 2, two vols, 1979, 1980; Music for Several Occasions, 1985; Case Book, 1987; Love and Science, 1990; A Sonare, 1994. Fiction: 2 + 12 (short stories), 1979. Play: Barometric Pressure 29.83 and Steady, 1965. Other: Mahler, 1975; The July Book, 1976. *Honours:* Nieman Award for Journalism, 1955; National Endowment for the Arts Grant, 1976. *Address:* RFD Box 289, Kansas Rd, Milbridge, MA 04658, USA.

ENZENSBERGER, Hans Magnus; Author, Poet, Dramatist, Trans., Ed. and Publisher; b. 11 Nov. 1929, Kaufbeuren, Germany; m. 1st Dagrun Christensen, one d.; m. 2nd Maria Makarowa; m. 3rd Katharina Bonitz, one d. *Education:* German Literature, Philosophy, and Linguistics, Universities of Erlangen, Hamburg, Freiburg im Breisgau, Sorbonne, Paris, 1949–54; DPhil, 1955. *Career:* Mem., Gruppe 47, 1955; Lecturer, Hochschule für Gestaltung, Ulm, 1956–57; Literary Consultant, Suhrkamp publishers, 1960–; Hon. Lecturer, University of Frankfurt am Main, 1964–65; Ed., 1965–75, Publisher, 1970–90, Kursbuch periodical; Ed., TransAtlantik periodical, 1980–82; Ed.-Publisher, Die Andere Bibliothek, 1985–; Artistic Dir, Renaissance Theatre, Berlin, 1995–. *Publications:* Verteidigung der wölfe (poems), 1957; Landessprache (poems), 1957; Museum der modernen Poesie (ed. and trans.), 1960; Clemens Brentanos Poetik (essay), 1961; Einzelheiten, 1964; Blindenschrift (poems), 1964; Politik und Verbrechen, 1964; Das Verhör von Habana (play), 1970; Klassenbuch (co-ed.), three vols, 1972; Der kurze Sommer der Anarchie: Buenaventura Durrutis Leben und Tod (novel), 1972; Gespräche mit Marx und Engels (ed.), 1973; Mausoleum: Siebenunddreissig Balladen aus der Geschichte des Fortschritts (poems), 1975; Der Untergang der Titanic (epic poem), 1978; Die Furie des Verschwindens (poems), 1980; Politische Brosamen (essays), 1982; Der Menschenfeind (play), 1984; Gedichte 1950–1985 (poems), 1986; Ach Europa!: Wahrnehmungen aus sieben Ländern (essays), 1987; Mittelmass und Wahn: Gesammelte Zerstreuungen (essays), 1988; Requiem für eine romantische Frau: Die Geschichte von Auguste Bussmann und Clemens Brentano (novel), 1988; Zukunftsmusik (poems), 1991; Die Grosse Wanderung: 33 Markierungen (essays), 1992; Aussichten des Bürgerkriegs (essay), 1993; Kiosk (poems), 1995; Der Zahlenteufel, 1997; Wo warst du, Robert (novel, trans. as Where Were You, Robert?), 1998; Leichter als Luft: Moralische Gedichte (poems), 1999; Zickzack, 1999; Einladung zu einem Poesie-Automaton, 2000; Die Elixiere der Wissenschaft, 2002. *Honours:* German Critics' Literature Prize, 1962; Georg Büchner Prize, 1963; Cultural Prize of the City of Nuremberg, 1967; Premio Pasolino, 1982; Heinrich Böll Prize, 1985; Bavarian Acad. of Fine Arts Literature Award, Munich, 1987; Erich Maria Remarque Peace Prize, Osnabrück, 1993; Cultural Prize of the City of Munich, 1994; Orden pour le mérite für Wissenschaften und Künste, 2000; Premio Príncipe de Asturias, 2002. *Address:* c/o Suhrkamp Verlag, Lindenstr 29–35, 60325 Frankfurt am Main, Germany.

EPHRON, Delia; American author and scriptwriter; b. 1945, Beverly Hills, Calif.; sister of Nora Ephron; m. Jerome Kass. *Career:* began career as journalist, New York Magazine and New York Times; co-writer of screenplays with sister, Nora Ephron. *Screenplays include:* This is My Life 1992, Sleepless in Seattle (exec. producer) 1993, Mixed Nuts, Michael 1996, You've Got Mail 1998, Lucky Numbers 1999, Hanging Up 2000. *Publications include:* How to Eat Like A Child, Teenage Romance or How to Die of Embarrassment, Big City Eyes 2000; numerous children's books. *Literary Agent:* Sam Cohn International Creative Management, 40 West 57th Street, New York, NY 10019, USA.

EPHRON, Nora, BA; American author and scriptwriter; b. 19 May 1941, New York; sister of Delia Ephron; m. 1st Dan Greenburg (divorced); m. 2nd Carl Bernstein (divorced); two s.; m. 3rd Nicholas Pileggi. *Education:* Wellesley Coll. *Career:* reporter, New York Post 1963–68; freelance writer 1968–; Contributing Ed. and columnist, Esquire Magazine 1972–73, Sr Ed. 1974–78; Contributing Ed., New York Magazine 1973–74; mem. American Writers' Guild, Authors' Guild, PEN, Acad. of Motion Picture Arts and Sciences. *Film appearances:* Crimes and Misdemeanors, Husbands and Wives. *Screenplays:* Silkwood (with Alice Arlen) 1983, Heartburn 1986, When Harry Met Sally... 1989, Cookie 1989 (co-exec. producer, co-screenwriter), My Blue Heaven 1990, This is My Day 1992 (dir, screenwriter, with Delia Ephron), Sleepless in Seattle (also dir) 1993, Mixed Nuts (also dir), Michael (also dir) 1996, You've Got Mail (also dir) 1998, Red Tails in Love: a Wildlife Drama in Central Park (also producer and dir) 2000, Lucky Numbers 1999, Hanging Up (also producer) 2000. *Publications:* Wallflower at the Orgy 1970, Crazy Salad 1975, Scribble, Scribble 1978, Heartburn 1983, Nora Ephron Collected 1991, Big City Eyes 2000. *Honours:* BAFTA for Best Screenplay 1989. *Literary Agent:* Sam Cohn, International Creative Management, 40 West 57th Street, New York, NY 10019, USA.

EPSTEIN, Barbara; American editor and publisher; *Editor, The New York Review of Books*; b. Boston, Mass. *Education:* Radcliffe Coll. *Career:* began publishing career at Doubleday & Co. as Jr Ed. 1949; worked in publishing at The Partisan Review –1963; Co-Founder and Co-Ed. The New York Review of Books 1963–. *Address:* The New York Review of Books, 1755 Broadway, 5th Floor, New York, NY 10019-3780, USA (Office). *Telephone:* (212) 757-8070 (Office). *Fax:* (212) 333-5374 (Office). *E-mail:* nyrev@nybooks.com (Office). *Website:* www.nybooks.com (Office).

EPSTEIN, Joseph, BA; editor, writer and lecturer; b. 9 Jan. 1937, Chicago, IL, USA; m. Barbara Maher 1976; one s. *Education:* University of Chicago. *Career:* Assoc. Ed., The New Leader, 1962–63; Senior Ed., Encyclopaedia Britannica, 1965–69, Quadrangle/New York Times Books, 1969–70; Lecturer, Northwestern University, 1974–; Ed., The American Scholar, 1975–. *Publications:* Divorced in America, 1975; Ambition, 1979; Familiar Territory, 1980; The Middle of My Tether, 1983; Plausible Prejudices, 1985; Once More Around the Block, 1987; Partial Payments, 1989; A Line Out for a Walk, 1991; The Golden Boys: Stories, 1991; Pertinent Players, 1993; With My Trousers Rolled, 1995; Life Sentences, 1997; Narcissus Leaves the Pool, 1999; Snobbery: The American Version, 2002. Editor: Masters: Portraits of Teachers, 1980; Best American Essays, 1993; Norton Book of Personal Essays, 1997. Contributions: many books and journals. *Address:* 522 Church Street, Evanston, IL 60201, USA.

EPSTEIN, Leslie, DipAnthro, MA, DFA; American writer; b. 1938, Los Angeles, CA; one s. *Education:* Yale, Merton Coll., Oxford, UCLA. *Career:* Dir of Creative Writing Programme, Univ. of Boston; Ed., Tikkun; writer-in-residence, Rockefeller Inst., Bellagio, Italy. *Publications:* P. D. Kimerakov 1975, The Steinway Quintet Plus Four 1976, King of the Jews 1978, The Elder 1979, Regina 1982, Goldkorn Tales 1986, Pinto and Sons 1990, Pandaemonium 1997, Ice Fire Water: A Leib Goldkorn Cocktail, San Remo Drive: a Novel from Memory 2003; contrib. to numerous magazines and newspapers. *Honours:* Rhodes scholar 1960–72, Fulbright scholar, NEA fellow 1972, 1981–82, Guggenheim fellow 1977–78 ; Award for Distinction in Literature, American Acad. and Inst. of Arts and Letters. *Address:* c/o Boston University Dept of English, 236 Bay Road, Boston, MA 02215, USA. *Telephone:* (617) 3532506. *E-mail:* leslieep@bu.edu.

EPSTEIN, Seymour (Sy); writer and academic; b. 2 Dec. 1917, New York, NY, USA; m. Miriam Kligman 1956; two s. *Career:* mem. Authors' Guild, PEN. *Publications:* Pillar of Salt, 1960; Leah, 1964; Caught in That Music, 1967; The Dream Museum, 1971; Looking for Fred Schmidt, 1973; A Special Destiny, 1986; September Faces, 1987; Light, 1989. Contributions: periodicals. *Honours:* Edward Lewis Wallant Memorial Award, 1965; Guggenheim Fellowship, 1965.

ERBA, Luciano, PhD; Italian poet, translator, writer and retd academic; b. 18 Sept. 1922, Milan. *Education:* Catholic Univ., Milan. *Career:* Prof. of Comparative Literature, Rutgers Univ., NB, USA 1964–65; Prof. of Italian and French Literature, Univ. of Washington at Seattle, USA 1965–66; Prof. of French Literature, Univ. of Padua 1973–82, Univ. of Verona 1982–87, Catholic Univ., Milan 1987–97. *Publications:* Linea K 1951, Il bel paese 1956, Il prete di Ratanà 1959, Il male minore 1960, Il prato più verde 1977, Il nastro di Moebius 1980, Il cerchio aperto 1983, L'ippopotamo 1989, L'ipotesi circense 1995, Negli spazi intermedi 1998, Nella terra di mezzo 2000; other: Françoise (novel) 1982, radio plays, translations. *Honours:* Viareggio Prize 1980, Bagutta Prize 1988, Librex-Guggenheim Eugenio Montale Prize 1989, Italian PEN Club Prize 1995. *Address:* Via Giason del Maino 16, 20146 Milan, Italy.

ERDRICH, (Karen) Louise; writer and poet; b. 7 June 1954, Little Falls, MN, USA; m. Michael Anthony Dorris 1981 (died 1997); seven c. *Education:* BA, Dartmouth College, 1976; MA, Johns Hopkins University, 1979. *Career:* Visiting Poet and Teacher, North Dakota State Arts Council, 1977–78; Writing Instructor, Johns Hopkins University, 1978–79; Communications Dir and Ed. of Circle of the Boston Indian Council, 1979–80. *Publications:* Fiction: Love Medicine, 1984; The Beet Queen, 1986; Tracks, 1988; The Crown of Columbus (with Michael Anthony Dorris), 1991; The Bingo Palace, 1994; The Bluejay's Dance, 1995; Tales of Burning Love, 1996; The Antelope Wife, 1998; The Birchbark House, 2000; The Last Report on the Miracles at Little No Horse, 2001; The Master Butcher's Singing Club, 2003. Poetry: Jacklight, 1984; Baptism of Desire, 1989. Other: Imagination (textbook), 1980. Contributions: anthologies; American Indian Quarterly; Atlantic; Frontiers; Kenyon Review; Ms; New England Review; New York Times Book Review; New Yorker; North American Review; Redbook; Others. *Honours:* MacDowell Colony Fellowship, 1980; Yaddo Colony Fellowship, 1981; Dartmouth College Visiting Fellow, 1981; National Magazine Fiction Awards, 1983, 1987; National Book Critics Circle Award for Best Work of Fiction, 1984; Virginia McCormick Scully Prize for Best Book of the Year, 1984; Best First Fiction Award, American Acad. and Institute of Arts and Letters, 1985; Guggenheim Fellowship, 1985–86; First Prize, O. Henry Awards, 1987. *Literary Agent:* The Wylie Agency, 250 W 57th Street, Suite 2114, New York, NY 10107, USA.

ERICKSON, Stephen (Michael), (Steve Erickson); Novelist; b. 20 April 1950, Santa Monica, CA, USA. *Education:* BA, 1972, MA, Journalism, 1973, University of California, Los Angeles. *Career:* Arts Ed., 1989–91, Film Ed., 1992–93, L.A. Weekly; Instructor, California Institute of the Arts, 2000–. *Publications:* Days Between Stations, 1985; Rubicon Beach, 1986; Tours of the Black Clock, 1989; Leap Year, 1989; Arc d'X, 1993; Amnesiascope, 1996; American Nomad, 1997; The Sea Came in at Midnight, 1999. Contributions:

New York Times; Esquire; Rolling Stone; Details; Elle; Los Angeles Times; Los Angeles Magazine; LA Weekly; LA Style; San Francisco Magazine; Salon; Conjunctions. *Honours:* Samuel Goldwyn Award, 1972; National Endowment for the Arts Fellowship, 1987.

ERNAUX, Annie; French writer; b. (Annie Duchesne), 1 Sept. 1940, Lillebonne, Seine-Maritime; m. Philippe Ernaux 1964 (divorced); two s. *Education:* Lycée Jeanne-d'Arc, Rouen, Univs of Rouen, Bordeaux and Grenoble. *Career:* teacher of literature 1966–2000. *Publications:* Les armoires vides 1974, La femme gelée 1984, La place 1984, Une femme 1988, Passion simple 1992, La honte 1997, Je ne suis pas sortie de ma nuit 1997, L'événement 2000, Se perdre 2001, L'occupation 2002, L'écriture comme un couteau 2003. *Honours:* Prix Renaudot 1984. *Address:* 23 rue des Lozères, 95000 Cergy, France. *Fax:* 1-30-31-27-74. *E-mail:* a.ernaux@infonie.fr (Home).

ERSKINE, Barbara; Writer; b. 10 Aug. 1944, Nottingham, England; m.; two s. *Education:* MA, Edinburgh University, 1967. *Career:* mem. Society of Authors; Scientific and Medical Network. *Publications:* Lady of Hay, 1986; Kingdom of Shadows, 1988; Encounters, 1990; Child of the Phoenix, 1992; Midnight is a Lonely Place, 1994; House of Echoes, 1996; Distant Voices, 1996; On the Edge of Darkness, 1998; Whispers in the Sand, 2000; Hiding from the Light, 2002; Sands of Time, 2003. Contributions: numerous short stories to magazines and journals. *Address:* c/o Blake Friedmann, 122 Arlington Rd, London NW1 7HP, England.

ESCANDELL, Noemi; Prof. of Spanish Language and Literature and Poet; b. 27 Sept. 1936, Havana, Cuba; m. Peter Knapp, 1 June 1957, divorced 1972, two s. two d. *Education:* BLitt, Instituto de la Vibora, 1955; BA, Queens College, CUNY, 1968; MA, 1971, PhD, 1976, Harvard University. *Career:* Asst Prof., Bard College, 1976–83; Language Programme Dir, Nuevo Instituto de Centroamerica, Esteli, Nicaragua, 1987–88; Prof. of Spanish, Westfield State College, 1983–93; Dir, Afterschool Programme, Ross School, Washington, DC, 1995–96; mem. Acad. Iberoamericana de Poesia, Washington, DC, Chapter. *Publications:* Cuadros, 1982; Ciclos, 1982; Palabras/Words, 1986. Contributions: anthologies and periodicals. *Honours:* Poet-in-Residence, Millay Colony for the Arts, Austerlitz, New York, 1983, 1991; Special Mention, Certamen Poetico Federico García Lorca Poetry Contest, 1995; First Prize in Poetry, XXXII Certamen Literario International Odon Betanzos Palacio, 1996.

ESHLEMAN, Clayton; Prof. of English, Poet, Writer and Trans; b. 1 June 1935, Indianapolis, IN, USA; m. 1st Barbara Novak, 1961, divorced 1967, one s.; m. 2nd Caryl Reiter, 1969. *Education:* BA, Philosophy, 1958, MA, Creative Writing, 1961, Indiana University. *Career:* Ed., Folio, 1959–60; Instructor, University of Maryland Eastern Overseas Division, 1961–62, New York University American Language Institute, 1966–68; Publisher, Caterpillar Books, 1966–68; Founder-Ed.-Publisher, Caterpillar magazine, 1967–73; Faculty, School of Critical Studies, California Institute of the Arts, Valencia, 1970–72; Dreyfuss Poet-in-Residence and Lecturer, California Institute of Technology, Pasadena, 1979–84; Visiting Lecturer in Creative Writing, Universities of California at San Diego, Los Angeles, Santa Barbara, and Riverside, 1979–86; Reviewer, Los Angeles Times Book Review, 1979–86; Founder-Ed., Sulfur magazine, 1981–; Prof. of English, Eastern Michigan University, 1986–. *Publications:* Mexico & North, 1962; Brother Stones, 1968; Indiana, 1969; The House of Ibuki, 1969; Altars, 1971; A Caterpillar Anthology: A Selection of Poetry and Prose from Caterpillar Magazine (ed.), 1971; Coils, 1973; The Gull Wall, 1975; Grotesca, 1975; On Mules Sent from Chavin, 1977; What She Means, 1977; Our Lady of the Three-Pronged Devil, 1977; Nights We Put the Rock Together, 1980; Hades in Manganese, 1981; Fracture, 1983; The Name Encanyoned River: Selected Poems, 1960–85, 1986; Hotel-Cro-Magnon, 1989; Antiphonal Swing: Selected Prose, 1962–87, 1989; Novices: A Study of Poetic Apprenticeship, 1989; Under World Arrest, 1994; Nora's Roar, 1996; From Scratch, 1998. Translations: 13 books, 1962–95. Contributions: numerous anthologies, magazines, and newspapers. *Honours:* PEN Trans. Prize, 1977; Guggenheim Fellowship, 1978; National Book Award for Trans., 1979; National Endowment for the Arts Fellowship, 1979; National Endowment for the Humanities Grant, 1980, and Fellowships, 1981, 1988; Michigan Arts Council Grant, 1988; Eastern Michigan University Research Grants, 1990, 1997. *Address:* 210 Washtenaw Ave, Ypsilanti, MI 48197, USA.

ESLER, Gavin William James, BA, MA, FRSA; Broadcaster and Author; b. 27 Feb. 1953, Glasgow, Scotland; m. Patricia Warner, one s. one d. *Education:* University of Kent, University of Leeds. *Career:* BBC Television News and Radio Presenter; Columnist, The Scotsman Newspaper. *Publications:* Fiction: Loyalties, 1990; Deep Blue, 1992; The Blood Brother, 1995. Non-Fiction: The United States of Anger, 1997. Contributions: anthologies, journals, periodicals, quarterlies, newspapers and magazines. *Honours:* MA hc, Kent. *Literary Agent:* Curtis Brown Ltd, Haymarket House, 28–29 Haymarket, London, SW1Y 4SP, England. *Telephone:* (20) 7393-4400. *Fax:* (20) 7393-4401. *E-mail:* info@curtisbrown.co.uk. *Website:* www.curtisbrown.co.uk.

ESMENARD, Francis; French publisher; b. 8 Dec. 1936, Paris; one s. *Career:* Pres., Dir-Gen. Editions Albin Michel 1982–, Paris; Vice-Pres. Nat. Publishing Syndicat 1979–; Prés. du Directoire 1999–. *Address:* Editions Albin Michel, 22 rue Huyghens, 75014 Paris, France (Office). *Telephone:* 1-42-79-10-00. *Fax:* 1-43-27-21-58.

ESMOND, Harriet (see Burke, John Frederick).

ESPADA, Martin, BA, JD; American poet and educator; b. 1957, Brooklyn, NY; m.; one s. *Education:* Univ. of Wisconsin, Northeastern Univ., Boston, MA. *Career:* Assoc. Prof. of English, Univ. of Massachusetts-Amherst; Poet Laureate of Northampton, MA. *Publications:* poetry: Trumpets From the Islands of their Eviction 1987, Rebellion is the Circle of a Lover's Hands 1990, City of Coughing and Dead Radiators 1993, A Mayan Imagine the Angels of Bread 1996, Astronomer in Hell's Kitchen 2000, Alabanza: New and Selected Poems 1982–2002 2003; editor: Poetry Like Bread: Poets of the Political Imagination 1994, El Coro: A Chorus of Latino and Latina Poets 1997; other: Zapata's Disciple: Essays 1998; contrib. to publications, including New York Times Book Review, Harpers, The Nation, The Best American Poetry. *Honours:* Nat. Endowment for the Arts Fellowships, PEN/Revson Fellowship, Massachusetts Artists Foundation Fellowship; American Book Award, PEN/Voelker Award for Poetry, Paterson Poetry Prize, Independent Publisher Book Award . *Address:* c/o University of Massachusetts, Amherst, MA 01003, USA. *E-mail:* martin@martinespada.net. *Website:* www.martinespada.net.

ESPOSITO, Nancy Giller, BA, MA; poet, writer, editor and academic; *Senior Lecturer, Bentley College*; b. 1 Jan. 1942, Dallas, TX, USA. *Education:* Univ. of Wisconsin, New York Univ. *Career:* Assoc. Prof., Illinois Central Coll., East Peoria 1968–70; Instructor, Harvard Univ. 1976–80, 1981–84, Wellesley Coll. 1980; Lecturer, Tufts Univ. 1986–93, Boston Coll. 1994; Sr Lecturer, Bentley Coll. 1986–; CIEE Seminar, Viet Nam 2002; mem. Acad. of American Poets, Associated Writing Programs, Poetry Soc. of America, Poets and Writers, PEN. *Publications:* Changing Hands 1984, Mêm' Rain 2002, Greatest Hits 1978–2001 2003; contrib. to anthologies, including Two Decades of New Poets 1984, Ixok-Amar-Go 1987, Quarterly Review of Literature 50th Anniversary Anthology 1993, Poetry from Sojourner 2004, and to reviews, journals and periodicals. *Honours:* Discovery/The Nation Award 1979, Virginia Center for the Creative Arts Fellow 1979–80, 1981, 1990, 2003–04, Yaddo Fellow 1981, Colladay Award 1984, MacDowell Colony Fellow 1986–87, Gordon Barber Memorial Award, Poetry Soc. of America 1987, Fulbright-Hays Grant, Egypt 1988, Publishing Award 1988, Faculty Development Fund Grants, Bentley Coll. 1997, 1999, 2003, Ragdale Foundation Fellow 1990, Bentley Coll. Faculty Grant, Viet Nam 1999–2000. *Address:* 34 Trowbridge Street, Belmont, MA 02478, USA.

ESQUIVEL, Laura; Novelist; b. 1950, México, DF, Mexico; m. 1st Alfonso Arau (divorced); m. 2nd Javier Valdez. *Publications:* Como agua para chocolate (Like Water for Chocolate, novel, screenplay), 1990; La ley del amor (The Law of Love), 1996; Estrellita Marinera, 1999; Libro de las emociones: Son de la razón sin corazón, 2000; Between Two Fires: Intimate Writings on Life, Love, Food and Flavor, 2001; Tan veloz como el deseo (Swift as Desire), 2001. *Honours:* American Booksellers Association ABBY Award, 1994. *Literary Agent:* Thomas Colchie. *Address:* c/o Random House, 1745 Broadway, Third Floor, New York, NY 10019, USA.

ESSOP, Ahmed, BA; writer; b. 1 Sept. 1931, Dabhel, India; m. 1960; one s. three d. *Education:* University of South Africa. *Publications:* The Hajii and Other Stories, 1978; The Visitation, 1980; The Emperor, 1984; Noorjehan and Other Stories, 1990; The King of Hearts and Other Stories, 1997; Narcissus and Other Stories, 2002; Suleiman M. Nana: A Biographical and Historical Record of His Life and Times, 2002. *Honours:* Olive Schreiner Award, English Acad. of Southern Africa, 1979. *Address:* PO Box 1747, Lenasia 1820, Johannesburg, South Africa.

ESTERHÁZY, Péter; Hungarian writer and essayist; b. 14 April 1950; m. Gitta Reén; two s. two d. *Education:* Budapest Univ. *Career:* full-time writer since 1978. *Publications:* short stories: Pápai vizeken ne kalózkodj! 1977; novels: Fancsikó és Pinta 1976, Termelési regény 1979, Függő 1981, Ki szavatol a lady biztonságáért? 1982, Kis magyar pornográfia 1984, A sziv segédigéi 1985, Bevezetés a szépirodalomba 1986, Tizenhét hattyúk (as Csokonai Lili) 1987, Hrabal könyve 1990, Hahn-Hahn grófnő pillantása (The Glance of Countess Hahn-Hahn Down the Danube) 1991, Egy nő (She Loves Me) 1995, Harmonia caelistis (trans. as Celestial Harmonies) 2000; essays: A kitömött hattyú 1988, Az elefántcsonttoronyból 1991, A halacska csodálatos élete 1991, Egy kékharisnya följegyzéseiből 1994, Egy kék haris 1996. *Honours:* Füst Milán, Déry, Kossuth, József Attila, Krúdy, Aszu, Márai, Magyar Irodalini Díj, Vilenica awards, Österreichische Staatspreis für europäische Literatur. *Address:* c/o Hungarian Writers Federation, 1062 Budapest, Bajza-utca 18, Hungary. *Telephone:* (1) 322-8840.

ESTLEMAN, Loren D., BA; writer; b. 15 Sept. 1952, Ann Arbor, MI, USA. *Education:* Eastern Michigan Univ. *Career:* mem. Western Writers of America, pres., 2000–02; MWA; Private Eye Writers of America; National Cowboy Hall of Fame. *Publications:* The Oklahoma Punk, 1976; The Hider, 1978; Sherlock Holmes vs Dracula, 1978; The High Rocks, 1979; Dr Jekyll and Mr Holmes, 1979; Stamping Ground, 1980; Motor City Blue, 1980; Aces and Eights, 1981; Angel Eyes, 1981; The Wolfer, 1981; Murdock's Law, 1982; The Midnight Man, 1982; Mister St John, 1983; This Old Bill, 1984; Kill Zone, 1984; Sugartown, 1984; Roses are Dead, 1985; Gun Man, 1985; Every Brilliant Eye, 1986; Any Man's Death, 1986; Lady Yesterday, 1987; Downriver, 1988; Bloody Season, 1988; Silent Thunder, 1989; Peeper, 1989; Sweet Women Lie, 1990; Whiskey River, 1990; Sudden Country, 1991; Motown, 1991; King of the Corner, 1992; City of Widows, 1994; Edsel, 1995; Stress, 1996; Billy Gashade, 1997; Never Street, 1997; The Witchfinder,

1998; Journey of the Dead, 1998; Jitterbug, 1998; The Hours of the Virgin, 1999; The Rocky Mountain Moving Picture Asscn, 1999; Thunder City, 1999; White Desert, 2000; A Smile on the Face of the Tiger, 2000; The Master Executioner, 2001; Sinister Heights, 2002; Something Borrowed, Something Black, 2002. Contributions: journals and magazines. *Honours:* Golden Spur Awards, 1981, 1987, 1999, Stirrup Award, 1983, Western Writers of America; Shamus Awards, 1984, 1985, 1988; Michigan Arts Foundation Award, 1987; American Mystery Awards, 1988, 1990; Golden Spur Award, 1996; Michigan Author Award, 1997; Western Heritage Award, 1999, 2000, 2001; Hon. Doctorate in Humane Letters, Eastern Michigan University, 2002. *Literary Agent:* Dominick Abel Literary Agency Inc, 5552 Walsh Road, Whitmore Lake, MI 48189, USA.

ESZTERHAS, Joseph A.; American scriptwriter; b. 23 Nov. 1944, Csakanydoroszlo, Hungary; m. 1st Geraldine Javer 1972 (divorced 1994); one s. one d.; m. 2nd Naomi Baka 1994; one s. *Education:* Ohio State Univ. *Career:* reporter, Plain Dealer, Cleveland; staff writer, Man. Ed. Rolling Stone, San Francisco 1971–75; screenwriter 1975–; writer and producer, Checking Out 1980, Betrayed 1989. *Publications:* novels: Thirteen Seconds: Confrontation at Kent State 1970, Charlie Simpson's Apocalypse 1974, Nark! 1974, Fist 1977, Hollywood Animal: A Memoir 2004; screenplays: Fist 1978, Flashdance 1983, Jagged Edge 1985, Big Shots 1987, The Music Box 1990, Basic Instinct 1991, Sliver 1993, Showgirls 1995, Telling Lies in America 1997, Original Sin 1997, One Night 1997, An Alan Smithee Film: Burn Hollywood Burn 1997, Hollywood Animal 2004. *Honours:* recipient of various awards. *Address:* c/o Hutchinson, 20 Vauxhall Bridge Road, London, SW1V 2SA, England.

ETCHEMENDY, Nancy Howell; Writer and Poet; b. 19 Feb. 1952, Reno, NV, USA; m. John W. Etchemendy 1973, one s. *Education:* BA, University of Nevada, Reno, 1974. *Career:* mem. Treasurer, 1996–97, Trustee, 1997–98, Horror Writers' Asscn; Society of Children's Book Writers; SFWA. *Publications:* The Watchers of Space, 1980; Stranger from the Stars, 1983; The Crystal City, 1985; The Power of UN, 2000. Contributions: numerous short stories, essays and individual poems to magazines and journals. *Honours:* The Bram Stoker Award, 1998. *Literary Agent:* Curtis Brown Ltd, 10 Astor Place, New York, NY 10003, USA. *E-mail:* etchemendy@sff.net.

ETTER, Dave, (David Pearson Etter); Poet, Writer and Ed.; b. 18 March 1928, Huntington Park, CA, USA; m. Margaret A. Cochran, 8 Aug. 1959, one s. one d. *Education:* BA, History, University of Iowa, 1953. *Career:* Promotion Dept, Indiana University, 1959–60; Rand McNally Publishing Co, 1960–61; Ed., Northwestern University Press, 1962–63; Asst Ed., Encyclopaedia Britannica, Chicago, 1964–73; Ed., Northern Illinois University Press, 1974–80; Freelance Writer, Poet and Ed., 1981–. *Publications:* Go Read the River, 1966; The Last Train to Prophetstown, 1968; Well You Needn't, 1975; Central Standard Time, 1978; Open to the Wind, 1978; Riding the Rock Island Through Kansas, 1979; Cornfields, 1980; West of Chicago, 1981; Boondocks, 1982; Alliance, IL, 1983; Home State, 1985; Live at the Silver Dollar, 1986; Selected Poems, 1987; Midlanders, 1988; Electric Avenue, 1988; Carnival, 1990; Sunflower County, 1994; How High the Moon, 1996; The Essential Dave Etter, 2001; Greatest Hits, 1960–2000, 2002. Contributions: Poetry; Nation; Chicago Review; Kansas Quarterly; Prairie Schooner; Poetry Northwest; TriQuarterly; Massachusetts Review; North American Review; Ohio Review; New Letters; Shenandoah; Beloit Poetry Journal; El Corno Emplumado; San Francisco Review; New Mexico Quarterly; Mark Twain Journal; Slow Dancer (England), among others. *Honours:* Society of Midland Authors Poetry Prize, 1967; Friends of Literature Poetry Prize, 1967; Bread Loaf Writers' Conference Fellowship in Poetry, 1967; Illinois Sesquicentennial Poetry Prize, 1968; Theodore Roethke Poetry Prize, 1971; Carl Sandburg Poetry Prize, 1982. *Address:* 628 E Locust St, Lanark, IL 61046, USA.

ETZIONI, Amitai; American sociologist, academic and writer; b. 4 Jan. 1929, Cologne, Germany; m. 1st Minerva Morales 1965 (died 1985); five s.; m. 2nd Patricia Kellogg 1992. *Education:* BA, 1954, MA, 1956, Hebrew University, Jerusalem; PhD in Sociology, University of California at Berkeley, 1958. *Career:* Faculty, 1958–67, Prof. of Sociology, 1967–78, Chair., Dept of Sociology, 1969–78, Columbia University; Fellow, Center for Advanced Study in the Behavioral Sciences, 1965–66; Founder-Dir, Center for Policy Research, 1968–; Guest Scholar, Brookings Institution, 1978–79; Senior Adviser, White House, Washington, DC, 1979–80; University Prof., 1980–, Dir, Center for Communitarian Studies, 1995–, George Washington University; Thomas Henry Carroll Ford Foundation Visiting Prof., Graduate School of Business, Harvard University, 1987–89; Ed., The Responsive Community: Rights and Responsibilities quarterly, 1990–; Founder-Dir, The Communitarian Network, 1993–; mem. American Acad. of Arts and Sciences, fellow; American Sociological Asscn, pres., 1995; Society for the Advancement of Socio-Economics, founder-pres., 1989–90, hon. fellow. *Publications:* A Comparative Analysis of Complex Organizations, 1961; Modern Organizations, 1964; Political Unification: A Comparative Study of Leaders and Forces, 1965; Studies in Social Change, 1966; The Active Society, 1968; Genetic Fix, 1973; Social Problems, 1975; An Immodest Agenda, 1982; Capital Corruption, 1984; The Moral Dimension, 1988; The Spirit of Community: Rights, Responsibilities and the Communitarian Agenda, 1993; The New Golden Rule: Community and Morality in a Democratic Society, 1996; The Limits of Privacy, 1999. Contributions: scholarly journals, newspapers, periodicals, and television. *Honours:* Social Science Research Council Fellowship, 1960–61; Guggenheim Fellowship, 1968–69; Certificate of Appreciation, American Revolution Bicentennial Commission, 1976; Tolerance Book Award, Simon Wiesenthal Center, 1997; Hon. doctorates. *Address:* c/o The Gelman Library, George Washington University, 2130 H Street NW, Washington, DC 20052, USA.

EUGENIDES, Jeffrey, MA; American novelist; b. 1960, Detroit, MI; m.; one d. *Education:* Brown Univ., Stanford Univ. *Career:* Fellow, Berliner Künstlerprogramm 2002. *Publications:* The Virgin Suicides 1993, Middlesex 2002; contrib. to The New Yorker, The Paris Review, The Yale Review, The Gettysburg Review, Best American Short Stories, Granta's Best of Young American Novelists. *Honours:* Guggenheim Foundation Fellowship, National Foundation for the Arts Fellowship, Whiting Writers' Award, American Acad. of Arts and Letters Harold D. Vursell Memorial Award, American Academy in Berlin Prize Fellowship 2000–01, Pulitzer Prize for Fiction 2003. *Address:* c/o Bloomsbury Publishing PLC, 38 Soho Square, London, W1D 3HB, England.

EULO, Ken; Playwright, Dir and Novelist; b. 17 Nov. 1939, Newark, NJ, USA; m.; one s. *Education:* University of Heidelberg, 1961–64. *Career:* Artistic Dir, Courtyard Playhouse, New York; Staff Writer, Paramount; mem. Dramatists' Guild; Italian Playwrights of America; Writers' Guild of America. *Publications:* Plays: Bang?, 1969; Zarf, I Love You, 1969; SRO, 1970; Puritan Night, 1971; Billy Hofer and the Quarterback Sneak, 1971; Black Jesus, 1972; The Elevator, 1972; 48 Spring Street, 1973; Final Exams, 1975; The Frankenstein Affair, 1979; Say Hello to Daddy, 1979. Fiction: Bloodstone, 1982; The Brownstone, 1982; The Deathstone, 1982; Nocturnal, 1983; The Ghost of Veronica, 1985; House of Caine, 1988. Other: Television scripts. Contributions: Magazines and newspapers. *Address:* 14633 Valley Vista Blvd, Sherman Oaks, CA 91403, USA.

EVANS, Alan (see Stoker, Alan).

EVANS, Aled Lewis; Poet, Teacher, Preacher and Broadcaster; b. 9 Aug. 1961, Machynlleth, Wales. *Education:* BA, Welsh and English, Univ. College of North Wales, Bangor; BTh, Theology, Univ. of Wales, Aberystwyth. *Career:* mem. Gorsedd of Bards; Chester Poets. *Publications:* Poetry: Tonnau, 1989; Ga'i ddarn o awyr las heddiw?, 1991; Sglefrfyrddio, 1994; Wavelengths (in trans.), 1995; Bro Maelor, 1996; Mendio Gondola, 1997; Llyfr Erchwyn Gwely, 1998; Troeon, 1998; Mixing the Colours (in trans.), 1999. Novels: Rhwng Dau Lanw Medi (Between Two September Tides), 1994; Y Caffi (The Cafe), 2002. Other: short stories. Contributions: Barn; Golwg; Y Traethodydd; Poetry Wales; other Welsh periodicals; anthologies incl.: A White Afternoon, 1998; The Bloodaxe Book of Modern Welsh Poetry, 2003. *Honours:* National Eisteddfod of Wales literary awards, 1991, 1998, 1999. *Address:* 28 Jubilee Rd, Pentrefelin, Wrexham, Wrexham County LL13 7NN, Wales.

EVANS, C. Stephen; Philosopher and Writer; b. 26 May 1948, Atlanta, GA, USA; m. Jan Walter, 6 Sept. 1969, one s. two d. *Education:* BA, Wheaton College, 1969; PhD, Yale University, 1974. *Career:* Asst Prof., 1974–78, Assoc. Prof., 1978–82, Prof., 1982–84, Wheaton College, IL; Prof., Philosophy, Psychology, Kierkegaard Library Curator, 1986–94, Division Chair, 1991–93, St Olaf College, Northfield, MN; Prof. of Philosophy, 1994–, William Spoelhof Teacher-Scholar, 1994–96, Calvin College, Grand Rapids, MI; Visiting positions; Lectures; mem. American Philosophical Asscn; Kierkegaard Society, pres., 1991; Society of Christian Philosophers. *Publications:* Despair: A Moment or a Way of Life?, 1971; Preserving the Person: A Look at the Human Sciences, 1977; Subjectivity and Religious Belief: An Historical Critical Study, 1978; Kierkegaard's Fragments, and Postscripts: The Religious Philosophy of Johannes Climacus, 1983; Contours of Christian Philosophy, Vol. IV: Philosophy of Religion: Thinking about Faith, 1985; The Quest for Faith: Reason and Mystery as Pointers to God, 1986; Wisdom and Humanness in Psychology, 1989; Søren Kierkegaard's Christian Psychology, 1990; Passionate Reason: Making Sense of Kierkegaard's Philosophical Fragments, 1992; Foundation of Kierkegaard's Vision of Community: Religion, Ethics, and Politics in Kierkegaard, 1992; The Historical Christ and the Jesus of Faith: The Incarnational Narrative as History, 1996; Faith Beyond Reason, 1998. Contributions: articles and reviews to journals. *Honours:* George C. Marshall Fellow, 1977–78; National Endowment for the Humanities Fellowships, 1988–89, 2000–01; Fellow, Center for Faith Development, Emory University, 1988–89; Pew Evangelical Senior Scholar, 1991–94. *Address:* 2600 Golfridge Dr. SE, Grand Rapids, MI 49546, USA. *E-mail:* sevans@calvin.edu.

EVANS, George, BA, MA; American writer, poet, translator and editor; b. Pittsburgh, PA. *Education:* Johns Hopkins Univ., Carnegie-Mellon Univ. *Career:* medical corpsman and sergeant in the US Air Force 1967–70; founder ed., Streetfare Journal project. *Publications include:* poetry: Wrecking, Nightvision, Eye Blade, Sudden Dreams: New & Selected Poems; editor: Charles Olson and Cid Corman: Complete Correspondence 1950–64. *Honours:* Lanann Foundation Fellowship, National Endowment of the Arts Fellowship, California Arts Fellowship, Monbusho Fellowship from the Japanese Ministry of Education. *Address:* c/o Curbstone Press, 321 Jackson Street, Willimantic, CT 06226-1738, USA. *E-mail:* info@curbstone.org. *Website:* www.curbstone.org.

EVANS, Harold Matthew, MA; American (b. British) publisher, fmr newspaper editor and writer; b. 28 June 1928, Manchester, England; m. 1st Enid

Parker 1953 (divorced 1978); one s. two d.; m. 2nd Tina Brown 1982; one s. one d. *Education:* Durham Univ. *Career:* Commonwealth Fund Fellow, Univ. of Chicago 1956–57; Ed. Sunday Times, London 1967–81, The Times 1981–82; mem. Bd Times Newspapers Ltd, Dir 1978–82; Int. Press Inst. 1974–80; Dir Goldcrest Films and Television 1982–85; Ed.-in-Chief Atlantic Monthly 1984–86, Contributing Ed. 1986–, Editorial Dir and Vice-Chair. 1998–; Ed. Dir U.S. News and World Report 1984–86, Contributing Ed. 1986–, Editorial Dir and Vice-Chair. 1998–; Vice-Pres. and Sr Ed. Weidenfeld and Nicolson 1986–87; Adviser to Chair. Condé Nast Publications 1986–; Founding Ed.-in-Chief, Condé Nast Traveler 1986–90; Pres. and Publr Random House Adult Trade Group 1990–97; Editorial Dir Mortimer Zuckerman's media properties 1997–; Editorial Dir and Vice-Chair. New York Daily News Inc. 1998–99, Fast Co. 1998–; author Little, Brown and Co., NY 2000–; Fellow, Soc. Industrial Artists, Inst. of Journalists; Hon. Visiting Prof. of Journalism City Univ. 1978–; Hon. DCL (Durham) 1998. *Publications:* Active Newsroom 1964, Editing and Design, Newsman's English 1970, Newspaper Design 1971, Newspaper Headlines 1973, Newspaper Text 1973, We Learned to Ski (co-author) 1974, Freedom of the Press 1974, Pictures on a Page 1978, Suffer the Children (co-author), How We Learned to Ski 1983, Good Times, Bad Times 1983, Front Page History 1984, The American Century 1998. *Honours:* Dr hc (Stirling); Journalist of the Year Prize 1973; Int. Ed. of the Year Award 1975, Inst. of Journalists Gold Medal Award 1979; Design and Art Dir, Pres.'s Award 1981, Ed. of Year Award, Granada 1982, Hood Medal, Royal Photographic Soc. 1981, Press Photographers of GB Award 1986; Gold Award for Achievement, British Press Awards 2000, World Press Freedom Hero, Int. Press Inst. 2000. *Address:* Little, Brown and Co., 1271 Avenue of the Americas, New York, NY 10020, USA (Office). *E-mail:* hevans@usnews.com (Office).

EVANS, Jonathan (see Freemantle, Brian (Harry)).

EVANS, Max; Writer and Painter; b. 29 Aug. 1925, USA. *Publications:* Southwest Wind (short stories), 1958; Long John Dunn of Taos, 1959; The Rounders, 1960; The Hi Lo Country, 1961; Three Short Novels: The Great Wedding, The One-Eyed Sky, My Pardner, 1963; The Mountain of Gold, 1965; Shadow of Thunder, 1969; Three West: Conversations with Vardis Fisher, Max Evans, Michael Straight, 1970; Sam Peckinpah, Master of Violence, 1972; Bobby Jack Smith, You Dirty Coward!, 1974; The White Shadow, 1977; Xavier's Folly and Other Stories, 1984; Super Bull and Other True Escapades, 1985. *Address:* 1111 Ridgecrest Dr. SE, Albuquerque, NM 87108, USA.

EVANS, Nicholas; British film and TV producer and writer; b. Bromsgrove, Worcestershire; pnr Charlotte Gordon Cumming; three s. one d. *Education:* Univ. of Oxford. *Career:* fmr journalist Evening Chronicle, Newcastle upon Tyne, producer documentaries for London Weekend TV, writer and producer films for TV and cinema. *Film:* Just Like a Woman 1991. *Television:* producer documentaries on artists, including David Hockney, Francis Bacon, Patricia Highsmith, David Lean. *Publications:* The Horse Whisperer 1995, The Loop 1998, The Smoke Jumper 2001. *Literary Agent:* AP Watt, 20 John Street, London, WC1N 2DR, England. *Website:* www.randomhouse.com/features/nickevans/.

EVANS, Richard John, FRHistS, FRSL, FBA; Prof. of Modern History and Writer; b. 29 Sept. 1947, Woodford, Essex, England; m. Elín Hjaltadóttir 1976 (divorced 1993); pnr Christine L. Corton; two s. *Education:* BA, Modern History, Jesus College, Oxford, 1969; MA, DPhil, 1973, St Antony's College, Oxford. *Career:* Lecturer in History, University of Stirling, 1972–76; Lecturer in European History, 1976–83, Prof. of European History, 1983–89, University of East Anglia; Visiting Assoc. Prof. of European History, Columbia University, 1980; Alexander von Humboldt Fellow, Free University of Berlin, 1981, 1985, 1989; Visiting Fellow, Australian National University, Canberra, 1986; Prof. of History, 1989–98, Vice-Master, 1993–98, Acting Master, 1997, Birkbeck College, London; Prof. of Modern History, University of Cambridge, 1998–; Fellow, Gonville and Caius College, Cambridge, 1998–. *Publications:* The Feminist Movement in Germany 1894–1933 1976, The Feminists 1977, Society and Politics in Wilhelmine Germany (ed.) 1978, Sozialdemokratie und Frauenemanzipation im deutschen Kaiserreich 1979, The German Family (co-ed.) 1981, The German Working Class (ed.) 1982, The German Peasantry (co-ed.) 1986, The German Unemployed (co-ed.) 1987, Comrades and Sisters 1987, Rethinking German History 1987, Death in Hamburg 1987, The German Underworld (ed.) 1988, Kneipengespräche im Kaiserreich (ed.) 1989, In Hitler's Shadow 1989, Proletarians and Politics 1990, The German Bourgeoisie (co-ed.) 1992, Rituals of Retribution: Capital Punishment in Germany 1600–1987 1996, Rereading German History 1997, In Defence of History 1997, Tales from the German Underworld 1998, Lying About Hitler 2001, The Coming of the Third Reich 2003. Contributions to scholarly journals, newspapers, magazines, radio and TV. *Honours:* Hon. Fellow, Jesus College Oxford 1998, Birkbeck College London 1999Wolfson Literary Award for History 1987, William H. Welch Medal American Asscn for the History of Medicine 1989, Medaille für Kunst und Wissenschaft der Hansestadt Hamburg 1993, Fraenkel Prize in Contemporary History Institute of Contemporary History 1994. *Address:* c/o Gonville and Caius College, Cambridge CB2 1TA, England.

EVANS, Robert John Weston; writer; b. 7 Oct. 1943, Leicester, England; m. Kati Róbert 1969; one s. one d. *Education:* BA, 1965, PhD, 1968, Jesus College, Cambridge. *Career:* Fellow, Brasenose College, Oxford, 1968–97; Lecturer, 1969–90, Reader in the Modern History of East Central Europe, 1990–92, Prof. of European History, 1992–97, Regius Prof. of Modern History, 1997–, University of Oxford; Mem., Institute for Advanced Study, Princeton, NJ, 1981–82; Co-Ed., English Historical Review, 1985–95; Fellow, Oriel College, Oxford, 1997–. *Publications:* Rudolf II and His World, 1973; The Wechel Presses, 1975; The Making of the Habsburg Monarchy, 1979; The Coming of the First World War (ed. with H. Pogge von Strandmann), 1988; Crown, Church and Estates: Central European Politics, 1991 (ed. with T. V. Thomas), 1991; The Revolutions in Europe, 1848–9 (ed. with H. Pogge von Strandmann), 2000. Contributions: Professional journals. *Honours:* Wolfson Literary Award for History, 1980; Fellow, British Acad., 1984; Anton Gindely Prize, Austria, 1986; František Palacký Medal, Czechoslovakia, 1991; Fellow, Hungarian Acad. of Sciences, 1995; Fellow, Austrian Acad. of Sciences, 1997. *Address:* Rowan Cottage, 45 Sunningwell, Abingdon, Oxfordshire OX13 6RD, England.

EVANS OF TEMPLE GUITING, Baron (Life Peer), cr. 2000, of Temple Guiting in the County of Gloucestershire; **Matthew Evans,** CBE, BSc Econs, FRSA; British publishing executive; b. 7 Aug. 1941; m. 1st Elizabeth Amanda Mead 1966 (divorced 1991); two s.; m. 2nd Caroline Michel 1991; two s. one d. *Education:* Friends' School, Saffron Walden and LSE. *Career:* bookselling 1963–64; with Faber & Faber 1964–, Man. Dir 1972–93, Chair. 1981–; Chair. Nat. Book League 1982–84, English Stage Co. 1984–90; mem. Council, Publishers' Asscn 1978–84; Gov. BFI 1982–97, Vice-Chair. 1996–97; Chair. Library and Information Comm. 1995–99; Chair. Museums, Libraries and Archives Council 2000–02; Dir Which? Ltd 1997–; mem. Arts Council Nat. Lottery Advisory Panel 1997–99, Univ. for Industry Advisory Group 1997, Royal Opera House Working Group 1997, Arts and Humanities Research Bd 1998–; mem. Franco-British Soc. 1981–; founder mem. Groucho Club (Dir 1982–97). *Honours:* Hon. FRCA 1999; Hon. FLA 1999. *Address:* Faber & Faber, 3 Queen Square, London, WC1N 3AU, England. *Telephone:* (20) 7465-0045. *Fax:* (20) 7465-0034.

EVENO, Bertrand; French publishing executive; b. 26 July 1944, Egletons; m. 2nd Brigitte Pery 1984; five d. (three d. from previous m.). *Education:* Lycée Condorcet and Law Faculty, Paris. *Career:* Treasury Inspector 1973–77; Tech. Consultant to Health Minister 1977–78; Cabinet Dir for Minister of Culture and Communication 1978–81; mem. Atomic Energy Comm. Control Bd 1981–83; Deputy Gen. Man. André Shoe Co. 1984–86; Chair. Editions Fernand Nathan 1987–2000; Pres. Conseil d'admin., Fondation nationale de la photographie 1981–95, Gens d'Image 1986–2000; Chair. Larousse-Nathan Int. 1988–90, Le Robert dictionaries 1989–2000, Editions Masson 1995–98; Dir-Gen. Groupe de la Cité 1988–2000, Presses de la Cité 1991–95; Pres., Dir-Gen. Larousse-Bordas 1996–2000; Pres., Dir-Gen. Havas Educ. et Référence 1999–; Dir Anaya Groupe 1999–2000; Pres. Agence France Presse 2000–; Zellidja Scholarship 1961. *Publication:* monograph on Willy Ronis in Les grands photographes 1983. *Address:* Agence France Presse, 11–25 place de la Bourse, BP 20, 75061 Paris Cédex 02 (Office); 80 rue de Rennes, 75006 Paris, France (Home). *Telephone:* 1-40-41-46-46. *Fax:* 1-40-41-46-32. *Website:* www.afp.com (Office).

EVENSON, Brian; Asst Prof., Writer and Ed.; b. 12 Aug. 1966, Ames, IA, USA; m. Connie Joyce Evenson, 16 Aug. 1989, two d. *Education:* BA, English, Brigham Young University, 1989; MA, English, 1990; PhD, Critical Theory/English Literature, University of Washington, 1994. *Career:* Asst Prof., English, Brigham Young University, 1994–96; Asst Prof., English, Oklahoma State University, 1996–; Fiction Ed., Cimarron Review, 1996–; Ed., Conjunctions, 1997–. *Publications:* Altmann's Tongue, 1994; The Din of Celestial Birds, 1997; Prophets and Brothers, 1997; Father of Lies, 1998. *Honours:* National Endowment for the Arts Grant, 1995. *Literary Agent:* Curtis Brown Ltd, 7 Queensferry St, Edinburgh EH2 4QS, Scotland.

EVERDELL, William R(omeyn); Educator and Writer; b. 25 June 1941, New York, NY, USA; m. Barbara Scott, 21 Dec. 1966, two s. *Education:* BA, Princeton University, 1964; Certificate, University of Paris, 1964; MA, 1965, PhD, 1971, New York University. *Career:* Chair, History Dept, 1972–73, Head, Upper School, 1973–75, Co-Chair, History Dept, 1975–84, Dean, Humanities, 1984–, St Ann's School; Adjunct Instructor, New York University, 1984–89; mem. International Society for Intellectual History; New York Acad. of Sciences; Society for Eighteenth-Century Studies; Society of French Historical Studies. *Publications:* Rowboats to Rapid Transit (co-author), 1974; The End of Kings: A History of Republics and Republicans, 1983; Christian Apologetics in France, 1730–1790: The Roots of Romantic Religion, 1987; The First Moderns: Profiles in the Origins of Twentieth-Century Thought, 1997. Contributions: periodicals. *Honours:* Woodrow Wilson Fellowships, 1964, 1970; National Endowment for the Humanities Fellowships, 1985, 1990; National Endowment for the Humanities/Wallace Foundation Teacher-Scholar, 1990–91; Honoree, New York Public Library Books to Remember, 1998. *Address:* c/o St Ann's School, 129 Pierrepont St, New York, NY 11201, USA.

EVERETT, Graham; Prof., Poet and Writer; b. 23 Dec. 1947, Oceanside, NY, USA; m. Elyse Arnow, 27 Dec. 1981, one s. *Education:* BA, English, Canisius College, 1970; MA, English, 1987, PhD, English, 1994, SUNY at

Stony Brook. *Career:* Ed. and Publisher, Street Press and Magazine, 1972–86; mem. MLA; National Council of Teachers of English. *Publications:* Trees, 1978; Strange Coast, 1979; Paumanok Rising: An Anthology of Eastern Long Island Aesthetics (co-ed.), 1981; Sunlit Sidewalk, 1985; Minus Green, 1992; Minus Green Plus, 1995; Corps Calleux, 2000. Contributions: anthologies, reviews, quarterlies, and journals. *Address:* PO Box 772, Sound Beach, NY 11789, USA.

EVERETT, Percival, BA, MA; writer and academic; b. 22 Dec. 1956, Fort Gordon, GA, USA. *Education:* University of Miami, University of Oregon, Brown University. *Career:* Assoc. Prof., University of Kentucky, Lexington, 1985–89, University of Notre Dame, IN, 1989–92; Prof., University of California at Riverside, 1992–99, University of Southern California at Los Angeles, 1999–; mem. MLA, Writers' Guild of America. *Publications:* Suder, 1983; Walk Me to the Distance, 1985; Cutting Lisa, 1986; The Weather and Women Treat Me Fair, 1989; Zulus, 1989; For Her Dark Skin, 1989; The One That Got Away, 1992; God's Country, 1994; The Body of Martin Aguilera, 1994; Big Picture, 1996; Watershed, 1996; Frenzy, 1996; Glyph, 1999; Erasure, 2001. Contributions: anthologies and periodicals. *Address:* c/o Department of English, University of Southern California at Los Angeles, Los Angeles, CA 90089, USA.

EXTON, Clive; Scriptwriter and Playwright; b. 11 April 1930, London, England; m. 1st Patricia Fletcher Ferguson, 1951, two d.; m. 2nd Margaret Josephine Reid, 1957, one s. two d. *Education:* Christ's Hospital. *Publications:* Television plays; Television series; Screenplays; Stage plays. *Honours:* Writers' Guild Award, 1994. *Address:* c/o Rochell Stevens & Co, 2 Terrets Pl., London N1 1QZ, England.

EYNON, Robert (Bob), BA; university lecturer and writer; b. 20 March 1941, Tynewydd, Rhondda, Wales. *Education:* Univ. of London. *Publications:* Bitter Waters, 1988; Texas Honour, 1988; Johnny One Arm, 1989; Gunfight at Simeons Ridge, 1991; Gun Law Legacy, 1991; Sunset Reckoning, 1993; Anderton Justice, 1997; Pecos Vengeance, 1998; Brothers Till Death, 1999; Dol Rhydian, 1999; Lladd Akamuro, 2000; Arizona Payback, 2001; Poison Valley, 2003. Other: Welsh novels and short stories for learners including: Perygl Yn Sbaen, 1987; Yr Asiant Cudd, 1997. *Address:* 5 Troedyrhiw Terrace, Treorchy, Rhondda CF42 6PG, Wales.

F

FABEND, Firth Haring, (Firth Haring); Writer and Historian; b. 12 Aug. 1937, Tappan, New York, USA; m. Carl Fabend, 12 Feb. 1966, two d. *Education:* BA, Barnard College, 1959; PhD, New York University, 1988. *Publications:* As Firth Haring: The Best of Intentions, 1968; Three Women, 1972; A Perfect Stranger, 1973; The Woman Who Went Away, 1981; Greek Revival, 1985. As Firth Haring Fabend: A Dutch Family in the Middle Colonies, 1660–1800. Contributions: de Halve Maen; New York History. *Honours:* Ms Award, New York State Historical Asscn, 1989; Hendricks Prize, 1989; Fellow, Holland Society of New York, 1993; Fellow, New Netherland Project, 1996.

FABER, Michel; Author; b. 1959, Holland; m. 2nd Eva Youren; two step-s. *Education:* Melbourne Univ. *Career:* emigrated to Australia, 1967; now lives in Scotland. *Publications:* Fish (short story); Some Rain Must Fall (short stories), 1996; Under the Skin (novel), 1999; The 199 Steps (short story); The Courage Consort (short story); The Crimson Petal and the White (novel), 2002. Contributions: Guardian. *Honours:* Macallan short story award; Saltire First Book of the Year Award, 1999. *Address:* c/o Canongate Books, 14 High St, Edinburgh EH1 1TE, Scotland.

FAES, Urs; Author, Poet and Dramatist; b. 13 Feb. 1947, Aarau, Switzerland. *Education:* MA, University of Zürich. *Career:* Journalist, 1979–81; Dramatist, 1982–86; Writer, 1982–; mem. Swiss Authors' Group; PEN. *Publications:* Eine Kerbe im Mittag (poems), 1975; Heidentum und Aberglaube (essay), 1979; Regenspur (poems), 1979; Webfehler (novel), 1983; Zugluft (play), 1983; Der Traum vom Leben (short stories), 1984; Kreuz im Feld (play), 1984; Bis ans Ende der Erinnerung (novel), 1986; Wartzimmer (play), 1986; Partenza (radio play), 1986; Sommerwende (novel), 1989; Alphabet des Abschieds, 1991; Eine andere Geschichte (radio play), 1993; Augenblicke im Paradies (novel), 1994; Ombra (novel), 1997; Und Ruth (novel), 2001. *Honours:* Prize, City of Zürich, 1986; Prize for Literature, 1991; Literary Prize, Kanton Soluthurn, 1999. *Address:* Urs Faes, Sirius Str 4, 8044 Zürich, Switzerland.

FAGAN, Brian Murray, BA, MA, PhD; academic and writer; b. 1 Aug. 1936, Birmingham, England; m. Lesley Ann Newhart 1985; two c. *Education:* Pembroke Coll., Cambridge. *Career:* Keeper of Prehistory, Livingstone Museum, Zambia 1959–65; Visiting Assoc. Prof., University of Illinois 1965–66; Assoc. Prof. 1967–69, Prof. of Anthropology 1969–, University of California at Santa Barbara. *Publications:* Victoria Falls Handbook, 1964; Southern Africa During the Iron Age (ed.), 1966; Iron Age Cultures in Zambia (with S. G. H. Daniels and D. W. Phillipson), 2 vols, 1967, 1969; A Short History of Zambia, 1968; The Hunter-Gatherers of Gwisho (with F. Van Noten), 1971; In the Beginning, 1972; People of the Earth, 1974; The Rape of the Nile, 1975; Elusive Treasure, 1977; Quest for the Past, Archaeology: A Brief Introduction, 1978; Return to Babylon, 1979; The Aztecs, Clash of Cultures, 1984; Adventures in Archaeology, Bareboating, Anchoring, 1985; The Great Journey, 1987; The Journey From Eden, 1990; Ancient North America, 1991; Kingdoms of Jade, Kingdoms of Gold, 1991; Time Detectives, 1995; Oxford Companion to Archaeology, 1996; Into the Unknown, 1997; From Black Land to Fifth Sun, 1998; Floods, Famines and Emperors, 1999; The Long Summer: How Climate Changed Civilisation 2004. *Address:* Department of Anthropology, University of California at Santa Barbara, CA 93106, USA.

FAGLES, Robert; Prof., Trans. and Poet; b. 11 Sept. 1933, Philadelphia, PA, USA; m. Marilyn Fagles, 17 June 1956, two c. *Education:* AB, summa cum laude, Amherst College, 1955; MA, 1956, PhD, 1959, Yale University. *Career:* Instructor, Yale University, 1959–60; Instructor, 1960–62, Asst Prof., 1962–65, Assoc. Prof., 1965–70, Dir, Program in Comparative Literature, 1966–75, Prof., 1970–2002, Chair., Dept of Comparative Literature, 1975–94, Arthur W. Marks Prof. of Comparative Literature, Emeritus, 2002–, Princeton University; mem. American Acad. of Arts and Letters; American Acad. of Arts and Sciences; American Philosophical Society. *Publications:* Translator: Complete Poems, by Bacchylides, 1961; The Oresteia, by Aeschylus, 1975; The Three Theban Plays, by Sophocles, 1984; The Iliad, by Homer, 1990; The Odyssey, by Homer, 1996. Poetry: I, Vincent: Poems from the Pictures of Van Gogh, 1978. Co-Editor: Homer: A Collection of Critical Essays, 1962; Pope's Iliad and Odyssey, 1967. Contributions: Books and journals. *Honours:* Harold Morton Landon Trans. Award, Acad. of American Poets, 1991; American Acad. of Arts and Letters Award in Literature, 1996; PEN/Ralph Manheim Medal for Life-time Achievement in Trans., 1997; Commander, Order of the Phoenix, Hellenic Republic, 1999; Hon. doctorates, Amhurst College, 1990, Bourdoin College, 2000, Yale University, 2002. *Address:* c/o Dept of Comparative Literature, Princeton University, Princeton, NJ 08544, USA. *E-mail:* fagles@princeton.edu.

FAINLIGHT, Ruth (Esther); Writer, Poet, Trans. and Librettist; b. 2 May 1931, New York, NY, USA; m. Alan Sillitoe 19 Nov. 1959; one s. one d. *Education:* Colleges of Arts and Crafts, Birmingham, Brighton. *Career:* Poet-in-Residence, Vanderbilt Univ., 1985, 1990; mem. PEN; Writers in Prison Committee. *Publications:* Poetry: Cages, 1966; To See the Matter Clearly, 1968; The Region's Violence, 1973; Another Full Moon, 1976; Sibyls and Others, 1980; Climates, 1983; Fifteen to Infinity, 1983; Selected Poems, 1987; The Knot, 1990; Sibyls, 1991; This Time of Year, 1994; Sugar-Paper Blue, 1997; Burning Wire, 2002. Translator: All Citizens Are Soldiers, from Lope de Vega, 1969; Navigations, 1983; Marine Rose: Selected Poems of Sophia de Mello Breyner, 1988. Short Stories: Daylife and Nightlife, 1971; Dr Clock's Last Case, 1994. Libretti: The Dancer Hotoke, 1991; The European Story, 1993; Bedlam Britannica, 1995; Poemas, 2000; Bleue Papier-Sucre, 2000. Contributions: Atlantic Monthly; Critical Quarterly; English; Hudson Review; Lettre Internationale; London Magazine; London Review of Books; New Yorker; Poetry Review; Threepenny Review; TLS. *Honours:* Cholmondeley Award for Poetry, 1994; Hawthornden Award for Poetry, 1994. *Address:* 14 Ladbroke Terrace, London W11 3PG, England.

FAIRBAIRNS, Zoe Ann; Writer; b. 20 Dec. 1948, England. *Education:* MA, University of St Andrews, Scotland, 1972. *Career:* C. Day-Lewis Fellowship, Rutherford School, London, 1977–78; Writer-in-Residence, Deakin University, Australia, 1983, Sunderland Polytechnic, 1983–85; mem. Writer's Guild. *Publications:* Live as Family, 1968; Down, 1969; Benefits, 1979; Stand We at Last, 1983; Here Today, 1984; Closing, 1987; Daddy's Girls, 1991; Other Names, 1998. Contributions: New Scientist; Guardian; Women's Studies International Quarterly; Spare Rib; Arts Express. *Honours:* Fawcett Book Prize, 1985. *Address:* c/o PFD, Drury House, 34–43 Russell St, London WC2B 5HA, England. *E-mail:* zoebridge@compuserve.com.

FAIRBURN, Eleanor M., (Catherine Carfax, Emma Gayle, Elena Lyons); author; b. 23 Feb. 1928, Ireland; m. Brian Fairburn, one d. *Career:* tutor, Practical Writing, Univ. of Leeds Adult Education Centre; mem. Middlesbrough Writers Group (pres. 1988, 1989, 1990). *Publications:* The Green Popinjays 1962, The White Seahorse 1964, The Golden Hive 1966, Crowned Ermine 1968, The Rose in Spring 1971, White Rose, Dark Summer 1972, The Rose at Harvest End 1975, Winter's Rose 1976, Edith Cavell (biog.) 1985, Mary Hornbeck Glyn (biog.) 1987, Grace Darling (biog.) 1988; as Catherine Carfax: A Silence with Voices 1969, The Semper Inheritance 1972, To Die a Little 1972, The Sleeping Salamander 1973; as Emma Gayle: Cousin Caroline 1980, Frenchman's Harvest 1980; as Elena Lyons: The Haunting of Abbotsgarth 1980, A Scent of Lilacs 1982. *Literary Agent:* S. Cashman, Wolfhound Press, Mountjoy Square, Dublin 1, Ireland. *Address:* 27 Minsterley Drive, Acklam, Middlesbrough, Cleveland TS5 8QU, England. *Telephone:* (1642) 821550.

FAIRCLOUGH, Troy Andrew; British playwright; b. 1976, Brixton, London. *Plays:* You Don't Kiss 2001, Justin Fashanu woz 'ere 2004. *Honours:* Newham Writing Out Award 2001. *Address:* c/o Oval House Theatre, 52–54 Kennington Oval, London, SE11 5SW, England. *Telephone:* (20) 7582-0080. *Website:* www.ovalhouse.com.

FAIRFAX, John; Writer and Poet; b. 9 Nov. 1930, London, England; two s. *Career:* Co-Founder and Mem. of Council of Management, Arvon Foundation; Dir, Phoenix Press, Arts Workshop, Newbury; Poetry Ed., Resurgence; mem. The Arvon Foundation, co-founder, 1968. *Publications:* The Fifth Horseman of the Apocalypse, 1969; Double Image, 1971; Adrift on the Star Brow of Taliesin, 1974; Bone Harvest Done, 1980; Wild Children, 1985; The Way to Write, 1981; Creative Writing, 1989; Spindrift Lp, 1981; 100 Poems, 1992; Zuihitsu, 1996; Poem Sent to Satellite E2F3, 1997; Poem on Sculpture, 1998; Poem in Hologram, 1998; Commissioned poems: Boots Herbal Garden, engraved on glass for several institutes, 1999, 2003; Poems for dance and art films, 2001–03. Contributions: Most major literary magazines. *Address:* The Thatched Cottage, Eling, Hermitage, Newbury, Berkshire RG16 9XR, England.

FAIRLEY, John Alexander, MA; broadcasting executive and writer; b. 15 April 1939, Liverpool, England; three d. *Education:* Queen's College, Oxford. *Career:* journalist, Bristol Evening Post, 1963, London Evening Standard, 1964; Producer, BBC Radio, 1965–68; Producer, 1968–78, Dir of Programmes, 1984–92, Managing Dir, 1992–95, Yorkshire TV; Chair., ITV Broadcast Board, 1995–. *Publications:* The Coup, 1975; The Monocled Mutineer (with W. Allison), 1975; Arthur C. Clarke's Mysterious World, 1980; Great Racehorses in Art, 1984; Chronicles of the Strange and Mysterious, 1987; Racing in Art, 1990; The Cabinet of Curiosities, 1991; A Century of Mysteries, 1993; The Art of the Horse, 1995.

FALCK, (Adrian) Colin, BA, MA, PhD; British academic, writer and poet; b. 14 July 1934, London, England; one d. one s. *Education:* University of Oxford, University of London. *Career:* Lecturer in Sociology, LSE, 1961–62; Assoc. Ed., The Review, 1962–72; Lecturer in Literature, Chelsea College, 1964–84; Poetry Ed., The New Review, 1974–78; Assoc. Prof., York College, Pennsylvania, 1989–99. *Publications:* The Garden in the Evening, 1964; Promises, 1969; Backwards into the Smoke, 1973; Poems Since 1900: An Anthology (ed. with Ian Hamilton), 1975; In This Dark Light, 1978; Robinson Jeffers: Selected Poems (ed.), 1987; Myth, Truth and Literature, 1989; Edna St Vincent Millay: Selected Poems (ed.), 1991; Memorabilia, 1992; Post-Modern Love, 1997; American and British Verse in the Twentieth Century 2004. Contributions: many professional journals and general periodicals. *Literary Agent:* Johnson & Alcock Ltd, Clerkenwell House, 45–47 Clerkenwell Green, London EC1R 0HT, England. *Address:* 20 Thurlow Road, London NW3 5PP, England. *Telephone:* (20) 7435-6806. *Fax:* (20) 7435-6806.

FALKENLÖWE, Michael Sixten Joachim, (Baron of Rütz); Writer; b. 2 Aug. 1942, Copenhagen, Denmark; m. Kiell Otto Falkenlöwe of Rütz, 15 Aug. 1998. *Education:* Historian, University of Århus; Journalist; Writer. *Career:* Pres., Falkenlöwe Group of Publishing Firms, Scandinavia and Netherlands. *Publications:* 20 books, 1964–, including Famous Gay, 1998. Contributions: numerous to magazines and journals. *Honours:* Brother, Danish Cullenton Society.

FALKIRK, Richard (see Lambert, Derek (William)).

FALLACI, Oriana; Writer and Journalist; b. 29 June 1930, Florence, Italy. *Education:* Liceo Classico Galileo Galilei; Faculty, Medicine, University of Florence, 1947–49. *Career:* Ed., Special Correspondent, Europeo Magazine, Milan, 1958–77; Special Correspondent, Corriere della Sera, Milan. *Publications:* The Seven Sins of Hollywood, 1958; The Useless Sex (Voyage Around the Woman), 1962; The Egotists, 1965; Penelope at War (novel), 1966; If the Sun Dies, 1967; Nothing and So Be It, 1972; Interview With History, 1976; Letter to a Child Never Born (novel), 1977; A Man (novel), 1979; Inshallah (novel), 1990; The Rage and the Pride, 2001; On Anti-semitism, 2002. Contributions: Look magazine; Life; Washington Post; New York Times; London Times; Corriere della Sera; El Mundo; La Nouveux Observateur; Der Spiegel; L'Express. *Honours:* St Vincent Awards for Journalism, 1971, 1973; two Bancarella Awards, 1972; Hon. LittD, Columbia College, Chicago, 1977; Viareggio Prize, 1979; Hemingway Prize for Literature, 1991; Super Bancarella Prize, 1991; Prix d'Antibes, 1993. *Address:* c/o RCS Rizzoli Corp, 31 W 57th St, Fourth Floor, New York, NY 10019, USA.

FALLON, Ivan Gregory, FRSA; Newspaper Exec. and Writer; b. 26 June 1944, Wexford, Ireland; m. 1st Susan Mary Lurring, 1967, divorced 1997, one s. two d.; m. 2nd Elizabeth Rees-Jones, 1997. *Education:* St Peter's College, Wexford, 1952–62; BBS, Trinity College, Dublin, 1966. *Career:* Staff Irish Times 1964–66, Thomson Provincial Newspapers 1966–67, Daily Mirror 1967–68; Staff Sunday Telegraph 1968–70, 1971–79, City Ed. 1979–84; Deputy City Ed. Sunday Express 1970–71; Deputy Ed. Sunday Times 1984–94; Editorial Dir Argus Group 1994–97; Dir N. Brown Group PLC 1994–, Independent Newspapers PLC Ireland 1995–97; Deputy Chief Exec. and Editorial Dir Independent Newspapers Holdings Ltd 1995–97, CEO Independent Newspaper Holdings of South Africa 1997–2002, Chief Exec. Ind. News & Media UK 2002–; Chair. Itouch PLC 2000–; mem. RSA, Beefsteak, Political Economy, Rand Club Johannesburg. *Publications:* Delorean: The Rise and Fall of a Dream Maker (with James L. Srodes), 1983; Takeovers (with James L. Srodes), 1987; The Brothers: The Rise of Saatchi and Saatchi, 1988; Billionaire: The Life and Times of Sir James Goldsmith, 1991; Paperchase, 1993; The Player: The Life of Tony O'Reilly, 1994. *Address:* Independent House, 191 Marsh Wall, London E14 9RSEngland.

FALLON, Martin (see Patterson, Henry (Harry)).

FALLON, Peter, BA, HDipEd, MA; Irish editor and poet; b. 26 Feb. 1951, Osnabrück, Germany; two c. *Education:* Trinity College, Dublin. *Career:* Founder, Ed., Gallery Press, Dublin, 1970–; Poet-in-Residence, Deerfield Acad., MA, 1976–77, 1996–97; International Writer-in-Residence at various Indiana Schools, 1979; Fiction Ed., O'Brien Press, Dublin, 1980–85; Teacher, Contemporary Irish Poetry, School of Irish Studies, Dublin, 1985–89; Writing Fellow, Poet-in-Residence, Trinity College, Dublin, 1994; Heimbold Prof. of Irish Studies, Villanova University, PA. *Publications:* Among the Walls, 1971; Co-incidence of Flesh, 1972; The First Affair, 1974; Finding the Dead, 1978; The Speaking Stones, 1978; Winter Work, 1983; The News and Weather, 1987; The Penguin Book of Contemporary Irish Poetry (ed. with Derek Mahon), 1990. Other: Eye to Eye, 1992; News of the World: Selected and New Poems, 1998, 1999. Contributions: Poetry anthologies, periodicals and journals. *Honours:* Irish Arts Council Bursary, 1981; National Poetry Competition, England, 1982; Meath Merit Award, Arts and Culture, 1987; O'Shaughnessy Poetry Award, 1993. *Address:* Gallery Press, Loughcrew, Oldcastle, County Meath, Ireland.

FALLOWELL, Duncan Richard; writer; b. 26 Sept. 1948, London, England. *Education:* Magdalen Coll., Oxford. *Publications:* Drug Tales 1979, April Ashley's Odyssey 1982, Satyrday 1986, The Underbelly 1987, To Noto 1989, Twentieth Century Characters 1994, One Hot Summer in St Petersburg 1994, A History of Facelifting 2003. *Address:* 44 Leamington Road Villas, London, W11 1HT, England.

FALLOWS, David (Nicholas); Prof. of Music, Writer and Ed.; b. 20 Dec. 1945, Buxton, England; m. Paulène Oliver, 1976, separated 1996, one s. one d. *Education:* BA, Jesus College, Cambridge, 1967; MMus, King's College, London, 1968; PhD, University of California at Berkeley, 1978. *Career:* Asst, Studio der Frühen Musik, Munich, 1967–70; Lecturer, University of Wisconsin at Madison, 1973–74; Lecturer, 1976–82, Senior Lecturer, 1982–92, Reader in Music, 1992–97, Prof. of Music, 1997–, University of Manchester; Reviews Ed., Early Music, 1976–95, 1999–2000; Visiting Assoc. Prof., University of North Carolina at Chapel Hill, 1982–83; Founder-Gen. Ed., Royal Musical Asscn Monographs, 1982–98; Visiting Prof. of Musicology, École Normale Supérieure, Paris, 1993; mem. American Musicological Society, corresponding mem., 1999–; International Musicological Society, vice-pres., 1997–2002, pres., 2002–; Royal Musical Asscn, vice-pres., 2000–; Fellow, British Acad., 1997–. *Publications:* Dufay, 1982; Chansonnier de Jean de Montchenu (co-author), 1991; Companion to Medieval and Renaissance Music (ed. with T. Knighton), 1992; The Songs of Guillaume Dufay, 1995; Oxford Bodleian Library MS Canon Misc. 213, Late Medieval and Early Renaissance Music in Facsimile, Vol. 1 (ed.), 1995; Songs and Musicians in the Fifteenth Century, 1996; The Songbook of Fridolin Sicher, 1996; A Catalogue of Polyphonic Songs, 1415–1480, 1999. Contributions: Reference works, scholarly books and professional journals. *Honours:* First Ingolf Dahl Prize in Musicology, 1971; Dent Medal, 1982; Chevalier, Ordre des Arts et des Lettres, 1994. *Address:* 10 Chatham Rd, Manchester M16 0DR, England. *E-mail:* david.fallows@man.ac.uk.

FANTHORPE, (Robert) Lionel, BA, FRSA, FCMI; priest, writer, broadcaster and academic; b. 9 Feb. 1935, Dereham, Norfolk, England; m. Patricia Alice Tooke 1957; two d. *Education:* FCP; Teaching Certificate with Advanced Mains Distinction; Anglican Ordination Certificate. *Career:* Consultant and Festival Co-ordinator, UK Year of Literature and Writing, 1995; Presenter, Fortean TV, Channel 4, 1997; The Real Nostradamus Channel 4, Stranger than Fiction Westcountry TV, Stations of the Cross HTV, Holy Quiz HTV 2000; Three Wise Men BBC Radio Wales 2000; Talking Stones 2002, 2003; Real Radio Reverend slot Real Radio 105FM; mem. MENSA; Equity; Society of Authors; Welsh Acad. *Publications:* The Black Lion, 1979; The Holy Grail Revealed, 1982; Life of St Francis, 1988; God in All Things, 1988; Thoughts and Prayers for Troubled Times, 1989; Birds and Animals of the Bible, 1990; Thoughts and Prayers for Lonely Times, 1990; The First Christmas, 1990; Rennes-le-Château, 1992; The Oak Island Mystery, 1995; The Abbot's Kitchen, 1995; The World's Greatest Unsolved Mysteries, 1997; The World's Most Mysterious People, 1998; The World's Most Mysterious Places, 1998; Mysteries of the Bible, 1999; Death, the Final Mystery 2000, The World's Most Mysterious Objects 2002, The World's Most Mysterious Murders 2003, Talking Stones (book of TV series) 2003. *Honours:* Electrical Development Asscn Diploma, 1958; Holder of Seven World Championships for Professional Authors: Prose, Drama, Poetry and Autobiography; Pres. ASSAP 1999; Pres. BUFORA, 2000; Grand Chaplain Gen. Knights Templar Priory of the Holy Lands 2002–; Guest Celebrity Poet at the Margate Poetry Festival, 2000. *Address:* Rivendell, 48 Claude Road, Roath, Cardiff, Wales. *E-mail:* Fanthorpe@aol.com. *Website:* www.lionel-fanthorpe.com.

FANTHORPE, Ursula Askham, CBE, BA, MA, FRSA, FRSL; British poet and writer; b. 22 July 1929, Kent, England; pnr R. V. Bailey. *Education:* St Catherine's School, Bramley, St Anne's Coll., Oxford, London Inst. of Educ., Univ. of Swansea. *Career:* Asst Mistress Cheltenham Ladies' Coll. 1954–62, Head of English 1962–70; English teacher Howells School, Llandaff 1972–73; temp. clerical work Bristol 1973–74; clerk/receptionist Burden Neurological Hosp. Bristol 1974–89; Arts Council writer-in-residence, St Martin's Coll. Lancaster 1983–85; Northern Arts Literary Fellow, Univs of Durham and Newcastle 1987–88; freelance writer 1989–; contrib. to radio and television programmes, various workshops and collaborations with artists and musicians; Hon. Fellow, Cheltenham & Glos. Coll. of Higher Education 1995, St Anne's Coll., Oxford 2003, Sarum Coll., Salisbury 2004; mem. Nat. Trust, Wildlife and Wetlands Trust, Council for the Protection of Rural England, Compassion in World Farming, Medical Foundation, Religious Soc. of Friends, PEN 1980, Soc. of Authors 1995. *Publications:* Side Effects 1978, Standing To 1982, Voices Off 1984, Selected Poems 1986, A Watching Brief 1987, Neck-Verse 1992, Safe as Houses 1995, Consequences 2000, Christmas Poems 2002, Queueing for the Sun 2003; contrib. to anthologies, including Selected Poems 1986, Penguin Modern Poets 6 1996, Double Act (audiobook with R. V. Bailey) 1997, Poetry Quartets 5 (audiobook) 1999; contrib. to journals and periodicals, including TLS, Encounter, Outposts, Firebird, Bananas, South West Review, Quarto, Tribune, Country Life, Use of English, Poetry Review, Poetry Book Society Supplement, Writing Women, Spectator, BBC. *Honours:* Hon. DLitt (West of England) 1995; Dr hc (Gloucestershire) 2000; Soc. of Authors' Travelling Fellowship 1983, Hawthornden Fellowships 1987, 1997, 2002, Arts Council Writers' Award 1994, Soc. of Authors Cholmondeley Award 1995, Queen's Gold Medal for Poetry 2003. *Address:* Culverhay House, Wotton-under-Edge, Gloucestershire GL12 7LS, England. *E-mail:* fanthorpe.bailey@virgin.net.

FARAH, Nuruddin; Writer; b. 24 Nov. 1945, Baidoa, Somalia; m. 1st, one s. one d.; m. 2nd Amina Mama, 18 Sept. 1992. *Education:* Panjab University, 1966–70; University of London, 1974–75; Essex University, 1975–76. *Career:* Writer-in-Residence, University of Jos, Nigeria, 1981–83, University of Minnesota, 1989, Brown University, 1991; Prof., Makerere University, Uganda, 1989–91; mem. Union of Writers of the African People; PEN International; Somali-Speaking PEN Centre. *Publications:* From a Crooked Rib, 1970; A Naked Needle, 1976; Sweet and Sour Milk, 1979; Sardines, 1981; Close Sesame, 1983; Maps, 1986; Gifts, 1992; Secrets, 1998; Yesterday, Tomorrow: Voices from the Somali Diaspora, 1999. Contributions: Guardian; New African; Transition Magazine; New York Times; Observer; TLS; London Review of Books. *Honours:* English Speaking Literary Award, 1980; Deutscher Akademischer Austauschdienst Residency, 1990; Tucholsky Award, 1991; Premio Cavour Award, 1992; Zimbabwe Annual Award, 1993; Neustadt International Prize for Literature, 1998; Festival Étonnant Voyageur St Malo, France, 1998. *Literary Agent:* Rogers, Coleridge & White Ltd, 20 Powis Mews, London W11 1JN, England. *Telephone:* (20) 7221-3717. *Fax:* (20) 7229-9084.

FARELY, Alison (see Poland, Dorothy Elizabeth Hayward).

FARHI, (Musa) Moris, MBE, BA, FRSL, FRGS; novelist and poet; b. 5 July 1935, Ankara, Turkey; m. Nina Ruth Gould 1978; one step-d. *Education:* Istanbul American Coll., RADA London. *Career:* mem. Soc. of Authors, Writers Guild, PEN, Int. PEN (vice-pres.). *Publications:* The Pleasure of Death 1972, The Last of Days 1983, Journey Through the Wilderness 1989, Children of the Rainbow 1999, Young Turk (novel) 2004; contrib. to Menard Press, Voices Within the Art: The Modern Jewish Poets, Men Cards, European Judaism, Modern Poetry in Translation, Frank, Jewish Quarterly, Steaua (Romania), Confrontation (USA), North Atlantic Review (USA), Reflections on the Universal Declaration of Human Rights. *Address:* 11 North Square, London, NW11 7AB, England.

FARICY, Robert; academic and writer; b. 29 Aug. 1926, St Paul, Minnesota, USA. *Education:* BS, United States Naval Acad., 1949; PhL, 1954, MA, 1955, St Louis University; STL, Lyon-Fourvière Seminaire des Missions, 1963; STD, Catholic University of America, 1966. *Career:* Society of Jesus; Asst Prof., Catholic University of America, 1965–71; Prof. of Spiritual Theology, 1971–96, Prof. Emeritus, 1996–, Pontifical Gregorian University, Rome; Visiting Prof., Pontifical Urbaniana University, Rome, 2000–02; Prof., Regina Mundi Institute, Rome, 2000–. *Publications:* Seeking Jesus in Contemplation and Discernment, 1983; Medjugorje Up Close: Mary Speaks to the World (with L. Rooney), 1985; Contemplating Jesus (with R. Wicks), 1986; The Contemplative Way of Prayer (with L. Rooney), 1986; The Healing of the Religious Life (with S. Blackborow), 1986; Lord, Teach Us to Pray (with L. Rooney), 1986; Wind and Sea Obey Him: Approaches to a Theology of Nature, 1986; Medjugorje Journal (with L. Rooney), 1987; Lord Jesus, Teach Me to Pray (with L. Rooney), 1988; The Lord's Dealing, 1988; Mary Among Us, 1989; Medjugorje Retreat (with L. Rooney), 1989; Pilgrim's Journal, 1990; Our Lady Comes to Scottsdale (with L. Rooney), 1991; Return to God (with L. Rooney), 1993; Knowing Jesus in the World (with L. Rooney), 1996; Your Wounds I Will Heal (with L. Rooney), 1998. Contributions: numerous theological and philosophical journals. *Address:* c/o Pontifical Gregorian University, Piazza della Pilotta 4, 00187 Rome, Italy. *E-mail:* faricy@unigre.it.

FARLEY, Carol; Children's Book Writer; b. 20 Dec. 1936, Ludington, Michigan, USA; m. 21 June 1954, one s., three d. *Education:* Western Michigan University, 1956; BA, Michigan State University, 1980; MA, Children's Literature, Central Michigan University, 1983. *Career:* mem. MWA; Authors' Guild; Children's Book Guild; Society of Children's Book Writers; Chicago Children's Reading Round Table. *Publications:* Mystery of the Fog Man, 1974; The Garden is Doing Fine, 1976; Mystery in the Ravine, 1976; Mystery of the Melted Diamonds, 1985; Case of the Vanishing Villain, 1986; Case of the Lost Look Alike, 1988; Korea, Land of the Morning Calm, 1991; Mr Pak Buys a Story, 1997. Contributions: The Writer; Society of Children's Book Writer's Bulletin; Cricket; Disney Adventures; Challenge; Spider; Pockets; Appleseeds. *Honours:* Best Book of Year, Child Study Asscn, 1976; Best Juvenile Book by Mid-West Writer, Friends of the Writer, 1978; IRA/CBC Children's Choice Book, 1987. *Address:* 5448 Desert Paradise Dr., Las Vegas, NV 89130, USA.

FARMER, Beverley; Novelist; b. 1941, Australia. *Publications:* Alone, 1980; Short stories: Milk, 1983; Home Time, 1985; A Body of Water: A Year's Notebook, 1990; Place of Birth, 1990; The Seal Woman, 1992; The House in the Light, 1995; Collected Stories, 1996. *Address:* c/o University of Queensland Press, PO Box 42, St Lucia, Qld 4067, Australia.

FARMER, David Hugh; Lecturer, Reader and Writer; b. 30 Jan. 1923, Ealing, London, England; m. Pauline Ann Widgery 1966 (died 1999); two s. *Education:* BLitt, Linacre College, Oxford, 1967. *Career:* Lecturer, 1967–77, Reader, 1977–88, Reading University. *Publications:* Life of St Hugh of Lincoln, 1961; The Monk of Farne, 1962; The Rule of St Benedict, 1968; The Oxford Dictionary of Saints, 1978; Benedict's Disciples, 1980; The Age of Bede, 1983; St Hugh of Lincoln, 1985; Bede's Ecclesiastical History, 1990; Christ Crucified and Other Meditations, 1994. Contributions: St Augustine's Abbey (English Heritage), 1997; Benedictines in Oxford, 1997; The Story of Christian Spirituality, 2001; Dictionnaire D'Histoire Ecclesiastique; New Catholic Encyclopedia; Bibliotheca Sanctorum; Lexikon der Christlichen Ikonographie; Studia Monastica; Studia Anselmiana; Journal of Ecclesistical History; English Historical Review; The Tablet. *Honours:* Fellow, Society of Antiquaries 1962; FRHistS, 1967. *Address:* 23 Hartstock Ct, Shooters Hill, Pangbourne, Berkshire RG8 7BJ, England.

FARMER, Penelope (Jane); Writer; b. 14 June 1939, Westerham, Kent, England; m. 1st Michael John Mockridge, 16 Aug. 1962, divorced 1977, one s. one d.; m. 2nd Simon Shorvon, 20 Jan. 1984. *Education:* Degree in History, St Anne's College, Oxford, 1960; Diploma in Social Studies, Bedford College, London, 1962. *Career:* mem. PEN; Society of Authors. *Publications:* Fiction: Standing in the Shadow, 1984; Eve: Her Story, 1985; Away from Home, 1987; Glasshouses, 1988; Snakes and Ladders, 1993. Children's Books: The China People, 1960; The Summer Birds, 1962; The Magic Stone, 1964; The Saturday Shillings, 1965; The Seagull, 1965; Emma in Winter, 1966; Charlotte Sometimes, 1969; Dragonfly Summer, 1971; A Castle of Bone, 1972; William and Mary, 1974; Heracles, 1975; August the Fourth, 1975; Year King, 1977; The Coal Train, 1977; Beginnings: Creation Myths of the World (ed.), 1979; The Runaway Train, 1980; Thicker Than Water, 1989; Stone Croc, 1991; Penelope, 1994; Twin Trouble, 1996. Other: Anthology: Two: The Book of Twins and Doubles, 1996; Short stories; Radio and television scripts. Contributions: periodicals. *Honours:* American Library Asscn Notable Book, 1962; Carnegie Medal Commendation, 1963. *Address:* 12 Dalling Rd, London W6 0JB, England.

FARRINGTON, David Philip; Psychologist and Criminologist; b. 7 March 1944, Ormskirk, Lancashire, England; m. Sally Chamberlain, 30 July 1966, three d. *Education:* BA, 1966, MA, 1970, PhD, 1970, University of Cambridge. *Career:* Institute of Criminology, Cambridge, England; mem. Fellow, British Acad.; British Society of Criminology; British Psychological Society; European Asscn of Psychology and Law; American Society of Criminology; American Psychological Asscn; Asscn for Child Psychology and Psychiatry; Fellow, Acad. of Medical Sciences. *Publications:* Who Becomes Delinquent, 1973; The Delinquent Way of Life, 1977; Psychology, Law and Legal Processes, 1979; Behaviour Modification with Offenders, 1979; Abnormal Offenders, Delinquency and the Criminal Justice System, 1982; Prediction in Criminology, 1985; Reactions to Crime, 1985; Aggression and Dangerousness, 1985; Understanding and Controlling Crime, 1986; Human Development and Criminal Behaviour, 1991; Offenders and Victims, 1992; Integrating Individual and Ecological Aspects of Crime, 1993; Psychological Explanations of Crime, 1994; Building a Safer Society, 1995; Understanding and Preventing Youth Crime, 1996; Biosocial Bases of Violence, 1997; Serious and Violent Juvenile Offenders, 1998; Evaluating Criminology and Criminal Justice, 1998; Antisocial Behaviour and Mental Health Problems, 1998; Crime and Justice in the United States and in England and Wales 1981–96, 1998; Costs and Benefits of Preventing Crime, 2001; Child Delinquents: Development, Intervention and Service Needs, 2001; Offender Rehabilitation in Practice, 2001; Sex and Violence, 2001; Evidence-Based Crime Prevention, 2002; Early Prevention of Adult Antisocial Behaviour, 2003. Contributions: over 340 journal articles and book chapters. *Honours:* Sellin Glueck Award for International Contributions to Criminology, 1984; Sutherland Award for Outstanding Contributions to Criminology, 2002. *Address:* Institute of Criminology, 7 West Rd, Cambridge CB3 9DT, England.

FARROW, James S. (see Tubb, Edwin Charles).

FARROW, John (see Ferguson, Trevor).

FARTHING, Michael J. G., PhD; British gastroenterologist and ethics spokesperson; *Chairman, Committee on Publication Ethics. Career:* Ed., Gut magazine; Chair., Cttee on Publication Ethics (COPE); Exec. Dean of Medicine, Univ. of Glasgow 2000–03; Principal, St George's Hospital Medical School, London 2003; mem. General Medical Council. *Publications:* non-fiction: Clinical Challenges in Gastroenterology 1996, Fraud and Misconduct in Biomedical Research (co-author) 2001, Drug Therapy for Gastrointestinal Disease (ed.) 2001. *Address:* c/o Ms Rachel Fetches, Secretary COPE, BMJ Publishing Group Ltd, BMA House, Tavistock Square, London, WC1H 9JR, England. *Website:* www.publicationethics.org .uk.

FASQUELLE, Jean-Claude; French publisher; *Chairman of the Board, Éditions Grasset et Fasquelle*; b. 29 Nov. 1930, Paris; m. 1st Solange de la Rochefoucauld; one d.; m. 2nd Nicola Jegher 1966. *Education:* Ecole des Roches, Verneuil-sur-Avre, Sorbonne and Faculté de Droit, Paris. *Career:* Pres.-Dir-Gen. Société des Editions Fasquelle 1953–60, Editions du Sagittaire 1958–; Admin.-Dir-Gen. Editions Grasset et Fasquelle 1960, Pres.-Dir-Gen. 1980–2000, Chair. of Bd 2000–; Dir Le Magazine littéraire (monthly) 1970–2004. *Address:* Éditions Grasset et Fasquelle, 61 rue des Saintes-Pères, 75006 Paris (Office); 13 Square Vergennes, 75015 Paris, France (Home). *Telephone:* 1-44-39-22-00 (Office). *Fax:* 1-44-39-22-18 (Office).

FATCHEN, Maxwell Edgar; Author and Poet; b. 3 Aug. 1920, Adelaide, SA, Australia; m. Jean Wohlers, 15 May 1942, two s. one d. *Career:* Journalist, Feature Writer, Adelaide News, 1946–55; Special Writer, 1955, 1981–84, Literary Ed., 1971–81, The Advertiser; mem. Australian Society of Authors; Australian Fellowship of Writers; South Australian Writers Centre; Media Alliance. *Publications:* The River Kings, 1966; Conquest of the River, 1970; The Spirit Wind, 1973; Chase Through the Night, 1977; Closer to the Stars, 1981; Wry Rhymes, 1987; A Country Christmas, 1990; Tea for Three, 1994. Contributions: Denver Post; Sydney Sun; Regional South Australian Histories. *Honours:* AM, 1980; Advance Australia Award for Literature, 1991; AMP-Walkley Award for Journalism, 1996; SA Great Award for Literature, 1999. *Address:* 15 Jane St, Box 6, Smithfield, SA 5114, Australia.

FAULKS, Sebastian, CBE, BA, FRSL; British writer and journalist; b. 20 April 1953, Newbury, Berkshire, England; m. Veronica Youlten 1989; two s. one d. *Education:* Emmanuel Coll., Cambridge. *Career:* reporter, Daily Telegraph 1979–83; feature writer, Sunday Telegraph 1983–86; Literary Ed., The Independent 1986–89; Deputy Ed. 1989–90, Assoc. Ed. 1990–91, The Independent on Sunday; columnist, The Guardian 1992–97, Evening Standard 1996–98, Mail on Sunday 1999–2000. *Publications:* A Trick of the Light 1984, The Girl at the Lion d'Or 1989, A Fool's Alphabet 1992, Birdsong 1993, The Fatal Englishman 1996, Charlotte Gray 1998, On Green Dolphin Street 2001. *Literary Agent:* Gillon Aitken Associates Ltd, 18–21 Cavaye Place, London, SW10 9PT, England. *Telephone:* (20) 7373-8672. *Fax:* (20) 7373-6002.

FAWKES, Richard Brian; Writer, Dramatist and Film Dir; b. 31 July 1944, Camberley, Surrey, England; m. Cherry Elizabeth Cole, 17 April 1971, two

s. one d. *Education:* BA, St David's University College, 1967. *Career:* mem. Society of Authors; Society for Theatre Research. *Publications:* The Last Corner of Arabia (with Michael Darlow), 1976; Fighting for a Laugh, 1978; Dion Boucicault: A Biography, 1979; Notes from a Low Singer (with Michael Langdon), 1982; Welsh National Opera, 1986. Other: Plays for stage, radio, and television; Documentary film scripts. Contributions: journals and magazines including, BBC Music Magazine, Opera Now, Classical Music and Daily Telegraph. *Honours:* West Midlands Arts Asscn Bursary, 1978. *Address:* 5–8 Lower John St, Golden Sq., London W1R 4HA, England.

FEDER, Kenneth, MA, PhD; archaeologist and writer; b. 1 Aug. 1952, New York, USA; m. Melissa Jean Kalogeros, 30 Aug. 1981, two s. *Education:* State University of New York, University of Connecticut. *Career:* Prof. of Anthropology, Central Conecticut State University, 1977–. *Publications:* Human Antiquity (with Michael Park), 1989; Frauds, Myths and Mysteries: Science and Pseudoscience in Archaeology, 1990; A Village of Outcasts: Historical Archaeology and Documentary Research at the Lighthouse, 1994; The Past In Perspective: An Introduction to Human Prehistory, 1996; Field Methods in Archaeology (with Tom Hester and Harry Shafer), 1997; Lessons From the Past, 1999; Dangerous Places: Health and Safety in Archaeology (ed. with David Poirier), 2001; Atlantis: Fact or Fiction, The Trojan War, Theseus and the Minotaur, Jason and the Argonauts (contributions to The Seventy Great Mysteries of the Ancient World, ed. by Brian Fagan, 2001), Linking to the Past 2004. *Honours:* Fellow Cttee for the Scientific Investigation of Claims of the Paranormal, Excellence in Teaching Central Connecticut State University. *Address:* c/o Dept of Anthropology, Central Conecticut State University, New Britain, CT 06050, USA. *E-mail:* feder@mail.ccsu.edu.

FEDERMAN, Raymond; Distinguished Prof., Novelist, Poet and Trans; b. 15 May 1928, Paris, France; m. Erica Hubscher, 14 Sept. 1960, one d. *Education:* BA cum laude, Columbia University, 1957; MA, 1958, PhD, 1963, University of California at Los Angeles. *Career:* Asst Prof., University of California at Los Angeles, 1960–64; Assoc. Prof. of French and Comparative Literature, 1964–68, Prof. of Comparative Literature, 1968–73, Prof. of English and Comparative Literature, 1973–90, Distinguished Prof., 1990–, SUNY at Buffalo; mem. American PEN Centre; Fiction Collective, board mem., 1988–, dir, 1989–94. *Publications:* Fiction: Double or Nothing, 1971; Amer Eldorado, 1974; Take It or Leave It, 1976; The Voice in the Closet, 1979; The Twofold Vibration, 1982; Smiles on Washington Square, 1985; To Whom It May Concern, 1990. Non-Fiction: Journey to Chaos, 1965; Samuel Beckett, 1970; Surfiction, 1976; Critifiction, 1992; The Supreme Indecision of the Writer, 1996. Poetry: Temporary Landscapes, 1965; Among the Beasts, 1967; Me Too, 1975; Duel, 1989; Autobiographic Poems, 1991. Contributions: Reviews, journals, and magazines. *Honours:* Guggenheim Fellowship, 1966–67; Frances Steloff Fiction Prize, 1971; Panache Experimental Prize, 1972; American Book Award, 1986.

FEIFFER, Jules (Ralph); Cartoonist, Writer, Dramatist and Screenwriter; b. 26 Jan. 1929, New York, NY, USA; m. Judith Sheftel, 1961, one d. *Education:* Art Students League; Pratt Institute. *Career:* Contributing cartoonist, Village Voice, New York City, 1956–97; Cartoons nationally syndicated in USA, 1959–. *Publications:* Sick, Sick, Sick, 1959; Passionella and Other Stories, 1960; The Explainers, 1961; Boy, Girl, Boy, Girl, 1962; Hold Me!, 1962; Harry, The Rat With Women (novel), 1963; Feiffer's Album, 1963; The Unexpurgated Memoirs of Bernard Mergendeiler, 1965; The Great Comic Book Heroes, 1967; Feiffer's Marriage Manual, 1967; Pictures at a Prosecution, 1971; Ackroyd (novel), 1978; Tantrum, 1980; Jules Feiffer's America: From Eisenhower to Reagan, 1982; Marriage is an Invasion of Privacy, 1984; Feiffer's Children, 1986; Ronald Reagan in Movie America, 1988; Elliott Loves, 1990. Other: Plays and screenplays. *Honours:* Acad. Award for Animated Cartoon, 1961; Special George Polk Memorial Award, 1962. *Address:* c/o Universal Press Syndicate, 4900 Main St, Kansas City, MO 64112, USA.

FEINSTEIN, (Allan) David; psychologist and writer; b. 22 Dec. 1946, New York, NY, USA; m. Donna Eden 1984. *Education:* BA, Whittier College, 1968; MA, US International University, 1970; PhD, Union Institute, 1973. *Career:* mem. American Psychological Asscn; Asscn for Humanistic Psychology. *Publications:* Personal Mythology, 1988; Rituals for Living and Dying, 1990; The Mythic Path, 1997; Energy Medicine, 1999; Energy Psychology Interactive, 2003. Contributions: The Futurist; Common Boundary; Psychotherapy; American Journal of Hypnosis; American Journal of Orthopsychiatry. *Honours:* William James Award, Whittier College, 1968; Outstanding Contribution Award, Asscn for Comprehensive Energy Psychology, 2002. *Literary Agent:* Margaret McBride Agency, San Diego, CA, USA. *Address:* 777 E Main Street, Ashland, OR 97520, USA.

FEIST, Raymond E., BA; American writer; b. 1945, Los Angeles, CA; m. Kathleen Starbuck; one c. *Education:* Univ. of California, San Diego, CA. *Publications include:* novels: Magician 1982, Silverthorn 1985, A Darkness at Sethanon 1986, Magician's Apprentice 1986, Master 1986, Daughter of the Empire 1987, Faerie Tale 1988, Prince of the Blood 1989, Servant of the Empire 1990, Mistress of the Empire 1992, The King's Buccaneer 1992, Shadow of a Dark Queen 1994, Rise of a Merchant Prince 1995, Rage of a Demon King 1997, Shards of a Broken Crown 1998, The Betrayal 1998, The Assassins 1999, Tear of the Gods 2000, The Atlas of Midkemia 2000, Krondor 2001, Murder in Lamut 2002, Birthright: The Book of Man 2002, Honoured Enemy 2002, Talon of the Silver Hawk 2002, King of Foxes 2003, Jimmy the Hand 2003, Exile's Return 2004. *Address:* c/o Voyager, Harper Collins Publishing, 10 E 53rd Street, New York, NY 10022, USA. *Website:* www.harpercollins.com.

FEKETE, John, BA, MA, PhD; professor of English and cultural studies and writer; b. 7 Aug. 1946, Budapest, Hungary. *Education:* McGill Univ., Univ. of Cambridge. *Career:* Visiting Asst Prof. of English, McGill Univ., Montréal, QC 1973–74; Assoc. Ed., Telos 1974–84; Visiting Asst Prof. of Humanities, York Univ., Toronto, ON 1975–76; Asst Prof. 1976–78, Assoc. Prof. 1978–84, Prof. of English and Cultural Studies 1984–, Trent Univ., Peterborough, ON. *Publications:* The Critical Twilight: Explorations in the Ideology of Anglo-American Literary Theory from Eliot to McLuhan, 1978; The Structural Allegory: Reconstructive Encounters With the New French Thought, 1984; Life After Postmodernism: Essays on Culture and Value, 1987; Moral Panic: Biopolitics Rising, 1994. Contributions: Canadian Journal of Political and Social Theory; Canadian Journal of Communications; Science-Fiction Studies. *Address:* 181 Wallis Drive, Peterborough, ON K9J 6C4, Canada. *E-mail:* jfekete@trentu.ca.

FELDMAN, Alan Grad; Writer, Poet and Teacher; b. 16 March 1945, New York, NY, USA; m. Nanette Hass, 22 Oct. 1972, one s. one d. *Education:* AB, Columbia College, 1966; MA, Columbia University, 1969; PhD, SUNY at Buffalo, 1973. *Publications:* The Household, 1966; The Happy Genius, 1978; Frank O'Hara, 1978; The Personals, 1982; Lucy Mastermind, 1985; Anniversary, 1992. Contributions: New Yorker; Atlantic; Kenyon Review; Mississippi Review; Ploughshares; North American Review; Threepenny Review; Boston Review; Tendril; College English. *Honours:* Award for Best Short Story in a College Literary Magazine, Saturday Review-National Student Asscn, 1965; Elliston Book Award for Best Book of Poems by a Small Press in US, 1978. *Address:* 399 Belknap Rd, Framingham, MA 01701, USA.

FELDMAN, Gerald D(onald); Prof. of History and Writer; b. 24 April 1937, New York, NY, USA; m. 1st, one s. one d.; m. 2nd Norma von Ragenfeld, 30 Nov. 1983. *Education:* BA, Columbia College, 1958; MA, 1959, PhD, 1964, Harvard University. *Career:* Asst Prof., 1963–68, Assoc. Prof., 1968–70, Prof. of History, 1970–, Dir, Center for German and European Studies, 1994–, Chancellor's Professorship, 1997–2000; University of California at Berkeley; Karl W. Deutsch Guest Prof., Wissenschaftszentrum Berlin, Oct.–Dec. 1997; Berlin Prize Fellow, American Acad. in Berlin, 1998–99; Dir, Institute of European Studies, University of California at Berkeley, 2000–. *Publications:* Army, Industry and Labor in Germany, 1914–1918, 1966; German Imperialism, 1914–1918, 1972; A Documentary History of Modern Europe (with Thomas G. Barnes), 4 vols, 1972; Iron and Steel in the German Inflation, 1916–1923, 1977; The German Inflation Reconsidered: A Preliminary Balance (with Carl-Ludwig Holtfrerich, Gerhard A Ritter, and Peter-Christian Witt), 1982; The Experience of Inflation: International Comparative Studies (with Carl-Ludwig Holtfrerich, Gerhard A Ritter, and Peter-Christian Witt), 1984; Die Anpassung and die Inflation/The Adaption to Inflation (with Carl-Ludwig Holtfrerich, Gerhard A Ritter, and Peter-Christian Witt), 1986; Konsequenzen der Inflation/Consequences of Inflation (with Carl-Ludwig Holtfrerich Gerhard A Ritter and Peter-Christian Witt), 1989; Arbeiter, Unternehmer und Staat im Bergbau: Industrielle Beziehungen im internationalen Vergleich (with Klaus Tenfelde), 1989, English trans. as Workers, Owners and Politics in Coal Mining: An International Comparison of Industrial Relations, 1990; Great Disorder: Politics, Economics, and Society in the German Inflation, 1916–1924, 1993; The Evolution of Financial Institutions and Markets in Twentieth-Century Europe (with Youssef Cassis and Ulf Olsson), 1995; How to Write the History of a Bank (with Martin M. G. Fase and Manfred Pohl), 1995; Hugo Stinnes: Biographie eines Industriellen, 1870–1914, 1998; Allianz and the German Insurance Business, 1933–1945, 2001; The Treaty of Versailles: A Reassessment after 75 Years (co-ed. with Manfred F. Boemeke and Elisabeth Glaser), 1998. Contributions: many scholarly books and journals. *Honours:* ACLS Fellowships, 1966–67, 1970–71; Guggenheim Fellowship, 1973–74; National Endowment for the Humanities Fellowship, 1977–78; German Marshall Fund Fellow, 1981–82; Rockefeller Foundation Center Residency, Bellagio, Italy, 1987; Woodrow Wilson Center Fellow, 1991–92; Book Prize, Conference Group for Central European History, American Historical Asscn, 1995; DAAD Book Prize, German Studies Asscn, 1995; Co-Winner, Financial Times/Booz-Allen & Hamilton Business Book Award, 1995; Commander's Cross of the Order of Merit of the Federal Republic of Germany, 2000; Co-winner, Hagley Prize for Best Book in Business History, 2002; Alexander von Humboldt Research Prize Fellow, 2002–2003. *Address:* c/o University of California at Berkeley, Dept of History, Berkeley, CA 94720, USA.

FELDMAN, Irving (Mordecai); Prof. of English and Poet; b. 22 Sept. 1928, New York, NY, USA; m. Carmen Alvarez del Olmo, 1955, one s. *Education:* BS, City College, CUNY, 1950; MA, Columbia University, 1953. *Career:* Teacher, University of Puerto Rico, Rio Piedras, 1954–56, University of Lyons, France, 1957–58, Kenyon College, Gambier, Ohio, 1958–64; Prof. of English, SUNY at Buffalo, 1964–. *Publications:* Poetry: Work and Days and Other Poems, 1961; The Pripet Marshes and Other Poems, 1965; Magic Papers and Other Poems, 1970; Lost Originals, 1972; Leaping Clear, 1976; New and Selected Poems, 1979; Teach Me, Dear Sister, and Other Poems, 1983; All of us Here and Other Poems, 1986; Beautiful False Things, 2000.

Other: The Life and Letters, 1994. *Honours:* Kovner Award, Jewish Book Council of America, 1962; Ingram Merrill Foundation Grant, 1963; American Acad. of Arts and Letters Grant, 1973; Guggenheim Fellowship, 1973; Creative Artists Public Service Grant, 1980; Acad. of American Poets Fellowship, 1986; John D. and Catherine T. MacArthur Foundation Fellowship, 1992. *Address:* c/o Dept of English, State University of New York at Buffalo, Buffalo, NY 14260, USA.

FELDMAN, Paula R.; Prof. of English and Writer; b. 4 July 1948, Washington, DC, USA; m. Peter Mugglestone; two c. *Education:* BA, Bucknell University, 1970; MA, 1971, PhD, 1974, Northwestern University. *Career:* Asst Prof., English, 1974–79, Assoc. Prof., English, 1979–89, Prof., English, 1989–, Dir, Graduate Studies in English, 1991–93, C. Wallace Martin Prof. of English, 1999–; Louise Fry Scudder Prof. of Liberal Arts, 2000–, University of South Carolina, Columbia. *Publications:* The Microcomputer and Business Writing (with David Byrd and Phyllis Fleishel), 1986; The Journals of Mary Shelley (ed. with Diana Scott-Kilvert), 2 vols, 1987; The Wordworthy Computer: Classroom and Research Applications in Language and Literature (with Buford Norman), 1987; Romantic Women Writers: Voices and Countervoices (ed. with Theresa Kelley), 1995; British Women Poets of the Romantic Era: An Anthology, 1997; A Century of Sonnets: The Romantic Era Revival 1750–1850 (ed. with Daniel Robinson), 1999; Records of Woman (ed.), 1999. Contributions: Studies in English Literature; Keats-Shelley Journal; Papers of the Bibliographical Society of America; ADE Bulletin, 1995; New Literary History, 2002; Approaches to Teaching Shelley's Frankenstein, 1990; Blake: An Illustrated Quarterly, 1994; Approaches to Teaching the Women Romantic Poets, 1997; Romanticism and Women Poets, 1997; Cambridge Guide to Women's Writing, 1999. *Address:* Dept of English, University of South Carolina, Columbia, SC 29208, USA. *Telephone:* (803) 777-4204. *Fax:* (803) 777-9064. *E-mail:* pfeldman@sc.rr.com. *Website:* www.cla.sc.edu/ENGL/faculty/bios/feldman/feldman.htm.

FELL, Alison; Writer and Poet; b. 4 June 1944, Dumfries, Scotland; m. Roger Coleman, 1964, divorced 1966, one s. *Education:* Diploma in Sculpture, Edinburgh College of Art, 1967; Postgraduate Certificate in Education, English, Media Studies, University of London, Institute of Education, 1981; National Film School, 1992. *Career:* Co-founder, Welfare State Theatre, Leeds-Bradford, 1970, Women's Street Theatre, London, 1971; Journalist, Underground Press, 1971–75; Fiction Ed., Spare Rib, 1975–79; C. Day-Lewis Fellow and Writer-in-Residence, London Borough of Brent, 1978; Writer-in-Residence, London Borough of Walthamstow, 1981–82, New South Wales Institute of Technology, Australia, 1986; Guest Writer, Female Eye Conference, Huddersfield, England, 1996; Writing Fellow, University of East Anglia, 1998; British Council tours to Germany, Canada and USA, 1996–97, 2000; Co-Judge, Presenter, New Blood Competition, Institute of Contemporary Arts, 1996; Royal Literary Fund Fellow, University College London, 2002–03; Research Fellow, Middlesex Univ., 2003–; has led writing workshops; readings from her works. *Publications:* Fiction: The Grey Dancer, 1981; Every Move You Make, 1984; The Bad Box, 1987; Mer de Glace, 1991; The Pillow Boy of the Lady Onogoro, 1994; The Mistress of Lilliput, 1999; Tricks of the Light, 2003. Poetry: Kisses for Mayakovsky, 1984; The Crystal Owl, 1988; Dreams, like heretics, 1997. Other: The Shining Mountain, 1989; Dionysus Day (prose poem), 1992; The Weaver (feature film), 1993; Whispers in the Dark, 1995; Medea: Mapping the Edge (play), 2001. Contributions: Books and magazines. *Honours:* Alice Hunt Bartlett Prize, National Poetry Society, 1984; Boardman Tasker Award for Mountain Literature, 1991. *Literary Agent:* Peake Associates, 14 Grafton Crescent, London NW1 8SL, England.

FELLOWES, Julian Alexander; British novelist, screenwriter, actor and producer; b. 6 Aug. 1949, Egypt; m. Emma Kitchener-Fellowes 1990; one s. *Education:* Magdalene Coll., Cambridge. *Career:* numerous television and film appearances. *Screenplays:* Little Lord Fauntleroy (Emmy Award) 1995, The Prince and the Pauper (also prod.) 1996, Gosford Park (also prod.) (New York Film Critic's Circle Best Screenplay, Nat. Soc. of Film Critics Best Screenplay, Acad. Award for Best Original Screenplay) 2001, Vanity Fair 2004. *Publications:* novel: Snobs: A Novel 2004; other: A viewer's guide to Aristocrats 1999; fiction as Rebecca Greville: Poison Presented 1975, Court in the Terror 1976. *Address:* c/o Weidenfield & Nicholson, Orion House, 5 Upper St Martin's Lane, London, WC2H 9EA, England. *Telephone:* (20) 7240-3444. *Fax:* (20) 7240-4822. *Website:* www.orionbooks.com.

FENDRICH, James Max; Sociologist and Writer; b. 31 Oct. 1938, Salem, SD, USA; m. 1st Judith Curtin-Ausman, 1963, divorced 1983; m. 2nd Mary E. Bryant, 22 Dec. 1985, two s. two d. *Education:* BA, Seattle University, 1960; MA, University of Notre Dame, 1962; PhD, Michigan State University, 1965. *Career:* Asst Prof., 1965–68, Assoc. Prof., 1968–74, Prof. of Sociology, 1974–94, Florida State University, Tallahassee; Consulting; mem. American Sociological Asscn; Southern Sociological Asscn; Society for the Study of Social Problems. *Publications:* Leadership in American Society: A Case Study of Black Leadership (co-author), 1969; Ideal Citizens: The Legacy of the Civil Rights Movement, 1993.

FENNARIO, David; Playwright; b. 26 April 1947, Verdun, QC, Canada; m. Elizabeth Fennario, 1976, one c. *Education:* Dawson College, Montréal, 1969–71. *Career:* Playwright-in-Residence, Centaur Theatre, Montréal, 1973–; Co-Founder, Cultural Workers Asscn; mem. International Socialist. *Publications:* Plays: On the Job, 1976; Nothing to Lose, 1977; Without a Parachute, 1978; Balconville, 1980; Changes, 1980; Moving, 1983; Joe Beef, 1991; Doctor Thomas Weill Cream, 1994; Placeville Marie, 1996. *Honours:* Canada Council Grant, 1973; Chalmers Awards, 1976, 1979; Prix Pauline Julien, 1986.

FENNELLY, Antonia, (Tony Fennelly); Author; b. 25 Nov. 1945, Orange, NJ, USA; m. James Richard Catoire, 24 Dec. 1972. *Education:* BA, Drama and Communications, University of New Orleans, 1976. *Career:* mem. MWA; Authors' Guild; International Asscn of Crime Writers; Sisters in Crime. *Publications:* The Glory Hole Murders, 1985; The Closet Hanging, 1987; Kiss Yourself Goodbye, 1989; Der Hippie in Der Wand, 1992; Hurenglanz, 1993; 1(900) D-E-A-D, 1997. *Honours:* Edgar Allan Poe Special Award, MWA, 1986. *Address:* 921 Clouet St, New Orleans, LA 70117, USA.

FENNER, Carol (Elizabeth); Children's Writer and Illustrator; b. 30 Sept. 1929, Almond, New York, USA; m. Jiles B. Williams, 3 July 1965. *Career:* mem. Society of Children's Book Writers and Illustrators. *Publications:* Tigers in the Cellar, 1963; Christmas Tree on the Mountain, 1966; Lagalag, the Wanderer, 1968; Gorilla, Gorilla, 1973; The Skates of Uncle Richard, 1978; Saving Amelia Earhart, 1982; A Summer of Horses, 1989; Randall's Wall, 1991; Yolonda's Genius, 1995; The King of Dragons, 1998. Contributions: Magazines. *Honours:* Notable Book Citations, 1963, 1973, Newbery Honor Book, 1996, American Library Asscn; Christopher Medal, 1973; Library of Congress Book of the Year, 1973; Michigan Council for the Arts Literature Grant, 1982; Readers' Choice Master Lists Citations, 1991–92; Maryland Children's Book Award, 1997; Patterson Prize, 1999. *Address:* 190 Rebecca Rd, Battle Creek, MI 49015, USA.

FENNER, James R. (see Tubb, Edwin Charles).

FENNO, Jack (see Calisher, Hortense).

FENTON, James (Martin); Prof. of Poetry, Poet and Writer; b. 25 April 1949, Lincoln, England. *Education:* MA, Magdalen College, Oxford, 1970. *Career:* Asst Literary Ed., 1971, Editorial Asst, 1972, Political Columnist, 1976–78, New Statesman; Freelance Correspondent, Indo-China, 1973–75; German Correspondent, Guardian, 1978–79; Theatre Critic, Sunday Times, 1979–84; Chief Book Reviewer, Times, 1984–86; Far East Correspondent, 1986–88, Columnist, 1993–95, Independent; Prof. of Poetry, University of Oxford, 1994–99. *Publications:* Our Western Furniture, 1968; Terminal Moraine, 1972; A Vacant Possession, 1978; A German Requiem, 1980; Dead Soldiers, 1981; The Memory of War, 1982; Rigoletto, by Giuseppe Verdi (trans.), 1982; You Were Marvellous, 1983; The Original Michael Frayn, 1983; Children in Exile, 1984; Poems 1968–83, 1985; Simon Boccanegra, by Giuseppe Verdi (trans.), 1985; The Fall of Saigon, 1985; The Snap Revolution, 1986; Cambodian Witness: The Autobiography of Someth May (ed.), 1986; Partingtime Hall (poems with John Fuller), 1987; All the Wrong Places: Adrift in the Politics of Asia, 1988; Manila Evelope, 1989; Underground in Japan, by Rey Ventura (ed.), 1992; Out of Danger (poems), 1993; Leonardo's Nephew: Essays on Art and Artists, 1998; The Strength of Poetry: Oxford Lectures, 2001; An Introduction to English Poetry, 2002; The Love Bomb and Other Musical Pieces, 2003. *Honours:* FRSL; Hon. Fellow, Magdalen College, Oxford, 1999. *Literary Agent:* PFD, Drury House, 34–43 Russell St, London WC2B 5HA, England.

FÉRAL, Josette, PhD; Canadian critic and dramaturg. *Education:* Université de Paris. *Career:* Prof., Univ. of Toronto 1978–81; Titular Prof., École Supérieure de Théâtre de l'Université du Québec 1981, Montréal; Dir Dept of Theatre, Université du Québec 1992–94; Vice-Pres. Int. Federation for Theatre Research (FIRT) 1995–99, Pres. 1999–2003. *Publications:* non-fiction: La Culture contre l'art 1990, Dresser un monument à l'éphémère 1995, Mise en scène et Jeu de l'acteur (two vols) 1997–98, Trajectoires du soleil 1998, Les Chemins de l'acteur, Acerca de la teatralidad 2004; editor: Théâtralité, écriture et mise en scène 1985, Substance 98/99 2002, L'école du jeu 2003, Ariane Mnouchkine und Das Théâtre du Soleil 2003, Theatre in France: Ten Years of Research; contrib. to numerous books and journals. *Honours:* Prix Jean Beraud 1989–90. *Address:* c/o École Supérieure de Théâtre, Université du Québec à Montréal, CP 8888, succursale Centre-Ville, Montréal, H3C 3P8, Canada. *Telephone:* (514) 987 4116. *E-mail:* feral .josette@uqam.ca. *Website:* www.josette-feral.org.

FERDINANDY, György, (Georges Ferdinandy); Prof. and Author; b. 11 Oct. 1935, Budapest, Hungary; m. 1st Colette Peyrethon, 27 May 1958; m. 2nd Maria Teresa Reyes-Cortes, 3 Jan. 1981, three s., one d. *Education:* Doctorate in Literature, University of Strasbourg, France, 1969. *Career:* Freelance Literary Critic, Radio Free Europe, 1977–86; Prof., University of Puerto Rico, Cayey, Puerto Rico; mem. Société des Gens de Lettres, France; Hungarian Writers' Asscn; International PEN. *Publications:* In French: L'ile sous l'eau, 1960; Famine au Paradis, 1962; Le seul jour de l'annèe, 1967; Itinéraires, 1973; Chica, Claudine, Cali, 1973; L'oeuvre hispanoaméricaine de Zs Remenyik, 1975; Fantomes magnétiques, 1979; Youri, 1983; Hors jeu, 1986; Mémoires d'un exil terminé, 1992; Entre chien et loup, 1996. In Hungarian: Latoszemueknek, 1962; Tizenharom Töredék, 1964; Futoszalagon, 1965; Nemezio Gonzalex, 1970; Valencianal a tenger, 1975; Mammuttemetö, 1982; A Mosoly Albuma, 1982; Az elveszett gyermek, 1984; A Vadak Utjan, 1986; Szerecsenségem Története, 1988; Furcsa, idegen szerelem, 1990; Uzenöfüzet, 1991; Szomorü Szigetek, 1992; A Francia Völegény, 1993; Ta'vlattan, 1994; Az Amerikai telefon, 1996. Contributions: Le

Monde; NRF; Europe; Elet és Irodalom; Kortars; Uj Hold; Magyar Naplo. *Honours:* Del Duca Prix, 1961; St Exupéry Literary Award, 1964; Book of the Year, 1993; Prize Jòzsef Attila, Budapest, 1995; Prize Ma'rai Sàndor, Budapest, 1997. *Address:* Joaquin Lopez Lopez 1056, Sta Rita, Rio Piedras, PR 00925, USA.

FERGUSON, Gillian K.; British poet and journalist; b. Edinburgh, Scotland. *Education:* Univ. of Edinburgh. *Career:* jewellery maker, artist. *Publications:* poetry: Air for Sleeping Fish 1997, Baby 2000; contrib. to anthologies, including Making for Planet Alice, journals, including Scotland on Sunday, The Scotsman, The Herald, Financial Times, Home Truths (BBC Radio 4). *Honours:* three Writers' Bursaries from the Scottish Arts Council ; prizewinner, Daily Telegraph Arvon International Poetry Competition. *Address:* c/o Bloodaxe Books Ltd, Highgreen, Tarset, Northumberland NE48 1RP, England. *Telephone:* (1434) 240500. *Fax:* (1434) 240505. *Website:* www.bloodaxebooks.com.

FERGUSON, Joseph (Francis); Critic, Writer and Poet; b. 11 Feb. 1952, Yonkers, New York, USA; m. Janice Robinson, 30 July 1986, one s. *Education:* BA, SUNY at New Paltz, 1979; MS (not completed), Pace University. *Career:* Critic for various publications. *Publications:* Contributions: fiction and poetry in many anthologies and other publications; Articles and columns in numerous publications. *Honours:* Honorable mention, American Poetry Asscn Contest, 1989; Honorable mention, World of Poetry Contest, 1990; Golden Poet, World of Poetry, 1990; Distinguished Poet of America, 1993. *Address:* 26 Bank St, Cold Spring, NY 10516, USA.

FERGUSON, Niall, MA, DPhil; British economic historian; *Herzog Professor of Financial History, Stern School of Business*; b. 18 April 1964, British; m. Susan M. Douglas 1994; two s. one d. *Education:* Univ. of Oxford, Univ. of Hamburg. *Career:* Fellow Christ's Coll., Cambridge 1989–90, Peterhouse, Cambridge 1990–92, Jesus Coll., Oxford, 1992–; Prof. of Political and Financial History Univ. of Oxford 2000–2002, Herzog Prof.of Financial History, Stern School of Business, Univ. of New York 2003–, Sr Fellow, Hoover Inst., Stanford Univ. 2003–. *Television:* Empire 2003. *Publications:* Paper and Iron: Hamburg Business and German Politics in the Era of Inflation 1897–1927 1995, (ed.) Virtual History: Alternatives and Counterfactuals 1997, The World's Banker: A History of the House of Rothschild, The Pity of War 1998, The Cash Nexus: Money and Power in the Modern World 1700–2000 2001, Empire: How Britain Made the Modern World 2003, Colossus: the Price of America's Empire 2004. *Honours:* Wadsworth Prize for Business History 1998. *Address:* Leonard N. Stern School of Business, Henry Kaufman Management Center, 44 West Fourth Street, Floor 7: Economics Department, KMC Room #7-79, New York, NY 10012, USA. *Telephone:* (212) 998-0062 (Office). *E-mail:* nferguso@stern.nyu.edu.

FERGUSON, Robert Thomas, BA; writer; b. 2 June 1948, Stoke on Trent, England; m. 1987. *Education:* Univ. Coll. London. *Publications:* Enigma: The Life of Knut Hamsun 1987, Henry Miller: A Life 1991, Henrik Ibsen: A New Biography 1996, Dr Ibsens Gjengangere (in Norwegian, Dr Ibsen's Ghosts, radio play) 1999, Siste Kjaerlighet (in Norwegian, Last Love, novel) 2002, The Short Sharp Life of T. E. Hulme 2002, Fleetwood (in Norwegian, novel) 2004; contrib. to Best Radio Drama 1984, Best Radio Drama 1986. *Honours:* BBC Methuen Giles Cooper Awards 1984, 1986, J. G. Robertson Prize 1985–87. *Address:* Trudvangvn 25, 0363 Oslo, Norway. *E-mail:* robert.ferguson@c2i.net.

FERGUSON, Trevor, (John Farrow); Author; b. 11 Nov. 1947, Seaforth, ON, Canada; m. Lynne Hill, 1985. *Career:* mem. Writers' Union of Canada, chair., 1990–91. *Publications:* High Water Chants, 1977; Onyx John, 1985; The Kinkajou, 1989; The True Life Adventures of Sparrow Drinkwater, 1993; The Fire Line, 1995; The Timekeeper, 1995. As John Farrow: City of Ice, 1999; Ice Lake, 2001. *Honours:* Hugh MacLennan Award for Fiction, Québec Writers' Federation, 1996. *Address:* c/o Anne McDermid and Assocs, 92 Willcocks St, Toronto, ON M5S 1C8, Canada.

FERGUSON, William Rotch; academic, writer and poet; b. 14 Feb. 1943, Fall River, MA, USA; m. Nancy King 1983. *Education:* BA, 1965, MA, 1970, PhD, 1975, Harvard University. *Career:* Instructor, 1971–75, Asst Prof., 1975–77, Boston University; Visiting Prof., 1977–79, Asst Prof., 1979–83, Assoc. Prof. of Spanish, 1983–, Adjunct Prof. of English, 1989–, Chair., Foreign Languages, 1990–98, Clark University, Worcester, Massachusetts; Visiting Lecturer in Spanish Renaissance Literature, University of Pennsylvania, 1986–87; Assoc. Ed., Hispanic Review, 1986–87; mem. American Asscn of University Profs; International Institute in Spain; MLA. *Publications:* Dream Reader (poems), 1973; Light of Paradise (poems), 1973; La versificación imitativa en Fernando de Herrera, 1981; Freedom and Other Fictions (short stories), 1984. Contributions: scholarly journals, anthologies, periodicals and magazines. *Address:* 1 Tahanto Road, Worcester, MA 01602, USA.

FERLINGHETTI, Lawrence (Monsanto); Poet, Writer, Dramatist, Publisher, Ed. and Painter; b. 24 March 1920, Yonkers, New York, USA; m. Selden Kirby-Smith, April 1951, divorced, one s. one d. *Education:* AB, University of North Carolina, 1941; MA, Columbia University, 1948; Doctorate, Sorbonne, University of Paris, 1951. *Career:* Co-Owner, City Lights Pocket Bookshop, later City Lights Books, San Francisco, 1953–; Founder-Ed., City Lights Books, publishing, San Francisco, 1955–; many poetry readings; Participation in many national and international literary conferences; Retrospective exhibition of paintings, Palazzo delle Esposizione, Rome, Italy, 1996. *Publications:* Poetry: Pictures of the Gone World, 1955; A Coney Island of the Mind, 1958; Berlin, 1961; Starting from San Francisco, 1961; Where is Vietnam?, 1965; An Eye on the World: Selected Poems, 1967; After the Cries of the Birds, 1967; The Secret Meaning of Things, 1969; Tyrannus Nix?, 1969; Back Roads to Far Places, 1971; Open Eye, Open Heart, 1973; Who Are We Now?, 1976; Landscapes of Living and Dying, 1979; A Trip to Italy and France, 1980; Endless Life: Selected Poems, 1984; Over All the Obscene Boundaries: European Poems and Transitions, 1985; Inside the Trojan Horse, 1987; When I Look at Pictures, 1990; These Are My Rivers: New and Selected Poems, 1955–1993, 1993. Fiction: Her, 1960; Love in the Days of Rage, 1988. Other Writings: The Mexican Night: Travel Journal, 1970; Northwest Ecolog, 1978; Literary San Francisco: A Pictorial History from the Beginning to the Present (with Nancy J. Peters), 1980; The Populist Manifestos, 1983; Seven Days in Nicaragua Libre, journal, 1985. Editor: Beatitude Anthology, 1960; City Lights Anthology, 1974; City Lights Review, No. 1, 1987, and No. 2, 1988. Plays: Unfair Arguments with Existence: Seven Plays for a New Theatre, 1963; Routines (13 short plays), 1964. Contributions: numerous books and periodicals. *Honours:* Notable Book of 1979 Citation, Library Journal, 1980; Silver Medal for Poetry, Commonwealth Club of California, 1986, 1998; Poetry Prize, City of Rome, 1993; First Poet Laureate of San Francisco, 1998; Lifetime Achievement Award, Los Angeles Times Book Expo, 2001. *Address:* c/o City Lights Books, 261 Columbus Ave, San Francisco, CA 94133, USA.

FERLITA, Ernest Charles; Jesuit Priest and Writer; b. 1 Dec. 1927, Tampa, FL, USA. *Education:* BS, Spring Hill College, 1950; STL, St Louis University, 1964; DFA, Yale University, 1969. *Career:* mem. Dramatists Guild; International Hopkins Society. *Publications:* The Theatre of Pilgrimage, 1971; Film Odyssey (co-author), 1976; The Way of the River, 1977; The Parables of Lina Wertmuller (co-author), 1977; Religion in Film (contributor), 1982; Gospel Journey, 1983; The Mask of Hiroshima in Best Short Plays, 1989; The Uttermost Mark, 1990; The Paths of Life, Cycles A, B, C, 1992, 1993, 1994; The Road to Bethlehem, 1997; Two Cities, 1999; In the Light of the Lord, 2002. *Honours:* First Prize, Christian Theatre Artists Guild, 1971; American Radio Scriptwriting Contest, 1985; Miller Award, 1986; Second Prize, International Competition of Religious Drama, 2000. *Address:* Loyola University, New Orleans, LA 70118, USA.

FERLOSIO, Rafael Sanchez; Spanish/Italian writer; b. 1927, Rome, Italy. *Publications:* The Adventures of the Ingenious Alfanhui 1951, The Jarama 1956, Mientrasno cambien los dioses, nada ha cambiado 1986, Ensayos y articulos 1992. *Honours:* Spanish National Critics' Prize. *Address:* c/o Dedalus Ltd, Langford Lodge, St Judith's Lane, Sawtry, Cambridgeshire PE28 5XE, England. *E-mail:* info@dedalusbooks.com. *Website:* www.dedalusbooks.com.

FERMOR, Sir Patrick Michael Leigh, Kt, DSO, OBE, CLit; British author; b. 11 Feb. 1915, London; m. Hon. Joan Eyres-Monsell 1968 (died 2003). *Education:* King's School, Canterbury. *Career:* travelled for four years in Cen. Europe, Balkans and Greece in 1930s; enlisted in Irish Guards 1939; 'I' Corps 1940; Lt British Mil. Mission, Greece 1940; Liaison Officer, Greek GHQ, Albania; with Cretan Resistance for two years in German-occupied Crete; Team-Commdr Special Allied Airborne Reconnaissance Force, N Germany 1945; Deputy Dir British Inst. Athens 1945–46; travelled in Caribbean and Cen. America 1947–48; Corresp. mem. Athens Acad. 1980. *Publications:* The Traveller's Tree (Heinemann Foundation Prize for Literature 1950, Kemsley Prize 1951), Colette's Chance Acquaintances (trans.) 1952, A Time to Keep Silence 1953, The Violins of Saint Jacques 1953, The Cretan Runner (trans.) 1955, Mani 1958 (Duff Cooper Prize), Roumeli 1966, A Time of Gifts 1977 (W.H. Smith Award 1978), Between the Woods and the Water 1986 (Thomas Cook Award 1986), Three Letters from the Andes 1991. *Honours:* Hon. Citizen of Heraklion, Crete 1947, Gytheion, Laconia 1966, Kardamyli, Messenia 1967; Chevalier, Ordre des Arts et des Lettres (France) 1995; Hon. DLitt (Kent) 1991, (American School of Greece) 1993, (Warwick) 1996; Int. PEN/Time Life Silver Pen Award 1986, Municipality of Athens Gold Medal of Honour 1988; Prix Jacques Audiberti, Ville d'Antibes 1992. *Address:* c/o John Murray, 50 Albemarle Street, London, W1X 4BD, England.

FERNANDEZ, Dominique; Author and Critic; b. 25 Aug. 1929, Neuilly-sur-Seine, France; m. Diana Jacquin de Margerie, divorced, one s. one d. *Education:* Lycée Buffon, Paris; École Normale Supérieure, Paris. *Career:* Prof., Institut Français, Naples, 1957–58; Literary critic, L'Express, 1959–84, Le Nouvel Observateur, 1985–; Prof. of Italian, University of Haute-Bretagne, 1966–89; Music critic, Diapason, 1977–85, Opera International, 1978, Classica, 2003. *Publications:* Le roman italien et la crise de la conscience moderne, 1958; L'écorce des pierres, 1959; L'aube, 1962; Mère Méditerranée, 1965; Les evénements de palerme, 1966; L'échec de pavèse, 1968; Lettre à Dora, 1969; Les enfants de Gogol, 1971; Il mito dell'America, 1969; L'arbre jusqu'aux racines, 1972; Porporino, 1974; Eisenstein, 1975; La rose des Tudors, 1976; Les Siciliens, 1977; Amsterdam, 1977; L'étoile rose, 1978; Une fleur de jasmin à l'oreille, 1980; Le promeneur amoureux, 1980; Signor Giovanni, 1981; Dans la main de l'ange, 1982; Le volcan sous la ville, 1983; Le banquet des anges, 1984; L'amour, 1986; La gloire du paria, 1987; Le rapt de Perséphone (opera libretto), 1987; Le radeau de la Gorgone, 1988; Le rapt de Ganymede, 1989; L'école du sud, 1991; Porfirio et Constance, 1992; Séville, 1992; L'or des tropiques, 1993; Le dernier des médicis, 1993; La magie blanche de Saint-Pétersbourg, 1994; Prague et la bohème (co-author), 1995; La perle et le croissant, 1995; Le musée idéal de Stendhal, 1995; Saint-Pétersbourg, 1996; Tribunal d'honneur, 1997; Le musee de Zola, 1997; Le voyage d'Italie, 1998; Rhapsodie roumaine, 1998; Palerme et la Sicile, 1998; Le loup et le chien, 1999; Le douze muses d'Alexandre Dumas, 1999; Bolivie, 1999; Nicolas, 2000; L'amour qui ase dire son nom, 2001; Syrie, 2002; La course à l'abîme, 2003. *Honours:* Prix Pierre de Monaco, 1986; Prix Méditerranée, 1988; Prix Oscar Wilde, 1988; Chevalier, Légion d'honneur; Commdr, Ordre nat. du Mérite. *Address:* c/o Editions Bernard Grasset, 61 rue des Saints-Peres, 75006 Paris, France.

FERNÁNDEZ-ARMESTO, Felipe Fermín Ricardo, BA, MA, DPhil, FRHistS; historian; b. 6 Dec. 1950, London, England; m. Lesley Patricia Hook 1977; two s. *Education:* Magdalen Coll., Oxford. *Career:* journalist, The Diplomatist 1972–74; Sr Visiting Fellow, John Carter Brown Library, Brown Univ., USA 1997–99; Professorial Fellow, Queen Mary Univ. of London 2000–; mem. Hakluyt Soc., Soc. of Authors, PEN, Athenaeum, Historical Asscn, Asscn of Hispanists, American Historical Asscn; Fellow, Soc. of Antiquaries, Netherlands Inst. *Publications:* The Canary Islands after the Conquest 1982, Before Columbus 1987, The Spanish Armada 1988, Barcelona 1991, The Times Atlas of World Exploration (general ed.) 1991, Columbus 1991, Edward Gibbon's Atlas of the World 1992, Millennium 1995, The Times Guide to the People of Europe 1995, The Times Illustrated History of Europe 1995, Reformation (with Derek Wilson) 1996, Truth 1997, Religion 1997, Civilizations 2000, The Americas: A History of the Continents 2003, So You Think You're Human 2004; contrib. to scholarly books, newspapers and periodicals. *Honours:* Hon. DLitt (La Trobe Univ., Australia) 1997; Arnold Modern History Prize 1971, Leverhulme Research Fellowship 1981, Library Asscn commendation 1992, Nat. Maritime Museum Caird Medal 1997, John Carter Brown Medal 1999. *Literary Agent:* David Higham Associates, 5–8 Lower John Street, Golden Square, London, W1F 9HA, England.

FERRANTI, Marie; Writer; b. 1964, Corsica, France. *Career:* fmr teacher in literature before becoming full-time novelist. *Publications:* Les Femmes de San Stefano (Prix François Mauriac) 1995, La Chambre des Défunts 1996, La Fuite aux Agriates 2000, Le Paradoxe de l'Ordre 2002, La Princess de Mantoue (Grand Prix du Roman, Acad. Française) 2002. *Address:* c/o Editions Gallimard, 5 rue Sébastian-Bottin, 75328 Paris Cedex 7, France.

FERRÉ, Rosario; Writer; b. 28 July 1942, Ponce, Puerto Rico, USA; m. Benigno Trigo, 1960, divorced, two s. one d. *Education:* MA, University of Puerto Rico; PhD, University of Maryland, 1986. *Career:* Founder-Dir, Zona de carga y descarga, Puerto Rican literary journal. *Publications:* (in English) The Youngest Doll, 1991; The House on the Lagoon, 1995; Sweet Diamond Dust and Other Stories, 1996; Flight of the Swan, 2001. Contributions: anthologies.

FERRIS, Paul Frederick; Writer and Dramatist; b. 15 Feb. 1929, Swansea, Wales. *Publications:* A Changed Man, 1958; The City, 1960; Then We Fall, 1960; The Church of England, 1962; A Family Affair, 1963; The Doctors, 1965; The Destroyer, 1965; The Nameless: Abortion in Britain Today, 1966; The Dam, 1967; Men and Money: Financial Europe Today, 1968; The House of Northcliffe, 1971; The New Militants, 1972; The Detective, 1976; Talk to Me about England, 1979; Richard Burton, 1981; A Distant Country, 1983; Gentlemen of Fortune, 1984; Children of Dust, 1988; Sex and the British, 1993; Caitlin, 1993; The Divining Heart, 1995; Dr Freud: A Life, 1997; Dylan Thomas: The Biography, 1999; Infidelity, 1999; New Collected Letters of Dylan Thomas, 2000; Cora Crane, 2003. Television Plays: The Revivalist, 1975; Dylan, 1978; Nye, 1982; The Extremist, 1983; The Fasting Girl, 1984. *Literary Agent:* Curtis Brown Ltd, Haymarket House, 28–29 Haymarket, London, SW1Y 4SP, England. *Telephone:* (20) 7393-4400. *Fax:* (20) 7393-4401. *E-mail:* info@curtisbrown.co.uk. *Website:* www .curtisbrown.co.uk.

FERRON, Madeleine; Writer; b. 24 July 1922, Louiseville, QC, Canada; m. Robert Cliche, 22 Sept. 1945, two s. one d. *Publications:* Short Stories: Coeur de Sucre, 1966; Le Chemin des Dames, 1977; Histoires Edifiantes, 1981; Un Singulier Amour, 1987; Le Grand Theatre, 1989. Fiction: La Fin des Loups-Garous, 1966; Le Baron Ecarlate, 1971; Sur le Chemin Craig, 1982. Essays: Quand le Peuple fait la loi, 1972; Les Beaucerons, ces insoumis, 1974; Adrienne, une saga familiale, 1993. *Honours:* Chevalier, Ordre nat. du Québec, 1992. *Address:* 1130 de la Tour, QC G1R 2W7, Canada.

FERRY, Charles Allen; Writer; b. 8 Oct. 1927, Chicago, IL, USA; m. Ruth Louise Merz 26 Sept. 1958; one step-s. *Education:* Attended University of Illinois. *Publications:* Children's Fiction: Up in Sister Bay, 1975; O Zebron Falls!, 1977; Raspberry One, 1983; One More Time!, 1985; Binge, 1992; A Fresh Start, 1996; Love, 1998. *Honours:* Best Book of 1983, Friends of American Writers; Best Book, American Library Asscn, 1983, 1992; Best Book, National Council of Teachers of English, 1983, 1992, 1996; Best Book of the Year, Daisy Hill Press, 1992; Best Book, New York Public Library, 1992, 1996. *Address:* PO Box 1681, Rochester, MI 48308, USA.

FERRY, David (Russell); Prof. of English Emeritus, Poet, Writer and Trans; b. 5 March 1924, Orange, NJ, USA; m. Anne Elizabeth Davidson 22 March 1958; one s. one d. *Education:* BA, Amherst College, 1948; MA, 1949, PhD, 1955, Harvard University. *Career:* Instructor, 1952–55, Asst Prof., 1955–61, Assoc. Prof., 1961–67, Prof. of English, 1967–71, Sophie Chautal Hart Prof. of English, 1971–89, Prof. Emeritus, 1989–, Wellesley College; Fannie Hurst Visiting Poet, Washington University, St Louis, 1999; mem. Fellow, Acad. of American Poets, 1994; Fellow, American Acad. of Arts and Sciences, 1998. *Publications:* The Limits of Mortality: An Essay on Wordsworth's Major Poems, 1959; On the Way to the Island (poems), 1960; British Literature (co-ed.), two vols, 1974; Strangers: A Book of Poems, 1983; Gilgamesh: A New Rendering in English Verse, 1992; Dwelling Places: Poems and Translations, 1993; The Odes of Horace: A Translation, 1997; The Eclogues of Virgil: A Translation, 1999; Of No Country I Know: New and Selected Poems and Translations, 1999; The Epistles of Horace: A Translation, 2001. Contributions: Literary journals. *Honours:* Pushcart Prize, 1988; Ingram Merrill Award for Poetry and Translation, 1993; Teasdale Prize for Poetry, 1995; Hon. Fellow, Acad. of American Poets, 1995; Guggenheim Fellowship, 1996–97; William Arrowsmith Translation Prize, AGNI, 1999; Bingham Poetry Prize, Boston Book Review, 2000; Lenore Marshall Poetry Prize, 2000; Rebekah Johnson Bobbitt National Prize for Poetry, Library of Congress, 2000; American Acad. of Arts and Letters Award for Literature, 2001; Harold Morton Landon Trans. Prize, Acad. of American Poets, 2002. *Address:* 8 Ellery St, Cambridge, MA 02138, USA. *E-mail:* dferry@wellesley.edu.

FERRY, Luc, Dr rer. pol; French philosopher, politician and university professor; b. 3 Jan. 1951, Colombes; m. Marie-Caroline Becq de Fouquières 1999; three d. (one from previous marriage). *Education:* Lycée Saint-Exupéry, Centre nat. de télé-enseignement, Sorbonne, Univ. of Heidelberg. *Career:* lecturer, Teacher Training Coll., Arras, Asst Lecturer, Univ. of Reims 1977–79; Asst Lecturer, Ecole Normale Supérieure, Paris 1977–79, 1980–82; Research Attaché Nat. CNRS 1980–82; Asst Lecturer, Univ. of Paris I-Panthéon Sorbonne and Paris X-Nanterre 1980–88; Prof. of Political Sciences, Inst. of Political Studies, Univ. of Lyon II–Lumière 1982–88; Prof. of Philosophy, Univ. of Caen 1989–97; Asst Lecturer, Paris I 1989; Prof. of Philosophy, Univ. of Paris VI-Jussieu 1996–; Founder-mem., Sec. Gen. College of Philosophy 1974–; responsible for Ideas section then Editorial Adviser, L'Express 1987–94; Pres. Nat. Curriculum Council (CNP) 1994–2002; Minister for Nat. Educ., Research and Technology 1997–2002; Minister of Youth, Nat. Educ. and Research 2002–2004; mem. Comm. for UNESCO 1997–2002; Dir Editions Grasset collection of Coll. of Philosophy; fmr mem. Saint-Simon Foundation; columnist for Le Point 1995–. *Publications include:* Philosophie politique (3 vols 1984–85), la Pensée 68, le Nouvel ordre écologique: l'arbre, l'animal et l'homme (Prix Jean-Jacques Rousseau) 1992, Homo aestheticus – L'Intervention du goût à l'âge démocratique 1990 (Prix Médicis 1992), l'Homme Dieu ou le sens de la vie (Prix Littéraire des Droits de l'Homme)1996, La Sagesse des Modernes 1998, Le Sens du Beau 1998, Philosopher à dix-huit ans (jtly) 1999, Qu'est-ce que l'homme? (jtly) 2000, Qu'est-ce qu-une vie réussie 2002, numerous articles on philosophy. *Honours:* Chevalier Légion d'honneur, Ordre des Arts et des Lettres. *Address:* c/o Ministry of Youth, National Education and Research, 110 rue de Grenelle, 75357 Paris, France (Office).

FEST, Joachim C.; German historian; b. 8 Dec. 1926, Berlin; m.; two s. one d. *Education:* Freiburg Univ., Frankfurt am Main Univ., Berlin Univ. *Career:* Ed., RIAS 1954–61; Ed.-in-Chief, NDR-TV Hamburg 1963–68; presenter, TV series Panorama; editorial bd mem. (culture), Frankfurter Allgemeine Zeitung 1973–93. *Publications:* non-fiction: The Face of the Third Reich 1963, Hitler 1973, Plotting Hitler's Death 1996, Speer: The Final Verdict 2001, Inside Hitler's Bunker: The Last Days of the Third Reich 2004. *Address:* c/o Macmillan Publishing Ltd, 25 Eccleston Place, London, SW1W 9NF, England. *Telephone:* (20) 7881-8000. *Fax:* (20) 7881-8001. *Website:* www.macmillan.co.uk.

FFORDE, Jasper; British novelist; b. 1961, London, England. *Education:* Dartington Hall School. *Career:* fmrly worked in the film industry. *Publications:* The Eyre Affair 2001, Lost in a Good Book 2002, The Well of Lost Plots (Bollinger Everyman Wodehouse Prize for Comic Writing 2004) 2003, Something Rotten 2004. *Honours:* Sherlock Award for Best Comic Detective 2002. *Literary Agent:* Sanklow & Nesbit UK, 29 Adam & Eve Mews, London, W8 6UG, England. *Website:* www.jasperfforde.com.

FICKERT, Kurt Jon; Prof. of Languages Emeritus and Writer; b. 19 Dec. 1920, Pausa, Germany; m. Lynn Barbara Janda, 8 Aug. 1946, two s. one d. *Education:* BA, Hofstra University, 1941; MA, 1947, PhD, 1952, New York University. *Career:* Instructor, Hofstra University, 1947–52; Asst Prof., Florida State University, 1953–54, Kansas State University, 1954–56; Asst Prof., Assoc. Prof., Prof., 1956–86, Prof. Emeritus, 1986–, Wittenberg University; mem. Ohio Poetry Day Asscn, pres., 1970–75. *Publications:* To Heaven and Back, 1972; Hermann Hesse's Quest, 1978; Kafka's Doubles, 1979; Signs and Portents, 1980; Franz Kafka: Life, Work, Criticism, 1984; Neither Left nor Right: The Politics of Individualism in Uwe Johnson's Work, 1987; End of a Mission, 1993; Dialogue With the Reader, 1995. Contributions: journals and magazines. *Address:* 33 S Kensington Pl., Springfield, OH 45504, USA.

FIDO, Martin (Austin); University Teacher, Writer, Broadcaster, Courier and Guide-Lecturer; b. 18 Oct. 1939, Penzance, Cornwall, England; m. 1st Judith Mary Spicer, 21 June 1961, divorced 1972; m. 2nd Norma Elaine Wilson, 16 Dec. 1972, divorced 1984; m. 3rd Karen Lynn Sandel, 17 Dec. 1994, one s. two d. *Education:* BA, 1961, BLitt, 1966, Lincoln College,

Oxford. *Career:* Andrew Bradley Junoir Research Fellow, Balliol College, Oxford, 1963–66; Lecturer in English, University of Leeds, 1966–72; Visiting Assoc. Prof., Michigan State University, 1971–72; Reader in English and Head, Dept of English and Linguistics, University of the West Indies, Barbados, 1973–83; Writing Instructor, Boston University, 2001–; Actor, Hoevec Investors Ltd, Barbados, 1981–83; Courier, Guide-Lecturer: Footprints Walks, City Walks, King Arthur Land Tours, 1983–2001; Broadcaster, BBC Radio 2, 1992, LBC Radion, 1987–. *Publications:* Charles Dickens: An Authentic Account of His Life and Times, 1970; Oscar Wilde, 1973; Rudyard Kipling, 1974; Shakespeare, 1978; Murder Guide to London, 1986; The Crimes, Detection and Death of Jack the Ripper, 1987; Body-snatchers: A History of the Resurrectionists, 1742–1832, 1989; Murders after Midnight, 1990; The Peasenhall Murder (co-author), 1990; The Jack the Ripper A to Z (co-author), 1991; The Chronicle of Crime: The Infamous Felons of Modern History and Their Hideous Crimes, 1993; Deadly Jealousy, 1993; Great Crimes and Trials of the Twentieth Century (co-author), 1994; Twentieth Century Murder, 1995; The World's Worst Medical Mistakes (co-author), 1996; Our Family (co-author), 1997; The World of Charles Dickens, 1997; The World of Sherlock Holmes, 1998; The World of Agatha Christie, 1999; The Official Encyclopedia of Scotland Yard (co-author), 1999; The Krays: Unfinished Business, 2000; To Kill and Kill Again, 2000, US edn as A History of British Serial Killers, 2001. Other: Writer and reader of audiotapes dealing with criminals and true crime stories. Contributions: Essays in Criticism; Notes and Queries; English Language Studies; Modern Language Review; Dutch Opera Yearbook; Ripperologist; Ripperana; Reviews to periodicals including: Times Educational Supplement; TLS; Oxford Review; Oxford Magazine. *Honours:* First Ripperana Annual Award, 1999. *Address:* c/o Dept of English, Boston University, 147 Bay State Rd, Boston, MA 02215, USA; c/o Richard Jeffs, Communications Consultants, Wigmore St, London W1H 9DL, England.

FIELD, D. M. (see Grant, Neil).

FIELD, Edward, (Bruce Elliot); Writer and Poet; b. 7 June 1924, New York, NY, USA. *Education:* New York Univ., 1946–48. *Career:* mem. American Acad. of Rome, fellow. *Publications:* Stand Up, Friend, With Me, 1963; Variety Photoplays, 1967; Eskimo Songs and Stories, 1973; A Full Heart, 1977; A Geography of Poets (ed.), 1979, revised edn as A New Geography of Poets, 1992; New and Selected Poems, 1987; Counting Myself Lucky, 1992; A Frieze for a Temple of Love, 1998; Magic Words, 1998; The Villagers, 2000. Contributions: reviews, journals and periodicals. *Honours:* Lamont Award, 1963; Shelley Memorial Award, 1978; Lambda Award, 1993. *Address:* 463 West St, A323, New York, NY 10014, USA. *E-mail:* fieldinski@yahoo.com.

FIELDING, Helen; British author and journalist; b. Yorkshire; pnr Kevin Curran; one s. *Education:* Univ. of Oxford. *Career:* began career working for BBC; fmr columnist The Independent. *Publications:* Cause Celeb 1994, Bridget Jones's Diary 1996, Bridget Jones: The Edge of Reason 2000, Bridget Jones's Guide to Life (for Comic Relief charity) 2001, Olivia Joules and the Overactive Imagination 2003. *Honours:* Nielsen BookScan and The Times Platinum Book Award, British Book Awards 2002. *Address:* c/o Picador, Macmillan Publishers Ltd, 25 Eccleston Place, London, SW1W 9NF, England.

FIENNES, Sir Ranulph (Twisleton-Wykeham); Explorer and Writer; b. 7 March 1944, Windsor, England; m. Virginia Pepper, 9 Sept. 1970. *Education:* Eton College. *Career:* British Army, 1965–70; Special Air Service, 1966; Sultan of Muscat's Armed Forces, 1968–70; Led British Expeditions to White Nile, 1969, Jostedalsbre Glacier, 1970, Headless Valley, BC, 1970; Transglobal expedition, first circumpolar journey round the world, 1979–82, North Pole (5 expeditions), 1985–90, Ubar Expedition (discovered the lost city of Ubar, Oman), 1992, First unsupported crossing of Antarctic continent, 1993; Lectures; Television and film documentary appearances; mem. Hon. Membership, Royal Institute of Navigation, 1997. *Publications:* A Talent for Trouble, 1970; Ice Fall on Norway, 1972; The Headless Valley, 1973; Where Soldiers Fear to Tread, 1975; Hell on Ice, 1979; To the Ends of the Earth: The Transglobe Expedition – The First Pole-to-Pole Circumnavigation of the Globe, 1983; Bothie the Polar Dog (with Virginia Fiennes), 1984; Living Dangerously (autobiog.), 1988; The Feather Men, 1991; Atlantis of the Sands, 1992; Mind Over Matter: The Epic Crossing of the Antarctic Continent, 1994; The Sett, 1996; Ranulph Fiennes: Fit For Life, 1998; Beyond the Limits, 2000; The Secret Hunters, 2001; Captain Scott (biog.), 2003. *Honours:* Dhofar Campaign Medal, 1969; Sultan of Muscat Bravery Medal, 1970; Krug Award for Excellence, 1980; Gold Medal and Hon. Life Membership, Explorer's Club of New York, 1983; Livingstone's Gold Medal, Royal Scottish Geographic Society, 1983; Founder's Medal, RGS, 1984; Guiness Hall of Fame, 1987; Polar Medal and Bar, 1987, 1994; ITN Award, 1990; OBE, 1993; British Chapter, The Explorers Club Millennium Award For Polar Exploration. *Address:* Greenlands, Exford, Somerset TA24 7NU, England.

FIFIELD, Christopher George, MusB, ARCO, ARMCM; British conductor and writer on music; *Music Director, Lambeth Orchestra*; b. 4 Sept. 1945, Croydon, Surrey, England; m. Judith Weyman 1972 (divorced); three c. *Education:* Manchester Univ., Royal Manchester Coll. of Music, Guildhall School, Cologne Musikhochschule. *Career:* fmrly Asst Dir of Music Capetown Opera, music staff Glyndebourne for 12 years, Music Dir London Contemporary Dance Theatre, Dir Northampton Symphony Orchestra, Central Festival Opera, Reigate and Redhill Choral Soc. and Jubilate Choir; frequent conductor at Trinity Coll. of Music; Dir of Music, Univ. Coll. London 1980–90; fmrly chorus master Chelsea Opera Group; currently Music Dir and Conductor, Lambeth Orchestra. *Publications:* Max Bruch: His Life and Works 1988, Wagner in Performance 1992, True Artist and True Friend: A Biography of Hans Richter 1993, Letters and Diaries of Kathleen Ferrier 2003; contrib. to reference books and journals, including Viking Opera Guide, International Opera Guide, New Grove Dictionary of Opera 1992, Grove 7, Dictionary of National Biography, Oxford Companion to Music. *Address:* 162 Venner Road, London, SE26 5JQ, England. *E-mail:* christopherfifield@ntlworld.com. *Website:* www.lambeth-orchestra.org.uk.

FIGES, Eva; Writer; b. 15 April 1932, Berlin, Germany; one s. one d. *Education:* BA, English Language and Literature, Univ. of London, 1953. *Career:* mem. Society of Authors. *Publications:* Winter Journey, 1967; Patriarchal Attitudes, 1970; B, 1972; Nelly's Version, 1977; Little Eden, 1978; Waking, 1981; Sex and Subterfuge, 1982; Light, 1983; The Seven Ages, 1986; Ghosts, 1988; The Tree of Knowledge, 1990; The Tenancy, 1993; The Knot, 1996; Tales of Innocence and Experience, 2003. *Honours:* Guardian Fiction Prize, 1967. *Address:* 24 Fitzjohns Ave, London NW3 5NB, England.

FIGES, Orlando; academic and writer; b. 20 Nov. 1959, UK; m. Stephanie Palmer 1990; two d. *Education:* Gonville and Caius Coll. Cambridge, Trinity Coll. Cambridge. *Career:* Fellow Trinity Coll., Cambridge 1984–89; Dir of Studies in History 1988–98, Lecturer in History, Univ. of Cambridge 1987–99; Prof. of History, Birkbeck Coll., London Univ. 1999–. *Publications:* Peasant Russia, Civil War: the Volga Countryside in Revolution 1917–21 1989, A People's Tragedy: the Russian Revolution 1891–1924 1996, Interpreting the Russian Revolution (jtly) 1999, Natasha's Dance: a Cultural History of Russia 2002; contrib. numerous review articles and contribs to other published books. *Honours:* Wolfson History Prize 1996, WHSmith Literary Award 1996, NCR Book Award 1996, Los Angeles Times Book Prize 1996. *Address:* School of History, Classics and Archaeology, Birkbeck College, Malet Street, London WC1E 7HX, England. *E-mail:* orlando.figes@ntlworld.com. *Website:* www.bbk.ac.uk.

FILIPETTI, Aurélie; French novelist; b. 1973, Lorraine. *Publications:* novels: Les derniers jours de la classe ouvrière 2003. *Address:* c/o Stock, 27 rue Cassette, 75006 Paris, France. *Telephone:* 1 42 84 87 00. *Fax:* 1 42 87 87 15. *Website:* www.editions-stock.fr.

FILIPPINI, Serge; French novelist, critic and philosopher; b. 1950, Pontarlier. *Publications:* L'Aquarium 1980, Angele 1986, La Vie en double 1987, L'Homme incendié (trans. as The Man in Flames) 1990, Comedia 1992, Haut mal 1993, LeRoi de Sicile 1998, L'Amant absolu 1999, Un Amour de Paul 2000, Érotique du mensonge 2003. *Address:* c/o Dedalus Ltd, Langford Lodge, St Judith's Lane, Sawtry, Cambridgeshire PE28 5XE, England. *E-mail:* info@dedalusbooks.com. *Website:* www.dedalusbooks.com.

FINCH, Matthew (see Fink, Merton).

FINCH, Merton (see Fink, Merton).

FINCH, Peter; Poet and Writer; b. 6 March 1947, Cardiff, Wales; two s. one d. *Education:* Glamorgan Polytechnic. *Career:* Ed., Second Aeon, 1966–75; mem. Welsh Acad.; Welsh Union of Writers. *Publications:* Wanted, 1967; Pieces of the Universe, 1968; How to Learn Welsh, 1977; Between 35 and 42 (short stories), 1982; Some Music and a Little War, 1984; How to Publish Your Poetry, 1985; Reds in the Bed, 1986; Selected Poems, 1987; How to Publish Yourself, 1988; Make, 1990; Poems for Ghosts, 1991; Five Hundred Cobbings, 1994; The Spe Ell, 1995; The Poetry Business, 1995; Antibodies, 1997; Useful, 1997; Food, 2001; Real Cardiff, 2002. Contributions: Magazines and journals. *Address:* 19 Southminster Rd, Roath, Cardiff CF23 5AT, Wales. *E-mail:* peter@peterfinch.co.uk. Website; www.peterfinch.co.uk.

FINCKE, Gary (William); Prof. of English, Poet and Writer; b. 7 July 1945, Pittsburgh, Pennsylvania, USA; m. Elizabeth Locker, 17 Aug. 1968, two s. one d. *Education:* BA, Thiel College, 1967; MA, Miami University, 1969; PhD, Kent State University, 1974. *Career:* Instructor in English, Pennsylvania State University of Monaca, 1969–75; Chair, Dept of English, LeRoy Central School, New York, 1975–80; Administrator, 1980–93, Prof. of English and Dir of the Writers' Institute, 1993–, Susquehanna University; Ed., The Apprentice Writer, 1982–98; Syndicated Columnist, 1996–. *Publications:* Poetry: Breath, 1984; The Coat in the Heart, 1985; The Days of Uncertain Health, 1988; Handing the Self Back, 1990; Plant Voices, 1991; The Public Talk of Death, 1991; The Double Negatives of the Living, 1992; Inventing Angels, 1994; The Technology of Paradise, 1998; The Almanac for Desire, 2000. Fiction: For Keepsies, 1993; Emergency Calls, 1996; The Inadvertent Scofflaw, 1999; Blood Ties, 2002. Contributions: many anthologies, reviews, quarterlies, journals, and magazines. *Honours:* various grants and fellowships; Beloit Fiction Journal Short Story Prize, 1990; Bess Hokin Prize, Poetry Magazine, 1991; Book-of-the-Month, Vietnam Veteran's Magazine, 1993; Notable Fiction Book of the Year, Dictionary of Literary Biography, 1993; Pushcart Prize, 1995; Rose Lefcowitz Prize, Poet Lore, 1997. *Address:* 3 Melody Lane, Selinsgrove, PA 17870, USA.

FINE, Anne, OBE, BA, FRSL; British writer; b. (Anne Laker), 7 Dec. 1947, Leicester; m. Kit Fine 1968 (divorced 1991); two d. *Education:* Northampton High School for Girls and Univ. of Warwick. *Career:* Children's Laureate 2001–03; mem. Soc. of Authors. *Publications:* for older children: The Summer House Loon 1978, The Other Darker Ned 1978, The Stone Menagerie 1980, Round Behind the Icehouse 1981, The Granny Project 1983, Madame Doubtfire 1987, Goggle-Eyes (Guardian Children's Fiction Prize, Carnegie Medal 1990) 1989, The Book of the Banshee 1991, Flour Babies (Whitbread Children's Book of the Year, Carnegie Medal 1993) 1992, Step by Wicked Step 1995, The Tulip Touch (Whitbread Children's Book of the Year) 1996, Very Different (short stories) 2001, Up on Cloud Nine 2002; for younger children: Scaredy-Cat 1985, Anneli the Art Hater 1986, Crummy Mummy and Me 1988, A Pack of Liars 1988, Stranger Danger 1989, Bill's New Frock (Smarties Prize 1990) 1989, The Country Pancake 1989, A Sudden Puff of Glittering Smoke 1989, A Sudden Swirl of Icy Wind 1990, Only a Show 1990, Design-a-Pram 1991, A Sudden Glow of Gold 1991, The Worst Child I Ever Had 1991, The Angel of Nitshill Road 1991, Poor Monty (picture book) 1991, The Same Old Story Every Year 1992, The Chicken Gave It to Me 1992, The Haunting of Pip Parker 1992, The Diary of a Killer Cat 1994, Press Play 1994, How to Write Really Badly 1996, Countdown 1996, Jennifer's Diary 1996, Care of Henry 1996, Loudmouth Louis 1998, Charm School 1999, Roll Over Roly 1999, Bad Dreams 2000, Ruggles (picture book) 2001, Notso Hotso 2001, The Jamie and Angus Stories 2002, How to Cross the Road and Not Turn Into a Pizza 2002, The More the Merrier 2003; adult fiction: The Killjoy 1986, Taking the Devil's Advice 1990, In Cold Domain 1994, Telling Liddy 1998, All Bones and Lies 2001; adult non-fiction: Telling Tales: an Interview with Anne Fine 1999. *Honours:* Scottish Arts Council Writer's Bursary 1986, Scottish Arts Council Book Award 1986, British Book Awards Children's Author of the Year 1990, 1993, Publishing News Children's Author of the Year 1990, 1993, Nasen Special Educational Needs Book Award 1996, Prix Sorcière 1998. *Literary Agent:* David Higham Associates, 5–8 Lower John Street, London, W1R 4HA, England. *Website:* www.annefine.co.uk.

FINK, Gerald R., PhD; American professor of genetics; *Professor of Molecular Genetics, Massachusetts Institute of Technology*; b. 1 July 1940, Brooklyn, New York; m. Rosalie Lewis 1961; two d. *Education:* Amherst Coll., Yale Univ. *Career:* Postdoctoral Fellow, NIH 1965–66, 1966–67; Instructor, NIH Grad. Program 1966; Instructor, Cold Spring Harbor Summer Program 1970–; Asst Prof. of Genetics Cornell Univ. 1967–71, Assoc. Prof. 1971–76, Prof. 1976–79, Prof. of Biochem. 1979–82; Prof. of Molecular Genetics, MIT 1982–; American Cancer Soc. Prof. of Genetics 1979–; mem. Whitehead Inst. for Biomedical Research 1982–, Dir 1990–; Sec. Genetics Soc. of America 1977–80, Vice-Pres. 1986–87, Pres. 1988–89; mem. NAS, American Acad. of Arts and Sciences. *Publications:* numerous scientific publs. *Honours:* Hon. DSc (Amherst Coll.) 1982; NAS-US Steel Prize in Molecular Biology 1981, Genetics Soc. of America Medal 1982, Yale Science and Eng Award 1984, Emil Christian Hansen Foundation Award for Microbiological Research 1986. *Address:* Whitehead Institute for Biomedical Research, 9 Cambridge Center, Cambridge, MA 02142, USA.

FINK, Merton, (Matthew Finch, Merton Finch); Author; b. 17 Nov. 1921, Liverpool, England; m. 1st 15 March 1953, one s. one d.; m. 2nd 24 Nov. 1981. *Education:* School of Military Engineers, 1942; School of Military Intelligence, 1943; LDS, Liverpool University, 1952. *Career:* mem. Civil Service Writers; Deputy Chair., Bath Literary Society; British Dental Asscn; Chair., Service Committee, Bath British Legion. *Publications:* Dentist in the Chair, 1953; Teething Troubles, 1954; The Third Set, 1955; Hang Your Hat on a Pension, 1956; The Empire Builder, 1957; Solo Fiddle, 1959; Matchbreakers, 1961; Five Are the Symbols, 1962; Chew this Over, 1965; Eye with Mascara, 1966; Eye Spy, 1967; The Succubus, 1968; Snakes and Ladders, 1969; Jones is a Rainbow, 1970; Simon Bar Cochba, 1971; A Fox Called Flavius, 1973; Open Wide, 1976. Contributions: Dental Practice, 1956–; Bath Chronicle, 1995. *Honours:* Richard Edwards Scholar, 1950. *Address:* 27 Harbutts, Bathampton, Bath BA2 6TA, England.

FINKEL, Donald; Poet and University Teacher (retd); b. 21 Oct. 1929, New York, NY, USA; m. Constance Urdang, 1956, one s. two d. *Education:* BA, 1952, MA, 1953, Columbia University. *Career:* Teacher, University of Iowa, 1957–58, Bard College, 1958–60; Faculty, 1960–92, Poet-in-Residence, 1965–92, Poet-in-Residence Emeritus, 1992–, Washington University, St Louis; Visiting Lecturer, Bennington College, 1966–67, Princeton University, 1985, University of Missouri-St Louis, 1998–99, Webster University, 1999–2000. *Publications:* The Clothing's New Emperor and Other Poems, 1959; Simeon, 1964; A Joyful Noise, 1966; Answer Back, 1968; The Garbage Wars, 1970; Adequate Earth, 1972; A Mote in Heaven's Eye, 1975; Going Under, and Endurance: An Arctic Idyll: Two Poems, 1978; What Manner of Beast, 1981; The Detachable Man, 1984; Selected Shorter Poems, 1987; The Wake of the Electron, 1987; Beyond Despair, 1994; A Question of Seeing, 1998. *Honours:* Helen Bullis Prize, 1964; Guggenheim Fellowship, 1967; National Endowment for the Arts Grants, 1969, 1973; Ingram Merrill Foundation Grant, 1972; Theodore Roethke Memorial Prize, 1974; Morton Dauwen Zabel Award, American Acad. of Arts and Letters, 1980; Dictionary of Literary Biography Yearbook Award, 1994. *Address:* 2051 Park Ave, Apt D, St Louis, MO 63104, USA.

FINLAY, William (see Mackay, James Alexander).

FINN, Pavel Konstantinovich; Russian scriptwriter; b. (Pavel Finn-Halfin), 28 June 1940, Moscow; m. Irina Chernova-Finn; one s. *Education:* All-Union State Inst. of Cinematography. *Career:* fmr journalist, documentary maker; freelance script writer 1968–; Head of Higher Workshop Course of Scriptwriters; Chair. Cinema Dramaturgy Council, Moscow Union of Cinematographers 2001; First Deputy Chair. Russian Union of Cinematographers 2001–. *Publications:* Scripts: Headless Horse Rider 1973, Armed and Very Dangerous 1977, 26 Days of Dostoyevsky's Life 1980, Icicle in a Warm Sea 1983, Witness 1985, Lady Macbeth of Mtsensk Region 1989, Accidental Waltz 1989, Sunset 1990, Myth about Leonid 1991, A Big Concert of Peoples 1991, Shylock 1993, Jester's Revenge 1994, For What 1995, Career of Arthur Whui 1996, Break Point, We Are Your Kids, Moscow, Eve's Gates, Death of Tairov or Princess Brambilla, Secrets of Court Coups. *Address:* 4th Rostovsky per. 2/1, apt 9, 119121 Moscow, Russia. *E-mail:* pavelfinn@mtu-net.ru.

FINNIGAN, (Helen) Joan, BA; Canadian poet, playwright and oral historian; b. 23 Nov. 1925, Ottawa, ON; m. Charles Grant MacKenzie 1949 (died 1965); two s. one d. *Education:* Lisgar Collegiate (Ottawa), Carleton and Queen's Univs. *Career:* Gen. Reporter Ottawa Journal; freelance journalist 1949–67; research, scriptwriting, idea production, interviewing Canadian Nat. Film Bd 1969–1976; scriptwriter CBC Radio 1976–84; four photography exhibitions, guest lectures, radio and TV appearances; mem. Writers' Union of Canada, League of Canadian Poets. *Plays:* A Prince of Good Fellows 1976, Up the Vallee! 1978, Songs from Both Sides of the River 1987. *Screenplay:* The Best Damn Fiddler from Calabogie to Kaladar (nine Genie Awards, Best Screenplay Canadian Film Awards) 1969. *Radio plays:* Songs for the Bible Belt, May Day Rounds, Children of the Shadows, There's No Good Time Left – None at All. *Publications:* poetry: A Dream of Lilies 1965, It Was Warm and Sunny When We Set Out 1970, Living Together 1976, The Watershed Collection 1988, Wintering Over 1992, Second Wind, Second Sight 1998; prose: Through the Glass, Darkly 1963, Entrance to the Greenhouse 1968, In the Brown Cottage on Loughborough Lake 1970, A Reminder of Familiar Faces 1978, This Series Has Been Discontinued 1980, Some of the Stories I Told You Were True (oral history) 1981, Legacies, Legends and Lies (Ottawa-Carleton Literary Award) 1985, Tell Me Another Story (oral history) 1988, The Dog Who Wouldn't Be Left Behind (juvenile) 1989, Old Scores: New Goals, History of Ottawa Senators 1891–1992 1992, A History of Lisgar Collegiate, 1843–1993 (ed.) 1993, Witches, Ghosts and Loups-Garous 1994, Dancing at the Crossroads 1995, Down the Unmarked Roads 1997, Tallying the Tales of the Old-Timers (oral/social history) 1998, Life Along the Opeongo Line 2004. *Honours:* Pres.'s Medal for Poetry, Univ. of Western Ontario 1969; Philemon Wright Award 1983. *Address:* Moore Farm, Hartington, ON K0H 1W0, Canada.

FINNIS, John (Mitchell); Prof. of Law and Legal Philosophy and Writer; b. 28 July 1940, Adelaide, SA, Australia; m. Marie Carmel McNally, 1964, three s., four d. *Education:* St Peter's College, Adelaide; LLB, St Mark's College, University of Adelaide, 1961; Rhodes Scholar, 1962, DPhil, 1965, University College, Oxford. *Career:* Assoc. in Law, University of California, Berkeley, 1965–66; Fellow and Praelector in Jurisprudence, 1966–, Stowell Civil Law Fellow, 1973–, Vice-Master, 2001–, University College, Oxford; Called to the Bar, Gray's Inn, 1970; Rhodes Reader in the Laws of the British Commonwealth and the United States, 1972–89, Prof. of Law and Legal Philosophy, 1989–, University of Oxford; Prof. and Head, Dept of Law, University of Malawi, 1976–78; Consultor, Pontifical Commission, Iustitia et Pax, 1977–89; Huber Distinguished Visiting Prof., Boston College, 1993–94; Biolchini Prof. of Law, University of Notre Dame, IN, 1995–; mem. Catholic Bishops' Joint Committee on Bio-Ethical Issues, 1981–88; International Theological Commission, Vatican, 1986–92; Pontifical Council de Iustitia et Pace, 1990–96; Pontifical Acad. for Life, 2001–; Fellow, British Acad., 1990. *Publications:* Commonwealth and Dependencies (Halsbury's Laws of England), Vol. 6, fourth edn, 1974; Natural Law and Natural Rights, 1980; Fundamentals of Ethics, 1983; Nuclear Deterrence, Morality and Realism (with Joseph Boyle and Germain Grisez), 1987; Moral Absolutes, 1991; Aquinas: Moral, Political and Legal Theory, 1998. *Address:* University College, Oxford, OX1 4BH, England.

FINSCHER, Ludwig; Prof. of Musicology (retd), Ed. and Lexicographer; b. 14 March 1930, Kassel, Germany. *Education:* PhD, University of Göttingen, 1954; Habilitation, University of Saarbrücken, 1967. *Career:* Asst Lecturer, University of Kiel, 1960–65, University of Saarbrücken, 1965–68; Ed., 1961–68, Co-Ed., 1968–74, Die Musikforschung; Prof. of Musicology, University of Frankfurt am Main, 1968–81, University of Heidelberg, 1981–95; mem. Akademie der Wissenschaften, Heidelberg; Akademie der Wissenschaften und der Literatur, Mainz; Academia Europaea; International Musicological Society, hon. mem.; Royal Musical Asscn, London, hon. foreign mem.; Gesellschaft für Musikforschung, hon. mem.; American Musicological Society, corresponding mem. *Publications:* Loyset Compère (c.1450–1518): Life and Works, 1964; Geschichte der Evangelischen Kirchenmusik (ed. with others), second edn, 1965, revised English trans. as Protestant Church Music: A History, 1974; Studien zur Geschichte des Streichquartetts: I, Die Entstehung des klassischen Streichquartetts: Von den Vorformen zur Grundlegung durch Joseph Haydn, 1974; Renaissance-Studien: Helmuth Osthoff zum 80. Geburtstag (ed.), 1979; Quellenstudien zu Musik der Renaissance (ed.), 2 vols, 1981, 1983; Ludwig van Beethoven (ed.), 1983; Claudio Monteverdi: Festschrift Reinhold Hammerstein zum

70. Geburtstag (ed.), 1986; Die Musik des 15. und 16. Jahrhunderts: Neues Handbuch der Musikwissenschaft (ed.), Vol. 3/1-2, 1989–90; Die Mannheimer Hofkapelle im Zeitalter Carl Theodors (ed.), 1992; Die Musik in Geschichte und Gegenwart (ed.), second edn, 26 vols, 1994–; Joseph Haydn, 2000. Other: Ed. of the works of Gaffurius, 2 vols, 1955, 1960, Complete works of Compère, 5 vols, 1958–72, and Hindemith (co-ed.), 1976 et seq. Contributions: Complete works of Mozart and Gluck, and scholarly books and journals. *Honours:* Akademie der Wissenschaften Prize, Göttingen, 1968; Order Pour le mérite, 1994; Great Order of Merit, Germany, 1997; Dr hc, Univ. of Athens, 2002, Univ. of Zürich, 2003. *Address:* Am Walde 1, 38302 Wolfenbüttel, Germany.

FINSTAD, Suzanne; Author and Attorney (non-practising); b. 14 Sept. 1955, Minneapolis, Minnesota, USA. *Education:* University of Texas, Austin, 1973–74; BA, French, University of Houston, 1976; University of Grenoble, France, 1979; JD, Bates College of Law, 1980; LSE, 1980. *Publications:* Heir Not Apparent, 1984; Ulterior Motives, 1987; Sleeping with the Devil, 1991. Contributions: Magazines. *Honours:* American Jurisprudence Award in Criminal Law, Bancroft-Whitney Publishing Co, 1979; Order of the Barons, 1980; Frank Wardlaw Award, 1985. *Address:* c/o Joel Gotler, 152 N La Peer Dr., Beverly Hills, CA 90048, USA.

FINZI, Sergio; Psychoanalyst and Writer; b. 15 May 1936, Brescia, Italy; m. Virginia Finzi Ghisi. *Education:* Degree in Philosophy, University of Pavia, 1959; Training in Psychoanalysis, École Freudienne de Paris. *Publications:* Co-author with Virgina Finzi: Un saggio in famiglia, 1971; Il principe splendente, 1973; Lavoro dell' inconscio e comunismo 1975; Nevrosi di guerra in tempo di pace, 1989; Gli Effetti Dell'Amore, 1995; La Scienza Dei Vincoli, 2000. Contributions: Il piccolo Hans, 1974–95; Il Cefalopodo. *Address:* Via Borgospesso 8, 20121 Milan, Italy.

FIRER, Susan; Adjunct Asst Prof. of English and Poet; b. 14 Oct. 1948, Milwaukee, Wisconsin, USA; one s. two d. *Education:* BA, 1973, MA, 1982, University of Wisconsin at Milwaukee. *Career:* Teaching Asst, 1981–82, Lecturer, 1982, Adjunct Asst Prof. of English, 1988–, University of Wisconsin at Milwaukee. *Publications:* My Life with the Tsar and Other Poems, 1979; The Underground Communion Rail, 1992; The Lives of the Saints and Everything, 1993. Contributions: numerous anthologies, reviews, journals, and magazines. *Honours:* Acad. of American Poets Prize, University of Wisconsin at Milwaukee, 1977; Best American Poetry, 1992; Cleveland State University Poetry Center Prize, 1992; Wisconsin Council of Writers Posner Poetry Award, 1993; First Place, Writer's Place Literary Awards, 1995; Milwaukee County Artist Fellowship, 1996; Work included in Midwest Express Center, 1998.

FIRST, Philip (see Williamson, Philip G.).

FIRTH, Anne Catherine, (Anne Valery); Scriptwriter, Autobiographer, Novelist and Theatre Playwright; b. 24 Feb. 1926, London, England. *Career:* mem. PEN International; Fawcett Society. *Publications:* Baron Von Kodak, Shirley Temple and Me, 1973; The Edge of a Smile, 1974; The Passing Out Parade (theatre), 1979; Tenko Reunion, 1984; Talking About the War... (non-fiction), 1991. Other: Over 50 television plays. Contributions: Radio Times. *Honours:* Book of the Month, Telegraph; BAFTA Award, Tenko (TV Series), 1984. *Address:* Flat 3, 28 Arkwright Rd, London NW3 6BH, England.

FISCHER, August A.; Swiss fmr publishing executive; b. 7 Feb. 1939, Zürich; m. Gillian Ann Fischer 1961; one s. one d. *Career:* various positions E.I. Du Pont De Nemours & Co. 1962–78; Man. Dir European subsidiary of Napp Systems Inc. 1978–81, Exec. Vice-Pres., then Pres. and COO Napp Systems Inc., San Diego, Calif. 1981–89; Gen. Man. Devt, News Int. PLC 1989–90, Man. Dir 1990–95, mem. Bd and COO News Corpn Ltd 1991–95, Chief Exec. News Int. PLC (UK subsidiary of News Corpn) 1993–95; mem. Supervisory Bd Ringier AG, Zürich, consultant 1995–97; Chair. Bd and CEO Axel Springer Verlag AG 1998–2001; mem. American Man. Asscn, The Pres.'s Asscn; Trustee St Katharine and Shadwell Trust. *Address:* c/o Axel Springer Verlag AG, Axel-Springer-str. 65, 10117 Berlin, Germany (Office).

FISCHER, Tibor; Journalist and Writer; b. 15 Nov. 1959, Stockport, England. *Education:* University of Cambridge. *Publications:* Under the Frog, 1992, US edn as Under the Frog: A Black Comedy, 1994; The Thought Gang, 1994; The Collector Collector, 1997; Don't Read This Book if You're Stupid (short stories, aka I Like Being Killed), 2000; Voyage to the End of the Room, 2003. *Honours:* Betty Trask Award for Best of Young British Novelists, 1993. *Literary Agent:* William Morris Agency (UK) Ltd, 52–53 Poland St, London W1F 7LX, England.

FISH, Joe (see Williamson, Philip G.).

FISH, Stanley Eugene, BA, MA, PhD; academic and writer; *Dean of the College of Liberal Arts and Sciences, University of Illinois at Chicago*; b. 19 April 1938, Providence, RI, USA; m. 1st Adrienne Aaron 1959 (divorced 1980); one d.; m. 2nd Jane Parry Tompkins 1982. *Education:* Univ. of Pennsylvania, Yale Univ. *Career:* Asst Prof. 1963–67, Assoc. Prof. of English 1967–69, Prof. of English 1969–74, Univ. of California at Berkeley; Visiting Asst Prof., Washington Univ., St Louis 1967; Visiting Prof., Sir George Williams Univ. 1969, Linguistics Inst., SUNY 1971, Columbia Univ. 1983–84; Visiting Prof. 1971, Prof. of English 1974–78, William Kenan Jr Prof. of English and Humanities 1978–85, Chair, Dept of English 1983–85, Johns Hopkins Univ.; Visiting Bing Prof. of English, Univ. of Southern California at Los Angeles 1973–74; Adjunct Prof., Univ. of Maryland Law School 1976–85; Arts and Sciences Prof. of English and Prof. of Law 1985–98, Duke Univ.; Exec. Dir, Duke Univ. Press 1993–98; Dean, Coll. of Liberal Arts and Sciences, Univ. of Illinois at Chicago 1999–; Distinguished Visiting Prof., John Marshall Law School 2000–02; Fellow, Humanities Research Inst., Univ. of California at Irvine 1989; mem. American Acad. of Arts and Sciences, Milton Soc. of America (pres. 1980). *Publications:* John Skelton's Poetry 1965, Surprised by Sin: The Reader in Paradise Lost 1967, Seventeenth Century Prose: Modern Essays in Criticism (ed.) 1971, Self-Consuming Artifacts: The Experience of Seventeenth Century Literature 1972, The Living Temple: George Herbert and Catechizing 1978, Is There a Text in This Class?: The Authority of Interpretive Communities 1980, Doing What Comes Naturally: Change, Rhetoric, and the Practice of Theory in Literary and Legal Studies 1989, There's No Such Thing as Free Speech, and It's a Good Thing, Too 1994, Professional Correctness: Literary Studies and Political Change 1995, The Stanley Fish Reader (ed. by H. Aram Veeser) 1998, The Trouble with Principle 1999, How Milton Works 2001; contrib. to scholarly books and journals. *Honours:* ACLS Fellowship 1966, Humanities Research Professorship, Univ. of California at Berkeley 1966, 1970, second place Explicator Prize 1968, Guggenheim Fellowship 1969–70, Honored Scholar, Milton Soc. of America 1991, PEN/Spielvogel-Diamonstein Award 1994, Hanford Book Award 1998. *Address:* c/o Office of the Dean, College of Liberal Arts and Sciences, University of Illinois at Chicago, 601 S Morgan Street, Chicago, IL 60607-7104, USA.

FISHER, Allen; Painter, Poet and Art Historian; b. 1 Nov. 1944, Norbury, Surrey, England. *Education:* BA, University of London; MA, University of Essex. *Career:* Head of Art, Professor of Poetry and Art, University of Surrey Roehampton. *Publications:* Over 100 books incl.: Place Book One, 1974; Brixton Fractals, 1985; Unpolished Mirrors, 1985; Stepping Out, 1989; Future Exiles, 1991; Fizz, 1994; Civic Crime, 1994; Breadboard, 1994; Now's the Time, 1995; The Topological Shovel (essays), 1999; Watusi, 2000; Ring Shout, 2001; Sojourns, 2001. Contributions: various magazines and journals. *Honours:* Co-Winner, Alice Hunt Bartlett Award, 1975. *Address:* 14 Hopton Rd, Hereford HR1 1BE, England. *E-mail:* a.fisher@roehampton.ac.uk.

FISHER, Carrie; American actress and author; b. 21 Oct. 1956, Beverly Hills; m. Paul Simon 1983 (divorced 1984); one d. *Education:* Beverly Hills High School and Cen. School of Speech and Drama, London. *Career:* appeared with her mother in nightclub act aged 13; appeared in chorus of Broadway production of Irene, starring Debbie Reynolds, aged 15; Broadway stage appearances in Censored Scenes from King Kong, Agnes of God; several TV credits; film début in Shampoo (Photoplay Award as Best Newcomer of the Year) 1974. *Films include:* Shampoo 1974, Star Wars 1977, The Empire Strikes Back 1980, The Blues Brothers 1980, Return of the Jedi 1983, Under the Rainbow, Garbo Talks, The Man With One Red Shoe 1985, Hannah and Her Sisters 1986, Amazing Women on the Moon 1987, Appointment With Death 1988, The 'Burbs 1989, Loverboy 1989, She's Back 1989, When Harry Met Sally... 1989, The Time Guardian 1990, Sibling Rivalry 1990, Drop Dead Fred 1991, Soapdish 1991, This is My Life 1992, Austin Powers: International Man of Mystery 2000, Scream 3 2000, Famous 2000, Heartbreakers 2001, Jay and Silent Bob Strike Back 2001, A Midsummer Night's Rave 2002. *Publications:* Postcards From the Edge (novel and screenplay, PEN Award for first novel 1987) 1987, Surrender the Pink 1990, Delusions of Grandma 1994 (novels), The Best Awful There Is 2003; short stories. *Literary Agent:* Creative Artists Agency, 9830 Wilshire Boulevard, Beverly Hills, CA 90212, USA.

FISHER, Leonard Everett; Artist and Author; b. 24 June 1924, New York, NY, USA; m. Margery Meskin, 21 Dec. 1952, one s. two d. *Education:* BFA, 1949, MFA, 1950, Yale University. *Career:* mem. PEN; Authors' Guild; Society of Illustrators; Society of Children's Book Authors and Illustrators. *Publications:* 88 books written and illustrated including: Non Fiction: Colonial Americans, 19 vols, 1964–76; Ellis Island, 1986; Look Around, 1987; The Tower of London, 1987; Galileo, 1992; Tracks Across America, 1992; Stars and Stripes, 1993; Marie Curie, 1994; Moses, 1995; Gandhi, 1995; Niagara Falls, 1996; Anasazi, 1997. Fiction: Death of Evening Star, 1972; Across the Sea from Galway, 1975; Sailboat Lost, 1991; Cyclops, 1991; Kinderdike, 1994; William Tell, 1996; The Jetty Chronicles, 1997; Gods and Goddesses of the Ancient Maya, 2000; Sky, Sea, the Jetty and Me, 2001; Gods and Goddesses of the Ancient Norse, 2001. Other: Illustrator of children's books. *Honours:* Premio Grafico Fiera di Bologno, Italy, 1968; Medallion, University of Southern Mississippi, 1979; Christopher Medal, 1980; National Jewish Book Award for Children's Literature, 1981; Children's Book Guild, Washington Post Non-Fiction Award, 1989; Regina Medal, Catholic Library Asscn, 1991; Kerlan Award, University of Minnesota, 1991; Arbuthnot Honour Lecture Citation, American Library Asscn, 1994. *Literary Agent:* William B. R. Reiss, c/o John Hawkins and Assocs, New York, NY 10010, USA. *Address:* 7 Twin Bridge Acres Rd, Westport, CT 06880, USA.

FISHER, Roy; Poet and Musician; b. 11 June 1930, Birmingham, England. *Education:* BA, 1951, MA, 1970, Birmingham University. *Career:* mem. Musicians Union; Society of Authors. *Publications:* City, 1961; Interiors, 1966; The Ship's Orchestra, 1967; The Memorial Fountain, 1968; Matrix, 1971; Cut Pages, 1971; Metamorphoses, 1971; The Thing About Joe

Sullivan, 1978; A Furnace, 1986; The Left-Handed Punch, 1987; Poems 1955–1987, 1988; Birmingham River, 1994; The Dow Low Drop: New and Selected Poems, 1996; Interviews Through Time, 2000. Contributions: numerous journals and magazines. *Honours:* Andrew Kelus Prize, 1979; Cholmondeley Award, 1981; Hamlyn Award, 1997; Hon. DLitt, University of Keele, 1999. *Address:* Four Ways, Earl Sterndale, Buxton, Derbyshire SK17 0EP, England.

FISHKIN, Shelley Fisher; Prof. of American Studies and English, Writer and Ed.; b. 9 May 1950, New York, NY, USA; m. James Steven Fishkin, 27 May 1973, two s. *Education:* Swarthmore College, 1967–69; BA in English, 1971, MA in English, 1974, MPhil in American Studies, 1974, PhD in American Studies, 1977, Yale University. *Career:* Visiting Lecturer, Yale University, 1981–84; Senior Lecturer, 1985–89, Assoc. Prof., 1989–92, Prof. of American Studies, 1993–, Prof. of American Studies and English, 1994–, University of Texas at Austin; Assoc. Ed., American National Biography, 1989–; mem. American Literature Asscn; American Studies Asscn; Authors' Guild; Charlotte Perkins Gilman Society, co-founder and exec. dir, 1990–; International Theodore Dreiser Society; Mark Twain Circle of America, pres., 1997–; MLA; Research Society for American Periodicals, board of dirs, 1991–94. *Publications:* From Fact to Fiction: Journalism and Imaginative Writing in America, 1985; Was Huck Black?: Mark Twain and African-American Voices, 1993; Listening to Silences: New Essays in Feminist Criticism (ed. with Elaine Hedges), 1994; The Oxford Mark Twain (ed.), 29 vols, 1996; Lighting Out for the Territory: Reflections on Mark Twain and American Culture, 1997. Contributions: Books, journals, newspapers and periodicals. *Honours:* Mellon Fellow, 1979, Rockefeller Humanist Fellow, 1984, Aspen Institute; Frank Luther Mott-Kappa Tau Alpha Research Book Award, National Journalism Scholarship Society, 1986; ACLS Fellowship, 1987–88; Humanities Scholar, Connecticut Humanities Council, 1987, 1989–91; Visiting Fellow, 1992–93; Life Mem., 1993–, Clare Hall, Cambridge; Outstanding Academic Book Citation, Choice, 1994. *Address:* c/o American Studies Program, University of Texas at Austin, Austin, TX 78712, USA.

FISHLOCK, Trevor; journalist and writer; b. 21 Feb. 1941, Hereford, England; m. Penelope Symon 1978. *Career:* Portsmouth Evening News 1957–62; freelance news agency reporter 1962–68; staff correspondent, Wales and W England 1968–77, South Asia correspondent 1980–83, New York correspondent 1983–86, Times; roving foreign correspondent 1986–89, 1993–96, Moscow correspondent 1989–91, Daily Telegraph; roving foreign correspondent, Sunday Telegraph 1991–93; mem. Travellers' Club, Soc. of Authors, World Press Inst. *Publications:* Wales and the Welsh 1972, Discovering Britain: Wales 1975, Talking of Wales 1975, Americans and Nothing Else 1980, India File 1983, The State of America 1986, Indira Gandhi (juvenile) 1986, Out of Red Darkness 1992, My Foreign Country 1997, Wild Tracks 1998, Cobra Road 1999, More Wild Tracks 2000, Fishlock's Sea Stories 2003, Conquerors of Time: Exploration and Invention in the Age of Daring 2004. *Honours:* David Holden Award for Foreign Reporting 1983, Int. Reporter of the Year 1986, British Press Awards. *Address:* 7 Teilo Street, Pontcanna, Cardiff CF11 9JN, Wales.

FISHMAN, Charles Munro, BA, MA, DA; American academic, poet and writer; b. 10 July 1942, Oceanside, NY; m. Ellen Marci Haselkorn 1967; two d. *Education:* Hofstra Univ., SUNY at Albany. *Career:* Founder-Dir, Visiting Writers Program, 1979–97, Distinguished Service Prof., 1989–, Prof. Emeritus, 1997–, Dir Distinguished Speakers Program, SUNY at Farmingdale; Founder-Ed., Xanadu, 1975–78; Poetry Ed., Gaia, 1993–95, The Genocide Forum, 1997–99, The Cistercian Studies Quarterly, 1998–99, Journal of Genocide Research, 1999; Assoc. Ed., The Drunken Boat, 1999–; Poetry Ed. New Works Review; mem. Associated Writing Programs; Poetry Society of America; Poets and Writers. *Publications:* An Index to Women's Magazines and Presses (ed.), 1977; Mortal Companions, 1977; The Death Mazurka, 1989; Zoom, 1990; Catlives, by Sarah Kirsch (trans. with Marina Roscher), 1991; Blood to Remember: American Poets on the Holocaust (ed.), 1991; As the Sun Goes Down in Fire, 1992; Nineteenth-Century Rain, 1994; The Firewalkers, 1996; An Aztec Memory, 1997, Time Travel Reports 2002. Contributions: many anthologies and over 300 periodicals. *Honours:* Gertrude B. Claytor Memorial Award, Poetry Society of America, 1987; Outstanding Academic Book of the Year, American Library Asscn, 1989; Firman Houghton Poetry Award, New England Poetry Club, 1995; New York Foundation for the Arts Fellowship in Poetry, 1995; Winner, Anabiosis Press Chapbook Competition, 1996; Ann Stanford Poetry Prize, Southern California Anthology, 1996; Eve of St Agnes Poetry Prize, 1999. *Address:* 56 Wood Acres Road, East Patchogue, NY 11772, USA.

FISK, Pauline, (Pauline Davies); Writer; b. 27 Sept. 1948, London, England; m. David Davies, 12 Feb. 1972, two s. three d. *Publications:* Midnight Blue, 1990; Telling the Sea, 1992; Tyger Pool, 1994; Beast of Whixall Moss, 1997; The Candle House, 1999; Sabrina Fludde, 2001; The Red Judge, 2004. Contributions: Homes and Gardens, 1989; Something to Do With Love (anthology), 1996. *Honours:* Smarties Grand Prix Prize, 1990. *Address:* c/o Laura Cecil, 17 Alwyne Villas, London N1 2HG, England.

FITZGERALD, Judith (Ariana); Poet and Critic; b. 11 Nov. 1952, Toronto, Ontario, Canada. *Education:* BA, 1976, MA, 1977, York University. *Career:* Teacher, Erindale College, 1978–81; Prof., Laurentian University, 1981–83; Poetry Ed., Black Moss Press, 1981–87; Entertainment Journalist, The Globe, 1983–84; Poetry Critic, The Toronto Star, 1984–88; Writer-in-Residence, University of Windsor, 1993–94; Creator, Today's Country, Satellite Radio Network, 1993–; Prof. of English, Université Canadienne en France, 1994–95; mem. League of Canadian Poets; Society of Composers, Authors and Music Publishers of Canada. *Publications:* Poetry: City Park, 1972; Journal Entries, 1975; Victory, 1975; Lacerating Heartwood, 1977; Easy Over, 1981; Split/Levels, 1983; Heart Attacks, 1984; Beneath the Skin of Paradise, 1984; Given Names, 1985; Diary of Desire, 1987; Rapturous Chronicles, 1991; Ultimate Midnight, 1992; Walkin' Wounded, 1993; River, 1995; AKA Paradise, 1996. Children's Poetry: My Orange Gorange, 1985; Whale Waddleby, 1986. Editor: Un Dozen: Thirteen Canadian Poets, 1982; Sp/Elles: Poetry by Canadian Women/Poesie de femmes canadiennes, 1986; First Person Plural, 1988. Contributions: various anthologies and other publications. *Honours:* Fiona Mee Award, 1983; Writers' Choice Award, 1986; several grants. *Address:* c/o League of Canadian Poets, 54 Wolseley St, Third Floor, Toronto, Ontario M5T 1AS, Canada.

FITZGERALD, Niall, KBE, FRSA, BComm; Irish business executive; *Chairman, Reuters Group PLC*; b. 13 Sept. 1945; m.; two s. two d. *Education:* Univ. Coll., Dublin. *Career:* joined Unilever 1967, various man. roles including CEO, Unilever Food Div., S Africa, early 1980s, later Treasurer, Unilever, London, Dir Unilever PLC and Unilever NV1987–2004, Financial Dir 1987–89, Co-ordinator, Edible Fats and Dairy 1989–90, mem. Foods Exec. 1989–91, Co-ordinator, Detergents 1991–95, Vice-Pres. Unilever PLC 1994–96, Chair. 1996–2004, also becoming Vice-Chair. Unilever NV 1996–2004; Dir Reuters Group 2003–, Chair. 2004–; Pres. Advertising Asscn, S Africa Int. Investment Advisory Council, Shanghai Major's Int. Business Leaders' Council; Vice-Chair. The Conf. Bd; mem. World Econ. Forum, Int. Advisory Bd, Council on Foreign Relations, Trilateral Comm., EU–China Cttee, US Business Council; Gov. Nat. Inst. of Econ. and Social Research; Trustee, Leverhulme Trust; fmr Dir Merck, Ericsson, Bank of Ireland, Prudential Corpn. *Address:* Reuters Group PLC, 85 Fleet Street, London, EC4P 4AJ, England (Office). *Telephone:* (20) 7250-1122 (Office). *Fax:* (20) 7542-4064 (Office). *Website:* www.reuters.com (Office).

FITZMAURICE, Gabriel John; Primary Teacher and Poet; b. 7 Dec. 1952, Moyvane, County Kerry, Ireland; m. Brenda Downey, 17 Aug. 1981, one s. one d. *Education:* Leaving Certificate, St Michael's College, Listowel, County Kerry, 1970; Diploma, Primary Teaching, Mary Immaculate College, Limerick, 1972. *Career:* Asst Teacher, Avoca National School, County Wicklow, 1972–74; Teacher, Christ the King National School, Limerick City, 1974–75, Moyvane National School, 1975–. *Publications:* Poetry in English: Rainsong, 1984; Road to the Horizon, 1987; Dancing Through, 1990; The Father's Part, 1992; The Space Between: New and Selected Poems 1984–92, 1993; The Village Sings, 1996; A Wrenboy's Carnival: Poems 1980–2000, 2000; I and the Village, 2002. Poetry in Irish: Nocht, 1989; Ag Síobshiúl Chun An Rince, 1995; Giolla na nAmhrán: Dánta 1988–1998, 1998. Essays: Kerry on My Mind, 1999. Other: Children's poetry in English and Irish. Translator: The Purge, by Míchéal Ó hAirtnéide, 1989; Poems I Wish I'd Written, 1996. Editor: The Flowering Tree, 1991; Between the Hills and Sea: Songs and Ballads of Kerry, 1991; Con Greaney: Traditional Singer, 1991; Homecoming/An Bealach 'na Bhaile: Selected Poems of Cathal Ó Searcaigh (Cló Iar-Chonnacnta, 1993; Irish Poetry Now: Other Voices, 1993; Kerry Through Its Writers, 1993; The Listowel Literary Phenomenon: North Kerry Writers – A Critical Introduction, 1994; Rusty Nails and Astronauts: A Wolfhound Poetry Anthology, 1999; 'The Boro' and 'The Cross': The Parish of Moyvane-Knockanure (with Áine Cronin and John Looney), 2000; The Kerry Anthology, 2000. Contributions: newspapers, reviews, and journals. *Honours:* Represented Ireland, Europees Poeziefestival, Leuven, Belgium, 1987, 1991; Award Winner, Gerard Manley Hopkins Centenary Poetry Competition, 1989. *Address:* Applegarth, Moyvane, County Kerry, Ireland.

FITZSIMMONS, Thomas; Poet, Writer, Trans., Ed., Publisher and Prof.; b. 21 Oct. 1926, Lowell, Massachusetts, USA; Emeritus of English and Comparative Literature. m. Karen Hargreaves, two s. *Education:* Fresno State College, 1947–49; Sorbonne and Institut de Sciences Politiques, Paris, 1949–50; BA, English Literature and Creative Writing, Stanford University, 1951; MA, English and Comparative Literature, Columbia University, 1952. *Career:* Writer and Ed., The New Republic magazine, 1952–55; Research Team Chair., 1955–56, Dir of Research for Publication, 1956–58, Dir and Ed., 1958–59, HRAF Press, Yale University; Asst Prof., 1959–61, Assoc. Prof., 1961–66, Prof. of English and Comparative Literature, 1966–89, Prof. Emeritus, 1989–, Oakland University, Rochester, Michigan; Fulbright Lecturer, Tokyo University of Education, 1962–64, Tsuda University, Tokyo, 1962–64, University of Bucharest, 1967–68, University of Nice, 1968; Visiting Lecturer, Japan National Women's University, Tokyo, 1973–75, Keio University, Tokyo, 1973–75, Detroit Institute of Arts, 1986; Visiting Prof., Tokyo University of Education, 1973–75, Kyushu National University, Fukuoka, 1979; Visiting Poet and Scholar, Sophia University, Tokyo, 1988–89; Ed.-Publisher, Katydid Books. *Publications:* Poetry: This Time This Place, 1969; Mooning, 1971; Meditation Seeds, 1971; With the Water, 1972; Playseeds, 1973; The Big Huge, 1975; The Nine Seas and the Eight Mountains, 1981; Rocking Mirror Daybreak, 1982; Water Ground Stone (poems and essays), 1994; The Dream

Machine, 1996; Fencing the Sky, 1998; Iron Harp, 1999; Build Me Ruins 2002. Other: Author, ed. or trans. of over 60 vols, 1955–98. *Honours:* National Endowment for the Arts Fellowships, 1967, 1982, 1989–90, and Grants, 1984, 1986; Oakland University Research Fellowship, 1982; Japan-US Friendship Foundation Grant, 1983; Michigan Council for the Arts Award, 1986; Fulbright Research Fellowship, Japan, 1988–89. *Address:* 1 Balsa Rd, Santa Fe, NM 87505, USA.

FLAGG, Fannie, (Patricia Neal); Writer and Actress; b. 21 Sept. 1941, Birmingham, AL, USA. *Education:* University of Alabama; Pittsburgh Playhouse; Town and Gown Theatre. *Publications:* Coming Attractions: A Wonderful Novel, 1981; Fried Green Tomatoes at the Whistle Stop Cafe, 1987; Welcome to the World, Baby Girl!, 1988. Other: Fried Green Tomatoes at the Whistle Stop Cafe (screenplay with Jon Avnet), 1991; Standing in the Rainbow, 2002. Contributions: Magazines and newspapers. *Address:* c/o Random House Inc, 201 E 50th St, New York, NY 10022, USA.

FLAM, Jack (Donald); Prof. of Art History and Writer; b. 2 April 1940, Paterson, NJ, USA; m. Bonnie Burnham, 7 Oct. 1972, one d. *Education:* BA, Rutgers University, 1961; MA, Columbia University, 1963; PhD, New York University, 1969. *Career:* Instructor in Art, Newark College of Arts and Sciences, Rutgers University, 1962–66; Asst Prof. of Art, 1966–69, Assoc. Prof. of Art, 1969–72, University of Florida; Assoc. Prof. of Art, 1975–79, Prof. of Art, 1980–91, Distinguished Prof. of Art, 1991–, Brooklyn College, CUNY; Assoc. Prof. of Art History, 1979–80, Prof. of Art History, 1980–91, Distinguished Prof. of Art History, 1991–, Graduate School and University Center, CUNY; Art Critic, The Wall Street Journal, 1984–92; mem. International Asscn of Art Critics; PEN. *Publications:* Matisse on Art, 1973; Zoltan Gorency, 1974; Bread and Butter, 1977; Henri Matisse Paper Cut-Outs (co-author), 1977; Robert Motherwell (co-author), 1983; Matisse: The Man and His Art 1869–1918, 1986; Fernand Léger, 1987; Matisse: A Retrospective, 1988; Motherwell, 1991; Richard Diebenkorn: Ocean Park, 1992; Matisse: The Dance, 1993; Western Artists/African Art, 1994; The Paine Webber Art Collection (co-author), 1995; Robert Smithson: The Collected Writings (ed.), 1996; Judith Rotheschild an Artist's Search, 1998; Les Peintures de Picasso: Un Théâtre Mentale, 1998; The Modern Drawing, 1999; Matisse and Picasso: The Story of Their Rivalry and Friendship, 2003; Primitivism and Twentieth-Century Art: A Documentary History, 2003. Contributions: Apollo; Art in America; Art News; New York Review of Books. *Honours:* Guggenheim Fellowship, 1979–80; National Endowment for the Humanities Fellowship, 1987–88. *Address:* c/o Georges Borchardt Inc., 136 E 57th St, New York, NY 10022, USA.

FLAMMARION, Charles-Henri, LèsL, LèsLet, MBA; French publishing executive; b. 27 July 1946, Boulogne-Billancourt; m. Marie-Françoise Mariani 1968; one s. two d. *Education:* Lycée de Sèvres, Sorbonne, Paris, Institut d'Etudes Politiques, Paris and Columbia Univ., USA. *Career:* Asst Man. Editions Flammarion 1972–81, Gen. Man. 1981–85, Pres. Flammarion SA 1985–; Pres. Editions J'ai Lu 1982–, Audie-Fluide Glacial 1990–; mem. Bureau du Syndicat Nat. de l'Édition 1979–88, 1996–; Vice-Pres. Cercle de la Librairie 1988–94, Pres. 1994–2003; Pres. Casterman 1999–. *Address:* Flammarion SA, 26 rue Racine, 75006 Paris (Office); 5 avenue Franco-Russe, 75007 Paris, France (Home).

FLANAGAN, Mary; Novelist and Critic; b. 20 May 1943, Rochester, NH, USA. *Education:* BA, History of Art, Brandeis University, Waltham, MA, USA. *Career:* Creative Writing Seminars (two terms), University of East Anglia, England; mem. PEN; Society of Authors. *Publications:* Bad Girls, 1984; Trust, 1987; Rose Reason, 1991; The Blue Woman, 1994; Adèle, 1997.

FLANAGAN, Richard; Australian writer and film director; b. 1961, Tasmania. *Education:* Univ. of Oxford, UK. *Career:* fmr river guide; scriptwriter, author of history books, novelist. *Film:* The Sound of One Hand Clapping (dir). *Publications include:* non-fiction: A Terrible Beauty: A History of the Gordon River County, Codename Iago: The Story of John Friedrich, Parish-Fed Bastards: A History of the Politics of the Unemployed in Britain 1884–1939 1994; novels: Death of a River Guide (Victorian Premier's Award for Fiction) 1995, The Sound of One Hand Clapping 1998, Gould's Book of Fish (Commonwealth Writer's Prize) 2002. *Honours:* Rhodes Scholar. *Address:* c/o Pan Macmillan Australia Pty Ltd, Level 18/ St Martin's Tower, 31 Market Street, Sydney, NSW 2000, Australia (Office).

FLANAGIN, Annette, RN, MA; American; *Managing Senior Editor, Journal of the American Medical Association. Career:* fmr pres., Council of Science Eds; Managing Sr Ed., Journal of the American Medical Asscn; mem., Council of Science Eds 1989–. *Address:* Journal of the American Medical Assocation (JAMA), 515 North State Street, Chicago, IL 60610, USA. *Telephone:* (342) 464-2432. *E-mail:* annette_flanagin@ama-assn.org. *Website:* jama.ama-assn.org.

FLEISCHMAN, Paul; Children's Writer and Poet; b. 5 Sept. 1952, Monterey, CA, USA; m. Becky Mojica, 15 Dec. 1978, two s. *Education:* University of California at Berkeley; BA, University of New Mexico. *Career:* mem. Authors' Guild; Society of Children's Book Writers. *Publications:* The Birthday Tree, 1979; The Half-a-Moon Inn, 1980; Graven Images, 1982; Path of the Pale Horse, 1983; Finzel the Farsighted, 1983; Coming-and-Going Men, 1985; I Am Phoenix: Poems for Two Voices, 1985; Rondo in C, 1988; Joyful Noise: Poems for Two Voices, 1989; Saturnalia, 1990; Shadow Play, 1990; The Borning Room, 1991; Time Train, 1991. *Honours:* Silver Medal, Commonwealth Club of California, 1980; Newberry Medals, American Library Asscn, 1983, 1989; Parents Choice Award, 1983; numerous citations by Society of Children's Book Writers, American Library Asscn, New York Times.

FLEISCHMAN, (Albert) Sidney, BA; American writer; b. 16 March 1920, New York, NY. *Education:* San Diego State Coll. *Publications:* 10 adult novels 1948–63, over 40 children's books 1962–. *Honours:* Newbery Award 1987. *Address:* 305 10th Street, Santa Monica, CA 90402, USA.

FLEISSNER, Robert F., MA, PhD; academic and writer; b. 17 Oct. 1932, Auburn, NY, USA; m. Judith Gerber 1966 (divorced 1967). *Education:* Hamilton College, Cornell University, Catholic University of America, Middlebury College; University of North Carolina at Chapel Hill, Ohio State University, New York University. *Career:* Instructor in English, Speech and Drama, Spring Hill College, Mobile, AL, 1958–59; Asst Instructor in English, Ohio State University, 1960–61; Lecturer in English, City College, CUNY, 1962–64; Asst Prof. of English, Dominican College, Blauvelt, New York, 1964–66; Instructor in English, University of New Mexico, Albuquerque, 1966–67; Asst Prof., then Assoc. Prof. of English, Central State University, Wilberforce, Ohio, 1967–; mem. MLA of America; T. S. Eliot Society; Shakespeare Asscn of America. *Publications:* Dickens and Shakespeare: A Study in Histrionic Contrasts 1969, Resolved to Love: The 1592 Edition of Henry Constable's 'Diana' Critically Considered 1980, The Prince and the Professor: The Wittenberg Connection in Marlowe, Shakespeare, Goethe and Frost – A Hamlet-Faust(us) Analogy 1986, Ascending the Prufrockian Stair: Studies in a Dissociatted Sensibility 1988, A Rose by Another Name: A Survey of Literary Flora from Shakespeare to Eco 1989, Shakespeare and the Matter of the Crux 1991, T. S. Eliot and the Heritage of Africa 1992, Frost's Road Taken 1996, Sources, Meaning, and Influences of Coleridge's 'Kubla Khan' 2000, Names, Titles and Characters by Literary Writers: Shakespeare, 19th- and 20th-Century Authors 2001, The Master Sleuth on the Trail of 'Edwin Drood': Sherlock Holmes and the Jasper Syndrome 2001, Shakespearean and Other Literary Investigations with the Master Sleuth (and Conan Doyle): Homing in on Holmes 2003; Shakespeare and Africa: The Dark Lady of his Sonnets Revamped and Other Africa-Related Associations 2004; contrib. to books and journals. *Address:* 367 E Cassilly Street, Springfield, OH 45503, USA.

FLEMING, Laurence William Howie; Author, Artist and Landscape Designer; b. 8 Sept. 1929, Shillong, Assam, India. *Education:* The New School, Darjeeling, India, 1941–44; Repton School, Derbyshire, 1945–47; Royal Air Force, 1947–49; St Catharine's College, Cambridge, 1949–52. *Career:* mem. International PEN; Writers Guild; Anglo-Brazilian Society. *Publications:* A Diet of Crumbs, 1959; The English Garden, 1979; The One Hour Garden, 1985; Old English Villages, 1986; Roberto Burle Marx: A Portrait, 1996. Contributions: journals. *Address:* c/o Lloyds Bank Plc, 112 Kensington High St, London W8 4SN, England.

FLETCHER, John (Walter James), (Jonathan Fune); Emeritus Prof. of European Literature, Writer and Trans; b. 23 June 1937, Barking, Essex, England; m. Beryl Sibley Connop, 14 Sept. 1961, two s. one d. *Education:* BA, 1959, MA, 1963, University of Cambridge; MPhil, 1961, PhD, 1964, University of Toulouse. *Career:* Lecturer, University of Toulouse, 1961–64, University of Durham, 1964–66; Lecturer in French, 1966–68, Reader in French, 1968–69, Prof. of Comparative Literature, 1969–89, Prof. of European Literature, 1989–98, Prof. Emeritus, 1998–, University of East Anglia. Hon. Senior Research Fellow, University of Kent at Canterbury, 1998; mem. Asscn of University Teachers; Society of Authors; Trans' Asscn. *Publications:* The Novels of Samuel Beckett, 1964; Samuel Beckett's Art, 1967; A Critical Commentary on Flaubert's Trois Contes, 1968; New Directions in Literature: Critical Approaches to a Contemporary Phenomenon, 1968; Samuel Beckett: Fin de Partie (ed. with Beryl S. Fletcher), 1970; Samuel Beckett: His Works and His Critics, An Essay in Bibliography (with Raymond Federman), 1970; Beckett: A Study of His Plays (with John Spurling), 1972; Claude Simon and Fiction Now, 1975; Novel and Reader, 1980; Alain Robbe-Grillet, 1983; The Nouveau Roman Reader (ed. with John Calder), 1986; Iris Murdoch: A Primary and Secondary Bibliography (with Cheryl Bove), 1994; About Beckett: The Playwright and the Work, 2003. Contributions: scholarly journals, newspapers and periodicals. *Honours:* Scott Moncrieff Prize, 1990; Honourable Mention, Florence Gould Foundation Trans. Prize, 1990. *Address:* 23 Rheims Ct, Canterbury CT2 8BL, England. *E-mail:* j.w.j.fletcher@kent.ac.uk.

FLINT, John (see Wells, Peter Frederick).

FLORA, Joseph Martin; Prof., Writer and Ed.; b. 9 Feb. 1934, Toledo, Ohio, USA; m. Glenda Christine Flora, 30 Jan. 1959, four s. *Education:* BA, English, 1956, MA, English, 1957, PhD, English, 1962, University of Michigan. *Career:* Teaching Fellow to Instructor, University of Michigan, 1957–62; Instructor, 1962–64, Asst Prof., 1964–66, Assoc. Prof., 1966–77, Prof., 1977–2001, Atlanta Prof. of Southern Culture, 2001–, University of North Carolina at Chapel Hill; Visiting Prof., University of New Mexico, 1976, 1996; Senior Ed., American Literature, 1915–1945, Twayne Publishers, 1989–; mem. American Literature Asscn; James Branch Cabell Society; Hemingway Society; MLA; Society for the Study of Southern Literature; South Atlantic MLA, pres., 1998–99; Thomas Wolfe Society, pres., 1995–97; Western Literature Asscn, pres., 1992. *Publications:* Vardis Fisher, 1965; William Ernest Henley, 1970; Frederick Manfred, 1974;

Southern Writers: A Biographical Dictionary (ed. with Robert Bain and Louis D. Rubin Jr), 1979; Hemingway's Nick Adams, 1982; The English Short Story 1880–1945: A Critical History (ed.), 1985; Fifty Southern Writers After 1900 (ed. with Robert Bain), 1987; Fifty Southern Writers Before 1900 (ed. with Robert Bain), 1987; Ernest Hemingway: A Study of the Short Fiction, 1989; Contemporary Fiction Writers of the South (ed. with Robert Bain), 1993; Contemporary Poets, Dramatists, Essayists, and Novelists of the South (ed. with Robert Bain), 1994; Rediscovering Vardis Fisher: Centennial Essays, 2000; The Companion to Southern Literature (ed. with Lucinda MacKethan). Contributions: Books and journals. *Honours:* Kenan Research Award, 1978; Mayflower Award, North Carolina Literary and Historical Asscn, 1982. *Address:* 505 Caswell Rd, Chapel Hill, NC 27514, USA.

FLOREN, Lee, (Brett Austin, Lisa Franchon, Claudia Hall, Wade Hamilton, Matt Harding, Matthew Whitman Harding, Felix Lee Horton, Stuart Jason, Grace Lang, Marguerite Nelson, Lew Smith, Maria Sandra Sterling, Lee Thomas, Len Turner, Will Watson, Dave Wilson); Author; b. 22 March 1910, Hinsdale, Montana, USA. *Education:* BA, Santa Barbara State College; Teacher's Certificate, Occidental College; MA, Texas Western College, 1964. *Publications:* Over 300 novels, 1944–. *Address:* c/o Hale, 45–47 Clerkenwell Green, London EC1R 0HT, England.

FLUSFEDER, David; Writer; b. Nov. 1960, Berkeley Heights, NJ, USA; m. Susan Flusfeder 1990; one s. one d. *Education:* BA, Philosophy with Literature, Sussex Univ., 1983; MA, Creative Writing, Univ. of East Anglia 1988. *Publications:* Novels: Man Kills Woman, 1993; Like Plastic, 1996; Morocco, 2000; The Gift, 2003. Contributions: short stories in anthologies, incl. New Writing 8, Fatherhood, The Agony and the Ecstasy; magazines and newspapers incl. Erotic Review, Arena, Esquire, Jewish Quarterly, The Times, Guardian, TLS, GQ, Frankfurter Allgemeine Zeitung, Literaturen, Jewish Chronicle, Daily Telegraph. *Honours:* Encore Award, 1997. *Address:* c/o Fourth Estate, 77–85 Fulham Palace Rd, London W6 8JB, England.

FLYNN, Robert (Lopez); Prof. and Writer; b. 12 April 1932, Chillicothe, TX, USA; m. Jean Sorrels 1 June 1953; two d. *Career:* Asst Prof., Baylor University, Waco, Texas, 1959–63; fmr Prof., Novelist-in-Residence, Trinity University, San Antonio, TX. *Publications:* North to Yesterday, 1967; In the House of the Lord, 1969; The Sounds of Rescue, The Signs of Hope, 1970; Seasonal Rain and Other Stories, 1986; Wanderer Springs, 1987; A Personal War in Vietnam, 1989; When I Was Just Your Age, 1992; The Last Klick, 1994; Living with the Hyenas, 1996; The Devil's Tiger; Tie-Fast Country; Growing Up a Sullen Baptist, and Other Lies; Paul Baker and the Integration of Abilities. *Address:* 101 Cliffside Dr., San Antonio, TX 78231, USA.

FO, Dario; Dramatist and Actor; b. 24 March 1926, Leggiuno-Sangiamo, Italy; m. Franca Rame, 1954. *Education:* Acad. of Fine Arts, Milan. *Career:* Dramatist and Actor in agitprog theatre and television; Co-Founder (with Franca Rame), Dramatist, Actor, Nuova Scena acting groupe, 1968, Collettivo Teatrale la Comune, 1970. *Publications:* numerous plays, including: Morte accidentale di un anarchico (Accidental Death of an Anarchist), 1974; Non si paga, non si paga! (We Can't Pay? We Won't Pay!), 1974; Tutta casa, letto e chiesa (Adult Orgasm Escapes From the Zoo), 1978; Female Parts (with Franca Rame), 1981; Il papa e la stega (The Pope and the Witch), 1989; Le commedie, I–IX, 1966–91, 1992; Il diavolo con le zinne, 1997. *Honours:* Nobel Prize for Literature, 1997.

FOER, Jonathan Safran; American writer; b. 1977, Washington, DC. *Education:* Princeton Univ. *Publications:* A Convergence of Birds: Original Fiction and Poetry Inspired by the Work of Joseph Cornell (ed.) 2001, Everything is Illuminated (novel) 2002, Amelia Bedelia, Bookworm 2003, I'm OK 2004; contrib. to Paris Review, Conjunctions, New Yorker. *Honours:* Zoetrope: All Story Fiction Prize 2000, National Jewish Book Award, Guardian First Book Award 2002. *Literary Agent:* The Marsh Agency, 11 Dover Street, London, W1S 4LJ, England. *Telephone:* (20) 7399-2800. *Fax:* (20) 7399-2801. *Website:* www.marsh-agency.co.uk. *Address:* c/o Houghton Mifflin Co, Trade Division, Adult Editorial, Eighth Floor, 222 Berkeley Street, Boston, MA 02116-3764, USA.

FOERSTER, Richard Alfons, BA, MA; editor, writer and poet; b. 29 Oct. 1949, New York, NY, USA; m. Valerie Elizabeth Malinowski 1972 (divorced 1985). *Education:* Fordham University, University of Virginia, Manhattanville College. *Career:* Asst Ed., Clarence L. Barnhart Inc, 1973–75; Ed., Prentice Hall Inc, 1976–78; Assoc. Ed., 1978–94, Ed., 1994–2001, Chelsea Magazine; Ed., Chautauqua Literary Journal, 2003–; mem. Acad. of American Poets; Maine Writers and Publishers Alliance; Poetry Society of America; Society for the Arts, Religion and Contemporary Culture. *Publications:* Transfigured Nights, 1990; Sudden Harbor, 1992; Patterns of Descent, 1993; Trillium, 1998; Double Going, 2002. Contributions: Boulevard; Epoch; Kenyon Review; Nation; New Criterion; Paris Review; Poetry; Shenandoah; Southern Review; Southwest Review. *Honours:* Discovery/The Nation Award, 1985; Bess Hokin Prize, 1992; Hawthornden Fellow, 1993; National Endowment for the Arts Creative Writing Fellowship, 1995; Maine Arts Commission Individual Artist Fellowship, 1997; Amy Lowell Poetry Travelling Scholarship, 2000–01; Hobart City International Writer-in-Residence, 2002. *Address:* PO Box 1040, York Beach, ME 03910, USA.

FOGEL, Robert William; economic historian and academic; b. 1 July 1926, New York, NY, USA; m. Enid Cassandra Morgan 1949; two s. *Education:* AB, Cornell University, 1948; AM, Columbia University, 1960; PhD, Johns Hopkins University, 1963. *Career:* Asst Prof., 1960–64, Prof. of Economics, 1968–71, Prof. of Economics and History, 1972–75, University of Rochester; Ford Foundation Visiting Research Prof., 1963–64, Assoc. Prof., 1964–65, Prof. of Economics, 1965–69, Prof. of Economics and History, 1970–75, Charles R. Walgreen Distinguished Service Prof. of American Institutions, 1981–, University of Chicago; Taussig Research Prof., 1973–74, Harold Hitchings Burbank Prof. of Political Economy and Prof. of History, 1975–81, Harvard University; Research Assoc., 1978–, Dir, DAE program, 1978–91, National Bureau of Economic Research; mem. American Acad. of Arts and Sciences; American Economic Society, pres., 1998–; American Historical Asscn; Asscn of American Historians; British Acad., corresponding fellow; Econometric Society, fellow; Economic History Asscn, pres., 1977–78; Economic History Society; National Acad. of Sciences; Royal Economic Society; Royal Historical Society; Social Science History Asscn, pres., 1980–81. *Publications:* The Union Pacific Railroad: A Case in Premature Enterprise, 1960; Railroads and American History (with others), 1971; The Dimensions of Quantitative Research in History (with others), 1972; Time on the Cross: The Economics of American Negro Slavery (with S. L. Engerman), 1974; Ten Lectures on the New Economic History, 1977; Which Road to the Past?: Two Views of History (with G. R. Elton), 1983; Without Consent or Contract: The Rise and Fall of American Slavery (with others), 4 vols, 1989, 1992; The Political Realignment of the 1850s: A Socioeconomic Analysis, 1996; Egalitarianism: The Fourth Great Awakening and the Future of Egalitarianism, 2000; The Escape from Hunger and Premature Death: Europe, America, and the Third World: 1700–2100, 2002. Contributions: numerous book and scholarly journals. *Honours:* National Science Foundation Grants, 1967, 1970, 1972, 1975–76, 1978, 1992–96; Fulbright Grant, 1968; Schumpeter Prize, 1971; Bancroft Prize, 1975; Gustavus Myers Prize, 1990; Nobel Prize in Economic Science, 1993; several hon. degrees. *Address:* c/o Graduate School of Business, University of Chicago, 1101 E 58th Street, Chicago, IL 60637, USA.

FOLEY, Jack, (John Wayne Harold Foley); Poet, Writer, Ed. and Radio Personality; b. 9 Aug. 1940, Neptune, NJ, USA; m. Adelle Joan Abramowitz, 21 Dec. 1961, one s. *Education:* BA, English, Cornell University, 1963; MA, 1965, Continuing graduate studies, 1960s, 1970s, University of California, Berkeley. *Career:* Host, Exec. Producer in charge of Poetry Programme, KPFA-FM, Berkeley, CA, 1988–; Guest Ed., Poetry: San Francisco, 1988–89; Ed.-in-Chief, Poetry USA, Oakland, CA, 1990–95; Contributing Ed., Poetry Flash, 1992–; Resident Artist, Djerassi Program, 1994; Performs poetry with wife; mem. MLA; Poets and Writers; National Poetry Asscn; PEN, Oakland, CA, Programme Dir, 1990–97. *Publications:* Poetry: Letters/Lights – Words for Adelle, 1987; Gershwin, 1991; Adrift, 1993; Exiles, 1996; Bridget, 1997; New Poetry from California: Dead/Requiem (with Ivan Argüelles), 1998; Some Songs by Georges Brassens (trans.), 2002. Prose: Inciting Big Joy, monograph, 1993; O Her Blackness Sparkles! – The Life and Times of the Batman Art Gallery, San Francisco, 1960–63, 1995; O Powerful Western Star (criticism), 2000; Foley's Books (criticism), 2000; The 'Fallen Western Star' Wars (criticism, ed.), 2001. Contributions: journals, including: Barque; Beloit Poetry Journal; Berkeley Poetry Review; Blue Beetle Press Magazine; Cafe Review; The Experioddicist; Exquisite Corpse; Galley Sail Review; Inkblot; MaLLife; Malthus; Meat Epoch; New York Quarterly; NRG; Outre; Talisman; Tight; Transmog; Wet Motorcycle; ELH; Heaven Bone; Konch; Linden Lane Magazine; Lower Limit Speech; Multicultural Review; Open Letter; Poetry Flash; Prosodia; Seattle Literary Quarterly; W'Orcs; Bright Lights; Journal of Popular Film; Artweek; East Bay Express; Poetry Flash; Anthologies, including: Poly: New Speculative Writing; The Love Project; Online column (criticism) at The Alsop Review (www.alsopreview.com). *Honours:* Full Scholarship to Cornell University, 1958–63; Woodrow Wilson Fellowship, University of California, 1963–65; Yang Poetry Prize, University of California at Berkeley, 1971; Poetry Grantee, Oakland Arts Council, 1992–95; The Artists Embassy Literary/Cultural Award, 1998–2000. *Address:* 2569 Maxwell Ave, Oakland, CA 94601-5521, USA. *E-mail:* jasfoley@aol.com.

FOLEY, (Mary) Louise Munro, BA; American novelist; b. 22 Oct. 1933, Toronto, ON, Canada; m. Donald J. Foley 1957; two s. *Education:* University of Western Ontario, Ryerson Institute of Technology, California State University, Sacramento. *Career:* Columnist, News-Argus, Goldsboro, NC, 1971–73; Ed. of Publications, Institute for Human Service Management, California State University, Sacramento, 1975–80; mem. Authors' Guild; California Writers Club; National League of American Pen Women; Society of Children's Book Writers and Illustrators; Novelists Inc. *Publications:* The Caper Club, 1969; No Talking, 1970; Sammy's Sister, 1970; A Job for Joey, 1970; Somebody Stole Second, 1972; Stand Close to the Door (ed.), 1976; Tackle 22, 1978; Women in Skilled Labor (ed.), 1980; The Train of Terror, 1982; The Sinister Studies of KESP-TV, 1983; The Lost Tribe, 1983; The Mystery of the Highland Crest, 1984; The Mystery of Echo Lodge, 1985; Danger at Anchor Mine, 1985; The Mardi Gras Mystery, 1987; Mystery of the Sacred Stones, 1988; Australia! Find the Flying Foxes, 1988; The Cobra Connection, 1990; Ghost Train, 1991; Poison! Said the Cat, 1992; Blood! Said the Cat, 1992; Thief! Said the Cat, 1992; In Search of the Hidden Statue, 1993; Moving Target, 1993; Stolen Affections, 1995; Running Into Trouble, 1996; The Vampire Cat Series: My Substitute Teacher's Gone

Baity, 1996, The Bird-Brained Fiasco, 1996, The Phoney Baloney Professor, 1996, The Cat-Nap Cat-Astrophe, 1997. *Address:* 5010 Jennings Way, Sacramento, CA 95819, USA.

FOLLETT, Kenneth (Ken) Martin, BA; writer; b. 5 June 1949, Cardiff, Wales; m. 1st 1968; one s. one d.; m. 2nd 1985. *Education:* University College London. *Career:* Pres., The Dyslexia Institute; Council Mem., National Literacy Trust; Chair, National Year of Reading, 1998–99; mem. National Union of Journalists, UK; Writers Guild, USA. *Publications:* The Shakeout, 1975; The Bear Raid, 1976; The Modigliani Scandal, 1976; The Power Twins and the Worm Puzzle, 1976; The Secret of Kellerman's Studio, 1976; Paper Money, 1977; Eye of the Needle, 1978; Triple, 1979; The Key to Rebecca, 1980; The Man from St Petersburg, 1982; On Wings of Eagles, 1983; Lie Down with Lions, 1986; The Pillars of the Earth, 1989; Night Over Water, 1991; A Dangerous Fortune, 1993; A Place Called Freedom, 1995; The Third Twin, 1996; The Hammer of Eden, 1998; Code to Zero, 2000; Jackdaws, 2001; Hornet Flight, 2002; Whiteout 2004; screenplays; contrib. to book reviews and essays. *Honours:* Edgar Award for Best Novel, MWA, 1979; Fellow, University College London, 1995. *Address:* PO Box 4, Knebworth, SG3 6UT, England. *Website:* www.ken-follett.co.uk.

FONER, Eric, BA, PhD; academic and writer; *Professor of History, Columbia University*; b. 7 Feb. 1943, New York, NY, USA; m. Lynn Garafola 1980; one d. *Education:* Columbia College, Oriel College, Oxford, Columbia University. *Career:* Prof., City College and Graduate School and University Center, CUNY, 1973–82; Pitt Prof. of American History and Institutions, University of Cambridge, 1980–81; Prof., 1982–88, DeWitt Clinton Prof. of History, 1988–, Columbia University; Fulbright Prof. of American History, Moscow State University, 1990; Harmsworth Prof. of American History, University of Oxford, 1993–94; mem. American Acad. of Arts and Sciences; British Acad., corresponding fellow; Organization of American Historians, pres., 1993–94; American Historical Asscn, pres., 2000. *Publications:* Free Soil, Free Labor, Free Men: The Ideology of the Republican Party Before the Civil War, 1970; Nat Turner, 1971; Tom Paine and Revolutionary America, 1976; Politics and Ideology in the Age of the Civil War, 1980; Nothing But Freedom: Emancipation and Its Legacy, 1983; Reconstruction: America's Unfinished Revolution 1863–1877, 1988; A Short History of Reconstruction, 1990; A House Divided: America in the Age of Lincoln (with Olivia Mahoney), 1990; Freedom's Lawmakers: A Directory of Black Officeholders During Reconstruction, 1993; Thomas Paine, 1995; America's Reconstruction: People and Politics After the Civil War (with Olivia Mahoney), 1995; The Story of American Freedom, 1998; Who Owns History?, 2002; Give Me Liberty!: An American History 2004. Contributions: scholarly journals and periodicals. *Honours:* ACLS Fellowship, 1972–73; Guggenheim Fellowship, 1975–76; National Endowment for the Humanities Senior Fellowships, 1982–83, 1996–97; Los Angeles Times Book Award for History, 1989; Bancroft Prize, 1989; Parkman Prize, 1989; Lionel Trilling Award, 1989; Owsley Prize, 1989; James Harvey Robinson Prize, American Historical Asscn, 1991; Literary Lion, New York Public Library, 1994; Scholar of the Year Award, New York Council for the Humanities, 1995. *Address:* 606 W 116th Street, New York, NY 10027, USA. *E-mail:* ef17@columbia.edu.

FONSECA, Rubem; Brazilian writer; b. 11 May 1925, Juiz de Fora, MG. *Education:* Escola de Policia, Rio de Janeiro, Fundação Getúlio Vargas, New York Univ. *Career:* commissioner of police, São Cristóvão (RJ) 1952. *Screenplays include:* Relatório de um homen casado, Stelinha, A grande arte. *Publications:* Os prisioneiros 1963, A coleira do cão 1965, Lucía McCartney 1967, O caso Morel 1973, O homen de fevereiro ou março 1973, Felis ano novo 1975, O cobrador (Prêmio Estácio de Sá) 1979, A grande arte (trans. as High Art) (Prêmio Goethe, Prêmio Jabuti) 1983, Buffo & Spallanzani 1986, Vastas emoções e pensamentos imperfeitos (Prêmio Pedro Nava) 1988, Agosto 1990, Romance negro e outras histórias 1992, Contos reunidos 1994, O selvagem da opera 1994, O buraco na parede (Prêmio Jabuti) 1995, Romance negro, Felis ano novo e outras histórias 1996, Histórias de amor 1997, E do meio do mundo prostitute só amores guardei ao meu charuto (Prêmio Machado de Assis) 1997, Confraria dos espadas (Prêmio Eça de Queiroz) 1998, O doente Molière (Prêmio de melhor romance do ano, Associação Paulista de Críticos de Arte) 2000, Secreções, excreções, desatinos 2001, Pequenas criaturas 2002, Diário de um fescenino 2003; contrib. to numerous anthologies. *Honours:* Prêmio Luis de Camões 2003, Premio Juan Rulfo 2003. *Address:* c/o Companhia das Letras, Rua Bandeira Paulista 702 cj. 32, 04532-002 São Paulo, SP, Brazil. *Telephone:* (11) 3707-3500. *Fax:* (11) 3707-3501. *Website:* www.ciadasletras.com.br.

FONTENEAU, Pascale; Belgian writer; b. 1963, Fougères, Ille-et-Vilaine. *Education:* Université libre de Bruxelles. *Career:* broadcast first story Chronique des polars on campus radio, Université libre de Bruxelles; writer of novels for Série noire, Gallimard 1992–; contrib. to Le Monde newspaper, Paris 2003–. *Publications include:* Confidences sur l'escalier 1992, Etats de lame 1993, Les Fils perdus de Sylvie Derijke 1995, Les Damnés de l'artère 1996, Otto 1997, La Puissance du désordre 1997, La Vanité des pions 2000. *Address:* c/o Éditions Gallimard, 5, rue Sébastien-Bottin, Paris 75328, France (Office).

FOOT, Philippa Ruth; academic and writer; b. 3 Oct. 1920, Owston Ferry, Lincolnshire, England; m. M. R. D. Foot 1945 (divorced 1960). *Education:* BA, 1942, MA, 1946, Somerville College, Oxford. *Career:* Lecturer in Philosophy, 1947, Fellow and Tutor, 1950–69, Vice-Principal, 1967–69, Senior Research Fellow, 1970–88, Hon. Fellow, 1988–, Somerville College, Oxford; Prof. of Philosophy, 1974–91, Griffin Prof., 1988–91, Prof. Emeritus, 1991–, University of California, Los Angeles; Fellow, Center for Advanced Studies in the Behavioral Sciences, Stanford, CA, 1981–82; various visiting professorships; mem. British Acad.; American Acad. of Arts and Sciences, fellow. *Publications:* Theories of Ethics (ed.), 1967; Virtues and Vices, 1978; Die Wirklichkeit des Guten, 1997, Natural Goodness, 2001; Moral Dilemmas, 2002. Contributions: scholarly journals and periodicals. *Honours:* Hon. Doctorate, Sofia University, 2000. *Address:* 15 Walton Street, Oxford OX1 2HG, England.

FOOT, Rt Hon. Michael Mackintosh; journalist and politician; b. 23 July 1913, Plymouth, England; m. Jill Craigie 1949 (died 1999). *Education:* Wadham College, Oxford. *Career:* Pres., Oxford Union, 1933; contested Monmouth, 1935; Asst Ed., 1937–38, Joint Ed., 1948–52, Ed., 1952–59, Man. Ed., 1952–74, Tribune; staff, 1938, Acting Ed., 1942–44, Evening Standard; political columnist, Daily Herald, 1944–64; MP, Labour Party, Devonport Division of Plymouth, 1945–55, Ebbw Vale, 1960–83, Blaenau Gwent, 1983–92; fmr Opposition Spokesman on European Policy; Sec. of State for Employment, 1974–76; Lord Pres. of Council, Leader of the House of Commons, 1976–79, Shadow Leader of the House of Commons, 1979–80; Deputy Leader, 1976–80, Leader, 1980–83, Labour Party. *Publications:* Guilty Men (with Frank Owen and Peter Howard), 1940; Armistice 1918–1939, 1940; Trial of Mussolini, 1943; Brendan and Beverley, 1944; Who Are the Patriots? (co-author), 1949; Still at Large, 1950; Full Speed Ahead, 1950; The Pen and the Sword, 1957; Parliament in Danger, 1959; Anuerin Bevan, Vol. I: 1897–1945, 1962, Vol. II: 1945–1960, 1973, (as one vol., 1997); Harold Wilson: A Political Biography, 1964; Debts of Honour, 1980; Another Heart and Other Pulses, 1984; Loyalists and Loners, 1986; The Politics of Paradise, 1988; H. G.: The History of Mr Wells, 1995; Dr Strangelove I Presume, 1999; The Uncollected Michael Foot, 2003. *Honours:* Hon. Fellow, Wadham College, 1969; Hon. mem., NUJ, 1985; Hon. DLitt, University of Wales, 1985, Nottingham, 1990, Plymouth, 1993; Hon. LLD, Exeter, 1990; Spanish Republican Order of Liberation, 1973. *Address:* c/o Tribune, 9 Arkwright Road, London NW3 6AN, England.

FOOTE, (Albert) Horton, Jr; dramatist and scriptwriter; b. 14 March 1916, Wharton, TX, USA; m. Lillian Valish 1945; two s. two d. *Education:* Pasadena Playhouse School Theatre, CA, 1933–35; Tamara Daykarhanova School Theatre, New York City, 1937–39. *Career:* Actor, American Actors Theatre, New York City, 1939–42; Theatre Workshop Dir and Producer, King-Smith School of Creative Arts, Washington, DC, 1944–45; Man., Productions Inc, Washington, DC, 1945–48; mem. American Acad. of Arts and Letters. *Publications:* Novel: The Chase, 1956. Plays: Texas Town, 1942; Out of My House, 1942; Only the Heart, 1944; Celebration, 1948; The Chase, 1952; The Trip to Bountiful, 1953; The Midnight Caller, 1953; A Young Lady of Property, 1954; The Traveling Lady, 1955; The Roads to Home, 1955; Tomorrow, 1960; Roots in a Parched Ground, 1962; The Road to the Graveyard, 1985; Blind Date, 1986; Habitation of Dragons, 1988; Dividing the Estate, 1989; Talking Pictures, 1990; The Young Man from Atlanta, 1994; Night Seasons, 1994; Laura Dennis, 1994. Screenplays: Storm Fear, 1956; To Kill a Mockingbird, 1962; Baby, the Rain Must Fall, 1965; Hurry Sundown, 1966; Tomorrow, 1971; Tender Mercies, 1983; 1918, 1984; On Valentine's Day, 1985; The Trip to Bountiful, 1985; Spring Moon, 1987; Convicts, 1991; Of Mice and Men, 1992. Other: Farewell: A Memoir of a Texas Childhood, 1999; Beginnings (memoir), 2001; many television scripts. *Honours:* Acad. Awards, 1962, 1983; Writers Guild of America Awards, 1962, 1989; Pulitzer Prize in Drama, 1995; American Acad. of Arts and Letters Gold Medal, 1998.

FOOTE, Shelby; Author, Historian and Dramatist; b. 17 Nov. 1916, Greenville, Mississippi, USA; m. Gwyn Rainer, 5 Sept. 1956, one s. one d. *Education:* University of North Carolina, 1935–37. *Career:* Guest Lecturer, University of Virginia, 1963; Playwright-in-Residence, Arena Stage, Washington, DC, 1963–64; Writer-in-Residence, Hollins College, Virginia, 1968; Academic Advisory Board, US Naval Acad., 1988–89; mem. American Acad. of Arts and Letters; Fellowship of Southern Writers; Society of American Historians. *Publications:* Fiction: Tournament, 1949; Follow Me Down, 1950; Love in a Dry Season, 1951; Shiloh, 1952; Jordan County: A Landscape in Narrative, 1954; September September, 1977. Non-Fiction: The Civil War: A Narrative: Vol. I: Fort Sumter to Perryville, 1958, Vol. II: Fredericksburg to Meridian, 1963, Vol. III: Red River to Appomattox, 1974; The Novelist's View of History, 1981; Stars in Their Courses, 1994; The Beleaguered City, 1995. Play: Jordan County: A Landscape in the Round, 1964. Editor: The Night Before Chancellorsville and Other Civil War Stories, 1957; Chickamauga and Other Civil War Stories, 1993. Other: The Civil War, adapted for PBS telecast, 1990. *Honours:* Guggenheim Fellowships, 1955–57; Ford Foundation Grant, 1963; Fletcher Pratt Awards, 1963, 1974; Distinguished Alumnus, University of North Carolina, 1975; Dos Passos Prize for Literature, 1988; Charles Frankel Award, 1992; St Louis Literary Award, 1992; Nevins-Freeman Award, 1992; several hon. doctorates. *Address:* 542 E Parkway S, Memphis, TN 38104, USA.

FORAN, Charles William; Writer; b. 2 Aug. 1960, North York, Ontario, Canada; m. Mary, two d. *Education:* BA, University of Toronto, 1983; MA, University College, Dublin, 1984. *Career:* Librarian and Freelance Journalist, New York State, 1985–88; Teacher, Beijing College, 1988–90; Freelance Writer and Journalist, 1990–; mem. PEN Canada; Writers Union of Canada. *Publications:* Coming Attractions (5 short stories), 1987; Sketches in Winter (non-fiction), 1992; Kitchen Music (novel), 1994; The Last House of Ulster (non-fiction), 1995; Butterfly Lovers (novel), 1996; The Story of My Life (So Far) (non-fiction), 1998; House on Fire (novel), 2001. Contributions: Globe and Mail; Montréal Gazette; Saturday Night Magazine. *Honours:* QSpell Award, Fiction, 1990, Non-Fiction, 1995. *Address:* 298 Boswell Ave, Peterborough, Ontario K9J 5G3, Canada.

FORBES, Bryan, CBE; British film executive, director, screenwriter and novelist; b. 22 July 1926, Stratford, London; m. Nanette Newman 1955; two d. *Education:* West Ham Secondary School, RADA. *Career:* first stage appearance 1942; served in Intelligence Corps 1944–48; entered films as actor 1948; Head of Production, Assoc. British Picture Corpn 1969–71, subsequently became EMI Film Productions Ltd; mem. Gen. Advisory Council of BBC 1966–69, Experimental Film Bd of British Film Acad.; Govt Nominee BBC Schools Broadcasting Council 1972; mem. Beatrix Potter Soc. (pres. 1982–96, now patron), Nat. Youth Theatre (pres. 1984–), Writers Guild of GB (pres. 1988–91); founder and fmr Dir Capital Radio Ltd. *Films:* wrote and co-produced The Angry Silence (British Film Acad. Award) 1959; dir Whistle Down the Wind 1961; writer and dir The L-Shaped Room (UN Award) 1962, Seance on a Wet Afternoon (Best Screenplay Award) 1963, King Rat 1964; writer Only Two Can Play (Best Screenplay Award) 1964; producer and dir The Wrong Box 1965; writer, producer and dir The Whisperers 1966, Deadfall 1967, The Madwoman of Chaillot 1968, The Raging Moon (Long Ago Tomorrow in USA) 1970; dir Macbeth 1980, Killing Jessica 1986, Star Quality 1986, The Living Room 1987, One Helluva Life 2002; writer, producer and dir filmed biography of Dame Edith Evans for Yorkshire TV 1973; filmed documentary on life style of Elton John for ATV 1974; wrote and dir The Slipper and the Rose 1975, Jessie (BBC) 1977, Ménage à trois (Better Late than Never in USA) 1981, The Endless Game 1989 (for Channel 4 TV); dir British segment of The Sunday Lovers 1980; dir The King in Yellow (for LWT Television) 1982, The Naked Face 1983; produced, wrote and dir International Velvet 1977. *Publications:* Truth Lies Sleeping (short stories) 1951, The Distant Laughter (novel) 1972, Notes for a Life (autobiog.) 1974, The Slipper and the Rose 1976, Ned's Girl (biog. of Dame Edith Evans) 1977, International Velvet (novel) 1978, Familiar Strangers (novel, aka Stranger) 1979, That Despicable Race – A History of the British Acting Tradition 1980, The Rewrite Man (novel) 1983, The Endless Game (novel) 1986, A Song at Twilight (novel) 1989, A Divided Life (autobiog.) 1992, The Twisted Playground (novel) 1993, Partly Cloudy (novel) 1995, Quicksand (novel) 1996, The Memory of All That 1999. *Honours:* Hon. DLitt (Council for Nat. Academic Awards) 1987, (Sussex) 1999; many film festival prizes. *Literary Agent:* Curtis Brown Ltd, Haymarket House, 28–29 Haymarket, London, SW1Y 4SP, England. *Telephone:* (20) 7393-4400. *Fax:* (20) 7393-4401. *E-mail:* info@curtisbrown.co.uk. *Website:* www.curtisbrown.co.uk. *Address:* The Gallery, Station Approach, Virginia Water, Surrey, GU25 4DP, England. *Fax:* (1344) 845174. *E-mail:* endlessgame@aol.com (Office).

FORBES, Calvin; poet, writer and academic; b. 6 May 1945, Newark, NJ, USA. *Education:* New School for Social Research; Rutgers University; MFA, Brown University, 1978. *Career:* Asst Prof. of English, Emerson College, 1969–73, Tufts University, 1973–74, 1975–77; Asst Prof. of Creative Writing, Washington College, 1988–89; Assoc. Prof., Art Institute of Chicago, 1991–; mem. College Language Asscn; MLA of America. *Publications:* Poetry: Blue Monday, 1974; From the Book of Shine, 1979; The Shine Poems, 2001. Contributions: many anthologies. *Honours:* Bread Loaf Writers' Conference Fellowship, 1973; Yaddo Residency, 1976–77; National Endowment for the Arts Fellowship, 1982–83; District of Columbia Commission on the Arts Fellowship, 1984; Illinois Arts Council Fellowship, 1999. *Address:* c/o School of the Art Institute of Chicago, 37 S Wabash Avenue, Chicago, IL 60603, USA.

FORBES, John, BA; Australian poet and writer; b. 1 Sept. 1950, Melbourne, Vic. *Education:* Univ. of Sydney. *Career:* Ed., Surfer's Paradise 1974–83; mem. Australian Soc. of Authors. *Publications:* Tropical Skiing 1976, On the Beach 1977, Drugs 1980, Stalin's Holidays 1981, The Stunned Mullet and Other Poems 1988, New and Selected Poems 1992; contrib. to newspapers and magazines. *Honours:* New Poetry Prize 1973, Southerly Prize 1976, Grace Leverson Prize 1993. *Address:* 91 Prospect Road, Summer Hill, 2130 NSW, Australia.

FORBES, Malcolm Stevenson, Jr, LHD; American publishing executive; b. 18 July 1947, Morristown, NJ; m. Sabina Beekman 1971. *Education:* Princeton Univ. and Lycoming Coll. Jacksonville Univ. *Career:* with Forbes Inc., New York 1970–, Pres. and COO 1980–90, Deputy Ed.-in-Chief 1982–90, Ed.-in-Chief, Pres. and CEO 1990–; Chair. Forbes Newspapers 1989–; mem. Bd for Int. Broadcasting 1983–93, Chair. 1985–93; mem. Advisory Council, Dept of Econs Princeton Univ. 1985–. *Wrote:* Some Call It Greed (film script) 1977. *Publication:* Fact and Comment (ed.) 1974. *Honours:* several hon. degrees. *Address:* Forbes Inc., 60 Fifth Avenue, New York, NY 10011, USA.

FORD, David (see Harknett, Terry).

FORD, Kirk (see Spence, William (John Duncan)).

FORD, Peter; Author and Editorial Consultant; b. 3 June 1936, Harpenden, Hertfordshire, England; Divorced, two s. one d. *Education:* St George's School, 1948–52. *Career:* Ed., Cassell, 1958–61; Senior Copy Ed., Penguin Books, 1961–64; Senior Ed., Thomas Nelson, 1964–70; mem. Society of Authors; New York Acad. of Sciences; Folklore Society. *Publications:* The Fool on the Hill, 1975; Scientists and Inventors, 1979; The True History of the Elephant Man, 1980; Medical Mysteries, 1985; The Picture Buyer's Handbook, 1988; A Collector's Guide to Teddy Bears, 1990; Rings and Curtains: Family and Personal Memoirs, 1992; The Monkey's Paw and Other Stories by W. W. Jacobs, 1994; A Willingness to Die: Memoirs of Brian Kingcome, 1999. *Address:* The Storehouse, Longhope, Orkney KW16 3PQ, Scotland.

FORD, Richard; Writer; b. 16 Feb. 1944, Jackson, Mississippi, USA; m. Kristina Hensley, 1968. *Education:* BA, Michigan State University, 1966; MFA, University of California, Irvine, 1970. *Career:* Lecturer, University of Michigan, Ann Arbor, 1974–76; Asst Prof. of English, Williams College, Williamstown, Massachusetts, 1978–79; Lecturer, Princeton University, 1979–80; mem. American Acad. of Arts and Letters; PEN; Writers Guild; American Acad. of Arts and Sciences. *Publications:* Fiction: A Piece of My Heart, 1976; The Ultimate Good Luck, 1981; The Sportswriter, 1986; Rock Springs: Stories, 1987; Wildlife, 1990; Independence Day, 1995; Women with Men, 1997; A Multitude of Sins (short stories), 2002. Play: American Tropical, 1983. Screenplay: Bright Angel, 1991. Editor: The Best American Short Stories (with Shannon Ravenal), 1990; The Granta Book of the American Short Story, 1992; The Granta Book of the American Long Story, 1999. Contributions: various periodicals. *Honours:* Guggenheim Fellowship, 1977–78; National Endowment for the Arts Fellowships, 1979–80, 1985–86; Mississippi Acad. of Arts and Letters Literature Award, 1987; American Acad. and Institute of Arts and Letters Award, 1989; Pulitzer Prize in Fiction, 1996; PEN-Faulkner Award, 1996; Award in Merit for the Novel, American Acad. of Arts and Letters, 1997; PEN-Malamud Award for Short Fiction, 2001. *Address:* c/o Amanda Urban, International Creative Management, 40 W 57th St, New York, NY 10019, USA.

FOREMAN, Amanda; Writer; b. 1968, London, England; m.; one d. *Education:* Sarah Lawrence College; Columbia Univ.; PhD, 18th Century British History, Univ. of Oxford, 1998. *Publications:* Georgiana, Duchess of Devonshire; Our American Cousins, 2004. *Honours:* Henrietta Jex Blake Senior Scholarship, Univ. of Oxford, 1993; Whitbread Biography Award, 1998. *Address:* c/o Flamingo, HarperCollins Publishers, 77–85 Fulham Palace Rd, London W6 8JB, England. *Website:* www.amanda-foreman.com.

FOREMAN, Richard; Dramatist and Dir; b. 10 June 1937, New York, NY, USA; m. 1st Amy Taubin 1961 (divorced 1972); m. 2nd Kate Manhelm 1986. *Education:* BA, Brown Univ., 1959; MFA, Yale Univ., 1962. *Career:* Artistic Dir, Ontological-Hysteric Theatre, New York City, 1968–, Theatre O H, Paris, 1973–85; Dir-in-Residence, New York Shakespeare Festival, 1975–76; Dir, Broadway and Off-Broadway plays; mem. Dramatists Guild: PEN; Society of Stage Dirs. *Publications:* Dr Selavy's Magic Theater, 1972; Rhoda in Potatoland, 1976; Theatre of Images, 1977; Reverberation Machines, 1985; Film is Evil: Radio is Good, 1987; Unbalancing Acts: Foundations for a Theater, 1992; My Head Was a Sledgehammer, 1995. *Honours:* Creative Artists Public Service Fellow, New York State Arts Council, 1971, 1974; Guggenheim Fellowship, 1972; Rockefeller Foundation Fellow, 1974; Lifetime Achievement Award, National Endowment for the Arts, 1990; American Acad. of Arts and Letters Prize in Literature, 1992; Hon. DArts, Brown Univ., 1993; John D. and Catherine T. MacArthur Foundation Fellow, 1995–2000; PEN Master American Dramatist Award, 2001. *Address:* 152 Wooster St, New York, NY 10012, USA.

FORKER, Charles Rush; academic and writer; b. 11 March 1927, Pittsburgh, Pennsylvania, USA. *Education:* AB, Bowdoin College, 1951; BA, 1953, MA, 1955, Merton College, Oxford; PhD, Harvard University, 1957. *Career:* Instructor, University of Wisconsin, 1957–59; Instructor, 1959–61, Asst Prof., 1961–65, Assoc. Prof., 1965–68, Prof., 1968–92, Prof. Emeritus, 1992–, Indiana University; Visiting Prof., University of Michigan, 1969–70, Dartmouth College, 1982–83, Concordia University, Montréal, 1989; mem. American Asscn of University Profs; Guild of Anglican Scholars, pres., 1993–94; International Shakespeare Asscn; Malone Society; Marlowe Society; MLA; Renaissance Society of America; Shakespeare Society of America; World Centre for Shakespeare Studies, advisory board. *Publications:* James Shirley: The Cardinal (ed.), 1964; William Shakespeare: Henry V (ed.), 1971; Edward Phillips's 'History of the Literature of England and Scotland': A Translation from the 'Compendiosa Enumeratio Poetarum' with an Introduction and Commentary (with Daniel G. Calder), 1973; Visions and Voices of the New Midwest (assoc. ed.), 1978; Henry V: An Annotated Bibliography (with Joseph Candido), 1983; Skull Beneath the Skin: The Achievement of John Webster, 1986; Fancy's Images: Contexts, Settings, and Perspectives in Shakespeare and His Contemporaries, 1990; Christopher Marlowe: Edward the Second (ed.), 1994; Richard II: The Critical Tradition, 1998; William Shakespeare: Richard II (ed.), 2002. Contributions: scholarly books and journals. *Honours:* Fulbright Fellowship, England, 1951–53; Folger Fellow, 1963; Huntington Library Fellow, 1969; National Endowment for the Humanities Senior Research Fellow, 1980–81. *Address:* 1219 E Maxwell Lane, Bloomington, IN 47401, USA.

FORMAN, Robert Kraus Conrad; academic and writer; b. 3 Aug. 1947, Baltimore, MD, USA; m. Yvonne Forman 1975; two c. *Education:* BA in Philosophy, University of Chicago, 1969; MA in Religion, 1981, MPhil in

Religion, 1985, PhD in Religion, 1988, Columbia University. *Career:* Adjunct Prof., New School for Social Research, New York City, 1985–88; Instructor, Union Theological Seminary, New York City, 1987; Visiting Asst Prof., Vassar College, 1989–90; Assoc. Prof. of Religion, Hunter College, CUNY, 1990–2001; Founder-Exec. Ed., Journal of Consciousness Studies: Controversies in Science and the Humanities, 1991–; mem. American Acad. of Religion; Asscn for Asian Studies; Asscn for Transpersonal Psychology; Institute for Noetic Sciences; Sankat Mocan (Save the Ganges) Foundation; Founder, CBO, The FORGE Institute, the FORGE Guild. *Publications:* The Problem of Pure Consciousness (ed.), 1990; Meister Eckhart: Mystic as Theologian: An Experiment in Methodology, 1991; The Religions of Asia, third edn (general ed.), 1993; Religions of the World, third edn (general ed.), 1993; The Innate Capacity (ed.), 1997; Mysticism, Mind, Consciousness, 2001. Contributions: More than 30 scholarly books and journals. *Honours:* New World Foundation Grants, 1992, 1993, 1994; Senior Fellow, Columbia University Writing Program, 1993; CUNY Research Grant, 1996; Fetzer Institute Grants, 1997, 2001, 2002; Bruss Prize for Scholarship in Religion, 2000. *Address:* 383 Broadway, Hastings-on-Hudson, NY 10706, USA. *E-mail:* forman@theforge.org.

FORNA, Aminatta; Sierra Leone/British journalist and writer; b. 1965, Sierra Leone. *Career:* documentary prod. and journalist. *Publications:* Mother of All Myths 1998, The Devil That Danced on the Water: A Daughter's Memoir 2002. *Address:* c/o HarperCollins Publishers Ltd, 77–85 Fulham Palace Road, London, W6 8JB, England. *Telephone:* (20) 8741-7070. *Fax:* (20) 8307-4440. *Website:* www.harpercollins.co.uk.

FORNÉS, María Irene; Playwright; b. 1931, Havana, Cuba. *Career:* managing dir, New York Theatre Strategy, 1973–79; fmr TCG/PEW Artist-in-Residence, Women's Project and Productions; Plays (many unpublished): The Widow, 1961; Tango Palace (aka There! You Died), 1963; The Office, 1964; Promenade, 1965; The Successful Life of 3, 1965; The Annunciation, 1967; A Vietnamese Wedding, 1967; The Red Burning Light (aka Mission XQ3), 1968; Dr Kheal, 1968; Molly's Dream, 1968; Baboon!!!, 1972; Aurora, 1974; Cap-a-Pie, 1975; Washing, 1976; Fefu and Her Friends, 1977; In Service, 1978; Evelyn Brown, 1979; Eyes on the Harem, 1979; A Visit, 1981; Sarita, 1982; The Danube, 1982; The Curse of the Langston House, 1983; Mud, 1983; Abingdon Square, 1984; The Conduct of Life, 1985; Drowning, 1985; The Trial of Joan of Arc on a Matter of Faith, 1986; Lovers and Keepers, 1986; The Mothers, 1986; Oscar and Bertha, 1987; Hunger, 1988; And What of the Night?, 1989; Enter the Night; The Summer in Gossensass; Letters from Cuba, 1999. Contributions: Performing Arts Journal; numerous anthologies. *Honours:* nine Obie awards; NEA awards, including Distinguished Artists Award; Rockefeller Foundation grants; Guggenheim grant; American Academy and Institute of Arts and Letters award; NY State Governor's Arts Award; PEN/Nabokov Award, 2002. *Address:* c/o Performing Arts Journal, The MIT Press, Five Cambridge Center, Cambridge, MA 02142-1493, USA.

FORREST, Richard (Stockton), (Stockton Woods); Writer; b. 8 May 1932, Orange, NJ, USA; m. 1st Frances Anne Reese 20 Dec. 1952 (divorced 1955); one s.; m. 2nd Mary Bolan Brumby 11 May 1955 (died 1996); five c.; m. 3rd Patricia Hale 26 June 1999. *Education:* New York Dramatic Workshop, 1950; University of South Carolina, 1953–55. *Career:* mem. MWA. *Publications:* Who Killed Mr Garland's Mistress?, 1974; A Child's Garden of Death, 1975; The Wizard of Death, 1977; Death Through the Looking Glass, 1978; The Death in the Willows, 1979; The Killing Edge, 1980; The Laughing Man, 1980; Death at Yew Corner, 1981; Game Bet, 1981; The Man Who Heard Too Much, 1983; Death Under the Lilacs, 1985; Lark, 1986; Death on the Mississippi, 1989; The Complete Nursing Home Guide (with Mary Forrest), 1990; Retirement Living (with Mary Forrest), 1991; Pied Piper of Death, 1997; Sign of the Beast, 1999; Sign of Blood, 1999; Sign of Terror, 1999. Contributions: periodicals. *Honours:* Edgar Allan Poe Award, MWA, 1975. *Address:* 108 Park Lane W, Charlottesville, VA 22903, USA.

FORSTER, Margaret, BA, FRSL; writer; b. 25 May 1938, Carlisle, Cumberland, England; m. Edward Hunter Davies 1960; one s. two d. *Education:* Sommerville College, Oxford, 1960. *Career:* chief non-fiction reviewer, London Evening Standard 1977–80; mem., Arts Council Literary Panel 1978–81. *Publications:* Dame's Delight, 1964; Georgy Girl, 1963; The Bogeyman, 1966; The Travels of Maudie Tipstaff, 1967; The Park, 1968; Miss Owen-Owen is at Home, 1969; Fenella Phizackerley, 1970; Mr Bone's Retreat, 1971; The Rash Adventurer: The Rise and Fall of Charles Edward Stuart, 1973; The Seduction of Mrs Pendlebury, 1974; William Makepeace Thackeray: Memoirs of a Victorian Gentleman, 1978; Mother, Can You Hear Me?, 1979; The Bride of Lowther Fell, 1980; Marital Rites, 1981; Significant Sisters: Grassroots of Active Feminism, 1839–1939, 1984; Private Papers, 1986; Elizabeth Barrett Browning: A Biography, 1988; Have the Men Had Enough?, 1989; Lady's Maid, 1989; The Battle for Christabel, 1991; Daphne du Maurier: The Authorised Biography, 1993; Mothers' Boys, 1994; Hidden Lives (memoir), 1995; Shadow Baby, 1996; Rich Desserts and Captain's Thin: A Family and Their Times, 1831–1931, 1997; Precious Lives (memoir), 1997; The Memory Box, 2000; Good Wives?: Mary, Fanny, Jeannie and Me, 1845–2001, 2001; Diary of an Ordinary Woman 1914–1995, 2003. *Honours:* RSL Award 1988, Fawcet Society Prize 1993. *Literary Agent:* The Sayle Literary Agency, Bickerton House, 25–27 Bickerton Road, London, N19 5JT, England. *Telephone:* (20) 7263-8681. *Fax:* (20) 7561-0529. *Address:* 11 Boscastle Road, London, NW5 1EE, England.

FORSYTH, Frederick, CBE; British writer; b. 25 Aug. 1938, Ashford, Kent; m. 1st Carole Cunningham 1973; two s.; m. 2nd Sandy Molloy. *Education:* Tonbridge School, Univ. of Granada, Spain. *Career:* with RAF 1956–58; reporter, Eastern Daily Press, Norfolk 1958–61; joined Reuters 1961, reporter, Paris 1962–63, Chief of Bureau, E Berlin 1963–64; radio and TV reporter, BBC 1965–66; Asst Diplomatic Corresp., BBC TV 1967–68; freelance journalist, Nigeria and Biafra 1968–69. *Television appearances include:* Soldiers (narrator) 1985, Frederick Forsyth Presents 1989. *Publications:* fiction: The Day of the Jackal 1971, The Odessa File 1972, The Dogs of War 1974, The Shepherd 1975, The Devil's Alternative 1979, No Comebacks (short stories) 1982, The Fourth Protocol 1984, The Negotiator 1988, The Deceiver 1991, Great Flying Stories (ed.) 1991, The Fist of God 1993, Icon 1996, The Phantom of Manhattan 1999, Quintet 2000, The Veteran and Other Stories 2001, Avenger 2003; non-fiction: The Biafra Story 1969 (revised edn as The Making of an African Legend: The Biafra Story 1977), Emeka 1982, I Remember: Reflections on Fishing in Childhood 1995. *Honours:* MWA Edgar Allan Poe Award 1971. *Address:* c/o Bantam Books, 62–63 Uxbridge Road, London, W5 5SA, England.

FORTE, Allen; Prof. of the Theory of Music and Writer; b. 23 Dec. 1926, Portland, OR, USA. *Education:* BA, 1950, MA, 1952, Columbia University. *Career:* Faculty, Teachers College, Columbia University, 1953–59, Manhattan School of Music, 1957, Mannes College of Music, 1957–59; Instructor, 1959–61, Asst Prof., 1961–64, Assoc. Prof., 1964–68, Prof., 1968–91, Battell Prof. of the Theory of Music, 1991–, Yale University; Ed., Journal of Music Theory, 1960–67; General Ed., Composers of the Twentieth Century, 1980–; mem. American Musicological Society; Society for Music Theory, pres., 1977–82. *Publications:* Contemporary Tone-Structure, 1955; The Compositional Matrix, 1961; Tonal Harmony in Concept and Practice, 1962; The Harmonic Organization of The Rite of Spring, 1978; Introduction to Schenkerian Analysis (with S. Gilbert), 1982; The American Popular Ballad of the Golden Era, 1924–1950, 1995; The Atonal Music of Anton Webern, 1998; Listening to Classic American Popular Songs, 2001. Contributions: learned books and journals. *Honours:* Guggenheim Fellowship, 1981; Hon. doctorate, Eastman School of Music, 1988; Fellow, American Acad. of Arts and Sciences, 1995; Festschrift published in his honour, 1997. *Address:* c/o Dept of Music, PO Box 208310, Yale University, New Haven, CT 06520, USA.

FORTEY, Richard Alan, PhD, ScD, FRS; British palaeontologist and writer; b. 15 Feb. 1946, London; m. 1st Bridget Elizabeth Thomas (divorced); one s.; m. 2nd Jacqueline Francis 1977; one. s. two d. *Education:* Ealing Grammar School for Boys, King's Coll. Cambridge. *Career:* Research Fellow, then Sr Scientific Officer, Natural History Museum, London 1970–77, Prin. Scientific Officer 1978–86, Sr Prin. Scientific Officer 1986–98, Merit Researcher 1998–; Howley Visiting Prof. Memorial Univ. of Newfoundland 1977–78; Visiting Prof. Palaeobiology, Oxford Univ. 2000–; Collier Chair in Public Understanding of Science and Tech., Univ. of Bristol 2002–03; mem. Geological Soc. of London 1972–, British Mycological Soc. 1980–. *Publications:* The Roderick Masters Book of Money Making Schemes (as Roderick Masters) 1981, Fossels: The Key to the Past 1982, The Hidden Landscape 1993, Life: An Unauthorised Biography 1997, Trilobite! 2000, The Earth: an Intimate History 2004. *Honours:* Natural World Book of the Year Award 1994; Lyell Medal, Geological Soc. of London 1996; Frink Medal Zoological Soc. of London 2001; Lewis Thomas Prize of the Rockefeller Foundation 2003. *Address:* Department of Palaeontology, Natural History Museum, Cromwell Road, London, SW7 5BD, England (Office). *Telephone:* (20) 7942-5493 (Office). *Fax:* (20) 7942-5546 (Office). *E-mail:* r.fortey@nhm.ac.uk (Office). *Website:* www.nhm.ac.uk/palaeontology (Office).

FOSSE, Jon; Author, Dramatist and Poet; b. 29 Sept. 1959, Haugesund, Norway. *Education:* Cand philol, Comparative Literature, University of Bergen. *Career:* Teacher of Creative Writing, Acad. of Writing, Bergen, 1987–93; Professional Writer, 1993–; mem. Norwegian Society of Authors; Norwegian Society of Dramatists; Norwegian Actors' Society, hon. mem. *Publications:* Fiction: Raudt, svart, 1983; Stengd gitar, 1985; Naustet, 1989; Flaskesamlaren, 1991; Bly og vatn, 1992; Melancholia I, 1995; Melancholia II, 1996; Morgen og kveld, 2000. Shorter prose: Blod. Steinen er. Forteljing, 1987; To forteljingar, 1993; Prosa frå ein oppvekst. Kortprosa, 1994; Eldre kortare prosa, 1997. Books of poems: Engel med vatn i augene, 1986; Hundens bevegelsar, 1990; Hund og engel, 1992; Nye dikt, 1997. Plays: Og aldri skal vi skiljast, 1994; Namnet, 1995; Nokon kjem til å komme, 1996; Barnet, Mor og barn, Sonen: Tre skodespel, 1997; Natta syng sine songar, Ein sommars dag: To skodespel, 1998; Draum om hausten, 1999; Besak, Vinter, Ettermiddag. Treskodespel, 2000; Vakkert, 2001; Dadsvariasjonar, 2002. Essays: Frå telling via showing til writing, 1989; Gnostiske essays, 1999. Other: Books for children. *Honours:* Noregs Mållags Prize for Children's Books, 1990; Andersson-Rysst Fondet, 1992; Prize for Literature in New Norwegian, 1993; Samlags Prize, 1994; Ibsen Prize, 1996; Sunnmoers Prize, 1996; Melsom Prize, 1997; Asehoug Prize, 1997; Dobloug Prize, 1999; Gyldendal Prize, 2000; Nordic Prize for Dramatists, 2000; Nestroy Prize, 2001; Scandinavian National Theatre Prize,

2002. *Literary Agent:* For books: Samlaget, Boks 4672 Sofienberg, 0506 Oslo, Norway; For plays: Colombine Teaterförlag, Gaffelgränd 1A, 11130 Stockholm, Sweden.

FOSTER, Cecil Adolphus; Writer and Journalist; b. 26 Sept. 1954, Barbados; three s. *Education:* Diploma, Mass Communications, University of the West Indies, 1978; BA, Administrative Studies, York University, Toronto, 1982; BA, Economics, York University, Toronto, 1984. *Career:* mem. PEN Canada. *Publications:* No Man in the House, 1992; Sleep on Beloved, 1994; Caribana: The Greatest Celebration, 1995; A Place Called Heaven: The Meaning of Being Black, 1996; Slammin' Tar, 1998; Island Wing, 1998. *Honours:* Gordon Mantador Award, 1997. *Address:* 111 Davisville Ave, Apt 208, Toronto, on M45 1G4, Canada.

FOSTER, David (Manning); Novelist; b. 15 May 1944, Sydney, NSW, Australia. *Education:* BSc, Chemistry, University of Sydney, 1967; PhD, Australian National University, Canberra, 1970. *Publications:* The Pure Land, 1974; The Empathy Experiment, 1977; Moonlite, 1981; Plumbum, 1983; Dog Rock: A Postal Pastoral, 1985; The Adventures of Christian Rosy Cross, 1986; Testostero, 1987; The Pale Blue Crochet Coathanger Cover, 1988; Mates of Mars, 1991; Self Portraits (ed.), 1991; A Slab of Fosters, 1994; The Glade Within the Grove, 1996; The Ballad of Erinungarah, 1997; Crossing the Blue Montain (contributor), 1997; In the New Country, 1999; The Land Where Stories End, 2001. Short Stories: North South West: Three Novellas, 1973; Escape to Reality, 1977; Hitting the Wall: Two Novellas, 1989. *Honours:* The Age Award, 1974; Australian National Book Council Award, 1981; New South Wales Premier's Fellowship, 1986; Keating Fellowship, 1991–94; James Joyce Foundation Award, 1996; Miles Franklin Award, 1997; Courier Mail Award, 1999; Australian Writers' Fellowship, 1999. *Address:* PO Box 57, Bundanoon, NSW 2578, Australia.

FOSTER, James Anthony (Tony); writer; b. 2 Aug. 1932, Winnipeg, Manitoba, Canada; m. 1964; one s. two d. *Education:* University of Brunswick. *Career:* mem. Canadian Authors Asscn; PEN; Writers Guild of America; Writers' Union of Canada. *Publications:* Zig Zag to Armageddon, 1978; By-Pass, 1982; The Money Burn, 1984; A coeur ouvert, 1985; Heart of Oak: A Pictorial History of the Royal Canadian Navy, 1985; Meeting of Generals, 1986; Sea Wings: A Pictorial History of Canada's Waterborne Defence Aircraft, 1986; Muskets to Missiles, 1987; Rue du Bac, 1987; For Love and Glory, 1989; The Bush Pilots: A Canadian Phenomena, 1990; Ransom for a God, 1990; The Sound and the Silence, 1990. *Address:* 67 Briarwood Crescent, Halifax, NS B3M 1P2, Canada.

FOSTER, Jeanne (see Williams, Jeanne R.).

FOSTER, Linda Nemec, BA, MFA; poet, writer and teacher; b. 29 May 1950, Garfield Heights, Ohio, USA; m. Anthony Jesse Foster 1974; one s. one d. *Education:* Aquinas College, Grand Rapids, Goddard College, Plainfield, VT. *Career:* Teacher of Creative Writing and Poetry, Michigan Council for the Arts, 1980–; Instructor of English Composition, Ferris State University, 1983–84; Dir of Literature Programming, Urban Institute for Contemporary Arts, Grand Rapids, 1989–96; Lecturer in Poetry, Aquinas College, 1999–; Guest Lecturer and Speaker, various schools, colleges, and conferences; mem. Acad. of American Poets; Detroit Women Writers; Poetry Resource Center of Michigan; Urban Institute for Contemporary Arts; Poetry Society of America. *Publications:* A History of the Body, 1987; A Modern Fairy Tale: The Baba Yaga Poems, 1992; Trying to Balance the Heart, 1993; Living in the Fire Nest, 1996; Contemplating the Heavens, 2001; Amber Necklace from Gdańsk, 2001. Contributions: Reviews, journals, and magazines. *Honours:* Creative Artist Grants in Poetry, Michigan Council for the Arts, 1984, 1990, 1996; Grand Prize, American Poetry Asscn, 1986; Hon. mention, Writers' Digest, 1987; Prizewinner, McGuffin Poetry Contest, 1987, 1994; Passages North National Poetry Competition, 1988; Poetry/Visual Art Selections, Sage College, New York, 1994, 1995; Arts Foundation of Michigan Fellowship in Poetry, 1996; Fellowship, National Writer's Voice Project, 1999; Grant in Poetry, Art Serve Michigan, 2001; first Poet Laureate of Grand Rapids, MI 2003. *Address:* 2024 Wilshire Drive SE, Grand Rapids, MI 49506, USA. *Website:* www.lindanemecfoster.com.

FOSTER, Paul; Dramatist and Screenwriter; b. 15 Oct. 1931, Pennsgrove, NJ, USA. *Education:* BA, Rutgers University; LLB, New York University Law School. *Career:* mem. Dramatists Guild; Society of Composers and Dramatic Authors, France; Players Club, New York City. *Publications:* 25 books of plays including: Tom Paine, 1971; Madonna in the Orchard, 1971; Satyricon, 1972; Elizabeth I, 1972; Marcus Brutus, 1976; Silver Queen Saloon, 1976; Mellon and the National Art Gallery, 1980; A Kiss is Just a Kiss, 1984; 3 Mystery Comedies, 1985; The Dark and Mr Stone, 1985; Odon von Horvath's Faith, Hope and Charity, trans., 1987; Make Believe (with music by Solt Dome), musical book and lyrics, 1994. Films: Smile, 1980; Cop and the Anthem, 1982; When You're Smiling, 1983; Cinderella, 1984; Home Port, 1984. Contributions: Off-Off Broadway Book, 1972; Best American Plays of the Modern Theatre, 1975; New Stages magazine. *Honours:* Rockefeller Foundation Fellowship, 1967; British Arts Council Award, 1973; Guggenheim Fellowship, 1974; Theater Heute Award, 1977.

FOSTER, Roy F.; Irish historian. *Career:* Carroll Professor of Irish History, Hertford Coll., Oxford. *Publications:* Modern Ireland 1600–1972, The Oxford Illustrated History of Ireland, biogs. of Charles Stewart Parnell and Lord Randolph Churchill, W. B. Yeats: A Life, Vol. I: The Apprentice Mage 1865–1914 2001, The Irish Story: Telling Tales and Making it Up in Ireland 2001, W. B. Yeats: A Life, Vol. II: The Arch-Poet 1915–1939 2003. *Address:* Hertford College, Catte Street, Oxford, OX1 3BW, England (Office). *Telephone:* (1865) 279400 (Office). *Website:* www.hertford.ox.ac.uk (Office).

FOUDA, Yosri; Journalist; b. t. *Education:* American Univ., Cairo. *Career:* producer Arabic-language TV Service, BBC, London, UK –1996; reporter Al Jazeera London Bureau, UK 1996–, presenter 'Top Secret' TV programme (interviewed April 2002 Khalid Shaikh Mohammed, Chief of Al-Qaeda Mil. Cttee, believed to have masterminded 9/11 US attacks).

FOULKE, Robert Dana; Prof., Author and Travel Writer; b. 25 April 1930, Minneapolis, USA; m. Patricia Ann Nelson, 29 Dec. 1953, one s. two d. *Education:* AB, Princeton University, 1952; MA, 1957, PhD, 1961, University of Minnesota. *Career:* Instructor in English, University of Minnesota, 1956–59, 1960–61; Asst Prof. of English, 1961–66, Assoc. Prof., 1966–70, Trinity College, Hartford; Prof. of English, 1970–92, Chair of Dept, 1970–80, Skidmore College; Visiting Assoc. and Life Mem., Clare Hall, Cambridge, 1976–77, 1990–91; Visiting Fellow, Dept of English, Princeton University, 1988; Literary Ed., The Oxford Encyclopedia of Maritime History, 1999–2004; mem. College English Asscn; MLA; Joseph Conrad Society; Melville Society; American Society of Journalists and Authors; Society of American Travel Writers; Travel Journalists Guild; Hakluyt Society; National Maritime Historical Society; North American Society for Oceanic History, exec. council, 1995–; Society for Nautical Research. *Publications:* An Anatomy of Literature (co-author and ed.) 1972; The Writer's Mind (co-ed.) 1983; The Sea Voyage Narrative 1997, 2002. Travel Guides: Europe Under Canvas 1980; Fielding's Motoring and Camping Europe 1986; Day Trips and Getaway Vacations in New England 1983; Day Trips and Getaway Vacations in Mid-Atlantic States 1986; Exploring Europe by Car 1991; Fielding's Great Sights of Europe 1994; Colonial America 1995; Romantic Weekends: New England 1998; Day Trips and Get Away Weekends: New England 1999; Day Trips and Get Away Weekends: Mid-Atlantic States 2000; Day Trips and Getaway Weekends: Connecticut, Rhode Island and Massachusetts 2002; Day Trips and Getaway Weekends: Vermont, New Hampshire and Maine 2002; An Adventure Guide to the Champkin and Hudson River Valleys 2003. Contributions: numerous articles in scholarly journals and some 500 travel articles in magazines and newspapers. *Honours:* Fulbright Fellow, University of London, 1959–60; Alexander O. Vietor Fellow, John Carter Brown Library, Brown University, 1993. *Address:* 25 Dark Bay Lane, Lake George, NY 12845, USA.

FOWLER, Alastair (David Shaw); Prof. of English, Writer and Ed.; b. 17 Aug. 1930, Glasgow, Scotland; m. Jenny Catherine Simpson, 23 Dec. 1950, one s. one d. *Education:* MA, University of Edinburgh, 1952; MA, 1955, DPhil, 1957, DLitt, 1972, University of Oxford. *Career:* Junior Research Fellow, Queen's College, Oxford, 1955–59; Instructor, Indiana University, 1957; Lecturer, University College, Swansea, 1959–61; Fellow and Tutor in English Literature, Brasenose College, Oxford, 1962–71; Visiting Prof., Columbia University, 1964; Mem., Institute for Advanced Study, Princeton, NJ, 1966, 1980; Visiting Prof., 1969, 1979, 1985–90, Prof. of English, 1990–98, University of Virginia; Regius Prof. of Rhetoric and English Literature, 1972–84, Prof. Emeritus, 1984–, University Fellow, 1985–87, University of Edinburgh; Advisory Ed., New Literary History, 1972–; Visiting Fellow, Council of the Humanities, Princeton University, 1974, Humanities Research Centre, Canberra, 1980, All Souls College, Oxford, 1984; General Ed., Longman Annotated Anthologies of English Verse, 1977–80; Mem., Editorial Board, English Literary Renaissance, 1978–2003, Word and Image, 1984–91, 1992–97, The Seventeenth Century, 1986–, Connotations, 1990–99, English Review, 1990–, Translation and Literature, 1990–; mem. Fellow, British Acad., 1974. *Publications:* De re poetica, by Richard Wills (ed. and trans.), 1958; Spenser and the Numbers of Time, 1964; Spenser's Images of Life, by C. S. Lewis (ed.), 1967; The Poems of John Milton (ed. with John Carey), 1968; Triumphal Forms, 1970; Silent Poetry (ed.), 1970; Topics in Criticism (ed. with Christopher Butler), 1971; Seventeen, 1971; Conceitful Thought, 1975; Catacomb Suburb, 1976; Edmund Spenser, 1977; From the Domain of Arnheim, 1982; Kinds of Literature, 1982; A History of English Literature, 1987; The New Oxford Book of Seventeenth Century Verse (ed.), 1991; The Country House Poem, 1994; Time's Purpled Masquers, 1996; Milton: Paradise Lost (ed.), 1998; Renaissance Realism, 2003. Contributions: scholarly books and journals. *Address:* 11 E Claremont St, Edinburgh EH7 4HT, Scotland.

FOWLER, Don D., BA, PhD; academic and writer; *Professor of Historic Preservation and Anthropology, University of Nevada*; b. 24 April 1936, Torrey, Utah, USA; m. Catherine Sweeney 1963. *Education:* Weber State College, University of Utah, University of Pittsburgh. *Career:* Instructor, 1964–65, Asst Prof., 1965–67, Assoc. Prof. of Anthropology and Exec. Dir of Human Systems Center of the Desert Research Institute, 1968–71, Research Prof. and Exec. Dir of the Social Sciences Center of the Desert Research Institute, 1971–78, Mamie Kleberg Prof. of Historic Preservation and Anthropology, 1978–, Chair., Dept of Anthropology, 1990–98, University of Nevada, Reno; Visiting Postdoctoral Fellow, 1967–68, Research Assoc., 1970–, Smithsonian Institution, Washington, DC; Fellow, American Anthropological Asscn; mem. Soc. for American Archaeology (pres. 1985–87). *Publications:* Down the Colorado: John Wesley Powell's Diary of the First Trip Through the Grand Canyon (with Eliot Porter), 1969; The

Anthropology of the Numa: John Wesley Powell's Manuscripts on Great Basin Indians, 1968–1980 (with C. S. Fowler), 1971; 'Photographed all the Best Scenery': Jack Hillers' Diary of the Powell Expedition, 1871–1875 (ed.), 1971; In Sacred Manner We Live: Edward S. Curtis' Indian Photographs, 1972; Material Culture of the Numa: The John Wesley Powell Collection, 1867–1880 (with J. F. Matley), 1979; American Archaeology Past and Future: A Celebration of the Society for American Archaeology, 1935–1985 (ed. with D. J. Meltzer and J. A. Sabloff), 1986; Anthropology of the Desert West: Essays in Honor of Jesse D. Jennings (ed. with Carol J. Condie), 1986; The Western Photographs of Jack Hillers, 'Myself in the Water', 1989; Others Knowing Others: Perspectives on Ethnographic Careers (ed. with Donald L. Hardesty), 1994; A Laboratory for Anthopology: Science and Romanticism in the American Southwest, 1946–1930, 2000. Contributions: many scholarly journals. *Honours:* many private and government grants; Distinguished Graduate Medal, University of Pittsburgh, 1986; Lifetime Achievement Award, Society for American Archaeology, 2003. *Address:* 1010 Foothill Road, Reno, NV 89511, USA.

FOWLER, Marian Elizabeth, BA, MA, PhD; writer; b. 15 Oct. 1929, Newmarket, ON, Canada; m. Dr Rodney Singleton Fowler 1953 (divorced 1977), one s. one d. *Education:* Univ. of Toronto. *Publications:* The Embroidered Tent: Five Gentlewomen in Early Canada 1982, Redney: A Life of Sara Jeannette Duncan 1983, Below the Peacock Fan: First Ladies of the Raj 1987, Blenheim: Biography of a Palace 1989, In a Gilded Cage: From Heiress to Duchess 1993, The Way She Looks Tonight: Five Women of Style 1996, Hope: Adventures of a Diamond 2003; contrib. to English Studies in Canada, University of Toronto Quarterly, Dalhousie Review, Ontario History, Dictionary of Canadian Biography, Oxford Companion to Canadian Literature, New Canadian Encyclopaedia. *Honours:* Gov.-Gen.'s Gold Medal in English 1951, Canadian Biography Award 1979. *Address:* Apt 503, 77 St Clair Avenue E, Toronto, ON M4T 1M5, Canada.

FOWLER, Rebecca, BSc; British newspaper editor; b. 1958; m. Niall Ferguson; one s. one d. *Education:* Univ. of Southampton. *Career:* Freelance journalist; Medical Corresp. Mail on Sunday, then Features Ed.; journalist Daily Mail; Assoc. Ed. Sunday Times 1991, then Deputy Ed.; fmr Ed. Sunday Express. *Address:* c/o Sunday Express, Ludgate House, 245 Blackfriars Road, London SE1 9UX, England.

FOWLES, John Robert; British writer and poet; b. 31 March 1926, Leigh-on-Sea, Essex; m. 1st Elizabeth Whitton 1954 (died 1990); m. 2nd Sarah Smith 1998. *Education:* Bedford School and Oxford Univ. *Career:* Lecturer in English Univ. of Poitiers, France 1950–51; Teacher Anargyrios Coll., Greece 1951–52, and London 1953–63; jt hon. curator Lyme Regis Museum 1978–79, hon. curator 1979–88; mem. British Humanist Asscn. *Publications:* The Collector 1963, The Aristos 1964, The Magus 1965, The French Lieutenant's Woman 1969 (WHSmith Literary Award), Poems 1973, Shipwreck 1974, The Ebony Tower 1974, Daniel Martin 1977, Islands (with Fay Godwin) 1978, The Tree (with Frank Horvat) 1979, The Enigma of Stonehenge 1980, John Aubrey's Monumenta Britannica (ed, Parts 1 and 2 1980, Part 3 and Index 1982), Mantissa 1982, Thomas Hardy's England 1984, Land 1985, A Maggot 1985, Wormholes 1998, Lyme Worthies 2000, The Journals Vol. 1 (ed. by Charles Drazin) 2003. *Honours:* Hon. Fellow New Coll., Oxford 1997Hon. DLitt (Exeter) 1983, Hon. LittD (E Anglia) 1997; PEN Silver Pen Award 1969. *Literary Agent:* Gillon Aitken Associates Ltd, 18–21 Cavaye Place, London, SW10 9PT, England. *Telephone:* (20) 7373-8672. *Fax:* (20) 7373-6002.

FOX, Hugh (Bernard), BS, MA, PhD; professor, author, poet and dramatist; b. 12 Feb. 1932, Chicago, IL, USA; m. 1st Lucia Alicia Ungaro 1957, divorced 1969, one s. two d.; m. 2nd Nona W. Werner 1970, one s. two d.; m. 3rd Maria Bernadette Costa 1988. *Education:* Loyola Univ., Chicago, Univ. of Illinois, Urbana-Champaign. *Career:* Prof. of American Literature Loyola Marymount Univ., Los Angeles 1958–68; Fulbright Prof., Mexico 1961, Venezuela 1964–66, Brazil 1978–80; Ed. Ghost Dance: The International Quarterly of Experimental Poetry 1968–95; Prof., Michigan State Univ. 1968–99; Lecturer Spain, Portugal 1975–76. *Publications:* Fiction: Honeymoon/Mom 1978, Leviathan 1980, Shaman 1993, The Last Summer 1995. Poetry: The Face of Guy Lombardo 1975, Almazora 42 1982, Jamais Vu 1991, The Sacred Cave 1992, Once 1995, Techniques 1997. Non-Fiction: Henry James 1968, Charles Bukowski: A Critical and Bibliographical Study 1969, The Gods of the Cataclysm 1976, First Fire: Central and South American Indian Poetry 1978, Lyn Lifshin: A Critical Study 1985, The Mythological Foundations of the Epic Genre: The Solar Voyage as the Hero's Journey 1989, Stairway to the Sun 1996, Strata 1998, Back 1999, Slides 2000, The Angel of Death: O Ango da Morte 2001, Boston: A Long Poem 2002, Voices 2002, Hugh Fox: Greatest Hits 1968–2001 2003. Contributions: many journals, reviews, quarterlies and periodicals. *Honours:* John Carter Brown Library Fellowship, Brown Univ. 1968, Organization of American States Grants, Argentina 1971, Chile 1986. *Address:* 340 Wildwood Drive, E Lansing, MI 48823, USA. *Telephone:* (517) 337-3129. *E-mail:* hughfox8@aol.com.

FOX, Levi; Author; b. 28 Aug. 1914, Leicestershire, England; m. Jane Richards, one s. two d. *Education:* BA, 1936, MA, 1938, Oriel College, Oxford; MA, University of Manchester, 1938. *Career:* General Ed., Dugdale Society, 1945–80; Dir and Secretary, 1945–89, Dir Emeritus, 1990–, Shakespeare Birthplace Trust. *Publications:* Leicester Abbey, 1938; Leicester Castle, 1943; Leicester Forest (with P. Russell), 1945; Coventry's Heritage, 1946; Stratford-upon-Avon, 1949; Shakespeare's Town, 1949; Oxford, 1951; Shakespeare's Stratford-upon-Avon, 1951; Shakespeare's Country, 1953; The Borough Town of Stratford-upon-Avon, 1953; Shakespeare's Town and Country, 1959; Stratford-upon-Avon: An Appreciation, 1963; The Shakespeare Book, 1969; Shakespeare's Sonnets (ed.), 1970; Shakespeare's England, 1972; In Honour of Shakespeare, 1972; Stratford: Past and Present, 1975; Shakespeare's Flowers, 1978; Shakespeare's Birds, 1978; Shakespeare in Medallic Art, 1982; Shakespeare's Magic, 1982; Historic Stratford-upon-Avon, 1986; Shakespeare's Town and Country, 1986; Minutes and Accounts of the Corporation of Stratford-upon-Avon (1592–96), 1990; The Shakespeare Birthplace Trust: A Personal Memoir, 1997. Contributions: English Historical Review; Shakespeare Survey. *Honours:* FRHistS, 1960; FRSA, 1960; FRSL, 1960; New York University medal, 1964; Hon. LHD, George Washington University, 1964; Hon. DLitt, Birmingham University, 1975. *Address:* The Shakespeare Centre, Stratford-upon Avon CV37 6QW, England.

FOX, Merrion (Mem) Frances; writer; b. 5 March 1946, Melbourne, Vic., Australia; m. Malcolm 1969; one d. *Education:* BA, Flinders University, 1978; BEd, Sturt College, 1979; Graduate Diploma, Underdale College, 1981. *Career:* mem. Australian Society of Authors; Australian Children's Book Council. *Publications:* Children's Books: Possum Magic, 1983; Wilfrid Gordon McDonald Partridge, 1984; How to Teach Drama to Infants, 1984; A Cat Called Kite, 1985; Zoo-Looking, 1986; Hattie and the Fox, 1986; Sail Away, 1986; Arabella, 1986; Just Like That, 1986; A Bedtime Story, 1987; The Straight Line Wonder, 1987; Goodnight Sleep Tight, 1988; Guess What?, 1988; Koala Lou, 1988; Night Noises, 1989; Shoes for Grandpa, 1989; Sophie, 1989; Memories, 1992; Tough Boris, 1994; Wombat Divine, 1995; Boo to a Goose, 1996; Feathers and Fools, 1996. Adult Books: Mem's the Word, 1990; Dear Mem Fox, I Have Read All Your Books, Even the Pathetic Ones, 1992. Co-Author: English Essentials: The Wouldn't-be-without-it Handbook on Writing Well, 1993; Radical Reflections: Passionate Opinions on Teaching, Learning, and Living, 1993. Contributions: Language Arts; Horn Book; Australian Journal of Language and Literacy; Reading Teacher; Reading and Writing Quarterly; Dragon Lode. *Honours:* New South Wales Premier's Literary Award, Best Children's Book, 1984; KOALA First Prize, 1987; Dromkeen Medal for Outstanding Services to Children's Literature, 1990; Advance Australia Award, 1990; AM, 1994; Alice Award, Fellowship of Australian Women Writers, 1994; Hon. Doctorate, University of Wollongong, 1996. *Literary Agent:* Australian Literary Management, 2A Booth Street, Balmain, NSW 2041, Australia.

FOX, Paula; Novelist; b. 22 April 1923, New York, NY, USA; m. 1st Howard Bird 1940 (divorced); one d.; m. 2nd Richard Sigerson 1948 (divorced); two s.; m. 3rd Martin Greenberg 1962. *Education:* Columbia Univ. *Publications:* Novels: Poor George, 1967; Desperate Characters, 1970; The Western Coast, 1972; The Widow's Children, 1976; A Servant's Tale, 1984; The God of Nightmares, 1990. Children's Books: Maurice's Room, 1966; A Likely Place, 1967; Dear Prosper, 1968; The Stone-Faced Boy, 1968; The King's Falcon, 1969; Blowfish Live in the Sea, 1970; The Slave Dancer, 1973; The Little Swinehead and Other Tales, 1978; A Place Apart, 1980; One-Eyed Cat, 1984; The Moonlight Man, 1986; The Village by the Sea (aka In a Place of Danger), 1988; Monkey Island, 1991; Western Wind, 1993; The Eagle Kite (aka The Gathering Darkness), 1995; Amzat and His Brothers: Three Italian Tales, 1999. Other: Borrowed Finery (memoir), 2001. *Address:* c/o Flamingo, 77–85 Fulham Palace Rd, London W6 8JB, England.

FOX-GENOVESE, Elizabeth Ann Teresa; historian and academic; b. 28 May 1941, Boston, Massachusetts, USA; m. Eugene Dominick Genovese 1969. *Education:* BA, Bryn Mawr College, 1963; Institut d'Etudes Politiques, Paris, 1961–62; MA, 1966, PhD, 1974, Harvard University; Special Candidate, Center for Psychoanalytic Training and Research, Columbia University, 1977–79; Institute in Quantitative Methods, Newberry Library, Chicago, 1979. *Career:* Teaching Fellow, Harvard University, 1965–66, 1967–69; Asst Prof., 1973–76, Assoc. Prof., 1976–80, University of Rochester; Prof., SUNY at Binghamton, 1980–86; Prof., 1986–, Eleonore Raoul Prof. of Humanities, 1988–, Emory University; Adjunct Prof., Auburn University, AL, 1987; Eudora Welty Prof., Millsaps College, 1990; mem. American Acad. of Liberal Education; American Antiquarian Society; American Comparative Literature Asscn; American Historical Asscn; American Political Science Asscn; American Studies Asscn; Asscn of Literary Scholars and Critics; MLA; Organization of American Historians, life mem.; Social Science Historical Asscn; Society for the Study of Southern Literature; Society of American Historians; Southern Asscn for Women Historians, life mem.; Southern Historical Asscn, life mem. *Publications:* The Origins of Physiocracy: Economic Revolution and Social Order in 18th Century France, 1976; Fruits of Merchant Capital: Slavery and Bourgeois Property in the Rise and Expansion of Capitalism (with Eugene Dominick Genovese), 1983; Within the Plantation Household: Black and White Women of the Old South, 1988; Feminism without Illusions: A Critique of Individualism, 1991; Feminism is Not the Story of My Life: How Today's Feminist Elite Has Lost Touch with the Real Concerns of Women, 1996. Contributions: Professional journals and general periodicals. *Honours:* Hon. LittD, Millsaps College, 1992. *Address:* c/o Dept of History, Emory University, Atlanta, GA 30322, USA.

FRAILE, Medardo; writer and academic; b. 21 March 1925, Madrid, Spain; m. Janet H. Gallagher; one d. *Education:* PhD, DLitt, University of Madrid, 1968. *Career:* mem. General Society of Spanish Authors; Working Community of Book Writers, Spain; Asscn of University Teachers. *Publications:* Cuentos con algún amor, 1954; A la luz cambian las cosas, 1959; Cuentos de verdad, 1964; Descubridor de nada y otros cuentos, 1970; Con los días contados, 1972; Samuel Ros hacia una generación sin crítica, 1972; La penúltima Inglaterra, 1973; Poesia y teatro españoles contemporáneos, 1974; Ejemplario, 1979; Autobiografía, 1986; Cuento español de posguerra, 1986; El gallo puesto en hora, 1987; Entre parentesis, 1988; Santa Engracia, numero dos o tres, 1989; Teatro español en un acto, 1989; El rey y el país con granos, 1991; Cuentos completos, 1991; Claudina y los cacos, 1992; La familia irreal inglesa, 1993; Los brazos invisibles, 1994; Documento nacional, 1997; Contrasombras, 1998; Ladrones del paraiso, 1999; Cuentos de verdad (anthology), 2000; Descontar y contar, 2000; La letra con sangre, 2001; Años de aprendizaje, 2001. Translator: El Weir de Hermiston by R. L. Stevenson, 1995. Contributions: many publications. *Honours:* Sesamo Award, 1956; Literary Grant, Fundación Juan March, 1960; Critics' Book of the Year, 1965; La estafeta literaria award, 1970; Hucha de Oro, 1971; Research Grant, Carnegie Trust for Universities of Scotland, 1975; Colegiado de Honor del Colegio Heraldico de España y de las Indias, 1995; Comendador con Placa de la Orden Civil de Alfonso X El Sabio, 1999; Orden venezolana de Don Balthasar de León de Primera Clase. *Address:* 24 Etive Crescent, Bishopbriggs, Glasgow G64 1ES, Scotland.

FRAJLICH, Anna; Poet and University Teacher; b. 10 March 1942, Katta Taldyk, Kyrgyzstan; m. Władysław Zajac 31 July 1965; one s. *Education:* MA, Polish Literature, Warsaw University, 1965; PhD, Slavic Studies, New York University, 1991. *Career:* Lecturer, Dept of Slavic Languages, Columbia University, 1982–; mem. PEN Club, Center for Writers in Exile, USA; Asscn of Polish Writers. *Publications:* Indian Summer, 1982; Który las, 1986; Between Dawn and the Wind, 1991; Ogrodem i ogrodzeniem (The Garden and the Fence), 1993; Jeszcze w drodze (Still on its Way), 1994; Wsłońcu listopada, 2000; Znów szuka mnie wiatr, 2001. Contributions: Terra Poetica; Artful Dodge; The Polish Review; Wisconsin Review; Mr Cogito; The Jewish Quarterly; Poésie Premiére; World Literature Today. *Honours:* Koscielski Foundation Award, Switzerland, 1981; Reader's Choice for Polish Book of the Year, Rzeczpospolita newspaper, Warsaw, 2001. *Address:* c/o Dept of Slavic Languages, Columbia University, New York, NY 10027, USA.

FRAME, Ronald William Sutherland, MA, MLITT; British author; b. 23 May 1953, Glasgow, Scotland. *Education:* The High School of Glasgow, Univ. of Glasgow, Jesus Coll. Oxford. *Career:* full-time author 1981–. *Publications:* Winter Journey 1984, Watching Mrs. Gordon 1985, A Long Weekend with Marcel Proust 1986, Sandmouth People 1987, Paris (TV play) 1987, A Woman of Judah 1987, Penelope's Hat 1989, Bluette 1990, Underwood and After 1991, Walking My Mistress in Deauville 1992, The Sun on the Wall 1994, The Lantern Bearers 1999, Permanent Violet 2002, All of It 2003, Time in Carnbeg 2004. *TV screenplays:* Paris 1985, Out of Time 1987, Ghost City 1994, A Modern Man 1996, Four Ghost Stories for Christmas (adaptation) 2000, Darien: Disaster in Paradise 2003, Cromwell 2003. *Radio scripts include:* Winter Journey 1985, Cara 1989, The Lantern Bearers 1997, The Hydro (serial) 1997–99, Havisham 1998, Maestro 1999, Pharos 2000, Don't Look Now (adaptation) 2001, Sunday at Sant' Agata 2001, Greyfriars 2002, The Garden of the Finzi-Continis (adaptation) 2003. *Honours:* Betty Trask Prize (jt first recipient) 1984, Samuel Beckett Prize 1986; TV Industries' Panel's Most Promising Writer New to Television Award 1986, Saltire Scottish Book of the Year 2000, American Library Asscn Stonewall Award in Literature 2003, Barbara Gittings Honor Prize for Fiction 2003. *Literary Agent:* Curtis Brown Ltd, Haymarket House, 28–29 Haymarket, London, SW1Y 4SP, England. *Telephone:* (20) 7393-4400. *Fax:* (20) 7393-4401. *E-mail:* info@curtisbrown.co.uk. *Website:* www.curtisbrown.co.uk.

FRANCE, (Evelyn) Christine, BA; art historian; b. 23 Dec. 1939, Sydney, NSW, Australia; m. Stephen Robert Bruce France 1962; one d. *Education:* University of Sydney. *Publications:* Justin O'Brien: Image and Icon, 1987; Margaret Olley, 1990; Marea Gazzard: Form and Clay, 1994; Jean Appleton: A Lifetime with Art, 1998. Contributions: Art and Australia; Australian newspapers. *Address:* Old Baerami, Baerami, NSW 2333, Australia.

FRANCHON, Lisa (see Floren, Lee).

FRANCIS, Clare, MBE; British writer; b. 17 April 1946, Surrey, England; one s. *Education:* University College London. *Career:* Chair, Advisory Committee on Public Lending Right 2000–03; mem. Society of Authors (chair. 1997–99). *Publications:* Come Hell or High Water, 1977; Come Wind or Weather, 1978; The Commanding Sea, 1981; Night Sky, 1983; Red Crystal, 1985; Wolf Winter, 1987; Requiem, 1991; Deceit, 1993; Betrayal, 1995; A Dark Devotion, 1997; Keep Me Close, 1999; A Death Divided, 2001; Homeland, 2003. *Honours:* University College London, fellow; Univ. of Manchester Institute of Technology, hon. fellow. *Literary Agent:* Johnson & Alcock Ltd, Clerkenwell House, 45–47 Clerkenwell Green, London EC1R 0HT, England. *Website:* www.clarefrancis.co.uk.

FRANCIS, Dick, (Richard Stanley Francis); Writer; b. 31 Oct. 1920, Tenby, South Wales; m. Mary Margaret Brenchley 1947 (died 2000); two s. *Career:* Pilot, RAF, 1940–45; Professional Steeple Chase Jockey, 1948–57; Champion Jockey, 1953–54; Racing Correspondent, Sunday Express, 1957–73. *Publications:* Fiction: Dead Cert, 1962; Nerve, 1964; For Kicks, 1965; Odds Against (Sid Halley series), 1965; Flying Finish, 1966; Blood Sport, 1967; Forfeit, 1968; Enquiry, 1969; Rat Race, 1970; Bonecrack, 1971; Smokescreen, 1972; Slayride, 1973; Knockdown, 1974; High Stakes, 1975; In the Frame, 1976; Risk, 1977; Trial Run, 1978; Whip Hand (Sid Halley series), 1979; Reflex, 1980; Twice Shy, 1981; Banker, 1982; The Danger, 1983; Proof, 1984; Break In (Kit Fielding series), 1985; Bolt (Kit Fielding series), 1986Hot Money, 1987; The Edge, 1988; Straight, 1989; Great Racing Stories (co-ed.), 1989; Longshot, 1990; Comeback, 1991; Driving Force, 1992; Decider, 1993; Wild Horses, 1994; Come to Grief (Sid Halley series), 1995; To the Hilt, 1996; 10 1b Penalty, 1997; Field of Thirteen, 1998; Second Wind, 1999; Shattered, 2000. Non-Fiction: The Sport of Queens (autobiog.), 1957; Lester, the Official Biography, 1986. *Honours:* CWA Silver Dagger Award, 1966, Golden Dagger Award, 1980, Cartier Diamond Dagger Award, 1990; MWA Edgar Allan Poe Awards, 1970, 1980, 1996, and Grand Master, 1996; Hon. LHD, Tufts Univ., 1991; FRSL, 1998. *Literary Agent:* Johnson & Alcock Ltd, Clerkenwell House, 45–47 Clerkenwell Green, London EC1R 0HT, England.

FRANCIS, Matthew, MA, PhD; British poet and novelist; m. Creina. *Education:* Univ. of Cambridge, Univ. of Southampton. *Career:* fmrly Lecturer in Creative Writing, St Mary's, Strawberry Hill; Sr Lecturer in Creative Writing, Univ. of Glamorgan, South Wales. *Publications:* poetry: Blizzard 1996, Dragons 2001; novel: Whom 1989. *Honours:* Southern Arts Literature Prize 1997, Gathering Swallows Prize 1997, Hawthornden Fellowship 1998, MFCAP Prize 1999, TLS/Blackwells Prize 2000. *Address:* c/o Faber and Faber Ltd, 3 Queen Square, London, WC1N 3AU, England. *Website:* www.7greenhill.freeserve.co.uk.

FRANCK, Thomas Martin; American academic and writer; b. 14 July 1931, Berlin, Germany. *Education:* BA, 1952, LLB, 1953, University of British Columbia; LLM, 1954, SJD, 1959, Harvard Law School. *Career:* Asst Prof., University of Nebraska College of Law, 1954–56; Assoc. Prof., 1960–62, Prof. of Law, 1962–, Dir, Center for International Studies, 1965–2002, New York University School of Law; Visiting Prof., Stanford Law School, 1963, University of East Africa Law School, Dar es Salaam, 1963–66, Osgood Hall Law School, York University, Toronto, 1972–76, Woodrow Wilson School, Princeton University, 1979; Lecturer, The Hague Acad. of International Law, 1993; Visiting Fellow, Trinity College, Cambridge, 1996–97; mem. Africa Watch; American Society of International Law; Canadian Council on International Law; Council on Foreign Relations; French Society of International Law; German Society of International Law; Institut du Droit International; International Law Asscn, vice-pres., 1973–94, hon. vice-pres., 1994–; International Peace Acad.; Acad. of Arts and Sciences, 2003. *Publications:* United States Foreign Relations Law: Documents and Sources (co-author), 5 vols, 1980–84; The Tethered Presidency, 1981; Human Rights in Third World Perspective, 3 vols, 1982; Foreign Relations and National Security Law, 1987; The Power of Legitimacy Among Nations, 1990; Political Questions/Judicial Answers: Does the Rule of Law Apply to Foreign Affairs?, 1992; Fairness in the International Legal and Institutional System, 1993; Fairness in International Law and Institutions, 1995; International Law Decisions in National Courts (co-ed.), 1996; The Empowered Self: Law and Society in the Age of Individualism, 1999; Delegating State Powers; The Effect of Treaty Regimes on Democracy and Sovereignty, 2000; Recourse to Force: State Action Against Threats and Armed Attacks, 2002. Contributions: scholarly journals. *Honours:* Guggenheim Fellowships, 1973–74, 1982–83; Christopher Medal, 1976; Certificates of Merit, American Society of International Law, 1981, 1986, 1994, 1996; John E. Read Medal, Canadian Council on International Law, 1994; Hon. LLD, University of British Columbia, 1995; Hon. DHL, Monterey Institute of International Studies, 2003; Hudson Medal, American Society of International Law, 2003. *Address:* c/o New York University School of Law, 40 Washington Square S, New York, NY 10012, USA.

FRANCO, Tomaso; Poet and Writer; b. 23 May 1933, Bologna, Italy; divorced, two s. *Education:* Classical Studies, 1952; Doctorate in Law, 1959; Art Studies. *Publications:* Poetry: Uno Scatto dell'Evoluzione 1984, Parole d'Archivio 1986, Il Libro dei Torti 1988, Casa di Frontiera 1990, Volavi Per Me 2000, In Un Luogo della Mente 2001. Novel: Soldato dei Sogni 1995. Essays: Sila-Torino 1961, Lettere a un Fuoruscito 1988, Antichità di Lavarone 2003. Anthology: Il Viaggiatore Indispensabile 2002. Contributions: various anthologies, newspapers, and journals. *Honours:* First Award, Clemente Rèbora, Milan, 1986; Gold Medal, City of Como, 1990; First Award, National, Associazione Promozione Cultura in Toscana, 1992. *Address:* Via San Domenico 2, 36100 Vicenza, Italy.

FRANK, Joseph Nathaniel; academic and writer; b. 6 Oct. 1918, New York, NY, USA; m. Marguerite J. Straus 1953; two d. *Education:* New York University, 1937–38; University of Wisconsin 1941–42; University of Paris, 1950–51; PhD, University of Chicago, 1960. *Career:* Ed., Bureau of National Affairs, Washington, DC, 1942–50; Asst Prof., Dept of English, University of Minnesota, 1958–61; Assoc. Prof., Rutgers University, 1961–66; Prof. of Comparative Literature, 1966–85, Dir of Christian Gauss Seminars, 1966–83, Princeton University; Visiting Mem., Institute for Advanced Study, 1984–87; Prof. of Comparative Literature and Slavic Languages and Literatures, 1985–89, Prof. Emeritus, 1989–, Stanford University; mem.

American Acad. of Arts and Sciences, fellow. *Publications:* The Widening Gyre: Crisis and Mastery in Modern Literature, 1963; Dostoevsky: The Seeds of Revolt, 1821–1849, 1976; Dostoevsky: The Years of Ordeal, 1850–1859, 1983; Dostoevsky: The Stir of Liberation, 1860–1865, 1986; Selected Letters of Fyodor Dostoevsky (co-ed.), 1987; Through the Russian Prism, 1989; The Idea of Spatial Form, 1991; Dostoevsky: The Miraculous Years, 1865–1871, 1995. Contributions: Southern Review; Sewanee Review; Hudson Review; Partisan Review; Art News; Critique; Chicago Review; Minnesota Review; Russian Review; Le Contrat Social; Commentary; Encounter; New York Review. *Honours:* Fulbright Scholar, 1950–51; Rockefeller Fellow, 1952–53, 1953–54; Guggenheim Fellowships, 1956–57, 1975–76; Award, National Institute of Arts and Letters, 1958; Research Grants, ACLS, 1964–65, 1967–68, 1970–71; James Russell Lowell Prize, 1977; Christian Gauss Awards, 1977, 1996; Rockefeller Foundation Fellowships, 1979–80, 1983–84; National Book Critics Circle Award, 1984. *Address:* c/o Dept of Slavic Languages and Literatures, Stanford University, Stanford, CA 94305, USA.

FRANK, Terence Francis (see Coleman, Terry).

FRANKE, William, BA, MA, PhD; academic and poet; b. 1 April 1956, Milwaukee, Wisconsin, USA. *Education:* Williams College, University of Oxford, University of California at Berkeley, Stanford University. *Career:* Adjunct Faculty Mem., Columbia College, 1984–86; Faculty Mem., 1991–96, Assoc. Prof. of Comparative Literature and Italian, 1996–, Vanderbilt University, Nashville, Tennessee; Lecturer, educational institutions including Stanford University, 1991, University of Tulsa, 1992, University of Reading, England, 1995. *Publications:* Dante's Interpretative Journey, 1996. Contributions: Books including Through a Glass Darkly: Essays in the Religious Imagination; Dante: Contemporary Perspectives, 1996; Articles and poems to journals including SEAMS: Cultural Arts Journal; California State Poetry Quarterly; Italian Quarterly; Religion and Literature; Yeats-Eliot Review; Symploke: Journal for the Intermingling of Literary, Cultural, and Theoretical Scholarship. *Honours:* John E. Moody Scholar, University of Oxford, 1978–80; Scholarship to W. B. Yeats International Summer School, Sligo, Ireland, 1979; Alexander von Humboldt Fellow, Germany, 1994–95; Grants, Istituto Italiano per gli studi filosifici, Naples, Italy, 1995, 1996; Robert Penn Warren Center for the Humanities Fellow, 1995–96. *Address:* c/o Vanderbilt University, PO Box 1709, Station B, Nashville, TN 37235, USA.

FRANKEL, Max, MA; American journalist; b. 3 April 1930, Gera, Germany; m. 1st. Tobia Brown 1956 (died 1987); two s. one d.; m. 2nd Joyce Purnick 1988. *Education:* Columbia Univ., New York. *Career:* mem. staff, The New York Times 1952, Chief Washington Corresp. 1968–72, Sunday Ed. 1973–76, Editorial Pages Ed. 1977–86, Exec. Ed. 1986–94, 1994–95, also columnist New York Times magazine 1995–2000. *Publication:* The Time of My Life and My Life with the Times 1999. *Honours:* Pulitzer Prize for Int. Reporting 1973. *Address:* c/o The New York Times Co., 15 West 67th Street, New York, NY 10023-6226, USA.

FRANKEL, Naomi; Israeli poet and writer. *Address:* c/o Hebron University, PO Box 40, Hebron, West Bank, via Israel.

FRANKFURT, Harry; Prof. of Philosophy and Writer; b. 29 May 1929, Langhorne, Pennsylvania, USA; m. Joan Gilbert. *Education:* BA, 1949, MA, 1953, PhD, 1954, Johns Hopkins University; Cornell University, 1949–51. *Career:* Instructor, 1956–59, Asst Prof., 1959–62, Ohio State University; Assoc. Prof., SUNY at Binghamton, 1962–63; Research Assoc., 1963–64, Assoc. Prof., 1964–71, Prof. of Philosophy, 1971–76, Rockefeller University, New York City; Visiting Fellow, All Souls College, Oxford, 1971–72; Visiting Prof., Vassar College, 1973–74, University of Pittsburgh, 1975–76, University of California at Los Angeles, 1990; Prof. of Philosophy, 1976–89, Chair., Dept of Philosophy, 1978–87, John M. Schiff Prof., 1989, Yale University; Prof. of Philosophy, 1990–2002, Prof. Emeritus, 2002–, Princeton Univ.; mem. American Acad. of Arts and Sciences, fellow. *Publications:* Demons, Dreamers, and Madmen: The Defense of Reason in Descartes's Meditations, 1970; Leibniz: A Collection of Critical Essays (ed.), 1972; The Importance of What We Care About, 1988; Necessity, Volition and Love, 1999; The Reasons of Love, 2004. Contributions: many scholarly books and journals. *Honours:* National Endowment for the Humanities Fellowships, 1981–82, 1994; Guggenheim Fellowship, 1993; American Philosophical Asscn (Eastern Division), pres., 1991–92. *Address:* c/o Dept of Philosophy, 1879 Hall, Princeton University, Princeton, NJ 08544, USA.

FRANKLAND, (Anthony) Noble, CBE, MA, DPhil; historian and writer; b. 4 July 1922, Ravenstonedale, England; m. 1st Diana Madeline Fovargue Tavernor 1944 (died 1981); one s. one d.; m. 2nd Sarah Katharine Davies 1982. *Education:* Trinity College, Oxford. *Career:* Official British Military Historian, Cabinet Office, 1951–58; Deputy Dir of Studies, Royal Institute of International Affairs, 1956–60; Dir, Imperial War Museum, 1960–82; Lees Knowles Lecturer, Trinity College, Cambridge, 1963. *Publications:* Documents on International Affairs, 1958, 1959, 1960; Crown of Tragedy: Nicholas II, 1960; The Strategic Air Offensive Against Germany, 1939–45 (with Sir Charles Webster), 4 vols, 1961; The Bombing Offensive Against Germany: Outlines and Perspectives, 1965; Bomber Offensive: The Devastation of Europe, 1970; The Politics and Strategy of the Second World War (co-ed.), eight vols, 1974–78; Decisive Battles of the Twentieth Century: Land, Sea, Air (co-ed.), 1976; Prince Henry, Duke of Gloucester, 1980; Encyclopedia of Twentieth Century Warfare (general ed. and contributor), 1989; Witness of a Century: Prince Arthur, Duke of Connaught, 1850–1942, 1993; History at War: The Campaigns of an Historian, 1998. Contributions: Encyclopaedia Britannica; TLS; The Times; Daily Telegraph; Observer; Military journals. *Honours:* Companion of the Order of the Bath, 1983; Holder of the Distinguished Flying Cross. *Address:* 26–27 Riverview Terrace, Abingdon, Oxfordshire OX14 5AE, England.

FRANKLIN, John Hope; Historian, Prof. and Author; b. 2 Jan. 1915, Rentiesville, Oklahoma, USA; m. Aurelia E. Whittington, 11 June 1940, one s. *Education:* AB, Fisk University, 1935; AM, 1936, PhD, 1941, Harvard University. *Career:* Prof. of History, St Augustine's College, 1939–43, North Carolina College at Durham, 1943–47, Howard University, 1947–56; Chair., Dept of History, Brooklyn College, CUNY, 1956–64; Prof. of American History, 1964–82, Chair., Dept of History, 1967–70, John Matthews Manly Distinguished Service Prof., 1969–82, University of Chicago; James B. Duke Prof. of History, 1982–85, Prof. of Legal History, 1985–92, Duke University; various visiting professorships; mem. American Acad. of Arts and Sciences, fellow; American Asscn of University Profs; American Historical Asscn, pres., 1978–79; American Philosophical Society; American Studies Asscn; Asscn for the Study of Negro Life and History; Organization of American Historians, pres., 1974–75; Southern Historical Asscn, pres., 1970–71. *Publications:* Free Negro in North Carolina, 1943; From Slavery to Freedom: A History of American Negroes, 1947; Militant South, 1956; Reconstruction After the Civil War, 1961; The Emancipation Proclamation, 1963; Illustrated History of Black Americans (with others), 1970; A Southern Odyssey, 1976; Racial Equality in America, 1976; George Washington Williams: A Biography, 1985; The Color Line: Legacy for the 21st Century, 1993. Editor: several books. Contributions: scholarly journals. *Honours:* Edward Austin Fellow, 1937–39; Guggenheim Fellowships, 1950–51, 1973–74; Pres.'s Fellow, Brown University, 1952–53; Center for Advanced Study in the Behavioral Sciences Fellow, 1973–74; Senior Mellon Fellow, National Humanities Center, 1980–82; Cleanth Brooks Medal, Fellowship of Southern Writers, 1989; Gold Medal, Encyclopaedia Britannica, 1990; North Carolina Medals, 1992, 1993; Charles Frankel Medal, 1993; Bruce Catton Award, Society of American Historians, 1994; Presidential Medal of Freedom, 1995; Spingarn Medal, 1995; Lincoln Prize, 2000; Over 100 hon. doctorates. *Address:* c/o Dept of History, Duke University, Durham, NC 27707, USA.

FRANZEN, Jonathan, BA; American author; b. 1959, Western Springs, IL; m. (divorced). *Education:* Swarthmore Coll., Free Univ. of Berlin, Germany. *Career:* fmrly worked in seismology lab., Harvard Univ. Dept of Earth and Planetary Sciences; currently full-time writer; columnist, The New Yorker, Harper's. *Publications:* The Twenty-Seventh City (Whiting Award) 1988, Strong Motion 1991, The Corrections (Nat. Book Award for Fiction, New York Times Ed.'s Choice, James Tait Black Memorial Prize for Fiction 2003) 2001, How to be Alone (essays) 2002; contrib. to New Yorker, Harper's. *Honours:* American Acad. Berlin Prize 2000, Granta Best Young American Novelist. *Literary Agent:* Steven Barclay Agency, 12 Western Avenue, Petaluma, CA 94952, USA. *Telephone:* (707) 773-0654. *Fax:* (707) 778-1868. *Website:* www.barclayagency.com. *Address:* c/o Farrar, Straus and Giroux, 19 Union Square W, New York, NY 10003 (Office); 875 Sixth Avenue, New York, NY 10001, USA. *Website:* www.jonathanfranzen.com.

FRASER, Lady Antonia, CBE, MA, FRSL; British author; b. 27 Aug. 1932, London; m. 1st Hugh Fraser 1956 (divorced 1977, died 1984); three s. three d.; m. 2nd Harold Pinter 1980. *Education:* Dragon School, Oxford, St Mary's Convent, Ascot and Lady Margaret Hall, Oxford. *Career:* mem. Cttee English PEN 1979–88 (Pres. 1988–89, Vice-Pres. 1990–), Crimewriters Asscn 1980–86, Writers in Prison Cttee, Chair. 1985–88, 1990. *TV plays:* Charades 1977, Mister Clay 1985. *Publications:* King Arthur 1954, Robin Hood 1955, Dolls 1963, History of Toys 1966, Mary, Queen of Scots 1969 (James Tait Black Memorial Prize), Cromwell: Our Chief of Men 1973, King James VI of Scotland and I of England 1974, Scottish Love Poems, A Personal Anthology 1974, Kings and Queens of England (ed.) 1975, Love Letters (anthology) 1976, Quiet as a Nun 1977, The Wild Island 1978, King Charles II 1979, Heroes and Heroines (ed.) 1980, A Splash of Red 1981, Cool Repentance 1982, Oxford In Verse (ed.) 1982, The Weaker Vessel 1984 (Wolfson History Prize), Oxford Blood 1985, Jemima Shore's First Case 1986, Your Royal Hostage 1987, Boadicea's Chariot: The Warrior Queens 1988, The Cavalier Case 1990, Jemima Shore at the Sunny Grave 1991, The Six Wives of Henry VIII 1992, Charles II: His Life and Times 1993, Political Death: A Jemima Shore Mystery 1994, The Gunpowder Plot (St Louis Literary Award 1996, CWA Non Fiction Gold Dagger 1996) 1996, The Lives of the Kings and Queens of England 1998, Marie Antoinette: the Journey 2001; ed. The Pleasure of Reading 1992; television adaptations of Quiet as a Nun 1978, Jemima Shore Investigates 1983. *Honours:* Hon. DLitt (Hull) 1986, (Sussex) 1990, (Nottingham) 1993, (St Andrew's) 1994; Prix Caumont-La Force 1985, Norten Medlicott Medal, Historical Asscn 2000. *Literary Agent:* Curtis Brown Group Ltd., Haymarket House, 28/29 Haymarket, London, SW1Y 4SP, England. *Telephone:* (20) 7396-6600. *Fax:* (20) 7396-0110.

FRASER, Sir David (William); General of the British Army (retd) and Author; b. 30 Dec. 1920, Camberley, England; m. 1st Anne Balfour, 26 Sept. 1947, divorced, one d.; m. 2nd Julia de la Hey, 11 Oct. 1957, two s. two d. *Education:* Christ Church, Oxford; British Army Staff College; Imperial

Defence College. *Career:* Career Officer, British Army, 1941–80, retiring with rank of Gen.; Vice-Lord-Lieutenant, Hampshire, 1988–96. *Publications:* Alanbrooke, 1982; And We Shall Shock Them, 1983; The Christian Watt Papers, 1983; August 1988, 1983; A Kiss for the Enemy, 1985; The Killing Times, 1986; The Dragon's Teeth, 1987; The Seizure, 1988; A Candle for Judas, 1989; In Good Company, 1990; Adam Hardrow, 1990; Codename Mercury, 1991; Adam in the Breach, 1993; The Pain of Winning, 1993; Knight's Cross: A Life of Field Marshal Erwin Rommel, 1993; Will: A Portrait of William Douglas Home, 1995; Frederick the Great, 2000. *Honours:* OBE, 1962; Knight Commander, 1973, Grand Cross, 1980, Order of the Bath. *Address:* Vallenders, Alton, Hants GU34 4PP, England.

FRASER, George MacDonald; Author and Journalist; b. 2 April 1925, Carlisle, England; m. Kathleen Margarette Hetherington 1949; two s. one d. *Education:* Glasgow Acad. *Career:* Deputy Ed., Glasgow Herald newspaper, 1964–69. *Publications:* Flashman, 1969; Royal Flash, 1970, screenplay, 1975; The General Danced at Dawn, 1970; Flash for Freedom, 1971; Steel Bonnets, 1971; Flashman at the Charge, 1973; The Three Musketeers (screenplay), 1973; The Four Musketeers (screenplay), 1974; McAuslan in the Rough, 1974; Flashman in the Great Game, 1975; The Prince and the Pauper (screenplay), 1976; Flashman's Lady, 1977; Mr American, 1980; Flashman and the Redskins, 1982; Octopussy (screenplay), 1983; The Pyrates, 1983; Flashman and the Dragon, 1985; Casanova (TV screenplay), 1987; The Hollywood History of the World, 1988; The Sheikh and the Dustbin, 1988; The Return of the Musketeers (screenplay), 1989; Flashman and the Mountain of Light, 1990; Quartered Safe Out Here, 1992; The Candlemass Road, 1993; Flashman and the Angel of the Lord, 1994; Black Ajax, 1997; Flashman and the Tiger, 1999; The Light's on at Signpost, 2002. *Honours:* OBE, 1999. *Address:* Baldrine, Isle of Man, Britain.

FRASER, Helen Jean Sutherland; Publisher; b. 8 June 1949, London, England; m. Grant James McIntyre 1982; two d. two step-d. *Education:* MA, St Anne's College, Oxford. *Career:* Ed., Methuen Academic Ltd, 1972–74, Open Books Ltd, 1974–76; Ed., Fontana non-fiction, then Editorial Dir, William Collins, 1977–87; Publr, William Heinemann, 1987–91, Reed Trade Books, 1991–96, Man. Dir, 1996–97; Man. Dir, Penguin General Division, 1997–2001, Man. Dir, Penguin UK, 2001–. *Address:* c/o Penguin Books Ltd, 80 Strand, London WC2R 0RL, England. *E-mail:* helen.fraser@penguin.co.uk.

FRASER, Jane (see Pilcher, Rosamunde).

FRASER, Kathleen; Prof. and Poet; b. 22 March 1937, Tulsa, Oklahoma, USA; m. Jack Marshall, 1961, divorced 1970, one s. *Education:* BA, Occidental College, Los Angles, 1959; Columbia University, 1960–61; New School for Social Research, New York City, 1960–61; Doctoral Equivalency in Creative Writing, San Francisco State University, 1976–77. *Career:* Visiting Prof., University of Iowa, 1969–71; Writer-in-Residence, Reed College, Portland, Oregon, 1971–72; Dir, Poetry Center, 1972–75, Assoc. Prof., 1975–78, Prof., 1978–92, San Francisco State University. *Publications:* Poetry: Change of Address and Other Poems, 1966; In Defiance of the Rains, 1969; Little Notes to You from Lucas Street, 1972; What I Want, 1974; Magritte Series, 1978; New Shoes, 1978; Each Next, 1980; Something (Even Human Voices) in the Foreground, A Lake, 1984; Notes Preceding Trust, 1987; Boundary, 1988; Giotto, Arena, 1991; When New Time Folds Up, 1993; Wing, 1995; Il Cuore: The Heart, New and Selected Poems 1970–95, 1997; Translating the Unspeakable (essays), 1999. Editor: Feminist Poetics: A Consideration of Female Construction of Language, 1984. *Honours:* YMM-YWHA Discovery Award, 1964; National Endowment for the Arts Grant, 1969, and Fellowship, 1978; Guggenheim Fellowship in Poetry, 1981. *Address:* 1936 Leavenworth St, San Francisco, CA 94133, USA.

FRASER, Sylvia Lois, BA; Canadian writer; b. 8 March 1935, Hamilton, ON; m. (divorced). *Education:* University of Western Ontario. *Career:* writer, Toronto Star Weekly, 1957–68; Guest Lecturer, Banff Centre, 1973–79, 1985, 1987–88; Writer-in-Residence, University of Western Ontario, 1980; Instructor, Maritime Writers' Workshop, 1986; Instructor, Huron College Young Writers' Workshop, 2003; mem. Writers' Development Trust. *Publications:* Pandora, 1972; The Candy Factory, 1975; A Casual Affair, 1978; The Emperor's Virgin, 1980; Berlin Solstice, 1984; My Father's House (memoir), 1987; The Book of Strange, 1992; The Ancestral Suitcase, 1996; A Woman's Place: Seventy Years in the Lives of Canadian Women (ed.), 1997; Tom and Francine (children's book), 1998; The Rope in the Water: A Pilgrimage to India, 2001; The Green Labyrinth: Exploring the Mysteries of the Amazon, 2003. *Honours:* Women Press Club Awards, 1967, 1968; Pres.'s Medal for Canadian Journalism, 1969; Canadian Authors' Asscn Award for Non-Fiction, 1987; National Magazine Awards, 1994, 1996, 2002. *Address:* 701 King Street W, No. 302, Toronto, ON M5V 2W7, Canada.

FRAYN, Michael, BA, FRSL; British playwright and author; b. 8 Sept. 1933, London; m. 1st Gillian Palmer 1960 (divorced 1989); three d.; m. 2nd Claire Tomalin 1993. *Education:* Kingston Grammar School and Emmanuel Coll., Cambridge. *Career:* reporter, The Guardian 1957–59, columnist 1959–62; columnist, The Observer 1962–68. *Stage plays:* The Two of Us 1970, The Sandboy 1971, Alphabetical Order 1975 (Evening Standard Best Comedy of the Year 1975), Donkeys' Years 1976 (Laurence Olivier Award for Best Comedy 1976, Society of West End Theatre Comedy of the Year 1976), Clouds 1976, Balmoral 1978, Liberty Hall (new version of Balmoral) 1980, Make and Break 1980 (Evening Standard Best Comedy of the Year 1980), Noises Off (Evening Standard Best Comedy of the Year 1982, Laurence Olivier Award for Best Comedy 1982, Society of West End Theatre Comedy of the Year 1982) 1982, Benefactors (Laurence Olivier/ BBC Award for Best New Play 1984) 1984, Look Look 1990, Here 1993, Now You Know 1995, Copenhagen (Evening Standard Award for Best Play of the Year 1998, West End Critics' Circle Best New Play Award 1998, Prix Molière Best New Play 1999, Tony Award for Best Play 2000) 1998, Alarms and Excursions 1998, Democracy (Evening Standard Theatre Award for Best Play) 2004. *TV includes:* plays: Jamie, on a Flying Visit (BBC) 1968, Birthday (BBC) 1969; documentary series: Second City Reports (with John Bird, Granada) 1964, Beyond a Joke (with John Bird and Eleanor Bron) 1972, Making Faces 1975; documentaries: One Pair of Eyes 1968, Laurence Sterne Lived Here 1973, Imagine a City Called Berlin 1975, Vienna: The Mask of Gold 1977, Three Streets in the Country 1979, The Long Straight (Great Railway Journeys of the World) 1980, Jerusalem 1984, Magic Lantern, Prague 1993, Budapest: Written in Water 1996 (all BBC documentaries); films: First and Last 1989, A Landing on the Sun 1994. *Cinema:* Clockwise 1986, Remember Me? 1997. *Plays translated include:* The Cherry Orchard, Three Sisters, The Seagull, Uncle Vanya, Wild Honey, The Sneeze (Chekhov), The Fruits of Enlightenment (Tolstoy), Exchange (Trifonov), Number One (Anouilh). *Publications:* novels: The Tin Men 1965 (Somerset Maugham Award 1966), The Russian Interpreter 1966 (Hawthornden Prize 1967), Towards the End of the Morning 1967, A Very Private Life 1968, Sweet Dreams 1973, The Trick of It 1989, A Landing on the Sun 1991 (Sunday Express Book of the Year), Now You Know 1992, Headlong 1999, Spies (Whitbread Award for Best Novel) 2002; non-fiction: Constructions (philosophy) 1974, Speak after the Beep 1995, Celia's Secret (with David Burke) 2000; several vols of collections of columns, plays and translations. *Honours:* Hon. Fellow Emmanuel Coll., Cambridge; Hon. DLitt (Cambridge) 2001; Heywood Hill Literary Prize 2002. *Address:* c/o Greene & Heaton Ltd, 37A Goldhawk Road, London, W12 8QQ, England.

FRAZER, Andrew (see Marlowe, Stephen).

FRAZEUR, Joyce Jaeckle; Poet and Writer; b. 17 Jan. 1931, Lewisburg, Pennsylvania, USA; m. Theodore C. Frazeur Jr, 24 July 1954, one s. two d. *Education:* BA, William Smith College, 1952. *Publications:* Poetry: A Slip of Greenness, 1989; The Bovine Affliction, 1991; Flower Soup, 1993; Chirruping, 1994; Cycles, 1996. Novel: By Lunar Light, 1995. Contributions: newspapers, reviews, magazines, and journals.

FRAZIER, Arthur (see Bulmer, Henry Kenneth).

FRAZIER, Charles; Author; b. 1950, Asheville, NC, USA; m. Katherine Frazier, one d. *Education:* PhD, University of North Carolina at Chapel Hill. *Career:* Former faculty mem., University of Colorado at Boulder and North Carolina State University. *Publications:* Adventuring in the Andes: The Sierra Club Travel Guide to Ecuador, Peru, Bolivia, the Amazon Basin, and the Galapagos Islands (with Donald Secreast), 1985; Cold Mountain: Odyssey in North Carolina (novel), 1997. *Honours:* National Book Award, 1997. *Address:* c/o The Atlantic Monthly Press, 19 Union Sq., New York, NY 10003, USA.

FREDERICKS, Frohm (see Kerner, Fred).

FREEBORN, Richard (Harry); Prof. of Russian Literature Emeritus, Writer and Trans; b. 19 Oct. 1926, Cardiff, Wales; m. Anne Davis 14 Feb. 1954; one s. three d. *Education:* BA, 1950, MA, 1954, DPhil, 1957, Univ. of Oxford. *Career:* Univ. Lecturer in Russian and Hulme Lecturer in Russian, Brasenose College, Oxford, 1954–64; Visiting Prof., Univ. of California at Los Angeles, 1964–65; Sir William Mather Chair of Russian Studies, Univ. of Manchester, 1965–67; Prof. of Russian Literature, 1967–88, Prof. Emeritus, 1988–, Univ. of London; mem. Kingston AE, Governor. *Publications:* Fiction: Two Ways of Life, 1962; The Emigration of Sergey Ivanovich, 1963; Russian Roulette, 1979; The Russian Crucifix, 1987. Non-Fiction: Turgenev: A Study, 1960; A Short History of Modern Russia, 1966; The Rise of the Russian Novel, 1974; Russian Literary Attitudes from Pushkin to Solzhenitsyn (ed.), 1976; Russian and Slavic Literature to 1917, Vol. I (ed. with Charles Ward), 1976; The Russian Revolutionary Novel: Turgenev to Pasternak, 1982; Ideology in Russian Literature (ed. with Jane Grayson), 1990; Furious Vissarion: Belinski's Struggle for Literature, Love and Ideas, 2003; Dostoevsky, 2003. Translator: Sketches from a Hunter's Album, by Turgenev, 1967; Home of the Gentry, by Turgenev, 1970; Rudin, by Turgenev, 1974; Love and Death: Six Stories by Ivan Turgenev, 1983; First Love and Other Stories, by Turgenev, 1989; Fathers and Sons, by Turgenev, 1991; A Month in the Country, by Turgenev, 1991; An Accidental Family, by Dostoevsky, 1994. Editor: Anton Chekhov: The Steppe and Other Stories, 1991; Ivan Goncharov: Oblomov, 1992; Reference Guide to Russian Literature: Articles on the Classic Russian Novel, Gor'kii, Kuzmin, Pasternak et al, 1998; The Cambridge Companion to Tolstoy (contributor), 2002. Contributions: various publications. *Honours:* Hon. DLitt, Univ. of London, 1984. *Address:* 24 Park Rd, Surbiton, Surrey KT5 8QD, England.

FREEDMAN, David N(oel); Prof. of Biblical Studies, Writer and Ed.; b. 12 May 1922, New York, NY, USA; m. Cornelia Anne Pryor, 16 May 1944, two s. two d. *Education:* City College, CUNY, 1935–38; BA, University of California at Los Angeles, 1938–39; BTh, Old Testament, Princeton Theological Seminary, 1944; PhD, Semitic Languages and Literature, Johns

Hopkins University, 1948. *Career:* Ordained Minister, Presbyterian Church, USA, 1944; State Supply Minister, Acme and Deming, Washington, Presbyterian Churches, 1944–45; Teaching Fellow, 1946–47, Asst Instructor, 1947–48, Johns Hopkins University; Asst Prof. of Old Testament, 1948–51, Prof. of Hebrew and Old Testament, 1951–60, Western Theological Seminary, Pittsburgh; Assoc. Ed., 1952–54, Ed., 1955–59, Journal of Biblical Literature; Prof. of Hebrew and Old Testament, 1960–61, James A. Kelso Prof. of Hebrew and Old Testament, 1961–64, Pittsburgh Theological Seminary; Prof. of Old Testament, 1964–70, Dean of Faculty, 1966–70, Gray Prof. of Old Testament Exegesis, 1970–71, San Francisco Theological Seminary; Prof. of Old Testament, Graduate Theological Union, 1964–71; Vice-Pres., 1970–82, Dir of Publications, 1974–82, American Schools of Oriental Research; Ed., Biblical Archaeologist, 1976–82; Prof. of Biblical Studies, 1971–92, Dir, Program on Studies in Religion, 1971–91, Arthur F. Thurnau Prof. in Old Testament Studies, 1984–92, University of Michigan; Visiting Prof. in Old Testament Studies, 1985–86, Prof. in Hebrew Biblical Studies, 1987, Endowed Chair. in Hebrew Biblical Studies, 1987–, University of California at San Diego; numerous visiting lectureships and professorships; mem. American Acad. of Religion; American Archaeological Institute; American Oriental Society; American Schools of Oriental Research; Explorers' Club; Society of Biblical Literature. *Publications:* God Has Spoken (with J. D. Smart), 1949; Studies in Ancient Yahwistic Poetry (with Frank M. Cross), 1950; Early Hebrew Orthography (with Frank M. Cross), 1952; The People of the Dead Sea Scrolls (with J. M. Allegro), 1958; The Secret Sayings of Jesus (with R. M. Grant), 1960; Ashdod I (with M. Dothan), 1967; The Published Works of W. F. Albright (with R. B. MacDonald and D. L. Mattson), 1975; William Foxwell Albright: Twentieth Century Genius (with L. G. Running), 1975; The Mountain of the Lord (with B. Mazar and G. Cornfeld), 1975; An Explorer's Life of Jesus (with W. Phillips), 1975; Hosea (Anchor Bible Series; with F. I. Andersen), 1980; Pottery, Poetry and Prophecy, 1981; The Paleo-Hebrew Leviticus Scroll (with K. A. Mathews), 1985; Amos (Anchor Bible Series; with F. I. Andersen), 1989; The Unity of the Hebrew Bible, 1991; Studies in Hebrew and Aramaic Orthography (with D. Forbes and F. I. Andersen), 1992; The Relationship Between Herodotus' History and Primary History (with Sara Mandell), 1993. Other: The Biblical Archaeologist Reader (co-ed.), four vols, 1961, 1964, 1970, 1982; Anchor Bible Series (co-ed.), 18 vols, 1964–72, 50 vols (general ed.), 1972–; Computer Bible Series (co-ed.), 18 vols, 1971–80; Anchor Bible Reference Library (general ed.), 16 vols, 1988–96; Anchor Bible Dictionary (ed.-in-chief), six vols, 1992. *Honours:* Guggenheim Fellowship, 1958–59; AATS Fellowship, 1965; Hon. doctorates. *Address:* c/o Dept of History, No. 0104, University of California, San Diego, 9500 Gilman Dr., La Jolla, CA 92093-0104, USA.

FREEDMAN, Lawrence (David); Prof. of War Studies, Writer and Ed.; b. 7 Dec. 1948, Northumberland, England; m. Judith Anne Hill, 1974, one s. one d. *Education:* BA, Economics, University of Manchester, 1970; BPhil, University of York, 1971; DPhil, University of Oxford, 1975. *Career:* Teaching Asst, University of York, 1971–72; Research Fellow, Nuffield College, Oxford, 1974–75; Lecturer in Politics, Balliol College, Oxford, 1975; Research Assoc., 1975–76, Mem. of the Council, 1983–92, 1993–, International Institute for Strategic Studies; Research Fellow, 1976–78, Head of Policy Studies, 1978–82, Royal Institute of International Affairs; Prof. of War Studies, 1982–, Head, School of Social and Public Policy, 2001–, King's College, University of London; Chair., Committee on International Peace and Security, Social Science Research Council, USA, 1993–96. *Publications:* US Intelligence and the Soviet Strategic Threat, 1977; Britain and Nuclear Weapons, 1980; The Evolution of Nuclear Strategy, 1981; Nuclear War and Nuclear Peace (with Edwina Moreton, Gerald Segal, and John Baylis), 1983; The Troubled Alliance: Atlantic Relations in the 1980s (ed.), 1983; The Atlas of Global Strategy, 1985; The Price of Peace: Living with the Nuclear Dilemma, 1986; Britain and the Falklands War, 1988; US Nuclear Strategy: A Reader (ed. with Philip Bobbitt and Gregory Treverton), 1989; Signals of War: The Falklands Conflict of 1982 (with Virginia Gamba-Stonehouse), 1990; Europe Transformed (ed.), 1990; Military Power in Europe: Essays in Memory of Jonathon Alford (ed.), 1990; Britain in the world (ed. with Michael Clarke), 1991; Population Change and European Security (ed. with John Saunders), 1991; War, Strategy and International Politics: Essays in Honour of Sir Michael Howard (ed. with Paul Hayes and Robert O'Neill), 1992; The Gulf Conflict 1990–91; Diplomacy and War in the New World Order (with Efraim Karsh), 1993; War: A Reader (ed.), 1994; Military Intervention in Europe (ed.), 1994; The Revolution in Strategic Affairs, 1998; Strategic Coercion (ed.), 1998; The Politics of British Defence, 1999; Kennedy's Wars, 2000; Cold War, 2001; Superterrorism (ed.), 2002. Contributions: various publications. *Honours:* FRSA, 1991; Fellow, King's College, University of London, 1992; Fellow, British Acad., 1995; CBE, 1996; FRHistS, 2000; KCMG, 2003. *Address:* c/o Dept of War Studies, King's College, University of London, Strand, London WC2R 2LS, England.

FREEMAN, Gillian, (Elisabeth von Stahlenberg); Writer; b. 5 Dec. 1929, London, England; m. Edward Thorpe, 12 Sept. 1955, two d. *Education:* BA, University of Reading, 1951. *Career:* mem. Arts Council; Writers Guild of Great Britain. *Publications:* The Liberty Man, 1955; Fall of Innocence, 1956; Jack Would be a Gentleman, 1959; The Story of Albert Einstein, 1960; The Leather Boys, 1961; The Campaign, 1963; The Leader, 1965; The Undergrowth of Literature, 1969; The Alabaster Egg, 1970; The Marriage Machine, 1975; The Schoolgirl Ethic: The Life and Work of Angela Brazil, 1976; Nazi Lady: The Diaries of Elisabeth von Stahlenberg, 1938–48, 1979; An Easter Egg Hunt, 1981; Lovechild, 1984; Life Before Man, 1986; Ballet Genius (with Edward Thorpe), 1988; Termination Rock, 1989; His Mistress's Voice, 2000. Other: Screenplays and adaptations; Ballet scenarios. Contributions: periodicals. *Address:* c/o Richard Scott Simon, 48 Doughty St, London WC1N 2LP, England.

FREEMAN, Gwendolen; Author; b. 4 April 1908, Ealing, London, England; one adopted s. *Education:* BA, English, Girton College, Cambridge, 1926–29. *Career:* Woman Ed., Birmingham Post; Public Relations Office, Birmingham Ministry of Labour; The Spectator. *Publications:* The Houses Behind, 1947; Children Never Tell, 1949; When You Are Old, 1951; Between Two Worlds, 1979; A Zeppelin in My Childhood, 1989; United Family Record, 1989; World of an Artist, 1990; Alma Mater, 1990; Scriptural Beasts, 1991; Whys of Loving, 1993; Flora at School, 1994; The Dodona Oak, 1995; Anna with Tristram, 1995; Midland Thirties, 1998; People of the Century, 2000; Harriet Without Conclusions, 2001. Contributions: newspapers. *Address:* c/o Brewin Books Ltd, Doric House, 56 Alcester Rd, Studley, Warwickshire B80 7LG, England.

FREEMAN, James M(ontague); Prof. of Anthropology and Writer; b. 1 Dec. 1936, Chicago, IL, USA. *Education:* BA, Northwestern University, 1958; MA, 1964, PhD, 1968, Harvard University. *Career:* Asst Prof. to Prof. of Anthropology, San Jose State University, 1966–; mem. Aid to Refugee Children Without Parents, 1988–95, and its successor, Aid to Children Without Parents, Inc, chair. of the board, 1995–; Southwestern Anthropological Asscn, pres., 1991–92. *Publications:* Scarcity and Opportunity in an Indian Village, 1977; Untouchable: An Indian Life History, 1979; Hearts of Sorrow: Vietnamese-American Lives, 1989; Changing Identities: Vietnamese Americans 1975–1995, 1996. Contributions: scholarly books and journals. *Honours:* Choice Outstanding Academic Book, 1979; National Endowment for the Humanities Fellowship, 1983–84; Pres.'s Scholar, San Jose State University, 1984; Before Columbus Foundation American Book Award, 1990; Asscn for Asian-American Studies Outstanding Book Award, 1990; Austin D. Warburton Award for Outstanding Scholarship, 1991. *Address:* c/o Dept of Anthropology, San Jose State University, San Jose, CA 95192, USA.

FREEMAN, Judith; Writer and Critic; b. 1 Oct. 1946, Ogden, Utah, USA; m. Anthony Hernandez, 1986, one s. *Career:* Contributing Critic, Los Angeles Times Book Review; mem. PEN West. *Publications:* Family Attractions, 1988; The Chinchilla Farm, 1989; Set for Life, 1991; A Desert of Pure Feeling, 1996. *Honours:* Western Heritage Award for Best Western Novel, 1991. *Literary Agent:* Lantz Office Ltd, 200 W 57th St, Suite 503, New York, NY 10019, USA.

FREEMAN-GRENVILLE, Greville Stewart Parker; Historian and Writer; b. 29 June 1918, Hook Norton, Oxfordshire, England; m. The Rt Hon. Lady Kinloss, 29 Aug. 1950, three c. *Education:* BLitt, 1940, MA, 1943, DPhil, 1957, Worcester College, Oxford. *Career:* Captain, Royal Berkshire Regiment, Personnel Selection Staff, 1939–46; HM Overseas Civil Service, Tanganyika, 1951–60; Educational Adviser, Aden Protectorate, 1961–64; Senior Research Fellow, University of Ghana, 1964–66, University of York, 1966–69; Hon. Fellow, University of York, 1969–; Prof. of History, State University of NY, 1969–74; mem. Society of Antiquaries, fellow; Royal Asiatic Society, fellow; Palestine Exploration Fund, exec. committee, 1992–2000; Catholic Union of Great Britain; Society for Arabian Studies; Royal Asiatic Society, vice-pres., 1997–2000. *Publications:* The Medieval History of the Coast of Tanganyika, 1962; The East African Coast: Select Documents (ed. and trans.), 1962; The Muslim and Christian Calendars, 1963; French at Kilwa Island, 1965; Chronology of African History, 1973; Chronology of World History, 1975; A Modern Atlas of African History, 1976; The Queen's Lineage, 1977; Atlas of British History, 1979; The Mombasa Rising Against the Portuguese 1631, 1980; The Beauty of Cairo, 1981; Buzurg ibn Shahriyar: The Book of Wonders of India (c 953) (ed. and trans.), 1982; Emily Said-Ruete: Memoirs of an Arabian Princess (1888) (ed.), 1982; The Beauty of Jerusalem and the Holy Places of the Gospels, 1982; The Stations of the Cross, 1982; The Beauty of Rome, 1988; The Swahili Coast: Islam, Christianity and Commerce in Eastern Africa, 1988; A New Atlas for African History, 1991; Historical Atlas of the Middle East, 1993; The Basilica of the Nativity at Bethlehem, 1993; The Basilica of the Holy Sepulchre in Jerusalem, 1993; The Basilica of the Annunciation at Nazareth and Other Nearby Shrines, 1993; The Holy Land: A Pilgrim's Guide to Israel, Jordan and the Sinai, 1995; Islamic and Christian Calendars, AD 622–2222, 1995; Wordsworth's Kings and Queens of Great Britain, 1997; The Land of Jesus: Then and Now, 1998; Historical Atlas of Islam (with Stuart Munro-Hay), 2002. Contributions: numerous journals, reviews and encyclopaedias including Journal of the Royal Asiatic Society; Numismatic Chronicle; Encyclopaedia of Islam; Encyclopaedia Britannica. *Address:* North View House, Sheriff Hutton, York Y060 6ST, England. *Telephone:* (1347) 878447. *Fax:* (1347) 878447.

FREEMANTLE, Brian (Harry), (Jonathan Evans, Richard Gant, John Maxwell, Jack Winchester); Author; b. 10 June 1936, Southampton, England; m. Maureen Hazel Tipney, 8 Dec. 1957, three d. *Education:* Secondary school, Southampton. *Career:* Reporter, New Milton Advertiser, 1953–58, Bristol Evening News, 1958, Evening News, London, 1959–61; Reporter,

1961–63, Asst Foreign Ed., 1963–69, Daily Express; Foreign Ed., Daily Sketch, London, 1969–70, Daily Mail, London, 1971–75. *Publications:* Fiction: The Touchables, 1968; Goodbye to an Old Friend, 1973; Face Me When You Walk Away, 1974; The Man Who Wanted Tomorrow, 1975; The November Man, 1976; Deaken's War, 1982; Rules of Engagement, 1984; Vietnam Legacy, 1984; The Lost American, 1984; The Laundryman, 1986; The Kremlin Kiss, 1986; The Bearpit, 1988; O'Farrell's Law, 1990; The Factory, 1990; The Choice of Eddie Franks, 1990; Betrayals, 1991; Little Grey Mice, 1992; The Button Man, 1993; No Time for Heroes, 1995. Other: 11 books in the Charlie Muffin mystery series. Non-Fiction: KGB, 1982; CIA, 1983; The Fix: Inside the World Drug Trade, 1985; The Steal: Counterfeiting and Industrial Espionage, 1987; The Octopus: Europe in the Grip of Organised Crime, 1996. Contributions: periodicals. *Address:* c/o Jonathan Clowes, 10 Iron Bridge House, Bridge Approach, London NW1 8BD, England.

FREIBERG, Stanley Kenneth, BA, MA, PhD; fmr teacher, poet and writer; b. 26 Aug. 1923, Wisconsin, USA; m. Marjorie Ellen Speckhard 1947; one s. one d. *Education:* University of Wisconsin. *Career:* Chair., English Dept, Cottey Cottage, Nevada, MO 1954–58; Chair., Board of Foreign Language Studies, Univ. of Baghdad 1964–65. *Publications:* The Baskets of Baghdad: Poems of the Middle East 1968, Plumes of the Serpent: Poems of Mexico 1973, The Caplin-Crowded Seas: Poems of Newfoundland 1975, Nightmare Tales: Ten Stories of Nova Scotia 1980, Mad Blake at Felpham (play) 1987, The Hidden City: A Poem of Peru 1988, Blake and Beethoven in the Tempest (play) 1997, The Dignity of Dust: Poems from the Four Directions 1997, Sverre, King of Norway: Drama of 12th Century Norway 1999, Jahanara, Daughter of the Taj Mahal: Drama of the Mogul Empire 1631–1681 1999, Black Madonna of the Deluge: Drama of 17th Century Poland 2000, Anaho of the Southstars: Novella of Pyramid Lake, Nevada 2003, On Gravel Roads: Tales of Early Ontario 2004; contrib. to Redlands Review, Christian Century, Dalhousie Review, Queen's Quarterly, Ariel, Parnassus of World Poets 1994. *Honours:* Canada Council Award 1978. *Address:* 202–268 Superior Street, Victoria, BC V8V 1T3, Canada.

FREIREICH, Valerie J.; Lawyer and Writer; b. 14 July 1952, Chicago, IL, USA; m. Jordan L. Kaplan, 15 June 1980, one s. *Education:* BA, Anthropology, 1974, JD, 1977, University of Illinois at Champaign-Urbana. *Career:* Lawyer, various law firms, 1977–84; Sole Practitioner in Small Business and Real Estate Law, 1984–; mem. American Bar Asscn; SFWA; American Asscn for the Advancement of Science; Illinois State Bar Asscn. *Publications:* Fiction: Becoming Human, 1995; Testament, 1995; Beacon, 1996; Sensations of the Mind (short story). Contributions: Short stories and novellas to periodicals including: Aboriginal Science Fiction; Asimov's Science Fiction; Tomorrow Speculative Fiction. *Honours:* Writers of the Future Quarterly prize, First Prize, for Short Story, 1990. *Literary Agent:* Merrilee Heifetz, Writer's House Inc, 21 W 26th St, New York, NY 10010, USA. *Address:* 2 Paddock, Lemont, IL 60439, USA.

FREISINGER, Randall Roy; academic and poet; b. 6 Feb. 1942, Kansas City, MO, USA; m.; two s. *Education:* BJ, Journalism, 1962, MA, English Literature, 1964, PhD, English Literature, 1975, University of Missouri. *Career:* Instructor, Jefferson College, 1964–68; Resident Lecturer, University of Maryland Overseas Program, 1968–69, 1975–76; Asst Prof., Columbia College, 1976–77; Asst, Assoc. Prof., 1977–93, Prof. of Rhetoric, Literature and Creative Writing, 1993–, Michigan Technological University; Assoc. Ed., Laurel Review, 1989–; mem. Associated Writing Programs; National Council of Teachers of English. *Publications:* Running Patterns, 1985; Hand Shadows, 1988; Plato's Breath, 1997. Contributions: anthologies, journals, reviews, and quarterlies. *Honours:* Winner, Flume Press National Chapbook Competition, 1985; May Swenson Poetry Award, 1996. *Address:* 200 Prospect Street, Houghton, MI 49931, USA.

FRENCH, Linda (see Mariz, Linda Catherine French).

FRENCH, Marilyn, BA, MA, PhD; American writer and critic; b. 21 Nov. 1929, New York, NY; m. Robert M. French Jr 1950 (divorced 1967); two c. *Education:* Hofstra University, Harvard University. *Career:* Lecturer, Hofstra University, 1964–68; Asst Prof., Holy Cross College, Worcester, Massachusetts, 1972–76; Mellon Fellow, Harvard University, 1976–77; mem. James Joyce Society; MLA; Virginia Woolf Society. *Publications:* Fiction: The Women's Room, 1977; The Bleeding Heart, 1980; Her Mother's Daughter, 1987; Our Father: A Novel, 1994; My Summer With George, 1996. Non-Fiction: The Book as World: James Joyce's Ulysses, 1976; Shakespeare's Division of Experience, 1981; Beyond Power: On Women, Men and Morals, 1986; The War Against Women, 1992; A Season in Hell, 1998. Contributions: Books and periodicals. *Address:* c/o Virago Press, Brettenham House, Lancaster Place, London WC2E 7EN, England.

FRENCH, Nicci (see Sean French, Nicci Gerrard).

FRENCH, Philip (Neville); Writer, Broadcaster and Film Critic; b. 28 Aug. 1933, Liverpool, England; m. Kersti Elisabet Molin, 1957, three s. *Education:* BA, Exeter College, Oxford; Indiana University. *Career:* Reporter, Bristol Evening Post, 1958–59; Producer, North American Service, 1959–61, Talks Producer, 1961–67, Senior Producer, 1968–90, BBC Radio; Theatre Critic, 1967–68, Arts Columnist, 1967–72, New Statesman; Film Critic, The Observer, 1978–. *Publications:* The Age of Austerity, 1945–51 (ed. with Michael Sissons), 1963; The Novelist as Innovator (ed.), 1966; The Movie Moguls, 1969; Westerns: Aspects of a Movie Genre, 1974; Three Honest Men: Portraits of Edmund Wilson, F. R. Leavis, Lionel Trilling, 1980; The Third Dimension: Voices from Radio Three (ed.), 1983; The Press: Observed and Projected (ed. with Deac Rossell), 1991; Malle on Malle (ed.), 1992; The Faber Book of Movie Verse (ed. with Ken Wlaschin), 1993; Wild Strawberries (with Kersti French), 1995; Cult Movies (with Karl French), 1999. Contributions: many anthologies and periodicals. *Address:* 62 Dartmouth Park Rd, London NW5 1SN, England.

FRENCH, Sean, (Nicci French), BA; writer; b. 28 May 1959, Bristol, England; m. Nicci Gerrard 1990; two s. two d. *Education:* Christ Church, Oxford. *Career:* Deputy Literary Ed., Sunday Times, London 1984–86; Deputy Ed., New Society 1986–87; columnist, New Statesman and Society 1987–2000. *Publications:* Fatherhood (ed.) 1992, The French Brothers' Wild and Crazy Film Quiz Book (with Karl and Patrick French) 1992, The Imaginary Monkey (novel) 1993, Patrick Hamilton: A Life (biog.) 1993, Bardot (biog.) 1994, Dreamer of Dreams (novel) 1995, The Terminator (criticism) 1996, Jane Fonda (biog.) 1997, The Faber Book of Writers on Writers (ed.) 1999, Start from Here (novel) 2004; with Nicci Gerrard under joint pseudonym of Nicci French: The Memory Game 1997, The Safe House 1998, Killing Me Softly 1999, Beneath the Skin 2000, The Red Room 2001, Land of the Living 2003, Secret Smile 2004. *Literary Agent:* PFD, Drury House, 34–43 Russell Street, London, WC2B 5HA, England. *Address:* The Old Rectory, Elmsett, Ipswich IP7 6NA, England. *E-mail:* seanicci@dircon.co.uk.

FRENCH, Warren Graham; academic and writer; b. 26 Jan. 1922, Philadelphia, Pennsylvania, USA. *Education:* BA, University of Pennsylvania, 1943; MA, 1948, PhD, American Literature 1954, University of Texas. *Career:* mem. International John Steinbeck Society; American Literature; MLA of America; American Studies Asscn; Western American Literature Asscn. *Publications:* John Steinbeck, 1961; Frank Norris, 1962; J. D. Salinger, 1963; The Social Novel at the End of an Era, 1966; Jack Kerouac, 1986; J. D. Salinger, Revisited, 1988; The San Francisco Poetry Renaissance, 1955–1960, 1991. Editor: The Thirties, 1967; The Forties, 1969; The Fifties, 1971; The South in Film, 1981; The Twenties, 1975. Contributions: numerous American academic journals. *Honours:* DHL, Ohio University, 1985. *Address:* 23 Beechwood Road, Uplands, Swansea, West Glamorgan SA2 0HL, Wales.

FREUD, Esther Lea; Novelist; b. 2 May 1963, London, England; Pnr David Morrissey; one s. one d. *Education:* Trained as an actress, Drama Centre, London, 1981–83. *Career:* Co-f., film production co, Tubedale Films. *Publications:* Hideous Kinky, 1991; Peerless Flats, 1993; Gaglow, 1997; The Wild, 2000; The Sea House, 2003. *Literary Agent:* AP Watt Ltd, 20 John St, London WC1N 2DR, England.

FREUDENBERGER, Nell; American writer; b. 1975, New York, NY. *Career:* English teacher in Bangkok and New Delhi. *Publications:* Lucky Girls 2003; contrib. to The New Yorker, Granta. *Honours:* PEN/Malamud Award 2004. *Address:* Ecco, Harper Collins Publishing, 10 E 53rd Street, New York, NY 10022, USA. *Telephone:* (212) 207-7000. *Website:* www.harpercollins.com.

FREWER, Glyn Mervyn Louis, (Mervyn Lewis); Author and Scriptwriter; b. 4 Sept. 1931, Oxford, England; m. Lorna Townsend, 11 Aug. 1956, two s. one d. *Education:* MA, English Language and Literature, St Catherine's College, Oxford, 1955. *Publications:* The Hitch-Hikers (BBC Radio Play), 1957; Adventure in Forgotten Valley, 1962; Adventure in the Barren Lands, 1964; The Last of the Wispies, 1965; Death of Gold (as Mervyn Lewis), 1970; The Token of Elkin, 1970; Crossroad, 1970; The Square Peg, 1972; The Raid, 1976; The Trackers, 1976; Tyto: The Odyssey of an Owl, 1978; Bryn of Brockle Hanger, 1980; Fox, 1984; The Call of the Raven, 1987. Other scripts for children's television series, industrial films, etc. Contributions: Birds; The Countryman. *Honours:* Junior Literary Guild of America Choice, 1964; Freeman of the City of Oxford, 1967. *Address:* Cottage Farm, Taston, Oxford OX7 3JN, England.

FRIEDA, Leonie; Swedish historian and biographer; b. 1956; one d., one s. *Career:* model, translator. *Publications:* Catherine de Medici: A Biography 2004. *Address:* c/o Weidenfeld & Nicholson, The Orion Publishing Group Ltd, Orion House, 5 Upper St Martin's Lane, London, WC2H 9EA, England. *Telephone:* (20) 7240-3444. *Fax:* (20) 7240-4822. *Website:* www.leoniefrieda.com.

FRIEDAN, Betty (Naomi); Feminist Activist and Writer; b. 4 Feb. 1921, Peoria, IL, USA; m. Carl Friedan, June 1947, divorced May 1969, two s. one d. *Education:* AB, Smith College, 1942. *Career:* Research Fellow, University of California at Berkeley, 1943; Founder-First Pres., National Organization for Women, 1966–70; Contributing Ed., McCall's magazine, 1971–74; Senior Research Assoc., Columbia University, 1979–81; Research Fellow, Harvard University, 1982–83; Chubb Fellow, Yale University, 1985; Guest Scholar, Woodrow Wilson Center for International Scholars, 1995–96; many other lectureships; mem. American Society of Journalists and Authors; American Sociology Asscn; Asscn of Humanistic Psychology; Authors' Guild; National Organizatioin for Women; National Press Club; PEN. *Publications:* The Feminine Mystique, 1963; It Changed My Life: Writings on the Women's Movement, 1976; The Second Stage, 1981; The Fountain of Age, 1993; Life So Far: A Memoir, 2000. Contributions: periodicals. *Honours:* Humanist of the Year Award, 1974; Mort Weisinger

Award for Outstanding Magazine Journalism, 1979; Author of the Year, 1982, American Society of Journalists and Authors Eleanor Roosevelt Leadership Award, 1989; various hon. doctorates.

FRIEDMAN, Alan Howard; Writer; b. 4 Jan. 1928, New York, USA; m. 1st Leonore Ann Helman, 1 Aug. 1950, divorced, one s.; m. 2nd Kate Miller Gilbert, 30 Oct. 1977. *Education:* BA, Harvard College, 1949; MA, Columbia University, 1950; PhD, University of California at Berkeley, 1964. *Publications:* The Turn of the Novel, 1966; Hermaphrodeity (novel), 1972. Contributions: Hudson Review; Mademoiselle; Partisan Review; New American Review; Paris Review; New York Times Book Review; American Literary Anthology; Twentieth Century Mind; Fiction International; Kansas Quarterly; Denver Quarterly; Raritan. *Honours:* D. H. Lawrence Fellowship, 1974; National Endowment for the Arts Award, 1975; Pen Syndicated Fiction Award, 1987; Grand Prize, National Library of Poetry, 1998, Best Actor Award Asscn of Community Theatres 2001. *Address:* 3530 Monte Real, Escondido, CA 92029, USA. *E-mail:* alanfman@post.harvard.edu.

FRIEDMAN, Bruce Jay; Writer, Dramatist and Screenwriter; b. 26 April 1930, New York, NY, USA; m. 1st Ginger Howard, 13 June 1954, divorced 1978, three s.; m. 2nd Patricia O'Donohue, 3 July 1983, one d. *Education:* BJ, University of Missouri, 1951. *Career:* Editorial Dir, Magazine Management Co, New York City, 1953–64; mem. PEN. *Publications:* Stern, 1962; Far From the City of Class, and Other Stories, 1963; A Mother's Kisses, 1964; Black Humour (ed.), 1965; Black Angels, 1966; Pardon Me, Sir, But Is My Eye Hurting Your Elbow? (with others), 1968; The Dick, 1970; About Harry Towns, 1974; The Lonely Guys Book of Life, 1978; Let's Hear It for a Beautiful Guy, and Other Works of Short Fiction, 1984; Tokyo Woes, 1985; Violencia, 1988; The Current Climate, 1990; Collected Short Fiction of Bruce Jay Friedman, 1995; The Slightly Older Guy, 1995. Other: Plays and screenplays including Have You Spoken to Any Jews Lately, 1995; A Father's Kisses, 1996. *Literary Agent:* Candida Denadio, 121 W 27th St, New York, NY 10001, USA.

FRIEDMAN, Dennis; Psychiatrist and Writer; b. 23 Feb. 1924, London, England; m. Rosemary Tibber, 2 Feb. 1949, four d. *Education:* Licentiate, Royal College of Physicians, London, 1948. *Career:* mem. Royal College of Psychiatrists, Fellow; Royal College of Psychiatrists; Royal Society of Medicine; Royal College of Surgeons, 1948. *Publications:* Inheritance: A Psychological History of the Royal Family, 1993; Darling Georgie: The Enigma of King George V, 1998; Ladies of the Bedchamber: The Role of the Royal Mistress, 2003. Contributions: books and other publications. *Address:* Apt 5, 3 Cambridge Gate, London NW1 4JX, England.

FRIEDMAN, Jane; American publishing executive; *President and CEO, HarperCollins Publishers Inc. Career:* joined Random House 1968; fmr Pres. Random House Audio; fmr Exec. Vice-Pres. Knopf Publishing Group, Random House Inc.; fmr Publr Vintage Books; fmr mem. Random House Exec. Cttee; Pres., CEO HarperCollins 1997–. *Address:* HarperCollins, 10 East 53rd Street, New York, NY 10022-5299, USA (Office). *Telephone:* (212) 207-7000 (Office). *Fax:* (212) 207-7759 (Office). *Website:* www.harpercollins.com (Office).

FRIEDMAN, Lawrence J.; Prof. of History and Writer; b. 8 Oct. 1940, Cleveland, Ohio, USA. *Education:* BA, University of California at Riverside, 1962; MA, 1965, PhD, 1967, University of California at Los Angeles; Postdoctoral Fellow, Menninger Foundation Interdisciplinary Studies Program, 1981. *Career:* Asst Prof., Arizona State University, 1967–71; Assoc. Prof., 1971–77, Prof. of History and American Studies, 1977–91, Distinguished University Prof., 1991–93, Bowling Green State University; Visiting Scholar, Harvard University, 1991; Prof. of History, Indiana University, 1993–; Fulbright Distinguished Chair, Germany, 2002–03; mem. American Asscn of University Profs; American Historical Asscn; Cheiron; Organization of American Historians; Society of American Historians. *Publications:* The White Savage: Racial Fantasies in the Postbellum South, 1970; Inventors of the Promised Land, 1975; Gregarious Saints: Self and Community in American Abolitionism, 1830–1870, 1982; Menninger: The Family and the Clinic, 1990; Identity's Architect: A Biography of Erik Erikson, 1999; Charity, Philanthropy and Civility in American History, 2003. Contributions: Books and professional journals. *Honours:* National Endowment for the Humanities Fellowships, 1979–80, 1986–87, 1994–95; Ohioana Library Asscn Book Award in History, 1983; Paul and Ruth Olscamp Distinguished Research Award, 1989–92; John Adams Fellow, Institute of United States Studies, University of London. *Address:* c/o Dept of History, Indiana University, Bloomington, IN 47405, USA. *E-mail:* LJFriedm@indiana.edu.

FRIEDMAN, Lawrence Meir; Prof. of Law and Writer; b. 2 April 1930, Chicago, IL, USA; m. Leah Feigenbaum, 27 March 1955, two d. *Education:* AB, 1948, JD, 1951, MLL, 1953, University of Chicago. *Career:* Asst to Assoc. Prof., 1957–61, Childress Memorial Lecturer, 1987, St Louis University; Assoc. Prof. to Prof. of Law, University of Wisconsin, Madison, 1961–68; Prof. of Law, 1968–76, Marion Rice Kirkwood Prof. of Law, 1976–, Stanford University; David Stouffer Memorial Lecturer, Rutgers University, 1969; Fellow, Center for Advanced Study in the Behavioral Sciences, 1973–74, Institute for Advanced Study, Berlin, 1985; Sibley Lecturer, University of Georgia, 1976; Wayne Morse Lecturer, University of Oregon, 1985; Jefferson Lecture, University of California at Berkeley, 1995; Ruston Lecture, Cumberland School of Law, 1997; Tucker Lecture, Washington and Lee University, 2000; mem. American Acad. of Arts and Sciences; Law and Society Asscn, pres., 1979–81; American Society for Legal History, pres., 1990–91; Society of American Historians. *Publications:* Contract Law in America, 1965; Government and Slum Housing: A Century of Frustration, 1968; Law and the Behavioral Sciences (with Stewart Macaulay), 1969; A History of American Law, 1973; The Legal System: A Social Science Perspective, 1975; Law and Society: An Introduction, 1978; The Roots of Justice: Crime and Punishment in Alameda County, CA, 1870–1910, 1981; American Law, 1984; Total Justice: What Americans Want from the Legal System and Why, 1985; Your Time Will Come: The Law of Age Discrimination and Mandatory Retirement, 1985; American Law and the Constitutional Order Historical Perspectives (ed. with Harry N. Schrieber), 1988; The Republic of Choice: Law, Authority and Culture, 1990; Crime and Punishment in American History, 1993; Law and Society: Readings on the Study of Law (co-ed.), 1995; Legal Culture and the Legal Profession (co-ed.), 1996; The Crime Conundrum (co-ed.), 1997; The Horizontal Society, 1999. *Honours:* Scribes Award, 1974; Triennial Award, Order of Coif, 1976; Willard Hurst Prize, 1982; Harry Kalven Prize, 1992; Silver Gavel Award, American Bar Asscn, 1994; Five Hon. Doctorates, 1977–98. *Address:* c/o School of Law, Stanford University, Stanford, CA 94305, USA.

FRIEDMAN, Milton; Prof. of Economics Emeritus, Senior Research Fellow and Writer; b. 31 July 1912, New York, NY, USA; m. Rose Director, 25 June 1938, one s. one d. *Education:* BA, Rutgers University, 1932; AM, University of Chicago, 1933; PhD, Columbia University, 1946. *Career:* Assoc. Economist, Natural Resources Committee, Washington, DC, 1935–37, National Bureau of Economic Research, New York, 1937–40; Principal Economist, Tax Research Division, US Treasury Dept, Washington, DC, 1941–43; Assoc. Dir, Statistical Research Group, Division of War Research, Columbia University, 1943–45; Prof. of Economics, 1948–82, Prof. Emeritus, 1982–, University of Chicago; Mem., Research Staff, National Bureau of Economic Research, 1948–81; Fulbright Lecturer, University of Cambridge, 1953–54; Columnist, 1966–84, Contributing Ed., 1974–84, Newsweek magazine; Senior Research Fellow, Hoover Institution, Stanford University, 1976–; mem. American Economic Asscn, pres., 1967; Mont Pelerin Society, pres., 1970–72; Royal Economic Society. *Publications:* Income from Independent Professional Practice (with Simon Kuznets), 1946; Sampling Inspection (with others), 1948; Essays in Positive Economics, 1953; Studies in the Quantity Theory of Money (ed.), 1956; A Theory of the Consumption Function, 1957; A Program for Monetary Stability, 1960; Capitalism and Freedom, 1962; Price Theory: A Provisional Text, 1962; A Monetary History of the United States 1867–1960 (with Anna J. Schwartz), 1963; Inflation: Causes and Consequences, 1963; The Balance of Payments: Free Versus Flexible Exchange Rates (with Robert V. Roosa), 1967; Dollars and Deficits, 1968; Optimum Quantity of Money and Other Essays, 1969; Monetary Policy Versus Fiscal Policy (with Walter W. Heller), 1969; Monetary Statistics of the United States (with Anna J. Schwartz), 1970; A Theoretical Framework for Monetary Analysis, 1971; Social Security: Universal or Selective? (with Wilbur J. Cohen), 1972; An Economist's Protest, 1972; Money and Economic Development, 1973; There's No Such Thing as a Free Lunch, 1975; Price Theory, 1976; Free to Choose (with Rose Friedman), 1980; Monetary Trends in the United States and the United Kingdom (with Anna J. Schwartz), 1982; Bright Promises, Dismal Performance, 1983; Tyranny of the Status Quo (with Rose Friedman), 1984; Monetarist Economics, 1991; Money Mischief, 1992; Two Lucky People: Memoirs (with Rose Friedman), 1998. *Honours:* John Bates Clark Medal, American Economic Asscn, 1951; Nobel Prize for Economic Science, 1976; Grand Cordon, Sacred Treasure, Japan, 1986; US Presidential Medal of Freedom, 1988; National Medal of Science, 1988; Institution of World Capitalism Prize, Jacksonville University, 1993; Goldwater Award, Goldwater Institute, 1997; Robert Maynard Hutchins History Maker Award for Distinction in Education, Chicago Historical Society, 1997; Templeton Honour Rolls Lifetime Achievement Award, 1997; James U. Blanchard Freedom Award, Jefferson Financial, 2001; Abraham Lincoln Award, American Hungarian Foundation, 2002; various fellowships, awards and hon. doctorates. *Address:* Hoover Institution, Stanford, CA 94305-6010, USA.

FRIEDMAN, (Eve) Rosemary, (Robert Tibber, Rosemary Tibber); writer; b. 5 Feb. 1929, London, England; m. Dennis Friedman 1949; four d. *Education:* Queen's College, Harley Street, London; Law Faculty, University College London. *Career:* mem. Fellow, PEN; RSL; Society of Authors; Writers' Guild of Great Britain; BAFTA; PEN, fellow; Writers' Guild of Great Britain. *Publications:* The Life Situation, 1977; The Long Hot Summer, 1980; Proofs of Affection, 1982; A Loving Mistress, 1983; Rose of Jericho, 1984; A Second Wife, 1986; To Live in Peace, 1987; An Eligible Man, 1989; Golden Boy, 1994; Vintage, 1996; Intensive Care, 2000; Tsunami, 2003. As Robert Tibber: No White Coat, 1957; Love on My List, 1959; We All Fall Down, 1960; Patients of a Saint, 1961; The Fraternity, 1963; The Commonplace Day, 1964; The General Practice, 1967; Practice Makes Perfect, 1969. Others: Home Truths (play), 1997; The Writing Game, 1999; Intensive Care, 2001. Other: several screenplays and television dramas. Contributions: Reviewer; Sunday Times; TLS; Guardian; Sunday Times; Jewish Quarterly. *Address:* Apt 5, 3 Cambridge Gate, London NW1 4JX, England. *E-mail:* rosemaryfriedman@hotmail.com.

FRIEDMAN, Thomas (Loren); Journalist; b. 20 July 1953, Minneapolis, MN, USA; m. Ann Louise Bucksbaum, 23 Nov. 1978, two d. *Education:* BA, Brandeis University, 1975; MPhil, St Anthony's College, Oxford, 1978. *Career:* Correspondent, London and Beirut, United Press International, 1978–81; Business Reporter, 1981–82, Beirut Bureau Chief, 1982–84, Jerusalem Bureau Chief, 1984–89, Chief Diplomatic Correspondent, Washington, DC, Bureau, 1989–92, Chief White House Correspondent, 1992–94, International Economics Correspondent, 1994–95, Foreign Affairs Columnist, 1995–, New York Times. *Publications:* War Torn, 1984; From Beirut to Jerusalem, 1989; The Lexus and the Olive Tree, 1999; Longitudes and Attitudes: Exploring the World After September 11, 2002. Contributions: New York Times Magazine; Golf Digest. *Honours:* Overseas Press Club Awards, 1980, 2000; George Polk Award, 1982; Livingston Award for Young Journalists, 1983; Pulitzer Prizes for Journalism, 1983, 1988; Page One Award, New York Newspaper Guild, 1984; Colonel Robert D. Heinl Jr Memorial Award in Marine Corps History, Marine Corps Historical Foundation, 1985; National Book Award, National Book Foundation, 1989; Pulitzer Prize for Distinguished Commentary, 2002. *Address:* c/o New York Times, Washington, DC, Bureau, 1627 I St NW, Washington, DC 20006, USA.

FRIEDMANN, Patricia Ann; Author; b. 29 Oct. 1946, New Orleans, LA, USA; m. 1st Robert Skinner, 17 March 1979, divorced, 1996, one s. one d.; m. 2nd Edward Muchmore, 11 Nov. 1999. *Education:* AB, Smith College, 1968; MEd, Temple University, 1970; ABD on Doctorate, University of Denver, 1975. *Career:* Managing Ed., Diplomat, 1980–82; Ed., Jewish Times, 1976–78; Adjunct Faculty, Loyola University, 1993–; Writer-in-Residence, Tulane University, 2001; mem. Authors' Guild; Society for the Study of the Short Story; National Writers Union. *Publications:* Too Smart to Be Rich, 1988; The Exact Image of Mother, 1991; The Accidental Jew (part of Native Tongues stage production), 1994; Eleanor Rushing, 1998; Lovely Rita (part of Native Tongues stage production), 2000; Odds (novel), 2000; Secondhand Smoke (novel), 2002. Contributions: Short stories in anthologies and periodicals. *Honours:* Discover Great New Writers, 1999; Original Voices, 1999. *Address:* 8330 Sycamore Pl., New Orleans, LA 70118, USA. *E-mail:* afreelunch@aol.com.

FRIEDRICH, Paul William; academic, writer and poet; b. 22 Oct. 1927, Cambridge, Massachusetts, USA; m. 1st Lore Bucher 1950 (divorced 1966); one s. two d.; m. 2nd Margaret Hardin 1966 (divorced 1974); m. 3rd Deborah Joanna Gordon 1975 (divorced 1996); two d.; m. 4th Domnica Radulescu 1996; one s. *Education:* Williams College, 1945–46; BA, Harvard College, 1951; MA, Harvard University, 1951; PhD, Yale University, 1957. *Career:* Asst Prof., University of Pennsylvania, 1959–62; Visiting Asst Prof., University of Michigan, 1960, 1961; Assoc. Prof., 1962–67, Prof. of Anthropology, Linguistics, Social Thought, 1992–, University of Chicago; Visiting Prof., Indiana University, 1964, Georgetown University, 1998, 1999, 2000, Washington and Lee University, 1999, University of Virginia, 2002; mem. Acad. of American Poets; American Acad. of Arts and Sciences; American Anthropological Asscn; American Asscn for Teachers of Slavic and East European Languages; American Asscn for the Advancement of Science; Linguistic Society of America, life mem.; Linguistic Society of India, life mem.; MLA; Poetry Society of America. *Publications:* Proto-Indo-European Trees, 1970; The Tarascan Suffices of a Locative Space: Meaning and Morphotactics, 1971; A Phonology of Tarascan, 1973; On Aspect Theory and Homeric Aspect, 1974; Proto-Indo-European Syntax: The Order of Meaningful Elements, 1975; Neighboring Leaves Ride This Wind (poems), 1976; The Meaning of Aphrodite, 1978; Bastard Moons (poems), 1978; Language, Context, and the Imagination: Essays by Paul Friedrich (ed. by A. S. Dil), 1979; Redwing (poems), 1982; The Language Parallax: Linguistic Relativism and Poetic Indeterminacy, 1986; The Princes of Naranja: An Essay in Anthrohistorical Method, 1987; Sonata (poems), 1987; Russia and Eurasia: Encyclopedia of World Cultures, Vol. 6 (co-ed.), 1994; Music in Russian Poetry, 1998. Contributions: Books and journals. *Honours:* Ford Foundation Grant, 1957; Social Science Research Council Grant, 1966–67; National Endowment for the Humanities Grant, 1974–76; Guggenheim Fellowship, 1982–83. *Address:* c/o Committee on Social Thought, University of Chicago, 1130 E 59th Street, Chicago, IL 60637, USA.

FRIEL, Brian; Writer and Dramatist; b. 9 Jan. 1929, Killyclogher, County Tyrone, Ireland; m. Anne Morrison, 1954, one s., four d. *Education:* St Columb's College, Derry; St Patrick's College, Maynooth; St Joseph's Training College, Belfast. *Career:* Taught in various schools, 1950–60; Writer, 1960–. *Publications:* Collected Stories: The Saucer of Larks, 1962; The Gold in the Sea, 1966. Plays: Philadelphia Here I Come!, 1965; The Loves of Cass McGuire, 1967; Lovers, 1968; The Mundy Scheme, 1969; Crystal and Fox, 1970; The Gentle Island, 1971; The Freedom of the City, 1973; Volunteers, 1975; Living Quarters, 1976; Aristocrats, 1979; Faith Healer, 1979; Three Sisters (trans.), 1981; The Communication Cord, 1983; Fathers and Sons (trans.), 1987; Making History, 1988; Dancing at Lughnara, 1990; The London Vertigo, adaptation of a play by Charles Macklin, 1992; A Month in the Country, adaptation of Turgenev, 1992; The Yalta Game, 2001. *Honours:* Hon. DLitt, National University of Ireland, 1983; Ewart Biggs Memorial Prize, British Theatre Asscn Award. *Address:* Drumaweir House, Greencastle, County Donegal, Ireland.

FRIGGIERI, Oliver, MA, PhD; writer, poet, critic and academic; b. 27 March 1947, Floriana, Malta; m. Eileen Cassar 1972; one d. *Education:* University of Malta. *Career:* Prof. and Head, Dept of Maltese, University of Malta, 1987–; Author of works trans. into various languages; Presenter, many television and radio cultural programmes; Guest author and scholar, numerous Int. congresses and recitals; mem. Academia Internationale Mihai Eminescu, Craiova, founder-mem., 1995; Asscn Internationale des Critiques Littéraire, Paris; PEN Club, Switzerland. *Publications:* Il-Gidba (novel), 1977; La cultura italiana a Malta: Storia e influenza letteraria e stilistica attraverso l'opera di Dun Karm (criticism), 1978; Storja tal-Letteratura Maltija (criticism), 1979; L-Istramb (novel), 1980, English trans. as A Turn of the Wheel, 1987; L'esperienza leopardiana di un poeta maltese: Karmenu Vassallo (criticism), 1983; Fil-Parlament ma Jikbrux Fjuri (novel), 1986; Stejjer ghal Qabel Jidlam (short stories), two vols 1986, English trans. as Koranta and Other Short Stories from Malta 1994; Storia della letteratura maltese (criticism), 1986; Il-Kuxjenza Nazzjonali Maltija (criticism), 1995; Dizzjunarju ta' Termini Letterarji, revised edn, 1996; Gizimin li qatt ma jiftah (novel), 1998; Poeziji (poems), 1998; It-tfal jigu bil-vapuri (novel) 2000, English trans. as Children Come by Ship 2004; Il-Poeziji Migbura, 2002. Contributions: many journals. *Honours:* National Order of Merit, Malta, 1999Premio Internazionale Mediterraneo, Palermo 1988, Malta Government Literary Awards 1988, 1996, 1997, 1999, Premio Int. Trieste Poesia 2002. *Address:* c/o Faculty of Arts, Department of Maltese, University of Malta, Msida-Malta.

FRIMAN, Alice (Ruth); Prof. of English, Poet and Writer; b. 20 Oct. 1933, New York, NY, USA; m. 1st Elmer Friman 3 July 1955; two s. one d.; m. 2nd Marshall Bruce Gentry 24 Sept. 1989. *Education:* BA, Brooklyn College, CUNY, 1954; Indiana University, 1964–66; MA, English, Butler University, 1971. *Career:* Lecturer of English, Indiana University-Purdue University of Indianapolis, 1971–74; Faculty, 1971–90, Prof. of English, 1990–93, Prof. Emerita, 1993–, University of Indianapolis; Visiting Prof. of Creative Writing, Indiana State University, 1982, Ball State University, 1996; Writer-in-Residence, Curtin University, Perth, Australia, 1989; mem. Associated Writing Programs; MLA; Poetry Society of America; Writers' Center of Indiana, board mem., 1984–89, hon. life mem., 1993–. *Publications:* A Question of Innocence, 1978; Song to My Sister, 1979; Loaves and Fishes: A Book of Indiana Women Poets (ed.), 1983; Reporting from Corinth, 1984; Insomniac Heart, 1990; Driving for Jimmy Wonderland, 1992; Inverted Fire, 1997; Zoo, 1999. Contributions: several anthologies and numerous reviews, quarterlies, and journals. *Honours:* Virginia Center for the Creative Arts Fellowships, 1983, 1984, 1993, 1996, 2000; Consuelo Ford Award, 1988, Cecil Hemley Memorial Award, 1990, Lucille Medwick Memorial Award, 1993, Poetry Society of America; Midwest Poetry Award, Society for the Study of Midwestern Literature, 1990; Erika Mumford Prize, 1990, Firman Houghton Award, 1996, Sheila Margaret Motton Prize, 2001, New England Poetry Club; Millay Colony for the Arts Fellowship, 1990; Yaddo Fellowship, 1991; Teacher of the Year Award, University of Indianapolis, 1993; First Prize, Abiko Quarterly International Poetry Contest, 1994; Individual Artist Fellowship, Indiana Arts Commission, 1996–97; Ezra Pound Poetry Award, Truman State University, 1998; Creative Renewal Fellowship, Arts Council of Indianapolis, 1999–2000; James Boatwright Prize for Poetry, Shenandoah, 2002; Georgia Poetry Circuit, 2001–02; Bernheim Writing Fellowship, 2003. *Address:* 109 Treanor Dr., Milledgeville, GA 31061, USA.

FRITZ, Walter Helmut; Author and Poet; b. 26 Aug. 1929, Karlsruhe, Germany. *Education:* Literature and Philosophy, University of Heidelberg, 1949–54. *Career:* mem. Acad. for Sciences and Literature; Bavarian Acad. of Fine Arts; German Acad. for Speech and Poetry; PEN; Union of German Writers. *Publications:* Achtsam sein, 1956; Veranderte Jahre, 1963; Umwege, 1964; Zwischenbemerkungen, 1965; Abweichung, 1965; Die Verwechslung, 1970; Aus der Nahe, 1972; Die Beschaffenheit solcher Tage, 1972; Bevor uns Horen und Sehen Vergeht, 1975; Schwierige Uberfahrt, 1976; Auch jetzt und morgen, 1979; Gesammelte Gedichte, 1979; Wunschtraum alptraum, 1981; Werkzeuge der Freiheit, 1983; Cornelias Traum und andere Aufzeichnungen, 1985; Immer einfacher, immer schwieriger, 1987; Zeit des Sehens, 1989; Die Schlüssel sind vertauscht, 1992; Gesammelte Gedichte 1979–94, 1994; Das offene Fenster, 1997; Zugelassen im Leben, 1999. Contributions: journals and periodicals. *Honours:* Literature Prize, City of Karlsruhe, 1960; Prize, Bavarian Acad. of Fine Arts, 1962; Heine-Taler Lyric Prize, 1966; Prize, Culture Circle, Federation of German Industry, 1971; Literature Prize, City of Stuttgart, 1986; Georg Trakl Prize, 1992. *Address:* Kolbergerstrasse 2a, 76139 Karlsruhe, Germany.

FROHM, Frederika (see Kerner, Fred).

FROST, Sir David Paradine, OBE, MA; television personality and writer; b. 7 April 1939, Beccles, Suffolk, England; m. 1st Lynn Frederick 1981 (divorced 1982); m. 2nd Lady Carina Fitzlan-Howard 1983; three s. *Education:* Gonville and Caius College, Cambridge. *Career:* various BBC TV series, 1962–; many ITV series, 1966–; Chair. and Chief Exec., David Paradine Ltd, 1966–; joint founder and Dir, TV-am, 1981–93; regular appearances on US television. *Publications:* That Was the Week That Was, 1963; How to Live Under Labour, 1964; Talking with Frost, 1967; To England With Love, 1967; The Presidential Debate 1968, 1968; The Americans, 1970; Whitlam and Frost, 1974; I Gave Them a Sword, 1978; I Could Have Kicked Myself, 1982; Who Wants to be a Millionaire?, 1983; The Mid-Atlantic Companion (jointly), 1986; The Rich Tide (jointly), 1986; The World's Shortest Books, 1987; David Frost: An Autobiography, Part I: From

Congregations to Audiences, 1993. *Honours:* Hon. DCL (Univ. of East Anglia) 2004; Golden Rose Award, Montreux 1967, Richard Dimbleby Award 1967, RTS Silver Medal 1967, Religious Heritage of America Award 1970, Emmy Awards 1970, 1971, Albert Einstein Award 1971. *Address:* David Paradine Ltd, 5 St Mary Abbots Place, London W8 6LS, England (Office).

FROST, Jason (see Obstfeld, Raymond).

FROST, Richard; Poet, Writer and Prof. of English; b. 8 April 1929, Palo Alto, CA, USA; m. 1st Frances Atkins, 2 Sept. 1951, one s. two d.; m. 2nd Carol Kydd, 23 Aug. 1969, two s. *Education:* BA, 1951, MA, 1957, San Jose State College. *Career:* Instructor in English, San Jose State College, 1956–57, Towson State College, 1957–59; Asst Prof., 1959–64, Assoc. Prof., 1964–71, Prof. of English, 1971–, SUNY at Oneonta. *Publications:* The Circus Villains, 1965; Getting Drunk With the Birds, 1971; Neighbor Blood, 1996. Contributions: Magazines, reviews, quarterlies and journals. *Honours:* Danforth Fellow, Bread Loaf Writers' Conference, 1961; Resident Fellow, Yaddo, 1979, 1981, 1983; Gustav Davidson Memorial Award, Poetry Society of America, 1982; National Endowment for the Arts Creative Writing Fellowship, 1992. *Address:* c/o Dept of English, State University of New York at Oneonta, Oneonta, NY 13820, USA. *Telephone:* (607) 988-7170. *E-mail:* frostrq@oneonta.edu.

FRUCHTMANN, Benno; Writer, Poet and Dramatist; b. 5 Sept. 1913, Meuselwitz, Germany; m. Mirjam David, 2 Nov. 1951, two s. *Career:* mem. Asscn of German Writers; Israel Writers Asscn. *Publications:* Poetry in anthologies in German and Hebrew trans.; short stories; ballads; metric prose. Other: Radio plays. Contributions: German and Hebrew newspapers and periodicals. *Honours:* Stipend Atelierhaus, Worpswede, Germany, 1986; Participant, International Colloquium of Jewish Authors, Osnabrück, 1991. *Address:* 10 Liesin St, 62977, Tel-Aviv, Israel.

FRY, Christopher; Dramatist; b. 18 Dec. 1907, Bristol, England; m. Phyllis Marjorie Hart 1936 (died 1987); one s. *Education:* Bedford Modern School. *Career:* mem. Garrick Club. *Publications:* The Boy with a Cart, 1939; The Firstborn, 1946; A Phoenix too Frequent, 1946; The Lady's Not for Burning, 1949; Thor, with Angels, 1949; Venus Observed, 1950; A Sleep of Prisoners, 1951; The Dark is Light Enough, 1954; The Lark, 1955; Tiger at the Gates, 1955; Duel of Angels, 1958; Curtmantle, 1961; Judith, 1962; A Yard of Sun, 1970; Peer Gynt, 1970. Television Plays: The Brontës of Haworth, 1973; Sister Dora, 1977; The Best of Enemies, 1977; Can You Find Me: A Family History, 1978; Selected Plays, 1985; Genius, Talent and Failure, 1986; One Thing More or Caedmon Construed, 1987; A Journey into Light, 1992. Films: The Queen is Crowned, 1953; The Beggar's Opera, 1953; Ben Hur, 1958; Barabbas, 1960; The Bible: In the Beginning, 1962. *Honours:* FRSL, 1950; Queen's Gold Medal for Poetry, 1962; Hon. Fellow, Manchester Metropolitan University, 1988; Hon. doctorates, Lambeth University, 1988, University of Sussex, 1994, De Montfort University, 1994; RSL Benson Medal, 2000. *Address:* The Toft, East Dean, Chichester, West Sussex PO18 0JA, England.

FRY, Stephen John, MA; actor and writer; b. 24 Aug. 1957. *Education:* Queens' Coll., Cambridge. *Career:* columnist, The Listener 1988–89, Daily Telegraph 1990–; wrote first play, Latin, performed at Edinburgh Festival 1980, Lyric Theatre, Hammersmith 1983; appeared with Cambridge Footlights in revue The Cellar Tapes, Edinburgh Festival 1981; re-wrote script of Me and My Girl, London, Broadway, Sydney 1984; appears in films, notably as Oscar Wilde in Wilde 1997, on stage, and on radio and television (Blackadder); film directorial debut: Bright Young Things 2003; mem. Amnesty International, Comic Relief, Friends for Life, Terrence Higgins Trust (pres.). *Publications:* Paperweight (collected essays) 1992, Stephen Fry Mixed Shrinkwrap 1993, X10 Hippopotamus Shrinkwrap, The Liar (novel), The Hippopotamus 1994, A Bit of Fry and Laurie (with Hugh Laurie), 3 Bits of Fry and Laurie (with Hugh Laurie), Fry and Laurie 4 (with Hugh Laurie) 1994, Paperweight Vol. II (collected essays) 1995, Making History 1996, Moab is my Washpot (autobiog.) 1997, The Star's Tennis Balls (novel) 2000, The Salmon of Doubt by Douglas Adams (ed.) 2002, Revenge (novel) 2002, Rescuing the Spectacled Bear (novel) 2002. *Honours:* Hon. LLD (Dundee) 1995, (East Anglia) 1999, Hon. DLitt. *Literary Agent:* Hamilton Asper Management, Ground Floor, 24 Hanway Street, London, W1P 9DD, England. *Website:* www.stephenfry.com.

FRYE, Roland Mushat; Literary and Theological Scholar; b. 3 July 1921, Birmingham, AL, USA; m. Jean Elbert Steiner, 11 Jan. 1947, one s. *Education:* AB, 1943, PhD, 1952, Princeton University; Special Student, Theology, Princeton Theological Seminary, 1950–52. *Career:* Emory University, 1952–61; L. P. Stone Foundation Lecturer, Princeton Theological Seminary, 1959; Faculty, 1965–83, Emeritus Prof., 1983–, National Phi Beta Kappa Visiting Scholar, 1985–86, University of Pennsylvania; Chair., 1989–91, Chair. Emeritus, 1991–, Center of Theological Inquiry, Princeton, NJ. *Publications:* God, Man and Satan: Patterns of Christian Thought and Life, 1960; Shakespeare and Christian Doctrine, 1963; Shakespeare's Life and Times: A Pictorial Record, 1967; Milton's Imagery and the Visual Arts: Iconographic Tradition in the Epic Poems, 1978; Is God a Creationist?: The Religious Case Against Creation-Science, 1983; The Renaissance Hamlet: Issues and Responses in 1600, 1984. Contributions: scholarly journals. *Address:* 226 W Valley Rd, Strafford-Wayne, PA 19087, USA.

FRYER, Jonathan, (G. L. Morton); Writer, Broadcaster and University Lecturer; b. 5 June 1950, Manchester, England. *Education:* Diplôme D'Etudes Françaises, Université de Poitiers, France, 1967; BA, Chinese with Japanese, 1973, MA, St Edmund Hall, University of Oxford, 1980. *Career:* Visiting Lecturer, School of Journalism, University of Nairobi, Kenya, 1976; Subject Teacher, School of Oriental and African Studies, University of London, 1993–; mem. English PEN; RSL; Society of Authors. *Publications:* The Great Wall of China, 1975; Isherwood, 1977, revised edn as Eye of the Camera, 1993; Brussels as Seen by Naif Artists (with Rona Dobson), 1979; Food for Thought, 1981; George Fox and the Children of the Light, 1991; Dylan, 1993; The Sitwells (with Sarah Bradford and John Pearson), 1994; André and Oscar, 1997; Soho in the Fifties and Sixties, 1998; Robbie Ross: Oscar Wilde's True Love, 2000; numerous political pamphlets, mainly on Third World themes. Contributions: Economist; Tablet; Geographical Magazine; London Magazine; Gay Times; The Wildean; Liberator. *Honours:* Chevalier, Ordre nat. du Mérite, Mauritania, 2000. *Literary Agent:* Andrew Lownie, 17 Sutherland St, London SW1V 4JU, England. *Address:* 140 Bow Common Lane, London E3 4BH, England. *E-mail:* jonathanfryer@hotmail.com.

FUENTES, Carlos; Prof. of Latin American Studies and Writer; b. 11 Nov. 1928, Panama City, Panama; m. 1st Rita Macedo, 1957, one d.; m. 2nd Sylvia Lemus, 24 Jan. 1973, one s. one d. *Education:* Law School, National University of Mexico; Institute de Hautes Études Internationales, Geneva. *Career:* Head, Cultural Relations Dept, Ministry of Foreign Affairs, Mexico, 1955–58; Mexican Ambassador to France, 1975–77; Prof. of English and Romance Languages, University of Pennsylvania, 1978–83; Prof. of Comparative Literature, 1984–86, Robert F. Kennedy Prof. of Latin American Studies, 1987–, Harvard University; Simon Bolivar Prof., University of Cambridge, 1986–87; Prof.-at-Large, Brown University, 1994–; mem. American Acad. and Institute of Arts and Letters; El Colegio Nacional, Mexico; Mexican National Commission on Human Rights. *Publications:* La Region Mas Transparente, 1958; Las Buenas Conciencias, 1959; Aura, 1962; La Muerte de Artemio Cruz, 1962; Cantar de Ciegos, 1964; Cambio de Piel, 1967; Zona Sagrada, 1967; Terra Nostra, 1975; Una Familia Lejana, 1980; Agua Quemada, 1983; Gringo Viejo, 1985; Cristóbal Nonato, 1987; Myself with Others (essays), 1987; Orchids in the Moonlight (play), 1987; The Campaign, 1991; The Buried Mirror, 1992; El Naranjo, 1993; Geography of the Novel: Essays, 1993; La frontera de cristal (short stories), 1995; Los años con Laura Diaz (novel), 1999; Los cinco soles de México, 2000; Instinto de Inez, 2003. Contributions: periodicals. *Honours:* Biblioteca Breva Prize, Barcelona, 1967; Rómulo Gallegos Prize, Caracas, 1975; National Prize for Literature, Mexico, 1984; Miguel de Cervantes Prize for Literature, Madrid, 1988; Légion d'Honneur, France, 1992; Premio Príncipe de Asturias, 1992; Latin Civilisation Prize, French and Brazilian Academies, 1999; Hon. doctorates, Universities of Ghent, 2000, Madrid, 2000. *Literary Agent:* Brandt & Hochman Literary Agents Inc, 1501 Broadway, New York, NY 10036, USA.

FUGARD, (Harold) Athol, FRSL; playwright, director and actor; b. 11 June 1932, Middelburg Cape, South Africa; m. Sheila Meiring 1956; one d. *Career:* mem. American Acad. of Arts and Sciences. *Publications:* Plays: Three Port Elizabeth Plays, 1974; Statements: Three Plays (co-author), 1974; Sizwi Banzzi is Dead, and The Island (co-author), 1976; Dimetos and Two Early Plays, 1977; Boesman and Lena and Other Plays, 1978; A Lesson from Aloes, 1981; Master Harold… and the Boys, 1982; The Road to Mecca, 1985; Notebooks 1960–1977, 1983; My Children! My Africa!, 1990; The Captain's Tiger, 1998. Film Scripts: The Guest, 1977; Marigolds in August, 1981; Playland, 1991. Novel: Tsotsi, 1980. Other: Cousins: A Memoir, 1997. *Honours:* New York Drama Critics' Circle Award for Best Play, 1981; Evening Standard Award, Best Play of the Year, 1984. *Address:* PO Box 5090 Walmer, Port Elizabeth 6065, South Africa.

FUKUYAMA, Francis, BA, PhD; American writer; *Bernard Schwartz Professor of International Political Economy, Johns Hopkins University*; b. 27 Oct. 1952, Chicago, IL, USA; m. Laura Holmgren 1986; two s. one d. *Education:* Cornell Univ., Yale Univ., Harvard Univ., 1981. *Career:* staff, RAND Corpn, 1979–89; Deputy Dir, Policy Planning Staff, US Dept of State, 1989–90; Prof., George Mason Univ., 1990–2001; Bernard Schwartz Prof. of International Political Economy, Johns Hopkins Univ., 2001–. *Publications:* The Soviet Union and the Third World: The Last Three Decades (ed. with Andrzej Korbonski), 1987; The End of History and the Last Man, 1992; Our Posthuman Future: Consequences of the Biotechnology Revolution, 2001; State Building: Governance and World Order in the 21st Century 2004. Contributions: books and journals. *Honours:* Los Angeles Times Book Award, 1992; Premio Capri International Award, 1992. *Address:* c/o Paul H. Nitze School of Advanced International Studies, Johns Hopkins University, 1619 Massachusetts Ave NW, Room 732, Washington, DC 20036-2213, USA. *E-mail:* fukuyama@jhu.edu.

FULFORD, Robert (Marshall Blount); Journalist and Writer; b. 13 Feb. 1932, Ottawa, Ontario, Canada; m. 1st Jocelyn Jean Dingman, 16 June 1956, divorced 1970, one s. one d.; m. 2nd Geraldine Patricia Sherman, 28 Nov. 1970, two d. *Education:* Malvern Collegiate, Toronto. *Career:* Reporter, 1950–53, 1956–57, Columnist, 1992–, Globe and Mail; Asst Ed., Canadian Homes and Gardens, 1955, Mayfair, 1956, Maclean's, 1962–64; Columnist, Toronto Star, 1958–62, 1964–68, 1971–87; Ed., Saturday Night, 1968–87; Barker Fairley Distinguished Visitor in Canadian Culture, University College, University of Toronto, 1987–88; Columnist and Contributing Ed., Financial Times, 1988–92; Chair, Banff Centre Program in Arts Journalism, 1989–91, Maclean Hunter Program in Communications Ethics, Ryerson Polytechnical Institute, Toronto, 1989–93; mem. Canadian Civil Liberties Asscn. *Publications:* This Was Expo, 1968; Crisis at the Victory Burlesk, 1968; Marshall Delaney at the Movies, 1974; An Introduction to the Arts in Canada, 1977; Canada: A Celebration, 1983; Best Seat in the House: Memoirs of a Lucky Man, 1988; Accidental City: The Transformation of Toronto, 1995. *Honours:* Prix d'Honneur, Canadian Conference of the Arts, 1981; Officer of the Order of Canada, 1984; Hon. doctorates, McMaster University, 1986, York University, 1987, University of Western Ontario, 1988, University of Toronto, 1994. *Address:* 19 Lynwood Ave, Toronto, ON M4V 1K3, Canada.

FULLER, Charles; Dramatist; b. 5 March 1939, Philadelphia, Pennsylvania, USA; m. Miriam A. Nesbitt, 4 Aug. 1962, two s. *Education:* Villanova University, 1956–58; LaSalle College, 1965–67. *Career:* Co-Founder and Co-Dir, Afro-American Arts Theatre, Philadelphia, 1967–71; Writer and Dir, The Black Experience, WIP Radio, Philadelphia, 1970–71; Prof. of African-American Studies, Temple University, until 1993; mem. Dramatists Guild; PEN; Writers Guild of America. *Publications:* Plays: The Village: A Party, 1968, revised version as The Perfect Party, 1969; In My Names and Days, 1972; Candidate, 1974; In the Deepest Part of Sleep, 1974; First Love, 1974; The Lay Out Letter, 1975; The Brownsville Raid, 1976; Sparrow in Flight, 1978; Zooman and the Sign, 1981; A Soldier's Play, 1982; We: Part I, Sally, 1988, Part II, Prince, Part III, Jonquil, 1989, Part IV, Burner's Frolic, 1990; Songs of the Same Lion, 1991. Other: Screenplays and television series. *Honours:* National Endowment for the Arts Grant, 1976; Rockefeller Foundation Grant, 1976; Guggenheim Fellowship, 1977–78; Obie Award, 1981; Pulitzer Prize in Drama, 1982; New York Drama Critics Circle Award, 1982; Edgar Allan Poe Mystery Award, 1985. *Literary Agent:* William Morris Agency, 1325 Avenue of the Americas, New York, NY 10019, USA.

FULLER, Cynthia Dorothy; Poet and Adult Education Tutor; b. 13 Feb. 1948, Isle of Sheppey, England; Divorced, two s. *Education:* BA, English, Sheffield University, 1969; Postgraduate Certificate of Education, University of Oxford, 1970; MLitt, Aberdeen University, 1979. *Career:* Teacher of English, Redborne School, 1970–72; Freelance in Adult Education, University Depts at Durham, Leeds and Newcastle Universities, also Open University and Workers' Education Asscn. *Publications:* Moving Towards Light, 1992; Instructions for the Desert, 1996; Only a Small Boat, 2001. Contributions: poems in various magazines including: Other Poetry; Iron; Poetry Durham; Literary Review. *Honours:* Northern Arts Financial Assistance. *Address:* 28 South Terrace, Esh Winning, Co Durham DH7 9PR, England.

FULLER, Jean Violet Overton; Author and Poet; b. 7 March 1915, Iver Heath, Bucks, England. *Education:* Brighton High School, 1927–31; RADA, 1931–32; BA, University of London, 1945; University College of London, 1948–50. *Career:* mem. Society of Authors. *Publications:* The Comte de Saint Germain, 1988; Blavatsky and Her Teachers, 1988; Dericourt: The Chequered Spy, 1989; Sickert and the Ripper Crimes, 1990; Cats and Other Immortals, 1992; Espionage as a Fine Art, 2002; Krishnamurti and the Wind, 2002. *Honours:* Writers Manifold Poems of the Decade, 1968. *Address:* Fuller D'Arch Smith Ltd, 37B New Cavendish St, London, England.

FULLER, John Leopold; Poet and Writer; b. 1 Jan. 1937, Ashford, Kent, England; m. Cicely Prudence Martin 20 July 1960; three d. *Education:* BA, BLitt, MA, New College, Oxford, 1957–62. *Career:* Fellow and Tutor, Magdalen College, Oxford; mem. FRSL; Emeritus Fellow, Magdalen College, Oxford. *Publications:* Fairground Music, 1961; The Tree That Walked, 1967; Cannibals and Missionaries, 1972; The Sonnet, 1972; Epistles to Several Persons, 1973; Penguin Modern Poets 22, 1974; The Mountain in the Sea, 1975; Lies and Secrets, 1979; The Illusionists, 1980; The Dramatic Works of John Gay (ed.), 1983; The Beautiful Inventions, 1983; Flying to Nowhere, 1983; The Adventures of Speedfall, 1985; Selected Poems, 1954–82, 1985; The Grey Among the Green, 1988; Tell it Me Again, 1988; The Burning Boys, 1989; Partingtime Hall (with James Fenton), 1989; The Mechanical Body and Other Poems, 1991; Look Twice, 1991; The Worm and the Star, 1993; The Chatto Book of Love Poetry, 1994; Stones and Fires 1996; Collected Poems, 1996; A Skin Diary, 1997; W. H. Auden: A Commentary, 1998; W. H. Auden: Poems Selected by John Fuller, 2000; The Oxford Book of Sonnets (ed.), 2000; The Memoirs of Laetitia Horsepole, 2001; Now and for a Time, 2002. Contributions: periodicals, reviews and journals. *Honours:* Newdigate Prize, 1960; Richard Hillary Award, 1962; E. C. Gregory Award, 1965; Geoffrey Faber Memorial Prize, 1974; Southern Arts Prize, 1980; Whitbread Prize, 1983; Forward Prize, 1996. *Address:* 4 Benson Pl., Oxford OX2 6QH, England.

FULLER, Lawrence Robert, BJ; American newspaper publisher; b. 9 Sept. 1941, Toledo; m. Suzanne Hovik 1967; one s. one d. *Education:* Univ. of Missouri. *Career:* reporter, Globe Gazette, Mason City, Ia 1963–67; reporter, later City Ed. Minneapolis Star 1967–75; Exec. Ed. Messenger-Inquirer, Owensborough, Ky 1975–77; Exec. Ed. Argus Leader, Sioux Falls, South Dakota 1977–78, Pres., Publr 1974–84, 1986–99; Pres. Gannett News Media, Washington, DC 1984–85; Dir Corp. Communications, Gannett Co. Inc. Washington 1985–86; Vice-Pres. Gannett/West Regional Newspaper Group 1986–, The Honolulu Advertisers 1986–; several directorships; mem. American Newspaper Publishers' Asscn, American Soc. of Newspaper Eds etc. *Address:* 605 Kapiolani Boulevard, Honolulu, HI 96813, USA.

FULLERTON, Alexander Fergus; Writer; b. 20 Sept. 1924, Saxmundham, Suffolk, England; m. Priscilla Mary Edelston, 10 May 1956, three s. *Education:* Royal Naval College, Dartmouth, 1938–41; School of Slavonic Studies, University of Cambridge, 1947. *Career:* Editorial Dir, Peter Davies Ltd, 1961–64; General Man., Arrow Books, 1964–67. *Publications:* Surface!, 1953; A Wren Called Smith, 1957; The White Men Sang, 1958; The Blooding of the Guns, 1976; Sixty Minutes for St George, 1977; Patrol to the Golden Horn, 1978; Storm Force to Narvik, 1979; Last Lift from Crete, 1980; All the Drowning Seas, 1981; A Share of Honour, 1982; The Torch Bearers, 1983; The Gatecrashers, 1984; Special Deliverance, 1986; Special Dynamic, 1987; Special Deception, 1988; Bloody Sunset, 1991; Look to the Wolves, 1992; Love for an Enemy, 1993; Not Thinking of Death, 1994; Into the Fire, 1995; Band of Brothers, 1996; Return to the Field, 1997; Final Dive, 1998; In at the Kill, 1999; Wave Cry, 1999; The Floating Madhouse, 2000; Single to Paris, 2001; Flight to Mons, 2003; Westbound, Warbound, 2003; Stark Realities, 2004. *Literary Agent:* Johnson & Alcock Ltd, Clerkenwell House, 45–47 Clerkenwell Green, London EC1R 0HT, England. *E-mail:* alexfullerton@tiscali.co.uk.

FULTON, Alice; Prof. of English and Poet; b. 25 Jan. 1952, Troy, New York, USA; m. Hank De Leo, 1980. *Education:* BA, Empire State College, Albany, New York, 1978; MFA, Cornell University, 1982. *Career:* Asst Prof., 1983–86, Willam Willhartz Prof., 1986–89, Assoc. Prof., 1989–92, Prof. of English, 1992–, University of Michigan; Visiting Prof. of Creative Writing, Vermont College, 1987, University of California at Los Angeles, 1991. *Publications:* Anchors of Light, 1979; Dance Script with Electric Ballerina, 1983; Palladium, 1986; Powers of Congress, 1990; Sensual Math, 1995; Feeling as a Foreign Language: The Good Strangeness of Poetry, 1999; Felt, 2001. *Honours:* Macdowell Colony Fellowships, 1978, 1979; Millay Colony Fellowship, 1980; Emily Dickinson Award, 1980; Acad. of American Poets Prize, 1982; Consuelo Ford Award, 1984; Rainer Maria Rilke Award, 1984; Michigan Council for the Arts Grants, 1986, 1991; Guggenheim Fellowship, 1986–87; Yaddo Colony Fellowship, 1987; Bess Hokin Prize, 1989; Ingram Merrill Foundation Award, 1990; John D. and Catherine T. MacArthur Foundation Fellowship, 1991–96; Elizabeth Matchett Stover Award, 1994. *Address:* 2370 Le Forge Rd, RR2, Ypsilanti, MI 48198, USA.

FULTON, Len; Author and Publisher; b. 15 May 1934, Lowell, Massachusetts, USA; one s. one d. *Education:* BA, University of Wyoming, 1961. *Career:* Mem., Literary Advisory Panel, National Endowment for the Arts, 1976–78; Mem., Advisory Board, Center for the Book, Library of Congress, 1978–80; mem. PEN. *Publications:* The Grassman, novel, 1974; Dark Other Adam Dreaming, novel, 1976, play, 1984; American Odyssey, travelogue, 1978; For the Love of Pete, play, 1988; Grandmother Dies, play, 1989; Headlines, play, 1990. *Address:* PO Box 100, Paradise, CA 95967, USA.

FULTON, Robin, MA, PhD; poet, writer, translator and editor; b. 6 May 1937, Arran, Scotland. *Education:* University of Edinburgh. *Career:* Ed., Lines Review 1967–76. *Publications:* Poetry: Instances, 1967; Inventories, 1969; The Spaces Between the Stones, 1971; The Man with the Surbahar, 1971; Tree-Lines, 1974; Following a Mirror, 1980; Selected Poems, 1963–78, 1980; Fields of Focus, 1982; Coming Down to Earth and Spring is Soon, 1990; Scottish Poetry (supplements) 2003. Criticism: Contemporary Scottish Poetry: Individuals and Contexts, 1974; The Way the Words are Taken, Selected Essays, 1989; Editor: Iain Crichton Smith: Selected Poems, 1955–80, 1982; Robert Garioch: The Complete Poetical Works with Notes, 1983; Robert Garioch: A Garioch Miscellany, Selected Prose and Letters, 1986. Translator: An Italian Quartet, 1966; Five Swedish Poets, 1972; Lars Gustafsson, Selected Poems, 1972; Gunnar Harding: They Killed Sitting Bull and Other Poems, 1973; Tomas Tranströmer: Selected Poems, 1974; Östen Sjöstrand: The Hidden Music & Other Poems, 1975; Toward the Solitary Star: Selected Poetry and Prose, 1988; Werner Aspenström: 37 Poems, 1976; Tomas Tranströmer: Baltics, 1980; Werner Aspenström: The Blue Whale and Other Prose Pieces, 1981; Kjell Espmark: Béla Bartók Against the Third Reich and Other Poems, 1985; Olav Hauge: Don't Give Me the Whole Truth and Other Poems, 1985; Tomas Tranströmer: Collected Poems, 1987; Stig Dagerman: German Autumn, 1988; Pär Lagervist: Guest of Reality, 1989; Preparations for Flight, and other Swedish Stories, 1990; Four Swedish Poets (Kjell Espmark, Lennart Sjögren, Eva Ström & Tomas Tranströmer), 1990; Olav Hauge: Selected Poems, 1990; Hermann Starheimsaeter: Stone-Shadows, 1991; Five Swedish Poets (Werner Aspenström, Kjell Espmark, Lennart Sjögren, Eva Ström, Staffan Söderblom), 1997; Tomas Tranströmer, New Collected Poems, 1997; Henrik Nordbrandt, My Life, My Dream 2002; Olav Hauge, Leaf-Huts and Snow-Houses 2003. *Honours:* Gregory Award, 1967; Writers Fellowship, University of Edinburgh, 1969; Scottish Arts Council Writers Bursary, 1972; Arthur Lundquist Award for Trans. from Swedish, 1977; Swedish Acad. Award, 1978, 1998. *Address:* Postboks 467, N 4002, Stavanger, Norway.

FUNDER, Anna, BA; Australian writer; b. 1966, Melbourne, Vic. *Education:* Univ. of Melbourne, Free Univ. of Berlin. *Career:* Co-Ed., Melbourne Univ. Law Review 1991; int. lawyer, researcher and trans., Deutsche Welle Television, Berlin; radio and television prod., ABC, Australia; writer-in-residence, Australia Centre, Potsdam. *Publications:* Stasiland: Stories from Behind the Berlin Wall (Samuel Johnson Prize 2004) 2002. *Honours:* DAAD Scholarship, Australian-German Asscn Fellowship, Arts Victoria Literary Grant ; Felix Meyer Creative Writing Award. *Address:* c/o Granta, 2–3 Hanover Yard, Noel Road, London, N1 8BE, England. *Telephone:* (20) 7704-9776. *Fax:* (20) 7704-0474. *Website:* www.granta.com.

FUNE, Jonathan (see Fletcher, John (Walter James)).

FURST, Alan; Writer; b. 20 Feb. 1941, New York, NY, USA. *Education:* BA, Oberlin College, 1962; MA, Pennsylvania State University, 1967. *Publications:* Your Day in the Barrel, 1976; The Paris Drop, 1980; The Caribbean Account, 1981; Shadow Trade, 1983; Night Soldiers, 1988; Dark Star, 1991; The Polish Officer, 1995; The World at Night, 1996; Red Gold, 1999; Kingdom of Shadows, 2001; Blood of Victory, 2002. Contributions: periodicals. *Address:* PO Box 2345, Sag Harbor, NY 11963, USA.

FURTWÄNGLER, Virginia Walsh, (Ann Copeland); Writer and Teacher; b. 16 Dec. 1932, Hartford, CT, USA; m. Albert Furtwangler, 17 Aug. 1968, two s. *Education:* BA, College of New Rochelle, 1954; MA, Catholic University of America, 1959; PhD, Cornell University, Kent, 1970. *Career:* Writer-in-Residence, College of Idaho, 1980, Linfield College, 1980–81, University of Idaho, 1982, 1986, Wichita State University, 1988, Mt Allison University, 1990, St Mary's University, 1993; Hallie Brown Ford Chair of English, Willamette University, 1996; mem. Authors' Guild; Writers Union of Canada; International Womens Writing Guild. *Publications:* At Peace, 1978; The Back Room, 1979; Earthen Vessels, 1984; The Golden Thread, 1989; Strange Bodies on a Stranger Shore, 1994; The ABC's of Writing Fiction, 1996; Season of Apples, 1996. Contributions: anthologies and magazines. *Honours:* Kent Fellowship; Canada Council Grant; National Endowment for the Arts Writing Fellowship, 1994; Ingram Merrill Foundation Award. *Address:* 235 Oak Way NE, Salem, OR 97301, USA. *E-mail:* vfurtwan@willamette.edu.

FUSSELL, Paul; academic and writer; b. 22 March 1924, Pasadena, CA, USA; m. 1st Betty Ellen Harper 1949 (divorced 1987); one s. one d.; m. 2nd Harriette Behringer 1987. *Education:* BA, Pomona College, 1947; MA, 1949, PhD, 1952, Harvard University. *Career:* Instructor, Connecticut College, 1951–55; Faculty, 1955–76, John DeWitt Prof. of English Literature, 1976–83, Rutgers University; Consultant Ed., Random House, 1963–64; Contributing Ed., Harper's, 1979–83, The New Republic, 1979–85; Donald T. Regan Prof. of English Literature, 1983–94, Prof. Emeritus, 1994–, University of Pennsylvania; Visiting Prof., King's College, London, 1990–92; mem. Acad. of Literary Studies; MLA; FRSL; Society of American Historians. *Publications:* The Rhetorical World of Augustan Humanism, 1965; Poetic Meter and Poetic Form, 1965; Samuel Johnson and the Life of Writing, 1971; The Great War and Modern Memory, 1975; Abroad: British Literary Traveling Between the Wars, 1980; The Boy Scout Handbook and Other Observations, 1982; Class: A Guide Through the American Status System, 1983; Thank God for the Atom Bomb and Other Essays, 1988; Wartime: Understanding and Behavior in the Second World War, 1989; BAD: Or the Dumbing of America, 1991; The Anti-Egoist: Kingsley Amis, Man of Letters, 1994; Doing Battle: The Making of a Skeptic, 1996; Uniforms, 2002. Contributions: scholarly journals. *Honours:* James D. Phelan Award, 1964; Lindback Foundation Award, 1971; Senior Fellow, National Endowment for the Humanities, 1973–74; Guggenheim Fellowship, 1977–78; Rockefeller Foundation Fellow, 1983–84. *Address:* 2020 Walnut Street, Philadelphia, PA 19103, USA.

FYFIELD, Frances (see Hegarty, Frances).

G

GAARDER, Jostein; writer; b. 1952, Oslo, Norway; m.; two s. *Publications:* Diagnosen og andre noveller (trans. as The Diagnosis and Other Stories), 1986; Froskeslottet (trans. as The Frog Castle, children's book), 1988; Kabalmysteriet (trans. as The Solitaire Mystery), 1990; Sofies verden: Roman on filosofiens historie (trans. as Sophie's World: A Novel about the History of Philosophy), 1991; Julemysteriet (trans. as The Christmas Mystery), 1992; I et speil, i en gåte (trans. as Through a Glass, Darkly), 1993; Hallo? Er det noen her? (trans. as Hello? Is Anybody There?, children's book), 1996; Vita Brevis (trans. as That Same Flower, novella), 1996; Maya, 1999; Sirkusdirektørens datter (trans. as The Ringmaster's Daughter), 2001; The Orange Girl (in trans.) 2004. *Honours:* Norwegian Literary Critics Award, 1991; Norwegian Ministry of Cultural and Scientific Affairs Literary Prize, 1991; Number One International Fiction Bestseller, Publishing Trends, 1995. *Address:* c/o H. Ashehoug & Co, Postboks 363 Sentrum, 0102 Oslo, Norway.

GAGLIANO, Frank; Playwright, Screenwriter, Novelist and Prof. of Playwriting; b. 18 Nov. 1931, New York, NY, USA. *Education:* Queens College, CUNY, 1949–53; BA, University of Iowa, 1954; MFA, Columbia University, 1957. *Career:* Playwright-in-Residence, RSC, London, 1967–69; Asst Prof. of Drama, Playwright-in-Residence, Dir of Contemporary Playwrights Center, Florida State University, Tallahassee, 1969–73; Lecturer in Playwriting, Dir of Conkie Workshop for Playwrights, University of Texas, Austin, 1973–75; Distinguished Visiting Prof., University of Rhode Island, 1975; Benedum Prof. of Theatre, West Virginia University, 1976–; Artistic Dir, Carnegie Mellon, Showcase of New Plays, 1986–99; Artistic Dir, University of Michigan's Festival of New Works, 2000–02. *Publications:* The City Scene (2 plays), 1966; Night of the Dunce, 1967; Father Uxbridge Wants to Marry, 1968; The Hide-and-Seek Odyssey of Madeleine Gimple, 1970; Big Sur, 1970; The Prince of Peasantmania, 1970; The Private Eye of Hiram Bodoni (television play), 1971; Quasimodo (musical), 1971; Anywhere the Wind Blows (musical), 1972; In the Voodoo Parlour of Marie Laveau, 1974; The Commedia World of Lafcadio Beau, 1974; The Resurrection of Jackie Cramer (musical), 1974; Congo Square (musical), 1975, revised, 1989; The Total Immersion of Madelaine Favorini, 1981; San Ysidro (dramatic cantata), 1985; From the Bodoni County Songbook Anthology, Book I, 1986, musical version, 1989; Anton's Leap (novel), 1987; The Farewell Concert of Irene and Vernon Palazzo, 1994; My Chekhov Light, 1998. *Address:* West Virginia University Creative Arts Center, Morgantown, WV 26506 USA.

GAGNON, Madeleine; Author and Poet; b. 27 July 1938, Amqui, QC, Canada; Divorced, two s. *Education:* BA, Literature, Université Saint-Joseph du Nouveau-Brunswick, 1959; MA, Philosophy, University of Montréal, 1961; PhD, Literature, Université d'Aix-en-Provence, 1968. *Career:* Teacher of Literature, Université du Québec à Montréal, 1969–82; various guest professorships and writer-in-residencies; mem. Union des écrivaines et des écrivains québécois; Académie des Lettres du Québec; PEN Canada, Québec section. *Publications:* Les morts-vivants, 1969; Pour les femmes et tous les autres, 1974; Poélitique, 1975; La venue à l'écriture (with Hélène Cixous and Annie Leclerc), 1977; Retailles (with Denise Boucher), 1977; Antre, 1978; Lueur: Roman archéologique, 1979; Au coeur de la lettre, 1981; Autographie 1 and 2: Fictions, 1982; Les fleurs du catapla, 1986; Toute écriture est amour, 1989; Chant pour un Québec lointain, 1991; La terre est remplie de langage, 1993; Les cathédrales sauvages, 1994; Le vent majeur, 1995; Le Deuil du Soleil, 1998; Rêve de Pierre, 1999; Les Femmes et la Guerre, 2000. Contributions: many periodicals. *Honours:* Grand Prize, Journal de Montréal, 1986; Governor-General's Award for Poetry, 1991. *Address:* c/o Union des écrivaines et des écrivains québécois, La Maison des écrivains, 3492 Ave Laval, Montréal, QC H2X 3C8, Canada.

GAILLARD, Frye; Journalist and Author; b. 23 Dec. 1946, Mobile, AL, USA; m. Nancy B. Gaillard, two d. *Education:* BA, History, Vanderbilt University. *Publications:* Watermelon Wine: The Spirit of Country Music, 1978; Race, Rock and Religion, 1982; The Catawba River, 1983; The Unfinished Presidency: Essays on Jimmy Carter, 1986; The Dream Long Deferral, 1988; The Secret Diary of Mikhail Gorbachev, 1990; Southern Voices, 1991; Kyle at 200 MPH, 1993; Lessons from the Big House, 1994; The Way We See It, 1995; If I Were a Carpenter: Twenty Years of Habitat for Humanity, 1996; Mobile and the Eastern Shore, 1997; As Long as the Waters Flow: Native Americans in the South and East, 1998; The S21 All-Stars, 1999. Contributions: The Oxford American; Saturday Review; Parade; Southern Accents; Southern Magazine; New West. *Honours:* Gustavus Myers Award, 1989; Small Press Award, 1997; Library of Congress Legacies Recognition, 1999. *Address:* 127 Indian Trail Rd, Indian Trail, NC 28079, USA.

GAIMAN, Neil Richard, BA; British writer and illustrator; b. 10 Nov. 1960, Portchester, Hants.; m.; three c. *Career:* creator and writer of Sandman comics (75 issues, collected in 10 vols); collaborations with Dave McKean, Terry Pratchett. *Television writing:* Neverwhere (BBC) 1996, Babylon 5 (episode) 1997. *Film writing:* Mirror Mask 2004. *Publications:* novels: Ghastly Beyond Belief 1985, Don't Panic 1987, Violent Cases 1987, Black Orchid 1988, Good Omens 1990, Miracleman: The Golden Age 1992, Signal to Noise 1992, Death: The High Cost of Living 1993, Neverwhere 1997, Stardust 1998, Sandman: The Dream Hunters 1999, American Gods 2001, Sandman: Endless Nights 2003; juvenile fiction: The Day I Swapped My Dad for Two Goldfish 1997, Coraline 2002, The Wolves in the Walls (with Dave McKean) (BSFA Best Short Fiction) 2003; anthologies: Angels and Visitations 1993, Smoke and Mirrors: Short Fictions and Illusions 1998; editor: Now We Are Sick 1991; contrib. to Time Out, The Sunday Times, Comic Relief, Punch, The Observer, The Face, BBC Radio 3. *Honours:* International Horror Critics' Guild Award for Best Collection, Eagle Award for Best Graphic Novel 1988, Best Writer of American Comics 1990, Will Eisner Comic Industry Award 1991–94, Diamond Distributors' Gem Award 1993, GLAAD Award for Best Comic 1996, Mythopoeic Award for Best Novel (France) 1999, Julia Verlanger Award 1999, Bram Stoker Award 1999, Hugo Nebula SFX Stoker and Locus Awards 2001. *Literary Agent:* Merrilee Heifetz, Writers House, 21 W 26th Street, New York, NY 10010, USA. *Telephone:* (212) 685-2400. *Website:* www.neilgaiman.com.

GAINES, Ernest J(ames); Prof. of English and Writer; b. 15 Jan. 1933, River Lake Plantation, Pointe Coupee Parish, LA, USA. *Education:* BA, San Francisco State College, 1957; Graduate Studies, Stanford University, 1958–59. *Career:* Writer-in-Residence, Denison University, 1971, Stanford University, 1981; Visiting Prof., 1983, Writer-in-Residence, 1986, Whittier College; Prof. of English and Writer-in-Residence, University of Southwestern Louisiana, 1983–; mem. American Acad. of Arts and Letters. *Publications:* Catherine Carmier, 1964; Of Love and Dust, 1967; Bloodline (short stories), 1968; The Autobiography of Miss Jane Pittman, 1971; In My Father's House, 1978; A Gathering of Old Men, 1983; A Lesson Before Dying, 1993. Contributions: anthologies and periodicals. *Honours:* National Endowment for the Arts Award, 1967; Rockefeller Grant, 1970; Guggenheim Fellowship, 1971; Black Acad. of Arts and Letters Award, 1972; Fiction Gold Medals, Commonwealth Club of California, 1972, 1984; 9 Emmy Awards, 1975; American Acad. and Institute of Arts and Letters Award, 1987; John D. and Catherine T. MacArthur Foundation Fellowship, 1993; National Book Critics Circle Award, 1994; Hon. doctorates. *Address:* 932 Divosadero St, San Francisco, CA 94115, USA.

GAINHAM, Sarah; Writer; b. 1 Oct. 1922, London, England; m. Kenneth Robert Ames 14 April 1964 (died 1975). *Publications:* Time Right Deadly, 1956; Cold Dark Night, 1957; The Mythmaker, 1957; Stone Roses, 1959; Silent Hostage, 1960; Night Falls on the City, 1967; A Place in the Country, 1968; Takeover Bid, 1970; Private Worlds, 1971; Maculan's Daughter, 1973; To the Opera Ball, 1975; The Habsburg Twlight, 1979; The Tiger, Life, 1983; A Discursive Essay on the Presentation of Recent History in English, 1998. Contributions: Encounter; Atlantic; BBC.

GALASSI, Jonathan White, MA; American publishing executive; *President, Farrar, Straus & Giroux Inc.*; b. 4 Nov. 1949, Seattle, Wash.; m. Susan Grace Galassi 1975; two d. *Education:* Harvard and Cambridge Univs. *Career:* Ed. Houghton Mifflin Co., Boston, New York 1973–81; Sr Ed. Random House, Inc., New York 1981–86; Exec. Ed. and Vice-Pres. Farrar, Straus & Giroux Inc., New York 1986–87, Ed.-in-Chief and Sr Vice-Pres. 1988–93, Exec. Vice-Pres. 1993–99, Publr 1999–, Pres. 2002–; Poetry Ed. Paris Review 1978–88; Guggenheim Fellow 1989; mem. Acad. of American Poets (Dir 1990–2002, Pres. 1994–99, Chair. 1999–2002, Hon. Chair. 2002–). *Publications:* Morning Run (poetry) 1988, The Second Life of Art: Selected Essays of Eugenio Montale (ed., trans.) 1982, Otherwise: Last and First Poems of Eugenio Montale (ed., trans.) 1986, Eugenio Montale, Collected Poems 1916–56 (ed., trans.) 1998, North Street (poetry) 2000, Eugenio Montale, Postumous Diary 2001. *Honours:* Fellow American Acad. of Arts and Sciences 2002; Roger Klein Award for Editing, PEN 1984, Award in Literature, American Acad. of Arts and Letters 2000. *Address:* Farrar, Straus & Giroux Inc., 19 Union Square W, New York, NY 10003 (Office); 239 Sackett Street, Brooklyn, NY 11231, USA (Home). *Telephone:* (212) 741-6900 (Office).

GALBRAITH, John Kenneth; American academic and writer; b. 15 Oct. 1908, Iona Station, ON, Canada; m. Catherine Atwater 1937; three s. *Education:* BS, University of Guelph, 1931; MS, 1933, PhD, 1934, University of California; Postgraduate Studies, University of Cambridge, 1937–38. *Career:* Research Fellow, University of California, 1931–34; Instructor and Tutor, 1934–39, Lecturer 1948–49, Prof. of Economics, 1949–75, Paul M. Warburg Prof. of Economics, 1959–75, Prof. Emeritus, 1975–, Harvard University; Asst Prof. of Economics, Princeton University, 1939–42; Economic Adviser, National Defense Advisory Commission, Washington, DC, 1940–41; Asst Administrator, Price Division, 1941–42, Deputy Administrator, 1942–43, Office of Price Administration, Washington, DC; Dir, US Strategic Bombing Survey, 1945, Office of Economic Security Policy, US State Dept, Washington, DC, 1946; US Ambassador to India, 1961–63; Adviser to Pres John F. Kennedy and Lyndon B. Johnson; mem. American Acad. of Arts and Sciences, fellow; American Acad. and Institute of Arts and Letters, pres., 1984–87; American Economic Asscn, pres., 1972; American Agricultural Economics Asscn; Americans for Democratic Action, chair., 1967–68. *Publications:* Modern Competition and Business Policy (with Henry Sturgis Dennison), 1938; American Capitalism: The Concept of Countervailing Power, 1952; A Theory of Price

Control, 1952; The Great Crash, 1929, 1955; Marketing Efficiency in Puerto Rico (with others), 1955; Journey to Poland and Yugoslavia, 1958; The Affluent Society, 1958; The Liberal Hour, 1960; Economic Development in Perspective, 1962, revised edn as Economic Development, 1964; The McLandress Dimension (satire published under the name Mark Epernay), 1963; The Scotch (memoir), 1964; The New Industrial State, 1967; How to Get Out of Vietnam: A Workable Solution to the Worst Problem of Our Time, 1967; The Triumph: A Novel of Modern Diplomacy, 1968; Indian Painting: The Scene, Themes and Legends (with Mohinder Singh Randhawa), 1968; How to Control the Military, 1969; Ambassador's Journal: A Personal Account of the Kennedy Years, 1969; Who Needs the Democrats, and What It Takes to Be Needed, 1970; A Contemporary Guide to Economics, Peace, and Laughter (essays), 1971; A China Passage, 1973; Economics and the Public Purpose, 1973; Money: Whence It Came, Where It Went, 1975; The Age of Uncertainty, 1977; Almost Everyone's Guide to Economics (with Nicole Salinger), 1978; Annals of an Abiding Liberal, 1979; The Nature of Mass Poverty, 1979; A Life in Our Times: Memoirs, 1981; The Anatomy of Power, 1983; The Voice of the Poor: Essays in Economic and Political Persuasion, 1983; A View from the Stands: Of People, Politics, Military Power, and the Arts, 1986; Economics in Perspective: A Critical History, 1987; Capitalism, Communism and Coexistence: From the Bitter Past to the Bitter Present (with Stanislav Menshikov), 1988; A Tenured Professor (novel), 1990; The Culture of Contentment, 1992; A Short History of Financial Euphoria, 1993; A Journey Through Economic Time, 1994; Name-Dropping from FDR on, 1999. Contributions: books and scholarly journals. *Honours:* Social Science Research Council Fellow, 1937–38; US Medal of Freedom, 1964; many hon. doctorates. *Address:* 30 Francis Avenue, Cambridge, MA 02138, USA.

GALEANO, Eduardo (Hughes); Author and Journalist; b. 3 Sept. 1940, Montevideo, Uruguay; m. 1st Silvia Brando, 1959, one d.; m. 2nd Graciela Berro, 1962, one s. one d.; m. 3rd Helena Villagra, 1976. *Career:* Ed.-in-Chief, Marcha, 1961–64, University Press, 1965–73, Montevideo; Dir, Épocha, Montevideo, 1964–66; Founder-Dir, Crisis, Buenos Aires, 1973–76. *Publications:* Los días siguientes, 1963; China 1964, 1964; Guatamala: Clave de Latinoamerica, 1967, English trans. as Guatemala: Occupied Country, 1969; Reportajes, 1967; Los fantasmas del día del léon, y otros relatos, 1967; Su majestad el fútbol, 1968; Las venas abiertas de América Latina, 1971, English trans. as The Open Veins of Latin America, 1973; Siete imágenes de Bolivia, 1971; Crónicas latinoamericanas, 1972; Vagamundo, 1973; La cancion de nosotros, 1975; Conversaciones con Ramón, 1977; Días y noches de amor y de guerra, 1978, English trans. as Days and Nights of Love and War, 2000; La piedra arde, 1980; Voces de nuestro tiempo, 1981; Memoria del fuego: Genesis, 1982, English trans. as Memory of Fire: Genesis, 1985; Memoria del fuego: Las caras y las máscaras, 1984, English trans. as Memory of Fire: Faces and Masks, 1987; Aventuras de los jóvenes dioses, 1984; Ventana sobre Sandino, 1985; Contraseña, 1985; Memoria del fuego: El siglo del viento, 1986, English trans. as Memory of Fire: Century of the Wind, 1988; El descubrimento de América que todavía no fue y otros escritos, 1986; El tigre azul y otros artículos, 1988; Entrevistas y artículos, 1962–1987, 1988; El libro de los abrazos, 1989, English trans. as The Book of Embraces, 1991; Nosostros decimos no, 1989, English trans. as We Say No, 1992; América Latina para entenderte mejor, 1990; Palabras: Antología personal, 1990; An Uncertain Grace: Essays by Eduardo Galeano and Fred Ritchin, 1990; Ser como ellos y otros artículos, 1992; Amares, 1993; Las palabras andantes, 1993, English trans. as Walking Woods, 1995; Uselo y tírelo, 1994; El fútbol a sol y sombra, 1995, English trans. as Football in Sun and Shadow, 1998; Patas arriba: La escuela del mundo al revés, 1998, English trans. as Upside Down: A Primer for the Looking-Glass World, 2000. *Honours:* Premio Casa de las Américas, 1975, 1978; American Book Award, 1989. *Address:* c/o Siglo XXI Editores, Avda Cerro del Agua, No. 240, Col. Romero de Terreros, 04310 México, DF, Mexico.

GALGUT, Damon; South African playwright and novelist; b. 1963, Pretoria. *Education:* Univ. of Cape Town. *Plays:* Echoes of Anger, Party for Mother, Alive and Kicking, The Green's Keeper. *Publications:* novels: A Sinless Season 1982, Small Circle of Beings 1988, The Beautiful Screaming of Pigs 1991, The Quarry 1995, The Good Doctor (Commonwealth Writers Prize Africa Region Best Book Award 2004) 2003. *Honours:* CNA Award 1992. *Literary Agent:* Peake Associates, 14 Grafton Crescent, London, NW1 8SL, England.

GALIN, Aleksandr, (Aleksandr Mikhailovich Pourer); Playwright, Actor and Film and Theatre Dir; b. 10 Sept. 1947, Rosvovskya oblast, USSR; m. Galina Alekseyevna Pourer 1970; one s. *Education:* Institute of Culture, Leningrad. *Career:* factory worker, later actor in puppet theatre; freelance writer, 1978–; Films: Casanova's Coat (scriptwriter and dir); Photo (scriptwriter, actor and dir), 2003. *Publications:* Plays: The Wall, 1971; Here Fly the Birds, 1974; The Hole, 1975; The Roof, 1976; Retro, 1979; The Eastern Tribute, 1980; Stars in the Morning Sky, 1982; The Toastmaster, 1983; Jeanne, 1986; Sorry, 1990; The Group, 1991; The Title, 1991; The Czech Photo, 1993; The Clown and the Bandit, 1996; The Anomaly, 1996; Sirena and Victoria, 1997; The Competition, 1998; Rendezvous, 2002. *Honours:* Ambassador of the Arts, Florida. *Address:* Gorohowsky pereulok 15, Apt. 11, 103064 Moscow, Russia. *Telephone:* (095) 267-70-21. *Fax:* (095) 267-70-21. *E-mail:* agalin@online.ru. *Website:* www.webcenter.ru/~agalin.

GALIOTO, Salvatore; Prof. of Humanities (retd) and Poet; b. 6 June 1925, Italy; m. Nancy Morris, 8 July 1978, one s. *Education:* BA, University of New Mexico, 1952; MA, University of Denver, 1955; John Hay Fellow, Yale University, 1959–60; Catskill Area Project Fellow, Columbia University, 1961–62; Mediaeval and Renaissance Doctoral Programme, University of New Haven. *Career:* mem. Long Island Historians' Society; Asian Society; California State Poetry Society; Poets and Writers of America; International Society of Poets. *Publications:* The Humanities: Classical Athens, Renaissance Florence and Contemporary New York, 1970; Bibliographic Materials on Indian Culture, 1972; Let Us Be Modern (poems), English, Italian, 1985; INAGO Newsletter (poems), 1988; Is Anybody Listening? (poems), English, 1990; Flap Your Wings (poems), 1992; Rosebushes and the Poor (poems), Italian, 1993. Contributions: anthologies and periodicals. *Honours:* Purple Heart, Bronze Star, 1944; John Hay Fellowship, 1958–59; Asian Studies Fellow, 1965–66; First Prize, Chapbook Competition, The Poet, 1985, 1986; Gold Medal, Istituto Carlo Capodieci, 1987; INAGO Newspaper Poet, 1989.

GALL, Henderson Alexander, (Sandy Gall); Television Journalist; b. 1 Oct. 1927, Penang, Malaysia; m. Aug. 1958, one s., three d. *Education:* MA, Aberdeen University, Scotland, 1952. *Publications:* Gold Scoop, 1977; Chasing the Dragon, 1981; Don't Worry about the Money Now, 1983; Behind Russian Lines: An Afghan Journal, 1983; Afghanistan: Agony of a Nation, 1988; Salang, 1989; George Adamson: Lord of the Lions, 1991; News From the Front: The Life of a Television Reporter, 1994; The Bushmen of Southern Africa: Slaughter of the Innocent, 2001. *Honours:* Rector, 1978–81, Hon. LLD, 1981, Aberdeen University; Sitara-i-Pakistan, 1986; Lawrence of Arabia Medal, 1987; CBE, 1988. *Literary Agent:* PFD, Drury House, 34–43 Russell St, London WC2B 5HA, England.

GALLAGHER, Tess; Poet and Writer; b. 21 July 1943, Port Angeles, Washington, USA; m. 1st Lawrence Gallagher, 1963, divorced 1968; m. 2nd Michael Burkard, 1973, divorced 1977; m. 3rd Raymond Carver, 1988, deceased. *Education:* BA, 1969, MA, 1970, University of Washington, Seattle; MFA, University of Iowa, 1974. *Career:* Instructor, St Lawrence University, Canton, New York, 1974–75; Asst Prof., Kirkland College, Clinton, New York, 1975–77; Visiting Lecturer, University of Montana, 1977–78; Asst Prof., University of Arizona, Tucson, 1979–80; Prof. of English, Syracuse University, 1980–89; Visiting Fellow, Williamette University, Salem, Oregon, 1981; Cockefair Chair Writer-in-Residence, University of Missouri, Kansas City, 1994; Poet-in-Residence, Trinity College, Hartford, CT, 1994; Edward F. Arnold Visiting Prof. of English, Whitman College, Walla Walla, Washington 1996–97; Poet-in-Residence Bucknell University 1998; mem. Writers Union, PEN, American Poetry Society, Poets and Writers. *Publications:* Poetry: Stepping Outside, 1974; Instructions to the Double, 1976; Under Stars, 1978; Portable Kisses, 1978; On Your Own, 1978; Willingly, 1984; Amplitude: New and Selected Poems, 1987; Moon Crossing Bridge, 1992; The Valentine Elegies, 1993; Portable Kisses Expanded, 1994; My Black Horse: New and Selected Poems, 1995. Short Stories: The Lover of Horses, 1986; At the Owl Woman Saloon, 1997, various magazine publs of stories written with Irish storyteller Jose Gray. Non-Fiction: A Concert of Tenses: Essays on Poetry, 1986; Soul Barnacles: Ten More Years with Ray, 2000. Translator: The Sky Behind the Forest, by Liliana Ursu (with Liliana Ursu and Adam Sorkin), 1997. Other: Screenplay: Dostoevsky (with Raymond Carver), 1985; many introductions to the works of Raymond Carver, 1988–2000, Introduction to Alfredo Arreguin, Patterns of Dreams and Nature. Contributions: many anthologies. *Honours:* Elliston Award, 1976; National Endowment for the Arts Grants, 1977, 1981, 1987; Guggenheim Fellowship, 1978; American Poetry Review Award, 1981; Washington State Governor's Awards, 1984, 1986, 1987, 1993; New York State Arts Grant, 1988; Maxine Cushing Gray Foundation Award, 1990; American Library Asscn Most Notable Book List, 1993; Lyndhurst Prize, 1993; Trans. Award, 1997; Hon. DHL, Whitman College, Walla Walla, Washington, 1998; Pryor Award for Literary Excellence, 1999. *Literary Agent:* International Creative Management, 40 W 57th Street, New York, NY 10019, USA.

GALLAHER, John Gerard, BA, MA, PhD; academic and writer; *Professor of History Emeritus, Southern Illinois University at Edwardsville*; b. 28 Dec. 1928, St Louis, MO, USA; m. C. Maia Hofacker 1956; one s. two d. *Education:* University of Paris, University of Grenoble, Washington University, St Louis University. *Career:* Prof. to Prof. of History Emeritus, Southern Illinois University at Edwardsville; mem. Napoleonic Alliance (pres. 2001–03). *Publications:* The Iron Marshal: A Biography of Louis N. Davout, 1976; The Students of Paris and the Revolution of 1848, 1980; Napoleon's Irish Legion, 1993; General Alexandre Dumas: Soldier of the French Revolution, 1997. Contributions: Reference works, books and scholarly journals. *Honours:* Fulbright Research Scholar, France 1959–60, University Research Fellow, Southern Illinois University at Edwardsville 1978–79, Chevalier, Ordre des Palmes Académiques, Int. Napoleonic Soc. Legion of Merit. *Address:* 8461 SE 71st Street, Mercer Island, WA 98040, USA.

GALLANT, Mavis, CC, OC, FRSL; Canadian writer and literary critic; b. 11 Aug. 1922, Montréal, QC. *Education:* schools in Montréal and New York, USA. *Career:* Employee Nat. Film Bd of Canada and Montréal Standard; emigrated to France 1950; short stories published The New Yorker 1951–; has written reviews and essays for New York Review of Books, The New

York Times Book Review; Writer-in-Residence Univ. of Toronto 1983–84; Hon. mem. American Acad. and Inst. of Arts and Letters 1989. *Publications:* short stories: The Other Paris 1956, My Heart is Broken 1964, The Pegnitz Junction 1973, The End of the World 1974, From the Fifteenth District 1978, Home Truths (Gov.-Gen. Award 1982) 1981, Overhead in a Balloon 1985, In Transit 1988, Across the Bridge 1993, Paris Notebooks 1997, The Selected Stories of Mavis Gallant 2004; novels: Green Water, Green Sky 1969, A Fairly Good Time 1970; play: What is to Be Done? 1984; non-fiction: Paris Journals: Selected Reviews and Essays 1986. *Honours:* Hon. degree (Univ. Sainte Anne), Pointe de Eglise, NS 1984, Hon. LLD (Queen's) 1991; Canada-Australia Literary Prize 1984, Canada Council Molson Prize for the Arts 1997; Tributee Int. Authors Festival, Harbourfront, Toronto 1993. *Address:* c/o McLelland & Stewart, Suite 900, 481 University Avenue, Toronto, ON M5G 2E9, Canada.

GALLANT, Roy Arthur; Author and Teacher; b. 17 April 1924, Portland, Maine, USA; m. Kathryn Dale, 1952, two s. *Education:* BA, 1948, Bowdoin College; MS, 1949, Columbia University; Doctoral work, Columbia University, 1953–59. *Career:* Managing Ed., Scholastic Teachers Magazine, 1954–57; Author-in-Residence, Doubleday, 1957–59; Editorial Dir, Aldus Books, London, 1959–62; Ed.-in-Chief, The Natural History Press, 1962–65; Consultant, The Edison Project, Israel Arts and Sciences Acad.; Dir, Southworth Planetarium, 1980–2000, Prof. Emeritus, 2001–, Univ. Southern Maine. *Publications:* Approximately 100 books, including: Our Universe, 1986; Private Lives of the Stars, 1986; Rainbows, Mirages and Sundogs, 1987; Before the Sun Dies, 1989; Ancient Indians, 1989; The Peopling of Planet Earth, 1990; Earth's Vanishing Forests, 1991; A Young Person's Guide to Science, 1993; The Day the Sky Split Apart, 1995; Geysers, 1997; Sand Dunes, 1997; Limestone Caves, 1998; Planet Earth, 1998; When the Sun Dies, 1998; Glaciers, 1999; The Ever-Changing Atom, 1999; Earth's Place in Space, 1999; Early Humans, 1999; Dance of the Continents, 1999; The Origins of Life, 2000; The Life Stories of Stars, 2000; Stars, 2000; Rocks, 2000; Minerals, 2000; Fossils, 2000; Comets and Asteroids, 2000; The Planets, 2000; Water, 2000; Space Station, 2000; Meteorite Hunter, 2002; Earth Structure, 2003; Earth History, 2003; Plate Tectonics, 2003; Natural Resources, 2003; Earth's Atmosphere, 2003; Earth's Water, 2003; Inheritance, 2003; Biodiversity, 2003. *Honours:* Thomas Alva Edison Foundation Mass Media Award, 1955; Distinguished Achievement Award, University of Southern Maine, 1981; John Burroughs Award for Nature Writing, 1995; Lifetime Achievement Award, Maine Library Asscn, 2001. *Address:* PO Box 228, Beaver Mountain Lake, Rangeley, ME 04970, USA.

GALLEGO, Rubén David González; Russian writer; b. 1968, Moscow. *Career:* emigrated to France, resident in Spain. *Publications:* Byeloye na chernom (trans. as White on Black) (Booker-Open Russia Prize) 2003. *Address:* c/o Alfaguara de Novela, Torrelaguna 60, 28043, Madrid, Spain. *Telephone:* (91) 7449060. *Fax:* (91) 7449224. *Website:* www.alfaguara.santillana.es.

GALLINER, Peter; British publisher; *Chairman, Peter Galliner Associates*; b. 19 Sept. 1920, Berlin, Germany; m. 1st Edith Marguerite Goldschmidt 1948; one d.; m. 2nd Helga Stenschke 1990. *Education:* in Berlin and London. *Career:* worked for Reuters, London 1942–45; Foreign Man. Financial Times, London 1945–61; Chair. of Bd and Man. Dir Ullstein Publishing Group, Berlin 1961–64; Vice-Chair. and Man. Dir British Printing Corpn Publishing Group, London 1967–70; Int. Publishing Consultant 1965–67, 1970–75; Chair. Peter Galliner Assocs 1970–; Dir Int. Press. Inst. 1975–93; Chair. Int. Encounters London/Zürich/Berlin 1995–. *Honours:* Fed. Cross of Merit, First Class (FRG) 1961, Encomienda, Orden de Isabel la Católica (Spain) 1982, Kt Commdr's Cross (Badge and Star) of Order of Merit (FRG) 1990, Press Freedom Award (Turkey) 1995, Europäischer Media and Communications Award (Poland) 1998. *Address:* Bregenzerstrasse 3, D-10707 Berlin, Germany; Untere Zäune 9, 8001 Zürich, Switzerland. *Telephone:* (30) 887-1166 (Berlin); (1) 2518664 (Zürich). *Fax:* (30) 887-11677 (Berlin).

GALLO, Max Louis, DenH, DèsSc; French politician, writer and university teacher; b. 7 Jan. 1932, Nice. *Education:* Univ. de Paris and Inst. d'Etudes Politiques. *Career:* teacher Lycée de Nice 1960–65; Sr Lecturer Univ. of Nice 1965–70; Gen. Ed. book series Ce Jour-là, l'Histoire que nous vivons, la Vie selon..., le Temps des révélations; contrib. to various newspapers; devised TV programme Destins du Siècle 1973; Deputy (Socialist) for Alpes-Maritimes 1981–83; jr minister and Govt spokesman 1983–84; Ed. Matin de Paris newspaper 1985–86; MEP 1984–94; Nat. Sec. (Culture) Parti Socialiste 1988–90. *Publications:* L'Italie de Mussolini 1964, La Grande Peur de 1989 (as Max Laugham) 1966, L'Affaire d'Ethiopie 1967, Maximilien Robespierre, Histoire d'une solitude 1968, Gauchisme, réformisme et révolution 1968, Histoire de l'Espagne franquiste 1969, Cinquième Colonne 1930–1940 1970, la Nuit des longs couteaux 1970, Tombeau pour la Commune, Histoire de l'Espagne franquiste 1971, Le Cortège des vainqueurs 1972, La Mafia, un pas vers la mer 1973, L'Affiche, miroir de l'Histoire (illustrated) 1973, L'Oiseau des origines 1974: La Baie des anges (Vol. I) 1975, Le Palais des fêtes (Vol. II) 1976, La Promenade des Anglais (Vol. III) 1976, Le Pouvoir à vif, Despotisme, démocratie et révolution, Que sont les siècles pour la mer 1977, Les hommes naissent tous le même jour: Aurore (Vol. I) 1978, Crépuscule (Vol. II) 1979, Une affaire intime 1979, L'Homme Robespierre: histoire d'une solitude 1978, Un crime très ordinaire 1982, Garibaldi 1982, La Demeure des puissants 1983, La Troisième alliance, pour un nouvel individualisme, Le Grand Jaurès 1984, Le Beau Rivage 1985, Lettre ouverte à Maximilien Robespierre sur les nouveaux Muscadins, Belle Epoque 1986, Que passe la justice du roi, la Route Napoléon 1987, Jules Vallès 1988, Une Affaire publique 1989, Les Clés de l'histoire contemporaine 1989, Manifeste pour une fin de siècle obscure 1989, La Gauche est morte, vive la gauche! 1990, Le Regard des femmes 1991, La Fontaine des innocents (Prix Carlton 1992), Une femme rebelle: Vie et mort de Rosa Luxembourg 1992, L'Amour au temps des solitudes 1993, Les Rois sans visage 1994, Le Condottiere 1994, Le Fils de Klara H. 1995, L'Ambitieuse 1995, La Part de Dieu 1996, Le Faiseur d'or 1996, La Femme derrière le miroir, Napoléon, Le chant du départ (biog., Vol. I) 1997, L'Immortel de Saint-Hélène (Vol. IV) 1997, De Gaulle: L'Appel du destin (Vol. I) 1998, La Solitude du combattant (Vol. II) 1998, Le Premier des Français (Vol. III) 1998, La Statue du Commandeur (Vol. IV) 1998, L'Amour de la France expliqué a mon fils, le Jardin des oliviers 1999, Bleu, blanc, rouge (Vol. I: Mariella) 2000, Les Patriotes (four vols) 2000–01. *Address:* Editions Robert Laffont, 24 avenue Marceau, 75008 Paris, France.

GALLOWAY, Janice; Writer; b. 2 Dec. 1956, Ayrshire, Scotland; one s. *Education:* Ardrossan Acad., Univ. of Glasgow, 1974–78. *Career:* Singing Waitress, 1972–74; Welfare Rights Worker, 1976; Teacher of English, 1980–90; mem. Society of Authors. *Publications:* The Trick is to Keep Breathing, 1990; Blood, 1991; Foreign Parts, 1994; Where You Find It, 1996; Pipelines (with Anne Bevan), 2000; Monster (opera with Sally Beamish), 2002; Clara, 2002; boy book see, 2003. *Honours:* MIND/Alan Lane Prize; Scottish Arts Council Award; Scottish Arts Council Award, 1994; McVitie's Prize, 1994; American Acad. of Arts and Letters E. M. Forster Award, 1994; Creative Scotland Award, 2001; Saltire Book of the Year, 2002. *Literary Agent:* AP Watt Ltd, 20 John St, London WC1N 2DR, England.

GALTON, Herbert; University Prof. and Writer; b. 1 Oct. 1917, Vienna, Austro-Hungary; m. 28 Jan. 1992. *Education:* High School, Vienna, 1935; University of Vienna, 1935–38; PhD, Russian Philology, University of London, 1951. *Career:* Prof., University of Kansas, 1962–88; mem. Austrian Writers' Union; Austrian PEN Club; Societas Linguistica Europaea. *Publications:* Aorist und Aspekt im Slavischen, 1962; The Main Functions of the Slavic Verbal Aspect, 1976; Freedom from Illusions, 1994; Der Einfluss des Altaischen auf die Entsehung des Slavischen, 1997; Reisetagebuch, (poems), 1990; Balkanisches Tagebuch, 1998. Contributions: The Equality Principle (anthology), 1974; Lyrische Annalen, 1994, 1995. Contributions: Over 100 linguistic articles in various periodicals. *Honours:* Gold Medal, Macedonian Acad. of Sciences, 1987. *Address:* Kaiserstrasse 12/18, 1070 Vienna, Austria.

GALVIN, Brendan; Prof. of English and Poet; b. 20 Oct. 1938, Everett, Massachusetts, USA; m. Ellen Baer, 1968, one s. one d. *Education:* BS, Boston College, 1960; MA, Northeastern University, 1964; MFA, 1967, PhD, 1970, University of Massachusetts. *Career:* Instructor, Northeastern University, 1964–65; Asst Prof., Slippery Rock State College, 1968–69; Asst Prof., 1969–74, Assoc. Prof., 1974–80, Prof. of English, 1980–, Central Connecticut State University; Visiting Prof., Connecticut College, 1975–76; Ed. (with George Garrett), Poultry: A Magazine of Voice, 1981–; Coal Royalty Chairholder in Creative Writing, University of Alabama, 1993. *Publications:* The Narrow Land, 1971; The Salt Farm, 1972; No Time for Good Reasons, 1974; The Minutes No One Owns, 1977; Atlantic Flyway, 1980; Winter Oysters, 1983; A Birder's Dozen, 1984; Seals in the Inner Harbour, 1985; Wampanoag Traveler, 1989; Raising Irish Walls, 1989; Great Blue: New and Selected Poems, 1990; Early Returns, 1992; Saints in Their Ox-Hide Boat, 1992; Islands, 1993; Hotel Malabar, 1998. *Honours:* National Endowment for the Arts Fellowships, 1974, 1988; Connecticut Commission on the Arts Fellowships, 1981, 1984; Guggenheim Fellowship, 1988; Sotheby Prize, Arvon International Foundation, 1988; Levinson Prize, Poetry magazine, 1989; O. B. Hardison Jr Poetry Prize, Folger Shakespeare Library, 1991; Charity Randall Citation, International Poetry Forum, 1994. *Address:* c/o Dept of English, Central Connecticut State University, New Britain, CT 06050, USA.

GAMBONE, Philip Arthur; Teacher and Writer; b. 21 July 1948, Melrose, Massachusetts, USA. *Education:* AB, Harvard University, 1970; MA, Episcopal Divinity School, 1976. *Career:* mem. PEN. *Publications:* Author or contributing author of 10 books including Men on Men III, 1990; Sister and Brother, 1994; Men on Men VI, 1996. Contributions: book reviews to New York Times; Lambda Book Report; Bay Windows. *Honours:* MacDowell Colony Fellow; Helene Wurlitzer Foundation Award, 1996. *Address:* 47 Waldeck St, Dorchester, MA 02124, USA.

GANDER, Forrest; Prof., Poet and Ed.; b. 21 Jan. 1956, Barstow, CA, USA; m. C. D. Wright, 1983, one s. *Career:* Co-Ed., Lost Road Publishers, 1982–; Prof., Dir of graduate programme in literary arts, Brown University; mem. Associated Writing Programs; PEN. *Publications:* Rush to the Lake, 1988; Eggplants and Lotus Root, 1991; Lynchburg, 1993; Mouth to Mouth: Poems by 12 Contemporary Mexican Women (ed.), 1993; Deeds of Utmost Kindness, 1994; Science of Steepleflower, 1998; Torn Awake, 2001; Immanent Visitor: Selected Poems of Jaime Saenz (trans. with Kent Johnson), 2001. *Address:* 351 Nayatt Rd, Barrington, RI 02806, USA. *Website:* www.brown.edu/Departments/English/Writing/people/gander/.

GANT, Richard (see Freemantle, Brian (Harry)).

GAO XINGJIAN, BA; French writer and dramatist; b. 4 Jan. 1940, Ganzhou, Jiangxi Prov., People's Republic of China. *Education:* Dept of Foreign Languages, Beijing. *Career:* translator China Reconstructs (magazine), later for Chinese Writers Asscn.; writer for People's Art Troupe; spent five years in "re-education" during Cultural Revolution; left China 1987 after work banned in 1985, living in Paris 1988–. *Publications:* plays: Wild Man 1990, Bus Stop, The Other Shore 1999, Fugitives 1993; novels: Soul Mountain 1999, Return to Painting 2001, One Man's Bible 2002; other: Snow in August (opera) 2002, Buying a Fishing Rod for my Grandfather (short stories) 2004. *Honours:* Chevalier des Arts et des Lettres 1992; Prix Communauté française de Belgium 1994, Prix du Nouvel An Chinois 1997, Nobel Prize for Literature 2000. *Address:* c/o Swedish Academy, PO Box 5232, Sturegatan 14, 10245 Stockholm, Sweden.

GAO YING; Chinese author and poet; b. 25 Dec. 1929, Jiaozuo, Henan; m. Duan Chuanchen 1954; one s. two d. *Career:* Vice-Chair. Sichuan Br. and mem. Council, Chinese Writers' Asscn; Deputy Dir Ed. Bd, Sichuan Prov. Broadcasting Station 1983–; mem. Sichuan Political Consultative Conf. *Publications:* The Song of Ding Youjun, Lamplights around the Three Gorges, High Mountains and Distant Rivers, Cloudy Cliff (novel), Da Ji and her Fathers (novel and film script), The Orchid (novel), Loving-Kindness of the Bamboo Storey (collection of prose), Mother in my Heart (autobiographical novel), Songs of Da Liang Mountains (poems), Frozen Snowflakes (poems), Reminiscences, Xue Ma (novel), Gao Ying (short stories). *Address:* Sichuan Branch of Chinese Association of Literary and Art Workers, Buhou-jie Street, Chengdu, Sichuan, People's Republic of China. *Telephone:* 66782836.

GARAFOLA, Lynn, AB, PhD; dance critic, historian and teacher; b. 12 Dec. 1946, New York, NY, USA; m. Eric Foner 1980; one d. *Education:* Barnard College, CUNY. *Career:* Ed., Studies in Dance History, 1990–99; Adjunct Prof., Dept of Dance, Barnard College, New York, 2000–; mem. Society of Dance History Scholars; Dance Critics Asscn. *Publications:* Diaghilev's Ballets Russes, André Levinson on Dance: Writings from Paris in the Twenties (ed. with Joan Acocella), The Diaries of Marius Petipa (ed. and trans.), Jose Limon: An Unfinished Memoir (ed.), Dance for a City: Fifty Years of the New York City Ballet (ed.), The Ballets Russes and Its World (ed.), Legacies of 20th-Century Dance; contrib. to Dance Magazine, Dance Research, Ballet Review, Nation, Women's Review of Books, TLS, New York Times Book Review. *Honours:* Torre de los Buenos Prize, 1989; CORD Award for Outstanding Publication, 1999; Kurt Weill Prize, 2001. *Address:* 606 W 116th Street, New York, NY 10027, USA. *E-mail:* lg97@columbia .edu.

GARCÍA MÁRQUEZ, Gabriel (Gabo) José; Colombian writer; b. 6 March 1928, Aracataca; m. Mercedes Barch March 1958; two s. *Education:* secondary school and Universidad Nacional de Colombia, Universidad de Cartagena. *Career:* began writing books 1946; lived in Baranquilla; corresp. El Espectador in Rome, Paris; first novel published while living in Caracas, Venezuela 1957; est. bureau of Prensa Latina (Cuban press agency) in Bogotá; worked for Prensa Latina in Havana, Cuba, then as Deputy Head of New York Office 1961; lived in Spain, contributing to magazines Mundo Nuevo, Casa de las Américas; went to Mexico; founder-Pres., Fundación Habeas 1979–; invited back to Colombia by Pres. July 1982; Hon. Fellow, American Acad. of Arts and Letters. *Publications:* fiction: La hojarasca (trans. as Leaf Storm and Other Stories) 1955, El coronel no tiene quien le escriba (trans. as No One Writes to the Colonel and Other Stories) 1961, La mala hora (trans. as In Evil Hour) 1962, Los funerales de la Mamá Grande (trans. as Funerals of the Great Matriarch) 1962, Cien años de soledad (trans. as One Hundred Years of Solitude) 1967, Isabel viendo llover en Macondo 1967, La increíble y triste historia de la cándida Eréndira y su abuela desalmada (trans. as Innocent Erendira and Other Stories) 1972, El negro que hizo esperar a los angeles 1972, Ojos de perro azul 1972, El otoño del patriarca (trans. as The Autumn of the Patriarch) 1975, Todos los cuentos de Gabriel García Márquez: 1947–1972 1975, Crónica de una muerte anunciada (trans. as Chronicle of a Death Foretold) 1981, El rastro de tu sangre en la nieve: El verano feliz de la señora Forbes 1982, María de mi corazón (screenplay, with J. H. Hermosillo) 1983, Collected Stories 1984, El amor en los tiempos del cólera (trans. as Love in the Time of Cholera) 1984, El General en su laberinto (trans. as The General in his Labyrinth) 1989, Amores difíciles 1989, Doce cuentos peregrinos (trans. as Strange Pilgrims: Twelve Stories) 1992, Del amor y otros demonios (trans. as Of Love and Other Demons) 1994, La bendita manía de contar 1998; non-fiction: La novela en América Latina: Diálogo (with Mario Vargas Llosa) 1968, Relato de un náufrago (trans. as The Story of a Shipwrecked Sailor) 1970, Cuando era feliz e indocumentado 1973, Crónicas y reportajes 1978, Periodismo militante 1978, De viaje por los países socialistas: 90 días en la 'cortina de hierro' 1978, Obra periodistica (four vols) 1981–83, El olor de la guayaba: Conversaciones con Plinio Apuleyo Mendoza (trans. as The Fragrance of Guava) 1982, Persecución y muerte de minorías: Dos perspectivas 1984, La aventura de Miguel Littín, clandestino en Chile: Un reportaje (trans. as Clandestine in Chile: The Adventures of Miguel Littín) 1986, Primeros reportajes 1990, Notas de prensa 1980–1984 1991, Elogio de la utopia: una entrevista de Nahuel Maciel 1992, Noticia de un secuestro (trans. as News of a Kidnapping) 1996, Vivir para contarla (memoir, vol. one, trans. as Living to Tell the Tale) 2002. *Honours:* Hon. LLD (Columbia Univ., New York) 1971; Colombian Asscn of Writers and Artists Award 1954, Premio Literario Esso (Colombia) 1961, Chianciano Award (Italy) 1969, Prix de Meilleur Livre Étranger (France) 1969, Books Abroad/ Neustadt International Prize for Literature 1972, Rómulo Gallegos Prize (Venezuela) 1972, Nobel Prize for Literature 1982, Los Angeles Times Book Prize for Fiction 1988, Serfin Prize 1989, Premio Príncipe de Asturias 1999. *Literary Agent:* Agencia Literaria Carmen Balcelos, Diagonal 580, Barcelona, Spain.

GARCÍA SÁNCHEZ, Javier; Spanish writer and poet; b. 1955, Barcelona. *Publications:* Lady of the South Wind 1990, La historia más triste 1991, La vida fosil 1998, Falta alma 2001, The Others 2002, Indurain: A Tempered Passion 2002, Dios se ha ido 2003. *Address:* c/o Dedalus Ltd, Langford Lodge, St Judith's Lane, Sawtry, Cambridgeshire PE28 5XE, England. *E-mail:* info@dedalusbooks.com. *Website:* www.dedalusbooks.com.

GARDAM, Jane Mary; Writer; b. 11 July 1928, Yorkshire, England; m. David Hill Gardam, 20 April 1954, two s. one d. *Education:* BA, Bedford College, London, 1949. *Career:* Sub-Ed., Weldon's Ladies Journal, 1952; Asst Literary Ed., Time and Tide, 1952–54; mem. PEN; FRSL. *Publications:* Fiction: A Long Way From Verona, 1971; The Summer After the Funeral, 1973; Bilgewater, 1977; God on the Rocks, 1978; The Hollow Land, 1981; Bridget and William, 1981; Horse, 1982; Kit, 1983; Crusoe's Daughter, 1985; Kit in Boots, 1986; Swan, 1987; Through the Doll's House Door, 1987; The Queen of the Tambourine, 1991; Faith Fox, 1995; Tufty Bear, 1996; The Green Man, 1998; The Flight of the Maidens, 2000. Short Stories: A Few Fair Days, 1971; Black Faces, White Faces, 1975; The Sidmouth Letters, 1980; The Pangs of Love, 1983; Showing the Flag, 1989; Going Into a Dark House, 1994; Missing the Midnight, 1997. Non-Fiction: The Iron Coast, 1994. Contributions: newspapers and magazines. *Honours:* David Higham Award, 1978; Winifred Holtby Award, 1978; Whitbread Literary Award, 1983, Novel Award, 1991, and Fiction Award, 1992; Katherine Mansfield Award, 1984; Silver Pen Award, PEN, 1995. *Address:* Haven House, Sandwich, Kent CT13 9ES, England.

GARDEL, Louis; French publishing editor, novelist and screenwriter; b. 8 Sept. 1939, Algiers, Algeria; m. 1st Béatrice Herr (deceased) 1963; m. 2nd Hélène Millerand 1990; two s. two d. *Education:* Lycée Bugeaud, Algiers, Lycée Louis-le-Grand, Paris and Institut d'Etudes Politiques, Paris. *Career:* Head of Dept Inst. des Hautes Etudes d'Outre-Mer 1962–64; Man. Soc. Rhône-Progil 1964–74; Head of Dept Conseil Nat. du Patronat 1974–80; Literary Consultant, Editions du Seuil 1980, Literary Ed. 1980–; mem. juries Prix Renaudot, Conseil Supérieur de la Langue Française. *Film screenplays:* Fort Saganne, Nocturne Indien, Indochine, La Marche de Radetzky 1996, Est.Ouest, Himalaya 1999. *Publications:* L'Eté Fracassé 1973, Couteau de chaleur 1976, Fort Saganne 1980 (Grand Prix du Roman de l'Acad. française), Notre Homme 1986, Le Beau Rôle 1989, Darbaroud 1993. L'Aurore des Bien-Aimés 1997, Grand-Seigneur 1999. *Address:* Editions du Seuil, 27 rue Jacob, 75004 Paris (Office); 25 rue de la Cerisaie, 75004, Paris, France (Home). *Telephone:* 1-40-46-50-50.

GARDEN, Bruce (see Mackay, James Alexander).

GARDEN, Nancy, BFA, MA; writer, editor and teacher; b. 15 May 1938, Boston, Massachusetts, USA. *Education:* Columbia University School of Dramatic Arts, Teachers College, Columbia University. *Career:* Actress, Lighting Designer, 1954–64; Teacher of Speech and Dramatics, 1961–64; Ed., educational materials, textbooks, 1964–76; Teacher of Writing, Adult Education, 1974; Correspondence School, 1974–; mem. Society of Children's Book Writers and Illustrators. *Publications:* What Happened in Marston, 1971; The Loners, 1972; Maria's Mountain, 1981; Fours Crossing, 1981; Annie on My Mind, 1982; Favourite Tales from Grimm, 1982; Watersmeet, 1983; Prisoner of Vampires, 1984; Peace, O River, 1986; The Door Between, 1987; Lark in the Morning, 1991; My Sister, the Vampire, 1992; Dove and Sword, 1995; My Brother, the Werewolf, 1995; Good Moon Rising, 1996; The Year They Burned the Books, 1999. The Monster Hunter series: Case No. 1, Mystery of the Night Raiders, 1987; Case No. 2: Mystery of the Midnight Menace, 1988; Case No. 3: Mystery of the Secret Marks, 1989; Case No. 4: Mystery of the Kidnapped Kidnapper, 1994; Case No. 5: Mystery of the Watchful Witches, 1995. Non-Fiction: Berlin: City Split in Two, 1971; Vampires, 1973; Werewolves, 1973; Witches, 1975; Devils and Demons, 1976; Fun with Forecasting Weather, 1977; The Kids' Code and Cipher Book, 1981. Contributions: Lambda Book Report.

GARDONS, S. S. (see Snodgrass, W. D.).

GARFINKEL, Patricia Gail; Poet and Writer; b. 15 Feb. 1938, New York, NY, USA; two s. *Education:* BA, New York University. *Career:* mem. Poets and Writers. *Publications:* Ram's Horn (poems), 1980; From the Red Eye of Jupiter (poems), 1990; Making the Skeleton Dance, 2000. Contributions: numerous anthologies and other publications. *Honours:* Poetry in Public Places Award for New York State, 1977; First Prize, Lip Service Poetry Competition, 1990; Book Competition, Washington Writers Publishing House, 1990; Winner, Moving Words competition. *Address:* 900 N Stuart St, Suite 1001, Arlington, Virginia, 22203, USA.

GARFITT, Roger; Poet and Writer; b. 12 April 1944, Melksham, Wiltshire, England. *Education:* BA, Merton College, Oxford, 1968. *Career:* Arts Council Creative Writing Fellow, University College of North Wales, Bangor, 1975–77, and Poet-in-Residence, Sunderland Polytechnic,

1978–80; Ed., Poetry Review, 1977–82; Welsh Arts Council Poet-in-Residence, Ebbw Vale, 1984; Poet-in-Residence, Pilgrim College, Boston, 1986–87, Blyth Valley Disabled Forum, 1992; mem. National Asscn of Writers in Education: Poetry Society; Welsh Acad. *Publications:* Caught on Blue, 1970; West of Elm, 1974; The Broken Road, 1982; Rowlstone Haiku (with Frances Horovitz), 1982; Given Ground, 1989; Border Songs, 1996. Contributions: journals, reviews, and magazines. *Honours:* Guinness International Poetry Prize, 1973; Gregory Award, 1974. *Address:* c/o Jane Turnbull, 13 Wendell Rd, London W12 9RS, England.

GARLAND, Alex, BA; British writer; b. 1970, London, England. *Education:* Univ. of Manchester. *Career:* occasionally works as an illustrator and a freelance journalist. *Publications:* The Beach (novel) 1996, The Tesseract (novel) 1999, 28 Days Later (screenplay) 2002, The Coma (novel) 2004. *Address:* c/o Faber and Faber Ltd, 3 Queen Square, London, WC1N 3AU, England.

GARLICK, Raymond; Poet and Lecturer (retd); b. 21 Sept. 1926, London, England; m. Elin Jane Hughes, 1948, one s. one d. *Education:* BA, University College of North Wales, Bangor, 1948. *Career:* Principal Lecturer, Trinity College, Carmarthen, 1972–86. *Publications:* Poetry: Poems from the Mountain-House, 1950; Requiem for a Poet, 1954; Poems from Pembrokeshire, 1954; The Welsh-Speaking Sea, 1954; Blaenau Observed, 1957; Landscapes and Figures: Selected Poems, 1949–63, 1964; A Sense of Europe: Collected Poems, 1954–68, 1968; A Sense of Time: Poems and Antipoems, 1969–72, 1972; Incense: Poems, 1972–75, 1975; Collected Poems, 1946–86, 1987; Travel Notes: New Poems, 1992; The Delphic Voyage, 2003. Other: An Introduction to Anglo-Welsh Literature, 1970; Anglo-Welsh Poetry, 1480–1980 (ed.), 1982. *Honours:* Welsh Arts Council Prizes; Hon. Fellow, Trinity College, Carmarthen; Fellow, Welsh Acad.; DLitt, Central University, Pella, IA, 1998. *Address:* 26 Glannant House, College Rd, Carmarthen SA31 3EF, Wales.

GARLINSKI, Jozef; Writer; b. 14 Oct. 1913, Poland. *Education:* MA, University of Warsaw, 1942; PhD, LSE, 1973. *Career:* Chair., Exec. Committee, Polish Home Army Circle, London, 1954–65; Cultural Vice-Chair., Polish Cultural and Social Centre, London, 1970–79; Chair., Union of Polish Writers Abroad, 1975–. *Publications:* Dramat i Opatrznosc, 1961; Matki i zony, 1962; Ziemia (novel), 1964; Miedzy Londynem i Warszawa, 1966; Polish SOE and the Allies, 1969; Fighting Auschwitz, 1975; Hitler's Last Weapons, 1978; Intercept: Secrets of the Enigma War, 1979; The Swiss Corridor, 1981; Polska w Drugiej Wojnie Swiatowej, 1982; Poland in the Second World War, 1985; Szwajcarski Kryterz, 1987; Niezapomniane lata, 1987; The Survival of Love, 1991; Swiat mojej pamięci, I, 1992; Swiat mojej pamięci, II, 1998. *Address:* 94 Ramillies Rd, London W4 1JA, England.

GARNER, Alan, OBE; writer; b. 17 Oct. 1934, Cheshire, England; m. 1st Ann Cook 1956 (divorced); one s. two d.; m. 2nd Griselda Greaves 1972; one s. one d. *Education:* Magdalen College, Oxford. *Career:* mem., International Editorial Board, Detskaya Literatura Publishers, Moscow, 1991–; mem. Portico Library, Manchester. *Publications:* The Weirdstone of Brisingamen, 1960; The Moon of Gomrath, 1963; Elidor, 1965; Holly from the Bongs, 1966; The Owl Service, 1967; The Book of Goblins, 1969; Red Shift, 1973; The Guizer, 1975; The Stone Book Quartet, 1976–78; Fairy Tales of Gold, 1979; The Lad of the Gad, 1980; British Fairy Tales, 1984; A Bag of Moonshine, 1986; Jack and the Beanstalk, 1992; Once Upon a Time, 1993; Strandloper, 1996; The Voice that Thunders, 1997; The Well of the Wind, 1998; Thursbitch, 2003. *Honours:* Carnegie Medal, 1967; Guardian Award, 1968; Lewis Carroll Shelf Award, USA, 1970; Gold Plaque, Chicago International Film Festival, 1981; Children's Literature Asscn International Phoenix Award, 1996. *Literary Agent:* Sheil Land Associates Ltd, 43 Doughty Street, London, WC1N 2LF, England. *Address:* Blackden, Holmes Chapel, Crewe, Cheshire CW4 8BY, England.

GARNER, Helen; novelist and journalist; b. 7 Nov. 1942, Geelong, Vic., Australia; m. 3rd Murray Bail 1992 (divorced 1998); one d. *Education:* BA, Melbourne University, 1965. *Publications:* Monkey Grip, 1977; Honour, and Other People's Children, 1980; The Children's Bach, 1984; Postcards from Surfers, 1985; Cosmo Cosmolino, 1992; The Last Days of Chez Nous, 1993; The First Stone, 1995; True Stories, 1996, The Feel of Steel 2001. *Honours:* Hon. DLitt (Newcastle) 2003, Hon. LLD (Melbourne) 2003. *Address:* c/o Barbara Mobbs, PO Box 126, Edgecliff, NSW 2027, Australia.

GARNETT, Richard (Duncan Carey); Writer, Publisher and Trans; b. 8 Jan. 1923, London, England. *Education:* BA, King's College, Cambridge, 1948; MA, 1987. *Career:* Production Man., 1955–59, Dir, 1957–66, Rupert Hart-Davis Ltd; Dir, Adlard Coles Ltd, 1963–66; Ed., 1966–82, Dir, 1972–82, Macmillan London; Dir, Macmillan Publishers, 1982–87. *Publications:* Goldsmith: Selected Works (ed.), 1950; Robert Gruss: The Art of the Aqualung (trans.), 1955; The Silver Kingdom (in US as The Undersea Treasure), 1956; Bernard Heuvelmans: On the Track of Unknown Animals (trans.), 1958; The White Dragon, 1963; Jack of Dover, 1966; Bernard Heuvelmans: In the Wake of the Sea-Serpents (trans.), 1968; Joyce (ed. with Reggie Grenfell), 1980; Constance Garnett: A Heroic Life, 1991; Sylvia and David, The Townsend Warner/Garnett Letters (ed.), 1994. *Literary Agent:* AP Watt Ltd, 20 John St, London WC1N 2DR, England. *Address:* Hilton Hall, Hilton, Huntingdon, Cambridgeshire PE28 9NE, England.

GARRÉTA, Anne F.; Novelist and Trans; b. 1962, Paris, France. *Career:* teacher, l'université de Rennes II; fmrly visiting Prof., Duke Univ., USA. *Publications:* Sphinx, 1986; Ciels liquides, 1990; La Décomposition, 1999;Pas un jour, 2002. *Honours:* Prix Médicis, 2002. *Address:* c/o Éditions Grasset, 61 rue des Saints-Pères, 75006 Paris, France.

GARRETT, George Palmer, Jr; Prof. of English, Writer, Poet and Ed.; b. 11 June 1929, Orlando, FL, USA; m. Susan Parrish Jackson, 1952, two s. one d. *Education:* BA, 1952, MA, 1956, PhD, 1985, Princeton University. *Career:* Asst Prof., Wesleyan University, 1957–60; US Poetry Ed., Transatlantic Review, 1958–71; Visiting Lecturer, Rice University, 1961–62; Assoc. Prof., 1962–67, Hoyns Prof. of English, 1984–, University of Virginia; Writer-in-Residence, Princeton University, 1964–65, Bennington College, Vermont, 1979, University of Michigan, 1979–80, 1983–84; Prof. of English, Hollins College, Virginia, 1967–71; Prof. of English and Writer-in-Residence, University of South Carolina, 1971–73; Senior Fellow, Council of the Humanities, Princeton University, 1974–78; Adjunct Prof., Columbia University, 1977–78; mem. Fellowship of Southern Letters; Cosmos Club. *Publications:* Fiction: The Finished Man, 1959; Which Ones Are the Enemy?, 1961; Do, Lord, Remember Me, 1965; Death of the Fox, 1971; The Succession: A Novel of Elizabeth and James, 1983; Poison Pen, or, Live Now and Pay Later, 1986; Entered from the Sun, 1990; The Old Army Game, 1994; The King of Babylon Shall Not Come Against You, 1996. Short Stories: King of the Mountain, 1958; In the Briar Patch, 1961; Cold Ground Was My Bed Last Night, 1964; A Wreath for Garibaldi and Other Stories, 1969; The Magic Striptease, 1973; To Recollect a Cloud of Ghosts: Christmas in England, 1979; An Evening Performance: New and Selected Short Stories, 1985. Poetry: The Reverend Ghost, 1957; The Sleeping Gypsy and Other Poems, 1958; Abraham's Knife and Other Poems, 1961; For a Bitter Season: New and Selected Poems, 1967; Welcome to the Medicine Show: Postcards, Flashcards, Snapshots, 1978; Luck's Shining Child: A Miscellany of Poems and Verses, 1981; The Collected Poems of George Garrett, 1984; Days of Our Lives Lie in Fragments, 1998. Other: James Jones, 1984; Understanding Mary Lee Settle, 1988; The Sorrows of Fat City, 1992; Whistling in the Dark, 1992; My Silk Purse and Yours, 1993; Bad Man Blues, 1998; Going to See the Elephant, 2002; Southern Excursions, 2003. Editor: 18 books, 1963–93. *Honours:* American Acad. in Rome Fellowship, 1958; Sewanee Review Fellowship in Poetry, 1958; Ford Foundation Grant, 1960; National Endowment for the Arts Grant, 1967; Guggenheim Fellowship, 1974; American Acad. of Arts and Letters Award, 1985; Cultural Laureate of Virginia, 1986; T. S. Eliot Award, 1989; PEN/Malamud Award for Short Fiction, 1989; Aiken Taylor Award for Poetry, 2000; Commonwealth of Virginia Gov.'s Award for the Arts, 2000; Poet Laureate of the Commonwealth of Virginia, 2002–04. *Address:* 1845 Wayside Pl., Charlottesville, VA 22903, USA.

GARRISON, Deborah, BA, MA; editor and poet; b. 12 Feb. 1965, Ann Arbor, MI, USA; m. Matthew C. Garrison 1986; two d. *Education:* Brown University, New York University. *Career:* Editorial Asst to Senior Ed., New Yorker, 1986–2000; Poetry Ed., Alfred A. Knopf, 2000–; Senior Ed., Pantheon Books, 2000–. *Publications:* A Working Girl Can't Win and Other Poems, 1998. Contributions: Elle; Slate; New York Times; New Yorker. *Address:* c/o Alfred A. Knopf, 1745 Broadway, Suite 81, New York, NY 10019-4305, USA.

GARROW, David Jeffries; writer and academic; b. 11 May 1953, New Bedford, Massachusetts, USA. *Education:* BA magna cum laude, Wesleyan University, 1975; MA, 1978, PhD, 1981, Duke University. *Career:* Senior Fellow, Twentieth Century Fund, 1991–93; Visiting Distinguished Prof., Cooper Union, 1992–93; James Pinckney Harrison Prof. of History, College of William and Mary, 1994–95; Distinguished Historian-in-Residence, American University, Washington, DC, 1995–96; Presidential Distinguished Prof., Emory University, 1997–. *Publications:* Protest at Selma, 1978; The FBI and Martin Luther King Jr, 1981; Bearing the Cross, 1986; The Montgomery Bus Boycott and the Women Who Started It (ed.), 1987; Liberty and Sexuality, 1994. Contributions: New York Times; Washington Post; Newsweek; Dissent; Journal of American History; Constitutional Commentary. *Honours:* Pulitzer Prize in Biography, 1987; Robert F. Kennedy Book Award, 1987; Gustavus Myers Human Rights Book Award, 1987. *Address:* Emory University Law School, Atlanta, GA 30322, USA.

GARTON ASH, Timothy John, BA, MA, FRSA; British writer; b. 12 July 1955, London, England; m. Danuta Maria 1982; two s. *Education:* Exeter Coll., Oxford, St Antony's Coll., Oxford. *Career:* editorial writer, The Times 1984–86; Foreign Ed., The Spectator 1984–90; Fellow, Woodrow Wilson Int. Center for Scholars, Washington, DC 1986–87; sr assoc. mem. 1987–89, Fellow and Sr Research Fellow in Contemporary European History 1990–, St Antony's Coll., Oxford; columnist, The Independent 1988–90; Sr Fellow, Hoover Institution, Stanford Univ. 2000–; Fellow, Acad. of Sciences, Berlin-Brandenburg, European Acad. of Arts and Sciences; corresponding Fellow, Inst. for Human Sciences, Vienna; mem. PEN, Soc. of Authors. *Publications:* 'Und willst du nicht mein Bruder sein...': Die DDR heute 1981, The Polish Revolution: Solidarity 1983, The Uses of Adversity: Essays on the Fate of Central Europe 1989, We the People: The Revolution of '89 Witnessed in Warsaw, Budapest, Berlin and Prague 1990, In Europe's Name: Germany and the Divided Continent 1993, Freedom for Publishing for Freedom: The Central and East European Publishing Project (ed.) 1995, The File: A Personal History 1997, History of the Present: Essays, Sketches and Despatches from Europe in the 1990s 1999, Free World: Why a Crisis of the West Reveals the Opportunity of Our Time 2004; contrib. books, newspapers and magazines. *Honours:* Somerset Maugham Award, Society of Authors, 1984; Prix Européen de l'Essai, Veillon Foundation, 1989; David Watt Memorial Prize, 1989; Commentator of the Year, Granada Awards, 1989; Friedrich Ebert Stiftung Prize, 1991; Golden Insignia of the Order of Merit, Poland, 1992; Knight's Cross of the Order of Merit, Germany, 1995; Imre Nagy Memorial Plaque, Hungary, 1995; Premio Napoli, 1995. *Address:* St Antony's College, Oxford, OX2 6JF, England.

GARWOOD, Julie; Writer; b. 26 Dec. 1946, Kansas City, MO, USA; m. Gerald Garwood, 10 June 1967, divorced, two s. one d. *Education:* Avila College. *Publications:* Gentle Warrior, 1985; Rebellious Desire, 1986; Honor's Splendor, 1987; The Lion's Lady, 1988; The Bride, 1989; Guardian Angel, 1990; The Gift, 1990; The Prize, 1991; The Secret, 1992; Castles, 1993; Saving Grace, 1993; Prince Charming, 1994; For the Roses, 1995; The Wedding, 1996; One Pink Rose, 1997; One White Rose, 1997; One Red Rose, 1997; Come the Spring, 1997; The Clayborne Brides, 1998; Ransom, 1999; Heartbreaker, 2000. *Address:* PO Box 7574, Leawood, KS 66211, USA.

GASCOIGNE, John; academic and writer; b. 20 Jan. 1951, Liverpool, England; m. Kathleen May Bock 1980; one s. one d. *Education:* BA, University of Sydney, 1972; MA, Princeton University, 1974; PhD, University of Cambridge, 1981. *Career:* Lecturer, St Paul's Teachers' College, Rabaul, 1973, University of Papua New Guinea, Port Moresby, 1977–78; Tutor, 1980–84, Lecturer, 1984–87, Senior Lecturer, 1987–96, Assoc. Prof. of History, 1997–2003, Prof. of History, 2003–, University of New South Wales; Reviews Ed., Journal of Religious History, 1996–. *Publications:* Cambridge in the Age of Enlightenment: Science, Religion and Politics from the Restoration to the French Revolution, 1988; Joseph Banks and the English Enlightenment: Useful Knowledge and Polite Culture, 1994; Science in the Service of Empire: Sir Joseph Banks and the British State in the Age of Revolution, 1998; Science, Politics and Universities in Europe 1600–1800, 1999; The Enlightenment and the Origins of European Australia, 2002. Contributions: scholarly books and journals. *Honours:* Hancock Prize, Australian Historical Society, 1991; FRHistS, London, 1992; Fellow, Australian Acad. of the Humanities. *Address:* c/o School of History, University of New South Wales, Sydney, NSW 2052, Australia.

GASCOIGNE, Marguerite (see Lazarus, Marguerite).

GASH, Jonathan (see Grant, John).

GASKELL, Jane; Writer; b. 7 July 1941, Lancashire, England. *Career:* Staff, Daily Express, 1961–65, Daily Sketch, 1965–71, Daily Mail, 1971–84. *Publications:* Strange Evil, 1957; King's Daughter, 1958; Attic Summer, 1958; The Serpent, 1963; The Shiny Narrow Grin, 1964; The Fabulous Heroine, 1965; Atlan, 1965; The City, 1966; All Neat in Black Stockings, 1966 (filmed); A Sweet Sweet Summer, 1969; Summer Coming, 1974; Some Summer Lands, 1977; Sun Bubble, 1990. *Honours:* Somerset Maugham Award, 1970. *Address:* c/o The Sharland Organization, The Manor House, Manor St, Raunds, Northants NN9 6JW, England.

GASKIN, Catherine Marjella; Novelist; b. 2 April 1929, County Louth, Dundalk, Ireland; m. Sol Cornberg 1 Dec. 1955 (died 1999). *Education:* Holy Cross College, Sydney, Australia; Conservatorium of Music, Sydney. *Career:* mem. Society of Authors; Authors' Guild of America. *Publications:* This Other Eden, 1946; With Every Year, 1947; Dust in Sunlight, 1950; All Else is Folly, 1951; Daughter of the House, 1952; Sara Dane, 1955; Blake's Reach, 1958; Corporation Wife, 1960; I Know My Love, 1962; The Tilsit Inheritance, 1963; The File on Devlin, 1965; Edge of Glass, 1967; Fiona, 1970; A Falcon for a Queen, 1972; The Property of a Gentleman, 1974; The Lynmara Legacy, 1975; The Summer of the Spanish Woman, 1977; Family Affairs, 1980; Promises, 1982; The Ambassador's Women, 1985; The Charmed Circle, 1988. *Address:* Villa 139, The Manors, 15 Hale Rd, Mosman, Sydney 2088, Australia.

GASKIN, John Charles Addison, BLitt, MA, DLitt; academic and writer; b. 4 April 1936, Hitchin, Hertfordshire, England; m. Diana Dobbin 1972; one s. one d. *Education:* St Peter's College, Oxford, Trinity College, Dublin, University of Dublin. *Career:* Lecturer 1965–78, Fellow 1978–, Prof. of Philosophy 1982–97, Trinity College, Dublin; Hon. Tutor, Hatfield College, Durham 1997; mem. Hume Society. *Publications:* Hume's Philosophy of Religion, 1978; The Quest for Eternity: An Outline of the Philosophy of Religion, 1984; Varieties of Unbelief From Epicurus to Sartre, 1989; David Hume: Dialogues Concerning Natural Religion and the Natural History of Religion (ed.), 1993; The Epicurean Philosophers (ed.), 1994; Thomas Hobbes: Human Nature and the De Corpore (ed.), 1994; Hobbes: Leviathan, 1996; The Dark Companion: Ghost Stories, 2001. Contributions: scholarly journals and periodicals. *Address:* c/o University of Dublin Trinity College, Dublin 2, Ireland.

GASS, William Howard, AB, PhD; academic, writer and critic; b. 30 July 1924, Fargo, ND, USA; m. 1st Mary Pat O'Kelly 1952; two s. one d.; m. 2nd Mary Henderson 1969; two d. *Education:* Kenyon College, Cornell University. *Career:* Instructor in Philosophy, College of Wooster, 1950–54; Asst Prof., 1955–58, Assoc. Prof., 1960–65, Prof. of Philosophy, 1966–69, Purdue University; Visiting Lecturer in English and Philosophy, University of Illinois, 1958–59; Prof. of Philosophy, 1969–78, David May Distinguished Prof. in the Humanities, 1979–2001, Dir, International Writers Centre, 1990–2001, Washington University; mem. American Acad. of Arts and Letters; American Acad. of Arts and Sciences. *Publications:* Fiction: Omensetter's Luck, 1966; Willie Masters' Lonesome Wife, 1968; The Tunnel, 1995. Stories: In the Heart of the Heart of the Country, 1968; Cartesian Sonata, 1998. Essays: Fiction and the Figures of Life, 1971; On Being Blue, 1976; The World Within the Word, 1978; The Habitations of the Word, 1984; Finding a Form, 1996; Tests of Time, 2002. Editor: The Writer in Politics (with Lorin Cuoco), 1996; The Writer and Religion (with Lorin Cuoco) 2000; Literary St Louis (with Lorin Cuoco) 2000. Translator: Reading Rilke, 1999. Contributions: Essays, criticism, poems, stories, and trans in various publications. *Honours:* Longview Foundation Prize for Fiction, 1959; Rockefeller Foundation Grant, 1965–66; Guggenheim Fellowship, 1970–71; American Acad. and Institute of Arts and Letters Award, 1975, and Medal of Merit, 1979; Pushcart Prizes, 1976, 1983, 1987, 1992; National Book Critics Circle Awards, 1985, 1996, 2003; Getty Scholar, 1991–92; American Book Award, Before Columbus Foundation, 1996; Lannan Lifetime Achievement Award, 1997; PEN-Nabokov Prize, 2000; PEN Spielvogel Diamondstein Award 2003. *Address:* 6304 Westminster Place, St Louis, MO 63130, USA.

GATENBY, Greg, BA; artistic director and poet; b. 5 May 1950, Toronto, ON, Canada. *Education:* York Univ. *Career:* Ed., McClelland and Stewart, Toronto 1973–75; Artistic Dir, Harbourfront Reading Series and concomitant festivals 1975, Humber Coll. School of Creative Writing 1992–93; mem. PEN Canadian Centre, Writers' Union of Canada. *Publications:* Imaginative Work: Rondeaus for Erica 1976, Adrienne's Blessing 1976, The Brown Stealer 1977, The Salmon Country 1978, Growing Still 1981; contrib. to anthologies, including 52 Pickup 1977, Whale Sound 1977, Whales: A Celebration 1983, The Definitive Notes 1991, The Wild is Always There 1993, Toronto Literary Guide 1999; translator: Selected Poems, by Giorgio Bassani 1980, The Wild Is Always There Vol. 2 1995, The Very Richness of that Past 1995. *Honours:* City of Toronto Arts Award for Literature 1989, hon. lifetime mem. League of Canadian Poets 1991, Jack Award for Lifetime Promotion of Canadian Books 1994, E. J. Pratt Lifetime Fellow 1995. *Address:* c/o The League of Canadian Poets, 920 Yonge Street, Suite 608, Toronto, ON M4W 3C7, Canada.

GATES, Henry Louis, Jr; Professor of Humanities and English, Writer and Editor; b. 16 Sept. 1950, Keyser, West Virginia, USA; m. Sharon Lynn Adams, 1 Sept. 1979, two d. *Education:* BA summa cum laude, History, Yale University, 1973; MA, English Language and Literature, 1974, PhD, English Language and Literature, 1979, Clare College, Cambridge. *Career:* Lecturer and Dir of Undergraduate Studies, 1976–79, Asst Prof., 1979–84, Assoc. Prof. of English and Afro-American Studies, 1984–85, Yale University; Prof. of English, Comparative Literature, and Africana Studies, 1985–88, W. E. B. Du Bois Prof. of Literature, 1988–90, Cornell University; Virginia Commonwealth Prof., 1987; Richard Wright Lecturer, University of Pennsylvania, 1990; John Spencer Bassett Prof. of English and Literature, Duke University, 1990–91; W. E. D. Du Bois Prof. of Humanities, 1991–, Prof. of English, 1991–, Chair, Dept of Afro-American Studies, 1991–, Dir, W. E. D. Du Bois Institute for Afro-American Research, 1991–, Harvard University; Clarendon Lecturer, University of Oxford, 1992; mem. African Literature Asscn; Afro-American Acad.; American Acad. of Arts and Letters; American Antiquarian Society; American Philosophical Society; American Studies Asscn; Asscn for the Study of Afro-American Life and History, life mem.; Caribbean Studies Asscn; College Language Asscn, life mem.; Council on Foreign Relations; MLA. *Publications:* Figures in Black: Words, Signs, and the Racial Self, 1987; The Signifying Monkey: Towards a Theory of Afro-American Literary Criticism, 1988; Loose Canons: Notes on the Culture Wars, 1992; Colored People: A Memoir, 1994; The Future of the Race (with Cornel West), 1996; Thirteen Ways of Looking at a Black Man, 1997; The African American Century: How Black Americans Have Shaped Our Country (with Cornel West), 2000. Editor: numerous books. Contributions: numerous scholarly and other publications. *Honours:* Ford Foundation National Fellowship, 1976–77; Rockefeller Foundation Fellowship for Minority Scholars, 1980–81; John D. and Catherine T. MacArthur Foundation Fellowship, 1981–86; Zora Neale Hurston Society Award for Cultural Scholarship, 1986; Woodrow Wilson National Fellowship, 1988–90; Anisfield-Wolf Book Award for Race Relations, 1989; American Book Award, American Jewish Committee, 1994; Chicago Tribune Heartland Award, 1994; Lillian Smith Book Award, 1994; West Virginian of the Year, 1995; Tikkun National Ethics Award, 1996; New England Award for Editorial Excellence, 1997; National Humanities Medal, 1998. numerous hon. degrees. *Address:* c/o Dept of Afro-American Studies, Harvard University, Barker Center, 12 Quincy St, Cambridge, MA 02128, USA.

GATHORNE-HARDY, Jonathan, BA; writer; b. 17 May 1933, Edinburgh, Scotland; m. 1st Sabrina Tennant 1962; one s. one d.; m. 2nd Nicolette Sinclair Loutit 1985. *Education:* Trinity Coll., Cambridge. *Publications:* One Foot in the Clouds (novel) 1961, Chameleon (novel) 1967, The Office (novel) 1970, The Rise and Fall of the British Nanny 1972, The Public School Phenomenon 1977, Love, Sex, Marriage and Divorce 1981, Doctors 1983, The Centre of the Universe is 18 Baedeker Strasse (short stories) 1985, The City Beneath the Skin (novel) 1986, The Interior Castle: A Life of Gerald Brenan (biog.) 1992, Particle Theory (novel) 1996, Alfred C. Kinsey – Sex the Measure of All Things, A Biography 1998; other: 11 novels for children; contrib. to numerous magazines and journals. *Address:* 31 Blacksmith's Yard, Binham, Fakenham, Norfolk NR21 0AL, England.

GATTEY, Charles Neilson; Author, Playwright and Lecturer; b. 3 Sept. 1921, London, England. *Education:* University of London. *Career:* mem. Society of Civil Service Authors, pres., 1980; The Garrick. *Publications:* The Incredible Mrs Van Der Eist, 1972; They Saw Tomorrow, 1977; Queens of Song, 1979; The Elephant that Swallowed a Nightingale, 1981; Peacocks on the Podium, 1982; Foie Gras and Trumpets, 1984; Excess in Food, Drink and Sex, 1987; Prophecy and Prediction in the 20th Century, 1989; Luisa Tetrazzini, 1995; Crowning Glory: The Merits of the Monarchy, 2003. Other: Television Play: The White Falcon, 1955. Film: The Love Lottery, 1954. *Address:* 15 St Lawrence Dr., Pinner, Middlesex HA5 2RL, England.

GATTI, Armand; French playwright; b. 26 Jan. 1924, Monaco. *Education:* Seminary of Saint Paul, near Cannes. *Publications:* Le Poisson noir 1958, La crapaud-buffle 1959, Le Voyage de Grand Chou 1960, Chant public devant deux chaises électriques 1966, V comme Vietnam 1967, Le Passion du général Franco 1968, Un homme seul 1969, Petit manuel de guérilla urbaine 1971, La colonne Durutti 1974, Die Hälfte des Himmels und wir 1975, Le labyrinthe 1982, Opéra avec titre long 1987, Oeuvres théâtrales, 3 tomes regroupant 44 pièces de 1958 à 1990 1991, Ces empereurs aux ombrelles trouées 1991, Le chant d'amour des alphabets d'Auschwitz 1992, Gatti à Marseille 1993, Adam quoi? 1993, La journée d'une infirmière 1995, Notre tranchée de chaque jour 1996, L'Inconnu no. 5 1996, Les personnages de théâtre meurent dans la rue 1997, La Parole errante 1999, L'anarchie comme un battement d'ailes (4 vols) 2001, 2003. *Honours:* Officier Ordre des Arts et des Lettres 1989, Chevalier de la Légion d'honneur 2000Prix Fénéon 1959, Grand prix national du théâtre 1988, Médaille de vermeil Picasso UNESCO 1994. *Address:* La Parole Errante, 9 rue François-Debergue, 93100 Montreuil-sous-Bois, France.

GAUDÉ, Laurent; French novelist and playwright; b. 6 July 1972, Paris. *Plays include:* Pluie de cendres 2001, Battle of Will 2002. *Publications include:* novels: La Mort du roi Tsongor (trans. as The Death of an Ancient King) 2004. *Honours:* Prix Goncourt des Lycéens. *Address:* c/o The Toby Press, PO Box 8531, New Milford, CT 06776-8531, USA. *Website:* www .tobypress.com.

GAUNT, Graham (see Grant, John).

GAY, Peter (Jack); Writer; b. 20 June 1923, Berlin, Germany; m. Ruth Slotkin 30 May 1959; three step-d. *Education:* AB, University of Denver, 1946; MA, 1947, PhD, 1951, Columbia University; Psychoanalytic training, Western New England Institute for Psychoanalysis, 1976–83. *Career:* Faculty, 1947–69, Prof. of History, 1962–69, Columbia University; Prof. of Comparative European Intellectual History, 1969–, Durfee Prof. of History, 1970–84, Sterling Prof. of History, 1984–93, Sterling Prof. Emeritus, 1993–, Yale University; Dir, Center for Scholars and Writers, New York Public Library, 1997–. *Publications:* The Dilemma of Democratic Socialism: Eduard Bernstein's Challenge to Marx, 1952; The Question of Jean Jacques Rousseau (ed.), 1954; Voltaire's Politics: The Poet as Realist, 1959; Voltaire: Philosophical Dictionary (trans.), 1962; Voltaire: Candide (trans.) 1963; The Party of Humanity: Essays in the French Enlightenment, 1964; John Locke on Education (ed.), 1964; The Enlightenment: An Interpretation, Vol. I: The Rise of Modern Paganism, 1966, Vol. II: The Science of Freedom, 1969; A Loss of Mastery: Puritan Historians in Colonial America, 1966; Weimar Culture: The Outsider as Insider, 1968; Deism: An Anthology, 1968; Columbia History of the World (with John A. Garraty), 1972; Modern Europe (with R. K. Webb), 2 vols, 1973; The Enlightenment: A Comprehensive Anthology, 1973; Style in History, 1974; Art and Act: On Causes in History – Manet, Gropius, Mondrian, 1976; The Bourgeois Experience, Victoria to Freud, Vol. I, Education of the Senses, 1984, Vol. II, The Tender Passion, 1986, Vol. III, The Cultivation of Hatred, 1993, Vol. IV, The Naked Heart, 1995, Vol. V, Pleasure Wars, 1998; Freud: A Life for Our Time, 1989; Reading Freud, 1990; My German Question: Growing Up in Nazi Berlin, 1998; Schnitzler's Century, 2001. *Honours:* Frederic G. Melcher Book Award, 1967; National Book Award, 1967; Guggenheim Fellowships, 1967–68, 1977–78; Gold Medal, American Acad. of Arts and Letters.

GAYLE, Emma (see Fairburn, Eleanor M.).

GEBAUER, Phyllis; Novelist, Writer and Teacher; b. 17 Oct. 1928, Chicago, IL, USA; m. Frederick A Gebauer, 2 Dec. 1950, deceased. *Education:* BS, Northwestern University, 1950; MA, University of Houston, 1966; Postgraduate, several universities. *Career:* Workshop Leader, Santa Barbara Writers' Conference, 1980–; Instructor, University of California at Los Angeles Extension Writers' Program, 1989–; Lecturer, San Diego State University Writers Conference, 1995–; mem. PEN Center, USA, West; Dorothy L. Sayers Society. *Publications:* The Pagan Blessing, 1979; The Cottage, 1985; The Final Murder of Monica Marlowe, 1986; Criticism, The Art of Give and Take, 1987. *Honours:* First Prize for Fiction, Santa Barbara City College, 1972; First and Second Prizes for Fiction, Santa Barbara City College, 1973; Outstanding Teacher in Creative Writing, UCLA Extension, 1993. *Address:* 515 West Scenic Dr., Monrovia, CA 91016-1511, USA.

GÉBLER, Carlo, BA; writer and film-maker; b. 21 Aug. 1954, Dublin, Ireland; m. Tyga Thomason 1990; three s. two d. *Education:* Univ. of York, National Film and Television School. *Career:* part-time teacher of creative writing, HMP Maze, Co Antrim 1993–95; writer-in-residence, HMP Magha-berry, Co Antrim 1997; mem. Aosdána (Ireland). *Publications:* The Eleventh Summer, 1985; August in July, 1986; Work & Play, 1987; Driving Through Cuba, 1988; Malachy and His Family, 1990; The Glass Curtain: Inside an Ulster Community, 1991; Life of a Drum, 1991; The Witch That Wasn't, 1991; The Cure, 1994; W9 and Other Lives, 1998; How to Murder a Man, 1998; Frozen Out, 1998; The Base, 1999; Father & I, 2000; Dance of Death, 2000; Caught on a Train, 2001; 10 Rounds, 2002; August '44, 2003; The Cup of Bitterness: The Siege of Derry 2005. *Literary Agent:* Antony Harwood, 103 Walton Street, Oxford, OX2 6EB, England.

GEDDES, Gary; Distinguished Prof. of Canadian Culture, Writer and Poet; b. 9 June 1940, Vancouver, BC, Canada; m. 1st Norma Joan Fugler, 1963, divorced 1969, one d.; m. 2nd Jan Macht, 2 May 1973, two d. *Education:* BA, University of British Columbia, 1962; Diploma in Education, University of Reading, 1964; MA, 1966, PhD, 1975, University of Toronto. *Career:* Lecturer, Carleton University, Ottawa, Ontario, 1971–72, University of Victoria, BC, 1972–74; Writer-in-Residence, 1976–77, Visiting Asst Prof., 1977–78, University of Alberta, Edmonton; Assoc. Prof., 1978–79, Prof. of English, 1979–98, Concordia University, Montréal, QC; Distinguished Prof. of Canadian Culture, Western Washington University, 1999–2001; mem. League of Canadian Poets; Writers' Union of Canada; Playwright's Union of Canada. *Publications:* Poetry: Poems 1971; Rivers Inlet 1972; Snakeroot 1973; Letter of the Master of Horse 1973; War and Other Measures 1976; The Acid Test 1980; The Terracotta Army 1984; Changes of State 1986; Hong Kong 1987; No Easy Exit/Salida difícil 1989; Light of Burning Towers 1990; Girl By the Water 1994; Perfect Cold Warrior 1995; Active Trading: Selected Poems 1970–95, 1996; Flying Blind 1998, Inspecting the Chickens 2004. Short Stories: The Unsettling of the West 1986. Non-Fiction: Letters from Managua: Meditations on Politics and Art 1990; Sailing Home: A Journey Through Time, Place and Memory 2001. Play: Les Maudits Anglais 1984. Criticism: Conrad's Later Novels 1980. Translator: I Didn't Notice the Mountain Growing Dark, by Li Bai and Du Fu (with George Liang) 1986. Editor: 20th Century Poetry and Poetics 1969 4th edn 1996; 15 Canadian Poets (with Phyllis Bruce) 1970, fourth edn as 15 Canadian Poets x 3 2001; Skookum Wawa: Writings of the Canadian Northwest 1975; Divided We Stand 1977; Chinada: Memoirs of the Gang of Seven 1983; The Inner Ear: An Anthology of New Canadian Poets 1983; Vancouver: Soul of a City 1986; Compañeros: Writings about Latin America 1990; The Art of Short Fiction: An International Anthology 1992. *Honours:* E. J. Pratt Medal, National Poetry Prize Canadian Authors Asscn, America's Best Book Award Commonwealth Poetry Competition 1985, Writers Choice Award, National Magazine Gold Award, Archibald Lampman Prize, Gabriela Mistral Prize 1996, Poetry Book Society Recommendation 1996. *Address:* 975 Seaside Dr., RR 2, Sooke, BC V0S 1N0, Canada.

GEDDES, John M., MA; American newspaper editor; *Managing Editor, The New York Times*; b. 1952. *Education:* Univs. of RI and WI. *Career:* reporter The Ansonia Evening Sentinel, Ansonia, CT 1976; reporter Associated Press-Dow Jones News Service, NY 1976–78, Bonn, Germany 1978–79; econs corresp. The Times, Bonn 1979–80; joined The Wall Street Journal 1980, various positions including Bureau Chief, Bonn, Deputy Man. Ed. then Man. Ed. European Edn, News Ed., Asst Man. Ed., Sr Ed. and Nat. News Ed. –1993; fmr Prin. Friday Holdings; CEO BIS Strategic Decisions (market research co.) 1993–94; Business and Financial Ed. The New York Times 1994–97, Deputy Man. Ed. 1997–2003, Man. Ed. for News Operations 2003–. *Address:* The New York Times, 229 West 43rd Street, New York, NY 10036, USA (Office). *Website:* www.nytco.com (Office).

GEDGE, Pauline Alice; writer; b. 1945, Auckland, New Zealand; two s. *Education:* University of Manitoba, one year. *Publications:* Child of the Morning, 1977; The Eagle and the Raven, 1978; Stargate, 1982; The Twelfth Transforming, 1984; Mirage, 1990, in US as Scroll of Saqqara, 1990; The Covenant, 1992; House of Dreams, 1994, in US as Lady of the Reeds, 1995; House of Illusions, 1997. *Honours:* Jeanne Boujassy Award, Société des Gens de Lettres, France; Winner, New Novelist Competition, Alberta Culture, 1978.

GEE, Maggie Mary, PhD, BLitt, PhD, FRSL; British author, journalist and lecturer; *Teaching Fellow, Sussex University*; b. 2 Nov. 1948, Poole, Dorset; m. Nicholas Rankin 1983; one d. *Education:* Horsham High School, Somerville Coll., Oxford. *Career:* Research Asst, Wolverhampton Polytechnic 1975–79; Eastern Arts Writing Fellow Univ. of E Anglia 1982; Visiting Fellow Sussex Univ. 1986–96, Teaching Fellow 1996–; Writer-in-Residence Northern Arts 1996; regular reviews in Daily Telegraph, Sunday Times; judge Booker Prize 1989; mem. RSL (mem. of council 1998–), Soc. of Authors (man. cttee 1991–94, council 1999–); Hawthornden Fellow 1989. *Publications:* novels: Dying, in Other Words 1981, The Burning Book 1983, Light Years 1985, Grace 1988, Where are the Snows? 1991, Christopher and Alexandra 1992, Lost Children 1994, How May I Speak in my Own Voice 1995, The Ice People 1998, The White Family 2002, The Flood 2003. *Honours:* Best of Young British Novelists 1982. *Literary Agent:* David Godwin Associates, 55 Monmouth Street, London, WC2H 9DG. *Telephone:* (20) 7240-9992. *Fax:* (20) 7395-6110. *Address:* c/o Society of Authors, 84 Drayton Gardens, London, SW10 9SB, England.

GEE, Maurice Gough, MA; New Zealand novelist; b. 22 Aug. 1931, Whakatane; m. Margaretha Garden 1970; one s. two d. *Education:* Avondale Coll.,

Auckland, Auckland Univ. *Career:* school teacher, librarian, other casual employment 1954–75; Robert Burns Fellow Univ. of Otago 1964; Writing Fellow Vic. Univ. of Wellington 1989; Katherine Mansfield Memorial Fellow, Menton, France 1992. *Publications include:* Plumb 1978, Meg 1981, Sole Survivor 1983, Collected Stories 1986, Prowlers 1987, The Burning Boy 1990, Going West 1992, Crime Story 1994, Loving Ways 1996, Live Bodies 1998, Ellie and the Shadow Man 2001, The Scornful Moon 2004; juvenile fiction includes: Under the Mountain 1979, The O Trilogy 1982–85, The Fat Man 1994; also scripts for film and TV. *Honours:* Hon. DLitt (Vic.) 1987; NZ Fiction Award 1976, 1979, 1982, 1991, 1993; NZ Book of the Year Award (Wattle Award) 1979, 1993; James Tait Black Memorial Prize 1979; NZ Children's Book of the Year Award 1986, 1995. *Address:* 41 Chelmsford Street, Ngaio, Wellington, New Zealand.

GEE, Shirley; Dramatist; b. 25 April 1932, London, England; m. Donald Gee, 30 Jan. 1965, two s. *Education:* Webber-Douglas Acad. of Music and Drama. *Career:* mem. Society of Authors; Writers Guild. *Publications:* Stones, 1974; Moonshine, 1977; Typhoid Mary, 1979; Bedrock, 1982; Never in My Lifetime, 1983; Flights, 1984; Long Live the Babe, 1985; Ask for the Moon, 1986; Against the Wind, 1988; Warrior, 1989. Other: Stage adaptations, including The Forsyte Saga (co-adapter); Children's poems, stories and songs. *Honours:* Radio Times Drama Bursary Award, 1974; Pye Award, 1979; Jury's Special Commendation, Prix Italia, 1979; Giles Cooper Awards, 1979, 1983; Sony Award, 1983; Samuel Beckett Award, 1984; Susan Smith Blackburn Prize, 1985. *Address:* c/o Shiel Land Assocs Ltd, 43 Doughty St, London WC1N 2LF, England.

GEERTZ, Clifford (James); Prof. of Social Science Emeritus and Writer; b. 23 Aug. 1926, San Francisco, CA, USA; m. 1st Hildred Storey, 30 Oct. 1948, divorced 1982, one s. one d.; m. 2nd Karen Blu, 1987. *Education:* AB, Antioch College, 1950; PhD, Harvard University, 1956. *Career:* Research Asst, 1952–56, Research Assoc., 1957–58, MIT; Instructor and Research Assoc., Harvard University, 1956–57; Fellow, Center for Advanced Study in the Behavioral Sciences, Stanford, 1958–59; Asst Prof. of Anthropology, University of California at Berkeley, 1958–60; Asst Prof., 1960–61, Assoc. Prof., 1962–64, Prof., 1964–68, Divisional Prof., 1968–70, University of Chicago; Senior Research Career Fellow, National Institute for Mental Health, 1964–70; Prof. of Social Science, 1970–82, Harold F. Linder Prof. of Social Science, 1982–2000, Prof. Emeritus, 2000–, Institute for Advanced Study, Princeton, NJ; Visiting Lecturer with Rank of Prof., Princeton University, 1975–2000; various guest lectureships; mem. American Acad. of Arts and Sciences, fellow; American Asscn for the Advancement of Science, fellow; American Philosophical Society, fellow; British Acad., corresponding fellow; Council on Foreign Relations, fellow; National Acad. of Sciences, fellow; Royal Anthropological Institute, hon. fellow. *Publications:* The Religion of Java, 1960; Old Societies and New States (ed.), 1963; Agricultural Involution: The Processes of Ecological Change in Indonesia, 1963; Peddlers and Princes, 1963; The Social History of an Indonesian Town, 1965; Person, Time and Conduct in Bali: An Essay in Cultural Analysis, 1966; Islam Observed: Religious Development in Morocco and Indonesia, 1968; The Interpretation of Cultures: Selected Essays, 1973; Myth, Symbol and Culture (ed.), 1974; Kinship in Bali (with Hildred Geertz), 1973; Meaning and Order in Moroccan Society (with Hildred Geertz and Lawrence Rosen), 1979; Negara: The Theatre State in Nineteenth Century Bali, 1980; Local Knowledge: Further Essays in Interpretive Anthropology, 1983; Bali, interprétation d'une culture, 1983; Works and Lives: The Anthropologist as Author, 1988; After the Fact: Two Countries, Four Decades, One Anthropologist, 1995; Available Light: Anthropological Reflections on Philosophical Topics, 2000. Contributions: scholarly books and journals. *Honours:* Talcott Parsons Prize, American Acad. of Arts and Sciences, 1974; Sorokin Prize, American Sociological Asscn, 1974; Distinguished Lecturer, American Anthropological Asscn, 1983; Huxley Memorial Lecturer and Medallist, Royal Anthropological Institute, 1983; Distinguished Scholar Award, Asscn for Asian Studies, 1987; National Book Critics Circle Prize in Criticism, 1988; Horace Mann Distinguished Alumnus Award, Antioch College, 1992; Fukuoka Asian Cultural Prize, 1992; Bintang Jasa Utama Distinguished Service Award, Republic of Indonesia. *Address:* c/o School of Social Science, Institute for Advanced Study, Einstein Dr., Princeton, NJ 08540, USA.

GEIER, Joan Austin, BS; poet and writer; b. 6 March 1934, New York, NY, USA; m. Walter Geier 1956; two s. one d. *Education:* Hunter College, CUNY. *Career:* mem. Brooklyn Poetry Circle, Poetry Soc. of America. *Publications:* Garbage Can Cat, 1976; Mother of Tribes, 1987; A Formal Feeling Comes, 1994. Contributions: Good Housekeeping; Christian Science Monitor; New York Newsday; Catholic Digest; Poetry Society of America Quarterly; SPSM&H; A Formal Feeling Comes; The Lyric; Poetpourri; Negative Capability; Hiram Poetry Review. *Honours:* Poetry Awards, World Order of Narrative Poets, 1980, 1987, 1990, 1992; Gustav Davidson Award, Poetry Society of America, 1982; John Masefield Award, World Order of Narrative Poets, 1983; Amelia Special Award for Haiku, 1985. *Address:* 556 H 102 Main Street, Roosevelt Island, NY 10044, USA.

GEIMAN, Leonid Mikhailovich, DrTechSci; Russian scientific publisher; b. 12 Aug. 1934, Moscow. *Education:* Moscow Ore Inst. *Career:* researcher ore industry research Orgs; Head of Div. Publishers' Sovietskaya Encyclopaedia 1963–88; Prof. Moscow Ore Inst.; researcher All-Union Inst. of Foreign Geology; f. Ind. Encyclopaedic Ed. House (ETA); Pres. Encyclopaedic Creative Asscn; mem. Russian Acad. of Natural Sciences 1992, Academician-Sec. Dept of Encyclopaedia. *Publications:* Russian Encyclopaedia of Banks 1995, Russian Nat. Electronic Encyclopaedia 1995, Encyclopaedia of Moscow Streets 1996, Encyclopaedia America 1997. *Address:* Russian Academy of Natural Sciences, Varshavskoye shosse 8, 113105 Moscow, Russia (Office). *Telephone:* (095) 954-26-11 (Office).

GEISMAR, Ludwig Leo, BA, MA, PhD; retd academic and writer; b. 25 Feb. 1921, Mannheim, Germany; m. Shirley Ann Cooperman 1948; three d. *Education:* University of Minnesota, Hebrew University, Jerusalem. *Career:* co-ordinator of Social Research, Ministry of Social Welfare, Israel, 1954–56; Research Dir, Family Centred Project, St Paul, Minnesota, USA, 1956–59; Assoc. Prof., 1959–62, Prof., Social Work and Sociology, Dir, Social Work Research Center, Graduate School of Social Work and Dept of Sociology, 1963–91, Rutgers University. *Publications:* Understanding the Multi-Problem Family: A Conceptual Analysis and Exploration in Early Identification (with M. A. LaSorte), 1964; The Forgotten Neighborhood: Site of an Early Skirmish in the War on Poverty (with J. Krisberg), 1967; Preventive Intervention in Social Work, 1969; Family and Community Functioning, 1971; Early Supports for Family Life, 1972; 555 Families: A Social Psychological Study of Young Families in Transition, 1973; Families in an Urban Mold (with S. Geismar), 1979; A Quarter Century of Social Work Education (ed. with M. Dinerman), 1984; Family and Delinquency: Resocializing the Young Offender (with K. Wood), 1986; Families at Risk (with K. Wood), 1989; The Family Functioning Scale: A Guide to Research and Practice (with M. Camasso), 1993. *Address:* 1050 George Street, Suite 9L, New Brunswick, NJ 08901, USA.

GELBART, Larry (Simon); Writer, Dramatist, Screenwriter and Producer; b. 25 Feb. 1928, Chicago, IL, USA; m. Pat Marshall, 25 Nov. 1956, three s., two d. *Education:* Chicago and Los Angeles public schools. *Career:* mem. American Society of Composers, Authors, and Publishers; Dramatists Guild; Writers Guild of America. *Publications:* Laughing Matters (memoir), 1998; Bedazzled (screenplay), 2000. Other: Dramatic: A Funny Thing Happened on the Way to the Forum, 1962; Sly Fox, 1976; One, Two, Three, Four, Five, 1988; City of Angels, 1989; Mastergate, 1989; Jerome Robbins' Broadway (co-author), 1989. Screenplays: The Notorious Landlady, 1962; The Thrill of It All, 1963; The Wrong Box, 1966; Not With My Wife You Don't, 1966; The Chastity Belt, 1968; A Fine Pair, 1969; Oh, God, 1977; Movie, Movie, 1978; Neighbors, 1981; Tootsie, 1982; Blame It On Rio, 1984; Barbarians at the Gate, 1993. Television: M*A*S*H, 1972–76; After M*A*S*H, 1983–84; Weapons of Mass Distraction, 1997. *Honours:* Tony Awards, 1963, 1990; Writers Guild Awards, 1972, 1974, 1977, 1978; Christopher Award, 1978; Los Angeles Film Critics Award, 1982; National Society of Film Critics Award, 1982; New York Film Critics Award, 1982; Drama Desk Award, 1989; Lee Strasberg Lifetime Achievement in the Arts and Sciences Award, 1990; Literary Award, PEN Center West, 1999. *Address:* 807 N Alpine Dr., Beverly Hills, CA 90210, USA.

GELBER, Jack; Prof., Dramatist and Dir; b. 12 April 1932, Chicago, IL, USA; m. Carol Westenberg, 22 Dec. 1957, one s. one d. *Education:* BS in Journalism, University of Illinois, 1953. *Career:* Adjunct Assoc. Prof., Columbia University, 1967–72; Prof., Brooklyn College, CUNY, 1972–. *Publications:* Plays: The Connection, 1959; The Apple, 1961; Square in the Eye, 1965; The Cuban Thing, 1968; Sleep, 1972; Barbary Shore (adapter), 1974; Jack Gelber's New Play: Rehearsal, 1976; Starters, 1982; Big Shot, 1988; Magic Valley, 1990. Other: On Ice (novel), 1964. *Honours:* Vernon Rice Award, 1959–60; Obie Awards, 1960, 1972, 1979; Guggenheim Fellowships, 1963–64, 1966–67; Rockefeller Grant, 1972; Directing Award, Village Voice, 1972–73; National Endowment for the Arts Fellow, 1974; CBS Fellow, Yale University, 1974–75. *Address:* 230 E 18th St, Apt 1C, New York, NY 10003, USA.

GELLIS, Roberta Leah, (Max Daniels, Priscilla Hamilton, Leah Jacobs); Author; b. 27 Sept. 1927, New York, NY, USA; m. Charles Gellis, 14 April 1947, one s. *Education:* BA, Hunter College, CUNY, 1947; MS, Brooklyn Polytechnic Institute, 1952. *Publications:* Knight's Honor, 1964; Bond of Blood, 1965; The Dragon and the Rose, 1977; The Sword and the Swan, 1977; The Space Guardian (as Max Daniels), 1978; The Roselynde Chronicles series: Roselynde, 1978, Alinor, 1978, Joanna, 1979, Gilliane, 1980, Rhiannon, 1982, Sybelle, 1983; Offworld (as Max Daniels), 1979; The Love Token (as Priscilla Hamilton), 1979; The Royal Dynasty series: Siren Song, 1980, Winter Song, 1982, Fire Song, 1984; A Silver Mirror, 1989; The Napoleonic Era series: The English Heiress, 1980, The Cornish Heiress, 1981, The Kent Heiress, 1982, Fortune's Bride, 1983, A Woman's Estate, 1984; The Tales of Jernaeve series: Tapestry of Dreams, 1985, Fires of Winter, 1986, Irish Magic, 1995, Shimmering Splendor, 1995, Enchanted Fire, 1996, Irish Magic II, 1997; Dazzling Brightness, 1994. *Literary Agent:* Ms Lucienne Diver, Spectrum Literary Agency, 111 Eighth Ave, New York, NY 10011, USA.

GEMMELL, David; British writer; b. 1 Aug. 1948, London. *Career:* fmrly labourer, bouncer, freelance journalist working for newspapers, including Daily Mail, Daily Mirror, Daily Express; full-time writer 1986–. *Publications:* Legend 1984, The King Beyond the Gate 1985, Waylander 1986, Wolf in Shadow 1987, Last Sword of Power 1988, Ghost King 1988, The Jerusalem Man 1988, The Last Guardian 1989, Knights of Dark Renown 1989, Quest for Lost Heroes 1990, The Drenai Tales 1991, The Lion of

Macedon 1991, Dark Prince 1991, Morningstar 1992, Stones of Power 1992, Waylander II: In the Realm of the Wolf 1992, The First Chronicles of Druss: The Legend 1993, Bloodstone 1994, The Hawk Eternal 1995, Ironhand's Daughter 1995, The Legend of Deathwalker 1996, Dark Moon 1996, Echoes of the Great Song 1997, Winter Warriors 1997, Sword in the Storm 1998, Midnight Falcon 1999, Hero in the Shadows 2000, Ravenheart 2001, The Drenai Tales Vol. 2 2002, Stormrider 2002, White Wolf 2003, The Swords of Night and Day 2004. *Address:* c/o Bantam Books, Transworld Publishers Ltd, 61–63 Uxbridge Road, London, W5 5SA, England. *Telephone:* (20) 8579-2652. *Fax:* (20) 8579-5479. *E-mail:* info@transworld-publishers.co.uk. *Website:* www.booksattransworld.co.uk.

GENOVESE, Eugene D(ominick); Prof. of History (retd) and Writer; b. 19 May 1930, New York, NY, USA; m. Elizabeth Ann Fox, 6 June 1969. *Education:* BA, Brooklyn College, CUNY, 1953; MA, 1955, PhD, 1959, Columbia University. *Career:* Asst Prof., Polytechnical Institute, Brooklyn, 1958–63; Assoc. Prof., Rutgers University, 1963–67; Prof. of History, 1967–69, Social Science Research Fellow, 1968–69, Sir George Williams University, Montréal; Visiting Prof., Columbia University, 1967, Yale University, 1969; Prof. of History, 1969–90, Distinguished Prof. of Arts and Sciences, 1985–90, University of Rochester; Pitt Prof. of American History and Institutions, University of Cambridge, England, 1976–77; Sunderland Fellow and Visiting Prof. of Law, University of Michigan, 1979; Visiting Mellon Prof., Tulane University, 1986; Distinguished Scholar-in-Residence, University Center, GA, 1990–95; mem. Historical Society, pres.; American Acad. of Arts and Sciences, fellow; National Asscn of Scholars. *Publications:* The Political Economy of Slavery, 1965; The World the Slaveholders Made, 1969; In Red and Black, 1971; Roll, Jordan, Roll, 1974; From Rebellion to Revolution, 1979; Fruits of Merchant Capital (with Elizabeth Fox-Genovese), 1983; The Slaveholder's Dilemma, 1991; The Southern Tradition, 1994; The Southern Front, 1995; A Consuming Fire, 1998. Contributions: scholarly journals. *Honours:* Richard Watson Gilder Fellow, Columbia University, 1959; Center for Advanced Study in the Behavioral Sciences Fellow, Stanford, CA, 1972–73; National Humanities Center Fellow, Research Triangle Park, North California, 1984–85; Mellon Fellow, 1987–88; Guggenheim Fellowship, 1987–88; Bancroft Prize, 1994. *Address:* 1487 Sheridan Walk NE, Atlanta, GA 30324, USA.

GENTLE, Mary Rosalyn, (Roxanne Morgan); Writer; b. 29 March 1956, Sussex, England. *Education:* BA, English, Politics, Geography, 1985, MA, 17th Century Studies, 1988; MA, War Studies, 1995. *Publications:* A Hawk in Silver, 1977; Golden Witchbreed, 1983; Ancient Light, 1987; Scholars and Soldiers, 1989; Rats and Gargoyles, 1990; The Architecture of Desire, 1991; Grunts!, 1992; Left to His Own Devices, 1994. Co-Editor: The Weerde Book 1, 1992; Villains!, 1992; The Weerde Book 2, The Book of the Ancients, 1993; A Secret History: The Book of Ash #1, 1999; Carthage Ascendant: The Book of Ash #2, 2000; The Wild Machines, The Book of Ash #2, 2000; Lost Burgundy, The Book of Ash #4, 2000; Ash: A Secret History, 2000; 1610: A Sundial in a Grave, 2003. As Roxanne Morgan: Dares, 1995; Bets, 1997; A Game of Masks, 1999; Degrees of Desire, 2001. Contributions: reviews. *Honours:* BSFA Award, Best Novel 2000; Sidewise Award for Alternative History, Best Long Fiction Award, 2000. *Literary Agent:* Maggie Noach, The Maggie Noach Literary Agency, 22 Dorville Cres., London W14 0AB, England. *Address:* 29 Sish Lane, Stevenage, Herts, England.

GEORGE, (Susan) Elizabeth, MS; American author; b. 26 Feb. 1949, Warren, OH; m. Ira Toibin 1971 (divorced 1995). *Education:* Foothill Community Coll., Univ. of California and California State Univ. *Career:* teacher, El Toro High School, Calif. 1975–87, Coastline Community Coll., Fountainvalley, Calif. 1988–; has lectured at Irvine Valley Coll., Irvine, Calif. 1989, Univ. of Calif. Extension 1990, Edinboro Univ. Summer School at Exeter Coll., Oxford, UK 1993, Univ. of British Columbia, Canada 1993, Univ. of Oklahoma 1995. *Publications:* A Great Deliverance (Anthony Award, Bouchercon XXI 1989, Agatha Award, Malice Domestic 1989, Le Grand Prix de Literature Policière, Mystery Writers of France 1990) 1988, Payment in Blood 1989, Well-Schooled in Murder (MIMI Award 1991) 1990, Sisters in Crime, Vol. II – The Evidence Exposed 1990, A Suitable Vengeance 1991, For the Sake of Elena 1992, Missing Joseph 1993, A Novel by Any Other Name 1994, Playing for the Ashes 1994, In the Presence of the Enemy 1996, Women on the Case (ed.) 1996, Deception on His Mind 1998, In Pursuit of the Proper Sinner 1999, A Traitor to Memory 2001, I, Richard 2002, Crime From the Mind of a Woman (ed.) 2002, A Place of Hiding 2003, Writing Away 2004. *Honours:* numerous honours and awards including the establishment of The Elizabeth George Collection at Boston Univ. 1989, One of Forty Graduates Who Have Made a Difference, Univ. of California, Riverside 1994, Visions and Visionaries, Honoring Six Graduates from California State Univ., Fullerton. *Literary Agent:* Deborah Schneider, 250 W 57th Street, New York, NY 10107, USA. *Address:* 4111 Shorebreak Drive, Huntington Beach, CA 92649, USA (Home). *Website:* www.elizabethgeorgeonline.com.

GEORGE, Jean Craighead; Author and Illustrator; b. 21 July 1919, Washington, DC, USA; m. John L. George, 28 Jan. 1944, divorced 1963, two s. one d. *Education:* BA, Pennsylvania State University. *Career:* Reporter, Washington Post, 1943–46; Roving Ed., Reader's Digest, 1965–84. *Publications:* My Side of the Mountain, 1959; Summer of the Falcon, 1962; The Thirteen Moons, 1967–69; Julie of the Wolves, 1972; Going to the Sun, 1976; Wounded Wolf, 1978; The American Walk Book, 1978; River Rats, 1979; The Grizzly Bear with the Golden Ears, 1982; The Cry of the Crow, 1982; Journey Inward, 1982; Talking Earth, 1983; How to Talk to Your Animals, 1985; Water Sky, 1987; One Day in the Woods, 1988, as musical, 1989; Shark Beneath the Reef, 1989; On the Far Side of the Mountain, 1990; One Day in a Tropical Rain Forest, 1990; Missing 'Gator of Gumbo Limbo, 1992; The Fire Bug Connection, 1993; Dear Rebecca Winter is Here, 1993; The First Thanksgiving, 1993; Julie, 1994; Animals Who Have Won Our Hearts, 1994; The Tarantula in My Purse, 1996; Look to the North, 1997; Julie's Wolf Pack, 1997. *Address:* 20 William St, Chappaqua, NY 10514, USA.

GEORGE, Jonathan (see Burke, John Frederick).

GEORGE, Kathleen (Elizabeth); Prof. of Theatre Arts, Dir, Dramatist and Writer; b. 7 July 1943, Johnstown, Pennsylvania, USA; m. Hilary Thomas Masters, 1994. *Education:* BA, English, 1964, MA, Theatre Arts, 1966, PhD, Theatre Arts, 1975; MFA, Creative Writing, 1988, University of Pittsburgh. *Career:* Asst Prof., Carlow College, 1968–76; Asst Prof., 1976–81, Assoc. Prof., 1981–2001, Prof., 2001–, University of Pittsburgh. *Publications:* Rhythm in Drama, 1980; Playwriting: The First Workshop, 1994; The Man in the Buick and Other Stories, 1999; Taken (novel), 2001. Other: various short fiction. Contributions: reviews and journals. *Honours:* Virginia Center for the Arts Fellowships, 1980–83; Pennsylvania Arts Council Grants, 1982, 1987; MacDowell Colony Fellowships, 1996, 2002; Mary Anderson Center Fellowship, 1996. *Literary Agent:* Ann Rittenberg. *Address:* 1213 Monterey St, Pittsburgh, PA 15212, USA. *Website:* www.geocities.com/taken_a_novel.

GERDES, Eckhard; Novelist, Playwright and Educator; b. 17 Nov. 1959, Atlanta, GA, USA; m. Persis Alisa Wilhelm, 30 Jan. 1988, three s. *Education:* BA, English, University of Dubuque, IA, 1988; MA, English, Roosevelt University, Chicago, 1994; MFA, Writing, School of the Art Institute of Chicago, 1998. *Career:* Ed., Journal of Experimental Fiction, 1994–; Instructor, Macon State College, 1998–. *Publications:* Projections, 1986; Truly Fine Citizen, 1989; Ring in a River, 1994. Contributions: Rampike; Oyez Review; Coe Review; Tomorrow Magazine; Planet Roc; Strong Coffee; No Magazine; Random Weirdness. *Honours:* Richard Pike Bissell Creative Writing Awards, 1987, 1988.

GERGELY, Ágnes; Hungarian poet and novelist; b. 1933, Budapest. *Career:* formerly secondary school teacher, radio prod., features ed. Nagyvilág (literary magazine), ed. of publishing house; teacher Int. Writing Program, Univ. of Iowa 1973–74. *Publications include:* novels: A tolmács (trans. as The Interpreter) 1973, A chicagöi változat (trans. as The Chicago Version) 1976, Stációk (trans. as Stages Along the Way) 1983, Őrizetlenek (trans. as The Unguarded) 2000; poetry: Fripress 1977, Requiem for a Sunbird: Forty Poems 1997. *Honours:* Attila Jözsef Prize, Déry Prize, Milán Füst Prize, Kossuth Prize, Getz Corporation Lifetime Achievement Award, USA 1996. *Address:* c/o Hungarian Cultural Centre, 10 Maiden Lane, Covent Garden, London, WC2E 7NA, England.

GERMAIN, Sylvie; French writer; b. 1948, Chateauroux. *Education:* Sorbonne, Paris. *Publications:* novels: Le Livre des nuits (trans. as The Book of Nights) 1985, Nuit d'Ambre (trans. as Night of Amber) 1987, Jours de colère (trans. as Days of Anger) 1989, La Pleurante des rues de Prague (trans. as The Weeping Woman of the Streets of Prague) 1992, Immensités 1993, Eclat du Sel (trans. as Invitation to a Journey) 1996, The Book of Tobias (in trans.) 2000, The Song of False Lovers (in trans.) 2004. *Address:* c/o Dedalus Ltd, Langford Lodge, St Judith's Lane, Sawtry, Cambridgeshire PE28 5XE, England. *E-mail:* info@dedalusbooks.com. *Website:* www.dedalusbooks.com.

GERRARD, Nicci, (Nicci French); writer; m. Sean French 1990; two s. two d. *Publications:* with Sean French under joint pseudonym of Nicci French: The Memory Game 1997, The Safe House 1998, Killing Me Softly 1999, Beneath the Skin 2000, The Red Room 2001, Land of the Living 2003, Secret Smile 2004, Things We Knew Were True 2004. *Literary Agent:* PFD, Drury House, 34–43 Russell Street, London, WC2B 5HA, England. *Address:* The Old Rectory, Elmsett, Ipswich IP7 6NA, England. *E-mail:* seanicci@dircon.co.uk.

GERRISH, Brian Albert; Theologian and Writer; b. 14 Aug. 1931, London, England; m. 1st one s. one d.; m. 2nd Dawn Ann De Vries, 3 Aug. 1990, one d. *Education:* BA, 1952, MA, 1956, Queens' College, Cambridge; STM, Union Theological Seminary, New York City, 1956; PhD, Columbia University, 1958. *Career:* Asst Pastor West End Presbyterian Church NY 1956–58; tutor philosophy of Religion Union Theological Seminary NY 1957–58; Asst Prof. McCormick Theological Seminary Chicago 1959–63, Assoc. Prof. 1963–65; Assoc. Prof., 1965–68, Prof., 1968–85, John Nuveen Prof., 1985–96, John Nuveen Prof. Emeritus, 1996–2002, Divinity School, University of Chicago; Co-Ed., Journal of Religion, 1972–85; Distinguished Service Prof. of Theology, Union Theological Seminary, Virginia, 1996–2002; mem. Fellow, American Acad. of Arts and Sciences. *Publications:* Grace and Reason: A Study in the Theology of Luther, 1962, Japanese trans., 1974; Tradition and the Modern World: Reformed Theology in the Nineteenth Century, 1978; The Old Protestantism and the New: Essays on the Reformation Heritage, 1982; A Prince of the Church: Schleiermacher and the Beginnings of Modern Theology, 1984, Korean trans., 1988; Grace and Gratitude: The Eucharistic Theology of John Calvin, 1993; Continuing the Reformation: Essays on Modern Religious

Thought, 1993; Saving and Secular Faith: An Invitation to Systematic Theology, 1999; The Pilgrim Road: Sermons on Christian Life, 2000. Editor: The Faith of Christendom: A Source Book of Creeds and Confessions, 1963; Reformers in Profile, 1967; Reformatio Perennis: Essays on Calvin and the Reformation in Honor of Ford Lewis Battles, 1981, Reformed Theology for the Third Christian Millennium: The 2001 Sprunt Lectures 2003. *Honours:* Guggenheim Fellowship, 1970; Hon. Doctorate, University of St Andrews, Scotland, 1984. *Address:* 9142 Sycamore Hill Pl., Mechanicsville, VA 23116, USA.

GERSTLER, Amy; Poet and Writer; b. 24 Oct. 1956, San Diego, CA, USA. *Education:* BA, Pitzer College. *Publications:* Poetry: Yonder, 1981; Christy's Alpine Inn, 1982; White Marriage/Recovery, 1984; Early Heavens, 1984; The True Bride, 1986; Bitter Angel, 1990; Nerve Storm, 1993; Crown of Weeds, 1997; Medicine, 2000. Fiction: Martine's Mouth, 1985; Primitive Man, 1987. Other: Past Lives (with Alexis Smith), 1989. Contributions: Magazines. *Honours:* National Book Critics Circle Award, 1991. *Address:* c/o Viking Penguin, 375 Hudson St, New York, NY 10014, USA.

GERVAIS, Charles Henry Martin; Poet, Writer and Ed.; b. 20 Oct. 1946, Windsor, Ontario, Canada; m. Donna Wright, 1968, two s. one d. *Education:* BA, University of Guelph, 1971; MA, University of Windsor, 1972. *Career:* Staff, Toronto Globe and Mail, 1966, Canadian Press, Toronto, 1967; Reporter, Daily Commercial News, Toronto, 1967, Chatham Daily News, 1972–73; Teacher of Creative Writing, St Clair College, Windsor, 1969–71; Publisher, Black Moss Press, Windsor, 1969–; Ed., Sunday Standard, Windsor, 1972; General News Reporter, 1973–74, 1976–81, Bureau Chief, 1974–76, Religion Ed., 1979–80, Book Ed., 1980–, Entertainment Writer, 1990–, Windsor Star. *Publications:* Poetry: Sister Saint Anne, 1968; Something, 1969; Other Marriage Vows, 1969; A Sympathy Orchestra, 1970; Bittersweet, 1972; Poems for American Daughters, 1976; The Believable Body, 1979; Up Country Lines, 1979; Silence Comes with Lake Voices, 1980; Into a Blue Morning: Selected Poems, 1982; Public Fantasy: The Maggie T. Poems, 1983; Letters From the Equator, 1986; Autobiographies, 1989; Playing God: New Poems, 1994. Other: The Rumrunners: A Prohibition Scrapbook, 1980; Voices Like Thunder, 1984; The Border Police: One Hundred and Twenty-Five Years of Policing in Windsor, 1992; Seeds in the Wilderness: Profiles of World Religious Leaders, 1994; From America Sent: Letters to Henry Miller, 1995. Editor: The Writing Life: Historical and Critical Views of the Tish Movement, 1976. Children's Books: How Bruises Lost His Secret, 1975; Doctor Troyer and the Secret in the Moonstone, 1976; If I Had a Birthday Everyday, 1983. *Honours:* Western Ontario Newspaper Awards, 1983, 1984, 1987.

GERVAIS, Ricky; British writer and comedian; b. 25 June 1961, Reading, Berkshire, England; pnr Jane Fallon. *Education:* Ashmead School, Univ. of London. *Career:* mem. pop duo Seona Dancing 1983–84; entertainments officer, Univ. of London; man. pop band Suede; music adviser, TV drama This Life (Island World/BBC2) 1996–97. *Plays:* Animals 2002, Politics 2004. *Television:* The 11 O'Clock Show (TalkBack/Channel 4) 1999–2000, Bruiser (BBC2) 2000, Meet Ricky Gervais (TalkBack/Channel 4) 2000, The Office (BBC2) 2001–03. *Radio:* BBC Radio 1, XFM London. *Publications:* The Office: Scripts Series 1 2002, The Office: Scripts Series 2 2003, Animals 2004. *Honours:* BAFTA Awards, British Comedy Awards, Golden Globes (USA). *Address:* c/o Faber and Faber Ltd, 3 Queen Square, London, WC1N 3AU, England. *Telephone:* (20) 7465-0045. *Fax:* (20) 7465-0034. *Website:* www.faber.co.uk.

GERY, John Roy Octavius; Research Prof. of English and Poet; b. 2 June 1953, Reading, PA, USA; m. Biljana D. Obradović; one s. *Education:* BA, Princeton University, 1975; MA, English, University of Chicago, 1976; MA, Creative Writing, Stanford University, 1978. *Career:* Lecturer, Stanford University and San Jose State University, 1977–79; Instructor, 1979–84, Asst Prof., 1984–88, Assoc. Prof., 1988–95, Prof. of English, 1995–2000, Research Prof. of English, 2000–, University of New Orleans; Founding Dir, Ezra Pound Center for Literature, Brunnenburg, Italy, 1990–; Visiting Prof., University of Iowa, 1991–92; mem. Acad. of American Poets; Assoc. Writing Programs; MLA; Poets and Writers. *Publications:* Charlemagne: A Song of Gestures, 1983; The Burning of New Orleans, 1988; Three Poems, 1989; The Enemies of Leisure, 1995; Nuclear Annihilation and Contemporary American Poetry, 1996; For the House of Torkom (co-trans.), 1999; American Ghost: Selected Poems, 1999; Davenport's Version, 2003. Contributions: Reviews and journals. *Honours:* Deep South Writers Poetry Award, 1987; Charles William Duke Long Poem Award, 1987; Wesleyan Writers' Conference Poetry Fellowship, 1989; National Endowment for the Arts Fellowship, 1992–93; Critics' Choice Award for Poetry, 1996; European Award Circle Franz Kafka, 2000; Louisiana Artist Fellowship, 2002; Summer Poet-in-Residence, Bucknell Univ., 2001, 2003. *Address:* c/o Dept of English, University of New Orleans, New Orleans, LA 70148-2315, USA.

GEVE, Thomas; Engineer and Writer; b. 1929, Germany; m. 1963, one s. two d. *Education:* National Diploma of Building, 1950; BSc, 1957. *Publications:* Youth in Chains, 1958; Guns and Barbed Wire, 1987; There Are No Children Here, 1997; Aufbrüche, 2000. *Address:* PO Box 4727, Haifa, Israel.

GEVIRTZ, Susan; Poet and Writer; b. 27 Oct. 1955, Los Angeles, CA, USA. *Education:* BA, Literature, Cultural Theory, Poetics, Evergreen State College, 1977; MA, Classical Literature, Philosophy, St John's Graduate Institute, Santa Fe, New Mexico, 1980; PhD, History of Consciousness, University of California at Santa Cruz, 1990. *Career:* Teaching Asst, University of California at Santa Cruz, 1983–87; Teacher-Poet, California Poets in the Schools, San Francisco, 1984–86; Teacher, Aegean College of Fine Arts, Paros, Greece, 1985; Assoc. Ed., HOW(ever) journal, 1985–90; Instructor, University of San Francisco, 1988–89, California College of Arts and Crafts, Oakland, 1989–91; Asst Prof., Hutchins School of Liberal Studies, Sonoma State University, Rohnert Park, CA, 1989–98; Prof., MFA in Poetry Programs, Univ. of San Francisco and San Francisco State Univ., 2000–; Prof. MA in Visual Criticism Program, California Coll. of the Arts, 2002–. *Publications:* Poetry: Korean and Milkhouse, 1991; Domino: Point of Entry, 1992; Linen minus, 1992; Taken Place, 1993; Prosthesis: Caesarea, 1994; Black Box Cutaway, 1998; Spelt (with Myung Mi Kim), 2000; Hourglass Transcripts, 2001. Other: Feminist Poetics: A Consideration of the 'Female' Construction of Language (assoc. ed.), 1984; Narrative's Journey: The Fiction and Film Writing of Dorothy Richardson, 1995. Contributions: anthologies, journals, and magazines. *Honours:* Awards, grants, and fellowships. *Address:* 1939 Jones St, San Francisco, CA 94133, USA. *E-mail:* susan@tsoft.com.

GEYER, Georgie Anne; Syndicated Columnist, Foreign Correspondent, Speaker and Author; b. 2 April 1935, Chicago, IL, USA. *Education:* BS, Journalism, Northwestern University, 1956. *Career:* Society Reporter, 1959–60, General Assignment Reporter, 1960–64, Foreign Correspondent, 1964–75, Roving Foreign Correspondent, 1967–75, Chicago Daily News; Syndicated Columnist, Los Angeles Times Syndicate, 1975–80, Universal Press Syndicate, 1980–; Lyle M. Spencer Prof. of Journalism, Syracuse University, 1977; mem. Council on Foreign Relations; International Press Institute; Cosmos Club; Gridiron Club; Tavern Club. *Publications:* The New Latins: Fateful Change in South and Central America, 1970; The New 100 Years' War, 1972; The Young Russians, 1976; Buying the Night Flight: Autobiography of a Woman Foreign Correspondent, 1983; Guerrilla Prince: The Untold Story of Fidel Castro, 1991; Waiting for Winter To End: An Extraordinary Voyage Through Soviet Central Asia, 1994; Americans No More: The Death of Citizenship, 1996. Contributions: books, newspapers, magazines and television. *Honours:* Fulbright Scholarship, University of Vienna, 1956–59; Weintal Prize Citation, Georgetown University, 1984; Chicago Foundation for Literature Award, 1984; Northwestern University Alumni Asscn Award, 1991; Society of Professional Journalists, Hall of Fame, 2000; many hon. doctorates. *Address:* The Plaza, 800 25th St NW, Washington, DC 20037, USA.

GHEZALI, Salima; Algerian newspaper editor; m. (divorced); two c. *Career:* fmr schoolteacher, Mitidja Hills; apptd Ed.-in-Chief La Nation weekly newspaper 1994, newspaper suspended by Algerian authorities 1996. *Honours:* Int. Press Club Award 1996, Sakharov Human Rights Prize. *Address:* c/o La Nation, Algiers, Algeria.

GHOSE, Zulfikar, BA; British academic, poet and writer; *Professor of English, University of Texas at Austin*; b. 13 March 1935, Sialkot, Pakistan. *Education:* Keele Univ. *Career:* Prof. of English, University of Texas at Austin 1969–. *Publications:* Poetry: The Loss of India, 1964; Jets from Orange, 1967; The Violent West, 1972; A Memory of Asia, 1984; Selected Poems, 1991. Fiction: The Contradictions, 1966; The Murder of Aziz Khan, 1967; The Incredible Brazilian the Native, 1972; The Beautiful Empire, 1975; Crump's Terms, 1975; A Different World, 1978; Hulme's Investigations into the Bogan Script, 1981; A New History of Torments, 1982; Don Bueno, 1983; Figures of Enchantment, 1986; The Triple Mirror of the Self, 1992. Criticism: Hamlet, Prufrock and Language, 1978; The Fiction of Reality, 1983; The Art of Creating Fiction, 1991; Shakespeare's Mortal Knowledge, 1993; Veronica and the Góngora Passion, 1998. Autobiography: Confessions of a Native-Alien, 1965. *Address:* c/o Dept of English, University of Texas at Austin, Austin, TX 78712, USA.

GHOSH, Amitav, BA, MA, DPhil; writer; b. 1956, Kolkata, India; m. Deborah Baker. *Education:* St Stephen's Coll., Delhi Univ., Institut Bourguiba des Langues Vivantes, Tunis, Univ. of Oxford. *Career:* Visiting Fellow, Centre for Social Sciences, Trivandrum, Kerala, India 1982–83; Research Assoc., Dept of Sociology, Delhi Univ. 1983–87; Lecturer, Dept of Sociology, Delhi Univ. 1987; Visiting Prof., Depts of Literature & Anthropology, Univ. of Virginia, Charlottesville 1988; Visiting Prof., South Asia Centre, Columbia Univ. 1989; Visiting Prof., Dept of Anthropology, Univ. of Pennsylvania 1989; Fellow, Centre for Studies in Social Science, Kolkata 1990–92; Adjunct Prof., Dept of Anthropology, Columbia Univ. 1993; Distinguished Visiting Prof., American Univ. in Cairo 1994; fiction workshop, Sarah Lawrence Coll., New York 1996; Visiting Prof., Dept of Anthropology, Columbia Univ. 1994–97; Distinguished Prof., Dept of Comparative Literature, Queens Coll., City Univ. of New York 1999–. *Publications:* The Circle of Reason 1986, The Shadow Lines 1988, In an Antique Land (non-fiction) 1992, The Calcutta Chromosome 1996, Dancing in Cambodia & At Large in Burma (essays) 1998, Countdown 1999, The Glass Palace 2000, The Hungry Tide 2004; contrib. articles in Ethnology, Granta, The New Republic, New York Times, Public Culture, Subaltern Studies, Letra Internacional, Cultural Anthropology, Observer Magazine, Wilson Quarterly, The New Yorker, Civil Lines, American Journal of Archaeology, Kenyon Review, Desh. *Honours:* Sahitya Akademi annual award 1990, Ananda Puraskar 1990, Prix Médicis Étranger 1990, Best American Essays award 1995, Arthur C. Clark Award 1996, Pushcart Prize 1999. *Address:* c/o HarperCollins Publishers, 77–85 Fulham Palace Road, London, W6 8JB, England. *E-mail:* info@amitavghosh.com. *Website:* www.amitavghosh.com.

GIBBONS, Kaye; Writer; b. 1960, Nash County, NC, USA; m. divorced, three d. *Education:* North Carolina State University; University of North Carolina at Chapel Hill. *Publications:* Ellen Foster, 1987; A Virtuous Woman, 1989; A Cure for Dreams, 1991; Charms for the Easy Life, 1993; Sights Unseen, 1995; On the Occasion of My Last Afternoon, 1998. *Honours:* Sue Kaufman Prize for First Fiction, American Acad. and Institute of Arts and Letters, 1988; Citation, Ernest Hemingway Foundation, 1988; National Endowment for the Arts Fellowship, 1989; Nelson Algren Heartland Award for Fiction, Chicago Tribune, 1991; PEN/Revson Foundation Fellowship, 1991. *Address:* c/o Penguin Putnam, 375 Hudson St, New York, NY 10014, USA.

GIBBONS, (William) Reginald, Jr; academic, poet, writer and translator; b. 7 Jan. 1947, Houston, TX, USA; m. Cornelia Maude Spelman 1983; one step-s. one step-d. *Education:* AB, Spanish and Portuguese, Princeton University, 1969; MA, English and Creative Writing, 1971, PhD, Comparative Literature, 1974, Stanford University. *Career:* Lecturer, Livingston College, Rutgers University, 1975–76, Princeton University, 1976–80, Columbia University, 1980–81; Ed., TriQuarterly magazine, 1981–97; Prof. of English, Northwestern University, 1981–; Core Faculty, MFA Program for Writers, Warren Wilson College, 1989–; mem. Associated Writing Programs; The Guild Complex, co-founder; PEN American Center; Poetry Society of America; Texas Institute of Letters; Society of Midland Authors. *Publications:* Poetry and Fiction: Roofs Voices Roads (poems), 1979; The Ruined Motel (poems), 1981; Saints (poems), 1986; Maybe It Was So (poems), 1991; Five Pears or Peaches (short stories), 1991; Sweetbitter (novel), 1994; Sparrow: New and Selected Poems, 1997; Homage to Longshot O'Leary (poems), 1999; It's Time (poems), 2002. Other: Criticism in the University (ed. with Gerald Graff), 1985; The Writer in Our World (ed.), 1986; Writers from South Africa (ed.), 1988; William Goyen: A Study of the Short Fiction, 1991; Thomas McGrath: Life and the Poem (ed. with Terrence Des Pres), 1991; New Writings from Mexico (ed. and principal trans.), 1992; Selected Poems of Luis Cernuda (trans.), 2000; Euripides' Bakkhai (trans.), 2001. Contributions: many journals, reviews, quarterlies, and magazines. *Honours:* Fulbright Fellowship, Spain, 1971–72; Co-Winner, Denver Quarterly Trans. Award, 1977; Guggenheim Fellowship, 1984; National Endowment for the Arts Fellowship, 1984–85; Texas Institute of Letters Short Story Award, 1986; Illinois Arts Council Fellowship, 1987; John Masefield Memorial Award, Poetry Society of America, 1991; Carl Sandburg Award, Friends of the Chicago Public Library, 1992; Anisfield-Wolf Book Award, 1995; Pushcart Prize XXII, 1997; Thomas H. Carter Prize, Shenandoah magazine, 1998; Balcones Poetry Prize, 1998. *Address:* 1428 Crain Street, Evanston, IL 60202, USA.

GIBSON, Charles E(dmund); Children's Writer; b. 16 Dec. 1916, England. *Education:* Wandsworth Training College, London. *Publications:* The Story of the Ship, 1948; The Secret Tunnel, 1948; Wandering Beauties, 1960; The Clash of Fleets, 1961; Knots and Splices, 1962; Plain Sailing, 1963; Daring Prows, 1963; Be Your Own Weatherman, 1963; The Two Olafs of Norway, 1964; With a Cross on Their Shields, 1964; The Ship with Five Names, 1965; Knots and Splices, 1979; Death of a Phantom Raider, 1987. *Literary Agent:* A. M. Heath & Co Ltd, 79 St Martin's Lane, London WC2N 4RE, England. *Address:* 59 Victoria Rd, Shoreham-by-Sea, Sussex BN43 5WR, England.

GIBSON, Graeme; Author; b. 9 Aug. 1934, London, Ontario, Canada; m. Margaret Atwood, two s. one d. *Education:* University of Waterloo, 1953–54; University of Edinburgh, 1955–56; BA, University of Western Ontario, 1958. *Career:* mem. International PEN, Canadian Centre, pres., 1987–89; Writers' Union of Canada, chair., 1974–75. *Publications:* Five Legs, 1969; Communion, 1971; Eleven Canadian Novelists, 1973; Perpetual Motion, 1982; Gentleman Death, 1993. *Honours:* Toronto Arts Award, 1990; Mem. of the Order of Canada, 1992; Harbourfront Festival Prize, 1993. *Address:* c/o McClelland and Stewart, 481 University Ave, Suite 900, Toronto, Ontario M5G 2E9, Canada.

GIBSON, Ian, BA; historian and writer; b. 1939, Dublin, Ireland. *Education:* Trinity Coll., Dublin. *Career:* Lecturer in Spanish, Queen's Univ., Belfast; Reader in Modern Spanish Literature, Univ. of London. *Publications:* La represión nacionalista de Granada en 1936 y la muerte de Federico García Lorca 1971, The Death of Lorca 1975, The English Vice: Beating, Sex and Shame in Victorian England and After 1979, The Assassination of Federico García Lorca 1983, Federico García Lorca: A Life 1989, Fire in the Blood 1992, Lorca's Granada: A Practical Guide 1992, Salvador Dalí: The Early Years (with others) 1995, The Shameful Life of Salvador Dalí 1997, Vida, Pasión y Muerte de Federico García Lorca 1998, Dalí-Lorca: La pasión que no pudo ser 1999, The Erotomaniac: The Secret Life of Henry Spencer Ashbee 2002, Viento del sur (novel) 2002, Yo, Rubén Darío: Memorias póstumas de un Rey de la Poesía (novel) 2002, Cela, el hombre que quiso ganar 2003, Dalí joven, Dalí genial 2004; contrib. to numerous magazines and newspapers. *Honours:* Duff Cooper Memorial Prize, James Tait Black Memorial Prize, Premio Así Fue, Univ. of Barcelona. *E-mail:* iangibson@arrakis.es.

GIBSON, Morgan, BA, MA, PhD; academic, poet and writer; b. 6 June 1929, Cleveland, OH, USA; m. 1st Barbara Gibson 1950 (divorced 1972); two d.; m. 2nd Keiko Matsui Gibson 1978; one s. *Education:* Oberlin College, University of Iowa. *Career:* Asst, then Assoc. Prof. of English, University of Wisconsin at Milwaukee, 1961–72; Chair, Graduate Faculty, Goddard College, Vermont, 1972–75, Osaka University, 1975–79; Visiting Prof., Michigan State University, 1979, University of Illinois, 1982, Knox College, 1989–91; Prof., Chukyo University, 1987–89, Japan Women's University, Tokyo, 1993–96, Kanda University of International Studies, 1997–2000; Lecturer, Pennsylvania State University, 1991–93. *Publications:* Stones Glow Like Lovers' Eyes, 1970; Crystal Sunlake, 1971; Kenneth Rexroth, 1972; Dark Summer, 1977; Wakeup, 1978; Speaking of Light, 1979; Kokoro: Heart-Mind, 1979; The Great Brook Book, 1981; Revolutionary Rexroth: Poet of East-West Wisdom, 1986, and online, 2000; Among Buddhas in Japan, 1988; Winter Pilgrim, 1993. Editor: several books and journals. Contributions: anthologies, books, journals and reviews. *Honours:* awards and grants. *Address:* 3-17-604 Sakashita-cho, Isogo-ku, Yokohama-shi, 235-0003, Japan. *E-mail:* nonzenpoet@mac.com.

GIBSON, Walter Samuel; Prof. of the Humanities Emeritus and Writer; b. 31 March 1932, Columbus, Ohio, USA. *Education:* BFA, 1957, MA, 1960, Ohio State University; PhD, Harvard University, 1969. *Career:* Asst Prof., 1966–71, Assoc. Prof., 1971–78, Acting Chair., 1970–71, Chair., 1971–79, Dept of Art, Andrew W. Mellon Prof. of the Humanities, 1978–97, Andrew W. Mellon Prof. of the Humanities Emeritus, 1997–, Case Western Reserve University; Murphy Lecturer, University of Kansas and the Nelson-Atkins Museum of Art, 1988; Clark Visiting Prof. of Art History, Williams College, 1989, 1992; mem. American Asscn of Netherlandic Studies; College Art Asscn; Historians of Netherlandish Art; Midwest Art History Society; Renaissance Society of America; Society for Emblem Studies. *Publications:* Hieronymus Bosch, 1973; The Paintings of Cornelis Engebrechtsz, 1977; Bruegel, 1977; Hieronymus Bosch: An Annotated Bibliography, 1983; 'Mirror of the Earth': The World Landscape in Sixteenth-Century Flemish Painting, 1989; Pieter Bruegel the Elder: Two Studies, 1991; Pleasant Places: The Rustic Landscape from Bruegel to Ruisdael, 2000. Contributions: scholarly books and journals. *Honours:* Fulbright Scholarships, 1960–61, 1984; Guggenheim Fellowship, 1978–79; Fellow-in-Residence, Netherlands Institute for Advanced Study, Wasenaar, 1995–96. *Address:* 938 Mason Hill Rd N, VT 05261-9767, USA.

GIBSON, William; Dramatist, Writer and Poet; b. 13 Nov. 1914, New York, NY, USA; m. 1st, divorced; m. 2nd Margaret Brenman, 6 Sept. 1940, two s. *Education:* College of the City of New York. *Career:* mem. Authors League of America; Dramatists Guild; PEN. *Publications:* Plays (with dates of production and publication): I Lay in Zion, 1943, 1947; A Cry of Players, 1948, 1969; The Ruby, 1955; The Miracle Worker, 1957, 1957; Two for the Seesaw, 1958, 1960; Dinny and the Witches, 1959, 1960; Golden Boy (with Clifford Odets), 1964, 1965; John and Abigail, 1969, 1972; The Body and the Wheel, 1974, 1975; The Butterfingers Angel, Mary and Joseph, Herod the Nut, and the Slaughter of 12 Hit Carols in a Pear Tree, 1974, 1975; Golda, 1977, 1977; Goodly Creatures, 1980, 1986; Monday After the Miracle, 1982, 1983; Handy Dandy, 1984, 1986; Raggedy Ann: The Musical Adventure, 1985, 1986. Novel: The Cobweb, 1954. Poetry: Winter Crook, 1948; A Mass for the Dead, 1968. Criticism: Shakespeare's Game, 1978. Contributions: Magazines. *Honours:* Harriet Monroe Memorial Prize for Poetry, 1945; Sylvania Award, 1957. *Address:* c/o Flora Roberts, 157 W 57th St, New York, NY 10022, USA.

GIBSON, William (Ford); Writer; b. 17 March 1948, Conway, South Carolina, USA; m. Deborah Thompson, June 1972, one s. one d. *Education:* BA, University of British Columbia, 1977. *Publications:* Neuromancer, 1984; Count Zero, 1986; Burning Chrome (short stories with John Shirley, Bruce Sterling, and Michael Swanwick), 1986; Mona Lisa Overdrive, 1988; The Difference Engine (with Bruce Sterling), 1990; Agrippa: A Book of the Dead (with Dennis Ashbaugh and Keven Begos Jr), 1992; Virtual Light, 1993; Pattern Recognition, 2002. Other: Dream Jumbo (performance art text), 1989; Johnny Mnemonic (screenplay), 1995. Contributions: anthologies and journals. *Honours:* Ditmar Award, Australian National Science Fiction Foundation, 1984; Hugo Award, World Science Fiction Society, 1984; Nebula Award, SFWA, 1984; Porgie Award, West Coast Review of Books, 1984. *Address:* c/o Martha Millard Literary Agency, 204 Park Ave, Madison, NJ 07940, USA.

GIFFORD, Barry Colby; Writer; b. 18 Oct. 1946, Chicago, IL, USA; m. Mary Lou Nelson, 23 Oct. 1970, one s. one d. *Education:* University of Missouri, 1964–65; University of Cambridge, 1966. *Publications:* Jack's Book (co-author, biog.), 1978; Port Tropique, 1980; Landscape with Traveler, 1980; The Neighborhood of Baseball, 1981; The Devil Thumbs a Ride, 1988; Ghosts No Horse Can Carry, 1989; Wild at Heart, 1990; Sailor's Holiday, 1991; New Mysteries of Paris, 1991; A Good Man to Know, 1992; Night People, 1992; Arise and Walk, 1994; Hotel Room Trilogy, 1995; Baby Cat-Face, 1995; The Phantom Father, 1997; Lost Highway (co-author), 1997; Flaubert at Key West, 1997; Perdita Durango, 1997; The Sinaloa Story, 1998; Bordertown, 1998; The Wild Life of Sailor & Lula, 1998; My Last Martini, 1999; Southern Nights, 1999; Wyoming, 2000; Replies to Wang Wei, 2001; American Falls, 2002; The Rooster Trapped in the Reptile Room: A Barry Gifford Reader, 2003; Brando Rides Alone, 2003; Do the Blind Dream?, 2004. Contributions: Punch; Esquire; Rolling Stone. *Honours:* Notable Book Awards, American Library Asscn, 1978, 1988; National

Endowment for the Arts Fellowship, 1982; Maxwell Perkins Award, 1983; Syndicated Fiction Award, PEN, 1987; Premio Brancati, Italy, 1993. *Literary Agent:* Curtis Brown Ltd, 10 Astor Pl., New York, NY 10003, USA.

GIGGAL, Kenneth, (Henry Marlin, Angus Ross); Writer; b. 19 March 1927, Dewsbury, Yorkshire, England. *Career:* mem. Savage Club; Arms and Armour Society. *Publications:* The Manchester Thing, 1970; The Huddersfield Job, 1971; The London Assignment, 1972; The Dunfermline Affair, 1973; The Bradford Business, 1974; The Amsterdam Diversion, 1974; The Leeds Fiasco, 1975; The Edinburgh Exercise, 1975; The Ampurias Exchange, 1976; The Aberdeen Conundrum, 1977; The Congleton Lark, 1979; The Hamburg Switch, 1980; A Bad April, 1980; The Menwith Tangle, 1982; The Darlington Jaunt, 1983; The Luxembourg Run, 1985; Doom Indigo, 1986; The Tyneside Ultimatum, 1988; Classic Sailing Ships, 1988; The Greenham Plot, 1989; The Leipzig Manuscript, 1990; The Last One, 1992; John Worsley's War, 1992. Other: Television scripts and films. Contributions: many magazines, national and international. *Honours:* Truth Prize for Fiction, 1954. *Address:* The Old Granary, Bishop Monkton, Near Harrogate, North Yorkshire, England.

GIGUERE, Diane Liliane; Author; b. 6 Dec. 1937, Montréal, QC, Canada. *Education:* Collège Marie de France, 1941; Conservatory of Dramatic Arts, 1954–56. *Career:* mem. Writers' Union, Québec; Asscn of French Speaking Writers at Home and Overseas. *Publications:* Le Temps des Jeux, 1961; L'eau est Profonde, 1965; Dans Les Ailes du vent, 1976; L'Abandon, 1993; Un Dieu fantôme, 2001. *Honours:* Prix du Cercle du Livre de France, 1961; Guggenheim Fellowship, 1969; France Québec Prize, 1977. *Address:* 60 rue William Paul 304, Ile des Soeurs, QC H3E 1N5, Canada.

GIKANDI, Simon; Ugandan writer. *Career:* Robert Haydon Prof. of English Language and Literature, Univ. of Michigan, USA. *Publications include:* non-fiction: Reading the African Novel 1987, Reading Chinua Achebe: Language and Ideology in Fiction 1991, Writing in Limbo: Modernism and Caribbean Literature 1992, Maps of Englishness: Writing Identity in the Culture of Colonialism 1997, Cambridge Studies in African and Caribbean Literature: Ngugi wa Thiong'o 2000, The Cambridge History of African and Caribbean Literature (with F. Abiola Irele) 2004; editor: Uganda's Katakiro in England (Exploring Travel) by Ham Mukasa 1998, Death and the King's Horsemen by Wole Soyinka 2002, Encyclopedia of African Literature 2002. *Honours:* Fellow of John Simon Guggenheim Memorial Foundation. *Literary Agent:* c/o Cambridge University Press, The Edinburgh Building, Shaftesbury Road, Cambridge, CB2 2RU, England. *Telephone:* (1223) 312393. *Fax:* (1223) 315052. *Website:* www.cup.cam.ac.uk.

GIL, David Georg; Prof. of Social Policy and Author; b. 16 March 1924, Vienna, Austria; m. Eva Breslauer, 2 Aug. 1947, two s. *Education:* Certificate in Psychotherapy with Children, Israeli Society for Child Psychiatry, 1952; Diploma in Social Work, School of Social Work, 1953, BA, 1957, Hebrew University, Jerusalem, Israel; MSW, 1958, DSW, 1963, University of Pennsylvania. *Career:* Prof. of Social Policy, Brandeis University; mem. National Asscn of Social Workers; American Orthopsychiatric Asscn; Asscn of Humanist Sociology. *Publications:* Violence Against Children, 1970; Unravelling Social Policy, 1973; The Challenge of Social Equality, 1976; Beyond the Jungle, 1979; Child Abuse and Violence (ed.), 1979; Toward Social and Economic Justice (ed. with Eva Gil), 1985; The Future of Work (ed. with Eva Gil), 1987; Confronting Injustice and Oppression, 1998. Contributions: Over 50 articles to professional journals, book chapters, book reviews. *Honours:* Leadership in Human Services, Brandeis University, Heller School, 1999; Social Worker of the Year, National Asscn of Social Workers, Massachusetts, 2000. *Address:* Heller School for Social Policy and Management, Brandeis University, Waltham, MA 02454-9110, USA.

GILB, Dagoberto G., BA, MA; writer; b. 31 July 1950, Los Angeles, CA, USA; m. Rebeca Santos 1978; two s. *Education:* University of California. *Career:* Visiting Writer, University of Texas, 1988–89, University of Arizona, 1992–93, University of Wyoming, 1994; mem. Texas Institute of Letters; PEN. *Publications:* Winners on the Pass Line, 1985; The Magic of Blood, 1993; The Last Known Residence of Mickey Acuña, 1994; The Magic of Blood, 2001; Woodcuts of Women (short stories), 2001. *Honours:* James D. Phelan Award; Dobie Paisano Fellowship; Creative Writing Fellowship, National Endowment for the Arts; Whiting Writers Award, 1993; Best Book of Fiction Award, Texas Institute of Letters, 1993; Ernest Hemingway Foundation Award, 1994. *Address:* PO Box 31001, El Paso, TX 79931, USA.

GILBERT, Anna (see Lazarus, Marguerite).

GILBERT, Bentley Brinkerhoff; Writer; b. 5 April 1924, Mansfield, Ohio, USA. *Education:* AB, History, Miami University, Oxford, Ohio, 1949; MA, University of Cincinnati, 1950; PhD, University of Wisconsin, 1954. *Career:* Faculty, University of Cincinnati, Colorado College, 1955–67; Faculty, 1967–70, Prof. of History, 1967–, University of Illinois at Chicago; Ed., Journal of British Studies, 1978–83; mem. North American Conference on British Studies; FRHistS. *Publications:* The Evolution of National Insurance in Great Britain: The Origins of the Welfare State, 1966; Britain Since 1918, 1967; British Social Policy, 1970; David Lloyd George: A Political Life, Vol. I, The Architect of Change 1863–1912, 1987, Vol. II, The Organiser of Victory, 1912–1916, 1992; Britain, 1914–1945: The Aftermath of Power, 1996. Contributions: Reference works and professional journals. *Honours:* Guggenheim Fellowship, 1973–74; Society of Midland Authors Biography Prize, 1993; various grants. *Address:* c/o Dept of History University of Illinois at Chicago, Chicago, IL 60607, USA.

GILBERT, Harriett Sarah; Writer; b. 25 Aug. 1948, London, England. *Education:* Diploma, Rose Bruford College of Speech and Drama, 1966–69. *Career:* Co-Books Ed., City Limits magazine, 1981–83; Deputy Literary Ed., 1983–86, Literary Ed., 1986–88, New Statesman; Presenter, Meridian Books Programme, BBC World Service Radio, 1991–; Lecturer in Journalism, City University, London, 1992–; mem. Writers Guild of Great Britain. *Publications:* I Know Where I've Been, 1972; Hotels with Empty Rooms, 1973; An Offence Against the Persons, 1974; Tide Race, 1977; Running Away, 1979; The Riding Mistress, 1983; A Women's History of Sex, 1987; The Sexual Imagination (ed.), 1993. Contributions: Time Out; City Limits; New Statesman; Guardian; BBC; Australian Broadcasting Corporation; Washington Post; BBC World Service Radio. *Address:* 2 Oaktree Ct, Valmar Rd, London SE5 9NH, England.

GILBERT, Jack; Poet and Writer; b. 17 Feb. 1925, Pittsburgh, Pennsylvania, USA. *Education:* BA, University of Pittsburgh, 1954; MA, San Francisco State University, 1962. *Career:* University of California at Berkeley, 1958–59, San Francisco State University, 1962–63, 1965–67, 1971, Syracuse University, 1982–83, University of San Francisco, 1985; Prof., Kyoto University, Tokyo, 1974–75; Chair, Creative Writing, University of Alabama, Tuscaloosa, 1986. *Publications:* Poetry: Views of Jeopardy, 1962; Monolithos, 1982; The Great Fires: Poems, 1982–1992, 1994. Contributions: various reviews, journals, and periodicals. *Honours:* Yale Younger Poet Award, 1962; Guggenheim Fellowship, 1964; National Endowment for the Arts Award, 1974; First Prize, American Poetry Review, 1983; Stanley Kunitz Prize, 1983; Lannan Award, 1995.

GILBERT, John (Raphael); Writer; b. 8 April 1926, London, England; m.; three s. *Education:* Columbia University, 1941–42; BA, King's College, London, 1945. *Publications:* Modern World Book of Animals, 1947; Cats, Cats, Cats, 1961; Famous Jewish Lives, 1970; Myths of Ancient Rome, 1970; Pirates and Buccaneers, 1971; Highwaymen and Outlaws, 1971; Charting the Vast Pacific, 1971; National Costumes of the World, 1972; World of Wildlife, 1972–74; Miracles of Nature, 1975; Knights of the Crusades, 1978; Vikings, 1978; Prehistoric Man, 1978; Leonardo da Vinci, 1978; La Scala, 1979; Dinosaurs Discovered, 1980; Macdonald Guide to Trees, 1983; Macdonald Encyclopedia of House Plants, 1986; Theory and Use of Colour, 1986; Macdonald Encyclopedia of Roses, 1987; Gardens of Britain, 1987; Macdonald Encyclopedia of Butterflies and Moths, 1988; Trekking in the USA, 1989; Macdonald Encyclopedia of Orchids, 1989; Macdonald Encyclopedia of Bulbs, 1989; Trekking in Europe, 1990; Macdonald Encyclopedia of Herbs and Spices, 1990; Macdonald Encyclopedia of Bonsai, 1990; Macdonald Encyclopedia of Amphibians and Reptiles, 1990; Macdonald Encyclopedia of Saltwater Fishes, 1992; Decorating Chinese Porcelain, 1994. *Address:* 28 Lyndale Ave, London NW2, England.

GILBERT, Sir Martin John, CBE, FRSL; historian; b. 25 Oct. 1936, London, England; m. 1st Helen Constance 1963; one d.; m. 2nd Susan Sacher; two s. *Education:* Magdalen Coll., Oxford. *Career:* Senior Research Scholar, St Antony's College, Oxford, 1960–62; Visiting Lecturer, University of Budapest, 1961; Research Asst to Randolph S. Churchill, 1962–67; Fellow, 1962–94, Hon. Fellow, 1994–, Merton College, Oxford; Visiting Prof., University of South Carolina, 1965, University of Tel-Aviv, 1979, Hebrew University of Jerusalem, 1980–, University College London, 1995–96, University of California, San Diego, 2002; Leslie Stephen Lecturer, University of Cambridge, 1988; Official Biographer of Sir Winston Churchill, 1968–. *Publications:* The Appeasers (with Richard Gott), 1963; Britain and Germany Between the Wars, 1964; The European Powers, 1900–1945, 1965; Plough My Own Furrow: The Life of Lord Allen of Hurtwood, 1965; Servant of India: A Study of Imperial Rule, 1905–1910, 1966; The Roots of Appeasement, 1966; Recent History Atlas 1860–1960, 1966; Winston Churchill, 1966; British History Atlas, 1968; American History Atlas, 1968; Jewish History Atlas, 1969; First World War Atlas, 1970; Winston S. Churchill, Vol. III, 1914–1916, 1971, companion vol., 1973, Vol. IV, 1917–1922, 1975, companion vol., 1977, Vol. V, 1922–1939, 1976, companion vols, 1980, 1981, 1982, Vol. VI, Finest Hour, 1939–1941, 1983, Vol. VII, Road to Victory, 1986, Vol. VIII, 'Never Despair', 1945–1965, 1988; Russian History Atlas, 1972; Sir Horace Rumbold: Portrait of a Diplomat, 1973; Churchill: A Photographic Portrait, 1974; The Arab-Israeli Conflict: Its History in Maps, 1974; The Jews in Arab Lands: Their History in Maps, 1975; The Jews of Russia: Illustrated History Atlas, 1976; Jerusalem Illustrated History Atlas, 1977; Exile and Return: The Emergence of Jewish Statehood, 1978; Children's Illustrated Bible Atlas, 1979; Final Journey, the Fate of the Jews of Nazi Europe, 1979; Auschwitz and the Allies, 1981; Churchill's Political Philosophy, 1981; Atlas of the Holocaust, 1982; The Jews of Hope: The Plight of Soviet Jewry Today, 1984; Jerusalem: Rebirth of a City, 1985; The Holocaust: The Jewish Tragedy, 1986; Shcharansky: Hero of Our Time, 1986; Second World War, 1989; Churchill: A Life, 1991; Atlas of British Charities, 1993; The Churchill War Papers, 3 vols, 1993, 1995, 2000; In Search of Churchill, 1994; First World War, a History, 1994; The Day the War Ended: VE Day, 1945, 1995; Jerusalem in the 20th Century, 1996; The Boys: Triumph Over Adversity, 1996; Never Again: A History of the Holocaust, 1999; The Jews in the Twentieth Century: An Illustrated History, 2001; Letters to Auntie Fori: The 5,000-Year History of the Jews and their Faith, 2002; The Righteous: The Unsung Heroes of the Holocaust, 2003; D-Day 2004. Contributions: periodicals. *Honours:* Acad. Award 1981, Wolfson Award 1983. *Literary Agent:* AP Watt Ltd, 20 John Street, London WC1N 2DR, England. *Address:* Merton College, Oxford OX1 4JD, England.

GILBERT, Michael (Francis); Author and Solicitor; b. 17 July 1912, Billinghay, Lincolnshire, England; m. Roberta Mary Marsden, 26 July 1947, two s. five d. *Career:* mem. Garrick Club; CWA; FRSL, 1999. *Publications:* Close Quarters, 1947; They Never Looked Inside, 1948; The Doors Open, 1949; Smallbone Deceased, 1950; Death has Deep Roots, 1951; Death in Captivity, 1952; Fear to Tread, 1953; Sky High, 1955; Be Shot for Sixpence, 1956; The Tichborn Claimant, 1957; Blood and Judgement, 1958; After the Fine Weather, 1963; The Crack in the Teacup, 1965; The Dust and the Heat, 1967; Game Without Rules (short stories), 1967; The Etruscan Net, 1969; The Body of a Girl, 1972; The Ninety Second Tiger, 1973; Amateur in Violence (short stories), 1973; Flash Point, 1975; The Night of the Twelfth, 1976; Petrella at Q (short stories), 1977; The Empty House, 1978; Death of a Favourite Girl (in US as The Killing of Katie Steelstock), 1980; Mr Calder and Mr Behrens (short stories), 1982; The Final Throw (in US as End-Game), 1982; The Black Seraphim, 1983; The Long Journey Home, 1985; The Oxford Book of Legal Anecdotes, 1986; Trouble, 1987; Paint Gold & Blood, 1989; Anything for a Quiet Life, 1991; Prep School (anthology), 1991; Roller-Coaster, 1993; Into Battle, 1997; Ring of Terror, 1998; Over and Out, 1998; The Curious Conspiracy, 2002. *Honours:* Lauréat de Grand Prix de Littérature Policière, 1957; Grand Master, Swedish DeKarademins, 1981; Grand Master, MWA, 1987; CWA Cartier Diamond Dagger, 1994. *Address:* Luddesdown Old Rectory, Gravesend, Kent DA13 0XE, England.

GILBERT, Robert Andrew; Antiquarian Bookseller, Ed. and Writer; b. 6 Oct. 1942, Bristol, England; m. Patricia Kathleen Linnell 20 June 1970; three s. two d. *Education:* BA, Philosophy, Psychology, Univ. of Bristol, 1964. *Career:* Ed., Ars Quatuor Coronatorum, 1994–2001; mem. Society of Authors; Societas Rosicruciana in Anglia. *Publications:* The Golden Dawn: Twilight of the Magicians, 1983; A. E. Waite: A Bibliography, 1983; The Golden Dawn Companion, 1986; A. E. Waite: Magician of Many Parts, 1987; The Treasure of Montsegur (with W. N. Birks), 1987; Elements of Mysticism, 1991; World Freemasonry: An Illustrated History, 1992; Freemasonry: A Celebration of the Craft (with J. M. Hamill), 1992; Casting the First Stone, 1993; The Golden Dawn Scrapbook, 1997. Editor: The Oxford Book of English Ghost Stories (with M. A. Cox), 1986; Victorian Ghost Stories: An Oxford Anthology (with M. A. Cox), 1991; The Rise of Victorian Spiritualism (series ed.), 2000. Contributions: Ars Quatuor Coronatorum; Avallaunius; Christian Parapsychologist; Gnosis; Hermetic Journal; Cauda Pavonis; Yeats Annual. *Address:* 4 Julius Rd, Bishopston, Bristol BS7 8EU, England.

GILBERT, Virginia; academic, poet and writer; b. 19 Dec. 1946, Elgin, IL, USA. *Education:* BA, English, Iowa Wesleyan College, 1969; MFA, Creative Writing and Poetry, University of Iowa, 1971; PhD, Creative Writing, Poetry and English, University of Nebraska, 1991. *Career:* Instructor, College of Lake County, IL, 1979; Teaching Asst, University of Nebraska, 1984–87; Asst Prof., 1990–92, Assoc. Prof., 1992–, of English, Alabama A & M University; mem. Associated Writing Programs; MLA; Peace Corps Volunteer Asscn; Peace Corps Volunteer Readers and Writers Asscn; Poetry Society of America; Poets and Writers. *Publications:* To Keep at Bay the Hounds, 1985; The Earth Above, 1993. That Other Brightness, 1996. Contributions: anthologies: Wordlens, Ordinary and Sacred as Blood, Claiming the Spirit Within: A Source Book of Women's Poetry; journals, reviews and quarterlies. *Honours:* National Endowment for the Arts Fellowship, 1976–77; Second Place, Hackney Awards, 1990; First Place, Sakura Festival Haiku Contest, 1992; Fulbright Fellow to China, 1993; First Place Alabama State Poetry Society's Poetry Slam, 1998. *Address:* c/o Department of English, Alabama A & M University, Box 453, Normal, AL 35762, USA.

GILCHRIST, Ellen; Author and Poet; b. 20 Feb. 1935, Vicksburg, MI, USA. *Education:* BA, Millsaps College, Jackson, Mississippi, 1967; Postgraduate Studies, University of Arkansas, 1976. *Career:* mem. Authors' Guild; Authors League of America. *Publications:* The Land Surveyor's Daughter (poems), 1979; The Land of Dreamy Dreams (short stories), 1981; The Annunciation (novel), 1983; Victory Over Japan: A Book of Stories, 1984; Drunk With Love (short stories), 1986; Riding Out the Tropical Depression (poems), 1986; Falling Through Space: The Journals of Ellen Gilchrist, 1987; The Anna Papers (novel), 1988; Light Can Be Both Wave and Particle: A Book of Stories, 1989; I Cannot Get You Close Enough (3 novellas), 1990; Net of Jewels (novel), 1992; Anabasis: A Journey to the Interior, 1994; Starcarbon: A Meditation on Love, 1994; An Age of Miracles (short stories), 1995; Rhoda: A Life in Stories, 1995; Sarah Conley, 1997; I, Rhoda Manning, Go Hunting with my Daddy and Other Stories (short stories), 2002. Contributions: many journals and periodicals. *Honours:* National Endowment for the Arts Grant in Fiction, 1979; Pushcart Prizes, 1979–80, 1983; Louisiana Library Asscn Honor Book, 1981; Mississippi Acad. of Arts and Sciences Awards, 1982, 1985; Saxifrage Award, 1983; American Book Award for Fiction, 1984; J. William Fulbright Award for Literature, University of Arkansas, 1985; Mississippi Institute of Arts and Letters Literature Award, 1985. *Address:* 834 Eastwood Dr., Fayetteville, AR 72701, USA.

GILES, Frank (Thomas Robertson); Journalist (retd) and Writer; b. 31 July 1919, London, England; m. Lady Katharine Sackville, 29 June 1946, one s. two d. *Education:* Wellington College; MA, Open Scholar in History, Brasenose College, Oxford, 1946. *Career:* Asst Correspondent, Paris Bureau, 1947–50, Chief Correspondent, Rome Bureau, 1950–53, and Paris Bureau, 1953–61, The Times, London; Foreign Ed., 1961–77, Deputy Ed., 1967–81, Ed., 1981–83, The Sunday Times, London; Dir, The Times Newspapers, 1981–85. *Publications:* A Prince of Journalists: The Life and Times of Henri de Blowitz, 1962; Sundry Times (autobiog.), 1986; Forty Years On (ed.), 1990; The Locust Years: History of the Fourth French Republic, 1991; Corfu: The Garden Isle (ed.), 1994; Napoleon Bonaparte, England's Prisoner, 2001. Contributions: books, newspapers and periodicals, including the Dictionary of National Biography. *Honours:* Franco-British Society Prize. *Address:* 42 Blomfield Rd, London W9 2PF, England.

GILES, Molly; academic and writer; b. 12 March 1942, California, USA; m. 1st Daniel Giles 1961 (divorced 1974); m. 2nd Richard King 1976 (divorced); three c. *Education:* University of California at Berkeley, 1960–61; BA, 1978, MA, 1980, San Francisco State University. *Career:* Lecturer in Creative Writing, San Francisco State University, 1980–99; Assoc. Prof. of Creative Writing, University of Arkansas, Fayetteville, 1999–. *Publications:* Rough Translations, 1985; Creek Walk and Other Stories, 1996; Iron Shoes, 2000. Contributions: periodicals. *Honours:* Flannery O'Connor Award for Short Fiction, 1986; National Book Critics Circle Citation for Excellence in Book Reviewing, 1991; Small Press Best Fiction/Short Story Award, 1998. *Address:* c/o Department of English, University of Arkansas, Fayetteville, AR 72701, USA.

GILES, Richard Lawrence; Teacher and Writer; b. 24 May 1937, Petersham, NSW, Australia; m. Faye Laurel, 3 May 1969. *Education:* BA, 1957; DipEd, 1969; ATCL, 1971; AMusA, 1973. *Career:* mem. Asscn for Good Government. *Publications:* Technology, Employment and the Industrial Revolution, 1984; For and Against, 1989; Debating, 1992; Understanding Our Economy, 1995. Contributions: Good Government; Progress; The Individual; Australian Land Economics Review. *Address:* PO Box 443, Enfield, NSW 2136, Australia.

GILL, Anton; Writer; b. 22 Oct. 1948, Essex, England; m. Nicola Susan Browne, 6 Nov. 1982. *Education:* Clare College, Cambridge, 1967–70. *Publications:* The Journey Back From Hell; Berlin to Bucharest; City of the Horizon; City of Dreams; A Dance Between Flames; City of the Dead; An Honourable Defeat; The Devil's Mariner, 1997; Peggy Guggenheim: The Life of an Art Addict, 2001; The Great Escape, 2002; The Egyptians: The Kingdom of the Pharaohs Brought to Life, 2003. *Honours:* H. H. Wingate Award. *Address:* c/o Mark Lucas, L.A.W., Elsinore House, 77 Fulham Rd, London W6 8JA, England.

GILL, David Lawrence William; Poet and Writer; b. 3 July 1934, Chislehurst, Kent, England; m. Irene Henry, 5 July 1958, two s. one d. *Education:* BA, German, University College London, 1955; Certificate in Education, Birmingham University, 1958; BA, English, London External, 1970. *Career:* Lecturer, 1971–79, Senior Lecturer, 1979–87, Newland Park College of Education, later incorporated into Bucks College of Higher Education. *Publications:* Men Without Evenings, 1966; The Pagoda and Other Poems, 1969; In the Eye of the Storm, 1975; The Upkeep of the Castle, 1978; Karel Klimsa, by Ondra Lysohorsky (trans.), 1984; One Potato, Two Potato (with Dorothy Clancy), 1985; Legends, Please, 1986; The White Raven, 1989; The New Hesperides, 1991. Contributions: many journals, reviews, and magazines. *Address:* 38 Yarnells Hill, Botley, Oxford OX2 9BE, England.

GILL, Elizabeth (see Hankin, Elizabeth Rosemary).

GILL, Stephen Matthew; Poet, Author and Ed.; b. 25 June 1932, Sialkot, Pakistan; m. Sarala Gill, 17 Feb. 1970, one s. two d. *Education:* BA, Punjab University, 1956; MA, Meerut College, Agra University, 1963; University of Ottawa, 1967–70; University of Oxford, 1971. *Career:* Ed., Canadian World Federalist, 1971–73, 1977–79, Writer's Lifeline, 1982–; Pres., Vesta Publications Ltd, 1974–90; mem. Christian Cultural Asscn of South Asians, vice-pres.; International Acad. of Poets, fellow; PEN International; World Acad. of Arts and Culture; World Federalists of Canada; Amnesty International; Writers Union of Canada. *Publications:* Poetry: Reflections and Wounds, 1978; Moans and Waves, 1989; The Dove of Peace, 1989; The Flowers of Thirst, 1991; Songs for Harmony, 1992; Flashes, 1994; Aman Di Ghuggi, 1994; Divergent Shades, 1995; Shrine, 1999. Fiction: Life's Vagaries (short stories), 1974; Why, 1976; The Loyalist City, 1979; Immigrants, 1982. Non-Fiction: Six Symbolist Plays of Yeats, 1974; Discovery of Bangladesh, 1975; Scientific Romances of H. G. Wells, 1975; English Grammar for Beginners, 1977; Political Convictions of G. B. Shaw, 1980; Sketches of India, 1980. Editor: various anthologies. Contributions: Over 250 publications. *Honours:* Hon. DLitt, World University, 1986, World Acad. of Arts and Culture, 1990; International Eminent Poet, International Poets Acad., Chennai, 1991; Pegasus International Poetry for Peace Award, Poetry in the Arts, Austin, Texas, 1991; Laureate Man of Letters, United Poets Laureate International, 1992; Poet of Peace Award, Pakistan Asscn, Orleans, Ontario, 1995; Mawaheb Culture Friendship Medal, Mawaheb Magazine, 1997; Sahir Award of Honour, 1999. *Address:* PO Box 32, Cornwall, ON K6H 5R9, Canada. *E-mail:* stefgill@hotmail.com.

GILLIES, Valerie, MA, MLitt; British poet and writer; b. 4 June 1948, Edmonton, AB, Canada; m. William Gillies 1972; one s. two d. *Education:* Univ. of Edinburgh. *Career:* writer-in-residence, Duncan of Jordanstone College of Art, Dundee 1988–90, University of Edinburgh 1995–98; mem. Soc. of Authors, Scotland (fellow). *Publications:* Trio: New Poets from Edinburgh, 1971; Each Bright Eye: Selected Poems, 1977; Bed of Stone, 1984; Leopardi: A Scottish Quair, 1987; Tweed Journey, 1989; The Chanter's Tune, 1990; The Jordanstone Folio, 1990; The Ringing Rock, 1995. Contributions: Radio, television, reviews, and journals. *Honours:* Scottish Arts Council Bursary, 1976, and Book Award, 1996; Eric Gregory Award, 1976. *Address:* c/o Society of Authors in Scotland, 84 Drayton Gardens, London, SW10 9SB, England.

GILLON, Adam; Professor of English Emeritus, Writer and Poet; b. 17 July 1921, Poland; m. Isabella Zamojre, 1946, one s. one d. *Education:* MA, Hebrew University of Jerusalem, 1949; PhD, English and Comparative Literature, Columbia University, 1954. *Career:* Prof. of English, Acadia University, NS, 1957–62, University of Haifa, 1979–84; Prof. of English and Comparative Literature, 1962–81, Prof. Emeritus, 1981–, SUNY at New Paltz; mem. Haiku Society of America; Joseph Conrad Society of America; MLA; Polish Institute of Arts and Sciences. *Publications:* Poetry: Selected Poems and Translations, 1962; In the Manner of Haiku: Seven Aspects of Man, 1967; Daily New and Old: Poems in the Manner of Haiku, 1971; Strange Mutations in the Manner of Haiku, 1973; Summer Morn... Winter Weather: Poems 'Twist Haiku and Senryu, 1975; The Withered Leaf: A Medley of Haiku and Snryu, 1982. Fiction: A Cup of Fury, 1962; Jared, 1986. Non-Fiction: The Eternal Solitary: A Study of Joseph Conrad, 1960; Joseph Conrad: Commemorative Essays (ed.), 1975; Conrad and Shakespeare and Other Essays, 1976; Joseph Conrad, 1982; Joseph Conrad: Comparative Essays, 1994. Other: Trans, radio plays, and screenplays. Contributions: journals, reviews, and periodicals. *Honours:* Alfred Jurzykowski Foundation Award, 1967; Joseph Fels Foundation Award, 1970; National Endowment for the Humanities Grant, 1985; Gold Award, Worldfest International Film Festival, 1993. *Address:* Lake Illyria, 490 Route 299 W, New Paltz, NY 12561, USA.

GILMAN, Dorothy, (Dorothy Gilman Butters); Author and Children's Writer; b. 25 June 1923, New Brunswick, NJ, USA; m. Edgar A Butters, 15 Sept. 1945, divorced 1965, two s. *Education:* Pennsylvania Acad. of Fine Arts, 1940–45; University of Pennsylvania and Art Students League, 1963–64. *Career:* mem. Authors' Guild. *Publications:* Fiction: The Unexpected Mrs Pollifax, 1966, in the UK as Mrs Pollifax, Spy, 1971; Uncertain Voyage, 1967; The Amazing Mrs Pollifax, 1970; The Elusive Mrs Pollifax, 1971; A Palm for Mrs Pollifax, 1973; A Nun in the Closet, 1975, in the UK as A Nun in the Cupboard, 1976; The Clairvoyant Countess, 1975; Mrs Pollifax on Safari, 1977; A New Kind of Country, 1978; The Tightrope Walker, 1979; Mrs Pollifax on the China Station, 1983; The Maze in the Heart of the Castle, 1983; Mrs Pollifax and the Hong Kong Buddha, 1985; Mrs Pollifax and the Golden Triangle, 1988; Incident at Badamya, 1989; Mrs Pollifax and the Whirling Dervish, 1990; Mrs Pollifax and the Second Thief, 1993; Mrs Pollifax Pursued, 1995. Children's Fiction: Enchanted Caravan, 1949; Carnival Gypsy, 1950; Ragamuffin Alley, 1951; The Calico Year, 1953; Four-Party Line, 1954; Papa Dolphin's Table, 1955; Girl in Buckskin, 1956; Heartbreak Street, 1958; Witch's Silver, 1959; Masquerade, 1961; Ten Leagues to Boston Town, 1962; The Bells of Freedom, 1963. Contributions: Magazines. *Honours:* Catholic Book Award, 1975. *Literary Agent:* Howard Morhaim Literary Agency, 841 Broadway, Suite 604, New York, NY 10003, USA.

GILMAN, George G. (see Harknett, Terry).

GILMAN, Rebecca; American playwright; b. Trussville, AL. *Plays:* My Sin and Nothing More 1997, The Land of Little Horses 1998, The Glory of Living 1999, Spinning into Butter 2000, Boy Gets Girl 2000, Blue Surge 2002, The Sweetest Swing in Baseball 2004. *Honours:* London Evening Standard Award for Most Promising Playwright 1999, American Theatre Critics' Asscn Osborn Award. *Address:* c/o Faber and Faber Ltd, 3 Queen Square, London, WC1N 3AU, England. *Telephone:* (20) 7465-0045. *Fax:* (20) 7465-0034. *Website:* www.faber.co.uk.

GILMAN, Sander L(awrence); Prof. and Writer; b. 21 Feb. 1944, Buffalo, NY, USA; m. Marina von Eckardt, 28 Dec. 1969. *Education:* BA, PhD, Tulane University; University of Munich; Free University of Berlin. *Career:* Prof. of German Language and Literature; Prof. of Psychiatry. *Publications:* Nietzchean Parody, 1976; The Face of Madness: Hugh W. Diamond and the Origin of Psychiatric Photography, 1976; Bertold Brecht's Berlin, 1976; Seeing the Insane, 1981; Sexuality: An Illustrated History, 1989; The Jew's Body, 1991; Freud, Race and Gender, 1993; The Case of Sigmund Freud: Medicine and Identity at Fin de Siècle, 1994; Re-emerging Jewish Culture in Today's Germany, 1994; Franz Kafka, The Jewish Patient, 1995; Jews in Today's German Culture, 1995; Also scholarly edns of German texts and monographs. *Address:* c/o Dept of Modern Languages, Cornell University, 203 Merrill Hall, Ithaca, NY 14853-0001, USA.

GILMOUR, David, BA; British writer; b. 14 Nov. 1952, London, England; m. Sarah Anne Bradstock 1975, one s. three d. *Education:* Balliol Coll., Oxford. *Career:* Deputy Ed. and Contributing Ed., Middle East International, London 1978–85; Research Fellow, St Antony's Coll., Oxford 1996–97. *Publications:* Dispossessed: The Ordeal of the Palestinians, 1980; Lebanon: The Fractured Country, 1983; The Transformation of Spain: From Franco to the Constitutional Monarchy, 1985; The Last Leopard: A Life of Giuseppe di Lampedusa, 1988; The Hungry Generations, 1991; Cities of Spain, 1992; Curzon, 1994; The Long Recessional: The Imperial Life of Rudyard Kipling, 2001. Contributions: periodicals. *Honours:* Marsh Biography Award, 1988; Scottish Arts Council Spring Book Award, 1988; Duff Cooper Prize, 1994; Elizabeth Longford Prize for Historical Biography, 2003. *Literary Agent:* Gillon Aitken Associates Ltd, 18–21 Cavaye Place, London, SW10 9PT, England. *Telephone:* (20) 7373-8672. *Fax:* (20) 7373-6002.

GILROY, Frank D(aniel); Dramatist, Screenwriter, Author, Producer and Dir; b. 13 Oct. 1925, New York, NY, USA; m. Ruth Dorothy Gaydos, 13 Feb. 1954, three s. *Education:* BA magna cum laude, Dartmouth College, 1950; Yale School of Drama, 1950–51. *Career:* mem. Dirs Guild of America; Dramatists Guild, pres., 1969–71; Writers Guild of America. *Publications:* Fiction: Private, 1970; Little Ego (with Ruth Gilroy), 1970; Little Ego (with Ruth Gilroy), 1970; From Noon Till Three, 1973. Non-Fiction: I Wake Up Screening: Everything You Need to Know About Making Independent Films Including a Thousand Reasons Not To, 1993. Other: Plays: Who'll Save the Plowboy?, 1957; The Subject was Roses, 1962; That Summer, That Fall, 1967; The Only Game in Town, 1968; The Next Contestant, 1978; Last Licks, 1979; Real to Reel, 1987; Match Point, 1990; A Way with Words, 1991; Give the Bishop My Faint Regards, 1992; Any Given Day, 1993. Films: The Fastest Gun Alive (with Russell House), 1956; Gallant Hours (with Beirne Lay Jr), 1960; Desperate Characters, 1970; From Noon till Three, 1977; Once in Paris, 1978; The Gig, 1985; The Luckiest Man in the World, 1989. *Honours:* Obie Award, 1962; Outer Circle Award, 1964; Drama Critics Circle Award, 1964; New York Theatre Club Award, 1964–65; Tony Award, 1965; Pulitzer Prize for Drama, 1965; Best Screenplay Award, Berlin Film Festival, 1970. *Address:* c/o Dramatists Guild, 1501 Broadway, New York, NY 10036, USA.

GINZBURG, Carlo; historian and academic; b. 1939, Turin, Italy; m. 1st (divorced); m. 2nd Luisa Ciammitti; two d. *Education:* Scuola Normale Superiore, Pisa, Warburg Institute, London. *Career:* Prof. of Modern History, University of Bologna, 1970–; several visiting fellowships. *Publications:* I benandanti: Stregoneria e culti agrari tra Cinquecento e Seicento, 1966, English trans. as The Night Battles: Witchcraft and Agrarian Cults in the Sixteenth and Seventeenth Centuries, 1983; Il nicodemismo: Simulazione e dissimulazione religiosa nell'Europa del '500, 1970; Giochi di pazienza: Un seminario sul Beneficio di Cristo (with Adriano Prosperi), 1975; Il formaggio e i vermi: Il cosmo di un mugnaio del '500, 1976, English trans. as The Cheese and the Worms: The Cosmos of a Sixteenth-Century Miller, 1980; Indagini su Piero: Il Battesimo, il Ciclo di Arezzo, la Flagellazione di Urbino, 1981, English trans. as Clues, Myths, and the Historical Method, 1989; Storia notturna: Una decifrazione del sabba, 1989, English trans. as Ecstacies: Deciphering the Witches' Sabbath, 1991; Il giudice e lo storico: Considerazioni in margine al processo sofri, 1991; Il registro: Carcere politico di Civitavecchia (ed. with Aldo Natoli and Vittorio Foa), 1994. *Honours:* Citta di Montesilvano, 1989. *Address:* c/o Departimento di Storia, Universita degli Studi, Piazza San Giovanni in Monte 2, 40124 Bologna, Italy.

GIOIA, (Michael) Dana, BA, MA, MBA; American writer and poet; *Chairman, National Endowment for the Arts*; b. 24 Dec. 1950, Los Angeles, CA; m. Mary Hiecke 1980; three s. (one deceased). *Education:* Stanford Univ., Harvard Univ. *Career:* fmr Exec., Vice-Pres. of Marketing, General Foods, New York; classical music critic, San Francisco magazine 1997–2002; visiting writer, Johns Hopkins Univ., Sarah Lawrence Coll., Mercer Univ., Wesleyan Univ.; Chair., National Endowment for the Arts 2003–. *Publications:* Daily Horoscope, 1986; Mottetti: Poems of Love, by Eugenio Montale (trans.), 1990; The Gods of Winter, 1991; Can Poetry Matter?: Essays on Poetry and American Culture, 1992; An Introduction to Poetry, 1994; The Madness of Hercules, by Seneca (trans.), 1995; Interrogations at Noon (poems), 2001; Nosferatu (opera libretto), 2001; The Barrier of a Common Language: Essays on Contemporary British Poetry, 2002. Editor: The Ceremony and Other Stories, 1984; Poems from Italy (with William Jay Smith), 1985; New Italian Poets (with Michael Palma), 1991; Formal Introductions: An Investigative Anthology, 1994; Certain Solitudes: Essays on the Poetry of Donald Justice (with William Logan), 1997; The Longman Anthology of Short Fiction: Stories and Authors in Context (with R. S. Gwynn), 2001; An Introduction to Poetry (with X. J. Kennedy), 2002; An Introduction to Fiction (with X. J. Kennedy), 2002; Literature: An Introduction to Fiction, Poetry and Drama (with X. J. Kennedy), 2002; The Misread City: New Literary Los Angeles (with Scott Timberg), 2003. Contributions: reviews, journals and periodicals. *Honours:* Esquire Best of New Generation Award 1984, Frederick Bock Prize for Poetry 1985, American Book Award 2002. *Address:* National Endowment for the Arts, 1100 Pennsylvania Avenue NW, Washington, DC 20506, USA. *Website:* arts.endow.gov.

GIOSEFFI, Daniela; Poet and Writer; b. 12 Feb. 1941, Orange, NJ, USA; m. 1st Richard J. Kearney, 5 Sept. 1965, divorced 1982, one d.; m. 2nd Lionel B. Luttinger, 1986. *Education:* BA, Montclair State College; MFA, Drama, Catholic University of America. *Career:* Editorial Board, VIA, magazine of literature and culture at Purdue University; Skylands Writers Asscn Inc, pres.; Wise Womans Web, ed.-in-chief: Electronic magazine of Literature and Graphics; Ed. literary websites: njpoets.com, poetsusa.com, italianamericanwriters.com, gioseffi.com; mem. PEN; Acad. of American

Poets; National Book Critics Circle; Poetry Society of America; Poets House, NYC. *Publications:* The Great American Belly Dance (novel), 1977; Eggs in the Lake (poems), 1979; Earth Dancing: Mother Nature's Oldest Rite, 1980; Women on War, 1990; On Prejudice: A Global Perspective, 1993; Words, Wounds and Flowers, 1995; Dust Disappears by Carilda Oliver Labra, (trans.), 1995; In Bed With the Exotic Enemy: Stories and Novella, 1997; Going On (poems), 2000; Symbiosis (poems), 2002; Women on War: International Writings (ed.), 2003. Contributions: Nation; Chelsea; Ambit; Poetry Review; Modern Poetry Studies; Anteus; The Paris Review; American Book Review; The Hungry Mind Review; Prairie Schooner; Independent publishers; Poetry East; The Cortland Review; Big City Lit. *Honours:* New York State Council on the Arts Award Grants in Poetry, 1972, 1977; American Book Award, 1990; PEN American Centre Short Fiction Award, 1990. *Address:* 57 Montague St, 8G, Brooklyn Heights, New York, NY 11201, USA.

GIOVANNI, Nikki, (Yolande Cornelia Giovanni); Poet, Writer and Prof. of Creative Writing; b. 7 June 1943, Knoxville, Tennessee, USA; one s. *Education:* BA, Fisk University, 1967; School of Social Work, University of Pennsylvania, 1967; Columbia University, 1968. *Career:* Asst Prof., Queens College, CUNY, 1968; Assoc. Prof., Livingston College, Rutgers University, 1968–72; Founder-Publisher, Niktom Publishers, 1970–74; Visiting Prof., Ohio State University, 1984; Prof. of Creative Writing, College of Mount St Joseph on the Ohio, 1985–87; Prof., Virginia Polytechnic Institute and State University, 1987–. *Publications:* Poetry: Black Judgement, 1968; Black Feeling, Black Talk, 1968; Re: Creation, 1970; Poem for Angela Yvonne Davis, 1970; My House, 1972; The Women and the Men, 1975; Cotton Candy on a Rainy Day, 1978; Those Who Ride the Night Winds, 1983; Blues: For All the Changes, 1999; Quilting the Black-Eyed Pea: Poems and Not-Quite Poems, 2002. Children's Poetry: Spin a Soft Black Dog, 1971; Ego Tripping and Other Poems for Young Readers, 1973; Vacation Time, 1980; Knoxville, Tennessee, 1994. Non-Fiction: Gemini: An Extended Autobiographical Statement on My First Twenty-Five Years of Being a Black Poet, 1971; A Dialogue: James Baldwin and Nikki Giovanni, 1973; A Poetic Equation: Conversations Between Nikki Giovanni and Margaret Walker, 1974; Sacred Cows... and Other Edibles, 1988; Conversations with Nikki Giovanni, 1992; Racism 101, 1994. Editor: Night Comes Softly: An Anthology of Black Female Voices, 1970; Appalachian Elders: A Warm Hearth Sampler (with Cathee Dennison), 1991; Grandmothers: Poems, Reminiscences, and Short Stories About the Keepers of Our Traditions, 1994. *Honours:* Ford Foundation Grant, 1968; National Endowment for the Arts Grant, 1969; Hon. doctorates. *Address:* c/o Dept of English, Shanks Hall, Virginia Polytechnic Institute and State University, Blacksburg, VA 24061, USA.

GIRARD, Keith; American editor; *Ed.-in-Chief, Billboard magazine. Career:* fmr reporter, The Washington Post; Ed. Daily Record and Investment News; Ed.-in-Chief, Billboard magazine 2003–. *Address:* Billboard, VNU eMedia Inc., 770 Broadway, Sixth Floor, New York, NY 10003, USA. *Website:* www.billboard.com.

GISCOMBE, C. S.; Poet, Writer and Prof. of English; b. 30 Nov. 1950, Dayton, OH, USA; m. Katharine Wright, 10 Aug. 1975, one d. *Education:* BA, SUNY at Albany, 1973; MFA, Cornell University, 1975. *Career:* Faculty, Syracuse University, 1977, Cornell University, 1980–89; Prof. of English, Illinois State University, 1989–98, Pennsylvania State University, 1998–; mem. Poets and Writers. *Publications:* Poetry: Postcards, 1977; Here, 1994; Giscombe Road, 1998; Two sections from 'Practical Geography: Five Poems', 2000; Inland, 2001. Other: Intro and Out of Dislocation, 2000. Contributions: periodicals. *Honours:* Creative Artists Public Service Fellowship, 1981–82; National Endowment for the Arts Fellowship, 1986–87; New York Foundation for the Arts Fellowship, 1988; Carl Sandburg Award for Poetry, 1998. *Address:* c/o Dept of English, Pennsylvania State University, State College, PA 16804, USA.

GIVNER, Joan (Mary); Prof. of English (retd) and Writer; b. 5 Sept. 1936, Manchester, England; m. David Givner, 15 April 1965, two d. *Education:* BA, 1958, PhD, 1972, University of London; MA, Washington University, St Louis, 1962. *Career:* Prof. of English, University of Regina, 1965–95; Ed., Wascana Review, 1984–92; mem. Saskatchewan Writers' Guild. *Publications:* Katherine Anne Porter: A Life, 1982; Tentacles of Unreason, 1985; Katherine Anne Porter: Conversations (ed.), 1987; Unfortunate Incidents, 1988; Mazo de la Roche: The Hidden Life, 1989; Scenes from Provincial Life, 1991; The Self-Portrait of a Literary Biographer, 1993; In the Garden of Henry James, 1996. *Address:* 2587 Seaview Rd, RR 1, Mill Bay, BC V0R 2P0, Canada.

GJESSING, Ketil; poet and writer; b. 18 Feb. 1934, Oslo, Norway. *Education:* University of Oslo. *Career:* teacher, Atlantic College (now United World College of the Atlantic), 1965–66; dramaturg at the Radio Drama Dept, Norwegian Broadcasting Corp, 1966–99; adviser, Klassisk Musikkmagasion, 2001; mem. Norwegian Authors' Asscn; Norwegian Authors' Centre; Norwegian Trans' Asscn. *Publications:* 10 collections of poetry, including: Dans på roser og glass (Dance on Roses and Glass), 1996. Contributions: Aftenposten (newspaper); Vinduet; Samtiden (magazines); others. *Honours:* Gyldendals Prize, 1983; Språklig Samlings Litteraturpris, 1996. *Address:* Dannevigsvn 12, 0463 Oslo, Norway.

GLAISTER, Lesley Gillian, MA, FRSL; writer; b. 4 Oct. 1956, Wellinborough, Northamptonshire, England; three s. *Education:* Univ. of Sheffield. *Publications:* novels: Honour Thy Father, Trick or Treat, Digging to Australia, Limestone and Clay 1993, Partial Eclipse 1994, The Private Parts of Women 1996, Easy Peasy 1997, Sheer Blue Bliss 1999, Now You See Me 2001, As Far As You Can Go 2004; plays: Bird Calls (Crucible Theatre, Sheffield) 2003. *Honours:* Somerset Maugham Award, Betty Trask Award, Yorkshire Author of the Year Award 1993. *Address:* 34 Stainton Road, Sheffield, S11 7AX, England.

GLAZEBROOK, Philip Kirkland; Writer; b. 3 April 1937, London, England; m. Clare Rosemary Gemmell, 5 Oct. 1968, two s. two d. *Education:* MA, Trinity College, Cambridge. *Publications:* Try Pleasure, 1968; The Eye of the Beholder, 1975; Byzantine Honeymoon, 1978; Journey to Kars, 1985; Captain Vinegar's Commission, 1988; The Walled Garden, 1989; The Gate at the End of the World, 1989; Journey to Khiva, 1992; The Electric Rock Garden, 2001. Contributions: Spectator; Sunday Times; New York Times; Washington Post; Daily Telegraph. *Address:* Mabledon Farm House, Vauxhall Lane, Tonbridge TN11 0NE, England.

GLEN, Duncan Munro; academic, poet and writer; b. 11 Jan. 1933, Cambuslang, Lanarkshire, Scotland; m. Margaret Eadie 1957; one s. one d. *Education:* Edinburgh College of Art. *Career:* Lecturer to Principal Lecturer, South Lancashire University, 1965–78; Prof. and Head of the Dept of Visual Communication, Nottingham Trent University, 1972–87; Ed., Akros, 1965–83, Scottish Poetry Library Newsletter, 1988–, Zed 2 O, 1991–; mem. Chartered Society of Designers, fellow. *Publications:* Hugh MacDiarmid and the Scottish Renaissance, 1964; Selected Essays of Hugh MacDiarmid (ed.), 1969; In Appearances: A Sequence of Poems, 1971; The Individual and the Twentieth Century Scottish Literary Tradition, 1971; Buits and Wellies: A Sequence of Poems, 1976; Gaitherings (poems), 1977; Realities (poems), 1980; The Turn of the Earth: A Sequence of Poems, 1985; The Autobiography of a Poet, 1986; Tales to Be Told, 1987; European Poetry in Scotland (ed.), 1990; Selected Poems, 1965–90, 1991; The Poetry of the Scots, 1991; Hugh MacDiarmid: Out of Langhoom and Into the World, 1992; Echoes: Frae Classical and Italian Poetry, 1992; The Bright Writers' Guides to Scottish Culture, 1995; A Nation in a Parish: A New Historical Prospect of Scotland, 1995; Splendid Lanarkshire, 1997; Selected New Poems 1987–1996, 1998; Illustrious Fife, 1998; A New History of Cambuslang, 1998; Selected Scottish and Other Essays, 1999; Scottish Literature: A New History from 1299 to 1999, 1999; Printing Type Designs: A New History from Gutenburg to 2000, 2001; Winter: A Poem, and Other Verses by James Thomson (ed.), 2002; Historic Fife Murders, 2002; Robert Louis Stevenson and the Covenanters on the Bass Rock and 'The Tale of Tod Lapraik', 2002; Ruined Rural Fife Churches, 2002; A Photographic Celebration at the Ruins of Bighty Farm, 2002; The Ruins of Newark Castle, St Monans, Autumn 2002, 2003; Crossing Schools of Art: An Illustrated Historical Memoir, 2003; Stevenson's Scotland (ed.), 2003. Contributions: numerous journals and magazines. *Honours:* Special Award for Services to Scottish Literature, Scottish Arts Council, 1975; Howard Sergeant Poetry Award, 1993; Hon. Doctorate, Paisley University, 2000. *Address:* 33 Lady Nairn Avenue, Kirkcaldy, Fife KY1 2AW, Scotland.

GLENDINNING, Victoria; Author and Journalist; b. 23 April 1937, Sheffield, England; m. 1st O. N. V. Glendinning, 1958, four s.; m. 2nd Terence de Vere White, 1981; m. 3rd K. P. O'Sullivan, 1996. *Education:* BA, Modern Languages, Somerville College, Oxford, 1959; Diploma, Social Administration, 1969. *Career:* Editorial Asst, TLS, 1970–74; mem. RSL, Vice-Pres.; English PEN, Pres., 2001–03. *Publications:* A Suppressed Cry: Life and Death of a Quaker Daughter, 1969; Elizabeth Bowen: Portrait of a Writer, 1977; Edith Sitwell: A Unicorn Among Lions, 1981; Vita: The Life of Victoria Sackville-West, 1983; Rebecca West: A Life, 1987; The Grown-ups (novel), 1989; Hertfordshire, 1989; Trollope, 1992; Electricity (novel), 1995; Sons and Mothers (co-ed.), 1996; Jonathan Swift, 1998; Flight (novel), 2001. Contributions: various journals, newspapers and magazines. *Honours:* Duff Cooper Memorial Award, 1981; James Tait Black Memorial Prize, 1981; Whitbread Awards, 1983, 1992; Whitbread Award for Biography, 1992; Hon. DLitt, Southampton University, 1994, University of Ulster, 1995, Trinity College, Dublin, 1995, University of York, 2000; CBE, 1998. *Literary Agent:* David Higham Associates, 5–8 Lower John St, Golden Sq., London W1F 9HA, England. *E-mail:* victoriag@f25.com.

GLENDOWER, Rose (see Harris, Marion Rose).

GLICKMAN, James A., BA, MFA; educator and writer; b. 29 Dec. 1948, Davenport, IA, USA; m. Elissa Deborah Gelfand 1982; one s. *Education:* University of Iowa Writers' Workshop. *Career:* Instructor, University of Arizona Law School, Tucson, 1972; English Teacher, Community College of Rhode Island, Lincoln, 1972–; Faculty Mem., Radcliffe Seminars, Cambridge, Massachusetts, 1985–88. *Publications:* Sounding the Waters, 1996; The Crossing Point, 1999. Contributions: Short stories to periodicals including Kansas Quarterly; Redbook; Ladies Home Journal; Worcester Review. *Literary Agent:* Aaron Priest Literary Agency, 708 Third Avenue, 23rd Floor, New York, NY 10017-4103, USA. *Address:* 51 McGilpin Road, Sturbridge, MA 01566-1230, USA.

GLISSANT, Édouard; Distinguished Prof., Writer, Dramatist and Poet; b. 21 Sept. 1928, Sainte-Marie, Martinique. *Education:* DPhil, 1953, State Doctorate, 1977, Sorbonne, Université de Paris; Musée de l'homme, Paris.

Career: Instructor in Philosophy, Lycée des Jeunes Filles, Fort-de-France, Martinique, 1965; Founder, 1967, Dir, 1967–78, Institut Martiniquais d'Etudes, Fort-de-France; Co-Founder, ACOMA Review, 1970; Ed., UNESCO, Paris, France, 1981–88; Distinguished Prof. and Dir of Center for French and Francophone Studies, Louisiana State University, Baton Rouge, USA, 1988–. *Publications:* Poetry: Un champ d'îles, 1953; La terre inquiète, 1954; Les Indes: Poèmes de l'une et l'autre terre, 1955; Le sel noir, 1959; Le sang rivé, 1960; Poèmes, 1963; Boises, 1979; Pays rêvé, pays réel, 1985; Fastes, 1992. Non-Fiction: Soleil de la conscience, 1956; L'intention poétique, 1969; Le discours antillais, 1981, English trans. as Caribbean Discourse: Selected Essays, 1989; Poétique de la relation, 1990. Fiction: La Lézarde, 1958; Le quatrième siècle, 1964; Malemort, 1975; La case du commandeur, 1981; Mahagony, 1987; Tout-monde, 1993. Play: Monsieur Toussaint, 1961, revised version, 1978. *Honours:* Ordre des Francophones d'Amérique, Québec; Prix Rénaudot, 1958; Prix Charles Veillon, 1965; Award, 12th Putterbaugh Conference, Norman, Oklahoma, 1989; Hon. LittD, York University, 1989; Roger Callois International Prize, 1991.

GLOAG, Julian, BA, MA, FRSL; novelist; b. 2 July 1930, London, England; one s. one d. *Education:* Magdalene College, Cambridge. *Career:* mem. Authors Guild. *Publications:* Our Mother's House, 1963; A Sentence of Life, 1966; Maundy, 1969; A Woman of Character, 1973; Sleeping Dogs Lie, 1980; Lost and Found, 1981; Blood for Blood, 1985; Only Yesterday, 1986; Love as a Foreign Language, 1991; Le passeur de la nuit, 1996; Chambre d'ombre, 1996. Teleplays: Only Yesterday, 1986; The Dark Room, 1988. *Address:* c/o Michelle Lapautre, 6 rue Jean Carriès, 75007 Paris, France.

GLOVER, Douglas (Herschel); Writer and Ed.; b. 14 Nov. 1948, Simcoe, Ontario, Canada. *Education:* BA, York University, 1969; MLitt, University of Edinburgh, 1971; MFA, University of Iowa, 1982. *Career:* various writer-in-residencies; Lecturer, Skidmore College, 1992, 1993; Visiting Prof., Colgate University, 1995; mem. Writers' Union of Canada. *Publications:* The Mad River, 1981; Precious, 1984; Dog Attempts to Drown Man in Saskatoon, 1985; The South Will Rise at Noon, 1988; A Guide to Animal Behaviour, 1991; Coming Attractions (co-ed.), 5 vols, 1991–95; The Life and Times of Captain N, 1993; The Journey Prize Anthology (ed.), 1994; Best Canadian Stories (ed.), 1996, 1997, 2000–03; Notes from a Prodigal Son, 1999; Sixteen Categories of Desire, 2000; Elle, 2003; Bad News of the Heart, 2003. Contributions: numerous journals and magazines. *Honours:* Contributor's Prize, Canadian Fiction Magazine, 1985; Literary Press Group Writers Choice Award, 1986; National Magazine Award for Fiction, 1990. *Address:* RR 1, Waterford, ON N0E 1Y0, Canada.

GLOVER, Judith; Author; b. 31 March 1943, Wolverhampton, England; two d. *Education:* Wolverhampton High School for Girls, 1954–59; Aston Polytechnic, 1960. *Publications:* Drink Your Own Garden (non-fiction), 1979; The Sussex Quartet: The Stallion Man, 1982, Sisters and Brothers, 1984, To Everything a Season, 1986; Birds in a Gilded Cage, 1987; The Imagination of the Heart, 1989; Tiger Lilies, 1991; Mirabelle, 1992; Minerva Lane, 1994; Pride of Place, 1995. *Address:* c/o Artellus Ltd, 30 Dorset House, Gloucester Pl., London NW1 5AD, England.

GŁOWACKI, Janusz; Writer and Playwright; b. 13 Sept. 1938, Poznań, Poland; m.; one d. *Education:* Warsaw Univ. *Career:* columnist, Kultura weekly, 1964–81; lecturer in many colleges and universities in USA, incl. Bennington, Yale, Cornell, Columbia; playwright-in-residence, New York Shakespeare Festival, 1984, Mark Taper Forum, Los Angeles, 1989; mem. American and Polish PEN Club; Polish Film Union. *Publications:* Short Stories: Nowy taniec la-ba-da, 1970; Paradis, 1973; Polowanie na muchy, 1974; My Sweet Raskolnikov, 1977; Opowiadania wybrane, 1978; Skrzek. Coraz trudniej kochac, 1980; Rose Café, 1997. Novels: Moc truchleje, 1981; Ostani ciec, 2001. Film Scripts: Rejs, 1970; Psychodrama (with Marek Piwowski), 1971; Polowanie na muchy, 1971; Trzeba zabic te milosc, 1974; No Smoking Section (co-author), 1987; Hairdo, 1999. Plays: Cudzolóstwo ukarane, 1971; Mecz, 1977; Obciach, 1977; Kopciuch, 1981; Fortinbras Gets Drunk, 1986; Hunting Cockroaches, 1986; Cinders; Antigone in New York, 1993; Czwarta siostra, 1999; Scieki, Skrzeki, karaluchy (selected works), 1996; The Fourth Sister, 2002. *Honours:* Fellow in Writing, Univ. of Iowa, 1977, 1982; Hon. mem., Univ. of Iowa, 1977, 1982; Premio Molière, Argentina, 1986; First Prize, American Theatre Critics Asscn, 1986; Joseph Kesserling Award, 1987; Drama League of New York Playwrighting Award, 1987; Guggenheim Award, 1988; Nat. Endowment for the Arts Fellowship, 1988; Hon. MA, Atlantic Center for the Arts, 1991; Alfred Jurzykowski Foundation Award, 1997; Tony Cox Award, Nantucket, USA, 1999. *Address:* ul. Bednarska 7 m. 4, 00-310 Warsaw, Poland; 845 West End Ave, Apt. 4B, New York, NY 10025, USA.

GLÜCK, Louise Elisabeth; American poet and author; *Poet Laureate*; b. 22 April 1943, New York, NY; m. 1st Charles Hertz (divorced); one s.; m. 2nd John Dranow 1977 (divorced 1996). *Education:* Sarah Lawrence Coll., Bronxville, New York and Columbia Univ., New York. *Career:* artist-in-residence, Goddard Coll., Plainfield, VT 1971–72, faculty mem. 1973–74; poet-in-residence, Univ. of North Carolina at Greensboro 1973; Visiting Prof. Univ. of Iowa 1976–77; Elliston Prof. of Poetry Univ. of Cincinnati, OH 1978; Visiting Prof. Columbia Univ. 1979; Holloway Lecturer Univ. of California at Berkeley 1982; faculty mem., bd mem., MFA Writing Program at Warren Wilson Coll., Swannoa, NC 1980–84; Visiting Prof. Univ. of California at Davis 1983; Scott Prof. of Poetry, Williams Coll., MA 1983, part-time Sr Lecturer in English 1984–97, Parrish Prof. 1997–; Regents Prof. of Poetry Univ. of California at Los Angeles 1985–88; Baccalaureate Speaker Williams Coll. 1993; Poet Laureate of Vermont 1994; visiting mem. faculty Harvard Univ., MA 1995; Hurst Prof. Brandeis Univ. 1996; Special Consultant in Poetry at Library of Congress, Washington, DC 1999–2000; Poet Laureate of the USA 2003–; Fellow, American Acad. of Arts and Sciences; mem. PEN, American Acad. and Institute of Arts and Letters, Acad. of American Poets (bd of chancellors 1999–). *Publications:* poetry: Firstborn 1968, The House on the Marshland 1975, The Garden 1976, Descending Figure 1980, The Triumph of Achilles 1985, Ararat 1990, The Wild Iris (Pulitzer Prize for Poetry 1993) 1992, Proofs and Theories: Essays on Poetry 1994, The First Four Books of Poems 1995, Meadowlands 1996, Vita Nova 1999, The Seven Ages 2001, October 2004; contrib. to many anthologies and periodicals. *Honours:* Rockefeller Foundation Grant 1968–69, Nat. Educ. Asscn grants 1969–70, 1979–80, 1988–89, National Endowment for the Arts Fellowships 1969–70, 1979–80, 1988–89, Vermont Council for the Arts Grant 1978–79; Hon. LLD (Williams Coll.) 1993, (Skidmore Coll.) 1995, (Middlebury Coll.) 1996; Acad. of American Poets Prize 1967, Eunice Tietjens Memorial Prize 1971, Guggenheim Foundation Grant 1975–76, 1987–88, American Acad. and Inst. of Arts and Letters Literary Award 1981, Nat. Book Critics' Circle Award for poetry 1985, Poetry Soc. of America Melville Cane Award 1986, Wellesley Coll. Sara Teasdale Memorial Prize 1986, Bobbitt Natil Prize, Library of Congress 1992, William Carlos Williams Award 1993, PEN/Martha Albrand Award 1995, New Yorker Magazine Award in Poetry 1999, English Speaking Union Ambassador Award 1999, Bollingen Prize 2001. *Literary Agent:* Steven Barclay Agency, 12 Western Avenue, Petaluma, CA 94952, USA. *Telephone:* (707) 773-0654. *Fax:* (707) 778-1868. *Website:* www.barclayagency.com. *Address:* 14 Ellsworth Park, Cambridge, MA 02139, USA. *Website:* www.artstomp.com/gluck/.

GOAD, Johnny (see Philanderson, Flavian Titus).

GODBER, John (Harry); Dramatist; b. 18 May 1956, Upton, Yorkshire, England; m. Jane Thornton, 1993, two d. *Education:* Bretton Hall College, West Bretton, Yorkshire, 1974–78; CertEd, 1977, BEd, 1978, MA, Theatre, 1979, PhD, 1979–83, Leeds University. *Career:* Artistic Dir, Hull Truck Theatre Co, 1984–. *Publications:* Up 'N' Under, 1985; Bouncers, 1986; Shakers (with Jane Thornton), 1986; John Godber: 5 Plays, 1989; Teachers, 1990; On the Piste, 1991; April in Paris, 1992; Blood, Sweat and Tears, 1995; Lucky Sods, 1995; Passion Killers, 1995; Gym and Tonic, 1996; Weekend Breaks, 1997; It Started With A Kiss!, 1997; Perfect Pitch, 1998; Up 'n' Under (feature film), 1998. Contributions: Stage, film, and television. *Honours:* Sunday Times Playwriting Award, 1981; Edinburgh Festival Awards, 1981, 1982, 1984, 1988; Olivier Award for Comedy of the Year, 1984; Los Angeles Drama Critics Circle Award, 1986; Hon. DLitt, Hull University, 1988, Humberside University, 1997. *Address:* 64 Riverview Ave, North Ferriby, Humberside HU14 3DT, England.

GODBOUT, Jacques; Author, Poet and Film-maker; b. 27 Nov. 1933, Montréal, QC, Canada; m. Ghislaine Reiher, 31 July 1954, two c. *Education:* BA, 1953, MA, 1954, University of Montréal. *Career:* Lecturer, 1969, Writer-in-Residence, 1991–92, University of Montréal; Visiting Lecturer, University of California at Berkeley, 1985. *Publications:* Fiction: L'aquarium, 1962; Le couteau sur la table, 1965, English trans. as Knife on the Table, 1968; Salut Galarneau!, 1967, English trans. as Hail Galarneau!, 1970; D'Amour, PQ, 1972; L'ile au dragon, 1976, English trans. as Dragon Island, 1979; Les tetes a Papineau, 1981; Une histoire americaine, 1986, English trans. as an American Story, 1988; Le temps des Galarneau, 1993. Poetry: Carton-pate, 1956; Les pavés secs, 1958; La chair est un commencement, 1959; C'est la chaude loi des hommes, 1960; La grande muraille de Chine (with J. R. Colombo), 1969. Essays: Le réformiste, 1975; Le murmure marchand, 1984; L'écran du bonheur, 1990; Journal: Ecrivain de province, 1991. Other: many films. *Honours:* Prix France-Canada, 1962; Prix de l'Académie Française, 1965; Governor-General's Award for Fiction, 1968; various film prizes. *Address:* 815 Pratt, Montréal, QC H2V 2T7, Canada.

GODFREY, (William) Dave; novelist; b. 9 Aug. 1938, Winnipeg, MB, Canada; m. Ellen Swartz 1963; two s. one d. *Education:* BA, 1960, MFA, 1963, PhD, 1966, University of Iowa; MA, Stanford University, 1963; University of Chicago, 1965. *Career:* General Ed., Canadian Writers Series, McClelland and Stewart, 1968–72; Co-Founding Ed., News Press, Toronto, 1969–73; Ed., Press Porcepic, Erin, Ontario, 1972–; Vice-Pres., Inter Provincial Asscn for Telematcis and Telidon, 1982–. *Publications:* The New Ancestors, 1970; Short Stories: Death Goes Better with Coca Cola, 1967; New Canadian Writing, 1968, 1969; Dark Must Yield, 1978. *Honours:* University of Western Ontario Pres.'s Medal, 1965; Canada Council Award, 1969; Governor-General's Award, 1971. *Address:* Porcepic Books, 4252 Commerce Circle, Vancouver, BC V87 4M2, Canada.

GODFREY, Paul; Playwright and Director; b. 16 Sept. 1960, Exeter, Devon, England. *Publications:* Inventing a New Colour, 1988; A Bucket of Eels, 1989; Once in a While the Odd Thing Happens, 1990; The Panic, 1991; The Blue Ball, 1993; The Modern Husband, 1994; The Candidate, 1995; The Invisible Woman, 1996; Catalogue of Misunderstanding, 1997; Collected Plays, Vol. One, 1998; Tiananmen Square, 1999; The Oldest Play, 2000; Linda, 2000; The Best Sex of my Life (screenplay), 2003. *Literary Agent:* AP Watt Ltd, 20 John St, London WC1N 2DR, England.

GODINE, David R., MA, EdM; American publisher; b. 4 Sept. 1944, Cambridge, Mass.; m. Sara Sangree Eisenman 1988; one s. one d. *Education:* Dartmouth Coll., Harvard Univ. *Career:* f. David R. Godine, Publisher and Pres. 1969–; mem. Bds. Massachusetts Historical Soc., Massachusetts Horticultural Soc.; Fellow Pierpoint Morgan Library. *Publications:* Renaissance Books of Science 1970. *Honours:* Dwiggins Award 1984. *Address:* David R. Godine Publishers Inc., 9 Hamilton Place, Boston, MA 02108 (Office); 196 School Street, Milton, MA 02186, USA (Home). *Telephone:* (617) 451-9600 (Office). *Fax:* (617) 350-0250 (Office). *E-mail:* info@godine .com (Office). *Website:* www.godine.com (Office).

GODWIN, Gail Kathleen; Writer; b. 18 June 1937, Birmingham, AL, USA; m. 1st Douglas Kennedy, 1960, divorced 1961; m. 2nd, Ian Marshall, 1965, divorced 1966. *Education:* Peace Junior College, Raleigh, NC, 1955–57; BA in Journalism, University of North Carolina, 1959; MA in English, 1968, PhD, 1971, University of Iowa. *Career:* Staff, Miami Herald, 1959–60, US Travel Service, London, 1961–65; Editorial Asst, Saturday Evening Post, 1966; Instructor, University of Iowa, 1967–71; Lecturer, Iowa Writer's Workshops, 1972–73, Vassar College, 1977, Columbia University Writing Program, 1978, 1981; mem. American Society of Composers, Authors, and Publishers; Authors' Guild; Authors League; PEN. *Publications:* Fiction: The Perfectionists, 1970; Glass People, 1972; The Odd Woman, 1974; Violet Clay, 1978; A Mother and Two Daughters, 1982; The Finishing School, 1984; A Southern Family, 1987; Father Melancholy's Daughter, 1991; The Good Husband, 1994; Evensong, 1998. Librettos: The Last Lover, 1975; Journals of a Songmaker, 1976; Apollonia, 1979; Anna Margarita's Will, 1981; Remembering Felix, 1987. Editor: The Best American Short Stories, 1985 (with Shannon Ravenel), 1985. *Honours:* Fellow, Center for Advanced Study, University of Illinois, 1971–72; National Endowment for the Arts Grant, 1974–75; Guggenheim Fellowship, 1975–76; American Acad. and Institute of Arts and Letters Award, 1981; Janet Kafka Award, University of Rochester, 1988; Thomas Wolfe Memorial Award, Lipinsky Endowment of the Western North Carolina Historical Asscn, 1988. *Address:* PO Box 946, Woodstock, NY 12498, USA.

GODWIN, Parke; Novelist; b. 28 Jan. 1929, New York, NY, USA. *Education:* American University, 1 year. *Publications:* The Masters of Solitude (co-author), 1978; Firelord, 1980; Wintermind (co-author), 1982; A Memory of Lions, 1983; A Cold Blue Light (co-author), 1983; Beloved Exile, 1984; The Fire When It Comes, 1984; The Last Rainbow, 1985; A Truce with Time (A Love Story with Occasional Ghosts), 1988; Invitation to Camelot: An Arthurian Anthology of Short Stories (ed.), 1988; Waiting for the Galactic Bus, 1988; The Snake Oil Wars: or, Scheherazade Ginsberg Strikes Again, 1989; Sherwood, 1991; Robin and the King, 1993; Limbo Search, 1995; The Tower of Beowulf, 1995; Lord of Sunset, 1998. As Kate Hawks: The Lovers, 1999; Watch by Moonlight, 2001. *Honours:* World Fantasy Award, 1982. *Literary Agent:* Writers House, 21 W 26th St, New York, NY 10010, USA. *Address:* 736 Auburn Ravine Terrace, No. 535, Auburn, CA 95603, USA.

GODWIN, Rebecca Thompson; Writer; b. 9 July 1950, Charleston, South Carolina, USA; m. 1st two d.; m. 2nd Deane Bogardus, 24 Aug. 1988. *Education:* BA, Coastal Carolina College, 1977; MA, Middlebury College, 1988. *Career:* Teacher, Bennington Writing Workshops, 1995; Wildacres Writing Workshops, 1996; mem. Associated Writing Programs. *Publications:* Private Parts, 1992; Keeper of the House, 1994. Contributions: South Carolina Review; Paris Review; Iris; Crescent Review; First Magazine. *Honours:* Winner, S. C. Fiction Project, 1988; National Endowment for the Arts Grant, 1994–95. *Literary Agent:* Colleen Mohyde, Doe Coover Agency, Winchester, MA, USA. *Address:* PO Box 211, Poestenkill, NY 12140, USA.

GOEDICKE, Patricia, (Patricia Ann McKenna); Prof. of Creative Writing and Poet; b. 21 June 1931, Boston, Massachusetts, USA; m. Leonard Wallace Robinson, 3 June 1971. *Education:* BA, Middlebury College, 1953; MA, Ohio University, 1965. *Career:* Lecturer in English, Ohio University, 1963–68, Hunter College, CUNY, 1969–71; Assoc. Prof. of Creative Writing, Instituto Allende, 1972–79; Visiting Writer-in-Residence, Kalamazoo College, 1977; Guest Faculty, Writing Programme, Sarah Lawrence College, 1980; Visiting Poet-in-Residence, 1981–83, Assoc. Prof., 1983–90, Prof. of Creative Writing, 1990–, University of Montana; mem. Acad. of American Poets; Associated Writing Programs; Poetry Society of America. *Publications:* Between Oceans, 1968; For the Four Corners, 1976; The Trail That Turns on Itself, 1978; The Dog That Was Barking Yesterday, 1980; Crossing the Same River, 1980; The King of Childhood, 1984; The Wind of Our Going, 1985; Listen Love, 1986; The Tongues We Speak: New and Selected Poems, 1989; Paul Bunyan's Bearskin, 1992; Invisible Horses, 1996; As Earth Begins to End, 2000. Contributions: Reviews, journals, and periodicals. *Honours:* National Endowment for the Arts Fellowship, 1976; Pushcart Prize, 1977–78; Honourable Mention, Arvon International Poetry Competition, 1987; Honourable Award, Memphis State Review, 1988; Research Grant, 1989, Distinguished Scholar, 1991, University of Montana; Residency, Rockefeller Center, Bellagio, Italy, 1993; Distinguished Alumna, Ohio University, 2002; Ohioana Poetry Award, 2002; Chad Walsh Poetry Prize, 2002; H. G. Merriam Award for Distinguished Contributions to Montana Literature, 2003. *Address:* 310 McLeod Ave, Missoula, MT 59801, USA. *Telephone:* (406) 549-0343. *E-mail:* goedicke@earthlink.net.

GOERKE, Natasza; Short Story Writer and Poet; b. 1960, Poznań, Poland. *Education:* Polish, Mickiewicz Univ., Poznań; Oriental Languages, Jagiellonian Univ., Kraków. *Publications:* Fractale, 1994; Ksiega Pasztetów, 1997; Pozegnania plazmy, 1999; various collections published in trans. in German and English. Contributions: The Eagle and the Crow (anthology), 1996; numerous magazines. *Honours:* Czas Kultury Prize, 1993; six-month stipendium at Akademie Schloss Solitude, Stuttgart, 1995. *Address:* c/o Twisted Spoon Press, PO Box 21, Preslova 12, Prague 5, 150 21, Czech Republic.

GOFF, Martyn, OBE, FIAL, FRSA; British; *Chairman, Man Booker Prize Advisory Committee*; b. 7 June 1923. *Education:* Clifton Coll. *Career:* served in the RAF 1941–46; worked in film 1946–48; book seller 1948–70; established Booker Prize (later Man Booker Prize) 1969, Chair. and Admin. Man Booker Prize Advisory Cttee 2002–(06); CEO, Book Trust 1970–88, Vice-Pres. 2000– (deputy chair. 1991–92, 1996–97, chair. 1992–96); fiction reviewer, Daily Telegraph 1975–88, non-fiction reviewer 1988– Dir, Exec. Chair. Sotherans antiquarian bookseller 1988–; mem. Arts Council Literature Panel 1973–81, British Nat. Bibliography Research Fund 1976–88, British Library Advisory Council 1977–82, PEN Exec. Cttee 1978–, Exec. Cttee Greater London Arts Council 1982–88, Library and Information Services Council 1984–86; bd mem. British Theatre Asscn 1983–85; Chair. Paternosters '73 Library Advisory Council 1972–74, New Fiction Soc. 1975–88, School Bookshop Asscn 1977–, Soc. of Bookmen 1982–84 (pres. 1997–), 1890s Soc. 1990–99, Nat. Life Story Collections 1996–, Poetry Book Soc. 1996–99 (bd mem. 1992–99), Wingate Scholarships, H. H. Wingate Foundation 1998–, Books for Keeps; Vice-Pres. Royal Overseas League 1996–; Dir National Book League, Battersea Arts Centre 1992–97 (trustee 1981–85); trustee Cadmean Trust 1981–99, Nat. Literary Trust 1993–. *Publications:* fiction: The Plaster Fabric 1957, A Season With Mammon 1958, A Sort of Peace 1960, The Youngest Director 1961, Red on the Door 1962, The Flint Inheritance 1965, Indecent Assault 1967, The Liberation of Rupert Bannister 1978, Tar and Cement 1988; non-fiction: A Short Guide to Long Play 1957, A Further Guide to Long Play 1958, LP Collecting 1960, Why Conform? 1968, Victorian and Edwardian Surrey 1972, Record Choice 1974, Royal Pavilion 1976, Organising Book Exhibitions 1982, Publishing 1988, Prize Writing: An Original Collection of Writings by Past Winners to Celebrate 21 Years of the Booker Prize (ed.) 1989. *Honours:* The Bookseller Services to Bookselling Award 2001. *Address:* c/o Man Booker Prize, Colman Getty PR, Middlesex House, 34–42 Cleveland Street, London, W1T 4JE, England (Office).

GOLD, Herbert; Author; b. 9 March 1924, Cleveland, Ohio, USA; m. 1st Edith Zubrin, April 1948, divorced 1956, two d.; m. 2nd Melissa Dilworth, Jan. 1968, divorced 1975, two s. one d. *Education:* BA, 1946, MA, 1948, Columbia University; Licences-Lettres, Sorbonne, University of Paris, 1951. *Career:* Lecturer, Western Reserve University, 1951–53; Faculty, Wayne State University, 1954–56; Visiting Prof., Cornell University, 1958, University of California at Berkeley, 1963, 1968, Harvard University, 1964, Stanford University, 1967; Mcguffey Lecturer in English, Ohio University, 1971; Regents Prof., 1973, Visiting Prof., 1974–79, 1985, University of California at Davis. *Publications:* Fiction: Birth of a Hero, 1951; The Prospect Before Us, 1954; The Man Who Was Not With It, 1956; 15 x 3 (short stories with R. V. Cassill and James B. Hall), 1957; The Optimist, 1959; Therefore Be Bold, 1960; Love and Like (short stories), 1960; Salt, 1963; Father: A Novel in the Form of a Memoir, 1967; The Great American Jackpot, 1969; Biafra Goodbye, 1970; The Magic Will: Stories and Essays of a Decade, 1971; My Last Two Thousand Years, 1972; Swiftie the Magician, 1974; Waiting for Cordelia, 1977; Slave Trade, 1979; He/She, 1980; Family: A Novel in the Form of a Memoir, 1981; True Love, 1982; Mister White Eyes, 1984; Stories of Misbegotten Love, 1985; A Girl of Forty, 1986; Lovers and Cohorts: Twenty Seven Stories, 1986; Dreaming, 1988; She Took My Arm as if She Loved Me, 1997; Daughter Mine, 2000. Non-Fiction: The Age of Happy Problems, 1962; A Walk on the West Side: California on the Brink, 1981; Travels in San Francisco, 1990; Best Nightmare on Earth: A Life In Haiti, 1991; Bohemia: Where Art, Angst, Love and Strong Coffee Meet, 1993. Contributions: various periodicals. *Honours:* Guggenheim Fellowship, 1957; Ohioana Book Award, 1957; National Institute of Arts and Letters Grant, 1958; Longview Foundation Award, 1959; California Literature Medal Award, 1968; Commonwealth Club Award for Best Novel, San Francisco, 1982; Hon. LHD, Baruch College, CUNY, 1988; Sherwood Anderson Prize for Fiction, 1989. *Address:* 1051-A Broadway, San Francisco, CA 94133, USA.

GOLD, Ivan; Writer; b. 12 May 1932, New York, NY, USA; m. Vera Cochran, 22 Oct. 1968, one s. *Education:* BA, Columbia College, New York City, 1953; MA, University of London. *Career:* Writer-in-Residence, Austin Peay State University, 1991, University of Massachusetts, Boston, 1992. *Publications:* Nickel Miseries; Sick Friends; Sams in a Dry Season. *Address:* c/o Many Yost Assocs, 59 E 54th St, New York, NY 10022, USA.

GOLDBARTH, Albert; Poet, Writer and Asst Prof. of Creative Writing; b. 31 Jan. 1948, Chicago, IL, USA. *Education:* BA, University of Illinois, 1969; MFA, University of Iowa, 1971; University of Utah, 1973–74. *Career:* Instructor, Elgin Community College, IL, 1971–72, Central YMCA Community College, Chicago, 1971–73, University of Utah, 1973–74; Asst Prof., Cornell University, 1974–76; Visiting Prof., Syracuse University, 1976; Asst Prof. of Creative Writing, University of Texas at Austin, 1977–. *Publications:* Poetry: Under Cover, 1973; Coprolites, 1973; Opticks: A Poem in Seven Sections, 1974; Jan. 31, 1974; Keeping, 1975; A Year of Happy,

1976; Comings Back: A Sequence of Poems, 1976; Curve: Overlapping Narratives, 1977; Different Flashes, 1979; Eurekas, 1980; Ink Blood Semen, 1980; The Smugglers Handbook, 1980; Faith, 1981; Who Gathered and Whispered Behind Me, 1981; Goldbarth's Book of Occult Phenomena, 1982; Original Light: New and Selected Poems 1973–1983, 1983; Albert's Horoscope Almanac, 1986; Arts and Sciences, 1986; Popular Culture, 1989; Delft: An Essay Poem, 1990; Heaven and Earth: A Cosmology, 1991; Across the Layers: Poems Old and New, 1993; The Gods, 1993. Fiction: Marriage and Other Science Fiction, 1994. Essays: A Sympathy of Souls, 1990; Great Topics of the World: Essays, 1994. Editor: Every Pleasure: The 'Seneca Review' Long Poem Anthology, 1979. *Honours:* Theodore Roethke Prize, 1972; Ark River Review Prizes, 1973, 1975; National Endowment for the Arts Grants, 1974, 1979; Guggenheim Fellowship, 1983. *Address:* c/o Dept of English, University of Texas at Austin, Austin, TX 78712, USA.

GOLDBERG, Barbara June, MA, MEd, MFA; writer, poet and editor; b. 26 April 1943, Wilmington, DE, USA; m. 1st J. Peter Kiers 1963, divorced 1970; m. 2nd Charles Goldberg 1971, divorced 1990, two s. *Education:* Mt Holyoke College, Yeshiva Univ., Columbia Univ., American Univ. *Career:* Man. speechwriters AARP 1998–; Dir Editorial Board, The Word Works publishers 1987–99; Dir Editorial Services American Speech-Language-Hearing Asscn 1988–98; Exec. Ed., Poet Lore 1990–98; mem. Poetry Society of America; individual mem. Associated Writing Programs. *Publications:* Berta Broad Foot and Pepin the Short: A Merovingian Romance 1985, Cautionary Tales (Camden Award) 1990, Marvelous Pursuits (Violet Reed Hass Award) 1995; 3 books in Hebrew translation including Night Watch; translations: The Stones Remember: Native Israeli Poetry 1996, After the First Rain: Israeli Poems on War and Peace 1998, The Fire Stays in Red: Poems of Ronny Someck (trans. with Moshe Dor) 2001; ed: The First Yes: Poems on Communication 1996. Contributions: American Poetry Review, American Scholar, Gettysburg Review, Paris Review, Poetry, Virginia Quarterly. *Honours:* 2 National Endowment for the Arts Fellowships, 4 Maryland State Art Council fellowships for poetry, Armand G. Erpf Award Columbia Univ.'s Translation Center, Witter Bynner Foundation Award. *Address:* 6703 Fairfax Rd, Chevy Chase, MD 20815, USA. *E-mail:* bjgoldberg@comcast.net.

GOLDEN, Arthur, MA; American writer; b. 1957, Chattanooga, TN; m.; two c. *Education:* Harvard Coll., Columbia Univ., Boston Univ. *Career:* magazine journalist, Tokyo 1980–82; tutor in literature and creative writing, Boston Univ.; mem. advisory council, Grub Street, Inc. *Publications:* Memoirs of a Geisha 1997. *Literary Agent:* Leigh Feldman, Darhansoff, Verrill & Feldman Literary Agents, 236 W 26th Street, Suite 802, New York, NY 10001, USA. *Telephone:* (917) 3051300. *Fax:* (917) 3051400.

GOLDEN, Mark, BA, MA, PhD; academic and writer; *Professor of Classics, University of Winnipeg*; b. 6 Aug. 1948, Winnipeg, MB, Canada; m. Monica Becker 1985; one s. *Education:* Univ. Coll., Toronto, Univ. of Toronto. *Career:* Lecturer, Asst Prof., Univ. of British Columbia 1980–82; Asst Prof., Prof. of Classics, Univ. of Winnipeg 1982–; Nat. Humanities Center Fellow, Research Triangle Park, NC 1987–88; Visiting Research Fellow, Univ. of New England, Armidale, NSW, Australia 1992; Visiting Fellow, Clare Hall, Cambridge 1995; Center for Hellenic Studies Summer Scholar, Washington, DC 1996; Ioannides Memorial Lecturer, Univ. of Western Ontario 1999; Fordyce Mitchel Memorial Lecturer, Univ. of Missouri, Columbia 2000; Stubbs Lecturer, Univ. Coll., Toronto 2004. *Publications:* Children and Childhood in Classical Athens 1990, Inventing Ancient Culture: Historicism, Periodization and the Ancient World (ed. with Peter Toohey) 1997, Sport and Society in Ancient Greece 1998, Sex and Difference in Ancient Greece and Rome (ed. with Peter Toohey) 2003, Sport in the Ancient World from A to Z 2004; contrib. to scholarly books and journals. *Honours:* Rogers Award for Excellence in Research and Scholarship, Univ. of Winnipeg 1998. *Address:* c/o Department of Classics, University of Winnipeg, Winnipeg, MB R3B 2E9, Canada.

GOLDIN, Barbara Diamond; Writer and Teacher; b. 4 Oct. 1946, New York, NY, USA; m. Alan Goldin, 31 March 1968, divorced 1990, one s. one d. *Education:* BA, University of Chicago, 1968; Teacher's Certificate, Primary and Secondary Education, Boston University, 1970; Western Washington University, 1970. *Publications:* Just Enough Is Plenty: A Hanukkah Tale, 1988; The World's Birthday: A Story About Rosh Hashanah, 1990; The Family Book of Midrash: Fifty-two Stories from the Sages, 1990; Cakes and Miracles: A Purim Tale, 1991; Fire!: The Beginnings of the Labor Movement, 1992; The Magician's Visit: A Passover Tale, 1993; The Passover Journey: A Seder Companion, 1994; Red Means Good Fortune: A Story of San Francisco's China Town, 1994; Night Lights: A Sukkot Story, 1994; Bat Mitzvah: A Jewish Girl's Coming of Age, 1995; Creating Angels: Stories of Tzedakah, 1996; Coyote and the Fire Stick: A Pacific Northwest Indian Tale, 1996; While the Candles Burn: Eight Stories for Hanukkah, 1996; The Girl Who Lived with the Bears, 1997. Contributions: various publications. *Honours:* National Jewish Book Award, 1989; Sydney Taylor Book Award, 1991, and Body-of-Work Award, 1997; Asscn of Jewish Libraries Award, 1992; American Library Asscn Notable Book Citation, 1995. *Address:* PO Box 981, Nothampton, MA 01061, USA.

GOLDMAN, Paul Henry Joseph, BA; art historian; b. 3 April 1950, London, England; m. Corinna Maroulis 1987. *Education:* University of London; Postgraduate Diploma in Art Gallery and Museum Studies, University of Manchester; Diploma, Museums Asscn in Art. *Career:* Asst Keeper, Dept of Prints and Drawings, British Museum, London, 1974–97; mem. FRSA; Museums Asscn, fellow; Society of Authors; Founder, committee mem., Imaginative Book Illustration Society; Trustee, Cartoon Art Trust; Mem. of Council, Friends of the British Library; Assoc. Fellow, Institute of English Studies, University of London. *Publications:* Sporting Life: An Anthology of British Sporting Prints, 1983; Looking at Prints, Drawings and Watercolours, 1988; Victorian Illustrated Books 1850–1870: The Heyday of Wood-Engraving, 1994; Victorian Illustration: The Pre-Raphaelites, the Idyllic School and the High Victorians, 1996; Retrospective Adventures, Forrest Reid, Author and Collector (ed. with Brian Taylor), 1998. Contributions: journals, reviews, and quarterlies. *Address:* Meadow View, East Orchard, Shaftesbury, Dorset SP7 0LG, England.

GOLDMAN, William; Author and Screenwriter; b. 12 Aug. 1931, Chicago, IL, USA; m. Ilene Jones, 15 April 1961, two d. *Education:* BA, Oberlin College, 1952; MA, Columbia University, 1956. *Publications:* The Temple of Gold, 1957; Your Turn to Curtsy, My Turn to Bow, 1958; Soldier in the Rain, 1960; Boys and Girls Together, 1964; No Way to Treat a Lady, 1964; The Thing of It Is, 1967; The Season: A Candid Look at the Broadway, 1969; Father's Day, 1971; The Princess Bride, 1973; Marathon Man, 1974; Wigger, 1974; Magic, 1976; Tinsel, 1979; Control, 1982; Adventures in the Screen Trade, 1983; The Silent Gondoliers, 1983; The Color of Light, 1984; Heat, 1985; Brothers, 1987; Wait Until Next Year, 1988; Hype and Glory, 1990; Four Screenplays, 1995. Screenplays: Masquerade, 1965; Harper, 1966; Butch Cassidy and the Sundance Kid, 1969; The Hot Rock, 1972; The Stepford Wives, 1974; The Great Waldo Pepper, 1975; Marathon Man, 1976; All the President's Men, 1976; A Bridge Too Far, 1977; Magic, 1978; The Princess Bridge, 1987; Heat, 1987; Misery, 1990; The Year of the Comet, 1992; Memoirs of an Invisible Man, 1992; Chaplin, 1992; Maverick, 1994; Ghost and the Darkness, 1996; Absolute Power, 1997; Which Lie Did I Tell?, 2000. Play: Blood, Sweat and Stanley Poole (with James Goldman), 1961. Musical Comedy: A Family Affair (with James Goldman and John Kander), 1962. *Honours:* Acad. Award for Best Original Screenplay, 1970, and for Best Screenplay Adaptation, 1977; Laurel Award for Lifetime Achievement in Screenwriting, 1983. *Address:* c/o CAA, 9830 Wilshire Blvd, Beverly Hills, CA 90212, USA.

GOLDMARK, Peter Carl, Jr, BA; American newspaper executive; b. 2 Dec. 1940, New York; m. Aliette Marie Misson 1964; three d. *Education:* Harvard Univ. *Career:* worked for US Office of Econ. Opportunity, Washington; fmr teacher of history Putney School, Vt; employed in Budget Office, City of New York for four years, later Asst Budget Dir Program Planning and Analysis then Exec. Asst to the Mayor 1971; Sec. Human Services, Commonwealth of Mass. 1972–75; Dir of Budget, NY State 1975–77; Exec. Dir Port Authority of NY and NJ 1977–85; joined Times Mirror Co., Los Angeles 1985, fmr Sr Vice-Pres. Eastern Newspapers Div.; Pres. Rockefeller Foundation 1988–97; Chair. and CEO Int. Herald Tribune 1998–2003; mem. Bd Dirs Financial Accounting Foundation, Lend Lease Corpn, Whitehead Inst. for Biomedical Research. *Address:* c/o International Herald Tribune, 6 bis rue des Graviers, 92521 Neuilly Cédex, France (Office).

GOLDSMITH, Howard, (Ward Smith, Dayle Courtney); Author and Ed.; b. 24 Aug. 1945, New York, NY, USA. *Education:* BA, CUNY, 1965; MA, University of Michigan, 1966. *Career:* Editorial Consultant, Mountain View Center for Environmental Education, University of Colorado, 1970–85; Senior Ed., Santillana Publishing Company, 1980–85; Contributing Ed., Children's Magic Window, 1987–; mem. Poets and Writers; SFWA; Society of Children's Book Writers and Illustrators. *Publications:* The Whispering Sea, 1976; What Makes a Grumble Smile?, 1977; The Shadow and Other Strange Tales, 1977; Terror by Night, 1977; Spine-Chillers, 1978; Sooner Round the Corner, 1979; Invasion: 2200 A.D., 1979; Toto the Timid Turtle, 1980; The Ivy Plot, 1981; Three-Ring Inferno, 1982; Plaf Le Paresseux, 1982; Ninon, Miss Vison, 1982; Toufou Le Hibou, 1982; Fourtou Le Kangourou, 1982; The Tooth Chicken, 1982; Mireille l'Abeille, 1982; Little Dog Lost, 1983; Stormy Day Together, 1983; The Sinister Circle, 1983; Shadow of Fear, 1983; Treasure Hunt, 1983; The Square, 1983; The Circle, 1983; The Contest, 1983; Welcome, Makoto!, 1983; Helpful Julio, 1984; The Secret of Success, 1984; Pedro's Puzzling Birthday, 1984; Rosa's Prank, 1984; A Day of Fun, 1984; The Rectangle, 1984; Kirby the Kangaroo, 1985; Ollie the Owl, 1985; The Twiddle Twins' Haunted House, 1985; Young Ghosts, 1985; Von Geistern Besessen, 1987; The Further Adventures of Batman, 1989; Visions of Fantasy, 1989; The Pig and the Witch, 1990; The Mind-Stalkers, 1990; Spooky Stories, 1990; Little Quack and Baby Duckling, 1991; The Proust Syndrome, 1992; The President's Train, 1991; The Future Light of the World, 1993; Evil Tales of Evil Things, 1991; The Twiddle Twins' Music Box Mystery, 1996; The Gooey Chewy Contest, 1996; The Twiddle Twins' Amusement Park Mystery, 1997; McGraw-Hill Science Through Stories Series, 1998; The Twiddle Twins' Single Footprint Mystery, 1999; The Tooth Fairy Mystery, 1999; Danger Zone, 1999; Strike up the Band, 2000; See It Fly, 2000; Thomas Edison to the Rescue, 2003; Mark Twain at Work, 2003. Contributions: periodicals, journals, magazines, reviews and newspapers. *Address:* 41-07 Bowne St, Suite 6B, Flushing, NY 11355-5629, USA.

GOLDSTEIN, Laurence Alan, BA, PhD; American academic, writer, poet and editor; *Professor of English, University of Michigan*; b. 5 Jan. 1943, Los Angeles, CA; m. Nancy Jo Copeland 1968; two s. *Education:* Univ. of

California at Los Angeles, Brown Univ. *Career:* instructor, Brown Univ. 1968–70; Asst Prof. 1970–78, Assoc. Prof. 1978–85, Prof. of English 1985–, Univ. of Michigan; Ed., Michigan Quarterly Review 1977–. *Publications:* Ruins and Empire: The Evolution of a Theme in Augustan and Romantic Literature 1977, Altamira 1978, The Automobile and American Culture (ed. with David L. Lewis) 1983, The Flying Machine and Modern Literature 1986, The Three Gardens 1987, Writers and Their Craft: Short Stories and Essays on the Narrative (ed. with Nicholas Delbanco) 1991, Seasonal Performances: A Michigan Quarterly Review Reader (ed.) 1991, The Female Body: Figures, Styles, Speculations (ed.) 1992, The American Poet at the Movies: A Critical History 1994, The Male Body: Features, Destinies, Exposures (ed.) 1994, Cold Reading 1995, The Movies: Texts, Receptions, Exposures (ed. with Ira Konigsberg) 1996, Robert Hayden: Essays on the Poetry (ed. with Robert Chrisman) 2001, A Room in California 2005; contrib. to books, anthologies, reviews and journals. *Honours:* Distinguished Service Award, Univ. of Michigan 1977, Univ. of Michigan Press Book Award 1995. *Address:* c/o Department of English, University of Michigan, Ann Arbor, MI 48109, USA. *E-mail:* lgoldste@umich.edu.

GOLDSTEIN, Rebecca; Author; b. 23 Feb. 1950, White Plains, NY, USA; m. Sheldon Goldstein, 25 June 1969, two d. *Education:* BA, Barnard College, 1972; PhD, Princeton University, 1976. *Career:* Prof. of Philosophy, Barnard College, 1976–86; Adjunct Asst Prof. of Writing, Columbia University, 1994–; mem. PEN. *Publications:* The Mind-Body Problem, 1983; The Late Summer Passion of a Woman of Mind, 1989; The Dark Sister, 1991; Strange Attractors, 1993; Mazel, 1995; Properties of Light: A Novel of Love, Betrayal, and Quantum Physics, 2000. *Honours:* Whiting Writers' Award, 1991; John D. and Catherine T. MacArthur Foundation Fellowship, 1996. *Address:* 15th N Seventh Ave, Highland Park, NJ 08904, USA.

GOLDSTEIN, Robert Justin, BA, MA, PhD; academic and writer; *Professor, Oakland University*; b. 28 March 1947, Albany, NY, USA. *Education:* Univ. of Illinois, Univ. of Chicago. *Career:* Research and Administrative Asst, Univ. of Illinois 1972–73; Lecturer, San Diego State Univ. 1974–76; Asst Prof., Assoc. Prof., Full Prof., Oakland Univ., Rochester, Michigan 1976–. *Publications:* Political Repression in Modern America 1978, Political Repression in Nineteenth Century Europe 1983, Political Censorship of the Press and the Arts in Nineteenth Century Europe 1989, Censorship of Political Caricature in Nineteenth Century France 1989, Saving 'Old Glory': The History of the American Flag Desecration Controversy 1995, Burning the Flag: The Great 1989–90 American Flag Desecration Controversy 1996, Desecrating the American Flag: Key Documents from the Controversy from the Civil War to 1995 1996, Flag Burning and Free Speech: The Case of Texas v. Johnson 2000, The War for the Public Mind: Political Censorship in Nineteenth-Century Europe 2000, Political Censorship: 'The New York Times' Twentieth Century in Review 2001. *Address:* Department of Political Science, Oakland University, Rochester, MI 48309, USA. *E-mail:* goldstei@oakland.edu.

GOLDSWORTHY, Peter; Poet and Writer; b. 12 Oct. 1951, Minlaton, SA, Australia; m. Helen Louise Wharldall, 1972, one s. two d. *Education:* BMed, BSurg, 1974, University of Adelaide. *Publications:* Number Three Friendly Street: Poetry Reader (co-ed.), 1979; Readings from Ecclesiastes, 1982; This Goes With This, 1988; Maestro (novel), 1989; This Goes With That: Poems 1974–2001, 2001. *Honours:* Commonwealth Poetry Prize, 1982; South Australia Poetry Award, 1988.

GOMERY, Douglas; Prof. and Writer; b. 5 April 1945, New York, NY, USA; m. Marilyn Moon, 1973. *Education:* BS, Lehigh University, 1967; MA, 1970, PhD, 1975, University of Wisconsin at Madison. *Career:* Instructor to Assoc. Prof., University of Wisconsin at Milwaukee, 1974–81; Visiting Prof., University of Wisconsin at Madison, 1977, Northwestern University, 1981, University of Iowa, 1982, University of Utrecht, 1990, 1992; Assoc. Prof., 1981–86, Prof., Dept of Radio-Television-Film, 1987–92, then College of Journalism, 1992–, University of Maryland; Senior Researcher, Woodrow Wilson Center for International Scholars, Washington, DC, 1988–92. *Publications:* High Sierra: Screenplay and Analysis, 1979; Film History: Theory and Practice (with Robert C. Allen), 1985; The Hollywood Studio System, 1986; The Will Hays Papers, 1987; American Media (with Philip Cook and Lawrence W. Lichty), 1989; The Art of Moving Shadows (with Annette Michelson and Patrick Loughney), 1989; Movie History: A Survey, 1991; Shared Pleasures, 1992; The Future of News (with Philip Cook and Lawrence W. Lichty), 1992; A Media Studies Primer (with Michael Cornfield and Lawrence W. Lichty), 1997; Media in America (ed.), 1998. Contributions: books and scholarly journals. *Honours:* Jeffrey Weiss Literary Prize, Theatre Historical Society, 1988; Prize, Theatre Library Asscn, 1992. *Address:* 4817 Drummond Ave, Chevy Chase, MD 20815, USA.

GOMEZ, Jewelle Lydia; Writer and Poet; b. 11 Sept. 1948, Boston, Massachusetts, USA. *Education:* BA, Northeastern University, 1971; MS, Columbia Graduate School of Journalism, 1973. *Career:* Assoc., 1984–91, Dir of Literature, 1991–93, New York State Council on the Arts; Adjunct Prof., New College of California, 1994, Menlo College, CA, 1994; Writer-in-Residence, California Arts Council, 1995–96; mem. American Center of Poets and Writers; PEN. *Publications:* The Gilda Stories, 1991; Forty-Three Septembers, 1993; Oral Tradition, 1995. Contributions: various publications. *Address:* c/o Frances Goldin Literary Agency, 57 E 11th St, New York, NY 10003, USA.

GÖNCZ, Árpád; Writer, Dramatist, Trans. and Former Pres. of Hungary; b. 10 Feb. 1922, Budapest, Hungary; m. Mária Zsuzsanna Göntér, 1947, two s. two d. *Education:* DJ, Pázmány Péter University, 1944. *Career:* Active with Independent Smallholders' Party, 1947–48; Imprisoned for political activities, 1957–63; Founding Mem., Free Initiative Network, Free Democratic Federation, Historic Justice Committee; Mem. and Speaker of Parliament, 1990; Acting Pres., 1990, Pres., 1990–2000, Hungary; mem. Hungarian Writers' Union, pres., 1989–90. *Publications:* Men of God (novel), 1974; Hungarian Medea (play), 1979; Iron Bars (play), 1979; Encounters (short stories), 1980; Six plays, 1990; Homecoming (short stories), 1991; Shavings (essays), 1991. *Honours:* Hon. Knight Commander of the Order of St Michael and St George, England, 1991. *Address:* c/o Office of the Pres., Kossuth tér 1–3, 1357 Budapest, Hungary.

GONZÁLEZ, Justo Luis, MA, PhD, DDL; American theologian, writer and editor; b. 9 Aug. 1937, Havana, Cuba; m. 1st Erlantina Ramos 1959 (divorced 1972); one d.; m. 2nd Catherine Gunsalus 1973. *Education:* University of Havana, Seminario Evangélico de Teología, Matanzas, Yale University, University of Strasbourg, Seminario Evangélico de Puerto Rico. *Career:* Prof. of Historical Theology, Seminario Evangélico de Puerto Rico, 1961–69; Research Fellow, Yale University, 1968; Asst Prof. of World Christianity, 1969–71, Assoc. Prof., 1971–77, Emory University; Visiting Prof. of Theology, Interdenominational Theological Center, 1977–88; Ed., Apuntes, 1980–2000; Adjunct Prof. of Theology, Columbia Theological Seminary, 1988–91; mem. United Methodist Church; many ecumenical commissions and task forces. *Publications:* The Development of Christianity in the Latin Caribbean, 1969; A History of Christian Thought, Vol. I, From the Beginnings to the Council of Chalcedon, 1970, Vol. II, From Saint Augustine to the Eve of the Reformation, 1971, Vol. III, From the Reformation to the Present, 1979; Their Souls Did Magnify the Lord: Studies on Biblical Women (with Catherine Gunsalus González), 1977; Rejoice in Your Saviour: A Study for Lent-Easter (with Catherine Gunsalus González), 1979; Liberation Preaching: The Pulpit and the Oppressed (with Catherine Gunsalus González), 1980; In Accord: Let Us Worship (with Catherine Gonsalus González), 1981; The Story of Christianity, Vol. I, Early and Medieval Christianity, 1984, Vol. II, From the Reformation to the Present, 1985; Paul: His Impact on Christianity (with Catherine Gunsalus González), 1987; The Crusades: Piety Misguided, 1988; Monasticism: Patterns of Piety, 1988; The Theological Education of Hispanics, 1988; Christian Thought Revisited: Three Types of Theology, 1989; A Faith More Precious Than Gold: A Study of 1 Peter (with Catherine Gunsalus González), 1989; Faith and Wealth: A History of Early Christian Ideas on the Origin, Significance, and Use of Money, 1990; Mañana: Christian Theology from a Hispanic Perspective, 1990; Each in Our Own Tongue: A History of Hispanic Methodism (ed.), 1991; Voces: Voices from the Hispanic Church (ed.), 1992; Out of Every Tribe and Nation: Christian Theology at the Ethnic Roundtable, 1992; The Liberating Pulpit (with Catherine Gunsalus González), 1994; Journey Through the Bible, Vol. 11, Luke, 1994, Vol. 13, Acts of the Apostles, 1995; When Christ Lives in Us, 1995; Santa Biblia: The Bible Through Hispanic Eyes, 1996; Church History: An Essential Guide, 1996; Revelation (with Catherine Gunsalus González), 1997; For the Healing of the Nations: The Book of Revelation in an Age of Cultural Conflict, 1999; Mark's Message for the New Millennium, 2000; Acts: The Gospel of the Spirit, 2001; The Changing Shape of Church History, 2003. Other: many books in Spanish. Contributions: numerous books, reference works, journals, periodicals, etc. *Address:* 336 S Columbia Drive, Decatur, GA 30030, USA.

GONZÁLEZ, Ray, MFA; American writer, poet, editor and essayist; b. El Paso, TX. *Education:* Univ. of Texas at El Paso, Southwest Texas State Univ. *Career:* Literary Dir, Guadaloupe Cultural Arts Centre, San Antonio; Poetry Ed., Bloomsbury Review for over 20 years; Ed., Guadaloupe Review; founder, Luna poetry journal 1998. *Publications include:* poetry: The Heat of Arrivals 1996, Cabato Sentora 1999, Memory Fever 1999, Turtle Pictures 2000; essays: The Underground Heart: Essays from Hidden Landscapes 2002; short story collections: Circling the Tortilla Dragon 2002; editor: Touching the Fire: 15 Poets of the Latino Renaissance 1998; contributor to Best American Poetry 1999–2000, The Pushcart Prize: Best of the Small Presses 2000, The Norton Anthology of Nature Writing. *Honours:* Illinois Arts Council Fellowship in Poetry 1998; Amercian Book Award for Excellence in Editing 1993, Josephine Miles Book Award for Excellence in Literature 1997, Minnesota Book Award for Poetry 2001. *Address:* c/o Curbstone Press, 321 Jackson Street, Willimantic, CT 06226-1738, USA. *E-mail:* info@curbstone.org. *Website:* www.curbstone.org.

GOOCH, John; Prof. of International History and Writer; b. 25 Aug. 1945, Weston Favell, England; m. Catharine Ann Staley, 1967, one s. one d. *Education:* BA, History, 1966, PhD, War Studies, 1969, King's College, University of London. *Career:* Asst Lecturer in History, 1966–67, Asst Lecturer in War Studies, 1969, King's College, University of London; Lecturer in History, 1969–81, Senior Lecturer, 1981–84, Reader in History, 1984–88, Prof. of History, 1988–92, University of Lancaster; Ed., Journal of Strategic Studies, 1978–; Secretary of the Navy Senior Research Fellow, US Naval War College, 1985–86; Visiting Prof. of Military and Naval History, Yale University, 1988; Prof. of International History, University of Leeds, 1992–; mem. Army Records Society, chair. of the council, 1983–; FRHistS, vice-pres., 1990–94. *Publications:* The Plans of War: The General

Staff and British Military Strategy c.1900–1916; Armies in Europe, 1980; The Prospect of War: Studies in British Defence Policy 1847–1942, 1981; Politicians and Defence: Studies in the Formulation of British Defence Policy 1847–1970, 1981; Strategy and the Social Sciences, 1981; Military Deception and Strategic Surprise, 1982; Soldati e Borghesi nell' Europa Moderna, 1982; Army, State and Society in Italy 1870–1915, 1989; Decisive Campaigns of the Second World War, 1989; Military Misfortunes: The Anatomy of Failure in War (with Eliot A Cohen), 1990; Airpower: Theory and Practice, 1995. Contributions: scholarly journals. *Honours:* Premio Internazionale di Cultura, Città di Anghiari, 1983; Knight, Royal Military Order of Vila Viçosa, Portugal, 1991. *Address:* Coverhill House, Coverhill Rd, Oldham OL4 5RE, England.

GOOCH, Stanley Alfred; Writer; b. 13 June 1932, London, England; m. Ruth Senior, 1 April 1961. *Education:* BA, Modern Languages, King's College, London, 1955; Diploma in Education, Institute of Education, London, 1957; BSc, Psychology, Birkbeck College, University of London, 1962. *Publications:* Four Years On, 1966; Total Man, 1972; Personality and Evolution, 1973; The Neanderthal Question, 1977; The Paranormal, 1978; Guardians of the Ancient Wisdom, 1979; The Double Helix of the Mind, 1980; The Secret Life of Humans, 1981; Creatures from Inner Space, 1984; The Child with Asthma, 1986; Cities of Dreams, 1989. Contributions: New Scientist; New Society; British Journal of Psychology; British Journal of Social and Clinical Psychology; British Journal of Educational Psychology; International Journal of Human Development. *Honours:* Royal Literary Fund Awards, 1984, 1987, 1994. *Address:* c/o David Percy, 25 Belsize Park, Hampstead, London NW3 4DU, England.

GOODALL, Jane; Ethnologist and Author; b. 3 April 1934, London, England; m. 1st Hugo Van Lawick 1964 (divorced 1974); one s.; m. 2nd M. Derek Bryceson 1975 (died 1980). *Education:* Uplands School; Univ. of Cambridge. *Career:* Sec. Oxford Univ.; Asst Ed. Documentary Film Studio; waitress; Asst Sec. to Louis Leakey, worked in Olduvai Gorge, then moved to Gombe Stream Game Reserve (now Gombe Nat. Park), camp became Gombe Stream Research Centre 1964; Scientific Dir Gombe Wildlife Research Inst. 1967–; Founder Jane Goodall Inst. for Wildlife Research 1977–; Founder Cttee for Conservation and Care of Chimpanzees 1986; Hon. Visiting Prof. in Zoology Dar es Salaam Univ. 1973–; A. D. White Prof.-at-Large Cornell Univ. 1996–; mem. advisory panel World Summit on Sustainable Devt 2002; UN(O) Messenger of Peace 2002; visiting lecturer numerous univs including Yale Univ., USA; speaker on conservation issues, appearing on numerous TV shows including: 20/20, Nightline, Good Morning America; mem. Hon. Foreign mem., American Acad. for Advancement of Sciences. *Publications:* Shadow of Man, Chimpanzees of Gombe, 1986; The Chimpanzee Family Book, 1989; Through a Window, 1990; The Chimpanzee: The Living Link Between Man and Beast, 1992; Visions of Caliban, 1993; Jane Goodall: With Love, 1994; Dr White, 1999; 40 Years at Gombe, 1999; Brutal Kinship, 1999; Reason for Hope, 1999; Africa in My Blood: An Autobiography in Letters, 2000; Beyond Innocence: An Autobiography in Letters, the Later Years, 2001; Chimpanzees I Love: Saving Their World and Ours, 2001; Performance and Evolution in the Age of Darwin, 2003. Contributions: New York Times. *Honours:* Conservation Award (New York Zoological Soc.), Franklin Burr Award (twice, Nat. Geographic Soc.), Nat. Geographic Soc. Centennial Award, Hubbard Medal 1995, Medal of Mt Kilimanjaro 1996, Public Service Award, Nat. Scientific Bd 1998, John Hay Award, Orion Soc. 1998, Int. Peace Award, Reorganized Church of the Latter Day Saints, Gandhi/King Peace Award 2001; CBE. *Address:* The Jane Goodall Institute for Wildlife Research, Education and Conservation, PO Box 14890, Silver Spring, MD 20911-4890, USA. *Website:* www.janegoodall.org.

GOODHEART, Eugene, BA, MA, PhD; academic and writer; *Edytha Macy Gross Professor of Humanities Emeritus, Brandeis University*; b. 26 June 1931, New York, NY, USA; m. Joan Bamberger; one s. one d. *Education:* Columbia College, University of Virginia, Sorbonne University of Paris, Columbia University. *Career:* Instructor, 1958–60, Asst Prof., 1960–62, Bard College; Asst Prof., University of Chicago, 1962–66; Assoc. Prof., Mount Holyoke College, 1966–67; Assoc. Prof., 1967–70, Prof., 1970–74, MIT; Visiting Prof., Wellesley College, 1968; Prof., Boston University, 1974–83; Corresponding Ed., Partisan Review, 1978–; Edytha Macy Gross Prof. of Humanities Emeritus, 1983–, Dir, Center for the Humanities, 1986–, Brandeis University; Adjunct Prof. of English, Columbia University, 1986; mem. PEN. *Publications:* The Utopian Vision of D. H. Lawrence, 1963; The Cult of the Ego: The Self in Modern Literature, 1968; Culture and the Radical Conscience, 1978; The Failure of Criticism, 1978; The Skeptic Disposition in Contemporary Criticism, 1984; Pieces of Resistance, 1987; Desire and Its Discontents, 1991; The Reign of Ideology, 1996; Does Literary Studies Have a Future?, 1999; Confessions of a Secular Jew, 2001; Novel Practices: Classic Modern Fiction 2004. Contributions: journals and periodicals. *Honours:* Fulbright Scholarship, Paris, 1956–57; ACLS Fellowship, 1965–66; Guggenheim Felowship, 1970–71; National Endowment for the Humanities Senior Fellowship, 1981; National Humanities Center Fellow, 1987–88; Rockefeller Foundation Fellowship, Bellagio, Italy, 1989. *Address:* c/o Department of English, Brandeis University, Waltham, MA 02254, USA.

GOODISON, Lorna (Gaye); poet, painter and writer; b. 1 Aug. 1947, Kingston, Jamaica; one d. *Education:* Art schools, Kingston and New York 1967–69. *Career:* teacher of Creative Writing, USA and Canada; has participated in literary festivals in New York, London and Erlangen. *Publications:* poetry: Poems 1974, Tamarind Season 1980, I Am Becoming My Mother 1986, Heartease 1988, Selected Poems 1992, To Us All Flowers Are Roses 1995; short stories: Baby Mother and the King of Swords 1989. *Honours:* Institute of Jamaica Centenary Prize 1981, Commonwealth Poetry Prize 1986. *Address:* 8 Marley Close, Kingston 6, Jamaica.

GOODMAN, Jonathan; Author, Poet, Publisher and Ed.; b. 17 Jan. 1931, London, England. *Career:* Theatre Dir and Television Prod., various companies, United Kingdom, 1951–64; Dir, Anmbar Publications Ltd, London, 1967–; Gen. Ed., Celebrated Trials Series, David & Charles (Publishers) Ltd, Newton Abbott, Devon, 1972–. *Publications:* Martinee Idylls (poems), 1954; Instead of Murder (novel), 1961; Criminal Tendencies (novel), 1964; Hello Cruel World Goodbye (novel), 1964; The Killing of Julia Wallace, 1969; Bloody Versicles, 1971; Posts-Mortem, 1971; Trial of Ian Brady and Myra Hindley (ed.), 1973; Trial of Ian Ruth Ellis (ed.), 1975; The Burning of Evelyn Foster, 1977; The Last Sentence (novel), 1978; The Stabbing of George Harry Storrs, 1982; Pleasure of Murder, 1983; Railway Murders, 1984; Who-He, 1984; Seaside Murders, 1985; The Crippen File (ed.) 1985; The Underworld (with I. Will), 1985; Christmas Murders (ed.) 1986; The Moors Murders, 1986; Acts of Murder, 1986; Murder in High Places, 1986; The Slaying of Joseph Bowne Elwell, 1987. *Address:* 43 Ealing Village, London W5 2LZ, England.

GOODWIN, Doris (Helen) Kearns; Historian; b. 4 Jan. 1943, Rockville Centre, New York, USA; m. Richard Goodwin, 1973, three s. *Education:* BA, Colby College, 1964; PhD, Harvard University, 1968. *Career:* Research Assoc., US Dept of Health, Education, and Welfare, 1966; Special Asst, US Dept of Labor, 1967, and to Pres. Lyndon B. Johnson, 1968; Asst Prof., 1969–71, Asst Dir, Institute of Politics, 1971, Assoc. Prof. of Government, 1972, Harvard University; Special Consultant to Pres. Lyndon B. Johnson, 1969–73; mem. Amnerican Political Science Asscn; Council on Foreign Relations; Group for Applied Psychoanalysis; Signet Society; Women Involved. *Publications:* Lyndon Johnson and the American Dream, 1976; The Fitzgeralds and the Kennedys: An American Saga, 1987; No Ordinary Time: Franklin and Eleanor Roosevelt: The Home Front in World War II, 1994; Wait Till Next Year: A Memoir, 1997; Every Four Years: Presidential Campaigns and the Media Since 1896, 2003. Contributions: books and television. *Honours:* Fulbright Fellow, 1966; White House Fellow, 1967; Pulitzer Prize for History, 1995. *Address:* c/o Simon & Schuster Trade Division, 1230 Ave of the Americas, New York, NY 10020, USA.

GOONERATNE, Malini Yasmine; writer, poet, editor and academic; b. 22 Dec. 1935, Colombo, Sri Lanka; m. Brendon Gooneratne 1962; one s. one d. *Education:* BA, Ceylon, 1959; PhD, English Literature, University of Cambridge, 1962; DLitt, English and Commonwealth Literature, Macquarie University, Australia, 1981. *Career:* Dir, Post-Colonial Literature and Language Research Centre, 1988–93, Personal Chair in English Literature, 1991–99, Emeritus Prof., 1999–, Macquarie University; mem. Australian Society of Authors; Fédération Internationales des Langues et Littératures Modernes, vice-pres., 1990–96; International Asscn of University Prof.s of English; Jane Austen Society of Australia, patron; New South Wales Writers Centre; South Asian Studies Asscn of Australia. *Publications:* English Literature in Ceylon 1815–1878: The Development of an Anglo-Ceylonese Literature, 1968; Jane Austen, 1970; Word Bird, Motif, 53 Poems, 1971; The Lizard's Cry and Other Poems, 1972; Alexander Pope, 1976; Diverse Inheritance: A Personal Perspective on Commonwealth Literature, 1980; 6000 Foot Death Dive (poems), 1981; Silence, Exile, and Cunning: The Fiction of Ruth Prawer Jhabvala, 1983; Relative Merits (memoir), 1986; Celebrations and Departures (poems), 1991; A Change of Skies (novel), 1991; The Pleasures of Conquest (novel), 1995; This Inscrutable Englishman: Sir John D'Oyly 1774–1824 (co-author), 1999; Masterpiece and Other Stories, 2002; Celebrating Sri Lankan Women's English Writing, 2002. Contributions: various publications. *Honours:* AM, 1990; Marjorie Barnard Literary Award for Fiction, 1992; Raja Rao Award, 2001; several research and travel grants. *Address:* c/o Dept of English, College of Humanities, Macquarie University, North Ryde, NSW 2109, Australia.

GOOS, Maria; Dutch playwright, screenwriter and director; b. 1956; m. Peter Blok; two d. *Education:* Acad. of Dramatic Art, Maastricht. *Career:* director with theatre companies; Artistic Man., De Kompaan theatre group. *Screenplays include:* Famille 2001, Cloaca 2003. *Television screenplays:* De Keizerin van België 1990, Oog in oog (series) 1990, Klokhuis 1991, Hartslag 1991, Pleidooi (series) 1991–94, Oud geld (series) 1995–97, Familie 1999, Icarus 1999, Ver van huis 2000, De Aanklacht 2000, Leef! 2002, Lieve Mensen (also dir) 2003. *Plays:* writer and director: En toen Mamma 1982, Blessuretijd 1983, Tussen Zussen 1983, Een avond in Extase 1984, De Keizerin van België 1985, Helden 1986, De Kuba Walbas 1998, Nu Even Niet 2001; writer only: Alles is liefde 1988, Eeuwig Jong 1988, Draaikonten 1997, Krambamboelie 1999, Familie 1999, Cloaca 2002, Nu Even Well 2003; director only: In het uiterste geval by Paul Binnerts 1987. *Honours:* Acad. Award Nederland for best series 1998–99, Lira Script Award 2001, Golden Gate Award 2002, Publieksprijs en de speciale juryprijs 2003. *Address:* Kik Productions, Postbus 13120, 3507 LC, Utrecht, Netherlands. *E-mail:* info@kikproductions.nl. *Website:* www.mariagoos.nl.

GORDIMER, Nadine, FRSL; South African writer; b. 20 Nov. 1923, Springs; m. 2nd Reinhold Cassirer 1954 (died); one s. one d. *Education:* convent school. *Career:* mem. ANC 1990–; Vice-Pres. Int. PEN; Goodwill Amb. CINDP; mem. Congress of S African Writers. *Publications:* The Soft Voice of the Serpent (stories), The Lying Days (novel) 1953, Six Feet of the Country (stories) 1956, A World of Strangers (novel) 1958, Friday's Footprint (stories) 1960, Occasion for Loving (novel) 1963, Not For Publication (stories) 1965, The Late Bourgeois World (novel) 1966, A Guest of Honour (novel) 1970, Livingstone's Companions (stories) 1972, The Black Interpreters (literary criticism) 1973, The Conservationist (novel) 1974, Selected Stories 1975, Some Monday for Sure (stories) 1976, Burger's Daughter 1979, A Soldier's Embrace (stories) 1980, July's People (novel) 1981, Something Out There (novella) 1984, A Sport of Nature (novel) 1987, The Essential Gesture (essays) 1988, My Son's Story (novel) 1990, Jump (short stories) 1991, Crimes of Conscience (short stories) 1991, None to Accompany Me (novel) 1994, Writing and Being (lectures) 1995, The House Gun 1997, Living in Hope and History: Notes on our Century (essays) 1999, The Pickup 2001, Loot and Other Stories 2003; co-ed. South African Writing Today 1967; ed. Telling Tales 2004. *Honours:* Hon.Fellow American Acad. of Arts and Letters, American Acad. of Arts and Sciences; Hon. mem. American Inst. of Arts and Letters; Officier Ordre des Arts et des Lettres 1987; Charles Eliot Norton Lecturer in Literature, Harvard Univ. 1994; Dr hc (Cambridge) 1992, (Oxford) 1994; W. H. Smith Literary Award 1961, Thomas Pringle Award (English Acad. of SA) 1969, James Tait Black Memorial Prize 1971, Booker Prize (co-winner) 1974, Grand Aigle d'Or Prize (France) 1975, CNA Literary Award (S Africa) 1974, 1979, 1981, 1991, Scottish Arts Council Neil M. Gunn Fellowship 1981, Modern Language Asscn Award (USA) 1981, Premio Malaparte (Italy) 1985, Nelly Sachs Prize (Germany) 1985, Bennett Award (USA) 1987, Benson Medal (Royal Soc. of Literature) 1990, Nobel Prize for Literature 1991, Primo Levi Award 2002, Mary McCarthy Award 2003, Bavarian State Premier's Hon. Award (part of the Corine Int. Book Prize). *Literary Agent:* A. P. Watt, 20 John Street, London, WC1N 2DR, England.

GORDON, Donald Ramsay; Writer; b. 14 Sept. 1929, Toronto, Ontario, Canada; m. Helen E. Currie, 21 Dec. 1952, three s. *Education:* BA, Political Science, Economics, Queen's University, Kingston, 1953; MA, Political Economy, University of Toronto, 1955; Predoctoral studies, Political Science, LSE, England, 1956–63. *Career:* Writer, Filing Ed., The Canadian Press, Toronto, Montréal, Edmonton, 1955; Asst Ed., The Financial Post, Toronto, 1955–57; European Correspondent, Canadian Broadcasting Corporation, London, 1957–63; Asst Prof., Assoc. Prof., Political Science, University of Calgary, Alberta, 1963–66, University of Waterloo, Ontario, 1966–75; Self-employed Writer, Consultant, 1975–81; Chief Writer, The Image Corporation, Waterloo, 1983–92; Instructor, Conestoga College, Kitchener, Ontario, 1991–, Long Ridge Writers Group, West Redding, CT, USA, 1992–. *Publications:* Language, Logic and the Mass Media, 1966; The New Literacy, 1971; The Media, 1972; Fineswine, 1984; The Rock Candy Bandits, 1984; S.P.E.E.D., 1984; The Prosperian Papers, 1989; The Choice, 1990; The Sex Shoppe, 1991. *Address:* 134 Iroquois Pl., Waterloo, Ontario N2L 2S5, Canada.

GORDON, Graeme, BA, DEJF; writer; b. 21 June 1966, Epsom, England. *Education:* University of Sussex, University of Strasbourg, III. *Career:* mem. Writers' Guild of Great Britain. *Publications:* Fiction: Bayswater Bodycount, 1995; Barking Mad.

GORDON, Jaimy; Prof. of English and Writer; b. 4 July 1944, Baltimore, MD, USA; m. Peter Blickle, 1988. *Education:* BA, Antioch College, 1966; MA, 1972, DA, 1975, Brown University. *Career:* Writer-in-Residence, Rhode Island State Council on the Arts, 1975–77; Dir, Creative Writing Program, Stephens College, Columbia, MO, 1980–81; Asst Prof., 1981–87, Assoc. Prof., 1987–92, Prof. of English, 1992–, Western Michigan University, Kalamazoo. *Publications:* Shamp of the City-Solo, 1974; The Bend, the Lip, the Kid (narrative poem), 1978; Circumspections from an Equestrian Statue, 1979; Maria Beig: Lost Weddings (trans. with Peter Blickle), 1990; She Drove Without Stopping, 1990; Bogeywoman, 1999. Contributions: Magazines. *Honours:* National Endowment for the Arts Fellowships, 1979, 1991; American Acad. and Institute of Arts and Letters Award, 1991. *Address:* 1803 Hazel St, Kalamazoo, MI 49008, USA.

GORDON, John William; Writer; b. 19 Nov. 1925, Jarrow-on-Tyne, England; m. Sylvia Young 9 Jan. 1954; one s. one d. *Career:* mem. Society of Authors. *Publications:* The Giant Under the Snow, 1968; The House on the Brink, 1970; The Ghost on the Hill, 1976; The Waterfall Box, 1978; The Spitfire Grave, 1979; The Edge of the World, 1983; Catch Your Death, 1984; The Quelling Eye, 1986; The Grasshopper, 1987; Ride the Wind, 1989; Secret Corridor, 1990; Blood Brothers, 1991; Ordinary Seaman (autobiog.), 1992; The Burning Baby, 1992; Gilray's Ghost, 1995; The Flesh Eater, 1998; The Midwinter Watch, 1998; Skinners, 1999; The Ghosts of Blacklode, 2002. *Address:* 99 George Borrow Rd, Norwich, Norfolk NR4 7HU, England.

GORDON, Lois, BA, MA, PhD; academic and writer; b. Englewood, NJ, USA; m. Alan Lee Gordon 1961; one s. *Education:* Univ. of Michigan, Univ. of Wisconsin. *Career:* Lecturer in English, City Coll., CUNY, 1964–66; Asst Prof. of English, Univ. of Missouri, Kansas City, 1966–68; Asst Prof., 1968–71, Assoc. Prof., 1971–75, Prof. of English, 1975–, Chair., Dept of English and Comparative Literature, 1982–90, Fairleigh Dickinson Univ.; Visiting Exchange Prof., Rutgers Univ., 1994; mem. Acad. of American Poets; Authors' Guild; Harold Pinter Society; International League for Human Rights; MLA; PEN; Samuel Beckett Society. *Publications:* Stratagems to Uncover Nakedness: The Dramas of Harold Pinter, 1969; Donald Barthelme, 1981; Robert Coover: The Universal Fictionmaking Process, 1983; American Chronicle: Six Decades in American Life, 1920–1980, 1987; American Chronicle: Seven Decades in American Life, 1920–1990, 1990; Harold Pinter Casebook, 1990; The Columbia Chronicle of American Life, 1910–1992, 1995; The Columbia World of Quotations, 1996; The World of Samuel Beckett, 1906–1946, 1996; American Chronicle: Year by Year Through the Twentieth Century, 1999; Pinter at 70, 2001; Reading Godot, 2002. Contributions: journals, reviews, and newspapers. *Address:* c/o Department of English, Fairleigh Dickinson University, Teaneck, NJ 07666, USA.

GORDON, Lyndall Felicity, BA, PhD; biographer and senior research fellow; b. 4 Nov. 1941, Cape Town, South Africa; m. Siamon Gordon 1963; two d. *Education:* Univ. of Cape Town, Columbia Univ. *Career:* Asst Prof. of English, Columbia Univ. 1975–76; Lecturer in English, Jesus Coll., Oxford 1977–84; tutor in English 1984–95, Sr Research Fellow 1995–, St Hilda's Coll., Oxford. *Publications:* Eliot's Early Years, 1977; Virginia Woolf: A Writer's Life, 1984; Eliot's New Life, 1988; Shared Lives, 1992; Charlotte Brontë: A Passionate Life, 1994; A Private Life of Henry James: Two Women and His Art, 1998; T. S. Eliot: An Imperfect Life, 1998; Mary Wollstonecraft 2005. *Honours:* Rose Mary Crawshay Prize, British Acad., 1978; James Tait Black Memorial Prize, 1985; Southern Arts Prize, 1989; Cheltenham Festival Prize, 1999. *Literary Agent:* PFD, Drury House, 34–43 Russell Street, London, WC2B 5HA, England.

GORDON, Mary (Catherine); Writer and Prof. of English; b. 8 Dec. 1949, Far Rockaway, Long Island, NY, USA; m. 1st James Brian, 1974, divorced; m. 2nd Arthur Cash, 1979, one s. one d. *Education:* BA, Barnard College, 1971; MA, Syracuse University, 1973. *Career:* Teacher of English, Dutchess Community College, Poughkeepsie, NY, 1974–78, Amherst College, MA, 1979; Millicent C. McIntosh Prof. of English, Barnard College, 1988–. *Publications:* Final Payments, 1978; The Company of Women, 1981; Men and Angels, 1985; Temporary Shelter, 1987; The Other Side, 1989; Good Boys and Dead Girls (essays), 1992; The Shadow Man (memoir), 1996; Spending: A Utopian Divertimento, 1998; Seeing Through Places: Reflections on Geography and Identity, 2000; Joan of Arc, 2000. Contributions: books and periodicals. *Honours:* Janet Heidinger Kafka Prizes, 1979, 1981; O. Henry Award, 1997. *Address:* c/o Dept of English, Barnard College, 3009 Broadway, New York, NY 10027, USA.

GÓREC-ROSINSKI, Jan; Poet, Writer, Essayist and Journalist; b. 6 Jan. 1920, Króglik, Poland; m. Maria Barbara Dobrzalska-Górec 15 Aug. 1938; three s. *Education:* Master of Law, Nicolai Copernici Univ., Torun, 1952. *Career:* journalist, Polish radio, 1957–58; Ed., Fakty, 1989–, Metafora (literary magazine), 1989–; mem. Union of Polish Writers in Warsaw. *Publications:* Jamark arlekinów, 1963; Ucieczka z Wiezy Babel, 1964; Bluznierstwo garncarza, 1965; Zaprzeszle horyzonty, 1968; Molitwa za dobrinu, 1968; Czas odnajdywania, 1970; Zywa galaz, 1971; W kamieniu, 1973; Poezje wybrane, 1976; Ulica Sokratesa, 1978; Eroica, 1980; Sen Syzyfa, 1982; Wzejscie slonc, 1985; Departures, 1985; Czyje bedzie królestwo, 1987; Kredowy Bóg, 1987; Czlowiek Podzielony, 1988; Czarnopis, poezje wybrane, 1989; Siedem wieczerników, 1990; Krzyczec beda kamienie, 1991; Czarna perla, 1992; Sloneczny splot, 1993; Demony, 1994; Przechodzien róz, 1995; Rajska jablon, 1995; Przychodzacy: sacrum et profanum, 1997; Mesjasz zbuntowany: dramat mityczny, 2001. Contributions: many publications. *Honours:* Council Award, Bydgoszcz People's Province, 1968; Workers' Publishing Co-operative Award, 1979; Klemens Janicki Award, 1986; International Poetic November Award, 1987; Prof. T. Kotarbinski Prize, 1989; Pres. of Bydgoszcz Artistic Award, 2000; Commander's Order and Star from Pres. of Poland, 2002. *Address:* Metafora, ul Siedlecka 70a, 85-412 Bydgoszcz, Poland.

GORES, Joseph (Nicholas); Writer, Novelist and Screenwriter; b. 25 Dec. 1931, Rochester, Minnesota, USA; m. Dori Corfitzen, 16 May 1976, one s. one d. *Education:* BA, University of Notre Dame, 1953; MA, Stanford University, 1961. *Career:* Story Ed., B. L. Stryker Mystery Movie Series, ABC-TV, 1988–89; mem. MWA, pres., 1986; International Asscn of Crime Writers; CWA; Private Eye Writers of America. *Publications:* A Time of Predators, 1969; Marine Salvage (non-fiction), 1971; Dead Skip, 1972; Final Notice, 1973; Interface, 1974; Hammett, 1975; Gone, No Forwarding, 1978; Come Morning, 1986; Wolf Time, 1989; Mostly Murder (short stories), 1992; 32 Cadillacs, 1992; Dead Man, 1993; Menaced Assassin, 1994; Contract Null and Void, 1996; Cases, 1998; Speak of the Devil (short stories), 1999; Stakeout on Page Street (short stories), 2000; Cons, Scams and Grifts, 2001. Contributions: numerous magazines and anthologies; Eight film scripts; Television drama. *Honours:* Best First Novel, 1969, Best Short Story, 1969, Edgar, Best Episodic TV Drama, 1975, MWA; Falcon, Maltese Falcon Society of Japan, 1986. *Address:* PO Box 446, Fairfax, CA 94978, USA.

GÖRGEY, Gábor; Hungarian poet, novelist and playwright. *Career:* Minister of Cultural Heritage for Hungary. *Publications:* Lilla-Cápák Nyugalom 1976, Légifolyosó 1977, Találkozás egy fél kutyával 1980, Egy vacsora anatómiája 1981, A fél kutya másik fele 1983, Munkavilágítás 1984, A diva bosszúja 1988, Meteoropata nemzet 1989, Mindig újabb kuty ák jönnek 1991, Waterloo kellos közepén 1994. *Address:* c/o Hungarian Cultural Centre, 10 Maiden Lane, Covent Garden, London, WC2E 7NA, England.

GOSLING(-HARE), Paula (Louise), (Ainslie Skinner); Writer; b. 12 Oct. 1939, Michigan, USA; m. 1st Christopher Gosling Sept. 1968 (divorced 1978); two d.; m. 2nd John Hare 1982. *Education:* BA, Wayne State Univ. *Career:* mem. CWA, chair., 1982; Society of Authors. *Publications:* A Running Duck, 1976; Zero Trap, 1978; The Woman in Red, 1979; Losers Blues, 1980; Minds Eye (as Ainslie Skinner), 1980; Monkey Puzzle, 1982; The Wychford Murders, 1983; Hoodwink, 1985; Backlash, 1987; Death Penalties, 1990; The Body in Blackwater Bay, 1992; A Few Dying Words, 1994; The Dead of Winter, 1995; Death and Shadows, 1999; Underneath Every Stone, 2000; Richochet, 2002. *Honours:* Gold Dagger, CWA; Arts Achievement Award, Wayne State Univ. *Literary Agent:* Greene & Heaton Ltd, 37 Goldhawk Rd, London W12 8QQ, England.

GOSSETT, Philip; Musicologist, Distinguished Service Prof., Writer and Ed.; b. 27 Sept. 1941, New York, NY, USA; m. Suzanne S. Gossett, 4 Aug. 1963, two s. *Education:* BA, summa cum laude, Amherst College, 1963; Columbia University, 1961–62; MFA, 1965, PhD, 1970, Princeton University. *Career:* Asst Prof., 1968–73, Assoc. Prof., 1973–77, Prof., 1977–84, Chair., Dept of Music, 1978–84, 1989, Robert W. Reneker Distinguished Service Prof., 1984–, Dean, Division of Humanities, 1989–99, University of Chicago; Visiting Assoc. Prof., Columbia University, 1975; Direttore dell'edizione, Edizione critica delle Opere di Gioachino Rossini, 1978–; Meadows Visiting Prof., Southern Methodist University, 1980; General Ed., The Works of Giuseppe Verdi, 1981–; Assoc. Prof., Universitá degli Studi, Parma, 1983, and Rome, 1994; Visiting Prof., University of Paris, 1988; Five-College Visiting Prof., 1989; Gauss Seminars, Princeton University, 1991; Hambro Visiting Prof. of Opera Studies, University of Oxford, 2001; Visiting Scholar, Phi Beta Kappa, 2002–03; mem. American Acad. of Arts and Sciences; American Institute of Verdi Studies; American Musicological Society, pres., 1994–96; International Musicological Society; Società Italiana di Musicologia; Society for Textual Scholarship, pres., 1993–95. *Publications:* The Operas of Rossini: Problems of Textual Criticism in Nineteenth-Century Opera, two vols, 1970; Treatise on Harmony by Jean-Philippe Rameau (trans. and ed.), 1971; The Tragic Finale of Tancredi, 1977; Early Romantic Opera (ed. with Charles Rosen), 1978–83; Le Sinfonie di Rossini, 1981; Italian Opera 1810–1840 (ed.), 25 vols, 1984–92; 'Anna Bolena' and the Maturity of Gaetano Donizetti, 1985; Il barbiere di Siviglia 1992, Don Pasquale 1999. Contributions: Reference works, scholarly books and professional journals. *Honours:* Fellow, American Acad. of Arts and Sciences, 1989–; Hon. Mem., Accademia Filarmonica di Bologna, 1992, Accademico Onorario Accademia di Santa Cecilia Rome 2003Grand Ufficiale dell'Ordine al Merito, 1997, Cavaliere di Gran Croce, 1998, Republic of Italy; Order of Rio Branca, Republic of Brazil, 1998; Socio Straniero, Ateneo Veneto, 2001Hon. Doctor of Humane Letters, Amherst College 1993Woodrow Wilson Fellowship, 1963–64; Fulbright Scholar, Paris, 1965–66; Martha Baird Rockefeller Fellowship, 1967–68; Alfred Einstein Award, American Musicological Society, 1969; Guggenheim Fellowship, 1971–72; National Endowment for the Humanities Senior Fellowship, 1982–83; Medaglio d'Oro, prima classe, Italian Government, 1985; Deems Taylor Award, American Acad. of Composers, Authors and Publishers, 1986. *Address:* c/o Dept of Music, University of Chicago, 1010 E 59th St, Chicago, IL 60637, USA. *E-mail:* phgs@midway.uchicago.edu.

GOTO, Hiromi; Writer; b. 31 Dec. 1966, Chiba-ken, Japan; two c. *Education:* BA, Humanities, University of Calgary, 1989. *Career:* mem. Writers Union of Canada, co-chair, racial minority committee, 1995–97. *Publications:* Chorus of Mushrooms, 1994; The Kappa Child, 2001; The Water of Possibility, 2001. *Honours:* Co-Winner, Canada-Japan Book Award, 1995; Commonwealth Writers Prize, Best First Book, Canada-Caribbean Region, 1995; James Tiptree Jr Memorial Award, 2001. *Literary Agent:* Anne McDermid and Assocs.

GOULD, Alan David; Poet and Novelist; b. 22 March 1949, London, England; m. Anne Langridge, 17 Jan. 1984, two s. *Education:* BA, 1971; DipEd, 1974. *Career:* Creative Fellow, Australian National University, 1978; Writer-in-Residence, Geelong College, 1978, 1980, 1982, 1985, Australian Defence Forces Acad., 1986, Lincoln Humberside Arts Centre, 1988. *Publications:* Poetry: Icelandic Solitaries, 1978; Astral Sea, 1981; The Pausing of the Hours, 1984; The Twofold Place, 1986; Years Found in Likeness, 1988; Former Light (selected poems), 1992; Momentum, 1992; Mermaid, 1996; Dalliance and Scorn, 1999; A Fold in the Light, 2001. Fiction: The Man Who Stayed Below, 1984; The Enduring Disguises, 1988; To The Burning City, 1991; Close Ups, 1994; The Tazyrik Year, 1998; The Schoonermaster's Dance, 2000. Essays: The Totem Ship, 1996. Contributions: various Australian publications. *Honours:* New South Wales Premier's Prize for Poetry, 1981; Prizes for Fiction, 1985, 1992; Philip Hodgins Memorial Medal, 1999; Royal Blind Society Audio Book of the Year, 1999; Co-winner, Courier-Mail Book of the Year, 2001; Co-winner, A.C.T. Book of the Year, 2001. *Address:* 6 Mulga St, O'Connor, ACT 2602, Australia.

GOULDEN, Joseph C., (Henry S. A. Becket); Writer; b. 23 May 1934, Marshall, Texas, USA; m. 1st, two s.; m. 2nd Leslie Cantrell Smith, 23 June 1979. *Education:* University of Texas, 1952–56. *Career:* Staff Writer, Dallas Morning News, Philadelphia Inquirer, 1958–68. *Publications:* The Curtis Caper, 1965; Monopoly, 1968; Truth is the First Casualty, 1969; The Money Givers, 1971; The Superlawyers, 1972; Meany: The Unchallenged Strong Man of American Labor, 1972; The Benchwarmers, 1974; Mencken's Last Campaign (ed.), 1976; The Best Years, 1976; The Million Dollar Lawyers, 1978; Korea: Untold Story of War, 1982; Myth-Informed (with Paul Dickson), 1983; The News Manipulators (with Reed Irvine and Cliff Kincaid), 1983; Jerry Wurf: Labor's Last Angry Man, 1982; The Death Merchant, 1984; There Are Alligators in Our Sewers (with Paul Dickson), 1984; Dictionary of Espionage (as Henry S. A. Becket), 1987; Fit to Print: A. M. Rosenthal and His Times, 1988. Contributions: Over 200 articles to magazines. *Address:* 1534 29th St NW, Washington, DC 20007, USA.

GOVIER, Katherine Mary; Writer; b. 4 July 1948, Edmonton, AB, Canada; m. John Allen, 27 Feb. 1981, two c. *Education:* BA, University of Alberta, 1970; MA, York University, 1972. *Career:* Lecturer in English, Ryerson Polytechnic, 1973–74; Contributing Ed., Toronto Life Magazine, 1975–77; Visiting Lecturer in Creative Writing, York University, 1982–85; Research Fellow, University of Leeds, 1986; Writer-in-Residence, Toronto Public Library, 1994–95; mem. PEN Canada; Writers Development Trust, chair., 1990–91; Writers in Electronic Residence, chair., 1991–94; Writers Union of Canada. *Publications:* Random Descent, 1979; Going Through the Motions, 1981; Fables of Brunswick Avenue, 1985; Between Men, 1987; Before and After, 1989; Hearts of Flame, 1991; The Immaculate Conception Photography Gallery, 1994; Without a Guide (ed.), 1994; Angel Walk, 1996. Contributions: numerous anthologies and periodicals. *Honours:* Authors Award, Foundation for the Advancement of Canadian Letters, 1979; National Magazine Award, 1979; City of Toronto Book Award, 1992.

GOW, Michael; Australian playwright and writer; b. 14 Feb. 1955, Sydney. *Plays:* Away 1986, Furious 1991, Sweet Phoebe 1994, Live Acts on Stage. *Publications:* fiction: The Kid 1983, The Astronaut's Wife 1984, On Top of the World 1986, Europe 1987, 1841 1988, All Stops Out (juvenile) 1991. *Literary Agent:* RGM Associates, PO Box 128, Surry Hills, NSW 2010, Australia. *Telephone:* (2) 9281-3911. *Fax:* (2) 9281-4705. *E-mail:* info@rgm.com.au. *Website:* www.rgm.com.au.

GOWDY, Barbara Louise; novelist and short story writer; b. 25 June 1950, Windsor, ON, Canada. *Education:* York Univ. *Career:* mem. PEN Canada, Writer's Union of Canada. *Publications:* Through the Green Valley (novel) 1988, Falling Angels (novel) 1989, We So Seldom Look on Love (short stories) 1992, Mister Sandman (novel) 1995, The White Bone (novel) 1998, The Romantic (novel) 2003; contrib. to Best American Short Stories, The New Oxford Book of Canadian Short Stories, The Penguin Anthology of Stories by Canadian Women. *Honours:* Marian Engel Award. *Literary Agent:* Westwood Creative Artists, 94 Harbord Street, Toronto, ON M5S 1G6, Canada.

GOYTISOLO, Juan; Spanish writer; b. 5 Jan. 1931, Barcelona; m. Monique Lange 1978 (died 1996). *Education:* Univs of Barcelona and Madrid. *Career:* emigrated to France 1957; reporter, Cuba 1965; assoc. with Gallimard Publishing Co.; Visiting Prof. at various univs in USA. *Writing for television:* Alquibla (TVE series). *Publications:* novels: Juegos de manos (trans. as The Young Assassins) 1954, Duelo en el paraíso (trans. as Children of Chaos) 1955, El circo 1957, Fiestas 1957, La resaca 1958, La isla 1961, La chanca 1962, Señas de identidad (trans. as Marks of Identity) 1966, Reivindicación del Conde don Julián (trans. as Count Julian) 1970, Juan sin tierra (trans. as John the Landless) 1975, Colera de Aquines 1979, Makbara 1980, Paisajes después de la batalla (trans. as Landscapes After the Battle) 1982, Las virtudes del pájaro solitario (trans. as The Virtues of the Solitary Bird) 1988, La cuarentena (trans. as Quarantine) 1991, La saga de los Marx (trans. as The Marx Family Saga) 1993, Campos de Níjar 1993, Las semanas del jardín (trans. as The Garden of Secrets) 1997, Carajicomedia (trans. as A Cock-Eyed Comedy) 2000; other: Crónicas Sarracinas (essays, trans. as Saracen Chronicles) 1982, Coto vedado (autobiog., trans. as Forbidden Territory) 1985, En los reinos de taifa (autobiog., trans. as Realms of Strife) 1986, Pájaro que ensucia su propio nido (essays) 2003, Cinema Eden: Essays from the Muslim Mediterranean 2004, short stories, travel narratives, literary criticism, essays. *Honours:* Premio Europalia 1985; numerous awards for novel Juegos de manos; Octavio Paz Essay and Poetry Prize 2002. *Address:* c/o Sickle Moon Books, Eland Publishing Ltd, Third Floor, 61 Exmouth Market, London, EC1R 4QL, England.

GRACE, Patricia (Frances); Writer; b. 1937, Wellington, New Zealand; m., seven c. *Education:* St Mary's College; Wellington Teachers College. *Career:* Teacher, Primary and Secondary Schools, King Country, Northland and Porirua; Writing Fellow, Victoria University, Wellington, 1985. *Publications:* Mutuwhenua: The Moon Sleeps, 1978; Potiki, 1986; Cousins, 1992; Baby No-Eyes, 1998. Short Stories: Waiariki, 1975; The Dream Sleepers and Other Stories, 1980; Electric City and Other Stories, 1980; Selected Stories, 1991; The Sky People, 1994; Collected Stories, 1994; Baby No-Eyes, 1998. Other: several books for children. *Honours:* New Zealand Fiction Award, 1987; HLD, Victoria University, 1989. *Address:* c/o Pearson Education New Zealand Ltd, Private Bag 102908, NSMC, Auckland, New Zealand.

GRACQ, Julien; French writer and professor (retd); b. 27 July 1910, St Florent-le-Vieil, Maine et Loire. *Education:* Ecole Normale Supérieure and Ecole des Sciences Politiques, Paris (Prof. agrégé d'histoire). *Career:* History teacher 1935–47; History teacher Lycée Claude Bernard, Paris

1947–70; retd. *Publications:* Au château d'Argol 1939, Un beau ténébreux 1945, Le roi pêcheur 1947, Liberté grande 1947, André Breton 1947, La littérature à l'estomac 1950, Le rivage des Syrtes 1951, Un balcon en forêt 1958, Préférences 1961, Lettrines 1967, La presqu'île 1970, Lettrines 2 1974, Les eaux étroites 1976, En lisant, En écrivant 1981, La forme d'une ville 1985, Autour des Sept Collines 1988, Carnets du Grand Chemin 1992, Le Roi pêcheur 1996, Entretiens 2002. *Address:* 3 rue du Grenier à Sel, 49410 St Florent-le-Vieil, France.

GRAEME, Roderic (see Jeffries, Roderic (Graeme)).

GRAFF, Henry F(ranklin); Prof. of History Emeritus and Writer; b. 11 Aug. 1921, New York, NY, USA; m. Edith Krantz, 16 June 1946, two d. *Education:* BSS, City College, CUNY, 1941; MA, 1942, PhD, 1949, Columbia University. *Career:* Fellow in History, 1941–42, Tutor in History, 1946, City College, CUNY; Lecturer, 1946–47, Instructor to Assoc. Prof., 1946–61, Chair., Dept of History, 1961–64, Prof. of History, 1961–91, Prof. Emeritus, 1991–, Columbia University; Lecturer, Vassar College, 1953, Yale School of Medicine, 1993; Presidential appointee, National Historical Publications Commission, 1965–71, Pres. John F. Kennedy Assassination Records Review Board, 1993–98; Senior Fellow, Freedom Foundation Media Studies Center, New York City, 1991–92; Dean's Distinguished Lecturer in the Humanities, Columbia University College of Physicians and Surgeons, 1992; mem. American Historical Asscn; Authors' Guild; Council on Foreign Relations; Organization of American Historians; PEN; Society of American Historians; Corresponding mem., Massachusetts Historical Society. *Publications:* Bluejackets with Perry in Japan, 1952; The Modern Researcher (with Jacques Barzun), 1962; American Themes (with Clifford Lord), 1963; Thomas Jefferson, 1968; American Imperialism and the Philippine Insurrection, 1969; The Tuesday Cabinet: Deliberation and Decision on Peace and War under Lyndon B. Johnson, 1970; The Call of Freedom (with Paul J. Bohannan), 1978; The Promise of Democracy, 1978; This Great Nation, 1983; The Presidents: A Reference History, 1984; America: The Glorious Republic, 1985; Grover Cleveland, 2002. Contributions: scholarly journals and to general periodicals. *Honours:* Townsend Harris Medal, City College, CUNY, 1966; Mark Van Doren Award, 1981, Great Teacher Award, 1982, Columbia University; Kidger Award, New England History Teachers Asscn, 1990; Presidential Medal, George Washington University, 1997; James Madison Award, American Library Asscn, 1999; Lifetime Achievement Award, Westchester Community College Foundation, 2000. *Address:* 47 Andrea Lane, Scarsdale, NY 10583, USA.

GRAFTON, Anthony T(homas); Historian, University Prof. and Writer; b. 21 May 1950, New Haven, CT, USA; m. Louise Ehrlich, 13 May 1972, one s. one d. *Education:* BA, 1970, MA, 1972, PhD, History, 1975, University of Chicago. *Career:* Instructor in History, Cornell University, 1974–75; Asst Prof., 1975, Assoc. Prof., 1976–85, Prof., 1985–88, Andrew Mellon Prof. of History, 1988–93, Dodge Prof. of History, 1993–2000, Henry Putnam University Prof., 2000–, Princeton University; Exhibit Curator, New York Public Library, New York, 1992; Meyer Schapiro Lecturer, Columbia University, 1996–96; mem. Renaissance Society of America; American Philosophical Society. *Publications:* Joseph Scaliger: A Bibliography, 1852–1982 (ed. with H. J. de Jonge), 1982; Joseph Scaliger: A Study in the History of Classical Scholarship, Vol. 1, Textual Criticism and Exegesis, 1983, Vol. 2, Historical Chronology, 1993; From Humanism to the Humanities: Education and the Liberal Arts in Fifteenth- and Sixteenth-Century Europe (with Lisa Jardine), 1986; Forgers and Critics: Creativity and Duplicity in Western Scholarship, 1990; The Transmission of Culture in Early Modern Europe (with Ann Blair), 1990; Defenders of the Text: The Traditions of Scholarship in an Age of Science, 1450–1800, 1991; New Worlds, Ancient Texts: The Power of Tradition and the Shock of Discovery (with April Shelford and Nancy Siraisi), 1992; The Foundations of Early Modern Europe, 1460–1559 (with Eugene F. Rice), 1994; The Footnote: A Curious History, 1997; Cardano's Cosmos: The Worlds and Works of a Renaissance Astrologer, 1999; Natural Particulars: Nature and the Disciplines in Renaissance Europe (ed. with Nancy Siraisi), 1999; Leon Battista Alberti: Master Builder of the Italian Renaissance, 2000; Bring Out Your Dead: The Past as Revelation, 2001. Contributions: periodicals including: Proceedings of the American Philosophical Society; History and Theory; Journal of the Warburg and Courtauld Institutes; Journal of Roman Studies. *Honours:* Danforth Fellow, 1971–75; Grant-in-Aid, ACLS, 1977; Rollins Bicentennial Professorship, Princeton University, 1978; Guggenheim Fellow, 1988–89; Fairchild Fellow, California Technical Institute, 1988–89; Prize for History, Los Angeles Times, 1993; Behrmann Fellow, Princeton University, 1994–95; Bainton Prize, Sixteenth-Century Studies Conference, 1999; Marron Prize, American Historical Asscn, 2000. *Address:* c/o Dept of History, Dickinson Hall, Princeton University, Princeton, NJ 08544, USA.

GRAFTON, Sue, BA; writer; b. 24 April 1940, Louisville, KY, USA; m. 1st; one c.; m. 2nd; two c.; m. 3rd Steven F. Humphrey 1978. *Education:* University of Louisville. *Career:* many guest lectureships at colleges and universities; mem. CWA, pres., 1989–90; Writers Guild of America. *Publications:* Keziah Dane 1967, The Lolly-Madonna War 1969, 'A' is for Alibi 1982, 'B' is for Burglar 1985, 'C' is for Corpse 1989, 'D' is for Deadbeat 1987, 'E' is for Evidence 1988, 'F' is for Fugitive 1989, 'G' is for Gumshoe 1990, 'H' is for Homicide 1991, 'I' is for Innocent 1992, Kinsey and Me 1992, 'J' is for Judgement 1994, 'K' is for Killer 1994, 'L' is for Lawless 1995, 'M' is for Malice 1996, 'N' is for Noose 1998, 'O' is for Outlaw 1999, 'P' is for Peril 2001, 'Q' is for Quarry 2003, 'R' is for Ricochet 2004; editor: Writing Mysteries 1992; contrib. to magazines, films and television. *Honours:* Shamus Awards, 1986, 1991, 1994; Anthony Awards, 1987, 1991; Doubleday Mystery Guild Awards, 1989, 1990, 1991, 1992; Falcon Award, 1990. *Address:* PO Box 41447, Santa Barbara, CA 93140, USA. *Website:* www.suegrafton.com.

GRAHAM, Charles S. (see Tubb, Edwin Charles).

GRAHAM, Donald Edward, BA; American newspaper publisher; b. 22 April 1945, Baltimore, Md; m. Mary L. Wissler 1967; one s. three d. *Education:* Harvard Univ. *Career:* joined the Washington Post 1971, Asst Man. Ed./Sports 1974–75, Asst Gen. Man. 1975–76, Exec. Vice-Pres. and Gen. Man. 1976–79, Publr 1979–; Pres., CEO Washington Post Co. 1991–93, Chair., CEO 1993–; fmrly reporter and writer for Newsweek. *Address:* The Washington Post, 1150 15th Street, NW, Washington, DC 20071, USA. *Telephone:* (202) 334-7138.

GRAHAM, Henry; Lecturer and Poet; b. 1 Dec. 1930, Liverpool, England. *Education:* Liverpool College of Art, 1950–52. *Career:* Poetry Ed., Ambit, London, 1969–. *Publications:* Good Luck to You Kafka/You'll Need It Boss, 1969; Soup City Zoo, 1969; Passport to Earth, 1971; Poker in Paradise Lost, 1977; Europe After Rain, 1981; Bomb, 1985; The Very Fragrant Death of Paul Gauguin, 1987; Jardin Gobe Avions, 1991; The Eye of the Beholder, 1997; Kafka in Liverpool, 2002. Contributions: Ambit; Transatlantic Review; Prism International Review; Evergreen Review; numerous anthrologies world-wide. *Honours:* Arts Council Literature Awards, 1969, 1971, 1975. *Address:* Flat 5, 23 Marmion Rd, Liverpool L17 8TT, England.

GRAHAM, James (see Patterson, Henry (Harry)).

GRAHAM, Jorie; Poet and Teacher; b. 9 May 1951, New York, NY, USA; m. James Galvin. *Education:* BFA, New York Univ., 1973; MFA, Univ. of Iowa, 1978. *Career:* Poetry Ed., Crazy Horse, 1978–81; Asst Prof., Murray State Univ., KY, 1978–79, Humboldt State Univ., Arcata, CA, 1979–81; Instructor, Columbia Univ., 1981–83; Staff, Univ. of Iowa, 1983–. *Publications:* Hybrids of Plants and of Ghosts, 1980; Erosion, 1983; The End of Beauty, 1987; The Best American Poetry (ed. with David Lehman), 1990; Region of Unlikeness, 1991; Materialism, 1993; The Dream of the Unified Field, 1995; Errancy, 1997; Swarm, 1999; Never, 2002. *Honours:* American Acad. of Poets Award, 1977; Young Poets Prize, Poetry Northwest, 1980; Pushcart Prizes, 1980, 1982; Ingram Merrill Foundation Grant, 1981; Great Lakes Colleges Asscn Award, 1981; American Poetry Review Prize, 1982; Bunting Fellow, Radcliffe Institute, 1982; Guggenheim Fellowship, 1983–84; John D. and Catherine T. MacArthur Foundation Fellowship, 1990; Pulitzer Prize in Poetry, 1996. *Address:* c/o Dept of Creative Writing, University of Iowa, Iowa City, IA 52242, USA.

GRAHAM, Robert (Bob) Donald; writer and illustrator; b. 20 Oct. 1942, Sydney, Australia; m. Carolyn Smith 1968; one s. one d. *Education:* Julian Ashton School of Fine Art, Sydney. *Career:* mem. Australian Soc. of Authors, British Soc. of Authors. *Publications:* Pete and Roland 1981, Here Comes John 1983, Here Comes Theo 1983, Pearl's Place 1983, Libby, Oscar and Me 1984, Bath Time for John 1985, First There Was Frances 1985, Where is Sarah? 1985, The Wild 1986, The Adventures of Charlotte and Henry 1987, Crusher is Coming! 1987, The Red Woollen Blanket 1987, Has Anyone Here Seen William? 1988, Bringing Home the New Baby 1989, Grandad's Magic 1989, Greetings from Sandy Beach 1990, Rose Meets Mr Wintergarten 1992, Brand New Baby 1992, Spirit of Hope 1993, Zoltan the Magnificent 1994, Queenie the Bantam 1997, Buffy 1999, Max (Smarties Prize Gold Medal for Picture Book) 2000, Charlotte and Henry 2000, Let's Get a Pup (Early Childhood CBC Picture Book of the Year 2002, Boston Globe Horn picture book award 2002) 2001, Jethro Byrde 2002, Tales From the Waterhole 2004. *Honours:* Australian Picture Book of the Year 1988, 1991, 1993, Highly Commended, Kate Greenaway Medals 1997, 2002. *Address:* 34 Melville Street, Hawthorn, Vic. 3122, Australia.

GRAHAM, Sonia (see Sinclair, Sonia Elizabeth).

GRAINVILLE, Patrick; Author; b. 1 June 1947, Villers-sur-mer, France; m. Françoise Lutgen, 1971. *Education:* Lycée Deauville; Sorbonne, Paris. *Publications:* La toison, 1972; La lisière, 1973; L'abîme, 1974; Les flamboyants, 1976; La Diane rousse, 1978; Le dernier viking, 1980; Les forteresses noires, 1982; La caverne céleste, 1984; Le paradis des orages, 1986; L'Atelier du peintre, 1988; L'Orgie, La Neige, 1990; Colère, 1992; Mathieu (co-author), 1993; Les anges et les faucons, 1994; Le lien, 1996; Le tyran éternal, 1998; Le tour de la fin du monde, une femme me chache, 2000. *Honours:* Officier, Ordre nat. du Mérite; Officier, Ordre des Arts et des Lettres; Prix Goncourt, 1976. *Address:* c/o Editions de Seuil, 27 rue Jacob, 75261 Paris cédex 06, France.

GRAN, Peter; academic and writer; b. 14 Dec. 1941, Jersey City, NJ, USA; m. Judith Abbott 1966. *Education:* BA, Yale University, 1964; MA, 1965, PhD, 1974, University of Chicago. *Career:* Core Faculty, Friends World College, 1974–75; Visiting Asst Prof. of History, University of California, Los Angeles, 1975–77, University of Texas, Austin, 1977–79; Asst, Assoc., Full Prof. of History, Temple University, 1979–. *Publications:* Islamic Roots of Capitalism: Egypt, 1760–1840, 1979, revised edn as Al-Judhur al-

Islamiyah li-l-ra'smaliya: Misr 1760–1840, 1992; Beyond Eurocentrism: A New View of Modern World History, 1996. Contributions: books and journals. *Honours:* National Endowment for the Humanities Award, American Research Center in Egypt, 1992; Senior Fulbright Fellow, Cairo, 1994. *Address:* Department of History, Temple University, 951 Gladfelter Hall, Philadelphia, PA 19122, USA. *E-mail:* pgran@astrs.temple.edu.

GRANADOS, Paul (see Kent, Arthur (William Charles)).

GRANDOWER, Elissa (see Waugh, Hillary Baldwin).

GRANGÉ, Jean-Christophe; French writer; b. 1961, Paris. *Career:* fmr independent journalist, established own news agency. *Publications:* Le Vol des cigognes (The Flight of the Storks) 1994, Les Rivières pourpres (Blood-Red Rivers) 1997, Le Concile de pierre (The Stone Council) 2000, L'Empire des loups (The Empire of the Wolves) 2003. *Address:* c/o Éditions Albin Michel, 22 rue Huyghens, 75014 Paris, France. *Website:* www.jc-grange .com.

GRANGE, Peter (see Nicole, Christopher (Robin)).

GRANN, Phyllis, BA; American publisher and editor; b. 2 Sept. 1937, London, England; m. Victor Grann 1962; two s. one d. *Education:* Barnard Coll. *Career:* Sec., Doubleday Publrs., New York 1958–60; Ed., William Morrow Inc., New York 1960–62, David McKay Co., New York 1962–70, Simon & Schuster Inc., New York 1970; Vice-Pres. Simon & Schuster Inc. 1976; Pres., Publr G. P. Putnam's & Sons, New York 1976–86; Pres. Putnam Publishing Group Inc. (now Penguin Putnam Inc.), New York 1986–96, CEO 1987–96, Chair. 1997–2001; Vice-Chair. Random House, Inc 2001–02. *Address:* c/o Random House Inc, 201 E 50th Street, New York, NY 10014, USA.

GRANT, Anne Underwood; Writer; b. 24 Feb. 1946, Savannah, GA, USA; m. Maxwell Berry Grant Jr, one s. one d. *Education:* AB, 1970, Graduate Studies, 1971, University of North Carolina at Chapel Hill; Warren Wilson College, 1994. *Career:* Community Assoc., North Carolina Arts Council, Raleigh, early 1970s; Communications Dir, Good Will Publishers, Gastonia, NC, early 1980s; Pres., Underwood Grant Advertising, Charlotte, NC, 1980s–mid-1990s; Pres., Tarra-diddle Players, 1990s; mem. MWA, Board of Dirs, 1977–, Pres., Southeast Chapter, 1997–; Southern Mystery Gathering, Chair. *Publications:* Multiple Listing, 1998; Smoke Screen, 1998; Cuttings, 1999. *Address:* 120 George Chastain Dr., Horse Shoe, NC 28742, USA. *E-mail:* annieug@sprynet.com.

GRANT, Charles; Writer; b. 12 Sept. 1942, Newark, NJ, USA. *Education:* BA, Trinity College, Hartford, CT, 1964. *Publications:* The Shadow of Alpha, 1976; The Curse, 1976; The Hour of the Oxrum Dead, 1977; Writing and Selling Science Fiction (ed.), 1977; The Ravens of the Moon, 1978; The Sound of Midnight, 1978; Shadows (ed.), 9 vols, 1978–86; Nightmares (ed.), 1979; The Last Call of Mourning, 1979; Legion, 1979; Tales from the Nightside, 1981; Glow of Candles and Other Stories, 1981; Nightmare Seasons, 1982; Night Songs, 1984; The Tea Party, 1985; The Pet, 1986; The Orchards, 1987; Something Stirs, 1992. *Address:* c/o Tor Books, 175 Fifth Ave, New York, NY 10010, USA.

GRANT, John, (Jonathan Gash, Graham Gaunt); Physician and Writer; b. 30 Sept. 1933, Bolton, Lancashire, England; m. Pamela Richard, 19 Feb. 1955, three d. *Education:* BM, 1958, BS, 1958, University of London. *Career:* GP, London, 1958–59; Pathologist, London and Essex, 1959–62; Clinical Pathologist, Hannover and Berlin, 1962–65; Lecturer in Clinical Pathology and Head of the Pathology Division, University of Hong Kong, 1965–68; Microbiologist, Hong Kong and London, 1968–71; Head, Bacteriology Unit, School of Hygiene and Tropical Medicine, University of London, 1971–88; mem. International College of Surgeons, fellow; Royal Society of Tropical Medicine, fellow; MRCS, 1958; LRCP, 1958. *Publications:* As Jonathan Gash: The Judas Pair, 1977; Gold by Gemini, 1978; The Grail Tree, 1979; Spend Game, 1981; The Vatican Rip, 1981; The Sleepers of Erin, 1983; Firefly Gadroom, 1984; The Gondola Scam, 1984; Pearlhanger, 1985; The Tartan Ringers, 1986; Moonspender, 1987; Jade Woman, 1989; The Very Last Gambado, 1990; The Great California Game, 1991; The Lies of Fair Ladies, 1992; Paid and Loving Eyes, 1993; The Sin Within Her Smile, 1994; The Grace of Older Women, 1995; The Possessions of a Lady, 1996; The Rich and the Profane, 1998; A Rag, a Bone, and a Hank of Hair, 2000; Bone Dancing, 2002. As Graham Gaunt: The Incomer, 1982. *Honours:* CWA Award, 1977. *Address:* Silver Willows, Chapel Lane, West Bergholt, Colchester, Essex C06 3EF, England.

GRANT, John (see Barnett, Paul (Le Page)).

GRANT, Linda; Journalist and Author; b. 15 Feb. 1951, Liverpool, England. *Education:* English, Univ. of York; MA, English, MacMaster Univ., Hamilton, ON, Canada; postgraduate studies, Simon Fraser Univ., Vancouver, Canada. *Career:* Journalist, 1985–; fmr columnist, Jewish Chronicle; Feature writer, Guardian, 1995–2000; Chair. of judges, Jewish Quarterly Prize, 1998; gave George Orwell Memorial Lecture, Sheffield Univ., 2000; mem., Advisory panel of the MA in Creative Writing, Middlesex Univ.; mem., Man. Cttee, Society of Authors. *Publications:* Fiction: The Cast Iron Shore, 1996; When I Lived in Modern Times, 2000; Still Here, 2002. Non-fiction: Sexing the Millennium: A Political History of the Sexual Revolution, 1993; Remind Me Who I Am Again (non-fiction), 1998. Contributions: The Guardian, essays in collections. *Honours:* David Higham First Novel Award, 1996; MIND/Allen Lane Book of the Year, 1998; Age Concern Book of the Year, 1998; Orange Prize for Fiction, 2000. *Literary Agent:* Derek Johns, AP Watt Ltd, 20 John St, London WC1N 2DR, England. *Address:* Virago Press, Brettenham House, Lancaster Pl., London WC2E 7EN, England. *Website:* www.lindagrant.co.uk.

GRANT, Maxwell (see Lynds, Dennis).

GRANT, Michael; Educator (retd) and Writer; b. 21 Nov. 1914, London, England; m. Anne Sophie Beskow, 2 Aug. 1944, two s. *Education:* BA, 1936, MA, 1940, Trinity College, Cambridge. *Career:* Fellow, Trinity College, Cambridge, 1938–49; Prof. of Latin Literature, University of Edinburgh, 1948–59; Vice-Chancellor, University of Khartoum, 1956–58; Pres. and Vice-Chancellor, Queen's University, Belfast, 1959–66; mem. British Institute of Archaeology at Ankara, vice-pres., 1961–; Classical Asscn, pres., 1977–78; Roman Society, vice-pres., 1961–; Royal Numismatic Society, pres., 1953–56; Virgil Society, pres., 1963–66. *Publications:* Ancient History, 1952; Roman Imperial Money, 1954; Roman Literature, 1954; Greeks (with Don Pottinger), 1958; Romans (with Don Pottinger), 1960; The World of Rome, 1960; Myths of the Greeks and Romans, 1962; The Birth of Western Civilization: Greece and Rome, 1964; The Civilizations of Europe, 1966; Cambridge, 1966; Gladiators, 1967; The Climax of Rome: The Final Achievements of the Ancient World, AD 161–337, 1968; The Ancient Mediterranean, 1969; Julius Caesar, 1969; The Ancient Historians, 1970; The Rome Forum, 1970; Nero: Emperor in Revolt, 1970; Cities of Vesuvius: Pompeii and Herculaneum, 1971; Herod the Great, 1971; Roman Myths, 1971; Cleopatra, 1972; The Jews in the Roman World, 1973; Gods and Mortals in Classical Mythology (with John Hazel), 1973; Caesar, 1974; The Army of the Caesars, 1974; The Twelve Caesars, 1975; Eros in Pompeii: The Secret Rooms of the National Museum of Naples, 1975; The Fall of the Roman Empire: A Reappraisal, 1976; Saint Paul, 1976; Jesus: An Historian's Review of the Gospels, 1977; The History of Rome, 1978; The Art and Life of Pompeii and Herculaneum, 1979; The Etruscans, 1980; Greek and Latin Authors, 800 BC-AD 1000, 1980; From Alexander to Cleopatra: The Hellenistic World, 1980; History of Ancient Israel, 1984; The Roman Emperors: A Biographical Guide to the Rulers of Ancient Rome, 31 BC-AD 476, 1985; Guide to the Classical World: A Dictionary of Place-Names, 1986; The Rise and Fall of the Greeks, 1988; The Classical Greeks, 1988; A Social History of Greece and Rome, 1992; Saint Peter, 1994; My First Eighty Years, 1994; The Antonines, 1994; Art in the Roman Empire, 1995; Greek and Roman Historians: Information and Misinformation, 1995; The Severans, 1996; From Rome to Byzantium, 1998; The Collapse and Recovery of the Roman Empire, 1999. Other: Ed. and trans. of various Roman writers. *Honours:* OBE, 1946; CBE, 1958; Leverhulme Research Fellow, 1958; Premio Latina, 1981. *Address:* Le Pitturacce, 351 Via Della Chiesa, Gattaiola, 55050 Lucca, Italy.

GRANT, Neil, (D. M. Field, David Mountfield, Gail Trenton); Writer; b. 9 June 1938, England; m. Vera Steiner, 23 Sept. 1977, two d. *Education:* MA, St John's College, Cambridge, 1961. *Career:* mem. RGS. *Publications:* A History of Polar Exploration, 1974; Neil Grant's Book of Spies and Spying, 1975; A History of African Exploration, 1976; Children's History of Britain, 1977; Greek and Roman Erotica, 1982; The White Bear, 1983; American Folktales and Legends, 1988; London's Villages, 1990; Scottish Clans and Tartans, 2000; Oxford Children's History of the World, 2000. *Address:* 2 Ave Rd, Teddington, Middlesex TW11 0BT, England.

GRANT, Nicholas (see Nicole, Christopher (Robin)).

GRANT, Roderick; Author; b. 16 Jan. 1941, Forres, Morayshire, Scotland. *Publications:* Adventure in My Veins, 1968; Seek Out the Guilty, 1969; Where No Angels Dwell, 1969; Gorbals Doctor, 1970; The Dark Horizon (with Alexander Highlands), 1971; The Lone Voyage of Betty Mouat, 1973; The Stalking of Adrian Lawford, 1974; The Clutch of Caution, 1975; The 51st Highland Division at War, 1976; Strathalder: A Highland Estate, 1978; A Savage Freedom, 1978; The Great Canal, 1978; A Private Vendetta, 1978; But Not in Anger (with C. Cole), 1979; Clap Hands for the Singing Molecatcher, 1989. *Address:* 3 Back Lane Cottages, Bucks Horn Oak, Farmham, Surrey, England.

GRASS, Günter Wilhelm; German writer, poet and artist; b. 16 Oct. 1927, Danzig, (now Gdańsk, Poland); m. 1st Anna Schwarz 1954 (divorced 1978); three s. one d.; m. 2nd Ute Grunert 1979. *Education:* Conradinum, Danzig, Kunstakademie, Düsseldorf, Höchschule für Bildende Künste, Berlin. *Career:* mem. Akad. der Künste, Berlin (pres. 1983–86), American Acad. of Arts and Sciences; mem. Social Democratic Party (resgnd Dec. 1992). *Plays:* Beritten, hin und zurück 1954, Hochwasser 1954, Die bösen Köche 1957, Noch Zehn Minuten bis Buffalo 1957, Onkel, Onkel 1958, Die Plebejer proben den Aufstand 1965, Davor 1968. *Publications:* Die Vorzüge der Windhühner (poems, prose and drawings) 1955, Die Blechtrommel (novel, trans. as The Tin Drum) 1959, Gleisdreieck (poems and drawings) 1960, Katz und Maus (novella, trans. as Cat and Mouse) 1961, Hundejahre (novel, trans. as Dog Years) 1963, Ausgefragt (poems and drawings) 1967, Über das Selbstverständliche 1968, Örtlich betäubt (novel) 1969, Aus dem Tagebuch einer Schnecke 1972, Dokumente zur politischen Wirkung 1972, Die Bürger und seine Stimme 1974, Der Butt (novel, trans. as The Flounder) 1976, Denkzettel 1978, Das Treffen in Telgte (novel, trans. as The Meeting in Telgte) 1979, Kopfgeburten oder Die Deutschen sterben aus (novel, trans. as Headbirths, or the Germans are Dying Out) 1980, Aufsätze zur Literatur

1980, Zeichnen und Schreiben Band I 1982, Widerstand lernen-Politische Gegenreden 1980–83 1984 Band II 1984, On Writing and Politics 1967–83 1985, Die Rättin (novel) 1986, Züngezeigen 1987, Werkansgabe (10 vols) 1987, Die Gedichte 1955–1986 1988, Deutscher Lastenausgleich: Wider das dumpfe Einheitsgebot 1990, Two States—One Nation? 1990, Vier Jahrzehnte: Ein Werkstattbericht (drawings and notes) 1991, Unkenrufe (novel, trans. as The Call of the Toad) 1992, Rede vom Verlust: Über den Niedergang der politischen Kultur im geiinten Deutschland 1992, Der Ruf der Kröte (novel) 1992, Studienausgabe (12 vols) 1994, Ein weites Feld (trans. as Too Far Afield) 1995, Fundsachen für Nichtleser (poems) 1997, Auf ein anderes Blatt 1999, Vom Abenteuer der Aufklärung (jtly) 1999, Mein Jahrhundert (trans. as My Century) 1999, Nie wieder schweigen 2000, Fünf Jahrzehnte 2001, Im Krebsgang (novel, trans. as Crabwalk) 2002. *Honours:* Dr hc (Kenyon Coll.) 1965, (Harvard) 1976; Lyric Prize, Süddeutscher Rundfunk 1955, Group 47 Prize 1959, Literary Prize, Asscn of German Critics 1960, Georg-Büchner Prize 1965, Theodor-Heuss Prize 1969, Int. Feltrinelli Prize 1982, Karel Čapek Prize 1994, Sonning Arts Prize (Denmark) 1996, Thomas Mann Prize 1996, Hermann Kestan Medal 1995, Nobel Prize for Literature 1999, Premio Príncipe de Asturias 1999. *Address:* Glockengiesserstrasse 21, 23552 Lübeck, Germany.

GRAU, Shirley Ann; Writer; b. 8 July 1929, New Orleans, LA, USA; m. James Feibleman, 4 Aug. 1955, two s. two d. *Education:* BA, Tulane University. *Publications:* The Black Prince, 1955; The Hard Blue Sky, 1958; The House on Coliseum Street, 1961; The Keepers of the House, 1964; The Condor Passes, 1971; The Wind Shifting West, 1973; Evidence of Love, 1977; Nine Women, 1985; Roadwalkers, 1994. Contributions: New Yorker; Saturday Evening Post; Others. *Honours:* Pulitzer Prize for Fiction, 1965. *Address:* c/o JCA, 27 W 20th St, New York, NY, 10011, USA. *E-mail:* s .grau@worldnet.att.net.

GRAVER, Elizabeth; Writer and Teacher; b. 2 July 1964, Los Angeles, CA, USA. *Education:* BA, Wesleyan University, 1986; MFA, Washington University, 1990. *Career:* Visiting Prof. of English and Creative Writing, 1993–95, Asst Prof. of Creative Writing and English, 1995–99, Assoc. Prof., 1999–, Boston College. *Publications:* Unravelling, 1997; The Honey Thief, 1999. Contributions: Best American Short Stories; Story; Southern Review; Antaeus; Southwest Review; O. Henry Prize Stories, 1994, 1996; Ploughshares; Best American Essays, 1998. *Honours:* Fulbright Fellowship; Drue Heinz Literature Prize; National Endowment for the Arts Fellowship; Writers Exchange Winner; Guggenheim Fellowship, 1997. *Address:* c/o Richard Parks Agency, 138 E 16th St, No. 5B, New York, NY 10003, USA.

GRAVER, Lawrence Stanley; Prof. of English; b. 6 Dec. 1931, New York, NY, USA; m. Suzanne Levy Graver, 28 Jan. 1960, two d. *Education:* BA, City College, CUNY, 1954; PhD, University of California, Berkeley, 1961. *Career:* Asst Prof., University of California, Los Angeles, 1961–64; Assoc. Prof., 1964–71, Prof., 1971–, Williams College; mem. MLA. *Publications:* Conrad's Short Fiction, 1968; Carson McCullers, 1969; Mastering the Film, 1974; Beckett: The Critical Heritage, 1979; Beckett: Waiting for Godot, 1989; An Obsession with Anne Frank: Meyer Levin and The Diary, 1995. Contributions: New York Times Book Review: Saturday Review: New Republic: New Leader; 19th Century Fiction. *Address:* Dept of English, Williams College, Williamstown, MA 01267, USA.

GRAVES, Keller (see Rogers, Evelyn).

GRAVES, Richard Perceval; Author; b. 21 Dec. 1945, Brighton, England; two s. one d. *Education:* St John's College Oxford, 1964–67; MA, Modern History. *Career:* Arnold Lodge School, 1968; Harrow School, 1969; Holme Grange School, 1969–71; Ellesmere College, 1971–73; mem. Housman Society; Powys Society; Society of Authors. *Publications:* Lawrence of Arabia and His World, 1976; A. E. Houseman: The Scholar-Poet, 1979; The Brothers Powys, 1983; Robert Graves: The Assault Heroic, 1986; Robert Graves: The Years with Laura Riding, 1990; Richard Hughes, 1994; Robert Graves and The White Goddess, 1995. *Honours:* Hawthornden Fellowship, 1999. *Literary Agent:* Rachel Calder of Tessa Sayle, 11 Jubilee Pl., London SW3 3TE, England. *Address:* 26 Hill's Lane, Shrewsbury SY1 1QU, England.

GRAVES, Roy Neil; Prof. of English, Poet and Writer; b. 2 Feb. 1939, Medina, Tennessee, USA; m. Sue Lain Hunt, 5 June 1965, divorced July 1982, one s. two d. *Education:* BA, English, Princeton University, 1961; MA, English, Duke University, 1964; DA, English, University of Mississippi, 1977. *Career:* Asst Prof. of English, Lynchburg Branch, University of Virginia, 1965–67; Asst Prof., 1967–68, Assoc. Prof. of English, 1968–69, Central Virginia Community College, Lynchburg; Asst Prof., 1969–77, Assoc. Prof., 1977–82, Prof. of English, 1982–, University of Tennessee at Martin. *Publications:* River Region Monographs: Reports on People and Popular Culture (ed.), 1975; 'Medina' and Other Poems, 1976; Hugh John Massey of the Royal Hall: The Lost Master Poet of Fourteenth-Century England and the Lost Runes, 1977; Out of Tennessee: Poems, with an Introduction, 1977; The Runic 'Beowulf' and Other Lost Anglo-Saxon Poems, Reconstructed and Annotated, 1979; Shakespeare's Lost Sonnets: The 154 Runic Poems Reconstructed and Introduced, 1979; Somewhere on the Interstate (poems), 1987; Shakespeare's Sonnets Upside Down, 1995; Always at Home Here: Poems and Insights from Six Tennessee Poets (edited by Ernest Lee), 1997, web publ. of Shakespeare's Lost Sonnets 2003. Contributions: articles in reference works and scholarly journals; Poems in anthologies and periodicals. *Honours:* National Endowment for the Humanities Grant, 1975; Cunningham Teacher/Scholar Award, University of Tennessee at Martin, 1997; First Place, Southern Poets over 50 Competition, Kennesaw State University, 2002. *Address:* c/o Dept of English, University of Tennessee at Martin, Martin, TN 38238, USA. *E-mail:* ngraves@utm.edu. *Website:* www.utm.edu/~ngraves; www.utm.edu/~ngraves/shakespeare.

GRAY, Alasdair James; British writer and painter; b. 28 Dec. 1934, Glasgow; m. 1st Inge Sørensen (divorced); one s.; m. 2nd Morag McAlpine 1991. *Education:* Glasgow School of Art. *Career:* art teacher, Glasgow and Lanarkshire 1958–62; scene painter, Pavilion and Citizens' theatres 1962–63; freelance writer and painter 1963–76; artist recorder, People's Palace Local History Museum, Glasgow 1976–77; Writer-in-Residence, Glasgow Univ. 1977–79; freelance writer and painter 1979–2001; Prof. of Creative Writing, Univ. of Glasgow 2001–2003; painter of mural decorations in Oran Mhor Leisure Centre, Glasgow, 2003–; works in collections of People's Palace Local History Museum, Glasgow, Collin's Gallery, Strathclyde Univ.; mural paintings in Palace Rigg Nature Reserve Exhibition Centre, New Cumbernauld, Abbot's House Local History Museum, Dunfermline, The Ubiquitous Chip Restaurant, Glasgow; mem. Soc. of Authors. *Exhibitions include:* Retrospective, Collins Gallery Glasgow 1974; Retrospective, Glasgow, Edinburgh and Aberdeen Art Galleries 1987–88. *Plays include:* Quiet People 1968, The Trial of Thomas Muir 1970, Dialogue 1971, Homeward Bound 1973, The Loss of the Golden Silence 1973, McGrothy and Ludmilla 1993, Working Legs 1998. *Television plays include:* The Fall of Kelvin Walker 1967, The Man Who Knew about Electricity 1973, The Story of a Recluse 1987. *Works include:* has designed and illustrated several books including Shoestring Gourmet 1986, Songs of Scotland 1997. *Publications include:* The Comedy of the White Dog (short story) 1979, Lanark: A Life in Four Books (novel) 1981, Unlikely Stories Mostly 1982, Janine (novel) 1984, The Fall of Kelvin Walker (novel) 1985, Lean Tales (co-writer) 1985, Five Scottish Artists (catalogue) 1986, Saltire Self-Portrait 4 (autobiographical sketch) 1988, Old Negatives (four verse sequences) 1989, Something Leather (novel) 1990, McGrotty and Ludmilla (novel) 1990, Poor Things (novel) 1992, Why Scots Should Rule Scotland (polemic) 1992, Ten Tales Tall and True (Short Stories) 1993, A History Maker (novel) 1994, Mavis Belfrage (novel) 1996, Working Legs (play) 1997, The Book of Prefaces 2000, Sixteen Occasional Poems 2000, A Study in Classic Scottish Writing 2001, The Ends of Our Tethers: 13 Sorry Stories 2003. *Honours:* Saltire Soc. Award 1981, Times Literary Supplement Award 1982, Whitbread and Guardian Awards 1992. *Literary Agent:* c/o Giles Gordon, 6 Ann Street, Edinburgh, EH4 1PJ. *Address:* 2 Marchmont Terrace, Glasgow, G12 9LT, Scotland. *Telephone:* (141) 339-0093.

GRAY, Angela (see Daniels, Dorothy).

GRAY, Caroline (see Nicole, Christopher (Robin)).

GRAY, Douglas; academic and writer; b. 17 Feb. 1930, Melbourne, Vic., Australia; m. 1959; one s. *Education:* MA, Victoria University of Wellington, New Zealand, 1952; BA, 1956, MA, 1960, Merton College, Oxford. *Career:* J. R. R. Tolkien Prof. of English, 1980–97, Prof. Emeritus, 1997–, University of Oxford; mem. Early English Text Society; Society for the Study of Medieval Languages and Literatures, pres., 1982–86. *Publications:* Themes and Images in the Medieval English Religious Lyric, 1972; Robert Henryson, 1979; The Oxford Book of Late Medieval Verse and Prose (ed.), 1985; Selected Poems of Robert Henryson and William Dunbar (ed.), 1998; The Oxford Companion to Chaucer, 2003. Contributions: scholarly journals. *Honours:* British Acad., fellow, 1989; Hon. DLitt, Victorian University of Wellington, 1995. *Address:* Lady Margaret Hall, Oxford OX2 6QA, England.

GRAY, Dulcie (Winifred Catherine); Actress, Dramatist and Writer; b. 20 Nov. 1920, England; m. Michael Denison, 29 April 1939. *Education:* England and Malaysia. *Career:* numerous stage, film, radio, and television appearances; mem. British Actors Equity; Linnean Society, fellow; FRSA; Society of Authors. *Publications:* Murder on the Stairs, 1957; Baby Face, 1959; For Richer, for Richer, 1970; Ride on a Tiger, 1975; Butterflies on My Mind, 1978; Dark Calypso, 1979; The Glanville Women, 1982; Mirror Image, 1987; Looking Forward, Looking Backward (autobiog.), 1991; J. B. Priestley (biog.), 2000. Contributions: periodicals. *Honours:* Queen's Silver Jubilee Medal, 1977; Times Educational Supplement Senior Information Book Prize, 1978; CBE, 1983. *Address:* Shardeloes, Amersham, Bucks HP7 0RL, England.

GRAY, Francine du Plessix; Author; b. 25 Sept. 1930, Warsaw, Poland; m. Cleve Gray, 23 April 1957, two s. *Education:* Bryn Mawr College, 1948–50; Black Mountain College, 1951, 1952; BA, Barnard College, 1952. *Career:* Reporter, United Press International, New York City, 1952–54; Asst Ed., Realites Magazine, Paris, 1954–55; Book Ed., Art in America, New York City, 1962–64; Visiting Prof., CUNY, 1975, Yale University, 1981, Columbia University, 1983; Ferris Prof., Princeton University, 1986; Annenberg Fellow, Brown University, 1997; Gladys Krieble Delmas Chair, Vassar College, 2001; mem. American Acad. of Arts and Letters. *Publications:* Divine Disobedience: Profiles in Catholic Radicalism, 1970; Hawaii: The Sugar-Coated Fortress, 1972; Lovers and Tyrants, 1976; World Without End, 1981; October Blood, 1985; Adam and Eve and the City, 1987; Soviet Women: Walking the Tightrope, 1991; Rage and Fire: A Life of Louise

Colet, 1994; At Home with the Marquis de Sade: A Life, 1998; Simone Weil, 2001. *Address:* c/o Georges Borchardt Inc, 136 E 57th St, New York, NY 10022, USA.

GRAY, John; British philosopher, academic and writer. *Career:* staff, Inst. of Economic Affairs (UK), Cato Inst., Inst. for Humane Studies, The Liberty Fund, Social Philosophy and Policy Center (all USA); Prof. of Politics, Univ. of Oxford; currently Prof. of European Thought, LSE. *Publications include:* non-fiction: Hayek on LIberty 1984, Liberalism 1986, Voltaire 1998, False Dawn: The Delusions of Global Capitalism 1998, Two Faces of Liberalism 2000, Straw Dogs: Thoughts on Humans and Other Animals 2003, Al Qaeda and What it Means to be Modern 2003, Heresies 2004; editor: On Liberty and other essays by John Stuart Mill 1998; contrib. to The Guardian, TLS, Granta (Granta 77: What We Think of America), Journal of Ethics, Demos. *Honours:* Fellow, Jesus Coll., Oxford. *Address:* c/o London School of Economics and Political Science, Houghton Street, London, WC2A 2AE, England. *Telephone:* (20) 7955-7905. *E-mail:* j.gray@lse.ac.uk. *Website:* www.lse.ac.uk.

GRAY, (John) Richard; academic and writer; b. 7 July 1929, Weymouth, England; m. Gabriella Gray 1957; one s. one d. *Education:* Downing College, Cambridge; BA, Cantab, 1951; PhD, University of London, 1957. *Career:* Lecturer, University of Khartoum, 1959–61; Resident Fellow, 1961–63, Reader, 1963–72, School of Oriental and African Studies, London; Visiting Prof., University of California at Los Angeles, 1967; Ed., Journal of African History, 1968–71; Prof. of African History, 1972–89; Prof. Emeritus, 1989–, University of London; mem. Pontifical Committee of the Historical Sciences, 1982–. *Publications:* The Two Nations: Aspects of the Development of Race Relations in the Rhodesias and Nyasaland, 1960; A History of the Southern Sudan, 1839–1889, 1961; Materials for West African History in Italian Archives (with D. Chambers), 1965; Pre-Colonial African Trade (ed. with D. Birmingham), 1970; The Cambridge History of Africa, Vol. 4 (ed.), 1975; Christianity in Independent Africa (ed. with others), 1978; Black Christians and White Missionaries, 1990; Religion and Conflict in Sudan (ed. with Yusuf Fadl Hasan), 2002. Contributions: Professional journals. *Honours:* Order of St Silvester, 1966. *Address:* 39 Rotherwick Road, London NW11 7DD, England.

GRAY, Simon James Holliday, (Hamish Reade), MA; British writer, playwright and teacher; b. 21 Oct. 1936, Hayling Island; m. 1st Beryl Mary Kevern 1965 (divorced); one s. one d.; m. 2nd Victoria Katherine Rothschild 1997. *Education:* Westminster School, Dalhousie Univ., Halifax, NS, Canada and Trinity Coll., Cambridge. *Career:* Supervisor in English, Univ. of BC, Canada 1960–63, Sr Instructor 1963–64; Lecturer in English, Queen Mary Coll., Univ. of London 1965–84; Co-Dir The Common Pursuit, Promenade Theatre, New York 1986; Dir Phoenix Theatre 1988. *Radio plays:* The Rector's Daughter (adaptation) 1992, Suffer the Little Children 1993, With a Nod and a Bow 1993, Cell Mates 1995. *Television:* After Pilkington 1987, Old Flames 1990, They Never Slept 1991, Running Late 1992, Unnatural Pursuits 1992 (Emmy Award, New York 1993), Femme Fatale 1993. *Film:* A Month in the Country 1997. *Publications:* novels: Colmain 1963, Simple People 1965, Little Portia 1967, A Comeback for Stark 1968, Breaking Hearts 1997; non-fiction: An Unnatural Pursuit and Other Pieces 1985, How's That for Telling 'Em, Fat Lady (memoirs) 1988, Fat Chance 1995, Enter a Fox (memoirs) 2001, The Smoking Diaries (memoirs) 2004; plays: Wise Child 1968, Sleeping Dog 1968, Dutch Uncle 1969, The Idiot 1971, Spoiled 1971, Butley 1971 (Evening Standard Award), Otherwise Engaged 1975 (Best Play, New York Drama Critics' Circle, Evening Standard Award), Plaintiffs and Defendants 1975, Two Sundays 1975, Dog Days 1976, Molly 1977, The Rear Column 1978, Close of Play 1979, Quartermaine's Terms 1981, Tartuffe 1982, Chapter 17 1982, Common Pursuit 1984, Melon 1987, The Holy Terror and Tartuffe 1990, Hidden Laughter 1990, Cell Mates 1994, Simply Disconnected 1996, Life Support 1997, Just the Three of Us 1997, The Late Middle Classes 1999, Japes 2001. *Honours:* Hon. Fellow, Queen Mary Coll., Univ. of London; several drama awards in UK and USA. *Literary Agent:* Judy Daish Associates, 2 St Charles Place, London, W10 6EG, England. *Telephone:* (20) 8964-8811. *Fax:* (20) 8964-8966.

GRAY, Tony (George Hugh); Writer; b. 23 Aug. 1922, Dublin, Ireland; m. Patricia Mary Walters, 1 Oct. 1946, one s. one d. *Education:* St Andrews College, Dublin, 1935–39. *Career:* Features Ed., Daily Mirror, London, 1959–62. *Publications:* Starting from Tomorrow, 1965; The Real Professionals, 1966; Gone the Time, 1967; The Irish Answer, 1967; The Record Breakers (with L. Villa), 1970; The Last Laugh, 1972; The Orange Order, 1972; Psalms and Slaughter, 1972; The White Lions of Timbavati (with C. McBride), 1977; Some of My Best Friends Are Animals (with T. Murphy), 1979; Operation White Lion (with C. McBride), 1981; Ireland This Century, 1985; The Road to Success: Alfred McAlpine, 1935–85, 1987; Fleet Street Remembered, 1990; Mr Smyllie, Sir, 1991; Ireland This Century, 1994; Saint Patrick's People, 1996; A Peculiar Man: A Life of George Moore. *Address:* 5 Crossways, Crookham Village, Hants GU51 5TA, England. *E-mail:* ghtonygray@onetel.net.uk.

GRAYLING, Anthony C., MA, DPhil; British philosopher and writer; m. Katie Hickman; two c. *Education:* Univ. of Oxford. *Career:* Coll. Lecturer 1985–91, Sr Research Fellow 1991–97, St Anne's Coll., Oxford; Lecturer, Inst. of Philosophy at the Chinese Acad. of Social Sciences 1984; Dir, Sino-British Summer School in Philosophy, Beijing 1988, 1993; Contributing Ed., Philosophical Annual of the Chinese Acad. of Social Sciences; Visiting Prof., Univ. of Tokyo 1997; Lecturer, Univs of Chiba, Nagoya and Hokkaido, Lublin Univ., Poland 1993; Reader in Philosophy, Birkbeck Coll., London; Jan Hus Visiting Fellow, Inst. of Philosophy at the Czech Acad. of Sciences 1994, 1996; Supernumerary Fellow, St Anne's Coll., Oxford 1997; mem. Aristotelian Soc. (hon. sec. 1993–2001). *Publications:* An Introduction to Philosophical Logic 1982, The Refutation of Scepticism 1985, Berkeley: The Central Arguments 1986, Wittgenstein 1988, William Hazlitt 1989, China: A Literary Companion (with Susan Whitfield) 1994, Philosophy: A Guide Through the Subject (ed.) 1995, Russell 1996, Moral Values 1998, The Quarrel of the Age: The Life and Times of William Hazlitt 2001, Wittgenstein: A Very Short Introduction 2001, Russell: A Very Short Introduction 2002, The Mystery of Things: Applying Philosophy to Life 2002, Meditations for the Humanist: Ethics for a Secular Age 2002, Life, Sex and Ideas: The Good Life Without God 2003, What is Good?: The Search for the Best Way to Live 2003, Cassell's Dictionary of Ideas 2005. *Literary Agent:* Felicity Bryan, 2a North Parade, Banbury Road, Oxford, OX2 6LX, England. *Address:* c/o School of Philosophy, Birkbeck College, Malet Street, London, WC1E 7HX, England. *Telephone:* (20) 7631-6383. *Fax:* (20) 7631-6564. *E-mail:* mail@acgrayling.com. *Website:* www.bbk.ac.uk/phil.

GREALY, Lucy; Writer and Poet; b. 1963, Dublin, Ireland. *Education:* BA, Sarah Lawrence College, Bronxville, NY; MFA, University of Iowa. *Publications:* Autobiography of a Face, 1994, UK edn as In the Mind's Eye, 1994; As Seen on TV: Provocations, 2000. Contributions: periodicals. *Honours:* Fine Arts Work Centre Fellow, Provincetown, MA, 1993; National Magazine Award, 1994. *Address:* c/o Houghton Mifflin Co, 2 Park St, Boston, MA 02107, USA.

GREAVES, Richard L(ee); Distinguished Prof. of History and Writer; b. 11 Sept. 1938, Glendale, CA, USA; m. Judith Rae Dieker 4 Sept. 1959; two d. *Education:* BA, Bethel College, 1960; MA, Berkeley Baptist Divinity School, 1962; PhD, Univ. of London, 1964; Postdoctoral Studies, Univ. of Missouri, 1965. *Career:* Assoc. Prof. of History, Florida Memorial College, 1964–65; Asst Prof. of History, William Woods College, 1965–66, Eastern Washington State College, 1966–69; Assoc. Prof. of Humanities, Michigan State Univ., 1969–72; Prof. of History, 1972–89, Robert O. Lawton Distinguished Prof. of History, 1989–, Florida State Univ.; mem. American Historical Asscn; American Philosophical Society; American Society of Church History, pres., 1991; Baptist Historical Society; Historians of Early Modern Europe; International John Bunyan Society, pres., 1992–95; FRHistS. *Publications:* The Puritan Revolution and Educational Thought: Background for Reform, 1969; John Bunyan, 1969; An Annotated Bibliography of John Bunyan Studies, 1972; Elizabeth I: Queen of England (ed.), 1974; The Miscellaneous Works of John Bunyan (ed.), Vol. 2, 1976, Vol. 8, 1979, Vol. 9, 1981, Vol. 11, 1985; Theology and Revolution in the Scottish Reformation: Studies in the Thought of John Knox, 1980; Society and Religion in Elizabethan England, 1981; John Bunyan: A Reference Guide (ed. with James Forrest), 1982; Biographical Dictionary of British Radicals in the Seventeenth Century (ed. with Robert Zaller), three vols, 1982, 1983, 1984; Saints and Rebels: Seven Nonconformists in Stuart England, 1985; Triumph Over Silence: Women in Protestant History (ed.), 1985; Deliver Us From Evil: The Radical Underground in Britain, 1660–1663, 1986; Civilizations of the World: The Human Adventure (with Robert Zaller, Philip Cannistrano and Rhoads Murphey), 1990; Enemies Under His Feet: Radicals and Nonconformists in Britain, 1664–1677, 1990; Civilization in the West (with Robert Zaller and Jennifer Roberts), 1992; Secrets of the Kingdom: British Radicals from the Popish Plot to the Revolution of 1688–89, 1992; John Bunyan and English Nonconformity, 1992; God's Other Children: Protestant Nonconformists and the Emergence of Denominational Churches in Ireland, 1660–1700, 1997; Dublin's Merchant-Quaker: Anthony Sharp and the Community of Friends, 1643–1707, 1998; Glimpses of Glory: John Bunyan and English Dissent, 2002. Contributions: scholarly books and journals. *Honours:* National Endowment for the Humanities Grants, 1967, 1980; Walter D. Love Memorial Prize, Conference on British Studies, 1970; Andrew W. Mellon Fellow, 1977; ACLS Fellow, 1977, 1983, 1987; American Philosophical Society Fellow, 1993; Albert C. Outler Prize, American Society of Church History, 1996; Rockefeller Foundation Fellow, Bellagio Center, Italy, 1998; Guggenheim Fellowship, 2000. *Address:* c/o Dept of History, Florida State University, Tallahassee, FL 32306-2200, USA. *Website:* mailer.fsu.edu/~rgreaves.

GREELEY, Andrew (Moran); Prof. and Author; b. 5 Feb. 1928, Oak Park, IL, USA. *Education:* AB, 1950, STB, 1952, STL, 1954, St Mary of the Lake Seminary; MA, 1961, PhD, 1962, University of Chicago. *Career:* Ordained, Roman Catholic Priest, 1954; Asst Pastor, Church of Christ the King, Chicago, 1954–64; Senior Study Dir, 1961–68, Program Dir for Higher Education, 1968–70, Dir of Center for the Study of American Pluralism, 1971–85, Research Assoc., 1985–, Prof. of Social Science, 1991–, University of Chicago; Prof. of Sociology, University of Arizona at Tucson, 1978–; mem. American Catholic Sociological Society; American Sociological Asscn; Religious Research Asscn; Society for the Scientific Study of Religion. *Publications:* Non-Fiction includes: The Catholic Experience: An Interpretation of the History of American Catholicism, 1967; Uncertain Trumpet: The Priest in Modern America, 1968; What Do We Believe?: The Stance of Religion in America (with Martin E. Marty and Stuart E. Rosenberg), 1968;

Life for a Wanderer: A New Look at Christian Spirituality, 1969; Come Blow Your Mind with Me (essays), 1971; The Jesus Myth, 1971; What a Modern Catholic Believes about God, 1971; The Denominational Society: A Sociological Approach to Religion in America, 1972; The Sinai Myth, 1972; The Devil, You Say! Man and His Personal Devils and Angels, 1974; The Sociology of the Paranormal: A Reconnaissance, 1975; Death and Beyond, 1976; The Great Mysteries: An Essential Catechism, 1976; The Mary Myth: On the Femininity of God, 1977; The Best of Times, The Worst of Times (with J. N. Kotre), 1978; Religion: A Secular Theory, 1982; Confessions of a Parish Priest: An Autobiography, 1986; God in Popular Culture, 1989; Myths of Religion, 1989; Complaints Against God, 1989; Andrew Greeley (autobiog.), 1990; The Bible and Us: A Priest and a Rabbi Read Scripture Together (with Jacob Neusner), 1990; Faithful Attraction: Discovering Intimacy, Love and Fidelity in American Marriage, 1991; Love Affair: A Prayer Journal, 1992; The Sense of Love, 1992; I Hope You're Listening God, 1997; Furthermore (autobiog.), 1999. Fiction includes: Nora Maeve and Sebi, 1976; The Magic Cup: An Irish Legend, 1979; The Cardinal Sins, 1981; Ascent into Hell, 1984; God Game, 1986; All About Women, 1989; Fall from Grace, 1993; Star Bright: A Christmas Story, 1997; The Bishop at Sea, 1997; A Midwinter's Tale, 1998; The Bishop and the Three Kings, 1998; Irish Mist, 1999; Younger Than Springtime, 1999; The Bishop and the Missing L Train, 2000; A Christmas Wedding, 2000; Irish Love, 2001; The Bishop and the Beggar Girl of St Germain, 2001; September Song, 2001; Irish Stew, 2002. *Honours:* C. Albert Kobb Award, National Catholic Education Asscn, 1977; Mark Twain Award, Society for the Study of Midwestern Literature, 1987; several hon. doctorates. *Address:* 1155 E 60th St, Chicago, IL 60637, USA.

GREEN, Brian (see Card, Orson Scott).

GREEN, Dan, BA; American book publishing executive; b. 28 Sept. 1935, Passaic, NJ; m. Jane Oliphant 1959; two s. *Education:* Syracuse Univ., NY. *Career:* Publicity Dir Dover Press 1957–58; Station WNAC-TV 1958–59; Bobbs-Merrill Co. 1959–62; Simon & Schuster Inc. 1962–85, Assoc. Publr 1976–80, Vice-Pres., Publr 1980–84; Pres. Trade Publishing Group 1984–85; Founder, Publr, Kenan Press 1979–80; CEO Grove Press and Weidenfeld & Nicolson, New York 1985–89; Pres. Kenan Books, New York 1989–, Pom Literary Agency 1989. *Address:* Pom Inc., 611 Broadway, New York, NY 10012; Kenan Books, 611 Broadway, New York, NY 10012, USA. *Telephone:* (212) 673-3835. *Fax:* (212) 673-4653 (Office). *E-mail:* pom-inc@att.net (Office).

GREEN, Debbie Tucker; British playwright. *Career:* fmr stage man. *Plays:* Born Bad 2003, Dirty Butterfly 2003. *Address:* c/o Nick Hern Books Ltd, The Glasshouse, 49a Goldhawk Road, London, W12 8QP, England. *Telephone:* (20) 8749-4953. *Fax:* (20) 8735-0250. *Website:* www.nickhernbooks.co.uk.

GREEN, Hannah (see Greenberg, Joanne).

GREEN, Jonathon; Writer and Broadcaster; b. 20 April 1948, Kidderminster, Worcestershire, England; two s. Educatioin: BA, Brasenose College, Oxford, 1969. *Publications:* Book of Rock Quotes I, 1977; Famous Last Words, 1979; The Book of Sports Quotes (with D. Atyeo), 1979; Directory of Infamy, 1980; Don't Quote Me: The Other Famous Last Words (with D. Atyeo), 1981; The Book of Royal Quotes (with D. Atyeo), 1981; Book of Political Quotes, 1982; Book of Rock Quotes II, 1982; Contemporary Dictionary of Quotations, 1982; What a Way to Go, 1983; Newspeak: A Dictionary of Jargon, 1983, revised edn as The Dictionary of Jargon, 1987; The Dictionary of Contemporary Slang, 1984; The Cynics' Lexicon, 1984; Sweet Nothings: A Book of Love Quotes, 1985; Consuming Passions: A Book of Food Quotes, 1985; It Takes All Sports: Sporting Anecdotes (with D. Atyeo), 1986; The Slang Thesaurus, 1986; The A to Z of Nuclear Jargon, 1986; Says You: A Twentieth-Century Quotation Finder, 1988; Day in the Life: Voices from the English Underground, 1961–71, 1988; The Bloomsbury Good Word Guide, 1988; The Encyclopedia of Censorship, 1990; Them: Voices from the Immigrant Community in Contemporary Britain, 1990; The Dictionary of Political Language, 1991; Neologisms: A Dictionary of Contemporary Coinage, 1991; It: The State of Sex Today, 1992; All Dressed Up: The Sixties and the Counter-Culture, 1998; Cassell Dictionary of Slang, 1998. *Literary Agent:* Lucas Alexander Whitey, Elsinore House, 77 Fulham Palace Rd, London W6 8JA, England. *Address:* 117 Ashmore Rd, London W9 3DA, England.

GREEN, Martin (Burgess); Prof. of English and Writer; b. 21 Sept. 1927, London, England; m. Carol Elizabeth Hurd, 1967, one s. two d. *Education:* BA, 1948, MA, 1952, St John's College, Cambridge; Teachers Diploma, King's College, London, 1951; Certificat d'Études Françaises, Sorbonne, Paris, 1952; PhD, University of Michigan, 1957. *Career:* Instructor, Wellesley College, Massachussetts, USA, 1957–61; Lecturer, Birmingham University, England, 1965–68; Prof. of English, Tufts University, Medford, Massachusetts, 1968–. *Publications:* Mirror for Anglo-Saxons, 1960; Reappraisals, 1965; Science and the Shabby Curate of Poetry, 1965; Yeats's Blessings on von Hugel, 1968; Cities of Light and Sons of the Morning, 1972; The von Richthofen Sisters, 1974; Children of the Sun, 1975; The Earth Again Redeemed (novel), 1976; Transatlantic Patterns, 1977; The Challenge of the Mahatmas, 1978; Dreams of Adventure, Deeds of Empire, 1980; The Old English Elegies, 1983; Tolstoy and Gandhi, 1983; The Great American Adventure, 1984; Montains of Truth, 1986; The Triumph of Pierrot (with J. Swan), 1986. *Address:* 8 Boylston Terrace, Medford, MA 02144, USA.

GREEN, Michael Frederick; Writer; b. 2 Jan. 1927, Leicester, England. *Education:* BA, Open University. *Career:* mem. Society of Authors; Equity; National Union of Journalists. *Publications:* The Art of Coarse Rugby, 1960; The Art of Coarse Sailing, 1962; Even Coarser Rugby, 1963; Don't Print my Name Upside Down, 1963; The Art of Coarse Acting, 1964; The Art of Coarse Golf, 1967; The Art of Coarse Moving, 1969 (TV serial, 1977); The Art of Coarse Drinking, 1973; Squire Haggard's Journal, 1976 (TV serial, 1990 and 1992); Four Plays For Coarse Actors, 1978; The Coarse Acting Show Two, 1980; Tonight Josephine, 1981; The Art of Coarse Sex, 1981; Don't Swing from the Balcony Romeo, 1983; The Art of Coarse Office Life, 1985; The Third Great Coarse Acting Show, 1985; The Boy Who Shot Down an Airship, 1988; Nobody Hurt in Small Earthquake, 1990; Coarse Acting Strikes Back, 2000. *Literary Agent:* Anthony Sheil Assocs. *Address:* 31 Clive Road, Twickenham, Middlesex, TW1 4SQ, England.

GREEN, Rose Basile, FRSA, MA, PhD; American poet and writer; b. 19 Dec. 1914, New Rochelle, NY; m. Raymond S. Green 1942; one d. one s. *Education:* Coll. of New Rochelle, Columbia Univ. (NY) and Univ. of Pennsylvania. *Career:* Teacher Torrington High School, CT 1936–42; Writer, Researcher Cavalcade of America, NBC 1940–42; Assoc. Prof. of English, Registrar Univ. of Tampa, FL 1942–43; Special Lecturer in English Temple Univ., PA 1953–57; Prof. of English Cabrini Coll., PA 1957–70; Exec. Dir American Inst. of Italian Studies; Vice-Pres., Dir Nat. Italian-American Foundation; Chair. Nat. Advisory Council for Ethnic Heritage Studies; mem. American Acad. of Political and Social Sciences, Acad. of American Poets, American Studies Asscn, Ethnic Studies Asscn, American Asscn of Univ. Women; Hon. LHD (Gwynedd-Mercy Coll) 1979, (Cabrini Coll) 1982; Cavalier of the Repub. of Italy; Daughters of the American Revolution Nat. Bicentennial Award for Poetry 1976; Nat. Amita Award for Literature 1976. *Publications:* Cabrinian Philosophy of Education 1967, Lauding the American Dream 1980, The Life of Mother Frances Cabrini 1984, The Pennsylvania People 1984, Challenger Countdown 1988, Five Hundred Years of America 1492–1992 1992, The Distaff Side 1995; Poetry: To Reason Why 1971, Primo Vino 1974, 76 for Philadelphia 1975, Woman, The Second Coming 1977, Century Four 1981, Songs of Ourselves 1982; Criticism: The Latin-American Novel 1974. *Address:* 308 Manor Rd, Lafayette Hill, PA 19444-1741, USA.

GREEN, Sharon; Writer; b. 6 July 1942, New York, NY, USA; divorced, three s. *Education:* BA, New York University, 1963. *Career:* mem. SFWA. *Publications:* The Crystals of Mida, 1982; The Warrior Within, 1982; The Warrior Enchained, 1983; An Oath to Mida, 1983; Chosen of Mida, 1984; The Warrior Rearmed, 1984; Mind Guest, 1984; Gateway to Xanadu, 1985; The Will of the Gods, 1985; To Battle the Gods, 1986; The Warrior Challenged, 1986; Rebel Prince, 1986; The Far Side of Forever, 1987; The Warrior Victorious, 1987; Lady Blade, Lord Fighter, 1987; Mists of the Ages, 1988; Hellhound Magic, 1989; Dawn Song, 1990; Haunted House, 1990; Silver Princess, Golden Knight, 1993; The Hidden Realms, 1993; Werewolfmoon, 1993; Fantasy Man, 1993; Flame of Fury, 1993; Dark Mirror, Dark Dreams, 1994; Silken Dreams, 1994; Enchanting, 1994; Wind Whispers, Shadow Shouts, 1995. Contributions: anthologies and magazines. *Address:* 110 Bellevue Rd, No. 28, Nashville, TN 37221, USA.

GREEN, Simon R(ichard); Writer; b. 25 Aug. 1955, Bradford-on-Avon, Wiltshire, England. *Education:* BA, Humanities, Thames Polytechnic, 1976; MA, Modern English and American Literature, Leicester University, 1978. *Publications:* Hawk and Fisher, 1990, UK edn as No Haven for the Guilty, 1990; Winner Takes All, 1991, UK edn as Devil Takes the Hindmost, 1991; The God Killer, 1991; Blue Moon Rising, 1991; Robin Hood: Prince of Thieves, 1991; Guard Against Dishonour, 1991; Wolf in the Fold, 1991, UK edn as Vengeance from a Lonely Man, 1992; Mistworld, 1992; Ghostworld, 1993; Blood and Honour, 1993; Down among the Dead Men, 1993; Shadows Fall, 1994; Hellworld, 1995; Deathstalker, 1995; Deathstalker Rebellion, 1996; Deathstalker War, 1997; Deathstalker Honour, 1998; Deathstalker Destiny, 1999; Beyond the Blue Moon, 2000; Drinking Midnight Wine, 2001. *Literary Agent:* Joshua Bilmes, Jabberwocky Literary Agency, PO Box 4558, Sunnyside, New York, NY 11104-0558, USA. *Address:* 40 St Laurence Rd, Bradford-on-Avon, Wiltshire BA15 1JQ, England.

GREEN, Terence Michael; Writer and Poet; b. 2 Feb. 1947, Toronto, ON, Canada; m. Merle Casci, 2 Sept. 1994, two s. *Education:* BA, 1967, BEd, 1973, University of Toronto; MA, University College, Dublin, 1972. *Career:* English Teacher, East York Collegiate Institute, Toronto, 1968; Juror for Philip K. Dick Award, 1995; mem. SFWA; Writers' Union of Canada; Crime Writers of Canada. *Publications:* The Woman Who Is the Midnight Wind (short stories), 1987; Barking Dogs (novel), 1988; Children of the Rainbow (novel), 1992; Shadow of Ashland (novel), 1996; Blue Limbo (novel), 1997. Contributions: anthologies including Northern Stars; Northern Frights; Ark of Ice; Dark Visions; Conversations with Robertson Davies; Tesseracts; The Writer's Voice 2; Aurora: The New Canadian Writing; Short stories, articles, interviews, reviews and poetry to periodicals including Globe and Mail; Books in Canada; Quarry; Magazine of Fantasy and Science Fiction; Isaac Asimov's SF Magazine; Twilight Zone; Unearth; Thrust; SF Review; SF Chronicle; Poetry Toronto; Leisure Ways. *Honours:* Canada Council

Grants; Ontario Art Council Grants; Participant, Harborfront Festival of Authors. *Address:* c/o Tor/Forge, 175 Fifth Avenue, New York, NY 10010, USA.

GREEN, Timothy (Seton); Writer; b. 29 May 1936, Beccles, England; m. Maureen Snowball, Oct. 1959, one d. *Education:* BA, Christ's College, Cambridge, 1957; Graduate Diploma in Journalism, University of Western Ontario, 1958. *Career:* London Correspondent, Horizon, and American Heritage, 1959–62, Life, 1962–64; Ed., Illustrated London News, 1964–66. *Publications:* The World of God, 1968; The Smugglers, 1969; Restless Spirit, UK edn as The Adventurers, 1970; The Universal Eye, 1972; World of Gold Today, 1973; How to Buy Gold, 1975; The Smuggling Business, 1977; The World of Diamonds, 1981; The New World of Gold, 1982; The Prospect for Gold, 1987; The World of Gold, 1993; The Good Water Guide, 1994; New Frontiers in Diamonds: The Mining Revolution, 1996; The Gold Companion, 1997; The Millennium in Gold, 1999; The Millennium in Silver, 1999. *Address:* 8 Ponsonby Pl., London SW1P 4PT, England.

GREEN, Vivian Hubert Howard; Writer; b. 18 Nov. 1915, Wembley, Middlesex, England. *Education:* BA, 1937, BD, 1941, University of Cambridge; DD, Oxford and Cambridge, 1957. *Career:* mem. FRHistS. *Publications:* Renaissance and Reformation, 1952; Oxford Common Room, 1957; The Young Mr Wesley, 1961; Religion at Oxford and Cambridge, 1964; The Commonwealth of Lincoln College 1427–1977, 1979; Love in a Cool Climate: The Letters of Mark Pattison and Meta Bradley, 1985; The Madness of Kings, 1993; A New History of Christianity, 1996; The European Reformation, 1998. *Honours:* Thirlwall Prize and Medal, University of Cambridge, 1940; Hon. Fellow, Lincoln College, Oxford. *Address:* Calendars, Sheep St, Burford, Oxford OX8 4LS, England.

GREENBERG, Alvin (David); Prof. of English, Poet and Writer; b. 10 May 1932, Cincinnati, Ohio, USA; m. 1st, two s. one d.; m. 2nd Janet Holmes, 1993. *Education:* BA, 1954, MA, 1960, University of Cincinnati; PhD, University of Washington, 1964. *Career:* Faculty, University of Kentucky, 1963–65; Prof. of English, 1965–, Chair, Dept of English, 1988–93, Macalester College; Fulbright Lecturer, University of Kerala, India, 1966–67; Ed., Minnesota Review, 1967–71. *Publications:* Poetry: The Metaphysical Giraffe, 1968; The House of the Would-Be Gardener, 1972; Dark Lands, 1973; Metaform, 1975; In/Direction, 1978; And Yet, 1981; Heavy Wings, 1988; Why We Live with Animals, 1990. Fiction: The Small Waves, 1965; Going Nowhere, 1971; The Invention of the West, 1976. Short Stories: The Discovery of America and Other Tales of Terror, 1980; Delta q, 1983; The Man in the Cardboard Mask, 1985; How the Dead Live, 1998. Play: A Wall, 1971. Opera Libretti: Horspfal, 1969; The Jealous Cellist, 1979; Apollonia's Circus, 1994. Contributions: many reviews, journals, and quarterlies. *Honours:* National Endowment for the Arts Fellowships, 1972, 1992; Bush Foundation Artist Fellowships, 1976, 1981; Associated Writing Programs Short Fiction Award, 1982; Nimrod/Pablo Neruda Prize in Poetry, 1988; Loft-McKnight Poetry Award, 1991, and Distinction in Poetry Award, 1994; Chelsea Award for Poetry, 1994; Minnesota State Arts Board Fellowship, 1996. *Address:* 1113 Lincoln Ave, St Paul, MN 55105, USA.

GREENBERG, Joanne, (Hannah Green); Author and Teacher; b. 24 Sept. 1932, New York, NY, USA; m. Albert Greenberg, 4 Sept. 1955, two s. *Education:* BA, American University. *Career:* mem. Authors' Guild; PEN; Colorado Authors League; National Asscn of the Deaf. *Publications:* The King's Persons, 1963; I Never Promised You a Rose Garden, 1964; The Monday Voices, 1965; Summering: A Book of Short Stories, 1966; In This Sign, 1970; Rites of Passage, 1972; Founder's Praise, 1976; High Crimes and Misdemeanors, 1979; A Season of Delight, 1981; The Far Side of Victory, 1983; Simple Gifts, 1986; Age of Consent, 1987; Of Such Small Differences, 1988; With the Snow Queen (short stories), 1991; No Reck'ning Made, 1993; Where the Road Goes, 1998. Contributions: articles, reviews, short stories to numerous periodicals. *Honours:* Harry and Ethel Daroff Memorial Fiction Award, 1963; William and Janice Epstein Fiction Award, 1964; Marcus L. Kenner Award, 1971; Christopher Book Award, 1971; Freida Fromm Reichman Memorial Award, 1971; Rocky Mountain Women's Institute Award, 1983; Denver Public Library Bookplate Award, 1990; Colorado Author of the Year. *Address:* 29221 Rainbow Hill Rd, Golden, CO 80401, USA.

GREENBERG, Martin; Prof. of English (retd), Writer and Trans; b. 3 Feb. 1918, Norfolk, Virginia, USA; m. Paula Fox, 9 June 1962, one s. *Education:* BA, University of Michigan. *Career:* Ed., Schocken Books, 1946–49, Commentary magazine, 1953–60; Lecturer, New School for Social Research, New York City, 1961–67; Asst Prof. to Prof. of English, C. W. Post College, 1963–88; mem. Acad. of American Poets. *Publications:* The Terror of Art: Kafka and Modern Literature, 1968; The Hamlet Vocation of Coleridge and Wordsworth, 1986. Translator: The Diaries of Franz Kafka 1914–23, 1948–49; The Marquise of O and Other Stories, 1960; Five Plays (von Kleist), 1988; Faust, Part One, 1992; Faust, Part Two, 1996. *Honours:* Literature Award, American Acad. and Institute of Arts and Letters, 1989; Harold Morton Landon Trans. Award, 1989. *Address:* 306 Clinton St, New York, NY 11201, USA.

GREENBLATT, Stephen Jay, BA, MA, MPhil, PhD; writer; *Cogan University Professor of the Humanities, Harvard University*; b. 7 Nov. 1943, Cambridge, Massachusetts, USA; m. Ellen Schmidt 1969; two s. *Education:* Yale University, Pembroke College, Cambridge. *Career:* Asst Prof., 1969–74, Assoc. Prof., 1974–79, Prof. of English, 1979–84, Class of 1932 Prof., 1984–97, University of California at Berkeley; Visiting Prof., University of California at Santa Cruz, 1981, University of Beijing, 1982, Northwestern University, 1984, University of Bologna, 1988, University of Chicago, 1989, École des Hautes en Sciences Sociales, Paris, 1989, Harvard University, 1990, 1991, 1993, 1994, University of Trieste, 1991, Dartmouth College, 1992, University of Florence, 1992, Wissenschaftskolleg zu Berlin, 1996–97, University of Turin, 1997; Clarendon Lecturer, University of Oxford, 1988; Prof. of English, 1997–, Cogan University Prof. of the Humanities, 2000–, Harvard University; mem. American Acad. of Arts and Sciences, fellow; International Asscn of University Profs of English; MLA; Renaissance Society of America; Wissenschaftskolleg zu Berlin, fellow. *Publications:* Three Modern Satirists: Waugh, Orwell and Huxley, 1965; Sir Walter Raleigh: The Renaissance Man and His Roles, 1973; Renaissance Self-Fashioning: From More to Shakespeare, 1980; Shakespearean Negotiations: The Circulation of Social Energy in Renaissance England, 1988; Learning to Curse: Essays in Early Modern Culture, 1990; Marvelous Possessions: The Wonder of the New World, 1991; Redrawing the Boundaries of Literary Study in English, 1992; New World Encounters, 1992; The Norton Shakespeare (ed.), 1997; The Norton Anthology of English Literature (ed.), 2000; Practising New Historicism, 2000; Hamlet in Purgatory, 2001; Will in the World 2004. Contributions: scholarly journals. *Honours:* Fulbright Scholarship, Cambridge, 1964–66; National Endowment for the Humanities Fellowship, 1971–72; Guggenheim Fellowships, 1975, 1983; British Council Prize in the Humanities, 1981; James Russell Lowell Prize, MLA, 1989. *Address:* c/o Department of English, Harvard University, Cambridge, MA 02138, USA.

GREENE, Alvin Carl, BA; academic, historian and writer; b. 4 Nov. 1923, Abilene, TX, USA; m. 1st Betty Jo Dozier 1950; three s. one d.; m. 2nd Judy Dalton 1990. *Education:* Phillips University, Kansas State College, Abilene Christian College, Hardin-Simmons University, University of Texas at Austin. *Career:* Co-Dir, Centre for Texas Studies, University of North Texas; mem. Texas Institute of Letters, pres., 1969–71, fellow 1981–; Writers Guild of America, West; PEN International. *Publications:* A Personal Country, 1969; The Santa Claus Bank Robbery, 1972; The Last Captive, 1972; Dallas: The Deciding Years, 1972; The Highland Park Woman, 1984; Taking Heart, 1990. Contributions: Atlantic; McCalls; Southwestern History Quarterly; New York Times Book Review. *Honours:* National Conference of Christians and Jews, 1964; Dobie-Paisano Fellow, 1968; Fellow, Texas State History Asscn, 1990. *Address:* 4359 Shirley Drive, Dallas, TX 75229, USA.

GREENE, Brian R., PhD; American physicist. *Education:* Harvard Univ., Univ. of Oxford. *Career:* post-doctoral fellow, Harvard Univ. 1987–90; Asst Prof. Cornell Univ. 1990, Assoc. Prof. 1995, later Prof.; now Prof. of Physics and Mathematics, Columbia Univ.; Dir Theoretical Advanced Study Inst. 1996; has lectured in more than 20 countries; mem. Editorial Bd Physical Review D, Advance in Theoretical and Mathematical Physics. *Television:* The Theory of Everything 2003. *Publications:* journal papers: Duality in Calabi-Yau Moduli Space (with M. R. Plesser) 1990, Calabi-Yau Moduli Space, Mirror Manifolds and Spacetime Topology Change in String Theory (with P. S. Aspinwall and D. R. Morrison) 1994, Black Hole Condensation and the Unification of String Vacua (with D. R. Morrison and A. Strominger) 1995, Orbifold Resolution by D-Branes (with M. R. Douglas and D. R. Morrison) 1997, D-Brane Topology Changing Transitions 1998; books: The Elegant Universe (Aventis Prize for Science Books 2000) 1999, The Fabric of the Cosmos: Space, Time and the Texture of Reality 2004. *Address:* Faculty of Science, Columbia University, New York, NY 10032, USA (Office). *Telephone:* (212) 854-3349 (Office). *E-mail:* greene@phys.columbia.edu. *Website:* www.phys.columbia.edu/faculty/greene.htm.

GREENE, Constance C(larke); Writer; b. 27 Oct. 1924, New York, NY, USA; m. Philip M. Greene, 8 June 1946, two s. three d. *Education:* Skidmore College, 1942–44. *Publications:* A Girl Called Al, 1969; Leo the Lioness, 1970; The Good-Luck Bogie Hat, 1971; Unmaking of Rabbit, 1972; Isabelle the Itch, 1973; The Ears of Louis, 1974; I Know You, Al, 1975; Beat the Turtle Drum, 1976; Getting Nowhere, 1977; I and Sproggy, 1978; Your Old Pal, Al, 1979; Dotty's Suitcase, 1980; Double-Dare O'Toole, 1981; Al(exandra) the Great, 1982; Ask Anybody, 1983; Isabelle Shows Her Stuff, 1984; Star Shine, 1985; Other Plans, 1985; The Love Letters of J. Timothy Owen, 1986; Just Plain Al, 1986; Isabelle and Little Orphan Frannie, 1988; Monday I Love You, 1988; Al's Blind Date, 1989; Funny You Should Ask, 1992; Odds on Oliver, 1992. Contributions: Magazines and newspapers. *Honours:* American Library Asscn Notable Books, 1970, 1977, 1987. *Address:* c/o Viking Press Inc, 375 Hudson St, New York, NY 10014, USA.

GREENE, Douglas G., BA, MA, PhD; editor, historian and educator; b. 24 Sept. 1944, Middletown, CT, USA; m. Sandra Virginia Stangland 1966; one s. one d. *Education:* University of Southern Florida, University of Chicago. *Career:* Instructor in History, University of Montana, Missoula, 1970–71; Prof. of History, 1971–83, Dir, Institute for Humanities, 1983–, Old Dominion University, Norfolk, Virginia; Publisher, Crippen and Landru Books, 1994–; mem. MWA. *Publications:* Bibliographia Oziana: A Concise Bibliographical Checklist of the Oz Books by L. Frank Baum and His Successors (co-author), 1976; W. W. Denslow (co-author), 1976; Diaries of the Popish Plot: Being the Diaries of Israel Tonge, Sir Robert Southwell, John Joyne, Edmund Warcup, and Thomas Dangerfield, and Including

Titus Oates's 'A True Narrative of the Horrid Plot' (1679) (compiler, author of introduction), 1977; The Meditations of Lady Elizabeth Delaval: Written between 1661 and 1671 (ed., author of introduction), 1978; John Dickson Carr, The Door to Doom, and Other Detections (ed., author of introduction), 1980; John Dickson Carr, The Dead Sleep Lightly (ed., author of introduction), 1983; Ruth Plumly Thompson, The Wizard of Way-Up and Other Wonders (co-ed.), 1985; Death Locked In: An Anthology of Locked Room Stories (co-ed.), 1987; The Collected Short Fiction of Ngaio March (ed., author of introduction), 1989; John Dickson Carr, Fell and Foul Play (ed., author of introduction), 1991; John Dickson Carr, Merrivale, March, and Murder (ed., author of introduction), 1991; John Dickson Carr: The Man Who Explained Miracles, 1995; Detection by Gaslight: Fourteen Victorian Detective Stories (ed., author of introduction), 1997. *Literary Agent:* Phyllis Westberg, Harold Ober Assocs, 425 Madison Avenue, New York, NY 10017, USA. *Address:* 627 New Hampshire Avenue, Norfolk, VA 23508-2132, USA. *E-mail:* Crippenl@pilot.infi.net.

GREENE, Graham Carleton, CBE, MA; British publisher; b. 10 June 1936, Berlin, Germany; m. 1st Judith Margaret Gordon Walker 1957 (divorced); m. 2nd Sally Georgina Horton 1976; one s.; also one step-s. one step-d. *Education:* Eton Coll. and Univ. Coll., Oxford. *Career:* Dir Jonathan Cape Ltd 1962–90, Man. Dir 1966–88; Dir Chatto, Virago, Bodley Head and Jonathan Cape Ltd 1969–88, Chair. 1970–88; Dir Book Reps (NZ) Ltd 1971–88, CVBC Services 1972–88, Australasian Publishing Co. Ltd (Chair. 1978–88) 1969–88, Guinness Peat Group PLC1973–87, Triad Paperbacks 1975–88, Greene King PLC 1979–, Statesman and Nation Publishing Co. (Chair. 1981–85) 1980–85, Statesman Publishing Co. Ltd (Chair. 1981–85) 1980–85, Random House Inc. 1987–88, Jupiter Int. Investment Trust PLC 1989–2001, Henry Sotheran Ltd 1990–, Ed Victor Ltd 1991–, Rosemary Sandberg Ltd 1991–2002, Libra KFT (Budapest) 1991–, London Merchant Securities PLC 1996– (Chair. 2000–); Chair. Random House UK Ltd 1988–90, British Museum Devt Trust 1986–93 (Vice-Chair. 1993–2004), British Museum Publications (now British Museum Co.) Ltd 1998–2002 (Chair. 1988–96), Museums and Galleries Comm. 1991–96, Vice Pres. 1997–; Chair. Nation Pty Co. Ltd 1981–87, New Society 1984–86, Great Britain–China Centre (Chair. 1986–1997); Dir Garsington Opera Ltd 1996–; mem. Bd of British Council 1977–88, mem. Council of Publishers Asscn (Pres. 1977–79) 1969–88; Trustee, British Museum 1978–2002 (Chair. 1996–2002), Open Coll. of the Arts 1990–97; Int. Cttee of Int. Publishers Asscn 1977–88, Groupe des Editeurs de Livres de la CEE (Pres. 1984–86) 1977–86; Chevalier, Ordre des Arts et Lettres. *Honours:* Hon.DLitt, (Keele Univesity) 2002; Hon.DCL, (Univ.E Anglia) 2002; Hon.DLitt, (Buckingham) 2004. *Address:* 6 Bayley Street, Bedford Square, London, WC1B 3HB, England. *Telephone:* (20) 7304-4101. *Fax:* (20) 7304-4102 (Office). *E-mail:* grahamc.greene@virgin.net (Office).

GREENE, Jonathan (Edward); Poet, Writer, Ed., Publisher and Book Designer; b. 19 April 1943, New York, NY, USA; m. 1st Alice-Anne Kingston, 5 June 1963, divorced, one d.; m. 2nd Dobree Adams, 23 May 1974. *Education:* BA, Bard College, 1965. *Publications:* The Reckoning, 1966; Instance, 1968; The Lapidary, 1969; A 17th Century Garner, 1969; An Unspoken Complaint, 1970; The Poor in Church, by Arthur Rimbaud (trans.), 1973; Scaling the Walls, 1974; Glossary of the Everyday, 1974; Peripatetics, 1978; Jonathan Williams: A 50th Birthday Celebration (ed.), 1979; Once a Kingdom Again, 1979; Quiet Goods, 1980; Idylls, 1983; Small Change for the Long Haul, 1984; Trickster Tales, 1985; Les Chambres des Poètes, 1990; The Man Came to Haul Stone, 1995; Of Moment, 1998; Inventions of Necessity: Selected Poems, 1998; Incidents of Travel in Japan, 1999; A Little Ink in the Paper Sea, 2001; Book of Correspondences, 2002; Watching Dewdrops Fall, 2003. Contributions: anthologies, reviews, quarterlies, and journals. *Honours:* National Endowment for the Arts Fellowships, 1969, 1978; Southern Federation of State Arts Agencies Fellowship, 1977; Kentucky Arts Council Fellowship, 2003. *Address:* PO Box 475, Frankfort, KY 40602-0475, USA.

GREENLAND, Colin; Writer; b. 17 May 1954, Dover, Kent, England. *Education:* MA, 1978, DPhil, 1981, Pembroke College, Oxford. *Career:* Writer-in-Residence, North East London Polytechnic, 1980–82; mem. Science Fiction Foundation; Science Fiction Writers' Conference, Milford; BSFA, Council Mem. *Publications:* The Entropy Exhibition, 1983; Daybreak on a Different Mountain, 1984; Magnetic Storm (with Roger and Martyn Dean), 1984; Interzone: The First Anthology (co-ed.), 1985; The Freelance Writer's Handbook (with Paul Kerton), 1986; The Hour of the Thin Ox, 1987; Storm Warnings (co-ed.), 1987; Other Voices, 1988; Take Back Plenty, 1990; Michael Moorcock: Death is No Obstacle, 1992; Harm's Way, 1993; Seasons of Plenty, 1995; The Plenty Principle, 1997; Mother of Plenty, 1998; Spiritfeather, 2000; Finding Helen, 2002. Contributions: many anthologies and periodicals. *Honours:* Eaton Award for Science Fiction Criticism, 1985; Arthur C. Clarke Award, 1992; BSFA Award, 1992; Eastercon Award, 1992; Guest of Honour, Evolution, National Science Fiction Easter Convention, 1996. *Literary Agent:* Maggie Noach Literary Agency, 22 Dorville Crescent, London W6 0HJ, England. *E-mail:* colin .greenland@networld.com.

GREENLEAF, Stephen (Howell); Writer; b. 17 July 1942, Washington, DC, USA; m. Ann Garrison, 20 July 1968, one s. *Education:* BA, Carleton College, 1964; JD, University of California at Berkeley, 1967; Creative Writing, University of Iowa, 1978–79. *Career:* Admitted to the Bar, California, 1968, Iowa, 1977; Instructor in Writing, University of Washington Extension, 1993–96, Iowa Summer Writing Festival, 1995–2000. *Publications:* Grave Error, 1979; Death Bed, 1980; Child Proof, 1981; State's Evidence, 1982; Fatal Obsession, 1983; The Ditto List, 1985; Beyond Blame, 1986; Toll Call, 1987; Impact, 1989; Book Case, 1991; Blood Type, 1992; Southern Cross, 1993; False Conception, 1994; Flesh Wounds, 1996; Past Tense, 1997; Strawberry Sunday, 1999; Ellipsis, 2000. *Honours:* Maltese Falcon Award, Japan, 1993. *Address:* c/o Scribner, 1230 Avenue of the Americas, New York, NY 10020, USA.

GREER, Bonnie; American writer, playwright and critic; b. 1948, Chicago, IL. *Education:* studied with David Mamet and Elia Kazan in New York. *Career:* theatre critic, Time Out, London; Gov., London Int. Film School; bd mem., Royal Opera House; judge for Orange Prize; regular contributor to radio, including Night Waves (BBC Radio 3), Front Row (BBC Radio 4) and television, including Booker Prize (Channel 4), Late Review and Newsnight Review (BBC2); Arts Council Playwright-in-Residence, Soho Theatre, Black Theatre Co-operative; Arts Council England Playwright-in-Residence, Pascal Theatre Co., London. *Plays:* Mundo Negra 1993, God Likes No Ugly. *Publications:* Hanging by her Teeth 1995, Ways into Shakespeare 1996, Riding the 903 2003. *Honours:* Verity Bargate Award for Best New Play. *Literary Agent:* Sheil Land Associates Ltd, 43 Doughty Street, London, WC1N 2LF, England. *Telephone:* (20) 7405-9351. *Fax:* (20) 7831-2127. *E-mail:* info@sheilland.co.uk.

GREER, Germaine, PhD; Australian feminist, author and broadcaster; b. 29 Jan. 1939, Melbourne. *Education:* Star of the Sea Convent, Vic., Melbourne and Sydney Univs and Cambridge Univ., England. *Career:* Sr Tutor in English, Sydney Univ. 1963–64; Asst Lecturer then Lecturer in English, Warwick Univ. 1967–72, Prof. of English and Comparative Studies 1998–2003; lecturer throughout N America with American Program Bureau 1973–78, to raise funds for Tulsa Bursary and Fellowship Scheme 1980–83; Visiting Prof., Grad. Faculty of Modern Letters, Univ. of Tulsa 1979, Prof. of Modern Letters 1980–83, Founder-Dir of Tulsa Centre for the Study of Women's Literature, Founder-Ed. Tulsa Studies in Women's Literature 1981; Dir Stump Cross Books 1988–; Special Lecturer and Unofficial Fellow, Newnham Coll., Cambridge 1989–98; broadcaster/journalist/columnist/reviewer 1972–; Jr Govt Scholarship 1952, Diocesan Scholarship 1956, Sr Govt Scholarship 1956, Teacher's Coll. Studentship 1956, Commonwealth Scholarship 1964; numerous television appearances and public talks including discussion with Norman Mailer in The Theatre of Ideas, New York. *Publications:* The Female Eunuch 1969, The Obstacle Race: The Fortunes of Women Painters and Their Work 1979, Sex and Destiny: The Politics of Human Fertility 1984, Shakespeare (co-ed.) 1986, The Madwoman's Underclothes (selected journalism 1964–85) 1986, Kissing the Rod: An Anthology of 17th Century Women's Verse (co-ed.) 1988, Daddy, We Hardly Knew You 1989 (J. R. Ackerly Prize and Premio Internazionale Mondello), The Uncollected Verse of Aphra Behn (ed.) 1989, The Change: Women, Ageing and the Menopause 1991, The Collected Works of Katherine Philips, the Matchless Orinda, Vol. III: The Translations (co-ed.) 1993, Slip-Shod Sybils: Recognition, Rejection and The Woman Poet 1995, The Surviving Works of Anne Wharton (co-ed.) 1997, The Whole Woman 1999, John Wilmot, Earl of Rochester 1999, 101 Poems by 101 Women (ed.) 2001, The Boy 2003, Poems for Gardeners (ed.) 2003, Whitefella Jump Up 2004; articles for Listener, Spectator, Esquire, Harper's Magazine, Playboy, Private Eye and other journals. *Honours:* Dr hc (Univ. of Griffith, Australia) 1996, (Univ. of York, Toronto) 1999, (UMIST) 2000; hon. degrees (Melbourne) 2003, (Essex) 2003. *Literary Agent:* Gillon Aitken Associates Ltd, 18–21 Cavaye Place, London, SW10 9PT, England. *Telephone:* (20) 7373-8672. *Fax:* (20) 7373-6002.

GREGOR-DELLIN, Martin; Writer, Poet, Dramatist and Ed.; b. 3 June 1926, Naumberg, Germany; m. Annemarie Dellin, 9 Nov. 1951, one d. *Education:* University of Leipzig. *Career:* Writer, Ed., Halle, 1951–58, Munich, 1962–66; Writer for Radio, Frankfurt am Main, 1961–62; Freelance Novelist, Ed., Biographer, Poet, 1966–; mem. German Acad. for Language and Literature; Bavarian Acad. for Fine Arts; Asscn of German Writers; PEN. *Publications:* Jakob Haferglanz (novel), 1956; Der Man mit der Stoppuhr (poems), 1957; Der Nullpunkte (novel), 1959; Der Kandelaber (novel), 1962; Einer (novel), 1965; Aufbruch ins Ungewisse, 1968; Richard Wagner, Die Revolution als Oper, 1973; Das Riesenrad Erzählungen, 1976; Im Zeitalter Kafkas, 1979; Richard Wagner: Sein Leben, sein Werk, sein Jahrhundert, 1980, in English trans. as Richard Wagner: His Life, His Work, His Century, 1983; Schlabrendorf, oder, Die Republik, 1982; Richard Wagner: Eine Biographie in Bildern, 1982; Luther: Eine Annäherung, 1983; Richard Wagner: Leben, Werk, Wirkung, 1983; Heinrich Schütz: Sein Leben, sein Werk, Seine Zeit, 1984; Was ist grösse?: Sieben Deutsche und ein deutsches Problem, 1985; Italienisches Traumbuch, 1986. Editor: Anthologies and various other books. Other: several radio plays. Contributions: essays and poetry to numerous anthologies. *Honours:* Förderpreis, Andreas-Gryphius Preis, 1963; Ostdeutscher Schrifttimuspreis, 1963; Stereo Radio Play Prize, 1967; Munich Literary Prize, 1971; Die Goldene Feder, Critics Prize, 1972; Grand Prix de la Critique Musicale Française, 1982; Fernseh-Kulturpreis, Eduard-Rhein-Stiftung, 1984; Cross of Merit, First Class, Federal Republic of Germany.

GREGORY, Richard (Langton); Prof. of Neuropsychology Emeritus and Writer; b. 24 July 1923, London, England; m. 1st Margaret Hope Pattison

Muir, 1953, divorced 1966, one s. one d.; m. 2nd Freja Mary Balchin, divorced 1976. *Education:* Downing College, Cambridge, 1947–50; DSc, University of Bristol, 1983. *Career:* Research, MRC Applied Psychology Research Unit, Cambridge, 1950–53; University Demonstrator, later Lecturer, Dept of Psychology, Cambridge, 1953–67; Fellow, Corpus Christi College, Cambridge, 1962–67; Prof. of Bionics, University of Edinburgh, 1967–70; Prof. of Neuropsychology and Dir of the Brain and Perception Laboratory, 1970–88, Prof. Emeritus, 1988–, University of Bristol; Founder-Ed., Journal of Perception, 1972–; Founder and Chair. of the Trustees, 1983–91, Pres., 1991–, Exploratory Hands-on Science Centre; mem. Royal Institution; Royal Society, fellow. *Publications:* Recovery from Early Blindness (with Jean Wallace), 1963; Eye and Brain, 1966; The Intelligent Eye, 1970; Illusion in Nature and Art (co-ed.), 1973; Concepts and Mechanisms of Perception, 1974; Mind in Science, 1981; Odd Perceptions (essays), 1986; The Oxford Companion to the Mind (ed.), 1987; Evolution of the Eye and Visual System (co-ed.), Vol. II of Vision and Visual Dysfunction, 1991; Even Odder Perceptions (essays), 1994; The Artful Eye, 1995; Mirrors in Mind, 1996; Mind-Makers, 1998. Contributions: Scientific journals. *Honours:* CBE, 1989; Michael Faraday Medal, Royal Society, 1993; Medawar Prize Lecture, Royal Society, 2001; Lord Crook Medal, Spectacle Makers' Co, 1996; Corpus Christi College, Cambridge, hon. fellowship; Hon. doctorates. *Literary Agent:* AP Watt Ltd, 20 John St, London WC1N 2DR, England. *Address:* 23 Royal York Crescent, Clifton, Bristol BS8 4JX, England.

GREIG, Andrew; poet and writer; b. 1951, Bannockburn, Scotland. *Education:* Univ. of Edinburgh. *Publications:* poetry: Men on Ice 1977, A Flame in Your Heart (with Kathleen Jamie) 1986, The Order of the Day 1990, Western Swing 1994, Into You 2000; novels: Surviving Passages 1982, Electric Brae 1992, The Return of John Macnab 1996, When They Lay Bare 1999, That Summer 2000, The Clouds Above 2002, In Another Light 2004; non-fiction: Summit Fever 1985, Kingdoms of Experience 1986. *Address:* c/o Bloodaxe Books Ltd, Highgreen, Tarset, Northumberland NE48 1RP, England.

GRENNAN, Eamon; Prof. and Poet; b. 13 Nov. 1941, Dublin, Ireland; one s. two d. *Education:* BA, 1963, MA, 1964, University College, Dublin; PhD, Harvard University, 1973. *Career:* Lecturer in English, University College, Dublin, 1966–67; Asst Prof., Lehman College, CUNY, 1971–74; Asst Prof., 1974–83, Assoc. Prof., 1983–89, Prof., 1989–, Vassar College. *Publications:* Wildly for Days, 1983; What Light There Is, 1987; Twelve Poems, 1988; What Light There Is and Other Poems, 1989; As If It Matters, 1991; So It Goes, 1995; Selected Poems of Giacomo Leopardi (trans.), 1995; Relations: New and Selected Poems, 1998; Facing the Music: Irish Poetry in the 20th Century, 1999; Still Life with Waterfall, 2001. Contributions: anthologies and periodicals. *Honours:* National Endowment for the Humanities Grant, 1986; National Endowment for the Arts Grant, 1991; Guggenheim Fellowship, 1995. *Address:* c/o Dept of English, Vassar College, Poughkeepsie, NY 12604, USA.

GRENVILLE, John Ashley Soames; historian and academic; b. 11 Jan. 1928, Berlin, Germany; m. 1st Betty Anne Rosenberg 1960 (died 1974); three s.; m. 2nd Patricia Carnie 1975; one d. one step-d. *Education:* Correspondence courses, Birkbeck College, London, LSE; BA, Yale University; PhD, University of London. *Career:* Postgraduate Scholar, University of London, 1951–53; Asst Lecturer to Lecturer, 1953–64, Reader in Modern History, 1964–65, Nottingham University; Commonwealth Fund Fellow, 1958–59; Postdoctoral Fellow, Yale University, 1960–63; Prof. of International History, Leeds University, 1965–69; Ed., Fontana History of War and Society, 1969–78, Leo Baeck Year Book, 1992–; Prof. of Modern History, 1969–94, Professorial Research Fellow, Institute of German Studies, 1994–, University of Birmingham. *Publications:* The Coming of the Europeans (with J. G. Fuller), 1962; Lord Salisbury and Foreign Policy, 1964; Politics, Strategy and American Diplomacy: Studies in Foreign Policy 1873–1917 (with G. B. Young), 1966; The Major International Treaties 1914–1973: A History and Guide, 1974, two-vol. edn, 1987; Europe Reshaped 1848–1878, 1975; Nazi Germany, 1976; World History of the Twentieth Century, Vol. I, 1900–1945, 1980; Collins World History of the Twentieth Century, 1994. Other: Films with N. Pronay: The Munich Crisis, 1968; The End of Illusion: From Munich to Dunkirk, 1970. Contributions: scholarly journals. *Address:* c/o Institute of German Studies, University of Birmingham, Birmingham B15 2TT, England.

GRENVILLE, Kate; Novelist and Writer; b. 1950, Sydney, Australia; m.; one s. one d. *Education:* BA, English Literature, Univ. of Sydney; MA, Creative Writing, Univ. of Colorado. *Publications:* Novels: Lilian's Story, 1985; Dreamhouse, 1986; Joan Makes History, 1988; Dark Places (aka Albion's Story), 1994; The Idea of Perfection, 1999. Short Stories: Bearded Ladies, 1984. Non-Fiction: The Writing Book, 1990; Making Stories (with Sue Woolfe), 1993; Writing From Start to Finish, 2001. *Honours:* Fellowship, Internatonal Asscn of Univ. Women; Fellowship, Literary Arts Board of the Australia Council; The Australian/Vogel Award, 1986; Talking Book of the Year award, 1986; Orange Prize for Fiction, 2001. *Literary Agent:* Australian Literary Management, 2A Booth St, Balmain, NSW 2041, Australia. *Address:* c/o Picador, 25 Eccleston Pl., London SW1W 9NF, England. *E-mail:* kgrenville@bigpond.com. *Website:* www.users.bigpond.com/kgrenville/.

GRENZ, Stanley J.; academic; b. 7 Jan. 1950, Alpena, MI, USA; m. Edna Sturhahn; one s. one d. *Education:* BA, University of Colorado, 1973; MDiv, Denver Conservative Baptist Seminary, 1976; DTheol magna cum laude, University of Munich, 1980. *Career:* Pioneer McDonald Prof. of Baptist Heritage, Theology and Ethics, Carey Theological College, Vancouver, 1990–2002; Affiliate Prof., Northern Baptist Theological Seminary, Lombard, IL, 1996–99; Distinguished Prof. of Theology, Baylor University, Waco, TX, 2002–03; Pioneer McDonald Prof. of Theology, Carey Theological Coll., Vancouver, BC, 2003–; mem. Baptist World Alliance; Canadian Evangelical Theological Society, Exec. Committee, 1996–2000; American Acad. of Religion, Regional Pres., 1986–87; National Asscn of Baptist Profs of Religion, Pres., 1989–90. *Publications:* Isaac Backus: Puritan and Baptist, 1983; The Baptist Congregation, 1985; Prayer: The Cry for the Kingdom, 1988; Reason for Hope: The Systematic Theology of Wolfhart Pannenberg, 1990; AIDS: Ministry in the Midst of an Epidemic (co-author), 1990; Sexual Ethics: A Biblical Perspective, 1990; Twentieth-Century Theology: God and the World in a Transitional Age (co-author), 1992; Revisioning Evangelical Theology, 1993; Theology for the Community of God, 1994; Betrayal of Trust: Sexual Misconduct in the Pastorate (co-author), 1995; Women and the Church: A Biblical Theology of Women in Ministry (co-author), 1995; A Primer on Postmodernism, 1996; Created for Community: Connecting Christian Belief with Christian Living, 1996; Who Needs Theology?: An Invitation to the Study of God (co-author), 1996; The Moral Quest: Foundations for Christian Ethics, 1997; What Christians Really Believe… and Why, 1998; Welcoming But Not Affirming: An Evangelical Response to Homosexuality, 1998; Pocket Dictionary of Theological Terms (co-author), 1999; Renewing the Center: Evangelical Theology in a Post-theological Era, 2000; Beyond Foundationalism: Shaping Theology in a Postmodern Context (co-author), 2001; The Social God and the Relational Self: A Trinitarian Theology of the Imago Dei, 2001. *Honours:* Fulbright Scholar in Germany, 1987–88; Christianity Today Book Awards, 1992, 1993, 1998, 1999, 2000; Theological Scholarship, Research Award, Asscn of Theological Schools in the United States and Canada, 1993; First Place, Christian Writing Awards, Faith Today and Evangelical Fellowship of Canada, 1995, 1997; Henry Luce III Fellow in Theology, 1999–2000. *Address:* Carey Theological College, 5920 Iona Drive, Vancouver, BC V6T 1J6, Canada. *E-mail:* sgrenz@stanleyjgrenz.com. *Website:* www.stanleyj.grenz.com.

GREY, Amelia (see Skinner, Gloria Dale).

GREY, Anthony (Keith); Author, Television and Radio Presenter/Reporter and Publisher; b. 5 July 1938, Norwich, England; m. Shirley McGuinn, 4 April 1970, two d. *Career:* Journalist, Eastern Daily Press, 1960–64; Foreign Correspondent, Reuters, East Berlin and Prague, 1965–67, Beijing, 1967–69; Established imprint, Tagman Press, Norfolk, UK, 1998; mem. PEN International; Royal Institute of International Affairs; Society of Authors; Groucho Club. *Publications:* Hostage in Peking, 1970; A Man Alone, 1971; Some Put Their Trust in Chariots, 1973; Crosswords from Peking, 1975; The Bulgarian Exclusive, 1976; Himself (radio play), 1976; The Chinese Assassin, 1978; Saigon, 1982; The Prime Minister was a Spy, 1983; Peking, 1988; The Naked Angels, 1990; The Bangkok Secret, 1990; Tokyo Bay, 1996. Other: BBC World Service radio documentary series, UFO's: Fact, Fiction or Fantasy, 1997. *Honours:* OBE, 1969; United Kingdom Journalist of the Year, 1970. *Literary Agent:* PFD, Drury House, 34–43 Russell St, London WC2B 5HA, England. *E-mail:* editorial@tagman-press.com.

GREY, Charles (see Tubb, Edwin Charles).

GRIBBIN, John R., MSc, PhD; British astrophysicist and writer; b. 1946; m. Mary Gribbin; two s. *Education:* Sussex Univ., Univ. of Cambridge. *Career:* Ed., Nature magazine 1970–75; science journalist, The Times; Visiting Fellow in Astronomy, Univ. of Sussex. *Publications include:* fiction: Brother Esau 1982, Double Planet 1988, Father to the Man 1989, Ragnarok 1991, Reunion 1991, Innervisions 1993; non-fiction: The Jupiter Effect 1974, Forecasts, Famines and Freezes 1976, Timewarps 1979, Our Changing Universe 1977, The Death of the Sun 1980, The Monkey Puzzle 1983, Spacewarps 1984, In Search of Schrodinger's Cat 1984, Amateur Astronomer 1985, In Search of the Double Helix 1985, The Hole in the Sky 1988, The Omega Point 1988, Winds of Change 1989, Cosmic Coincidence 1989, Hothouse Earth 1990, Blinded by the Light 1991, The Matter Myth 1992, In Search of the Big Bang 1992, Being Human 1993, In the Beginning 1993, Einstein: a Life in Science (with Michael White) 1994, In Search of the Edge of Time 1995, Companion to the Cosmos 1996, Schrodinger's Kittens and the Search for Reality 1996, Fire on Earth (with Mary Gribbin) 1996, Mendel in 90 Minutes (with Mary Gribbin) 1997, Richard Feynman: A Life in Science (with Michael White) 1998, Almost Everyone's Guide to Science 1999, Q is for Quantum 1999, The Search for Superstrings, Symmetry and the Theory of Everything 2000, The Case of the Missing Neutrinos 2000, Darwin: A Life in Science (with Michael White) 2000, The Birth of Time 2000, Stardust (with Mary Gribbin) 2001, Space: Our Final Frontier 2001, Science: A History 1534–2001 2002, Ice Age: How a Change of Climate Made Us Human (with Mary Gribbin) 2003, Stephen Hawking: A Life in Science (with Michael White) 2003, Deep Simplicity: Chaos, Complexity and the Emergence of Life 2004, The Men who Measured the Universe 2004, Fitzroy: The Remarkable Story of Darwin's Captain and the Invention of the Weather Forecast (with Mary Gribbin) 2004; contrib. to New Destinies

VII 1988, What's the Big Idea? Chaos and Uncertainty 1999, The Science of Philip Pullman's 'His Dark Materials' 2003, numerous journals, magazines and newspapers. *Honours:* Annual Award of the Gravity Research Foundation. *Literary Agent:* Bruce Hunter, David Higham Associates, 5–8 Lower Street, Golden Square, London, W1F 9HA, England. *Telephone:* (20) 7434-5900. *Fax:* (20) 7437-1072. *Website:* www.biols.susx.ac.uk/home/John_Gribbin/.

GRICHKOVETS, Evguéni; Playwright; b. 1966, Kémérovo, Siberia. *Publications:* plays incl. Zima. *Honours:* Innovation Prize, Moscow Festival, 2000. *Address:* c/o Editions Les Solitaires Intempestifs, 14 rue de la république, 25000 Besançon, France.

GRIDBAN, Volsted (see Tubb, Edwin Charles).

GRIFFIN, Jasper; university professor and writer; *Professor of Classical Literature, Public Orator, Balliol College Oxford*; b. 29 May 1937, London, England; m. Miriam Tamara Dressler, 1960, three d. *Education:* BA, 1958, MA, 1960, Balliol College, Oxford. *Career:* Jackson Fellow, Harvard University, 1960–61; Dyson Research Fellow, 1961–63, Fellow and Tutor in Classics, 1963–, Reader in Classical Literature, 1990–92, Prof. of Classical Literature, 1992–, Public Orator, 1992–, Balliol College, Oxford; T. S. Eliot Memorial Lecturer, University of Kent at Canterbury, 1984; mem. Fellow, British Acad. *Publications:* Homer on Life and Death, 1980; Homer, 1980; Snobs, 1982; Latin Poets and Roman Life, 1985; The Mirror of Myth, 1986; The Oxford History of the Classical World (ed. with J. Boardman and O. Murray), 1986; Virgil, 1986; Homer: The Odyssey, 1987; The Oxford History of Greece and the Hellenistic World (co-ed.), 1991; Homer: The Iliad, Book IX, 1995. Contributions: scholarly books and journals. *Address:* c/o Balliol College, Oxford OX1 3BJ, England.

GRIFFIN, Keith Broadwell; British academic and writer; *Distinguished Professor of Economics, University of California at Riverside*; b. 6 Nov. 1938, Colón, Panama; m. Dixie Beth Griffin 1956; two d. *Education:* BA, Williams College, Williamstown, Massachusetts, 1960; BPhil, 1962, DPhil, 1965, University of Oxford. *Career:* Fellow and Tutor in Economics, 1965–76, Pres., 1979–88, Magdalen College, Oxford; Cecil and Ida Green Visiting Prof., University of British Columbia, 1986; Distinguished Prof. of Economics, 1988–, Chair, Dept of Economics, 1988–93, University of California at Riverside. *Publications:* The Green Revolution: An Economic Analysis, 1972; The Political Economy of Agrarian Change, 1974; Land Concentration and Rural Poverty, 1976; International Inequality and National Poverty, 1978; The Transition to Egalitarian Development (with Jeffrey James), 1981; Growth and Equality in Rural China (with Ashwani Saith), 1981; World Hunger and the World Economy, 1987; Alternative Strategies for Economic Development, 1989; Implementing a Human Development Strategy (with Terry McKinley), 1994; Studies in Globalization and Economic Transitions, 1996; Economic Reform in Vietnam (ed.), 1998; Studies in Development Strategy and Systemic Transformation, 2000; Poverty Reduction in Mongolia (ed.), 2003. Contributions: scholarly books and journals. *Honours:* Hon. DLitt, Williams College, 1980; Hon. Fellow, Magdalen College, Oxford, 1988; American Asscn for the Advancement of Science, Fellow, 1997. *Address:* c/o Department of Economics, University of California at Riverside, Riverside, CA 92521, USA.

GRIFFITH, Patricia Browning; Writer and Dramatist; b. 9 Nov. 1935, Ft Worth, Texas, USA; m. William Byron Griffith, 6 June 1960, one d. *Education:* BA, Baylor University, 1958. *Career:* Assoc. Adjunct Prof., George Washington University; Pres., PEN/Faulkner Foundation Award for Fiction. *Publications:* Fiction: The Future is Not What it Used to Be, 1970; Tennessee Blue, 1981; The World Around Midnight, 1991; Supporting the Sky, 1996. Plays: Outside Waco, 1984; Safety, 1987; Risky Games, 1992. Contributions: anthologies and periodicals. *Honours:* National Endowment for the Arts Grant, 1978; American Library Asscn Notable Book, 1992. *Address:* 1215 Geranium St NW, Washington, DC 20012, USA.

GRIFFITHS, Helen, (Helen Santos); Writer and Lay Reader, Church of England; b. 8 May 1939, London, England. *Publications:* Horse in the Clouds, 1957; Wild and Free, 1958; Moonlight, 1959; Africano, 1960; The Wild Heart, 1962; The Greyhound, 1963; Wild Horse of Santander, 1965; Dark Swallows, 1965; Leon, 1966; Stallion of the Sands, 1967; Moshie Cat, 1968; Patch, 1969; Federico, 1970; Russian Blue, 1973; Just a Dog, 1974; Witch Fear, 1975; Pablo, 1976; Kershaw Dogs, 1978; The Last Summer, 1979; Blackface Stallion, 1980; Dancing Horses, 1981; Hari's Pigeon, 1982; Rafa's Dog, 1983; Jesus, As Told By Mark, 1983; Dog at the Window, 1984. As Helen Santos: Caleb's Lamb, 1984; If Only, 1987; Pepe's Dog, 1996. *Honours:* Daughter of Mark Twain, 1966; Highly Commended, Carnegie Medal Award, 1966; Silver Pencil Award for Best Children's Book, Netherlands, 1978. *Address:* 9 Ashley Terrace, Bath, Avon BA1 3DP, England. *E-mail:* helensantos@lineone.net.

GRIFFITHS, Jay; British writer and journalist; b. Manchester. *Education:* Univ. of Oxford. *Publications:* non-fiction: Pip Pip: A Sideways Look at Time (Discover Award for Non-Fiction, USA 2003) 1999, Wilderness 2005; contrib. to The Guardian, Resurgence, Artists Newsletter. *Literary Agent:* David Godwin Associates, 55 Monmouth Street, London, WC2H 9DG, England. *Telephone:* (20) 7240-9992. *Fax:* (20) 7395-6110.

GRIFFITHS, Paul (Anthony); Music Critic and Writer; b. 24 Nov. 1947, Bridgend, Glamorgan, Wales; m. Sally Mclaughlin, 1979. *Education:* BA, MSc, Lincoln College, Oxford. *Career:* Area Ed., The New Grove Dictionary of Music and Musicians, 1973–76; Music Critic, The Times, 1982–92, The New Yorker, 1992–. *Publications:* A Concise History of Modern Music, 1978; Boulez, 1978; A Guide to Electronic Music, 1979; Modern Music, 1980; Cage, 1981; Peter Maxwell Davies, 1982; The String Quartet, 1983; György Ligeti, 1983; Bartók, 1984; Olivier Messiaen, 1985; New Sounds, New Personalities, 1985; The Thames & Hudson Encyclopedia of 20th Century Music, 1986; Myself and Marco Polo (novel), 1987; The Life of Sir Tristram (novel), 1991; The Jewel Box (opera libretto), 1991; Stravinsky, 1992; Modern Music and After, 1995.

GRIFFITHS, Trevor; Playwright; b. 4 April 1935, Manchester, Lancashire, England; m. 1st Janice Elaine Stansfield 1960 (died 1977); one s. two d.; m. 2nd Gillian Cliff 1992. *Education:* St Bede's College, Manchester, 1945–52; BA, English, Manchester University, 1955. *Career:* Lecturer in Liberal Studies, Stockport Technical College, Cheshire, 1962–65; Co-Ed., Labour's Northern Voice, 1962–65; Series Ed., Workers Northern Publishing Society; Further Education Officer, BBC, Leeds, 1965–72. Plays: Occupations, 1970; The Party, 1973; Comedians, 1975; The Cherry Orchard, 1977; Oi for England, 1982; Real Dreams, 1984; Piano, 1990; The Gulf between Us, 1992; Thatcher's Children, 1993; Who Shall Be Happy.?, 1995. Television and film screenplays: All Good Men, 1974; Through the Night, 1975; Bill Brand, 1976; Sons and Lovers, 1981; Country, 1981; The Last Place on Earth, 1985; Hope in the Year Two, 1994; Food for Ravens, 1997. Cinema: Reds, 1981; Fatherland, 1986. Other publications include; Collected Plays for Television, 1988; Trevor Griffiths: Plays, 1996. *Honours:* BAFTA Writer's Award, 1982; Writers' Guild of America Award for Best Screenplay, 1982; RTS Award for the Best Regional Programme, 1998; BAFTA Wales, Gwyn A Williams Special Award, 1998. *Literary Agent:* PFD, Drury House, 34–43 Russell St, London WC2B 5HA, England.

GRISEZ, Germain; Prof. of Christian Ethics and Writer; b. 30 Sept. 1929, University Heights, Ohio, USA; m. Jeannette Selby, 9 June 1951, four s. *Education:* BA, John Carroll University, University Heights, Ohio, 1951; MA and PhL, Dominican College of St Thomas Aquinas, River Forest, IL, 1951; PhD, University of Chicago, 1959. *Career:* Asst Prof. to Prof., Georgetown University, 1957–72; Lecturer in Medieval Philosophy, University of Virginia at Charlottesville, 1961–62; Special Asst to Patrick Cardinal O'Boyle, Archbishop of Washington, DC, 1968–69; Consultant, Archdiocese of Washington, DC, 1969–72; Prof. of Philosophy, Campion College, University of Regina, Saskatchewan, Canada, 1972–79; Archbishop Harry J. Flynn Prof. of Christian Ethics, Mount Saint Mary's College, Emmitsburg, MD, 1979–; mem. American Catholic Philosophical Asscn, pres., 1983–84; Catholic Theological Society of America. *Publications:* Contraception and the Natural Law, 1964; Abortion: The Myths, the Realities, and the Arguments, 1970; Beyond the New Morality: The Responsibilities of Freedom (with Russell Shaw), 1974; Beyond the New Theism: A Philosophy of Religion, 1975; Free Choice: A Self-Referential Argument (with Joseph M. Boyle Jr and Olaf Tollefsen), 1976; Life and Death with Liberty and Justice: A Contribution to the Euthanasia Debate (with Joseph M. Boyle Jr), 1979; The Way of the Lord Jesus, Vol. I, Christian Moral Principles (with others), 1983, Vol. II, Living a Christian Life (with others), 1993, Vol. III, Difficult Moral Questions (with others), 1997; Nuclear Deterrence, Morality and Realism (with John Finnis and Joseph M. Boyle Jr), 1987; Fulfilment in Christ: A Summary of Christian Moral Principles (with Russell Shaw), 1991. Contributions: many scholarly journals. *Honours:* Pro ecclesia et pontifice Medal, 1972; Special Award for Scholarly Work, 1981, Cardinal Wright Award for Service to the Church, 1983, Fellowship of Catholic Scholars; various other fellowships and grants. *Address:* Mount Saint Mary's College, Emmitsburg, MD 21727, USA. *E-mail:* grisez@msmary.edu.

GRISHAM, John, BS, JD; American writer and lawyer; b. 8 Feb. 1955, Jonesboro, AR; m. Renée Jones; one s. one d. *Education:* Mississippi State Univ., Univ. of Mississippi, law school. *Career:* called to the Bar, Miss. 1981; attorney in Southaven, Miss. 1981–90; mem. Miss. House of Representatives 1984–90. *Film screenplay:* The Gingerbread Man 1998. *Publications:* A Time to Kill 1989, The Firm 1991, The Pelican Brief 1992, The Client 1993, The Chamber 1994, The Rainmaker 1995, The Runaway Jury 1996, The Partner 1997, The Street Lawyer 1998, The Testament 1999, The Brethren 2000, A Painted House 2001, Skipping Christmas 2001, The Summons 2002, The King of Torts 2003, Bleachers 2003, The Last Juror 2004. *Address:* Doubleday & Co. Inc., 1540 Broadway, New York, NY 10036, USA. *Website:* www.jgrisham.com.

GROSS, Claudia; German novelist; b. 26 July 1956, Arolsen, Hesse. *Publications include:* Scholarium 2002. *Address:* c/o The Toby Press, PO Box 8531, New Milford, CT 06776-8531, USA. *Website:* www.tobypress.com.

GROSS, John (Jacob); Writer, Critic and Ed.; b. 12 March 1935, London, England; m. Miriam May, 1965, divorced 1988, one s. one d. *Education:* MA, Wadham College, Oxford, 1955; Graduate Studies, Princeton University, 1958–59. *Career:* Ed., Victor Gollancz Ltd, 1956–58, TLS, 1974–81; Asst Lecturer, Queen Mary College, University of London, 1959–62; Fellow, King's College, Cambridge, 1962–65; Literary Ed., New Statesman, 1973; Dir, Times Newspapers Holdings, 1982; Staff, New York Times, 1983–89; Theatre Critic, Sunday Telegraph, 1989–. *Publications:* Dickens and the Twentieth Century (ed. with Gabriel Pearson), 1962; John P. Marquand,

1963; The Rise and Fall of the Man of Letters: Aspects of English Literary Life since 1800, 1969; James Joyce, 1970; Rudyard Kipling: The Man, His Work, and His World (ed.), 1972; The Oxford Book of Aphorisms (ed.), 1983; The Oxford Book of Essays (ed.), 1991; Shylock, 1992; The Modern Movement (ed.), 1992; The Oxford Book of Comic Verse (ed.), 1994. Contributions: periodicals and newspapers. *Honours:* Harkness Fellow, Princeton University, 1958–59; Duff Cooper Memorial Prize, 1969; Hon. DHL, Adelphi University, 1995. *Address:* 74 Princess Ct, Queensway, London W2 4RE, England.

GROSSKURTH, Phyllis, BA, MA, PhD; academic and writer; b. 16 March 1924, Toronto, ON, Canada; m. 1st Robert A. Grosskurth; two s. one d.; m. 2nd Mavor Moore 1968 (divorced 1980); m. 3rd Robert McMullan 1986. *Education:* Univ. of Toronto, Univ. of Ottawa, Univ. of London. *Career:* Lecturer, Carleton Univ., 1964–65; Prof. of English, 1965–87, Faculty, Humanities and Psychoanalysis Programme, 1987–95, Univ. of Toronto; mem. PEN. *Publications:* John Addington Symonds: A Biography, 1964; Notes on Browning's Works, 1967; Leslie Stephen, 1968; Gabrielle Roy, 1969; Havelock Ellis: A Biography, 1980; The Memoirs of John Addington Symonds (ed.), 1984; Melanie Klein: Her World and Her Work, 1986; Margaret Mead: A Life of Controversy, 1988; The Secret Ring: Freud's Inner Circle and the Politics of Psychoanalysis, 1991; Byron: The Flawed Angel, 1997. Contributions: periodicals. *Honours:* Hon. DSL (Trinity Coll., Univ. of Toronto) 1992, Dr hc (St Mary's Univ., Halifax) 2002; Gov.-Gen.'s Award for Non-Fiction, 1965; Univ. of British Columbia Award for Biography, 1965; Guggenheim Fellowships, 1977–78, 1983; Rockefeller Foundation Fellowship, 1982; Canada Council Arts Award, 1989–90; Social Science and Humanities Research Grant, 1982–92. *Address:* 147 Spruce Street, Toronto, ON M5A 26J, Canada.

GROSSMAN, David, BA; Israeli writer; b. 25 Jan. 1954, Jerusalem; m. Michal Grossman, two s. one d. *Education:* Hebrew Univ., Jerusalem. *Publications:* Hiyukh ha-gedi (trans. as The Smile of the Lamb) 1983, 'Ayen 'erekh–ahavah (trans. as See Under: Love) 1986, Ha-Zeman ha-tsahov (non-fiction, trans. as The Yellow Wind) 1987, Gan Riki: Mahazeh bi-shete ma'arakhot (play, trans. as Rikki's Kindergarten) 1988, Sefer hakikduk hapnimi (trans. as The Book of Intimate Grammar) 1991, Hanochachim hanifkadim (non-fiction, trans. as Sleeping on a Wire: Conversations with Palestinians in Israel) 1992, The Zigzag Kid (trans., Premio Mondelo, Premio Grinzane), Duel (trans.), Be My Knife (trans.) 2002, Someone to Run With (trans.) 2003, Death as a Way of Life: Dispatches from Jerusalem (non-fiction, trans.) 2003, Her Body Knows (novel in trans.); also short stories, children's books, contribs to periodicals. *Honours:* Ministry of Education Children's Literature Prize1983, Prime Minister's Hebrew Literature Prize 1984, Israeli Publisher's Asscn Prize for Best Novel 1985, Vallombrosa Prize, Italy 1989, Nelly Sachs Prize, Germany 1992. *Address:* c/o Bloomsbury Publishing PLC, 38 Soho Square, London, W1D 3HB, England.

GRUFFYDD, Peter; Writer, Poet, Trans. and Actor; b. 12 April 1935, Liverpool, England; m. 1st, one s. one d.; m. 2nd Susan Soar, 28 Dec. 1974, two s. *Education:* BA, University of Wales, Bangor, 1960. *Career:* mem. Equity; PEN International, founder-mem., Welsh Branch, 1993; Welsh Union of Writers; Yr Academi Gymraeg. *Publications:* Triad, 1963; Welsh Voices, 1967; Poems, 1969; The Lilting House, 1970; Poems, 1972; The Shivering Seed, 1972; On Censorship, 1985; Environmental Teletex, 1989; Damned Braces, 1993. Contributions: anthologies and periodicals. *Honours:* Eric Gregory Trust, 1963; Second Prize, Young Poets Competition, Welsh Arts Council, 1969; First Prizes, 1984, 1994, Third Prizes, 1986, 1991, 1993, Aberystwyth Open Poetry Competitions; Duncan Lawrie Prize, Arvon-Observer International Poetry Competition, 1993. *Address:* 21 Beech Rd, Norton, Stourbridge, West Midlands DY8 2AS, England.

GRUMBACH, Doris (Isaac); Author, Critic and Prof. of English (retd); b. 12 July 1918, New York, NY, USA; m. Leonard Grumbach, 15 Oct. 1941, divorced 1972, four d. *Education:* AB, Washington Square College, 1939; MA, Cornell University, 1940. *Career:* Assoc. Ed., Architectural Forum, 1942–43; Teacher of English, Albany Acad. for Girls, New York, 1952–55; Instructor, 1955–58, Asst Prof., 1958–60, Assoc. Prof., 1960–69, Prof. of English, 1969–73, College of Saint Rose, Albany; Visiting University Fellow, Empire State College, 1972–73; Literary Ed., New Republic, 1973–75; Adjunct Prof. of English, University of Maryland, 1974–75; Prof. of American Literature, American University, Washington, DC, 1975–85; Columnist and reviewer for various publications, radio, and television; mem. PEN. *Publications:* The Spoil of the Flowers, 1962; The Short Throat, the Tender Mouth, 1964; The Company She Kept (biog. of Mary McCarthy), 1967; Chamber Music, 1979; The Missing Person, 1981; The Ladies, 1984; The Magician's Girl, 1987; Coming Into the End Zone, 1992; Extra Innings: A Memoir, 1993; Fifty Days of Solitude, 1994; The Book of Knowledge: A Novel, 1995; The Presence of Absence, 1998; The Pleasure of Their Company, 2000. Contributions: books and periodicals. *Address:* c/o Maxine Groffsky, 2 Fifth Ave, New York, NY 10011, USA.

GRUN, Max von der; Author; b. 25 May 1926, Bayreuth, Germany; m. Elke Hüser, one s. one d. *Education:* Commercial Studies; Bricklayer Apprenticeship. *Career:* mem. PEN Club; Verband Deutscher Schriftsteller. *Publications:* Männer in zweifacher Nacht, 1962; Irrlicht und Feuer, 1963; Zwei Briefe an Pospischiel, 1968; Stellenweise Glatteis, 1973; Menschen in Deutschland, 1973; Leben im gelobten Land, 1975; Wenn der rote Rabe von Baum fällt, 1975; Vorstadtkrokodile, 1976; Wie war das eigentlich?: Kindheit und Jugend im Dritten Reich, 1979; Flächenbrand, 1979; Etwas ausserhalb der Legalität, 1980; Meine Fabrik, 1980; Klassengespräche, 1981; Späte Liebe, 1982; Friedrich und Friederlike, 1983; Die Lawine, 1986; Springflut, 1990; Die Saujagd und andere Vorstadtgeschichten, 1995. *Honours:* Grand Cultural Prize of the City of Nuremberg, 1974; Wilhelm Lubke Prize, 1979; Gerrit Engelke Prize, Hannover, 1985. *Address:* Bremsstrasse 40, 44239, Dortmund, Germany.

GRÜNBAUM, Adolf; American academic and writer; b. 15 May 1923, Cologne, Germany; m. Thelma Braverman 1949; one d. *Education:* BA, Wesleyan University, 1943; MS, Physics, 1948, PhD, Philosophy, 1951, Yale University. *Career:* Faculty, 1950–55, Prof. of Philosophy, 1955–56, Selfridge Prof. of Philosophy, 1956–60, Lehigh University; Visiting Research Prof., Minnesota Center for the Philosophy of Science, 1956, 1959; Andrew Mellon Prof. of Philosophy of Science, 1960–, Dir, 1960–78, later Chair., Center for the Philosophy of Science, Research Prof. of Psychiatry, 1979–, University of Pittsburgh; Werner Heisenberg Lecturer, Bavarian Acad. of Sciences, 1985; Gifford Lecturer, University of St Andrews, 1985; Visiting Mellon Prof., California Institute of Technology, 1990; Leibniz Lecturer, Univ. of Hannover, 2003; mem. American Acad. of Arts and Sciences; American Philosophical Asscn; Académie Internationale de Philosophie des Sciences; International Acad. of Humanism; Philosophy of Science Asscn, pres., 1965–70; American Asscn for the Advancement of Science. *Publications:* Philosophical Problems of Space and Time, 1963; Modern Science and Zeno's Paradoxes, second edn, 1968; Geometry and Chronometry in Philosophical Perspective, 1968; The Foundations of Psychoanalysis: A Philosophical Critique, 1984; Psicoanalisi: Obiezioni e Risposte, 1988; Validation in the Clinical Theory of Psychoanalysis, 1993; La Psychanalyse à l'Épreuve, 1993. Contributions: books and scholarly journals. *Honours:* J. Walker Tomb Prize, Princeton University, 1958; Honour Citation, Wesleyan University, 1959; Festschriften published in his honour, 1983, 1993; Senior US Scientist Prize, Alexander von Humboldt Foundation, 1985; Fregene Prize for Science, Italian Parliament, 1989; Master Scholar and Prof. Award, University of Pittsburgh, 1989; Wilbur Lucius Cross Medal, Yale University, 1990; Hon. Doctorate, University of Konstanz, Germany, 1995. *Address:* 7141 Roycrest Place, Pittsburgh, PA 15208, USA.

GU HUA; Chinese novelist; b. ((Luo Hongyu)), 20 June 1942, Jiahe County, Hunan. *Education:* Chenzhou Agricultural School, Coll. for Young Writers. *Career:* research worker, Chenzhou Agricultural Research Inst. 1961–75; mem. writing staff, Chenzhou Song and Dance Ensemble 1975–79; mem. Writers' Asscn of Hunan Prov. 1981–87; Hon. Fellow Univ. of Iowa, Int. Writing Program 1987–. *Publications include:* A Log Cabin Overgrown with Creepers, A Small Town Called Hibiscus, The Prison for the Scholars, Virgin Widows, Pagoda Ridge. *Address:* Chenzhou Association of Literary and Art Workers, Chenzhou, People's Republic of China.

GUARE, John; Dramatist; b. 5 Feb. 1938, New York, NY, USA; m. Adele Chatfield-Taylor, 20 May 1981. *Education:* AB, Georgetown University, 1961; MFA, Yale University, 1963. *Career:* Co-Founder, Eugene O'Neill Theater Center, Waterford, CT, 1965; Resident Playwright, New York Shakespeare Festival, 1976; Seminar-in-Writing Fellow, 1977–78, Adjunct Prof., 1978–81, Yale University; Co-Ed., Lincoln Center New Theatre Review, 1977–; Visiting Artist, Harvard University, 1990–91; Fellow, Juilliard School, 1993–94; mem. American Acad. of Arts and Letters; Dramatists Guild. *Publications:* Plays: Theatre Girl, 1959; The Toadstool Boy, 1960; The Golden Cherub, 1962; Did You Write My Name in the Snow?, 1962; To Wally Pantoni, We Leave a Credenza, 1964; The Loveliest Afternoon of the Year, 1966; Something I'll Tell You Tuesday, 1966; Muzeeka, 1967; Cop-Out, 1968; A Play by Brecht, 1969; Home Fires, 1969; Kissing Sweet, 1969; The House of Blue Leaves, 1971, as a musical, 1986; Two Gentlemen of Verona, 1971; A Day for Surprises, 1971; Un Pape a New York, 1972; Marco Polo Sings a Solo, 1973; Optimism, or the Adventures of Candide, 1973; Rich and Famous, 1974; Landscape of the Body, 1977; Take a Dream, 1978; Bosoms and Neglect, 1979; In Fireworks Lie Secret Codes, 1981; Lydie Breeze, 1982; Gardenia, 1982; Stay a While, 1984; Women and Water, 1984; Gluttony, 1985; The Talking Dog, 1985; Moon Over Miami, 1989, revised version as Moon Under Miami, 1995; Six Degrees of Separation, 1990; Four Baboons Adoring the Sun, 1992; Chuck Close, 1995; The War Against the Kitchen Sink (vol. of plays), 1996. *Honours:* Obie Awards, 1968, 1971, 1990; New York Drama Critics Circle Awards, 1969, 1971, 1972, 1990; Drama Desk Awards, 1972; Tony Awards, 1972, 1986; Joseph Jefferson Award, 1977; Award of Merit, American Acad. of Arts and Letters, 1981; Los Angeles Film Critics Award, 1981; National Society of Film Critics Circle Award, 1981; New York Film Critics Award, 1981; Venice Film Festival Grand Prize, 1981; Olivier Best Play Award, 1993; New York State Governor's Award, 1996. *Address:* c/o R. Andrew Boose, 1 Dag Hammarskjöld Plaza, New York, NY 10017, USA.

GUARNIERI, Patrizia; Historian, Lecturer in Italian and History of Science and Narrative Trans; b. 16 June 1954, Florence, Italy; m. Franco Cardini, 2 Aug. 1991, one s. one d. *Education:* MA, Philosophy, University of Florence, 1977; PhD, University of Urbino, 1979; Fulbright Visiting Scholar, Harvard University, Massachusetts, 1981. *Career:* Lecturer in Italian Culture and Language, University of Florence, 1978–81, Stanford University Programme in Italy, 1982–93; Prof., History of Science, University of Trieste, 1988–91; mem. Scientific Council, European Asscn of the

History of Psychiatry. *Publications:* Introduzione a James, 1985; Individualita' Difformi, 1986; L'Ammazzabambini, 1988, English edn as A Case of Child Murder, 1992; Between Soma and Psyche, 1988; Theatre and Laboratory, 1988; The Psyche in Trance, 1990; Carta Penna e Psiche, 1990; La Storia della Psichiatria, 1991; Per Una Storia delle Scienze del Bambino, 1996; Dangerous Girls, Family Secrets and Incest Law in Italy, 1998. Contributions: Kos; Physis; Nuncius; Belfagor. *Honours:* CNR-NATO Fellow, 1983; Jean Monnet Fellow, 1989. *Address:* Via A. Baldesi 12, 50131 Florence, Italy.

GUCCIONE, Robert Charles Joseph Edward Sabatini; American publisher; *Chairman, CEO and Publisher, General Media Inc.*; b. 17 Dec. 1930, Brooklyn; m. Kathy Keeton 1988; five c. from previous m. *Career:* artist 1948–55, 1992–; fmr cartoonist and greetings card designer; Man. London American; founder and publr Penthouse Magazine, 1965–; also Publr Forum, Variations, Penthouse Letters, Omni, Saturday Review, Four Wheeler, Longevity, Girls of Penthouse, Compute, Open Wheel, Stock Car Racing, Superstock and Drag, Hot Talk; Chair. CEO Gen. Media Inc. 1988–; producer of film Caligula 1979; exec. producer, TV show Omni: The New Frontier, Omni: Visions of Tomorrow. *Address:* General Media Inc., 11 Penn Plaza, New York, NY 10001, USA (Office). *Telephone:* (212) 702-6000 (Office). *Fax:* (212) 702-6262 (Office).

GUERARD, Albert Joseph; Prof. of English (retd) and Writer; b. 2 Nov. 1914, Houston, Texas, USA; m. 11 July 1941, three d. *Education:* BA, 1934, PhD, 1938, Stanford University; MA, Harvard University, 1996. *Career:* Instructor, Amherst College, 1935–36; Instructor to Prof. of English, Harvard University, 1938–61; Prof. of English, Stanford University, 1961–85; mem. American Acad. of Arts and Sciences. *Publications:* The Past Must Alter, 1937; The Hunted, 1944; Maguisard, 1945; Robert Bridges, 1942; Joseph Conrad, 1947; Thomas Hardy, 1949; Night Journey, 1950; André Gide, 1951; Conrad The Novelist, 1958; The Touch of Time, 1980; Christine/Annette, 1985; Gabrielle, 1993; The Hotel in the Jungle, 1995; Suspended Sentences, 1999. Contributions: journals, periodicals, reviews and magazines. *Address:* c/o Dept of English, Stanford University, Stanford, CA 94305, USA.

GUEST, Harry, (Henry Bayly Guest); Poet and Writer; b. 6 Oct. 1932, Glamorganshire, Wales; m. Lynn Doremus Dunbar, 28 Dec. 1963, one s. one d. *Education:* BA, Trinity Hall, Cambridge, 1954, DES, Sorbonne, University of Paris, 1955. *Career:* Lecturer, Yokohama National University, 1966–72; Head of Modern Languages, Exeter School, 1972–91; Teacher of Japanese, Exeter University, 1979–95; mem. Poetry Society, General Council, 1972–76. *Publications:* Arrangements, 1968; The Cutting-Room, 1970; Post-War Japanese Poetry (ed. and trans.), 1972; A House Against the Night, 1976; Days, 1978; The Distance, the Shadows, 1981; Lost and Found, 1983; The Emperor of Outer Space (radio play), 1983; Lost Pictures, 1991; Coming to Terms, 1994; Traveller's Literary Companion to Japan, 1994; So Far, 1998; The Artist on the Artist, 2000; A Puzzling Harvest, 2002. Contributions: reviews, quarterlies, and journals. *Honours:* Hawthornden Fellow, 1993; Hon. Research Fellow, Exeter University, 1994–; Hon. Doctor of Letters, Plymouth University, 1998. *Address:* 1 Alexandra Terrace, Exeter, Devon EX4 6SY, England.

GUILLOU, Jan; Writer and Journalist; b. 17 Jan. 1944, Södertälje, Sweden. *Career:* fmr journalist; writer, 1970s–. *Publications:* Om Kriget Kommer, 1971; Det Stora Avslöjandet, 1974; Journalistik, 1976; Irak—Det Nya Arabien, 1977; Artister, 1979; Reporter, 1979; Ondskan, 1981; Berättelser Från Det Nya Riket, 1982; Jiristiemord, 1983; Nya Berättelser, 1984; Coq Rouge: Berättelsen On En Svensk Spion, 1986; Den Demokratiske Terroristen, 1987; I Nationens Intresse, 1988; Fiendens Fiende, 1989; Reporter, 1989; Åsikter, 1990; En Hedervärde Mördaren, 1990; Gudarnas Berg, 1990; Stora Machoboken, 1991; Vendetta, 1991; Grabbarnas Kokbok, 1992; Ingen Mans Land, 1992; Den Enda Segern, 1993; I Hennes Majestäts Tjänst, 1994; En Medborgare Höjd Över Varje Misstanke, 1995; Hamlon: Skiss Till En Möjlig Fortsättning, 1995; On Jakt Och Jägare: Från Fagerhult Till Sibirien, 1996; Svenskarna, Invandrarna Och Svartskallarna: Mitt Livs Viktigaste Reportage, 1996; Antirasistiskt Lexikon, 1997; Vägen Till Jerusalem, 1998; Tempelriddaren, 1999; Riket Vid Vägens Slut, 2000; Arvet Efter Arn, 2001; Häxornas Försvarare, 2002. Other: Talismanen (TV series, with Henning Mankell), 2001. Contributions: Folket i Bild/Kulturfront. *Address:* c/o Orion House, 5 Upper St Martin's Lane, London WC2H 9EA, England.

GUNESEKERA, Romesh; Writer and Poet; b. 1954, Colombo, Sri Lanka. *Publications:* Monkfish Moon, 1992; Reef, 1995; The Sandglass, 1998; Heaven's Edge, 2002. *Honours:* Notable Book of the Year, New York Times, 1993; Best First Work Award, Yorkshire Post, 1994; Premio Mondello, 1997. *Address:* c/o Granta USA Ltd, 250 W 57th St, 13th Floor, New York, NY 10107, USA.

GUNNARS, Kristjana, MA; Icelandic writer, poet, translator and professor of English; b. 19 March 1948, Reykjavík; one c. *Education:* Oregon State Univ. (USA) and Univ. of Regina (SK). *Career:* Asst Ed. Iceland Review, Iceland 1980–81; freelance writer, translator and ed. 1981–; Writer-in-Residence Regina Public Library, Canada 1988–89, Univ. of Alberta, Edmonton, Canada 1989–90, Assoc. Prof. of English 1991, Prof. 1991–; Lecturer Okanagan Coll., BC, Canada 1990–91; mem. PEN, Writers' Union of Canada, League of Canadian Poets, Composers', Authors' and Publishers' Asscn of Canada, Alliance of Canadian Cinema, TV and Radio Artists. *Publications:* Settlement Poems I and II 1980, 1981, One-Eyed Moon Maps 1981, Wake-Pick Poems 1982, Stephan G. Stephansson, In Retrospect (trans) 1982, The Axe's Edge 1983, The Night Workers of Ragnarök 1985, The Papers of Dorothy Livesay (jtly) 1985, Crossing the River: Essays in Honor of Margaret Laurence (ed) 1988, Stephan G. Stephansson, Selected Prose and Poetry (trans) 1988, The Prowler 1989, Carnival of Longing 1989, Zero Hour 1991, Unexpected Fictions, New Icelandic Canadian Writing (ed), The Guest House and Other Stories 1992, The Substance of Forgetting 1992, The Rose Garden 1993, Exiles Among You 1996, Night Train to Nykøbing 1996, When Chestnut Trees Blossom 2002. *Address:* University of Alberta, Dept of English, Edmonton, AB T6G 2E2, Canada.

GUNSTON, Bill, (William Tudor Gunston); Author; b. 1 March 1927, London, England; m. Margaret Anne, 10 Oct. 1964, two d. *Education:* University College, Durham, 1945–46; City University, London, 1948–51. *Career:* Pilot, Royal Air Force, 1946–48; Editorial Staff, 1951–55, Technical Ed., 1955–64, Flight; Technology Ed., Science Journal, 1964–70; Freelance author, 1970–; Dir, So Few Ltd; Ed., Jane's Aero-Engines, 1995–. *Publications:* Over 370 books including: The Development of Piston Aero Engines, 1999; Modern Fighting Helicopters, 1999; Aerospace Dictionary, 1999; The Illustrated History of McDonnell Douglas Aircraft, 2000; Hamlyn History of Military Aviation, 2000; Soviet X-planes, 2000; The Encyclopedia of Modern Warplanes, 2001; Aviation Year by Year, 2001; Rolls-Royce Aero Engines, 2001; Aviation: The First 100 Years, 2002; The Development of Jet and Turbine Aero Engines, 2002; Flight Path (biog.), 2002. Contributions: 188 periodicals; 18 partworks; 75 video scripts. *Honours:* Royal Aeronautical Society, fellow; OBE. *Address:* High Beech, Kingsley Green, Haslemere, Surrey GU27 3LL, England.

GUPPY, Stephen Anthony; Writer, Poet and Teacher; b. 10 Feb. 1951, Nanaimo, BC, Canada; m. Nelinda Kazenbroot, 1986, one s. one d. *Education:* BA, 1971, Teaching Certificate, 1982, MA, 1988, University of Victoria. *Career:* Teacher, School District No. 69, Qualicum, BC, 1982–85; Instructor of English and Creative Writing, Malaspina University College, Nanaimo, 1986–. *Publications:* Ghostcatcher (poems), 1979; Rainshadow: Stories from Vancouver Island (anthology, co-ed.), 1982; Another Sad Day at the Edge of the Empire (short stories), 1985; Blind Date with the Angel (poems), 1998. Contributions: Short stories to anthologies including: Best Canadian Short Stories; The Journey Prize Anthology. *Honours:* Second Prize, Scottish International Open Poetry Competition, 1997. *Address:* 2184 Michigan Way, Nanaimo, BC V9R 5S5, Canada. *E-mail:* guppy@mala.bc.can.

GUPTA, Tanika; British playwright; b. 1963, London. *Education:* Univ. of Oxford. *Plays include:* The Good Woman of Szechuan, Voices in the Wind, Skeleton 1998, The Waiting Room 2000, Sanctuary 2002, Inside Out 2002, Fragile Land 2003, Hobson's Choice by Harold Brighouse (adaptation) 2003. *Films include:* Bideshi 1995, Flight 1995. *Television:* EastEnders (BBC1), The Bill (Thames/ITV), A Suitable Boy (adaptation, BBC2). *Literary Agent:* The Agency (London) Ltd, 24 Pottery Lane, Holland Park, London, W11 4LZ, England. *Telephone:* (20) 7727-1346. *Fax:* (20) 7727-9037. *E-mail:* info@theagency.co.uk. *Website:* www.theagency.co.uk.

GURGANUS, Allan; Writer and Artist; b. 11 June 1947, Rocky Mount, NC, USA. *Education:* Monterey Language School, 1966; Radioman and Cryptography School, 1966; University of Pennsylvania, 1966–67; Pennsylvania Acad. of Fine Arts, 1966–67; Harvard University, 1969–70; BA, Sarah Lawrence College, 1972; MFA, University of Iowa Writers' Workshop, 1974; Stanford University, 1974–76. *Career:* Prof. of Fiction Writing, 1972–74, Writer's Workshop, 1989–90, University of Iowa: Prof. of Fiction Writing, Stanford University, 1974–76, Duke University, 1976–78, Sarah Lawrence College, 1978–86; Artist. *Publications:* Oldest Living Confederate Widow Tells All, 1989; White People: Stories and Novellas, 1991; Practical Heart, 1993; Plays Well With Others, 1997; The Practical Heart: Four Novellas, 2001. Contributions: periodicals. *Honours:* National Endowment for the Arts Grants, 1976–77, 1987–88; Ingram Merrill Grant, 1986; Sue Kaufman Prize for First Fiction, American Acad. and Institute of Arts and Letters, 1990; Books Across the Sea Ambassador Book Award, English-Speaking Union of the United States, 1990; Los Angeles Times Book Prize, 1991. *Address:* c/o Amanda Urban, International Creative Management, 40 W 57th St, New York, NY 10019, USA.

GURNAH, Abdulrazak; Novelist, Literary Critic and Editor; b. 1948, Zanzibar, Tanzania. *Career:* Lecturer in English Literature, Univ. of Kent; Assoc. Ed., journal Wasafiri. *Publications:* Memory of Departure, 1987; Pilgrim's Way, 1988; Dottie, 1990; Essays on African Writing: A Re-Evaluation (ed.), 1993; Paradise, 1994; Essays on African Writing: Contemporary Literature (ed.), 1995; Admiring Silence, 1996; By the Sea, 2001; numerous works for radio. Contributions: Wole Soyinka: An Appraisal, 1994; Modernism and Empire, 1998; Essays and Criticism, 2000; New Writing 9. *Address:* c/o School of English, Rutherford College, University of Kent, Canterbury, Kent CT2 7NX, England. *Telephone:* (1227) 764000. *Fax:* (1227) 827001. *E-mail:* A.S.Gurnah@ukc.ac.uk.

GURNEY, Albert Ramsdell, BA, MFA; academic, dramatist and writer; b. 1 Nov. 1930, Buffalo, NY, USA; m. Mary Goodyear 1957; two s. two d. *Education:* Williams College, Yale University School of Drama. *Career:* Faculty, 1960–70, Prof. of Literature, 1970–96, MIT. *Publications:* Plays: Children, 1974; The Dining Room, 1982; The Perfect Party, 1986; Another

Antigone, 1986; Sweet Sue, 1986; The Cocktail Hour, 1988; Love Letters, 1989; The Old Boy, 1991; The Fourth Wall, 1992; Later Life, 1993; A Cheever Evening, 1994; Sylvia, 1995; Overtime, 1995; Labor Day, 1998; The Guest Lecturer, 1999; Far East, 1999; Ancestral Voices, 1999; Human Events, 2000; Buffalo Gal, 2001; O Jerusalem, 2002; Big Bill, 2003. Fiction: The Gospel According to Joe, 1974; The Snow Ball, 1985. Screenplay: The House of Mirth, 1972. Television Play: O Youth and Beauty (from a story by John Cheever), 1979. *Honours:* Drama Desk Award, 1971; Rockefeller Foundation Grant, 1977; National Endowment for the Arts Award, 1982; Theatre Award, American Acad. of Arts and Sciences, 1990; Lucille Lortel Award, 1992; Hon. doctorates. *Address:* 40 Wellers Bridge Road, Roxbury, CT 06783, USA.

GURR, Andrew (John); Prof. and Writer; b. 23 Dec. 1936, Leicester, England; m. Elizabeth Gordon, 1 July 1961, three s. *Education:* BA, 1957, MA 1958, University of Auckland, New Zealand; PhD, University of Cambridge, 1963. *Career:* Lecturer, Leeds University, 1962; Prof., University of Nairobi, 1969; University of Reading, 1976–; mem. International Shakespeare Asscn; Asscn of Commonwealth Literature and Language Studies; Society for Theatre Research; Malone Society. *Publications:* The Shakespeare Stage 1574–1642, 1970; Writers in Exile, 1982; Katherine Mansfield, 1982; Playgoing in Shakespeare's London, 1987; Studying Shakespeare, 1988; Rebuilding Shakespeare's Globe, 1989; The Shakespearian Playing Companies, 1996. Editor: Plays of Shakespeare and Beaumont and Fletcher. Contributions: scholarly journals and periodicals. *Address:* c/o Dept of English, University of Reading, PO Box 218, Reading, Berkshire RG6 2AA, England.

GURR, David; Writer; b. 5 Feb. 1936, London, England; m. Judith Deverell, 30 Aug. 1958, divorced 1991, two s. one d. *Education:* Canadian Naval College, 1954–56; BSc, University of Victoria, BC, 1965. *Career:* Career Officer, Royal Canadian Navy, 1954–70; House Designer and Builder, 1972–81; mem. Crime Writers of Canada; Writers' Guild of America; Writers' Union of Canada. *Publications:* Troika, 1979; A Woman Called Scylla, 1981; An American Spy Story, 1984; The Action of the Tiger, 1984; On the Endangered List, 1985; The Ring Master, 1987; The Voice of the Crane, 1989; Arcadia West: The Novel, 1994; The Charlatan, 2000. *Address:* c/o Henry Morrison, Henry Morrison Inc, Box 235, Bedford Hills, NY 10507, USA.

GUSTAFSSON, Lars Erik Einar; writer, poet, dramatist and academic; b. 17 May 1936, Västeras, Sweden. *Education:* Licentiate, Philosophy, 1960, DPhil, 1978, University of Uppsala. *Career:* Assoc. Ed., 1960–65, Ed.-in-Chief, 1965–72, Bonniers Litterära Magasin; Deutscher Akademischer Austauschdienst Fellow, Berlin, 1972–73; Research Fellow, Bielefeld Institute of Advanced Studies, Germany, 1981–82; Adjunct Prof. of German Studies, 1982–98, Jamail Distinguished Prof., 1998–, University of Austin at Texas; Aby Warburg Foundation Prof., Warburg Stiftung, Hamburg, 1997; mem. Akademie der Künste, Berlin; Akademie der Wissenschaften und der Literatur, Mainz; Akademie der Schönen Künste, Munich Royal Swedish Acad. of Engineering; Authors' Guild of America; PEN International, Sweden. *Publications:* more than 50 works, including fiction, non-fiction, poetry, and drama 1957–99. Contributions: various publications. *Honours:* Swedish Novel Prize, 1979; Prix International Charles Veillon des Essais, 1983; Officier, Ordre des Arts et des Lettres, 1986; Heinrich Steffens Prize, Germany, 1986; Kommendör des Bundesverdienstzeichens, Germany, 1988; Bellman Prize, Royal Swedish Acad., 1990; Poetry Prize, Swedish Broadcasting Corp, 1993; Guggenheim Fellowship, 1994; Pilot Prize, Sweden, 1996. *Address:* 2312 Tower Drive, Austin, TX 78703, USA.

GUTCHEON, Beth R(ichardson); Writer; b. 18 March 1945, Sewickley, PA, USA; m. Jeffrey Gutcheon, 18 March 1968, one s. *Education:* BA, Radcliffe College, 1967. *Publications:* Fiction: The New Girls, 1979; Still Missing, 1981; Domestic Pleasures, 1991; Saying Grace, 1995; Five Fortunes, 1998; More Than You Know, 2000. Non-Fiction: The Perfect Patchwork Primer, 1973; Abortion: A Woman's Guide, 1973; The Quilt Design Workbook (with Jeffrey Gutcheon), 1975. Film Scripts: The Children of Theatre Street, 1977; Without a Trace, 1983; The Good Fight, 1992. Contributions: periodicals. *Address:* c/o HarperTrade, 10 E 53rd St, New York, NY 10022, USA.

GUTERSON, David, BA, MFA; American author; b. 4 May 1956, Seattle; m. Robin Ann Radwick 1979; three s. one d. *Education:* Univ. of Washington, Brown Univ. *Career:* high school English teacher Bainbridge Island, Washington 1984–94; contrib. sports journalism for Sports Illustrated and Harper's, fmr Contributing Ed. Harper's. *Publications:* The Country Ahead of Us, The Country Behind (short stories) 1989, Family Matters: Why Home Schooling Makes Sense 1992, Snow Falling on Cedars (PEN/Faulkner Award for Ficition, Barnes & Noble Discovery Award, Pacific NW Booksellers Award 1995) 1994, East of the Mountains 1998, Our Lady of the Forest 2003. *Literary Agent:* Georges Borchardt Inc., 136 East 57th Street, New York, NY 10020, USA.

GUTHRIE, Alan (see Tubb, Edwin Charles).

GUTIÉRREZ, Pedro Juan; Novelist, Journalist and Poet; b. 1950, Matanzas, Cuba. *Education:* Journalism, Universidad de la Habana. *Career:* fmrly diverse range of employment, incl. ice-cream seller, soldier, sugar cane cutter, and many others; currently journalist, Bohemia journal, Havana. *Publications:* Trilogía sucia de La Habana (Dirty Havana Trilogy, short story collections): Anclado en Tierra de Nada, Nada que hacer, Sabor a mí; El rey de la Habana (novel); Animal tropical (Tropical Animal, novel); El insaciable hombre araña (novel); Dime algo sobre Cuba; Antes que anochezca; El libro de la realidad; Carne de perro; numerous collections of poetry. *Honours:* Premio Alfonso García-Ramos, Spain, 2000. *Address:* Apdo Postal 6239, 10600 Havana, Cuba.

GUTTERIDGE, Donald George; poet, writer and academic; b. 30 Sept. 1937, Sarnia, ON, Canada; m. Anne Barnett 1961; one s. one d. *Education:* Chatham College Institute, Ontario, 1956; BA, University of Western Ontario, London, 1960. *Career:* Asst Prof., 1968–75, Assoc. Prof., 1975–77, Prof. of English Methods, 1977–93, Prof. Emeritus, 1993–, University of Western Ontario. *Publications:* Poetry: Riel: A Poem for Voices, 1968; The Village Within, 1970; Death at Quebec and Other Poems, 1972; Saying Grace: An Elegy, 1972; Coppermine: The Quest for North, 1973; Borderlands, 1975; Tecumseh, 1976; A True History of Lambton County, 1977; God's Geography, 1982; The Exiled Heart: Selected Narratives, 1986; Love in the Wintertime, 1982; Flute Music in the Cello's Belly, 1997; Bloodlines, 2001. Fiction: Bus-Ride, 1974; All in Good Time, 1980; St Vitus Dance, 1986; Shaman's Ground, 1988; How the World Began, 1991; Summer's Idyll, 1993; Winter's Descent, 1996; Bewilderment, 2001; Turncoat, 2003; Solemn Vows, 2003. *Honours:* Pres.'s Medal, University of Western Ontario, 1971; Canada Council Travel Grant, 1973. *Address:* 114 Victoria Street, London, ON N6A 2B5, Canada. *E-mail:* dongutteridge@rogers.com.

GUY, Rosa (Cuthbert); Writer; b. 9 Jan. 1928, Trinidad. *Career:* Writer-in-Residence, Michigan Technical University; mem. Harlem Writers Guild, pres.; PEN. *Publications:* The Friends, 1973; Ruby, 1976; Edith Jackson, 1978; The Disappearance, 1979; A Measure of Time, 1983; New Guys Around the Block, 1983; Pee Wee and Big Dog, 1984; I Heard a Bird Sing, 1986; Music of Summer, 1992; My Love My Love, 1996. Play: Once on This Island (adaptation of My Love My Love), 1990. Contributions: New York Times Sunday Magazine; Red Book; Cosmopolitan. *Honours:* The Other Award, England; Best of the Best, New York Times. *Literary Agent:* Ellen Levine Literary Agency. *Address:* 20 W 72nd St, New York, NY 10023, USA.

GWYNN, Robert Samuel; Professor of English, Writer, Poet and Ed.; b. 13 May 1948, Leaksville, NC, USA; m. 1st Faye La Prade, 1969, divorced 1977; m. 2nd Donna Kay Skaggs Simon, 1 June 1977, one s. *Education:* BA, Davidson College, 1969; MA, MFA, University of Arkansas, 1973. *Career:* Instructor in English, Southwest Texas State University, San Marcos, 1973–76; University Prof. of English, Lamar University, Beaumont, TX, 1976–; many poetry readings throughout the USA; mem. Associated Writing Programs; Poetry Society of America; Conference of College Teachers of English; South Central MLA; Texas Asscn of Creative Writing Teachers; Texas Institute of Letters. *Publications:* Bearing and Distance (poems), 1977; The Narcissiad (poems), 1981; The Drive-In, 1986; Dictionary of Literary Biography, Second Series, Vol. 105: American Poets Since World War II (ed., contributor), 1991; Drama: A HarperCollins Pocket Anthology (ed.), 1993; Fiction: A HarperCollins Pocket Anthology (ed.), 1993; Poetry: A HarperCollins Pocket Anthology (ed.), 1993; The Area Code of God (poems), 1994; The Advocates of Poetry: A Reader of American Poet-Critics of the Modern Era, 1996; No Word of Farewell (poems), 1996; Fiction: A Longman Pocket Anthology (ed., contributor), 1997. Contributions: anthologies including: Texas Poets in Concert: A Quartet; Rebel Angels: Twenty-Five Poets of the New Formation; The Store of Joys; More than 70 articles, poems and reviews to periodicals including: Sparrow; Tar River Poetry; Sewanee Review; Hudson Review; Poetry Northwest; Texas Monthly. *Address:* 225 Canterbury Drive, Beaumont, TX 77707, USA. *E-mail:* rsgwynn@mail.com.

H

HA JIN, BA, MA, PhD; writer and poet; b. (Xuefei Jin), 21 Feb. 1956, Jinzhou, People's Republic of China; m. Lisah Bian 1982; one c. *Education:* Heilongjian Univ., Harbin, Shangdong Univ., Jinan, Brandeis Univ. *Career:* Faculty, Dept of English, Emory Univ., 1993–2002, Boston Univ., 2002–. *Publications:* Fiction: Ocean of Words: Army Stories, 1996; Under the Red Flag, 1997; In the Pond, 1998; Waiting, 1999; The Bridegroom (short stories), 2000; The Crazed, 2002; War Trash (novel), 2004. Poetry: Between Silences, 1990; Facing Shadows, 1996; Wreckage, 2001. *Honours:* PEN/Hemingway Award, 1997; Flannery O'Connor Award, 1997; National Book Award, 1999; PEN/Faulkner Award, 2000; Asian American Literary Award, 2001. *Address:* c/o Dept of English, 236 Bay State Road, Boston University, Boston, MA 02215, USA.

HAAVIKKO, Paavo (Juhani); Poet, Author, Dramatist and Publisher; b. 25 Jan. 1931, Helsinki, Finland; m. 1st Marja-Liisa Vartio 1955 (died 1966); one s. one d.; m. 2nd Ritva Rainio 1971. *Career:* Literary Dir, Otava Publishing Co, 1967–83; Publisher, Art House Publishing Group, 1983–; mem. Finnish Writers' Asscn, board mem., 1962–66. *Publications:* Tiet etäisyyksiin, 1951; Tuuliönä, 1953; Synnyinmaa, 1955; Lehdet lehtiä, 1958; Talvipalatsi, 1959; Yksityisiä Asioita, 1960; Toinen taivas ja maa, 1961; Runot, 1962; Vuodet, 1962; Lasi Claudius Civiliksen salaliittolaisten pöydällä, 1964; Puut, kaikki heidän vihreytensä, 1966; Selected Poems, 1968; Neljätoista hallitsijaa, 1970; Puhua vastata opettaa, 1972; Runoja matkalta salmen ylitse, 1973; Kaksikymmentä ja yksi, 1974; Runot 1949–1974, 1975; Runoelmat, 1975; Viiniä, Kirjoitusta, 1976; Kansakuninan linja, 1977; Yritys omaksikuvaksi, 1987; Toukokuu, ikuinen, 1988; Prospero, 1967–1995, 1996. *Honours:* Six Finnish State Prizes for Literature; Pro Finlandia Medal; Neustadt International Prize for Literature, 1984. *Address:* c/o Art House Publishing Group, Blvd 19C, 00120 Helsinki, Finland.

HABERMAS, Jürgen; Prof. of Philosophy Emeritus and Writer; b. 18 June 1929, Düsseldorf, Germany; m. Ute Wesselhoeft, 1955, one s. two d. *Education:* PhD, University of Bonn, 1954; Habilitation, University of Marburg, 1961. *Career:* Asst, Institute of Social Research, Frankfurt am Main, 1956–59; Assoc. Prof., University of Heidelberg, 1961–64; Prof. of Philosophy and Sociology, 1964–71, Prof. of Philosophy, 1983–94, Prof. Emeritus, 1994–, University of Frankfurt am Main; Dir, Max Planck Institute, Starnberg, 1971–81; mem. Academia Europaea, London; American Acad. of Arts and Sciences; British Acad. of Science; Deutsche Akademie für Sprache und Dichtung e. v. Darmstadt. *Publications:* Das Absolute und die Geschichte: Von der Zwiespältigkeit in Schellings Denken, 1954; Student und Politik: Eine soziologische Untersuchung zum politischen Bewusstsein Frankfurter Studenten (with Ludwig von Friedeburg, Christoph Oehler, and Friedrich Weltz), 1961; Strukturwandel der Offentlichkeit: Untersuchungen zu einer Katergorie der bürgerlichen Gesellschaft, 1962; Theorie und Praxis: Sozialphilosophische Studien, 1963; Technik und Wissenschaft als Ideologie, 1968; Erkenntnis und Interesse, 1968; Protestbewegung und Hochschulreform, 1969; Zur Logik der Sozialwissenschaften, 1970; Philosophisch-politische Profile, 1971; Theorie der Gesellschaft oder Sozialtechnologie (with Niklas Luhmann), 1971; Legitimationsprobleme im Spätkapitalismus, 1973; Zur Rekonstruktion des Historischen Materialismus, 1976; Politik, Kunst, Religion, 1978; Kleine Politische Schriften I–IV, 1981; Theorie des kommunikativen Handelns, 1981; Moralbewusstsein und kommunikatives Handeln, 1983; Vorstudien und Ergänzungen zur Theorie des kommunikativen Handelns, 1984; Der Philosophische Diskurs der Moderne, 1985; Die Neue Unübersichtlichkeit, 1985; Eine Art Schadensabwicklung, 1987; Nachmetaphysisches Denken, 1988; Die nachholende Revolution, 1990; Texte und Kontexte, 1991; Erläuterungen zur Diskursethik, 1991; Faktizität und Geltung, 1992; Vergangenheit als Zukunft, 1993; Die Normalität einer Berliner Republik, 1995; Die Einbeziehung des Anderen, 1996; Vom sinnlichen Eindruck zum symbolischen Ausdruck, 1997; Die postnationale Konstellation, 1998; Wahrheit und Rechtfertigung, 1999; Die Zukunft der menschlichen Natur, 2001; Zeit der Übergänge, 2001; Glauben und Wissen, 2001. Contributions: scholarly journals. *Honours:* Hegel Prize, Stuttgart, 1973; Sigmund Freud Prize, 1976; Theodor W. Adorno Prize, 1980; Geschwister Scholl Prize, 1985; Leuschner Medal, 1985; Leibniz Prize of the German Science Foundation, 1986; Sonning Prize, 1987; Karl Jaspers Prize, University of Heidelberg, 1995; Helmholtz Medal, Berlin-Brandenburg Acad. of Science, 2000; Friedenspreis des Deutschen Buchhandels, 2001; Premio Príncipe de Asturias, 2003; various hon. doctorates from German and foreign universities. *Address:* Ringstrasse 8b, 82319 Starnberg, Germany.

HABGOOD, Baron (Life Peer), cr. 1995, of Calverton in the County of Buckinghamshire; **Rt Rev. and Rt Hon. John Stapylton Habgood,** PC, DD, MA, PhD; British ecclesiastic (retd); b. 23 June 1927, Stony Stratford; m. Rosalie Mary Anne Boston 1961; two s. two d. *Education:* Eton Coll., King's Coll. Cambridge Univ. and Cuddesdon Coll., Oxford. *Career:* Demonstrator in Pharmacology, Univ. of Cambridge 1950–53; Fellow, King's Coll. Cambridge 1952–55, Hon. Fellow 1984; Curate, St Mary Abbott's Church, Kensington 1954–56; Vice-Prin. Westcott House, Cambridge 1956–62; Rector, St John's Church, Jedburgh, Scotland 1962–67; Prin. Queen's Coll., Birmingham 1967–73; Bishop of Durham 1973–83; Archbishop of York 1983–95; Pres. (UK) Council on Christian Approaches to Defence and Disarmament 1976–95; Chair. World Council of Churches' Int. Hearing on Nuclear Weapons 1981; mem. Council for Science and Society 1975–90, Council for Arms Control 1981–95; Moderator of Church and Soc. Sub-Unit, World Council of Churches 1983–90; Chair. UK Xenotransplantation Interim Regulatory Authority 1997–2003. *Publications:* Religion and Science 1964, A Working Faith 1980, Church and Nation in a Secular Age 1983, Confessions of a Conservative Liberal 1988, Making Sense 1993, Faith and Uncertainty 1997, Being a Person 1998, Varieties of Unbelief 2000, The Concept of Nature 2002. *Honours:* Hon. DD (Durham) 1975, (Cambridge) 1984, (Aberdeen) 1988, (Huron) 1990, (Hull) 1991, (Oxford) 1996, (Manchester) 1996; Hon. DUniv (York) 1996; Hon. DHL (York, Pa) 1995; Bampton Lecturer, Univ. of Oxford 1999, Gifford Lecturer, Univ. of Aberdeen 2000. *Address:* 18 The Mount, Malton, North Yorkshire, YO17 7ND, England.

HABILA, Helon; Writer; b. 1967, Kaltungo, Gombe State, Nigeria. *Education:* Univ. of Jos. *Career:* Lecturer in English and Literature, Fed. Polytechnic, Bauchi, 1997–99; fmr contributor to Hints magazine, Lagos; Arts Ed., Vanguard newspaper, Lagos; Writing fellowship, Univ. of East Anglia, 2002–(04). *Publications:* Mai Kaltungo (biog.), 1997; Prison Stories (short stories), 2000; Love Poems (short story), 2001; Waiting for an Angel (novel), 2002; short stories and poems in anthologies. Honours and awards: First Prize, MUSON Festival Poetry Competition, for poem Another Age, 2000; Caine Prize for African Writing, 2001; Commonwealth Writers Prize for Best First Book, 2003. *Address:* c/o Vanguard, Kirikiri Canal, PMB 1007, Apapa, Nigeria. *Website:* vanguard@linkserve.com.ng.

HACHETTE, Jean-Louis, LenD; French publisher; b. 30 June 1925, Paris; m. Y. de Bouillé 1954; one s. two d. *Education:* Collège Stanislas, Paris and Faculté de Droit, Paris. *Career:* joined Librairie Hachette (f. by great-grandfather in 1826) 1946 (now Hachette Livre); entire career spent with Librairie Hachette, Admin. Dir 1971–; Pres. Librairie Générale Française 1954–. *Address:* Librairie Générale Française, 43 quai de Grenelle, 75905 Paris, Cédex 15, France. *Website:* www.hachette.com.

HACKER, Katharina; German writer; b. 1967, Frankfurt. *Education:* Freiburg Univ., Hebrew Univ., Jerusalem. *Publications include:* Morpheus (novel) 1998, Der Bademeister (novel, trans. as The Lifeguard) 2000. *Address:* c/o The Toby Press, PO Box 8531, New Milford, CT 06776-8531, USA. *Website:* www.tobypress.com.

HACKER, Marilyn; Poet, Writer, Critic, Ed. and Teacher; b. 27 Nov. 1942, New York, NY, USA; one d. *Education:* BA, Romance Languages, New York University, 1964. *Career:* Ed., Quark: A Quarterly of Speculative Fiction, 1969–71, The Kenyon Review, 1990–94; Jenny McKean Moore Chair in Writing, George Washington University, 1976–77; Mem., Editorial Collective, 1977–80, Ed.-in-Chief, 1979, The Little Magazine; Teacher, School of General Studies, Columbia University, 1979–81; Visiting Artist, Fine Arts Work Center, Provincetown, Massachusetts, 1981; Visiting Prof., University of Idaho, 1982; Ed.-in-Chief, Thirteenth Moon: A Feminist Literary Magazine, 1982–86; Writer-in-Residence, SUNY at Albany, 1988, Columbia University, 1988; George Elliston Poet-in-Residence, University of Cincinnati, 1988; Distinguished Writer-in-Residence, American University, Washington, DC, 1989; Visiting Prof. of Creative Writing, SUNY at Binghamton, 1990, University of Utah, 1995, Barnard College, 1995, Princeton University, 1997; Fannie Hurst Poet-in-Residence, Brandeis University, 1996. *Publications:* Presentation Piece, 1974; Separations, 1976; Taking Notice, 1980; Assumptions, 1985; Love, Death and the Changing of the Seasons, 1986; The Hang-Glider's Daughter: New and Selected Poems, 1990; Going Back to the River, 1990; Selected Poems: 1965–1990, 1994; Winter Numbers, 1994; Edge (trans. of poems by Claire Malroux), 1996; Squares and Courtyards, 2000; A Long-Gone Sun, by Claire Malroux (trans.), 2000; Here There Was Once a Country, by Vénus Khoury-Ghata (trans.), 2001. Contributions: numerous anthologies and other publications. *Honours:* National Endowment for the Arts Grants, 1973–74, 1985–86, 1995; National Book Award in Poetry, 1975; Guggenheim Fellowship, 1980–81; Ingram Merrill Foundation Grant, 1984–85; Robert F. Winner Awards, 1987, 1989, John Masefield Memorial Award, 1994, Poetry Society of America; Lambda Literary Awards, 1991, 1995; Lenore Marshall Award, Acad. of American Poets, 1995; Poets' Prize, 1995. *Address:* 230 W 105th St, New York, NY 10025, USA.

HACKER, Peter Michael Stephen; Philosopher, Librarian and Writer; b. 15 July 1939, London, England; m. Sylvia Imhoff 31 Aug. 1963; two s. one d. *Education:* BA, MA, Queen's College, Oxford; DPhil, St Antony's College, Oxford, 1966. *Career:* Junior Research Fellow, Balliol College, Oxford, 1965–66; Fellow and Tutor in Philosophy, 1966–, Librarian, 1986–, St John's College, Oxford; Visiting Prof., Swarthmore College, 1973, 1986, Univ. of Michigan, Ann Arbor, 1974, Queen's Univ., Kingston, ON, 1985. *Publications:* Insight and Illusion: Wittgenstein and the Metaphysics of Experience, 1972, second edn as Insight and Illusion: Themes in the Philosophy of Wittgenstein, 1986; Law, Morality, and Society: Essays in

Honour of H. L. A. Hart (co-ed. and contributor), 1977; Wittgenstein: Understanding and Meaning (with G. P. Baker), 1980; Frege: Logical Excavations (with G. P. Baker), 1984; Language, Sense and Nonsense: A Critical Investigation into Modern Theories of Language (with G. P. Baker), 1984; Scepticism, Rules and Language (with G. P. Baker), 1984; Wittgenstein: Rules, Grammar and Necessity (with G. P. Baker), 1985; Appearance and Reality: A Philosophical Investigation into Perception and Perceptual Qualities, 1987; The Renaissance of Gravure: The Art of S. W. Hayter (ed. and contributor), 1988; Wittgenstein: Meaning and Mind, 1990; Gravure and Grace: The Engravings of Roger Vieillard (ed. and contributor), 1993; Wittgenstein: Mind and Will, 1996; Wittgenstein's Place in Twentieth Century Analytic Philosophy, 1996; Wittgenstein on Human Nature, 1997; Wittgenstein: Connections and Controversies, 2001; Philosophical Foundations of Neuroscience (with M. R. Bennett), 2002. Contributions: reference works, scholarly books and professional journals. *Honours:* British Acad. Research Reader, 1985–87; Leverhulme Senior Research Fellow, 1991–94. *Address:* c/o St John's College, Oxford OX1 3JP, England.

HADAS, Rachel; Prof. of English, Poet and Writer; b. 8 Nov. 1948, New York, NY, USA; m. 1st Stavros Kondilis, 7 Nov. 1970, divorced 1978; m. 2nd George Edwards, 22 July 1978, one s. *Education:* BA, Classics, Radcliffe College, 1969; MA, Poetry, Johns Hopkins University, 1977; PhD, Comparative Literature, Princeton University, 1982. *Career:* Asst Prof., 1982–87, Assoc. Prof., 1987–92, Prof. of English, 1992–2001, Board of Govs Prof. of English, 2001–, Rutgers University; Adjunct Prof., Columbia University, 1992–93; Visiting Prof., Princeton University, 1995, 1996; mem. American Acad. of Arts and Sciences, fellow; Modern Greek Studies Asscn; MLA; PEN; Poetry Society of America. *Publications:* Starting From Troy, 1975; Slow Transparency, 1983; A Son from Sleep, 1987; Pass It On, 1989; Living in Time, 1990; Unending Dialogue, 1991; Mirrors of Astonishment, 1992; Other Worlds Than This, 1994; The Empty Bed, 1995; The Double Legacy, 1995; Halfway Down the Hall (New and Selected Poems), 1998; Merrill, Cavafy, Poems and Dreams, 2000; Indelible, 2001; Laws, 2004. Contributions: periodicals. *Honours:* Ingram Merrill Foundation Fellowship, 1976–77; Guggenheim Fellowship, 1988–89; American Acad. and Institute of Arts and Letters Award, 1990; O. B. Hardison Award, 2000; Scholars and Writers, New York Public Library, 2000–01. *Address:* 838 West End Ave, No. 3A, New York, NY 10025, USA.

HADDON, Mark, MA; British writer and illustrator; b. 1962, Northampton; m. Sos Eltis; one s. *Education:* Merton Coll., Oxford, Edinburgh Univ. *Career:* positions at Mencap and other charity orgs; illustrator and cartoonist; painter; television work. *Screenwriting:* Microsoap (Royal Television Soc. Best Children's Drama), episodes of Starstreet, Fungus and the Bogeyman (adaptation). *Publications:* fiction: Gilbert's Gobstopper 1988, A Narrow Escape for Princess Sharon 1989, Toni and the Tomato Soup 1989, Agent Z Meets the Masked Crusader 1993, Gridzbi Spudvetch! 1993, In the Garden 1994, On Holiday (aka On Vacation) 1994, At Home 1994, At Playgroup 1994, Titch Johnson 1994, Agent Z Goes Wild 1994, Agent Z and the Penguin from Mars 1995, Real Porky Philips 1995, The Sea of Tranquillity 1996, Secret Agent Handbook 1999, Ocean Star Express 2001, Agent Z and the Killer Bananas 2001, The Ice Bear's Cave 2002, The Curious Incident of the Dog in the Night Time (Booktrust Teenage Prize, Guardian Children's Fiction Prize, South Bank Show Best Book Prize 2004, Whitbread Best Novel and Book of the Year 2004, Commonwealth Prize for best first book 2004, Soc. of Authors McKitterick Prize 2004, WHSmith Children's Book of the Year 2004, Waterstones Literary Fiction award 2004) 2003. *Address:* c/o Jonathan Cape Ltd, 20 Vauxhall Bridge Road, London, SW1V 2SA, England. *Telephone:* (20) 7840-8400.

HADLOW, Janice; British broadcasting executive; *Controller, BBC Four. Career:* production trainee, BBC 1986, later producer on Radio 4, Ed. Late Show, Deputy Head music and arts dept, Jt Head of history dept –1999; Head of History, Arts and Religion, Channel 4 1999, later Head of Specialist Factual Group, Channel 4 –2004; Controller, BBC Four 2004–. *Publication:* The Nunnery: The Six Daughters of George III (with Martin Davidson) 2004. *Address:* BBC Four, BBC Television Centre, Wood Lane, London, W12 7RJ, England. *Website:* www.bbc.co.uk/bbcfour.

HAGGER, Nicholas Osborne, MA; British poet, verse dramatist, lecturer, writer, philosopher and cultural historian; b. 22 May 1939, London, England; m. 1st Caroline Virginia Mary Nixon 1961; one d.; m. 2nd Madeline Ann Johnson 1974; two s. *Education:* Worcester Coll., Oxford. *Career:* Lecturer in English, Univ. of Baghdad 1961–62; Prof. of English Literature, Tokyo Univ. of Education and Keio Univ., Tokyo 1963–67, Tokyo Univ. 1964–65; Lecturer in English, Univ. of Libya, Tripoli 1968–70; freelance feature writer for The Times 1970–72; mem. Soc. of Authors. *Publications:* The Fire and the Stones: A Grand Unified Theory of World History and Religion 1991, Selected Poems: A Metaphysical's Way of Fire 1991, The Universe and the Light: A New View of the Universe and Reality 1993, A White Radiance: The Collected Poems 1958–93 1994, A Mystic Way: A Spiritual Autobiography 1994, Awakening to the Light: Diaries, Vol. 1 1958–67 1994, A Spade Fresh with Mud: Collected Stories, Vol. 1 1995, The Warlords: From D-Day to Berlin, A Verse Drama 1995, A Smell of Leaves and Summer: Collected Stories, Vol. 2 1995, Overlord, The Triumph of Light 1944–1945: An Epic Poem, Books 1–2 1995, Books 3–6 1996, Books 7–9, 10–12 1997, The One and the Many 1999, Wheeling Bats and a Harvest Moon: Collected Stories, Vol. 3 1999, Prince Tudor, A Verse Drama 1999, The Warm Glow of the Monastery Courtyard: Collected Stories, Vol. 4 1999, The Syndicate: The Story of the Coming World Government 2004. *Fax:* (20) 8502-0432. *E-mail:* nicholashagger@hotmail.com.

HAHN (GARCES), Oscar Arturo, MA, PhD; American poet, writer and academic; b. 5 July 1938, Iquique, Chile; m. Nancy Jorquera 1971; one d. *Education:* University of Chile, University of Iowa, University of Maryland at College Park. *Career:* Prof. of Hispanic Literature, University of Chile, 1965–73; Instructor, University of Maryland at College Park, 1974–77; Asst Prof., 1977–79, Assoc. Prof. of Spanish-American Literature, 1979–, University of Iowa; mem. Instituto Internacional de Literatura Iberoamericana; MLA of America. *Publications:* Esta rosa negra (poems), 1961; Agua final (poems), 1967; Arte de morir (poems), 1977, English trans. as The Art of Dying, 1987; El cuento fantástico hispanoamericano en el siglo XIX, 1978; Mal de amor, 1981, English trans. as Love Breaks, 1991; Imagenes nucleares, 1983; Texto sobre texto, 1984; Tratado de sortilegios, 1992; Antología poética, 1993; Antología virtual, 1996; ¿Qué hacia yo el once de septiembre de 1973? (with Matias Rivas and Roberto Merino), 1997; Antología retroactiva, 1998; Versos robados/Stolen Verses and Other Poems, 2000. Contributions: Literary journals. *Honours:* Premio Alerce, 1961; Poetry Award, University of Chile, 1966; Hon. Fellow, International Writing Program, 1972. *Address:* c/o Department of Spanish, University of Iowa, Iowa City, IA 52240, USA.

HAHN, Susan; poet, playwright and editor; b. 11 Nov. 1947, Chicago, IL, USA; m. Frederic L. Hahn 1967; one s. *Career:* staff 1980–, Ed. 1997–, TriQuarterly literary magazine; Co-Founder/Co-Ed., TriQuarterly Books 1988–. *Publications:* Harriet Rubin's Mother's Wooden Hand 1991, Incontinence 1993, Melancholia et cetera 1995, Confession 1997, Holiday 2001, Mother in Summer 2002, Golf (play); contrib. to many reviews, quarterlies and journals. *Honours:* Illinois Arts Council Literary Awards, 1985, 1990, 1996, 1997; Society of Midland Authors Award for Poetry, 1994; Pushcart Prizes for Poetry, 2000, 2003; George Kent Prize, Poetry magazine, 2000; Guggenheim Fellowship, 2003. *Address:* 1377 Scott Avenue, Winnetka, IL 60093, USA.

HAIBLUM, Isidore; Writer; b. 23 May 1935, New York, NY, USA. *Education:* BA, City College, CUNY, 1958. *Publications:* The Tsaddik of the Seven Wonders, 1971; The Return, 1973; Transfer to Yesterday, 1973; The Wilk Are Among Us, 1975; Interworld, 1977; Outerworld, 1979; Nightmare Express, 1979; Faster Than a Speeding Bullet: An Informal History of Radio's Golden Age (with Stuart Silver), 1980; The Mutants Are Coming, 1984; The Identity Plunderers, 1984; The Hand of Gantz, 1985; Murder in Yiddish, 1988; Bad Neighbors, 1990; Out of Sync, 1990; Specterworld, 1991; Crystalword, 1992. Contributions: periodicals. *Address:* 160 W 77th St, New York, NY 10024, USA.

HAIGH, Christopher; Lecturer in Modern History and Writer; b. 28 Aug. 1944, Birkenhead, England; two d. *Education:* BA, University of Cambridge, 1966; PhD, Victoria University of Manchester, 1969. *Career:* Lecturer in History, Victoria University of Manchester, 1969–79; Lecturer in Modern History, Christ Church, Oxford, 1979–; mem. FRHistS. *Publications:* The Last Days of the Lancashire Monasteries, 1969; Reformation and Resistance in Tudor Lancashire, 1975; The Cambridge Historical Encyclopaedia of Great Britain and Ireland, 1984; The Reign of Elizabeth l, 1985; The English Reformation Revised, 1987; Elizabeth l: A Profile in Power, 1988; English Reformations: Religion, Politics and Society Under the Tudors, 1993. *Address:* c/o Christ Church, Oxford OX1 1DP, England.

HAILEY, Arthur; British/Canadian writer and screenwriter; b. 5 April 1920, Luton, England; m. 1st Joan Fishwick 1944 (divorced 1950); three s.; m. 2nd Sheila Dunlop 1951; one s. two d. *Education:* British elementary schools. *Career:* Pilot, Flight Lieutenant, Royal Air Force, 1939–47; Flight Lieutenant, Royal Canadian Air Force Reserve, 1951; Industry and sales positions; Writer, 1956–; mem. Alliance of Canadian Cinema, Television and Radio Artists, hon. life mem.; Authors League of America; Writers Guild of America, life mem. *Publications:* Runway-Zero Eight (with John Castle), 1958; The Final Diagnosis, 1959; Close-up (collected plays), 1960; In High Places, 1962; Hotel, 1965; Airport, 1968; Wheels, 1971; The Moneychangers, 1975; Overload, 1979; Strong Medicine, 1984; The Evening News, 1990; Detective, 1997. Films: Zero Hour, 1956; Time Lock, 1957; The Young Doctors, 1961; Hotel, 1966; Airport, 1970; The Moneychangers, 1976; Wheels, 1978; Strong Medicine, 1986. *Honours:* Royal Air Force Air Efficiency Award; Canadian Council of Artists and Authors Award, 1956; Best Canadian TV Playwright Awards, 1957, 1959; Doubleday Prize Novel Award, 1962. *Address:* Lyford Cay, PO Box N7776, Nassau, Bahamas. *E-mail:* ahailey@coralwave.com.

HAILEY, Elizabeth Forsythe; Writer and Dramatist; b. 31 Aug. 1938, Dallas, Texas, USA; m. Oliver Daffan Hailey, 25 June 1960, deceased 1993, two d. *Education:* Diploma, Sorbonne, University of Paris, 1959; BA, Hollins College, Virginia, 1960. *Career:* mem. Authors League of America; PEN; Writers Guild of America West. *Publications:* Fiction: A Woman of Independent Means, 1978; Life Sentences, 1982; Joanna's Husband and David's Wife, 1986; Home Free, 1991. Plays: A Woman of Independent Means, 1984; Joanna's Husband and David's Wife, 1989. Contributions: books and periodicals. *Honours:* Silver Medal for Best First Novel, Commonwealth Club of California, 1978; Los Angeles Drama Critics Award, 1983. *Address:* 11747 Canton Pl., Studio City, CA 91604, USA.

HAINES, John (Meade); Poet, Writer and Teacher; b. 29 June 1924, Norfolk, Virginia, USA; m. 1st Jo Ella Hussey, 10 Oct. 1960; m. 2nd Jane McWhorter, 23 Nov. 1970, divorced 1974; m. 3rd Leslie Sennett, Oct. 1978, divorced, four c. *Education:* National Art School, Washington, DC, 1946–47; American University, 1948–49; Hans Hoffman School of Fine Art, New York City, 1950–52; University of Washington, 1974. *Career:* Poet-in-Residence, University of Alaska, 1972–73; Visiting Prof. in English, University of Washington, 1974; Visiting Lecturer in English, University of Montana, 1974; Writer-in-Residence, Sheldon Jackson College, 1982–83, Ucross Foundation, 1987, Montalvo Center for the Arts, 1988, Djerassi Foundation, 1988; Visiting Lecturer, University of California at Santa Cruz, 1986, Wordsworth Conference, Grasmere, England, 1996; Visiting Writer, The Loft Mentor Series, 1987, George Washington University, 1991–92; Visiting Prof., Ohio University, 1989–90; Elliston Fellow in Poetry, University of Cincinnati, 1992; Chair in Creative Arts, Austin Peay State University, Clarksville, Tennessee, 1993; mem. Acad. of American Poets; Alaska Conservation Society; Natural Resources Defense Council; PEN American Center; Poetry Society of America; Sierra Club; Wilderness Society. *Publications:* Poetry: Winter News, 1966; Suite for the Pied Piper, 1968; The Legend of Paper Plates, 1970; The Mirror, 1970; The Stone Harp, 1971; Twenty Poems, 1971; Leaves and Ashes, 1975; In Five Years, 1976; Cicada, 1977; In a Dusty Light, 1977; The Sun on Your Shoulder, 1977; News From the Glacier: Selected Poems, 1960–80, 1982; New Poems: 1980–1988, 1990; Rain Country, 1990; The Owl in the Mask of a Dreamer, 1993. Non-Fiction: Minus Thirty-One and the Wind Blowing: Nine Reflections About Living on the Land (with others), 1980; Living Off the Country: Essays on Poetry and Place, 1981; Other Days, 1982; Of Traps and Snares, 1982; Stories We Listened To, 1986; You and I and the World, 1988; The Stars, the Snow, the Fire, 1989; Fables and Distances: New and Selected Essays, 1996; A Guide to the Four-Chambered Heart, 1996. Contributions: periodicals. *Honours:* Guggenheim Fellowships, 1965–66, 1984–85; National Endowment for the Arts Grant, 1967–68; Amy Lowell Scholarship, 1976–77; Governor's Award for lifetime contributions to the arts in Alaska, 1982; Hon. LD, University of Alaska, 1983; Ingram Merrill Foundation Grant, 1987; Lenore Marshall Nation Award, 1991; Literary Award, American Acad. of Arts and Letters, 1995.

HAINING, Peter (Alexander), (Peter Alex, Jim Black, Richard De'ath, William Patrick, Richard Peters, Richard Peyton, Sean Richards); Writer; b. 2 April 1940, Enfield, Middlesex, England; m., three c. *Career:* Former Publishing Dir, New English Library, London; mem. PEN International. *Publications:* The Ghost Ship, 1985; Tune in for Fear, 1985; Vampire, 1985; Stories of the Walking Dead, 1986; Supernatural Sleuths, 1986; Tales of Dungeons and Dragons, 1986; Poltergeist, 1987; Werewolf, 1987; Irish Tales of Terror, 1988; The Mummy, 1988; The Scarecrow: Fact and Fable, 1988; Bob Hope: Thanks for the Memory, 1989; The Day War Broke Out, 1989; Hook, Line and Laughter, 1989; The Legend of Garbo, 1990; The Legend That is Buddy Holly, 1990; Spitfire Summer, 1990; The English Highwayman, 1991; Sinister Gambits, 1991; Great Irish Stories of the Supernatural, 1992; The Supernatural Coast, 1992; The Television Detectives Omnibus, 1992; The Armchair Detectives, 1993; Great Irish Detective Stories, 1993; The MG Log, 1993; Masters of the Macabre, 1993; Tombstone Humour, 1993; The Complete Maigret, 1994; London After Midnight, 1995; Murder at the Races, 1995; Agatha Christie's Poirot, 1996; Murder on the Railways, 1996; The Wizards of Odd, 1997; The Un-Dead: The Legend of Bram Stoker and Dracula, 1997; Great Irish Humorous Stories, 1998; Sweeney Todd: The Real Story of the Demon Barber of Fleet Street, 1998; Invasion: Earth, 1998; The Nine Lives of Doctor Who, 1999; The Classic Era of American Pulp Magazines, 2000; The Wizard's Den, 2001; The Classic Era of Crime Fiction, 2002. *Address:* Peyton House, Boxford, Suffolk, England.

HAKIM, Seymour, (Sy Hakim); Poet, Writer, Artist and Educator; b. 23 Jan. 1933, New York, NY, USA; m. Odetta Roverso, 18 Aug. 1970. *Education:* AB, Eastern New Mexico University, 1954; MA, New York University, 1960; Postgraduate work, various universities. *Career:* Consultant Ed., Poet Gallery Press, New York, 1970; Ed., Overseas Teacher, 1977; mem. Asscn of Poets and Writers; National Photo Instructors' Asscn; Italo-Brittanica Asscn. *Publications:* The Sacred Family, 1970; Manhattan Goodbye (poems), 1970; Under Moon, 1971; Museum of the Mind, 1971; Wine Theorem, 1972; Substituting Memories, 1976; Iris Elegy, 1979; Balancing Act, 1981; Birth of a Poet, 1985; Eleanor, Goodbye, 1988; Michaelangelo's Call, 1999. Other: Exhibits with accomanying writings: 1970, 1973, 1982–83, 1985. Contributions: Overseas Educator; California State Poetry Quarterly; American Writing; Dan River Anthology; Its On My Wall; Older Eyes; Art Exhibition and Reading, New York, 1999; Life Shards, 2000; Artwork/readings NYC, 2000. *Address:* Via Chiesanuova No. 1, 36023 Langare, VI 36023, Italy.

HALAM, Ann (see Jones, Gwyneth).

HALBERSTAM, David, AB; American writer; b. 10 April 1934, New York, NY, USA; m. 1st Elizabethj Tchizerska 1965 (divorced); m. 2nd Jean Sanders 1979; one d. *Education:* Harvard University. *Career:* staff, Daily Times Leader, West Point, Mississippi, 1955–56; Nashville Tennessean, 1956–60; Foreign Correspondent, New York Times, 1960–67; Contributing Ed., Harper's Magazine, 1967–71. *Publications:* The Noblest Roman, 1961; The Making of a Quagmire, 1965, second edn as The Making of a Quagmire: America and Vietnam During the Kennedy Era, 1987; One Very Hot Day, 1968; The Unfinished Odyssey of Robert Kennedy, 1969; Ho, 1971; The Best and the Brightest, 1972; The Powers That Be, 1979; The Breaks of the Game, 1981; The Amateurs, 1985; The Reckoning, 1986; The Summer of '49, 1989; The Next Century, 1991; The Fifties, 1993; October 1964, 1994; The Children, 1998; Playing for Keeps: Michael Jordan and the World He Made, 1999; The Best American Sports Writings of the Century (ed.), 1999. Contributions: newspapers and magazines. *Honours:* Page One Award, Newspaper Guild of America, 1962; Co-Winner, Pulitzer Prize for International Reporting, 1964; George Polk Award, 1964; Louis M. Lyons Award, 1964; Overseas Press Club Award, 1973. *Literary Agent:* William Morrow Inc., 1350 Avenue of the Americas, New York, NY 10019-4702, USA.

HALDEMAN, Joe William; Novelist; b. 9 June 1943, Oklahoma City, Oklahoma, USA; m. Mary Gay Potter, 21 Aug. 1965. *Education:* BS, Physics and Astronomy, University of Maryland, 1967; MFA, English, University of Iowa, 1975. *Career:* Assoc. Prof., writing programme, MIT, 1983–; mem. SFWA; Authors' Guild; Poets and Writers National Space Institute; Writers Guild. *Publications:* War Year, 1972; Cosmic Laughter (ed.), 1974; The Forever War 1975; Mindbridge, 1976; Planet of Judgement, 1977; All My Sins Remembered, 1977; Study War No More (ed.), 1977; Infinite Dreams, 1978; World Without End, 1979; Worlds, 1981; There is No Darkness (co-author), 1983; Worlds Apart, 1983; Nebula Awards 17 (ed.), 1983; Dealing in Futures, 1985; Body Armour 2000 (co-ed.), 1986; Tool of the Trade, 1987; Supertanks (co-ed.), 1987; Starfighters (co-ed.), 1988; The Long Habit of Living, 1989; The Hemingway Hoax, 1990; Worlds Enough and Time, 1992; 1968, 1995; None So Blind, 1996; Forever Peace, 1997; Saul's Death and Other Poems, 1997; Forever Free, 1999; The Coming, 2000; Guardian, 2002. *Honours:* Purple Heart, US Army, 1969; Nebula Awards, 1975, 1990, 1993, 1998; Hugo Awards, 1976, 1977, 1991, 1995, 1998; Rhysling Awards, 1984, 1990, 2001; World Fantasy Award, 1993; John Campbell Award, 1998. *Address:* 5412 NW 14th Ave, Gainesville, FL 32605, USA.

HALIM, Huri (see Offen, Yehuda).

HALL, Angus; Author and Ed.; b. 24 March 1932, Newcastle upon Tyne, England. *Career:* Ed., IPC Publishers, London, 1971–, BPC Publishers, London, 1972–. *Publications:* London in Smoky Region, 1962; High-Bouncing Lover, 1966; Live Like a Hero, 1967; Comeuppance of Arthur Hearne, 1967; Qualtrough, 1968; Late Boy Wonder, 1969; Devilday, 1970; To Play the Devil, 1971; Scars of Dracula, 1971; Long Way to Fall, 1971; On the Run, 1974; Signs of Things to Come: A History of Divination, 1975; Monsters and Mythic Beasts, 1976; Strange Cults, 1977; The Rigoletto Murder, 1978; Self-Destruct, 1985. *Address:* 96 High St, Old Town, Hastings, Sussex, England.

HALL, Claudia (see Floren, Lee).

HALL, Donald Andrew, Jr; Poet, Writer and Prof. of English (retd); b. 20 Sept. 1928, New Haven, CT, USA; m. 1st Kirby Thompson, 1952, divorced 1969, one s. one d.; m. 2nd Jane Kenyon, 1972, deceased 1995. *Education:* BA, Harvard University, 1951; BLitt, University of Oxford, 1953; Stanford University, 1953–54. *Career:* Poetry Ed., Paris Review, 1953–62; Asst Prof., 1957–61, Assoc. Prof., 1961–66, Prof. of English, 1966–75, University of Michigan. *Publications:* Poetry: Poems, 1952; Exile, 1952; To the Loud Wind and Other Poems, 1955; Exiles and Marriages, 1955; The Dark Houses, 1958; A Roof of Tiger Lilies, 1964; The Alligator Bride: Poems New and Selected, 1969; The Yellow Room: Love Poems, 1971; A Blue Wing Tilts at the Edge of the Sea: Selected Poems 1964–1974, 1975; The Town of Hill, 1975; Kicking the Leaves, 1978; The Toy Bone, 1979; The Twelve Seasons, 1983; Brief Lives, 1983; Great Day at the Cows' House, 1984; The Happy Man, 1986; The One Day: A Poem in Three Parts, 1988; Old and New Poems, 1990; The One Day and Poems (1947–1990), 1991; The Museum of Clear Ideas, 1993; The Old Life, 1996; Without, 1998; The Painted Bed, 2000. Short Stories: The Ideal Bakery, 1987. Other: Henry Moore: The Life and Work of a Great Sculptor, 1966; Marianne Moore: The Cage and the Animal, 1970; The Gentleman's Alphabet Book, 1972; Writing Well, 1973; Remembering Poets: Reminiscences and Opinions – Dylan Thomas, Robert Frost, T. S. Eliot, Ezra Pound, 1978; Goatfoot Milktongue Twinbird: Interviews, Essays and Notes on Poetry 1970–76, 1978; To Read Literature: Fiction, Poetry, Drama, 1981; The Weather for Poetry: Essays, Reviews and Notes on Poetry 1977–81, 1982; Poetry and Ambition: Essays 1982–1988, 1988; Anecdotes of Modern Art (with Pat Corrigan Wykes), 1990; Here at Eagle Pond, 1990; Their Ancient Glittering Eyes, 1992; Life Work, 1993; Death to Death of Poetry, 1994; Principal Products of Portugal, 1995. *Honours:* Edna St Vincent Millay Memorial Prize, 1956; Longview Foundation Award, 1960; Guggenheim Fellowships, 1963, 1972; Sarah Josepha Hale Award, 1983; Poet Laureate of New Hampshire, 1984–89; Lenore Marshall Award, 1987; National Book Critics Circle Award, 1989; Los Angeles Times Book Award, 1989; Robert Frost Silver Medal, Poetry Society of America, 1991; Lifetime Achievement Award, New Hampshire Writers and Publishers Project, 1992; New England Book Award for Non-Fiction, 1993; Ruth Lilly Prize for Poetry, 1994; Hon. doctorates. *Address:* Eagle Pond Farm, 24 US Route 4, Wilmot, NH 03287-4438, USA.

HALL, James B(yron); Author, Poet and University Provost Emeritus; b. 21 July 1918, Midland, Ohio, USA; m. Elizabeth Cushman, 14 Feb. 1946, one s., four d. *Education:* Miami University, Oxford, Ohio, 1938–39; University of Hawaii, 1938–40; BA, 1947, MA, 1948, PhD, 1953, University of Iowa; Postgraduate Studies, Kenyon College, 1949. *Career:* Writer-in-Residence, Miami University, Oxford, Ohio, 1948–49, University of North Carolina at Greensville, 1954, University of British Columbia, 1955, University of Colorado, 1963; Instructor, Cornell University, 1952–54; Asst Prof., 1954–57, Assoc. Prof., 1958–60, Prof. of English, 1960–65, University of Oregon; Prof. of English and Dir, Writing Center, University of California at Irvine, 1965–68; Provost, 1968–75, Provost Emeritus, 1983–88, University of California at Santa Cruz; mem. Associated Writing Programs, pres., 1965–66; American Assn of University Profs; National Writers' Union; Oregon Book Awards, trustee, 1992–2001. *Publications:* Fiction: Not by the Door, 1954; Racers to the Sun, 1960; Mayo Sergeant, 1968. Short Story Collections: 15 x 3 (with Herbert Gold and R. V. Cassill), 1957; Us He Devours, 1964; The Short Hall, 1980; I Like It Better Now, 1992. Poetry: The Hunt Within, 1973; Bereavements (collected and selected poems), 1991. Non-Fiction: Perspectives on William Everson (co-ed.), 1992; Art and Craft of the Short Story, 1995; The Extreme Stories +3. Contributions: anthologies and other publications. *Honours:* Octave Thanet Prize, 1950; Rockefeller Foundation Grant, 1955; Oregon Poetry Prize, 1958; Emily Clark Balch Fiction Prize, 1967; Chapelbrook Award, 1967; James B. Hall Gallery named in his honour, University of California Regents, 1985; James B. Hall Traveling Fellowship founded in his honour, University of California at Santa Cruz, 1985.

HALL, Jane Anna; Writer, Poet and Artist; b. 4 April 1959, New London, CT, USA. *Education:* Professional Model, Barbizon School, 1976; Graduate, Westbrook High School, 1977. *Career:* Founder-Ed., Poetry in Your Mailbox Newsletter, 1989–; mem. Romance Writers of America; Connecticut Poetry Society. *Publications:* Cedar and Lace, 1986; Satin and Pinstripe, 1987; Fireworks and Diamonds, 1988; Stars and Daffodils, 1989; Sunrises and Stonewalls, 1990; Mountains and Meadows, 1991; Moonlight and Water Lilies, 1992; Sunset and Beaches, 1993; Under Par Recipes, 1994; New and Selected Poems 1986–1994, 1994; Poems for Children 1986–1995, 1995; Butterflies and Roses, 1996; Hummingbirds and Hibiscus, 1997; Swans and Azaleas, 1998; Damselflies and Peonies, 1999; Egrets and Cattails, 2000; Doves and Rhododendron, 2001; Bluebirds and Mountain Laurel, 2002; The Full Moon Looks Like (children's book), 2002, Beach Poems Vol. I 2002, Spring Poems Vol. I 2003, Summer Poems Vol. I 2003, Autumn Poems Vol. I 2003 Winter Poems Vol. I 2003, Cardinals and Maples 2003. Contributions: several publications. *Honours:* Second Prizes, Connecticut Poetry Society Contest, 1983, 1986; various certificates. *Address:* PO Box 629, Westbrook, CT 06498, USA.

HALL, Oakley Maxwell, (Jason Manor); Author; b. 1 July 1920, San Diego, CA, USA; m. Barbara Erdinger, 28 June 1945, one s., three d. *Education:* BA, University of California, Berkeley, 1943; MFA, University of Iowa, 1950. *Career:* Dir, Programs in Writing, University of California, Irvine, 1969–89, Squaw Valley Community of Writers, 1969–. *Publications:* So Many Doors, 1950; Corpus of Joe Bailey, 1953; Mardios Beach, 1955; Warlock, 1958; The Downhill Racers, 1962; The Pleasure Garden, 1962; A Game for Eagles, 1970; Report from Beau Harbor, 1971; The Adelita, 1975; The Badlands, 1978; Lullaby, 1982; The Children of the Sun, 1983; The Coming of the Kid, 1985; Apaches, 1986; The Art and Craft of Novel Writing, 1989. *Honours:* Commonwealth Club of California Silver Medal, 1954; Western Writers of America Golden Spur Award, 1984; Cowboy Hall of Fame Wrangler Award, 1989. *Address:* Dept of English, University of California at Irvine, CA 92717, USA.

HALL, Peter (Geoffrey); Prof. of Planning and Writer; b. 19 March 1932, London, England; m. 1st Carla Maria Wartenberg, 1962, divorced 1966; m. 2nd Magdalena Mróz, 1967. *Education:* MA, PhD, St Catharine's College, Cambridge. *Career:* Asst Lecturer, 1957–60, Lecturer, 1960–66, Birkbeck College, University of London; Reader in Geography, LSE, 1966–68; Prof. of Geography, 1968–89, Prof. Emeritus, 1989–, University of Reading; Prof. of City and Regional Planning, 1980–92, Prof. Emeritus, 1992–, University of California at Berkeley; Prof. of Planning, 1992–, Dir, School of Public Policy, 1995–96, University College London; Dir, Institute of Community Studies, 2001–; mem. Fabian Society, chair., 1971–72; Tawney Society, chair., 1983–85. *Publications:* The Industries of London, 1962; London 2000, 1963; Labour's New Frontiers, 1964; Land Values (ed.), 1965; The World Cities, 1966; Von Thunen's Isolated State (ed.), 1966; An Advanced Geography of North West Europe (co-author), 1967; Theory and Practice of Regional Planning, 1970; Containment of Urban England: Urban and Metropolitan Growth Processes or Megapolis Denied (co-author), 1973; Containment of Urban England: The Planning System: Objectives, Operations, Impacts (co-author), 1973; Planning and Urban Growth: An Anglo-American Comparison (with M. Clawson), 1973; Urban and Regional Planning: An Introduction, 1974; Europe 2000, 1977; Great Planning Disasters, 1980; Growth Centres in the European Urban System, 1980; Transport and Public Policy Planning (ed. with D. Banister), 1980; The Inner City in Context (ed.), 1981; Silicon Landscapes (ed.), 1985; Can Rail Save the City? (co-author), 1985; High-Tech America (co-author), 1986; Western Sunrise (co-author), 1987; The Carrier Wave (co-author), 1988; Cities of Tomorrow, 1988; London 2001, 1989; The Rise of the Gunbelt, 1991; Technoples of the World, 1994; Sociable Cities (co-author), 1998; Cities in Civilisation, 1998; Urban Future 21 (co-author), 2000; Working Capital (co-author), 2002. *Honours:* Hon. Fellow, St Catharine's College, Cambridge, 1988; British Acad., fellow, 1983; Mem. of the Academia Europea, 1989; Knight Bachelor, 1998. *Address:* c/o Institute of Community Studies, 18 Victoria Park Sq., London E2 9PF, England. *Telephone:* (20) 8980-6263. *E-mail:* phall@icstudies.ac.uk.

HALL, Sir Peter Reginald Frederick, BA; British director, producer and academic; b. 22 Nov. 1930, Bury St Edmunds, Suffolk, England; m. 1st Leslie Caron 1956 (divorced 1965); one s. one d.; m. 2nd Jacqueline Taylor 1965 (divorced 1981); one s. one d.; m. 3rd Maria Ewing 1982 (divorced 1990); one d.; m. 4th Nicola Frei 1990; one d. *Education:* St Catharine's Coll., Cambridge. *Career:* Dir, Arts Theatre, London, 1955–56, Royal Shakespeare Theatre, 1960, National Theatre, 1973–88; Founder-Dir-Producer, International Playwright's Theatre, 1957, Peter Hall Co, 1988; Managing Dir, Stratford-on-Avon and Aldwych Theatre, London, 1960–68; Assoc. Prof. of Drama, Warwick University, 1966–; Co-Dir, RSC, 1968–73; Artistic Dir, Glyndebourne Festival, 1984–90, Old Vic, 1997; mem. Theatre Dirs' Guild of Great Britain, founder-mem., 1983–. *Publications:* The Wars of the Roses, adaptation after Shakespeare (with John Barton), 1970; John Gabriel Borkman, by Ibsen (trans. with Inga-Stina Ewbank), 1975; Peter Hall's Diaries: The Story of a Dramatic Battle (edited by John Goodwin), 1983; Animal Farm, adaptation after Orwell, 1986; The Wild Duck, by Ibsen (trans. with Inga-Stina Ewbank), 1990; Making an Exhibition of Myself (autobiog.), 1993; An Absolute Turkey, by Feydeau (trans. with Nicola Frei), 1994. *Honours:* Hon. Fellow, St Catharine's College, Cambridge, 1964; Chevalier, Ordre des Arts et des Lettres, 1965; Tony Award, USA, 1966; Shakespeare Prize, University of Hamburg, 1967; Knighted, 1977; Standard Special Award, 1979; Special Award for Outstanding Achievement in Opera, 1981, and Awards for Best Dir, 1981, 1987; several hon. doctorates. *Address:* c/o Old Vic, Waterloo Road, London SE1 8NB, England.

HALL, Rodney; Writer and Poet; b. 18 Nov. 1935, Solihull, Warwickshire, England; m. Bet MacPahil, three d. *Education:* BA, University of Queensland, Brisbane, 1971. *Career:* Poetry Ed., The Australian, 1967–78; Creative Arts Fellow, Australian National University, 1968–69. *Publications:* Fiction: The Ship on the Coin, 1972; A Place Among People, 1975; Just Relations, 1982; Kisses of the Enemy, 1987; Captivity Captive, 1988; The Second Bridegroom, 1991; The Grisly Wife, 1993; The Island in the Mind, 1998; Return to the Brink (play), 1999; The Day We Had Hitler Home, 2000; The Owner of My Face, 2002. Poetry: Penniless Till Doomsday, 1962; The Law of Karma: A Progression of Poems, 1968; A Soapbox Omnibus, 1973; Selected Poems, 1975; Black Bagatelles, 1978; The Most Beautiful World: Fictions and Sermons, 1981; Journey Through Australia, 1989. Contributions: newspapers, magazines, reviews, and journals. *Honours:* Grace Leven Prize for Poetry, 1973; Miles Franklin Awards, 1982, 1994; AM, 1990. *Literary Agent:* Australian Literary Management, 2A Booth St, Balmain, NSW 2041, Australia. *Address:* PO Box 7, Bermagui South, NSW 2546, Australia.

HALL, Roger Leighton, BA, MA, DipEd, QSO; dramatist; b. 17 Jan. 1939, Woodford, Wells, Essex, England; m. Dianne Sturm 1968; one s. one d. *Education:* Victoria Univ., Wellington, New Zealand. *Career:* Robert Burns Fellow, Otago Univ. 1977, 1978; Fullbright Visiting Lecturer, Georgetown Univ., DC 2000; mem. PEN New Zealand; Scriptwriters Guild; Arts Foundation of New Zealand, gov. *Publications:* Plays: Glide Time, 1976; Middle Age Spread, 1977; State of the Play, 1978; Prisoners of Mother England, 1979; The Rose, 1981; Hot Water, 1982; Fifty-Fifty, 1982; Multiple Choice, 1984; Dream of Sussex Downs, 1986; The Hansard Show, 1986; The Share Club, 1987; After the Crash, 1988; Conjugal Rites, 1990; By Degrees, 1993; Market Forces, 1995; Social Climbers, 1995; C'mon Black, 1996; The Book Club, 1999; You Gotta Be Joking, 1999; Take a Chance on Me, 2001; A Way of Life, 2001; Spreading Out 2004. Other: Musicals with Philip Norman and A. K. Grant; many plays for radio, television, and children. *Honours:* Hon. DLitt (Victoria Univ.) 1996; Fulbright Travel Award 1982, Turnovsky Award, Outstanding Contribution to the Arts 1987, CNZM 2003. *Address:* c/o Playmarket, PO Box 9767, Wellington, New Zealand. *E-mail:* roger.h@xtra.co.nz.

HALL, Sarah, MLitt; British writer; b. 1974, Cumbria. *Education:* Univ. of Wales, Aberystwyth, St Andrews Univ. *Career:* tutor in creative writing, St Andrews Univ.; emigrated to North Carolina, USA. *Publications:* Haweswater (Betty Trask Award, Commonwealth First Novel Prize 2003) 2002, Electric Michelangelo 2004. *Address:* c/o Faber & Faber, 3 Queen Square, London, WC1N 3AU, England. *Telephone:* (20) 7465-0045. *Fax:* (20) 7465-0034. *Website:* www.faber.co.uk.

HALL, Willis; Writer and Dramatist; b. 6 April 1929, Leeds, England; m. Valerie Shute 1973; one s., three s. by previous marriages. *Education:* Cockburn High School, Leeds. *Publications:* Football Classified (with Michael Parkinson), 1974; My Sporting Life, 1975; Football Final, 1975. Children's Books: The Royal Astrologers, 1960; The Incredible Kidnapping, 1975; The Last Vampire, 1982; The Inflatable Shop, 1984; The Return of the Antelope, 1985; Dragon Days, 1986; The Antelope Company Ashore, 1987; Spooky Rhymes, 1987; The Antelope Company at Large, 1987; Doctor Jekyll and Mr Hollins, 1988; The Vampire's Holiday, 1992; The Vampire's Christmas, 1994; The Vampire Vanishes, 1995; Vampire Park, 1996; The Vampire Hunt, 1998; Vampire Island, 1999. Plays: The Long and the Short and the Tall, 1959; The Play of the Royal Astrologers, 1960; Kidnapped at Christmas, 1975; Christmas Crackers, 1976; Walk On, Walk On, 1976; A Right Christmas Caper, 1978; Jane Eyre (adaptation from C. Brontë), 1992;

Mansfield Park (adaptation from Jane Austen), 1993; The Three Musketeers (adaptation from Dumas), 1994; The Magicians, 2003. Plays written in collaboration with Keith Waterhouse: Billy Liar, 1960; Celebration, 1961; All Things Bright and Beautiful, 1962; Squat Betty and the Sponge Room, 1963; Say Who You Are, 1965; Whoops A Daisy, 1968; Children's Day, 1969; Who's Who, 1972; Saturday, Sunday, Monday (adaptation from de Filippo), 1973; Filumena (adaptation from de Filippo), 1978. Musicals: Worzel Gummidge (with Keith Waterhouse and Denis King), 1981; Treasure Island (with Denis King), 1985; The Wind in the Willows (with Denis King), 1985; The Water Babies (with John Cooper) 1987; The Card (with Keith Waterhouse, Tony Hatch and Anthony Drewe), 1994; Peter Pan (with George Stiles and Anthony Drewe), 1998. *Address:* c/o Alexandra Cann Representation, 12 Abingdon Rd, London W8 6AF, England.

HALLIBURTON, David (Garland); Prof. of English and Writer; b. 24 Sept. 1933, San Bernardino, CA, USA; m. 1960, three c. *Education:* BA, 1955, MA, 1963, PhD, English, 1966, University of California-Riverside. *Career:* Asst Prof. of English, 1966–72, Assoc. Prof. of English, Comparative Literature, Modern Thought and Literature, 1972–80, University of California-Riverside, Riverside; Prof. of English, Stanford University, Stanford, CA, 1980–; mem. MLA. *Publications:* Edgar Allan Poe: A Phenomenological View, 1973; Poetic Thinking: An Approach to Heidegger, 1982; The Color of the Sky: A Study of Stephen Crane, 1989; The Fateful Discourse of Worldly Things, 1997. Contributions: periodicals including: Modern Fiction Studies; Papers in Language and Literatures; Studies in Romanticism. *Honours:* Grant, American Philosophical Society, 1970; Fellow, ACLS, 1971–72. *Address:* Dept of English, Stanford University, Stanford, CA 94305, USA.

HALLIDAY, Mark, PhD; American poet and academic; b. 1949. *Education:* Brandeis Univ. *Career:* teacher, Wellesley Coll., Univ. of Pennsylvania, West Michigan Univ., Indiana Univ.; teacher of creative writing, Ohio Univ. 1996–. *Publications:* poetry: Little Star 1987, Tasket Street 1992, Selfwolf 1999; non-fiction: The Sighted Singer (with Allen Grossman) 1991, Stevens and the Interpersonal 1991; contrib. to Slate magazine (online). *Honours:* Juniper Prize. *Address:* English Department, 360 Ellis Hall, Ohio University, Athens, OH 45701, USA. *Telephone:* (740) 593-2838. *Fax:* (740) 593-2818. *E-mail:* English.Department@ohio.edu.

HALLIGAN, Marion; Writer; b. 16 April 1940, Newcastle, NSW, Australia; m. Graham James Halligan 8 June 1963 (died Nov. 1998); one s. one d. *Education:* BA, 1961, DipEd, 1962, University of Newcastle. *Career:* several writer-in-residencies; Chair, Literature Board, Australia Council, 1992–95; mem. Australian Society of Authors; Australian Symposium of Gastronomy. *Publications:* Self Possession, 1987; The Living Hothouse, 1988; The Hanged Man in the Garden, 1989; Spider Cup, 1990; Eat My Words (essays), 1990; Lovers' Knots: A Hundred-Year Novel, 1992; The Worry Box, 1993; Wishbone, 1994; Cockles of the Heart (essays), 1996; Out of the Picture, 1996; Collected Stories, 1997; Those Women Who Go to Hotels (co-author), 1997; The Midwife's Daughters (children's), 1997; The Golden Dress (novel), 1998; The Fog Garden (novel), 2001; The Point (novel), 2003. Contributions: anthologies and periodicals. *Honours:* Australian Literature Board Grants, 1981, 1987; Braille Book of the Year Award, 1989; Age Book of the Year Award, 1992; Australian Capital Territory Book of the Year Award, 1993; 3M Talking Book of the Year Award, 1993. *Address:* 6 Caldwell St, Hackett, ACT 2602, Australia.

HALPERN, Daniel; academic, poet and writer; b. 11 Sept. 1945, Syracuse, NY, USA; m. Jeanne Catherine Carter 1982; one d. *Education:* San Francisco State College, 1963–64; BA, California State University at Northridge, 1969; MFA, Columbia University, 1972. *Career:* Founder-Ed., Antaeus literary magazine, 1969–95; Instructor, New School for Social Research, New York City, 1971–76; Ed.-in-Chief, Ecco Press, 1971–; Visiting Prof., Princeton University, 1975–76, 1987–88, 1995–96; Assoc. Prof., Columbia University, 1976–. *Publications:* Poetry: Traveling on Credit, 1978; Seasonal Rights, 1982; Tango, 1987; Foreign Neon, 1991; Selected Poems, 1994; Antaeus 1970, 1996; Something Shining, 1998. Other: The Keeper of Height, 1974; Treble Poets, 1975; Our Private Lives: Journals, Notebooks and Diaries, 1990; Not for Bread Alone: Writers on Food, Wine, and the Art of Eating, 1993; The Autobiographical Eye, 1993; Holy Fire: Nine Visionary Poets and the Quest for Enlightenment, 1994. Editor: Borges on Writing (co-ed.), 1973; The American Poetry Anthology, 1975; The Antaeus Anthology, 1986; The Art of the Tale: An International Anthology of Short Stories, 1986; On Nature, 1987; Writers on Artists, 1988; Reading the Fights (with Joyce Carol Oates), 1988; Plays in One Act, 1990; The Sophisticated Cat (with Joyce Carol Oates), 1992; On Music (co-ed.), 1994. Contributions: various anthologies, reviews, journals, and magazines. *Honours:* Jesse Rehder Poetry Award, Southern Poetry Review, 1971; YMHA Discovery Award, 1971; Great Lakes Colleges National Book Award, 1973; Borestone Mountain Poetry Award, 1974; Robert Frost Fellowship, Bread Loaf, 1974; National Endowment for the Arts Fellowships, 1974, 1975, 1987; Pushcart Press Prizes, 1980, 1987, 1988; Carey Thomas Award for Creative Publishing, Publishers Weekly, 1987; Guggenheim Fellowship, 1988; PEN Publisher Citation, 1993. *Address:* c/o The Ecco Press, 100 W Broad Street, Hopewell, NJ 08525, USA.

HALSEY, Alan, BA; bookseller and poet; b. 22 Sept. 1949, Croydon, Surrey, England. *Career:* mem. Thomas Lovell Beddoes Soc., David Jones Soc. *Publications:* Yearspace, 1979; Another Loop in Our Days, 1980; Present State, 1981; Perspectives on the Reach, 1981; The Book of Coming Forth in Official Secrecy, 1981; Auto Dada Cafe, 1987; A Book of Changes, 1988; Five Years Out, 1989; Reasonable Distance, 1992; The Text of Shelley's Death, 1995; A Robin Hood Book, 1996; Fit to Print (with Karen McCormack), 1998; Days of '49 (with Gavin Selerie), 1999; Wittgenstein's Devil: Selected Writings, 1978–98, 2000; Sonatas and Preliminary Sketches, 2000; Dante's Barber Shop, 2001; Lives of the Poets: A Preliminary Count (with Martin Corless-Smith), 2002; Death's Jest Book, by Thomas Lovell Beddoes (ed.), 2003. Contributions: Critical Quarterly; Conjunctions; North Dakota Quarterly; Writing; Ninth Decade; Poetica; South West Review; Poetry Wales; Poesie Europe; O Ars; Figs; Interstate; Prospice; Reality Studios; Fragmente; Screens and Tasted Parallels; Avec; Purge; Grille; Acumen; Shearsman; Oasis; New American Writing; Agenda; Colorado Review; Talisman; PN Review; Resurgence; West Coast Line; The Gig; Boxkite; The Paper; Chicago Review; Envelope; Ecorché; Fence; Kiosk; New Arcadians Journal; Queen Street Quarterly. *Address:* 40 Crescent Road, Nether Edge, Sheffield S7 1HN, England. *E-mail:* alan@nethedge.demon.co.uk.

HAMAD, Turki-al; Saudi Arabian writer and academic; b. Buraida. *Publications:* Adama 2003, Shumaisi 2004. *Address:* c/o Saqi Books, 26 Westbourne Grove, London, W2 5RH, England. *Telephone:* (20) 7221-9347. *Fax:* (20) 7229-7492. *Website:* www.saqibooks.com.

HAMBRICK-STOWE, Charles Edwin; Writer; b. 4 Feb. 1948, Worcester, Massachusetts, USA; m. Elizabeth Anne Hambrick-Stowe, 11 Sept. 1971, two s. one d. *Education:* BA, Hamilton College, 1970; MA and MDiv, Pacific School of Religion, 1973; PhD, Boston University Graduate School, 1980. *Career:* Religion Columnist, Evening Sun Newspaper, Carrol County, MD, 1982–85; mem. American Historical Asscn; American Society of Church History; American Acad. of Religion. *Publications:* Massachusetts Militia Companies and the Officers of the Lexington Alarm, 1976; Practice of Piety: Puritan Devotional Disciplines in 17th Century New England, 1982; Early New England Meditative Poetry: Anne Bradstreet and Edward Taylor, 1988; Theology and Identity: Traditions, Movements and Issues in the United Church of Christ, 1990; Charles G. Finney and The Spirit of American Evangelicalism, 1996; Living Theological Heritage: Colonial and Early National Beginnings, 1998. Contributions: Reference works, books and journals. *Honours:* Jamestown Prize for Early American History, 1980.

HAMBURGER, Anne (Ellen), (Anne Beresford); Poet, Writer, Actress and Teacher; b. 10 Sept. 1928, Redhill, Surrey, England; m. Michael Hamburger 28 July 1951; one s. two d. *Education:* Central School of Dramatic Art, London, 1944–46. *Career:* Actress, various repertory companies, 1946–48, BBC Radio, 1960–78; Teacher; General Council, Poetry Society, 1976–78; Committee Mem., 1989, Adviser on Agenda, Editorial Board, 1993–96, Aldeburgh Poetry Festival. *Publications:* Poetry: Walking Without Moving, 1967; The Lair, 1968; The Courtship, 1972; Footsteps on Snow, 1972; The Curving Shore, 1975; Songs a Thracian Taught Me, 1980; The Songs of Almut, 1980; The Sele of the Morning, 1988; Charm with Stones (Lyrik im Hölderlinturm), 1993; Landscape With Figures, 1994; Selected and New Poems, 1997; No Place for Cowards, 1998; Hearing Things, 2002. Other: Struck by Apollo (radio play, with Michael Hamburger), 1965; The Villa (radio short story), 1968; Alexandros Poems of Vera Lungu (trans.), 1974; Duet for Three Voices (dramatized poems for Anglia TV), 1982; Snapshots from an Album, 1884–1895, 1992. Contributions: periodicals. *Address:* Marsh Acres, Middleton, Saxmundham, Suffolk IP17 3NH, England.

HAMBURGER, Michael Peter Leopold, MA; British poet, writer, translator and editor; b. 22 March 1924, Berlin, Germany; m. Anne Ellen File 1951; one s. two d. *Education:* Christ Church Coll., Oxford. *Career:* Asst Lecturer in German, University College London, 1952–55; Lecturer, then Reader in German, University of Reading, 1955–64; Florence Purington Lecturer, Mount Holyoke College, South Hadley, Massachusetts, 1966–67; Visiting Prof., SUNY at Buffalo, 1969, and at Stony Brook, 1971, University of South Carolina, 1973, Boston University, 1975–77; Visiting Fellow, Wesleyan University, Middletown, CT, 1970; Regent's Lecturer, University of California at San Diego, 1973; Prof. (part-time), University of Essex, 1978. *Publications:* Poetry: Flowering Cactus, 1950; Poems 1950–51, 1952; The Dual Site, 1958; Weather and Season, 1963; Feeding the Chickadees, 1968; Penguin Modern Poets (with A Brownjohn and C. Tomlinson), 1969; Travelling, 1969; Travelling I–V, 1973; Ownerless Earth, 1973; Travelling VI, 1975; Real Estate, 1977; Moralities, 1977; Variations, 1981; Collected Poems, 1984; Trees, 1988; Selected Poems, 1988; Roots in the Air, 1991; Collected Poems, 1941–94, 1995; Late, 1997; Mr Littlejoy's Rattlebag for the New Millennium, 1999; Intersections: Shorter Poems, 1994–2000, 2000; From a Diary of Non-Events, 2002. Prose: Reason and Energy, 1957; From Prophecy to Exorcism, 1965; The Truth of Poetry, 1970; A Mug's Game (memoirs), 1973, revised edn as String of Beginnings, 1991; Hugo von Hofmannsthal, 1973; Art as a Second Nature, 1975; A Proliferation of Prophets, 1983; After the Second Flood: Essays in Modern German Literature, 1986; Testimonies: Selected Shorter Prose 1950–1987, 1989; Michael Hamburger in Conversation with Peter Dale, 1998; The Take-Over (fiction), 2000; Philip Larkin: A Retrospect (memoir), 2002. Translator: many books, including: Poems of Hölderin, 1943, revised edn as Hölderlin: Poems, 1952; JCF Hölderin: Selected Verse, 1961; H. von Hofmannsthal: Poems and Verse Plays (with others), 1961; H. von Hofmannsthal: Selected Plays and Libretti (with others), 1964; J. C. F. Hölderlin: Poems and Fragments, 1967; The Poems of Hans Magnus Enzenberger (with others), 1968; The Poems of Günter Grass (with C. Middleton), 1969; Paul Celan: Poems, 1972, revised edn as Poems of Paul Celan, 1988; Kiosk, 1997; Günter Grass: Selected Poems, 1998. Contributions: numerous publications. *Honours:* Bollingen Foundation Fellow, 1959–61, 1965–66; Trans. Prizes, Deutsche Akademie für Sprache und Dichtung, Darmstadt, 1964, Arts Council of Great Britain, 1969; Medal, Institute of Linguistics, 1977; Schlegel-Tieck Prizes, 1978, 1981; Goethe Medal, 1986; Austrian State Prize for Literary Trans., 1988; Hon. LittD, University of East Anglia, 1988; European Trans. Prize, 1990; OBE, 1992; Hon. DPhil, Technical University, Berlin, 1995; Cholmondeley Award for Poetry, 2000; Horst Bienek Prize, Munich, 2001. *Literary Agent:* Johnson & Alcock Ltd, Clerkenwell House, 45–47 Clerkenwell Green, London EC1R 0HT, England.

HAMBURGER, Philip (Paul); Writer; b. 2 July 1914, Wheeling, West Virginia, USA; m. 1st Edith Iglauer, 24 Dec. 1942; m. 2nd Anna Walling Matson, 27 Oct. 1968, two s. *Education:* BA, Johns Hopkins University, 1935; MS, Graduate School of Journalism, Columbia University, 1938. *Career:* Staff Writer, The New Yorker, 1939–; mem. Authors League of America; PEN USA; Board of Dirs, Authors League Fund; National Press Club, Washington; Century Asscn; Fellow, American Acad. of Arts and Sciences. *Publications:* The Oblong Blur and Other Odysseys, 1949; J. P. Marquand, Esquire, 1952; Mayor Watching and Other Pleasures, 1958; Our Man Stanley, 1963; An American Notebook, 1965; Curious World, A New Yorker at Large, 1987; Friends Talking in the Night, 1999; Matters of State – A Political Excursion, 2000. Contributions: The New Yorker. *Honours:* New York Public Library Literary Lion Award, 1986; George Polk Career Award, 1994; Columbia Journalism Alumni Award, 1997. *Address:* c/o The New Yorker, 4 Times Sq., New York, NY 10036, USA.

HAMELIN, Claude; Poet, Writer and Scientist; b. 25 Aug. 1943, Montréal, QC, Canada; m. Renée Artinian, 11 Sept. 1970, one s. one d. *Education:* BPed, 1965; BSc, 1970; MSc, 1972; PhD, 1975. *Publications:* Poetry: Fables des quatre-temps, 1990; Lueurs froides, 1991; Nef des fous, 1992; Néant bleu/Nada azul/Blue Nothingness, 1994. Novel: Roman d'un quartier, 1993. Contributions: anthologies and journals.

HAMILL, (William) Pete; journalist and writer; b. 24 June 1934, New York, NY, USA; m. 1st Ramona Negron 1962 (divorced 1970); two d.; m. 2nd Fukiko Aoki 1987. *Education:* Pratt Institute, Mexico City College. *Career:* reporter, later columnist, 1960–74, 1988–93, New York Post; Contributing Ed., Saturday Evening Post, 1963–64; Contributor, Village Voice and New York Magazine, 1974–; Columnist, New York Daily News, 1975–79, 1982–84, Esquire Magazine, 1989–91; Ed., Mexico City News, 1986–87; mem. Writers Guild of America. *Publications:* Fiction: A Killing for Christ, 1968; The Gift, 1973; Flesh and Blood, 1977; Loving Women, 1990; Tokyo Sketches, 1993. Non-Fiction: Irrational Ravings, 1972; The Invisible City: A New York Sketchbook, 1980; A Drinking Life: A Memoir, 1994; News is a Verb, 1998; Why Sinatra Matters, 1998. Screenplays: Doc, 1971; Badge 373, 1973; Liberty, 1986; Neon Empire, 1987. Contributions: many periodicals. *Honours:* Meyer Berger Award, Columbia School of Journalism, 1962; Newspaper Reporters Asscn Award, 1962; 25 Year Achievement Award, Society of Silurians, 1989; Peter Kihss Award, 1992. *Address:* c/o New York Magazine, 755 Second Avenue, New York, NY 10017, USA.

HAMILL, Sam P(atrick); Poet, Publisher, Ed. and Trans; b. 9 May 1943, California, USA; m. 1st Nancy Larsen, 1964, divorced, one d.; m. 2nd Tree Swenson, 1973, divorced; m. 3rd Gray Foster. *Education:* Journalism, Los Angeles Valley College, 1966–69; English Literature, University of California at Santa Barbara, 1970–72. *Career:* Co-Founder, Copper Canyon Press, 1972–; Writer-in-Residence, Reed College, University of Alaska, South Utah State University, South Oregon College, Austin College, Trinity College, 1974–, Dept of Correction, Washington, Alaska, California, 1976–88; Columnist, Port Townsend Leader, 1990–93; mem. PEN American Center; Poetry Society of America; Acad. of American Poets. *Publications:* Poetry: Heroes of the Teton Mythos, 1973; Petroglypics, 1975; Uintah Blue, 1975; The Calling Across Forever, 1976; The Book of Elegaic Geography, 1978; Triada, 1978; Animae, 1980; Fatal Pleasure, 1984; The Nootka Rose, 1987; Passport, 1988; A Dragon in the Clouds, 1989; Mandala, 1991; Destination Zero: Poems 1970–1995, 1995. Essays: At Home in the World, 1980; Basho's Ghost, 1989; A Poet's Work: The Other Side of Poetry, 1990. Ed. or co-ed., anthologies, selected poems, collections, including: Endless River: Li Po and Tu Fu: A Friendship in Poetry, 1993; Love Poems from the Japanese, 1994; Twenty-Five Years of Poetry from Copper Canyon Press, 1996. Trans. or co-trans. of Chinese, Estonian, Latin, Japanese and ancient Greek works. Contributions: Poetry, essays and trans to numerous anthologies and literary magazines. *Honours:* College Ed.'s Award, Best College Journal, Co-ordinating Council of Literary Magazines, 1972; Washington Gov.'s Arts Awards to Copper Canyon Press, 1975, 1990; National Endowment for the Arts Fellowship, 1980; Pacific Northwest Booksellers' Award, 1980; Guggenheim Fellowship, 1983; Pushcart Prizes, 1989, 1996; Lila Wallace-Reader's Digest Writing Fellowship, 1992–93. *Address:* PO Box 468, Port Townsend, WA 98368, USA.

HAMILTON, Carol Jean Barber, BS, MA; writer, poet and educator; b. 23 Aug. 1935, Enid, Oklahoma, USA; m. (divorced); two s. one d. *Education:* Phillips Univ., Univ. of Central Oklahoma. *Career:* English Prof., Rose State Coll.; Prof. in Creative Studies, Univ. of Central Oklahoma; Poet Laureate of Oklahoma 1995–97; mem. Poetry Soc. of Oklahoma, Individual Artists of Oklahoma, Mid Oklahoma Writers, American Acad. of Poetry, Soc. of Children's Book Writers and Illustrators. *Publications:* juvenile: The Dawn Seekers 1987, Legends of Poland 1993, The Mystery of Black Mesa 1995, I'm Not From Neptune 2003; poetry: Daring the Wind 1988, Once the Dust 1992, Breaking Bread, Breaking Silence, Legerdemain, Gold: Greatest Hits, I, People of the Llano; contrib. to Christian Science Monitor, Commonweal, New York Quarterly, Christian Century, Arizona Quarterly, Hawaii Review, Midwest Quarterly Review, Oklahoma Today, Kansas Quarterly, Arkansas Review, New Orleans Review, Southern Poetry Review, Chariton Review, Windsor Review. *Honours:* Oklahoma Book Award for Poetry 1992, Byline Literary Award for poetry 1994, for short story 1987, Pegasus Award 1995, Chriron Review Chapbook Award 2000, David Ray Poetry Award 2000, Warren Keith Lewis Poetry Award 2002. *Address:* 9608 Sonata Court, Midwest City, OK 73130, USA.

HAMILTON, Donald B(engtsson); Writer; b. 24 March 1916, Uppsala, Sweden; m. Kathleen Stick, 12 Sep 1941, deceased Oct. 1989, two s. two d. *Education:* BS, University of Chicago, 1938. *Career:* mem. Authors' Guild; MWA; Western Writers of America; Outdoor Writer's Asscn of America. *Publications:* 5 mystery novels, 1947–56; 4 western novels, 1954–60; The Big Country, 1958; 25 novels featuring agent Matt Helm, 1960–93; On Guns and Hunting, 1970; Cruises with Kathleen, 1980. Contributions: periodicals. *Honours:* Western Writers of America Spur, 1967. *Address:* PO Box 1141, Old Saybrook, CT 06475, USA.

HAMILTON, Jane; Writer; b. 1957, Oak Park, IL, USA; m. Robert Willard, June 1982, two c. *Education:* BA, Carleton College, Northfield, Minnesota, 1979. *Publications:* The Book of Ruth, UK edn as The Frogs Are Still Singing, 1989; A Map of the World, 1994; The Short History of a Prince, 1998; Disobedience, 2000. *Honours:* Ernest Hemingway Foundation Award, PEN American Center, 1989. *Address:* c/o Doubleday Publishers, 1540 Broadway, New York, 10036, USA.

HAMILTON, John Maxwell; University Dean, Prof. and Writer; b. 28 March 1947, Evanston, IL, USA; m. Regina Frances Nalewajek, 19 Aug. 1975, one s. *Education:* BA, Journalism, Marquette University, 1969; Postgraduate Studies, University of New Hampshire, 1971–73; MS, Journalism, Boston University, 1974; PhD, American Civilization, George Washington University, 1983. *Career:* Reporter, Milwaukee Journal, 1967–69; Journalist, Washington, DC, 1973–75; Foreign Correspondent, Latin America, 1976–78; Special Asst, Asst Administrator, Agency for International Development, Washington, DC, 1978–81; Staff Assoc., Foreign Affairs Subcommittee on International Economic Policy and Trade, US House of Representatives, Washington, DC, 1981–82; Chief US Foreign Policy Correspondent, International Reporting Information Systems, Washington, DC, 1982–83; Dir, Main Street America and the Third World, Washington, DC, 1985–87; Senior Counsellor, World Bank, Washington, DC, 1983–85, 1987–92; Dean and Prof., 1992–, Manship School of Mass Communication, Hopkins Breazeale Foundation Prof., 1998, Louisiana State University at Baton Rouge; Fellow, Shorenstein Center, Kennely School, Harvard, 2002; mem. Asscn of Schools of Journalism and Mass Communication; Society of Professional Journalists. *Publications:* Main Street America and the Third World, 1986; Edgar Snow: A Biography, 1988; Entangling Alliances: How the Third World Shapes Our Lives, 1990; Hold the Press: The Inside Story on Newspapers (with George Krimsky), 1996; Casanova Was a Book Lover: And Other Naked Facts and Provocative Curiosities About Reading, Writing and Publishing, 2000. Contributions: books, scholarly journals and general periodicals and newspapers. *Honours:* many grants; Critic's Choice, Los Angeles Times, 1988; Frank Luther Mott-Kappa Tau Alpha Research Award, 1988; By-line Award, Marquette University, 1993; Second Place, Green Eyeshade Awards, 1999, 2000; Freedom Forum Journalism Administrator of the Year, 2003. *Address:* c/o Office of the Dean, Manship School of Mass Communication, Louisiana State University, Baton Rouge, LA 70803-0001, USA. *E-mail:* jhamilt@lsu.edu.

HAMILTON, Peter F.; Author; b. 1960, Rutland, England. *Career:* writer, 1987–. *Publications:* Greg Mandel series: Mindstar Rising, 1993; A Quantum Murder, 1994; The Nano Flower, 1995; Night's Dawn Trilogy: The Reality Dysfunction, 1996; The Neutronium Alchemist, 1997; The Naked God, 1999; Other: Escape Route (novella), 1997; The Web: Lightstorm (children's), 1998; A Second Chance at Eden (short stories), 1998; The Confederation Handbook, 2000; Futures, 2001; Fallen Dragon, 2001; Watching Trees Grow, 2002; Misspent Youth, 2002; short stories. Contributions: magazines incl. Fear, Interzone; anthologies incl. In Dreams, New Worlds. *Address:* c/o Pan Macmillan, 20 New Wharf Rd, London N1 9RR, England. *Website:* www.peterhamilton.com.

HAMILTON, Priscilla (see Gellis, Roberta Leah).

HAMILTON, Wade (see Floren, Lee).

HAMILTON-PATERSON, James, BA; British writer and poet; b. 6 Nov. 1941, London, England. *Education:* Windlesham House, Sussex, Bickley Hall, Kent, King's School, Canterbury, Exeter Coll., Oxford, King's Coll., London. *Career:* teacher in Hertfordshire –1961, in Tripoli, Libya 1966; orderly, St Stephen's Hospital, London 1966–68; staff, New Statesman 1969–74; features ed., Nova magazine 1974–75; science columnist, Das Magazin, Zurich 2000–02, Die Weltwocher 2002–; currently resides in the

Philippines and Tuscany, Italy. *Publications:* poetry: Option Three 1974, Dutch Alps 1984; novels: Playing with Water 1987, Gerontius (Whitbread First Novel Award) 1989, The Bell-Boy (aka That Time in Malomba) 1990, Griefwork 1993, Ghosts of Manila 1994, Loving Monsters 2001, Cooking with Fernet Branca 2004; short story collections: The View from Mount Dog 1986, The Music 1995; juvenile: Flight Underground 1969, The House in the Waves 1970, Hostage! 1980; non-fiction: Very Personal War: The Story of Cornelius Hawkridge 1971, Mummies: Death and Life in Ancient Egypt (with Carol Andrews) 1978, Seven-Tenths 1992, The Great Deep: The Sea and Its Thresholds 1993, America's Boy: A Century of Colonialism in the Philippines 1998, Three Miles Down 1998. *Honours:* Oxford Newdigate prize 1964. *Address:* c/o Faber and Faber Ltd, 3 Queen Square, London, WC1N 3AU, England.

HAMLYN, David W(alter); Prof. of Philosophy Emeritus and Writer; b. 1 Oct. 1924, Plymouth, England; m. Eileen Carlyle Litt, 2 July 1949, one s. one d. *Education:* BA, Literae Humanores, 1948, BA, Philosophy and Psychology, 1950, MA, 1949, Exeter College, Oxford. *Career:* Research Fellow, Corpus Christi College, Oxford, 1950–53; Lecturer, Jesus College, Oxford, 1953–54; Lecturer, 1954–63, Reader, 1963–64, Prof. of Philosophy and Head of the Dept of Philosophy, 1964–88, Head of the Dept of Classics, 1981–86, Vice-Master, 1983–88, Fellow, 1988, Prof. of Philosophy Emeritus, 1988–, Birkbeck College, University of London; Ed., Mind, 1972–84; Consulting Ed., Journal of Medical Ethics, 1981–90; mem. Aristotelian Society, pres., 1977–78; University of London Senate, 1981–87; National Committee for Philosophy, 1986–92, hon. vice-pres., 1992–2003; Royal Institute of Philosophy, council, 1968–, exec. committee, 1971–97, vice-chair., 1991–95. *Publications:* The Psychology of Perception, 1957; Sensation and Perception, 1961; Aristotle's De Anima, Books II–III, 1968; The Theory of Knowledge, 1970; Experience and the Growth of Understanding, 1978; Schopenhauer, 1980; Perception, Learning and the Self, 1983; Metaphysics, 1984; History of Western Philosophy, 1987; In and Out of the Black Box, 1990; Being a Philosopher, 1992; Understanding Perception, 1996. Contributions: books and professional journals. *Address:* 38 Smithy Knoll Rd, Hope Valley, Calver, Derbyshire S32 3XW, England.

HAMMER, David Lindley, BA, JD; advocate and writer; b. 6 June 1929, Newton, IA, USA; m. Audrey Lowe Hammer 1953; one s. two d. *Education:* Grinnell Coll., Univ. of Iowa Law School. *Publications:* Poems From the Ledge 1980, The Game is Afoot 1983, For the Sake of the Game 1986, The 22nd Man 1989, To Play the Game 1990, Skewed Sherlock 1992, The Worth of the Game 1992, The Quest 1993, My Dear Watson 1994, The Before Breakfast Pipe 1995, A Dangerous Game 1997, The Vital Essence 1999, A Talent for Murder 2000, Yonder in the Gaslight 2000, Straight Up With a Twist 2001, You Heard What Jesse Said 2002; contrib. to American Journal of Philately, Baker Street Journal, Sherlock Holmes Journal. *Address:* Laurel Cottage, 720 Laurel Park Road, Dubuque, IA 52003; Hammer, Simon & Jensen, 770 Main Street, The Steele Centre, Dubuque, IA 52001-6820, USA (Office).

HAMMES, Gordon G., PhD; American fmr university vice-chancellor, professor of chemistry and editor; *University Distinguished Service Professor of Biochemistry, Duke University Medical Center*; b. 10 Aug. 1934, Fond du Lac, Wis.; m. Judith Ellen Frank 1959; one s. two d. *Education:* Princeton Univ. and Univ. of Wisconsin. *Career:* Postdoctoral Fellow, Max Planck Inst. für physikalische Chemie, Göttingen, FRG 1959–60; instructor, subsequently Assoc. Prof., MIT, Cambridge, Mass. 1960–65; Prof., Cornell Univ. 1965–88, Chair. Dept of Chem. 1970–75, Horace White Prof. of Chem. and Biochemistry 1975–88, Dir Biotechnology Program 1983–88; Prof., Univ. of Calif., Santa Barbara 1988–91, Vice-Chancellor for Academic Affairs 1988–91; Prof., Duke Univ., Durham, NC 1991–, Vice-Chancellor Duke Univ. Medical Center 1991–98, Univ. Distinguished Service Prof. of Biochemistry 1996–; mem. Physiological Chem. Study Section, Physical Biochemistry Study Section, Training Grant Cttee, NIH; mem. Bd of Counsellors, Nat. Cancer Inst. 1976–80, Advisory Council, Chem. Dept, Princeton 1970–75, Polytechnic Inst., New York 1977–78, Boston Univ. 1977–85; mem. Nat. Research Council, US Nat. Comm. for Biochemistry 1989–95; mem. ACS, American Soc. of Biochemistry and Molecular Biology (Pres. 1994–95), NAS, American Acad. of Arts and Sciences; Ed. Biochemistry 1992–. *Publications:* Principles of Chemical Kinetics, Enzyme Catalysis and Regulation, Chemical Kinetics: Principles and Selected Topics (with I. Amdur), Thermodynamics and Kinetics for the Biological Sciences 2000; numerous learned articles. *Honours:* ACS Award in Biological Chem. 1967, William C. Rose Award, American Soc. of Biochemistry and Molecular Biology 2002. *Address:* 11 Staley Place, Durham, NC 27705, USA. *Telephone:* (919) 684-8848 (Office). *E-mail:* hamme001@mc.duke.edu (Office).

HAMMICK, Georgina; writer and poet; b. 24 May 1939, Hampshire, England; m. 1961; one s. two d. *Education:* Académie Julian, Paris, Salisbury Art School. *Career:* mem. Writers' Guild. *Publications:* A Poetry Quintet (poems) 1976, People for Lunch 1987, Spoilt (short stories) 1992, The Virago Book of Love and Loss (ed.) 1992, The Arizona Game 1996; contrib. to journals and periodicals. *Literary Agent:* The Sayle Literary Agency, Bickerton House, 25–27 Bickerton Road, London, N19 5JT, England. *Telephone:* (20) 7263-8681. *Fax:* (20) 7561-0529. *Address:* Bridgewalk House, Brixton, Deverill, Warminster, Wiltshire BA12 7EJ, England.

HAMMOND, Jane (see Poland, Dorothy Elizabeth Hayward).

HAMPSHIRE, Susan; Actress and Writer; b. 12 May 1942, London, England; m. 1st Pierre Granier-Deferre, divorced 1974, one s.; m. 2nd Eddie Kulukundis, 1980. *Education:* Knightsbridge, England. *Career:* Actress on the London stage, 1959–; Film and television appearances; Writer; mem. Dyslexia Institute; Royal Society of Authors. *Publications:* Susan's Story: An Autobiographical Account of My Struggle with Dyslexia, 1982; The Maternal Instinct, 1985; Lucy Jane at the Ballet, 1987; Trouble Free Gardening, 1989; Lucy Jane on Television, 1989; Every Letter Counts, 1990; Lucy Jane and the Dancing Competition, 1990; Easy Gardening, 1992; Lucy Jane and the Russian Ballet, 1993; Rosie's First Ballet Lesson, 1995. *Honours:* Emmy Awards, 1970, 1971, 1973; Hon. doctorates, University of London, 1984, St Andrew's University, 1986, Kingston University, 1994, Pine Manor College, Boston, Massachusetts, 1994, Exeter University, 2001; OBE, 1995. *Address:* c/o Chatto and Linnit Ltd, 123a Kings Rd, London SW3 4PL, England.

HAMPSON, Norman; Prof. of History (retd) and Writer; b. 8 April 1922, Leyland, Lancashire, England; m. Jacqueline Gardin, 22 Apr 1948, two d. *Education:* BA, MA, 1947, University College, Oxford; Doctorat de l'Université, Paris, 1955. *Career:* Lecturer, 1948–62, Senior Lecturer in French History, 1962–67, University of Manchester; Prof. of Modern History, University of Newcastle upon Tyne, 1967–74; Prof. of History, University of York, 1974–89; mem. Fellow, British Acad., 1980. *Publications:* La Marine de l'an II, 1959; A Social History of The French Revolution, 1963; The Enlightenment, Volume IV of the Pelican History of European Thought, 1968, US edn as A Cultural History of the Enlightenment, 1968; The First European Revolution, 1776–1815, 1969; The Life and Opinions of Maximilien Robespierre, 1974; A Concise History of the French Revolution, 1975; Danton, 1978; Will and Circumstance: Montesquieu, Rousseau and The French Revolution, 1983; Prelude to Terror, 1988; Saint-Just, 1991; The Perfidy of Albion, 1998; Not Really What You'd Call a War, 2001. *Honours:* Hon. Dlitt, University of Edinburgh, 1989. *Address:* 305 Hull Rd, York Y010 3LU, England.

HAMPTON, Angeline Agnes, (A A Kelly); Writer; b. 28 Feb. 1924, London, England; m. George Hughan Hampton, 31 Dec. 1944, one s., three d. *Education:* BA, External, English, University of London, 1965; Licencié è lettres, 1969, Docteur ès lettres, 1973, University of Geneva, Switzerland. *Career:* mem. International Asscn for the Study of Anglo-Irish Literature; Society of Authors; PEN International. *Publications:* Liam O'Flaherty the Storyteller, 1976; Mary Lavin: Quiet Rebel, 1980; Joseph Campbell, 1879–1944, Poet and Nationalist, 1988; The Pillars of the House (ed.), 1987; Wandering Women, 1994; The Letters of Liam O'Flaherty (ed.), 1996. Contributions: English Studies; Comparative Education; Eire, Ireland; Hibernia; Linen Hall Review; Geneva News and International Report; Christian. *Honours:* British Acad. Grant, 1987.

HAMPTON, Christopher (James); Playwright; b. 26 Jan. 1946, Fayal, The Azores; m. Laura de Holesch, 1971, two d. *Education:* BA, Modern Languages, 1968, MA, New College, Oxford. *Career:* Resident Dramatist, Royal Court Theatre, London, 1968–70; mem. FRSL. *Publications:* Tales from Hollywood, 1983; Tartuffe or The Imposter (adaptation of Moliére's play), 1984; Les Liaisons Dangereuses (adaptation of C. de Laclos's novel), 1985; Hedda Gabler and A Doll's House (trans. of Ibsen's plays), 1989; Faith, Hope and Charity by Ödön von Horváth (trans.), 1989; The Ginger Tree (adaptation of Oswald Wynd's novel), 1989; White Chameleon, 1991; The Philanthropist and Other Plays, 1991; Alice's Adventures Underground (with Martha Clarke), 1994. Other: Screenplays, radio and television plays. *Honours:* CBE, 1999. *Address:* National House, 60–66 Wardour St, London W1V 3HP, England.

HAN SUYIN, MB, BS, LRCP, MRCS; British author and medical practitioner; b. 12 Sept. 1916, Xinyang, China; m. 1st Gen. P. H. Tang 1938 (died 1947); m. 2nd L. F. Comber 1952 (divorced 1968); m. 3rd Col Vincent Ruthnaswamy 1971; two adopted d. *Education:* Yenching Univ., Peking, China, Univ. of Brussels, Belgium, Royal Free Hospital, Univ. of London. *Career:* in London 1945–49; employed Queen Mary Hospital, Hong Kong 1948–52, Johore Bahru Hospital, Malaya 1952–55; pvt. medical practice 1955–64; Lecturer in Contemporary Asian Literature, Nanyang Univ., Singapore 1958–60; Hon. Prof., Univ. of Alberta and six Chinese univs. *Publications:* Destination Chungking 1942, A Many-Splendoured Thing 1952, ...And the Rain My Drink 1956, The Mountain is Young 1958, Cast but One Shadow 1962, Winter Love 1962, The Four Faces 1963, The Crippled Tree 1965, A Mortal Flower 1966, China in the Year 2001 1967, Birdless Summer 1968, Morning Deluge – Mao Tse-tung and the Chinese Revolution 1972, Wind in the Tower 1976, Lhasa, the Open City 1977, My House has Two Doors 1980, Phoenix Harvest 1980, Till Morning Comes 1982, The Enchantress (novel) 1985, A Share of Loving 1987, Tigers and Butterflies 1990, Fleur de Soleil, Les Yeux de Demain, La Peinture Chinoise, Chine Insolite, Wind in My Sleeve (autobiog.) 1992, Eldest Son: Zhou Enlai and the making of Modern China (1898–1976) 1994; three photography books. *Address:* c/o Jonathan Cape, 32 Bedford Square, London, WC1, England. *Address:* 37 Montoie, Lausanne 1007, Switzerland.

HAN UNG-BIN; South Korean writer. *Publications:* Second Thoughts 2002. *Address:* c/o Academia Koreana, 1000 Sindang-Dong, Dalseo-Gu 704–701, Republic of Korea.

HANBURY-TENISON, (Airling) Robin; writer and farmer; b. 7 May 1936, London, England. *Education:* BA, MA, Magdalen College, Oxford. *Career:* Chief Exec., British Field Sports Society/Countryside Alliance, 1995–98; mem. RGS, council mem., 1968–82, 1995– vice-pres., 1982–86; Survival International, pres., 1969–; Society of Authors. *Publications:* The Rough and the Smooth, 1969; A Question of Survival for the Indians of Brazil, 1973; A Pattern of Peoples: A Journey Among the Tribes of the Outer Indonesian Islands, 1975; Mulu: The Rain Forest, 1980; The Aborigines of the Amazon Rain Forest: The Yanomami, 1982; Worlds Apart (autobiog.), 1984; White Horses Over France, 1985; A Ride Along the Great Wall, 1987; Fragile Eden: A Ride Through New Zealand, 1989; Spanish Pilgrimage: A Canter to St James, 1990; The Oxford Book of Exploration, 1993; Jake's Escape, 1996; Jake's Treasure, Jake's Safari, 1998. Contributions: Frontiers Column, Geographical Magazine, 1995–98. *Honours:* RGS Gold Medal, 1979; OBE, 1981; Thomas Cook Travel Book Award, 1984. *Address:* Cabilla Manor, Cardinham, Bodmin, Cornwall PL30 4DW, England.

HANCOCK, Geoffrey White; Writer and Literary Journalist; b. 14 April 1946, New Westminster, NB, Canada; m. Gay Allison, 6 Aug. 1983, one d. *Education:* BFA, 1973, MFA, University of British Columbia, 1975. *Career:* Ed.-in-Chief, Canadian Fiction Magazine, 1975; Consulting Ed., Canadian Author and Bookman, 1978; Fiction Ed., Cross-Canada Writers Quarterly, 1980; Literary Consultant, CBC Radio, 1980; mem. Periodical Writers of Canada. *Publications:* Magic Realism, 1980; Illusion: Fables, Fantasies and Metafictions, 1983; Metavisions, 1983; Shoes and Shit: Stories for Pedestrians, 1984; Moving Off the Map: From Story to Fiction, 1986; Invisible Fictions: Contemporary Stories from Quebec, 1987; Canadian Writers at Work: Interviews, 1987; Singularities, 1990; Fast Travelling, 1995. Contributions: Toronto Star; Writer's Quarterly; Canadian Author and Bookman; Books In Canada; Canadian Forum. *Honours:* Fiona Mee Award for Literary Journalism, 1979. *Address:* c/o Canadian Fiction Magazine, PO Box 1061, Kingston, ON K7L 4Y5, Canada.

HANDKE, Peter; Writer, Dramatist and Poet; b. 6 Dec. 1942, Griffen-Altenmarkt, Austria; one d. *Education:* Law Studies, University of Graz. *Publications:* Die Hornissen, 1966; Publikumsbeschimpfung, 1966; Der Hausierer, 1967; Kaspar, 1968, English trans. as Kaspar and Other Plays, 1969; Deutsche Gedichte, 1969; Die Innenwelt der Aussenwelt der Innenwelt, 1969, English trans. as The Innerworld of the Outerworld of the Innerworld, 1974; Die Angst des Tormanns beim Elfmeter, 1970, English trans. as The Goalie's Anxiety at the Penalty Kick, 1972; Ich bin ein Bewohner des Elfenbeinturms, 1972; Der kurze Brief zum langen Abschied, 1972, English trans. as Short Letter, Long Farewell, 1974; Stücke, 2 vols, 1972–73; Wunschloses Unglück, 1972, English trans. as A Sorrow Beyond Dreams, 1975; Als das Wünschen noch geholfen hat, 1974, English trans. as Nonsense and Happiness, 1976; Falsche Bewegung, 1975; Der Rand der Wörter, 1975; Die linkshändige Frau, 1975, English trans. as The Left-Handed Woman, 1978; Die Stunde der wahren Empfindung, 1975, English trans. as A Moment of True Feeling, 1977; Das Ende des Flanierens, 1977; Das Gewicht der Welt: Ein Journal, 1977; Langsame Heimkehr, 1979; Die Lehre der Sainte-Victoire, 1980; Kindergeschichte, 1981; Über die Dörfer, 1981; Die Geschichte des Bleistifts, 1982; Der Chinese des Schmerzes, 1983; Die Wiederholung, 1986; Die Abwesenheit, 1987, English trans. as Absence, 1990; Nachmittag eines Schriftstellers, 1987; Versuch über die Müdigkeit, 1989; Noch einmal für Thukydides, 1990; Versuch über die Jukebox, 1990; Versuch über den geglückten Tag: Ein Wintertagtraum, 1991; Abschied des Träumers von Neunten Land: Eine Wirklichkeit, die vergangen ist: Erinnerung an Slowenien, 1991; Langsam in Schatten: Gesammelte Verzettelungen 1980–91, 1992; Theaterstücke in einem Band, 1992; Mein Jahre in der Niemandsbucht, 1994; Eine winterliche Reise zu den Flüssen Donau, Save, Morawa und Drina oder Gerechtigkeit für Serbien, 1996, English trans. as A Journey to the Rivers: Justice for Serbia, 1997; Die Fahrt im Einbaum, oder, Das Stück zum Film vom Krieg, 1999. *Honours:* Gerhart Hauptmann Prize, 1967; Peter-Rosegger-Literary-Prize, 1972; Schiller Prize, Mannheim, 1972; Büchner Prize, 1973; Prix Georges Sadoul, 1978; Kafka Prize, 1979; Salzburg Literary Prize, 1986; Great Austrian (state) Prize, 1987; Bremen Literary Prize, Hamburg, 1991; Franz Grillparzer Prize, Hamburg, 1991; Drama Prize, Goethe Institute, Munich, 1993; Prize of Honour of the Schiller Memorial Prize, 1995. *Address:* c/o Suhrkamp Verlag, Lindenstrasse 29, 60325 Frankfurt am Main, Germany.

HANDLIN, Oscar; Prof. of History and Writer; b. 29 Sept. 1915, New York, NY, USA; m. 1st Mary Flug, 18 Sept. 1937, one s. two d.; m. 2nd Lilian Bombach, 17 June 1977. *Education:* AB, Brooklyn College, CUNY, 1934; AM, 1935, LLD, 1940, Harvard University. *Career:* Instructor, 1939–44, Asst Prof., 1944–48, Assoc. Prof., 1948–54, Prof., 1954–, of History, Dir, Center for the Study of Liberty in America, 1958–66, Winthrop Prof. of History, 1962–65, Charles Warren Prof. of History, 1965–72, Dir, Charles Warren Center for Studies in American History, 1965–72, Carl H. Pforzheimer University Prof., 1972–84, Dir, University Library, 1979–84, Carl M. Loeb University Prof., 1984–86, Harvard University; Harmsworth Prof., University of Oxford, 1972–73; mem. American Acad. of Arts and Sciences, fellow; American Jewish Historical Society; Colonial Society of Massachusetts; Massachusetts Historical Society. *Publications:* Boston's Immigrants, 1941; Commonwealth, 1947; This Was America, 1949; The Uprooted, 1951; The American People in the Twentieth Century, 1954; Adventure in Freedom, 1954; Chance or Destiny, 1955; Race and Nationality in American Life, 1956; Readings in American History, 1957; Al Smith and His America, 1958; Immigration as a Factor in American History, 1959; The Newcomers: Negroes and Puerto Ricans in a Changing Metropolis, 1959; American Principles and Issues, 1961; The Dimensions of Liberty, 1961; The Americans, 1963; Fire-Bell in the Night, 1964; Children of the Uprooted, 1966; Popular Sources of Political Authority, 1967; History of the United States, 1967; America: A History, 1968; The American College and American Culture, 1970; Statue of Liberty, 1971; Facing Life: Youth and the Family in American History, 1971; A Pictorial History of Immigration, 1972; The Wealth of the American People, 1975; Truth in History, 1979; Abraham Lincoln and the Union, 1980; The Distortion of America, 1981; Liberty and Power, 1986; Liberty in Expansion, 1989; Liberty in Peril, 1992; Liberty and Equality, 1994; From the Outer Worlds, 1997. Contributions: scholarly journals. *Honours:* J. H. Dumming Prize, American History Asscn, 1941; Award of Honor, Brooklyn College, CUNY, 1945; Pulitzer Prize in History, 1952; Guggenheim Fellowship, 1954; Christopher Award, 1958; Robert H. Lord Award, 1972; many hon. doctorates. *Address:* 18 Agassiz St, Cambridge, MA 02140, USA.

HANKIN, Elizabeth Rosemary, (Elizabeth Gill); Writer and Journalist; b. 16 Oct. 1950, Newcastle upon Tyne, England; m. Richard Hankin, 6 July 1973, divorced 1988, one d. *Education:* Emma Willard School, 1968–69. *Publications:* Fiction: The Singing Winds, 1995; Far from My Father's House, 1995; Under a Cloud-Soft Sky, 1996; The Road to Berry Edge, 1997. *Literary Agent:* Judith Murdoch, 19 Challot Sq., London NW1 8YA, England. *Address:* 6 Watling Way, Lanchester, Durham DH7 0HN, England.

HANKINSON, Alan, MA; writer; b. 25 May 1926, Gatley, Cheshire, England; m. Roberta Lorna Gibson 1951 (divorced 1985); one s. *Education:* Magdalen Coll., Oxford. *Publications:* The First Tigers 1972, Camera on the Crags 1975, The Mountain Men 1977, Man of Wars 1982, The Blue Box 1983, The Regatta Men 1988, A Century on the Crags 1988, Coleridge Walks the Fells 1991, Geoffrey Winthrop Young 1995, Twelve Miles from a Lemon 1996; contrib. to Cumbria Life. *Honours:* Portico Prize 1991, Cumbria Book of the Year 1992, Boardman Tasker Award 1995. *Address:* 30 Skiddaw Street, Keswick, Cumbria CA12 4BY, England.

HANLEY, Clifford (Henry Calvin); Writer and Dramatist; b. 28 Oct. 1922, Glasgow, Scotland; m. Anna Clark, 10 Jan. 1948, one s. two d. *Education:* Eastbank Acad., Glasgow. *Career:* Prof. of Creative Writing, York University, Toronto, 1979; mem. Ours Club, Glasgow, pres.; PEN, Scottish pres., 1975. *Publications:* Dancing in the Streets, 1958; The Taste of Too Much, 1960; Nothing But the Best, 1964; Prissy, 1978; The Scots, 1980; Another Street Another Dance, 1983. Plays: The Durable Element, 1961; Oh For an Island, 1966; Dick McWhittie, 1967; Jack O'The Cudgel, 1969; Oh Glorious Jubilee, 1970; The Clyde Moralities, 1972. Contributions: numerous articles in magazines and journals. *Honours:* Oscar for Best Foriegn Documentary, 1960.

HANNAH, Barry; Author; b. 23 April 1942, Meridian, Mississippi, USA; Divorced, three s. *Education:* BA, Mississippi College, Clinton, 1964; MA, 1966, MFA, 1967, University of Arkansas. *Career:* Teacher, Clemson University, 1967–73, University of Alabama, Tuscaloosa, 1975–80; Writer-in-Residence, Middlebury College, Vermont, 1974–75, University of Iowa, 1981, University of Mississippi, University, 1982, 1984–85, University of Montana, Missoula, 1982–83. *Publications:* Geronimo Rex, 1972; Nightwatchmen, 1973; Airships, 1978; Ray, 1981; Two Stories, 1982; Black Butterfly, 1982; Power and Light, 1983; The Tennis Handsome, 1983; Captain Maximus, 1985; Hey Jack!, 1987; Boomerang, 1989; Never Die, 1991; Bats Out of Hell, 1993. Contributions: Magazines. *Honours:* Bellaman Foundation Award, 1970; Atherton Fellowship, Bread Loaf Writers Conference, 1971; Arnold Gingrich Award, Esquire Magazine, 1978; American Acad. of Arts and Letters Award, 1978. *Address:* c/o NAL/Dutton, 375 Hudson St, New York, NY 10014, USA.

HANNAH, Sophie; British poet and writer; b. 1971, Manchester. *Education:* Univ. of Manchester. *Career:* Fellow Commoner, Trinity Coll., Cambridge; Fellow, Wolfson Coll., Oxford; tutor, Writing School, Manchester Metropolitan Univ. *Publications:* poetry: Hero and the Girl Next Door 1995, Hotels Like House (Arts Council Writers' Award) 1996, Leaving and Leaving You 1999, First of the Last Chances 2003; fiction: Carrot the Goldfish 1992, Early Bird Blues 1993, Gripless 1999, Cordial and Corrosive 2000, The Superpower of Love 2001; pamphlet: Second Helping of Your Heart 1994; contrib. to The Box Room 2001, Hyphen: An Anthology of Short Stories by Poets 2003. *Honours:* Eric Gregory Award 1995. *Address:* c/o Carcanet Press, Fourth Floor, Alliance House, Cross Street, Manchester, M2 7AP, England. *Telephone:* (161) 834-8730. *Fax:* (161) 832-0084. *Website:* www.carcanet.co.uk.

HANNON, Ezra (see Hunter, Evan).

HANSEN, Erik Fosnes; Norwegian novelist; b. 6 June 1965, New York, USA; m. *Publications:* Falketårnet 1985, Salme ved reisens slutt (novel, Psalm at Journey's End) 1990, Beretninger om beskyttelse (novel) 1998, Underveis. Et portrett av Prinsesse Märtha Louise (non-fiction) 2001; contrib. articles in numerous magazines and newspapers. *Honours:* Riksmålsprisen 1998, Bokhandlerprisen 1998, NRK P2-lytternes pris 1999. *Address:* c/o Secker & Warburg, Random House, 20 Vauxhall Bridge Road, London SW1V 2SA, England.

HANSEN, Joseph, (Rose Brock, James Colton, James Coulton); Author; b. 19 July 1923, Aberdeen, SD, USA; m. Jane Bancroft, 4 Aug. 1943, one d. *Education:* Public Schools. *Career:* mem. MWA; PEN; Private Eye Writers of America. *Publications:* Lost on Twilight Road, 1964; Strange Marriage, 1965; The Corruptor and Other Stories, 1968; Known Homosexual, 1968, revised edn as Stranger to Himself, 1977, republished as Pretty Boy Dead, 1984; Cocksure, 1969; Gard, 1969; Hang-Up, 1969; Fadeout, 1970; The Outward Side, 1971; Tarn House, 1971; Todd, 1971; Death Claims, 1973; Longleaf, 1974; Troublemaker, 1975; One Foot in the Boat (poems), 1977; The Man Everybody Was Afraid Of, 1978; Skinflick, 1979; The Dog and Other Stories, 1979; A Smile in His Lifetime, 1981; Gravedigger, 1982; Backtrack, 1982; Job's Year, 1983; Nightwork, 1984; Brandsetter and Others: Five Fictions, 1984; Steps Going Down, 1985; The Little Dog Laughed, 1986; Early Graves, 1987; Bohannon's Book: Five Mysteries, 1988; Obedience, 1988; The Boy Who Was Buried This Morning, 1990; A Country of Old Men, 1991; Living Upstairs, 1993; Bohannon's Country (short stories), 1993. Contributions: anthologies and periodicals. *Honours:* National Endowment for the Arts Grant, 1974; Outstanding Literary Contribution to the Lesbian and Gay Communities Citation, Out/Look Foundation, San Francisco, 1991. *Address:* 2638 Cullen St, Los Angeles, CA 90034, USA.

HANSEN, Ron; Writer; b. 8 Dec. 1947, Omaha, NE, USA. *Education:* BA, Creighton University, 1970; MFA, University of Iowa, 1974; Stanford University, 1977–78. *Career:* Former Prof. of English, Cornell University. *Publications:* The Desperadoes, 1979; The Assassination of Jesse James by the Coward Robert Ford, 1983; The Shadowmaker, 1986; You Don't Know What Love Is, 1987; Nebraska Stories, 1989; Mariette in Ecstacy: A Novel, 1992; Atticus, 1996; Hitler's Niece, 1999; Isn't it Romantic?, An Entertainment, 2003. *Address:* c/o Grove-Atlantic, 841 Broadway, Fourth Floor, New York, NY 10003, USA.

HANSON, William Stewart; Prof. of Roman Archaeology and Writer; b. 22 Jan. 1950, Doncaster, Yorkshire, England; m. Lesley Macinnes. *Education:* BA Ancient History/Archaeology, 1972, PhD Archaeology, 1982, University of Manchester. *Career:* Prof. of Roman Archaeology, University of Glasgow, 2000–; mem. Fellow, Societies of Antiquaries of London and Scotland. *Publications:* Rome's North-West Frontier: The Antonine Wall (co-author), 1983; Agricola and the Conquest of the North, 1987; Scottish Archaeology: New Perceptions (co-ed.), 1991. Contributions: Major academic archaeological and antiquarian journals and collected works. *Address:* 10 Royal Gardens, Stirling, Scotland. *Website:* www.gla.ac.uk/archaeology/staff/wsh/index.html.

HAO, Tran Manh; Vietnamese poet, writer and critic; b. 21 July 1949, Nam Dinh Province. *Education:* Gorky Inst. of Literature, Moscow, Russia. *Career:* mem. Viet Nam Writers' Union. *Publications include:* poetry: Truong Son cua be (trans. as Baby's Truong Son) 1974, Giai Phong (trans. as Liberation) 1974, Tieng chim go cua (trans. as The Sound of the Bird Knocking at the Door) 1976, Van Nghe Giai Phong (trans. as Liberation and Arts) 1976, Hoa vua di vua no (trans. as The Flowers are Walking and Blooming at the Same Time) 1981, Mat troi trong long dat (trans. as The Underground Sun) 1981, Ba cap nui va mot hon nui le (trans. as Three Pairs of Mountains and One Standing-Alone Mountain) 1981, Tu chiec o troi cua me (trans. as From Mother's Heavenly Umbrella) 1987, Cuoc chien tranh khon nguoi (trans. as The Endless War) 1988, Minh anh trong mot the gioi (trans. as One You in One World) 1991, Dat nuoc hinh tia chop (trans. as Lightning-Shaped Country) 1994, Chuon chuon can ron (trans. as Dragonfly Biting the Navel) 1995, Tho tu tuyet (trans. as Four-Line Poems) 1995, Tho luc bat Tran Manh Hao (trans. as Tran Manh Hao's Six-Eight-Word-Metre Poetry) 2001; novels: Chia khoa cua moi nguoi (trans. as Everybody's Key) 1987, Trang mat (trans. as Honeymoon) 1989, Ly than (trans. as Separated) 1989, Sinh ra de yeu nhau (trans. as Born to Love Each Other) 1989; juvenile short stories: Cay trong vuon (trans. as Trees in the Garden) 1980, Chu heo dat (trans. as The Earthen Pig) 1981; criticism: Tho phan tho (trans. as Poetry against Poetry) 1995, Phe binh phan phe binh (trans. as Criticism against Criticism) 1996. *Honours:* Nat. Poetry Award for Children's Literature 1995, Nat. Poetry Awards 1996, 1999. *Address:* c/o Thanh Nien, 5 Ly Thuong Kiet, Hanoi, Viet Nam. *Website:* www.thanhnien.com.vn.

HARADA, Masako, (Satoko Kizaki); Writer; b. 14 Nov. 1939, Changchung, China; m. Hiroshi Harada, 1 Aug. 1962, two d. *Education:* Tokyo Women's University Junior College, 1957–59. *Publications:* Rasoku, 1982; Umi-to Rosoku, 1985; Aogiri, 1985, English trans. as The Phoenix Tree and Other Stories, 1990; Shizumeru tera, 1987, English trans. as The Sunken Temple, 1993; Nami-Half-way, 1988; Sanzoku-no-Haka, 1989; Kagami-no-Tani, 1990; Toki-no-Shizuku, 1991; Atonaki-Niwa-ni, 1991; Shiawase no chiisana tobira, 1994. *Honours:* Akutagawa Prize, 1985.

HARBINSON-BRYANS, Robert, (Robin Bryans); Author; b. 24 April 1928, Belfast, Northern Ireland. *Publications:* Gateway to the Khyber, 1959; Madeira, 1959; Summer Saga, 1960; No Surrender, 1960; Song of Erne, 1960; Up Spake the Cabin Boy, 1961; Danish Episode, 1961; Tattoo Lily, 1962; Fanfare for Brazil, 1962; The Protégé, 1963; The Azores, 1963; Ulster, 1964; Lucio, 1964; Malta and Gozo, 1966; The Field of Sighing, 1966; Trinidad and Tobago, 1967; Faber Best True Adventure Stories (ed.), 1967; Sons of El Dorado, 1968; Crete, 1969; The Dust Has Never Settled, 1992; Let the Petals Fall, 1993; Checkmate, 1994, Blackmail and Whitewash, 1996. *Address:* 90 Ferrymead Ave, Greenford, Middlesex UB6 9TN, England.

HARCOURT, Geoffrey Colin; writer and academic; b. 27 June 1931, Melbourne, Vic., Australia; m. Joan Margaret Bartrop 1955; two s. two d. *Education:* BCom, 1954, MCom, 1956, Univ. of Melbourne; PhD, 1960, LittD, 1988, Univ. of Cambridge. *Career:* Lecturer, 1958–62, Senior Lecturer, 1963–65, Reader, 1965–67, Prof., 1967–85, of Economics, Prof. Emeritus, 1988, Univ. of Adelaide; Univ. Lecturer in Economics and Politics, Dir of Studies in Economics and Fellow of Trinity Hall, Cambridge, 1964–66; Lecturer in Economics and Politics, 1964–66, 1982–90, Reader in the History of Economic Theory, 1990–98, Reader Emeritus, 1998–, Univ. of Cambridge; Leverhulme Exchange Fellow, Keio Univ., Toyko, 1967–70; Visiting Fellow, Clare Hall, Cambridge, 1972–73; Visiting Prof., Scarborough College, Univ. of Toronto, 1977, 1980; Fellow and Lecturer in Economics, 1982–98, Pres., 1988–89, 1990–92, Fellow Emeritus, 1998–, Jesus College, Cambridge; Visiting Fellow, Australian National Univ., 1997; Sugden Fellow, Queens College, Univ. of Melbourne, 2002; numerous university lectureships; mem. Economic Society of Australia and New Zealand, pres., 1974–77; Royal Economic Society, council, 1990–95, life mem., 1998–. *Publications:* Economic Activity (with P. H. Karmel and R. H. Wallace), 1967; Readings in the Concepts and Management of Income (ed. with R. H. Parker), 1969; Capital and Growth: Selected Readings (ed. with N. F. Laing), 1971; Some Cambridge Controversies in the Theory of Capital, 1972; The Microeconomic Foundations of Macroeconomics (ed.), 1977; The Social Science Imperialists (selected essays), 1982; Keynes and His Contemporaries: The Sixth and Centennial Keynes Seminar Held in the University of Kent at Canterbury (ed.), 1985; Controversies in Political Economy (selected essays), 1986; International Monetary Problems and Suppy-Side Economics: Essays in Honour of Lorie Tarshis (ed. with Jon Cohen), 1986; On Political Economists and Modern Political Economy (selected essays), 1992; Post-Keynesian Essays in Biography: Portraits of Twentieth Century Political Economists, 1993; The Dynamics of the Wealth of Nations: Growth, Distribution and Structural Change: Essays in Honour of Luigi Pasinetti (ed. with Mauro Baranzini), 1993; Income and Employment in Theory and Practice (ed. with Alessandro Roncaglia and Robin Rowley), 1994; Capitalism, Socialism and Post-Keynesianism: Selected Essays, 1995; A 'Second Edition' of The General Theory (ed. with P. A. Riach), two vols, 1997; Selected Essays on Ecomomic Policy, 2001; 50 Years a Keynsian and Other Essays, 2001; L'Economie Rebelle de Joan Robinson (ed.), 2001; Editing Economics: Essays in Honour of Mark Perlman (ed. with Hank Lim and Ungsuh K. Park), 2002; Joan Robinson: Critical Assessments of Leading Economists (with Prue Kerr), five vols, 2002. Contributions: scholarly books and professional journals. *Honours:* Fellow, Acad. of the Social Sciences in Australia, 1971–; AO, 1994; Distinguished Fellow, Economic Society of Australia, 1996; Hon. LittD, De Montfort Univ., 1997; Hon. Prof., Univ. of New South Wales, 1997, 1999; Hon. Fellow, Queens College, Melbourne, 1998; Hon. DCom, Univ. of Melbourne, 2003. *Address:* 43 New Square, Cambridge CB1 1EZ, England.

HARDEN, Blaine (Charles); Journalist; b. 4 April 1952, Moses Lake, Washington, USA. *Education:* BA, Philosophy and Political Science, Gonzaga University, 1974; MA, Journalism, Syracuse University, 1976. *Career:* Africa Correspondent, 1985–89, East European Correspondent, 1989–93, Reporter, 1995–, Washington Post. *Publications:* Africa: Dispatches From a Fragile Continent, 1990; A River Lost: The Life and Death of Columbia, 1996. Contributions: Washington Post. *Honours:* Livingston Award for Young Journalists, 1986; Martha Albrand Citation for First Book of Non-Fiction, PEN, 1991; Ernie Pyle Award for Human Interest Reporting, 1993. *Address:* c/o Washington Post, 1150 15th St NW, Washington, DC 20071, USA.

HARDING, James; Writer; b. 1929, England. *Career:* Senior Lecturer in French, University of Greenwich, 1966–94; mem. FRSL. *Publications:* Saint-Saëns and His Circle, 1965; The Duke of Wellington, 1968; Sacha Guitry, 1968; Massenet, 1970; Rossini, 1971; The Ox on the Roof, 1972; Lord Chesterfield's Letters to his Son, 1973; Gounod, 1974; Lost Illusions: Paul Léautaud and His World, 1974; Erik Satie, 1975; The Astonishing Adventure of General Boulanger, 1976; Poulenc: My Friends and Myself (trans.), 1978; Folies de Paris: The Rise and Fall of French Operetta, 1979; Offenbach, 1980; Maurice Chevalier, 1982; Jacques Tati: Frame by Frame, 1984; James Agate, 1986; Ivor Novello, 1987; The Rocky Horror Show Book, 1987; Cochran, 1988; Gerald du Maurier, 1989; George Robey and the Music Hall, 1991; Emlyn Williams, A Life, 1993; P. Ramlee, Bright Star, 2002. *Address:* 100 Ridgmount Gardens, Torrington Pl., London WC1E 7AZ, England.

HARDING, Matthew Whitman (see Floren, Lee).

HARDWICK, Elizabeth; Writer, Critic and Teacher; b. 27 July 1916, Lexington, KY, USA; m. Robert Lowell, 28 July 1949, divorced 1972, one d. *Education:* AB, 1938, MA, 1939, University of Kentucky; Columbia University. *Career:* Co-Founder and Advisory Ed., New York Review of Books, 1963–; Adjunct Assoc. Prof. of English, Barnard College. *Publications:* Fiction: The Ghostly Lover, 1945; The Simple Truth, 1955; Sleepless Nights, 1979. Non-Fiction: The Selected Letters of William James (ed.), 1960; A View of My Own: Essays on Literature and Society, 1962; Seduction and Betrayal: Women and Literature, 1974; Rediscovered Fiction by American Women: A Personal Selection (ed.), 18 vols, 1977; Bartleby in Manhattan (essays), 1984; The Best American Essays 1986 (ed.), 1986; Sight Readings: American Fictions (essays), 1998; Herman Melville, 2000. Contributions: periodicals. *Honours:* Gold Medal, American Acad. and Institute of Arts and Letters, 1993. *Address:* 15 W 67th St, New York, NY 10023, USA.

HARDY, Adam (see Bulmer, Henry Kenneth).

HARDY, Barbara (Gladys); Prof. of English Literature Emeritus and Writer; b. 27 June 1924, England; m. Ernest Dawson Hardy (deceased); two d. *Education:* BA, MA, University College London. *Career:* Prof. of English, Royal Holloway College, University of London, 1965–70; Prof. of English Literature, 1970–89, Prof. Emeritus, 1989–, Birkbeck College, University of London; mem. Dickens Society, pres., 1987–88; FRSL, 1997; Thomas Hardy Society, vice-pres., 1991–; Welsh Acad. *Publications:* The Novels of George Eliot: A Study in Form, 1959; The Appropriate Form: An Essay on the Novel, 1964; Middlemarch: Critical Appoaches to the Novel (ed.), 1967; Charles Dickens: The Later Novels, 1968; Critical Essays on George Elliot (ed.), 1970; The Exposure of Luxury: Radical Themes in Thackeray, 1970; Tellers and Listeners: The Narrative Imagination, 1975; A Reading of Jane Austen, 1975; The Advantage of Lyric: Essays on Feeling in Poetry, 1977; Particularities: Readings in George Eliot, 1982; Forms of Feeling in Victorian Fiction, 1985; Narrators and Novelists: Collected Essays, 1987; Swansea Girl, 1993; London Lovers (novel), 1996; Henry James: The Later Writing, 1996; Shakespeare's Storytellers, 1997; Thomas Hardy: Imagining Imagination, 2000. *Honours:* Hon. degrees; Rose Mary Cranshaw Prize, 1962; Hon. Fellow, Birkbeck College, University of London, 1991; Hon. Prof. of English, University College, Swansea, 1991; Sagittarius Prize, 1997. *Address:* Birkbeck College, Malet St, London WC1E 7HX, England.

HARDY, Frank; novelist; b. 21 March 1917, Southern Cross, Vic., Australia. *Career:* Pres., Realist Writers Group, Melbourne, Sydney, 1954–74; Co-Founder, Australian Society of Authors, Sydney, 1968–74; Pres., Carringbush Writers, Melbourne, 1980–83. *Publications:* The Four Legged Lottery, 1958; Power Without Glory, 1962; The Outcasts of Follgarah, 1971; Who Shot George Kirkland?, 1981; Warrant of Distress, 1983; The Obsession of Oscar Oswald, 1983. Short Stories: The Loser Now Will be Later to Win, 1985; Hardy's People, 1986. Plays: Black Diamonds, 1956; The Ringbolter, 1964; Who Was Harry Larse?, 1985; Faces in the Street: An Epic Drama, 1990. *Address:* 9/76 Elizabeth Bay Road, Elizabeth Bay, NSW 2011, Australia.

HARDY, Jules; British novelist; b. Bristol, England. *Career:* publishing, teaching, carpentry. *Publications:* novels: Altered Land 2001, Mister Candid 2003. *Honours:* WHSmith Fresh Talent Award. *Literary Agent:* Ed Victor Ltd, 6 Bayley Street, Bedford Square, London, WC1B 3HB, England.

HARE, Sir David, Kt, MA, FRSL; British playwright and theatre director; b. 5 June 1947, Hastings, Sussex; m. 1st Margaret Matheson 1970 (divorced 1980); two s. one d.; m. 2nd Nicole Farhi 1992. *Education:* Lancing Coll., Jesus Coll., Cambridge. *Career:* Literary Man. and Resident Dramatist, Royal Court 1969–71; Resident Dramatist, Nottingham Playhouse 1973; f. Portable Theatre 1968, Joint Stock Theatre Group 1975, Greenpoint Films 1983; Assoc. Dir Nat. Theatre 1984–88, 1989–; UK/US Bicentennial Fellowship 1978; Hon. Fellow Jesus Coll. Cambridge 2001. *Plays:* Slag, Hampstead 1970, Royal Court 1971, New York Shakespeare Festival (NYSF) 1971, The Great Exhibition, Hampstead 1972, Brassneck (with Howard Brenton), Nottingham Playhouse 1973 (also Dir), Knuckle, Comedy Theatre 1974, Fanshen, Inst. of Contemporary Arts 1975, Hampstead 1975, Nat. Theatre 1992, Teeth 'n' Smiles, Royal Court 1975 (also Dir), Wyndhams 1976 (also Dir), Plenty, Nat. Theatre 1978 (also Dir), NYSF and Broadway 1982 (also Dir), Albery 1999, A Map of the World, Nat. Theatre 1983 (also Dir) NYSF 1985 (also Dir), Pravda: A Fleet Street Comedy (with Howard Brenton), Nat. Theatre 1985 (also Dir), The Bay at Nice, Nat. Theatre 1986 (also Dir), The Secret Rapture, Nat. Theatre 1988, NYSF and Broadway 1989 (also Dir), Racing Demon, Nat. Theatre 1990, 1993, Broadway 1995, Murmuring Judges, Nat. Theatre 1992, 1993, The Absence of War, Nat. Theatre 1993, Skylight, Nat. Theatre 1995, Wyndhams and Broadway 1996, Vaudeville 1997, Amy's View, Nat. Theatre 1997, Aldwych 1998, Broadway 1999, The Judas Kiss, Almeida and Broadway 1998 (Dir on radio only), Via Dolorosa, Royal Court 1998 (also acted), Almeida and Broadway 1999 (also acted), My Zinc Bed, Royal Court 2000 (also Dir), The Breath of Life, Theatre Royal, Haymarket 2002, The Permanent Way, Nat. Theatre 2003, Stuff Happens, Nat. Theatre 2004. *Plays adapted:* The Rules of the Game, Nat. Theatre 1971, Almeida 1992, The Life of Galileo, Almeida 1994, Mother Courage and Her Children, Nat. Theatre 1995, Ivanov, Almeida and Broadway 1997 (Dir on radio only), The Blue Room, Donmar and Broadway 1998, Theatre Royal 2000, Platonov, Almeida 2001. *Plays directed:* Christi in Love, Portable Theatre 1969, Fruit, Portable Theatre 1970, Blowjob, Portable Theatre 1971, England's Ireland, Portable Theatre 1972 (co-Dir), The Provoked Wife, Palace, Watford 1973, The Pleasure Principle, Theatre Upstairs 1973, The Party, Nat. Theatre 1974, Weapons of Happiness, Nat. Theatre 1976, Devil's Island, Joint Stock 1977, Total Eclipse, Lyric 1981, King Lear, Nat. Theatre 1986, The Designated Mourner, Nat. Theatre 1996, Heartbreak House, Almeida 1997. *TV screenplays:* Licking Hitler (BBC) 1978 (also Dir), Dreams of Leaving (BBC) 1979 (also Dir), Saigon: Year of the Cat (Thames) 1983 (also assoc. producer), Heading Home (BBC) 1991 (also Dir), The Absence of War (BBC) 1995. *Film screenplays:* Wetherby 1985 (also Dir), Plenty 1985, Paris by Night 1989 (also Dir), Strapless 1990 (also Dir), Damage 1992, The Secret Rapture 1993 (also assoc. producer), Via Dolorosa 2000 (also actor), The Hours (adaptation of Michael Cunningham's novel) 2001, Lee Miller 2002. *Film directed:* The Designated Mourner 1996 (also produced). *Opera libretto:* The Knife, New York Shakespeare Festival 1988 (also Dir). *Publications:* Writing Lefthanded 1991, Asking Around 1993, Acting Up: A Diary 1999. *Honours:* Evening Standard Drama Award 1970, John Llewelyn Rhys Prize 1974, BAFTA Best Play of the Year 1978, New York Critics' Circle Awards 1983, 1990, 1997, 1999, Golden Bear Award for Best Film 1985, Evening Standard Drama Award for Best Play 1985, Plays and Players Best Play Awards 1985, 1988, 1990, City Limits Best Play 1985, Drama Magazine Awards Best Play 1988, Laurence Olivier Best Play of the Year 1990, 1996, Time Out Award 1990, Dramalogue Award 1992, Time Out Award for Outstanding Theatrical Achievement 1998, Outer Critics' Circle Award 1999, Drama League Award 1999, Drama Desk Award 1999, Joan Cullman Award 1999; Officier, Ordre des Arts et des Lettres 1997. *Literary Agent:* Casarotto Ramsay Ltd, 60–66 Wardour Street, London, W1V 3HP, England.

HARGITAI, Peter; writer; b. 28 Jan. 1947, Budapest, Hungary; m. Dianne Kress, 24 July 1967, one s. one d. *Education:* MFA, University of Massachusetts, 1988. *Career:* Lecturer in English, University of Miami, 1980–85, University of Massachusetts, 1987–88; Prof. and Writing Specialist, Florida International University, 1990–; mem. PEN International; Literary Network, New York. *Publications:* Forum: Ten Poets of the Western Reserve, 1976; Perched on Nothings Branch, 1986; Magyar Tales, 1989; Budapest to Bellevue, 1989; Budapesttöl New Yorkig és tovább..., 1991; Fodois Budget Zion, 1991; The Traveler, 1994; Attila: A Barbarian's Bedtime Story, 1994. Contributions: North Atlantic Review; Colorado Quarterly; Nimrod; College English; California Quarterly; Spirit; Prairie Schooner; Poetry East; Cornfield Review; Blue Unicorn. *Honours:* Acad. of American Poets Trans. Award, 1988; Fulbright Grant, 1988; Florida Arts Council Fellowship, 1990; Fust Milan Award, Hungarian Acad. of Sciences, 1994.

HARGRAVE, Leonie (see Disch, Thomas Michael).

HARING, Firth (see Fabend, Firth Haring).

HARJO, Joy; Poet, Author, Educator and Musician; b. 9 May 1951, Tulsa, Oklahoma, USA; one s. one d. *Education:* BA, University of New Mexico, 1976; MFA, University of Iowa, 1978; Anthropology Film Center, 1982. *Career:* Instructor, Institute of American Indian Arts, 1978–79, 1983–84, Santa Fe Community College, 1983–84; Lecturer, Arizona State University, 1980–81; Asst Prof., University of Colorado at Boulder, 1985–88; Assoc. Prof., University of Arizona at Tucson, 1988–90; Prof., University of New Mexico, 1991–97, UCLA, 2001–; mem. PEN, advisory board; National Council of the Arts. *Publications:* The Last Song, 1975; What Moon Drove Me To This?, 1980; She Had Some Horses, 1983; Secrets From the Center of the World (with Stephen Strom), 1989; In Mad Love and War, 1990; Fishing, 1992; The Woman Who Fell From the Sky, 1994; Reinventing the Enemy's Language, 1997; A Map to the Next World, 2000; The Good Luck Cat, 2000; How We Became Human, 2002; Joy Harjo and Poetic Justice: Letter from the End of the 20th Century (CD). Contributions: many anthologies, magazines, and recordings. *Honours:* National Endowment for the Arts Creative Writing Fellowships, 1978, 1992; Pushcart Prize, Poetry XIII, 1987–88, and Poetry Anthology XV, 1990; Arizona Commission on the Arts Poetry Fellowship, 1989; American Indian Distinguished Achievement in the Arts Award, 1990; American Book Award, Before Columbus Foundation, 1991; Delmore Schwartz Memorial Award, New York University, 1991; Mountains and Plains Booksellers Award for Best Book of Poetry, 1991; William Carlos Williams Award, Poetry Society of America, 1991; Hon. Doctorate, Benedictine College, 1992; Woodrow Wilson Fellowship, 1993; Witter Bynner Poetry Fellowship, 1994; Lifetime Achievement Award, Native Writers Circle of the Americas, 1995; Oklahoma Book Arts Awards, 1995; Governor's Award for Excellence in the Arts, State of New Mexico, 1997; Lila Wallace-Reader's Digest Writers Award, 1998–2000. *Address:* c/o Mekko Productions Inc, 1140 Alewa Dr., Honolulu, HI 96817, USA. *E-mail:* mekkopoet@earthlink.net.

HARKNETT, Terry, (Frank Chandler, David Ford, George G. Gilman, William M. James, Charles R. Pike, James Russell, William Terry); Writer; b. 14 Dec. 1936, Rainham, Essex, England. *Career:* Ed., Newspaper Features Ltd, 1958–61; Reporter and Features Ed., National Newsagent, 1961–72. *Publications:* (as George G. Gilman), Edge series: The Godforsaken, 1982; Arapaho Revenge, 1983; The Blind Side, 1983; House of the Range, 1983; Edge Meets Steele No. 3 Double Action, 1984; The Moving Cage, 1984; School for Slaughter, 1985; Revenge Ride, 1985; Shadow of the Gallows, 1985; A Time for Killing, 1986; Brutal Border, 1986; Hitting Paydirt, 1986; Backshort, 1987; Uneasy Riders, 1987. Adam Steele series: Canyon of Death, 1985; High Stakes, 1985; Rough Justice, 1985; The Sunset Ride, 1986; The Killing Strain, 1986; The Big Gunfight, 1987; The Hunted, 1987; Code of the West, 1987. The Undertaker series: Three Graves to a Showdown, 1982; Back from the Dead, 1982; Death in the Desert, 1982. As William Terry: Red Sun (novelization of screenplay), 1972. As Frank

Chandler: A Fistful of Dollars (novelization of screenplay), 1972. As Charles R. Pike: Jubal Cade series: The Killing Trail, 1974; Double Cross, 1974; The Hungary Gun, 1975. As William M. James: Apache series: The First Death, 1974; Duel to the Death, 1974; Fort Treachery, 1975. As Terry Harknett: The Caribbean, 1972. As James Russell: The Balearic Islands, 1972. As David Ford: Cyprus, 1973. *Address:* Spring Acre, Springhead Rd, Uplyme, Lyme Regis, Dorset DT7 3RS, England.

HARLAN, Louis Rudolph; academic and historian; b. 13 July 1922, West Point, Mississippi, USA; m. Sadie Morton 1947; two s. *Education:* BA, Emory University, 1943; MA, Vanderbilt University, 1948; PhD, Johns Hopkins University, 1955. *Career:* Asst to Assoc. Prof., East Texas State College, 1950–59; Assoc. Prof. to Prof., University of Cincinnati, 1959–66; Prof. of History, 1966–84, Distinguished Prof. of History, 1984–92, Prof. Emeritus, 1992–, University of Maryland, College Park; mem. American Historical Asscn, pres., 1989; Asscn for the Study of Afro-American Life and History; National Historical Publications and Records Commission; Organization of American Historians, pres., 1989–90; Society of American Historians, fellow. *Publications:* Separate and Unequal, 1958; The Booker T. Washington Papers (ed.), 14 vols, 1972–89; Booker T. Washington: Vol. I, The Making of a Black Leader, 1972, Vol. II, The Wizard of Tuskegee, 1983; Booker T. Washington in Perspective, 1988; All at Sea, 1998. Contributions: periodicals. *Honours:* Bancroft Prizes, 1973, 1984; Guggenheim Fellowship, 1975; Pulitzer Prize in Biography, 1984; Albert J. Beveridge Award, 1984; Julian P. Boyd Award, 1989; National Historical Publications and Records Commission Award, 1991. *Address:* 160 Kendal Drive, Cottage 1022, Lexington, VA 24450, USA.

HARLE, Elizabeth (see Roberts, Irene).

HARLEMAN, Ann; Writer and Educator; b. 28 Oct. 1945, Youngstown, Ohio, USA; m. Bruce A Rosenberg, 20 June 1981, one d. *Education:* BA, English Literature, Rutgers University, 1967; PhD, Linguistics, Princeton University, 1972; MFA, Creative Writing, Brown University, 1988. *Career:* Asst Prof. of English, Rutgers University, 1973–74; Asst Prof., 1974–79, Assoc. Prof. of English, 1979–84, University of Washington; Visiting Prof. of Rhetoric, MIT, 1984–86; Visiting Scholar, Program in American Civilization, Brown University, 1986–; Cole Distinguished Prof. of English, Wheaton College, 1992; Prof. of English, Rhode Island School of Design, 1994–; mem. MLA, chair., general linguistics exec. committee; Poets and Writers; PEN American Center. *Publications:* Graphic Representation of Models in Linguistic Theory, 1976; Ian Fleming: A Critical Biography (with Bruce A Rosenberg), 1989; Mute Phone Calls (trans. of fiction by Ruth Zernova), 1992; Happiness, 1994; Bitter Lake, 1996. Contributions: More than 50 scholarly articles, short stories, poems, reviews. *Honours:* Guggenheim Fellowship, 1976; Fulbright Fellowship, 1980; MacDowell Colony Fellow, 1988; National Endowment for the Humanities Fellowship, 1989; Rhode Island State Council on the Arts Fellowship, 1990, 1997; PEN Syndicated Fiction Award, 1991; Iowa Short Fiction Prize, 1993; Senior Fellow, ACLS, 1993; Bogliasco Foundation Fellowship, 1998.

HARMAN, Gilbert Helms, BA, PhD; American academic and writer; *Professor of Philosophy, Princeton University*; b. 26 May 1938, E Orange, NJ; m. Lucy Newman 1970; two d. *Education:* Swarthmore Coll. and Harvard Univ. *Career:* faculty mem. Dept of Philosophy, Princeton Univ. 1963–, Prof. of Philosophy 1971–, Co-Dir Cognitive Science Lab. 1986–2000; Fellow Cognitive Science Soc. 2003; mem. American Philosophical Asscn, Philosophy of Science Asscn, Soc. for Philosophy and Psychology, American Psychological Soc., Linguistic Soc. of America. *Publications:* Semantics of Natural Language (ed. with Donald Davidson) 1971, Thought 1973, On Noam Chomsky (ed.) 1974, The Logic of Grammar (ed. with Donald Davidson) 1975, The Nature of Morality: An Introduction to Ethics 1977, Change in View: Principles of Reasoning 1986, Skepticism and the Definition of Knowledge 1990, Conceptions of the Human Mind (ed.) 1993, Moral Relativism and Moral Objectivity (with Judith Jarvis Thomson) 1996, Reasoning, Meaning and Mind 1999, Explaining Values and other Essays in Moral Philosophy 2000; contrib. to scholarly journals. *Address:* Department of Philosophy, Princeton University, Princeton, NJ 08544-1006 (Office); 106 Broadmead Street, Princeton, NJ 08540, USA (Home). *Telephone:* (609) 258-4301. *Fax:* (609) 258-1502. *E-mail:* harman@princeton.edu (Office). *Website:* www.princeton.edu/~harman.

HARMON, Maurice; academic, writer and editor; b. 21 June 1930, Dublin, Ireland. *Education:* BA, 1951, HDE, 1953, MA, 1955, PhD, 1961, University College, Dublin; AM, Harvard Univ., 1957. *Career:* Lecturer in English, 1964–76, Assoc. Prof. of Anglo-Irish Literature and Drama, 1976–90, Prof. Emeritus, 1990–, University College, Dublin; Ed., University Review, 1964–68, Irish University Review, 1970–, Poetry Ireland Review, 2000–01. *Publications:* Sean O'Faolain: A Critical Introduction, 1966; Modern Irish Literature 1800–1967: A Reader's Guide, 1967; Fenians and Fenianism: Centenary Papers (ed.), 1968; The Celtic Master: Contributions to the First James Joyce Symposium, 1969; Romeo and Juliet, by Shakespeare (ed.), 1970; J. M. Synge Centenary Papers 1971 (ed.), 1971; King Richard II, by Shakespeare (ed.), 1971; Coriolanus, by Shakespeare (ed.), 1972; The Poetry of Thomas Kinsella, 1974; The Irish Novel in Our Time (ed. with Patrick Rafroidi), 1976; Select Bibliography for the Study of Anglo-Irish Literature and Its Backgrounds, 1976; Richard Murphy: Poet of Two Traditions (ed.), 1978; Irish Poetry After Yeats: Seven Poets (ed.), 1979; Image and Illusion: Anglo-Irish Literature and Its Contexts (ed.), 1979; A Short History of Anglo-Irish Literature From Its Origins to the Present (with Roger McHugh), 1982; The Irish Writer and the City (ed.), 1985; James Joyce: The Centennial Symposium (with Morris Beja et al), 1986; Austin Clarke: A Critical Introduction, 1989; The Book of Precedence (poems), 1994; Sean O'Faolain: A Life, 1994; A Stillness at Kiawah (poems), 1996; No Author Better Served: The Correspondence of Samuel Beckett and Alan Schneider, 1998; The Last Regatta (poems), 2000; Tales of Death (poems), 2001; The Colloquy of the Old Men (trans.), 2001; The Dolmen Press: A Celebration, 2001. *Address:* 20 Sycamore Road, Mount Merrion, Blackrock, Co Dublin, Ireland.

HARPER, Michael S(teven); Prof. of English and Poet; b. 18 March 1938, New York, NY, USA; m.; three c. *Education:* BA, 1961, MA, 1963, California State University at Los Angeles; MA, University of Iowa Writers Workshop, 1963; ad eundem, Brown University, 1972. *Career:* Visiting Prof., Lewis and Clark College, 1968–69, Reed College, 1968–69, Harvard University, 1974–77, Yale University, 1976; Prof. of English, Brown University, 1970–; Benedict Distinguished Prof., Carleton College, 1979; Elliston Poet and Distinguished Prof., University of Cincinnati, 1979; National Endowment for the Humanities Prof., Colgate University, 1985; Distinguished Minority Prof., University of Delaware, 1988, Macalester College, 1989; First Poet Laureate of the State of Rhode Island, 1988–93; Phi Beta Kappa Visiting Scholar, 1991; Berg Distinguished Visiting Prof., New York University, 1992; mem. American Acad. of Arts and Sciences. *Publications:* Dear John, Dear Coltrane, 1970; History is Your Own Heartbeat, 1971; History as Apple Tree, 1972; Song: I Want a Witness, 1972; Debridement, 1973; Nightmare Begins Responsibility, 1975; Images of Kin, 1977; Chant of Saints (co-ed.), 1979; Healing Song for the Inner Ear, 1985; Songlines: Mosaics, 1991; Every Shut Eye Ain't Asleep, 1994; Honorable Amendments, 1995; Collected Poems, 1996; Selected Poems, 2003. *Honours:* Black Acad. of Arts and Letters Award, 1972; National Institute of Arts and Letters Grants, 1975, 1976, 1985; Guggenheim Fellowship, 1976; Melville Cane Award, Poetry Society of America, 1978; Governor's Poetry Award, Rhode Island Council of the Arts, 1987; Robert Hayden Memorial Poetry Award, United Negro College Fund, 1990; Literary Lion, New York Public Library, 1992; Hon. doctorates. *Address:* c/o Dept of English, Brown University, Providence, RI 02912, USA.

HARPER, Stephen (Dennis); Journalist, Foreign Correspondent and Writer; b. 15 Sept. 1924, Newport, Monmouthshire, Wales. *Career:* mem. Society of Authors. *Publications:* Fiction: A Necessary End, 1975; Mirror Image, 1976; Live Till Tomorrow, 1977; White Christmas in Saigon, 1990. Non-Fiction: Last Sunset, 1978; Miracle of Deliverance, 1985; Capturing Enigma, 1999; Imperial War Museum Book of Modern Warfare (contributor), 2002. *Address:* Green Dene Lodge, Green Dene, East Horsley, Surrey KT24 5RG, England. *E-mail:* stephen@greendene.freeserve.co.uk.

HARRIS, Jana; Writer, Poet and Instructor; b. 21 Sept. 1947, San Francisco, CA, USA; m. Mark Allen Bothwell. *Education:* BS, University of Oregon, 1969; MA, San Francisco State University, 1972. *Career:* Instructor, Creative Writing, New York University, 1980, University of Washington, 1986–, Pacific Lutheran University, 1988; Founder, Ed., Switch-on Gutenberg, cyberspace poetry journal; mem. Feminist Writers' Guild; Assoc. Writing Programs; Women's Salon; PEN; Poetry Society of America; National Book Critics Circle. *Publications:* This House That Rocks with Every Truck on the Road, 1976; Pin Money, 1977; The Clackamas, 1980; Alaska (novel), 1980; Who's That Pushy Bitch?, 1981; Running Scared, 1981; Manhattan as a Second Language, 1982; The Sourlands: Poems by Jana Harris, 1989; Oh How Can I Keep on Singing: Voices of Pioneer Women (poems), 1993; The Dust of Everyday Life (poems); The Pearl of Ruby City (novel), 1998. Contributions: periodicals. *Honours:* Berkeley Civic Arts Commemoration Grant, 1974; Washington State Arts Council Fellowship, 1993. *Address:* 32814 120th St SE, Sultan, WA 98294, USA.

HARRIS, Joanne; British author; b. 1964, Yorkshire, England; m. Kevin; one d. *Education:* Saint Catharine's Coll., Cambridge. *Career:* fmr French teacher, Leeds Grammar School. *Publications:* The Evil Seed 1989, Sleep Pale Sister 1993, Chocolat 1999, Blackberry Wine 2000, Five Quarters of the Orange 2001, Coastliners 2002, The French Kitchen: A Cookbook, Holy Fools 2003, Jigs & Reels (short stories) 2004. *Address:* c/o Transworld Publishers, 61–63 Uxbridge Road, London W5 5SA, England. *Website:* www.joanne-harris.co.uk.

HARRIS, Jocelyn Margaret; University Teacher and Writer; b. 10 Sept. 1939, Dunedin, New Zealand; one s. one d. *Education:* MA, University of Otago; PhD, University of London. *Career:* Personal Chair, Dept of English, University of Otago; mem. Australian and South Pacific 18th Century Society. *Publications:* Samuel Richardson: Sir Charles Grandison (ed.), 1972; Samuel Richardson, 1989; Jane Austen's Art of Memory, 1989; Samuel Richardson's Published Commentary on Clarissa, 1747–1765, Vol. I (ed. with Tom Keymer). Contributions: scholarly journals. *Address:* c/o Dept of English, University of Otago, Box 56, Dunedin, New Zealand.

HARRIS, Marion Rose, (Rose Glendower, Rosie Harris, Marion Rose, Rose Young); Author; b. 12 July 1925, Cardiff, South Wales; m. Kenneth Mackenzie Harris, 18 Aug. 1943, two s. one d. *Career:* Ed./Owner, Regional Feature Service, 1964–74; Editorial Controller, W. Foulsham and Co Ltd, 1974–82; mem. Society of Authors; Romantic Novelists Asscn; Welsh Acad.

Publications: as Marion Harris: Captain of Her Heart, 1976; Just a Handsome Stranger, 1983; The Queen's Windsor, 1985; Soldiers' Wives, 1986; Officers' Ladies, 1987; Nesta, 1988; Heart of the Dragon, 1988; Amelda: Heart of the Dragon Vol. II, The Old Dragon, 1989; Sighing for the Moon (also as Rose Glendower), 1991. As Rosie Harris: Turn of the Tide, 2002; Troubled Waters (also as Marion Harris), 2002; Patsy of Paradise Place, 2003; One Step Forward, 2003; Looking for Love, 2003. As Rose Young: To Love and Love Again, 1993; Secret of Abbey Place, 1999; Love Can Conquer, 1999. *Address:* Walpole Cottage, Long Dr., Burnham, Slough SL1 8AJ, England. *E-mail:* marionharris@btinternet.com.

HARRIS, Mark; Prof. of English (retd) and Author; b. 19 Nov. 1922, Mount Vernon, New Hork, USA; m. Josephine Horen, 17 March 1946, two s. one d. *Education:* BA, 1950, MA, 1951, University of Denver; PhD, University of Minnesota, 1956. *Career:* Faculty, Dept of English, University of Minnesota, 1951–54, San Francisco State College, 1954–68, Prudue University, 1968–70, California Institute of the Arts, 1970–73, Immaculate Heart College, 1973–74, University of Southern California at Los Angeles, 1974–75; Fulbright Prof., University of Hiroshima, 1957–58; Visiting Prof., Brandeis University, 1963; Prof. of English, University of Pittsburgh, 1975–80, Arizona State University, Tempe, 1980–94. *Publications:* Trumpet to the World, 1946; City of Discontent: An Interpretive Biography of Vachel Lindsay, Being Also the Story of Springfield, IL, USA, and of the Love of the Poet for That City, That State, and That Nation, 1952; Wake Up, Stupid, 1959; Mark the Glove Boy, or, The Last Days of Richard Nixon, 1964; Twentyone Twice: A Journal, 1966; The Goy, 1970; Killing Everybody, 1973; Best Father Ever Invented: The Autobiography of Mark Harris, 1976; The Design of Fiction (ed. with Josephine Harris and Hester Harris), 1976; It Looked Like for Ever, 1979; Short Work of It: Selected Writings by Mark Harris, 1980; The Heart of Boswell: Six Journals in One Vol. (ed.), 1980; Saul Bellow: Drumlin Woodchuck, 1980; Lying in Bed, 1984; Speed, 1990; The Tale Maker, 1994; Diamond: Baseball Writings of Mark Harris, 1994. *Honours:* Ford Foundation Grant, 1960; National Institute of Arts and Letters Award, 1961; Guggenheim Fellowships, 1965–66, 1974; National Endowment for the Arts Grant, 1966; Hon. DHL, Illinois Wesleyan University, 1974.

HARRIS, Randy Allen; Prof. and Author; b. 6 Sept. 1956, Kitimat, BC, Canada; m. Indira Naidoo-Harris, 4 Aug. 1984. *Education:* BA, English Literature, Queen's University, 1980; MA, English Literature, Dalhousie University, 1982; MSc, Linguistics, University of Alberta, 1985; MS, Technical Communication, 1986; PhD, Communication and Rhetoric, 1990, Rensselaer Polytechnic Institute. *Publications:* Acoustic Dimensions of Functor Comprehension in Broca's Aphasia, 1988; Linguistics Wars, 1993; Landmark Essays in Rhetoric of Science, 1997. Contributions: College English; Perspectives on Science; Rhetoric Review; Historiographia Linguistica; Rhetoric Society Quarterly; Neuropsychologia. *Honours:* Heritage Scholar; Rensselaer Scholar; Killam Scholar; Killam Fellow. *Address:* Dept of English, University of Waterloo, Waterloo, Ontario N2L 3G1, Canada.

HARRIS, Robert Dennis, BA; journalist and writer; b. 7 March 1957, Nottingham, England; m. Gillian Hornby 1988; one s. two d. *Education:* Selwyn Coll., Cambridge. *Career:* Dir and reporter, BBC 1978–86; Political Ed., Observer 1987–89; columnist, Sunday Times 1989–92, 1996–97. *Publications:* A Higher Form of Killing (with Jeremy Paxman) 1982, Gotcha! 1983, The Making of Neil Kinnock 1984, Selling Hitler 1986, Good and Faithful Servant: The Unauthorized Biography of Bernard Ingham 1990, Fatherland (novel) 1992, Enigma (novel) 1995, Archangel (novel) 1998, Pompeii 2003; contrib. to periodicals. *Address:* Old Vicarage, Kintbury, Berkshire RG17 9TR, England.

HARRIS, Rosemary Jeanne; British author; b. 20 Feb. 1923, London, England. *Career:* children's book reviewer, The Times, London 1970–73; mem. Soc. of Authors. *Publications:* The Summer-House, 1956; Voyage to Cythera, 1958; Venus with Sparrows, 1961; All My Enemies, 1967; The Nice Girl's Story, 1968 (in USA as Nor Evil Dreams, 1974); The Moon in the Cloud, 1968; A Wicked Pack of Cards, 1969; The Shadow on the Sun, 1970; The Seal-Singing, 1971; The Child in the Bamboo Grove, 1972; The Bright and Morning Star, 1972; The King's White Elephant, 1973; The Double Snare, 1974; The Lotus and the Grail: Legends from East to West, 1974, US edn as Sea Magic and Other Stories of Enchantment; The Flying Ship, 1975; The Little Dog of Fo, 1976; Three Candles for the Dark, 1976; I Want to Be a Fish, 1977; A Quest for Orion, 1978; Beauty and the Beast (folklore), 1979; Green Finger House, 1980; Tower of the Stars, 1980; The Enchanted Horse, 1981; Janni's Stork, 1981; Zed, 1982; Summers of the Wild Rose, 1987; Love and the Merry-Go-Round, 1988; Ticket to Freedom, 1991; The Wildcat Strike, 1995; The Haunting of Joey M'basa, 1996. *Honours:* Library Asscn Carnegie Medal 1967. *Literary Agent:* AP Watt Ltd, 20 John Street, London, WC1N 2DR, England.

HARRIS, Ruth Elwin; Writer; b. 22 June 1935, Bristol, England; m. Christopher J. L. Bowes, 24 July 1964, two s. one d. *Education:* Bristol, England. *Career:* mem. Society of Authors. *Publications:* The Quantocks Quartet: The Silent Shore, 1986; The Beckoning Hills, 1987; The Dividing Sea, 1989; Billie: The Nevill Letters 1914–1916, 1991; Beyond the Orchid House, 1994. *Address:* c/o Random House, 20 Vauxhall Bridge Rd, London SW1V 2SA, England.

HARRIS, Thomas; Writer; b. 1940, Jackson, TN, USA; Divorced, one d. *Education:* Baylor University. *Publications:* Black Sunday, 1975; Red Dragon, 1981; Silence of the Lambs, 1988; Hannibal, 1999. *Address:* c/o St Martin's Press, 175 Fifth Ave, New York, NY 10010, USA. *Website:* www.thomasharris.com.

HARRIS, (Theodore) Wilson; poet and novelist; b. 24 March 1921, New Amsterdam, British Guiana; m. 1st Cecily Carew 1945; m. 2nd Margaret Whitaker 1959. *Education:* Queen's College, Georgetown. *Career:* Visiting Lecturer, SUNY at Buffalo, 1970; Writer-in-Residence, University of the West Indies, Jamaica, Scarborough College, University of Toronto, 1970, University of Newcastle, NSW, 1979; Commonwealth Fellow in Caribbean Literature, Leeds University, Yorkshire, 1971; Visiting Prof., University of Texas, Austin, 1972, 1981–82, University of Mysore, 1978, Yale University, 1979; Regents Lecturer, University of California, Santa Cruz, 1983. *Publications:* Poetry: Fetish, 1951; The Well and the Land, 1952; Eternity to Season, 1954. Fiction: The Guyana Quartet, 1960–63; Tumatumari, 1968; Black Marsden, 1972; Companions of the Day and Night, 1975; Da Silva's Cultivated Wilderness, 1977; Genesis of the Clowns, 1977; The Tree of the Sun, 1978; The Angel at the Gate, 1982; The Carnival Trilogy, 1985–90; Resurrection at Sorrow Hill, 1993; The Dark Jester, 2001; The Mask of the Beggar, 2003. Other: short stories and other publications. *Address:* c/o Faber and Faber Ltd, 3 Queen Square, London WC1N 3AU, England.

HARRIS, Zinnie; British playwright; b. 1973. *Plays:* By Many Wounds 1998, Further than the Furthest Thing 2000, Nightingale and Chase 2001. *Honours:* Peggy Ramsay New Writer Award. *Literary Agent:* Mel Kenyon, Casarotto Ramsay & Associates Ltd, National House, 60–66 Wardour Street, London, W1V 4ND, England. *Telephone:* (20) 7287-4450. *Fax:* (20) 7287-9128. *E-mail:* mel@casarotto.uk.com. *Website:* www.casarotto.uk.com.

HARRISON, Elizabeth Fancourt; Author; b. 12 Jan. 1921, Watford, Hertfordshire, England. *Career:* mem. Society of Authors; Romantic Novelists Asscn. *Publications:* Coffee at Dobree's, 1965; The Physicians, 1966; The Ravelston Affair, 1967; Corridors of Healing, 1968; Emergency Call, 1970; Accident Call, 1971; Ambulance Call, 1972; Surgeon's Call, 1973; On Call, 1974; Hospital Call, 1975; Dangerous Call, 1976; To Mend a Heart, 1977; Young Dr Goddard, 1978; A Doctor Called Caroline, 1979; A Surgeon Called Amanda, 1982; A Surgeon's Life, 1983; Marrying a Doctor, 1984; Surgeon's Affair, 1985; A Surgeon at St Mark's, 1986; The Surgeon She Married, 1988; The Faithful Type, 1993; The Senior Partner's Daughter, 1994; Made for Each Other, 1995. *Address:* 71 Wingfield Rd, Kingston on Thames, Surrey KT2 5LR, England.

HARRISON, James (Thomas); Author and Poet; b. 11 Dec. 1937, Grayling, Michigan, USA; m. Linda May King, 10 Oct. 1959, two d. *Education:* BA, 1960, MA, 1964, Michigan State University. *Career:* Instructor, SUNY at Stony Brook, 1965–66. *Publications:* Fiction: Wolf: A False Memoir, 1971; A Good Day to Die, 1973; Farmer, 1976; Legends of the Fall, 1979; Warlock, 1981; Sundog, 1984; Dalva, 1988; The Woman Lit by Fireflies, 1990; Sunset Limited, 1990; Julip, 1994; The Road Home, 1998. Poetry: Plain Song, 1965; Locations, 1968; Walking, 1969; Outlyer and Ghazals, 1971; Letters to Yesinin, 1973; Returning to Earth, 1977; New and Selected Poems, 1961–81, 1982; The Theory and Practice of Rivers, 1986; Country Stores, 1993. Screenplays: Cold Feet (with Tom McGuane), 1989; Revenge (with Jeffrey Fishkin), 1990; Wolf (with Wesley Strick), 1994. Non-Fiction: Just Before Dark, 1991. *Honours:* National Endowment for the Arts Grant, 1967–69; Guggenheim Fellowship, 1968–69. *Address:* PO Box 135, Lake Leelanau, MI 49653, USA.

HARRISON, Raymond Vincent; Inspector of Taxes, Financial Consultant and Writer; b. 28 Oct. 1928, Chorley, Lancashire, England; m. 7 April 1977. *Education:* BA, 1952; MA, 1954, Magdalene College, Cambridge. *Publications:* French Ordinary Murder, 1983; Death of An Honourable Member, 1984; Deathwatch, 1985; Death of a Dancing Lady, 1985; Counterfeit of Murder, 1986; A Season for Death, 1987; Harvest of Death, 1988; Tincture of Death, 1989; Sphere of Death, 1990; Patently Murder, 1991; Akin to Murder, 1992; Murder in Petticoat Square, 1993; Murder by Design, 1996.

HARRISON, Sarah; Author; b. 7 Aug. 1946, Exeter, England. *Education:* BA, University of London, 1967. *Career:* Journalist, IPC Magazines, London, 1967–71. *Publications:* Fiction: Flowers of the Field, 1980; A Flower That's Free, 1984; Hot Breath, 1985; An Imperfect Lady, 1987; Cold Feet, 1989; Foreign Parts, 1991; The Forests of the Night, 1992; Be An Angel, 1993; Both Your Houses, 1995; Life After Lunch, 1996; Flowers Won't Fax, 1997; That Was Then, 1998; Heaven's On Hold, 1999; The Grass Memorial, 2002; The Dreaming Stones, 2002; A Dangerous Thing, 2003; The Divided Heart, 2003. Children's Fiction: In Granny's Garden, 1980; Lark Rise series: Laura and Edmond, 1986; Laura and Old Lumber, 1986; Laura and the Lady, 1986; Laura and the Squire, 1986. Non-Fiction: How to Write a Blockbuster, 1995. *Literary Agent:* AP Watt Ltd, 20 John St, London WC1N 2DR, England.

HARRISON, Sue (Ann McHaney); Novelist; b. 29 Aug. 1950, Lansing, Michigan, USA; m. Neil Douglas Harrison 22 Aug. 1969; one s. two d. (one deceased). *Education:* BA, English, 1971. *Career:* mem. Society of Midland Authors. *Publications:* Mother Earth, Father Sky, 1990; My Sister the

Moon, 1992; Brother Wind, 1994; Sisu, 1997; Song of the River, 1997; Cry of the Wind, 1998; Call Down the Stars, 2001. *Address:* 23382 S Rocky Point Rd, Pickford, MI 49774, USA.

HARRISON, Tony; British poet and dramatist; b. 30 April 1937, Leeds. *Education:* Leeds Grammar School and Univ. of Leeds. *Writing for television and film:* Yan Tan Tethera 1983, The Big H 1984, 'V' 1987, Loving Memory 1987, The Blasphemers' Banquet 1989, Black Daisies for the Bride 1993, A Maybe Day in Kazakhstan 1994, The Shadow of Hiroshima 1995, Prometheus 1998, Crassingo 2002. *Plays:* Aikin Mata (with J. Simmons) 1965, The Misanthrope (trans. of Molière's play) 1973, Phaedra Britannica (trans. of Racine's Phèdre) 1975, The Passion 1977, Bow Down 1977, The Bartered Bride (libretto) 1978, The Oresteia (trans.) 1981, The Mysteries 1985, The Trackers of Oxyrhynchus 1990, The Common Chorus 1992, Square Rounds 1992, Poetry or Bust 1993, The Kaisers of Carnuntum 1995, The Labourers of Herakles 1995, The Prince's Play 1996, Fire and Poetry 1999. *Publications include:* poetry: Earthworks 1964, Newcastle is Peru 1969, The Loiners 1970, Poems of Palladas of Alexandria (ed. and trans.) 1973, From the School of Eloquence and Other Poems 1978, Continuous 1981, A Kumquat for John Keats 1981, US Martial 1981, Selected Poems 1984, Fire-Gap 1985, 'V' 1985, Dramatic Verse, 1973–1985 1985, 'V' and Other Poems 1990, A Cold Coming: Gulf War Poems 1991, The Gaze of the Gorgon and other poems 1992, The Shadow of Hiroshima and other film/poems 1995, Permanently Bard 1995, Laureate's Block and other poems 2000; collections of plays: Plays 1 1985, Theatre Works 1973–1985 1986, Plays 2 2002, Plays 3 1996, Plays 4 2002. *Honours:* Cholmondeley Award for Poetry, Geoffrey Faber Memorial Award, European Poetry Translation Prize, Whitbread Poetry Prize 1993, Mental Health Award 1994, Prix Italia 1994, Northern Rock Foundation Writer's Award 2004. *Address:* c/o Gordon Dickerson, 2 Crescent Grove, London, SW4 7AH; 2 Crescent Grove, London, SW4 7AH, England.

HARRISON, William (Neal); Writer and University Teacher; b. 29 Oct. 1933, Dallas, TX, USA; m. Merlee Kimsey, 2 Feb. 1957, two s. one d. *Education:* BA, Texas Christian University, 1955; MA, Vanderbilt University, 1959; Graduate Studies, University of Iowa, 1962. *Career:* Faculty, Dept of English, University of Arkansas at Fayetteville, 1964–99. *Publications:* The Theologian, 1965; In a Wild Sanctuary, 1969; Lessons in Paradise, 1971; Roller Ball Murder and Other Stories, 1974; Africana, 1977; Savannah Blue, 1981; Burton and Speke, 1982; Three Hunters, 1989; The Buddha in Malibu: New and Selected Stories, 1998; The Blood Latitudes, 1999. Other: Screenplays. Contributions: anthologies and periodicals. *Honours:* Guggenheim Fellowship, 1973–74; National Endowment for the Arts Grant, 1977; Christopher Award, 1979. *Address:* c/o Dept of English, University of Arkansas at Fayetteville, Fayetteville, AR 72701, USA.

HARROWER, David; British playwright; b. 1967. *Plays:* Knives in Hens 1995, Kill the Old, Torture their Young 1998, Begin Again 1999, Presence 2001, The Chysalids 2001, Ivanov, by Anton Chekhov (adaptation) 2002, The Girl on the Sofa, by Jon Fosse (adaptation) 2002, Dark Earth 2003, Tales from the Vienna Woods 2003, Purple, by Jon Fosse (adaptation) 2003. *Publications:* Six Characters Looking for an Author (ed.) 2001. *Literary Agent:* Casarotto Ramsay & Associates Ltd, National House, 60–65 Wardour Street, London, W1V 3HP, England. *Telephone:* (20) 7287-4450. *Fax:* (20) 7287-9128. *E-mail:* agents@casarotto.co.uk. *Website:* www.casarotto.co.uk.

HARRS, (Margaret) Norma; writer; b. 15 Sept. 1935, Releast, Northern Ireland; m. Leonard Michael Harrs; two s. *Career:* mem. Writers' Union of Canada, Playwrights' Union of Canada (treasurer 1997–99). *Publications:* A Certain State of Mind 1980, Love Minus One & Other Stories 1994, Where Dreams Have Gone 1997, Sonya (play), The 40th Birthday Party (play), Essential Conflict (play); contrib. to anthologies, including Ladies Start Your Engines 1997, Elements of English 1999; contrib. to journals, including Pittsburgh Review, Kairos, Antigonish Review, Room of One's Own. *Honours:* Ontario Literary Grant 1988, Canada Council Travel Grant 1997. *Address:* 171 Fifth Line, Fraserville, South Monoghan, ON K0L 1V0, Canada. *E-mail:* norharrs@nexicom.net. *Website:* www.normaharrs.com.

HARSENT, David; Poet and Writer; b. 9 Dec. 1942, Devonshire, England; m. 1st (divorced); two s. one d.; m. 2nd; one d. *Career:* Fiction Critic, TLS, London, 1965–73; Poetry Critic, Spectator, London, 1970–73. *Publications:* Poetry: Tonight's Lover, 1968; A Violent Country, 1969; Ashridge, 1970; After Dark, 1973; Truce, 1973; Dreams of the Dead, 1977; Mister Punch, 1984; Selected Poems, 1989; Storybook Hero, 1992; News From the Front, 1993; Playback, 1997; A Bird's Idea of Flight, 1998; Marriage, 2002. Novel: From an Inland Sea, 1985. Libretto: Gawain (for Harrison Birtwistle's opera), 1991; When She Died (opera for TV, music by Jonathan Dove). Music Theatre: Serenade the Silkie (music by Julian Grant), 1989; The Woman and the Hare (music by Harrison Birtwistle), 1998; The Ring Dance of the Nazarene (music by Harrison Birtwistle). Editor: New Poetry 7, 1981; Poetry Book Society Supplement, 1983; Savremena Britanska Poezija, 1988; Another Round at the Pillars, a festschrift for Ian Hamilton, 1999. Other: Sprinting from the Graveyard (trans. of poems by Goran Simic), 1997; The Sorrow of Sarajevo (trans. of poems by Goran Simic), 1996. *Honours:* Eric Gregory Award, 1967; Cheltenham Festival Prize, 1968; Arts Council Bursaries, 1969, 1984; Geoffrey Faber Memorial Prize, 1978; Society of Authors Travel Fellowship, 1989; FRSL, 1998. *Address:* c/o Jonathan Clowes Literary Agency, 10 Iron Bridge House, Bridge Approach, London NW1 8BD, England.

HART, Ellen; Writer; b. 10 Aug. 1949, Minneapolis, Minnesota, USA; two d. *Education:* BA, Theology, Ambassador University. *Career:* mem. Sisters in Crime. *Publications:* Hallowed Murder, 1989; Vital Lies, 1991; Stage Fright, 1992; A Killing Cure, 1993; The Little Piggy Went to Murder, 1994; A Small Sacrifice, 1994; Faint Praise, 1995; For Every Evil, 1995; Robber's Wine, 1996; The Oldest Sin, 1996; Murder in the Air, 1997; Wicked Games, 1998. *Honours:* Lambda Literary Award, 1994, 1996; Minnesota Book Award, 1995, 1996. *Address:* 4623 Blaisdell Ave S, Minneapolis, MN 55409, USA.

HART, Kevin; Australian academic and poet; b. 5 July 1954, London, England. *Education:* Australian National University; Stanford University, CA, and University of Melbourne; PhD, 1987. *Career:* Lecturer in English, Melbourne University, Australia, 1986–87; Lecturer to Sr Lecturer in Literary Studies, Deakin University, Victoria, 1987–91; Assoc. Prof., 1991–95, Prof. of English, 1995–2002, Monash University; Foundation Prof. of Australian and New Zealand Studies, Georgetown University, Washington, DC, 1996–97; Visiting Prof., Villanova University, 2001; Prof. of English, University of Notre Dame, IN, 2002–; mem. Vice-Pres., Johnson Society of Australia; Fellow, Australian Acad. of the Humanities; Fellow, Nanovic Institute. *Publications:* Nebuchadnezzar, 1976; The Departure, 1978; The Lines of the Hand: Poems 1976–79; Your Shadow, 1984; The Trespass of the Sign, 1989; Peniel, 1990; The Buried Harbour (trans.), 1990; A D. Hope, 1992; The Oxford Book of Australian Religious Verse (ed.), 1994; New and Selected Poems, 1995; Dark Angel, 1996; Samuel Johnson and the Culture of Property, 1999; Wicked Heat, 1999; Flame Tree: Selected Poems, 2002; The Impossible, 2003; The Dark Gaze: Maurice Blanchot and the Sacred, 2004. Contributions: Arena Journal, The Critical Review, Boxkite, Heat, Verse. *Honours:* Australian Literature Board Fellowship, 1977; New South Wales Premier's Award, 1985; Victorian Premier's Award for Poetry, 1985; Grace Levin Awards for Poetry, 1991, 1995; Christopher Brennan Award for Poetry, 1999. *Address:* Dept of English, University of Notre Dame, Notre Dame, IN 46556, USA. *E-mail:* khart2@nd.edu.

HART, Veronica (see Kelleher, Victor).

HART-DAVIS, Duff; Author; b. 3 June 1936, London, England. *Education:* BA, Univ. of Oxford, 1960. *Career:* Feature Writer, 1972–76, Literary Ed., 1976–77, Asst Ed., 1977–78, Sunday Telegraph; Country Columnist, Independent, 1986–2001. *Publications:* The Megacull, 1968; The Gold of St Matthew (US edn as The Gold Trackers), 1968; Spider in the Morning, 1972; Ascension: The Story of a South Atlantic Island, 1972; Peter Fleming (biog.), 1974; Monarchs of the Glen, 1978; The Heights of Rimring, 1980; Fighter Pilot (with C. Strong), 1981; Level Five, 1982; Fire Falcon, 1984; The Man-Eater of Jassapur, 1985; Hitler's Games, 1986; Armada, 1988; The House the Berrys Built, 1990; Horses of War, 1991; Country Matters, 1991; Wildings: The Secret Garden of Eileen Soper, 1992; Further Country Matters, 1993; When the Country Went to Town, 1997; Raoul Millais, 1998; Fauna Britannica, 2002; Audubon's Elephant, 2003. *Address:* Owlpen Farm, Uley, Dursley, Gloucestershire GL11 5BZ, England.

HARTCUP, Adeline; Writer; b. 26 April 1918, Isle of Wight, England; m. John Hartcup, 11 Feb. 1950, two s. *Education:* MA, Classics and English Literature, Oxon. *Career:* Editorial Staff, Times Educational Supplement; Hon. Press Officer, Kent Voluntary Service Council. *Publications:* Angelica, 1954; Morning Faces, 1963; Below Stairs in the Great Country Houses, 1980; Children of the Great Country Houses, 1982; Love and Marriage in the Great Country Houses, 1984; Spello: Life Today in Ancient Umbria, 1985. Contributions: Times Educational Supplement; Harper's & Queen; Times Higher Educational Supplement. *Address:* 8F Compton Rd, London N1 2PA, England. *Telephone:* (20) 7226-1924.

HARTILL, Rosemary Jane, BA, FRSA; writer, broadcaster and producer; b. 11 Aug. 1949, Oswestry, England. *Education:* University of Bristol. *Career:* BBC Religious Affairs Correspondent, 1982–88, Presenter, BBC World Service Meridian Books Programme, 1990–92, 1994. *Publications:* Emily Brontë: Poems (ed.), 1973; Wild Animals, 1976; In Perspective, 1988; Writers Revealed, 1989; Were You There?, 1995; Visionary Women: Florence Nightingale (ed.), 1996. Contributions: periodicals. *Honours:* Sandford St Martin Trust Personal Award, 1994; Hon. doctorates, Universities of Hull, 1995, Bristol, 2000. *Address:* Old Post Office, 24 Eglingham Village, Alnwick, Northumberland NE66 2TX, England.

HARTLEY, Aidan; writer; b. 1965. *Education:* Univ. of Oxford, Univ. of London. *Career:* grew up in Africa; foreign correspondent, Reuters, then freelance 1996–. *Publications:* The Zanzibar Chest: A Memoir of Love and War 2003. *Literary Agent:* c/o Grove/Atlantic, 841 Broadway, Fourth Floor, New York, NY 10003, USA. *Telephone:* (212) 614-7874. *Fax:* (212) 614-7886. *E-mail:* dseager@groveatlantic.com. *Website:* www.thezanzibarchest.com.

HÄRTLING, Peter; Author, Poet and Critic; b. 13 Nov. 1933, Chemnitz, Germany; m. Mechthild Maier, 1959, two s. two d. *Education:* Grammar School, Nürtingen. *Career:* Ed. and Co-Publisher, Der Monat, 1967–70; Ed. and Managing Dir, S. Fischer Verlag, Frankfurt am Main, 1968–74; Prof. of Poetry, University of Frankfurt am Main, 1984; mem. Acad. of Arts, Berlin; Acad. of Science and Literature, Mainz; Deutsche Akademie für

Sprache und Dichtung eV, Darmstadt; PEN. *Publications:* Yamins Stationen, 1955; Spielgeist, Spielgeist, 1962; Niembsch oder Der Stillstand: Eine Suite, 1964; Janek: Porträt einer Erinnerung, 1966; Das Familienfest oder Das Ende einer Geschichte, 1969; Neue Gedichte, 1972; Zwettl: Nachprüfung einer Erinnerung, 1973; Eine Frau, 1974; Hölderlin, 1976; Hubert oder Die Rückkehr nach Casablanca, 1978; Meine Lekture: Literatur als Widerstand, 1980; Nachgetragene Liebe, 1980; Die dreifache Maria, 1982; Vorwarnung, 1983; Sätze von Liebe, 1983; Das Windrad, 1983; Ich rufe die Wörter zusammen, 1984; Der spanische Soldat oder Finden und Erfinden: Frankfurter Poetik-Vorlesungen, 1984, 1984; Die Mörsinger Pappel, 1987; Waiblingers Augen, 1987; Gedichte 1953–1987, 1989; Herzwand: Mein Roman, 1990; Zwischen Untergang und Aufbruch: Aufsätze, Reden, Gespräche, 1990; Brüder und Schwestern: Tagebuch eines Synodalen, 1991; Schubert, 1992; Bozena, 1994; Schumanns Schatten, 1996; Grosse, kleine Schwester, 1998; Hoffmann oder Die vielfältige Liebe, 2000. *Honours:* Literary Prize, German Critics' Asscn, 1964; Gerhart Hauptmann Prize, 1971; Friedrich Hölderlin Prize, 1987; Andreas Gryphius Prize, 1990; Lion Feuchtwanger Prize, Acad. of Arts, Berlin, 1992; Hon. Prof., Stuttgart, 1994; Grand Cross of Merit, Federal Republic of Germany, 1995; Eichendorff Prize, 2000. *Address:* Finkenweg 1, 46546 Mörfelden-Walldorf, Germany.

HARTMAN, Geoffrey H., BA, PhD; American fmr academic and writer; b. 11 Aug. 1929, Frankfurt am Main, Germany; m. Renee Gross 1956; one s. one d. *Education:* Queens College, CUNY, Yale Univ. *Career:* Fulbright Fellow Univ. of Dijon 1951–52; Faculty Yale Univ. 1955–62; Assoc. Prof. Univ. of Iowa 1962–64, Prof. of English 1964–65; Prof. of English and Comparative Literature Cornell Univ. 1965–67; Karl Young Prof. Yale Univ. 1974–94, Sterling Prof. 1994–97; Gauss Seminarist Princeton Univ. 1968; Dir School of Theory and Criticism, Dartmouth College 1982–87; Assoc. Fellow Center for Research in Philosophy and Literature, Univ. of Warwick 1993; Fellow Woodrow Wilson International Center 1995; mem. American Acad. of Arts and Sciences, MLA. *Publications:* The Unmediated Vision 1954, André Malraux 1960, Wordsworth's Poetry 1964, Beyond Formalism 1970, The Fate of Reading 1975, Akiba's Children 1978, Criticism in the Wilderness 1980, Saving the Text 1981, Easy Pieces 1985, The Unremarkable Wordsworth 1987, Minor Prophecies 1991, A Critic's Journey 1999, Scars of the Spirit 2003; editor: Romanticism: Vistas, Instances, Continuities 1973, Psychoanalysis and the Question of the Text 1978, Shakespeare and the Question of Theory 1985, Bitburg in Moral and Political Perspective 1986, Midrash and Literature 1986, Holocaust Remembrance: The Shapes of Memory 1993. Monographs: The Longest Shadow: In the Aftermath of the Holocaust 1996, The Fateful Question of Culture 1997 (ACLA Renee Wellek Prize 1997), A Critic's Journey 1999, Scars of the Spirit: The Struggle Against Inauthenticity 2002. *Honours:* Guggenheim Fellowships 1969, 1986; Hon. LHD (Queens College, CUNY) 1990, (Hebrew Union Coll., Cincinnatti) 2003; Keats-Shelley Asscn Distinguished Scholar Award 1997; Tanner Lectures, 1999; Haskins Lecturer, 2000. *Address:* 260 Everit Street, New Haven, CT 06511, USA.

HARTMAN, Jan; Dramatist and Writer; b. 23 May 1938, Stockholm, Sweden. *Education:* Phillips Andover Academy, 1956; BA, Harvard College, 1960. *Career:* Resident Playwright, Theatre of The Living Arts, Philadelphia, 1964–65, Theatre St Clements, 1977–78; Founder-Dir, Playwrights Theatre Project Circle in the Square, 1967–69, Eleventh Hour Productions, 1977; Adjunct Prof. of Dramatic Writing and Shakespeare, New York University, 1981–93; Visiting Prof., Syracuse University, 1985–94; mem. PEN, Writers' Guild of America, Eugene O'Neill Memorial Theatre Foundation, Dramatists' Guild, BAFTA, Foreign Press Asscn UK. *Publications:* Fiction: Joshua; Envy; The Wail, 1998. Plays: (for film, television and radio) Into Exile, BBC Radio, 1999–2000; The Protégé, BBC Radio, 2000; The Albanian Women: Westdeutsche Randfunk; Mother Teresa: In the Name of God's Poor; The Next War; Genealogy of Evil; The Great Wallendas; Second Sight; Song of Myself; Kepler's Room; Abelard and Heloise; Flight 981; The American War Crimes Trial; Fragment of a Last Judgement; Freeman! Freeman!; The Legend of Daniel Boone. Contributions: Dramatists Guild Quarterly, The Observer, New York Times, Our Generation. *Honours:* Guggenheim Fellowship for Playwriting; Two Emmy Awards; Two Christopher Awards; Writers' Guild of America Award; numerous grants. *Address:* 5 Tatlintown, Wareside, Herts SG12 7RP, England. *E-mail:* jhartman_uk@yahoo.co.uk.

HARTNETT, David William; Writer, Poet and Ed.; b. 4 Sept. 1952, London, England; m. Margaret R. N. Thomas, 26 Aug. 1976, one s. one d. *Education:* Scholarship, English Language and Literature, 1971, Honour Moderations, 1973, BA, English Language and Literature, 1975, MA, 1981, DPhil, 1987, University of Oxford. *Career:* Co-Ed., Poetry Durham magazine; Dir, Contributing Ed., Leviathan Publishing Ltd, Leviathan Quarterly. *Publications:* Poetry: A Signalled Love, 1985; House of Moon, 1988; Dark Ages, 1992; At the Wood's Edge, 1997. Fiction: Black Milk, 1994; Brother to Dragons, 1998. Contributions: TLS. *Honours:* TLS/Cheltenham Festival Poetry Competition, 1989. *Literary Agent:* David Higham Associates, 5–8 Lower John St, Golden Sq., London W1F 9HA, England.

HARTNETT, Sonya, BA; Australian writer; b. 23 March 1968, Melbourne, Vic. *Education:* Royal Melbourne Institute of Technology. *Career:* mem. St Martin's Theatre, Melbourne (board mem.). *Publications:* Trouble All the Way 1984, Sparkle and Nightflower 1986, The Glass House 1990, Wilful Blue 1994, Sleeping Dogs 1995, The Devil Latch 1996, Black Foxes 1996, Princes 1997, Thursday's Child 2002, What the Birds See 2003, Stripes of the Sidestep Wolf 2004. *Honours:* International Books for Youth Prize 1996, Children's Book Council of Australia Honor Book 1996, Guardian Children's Fiction Prize 2002. *Address:* c/o Penguin Books, PO Box 257, Ringwood, Vic. 3134, Australia.

HARTUNG, Harald; German poet, professor and critic; b. 29 Oct. 1932, Herne; m. Freia Schnackenburg 1979; two s. *Career:* secondary school teacher 1960–66; Prof., Pädagogische Hochschule Berlin 1971–80, Tech. Univ. Berlin 1980–; mem. Akad. der Künste, Berlin, PEN. *Publications:* Experimentelle Literatur und Konkrete Poesie 1975, Das Gewöhnliche Licht 1976, Augenzeit 1978, Deutsche Lyrik seit 1965 1985, Traum im Deutschen Museum 1986, Luftfracht 1991, Jahre mit Windrad 1996, Masken und Stimmen 1996. *Honours:* Kunstpreis Berlin, Drostepreis 1987, Premio Antico Fattore 1999. *Address:* Rüdesheimer Platz 4, 14197 Berlin, Germany.

HARUF, Kent; Writer; b. 24 Feb. 1943, Pueblo, CO, USA; m. 1st Virginia Koon, divorced; m. 2nd Cathy Dempsey, three d. *Education:* BA, Nebraska Wesleyan University, 1965; MFA, University of Iowa, 1973. *Career:* Asst Prof., Nebraska Wesleyan University, 1986–91; Assoc. Prof., Southern Illinois University, 1991–2000. *Publications:* The Tie That Binds, 1984; Where You Once Belonged, 1991; Plainsong, 1999. Contributions: anthologies and periodicals. *Honours:* Whiting Writer's Award, 1986; Maria Thomas Award, 1991; Mt Plains Booksellers Award, 2000; Alex Award, 2000. *Address:* PO Box 1580, Salida, CO 81201, USA.

HARVEY, Anne (Berenice); Actress, Writer, Poet and Ed.; b. 27 April 1933, London, England; m. Alan Harvey, 13 April 1957, one s. one d. *Education:* Guildhall School of Music and Drama, London, 1950–54. *Career:* mem. Poetry Society; Friends of the Dymock Poets; Eighteen Nineties Society; Imaginative Book Illustration Society; Walter de la Mare Society, founder mem.; Wilfred Owen Society; John Masefield Society; Edward Thomas Fellowship; Charlotte Mary Yonge Fellowship. *Publications:* A Present for Nellie, 1981; Poets in Hand, 1985; Of Caterpillars, Cats and Cattle, 1987; In Time of War: War Poetry, 1987; Something I Remember (selected poetry of Eleanor Farjeon), 1987; A Picnic of Poetry, 1988; The Language of Love, 1989; Six of the Best, 1989; Faces in the Crowd, 1990; Headlines from the Jungle (with Virginia McKenna), 1990; Occasions, 1990; Flora's Red Socks, 1991; Shades of Green, 1991; Elected Friends (poems for and about Edward Thomas), 1991; He Said, She Said, They Said (conversation poems, ed.), 1993; Solo Audition: Speeches for Young Actors, 1993; Criminal Records: Poetry of Crime (ed.), 1994; Methuen Book of Duologues, 1995; Starlight, Starbright: Poems of Night, 1995; Swings and Shadows: Poems of Times Past and Present, 1996; Words Aloud, two vols (ed.), 1998; Eleanor Farjeon, The Last Four Years (ed.); Blackbird Has Spoken: Selected Poems of Eleanor Farjeon (ed.), 1999; Eleanor Farjeon, Come Christmas (ed.), 2000; Adlestrop Revisited (ed.), 2000; When Christmas Comes (anthology, ed.), 2002. Series Editor: Poetry Originals, 1992–95. Contributions: Radio, journals, and magazines. *Honours:* Signal Poetry Award, 1992. *Address:* 37 St Stephen's Rd, Ealing, London W13 8HJ, England.

HARVEY, Brett; Writer and Critic; b. 28 April 1936, New York, NY, USA; one s. one d. *Education:* Northwestern Univ., 1956–59. *Career:* Drama and Literature Dir, WBAI-FM, 1971–74; Publicity and Promotion Dir, The Feminist Press, Old Westbury, NY, 1974–80; Exec. Dir American Soc. of Journalists & Authors 2000–. *Publications:* My Prairie Year, 1986; Immigrant Girl, 1987; Cassie's Journey, My Prairie Christmas, 1990; The Fifties: A Women's Oral History, 1993. Contributions: Village Voice; New York Times Book Review; Psychology Today; Voice Literary Supplement; Mirabella; Mother Jones; Mademoiselle. *Address:* 305 Eighth Ave, Brooklyn, NY 11215, USA.

HARVEY, Caroline (see Trollope, Joanna).

HARVEY, Jack (see Rankin, Ian James).

HARVEY, John Barton, MA; writer and poet; b. 21 Dec. 1938, London, England; three c. *Education:* Goldsmiths Coll., London, Hatfield Polytechnic, Univ. of Nottingham. *Career:* teacher of English in secondary schools 1965–75; part-time lecturer in film and literature, Univ. of Nottingham 1980–86; fmrly tutor on residential writing courses, Arvon Foundation; teacher, Squaw Valley Community of Writers Fiction Workshop, Northern California 1995; Man., Slow Dancer Press 1977–99, ed. Slow Dancer magazine –1993. *Radio:* Wasted Years 1995, Cutting Edge 1996, Slow Burn 1997, Cheryl 2001; adaptations of works by A. S. Byatt, Richard Ford, Bobbie Ann Mason, Jayne Anne Phillips and Graham Greene (including The End of the Affair, winner of Silver Sony Radio Drama Award 1998. *Television:* Lonely Hearts (New York Festivals bronze medal for Screenplay for Best TV Drama Series 1992) 1991, Rough Treatment 1992, Hard Cases (series, Central TV); adaptations of Arnold Bennett works Anna of the Five Towns, Sophia and Constance. *Publications:* novels: Avenging Angel (as Thom Ryder) 1975, Angel Alone (as Thom Ryder) 1975, Kill Hitler! (as Jon Barton) 1976, Amphetamines and Pearls 1976, The Geranium Kiss 1976, River of Blood (as John J. McLaglen) 1976, Forest of Death (as Jon Barton) 1977, Lightning Strikes (as Jon Barton) 1977, The Raiders (as L. J. Coburn) 1977, Evil Breed (as J. B. Dancer) 1977, Black Blood (as Jon Hart) 1977, High Slaughter (as Jon Hart) 1977, Triangle of Death (as Jon

Hart) 1977, Guerilla Attack (as Jon Hart) 1977, Shadow of Vultures (as John J. McLaglen) 1977, Death in Gold (as John J. McLaglen) 1977, Junkyard Angel 1977, Neon Madman 1977, Cross-Draw (as John J. McLaglen) 1978, Death Raid (as Jon Hart) 1978, Judgement Day (as J. B. Dancer) 1978, Bloody Shiloh (as L. J. Coburn) 1978, Blood Rising (as William M. James) 1979, Cannons in the Rain (as J. D. Sandon) 1979, Border Affair (as J. D. Sandon) 1979, The Hanged Man (as J. B. Dancer) 1979, Vigilante! (as John J. McLaglen) 1979, Frame 1979, Blood Money (as William S. Brady) 1979, Killing Time (as William S. Brady) 1980, Blood Kin (as William S. Brady) 1980, Cherokee Outlet (as John B. Harvey) 1980, Blood Trail (as John B. Harvey) 1980, Tago (as John B. Harvey) 1980, The Silver Lie (as John B. Harvey) 1980, Sun Dance (as John J. McLaglen) 1980, Billy the Kid (as John J. McLaglen) 1980, Till Death... (as John J. McLaglen) 1980, Blood Brother (as William M. James) 1980, Mazatlan (as J. D. Sandon) 1980, Death Dragon (as William M. James) 1981, Wheels of Thunder (as J. D. Sandon) 1981, Blind 1981, Blood on the Border (as John B. Harvey) 1981, Ride the Wide Country (as John B. Harvey) 1981, Desperadoes (as William S. Brady) 1981, Dead Man's Hand (as William S. Brady) 1981, Whiplash (as William S. Brady) 1981, Sierra Gold (as William S. Brady) 1982, Death and Jack Shade (as William S. Brady) 1982, Endgame (as James Mann) 1982, Arkansas Breakout (as John B. Harvey) 1982, John Wesley Hardin (as John B. Harvey) 1982, Dying Ways (as John J. McLaglen) 1982, Hearts of Gold (as John J. McLaglen) 1982, Durango (as J. D. Sandon) 1982, Death Ride (as William M. James) 1983, The Hanging (as William M. James) 1983, Border War (as William S. Brady) 1983, Killer! (as William S. Brady) 1983, War-Party (as William S. Brady) 1983, Wild Blood (as John J. McLaglen) 1983, California Bloodlines (as John B. Harvey) 1983, The Skinning Place (aka The Fatal Frontier) (as John B. Harvey) 1983, Dancer Draws a Wild Card (as Terry Lennox) 1985, Lonely Hearts 1989, Rough Treatment 1990, Cutting Edge 1991, Off Minor 1992, Wasted Years 1993, Cold Light (Grand Prix du Roman Noir Etranger du Cognac 2000) 1994, Living Proof 1995, Easy Meat 1996, Still Water 1997, Last Rites (Sherlock Award Winner for Best British Detective 1999) 1998, In a True Light 2001, Flesh and Blood 2004; juvenile: What About It, Sharon? 1979, Reel Love 1982, Sundae Date 1983, What Game Are You Playing? 1983, Footwork 1984, Wild Love 1986, Last Summer 1986, Kidnap! 1987, Daylight Robbery! 1987, Hot Property! 1987, Terror Trap! 1988, Downeast to Danger 1988, Runner! Beaver 1988; poetry: Provence (chapbook) 1978, The Old Postcard Trick (chapbook) 1985, Neil Sedaka Lied (chapbook) 1987, The Downeast Poems (chapbook) 1989, Sometime Other Than Now (with Sue Dymoke) (chapbook) 1989, Territory (chapbook) 1992, Ghosts of a Chance 1992, Bluer Than This 1998. *Literary Agent:* Lutyens & Rubinstein, 231 Westbourne Park Road, London, W11 1EB, England. *Telephone:* (20) 7792-4855. *Website:* www.mellotone.co.uk.

HARVEY, John Robert; University Lecturer and Writer; b. 25 June 1942, Bishops Stortford, Hertfordshire, England; m. Julietta Chloe Papadopoulou, 1968, one d. *Education:* BA, English, 1964, MA, 1967, PhD, 1969, University of Cambridge. *Career:* English Faculty, Emmanuel College, Cambridge; Ed., Cambridge Quarterly, 1978–86. *Publications:* Victorian Novelists and Their Illustrators 1970, Men in Black 1995. Fiction: The Plate Shop 1979, Coup d'Etat 1985, The Legend of Captain Space 1990. Contributions: London Review of Books, Sunday Times, Sunday Telegraph, Listener, Encounter, Cambridge Quarterly, Essays in Criticism, Royal Academy Magazine. *Honours:* David Higham Prize, 1979. *Address:* Emmanuel College, St Andrew's St, Cambridge CB2 3AP, England.

HARVEY, Steven; Prof. of English, Writer and Poet; b. 9 June 1949, Dodge City, KS, USA; m. Barbara Hupfer, 8 May 1971, two s. two d. *Education:* BA, Wake Forest University, 1971; MA, Writing Seminars, Johns Hopkins University, 1973; MA, Literature, Middlebury College, 1984; PhD, University of Virginia, 1989. *Career:* Prof. of English, Young Harris College, GA, 1976–; Instructor in Writing, John C. Campbell Folk School, 1995–; mem. Associated Writing Programs. *Publications:* Powerlines (poems), 1976; A Geometry of Lilies (non-fiction), 1993; Lost in Translation (non-fiction), 1997; In a Dark Wood: Personal Essays by Men on Middle Age, 1997; Bound for Shady Grove (non-fiction), 2000. Contributions: periodicals. *Honours:* MacDowell Colony Fellowship, 1994. *Address:* PO Box 356, Young Harris, GA 30582, USA. *E-mail:* sharvey@yhc.edu.

HARVOR, Elisabeth, (Erica Elisabeth Arendt); Poet and Writer; b. 26 June 1936, Saint John, NB, Canada; m. Stig Harvor, 16 Nov. 1957, divorced 1977, two s. *Education:* MA, Concordia University, 1986. *Career:* Teacher, various creative writing programs; Writer-in-Residence, Ottawa Public Library, 1993. *Publications:* Women and Children, 1973, revised edn as Our Lady of All the Distances, 1991; If Only We Could Drive Like This Forever, 1988; Fortress of Chairs, 1992; Let Me Be the One, 1996; The Long Cold Green Evenings of Spring, 1997; A Room at the Heart of Things (ed.), 1998; Excessive Joy Injures the Heart, 2002. *Honours:* League of Canadian Poets' National Poetry Prizes, 1989, 1991; Malahat Long Poem Prize, 1990; Gerald Lampert Memorial Award, 1992.

HARWOOD, Lee, BA; poet, writer and translator; b. 6 June 1939, Leicester, England; (divorced), two s. one d. *Education:* Queen Mary Coll., London. *Career:* mem. National Poetry Secretariat (chair. 1974–76), Poetry Soc., London (chair. 1976–77). *Publications:* Title Illegible, 1965; The Man with Blue Eyes, 1966; The White Room, 1968; The Beautiful Atlas, 1969; Landscapes, 1969; The Sinking Colony, 1970; Penguin Modern Poets 19 (with John Ashbery and Tom Raworth), 1971; The First Poem, 1971; New Year, 1971; Captain Harwood's Log of Stern Statements and Stout Sayings, 1973; Freighters, 1975; HMS Little Fox, 1976; Boston-Brighton, 1977; Old Bosham Bird Watch and Other Stories, 1977; Wish You Were Here (with A Lopez), 1979; All the Wrong Notes, 1981; Faded Ribbons, 1982; Wine Tales (with Richard Caddel), 1984; Crossing the Frozen River: Selected Poems 1965–1980, 1984; Monster Masks, 1985; Dream Quilt (short stories), 1985; Rope Boy to the Rescue, 1988; The Empty Hill: Memories and Praises of Paul Evans 1945–1991 (ed. with Peter Bailey), 1992; In the Mists: Mountain Poems, 1993; Morning Light 1998. Other: Trans of works by Tristan Tzara. Contributions: journals, reviews, and magazines. *Honours:* Poetry Foundation Award, New York 1966, Alice Hunt Bartlett Prize, Poetry Soc., London 1976.

HARWOOD, Ronald, CBE, FRSL; British author and playwright; b. ((Ronald Horwitz)), 9 Nov. 1934, Cape Town, South Africa; m. Natasha Riehle 1959; one s. two d. *Education:* Sea Point Boys' High School, Cape Town and Royal Acad. of Dramatic Art. *Career:* actor 1953–60; author 1960–; Artistic Dir Cheltenham Festival of Literature 1975; presenter, Kaleidoscope, BBC Radio 1973, Read All About It, BBC TV 1978–79, All The World's A Stage, BBC TV; Chair. Writers' Guild of GB 1969; Visitor in Theatre, Balliol Coll. Oxford 1986; Pres. PEN (England) 1989–93, Int. PEN 1993–97; Gov. Cen. School of Speech and Drama; author of numerous TV plays and screenplays; mem. Council Royal Soc. of Literature 1998–2001, chair. 2001–04; Trustee Booker Foundation 2002. *TV plays include:* The Barber of Stamford Hill 1960, Private Potter (with Casper Wrede) 1961, The Guests 1972, Breakthrough at Reykjavik 1987, Countdown to War 1989. *Screenplays include:* A High Wind in Jamaica 1965, One Day in the Life of Ivan Denisovich 1971, Evita Perón 1981, The Dresser 1983, Mandela 1987, The Browning Version 1994, Cry, Beloved Country 1995, Taking Sides 2002, The Pianist 2002 (Acad. Award for Best Adapted Screenplay 2003), The Statement, Being Julia. *Plays include:* Country Matters 1969, The Good Companions (musical libretto) 1974, The Ordeal of Gilbert Pinfold 1977, A Family 1978, The Dresser 1980, After the Lions 1982, Tramway Road 1984, The Deliberate Death of a Polish Priest 1985, Interpreters 1985, J. J. Farr 1987, Ivanov (from Chekhov) 1989, Another Time 1989, Reflected Glory 1992, Poison Pen 1994, Taking Sides 1995, The Handyman 1996, Equally Divided 1998, Quartet 1999, Mahler's Conversion 2002. *Publications include:* fiction: All the Same Shadows 1961, The Guilt Merchants 1963, The Girl in Melanie Klein 1969, Articles of Faith 1973, The Genoa Ferry 1976, César and Augusta 1978, Home 1993; non-fiction: Sir Donald Wolfit, CBE: His Life and Work in the Unfashionable Theatre (biog.) 1971; editor: A Night at the Theatre 1983, The Ages of Gielfud 1984, Dear Alec: Guinness at Seventy-Five 1989, The Faber Book of the Theatre 1994; vols of essays and short stories. *Honours:* Chevalier des Arts et des Lettres 1996; Hon. DLitt (Keele) 2002; New Standard Drama Award 1981, Drama Critics Award 1981, Molière Award for Best Play, Paris 1993. *Literary Agent:* Judy Daish Associates, 2 St Charles Place, London, W10 6EG, England. *Telephone:* (020) 8964-8811.

HASHMI, (Aurangzeb) Alamgir, MA; Pakistani professor, poet, writer, editor and broadcaster; b. 15 Nov. 1951, Lahore; m. Beatrice Stoerk 1978; two s. one d. *Education:* Univ. of Louisville. *Career:* Lecturer, Forman Christian Coll., Lahore 1973–74, Univ. of Berne, Univ. of Basel 1982; Davidson Int. Visiting Scholar from Pakistan, Univ. of North Carolina 1974–75; Lecturer in English, Univ. of Louisville 1975–78, Univ. of Zürich and Volkshochschule, Zürich 1980–85; Asst Prof. of English, Univ. of Bahawalpur, Pakistan 1979–80; Assoc. Prof. of English, Int. Islamic Univ., Islamabad 1985–86; Prof. of English and Comparative Literature, Pakistan Futuristics Inst., Islamabad 1990; mem. Associated Writing Programs, Asscn for Asian Studies, Commonwealth Club, Asscn for Commonwealth Literature and Language Studies, Int. Asscn of Univ. Profs of English, Int. Centre for Asian Studies (fellow), Int. PEN (fellow), MLA of America. *Publications:* poetry: The Oak and Amen: Love Poems 1976, America is a Punjabi Word 1979, An Old Chair 1979, My Second in Kentucky 1981, This Time in Lahore 1983, Neither This Time/Nor That Place 1984, Inland and Other Poems 1988, The Poems of Alamgir Hashmi 1992, Sun and Moon and Other Poems 1992, Others to Sport with Amaryllis in the Shade 1992; other: Pakistani Literature (ed.), two vols 1978, second edn as Pakistani Literature: The Contemporary English Writers 1987, Commonwealth Literature 1983, The Commonwealth, Comparative Literature and the World 1988, Pakistani Short Stories in English (ed.) 1992, Encyclopedia of Post-Colonial Literatures (co-ed.) 1994, Where Coyotes Howl and Wind Blows Free (ed. with Alexandra Haslam) 1995, The Great Tejon Club Jubilee 1996; contrib. to many books, journals and periodicals. *Honours:* Hon. DLitt (Centre Universitaire de Luxembourg) 1984, (San Francisco State Univ.) 1984, Rockefeller Foundation Fellow 1994; Patras Bokhari Award, Pakistan Acad. of Letters 1985, Roberto Celli Memorial Award 1994. *Address:* 1542 Service Road West, G-11/2, Islamabad, Pakistan. *E-mail:* alamgirhashmi@yahoo.co.uk.

HASLAM, Gerald W(illiam); Writer and Prof. of English Emeritus; b. 18 March 1937, Bakersfield, CA, USA; m. Janice E. Pettichord, 1 July 1961, three s., two d. *Education:* AB, 1963, MA, 1965, San Francisco State College; Washington State University, 1965–66; PhD, Union Graduate School, 1980. *Career:* Instructor in English, San Francisco State College, 1966–67; Prof. of English, 1967–97, Prof. Emeritus, 1997–, Sonoma State University;

mem. California Studies Asscn; Yosemite Asscn, board of trustees; Western Literature Asscn, pres., 1984. *Publications:* Fiction: Okies: Selected Stories, 1973; Masks: A Novel, 1976; The Wages of Sin: Stories, 1980; Hawk Flights: Visions of the West: Short Stories, 1983; Snapshots: Glimpses of the Other California: Selected Stories, 1985; The Man Who Cultivated Fire and Other Stories, 1987; That Constant Coyote: California Stories, 1990; Condor Dreams and Other Fictions, 1994; The Great Tejon Club Jubilee: Stories, 1995; Manuel and the Madman (with Janice E. Haslam), 2000; Straight White Male, 2000. Other: Forgotten Pages of American Literature (ed.), 1970; The Language of the Oilfields: Examination of an Industrial Argot, 1972; Western Writings (ed.), 1974; Afro-American Oral Literature (ed.), 1974; California Heartland: Writing from the Great Central Valley (ed. with James D. Houston), 1978; Voices of a Place: The Great Central Valley, 1986; A Literary History of the American West (ed. with J. Golden Taylor), 1987; Baiting the Hook, 1990; Coming of Age in California: Personal Essays, 1990; The Other California: The Great Central Valley in Life and Letters, 1990; Many Californias: Literature from the Golden State (ed.), 1992; Out of the Slush Pile (with Stephen Glasser), 1993; The Horned Toad, 1995; Where Coyotes Howl and Wind Blows Free: Growing Up in the West (ed. with Alexandra Russell), 1995; Workin' Man Blues: Country Music in California (with Alexandra Russell and Richard Chon), 1999. *Honours:* California Arts Council Fellowship, 1989; Josephine Miles Award, PEN, 1990; Bay Area Book Reviewers' Award, 1993; Benjamin Franklin Award, Publishers' Marketing Asscn, 1993; Commonwealth Club Medal, 1994; Award of Merit, Asscn for State and Local Historians, 1994; Distinguished Achievement Award, Western Literature Asscn, 1999; Laureate, San Francisco Public Library, 1998; Ralph J. Gleason Award, 2000; Carey McWilliams Award, 2000; Western States Book Award for Fiction, 2000; Certificate for Citation, Asscn for State and Local History, 2001; Sequoia: Giant of the Valley Award, 2003. *Address:* PO Box 969, Penngrove, CA 94951, USA.

HASLUCK, Nicholas (Paul); Writer and Poet; b. 17 Oct. 1942, Canberra, ACT, Australia. *Education:* University of Western Australia, 1960–63; University of Oxford, 1964–66. *Career:* Barrister, Solicitor, Supreme Court of Western Australia, 1968; Deputy Chair., Australia Council, 1978–82; Chair., Literature Board, 1998–2001. *Publications:* Fiction: Quarantine 1978, The Blue Guitar 1980, The Hand that Feeds You: A Satiric Nightmare 1982, The Bellarmine Jug 1984, The Country without Music 1990, The Blosseville File 1992, Offcuts From a Legal Literary Life 1993, A Grain of Truth 1994, Our Man K 1999, The Legal Labyrinth 2003. Stories: The Hat on the Letter O and Other Stories, 1978. Poetry: Anchor and Other Poems, 1976; On the Edge, 1980; Chinese Journey, 1985. *Honours:* Age Book of the Year Award, 1984; AM, 1986. *Address:* 14 Reserve St, Claremont, WA 6010, Australia.

HASS, Robert Louis, BA, MA, PhD; poet, writer, translator, editor and academic; b. 1 March 1941, San Francisco, CA, USA; m. Earlene Joan Leif 1962 (divorced 1986); two s. one d. *Education:* St Mary's Coll. of California, Stanford Univ. *Career:* Asst Prof., SUNY at Buffalo 1967–71; Prof. of English, St Mary's Coll. of California 1971–89, Univ. of California, Berkeley 1989–; Visiting Lecturer, Univ. of Virginia 1974, Goddard Coll. 1976, Columbia Univ. 1982, Univ. of California, Berkeley 1983; poet-in-residence, The Frost Place, Franconia, NH 1978; Poet Laureate of the USA 1995–97. *Publications:* Poetry: Field Guide, 1973; Winter Morning in Charlottesville, 1977; Praise, 1979; The Apple Tree at Olema, 1989; Human Wishes, 1989; Sun under Wood, 1996. Other: Twentieth Century Pleasures: Prose on Poetry, 1984; Into the Garden – A Wedding Anthology: Poetry and Prose on Love and Marriage, 1993. Translations: Czesław Miłosz's The Separate Notebooks (with Robert Pinsky), 1983; Czesław Miłosz's Unattainable Earth (with Czesław Miłosz), 1986; Czesław Miłosz's Collected Poems, 1931–1987 (with Louis Iribane and Peter Scott), 1988. Editor: Rock and Hawk: A Selection of Shorter Poems by Robinson Jeffers, 1987; The Pushcart Prize Xll (with Bill Henderson and Jorie Graham), 1987; Tomaz Salamun: Selected Poems (with Charles Simic), 1988; Selected Poems of Tomas Tranströmer, 1954–1986 (with others), 1989; The Essential Haiku: Versions of Basho, Buson and Issa, 1994. Contributions: anthologies and other publications. *Honours:* Woodrow Wilson Fellowship, 1963–64; Danforth Fellowship, 1963–67; Yale Series of Younger Poets Award, Yale University Press, 1972; US-Great Britain Bicentennial Exchange Fellow in the Arts, 1976–77; William Carlos Williams Award, 1979; National Book Critics Circle Award, 1984; Award of Merit, American Acad. of Arts and Letters, 1984; John D. and Catherine T. MacArthur Foundation Grant, 1984. *Literary Agent:* Steven Barclay Agency, 12 Western Avenue, Petaluma, CA 94952, USA. *Telephone:* (707) 773-0654. *Fax:* (707) 778-1868. *Website:* www.barclayagency.com. *Address:* PO Box 807, Inverness, CA 94937, USA.

HASSNER, Pierre; writer and academic; b. 31 Jan. 1933, Bucharest, Romania. *Education:* École Normale Supérieure. *Career:* Lecturer in Int. Relations and History of Political Thought, Institut d'Études Politiques, Paris, European Center of John Hopkins Univ. Bologna; Emeritus Research Dir, Center for Int. Studies and Research (CERI), Paris. *Publications:* La violence et la paix (trans. as Violence and Peace: From the Atomic Bomb to Ethnic Cleansing) 1995, La terreur et l'empire: La violence et la paix II 2003, Washington et le monde: Dilemmes d'une superpuissance (with Justin Vaisse) 2003, Guerre et Sociétés: Etats et violence aprés la guerre froide (ed. with Roland Marchal) 2003; contrib. articles to Revue de Synthèse, Critique Internationale, Commentaire, The Natinoal Interst, Cahiers de Chaillot, Esprit, Europe Unbound, Le Débat, Politique Internationale. *Honours:* Prix Tocqueville 2003. *Address:* Center for International Studies and Research—Sciences Po, 56 rue Jacob, 75006 Paris, France. *Telephone:* 1 58 71 70 00. *Fax:* 1 58 71 70 90. *E-mail:* hassner@ceri-sciences-po.org. *Website:* www.ceri-sciences-po.org.

HASTINGS, Graham (see Jeffries, Roderic (Graeme)).

HASTINGS, March (see Levinson, Leonard).

HASTINGS, Sir Max Macdonald; Author, Broadcaster and Journalist; b. 28 Dec. 1945, London, England; m. 1st Patricia Edmondson, 27 May 1972, divorced, two s. one deceased, one d.; m. 2nd Penelope Grade, 1999. *Education:* Exhibitioner, University College, Oxford, 1964–65; Fellow, World Press Institute, St Paul, Minnesota, USA, 1967–68. *Career:* Researcher, BBC TV, 1963–64; Reporter, London Evening Standard, 1965–67, BBC TV Current Affairs, 1970–73; Ed., Evening Standard Londoner's Diary, 1976–77, Daily Telegraph, 1986–95, Evening Standard, 1996–2002; Columnist, Daily Express, 1981–83, Sunday Times, 1985–86; Ed.-in-Chief and a Dir, Daily Telegraph Plc, 1989–96; Dir, Associated Newspapers PLC, 1996–2002, Evening Standard Ltd, 1996–. *Publications:* The Fire This Time, 1968; Ulster, 1969; The Struggle for Civil Rights in Northern Ireland, 1970; Montrose: The King's Champion, 1977; Yoni: The Hero of Entebbe, 1979; Bomber Command, 1979; The Battle of Britain (with Lee Deighton), 1980; Das Reich, 1981; Battle for the Falklands (with Simon Jenkins), 1983; Overlord: D-Day and the Battle for Normandy, 1984; Oxford Book of Military Anecdotes (ed.), 1985; Victory in Europe, 1985; The Korean War, 1987; Outside Days, 1989; Scattered Shots, 1999; Going to the Wars, 2000; Editor: A Memoir, 2002; Armageddon, 2004. *Honours:* Somerset Maugham Prize, 1979; British Press Awards, Journalist of the Year, 1982; Granada TV Reporter of the Year, 1982; Yorkshire Post Book of the Year Awards, 1983, 1984; Ed. of the Year, 1988; Hon. DLitt, Leicester University, 1992; FRSL, 1996; KBE, 2002. *Literary Agent:* PFD, Drury House, 34–43 Russell St, London WC2B 5HA, England. *Address:* Northcliffe House, 2 Derry St, London W8 5EE, England.

HASTINGS, Michael (Gerald); Dramatist and Author; b. 2 Sept. 1938, London, England; m. 1st, two s. one d.; m. 2nd Victoria Hardie, 1975. *Publications:* Plays: Three Plays (Don't Destroy Me, Yes and After, and The World's Baby), 1966; The Silence of Saint-Just, 1970; Tom and Viv, 1985; Three Political Plays (The Silence of Lee Harvey Oswald, For the West, and the Emperor), 1990; A Dream of People, 1992; Unfinished Business and Other Plays, 1994. Fiction: The Game, 1957; The Frauds, 1960; Tussy Is Me: A Romance, 1970; The Nightcomers, 1972; And in the Forest the Indians, 1975; Bart's Mornings and Other Tales from Modern Brazil, 1975; A Spy in Winter, 1984. Poetry: Love Me Lambeth and Other Poems, 1961. Non-Fiction: The Handsomest Young Man in England: Rupert Brooke, 1967; Sir Richard Burton: A Biography, 1978. Contributions: Films and television. *Honours:* Arts Council Award, 1956; Emmy Award, 1972; Writers Guild Award, 1972; Somerset Maugham Award, 1972; Comedy of the Year Award, Evening Standard, 1978. *Address:* 2 Helix Gardens, Brixton Hill, London SW2, England.

HASTINGS, Lady Selina; British writer; b. 5 March 1945, Oxford, England. *Education:* St Hugh's Coll., Oxford. *Career:* books page, Daily Telegraph 1968–82; Literary Ed., Harper's & Queen 1986–94. *Publications:* biographies: Nancy Mitford 1985, Evelyn Waugh 1994, Rosamond Lehmann: A Life 2002; other: various children's books; contrib. to newspapers and periodicals. *Honours:* Marsh Biography Award 1993–96. *Literary Agent:* Rogers, Coleridge & White Ltd, 20 Powis Mews, London, W11 1JN, England.

HASWELL, Chetwynd John Drake; Soldier and Author; b. 18 July 1919, Penn, Buckinghamshire, England; m. Charlotte Annette Petter 25 Oct. 1947; two s. one d. *Education:* Winchester College, 1933–37; Royal Military College, Sandhurst, 1938–39. *Career:* Soldier, 1939–60; Author, Service Intelligence, Intelligence Centre, Ashford, 1966–84; Regimental Historian for the Queen's Regiment. *Publications:* As George Foster: Indian File, 1960; Soldier on Loan, 1961. As Jock Haswell: The Queen's Royal Regiment, 1967; The First Respectable Spy, 1969; James II, Soldier and Sailor, 1972; British Military Intelligence, 1973; Citizen Armies, 1973; The British Army, 1975; The Ardent Queen, Margaret of Anjou, 1976; The Battle for Empire, 1976; Spies and Spymasters, 1977; The Intelligence and Deception of the D-Day Landings, 1979; The Tangled Web, 1985; The Queen's Regiment, 1986; Spies and Spying, 1986. *Address:* The Grey House, Lyminge, Folkestone, Kent CT18 8ED, England.

HATÁR, Victor Gyözö; Hungarian poet, playwright, philosopher and novelist; b. 1914, Budapest. *Publications:* The Right to Sanity: A Victor Határ Reader 1999. *Address:* c/o Hungarian Cultural Centre, 10 Maiden Lane, Covent Garden, London, WC2E 7NA, England.

HATCHER, Robin Lee; Novelist; b. 10 May 1951, Payette, ID, USA; m. Jerrold W. Neu, 6 May 1989, two d. *Education:* General High School Diploma, 1969. *Career:* mem. Romance Writers of America, pres., 1992–94; The Authors' Guild. *Publications:* Stormy Surrender, 1984; Heart's Landing, 1984; Thorn of Love, 1985; Passion's Gamble, 1986; Heart Storm, 1986; Pirate's Lady, 1987; Gemfire, 1988; The Wager, 1989; Dream Tide, 1990; Promised Sunrise, 1990; Promise Me Spring, 1991; Rugged Splendor,

1991; The Hawk and the Heather, 1992; Devlin's Promise, 1992; Midnight Rose, 1992; A Frontier Christmas, 1992; The Magic, 1993; Where the Heart Is, 1993; Forever, Rose, 1994; Remember When, 1994; Liberty Blue, 1995; Chances Are, 1996; Kiss me Katie, 1996; Dear Lady, 1997; Patterns of Love, 1998; In His Arms, 1998; The Forgiving Hour, 1999; Hometown Girl; Taking Care of the Twins; Whispers from Yesterday; Daddy Claus, 1999; The Shepherd's Voice, 2000; The Story Jar, 2001; Ribbon of Years, 2001; Firstborn, 2002. Contributions: various publications. *Honours:* Emma Merritt Award, 1998; Heart of Romance Readers Choice Award, 1996; RITA Awards, 1999, 2001; Christy Award for Excellence in Christian Fiction, 2000; RWA Lifetime Achievement Award, 2001. *Address:* PO Box 4722, Boise, ID 83711, USA.

HATOUM, Milton; Prof. of French Literature, Poet, Writer and Trans; b. 19 Aug. 1952, Manaus, Brazil. *Education:* Diploma in Urban Architecture, State University of São Paulo; MA, Sorbonne, University of Paris, 1983. *Career:* Prof. of French Literature, University of Amazonas Manaus, 1983–. *Publications:* Um rio entre ruinas (poems), 1978; Relato de um Certo Oriente (novel), 1989, English translation as The Tree of the Seventh Heaven, 1994; Dois Irmãos (novel), 2000, English trans. as The Brothers, 2002. Other: Trans. into Portuguese: La Croisade des enfants, Marcel Schwob; Trois Contes, Gustave Flaubert; Representations of the Intellectual, Edward Said. Contributions: periodicals. *Honours:* Jabuti Award, 2000. *Address:* Rua Dr Veiga Filho, 83/131, 012229-001, São Paulo, SP, Brazil. *E-mail:* mhatoum@uol.com.br.

HATTENDORF, John Brewster; Prof. of Maritime History and Writer; b. 22 Dec. 1941, Hinsdale, IL, USA; m. Berit Sundell, 15 April 1978, three d. *Education:* AB, Kenyon College, 1964; AM, Brown University, 1971; DPhil, University of Oxford, 1979. *Career:* Serving Officer, US Navy, 1964–73; Prof. of Military History, National University of Singapore, 1981–83; Ernest J. King Prof. of Maritime History, US Naval War College, 1984–; mem. Navy Records Society; Hakluyt Society; Academie du Var; FRHistS; Royal Swedish Acad. of Naval Science; Society for Nautical Research. *Publications:* The Writings of Stephen B. Luce, 1975; On His Majesty's Service, 1983; Sailors and Scholars, 1984; A Bibliography of the Works of A. T. Mahan, 1986; England in the War of the Spanish Succession, 1987; Maritime Strategy and the Balance of Power, 1989; The Limitations of Military Power, 1990; Mahan on Naval Strategy, 1990; Mahan is Not Enough, 1993; British Naval Documents (co-ed.), 1993; Ubi Sumnus: The State of Maritime and Naval History, 1994; Doing Naval History, 1995; Sea of Words (with Dean King), 1995; Maritime History: The Age of Discovery, 1996; Maritime History: The Eighteenth Century, 1996. Contributions: Naval War College Review; International History Review. *Address:* 28 John St, Newport, RI 02840, USA.

HATTERSLEY, Roy Sydney George, (Baron Hattersley of Sparkbrook in the County of West Midlands); Politician and Writer; b. 28 Dec. 1932, Sheffield, England; m. Molly Hattersley, 1956. *Education:* BSc, Economics, University of Hull. *Career:* Journalist and Health Service Exec., 1956–64; Mem., City Council, Sheffield, 1957–65; MP, Labour Party, Sparkbrook Division, Birmingham, 1964–97; Parliamentary Private Secretary, Minister of Pensions and National Insurance, 1964–67; Dir, Campaign for a European Political Community, 1966–67; Joint Parliamentary Secretary, Ministry of Labour, 1967–69, Minister of Defence for Administration, 1969–70; Visiting Fellow, Harvard University, 1971, 1972, Nuffield College, Oxford, 1984–; Labour Party Spokesman on Defence, 1972, and on Education and Science, 1972–74; Minister of State, Foreign and Commonwealth Office, 1974–76; Secretary of State for Prices and Consumer Protection, 1976–79; Principal Opposition Spokesman on the Environment, 1979–80, Home Affairs, 1980–83, Treasury and Economics Affairs, 1983–87, Home Affairs, 1987–92; Deputy Leader, Labour Party, 1983–92. *Publications:* Nelson: A Biography, 1974; Goodbye to Yorkshire (essays), 1976; Politics Apart, 1982; Press Gang, 1983; A Yorkshire Boyhood, 1983; Choose Freedom: The Future for Democratic Socialism, 1987; Economic Priorities for a Labour Government, 1987; The Maker's Mark (novel), 1990; In That Quiet Earth (novel), 1991; Skylark Song (novel), 1994; Between Ourselves (novel), 1994; Who Goes Home?, 1995; 50 Years On, 1997; Buster's Diaries: As Told to Roy Hattersley, 1998; Blood and Fire: The Story of William and Catherine Booth and Their Salvation Army, 1999; A Brand From the Burning, 2002. Contributions: newspapers and journals. *Honours:* Privy Counsellor, 1975; Columnist of the Year, Granada, 1982; Created Life Peer, 1997; Hon. doctorates. *Address:* House of Lords, London SW1A 0PW, England.

HAUGAARD, Erik Christian; Author; b. 13 April 1923, Copenhagen, Denmark; m. 1st Myra Seld, 23 Dec. 1949, deceased 1981, one s. one d.; m. 2nd Masako Taira, 27 July 1986, deceased 1996. *Career:* mem. Authors' Guild; Society of Authors; British PEN; Danish Authors Union. *Publications:* The Little Fishes, 1967; Orphas of the Wind, 1969; The Untold Tale, 1972; Hans Christian Andersen's Fairy Tales (trans.), 1973; Chase Me Catch Nobody, 1980; Leif the Unlucky, 1982; The Samurai's Tale, 1984; Princess Horrid, 1990; The Boy and the Samurai, 1991; The Death of Mr Angel, 1992; Under the Black Flag, 1993; The Revenge of the Forty-Seven Samurai, 1995. *Honours:* Herald Tribune Award; Boston Globe-Horn Book Award; Jane Addams Award; Danish Cultural Ministry Award; Phoenix Award. *Literary Agent:* Dorothy Markinko Mcintosh and Otis, 353 Lexington Ave, New York, NY 10016, USA. *Address:* Toad Hall, Ballydehob, West Cork, Ireland.

HAUGEN, Paal-Helge; Poet, Writer and Dramatist; b. 26 April 1945, Valle, Norway. *Career:* Chair., Norwegian State Film Production Board, 1980–85, Board of Literary Advisers, Asscn of Norwegian Authors, 1984–88, International Pegasus Prize Committee, 1988. *Publications:* 30 books including: Anne (novel), 1968; Stone Fences, 1986; Meditasjonar over Georges de la Tour (poems), 1990; Sone O (poems), 1992; Wintering with the Light, 1995; Poesi: Collected Poems, 1965–1995, 1995. Other: Plays for stage, radio and television; Opera libretti. Contributions: Professional journals. *Honours:* Dobloug Prize, 1986; Richard Wilbur Prize, USA, 1986; Norwegian Literary Critics Prize, 1990; Norwegian National Brage Prize, 1992; Grieg Prize for texts set to music, 2000. *Address:* Skrefjellv 5, 4645 Nodeland, Norway. *E-mail:* phaugen@online.no.

HAUPTMAN, William (Thornton); Dramatist and Writer; b. 26 Nov. 1942, Wichita Falls, Texas, USA; m. 1st Barbara Barbat, 1968, divorced 1977, one d.; m. 2nd Marjorie Endreich, 1985, one s. *Education:* BFA, Drama, University of Texas at Austin, 1966; MFA, Playwrighting, Yale University School of Drama, 1973. *Publications:* Plays: Hear, 1977; Domino Courts/Comanche Cafe, 1977; Big River (with Roger Miller), 1986; Gillette, 1989. Television Drama: A House Divided (series), 1981. Fiction: Good Rockin' Tonight and Other Stories, 1988; The Storm Season, 1992. *Honours:* National Endowment for the Arts Grant, 1977; Boston Theatre Critics Circle Award, 1984; Tony Award, 1985; Drama-Lounge Award, 1986; Jesse Jones Award, Texas Institute of Letters, 1989. *Address:* 240 Warren St, Apt E, New York, NY 11201, USA.

HAVEL, Václav; Pres. of the Czech Republic, Writer and Dramatist; b. 5 Oct. 1936, Prague, Czechoslovakia; m. 1st Olga Splichová, 1964, deceased 27 Jan. 1996; m. 2nd Dagmar Havlová, 4 Jan. 1997. *Education:* Faculty of Economy, 1955–57; Drama Dept, Acad. of Arts, Prague, 1966. *Career:* ABC Theatre Prague, 1959–68, Editorial Board, Tvár, 1965, Lidové noviny, 1987–89; Co-founder, Charter 77, 1977, VONS, 1978, Civic Forum, 1989; Pres. of Czechoslovakia, 1989–1992; Pres., Czech Republic, 1993–; mem. Czech PEN, 1989; PEN-Centre, Germany; PEN, Sweden; Hamburg Acad. of Liberal Arts; Austrian PEN; Royal British Legion; Associé éntranger Académie des sciences morales et politiques, Institut de France. *Publications:* 13 plays; 10 books; Essays; English trans, including: The Garden Party, 1969; The Increased Difficulty of Concentration, 1972; Václav Havel or Living in Truth, 1986; Letters to Olga, 1988; Disturbing the Peace, 1990; Open Letters: Selected Writings 1965–90, 1991; Selected Plays by Václav Havel, 1991; Summer Meditations, 1992; Toward a Civil Society, 1994; The Art of the Impossible, 1997. *Honours:* Olof Palme Prize, 1989; Simon Bolívar Prize, UNESCO, 1990; Political Book of the Year, 1990. *Literary Agent:* Aura Pont Agency, Prague. *Address:* Kancelár prezidenta republiky, 119 08 Praha-Hrad, Czech Republic. *E-mail:* president@hrad.cz. *Website:* old.hrad.cz/president/Havel/cv_uk.html.

HAVIARAS, Stratis; Librarian, Poet, Writer and Ed.; b. 28 June 1935, Nea Kios, Greece; m. Heather E. Cole, 30 March 1990, one d. *Education:* BA, 1973, MFA, 1976, Goddard College. *Career:* Librarian, Harvard University Library; Ed., Harvard Review, 1992–; mem. PEN New England; Signet; Societe Imaginaire. *Publications:* Poetry: 4 books in Greek, 1963, 1965, 1967, 1972; Crossing the River Twice, 1976. Fiction: When the Tree Sings, 1979; The Heroic Age, 1984. Editor: Seamus Heaney: A Celebration, 1996. Contributions: newspapers and magazines. *Honours:* National Book Critics Circle Awards. *Address:* c/o Poetry Room, Harvard University Library, Cambridge, MA 02138, USA.

HAWKING, Stephen (William); Lucasian Prof. of Mathematics and Writer; b. 8 Jan. 1942, Oxford, England; m. Jane Wilde, 1965, divorced, two s. one d. *Education:* BA, University College, Oxford; PhD, Trinity Hall, Cambridge. *Career:* Research Fellow, 1965–69, Fellow for Distinction in Science, 1969–, Gonville and Caius College, Cambridge; Mem., Institute of Theoretical Astronomy, Cambridge, 1968–72; Research Asst, Institute of Astronomy, Cambridge, 1972–73; Research Asst, Dept of Applied Mathematics and Theoretical Physics, 1973–75, Reader in Gravitational Physics, 1975–77, Prof., 1977–79, Lucasian Prof. of Mathematics, 1979–, University of Cambridge; mem. American Acad. of Arts and Sciences; American Philosophical Society; Pontifical Acad. of Sciences; Fellow, Royal Society. *Publications:* The Large Scale Structure of Spacetime (with G. F. R. Ellis), 1973; General Relativity: An Einstein Centenary Survey (ed. with W. Israel), 1979; Is the End in Sight for Theoretical Physics?: An Inaugural Lecture, 1980; Superspace and Supergravity: Proceedings of the Nuffield Workshop (ed. with M. Rocek), 1981; The Very Early Universe: Proceedings of the Nuffield Workshop (co-ed.), 1983; 300 Years of Gravitation (with W. Israel), 1987; A Brief History of Time: From the Big Bang to Black Holes, 1988; Hawking on the Big Bang and Black Holes, 1992; Black Holes and Baby Universes and Other Essays, 1993; The Cambridge Lectures: Life Works, 1995; The Nature of Space and Time (with Roger Penrose), 1996; The Universe in a Nutshell, 2001; The Theory of Everything: The Origin and Fate of the Universe, 2002; The Future of Spacetime (ed. with others), 2002; On the Shoulders of Giants, 2002. Other: Individual lectures. Contributions: scholarly books and journals. *Honours:* Eddington Medal, 1975, Gold Medal, 1985, Royal Acad. of Science; Pius XI Gold Medal, Pontifical

Acad. of Sciences, 1975; William Hopkins Prize, Cambridge Philosophical Society, 1976; Maxwell Medal, Institute of Physics, 1976; Dannie Heinemann Prize for Mathematical Physics, American Physical Society and American Institute of Physics, 1976; Hon. Fellow, University College, Oxford, 1977, Trinity Hall, Cambridge, 1984; CBE, 1982; Paul Dirac Medal and Prize, Institute of Physics, 1987; Wolf Foundation Prize for Physics, 1988; Companion of Honour, 1989; Aventis Prize, 2002; 12 hon. doctorates. *Address:* c/o Dept of Applied Mathematics and Theoretical Physics, University of Cambridge, Silver St, Cambridge CB3 9EW, England. *Website:* www.hawking.org.uk.

HAWKINS, Loretta; Writer, Dramatist, Poet and Teacher; b. 1 Jan. 1942, Winston-Salem, NC, USA; m.; three d. *Education:* BS, Education, Illinois Teachers College, 1965; MA, Literature, 1977, MA, African Cultures, 1978, Governors State University; MLA, Humanities, University of Chicago, 1998. *Career:* Teacher, Chicago Public Schools, 1967–; Lecturer, Chicago City Colleges, 1987–90; mem. American Asscn of University Women; Dramatists' Guild of America; International Women's Writing Guild; National Council of Teachers of English; Women's Theatre Alliance. *Publications:* Contributions: numerous periodicals. *Honours:* several grants; First Place, James H. Wilson Full-Length Play Award, 1993; Zora Neale Hurston-Bessie Head Fiction Award, 1993; Third Place, Fiction, Feminist Writers Contest, 1993. *Address:* 8928 S Oglesby, Chicago, IL 60617, USA.

HAWLICEK, Hilde; Austrian politician; *President, International Institute for Children's Literature and Reading Research*; b. 14 April 1942, Vienna. *Career:* fmr Minister of Educ. and the Arts; MEP (Vice-Pres. PSE); mem. Cttee on Culture, Youth, Educ. and the Media, del. for relations with the Maghreb Countries and the Arab Maghreb Union; Pres., Int. Inst. for Children's Literature and Reading Research. *Address:* 1040 Vienna, Mayerhofgasse 6, Austria. *Telephone:* (1) 50503-59. *Fax:* (1) 50503-5917. *E-mail:* office@jugendliteratur.net. *Website:* www.jugendliteratur.net.

HAWTHORNE, Susan; University Lecturer, Publisher, Poet and Writer; b. 30 Nov. 1951, Wagga Wagga, NSW, Australia. *Education:* Diploma, Primary Teaching, Melbourne Teachers College, 1972; BA, Philosophy, La Trobe University, 1976; MA, Prelim, Classics, University of Melbourne, 1981. *Career:* Tutor, Koori Teacher Education Programme, Deakin University, 1986; Ed. and Commissioning Ed., Penguin Books, Australia, 1987–91; Publisher, Spinifex Press, 1991–; Lecturer, Dept of Communication and Language Studies, Victoria University of Technology, 1995–; mem. Australian Society of Authors; Fellowship of Australian Authors; PEN International; Victoria Writers Centre. *Publications:* Difference (ed.), 1985; Moments of Desire, 1989; The Exploring Frangipani, 1990; Angels of Power, 1991; The Falling Woman, 1992; The Language in My Tongue: Four New Poets, 1993; The Spinifex Quiz Book, 1993; Australia for Women (co-ed.), 1994; Car Maintenance, Explosives and Love (co-ed.), 1997; CyberFeminism (co-ed.), 1999; Bird, 1999. Contributions: journals, reviews, and periodicals. *Address:* c/o Spinifex Press, 504 Queensbury St, North Melbourne, Vic. 3051, Australia.

HAYCRAFT, Anna (Margaret), (Alice Thomas Ellis, Brenda O'Casey); Writer; b. 9 Sept. 1932, Liverpool, England; m. Colin Haycraft 1956 (deceased 1994); five s. (one deceased) two d. (one deceased). *Career:* Columnist, The Spectator, 1984–90, The Universe, 1989–90, The Catholic Herald, 1990–95, 1998–, The Oldie, 1995–; mem. FRSL, 1998. *Publications:* Natural Baby Food: A Cookery Book (as Brenda O'Casey), 1977; The Sin Eater (novel), 1977; Darling You Shouldn't Have Gone to So Much Trouble (cookery) (as Anna Haycraft with Caroline Blackwood), 1980; The Birds of the Air (novel), 1980; The 27th Kingdom (novel), 1982; The Other Side of the Fire (novel), 1983; Unexplained Laughter (novel), 1985; Home Life (collected columns from the Spectator), 1986; Secrets of Strangers (with Tom Pitt Aikens) (psychiatry), 1986; The Clothes in the Wardrobe (novel), 1987; More Home Life (collection), 1987; The Skeleton in the Cupboard (novel), 1988; Home Life III (collection), 1988; The Loss of the Good Authority (with Tom Pitt Aikens) (psychiatry), 1989; Wales: An Anthology, 1989; The Fly in the Ointment (novel), 1989; Home Life IV (collection), 1989; The Inn at the Edge of the World (novel), 1990; A Welsh Childhood (autobiog.), 1990; Pillars of Gold, 1992; Serpent on the Rock, 1994; The Evening of Adam, 1994; Cat Among the Pigeons: Collected Columns from the Catholic Herald, 1994; Fairy Tale, 1996; Valentine's Day, 2000. *Honours:* Welsh Arts Council Award, 1977; Yorkshire Post Novel of the Year, 1983; Writers Guild Award for Best Fiction, 1991. *Literary Agent:* PFD, Drury House, 34–43 Russell St, London WC2B 5HA, England. *Address:* 22 Gloucester Crescent, London NW1 7DS, England.

HAYDEN, Dolores; Architect, Prof. and Author; b. 15 March 1945, New York, NY, USA; m. Peter Marris, 18 May 1975, one d. *Education:* BA, Mount Holyoke College, 1966; Diploma, English Studies, Girton College, Cambridge, 1967; MArch, Harvard Graduate School of Design, 1972. *Career:* Lecturer, University of California at Berkeley, 1973; Assoc. Prof., MIT, 1973–79; Prof., University of California at Los Angeles, 1979–91, Yale University, 1991–; mem. American Studies Asscn; Organization of American Historians. *Publications:* Seven American Utopias, 1976; The Grand Domestic Revolution, 1981; Redesigning the American Dream, 1984; The Power of Place: Urban Landscapes as Public History, 1995; Playing House, 1998; Line Dance, 2001. Contributions: numerous journals. *Honours:* National Endowment for the Humanities Fellowship, 1976; National Endowment for the Arts Fellowship, 1980; Guggenheim Fellowship, 1981; Rockefeller Foundation Fellowship, 1981; ACLS-Ford Foundation Fellowship, 1988; Asscn of American Publishers Award, 1995. *Address:* School of Architecture, Yale University, PO Box 208242, New Haven, CT 06520, USA. *E-mail:* dolores.hayden@yale.edu.

HAYES, Charles Langley (see Holmes, Bryan John).

HAYLOCK, John Mervyn; Writer; b. 22 Sept. 1918, Bournemouth, England. *Education:* Diplôme français, Institut de Touraine, Tours, France, 1937; Certificat d'Immatriculation, Grenoble University, France, 1938; BA, 1940, MA, 1946, Pembroke College, Cambridge. *Career:* mem. FRSL; Oriental Club, London. *Publications:* New Babylon, A Portrait of Iraq (with Desmond Stewart), 1956; See You Again, 1963; It's All Your Fault, 1964; Robert de Montesquiou, A Prince of the Nineties (trans. with Francis King), 1967; Flight into Egypt, by Philippe Jullian (trans.), 1970; Choice and Other Stories, 1979; One Hot Summer in Kyoto, 1980; Tokyo Sketch Book, 1980; Japanese Excursions 1981; Japanese Memories, 1987; Romance Trip and Other Stories, 1988; A Touch of the Orient, 1990; Uneasy Relations, 1993; Eastern Exchange: Memoirs of People and Places, 1997; Doubtful Partners, 1998; Body of Contention, 1999; Loose Connections, 2003. Contributions: magazines and periodicals. *Literary Agent:* Rivers Scott, 15 Gledhow Gardens, London SW5 0AY, England. *Address:* Flat 28, 15 Grand Ave, Hove, BN3 2NG, England.

HAYMAN, David; Prof. of Comparative Literature Emeritus, Writer and Ed.; b. 7 Jan. 1927, New York, NY, USA; m. Loni Goldschmidt, 28 June 1951, two d. *Education:* BA, New York University, 1948; PhD, University of Paris, 1955. *Career:* Instructor, 1955–57, Asst Prof., 1957–58, Assoc. Prof. of English, 1958–65, University of Texas; Prof. of English and Comparative Literature, University of Iowa, 1965–73; Prof. of Comparative Literature, 1973–96, Eujire-Bascon Prof. in the Humanities, 1990–96, Prof. Emeritus, 1997–, University of Wisconsin, Madison. *Publications:* Joyce et Mallarmé, 1956; A First-Draft Version of Finnegans Wake, 1963; Configuration Critique de James Joyce (ed.), 1965; Ulysses: The Mechanics of Meaning, 1970; Form in Fiction (with Eric Rabkin), 1974; Ulysses: Critical Essays (with Clive Hart), 1974; The James Joyce Archive (ed.), 1978; Philippe Sollers: Writing and the Experience of Limits (ed. and co-trans.), 1980; Reforming the Narrative, 1987; The Wake in Transit, 1990; Probes: Genetic Studies in Joyce (with Sam Slote), 1994; James Joyce: Epiphanias (ed.), 1996. Contributions: many scholarly books and journals. *Honours:* Guggenheim Fellowship, 1958–59; National Endowment for the Humanities Fellowship, 1979–80; Harry Levin Prize, American Comparative Literature Asscn, 1989. *Address:* 2913 Columbia Rd, Madison, WI 53705, USA.

HAYMAN, Ronald, BA, MA; writer; b. 4 May 1932, Bournemouth, England. *Education:* Trinity Hall, Cambridge. *Career:* mem. Soc. of Authors. *Publications:* Harold Pinter, 1968; Samuel Beckett, 1968; John Osborne, 1968; John Arden, 1968; Robert Bolt, 1969; John Whiting, 1969; Collected Plays of John Whiting (ed.), two vols, 1969; Techniques of Acting, 1969; The Art of the Dramatist and Other Pieces, by John Whiting (ed.), 1970; Arthur Miller, 1970; Tolstoy, 1970; Arnold Wesker, 1970; John Gielgud, 1971; Edward Albee, 1971; Eugène Ionesco, 1972; Playback, 1973; The Set-Up, 1974; Playback 2, 1974; The First Thrust, 1975; The German Theatre (ed.), 1975; How to Read a Play, 1977; The Novel Today, 1967–75, 1976; My Cambridge (ed.), 1977; Tom Stoppard, 1977; Artaud and After, 1977; De Sade, 1978; Theatre and Anti-Theatre, 1979; British Theatre Since 1955: A Reassessment, 1979; Nietzsche: A Critical Life, 1980; K: A Biography of Kafka, 1981; Brecht: A Biography, 1983; Fassbinder: Film Maker, 1984; Brecht: The Plays, 1984; Günter Grass, 1985; Secrets: Boyhood in a Jewish Hotel, 1932–54, 1985; Writing Against: A Biography of Sartre, 1986; Proust: A Biography, 1990; The Death and Life of Sylvia Plath, 1991; Tennessee Williams: Everyone Else Is an Audience, 1994; Thomas Mann, 1995; Hitler and Geli, 1997; Nietzsche's Voices, 1997; A Life of Jung, 1999. *Literary Agent:* Gillon Aitken Associates Ltd, 18–21 Cavaye Place, London, SW10 9PT, England. *Telephone:* (20) 7373-8672. *Fax:* (20) 7373-6002. *Address:* 25 Church Row, London, NW3 6UP, England.

HAYS, Robert Glenn, BS, MS, PhD; journalism educator and writer; b. 23 May 1935, Carmi, IL, USA; m. Mary Elizabeth Corley 1957; two s. *Education:* Southern Illinois Univ. *Career:* reporter, Granite City Press-Record 1961–63; public relations writer 1963–66, Alumni Ed. 1966–71, Southern Illinois Univ.; Asst Scientist, Illinois Board of Natural Resources and Conservation 1971–73; Journalism Faculty, Sam Houston State Univ. 1974–75, Univ. of Illinois 1975–86, 1987–; Chair, Dept of Mass Communications, Southeast Missouri Univ. 1986–87; founding mem. Research Soc. of American Periodicals; mem., Asscn for Education in Journalism and Mass Communications, Illinois Press Asscn, Investigative Reporters and Eds, Missouri Press Asscn, Soc. of Professional Journalists, American Civil Liberties Union (chapter steering cttee 1991–93), Nat. Organization for Women. *Publications:* G-2: Intelligence for Patton 1971, Country Ed 1974, State Science in Illinois 1980, Early Stories From the Land 1995, A Race at Bay: New York Times Editorials on the 'Indian Problem' 1860–1900 1997; contrib. to periodicals and journals. *Honours:* Int. ACE Award of Excellence 1993, 1994, University of Illinois Acad. of Teaching Excellence Award 1996. *Address:* 2314 Glenoak Drive, Champaign, IL 61821, USA. *E-mail:* r-hays1@uiuc.edu.

HAYTER, Alethea Catharine; Writer; b. 7 Nov. 1911, Cairo, Egypt. *Education:* BA, MA, University of Oxford. *Career:* mem. FRSL; Society of Authors, committee of management, 1975–79; PEN. *Publications:* Mrs Browning: A Poet's Work and Its Setting, 1962; A Sultry Month: Scenes of London Literary Life in 1846, 1965; Elizabeth Barrett Browning, 1965; Opium and the Romantic Imagination, 1968; Horatio's Version, 1972; A Voyage in Vain, 1973; Fitzgerald to His Friends: Selected Letters of Edward Fitzgerald, 1979; Portrait of a Friendship, Drawn From New Letters of James Russell Lowell to Sybella Lady Lyttelton 1881–1891, 1990; The Backbone: Diaries of a Military Family in the Napoleonic Wars, 1993; Charlotte Yonge, 1996; A Wise Woman: A Memoir of Lavinia Mynors from her Diaries and Letters, 1996; The Wreck of the Abergavenny, 2002. Contributions: Oxford Companion to English Literature; Sunday Times; TLS; Spectator; New Statesman; History Today; Ariel; London Review of Books; Longman Encyclopedia. *Honours:* W. H. Heinemann Prize, RSL, 1963; Rose Mary Crawshay Prize, British Acad., 1968; OBE. *Address:* 22 Aldebert Terrace, London SW8 1BJ, England.

HAZEN, Robert M(iller); Scientist, Musician and Writer; b. 1 Nov. 1948, Rockville Centre, New York, USA; m. Margaret Hindle, 9 Aug. 1969, one s. one d. *Education:* BS, SM, MIT, 1971; PhD, Harvard University, 1975. *Career:* NATO Fellow, University of Cambridge, 1975–76; Research Scientist, Geophysical Laboratory, Carnegie Institution, Washington, DC, 1976–; Clarence Robinson Prof., George Mason University; Trumpeter with many orchestras; mem. American Chemistry Society; American Geophysical Union; History of Science Society; International Guild of Trumpeters; Mineralogical Society of America. *Publications:* Comparative Crystal Chemistry, 1982; Poetry of Geology, 1982; Music Men, 1987; The Breakthrough, 1988; Science Matters, 1990; Keepers of the Flame, 1991; The New Alchemist, 1993; The Sciences, 1995; Why Aren't Black Holes Black?, 1997; The Diamond Makers, 1999. Contributions: many scientific journals and to periodicals. *Honours:* Mineralogical Society of America Award, 1981; Ipatief Prize, 1984; ASCAP-Deems Taylor Award, 1988; Education Press Asscn Award, 1992; Elizabeth Wood Science Writing Award, 1998. *Address:* c/o Geophysical Laboratory, Carnegie Institution, 5251 Broad Branch Rd NW, Washington, DC 20015, USA.

HAZLETON, Lesley; Writer; b. 20 Sept. 1945, Reading, England. *Education:* BA, Psychology, Manchester University, 1966; MA, Psychology, Hebrew University of Jerusalem, 1972. *Career:* mem. PEN American Center. *Publications:* Israeli Women, 1978; Where Mountains Roar, 1980; In Defence of Depression, 1984; Jerusalem, Jerusalem, 1986; England, Bloody England, 1989; Confessions of a Fast Woman, 1992; Everything Women Always Wanted to Know About Cars, 1995; Driving to Detroit, 1998. Contributions: many periodicals and magazines. *Literary Agent:* Watkins Loomis Agency Inc, 133 E 35th St, Suite 1, New York, NY 10016, USA.

HAZO, Samuel (John); Prof. of English, Writer and Poet; b. 19 July 1928, Pittsburgh, Pennsylvania, USA. *Education:* BA, University of Notre Dame, 1948; MA, Duquesne University, 1955; PhD, University of Pittsburgh, 1957. *Career:* Faculty, 1955–65, Dean, College of Arts and Sciences, 1961–66, Prof. of English, 1965–, Duquesne University; Dir, International Forum, 1966–; State Poet, Commonwealth of Pennsylvania. *Publications:* Discovery and Other Poems, 1959; The Quiet Wars, 1962; Hart Crane: An Introduction and Interpretation, 1963, revised edn as Smithereened Apart: A Critique of Hart Crane, 1978; The Christian Intellectual Studies in the Relation of Catholicism to the Human Sciences (ed.), 1963; A Selection of Contemporary Religious Poetry (ed.), 1963; Listen With the Eye, 1964; My Sons in God: Selected and New Poems, 1965; Blood Rights, 1968; The Blood of Adonis (with Ali Ahmed Said), 1971; Twelve Poems (with George Nama), 1972; Seascript: A Mediterranean Logbook, 1972; Once for the Last Bandit: New and Previous Poems, 1972; Quartered, 1974; Inscripts, 1975; The Very Fall of the Sun, 1978; To Paris, 1981; The Wanton Summer Air, 1982; Thank a Bored Angel, 1983; The Feast of Icarus, 1984; The Color of Reluctance, 1986; The Pittsburgh That Starts Within You, 1986; Silence Spoken Here, 1988; Stills, 1989; The Rest is Prose, 1989; Lebanon, 1990; Picks, 1990; The Past Won't Stay Behind You, 1993; The Pages of Day and Night, 1995; The Holy Surprise of Right Now, 1996; As They Sail, 1999; Spying for God, 1999; Mano a Mano: The Life of Manolete, 2001. *Address:* 785 Somerville Dr., Pittsburgh, PA 15243, USA.

HAZZARD, Shirley, FRSL; Australian/American writer; b. 30 Jan. 1931, Sydney, Australia; m. Francis Steegmuller 1963 (died 1994). *Education:* Queenwood School, Sydney. *Career:* Combined Services Intelligence, Hong Kong 1947–48; UK High Commr's Office, Wellington, NZ 1949–50; UN, New York (Gen. Service Category) 1952–61; novelist and writer of short stories and contrib. to The New Yorker 1960–; Guggenheim Fellow 1974; mem. American Acad. of Arts and Letters, American Acad. of Arts and Sciences; Boyer Lecturer, Australia 1984, 1988; Hon. Citizen of Capri 2000. *Publications:* short stories: Cliffs of Fall 1963; novels: The Evening of the Holiday 1966, People in Glass Houses 1967, The Bay of Noon 1970, The Transit of Venus (Nat. Critics Circle Award for Fiction 1981) 1980, The Great Fire (Nat. Book Award for Fiction) 2003; non-fiction: Defeat of an Ideal: A Study of the Self-destruction of the United Nations 1973, Countenance of Truth: The United Nations and the Waldheim Case 1990, Greene on Capri (memoir) 2000. *Honours:* Hon. Citizen of Capri; American Acad. of Arts and Letters Award in Literature 1966, First Prize, O. Henry Short Story Awards 1976, Nat. Book Critics Award for Fiction, USA 1981, Clifton Fadiman Medal for Literature 2001. *Address:* Apt. c-1705, 200 East 66th Street, New York, NY 10021, USA.

HEADLEY, John Miles; historian and academic; b. 23 Oct. 1929, New York, NY, USA. *Education:* BA, Princeton University, 1951; MA, 1953, PhD, 1960, Yale University. *Career:* Instructor, University of Massachusetts, Amherst, 1959–61; Instructor to Asst Prof., University of British Columbia, Vancouver, 1962–64; Asst Prof., 1964–66, Assoc. Prof., 1966–69, Prof., 1969–, University of North Carolina at Chapel Hill. *Publications:* Luther's View of Church History, 1963; Medieval and Renaissance Studies, Vol. III (ed.), 1968; Responsio ad Lutherum, Complete Works of St Thomas More, Vol. V (ed.), 1969; The Emperor and his Chancellor: A Study of the Imperial Chancellery under Gattinara, 1983; San Carlo Borromeo: Catholic Reform and Ecclesiastical Politics in the Second Half of the Sixteenth Century (ed. and contributor), 1988; The Oxford Encyclopedia of the Reformation (assoc. ed.), 1996; Tommaso Campanella and the Transformation of the World, 1997; Empire, Church and World: The Quest for Universal Order, 1997. Contributions: various scholarly books and journals. *Honours:* Guggenheim Fellowship, 1974; Institute for Arts and Humanities Fellowship, 1989. *Address:* c/o Dept of History, University of North Carolina at Chapel Hill, Chapel Hill, NC 27599, USA.

HEALD, Tim(othy Villiers), (David Lancaster); Journalist and Writer; b. 28 Jan. 1944, Dorset, England; m. 1st Alison Martina Leslie 30 March 1968 (divorced); two s. two d.; m. 2nd Penelope Byrne 1999. *Education:* MA, Balliol College, Oxford, 1965. *Career:* Reporter, Sunday Times, 1965–67; Feature Ed., Town magazine, 1967; Feature Writer, Daily Express, 1967–72; Assoc. Ed., Weekend Magazine, Toronto, 1977–78; Columnist, Observer, 1990; Visiting Fellow, Jane Franklin Hall, 1997, 1999, Univ. Tutor in Creative Writing, 1999, 2000, Univ. of Tasmania; Writer-in-Residence, Univ. of South Australia, 2001; mem. CWA, chair., 1987–88; PEN; Society of Authors. *Publications:* It's a Dog's Life, 1971; Unbecoming Habits, 1973; Blue Book Will Out, 1974; Deadline, 1975; Let Sleeping Dogs Die, 1976; The Making of Space, 1976; John Steed: An Authorized Biography, 1977; Just Desserts, 1977; H.R.H.: The Man Who Will be King (with M. Mohs), 1977; Murder at Moose Jaw, 1981; Caroline R, 1981; Masterstroke, 1982; Networks, 1983; Class Distinctions, 1984; Red Herrings, 1985; The Character of Cricket, 1986; Brought to Book, 1988; The Newest London Spy (ed.), 1988; Business Unusual, 1989; By Appointments: 150 Years of the Royal Warrant, 1989; A Classic English Crime (ed.), 1990; My Lord's (ed.), 1990; The Duke: A Portrait of Prince Philip, 1991; Honorable Estates, 1992; Barbara Cartland: A Life of Love, 1994; Denis: The Authorized Biography of the Incomparable Compton, 1994; Brian Johnston: The Authorized Biography, 1995; A Classic Christmas Crime (ed.), 1995; Beating Retreat: Hong Kong Under the Last Governor, 1997; Stop Press, 1998; A Peerage for Trade, 2001. Contributions: newspapers and periodicals. *Honours:* FRSL. *Address:* 66 The Esplanade, Fowey, Cornwall PL23 1JA, England. *Telephone:* (1726) 832781. *Fax:* (1726) 833246. *E-mail:* timheald@compuserve .com. *Website:* www.timheald.com.

HEALEY, Denis (Winston), (Baron Healey of Riddlesden in the County of West Yorkshire); Politician and Writer; b. 30 Aug. 1917, Mottingham, England. *Education:* BA, 1940, MA, 1945, Balliol College, Oxford. *Career:* Sec., International Dept, Labour Party, 1945–52; MP, Labour Party, South East Leeds, 1951–55, Leeds East, 1955–92; Shadow Cabinet, 1959–64, 1970–74, 1979–87; Sec. of State for Defence, 1964–70; Chancellor of the Exchequer, 1974–79; Deputy Leader, Labour Party, 1980–83; Pres., Birkbeck College, 1993; mem. FRSL. *Publications:* The Curtain Falls, 1951; New Fabian Essays, 1952; Neutralism, 1955; Fabian International Essays, 1956; A Neutral Belt in Europe, 1958; NATO and American Security, 1959; The Race Against the H Bomb, 1960; Labour Britain and the World, 1963; Healey's Eye, 1980; Labour and a World Society, 1985; Beyond Nuclear Deterrence, 1986; The Time of My Life (autobiog.), 1989; When Shrimps Learn to Whistle (essays), 1990; My Secret Planet, 1992; Denis Healey's Yorkshire Dales, 1996; Healey's World, 2002. *Honours:* MBE, 1945; Companion of Honour, 1979; Grand Cross of the Order of Merit, Federal Republic of Germany, 1979; Created Life Peer, 1992; Freeman, City of Leeds, 1992; Hon. doctorates. *Address:* Pingles Pl., Alfriston, East Sussex BN26 5TT, England.

HEALEY, Robin Michael, BA, MA; historian and biographer; b. 16 Feb. 1952, London, England. *Education:* Univ. of Birmingham. *Career:* Documentation Officer, Tamworth Castle and Cambridge Museum of Archaeology and Anthropology 1977–79; Research Asst, History of Parliament 1985–92; Ed., Hertfordshire Soc. Jubilee Yearbook 1986; Visiting Research Fellow, Manchester Univ. 1997–; Ed., Lewisletter 2001–; mem. Charles Lamb Soc. (exec. 1987–), Alliance of Literary Socs (press officer 1997–), Wyndham Lewis Soc. *Publications:* Hertfordshire: A Shell Guide 1982, Diary of George Mushet (1805–13) 1982, Grigson at Eighty 1985, A History of Barley School 1995, My Rebellious and Imperfect Eye: Observing Geoffrey Grigson 2002; contrib. to Biographical Dictionary of Modern British Radicals 1984, Domesday Book 1985, Secret Britain 1986, Dictionary of Literary Biography 1991, Encyclopaedia of Romanticism 1992, Consumer Magazines of the British Isles 1993, Postwar Literatures in English 1998–, New Dictionary of National Biography, Country Life, Hertfordshire Countryside, Guardian, Literary Review, Book and Magazine Collector, Independent, TLS, Art Newspaper, Mensa Magazine, Charles Lamb Bulletin, Cobbett's

New Political Register, Antiquarian Book Review. *Honours:* First Prize, Birmingham Post Poetry Contest 1974. *Address:* 80 Hall Lane, Great Chishill, Royston, Hertfordshire SG8 8SH, England. *Telephone:* (1763) 837058. *E-mail:* robin@pitmaston.freeserve.co.uk.

HEALY, Jeremiah, (Terry Devane); American novelist. *Education:* Rutgers Coll., Harvard Law School. *Career:* Prof., New England School of Law, 18 years; mem. Private Eye Writers of America (fmr pres.) Shamus Awards (fmr chair.), Int. Asscn of Crime Writers (pres. 2000–). *Publications:* as Jeremiah Healy: Blunt Darts 1984, The Staked Goat 1986, So Like Sleep 1987, Swan Dive 1988, Yesterday's News 1989, Right to Die 1991, Shallow Graves 1992, Foursome 1993, Act of God 1994, Rescue 1995, Invasion of Privacy 1996, The Only Good Lawyer 1998, The Stalking of Sheilah Quinn 1998, The Concise Cuddy (short stories) 1998, Spiral 1999, Turnabout 2001, Cuddy Plus One (short stories) 2003; as Terry Devane: Uncommon Justice 2001, Juror Number Eleven 2002, A Stain Upon the Robe 2003; contrib. shorts stories to collections, including Irreconcilable Differences, Blonde & Blue: Classic Private Eyes, Mom, Apple Pie, and Murder. *Honours:* Shamus Award 1986. *Literary Agent:* Sandy Balzo, Balzo Communications, 750 E Briar Ridge Drive, Brookfield, WI 53045, USA. *Telephone:* (262) 784-2591. *Fax:* (262) 784-3468. *E-mail:* balzocom@aol.com. *Address:* c/o Penguin Putnam, 375 Hudson Street, New York, NY 10014, USA. *E-mail:* jeremiah_healy@yahoo.com. *Website:* www.jeremiahhealy.com.

HEANEY, Seamus, CLit; Irish poet and author; *Ralph Waldo Emerson Poet in Residence, Harvard University*; b. 13 April 1939, Northern Ireland; m. Marie Devlin 1965; two s. one d. *Education:* St Columb's Coll., Londonderry, Queen's Univ., Belfast. *Career:* Lecturer, St Joseph's Coll. of Educ., Belfast 1963–66, Queen's Univ., Belfast 1966–72; freelance writer 1972–75, Lecturer, Carysfort Coll. 1975–81, Sr Visiting Lecturer, Harvard Univ. 1982–84, Boylston Prof. of Rhetoric and Oratory 1985–97, Ralph Waldo Emerson Poet in Residence 1998–; Prof. of Poetry, Univ. of Oxford 1989–94. *Poems:* Eleven Poems 1965, Death of a Naturalist 1966, Door into the Dark 1969, Wintering Out 1972, North 1975, Field Work 1979, Selected Poems 1965–1975 1980, Station Island 1984, The Haw Lantern 1987, New Selected Poems 1966–1987 1990, Seeing Things 1991, The Spirit Level 1996 (Whitbread Book of the Year Award 1997), Opened Ground: Poems 1966–96 1998 (Irish Times Literary Award 1999), Beowulf: A New Verse Translation 1999, Electric Light 2001. *Prose:* Preoccupations: Selected Prose 1968–1978 1980, The Government of the Tongue 1988, The Place of Writing 1990, The Redress of Poetry (lectures) 1995, Finders Keepers: Selected Prose 1971–2001 2002, The Midnight Verdict 2002. *Anthology:* The School Bag 1997 (co-ed. with Ted Hughes). *Plays:* The Cure at Troy 1991, The Burial at Thebes (Abbey Theatre, Dublin) 2004. *Translations:* Sweeney Astray 1984, Sweeney's Flight 1992, Laments, by Jan Kochanowski (with Stanislaw Baranczak); Beowulf: a New Verse Translation (Whitbread Book of the Year 1999) 1999. *Honours:* Hon. DLitt (Oxford) 1997, (Birmingham) 2000; Commdr des Arts et Lettres; WH Smith Prize 1975, Bennet Award 1982, Sunday Times Award for Excellence in Writing 1988, Lannan Literary Award 1990, Nobel Prize for Literature 1996. *Literary Agent:* Steven Barclay Agency, 12 Western Avenue, Petaluma, CA 94952, USA. *Telephone:* (707) 773-0654. *Fax:* (707) 778-1868. *Website:* www.barclayagency.com. *Address:* c/o Faber and Faber, 3 Queen Square, London, WC1N 3AU, England. *Telephone:* (20) 7465-0045. *Fax:* (20) 7465-0034.

HEARON, Shelby; Author; b. 18 Jan. 1931, Marion, KY, USA; m. 1st Robert Hearon Jr, 15 June 1953, divorced 1976, one s. one d.; m. 2nd Billy Joe Lucas, 19 April 1981, divorced 1995; m. 3rd William Halpern, 19 Aug. 1995. *Education:* BA, University of Texas at Austin, 1953. *Career:* Visiting Lecturer, University of Texas at Austin, 1978–80; Visiting Assoc. Prof., University of Houston, 1981, Clark University, 1985, University of California at Irvine, 1987; Visiting Prof., University of Illinois at Chicago, 1993, Colgate University, 1993, University of Massachusetts at Amherst, 1994–96, Middlebury College, 1996–98; mem. Associated Writing Programs; Authors' Guild; Authors League; PEN American Centre; Poets and Writers; Texas Institute of Letters. *Publications:* Armadillo in the Grass, 1968; The Second Dune, 1973; Hannah's House, 1975; Now and Another Time, 1976; A Prince of a Fellow, 1978; Painted Dresses, 1981; Afternoon of a Faun, 1983; Group Therapy, 1984; A Small Town, 1985; Five Hundred Scorpions, 1987; Owning Jolene, 1989; Hug Dancing, 1991; Life Estates, 1994; Footprints, 1996; Ella in Bloom, 2001. Other: Best Friends for Life (based on Life Estates), CBS-TV, 1998. Contributions: Magazines. *Honours:* Guggenheim Fellowship in Fiction, 1982; National Endowment for the Arts Fellowship in Fiction, 1983; Ingram Merrill Foundation Grant, 1987; American Acad. of Arts and Letters Literature Award, 1990. *Address:* 246 S Union St, Burlington, VT 05401, USA.

HEAT-MOON, William Least, (William Lewis Trogdon); Writer; b. 27 Aug. 1939, Kansas City, MO, USA; m. 1st Lezlie, divorced 1978; m. 2nd Linda. *Education:* BA, 1961, MA, 1962, PhD, 1973, BA in Photojournalism, 1978, University of Missouri at Columbia. *Career:* Teacher of English, Stephens College, Columbia, MO, 1965–68, 1972, 1978; Lecturer, School oif Journalism, University of Missouri, 1984–87. *Publications:* Blue Highways: A Journey into America, 1982; PrairyErth (a deep map), 1991; River Horse, 1999. Contributions: newspapers and magazines. *Honours:* New York Times Notable Book Citations, 1983, 1991; Books-Across-the-Sea Award, 1984; Christopher Award, 1984; American Library Asscn Best Non-Fiction Work, 1991.

HEATER, Derek Benjamin; Writer; b. 28 Nov. 1931, Sydenham, England; m. Gwyneth Mary Owen 12 March 1982; one s. one d. *Education:* BA, History, University College London, 1953; PGCE, Institute of Education, Univ. of London, 1954. *Career:* Ed., Teaching Politics, 1973–79; Co-Ed. (with Bernard Crick), Political Realities Series, 1974–93; mem. Politics Asscn, co-f., 1969; Council for Education in World Citizenship, hon. life mem. *Publications:* Political Ideas in the Modern World, 1960; Order and Rebellion, 1964; World Affairs (with Gwyneth Owen), 1972; Contemporary Political Ideas, 1974; Britain and the Outside World, 1976; Essays in Political Education (with Bernard Crick), 1977; World Studies, 1980; Our World This Century, 1982; Peace Through Education, 1984; Reform and Revolution, 1987; Refugees, 1988; Case Studies in Twentieth-Century World History, 1988; Citizenship: The Civic Ideal in World History, Politics and Education, 1990; The Idea of European Unity, 1992; The Remarkable History of Rottingdean, 1993; Introduction to International Politics (with G. R. Berridge), 1993; Foundations of Citizenship (with Dawn Oliver), 1994; National Self-Determination, 1994; World Citizenship and Government, 1996; The Theory of Nationhood: A Platonic Symposium, 1998; History of Sutton Grammar School, 1998; Keeping Faith 1899–1999, 1999; What is Citizenship?, 1999; World Citizenship: Cosmopolitan Thinking and Its Opponents, 2002; A History of Education for Citizenship, 2003. Contributions: reference works, scholarly journals. *Honours:* Children's Book of the Year Award for Refugees, 1988; Fellow, Politics Asscn, 1994. *Address:* 3 The Rotyngs, Rottingdean, Brighton BN2 7DX, England.

HEATH, Roy Aubrey Kelvin, BA; writer and dramatist; b. 13 Aug. 1926, Georgetown, British Guiana; m. Aemilia Oberli; three c. *Education:* University of London. *Career:* teacher, London, 1959–; called to the Bar, Lincoln's Inn, 1964. *Publications:* Fiction: A Man Come Home, 1974; The Murderer, 1978; From the Heat of the Day, 1979; One Generation, 1980; Genetha, 1981; Kwaku, or, The Man Who Could Not Keep His Mouth Shut, 1982; Orealla, 1984; The Shadow Bridge, 1988. Non-Fiction: Art and History, 1983; Shadows Round the Moon (memoirs), 1990. Play: Inez Combray, 1972. *Honours:* Drama Award, Theatre Guild of Guyana, 1971; Fiction Prize, The Guardian, London, 1978; Guyana Award for Literature, 1989. *Address:* c/o Harper/Collins, 77 Fulham Palace Road, London W6 8J, England.

HEATH-STUBBS, John (Francis Alexander); Poet, Writer, Trans. and Ed.; b. 9 July 1918, London, England. *Education:* Worcester College for the Blind; Queen's College, Oxford. *Career:* English Master, Hall School, Hampstead, 1944–45; Editorial Asst, Hutchinson's 1945–46; Gregory Fellow in Poetry, University of Leeds, 1952–55; Visiting Prof. of English, University of Alexandria, 1955–58, University of Michigan, 1960–61; Lecturer in English Literature, College of St Mark and St John, Chelsea, 1963–73; mem. FRSL. *Publications:* Poetry: Wounded Thammuz, 1942; Beauty and the Beast, 1943; The Divided Ways, 1946; The Swarming of the Bees, 1950; A Charm Against the Toothache, 1954; The Triumph of the Muse, 1958; The Blue Fly in His Head, 1962; Selected Poems, 1965; Satires and Epigrams, 1968; Artorius, 1973; A Parliament of Birds, 1975; The Watchman's Flute, 1978; Mouse, the Bird and the Sausage, 1978; Birds Reconvened, 1980; Buzz Buzz, 1981; Naming the Beasts, 1982; The Immolation of Aleph, 1985; Cat's Parnassus, 1987; Time Pieces, 1988; Collected Poems, 1988; A Partridge in a Pear Tree, 1988; A Ninefold of Charms, 1989; Selected Poems, 1990; The Parson's Cat, 1991; Sweetapple Earth, 1993; Chimeras, 1994; Galileo's Salad, 1996; The Torriano Sequences, 1997; The Sound of Light, 2000; The Return of the Cranes, 2002. Play: Helen in Egypt, 1958. Autobiography: Hindsights, 1993. Criticism: The Darkling Plain, 1950; Charles Williams, 1955; The Pastoral, 1969; The Ode, 1969; The Verse Satire, 1969. Translator: Hafiz of Shiraz (with Peter Avery), 1952; Leopardi: Selected Prose and Poetry (with Iris Origo), 1966; The Poems of Anyte (with Carol A Whiteside), 1974; The Rubaiyat of Omar Khayyam (with Peter Avery), 1979; Sulpicia, 2000. Editor: several books, including: Faber Book of Twentieth Century Verse (with David Wright), 1953; Poems of Science (with Phillips Salman), 1984. *Honours:* Queen's Gold Medal for Poetry, 1973; Oscar Williams/Jean Durwood Award, 1977; OBE, 1989; Commonwealth Poetry Prize, 1989; Cholmondeley Award, 1989; Howard Sargeant Award, 1989; Cross of St Augustine, 1999; Fellow, English Asscn, 1999. *Address:* 22 Artesian Rd, London W2 5AR, England.

HEATHCOTT, Mary (see Keegan, Mary Constance).

HEBALD, Carol; Writer; b. 6 July 1934, New York, NY, USA. *Education:* MFA, University of Iowa, 1971; BA, City College, CUNY, 1969. *Career:* mem. PEN American Centre; Authors' Guild of America. *Publications:* Three Blind Mice, 1989; Clara Kleinschmidt, 1989; Martha (play), 1991; The Heart Too Long Suppressed, 2001. Contributions: Antioch Review; Kansas Quarterly; Texas Quarterly; Massachusetts Review; The Humanist; New Letters; Confrontation; North American Review; New York Tribune; PEN International. *Literary Agent:* Thomas C. Wallace Ltd. *Address:* 425 Madison Ave, Suite 1001, New York, NY 10017, USA.

HECHT, Anthony Evan; poet and academic; b. 16 Jan. 1923, New York, NY, USA; m. 1st Patricia Harris 1954 (divorced 1961); two s.; m. 2nd Helen D'Alessandro 1971; one s. *Education:* BA, Bard College, 1944; MA, Columbia University, 1950. *Career:* Teacher, Kenyon College, 1947–48, State University of Iowa, 1948–49, New York University, 1949–56, Smith College, 1956–59; Assoc. Prof. of English, Bard College, 1961–67; Faculty,

1967–68, John D. Deane Prof. of English of Rhetoric and Poetry, 1968–85, University of Rochester, New York; Hurst Prof., Washington University, St Louis, 1971; Visiting Prof., Harvard University, 1973, Yale University, 1977; Faculty, Salzburg Seminar in American Studies, 1977; Consultant in Poetry, Library of Congress, Washington, DC, 1982–84; Prof., Georgetown University, 1985–93; Andrew Mellon Lecturer in Fine Arts, National Gallery of Art, Washington, DC, 1992; mem. Acad. of American Poets, hon. chancellor, 1971–97; American Acad. of Arts and Sciences; American Acad. of Arts and Letters. *Publications:* A Summoning of Stones, 1954; The Seven Deadly Sins, 1958; A Bestiary, 1960; The Hard Hours, 1968; Millions of Strange Shadows, 1977; The Venetian Vespers, 1977; Obbligati: Essays in Criticism, 1986; The Transparent Man, 1990; Collected Earlier Poems, 1990; The Hidden Law: The Poetry of W. H. Auden, 1993; On the Laws of the Poetic Art, 1995; The Presumption of Death, 1995; Flight Among the Tombs, 1996; The Darkness and the Light, 2001. Co-Author and Co-Editor: Jiggery-Pokery: A Compendium of Double Dactyls (with John Hollander), 1967. Editor: The Essential Herbert, 1987. Translator: Seven Against Thebes (with Helen Bacon), 1973. Contributions: many anthologies; Hudson Review; New York Review of Books; Quarterly Review of Literature; Transatlantic Review; Voices. *Honours:* Prix de Rome Fellowship, 1950; Guggenheim Fellowships, 1954, 1959; Hudson Review Fellowship, 1958; Ford Foundation Fellowships, 1960, 1968; Acad. of American Poets Fellowship, 1969; Bollingen Prize, 1983; Eugenio Montale Award, 1983; Harriet Monroe Award, 1987; Ruth Lilly Award, 1988; Aiken Taylor Award, Sewanee Review, 1988; National Endowment for the Arts Grant, 1989. *Address:* 4256 Nebraska Avenue NW, Washington, DC 20016, USA.

HECKLER, Jonellen; Writer and Poet; b. 28 Oct. 1943, Pittsburgh, Pennsylvania, USA; m. Lou Heckler, 17 Aug. 1968, one s. *Education:* BA, English Literature, University of Pittsburgh, 1965. *Career:* mem. Authors' Guild. *Publications:* Safekeeping, 1983; A Fragile Peace, 1986; White Lies, 1989; Circumstances Unknown, 1993; Final Tour, 1994. Contributions: numerous poems and short stories in Ladies Home Journal Magazine, 1975–83.

HEDIN, Mary Ann; Writer and Poet; b. 3 Aug. 1929, Minneapolis, MN, USA; m. Roger Willard Hedin, three s., one d. *Education:* BS, University of Minnesota; MA, University of California. *Career:* Fellow, Yaddo, 1974; Writer-in-Residence, Robinson Jeffers Town House Foundation, 1984–85; mem. Authors' Guild; PEN; American Poetry Society. *Publications:* Fly Away Home, 1980; Direction, 1983. Contributions: anthologies and journals. *Honours:* John H. McGinnis Memorial Award, 1979; Iowa School of Letters Award for Short Fiction, 1979. *Address:* 182 Oak Ave, San Anselmo, CA 94960, USA.

HEDRICK, Joan Doran; academic and writer; b. 1 May 1944, Baltimore, MD, USA; m. Travis K. Hedrick 1967; two d. *Education:* AB, Vassar College, 1966; PhD, Brown University, 1974. *Career:* Prof. of History, Trinity College, Hartford, CT; mem. American Studies Asscn; MLA. *Publications:* Solitary Comrade: Jack London and His Work, 1982; Harriet Beecher Stowe: A Life, 1994; The Oxford Harriet Beecher Stowe Reader, 1999. *Honours:* Pulitzer Prize in Biography, 1995. *Address:* c/o Department of History, Trinity College, Hartford, CT 06106, USA.

HEFFERNAN, Thomas (Patrick Carroll); American and English Studies Educator, Writer and Poet; b. 19 Aug. 1939, Hyannis, Massachusetts, USA; m. Nancy E. Iler, 15 July 1972, divorced 1977. *Education:* AB, Boston College, 1961; MA, English Literature, University of Manchester, England, 1963; Universita per Stranieri, Perugia, Italy, 1965; PhD, English Literature, Sophia University, Tokyo, 1990. *Career:* Poet in Schools, North Carolina Dept of Public Instruction, Raleigh, 1973–77; Visiting Artist, Poetry, North Carolina Dept of Community Colleges, 1977–81, South Carolina Arts Commission, 1981–82; Co-Ed., The Plover (Chidori), bilingual haiku journal, Japan, 1989–92; Prof. of English, Kagoshima Prefectural University, Japan; mem. MLA; Japan English Literary Society; Japan American Literary Society. *Publications:* Mobiles, 1973; A Poem is a Smile You Can Hear (ed.), 1976; A Narrative of Jeremy Bentham, 1978; The Liam Poems, 1981; City Renewing Itself, 1983; Art and Emblem: Early Seventeenth Century English Poetry of Devotion, 1991; Gathering in Ireland, 1996; Mutiny on the Globe: The Fatal Voyage of Samuel Comstock, 2002. Contributions: anthologies and other publications. *Honours:* National Endowment for the Arts Fellowship, 1977; Gordon Barber Memorial Award, 1979; Portfolio Award, 1983; Roanoke Chowan Prize, 1982. *Address:* Kagoshima Prefectural University, 1-52-1 Shimo-Ishiki-cho, Kagoshima-shi, 890-0005, Japan.

HEFFRON, Dorris; Writer; b. 18 Oct. 1944, Noranda, QC, Canada; m. 1st William Newton-Smith, 29 June 1968, divorced, two d.; m. 2nd D. L. Gauer, 29 Oct. 1980, one s. one d. *Education:* BA, 1967, MA, 1969, Queen's University, Kingston, Ontario. *Career:* Tutor, University of Oxford, 1970–80, The Open University, 1975–78, University of Malaysia, 1978; Writer-in-Residence, Wainfleet Public Library, 1989–90; mem. Authors Society; PEN; Writers Union of Canada. *Publications:* A Nice Fire and Some Moonpennies, 1971; Crusty Crossed, 1976; Rain and I, 1982; A Shark in the House, 1996. Contributions: various publications. *Honours:* Canada Council Arts Grant, 1974. *Address:* Little Creek Wolf Range, RR No. 1 Clarksburg, ON N0H 1J0, Canada. *E-mail:* dheffron@sympatico.ca. *Website:* ww3.sympatico.ca/dheffron.

HEFNER, Hugh Marston, BS; American publisher; *Chairman Emeritus, Playboy Enterprises, Inc.*; b. 9 April 1926, Chicago, Ill.; m. 1st Mildred Williams 1949 (divorced 1959); one s. one d.; m. 2nd Kimberley Conrad 1989; two s. *Education:* Univ. of Illinois. *Career:* Ed.-in-Chief Playboy Magazine 1953–, Oui Magazine 1972–81; Chair. Emer. Playboy Enterprises 1988–; Pres. Playboy Club Int. Inc. 1959–86. *Honours:* Int. Press Directory Int. Publisher Award 1997. *Address:* Playboy Enterprises Inc., 680 North Lake Shore Drive, Chicago, IL 60611, USA (Office). *Telephone:* (312) 751-8000 (Office). *Fax:* (312) 751-2818 (Office). *Website:* www.playboyenterprises.com (Home).

HEGARTY, Frances; British writer and lawyer; b. 1949. *Career:* part-time lawyer 1987–2000; novelist 1987–. *Publications include:* as Frances Fyfield: A Question of Guilt 1988, Deep Sleep (Silver Dagger Award) 1991, A Clear Conscience 1994 (Grand Prix de Littérature Policière 1998), Without Consent 1996, Blind Date 1998, Staring at the Light 1999, Undercurrents 2000, Helen West Omnibus 2001, The Nature of the Beast 2001, Looking Down 2004; as Frances Hegarty: The Playroom 1991, Half Light 1992, Let's Dance 1995. *Literary Agent:* Rogers Coleridge White, 20 Powis Mews, London, W11 1JN, England.

HEGI, Ursula (Johanna); Prof. of English, Writer, Poet and Critic; b. 23 May 1946, Büderich, Germany; two s. *Education:* BA, 1978, MA, 1979, University of New Hampshire. *Career:* Instructor, University of New Hampshire, 1980–84; Book Critic, Los Angeles Times, New York Times, Washington Post, 1982–; Asst Prof., 1984–89, Assoc. Prof., 1989–95, Prof. of English, 1995–, Eastern Washington University; Visiting Writer, various universities; mem. Associated Writing Programs; National Book Critics Circle, board of dirs, 1992–94. *Publications:* Fiction: Intrusions, 1981; Unearned Pleasures and Other Stories, 1988; Floating in My Mother's Palm, 1990; Stones from the River, 1994; Salt Dancers, 1995; The Vision of Emma Blau, 1999; Hotel of the Saints (short stories), 2001. Non-Fiction: Tearing the Silence: On Being German in America, 1997. Contributions: anthologies, newspapers, journals and magazines. *Honours:* Indiana Fiction Award, 1988; National Endowment for the Arts Fellowship, 1990; New York Times Best Books Selections, 1990, 1994; Pacific Northwest Booksellers Asscn Award, 1991; Governor's Writers Awards, 1991, 1994. *Address:* c/o Dept of English, Eastern Washington University, Cheney, WA 99004, USA.

HEIGHTON, (John) Steven; writer, poet, editor and translator; b. 1961, Toronto, ON, Canada. *Education:* BA, 1985, MA, 1986, Queen's University. *Career:* Ed., Quarry Magazine, 1988–94; mem. League of Canadian Poets; PEN; Writers' Union of Canada. *Publications:* Fiction: Flight Paths of the Emperor, 1992; On Earth As It Is, 1995; The Shadow Boxer, 2000. Non-Fiction: The Admen Move on Lhasa (writing and culture in a virtual world), 1997. Poetry: Stalin's Carnival, 1989; Foreign Ghosts, 1989; The Ecstasy of Skeptics, 1994. *Honours:* Air Canada Award, 1988; Gerald Lampert Award, 1990; Gold Medal for Fiction, National Magazine Awards, 1991; Petra Kenney Prize, 2002. *Address:* PO Box 382, Kingston, ON K7L 4W2, Canada. *E-mail:* sheighton@kos.net.

HEILBRONER, Robert L(ouis); Prof. of Economics and Writer; b. 24 March 1919, New York, NY, USA; m. 1st Joan Knapp, divorced, two s.; m. 2nd Shirley E. T. Davis. *Education:* BA, Harvard University, 1940; PhD, New School for Social Research, New York City. *Career:* Economist in government and business; Norman Thomas Prof. of Economics, New School for Social Research, New York City, 1972–; Lecturer to various organizations; mem. American Economic Asscn; Council on Economic Priorities. *Publications:* The Worldly Philosophers, 1953; The Quest for Wealth, 1956; The Future as History, 1960; The Making of Economic Society, 1962; The Great Ascent, 1963; Understanding Macroeconomics (with James Galbraith), 1965; The Limits of American Capitalism, 1966; The Economic Problem (with James Galbraith), 1968; Understanding Microeconomics (with James Galbraith), 1968; Between Capitalism and Socialism: Essays in Political Economics, 1970; An Inquiry into the Human Prospect, 1975; Business Civilization in Decline, 1976; Economic Relevance: A Second Look (with A. M. Ford), 1976; The Economic Transformation of America (with Aaron Singer), 1977; Beyond Boom and Crash, 1978; Marxism: For and Against, 1980; Economics Explained (with Lester C. Thurow), 1982; The Nature and Logic of Capitalism, 1985; Beyond the Veil of Economics, 1988; Twenty-First Century Capitalism, 1993; The Crisis of Vision in Modern Economic Thought (with William Milberg), 1995; Teachings from the Worldly Philosophy (ed.), 1996. Contributions: many periodicals. *Honours:* Guggenheim Fellowship, 1983; Scholar of the Year, 1995; Hon. doctorates.

HEIM, Scott; Writer and Poet; b. 26 Sept. 1966, Hutchinson, KS, USA. *Education:* BA, 1989, MA, 1991, University of Kansas; MFA, Columbia University, 1993. *Publications:* Saved from Drowning: Poems, 1993; Mysterious Skin (novel), 1995; In Awe (novel), 1997. *Honours:* William Herbert Carruth Award for Poetry, 1991; Edna Osborne Whitcomb Fiction Prize, 1991. *Address:* c/o Harper Collins, 10 E 53rd St, New York, NY 10022, USA.

HEIN, Christoph; Novelist and Playwright; b. 8 April 1944, Heinzendorf/Schlesien, Germany. *Education:* University of Leipzig, Humboldt University Berlin. *Career:* Dramaturg and Playwright, Volksbühne Berlin 1971–79. *Plays:* . *Publications:* Fiction: Nachfahrt und früher Morgen 1980, The Distant Lover 1982, Horns Ende 1985, Der Tangospieler, 1989, Bridge freezes before roadway 1990, Die Vergewaltigung 1991, Das Napoleon-

Spiel 1993, Exekution eines Kalbes 1994, Von allem Anfang an 1997, Willenbrock 2000. Plays: Schlötel oder Was solls 1974, Cromwell 1980, Lassalle fragt Herrn Herbert nach Sonja 1981, Die wahre Geschichte des Ah Q 1983, Passage 1987, Die Ritter der Tafelrunde 1989, Randow 1994, Bruch 1998, Himmel auf Erden 1998, In Acht und Bann 1998, Mutters Tag 2000, Noach (opera) 2001, Zur Geschichte des menschlichen Herzens 2002. For children: Jamie and his Friends 1984, Mama ist gegangen 2003; Essays: I Saw Stalin as a Child 1990, Die 5 Grundrechenart 1990, Die Mauern von Jerichow 1996. *Honours:* Heinrich Mann-Preis der Akad. der Künste Berlin 1982, (westdeutscher) Kritikerpreis für Literatur Berliln 1983, Literaturpreis Hamburg 1985, Lessing Prize 1989, Berliner Literaturpreis der Stiftung Preussische Seehandlung 1992, Norddt. Literaturpreis 1998, Peter-Weiss-Preis 1998, Solothurner Literaturpreis 2000, Premio Grinzane Cavour Turin 2002, State Prize for European Literature Austria 2002. *Address:* c/o Suhrkamp-Verlag, Postfach 10 19 45, 60019 Frankfurt am Main, Germany.

HEJINIAN, Lyn; Poet and Writer; b. 17 May 1941, Alameda, CA, USA; m. 1st John P. Hejinian, 1961, divorced 1972, one s. one d.; m. 2nd Larry Ochs, 1977. *Education:* BA, Harvard University, 1963. *Career:* Founder-Ed., Tuumba Press, 1976–84; Co-Founder and Co-Ed., Atelos; Prof., Dept of English, University of California at Berkeley; mem. Fellow, Acad. of American Poets. *Publications:* A Great Adventure, 1972; A Thought is the Bride of What Thinking, 1976; A Mask of Motion, 1977; Gesualdo, 1978; Writing is an Aid to Memory, 1978; My Life, 1980; The Guard, 1984; Redo, 1984; Individuals, 1988; Leningrad: American Writers in the Soviet Union (with Michael Davidson, Ron Silliman, and Barrett Watten), 1991; The Hunt, 1991, revised edn as Oxota: A Short Russian Novel, 1991; The Cell, 1992; The Cold of Poetry, 1994; Two Stein Talks, 1995; Guide, Grammar, Watch and the Thirty Nights, 1996; The Little Book of a Thousand Eyes, 1996; Wicker (with Jack Collom), 1996; The Traveler and the Hill (with Emilie Clark), 1998; Sight, 1999; Sunflower (with Jack Collom), 2000; Chartings, 2000; Happily, 2000; The Beginner, 2000; The Language of Enquiry, 2000; A Border Comedy, 2001; Slowly, 2002. Contributions: journals. *Address:* 2639 Russell St, Berkeley, CA 94705, USA.

HELD, Michael J., MA; American; *Executive Director, Rockefeller Univ. Press. Career:* Pres., Council of Science Edition; Exec. Dir, Rockefeller Univ. Press. *Address:* c/o The Rockefeller University Press, 1114 First Avenue, Third Floor, New York, NY 10021, USA. *Website:* www.rockefeller.edu/rupress/.

HELLENGA, Robert; Teacher and Writer; b. 5 Aug. 1941, USA; m. Virginia Killion, 31 Aug. 1963, three d. *Education:* BA, University of Michigan, 1963; Queen's University, Belfast, 1963–64; PhD, Princeton University, 1969. *Career:* Knox College, 1968–; mem. Society of Midland Authors; Illinois Arts Alliance. *Publications:* Fiction: The Sixteen Pleasures, 1994; The Fall of a Sparrow, 1998; Blues Lessons, 2002. Contributions: Iowa Review; Chicago Review; California Quarterly; Columbia; Ascent; Farmer's Market; Chicago Tribune Magazine; TriQuarterly; Crazyhorse; Mississippi Valley Review; Black Warrior Review; New York Times Magazine; The Gettysburg Review. *Honours:* several fellowships and grants; Illinois Arts Council Artist's Literary Award, 1985; PEN Syndicated Fiction Award, 1988; Society of Midland Authors Award for Fiction, 1995; Knox College Faculty Achievement Award, 1997–98. *Address:* 343 N Prairie St, Galesburg, IL 61401, USA.

HELLER, Agnes; Prof. of Philosophy and Writer; b. 12 May 1929, Budapest, Hungary; m. 1st Istvan Hermann, 9 Sept. 1949, one d.; m. 2nd Ferenc Feher, 15 March 1963, one s. *Education:* University of Budapest; MA, PhD, Hungarian Acad. of Sciences. *Career:* Reader in Sociology, La Trobe University, Bundoora, Vic., Australia; Prof. of Philosophy, New School for Social Research, New York, 1985–; mem. Société Européenne. *Publications:* Renaissance Man, 1978; A Theory of History, 1981; Hungary 1956 Revisited: The Message of a Revolution – A Quarter-Century After (co-author), 1983; Dictatorship Over Needs (co-author), 1983; Lukacs Reappraised, 1983, UK edn as Lukacs Revalued, 1983; The Power of Shame: A Rational Perspective, 1985; Reconstructing Aesthetics: Writings of the Budapest School (co-ed.), 1986; Doomsday or Deterrence?: On the Antinuclear Issue (co-author), 1986; Eastern Left, Western Left: Totalitarianism, Freedom and Democracy (co-author), 1987; Beyond Justice, 1987; The Postmodern Political Condition (co-author), 1988; General Ethics, 1988; A Philosophy of Morals, 1990; Can Modernity Survive?, 1990; From Yalta to Glasnost: The Dismantling of Stalin's Empire (co-author), 1991; The Grandeur and Twilight of Radical Universalism (co-author), 1991; A Philosophy of History in Fragments, 1993; The Limits to Natural Law and the Paradox of Evil, 1993; An Ethics of Personality, 1995. Contributions: Academic journals. *Honours:* Lessing Prize, Hamburg, 1991. *Address:* c/o New School for Social Research, New York, NY.

HELLER, (Franz) André; Austrian poet, writer, singer and theatre producer; b. 22 March 1947, Vienna. *Career:* actor 1965–67; co-founder, Ö3 radio station 1967; recording artist 1968–83; dir. TV documentaries 1978–. *Publications include:* short story collections: Die Ernte der Schlaflosigkeit in Wien 1976, Auf und davon: Erzähites, Schlamassel, Als ich ein Hund war; novel: Schättentaucher; poetry: Sitzt ana und glaubt er is zwa (with Helmut Qualtinger); picture books: Jagmandir: Traum und Wiklichkeit, Die Zaubergärten des André Heller. *Address:* c/o Verlagsgruppe Random House, Neumarkter str. 28, 81673 Munich, Germany; Artevent, Singerstr. 8, 1010 Vienna, Austria. *E-mail:* contact@andreheller.com. *Website:* www.andreheller.com.

HELLER, Michael, BS, MA; poet, writer and teacher; b. 11 May 1937, New York, NY, USA; m. 1st Doris Whytal 1962 (divorced 1978); m. 2nd Jane Augustine 1979; one s. *Education:* Rensselaer Polytechnic Institute, New York Univ. *Career:* Faculty, 1967, Acting Dir, 1986–87, Academic Coordinator, 1987–91, American Language Institute, New York Univ.; Poet and Teacher, New York State Poets in the Schools, 1970–; mem. American Acad. of Poets; MLA; New York State Poets in Public Service; PEN; Poetry Society of America; Poets and Writers; Poets House. *Publications:* Two Poems, 1970; Accidental Center, 1972; Figures of Speaking, 1977; Knowledge, 1979; Marble Snows, Origin, 1979; Conviction's Net of Branches: Essays on the Objectivist Poets and Poetry, 1985; Marginalia in a Desperate Hand, 1986; In the Builded Place, 1990; Carl Rakosi: Man and Poet (ed.), 1993; Wordflow: New and Selected Poems, 1997; Living Root: A Memoir, 2000; Exigent Futures: New and Selected Poems, 2003. Contributions: anthologies, reference books, journals. *Honours:* Coffey Poetry Prize, New School for Social Research, 1964; Poetry in Public Places Award, 1975; New York State Creative Artists Public Service Fellowship in Poetry, 1975–76; National Endowment for the Humanities Grant, 1979; Di Castagnola Award, Poetry Society of America, 1980; Outstanding Writer Citations, Pushcart Press, 1983, 1984, 1992; New York Fellowship in the Arts, 1989; Fund for Poetry Award 2003. *Address:* 346 E 18th Street, New York, NY 10003, USA.

HELLER, Zoë, BA; British novelist and journalist; b. 1965, London, England; one d. *Education:* St Anne's Coll., Oxford, Columbia Univ., NY, USA. *Career:* fmrly journalist, Independent on Sunday; columnist, fmrly Sunday Times, currently Daily Telegraph. *Publications:* Everything You Know 1999, Notes on a Scandal (aka What Was She Thinking?) 2003; contrib. to Harper's Bazaar, The Independent, City Limits, Granta, Vogue, Vanity Fair. *Honours:* British Press Awards Columnist of the Year 2001. *Address:* c/o Viking, 80 Strand, London, WC2R 0RL, England.

HELLIER, Trudy; Australian playwright, film-maker and actress. *Education:* RMIT Univ., Melbourne. *Television appearances:* MDA, Welcher & Welcher, Marshall Law, Frontline, Round the Twist, SeaChange, The Games, Guinevere Jones, Blue Heelers, Halifax fp. *Plays as writer:* Trapped 1996, Blind Faith 2001. *Screenplays:* Break and Enter 1997, Trapped 2002. *Honours:* AFI Award 1999. *Literary Agent:* RGM Associates, PO Box 128, Surry Hills, NSW 2010, Australia. *Telephone:* (2) 9281-3911. *Fax:* (2) 9281-4705. *E-mail:* info@rgm.com.au. *Website:* www.rgm.com.au.

HELPRIN, Mark; Writer; b. 28 June 1947, New York, NY, USA; m. Lisa Kennedy, 28 June 1980, two d. *Education:* AB, 1969, AM, 1972, Harvard University; Postgraduate Studies, Magdalen College, Oxford, 1976–77. *Career:* Contributing Ed., The Wall Street Journal; Speechwriter for Senator Robert J. Dole, 1996; mem. Council on Foreign Relations. *Publications:* A Dove of the East and Other Stories, 1975; Refiner's Fire, 1977; Ellis Island and Other Stories, 1981; Winter's Tale, 1983; Swan Lake, 1989; A Soldier of the Great War, 1991; Memoir from Antproof Case, 1995; A City in Winter, 1996. *Honours:* Prix de Rome, American Acad. and Institute of Arts and Letters, 1982; National Jewish Book Award, 1982. *Address:* c/o The Wall Street Journal, 200 Liberty St, New York, NY 10281, USA.

HELWIG, David (Gordon); Poet, Writer and Ed.; b. 5 April 1938, Toronto, Ontario, Canada; m. Nancy Keeling, 1959, two d. *Education:* Graduated, Stamford Collegiate Institute, 1956; BA, University of Toronto, 1960; MA, University of Liverpool, 1962. *Career:* Faculty, Dept of English, Queen's University, Kingston, Ontario, 1962–80; Co-Ed., Quarry magazine. *Publications:* Poetry: Figures in a Landscape, 1967; The Sign of the Gunman, 1969; The Best Name of Silence, 1972; Atlantic Crossings, 1974; A Book of the Hours, 1979; The Rain Falls Like Rain, 1982; Catchpenny Poems, 1983; The Hundred Old Names, 1988; The Beloved, 1992; Telling Stories, 2001. Fiction: The Day Before Tomorrow, 1971; The Glass Knight, 1976; Jennifer, 1979; The King's Evil, 1981; It Is Always Summer, 1982; A Sound Like Laughter, 1983; The Only Son, 1984; The Bishop, 1986; A Postcard From Rome, 1988; Old Wars, 1989; Of Desire, 1990; Blueberry Cliffs, 1993; Just Say the Words, 1994; Close to the Fire, 1999. Editor: Fourteen Stories High: Best Canadian Stories of 71 (with Tom Marshall), 1971; 72, 73, 74 and 75: New Canadian Stories (with Joan Harcourt), 4 vols, 1972–75; Words From Inside, 1972; The Human Elements: Critical Essays, 2 vols, 1978, 1981; Love and Money: The Politics of Culture, 1980; 83, 84, 85 and 86: Best Canadian Stories (with Sandra Martin), 4 vols, 1983–86; Coming Attractions 1983, 1984, 1985, and 1986 (with Sandra Martin), 4 vols, 1983–86; Coming Attractions 1987 and 1988 (with Maggie Helwig), 2 vols 1987, 1988; 87, 88, 89, and 91: Best Canadian Stories (with Maggie Helwig), 4 vols, 1987–91. *Honours:* CBC Literary Prize, 1983. *Address:* c/o Viking Penguin, 375 Hudson St, New York, NY 10014, USA.

HELY-HUTCHINSON, Timothy Mark, MA; British publisher; *Group Chief Executive, Hodder Headline PLC;* b. 26 Oct. 1953, London. *Education:* Eton Coll., Oxford Univ. *Career:* Man. Dir Macdonald & Co. (Publrs) Ltd 1982–86, Headline Book Publishing PLC 1986–93; Group Chief Exec. Hodder Headline PLC 1993–; Dir W. H. Smith PLC 1999–, Chair. W. H. Smith News Ltd. *Honours:* Venturer of the Year (British Venture Capital

Asscn) 1990, Publr of the Year (British Book Awards) 1992. *Address:* Hodder Headline PLC, 338 Euston Road, London, NW1 3BH (Office). *Telephone:* (20) 7873-6011 (Office). *Fax:* (20) 7873-6012 (Office).

HELYAR, Jane Penelope Josephine, (Josephine Poole); writer; b. 12 Feb. 1933, London, England; m. 1st T. R. Poole 1956; m. 2nd V. J. H. Helyar 1975; one s. five d. *Television scripts:* The Harbourer 1975, The Sabbatical 1981, The Breakdown 1981, Miss Constantine 1981, Ring a Ring a Rosie 1983, With Love, Belinda 1983, The Wit to Woo 1983, Fox 1984, Buzzard 1984, Dartmoor Pony 1984. *Publications:* A Dream in the House 1961, Moon Eyes 1965, The Lilywhite Boys 1967, Catch as Catch Can 1969, Yokeham 1970, Billy Buck 1972, Touch and Go 1976, When Fishes Flew 1978, Hannah Chance 1980, Diamond Jack 1983, The Country Diary Companion (to accompany Central TV series) 1983, Three for Luck 1985, Wildlife Tales 1986, The Loving Ghosts 1988, Angel 1989, This is Me Speaking 1990, Snow White (picture book) 1991, Paul Loves Amy Loves Christo 1992, Scared to Death 1994, Pinocchio (re-written) 1994, Deadly Inheritance 1995, The Water Babies (re-written) 1996, Hero 1997, Jack and the Beanstalk (picture book) 1997, Joan of Arc (picture book) 1998, Run Rabbit 1999, Fair Game 2000, Scorched 2003, Anne Frank (picture book) 2005. *Address:* Poundisford Lodge, Poundisford, Taunton, Somerset TA3 7AE, England.

HEMLEY, Robin; Asst Prof. of English and Writer; b. 28 May 1958, New York, NY, USA; m. Beverly Bertling Hemley, 18 July 1987, two d. *Education:* BA, Indiana University, 1980; MFA, University of Iowa, 1982. *Career:* Assoc. Prof. of English, University of North Carolina at Charlotte, 1986–94; Asst Prof. of English, Western Washington University, Bellingham, 1994–. *Publications:* The Mouse Town, 1987; All You Can Eat, 1988; The Last Studebaker, 1992; Turning Life Into Fiction, 1994. *Literary Agent:* Sterling Lord Literistic Inc, 65 Bleecker St, New York, NY 10012, USA.

HEMMING, John Henry; Author and Publisher; b. 5 Jan. 1935, Vancouver, BC, Canada; m. Sukie Babington-Smith, 1979, one s. one d. *Education:* McGill and Oxford Universities; MA; D.Litt. *Career:* Explorations in Peru and Brazil, 1960, 1961, 1971, 1972, 1986–87; Dir and Sec., RGS, 1975–96; Joint Chair., Hemming Group Ltd, 1976–; Chair, Brintex Ltd., Newman Books Ltd. *Publications:* The Conquest of the Incas, 1970; Tribes of the Amazon Basin in Brazil (with others), 1973; Red Gold: The Conquest of the Brazilian Indians, 1978; The Search for El Dorado, 1978; Machu Picchu, 1982; Monuments of the Incas, 1983; Change in the Amazon Basin (ed.), two vols, 1985; Amazon Frontier: The Defeat of the Brazilian Indians, 1987; Maracá, 1988; Roraima: Brazil's Northernmost Frontier, 1990; The Rainforest Edge (ed.), 1994; The Golden Age of Discovery, 1998; Die If You Must, 2003. *Honours:* Pitman Literary Prize, 1970; Christopher Award, New York, 1971; Order of Merit, Peru, 1991; Companion of St Michael and St George, 1994; Order of the Southern Cross, Brazil, 1998; Medals from RGS, Boston Museum of Science, Royal Scottish Geographical Society; Citation of Merit, New York Explorers' Club, Instituto Nacional de Cultura, Peru; Hon. doctorates, University of Warwick, University of Stirling. *Address:* Hemming Group Ltd, 32 Vauxhall Bridge Rd, London SW1V 2SS, England. *Telephone:* (20) 7973-6634. *E-mail:* j.hemming@hgluk.com.

HEMON, Aleksandar; Bosnian/American writer and journalist; b. 1965, Sarajevo. *Career:* fmr Cultural Ed. Dani magazine, Sarajevo; emigrated to Chicago, USA 1992. *Publications:* fiction: The Question of Bruno (Los Angeles Times Book Review book of the year) 2000, Nowhere Man (novel) 2003, Pretext 7: Cut That Fence (ed.) 2003. *Address:* c/o Picador USA, 175 Fifth Avenue, New York, NY 10010, USA.

HENDERSON, Hamish Scott; poet and songwriter; b. 11 Nov. 1919, Blairgowrie, Perthshire, Scotland; m. Felicity Schmidt 1959; two d. *Education:* Downing College, Cambridge; Musical tuition with traditional singers, Perthshire and Aberdeenshire. *Career:* Collection of soldiers songs in WWII, published in Ballads of World War II, 1947; Collection of North-East Scottish folk songs with Alan Lomax, 1951; Joined School of Scottish Studies, Edinburgh University, 1952; Collection of Gaelic and Lowland Scottish Songs and Tales; mem, Hon. Mem., Saltire Society, Edinburgh; Hon. Mem., Folklore Fellows, Helsinki; Hon. Fellow, School of Scottish Studies. *Compositions:* numerous songs popular with Scottish folk revival include: The Freedom Come-All-Ye; The 51st Highland Division's Farewell To Sicily; The Gillie More; The Men of Knoydart. *Recordings:* album: Freedom Come-All-Ye. *Publications:* Elegies For The Dead In Cyrenaica 1948, Alias MacAlias (essays on folklore) 1992, The Armstrong Nose (selected letters) 1996, Gramsci's Prison Letters 1996. *Honours:* Somerset Maugham Award, 1949.

HENDERSON, Neil Keir; Poet and Writer; b. 7 March 1956, Glasgow, Scotland. *Education:* MA, English Language, English Literature and Scottish Literature, University of Glasgow, 1977. *Publications:* Maldehyde's Discomfiture, or A Lady Churned, 1997; Fish-Worshipping—As We Know It, 2001. Contributions: anthologies, incl.: Mystery of the City; Red Candle Treasury; Loveable Warts: A Defence of Self-Indulgence, Chapman 87, 1997; Mightier Than the Sword: The Punch-Up of the Poses, Chapman 91, 1998; Haggis: The Thinking Man's Buttock, Chapman 98, 2001; Labyrinths 6 (showcased), 2002. *Address:* 46 Revoch Dr., Knightswood, Glasgow G13 4SB, Scotland.

HENDRIKS, Arthur Lemiere; poet and writer; b. 17 April 1922, Kingston, Jamaica. *Education:* Open University. *Publications:* The Independence Anthology of Jamaican Literature (ed. with C. Lindo), 1962; On This Mountain and Other Poems, 1965; These Green Islands, 1971; Muet, 1971; Madonna of the Unknown Nation, 1974; The Islanders and Other Poems, 1983; Archie and the Princess and the Everythingest Horse (for children), 1983; The Naked Ghost and Other Poems, 1984; Great Families of Jamaica, 1984; To Speak Simply: Selected Poems, 1961–86, 1988. *Address:* 93 Victoria Mansions, London SW8, England.

HENDRY, Diana (Lois); Poet and Children's Writer; b. 2 Oct. 1941, Meols, Wirral, Cheshire, England; m. George Hendry 9 Oct. 1965 (divorced 1981); one s. one d. *Education:* BA, 1984, MLitt, 1986, Univ. of Bristol. *Career:* Asst to Literature Ed., Sunday Times, London, 1958–60; Reporter and Feature Writer, Western Mail, Cardiff, 1960–65; Freelance journalist, 1965–80; Part-time English Teacher, Clifton College, 1984–87; Part-time Lecturer, Bristol Polytechnic, 1987; WEA, Modern Poets Course, 1987–; Tutor, Open Univ., 1991–92; Part-time Tutor, Creative Writing, Univ. of Bristol, 1993–1997; Writer-in-Residence, Dumfries and Galloway Royal Infirmary, 1997–98; mem. Society of Authors; PEN. *Publications:* Poetry: Making Blue, 1995; Strange Goings-On (children's), 1995; Borderers, 2001; Twelve Lilts: Psalms and Responses, 2003; No Homework Tomorrow (children's), 2003. Children's Fiction: Midnight Pirate, 1984; Fiona Finds Her Tongue, 1985; Hetty's First Fling, 1985; The Not Anywhere House, 1989; The Rainbow Watchers, 1989; The Carey Street Cat, 1989; Christmas on Exeter Street, 1989; Sam Sticks and Delilah, 1990; A Camel Called April, 1990; Double Vision, 1990; Harvey Angell, 1991; Kid Kibble, 1992; The Thing-in-a-Box, 1992; Wonderful Robert and Sweetie-Pie Nell, 1992; Back Soon, 1993; The Awesome Bird, 1995; The Thing on Two Legs, 1995; Harvey Angell and the Ghost Child, 1997; Minders, 1998; Harvey Angell Beats Time, 2001; You Can't Kiss it Better, 2003. Contributions: anthologies and periodicals incl. Poetry Review, The Spectator, The North, The London Magazine. *Honours:* Stroud Festival International Poetry Competition, 1976; Third Prize, 1991, Second Prize, 1993, Peterloo Poetry Competition; Whitbread Award for Children's Novel, 1991; First Prize, Housman Poetry Society competition, 1996; Scottish Arts Council Children's Book Award, 2001. *Address:* 23 Dunrobin Pl., Edinburgh EH3 5HZ, Scotland.

HENLEY, Elizabeth Becker; Playwright; b. 8 May 1952, Jackson, Mississippi, USA. *Education:* BFA, Southern Methodist University. *Publications:* Crimes of the Heart, 1981; The Wake of Jamey Foster, 1982; Am I Blue, 1982; The Miss Firecracker Contest, 1984; The Lucky Spot, 1987; The Debutante Ball, 1988; Abundance, 1990; Control Freaks, 1993. *Honours:* Pulitzer Prize for Drama, 1981; New York Drama Critics Circle Best Play Award, 1981; George Oppenheimer/Newsday Playwriting Award, 1981. *Literary Agent:* William Morris Agency, 1325 Avenue of the Americas, New York, NY 10019, USA.

HENNESSY, Helen (see Vendler, Helen).

HENNESSY, Peter (John); Prof. of Contemporary History and Writer; b. 28 March 1947, London, England; m. Enid Mary Candler, 14 June 1969, two d. *Education:* BA, St John's College, Cambridge, 1969; LSE, 1969–71; Kennedy Memorial Scholar, Harvard University, 1971–72; PhD, Cantab, 1990. *Career:* Senior Fellow, 1984–85, Visiting Fellow, 1986–91, Policy Studies Institute; Columnist, New Statesman, 1986–87, The Independent, 1987–91; Co-Founder and Co-Dir, 1986–89, Mem. of the Board, 1989–98, Institute of Contemporary British History; Visiting Fellow, University of Reading, 1988–94, Royal Institute of Public Administration, 1989–92, University of Nottingham, 1989–95; Visiting Prof. of Government, University of Strathclyde, 1989–; Partner, Intellectual R and D, 1990–; Prof. of Contemporary History, Queen Mary and Westfield College, University of London, 1992–; Gresham Prof. of Rhetoric, Gresham College, London, 1994–97; Chair., Kennedy Memorial Trust, 1995–2000; mem. Fellow, Royal Historial Society, vice-pres., 1996–; FRSA; Johnian Society, pres., 1995. *Publications:* States of Emergency (with Keith Jeffery), 1983; Sources Close to the Prime Minister (with Michael Cockerell and David Walker), 1984; What the Papers Never Said, 1985; Cabinet, 1986; Whitehall, 1989; Never Again: Britain, 1945–51, 1992; The Hidden Wiring: Unearthing the British Constitution, 1995; Muddling Through: Power, Politics and the Quality of Government in Postwar Britain, 1996; The Prime Minister: The Office and Its Holders Since 1945, 2001; The Secret State: Whitehall and the Cold War 1945–70, 2002. Contributions: scholarly books and journals, and to radio and television. *Honours:* Duff Cooper Prize, 1993; NCR Book Award for Non-Fiction, 1994; Hon. doctorates, University of West of England 1995, University of Westminster, 1996, Kingston University, 1998. *Address:* c/o Dept of History, Queen Mary and Westfield College, University of London, Mile End Rd, London E1 4NS, England.

HENNING JOCELYN, Ann Margareta Maria, (Countess of Roden), BA; writer, dramatist, translator and broadcaster; b. 5 Aug. 1948, Göteborg, Sweden; m. Earl of Roden 1986; one s. *Education:* University of Lund. *Career:* Artistic Dir, Connemara Theatre Co; mem. Irish Playwrights' and Scriptwriters' Guild; Irish Writers' Union. *Publications:* Modern Astrology, 1983; The Connemare Whirlwind Trilogy, 1990–94; Keylines, 2000. Plays: Smile, 1972; Baptism of Fire, 1997; The Alternative, 1998. Contributions: Swedish and Irish radio and television.

HENRY, Desmond Paul; Philosopher, Artist and Inventor; b. 5 July 1921, Huddersfield, Yorkshire, England; m. Louise H. J. Bayen 19 May 1945; three d. *Education:* BA, Philosophy, Univ. of Leeds, 1949; PhD, Univ. of

Manchester, 1960. *Career:* Philosophy Teacher, Univ. of Manchester, 1949–82; Visiting Prof., Brown Univ., 1966, Univ. of Pennsylvania, 1970; mem. Manchester Medieval Society. *Publications:* The Logic of St Anselm, 1967; Medieval Logic and Metaphysics, 1972; Commentary on De Grammatico, 1974; That Most Subtle Question, 1984; Medieval Meréology, 1991. Contributions: various publications; exhibitions in London and Manchester. *Address:* 15 Oakwood House, Corkland Rd, Chorlton-cum-Hardy, Manchester M21 8TX, England.

HENRY, Stuart (Dennis); Prof. of Sociology, Writer and Ed.; b. 18 Oct. 1949, London, England; m. Lee Doric, 5 March 1988. *Education:* BA, Sociology, 1972, PhD, Sociology, 1976, University of Kent. *Career:* Research Sociologist, University of London, 1975–78; Research Fellow, Middlesex University, 1978–79; Senior Lecturer, Nottingham Trent University, 1979–83; Asst Prof., Old Dominion University, Norfolk, Virginia, 1984–87; Prof., Eastern Michigan University, 1987–98; Co-Ed., Critical Criminologist, 1997–; Prof. of Sociology and Chair. of Dept of Sociology, Valparaiso University, 1998–; mem. American Sociological Asscn; American Society of Criminology. *Publications:* Self-help and Health: Mutual Aid for Modern Problems (with D. Robinson), 1977; The Hidden Economy: The Context and Control of Borderline Crime, 1978; Private Justice: Toward Integrated Theorizing in the Sociology of Law, 1983; Making Markets: An Interdisciplinary Perspective on Economic Exchange (with R. Cantor and S. Rayner), 1992; The Deviance Process (with E. H. Pfuhl), third edn, 1993; Criminological Theory (with W. Einstadter), 1995; Constitutive Criminology: Beyond Postmodernism (with D. Milovanovic), 1996; Essential Criminology (with M. Lanier), 1998. Editor: Informal Institutions: Alternative Networks in the Corporate State, 1981; The Informal Economy (with L. Ferman and M. Hoyman), 1987; Degrees of Deviance: Student Accounts of their Deviant Behavior, 1989; Work Beyond Employment in Advanced Capitalist Countries: Classic and Contemporary Perspectives on the Informal Economy (with L. Ferman and L. Berndt), 2 vols, 1993; Social Control: Aspects of Non-State Justice, 1994; Employee Dismissal: Justice at Work, 1994; Inside Jobs: A Realistic Guide to Criminal Justice Careers for College Graduates, 1994; The Criminology Theory Reader (with W. Einstadter), 1998; The Criminology Theory Reader, 1998. Contributions: scholarly books and journals. *Address:* c/o Dept of Sociology, Valparaiso University, Valparaiso, IN 46383, USA.

HENSHER, Philip Michael, BA, PhD, FRSL; British novelist; b. 20 Feb. 1965, London, England. *Education:* Lady Margaret Hall, Oxford, Jesus Coll., Cambridge. *Career:* clerk, House of Commons 1990–96; chief book reviewer, Spectator 1994–; art critic, Mail on Sunday 1996–; columnist, Independent; mem. RSL (mem. of Council 2000–). *Publications:* Other Lulus 1994, Kitchen Venom 1996, Pleasured 1998, The Bedroom of the Master's Wife (short stories) 1999, The Mulberry Empire 2002, The Fit 2004; other: libretto for opera Powder Her Face, by Thomas Adès. *Honours:* Somerset Maugham Award 1996. *Literary Agent:* AP Watt Ltd, 20 John Street, London, WC1N 2DR, England. *Address:* 83A Tennyson Street, London, SW8 3TH, England.

HEPBURN, Ronald William, MA, PhD; academic (retd) and writer; b. 16 March 1927, Aberdeen, Scotland; m. Agnes Forbes Anderson 1953; two s. one d. *Education:* Univ. of Aberdeen. *Career:* Asst 1952–55, Lecturer 1955–60, Dept of Moral Philosophy, Univ. of Aberdeen; Visiting Assoc. Prof., New York Univ. 1959–60; Prof. of Philosophy, Univ. of Nottingham 1960–64; Prof. of Philosophy 1964–75, Prof. of Moral Philosophy 1975–96, Univ. of Edinburgh; Stanton Lecturer in the Philosophy of Religion, Univ. of Cambridge 1965–68. *Publications:* Metaphysical Beliefs (jtly) 1957, Christianity and Paradox: Critical Studies in Twentieth-Century Theology 1958, Wonder and Other Essays: Eight Studies in Aesthetics and Neighbouring Fields 1984, The Reach of the Aesthetic 2001; contrib. to scholarly books and journals. *Address:* 8 Albert Terrace, Edinburgh, EH10 5EA, Scotland.

HERALD, Kathleen (see Peyton, Kathleen Wendy).

HERBERT, Brian Patrick; Author; b. 29 June 1947, Seattle, WA, USA. *Education:* BA, Sociology, University of California at Berkeley, 1968. *Career:* mem. L-5 Society; National Writers Club; SFWA; Horror Writers Asscn. *Publications:* Classic Comebacks, 1981; Incredible Insurance Claims, 1982; Sidney's Comet, 1983; The Garbage Chronicles, 1984; Sudanna, Sudanna, 1985; Man of Two Worlds (with Frank Herbert), 1986; Prisoners of Arionn, 1987; The Notebooks of Frank Herbert's Dune (ed.), 1988; Memorymakers (with Marie Landis), 1991; The Race for God, 1990; Never As It Seems (ed.), 1992; Songs of Muad' Dib (ed.), 1992; Blood on the Sun (with Marie Landis), 1996; House Atreides (with Kevin J. Anderson), 1999; A Whisper of Caladan Seas (with Kevin J. Anderson), 1999; House Harkonnen (with Kevin J. Anderson), 2001. Contributions: Short stories in various anthologies and other publications. *Address:* PO Box 10164, Bainbridge Island, WA 98110, USA.

HERBERT, James John; writer; b. 8 April 1943, London, England. *Education:* Hornsey College of Art. *Publications:* The Rats, 1974; The Fog, 1975; The Survivor, 1976; Fluke, 1977; The Spear, 1978; Lair, 1979; The Dark, 1980; The Jonah, 1981; Shrine, 1983; Domain, 1984; Moon, 1985; The Magic Cottage, 1986; Sepulchre, 1987; Haunted, 1988; Creed, 1990; Portent, 1992; James Herbert: By Horror Haunted, 1992; James Herbert's Dark Places, 1993; The City, 1994; The Ghosts of Sleath, 1994; '48, 1996; Others, 1999; Once..., 2001; Devil in the Dark: Biography, 2003; Nobody True, 2003. Films: The Rats, 1982; The Survivor, 1986; Fluke, 1995; Haunted, 1995. *Literary Agent:* David Higham Associates, 5–8 Lower John Street, Golden Square, London W1F 9HA, England. *Website:* www.jamesherbert.net.

HERBST, Philip H., BA, PhD; editor, writer and researcher; b. 1 June 1944, Peoria, IL, USA. *Education:* University of Illinois, Cornell University. *Career:* Instructor in Anthropology, SUNY at Potsdam, 1971–74; Visiting Scholar, Northwestern University, 1989–92. *Publications:* A Multicultural Dictionary: A Guide to Ethnic and Racial Words, 1993; The Color of Words: An Encyclopedic Dictionary of Ethnic Bias in the United States, 1997. Contributions: several publications. *Address:* 2415 Central Street, Evanston, IL 60201, USA.

HERDMAN, John Macmillan; Writer; b. 20 July 1941, Edinburgh, Scotland; m. 1st Dolina Maclennan 30 July 1983 (divorced); m. 2nd Mary Ellen Watson 17 Aug. 2002. *Education:* BA, 1963, MA, 1967, PhD, 1988, Magdalene College, Cambridge. *Career:* Creative Writing Fellow, Edinburgh University, 1977–79; William Soutar Fellow, Perth, Scotland, 1990–91. *Publications:* Descent, 1968; A Truth Lover, 1973; Memoirs of My Aunt Minnie/Clapperton, 1974; Pagan's Pilgrimage, 1978; Stories Short and Tall, 1979; Voice Without Restraint: Bob Dylan's Lyrics, 1982; Three Novellas, 1987; The Double in Nineteenth-Century Fiction, 1990; Imelda and Other Stories, 1993; Ghostwriting, 1996; Cruising (play), 1997; Poets, Pubs, Polls and Pillarboxes, 1999; Four Tales, 2000; The Sinister Cabaret, 2001. *Honours:* Scottish Arts Council Book Awards, 1978, 1993. *Address:* Roselea, Bridge of Tilt, Pitlochry, Perthshire PH18 5SX, Scotland.

HERMANN, Judith; German writer; b. 1970, Berlin. *Publications:* Sommerhaus Spaeter (short stories) 1999, Nothing But Ghosts (novel, in trans.) 2004. *Address:* c/o Flamingo, HarperCollins Publishers Ltd, 77–85 Fulham Palace Road, London, W6 8JB, England.

HERNDON, Nancy Ruth; Writer; b. 29 May 1934, St Louis, MO, USA; m. William C. Herndon, 27 Dec. 1956, two s. *Education:* BA, English; BJ, 1956; MA, English, 1958, Rice University. *Career:* Lecturer in English, Rice University, 1956–58, New York University, 1959–61, University of Mississippi, 1963–63, Florida Atlantic University, 1966, University of Texas at El Paso, 1976–81; mem. Sisters in Crime; South West Writer's Workshop. *Publications:* Wanton Angel, 1989; Widow's Fire, 1990; Virgin Fire, 1991; Bride Fire, 1992; The Fourth Gift, 1993; Elusive Lovers, 1994; Acid Bath, 1995; Lethal Statues, 1996; Time Bombs, 1997; C.O.P. Out, 1998; Casanova Crimes, 1999; Crime Brulee, 2001. *Honours:* El Paso Writers Hall of Fame, 1997. *Address:* 6504 Pino Dr., El Paso, TX 79912, USA.

HERRA, Maurice (see Asselineau, Roger Maurice).

HERRERA, Juan Felipe; American poet and writer; b. 27 Dec. 1948, Fowler, CA. *Career:* Assoc. Prof. of Chicano and Latin American Studies, California State Univ., Fresno. *Publications include:* poetry: Facegames 1987, Akrilika 1989, Love After the Riots 1996, Night Train to Tuxlta, Mayan Drifter: Chicano Poet in the Lowlands of America 1997, Laughing Out Loud I Fly: Poems in Spanish and English 1998; novels: Crashboomlove: A Novel in Verse 1999; juvenile: The Upside Down Boy 2000, Calling the Doves 2001. *Address:* c/o Curbstone Press, 321 Jackson Street, Willimantic, CT 06226-1738, USA. *Website:* www.curbstone.org.

HERSH, Burton David; Author and Biographer; b. 18 Sept. 1933, Chicago, IL, USA; m. Ellen Eiseman, 3 Aug. 1957, one s. one d. *Education:* BA magna cum laude, Harvard College, 1955; Fulbright Scholar, 1955–56. *Career:* mem. Authors' Guild; American Society of Journalists and Authors; PEN. *Publications:* The Ski People, 1968; The Education of Edward Kennedy, 1972; The Mellon Family, 1978; The Old Boys, 1992; The Shadow Pres., 1997. Contributions: many magazines. *Honours:* Book Find Selection, 1972; Book-of-the-Month Club, 1978. *Address:* PO Box 433, Bradford, NH 03221, USA.

HERSH, Seymour M., BA; American journalist and writer; b. 8 April 1937, Chicago, IL; m. Elizabeth Sarah Klein 1964; two s. one d. *Education:* Univ. of Chicago. *Career:* corresp. United Press International 1962–63, Associated Press 1963–67, The New Yorker 1992–; mem. of staff New York Times 1972–79; nat. corresp. Atlantic Monthly 1983–86. *Publications:* Chemical and Biological Warfare: America's Hidden Arsenal 1968, My Lai 4: A Report on the Massacre and Its Aftermath 1970, Cover-Up: The Army's Secret Investigation of the Massacre of My Lai 1972, The Price of Power: Kissinger in the Nixon White House 1983, The Target is Destroyed: What Really Happened to Flight 007 and What America Knew About It 1986, The Samson Option: Israel's Nuclear Arsenal and America's Foreign Policy 1991, The Dark Side of Camelot 1997, Against All Enemies: Gulf War Syndrome: The War Between America's Ailing Veterans and Their Government 1999; contribs to various magazines. *Honours:* Pulitzer Prize for International Reporting 1970, George Polk Memorial Awards 1970, 1973, 1974, 1981, Scripps-Howard Public Service Award 1973, Sidney Hillman Award 1974, John Peter Zenger Freedom of the Press Award 1975, Los Angeles Times Book Prize 1983, National Book Critics Circle Award 1983, Investigative Reporters and Eds Prizes 1983, 1992. *Address:* 1211 Connecticut Ave NW, Suite 320, Washington, DC 20036, USA.

HERTMANS, Stefan; Belgian novelist and poet; b. 31 March 1951, Ghent. *Career:* Prof. of Academy of Fine Arts, Ghent. *Publications:* Ruimte (trans.

as Space) 1981, Melksteen 1986, Zoutsneeuw 1987, Gestolde wolken 1987, Bezoekingen Gedichten 1988, Oorverdovende Steen: Essays over literatuur 1988, Steden: Verhalen onderweg 1988, Sneeuwdoosjes 1989, De grenzen van woestijnen Verhalen 1989, Kopnaad: Eentekstvoor vier stemmen 1992, Muziek voor de overtocht: Gedichten 1994, Naar Merelbeke 1994, Francescos paradox: Gedichten 1995, Fugas en pimpelmezen: Over actualiteit, kunst en Kritiek 1995, Annunciaties 1997, Het bedenkelijke 1999, Goya als hond 1999, Mind the Gap 2000, Intercities: Topographics 2001, Als op de eerste dag (trans. as Like the First Day) 2001. *Address:* c/o J.M. Meulenhoff BV, PO Box 100, 1000 AC, Amsterdam, Netherlands.

HERVEY, Evelyn (see Keating, Henry Reynard Fitzwalter).

HERZBERG, Judith; Poet and Playwright; b. 4 Nov. 1934, Amsterdam, Netherlands. *Education:* Graduated, Montessori Lyceum, 1952. *Career:* Teacher at film schools in Netherlands and Israel. *Publications:* Slow Boat, 1964; Meadow Grass, 1968; Flies, 1970; Grazing Light, 1971; 27 Love Songs, 1973; Botshol, 1980; Remains of the Day, 1984; Twenty Poems, 1984; But What: Selected Poems, 1988; The Way, 1992; What She Meant to Paint, 1998; Small Catch, 1999. Plays: Near Archangel, 1971; It Is Not a Dog, 1973; That Day May Dawn, 1974; Lea's Wedding, 1982; The Fall of Icarus, 1983; And/Or, 1984; The Little Mermaid, 1986; Scratch, 1989; Lulu (adaptation of Wedekind), 1989; A Good Head, 1991; Rijgraad, 1995; The Nothing-factory, 1997; Wie Is Van Wie, 1999; Simon, 2002. Other: Texts for the stage and film, 1972–88; Screenplays and television plays; Trans, including The Trojan Women, by Euripides, and Ghosts, by Ibsen. *Honours:* Netherlands-Vlaamse Drama Prize, 1989; Constantijn Huyens Prize, 1995; P. C. Hooft Prize for Poetry, 1997. *Address:* c/o De Harmonie, PO Box 3547, 1001 AH Amsterdam, Netherlands.

HESKETH, Phoebe; Lecturer (retd), Poet and Writer; b. 29 Jan. 1909, Preston, Lancashire, England. *Career:* Lecturer, Bolton Women's College, 1967–69; Teacher of Creative Writing, Bolton School, 1977–79. *Publications:* Poetry: Lean Forward, Spring, 1948; No Time for Cowards, 1952; Out of the Dark, 1954; Between Wheels and Stars, 1956; The Buttercup Children, 1958; Prayer for Sun, 1966; A Song of Sunlight, 1974; Preparing to Leave, 1977; The Eighth Day, 1980; A Ring of Leaves, 1985; Over the Brook, 1985; Netting the Sun: New and Collected Poems, 1989; Sundowner, 1992; The Leave Train, New and Selected Poems, 1994; A Box of Silver Birch, 1997. Prose: My Aunt Edith, 1966; Rivington: The Story of a Village, 1972; What Can the Matter Be?, 1985; Rivington: Village of the Mountain Ash, 1989. *Honours:* Hon. Fellow, University of Central Lancashire, 1992. *Address:* Craig yr Ysgol, Gwaenysgor, Rhyl, Clwyd LL18 6EP, Wales.

HESSAYON, David Gerald, BSc, PhD; writer; b. 13 Feb. 1928, Manchester, England; m. Joan Parker Gray 1951; two d. *Education:* Leeds University, Manchester University. *Career:* mem. Society of Authors. *Publications:* The House Plant Expert, 1980; The Armchair Book of the Garden, 1983; The Tree and Shrub Expert, 1983; The Flower Expert, 1984; The Indoor Plant Spotter, 1985; The Garden Expert, 1986; The Home Expert, 1987; The Fruit Expert, 1990; Be Your Own Greenhouse Expert, 1990; The New House Plant Expert, 1991; The Garden DIY Expert, 1992; The Rock and Water Garden Expert, 1993; The Flowering Shrub Expert, 1994; The Greenhouse Expert, 1994; The Flower Arranging Expert, 1994; The Container Expert, 1995; The Bulb Expert, 1995; The Easy-Care Gardening Expert, 1996; The New Bedding Plant Expert, 1996; The New Rose Expert, 1996; The New Vegetable and Herb Expert, 1997; The New Lawn Expert, 1997; The Evergreen Expert, 1998; The New Flower Expert, 1999; The Pocket Flower Expert, 2001; The Pocket Garden Troubles Expert, 2001; The Pocket Tree and Shrub Expert, 2001; The Pocket House Plant Expert, 2002; The Pocket Vegetable Expert, 2002. *Honours:* Lifetime Achievement Trophy, National British Book Awards, 1992; Gold Veitch Memorial Medal, Royal Horticultural Society, 1992; Gardening Book of the Year Award, 1993; Roy Hay Memorial Award, 1998. *Address:* c/o Transworld Publishers, 61–63 Uxbridge Road, London W5 5SA, England.

HETHERINGTON, Norriss Swigart; University Research Assoc. and Writer; b. 30 Jan. 1942, Berkeley, CA, USA; m. Edith Wiley White, 10 Dec. 1966, one s. one d. *Education:* BA, 1963, MA, 1965, MA, 1967, University of California, Berkeley; PhD, Indiana University, 1970. *Career:* Lecturer in Physics and Astronomy, Agnes Scott College, Decatur, GA, 1967–68; Asst Prof. of Mathematics and Science, York University, Toronto, Ontario, 1970–72; Administrative Specialist, National Aeronautics and Space Aministration, 1972; Asst Prof. of History, University of Kansas, 1972–76; Asst Prof. of Science, Technology and Society, Razi University, Sanandaj, Iran, 1976–77; Visiting Scholar, University of Cambridge, 1977–78; Research Assoc., Office for History of Science and Technology, University of Calfornia, Berkeley, 1978–; Assoc. Prof. of the History of Science, University of Oklahoma at Norman, 1981; Dir, Institute for the History of Astronomy, 1988–. *Publications:* Ancient Astronomy and Civilization, 1987; Science and Objectivity: Episodes in the History of Astronomy, 1988; The Edwin Hubble Papers, 1990; Encyclopedia of Cosmology, 1993; Cosmology: Historical, Literary, Philosophical, Religious and Scientific Perspectives, 1993; Hubble's Cosmology: A Guided Study of Selected Texts, 1996. *Honours:* Goddard Historical Essay Award, 1974. *Address:* Office for History of Science and Technology, 543 Stephens Hall, University of California at Berkeley, Berkeley, CA 94720, USA.

HETTICH, Michael; Prof. and Writer; b. 25 Sept. 1953, New York, NY, USA; m. Colleen Ahern, 7 Feb. 1980, one s. one d. *Education:* BA, Hobart College, 1975; MA, University of Denver, 1979; PhD, University of Miami, 1990. *Publications:* Lathe, 1987; White Birds, 1989; A Small Boat, 1990; Immaculate Bright Rooms, 1994; Many Simple Things, 1997; Sleeping With The Light On; The Point of Touching. Contributions: Poetry East; Witness; Literary Review; Miami Herald; Salt Hills Journal. *Honours:* State of Florida Artist Fellowship. *Address:* 561 NE 95th St, Miami Shores, FL 33138, USA.

HEWETT, Dorothy (Coade); Poet, Writer and Dramatist; b. 21 May 1923, Perth, WA, Australia. *Education:* BA, 1961, MA, 1963, University of Western Australia. *Publications:* Bobbin Up (novel), 1959; What About the People? (poems with Merv Lilly), 1962; The Australians Have a Word for It (short stories), 1964; Windmill Country (poems), 1968; The Hidden Journey (poems), 1969; The Chapel Perilous, or The Perilous Adventures of Sally Bonner, 1971; Sandgropers: A Western Australian Anthology, 1973; Rapunzel in Suburbia (poems), 1975; Miss Hewett's Shenanigans, 1975; Greenhouse (poems), 1979; The Man from Mukinupin (play), 1979; Susannah's Dreaming (play), 1981; The Golden Oldies (play), 1981; Selected Poems, 1990; Wild Card (autobiog.), 1990. *Honours:* AM, 1986. *Address:* 195 Bourke St, Darlinghurst, NSW 2011, Australia.

HEYEN, William (Helmuth); Prof. of English, Poet and Writer; b. 1 Nov. 1940, New York, NY, USA; m. Hannelore Greiner, 7 July 1962, one s. one d. *Education:* BS, Education, SUNY at Brockport, 1961; MA, English, 1963, PhD, English, 1967, Ohio University. *Career:* Asst Prof. to Prof. of English and Poet-in-Residence, SUNY at Brockport, 1967–2000; Senior Fulbright Lecturer in American Literature, 1971–72; Visiting Creative Writer, University of Wisconsin at Milwaukee, 1980; Visiting Writer, Hofstra University, 1981, 1983, Southampton College, 1984, 1985; Visiting Prof. of English, University of Hawaii, 1985. *Publications:* Depth of Field, 1970; Noise in the Trees: Poems and a Memoir, 1974; American Poets in 1976 (ed.), 1976; The Swastika Poems, 1977; Long Island Light: Poems and a Memoir, 1979; The City Parables, 1980; Lord Dragonfly: Five Sequences, 1981; Erika: Poems of the Holocaust, 1984; The Generation of 2000: Contemporary American Poets (ed.), 1984; Vic Holyfield and the Class of 1957: A Romance, 1986; The Chestnut Rain: A Poem, 1986; Brockport, New York: Beginning with 'And', 1988; Falling From Heaven (co-author), 1991; Pterodactyl Rose: Poems of Ecology, 1991; Ribbons: The Gulf War, 1991; The Host: Selected Poems 1965–1990, 1994; With Me Far Away: A Memoir, 1994; Crazy Horse in Stillness: Poems, 1996; Pig Notes and Dumb Music: Prose on Poetry, 1998; Diana, Charles and the Queen: Poems, 1998; September 11, 2001: American Writers Respond, 2002; The Hummingbird Corporation: Stories, 2002; Home: Autobiographies, Etc., 2002. Contributions: many books, chapbooks, journals and magazines. *Honours:* Borestone Mountain Poetry Prize, 1965; National Endowment for the Arts Fellowships, 1973–74, 1984–85; American Library Asscn Notable American Book, 1974; Ontario Review Poetry Prize, 1977; Guggenheim Fellowship, 1977–78; Eunice Tietjens Memorial Award, 1978; Witter Bynner Prize for Poetry, 1982; New York Foundation for the Arts Poetry Fellowship, 1984–85; Lillian Fairchild Award, 1996; Small Press Book Award for Poetry, 1997. *Address:* c/o Dept of English, State University of New York at Brockport, Brockport, NY 14420, USA.

HIBBERT, Christopher, MA; writer; b. 5 March 1924, Enderby, Leicestershire, England; m. Susan Piggford 1948; two s. one d. *Education:* Oriel College, Oxford. *Career:* served in Italy, 1944–45; Captain, London Irish Rifles; Military Cross; partner, firm of land agents, auctioneers and surveyors 1948–59. *Publications:* The Road to Tyburn, 1957; King Mob, 1958; Wolfe at Quebec, 1959; The Destruction of Lord Raglan, 1961; Corunna, 1961; Benito Mussolini, 1962; The Battle of Arnhem, 1962; The Roots of Evil, 1963; The Court at Windsor, 1964; Agincourt, 1964; The Wheatley Diary (ed.), 1964; Garibaldi and His Enemies, 1965; The Making of Charles Dickens, 1967; Waterloo: Napoleon's Last Campaign (ed.), 1967; An American in Regency England: The Journal of Louis Simond (ed.), 1968; Charles I, 1968; The Grand Tour, 1969; London: Biography of a City, 1969; The Search for King Arthur, 1970; Anzio: The Bid for Rome, 1970; The Dragon Wakes: China and the West, 1793–1911, 1970; The Personal History of Samuel Johnson, 1971; George IV, Prince of Wales 1762–1811, 1972; George IV, Regent and King 1812–1830, 1973; The Rise and Fall of the House of Medici, 1974; Edward VII: A Portrait, 1976; The Great Mutiny: India, 1857, 1978; The French Revolution, 1981; Africa Explored: Europeans in the Dark Continent, 1796–1889, 1982; The London Encyclopaedia (ed.), 1983; Queen Victoria in Her Letters and Journals, 1984; Rome: The Biography of a City, 1985; Cities and Civilizations, 1985; The English: A Social History, 1987; Venice: Biography of a City, 1988; The Encyclopaedia of Oxford (ed.), 1988; Redcoats and Rebels: The War for America 1760–1781, 1990; The Virgin Queen: The Personal History of Elizabeth I, 1990; Captain Gronow: His Reminiscences of Regency and Victorian Life (ed.), 1991; Cavaliers and Roundheads: The English at War 1642–1649, 1993; Florence: Biography of a City, 1993; Nelson: A Personal History, 1994; Wellington: A Personal History, 1997; George III: A Personal History, 1998; Queen Victoria: A Personal History, 2000; The Marlboroughs: John and Sarah Churchill 1650–1744, 2001; Napoleon: His Wives and Women, 2002; Disraeli: A Personal History 2004. *Honours:* Heinemann Award for Literature, 1962; McColvin Medal, 1989; Hon. DLitt, Leicester University, 1996. *Literary Agent:* David Higham Associates, 5–8 Lower John Street, Golden Square, London W1F 9HA, England.

HICK, John Harwood, MA, DLitt, DPhil, PhD; academic and writer; b. 20 Jan. 1922, Scarborough, Yorkshire, England; m. Joan Hazel Bowers 1953; three s. one d. *Education:* Univ. of Edinburgh, Univ. of Oxford, Westminster Theological Coll., Univ. of Cambridge. *Career:* Ordained to the Ministry, Presbyterian Church of England 1953; Minister, Belford Presbyterian Church, Northumberland, England 1953–56; Asst Prof. of Philosophy, Cornell Univ. 1956–59; Stuart Prof. of Christian Philosophy, Princeton Theological Seminary 1959–64; Lecturer 1964–67, Arthur Stanley Eddington Memorial Lecturer 1972, Stanton Lecturer 1974–77, Univ. of Cambridge; H. G. Wood Prof. of Theology, Birmingham Univ. 1967–82; Ingersoll Lecturer, Harvard Univ. 1977; Danforth Prof. of the Philosophy of Religion, Claremont Graduate Univ., CA 1979–92; Gifford Lecturer, Univ. of Edinburgh 1986–87; numerous other lectureships; mem. American Acad. of Religion, American Philosophical Asscn, British Soc. for the Philosophy of Religion (vice-pres. 1994–), World Congress of Faiths (vice-pres. 1993–). *Publications:* Faith and Knowledge 1957, The Philosophy of Religion 1963, Evil and the God of Love 1966, God and the Universe of Faiths 1973, Death and Eternal Life 1976, God Has Many Names 1980, Problems of Religious Pluralism 1985, An Interpretation of Religion 1989, Disputed Questions in Theology and the Philosophy of Religion 1993, The Metaphor of God Incarnate 1993, The Rainbow of Faiths 1995, The Fifth Dimension 1999, Dialogues in the Philosophy of Religion 2001, John Hick: An Autobiography 2003. *Honours:* Guggenheim Fellowships 1963–64, 1985–86, Leverhulme Research Fellowships 1976, 1990, Hon. DTheol (Uppsala Univ.) 1977, Hon. DD (Glasgow Univ.) 2002, Grawemeyer Award in Religion 1991. *Address:* 144 Oak Tree Lane, Selly Oak, Birmingham B29 6HU, England. *E-mail:* j.h.hick@bham.ac.uk. *Website:* www.johnhick.org.uk.

HICKOK, Gloria Vando (see Vando (Hickok), Gloria).

HICKSON, Jill Lesley Norton, MBA; Australian literary agent and business executive; b. 28 Sept. 1948; m. Neville K. Wran 1976; one d. *Education:* Univ. of Sydney and Australian Graduate School of Management. *Career:* Programmer/Announcer 2MBS FM 1975–76; Int. Relations Man. Quantas Airways 1976–81; Literary Agent and Man. Dir Hickson Assocs Pty Ltd 1983–99; consultant Curtis Brown Australia Pty Ltd 1999–; mem. Bd Dirs Ansett NZ, NSW Conservatorium of Music 1984–89, Sydney Opera House Trust 1985–89, Sydney Symphony Orchestra 1986; mem. Australian Inst. of Int. Affairs, Australian Soc. of Authors, Australian Writers' Guild, Grad. Man. Asscn; Patron Fellowship of Australian Writers, United Music Teachers' Asscn of NSW, 2MBS FM Music Foundation, Domestic Animal Birth Control Soc.; mem. Cttee State Library NSW Foundation, Art Gallery NSW Foundation; Cecil Hall Prize, Australian Inst. of Man. 1972; Schroder Darling Finance Prize; Inst. of Dirs Prize. *Address:* POB 271, Woollahra, NSW 2025, Australia.

HIGGINBOTHAM, (Prieur) Jay; archivist and writer; b. 16 July 1937, Pascagoula, MS, USA; m. Alice Louisa Martin 1970; two s. one d. *Education:* BA, University of Mississippi, 1960; Graduate Studies, Hunter College, CUNY, American University, Washington, DC. *Career:* Head, Local History Dept, Mobile Public Library, 1973–83; Dir, Mobile Municipal Archives, 1983–; mem. Chair., Mobile Assembly of Sages and Savants, 1983–2001. *Publications:* The Mobile Indians, 1966; The World Around, 1966; Family Biographies, 1967; The Pascagoula Indians, 1967; Pascagoula: Singing River City, 1968; Mobile: City by the Bay, 1968; The Journal of Sauvole, 1969; Fort Maurepas: The Birth of Louisiana, 1969, re-published, 1998; Brother Holyfield, 1972; A Voyage to Dauphin Island, 1974; Old Mobile: Fort Louis de la Louisiane, 1702–1711, 1977; Fast Train Russia, 1983; Autumn in Petrishchevo, 1986; Discovering Russia, 1989; Mauvila, 1990; Kazula (play), 1991; Man, Nature and the Infinite, 1998; Alma, 2002. Contributions: Library Journal; The Humanist; Harvard International Review; Soviet Literature; Louisiana History; Encyclopaedia Britannica. *Honours:* General L. Kemper Williams Prize, Louisiana Historical Asscn, 1977; Award of Merit, Mississippi Historical Society, 1978; Alabama Library Asscn, Non-Fiction Award, 1978; Gilbert Chinard Prize, 1978. *Address:* 60 N Monterey Street, Mobile, AL 36604, USA.

HIGGINS, Aidan; writer; b. 3 March 1927, Celbridge, County Kildare, Ireland. *Education:* Clongowes Wood College, County Kildare. *Publications:* Stories Felo De Se, 1960; Langrishe, Go Down, 1966; Balcony of Europe, 1972; Scenes from a Receding Past, 1977; Bornholm Night Ferry, 1983; Helsingor Station and Other Departures, 1989; Ronda Gorge and Other Precipices: Travel Writings, 1959–90; Lions of The Grunewald (novel), 1993; Donkey's Years (Memories of a Life as Story Told), 1995; Secker, Flotsam and Jetsam (collected stories), 1997; Dog Days, 1998. *Honours:* British Arts Council Grant; James Tait Black Memorial Prize, 1967; Irish Acad. of Letters Award, 1970; American Ireland Fund, 1977.

HIGGINS, Jack (see Patterson, Henry (Harry)).

HIGGINS, Rita Ann; Irish poet and playwright; b. 1955, Galway. *Career:* writer-in-residence, Galway County 1987, National Univ. of Ireland, Galway 1994–95, Offaly County Council 1998–99; Green Honors Prof., Texas Christian Univ., USA 2000. *Plays:* Face Licker Come Home 1991, God of the Hatch Man 1992, Colie Lally Doesn't Live in a Bucket 1993, Down All the Roundabouts 1999. *Publications:* poetry: Goddess on the Mervue Bus 1986, Witch in the Bushes 1988, Goddess and Witch 1990, Philomena's Revenge 1992, Higher Purchase 1996, Sunny Side Plucked: New and Selected Poems 1996, An Awful Racket 2001; editor: Out the Clara Road: The Offaly Anthology 1999. *Honours:* Peadar O'Donnell Award 1989. *Address:* c/o Bloodaxe Books Ltd, Highgreen, Tarset, Northumberland NE48 1RP, England. *Website:* www.bloodaxebooks.com.

HIGH, Peter Brown; Prof. and Writer; b. 6 Sept. 1944, New York, NY, USA; m. 21 Oct. 1972, one s. *Education:* BA, American University, 1966; MA, California State University, 1982; PhD, Nagoya University, 1985. *Career:* Columnist, Asahi Shimbun, Japanese Language, 1987–92; Prof. of Film and Literature, Nagoya University, 1987–. *Publications:* An Outline of American Literature, 1985; Read All About It, 1986; A Journalist Looks at Popular Culture, 1991; The Imperial Screen: Japanese Cinema and the 15-Year War, 1995; A History of Cinema, 1997; Assorted language textbooks in the ESL field. Contributions: journals. *Address:* 43 Meidai Shukusha, Kogawa-cho, Chikusa-ku, Nagoya, Japan.

HIGHAM, Charles; Writer; b. 18 Feb. 1931, London, England. *Career:* Film Critic, Nation, Sydney, 1961–63; Literary Ed., The Bulletin, Sydney, 1963–68; Hollywood Feature Writer, New York Times, 1971–80; Visiting Regents' Prof., University of California at Santa Cruz, 1990. *Publications:* The Earthbound and Other Poems, 1959; Noonday Country: Poems 1954–1865, 1966; The Celluloid Muse: Hollywood Directors Speak (ed. with J. Greenberg), 1969; Hollywood in the Forties (ed. with J. Greenberg), 1969; The Films of Orson Welles, 1970; The Voyage to Brindisi and Other Poems 1966–1969, 1970; Ziegfeld, 1972; Cecil B. DeMille, 1973; The Art of the American Film, 1900–1971, 1973; Ava, 1974; Kate: The Life of Katharine Hepburn, 1975; Warner Brothers, 1975; Charles Laughton: An Intimate Biography, 1976; Marlene: The Life of Marlene Dietrich, 1977; Errol Flynn: The Untold Story, 1980; Star Maker: The Autobiography of Hal B. Wallis, 1980; Bette: The Life of Bette Davis, 1981; Trading with the Enemy: An Exposae of the Nazi-American Money Plot 1933–1949, 1983; Princess Merle (with Roy Moseley), 1983; Sisters: The Story of Olivia de Haviland and Joan Fontaine, 1984; Audrey: The Life of Audrey Hepburn, 1984; American Swastika, 1985; Orson Welles: The Rise and Fall of an American Genius, 1986; Palace: My Life in the Royal Family of Monaco (with Baron C. de Massy), 1986; Brando: The Unauthorized Biography, 1987; Wallis: The Secret Lives of the Duchess of Windsor, 1988; Cary Grant: The Lonely Heart (with Roy Moseley), 1989; Elizabeth and Philip: The Untold Story of the Queen of England and Her Prince (with Roy Moseley), 1991; Rose: The Life of Rose Fitzgerald Kennedy, 1994; The Civilization of Angkor, 2001. Contributions: newspapers, reviews, and magazines. *Address:* John Hawkins and Sons, 71 W 23rd St, New York, NY 100010, USA.

HIGHAM, Robin David Stewart; American academic, writer and editor; b. 20 June 1925, London, England; m. Barbara Davies 1950; one s. three d. (two deceased). *Education:* AB, 1950, PhD, 1957, Harvard University; MA, Claremont Graduate School, CA, 1953. *Career:* Instructor, University of Massachusetts, 1954–57; Asst Prof., University of North Carolina at Chapel Hill, 1957–63; Assoc. Prof., 1963–66, Prof. of History, 1966–, Kansas State University; Ed., 1968–88, Ed. Emeritus, 1989–, Military Affairs; Ed., 1970–88, Ed. Emeritus, 1989–, Aerospace Historian; Founder-Pres., Sunflower University Press, 1977–; Ed. and Co-Publisher, Journal of the West, 1977–; mem. International Commission of Military History. *Publications:* Britain's Imperial Air Routes, 1918–39, 1960; The British Rigid Airship, 1908–31, 1961; Armed Forces in Peacetime: Britain, 1918–39, 1963; The Military Intellectuals in Britain, 1918–39, 1966; A Short History of Warfare (with David H. Zook), 1966; Air Power: A Concise History, 1973; The Compleat Academic, 1975; A Brief Guide to Scholarly Editing (with Mary Cisper and Guy Dresser), 1982; Diary of a Disaster: British Aid to Greece, 1940–41, 1986; The Bases of Air Strategy 1915–1945, 1998. Editor: various books, including: Civil Wars in the Twentieth Century, 1972; A Guide to the Sources of British Military History, 1971; A Guide to the Sources of US Military History, 1975; The Rise of the Wheat State: A History of Kansas Agriculture (with George E. Ham), 1986; Russian Aviation and Air Power (with John T. Greenwood and Von Handesty), 1998; A Military History of Tsarist Russia (with Frederick W. Kagan), 2001; A Military History of the Soviet Union (with Frederick W. Kagan), 2001; A Military History of China (with David Graff), 2001. Contributions: Reference works, scholarly books, and professional journals. *Honours:* Social Science Research Council National Security Policy Research Fellow, 1960–61; Victor Gondos Award, 1983, Samuel Eliot Morison Award, 1986, American Military Institute; Kansas Governor's Aviation Honor Award, 2000. *Address:* 2961 Nevada Street, Manhattan, KS 66502, USA.

HIGHLAND, Monica (see See, Carolyn).

HIGSON, Philip John Willoughby-, BA, MA, PhD, PGCE, FRHistS, FRSA, FSA; British poet, translator, editor, historian, art historian and playwright; b. 21 Feb. 1933, Newcastle-under-Lyme, Staffordshire, England. *Education:* Liverpool Univ., Keele Univ. *Career:* Lecturer, Sr Lecturer in History 1972–89, Visiting Lecturer 1989–90, Univ. Coll., Chester; Chair., Pres., Anthology Ed., Chester Poets 1974–92; Pres., The Baudelaire Soc., Chester and Paris 1992–; mem. Soc. of Authors. *Publications:* The Riposte and Other Poems 1971, Sonnets to My Goddess 1983 (re-published as Sonnets to My

Goddess in This Life and the Next 2002), Maurice Rollinat's Les Névroses: Selected English Versions (trans.) 1986 (re-published as Maurice Rollinat: A Hundred Poems from Les Névroses 2003), A Warning to Europe: The Testimony of Limouse (co-author) 1992, The Complete Poems of Baudelaire with Selected Illustrations by Limouse (ed. and principal trans.) 1992, Limouse Nudes 1994, Childhood in Wartime Keele: Poems of Reminiscence 1995, Poems on the Dee 1997, Inner City Love-Revolt: Footage from a Fifties Affair 2000, A Poet's Pilgrimage: The Shaping of a Creative Life 2000, The Jewelled Nude: A Play About Baudelaire and Queen Pomaré 2002, Poems of Sauce and Satire: A Humorous Selection 2002, Ut Pictura Poesis: Pictorial Poems 2004, Manichaean Contrasts (poems) 2004; contrib. historical articles to Oxford Dictionary of National Biography and to journals, including Antiquaries Journal, Genealogists' Magazine, Coat of Arms, Northern History, Transactions of the Historic Society of Lancashire and Cheshire, and of the Lancashire and Cheshire Antiquarian Society; poems to The Picador Book of Erotic Verse 1978, Rhyme Revival 1982, Poet's England: Staffordshire 1987, Red Candle Treasury 1998, and to journals, including Critical Quarterly, Chester Poets Anthologies, Collegian, Candelabrum, The Eclectic Muse, Mandrake Poetry Review, Cadmium Blue Literary Journal, Lexikon, Rebirth, Solar Flame, Romantic Renaissance, Rubies in the Darkness. *Honours:* First Prize for an Established Poet, The Eclectic Muse, Vancouver 1990, David St John Thomas Poetry Publication Prize 1996, prizewinner Lexikon Poetry Competition 1996, first prize Rubies in the Darkness Poetry Competition 2003. *Address:* 1 Westlands Avenue, Newcastle-under-Lyme, Staffordshire ST5 2PU, England.

HIJUELOS, Oscar, BA, MA; American writer; b. 24 Aug. 1951, New York, NY. *Education:* City Coll., CUNY. *Publications:* Our House in the Last World 1983, The Mambo Kings Play Songs of Love 1989, The Fourteen Sisters of Emilio Montez O'Brien 1993, Mr Ive's Christmas 1995, Empress of the Splendid Season 1999, A Simple Habana Melody (From When the World Was Good) 2002. *Honours:* Pushcart Press Outstanding Writer 1978, Bread Loaf Writers' Conference Scholarship 1980, Ingram Merrill Foundation Grant 1983, Nat. Endowment for the Arts Fellowship 1985, American Acad. in Rome Fellowship 1985, Pulitzer Prize in Fiction 1990. *Literary Agent:* Harriet Wasserman Literary Agency, E 36th Street, New York, NY 10016, USA.

HILDEBIDLE, John; Poet, Writer and Asst Prof. of Literature; b. 2 Feb. 1946, Hartford, CT, USA; m. Nichola Gilsdorf, 27 May 1978, one s. one d. *Education:* BA, 1967, MA, 1969, PhD, 1981, Harvard University. *Career:* Lecturer in English and American Literature, 1980–83, Mem., Extension Faculty, 1981–, Harvard University; Asst Prof. of Literature, MIT, 1983–; mem. MLA of America; National Council of Teachers of English; Thoreau Society. *Publications:* Poetry: The Old Chore, 1981; One Sleep, One Waking, 1994; Defining Absence, 1999. Other: Modernism Reconsidered (ed. with Robert J. Kiely), 1983; Thoreau: A Naturalist's Liberty, 1983; Stubborness: A Field Guide, 1986; Five Irish Writers: The Errand of Keeping Alive, 1989; A Sense of Place; Poetry from Ireland (with Dorys Crow Grover and Michael D. Riley), 1995. Contributions: anthologies and periodicals. *Honours:* Book Award, San Francisco Poetry Center, 1982; Katherine Anne Porter Prize, Tulsa Arts and Humanities Council, 1984; Anniversary Award for Poetry, Associated Writing Programs, 1984; John Gardner Short Fiction Prize, 1987. *Address:* c/o Dept of Humanities, MIT, Cambridge, MA 02139, USA.

HILL, Anthony Robert; writer and journalist; b. 24 May 1942, Melbourne, Vic., Australia; m. Gillian Mann 1965; one d. *Career:* mem. Australian Soc. of Authors. *Publications:* The Bunburyists, 1985; Antique Furniture in Australia, 1985; Birdsong, 1988; The Burnt Stick, 1994; Spindrift, 1996; The Grandfather Clock, 1996; Growing Up and Other Stories, 1999; Soldier Boy, 2001; Forbidden, 2002; Young Digger, 2002; The Shadow Dog, 2003. *Honours:* Children's Book Council of Australia Honour Book 1995, 2002; NSW Premier's Award, 2002. *Address:* PO Box 7085, Yarralumla, ACT 2600, Australia.

HILL, Douglas Arthur, (Martin Hillman); Author; b. 6 April 1935, Brandon, Manitoba, Canada; m. Gail Robinson, 8 April 1958, divorced, one s. *Education:* BA, University of Saskatchewan, 1957. *Career:* Literary Ed., Tribune, London, 1971–84; mem. Society of Authors; Children's Book Circle. *Publications:* The Supernatural, 1965; The Opening of the Canadian West, 1967; John Keats, 1969; The Scots to Canada, 1972; Galactic Warlord, 1980; The Huntsman, 1982; The Last Legionary Quartet, 1985; Penelope's Pendant, 1990; The Unicorn Dream, 1992; The Lightless Dome, 1993; The Voyage of Mudjack, 1993; World of the Stiks, 1994; The Leafless Forest, 1994; CADE: Galaxy's Edge, 1996; The Dragon Charmer, 1997; Eyewitness Witch and Wizard, 1997; Space Girls Don't Cry, 1998; Melleron's Monsters, 2000. *Address:* 3 Hillfield Ave, London N8 7DU, England.

HILL, Geoffrey (William); Prof. of Literature and Religion, Poet and Writer; b. 18 June 1932, Bromsgrove, Worcestershire, England; m. 1st Nancy Whittaker, 1956, divorced 1983, three s., one d.; m. 2nd Alice Goodman, 1987, one d. *Education:* BA, 1953, MA, 1959, Keble College, Oxford. *Career:* Staff, 1954–76, Prof. of English Literature, 1976–80, University of Leeds; Churchill Fellow, University of Bristol, 1980; University Lecturer in English and Fellow, Emmanuel College, Cambridge, 1981–88; Clark Lecturer, Trinity College, Cambridge, 1986; University Prof. and Prof. of Literature and Religion, Boston University, 1988–; mem. FRSL; American Acad. of Arts and Sciences, fellow. *Publications:* Poetry: Poems, 1952; For the Unfallen: Poems, 1952–58, 1959; Preghiere, 1964; King Log, 1968; Mercian Hymns, 1971; Somewhere is Such a Kingdom: Poems 1952–72, 1975; Tenebrae, 1978; The Mystery of the Charity of Charles Péguy, 1983; New and Collected Poems 1952–92, 1994; Canaan, 1996; Speech! Speech!, 2000. Criticism: The Lords of Limit, 1984; The Enemy's Country, 1991. Other: Brand (adaptation of Henrik Ibsen's play), 1978. *Honours:* Gregory Award, 1961; Hawthornden Prize, 1969; Alice Hunt Bartlett Award, 1971; Geoffrey Faber Memorial Prize, 1971; Whitbread Award, 1971; Duff Cooper Memorial Prize, 1979; Hon. Fellow, Keble College, Oxford, 1981, Emmanuel College, Cambridge, 1990; Loines Award, American Acad. and Institute of Arts and Letters, 1983; Ingram Merrill Foundation Award, 1988; Hon. DLitt, University of Leeds, 1988. *Address:* The University Profs, Boston University, 745 Commonwealth Ave, Boston, MA 02215, USA.

HILL, Jane (Bowers); Asst Prof., Ed., Writer and Poet; b. 17 Oct. 1950, Seneca, SC, USA; m. Robert W. Hill, 16 Aug. 1980, one d. *Education:* BA, 1972, MA, 1978, Clemson University; PhD, University of Illinois, 1985. *Career:* Assoc. Ed., Peachtree Publishers, 1986–88; Senior Ed., Longstreet Press, 1988–91; Dir, Kennesaw Summer Writers' Workshop, 1988–92; Asst Prof., West Georgia College, 1992–; mem. MLA. *Publications:* Gail Godwin, 1992. Editor: An American Christmas: A Sampler of Contemporary Stories and Poems, 1986; Our Mutual Room: Modern Literary Portraits of the Opposite Sex, 1987; Songs: New Voices in Fiction, 1990; Cobb County: At the Heart of Change, 1991. Contributions: numerous stories, poems, essays and reviews. *Honours:* Frank O'Connor Prize for Fiction, 1989; Syvenna Foundation Fellow, 1991; Monticello Fellowship for Female Writers, 1992. *Address:* 1419 Arden Dr., Marietta, GA 30060, USA.

HILL, John (see Koontz, Dean Ray).

HILL, John Spencer; Prof. of English Literature and Writer; b. 22 Oct. 1943, Brantford, ON, Canada; m. 25 June 1966, two s. one d. *Education:* BA, 1966, MA, 1968, Queen's University; PhD, University of Toronto, Canada, 1972. *Career:* Asst Prof. of English, Royal Military College of Canada, 1967–69, 1972–73; Lecturer, University of Western Australia, 1973–79; Prof. of English Literature, University of Ottawa, 1979–. *Publications:* Imaginations in Coleridge, 1978; John Milton: Poet, Priest and Prophet, 1979; The Last Castrato (novel), 1995; Ghirlandaio's Daughter (novel), 1996; Infinity, Faith and Time, 1997. Contributions: scholarly journals. *Honours:* Critics' Choice Award, San Francisco Review of Books, 1995; Arthur Ellis Award, Crime Writers of Canada, 1996. *Address:* Dept of English, University of Ottawa, Ottawa, ON K1N 6N5, Canada.

HILL, Pamela, (Sharon Fiske); Writer; b. 26 Nov. 1920, Nairobi, Kenya. *Education:* DA, Glasgow School of Art, 1943; BSc, Equivalent, University of Glasgow, 1952. *Career:* mem. RSL; Society of Authors. *Publications:* Flaming Janet, 1954; The Devil of Aske, 1972; The Malvie Inheritance, 1973; Homage to a Rose, 1979; Fire Opal, 1980; This Rough Beginning, 1981; My Lady Glamis, 1981; Summer Cypress, 1981; The House of Cray, 1982; The Governess, 1985; Venables, 1988; The Sutburys, 1987; The Brocken, 1991; The Sword and the Flame, 1991; Mercer, 1992; The Silver Runaways, 1992; O Madcap Duchess, 1993; The Parson's Children, 1993; The Man from the North, 1994; Journey Beyond Innocence, 1994; The Charmed Descent, 1995; The Inadvisable Marriages, 1995; Saints' Names for Confirmation, 1995; Alice the Palace, 1996; Murder in Store, 1996; Widow's Veil, 1997. Contributions: periodicals.

HILL, Peter; British journalist and newspaper editor. *Career:* Ed., Daily Star 1998–2003, Daily Express 2003–; mem. Press Complaints Commission (PCC) 2003–. *Honours:* Editor of the Year, What the Papers Say Awards 2002. *Address:* Daily Express, Ludgate House, 245 Blackfriars Road, London, SE1 9UX, England.

HILL, Reginald Charles, (Dick Morland, Patrick Ruell, Charles Underhill), BA; British novelist and playwright; b. 3 April 1936, West Hartlepool, Co Durham, England. *Education:* St Catherine's Coll., Oxford. *Publications:* A Clubable Woman, 1970; An Advancement of Learning, 1971; Fell of Dark, 1971; A Fairly Dangerous Thing, 1972; An Affair of Honour (play), 1972; Ruling Passion, 1973; A Very Good Hater, 1974; An April Shroud, 1975; Another Death in Venice, 1976; A Pinch of Snuff, 1978; The Spy's Wife, 1980; A Killing Kindness, 1980; Who Guards the Prince, 1982; Traitor's Blood, 1983; Dead Heads, 1983; Exit Lines, 1984; No Man's Land, 1985; Child's Play, 1987; The Collaborators, 1987; There Are No Ghosts in the Soviet Union (short stories), 1987; Underworld, 1988; Pascoe's Ghost (short stories), 1989; Bones and Silence, 1990; One Small Step, 1990; Recalled to Life, 1992; Pictures of Perfection, 1994; Blood Sympathy, 1994; The Woods Beyond, 1995; Born Guilty, 1995; Asking for the Moon, 1996; Killing the Lawyers, 1997; On Beulah Height, 1998; Singing the Sadness, 1999; Arms and the Women, 2000; Beyond the Bone, 2000; Dialogues of the Dead, 2001; Death's Jest-Book, 2002; Good Morning, Midnight, 2003; as Dick Morland: Heart Clock, 1973; Albion! Albion!, 1974; as Patrick Ruell: The Castle of Demon, 1971; Red Christmas, 1972; Death Takes the Low Road, 1974; Urn Burial, 1975; The Long Kill, 1986; Death of a Dormouse, 1987; Dream of Darkness, 1989; The Only Game, 1991; as Charles Underhill: Captain Fantom, 1978; The Forging of Fantom, 1979. *Honours:* Gold Dagger Award 1990, Diamond Dagger Award 1995. *Literary Agent:* AP Watt Ltd, 20 John Street, London, WC1N 2DR, England.

HILL, Susan Elizabeth, BA; British writer, dramatist, literary critic and publisher; b. 5 Feb. 1942, Scarborough, Yorkshire; m. Stanley W. Wells 1975; three d. (one deceased). *Education:* King's College, London. *Career:* Fellow King's College, London 1978; Presenter Bookshelf, BBC Radio 1986–87; Founder-Publisher Long Barn Books 1996–; Ed. Books and Company magazine; scriptwriter The Archers; regular contrib. to Kaleidoscope (now Front Row). *Publications:* The Enclosure 1961, Do Me a Favour 1963, Gentleman and Ladies 1969, A Change for the Better 1969, I'm the King of the Castle (Somerset Maugham Award) 1970, The Albatross (John Llewelyn Rhys Memorial Prize) 1971, Strange Meeting 1971, The Bird of Night (Whitbread Award 1972) 1972, A Bit of Singing and Dancing 1973, In the Springtime of the Year 1974, The Cold Country and Other Plays for Radio 1975, The Magic Apple Tree 1982, The Woman in Black 1983, One Night at a Time 1984, Through the Kitchen Window 1984, Through the Garden Gate 1986, Mother's Magic 1986, The Lighting of the Lamps 1987, Lanterns Across the Snow 1987, Shakespeare Country 1987, The Spirit of the Cotswolds 1988, Can it be True? (Smarties Prize) 1988, Family (autobiog.) 1989, Susie's Shoes 1989, Stories From Codling Village 1990, I've Forgotten Edward 1990, I Won't Go There Again 1990, Pirate Roll 1991, The Glass Angels 1991, The Mist in the Mirror 1992, Beware! Beware! 1993, King of Kings 1993, Mrs de Winter 1993, Reflections From a Garden (with Rory Stuart) 1995, Contemporary Women's Short Stories (ed. with Rory Stuart) 1995, Listening to the Orchestra 1996, The Second Penguin Book of Women's Short Stories (ed.) 1997, The Service of Clouds 1998, Air and Angels 1998, Diana: the Secret Years (co-author) 1998, The Boy Who Taught the Beekeeper to Read and Other Stories 2003, The Various Haunts of Men 2004. Contributions: many journals, radio. *Address:* Longmoor Farmhouse, Ebrington, Chipping Campden, Gloucestershire GL55 6NW, England. *Website:* www.susan-hill.com.

HILL, Tobias, BA; British writer, poet, editor and music critic; b. 30 March 1970, London, England. *Education:* Sussex Univ. *Career:* teacher, Apex School, Anjo, Aichi, Japan 1993–94; music critic, Telegraph on Sunday 1994–; Poetry Ed., Richmond Review 1995–96; Books Ed., Don't Tell It magazine 1995–96. *Publications:* Year of the Dog (poems) 1995, Midnight in the City (poems) 1996, Skin (short stories) 1997, Zoo (poems) 1998, Underground (novel) 1999, The Love of Stones (novel) 2002, The Cryptographer (novel) 2003; contrib. to Observer, Times, Telegraph. *Honours:* Poetry Book Society Recommendation 1996, University of Cambridge Harper-Wood Studentship for Literature 1996, Eric Gregory Award, National Poetry Foundation 1996, PEN-Macmillan Award for Fiction 1997, Ian St James Award 1997. *Address:* Flat 4, 1 Minster Road, London, NW2 3SD, England.

HILLERMAN, Tony; Prof. of Journalism Emeritus and Author; b. 27 May 1925, USA; m. Mary Unzner, 16 Aug. 1948, three s., three d. *Education:* Oklahoma State University, 1943; BA, University of Oklahoma, 1946; MA, University of New Mexico, 1966. *Career:* Reporter, Borger News Herald, Texas, 1948; City Ed., Morning Press-Constitution, Lawton, Oklahoma, 1948–50; Political Reporter, Oklahoma City, 1950–52, Bureau Man., Santa Fe, 1952–54, United Press International; Political Reporter and Exec. Ed., New Mexican, Santa Fe, 1954–63; Assoc. Prof., 1965–66, Prof. of Journalism, 1966–85, Prof. Emeritus, 1985–, University of New Mexico. *Publications:* Fiction: The Blessing Way, 1970; The Fly on the Wall, 1971; Dance Hall of the Dead, 1973; Listening Woman, 1977; The People of Darkness, 1978; The Dark Wind, 1981; Ghostway, 1984; A Thief of Time, 1985; Skinwalkers, 1986; The Joe Leaphorn Mysteries (collection), 1989; Talking God, 1989; Coyote Waits, 1990; Best of the West: An Anthology of Classic Writing from the American West (ed.), 1991; The Jim Chee Mysteries (collection), 1992; Sacred Clowns, 1993; Finding Moon, 1994; The Fallen Man, 1996; The First Eagle, 1998; Hunting Badger, 1999; The Wailing Wind, 2002. Non-Fiction: The Spell of New Mexico (ed.), 1984; Indian Country: America's Sacred Land, 1987; Hillerman Country: A Journey through the Southwest with Tony Hillerman, 1991; Talking Mysteries: A Conversation with Tony Hillerman (with Ernie Bulow), 1991; New Mexico, Rio Grande, and Other Essays, 1992; Seldom Disappointed: A Memoir, 2001. Other: The Oxford Book of the American Detective Story, 1996; The Best American Mystery Stories of the Century, 2000. Contributions: Magazines. *Honours:* Edgar Allan Poe Award, MWA, 1974. *Address:* 1632 Francisca N, Albuquerque, NM 87107, USA.

HILLES, Robert Edward; poet, writer and academic; b. 13 Nov. 1951, Kenora, ON, Canada; m. Rebecca Susan Knight 1980; two c. *Education:* BA, 1976, MSc, 1984, University of Calgary. *Career:* Prof. of Computer Programming, 1983–, Senior Prof., 1994–, DeVry Institute of Technology, Calgary, AB; mem. League of Canadian Poets; Writers' Union of Canada; Writers' Guild of Alberta. *Publications:* Look the Lovely Animal Speaks, 1980; The Surprise Element, 1982; An Angel in the Works, 1983; Outlasting the Landscape, 1989; Finding the Lights On, 1991; A Breath at a Time, 1992; Cantos From a Small Room, 1993; Raising of Voices, 1993; Near Morning, 1995; Kissing the Smoke, 1996; Nothing Vanishes, 1996; Breathing Distance, 1997. Contributions: anthologies and periodicals. *Honours:* Gov.-Gen.'s Literary Award for Poetry, 1994; Best Novel Award, Writers' Guild of Alberta, 1994. *Address:* c/o League of Canadian Poets, 54 Wolseley Street, Third Floor, Toronto, ON M5T 1AS, Canada.

HILLIS, Rick; Writer, Poet and Teacher; b. 3 Feb. 1956, Nipawin, Saskatchewan, Canada; m. Patricia Appelgren, 29 Aug. 1988, one s. one d. *Education:* University of Victoria, 1977–78; BEd, University of Saskatchewan, 1979; Graduate Studies, Concordia University, 1983; MFA, University of Iowa, 1984; Stanford University, 1988–90. *Career:* Stegner Fellow, 1988–90, Jones Lecturer, 1990–92, Stanford University; Lecturer, California State University at Hayward, 1990; Chesterfield Film Writer's Fellowship, 1991–92; Visiting Asst Prof. of English, Reed College, 1992–96. *Publications:* The Blue Machines of Night (poems), 1988; Coming Attractions (co-author), 1988; Canadian Brash (co-author), 1990; Limbo Stories, 1990. Contributions: anthologies and periodicals. *Honours:* Canada Council Grants, 1985, 1987, 1989; Drue Heinz Literature Prize, 1990.

HILLMAN, Martin (see Hill, Douglas Arthur).

HILTON, Suzanne McLean; Writer; b. 3 Sept. 1922, Pittsburgh, Pennslyvania, USA; m. Warren Mitchell Hilton, 15 June 1946, one s. one d. *Education:* BA, Beaver College, 1946. *Career:* Ed., Bulletin of Old York Road Historical Society, 1976–92, Bulletin of Historical Society of Montgomery County, 1987–89; Assoc. Ed., Montgomery County History, 1983; mem. Society of Children's Book Writers and Illustrators; Philadelphia Children's Reading Round Table. *Publications:* How Do They Get Rid of It?, 1970; How Do They Cope with It?, 1970; Beat It, Burn It and Drown It, 1974; Who Do You Think You Are?, 1976; Yesterday's People, 1976; Here Today and Gone Tomorrow, 1978; Faster than a Horse: Moving West with Engine Power, 1983; Montgomery County: The Second Hundred Years, 1983; The World of Young Tom Jefferson, 1986; The World of Young George Washington, 1986; The World of Young Herbert Hoover, 1987; The World of Young Andrew Jackson, 1988; A Capital Capitol City, 1991; Miners, Merchants and Maids, 1995. Contributions: Historical journals. *Honours:* Legion of Honour, Chapel of the Four Chaplains, 1978; Award for Excellence in Non-Fiction, Drexel University, 1979; Golden Spur, Western Writers of America, 1980; Gold Disc, Beaver College, 1981. *Address:* 3320 108th St NW, Gig Harbour, WA 98332, USA.

HILTON, Tessa; British newspaper editor; b. 18 Feb. 1951; m. Graham Ball 1976; two s. one d. *Education:* St Mary's School (Gerrards Cross). *Career:* Journalist Sunday Mirror 1970–78, Ed. 1994–; freelance writer 1978–85; Ed. Mother magazine 1985–87; Exec. Today 1987–91; Ed. Femail, Daily Mail 1991–94; Asst Ed. Sun 1994; Deputy Ed. Express then Ed. Express on Sunday magazine 1996–99. *Publication:* Great Ormond Street Book of Child Health 1990. *Address:* c/o Express Newspapers, 245 Blackfriars Road, London SE1, England.

HIMMELFARB, Gertrude, BA, MA, PhD, FBA, FRHistS; academic and writer; *Professor of History Emerita, City University of New York*; b. 8 Aug. 1922, New York, NY, USA; m. Irving Kristol 1942; one s. one d. *Education:* Jewish Theological Seminary, Brooklyn Coll., CUNY, Univ. of Chicago, Girton Coll., Cambridge. *Career:* Prof. 1965–78, Distinguished Prof. of History 1978–88, Prof. of History Emerita 1988–, Graduate School and Univ. Center, CUNY; mem. American Acad. of Arts and Sciences, American Historical Asscn, American Philosophical Soc., Soc. of American Historians. *Publications:* Lord Acton: A Study in Conscience and Politics 1952, Darwin and the Darwinian Revolution 1959, Victorian Minds: Essays on Nineteenth Century Intellectuals 1968, On Liberty and Liberalism: The Case of John Stuart Mill 1974, The Idea of Poverty: England in the Industrial Age 1984, Marriage and Morals Among the Victorians and Other Essays 1986, The New History and the Old 1987, Poverty and Compassion: The Moral Imagination of the Late Victorians 1991, On Looking Into the Abyss: Untimely Thoughts on Culture and Society 1994, The De-Moralization of Society: From Victorian Virtues to Modern Values 1995, One Nation, Two Cultures 1999, The Roads to Modernity: The British, French, and American Enlightenments 2004; contrib. to scholarly books and journals. *Honours:* American Asscn of University Women Fellowship 1951–52, American Philosophical Soc. Fellowship 1953–54, Guggenheim Fellowships 1955–56, 1957–58, Nat. Endowment for the Humanities Senior Fellowship 1968–69, ACLS Fellowship 1972–73, Phi Beta Kappa Visiting Scholarship 1972–73, Woodrow Wilson Center Fellowship 1976–77, Rockefeller Humanities Fellowship 1980–81, Jefferson Lectureship, Nat. Endowment for the Humanities 1991, Templeton Foundation Award 1997, Professional Achievement Citation, Univ. of Chicago Alumni Asscn 1998. *Address:* 2510 Virginia Avenue NW, Washington, DC 20037, USA.

HINDE, Thomas (see Chitty, Sir Thomas Wiles).

HINE, (William) Daryl; poet, writer and translator; b. 24 Feb. 1936, Burnaby, BC, Canada. *Education:* McGill University, 1954–58; MA, 1965, PhD, 1967, University of Chicago. *Career:* Asst Prof. of English, University of Chicago, 1967–69; Ed., Poetry magazine, Chicago, 1968–78. *Publications:* Poetry: Five Poems 1954; The Carnal and the Crane, 1957; The Devil's Picture Book, 1960; Heroics, 1961; The Wooden Horse, 1965; Minutes, 1968; Resident Alien, 1975; In and Out: A Confessional Poem, 1975; Daylight Saving, 1978; Selected Poems, 1980; Academic Festival Overtures, 1985; Arrondissements, 1988; Postscripts, 1992. Novel: The Prince of Darkness and Co, 1961. Other: Polish Subtitles: Impressions from a Journey, 1962; The 'Poetry' Anthology 1912–1977 (ed. with Joseph Parisi), 1978. Translator: The Homeric Hymns and the Battle of the Frogs and the Mice, 1972; Theocritus: Idylls and Epigrams, 1982; Ovid's Heroines: A Verse Translation of the Heroides, 1991; Hesiod's Works, 2000; Puerilities from the Greek Anthology, 2001. *Honours:* Canada Foundation-Rockefeller Fellowship, 1958; Canada Council Grants, 1959, 1979; Ingram Merrill Foundation

Grants, 1962, 1963, 1983; Guggenheim Fellowship, 1980; American Acad. of Arts and Letters Award, 1982; John D. and Catherine T. MacArthur Foundation Fellowship, 1986. *Address:* 2740 Ridge Avenue, Evanston, IL 60201, USA.

HINES, Donald (Merrill); Writer and Teacher; b. 23 Jan. 1931, St Paul, Minnesota, USA; m. Linda Marie Arnold, 10 June 1961, three s. *Education:* BS, Lewis and Clark College, Portland, Oregon, 1953; MAT, Reed College, Portland, Oregon, 1960; PhD, Indiana University, 1969. *Career:* Faculty, Washington State University, 1968–77, King Saud University, Abha, Saudi Arabia, 1982–90, Blue Mountain Community College, Pendleton, Oregon, 1990–91; mem. American Folklore Society. *Publications:* Cultural History of the Inland Pacific Northwest Frontier, 1976; Tales of the Okanogans, 1976; Tales of the Nez Perce, 1984; The Forgotten Tribes: Oral Tales of the Tenino and Adjacent Mid-Columbia River Indian Nations, 1991; Ghost Voices: Yakima Indian Myths, Legends, Humor and Hunting Stories, 1992; Celilo Tales: Wasco Myths, Legends, Tales of Magic and the Marvelous, 1996. Contributions: journals. *Honours:* Ford Foundation Fellowship, 1965; Third Prize, Chicago Folklore Contest, University of Chicago, 1970.

HINOJOSA-SMITH, Rolando; writer and academic; b. 21 Jan. 1929, Mercedes, TX, USA; one s. two d. *Education:* BS, University of Texas at Austin, 1953; MA, New Mexico Highlands University, Las Vegas, 1963; PhD, University of Illinois, 1969. *Career:* Asst Prof., Trinity University, San Antonio, 1968–70; Assoc. Prof., 1970–74, Dean, College of Arts and Sciences, 1974–76, Vice-Pres. for Academic Affairs, 1976–77, Texas A and I University, Kingsville; Chair, Dept of Chicano Studies, 1977–80, Prof., 1980–81, University of Minnesota; Prof., University of Texas at Austin, 1981–; mem. MLA; PEN; Salado Institute. *Publications:* Estampas del valle y otras obras, 1972, English trans as Sketches of the Valley and Other Works, 1980, The Valley, 1983; Klail City y sus alrededores, 1976, English trans. as Klail City, 1987; Korean Love Songs from Klail City Death Trip, 1978; Claros varones de Belken, 1981, English trans. as Fair Gentlemen of Belken County, 1987; Mi querido Rafa, 1981, English trans. as Dear Rafe, 1985; Rites and Witnesses, 1982; Partners in Crime, 1985; Los amigos de Becky, 1990, English trans. as Becky and Her Friends, 1990; The Useless Servants, 1993; Ask a Policeman, 1998. Contributions: anthologies, reviews, journals, and periodicals. *Honours:* Quinto Sol Literary Award for Best Novel, 1972; Casa de las Américas Award for Best Novel, 1976; Southwest Studies on Latin America Award for Best Writing in the Humanities, 1981; University of Illinois College of Liberal Arts Award, 1987, and Alumni Achievement Award, 1998; Lon C. Tinkle Award, Texas Institute of Letters, 1998. *Address:* c/o Dept of English, PAR 108, University of Texas at Austin, Austin, TX 78712, USA.

HINSON, Edward Glenn; academic and writer; b. 27 July 1931, St Louis, MO, USA; m. Martha Anne Burks 1956; one s. one d. *Education:* BA, Washington University, St Louis, 1954; BD, 1957, ThD, 1962, Southern Baptist Theological Seminary, Louisville; DPhil, University of Oxford, 1973. *Career:* Prof., Southern Baptist Theological Seminary, 1959–92, Wake Forest University, 1982–84; Visiting Prof., St John's University, Collegeville, Minnesota, 1983, Catholic University of America, 1987, University of Notre Dame, 1989; Prof. of Spirituality and John F. Loftis Prof. of Church History, Baptist Theological Seminary, Richmond, Virginia, 1992–; mem. American Society of Church History; Asscn Internationale des Patristique; International Thomas Merton Society; National Asscn of Baptist Profs of Religion, pres., 1993–94; North American Patristics Society; Societas Liturgica. *Publications:* The Church: Design for Survival, 1967; Seekers after Mature Faith, 1968; A Serious Call to a Contemplative Life-Style, 1974; Soul Liberty, 1975; The Early Church Fathers, 1978; The Reaffirmation of Prayer, 1979; A History of Baptists in Arkansas, 1980; The Evangelization of the Roman Empire, 1981; Are Southern Baptists Evangelicals?, 1983; Religious Liberty, 1991; Spirituality in Ecumenical Perspective, 1993; The Church Triumphant: A History of Christianity up to 1300, 1995; The Early Church, 1996; Love at the Heart of Things: A Biography of Douglas V. Steere, 1998. Contributions: Festschriften, reference works, and journals. *Honours:* American Asscn of Theological Schools Fellowship, 1966–67; Prof. of the Year, Southern Baptist Theological Fellowship, 1975–76; Johannes Quasten Medal, Catholic University of America; Cuthbert Allen Award, Ecumenical Institute of Belmont Abbey/ Wake Forest University, 1992. *Address:* 3400 Brook Road, Richmond, VA 23227, USA.

HINTON, Susan Eloise, BS; writer; b. 1948, Tulsa, Oklahoma, USA; m. David Inhofe 1970; one s. *Education:* University of Tulsa. *Publications:* The Outsiders, 1967; That Was Then, This is Now, 1971; Rumble Fish, 1975; Tex, 1979; Taming the Star Runner, 1988; Big David, Little David, 1994. Screenplay: Rumble Fish (with Francis Ford Coppola), 1983. *Honours:* Media and Methods Maxi Award, 1975; Golden Archer Award, 1983; Sue Hefly Award, 1983; Author's Award, American Library Asscn Young Adult Services Division/School Library Journal, 1988. *Address:* c/o Delacorte Press, 1540 Broadway, New York, NY 10036, USA.

HIRSCH, Edward Mark, BA, PhD; academic, poet and writer; b. 20 Jan. 1950, Chicago, IL, USA; m. Janet Landay 1977; one s. *Education:* Grinnell College, University of Pennsylvania. *Career:* teacher, Poetry in the Schools Program, New York and Pennsylvania, 1976–78; Asst Prof., 1978–82, Assoc. Prof. of English, 1982–85, Wayne State University; Assoc. Prof., 1985–88, Prof. of English, 1988–, University of Houston; mem. Authors' Guild; MLA; PEN; Poetry Society of America; Texas Institute of Letters. *Publications:* For the Sleepwalkers, 1981; Wild Gratitude, 1986; The Night Parade, 1989; Earthly Measures, 1994; Transforming Vision (ed.), 1994; On Love, 1998; How to Read a Poem and Fall in Love with Poetry, 1999; Responsive Reading, 1999. Contributions: many anthologies, books, journals, and periodicals. *Honours:* Awards, 1975–77, Peter I B. Lavan Younger Poets Award, 1983, Acad. of American Poets; Ingram Merrill Foundation Award, 1978; ACLS Fellow, 1981; National Endowment for the Arts Fellowship, 1982; Delmore Schwartz Memorial Poetry Award, New York University, 1985; Guggenheim Fellowship, 1986–87; Texas Institute of Letters Award in Poetry, 1987; National Book Critics Circle Award, 1987; Rome Prize, American Acad. and Institute of Arts and Letters, 1988; Robert and Hazel Ferguson Memorial Award for Poetry, Friends of Chicago Literature, 1990; Lila Wallace-Reader's Digest Writing Fellow, 1993; Woodrow Wilson Fellow, 1994, 1995; Lyndhurst Prize, 1994–96. *Address:* 315 W 98th Street, Apt 5B, New York, NY 10025-5556, USA.

HIRSCHMAN, Jack, BA, AM, PhD; American poet and translator; b. 13 Dec. 1933, New York, NY; m. Ruth Epstein 1954; one s. one d. *Education:* City Coll. CUNY, Indiana Univ. *Career:* editorial team of journal Left Curve, correspondent for The People's Tribune. *Publications:* poetry: Fragments, 1952; Correspondence of Americans, 1960; Two, 1963; Interchange, 1964; Kline Sky, 1965; Yod, 1966; London Seen Directly, 1967; Wasn't Like This in the Woodcut, 1967; William Blake, 1967; A Word in Your Season (with Asa Benveniste), 1967; Ltd Interchangeable in Eternity: Poems of Jackruthdavidcelia Hirschman, 1967; Jerusalem, 1968; Aleph, Benoni and Zaddik, 1968; Jerusalem Ltd, 1968; Shekinah, 1969; Broadside Golem, 1969; Black Alephs: Poems 1960–68, 1969; NHR, 1970; Scintilla, 1970; Soledeth, 1971; DT, 1971; The Burning of Los Angeles, 1971; HNYC, 1971; Les Vidanges, 1972; The R of the Ari's Raziel, 1972; Adamnan, 1972; K'wai Sing: The Origin of the Dragon, 1973; Cantillations, 1973; Aur Sea, 1974; Djackson, 1974; Cockroach Street, 1975; The Cool Boyetz Cycle, 1975; Kashtaniyah Segodnyah, 1976; Lyripol, 1976; The Arcanes of Le Comte de St Germain, 1977; The Proletarian Arcane, 1978; The Jonestown Arcane, 1979; The Caliostro Arcane, 1981; The David Arcane, 1982; Class Questions, 1982; Kallatumba, 1984; The Necessary Is, 1984; The Bottom Line, 1988; Sunsong, 1988; The Tirana Arcane, 1991; The Satin Arcane, 1991; Endless Threshold, 1992; The Back of a Spoon, 1992; The Heartbeat Arcane, 1993; The Xibalba Arcane, 1994. Editor: Artaud Anthology, 1965; Would You Wear My Eyes: A Tribute to Bob Kaufman, 1989. Translator: Over 25 vols, 1970–95. *Address:* PO Box 26517, San Francisco, CA 94126, USA.

HIRSHFIELD, Jane, AB; poet, writer, editor and lecturer; b. 24 Feb. 1953, New York, NY, USA. *Education:* Princeton Univ. *Career:* California Poet in the Schools 1980–85; faculty, various writers' conferences 1984–; Lecturer, Univ. of San Francisco 1991–; Visiting Poet-in-Residence, Univ. of Alaska, Fairbanks 1993; Adjunct Prof., Northern Michigan Univ. 1994; Assoc. Faculty, Bennington Coll. 1995; Visiting Assoc. Prof., Univ. of California at Berkeley 1995; Core Faculty, Bennington Coll., MFA Writing Seminars 1999–; Elliston Visiting Poet, Univ. of Cincinnati 2000; Fellow, Lindisfarne Asscn 1995–; mem. Associated Writing Programs, Authors' Guild, Djerassi Resident Artist Program (bd mem. 1996–), PEN American Center. *Publications:* Poetry: Alaya, 1982; Of Gravity and Angels, 1988; The October Palace, 1994; The Lives of the Heart, 1997; Given Sugar, Given Salt, 2001. Other: The Ink Dark Moon: Poems by Ono no Komachi and Izumi Shikibu (trans. with Aratani), 1988; Women in Praise of the Sacred: 43 Centuries of Spiritual Poetry by Women (ed.), 1994; Nine Gates: Entering the Mind of Poetry (essays), 1997; Mirabai: Ecstatic Poems (trans. with Bly) 2004. Contributions: many anthologies, journals, and reviews. *Honours:* Yaddo Fellowships, 1983, 1985, 1987, 1989, 1992, 1996, 2002; Guggenheim Fellowship, 1985; Joseph Henry Jackson Award, San Francisco Foundation, 1986; Columbia University Trans. Center Award, 1987; Poetry Society of America Awards, 1987, 1988; Artist-in-Residence, Djerassi Foundation, 1987–90; Pushcart Prize, 1988; Commonwealth Club of California Poetry Medals, 1988, 1994; Dewar's Young Artists Recognition Award in Poetry, 1990; MacDowell Colony Fellowship, 1994; Bay Area Book Reviewers Awards, 1994, 2001; Poetry Center Book Award, 1995; Rockefeller Foundation Fellowship, Bellagio Study Center, Italy, 1995. *Literary Agent:* Steven Barclay Agency, 12 Western Avenue, Petaluma, CA 94952, USA. *Telephone:* (707) 773-0654. *Fax:* (707) 778-1868. *Website:* www.barclayagency.com. *Address:* c/o Michael Katz, 367 Molino Avenue, Mill Valley, CA 94941, USA.

HISLOP, Ian David, BA; editor, writer and broadcaster; b. 13 July 1960, England; m. Victoria Hamson 1988; one s. one d. *Education:* Magdalen College, Oxford. *Career:* Staff, 1981–85, Deputy Ed., 1985–86, Ed., 1986–, Private Eye; Columnist, The Listener, 1985–89, Sunday Telegraph, 1996–; Television Critic, The Spectator, 1994–96. *Publications:* Private Eye collections, 1985–. Other: Television scripts. Contributions: newspapers, magazines, radio, television. *Honours:* Ed.'s Ed. Award, British Society of Magazine Eds, 1991; Magazine of the Year, What the Papers Say, 1991; Ed. of the Year, British Society of Magazine Eds, 1998. *Address:* c/o Private Eye, 6 Carlisle Street, London W1V 5RG, England.

HITCHCOCK, H(ugh) Wiley; Musicologist, Writer, Ed. and Distinguished Prof. of Music (retd); b. 28 Sept. 1923, Detroit, MI, USA. *Education:* BA, Dartmouth College, 1944; MMus, 1948, PhD, 1954, University of Michigan.

Career: Faculty, University of Michigan, 1947–61; Prof. of Music, Hunter College, CUNY, 1961–71; Ed., Prentice-Hall History of Music Series, 1965–, Earlier American Music, 1972–98, Recent Researches in American Music, 1976–94; Prof. of Music, 1971–80, Distinguished Prof. of Music, 1980–93, Founder-Dir, Institute for Studies in American Music, 1971–93, Brooklyn College, CUNY; mem. American Musicological Society, pres., 1991–92, hon. mem., 1994–; Charles Ives Society, pres., 1973–93; Music Library Asscn, pres., 1966–68. *Publications:* Music in the United States: A Historical Introduction, 1969; Charles Ives Centennial Festival-Conference 1974, 1977; Ives, 1977; An Ives Celebration: Papers and Panels of the Charles Ives Centennial Festival-Conference (ed. with Vivian Perlis), 1977; The Phonograph and Our Musical Life, 1980; The Music of Ainsworth's Psalter (1612) (with L. Inserra), 1981; The Works of Marc-Antoine Charpentier: A Catalogue Raisonné, 1982; Ives: A Survey of the Music, 1983; The New Grove Dictionary of American Music (co-ed.), four vols, 1986; Marc-Antoine Charpentier, 1990. Contributions: scholarly books and professional journals. *Honours:* Fulbright Senior Research Fellowships, 1954–55, 1968–69; Guggenheim Fellowship, 1968–69; Festschrift published in his honour, 1989; Chevalier, Ordre des Arts et des Lettres, 1995; Inducted, American Classical Music Hall of Fame, 1999. *Address:* 1192 Park Ave, No. 10-E, New York, NY 10128, USA.

HITCHENS, Christopher (Eric); Journalist and Writer; b. 13 April 1949, Portsmouth, England; m. 1st Eleni Meleagrou, 1981, one s. one d.; m. 2nd Carol Blue, 1991, one d. *Education:* BA, PPE, 1970, Balliol College, Oxford. *Career:* Social Science Correspondent, THES, 1971–73; Writer and Asst Ed., 1973–81, Columnist and Washington Correspondent, 1982–, New Statesman; Columnist, The Nation, 1982–, Vanity Fair, 1982–; Contributor, London Review of Books, 1989–; Mellon Prof. of English, University of Pittsburgh, 1997. *Publications:* Karl Marx and the Paris Commune, 1971; James Callaghan, 1976; Hostage to History: Cyprus From the Ottomans to Kissinger, 1984; Imperial Spoils: The Curious Case of the Elgin Marbles, 1986; Prepared for the Worst: Selected Essays, 1989; Blood, Class and Nostalgia: Anglo-American Ironies, 1990; For the Sake of Argument: Selected Essays, 1993; When the Borders Bleed: The Struggle of the Kurds, 1994; The Missionary Position: Mother Teresa in Theory and Practice, 1995; No One Left to Lie to, 1999; Letters to a Young Contrarian, 2001; Orwell's Victory, 2001. *Address:* 2022 Columbia Rd NW, Washington, DC 20009, USA.

HJÖRNE, Lars Goran; Swedish newspaper editor and publisher; b. 20 Oct. 1929, Gothenburg; m. Lena Hjörne (née Smith); one s. one d. *Career:* Chief Ed. Göteborgs-Posten 1969–89, Chair. 1969–95, Hon. Chair. 1995–; Hon. British Consul-Gen. in Gothenburg 1991–98. *Honours:* Hon. OBE. *Address:* Polhemsplatsen 5, 405 02 Gothenburg (Office); Stora Vägen 43, 26043 Arild, Sweden (Home). *Telephone:* (31) 62-40-00 (Office); (42) 34-68-03 (Home).

HJÖRNE, Peter Lars; Newspaper Editor and Publisher; b. 7 Sept. 1952, Gothenburg, Sweden; m. 2nd Karin Linnea Tufvesson Hjörne 1995; four d. *Education:* Göteborgs Högre Samskola; Univ. of Gothenburg. *Career:* Man. Trainee John Deere Co., USA 1978–79; Exec. Asst Göteborgs-Posten 1979–82, Deputy Man. Dir 1983–85, Man. Dir 1985–93, Publisher and Chief Ed. 1993–. *Address:* Göteborgs-Posten, Polhemsplatsen 5, 405 02 Gothenburg, Sweden.

HO ANH THAI; Vietnamese novelist and diplomatist. *Career:* served in India and the Middle East as a diplomat; Ed., World Affairs Weekly. *Publications include:* Behind the Red Mist: Short Fiction 1988, The Women on the Island 2001; co-editor: Love After War: Contemporary Fiction from Viet Nam 2003. *Address:* c/o Curbstone Press, 321 Jackson Street, Willimantic, CT 06226-1738, USA. *E-mail:* info@curbstone.org. *Website:* www.curbstone.org.

HOAGLAND, Edward, AB; American author; b. 21 Dec. 1932, New York; m. 1st Amy J. Ferrara 1960 (divorced 1964); m. 2nd Marion Magid 1968 (died 1993); one d. *Education:* Harvard Univ. *Career:* faculty mem. New School for Social Research, New York 1963–64, Rutgers Univ. 1966, Sarah Lawrence Coll., Bronxville, New York 1967, 1971, City Univ. 1967, 1968, Univ. of Iowa 1978, 1982, Columbia Univ. 1980, 1981, Brown Univ. 1988, Bennington Coll., Bennington, Vt 1987–2002, Univ. of Calif. at Davis 1990, 1992, Beloit Coll., Wis. 1995; Gen. Ed. Penguin Nature Library 1985–; Houghton Mifflin Literary Fellow 1954; American Acad. of Arts and Letters Travelling Fellow 1964; Guggenheim Fellow 1964, 1975; mem. American Acad. of Arts and Letters. *Publications:* Cat Man 1956, The Circle Home 1960, The Peacock's Tail 1965, Notes from the Century Before: A Journal from British Columbia 1969, The Courage of Turtles 1971, Walking the Dead Diamond River 1973, The Moose on the Wall: Field Notes from the Vermont Wilderness 1974, Red Wolves and Black Bears 1976, African Calliope: A Journey to the Sudan 1979, The Edward Hoagland Reader 1979, The Tugman's Passage 1982, City Tales 1986, Seven Rivers West 1986, Heart's Desire 1988, The Final Fate of the Alligators 1992, Balancing Acts 1992, Tigers and Ice 1999, Compass Points 2001, How I Lived 2001; numerous essays and short stories. *Honours:* Longview Foundation Award 1961, Prix de Rome 1964, O. Henry Award 1971, Brandeis Univ. Citation in Literature 1972, New York State Council on Arts Award 1972, Nat. Book Critics' Circle Award 1980, American Acad. of Arts and Letters Harold D. Vursell Memorial Award 1981, Nat. Endowment for the Arts Award 1982, NY Public Library Literary Lion Award 1988, Nat. Magazine Award 1989, Lannan Foundation Literary Award 1993, Boston Public Library Literary Lights Award 1995. *Address:* PO Box 51, Barton, VT 05822, USA (Home).

HOBAN, Russell Conwell, FRSL; American writer; b. 4 Feb. 1925, Lansdale, PA; m. 1st Lillian Aberman 1944 (divorced); one s. three d.; m. 2nd Gundula Ahl 1975; three s. *Education:* High School, Philadelphia. *Career:* General Illustrator, Wexton Co, New York, 1950–52; Television Art Dir, Batten, Barton, Durstine & Osborne, New York, 1952–57; Copywriter, Doyle Dane Bernbach, New York, 1965–67; mem. PEN, Society of Authors. *Publications:* Novels: The Lion of Boaz-Jachin and Jachin-Boaz, 1973; Kleinzeit, 1974; Turtle Diary, 1975; Riddley Walker, 1980; Pilgermann, 1983; The Medusa Frequency, 1987; Angelica's Grotto, 1991; The Moment Under the Moment, 1992; Fremder, 1996; Mr Rinyo-Clacton's Offer, 1998; Amaryllis Night and Day, 2001; The Bat Tattoo, 2002; Her Name Was Lola, 2003. Children's Books: over 65 books, incl.: Bedtime for Frances, 1960; Baby Sister for Frances, 1964; The Mouse and His Child, 1967; Best Friends for Frances, 1969; The Pedalling Man, 1970; The Sea-thing Child, 1972; How Tom Beat Captain Najork and His Hired Sportsmen, 1974; Dinner at Alberta's, 1975; A Near Thing for Captain Najork, 1975; The Twenty-Elephant Restaurant, 1978; Ace Dragon, 1980; The Marzipan Pig, 1986; The Rain Door, 1986; Ponders, 1988; Bread and Jam for Frances, 1993; Birthday for Frances, 1994; The Trokeville Way, 1996; Trouble on Thunder Mountain, 1999; Jim's Lion, 2001. Poetry: The Last of the Wallendas and Other Poems. Libretto: The Second Mrs Kong (for Harrison Birtwistle's Opera), 1994. *Honours:* Whitbread Children's Book Award, 1974; John W. Campbell Memorial Award for Best Science Fiction Novel, 1981; Science Fiction Achievement Award, 1981; Ditmar Award, 1983. *Literary Agent:* David Higham Associates, 5–8 Lower John Street, Golden Square, London W1F 9HA, England.

HOBB, Robin (see Ogden, Margaret (Astrid) Lindholm).

HOBSBAUM, Philip (Dennis); Writer, Poet and Emeritus Prof. of English Literature; b. 29 June 1932, London, England; m. 1st Hannah Hobsbaum, 1957, divorced 1968; m. 2nd Rosemary Phillips, 20 July 1976. *Education:* BA, 1955, MA, 1961, Downing College, Cambridge; Licentiate, Royal Acad. of Music, London, 1956, Guildhall School of Music, 1957; PhD, University of Sheffield, 1968. *Career:* Ed., Delta, 1954–55; Co-Ed., Poetry from Sheffield, 1959–61; Lecturer in English, Queen's University, Belfast, 1962–66; Lecturer, 1966–72, Senior Lecturer, 1972–79, Reader, 1979–85, Prof. of English Literature, 1985–97, Hon. Professorial Research Fellow, 1997–, University of Glasgow. *Publications:* A Group Anthology (ed. with E. Lucie-Smith), 1963; The Place's Fault and Other Poems, 1964; Snapshots, 1965; In Retreat and Other Poems, 1966; Ten Elizabethan Poets (ed.), 1969; Coming Out Fighting, 1969; Some Lovely Glorious Nothing, 1969; A Theory of Communication: A Study of Value in Literature, 1970; Women and Animals, 1972; A Reader's Guide to Charles Dickens, 1973; Tradition and Experiment in English Poetry, 1979; A Reader's Guide to D. H. Lawrence, 1981; Essentials of Literary Criticism, 1983; A Reader's Guide to Robert Lowell, 1988; Wordsworth: Selected Poetry and Prose (ed.), 1989; Channels of Communication (ed. with P. Lyons and J. McGhie), 1993; Metre, Rhythm and Verse Form, 1996. Contributions: anthologies, journals, reviews, and magazines. *Honours:* Hon. DLitt, University of Glasgow, 1994, University of Sheffield, 2003. *Address:* c/o Dept of English Literature, University of Glasgow, Glasgow G12 8QQ, Scotland.

HOBSBAWM, Eric John Ernest, BA, MA, PhD; British academic and writer; b. 9 June 1917, Alexandria, Egypt; m. Marlene Schwarz 1962; one s. one d. *Education:* University of Cambridge. *Career:* Lecturer in History, 1947–59, Reader in History, 1959–70, Prof. of Economic and Social History, 1970–82, Prof. Emeritus, 1982–, Pres., 2002, Birkbeck College, University of London; Fellow, King's College, Cambridge, 1949–55; Andrew D. White Prof.-at-Large, Cornell University, 1976–82; Prof., New School for Social Research, New York, 1984–97; mem. American Acad. of Arts and Sciences, hon. foreign mem.; British Acad., fellow; Hungarian Acad. of Sciences, foreign mem.; Acad. of Sciences, Turin. *Publications:* Labour's Turning Point, 1880–1900 (ed.), 1948; Primitive Rebels, 1959, US edn as Social Bandits and Primitive Rebels, 1959; The Jazz Scene, 1959; The Age of Revolution, 1789–1848, 1962; Labouring Men, 1964; Industry and Empire: An Economic History of Britain since 1750, 1968, US edn as Industry and Empire: The Making of Modern English Society, 1968; Captain Swing (with George Rudé), 1969; Bandits, 1969; Revolutionaries, 1973; The Age of Capital, 1848–1875, 1975; Marxism in Marx's Day (ed.), 1982; The Invention of Tradition (ed. with Terence Ranger), 1983; Worlds of Labour: Further Studies in the History of Labour, 1984, US edn as Workers: Worlds of Labor, 1984; The Age of Empire, 1875–1914, 1987; Politics for a Rational Left: Political Writing, 1977–1988, 1989; Echoes of the Marseillaise: Two Centuries Look Back on the French Revolution, 1990; Nations and Nationalism since 1780: Programme, Myth, Reality, 1990; Age of Extremes: The Short Twentieth Century, 1914–1991, 1994, US edn as The Age of Extremes: A History of the World, 1914–1991, 1994; On History, 1997; Uncommon People, 1998; W. A. Polito: On the Edge of the New Century, 2000; Interesting Times: A 20th Century Life (autobiog.), 2002. Contributions: scholarly journals and general publications. *Honours:* Hon. Fellow, King's College, London, 1971; Palmes Académiques, France, 1993; Commander,

Order of the Southern Cross, Brazil, 1996; Companion of Honour, 1998; various hon. degrees. *Address:* School of History, Birkbeck College, University of London, Malet Street, London WC1E 7HX, England.

HOBSON, Charlotte; British writer. *Education:* Univ. of Edinburgh. *Publications:* Black Earth City: When Russia Ran Wild (And So Did We) 2002; contrib. to Virgin Soil 2001, Granta 64: The Wild East. *Honours:* Somerset Maugham Award 2002. *Address:* c/o Granta Books, 2–3 Hanover Yard, Noel Road, London, N1 8BE, England. *Website:* www.granta.com.

HOBSON, Fred Colby, Jr; Prof. of Literature and Writer; b. 23 April 1943, Winston-Salem, NC, USA; m. 17 June 1967, divorced, one d. *Education:* BA, English, 1965, PhD, English, 1972, University of North Carolina; MA, History, Duke University, 1967. *Career:* Prof. of English, University of Alabama, 1972–86; Prof. of English and Co-Ed., Southern Review, Louisiana State University, 1986–89; Prof. of English, Lineberger Prof. in the Humanities and Co-Ed., Southern Literary Journal, University of North Carolina at Chapel Hill, 1989–. *Publications:* Serpent in Eden: H. L. Mencken and the South, 1974; Literature at the Barricades: The American Writer in the 1930s (co-ed.), 1983; Tell About the South: The Southern Rage to Explain, 1984; South-Watching: Selected Essays of Gerald W. Johnson (ed.), 1984; The Southern Writer in the Post-Modern World, 1990; Mencken: A Life, 1994; Thirty-Five Years of Newspaper Work by H. L. Mencken (co-ed.), 1994; The Literature of the American South: A Norton Anthology (co-ed.), 1998; But Now I See: The Southern White Racial Conversion Narrative, 1999; South to the Future: An American Region in the Twenty-First Century (ed.), 2002; Faulkner's Absalom, Absalom!: An Oxford Casebook (ed.), 2003. Contributions: Virginia Quarterly Review; Sewanee Review; Atlantic Monthly; Kenyon Review; New York Times Book Review; American Literature; TLS. *Honours:* Lillian Smith Award, 1984; Jules F. Landry Awards, 1984, 1999. *Address:* Dept of English, University of North Carolina at Chapel Hill, NC 27599-3520, USA. *E-mail:* fhobson@email.unc.edu.

HOCH, Edward D(entinger); Writer; b. 22 Feb. 1930, Rochester, NY, USA; m. Patricia McMahon 5 June 1957. *Education:* Univ. of Rochester, 1947–49. *Career:* mem. Authors' Guild: CWA; MWA, pres., 1982–83; Science Fiction Writers of America. *Publications:* The Shattered Raven, 1969; The Transvection Machine, 1971; The Judges of Hades and Other Simon Ark Stories, 1971; The Spy and the Thief, 1971; City of Brass and Other Simon Ark Stories, 1971; The Fellowship of the Hand, 1973; The Frankenstein Factory, 1975; The Thefts of Nick Velvet, 1978; The Quests of Simon Ark, 1984; Leopold's Way, 1985; The Night My Friend, 1991; Diagnosis Impossible: The Problems of Dr Sam Hawthorne, 1996; The Ripper of Storyville and Other Ben Snow Tales, 1997; The Velvet Touch, 2000; The Old Spies Club, 2001; The Night People, 2001; The Iron Angel, 2003. Contributions: Ellery Queen's Mystery Magazine. *Honours:* Edgar Allan Poe Award, 1967, Grand Master, 2001, MWA; Boucheron Awards, 1998, Lifetime Achievement Award, 2001. *Address:* 2941 Lake Ave, Rochester, NY 14612, USA.

HOCHHUTH, Rolf; Dramatist, Writer, Poet and Critic; b. 1 April 1931, Eschwege, Germany; m.; three s. *Education:* Extramural Studies, University of Heidelberg, University of Munich. *Career:* Chief Cultural Correspondent, Die Welt newspaper, Berlin, 1989–; mem. Acad. of Fine Arts; PEN Club. *Publications:* Der Stellvertreter, 1963; Die Berliner Antigone, 1966; Soldaten, 1967; Guerrillas, 1970; Die Hebamme, 1971; Lysistrate und die NATO, 1973; Tod eines Jägers, 1976; Eine Liebe in Deutschland, 1978; Juristen, 1979; Arztinnen, 1980; Spitze des Eisbergs: Ein Reader, 1982; Judith, 1984; Atlantik, 1985; Der Berliner Antiogone: Erzählungen und Gedichte, 1986; War hier Europa?: Reden, Gedichte, Essays, 1987; Tater und Denker: Profile und Probleme von Cäaser bis Jünger, 1987; Unbefleckte Empfängnis: Ein Kreidekreis, 1988; Sommer 14: Ein Totentan, 1989; Alle Dramen, 2 vols, 1991; Panik im Mai: Sämtliche Gedichte und Erzählungen, 1991; Wessis in Weimar: Szenen aus einem besetzten Land, 1993; Julia oder Weg zur Macht, 1994. *Honours:* Gerhart Hauptmann Prize, 1962; Berlin Art Prize, 1963; Basel Art Prize, 1976; Literature Prize, City of Munich and Asscn of Bavarian Publishers, 1980; Lessing Prize, Hamburg, 1981; Jacob Burckhardt Prize, 1991. *Address:* c/o Die Welt, Kochstrasse 50, 10069 Berlin, Germany.

HOCHSCHILD, Adam; Writer; b. 5 Oct. 1942, New York, NY, USA; m. Arlie Russell, 26 June 1965, two s. *Education:* AB cum laude, Harvard University, 1963. *Career:* Reporter, San Francisco Chronicle, 1965–66; Ed. and Writer, Ramparts Magazine, 1966–68, 1973–74; Co-Founder, Ed., Writer, Mother Jones Magazine, 1974–81, 1986–87; Commentator, National Public Radio, 1982–83, Public Interest Radio, 1987–88; Regents Lecturer, University of California at Santa Cruz, 1987; Lecturer, Graduate School of Journalism, University of California at Berkeley, 1992–; Fulbright Lecturer, India, 1997–98; mem. PEN; National Writers Union; National Book Critics Circle. *Publications:* Half the Way Home: A Memoir of Father and Son, 1986; The Mirror at Midnight: A South African Journey, 1990; The Unquiet Ghost: Russians Remember Stalin, 1994; Finding the Trapdoor: Essays, Portraits, Travels, 1997; King Leopold's Ghost: A Story of Greed, Terror and Heroism In Colonial Africa, 1998. Contributions: New Yorker; Harper's; New York Times; Los Angeles Times; Washington Post; Progressive; Village Voice; New York Review of Books; Mother Jones. *Honours:* Thomas Storke Award, World Affairs Council, 1987; Madeleine Dane Ross Award, Overseas Press Club of America, 1995; Lowell Thomas Award, Society of American Travel Writers, 1995; PEN/Spielvogel-Diamonstein Award for the Art of the Essay, 1998; Gold Medal, California Book Awards, 1999; J. Anthony Lukas Prize, 1999; Lionel Gelber Prize, Canada, 1999; Duff Cooper Prize, UK, 2000; Best Magazine Article, Society of Professional Journalists Awards, 2000. *Literary Agent:* Georges Borchardt Inc, 136 E 57th St, New York, NY 10022, USA. *Address:* 84 Seward St, San Francisco, CA 94114, USA.

HOCKING, Mary (Eunice); Writer; b. 8 April 1921, London, England. *Career:* Local government officer, 1946–70; mem. FRSL; Society of Authors. *Publications:* The Winter City, 1961; Visitors to the Crescent, 1962; The Sparrow, 1964; The Young Spaniard, 1965; Ask No Question, 1967; A Time of War, 1968; Checkmate, 1969; The Hopeful Traveller, 1970; The Climbing Frame, 1971; Family Circle, 1972; Daniel Come to Judgement, 1974; The Bright Day, 1975; The Mind Has Mountains, 1976; Look, Stranger!, 1978; He Who Plays the King, 1980; March House, 1981; Good Daughters, 1984; Indifferent Heroes, 1985; Welcome Strangers, 1986; An Irrelevant Woman, 1987; A Particular Place, 1989; Letters from Constance, 1991; The Very Dead of Winter, 1993; The Meeting Place, 1996. *Address:* 3 Church Row, Lewes, Sussex, England.

HODGE, Jane Aiken; Author; b. 4 Dec. 1917, Watertown, Massachusetts, USA; m. Alan Hodge, 3 Jan. 1948, deceased 1979, two d. *Education:* BA, Somerville College, Oxford, 1938; AM, Radcliffe College, 1939. *Career:* mem. Society of Authors. *Publications:* Fiction: Maulever Hall, 1964; The Adventurers, 1965; Watch the Wall, My Darling, 1966; Here Comes a Candle, 1967; The Winding Stair, 1968; Marry in Haste, 1970; Greek Wedding, 1970; Savannah Purchase, 1971; Strangers in Company, 1973; Shadow of a Lady, 1974; One Way to Venice, 1975; Rebel Heiress, 1975; Runaway Bride, 1976; Judas Flowering, 1976; Red Sky at Night: Lover's Delight?, 1978; Last Act, 1979; Wide is the Water, 1981; The Lost Garden, 1981; Secret Island, 1985; Polonaise, 1987; First Night, 1989; Leading Lady, 1990; Windover, 1992; Escapade, 1993; Whispering, 1995; Bride of Dreams, 1996; Unsafe Hands, 1997; Susan in America, 1998; Caterina, 1999; A Death in Two Parts, 2000. Non-Fiction: The Double Life of Jane Austen, 1972; The Private World of Georgette Heyer, 1984; Passion and Principle: The Loves and Lives of Regency Women, 1996. Contributions: newspapers and journals. *Address:* 23 Eastport Lane, Lewes, East Sussex BN7 1TL, England.

HODGINS, Jack Stanley; Novelist and Teacher; b. 3 Oct. 1938, Vancouver Island, BC, Canada; m. Dianne Child, 17 Dec. 1960, two s. one d. *Education:* BEd, University of British Columbia. *Career:* mem. PEN; Writers Union of Canada. *Publications:* Spit Delaney's Island, 1976; The Invention of the World, 1977; The Resurrection of Joseph Bourne, 1979; The Honorary Patron, 1987; Innocent Cities, 1990; Over Forty in Broken Hill, 1992; A Passion for Narrative, 1993; The Macken Charm, 1995; Broken Ground, 1998. *Honours:* Gibson First Novel Award, 1978; Gov.-Gen.'s Award for Fiction, 1980; Canada-Australia Literature Prize, 1986; Commonwealth Literature Prize, 1988; DLitt, University of British Columbia, 1995; DLitt, Malaspina University, 1998; Ethel Wilson Award, British Columbian Book Prize, 1999; Fellow, Royal Society of Canada, 1999. *Address:* Dept of Writing, University of Victoria, PO Box 1700, Victoria, BC V8W 2Y2, Canada.

HOE, Susanna Leonie, BA; historian; b. 14 April 1945, Southampton, England; m. Derek Roebuck 1981. *Education:* LSE, Univ. of Papua, New Guinea. *Career:* campaign co-ordinator, British Section, Amnesty Int. 1977–80; Tutor, Dept of Anthropology and Sociology, Univ. of Papua New Guinea 1985–86; TEFL teacher, Women's Centre, Hong Kong 1991–97. *Publications:* Lady in the Chamber (novel) 1971, God Save the Tsar (novel) 1978, The Man Who Gave his Company Away (biog.) 1978, The Private Life of Old Hong Kong (history) 1991, Chinese Footprints (history) 1996, Stories for Eva (reader for learning English) 1997, The Taking of Hong Kong (history, with Derek Roebuck) 1999, Women at the Siege, Peking 1900 (history) 2000, At Home in Paradise (travel, autobiog.) 2003; contrib. to Times (Papua New Guinea), Liverpool Post, Women's Feature Service. *Honours:* Rangi Hiroa Pacific History Prize 1984, Hon. Research Fellow, Centre of Asian Studies, Univ. of Hong Kong. *Address:* 20A Plantation Road, Oxford, OX2 6JD, England.

HØEG, Peter; Danish writer; b. 1957, Copenhagen; m.; two d. *Education:* Univ. of Copenhagen. *Career:* worked as sailor, ballet dancer, athlete and actor before becoming full-time writer; f., Lolwe Foundation 1996. *Publications:* The History of Danish Dreams 1988, Tales of the Night (short stories) 1990, Miss Smilla's Feeling for Snow 1992, Borderliners 1994, The Woman and the Ape 1996.

HOFFMAN, Adina; American writer and journalist; b. 1967, Mississippi; m. Peter Cole. *Career:* Visiting Prof., Wesleyan Univ., Middlebury Coll.; editorial bd mem., Ibis Editions; film critic for American Prospect, Jerusalem Post. *Publications:* House of Windows: Portraits from a Jerusalem Neighbourhood 2000; contrib. to The Washington Post, TLS, Boston Globe, New York Newsday, Tin House, Co-Exist Magazine, The Forward, BBC World Service. *Address:* c/o Ibis Editions, PO Box 8074, German Colony, Jerusalem, Israel. *E-mail:* ibis@netvision.net.il. *Website:* www.ibiseditions.com.

HOFFMAN, Alice; Author and Screenwriter; b. 16 March 1952, New York, NY, USA; m. Tom Martin, two s. *Education:* BA, Adelphi University, 1973;

MA, Stanford University, 1975. *Publications:* Property Of, 1977; The Drowning Season, 1979; Angel Landing, 1980; White Horses, 1982; Fortune's Daughter, 1985; Illumination Night, 1987; At Risk, 1988; Seventh Heaven, 1990; Turtle Moon, 1992; Second Nature, 1994; Practical Magic, 1996; Here on Earth, 1997; Local Girls, 1999; The River King, 2001; Blue Diary, 2001; Aquamarine, 2003; The Probable Future, 2003. Other: various screenplays. Contributions: Redbook; American Review; Playgirl. *Address:* c/o Penguin Putnam, 375 Hudson St, New York, NY 10014, USA. *Website:* www.alicehoffman.com.

HOFFMAN, Daniel (Gerard); Prof. of English Emeritus, Poet and Writer; b. 3 April 1923, New York, NY, USA; m. Elizabeth McFarland, 1948, two c. *Education:* AB, 1947, MA, 1949, PhD, 1956, Columbia University. *Career:* Visiting Prof., University of Dijon, 1956–57; Asst Prof., 1957–60, Assoc. Prof., 1960–65, Prof. of English, 1965–66, Swarthmore College; Elliston Lecturer, University of Cincinnati, 1964; Lecturer, International School of Yeats Studies, Sligo, Ireland, 1965; Prof. of English, 1966–83, Poet-in-Residence, 1978–, Felix E. Schelling Prof. of English, 1983–93, Prof. Emeritus, 1993–, University of Pennsylvania; Consultant in Poetry, 1973–74, Hon. Consultant in American Letters, 1974–77, Library of Congress, Washington, DC; Poet-in-Residence, Cathedral of St John the Divine, New York City, 1988–; Visiting Prof. of English, King's College, London, 1991–92; mem. Acad. of American Poets, chancellor, 1973–97, chancellor emeritus, 1997–. *Publications:* Poetry: An Armada of Thirty Whales, 1954; A Little Geste and Other Poems, 1960; The City of Satisfactions, 1963; Striking the Stones, 1968; Broken Laws, 1970; Corgi Modern Poets in Focus 4 (with others), 1971; The Center of Attention, 1974; Able Was I Ere I Saw Elba: Selected Poems 1954–1974, 1977; Brotherly Love, 1981; Hang-Gliding from Helicon: New and Selected Poems 1948–1988, 1988; Middens of the Tribe, 1995. Other: The Poetry of Stephen Crane, 1957; Form and Fable in American Fiction, 1961; Barbarous Knowledge: Myth in the Poetry of Yeats, Graves and Muir, 1967; Poe Poe Poe Poe Poe Poe Poe, 1972. Others: Shock Troops of Stylistic Change, 1975; 'Moonlight Dries No Mittens': Carl Sandburg Reconsidered, 1979; Faulkner's Country Matters: Folklore and Fable in Yoknapatawpha, 1989; Words to Create a World: Interviews, Essays and Reviews of Contemporary Poetry, 1993. Editor: several books. *Honours:* Yale Series of Younger Poets Award, 1954; Ansley Prize, 1957; ACLS Fellowships, 1961–62, 1966–67; Columbia University Medal for Excellence, 1964; American Acad. of Arts and Letters Grant, 1967; Ingram Merrill Foundation Grant, 1971; National Endowment for the Humanities Fellowship, 1975–76; Hungarian PEN Medal, 1980; Guggenheim Fellowship, 1983; Hazlett Memorial Award, 1984; Paterson Poetry Prize, 1989. *Address:* c/o Dept of English, University of Pennsylvania, Philadelphia, PA 19104, USA.

HOFFMAN, Eva Alfreda; writer; b. 1 July 1945, Kraków, Poland. *Career:* Ed., The New York Times Book Review 1987–90; Visiting Prof., Dept of the Humanities, MIT; mem. PEN, New York Univ. Inst. for the Humanities. *Publications:* Lost in Translation: A Life in a New Language 1989, Exit Into History: A Journey Through the New Eastern Europe 1993, Shtetl: A History of a Small Town and an Extinguished World 1997, The Secret: A Fable for Our Time 2001, After Such Knowledge: Where Memory of the Holocaust Ends and History Begins 2004; contrib. to newspapers and periodicals. *Honours:* American Acad. of Arts and Letters Award 1990, Whiting Award 1992, Guggenheim Fellowship 1993. *Literary Agent:* Georges Borchardt, 136 E 57th Street, New York, NY 10022, USA. *Address:* Gill Coleridge, Rogers, Coleridge & White Ltd, 20 Powis Mews, London, W11 1JN, England.

HOFFMAN, Mary Margaret Lassiter, BA, MA; writer and journalist; b. 20 April 1945, Eastleigh, Hampshire, England; m. Stephen James Barber 1972; three d. *Education:* Newnham College, Cambridge; University College London. *Career:* mem. Society of Authors. *Publications:* 80 Children's Books, including: Amazing Grace, 1991; Henry's Baby, 1993; Grace and Family, 1995; Song of the Earth, 1995; An Angel Just Like Me, 1997; Sun, Moon and Stars, 1998; Three Wise Women, 1999; Starring Grace, 2000; Stravaganza: City of Masks, 2002; Lines in the Sand (ed.), 2003; Stravaganza: City of Stars, 2003; Encore, Grace!, 2003. Contributions: Daily Telegraph; Guardian; Independent; Sunday Times; Specialist Children's Book Press. *Honours:* Waldenbooks Best Children's Book Honor Award, 1991; Primary English Award, 1995; Hon. Fellow, Library Asscn, 1998. *Literary Agent:* Rogers, Coleridge & White Ltd, 20 Powis Mews, London, W11 1JN, England.

HOFFMAN, William; Writer; b. 12 April 1939, New York, NY, USA. *Education:* BA, City College, CUNY. *Career:* mem. American Society of Composers, Authors, and Publishers; Dramatists Guild; PEN; Writers Guild of America. *Publications:* As Is, 1985; The Ghosts of Versailles (libretto for opera by John Corigliano), 1991. Editor: New American Plays 2, 3, 4, 1968, 1970, 1971; Gay Plays, 1977. Contributions: journals and magazines. *Honours:* Drama Desk Award, 1985; Obie, 1985; International Classical Music Award, 1991; Emmy, 1992; WGA Award, 1992; Erwin Piscator Award, 1994. *Address:* c/o International Creative Management, 40 W 57th St, New York, NY 10019, USA.

HOFFMANN, Donald; Architectural Critic and Historian; b. 24 June 1933, Springfield, IL, USA; m. Theresa McGrath, 12 April 1958, four s., one d. *Education:* University of Chicago, University of Kansas City. *Career:* General Assignment Reporter, 1956–65, Art Critic, 1965–90, Kansas City Star; Asst Ed., Journal of the Society of Architectural Historians, 1970–72; mem. Art Institute of Chicago, life mem. *Publications:* The Meanings of Architecture: Buildings and Writings by John Wellborn Root (ed.), 1967; The Architecture of John Wellborn Root, 1973; Frank Lloyd Wright's Fallingwater, 1978; Frank Lloyd Wright's Robie House, 1984; Frank Lloyd Wright: Architecture and Nature, 1986; Frank Lloyd Wright's Hollyhock House, 1992; Understanding Frank Lloyd Wright's Architecture, 1995; Frank Lloyd Wright's Dana House, 1996; Frank Lloyd Wright, Louis Sullivan and the Skyscraper, 1998; Frank Lloyd Wright's House on Kentuck Knob, 2000. *Honours:* National Endowment for the Humanities Fellowship, 1970–71; National Endowment for the Arts Fellowship, 1974; Graham Foundation Grant, 1981. *Address:* 6441 Holmes St, Kansas City, MO 64131-1110, USA. *Telephone:* (816) 333-0355. *E-mail:* donhoff@homerelay.net.

HOFMANN, Michael; Poet, Dramatist and Trans; b. 25 Aug. 1957, Freiburg, Germany. *Education:* BA, Magdalene College, Cambridge, 1979. *Career:* Visiting Assoc. Prof., Creative Writing Dept, University of Michigan, Ann Arbor, 1994; Visiting Distinguished Lecturer, University of Florida, Gainesville, 1994–. *Publications:* Nights in the Iron Hotel, 1983; Acrimony, 1986; K.S. in Lakeland: New and Selected Poems, 1990; Corona, Corona, 1993; After Ovid: New Metamorphoses (co-ed. with James Lasdun), 1994; Penguin Modern Poets 13, 1998; Approximately Nowhere, 1999; Behind the Lines, 2002. Plays: The Double Bass (adaptation of a play by Patrick Suskind), 1987; The Good Person of Sichuan (adaptation of a play by Brecht), 1989. Other: Trans. Contributions: The London Review of Books; TLS. *Honours:* Cholmondeley Award, 1984; Geoffrey Faber Memorial Prize, 1988; Schlegel Tieck Prizes, 1988, 1992; Arts Council Writers Bursary, 1997–98; PEN/Book of the Month Club Trans. Prize, 1999; Helen and Kurt Wolff Prize, 2000. *Address:* c/o Faber and Faber, 3 Queen Sq., London WC1N 3AU, England.

HOFSTADTER, Douglas Richard; academic and writer; b. 15 Feb. 1945, New York, NY, USA; m. Carol Ann Brush 1985 (died 1993); one s. one d. *Education:* BS in Mathematics, Stanford University, 1965; MS in Physics, 1972, PhD in Physics, 1975, University of Oregon. *Career:* Visiting Scholar, Stanford University, 1975–77, 1980–81, 1997; Asst Prof. of Computer Science, 1977–80, Assoc. Prof. of Computer Science, 1980–83, College Prof. of Computer Science and Cognitive Science, and Dir, Center for Research on Concepts and Cognition, 1988–, Indiana University; Visiting Scientist, MIT, 1983–84, Istituto per la Ricerca Scientifica e Technologica, Povo, Trento, 1993–94; Walgreen Prof. for the Study of Human Understanding and Prof. of Psychology and Cognitive Science, University of Michigan, 1984–88; mem. American Asscn for Artificial Intelligence; Committee for the Scientific Investigation of Claims of the Paranormal; Cognitive Science Society; Golden Key National Honor Society. *Publications:* Gödel, Escher, Bach: An Eternal Golden Braid, 1979; The Mind's I: Fantasies and Reflections on Self and Soul (ed. with Daniel C. Dennett), 1981; Metamagical Themas: Questing for the Essence of Mind and Pattern, 1985; Ambigrammi: Un microcosmo ideale per lo studio della creativita, 1987; Fluid Concepts and Creative Analogies: Computer Models of the Fundamental Mechanisms of Thought, 1995; Rhapsody on a Theme by Clément Marot, 1996; Le Ton beau de Marot: In Praise of the Music of Language, 1997; Eugene Onegin: A Novel in Verse, by Alexander Sergeevich Pushkin, A Novel Versification by Douglas Hofstadter, 1999. Contributions: scholarly books and journals. *Honours:* Pulitzer Prize for General Non-Fiction, 1980; American Book Award, 1980; Guggenheim Fellowship, 1980–81; Senior Fellow, Michigan Society of Fellows, 1985; Arts and Sciences Alumni Fellows Award, University of Oregon, 1997. *Address:* c/o Center for Research on Concepts and Cognition, Indiana University, 510 N Fess Street, Bloomington, IN 47408, USA.

HOGAN, Desmond; Writer and Teacher; b. 10 Dec. 1950, Ballinasloe, Ireland. *Education:* BA, 1972, MA, 1973, University College, Dublin. *Career:* Strode Fellow, University of Alabama, 1989. *Publications:* The Ikon Maker, 1976; The Leaves on Grey, 1980; A Curious Street, 1984; A New Shirt, 1984; A Link with the River, 1989; The Edge of the City, 1993. *Honours:* John Llewellyn Memorial Prize, 1980; Irish Post Award, 1985; Deutscher Akademischer Austauschdienst Fellowship, Berlin, 1991.

HOGAN, James P(atrick); Writer; b. 27 June 1941, London, England; m. 1st Iris Crossley, 1961, divorced 1977, three d.; m. 2nd Lynda Shirley Dockerty, divorced 1980; m. 3rd Jackie Price, 1983, three s. *Education:* Certificates, Royal Aircraft Establishment Technical College, 1963, Reading Technical College, 1965. *Publications:* Inherit the Stars, 1977; The Genesis Machine, 1978; The Gentle Giants of Ganymede, 1978; The Two Faces of Tomorrow, 1979; Thrice Upon a Time, 1980; Giants' Star, 1981; Voyage from Yesteryear, 1982; Code of the Lifemaker, 1983; The Proteus Operation, 1985; Minds, Machines and Evolution (short stories), 1986; Endgame Enigma, 1987; The Mirror Maze, 1989; The Infinity Gambit, 1991; The Multiplex Man, 1992; Entoverse, 1992; Realtime Interrupt, 1995; The Immortality Option, 1995; Paths to Otherwhere, 1996; Bug Park, 1997; Mind Matters, 1998. Contributions: anthologies and magazines.

HOGAN, Kathleen Margaret, (Kay Hogan); Writer; b. 13 Feb. 1935, New York, NY, USA; m. James P. Hogan, four s., one d. *Education:* High School Graduate, 1952. *Publications:* The El Train, 1882; The Silent Men, 1984;

Widow Women, 1985; Little Green Girl, 1986; Of Saints and Other Things, 1992; The Women Wore Black, 1993. Contributions: Descant; Long Pond Review; Journal of Irish Literature; North Country Anthology; Catholic Girls Anthology; Glens Falls Review. *Address:* 154 East Ave, Saratoga Springs, NY 12866, USA.

HOGAN, Linda Chickasaw Nation, MA; poet, novelist, essayist and academic; b. 16 July 1947, Denver, CO, USA; m. Pat Hogan (divorced); two d. *Education:* University of Colorado at Boulder. *Career:* Assoc., Rocky Mountain Women's Institute, University of Denver, 1979–80; Poet-in-the-Schools, Colorado and Oklahoma, 1980–84; Asst Prof., Tribes Program, Colorado College, 1982–84; Assoc. Prof. of American and American Indian Studies, University of Minnesota, 1984–89; Prof. of English, University of Colorado at Boulder, 1989–; mem. Authors' Guild; MLA; National American Studies Program; National Council of Teachers of English; PEN West; Writers Guild. *Publications:* Poetry: Calling Myself Home, 1979; Eclipse, 1983; Seeing Through the Sun, 1985; Savings, 1988; The Book of Medicines, 1993. Fiction: That Horse, 1985; Mean Spirit, 1990; Solar Storms, 1995; Power, 1998. Other: A Piece of Moon (play), 1981; The Stories We Hold Secret: Tales of Women's Spiritual Development (ed. with Carol Bruchac and Judith McDaniel), 1986; Dwellings: A Spiritual History of the Natural World, 1995; Intimate Nature: The Bond Between Women and Animals, 1998. *Honours:* Guggenheim Fellowship; Lannan Award for Poetry; National Endowment for the Arts Grant; American Book Award, 1986; Oklahoma Book Award for Fiction, 1990; Colorado Book Awards, 1994, 1997. *Address:* c/o Dept of English, University of Colorado at Boulder, Boulder, CO 80302, USA.

HOGAN, Robert (Goode); Prof. of English and Writer; b. 29 May 1930, Boonville, MO, USA; m. 1st Betty Mathews, 1 Dec. 1950, divorced 1978, two s. three d.; m. 2nd Mary Rose Callaghan, 21 Dec. 1979. *Education:* BA, 1953, MA, 1954, PhD, 1956, University of Missouri. *Career:* Publisher, Proscenium Press, 1964–; Prof. of English, University of Delaware, 1970–; Ed., Journal of Irish Literature, 1972–, George Spelvin's Theatre Book, 1978–85. *Publications:* Experiments of Sean O'Casey, 1960; Feathers from the Green Crow, 1962; Drama: The Major Genres (ed. with S. Molin), 1962; Arthur Miller, 1964; Independence of Elmer Rice, 1965; Joseph Holloway's Abbey Theatre (ed. with M. J. O'Neill), 1967; The Plain Style (with H. Bogart), 1967; After the Irish Renaissance, 1967; Seven Irish Plays (ed.), 1967; Joseph Holloway's Irish Theatre (ed. with M. J. O'Neill), 3 vols, 1968–70; Dion Boucicault, 1969; The Fan Club, 1969; Betty and the Beast, 1969; Lost Plays of the Irish Renaissance (with J. Kilroy), 1970; Crows of Mephistopheles (ed.), 1970; Towards a National Theatre (ed.), 1970; Eimar O'Duffy, 1972; Mervyn Wall, 1972; Conor Cruise O'Brien (with E. Young-Bruehl), 1974; A History of the Modern Irish Drama, Vol. 1, The Irish Literary Theatre (with J. Kilroy), 1975, Vol. II, Laying the Foundation (with J. Kilroy), 1976, Vol. III, The Abbey Theatre 1905–09 (with J. Kilroy), 1978, Vol. IV, The Rise of the Realists, 1910–1915 (with R. Burnham and D. P. Poteet), 1979, Vol. V, The Art of the Amateur 1916–1920 (with R. Burnham), 1984, Vol. VI, The Years of O'Casey (with R. Burnham), 1992; The Dictionary of Irish Literature (ed.), 1979; Since O'Casey, 1983; The Plays of Frances Sheridan (ed. with J. C. Beasley), 1984; Guarini's The Faithful Shepherd (trans. by Thomas Sheridan, ed. and completed with E. Nickerson), 1990; Murder at the Abbey (with J. Douglas), 1993. *Address:* PO Box 361, Newark, DE 19711, USA.

HOGGARD, James (Martin); Prof. of English, Poet, Writer and Trans; b. 21 June 1941, Wichita Falls, Texas, USA; m. Lynn Taylor Hoggard, 23 May 1976, one s. one d. *Education:* BA, Southern Methodist University, 1963; MA, University of Kansas, 1965. *Career:* Teaching Asst, University of Kansas, 1963–65; Instructor to Prof. of English, Midwestern State University, 1966–; Guest Prof., Instituto Allende, San Miguel de Allende, Mexico, 1977, 1978; University of Mosul, Iraq, 1990; Exchange Prof., Instituto Tecnologico de Estudias Superiores de Monterrey, Chihuahua, Mexico, 1993; mem. American Literary Trans Asscn; American Studies Asscn of Texas; PEN; Conference of College Teachers of English; Texas Institute of Letters, pres., 1994–98. *Publications:* Poetry: Eyesigns: Poems on Letters and Numbers, 1977; The Shaper Poems, 1983; Two Gulls, One Hawk, 1983; Breaking an Indelicate Statue, 1986; Medea in Taos, 2000; Rain In A Sunlit Sky, 2000. Fiction: Trotter Ross, 1981; Riding the Wind and Other Tales, 1997; Patterns of Illusion: Stories and a Novella. Non-Fiction: Elevator Man, 1983. Contributions: anthologies, reviews, quarterlies, journals, and magazines. *Honours:* Soeurette Diehl Fraser Award; Stanley Walker Award; Brazos Bookstore (Houston) Short Story Award; NEA Creative Writing Fellowship; grants and citations. *Address:* c/o Dept of English, Midwestern State University, Wichita Falls, TX 76308, USA.

HOGGART, Richard Herbert, MA, DLitt; British educator (retd) and writer; b. 24 Sept. 1918, Leeds; m. Mary Holt France 1942; two s. one d. *Education:* Cockburn Grammar School and Univ. of Leeds. *Career:* RA 1940–46; Staff Tutor and Sr Staff Tutor, Univ. Coll. of Hull and Univ. of Hull 1946–59; Sr Lecturer in English, Univ. of Leicester 1959–62; Visiting Prof., Univ. of Rochester, NY 1956–57; Prof. of English, Univ. of Birmingham 1962–73; Pres. British Asscn of fmr UN Civil Servants 1978–86; Chair. European Museum of the Year Award Cttee 1977–, Broadcasting Research Unit 1980–90; mem. Albemarle Cttee on Youth Services 1958–60, Youth Service Devt Council 1960–62, Pilkington Cttee on Broadcasting 1960–62; Gov. Birmingham Repertory Theatre 1963–70; Dir Centre for Contemporary Cultural Studies 1964–73; mem. BBC Gen. Advisory Council 1959–60, 1964–70, Arts Council of GB 1976–81, Culture Advisory Cttee of UK Nat. Comm. to UNESCO 1966–70, Communications Advisory Cttee of UK Nat. Comm. to UNESCO 1977–79, Wilton Park Academic Council 1983–; Chair. Arts Council Drama Panel 1977–80, Vice-Chair. Arts Council 1980–81, Chair. Advisory Council for Adult and Continuing Educ. 1977–83, The Statesman and Nation Publishing Co. Ltd 1978–81; Gov. Royal Shakespeare Theatre 1966–88; Asst Dir-Gen. for Social Sciences, Humanities and Culture UNESCO 1970–75; Warden of Goldsmiths' Coll., London 1976–84; Chair. Book Trust 1995–97; Pres. Nat. Book Cttee 1997–. *Publications:* Auden 1951, The Uses of Literacy 1957, W. H. Auden – A Selection 1961, Teaching Literature 1963, The Critical Moment 1964, How and Why Do We Learn 1965, Technology and Society 1966, Essays in Literature and Culture 1969, Speaking to Each Other 1970, Only Connect (Reith Lectures) 1972, An Idea and Its Servants 1978, An English Temper 1982, The Future of Broadcasting (ed. with Janet Morgan) 1978, An Idea of Europe (with Douglas Johnson) 1987, A Local Habitation (autobiog.) 1988, Liberty and Legislation (ed.) 1989, A Sort of Clowning 1990, An Imagined Life 1992, Townscape with Figures 1994, The Way We Live Now 1995, First and Last Things 1999, Hoggart en France 1999, Between Two Worlds 2001, Everyday Language and Everyday Life 2003, Mass Media in a Mass Society 2004. *Honours:* Hon. Visiting Prof., Univ. of E Anglia 1985–, Univ. of Surrey 1985–; Hon. Fellow Sheffield City Polytechnic 1983, Goldsmiths' Coll. 1987, Ruskin Coll. Oxford 1994; Hon. DUniv (Open Univ.) 1972, (Surrey) 1981; Hon. DèsSc (Bordeaux) 1974, (Paris) 1987; Hon. LLD (CNAA) 1982, (York Univ., Toronto) 1988; Hon. LittD (E Anglia) 1986, (Metropolitan Univ. of London) 2003; Hon. DLitt (Leicester), (Hull) 1988, (Keele) 1995, (Metropolitan Univ. of Leeds) 1995, (Westminster) 1996, (Sheffield) 1999, (London) 2000; Hon. EdD (E London) 1998; BBC Reith Lecturer 1971. *Literary Agent:* Curtis Brown Ltd, Haymarket House, 28–29 Haymarket, London, SW1Y 4SP, England. *Telephone:* (20) 7393-4400. *Fax:* (20) 7393-4401. *E-mail:* info@curtisbrown.co.uk. *Website:* www.curtisbrown.co.uk. *Address:* 19 Mount Pleasant, Norwich, NR2 2DH, Norfolk, England (Home). *Telephone:* (1603) 250398. *Fax:* (1603) 250398. *E-mail:* richard.hoggart@onetel.net.uk.

HOGWOOD, Christopher (Jarvis Haley); Harpischordist, Conductor, Musicologist, Writer, Ed. and Broadcaster; b. 10 Sept. 1941, Nottingham, England. *Education:* BA, Pembroke College, Cambridge, 1964; Charles University, Prague; Acad. of Music, Prague. *Career:* Founder-Mem., Early Music Consort of London, 1967–76; Founder-Dir, The Acad. of Ancient Music, 1973–; Faculty, University of Cambridge, 1975–; Artistic Dir, 1986–2000, Conductor Laureate, 2001–, Handel and Haydn Society, Boston; Hon. Prof. of Music, University of Keele, 1986–89; Music Dir, 1988–92, Principal Guest Conductor, 1992–98, St Paul Chamber Orchestra, Minnesota; International Prof. of Early Music Performance, Royal Acad. of Music, London, 1992–; Visiting Prof., King's College, London, 1992–96; Principal Guest Conductor, Kammerorchester Basel, 2000–, Orquesta Ciudad de Granada, 2001–; mem. Royal Society of Authors, fellow. *Publications:* Music at Court, 1977; The Trio Sonata, 1979; Haydn's Visits to England, 1980; Music in Eighteenth-Century England (ed.), 1983; Handel, 1984; Holme's Life of Mozart (ed.), 1991. Contributions: The New Grove Dictionary of Music and Musicians, 1980. *Honours:* Walter Wilson Cobbett Medal, 1986; CBE, 1989; Hon. Fellow, Jesus College, Cambridge, 1989, Pembroke College, Cambridge, 1992; Hon. Prof., Univ. of Cambridge, 2002–; Freeman, Worshipful Company of Musicians, 1989; Incorporated Society of Musicians Distinguished Musician Award, 1997; Martinů Medal, Bohuslav Martinů Foundation, Prague, 1999. *Address:* 10 Brookside, Cambridge CB2 1JE, England.

HOLBROOK, David (Kenneth); Author and Poet; b. 9 Jan. 1923, Norwich, England; m. 23 April 1949, two s. two d. *Education:* BA, English, 1946, MA, 1951, Downing College, Cambridge. *Career:* Fellow, King's College, Cambridge, 1961–65; Senior Leverhulme Research Fellow, 1965, Leverhulme Emeritus Research Fellow, 1988–90; Writer-in-Residence, Dartington Hall, 1972–73; Fellow and Dir of English Studies, 1981–88, Emeritus Fellow, 1988, Downing College; mem. English Asscn, founding fellow, 2000; Society of Authors. *Publications:* English for Maturity, 1961; Imaginings, 1961; Against the Cruel Frost, 1963; English for the Rejected, 1964; The Secret Places, 1964; Flesh Wounds, 1966; Children's Writing, 1967; The Exploring Word, 1967; Object Relations, 1967; Old World New World, 1969; English in Australia Now, 1972; Chance of a Lifetime, 1978; A Play of Passion, 1978; English for Meaning, 1980; Selected Poems, 1980; Nothing Larger than Life, 1987; The Novel and Authenticity, 1987; A Little Athens, 1990; Edith Wharton and the Unsatisfactory Man, 1991; Jennifer, 1991; The Gold in Father's Heart, 1992; Where D. H. Lawrence Was Wrong About Women, 1992; Creativity and Popular Culture, 1994; Even If They Fail, 1994; Tolstoy, Women and Death, 1996; Wuthering Heights: A Drama of Being, 1997; Getting it Wrong with Uncle Tom, 1998; Bringing Everything Home (poems), 1999; A Study of George MacDonald and the Image of Woman, 2000; Lewis Carroll: Nonsense Against Sorrow, 2001. Contributions: numerous professional journals. *Honours:* Festschrift, 1996. *Address:* 1 Tennis Court Terrace, Cambridge CB2 1QX, England. *E-mail:* dkh1000@cam.ac.uk.

HOLDEN, Anthony Ivan, MA; journalist and writer; b. 22 May 1947, Southport, England; m. 1st Amanda Warren 1971 (divorced 1988); m. 2nd

Cynthia Blake 1990. *Education:* Merton College, Oxford. *Career:* correspondent, Sunday Times 1973–77; columnist (Atticus) 1977–79, Chief US correspondent 1979–81, The Observer; Features Ed. and Asst Ed., The Times 1981–82; freelance journalist and author, broadcaster on radio and television. *Publications:* Agememnon of Aeschylus 1969, The Greek Anthology 1973, The St Albans Poisoner 1974, Charles, Prince of Wales 1979, Their Royal Highnesses 1981, Of Presidents, Prime Ministers and Princes 1984, The Queen Mother 1985, Charles 1988, Olivier 1988, Big Deal 1990, The Last Paragraph (ed.) 1990, A Princely Marriage 1991, The Oscars 1993, The Tarnished Crown 1993, Tchaikovsky 1995, Diana: A Life, A Legacy 1997, Charles at Fifty 1998, William Shakespeare 2000, The Wit in the Dungeon: Leigh Hunt and his Circle 2005. *Honours:* Columnist of the Year, British Press Awards 1977, Fellow, Center for Scholars and Writers, New York Public Library 1999–2000. *Literary Agent:* Rogers, Coleridge & White Ltd, 20 Powis Mews, London W11 1JN, England.

HOLDEN, Joan; Dramatist; b. 18 Jan. 1939, Berkeley, CA, USA; m. 1st Arthur Holden, 1958, divorced; m. 2nd Daniel Chumley, 1968, three d. *Education:* BA, Reed College, Portland, Oregon, 1960; MA, University of California at Berkeley, 1964. *Career:* Ed., Pacific News Service, 1973–75; Instructor in Playwriting, University of California at Davis, 1975, 1977, 1979, 1983, 1985, 1987. *Publications:* Americans, or, Last Tango in Huahuatenango (with Daniel Chumley), 1981; Factwindo Meets the Moral Majority (with others), 1981; Factwindo vs Armaggedonman, 1982; Steeltown, 1984; Spain/36, 1986; The Mozangola Caper (with others), 1986; Seeing Double, 1989; Back to Normal, 1990; Offshore, 1993. *Honours:* Obie Awards, 1973, 1990; Rockefeller Foundation Grant, 1985; Edward G. Robbins Playwriting Award, 1992. *Address:* c/o San Francisco Mime Troupe, 855 Treat St, San Francisco, CA 94110, USA.

HOLDSTOCK, Robert; Writer; b. 2 Aug. 1948, Hythe, Kent, England. *Education:* BSc, University College of North Wales, 1970; MSc, London School of Hygiene and Tropical Medicine, 1971. *Publications:* Eye Among the Blind, 1976; Earthwind, 1977; Necromancer, 1978; Stars of Albion, 1979; Alien Landscapes, 1979; Tour of the Universe, 1980; Where Time Winds Blow, 1981; Mythago Wood, 1984; Emerald Forest, 1985; The Labyrinth, 1987; Other Edens, 1987; Lavondyss, 1988; The Fetch, 1991; The Bone Forest, 1992; The Hollowing, 1993; Merlin's Wood, 1994; Ancient Echoes, 1996; Gate of Ivory, Gate of Horn, 1997; Celtika, 2000; The Iron Grail, 2002. *Honours:* World Fantasy Awards, 1985, 1993. *Address:* 54 Raleigh Rd, London N8 0HY, England. *Website:* www.mythago.tuath.org.

HOLLAND, Cecelia (Anastasia); Author; b. 31 Dec. 1943, Henderson, Nevada, USA. *Education:* Pennsylvania State University; BA, Connecticut College, 1965. *Publications:* The Firedrake, 1966; Rakosy, 1967; Kings in Winter, 1968; Until the Sun Falls, 1969; Ghost on the Steppe, 1969; The King's Road, 1970; Cold Iron, 1970; Antichrist, 1970; Wonder of the World, 1970; The Earl, 1971; The Death of Attila, 1973; The Great Maria, 1975; Floating Worlds, 1976; Two Ravens, 1977; The Earl, 1979; Home Ground, 1981; The Sea Beggars, 1982; The Belt of Gold, 1984; Pillar of the Sky, 1985; The Bear Flag, 1992; Jerusalem, 1996; The Soul Thief, 2002. *Honours:* Guggenheim Fellowship, 1981–82. *Address:* c/o Alfred A. Knopf, 299 Park Ave, New York, NY 10171, USA.

HOLLAND, Norman N(orwood); Scholar and Writer; b. 29 Sept. 1927, New York, NY, USA; m. Jane Kelley, 17 Dec. 1954, one s. one d. *Education:* BS, MIT, 1947; LLB, 1950, PhD, 1956, Harvard University. *Career:* Instructor to Assoc. Prof., MIT, 1955–66; McNulty Prof. of English, SUNY at Buffalo, 1966–83; Assoc. Prof., University of Paris, 1971–72, 1985; Marston-Milbauer Eminent Scholar, University of Florida at Gainesville, 1983–; mem. American Acad. of Psychoanalysis; Boston Psychoanalytic Society; MLA. *Publications:* The First Modern Comedies, 1959; The Shakespearean Imagination, 1964; Psychoanalysis and Shakespeare, 1966; The Dynamics of Literary Response, 1968; Poems in Persons: An Introduction to the Psychoanalysis of Literature, 1973; 5 Readers Reading, 1975; Laughing: A Psychology of Humor, 1982; The I, 1985; The Brain of Robert Frost: A Cognitive Approach to Literature, 1988; Holland's Guide to Psychoanalytic Psychology and Literature-and-Psychology, 1990; The Critical I, 1992; Death in a Delphi Seminar, 1995. *Honours:* ACLS Fellow, 1974–75; Guggenheim Fellowship, 1979–80. *Address:* c/o Dept of English, University of Florida at Gainesville, Gainesville, FL 32611, USA.

HOLLAND, Tom, BA, PhD; British writer; b. 1947, Broadchalke, Salisbury, Hants. *Education:* Univ. of Cambridge. *Career:* previously worked in radio. *Publications:* Doomed Range 1973, Rustler Range 1989, Fugitive Trail 1990, Bullet Bounty 1991, Attis 1995, Lord of the Dead: The Secret History of Byron 1995, The Vampyre: Being the True Pilgrimage of George Gordon, Sixth Lord Byron 1995, Supping with Panthers 1996, Supping with Vampyres 1996, Deliver Us from Evil 1997, Importance of Being Frank 1997, The Libertine 1997, Slave of my Thirst 1997, Banquete de sangre 1998, Sleeper in the Sands 1998, Talking it Over 1998, The Bonehunter 2001, Rubicon: The Last Years of the Roman Republic (Hessel-Tiltman Prize 2004) 2003. *Address:* c/o Little, Brown & Co., Time Warner Book Group, Brettenham House, Lancaster Place, London, WC2E 7EN, England. *Website:* www.twbookmark.com.

HOLLANDER, John; Prof. of English, Poet, Critic and Ed.; b. 28 Oct. 1929, New York, NY, USA; m. 1st Anne Loesser, 15 June 1953, divorced, two d.; m. 2nd Natalie Charkow, 17 Dec. 1982. *Education:* AB, 1950, MA, 1952, Columbia University; PhD, Indiana University, 1959. *Career:* Lecturer, Connecticut College, 1957–59; Poetry Ed., Partisan Review, 1959–65; Instructor to Assoc. Prof., 1959–66, Prof. of English, 1977–86, A Bartlett Giametti Prof. of English, 1986–95, Sterling Prof. of English, 1995–, Yale University; Christian Gauss Seminarian, Princeton University, 1962; Visiting Prof., 1964, Patten Lecturer, 1986, Fellow, Institute for Advanced Study, 1986, Indiana University; Prof. of English, Hunter College and the Graduate School and University Center, CUNY, 1966–77; Elliston Prof. of Poetry, University of Cincinnati, 1969; mem. Acad. of American Poets, board of chancellors, 1980–2000; American Acad. of Arts and Letters, sec., 2000–; Asscn of Literary Scholars and Critics, pres., 2000–01. *Publications:* Poetry: A Crackling of Thorns, 1958; Movie-Going and Other Poems, 1962; Visions from the Ramble, 1965; Types of Shape, 1968; The Night Mirror, 1971; Town and Country Matters, 1972; Selected Poems, 1972; Tales Told of the Fathers, 1975; Reflections on Espionage, 1976; Spectral Emanations: New and Selected Poems, 1978; Blue Wine, 1979; Flowers of Thirteen, 1983; In Time and Place, 1986; Harp Lake, 1988; Selected Poetry, 1993; Tesserae, 1993; Figurehead and Other Poems, 1999; War Poems, 1999; Sonnets, 2000. Criticism: The Untuning of the Sky, 1960; Images of Voice, 1970; Vision and Resonance, 1975; The Figure of Echo, 1981; Rhyme's Reason, 1981; Melodious Guile, 1988; William Bailey, 1990; The Gazer's Spirit, 1995; The Work of Poetry, 1997; The Poetry of Everyday Life, 1998; Figurehead, 1998. Editor: The Wind and the Rain (with Harold Bloom), 1961; Jiggery-Pokery (with Anthony Hecht), 1966; Poems of Our Moment, 1968; Modern Poetry: Essays in Criticism, 1968; The Oxford Anthology of English Literature (with Frank Kermode, Harold Bloom, J. B. Trapp, Martin Price and Lionel Trilling), 1973; Nineteenth-Century American Poetry, 2 vols, 1993; Committed to Memory, 1997; The Best American Poetry, 1998. Other: The Death of Moses (libretto for Alexander Goehr's opera), 1992. *Honours:* Poetry Chapbook Award, 1962, Melville Cane Award, 1990, Poetry Society of America; National Institute of Arts and Letters Award, 1963; National Endowment for the Humanities Senior Fellowship, 1973–74; Levinson Prize, 1974; Washington Monthly Prize, 1976; Guggenheim Fellowship, 1979–80; Mina P. Shaughnessy Award, MLA, 1982; Bollingen Prize, 1983; Shenandoah Prize, 1985; John D. and Catherine T. MacArthur Foundation Fellowship, 1990–95; Robert Penn Warren-Cleanth Brooks Award, 1998. *Address:* c/o Dept of English, Yale University, PO Box 208302, New Haven, CT 06520, USA.

HOLLANDER, Paul, BA, MA, PhD; American academic and writer; *Professor Emeritus, University of Massachusetts*; b. 3 Oct. 1932, Budapest, Hungary; m. Mina Harrison 1977; one d. *Education:* LSE, Univ. of Illinois, Princeton Univ. *Career:* Asst Prof. 1963–68, Research Fellow, Assoc., Russian Research Center 1963–, Harvard Univ.; Assoc. Prof. 1968–73, Prof. of Sociology 1973–2000, Prof. Emeritus 2000–, Univ. of Massachusetts at Amherst; scholar-in-residence, Rockefeller Study and Conference Center, Bellagio, Italy 1984; Visiting Scholar, Hoover Institution 1985, 1986, 1993; mem. Nat. Asscn of Scholars. *Publications:* American and Soviet Society: A Reader in Comparative Sociology and Perception (ed.) 1969, Soviet and American Society: A Comparison 1973, Political Pilgrims: Travels of Western Intellectuals to the Soviet Union, China and Cuba 1928–1978 1981, The Many Faces of Socialism 1983, The Survival of the Adversary Culture 1988, Decline and Discontent: Communism and the West Today 1992, Anti-Americans: Critiques at Home and Abroad 1965–1990 1992, Anti-Americanism: Irrational and Rational 1995, Political Will and Personal Belief: The Decline and Fall of Soviet Communism 1999, Discontents: Postmodern and Postcommunist 2002, Understanding Anti-Americanism: Its Origins and Impact at Home and Abroad (ed.) 2004; contrib. to scholarly and general publications. *Honours:* Guggenheim Fellowship 1974–75, Peter Shaw Award, Nat. Asscn of Scholars 2002. *Address:* 35 Vernon Street, Northampton, MA 01060, USA. *E-mail:* Hollander@soc.umass.edu.

HOLLERAN, Andrew; Author; b. 1942, USA. *Education:* Harvard University; University of Iowa. *Publications:* Dancer from the Dance, 1978; Nights in Aruba, 1983; Ground Zero, 1988; The Beauty of Men, 1996; In September, the Light Changes, 1999. Contributions: anthologies and periodicals. *Address:* c/o Hyperion, 114 Fifth Ave, NY 10011, USA.

HOLLINGHURST, Alan James, BA, MLitt, FRSL; British writer; b. 26 May 1954, Stroud. *Education:* Canford School, Dorset, Magdalen Coll., Oxford. *Career:* Asst Ed. Times Literary Supplement 1982–84, Deputy Ed. 1985–90, Poetry Ed. 1991–95. *Publications include:* fiction: The Swimming-Pool Library 1988, The Folding Star 1994, The Spell 1998, The Line of Beauty 2004; poetry: Confidential Chats with Boys 1982; trans.: Bajazet (Racine) 1991. *Honours:* Somerset Maugham Award 1988, American Acad. of Arts and Letters E. M. Forster Award 1989, James Tait Black Memorial Prize 1994. *Literary Agent:* Antony Harwood Ltd, 103 Walton Street, Oxford, OX2 6EB, England.

HOLLINGSHEAD, Greg(ory Albert Frank); Prof. of English and Writer; b. 25 Feb. 1947, Toronto, Ontario, Canada; m. Rosa Spricer, one s. *Education:* BA, 1968, MA, 1970, University of Toronto; PhD, University of London, 1974. *Career:* Asst Prof., 1975–81, Assoc. Prof., 1981–93, Prof. of English, 1993–, University of Alberta; mem. PEN Canada; Writers Guild of Alberta; Writers' Union of Canada. *Publications:* Famous Players, 1982; White Buick, 1992; Spin Dry, 1992; The Roaring Girl, 1995; The Healer, 1998. *Honours:* George Bugnet Awards for Excellence in the Novel, 1993,

1999; Howard O'Hagan Awards for Excellence in Short Fiction, 1993, 1996; Gov.-Gen.'s Award for Fiction, 1995; Rogers Fiction Prize, 1999. *Address:* c/o Dept of English, University of Alberta, Edmonton, AB T6G 2E5, Canada.

HOLLINGWORTH, Clare, OBE; British journalist; b. 10 Oct. 1911; m. 1st Vyvyan Derring Vandeleur Robinson 1936 (divorced 1951); m. 2nd Geoffrey Spence Hoare 1952 (died 1966). *Education:* Girls' Collegiate School, Leicester, Grammar School, Ashby-de-la-Zouch, School of Slavonic Studies, Univ. of London. *Career:* mem. staff League of Nations Union 1935–38; worked in Poland for Lord Mayor's Fund for Refugees from Czechoslovakia 1939; Corresp. for Daily Telegraph Poland, Turkey, Cairo (covered Desert Campaigns, troubles in Persia and Iraq, Civil War in Greece and events in Palestine) 1941–50, for Manchester Guardian (covered Algerian War and trouble spots including Egypt, Aden and Viet Nam), based in Paris 1950–63; Guardian Defence Corresp. 1963–67; foreign trouble-shooter for Daily Telegraph (covering war in Viet Nam) 1967–73, Corresp. in China 1973–76, Defence Corresp. 1976–81; Far Eastern Corresp. in Hong Kong for Sunday Telegraph 1981–; Research Assoc. (fmrly Visiting Scholar), Centre for Asian Studies, Univ. of Hong Kong 1981–. *Publications:* Poland's Three Weeks War 1940, There's A German Just Behind Me 1945, The Arabs and the West 1951, Mao and the Men Against Him 1984, Front Line 1990. *Honours:* Hon. DLitt (Leicester) 1993; Granada Journalist of the Year Award and Hannan Swaffer Award 1963; James Cameron Award for Journalism 1994. *Address:* 302 Ridley House, 2 Upper Albert Road, Hong Kong Special Administrative Region, People's Republic of China. *Telephone:* 2868-1838 (Hong Kong).

HOLLO, Anselm; Prof. of Poetry, Poetics, and Trans., Poet, Writer, Trans. and Ed.; b. 12 April 1934, Helsinki, Finland; m. Jane Dalrymple-Hollo. *Education:* Modern Languages and Literature, University of Helsinki, University of Tübingen. *Career:* Visiting Prof., SUNY at Buffalo, 1967, University of Iowa, 1968–73, Bowling Green State University, Ohio, 1971–73, Hobart and William Smith Colleges, Geneva, New York, 1973–75, Southwest Minnesota State College, Marshall, 1977–78; Distinguished Visiting Poet, Michigan State University, 1974; Assoc. Prof. of Literature and Creative Writing, University of Maryland, 1975–77; Margaret Bannister Distinguished Writer-in-Residence, Sweet Briar College, 1978–81; Poet-in-Residence, 1981, Visiting Lecturer, 1985–89, Kerouac School of Poetics, Boulder; Visiting Lecturer in Poetics, New College of California, San Francisco, 1981–82; Book Reviewer, Baltimore Sun, 1983–85; Distinguished Visiting Prof. of Poetry, University of Colorado at Boulder, 1985; Contributing Ed., The New Censorship, 1989–; Assoc. Prof. of Poetry, Poetics and Trans., Naropa University, Boulder, 1989–. *Publications:* Poetry: Sojourner Microcosms: New and Selected Poems, 1959–77, 1978; Finite Continued, 1981; Pick Up the House: New and Selected Poems, 1986; Outlying Districts: New Poems, 1990; Near Miss Haiku, 1990; Blue Ceiling, 1992; High Beam: 12 Poems, 1993; West is Left on the Map, 1993; Survival Dancing, 1995; Corvus: New Poems, 1995; Hills Like Purple Pachyderms, 1997; AHOE: And How on Earth, 1997; Rue Wilson Monday, 2000; Notes on the Possibilities and Attractions of Existence: New and Selected Poems, 1965–2000, 2001. Prose: Caws and Causeries: Around Poetry and Poets, 1999. *Honours:* Yaddo Residency Fellowship, 1978; National Endowment for the Arts Fellowship in Poetry, 1979; PEN/American-Scandinavian Foundation Award for Poetry in Trans., 1980; American-Scandinavian Foundation Award for Poetry in Trans., 1989; Fund for Poetry Award for Contributions to Contemporary Poetry, 1989, 1991; Stein Award in Innovative American Poetry, 1996; Grez-sur-Loing Foundation Fellowship, 1998; Baltic Centre for Writers and Trans Residency Fellowship, 2002. *Address:* 3336 14th St, Boulder, CO 80304, USA.

HOLLOWAY, John; Prof. of Modern English (retd), Writer and Poet; b. 1 Aug. 1920, Croydon, Surrey, England; m. 1st Audrey Gooding, 1946, one s. one d.; m. 2nd Joan Black, 1978. *Education:* BA, Modern Greats, New College, Oxford, 1941; DPhil, Oxon, 1947. *Career:* Temporary Lecturer in Philosophy, New College, Oxford, 1945; Fellow, All Souls College, Oxford, 1946–60; Lecturer in English, University of Aberdeen, 1949–54, University of Cambridge, 1954–66; Fellow, 1955–82, Life Fellow, 1982–, Queens' College, Cambridge; Reader, 1966–72, Prof. of Modern English, 1972–82, University of Cambridge; various visiting lectureships and professorships; mem. FRSL, 1956. *Publications:* Language and Intelligence, 1951; The Victorian Sage, 1953; Poems of the Mid-Century (ed.), 1957; The Charted Mirror (essays), 1960; Selections from Shelley (ed.), 1960; Shakespeare's Tragedies, 1961; The Colours of Clarity (essays), 1964; The Lion Hunt, 1964; Widening Horizons in English Verse, 1966; A London Childhood, 1966; Blake: The Lyric Poetry, 1968; The Establishment of English, 1972; Later English Broadside Ballads (ed. with J. Black), 2 vols, 1975, 1979; The Proud Knowledge, 1977; Narrative and Structure, 1979; The Slumber of Apollo, 1983; The Oxford Book of Local Verses (ed.), 1987. Poetry: The Minute, 1956; The Fugue, 1960; The Landfallers, 1962; Wood and Windfall, 1965; New Poems, 1970; Planet of Winds, 1977; Civitatula: Cambridge, the Little City, 1994. Contributions: Professional journals. *Address:* c/o Queens' College, Cambridge CB3 9ET, England.

HOLLOWAY, Robin Greville, PhD, DMus; British composer, writer and academic; *Professor of Musical Composition*; b. 19 Oct. 1943, Leamington Spa. *Education:* St Paul's Cathedral Choir School, King's Coll. School, Wimbledon, King's Coll., Cambridge and New Coll., Oxford. *Career:* Lecturer in Music, Univ. of Cambridge 1975–, Reader in Musical Composition 1999–, Prof. 2001–; Fellow of Gonville and Caius Coll., Cambridge 1969–. *Compositions include:* Garden Music opus 1 1962, Scenes from Schumann opus 13 1970, Evening with Angels opus 17 1972, Domination of Black opus 23 1973, Clarissa opus 30 1976, Second Concerto for Orchestra opus 40 1979, Brand opus 48 1981, Women in War opus 51 1982, Seascape and Harvest opus 55 1983, Viola Concerto opus 56 1984, Double Concerto opus 68, The Spacious Firmament opus 69, Violin Concerto opus 70 1990, Boys and Girls Come Out To Play 1991, Frost at Midnight opus 78, Third Concerto for Orchestra opus 80 1994, Clarinet Concerto opus 82 1996, Peer Gynt opus 84 1984–97, Scenes from Antwerp opus 85 1997, Symphony 1999, Missa Caiensis 2001, Spring Music opus 96 2002. *Publications:* Wagner and Debussy 1978, On Music: Essays and Diversions 1963–2003 2004; numerous articles and reviews. *Address:* Gonville and Caius College, Cambridge, CB2 1TA, England. *Telephone:* (1223) 335424. *E-mail:* rgh1000@cam.ac.uk (Home).

HOLME OF CHELTENHAM, Baron (Life Peer), cr. 1990, of Cheltenham in the County of Gloucestershire; **Richard Gordon Holme,** CBE, PC, MA; British politician, publisher and business executive; b. 27 May 1936, London; m. Kay Powell 1958; two s. two d. *Education:* Royal Masonic School, St John's Coll. Oxford, Harvard Business School, USA. *Career:* served in 10th Gurkha Rifles in Malaya 1954–56; Marketing Man., Unilever 1959–64; Dir Penguin Books 1964–66; Chair. BPC Publishing 1966–70; Pres. CRM Books, Calif., USA 1970–74; Dir Nat. Cttee for Electoral Reform 1976–84; Chair. Constitutional Reform Centre 1985, Threadneedle Publishing Group 1988–, Hollis Directories 1989–98, Prima Europe 1992–1995, Brasseys Ltd 1996–98; Pres. Liberal Party 1980–81; Liberal Democrat Parl. Spokesman on NI, House of Lords 1992–99; Chair. Broadcasting Standards Comm. 1999–2000; Chair. of Govs English Coll., Prague; Chair. Hansard Soc. for Parl. Govt2000–; Dir Rio Tinto PLC 1995–98; Chancellor Univ. of Greenwich 1998–; Vice-Chair. LEAD Int. 2003–; Chair. Advisory Bd British-American Project 2000–. *Publications:* No Dole for the Young 1975, A Democracy Which Works 1978, The People's Kingdom (jt ed.) 1987, 1688–1988: Time for a New Constitution 1988. *Address:* House of Lords, London, SW1A 0PW, England. *Telephone:* (20) 7753-2454.

HOLMES, Bryan John, (Charles Langley Hayes, Ethan Wall); Lecturer (retd) and Writer; b. 18 May 1939, Birmingham, England; m. 1962, two s. *Education:* BA, University of Keele, 1968. *Publications:* The Avenging Four, 1978; Hazard, 1979; Blood, Sweat and Gold, 1980; Gunfall, 1980; A Noose for Yanqui, 1981; Shard, 1982; Bad Times at Backwheel, 1982; Guns of the Reaper, 1983; On the Spin of a Dollar, 1983; Another Day, Another Dollar, 1984; Dark Rider, 1987; I Rode with Wyatt, 1989; Dollars for the Reaper, 1990; A Legend Called Shatterhand, 1990; Loco, 1991; Shatterhand and the People, 1992; The Last Days of Billy Patch, 1992; Blood on the Reaper, 1992; All Trails Lead to Dodge, 1993; Montana Hit, 1993; A Coffin for the Reaper, 1994; Comes the Reaper, 1995; Utah Hit, 1995; Dakota Hit, 1995; Viva Reaper, 1996; The Shard Brand, 1996; High Plains Death, 1997; Smoking Star, 1997; Crowfeeders, 1999; North of the Bravo, 2000; Bradford's Pocket Crossword Dictionary, 2001. Contributions: Professional and academic journals. *Address:* c/o Robert Hale Ltd, Clerkenwell Green, London EC1R 0HT, England.

HOLMES, Charlotte Amalie; academic and writer; b. 26 April 1956, Georgia, USA; m. James Brasfield 1983; one s. *Education:* BA, Louisiana State University, 1977; MFA, Columbia University, 1980. *Career:* Editorial Asst, Paris Review, 1979–80; Assoc. and Managing Ed., Ecco Press, 1980–82; Instructor, Western Carolina University, 1984–87; Asst Prof., 1987–93, Assoc. Prof., 1993–, Pennsylvania State University; mem. Associated Writing Programs. *Publications:* Gifts and Other Stories, 1994. Contributions: periodicals. *Honours:* Stegner Fellowship, Stanford University, 1982; North Carolina Arts Council Grant, 1986; Pennsylvania Council on the Arts Fellowships, 1988, 1993; Bread Loaf Writer's Conference National Arts Club Scholarship, 1990; Poets and Writers Award, 1993; DH Lawrence Fellowship, 2000. *Literary Agent:* Neil Olson, Donadio and Olson. *Address:* c/o Department of English, Pennsylvania State University, University Park, PA 16802, USA.

HOLMES, Diana; Prof. of French, Writer and Ed.; b. 28 Jan. 1949, Preston, Lancashire, England; m. Nicolas W. Cheesewright, 18 June 1983, one s. one d. *Education:* BA, 1971, DPhil, 1977, University of Sussex; La Nouvelle Sorbonne, Université de Paris III, 1972. *Career:* Lecturer in French, 1975–80, Senior Lecturer in French, 1984–90, Principal Lecturer in French, 1990, Wolverhampton Polytechnic; Part-time Lecturer in French, North London Polytechnic, 1981–84; Lecturer, 1992–94, Senior Lecturer, 1994–95, Prof. of French, Head of French Studies, 1995–, Keele University; Visiting Lecturer, University of Birmingham, 1986–87; Ed., Modern and Contemporary France, 1996–; mem. Asscn for the Study of Modern and Contemporary France, Exec. Committee, 1987–91; Women in French. *Publications:* Colette, 1991; Women in Context: French Women Writers, 1848–1994, 1996; French Film Directors series (co-ed.). Contributions: periodicals including Cross-Currents; Books. *Address:* 151 Compton Rd, Wolverhampton, West Midlands WV3 9JT, England.

HOLMES, George Arthur; Historian and Writer; b. 22 April 1927, Aberystwyth, Wales; m. Evelyn Anne Klein, 1953, two s. one deceased, two d. *Education:* University College, Aberystwyth; MA, PhD, 1952, St John's

College, Cambridge. *Career:* Fellow, St John's College, Cambridge, 1951–54, All Souls College, Oxford, 1989–94; Tutor, St Catherine's Society, Oxford, 1954–62; Fellow and Tutor, 1962–89, Vice-Master, 1969–71, Emeritus Fellow, 1990, St Catherine's College, Oxford; Mem., Institute for Advanced Study, Princeton, NJ, 1967–68; Co-Ed., English Historical Review, 1974–81; Delegate, OUP, 1982–91; Chichele Prof. of Medieval History, University of Oxford, 1989–94; Visiting Prof., Harvard University Centre for Italian Renaissance Studies, Florence, 1995–; mem. Fellow, British Acad., 1985. *Publications:* The Estates of the Higher Nobility in Fourteenth-Century England, 1957; The Later Middle Ages, 1962; The Florentine Enlightenment, 1400–1450, 1969; Europe: Hierarchy and Revolt, 1320–1450, 1975; The Good Parliament, 1975; Dante, 1980; Florence, Rome and the Origins of the Renaissance, 1986; The Oxford Illustrated History of Medieval Europe (ed.), 1988; The First Age of the Western City, 1300–1500, 1990; Art and Politics in Renaissance Italy (ed.), 1993; Renaissance, 1996; The Oxford Illustrated History of Italy (ed.), 1997. Contributions: scholarly journals. *Honours:* Serena Medal for Italian Studies, British Acad., 1993; Emeritus Fellow, Leverhulme Trust, 1996–98. *Address:* Highmoor House, Bampton, Oxfordshire OX18 2HY, England.

HOLMES, John (see Souster, (Holmes) Raymond).

HOLMES, Leslie Templeman; Prof. of Political Science and Writer; b. 5 Oct. 1948, London, England; m. Susan Mary Bleasby, 4 Sept. 1971, divorced Oct. 1989. *Education:* BA, Russian Studies and German, Hull University, 1971; MA, Soviet Government and Politics, 1974, PhD, Comparative Government, 1979, Essex University. *Career:* Prof. of Political Science, University of Melbourne. *Publications:* The Policy Progress in Communist States, 1981; The Withering Away of the State? (ed.), 1981; Politics in the Communist World, 1986; The End of Communist Power, 1993; Post-Communism, 1997; Europe: Rethinking the Boundaries (co-ed.), 1998; Citizenship and Identity in Europe (co-ed.), 1999. *Honours:* Fellow, Acad. of the Social Sciences in Australia, 1995. *Address:* Dept of Political Science, University of Melbourne, Parkville, Vic. 3052, Australia.

HOLMES, Richard Gordon Heath, OBE, BA, FRSL; British writer, poet and academic; b. 5 Nov. 1945, London, England; pnr Rose Tremain. *Education:* Churchill College, Cambridge. *Career:* reviewer and historical features writer, The Times, London 1967–92; Earnest Jones Memorial Lecturer, British Inst. of Psycho-Analysis 1990; John Keats Memorial Lecturer, Royal Coll. of Surgeons 1995; Visiting Fellow, Trinity Coll., Cambridge 2000; Prof. of Biographical Studies, Univ. of East Anglia 2001–. *Publications:* Thomas Chatterton: The Case Re-Opened 1970, One for Sorrows (poems) 1970, Shelley: The Pursuit 1974, Shelley on Love (ed.) 1980, Coleridge 1982, Nerval: The Chimeras (with Peter Jay) 1985, Footsteps: Adventures of a Romantic Biographer 1985, Mary Wollstonecraft and William Godwin (ed.) 1987, Kipling: Something Myself (ed. with Robert Hampson) 1987, Coleridge: Early Visions 1989, Dr Johnson and Mr Savage 1993, Coleridge: Selected Poems (ed.) 1996, The Romantic Poets and Their Circle 1997, Coleridge: Darker Reflections 1998, Sidetracks: Explorations of a Romantic Biographer 2000, Tommy: the British Soldier on the Western Front 1914–1918 2004. *Honours:* Dr hc (Univ. of East Anglia) 2000, (Tavistock Inst.) 2001; Somerset Maugham Award 1977, Whitbread Book of the Year Prize 1989, James Tait Black Memorial Prize 1994, Duff Cooper Prize 1998. *Address:* c/o HarperCollins, 77 Fulham Palace Road, London, W6 8JB, England.

HOLROYD, Michael, CBE, FRHistS; British writer; *President, Royal Society of Literature*; b. 27 Aug. 1935, London; m. Margaret Drabble 1982. *Education:* Eton Coll. *Career:* Chair. Soc. of Authors 1973–74, Nat. Book League 1976–78; Pres. English Centre of PEN 1985–88; Chair. Strachey Trust 1990–95, Public Lending Right Advisory Cttee 1997–2000, Royal Soc. of Literature 1998–2001 (Pres. 2003–); Vice-Pres. Royal Literary Fund 1997–; mem. Arts Council (Chair. Literature Panel) 1992–95; Gov. Shaw Festival Theatre, Niagara-on-the-Lake 1993–; Trustee Laser Foundation 2001–03. *Publications:* Hugh Kingsmill: A Critical Biography 1964, Lytton Strachey: A Critical Biography 1967–68 (new edn 1994), A Dog's Life (novel) 1969, The Best of Hugh Kingsmill (ed) 1970, Lytton Strachey by Himself: A Self-Portrait (ed) 1971, Unreceived Opinions (essays) 1973, Augustus John 1974–75 (new edn 1996), The Art of Augustus John (with Malcolm Easton) 1974, The Genius of Shaw (ed) 1979, The Shorter Strachey (ed with Paul Levy) 1980, William Gerhardie's God's Fifth Column (ed with Robert Skidelsky) 1981, Essays by Diverse Hands (ed) Vol. XLII 1982, Peterley Harveset: The Private Diary of David Peterley (ed) 1985, Bernard Shaw: Vol. 1: The Search for Love 1988, Vol. II: The Pursuit of Power 1989, Vol. III: The Lure of Fantasy 1991, Vol. IV: The Last Laugh 1992, Vol. V: The Shaw Companion 1992, Bernard Shaw 1997 (one-vol. biog.), Basil Street Blues 1999, Works on Paper: The Craft of Biography and Autobiography 2002, Mosaic: Portraits in Fragments 2004. *Honours:* Hon. DLitt (Ulster) 1992, (Sheffield, Warwick) 1993, (East Anglia) 1994, (LSE) 1998; Saxton Memorial Fellowship 1964, Bollingen Fellowship 1966, Winston Churchill Fellowship 1971, Irish Life Arts Award 1988, Meilleur Livre Etranger 1995, Heywood Hill Prize 2001. *Literary Agent:* A. P. Watt Ltd, 20 John Street, London, WC1N 2DL, England. *Telephone:* (20) 7405-6774. *Fax:* (20) 7831-2154.

HOLT, George (see Tubb, Edwin Charles).

HOLT, Hazel; Writer; b. 3 Sept. 1928, Birmingham, England; m. Geoffrey Louis Holt, 1951, one s. *Education:* BA, Newnham College, Cambridge, 1950. *Career:* Ed., International African Institute, London, 1950–74; Reviewer, Feature Writer, Stage and Television Today, London, 1975–80; Writer, 1989–. *Publications:* A Very Private Eye: An Autobiography in Diaries and Letters (co-ed. and annotator), 1984; Barbara Pym, Civil to Strangers and Other Writings (ed.), 1988; Mrs Malory Investigates, 1989; Gone Away, 1989; The Cruellest Month, 1991; A Lot to Ask: A Life of Barbara Pym, 1991; Mrs Malory and the Festival Murders, 1993, also as Uncertain Death; Mrs Malory: Detective in Residence, 1994; The Shortest Journey, 1994; Mrs Malory Wonders Why, 1995; Superfluous Death, 1995; Mrs Malory: Death of a Dean, 1996; Mrs Malory and the Only Good Lawyer, 1997; Dead and Buried, 1998; Fatal Legacy, 1999; Lilies that Fester, 2000; Delay of Execution, 2001; Leonora, 2002; Death in Practice, 2003. *Literary Agent:* James Hale, 47 Peckham Rye, London SE15 3NX, England. *Address:* Tivington Knowle, Nr Minehead, Somerset TA24 8SX, England.

HOLT, Samuel (see Westlake, Donald Edwin).

HOMBERGER, Eric (Ross); Reader in American Literature and Writer; b. 30 May 1942, Philadelphia, Pennsylvania, USA; m. Judy Jones, 2 June 1967, two s. one d. *Education:* BA, University of California at Berkeley, 1964; MA, University of Chicago, 1965; PhD, University of Cambridge, 1972. *Career:* Temporary Lecturer in American Literature, University of Exeter, 1969–70; Lecturer, 1970–88, Reader in American Literature, 1988–, University of East Anglia; Visiting Faculty, University of Minnesota, 1977–78; Visiting Prof. of American Literature, University of New Hampshire, 1991–92; mem. British Asscn for American Studies. *Publications:* The Cambridge Mind: Ninety Years of the 'Cambridge Review', 1879–1969 (ed. with William Janeway and Simon Schama), 1970; Ezra Pound: The Critical Heritage (ed.), 1972; The Art of the Real: Poetry in England and America since 1939, 1977; The Second World War in Fiction (ed. with Holger Klein and John Flower), 1984; John le Carre, 1986; American Writers and Radical Politics, 1900–1939: Equivocal Commitments, 1987; The Troubled Face of Biography (ed. with John Charmley), 1987; John Reed, 1990; John Reed and the Russian Revolution: Uncollected Articles, Letters and Speeches in Russia, 1917–1920 (ed. with John Biggart), 1992; The Historical Atlas of New York City, 1994; Scenes from the Life of a City: Corruption and Conscience in Old New York, 1994; The Penguin Historical Atlas of North America, 1995; New York City, 2002; Mrs Astor's New York: Money and Social Power in a Gilded Age, 2002. Contributions: periodicals. *Honours:* Leverhulme Fellowship, 1978–79; Gilder Lehrman Institute Fellowship in American History, 1999. *Address:* 74 Clarendon Rd, Norwich NR2 2PW, England. *E-mail:* e.homberger@uea.ac.uk.

HOME, Stewart Ramsay, (Harry Bates, Monty Cantsin, Karen Eliot); Writer; b. 24 March 1962, Merton, South London, England. *Career:* mem. Society of Authors. *Publications:* Assault on Culture, 1988; Pure Mania, 1989; Defiant Pose, 1991; No Pity, 1993; Red London, 1994; Neoism, Plagiarism & Praxis, 1995; Cranked Up Really High, 1995; Slow Death, 1996; Come Before Christ & Murder Love, 1997; Blow Job, 1997; Cunt, 1999; Confusion Incorporated: A Collection of Lies, Hoaxes and Hidden Truths, 1999; Whips and Furs: My Life as a Bon Vivant Gambler and Love Rat, 2000; 69 Things to Be Done with a Dead Princess, 2002. Contributions: Big Issue; Independent; Art Monthly; Edinburgh Review; New Art Examiner; Konkret. *Address:* BM Senior, London WC1N 3XX, England. *Website:* stewarthomesociety.org.

HOMEL, David; American/Canadian writer, journalist and translator; b. 1952, Chicago; two s. *Education:* Concordia Univ., Toronto. *Career:* tutor in translation at Concordia Univ., Toronto. *Screenplay:* Great North. *Publications:* fiction: Electrical Storms 1988, Rat Palms (Canadian Book and Periodical Marketers, Paperback of the Year 1993) 1992, Sonya and Jack (Prix Millepages for Best Foreign Literary Fiction, France) 1995, Get on Top 1999, The Speaking Cure (Hugh McLennan Prize for Fiction) 2003; non-fiction: Mapping Literature: The Art and Politics of Literary Translation 1988; contrib. to Talking it Out: The October Crisis from Inside 1987, Postmodernism and the Quebec Novel 1995, The Gazette. *Honours:* Governor General's Award for Translation 1995, 2001, QWF Prize for translation 2003. *Literary Agent:* Anne McDermid & Associates Ltd, 92 Willcocks Street, Toronto, ON M5S 1C8, Canada. *E-mail:* dhomel@alcor.concordia.ca.

HOMES, Amy M.; American writer; b. 1962, Chevy Chase, MD. *Career:* Judge Nat. Book Award, Fiction 2000, NY Public Library Award 2001; mem. Bd of Dirs Yaddo. *Publications:* Jack (Deutscher Jugendliteraturpreis) 1989, The Safety of Objects 1990, In a Country of Mothers 1993, The End of Alice 1995, Appendix A 1995, Music for Torching 1999, Things You Should Know (short stories) 2002, Los Angeles 2002. *Honours:* fellowships from The Center for Scholars and Writers, NY Public Library, Guggenheim Foundation, Nat. Endowment for the Arts and NY Foundation for the Arts; Benjamin Franklin Award 2000. *Address:* c/o Anchor Books, Transworld Publishers, 61 Uxbridge Road, London, W5, England.

HONAN, Park; Biographer, Writer and Ed.; b. 17 Sept. 1928, Utica, New York, USA. *Education:* MA, University of Chicago, 1951; PhD, University of London, 1959. *Career:* Prof. of English and American Literature, University of Leeds, 1984–93. *Publications:* Browning's Characters: A Study in Poetic Technique, 1961; Shelley (ed.), 1963; Bulwer Lytton's Falkland (ed.),

1967; The Complete Works of Robert Browning (co-ed.), 9 vols, 1969–; The Book, The Ring and The Poet: A Biography of Robert Browning (co-author), 1975; Matthew Arnold: A Life, 1981; Jane Austen: Her Life, 1987; The Beats: An Anthology of 'Beat' Writing (ed.), 1987; Authors' Lives: On Literary Biography and the Arts of Language, 1990; Shakespeare: A Life, 1998. *Honours:* British Acad. Awards; Leverhulme Award; Huntington Library Fellowship; Folger Shakespeare Library Fellowship, 1991; FRSL, 1998. *Address:* School of English, University of Leeds, Leeds LS2 9JT, England.

HONAN, William Holmes; Journalist and Writer; b. 11 May 1930, New York, NY, USA; m. Nancy Burton, 22 June 1975, two s. one d. *Education:* BA, Oberlin College, 1952; MA, University of Virginia, 1955. *Career:* Ed., The Villager, New York, 1957–60; Asst Ed., New Yorker Magazine, 1960–64, New York Times Magazine, 1969–70; Assoc. Ed., Newsweek, New York City, 1969; Travel Ed., 1970–72, 1973–74, Arts and Leisure Ed., 1974–82, Culture Ed., 1982–88, Chief Cultural Correspondent, 1988–93, National Higher Education Correspondent, 1993–2000, General Assignment, 2000–, New York Times; Managing Ed., Saturday Review, 1972–73. *Publications:* Greenwich Village Guide, 1959; Ted Kennedy: Profile of a Survivor, 1972; Bywater: The Man Who Invented the Pacific War, 1990; Visions of Infamy: The Untold Story of How Journalist Hector C. Bywater Devised the Plans that Led to Pearl Harbour, 1991; Fire When Ready, Gridley! – Great Naval Stories from Manila Bay to Vietnam (ed.), 1992; Treasure Hunt: A New York Times Reporter Tracks the Quedlinburg Treasures, 1997; Zingers (a play), 2002. Contributions: periodicals. *Address:* c/o New York Times, 229 W 43rd St, New York, NY 10036. USA.

HONE, Joseph; writer and broadcaster; b. 25 Feb. 1937, London, England; m. Jacqueline Mary Yeend 1963; one s. one d. *Education:* Kilkenny College, Sandford Park School, Dublin; St Columba's College, Dublin. *Career:* mem. Upton House Cricket Club. *Publications:* The Flowers of the Forest, 1982; Children of the Country, 1986; Duck Soup in the Black Sea, 1988; Summer Hill, 1990; Firesong, 1997. Contributions: periodicals. *Literary Agent:* Gillon Aitken Associates Ltd, 18–21 Cavaye Place, London, SW10 9PT, England. *Telephone:* (20) 7373-8672. *Fax:* (20) 7373-6002.

HONEYMAN, Brenda (see Clarke, Brenda (Margaret Lilian)).

HONIG, Edwin; academic, poet, writer, dramatist and translator; b. 3 Sept. 1919, New York, NY, USA; m. 1st Charlotte Gilchrist 1940 (deceased 1963); m. 2nd Margot Dennes 1963 (divorced 1978); two s. *Education:* BA, 1939, MA, 1947, University of Wisconsin at Madison. *Career:* Poetry Ed., New Mexico Quarterly, 1948–52; Instructor, Claremont College, CA, 1949; Faculty, 1949–57, Asst Prof. of English, Harvard University; Faculty, 1957–60, Prof. of English, 1960–82, Prof. of Comparative Literature, 1962–82, Brown University; Visiting Prof., University of California at Davis, 1964–65; Mellon Prof., Boston University, 1977; mem. Dante Society of America; Poetry Society of America. *Publications:* Poetry: The Moral Circus, 1955; The Gazabos: 41 Poems, 1959; Survivals, 1964; Spring Journal, 1968; Four Springs, 1972; At Sixes, 1974; Shake a Spear with Me, John Berryman, 1974; Selected Poems 1955–1976, 1979; Interrupted Praise, 1983; Gifts of Light, 1983; The Imminence of Love: Poems 1962–1992, 1993. Stories: Foibles and Fables of an Abstract Man, 1979. Non-Fiction: García Lorca, 1944; Dark Conceit: The Making of Allegory, 1959; Calderón and the Seizures of Honor, 1972; The Poet's Other Voice: Conversations on Literary Translation, 1986. Plays: Ends of the World and Other Plays, 1984. Translations: Over 10 books, 1961–93. Contributions: books, anthologies, reviews, journals, and periodicals. *Honours:* Guggenheim Fellowships, 1948, 1962; National Acad. of Arts and Letters Grant, 1966; Amy Lowell Traveling Poetry Fellowship, 1968; Rhode Island Governor's Award for Excellence in the Arts, 1970; National Endowment for the Humanities Fellowship, 1975, and Grants, 1977–80; National Endowment for the Arts Fellowship, 1977; Trans. Award, Poetry Society of America, 1984; National Award, Columbia University Trans. Center, 1985; Decorated by the Portuguese Pres. for trans. of Pessoa, 1989; Decorated by the King of Spain for trans. of Calderón, 1996. *Address:* 229 Medway Street, Apt 305, Providence, RI 02906, USA.

HOOD, Daniel; Writer and Ed.; b. 3 Nov. 1967, New Rochelle, New York, USA. *Education:* BA, History, Georgetown University, 1989. *Career:* Art Dir, IMP, publishers, New York City, 1989–94; Desktop Man., Wall Street Journal Europe, Brussels, Belgium, 1994–96; Managing Ed., Faulkner and Gray, publishers, New York City, 1996–2000; Business Ed., Daily News Express, New York, 2000–01; mem. SFWA. *Publications:* Fantasy Fiction: Fanuilh, 1994; Wizard's Heir, 1996; Beggar's Banquet, 1997; Scales of Justice, 1998; King's Cure, 2000. *Literary Agent:* Donald Maass Literary Agency, 157 W 57th St, Suite 1003, New York, NY 10019, USA. *Address:* 315 E 92nd St, No. 2E, New York, NY 10128, USA. *E-mail:* danhood@earthlink.net.com.

HOOKER, Jeremy Peter; lecturer, poet and writer; *Reader in English Literature, Professor, University of Glamorgan*; b. 23 March 1941, Warsash, Hampshire, England. *Education:* BA, 1963, MA, 1965, University of Southampton. *Career:* Arts Council Creative Writing Fellow, Winchester School of Art, 1981–83; fmr Lecturer in English, Bath College of Higher Education, and Netherlands and USA; currently Reader in English Literature, Prof. Univ. of Glamorgan; mem. Fellow, Academi Gymreig, 2000; Richard Jefferies Society, pres., 1999. *Publications:* The Elements, 1972; Soliloquies of a Chalk Giant, 1974; Solent Shore: New Poems, 1978; Landscape of the Daylight Moon, 1978; Englishman's Road, 1980; Itchen Water, 1982; Poetry of Place, 1982; A View from the Source: Selected Poems, 1982; Master of the Leaping Figures, 1987; The Presence of the Past, 1987; In Praise of Windmills, 1990; Their Silence a Language (with Lee Grandjean), 1994; Writers in a Landscape, 1996; Our Lady of Europe, 1997; Groundwork (with Lee Grandjean), 1998. Contributions: Reviews and journals. *Honours:* Eric Gregory Award, 1969; Welsh Arts Council Literature Prize, 1975. *Address:* Old School House, 7 Sunnyside, Frome, Somerset BA11 1LD, England.

HOOKS, Bell, MA, PhD; American critic, writer, cultural theorist and activist; b. (Gloria Jean Watkins), 25 Sept. 1952, Hopkinsville, KY. *Education:* Crispus Attucks High School, Hopkinsville, Stanford Univ., Univ. of Wisconsin, Univ. of California at Santa Cruz. *Career:* English Prof. and Sr Lecturer in Ethnic Studies, Univ. of Southern California; lead numerous courses at Univ. of California and San Fransisco State Univ. 1980s; tutor in African and Afro-American Studies, Yale Univ. 1985; Assoc. Prof. of Women's Studies and American Literature, Oberlin Coll., OH 1988; Distinguished Prof. of English, City Coll., New York 1994; f. Hambone magazine. *Publications include:* poetry: And There We Wept (chapbook) 1978, The Woman's Mourning Song 1993; non-fiction: Ain't I a Woman: Black Women and Feminism 1981, Feminist Theory from Margin to Center 1984, Talking Back: Thinking Feminist, Thinking Black 1989, Yearning: Race, Gender and Cultural Politics 1990, Breaking Bread: Insurgent Black Intellectual Life (with Cornel West) 1991, Black Looks: Race and Representation 1992, Sisters of the Yam: Black Women and Self-recovery 1993, Teaching to Transgress: Education as the Practice of Freedom 1994, Outlaw Culture: Resisting Representations 1994, Art on my Mind: Visual Politics 1995, Killing Rage: Ending Racism 1995, Bone Black: Memories of Girlhood 1996, Reel to Real: Race, Sex and Class at the Movies 1996, Seduction and Surrender 1997, Wounds of Passion: A Writing Life 1997, Remembered Rapture: The Writer at Work 1999, Feminism is for Everybody: Passionate Politics 2000, Where We Stand: Class Matters 2000, Salvation: Black People and Love 2001, All About Love 2001, Communion: The Female Search for Love 2002, Rock my Soul: Black People and Self-Esteem 2002, Teaching Community: A Pedagogy of Hope 2003, We Real Cool: Black Men and Masculinity 2003, The Will to Change 2004; juvenile: Happy to be Nappy (with Christopher Raschka) 1999, Be Boy Buzz 2002, Homemade Love 2002; contrib. to numerous journals. *Honours:* Lila Wallace-Reader's Digest Fund Writer's Award 1994. *Address:* c/o The City College of New York, 138th Street and Convent Avenue, New York, NY 10031, USA.

HOOVER, Paul (Andrew); Poet, Writer, Ed. and Educator; b. 30 April 1946, Harrisonburg, VA, USA; m. Maxine Chernoff, 5 Oct. 1974, two s. one d. *Education:* BA, English, Manchester College, 1968; MA, English, University of Illinois, 1973. *Career:* Ed., OINK!, 1971–85; Founder-Mem., 1974, Mem., Board of Dirs, 1974–87, Pres., 1975–78, School of the Art Institute of Chicago; Poet-in-Residence, Columbia College, 1974–; Co-Founder and Ed., New American Writing, 1986–; Fellow, Simon's Rock of Bard College, 1988–; Lecturer in Creative Writing, San Francisco State University, 1999–2000; mem. Associated Writing Programs; Co-ordinating Council of Literary Magazines; MLA of America. *Publications:* Hairpin Turns (poems), 1973; The Monocle Thugs, 1977; Letter to Einstein Beginning Dear Albert (poems), 1979; Somebody Talks a Lot (poems), 1983; Nervous Songs (poems), 1986; Idea (poems), 1987; Saigon, Illinois (novel), 1988; The Novel: A Poem, 1990; Postmodern American Poetry: A Norton Anthology (ed.), 1993; Viridian (poems), 1997; Totem and Shadow: New and Selected Poems, 1999; Rehearsal in Black, 2001; Winter (Mirror), 2002; Fables of Representation (essays), 2004. Contributions: numerous anthologies, reviews, quarterlies and journals. *Honours:* National Endowment for the Arts Poetry Fellowship, 1980; Illinois Arts Council Artist's Fellowships, 1983, 1984, 1986; General Electric Foundation Award for Younger Writers, 1984; Carl Sandburg Award, Friends of the Chicago Public Library, 1987; Gwendolyn Brooks Poet Laureate Award, 1988; Shifting Foundation Grants, 1990, 1991; Gertrude Stein Award in Innovative American Poetry, 1994–95; Winner, Contemporary Poetry Series Competition, University of Georgia, 1997; San Francisco Literary Laureate Award, Friends of the San Francisco Public Library, 2000; Jerome J. Shestack Prize, American Poetry Review, 2003. *Address:* 369 Molino Ave, Mill Valley, CA 94941, USA. *Website:* www.previewport.com.

HOPCRAFT, Arthur (Edward); Writer and Dramatist; b. 29 Nov. 1932, Essex, England. *Career:* Staff, Daily Mirror, 1956–59, Guardian, 1959–64; mem. Writers Guild of Great Britain. *Publications:* Born to Hunger, 1968; The Football Man, 1968; The Great Apple Raid, 1970; World Cup 70 (ed. with H. McIlvanney), 1970; Mid-Century Men, 1982. Other: Screenplay: Agatha (with K. Tynan), 1979. Television Dramatisations: The Mosedale Horseshoe, 1971; The Panel, 1971; The Birthday Run, 1972; Buggins Ermine, 1972; The Reporters, 1972; Said the Preacher, 1972; Jingle Bells, 1973; Katapult, 1973; The Nearly Man, 1974; Humbug, Finger or Thumb?, 1974; Journey to London, 1974; Baa, Baa, Blacksheep, 1974; Wednesday Love, 1975; Nightingale's Boys, 1975; Hannah, 1976; Hard Times, 1977; Tinker, Tailor, Soldier, Spy, 1979; Bleak House, 1985; A Perfect Spy, 1987; A Tale of Two Cities, 1988; Hostage, 1992; Rebecca, 1997. *Honours:* several drama awards. *Address:* c/o The Rod Hall Agency, 7 Goodge Pl., London W1P 1FL, England.

HOPE, Christopher David Tully, MA, FRSL; South African writer; b. 26 Feb. 1944, Johannesburg; m. Eleanor Marilyn Margaret Klein; two s. *Education:* Natal Univ., Univ. of the Witwatersrand. *Career:* mem. Soc. of Authors. *Publications:* A Separate Development 1981, Private Parts 1982, The King, the Cat and the Fiddle (with Yehudi Menuhin) 1983, Kruger's Alp (Whitbread Prize for Fiction 1985) 1984, The Dragon Wore Pink 1985, The Hottentot Room 1986, Black Swan 1987, White Boy Running 1988, My Chocolate Redeemer 1989, Moscow! Moscow! 1990, Serenity House 1992, The Love Songs of Nathan J. Swirsky 1993, Darkest England 1996; poetry: Cape Drives 1974, In the Country of the Black Pig 1981, Englishman 1985, Me, the Moon and Elvis Presley 1997, Signs of the Heart 1999, Heaven Forbid 2002, Brothers Under the Skin 2003; contrib. to TLS, London Magazine, Les Temps Modernes. *Honours:* Cholmondeley Award 1972, David Higham Award 1981, Int. PEN Award 1983, CNA Literary Award (S Africa) 1989. *Literary Agent:* Rogers, Coleridge & White Ltd, 20 Powis Mews, London, W11 1JN, England. *Telephone:* (20) 7221-3717. *Fax:* (20) 7229-9084.

HOPE, Ronald (Sidney); Writer; b. 4 April 1921, London, England. *Education:* BA, 1941, MA, 1946, DPhil, New College, Oxford. *Career:* Fellow, Brasenose College, Oxford, 1945–47, Dir, Seafarer's Education Service, London, 1947–76; Dir, The Marine Society, 1976–86. *Publications:* Spare Time at Sea, 1954; Economic Geography, 1956; Dick Small in the Half Deck, Ships, 1958; The British Shipping Industry, 1959; The Shoregoer's Guide to World Ports, 1963; Seamen and the Sea, 1965; Introduction to the Merchant Navy, 1965; Retirement from the Sea, 1967; In Cabined Ships at Sea, 1969; Twenty Singing Seamen, 1979; The Seamen's World, 1982; A New History of British Shipping, 1990; Poor Jack: The Perilous History of the Merchant Seaman, 2001. *Address:* 2 Park Pl., Dollar FK14 7AA, England.

HOPE-SIMPSON, Jacynth (Ann), (Helen Dudley); Writer; b. 10 Nov. 1930, Birmingham, England. *Education:* University of Lausanne, 1949; MA and Diploma in Education, University of Oxford, 1953. *Publications:* The Stranger in the Train, 1960; The Bishop of Kenelminster, 1961; The Man Who Came Back, 1962; The Bishop's Picture, 1962; The Unravished Bridge, 1963; The Witch's Cave, 1964; The Hamish Hamilton Book of Myths and Legends, 1965; The Hamish Hamilton Book of Witches, 1966; Escape to the Castle, 1967; The Unknown Island, 1968; They Sailed from Plymouth, 1970; Elizabeth I, 1971; Tales in School, 1971; The Gunner's Boy, 1973; Save Tarranmoor!, 1974; Always on the Move, 1975; The Hijacked Hovercraft, 1975; Black Madonna, 1976; Vote for Victoria, 1976; The Making of the Machine Age, 1978; The Hooded Falcon, 1979; Island of Perfumes, 1985; Cottage Dreams, 1986. *Address:* Franchise Cottage, Newtown, Milborne, Port Sherborne, Dorset, England.

HOPKINS, Antony; Composer, Conductor, Lecturer and Writer; b. 21 March 1921, London, England; m. Alison Purves, 1947, deceased 1991. *Education:* Royal College of Music, London. *Career:* Dir, Intimate Opera Co, 1952–64; Presenter, Talking About Music, BBC, 1954–92; Lecturer, Royal College of Music, London. *Publications:* Talking About Symphonies, 1961; Talking About Concertos, 1964; Music All Around Me, 1967; Music Face to Face, 1971; Talking About Sonatas, 1971; Downbeat Guide, 1977; Understanding Music, 1979; The Nine Symphonies of Beethoven, 1980; Songs for Swinging Golfers, 1981; Sounds of Music, 1982; Beating Time, 1982; Pathway to Music, 1983; The Concertgoer's Companion, 2 vols, 1984, 1986, one vol. edn, 1994; The Seven Concertos of Beethoven, 1996. *Honours:* Gold Medal, Royal College of Music, 1943; Italia Prizes, 1951, 1957; Medal for Services to Music, City of Tokyo, 1973; CBE, 1976. *Address:* Woodyard, Ashridge, Berkhamsted, Hertfordshire HP4 1PS, England.

HOPKINSON, Simon; Australian playwright, director and writer. *Career:* Artistic Dir, Australian Theatre for Young People, New England Theatre Co., Darwin Theatre Group; fmr resident dramatist and Assoc. Dir, Melbourne Theatre Co.; founder, Theatre-in-Education Co., Australia; specialist consultant for children's television, Australian Broadcasting Authority. *Theatre includes:* Lipstick Dreams, Wedding Games, Happy Families. *Television includes:* Bananas in Pyjamas (co-creator, writer) 1991 (also subsequent stage shows), Driven Crazy, Chuck Finn, Fast Tracks, Gloria's House, Petals. *Films include:* The Magic Pudding. *Publications (on CD-ROM):* Oz – The Magical Adventure 2000, Bananas in Pyjamas: It's Fun Time, It's Party Time. *Literary Agent:* RGM Associates, PO Box 128, Surry Hills, NSW 2010, Australia. *Telephone:* (2) 9281 3911. *Fax:* (2) 9281 4705. *E-mail:* info@rgm.com.au. *Website:* www.rgm.com.au.

HORNBY, Nick; British journalist and novelist; b. 1957, London, England. *Publications:* Contemporary American Fiction (essays) 1992, Fever Pitch (memoir) 1992, (screenplay) 1997, My Favourite Year: A Collection of New Football Writing (ed.) 1993, High Fidelity (novel) 1995, Speaking With the Angel (ed.) 2000, About a Boy (novel) 2000, How to be Good (novel) 2001, 31 Songs (non-fiction) 2003; contrib. to Sunday Times, TLS, Literary Review, New York Times, New Yorker, the Believer. *Honours:* William Hill Sports Book of the Year Award 1992, Writers' Guild Best Fiction Book Award 1995, American Acad. of Arts and Letters E. M. Forster Award 1999, WHSmith Fiction Award 2002, London Award 2003. *Literary Agent:* PFD, Drury House, 34–43 Russell Street, London, WC2B 5HA, England.

HORNE, Sir Alistair Allan, Kt, MA; British author, journalist and lecturer; b. 9 Nov. 1925, London, England; m. 1st Renira Margaret Hawkins; three d.; m. 2nd The Hon. Mrs Sheelin Eccles 1987. *Education:* Jesus Coll., Cambridge. *Career:* foreign correspondent, Daily Telegraph 1952–55; official biographer for Prime Minister Harold Macmillan 1979; mem. Soc. of Authors, RSL. *Publications:* Back into Power 1955, The Land is Bright 1958, Canada and the Canadians 1961, The Fall of Paris 1870–1871 1965, To Lose a Battle: France 1940 1969, Death of a Generation 1970, The Paris Commune 1971, Small Earthquake in Chile 1972, Napoleon, Master of Europe 1805–1807 1979, The French Army and Politics 1870–1970 1984, Macmillan, Vol. I 1894–1956 1985, Vol. II 1957–1986 1989, A Bundle from Britain 1993, The Lonely Leader: Monty 1944–45 1994, How Far from Austerlitz: Napoleon 1805–1815 1996, Telling Lives (ed.) 2000, Seven Ages of Paris: Portrait of a City 2002, The Age of Napoleon 2004; contrib. to various periodicals. *Honours:* Hawthornden Prize 1963, Yorkshire Post Book of Year Prize 1978, Wolfson Literary Award 1978, Enid Macleod Prize 1985; Chevalier, Légion d'honneur 1993. *Literary Agent:* The Wylie Agency, 4–8 Rodney Street, London, N1 9JH, England. *Address:* The Old Vicarage, Turville, Nr Henley on Thames, Oxfordshire RG9 6QU, England.

HORNE, Donald Richmond; writer and academic; b. 26 Dec. 1921, Sydney, NSW, Australia; m. 1960; one s. one d. *Education:* Sydney University, Canberra University College, 1944–45. *Career:* Ed., The Observer, 1958–61, The Bulletin, 1961–62, 1967–72, Quadrant, 1963–66; Contributing Ed., Newsweek International, 1973–76; Chancellor, University of Canberra, 1992–96; mem. Australian Society of Authors; Copyright Agency Ltd. *Publications:* The Lucky Country, 1964; The Permit, 1965; The Education of Young Donald, 1967; God is an Englishman, 1969; The Next Australia, 1970; But What If There Are No Pelicans?, 1971; Money Made Us, 1976; The Death of the Lucky Country, 1976; His Excellency's Pleasure, 1977; Right Way Don't Go Back, 1978; In Search of Billy Hughes, 1979; Time of Hope, 1980; Winner Take All, 1981; The Great Museum, 1984; Confessions of New Boy, 1985; The Story of the Australian People, 1985; The Public Culture, 1986; The Lucky Country Revisited, 1987; Portrait of an Optimist, 1988; Ideas for a Nation, 1989; The Intelligent Tourist, 1993; The Avenue of the Fair Go, 1997; An Interrupted Life, 1998; Into the Open: Memoirs 1958–99, 2000; Looking for Leadership, 2000; Ten Steps to a More Tolerant Australia, 2003. Contributions: numerous professional journals. *Honours:* AO, 1982; Hon. doctorates; Fellow, Australian Acad. of Humanities. *Address:* 53 Grosvenor Street, Woollahra, Sydney, NSW 2025, Australia.

HOROVITZ, Michael, BA, MA; writer, poet, editor and publisher; b. 4 April 1935, Frankfurt am Main, Germany. *Education:* Brasenose Coll., Oxford. *Career:* Ed. and Publisher, New Departures International Review 1959–; founder, co-ordinator, and torchbearer, Poetry Olympics Festivals 1980–. *Publications:* Europa (trans.), 1961; Alan Davie, 1963; Declaration, 1963; Strangers: Poems, 1965; Poetry for the People: An Essay in Bop Prosody, 1966; Bank Holiday: A New Testament for the Love Generation, 1967; Children of Albion (ed.), 1969; The Wolverhampton Wanderer: An Epic of Football, Fate and Fun, 1970; Love Poems, 1971; A Contemplation, 1978; Growing Up: Selected Poems and Pictures 1951–1979, 1979; The Egghead Republic (trans.), 1983; A Celebration of and for Frances Horovitz, 1984; Midsummer Morning Jog Log, 1986; Bop Paintings, Collages and Drawings, 1989; Grandchildren of Albion (ed.), 1992; Wordsounds and Sightlines: New and Selected Poems, 1994; Grandchildren of Albion Live (ed.), 1996; The POW! Anthology, 1996; A New Waste Land: Britain at the Millennium, 2004. *Address:* c/o New Departures International Review, PO Box 9819, London, W11 2GQ, England.

HOROWITZ, Anthony; British writer and screenwriter; b. 5 April 1955, London; m. Jill Green; two s. *Education:* Orley Farm School London, Rugby School, Univ. of York. *Writing for television:* Dramarama, Boon, Robin of Sherwood, Poirot, The Gift (adaptation), Murder Most Horrid, The Last Englishman, Chiller, Crime Traveller, Midsomer Murders, Murder in Mind (also creator), Menace, Foyle's War (also creator). *Film screenplay:* The Gathering 2002. *Play:* Mindgame 2000. *Publications:* The Sinister Secret of Frederick K. Bower 1979, Misha, the Magician and the Mysterious Amulet 1981, Devil's Door Bell 1983, Enter Frederick K. Bower 1985, Night of the Scorpion 1985, The Myths and Mythology 1985, Robin the Hooded Man (with Richard Carpenter) 1986, The Silver Citadel 1986, Public Enemy #2 1987, Adventurer 1987, Crossbow: The Adventures of William Tell 1987, The Falcon's Malteser 1987, Groosham Grange 1988, Just Ask for Diamond 1989, Day of the Dragon 1989, Groosham Grange II: The Unholy Grail 1991, South by South East 1991, The Puffin Book of Horror Stories (ed.) 1994, Granny 1994, The Switch 1996, Death Walks Tonight: Horrifying Stories 1996, The Devil and his Boy 1998, Horowitz Horror 1999, More Horowitz Horror 2000, Stormbreaker 2000, Point Blank 2001, Skeleton Key 2002, Eagle Strike 2003, Alex Rider 2003, I Know What You Did Last Wednesday 2003, Return to Groosham Grange 2003, The Blurred Man 2003, Scorpia 2004, Three of Diamonds 2004, The Killing Joke 2004. *Address:* c/o Orchard Books, The Watts Publishing Group, 96 Leonard Street, London, EC2A 4XD, England. *Website:* www.orchardbooks.co.uk.

HOROWITZ, Irving (Louis); Prof. of Social and Political Theory, Writer, Ed. and Publisher; b. 25 Sept. 1929, New York, NY, USA; m. 1st Ruth Lenore Horowitz, 1950, divorced 1964, two s.; m. 2nd Mary Curtis Horowitz, 9 Oct. 1979. *Education:* BSS, City College, CUNY, 1951; MA, Columbia University, 1952; PhD, University of Buenos Aires, 1957; Postgraduate Fellow, Brandeis University, 1958–59. *Career:* Assoc. Prof., University of

Buenos Aires, 1955–58; Asst Prof., Bard College, 1960; Chair., Dept of Sociology, Hobart and William Smith Colleges, 1960–63; Ed.-in-Chief, Transaction Society, 1962–94; Assoc. Prof. to Prof. of Sociology, Washington University, St Louis, 1963–69; Pres., Transaction Books, 1966–94; Chair., Dept of Sociology, Livingston College, Rutgers University, 1969–73; Prof. of Sociology, Graduate Faculty, 1969–, Hannah Arendt Prof. of Social and Political Theory, 1979–, Rutgers University; Bacardi Chair of Cuban Studies, Miami University, 1992–93; Editorial Chair. and Pres. Emeritus, Transaction/USA and Transaction/UK; Bd Chair. ILH Foundation for Social Policy 1998–2004mem. American Acad. of Arts and Sciences; American Asscn of University Profs; American Political Science Asscn; Authors' Guild; Council on Foreign Relations; International Society of Political Psychology, founder; National Asscn of Scholars. *Publications:* Idea of War and Peace in Contemporary Philosophy, 1957; Philosophy, Science and the Sociology of Knowledge, 1960; Radicalism and the Revolt Against Reason: The Social Theories of Georges Sorel, 1962; The War Game: Studies of the New Civilian Militarists, 1963; Professing Sociology: The Life Cycle of a Social Science, 1963; Revolution in Brazil: Politics and Society in a Developing Nation, 1964; The Rise and Fall of Project Camelot, 1967; Three Worlds of Development: The Theory and Practice of International Stratification, 1967; Latin American Radicalism: A Documentary Report on Nationalist and Left Movements, 1969; Sociological Self-Images, 1969; The Knowledge Factory: Masses in Latin America, 1970; Cuban Communism, 1970; Foundations of Political Sociology, 1972; Social Science and Public Policy in the United States, 1975; Ideology and Utopia in the United States, 1977; Dialogues on American Politics, 1979; Taking Lives: Genocide and State Power, 1979; Beyond Empire and Revolution, 1982; C. Wright Mills: An American Utopian, 1983; Winners and Losers, 1985; Communicating Ideas, 1987; Daydreams and Nightmares: Reflections of a Harlem Childhood, 1990; The Decomposition of Sociology, 1993; Behemoth: Main Currents in the History and Theory of Political Sociology, 1999; Searching for the Soul of American Foreign Policy: The Cuban Embargo and the National Interest, 2000, Tributes: An Informal History of Social Science in the Twentieth Century. Contributions: Professional journals. *Honours:* Harold D. Lasswell Award; Festschrift, 1994; National Jewish Book Award in Biography/Autobiography; Lifetime Service Award, Inter-University Armed Forces Society. *Literary Agent:* Brandt & Hochman Literary Agents Inc, 1501 Broadway, New York, NY 10036, USA. *Address:* 1247 State Rd, Route 206, Blanwenberg Rd, Rocky Hill Intersection, Princeton, NJ 08540, USA.

HORROCKS, Paul John; Editor; b. 19 Dec. 1953, UK; m. Linda Jean Walton 1976; two s. one d. *Education:* Bolton School. *Career:* reporter Daily Mail 1974–75; reporter Manchester Evening News 1975–80, crime corresp. 1980–87, news ed. 1987–91, Asst Ed. 1991–95, Deputy Ed. 1995–97, Ed. 1997–; mem. UK Soc. of Eds, mem., board of dirs; mem., Organizing Cttee, Commonwealth Games Manchester, 2002; Community Foundation for Greater Manchester, vice-pres.; Francis House Children's Hospice, patron; Manchester Enterprises Partners' Council. *Address:* c/o Manchester Evening News, 164 Deansgate, Manchester M60 2RD, England. *E-mail:* joanne.watchorn@man.news.co.uk. *Website:* www.manchesteronline.co.uk.

HORTON, Felix Lee (see Floren, Lee).

HORTON, Richard C., FRCP; British physician; *Editor, The Lancet. Career:* Visting Prof., London School of Hygiene and Tropical Medicine; Ed., publisher, The Lancet; bd mem. Council of Science Editors 1994–. *Publications:* non-fiction: Prostglandins and the Kidney (with Michael Dunn) 1981, Preventing Coronary Artery Disease (with Martin Kendall) 1997, How to Publish in Biomedicine 1997, Second Opinion: Doctors and Diseases 2003, A Life in Medical Research and Teaching: An Endocrinologist's Tale 2003, Health Wars: On the Global Front Lines of Modern Medicine 2003, MMR: Science and Fiction 2004; contrib. to New York Review of Books, London Review of Books, The Lancet, journals. *Address:* The Lancet, 32 Jamestown Road, London, NW1 7BY, England. *Telephone:* (20) 7424-4910. *Fax:* (20) 7424-4911. *E-mail:* r.horton@elsevier.co.uk.

HORWITZ, Allan Kolski; writer and performance poet; b. South Africa. *Career:* f. and co-ordinator, Botsotso Publishing, mem. editorial board, Botsotso Magazine; f., Botsotso Jesters performance poetry group. *Publications:* Call from the Free State (poems), 1979. Contributions: short story 'Courageous and Steadfast', in Unity in Flight anthology, 2001; Donga; The Literate Gymnast; LitNet. *Address:* Postnet Suit 136, Private Bag X2600, Houghton, South Africa. *Telephone:* (011) 648 7996. *Fax:* (011) 487 2112. *E-mail:* artstudio@artslink.co.za. *Website:* www.111.co.za/botsotso.htm.

HORWOOD, Harold (Andrew); Author; b. 2 Nov. 1923, St John's, NF, Canada; m. Cornelia Lindismith, 1 July 1973, one s. one d. *Education:* Prince of Wales College, St John's, NF. *Career:* Mem., House of Assembly, NF, Liberal Party, 1949–51; Columnist, Evening Telegram, St John's, NF, 1952–58; Writer-in-Residence, University of Western Ontario, 1976–77, University of Waterloo, 1980–82; mem. Writers' Union of Canada, chair., 1980–81. *Publications:* Tomorrow Will be Sunday (novel), 1966; The Foxes of Beachy Cove, 1967; Newfoundland, 1969; White Eskimo: A Novel of Labrador, 1972; Beyond the Road: Portraits and Visions of Newfoundlands, 1976; Bartlett: The Great Canadian Explorer, 1977; The Colonial Dream 1497/1760, 1978; Only the Gods Speak (short stories), 1979; Tales of the Labrador Indians, 1981; A History of Canada, 1984; Pirates and Outlaws of Canada 1610–1932 (with E. Butts), 1984; A History of the Newfoundland Ranger Force, 1986; Corner Brook: A Social History of a Paper Town, 1986; Historic Newfoundland (with John de Visser), 1986; Remembering Summer (novel), 1987; Dancing on the Shore, 1987; Bandits and Privateers: Canada in the Age of Gunpowder (with E. Butts), 1987; Joey: The Life and Political Times of Joey Smallwood, 1989; The Magic Ground, 1996; A Walk in the Dream Time: Growing Up in Old St John's, 1997; Evening Light (novel), 1998; Among the Lions, a Lamb in the Literary Jungle, 2000; Cycle of the Sun (poetry), 2003. Contributions: numerous journals and magazines. *Honours:* Best Scientific Book of the Year, 1967; Canada Council Senior Arts Award, 1975; Mem. of the Order of Canada, 1980. *Address:* PO Box 489, Annapolis Royal, NS BOS 1A0, Canada.

HORWOOD, William; British novelist; b. 1944, Oxford, England; m. 1st; m. 2nd; m. 3rd; six c. *Education:* Sir Roger Manwood's School, Sandwich, Univ. of Bristol. *Career:* frmly worked at trade magazine Campaign, feature ed. Daily Mail –1978. *Publications:* Duncton Wood 1980, The Stonor Eagles 1982, Callanish 1984, Skallagrigg 1987, Duncton Quest 1988, Duncton Found 1989, Duncton Tales 1991, The Book of Silence 1992, Duncton Rising 1993, Duncton Stone 1993, The Willows in Winter 1993, Toad Triumphant 1995, Journeys to the Heartland 1995, The Willows and Beyond 1996, Seekers at the Wulfrock 1997, Mole Gets Lost 1997, Flying into Danger 1997, Toad in Trouble 1997, Willows at Christmas 1998, The Boy With No Shoes (autobiog.) 2004. *Address:* c/o Hodder Headline, 338 Euston Road, London, NW1 3BH, England.

HOSKING, Geoffrey Alan, MA, PhD, FRHistS; historian and academic; b. 28 April 1942, Troon, Ayrshire, Scotland; m. Anne Lloyd Hirst 1970; two d. *Education:* King's College, Cambridge, St Antony's College, Oxford, Moscow State University. *Career:* Asst Lecturer in Government, 1966–68, Lecturer in Government, 1968–71, Lecturer in History, 1972–76, Senior Lecturer and Reader in Russian History, 1976–84, University of Essex; Visiting Lecturer in Political Science, University of Wisconsin at Madison, 1971–72; Senior Research Fellow, Russian Institute, Columbia University, 1976; Visiting Prof., Slavisches Institut, University of Cologne, 1980–81; Prof. of Russian History, 1984–99, Deputy Dir, School of Slavonic and East European Studies, 1996–98, Leverhulme Research Prof., 1999–, University of London; BBC Reith Lecturer, 1988. *Publications:* The Russian Constitutional Experiment: Government and Duma, 1907–14, 1973; Beyond Socialist Realism: Soviet Fiction Since Ivan Denisovich, 1980; The First Socialist Society: A History of the Soviet Union from Within, 1985; The Awakening of the Soviet Union, 1990; The Road to Post-Communism: Independent Political Movements in the Soviet Union, 1985–91 (with J. Aves and P. J. S. Duncan), 1992; Russia: People and Empire, 1552–1917, 1997; Myths and Nationhood (ed. with George Schöpflin), 1997; Russian Nationalism Past and Present (ed. with Robert Service), 1998; Reinterpreting Russia (ed. with Robert Service), 1999; Russia and the Russians: A History, 2001. Contributions: scholarly books and journals. *Honours:* Los Angeles Times History Books Prize, 1986; Fellow, British Acad., 1993; US Independent Publishers History Book Prize, 2002. *Address:* c/o School of Slavonic and East European Studies, University College London, Senate House, Malet Street, London WC1E 7HU, England.

HOSPITAL, Janette Turner; novelist; b. 12 Nov. 1942, Melbourne, Vic., Australia. *Education:* BA, University of Queensland, Brisbane, 1965; MA, Queen's University, Canada, 1973. *Career:* Lecturer, Queen's University, St Lawrence College, Kingston, Ontario, 1971–82; Writer-in-Residence, MIT, 1985–89; Adjunct Prof., La Trobe University, 1991–93; Visiting Fellow and Writer-in-Residence, University of East Anglia, Norwich, 1996; O'Connor Chair in Literature, Colgate University, Hamilton, NY, 1999–. *Publications:* The Ivory Swing, 1982; The Tiger in the Tiger Pit, 1983; Borderline, 1985; Charades, 1988; A Very Proper Death, 1990; The Last Magician, 1992; Collected Stories, 1995; Oyster, 1996. Contributions: TLS; London Review of Books; Independent; New York Times; Boston Globe. *Honours:* Seal Award, 1982; Fellowship of Australian Writers Award, 1988. *Address:* c/o Mic Cheetham, 138 Buckingham Palace Road, London SW1W 9SA, England.

HOTCHNER, Aaron Edward; Author and Dramatist; b. 28 June 1920, St Louis, MO, USA. *Education:* LLB, Washington University, St Louis, 1941. *Career:* mem. Authors League; Dramatists Guild; PEN. *Publications:* The Dangerous American, 1958; The White House (play), 1964; Papa Hemingway: A Personal Memoir, 1966; The Hemingway Hero (play), 1967; Treasure, 1970; Do You Take This Man? (play), 1970; King of the Hill, 1972; Looking for Miracles, 1974; Doris Day: Her Own Story, 1976; Sophia: Living and Loving, 1979; Sweet Prince (play), 1980; The Man Who Lived at the Ritz, 1982; Choice People, 1984; Hemingway and His World, 1988; Welcome to the Club (musical), 1989; Blown Away, 1990; Louisiana Purchase, 1996; Exactly Like You (musical), 1998; After the Storm, 2001; The Day I Fired Alan Ladd and Other World War Two Adventures, 2002. Contributions: Magazines. *Honours:* Hon. DHL, Washington University, 1992; Distinguished Alumni Award, Washington University Law School, 1992. *Address:* 14 Hillandale Rd, Westport, CT 06880, USA.

HOUELLEBECQ, Michel; Poet and Novelist; b. 26 Feb. 1958, Réunion. *Education:* DipAgr. m. 1st 1980 (divorced); one s.; m. 2nd Marie-Pierre Gauthier 1998. *Publications:* H. P. Lovecraft, contre le monde, contre la vie, 1991; Rester Vivant—méthode, 1991; La Poursuite du bonheur, 1992;

Extension du domaine à la lutte (novel, trans. as Whatever), 1994; Le Sens du combat, 1996; Les Particules élémentaires (novel, trans. as Atomised), 1998; Interventions, 1998; Renaissance (poems), 1999; Plateforme (novel, trans. as Platform), 1999; Poésies, 2000; Lanzarote (photos and text), 2000. Recording: Presence humaine (poems to music of Bertrand Burgalat), 2000. Contributions: first works (poetry) published in Nouvelle Revue de Paris 1985; Literary reviews, incl. L'atelier du roman, Perpendiculaires. *Honours:* Prix Tristan Tzara, 1992; Prix de Flore, 1996; Grand Prix National des Lettres Jeunes Talents, 1998; Prix Novembre, 1998; International IMPAC Dublin Literary Award, 2002. *Address:* c/o Flammarion, 26 rue Racine, 75006 Paris, France. *Website:* www.houellebecq.info.

HOUGH, (Helen) Charlotte; writer; b. 24 May 1924, Hampshire, England; m. 1st Richard Hough 1941 (divorced 1973); four d.; m. 2nd Louis Ackroyd 1997. *Career:* mem. CWA; PEN; Society of Authors. *Publications:* Jim Tiger, 1956; Morton's Pony, 1957; The Hampshire Pig, 1958; The Story of Mr Pinks, 1958; The Animal Game, 1959; The Homemakers, 1959; The Trackers, 1960; Algernon, 1962; Three Little Funny Ones, 1962; The Owl in the Barn, 1964; More Funny Ones, 1965; Red Biddy, 1966; Anna and Minnie, 1967; Sir Frog, 1968; My Aunt's Alphabet, 1969; A Bad Child's Book of Moral Verse, 1970; The Bassington Murder, 1980. *Address:* 1A Ivor Street, London NW1 9PL, England.

HOUGH, Julia Marie (see Taylor, Judy).

HOUGHTON, Eric; Teacher and Author; b. 4 Jan. 1930, West Yorkshire, England; m. Cecile Wolffe, 4 June 1954, one s. one d. *Education:* Sheffield City College of Education, 1952. *Career:* mem. Society of Authors; Children's Writers Group. *Publications:* The White Wall, 1961; Summer Silver, 1963; They Marched with Spartacus, 1963; Boy Beyond the Mist, 1966; A Giant Can Do Anything, 1975; The Mouse and the Magician, 1976; The Remarkable Feat of King Caboodle, 1978; Steps Out of Time, 1979; Gates of Glass, 1987; Walter's Wand, 1989; The Magic Cheese, 1991; The Backwards Watch, 1991; Vincent the Invisible, 1993; Rosie and the Robbers, 1997; The Crooked Apple Tree, 1999. *Honours:* American Junior Book Award, 1964. *Address:* The Crest, 42 Collier Rd, Hastings, East Sussex TN34 3JR, England.

HOUSTON, James D., BA, MA; writer; b. 10 Nov. 1933, San Francisco, CA, USA; m. Jeanne Toyo Wakatsuki 1957; one s. two d. *Education:* San Jose State Coll., Stanford Univ. *Career:* Lecturer in English, Stanford Univ. 1967–68; Lecturer in Writing 1969–88, Visiting Prof. in Literature 1989–93, Univ. of California at Santa Cruz; writer-in-residence, Villa Montalvo, Saratoga, CA 1980, 1992, Centrum Foundation, Port Townsend, Washington 1992; Distinguished Visiting Writer, Univ. of Hawaii 1983; Allen T. Gilliland Chair in Telecommunications, San Jose State Univ. 1985; Visiting Writer, Univ. of Michigan 1985, Univ. of Oregon 1994, George Mason Univ., Fairfax 1999; writer-in-residence, Deutsche Bundesbank, Frankfurt 2002; mem. PEN Center West. *Films:* Farewell to Manzanar (with Jean Wakatsuki Houston and John Korty) 1976, Li'a: The Legacy of a Hawaiian Man 1988, Listen to the Forest 1991, The Hawaiian Way: The Art and Family Tradition of Slack Key 1993, Words, Earth and Aloha: The Sources of Hawaiian Music 1995. *Publications:* fiction: Between Battles 1968, Gig 1969, A Native Son of the Golden West 1971, Continental Drift 1978, Gasoline: The Automotive Adventures of Charlie Bates (short stories) 1980, Love Life 1987, The Last Paradise 1998, Snow Mountain Passage 2001; non-fiction: Farewell to Manzanar (with Jeanne Wakatsuki Houston) 1973, Open Field (with John R. Brodie) 1974, Three Songs for My Father 1974, Californians: Searching for the Golden State 1982, One Can Think About Life After the Fish is in the Canoe, and Other Coastal Sketches 1985, The Men in My Life, and Other More or Less True Recollections of Kinship 1987, In the Ring of Fire: A Pacific Basin Journey 1997, Hawaiian Son: The Life and Music of Eddie Kamae 2004; editor: The Literature of California Vol. 1 (with Jack Hicks, Maxine Hong Kingston and Al Young) 2000; contrib. to various anthologies. *Honours:* Wallace Stegner Writing Fellow, Stanford Univ. 1966–67, Joseph Henry Jackson Award 1967, Humanitas Prize 1976, Nat. Endowment for the Arts grants 1976–77, Research Fellow, East-West Center, Honolulu 1984, American Book Award 1983, Hawaii Int. Film Festival Special Award 1989, Rockefeller Foundation Writer's Residency, Bellagio, Italy 1995, American Book Award 1999, Distinguished Achievement Award, Western Literature Asscn 1999, Carey McWilliams Award 2000, Commonwealth Club Californiana Silver Medal 2001. *Address:* 2-1130 East Cliff Drive, Santa Cruz, CA 95062, USA. *Website:* www.jamesdhouston.com.

HOUSTON, R. B. (see Rae, Hugh Crauford).

HOVANNISIAN, Richard G.; academic and writer; b. 9 Nov. 1932, Tulare, CA, USA; m. Vartiter Kotcholosian 1957; four c. *Education:* BA in History, 1954, MA in History, 1958, University of California at Berkeley; Certificate in Armenian, Collège Arménien, Beirut, 1956; PhD in History, University of California at Los Angeles, 1966. *Career:* Lecturer, 1962–69, Prof. of Armenian and Near Eastern History, 1969–, Assoc. Dir, G. E. von Grunebaum Center of Near Eastern Studies, 1979–95, University of California at Los Angeles; Assoc. Prof. of History, St Mary's College, Los Angeles, 1965–69; Chair., Modern Armenian History, Armenian Educational Foundation, 1987–; Guest Lecturer; Consultant; mem. American Asscn for the Advancement of Slavic Studies; American Historical Asscn; Armenian Acad. of Science; Middle East Studies Asscn, fellow; National Asscn of Armenian Studies; Oral History Asscn; Society for Armenian Studies, founder-pres., 1974–75, 1990–92. *Publications:* Armenia on the Road to Independence, 1967; The Republic of Armenia, Vol. I, 1971, Vol. II, 1982, Vols III–IV, 1996; The Armenian Holocaust, 1980; The Armenian Genocide in Perspective, 1986; The Armenian Genocide: History, Politics, Ethics, 1992; The Armenian People from Ancient to Modern Times, Vol. I, The Dynastic Periods: From Antiquity to the Fourteenth Century, Vol. II, Foreign Dominion to Statehood: The Fifteenth to Twentieth Century, 1997. Co-Author: Transcaucasia: Nationalism and Social Change, 1983; Le Crime de Silence: Le Gènocide des Armèniens, 1984; Toward the Understanding and Prevention of Genocide, 1984; A Crime of Silence, 1985; Genocide: A Critical Bibliographic Review, 1988; Embracing the Other: Philosophical, Psychological, and Historical Perspectives on Altruism, 1992; Diasporas in World Politics, 1993; Genocide and Human Rights, 1993; Genocide: Conceptual and Historical Dimensions, 1994; The Legacy of History in Russia and the New States of Eurasia, 1994. Contributions: many professional journals and to periodicals. *Honours:* Humanities Institute Fellow, 1972; Guggenheim Fellowship, 1974–75; National Endowment for the Humanities Grant, 1981–82; California Council for the Humanities Grant, 1985–86; numerous awards, citations, and recognitions. *Address:* 101 Groverton Place, Los Angeles, CA 90077, USA.

HOWARD, Anthony Michell; Biographer, Reviewer and Writer; b. 12 Feb. 1934, London, England; m. Carol Anne Gaynor, 26 May 1965. *Education:* BA, Christ Church, Oxford, 1955. *Career:* Called to the Bar, Inner Temple, 1956; Political Correspondent, Reynolds News, 1958–59; Editorial Staff, Manchester Guardian, 1959–61; Political Correspondent, 1961–64, Asst Ed., 1970–72, Ed., 1972–78, New Statesman; Whitehall Correspondent, 1965, Sunday Times; Washington Correspondent, 1966–69, Deputy Ed., 1981–88, Observer; Ed., The Listener, 1979–81; Reporter, BBC TV News and Current Affairs, 1989–92; Obituaries Ed., The Times, 1993–99. *Publications:* The Making of the Prime Minister (with Richard West), 1965; The Crossman Diaries: Selections from the Diaries of a Cabinet Minister (ed.), 1979; Rab: The Life of R. A. Butler, 1987; Crossman: The Pursuit of Power, 1990; The Times Lives Remembered (ed. with David Heaton), 1993. Contributions: books, newspapers, and journals. *Honours:* Harkness Fellowship, USA, 1960; CBE, 1997; Hon. LLD, Nottingham Univ., 2001; Hon. DLitt, Leicester Univ., 2003. *Address:* 11 Campden House Ct, 42 Gloucester Walk, London W8 4HU, England.

HOWARD, Clark; Author; b. 1934, USA. *Career:* mem. MWA. *Publications:* The Arm, 1967; A Movement Toward Eden, 1969; The Doomsday Squad, 1970; The Killings, 1973; Last Contract, 1973; Summit Kill, 1975; Mark the Sparrow, 1975; The Hunters, 1976; The Last Great Death Stunt, 1976; Six Against the Rock, 1977; The Wardens, 1979; Zebra: The True Account of the 179 Days of Terror in San Francisco, 1979, UK edn as The Zebra Killings, 1980; American Saturday, 1981; Brothers in Blood, 1983; Dirt Rich, 1986; Hard City, 1990; Love's Blood, 1993; City Blood, 1994; Crowded Lives and Other Stories of Desperation and Danger, 2000; Challenge the Widow-Maker and Other Stories of People in Peril, 2000. *Honours:* Edgar Allan Poe Award, 1980; Ellery Queen Awards, 1985, 1986, 1988, 1990, 1999. *Address:* Box 1527, Palm Springs, CA 92263, USA. *E-mail:* 72002.2040@compuserve.com.

HOWARD, Deborah (Janet); Architectural Historian and Writer; b. 26 Feb. 1946, London, England; m. Malcolm S. Longair, 26 Sept. 1975, one s. one d. *Education:* BA, 1968, MA, 1972, Newnham College, Cambridge; MA, 1969, PhD, 1973, University of London. *Career:* Prof. of Architectural History, University of Cambridge; Fellow, St John's College, Cambridge; mem. Society of Antiquarians of Scotland, fellow; Society of Antiquaries, fellow. *Publications:* Jacopo Sansovino: Architecture and Patronage in Renaissance Venice, 1975; The Architectural History of Venice, 1980, revised and enlarged edn, 2002; Scottish Architecture from the Reformation to the Restoration, 1560–1660, 1995; La Scuola Grande della Misericordia di Venezia (with G. Fabbri and S. Mason), 1999; Venice and the East: The Impact on the Islamic World on Venetian Architecture 1100–1500, 2000. Contributions: Professional journals. *Honours:* Hon. Fellow, Royal Incorporation of Architects of Scotland. *Address:* St John's College, Cambridge CB2 1TP, England.

HOWARD, Elizabeth Jane; Author; b. 26 March 1923, London, England; m. 1st Peter Scott, 1941, one d.; m. 2nd Kingsley Amis, 1965, divorced 1983. *Education:* Trained as Actress, London Mask Theatre School, Scott Thorndike Student Repertory. *Career:* mem. FRSL; Authors Lending and Copyright Society. *Publications:* The Beautiful Visit, 1950; The Long View, 1956; The Sea Change, 1959; After Julius, 1965; Odd Girl Out, 1972; Mr Wrong, 1975; Getting It Right, 1982; The Light Years, 1990; Marking Time, 1991; Confusion, 1993; Casting Off, 1995; Falling, 1999; Slipstream (memoir), 2002. Other: 14 TV plays; three film scripts. Contributions: The Times; Sunday Times; Telegraph; Encounter; Vogue; Harper's; Queen. *Honours:* CBE; Yorkshire Post Novel of the Year, 1982; CBE, 2000. *Address:* c/o Jonathan Clowes, Ivan Bridge House, Bridge Approach, London NW1 8BD, England.

HOWARD, Ellen; Writer; b. 8 May 1943, New Bern, NC, USA; m. Charles Howard Jr, 29 June 1975, four d. *Education:* University of Oregon, 1961–63; BA, English, Portland State University, 1979. *Career:* mem. Authors' Guild; Society of Children's Book Writers and Illustrators. *Publications:* Circle of

Giving, 1984; When Daylight Comes, 1985; Gillyflower, 1986; Edith Herself, 1987; Her Own Song, 1988; Sister, 1990; The Chickenhouse House, 1991; The Cellar, 1992; The Tower Room, 1993; The Big Seed, 1993; Murphy and Kate, 1995; The Log Cabin Quilt, 1996; A Different Kind of Courage, 1996. *Honours:* Golden Kite Honor Book, 1984; Christopher Award, 1997. *Address:* 1811 Montview Blvd, Greeley, CO 80631, USA.

HOWARD, Lynette Desley (see Stevens, Lynsey).

HOWARD, Maureen; Lecturer and Writer; b. 28 June 1930, Bridgeport, CT, USA; m. 1st Daniel F. Howard, 28 Aug. 1954, divorced 1967, one d.; m. 2nd David J. Gordon, 2 April 1968, divorced; m. 3rd Mark Probst, 1981. *Education:* BA, Smith College, 1952. *Career:* Lecturer, New School for Social Research, New York, 1967–68, 1970–71, 1974–, University of California at Santa Barbara, 1968–69, Amherst College, Brooklyn College, CUNY, Columbia University. *Publications:* Fiction: Not a Word About Nightingales, 1961; Bridgeport Bus, 1966; Before My Time, 1975; Grace Abounding, 1982; Expensive Habits, 1986; Natural History, 1992; A Lover's Almanac, 1998; Big as Life: Three Tales for Spring, 2001. Non-Fiction: Facts of Life (autobiog.), 1978. Editor: Seven American Women Writers of the Twentieth Century, 1977; Contemporary American Essays, 1984. *Honours:* Guggenheim Fellowship, 1967–68; Radcliffe Institute Fellow, 1967–68; National Book Critics Circle Award, 1980; Ingram Merrill Foundation Fellow, 1988; Literary Lion Award, New York Public Library, 1993.

HOWARD, Sir Michael Eliot, Kt, CBE, CH, MC, MA, DLitt, FBA, FRHistS; British historian; b. 29 Nov. 1922, London. *Education:* Wellington Coll., Christ Church, Oxford. *Career:* served in army 1942–45; Asst Lecturer, Lecturer in History, King's Coll., London 1947–53; Lecturer, Reader in War Studies, Univ. of London 1953–63; Prof. of War Studies, Univ. of London 1963–68; Fellow in Higher Defence Studies, All Souls Coll., Oxford 1968–77; Chichele Prof. of the History of War, Univ. of Oxford 1977–80; Regius Prof. of Modern History, Univ. of Oxford 1980–89, Prof. Emer. 1989–; Hon. Fellow, Oriel Coll. 1990; Hon. Student Christ Church 1990; Robert A. Lovett Prof. of Mil. and Naval History, Yale Univ. 1989–93; Leverhulme Lecturer 1996; Lee Kuan Yew Distinguished Visitor, Nat. Univ. of Singapore 1996; Founder and Pres. Emer. Int. Inst. for Strategic Studies; mem. The Literary Soc. (Pres. -2004); Foreign mem. American Acad. of Arts and Sciences. *Publications:* The Coldstream Guards 1920–1946 (with John Sparrow) 1951, Disengagement in Europe 1958, Wellingtonian Studies 1959, The Franco-German War 1961, The Theory and Practice of War 1965, The Mediterranean Strategy in the Second World War 1967, Studies in War and Peace 1970, Grand Strategy, Vol. IV (in UK History of Second World War) 1972, The Continental Commitment 1973, War in European History 1976, Clausewitz on War (trans. with Peter Paret) 1976, War and the Liberal Conscience 1978, Restraints on War (ed.) 1979, The Causes of Wars 1983, Clausewitz 1983, Strategic Deception: British Intelligence in the Second World War 1990, The Lessons of History (essays) 1991, The Oxford History of the Twentieth Century (co-ed. with W. R. Louis) 1998, The Invention of Peace 2000, The First World War 2001. *Honours:* Hon. Fellow Oriel Coll., Oxford 1990; Hon. LittD (Leeds) 1979; Hon. DLitt (London) 1988; Duff Cooper Memorial Prize 1961, Wolfson Foundation History Award 1972, NATO Atlantic Award 1989, Chesney Memorial Gold Medal, Royal United Services Inst., Samule Eliot Morrison Prize, Soc. for Mil. History 1992, Paul Nitze Award, Center for Naval Analysis 1994, Political Book Prize, Friedrich Ebert Stiftung 2002. *Address:* The Old Farm, Eastbury, Hungerford, Berks., RG17 7JN, England (Home). *Telephone:* (1488) 71387. *Fax:* (1488) 71387.

HOWARD, Philip Nicholas Charles, MA, FRSL; editor, columnist and writer; b. 2 Nov. 1933, London, England; m. Myrtle Janet Mary Houldsworth 1959; two s. one d. *Education:* Trinity College, Oxford. *Career:* Staff, Glasgow Herald, 1959–64; Staff, 1964–, Literary Ed., 1978–92, Leader Writer and Columnist, 1992–, The Times; London Ed., Verbatim, 1977–; mem. Classical Asscn, pres., 2002; Friends of Classics, founder-patron; Horatian Society; Literary Society; Society of Bookmen. *Publications:* The Black Watch, 1968; The Royal Palaces, 1970; London's River, 1975; New Words for Old, 1977; The British Monarchy, 1977; Weasel Words, 1978; Words Fail Me, 1980; A Word in Your Ear, 1983; The State of the Language: English Observed, 1984; The Times Bicentenary Stamp Book (co-author), 1985; We Thundered Out: 200 Years of the Times, 1785–1985, 1985; Winged Words, 1988; Word-Watching, 1988; London: The Evolution of a Great City (co-author), 1989; A Word in Time, 1990; The Times Bedside Book (ed.), 1991; Reading a Poem, 1992. *Address:* Flat 1, 47 Ladbroke Grove, London W11 3AR, England. *E-mail:* philipnchoward@compuserve.com.

HOWARD, Richard (Joseph); Poet, Critic, Editor and Trans; b. 13 Oct. 1929, Cleveland, OH, USA. *Education:* BA, 1951, MA, 1952, Columbia Univ.; Postgraduate Studies, Sorbonne, Univ. of Paris, 1952–53. *Career:* Lexicographer, World Publishing Co, 1954–58; Poetry Ed., New American Review, New Republic, Paris Review, Shenandoah, Western Humanities Review; Rhodes Prof. of Comparative Literature, Univ. of Cincinnati. *Publications:* Poetry: Quantities, 1962; The Damages, 1967; Untitled Subjects, 1969; Findings, 1971; Two-Part Inventions, 1974; Fellow Feelings, 1976; Misgivings, 1979; Lining Up, 1984; Quantities/Damages, 1984; No Traveller, 1989; Like Most Revelations: New Poems, 1994; Trappings, 1999; Talking Cures, 2002. Criticism: Alone with America: Essays on the Art of Poetry in the United States Since 1950, 1969; Passengers Must Not Ride on Fenders, 1974. Editor: Preferences: Fifty-One American Poets Choose Poems from Their Own Work and from the Past, 1974; The War in Algeria, 1975. Translator: numerous books, from French. Contributions: Magazines and journals. *Honours:* Guggenheim Fellowship, 1966–67; Harriet Monroe Memorial Prize, 1969; Pulitzer Prize in Poetry, 1970; Levinson Prize, 1973; Cleveland Arts Prize, 1974; American Acad. and Institute of Arts and Letters Medal for Poetry, 1980; American Book Award for Trans., 1983; PEN American Center Medal for Trans., 1986; France-American Foundation Award for Trans., 1987; National Endowment for the Arts Fellowship, 1987; MacArthur Fellowship, 1996. *Address:* c/o Turtle Point Press, 233 Broadway, Room 946, New York, NY 10279, USA.

HOWARD, Roger; Dramatist, Poet, Author and Sr Lecturer in Literature; b. 19 June 1938, Warwick, England; m. Anne Mary Zemaitis 13 Aug. 1960; one s. *Education:* RADA, London, 1956–57; Univ. of Bristol, 1958; MA, Univ. of Essex, 1976. *Career:* Teacher, Nankai Univ., Tientsin, People's Republic of China, 1965–67; Lecturer, Univ. of Beijing, 1972–74; Fellow in Creative Writing, Univ. of York, 1976–78; Writing Fellow, Univ. of East Anglia, 1979; Lecturer, 1979–93, Founder-Dir, Theatre Underground, 1979–, Lecturer in Literature, 1979–93, Ed., New Plays series, 1980–, Senior Lecturer in Literature, 1993–2003, Univ. of Essex. *Publications:* A Phantastic Satire (novel), 1960; From the Life of a Patient (novel), 1961; To the People (poems), 1966; Praise Songs (poems), 1966; The Technique of the Struggle Meeting, 1968; The Use of Wall Newspapers, 1968; New Short Plays I, 1968; Fin's Doubts, 1968; Episodes from the Fighting in the East, 1971; The Hooligan's Handbook, 1971; Slaughter Night and Other Plays, 1971; Method for Revolutionary Writing, 1972; Culture and Agitation: Theatre Documents (ed.), 1972; Contemporary Chinese Theatre, 1977; Mao Tse-tung and the Chinese People, 1978; The Society of Poets, 1979; A Break in Berlin, 1980; The Siege, 1981; Partisans, 1983; Ancient Rivers, 1984; The Speechifier, 1984; Contradictory Theatres, 1985; Senile Poems, 1988; The Tragedy of Mao and Other Plays, 1989; Britannia and Other Plays, 1990; Selected Poems 1966–96, 1997. Contributions: anthologies, newspapers and journals. *Address:* c/o Theatre Underground, Dept of Literature, University of Essex, Wivenhoe Park, Colchester, Essex CO4 3SQ, England.

HOWATCH, Susan, LLB; British writer; b. 14 July 1940, Leatherhead, Surrey; m. Joseph Howatch 1964 (divorced 1975); one d. *Education:* Sutton High School, King's Coll., London. *Career:* emigrated to USA 1964, lived in Ireland 1976–80, returned to UK 1980; first book published 1965; Fellow King's Coll. London 1999–; mem. Soc. of Authors. *Publications:* novels: The Dark Shore 1965, The Waiting Sands 1966, Call in the Night 1967, The Shrouded Walls 1968, April's Grave 1969, The Devil on Lammas Night 1970, Penmarric 1971, Cashelmara 1974, The Rich are Different 1977, Sins of the Fathers 1980, The Wheel of Fortune 1984, Glittering Images 1987, Glamorous Powers 1988, Ultimate Prizes 1989, Scandalous Risks 1991, Mystical Paths 1992, Absolute Truths 1994, A Question of Integrity (US title: The Wonder Worker) 1997, The High Flyer 1999, The Heartbreaker 2003. *Honours:* Winifred Mary Stanford Memorial Prize 1991. *Literary Agent:* Gillon Aitken Associates, 18–21 Cavaye Place, London, SW10 9PT, England. *Telephone:* (20) 7373-8672. *Fax:* (20) 7373-6002. *E-mail:* reception@aitkenassoc.demon.co.uk.

HOWE, Fanny; Prof. of Writing and American Literature, Author, Poet and Dramatist; b. 15 Oct. 1940, Buffalo, NY, USA; one s. two d. *Education:* Stanford University, 1958–61. *Career:* Lecturer, Tufts University, 1968–71, Emerson College, 1974, Columbia University Extension and School of the Arts, 1975–78, Yale University, 1976, Harvard University Extension, 1977, MIT, 1978–87; Prof. of Writing and American Literature, University of California at San Diego, 1987–; Assoc. Dir, Study Center, University College London, 1993–95; Distinguished Visiting Writer-in-Residence, Mills College, 1996–97. *Publications:* Fiction: Forty Whacks, 1969; First Marriage, 1975; Bronte Wilde, 1976; Holy Smoke, 1979; The White Slave, 1980; In the Middle of Nowhere, 1984; Taking Care, 1985; The Lives of a Spirit, 1986; The Deep North, 1988; Famous Questions, 1989; Saving History, 1992; Nod, 1998. Young Adult Fiction: The Blue Hills, 1981; Yeah, But, 1982; Radio City, 1983; The Race of the Radical, 1985. Poetry: Eggs, 1980; The Amerindian Coastline Poem, 1976; Poem from a Single Pallet, 1980; Alsace Lorraine, 1982; For Erato, 1984; Introduction to the World, 1985; Robeson Street, 1985; The Vineyard, 1988; The Quietist, 1992; The End, 1992; O'Clock, 1995; One Crossed Out, 1997; Q, 1998. Contributions: many anthologies, reviews, quarterlies, journals, and magazines. *Honours:* MacDowell Colony Fellowships, 1965, 1990; National Endowment for the Arts Fellowships in Fiction, 1969, and in Poetry, 1991; Bunting Institute Fellowship, 1974; St Botolph Award for Fiction, 1976; Writer's Choice Award for Fiction, 1984; Village Voice Award for Fiction, 1988; California Council on the Arts Award for Poetry, 1993; Lenore Marshall Poetry Prize, Acad. of American Poets, 2001.

HOWE, Susan; Poet and Prof. of English; b. 10 June 1937, USA. *Education:* BFA, Painting, Museum of Fine Arts, Boston, 1961. *Career:* Butler Fellow in English, 1988, Prof. of English, 1991–, SUNY at Buffalo; Visiting Scholar and Prof. of English, Temple University, Philadelphia, 1990, 1991; Visiting Poet and Leo Block Prof., University of Denver, 1993–94; Visiting Brittingham Scholar, University of Wisconsin at Madison, 1994; Visiting Poet, University of Arizona, 1994; Visiting Prof., Stanford University, 1998; mem. Acad. of American Poets, board of chancellors, 2000–; American Acad. of Arts and Sciences. *Publications:* Poetry: Hinge Picture, 1974; The

Western Borders, 1976; Secret History of the Dividing Line, 1978; Cabbage Gardens, 1979; The Liberties, 1980; Pythagorean Silence, 1982; Defenestration of Prague, 1983; Articulation of Sound Forms in Time, 1987; A Bibliography of the King's Book, or Eikon Basilike, 1989; The Europe of Trusts: Selected Poems, 1990; Singularities, 1990; The Nonconformist's Memorial, 1993; Frame Structures: Early Poems 1974–1979, 1996; Pierce-Arrow, 1999; Bad-Hangings, 2000. Other: My Emily Dickinson, 1985; Incloser, 1990; The Birthmark: Unsettling the Wilderness in American Literary History, 1993. *Honours:* Before Columbus Foundation American Book Awards, 1980, 1986; New York State Council of the Arts Residency, 1986; Pushcart Prize, 1987; New York City Fund for Poetry Grant, 1988; Roy Harvey Pearce Award, 1996; Guggenheim Fellowship, 1996–97; Distinguished Fellow, Stanford Humanities Centre, 1998; Hon. degrees, National Univ. of Ireland, 2000, St Joseph Coll., Hartford, CT, 2003; State of New York Distinguished Prof., 2002. *Address:* 115 New Quarry Rd, Guilford, CT 06437, USA.

HOWE, Tina; playwright and academic; b. 21 Nov. 1937, New York, NY, USA; m. Norman Levy 1961; one s. one d. *Education:* BA, Sarah Lawrence College, Bronxville, New York, 1959. *Career:* Adjunct Prof., New York University, 1983–; Visiting Prof., Hunter College, CUNY, 1990–; mem. Dramatists Guild, council, 1990–; PEN. *Publications:* The Nest, 1969; Museum, 1979; The Art of Dining, 1980; Painting Churches, 1984; Coastal Disturbances, 1987. Productions: One Shoe Off, New York, 1993; Approaching Zanzibar and Other Plays, Theatre Communications Group, 1995; Birth and After Birth, Philadelphia and Washington, DC, 1995–96; Prides Crossing, 1997. *Honours:* Obie for Distinguished Playwriting, 1983; Outer Critics Circle Award, 1983; Rockefeller Grant, 1984; National Endowment for the Arts Fellowships, 1985, 1995; Guggenheim Fellowship, 1990; American Acad. of Arts and Letters Award in Literature, 1993; Hon. doctorates, Whittier College, 1997, Bowdoin College, 1998. *Address:* Flora Roberts Inc, 157 W 57th Street, New York, NY 10019, USA.

HOWELL, Anthony; Poet, Writer and Ed.; b. 20 April 1945, London, England. *Education:* Leighton Park School; Royal Ballet School, London. *Career:* Lecturer, Grenoble University, Cardiff School of Art; Ed., Softly, Loudly Books, London, Grey Suit. *Publications:* Poetry: Inside the Castle, 1969; Femina Deserta, 1971; Oslo: A Tantric Ode, 1975; The Mekon, 1976; Notions of a Mirror: Poems Previously Uncollected, 1964–82, 1983; Winter's Not Gone, 1984; Why I May Never See the Walls of China, 1986; Howell's Law, 1990; Near Cavalry: Selected Poems of Nick Lafitte (ed.), 1992. Fiction: In the Company of Others, 1986; First Time in Japan, 1995. *Honours:* Welsh Arts Council Bursary, 1989. *Address:* 21 Augusta St, Adamsdown, Cardiff CF2 1EN, Wales.

HOWELLS, Coral Ann; Prof. of English and Canadian Literature and Writer; b. 22 Oct. 1939, Maryborough, Qld, Australia; m. Robin Jonathan Howells, 17 Dec. 1963, two d. *Education:* BA, 1962, MA, 1965, University of Queensland; PhD, University of London, 1969. *Career:* Prof. of English and Canadian Literature, University of Reading, 1996–; mem. British Asscn for Canadian Studies, pres., 1992–94; Assoc. Ed., International Journal for Canadian Studies, 1998–; Council Mem., Foundation for Canadian Studies in the UK, 1998–. *Publications:* Love, Mystery and Misery: Feeling in Gothic Fiction, 1978; Private and Fictional Words: Canadian Women Novelists of the 1970s and 80s, 1987; Jean Rhys, 1991; Margaret Atwood, 1996; Alice Munro, 1998. Contributions: many academic journals. *Address:* Dept of English, University of Reading, Whiteknights, Reading RG6 6AA, Berkshire, England.

HOYLAND, Michael (David); Art Lecturer (retd), Author and Poet; b. 1 April 1925, Nagpur, India; m. Marette Nicol Fraser, 21 July 1948, two s. two d. *Career:* School Teacher, 1951–63; Lecturer, 1963–65, Senior Lecturer in Art, 1963–80, Kesteven College of Education; mem. Stamford Writers Group; PEN; Welland Valley Art Society; East Anglian Potters Asscn. *Publications:* Introduction Three, 1967; Art for Children, 1970; Variations: An Integrated Approach to Art, 1975; A Love Affair with War, 1981; The Bright Way In, 1984; Dominus-Domina (play); Poems in journals and a collection; 6 Short Stories. Contributions: Reviewing for Ore; Jade. *Address:* Foxfoot House, South Luffenham, Nr Oakham Rutland, Leicestershire LE15 8NP, England.

HOYLE, Peter; Writer; b. 25 Oct. 1939, Accrington, Lancashire, England; m. Barbara Croop; one s. one d. *Education:* BA, English Literature, Univ. of Liverpool, 1962. *Publications:* The Man in the Iron Mask, 1984; Brantwood, 1986. Contributions: Stand; PN Review. *Address:* 19 Hexham Ave, Bolton, Lancs BL1 5PP, England.

HOYLE, Trevor; writer; b. Rochdale, England; m. 1962; one s. one d. *Career:* mem. Society of Authors. *Publications:* The Relatively Constant Copywriters, 1972; The Adulterer, 1972; Rule of Night, 1975; Rock Fix, 1977; Seeking the Mythical Future, 1977; Through the Eye of Time, 1977; The Gods Look Down, 1978; The Man Who Travelled on Motorways, 1979; Earth Cult, 1979; The Stigma, 1980; Bullet Train, 1980; The Last Gasp, 1983; Vail, 1984; K.I.D.S., 1988; Blind Needle, 1994; Mirrorman, 1999. Other: several film and television adaptations. Contributions: periodicals; Oxford Good Fiction Guide, 2001. *Honours:* Radio Times Drama Award 1991. *Literary Agent:* Tanja Howarth Literary Agency, 19 New Row, London WC2N 4LA, England.

HUCKER, Hazel (Zoë); Novelist and Justice of the Peace; b. 7 Aug. 1937, London, England; m. Michael Hucker, 7 Jan. 1961, two s. one deceased, one d. *Education:* BSc, Economics, LSE, 1960. *Career:* mem. Society of Authors. *Publications:* The Aftermath of Oliver, 1993; La Herencia del Recuerdo, 1994; A Dangerous Happiness, 1994; Cousin Susannah, 1995; Trials of Friendship, 1996; The Real Claudia Charles, 1998; Changing Status, 2000. *Literary Agent:* MBA Literary Agents Ltd, 62 Grafton Way, London W1T 5DW, England.

HUDDLE, David, BA, MA, MFA; academic, writer and poet; b. 11 July 1942, Ivanhoe, VA, USA; m. Lindsey M. Huddle; two d. *Education:* University of Virginia, Hollins College, Columbia University. *Career:* Faculty, Warren Wilson College, 1981–85; Prof. of English, University of Vermont, 1982–; Ed., New England Review, 1993–94. *Publications:* A Dream With No Stump Roots In It, 1975; Paper Boy, 1979; Only the Little Bone, 1986; Stopping by Home, 1988; The High Spirits, 1992; The Writing Habit: Essays on Writing, 1992; The Nature of Yearning, 1992; Intimates, 1993; Tenormen, 1995; Summer Lake: New and Selected Poems, 1999; The Story of a Million Years, 1999; Not: A Trio – A Novella and Two Stories, 2000; La Tour Dreams of the Wolf Girl, 2002. Contributions: Esquire; Harper's; New York Times Book Review; Kentucky Poetry Review; Texas Quarterly; Poetry; Shenandoah; American Poetry Review. *Honours:* Hon. Doctorate of Humanities, Shenandoah College and Conservatory, Virginia, 1989; Bread Loaf School of English Commencement Speaker, 1989; Robert Frost Prof. of American Literature, 1991. *Address:* Department of English, University of Vermont, Burlington, VT 05405, USA.

HUDGINS, Andrew Leon, Jr; Prof. of English, Poet and Writer; b. 22 April 1951, Killeen, Texas, USA. *Education:* BA, Huntingdon College, 1974; MA, University of Alabama, 1976; Postgraduate Studies, Syracuse University, 1976–78; MFA Writers' Workshop, University of Iowa, 1981–83. *Career:* Adjunct Instructor, Auburn University, 1978–81; Teaching-Writing Fellow, University of Iowa, 1981–83; Lecturer, Baylor University, 1984–85; Prof. of English, University of Cincinnati, 1985–; mem. Texas Institute of Letters. *Publications:* Poetry: Saints and Strangers, 1985; After the Lost War: A Narrative, 1988; The Never-Ending: New Poems, 1991; The Glass Hammer: A Southern Childhood, 1994; Babylon in a Jar, 1998. Non-Fiction: The Glass Anvil (essays), 1997. Contributions: numerous journals. *Honours:* Wallace Stegner Fellow in Poetry, Stanford University, 1983–84; Yaddo Fellowships, 1983, 1985, 1987, 1988, 1991; Acad. of American Poets Award, 1984; MacDowell Colony Fellowship, 1986; National Endowment for the Arts Fellowships, 1986, 1992; Ingram Merrill Foundation Grant, 1987; Poets' Prize, 1988; Witter Bynner Award, American Acad. and Institute of Arts and Letters, 1988; Alfred Hodder Fellow, Princeton University, 1989–90; Poetry Award, Texas Institute of Letters, 1991; Ohioana Poetry Award, 1997. *Address:* c/o Dept of English, ML 69, University of Cincinnati, Cincinnati, OH 45221, USA.

HUDSON, Christopher; Writer; b. 29 Sept. 1946, England; m. Kirsty McLeod, 10 March 1978, one s. *Education:* Scholar, Jesus College, Cambridge. *Career:* Ed., Faber and Faber, 1968; Literary Ed., The Spectator, 1971, The Standard, 1981; Editorial Page Ed., The Daily Telegraph, 1992, 1994. *Publications:* Overlord, 1975; The Final Act, 1980; Insider Out, 1982; The Killing Fields, 1984; Colombo Heat, 1986; Playing in the Sand, 1989; Spring Street Summer, 1993. *Address:* Little Dane, Biddenden, Kent TN27 8JT, England.

HUDSON, Helen (see Lane, Helen).

HUDSON, Jeffrey (see Crichton, (John) Michael).

HUDSON, Liam, MA, PhD; psychologist and writer; b. 20 July 1933, London, England; m. Bernadine Jacot de Boinod 1965; three s. one d. *Education:* Exeter College, Oxford, University of Cambridge. *Publications:* Contrary Imaginations, 1966; Frames of Mind, 1968; The Ecology of Human Intelligence, 1970; The Cult of the Fact, 1972; Human Beings, 1975; The Nympholepts, 1978; Bodies of Knowledge, 1982; Night Life, 1985; The Way Men Think, 1991; Intimate Relations, 1995. Contributions: TLS. *Honours:* Tanner Lectures, Yale University, 1997.

HUFANA, Alejandrino, AB, MA, MS; editor, writer, poet and dramatist; b. 22 Oct. 1926, San Fernando, Philippines. *Education:* University of the Philippines, University of California at Berkeley, Columbia University. *Career:* Co-Founding Ed., Signatures Magazine, 1955, Comment Magazine, 1956–67; Co-Founding Ed., 1967–68, Literary Ed., 1987–, Heritage Magazine; Dir, Cultural Center of the Philippines Library, 1970–85; Prof., 1975, Dir, Creative Writing Center, 1981–85, University of the Philippines. *Publications:* 13 Kalisud, 1955; Man in the Moon, 1956; Sickle Season, 1948–58, 1959; Poro Point, 1955–60, 1961; Curtain Raisers: First Five Plays, 1964; A Philippine Cultural Miscellany, 1970; The Wife of Lot and Other New Poems, 1971; Notes on Poetry, 1973; Sieg Heil, 1975; Philippine Writing, 1977; Shining On, 1985; Dumanon, 1994; No Facetious Claim: Notes on Writers and Writing, 1995; Enuegs, 1999; Survivor, 1999; Kaputt, 1999. *Address:* c/o Heritage Magazine, 20218 Tajauta Avenue, Carson, CA 90746, USA.

HUGHES, David John, MA, FRSL; British writer, critic and editor; b. 27 July 1930, Alton, Hampshire, England; m. 1st Mai Zetterling 1957; m. 2nd Elizabeth Westoll 1980; one s. one d. *Education:* Christ Church, Oxford. *Career:* Editorial Asst, London Magazine 1953–55; reader, Rupert Hart-

Davis 1956–60; Ed., Town Magazine 1960–61, New Fiction Soc. 1975–78, 1981–82, Letters, Journal of the RSL 1992–96; Asst Visiting Prof., Univ. of Iowa 1978–79, 1987, Univ. of Alabama 1979; film critic, Sunday Times 1982–83; fiction critic, Mail on Sunday 1982–98; Visiting Assoc. Prof., Univ. of Houston 1986; ed., letters 1992–96, theatre critic 1996, Mail on Sunday; mem. FRSL (vice-pres.). *Publications:* fiction: A Feeling in the Air 1957, Sealed with a Loving Kiss 1958, The Horsehair Sofa 1961, The Major 1964, The Man Who Invented Tomorrow 1968, Memories of Dying 1976, A Genoese Fancy 1979, The Imperial German Dinner Service 1983, The Pork Butcher 1984, But for Bunter 1985; non-fiction: J. B. Priestley: An Informal Study 1958, The Road to Stockholm 1964, The Seven Ages of England 1967, The Rosewater Revolution 1971, Evergreens 1976, The Little Book 1996, Himself and Other Animals 1997, The Lent Jewels 2002, The Hack's Tale 2004; editor: Winter's Tales: New Series I 1985, Best Short Stories (with Giles Gordon, 10 vols) 1986–95, The Best of Best Short Stories 1986–1995 1995. *Honours:* Welsh Arts Council Fiction Prize 1984, WHSmith Literary Award 1985. *Literary Agent:* Curtis Brown Ltd, Haymarket House, 28–29 Haymarket, London, SW1Y 4SP, England. *Telephone:* (20) 7393-4400. *Fax:* (20) 7393-4401. *E-mail:* info@curtisbrown.co.uk. *Website:* www.curtisbrown.co.uk. *Address:* 163 Kennington Road, London, SE11 6SF, England.

HUGHES, Frieda, BA; British/Australian poet, artist and children's cuthor; b. 1960, England; m. Laszlo Lukacs. *Education:* North Devon College of Art, St Martin's School of Art, London. *Career:* three-year project of poetry and painting, Forty Years 2001–. *Exhibitions:* numerous solo, joint and group exhibitions as painter 1989–. *Publications:* poetry: Wooroloo 1999, Stonepicker 2001, Waxworks 2002; juvenile fiction: Getting Rid of Aunt Edna (short stories) 1986, The Meal a Mile Long, Waldorf and the Sleeping Granny, The Thing in the Sink, Rent a Friend, The Tall Story, Three Scary Stories. *Address:* c/o Bloodaxe Books Ltd, Highgreen, Tarset, Northumberland NE48 1RP, England.

HUGHES, Glyn; Author and Poet; b. 25 May 1935, Middlewich, Cheshire, England; one s. *Education:* Regional College of Art, Manchester, 1952–56; Qualified Art Teacher, 1959. *Career:* Teacher, Lancashire and Yorkshire, 1956–72; Arts Council Fellow, Bishop Grosseteste College, Lincoln, 1979–81; Southern Arts Writer-in-Residence, Farnborough, 1982–84; Arts Council Writer-in-Residence, D. H. Lawrence Centenary Festival, 1985. *Publications:* Fiction: Where I Used to Play on the Green, 1982; The Hawthorn Goddess, 1984; The Antique Collector, 1990; Roth, 1992; Brontë, 1996; Autobiography: Millstone Grit, 1975; Fair Prospects, 1976. Poetry: Neighbours, 1970; Rest the Poor Struggler, 1972; Best of Neighbours, 1979. Plays: Mary Hepton's Heaven, 1984; Pursuit, BBC Radio 4, 1999; Mr Lowry's Loves, BBC Radio 4, 2001; Glorious John, BBC Radio 4, 2002. various plays for BBC school broadcasts on radio and television. *Honours:* Welsh Arts Council Poets Prize, 1970; Guardian Fiction Prize, 1982; David Higham Fiction Prize, 1982. *Literary Agent:* Mic Cheetham Agency, 11–12 Dover St, London W1X 3PH, England. *Address:* Mors House, 1 Mill Bank Rd, Mill Bank, Sowerby Bridge, West Yorkshire HX6 3DY, England. *E-mail:* glyn-hughes@novelist-poet.freeserve.co.uk. *Website:* www.novelist-poet.freeserve.co.uk.

HUGHES, Gwyneth, BA; poet, playwright and short story writer; b. 10 May 1929, Berkeley, CA, USA; m. Henri Lasry 1951; two s. one d. *Education:* Univ. of California, Berkeley. *Career:* mem. Society of Authors, UK, Dramatists' Guild, USA. *Publications:* Augmented Seventh (poems), After Gladys Adams (short stories), Henry's Navy Blue Hair (short stories), Escapements (plays in verse); contrib. to numerous journals and magazines. *Address:* c/o Lasry, 106 blvd Diderot, 75012 Paris, France. *E-mail:* gwyneth.hughes@wanadoo.fr.

HUGHES, Ian (see Paterson, Alistair (Ian)).

HUGHES, John Lawrence, BA; American publisher; b. 13 March 1925, New York; m. Rose M. Pitman 1947; three s. one d. *Education:* Yale Univ. *Career:* reporter, Nassau Review Star, Rockville Centre, Long Island, NY 1949; Asst Sr Ed., Pocket Books, Inc. New York 1949–59; Vice-Pres. Washington Square Press 1958; Sr Ed., Vice-Pres., Dir William Morrow & Co. 1960–65, Pres. and CEO 1965–85; Pres. The Hearst Trade Book Group 1985–87, Chair., CEO 1988–90, Ed.-at-Large, Group Adviser 1990–; Consultant, Ed.-at-Large HarperCollins Publrs., NY 1999–; Trustee, Yale Univ. Press, Pierpont Morgan Library, Library of America, Acad. of American Poets; mem. Bd Asscn of American Publishers 1986–90 (Chair. 1988–90); mem. Bd Nat. Book Awards 1982–94 (Chair. 1988–89); mem. Publrs Hall of Fame 1989. *Address:* HarperCollins Publishers, 10 East 53rd Street, New York, NY 10022-5299 (Office); PO Box 430, Southport, CT 06490, USA (Home). *Telephone:* (212) 207-7569 (Office); (203) 259-8957 (Home). *Fax:* (212) 207-7506 (Office); (203) 259-8142 (Home). *E-mail:* larry.hughes@harpercollins.com (Office). *Website:* www.harpercollins.com (Office).

HUGHES, John W.; American film producer, screenplay writer and director; b. 18 Feb. 1950, Lansing, Mich.; m. Nancy Ludwig; two s. *Education:* Univ. of Arizona. *Career:* copywriter and Creative Dir Leo Burnett Co.; Ed. Nat. Lampoon magazine which led to writing screenplay of Nat. Lampoon's Class Reunion; Founder and Pres. Hughes Entertainment 1985–. *Films:* National Lampoon's Class Reunion (screenplay) 1982, National Lampoon's Vacation (screenplay) 1983, Mr. Mom (screenplay) 1983, Nate and Hayes (screenplay) 1983, Sixteen Candles (screenplay and dir) 1984, National Lampoon's European Vacation (screenplay) 1985, Weird Science (screenplay and dir) 1985, The Breakfast Club (screenplay, dir and producer) 1985, Ferris Bueller's Day Off (screenplay, dir and producer) 1986, Pretty in Pink (screenplay and producer) 1986, Some Kind of Wonderful (screenplay and producer) 1987, Planes, Trains and Automobiles (screenplay, dir and producer) 1987, The Great Outdoors (screenplay and producer) 1988, She's Having a Baby (screenplay, dir and producer) 1988, National Lampoon's Christmas Vacation (screenplay and producer) 1989, Uncle Buck (screenplay, dir and producer) 1989, Home Alone (screenplay and producer) 1990, Career Opportunities (screenplay and producer) 1990, Dutch (screenplay and producer) 1991, Curly Sue (screenplay, dir and producer) 1991, Only the Lonely (co-producer) 1991, Beethoven (screenplay, as Edmond Dantès) 1992, Home Alone 2: Lost in New York (screenplay and producer) 1992, Dennis the Menace (screenplay and producer) 1993, Baby's Day Out (screenplay and producer) 1994, Miracle on 34th Street (screenplay and producer) 1994, 101 Dalmatians (screenplay) 1996, Home Alone 1997, Reach the Rock 1998, New Port South 1999, 102 Dalmatians 2000, Just Visiting 2001. *Honours:* Commitment to Chicago Award 1990, NATO/ShoWest Producer of the Year 1990. *Literary Agent:* Jacob Bloom, Bloom and Dekom, 150 South Rodeo Drive, Beverly Hills, CA 90212; Hughes Entertainment, 10201 West Pico Boulevard, Los Angeles, CA 90064, USA.

HUGHES, Linda Jean, BA; Canadian newspaper publisher; b. 27 Sept. 1950; m. George Ward 1978; one s. one d. *Education:* Univs of Victoria and Toronto. *Career:* Reporter on Victoria Times 1972–73, Head Legislature Bureau 1974–76; City Hall Reporter, Copy Ed. on The Edmonton Journal 1976–77, Editorial Writer 1978–80, Head Legislature Bureau, Asst City Ed. 1980, City Ed. 1981–84, Asst Man. Ed. 1984–87, Ed. 1987–91, Publr 1992–; Southam News Services, Ottawa 1979; Southam Fellow Univ. of Toronto 1977–78. *Honours:* Hon. DLitt (Athabasca) 1997. *Address:* The Edmonton Journal, POB 2421, Edmonton, Alberta, T5J 2S6, Canada (Office). *Telephone:* (403) 429-5129 (Office). *Fax:* (403) 429-5536 (Office).

HUGHES, Matilda (see Macleod, Charlotte).

HUGHES, Richard (Edward); Writer, Poet and Teacher; b. 31 Oct. 1950, Los Angeles, CA, USA; m. Dalcy Beatriz Camacho, 24 June 1989, one c. *Education:* BA, California State University, 1982; MEd, University of Hawaii, 1985. *Career:* Prof. of English as a Second Language, American Samoa Community College, Pago Pago, 1984–86; Instructor in English, Cambria English Institute, Los Angeles, 1986–88; Freelance Writer, 1988–; mem. PEN; Poets and Writers. *Publications:* Isla Grande (novel), 1994; Legends of the Heart (novel), 1997. Contributions: poems to magazines and anthologies. *Honours:* Henri Coulette Award for Poetry, Acad. of American Poets, 1981.

HUGHES, Robert Studley Forrest; art critic and writer; b. 28 July 1938, Sydney, NSW, Australia; m. Victoria Whistler 1981; one s. *Education:* Saint Ignatius College, Sydney, University of Sydney. *Career:* staff, Time magazine, New York 1970–; writer and narrator, art documentaries, BBC-TV, London, 1974–. *Publications:* The Art of Australia, 1966; Heaven and Hell in Western Art, 1970; The Fatal Shore, 1987; Nothing If Not Critical, 1990; Frank Auerbach, 1990; Barcelona, 1992; Culture of Complaint, 1993; American Visions: The Epic History of Art in America, 1997; Goya (biog.), 2003. Contributions: various publications. *Honours:* Frank Jewett Mather Awards, College Art Asscn of America, 1982, 1985; Duff Cooper Prize, 1987; WHSmith Literary Award, 1987; AO, 1991; First Prize, Olimpiada Cultural, Spain, 1992. *Address:* c/o Time Magazine, Time-Life Building, Rockefeller Center, New York, NY 10020, USA.

HUGHES, Shirley, OBE, FRSL; British writer and illustrator; b. 16 July 1927, Hoylake, England; m John Sebastian Papendrek Vulliamy 1952; two s. one d. *Education:* West Kirby High School for Girls, Liverpool Art School and Ruskin School of Drawing and Fine Art, Oxford. *Career:* freelance writer and illustrator; lecturer in field; Advisory Cttee Public Lending Rights Registrar 1984–88; Library and Information Services Council 1989–92; mem. Soc. of Authors (man. cttee 1983–86). *Publications:* Lucy & Tom Series: Lucy & Tom's Day, Lucy & Tom's Christmas, Lucy & Tom at the Seaside, Lucy & Tom Go To School, Lucy & Tom's abc, Lucy & Tom's 123 1960–87; Dogger, The Trouble with Jack 1970, Sally's Secret 1973, Helpers, It's Too Frightening for Me 1977, Moving Molly 1978, Up and Up 1979, Here Comes Charlie Moon, Charlie Moon and the Big Bonanza Bust Up 1982, Alfie Gets in First, Alfie's Fee, Alfie Gives a Hand 1983, An Evening at Alfie's 1984, The Nursery Collection (six vols) 1985–86, Chips and Jessie 1985, Another Helping of Chips 1986, The Big Alfie and Annie Rose Story Book 1988, Out and About 1988, Angel Mae 1989, The Big Concrete Lorry 1989, The Snow Lady 1990, Wheels 1991, The Big Alfie Out of Doors Story Book 1992, Stories by Firelight 1993, Giving, Bouncing, Chatting, Hiding 1994, Rhymes for Annie Rose 1995, Enchantment in the Garden 1996, Alfie and the Birthday Surprise 1997, The Lion and the Unicorn 1998, Mother and Child Treasury (ed.) 1998, Abel's Moon 1999, Alfie's Numbers 1999, The Shirley Hughes Collection 2000, Alfie Weather 2001, Annie Rose is My Little Sister 2002, A Life Drawing: Recollections of an Illustrator (autobiog.) 2002, Ella's Big Chance: A Fairy Tale Retold (Kate Greenaway Medal) 2003, Olly and Me 2004. *Honours:* Hon. DLitt (Univ. of East Anglia) 2003; Children's Rights Award 1976, Kate Greenaway Medal 1978, Silver Pencil Award, Netherlands 1980, Eleanor Farjeon Award 1984; Hon. Fellow

Library Asscn 1997, Hon. Fellow Liverpool John Moores Univ. 2003. *Address:* c/o Random House Children's Books, 61–63 Uxbridge Road, London, W5 5SA, England (Office).

HULME, Keri; Writer; b. 9 March 1947, Christchurch, New Zealand. *Education:* Canterbury University, Christchurch. *Career:* mem. New Zealand Society of Authors; Nga Puna Wailhanga. *Publications:* The Silences Between, 1982; The Bone People, 1984; Lost Possessions, 1986; Te Kaihau, the Windeater, 1986; Homeplaces, 1989; Strands, 1992; Bait, 1996. Contributions: various publications. *Honours:* New Zealand Writing Bursary, 1983; New Zealand Book of the Year, 1984; Mobil Pegasus Prize, 1984; Booker McConnell Award, 1985; Special Scholarship in Letters, 1990. *Address:* PO Box 1, Whataroa, South Westland, Aotearoa, New Zealand.

HULSE, Michael William, MA; British poet, writer, translator, editor and publisher; b. 12 June 1955, Stoke-on-Trent, Staffordshire, England. *Education:* University of St Andrews. *Career:* Lecturer, University of Erlangen-Nuremberg, 1977–79, Catholic University of Eichstätt, 1981–83; Part-time Lecturer, University of Cologne, 1985–95; Trans., Deutsche Welle TV, Cologne, 1986–2000; Assoc. Ed., Littlewood Arc, Todmorden, 1992–98; Visiting Lecturer, University of Zürich, 1994; Founder-Editorial Dir, Leviathon publishing house, Amsterdam, 2000–; mem. Poetry Society; Society of Authors. *Publications:* poetry: Monochrome Blood 1980, Dole Queue 1981, Knowing and Forgetting 1981, Propaganda 1985, Eating Strawberries in the Necropolis 1991, Monteverdi's Photographs 1995; other: The New Poetry (with David Kennedy and David Morley) 1993; numerous trans.; contrib. to anthologies. *Honours:* First Prize, National Poetry Competition, 1978; Second Prize, TLS/Cheltenham Literature Festival Poetry Competition, 1987; First Prizes, Bridport Poetry Competition, 1988, 1994; Hawthornden Castle Fellowship, 1991. *Address:* c/o Bloodaxe Books Ltd, Highgreen, Tarset, Northumberland NE48 1RP, England.

HUMPHREYS, Emyr Owen; Author and Poet; b. 15 April 1919, Clwyd, Wales; m. Elinor Myfanwy, 1946, three s., one d. *Education:* University College, Aberystwyth; University College, Bangor. *Career:* mem. FRSL, 1991. *Publications:* The Little Kingdom, 1946; The Voice of a Stranger, 1949; A Change of Heart, 1951; Hear and Forgive, 1952; A Man's Estate, 1955; The Italian Wife, 1957; A Toy Epic, 1958; The Gift, 1963; Outside the House of Baal, 1965; Natives, 1968; Ancestor Worship, 1970; National Winner, 1971; Flesh and Blood, 1974; Landscapes, 1976; The Best of Friends, 1978; The Kingdom of Bran, 1979; The Anchor Tree, 1980; Pwyll a Riannon, 1980; Miscellany Two, 1981; The Taliesin Tradition, 1983; Salt of the Earth, 1985; An Absolute Hero, 1986; Open Secrets, 1988; The Triple Net, 1988; Bonds of Attachment, 1990; Outside Time, 1991; Unconditional Surrender, 1996; The Gift of a Daughter, 1998; Collected Poems, 1999; Dal Pen Rheswm, 1999; Ghosts and Strangers, 2001; Conversations and Reflections, 2002; Old People are a Problem, 2003. *Honours:* Somerset Maugham Award, 1953; Hawthornden Prize, 1959; Society of Authors Travel Award, 1978; Welsh Arts Council Prize, 1983; Hon. DLitt, University of Wales, 1990; Welsh Book of the Year, 1992, 1999; Hon. Prof. of English, University College of North Wales, Bangor. *Address:* Llinon, Penyberth, Llanfairpwll, Ynys Môn, Gwynedd LL61 5YT, Wales.

HUMPHREYS, Josephine; Novelist; b. 2 Feb. 1945, Charleston, South Carolina, USA; m. Thomas A Hutcheson, 30 Nov. 1968, two s. *Education:* AB, Duke University, 1967; MA, Yale University, 1968. *Publications:* Dreams of Sleep, 1984; Rich in Love, 1987; The Fireman's Fair, 1991; Nowhere Else on Earth, 2000. Contributions: newspapers and periodicals. *Honours:* PEN, Ernest Hemingway Foundation, 1985; Guggenheim Fellowship, 1985; Lyndhurst Prize, 1986. *Address:* c/o Harriet Wasserman, 137 E 36th St, New York, NY 10016, USA.

HUMPHRIES, (John) Barry; Australian writer and actor; b. 17 Feb. 1934, Kew, Melbourne, Vic.; m.; two s. *Education:* University of Melbourne. *Career:* various one-man shows, including as alter ego, Dame Edna Everage. *Television:* Dr Fischer of Geneva 1985, Selling Hitler (series) 1991, The Life and Death of Sandy Stone (series) 1991, Seriously Funny: an Argument for Comedy (series) 1996, Ally McBeal (series) 2001–02; numerous chat shows and special shows. *Films:* Bedazzled 1967, The Bliss of Mrs Blossom 1968, The Naked Bunyip 1970, The Adventures of Barry McKenzie 1972, Percy's Progress 1974, Barry McKenzie Holds His Own 1974, The Great McCarthy 1975, Side by Side 1975, The Getting of Wisdom 1977, Shock Treatment 1981, Les Patterson Saves the World 1987, Howling III 1987, Immortal Beloved 1994, Pterodactyl Woman from Beverly Hills 1994, The Leading Man 1996, Napoleon (voice) 1996, Welcome to Woop Woop 1997, Spice World 1997, Nicholas Nickleby 2002, Finding Nemo (voice) 2003. *Publications:* Bizarre I 1965, Innocent Australian Verse 1968, Wonderful World of Barry McKenzie 1968, Bazza Pulls It Off 1972, Adventures of Barry McKenzie 1973, Bazza Holds His Own 1974, Dame Edna's Coffee Table Book 1976, Bazza Comes into his Own 1978, Les Patterson's Australia 1979, Barry Humphries' Treasury of Australian Kitsch 1980, Dame Edna's Bedside Companion 1982, Les Patterson: The Traveller's Tool 1985, Dame Edna: My Gorgeous Life 1989, Women in the Backyard 1996, My Life as Me: A Memoir 2003. *Honours:* Society of West End Managements Award 1979. *Literary Agent:* David Higham Associates, 5–8 Lower John Street, Golden Square, London, W1F 9HA, England. *Telephone:* (20) 7434-5900. *Fax:* (20) 7437-1072. *E-mail:* dha@davidhigham .co.uk.

HUMPHRY, Derek John; Journalist, Author and Broadcaster; b. 29 April 1930, Bath, England. *Career:* Messenger Boy, Yorkshire Post, London, 1945–46; Cub Reporter, Evening World, Bristol, 1946–51; Junior Reporter, Evening News, Manchester, 1951–55; Reporter, Daily Mail, 1955–61; Deputy Ed., The Luton News, 1961–63; Ed., Havering Recorder, 1963–67, World Federation of Right-To-Die Societies Newsletter, 1980; Hemlock Quarterly, 1983–92, Euthanasia Review, 1986–88, World Right to Die Newsletter, 1992–94; Home Affairs Correspondent, The Sunday Times, 1966–78; Special Writer, Los Angeles Times, 1978–79; Founder, 1980, Exec. Dir, 1980–92, Hemlock Society, USA; Founder, Euthanasia Research and Guidance Organization, 1993, Pres., 1993–; Dir, World Federation of Right-To-Die Societies, 1980–. *Publications:* Because They're Black, 1971; Police Power and Black People, 1972; Passports and Politics, 1974; The Cricket Conspiracy, 1976; False Messiah, 1977; Jean's Way, 1978; Let Me Die Before I Wake, 1982; The Right to Die!: Understanding Euthanasia, 1986; Final Exit, 1991; Dying with Dignity, 1992; Lawful Exit, 1993; Freedom to Die, 1998. Contributions: New Statesman; Independent, London; USA Today. *Honours:* Martin Luther King Memorial Prize, UK, 1972; Saba Medal for contribution to the World Right-to-Die Movement, 2000. *Literary Agent:* Robert I Ducas, The Barn House, 244 Westside Rd, Norfolk, CT 06058, USA. *Address:* 24829 Norris Lane, Junction City, OR 97448-9559, USA. *E-mail:* ergo@efn.org. *Website:* www.finalexit.org/dhumphry.

HUNT, Gill (see Tubb, Edwin Charles).

HUNTER, Alan James Herbert; Author; b. 25 June 1922, Hoveton St John, Norwich, England; m. Adelaide Elizabeth Cecily Cubitt, 6 March 1944, one d. *Education:* Wroxham School; Royal Air Force, 1940–46. *Career:* Crime Reviewer, Eastern Daily Press, 1955–71; mem. Society of Authors; CWA; Authors Licensing and Collecting Society. *Publications:* The Norwich Poems, 1945; Gently Does It, 1955; Gently Go Man, 1961; Vivienne: Gently Where She Lay, 1972; The Honfleur Decision, 1980; Gabrielle's Way, 1981; The Unhung Man, 1984; Traitor's End, 1988; Bomber's Moon, 1994; Jackpot!, 1995; The Love of Gods, 1997; Over Here, 1998. Other: 46 crime novels featuring Chief Superintendent George Gently, to 1999. Contributions: Magazines and journals. *Address:* 3 St Laurence Ave, Brundall, Norwich NR13 5QH, England.

HUNTER, Elizabeth (see De Guise, Elizabeth (Mary Teresa)).

HUNTER, Evan, (Curt Cannon, Hunt Collins, Ezra Hannon, Richard Marsten, Ed McBain), BA; American writer, dramatist and editor; b. (Salvatore Lombino), 15 Oct. 1926, New York, NY; m. 1st Anita Melnick 1949 (divorced); three s.; m. 2nd Mary Vann Finley 1973 (divorced); one step-d.; m. 3rd Dragica Dimitrijevic 1997. *Education:* Cooper Union, Hunter College, CUNY. *Publications:* The Evil Sleep 1952, The Big Fix 1952, Don',t Crowd Me 1953, The Blackboard Jungle 1954, Second Ending 1956, The Jungle Kids 1956, Strangers When We Meet 1958, A Matter of Conviction 1959, The Last Spin and Other Stories 1960, Mothers and Daughters 1961, Happy New Year Herbie and Other Stories 1963, Buddwing 1964, The Paper Dragon 1966, A Horse',s Head 1967, Last Summer 1968, Sons 1969, Nobody Knew They Were There 1971, The Beheading and Other Stories 1971, Every Little Crook and Nanny 1972, Seven 1972, Come Winter 1973, Streets of Gold 1974, The Chisholms: A Novel of the Journey West 1976, Walk Proud 1979, Love Dad 1981, Far from the Sea 1983, Lizzie 1984, Criminal Conversation 1994, Privileged Conversation 1996, Me and Hitch 1997, Barking at Butterflies and Other Stories 2000, Candyland: A Novel in Two Parts (as Evan Hunter and Ed McBain) 2001, The Moment She Was Gone 2002; juvenile fiction: Find the Feathered Serpent 1952, Danger: Dinosaurs! 1953, The Remarkable Harry 1959, The Wonderful Button 1961, Me and Mr Stenner 1976; as Ed McBain: Cop Hater 1956, The Mugger 1956, The Pusher 1956, The Con Man 1957, Killer',s Choice 1957, April Robin Murders (with Craig Rice) 1958, Killer',s Payoff 1958, Lady Killer 1958, Killer',s Wedge 1958, ',Til Death 1959, King',s Ransom 1959, Give the Boys a Great Big Hand 1960, The Heckler 1960, See Them Die 1960, Lady Lady I Did It! 1961, Like Love 1962, The Empty Hours 1962, Ten Plus One 1963, Ax 1964, He Who Hesitates 1965, Doll 1965, The Sentries 1965, Eighty Million Eyes 1966, Fuzz 1968, Shotgun 1969, Jigsaw 1970, Hail Hail the Gang',s All Here 1971, Sadie When She Died 1972, Let',s Hear It for the Deaf Man 1972, Hail to the Chief 1973, Bread 1974, Blood Relatives 1975, Where There',s Smoke 1975, Guns 1976, So Long as You Both Shall Live 1976, Long Time No See 1977, Calypso 1979, Ghosts 1980, Heat 1981, The McBain Brief 1982, Ice 1983, Lightning 1984, Eight Black Horses 1985, Another Part of the City 1987, Poison 1987, Tricks 1987, McBain',s Ladies: The Women of the 87th Precinct 1988, Downtown 1989, Gangs 1989, Lullaby 1989, McBain',s Ladies Too 1989, Vespers 1990, Widows 1991, Kiss 1992, Mischief 1993, Romance 1995, Nocturne 1997, The Big Bad City 1998, The Last Dance 2000, Driving Lessons 2000, Money Money Money 2001, Fat Ollie',s Book 2002, The Frumious Bandersnatch 2003, Hark! 2004; as Curt Cannon: Good and Dead/Deadlier Than the Mail 1953, I',m Cannon –, For Hire 1958, Now Die In It 1958, The Death of Me 1958, Dead Men Don',t Dream/Die Hard 1958; as Hunt Collins: Sucker 1958; as Ezra Hannon: Doors 1975; as Richard Marsten: Rocket to Luna 1952, Murder in the Navy 1955, Vanishing Ladies 1957, Big Man 1959; several plays and television scripts. *Honours:* Grand Master Award, MWA, 1986; Diamond Dagger Award, CWA, 1998. *Address:* c/o Gelfman Schneider, 250 W 57th Street, New York, NY 10107, USA.

HUNTINGTON, Samuel Phillips, BA, MA, PhD; political scientist and writer; b. 18 April 1927, New York, NY, USA; m. Nancy Alice Arkelyan 1957; two s. *Education:* Yale University, University of Chicago, Harvard University. *Career:* Instructor, 1950–53, Asst Prof., 1953–58, Prof. of Government, 1962–, Research Assoc., 1963–64, Faculty, 1964–, Assoc. Dir, 1973–78, Acting Dir, 1975–76, Dir, 1978–89, Center for International Affairs, Thomson Prof. of Government, 1967–81, Clarence Dillon Prof. of International Affairs, 1981–82, Eaton Prof. of the Science of Government, 1982–, Dir, John M. Olin Institute for Strategic Studies, 1989–2000, Albert J. Weatherhead University Prof., 1995–, Harvard University; Research Assoc., Brookings Institution, Washington, DC, 1952–53; Research Fellow, Social Science Research Council, New York City, 1954–57; Asst Dir, 1958–59, Research Assoc., 1958–63, Assoc. Dir, 1959–62, Assoc. Prof. of Government, 1959–62, Institute of War and Peace Studies, Columbia University; Fellow, Center for Advanced Study in the Behavioral Sciences, Stanford, CA, 1969–70; Co-Ed., Foreign Policy Quarterly, 1970–77; Visiting Fellow, All Souls College, Oxford, 1973; Co-ordinator, Security Planning, National Security Council, 1977–78; Chair., Havard Acad. for International and Area Studies, 1996–; mem. American Acad. of Arts and Sciences, fellow; American Political Science Asscn, pres., 1986–87; Council on Foreign Relations; International Institute for Strategic Studies; International Political Science Asscn. *Publications:* The Soldier and the State: The Theory and Politics of Civil-Military Relations, 1957; The Common Defense: Strategic Programs in National Politics, 1961; Changing Patterns of Military Politics (co-ed.), 1962; Political Power: USA/USSR (co-author), 1964; Political Order in Changing Societies, 1968; Authoritarian Politics in Modern Society: The Dynamics of Established One-Party Systems (co-ed.), 1970; The Crisis of Democracy (co-author), 1975; No Easy Choice: Political Participation in Developing Countries (with J. M. Nelson), 1976; American Politics: The Promise of Disharmony, 1981; The Strategic Imperative: New Policies for American Security, 1982; Living with Nuclear Weapons (co-author), 1983; Global Dilemmas (co-ed.), 1985; Reorganizing America's Defense (co-ed.), 1985; Understanding Political Development (co-ed.), 1987; The Third Wave: Democratization in the Late Twentieth Century, 1991; The Clash of Civilizations and the Remaking of the World Order, 1996; Culture Matters: How Values Shape Human Progress, 2000; Who Are We?: The Challenges to America's National Identity 2004; contrib. to professional journals. *Honours:* Silver Pen Award, 1960; Grawemayer World Order Award, 1992. *Address:* c/o Harvard University, 1737 Cambridge Street, Cambridge, MA 02138, USA.

HURD, Douglas (Richard), (Baron Hurd of Westwell); Politician, Diplomat (retd) and Writer; b. 8 March 1930, Marlborough, England; m. 1st Tatiana Elizabeth Michelle, 1960, divorced, three s.; m. 2nd Judy Smart, 1982, one s. one d. *Education:* Eton; Trinity College, Cambridge. *Career:* HM Diplomatic Service, 1952–66; Joined Conservative Research Dept, 1966, Head, Foreign Affairs Section, 1968; Private Secretary to the Leader of the Opposition, 1968–70; Political Secretary to the Prime Minister, 1970–74; MP, Conservative Party, Mid-Oxon, 1974–83, Witney, 1983–97; Opposition Spokesman on European Affairs, 1976–79; Visiting Fellow, Nuffield College, 1978–86; Minister of State, Foreign and Commonwealth Office, 1979–83, Home Office, 1983–84; Secretary of State for Northern Ireland, 1984–85, Home Secretary, 1985–89, for Foreign and Commonwealth Affairs, 1989–95; Dir NatWest Group, 1995–99; Deputy Chair., NatWest Markets, 1995–98, Coutts & Co, 1998–; Chair., Hawkpoint Advisory Committee, 1998–, British Invisibles, 1998–2000, Prison Reform Trust, 1998–2001, Pres., 2002–; Chair., Centre for Dispute Resolution, 2000–, German-British Forum, 2000–; Co-Pres., Royal Institute of International Affairs, 2001–; Chair., The Booker Prize Panel, 1998; Mem., Appointments Commission, 2000–; High Steward, Westminster Abbey, 2000–. *Publications:* The Arrow War, 1967; Send Him Victorious (with Andrew Osmond), 1968; The Smile on the Face of the Tiger (with Andrew Osmond), 1969; Scotch on the Rocks (with Andrew Osmond), 1971; Truth Game, 1972; Vote to Kill, 1975; An End to Promises, 1979; War Without Frontiers (with Andrew Osmond), 1982; Palace of Enchantments (with Stephen Lamport), 1985; The Search for Peace, 1997; The Shape of Ice, 1998; Ten Minutes to Turn the Devil, 1999; Image in the Water, 2001; Memoirs, 2003. *Honours:* CBE, 1974; Privy Councillor, 1982; Companion of Honour, 1996; Life Peer, 1997. *Address:* c/o House of Lords, London SW1A OPW, England.

HURD, Michael John; Composer and Author; b. 19 Dec. 1928, Gloucester, England. *Education:* BA, 1953, MA, 1957, Pembroke College, Oxford. *Career:* Prof. of Theory, Royal Marines School of Music, 1953–59. *Publications:* Immortal Hour: The Life and Period of Rutland Boughton, 1962, revised edn as Rutland Boughton and the Glastonbury Festivals, 1993; The Composer, 1968; An Outline History of European Music, 1968; Elgar, 1969; Vaughan Williams, 1970; Mendelssohn, 1970; The Ordeal of Ivor Gurney, 1978; The Oxford Junior Companion to Music, 1979; Vincent Novello and Company, 1981; The Orchestra, 1981; Letters of Gerald Finzi and Howard Ferguson, 2001. Contributions: Reference books. *Address:* 4 Church St, West Liss, Hampshire GU33 6JX, England.

HURST, Frances (see Mayhar, Ardath).

HUSTON, Nancy Louise; Writer; b. 16 Sept. 1953, Calgary, AB, Canada; m. Tzvetan Todorov, 18 May 1981, one s. one d. *Education:* BA, Sarah Lawrence College, 1975; Diploma, École des Hautes Études, 1977. *Career:* Writer-in-Residence, American University, Paris, 1989; Facilitator, South African Writers Workshop, 1994; Visiting Prof., Harvard University, 1994. *Publications:* Les Variations Goldberg, 1981; The Goldberg Variations, 1981; Histoire d'Omaya, 1985; The Story of Omaya 1987; Journal de la Création, 1990; Cantique des Plaines, 1993; Plainsong, 1993; La Virevolte, 1994; The Goldberg Variations: Slow Emergencies, 1996; Instruments of Darkness, 1997; L'Empreinte de l'ange, 1998; The Mark of the Angel, 1999; Dolce Agonia, 2001. *Honours:* Prix, Binet Sangle de l'Académie Française, 1980; Prix Contrepoint, 1981; Prix du Gouverneur-Général, 1993; Prix Louis Hémon, 1995; Prix Goncourt des Lycéens, 1996; Prix du Livre Inter, 1997. *Address:* c/o Mary Kling, La Nouvelle Agence, 7 Rue Corneille, 75006 Paris, France.

HUSTVEDT, Siri, PhD; American poet and writer; b. 1955, MN; m. Paul Auster 1981; one d. *Education:* Columbia Univ. *Career:* worked as ed. and trans. *Publications:* Reading to You (poems) 1982, The Blindfold (novel) 1990, The Enchantment of Lily Dahl (novel) 1996, Yonder: Essays 1998, What I Loved (novel) 2003; contrib. to Paris Review. *Literary Agent:* The Marsh Agency, 11 Dover Street, London, W1S 4LJ, England. *Telephone:* (20) 7399-2800. *Fax:* (20) 7399-2801. *Website:* www.marsh-agency.co.uk.

HUTCHEON, Linda (Ann Marie); Prof. and Writer; b. 24 Aug. 1947, Toronto, Ontario, Canada; m. Michael Alexander Hutcheon, 30 May 1970. *Education:* BA, Modern Language and Literature, 1969, PhD, Comparative Literature, 1975, University of Toronto; MA, Romance Studies, Cornell University, 1971. *Career:* Asst, Assoc. and Full Prof. of English, McMaster University, 1976–88; Prof. of English and Comparative Literature, 1988–96, University Prof., 1996–, University of Toronto; mem. MLA of America. *Publications:* Narcissistic Narrative, 1980; Formalism and the Freudian Aesthetic, 1984; A Theory of Parody, 1985; A Poetics of Postmodernism, 1988; The Canadian Postmodern, 1988; The Politics of Postmodernism, 1989; Splitting Images, 1991; Irony's Edge, 1995; Opera: Desire, Disease, Death (with Michael Hutcheon), 1996; Bodily Charm: Living Opera (with Michael Hutcheon), 2000; Opera: The Art of Dying (with Michael Hutcheon), 2004. Editor: Other Solitudes, 1990; Double-Talking, 1992; Likely Stories, 1992; A Postmodern Reader, 1993; Rethinking Literary History: A Forum on Theory, 2002. Contributions: Diacritics; Textual Practice; Cultural Critique and other journals. *Honours:* Fellow, Royal Society of Canada, 1990; LLD, 1995. *Address:* University of Toronto, Toronto, ON M5S 1A1, Canada.

HUTCHINSON, Gregory Owen; Writer; b. 5 Dec. 1957, London, England; m. Yvonne Downing, 4 Aug. 1979, one d. *Education:* BA, MA, DPhil, Balliol and Christ Church Colleges, Oxford, 1975–83. *Publications:* Aeschylus, Septem Contra Thebas (ed.), 1985; Hellenistic Poetry, 1988; Latin Literature from Seneca to Juvenal: A Critical Study, 1993; Cicero's Correspondence: A Literary Study, 1998; Greek Lyric Poetry: A Commentary on Selected Larger Pieces, 2001. *Address:* Exeter College, Oxford OX1 3DP, England.

HUTTERLI, Kurt; Writer, Poet and Artist; b. 18 Aug. 1944, Bern, Switzerland; m. Marianne Büchler, 7 July 1966, one s. one d. *Education:* Secondary School Teacher Diploma, University of Bern, 1966. *Career:* mem. PEN Switzerland; Autorinnen und Autoren der Schweiz; Berner Schriftsteller-Verein. *Publications:* Aber, 1972; Herzgrün, 1974; Felsengleich, 1976; Die Faltsche, 1977; Das Matterköpfen, 1978; Ein Hausmann, 1980; Finnlandisiert, 1982; Überlebenslust, 1984; Elchspur, 1986; Baccalà, 1989; Gaunerblut, 1990; Mir kommt kein Tier ins Haus, 1991; Stachelflieder, 1991; Katzensprung, 1993; Die sanfte Piratin, 1994; Im Fischbauch, 1998; Hotel Goldtown, 2000; Der Clown im Mond, 2000; Arche Titanic, 2000; Das Centovalli Brautgeschenk, 2003, Der Rocky Mountain King 2003. Contributions: Der Bund; Stuttgarter Zeitung; Drehpunkt; Einspruch. *Honours:* Poetry Prize, City of Bern, 1971; Book Prizes, City of Bern, 1972, 1978; Theatre Awards, 1976, 1982, 1987. *Address:* RR2, S53/C9, Oliver, BC V0H 1T0, Canada.

HUTTON, Ronald Edmund; Historian; b. 19 Dec. 1953, Ootacamund, India; m. Lisa Radulovic 5 Aug. 1988 (divorced 19 March 2003). *Education:* BA, Cantab, 1976; MA, 1980; DPhil, 1980. *Career:* Prof. of British History, Bristol University, 1996–; mem. Royal Historical Society; Folklore Society; Fellow, Society of Antiquaries. *Publications:* The Royalist War Effort, 1981; The Restoration, 1985; Charles II, 1989; The British Republic, 1990; The Pagan Religions of the Ancient British Isles, 1991; The Rise and Fall of Merry England, 1994; The Stations of the Sun, 1996; The Triumph of the Moon: A History of Modern Pagan Witchcraft, 1999; Shamans, 2001; Witches, Druids and King Arthur: Studies in Paganism, Myth and Magic, 2003. Contributions: journals. *Honours:* Benjamin Franklin Prize, 1993. *Address:* 13 Woodland Rd, Bristol BS8 1TB, England.

HUTTON, Will Nicholas, MBA; British newspaper editor and business executive; *Chief Executive, The Work Foundation*; b. 21 May 1950, London; m. Jane Atkinson 1978; one s. two d. *Education:* Chislehurst and Sidcup Grammar School, Univ. of Bristol and INSEAD. *Career:* with Phillips & Drew (stockbrokers) 1971–77; Sr Producer Current Affairs, BBC Radio 4 1978–81; Dir and Producer The Money Programme, BBC2 1981–83; Econs Corresp. Newsnight, BBC2 1983–88; Ed. European Business Channel 1988–90; Econs Ed. The Guardian 1990–95, Asst Ed. 1995–96; Ed. The Observer 1996–98, Ed.-in-Chief 1998–2000; Chief Exec. The Work Foundation (fmrly The Industrial Soc. –2002) 2000–; Gov. LSE 2000–. *Publications:* The Revolution That Never Was: An Assessment of Keynesian Economics

1986, The State We're In 1994, The State to Come 1997, The Stakeholding Society 1998, The World We're In 2002. *Honours:* Hon. DLitt (Kingston) 1995, (De Montfort) 1996; Political Journalist of the Year, What the Papers Say 1993. *Address:* The Work Foundation, Peter Runge House, 3 Carlton Terrace, London, SW1Y 5DG (Office); 34 Elms Avenue, London, N10 2JP, England (Home). *Telephone:* (20) 7004-7103 (Office). *Fax:* (20) 7004-7111 (Office). *E-mail:* roconnor@theworkfoundation.com (Office); whutton@virgin.net (Home). *Website:* www.theworkfoundation.com (Office).

HWANG, David Henry, BA; dramatist and screenwriter; b. 11 Aug. 1957, Los Angeles, CA, USA; m. 1st Ophelia Chong 1985; m. 2nd Kathryn Layng 1993; one s. *Education:* Stanford Univ., Yale Drama School. *Career:* dramaturg, Asian American Theatre Centre, San Francisco 1987–; mem. Dramatists' Guild (bd of dirs 1988–). *Plays:* FOB 1980, The Dance and the Railroad 1981, Family Devotions 1981, Sound and Beauty 1983, The Sound of a Voice 1984, As the Crow Flies 1986, Rich Relations 1986, M Butterfly 1988, Bondage 1992, Face Value 1993, Trying to Find Chinatown 1996, Golden Child 1996. *Screenplays:* M Butterfly 1993, Golden Gate 1993. *Other works:* 1000 Airplanes on the Roof (musical) 1988, Forbidden Nights (TV play) 1990, The Voyage (libretto) 1992, Elton John and Tim Rice's Aida (co-librettist, Broadway) 2000, Flower Drum Song (revised libretto, Broadway) 2002. *Honours:* Drama-Logue Awards 1980, 1986, Obie Award 1981, Rockefeller Foundation Fellowship 1983, Guggenheim Fellowship 1984, Nat. Endowment for the Arts Fellowship 1987, Tony Award for Best Play 1988, Outer Critics Circle Award for Best Broadway Play 1988, John Gassner Award 1988. *Literary Agent:* Writers and Artists Agency, 19 W 44th Street, Suite 1410, New York, NY 10036, USA.

HYDE, Lewis; Prof. of Creative Writing, Author, Poet, Ed. and Trans; b. 16 Oct. 1945, Boston, MA, USA; m. Patricia Auster Vigderman 27 Nov. 1981; one step-s. *Education:* BA, Sociology, University of Minnesota, 1967; MA, Comparative Literature, University of Iowa, 1972. *Career:* Instructor in Literature, University of Iowa, 1969–71; Lecturer in Expository Writing, 1983–85, Briggs-Copeland Asst Prof. of English, 1985–89, Dir, Creative Writing Programme, 1988–89, Harvard University; Henry R. Luce Prof. of Art and Politics, 1989–2001, Richard L. Thomas Prof. of Creative Writing, 2001–, Kenyon College. *Publications:* Twenty Poems of Vicente Aleixandre (ed. and trans. with Robert Bly), 1977; A Longing for the Light: Selected Poems of Vicente Aleixandre (ed. and trans. with others), 1979; World Alone, by Vicente Aleixandre (trans. with David Unger), 1982; The Gift: Imagination and the Erotic Life of Property, 1983; On the Work of Allen Ginsberg (ed.), 1984; Alcohol and Poetry: John Berryman and the Booze Talking, 1986; This Error is the Sign of Love (poems), 1988; Trickster Makes This World: Mischief, Myth, and Art, 1998; Selected Essays of Henry D. Thoreau (ed. and annotator), 2002. Contributions: numerous journals, quarterlies, reviews. *Honours:* Acad. of American Poets Prize, 1966; National Endowment for the Arts Creative Writing Fellowships, 1977, 1982, 1987; Columbia University Trans. Center Award, 1979; National Endowment for the Humanities Fellowship for Independent Study and Research, 1979; Massachusetts Council on the Arts and Humanities Fellowship In Poetry, 1980; MacDowell Colony Fellowships, 1989, 1991, 1996, 1999, 2000; Scholar-in-Residence, Rockefeller Study and Conference Center, Bellagio, Italy, 1991; John D. and Catherine T. MacArthur Foundation Fellowship, 1991–96; Getty Scholar, 1993–94; Hon. DFA, San Francisco Art Institute, 1997; Osher Fellow, 1998. *Address:* PO Box 613, Gambier, OH 43022, USA.

HYLAND, Paul, BSc; poet and travel writer; b. 15 Sept. 1947, Poole, Dorset, England. *Education:* Bristol Univ. *Career:* mem. Soc. of Authors, Poetry Soc., PEN. *Publications:* Purbeck: The Ingrained Island, 1978; Wight: Biography of an Island, 1984; The Black Heart, 1988; Indian Balm, 1994; Backwards Out of the Big World, 1996; Discover Dorset: Isle of Purbeck, 1998; Ralegh's Last Journey, 2003. Poetry: Poems of Z, 1982; The Stubborn Forest, 1984; Getting into Poetry, 1992; Kicking Sawdust, 1995; Art of the Impossible, 2004. *Honours:* Eric Gregory Award 1976, Alice Hunt Bartlett Award 1985, Authors' Foundation 1995. *Literary Agent:* David Higham Associates, 5–8 Lower John Street, Golden Square, London, W1F 9HA, England. *Address:* 32 Colliton Street, Dorchester, Dorset DT1 1XH, England. *E-mail:* write@paul-hyland.co.uk.

HYMAN, Harold M(elvin); Prof. of History Emeritus and Author; b. 24 July 1924, New York, NY, USA; m. Ferne Beverly Handelsman, 11 March 1946, two s. one d. *Education:* BA, University of California at Los Angeles, 1948; MA, 1950, PhD, 1952, Columbia University. *Career:* Asst Prof., Earlham College, 1952–55; Visiting Asst Prof., 1955–56, Prof., 1963–68, University of California at Los Angeles; Assoc. Prof., Arizona State University, Tempe, 1956–57; Prof. of History, University of Illinois, 1963–68; William P. Hobby Prof. of History, 1968–96, Prof. Emeritus, 1997–, Rice University; Graduate Faculty in Political Science, University of Tokyo, 1973; Faculty of Law, Keio University, 1973; Adjunct Prof. of Legal History, Bates College of Law, University of Houston, 1977, and of American Legal History, School of Law, University of Texas, 1986; Meyer Visiting Distinguished Prof. of Legal History, School of Law, New York University, 1982–83; mem. American Historical Asscn; American Society of Legal History, pres., 1994–95; Organization of American Historians; Southern Historical Asscn. *Publications:* Era of the Oath: Northern Loyalty Tests During the Civil War and Reconstruction, 1954; To Try Men's Souls: Loyalty Tests in American History, 1959; Stanton: The Life and Times of Lincoln's Secretary of War (with Benjamin P. Thomas), 1962; Soldiers and Spruce: The Loyal Legion of Loggers and Lumbermen, the Army's Labor Union of World War I, 1963; A More Perfect Union: The Impact of the Civil War and Reconstruction on the Constitution, 1973; Union and Confidence: The 1860s, 1976; Equal Justice Under Law: Constitutional History, 1835–1875 (with William Wiecek), 1982; Quiet Past and Stormy Present?: War Powers in American History, 1986; American Singularity: The 1787 Northwest Ordinance, the 1862 Homestead-Morrill Acts, and the 1944 G.I. Bill, 1986; Oleander Odyssey: The Kempners of Galveston, 1870–1980, 1990; The Reconstruction Justice of Salmon P. Chase: In Re Turner and Texas v White, 1997; Craftsmanship and Character: A History of the Vinson & Elkins Law Firm of Houston, 1917–1990s, 1998. Editor: several books. Contributions: scholarly journals. *Honours:* Albert J. Beveridge Award, American Historical Asscn, 1952; Coral H. Tullis Memorial Prize, Texas A & M University Press, 1990; T. R. Fehrenbach Book Award, Texas Historical Commission, 1990; Ottis Lock Endowment Award, East Texas Historical Asscn, 1991. *Address:* c/o Dept of History, M5 42, Rice University, 6100 Main St, Houston, TX 77005, USA.

HYMAN, Timothy; British painter and writer on art; b. 17 April 1946, Hove; m. Judith Ravenscroft 1982. *Education:* Charterhouse and Slade School of Fine Art. *Career:* Curator Narrative Paintings at Arnolfini and ICA Galleries, etc. 1979–80; public collections include Arts Council, Bristol City Art Gallery, Museum of London, Contemporary Art Soc., British Museum, Govt Art Collection, Los Angeles Co. Museum; Visiting Prof. at Baroda, India, two British Council lecture tours 1981–83; Artist in Residence at Lincoln Cathedral 1983–84, Sandown Racecourse 1992; Purchaser for Arts Council Collection 1985; selector, John Moores Prize 1995; Lead curator Stanley Spencer retrospective exhbn, Tate Gallery, London 2001–. *Exhibitions:* started to exhibit at Blond 1980, one-man exhbns 1981, 1983 and 1985; Austin/Desmond (one-man exhbn 1990, 2000, 2003), Castlefield Gallery, Manchester 1993, Gallery Chemould, Bombay 1994, Gallery M, Flowers East 1994; group exhbns at Royal Acad., Hayward Gallery, Whitechapel Art Gallery, Nat. Portrait Gallery. *Publications:* Hodgkin 1975, Kitaj 1977, Beckmann 1978, Balthus 1980, Narrative Paintings 1979, English Romanesque 1984, Kiff 1986, Domenico Tiepolo 1987, Bhupen Khakhar (monograph) 1998, Bonnard (monograph) 1998, Carnivalesque (catalogue) 2000, Stanley Spencer (catalogue) 2001, Sienese Painting (monograph) 2003; numerous articles on contemporary figurative painting in London Magazine, Artscribe, Times Literary Supplement 1975–. *Honours:* Leverhulme Award 1992, Rootstein Hopkins Foundation Award 1995, Wingate Award 1998. *Address:* 62 Myddelton Square, London, EC1, England. *Telephone:* (20) 7837-1933.

HYNES, Samuel; Prof. of Literature Emeritus, Writer and Ed.; b. 29 Aug. 1924, Chicago, IL, USA; m. Elizabeth Igleheart 28 July 1944; two d. *Education:* BA, Univ. of Minnesota, 1947; MA, 1948, PhD, 1956, Columbia Univ. *Career:* Faculty, 1949–65, Prof. of English Literature, 1965–68, Swarthmore Coll.; Prof. of English, Northwestern Univ., 1968–76; Prof. of English, 1976–90, Woodrow Wilson Prof. of Literature, 1978–90, Prof. Emeritus, 1990–, Princeton Univ.; mem. FRSL. *Publications:* Further Speculations by T. E. Hulme (ed.), 1955; The Pattern of Hardy's Poetry, 1961; William Golding, 1964; The Edwardian Turn of Mind, 1968; The Author's Craft and Other Critical Writings of Arnold Bennett (ed.), 1968; Romance and Realism (ed.), 1970; Edwardian Occasions, 1972; The Auden Generation, 1976; The Complete Poetical Works of Thomas Hardy (ed.), Vol. I, 1982, Vol. II, 1984, Vol. III, 1985, Vol. IV, 1995, Vol. V, 1995; Thomas Hardy, 1984; Flights of Passage: Recollections of a World War Two Aviator, 1988; A War Imagined: The First World War and English Culture, 1990; The Complete Short Fiction of Joseph Conrad (ed.), Vols I–III, 1992, Vol. IV, 1993; The Soldiers' Tale, 1997; The Growing Seasons: An American Boyhood Before the War, 2003. Contributions: scholarly journals. *Honours:* Fulbright Fellowship, 1953–54; Guggenheim Fellowships, 1959–60, 1981–82; Explicator Award, 1962; Bollingen Fellowship, 1964–65; ACLS Fellowships, 1973–74, 1977–78, 1989, 1991; Robert F. Kennedy Book Award, 1998. *Address:* 130 Moore St, Princeton, NJ 08540, USA.

I

IBBOTSON, Eva; Austrian writer; b. 1925, Vienna; m. Alan Ibbotson; four c. *Education:* Univ. of London, Univ. of Cambridge. *Publications include:* juvenile: The Great Ghost Rescue 1975, Which Witch 1979, Magic Flutes 1982, A Countess Below Stars 1983, The Worm and the Toffee-Nosed Princess 1983, Glove Shop in Vienna and other stories 1984, A Company of Swans 1985, The Haunting of Hiram C. Hopgood 1987, Madensky Square 1988, Not Just a Witch 1989, The Morning Gift 1993, Native: The Beauty and the Wonder 1994, The Secret of Platform 13 1995, Dial-A-Ghost 1996, A Song for Summer 1997, Island of the Aunts 2000, Monster Mission 2001, Journey to the River Sea 2001, The Emperor's Horse 2004, The Star of the Kazan 2004, The Haunting of Granite Falls 2005. *Address:* c/o Puffin Books, Penguin Books UK, 80 Strand, London, WC2R 0LR, England. *E-mail:* puffin@penguin.co.uk. *Website:* www.puffin.co.uk.

IBRAHIM, Sonallah; Writer; b. 1937, Cairo, Egypt. *Education:* Law and Drama, Cairo Univ. *Career:* fmr journalist; Visiting Assoc. Prof., Dept of Near Eastern Studies, Univ. of California at Berkeley, 1999. *Publications:* Tilka Al Raiha (The Smell of It), 1966; Star of August, 1974; The Committee, 1981; Beirut Beirut, 1984; Zaat, 1992; Sharaf, 1997; Warda, 2000. *Honours:* Best Egyptian novel, 1998. *Address:* c/o Syracuse University Press, 621 Skytop Rd, Suite 110, Syracuse, NY 13244-5290, USA.

IGGERS, Georg Gerson; Historian, Distinguished Prof. and Writer; b. 7 Dec. 1926, Hamburg, Germany; m. Wilma Abeles, 23 Dec. 1948, three s. *Education:* BA, University of Richmond, Virginia, 1944; AM, 1945, PhD, 1951, University of Chicago; Graduate Studies, New School for Social Research, New York, 1945–46. *Career:* Instructor, University of Akron, 1948–50; Assoc. Prof., Philander Smith College, 1950–56; Visiting Prof., University of Arkansas, 1956–57, 1964, University of Rochester, New York, 1970–71, University of Leipzig, 1992; Assoc. Prof., Dillard University, New Orleans, 1957–63; Visiting Assoc. Prof., Tulane University, 1957–60, 1962–63; Assoc. Prof., Roosevelt University, Chicago, 1963–65; Prof., 1965–, Distinguished Prof., 1978–, SUNY at Buffalo; Visiting Scholar, Technische Hochschule, Darmstadt, 1991, Forschungsschwerpunkt Zeithistorische Studien, Potsdam, 1993, 1998, University of Århus, Denmark, 1998, University of New England, Australia, 1999, University of Vienna, 2002; Fellow, International Institute of Cultural Studies, Vienna, 2000; mem. International Commission for the History and Theory of Historiography, pres., 1995–2000. *Publications:* Cult of Authority: Political Philosophy of the Saint Simonians, 1958; German Conception of History, 1968; Leopold von Ranke: The Theory and Practice of History (co-ed.), 1973; New Directions in European Historiography, 1975; International Handbook of Historical Studies (co-ed.), 1979; Social History of Politics (ed.), 1985; Aufklärung und Geschichte (co-ed.), 1986; Leopold von Ranke and the Shaping of the Historical Discipline (co-ed.), 1990; Marxist Historiography in Transition: Historical Writings in East Germany in the 1980s (ed.), 1991; Geschichtswissenschaft 20. Jahrhundert, 1993; Historiography in the Twentieth Century: From Scientific Objectivity to the Postmodern Challenge, 1997; Zwei Seiten der Geschichte (autobiog. with Wilma Iggers), 2002; Turning Points in Historiography (co-ed.), 2002. Contributions: scholarly journals. *Honours:* Foreign Mem., Acad. of Sciences of German Democratic Republic, 1990–92; Research Prize, Alexander von Humboldt Foundation, 1995–96. *Address:* c/o Dept of History, State University of New York at Buffalo, Buffalo, NY 14260, USA.

IGGULDEN, John Manners, (Jack Iggulden); writer and industrialist; b. 12 Feb. 1917, Brighton, Vic., Australia; m. Helen Carroll Schapper; one s. (deceased) two d. *Career:* man., family-owned manufacturing companies, 1940–59; Writer, 1959–70; Businessman, 1970–; Part-time writer, 1980–; Currently, Chief Exec., Planet Lighting, Lucinda Glassworks, Bellingen, NSW, Australia. *Publications:* Breakthrough, 1960; The Storms of Summer, 1960; The Clouded Sky, 1964; Dark Stranger, 1965; Summer's Tales 3, 1966; Manual of Standard Procedures, Gliding Federation of Australia, 1964; Gliding Instructor's Handbook, 1968; The Promised Land Papers Vol. 1, The Revolution of the Good, 1986, Vol. 2, How Things Are Wrong and How to Fix Them, 1988, Vol. 3, The Modification of Freedom, 1993; Silent Lies, 1997; Good World, 1998. *Address:* 'Evandale', Promised Land, Bellingen, NSW 2454, Australia.

IGNATIEFF, Michael, BA, MA, PhD; Canadian writer and historian; *Director, Carr Center for Human Rights Policy at Harvard University*; b. 12 May 1947, Toronto, ON; m. 1st Susan Barrowclough 1977; one s. one d.; m. 2nd Zsuzsanna Zsohar. *Education:* Univ. of Toronto, Harvard Univ., Univ. of Cambridge. *Career:* reporter, Globe and Mail, Toronto 1966–67; teaching Fellow, Harvard Univ. 1971–74; Asst Prof., Univ. of British Columbia, Vancouver 1976–78; Sr Research Fellow, King's Coll., Cambridge 1978–84; Visiting Prof., École des Hautes Études, Paris 1985; editorial columnist, The Observer, London 1990–93; correspondent for the BBC, the Observer and the New Yorker 1984–2000; mem., Int. Commission on Sovereignty and Intervention; Carr Prof. of Human Rights Practice 2000–, Carr Center for Human Rights Policy, John F. Kennedy School of Government at Harvard Univ., Dir 2001–. *Television:* host Thinking Aloud (BBC) 1986–, Voices (Channel Four) 1986, The Late Show (BBC 2) 1989–. *Publications:* A Just Measure of Pain: The Penitentiary in the Industrial Revolution 1978, Wealth and Virtue: The Shaping of Classical Political Economy in the Scottish Enlightenment (ed. with Istvan Hont) 1983, The Needs of Strangers: An Essay on the Philosophy of Human Needs 1984, The Russian Album: A Family Memoir (RSL W. H. Heinemann Award, UK, Governor-General Award, Canada 1988) 1987, Asya 1991, Scar Tissue (novel) 1993, Blood and Belonging: Journeys into the New Nationalism 1993, Isaiah Berlin: A Life 1998, The Warrior's Honor: Ethnic War and the Modern Conscience 1998, Virtual War: Kosovo and Beyond 2000, The Rights Revolution (Massey Lectures 2000) 2001, Human Rights as Politics and Idolatry (Tanner Lectures) 2001, Charlie Johnson in the Flames 2003, The Lesser Evil: Political Ethics in an Age of Terror 2004, After Paradise 2005; contrib. to New York Times, New Yorker, New York Review of Books. *Honours:* Hon. doctorate (Bishop's Univ.) 1995; Lionel Gelber Award 1994. *Literary Agent:* AP Watt Ltd, 20 John Street, London, WC1N 2DR, England. *Address:* Carr Center for Human Rights Policy, John F. Kennedy School of Government, 79 JFK Street, Cambridge, MA 02138, USA. *E-mail:* Michael_Ignatieff@harvard.edu.

IGNATIUS, David; Journalist, Editor and Novelist; b. 1950, Cambridge, MA, USA; m. Eve Ignatius; three d. *Education:* Harvard Univ. and King's Coll. Cambridge. *Career:* Ed. The Washington Monthly magazine 1975; reporter The Wall Street Journal 1976–86, assignments included Steelworkers Corresp., Pittsburgh, Senate Corresp., Washington DC, Middle East Corresp., Chief Diplomatic Corresp.; Ed. Sunday Outlook, The Washington Post 1986–90, Foreign Ed. 1990–93, apptd Asst Managing Business Ed. 1993, then Assoc. Ed.; Exec. Ed. International Herald Tribune 2000–03; mem. Washington Post Writer's Group 2003–; Contrib. to The New York Times Magazine, The Atlantic Monthly, Foreign Affairs and The New Republic. *Publications:* Agents of Innocence 1987, SIRO 1991, The Bank of Fear 1994, A Firing Offense 1997, The Sun King 1999. *Honours:* Frank Knox Fellow, Harvard–Oxford Univs. 1973–75; Edward Weintal Prize for Diplomatic Reporting 1985, Gerald Loeb Award for Commentary 2000. *Address:* Washington Post Writers Group, 1150 15th St, NW Washington, DC 20071, USA. *E-mail:* writersgrp@washpost.com. *Website:* www .postwritersgroup.com.

IHIMAERA, Witi; Author; b. 7 Feb. 1944, Gisborne, New Zealand. *Education:* University of Auckland, 1963–66; Victoria University, 1968–72. *Publications:* Pounamu, Pounamy, 1972; Tangi, 1973; Whanau, 1974; Maori, 1975; The New Net Goes Fishing, 1977; Into the World of Light, 1980; The Matriarch, 1986; The Whale Rider, 1987; Dear Miss Mansfield, 1989. *Address:* c/o Ministry of Foreign Affairs, Private Bag, Wellington 1, New Zealand.

IKEDA, Daisaku; Buddhist philosopher, writer and Poet; b. 2 Jan. 1928, Tokyo, Japan; m. Kaneko Shiraki, 1952, two s. *Education:* Fuji College. *Career:* Pres., Soka Gakkai Int., 1975–; Founder, Soka University, Soka University of America, Soka Women's College, Tokyo, Kansai Soka Schools, Soka Kindergartens, Makiguchi Foundation for Education, Institute of Oriental Philosophy, Boston Research Center for the 21st Century, Toda Institute for Global Peace and Policy Research, Tokyo, Shizuoka Fuji Art Museum, Min-On Concert Asscn, Victor Hugo House of Literature, Komeito Party; mem. Brazilian Acad. of Letters, non-resident mem. *Publications:* The Human Revolution, six vols, 1972–99; Choose Life: A Dialogue with Arnold Toynbee, 1976; The Living Buddha, 1976; Buddhism: The First Millennium, 1977; Songs From My Heart, 1978; Glass Children and Other Essays, 1979; La nuit appelle l'aurore (with René Huyghe) 1980; Letters of Four Seasons (with Yasushi Inoue) 1980; A Lasting Peace, two vols, 1981, 1987; Life: An Enigma, a Precious Jewel, 1982; Before it is too Late (with Aurelio Peccei) 1984; Buddhism and the Cosmos, 1985; The Flower of Chinese Buddhism, 1986; Human Values in a Changing World (with Bryan Wilson), 1987; Unlocking the Mysteries of Birth and Death, 1988; The Snow Country Prince, 1990; A Lifelong Quest for Peace (with Linus Pauling), 1992; Choose Peace (with Johan Galtung), 1995; A New Humanism: The University Addresses of Daisaku Ikeda, 1996; The Wisdom of the Lotus Sutra (in Japanese), six vols, 1996–2000; The New Human Revolution (in Japanese), 11 vols, 1998–2002; The Way of Youth, 2000; For the Sake of Peace, 2000; Soka Education, 2001; Dialogue pour la paix (with Mikhail Gorbachev) 2001; The World is Yours to Change, 2002; Selected Poetry: Journey of Life (in Japanese) 2003; Golbal Civilization: A Buddhist-Islamic Dialogue (with Majid Tehranian) 2003. Other: Writings on Buddhism, civilization, life and peace. Contributions: newspapers, magazines and books. *Honours:* Hon. Senator European Acad. of Sciences and Arts; Hon. Founding mem. Pan-African Writers' Asscn; Hon. mem. International Poetry for Peace Asscn, Writers' Asscn of Kenya, The Club of Rome; Hon. Life mem. The Thoreau Soc.Poet Laureate, World Acad. of Arts and Culture, 1981; UN Peace Award, 1983; Kenya Oral Literature Award, 1986; World Poet Laureate Award, World Poetry Society, 1995; Tagore Peace Award, 1997; Hon. doctorates, Moscow State University, 1975, University of Sofia, 1981, University of Buenos Aires, 1990, University of the Philippines, 1991, University of Glasgow, 1994, University of Hong Kong, 1996, University of Havana, 1996, University of Ghana, 1996, University of Delhi, 1999, Queens College, CUNY, 2000, Morehouse College, 2002; Hon. Profs, National University of San Marcos, 1981, University of Beijing, 1984.

Address: 32 Shinano-machi, Shinjuku-ku, Tokyo 160-8583, Japan. *Telephone:* (3) 5360-9831. *Fax:* (3) 5360-9885. *Website:* www.sgi.org.

IMALAYEN, Fatima-Zohra (see Djebar, Assia).

IMPEY, Rose(mary June); Writer; b. 7 June 1947, Northwich, Cheshire, England; two d. *Education:* Teacher's Certificate, 1970. *Publications:* Who's a Clever Girl, Then, 1985; The Baked Bean Queen, 1986; The Girls Gang, 1986; Desperate for a Dog, 1988; The Flat Man, 1988; Letter to Father Christmas, 1988; Instant Sisters, 1989; Joe's Cafe, 1990; Revenge of the Rabbit, 1990; First Class, 1992; Trouble with the Tucker Twins, 1992; Orchard Book of Fairytales, 1992; Animal Crackers, 1993; Sir Billy Bear and Other Friends, 1996; Potbelly and the Haunted House, 1996; Fireballs from Hell, 1996; Sleepover Club, 1997; Feather Pillows, 1997.

INGALLS, Rachel (Holmes); Author; b. 13 May 1940, Boston, Massachusetts, USA. *Education:* BA, Radcliffe College, 1964. *Career:* mem. American Acad. and Institute of Arts and Letters, fellow. *Publications:* Theft, 1970; The Man Who Was Left Behind, 1974; Mediterranean Cruise, 1973; Mrs Caliban, 1982; Binstead's Safari, 1983; I See a Long Journey, 1985; The Pearlkillers, 1986; The End of the Tragedy, 1987; Something to Write Home About, 1990; Black Diamond, 1992; Be My Guest, 1992; Days Like Today, 2001. *Honours:* First Novel Award, Author's Club, England, 1971; British Book Marketing Council Best Book Award, 1986. *Address:* c/o Georges Borchardt Inc, 136 E 57th St, New York, NY 10022, USA.

INGHAM, Daniel (see Lambot, Isobel Mary).

INGHAM, Kenneth; Prof. of History Emeritus and Writer; b. 9 Aug. 1921, Harden, England; m. Elizabeth Mary Southall, 18 June 1949, one s. one d. *Education:* Exhibitioner, Keble College, Oxford, 1940; Frere Exhibitioner in Indian Studies, 1947, DPhil, 1950, University of Oxford. *Career:* Lecturer, 1950–56, Prof., 1956–62, Makerere College, Uganda; Dir of Studies, Royal Military Acad., Sandhurst, 1962–67; Prof. of History, 1967–84, Head, Dept of History, 1970–84, Part-time Prof. of History, 1984–86, Prof. Emeritus, 1986–, University of Bristol; mem. British Institute in Eastern Africa; Royal African Society; Royal Historical Society. *Publications:* Reformers in India, 1956; The Making of Modern Uganda, 1958; A History of East Africa, 1962; The Kingdom of Toro in Uganda, 1975; Jan Christian Smuts: The Conscience of a South African, 1986; Politics in Modern Africa, 1990; Obote: A Political Biography, 1994. Contributions: Reference books and professional journals. *Honours:* Military Cross, 1946; OBE, 1961. *Address:* The Woodlands, 94 W Town Lane, Bristol BS4 5DZ, England.

INGLE, Stephen James; University Prof. and Writer; b. 6 Nov. 1940, Ripon, Yorkshire, England; m. Margaret Anne Farmer, 5 Aug. 1964, two s. one d. *Education:* BA, 1962, DipEd, 1963, MA, 1965, University of Sheffield; PhD, Victoria University, New Zealand, 1967. *Career:* Prof., University of Stirling; mem. Political Studies Asscn. *Publications:* Socialist Thought in Imaginative Literature, 1979; Parliament and Health Policy, 1981; British Party System, 1989; George Orwell: A Political Life, 1993; Narratives of British Socialism, 2002. Contributions: many in Fields of Politics and Literature. *Honours:* Commonwealth Scholar, 1964–67; Erasmus Scholar, 1989; Visiting Research Fellow, Victoria University, New Zealand, 1993. *Address:* Dept of Politics, University of Stirling, Stirling FK9 4LA, Scotland. *E-mail:* s.j.ingle@stir.ac.uk.

INGRAMS, Richard Reid, (Philip Reid); Journalist and Writer; b. 11 Aug. 1937, London, England; m. Mary Morgan, 1962, divorced, 1993, two s. one deceased, one d. *Education:* University College, Oxford. *Career:* Ed., 1963–86, Chair., 1974–, Private Eye; TV Critic, The Spectator, 1976–84; Columnist, The Observer, 1988–90, 1992–; Ed., The Oldie, 1992–. *Publications:* Private Eye on London (with Christopher Booker and William Rushton), 1962; Private Eye's Romantic England, 1963; Mrs Wilson's Diary (wih John Wells), 1965; Mrs Wilson's Second Diary, 1966; The Tale of Driver Grope, 1968; The Bible for Motorists (with Barry Fantoni), 1970; The Life and Times of Private Eye (ed.), 1971; Harris in Wonderland (as Philip Reid with Andrew Osmond), 1973; Cobbet's Country Book (ed.), 1974; Beachcomber: The Works of J. B. Morton (ed.), 1974; The Best of Private Eye, 1974; God's Apology, 1977; Goldenballs, 1979; Romney Marsh (with Fay Godwin), 1980; Dear Bill: The Collected Letters of Denis Thatcher (with John Wells), 1980; The Other Half, 1981; Piper's Places (with John Piper), 1983; Dr Johnson by Mrs Thrale (ed.), 1984; Down the Hatch (with John Wells), 1985; Just the One (with John Wells), 1986; John Stewart Collis: A Memoir, 1986; The Best of Dear Bill (with John Wells), 1986; Mud in Your Eye (with John Wells), 1987; The Eye Spy Look-alike Book (ed.), 1988; The Ridgeway, 1988; You Might as Well Be Dead, 1988; England: An Anthology, 1989; Number 10, 1989; On and On...Further Letters of Denis Thatcher (with John Wells), 1990; The Oldie Annual (ed.), 1993; The Oldie Annual II (ed.), 1994; Malcolm Muggeridge, 1995; I Once Met (ed.), 1996; The Oldie Annual III (ed.), 1997; Jesus: Authors Take Sides (ed.), 1999; The Oldie Annual IV (ed.), 1999. *Address:* c/o Private Eye, 6 Carlisle St, London W1, England; c/o The Oldie, 45 Poland St, London W1V 3DF, England.

INKSTER, Tim; Poet, Printer, Designer and Publisher; b. 26 Sept. 1949, Toronto, ON, Canada; m. Elke Inkster. *Education:* University of Toronto. *Career:* Designer, Printer, Press Porcepic, Erin, Ontario, 1971–74; Co-owner, The Porcupine's Quill, Erin, 1974–; mem. League of Canadian Poets; American Institute of Graphic Arts; Society of Graphic Designers of Canada. *Publications:* Poetry: For Elke, 1971; The Topolobampo Poems and Other Memories, 1972; Mrs Grundy, 1983; The Coach House Press, 1974; The Crown Prince Waits for a Train, 1976; Blue Angel, 1981; Other: Letters, Riddles and Miscellany, 1976; The Porcupine's Quill Reader (co-ed.), 1997; Autobiographic films: Print Shop, 1976; Tin Inkster: Colours of a Poet, 1976. *Address:* 68 Main Street, Erin, ON N0B 1T0, Canada.

INNAURATO, Albert (Francis); Playwright, Writer and Dir; b. 2 June 1947, Philadelphia, Pennsylvania, USA. *Education:* BA, Temple University; BFA, California Institute of the Arts, 1972; MFA, Yale University, 1975. *Career:* Playwright-in-Residence, Public Theatre, New York City, 1977, Circle Repertory Theatre, New York City, 1979, Playwright's Horizons, New York City, 1983; Adjunct Prof., Columbia University, Princeton University, 1987–89; Instructor, Yale School of Drama, 1993; mem. Dramatists Guild; Writers Guild of America. *Publications:* Plays: Earthworms, 1974; Gemini, 1977; The Transfiguration of Bennon Blimpie, 1977; Verna the USO Girl, 1980; Gus and Al, 1988; Magda and Callas, 1988. Other: Coming of Age in Soho, 1985. Contributions: newspapers and journals. *Honours:* Guggenheim Fellowship, 1976; Rockefeller Foundation Grant, 1977; Obie Awards, 1977, 1978; Emmy Award, 1981; National Endowment for the Arts Grants, 1986, 1989; Drama League Award, 1987.

INNES, Brian; Writer and Publisher; b. 4 May 1928, Croydon, Surrey, England; m. 1st Felicity McNair Wilson 5 Oct. 1956; m. 2nd Eunice Lynch 2 April 1971; three s. *Education:* BSc, MRSc, King's College, London, 1946–49. *Career:* Asst Ed., Chemical Age, 1953–55; Assoc. Ed., The British Printer, 1955–60; Art Dir, Hamlyn Group, 1960–62; Dir, Temperance Seven Ltd, 1961–; Proprietor, Brian Innes Agency, 1964–66, Immediate Books, 1966–70, FOT Library, 1970–; Creative Dir, Deputy Chair., Orbis Publishing Ltd, 1970–86; Editorial Dir, Mirror Publishing, 1986–88; mem. Arts Club, Chartered Society of Designers; RSA; Institute of Printing; CWA; British Actors' Equity; RSL; Royal Society of Chemistry. *Publications:* Book of Pirates, 1966; Book of Spies, 1967; Book of Revolutions, 1967; Book of Outlaws, 1968; Flight, 1970; Saga of the Railways, 1972; Horoscopes, 1976; The Tarot, 1977; Book of Change, 1979; The Red Baron Lives, 1981; Red Red Baron, 1983; The Havana Cigar, 1983; Crooks and Conmen, 1993; Catalogue of Ghost Sightings, 1996; The History of Torture, 1998; Death and The Afterlife, 1999; Dreams, 1999; Bodies of Evidence, 2000; A Long Way from Pasadena, 2001; Snapshots of the Sixties, 2002; United Kingdom, 2002; Myths of Ancient Rome, 2002; Profile of a Criminal Mind, 2003. Contributions: Man, Myth & Magic; Take Off; Real Life Crimes; Fire Power; The Story of Scotland; Discover Scotland; Marshall Cavendish Encyclopaedia of Science; numerous recordings, films, radio and television broadcasts; many photographs published. *Honours:* Royal Variety Command Performance, 1961. *Address:* Les Forges de Montgaillard, 11330 Montgaillard, France. *E-mail:* binnes1@compuserve.com.

INNESS-BROWN, Elizabeth (Ann); Writer, Ed. and Educator; b. 1 May 1954, Rochester, NY, USA; m. Keith Calvert Monley 1 Aug. 1987; one s. *Education:* English, Fine Arts cum laude, St Lawrence Univ., 1976; MFA, Creative Writing, Columbia Univ., 1978. *Career:* Asst Prof. of English, 1979–84, Acting Dir, Center for Writers Graduate Program in Creative Writing, 1983, Assoc. Prof. of English, 1985–86, Univ. of Southern Mississippi, Hattiesburg; Ed., English News, 1980–84, 1985–86, Mississippi Review, 1983; Contributing Ed., Pushcart Prize, 1983–, Boulevard, 1985–; Visiting Writer, St Lawrence Univ., Canton, NY, 1984–85, Purdue Univ., West Lafayette, IN, 1987, Univ. of Hartford, Hartford, CT, 1987–88; English Lecturer, 1988–90, Dir, Writing Center, 1988–, Asst Prof., 1990–94, Assoc. Prof. of English, 1994–2001, Prof. of English, 2001–, St Michael's College, Colchester, VT; Adjunct and Field Faculty, Vermont College, 1988–90. *Publications:* Satin Palms, 1981; Here, 1994; Burning Marguerite (novel), 2002. Contributions: anthologies and periodicals. *Honours:* Youth Foundation Fellowship, 1977; Research Grant, Univ. of Southern Mississippi, 1980; Listed as Outstanding Writer, Pushcart Prize, 1980, 1981, 1989, 1992; Award in Short Fiction, Associated Writing Programs, 1981; St Lawrence Award for Short Fiction, St Lawrence Univ., 1982; Millay Council for the Arts Fellow, 1982; Grant, National Endowment for the Arts, 1982; Pushcart Prize, 1982; Yaddo Fellow, 1982. *Literary Agent:* Emma Parry, Carlisle & Co, 6 W 18th St, New York, NY 10011, USA. *Address:* St Michael's College, Colchester, VT 05439, USA. *E-mail:* einness-brown@smcvt.edu.

IOANNOU, Susan, BA, MA; writer and poet; b. 4 Oct. 1944, Toronto, ON, Canada; m. Lazaros Ioannou 1967; one s. one d. *Education:* Univ. of Toronto. *Career:* Managing Ed., Coiffure du Canada 1979–80; Assoc. Ed., Cross-Canada Writers' Magazine 1980–89; Poetry Ed., Arts Scarborough Newsletter 1980–85; Poetry Instructor, Toronto Board of Education 1982–94, Univ. of Toronto 1989–90; Dir, Wordwrights Canada 1985–; mem. League of Canadian Poets, Writers' Union of Canada, Arts and Letters Club of Toronto, Canadian Poetry Asscn. *Publications:* Spare Words 1984, Motherpoems 1985, The Crafted Poem 1985, Familiar Faces, Private Griefs 1986, Ten Ways to Tighten Your Prose 1988, Writing Reader-Friendly Poems 1989, Clarity Between Clouds 1991, Read-Aloud Poems: For Students from Elementary through Senior High School 1993, Polly's Punctuation Primer 1994, Where the Light Waits 1996, A Real Farm Girl 1998, A Magical Clockwork: The Art of Writing the Poem 2000, Coming Home 2004. *Honours:* Arts Scarborough Poetry Award 1987, Media Club of Canada

Memorial Award 1990, Okanagan Short Story Award 1997. *Address:* c/o Wordwrights Canada, PO Box 456, Station O, Toronto, ON M4A 2P1, Canada.

IPARRAGUIRRE, Sylvia; Argentine novelist; b. 4 July 1947, Junín, Buenos Aires; m. Abelardo Castillo 1976. *Career:* Prof. of Modern Literature, Instituto de Literatura Hispanoamericana de la Facultad de Filosofía y Letras, Universidad de Buenos Aires 1986–; co-founder of literary journal El Ornitorrinco. *Publications:* En el invierno de las ciudades (short stories) (Premio Municipal de Literatura) 1988, Probables lluvias por la noche (short stories) 1993, El Parque (novel) 1996, Tierra del Fuego: una biografía del fin del mundo (novel) (Sor Juana Inés de la Cruz Prize) 2000; contrib. short stories and essays to newspapers and literary journals, including El Escarabajo de Oro, Clarín, Página\12, ETC, Contexto, Puro Cuento, Tramas, Cuadernos Hispanoamericanos, and short stories to numerous anthologies. *Address:* c/o Curbstone Press, 321 Jackson Street, Willimantic, CT 06226-1738, USA. *E-mail:* info@curbstone.org. *Website:* www.curbstone.org.

IRBY, Kenneth (Lee); Writer, Poet and Teacher; b. 18 Nov. 1936, Bowie, TX, USA. *Education:* BA, University of Kansas; MA, 1960, PhD, 1962–63, Harvard University; MLS, University of California, 1968. *Career:* Assoc. Prof. of English, University of Kansas, Lawrence. *Publications:* The Roadrunner Poem, 1964; Kansas-New Mexico, 1965; Movements/Sequences, 1965; The Flower of Having Passed Through Paradise in a Dream, 1968; Relation, 1970; To Max Douglas, 1971; Archipelago, 1976; Catalpa, 1977; Orexis, 1981; Riding the Dog, 1982; A Set, 1983; Call Steps, 1992; Antiphonal and Fall to Fall, 1994. Contributions: anthologies and magazines. *Address:* N-311 Regency Pl., Lawrence, KS 66049, USA.

IRELAND, David; Novelist; b. 24 Aug. 1927, Lakemba, NSW, Australia. *Education:* State Schools, NSW. *Publications:* The Chantic Bird, 1968; The Unknown Industrial Prisoner, 1971; The Flesheaters, 1972; Burn, 1974; The Glass Canoe, 1976; A Woman of the Future, 1979; City of Women, 1981; Archimedes and the Eagle, 1984; Bloodfather, 1987. Short Story: The Wild Colonial Boy, 1979. Play: Image in the Clay, 1962. *Honours:* Adelaide Advertiser Award, 1966; Age Book of the Year Award, 1980; AM, 1981.

IRELAND, Kevin Mark; Writer and Poet; b. 18 July 1933, Auckland, New Zealand; m. Phoebe Caroline Dalwood, two s. *Career:* Writer-in-Residence, Canterbury University, 1986; Sargeson Fellow, 1987, Literary Fellow, 1989, Auckland University; mem. NZSA (PEN). *Publications:* Poetry: Face to Face, 1964; Educating the Body, 1967; A Letter From Amsterdam, 1972; Orchids, Hummingbirds and Other Poems, 1974; Poems, 1974; A Grammar of Dreams, 1975; Literary Cartoons, 1978; The Dangers of Art: Poems 1975–80, 1980; Practice Night in the Drill Hall, 1984; The Year of the Comet, 1986; Selected Poems, 1987; Tiberius at the Beehive, 1990; Skinning a Fish, 1994; Anzac Day: Selected Poems, 1997; Fourteen Reasons for Writing, 2001; Walking the Land, 2003. Other: Sleeping with the Angels (short stories), 1995; Blowing My Top (novel), 1996; The Man Who Never Lived (novel), 1997; Under the Bridge and Over the Moon (memoir), 1998; The Craymore Affair (novel), 2000; Backwards to Forewards (memoir), 2002. *Honours:* New Zealand National Book Award for Poetry, 1979; Commemorative Medal, 1990; OBE, 1992; Montana Award for History and Biography, 1999; Hon. DLitt, 2000. *Address:* 8 Domain St, Devonport, Auckland 9, New Zealand. *E-mail:* kireland@xtra.co.nz.

IRVING, Clifford (Michael), (John Luckless); Author and Screenwriter; b. 5 Nov. 1930, New York, NY, USA. *Education:* BA, Cornell University, 1951. *Publications:* On a Darkling Plain, 1956; The Losers, 1957; The Valley, 1962; The 38th Floor, 1965; Spy, 1969; The Battle of Jerusalem, 1970; Fake, 1970; Global Village Idiot, 1973; Project Octavio, 1978; The Death Freak, 1979; The Hoax, 1981; Tom Mix and Pancho Villa, 1982; The Sleeping Spy, 1983; The Angel of Zin, 1984; Daddy's Girl, 1988; Trial, 1990; Final Argument, 1993. *Address:* c/o Frank Cooper, 10100 Santa Monica Blvd, Los Angeles, CA 90067, USA.

IRVING, Janet Turnbull, MA; Canadian literary agent; b. 16 April 1954, Toronto; m. John Irving 1987. *Education:* Univ. of Toronto. *Career:* Ed Authors' Marketing Services Ltd 1979; Ed. Doubleday Canada Ltd 1980, Man. Ed. 1981; Vice-Pres., Publr and Dir Seal Books 1984–87; Pres. The Turnbull Agency 1987–, Curtis Brown Canada Ltd 1989–99; Ed. Bantam Canada Inc.; Founding Pres. The Canadian Business Task Force on Literacy. *Address:* POB 1048, Manchester Centre, VT 05255, Canada.

IRVING, John Winslow, BA, MFA; American novelist; b. 2 March 1942, Exeter, NH; m. 1st Shyla Leary 1964 (divorced 1981); two s.; m. 2nd Janet Turnbull 1987; one s. *Education:* University of New Hampshire, University of Iowa. *Career:* mem. Acad. of Motion Picture Arts and Sciences, National Wrestling Hall of Fame. *Publications:* Setting Free the Bears, 1969; The Water-Method Man, 1972; The 158 Pound Marriage, 1974; The World According to Garp, 1978; The Hotel New Hampshire, 1981; The Cider House Rules, 1985; A Prayer for Owen Meany, 1989; A Son of the Circus, 1994; Trying to Save Piggy Sneed, 1996; A Widow for One Year, 1998; My Movie Business, 1999; The Cider House Rules (screenplay), 1999; The Fourth Hand, 2001. Contributions: New York Times Book Review; New Yorker; Rolling Stone; Esquire; Playboy. *Honours:* Pushcart Prize, Best of the Small Presses, 1978; National Book Award, 1980; O. Henry Prize, 1981; Acad. Award for Best Adapted Screenplay, 1999. *Literary Agent:* Turnbull Agency, PO Box 757, Dorset, VT 05251, USA.

ISAACS, Anne; Writer; b. 2 March 1949, Buffalo, NY, USA; one s. two d. *Education:* BA, 1971, MS, 1975, University of Michigan; SUNY at Buffalo, 1971–72. *Career:* numerous positions in environmental education, 1975–90. *Publications:* Swamp Angel, 1994, (broadcast adaptation, 1995); Treehouse Tales, 1997; Cat up a Tree, 1998; Torn Thread, 2000. *Honours:* Ralph Caldecott Honor Book, American Library Asscn Notable Books Selection, New York Times Best Illustrated Books Citation, School Library Journal Best Books, Publishers Weekly Best Books, Honor Book, Boston Globe-Horn Book, Children's Book of the Year List, Child Study Children's Book Committee, National Council of Teachers of English Notable Trade Book in Language Arts. *Literary Agent:* Brandt & Hochman Literary Agents Inc, 1501 Broadway, New York, NY 10036, USA.

ISAACS, Susan; Novelist and Screenwriter; b. 7 Dec. 1943, New York, NY, USA; m. 11 Aug. 1968, one s. one d. *Education:* Queens College, CUNY. *Career:* mem. Authors' Guild; International Asscn of Crime Writers; MWA; National Book Critics Circle; PEN; Poets and Writers, Chair. of the Board; Creative Coalition; American Society of Journalists and Authors. *Publications:* Compromising Positions, 1978; Close Relations, 1980; Almost Paradise, 1984; Shining Through, 1988; Magic Hour, 1991; After All These Years, 1993; Lily White, 1996; Red, White and Blue, 1998; Brave Dames and Wimpettes: What Women are really doing on Page and Screen, 1999; Long Time No See, 2001. Contributions: newspapers and magazines. *Honours:* Hon. Doctor of Letters, Dowling College, 1988; Hon. Doctor of Humane Letters, Queens College, CUNY, 1996; Barnes & Noble Writers for Writers Award, 1996; John Steinbeck Award, 1999. *Address:* c/o Scribner, 1230 Avenue of the Americas, New York, NY 10020, USA.

ISEGAWA, Moses; Dutch writer; b. 1963, Kampala, Uganda. *Career:* resettled in Netherlands 1990. *Publications:* Abyssinian Chronicles (in trans.) 1999, Slangenkuil (trans. as Nest of Snakes) 1999, Twee chimpansees (trans. as Two Chimpanzees, non-fiction) 2001. *Address:* c/o Picador, 20 New Wharf Road, London, N1 9RR, England.

ISHIGURO, Kazuo, OBE, MA, DLitt, FRSL; British author; b. 8 Nov. 1954, Nagasaki, Japan; m. Lorna Anne Macdougall 1986; one d. *Education:* Woking Grammar School, Univs of Kent and East Anglia. *Career:* fmr community worker, Renfrew; writer 1980–. *Publications include:* A Pale View of Hills (RSL Winifred Holtby Prize 1983) 1982, A Profile of Arthur J. Mason (TV play) 1985, An Artist of the Floating World (Whitbread Book of the Year Fiction Prize 1986) 1986, The Gourmet (TV play) 1987, The Remains of the Day (Booker Prize 1989) 1989, The Unconsoled (Cheltenham Prize 1995) 1995, When We Were Orphans (novel) 2000, The Saddest Music in the World (screenplay, co-author) 2003, Never Let Me Go (novel) 2005. *Honours:* Chevalier des Arts et Lettres 1998; Hon. DLit (Kent) 1990, (East Anglia) 1995, (St Andrews) 2003; Premio Scanno 1995, Premio Mantova 1998. *Literary Agent:* Rogers, Coleridge and White Ltd, 20 Powis Mews, London, W11 1JN, England. *Telephone:* (20) 7221-3717. *Fax:* (20) 7229-9084.

ISITT, Samuel John, BA, MBIM, IPM, MInstM, MInstEx; Artist, Writer, Poet and Actor; b. 9 Feb. 1935, Newport, Monmouthshire, Wales; three s., one d. *Education:* University of London. *Career:* Teacher, Norfolk Authority, 1958–59; Brand Man., Distillers Biochem, 1959–63; Export Exec., Glaxo, 1963–66; Overseas Marketing Dir, Norcos Group, 1966–74; Artist, Actor, Writer, 1974–; mem. Oxbridge Artists and Writers, Dir. *Publications:* Act of Love, 1980; The Propitiation, 1981; Mary's Song, 1990; Seven Deadly Sins, 1992; Love Bytes, 1998. Contributions: numerous articles and verse for magazines and journals. *Honours:* Koestler Prize, 1980. *Address:* 24 Jericho Street, Oxford OX2 6BU, England. *E-mail:* taff.isitt@hot-toast.com.

ISLER, Alan David; American academic; b. (writer), 12 Sept. 1934, London, England. *Education:* BA, Hunter College, CUNY, 1961; MA, 1962, PhD, 16th Century Literature, 1966, Columbia University. *Career:* Asst Prof. of English, Huron College, University of Western Ontario, Canada, 1965–67; Assoc. Prof. of English, Queens College, CUNY, 1967–; Visiting Lecturer, University of Tel-Aviv, 1971–72; mem. Renaissance Society of America. *Publications:* The Prince of West End Ave, 1994; Kraven Images, 1996. Contributions: periodicals including University of Toronto Quarterly. *Honours:* National Jewish Book Award 1994. *Address:* Department of English, Queens College, City University of New York, Flushing, NY 11367, USA.

ISRAEL, Jonathan Irvine; Prof. of Dutch History and Institutions and Writer; b. 22 Jan. 1946, London, England; m. Jenny Tatjana Winckel, 1985, one s. one d. *Education:* Queens' College, Cambridge; DPhil, St Antony's College, Oxford, 1972. *Career:* Lecturer, University of Hull, 1972–74; Lecturer, 1974–81, Reader, 1981–84, Prof. of Dutch History and Institutions, 1985–, University College London. *Publications:* Race, Class and Politics in Colonial Mexico, 1975; The Dutch Republic and the Hispanic World, 1982; European Jewry in the Age of Mercantilism, 1550–1750, 1985; Dutch Primacy in World Trade, 1585–1740, 1989; Empires and Entrepots: The Dutch, the Spanish Monarchy and the Jews, 1585–1713, 1990; The Anglo-Dutch Movement: Essays on the Glorious Revolution and its World Impact (ed.), 1991; The Dutch Republic, 1995; Conflict of Empires: Spain, the Low Countries and the Struggle for World Supremacy, 1585–1713,

1997; Radical Enlightenment, 2001. Contributions: scholarly books and journals. *Honours:* Fellow, British Acad., 1992. *Address:* c/o Dept of History, University College London, Gower St, London WC1E 6BT, England.

ITANI, Frances, BA, MA; Canadian novelist and poet; b. Belleville, ON. *Education:* Univ. of Alberta, Univ of New Brunswick. *Career:* nursing, then teaching and writer-in-residence positions at Univ. of Ottawa, Trent Univ., The Banff Centre, Nepean Public Library. *Publications:* novels: Linger by the Sea 1979, Deafening 2003, poetry: No Other Lodgings 1978, Rentee Bay 1983, A Season of Mourning 1988; short story collections: Pack Ice 1989, Truth or Lies 1989, Man Without Face 1994, Leaning, Leaning Over Water 1998, Poached Egg on Toast 2004. *Honours:* Best Short Story, Canadian Fiction Magazine 1987, Ottawa-Carleton Book Award (Fiction) 1994, Tilden/CBC/Saturday Night Literary Award First Prize (Fiction) 1995, 1996, Drummer General's Award for Fiction 2004, Commonwealth Writers Prize (Caribbean and Canada Region) Best Book Award 2004. *Literary Agent:* Harper Flamingo Canada, Harper Collins Publishers Ltd, 2 Bloor Street E, 20th FloorToronto, ON M4W 1A8, Canada. *Telephone:* 416 975 9334. *Fax:* 416 975 5223. *Website:* www.harpercanada.com.

IVIMY, May (see Badman, May Edith).

IYAYI, Festus; Novelist; b. 29 Sept. 1947, Ibadan, Nigeria. *Education:* Annunciation Catholic College; Kiev Institute of Economics; PhD, University of Bradford, Yorkshire, 1980. *Career:* Lecturer, University of Benin. *Publications:* Violence, 1979; The Contract, 1982; Heroes, 1986; Awaiting Court Martial, 1996. *Honours:* Asscn of Nigerian Authors Prize, 1987; Commonwealth Writers Prize, 1988; Pius Okigbo Africa Prize for Literature, 1996; Nigerian Author of the Year, 1996. *Address:* Dept of Business Administration, University of Benin, PMB 1145, Ugbowo Campus, Benin City, Nigeria.

J

JACCOTTET, Philippe; poet and writer; b. 30 June 1925, Moudon, Switzerland. *Education:* University of Lausanne. *Publications:* Poetry: Requiem, 1947; L'Effraie et autres poésies, 1953; L'ignorant: Poèmes 1952–56. Airs: Poèmes 1961–64; Poésie 1946–67; Leçons, 1969; Chants d'en bas, 1974; Breathings, 1974; Pensées sous les nuages, 1983; Selected Poems, 1987; Cahier de verdure, 1990; Libretto, 1990. Other: Through the Orchard, 1975; Des Histoires de passage: Prose 1948–78; Autres Journées, 1987; Trans. of works by Robert Musil, Thomas Mann, Leopardi, Homer and Hölderlin. *Honours:* Larbaud Prize 1978. *Address:* c/o Editions Gallimard, 5 rue Sebastien-Bottin, 75007 Paris, France.

JACK, Ian; British editor, writer and journalist. *Career:* journalist, Scotland 1960s; variously reporter, feature writer, foreign correspondent, Sunday Times 1970–86; co-f., Independent on Sunday 1989, ed. 1991–95; Ed., Granta magazine 1995–. *Publications:* Before the Oil Ran Out, 1987; The Granta Book of Reportage (ed.), 1998; The Granta Book of Travel (ed.), 1998; The Granta Book of the Family (ed.), 1998; Granta: The First 21 Years (ed.), 2001; The Crash that Stopped Britain, 2001; Granta 81: Best of Young British Novelists (ed.), 2003; Granta 83: This Overheating World 2003. *Address:* 2/3 Hanover Yard, Noel Road, London N1 8BE, England. *Telephone:* (20) 7704-9776. *Fax:* (20) 7704-0474. *E-mail:* ijack@granta.com. *Website:* www.granta.com.

JACK, Ian (Robert James); Prof. of English Literature Emeritus, Writer and Ed.; b. 5 Dec. 1923, Edinburgh, Scotland; m. 1st Jane Henderson MacDonald, 1948, divorced, two s. one d.; m. 2nd Margaret Elizabeth Crone, 1972, one s. *Education:* George Watson's College; MA, University of Edinburgh, 1947; DPhil, Merton College, Oxford, 1950. *Career:* Lecturer in English Literature, 1950–55, Senior Research Fellow, 1955–61, Brasenose College, Oxford; Visiting Prof., University of Alexandria, 1960, University of Chicago, 1968–69, University of California at Berkeley, 1968–69, University of British Columbia, 1975, University of Virginia, 1980–81, Tsuda College, Tokyo, 1981, New York University, 1989; Lecturer in English Literature, 1961–73, Reader in English Poetry, 1973–76, Prof. of English Literature, 1976–89, Prof. Emeritus, 1989–, University of Cambridge; Fellow, 1961–89, Librarian, 1965–75, Fellow Emeritus, 1989–, Pembroke College, Cambridge; de Carle Lecturer, University of Otago, 1964; Warton Lecturer in English Poetry, British Acad., 1967; mem. British Acad., fellow; Brontë Society, vice-pres., 1973–; Browning Society, pres., 1980–83; Charles Lamb Society, pres., 1970–80; Johnson Society, Lichfield, pres., 1986–87. *Publications:* Augustan Satire, 1952; English Literature 1815–1832, Vol. X of The Oxford History of English Literature, 1963; Keats and the Mirror of Art, 1967; Browning's Major Poetry, 1973; The Poet and His Audience, 1984. Editor: Brontë novels, Clarendon edn, 7 vols, 1969–72; The Poetical Works of Browning, 1983, Vols I–V, 1983–95. Contributions: scholarly books and professional journals. *Honours:* Leverhulme Emeritus Fellow, 1990–91; Hon. Fellow, Merton College, Oxford, 1997. *Address:* Highfield House, High St, Fen Ditton, Cambridgeshire CB5 8ST, England.

JACK, Ronald Dyce Sadler; academic and writer; b. 3 April 1941, Ayr, Scotland; m. Kirsty Nicolson 1967; two d. *Education:* MA, 1964, DLitt, 1990, Univ. of Glasgow; PhD, Univ. of Edinburgh, 1968. *Career:* Lecturer, 1965–78, Reader, 1978–87, Prof., 1987–, Univ. of Edinburgh; Visiting Prof., Univ. of Virginia, 1973–74, Univ. of Strathclyde, 1993; Distinguished Visiting Prof., Univ. of Connecticut, 1998; W. Ormiston Roy Fellow, Univ. of South Carolina, 2003; mem. Medieval Acad. of America; Scottish Text Society. *Publications:* Scottish Prose 1550–1700, 1972; The Italian Influence on Scottish Literature, 1972; A Choice of Scottish Verse 1560–1660, 1978; The Art of Robert Burns (co-author), 1982; Sir Thomas Urquhart (co-author), 1984; Alexander Montgomerie, 1985; Scottish Literature's Debt to Italy, 1986; The History of Scottish Literature, Vol. I, 1988; Patterns of Divine Comedy, 1989; The Road to the Never Land, 1991; Of Lion and Unicorn, 1993; The Poems of William Dunbar, 1997; Mercat Anthology of Early Scottish Literature, 1997. Contributions: Review of English Studies; Modern Language Review; Comparative Literature; Studies in Scottish Literature. *Honours:* Fellow, Royal Society of Edinburgh, 2000; Fellow, English Asscn, 2000. *Address:* c/o University of Edinburgh, David Hume Tower, George Square, Edinburgh EH8 9JX, Scotland.

JACKMAN, Brian; journalist and writer; b. 25 April 1935, Epsom, Surrey, England; m. 1st 1964 (divorced 1992); one d.; m. 2nd 1993. *Education:* grammar school. *Career:* staff, Sunday Times, 1970–90; Contributing Ed., Condé Nast Traveller; mem. RGS; Fauna and Flora Preservation Society. *Publications:* We Learned to Ski, 1974; Dorset Coast Path, 1977; The Marsh Lions, 1982; The Countryside in Winter, 1986; My Serengeti Years, 1987; Roaring at the Dawn, 1996; The Big Cat Diary, 1996; Touching the Wild, 2003. Contributions: Sunday Times; The Times; Daily Telegraph; Daily Mail; Country Living; Country Life; BBC Wildlife. *Honours:* TTG Travel Writer of Year, 1982; Wildscreen Award, 1982. *Address:* Spick Hatch, West Milton, Nr Bridport, Dorset DT6 3SH, England. *E-mail:* brian@spickhatck .freeserve.co.uk.

JACKMAN, Stuart Brooke; Clergyman, Editor and Writer; b. 22 June 1922, Manchester, England. *Career:* Congregational Minister, Barnstaple, Devon, 1948–52, Pretoria, 1952–55, Caterham, Surrey, 1955–61, Auckland, 1961–65, Upminster, Essex, 1965–67, Oxford, Surrey, 1969–; Ed., Council for World Mission, 1967–71, Oxted, Surrey, 1969–81, Melbourne, Cambridgeshire, 1981–87. *Publications:* Portrait in Two Colours, 1948; But They Won't Lie Down, 1954; The Numbered Days, 1954; Angels Unawares, 1956; One Finger for God, 1957; The Waters of Dinyanti, 1959; The Daybreak Boys, 1961; The Desirable Property, 1966; The Davidson Affair, 1966; The Golden Orphans, 1968; Guns Covered with Flowers, 1973; Slingshot, 1975; The Burning Men, 1976; Operation Catcher, 1980; A Game of Soldiers, 1981; The Davidson File, 1981; Death Wish, 1998. *Literary Agent:* Curtis Brown Ltd, Haymarket House, 28–29 Haymarket, London, SW1Y 4SP, England. *Telephone:* (20) 7393-4400. *Fax:* (20) 7393-4401. *E-mail:* info@curtisbrown.co.uk. *Website:* www.curtisbrown.co.uk.

JACKOWSKA, Nicki; Poet, Novelist, Writer and Teacher; b. 6 Aug. 1942, Brighton, Sussex, England; m. Andrzej Jackowski, 1 May 1970, divorced, one d. *Education:* ANEA Acting Diploma, 1965; BA, 1977, MA, 1978, University of Sussex. *Career:* Founder-Tutor, Brighton Writing School; Writer-in-Residence at various venues; Readings; Radio and television appearances; mem. Poetry Society. *Publications:* The House That Manda Built, 1981; Doctor Marbles and Marianne, 1982; Earthwalks, 1982; Letters to Superman, 1984; Gates to the City, 1985; The Road to Orc, 1985; The Islanders, 1987; News from the Brighton Front, 1993; Write for Life, 1997; Lighting a Slow Fuse, New and Selected Poems, 1998. Contributions: various publications. *Honours:* Winner, Stroud Festival Poetry Competition, 1972; Continental Bursary, South East Arts, 1978; C. Day-Lewis Fellowship, 1982; Arts Council Writer's Fellowship, 1984–85; Arts Council of England Writer's Bursary, 1994. *Address:* c/o Judy Martin Agency, 94 Goldhurst Terrace, London, NW6 3HS, England.

JACKSON, E. F. (see Tubb, Edwin Charles).

JACKSON, Everatt (see Muggeson, Margaret Elizabeth).

JACKSON, Jane (see Pollard, Jane).

JACKSON, Keith (see Kelly, Tim).

JACKSON, Kenneth T(erry); Prof. of History and Writer; b. 27 July 1939, Memphis, Tennessee, USA; m. Barbara Ann Bruce, 25 Aug. 1962, two s. one deceased. *Education:* BA, University of Memphis, 1961; MA, 1963, PhD, 1966, University of Chicago. *Career:* Asst Prof., 1968–71, Assoc. Prof., 1971–76, Prof., 1976–87, Mellon Prof., 1987–90, Barzun Prof. of History and Social Sciences, 1990–, Chair., Dept of History, 1994–97, Columbia University; Visiting Prof., Princeton University, 1973–74, George Washington University, 1982–83, University of California at Los Angeles, 1986–87; Chair., Bradley Commission on History in the Schools, 1987–90, National Council for History Education, 1990–92; mem. American Historical Asscn; Organization of American Historians, pres., 2000–01; Urban History Asscn, pres., 1994–95; Society of American Historians, pres., 1998–2000. *Publications:* The Ku Klux Klan in the City 1915–1930, 1967; American Vistas (ed. with L. Dinnerstein), 2 vols, 1971; Cities in American History (ed. with S. K. Schultz), 1972; Atlas of American History, 1978; Columbia History of Urban Life (general ed.), 1980–; Crabgrass Frontier: The Suburbanization of the United States, 1985; Silent Cities: The Evolution of the American Cemetery (with Camilo Verqara), 1989; Dictionary of American Biography (ed.-in-chief), 1991–95; Encyclopaedia of New York City, 1995. Contributions: scholarly books and professional journals. *Honours:* Woodrow Wilson Foundation Fellow, 1961–62; National Endowment for the Humanities Senior Fellow, 1979–80; Guggenheim Fellowship, 1983–84; Bancroft Prize, 1986; Francis Parkman Prize, 1986; Mark Van Doren Great Teaching Award, Columbia University, 1989; Outstanding Alumni Award, University of Memphis, 1989. *Address:* c/o Dept of History, 603 Fayerweather Hall, Columbia University, New York, NY 10027, USA.

JACKSON, Richard Paul; Writer, Poet, College Prof. and Ed.; b. 17 Nov. 1946, Lawrence, Massachusetts, USA; m. Theresa Harvey, 19 June 1999, one d. *Education:* BA, Merrimack College, 1969; MA, Middlebury College, 1972; PhD, Yale University, 1976. *Career:* Journal Ed., University of Tennessee at Chattanooga; Faculty, Vermont College, MFA, 1988–; mem. Sarajevo Committee of Slovene; PEN; Associated Writing Programs. *Publications:* Part of the Story, 1983; Acts of Mind, 1983; Worlds Apart, 1987; Dismantling Time in Contemporary Poetry, 1989; Alive All Day, 1993; Heart's Bridge, 1999; Heartwall, 2000; Half Lives, 2001. Contributions: Georgia Review; Antioch Review; North American Review; New England Review. *Honours:* National Endowment for the Humanities Fellowship, 1980; National Endowment for the Arts Fellowship, 1985; Fulbright Exchange Fellowships, 1986, 1987; Agee Prize, 1989; CSU Poetry Award, 1992; Juniper Prize, 2000; 4 Pushcart Prizes. *Address:* 3413 Alta Vista Dr., Chattanooga, TN 37411, USA.

JACKSON, Robert Louis; academic, writer and editor; b. 10 Nov. 1923, New York, NY, USA; m. Elizabeth Mann Gillette 1951; two d. *Education:* BA, Cornell University, 1944; MA, 1949, Certificate, Russian Institute, 1949, Columbia University; PhD, University of California at Berkeley, 1956. *Career:* Instructor, 1954–58, Asst Prof., 1958–67, Prof. of Russian Literature, 1967–91, B. E. Bensinger Prof. of Slavic Languages and Literatures,

1991–, Yale University; mem. North American Dostoevsky Society, pres., 1971–77; International Dostoevsky Society, pres., 1977–83; North American Chekhov Society, founder and pres., 1988–; Vyacheslav Ivanov Convivium, founder and pres., 1981–. *Publications:* Dostoevsky's Underground Man in Russian Literature, 1958; Dostoevsky's Quest for Form: A Study of His Philosophy of Art, 1966; The Art of Dostoevsky, 1981; Dialogues with Dostoevsky: The Overwhelming Questions, 1993. Editor: Chekhov: Collected Critical Essays, 1967; Crime and Punishment: Collected Critical Essays, 1974; Dostoevsky: Collected Critical Essays, 1984; Reading Chekhov's Text, 1993. Contributions: Professional journals. *Honours:* Distinguished Scholarly Career Award, 1993, Prize for Outstanding Work in the field of Slavic Languages and Literature, 1994, American Asscn of Teachers of Slavic and East European Languages; Hon. Doctorate, Moscow State University, 1994. *Address:* c/o Dept of Slavic Languages and Literatures, Yale University, PO Box 208236, New Haven, CT 06520, USA.

JACOBS, Barbara; Journalist and Writer; b. 6 Feb. 1945, St Helens, England; m. Mark Jacobs, 26 Feb. 1968, divorced, one s. *Education:* BA, 1966, PGCE, 1967, Leicester University. *Career:* Freelance journalist, 1978–. *Publications:* Ridby Graham, 1982; Two Times Two, 1984; The Fire Proof Hero, 1986; Desperadoes, 1987; Listen to My Heartbeat, 1988; Stick, 1988; Goodbye My Love, 1989; Just How Far, 1989; Loves a Pain, 1990; Not Really Working, 1990. Contributions: periodicals. *Address:* 29 Gotham St, Leicester LE2 0NA, England.

JACOBS, Jane; American writer; b. 1916, Scranton, PA; m. Robert Jacobs. *Career:* community activist and conservationist; began career as asst to women's page ed., local newspaper, Scranton; writer for a metals trade magazine, New York; freelance journalist, The New York Herald Tribune and Vogue magazine; fmr staff mem. Office of War Information and Architectural Forum; written works focus on role of cities and urban planning. *Publications include:* The Death and Life of Great American Cities 1961, The Economy of Cities 1969, A Question of Separatism: Quebec and the Struggle for Sovereignty 1980, Cities and the Wealth of Nations 1984, Systems of Survival: A Dialogue on the Moral Foundations of Commerce and Politics 1992; contrib. articles to journals, including Fortune, Places, Openair-Market Net, various websites. *Address:* c/o Vintage Books, Random House, 1745 Broadway, New York, NY 10019, USA (Office).

JACOBS, Leah (see Gellis, Roberta Leah).

JACOBS, Steve; writer; b. 1955, Port Elizabeth, South Africa. *Education:* Univ. of Cape Town. *Career:* sub-ed. and web producer, The Sydney Morning Herald, The Sun-Herald, Sydney, Australia. *Publications:* Light in a Stark Age (short stories) 1984, Diary of an Exile (two novellas) 1986, Under the Lion (novel) 1993, The Enemy Within (novel) 1995. *Address:* c/o African Writers Series, Heinemann Educational Publishers, Halley Court, Jordan Hill, Oxford OX2 8EJ, England.

JACOBSON, Dan; British academic; b. (writer), 7 March 1929, Johannesburg, South Africa; m. Margaret Pye; three s. one d. *Education:* BA, University of the Witwatersrand. *Career:* Prof., Syracuse University, New York, 1965–66; Lecturer, 1975–80, Reader, 1980–87, Fellow, 1981, Australian National University; Prof., 1988–94, Prof. Emeritus, 1994–, University College London. *Publications:* The Trap, 1955; A Dance in the Sun, 1956; The Price of Diamonds, 1957; The Evidence of Love, 1960; The Beginners, 1965; The Rape of Tamar, 1970; The Confessions of Josef Baisz, 1979; The Story of the Stories, 1982; Time and Time Again, 1985; Adult Pleasures, 1988; Hidden in the Heart, 1991; The God Fearer, 1992; The Electronic Elephant, 1994; Heshel's Kingdom, 1998; A Mouth Full of Glass, 2000; Ian Hamilton in Conversation with Dan Jacobson, 2002. Contributions: periodicals and newspapers. *Honours:* John Llewelyn Rhys Memorial Award, 1958; W. Somerset Maugham Award, 1964; H. H. Wingate Award, 1979; J. R. Ackerley Award, 1986; Hon. DLitt, University of the Witwatersrand, 1987; Mary Elinore Smith Prize, 1992. *Literary Agent:* A. M. Heath & Co Ltd, 79 St Martin's Lane, London WC2N 4RE, England.

JACOBSON, Howard, BA; writer; b. 25 Aug. 1942, Manchester, England; m. Rosalin Sadler 1978; one s. *Education:* Downing Coll., Cambridge. *Career:* Lecturer, Univ. of Sydney, 1965–68; Supervisor, Selwyn College, Cambridge, 1969–72; Senior Lecturer, Wolverhampton Polytechnic, 1974–80; Television Critic, The Sunday Correspondent, 1989–90; Writer, Presenter, TV: Yo, Mrs Askew! (BBC2), 1991, Roots Schmoots (Channel 4), 1993, Sorry, Judas (Channel 4), 1993, Seriously Funny: An Argument for Comedy (Channel 4), 1997; Howard Jacobson Takes on the Turner (Channel 4), 2000; Why the Novel Matters (South Bank Show special, LWT), 2002; Columnist, The Independent, 1998–; mem. Modern Painters, editorial board. *Publications:* Shakespeare's Magnanimity: Four Tragic Heroes, Their Friends and Families, 1978; Coming From Behind, 1983; Peeping Tom, 1984; Redback, 1986; In the Land of Oz, 1987; The Very Model of a Man, 1992; Roots Schmoots, 1993; Seeing With the Eye: The Peter Fuller Memorial Lecture, 1993; Seriously Funny, 1997; No More Mister Nice Guy, 1998; The Mighty Walzer, 1999; Who's Sorry Now, 2002; The Making of Henry 2004. *Honours:* Jewish Quarterly and Wingate Prize, 2000; Bollinger Everyman Wodehouse Prize, 2000. *Literary Agent:* PFD, Drury House, 34–43 Russell Street, London, WC2B 5HA, England.

JACOBUS, Lee A.; Prof. of English and Writer; b. 20 Aug. 1935, Orange, NJ, USA; m. Joanna Jacobus, 1958, two c. *Education:* BA, 1957, MA, 1959, Brown University; PhD, Claremont Graduate University, 1968. *Career:* Faculty, Western Connecticut State University, 1960–68; Asst Prof., 1968–71, Assoc. Prof., 1971–76, Prof. of English, 1976–, University of Connecticut; Visiting Prof., Brown University, 1981; Visiting Fellow, Yale University, 1983, 1996. *Publications:* Improving College Reading, 1967; Issues and Responses, 1968; Developing College Reading, 1970; Humanities Through the Arts (with F. David Martin), 1974; John Cleveland: A Critical Study, 1975; Sudden Apprehension: Aspects of Knowledge in Paradise Lost, 1976; The Paragraph and Essay Book, 1977; The Sentence Book, 1980; Humanities: The Evolution of Values, 1986; Writing as Thinking, 1989; Shakespeare and the Dialectic of Certainty, 1993; Substance, Style and Strategy, 1998. Editor: Aesthetics and the Arts, 1968; 17 From Everywhere: Short Stories from Around the World, 1971; Poems in Context (William T. Moynihan), 1974; Longman Anthology of American Drama, 1982; The Bedford Introduction to Drama, third edn, 1997; A World of Ideas, fourth edn, 1994; Teaching Literature: An Introduction to Critical Reading, 1996. Contributions: scholarly books, journals, and other publications. *Address:* Dept of English, U-25, University of Connecticut, Storrs, CT 06269, USA.

JACOBUS, Mary; Prof. of English and Writer; b. 4 May 1944, Cheltenham, Gloucestershire, England. *Education:* BA, 1965, MA, 1970, DPhil, 1970, University of Oxford. *Career:* Lecturer, Dept of English, Manchester University, 1970–71; Fellow, Tutor in English, Lady Margaret Hall, Oxford, 1971–80; Lecturer in English, University of Oxford, 1971–80; Assoc. Prof., 1980–82, Prof., 1982–, John Wendell Anderson Prof. of English, 1989, Cornell University, Ithaca, NY; Grace Prof. of English, University of Cambridge, 2000–; Fellow, Churchill Coll., Cambridge; mem. MLA. *Publications:* Tradition and Experiment in Wordsworth's Lyrical Ballads (1798), 1976; Women Writing and Women about Women (ed.), 1979; Reading Women, 1986; Romanticism, Writing, and Sexual Difference: Essays on The Prelude, 1989; Body/Politics: Women and the Discourses of Science (co-ed.), 1989; First Things: The Maternal Imaginary, 1995; Psychoanalysis and the Scene of Reading, 1999. Contributions: numerous magazines and journals. *Honours:* Guggenheim Fellowship, 1988–89; National Endowment for the Humanities Award, 2000–01; Hon. Fellow, Lady Margaret Hall, Oxford, 2000–. *Address:* Churchill College, University of Cambridge, Cambridge CB3 0AS, England.

JACOBY, Russell; Historian and Writer; b. 23 April 1945, New York, NY, USA; m. Naomi Glauberman, one s. one d. *Education:* University of Chicago, 1963–64; BA, University of Wisconsin at Madison, 1967; MA, 1968, PhD, 1974, University of Rochester; Graduate Studies, École Pratique des Hautes Études, Paris, 1969–70. *Career:* Lecturer in Social Science, Boston University, 1974–75; Scholar-in-Residence, Brandeis University, 1975–76; Lecturer in History, 1976–79, Visiting Assoc. Prof. of History, 1992–, University of California at Los Angeles; Visiting Asst Prof. of History, University of California at Irvine, 1979–80; Visiting Assoc. Prof. of Humanities, Simon Fraser University, 1983–84; Visiting Scholar-Assoc. Prof., Longergan University College-Liberal Arts College, Concordia University, 1985–86; Visiting Senior Lecturer, University of California at San Diego, 1986–87; Visiting Assoc. Prof. of History, University of California at Riverside, 1988–90. *Publications:* Social Amnesia: A Critique of Conformist Psychology from Adler to Laing, 1975; Dialectic of Defeat: Contours of Western Marxism, 1981; The Repression of Psychoanalysis: Otto Fenichel and the Political Freudians, 1983; The Last Intellectuals: American Culture in the Age of Academe, 1987; Dogmatic Wisdom: How the Culture Wars Divert Education and Distract America, 1994; The Bell Curve Debate: History, Documents, Opinions (ed. with Naomi Glauberman), 1995; The End of Utopia: Politics and Culture in an Age of Apathy, 1999. Contributions: anthologies, reviews, quarterlies and journals. *Honours:* National Endowment for the Humanities Fellowship, 1976; Mellon Postdoctoral Fellowship, 1976–77; Guggenheim Fellowship, 1980–81. *Address:* 32 Breeze Ave, Venice, CA 90291, USA.

JACQUEMARD, Simonne; French novelist, poet and essayist; b. 6 May 1924, Paris; m. 2nd Jacques Brosse 1955. *Education:* Inst. Saint-Pierre, Univ. of Paris. *Career:* teacher of music; collaborator, Laffont-Bompiani Dictionaries; contributor to Figaro Littéraire, La Table Ronde; travelled in USSR, Egypt, Greece, Italy, N Africa and Spain. *Dance:* 23 Native American and flamenco dance shows 1982–2000. *Publications:* Les fascinés 1951, Sable 1952, La leçon des ténèbres 1954, Judith Albarès 1957, Planant sur les airs 1960, Compagnons insolites 1961, Le veilleur de nuit 1962 (Prix Renaudot 1962), L'oiseau 1963, L'orangerie 1963, Les derniers rapaces 1965, Dérive au zénith 1965, Exploration d'un corps 1965, Navigation vers les îles 1967, A l'état sauvage 1967, L'éruption du Krakatoa 1969, La thessalienne 1973, Des roses pour mes chevreuils 1974, Le mariage berbère 1975, Danse de l'orée 1979, Le funambule 1981, Lalla Zahra 1983, La fête en éclats 1985, Les belles échappées 1987, L'huître dans la perle 1993, Le Jardin d'Hérodote 1995, L'Éphèbe couronné de lierre 1995, La Gloire d'Ishwara 1996, Vers l'estuaire ébloui 1996, Trois mystiques grecs 1997, Orphée ou l'initiation mystique (jtly) 1998, L'Oiseau 1998 (Prix Jacques Lacroix, l'Académie française 1999), Héraclite d'Ephèse 2003, Rituels 2004.

Honours: Prix Renaudot 1962, Grand prix Thyde-Monnier 1984; Officier Ordre des Arts et des Lettres 1993, Chevalier Légion d'honneur 1999. *Address:* Le Verdier, 24620 Sireuil, France.

JACQUES, Paula; French author and broadcaster; b. 8 May 1949, Cairo; m. (divorced 1970). *Career:* worked as comedienne in Africa; joined Radio France Internationale as reporter, worked on Après-midi de France-Culture, L'Oreille en coin 1975–90; presenter Nuits-noires France-Inter radio 1997–, Cosmopolitaine 2000–; sometime writer F Magazine; mem. Prix Femina jury 1996–. *Play:* Zanouba. *Publications:* Lumière de l'oeil 1980, Un baiser froid comme la lune 1983, L'Heritage de Tante Carlotta 1987, Deborah et les anges dissipés (Prix Femina 1991), La Déscente au Paradis 1995, Les femmes avec leur amour 1997, Gilda Stambouli souffre et se plaint... 2001. *Address:* France-Inter, 116 avenue du Président Kennedy, 75220 Paris cédex 16, France.

JAFFE, Harold; American writer and academic. *Career:* Prof. of Creative Writing and Literature, San Diego State Univ.; Ed.-in-Chief, Fiction Int. *Publications:* Mourning Crazy Horse 1982, Dos Indios 1983, Beasts 1986, Madonna and Other Spectacles 1988, Eros Anti-Eros 1990, Straight Razor 1995, Othello Blues 1996, Sex for the Millennium 1999, False Positive 2002, 15 Serial Killers 2003. *Honours:* two Nat. Endowment of the Arts grants, California Arts Council grant, Rockefeller Fellowship, NY CAPS grant, two Fulbright grants. *Address:* c/o Curbstone Press, 321 Jackson Street, Willimantic, CT 06226-1738, USA. *E-mail:* info@curbstone.org. *Website:* www.curbstone.org.

JAFFEE, Annette Williams; Novelist; b. 10 Jan. 1945, Abilene, Texas, USA; Divorced, one s. one d. *Education:* BS, Boston University, 1966. *Career:* mem. PEN. *Publications:* Adult Education, 1981; Recent History, 1988; The Dangerous Age, 1999. Contributions: Ploughshares; Missouri Review; Ontario Review. *Honours:* New Jersey Arts Council Grant, 1986; Dodge Fellow, Yaddo, 1991. *Address:* PO Box 26, River Rd, Lumberville, PA 18933, USA.

JAINS, Jessica (see Richeson, Cena Golder).

JAKES, John (William); Author; b. 31 March 1932, Chicago, IL, USA; m. Rachel Ann Payne, 15 June 1951, one s., three d. *Education:* AB, DePauw University, 1953; MA, Ohio State University, 1954. *Career:* Research Fellow, University of South Carolina, 1989; mem. Authors' Guild; Authors League of America; Dramatists Guild; PEN; Western Writers of America; Century Asscn. *Publications:* Brak the Barbarian, 1968; Brak the Barbarian Versus the Sorceress, 1969; Brak Versus the Mark of the Demons, 1969; Six Gun Planet, 1970; On Wheels, 1973; The Bastard, 1974; The Rebels, 1975; The Seekers, 1975; The Titans, 1976; The Furies, 1976; The Best of John Jakes, 1977; The Warriors, 1977; Brak: When the Idols Walked, 1978; The Lawless, 1978; The Americans, 1980; Fortunes of Brak, 1980; North and South, 1982; Love and War, 1984; Heaven and Hell, 1988; California Gold, 1989; The Best Western Stories of John Jakes, 1991; Homeland, 1993; New Trails (co-ed.), 1994; American Dreams, 1998; On Secret Service, 2000; Charleston, 2002. Contributions: Magazines. *Honours:* Hon. LLD, Wright State University, 1976; Hon. LittD, DePauw University, 1977; Porgie Award, 1977; Ohioana Book Award, 1978; Hon. LDH, Winthrop College, 1985, University of South Carolina, 1993; Distinguished Alumni Award, Ohio State University, 1995; Western Heritage Literature Award, Cowboy Hall of Fame, 1995; Hon. Doctor of Humanities, Ohio State University, 1996; Professional Achievement Award, Ohio State University Alumni Asscn, 1997; Career Achievement Award, South Carolina Humanities Asscn, 1998; Thomas Cooper Society Medal, Thomas Cooper Library, University of South Carolina, 2002. *Address:* c/o Rembar and Curtis, 19 W 44th St, New York, NY 10036, USA.

JAMES, Anthony Stephen; Writer and Poet; b. 27 Oct. 1956, Penllergaer, South Wales; m. Penny Windsor, 24 May 1987, divorced 1994, one d. *Education:* BA, University College of Swansea, 1991. *Career:* mem. Literature for More than One Year Group. *Publications:* Novel: A House with Blunt Knives. Poetry: All That the City Has to Offer; Introducing Kivi; We Rescued a Dog Called Gordon, 1997. As Antonia James: The Serpent in April. Contributions: numerous publications. *Honours:* Eileen Illtyd David Award, 1983.

JAMES, Clive Vivian Leopold; Australian writer, broadcaster, journalist and poet; b. 7 Oct. 1939, Kogarah, NSW. *Education:* Sydney Technical High School, Sydney Univ. and Pembroke Coll. Cambridge. *Career:* Asst Ed. Morning Herald, Sydney 1961; Pres. of Footlights at Cambridge, UK; television critic, The Observer 1972–82, feature writer 1972–; Dir Watchmaker Productions 1994–; as lyricist for Pete Atkin, record albums include: Beware of the Beautiful Stranger, Driving Through Mythical America, A King at Nightfall, The Road of Silk, Secret Drinker, Live Libel, The Master of the Revels; also songbook, A First Folio (with Pete Atkin). *Television series include:* Cinema, Up Sunday, So It Goes, A Question of Sex, Saturday Night People, Clive James on Television, The Late Clive James, The Late Show with Clive James, Saturday Night Clive, Fame in the 20th Century, Sunday Night Clive, The Clive James Show, Clive James on Safari; numerous TV documentaries including Clive James meets Katharine Hepburn 1986, Clive James meets Jane Fonda, Clive James meets Mel Gibson 1998, Clive James meets the Supermodels 1998, Postcard series 1989–. *Publications:* non-fiction: The Metropolitan Critic 1974, The Fate of Felicity Fark in the Land of the Media 1975, Peregrine Prykke's Pilgrimage through the London Literary World 1976, Britannia Bright's Bewilderment in the Wilderness of Westminster 1976, Visions Before Midnight 1977, At the Pillars of Hercules 1979, First Reactions 1980, The Crystal Bucket 1981, Charles Charming's Challenges on the Pathway to the Throne 1981, From the Land of Shadows 1982, Glued to the Box 1982, Flying Visits 1984, Snakecharmers in Texas 1988, The Dreaming Swimmer 1992, Fame 1993, The Speaker in Ground Zero 1999; novels: Brilliant Creatures 1983, The Remake 1987, The Silver Castle 1996; autobiography: Unreliable Memoirs 1980, Falling Towards England: Unreliable Memoirs Vol. II 1985, Unreliable Memoirs Vol. III 1990, May Week was in June 1990, Brrm! Brrm! or The Man from Japan or Perfume at Anchorage 1991, Fame in the 20th Century 1993, The Metropolitan Critic 1993; poetry: Fanmail 1977, Poem of the Year 1983, Other Passports: Poems 1958–85 1986, The Book of My Enemy: Collected Verse 1958–2003 2004; other: Clive James on Television 1993, Even as we Speak (essays) 2000, Reliable Essays 2001; contribs to numerous publs including Commentary, Encounter, Listener, London Review of Books, Nation, New Review, New Statesman, New York Review of Books, New Yorker, TLS. *Literary Agent:* PFD, Drury House, 34–43 Russell Street, London, WC2B 5HA, England. *Telephone:* (20) 7344-1000.

JAMES, Dana (see Pollard, Jane).

JAMES, Michael Leonard, (Ruth Carrington, Michael Hartland); Writer and Broadcaster; b. 7 Feb. 1941, Cornwall, England; m. Jill Tarján 1975; two d. *Education:* Christ's College, Cambridge. *Career:* British government service, 1963–78; Dir, International Atomic Energy Agency, Vienna, 1978–83; Chair., Hartland Press Ltd, 1985–2001, Wade Hartland Films, 1991–2000; mem. FRSA. *Publications:* Internationalization to Prevent the Spread of Nuclear Weapons (co-author), 1980. As Ruth Carrington: Dead Fish, 1998. As Michael Hartland: Down Among the Dead Men, 1983; Seven Steps to Treason, 1985; The Third Betrayal, 1986; Frontier of Fear, 1989; The Year of the Scorpion, 1991. Contributions: newspapers, journals and television. *Honours:* Hon. Fellow, University of Exeter, 1985. *Address:* Cotte Barton, Branscombe, Devon EX12 3BH, England.

JAMES, P. D. (see James of Holland Park).

JAMES, Russell; Writer; b. 5 Oct. 1942, Gillingham, Kent, England; m. Jill Redfern 1978; two d. one s. *Publications:* Undergound, 1989; Daylight, 1990; Payback, 1991; Slaughter Music, 1995; Count Me Out, 1996; Oh, No, Not My Baby: A Noir Mystery, 1999; Painting in the Dark, 2000; Pick Any Title, 2002; The Annex, 2002; No One Gets Hurt, 2003. Contributions: periodicals. *Address:* c/o Jane Conway-Gordon, 1 Old Compton St, London W1V 5PH, England. *E-mail:* news@russelljames.co.uk. *Website:* www.russelljames.co.uk.

JAMES, William M. (see Harknett, Terry).

JAMIESON, Kathleen Hall; Prof. of Communications and Writer; b. 24 Nov. 1946, Minneapolis, Minnesota, USA; m. Robert Jamieson, 1968, two s. *Education:* BA, Marquette University, 1967; MA, 1968, PhD, 1972, University of Wisconsin. *Career:* Prof. of Communications, University of Maryland, 1971–86, University of Texas at Austin, 1986–89; Prof. of Communications, 1989–, Dir, Annenberg School of Communications, 1993–, University of Pennsylvania, Philadelphia; Assoc. Ed., several journals; Television news appearances as Political Analyst. *Publications:* Debating Crime Control (co-author), 1967; A Critical Anthology of Public Speeches (compiler), 1978; Form and Genre: Shaping Rhetorical Action (co-ed.), 1978; Age Stereotyping and Television (ed.), 1978; Televised Advertising and the Elderly, 1978; The Interplay of Influence: Mass Media and Their Publics in News, Advertising, and Politics (co-author), 1982; Packaging the Presidency: A History and Criticism of Presidential Campaign Advertising, 1984; Eloquence in an Electronic Age: The Transformation of Political Speechmaking, 1988; Presidential Debates: The Challenge of Creating an Informed Electorate (co-author), 1988; Deeds Done in Words: Presidential Rhetoric and the Genres of Governance (co-author), 1990; Dirty Politics: Deception, Distraction, and Democracy, 1992; 1-800-President: The Report of the Twentieth Century Fund Task Force on Television and the Campaign of 1992 (co-author), 1993; Beyond the Double Bind: Women and Leadership, 1995; Spiral of Cynicism: The Press and the Public Good, 1996. Contributions: periodicals and professional journals. *Honours:* numerous fellowships, grants and teaching, research and academic awards; Golden Anniversary Book Award, 1984, Winans-Wichelns Book Award, 1989, Speech Communication Asscn. *Address:* Annenberg School of Communications, University of Pennsylvania, 3620 Walnut St, Philadelphia, PA 19104-6220, USA.

JANES, Joseph Robert, BSc, MEng; writer; b. 23 May 1935, Toronto, ON, Canada; m. Gracia Joyce Lind 1958; two s. two d. *Education:* Univ. of Toronto. *Career:* mem. Crime Writers of Canada, Crime Writers of the United Kingdom, Historical Novel Society, International Asscn of Crime Writers (North American Branch), MWA, Historical Novel Society (UK). *Publications:* Children's Books: The Tree-Fort War, 1976; Theft of Gold, 1980; Danger on the River, 1982; Spies for Dinner, 1984; Murder in the Market, 1985. Adult Books: The Toy Shop, 1981; The Watcher, 1982; The Third Story, 1983; The Hiding Place, 1984; The Alice Factor, 1991; Mayhem, 1992; Carousel, 1992; Kaleidoscope, 1993; Salamander, 1994; Mannequin, 1994; Dollmaker, 1995; Stonekiller, 1995; Sandman, 1996;

Gypsy, 1997; Madrigal, 1999; Beekeeper, 2001; Flykiller, 2002. Non-Fiction: The Great Canadian Outback, 1978. Textbooks: Holt Geophoto Resource Kits, 1972; Rocks, Minerals and Fossils, 1973; Earth Science, 1974; Geology and New Global Tectonics, 1976; Searching for Structure (co-author), 1977. Teachers' Guide: Searching for Structure (co-author), 1977; Airphoto Interpretation and the Canadian Landscape (with J. D. Mollard), 1984. Contributions: Toronto Star; Toronto Globe and Mail; The Canadian; Winnipeg Free Press; Canadian Children's Annual. *Honours:* grants from Canada Council, Ontario Arts Council, J. P. Bicknell Foundation; Thesis Award, Canadian Institute of Mining and Metallurgy; Canada Council Travel Grant, 2002. *Literary Agent:* Acacia House, 51 Acacia Road, Toronto, ON M4S 2K6, Canada. *Address:* PO Box 1590, Niagara-on-the-Lake, ON L0S 1J0, Canada.

JÁNOSHÁZY, György; editor; b. 20 June 1922, Cluj, Romania; m. Annamária Biluska 1980; one s. *Education:* LLB, Bolyai University, Cluj, 1946; Acad. of Dramatic Arts, Tg Mures, 1952; Studies in Aesthetics and History of Arts, Bolyai University. *Career:* Journalist, 1945–48; Art Secretary, Stage Man., Hungarian Opera, Cluj, 1949–59; Ed., Korunk, monthly, 1958–63, Igaz Szó, monthly, 1963–90, Deputy General Ed., 1969–; mem. Writers' Union of Romania; Tg Mures Asscn, secretary, 1981–90; Hungarian Writers' Union. *Publications:* Lepkék szekrényben (trans. as Butterflies in a Glass Case), 1994; Innen semerre (trans. as From Here In No Direction), 1995; Böllérek miséje (trans. as Butchers' Mass), 1999; Úszó sziget (trans. as Floating Island), 2002; Bagolytükör (trans. as Owe Mirror), 2003. Other: numerous trans; Essays on literature and the arts. Contributions: anthologies, reviews and journals. *Honours:* Order of Labour, 1968; Prize, Tg Mures Writers' Asscn, 1974; Cultural Merit Medal, 1981; Prize, Látó, monthly, 1992, 1999; Prize, Szentgyörgyi Albert Society, 1995; Gold Merit Cross of the Republic of Hungary, 1997; Prize, Writers' Union of Romania, 2000; Golden Feather, Hungarian Journalists' Asscn, Romania, 2002. *Address:* Str Parangului 24/9, 4300 Tg Mures, Romania.

JANSSON, Jan-Magnus, PhD; Finnish professor and publisher; b. 24 Jan. 1922, Helsinki; m. 1st Kerstin Edgren 1948 (divorced 1970); m. 2nd Marita Hausen 1970 (divorced 1975); m. 3rd Siv Dahlin 1976; two d. *Education:* Helsinki Univ. *Career:* Prof. of Political Science, Helsinki Univ. 1954–74; Minister of Trade and Industry 1973–74; Ed.-in-Chief Hufvudstadsbladet 1974–87; Chair. Bd Finnish Inst. of Foreign Affairs 1959–85; Chair. Paasikivi Soc. 1964–66, 1975–85, Swedish People's Party in Finland 1966–73, Parl. Defence Comms. 1970–71, 1975–76, 1980–81, mem. Governmental Comms. for Constitutional Reform 1983–90; mem. Bd Int. Political Science Assoc. 1958–61; Chancellor Åbo Akad. (Swedish Univ. of Finland) 1985–90; mem. Regia Societas Humaniorum Litterarum, Lund. *Publications:* Hans Kelsens statsteori 1950, Frihet och jämlikhet 1952, Politikens teori 1969, Idé och verklighet i politiken 1972, Ledare 1981, Från splittring till samverkan: parlamentarismen i Finland 1992, Tidiga Möten (memoirs) 1996, Från Regeringsformen till Grundlagen 2000; and two collections of poetry. *Honours:* Commdr Order of the White Rose of Finland, Commdr Grand Cross of the Order of the Lion of Finland, Cross of Liberty; Hon. LLD (Helsinki) 1990. *Address:* Mannerheimvägen 42 B 27, 00260 Helsinki 26, Finland (Home). *Telephone:* (9) 493424 (Home). *Fax:* (9) 493424 (Home).

JARMAN, Mark (Foster); Prof. of English and Poet; b. 5 June 1952, Mt Sterling, KY, USA; m. Amy Kane Jarman, 28 Dec. 1974, two d. *Education:* BA, University of California at Santa Cruz, 1974; MFA, University of Iowa, 1976. *Career:* Teacher and Writing Fellow, University of Iowa, 1974–76; Instructor, Indiana State University, Evansville, 1976–78; Visiting Lecturer, University of California at Irvine, 1979–80; Asst Prof., Murray State University, KY, 1980–83; Asst Prof., 1983–86, Assoc. Prof., 1986–92, Prof. of English, 1992–, Vanderbilt University; mem. Associated Writing Programs; MLA; Poetry Society of America; Poets Prize Committee. *Publications:* Poetry: North Sea, 1978; The Rote Walker, 1981; Far and Away, 1985; The Black Riviera, 1990; Iris, 1992; Questions for Ecclesiastes, 1997; Unholy Sonnets, 2000; To the Green Man, 2004. Other: The Reaper Essays (with Robert McDowell), 1996; Rebel Angels: 25 Poets of the New Formalism (ed. with David Mason), 1996; The Secret of Poetry, 2001; Body and Soul: Essays on Poetry, 2002. Contributions: journals, periodicals, and magazines. *Honours:* Joseph Henry Jackson Award, 1974; Acad. of American Poets Prize, 1975; National Endowment for the Arts Grants, 1977, 1983, 1992; Robert Frost Fellowship, Bread Loaf Writers' Conference, 1985; Guggenheim Fellowship, 1991–92; Lenore Marshall Poetry Prize, 1998. *Address:* 509 Broadwell Dr., Nashville, TN 37220, USA.

JARVIS, Sharon; Literary Agent, Publisher, Ed. and Writer; b. 1 Oct. 1943, New York, NY, USA. *Education:* BFA, Hunter College, CUNY, 1964. *Career:* Copy Ed., Ace Books, 1969; Asst Managing Ed., Popular Library, 1971; Ed., Ballantine Books, 1972, Doubleday and Co, 1975; Senior Ed., Playboy Books, 1978; mem. International Fortean Organization; The Holistic Consortium; American Booksellers Asscn; Artists for Art. *Publications:* The Alien Trace (with K. Buckley), 1984; Time Twister, 1984; Inside Outer Space, 1985; True Tales of the Unknown, 1985; True Tales of the Unknown: The Uninvited, 1989; True Tales of the Unknown: Beyond Reality, 1991; Dead Zones, 1992; Dark Zones, 1992; Pitching Your Project, 1999; The Cosmic Countdown, 2003. *Address:* RR2, Box 2090, Laceyville, PA 18623, USA.

JASON, Kathrine; Instructor and Writer; b. 9 Feb. 1953, New York, NY, USA; m. Peter Rondinone, 23 April 1984. *Education:* AB, Bard College, 1975; MFA, Columbia University, 1978; Doctoral Study, Graduate School and Univ. Center, CUNY, 1980–81. *Career:* Instructor, Hunter College, CUNY, 1981–. *Publications:* Racers, What People, 1984; Words in Commotion and Other Stories, 1986; Name and Tears: Forty Years of Italian Fiction, 1990. Contributions: anthologies and periodicals. *Honours:* Fulbright Fellowship, 1978–79.

JASON, Stuart (see Floren, Lee).

JASPER, David; Prof. of Literature and Theology, Clergyman and Writer; b. 1 Aug. 1951, Stockton on Tees, England; m. Alison Elizabeth Collins, 29 Oct. 1976, three d. *Education:* Jesus College, Cambridge, 1969–72; BA, 1976, MA, 1979, St Stephen's House, Oxford; BD, 1980, DD, 2002, Keble College, Oxford; PhD, Hatfield College, Durham, 1983. *Career:* Dir, Centre for the Study of Literature and Theology, Durham University, 1986–91; Dir, Centre for the Study of Literature and Theology, 1991–, Prof. of Literature and Theology, 1998–, University of Glasgow; Ed., Literature and Theology; mem. European Society for Literature and Religion, Sec.; American Acad. of Religion; MLA; Fellow and Dir, Society for Arts, Religion and Culture, 2000. *Publications:* Coleridge as Poet and Religious Thinker, 1985; The New Testament and the Literary Imagination, 1987; The Study of Literature and Religion, 1989; Rhetoric Power and Community, 1992; Reading in the Canon of Scripture, 1995; The Sacred and Secular Canon in Romanticism, 1999; General Ed., Macmillan Series, Studies in Religion and Culture. *Honours:* Dana Fellow, Emory University, Atlanta, 1991; Hon. Fellow, Research Foundation, Durham University, 1991; Ida Cornelia Beam Distinguished Visiting Prof., 2002–03, University of Iowa. *Address:* Netherwood, 124 Old Manse Rd, Wishaw, Lanarkshire ML2 0EP, Scotland.

JAUDEL, Jean Emmanuel; French publisher; b. 6 Jan. 1910, Strasbourg; m. Nicole Weill 1946; one s. one d. *Education:* Faculty of Law, Paris Univ., Ecole libre des sciences politiques, Ecole des hautes études internationales, Geneva, Switzerland. *Career:* Man. Dir Atlantique française 1945–; Chair. La Revue des Deux Mondes, publrs of La Revue des Deux Mondes (monthly review) 1969, Pres. Supervisory Bd 1988–; Pres. Asscn Presse-Enseignement 1981–. *Honours:* Officier Légion d'honneur, Commdr Ordre nat. du Mérite, Médaille militaire, Croix de guerre, other French and foreign awards. *Address:* 31 rue de Penthièvre, 75008 Paris, France (Home).

JAY, Sir Antony (Rupert); Writer and Producer; b. 20 April 1930, London, England; m. Rosemary Jill Watkins, 15 June 1957, two s. two d. *Education:* BA, Classics and Comparative Philology, 1952, MA, 1955, Magdalene College, Cambridge. *Career:* Staff, BBC, 1955–64; Chair., Video Arts Ltd, 1972–89; Writer (with Jonathan Lynn), Yes, Minister and Yes, Prime Minister, BBC TV series, 1980–88. *Publications:* Management and Machiavelli, 1967; To England With Love (with David Frost), 1967; Effective Presentation, 1970; Corporation Man, 1972; The Householder's Guide to Community Defence Against Bureaucratic Aggression, 1972; Yes, Minister (with Jonathan Lynn), 3 vols, 1981–83; The Complete Yes, Minister (with Jonathan Lynn), 1984; Yes, Prime Minister (with Jonathan Lynn), 2 vols, 1986–87; The Complete Yes, Prime Minister (with Jonathan Lynn), 1989; Elizabeth R, 1992; Oxford Dictionary of Political Quotations (ed.), 1996; How to Beat Sir Humphrey, 1997. *Honours:* Hon. MA, Sheffield University, 1987; Knighted, 1988; Doctor of Business Administration, International Management Centre, Buckingham, 1988; FRSA, 1992; Companion, Institute of Management, 1992; CVO, 1993. *Address:* c/o Video Arts Ltd, 68 Oxford St, London W1N 9LA, England.

JAY, Martin (Evan); Prof. of History and Writer; b. 4 May 1944, New York, NY, USA; m. Catherine Gallagher, 6 July 1974, two d. *Education:* BA, Union College, 1965; PhD, Harvard University, 1971. *Career:* Asst Prof., 1971–76, Assoc. Prof., 1976–82, Prof. of History, 1982–, Sidney Hellman Ehrman Prof., 1997–, University of California at Berkeley; mem. American Historical Asscn; Society for Exile Studies. *Publications:* The Dialectical Imagination: A History of the Frankfurt School and the Institute of Social Research, 1923–1950, 1973; Adorno, 1984; Marxism and Totality, 1984; Permanent Exiles, 1985; Fin de Siècle Socialism, 1989; Downcast Eyes, 1993; Force Fields, 1993; Cultural Semantics, 1997–98; Refractions of Violence, 2003. Contributions: Salmagundi. *Honours:* Herbert Baxter Adams Award, American Acad. of Arts and Sciences, 1996; Wissenschaftspreis of the Aby Warburg Stiftung, Hamburg, 2003. *Address:* 718 Contra Costa Ave, Berkeley, CA 94707, USA.

JEAL, Tim, MA; British author; b. 27 Jan. 1945, London, England; m. Joyce Timewell 1969; three d. *Education:* Christ Church, Oxford. *Career:* mem. Soc. of Authors. *Publications:* For Love of Money 1967, Somewhere Beyond Reproach 1969, Livingstone 1973, Cushing's Crusade 1974, Until the Colours Fade 1976, A Marriage of Convenience 1979, Baden-Powell 1989, The Missionary's Wife 1997, Deep Water 2000, Swimming with my Father 2004. *Honours:* joint winner, Llewelyn Rhys Memorial Prize 1974, Writers' Guild Laurel Award. *Address:* 29 Willow Road, London, NW3 1TL, England.

JEFFERSON, Alan (Rigby); Writer; b. 20 March 1921, Ashtead, Surrey, England; m. 1st, one s.; m. 2nd two s. one d.; m. 3rd Antonia Dora Raeburn, 24 Sept. 1976, two s. *Education:* Rydal School, Colwyn Bay, 1935–37; Old Vic Theatre School, 1947–48. *Career:* Administrator, London Symphony

Orchestra, 1968–69; Visiting Prof. of Vocal Interpretation, Guildhall School of Music and Drama, London, 1968–74; Man., BBC Concert Orchestra, London, 1969–73; Ed., The Monthly Guide to Recorded Music, 1980–82; mem. Royal Society of Musicians; Society of Authors. *Publications:* The Operas of Richard Strauss in Great Britain 1910–1963, 1964; The Lieder of Richard Strauss, 1971; Delius, 1972; The Life of Richard Strauss, 1973; Inside the Orchestra, 1974; Strauss, 1975; Discography of Richard Strauss's Operas, 1975; The Glory of Opera, 1976; Strauss, 1978; Sir Thomas Beecham, 1979; The Complete Gilbert and Sullivan Opera Guide, 1984; Der Rosenkavalier, 1986; Lotte Lehmann: A Centenary Biography, 1989; CD ROM: An Introduction to Classical Music, 1996. Contributions: periodicals. *Address:* c/o Society of Authors, 84 Drayton Gardens, London SW10 9SB, England. *E-mail:* alan.jefferson@virgin.net.

JEFFRIES, Roderic (Graeme), (Peter Alding, Jeffrey Ashford, Hastings Draper, Roderic Graeme, Graham Hastings); Writer; b. 21 Oct. 1926, London, England; m. Rosemary Powys Woodhouse, 13 March 1958, one s. one d. *Education:* University of Southampton, 1942–43; Barrister-at-Law, Gray's Inn, 1953. *Publications:* Evidence of the Accused, 1961; Exhibit No. Thirteen, 1962; Police and Detection, 1962; The Benefits of Death, 1963; An Embarrassing Death, 1964; Dead Against the Lawyers, 1965; Police Dog, 1965; Death in the Coverts, 1966; A Deadly Marriage, 1967; Police Car, 1967; A Traitor's Crime, 1968; River Patrol, 1969; Dead Man's Bluff, 1970; Police Patrol Boat, 1971; Trapped, 1972; Mistakenly in Mallorca, 1974; Two Faced Death, 1976; The Riddle in the Parchment, 1976; The Boy Who Knew Too Much, 1977; Troubled Deaths, 1977; Murder Begets Murder, 1978; Eighteen Desperate Hours, 1979; The Missing Man, 1980; Just Desserts, 1980; Unseemly End, 1981; Voyager into Danger, 1981; Peril at Sea, 1983; Deadly Petard, 1983; Three and One Make Five, 1984; Layers of Deceit, 1985; Sunken Danger, 1985; Meeting Trouble, 1986; Almost Murder, 1986; Relatively Dangerous, 1987; The Man Who Couldn't Be, 1987; Death Trick, 1988; Dead Clever, 1989; Too Clever by Half, 1990; A Fatal Fleece, 1991; Murder's Long Memory, 1992; Murder Confounded, 1993; Death Takes Time, 1994; An Arcadian Death, 1995; An Artistic Way to Go, 1996; A Maze of Murders, 1997; The Ambiguity of Murder 1999, An Enigmatic Disappearance 2000, Definitely Deceased 2001, Seeing is Deceiving 2002, An Intriguing Murder 2002. As Peter Alding: The C.I.D. Room, 1967; Circle of Danger, 1968; Murder Among Thieves, 1969; Guilt Without Proof, 1971; Despite the Evidence, 1971; Call Back to Crime, 1972; Field of Fire, 1973; The Murder Line, 1974; Six Days to Death, 1975; Murder Is Suspected, 1978; Ransom Town, 1979; A Man Condemned, 1981; Betrayed by Death, 1982; One Man's Justice, 1983. As Jeffrey Ashford: Counsel for the Defence, 1960; Investigations Are Proceeding, 1961; The Burden of Proof, 1962; Will Anyone Who Saw the Accident..., 1963; Enquiries Are Continuing, 1964; The Hands of Innocence, 1965; Consider the Evidence, 1966; Hit and Run, 1966; Forget What You Saw, 1967; Grand Prix Monaco, 1968; Prisoner at the Bar, 1969; Grand Prix Germany, 1970; To Protect the Guilty, 1970; Bent Copper, 1971; Grand Prix United States, 1971; A Man Will Be Kidnapped Tomorrow, 1972; Grand Prix Britain, 1973; The Double Run, 1973; Dick Knox at Le Mans, 1974; The Color of Violence, 1974; Three Layers of Guilt, 1975; Slow Down the World, 1976; Hostage to Death, 1977; The Anger of Fear, 1978; A Recipe for Murder, 1979; The Loss of the Culion, 1981; Guilt with Honour, 1982; A Sense of Loyalty, 1983; Presumption of Guilt, 1984; An Ideal Crime, 1985; A Question of Principle, 1986; A Crime Remembered, 1987; The Honourable Detective, 1988; A Conflict of Interests, 1989; An Illegal Solution, 1990; Deadly Reunion, 1991; Twisted Justice, 1992; Judgement Deferred, 1993; The Bitter Bite, 1994; The Price of Failure, 1995; Loyal Disloyalty, 1996, A Web of Circumstances 1997, The Cost of Innocence 1998, An Honest Betrayal 1999, Murder Will Out 2000, Lookingglass Justice 2001, A Truthful Injustice 2002. As Hastings Draper: Wiggery Pokery, 1956; Wigged and Gowned, 1958; Brief Help, 1961. As Roderic Graeme: Brandy Ahoy!, 1951; Concerning Blackshirt, 1952; Where's Brandy?, 1953; Blackshirt Wins the Trick, 1953; Blackshirt Passes By, 1953; Salute to Blackshirt, 1954; Brandy Goes a Cruising, 1954; The Amazing Mr Blackshirt, 1955; Blackshirt Meets the Lady, 1956; Paging Blackshirt, 1957; Blackshirt Helps Himself, 1958; Double for Blackshirt, 1958; Blackshirt Sets the Pace, 1959; Blackshirt Sees it Through, 1960; Blackshirt Finds Trouble, 1961; Blackshirt Takes the Trail, 1962; Blackshirt on the Spot, 1963; Call for Blackshirt, 1963; Blackshirt Saves the Day, 1964; Danger for Blackshirt, 1965; Blackshirt at Large, 1966; Blackshirt in Peril, 1967; Blackshirt Stirs Things Up, 1969. As Graham Hastings: Twice Checked, 1959; Deadly Game, 1961. *Address:* Apdo 5, Ca Na Paiaia, 07460 Pollensa, Mallorca, Spain.

JELINEK, Elfriede; Author, Dramatist and Poet; b. 20 Oct. 1946, Mürzzuschlag, Austria; m. Gottfried Hüngsberg. *Education:* Piano and Organ, Vienna Conservatory; Theatre and Art History, University of Vienna. *Career:* mem. Graz Writers' Asscn. *Publications:* Lisas Schatten, 1967; Wir sind lockvögel baby!, 1970; Michael: Ein Jugendbuch für die Infantilgesellschaft, 1973; Die Liebhaberinnen, 1975; Bukolit, 1979; Ende: gedichte, 1966–1968, 1980; Die Ausgesperrten, 1980; Die Klavierspielerin, 1983; Burgtheater, 1984; Clara S, 1984; Was geschah, nachdem Nora ihren Mann verlassen hatte oder Stützen der Gesellschaft, 1984; Oh Wildnis, oh Schutz vor ihr, 1985; Krankeit oder Moderne Frauen, 1987; Lust, 1989; Wolken: Heim, 1990; Malina, 1991; Totenauberg, 1991; Die Kinder der Toten, 1995; Gier, 2000. *Honours:* Prize for Poetry and Prose, Innsbrucker Jugendkulturwoche, 1969; National Scholarship for Writers, Austria, 1972; Roswitha von Gandersheim Memorial Medal, 1979; Drehbuchpreis, Ministry of the Interior, Austria, 1979; Heinrich Böll Prize, 1986; Styrian Literature Prize, 1987; Bremen Prize for Literature, Rudolf Alexander Schroder Foundation, 1996; Büchner Prize, 1998; Dramatist of the Year, Festival of Theatre of Muelheim and der Ruhr, 2002. *Address:* Sendlingerstr 43, 80331 Munich, Germany; Jupiterweg 40, 1140 Vienna, Austria.

JELLICOE, (Patricia) Ann, OBE; dramatist and director; b. 15 July 1927, Middlesborough, Yorkshire, England; m. 1st C. E. Knight-Clarke 1950 (divorced 1961); m. 2nd Roger Mayne 1962; one s. one d. *Education:* Polam Hall, Darlington, Queen Margaret's, York, Central School of Speech and Drama. *Career:* Actress, stage man., and dir, 1947–51; Founder-Dir, Cockpit Theatre Club, 1952–54; Teacher and Dir of Plays, Central School of Speech and Drama, 1954–56; Literary Man., Royal Court Theatre, 1973–75; Founder-Dir, 1979–85, Pres., 1986, Colway Theatre Trust. *Publications:* Plays: The Sport of My Mad Mother, 1958; The Knack, 1962; Shelley or The Idealist, 1966; The Rising Generation, 1969; The Giveaway, 1970; 3 Jelliplays, 1975. Other: Some Unconscious Influences in the Theatre, 1967; Shell Guide to Devon (with Roger Mayne), 1975; Community Plays: How to Put Them On, 1987. *Address:* Colway Manor, Lyme Regis, Dorset DT7 3HD, England.

JENCKS, Charles Alexander; writer, architect and academic; b. 21 June 1939, Baltimore, MD, USA; m. Margaret Keswick; three s. one d. *Education:* BA, 1961, BA, MA, 1965, Harvard University; PHP, University of London. *Career:* Editorial Adviser, Architectural Design, London, 1979. *Publications:* Ad Hocism, 1972; Modern Movements in Architecture, 1973; Le Corbusier and the Tragic View of Architecture, 1974; The Language of Post Modern Architecture, 1977; Daydream Houses of Los Angeles, 1978; Late Modern Architecture, 1980; Architecture Today, 1982; The New Paradigm in Architecture: The Language of Post-Modernism, 2002. Contributions: Architectural Design; TLS; Encounter. *Honours:* Melbourne Oration, 1974; Boston Lectures, RSA. *Address:* Architectural Asscn, 36 Bedford Square, London WC1, England.

JENKINS, Beverly; Writer; b. 15 Feb. 1951, Detroit, Michigan, USA; m. Mark Jenkins, one s. one d. *Education:* Michigan State University. *Career:* Assoc., Michigan State University Graduate Library, 1974–80; Founded theatre company, Michigan State University; Poetry readings in library shows, East Lansing, MI; Librarian, Belleville, MI; mem. Romance Writers Asscn. *Publications:* Night Song, 1994; Vivid, 1995; Indigo, 1996; Topaz, 1997. *Honours:* Night Song named a Waldenbooks Bestseller, 1994. *Address:* c/o Avon Books, 1350 Avenue of the Americas, New York, NY 10019, USA.

JENKINS, Catherine Anne May, BA, MA; writer and poet; b. 18 Feb. 1962, Hamilton, ON, Canada. *Education:* Trent University, Peterborough, ON. *Career:* mem. The Writers' Union of Canada; Eds' Asscn of Canada. *Publications:* Submerge (chapbook) 1997, Written in the Skin (anthology, contributor) 1998, Blood, Love and Boomerangs (poems) 1999, Swimming in the Ocean (novel) 2002; contrib. to Descant, Pottersfield Portfolio, Lichen, Rampike, Queen Street Quarterly, Room of One's Own, Blood and Aphorisms, Carleton Arts Review, Quill and Quire, The Toronto Star, The Globe and Mail, Dream Catcher, Magma Poetry Magazine, Poetry Croydon, Books in Canada, Canadian Bookseller. *E-mail:* solidus@sympatico.ca. *Website:* www.catherinejenkins.com.

JENKINS, (John) Robin, BA; retd teacher and writer; b. 11 Sept. 1912, Cambusland, Lanarkshire, England. *Education:* Glasgow University. *Career:* Teacher, Gjazi College, Khabul, 1957–59, British Institute, Barcelona, 1959–61, Gaya School, Sabah, 1963–68. *Publications:* Go Gaily Sings the Lark, 1951; Happy for the Child, 1953; The Thistle and the Grail, 1954; The Cone-Gatherers, 1955; Guests of War, 1956; The Missionaries, 1957; The Changeling, 1958; Love is a Fervent Fire, 1959; Some Kind of Grace, 1960; Dust on the Paw, 1961; The Tiger of Gold, 1962; A Love of Innocence, 1963; The Sardana Dancers, 1964; A Very Scotch Affair, 1968; The Holly Tree, 1969; The Expatriates, 1971; A Toast to the Lord, 1972; A Figure of Fun, 1974; A Would-Be-Saint, 1978; Fergus Lamont, 1979; The Awakening of George Darroch, 1985; Poverty Castle, 1991. *Address:* Fairhaven, Toward by Dunoon, Argyll PA23 7UE, Scotland.

JENKINS, Simon David; Journalist, Ed. and Writer; b. 10 June 1943, Birmingham, England; m. Gayle Hunnicutt 1978; one s. one step-s. *Education:* BA, St John's College, Oxford. *Career:* Staff, Country Life Magazine, 1965; News Ed., Times Educational Supplement, 1966–68; Leader-Writer, Columnist, Features Ed., 1968–71, Ed., 1977–78, Evening Standard; Insight Ed., Sunday Times, 1974–76; Political Ed., The Economist, 1979–86; Dir, The Municipal Journal, 1980–90, Faber and Faber Ltd., 1981–90; Columnist, Sunday Times, 1986–90, The Spectator, 1992–95; Ed., 1990–92, Columnist, 1992–, The Times. *Publications:* A City at Risk, 1971; Landlords to London, 1974; Newspapers: The Power and the Money, 1979; The Companion Guide to Outer London, 1981; Images of Hampstead, 1982; The Battle for the Falklands, 1983; With Respect, Ambassador, 1985; The Market for Glory, 1986; The Selling of Mary Davies and Other Writings, 1993; Against the Grain, 1994; Accountable to None: The Tory Nationalization of Britain, 1995; The Thousand Best Churches in England, 1999; England's Thousand Best Houses, 2003. *Honours:* Hon. Doctorates; Rio

Tinto David Memorial Prize, 1998. *Address:* c/o The Times, 1 Pennington St, London E98 1TT, England; 174 Regents Park Rd, London NW1, England.

JENKINS, Terence Andrew, BA, PhD; historian, writer and editor; b. 30 May 1958, England. *Education:* University of East Anglia, University of Cambridge. *Career:* British Acad. Postdoctoral Fellow, University of Cambridge, 1987–90; Lecturer, University of East Anglia, Norwich, 1990–91, 1992–93, 1995–96, University of Exeter, 1991–92, University of Bristol, 1996–97; Senior Research Officer, History of Parliament, London, 1998–; mem. FRHistS. *Publications:* Gladstone, Whiggery, and the Liberal Party, 1874–1886, 1988; The Parliamentary Diaries of Sir John Trelawny (ed.), Vol. 1, 1858–1865, 1990, Vol. 2, 1868–1873, 1994; The Liberal Ascendency, 1830–1886, 1994; Disraeli and Victorian Conservatism, 1996; Parliament, Party, and Politics in Victorian Britain, 1996; Sir Robert Peel, 1999; Britain: A Short History, 2001. Contributions: periodicals including: Historical Journal; English Historical Review; History Today; Parliamentary History. *Honours:* Prince Consort Prize for History, for Gladstone, Whiggery, and the Liberal Party, 1874–1886, University of Cambridge, 1988. *Address:* History of Parliament, Wedgwood House, 15 Woburn Square, London WC1H 0NS, England. *E-mail:* tjenkins@histparl.ac.uk.

JENS, Walter; academic, writer, dramatist, critic and translator; b. 8 March 1923, Hamburg, Germany; m. Inge Puttfarcken 1951; two s. *Education:* University of Hamburg; University of Freiburg im Breisgau. *Career:* docent, 1949–56, Prof. of Classical Philology and Rhetoric, 1956–88, Prof. Emeritus, 1988–, University of Tübingen; Visiting Prof., University of Stockholm, 1964, University of Vienna, 1984; mem. Akademie der Künste, Berlin-Brandenburg, pres., 1989–97, hon. pres., 1997–; Deutsche Akademie für Sprache und Dichtung; Freie Akademie der Künste, Hamburg; PEN, Germany, pres., 1976–82, hon. pres., 1982–. *Publications:* Nein: Die Welt der Angeklagten (novel), 1950; Der Blinde (novel), 1951; Vergessene Gesichter (novel), 1952; Der Mann, der nicht alt werden wollte (novel), 1955; Die Stichomythie in der frühen griechischen Tragodie, 1955; Hofmannsthal und die Griechen, 1955; Das Testament des Odysseus (novel), 1957; Statt einer Literaturgeschichte, 1957; Die Götter sind sterblich, 1959; Deutsche Literatur der Gegenwart, 1961; Herr Meister: Dialog über einen Roman, 1963; Von deutscher Rede, 1969; Die Verschwörung (TV play), 1970; Am Anfang der Stall: Am Ende der Galgen, 1972; Der barmherzige Samariter, 1973; Der tödliche Schlag (TV play), 1974; Der Prozess Judas (novel), 1975; Republikanische Reden, 1976; Zur Antike, 1979; Ort der Handlung ist Deutschland, 1981; Der Untergang (play), 1982; In Sachen Lessing, 1983; Kanzel und Katheder, 1984; Dichtung und Religion (with Hans Küng), 1985; Die Friedensfrau, 1986; Theologie und Literatur, 1986; Deutsche Lebensläufe, 1987; Feldzüge eines Republikanders, 1988; Juden und Christen in Deutschland, 1988; Reden, 1989; Die Zeit ist erfüllt: Die Stunde ist da, 1990; Und ein Gebot ging aus, 1991; Die sieben letzen Worte am Kreuz, 1992; Die Friedensfrau, 1992; Mythen der Dichter, 1993; Am Anfang das Wort, 1993; Menschenwürdig sterben, 1995; Macht der Erinnerung, 1997; Aus gegebenem Anlass, 1998; Wer am besten red't ist der reinste Mensch, 2000. *Honours:* Prix Amis de la Liberté, 1951; Lessing Prize, 1968; University of Tübingen Medal, 1979; Heine Prize, 1981; Theodor Heuss Prize, 1988; Austrian State Prize, 1990. *Address:* Sonnenstr 5, 72076 Tübingen, Germany.

JENSEN, Liz; British novelist; b. Oxfordshire; two s. *Career:* fmrly journalist in the Far East, BBC journalist and producer, sculptor. *Publications:* novels: Egg Dancing 1995, Ark Baby 1998, The Paper Eater 2000, War Crimes for the Home 2002, The Ninth Life of Louis Drax 2004. *Address:* c/o Bloomsbury Publishing, 38 Soho Square, London, W1D 3HB, England. *Website:* www.lizjensen.com.

JENSEN, Ruby Jean; Author; b. 1 March 1930, USA; m. Vaughn Jensen, one d. *Publications:* The House That Samuel Built, 1974; The Seventh All Hallows Eve, 1974; Dark Angel, 1978; Hear the Children Cry, 1981; Such a Good Baby, 1982; Mama, 1983; Home Sweet Home, 1985; Annabelle, 1987; Chain Letter, 1987; House of Illusions, 1988; Jump Rope, 1988; Death Stone, 1989; Baby Dolly, 1991; Celia, 1991; The Reckoning, 1992; The Living Exile, 1993; The Haunting, 1994.

JERSILD, Per Christian; writer; b. 1935, Katrineholm, Sweden; m. Ulla Flyxe 1960; two s. *Education:* Karolinska Institute. *Career:* Staff, Institute of Social Medicine, Stockholm, 1963–66; Stockholm Civil Service Welfare Dept; social psychiatrist, Huddinge hospital, 1974–78; Asst Prof. of Social and Preventive Medicine and medical adviser, National Govt Administration Board; writer, 1977–. *Publications:* Räknelära (short stories), 1960; Till Varmare Länder, 1961; Ledig Lördag, 1963; Calvinols Resa Genom Världen, 1965; Pyton (with Lars Ardelius), 1966; Prins Valiant Ock Konsum, 1966; Till Varmare Länder, 1967; Obs! Sammanträde Pågår, 1967; Sammanträde Pågor (TV play), 1967; Grisjakten, 1968; Fänrik Duva, 1969; Vi Ses I Song My, 1970; Drömpojken: En Paranoid Historia (Recovery in Schizophrenia), 1970; Uppror Bland Marsinen, 1972; Stumpen, 1973; Djurdoktorn (The Animal Doctor), 1973; Den Elektriska Kaninen, 1974; Barnens Ö (Children's Island), 1976; Moskvafeber, 1977; Babels Hus (House of Babel), 1978; Gycklarnas Hamlet. Och Monologerna Balans Och En Rolig Halvtimme, 1980; En Levande Själ (A Living Soul), 1980; Professionella Bekännelser, 1981; Efter Floden (After the Flood), 1982; Lit De Parade, 1983; Den Femtionde Frälsaren, 1984; Geniernas Återkomst, 1987; Svarta Villan, 1987; Ryktet Smittar: En Monolog An Aids, 1988; Ett Ensamt Öra, 1989; Fem Hjärtan In En Tändsticsask, 1989; Humpty-Dumpty's Fall, En Livsåskådsningsbok, 1990; Alice Och Nisse I Lustiga Huset, 1991; Holgerssons, 1991; Röda Hund, 1991; Hymir, 1993; En Gammal Kärlek, 1995; En Gammal Kylskåp Och Enförkyld Hund, 1995; Sena Sagor, 1998; Darwins Ofullbordade: Om Människans Biologiska Natur, 1999; Ljusets Drottning, 2000; Hundra Fristående Kolumner I Dagens Nyheter, 2002. Contributions: Dagens Nyheter; FIB/Kulturfront. *Honours:* Swedish Society for Promotion of Literature grand prize, 1981; De Nio prize, 1998. *Address:* c/o University of Nebraska Press, 233 N Eighth Street, Lincoln, NE 68588-0255, USA.

JESSUP, Frances; Novelist, Poet and Playwright; b. 29 July 1936, England; m. Clive Turner, 1960, divorced 1996, one s., three d. *Education:* BA, Philosophy, King's College, University of London, 1958. *Career:* Organiser, Theatre Writing, Haslemere, UNA, 1992; Programme Secretary, Wey Poets, 2000; Healthy Planet Poems, Electric Theatre, 2001; Signing the Charter, Haslemere UNA Branch Theatre; mem. PEN. *Publications:* The Fifth Child's Conception 1970, Deutsch Penguin 1972, The Car: A Fable for Voices 1999, Three Short Plays. Contributions: anthologies and magazines including Hard Lines 3, Acumen, Weyfarers. *Honours:* First Prize for Fiction and Poetry, Moor Park College, 1972; UNA Trust Award, 1988; University of Surrey Arts Committee Literary Festival Award, 1991. *Address:* 20 Heath Rd, Haslemere, GU27 3QN England. *E-mail:* francesjess@clara.co.uk.

JETER, K. W.; Novelist; b. 1950, Los Angeles, CA, USA; m. Geri Jeter. *Education:* BA, MA, San Francisco State University. *Publications:* Seeklight, 1975; The Dreamfields, 1976; Morlock Night, 1979; Soul Eater, 1983; Dr Adder, 1984; The Glass Hammer, 1985; Night Vision, 1985; Death Arms, 1987; Infernal Devices: A Mad Victorian Fantasy, 1987; Mantis, 1987; Dark Seeker, 1987; Farewell Horizontal, 1989; In the Land of the Dead, 1989; The Night Man, 1990; Madlands, 1991; Wolf Flow, 1992; Dark Horizon: Alien Nation, 1993; Warped: Star Trek, Deep Space Nine, 1995; Blade Runner 2: The Edge of Human, 1995; Blade Runner: Replicant Night, 1996. *Address:* c/o Russ Galen, Scott Meredith Literary Agency, 845 Third Ave, New York, NY 10022, USA.

JHA, Raj Kamal; Indian writer and journalist; *Executive Editor, Indian Express, New Delhi;* b. 1966, Kolkata. *Education:* Indian Inst. of Technology, Kharagpur, Univ. of Southern California, USA. *Career:* journalist, The Statesman, India Today; Deputy Ed., currently Exec. Ed., Indian Express, New Delhi. *Publications:* novels: The Blue Bedspread 1999, If You are Afraid of Heights 2003. *Address:* c/o The Indian Express Group, C-6, Qutab Institutional Area, New Delhi 110 016, India. *E-mail:* editor@expressindia.com. *Website:* www.expressindia.com.

JHABVALA, Ruth Prawer, CBE, BA, MA, DLitt, FRSL; British/American writer; b. 7 May 1927, Cologne, Germany; m. C. S. H. Jhabvala 1951; three d. *Education:* University of London. *Career:* mem. Authors' Guild, Writers' Guild of America. *Film screenplays:* Shakespeare Wallah, 1965; The Guru, 1969; Bombay Talkie, 1971; Autobiography of a Princess, 1975; Roseland, 1977; Hullabaloo Over Georgie and Bonnie's Pictures, 1978; The Europeans, 1979; Jane Austen in Manhattan, 1980; Quartet, 1981; The Bostonians, 1984; A Room With a View, 1986; Madame Sousatzka, 1988; Mr and Mrs Bridge, 1989; Howard's End, 1992; The Remains of the Day, 1993; Jefferson in Paris, 1995; Surviving Picasso, 1996; The Golden Bowl, 2000. *Publications:* Fiction: To Whom She Will, 1955; Nature of Passion, 1956; Esmond in India, 1958; The Householder, 1960; Get Ready for Battle, 1962; A Backward Place, 1962; A New Dominion, 1971; Heat and Dust, 1975; In Search of Love and Beauty, 1983; Three Continents, 1987; Poet and Dancer, 1993; Shards of Memory, 1995; My Nine Lives: Chapters of a Possible Past 2004. Short Stories: Like Birds, Like Fishes, 1963; A Stronger Climate, 1968; An Experience of India, 1970; How I Became a Holy Mother, 1976; Out of India: Selected Stories, 1986; East into Upper East, 1998. *Honours:* Booker Prize, 1975; Guggenheim Fellowship, 1976; Neil Gunn International Fellowship, 1979; John D. and Catherine T. MacArthur Foundation Fellowship, 1984–89; Acad. Awards for Best Screenplay, 1987, 1993; American Acad. of Arts and Letters Literature Award, 1992. *Address:* 400 E 52nd Street, New York, NY 10022, USA.

JIANG AN DAO (see Parkin, Andrew Terence Leonard).

JIANG ZILONG; Chinese writer; *Vice-Chairman, Chinese Writers' Association;* b. 2 June 1941, Cang Xian, Hebei; m. Zhang Qinglian 1968; one s. one d. *Career:* worker Tianjin Heavy Machinery Plant 1958; navy conscript 1960–65; Vice-Chair. Chinese Writers' Assn 1996–. *Publications:* A New Station Master 1965, One Day for the Chief of the Bureau of Electromechanics 1976, Manager Qiao Assumes Office 1979, Developer 1980, Diary of a Plant Secretary 1980, All the Colours of the Rainbow 1983, Yan-Zhao Dirge 1985, Serpent Deity 1986, Jiang Zilong Works Collection (eight vols) 1996, Human Vigour 2000, Ren Qi 2000, Empty Hole 2001. *Honours:* Nat. Short Story Prize 1979. *Address:* No. 7 Dali Road, Heping District, Tianjin (Home); Tianjin Writers' Association, Tianjin, People's Republic of China. *Telephone:* (22) 23304153 (Office); (22) 23306250 (Home). *Fax:* (22) 23304159 (Office); (22) 23306250 (Home). *E-mail:* jzltj@hotmail.com (Home).

JILES, Paulette; Poet and Writer; b. 1943, Salem, MO, USA. *Education:* BA, University of Missouri, 1968. *Career:* Teacher, David Thompson University, Nelson, BC, 1984–85; Writer-in-Residence, Phillips Acad., Andover, Massachusetts, 1987–; mem. Writers' Union of Canada. *Publications:* Poetry: Waterloo Express, 1973; Celestial Navigation, 1983; The Jesse James Poems, 1987; Flying Lessons: Selected Poems, 1995. Other: Sitting in the Club Car Drinking Rum & Karma-Kola, 1986; The Late Great Human Roadshow, 1986; Blackwater, 1988; Song to the Rising Sun, 1989; Cousins, 1991; North Spirit, 1995; Enemy Women, 2001. *Honours:* Governor-General's Award, 1984; Gerald Lampert Award, 1984; Pat Lowther Award, 1984; ACTRA Award for Best Original Drama, 1989.

JIN YONG; Chinese writer, journalist and newspaper publisher; b. (Louis Cha Liang Yong), 1923, Haining, Zhejiang Prov. *Education:* Dongwu Law School. *Career:* writer, Ta Kung Pao newspaper, Shanghai, later Hong Kong; later became film reviewer and screenwriter; first martial arts novel serialised in Xin Wan Bao newspaper, Hong Kong 1955; f. newspaper Ming Bao Daily, Hong Kong; ceased writing novels in 1972. *Publications:* (titles translated) Legend of the Book and the Sword, The Sword Stained With Royal Blood (vol. I Crimson Saber Saga), Fox Volant of the Snowy Mountain, The Young Flying Fox, Legend of the Condor Heroes (vol. I Condor trilogy), Return of the Condor Heroes (vol. II Condor trilogy), Heavenly Sword Dragon Saber (vol. III Condor trilogy), Demi Gods Semi Devils, Way of the Heroes, Requiem of Ling Sing, The Proud Smiling Wanderer, The Duke of Mount Deer (vol. II Crimson Saber Saga). *Address:* c/o The Chinese University Press, The Chinese University of Hong Kong, Sha Tin, N.T., Hong Kong. *Website:* www.chineseupress.com.

JOAQUIN, Nick; Novelist, Poet, Playwright and Essayist; b. 4 May 1917, Paco, Manila, Philippines. *Career:* proofreader, Philippines Free Press, later contributing ed. and essayist (under pen name Quijano de Manila); journalist, Philippines Free Press, –1970; Ed., Asia-Philippine Leader; Ed., Philippine Graphic magazine; Publisher, Women's Weekly. *Publications:* Prose and Poems, 1952; The Woman Who Had Two Navels, 1961; Selected Stories, 1962; La Naval de Manila and Other Essays, 1964; A Portrait of the Artist as Filipino (play), 1966; Tropical Gothic, 1972; Reportage on Crime, 1977; Reportage on Lovers, 1977; Nora Aunor and Other Profiles, 1977; A Question of Heroes, 1977; Stories for Groovy Kids, 1979; Tropical Baroque, 1979; Manila: Sin City and Other Chronicles, 1980; Reportage on the Marcoses, 1979; The Ballad of the Five Battles, 1981; Cave and Shadows, 1983; The Aquinos of Tarlac (biog.), 1983; Collected Verse, 1987; Manila, My Manila, 1990; La Orosa: The Dance-Drama That is Leonor Goquingco, 1994; One Woman's Liberating: The Life and Career of Dr Estefania Aldaba-Lim, 1996. Contributions: Tribune; numerous anthologies. *Honours:* Jose Garcia Villa's honour roll, 1940; First prize, Philippines Free Press Short Story Contest, 1949; First prize, Palance Memorial Award, 1957–58; Republic Cultural Heritage Award, 1961; Harry Stonehill Award for the Novel, 1961; Araw ng Maynila Award, 1963; Ramon Magsaysay Award for Literature, Broadcast and Journalism, 1966; National Artist Award, 1976. *Address:* c/o De La Salle University Press, Inc, #2504 Leon Guinto St, Malate 1004, Manila, Philippines.

JOFFE, Josef, PhD; German journalist, editor and international relations scholar; *Editor, Die Zeit*; b. 15 March 1944. *Education:* Harvard Univ. *Career:* Foreign and Editorial Page Dir Suddeutsche Zeitung; foreign correspondent, Die Zeit newspaper, Ed. and Publr 2000–; Visiting Lecturer, Harvard Univ., Princeton Univ., Stanford Univ., Dartmouth Univ., USA; Contrib. The National Interest, Foreign Affairs; Assoc. Olin Inst. for Strategic Studies, Harvard Univ.; Research Fellow, Hoover Inst., Stanford Univ.; mem. Editorial Bd International Security. *Publications include:* The Limited Partnership: Europe, the United States and the Burdens of Alliance 1987, The Great Powers 1998; numerous articles in scholarly journals and chapters in books. *Honours:* Order of Merit, Germany 1998; hon. degree (Swarthmore) 2002. *Address:* Die Zeit, Speersort 1, Pressehaus, 20095 Hamburg, Germany (Office). *Telephone:* (40) 32800 (Office). *Fax:* (40) 32711 (Office). *E-mail:* gentsch@zeit.de (Office). *Website:* www.zeit.de (Office).

JOHN, Katherine (see Watkins, Karen Christna).

JOHNS, Kenneth (see Bulmer, Henry Kenneth).

JOHNSON, Alison Findlay; Author; b. 19 Nov. 1947, Stafford, England; m. Andrew J. D. Johnson, 1973, one d. *Education:* MA, Aberdeen University, 1968; BPhil, University of Oxford, 1970. *Publications:* A House by the Shore, 1986; Scarista Style, 1987; Children of Disobedience, 1989; Islands in the Sound, 1989; The Wicked Generation, 1992. Contributions: West Highland Press; The Times. *Address:* c/o Vivien Green, 43 Doughty St, London WC1N 2LF, England.

JOHNSON, Boris (Alexander Boris de Pfeffel); British politician and journalist; *Shadow Minister for the Arts; Editor, The Spectator*; b. 19 June 1964; m. 1st Allegra Mostyn-Owen; m. 2nd Marina Wheeler 1993; two s. two d. *Education:* Eton Coll. and Balliol Coll., Oxford. *Career:* journalist with The Times 1987–88; EC Corresp., The Daily Telegraph 1989–94, Asst Ed. and Chief Political Columnist 1994–99; Ed. The Spectator 1999–; MP (Conservative) for Henley 2001–; Vice-Chair. Conservative Party, Shadow Minister for the Arts 2004–. *Publication:* Friends, Voters, Countrymen 2001. *Address:* The Spectator, 56 Doughty Street, London, WC1N 2LL, (Office); House of Commons, London, SW1A 0AA, England. *Telephone:* (20) 7405-1706 (Office). *Fax:* (20) 7242-0603 (Office). *E-mail:* editor@spectator.co.uk (Office). *Website:* www.spectator.co.uk (Office).

JOHNSON, Charles (Richard); Prof. of English and Writer; b. 23 April 1948, Evanston, IL, USA; m. Joan New, June 1970, one s. one d. *Education:* BA, 1971, MA, 1973, Southern Illinois University; Postgraduate Studies, SUNY at Stony Brook, 1973–76. *Career:* Asst Prof., 1976–79, Assoc. Prof., 1979–82, Prof. of English, 1982–, University of Washington, Seattle. *Publications:* Faith and the Good Thing, 1974; Oxherding Tale, 1982; The Sorcerer's Apprentice: Tales and Conjurations, 1986; Being and Race: Black Writing Since 1970, 1988; Middle Passage, 1990; All This and Moonlight, 1990; In Search of a Voice (with Ron Chernow), 1991; Dreamer, 1998. *Honours:* Governor's Award for Literature, State of Washington, 1983; National Book Award, 1990. *Address:* c/o Dept of English, University of Washington, Seattle, WA 98105, USA.

JOHNSON, Colin; Novelist; b. 23 July 1939, Beverley, WA, Australia. *Career:* Lecturer, University of Queensland, St Lucia. *Publications:* Wild Cat Falling, 1965; Long Live Sandawara, 1979; Before the Invasion: Aboriginal Life to 1788, 1980; Doctor Wooreddy's Prescription for Enduring the End of the World, 1983; Doin' Wildcat, 1988; Dalwurra: The Black Bittern, 1988; Writing from the Fringe, 1990. *Honours:* Wieckhard Prize, 1979; Western Australia Literary Award, 1989.

JOHNSON, David; historian; b. 26 Aug. 1927, Meir, Staffordshire, England. *Education:* Repton, Sandhurst. *Publications:* Sabre General, 1959; Promenade in Champagne, 1960; Lanterns in Gascony, 1965; A Candle in Aragon, 1970; Regency Revolution, 1974; Napoleon's Cavalry and its Leaders, 1978; The French Cavalry 1792–1815, 1989. Contributions: The Armourer (1914: The Riddle of the Marne); Skirmish Magazine.

JOHNSON, Denis; Writer and Poet; b. 1949, Munich, Germany. *Publications:* Poetry: The Man Among the Seals, 1969; Inner Weather, 1976; The Incognito Lounge and Other Poems, 1982; The Veil, 1987; The Throne of the Third Heaven of the Nations Millennium General Assembly: Poems Collected and New, 1995. Other: Angels, 1983; Fiskadoro, 1985; The Stars at Noon, 1986; Resuscitation of a Hanged Man, 1991; Jesus' Son, 1993; Already Dead: A Californian Gothic, 1997; The Name of the World, 2000; Seek: Reports from the Edges of America & Beyond, 2001. *Honours:* Whiting Writers' Award, 1986; American Acad. of Arts and Letters Literature Award, 1993; several grants. *Address:* c/o Robert Cornfield, 145 W 79th St, New York, NY 10024, USA.

JOHNSON, Diane Lain, AA, BA, MA, PhD; American writer; b. 28 April 1934, Moline, IL; m. 1st B. Lamar Johnson Jr 1953; four c.; m. 2nd John Frederick Murray 1969. *Education:* Stephens College, University of Utah, University of California at Los Angeles. *Career:* Asst Prof. to Prof. of English, University of California at Davis 1968–87; mem. International PEN, Writers' Guild of America. *Publications:* Fair Game 1965, Loving Hands at Home 1968, Burning 1971, Lesser Lives: The True History of the First Mrs Meredith 1972, The Shadow Knows 1975, Lying Low 1978, Terrorists and Novelists 1982, Dashiell Hammett: A Life 1983, Persian Nights 1987, Health and Happiness 1990, Natural Opium: Some Travelers' Tales 1993, Le Divorce 1997, Le Mariage 2000, L'Affaire 2003; contrib. to newspapers, periodicals and magazines. *Honours:* Guggenheim Fellowship, 1977–78; Rosenthal Award, 1979, Harold and Mildred Strauss Living Stipend, 1988–92, American Acad. of Arts and Letters; Los Angeles Times Medal, 1994. *Address:* 24 Edith Street, San Francisco, CA 94133, USA.

JOHNSON, Elizabeth Ann; Theologian and Writer; b. 6 Dec. 1941, New York, NY, USA. *Education:* BA, Brentwood College, 1964; MA, Manhattan College, 1970; PhD, Catholic University of America, 1981. *Career:* Prof. of Theology, Catholic University of America, 1981–91; Distinguished Prof. of Theology, Fordham University, 1991–; mem. Catholic Theological Society of America, Pres., 1996–97; American Acad. of Religion; College Theology Society; American Theological Society. *Publications:* Consider Jesus: Waves of Renewal in Christology 1990, She Who Is: The Mystery of God in Feminist Theological Discourse 1992, Women, Earth, and Creator Spirit 1993, Friends of God and Prophets: A Feminist Theological Reading of the Communion of Saints 1998, The Church Women Want 2002, Truly Our Sister: A Theology of Mary in the Communion of Saints 2003. Contributions: scholarly books and journals. *Honours:* Grawemeyer Award in Religion, University of Louisville, and Crossroad Women's Studies Award, 1992; Hon. Doctorates, St Mary's College, 1992, Maryknoll School of Theology, 1994, Chicago Theological Union, 1997, Siena College, 1998; Hon. DHumLitt (Le Moyne Coll. Syracuse NY 1999, St Joseph Coll. Brooklyn NY 2001), Hon. Dr of Pedagogy (Manhattan Coll. Riverdale NY 2002), Hon. DD (Jesuit School of Theology Berkeley Calif. 2003). *Address:* Dept of Theology, Fordham University, Bronx, NY 10458, USA.

JOHNSON, George (Laclede); Writer; b. 20 Jan. 1952, Fayetteville, AR, USA. *Education:* BA, University of New Mexico, 1975; MA, American University, 1979. *Publications:* Architects of Fear, 1984; Machinery of the Mind, 1986; In the Places of Memory, 1991. Contributions: newspapers and magazines. *Honours:* Alicia Patterson Journalism Fellow, 1984. *Address:* c/o International Creative Management, 40 W 57th St, New York, NY 10019, USA.

JOHNSON, Haynes (Bonner); Journalist, Television Commentator, Prof. of Journalism and Writer; b. 9 July 1931, New York, NY, USA; m. Julia Ann Erwin, 21 Sept. 1954, divorced, two s. three d. *Education:* BJ, University of Missouri, 1952; MS, University of Wisconsin, 1956. *Career:* Reporter, Wilmington News-Journal, DE, 1956–57; Reporter to Special Assignments Correspondent, Washington Star, 1957–69; Commentator, Washington Week in Review, 1967–94, The News Hour with Jim Lehrer, 1994–, PBS TV; National Correspondent, 1969–73, Asst Managing Ed., 1973–77, Columnist, 1977–94, Washington Post; Ferris Prof. of Journalism and Public Affairs, Princeton University, 1975–78; Guest Scholar, Brookings Institution, 1987–91; Regents Lecturer, University of California at Berkeley, 1992; Prof. of Political Commentary and Journalism, George Washington University, 1994–96; Prof. of Journalism, University of Maryland at College Park, 1998–; mem. National Acad. of Public Administration. *Publications:* Dusk at the Mountain, 1963; The Bay of Pigs, 1964; Fulbright: The Dissenter (with Bernard M. Gwertzman), 1968; Army in Anguish (with George C. Wilson), 1972; Lyndon (with Richard Harwood), 1973; The Fall of a President (ed.), 1974; The Working White House, 1975; In the Absence of Power, 1980; The Landing (with Howard Simons), 1986; Sleepwalking Through History, 1991; Divided We Fall, 1994; The System (with David S. Broder), 1996; The Best of Times: America in the Clinton Years, 2001. *Honours:* Pulitzer Prize for National Reporting, 1966; Hon. Doctorates, Wheeling Jesuit University, 1997, University of Missouri, 1999. *Address:* 3900 Watson Pl. NW, Apt 3D, Washington, DC 20016, USA.

JOHNSON, John H.; American publisher; *Chairman and Publisher, Johnson Publishing Company Inc.*; b. 19 Jan. 1918, Arkansas; m. Eunice Johnson; one s. (deceased) one d. *Education:* DuSable High School and Chicago and Northwestern Univs. *Career:* Asst Ed. 1936, later Man. Ed. of employees' publication, Supreme Life Insurance Co. of America; CEO, Chair. Johnson Publishing Co. 1942–; f. Ebony 1945, Jet 1951; first Black businessman to be selected as one of the "ten outstanding young men of the year" by US Jr Chamber of Commerce 1951; accompanied Vice-Pres. Nixon at Ghana Independence celebrations 1957, appointed Special Amb. representing the US at Ivory Coast Independence celebrations 1961 and Kenya Independence ceremony 1963; Chair. and CEO Supreme Life Insurance Co.; Dir Marina City Bank of Chicago, Service Fed. Savings and Loan Asscn, Chicago, Greyhound Corpn, Zenith, Bell & Howell, Arthur D. Little Corpn, 20th Century-Fox Corpn, United Negro Coll. Fund, etc.; Trustee, Inst. of Int. Educ., Tuskegee Inst., Howard and Fisk Univs; Dir Chicago Asscn of Commerce. *Publication:* Succeeding Against the Odds 1989. *Honours:* Hon. LLD of several univs and colls; Horatio Alger Award 1966, named Publr of the Year by Magazine Publrs' Asscn 1972, Presidential Medal of Freedom 1996, Lifetime Achievement Award, American Advertising Foundation 1996 and numerous other awards. *Address:* 820 South Michigan Avenue, Chicago, IL 60605, USA. *Telephone:* (312) 322-9200. *Fax:* (312) 322-0918. *Website:* www.ebony.com.

JOHNSON, Linton Kwesi, BA; poet and writer; b. 24 Aug. 1952, Chapeltown, Jamaica. *Education:* Goldsmiths Coll., London. *Career:* family emigrated to London 1963; involved in Black Panther movement, London; wrote for NME and Melody Maker in 1970s and 1980s; regular TV/radio apppearances as an authority on reggae; C. Day-Lewis Fellowship 1977, Assoc. Fellow, Warwick Univ. 1985;. *Albums:* Dread Beat An' Blood, Forces of Victory, More Time. *Publications:* Voices of the Living and the Dead 1974, Dread Beat an' Blood 1975, Inglan is a Bitch 1980, Tings an' Times: Selected Poems 1991, Mi Revalueshanary Fren: Selected Poems 2002; contrib. to recordings, television. *Honours:* Hon. Fellow, Wolverhampton Polytechnic 1987, Goldsmiths Coll., London 2002; Italian literary awards 1990, 1998. *Address:* PO Box 623, Herne Hill, London, SE24 OLS, England.

JOHNSON, Mel (see Malzberg, Barry).

JOHNSON, Nora; Author; b. 31 Jan. 1933, Los Angeles, CA, USA; m. 1st Leonard Siwek, 1955; m. 2nd John A Milici, 1965, two s. two d. *Education:* BA, Smith College, 1954. *Career:* mem. Authors' Guild; PEN. *Publications:* The World of Henry Orient, 1958; A Step Beyond Innocence, 1961; Love Letter in the Dead Letter Office, 1966; Flashback, 1979; You Can Go Home Again, 1982; The Two of Us, 1984; Tender Offer, 1985; Uncharted Places, 1988; Perfect Together, 1991. Contributions: newspapers and magazines. *Honours:* McCall's Short Story Prize, 1962; O. Henry Award Story, 1982; New York Times Best Book Citations, 1982, 1984. *Address:* c/o PEN American Center, 568 Broadway, New York, NY 10012, USA.

JOHNSON, Paul (Bede); Historian, Journalist and Broadcaster; b. 2 Nov. 1928, Barton, England; m. Marigold Hunt 1957; three s. one d. *Education:* BA, Magdalen College, Oxford. *Career:* Asst Exec. Ed., Realites, Paris, 1952–55; Asst Ed., 1955–60, Deputy Ed., 1960–64, Ed., 1965–70, Dir, 1965–75, New Statesman; DeWitt Wallace Prof. of Communications, American Enterprise Institute, Washington, DC, 1980; Freelance Writer; Daily Mail Columnist; mem. Royal Commission on the Press, 1974–77; Cable Authority, 1984–. *Publications:* The Offshore Islanders, 1972; Elizabeth I: A Study in Power and Intellect, 1974; Pope John XXIII, 1975; A History of Christianity, 1976; Enemies of Society, 1977; The National Trust Book of British Castles, 1978; The Civilization of Ancient Egypt, 1978; Civilizations of the Holy Land, 1979; British Cathedrals, 1980; Ireland: Land of Troubles, 1980; The Recovery of Freedom, 1980; Pope John Paul II and the Catholic Restoration, 1982; History of the Modern World: From 1917 to the 1980s, 1984; The Pick of Paul Johnson, 1985; A History of the Jews, 1986; The Oxford Book of Political Anecdotes (ed.), 1986; The Intellectuals, 1989; The Birth of the Modern World Society, 1815–30, 1991; 20th Century Britain: Economic, Social and Cultural Change, 1994; Wake Up Britain!, 1994; The Quest for God, 1996; To Hell with Picasso and Other Essays, 1996; A History of the American People, 1997; The Renaissance, 2000; Napoleon, 2002; Art: A New History, 2003. *Honours:* Book of the Year Prize, Yorkshire Post, 1975; Francis Boyer Award for Services to Public Policy, 1979; Krag Award for Excellence, Literature, 1980. *Address:* 29 Newton Rd, London W2, England.

JOHNSON, (John) Stephen, MA, DPhil; writer; b. 3 June 1947, Mansfield, England. *Education:* University of Oxford. *Publications:* The Roman Fort of the Saxon Shore, 1976; Later Roman Britain, 1980; Late Roman Fortifications, 1983; Hadrian's Wall, 1989; Rome and its Empire, 1989. *Address:* 50 Holmdere Avenue, London SE24 9LF, England.

JOHNSON, Susan Ruth; Writer; b. 30 Dec. 1956, Brisbane, Australia; m. 1st John Patrick Burdett 1989 (divorced 1991); m. 2nd Leslie William Webb 1994; one s. *Education:* Clayfield College, Brisbane, 1974; BA, English and Journalism, Univ. of Queensland. *Career:* Journalist, The Courier-Mail, 1975, The Australian Women's Weekly, 1977–78, The Sun-Herald, 1980–81, The Sydney Morning Herald, 1981–82, The National Times, 1982–84; full-time writer, 1984–; resident, Keesing Studio, Cité International des Arts, Paris (awarded by Literature Bd, Australia Council) –1992; Ed., Saturday Extra, in The Age, 1999–2001; mem. Australian Society of Authors. *Publications:* Fiction: Messages from Chaos, 1987; Flying Lessons, 1990; A Big Life, 1993; Hungry Ghosts, 1996. Non-Fiction: A Better Woman (memoir), 1999. Edited: WomenLoveSex (short stories), 1996; Latitudes: New Writing from the North (with Mary Roberts), 1986. *Honours:* several fellowships awarded by Australia Council, 1986–92. *Address:* c/o Margaret Connolly and Assocs, POB 48, Paddington, NSW 2021, Australia. *E-mail:* sjreaders@hotmail.com. *Website:* www.abetterwoman.net.

JOHNSON, Terry; Dramatist and Screenwriter; b. 20 Dec. 1955, England. *Education:* BA, Drama, Univ. of Birmingham, 1976. *Publications:* Plays: Insignificance, 1982; Cries from the Mammal House, 1984; Unsuitable for Adults, 1985; Tuesday's Child (with Kate Lock), 1987; Imagine Drowning, 1991; Hysteria, 1993; Dead Funny, 1994; Cleo, Camping, Emmanuelle and Dick, 1998; The London Cuckolds, 1998; Hitchcock Blonde, 2003. Screenplays: Insignificance, 1985; Absolute Beginners (with others), 1986; Killing Time, 1985; Way Upstream, 1987. TV Screenplays: Time Trouble, 1985; Tuesday's Child (with Kate Lock), 1985; Way Upstream, 1987; 99-1 (with others), 1994; Blood and Water, 1995; The Bite, 1996; Cor Blimey!, 2000. *Honours:* Evening Standard Drama Award, 1983. *Literary Agent:* Curtis Brown Ltd, Haymarket House, 28–29 Haymarket, London, SW1Y 4SP, England. *Telephone:* (20) 7393-4400. *Fax:* (20) 7393-4401. *E-mail:* info@curtisbrown.co.uk. *Website:* www.curtisbrown.co.uk.

JOHNSON, William Stacy; Theologian and Lawyer; b. 13 July 1956, Pinehurst, NJ, USA. *Education:* AB, Davidson College, 1978; JD, Wake Forest University, 1981; MDiv, Union Theological Seminary, 1988; PhD, Harvard University, 1992. *Career:* Assoc. Prof. of Theology, Austin Presbyterian Theological Seminary, Austin, Texas, 1992–; Attorney-at-Law; mem. Karl Barth Society of North America; American Acad. of Religion; American Asscn for the Advancement of Science. *Publications:* Theology, History, and Culture (ed.), 1996; The Mystery of God: Karl Barth and the Postmodern Foundations of Theology, 1997. *Address:* Austin Presbyterian Theological Seminary, 100 E 27th St, Austin, TX 78705, USA. *E-mail:* wsjnson@ix.netcom.com.

JOHNSTON, George (Benson); Poet and Trans; b. 7 Oct. 1913, Hamilton, Ontario, Canada; m. Jeanne McRae, 1944, three s., three d. *Education:* BA, 1936, MA, 1945, University of Toronto. *Career:* Faculty, Dept of English, Mount Allison University, Sackville, New Brunswick, 1947–49, Carleton College, later University, Ottawa, 1949–79. *Publications:* Poetry: The Cruising Auk, 1959; Home Free, 1966; Happy Enough: Poems 1935–1972, 1972; Between, 1976; Taking a Grip, 1979; Auk Redivivus: Selected Poems, 1981; Ask Again, 1984; Endeared by Dark: The Collected Poems, 1990; What is to Come: Selected and New Poems, 1996. Prose: Carl: Portrait of a Painter, 1986. Translator: Over 10 vols, 1963–94. *Honours:* Hon. doctorates. *Address:* PO Box 1706, Huntingdon, QC J0S 1H0, Canada.

JOHNSTON, Jennifer; Author and Dramatist; b. 12 Jan. 1930, Dublin, Ireland; m. 1st Ian Smyth, 1951, two s. two d.; m. 2nd David Gilliland, 1976. *Publications:* Fiction: The Captains and the Kings, 1972; The Gates, 1973; How Many Miles to Babylon?, 1974; Shadows on our Skin, 1978 (dramatised for TV, 1979); The Old Jest, 1979; The Invisible Worm, 1991. Plays: Nightingale and Not the Lark, 1980; Indian Summer, 1983; The Porch, 1986; The Invisible Man, 1986; The Desert Lullaby, 1996. Monologues: The Illusionist, 1995. Contributions: BBC Radio. *Honours:* Hon. doctorates. *Address:* Brook Hall, Culmore Rd, Derry BT48 8JE, Northern Ireland.

JOHNSTON, Julia (Ann); Writer; b. 21 Jan. 1941, Smith Falls, Ontario, Canada; m. Basil W. Johnston, 12 Oct. 1963, four d. *Education:* University of Toronto, 1963; Trent University, 1984. *Career:* mem. Canadian Society of Children's Authors; Writers' Union of Canada. *Publications:* There's Going to be a Frost 1979, Don't Give Up the Ghosts 1981, Tasting the Alternative 1982, After 30 Years of Law, Ken Starvis Sculpts New Career

1990, Hero of Lesser Causes 1992, The Interiors of Pots 1992, Adam and Eve and Pinch Me 1994, The Only Outcast 1998, Love Ya Like A Sister (Ed.) by Katie Ouniour, In Spite of Killer Bees 2001. *Honours:* Hon. DLitt (Trent) 1996Governor-General's Literary Award 1992, School Library Best Book 1993, Joan Fassler Memorial Award 1994, Ruth Schwartz Young Adult Book Award 1995, Canadian Library Asscn Young Adult Book Award 1995, Vicky Metcalf Award for body of work inspirationial to youth 2003. *Address:* 463 Hunter St W, Peterborough, Ontario K9H 2M7, Canada.

JOHNSTON, Kenneth Richard, BA, MA, PhD; academic and writer; *Professor of English, Indiana University*; b. 20 April 1938, Marquette, MI, USA; m. 1st Elizabeth Louise Adolphson (divorced); two s. one d.; m. 2nd Ilinca Marina Zarifopol; one s. *Education:* Augustana College, University of Chicago, Yale University. *Career:* Instructor in English, Augustana College, 1962–63; Asst Prof., 1966–70, Assoc. Prof., 1970–75, Prof. of English, 1975–, Indiana University; Senior Fulbright Lecturer, University of Bucharest, 1974–75; mem. British Asscn for Romantic Studies; MLA; North American Society for the Study of Romanticism; Wordsworth-Coleridge Asscn. *Publications:* The Rhetoric of Conflict (ed.), 1969; Wordsworth and 'The Recluse', 1984; Wordsworth and Romanticism (with Gene W. Ruoff), 1987; The Age of William Wordsworth: Critical Essays on the Romantic Tradition (ed. with Gene W. Ruoff), 1988; Romantic Revolutions: Criticism and Theory (ed. with Karen Hanson), 1990; The Hidden Wordsworth: Poet, Lover, Rebel, Spy, 1998. Contributions: scholarly books and journals. *Honours:* Guggenheim Fellowship; National Endowment for the Humanities Fellowships; Hon. Fellow, Institute for Advanced Study in the Humanities, University of Edinburgh, 1998. *Address:* c/o Department of English, Indiana University, Bloomington, IN 47405, USA.

JOHNSTON, Ronald John; Prof. of Geography and Writer; b. 30 March 1941, Swindon, Wiltshire, England; m. Rita Brennan, 16 April 1963, one s. one d. *Education:* BA, 1962, MA, 1964, University of Manchester; PhD, Monash University, 1967. *Career:* Teaching Fellow, 1964, Senior Teaching Fellow, 1965, Lecturer, 1966, Monash University; Lecturer, 1967–68, Senior Lecturer, 1969–72, Reader, 1973–74, University of Canterbury, New Zealand; Prof. of Geography, 1974–92, Pro-Vice-Chancellor for Academic Affairs, 1989–92, University of Sheffield; Vice-Chancellor, Essex University, 1992–95; Prof. of Geography, Bristol University, 1995–; mem. Institute of British Geographers, secretary, 1982–85, pres., 1990. *Publications:* The World Trade System: Some Enquiries Into Its Spatial Structure, 1976; Geography and Geographers: Anglo-American Human Geography Since 1945, 1979; Geography and the State, 1982; Philosophy and Human Geography: An Introduction to Contemporary Approaches, 1983; On Human Geography, 1986; Bell-Ringing: The English Art of Change-Ringing, 1986; Money and Votes: Constituency Campaign Spending and Election Results, 1987; The United States: A Contemporary Human Geography (co-author), 1988; A Nation Dividing?: The Electoral Map of Great Britain, 1979–1987 (with C. J. Pattie and J. G. Allsopp), 1988; Environmental Problems: Nature, Economy and State, 1989; The Dictionary of Human Geography (ed.), 1989; An Atlas of Bells (co-author), 1990; A Question of Place: Exploring the Practice of Human Geography, 1991; The Boundary Commissions, 1999; From Votes to Seats, 2001. Contributions: various books and professional journals. *Honours:* Murchison Award, 1985; Victoria Medal, RGS, 1990; Honors Award for Distinction in Research, Asscn of American Geographers, 1991; Hon. doctorates, University of Essex, 1996, Monash University, 1999, University of Sheffield, 2002; Fellow, British Acad., 1999. *Address:* School of Geographical Sciences, Bristol University, Bristol BS8 1SS, England.

JOHNSTON, William; Jesuit Roman Catholic Priest, Prof. of Theology and Writer; b. 30 July 1925, Belfast, Northern Ireland. *Education:* Theological studies. *Career:* Ordained a Roman Catholic Priest, 1957; Prof. of Theology, Sophia University, Tokyo, 1960–. *Publications:* The Mysticism of the Cloud of Unknowing, 1967; S. Endo: Silence (trans.), 1969; The Still Point: On Zen and Christian Mysticism, 1970; Christian Zen, 1971; The Cloud of Unknowing and the Book of Privy Counselling (ed.), 1973; Silent Music, 1974; The Inner Eye of Love, 1978; The Mirror Mind, 1981; T. Nagai, The Bells of Nagasaki (trans.), 1984; The Wounded Stag, 1985; Being in Love: The Practice of Christian Prayer, 1988; Letters to Contemplatives, 1991; Mystical Theology, 1995; Arise My Love.: Mysticism for a New Era, 2000. *Address:* c/o S. J. House, 7 Kioi-Cho, Chiyodaku, Tokyo 102, Japan.

JOLLEY, Elizabeth Monica, AO; British/Australian writer and professor of creative writing; b. 4 June 1923, Birmingham; m. Leonard Jolley 1945 (died 1994); one s. two d. *Education:* Friends' School, Sibford. *Career:* trained as nurse, Queen Elizabeth Hosp., Birmingham 1940–46; moved to Western Australia with family 1959; held a variety of occupations; Writer-in-Residence Western Australia Inst. of Tech. (later Curtin Univ. of Tech.), Perth, then Lecturer, School of Communication and Cultural Studies 1978–, Prof. of Creative Writing 1998–. *Publications:* Five Acre Virgin and Other Stories 1976, The Travelling Entertainer 1979, Palomino 1980, The Newspaper of Claremont Street 1981, Mr Scobie's Riddle (Age Book of the Year Award) 1983, Woman in a Lampshade 1983, Miss Peabody's Inheritance 1983, Milk and Honey (Premier of NSW Prize) 1984, The Well (Miles Franklin Award) 1986 (film 1997), The Sugar Mother (France-Australia Literary Translation Award) 1988, My Father's Moon (Age Book of the Year Award) 1989, Cabin Fever 1990, Central Mischief (essays, Premier of WA Prize) 1992, The Georges' Wife 1993, Diary of a Weekend Farmer (poems) 1993, The Orchard Thieves 1995, Lovesong 1997, An Accommodating Spouse 1999; one vol. of poetry and one vol. of radio plays. *Honours:* Hon. DTech (WAIT), Hon. DLitt (Macquarie Univ.) 1995, (Queensland) 1997, (Univ. of NSW) 2000; ASAL Gold Medal for Contrib. to Australian Literature. *Address:* School of English, Curtin University of Technology, PO Box U1987, Perth, WA 6001; 28 Agett Road, Claremont WA 6010, Western Australia. *Telephone:* (8) 9384-7879.

JOLLY, James; British writer; *Editor, Gramophone*. *Education:* Univ. of Bristol, Univ. of Reading. *Career:* producer, Record Review (BBC Radio 3); Asst Ed., Gramophone –1989, Ed. 1990–. *Publications as editor:* The Greatest Classical Recordings of All Time 1995, The Gramophone Opera 75: The 75 Best Opera Recordings of All Time 1997, The Gramophone Opera Good CD Guide 1998, The Gramophone Classical 2001 Good CD Guide (co-ed.) 2002. *Address:* Gramophone, Haymarket Magazines Ltd, PO Box 568, Haywards Heath, Sussex RH16 3XQ, England (Office). *Website:* www.gramophone.co.uk.

JONAS, Manfred; Historian; b. 9 April 1927, Mannheim, Germany; m. Nancy Jane Greene, 19 July 1952, two s. two d. *Education:* BS, City College, CUNY, 1949; AM, 1951, PhD, 1959, Harvard University. *Career:* Visiting Prof. for North American History, Free University of Berlin, 1959–62; Asst Prof. to Prof. of History, 1963–81, Washington Irving Prof. in Modern Literary and Historical Studies, 1981–86, John Bigelow Prof. of History, 1986–96, Union College, Schenectady, NY; Dr Otto Salgo Visiting Prof. of American Studies, Eötvös Lorand University, Budapest, 1983–84. *Publications:* Die Unabhängigkeitserklärung der Vereingten Staaten, 1964; Isolationism in America 1935–1941, 1966; American Foreign Relations in the 20th Century, 1967; Roosevelt and Churchill: Their Secret Wartime Correspondence, 1975; New Opportunities in the New Nation, 1982; The United States and Germany: A Diplomatic History, 1984. Contributions: Diplomatic History; The Historian; Mid-America; American Studies; Maryland Historical Magazine; Essex County Historical Collections; Jahrbuch für Amerikastudien. *Address:* Dept of History, Union College, Schenectady, NY 12308, USA. *E-mail:* jonasm@union.edu.

JONES, Alun Arthur Gwynne (see Chalfont).

JONES, Alys, BA; writer; b. 15 Sept. 1944, Newborough, Anglesey, North Wales; m. Robin Jones 1973; one s. one d. *Education:* Univ. Coll., Bangor, North Wales. *Career:* teacher in Welsh, Maesteg Comprehensive School 1966–67, Machynlleth Secondary School, Powys 1967–70, Ysgol Dyffryn Conwy, Llanrwst 1970–74, Ysgol Glan Clwyd, Llanelwy 1974–75. *Publications:* Ysbrydion y Môr, 1982; Storiau Non, 1982; Storiau Huw a'i Ffrindiau, 1987; Dirgelwch Neuadd Henffordd, 1987; Mac Pync, 1987; Storiau Cornel y Cae, 1988; Yr Ysbryd Arian, 1989; Y Gadwyn, 1989; Jetsam, 1991; Straeon Cornel y Stryd, 1994; Cuthbert Caradog, 1998; Pwtyn Escapes, 1998; Pwtyn ar Goll, 2001; Clymau Ddoe, 2001; Pwtyn and Pwtan go to School, 2001; Pwytn and Pwtan Meet, 2002. Contributions: CIP; Heno Heno (short story anthology), 1990; group reading booklet, Isle of Anglesey County Council, 2000. *Address:* Llys Alaw, 18 Ystad Eryri, Bethel, Caernarfon, Gwynedd, North Wales.

JONES, Brian; Poet and Writer; b. 1938, London, England. *Publications:* Poems, 1966; A Family Album, 1968; Interior, 1969; The Mantis Hand and Other Poems, 1970; For Mad Mary, 1974; The Spitfire on the Northern Line, 1975; The Island Normal, 1980; The Children of Separation, 1985; Freedom John, 1990. *Honours:* Cholmondeley Award, 1967; Eric Gregory Award, 1968. *Address:* c/o Carcanet Press, Fourth Floor, Alliance House, Cross St, Manchester M2 7AP, England.

JONES, Charlotte; British playwright and writer; m. Paul Bazely. *Education:* Balliol Coll., Oxford. *Career:* fmr actress. *Plays:* Airswimming (Battersea Arts Centre, London) 1997, In Flame (Bush Theatre, London) 1999, Martha, Josie and the Chinese Elvis (Octagon, Bolton) 1999, Humble Boy (Royal Nat. Theatre, London) 2001, The Principle of Eve (Royal Court Theatre) 2001, The Dark (Donmar Warehouse, London) 2004. *Radio:* for BBC Radio 4: Mary Something Takes the Veil, Future Perfect, A Seer of Sorts, Sea Symphony for Piano and Child 2001, Blue Air Love and Flowers. *Television:* Bessie and the Bell (Carlton) 2000, Mother's Ruin (Carlton) 2001. *Film:* Dogstar 2000. *Publications:* In Flame 2001, Martha, Josie and the Chinese Elvis 1999, Humble Boy 2001. *Honours:* Manchester Evening News Best Play Award 1999, Pearson TV Best Play Award 1999, Critics' Circle Award for Most Promising Playwright 2000, Susan Smith Blackburn Award 2001, Critics' Circle Best New Play Award 2002, People's Choice Best New Play Award 2002. *Literary Agent:* PFD, Drury House, 34–43 Russell Street, London, WC2B 5HA, England.

JONES, Christopher Dennis; Playwright; b. 13 Dec. 1949, New York, USA; m. Gwendoline Shirley Rose, 18 Aug. 1979. *Education:* BA, English Literature, University of Pittsburgh. *Career:* Resident Playwright, Carnaby Street Theatre, London, 1975–76, New Hope Theatre, London, 1977– 78; mem. Writer's Guild of Great Britain. *Publications:* Plays: Passing Strangers, 1975; Nasty Corners, 1977; New Signals, 1978; In Flight Reunion, 1979; Sterile Landscape, 1982; Ralph Bird's River Race, 1985; Dying Hairless With a Rash, 1985; Bitter Chalice, 1987; Begging the Ring, 1989; Burning Youth, 1989. Contributions: Country Life; Arts Review. *Literary Agent:* PFD, Drury House, 34–43 Russell St, London WC2B 5HA, England.

JONES, David James (see Annwn, David).

JONES, Diana Wynne; Writer; b. 16 Aug. 1934, London, England; m. J. A. Burrow 22 Dec. 1956; three s. *Education:* BA, Univ. of Oxford, 1956. *Career:* mem. Society of Authors; BSFA. *Publications:* Wilkin's Tooth, 1973; The Ogre Downstairs, 1974; Cart and Cwidder, 1975; Dogsbody, 1975; Eight Days of Luke, 1975; Power of Three, 1976; Charmed Life, 1977; Drowned Ammet, 1977; Who Got Rid of Angus Flint?, 1978; The Spellcoats, 1979; The Magicians of Caprona, 1980; The Four Grannies, 1980; The Homeward Bounders, 1981; The Time of the Ghost, 1981; Witch Week, 1982; Archer's Goon, 1984; Warlock at the Wheel, 1984; The Skiver's Guide, 1984; Fire and Hemlock, 1985; Howl's Moving Castle, 1986; A Tale of Time City, 1987; The Lives of Christopher Chant, 1988; Chair Person, 1989; Hidden Turnings (ed.), 1989; Wild Robert, 1989; Castle in the Air, 1990; Black Maria, 1991; Yes Dear, 1992; A Sudden Wild Magic, 1992; The Crown of Dalemark, 1993; Hexwood, 1993; Fantasy Stories (ed.), 1994; Everard's Ride, 1995; The Tough Guide to Fantasyland, 1996; Minor Arcana, 1996; Deep Secret, 1997; Dark Lord of Derkholm, 1998; Mixed Magics, 2000; Year of the Griffin, 2000; The Merlin Conspiracy, 2003; Stealer of Souls, 2004. Contributions: newspapers and magazines. *Honours:* Guardian Award for Children's Books, 1978; Honour Book, Boston Globe/Horn Book Award, 1986; Mythopogic Fantasy Awards, 1995, 1999; Karl Edward Wagner Fantasy Award, 1999. *Address:* 9 The Polygon, Bristol BS8 4PW, England.

JONES, Douglas Gordon, MA; poet and retd academic; b. 1 Jan. 1929, Bancroft, ON, Canada. *Education:* Queen's University, Kingston, ON. *Career:* Prof., University of Sherbrooke, Québec 1963–94. *Publications:* Poetry: Frost on the Sun, 1957; The Sun Is Axeman, 1961; Phrases from Orpheus, 1967; Under the Thunder the Flowers Light Up the Earth, 1977; A Throw of Particles: Selected and New Poems, 1983; Balthazar and Other Poems, 1988; The Floating Garden, 1995; Wild Asterisks in Cloud, 1997; Grounding Sight, 1999. Other: Butterfly on Rock: A Study of Themes and Images in Canadian Literature, 1970. *Honours:* Pres.'s Medal, University of Western Ontario, 1976; Gov.-Gen.'s Award for Poetry, 1977, and for Trans., 1993; Hon. DLitt, Guelph University, 1982. *Address:* 120 Houghton Street, North Hatley, QC JOB 2CO, Canada.

JONES, Edward P.; American author; b. Washington DC. *Education:* Holy Cross Coll., Univ. of Virginia. *Career:* worked as a magazine proofreader while writing his second novel. *Publications:* short story collection: Lost In The City 1992; novel: The Known World (Pulitzer Prize for Fiction 2004) 2003. *Honours:* PEN/Hemingway Award 1993, National Book Critics' Circle Award for Fiction, recipient, Lannan Foundation Grant. *Address:* c/o HarperCollins Publishers Inc., 10 E 53rd Street, New York, NY 10022, USA (Office). *Telephone:* (212) 207-7000. *Website:* www.harpercollins.com.

JONES, Evan Lloyd; poet and writer; b. 20 Nov. 1931, Preston, Vic., Australia; m. 1st Judith Anne Dale 1954; one s.; m. 2nd Margot Sanguinetti 1966; three d. *Education:* BA, History, MA, History, University of Melbourne; AM, Creative Writing, Stanford University. *Publications:* Poetry: Inside the Whale, 1960; Understandings, 1967; Recognitions, 1978; Left at the Post, 1984. Other: Kenneth Mackenzie, 1969; The Poems of Kenneth Mackenzie (ed. with Geoffrey Little), 1972. Contributions: Innumerable essays and reviews in venues ranging from learned journals to newspapers, on topics ranging from literature to physics. *Address:* PO Box 122, North Carlton, Vic. 3054, Australia.

JONES, Frederick Malcolm Anthony; academic, writer and poet; b. 14 Feb. 1955, Middlesex, England; m. Christina Jones; two s. *Education:* BA, Classics, University of Newcastle upon Tyne, 1977; MA, Medieval Studies, University of Leeds, 1979; PhD, St Andrews University, 1987. *Career:* Asst Lecturer, University of Cape Town, 1982–86; Teacher of Classics, Cobham Hall, Kent, 1987–89; Lecturer in Classics and Ancient History, University of Liverpool, 1989–; mem. Cambridge Philological Society; Society for the Promotion of Roman Studies. *Publications:* Congreve's Balsamic Elixir, 1995. Contributions: journals, reviews, and periodicals. *Honours:* 1 of 10 joint winners, Northern Poetry Competition, 1991; Felicia Hemans Prize for Lyrical Poetry, 1991. *Address:* c/o Dept of Classics and Ancient History, University of Liverpool, Liverpool L69 3BX, England.

JONES, Gwyneth, (Ann Halam); British writer and critic; b. 14 Feb. 1952, Manchester; m.; one s. *Education:* Univ. of Sussex. *Publications:* novels: Divine Endurance 1984, Escape Plans 1986, The Hidden Ones 1988, Kairos 1988, White Queen 1991, Flowerdust 1993, North Wind 1994, Seven Tales and a Fable 1995, Phoenix Cafe 1997, Bold as Love 2001, Castles Made of Sand 2002, Midnight Lamp 2003, Band of Gypsies 2004, Stone Free 2005; criticism: Deconstructing The Starships - Science Fiction and Reality 1999; juvenile: The Haunting of Jessica Raven 1997, Don't Open Your Eyes 2000; other: Identifying the Object - A Collection of Short Stories 1993; as Ann Halam: novels: Ally Ally Aster 1981, The Alder Tree 1982, King Death's Garden 1986, The Daymaker 1987, Transformations 1988, The Skybreaker 1990, Dinosaur Junction 1991, The Haunting of Jessica Raven 1993, The Fear Man 1995, The Powerhouse - A Horror Story 1997, Crying in the Dark 1998, The N.I.M.R.O.D. Conspiracy 1999, Don't Open Your Eyes 2000, The Shadow on the Stairs 2000, Dr Franklin's Island 2001, Taylor Five 2002, The Seed Savers 2004. *Honours:* two World Fantasy Awards, BFSA Short Story Award, Arthur C. Clarke Award 2001. *Literary Agent:* David Higham Associates, 5–8 Lower John Street, Golden Square, London, W1F 9HA, England. *Telephone:* (20) 7434-5900. *Fax:* (20) 7437-1072. *E-mail:* dha@davidhigham.co.uk. *Website:* www.davidhigham.co.uk. *E-mail:* gwyneth.jones@ntlworld.com. *Website:* www.boldaslove.co.uk.

JONES, Ivor Wynne; Journalist, Author and Lecturer; b. 28 March 1927, Liverpool, England; m. Marion-Jeannette Wrighton, 19 July 1958, one s. one d. *Education:* BBC Engineering Training School. *Career:* A founder of broadcasting in Cyprus; Ed., Caernarvon and Denbigh Herald, 1953; Columnist, 1955–, Welsh Political Correspondent, 1969–92, Chief Welsh Correspondent, 1980–92, Liverpool Daily Post; Research Ed., Llechwedd Slate Caverns, Blaenau Ffestiniog, 1972–; mem. Yr Academi Gymreig (Welsh Acad.); Lewis Carroll Society, UK; Lewis Carroll Society of North America; Lewis Carroll Society of Japan. *Publications:* Money for All, 1969; Arian I Bawb, 1969; Betws-y-coed, The Mountain Resort, 1972; Shipwrecks of North Wales, 1973; Betws-y-coed and the Conway Valley, 1974; Llandudno, Queen of the Welsh Resorts, 1975; America's Secret War in Welsh Waters, 1976; Luftwaffe Over Clwyd, 1977; U-Boat Rendezvous at Llandudno, 1978; Minstrels and Miners, 1986; Wales and Israel, 1988; Baden-Powell, The Welsh Dimension, 1992; The Order of St John in Wales, 1993; Colwyn Bay: A Brief History, 1995; Gold, Frankenstein and Manure, 1997; BFBS Cyprus 1948–98, 1998; Alice's Welsh Wonderland, 1999; Wilder Wales, 2001; Llandudno Queen of Welsh Resorts, 2002; Victorian Slate Mining, 2003; The Cairo Eisteddfod, 2003; Money Galore, 2003. Contributions: various historical journals. *Honours:* European Architectural Year Book Design Award, 1975. *Address:* Pegasus, Llandudno Rd, Penrhyn Bay, Llandudno LL30 3HN, Wales.

JONES, J. Farragut (see Levinson, Leonard).

JONES, Joanna (see Burke, John Frederick).

JONES, J(on) Sydney; Writer and Teacher; b. 6 April 1948, Britton, SD, USA. *Education:* Williamette University, 1966–67; BA, Communications, University of Oregon, 1970; University of Vienna, Austria. *Career:* Journalist, 1971–76; Instructor, English as a Second Language and Writing, 1977–; mem. American Society of Journalists and Authors; Authors' Guild. *Publications:* Bike and Hike: Sixty Tours around Great Britain and Ireland, 1977; Vienna Inside-Out: Sixteen Walking Tours, 1979; Hitler in Vienna, 1983; Tramping in Europe: A Walking Guide, 1984; Viennawalks, 1985; Time of the Wolf, 1990; The Hero Game, 1992; Frankie, 1997. Contributions: articles to over 100 newspapers in the USA and Europe. *Literary Agent:* Evan Marshall, 6 Tristam Pl., Pine Brook, NJ 07058, USA. *E-mail:* sjones@cats.ucsc.edu.

JONES, Julia; Writer and Dramatist; b. 27 March 1923, Liverpool, England; m. Edmund Bennett, 10 Oct. 1950, one s. one d. *Education:* RADA, London, 1946–48. *Career:* mem. Dramatist Club; Writers Guild of Great Britain. *Publications:* The Navigators, 1986. Other: Over 50 plays for stage, film, radio and television. *Honours:* First Prize for Drama, Prague Television Festival, 1970. *Address:* c/o Jill Foster Ltd, 35 Brompton Rd, London SW3 1DE, England.

JONES, (Everett) LeRoi, (Amiri Baraka), BA; American academic, poet, dramatist and writer; b. 7 Oct. 1934, Newark, NJ; m. 1st Hettie Robert Cohen (divorced 1965); two d.; m. 2nd Sylvia Robinson 1967; six c. two step-d. *Education:* Rutgers University, Howard University. *Career:* Founder-Dir, Yugen magazine and Totem Press, New York, 1958–62; Co-Ed., Floating Bear magazine, New York, 1961–63; Teacher, New School for Social Research, New York City, 1961–64, 1977–79, SUNY at Buffalo, 1964, Columbia University, 1964, 1980; Founder-Dir, Black Arts Repertory Theatre, Harlem, New York, 1964–66, Spirit House, Newark, 1966–; Visiting Prof., San Francisco State College, 1966–67, Yale University, 1977–78, George Washington University, 1978–79; Chair, Congress of Afrikan People, 1972–75; Asst Prof., 1980–82, Assoc. Prof., 1983–84, Prof. of Africana Studies, 1985–, SUNY at Stony Brook; mem. Black Acad. of Arts and Letters. *Publications:* Poetry: April 13, 1959; Spring and Soforth, 1960; Preface to a Twenty Volume Suicide Note, 1961; The Disguise, 1961; The Dead Lecturer, 1964; Black Art, 1966; A Poem for Black Hearts, 1967; Black Magic: Collected Poetry 1961–67, 1970; It's Nation Time, 1970; In Our Terribleness: Some Elements and Meaning in Black Style (with Billy Abernathy), 1970; Spirit Reach, 1972; African Revolution, 1973; Hard Facts, 1976; Selected Poetry, 1979; AM/TRAK, 1979; Spring Song, 1979; Reggae or Not!, 1982; Thoughts for You!, 1984; The LeRoi Jones/Amiri Baraka Reader, 1993. Plays: A Good Girl is Hard to Find, 1958; Dante, 1961; The Toilet, 1964; Dutchman, 1964; The Slave, 1964; The Baptism, 1964; Jello, 1965; Experimental Death Unit #1, 1965; A Black Mass, 1966; Arm Yrsell or Harm Yrsell, 1967; Slave Ship: A Historical Pageant, 1967; Madheart, 1967; Great Goodness of Life (A Coon Show), 1967; Home on the Range, 1968; Police, 1968; The Death of Malcolm X, 1969; Rockgroup, 1969; Insurrection, 1969; Junkies Are Full of (SHHH...), 1970; BA-RA-KA, 1972; Black Power Chant, 1972; Columbia the Gem of the Ocean, 1973; A Recent Killing, 1973; The New Ark's a Moverin, 1974; The Sidnee Poet Heroical, 1975; S-1, 1976; The Motion of History, 1977; What Was the Relationship of the Lone Ranger to the Means of Production?, 1979; At the Dim'cracker Convention, 1980; Boy and Tarzan Appear in a Clearing, 1981; Weimar 2, 1981; Money: A Jazz Opera (with George Gruntz), 1982; Primitive World, 1984; General Hag's Skeezag, 1992. Fiction: The System of Dante's Hell (novel), 1965; Tales (short stories), 1967. Other: Selected Plays and Prose, 1979; Daggers and Javelins: Essays 1974–1979, 1984; The Autobiography of LeRoi Jones/Amiri Baraka, 1984; The Artist and Social Responsibility, 1986; The Music: Reflections on Jazz and Blues (with Amina Baraka), 1987; A Race Divided, 1991; Conversations with Amiri Baraka, 1994. *Honours:* Obie Award, 1964; Guggenheim Fellowship, 1965; Yoruba Acad. Fellowship, 1965; Dakar Festival Prize, 1966; Grant, 1966, Award, 1981, National Endowment for the Arts; DHL, Malcolm X College, Chicago, 1972; Rockefeller Foundation Grant, 1981; American Book Award, Before Columbus Foundation, 1984. *Address:* c/o Department of Africana Studies, State University of New York at Stony Brook, Stony Brook, NY 11794, USA.

JONES, Madison Percy; Author and Prof. of English (retd); b. 21 March 1925, Nashville, Tennessee, USA; m. Shailah McEvilley, 5 Feb. 1951, three s., two d. *Education:* BA, Vanderbilt University, 1949; MA, University of Florida, 1953. *Career:* Instructor, Miami University of Ohio, 1953–54, University of Tennessee, 1955–56; Prof. of English and Writer-in-Residence, Auburn University, 1956–87; mem. Alabama Acad. of Distinguished Authors; Fellowship of Southern Writers. *Publications:* The Innocent, 1957; Forest of the Night, 1960; A Buried Land, 1963; An Exile, 1967; A Cry of Absence, 1971; Passage Through Gehenna, 1978; Season of the Stranger, 1983; Last Things, 1989; To the Winds, 1996; Nashville 1864: The Dying of the Light, 1997; Herod's Wife, 2003. Contributions: journals and magazines. *Honours:* Sewanee Review Writing Fellowship, 1954–55; Rockefeller Foundation Fellowship, 1968; Alabama Library Asscn Book Award, 1968; Guggenheim Fellowship, 1973–74; Lytle Annual Short Story Prize, Sewanee Review, 1994; T. S. Eliot Award, Ingersol Foundation, 1998; Michael Shaara Award, United States Civil War Center, 1998; Harper Lee Award, Alabama Arts Foundation, 1999. *Address:* 800 Kuderna Acres, Auburn, AL 36830, USA.

JONES, Malcolm Vince; Emeritus Prof. of Slavonic Studies and Writer; b. 7 Jan. 1940, Stoke-sub-Hamdon, England; m. Jennifer Rosemary Durrant, 27 July 1963, one s. one d. *Education:* Graduate, 1962, Postgraduate Studies, 1962–65, University of Nottingham. *Career:* Emeritus Prof. of Slavonic Studies, University of Nottingham; mem. British Asscn for Slavonic and East European Studies, vice-pres., 1988–91; British Universities' Asscn of Slavists, pres., 1986–88; International Dostoyevsky Society, pres., 1995–98. *Publications:* Dostoyevsky: The Novel of Discord, 1976; New Essays on Tolstoy (ed.), 1978; New Essays on Dostoyevsky (ed. with Garth M. Terry), 1983; Dostoyevsky After Bakhin, 1990; The Cambridge Companion to the Classic Russian Novel (ed. with Robin Feuer Miller), 1998. Contributions: scholarly journals. *Address:* c/o Dept of Russian and Slavonic Studies, University of Nottingham, University Park, Nottingham NG7 2RD, England.

JONES, (Sarah) Marie, OBE; Northern Irish playwright and actor; b. 1951, Belfast; three c. *Career:* co-founder, writer-in-residence, Charabanc Theatre Co. 1983–90; co-founder, Double Joint Theatre Co. 1991. *Film appearances include:* In the Name of the Father, Best, Rebel Heart. *Plays:* Lay Up Your Ends 1983, Oul' Delf and False Teeth 1984, Now You're Talking 1985, Gold on the Streets 1986, Girls in the Big Picture 1987, Somewhere over the Balcony 1988, Under Napoleon's Nose 1988, The Hamster Wheel 1990, Weddings Wee'ins and Wakes 1990, The Government Inspector (adaptation of Gogol) 1994, A Night in November 1994, Ethel Workman is Innocent 1995, Women on the Verge of HRT 1996, A Night to Remember 1998, Stones in his Pockets 1999. *Writing for television:* Tribes 1990, The Hamster Wheel 1991, Fighting the Shadows 1992, Wingnut and the Sprog 1994. *Honours:* Evening Standard Award for Best West End Comedy, John Hewitt Award, Olivier Award, Irish Times Theatre Award, Glasgow Mayfest Award. *Address:* c/o Nick Hern Books, The Glasshouse, 49a Goldhawk Road, London, W12 8QP, England. *Website:* www.nickhernbooks.co.uk.

JONES, Mervyn; Writer; b. 27 Feb. 1922, London, England. *Education:* New York University, 1939–41. *Career:* Asst Ed., 1955–60, Drama Critic, 1958–66, Tribune; Asst Ed., New Statesman, London, 1966–68. *Publications:* No Time to Be Young, 1952; The New Town, 1953; The Last Barricade, 1953; Helen Blake, 1955; Guilty Men (with Michael Foot), 1957; Suez and Cyprus, 1957; On the Last Day, 1958; Potbank, 1961; Big Two (in US as The Antagonists), 1962; Two Ears of Corn: Oxfam in Action (in US as In Famine's Shadow: A Private War on Hunger), 1965; A Set of Wives, 1965; John and Mary, 1966; A Survivor, 1968; Joseph, 1970; Mr Armitage Isn't Back Yet, 1971; Life on the Dole, 1972; Holding On (in US as Twilight of the Day), 1973; The Revolving Door, 1973; Lord Richard's Passion, 1974; Strangers, 1974; K. S. Karol: The Second Chinese Revolution (trans.), 1974; The Pursuit of Happiness, 1975; The Oil Rush (with Fay Godwin), 1976; Scenes from Bourgeois Life, 1976; Nobody's Fault, 1977; Today the Struggle, 1978; The Beautiful Words, 1979; A Short Time to Live, 1980; Two Women and Their Men, 1982; Joanna's Luck, 1985; Coming Home, 1986; Chances, 1987; That Year in Paris, 1988; A Radical Life, 1991; Michael Foot, 1994. *Address:* 1 Evelyn Mansions, Carlisle Pl., London SW1P 1NH, England.

JONES, Owen Marshall (see Marshall, Owen).

JONES, Richard Andrew, III; academic, poet, writer and editor; b. 8 Aug. 1953, London, England. *Education:* BA, English, 1975, MA, English, 1976, University of Virginia; MFA, Poetry, Vermont College, 1987. *Career:* Production Ed., CBS Books, 1978–80; Ed., Poetry East, 1979–, Scandinavian Review, 1982–83; Adjunct Faculty, Piedmont College, 1981–82; Dir of Publications, American-Scandinavian Foundation, 1982–83; Lecturer, University of Virginia, 1982–86; Teaching Fellow, Vermont College, 1985–87; Asst Prof., Ripon College, 1986–87; Prof. of English, DePaul University, 1987–; mem. Co-ordinating Council of Literary Magazines; Poetry Society of America. *Publications:* Windows and Walls, 1982; Innocent Things, 1985; Walk On, 1986; Country of Air, 1986; Sonnets, 1990; At Last We Enter Paradise, 1991; A Perfect Time, 1994; The Abandoned Garden, 1997; 48 Questions, 1998; The Stone It Lives On, 1999; The Blessing: New and Selected Poems, 2000. Editor: Of Solitude and Silence: Writings on Robert Bly (with Kate Daniels), 1982; Poetry and Politics, 1984; The Inward Eye: The Photographs of Ed Roseberry (with S. Margulies), 1986; The Last Believer in Words, 1998. Contributions: numerous publications. *Honours:* many grants; Swedish Writers Union Excellence Prize, 1982; Co-ordinating Council of Literary Magazines Eds' Award, 1985, and Citation of Special Commendation, 1988; Posner Award for Best Book of Poetry, Council for Wisconsin Writers, 1986; Illinois Artists Fellowship, 1990–91; Illinois Arts Council Awards, 1991, 1995, 1996, 1997, 2000, 2002; Society of Midland Authors Award for Best Book of Poetry, 2000; Via Sapentia Lifetime Achievement Award, 2000. *Address:* c/o Dept of English, DePaul University, 802 W Belden Avenue, Chicago, IL 60614, USA.

JONES, Robert Maynard, BA, MA, PhD, DLitt; academic and writer; b. 20 May 1929, Cardiff, Wales; m. Anne Elizabeth James 1952; one s. one d. *Education:* University of Wales, Cardiff. *Career:* Lecturer, Trinity College Carmarthen, 1956–58; Lecturer, 1959–67, Senior Lecturer to Reader, 1967–79, Prof. of Welsh and Head of Dept, 1980–89, Prof. Emeritus, 1989–, University of Wales, Aberystwyth; mem. Chair., Yr Academi Gymreig, 1975–79. *Publications:* Y Gân Gyntaf, 1956; Nid yw Dwr Yn Plygu, 1958; Rhwng Taf A Thaf, 1960; Allor Wydn, 1971; Tafod Y Llenor, 1974; Llên Cymru A Chrefydd, 1977; Seiliau Beirniadaeth, 1984–85; Hunllef Arthur, 1986; Llenyddiaeth Gymraeg, 1902–1936, 1987; Casgliad o Gerddi, 1989; Crio Chwerthin, 1990; Cyfriniaeth Gymraeg, 1994; Canu Arnaf, 1994, 1995; Ysbryd Y Cwlwm, 1998; Ynghylch Tawelwch, 1998; Tair Rhamant Arthuraidd, 1998; O'r Bedd i'r Crud, 2000; Mawl a'i Gyfeillion, 2000; Mawl a Gelynion ei Elynion, 2002; Ôl Troed, 2003; Beirniadaeth Gyfansawdd, 2003. *Honours:* Welsh Arts Council Prizes, 1956, 1959, 1971, 1987, 1990, 1998; Fellow, British Acad., 1992. *Address:* Tandderwen, Ffordd Llanbadarn, Aberystwyth, SY23 1HB, Wales.

JONES, Rodney; Poet and Writer; b. 11 Feb. 1950, Hartselle, AL, USA; m. 1st Virginia Kremza, 1972, divorced 1979; m. 2nd Gloria Nixon de Zepeda, 21 June 1981, two c. *Education:* BA, University of Alabama, 1971; MFA, University of North Carolina at Greensboro, 1973. *Career:* mem. Associated Writing Programs; MLA. *Publications:* Going Ahead, Looking Back, 1977; The Story They Told Us of Light, 1980; The Unborn, 1985; Transparent Gestures, 1989; Apocalyptic Narrative and Other Poems, 1993. Contributions: periodicals. *Honours:* Lavan Younger Poets Award, Acad. of American Poets, 1986; Younger Writers Award, General Electric Foundation, 1986; Jean Stein Prize, American Acad. and Institute of Arts and Letters, 1989; National Book Critics Circle Award, 1989. *Address:* c/o Houghton Mifflin Co, 222 Berkeley St, Boston, MA 02116, USA.

JONES, Russell Celyn; British novelist; b. 1955, Swansea, Wales. *Career:* Lecturer in Creative Writing, Univ. of East Anglia, Warwick Univ., Western Cape Univ., South Africa; book reviewer, The Times; judging panel mem. for The Booker Prize 2002. *Publications:* novels: Soldiers and Innocents 1990, Small Times 1992, An Interference of Light 1995, The Eros Hunter 1998, Surface Tension 2001. *Honours:* Fellowships at Iowa Univ., USA, Univ. of East Anglia ; David Higham Prize for Best First Novel 1990, Welsh Arts Council Fiction Award, Soc. of Authors Award 1996. *Address:* c/o Abacus, Brettenham House, Lancaster Place, London, WC2E 7EN, England.

JONES, Sally Roberts; Author and Publisher; b. 30 Nov. 1935, London, England. *Education:* BA, University College of North Wales, 1957; ALA, North-Western Polytechnic, 1964. *Career:* Senior Asst, Reference Library, London Borough of Havering, 1964–67; Reference Librarian, Borough of Port Talbot, Wales, 1967–70; Publisher, Alun Books, 1977–; Royal Literary Fund Fellow, University of Wales, Swansea, 1999–2001, Assoc. Fellow, 2002–02; mem. Welsh Union of Writers; Port Talbot Historical Society. *Publications:* Turning Away, 1969; Elen and the Goblin, 1977; The Forgotten Country, 1977; Books of Welsh Interest, 1977; Allen Raine, 1979; Relative Values, 1985; The History of Port Talbot, 1991; Pendarvis, 1992. *Honours:* Welsh Arts Council Literature Prize, 1970. *Address:* 3 Crown St, Port Talbot SA13 1BG, Wales.

JONES, Volcano (see Mitchell, Adrian).

JONG, Erica Mann, BA, MA; American writer and poet; b. 26 March 1942, New York, USA; m. 1st Michael Werthmann 1963 (divorced 1965); m. 2nd Allan Jong 1966 (divorced 1975); m. 3rd Jonathan Fast 1977 (divorced 1983); one d.; m. 4th Kenneth David Burrows 1989. *Education:* Barnard Coll., Columbia Univ. *Career:* Lecturer in English, City College, CUNY, 1964–65, 1969–70; Lecturer in English, University of Maryland Overseas Division 1967–69; Mem., Literary Panel, NY State Council on Arts, 1972–74; Faculty, Bread Loaf Writers Conference, Middlebury, VT, 1982; Faculty, Salzburg Seminar, Austria, 1993. *Publications:* poetry: Fruits and Vegetables 1971, Half Lives 1973, Loveroot 1975, At the Edge of the Body 1979, Witches 1981, Ordinary Miracles 1983, Becoming Light: Poems New and Selected 1992; prose: Fear of Flying 1973, How to Save Your Own Life

1977, Fanny: Being the True History of Fanny Hackabout-Jones 1980, Parachutes and Kisses 1984, Serenissima: A Novel of Venice (revised edn as Shylock's Daughter: A Novel of Love in Venice) 1987, Any Woman's Blues 1990, The Devil at Large: Erica Jong on Henry Miller 1993, Fear of Fifty: A Midlife Memoir 1994, Composer Zipless: Songs of Abandon from the Erotic Poetry of Erica Jong 1995, Inventing Memory: A Novel of Mothers and Daughters 1997, What Do Women Want? Bread. Roses. Sex. Power. 1998, Sappho's Leap 2004. *Honours:* Acad. of American Poets Prize, 1971; New York State Council on the Arts Grants, 1971; Woodrow Wilson Fellow; Recipient Bess Hokin Prize Poetry Magazine, 1971; Alice Faye di Castagnola Award, Poetry Society of America, 1972; National Endowment of the Arts Grant, 1973; Named Mother of the Year, 1982; Hon. Fellow, Welsh College of Music and Drama, 1994; Prix Littéraire, Deuville Film Festival, 1997. *Literary Agent:* Kenneth D. Burrows, Erica Jong Productions, 425 Park Avenue, New York, NY 10022-3506, USA. *E-mail:* erica@ericajong .com. *Website:* www.ericajong.com.

JORDAN, Leonard (see Levinson, Leonard).

JORDAN, Neil Patrick, BA; Irish writer and director; b. 25 Feb. 1950, Sligo; two d. three s. *Education:* St Paul's Coll. Raheny, Dublin and Univ. Coll. Dublin. *Career:* co-f. Irish Writers' Co-operative, Dublin 1974. *Films directed:* Angel 1981, Company of Wolves 1984, Mona Lisa 1986, High Spirits 1988, We're No Angels 1989, The Miracle 1990, The Crying Game 1992, Interview with the Vampire 1994, Michael Collins (Golden Lion, Venice 1996) 1995, The Butcher Boy 1997, In Dreams 1999, The End of the Affair 1999, Not I 2000, The Good Thief 2002. *Publications:* Night in Tunisia and Other Stories 1976, The Past 1979, The Dream of a Beast 1983, Sunrise with Sea Monster 1994, Nightlines 1995, Shade (novel) 2004. *Honours:* Guardian Fiction Award 1979, London Film Critics' Circle Award 1984, London Evening Standard Most Promising Newcomer Award 1982, Los Angeles Film Critics' Circle Award 1992, NY Film Critics' Circle Award 1992, Writers Guild of America Award 1992, BAFTA Awards 1992, 2000, Golden Lion, Venice Film Festival 1996, Silver Bear, Berlin Film Festival 1997. *Literary Agent:* Jenne Casarotto Co. Ltd, National House, 60–66 Wardour Street, London, WIV 3HP, England. *Address:* 2 Martello Terrace, Bray, Co. Wicklow, Ireland.

JOSE, F(rankie) Sionil; Writer and Social Activist; b. 4 Dec. 1924, Rosales, Philippines; m. Teresita 1949. *Education:* Univ. of Santo Tomas. *Career:* fmr journalist, Manila; f., publishing house, Solidaridad, 1965–, journal Solidarity, 1966–; mem. PEN, Philippines branch, f. *Publications:* Novels: Rosales Saga: The Pretenders, 1962, Tree, 1978, My Brother, My Executioner, 1979, Mass, 1982, Po-on (Dusk), 1984; Two Filipino Women, 1981; Ermita, 1988; Gagamba, 1991; Three Filipino Women, 1992; Viajero, 1993; Sin, 1994; Sins, 1996; Ben Singkol, 2002. Short Story Collections: The God Stealer and Other Stories, 1968; Waywaya, Eleven Filipino Short Stories, 1980; Platinum, Ten Filipino Stories, 1983; Olvidon and Other Short Stories, 1988; Puppy Love, 1999. Poetry: Questions, 1988. Non-Fiction: In Search of the Word: Selected Essays of F. Sionil Jose; Selected Essays of F. Sionil Jose; We Filipinos: Our Moral Malaise, Our Moral Heritage, 1999. *Honours:* Ramon Magsaysay Award for Journalism, Literature, and Creative Communication Arts, 1980; National Artist for Literature, Philippines, 2001. *Address:* c/o De La Salle University Press Inc, #2504 Leon Guinto St, Malate 1004, Manila, Philippines.

JOSEPH, Jenny, FRSL; Writer, Poet and Lecturer; b. 7 May 1932, Birmingham, England; m. C. A. Coles, 29 April 1961, deceased 1985, one s. two d. *Education:* BA, English, St Hilda's College, Oxford, 1953. *Career:* Patron Pennell Initiative; mem. Centre for the Spoken Word, Patron; council National Poetry Society of Great Britain 1975–78;. *Publications:* The Unlooked-for Season 1960, Warning" 1961, Boots 1966, Rose in the Afternoon 1974, The Thinking Heart 1978, Beyond Descartes 1983, Persephone 1986, The Inland Sea 1989, Beached Boats 1991, Selected Poems 1992, Ghosts and Other Company 1995, Extended Smiles 1997, Warning 1997, All the Things I See (poems for children) 2000, Led by the Nose: a garden of smells 2002. Contributions: anthologies and magazines. *Honours:* Eric Gregory Award, 1962; Cholmondeley Award, 1974; Arts Council of Great Britain Award, 1975; James Tait Black Memorial Prize for Fiction, 1986; Society of Authors Travelling Scholarship, 1995; Forward Prize, 1995. *Literary Agent:* Johnson & Alcock Ltd, Clerkenwell House, 45–47 Clerkenwell Green, London EC1R 0HT, England. *Address:* 17 Windmill Rd, Minchinhampton, Gloucestershire GL6 9DX, England.

JOSEPH, Lawrence; Poet, Essayist, Critic and Prof. of Law; b. 10 March 1948, Detroit, Michigan, USA; m. 10 April 1976. *Education:* BA 1970, JD 1975, University of Michigan; BA 1972, MA 1976, University of Cambridge. *Career:* Law Clerk, Michigan Supreme Court, Justice G. Mennen Williams; Litigator, Shearman Sterling, New York City; Creative Writing Prof., Princeton University, NJ; Prof. of Law, St John's University School of Law, Jamaica, New York, 1987–; mem. PEN American Centre; Poetry Society of America; Poets House; National Writers Voice. *Publications:* Shouting at No One, 1983; Curriculum Vitae, 1988; Before Our Eyes, 1993; Lawyerland: What Lawyers Talk about When They Talk about Law, 1997. Contributions: Paris Review; Nation; Village Voice; Partisan Review; Poetry; Boulevard; Kenyon Review. *Honours:* Hopwood Award for Poetry, 1970; Agnes Lynch Starrett Poetry Prize, 1982; National Endowment for the Arts Poetry Award, 1984; Fellowship, University of Cambridge. *Address:* c/o Law School, St John's University, Jamaica, NY 11439, USA.

JOSIPOVICI, Gabriel David; Prof. of English, Writer and Dramatist; b. 8 Oct. 1940, Nice, France. *Education:* BA, St Edmund Hall, Oxford, 1961. *Publications:* Fiction: The Inventory, 1968; Words, 1971; The Present, 1975; Migrations, 1977; The Air We Breathe, 1981; Contre-Jour, 1986; The Big Glass, 1990; In a Hotel Garden, 1993; Moo Pak, 1994; Now, 1997; Goldberg: Variations, 2002. Essays: The World and the Book, 1971; The Book of God: A Response to the Bible, 1988; Text and Voice, 1992; Touch, 1996; On Trust, 1998; A Life, 2001; Goldberg: Variations, 2001. Contributions: Encounter; New York Review of Books; London Review of Books; TLS. *Honours:* Lord Northcliffe Lectures, Univ. of London, 1981; Lord Weidenfeld Visiting Prof. of Comparative Literature, Univ. of Oxford, 1996–97; FRSL, 1997; Fellow, British Acad., 2000. *Literary Agent:* Johnson & Alcock Ltd, Clerkenwell House, 45–47 Clerkenwell Green, London EC1R 0HT, England. *Address:* 60 Prince Edwards Rd, Lewes, Sussex, England.

JOYAUX, Philippe (see Sollers, Philippe).

JOYCE, Graham; Author; b. 22 Oct. 1954, Keresley, Coventry, England; m. Suzanne Lucy Johnsen, 6 May 1988, one d., one s. *Education:* MA, BEd, Cert Ed, Leicester University. *Career:* mem. Society of Authors. *Publications:* Dreamside, 1991; Dark Sister, 1992; House of Lost Dreams, 1993; Requiem, 1995; The Tooth Fairy, 1996; The Stormwatcher, 1998; Indigo, 1999; Smoking Poppy, 2001. *Honours:* Derleth Awards, 1993, 1996, 1997, 1999. *Address:* c/o Sheil Land Assocs, 43 Doughty St, London WC1N 2LF, England.

JUDD, Alan, (Holly Budd); Writer; b. 1946, Kent, England. *Education:* University of Oxford. *Career:* fmr diplomat and teacher; mem. FRSL, 1990. *Publications:* as Alan Judd: A Breed of Heroes, 1981; Short of Glory, 1984; The Noonday Devil, 1987; Tango, 1989; Ford Madox Ford, 1990; The Devil's Own Work, 1991; First World War Poets (with David Crane), 1997; The Quest for 'C': Sir Mansfield Cumming and the Founding of the British Secret Service, 1999; Legacy, 2001; The Kaiser's Last Kiss, 2003. As Holly Budd: The Office Life Little Instruction Book, 1996. Contributions: newspapers and magazines. *Honours:* RSL Award, 1982; W. H. Heinemann Literature Award, 1990; Guardian Fiction Award, 1991. *Literary Agent:* David Higham Associates, 5–8 Lower John St, Golden Sq., London W1F 9HA, England.

JUDD, Denis (O'Nan); Historian and Writer; b. 28 Oct. 1938, Byfield, Northamptonshire, England; m. Dorothy Woolf, 10 July 1964, three s., one d. *Education:* BA, Modern History, University of Oxford, 1961; PGCEd, 1962, PhD, 1967, University of London. *Publications:* Balfour and the British Empire, 1968; The Boer War, 1977; Radical Joe: Joseph Chamberlain, 1977; Prince Philip, 1981; Lord Reading, 1982; Alison Uttley, 1986; Jawaharlal Nehru, 1993; Empire: The British Imperial Experience, 1996; The Boer War, 2002. Other: Two books for children; Other history books and biographies. Contributions: History Today; History; Journal of Imperial and Commonwealth History; Literary Review; Daily Telegraph; New Statesman; International Herald Tribune; Independent; BBC History Magazine; Mail on Sunday. *Honours:* FRHistS, 1977; Awarded Professorship, 1990. *Address:* 20 Mount Pleasant Rd, London NW10 3EL, England. *E-mail:* d.judd@unl.ac.uk.

JUDSON, John; Educator, Ed., Writer and Poet; b. 9 Sept. 1930, Stratford, CT, USA. *Education:* BA, Colby College, 1958; University of Maine, 1962–63; MFA, University of Iowa, 1965. *Career:* Ed., Juniper Press, Northeast/Juniper Books, literary magazine and chapbook series, 1961–; Prof. of English, University of Wisconsin, La Crosse, 1965–93. *Publications:* Two From Where It Snows (co-author), 1963; Surreal Songs, 1968; Within Seasons, 1970; Voyages to the Inland Sea, six vols, 1971–76; Finding Worlds in Winter; West of Burnam South of Troy, 1973; Ash Is the Candle's Wick, 1974; Roots from the Onion's Dark, 1978; A Purple Tale, 1978; North of Athens, 1980; Letters to Jirac II, 1980; Reasons Why I Am Not Perfect, 1982; The Carrabassett Sweet William Was My River, 1982; Suite for Drury Pond, 1989; Muse(sic), 1992; The Inardo Poems, 1996. *Address:* 1310 Shorewood Dr., La Crosse, WI 54601, USA.

JUERGENSMEYER, Mark (Karl); Prof. of Sociology and Writer; b. 13 Nov. 1940, Carlinville, IL, USA; m. Sucheng Chan, 21 Sept. 1969. *Education:* BA, Philosophy, University of Illinois at Urbana-Champaign, 1962; Columbia University, 1963–65; MDiv, Union Theological Seminary, New York, 1965; MA, 1968, PhD, 1974, Political Science, University of California at Berkeley. *Career:* Lecturer, 1971–72, Dir, Religious Studies Program, 1977–89, University of California at Berkeley; Lecturer, 1973–74, Assoc. Prof., 1974–84, Prof., 1984–89, Dir, Comparative Religion Program, 1984–89, Graduate Theological Union, Berkeley; Distinguished Visiting Prof., University of California at Santa Cruz, 1988; Dean, Asian and Pacific Studies, and Prof. of Religion and Political Science, University of Hawaii, 1989–93; Prof. of Sociology, 1993–, Dir, Global and International Studies, 1995–, University of California at Santa Barbara; Chair, Pacific Rim Research Program, University of California System, 1994–97; Halle Distinguished Visiting Prof. of Global Learning, Emory University, 2002. *Publications:* Sikh Studies: Comparative Perspectives on a Changing Tradition (co-ed.), 1979; Religion as Social Vision: The Movement Against Untouchability in

20th-Century Punjab, 1982; Fighting with Gandhi, 1984, revised edn as Gandhi's Way: A Handbook of Conflict Resolution, 2002; Songs of the Saints of India (co-trans.), 1988; Imagining India: Essays on Indian History by Ainslie Embres (ed.), 1989; Teaching the Introductory Course in Religious Studies (ed.), 1991; A Bibliographic Guide to the Comparative Study of Ethics (co-ed.), 1991; Radhasoami Reality: The Logic of a Modern Faith, 1991; Violence and the Sacred in the Modern World (ed.), 1992; The New Cold War?: Religious Nationalism Confronts the Secular State, 1993; Terror in the Mind of God: The Global Rise of Religious Violence, 2000. Contributions: Reference works, scholarly books and professional journals. *Honours:* International Fellow, Columbia University, 1963–65; Indo-American Fellowship, India, 1978; American Institute of Indian Studies Senior Research Grants, 1979, 1983, 1985, 1986; Fellow, Woodrow Wilson International Center for Scholars, Washington, DC, 1986; Guggenheim Fellowship, 1988–90; Fellow, United States Institute of Peace, 1989–91; Fellow, ACLS, 1996. *Address:* c/o Global and International Studies, 3042 Humanities and Social Sciences Bldg, University of California at Santa Barbara, Santa Barbara, CA 93106, USA.

JULIAN, Jane (see Wiseman, David).

JUNGER, Sebastian; American novelist and journalist; b. 1962, Belmont, MA. *Publications:* novels: The Perfect Storm 1997, Deception on his Mind 1998, Fire 2001; contrib. to Outside, City Paper, American Heritage, Men's Journal, Vanity Fair. *Honours:* Nat. Magazine Award. *Address:* c/o Fourth Estate, HarperCollins Publishers Ltd, 77–85 Fulham Palace Road, London, W6 8JB, England. *Website:* www.harpercollins.co.uk.

JUNGK, Peter Stephan; writer; b. Germany. *Publications:* Franz Werfel: A Life in Prague, Vienna, and Hollywood, 1990; Shabbat: A Rite of Passage in Jerusalem; A Life Torn by History: Franz Werfel 1890–1945, 1990; The Snowflake Constant, 2002. *Address:* c/o Faber and Faber Ltd, 3 Queen Square, London WC1N 3AU, England.

JUNKINS, Donald (Arthur); Poet, Writer and Prof. of English Emeritus; b. 19 Dec. 1931, Saugus, Massachusetts, USA; m. 1st; two s. one d.; m. 2nd Kaimei Zheng 18 Dec. 1993; one step-s. *Education:* BA, University of Massachusetts, 1953; STB, 1956, STM, 1957, AM, 1959, PhD, 1963, Boston University. *Career:* Instructor, 1961–62, Asst Prof., 1962–63, Emerson College, Boston; Asst Prof., Chico State College, CA, 1963–66; Asst Prof., 1966–69, Assoc. Prof., 1969–74, Dir, Master of Fine Arts Program in English, 1970–78, 1989–90, Prof. of English, 1974–95, Prof. Emeritus, 1995–, University of Massachusetts, Amherst; mem. PEN; Hemingway Society; Fitzgerald Society. *Publications:* The Sunfish and the Partridge, 1965; The Graves of Scotland Parish, 1969; Walden, One Hundred Years After Thoreau, 1969; And Sandpipers She Said, 1970; The Contemporary World Poets (ed.), 1976; The Uncle Harry Poems and Other Maine Reminiscences, 1977; Crossing By Ferry: Poems New and Selected, 1978; The Agamenticus Poems, 1984; Playing for Keeps: Poems, 1978–1988, 1989; Andromache, by Euripides (trans.), 1998; Journey to the Corrida, 1998; Lines from Bimini Waters, 1998. Contributions: Longman Anthology of American Poetry: Colonial to Contemporary; reviews, journals and magazines. *Honours:* Bread Loaf Writers Conference Poetry Scholarship, 1959; Jennie Tane Award for Poetry, 1968; John Masefield Memorial Award, 1973; National Endowment for the Arts Fellowships, 1974, 1979. *Address:* 63 Hawks Rd, Deerfield, MA 01342, USA.

JUST, Ward (Swift); Writer; b. 5 Sept. 1935, Michigan City, IN, USA. *Education:* Lake Forest Acad., IL, 1949–51; Cranbrook School, Michigan, 1951–53; Trinity College, Hartford, CT, 1953–57. *Career:* Reporter, Waukegan News-Sun, IL, 1957–59; Reporter, 1962–63, Correspondent, 1963–65, Newsweek magazine; Correspondent, Washington Post, 1965–70. *Publications:* To What End: Report from Vietnam, 1968; A Soldier of the Revolution, 1970; Military Men, 1970; The Congressmen Who Loved Flaubert and Other Washington Stories, 1973; Stringer, 1974; Nicholson at Large, 1975; A Family Trust, 1978; Honor, Power, Riches, Fame and the Love of Women, 1979; In the City of Fear, 1982; The American Blues, 1984; The American Ambassador, 1987; Jack Glance, 1989; Twenty-One Selected Stories, 1990; The Translator, 1991; Ambition and Love, 1994; Echo House, 1997; A Dangerous Friend, 1999; Lowell Limpett, 2001; The Weather in Berlin, 2002. Contributions: anthologies and periodicals. *Honours:* O. Henry Awards, 1985, 1986; Berlin Prize Fellowship, 1998. *Address:* Vineyard Haven, MA 02568, USA.

JUSTICE, Donald Rodney; poet, writer and retd academic; b. 12 Aug. 1925, Miami, FL, USA; m. Jean Catherine Ross 1947; one s. *Education:* BA, University of Miami, 1945; MA, University of North Carolina, 1947; Postgraduate Studies, Stanford University, 1948–49; PhD, University of Iowa, 1954. *Career:* Instructor, University of Miami, 1947–51; Asst Prof., Hamline University, 1956–57; Lecturer, 1957–60, Asst Prof., 1960–63, Assoc. Prof., 1963–66, Prof., 1971–82, University of Iowa; Prof., Syracuse University, 1966–70, University of Florida at Gainesville, 1982–92; mem. Acad. of American Poets, board of chancellors, 1997–; American Acad. of Arts and Letters. *Publications:* Poetry: The Summer Anniversaries, 1960; Night Light, 1967; Departures, 1973; Selected Poems, 1979; The Sunset Maker, 1987; A Donald Justice Reader, 1992; New and Selected Poems, 1995. Other: The Collected Poems of Weldon Kees (ed.), 1962; Platonic Scripts (essays), 1984; Oblivion: On Writers and Writing, 1998; Orpheus Hesitated Beside the Black River, 1998. Contributions: journals and magazines. *Honours:* Rockefeller Foundation Fellowship, 1954; Lamont Award, 1959; Ford Foundation Fellowship, 1964; National Endowment for the Arts Grants, 1967, 1973, 1980, 1989; Guggenheim Fellowship, 1976; Pulitzer Prize in Poetry, 1980; Acad. of American Poets Fellowship, 1988; Co-Winner, Bollingen Prize, 1991; Lannan Literary Award, 1996. *Address:* 338 Rocky Shore Drive, Iowa City, IA 52246, USA.

JUTEAU, Monique; Poet and Author; b. 8 Jan. 1949, Montréal, QC, Canada. *Education:* MA, French Literature, 1987. *Career:* mem. Société des Écrivains de la Mauricie; Union des écrivaines et des écrivains québécois. *Publications:* Poetry: La Lune Aussi, 1975; Regard Calligraphes, 1986; Trop Plein D'Angles, 1990; Des jours de chemins perdus et retrouvés, 1997. Fiction: En Moins de Deux, 1990; L'Emporte-Clé, 1994; La Fin des Terres, 2001. Contributions: various publications. *Honours:* Prix Gerald-Godin, 1998; Prix Félix-Antoine-Savard, 2001; Télé-Québec Prix Daring, 2002; Second Prize, Grands Prix Littéraires, Radio-Canada, 2002. *Address:* 19200 Forest, Bécancour, QC G9H 1P9, Canada. *E-mail:* monique_juteau@uqtr.ca. *Website:* www.litterature.org/ile32000.asp?numero=265.

K

KAAVERI (see Kannan, Lakshmi).

KADARÉ, Ismail; Writer and Poet; b. 28 Jan. 1936, Gjirokastër, Albania; m. Elena; two d. *Education:* Univ. of Tirana; Gorky Institute of World Literature, Moscow. *Publications:* Fiction: Gjenerali i ushtërisë së vdekur (trans. as The General of the Dead Army), 1963; Kështjella (trans. as The Castle), 1970; Kronikë në gur (trans. as Chronicle in Stone), 1971; Ura më tri harque (trans. as The Three-Arched Bridge), 1978; Kush e solli doruntinen (trans. as Doruntine), 1980; Prilli i thyer (trans. as Broken April), 1980; Nëpunësi i pallatit të ëndrrave (trans. as The Palace of Dreams), 1980; Nje dosje per Homerin (trans. as The File on H), 1980; Koncert në fund të dimrit (trans. as The Concert), 1988; Piramida (trans. as The Pyramid), 1992; Oeuvres, 1993–97, five vols, 1997; Il a fallu ce deuil pour se retrouver, 2000; Spring Flowers, Spring Frost (in trans.), 2002. Poetry: six vols, 1954–80. Other: short stories, criticism, essays. *Address:* c/o Librairie Artheme Fayard, 75 rue des Saints-Pères, 75006 Paris, France.

KADMON, Jean Ball Kosloff; Poet, Novelist and Painter; b. 1 Aug. 1922, Denver, CO, USA; m. 18 Aug. 1945, two s. *Education:* BA, University of Alberta, 1943; Graduate Studies, Anthropology, University of Chicago, 1944–46. *Career:* Anthropologist, International Centre for Community Development, Haifa, Israel, 1964–65; Sociologist, Jewish Agency, Israel, 1966–68; mem. Israel Asscn of Writers in English; Voices Israel Poetry Asscn. *Publications:* Moshav Segev, 1972; Clais and Clock, 1988; Peering Out, 1996; MacKenzie Breakup, 1997. Contributions: anthologies and periodicals. *Honours:* Second Prize, New Zealand International Writers Workshop, 1981; First prize, Ruben Rose International Poetry Contest, 2001. *Address:* 12 Zerubbabel St, Jerusalem 93505, Israel.

KADOHATA, Cynthia Lynn; Writer; b. 7 Feb. 1956, Chicago, IL, USA; m. 30 Aug. 1992. *Education:* Los Angeles City College; University of South Carolina; University of Pittsburgh; Columbia University. *Publications:* The Floating World, 1989; In the Heart of the Valley of Love, 1992. Contributions: newspapers and magazines. *Honours:* National Endowment for the Arts Grant, 1991; Whiting Writers Award, 1991. *Literary Agent:* The Wylie Agency, 250 W 57th St, Suite 2114, New York, NY 10107, USA.

KAGAN, Andrew Aaron; Art Historian, Art Adviser and Writer; b. 22 Sept. 1947, St Louis, MO, USA; m. Jayne Wilner, 17 May 1987. *Education:* BA, Washington University; MA, 1971, PhD, 1977, Harvard University. *Career:* Advisory Ed., Arts Magazine, 1975–89; Critic of Art, Music, Architecture, St Louis Globe Democrat, 1978–81; mem. Wednesday Night Society, founder, dir. *Publications:* Paul Klee/Art and Music, 1983; Rothko, 1987; Trova, 1988; Marc Chagall, 1989; Paul Klee at the Guggenheim, 1993; Absolute Art, 1995. Contributions: McMillan Dictionary of Art; Arts Magazine; Burlington Magazine; Others. *Honours:* Harvard Prize Fellowship, 1970–77; Kingsbury Fellowship, 1977–78; Goldman Prize, 1985.

KAGAN, Donald; American academic and writer; b. 1 May 1932, Kurshan, Lithuania; m. Myrna Dabrusky 1955; two s. *Education:* BA, History, Brooklyn College, CUNY, 1954; MA, Classics, Brown University, 1955; PhD, History, Ohio State University, 1958. *Career:* Part-time Instructor in History, Capital University, Columbus, Ohio, 1957–58; Instructor in History, Pennsylvania State University, 1959–60; Asst Prof. of History, 1960–63, Assoc. Prof. of History, 1964–66, Prof. of History, 1967–69, Cornell University; Prof. of History and Classics, 1969–, Chair., 1972–75, Acting Chair., 1986–87, Dept of Classics, Master, Timothy Dwight College, 1976–78, Richard M. Colgate Prof. of History and Classics, 1979–90, Dean, Yale College, 1989–92, Bass Prof. of History and Western Civilization, 1991–95, Hillhouse Prof. of History and Classics, 1995–, Yale University; Fellow, Center for Advanced Study in the Behavioural Sciences, Stanford, CA, 1992–93; Guest Scholar, Woodrow Wilson International Center for Scholars, 1996. *Publications:* The Decline and Fall of the Roman Empire in the West (ed.), 1962, third edn as The End of the Roman Empire, Decline or Transformation?, 1992; The Great Dialogue: A History of Greek Political Thought From Homer to Polybius, 1965; Readings in Greek Political Thought (ed.), 1965; Problems in Ancient History (ed.), two vols, 1966; Great Issues in Western Civilization (ed. with L. P. Williams and Brian Tierney), two vols, 1967; The Outbreak of the Peloponnesian War, 1969; Hellenic History, by Botsford and Robinson, revised edn, 1969; The Archidamian War, 1974; The Western Heritage (with Steven Ozment and Frank M. Turner), 1979; The Peace of Nicias and the Sicilian Expedition, 1981; The Heritage of World Civilizations (with Albert Craig, William Graham, Steven Ozment and Frank M. Turner), 1986; The Fall of the Athenian Empire, 1987; Pericles of Athens and the Birth of Democracy, 1990; On the Origins of War and Preservation of Peace, 1995; While America Sleeps (with Frederick W. Kagan), 2000; The Peloponnesian War, 2003. Contributions: scholarly books and professional journals, and to general periodicals. *Honours:* Fulbright Fellowship, 1958–59; Center for Hellenic Studies Fellowship, Washington, DC, 1966–67; National Endowment for the Humanities Senior Fellowship, 1971–72; Hon. doctorates, University of New Haven, 1988, Adelphi University, 1990, University of Dallas, 2001; Sidney Hook Memorial Award, National Asscn of Scholars, 1994: Harwood Byrnes '08/Richard B. Sewall Teaching Prize, Yale College, 1998; National Humanities Medal, 2002. *Address:* 37 Woodstock Road, Hamden, CT 06517, USA.

KAGAN, Robert, BA, MA; American author and journalist; b. 28 Sept. 1958, Athens, Greece; m. Victoria Nuland; one s. one d. *Education:* Yale Coll., Harvard Univ. *Career:* foreign policy adviser to Congressman Jack Kemp 1983; policy planning staff at US State Dept and principal speechwriter to Sec. of State George P. Schultz 1984–88; Sr Assoc. at the Carnegie Endowment for International Peace 1997–, Dir, US Leadership Project; mem., Council on Foreign Relations. *Publications:* non-fiction: A Twilight Struggle - American Power and Nicaragua (1977–1990) 1996, Present Dangers - Crisis and Opportunity in American Foreign and Defense Policy (ed. with William Kristol) 2000, Of Paradise and Power - America and Europe in the New World Order 2003; contrib. journalism to Foreign Affairs, Foreign Policy Commentary, New York Times, New Republic, Wall Street Journal, National Interest, Policy Review, Weekly Standard (contrib. ed.); columnist, The Washington Post. *Address:* c/o Carnegie Endowment for International Peace, 1779 Massachusetts Avenue NW, Washington, DC 20036, USA. *Telephone:* (202) 483-7600. *Fax:* (202) 483-1840. *E-mail:* info@ceip.org. *Website:* www.ceip.org.

KAHN, James; Physician and Writer; b. 30 Dec. 1947, Chicago, IL, USA. *Education:* BA, 1970, MD, 1974, University of Chicago. *Career:* Resident, Los Angeles County Hospital, 1976–77; University of California at Los Angeles, 1978–79; Physician, Emergency Room, Rancho Encino Hospital, Los Angeles, 1978–. *Publications:* Diagnosis Murder 1978, Nerves in Patterns (with Jerome McGann) 1978, World Enough and Time 1982, Time's Dark Laughter 1982, Poltergeist 1982, Return of the Jedi 1983, Indiana Jones and the Temple of Doom 1984, Goonies 1985, Timefall 1986, Poltergeist II 1986, Melrose Place (writer-producer) 1995–1999, Star Trek: Vogayer (writer-producer) 2001–02. *Address:* c/o Danielle Egan-Miller, 410 S Michigan Ave, Suite 460, Chicago, IL 60605, USA.

KAHN, Sy; academic, writer and poet; b. 15 Sept. 1924, New York, NY, USA; m. Janet Baker; one s. *Education:* BA, University of Pennsylvania, 1948; MA, University of Connecticut, 1951; PhD, University of Wisconsin, 1957. *Career:* Asst Prof., Beloit College, 1955–60, University of South Florida, 1960–63; Fulbright Prof. of American Literature, University of Salonika, Greece, 1958–59, University of Warsaw, 1966–67, University of Vienna, 1970–71, University of Porto, Portugal, 1985–86; Prof. of English and Humanities, Raymond College, 1963–68; Prof. of Drama and English, 1968–86, Chair., Dept of Drama, 1970–81, Prof. Emeritus, 1986–, University of the Pacific; mem. MLA. *Publications:* Our Separate Darkness, 1963; Triptych, 1964; The Fight is With Phantoms, 1966; A Later Sun, 1966; Another Time, 1968; Facing Mirrors, 1981; Devour the Fire: Selected Poems of Harry Crosby (ed.), 1984; Between Tedium and Terror: A Soldier's World War II Diary, 1993. Contributions: various anthologies, journals, reviews and quarterlies. *Honours:* Gardner Writing Awards, University of Wisconsin, 1954, 1955; Crosby Writing Fellowships, 1962, 1963; Borestone Poetry Award, 1964; Promethean Lamp Prize, 1966; Grand Prize in Poetry, University of the Pacific, 1985. *Address:* Ravenshill House, 1212 Holcomb Street, Port Townsend, WA 98368, USA.

KAISER, Philip M., AB, MA; American diplomatist, publisher and banker; b. 12 July 1913, New York; m. Hannah Greeley 1939; three s. *Education:* Univ. of Wisconsin and Balliol Coll., Oxford (Rhodes Scholar). *Career:* Fed. Reserve System 1939–42, Bd of Econ. Warfare 1942–46; joined Research Planning Div. Dept of State 1946; Exec. Asst to Asst Sec. of Labor (Int. Labor Affairs) 1946–47; Dir Office of Int. Labor Affairs, Dept of Labor 1947–49; Asst Sec. of Labor 1949–53; US Govt mem., Governing Body, Int. Labor Org. 1949–53; Labor Adviser, Comm. for Free Europe 1953–54; Special Asst to Gov. of New York 1955–58; Prof. of Int. Relations, American Univ. 1958–61; Amb. to Senegal and Mauritania 1961–64; President Kennedy's Special Amb. to Rwanda's Independence Day July 18 1962; Minister, American Embassy in London 1964–69; Amb. to Hungary 1977–80, to Austria 1980–81; Professorial Lecturer Johns Hopkins School for Advanced Int. Studies 1981–83; Chair. and Man. Dir Encyclopaedia Britannica Int. Ltd, London 1969–75; Sr Consultant SRI Int. 1981–97; mem. Bd, Guinness Mahon Holdings Ltd 1975–77, Weidenfeld and Nicolson 1969–77, American Ditchley Foundation 1981–, Council of American Ambs 1984–, Franklin & Eleanor Roosevelt Inst. 1985–, Weizmann Inst. of Science, Asscn of Diplomatic Studies 1987–, Partners for Democratic Change, American Acad. of Diplomacy 1996–; mem. Council on Foreign Relations, Washington Inst. of Foreign Affairs. *Publication:* Journeying Far and Wide: A Political and Diplomatic Memoir 1993. *Honours:* Kt Commdr Order of Austria 1992, Order of Merit, Return of Crown of St. Stephen (Hungary) 1998. *Address:* 2101 Connecticut Avenue, NW, Washington, DC 20008, USA (Home). *Telephone:* (202) 667-6095 (Home). *Fax:* (202) 332-6124 (Home).

KALB, Jonathan; Theatre Critic and Prof. of Theatre; b. 30 Oct. 1959, Englewood, NJ, USA; m. Julie Heffernan 18 June 1988; two s. *Education:* BA, English, Wesleyan University; MFA, Dramaturgy, Dramatic Criticism, 1985, DFA, Dramaturgy, Dramatic Criticism, 1987, Yale School of Drama. *Career:* Theatre Critic, The Village Voice, 1987–97; Asst Prof. of Performance Studies, 1990–92, Asst Prof. of Theatre, 1992–95, Assoc. Prof. of

Theatre, 1996–2002, Prof. of Theatre, 2003–, Hunter College, CUNY; Chief Theatre Critic, New York Press, 1997–2001; mem. MLA; PEN American Centre. *Publications:* Beckett in Performance, 1989; Free Admissions: Collected Theater Writings, 1993; The Theater of Heiner Müller, 1998; Play by Play: Theater Essays and Reviews 1993–2002, 2003. Contributions: newspapers and journals. *Honours:* Fulbright Hays Grant, 1988–89; T. C. G. Jerome Fellowship, 1989–90; George Jean Nathan Award for Dramatic Criticism, 1990–91. *Address:* c/o Dept of Theatre, Hunter College, City University of New York, 695 Park Ave, New York, NY 10021, USA.

KALECHOFSKY, Roberta; Writer and Publisher; b. 11 May 1931, New York, NY, USA; m. Robert Kalechofsky, 7 June 1953, two s. *Education:* BA, Brooklyn College, CUNY, 1952; MA, 1957, PhD, 1970, English, New York University. *Career:* Literary Ed., Branching Out, Canada, 1973–74; Contributing Ed., Margins, 1974–77, On the Issues, 1987–94; mem. National Writers Union, charter mem.; Authors' Guild. *Publications:* Stephen's Passion, 1975; La Hoya, 1976; Orestes in Progress, 1976; Solomon's Wisdom, 1978; Rejected Essays and Other Matters, 1980; The 6th Day of Creation, 1986; Bodmin 1349, 1988; Haggadah for the Liberated Lamb, 1988; Autobiography of a Revolutionary: Essays on Animals and Human Rights, 1991; Justice, My Brother, 1993; Haggadah for the Vegetarian Family, 1993; K'tia: A Savior of the Jewish People, 1995; A Boy, a Chicken and the Lion of Judah: How Ari Became a Vegetarian (children's book), 1995; Vegetarian Judaism: A Guide for Everyone, 1998. Contributions: Confrontation; Works; Ball State University Forum; Western Humanities Review; Rocky Mountain Review; Between the Species; So'western; Response; Reconstructionist. *Honours:* National Endowment for the Arts Fellowship, 1962; Hon. Mem., Israel Bibliophile Society, 1982; Literary Fellowship in Fiction, Massachusetts Council on the Arts, 1987. *Address:* 255 Humphrey St, Marblehead, MA 01945, USA.

KAMANDA, Kama Sywor; writer, poet, novelist and playwright; b. 11 Nov. 1952, Luebo, Congo. *Education:* Journalism School Kinshasa, Political Science Degree, Univ. of Kinshasa, 1973; Law Degrees Univ. of Liège, 1981. *Career:* Lecturer at various univs, schools etc; literary critic for several newspapers; mem. jury Louise Labé award; mem. Soc. de Poètes Français, French Soc. Men of Letters, Asscn of African Writers, Int. PEN, Asscn of French-Speaking Writers, Int. Council of French-Speaking Studies, Sabam. *Television:* subject of Kama Kamanda au Pays du Conte 1993, Kama Kamanda, Poète de l'exil 1994, Kama Sywor Kamana, chantre de la mémoire égyptienne 2003. *Publications:* Chants de brumes 1986, Les Résignations 1986, Éclipse d'étoiles 1987, Les Contes du griot Vol. 1 1988, Vol. 2: La Nuit des griots 1992, Vol. 3: Les Contes des veillées africaines 1998, La Somme du néant 1989, L'Exil des songes 1992, Les Myriades des temps vécus 1992, Les Vents de l'épreuve 1993, Lointaines sont les rives du destin 1994, Quand dans l'âme les mers s'agitent 1994, L'Étreinte des mots 1995, Chants de brumes 1997, Oeuvre Poétique 1999, Les Contes du crépuscule 2000, Le Sang des solitudes 2002, Contes 2003. *Honours:* Paul Verlaine Award Académie Française 1987, Théophile Gautier Award 1993, Literary Award Black Africa Asscn of French-Speaking Writers 1991, Special Poetry Award Acad. Inst. Paris 1992, Silver Jasmine for Poetic Originality 1992, Special Prize French-Speaking Countries Gen. Council Agen 1992, Melina Mercouri Award Asscn of Greek Writers and Poets 1999, Poet of the Millennium Award Int. Poets Acad., India 2000. *Address:* 18 Am Moul, 7418 Buschdorf, Luxembourg (Home). *Telephone:* 26610299. *E-mail:* kamanda@pt.lu.

KAMINER, Wladimir; German writer, journalist and DJ; b. 1967, Moscow, USSR. *Career:* moved to Germany 1990; DJ, Russian Disco, Berlin. *Publications:* Russendisko (short stories), 2000; Frische Goldjungs (ed.), 2001; Schönhauser Allee, 2001; Militärmusik, 2001; Die Reise nach Trulala, 2002; Helden des Alltags (with Helmut Höge), 2002; Dschungelbuch, 2003. Contributions: FAZ, taz and the Frankfurter Rundschau. *Address:* c/o Random House UK Ltd, Random House, 20 Vauxhall Bridge Road, London SW1V 2SA, England. *Website:* www.russendisko.de.

KAMINSKY, Stuart M(elvin); Prof. of Radio, Television and Film and Writer; b. 29 Sept. 1934, Chicago, IL, USA. *Education:* BS, 1957, MA, 1959, University of Illinois; PhD, Northwestern University, 1972. *Career:* Dir of Public Relations and Asst to the Vice-Pres. for Public Affairs, University of Chicago, 1969–72; Faculty, later Prof. of Radio, Television, and Film, Northwestern University, 1972–. *Publications:* Non-Fiction: Don Siegal: Director, 1973; Clint Eastwood, 1974; American Film Genres: Approaches to a Critical Theory of Popular Film, 1974; Ingmar Bergman: Essays in Criticism (ed. with Joseph Hill), 1975; John Huston: Maker of Magic, 1978; Basic Filmmaking (with Dana Hodgdon), 1981; American Television Genres (with Jeffrey Mahan), 1984. Fiction: Bullet for a Star, 1977; Murder on the Yellow Brick Road, 1978; You Bet Your Life, 1979; The Howard Hughes Affair, 1979; Never Cross a Vampire, 1980; Death of a Dissident, 1981; High Midnight, 1981; Catch a Falling Clown, 1981; He Done Her Wrong, 1983; When the Dark Man Calls, 1983; Black Knight on Red Square, 1983; Down for the Count, 1985; Red Chameleon, 1985; Exercise in Terror, 1985; Smart Moves, 1987; A Fine Red Rain, 1987; Lieberman's Day, 1994; Vengeance, 1999; Murder on the Trans-Siberian Express, 2001; Retribution, 2001.

KAN, Sergei; American academic and writer; b. 31 March 1953, Moscow, Russia; m. Alla Glazman 1976; one d. *Education:* Moscow State University, 1970–73; BA, Boston University, 1976; MA, 1978, PhD, 1982, University of Chicago. *Career:* Lecturer, Sheldon Jackson College, Sitka, AK, 1979–80, University of Massachusetts, Boston, 1982–83; Part-time Asst Prof., Northeastern University, 1981–83; Asst Prof., University of Michigan, 1983–89; Asst Prof., 1989–92, Assoc. Prof. of Anthropology and of Native American Studies, 1992–98, Prof. of Anthropology and Native American Studies, 1998–, Dartmouth College; mem. Alaska Anthropological Asscn; American Asscn for the Advancement of Slavic Studies; American Ethnological Society; American Society for Ethnohistory; International Arctic Social Science Asscn. *Publications:* Symbolic Immortality: The Tlingit Potlatch of the Nineteenth Century, 1989; Memory Eternal: Tlingit Culture and Russian Orthodox Christianity Through Two Centuries, 1999. Contributions: books and scholarly journals. *Honours:* Robert F. Heizer Prize, American Society for Ethnohistory, 1987; American Book Award, Before Columbus Foundation, 1990; ACLS Fellowship, 1993–94; National Endowment for the Humanities Fellowships, 1993–94, 1999–2000. *Address:* 18 Wellington Circle, Lebanon, NH 03766, USA.

KANDEL, Michael, PhD; editor and writer; b. 24 Dec. 1941, Baltimore, MD, USA. *Education:* Indiana Univ. *Career:* Asst Ed., MLA; Consultant Science Fiction Ed., Harcourt; Trans. of Stanislaw Lem; mem. PEN Club; SFWA. *Publications:* Strange Invasion, 1989; In Between Dragons, 1991; Captain Jack Zodiac, 1993; Panda Ray, 1996. *Address:* Modern Language Association, 26 Broadway, Third Floor, New York, NY 10004-1789, USA. *E-mail:* mkandel@mla.org.

KANE, Cheikh Hamidou; Novelist; b. 1928, Mataru, Senegal. *Education:* Philosophy and Law, Univ. of Paris; trained as administrator, Ecole Nationale de la France d'Outre-Mer. *Career:* frmly, Dir, Dept of Economic Planning and Development, Governor, Thies Region, Commissioner of Planning; worked for UNICEF. *Publications:* L'Aventure Ambiguë (Ambiguous Adventure), 1961; Les Gardiens du Temple, 1995. *Honours:* Grand Prix Litteraire de l'Afrique Noir, 1962. *Address:* c/o African Writers Series, Heinemann Educational Publishers, Halley Ct, Jordan Hill, Oxford OX2 8EJ, England.

KANE, Paul; Poet, Critic and Prof. of English; b. 23 March 1950, Cobleskill, New York, USA; m. Christine Reynolds, 21 June 1980. *Education:* BA, 1973, MA, 1987, MPhil, 1988, PhD, 1990, Yale University; MA, University of Melbourne, 1985. *Career:* Instructor, Briarcliff College, 1975–77; Assoc., Institute for World Order, 1982; Dir of Admissions and Instructor, Wooster School, 1982–84; Part-time Instructor, Yale University, 1988–90; Prof. of English, Vassar College, 1990–; mem. Acad. of American Poets; PEN; Poetry Society of America. *Publications:* The Farther Shore, 1989; A Hudson Landscape (with William Cliff), 1993; Ralph Waldo Emerson: Collected Poems and Translations, 1994; Poetry of the American Renaissance, 1995; Australian Poetry: Romanticism and Negativity, 1996; Emerson: Essays and Poems, 1996; Drowned Lands, 2000. Contributions: articles, poems, and reviews in New Republic; Paris Review; Poetry; Sewanee Review; Partisan Review; Raritan; Antipodes; The New Criterion. *Honours:* Fulbright Scholar, 1984–85; National Endowment for the Humanities Grant, 1998; Guggenheim Fellowship, 1999. *Address:* 8 Big Island, Warwick, NY 10990, USA.

KANEHARA, Hitomi; Japanese novelist; b. 1983, Tokyo. *Publications:* Hebi ni Piasu (trans. as Snakes and Earrings) (Akutagawa Prize (jtly) 2004) 2003; contrib. to Subaru magazine. *Address:* c/o Shueisha Inc, 2-5-10, Hitotsubashi, Chiyoda-ku, Tokyo 101-8050, Japan.

KANENGONI, Alexander; Author; b. 1951, Chivhu, Zimbabwe. *Education:* Saint Paul's Teacher Training College; English Literature, Univ. of Zimbabwe. *Career:* Project Officer, Ministry of Education and Culture, 1983; Head of Research Services, Zimbabwe Broadcasting Corpn, 1988–. *Publications:* Vicious Circle (novel), 1983; When the Rainbird Cries (novel), 1988; Effortless Tears (short stories), 1993; Echoing Silences (novel), 1998. *Honours:* Zimbabwe Book Publishers' Literary Awards, 1994. *Address:* c/o African Writers Series, Heinemann Educational Publishers, Halley Ct, Jordan Hill, Oxford OX2 8EJ, England.

KANIGEL, Robert; writer and academic; b. 28 May 1946, New York, NY, USA; m. Judith Schiff Pearl 1981 (divorced); one s. *Education:* BS, Rensselaer Polytechnic Institute, Troy, New York. *Career:* Freelance Writer, 1970–; Instructor, Johns Hopkins University School of Continuing Studies, 1985–91; Visiting Prof. of English, University of Baltimore, and Senior Fellow, Institute of Publications Design, 1991–99; Prof. of Science Writing, 1999–, Dir, Graduate Program in Science Writing, 2001–, MIT; mem. Authors' Guild; American Society of Journalists and Authors. *Publications:* Apprentice to Genius: The Making of a Scientific Dynasty, 1986; The Man Who Knew Infinity: A Life of the Genius Ramanujan, 1991; The One Best Way: Frederick Winslow Taylor and the Enigma of Efficency, 1997; Vintage Reading: From Plato to Bradbury, a Personal Tour of Some of the World's Best Books, 1998; High Season: How One French Riviera Town Has Seduced Traders for Two Thousand Years, 2002. Contributions: New York Times Magazine; The Sciences; Health; Psychology Today; Science 85; Johns Hopkins Magazine; Washington Post; Civilization. *Honours:* Grady-Stack Award, 1989; Alfred P. Sloan Foundation Grant, 1991; Elizabeth Eisenstein Prize, 1994; Author of the Year, American Society of Journalists and Authors, 1998. *Address:* 14N-420, Massachusetts Institute of Technology, 77 Massachusetts Avenue, Cambridge, MA 02139, USA.

KANN, Mark E.; Prof. of Political Science and Writer; b. 24 Feb. 1947, Chicago, IL, USA; m. Kathy Michael, 13 Feb. 1969, one s. *Education:* BA, 1968, MA, 1972, PhD, 1975, University of Wisconsin, Madison. *Career:* Asst Prof., 1975–81, Assoc. Prof., 1981–88, Prof. of Political Science, 1988–, University of Southern California at Los Angeles. *Publications:* Thinking About Politics: Two Political Sciences, 1980; The American Left: Failures and Fortunes, 1983; Middle Class Radicals in Santa Monica, 1986; On the Man in Question: Gender and Civic Virtue in America, 1991; A Republic of Men: The American Founders, Gendered Language, and Political Patriachy, 1998. Contributions: numerous newspapers, journals and magazines. *Honours:* various research and teaching awards. *Address:* Dept of Political Science, University of Southern California, Los Angeles, CA 90089, USA.

KANN, Peter Robert; American publisher, business executive and journalist; *Chairman and CEO, Dow Jones & Company, Inc.*; b. 13 Dec. 1942, New York; m. 1st Francesca Mayer 1969 (died 1983); m. 2nd Karen House 1984; one s. three d. *Education:* Harvard Univ. *Career:* with The Wall Street Journal 1964–; journalist, New York 1964–67, Viet Nam 1967–68, Hong Kong 1968–75, Publr and Ed. Asian Edn 1976–79, Assoc. Publr 1979–88; Exec. Vice-Pres. Dow Jones & Co. 1986, Pres. int. and magazine groups 1986–89, mem. Bd of Dirs. 1987; Publr and Editorial Dir The Wall Street Journal 1989–2002; Pres. Dow Jones & Co. New York 1989–91, Chair., CEO 1991–; Chair. Bd Far Eastern Econ. Review 1987–89; Trustee Asia Soc. 1989–94, Inst. for Advanced Study, Princeton 1990–, Aspen Inst. 1994–; mem. Pulitzer Prize Bd 1987–96. *Honours:* recipient, Pulitzer Prize for int. reporting 1972. *Address:* Wall Street Journal, 200 Liberty Street, New York, NY 10281, USA (Office). *Telephone:* (212) 416-2000 (Office). *Fax:* (212) 416-4348 (Office). *Website:* www.dj.com (Office).

KANNAN, Lakshmi, (Kaaveri), MA, PhD; writer and poet; b. 13 Aug. 1947, Mysore, India; m. L. V. Kannan (deceased); two s. *Career:* participant Int. Writing Program, Iowa Univ. USA; writer-in-residence on Charles Wallace Trust Fellowship, Univ. of Kent at Canterbury, UK 1993; Fellow, Indian Inst. of Advanced Study, Shimla, India; convenor for Tamil Bhasha Samiti, K. K. Birla Foundation, Delhi; scholar-in-residence, American Studies Research Centre, Hyderabad; Group Chief, Bharat Soka Gakkai, Indian chapter Soka Gakkai Int.; f. mem., governing body, Poetry Soc. of India, New Delhi; mem. of jury for the Commonwealth Writers Prize, Eurasia; mem., India Int. Centre, Delhi. *Publications include:* Impressions (poems) 1974, The Glow and the Grey (poems) 1976, Exiled Gods (poems) 1985, Rhythms (short stories) 1986, Parijata (short stories) 1992, India Gate (short stories) 1993, Going Home (novel) 1998; other works in Tamil and in Hindi trans. *Honours:* Hon. Fellow in Writing, Univ. of Iowa, USA, Ilakkiya Chintani Award for best short story in Tamil, Chennai, Katha Award for Best Translation, New Delhi. *Address:* B–XI/8193, Vasant Kunj, New Delhi 110 070, India. *Telephone:* (11) 26897793. *E-mail:* kannan01lakshmi@sify.com.

KANT, Hermann Paul Karl; Writer; b. 14 June 1926, Hamburg, Germany; m. Marion Meyer, 1 March 1982, two s. two d. *Education:* BA, Philosophy, University of Berlin, 1956. *Career:* mem. PEN Centre, Germany; Writers Asscn, pres., 1979–89. *Publications:* Ein bisschen Südsee 1962, Die Aula 1965, In Stockholm 1971, Eine Übertretung 1971, Das Impressum 1972, Der Aufenthalt 1977, Der dritte Nagel 1980, Zu den Unterlagen 1981, Bronzezeit 1986, Die Summe 1988, Abspann (memoir) 1991, Kormoran 1992, Escape 1994, Okarina 2002. *Honours:* Heinrich Heine Prize, 1962; Heinrich Mann Prize, 1967; National Prizes, 1973, 1977; Goethe Prize, 1985. *Address:* Prälank-Dorf 4, 17235 Neustrelitz, Germany.

KANTARIS, Sylvia; Poet, Writer and Teacher; b. 9 Jan. 1936, Grindleford, Derbyshire, England; m. Emmanuel Kantaris, 11 Jan. 1958, one s. one d. *Education:* Diplome d'Etudes Civilisation Française, Sorbonne, University of Paris, 1955; BA, 1957, CertEd, 1958, Bristol University; MA, 1967, PhD, 1972, University of Queensland, Australia. *Career:* Tutor, University of Queensland, Australia, 1963–66, Open University, England, 1974–84; Extra-Mural Lecturer, Exeter University, 1974–; Writer in the Community, Cornwall, 1986–87; mem. Poetry Society of Great Britain; South West Arts, literature panel, 1983–87, literary consultant, 1990–. *Publications:* Time and Motion, 1975; Stocking Up, 1981; The Tenth Muse, 1983; News From the Front (with D. M. Thomas), 1983; The Sea at the Door, 1985; The Air Mines of Mistila (with Philip Gross), 1988; Dirty Washing: New and Selected Poems, 1989; Lad's Love, 1993. Contributions: many anthologies, newspapers, and magazines. *Honours:* National Poetry Competition Award, 1982; Hon. Doctor of Letters, Exeter University, 1989; Major Arts Council Literature Award, 1991; Society of Authors Award, 1992. *Address:* 14 Osborne Parc, Helston, Cornwall TR13 8PB, England.

KANTOR, Peter, MA; poet and editor; b. 5 Nov. 1949, Budapest, Hungary. *Education:* Budapest ELTE University. *Career:* Literary Ed., Kortars magazine, 1984–86; Poetry Ed., Élet és Irodalom, magazine, 1997–2000; mem. Hungarian Writers Union; International PEN Club. *Publications:* Kavics, 1976; Halmadar, 1981; Sebbel Lobbal, 1982; Gradicsok, 1985; Hogy no az eg, 1988; Naplo, 1987–89, 1991; Font lomb, lent avar, 1994; Mentafü (selected poems), 1994; Bucsu és Megérkezés, 1997; Lóstaféta, 2002. Contributions: various publications. *Honours:* George Soros Fellowship, 1988–89; Wessely Laszlo Award, 1990; Dery Tibor Award, 1991; Fulbright Fellowship, 1991–92; Fust Milan Award, 1992; József Attila Award, 1994; George Soros Award, 1999. *Address:* Stollar Bela u 3/a, Budapest 1055, Hungary. *E-mail:* peterkantor@freemail.hn.

KAPLAN, Harold; academic and writer; b. 3 Jan. 1916, Chicago, IL, USA; m. Isabelle M. Ollier 1962; one s. two d. *Education:* BA, 1937, MA, 1938, University of Chicago. *Career:* Instructor of English, Rutgers University, 1946–49; Prof. of English, Bennington College, 1950–72; Prof. of English, 1972–86, Prof. Emeritus, 1986–, Northwestern University. *Publications:* The Passive Voice, 1966; Democratic Humanism and American Literature, 1972; Power and Order, 1981; Conscience and Memory: Meditations in a Museum of the Holocaust, 1994. *Honours:* Fulbright Lecturer, 1967, 1981; Rockefeller Foundation Humanities Fellowship, 1982. *Address:* 219 Meadowbrook Drive, Bennington, VT 05201, USA.

KAPLAN, Jeremiah; American publishing executive; b. 15 July 1926, New York; m. Charlotte R. Larsen 1945; one s. three d. *Career:* Vice-Pres. Free Press Glencoe Inc., Ill. 1947–60, Pres. 1960–64; Editorial Dir Gen. Publishing Div. Crowell Collier Publishing Co. 1960–62, Vice-Pres. 1962–67, Sr Vice-Pres. 1967–; Chair. Bd Science Materials Inc. 1962–63; Vice-Pres. Macmillan Co. 1960–63, Exec. Vice-Pres. 1963–65, Pres. 1965–73, 1977–86, Chair. 1983–87; Exec. Vice-Pres. Crowell Collier Div. Macmillan Inc. 1968–86; Head, Product Devt Corp. Marketing Planning, Crowell Collier & Macmillan Inc. 1972–, also mem. Bd Dirs; Chair. Collier Macmillan Int. 1973; Exec. Vice-Pres. and Dir Macmillan Inc. 1979–86; Chair. Bd Macmillan Publishing Co., Inc. 1980–86; Special Adviser to Chair. Simon & Schuster, Inc. New York 1987, Pres. 1987–90.

KAPLAN, Justin; Biographer and Ed.; b. 5 Sept. 1925, New York, NY, USA; m. Anne F. Bernays, 29 July 1954, three d. *Education:* BS, 1944, Postgraduate Studies, 1944–46, Harvard University. *Career:* Senior Ed., Simon & Schuster Inc, New York City, 1954–59; Lecturer in English, Harvard University, 1969, 1973, 1976, 1978; Writer-in-Residence, Emerson College, Boston, 1977–78; Visiting Lecturer, Griffith University, Brisbane, Australia, 1983; Jenks Prof. of Contemporary Letters, College of the Holy Cross, Worcester, Massachusetts, 1992–95; mem. American Acad. of Arts and Letters; American Acad. of Arts and Sciences, fellow; Society of American Historians, fellow. *Publications:* Mr Clemens and Mark Twain, 1966; Lincoln Steffens: A Biography, 1974; Mark Twain and His World, 1974; Walt Whitman: A Life, 1980; The Language of Names (with Anne Bernays), 1997; Back Then (with Anne Bernays), 2002. Editor: Dialogues of Plato, 1948; With Malice Toward Women, 1949; The Pocket Aristotle, 1956; The Gilded Age, 1964; Great Short Works of Mark Twain, 1967; Mark Twain: A Profile, 1967; Walt Whitman: Complete Poetry and Collected Prose, 1982; The Harper American Literature, 1987; Best American Essays, 1990. General Editor: Bartlett's Familiar Quotations, 17th edn, 2002. Contributions: newspapers, journals and magazines. *Honours:* Pulitzer Prize for Biography, 1967; National Book Award, 1967; Guggenheim Fellowship, 1975–76; American Book Award, 1981; Hon. DHL, Marlboro College, 1984; Bellagio Study and Conference Center Residency, 1990.

KAPLAN, Morton A.; political scientist, academic, writer, editor and publisher; b. 9 May 1921, Philadelphia, PA, USA; m. Azie Mortimer 1967. *Education:* BS, Temple Univ., 1943; PhD, Columbia Univ., 1951. *Career:* Fellow 1952–53, Research Assoc., 1958–62, Center of International Studies, Princeton, NJ; Asst Prof., Haverford College, 1953–54; Fellow, Center for Advanced Study in the Behavioral Sciences, Stanford, CA, 1955–56; Asst Prof., 1956–61, Assoc. Prof., 1961–65, Prof. of Political Science, 1965–89, Distinguished Service Prof., 1989–91, Prof. Emeritus, 1991–, Univ. of Chicago; Visiting Assoc. Prof., Yale Univ., 1961–62; Staff, 1961–78, Consultant, 1978–80, Hudson Institute; Dir, Center for Strategic and Foreign Policy Studies, 1976–85; Ed. and Publisher, The World and I, 1985–; mem. American Political Science Asscn; Institute of Strategic Studies, London. *Publications:* System and Process in International Politics, 1957; Some Problems in the Strategic Analysis of International Politics, 1959; The Communist Coup in Czechoslovakia (co-author), 1960; The Political Foundations of International Law, 1961; Macropolitics: Essays on the Philosophy and Science of Politics, 1969; On Historical and Political Knowing: An Enquiry into Some Problems of Universal Law and Human Freedom, 1971; On Freedom and Human Dignity: The Importance of the Sacred in Politics, 1973; The Rationale for NATO: Past and Present, 1973; Alienation and Identification, 1976; Justice, Human Nature and Political Obligation (co-author), 1976; Towards Professionalism in International Theory: Macrosystem Analysis, 1979; Science, Language and the Human Condition, 1984; The Soviet Union and the Challenge of the Future (co-ed.), four vols, 1988–89; Morality and Religion (co-ed.), 1992; Law in a Democratic Society, 1993; The World of 2044: Technological Development and the Future of Society (co-ed.), 1994; Character and Identity: Philosophical Foundations of Political and Sociological Perspectives (ed. and co-author), 1998; Character and Identity: Sociological Foundations of Literary and Historical Perspectives, 2000. Contributions: many books and professional journals. *Address:* 5446 S Ridgewood Court, Chicago, IL 60615, USA.

KAPLAN, Robert D., BA; writer; b. 23 June 1952, New York, NY, USA; m. Maria Cabral; one s. *Education:* University of Connecticut. *Publications:* Surrender or Starve: The Wars Behind the Famine, 1988; Soldiers of God: With the Mujahidin in Afghanistan, 1990; Balkan Ghosts; A Journey

Through History, 1993; The Arabists: The Romance of an American Elite, 1993; The Ends of the Earth: A Journey at the Dawn of the Twenty-First Century, 1996; An Empire Wilderness: Travels Into America's Future, 1998; The Coming Anarchy: Shattering the Dreams of the Post Cold War, 2000; Eastward to Tartary: Travels in the Balkans, the Middle East, and the Caucasus, 2000. Contributions: periodicals. *Address:* c/o Random House, 299 Park Avenue, New York, NY 10171, USA.

KAPLINSKI, Jaan; Estonian poet, writer and translator; b. 22 Jan. 1941, Tartu (Dorpat). *Education:* Univ. of Tartu. *Career:* mem. of Estonian parliament 1992–95; Lecturer in History of Western Civilization, Univ. of Tartu; columnist various Estonian and Scandinavian newspapers; has written around 900 poems, 20 stories and some plays; mem. Universal Acad. of Cultures, Estonian Writers' Union. *Publications include:* poetry: Ma vaatasin päikas ak nasse 1976, Uute kivide kasvamine 1977, The New Heaven & Earth of Jaan Kaplinski 1981, Raske on kergeks saada 1982, Tule tagasi helmemänd 1984, Õhtu toob tagasi kõik 1985, Käoraamat: Luulet 1956–80 1986, The Wandering Border 1987, Same Sea in Us All 1990, Sjunger näktergalen än i Dorpat?: En brevväxling 1990, I Am The Spring in Tartu and other poems in English 1991, Non-Existent Frontier 1995, Võimaluste võimalikkus 1997, Öölinnud, oomõtted yö lintuja, yöajatusksia: Luuletusi 1995–97 1998, Evening Brings Everything Back 2004. *Honours:* IV Class Order of Nat. Coat of Arms 1997. *Address:* c/o Bloodaxe Books Ltd, Highgreen, Tarset, Northumberland NE48 1RP, England. *Website:* www.bloodaxebooks.com.

KAPUSCINSKI, Ryszard, MA; Polish journalist and writer; b. 4 March 1932, Pinsk; m. Alicja Mielczarek 1952; one d. *Education:* Warsaw Univ. *Career:* journalist with Sztandar Mlodych 1951, Polityka 1957–61; correspondent, Polish Press Agency (PAP) in Africa and Latin America 1962–72, Kultura 1974–81; Deputy Chair., Poland 2000 Cttee, Polish Acad. of Sciences 1981–85; Visiting Scholar, Bangalore Univ. 1973, Univ. of Caracas 1978, Columbia Univ. 1983, Temple Univ., Philadelphia 1988; sr assoc. mem., St Antony's Coll., Oxford 1985; mem. Presidential Council of Culture 1992–95; mem. New Perspectives Quarterly (bd of advisers), European Acad. of Science and Art, Polish Acad. of Art and Science, Polish PEN Club. *Publications:* Busz po polsku 1962, Czarne gwiazdy 1963, Kirgiz schodzi z konia 1968, Gdyby cala Afryka… 1969, Dlaczego zginal Karl von Spreti 1970, Chrystus z karabinem na ramieniu 1975, Jeszcze dzien zycia 1976, Cesarz 1978, Wojna futbolowa 1978, Szachinszach 1982, Notes (poems) 1986, Lapidarium 1990, Imperium 1992, Vol. II 1995, Vol. III 1997, Lapidaria 1993, Heban 1998. *Honours:* hon. doctorate (Silesian Univ.) 1997; B. Prus Prize 1975, five Julian Brun Prizes, International Prize of International Journalists Organization, Prize of German Publishers and Booksellers for European Understanding, Leipzig 1994, Prix d'Astrolab, Paris 1995, Jan Parandowski PEN Club Prize 1996, J. W. Goethe Prize, Hamburg 1999, S. B. Linde Literary Prize, Torun-Göttingen 1999, Alfred Jurzykowski Foundation Award in the Field of Literature, New York 1994, Turanski Foundation Award, Toronto 1996, Josef Conrad Literature Award, J. Pilsudski Inst. of America 1997, Tkar Award, Journalist of the Century, 'Press' monthly 1999; State Prize (Second Class) 1976, Gold Cross of Merit, Knight's Cross Order of Polonia Restituta 1974. *Address:* ul. Prokuratorska 11 m. 2, 02-074 Warsaw, Poland.

KARAHASAN, Dževad; Bosnian writer, dramatist and poet; b. 1953, Duvno, Yugoslavia. *Education:* Univ. of Sarajevo. *Career:* worked at Zenica theatre 1976–78; Ed., Odjek magazine, Sarajevo 1979–86; Prof. of Drama, Univ. of Sarajevo 1986–93; Visiting Prof., Univ. of Salzburg, Austria 1994–95. *Plays:* Snow and Death 2002. *Publications:* novels: Schajrijar's Ring 1994, Sara und Serafina 1999, The Nocturnal Council 2003; non-fiction: Sarajevo: Exodus of a City 1994, Knjiga vrtova (trans. as The Book of Gardens) 2001. *Honours:* Leipzig European Understanding Literary Award. *Address:* c/o Antibarbarus, Nova Ves 4, Hrvatska, Zagreb, Croatia.

KARBO, Karen (Lee); Writer; b. 1956, Detroit, MI, USA; m. 1st (divorced); m. 2nd Kelley Baker 1988. *Education:* BA, 1977, MA, 1980, University of Southern California at Los Angeles. *Publications:* Trespassers Welcome Here, 1989; The Diamond Lane, 1991; Motherhood Made a Man Out of Me, 2000; Generation Ex: Tales from the Second Wives Club, 2001. Contributions: periodicals. *Address:* c/o Bloomsbury Publishing, 175 Fifth Ave, Suite 300, New York, NY 10010, USA.

KARIM, Fawzi, BA; poet, writer, editor and publisher; b. 1 July 1945, Baghdad, Iraq; m. 1980; two s. *Education:* Coll. of Arts, Baghdad. *Career:* Ed.-in-Chief and Publisher, Al-Lahda Al-Shiriya quarterly, London; mem. Poetry Soc., England, Union of Iraqi Writers. *Publications:* Where Things Begin 1968, I Raise My Hand in Protest 1973, Madness of Stone 1977, Stumbling of a Bird 1985, We Do Not Inherit the Earth 1988, Schemes of Adam 1991, Pestilential Continents 1995, Selected Poems, 1968–95 1995, Collected Poems (two vols) 2000, The Foundling Years 2003, Continent de douleurs (in French) 2003, The Last Gypsies 2004; other: From Exile to Awareness 1972, City of Copper 1995, The Emperor's Clothes 2000, The Musical Values 2002, Return to Gardenia 2004; essays and short stories; contrib. to reviews and periodicals. *E-mail:* fawzi46@hotmail.com. *Website:* www.iraqiwriter.com.

KARIM, Mustai; Russian (Bashkir) writer and poet; b. 20 Oct. 1919, Kliashevo, Bashkiria; m. Rauza Saubanova 1941; one s. one d. *Education:* Bashkir Pedagogical Inst. *Career:* first Publ 1935; mem. CPSU 1944–91, Soviet Army 1941–45; mem. Bashkir Writers' Union, chair., 1951–62; Russian Writer's Union, sec., 1964–80; Hon. mem., Acad. of Sciences of Bashkortostan, 1991. *Publications:* The Detachment Moves Off, 1938; Spring Voices, 1941; December Song, 1942; The Girls from Our Kolkhoz, 1948; Sabantui, 1953; Europe-Asia, 1951–54; Poems on Viet Nam, 1956–57; Viet Nam Is Not Far, 1958; Selected Works (two vols), 1969; Year by Year, 1971; A Long-Long Childhood, 1972–78; Collected Works, 1983; Homeland, Bread, Love, 1985; Forgiveness, 1985; The Village Advocates, 1989; Flashes of Life, 1991; Evening Meal, 1993; The Return, 1994; Daddy Yalaletdin, 1996; Collected Works (five vols), 1996–99; Memoirs, 2002. Plays: The Wedding Feast Goes On, 1947; Lonely Birch, 1950; Abduction of a Girl, 1959; A Song Unsung, 1961; On the Night of the Lunar Eclipse, 1964; Salavat, 1973; Prometheus, 1975; A Horse to Dictator!, 1980; Evening Meal, 1993. *Honours:* People's Poet of Bashkortostan, 1963; State Prize (USSR), 1972; Hero of Socialist Labour, 1979; Lenin Prize, 1984; Int. Sholokhov Prize, 1999; 10 state orders of USSR and Russia. *Address:* Engels Street. 5, Fl. 17, Ufa 450077, Russia. *E-mail:* karim@anrb.ru.

KARL, Frederick R(obert); Prof. and Literary Scholar; b. 10 April 1927, New York, NY, USA; m. Dolores Mary Oristaglio, 8 June 1951, three d. *Education:* BA, Columbia College, 1948; MA, Stanford University, 1949; PhD, Columbia University, 1957. *Career:* Faculty, 1957–81, Dir of Graduate Programs in English, 1970–76, City College, CUNY; Prof., New York University, 1982–; several guest professorships and lectureships. *Publications:* A Reader's Guide to Joseph Conrad, 1960; The Quest (novel), 1961; The Contemporary English Novel, 1962; The Adversary Literature, 1974; Joseph Conrad: The Three Lives, 1979; American Fictions: 1940–1980, 1983; Modern and Modernism: The Sovereignty of the Artist, 1885–1925, 1985; The Collected Letters of Joseph Conrad (general ed.), 1983 et seq.; William Faulkner: American Writer, 1989; Franz Kafka: Representative Man, 1991; George Eliot: Voice of a Century, 1995; American Fictions: 1980–2000, 2001; Quest for Biography, 2002; A Chronicle of Wasted Time: America in the Seventies, 2002. Contributions: scholarly books and journals. *Honours:* Fulbright Grant, 1965–66; Guggenheim Fellowship, 1966–67; National Endowment for the Humanities Senior Research Grants, 1979, 1988. *Address:* 2 Settlers Landing Lane, East Hampton, NY 11937, USA.

KARLIN, Wayne Stephen, BA, MA; American writer, teacher and editor; b. 13 June 1945, Los Angeles, CA; m. Ohnmar Thein 1977; one s. *Education:* American Coll., Jerusalem, Goddard Coll. *Career:* Pres., co-Ed., First Casualty Press 1972–73; Prof. of Languages and Literature, Coll. of Southern Maryland 1984–; visiting writer, William Joiner Center for the Study of War and Social Consequences, Univ. of Massachusetts, Boston 1989–93; Dir of Fiction, Literary Festival, St Mary's Coll. 1994–; Ed., Curbstone Press Vietnamese Writers series 1996–; mem. Associated Writing Programs. *Publications:* Crossover 1984, Lost Armies 1988, The Extras 1989, US 1993, Rumors and Stones: A Journey 1996, Prisoners (Paterson Prize for Fiction 1999) 1998, The Wished-for Country 2002. Contributions: anthologies and periodicals. *Honours:* Fellowship in Fiction and Individual Artist Award, Maryland State Arts Council, 1988, 1991, 1993, 2001; National Endowment for the Arts Fellowship, 1993; The Critics' Choice Award, 1995–96. *Literary Agent:* Harold Ober Associates, 425 Madison Avenue, New York, NY 10017, USA. *Address:* PO Box 239, St Mary's City, MD 20686, USA. *Address:* c/o Curbstone Press, 321 Jackson Street, Willimantic, CT 06226-1738, USA.

KARNOW, Stanley; Journalist and Writer; b. 4 Feb. 1925, New York, NY, USA; m. 1st Claude Sarraute, 15 July 1948, divorced 1955; m. 2nd Annette Kline, 21 April 1959, two s. one d. *Education:* BA, Harvard University, 1947; University of Paris, 1948–50. *Career:* Correspondent, Time magazine, Paris, 1950–57; Bureau Chief, North Africa, 1958–59, Hong Kong, 1959–62, Time-Life; Special Correspondent, Observer, London, 1961–65, Time Inc, 1962–63, NBC News, 1973–75; Far East Correspondent, Saturday Evening Post, 1963–65; Far East Correspondent, 1965–71, Diplomatic Correspondent, 1971–72, Washington Post; Assoc. Ed., New Republic, 1973–75; Columnist, King Features, 1975–88, Le Point, Paris, 1976–83, Newsweek International, 1977–81; Ed., International Writers Service, 1976–86; Chief Correspondent, PBS series, Viet Nam: A Television History, 1983; Chief Correspondent and Narrator, PBS series The US and the Philippines: In Our Image, 1989; mem. Asia Society; Council on Foreign Relations; PEN American Centre; Society of American Historians. *Publications:* Southeast Asia, 1963; Mao and China: From Revolution to Revolution, 1972; Vietnam: A History, 1983; In Our Image: America's Empire in the Philippines, 1989; Asian Americans in Transition (co-author), 1992; Paris in the Fifties, 1997. Contributions: books, newspapers, journals, and magazines. *Honours:* Neiman Fellow, 1957–58; East Asian Research Center Fellow, 1970–71; Peabody Award, 1984; Pulitzer Prize in History, 1990. *Address:* 10850 Spring Knowlls Dr., Rockville, MD 20854, USA.

KAROL, Alexander (see Kent, Arthur (William Charles)).

KARPOV, Vladimir Vasilyevich; Author and Editor; b. 28 July 1922, Orenburg, Russia; m. Evgenia Vasilievna Karpov 1956; one s. two d. *Education:* Military Acad., Moscow; Gorky Literary Inst. *Career:* arrested 1941, sent to camp, released to join a penal Bn, subsequently distinguishing himself in mil. reconnaissance work; mem. CPSU 1943–91; started publishing (novels, stories, essays) 1948–; Deputy Ed. of Oktyabr 1974–77; Sec.

of Presidium of USSR Union of Writers 1981–86, First Sec. 1986–91; Chief Ed. of Novy mir 1981–86; Deputy to the Presidium of the USSR Supreme Soviet 1984–89; mem. CPSU Cen. Cttee 1988–90, USSR People's Deputy 1989–91; mem. Acad. of Mil. Sciences. *Publications:* The Marshal's Baton, 1970; Take Them Alive, 1975; The Regimental Commander, 1982–84; The Eternal Struggle, 1987; Marshal Zhukov Vol. I, 1989, Vol. II, 1992, Vol. III, 1995; Selected Works (three vols); The Destiny of a Scout (novel), 1999; The Executed Marshals, 2000. *Honours:* Hon. DLitt, Strathclyde Univ.; State Prize, 1986; Hero of Soviet Union, 1944. *Address:* Kutozovsky prosp. 26, Apt 94, Moscow, Russia.

KASHU'A, Said; Israeli writer and journalist; b. Tira. *Education:* Israel Arts and Sciences Acad. High School, Jerusalem. *Publications include:* short stories: Dancing Arabs 2002. *Honours:* Fellow, John Simon Guggenheim Memorial Foundation. *Address:* c/o Grove Press, 841 Broadway, New York, NY 10003-4793, USA.

KASISCHKE, Laura; Poet, Writer and Teacher; b. 5 Dec. 1961, Lake Charles, LA, USA; m. William Abernethy, Aug. 1994, one s. *Education:* BA, 1984, MFA, 1987, University of Michigan; Graduate Studies, Columbia University. *Career:* Instructor in Writing, South Plains College, Levelland, Texas, 1987–88; Visiting Lecturer in Creative Writing and Literature, Eastern Michigan University, 1989–90; Instructor in Creative Writing and Literature, Washtenaw Community College, Ann Arbor, 1990–; Assoc. Prof., University of Nevada, Las Vegas, 1994–95. *Publications:* Poetry: Brides, Wives, and Widows, 1990; Wild Brides, 1992; Housekeeping in a Dream, 1995. Fiction: Suspicious River, 1996; The Life Before Her Eyes, 2001. Contributions: numerous periodicals. *Honours:* Michael Gutterman Poetry Award, 1983; Marjorie Rapaport Poetry Award, 1986; Michigan Council for the Arts Individual Artist Grant, 1990; Ragdale Foundation Fellowships, 1990–92; Elmer Holmes Bobst Award for Emerging Writers, 1991; Bread Loaf Fellow in Poetry, 1992; MacDowell Colony Fellow, 1992; Creative Artists Award, Arts Foundation of Michigan, 1993; Alice Fay DiCastagnola Award, 1993; Pushcart Prize, 1993; Barbara Deming Memorial Award, 1994; National Endowment for the Arts Fellowship, 1994; Poets & Writers Exchange Fellowship, 1994. *Address:* 2997 S Fletcher Rd, Chelsea, MI 48118, USA.

KASSABOVA, Kapka, BA, MA; Bulgarian poet, novelist and journalist; b. 1973, Sofia. *Education:* Univ. of Otago, Dunedin, Victoria Univ. of Wellington, New Zealand. *Career:* teacher of English, Marseilles, France 1998. *Publications:* poetry: All Roads Lead to the Sea 1997, Dismemberment 1998, Someone Else's Life 2003; novels: Reconnaissance 1999, Love in the Land of Midas 2000; travel writing: Globetrotter's Guide to Dheli, Jaipur and Agra 2002; contrib. to Critic, NZ Listener. *Honours:* Buddie Finlay Sargeson Fellowship 1999 ; New Zealand Soc. of Authors Jessie McKay Award for the Best First Book of Poetry, Commonwealth Writers' Prize for Best First Book in the SE Asia-Pacific Region 2000, Cathay Pacific NZ Travel Writer of the Year Award 2002. *Address:* c/o Bloodaxe Books Ltd, Highgreen, Tarset, Northumberland NE48 1RP, England. *Website:* www .bloodaxebooks.com.

KASSEM, Louise (Lou) Sutton Morrell; writer; b. 10 Nov. 1931, Elizabethton, Tennessee, USA; m. Shakeep Kassem 1951; four d. *Education:* East Tennessee State Univ., Univ. of Virginia, Vassar Coll. *Career:* mem. Soc. of Children's Book Writers, Writers in Virginia, Appalachian Writers, Nat. League of American Pen Women. *Publications:* Dance of Death 1984, Middle School Blues 1986, Listen for Rachel 1986, Secret Wishes 1989, A Summer for Secrets 1989, A Haunting in Williamsburg 1990, The Treasures of Witch Hat Mountain 1992, Odd One Out 1994, The Druid Curse 1994, The Innkeeper's Daughter 1996, Sneeze on Monday 1997; contrib. to Alan Review, Signal, Chicken Soup for Kids' Souls, Chicken Soup for Pre-Teen Souls. *Honours:* Notable Book in Social Studies, American Library Asscn 1986, Best Book for Young Readers, Virginia State Reading Asscn. *Address:* 715 Burruss Drive NW, Blacksburg, VA 24060, USA. *Telephone:* (540) 552-2241. *E-mail:* lmk1939@aol.com.

KATTAN, Naïm; Canadian writer, dramatist, critic and academic; b. 26 Aug. 1928, Baghdad, Iraq; m. Gaétane Laniel 1961; one s. *Education:* University of Baghdad, Sorbonne, University of Paris. *Career:* Head, Writing and Publishing Section, 1967–90, Assoc. Dir, 1990–91, Canada Council; Writer-in-Residence, 1992–94, Assoc. Prof., 1994–, University of Québec; Pres., Prix littéraire of the City of Montréal, 1994–96; Dir, Les écrits literary periodical, 2001–; mem. Académie Canadienne Française des Lettres du Québec; Royal Society of Canada. *Publications:* Fiction: Dans les désert, 1974; Adieu, Babylone, 1975, English trans. as Farewell, Babylon, 1976; La traversée, 1976; Les fruits arrachés, 1977, English trans. as Paris Interlude, 1979; Le rivage, 1979; Le sable de l'île, 1979; The Neighbour and Other Stories, 1982; La fiancée promise, 1983; La reprise, 1985; La fortune du passager, 1989; Farida, 1991; A. M. Klein, 1994; La distraction, 1994; La célébration, 1997; L'amour reconnu, 1999; Le silence des adieux, 1999; L'anniversaire, 2000. Plays: La discrétion et autres pièces, 1974. Non-fiction: Le réel et le théatral, 1970, English trans. as Reality and Theatre, 1972; Ecrivains des Amériques, three vols, 1972, 1976, 1980; La mémoire et la promesse, 1978; Le désir et le pouvoir, 1983; Le repos et l'oubli, 1987; Le père, 1990; La réconciliation, 1993; Portaits d'un pays, 1994; Culture: Alibi ou liberté, 1996; Idoles et images, 1996; Figures bibliques, 1997; Les villes de naissance, 2001; L'Ecrivain migrant, 2001. Contributions: many periodicals, radio and television. *Honours:* Prix France-Canada, 1971; Officer of the Order of Canada, 1976; Officier, Ordre des Arts et des Lettres, 1989. *Address:* 3463 Ste-Famille, No. 2114, Montréal, QC H2X 2K7, Canada. *E-mail:* kattan.naim@uqam.ca.

KATZ, Steve, BA, MA; writer, poet, screenwriter and academic; b. 14 May 1935, New York, NY, USA; m. Patricia Bell 1956 (divorced); three s. *Education:* Cornell University, University of Oregon. *Career:* English Language Institute, Lecce, Italy, 1960; Overseas Faculty, University of Maryland, Lecce, Italy, 1961–62; Asst Prof. of English, Cornell University, 1962–67; Lecturer in Fiction, University of Iowa, 1969–70; Writer-in-Residence, 1970–71, Co-Dir, Projects in Innovative Fiction, 1971–73, Brooklyn College, CUNY; Adjunct Asst Prof., Queens College, CUNY, 1973–75; Assoc. Prof. of English, University of Notre Dame, 1976–78; Assoc. Prof. of English, 1978–82, Prof. of English, 1982–, University of Colorado at Boulder; mem. Authors' League of America; PEN International; Writers' Guild. *Publications:* Fiction: The Lestriad, 1962; The Exagggerations of Peter Prince, 1968; Posh, 1971; Saw, 1972; Moving Parts, 1977; Wier and Pouce, 1984; Florry of Washington Heights, 1987; Swanny's Ways, 1995; Antonell's Lion, 2003. Short Stories: Creamy and Delicious: Eat my Words (in Other Words), 1970; Stolen Stories, 1985; 43 Fictions, 1991. Poetry: The Weight of Antony, 1964; Cheyenne River Wild Track, 1973; Journalism, 1990. Screenplay: Grassland, 1974. *Honours:* PEN Grant, 1972; Creative Artists Public Service Grant, 1976; National Educational Asscn grants, 1976, 1982; GCAH Book of the Year, 1991; America Award in Fiction, 1995. *Address:* 669 Washington Street, No. 602, Denver, CO 80203, USA. *E-mail:* elbonoz@earthlink.net.

KAUFMAN, Alan; Writer, Poet and Ed.; b. 12 Jan. 1952, New York, NY, USA; m. Diane Spencer, one d. *Education:* BA, City College, CUNY, 1975; Columbia University, 1986–87. *Career:* Founder-Ed., Jewish Arts Quarterly, 1974–75, Jewish Cultural Revolution, 1996–97, TATTOOJEW.COM, 1998–2001; many poetry performances. *Publications:* The End of Time (short stories), 1985; The New Generation: Fiction for Our Time from America's Writing Programs (ed.), 1987; Who Are We? (poems), 1997; The Outlaw Bible of American Poetry (ed.), 1999; Jew Boy: A Memoir, 2000. Contributions: anthologies and periodicals. *Honours:* Firecracker Alternative Book Award, 2000. *Address:* 1126 Bush St, Apt 605, San Francisco, CA 94109, USA.

KAUFMAN, Charles (Charlie) Stewart; American screenwriter; b. Nov. 1958, W Hartford, CT; m. Denise Kaufman. *Education:* Boston Univ., NY Univ. *Career:* worked in newspaper circulation dept, The Star Tribune, Minneapolis, MN 1986–90; contrib. articles National Lampoon, LA 1991; began scriptwriting 1991; cr. short films shown on Late Night with David Letterman TV show 1990s; writer 30 episodes for TV shows 1991–1996; producer Misery Loves Company (TV series) 1995. *Screenplays include:* films: Being John Malkovich 1999, Human Nature 2001, Adaptation 2002, Confessions of a Dangerous Mind 2002, Eternal Sunshine of the Spotless Mind 2003; television: Get A Life 1991–92, The Edge 1992–93, The Trouble with Larry 1993, Ned and Stacey 1996–97, The Dana Carvey Show 1996. *Literary Agent:* United Talent Agency, 9560 Wilshire Boulevard, Fifth Floor, Beverly Hills, CA 90212, USA.

KAUFMAN, Gerald (Bernard); MP and Writer; b. 21 June 1930, Leeds, England. *Education:* MA, Queen's College, Oxford, 1953. *Career:* Asst General Secretary, Fabian Society, 1954–55; Staff, Daily Mirror, 1955–64; Political Correspondent, New Statesman, 1964–65; Parliamentary Press Liaison Officer, Labour Party, 1965–70, MP, Manchester, Ardwick, 1970–83, Manchester, Gorton, 1983–, Labour Party; Parliamentary Under-Secretary of State, Dept of the Environment, 1974–75, Dept of Industry, 1975; Minister of State, Dept of Industry, 1975–79; Shadow Environment Secretary, 1980–83; Shadow Home Secretary, 1983–87; Shadow Foreign Secretary, 1987–92; Chair., Select Committee on the National Heritage, 1992–97, and on Culture, Media and Sport, 1997–; Chair., Booker Prize Judges, 1999. *Publications:* How to Live Under Labour (co-author), 1964; The Left (ed.), 1966; To Build the Promised Land, 1973; How to Be a Minister, 1980; Renewal: Labour's Britain in the 1980s, 1983; My Life in the Silver Screen, 1985; Inside the Promised Land, 1986; Meet Me in St Louis, 1994. *Honours:* Privy Councillor, 1978. *Address:* 87 Charlbert Ct, Eamont St, London NW8 7DA, England.

KAUFMANN, Myron S.; Novelist; b. 27 Aug. 1921, Boston, Massachusetts, USA; m. Paula Goldberg, 6 Feb. 1960, divorced 1980, one s. two d. *Education:* AB, Harvard University, 1943. *Publications:* Fiction: Remember Me To God, 1957; Thy Daughter's Nakedness, 1968; The Love of Elspeth Baker, 1982. *Address:* 111 Pond St, Sharon, MA 02067, USA.

KAUFMANN, Thomas DaCosta; Prof. of Art History and Writer; b. 7 May 1948, New York, NY, USA; m. Virginia Burns Roehrig, 1 June 1974, divorced 17 July 1998, one d. *Education:* BA, MA, 1970, Yale University; MPhil, Warburg Institute, University of London, 1972; PhD, Harvard University, 1977. *Career:* Asst Prof., 1977–83, Assoc. Prof., 1983–89, Prof. of Art History, 1989–, Princeton University; Visiting professorships and curatorships; mem. College Art Asscn of America; Renaissance Society of America; Verband Deutscher Kunsthistorien. *Publications:* Variations on the Imperial Theme, 1978; Drawings From the Holy Roman Empire 1540–1650, 1982; L'Ecole de Prague, 1985; Art and Architecture in Central Europe 1550–1620, 1985; The School of Prague: Painting at the Court of

Rudolf II, 1988; Central European Drawings 1680–1800, 1989; The Mastery of Nature, 1993; Court, Cloister and City, 1995. Contributions: books and professional journals. *Honours:* Marshall-Allison Fellow, 1970; David E. Finley Fellow, National Gallery of Art, Washington, DC, 1974–77; ACLS Award, 1977–78, and Fellowship, 1982; Senior Fellow, Alexander von Humboldt Stiftung, Berlin and Munich, 1985–86, 1989–90; Guggenheim Fellowship, 1993–94; Herzog August Bibliothek Fellow, Wolfenbüttel, 1994. *Address:* c/o Dept of Art and Archeology, McCormick Hall, Princeton University, Princeton, NJ 08544, USA.

KAVALER, Lucy Estrin, BA; writer; b. 29 Aug. 1930, New York, NY, USA; m. 1948; one s. one d. *Education:* Oberlin College, OH; Fellowship, Advanced Science Writing, Columbia University Graduate School. *Publications:* Private World of High Society, 1960; Mushrooms, Molds and Miracles, 1965; The Astors, 1966; Freezing Point, 1970; Noise the New Menace, 1975; A Matter of Degree, 1981; The Secret Lives of the Edmonts, 1989; Heroes and Lovers, 1995. Contributions: Smithsonian; Natural History; McCall's; Reader's Digest; Redbook; Primary Cardiology; Woman's Day (encyclopaedia); Skin Cancer Foundation Journal; Memories; Female Patient.

KAVALER, Rebecca; Writer; b. 26 July 1930, Atlanta, GA, USA; m. Frederic Kavaler 1955; two s. *Education:* AB, University of Georgia. *Career:* mem. PEN. *Publications:* Further Adventures of Brunhild, 1978; Doubting Castle, 1984; Tigers in the Woods, 1986; A Little More Than Kin, 2002. Contributions: anthologies and magazines. *Honours:* Short stories included in Best of Nimrod, 1957–69; Best American Short Stories, 1972; Award for Short Fiction, Associated Writing Programs, 1978; National Endowment for the Arts Fellowships, 1979, 1985. *Address:* 425 Riverside Dr., New York, NY 10025, USA. *E-mail:* rkavaler@msn.com.

KAVANAGH, Dan (see Barnes, Julian Patrick).

KAVANAGH, Patrick Joseph, MA, FRSL; poet, writer and editor; b. 6 Jan. 1931, Worthing, Sussex, England; m. 1st Sally Philipps 1956 (died 1958); m. 2nd Catherine Ward 1965; two s. *Education:* Merton College, Oxford. *Career:* Columnist, The Spectator, 1983–96, TLS, 1996–2002. *Publications:* Poetry: One and One, 1960; On the Way to the Depot, 1967; About Time, 1970; Edward Thomas in Heaven, 1974; Life Before Death, 1979; Selected Poems, 1982; Presences: New and Selected Poems, 1987; An Enchantment, 1991; Collected Poems, 1992. Fiction: A Song and Dance, 1968; A Happy Man, 1972; People and Weather, 1978; Scarf Jack: The Irish Captain, 1978; Rebel for Good, 1980; Only By Mistake, 1980. Non-Fiction: The Perfect Stranger, 1966; People and Places, 1988; Finding Connections, 1990; Voices in Ireland: A Traveller's Literary Companion, 1994; A Kind of Journal, 2003; A Poet's Country: Selected Prose, 2003. Editor: The Collected Poems of Ivor Gurney, 1982; The Oxford Book of Short Poems (with James Michie), 1985; The Bodley Head G. K. Chesterton, 1985; Selected Poems of Ivor Gurney, 1990; A Book of Consolations, 1992. *Honours:* Richard Hillary Prize, 1966; Guardian Fiction Prize, 1968; Cholmondeley Poetry Prize, 1993. *Literary Agent:* PFD, Drury House, 34–43 Russell Street, London WC2B 5HA, England.

KAVANAUGH, Cynthia (see Daniels, Dorothy).

KAWAMOTO, Koji; Japanese author and critic. *Career:* Pres., International Comparative Literary Asscn (ICLA); Vice-Pres., Oternae Univ.; teaches literature at the Univ. of Tokyo. *Publications:* non-fiction: The Poetics of Japanese Verse - Imagery, Structure and Meter 1999. *Address:* c/o Paola Mildonian, Letterature Comparate, Dipartim. di Studi Anglo-Americani e Ibero-Americani, Universitè Ca' Foscari-Venezia, Ca' Garzoni, S. Marco 3417, 30124, Venice, Italy.

KAY, Guy Gavriel; Author; b. 7 Nov. 1954, Weyburn, Saskatchewan, Canada; m. Laura Beth Cohen, 15 July 1984, two s. *Education:* BA, University of Manitoba, 1975; LLB, University of Toronto, 1978. *Career:* Principal Writer and Assoc. Producer, The Scales of Justice, CBC Radio Drama, 1981–90; mem. Asscn of Canadian Radio and TV Artists; Law Society of Upper Canada. *Publications:* The Summer Tree, 1984; The Darkest Road, 1986; The Wandering Fire, 1986; Tigana, 1990; A Song for Arbonne, 1992; The Lions of Al-Rassan, 1995. Contributions: journals. *Honours:* Aurora Prizes, 1986, 1990. *Literary Agent:* Curtis Brown Ltd, Haymarket House, 28–29 Haymarket, London, SW1Y 4SP, England. *Telephone:* (20) 7393-4400. *Fax:* (20) 7393-4401. *E-mail:* info@curtisbrown.co.uk. *Website:* www.curtisbrown.co.uk.

KAYE, Geraldine (Hughesdon); Writer; b. 14 Jan. 1925, Watford, Herts, England; m. 1948, divorced 1975, one s. two d. *Education:* BSc, Economics, LSE, 1949. *Career:* mem. PEN; West Country Writers; Society of Authors. *Publications:* Comfort Herself, 1985; A Breath of Fresh Air, 1986; Summer in Small Street, 1989; Someone Else's Baby, 1990; A Piece of Cake, 1991; Snowgirl, 1991; Stone Boy, 1991; Hands Off My Sister, 1993; Night at the Zoo, 1995; Forests of the Night, 1995; Late in the Day, 1997; The Dragon Upstairs, 1997; My Second Best Friend, 1998; Between Us (adult novel), 1998. *Honours:* The Other Award, 1986. *Address:* 39 High Kingsdown, Bristol BS2 8EW, England.

KAYE, Marvin (Nathan); Writer; b. 10 March 1938, Philadelphia, Pennsylvania, USA; m. Saralee Bransdorf, 4 Aug. 1963, one d. *Education:* BA, 1960, MA, 1962, Pennsylvania State University; Graduate Studies, University of Denver, 1960. *Career:* Senior Ed., Harcourt Brace Jovanovich; Artistic Dir, Open Book Theatre Company 1975–; Adjunct Prof. of Creative Writing, New York University, 1975–; Seminar Dir, Smithsonian Institution, Washington, DC, 1998–; mem. several professional organizations. *Publications:* The Histrionic Holmes, 1971; A Lively Game of Death, 1972; A Toy is Born, 1973; The Stein and Day Handbook of Magic, 1973; The Grand Ole Opry Murders, 1974; The Handbook of Mental Magic, 1974; Bullets for Macbeth, 1976; The Incredible Umbrella, 1977; Catalog of Magic, 1977; My Son the Druggist, 1977; The Laurel and Hardy Murders, 1977; My Brother the Druggist, 1979; The Amorous Umbrella, 1981; The Possession of Immanuel Wolf, 1981; The Soap Opera Slaughters, 1982; Ghosts of Night and Morning, 1985; Fantastique, 1993. With Parke Godwin: The Masters of Solitude, 1978; Wintermind, 1982; A Cold Blue Light, 1983. Editor: Fiends and Creatures, 1975; Brother Theodore's Chamber of Horrors, 1975; Ghosts, 1981; Masterpieces of Terror and the Supernatural, 1985; Ghosts of Night and Morning, 1987; Devils and Demons, 1987; Weird Tales, the Magazine That Never Dies, 1988; Witches and Warlocks, 1989; 13 Plays of Ghosts and the Supernatural, 1990; Haunted America, 1991; Lovers and Other Monsters, 1991; Sweet Revenge, 1992; Masterpieces of Terror and the Unknown, 1993; Frantic Comedy, 1993; The Game is Afoot, 1994; Angels of Darkness, 1995; Readers Theatre: How to Stage It, 1995; The Resurrected Holmes, 1996; Page to Stage, 1996; The Best of Weird Tales, 1923, 1997; The Confidential Casebook of Sherlock Holmes, 1998; Don't Open This Book, 1998. Contributions: Amazing; Fantastic; Galileo; Family Digest; Columnist, Science Fiction Chronicle. *Address:* c/o Donald C. Maass, 157 W 57th St, Suite 703, New York, NY 10019, USA.

KAYSEN, Susanna; Writer; b. 11 Nov. 1948, Cambridge, MA, USA. *Publications:* Asa, as I Knew Him, 1987; Far Afield, 1990; Girl, Interrupted, 1993; The Camera My Mother Gave Me, 2001. *Address:* c/o Jonathan Matson, Harold Matson Co Inc, 276 Fifth Ave, New York, NY 10001, USA.

KAZANTZIS, Judith; Poet and Novelist; b. 14 Aug. 1940, Oxford, England; m. 2nd Irving Weinman; one d., one s. (from previous marriage). *Education:* Degree, Modern History, Oxford 1961. *Career:* mem. Society of Authors, English PEN, Palestine Solidarity Campaign, Nicaragua Solidarity Campaign, Campaign for Nuclear Disarmament. *Publications:* Minefield 1977, The Wicked Queen 1980, Touch Papers (co-author) 1982, Let's Pretend 1984, Flame Tree 1988, A Poem for Guatemala (pamphlet) 1988, The Rabbit Magician Plate 1992, Selected Poems 1977–92 1995, Swimming Through the Grand Hotel 1997, The Odysseus Papers: Fictions on the Odyssey of Homer 1999, In Cyclop's Cave (trans. of book IX of The Odyssey) 2002, Of Love and Terror (novel) 2002, Just After Midnight (poetry) 2004; contribs to anthologies and periodicals. *E-mail:* jktropic@aol.com.

KEARNS, Marguerite, (Marguerite Culp); Writer; b. 17 Feb. 1943, Norristown, PA, USA. *Education:* BA, Sociology, Beaver College, Glenside, Pennsylvania, 1964; Graduate Studies, Temple University, Philadelphia, 1965–67. *Career:* mem. National Writers' Union; PEN. *Publications:* Freedom Deferred (online), 2002; Big Brother, 2002; For Love's Sake Only, 2002. Contributions: newspapers and journals. *Honours:* Award in Journalism, New York State Bar Asscn, 1974. *Address:* PO Box 23316, Santa Fe, NM 87502, USA.

KEATING, Henry Reynard Fitzwalter, (Evelyn Hervey); author; b. 31 Oct. 1926, St Leonards-on-Sea, Sussex, England; m. Sheila Mary Mitchell 1953; three s. one d. *Education:* BA, Trinity College, Dublin, 1952. *Career:* mem. CWA, chair., 1970–71; Detection Club, pres., 1985–2001; FRSL; Society of Authors, chair., 1983–84. *Publications:* Death and the Visiting Firemen, 1959; Zen There was Murder, 1960; A Rush on the Ultimate, 1961; The Dog it was That Died, 1962; Death of a Fat God, 1963; The Perfect Murder, 1964; Is Skin-Deep, Is Fatal, 1965; Inspector Ghote's Good Crusade, 1966; Inspector Ghote Caught in Meshes, 1967; Inspector Ghote Hunts the Peacock, 1968; Inspector Ghote Plays a Joker, 1969; Inspector Ghote Breaks and Egg, 1970; Inspector Ghote Goes by Train, 1971; The Strong Man, 1971; Blood on My Mind (ed.), 1972; Inspector Ghote Trusts the Heart, 1972; The Underside, 1974; Bats Fly Up for Inspector Ghote, 1974; A Remarkable Case of Burglary, 1975; Filmi, Filmi, Inspector Ghote, 1976; Murder Must Appetize, 1976; Agatha Christie: First Lady of Crime (ed.), 1977; A Long Walk to Wimbledon, 1978; Inspector Ghote Draws a Line, 1979; Sherlock Holmes: The Man and His World, 1979; The Murder of the Maharajah, 1980; Go West, Inspector Ghote, 1981; Whodunit (ed.), 1982; The Lucky Alphonse, 1982; The Sheriff of Bombay, 1984; Mrs Craggs, Crimes Cleaned Up, 1985; Under a Monsoon Cloud, 1986; Writing Crime Fiction, 1986; The Body in the Billiard Room, 1987; Crime and Mystery: The 100 Best Books, 1987; Dead on Time, 1988; Inspector Ghote: His Life and Crimes, 1989; Bedside Companion to Crime (ed.), 1989; The Iciest Sin, 1990; Crime Wave 1 (ed.), 1991; Cheating Death, 1992; The Man Who (ed.), 1992; The Rich Detective, 1993; Doing Wrong, 1994; The Good Detective, 1995; The Bad Detective, 1996; Asking Questions, 1996; The Soft Detective, 1997; In Kensington Gardens Once, 1997; Bribery, Corruption Also, 1999; Jack, the Lady Killer, 1999; The Hard Detective, 2000; Breaking and Entering, 2000; A Detective in Love, 2001; A Detective Under Fire, 2002. *Honours:* CWA Gold Dagger Awards, 1964, 1980, Diamond Dagger Award, 1996; FRSL, 1990. *Address:* 35 Northumberland Place, London W2 5AS, England.

KEAY, John (Stanley Melville); Author and Broadcaster; b. 18 Sept. 1941, Devon, England; m. Julia; four c. *Education:* Ampleforth Coll., York; BA, Magdalen Coll., Oxford, 1963. *Publications:* Into India, 1973; When Men and Mountains Meet, 1977; The Gilgit Game, 1979; India Discovered, 1981; Eccentric Travellers, 1982; Highland Drove, 1984; Explorers Extraordinary, 1985; The Royal Geographical Society's History of World Exploration, 1991; The Honourable Company, 1991; Collins Encyclopaedia of Scotland (with Julia Keay), 1994; Indonesia: From Sabang to Merauke, 1995; The Explorers of the Western Himalayas, 1996; Last Post: Empire's End, 1997; India: A History, 2000; The Great Arc, 2000; Sowing the Wind: The Seeds of Conflict in the Middle East, 2003. *Address:* Succoth, Dalmally, Argyll, Scotland.

KEEBLE, Neil Howard; University Prof., Writer and Ed.; b. 7 Aug. 1944, London, England; m. Jenny Bowers, 20 July 1968, two s. one d. *Education:* BA, University of Lampeter, 1966; DPhil, University of Oxford, 1974; DLitt, University of Stirling, 1994. *Career:* Lecturer in English, University of Århus, 1969–74; Lecturer, 1974–88, Reader in English, 1988–, University of Stirling. *Publications:* Richard Baxter: Puritan Man of Letters, 1982; The Literary Culture of Nonconformity, 1987; Calendar of the Correspondence of Richard Baxter (co-author), 1991. Editor: The Autobiography of Richard Baxter, 1974; The Pilgrim's Progress, 1984; John Bunyan: Conventicle and Parnassus, 1988; The Cultural Identity of Seventeenth-Century Woman, 1994; Lucy Hutchinson, Memoirs of the Life of Colonel Hutchinson, 1995; The Cambridge Companion to Writing of the English Revolution, 2001. Contributions: numerous articles on cultural history 1500–1700, in academic journals. *Honours:* FRHistS, 1990, English Asscn, 2000, Royal Society of Edinburgh; FRSA; Hon. Fellow, University of Wales, Lampeter, 2000. *Address:* Duncraggan House, Airthrey Rd, Stirling FK9 5JS, Scotland. *E-mail:* n.h.keeble@stir.ac.uk.

KEEFFE, Barrie (Colin); Playwright; b. 31 Oct. 1945, London, England; m. 1st Dee Truman 1969 (divorced 1979); m. 2nd Verity Bargate 1981 (died 1981); two step-s.; m. 3rd Julia Linday 1983 (divorced 1993). *Career:* Actor; Dramatist-in-Residence, Shaw Theatre, London, 1977, RSC, 1978; Assoc. Writer, Theatre Royal Stratford East, London, 1986–91; tutor, City Univ. of London, 2002–03; Judith E. Wilson Fellowship, Christ's College, Cambridge, 2003–(04). *Publications:* Plays: A Mad World, My Masters, 1977; Methuen, 1977; Gimme Shelter, 1977; Barbarians, 1977; Frozen Assets, 1978; Sus, 1979; Heaven Scent, 1979; Bastard Angel, 1980; Black Lear, 1980; She's So Modern, 1980; Chorus Girls (with Ray Davies), 1981; A Gentle Spirit (with Jules Croiset), 1981; The Long Good Friday (screenplay), 1984; Better Times, 1985; King of England, 1986; My Girl, 1989; Not Fade Away, 1990; Wild Justice, 1990; I Only Want to Be With You, 1997; Shadows on the Sun, 2001. Director: The Gary Oldman Fan Club, 1998. Radio Plays: Good Old Uncle Jack, 1975; Pigeon Skyline, 1975; Self-Portrait, 1977; Paradise, 1990; On the Eve of the Millennium, 1999; Tales, 2000; Feng Shui and Me, 2000; Barrie Keeffe Plays I, 2001; The Five of Us, 2002. Television Plays: Gotcha, 1977; Champions, 1978; Hanging Around, 1978; Waterloo Sunset, 1979; No Excuses Series, 1983; King, 1984. *Honours:* French Critics Prix Revelation, 1978; Giles Cooper Award, Best Radio Plays, 1978; Edgar Allan Poe Award, MWA, 1982; Ambassador for UN 50th Anniversary, 1995. *Address:* 110 Annandale Rd, London SE10 0JZ, England.

KEEGAN, Sir John (Desmond Patrick); Military Historian, Author, Ed. and Lecturer; b. 15 May 1934, London, England; m. Susanne Ingeborg Everett, 1960, two s. two d. *Education:* BA, 1957, MA, 1962, Balliol College, Oxford. *Career:* Political Analyst, US Embassy, London, 1958–60; Senior Lecturer in Military History, Royal Military Acad., Sandhurst, 1960–68; Contributing Ed., The New Republic, 1980–90, US News and World Report, 1986–; Visiting Fellow, Princeton University, 1984; Defence Ed., The Daily Telegraph, 1986–; Delmas Visiting Distinguished Prof. of History, Vassar College, 1997–98; mem. FRHistS; FRSL. *Publications:* The Face of Battle, 1976; Who's Who in Miltary History (co-author), 1976; World Armies (ed.), 1978; Six Armies in Normandy, 1982; Zones of Conflict (co-author), 1986; The Mask of Command, 1987; The Price of Admiralty, 1988, revised edn as Battle at Sea, 1993; The Second World War, 1989; The Times Atlas of the Second World War (ed.), 1989; Churchill's Generals (ed.), 1991; A History of Warfare, 1993; Warpaths: Travels of a Military Historian in North America, 1995; The Battle for History, 1996; The First World War, 1998; War and Our World: The Reith Lectures, 1998; The Penguin Book of War: Great Military Writings (ed.), 1999; Winston Churchill, 2002; Intelligence in War, 2003. Contributions: Dictionary of National Biography; Encyclopaedia Britannica. *Honours:* OBE, 1991; Duff Cooper Prize, 1994; Samuel Eliot Morrison Prize, 1996; Hon. Fellow, Balliol College, Oxford, 1999; Westminster Medal, 1999; Knighted, 2000. *Address:* The Manor House, Kilmington, near Warminster, Wiltshire BA12 6RD, England.

KEEGAN, Mary Constance, (Mary Heathcott, Mary Raymond); Author; b. 30 Sept. 1914, Manchester, England. *Career:* Editorial positions, London Evening News, 1934–40, Straits Times and Singapore Free Press, 1940–42, MOI All-India Radio, 1944, Time and Tide, 1945, John Herling's Labor Letter, 1951–54. *Publications:* As Mary Keegan, Mary Heathcott or Mary Raymond: If Today Be Sweet, 1956; Island of the Heart, 1957; Love Be Wary, 1958; Her Part of the House, 1960; Hide My Heart, 1961; Thief of My Heart, 1962; Never Doubt Me, 1963; Shadow of a Star, 1963; Take-Over, 1965; Girl in a Mask, 1965; The Divided House, 1966; The Long Journey Home, 1967; I Have Three Sons, 1968; That Summer, 1970; Surety for a Stranger, 1971; The Pimpernel Project, 1972; The Silver Girl, 1973; Villa of Flowers, 1976; April Promise, 1980; Grandma Tyson's Legacy, 1982. *Address:* Cockenskell, Blawith, Ulverston, Cumbria, England.

KEEGAN, William James; Journalist and Writer; b. 3 July 1938, London, England; m. 1st Tessa Ashton, 7 Feb. 1967, divorced 1982, two s. two d.; m. 2nd Hilary Stonefrost, 1992, one s. two d. *Career:* Economics Ed., 1977, Assoc. Ed., 1983–, The Observer; Visiting Prof. of Journalism, Sheffield University, 1989–; mem. Dept of Applied Economics, Cambridge, advisory board, 1988–93. *Publications:* Consulting Father Wintergreen (novel), 1974; A Real Killing (novel), 1976; Who Runs the Economy?, 1979; Mrs Thatcher's Economic Experiment, 1984; Britain Without Oil, 1985; Mr Lawson's Gamble, 1989; The Spectre of Capitalism, 1992; 2066 and All That, 2000. Contributions: The Tablet; Frequent Broadcaster. *Honours:* Hon. doctorates. *Address:* 76 Lofting Rd, London N1 1JB, England.

KEELEY, Edmund Leroy, BA, DPhil; American academic, writer and translator; b. 5 Feb. 1928, Damascus, Syria; m. Mary Stathatos-Kyris 1951. *Education:* Princeton University, University of Oxford. *Career:* Instructor, Brown University, 1952–53; Fulbright Lecturer, University of Thessaloniki, 1953–54, 1986; Instructor, 1954–57, Asst Prof., 1957–63, Assoc. Prof., 1963–70, Prof. of English and Creative Writing, 1970–92, Charles Branwell Straut Class of 1923 Prof. of English, 1992–94, Prof. Emeritus, 1994–, Princeton University; Visiting Lecturer, University of Iowa, 1962–63, University of the Aegean, 1988; Writer-in-Residence, Knox College, 1963; Visiting Prof., New School for Social Research, New York, 1980, Columbia University, 1981, King's College, University of London, 1996; Fulbright Lecturer, 1985, and Research Fellow, 1987, University of Athens; Senior Assoc. Mem., St Antony's College, Oxford, 1996; mem. American Acad. of Arts and Sciences; Acad. of Athens; American Literary Trans Asscn; Authors' Guild; Modern Greek Studies Asscn, pres., 1969–73, 1982–84; PEN American Center, pres., 1991–93; Poetry Society of America. *Publications:* Fiction: The Libation, 1958; The Gold-Hatted Lover, 1961; The Impostor, 1970; Voyage to a Dark Island, 1972; A Wilderness Called Peace, 1985; School for Pagan Lovers, 1993; Some Wine for Remembrance, 2001. Non-Fiction: Cavafy's Alexandria, 1976; Modern Greek Poetry: Voice and Myth, 1982; The Salonika Bay Murder: Cold War Politics and the Polk Affair, 1989; Albanian Journal: The Road to Elbasan, 1996; George Seferis and Edmund Keeley: Correspondence, 1951–1971, 1997; Inventing Paradise: The Greek Journey, 1937–1947, 1999; On Translation: Reflections and Conversations, 2000. Translator: George Seferis: Collected Poems (with Philip Sherrard), 1967; Odysseus Elytis: The Axion Esti (with George Savidis), 1974; C. P. Cavafy: Collected Poems (with Philip Sherrard and George Savidis), 1975; Angelos Sikelianos: Selected Poems (with Philip Sherrard), 1979; Odysseus Elytis: Selected Poems (with Philip Sherrard), 1981; Yannis Ritsos: Repetitions, Testimonies, Parentheses, 1991; A Greek Quintet (with Philip Sherrard), 1992. Contributions: books and journals. *Honours:* Rome Prize Fellow, 1959–60, Award in Literature, 1999, American Acad. of Arts and Letters; Guggenheim Fellowships, 1959–60, 1973; Columbia University Trans. Center-PEN Award, 1975; Harold Morton Landon Trans. Award, 1980; National Endowment for the Arts Fellowships, 1981, 1988–89; Rockefeller Foundation Scholar, Bellagio Study Center, Italy, 1982, 1989; Research Fellow, Virginia Center for the Creative Arts, 1983, 1984, 1986, 1990; Pushcart Prize Anthology, 1984; First European Prize for Trans. of Poetry, 1987; Hon. Doctorate, University of Athens, 1994; PEN-Ralph Manheim Medal for Trans., 2000; Commander, Order of the Phoenix (Greece), 2001. *Address:* 140 Littlebrook Road, Princeton, NJ, USA.

KEEN, Geraldine (see Norman, Geraldine (Lucia)).

KEENAN, Brian; Author; b. 28 Sept. 1950, Belfast, Northern Ireland; m. Audrey Doyle, 20 May 1993. *Education:* BA, 1974, MA, 1984, Ulster University; PhD, Queen's University, Belfast, 1993. *Career:* Instructor in English, American University, Beirut, Lebanon, 1985–86; Writer-in-Residence, Trinity College, Dublin, 1993–94. *Publications:* An Evil Cradling: The Five-Year Ordeal of a Hostage, 1992; Blind Fight (screenplay), 1995; Between Extremes, 1999; Turlough, 2000. *Honours:* Time/Life International PEN Award, 1992; Ewart Biggs Award, 1992; Irish Times Award, 1992; Christopher Award, New York, 1993. *Address:* c/o Elaine Steel, 110 Gloucester Ave, London NW1 8JA, England.

KEENE, Dennis; Prof. of English Literature (retd), Poet, Writer and Trans; b. 10 July 1934, London, England; m. Keiko Kurose 5 May 1962; one d. *Education:* BA, English Literature and Language, 1957, MA, 1961, DPhil, Oriental Studies, 1973, Univ. of Oxford. *Career:* Asst Lecturer in English Literature, Univ. of Malaya, 1958–60; Lecturer in English Language and Literature, Kyoto Univ., 1961–63; Invited Prof. of English Literature, Haile Selassie I Univ., Ethiopia, 1964–65; Lecturer in English Literature, Kyushu Univ., 1965–69; Asst Prof., 1970–76, Prof. of English Literature, 1976–81, 1984–93, Japan Women's Univ. *Publications:* Poetry: Surviving, 1980; Universe and Other Poems, 1984. Prose: Problems in English, 1969; Yokomitsu Riichi, Modernist, 1980; Wasurerareta Kuni, Nippon, 1995. Editor: Selected Poems of Henry Howard, Earl of Surrey, 1985. Translator: Grass For My Pillow (novel by Saiichi Maruya), 2002; Over 10 books of

Japanese poems, novels and short stories, 1974–2002. *Honours:* Independent Foreign Fiction Special Award, 1990; Noma Trans. Prize, 1992. *Address:* 77 Staunton Rd, Headington, Oxford OX3 7TL, England.

KEENE, Donald; Prof. of Japanese Emeritus, Writer and Trans; b. 18 June 1922, New York, NY, USA. *Education:* BA, 1942, MA, 1947, PhD, 1951, Columbia University; MA, 1949, DLitt, 1978, University of Cambridge. *Career:* Lecturer, University of Cambridge, 1948–53; Guest Ed., Asahi Shimbun, Tokyo, Japan; Prof., Columbia University, 1953–1992; Shincho Prof. Emeritus of Japanese, Columbia University; mem. Japan Society, New York, dir, 1979–82; American Acad. of Arts and Letters; Japan Acad., foreign mem. *Publications:* The Battles of Coxinga, 1951; The Japanese Discovery of Europe, 1952; Japanese Literature: An Introduction for Western Readers, 1953; Living Japan, 1957; Bunraku, the Puppet Theater of Japan, 1965; No: The Classical Theatre of Japan, 1966; Landscapes and Portraits, 1971; Some Japanese Portraits, 1978; World Within Walls, 1978; Meeting with Japan, 1978; Travels in Japan, 1981; Dawn to the West, 1984; Travellers of a Hundred Ages, 1990; Seeds in the Heart, 1993; On Familiar Terms, 1994; Modern Japanese Diaries, 1995; Emperor of Japan, 2002. Editor: Anthology of Japanese Literature, 1955; Modern Japanese Literature, 1956; Sources of Japanese Tradition, 1958; Twenty Plays of the No Theater, 1970. Translator: The Setting Sun, 1956; Five Modern No Plays, 1957; No Longer Human, 1958; Major Plays of Chikamatsu, 1961; The Old Woman, the Wife and the Archer, 1961; After the Banquet, 1965; Essays in Idleness, 1967; Madame de Sade, 1967; Friends, 1969; The Man Who Turned into a Stick, 1972; Three Plays of Kobo Abe, 1993; The Narrow Road to Oku, 1997; The Tale of the Bamboo Cutter, 1998. *Honours:* DLitt, Tohoku, 1997, Waseda, 1998, Tokyo University of Foreign Languages, 1999, Keiwa, 2000. *Address:* 407 Kent Hall, Columbia University, New York, NY 10027, USA.

KEILLOR, Garrison Edward, BA; American writer and broadcaster; b. (Gary Edward Keillor), 7 Aug. 1942, Anoka, MN; m. 1st Mary Guntzel (divorced 1976, died 1998); one s.; m. 2nd Ulla Skaerved (divorced); m. 3rd Jenny Lind Nilsson; one d. *Education:* Anoka High School and Univ. of Minnesota. *Career:* journalist 1962–63; radio announcer and presenter 1969–73; cr. and host A Prairie Home Companion radio show 1974–87, 1993–; host American Radio Co. 1989–93; staff writer The New Yorker 1987–92. *Publications:* Happy to Be Here 1982, Lake Wobegon Days (Grammy Award for best non-musical recording 1987) 1985, Leaving Home 1987, We Are Still Married: Stories and Letters 1989, WLT: A Radio Romance 1991, Wobegon Boy The Book of Guys 1993, Cat, You Better Come Home (children's book) 1995, The Old Man Who Loved Cheese 1996, The Sandy Bottom Orchestra 1996, Wobegon Boy 1997, ME by Jimmy (Big Boy) Valente as told to Garrison Keillor 1999, Lake Wobegon Summer 1956 2001, Love Me 2004; contrib. to newspapers and magazines. *Honours:* George Foster Peabody Award 1980, Ace Award for best musical host (A Prairie Home Companion) 1988, Best Music and Entertainment Host Awards 1988, 1989, American Acad. and Institute of Arts and Letters Medal 1990, Music Broadcast Communications Radio Hall of Fame 1994, Nat. Humanities Medal 1999. *Address:* A Prairie Home Companion, Minnesota Public Radio, 45 Seventh Street E, St Paul, MN 55101, USA (Office).

KEIN, Sybil; Prof. of English, Poet, Dramatist and Musician; b. 29 Sept. 1939, New Orleans, LA, USA; m. Felix Provost, 1960, divorced 1969, one s. two d. *Education:* BS, Xavier University, 1964; Aspen School of Arts, 1964; MA, Louisiana State University, 1972; PhD, University of Michigan, 1975. *Career:* Instructor, 1972–75, Asst Prof., 1975–78, Assoc. Prof., 1979–88, Prof. of English, 1988–, University of Michigan at Flint. *Publications:* Bessie, Bojangles and Me, 1975; Visions from the Rainbow, 1979; Gombo People: Poésies Créoles de la Nouvelle Orleans, 1981; Delta Dancer, 1984; An American South, 1997. Contributions: anthologies and journals. *Honours:* several teaching awards; Creative Artist Awards for Poetry, Michigan Council for the Arts, 1981, 1984, 1989; Chercheur Associé, Centre d'Etudes Afro-Americaines, Université de la Sorbonne Nouvelle, 1990. *E-mail:* sybkein@aol.com.

KEITH, William John, BA, MA, PhD, FRSC; Canadian academic, literary critic and poet; b. 9 May 1934, London, England; m. Hiroko Teresa Sato 1965. *Education:* Jesus Coll., Cambridge, Univ. of Toronto. *Career:* Lecturer, 1961–62, Asst Prof., 1962–66, McMaster University; Assoc. Prof., 1966–71, Prof. of English, 1971–95, Prof. Emeritus, 1995–, University of Toronto; Ed., University of Toronto Quarterly, 1976–85; mem. Richard Jefferies Society, hon. pres., 1974–91. *Publications:* Richard Jefferies: A Critical Study, 1965; Charles G. D. Roberts, 1969; The Rural Tradition, 1974; Charles G. D. Roberts: Selected Poetry and Critical Prose (ed.), 1974; The Poetry of Nature, 1980; The Arts in Canada: The Last Fifty Years (co-ed.), 1980; Epic Fiction: The Art of Rudy Wiebe, 1981; A Voice in the Land: Essays by and About Rudy Wiebe (ed.), 1981; Canadian Literature in English, 1985; Regions of the Imagination, 1988; Introducing The Edible Woman, 1989; A Sense of Style: Studies in the Art of Fiction in English-Speaking Canada, 1989; An Independent Stance: Essays on English-Canadian Criticism and Fiction, 1991; Echoes in Silence (poems), 1992; Literary Images of Ontario, 1992; The Jefferies Canon, 1995; In the Beginning and Other Poems, 1999; Canadian Odyssey: A Reading of Hugh Hood's The New Age/Le nouveau siècle, 2002. Contributions: journals. *Address:* University College, University of Toronto, Toronto, ON M5S 3H7, Canada.

KELL, Richard (Alexander); Senior Lecturer in English (retd), Poet and Ed.; b. 1 Nov. 1927, Youghal, County Cork, Ireland; m. Muriel Adelaide Nairn, 31 Dec. 1953, two s. two d. *Education:* BA, 1952, Higher Diploma in Education, 1953, University of Dublin. *Career:* Lecturer in English, Isleworth Polytechnic, England, 1960–70; Senior Lecturer in English, Newcastle upon Tyne Polytechnic, 1970–83; Joint Ed., Other Poetry, 1995–2003. *Publications:* Poems, 1957; Control Tower, 1962; Six Irish Poets, 1962; Differences, 1969; Humours, 1978; Heartwood, 1978; The Broken Circle, 1981; Wall (with others), 1981; In Praise of Warmth, 1987; Rock and Water, 1993; Collected Poems, 2001; Under the Rainbow, 2003. Contributions: newspapers and magazines. *Address:* 18 Rectory Grove, Gosforth, Newcastle upon Tyne NE3 1AL, England.

KELLEHER, Victor, (Veronica Hart); Writer; b. 19 July 1939, London, England; m. Alison Lyle, 2 Jan. 1962, one s. one d. *Education:* BA, University of Natal, 1961; Diploma in Education, University of St Andrews, 1963; BA, University of the Witwatersrand, 1969; MA 1970, DLitt et Phil 1973, University of South Africa. *Career:* Junior Lecturer in English, University of the Witwatersrand, 1969; Lecturer, 1970–71, Senior Lecturer in English, 1972–73, University of South Africa, Pretoria; Lecturer in English, Massey University, Palmerston North, New Zealand, 1973–76; Lecturer, 1976–79, Senior Lecturer, 1980–83, Assoc. Prof. of English, 1984–87, University of New England, Armidale, Australia; mem. Australian Society of Authors. *Publications:* Voices from the River, 1979; Forbidden Paths of Thual, 1979; The Hunting of Shadroth, 1981; Master of the Grove, 1982; Africa and After, 1983; The Beast of Heaven, 1983 Papio, 1983; The Green Piper, 1984; Taronga, 1986; The Makers, 1987; Em's Story, 1988; Baily's Bones, 1988; The Red King, 1989; Wintering, 1990; Brother Night, 1990; Del-Del, 1991; To the Dark Tower, 1992; Micky Darlin, 1992; Where the Whales Sing, 1994; Parkland, 1994; Double God (as Veronica Hart), 1994; The House that Jack Built (as Veronica Hart), 1994; Earthsong, 1995; Storyman, 1996; Fire Dancer, 1996; Slow Burn, 1997; Into the Dark, 1999; The Ivory Trail, 1999. Contributions: anthologies and magazines. *Address:* 1 Ave Rd, Glebe, NSW 2037, Australia.

KELLENBERGER, James; Prof. of Philosophy and Writer; b. 4 May 1938, San Francisco, CA, USA; m. Anne Dunn, 7 July 1981, one s. one d. *Education:* BA, Philosophy, San Jose State University, 1960; MA, Philosophy, University of California at Berkeley, 1963; PhD, Philosophy, University of Oregon, 1967. *Career:* Lecturer in Logic, Cameroon College of Arts and Science, 1962–64; Asst Prof., 1967–71, Assoc. Prof., 1971–75, Prof., 1975–, of Philosophy, California State University at Northridge; Visiting Prof., Albion College, Michigan, 1971–72; Adjunct Prof. of Religion, Claremont Graduate School, 1991; mem. American Philosophical Asscn; Society of Christian Philosophers. *Publications:* Religious Discovery, Faith and Knowledge, 1972; The Cognitivity of Religion: Three Perspectives, 1985; God-Relationships With and Without God, 1989; Inter-Religious Models and Criteria (ed.), 1993; Relationship Morality, 1995; Kierkegaard and Nietzsche: Faith and Eternal Acceptance, 1997; Moral Relativism, Moral Diversity, and Human Relationships, 2001. Contributions: scholarly books, reviews, quarterlies and journals. *Address:* c/o Dept of Philosophy, California State University at Northridge, 18111 Nordhoff St, Northridge, CA 91330, USA.

KELLER, Bill; Editor and Journalist; b. 18 Jan. 1949, USA; m. Emma Gilbey; two d. one s. *Education:* BA, Pomona College, 1970; Advanced Management Program, Wharton School, Univ. of Pennsylvania, 2000. *Career:* reporter, Portland Oregonian, 1970–79, Congressional Quarterly Weekly Report, Washington, 1980–82, Dallas Times Herald, 1982–84; domestic correspondent, Washington bureau, 1984–86, foreign correspondent, Moscow bureau, 1986–89, bureau chief, Moscow, 1989–91, bureau chief, Johannesburg, South Africa, 1992–95, Foreign Ed., 1995–97, Managing Ed., 1997–2001, columnist for Op-Ed page and sr writer for New York Times Magazine, 2001–03, Exec. Ed., 2003–, The New York Times; mem. mem. of board of trustees, Pomona College. *Honours:* Pulitzer Prize, 1989. *Address:* The New York Times, 229 W 43rd St, New York, NY 10036, USA. *Telephone:* (212) 556-1234. *E-mail:* executive-editor@nytimes.com. *Website:* www.nytimes.com.

KELLER, Evelyn Fox; academic and writer; b. 20 March 1936, New York, NY, USA; one s. one d. *Education:* BA, Brandeis University, 1957; MA, Radcliffe College, 1959; PhD, Harvard University, 1963. *Career:* Prof. of Mathematics and Humanities, Northeastern University, 1982–88; Senior Fellow, Cornell University, 1987; Mem., Institute for Advanced Study, Princeton, NJ, 1987–88; Prof., University of California at Berkeley, 1988–92; Prof. of History and Philosophy of Science, MIT, 1992–. *Publications:* A Feeling for the Organism: The Life and Work of Barbara McClintock, 1983; Reflections on Gender and Science, 1985; Women, Science and the Body (ed. with Mary Jacobus and Sally Shuttleworth), 1989; Conflicts in Feminism (ed. with Marianne Hirsch), 1990; Keywords in Evolutionary Biology (ed. with Elisabeth Lloyd), 1992; Secrets of Life, Secrets of Death: Essays on Language, Gender, and Science, 1992; Refiguring Life: Metaphors of Twentieth Century Biology, 1995; Feminism and Science (ed. with Helen Longino), 1996; The Century of the Gene, 2000; Making Sense of Life: Explaining Biological Development with Models, Metaphors, and Machines, 2002. Contributions: scholarly journals. *Honours:* Distinguished Publication Award, Asscn for Women in Psychology, 1986; Alumni Achievement Award, Brandeis University, 1991; Hon. doctorates, Holyoke College, 1991, University of Amsterdam, 1995, Simmons College, 1995, Rensselaer Polytechnic Institute, 1995, Technical University of Lulea, Sweden, 1996, New School, 2000; John D. and Catherine T. MacArthur Foundation Fellowship, 1992–97. *Address:* c/o Program in Science, Technology and Society, MIT, 77 Massachusetts Avenue, Cambridge, MA 02139, USA.

KELLERMAN, Jonathan Seth, AB, AM, PhD; American writer, clinical child psychologist and medical school professor; b. 9 Aug. 1949, New York, NY; m. Faye Kellerman; one s. three d. *Education:* University of California at Los Angeles, University of Southern California at Los Angeles. *Career:* freelance illustrator 1966–72, Dir, Psychsocial Program 1976–81, Staff Psychologist 1975–81, Children's Hospital of Los Angeles; Clinical Assoc. Prof., University of Southern California School of Medicine, Los Angeles 1979–; Head, Jonathan Kellerman PhD and Assocs, Los Angeles 1981–88. *Publications:* fiction: When the Bough Breaks 1985, Blood Test 1986, Over the Edge 1987, The Butcher's Theatre 1988, Silent Partner 1989, Time Bomb 1990, Private Eyes 1992, Devil's Waltz 1993, Bad Love 1994, Daddy, Daddy Can You Touch the Sky? 1994, Self-Defense 1995, The Web 1996, Survival of the Fittest 1997, Billy Straight 1999, Monster 2000, On Death 2000, Flesh and Blood 2001, The Murder Book 2002, The Conspiracy Club 2003, Therapy 2004, Twisted 2004; non-fiction: Psychological Aspects of Childhood Cancer 1980, Helping the Fearful Child: A Parents' Guide to Everyday Problem Anxieties 1981. *Honours:* MWA Edgar Allen Poe Award 1985, Anthony Boucher Award 1986. *Address:* c/o Headline, 338 Euston Road, London, NW1 3BH, England. *Website:* authorpages.hoddersystems .com/JonathanKellerman/.

KELLEY, Kitty; American writer; b. 1943; m. Michael Edgley (divorced). *Career:* fmr Press Asst; researcher Washington Post; freelance journalist and writer of biographies 1971–; currently developing TV show The Kitty Kelley Show. *Publications:* Jackie Oh! 1979, Elizabeth Taylor: The Last Star, His Way: The Unauthorized Biography of Frank Sinatra 1986, Nancy Reagan: The Unauthorized Biography 1991, The Royals 2001, The Family: The Real Story of the Bush Dynasty 2004; contrib. articles to magazines and newspapers, including New York Times, Newsweek, McCall's, Los Angeles Times, Chicago Tribune. *Honours:* Outstanding Author Award (American Soc. of Journalists and Authors) 1987, Philip M. Stern Award. *Address:* c/o Doubleday, 1745 Broadway, New York, NY 10019, USA.

KELLEY, Leo P(atrick); Author; b. 10 Sept. 1928, Wilkes Barre, Pennsylvania, USA. *Education:* BA, New School for Social Research, New York City, 1957. *Publications:* The Counterfeits, 1967; Odyssey to Earthdeath, 1968; Time Rogue, 1970; The Coins of Murph, 1971; Brother John, 1971; Mindmix, 1972; Time: 110100, 1972, UK edn as The Man From Maybe, 1974; Themes in Science Fiction: A Journey Into Wonder (ed.), 1972; The Supernatural in Fiction (ed.), 1973; Deadlocked (novel), 1973; The Earth Tripper, 1973; Fantasy: The Literature of the Marvellous (ed.), 1974. Science fiction novels for children: The Time Trap, 1977; Backward in Time, 1979; Death Sentence, 1979; Earth Two, 1979; Prison Satellite, 1979; Sunworld, 1979; Worlds Apart, 1979; Dead Moon, 1979; King of the Stars, 1979; On the Red World, 1979; Night of Fire and Blood, 1979; Where No Star Shines, 1979; Vacation in Space, 1979; Star Gold, 1979; Goodbye to Earth, 1979. Western novels: Luke Sutton series, 9 vols, 1981–90; Cimarron series, 20 vols, 1983–86; Morgan, 1986; A Man Named Dundee, 1988; Thunder Gods Gold, 1988.

KELLMAN, Steven G., BA, MA, PhD; critic and academic; *Professor of Comparative Literature, University of Texas*; b. 15 Nov. 1947, New York, NY, USA. *Education:* SUNY at Binghamton, Univ. of California, Berkeley. *Career:* Ed.-in-Chief, Occident 1969–70; Asst Prof., Bemidji State Univ., Minnesota 1972–73; Lecturer, Univ. of Tel-Aviv 1973–75; Visiting Lecturer, Univ. of California, Irvine 1975–76; Asst Prof. 1976–80, Assoc. Prof. 1980–85, Prof. 1985–, Ashbel Smith Prof. of Comparative Literature 1995–2000, Univ. of Texas, San Antonio; Fulbright Senior Lecturer, USSR 1980; Visiting Assoc. Prof., Univ. of California, Berkeley 1982; Literary Scene Ed., USA Today; Partners of the Americas Lecturer, Peru 1988, 1995; Fulbright Travel Grant, People's Republic of China 1995; Nat. Endowment for the Humanities Summer Seminar, Natal, South Africa 1996; John E. Sawyer Fellow, Longfellow Inst., Harvard Univ. 1997; Fulbright Distinguished Chair, Bulgaria 2000; mem. Nat. Book Critics Circle (bd of dirs 1996–2002). *Publications:* The Self-Begetting Novel 1980, Approaches to Teaching Camus's The Plague (ed.) 1985, Loving Reading: Erotics of the Text 1985, The Modern American Novel 1991, The Plague: Fiction and Resistance 1993, Perspectives on Raging Bull 1994, Into The Tunnel (co-ed.) 1998, Leslie Fiedler and American Culture (co-ed.) 1999, The Translingual Imagination 2000, UnderWords: Perspectives on Don DeLillo's Underworld (co-ed.) 2002, Switching Languages: Translingual Writers Reflect on Their Craft (ed.) 2003; contrib. to Chicago Tribune, San Antonio Light, Nation, Georgia Review, Newsweek, Modern Fiction Studies, Midstream, New York Times Book Review, Washington Post Book World, Gettysburg Review, The American Scholar, Atlantic Monthly, Forward, Atlanta Journal and Constitution, San Francisco Chronicle, Film Critic, Texas Observer, San Antonio Current. *Honours:* H. L. Mencken Award 1986. *Address:* 302 Fawn Drive, San Antonio, TX 78231, USA. *E-mail:* kellman@lonestar.utsa.edu.

KELLOGG, Marjorie Bradley; academic and writer; b. 30 Aug. 1946, Cambridge, MA, USA. *Education:* BA, summa cum laude, Vassar College, 1967; University of California at Los Angeles, 1967–68. *Career:* Scenic Designer, on and off Broadway, regional theatres and films, 1970–; Visiting Prof., Princeton University, 1983–84, 1985–86; Resident Designer, Alliance Theater, 1992–94; Adjunct Prof., Columbia University, 1993–95; Assoc. Prof. of Design, Colgate University, 1995–; mem. Science Fiction Writers of America; United Scenic Artists. *Publications:* A Rumor of Angels, 1983; Lear's Daughters, two vols, 1986; The Book of Earth, 1995; The Book of Water, 1997. *Honours:* several awards for design. *Address:* RD 1, PO Box 62-A, Sidney Center, NY 13839, USA. *E-mail:* mkellogg@wpe.com.

KELLS, Susannah (see Cornwell, Bernard).

KELLY, A. A. (see Hampton, Angeline Agnes).

KELLY, Christopher Paul, MA; British novelist and producer; b. 24 April 1940, Cuddington, Cheshire, England; m. Vivien Ann Day 1962; one s. one d. *Education:* Clare Coll., Cambridge. *Career:* mem. Writer's Guild. *Publications:* The War of Covent Garden 1989, The Forest of the Night 1991, Taking Leave 1995, A Suit of Lights 2000. *Address:* 37 Camden Square, London, NW1 9XA, England. *E-mail:* xtopherkelly@aol.com.

KELLY, Jim; Journalist; b. 15 Dec. 1953, Brooklyn, New York, NY, USA; m. Lisa Henricksson; one s. *Education:* Princeton Univ. *Career:* joined Time magazine 1977 as writer Nation section, Foreign Ed. early 1990s, Deputy Man. Ed. 1996–2000, Man. Ed. 2001–, Ed. Corporate Welfare series 1998, Visions 21 series 1999–2000. *Address:* Office of the Managing Editor, Time, Time-Life Bldg, Rockefeller Center, 1271 Avenue of the Americas, New York, NY 10020-1393, USA. *Website:* www.time.com.

KELLY, Milton Terrence, BA, BEd; writer, poet and dramatist; b. 30 Nov. 1946, Toronto, ON, Canada. *Education:* York University, University of Toronto. *Career:* Reporter, Moose Jaw Times Harald, 1974–75; Columnist, Globe and Mail, 1979–80; Teacher of Creative Writing, York University, 1987–92, 1995; Writer-in-Residence, North York Public Library, 1992, Metropolitan Toronto Reference Library, 1993; mem. International PEN; Writers' Union of Canada. *Publications:* Fiction: I Do Remember the Fall, 1978; The More Loving One, 1980; The Ruined Season, 1982; A Dream Like Mine, 1987; Breath Dances Between Them, 1990; Out of the Whirlwind, 1995; Save Me, Joe Louis, 1998. Poetry: Country You Can't Walk In, 1979; Country You Can't Walk In and Other Poems, 1984. Other: The Green Dolphin (play), 1982; Wildfire: The Legend of Tom Longboat (screenplay), 1983. Contributions: many anthologies, reviews, quarterlies, and journals. *Honours:* Canada Council Grants; Ontario Arts Council Grants; Toronto Arts Council Award for Poetry, 1986; Governor-General's Award for Fiction, 1987; Award for Journalism, 1995. *Address:* 60 Kendal, Toronto, ON M5R 1L9, Canada.

KELLY, Patrick (see Allbeury, Theodore Edward Le Bouthillier).

KELLY, Robert; Prof. of Literature, Poet and Writer; b. 24 Sept. 1935, New York, NY, USA. *Education:* AB, City College, CUNY, 1955; Columbia University, 1955–58. *Career:* Ed., Chelsea Review, 1957–60, Matter magazine and Matter publishing, 1964–, Los 1, 1977; Lecturer, Wagner College, 1960–61; Founding Ed. (with George Economou), Trobar magazine, 1960–64, Trobar Books, 1962–65; Instructor, 1961–64, Asst Prof., 1964–69, Assoc. Prof., 1969–74, Prof. of English, 1974–86, Dir, Writing Programme, 1980–93, Asher B. Edelman Prof. of Literature, 1986–, Bard College; Asst Prof., SUNY at Buffalo, 1964; Visiting Lecturer, Tufts University, 1966–67; Poet-in-Residence, California Institute of Technology, Pasadena, 1971–72, University of Kansas, 1975, Dickinson College, 1976. *Publications:* Poetry: Armed Descent, 1961; Her Body Against Time, 1963; Round Dances, 1964; Tabula, 1964; Entasy, 1964; Matter/Fact/Sheet/1, 1964; Matter/Fact/Sheet/2, 1964; Lunes, 1964; Lectiones, 1965; Words in Service, 1966; Weeks, 1966; Songs XXIV, 1967; Twenty Poems, 1967; Devotions, 1967; Axon Dendron Tree, 1967; Crooked Bridge Love Society, 1967; A Joining: A Sequence for H D, 1967; Alpha, 1968; Finding the Measure, 1968; From the Common Shore, Book 5, 1968; Songs I–XXX, 1969; Sonnets, 1969; We Are the Arbiters of Beast Desire, 1969; A California Journal, 1969; The Common Shore, Books I–V: A Long Poem About America in Time, 1969; Kali Yuga, 1971; Flesh: Dream: Book, 1971; Ralegh, 1972; The Pastorals, 1972; Reading Her Notes, 1972; The Tears of Edmund Burke, 1973; Whaler Frigate Clippership, 1973; The Bill of Particulars, 1973; The Belt, 1974; The Loom, 1975; Sixteen Odes, 1976; The Lady of, 1977; The Convections, 1978; The Book of Persephone, 1978; The Cruise of the Pnyx, 1979; Kill the Messenger Who Brings the Bad News, 1979; Sentence, 1980; The Alchemist to Mercury, 1981; Spiritual Exercises, 1981; Mulberry Women, 1982; Under Words, 1983; Thor's Thrush, 1984; Not This Island Music, 1987; The Flowers of Unceasing Coincidence, 1988; Oahu, 1988; A Strange Market, 1992; Mont Blanc, 1994. Fiction: The Scorpions, 1967; Cities, 1971; Wheres, 1978; A Transparent Tree: Ten Fictions, 1985; Doctor of Silence, 1988; Cat Scratch Fever: Fictions, 1990; Queen of Terrors: Fictions, 1994. Other: A Controversy of Poets: An Anthology of Contemporary American Poetry (ed. with Paris Leary), 1965; Statement, 1968; In Time, 1971; Sulphur, 1972; A Line of Sight, 1974. *Honours:* Los Angeles Times Book Prize, 1980; American Acad. of Arts and Letters Award, 1986. *Address:* c/o Dept of English, Bard College, Annandale-on-Hudson, NY 12504, USA.

KELLY, Tim, (Keith Jackson, J. Moriarty, Vera Morris, Robert Swift); Playwright and Screenwriter; b. 2 Oct. 1937, Saugus, Massachusetts, USA. *Education:* BA, 1956, MA, 1957, Emerson College; American Broadcasting

Fellow, Yale University, 1965. *Career:* mem. Authors League; Dramatists Guild; Writers Guild of America; College of Fellows of the American Theatre. *Publications:* Over 300 plays. *Honours:* numerous awards and grants. *Literary Agent:* William Talbot, Samuel French Inc., W 25th St, New York NY 10010, USA. *Address:* 8730 Lookout Mountain Ave, Los Angeles, CA 90046, USA.

KELMAN, James; British writer, dramatist and essayist; b. 9 June 1946, Glasgow, Scotland; m. Marie Connors; two d. *Education:* Univ. of Strathclyde. *Plays:* The Busker 1985, In the Night 1988, Hardie and Baird, The Last 1990, One, Two – Hey 1994, The Art of the Big Bass Drum 1998. *Film screenplay:* The Return 1990. *Publications:* fiction: The Busconductor Hines 1984, A Chancer 1985, A Disaffection 1989, How Late it Was, How Late 1994, Translated Accounts 2001, You Have to be Careful in the Land of the Free 2004; short story collections: An Old Pub Near the Angel 1973, Short Tales from the Nightshift 1978, Not Not While the Giro and Other Stories 1983, Lean Tales 1985, Greyhound for Breakfast 1987, The Burn 1991, Busted Scotch 1997, The Good Times 1998; essays: Some Recent Attacks 1991, Seven Stories (CD) 1997, 'And the Judges Said...': Essays 2002. *Honours:* Scottish Arts Council Fellowships, Scottish Arts Council Bursaries, Book Awards 1983, 1987, 1989, Cheltenham Prize 1987, James Tait Black Memorial Prize 1989, Booker Prize 1994, Spirit of Scotland Award, Scottish Writer of the Year 1998. *Literary Agent:* Rogers, Coleridge & White Ltd, 20 Powis Mews, London W11 1JN, England.

KELMAN, Judith (Ann); Writer; b. 21 Oct. 1945, New York, NY, USA; m. Edward Michael Kelman, 28 June 1970, two s. *Education:* BS, Cornell University, 1967; MA, New York University, 1968; MS, Southern Connecticut State College, 1977. *Career:* mem. American Society of Journalists and Authors; MWA; Authors' Guild. *Publications:* Prime Evil, 1986; Where Shadows Fall, 1988; While Angels Sleep, 1990; Hush Little Darlings, 1991; Someone's Watching, 1992; The House on the Hill, 1993; If I Should Die, 1994; One Last Kiss, 1995; More Than You Know, 1996; Fly Away Home, 1997. Contributions: anthologies and periodicals. *Literary Agent:* c/o Bantam Books, 1540 Broadway, New York, NY 10036, USA. *Address:* 60 Thornwood Rd, Stamford, CT 06903, USA. *E-mail:* jkelman@jkelman.com.

KELSALL, Malcolm Miles; Prof. of English, Writer and Ed.; b. 27 Feb. 1938, London, England; m. Mary Emily Ives, 5 Aug. 1961. *Education:* BA, 1961; BLitt, 1964, MA, 1965, Oxon. *Career:* Asst Lecturer, University of Exeter, 1963–64; Lecturer, University of Reading, 1964–75; Prof. of English, University of Wales, Cardiff, 1975–. *Publications:* Christopher Marlowe, 1981; Studying Drama, 1985; Byron's Politics, 1987; Encyclopedia of Literature and Criticism (ed.), 1990; The Great Good Place: The Country House and English Literature, 1992; Jefferson and the Iconography of Romanticism, 1999; Literary Representations of the Irish Country House, 2003. Editor: several plays. Contributions: scholarly journals. *Honours:* Elma Dangerfield Prize, 1991; British Acad. Warton Lecturer, 1992. *Address:* c/o School of English, University of Wales, PO Box 94, Cardiff CF10 3XB, Wales.

KELTON, Elmer Stephen, (Lee McElroy); Novelist and Agricultural Journalist; b. 29 April 1926, Andrews, Texas, USA; m. Anna Lipp, 3 July 1947, two s. one d. *Education:* BA, Journalism, University of Texas, 1948. *Career:* mem. Western Writers of America, pres., 1963–64; Texas Institute of Letters. *Publications:* The Day the Cowboys Quit, 1971; The Time It Never Rained, 1973; The Good Old Boys, 1978; The Wolf and the Buffalo, 1980; Stand Proud, 1984; The Man Who Rode Midnight, 1987; Honor at Daybreak, 1991; Slaughter, 1992; The Far Canyon, 1994; The Pumpkin Rollers, 1996; Cloudy in the West, 1997; The Smiling Country, 1998; The Buckskin Line, 1999; Badger Boy, 2001; The Way of the Coyote, 2001; Ranger's Trail, 2002; Texas Vendetta, 2003. Contributions: numerous articles to magazines and newspapers. *Honours:* seven Spur Awards, Western Writers of America; 4 Western Heritage Awards, National Cowboy Hall of Fame; Tinkle-McCombs Achievement Award, Texas Institute of Letters; Lifetime Achievement, Western Literature Asscn; Larry McMurtry Lone Star Lifetime Achievement Award. *Address:* 2460 Oxford, San Angelo, TX 76904, USA.

KEMAL, Yashar; Writer and Journalist; b. 1923, Adana, Turkey; m. Thilda Serrero, 1952, one s. *Education:* Self-educated. *Publications:* (in English) Memed, My Hawk, 1961; The Wind From the Plain, 1963; Anatolian Tales, 1968; They Burn the Thistles, 1973; Iron Earth, Copper Sky, 1974; The Legend of Ararat, 1975; The Legend of a Thousand Bulls, 1976; The Undying Grass, 1977; The Lords of Akchasaz, Part I, Murder in the Ironsmiths Market, 1979; The Saga of a Seagull, 1981; The Sea-Crossed Fisherman, 1985; The Birds Have Also Gone, 1987; To Crush the Serpent, 1991; Salman The Solitary, 1997; novels, short stories, plays and essays in Turkish. *Honours:* Commander, Légion d'honneur, 1984; Dr hc, Université de Sciences Humaines, Strasbourg, 1991; VIIIe Premi International Catalunya, Barcelona, 1996; Hellman-Hammett Award, 1996; Peace Prize of the German Book Trade, Frankfurt Book Fair, 1997; Stig Dagerman Prize, Sweden, 1997; Nonio Prize, Italy, 1997; Kenne Fant Foundation Award, Sweden, 1997; Norwegian Authors Prize, 1997; Prix Ecureuil, 1998. *Address:* PK 14, Basinkoy, Istanbul, Turkey.

KEMP, Anthony Eric; Priest, Music Educator, Chartered Psychologist and Counsellor; b. 2 Jan. 1934, Tanga, Tanzania; m. Valerie Francis, 8 Aug. 1964, one s. one d. *Education:* Cert Ed, College of St Mark and St John, 1957; LTCL, 1961, FTCL, 1963, Trinity College of Music; Dip Ed, University of London, 1970; MA, 1971, DPhil, 1979, University of Sussex. *Career:* Lecturer in Music, 1964, Senior Lecturer, 1967, Brighton College of Education; Principal Lecturer, Head of Music, College of St Mark and St John, 1972; Lecturer, 1973, Senior Lecturer, 1987, Prof., 1996, Emeritus Prof., 1999, University of Reading; Senior Research Fellow, University of Surrey, Roehampton, 1999; mem. Incorporated Society of Musicians; International Society for Music Education, Chair. of Research Commission, 1988–90; Music Education Council, Chair., 1989–92. *Publications:* Fun to Make Music, 1975; Considering the Mind's Ear, 1984; Research in Music Education; Festschrift for Arnold Bentley, 1988; Some Approaches to Research in Music Education, 1992; The Musical Temperament: Psychology and Personality of Musicians, 1996. Contributions: Psychology of Music, 1981, 1982, 1999; International Journal of Music Education, 1984, 1986, 1988; Council for Research in Music Education Bulletin, 1985, 1987; British Journal of Music Education, 1987, 1990; Quarterly Journal of Music Teaching and Learning, 1995; Musical Performance: An International Journal, 2000. *Honours:* Raysen Huang Fellowship, University of Hong Kong, 1989; Distinguished Scholars Fellowship, University of British Columbia, 1990; Hon. Fellow of London College of Music, 1983; Fellow of British Psychological Society, 1997; FRSA, 2001. *Address:* 18 Blagrove Lane, Wokingham, Berkshire RG41 4BA, England. *E-mail:* a.e.kemp@reading.ac.uk.

KEMP, Harry Vincent; Poet and Mathematician; b. 11 Dec. 1911, Singapore; m. Alix Eiermann, 9 July 1941, one s. one d. *Education:* Clare College, Cambridge, 1931–34. *Publications:* The Left Hersey (with Laura Riding and Robert Graves), 1939; Ten Messengers (with Witold Kawalec), 1977; Verses for Heidi, 1978; Poems for Erato, 1980; Collected Poems, 1985; Poems for Mnemosyne, 1993. *Address:* 6 Western Villas, Western Rd, Crediton, Devon EX17 3NA, England.

KEMP, Martin (John); Prof. of the History of Art and Writer; b. 5 March 1942, Windsor, England; m. Jill Lightfoot, 1966, separated 1995, one s. one d. *Education:* BA, 1963, MA, 1964, Downing College, Cambridge; Diploma, Courtauld Institute of Art, 1965. *Career:* Lecturer in the History of Western Art, Dalhousie University, Halifax, NS, 1965–66; Lecturer in the History of Fine Art, University of Glasgow, 1966–81; Prof. of Fine Arts, later of History and the Theory of Art, 1981–95, Assoc. Dean of Graduate Studies, Faculty of Arts, 1983–87, Provost, St Leonard's College, 1991–95, University of St Andrews; Fellow, Institute for Advanced Study, Princeton, NJ, 1984–85; Prof. of History and Hon. Mem., Royal Scottish Acad., 1985–; Slade Prof. of Fine Art, University of Cambridge, 1987–88; Benjamin Sonnenberg Visiting Prof., Institute of Fine Arts, New York University, 1988; Wiley Visiting Prof., University of North Carolina at Chapel Hill, 1993; Wofson Research Prof., British Acad., 1993–98; Prof. of the History of Art, University of Oxford, 1995–; Fellow, Trinity College, Oxford, 1995; mem. American Acad. of Arts and Sciences, foreign mem., 1996–; Asscn of Art Historians, chair., 1989–92; British Society for the History of Science, council, 1994–97; Leonardo da Vinci Society, pres., 1987–96. *Publications:* Leonardo da Vinci, The Marvellous Works of Nature and Man, 1981; Leonardo da Vinci (co-author), 1989; Leonardo on Painting (co-author), 1989; The Science of Art, 1990; Behind the Picture, 1997; The Oxford History of Western Art (ed.), 2000. Contributions: scholarly books and journals. *Honours:* Mitchell Prize for Best First Book in English on Art History, 1981; FRSA, 1983–98; Fellow, British Acad., 1991; Fellow, Royal Society of Edinburgh, 1992; Armand Hammer Prize for Leonardo Studies, 1992; Pres.'s Prize, Italian Asscn of America, 1998; Hon. Fellow, Downing College, Cambridge, 1999. *Address:* c/o Trinity College, Oxford OX1 3BH, England.

KEMP, (Patricia) Penn, BA, MEd; writer and poet; b. 1944, Strathroy, ON, Canada; m. Gavin Stairs; two c. *Education:* Univ. of Toronto. *Career:* various writer-in-residencies; Publisher, Pendas Productions; Series Ed., Pendas Poets Series; Asscn of Canadian Studies speaker in Brazil, India; mem. League of Canadian Poets, Playwrights' Guild of Canada, Writers' Union. *Publications:* Bearing Down 1972, Binding Twine 1984, Some Talk Magic 1986, Eidolons 1990, Throo 1990, The Universe is One Poem 1990, What the Ear Hears Last 1994, Four Women 1999, Vocal Braidings 2001, Sarasvati Scapes 2002, Poem for Peace in Two Voices 2003, C'Loud 2004, Gathering Voice 2004. *Honours:* Canada Council Arts grants 1979–80, 1981–82, 1991–92, 1994, 1999, 2001, Ontario's Graduate Scholarship 1987–88. *Address:* Pendas Productions, 525 Canterbury Road, London, ON N6G 2N5, Canada. *E-mail:* pendas@pennkemp.ca. *Website:* www.pennkemp.ca.

KEMSKE, Floyd; Writer; b. 11 March 1947, Wilmington, DE, USA; m. Alice Geraldine Morse, 21 Dec. 1968. *Education:* BA, University of Delaware, 1970; MA, Michigan State University, 1971. *Career:* mem. National Writers Union. *Publications:* Lifetime Employment, 1992; The Virtual Boss, 1993; Human Resources, 1995; The Third Lion, 1997; Jigsaw Puzzles: Hole in One, 1997; Unbridled Fear, 1997; Cooking Commando, 1997; Purrfect Medicine, 1998; Murder on the Hindenburg, 1999; Labor Day, 2000. *Address:* PO Box 563, Pepperell, MA 01463, USA.

KENDALL, Carol (Seeger); Writer; b. 13 Sept. 1917, Bucyrus, Ohio, USA; m. Paul Murray Kendall, 15 June 1939, two d. *Education:* AB, Ohio University, 1939. *Career:* mem. PEN American Center; Authors League of

America; Authors' Guild. *Publications:* The Black Seven 1946, The Baby Snatcher 1952, The Other Side of the Tunnel 1956, The Gammage Cup 1959, as The Minnipins 1960, The Big Splash 1960, The Whisper of Glocken 1965, Sweet and Sour Tales from China, retold by Carol Kendall and Yao-Wen Li 1978, The Firelings 1981, Haunting Tales from Japan 1985, The Wedding of the Rat Family 1988. *Honours:* Ohioana Award, 1960; Newbery Honour Book, 1960; American Library Assn Notable Book, 1960; Parents Choice Award, 1982; Aslan Award, Mythopoeic Society, 1983. *Address:* 1501 Inverness Drive, Apt 201, Lawrence, KS 66047, USA.

KENEALLY, Thomas Michael, AO, FRSL; Australian writer; b. 7 Oct. 1935, Sydney; m. Judith Mary Martin 1965; two d. *Education:* St Patrick's Coll., Strathfield, NSW. *Career:* Lecturer in Drama, Univ. of New England, Armidale, NSW 1968–70; Visiting Prof. Univ. of Calif., Irvine 1985, Prof. Dept of English and Comparative Literature 1991–95; Berg Prof. Dept of English, New York Univ. 1988; Pres. Nat. Book Council of Australia –1987; Chair. Australian Soc. of Authors 1987–90, Pres. 1990–; mem. Literary Arts Bd 1985–; mem. Australia-China Council; mem. American Acad. of Arts and Sciences; Founding Chair. Australian Republican Movt 1991–93. *Publications:* The Place at Whitton 1964, The Fear 1965, Bring Larks and Heroes 1967, Three Cheers for the Paraclete 1968, The Survivor 1969, A Dutiful Daughter 1970, The Chant of Jimmie Blacksmith 1972, Blood Red, Sister Rose 1974, Gossip from the Forest 1975, Moses and the Lawgiver 1975, Season in Purgatory 1976, A Victim of the Aurora 1977, Ned Kelly and the City of Bees 1978, Passenger 1978, Confederates 1979, Schindler's Ark (Booker Prize 1982) 1982, Outback 1983, The Cut-Rate Kingdom 1984, A Family Madness 1985, Australia: Beyond the Dreamtime (contrib.) 1987, The Playmaker 1987, Towards Asmara 1989, Flying Hero Class 1991, Now and in Time to Be: Ireland and the Irish 1992, Woman of the Inner Sea 1992, The Place Where Souls Are Born: A Journey into the American Southwest 1992, Jacko: The Great Intruder 1993, The Utility Player – The Story of Des Hassler (non-fiction) 1993, Our Republic (non-fiction) 1993, A River Town 1995, Homebush Boy: A Memoir 1995, The Great Shame: And the Triumph of the Irish in the English-Speaking World 1998, Bettany's Book 2000, An American Scoundrel: The Life of the Notorious Civil War General Dan Sickles (non-fiction) 2002, An Angel in Australia 2002, Abraham Lincoln (biog.) 2003, The Office of Innocence 2003, The Tyrant's Novel 2004. *Honours:* Hon. DLit (Univ. of Queensland), (Nat. Univ. of Ireland) 1994; Hon. DLitt (Fairleigh Dickenson Univ., USA) 1996, (Rollins Coll., USA) 1996; Royal Soc. of Literature Prize, Los Angeles Times Fiction Prize 1983. *Literary Agent:* Curtis Brown (Australia) Pty Ltd, PO Box 19, Paddington, NSW 2021, Australia.

KENNAN, George Frost; retd diplomat, academic and writer; b. 16 Feb. 1904, Milwaukee, Wisconsin, USA; m. Annelise Sorenson; one s. three d. *Education:* AB, Princeton University, 1925. *Career:* various diplomatic posts, 1926–45; Deputy for Foreign Affairs, National War College, Washington, DC, 1946; Dir, Policy Planning Staff, US Dept of State, 1947; Deputy Counselor and Chief Long Range Adviser to the US Secretary of State, 1949–50; Mem., 1950–53, Prof., 1956–74, Prof. Emeritus, 1974–, Institute for Advanced Study, Princeton, NJ; US Ambassador to the USSR, 1952, Yugoslavia, 1961–63; George Eastman Visiting Prof., University of Oxford, 1957–58; Fellow, Harvard University, 1965–70, All Souls College, Oxford, 1969; mem. American Acad. of Arts and Letters, pres., 1967–71; American Philosophical Society; National Institute of Arts and Letters, pres., 1964–67; RSA. *Publications:* American Diplomacy 1900–1950, 1951; Realities of American Foreign Policy, 1954; Soviet-American Relations 1917–1920, 2 vols, 1956, 1958; Russia, the Atom and the West, 1958; Soviet Foreign Policy 1917–1945, 1960; Russia and the West Under Lenin and Stalin, 1961; On Dealing with the Communist World, 1963; Memoirs 1925–1950, 1967; Democracy and the Student Left, 1968; From Prague After Munich: Diplomatic Papers 1938–1940, 1968; The Marquis de Custine and His Russia in 1839, 1971; Memoirs 1950–1963, 1972; The Cloud of Danger: Current Realities of American Foreign Policy, 1977; The Decline of Bismarck's European Order: Franco-Russian Relations 1875–1890, 1979; The Nuclear Delusion: Soviet-American Relations in the Atomic Age, 1982; The State Department Policy Planning Staff Papers, 1983; The Fateful Alliance: France, Russia and the Coming of the First World War, 1984; Sketches from a Life, 1989; Around the Cragged Hill, 1993; At a Century's Ending: Reflections, 1982–1995, 1996. Contributions: scholarly journals. *Honours:* Freedom House Award, 1951; Bancroft Prize, 1956; National Book Awards, 1957, 1968; Francis Parkman Prize, 1957; Pulitzer Prizes, 1957, 1968; Albert Einstein Peace Prize, 1981; Gold Medal in History, American Acad. and Institute of Arts and Letters, 1984; Literary Lion Award, New York Public Library, 1985; Creative Arts Award, Brandeis University, 1986; Toynbee Prize, 1988; Presidential Medal of Freedom, 1989; Ambassador Book Award, 1993; Distinguished Service Award, US Dept of State, 1994; Excellence in Diplomacy Award, 1997; numerous hon. doctorates. *Address:* 146 Hodge Road, Princeton, NJ 08540, USA.

KENNEDY, Adrienne (Lita); Dramatist; b. 13 Sept. 1931, Pittsburgh, Pennsylvania, USA; m. Joseph C. Kennedy, 15 May 1953, divorced 1966, two s. *Education:* BS, Ohio State University, 1953; Columbia University, 1954–56; New School for Social Research, American Theatre Wing, Circle in the Square Theatre School, New York City, 1957–58, 1962. *Career:* Playwright, Actors Studio, New York City, 1962–65; Lecturer, Yale University, 1972–74, Princeton University, 1977; CBS Fellow, School of Drama, New York City, 1973; Visiting Assoc. Prof., Brown University, 1979–80; Distinguished Lecturer, University of California, Berkeley, 1980, 1986; Visiting Lecturer, 1990, 1991, Visiting Prof., 1997–2000, Harvard University; mem. PEN. *Publications:* Plays: Funnyhouse of a Negro, 1964; Cities in Bezique, 1965; A Rat's Mass, 1966; A Lesson in Dead Language, 1966; The Lennon Plays, 1968; Sun, 1969; An Evening With Dead Essex, 1972; A Movie Star Has to Star in Black and White, 1976; In One Act, 1988; Deadly Triplets, 1990; She Talks to Beethoven, 1990; Ohio State Murders, 1992; The Alexander Plays, 1992; Sleep Deprivation Chamber: A Theatre Piece (with Adam Kennedy), 1996; Adrienne Kennedy Reader, 2001. Other: People Who Led to My Plays, 1987; Letter to My Students, 1992. Contributions: anthologies. *Honours:* Obie Awards, 1964, 1996; Guggenheim Fellowship, 1968; Rockefeller Foundation Fellowships, 1968, 1974; National Endowment for the Arts Fellowships, 1973, 1993; Manhattan Borough Pres.'s Award, 1988; American Acad. of Arts and Letters Award, 1994; Lila Wallace-Reader's Digest Award, 1994; Pierre Lecomte du Novy Award, Lincoln Center for the Performing Arts, New York, 1994. *Address:* c/o University of Minnesota Press, 111 Third Ave S, Suite 290, Minneapolis, MN 55401, USA.

KENNEDY, Alison Louise (A. L.), BA; writer; b. 22 Oct. 1965, Dundee, Scotland. *Education:* Warwick University. *Career:* Community Arts Worker for Clydebank & District, 1988–89; Writer-in-Residence, Hamilton & East Kilbride Social Work Dept, 1989–91; Writer-in-Residence for Project Ability, Arts & Special Needs, 1989–95; Book Reviewer for Scotsman, Glasgow Herald, BBC, STV, Telegraph, 1990–; Writer-in-Residence, Copenhagen University, 1995; Ed. of New Writing Scotland, 1993–95; Booker Prize Judge, 1996. *Television:* Ghostdancing (BBC TV drama/documentary, writer and presenter) 1995, Dice (series I and II, with John Burnside) (Canadian television). *Radio:* Born a Fox (BBC Radio 4 drama) 2002. *Plays:* Delicate (performance piece for Motionhouse dance co.) 1995, True (performance project for Fierce Productions and Tramway Theatre) 1998. *Publications:* Night Geometry and the Garscadden Trains 1991, Looking for the Possible Dance 1993, Now That You're Back 1994, So I Am Glad 1995, Tea and Biscuits 1996, Original Bliss 1997, The Life and Death of Colonel Blimp 1997, Everything You Need 1999, On Bullfighting 1999, Indelible Acts 2002, Paradise 2004. *Honours:* Somerset Maugham award; Encore Award; Saltire Scottish Book of the Year. *Literary Agent:* Antony Harwood Ltd, 103 Walton Street, Oxford, OX2 6EB, England. *Telephone:* (1865) 559615. *Fax:* (1865) 554173. *Website:* www.a-l-kennedy.co.uk.

KENNEDY, David Michael, BA, MA, PhD; academic and writer; *Donald J. McLachlan Professor of History, Stanford University*; b. 22 July 1941, Seattle, WA, USA; m. Judith Ann Osborne 1970; two s. one d. *Education:* Stanford Univ., Yale Univ. *Career:* Asst Prof. 1967–72, Assoc. Prof. 1972–80, Prof. 1980–, William Robertson Coe Prof. of History and American Studies 1988–93, Chair, Dept of History 1990–94, Donald J. McLachlan Prof. of History 1993–, Stanford Univ.; Harmsworth Prof. of American History, Univ. of Oxford 1995–96; Ed., The Oxford History of the United States 1999–; Fellow, American Acad. of Arts and Sciences, American Philosophical Soc. *Publications:* Birth Control in America: The Career of Margaret Sanger 1970, Social Thought in America and Europe (ed. with Paul A. Robinson) 1970, Progressivism: The Critical Issues (ed.) 1971, The American People in the Depression 1973, The American People in the Age of Kennedy 1973, The American Pageant: A History of the Republic (with Thomas A. Bailey and Lizabeth Cohen, sixth to 12th edns) 1979–2002, Over Here: The First World War and American Society 1980, The American Spirit: United States History as Seen by Contemporaries (ed. with Thomas A. Bailey, fifth to 10th edns) 1983–2002, Power and Responsibility: Case Studies in American Leadership (ed. with Michael Parrish) 1986, Freedom from Fear: The American People in Depression and War, 1929–1945 1999; contrib. to reference works, scholarly books, learned journals, periodicals, etc. *Honours:* Guggenheim Fellowship 1975–76, Center for Advanced Study in the Behavioural Sciences Fellowship 1986–87, Stanford Humanities Center Fellowship 1989–90, Hon. DLitt (LaTrobe Univ.) 2001; John Gilmary Shea Prize 1970, Bancroft Prize 1971, Ambassador's Book Award, English-Speaking Union 2000, Francis Parkman Prize, Soc. of American Historians 2000, Pulitzer Prize in History 2000. *Address:* c/o Department of History, Stanford University, Stanford, CA 94305, USA. *Website:* history.stanford.edu/faculty/dkennedy.

KENNEDY, Donald, MA, PhD; American academic and editor; b. 18 Aug. 1931, New York; m. 1st Barbara J. Dewey 1953; two d.; m. 2nd Robin Beth Wiseman 1987; two step-s. *Education:* Harvard Univ. *Career:* Asst Prof. Syracuse Univ. 1956–59, Assoc. Prof. 1959–60; Asst Prof. Stanford Univ. 1960–62, Assoc. Prof. 1962–65, Prof. 1965–77, Chair. Dept of Biological Sciences 1965–72, Benjamin Crocker Prof. of Human Biology 1974–77, Vice-Pres. and Provost 1979–80, Pres. 1980–92, Pres. Emer. and Bing Prof. of Environmental Science 1992–; Sr Consultant, Office of Science and Tech. Policy, Exec. Office of the Pres. 1976–77; Commr of Food and Drug Admin. 1977–79; Ed.-in-Chief Science 2000–; Fellow, American Acad. of Arts and Sciences; mem. NAS. *Publications:* The Biology of Organisms (with W. M. Telfer) 1965, Academic Duty 1997; over 60 articles in scientific journals. *Honours:* Hon. DSc (Columbia Univ., Williams Coll., Michigan, Rochester, Ariz., Whitman Coll., Coll. of William and Mary); Dinkelspiel Award 1976.

Address: Stanford University, Institute for International Studies, Encina Hall 401, Stanford, CA 94305 (Office); 532 Channing Avenue, #302, Palo Alto, CA 94301, USA (Home). *E-mail:* kennedyd@stanford.edu (Office).

KENNEDY, James C., BBA; American publishing and media executive; *Chairman and CEO, Cox Enterprises Inc.*; b. 1947; m. *Education:* Univ. of Denver. *Career:* with Atlanta Newspapers 1976–79; Pres. Grand Junction Newspapers 1979–80; Publr Grand Junction Daily Sentinel 1980–85; Vice-Pres. newspaper Div. Cox Enterprises Inc. 1985–86, Exec. Vice-Pres., Pres. 1986–87, COO, Chair. 1987–; Chair., CEO Cox Enterprises Inc. 1988–. *Address:* Cox Enterprises Inc., PO Box 105357, Atlanta, GA 30348 (Office); 1601 W Peachtree Street NE, Atlanta, GA 30309, USA (Home). *Telephone:* (678) 645-0000 (Office). *Fax:* (678) 645-1079 (Office). *Website:* www.coxenterprises.com (Office).

KENNEDY, Joseph Charles, (X. J. Kennedy); Poet and Writer; b. 21 Aug. 1929, Dover, NJ, USA; m. Dorothy Mintzlaff, 31 Jan. 1962, four s., one d. *Education:* BSc, Seton Hall University, 1950; MA, Columbia University, 1951; University of Paris, 1956. *Career:* Teaching Fellow, 1956–60, Instructor, 1960–62, University of Michigan; Poetry Ed., The Paris Review, 1961–64; Lecturer, Women's College of the University of North Carolina, 1962–63; Asst Prof. to Prof., Tufts University, 1963–79; mem. Authors' Guild; John Barton Wolgamot Society; MLA; PEN. *Publications:* Nude Descending a Staircase, 1961; An Introduction to Poetry (with Dana Gioia), 1968; The Bedford Reader, 1982; Cross Ties, 1985; Dark Horses, 1992; The Lords of Misrule: Poems 1992–2001, 2003. Contributions: newspapers and journals. *Honours:* Lamont Award, 1961; Los Angeles Times Book Award, 1985.

KENNEDY, Sir Ludovic (Henry Coverley); Writer and Broadcaster; b. 3 Nov. 1919, Edinburgh, Scotland; m. Moira Shearer King, 1950, one s., three d. *Education:* MA, Christ Church, Oxford. *Career:* Broadcaster, numerous radio and television programmes, 1955–90; Columnist, Newsweek International, 1974–75, Sunday Standard, 1981–82; Dir, The Spectator, 1988–90; mem. Russian Convoy Club, patron, 1989–2000; Voluntary Euthanasia Society, pres., 1995–. *Publications:* Sub-Lieutenant, 1942; Nelson's Band of Brothers, 1951; One Man's Meat, 1953; Murder Story, 1956; Ten Rillington Place, 1961; The Trial of Stephen Ward, 1964; Very Lovely People, 1969; The British War (general ed.), 1973–77; Pursuit: The Chase and Sinking of the Bismarck, 1974; A Presumption of Innocence: The Amazing Case of Patrick Meehan, 1979; Menace: The Life and Death of the Tirpitz, 1979; The Portland Spy Case, 1979; Wicked Beyond Belief, 1980; A Book of Railway Journeys (ed.), 1980; A Book of Sea Journeys (ed.), 1981; A Book of Air Journeys (ed.), 1982; The Airman and the Carpenter, 1985; On My Way to the Club (autobiog.), 1989; Euthanasia: The Good Death, 1990; Truth to Tell (collected writings), 1991; In Bed with an Elephant: A Journey Through Scotland's Past and Present, 1995; All in the Mind: A Farewell to God, 1999; 36 Murders and Two Immoral Earnings, 2002. *Honours:* Rockefeller Foundation Atlantic Award in Literature, 1950; Winner, Open Finals Contest, English Festival of Spoken Poetry, 1953; Cross, First Class, Order of Merit, Germany, 1979; Richard Dimbleby Award, BAFTA, 1988; Knighted, 1994; FRSL, 1998; several hon. doctorates. *Literary Agent:* Rogers, Coleridge & White Ltd, 20 Powis Mews, London W11 1JN, England.

KENNEDY, (George) Michael Sinclair; music critic and author; b. 19 Feb. 1926, Manchester, England; m. 1st Eslyn Durdle 1947 (died 1999); m. 2nd Joyce Bourne 1999. *Education:* Berkhamsted School. *Career:* Staff, 1941–, Northern Music Critic, 1950–, Northern Ed., 1960–86, Joint Chief Music Critic, 1986–89, The Daily Telegraph; Music Critic, The Sunday Telegraph, 1989–. *Publications:* The Hallé Tradition: A Century of Music, 1960; The Works of Ralph Vaughan Williams, 1964; Portrait of Elgar, 1968; Elgar: Orchestral Music, 1969; Portrait of Manchester, 1970; A History of the Royal Manchester College of Music, 1971; Barbirolli: Conductor Laureate, 1971; Mahler, 1974; The Autobiography of Charles Hallé, with Correspondence and Diaries (ed.), 1976; Richard Strauss, 1976; The Concise Oxford Dictionary of Music (ed.), 1980; Britten, 1981; The Hallé 1858–1983, 1983; Strauss: Tone Poems, 1984; The Oxford Dictionary of Music (ed.), 1985; Adrian Boult, 1987; Portrait of Walton, 1989; Music Enriches All: The First 21 Years of the Royal Northern College of Music, Manchester, 1994; Richard Strauss, Man, Musician, Enigma, 1999; The Life of Elgar, 2004. Contributions: newspapers and magazines. *Honours:* Fellow, Institute of Journalists, 1967; Hon. MA, Univ. of Manchester, 1975; OBE, 1981; Fellow, Royal Northern College of Music, 1981; CBE, 1997; Companion, Royal Northern College of Music, 1999; Hon. DMus, Univ. of Manchester, 2003. *Address:* The Bungalow, 62 Edilom Road, Manchester M8 4HZ, England. *E-mail:* majkennedy@bungalow62.fsnet.co.uk.

KENNEDY, Moorhead; Foundation Administrator and Writer; b. 5 Nov. 1930, New York, NY, USA; m. Louisa Livingston, 8 June 1955, four s. *Education:* AB, Princeton University, 1952; JD, Harvard University, 1959; National War College, 1974–75. *Career:* Foreign Service Officer, 1961–69, 1975–78, Dir, Office of Investment Affairs, 1971–74, US Dept of State; Exec. Dir, Cathedral Peace Institute, New York City, 1981–83, Council for International Understanding, New York City, 1983–90; Pres., Moorhead Kennedy Institute, New York City, 1990–97; mem. American Foreign Service Asscn; Americans for Middle East Understanding; International Advisory Committee, International Centre, New York. *Publications:* The Ayatollah in the Cathedral, 1986; Terrorism: The New Warfare, 1988; Hostage Crisis, 1989; Death of a Dissident, 1990; Fire in the Forest, 1990; Metalfabriken, 1993; Grocery Store, 1993; Nat-Tel, 1995; The Moral Authority of Government, 2000. Contributions: books and professional journals. *Honours:* Medal for Valor, US Dept of State, 1981; Gold Medal, National Institute of Social Sciences, 1991; many hon. doctorates. *Address:* POB 751, Mount Desert, ME 04660, USA.

KENNEDY, Paul M(ichael); Prof. of History and Writer; b. 17 June 1945, Wallsend, Northumberland, England; m. 1st Catherine Urwin, 2 Sept. 1967, deceased 1998, three s.; m. 2nd Cynthia Farrar, 16 Aug. 2001. *Education:* BA, University of Newcastle, 1966; DPhil, University of Oxford, 1970. *Career:* Research Asst to Sir Basil Liddell Hart, 1966–70; Lecturer, 1970–75, Reader, 1975–82, Prof., 1982–83, University of East Anglia; Visiting Fellow, Institute for Advanced Study, Princeton, NJ, 1978–79; J. Richardson Dilworth Prof. of History, 1983–, Dir, International Security Studies, 1990–, Yale University; various guest lectureships including the first Nobel Peace Foundation Lecture, Oslo, 1992; mem. American Acad. of Arts and Sciences; American Philosophical Society; FRHistS; Society of American Historians; Fellow, British Acad. *Publications:* Pacific Onslaught 1941–1943, 1972; Conquest: The Pacific War 1943–1945, 1973; The Samoan Tangle: A Study in Anglo-German-American Relations 1878–1900, 1974; The Rise and Fall of British Naval Mastery, 1976; The Rise of the Anglo-German Antagonism 1860–1914, 1980; The Realities Behind Diplomacy: Background Influences on British External Policy 1865–1980, 1981; Strategy and Diplomacy 1870–1945: Eight Essays, 1983; The Rise and Fall of the Great Powers: Economic Change and Military Conflict from 1500–2000, 1988; Preparing for the Twenty-First Century, 1993. Editor: Germany in the Pacific and Far East 1870–1914 (with John A Moses), 1977; The War Plans of the Great Powers 1880–1914, 1979; Appeasement (with Jack Spence), 1980; Nationalist and Racialist Movements in Britain and Germany Before 1914 (with A. J. Nicholls), 1981; Grand Strategies in War and Peace, 1991; Global Trends: The World Almanac of Development and Peace (with Ingomar Hauchler), 1994; The Pivotal States (with R. Chase and E. Hill), 1998. Contributions: Professional journals and to general magazines and newspapers. *Honours:* various research awards, fellowships, and hon. doctorates; CBE, 2000. *Address:* 409 Humphrey St, New Haven, CT 06511, USA.

KENNEDY, Thomas Eugene; Writer, Ed., Trans., Teacher and Administrator; b. 9 March 1944, New York, USA; m. Monique M. Brun, 28 Dec. 1974, divorced 1997, one s. one d. *Education:* BA, Fordham University, New York, 1974; MFA, Vermont College, Norwich University, USA, 1985; PhD, Copenhagen University, 1988. *Career:* Guest Ed., Nordic Section, Frank magazine, 1987; European Ed., Rohwedder, 1988–89; International Ed., Cimarron Review, 1989–, Potpourri, 1993–; Contributing Ed., Pushcart Prize, 1990–; Advisory Ed., Short Story, 1990–, Literary Review, 1996–; Editorial Board, International Quarterly, 1994. *Publications:* Andre Dubus: A Study, 1988; Crossing Borders (novel), 1990; The American Short Story Today, 1991; Robert Coover: A Study, 1992; Index, American Award Stories, 1993; A Weather of the Eye (novel), 1996; Unreal City (short stories) 1996; New Danish Fiction (ed.), 1995; The Book of Angels (novel), 1997; Drive, Dive, Dance and Fight (short stories), 1997; New Irish Writing (ed.), 1997; Stories and Sources (ed.), 1998; Poems and Sources (ed.), 2000; Realism and Other Illusions (essays), 2002; Kerrigan's Copenhagen, A Love Story (novel), 2002; The Secret Life of the Writer (co-ed.), 2002. Other: The Literary Traveller (online column), 2001–. *Honours:* Pushcart Prize, 1990; O. Henry Prize, 1994. *Address:* Strandboulevarden 118, 2100 Copenhagen, Denmark.

KENNEDY, William (Joseph); Novelist and Prof. of English; b. 16 Jan. 1928, Albany, New York, USA; m. Ana Daisy Dana Segarra, 31 Jan. 1957, one s. two d. *Education:* BA, Siena College, Loudonville, New York, 1949. *Career:* Asst Sports Ed. and Columnist, Glens Falls Post Star, 1949–50; Reporter, 1952–56, Special Writer, 1963–70, Albany Times-Union; Asst Managing Ed. and Columnist, Puerto Rico World Journal, San Juan, 1956; Reporter, Miami Herald, 1957, Knight Newspapers, 1957–59; Correspondent, Time-Life Publishers in Puerto Rico, 1957–59; Founding Managing Ed., San Juan Star, 1959–61; Lecturer, 1974–82, Prof. of English, 1983–, SUNY at Albany; Visiting Prof., Cornell University, 1982–83; Founder, New York State Writers Institute, 1983; mem. American Acad. of Arts and Letters; American Acad. of Arts and Sciences, 2002; Writers Guild of America. *Publications:* The Ink Truck, 1969; Legs, 1975; Billy Phelan's Greatest Game, 1978; O Albany!, 1983; Ironweed, 1983; The Cotton Club (with Francis Ford Coppola), film script, 1984; Charlie Malarkey and the Belly Button Machine (with Brenden Christopher Kennedy), 1986; Quinn's Book, 1988; Very Old Bones, 1992; Riding the Yellow Trolley Car, 1993; Charlie Malarkey and the Singing Moose (with Brenden Christopher Kennedy), 1994; The Flaming Corsage, 1996; Roscoe, 2002; The Albany Cycle, two vols, 2002. Contributions: numerous periodicals. *Honours:* National Endowment for the Arts Fellowship, 1981; John D. and Catherine T. MacArthur Foundation Fellowship, 1983; Pulitzer Prize in Fiction, 1984; National Book Critics Circle Award in Fiction, 1984; Creative Arts Award, Brandeis University, 1986; Commander of the Order of Arts and Letters, France, 1993. *Address:* New York State Writers Institute, 1400 Washington Ave, Albany, NY 12222, USA.

KENNEDY, X. J. (see Kennedy, Joseph Charles).

KENNEDY OF THE SHAWS, Baroness (Life Peer) cr. 1997, of Cathcart in the City of Glasgow; **Helena Ann Kennedy,** QC, FRSA; British lawyer; b. 12 May 1950, Glasgow; one s.; m. Dr Iain L. Hutchison 1986; one s. one d. *Education:* Holyrood Secondary School, Glasgow and Council of Legal Educ. *Career:* called to the Bar, Gray's Inn 1972; mem. Bar Council 1990–93; mem. CIBA Comm. into Child Sexual Abuse 1981–83; mem. Bd City Limits Magazine 1982–84, New Statesman 1990–96, Counsel Magazine 1990–93; mem. Council, Howard League for Penal Reform 1989–, Chair. Comm. of Inquiry into Violence in Penal Insts for Young People (report 1995); Commr BAFTA inquiry into future of BBC 1990, Hamlyn Nat. Comm. on Educ. 1991–; Visiting lecturer, British Postgrad. Medical Fed. 1991–; Adviser, Mannheim Inst. on Criminology, LSE 1992–; Leader of inquiry into health, environmental and safety aspects of Atomic Weapons Establishment, Aldermaston (report 1994); Chancellor, Oxford Brookes Univ. 1994–2001; Chair. British Council 1998–, Human Genetics Comm. 2000–; author of official report (Learning Works) for Further Educ. Funding Council on widening participation in further educ. 1997; Pres. School of Oriental and African Studies, London Univ. 2002–; mem. Advisory Bd, Int. Centre for Prison Studies 1998; Chair. London Int. Festival of Theatre, Standing Cttee for Youth Justice 1992–97; Chair. Charter 88 1992–97; Pres. London Marriage Guidance Council, Birth Control Campaign, Nat. Children's Bureau, Hillcroft Coll.; Vice-Pres. Haldane Soc., Nat. Ass. of Women; mem. British Council's Law Advisory Cttee Advisory Bd for Study of Women and Gender, Warwick Univ., Int. Bar Asscn's Task Force on Terrorism; presenter of various programmes on radio and TV and creator of BBC drama series Blind Justice 1988; Patron, Liberty; mem. Acad. de Cultures Internationales. *Publications:* The Bar on Trial (jtly) 1978, Child Abuse within the Family (jtly) 1984, Balancing Acts (jtly) 1989, Eve was Framed 1992, Just Law: the Changing Face of Justice and Why it Matters to Us All 2004; articles on legal matters, civil liberties and women. *Honours:* Hon. Fellow Inst. of Advanced Legal Studies, Univ. of London 1997; Hon. mem. Council, Nat. Soc. for Prevention of Cruelty to Children; 18 hon. LLDs from British and Irish Univs; Women's Network Award 1992, UK Woman of Europe Award 1995; Campaigning and Influencing Award, Nat. Fed. of Women's Insts 1996, Times Newspaper Lifetime Achievement Award in the Law (jtly) 1997; Spectator Magazine's Parl. Campaigner of the Year 2000. *Address:* House of Lords, London, SW1A 0PW, England. *Telephone:* (1708) 379482. *Fax:* (1708) 379482.

KENNELL, Nigel M.; Classicist; b. 29 Nov. 1955, London, England; m. Stefanie Adelaide Hillert Suszko, 1985. *Education:* BA, University of British Columbia, 1977; MA, 1978, PhD, 1985, University of Toronto; American School of Classical Studies, Athens, Greece, 1978–79, 1981–82. *Career:* Lecturer in Classics, Brock University, St Catherine's, Ontario, Canada, 1985–86; Asst Prof., 1986–92, Assoc. Prof. of Classics, 1992–, Memorial University, St John's University, NF; Research Asst, Institute for Advanced Study, Princeton, NJ, 1992–93; Research Assoc., Collège de France, Paris, 1993; mem. Archeological Institute of America; Classical Asscn of Canada; Society for the Promotion of Hellenic Studies; Canadian Academic Centre in Athens; Asscn of Ancient Historians; American School of Classical Studies Alumni Asscn. *Publications:* The Gymnasium of Virtue, 1996. Contributions: American Journal of Archaeology; American Journal of Philology; Epigraphica Anatolica; Hesperia; Phoenix; Zeitschrift für Papyrologie und Epigraphik. *Honours:* Outstanding Academic Book, Choice, 1996. *Address:* 117 Queen's Rd, Apt 20, St John's, NF A1C 5S7 Canada.

KENNELLY, (Timothy) Brendan, BA, MA, PhD; academic, poet, writer and dramatist; b. 17 April 1936, Ballylongford, County Kerry, Ireland. *Education:* Trinity College, Dublin. *Career:* Prof. of Modern Literature and Senior Fellow, Trinity College, Dublin, 1973–. *Publications:* Poetry: Cast a Cold Eye (with Rudi Holzapfel), 1959; The Rain, The Moon (with Rudi Holzapfel), 1961; The Dark About Our Loves (with Rudi Holzapfel), 1962; Green Townlands: Poems (with Rudi Holzapfel), 1963; Let Fall No Burning Leaf, 1963; My Dark Fathers, 1964; Up and At It, 1965; Collection One: Getting Up Early, 1966; Good Souls to Survive, 1967; Dream of a Black Fox, 1968; Selected Poems, 1969; A Drinking Cup: Poems From the Irish, 1970; Bread, 1971; Love Cry, 1972; Salvation, the Stranger, 1972; The Voices, 1973; Shelley in Dublin, 1974; A Kind of Trust, 1975; New and Selected Poems, 1976; Islandman, 1977; The Visitor, 1978; A Girl: 22 Songs, 1978; A Small Light, 1979; In Spite of the Wise, 1979; The Boats Are Home, 1980; The House That Jack Didn't Build, 1982; Cromwell: A Poem, 1983; Moloney Up and At It, 1984; Selected Poems, 1985; Mary: From the Irish, 1987; Love of Ireland: Poems From the Irish, 1989; A Time for Voices: Selected Poems 1960–1990, 1990; The Book of Judas: A Poem, 1991; Breathing Spaces: Early Poems, 1992; Poetry My Arse, 1995; The Man Made of Rain, 1998; The Singing Tree, 1998; Begin, 1999; Glimpses, 2001; The Little Book of Judas, 2002; Martial Art 2004. Fiction: The Crooked Cross, 1963; The Florentines, 1967. Plays: Medea, 1991; The Trojan Women, 1993; Antigone, 1996; Blood Wedding, 1996. Criticism: Journey into Joy: Selected Prose, 1994. Anthologies: The Penguin Book of Irish Verse, 1970; Landmarks of Irish Drama, 1988; Joycechoyce: The Poems in Verse and Prose of James Joyce (with A Norman Jeffares), 1992; Irish Prose Writings: Swift to the Literary Renaissance (with Terence Brown), 1992; Between Innocence and Peace: Favourite Poems of Ireland, 1993; Dublines (with Katie Donovan), 1994; Ireland's Women: Writings Past and Present (with Katie Donovan and A Norman Jeffares), 1994. Other: Real Ireland, 1984; Ireland Past and Present (ed.), 1985. *Honours:* AE Monorial Prize for Poetry, 1967; Fellow, Trinity College, Dublin, 1967; Critics' Special Harveys Award, 1988; American Ireland Funds Literary Award, 1999. *Address:* c/o School of English, Trinity College, Dublin 2, Ireland.

KENNELLY, Laura B., BA, MA, PhD; writer and poet; b. 28 July 1941, Denton, TX, USA; m. 1st Kevin Kennelly 1961 (divorced 1996); m. 2nd Robert Mayerovitch 1996; four s. one d. two step-d. *Education:* Univ. of North Texas. *Career:* Adjunct Prof., Univ. of North Texas, 1976–94, Texas Woman's Univ., 1995; Ed., Grasslands Review, 1989; Asst Ed., Bach: Journal of the Riemenschneider Bach Institute, Baldwin-Wallace Coll.; mem. Texas Asscn of Creative Writing Teachers, pres., 1993–95. *Publications:* The Passage of Mrs Jung, 1990; A Certain Attitude, 1995. Contributions: San Jose Studies; Studies in Contemporary Satire; Exquisite Corpse; New Mexico Humanities Review; Australian Journal of Communication. *Honours:* First Place, North Central Texas College Poetry Contest, 1988; First Place, University of North Texas Centennial Poem Award, 1990. *Address:* PO Box 626, Berea, OH 44017, USA. *E-mail:* LKennell@bw.edu.

KENNET, 2nd Baron, cr. 1935; **Wayland Kennet** (see Young, Wayland Hilton).

KENNEY, Catherine, BA, MA, PhD; writer, academic and arts administrator; b. 3 Oct. 1948, Memphis, Tennessee, USA; one s. *Education:* Siena College, Loyola University, Chicago. *Career:* currently Exec. Dir, Irish American Heritage Center, Chicago, Faculty of the American Managment Asscn. *Publications:* Thurber's Anatomy of Confusion, 1984; The Remarkable Case of Dorothy L. Sayers, 1990; Dorothy L. (play), 1993. Contributions: books, scholarly journals and newspapers. *Honours:* American Asscn of University Women Grant 1983. *Address:* 228 Stanley Avenue, Park Ridge, IL 60068, USA. *E-mail:* proudfootproductions@yahoo.com.

KENNY, Adele; Poet, Writer, Ed. and Consultant; b. 28 Nov. 1948, Perth Amboy, NJ, USA. *Education:* BA, English, Kean University, 1970; MS, Education, College of New Rochelle, 1982. *Career:* Artist-in-Residence, Middlesex County Arts Council, 1979–80; Poetry Ed., New Jersey ArtForm, 1981–83; Assoc. Ed., Muse-Pie Press, 1988–; Dir Carriage House Poetry Reading Series 1998–; Cultural Arts Dir Kuran Arts Center 1999–; mem. Haiku Society of America, pres., 1987–88, 1990; Poetry Society of America; Poets and Writers Inc. *Publications:* An Archeology of Ruins, 1982; Illegal Entries, 1984; The Roses Open 1984; Between Hail Marys, 1986; Migrating Geese, 1987; The Crystal Keepers Handbook, 1988; Counseling Gifted, Creative and Talented Youth Through the Arts, 1989; Castles and Dragons, 1990; Questi Momenti, 1990; Starship Earth, 1990; We Become By Being, 1994; Staffordshire Spaniels, 1997; At the Edge of the Woods, 1997; Staffordshire Animals, 1998, Photographic Cases: Victorian Design Sources 2001, Chosen Ghosts 2001. Contributions: periodicals. *Honours:* Writer's Digest Award, 1981; New Jersey State Council on the Arts Fellowships, 1982, 1987; Merit Book Awards, 1983, 1986, 1987, 1991; Henderson Award, 1984; Roselip Award, 1988; Haiku Quarterly Award, 1989; Allen Ginsberg Poetry Award, 1993. *Address:* 207 Coriell Ave, Fanwood, NJ 07023, USA.

KENNY, Sir Anthony (John Patrick); Philosopher and Writer; b. 16 March 1931, Liverpool, England; m. Nancy Caroline Gayley, 1966, two s. *Education:* STL, Gregorian University, Rome; St Benet's Hall, Oxford; DPhil, 1961; DLitt, 1980. *Career:* Ordained Roman Catholic priest, 1955; Curate, Liverpool, 1959–63; Asst Lecturer, University of Liverpool, 1961–63; Resumed lay status, 1963; Lecturer in Philosophy, Exeter and Trinity Colleges, Oxford, 1963–64; Tutor in Philosophy, 1964, Fellow, 1964–78, Senior Tutor, 1971–72, 1976–78, Master, 1978–89, Balliol College, Oxford; University Lecturer, 1965–78, Wilde Lecturer in Natural and Comparative Religion, 1969–72, Speaker's Lecturer in Biblical Studies, 1980–83, Pro-Vice-Chancellor, 1984–99, Pres., Development Programme, 1999–2001, University of Oxford; Joint Gifford Lecturer, University of Edinburgh, 1972–73; Stanton Lecturer, University of Cambridge, 1980–83; Bampton Lecturer, Columbia University, 1983; Warden, Rhodes House, Oxford, 1989–99; Professional Fellow, 1989–99, Emeritus Fellow, 1999–, St John's College, Oxford; mem. American Acad. of Arts and Sciences, 2003; American Philosophical Society, 1993–; British Acad., fellow, 1974–, pres., 1989–93; Norwegian Acad. of Sciences, 1993–; Society for the Protection of Science and Learning, chair., 1989–93. *Publications:* Action, Emotion and Will, 1963; Responsa Alumnorum of English College, Rome, two vols, 1963; Descartes, 1968; The Five Ways, 1969; Wittgenstein, 1973; The Anatomy of the Soul, 1974; Will, Freedom and Power, 1975; The Aristotelian Ethics, 1978; Freewill and Responsibility, 1978; Aristotle's Theory of the Will, 1979; The God of the Philosophers, 1979; Aquinas, 1980; The Computation of Style, 1982; Faith and Reason, 1983; Thomas More, 1983; The Legacy of Wittgenstein, 1984; A Path from Rome (autobiog.), 1985; Wyclif, 1985; The Logic of Deterrence, 1985; The Ivory Tower, 1985; A Stylometric Study of the New Testament, 1986; The Road to Hillsborough, 1987; Reason and Religion, 1987; The Heritage of Wisdom, 1987; God and Two Poets, 1988; The Metaphysics of Mind, 1989; The Oxford Diaries of Arthur Hugh Clough, 1990; Mountains: An Anthology, 1991; Aristotle on the Perfect Life, 1992; What is Faith?, 1992; Aquinas on Mind, 1993; The Oxford Illustrated History of Western Philosophy (ed.), 1994; Frege, 1995; A Life in Oxford (autobiog.), 1997; A Brief History of Western Philosophy, 1998; Essays on the Aristotelian Tradition, 2001; Aquinas on Being, 2002. *Honours:* several hon. doctorates; Knighted, 1992; Hon. Fellow, Harris Manchester College, Oxford, 1996. *Address:* The Old Bakery, 1A Larkins Lane, Oxford OW3 9DW, England.

KENRICK, Tony; Author; b. 23 Aug. 1935, Sydney, NSW, Australia,. *Career:* Advertising Copywriter, Sydney, Toronto, San Francisco, New York, London, 1953–72. *Publications:* The Only Good Body's a Dead One, 1970; A Tough One to Lose, 1972; Two for the Price of One, 1974; Stealing Lillian, 1975; The Seven Day Soldiers, 1976; The Chicago Girl, 1976; Two Lucky People, 1978; The Nighttime Guy, 1979; The 81st Site, 1980; Blast, 1983; Faraday's Flowers, 1985; China White, 1986; Neon Tough, 1988; Glitterbug, 1991; Round Trip, 1996. *Address:* c/o 216 E 75th St, New York, NY 10021, USA.

KENT, Alexander (see Reeman, Douglas Edward).

KENT, Arthur (William Charles), (James Bradwell, M. DuBois, Paul Granados, Alexander Karol, Alex Stamper, Brett Vane); Author; b. 31 Jan. 1925, London, England. *Education:* City Literary Institute, London. *Career:* Journalist, News Chronicle, London, 1943–46, Australian Daily Mirror, 1947–53, Beaverbook Newspapers, UK, 1957–69, BBC, London, 1970–71. *Publications:* Sunny (as Bret Vane), 1953; Gardenia (as Bret Vane), 1953; Broadway Contraband (as Paul Granados), 1954; El Tafile (as M. DuBois), 1954; Légion Étrangere (as M. DuBois), 1954; March and Die (as M. DuBois), 1954; Revolt at Zaluig (as Alex Stamper), 1954; Inclining to Crime, 1957; Special Edition Murder, 1957; Kansas Fast Gun, 1958; Stairway to Murder, 1958; Wake Up Screaming, 1958; The Camp on Blood Island (with G. Thomas), 1958; Last Action, 1959; Broken Doll, 1961; Action of the Tiger, 1961; The Weak and the Strong, 1962; The Counterfeiters, 1962; Long Horn, Long Grass, 1964; Black Sunday, 1965; Plant Poppies on My Grave, 1966; Red Red Red, 1966; Fall of Singapore (with I Simon), 1970; The Mean City (as James Bradwell), 1971; A Life in the Wind (with Z. de Tyras), 1971; Sword of Vengeance (as Alexander Karol), 1973; Dark Lady (as Alexander Karol), 1974; The King's Witchfinder (as Alexander Karol), 1975; Maverick Squadron, 1975; The Nowhere War, 1975. *Address:* 26 Verulam Ave, London E17, England.

KENT, Helen (see Polley, Judith Anne).

KENT, Philip (see Bulmer, Henry Kenneth).

KENYON, Bruce (Guy), (Meredith Leigh); Writer; b. 16 Aug. 1929, Cadillac, Michigan, USA; m. Marian Long, 1950, divorced 1954. *Career:* mem. Authors' Guild; Authors League. *Publications:* Rose White, Rose Red, 1983; The Forrester Inheritance, 1985; Fair Game, 1986; A Marriage of Inconvenience, 1986; Wild Rose, 1986; The Counterfeit Lady, 1987; An Elegant Education, 1987; A Lady of Qualities, 1987; Return to Cheyne Spa, 1988; A Certain Reputation, 1990. Contributions: periodicals. *Address:* c/o Kearns and Orr, 686 Lexington Ave, New York, NY 10022, USA.

KENYON, Michael; Author; b. 26 June 1931, Huddersfield, Yorkshire, England; three d. *Education:* Wadham College, Oxford, 1951–54; MA (Oxon), History. *Career:* mem. Detection Club. *Publications:* May You Die in Ireland, 1965; The 100,000 Welcomes, 1970; Mr Big, 1973; The Rapist, 1976; A Healthy Way to Die, 1986; Peckover Holds the Baby, 1988; Kill the Butler!, 1991; Peckover Joins the Choir, 1992; A French Affair, 1992; Peckover and the Bog Man, 1994. Contributions: 40 articles to Gourmet Magazine. *Address:* 164 Halsey St, Southampton, NY 11968, USA.

KEOGH, Dermot Francis; Prof. and Historian; b. 12 May 1945, Dublin, Ireland; m. Ann, 22 Aug. 1973, two s. two d. *Education:* BA, 1970, MA, 1974, University College, Dublin; PhD, 1980, European University Institute, Florence, 1980. *Career:* Lecturer, Dept of History, 1970–, Jean Monnet Prof. of Modern Integration, 1990–, University College, Cork. *Publications:* The Vatican, the Bishops and Irish Politics 1919–1939, 1985; The Rise of the Irish Working Class 1890–1914, 1983; Ireland and Europe 1919–1989, 1989; Church and Politics in Latin America, 1990; Ireland, 1922–1993, 1993; Jews in Twentieth Century Ireland, 1998. Contributions: Academic journals and national press. *Honours:* Fellow, Woodrow Wilson Centre for Scholars, Washington, DC, 1988. *Address:* Dept of Modern History, University College, Cork, Ireland.

KEOHANE, Robert Owen; Prof. of Political Science; b. 3 Oct. 1941, Chicago, IL, USA; m. Nannerl Overholser 1970; three s. one d. *Education:* Shimer Coll., IL; PhD, Harvard Univ. *Career:* Fellow Harvard Univ., Woodrow Wilson School of Public and Int. Affairs, Princeton Univ. 1961–62; mem. Woodrow Wilson Award Cttee 1982, Chair. Nominating Cttee 1990–91, Chair. Minority Identification Project 1990–92; Instructor, then Assoc. Prof. Swathmore Coll. 1965–73; Assoc. Prof., then Prof. Stanford Univ. 1973–81; Ed. Int. Org. 1974–80, mem. Bd Eds 1968–77, 1982–88, 1992–97, 1998–, Chair. 1986–87; Prof. Brandeis Univ. 1981–85; Pres. Int. Studies Asscn 1988–89, Chair. Nominations Cttee 1985; Prof., then Stanfield Prof. of Int. Peace, Harvard Univ. 1985–96, Chair. Dept of Govt 1988–92; Pres. American Political Science Asscn 1999–2000; currently James B. Duke Prof. of Political Science, Duke Univ.; Sherill Lecturer Yale Univ. Law School 1996. *Publications:* After Hegemony: Cooperation and Discord in the World Political Economy 1984, Neorealism and Its Critics 1986, International Institutions and State Power: Essays in International Relations Theory 1989; (as co-Ed.): Transnational Relations and World Politics 1972, The New European Community: Decision-Making and Institutional Change 1991, Ideas and Foreign Policy 1993, From Local Commons to Global Interdependence 1994, Institutions for Environmental Aid: Pitfalls and Promises 1996, Internationalization and Domestic Politics 1996, Imperfect Unions: Security Institutions Across Time and Space 1999, Exploration and Contestation in the Study of World Politics 1998, Legalization and World Politics 2000; (as co-author): Power and Interdependence: World Politics in Transition 1977, Institutions for the Earth: Sources of Effective International Environmental Protection 1993, After the Cold War: State Strategies and International Institutions in Europe, 1989–91 1993, Designing Social Inquiry: Scientific Inference in Qualitative Research 1994. *Honours:* Research Fellow German Marshall Fund 1977–78; Fellow Council on Foreign Relations 1967–69, Center for Advanced Study in Behavioral Sciences 1977–78, 1987–88, American Acad. of Arts and Sciences 1983–, Guggenheim Foundation 1992–93; Sr Foreign Policy Fellow Social Science Research Council 1986–88; Bellagio Resident Fellow 1993; Frank Kenan Fellow Nat. Endowment for the Humanities 1995–96; Hon. PhD (Univ. of Aarhus, Denmark) 1988; Grawemeyer Award for Ideas Improving World Order 1989, First Mentorship Award, Soc. for Women in Int. Political Economy 1997. *Address:* Department of Politics, Duke University, Durham, NC 27708-0204, USA; 1508 Pinecrest Road, Durham, NC 27705-5817, USA. *E-mail:* rkeohane@acpub.duke.

KEPEL, Gilles; French sociologist and writer. *Education:* Prof. of the Middle East, Institut d'Études Politiques, Paris. *Publications:* non-fiction: Muslim Extremism in Egypt: The Prophet and Pharaoh 1985, The Revenge of God: Resurgence of Islam, Christianity and Judaism in the Modern World 1993, Allah in the West: Islamic Movements in America and Europe 1997, Jihad: The Trail of Political Islam 2002, Bad Moon Rising: A Chronicle of the Middle East Today 2003, Islam and the West in the New World Order 2004. *Honours:* Tel-Aviv Prize for Literature 1990, Newman Prize 2003. *Address:* Institut d'Études Politiques de Paris, 2002 - 27 rue Saint-Guillaume, 75337 Paris Cédex 07, France.

KERBER, Linda K(aufman); Prof. of History and Writer; b. 23 Jan. 1940, New York, NY, USA; m. Richard Kerber 5 June 1960; two s. *Education:* AB, cum laude, Barnard College, 1960; MA, New York University, 1961; PhD, Columbia University, 1968. *Career:* Lecturer, 1963–67, Asst Prof., 1968, Stern College for Women, Yeshiva University; Asst Prof., San Jose State College, 1969–70; Visiting Asst Prof., Stanford University, 1970–71; Assoc. Prof., 1971–75, Prof. of History, 1975–85, May Brodbeck Prof. of Liberal Arts, 1985–, University of Iowa; Visiting Prof., University of Chicago, 1991–92; mem. American Acad. of Arts and Sciences; American Antiquarian Society; American Studies Asscn, pres., 1988; Organization of American Historians, pres., 1997; Society of American Historians; PEN American Center. *Publications:* Federalists in Dissent: Imagery and Ideology in Jeffersonian America, 1970; Women of the Republic: Intellect and Ideology in Revolutionary America, 1980; Women's America: Refocusing the Past (co-ed.), 1982; The Impact of Women on American Education, 1983; History Will Do It No Justice: Women's Lives in Revolutionary America, 1987; US History as Women's History: New Feminist Essays (co-ed.), 1995; Toward an Intellectual History of Women: Essays, 1997; No Constitutional Right to Be Ladies: Women and the Obligations of Citizenship, 1998. Contributions: Professional journals. *Honours:* National Endowment for the Humanities Fellowships, 1976, 1983–84, 1994; National Humanities Center Fellowship, 1990–91; Guggenheim Fellowship, 1990–91. *Address:* c/o Dept of History, University of Iowa, Iowa City, IA 52242, USA.

KERMAN, Joseph Wilfred, BA, PhD; American musicologist, writer, critic and editor; b. 3 April 1924, London, England; m. Vivian Shaviro 1945; two s. one d. *Education:* New York Univ., Princeton Univ. *Career:* Dir of Graduate Studies, Westminster Choir Coll. 1949–51; Asst Prof. 1951–56, Assoc. Prof. 1956–60, Prof. of Music 1960–71, 1974–94, Chair., Dept of Music 1960–63, 1991–93, Univ. of California at Berkeley; Heather Prof. of Music, Univ. of Oxford 1971–74; Fellow, Wadham Coll., Oxford 1972–74; founder/Co-Ed., 19th Century Music 1977–89; Charles Eliot Norton Prof. of Poetry, Harvard Univ. 1997–98; Fellow, American Acad. of Arts and Sciences 1973, American Philosophical Soc. 2001. *Publications:* Opera as Drama 1956, The Elizabethan Madrigal: A Comparative Study 1962, A History of Art and Music (with Horst W. Janson and Dora Jane Janson) 1968, Listen (with Vivian Kerman) 1972, Beethoven Studies (ed. with Alan Tyson) 1973, The Masses and Motets of William Byrd 1981, The New Grove Beethoven (with Alan Tyson) 1983, Contemplating Music: Challenges to Musicology 1985, Music at the Turn of the Century: A '19th Century Music' Reader (ed.) 1990, Write All These Down: Essays on Music 1994, Concerto Conversations 1999, The Art of Fugue: Bach Fugues for Keyboard 1715–1750 2005; contrib. to scholarly journals, including New York Review of Books. *Honours:* Guggenheim Fellowship 1960, Fulbright Fellowship 1966; National Inst. and American Acad. of Arts and Letters Award 1956, Hon. Fellow, Royal Acad. of Music, London 1972, hon. mem. American Musicological Soc. 1995. *Address:* 107 Southampton Avenue, Berkeley, CA 94707, USA.

KERMODE, Sir (John) Frank, BA, MA, FBA, FRSL; retd academic, writer and editor; b. 29 Nov. 1919, Douglas, Isle of Man, England; m. Maureen Eccles 1947 (divorced 1970); one s. one d. *Education:* Univ. of Liverpool. *Career:* Lecturer, King's College, Newcastle, 1947–49, University of Reading, 1949–58; John Edward Taylor Prof. of English Literature, University of

Manchester, 1958–65; Winterstoke Prof. of English, University of Bristol, 1965–67; Co-Ed., Encounter journal, 1966–67; Lord Northcliffe Prof. of Modern English Literature, 1967–74, University College London; Ed., Fontana Masterguides and Modern Masters series, 1969–, Oxford Authors, 1984–; columnist, Daily Telegraph, 1970–74; King Edward VII Prof. of English Literature, University of Cambridge, 1974–82; Fellow, 1974–87, King's College, Cambridge; Charles Eliot Norton Prof. of Poetry, Harvard University, 1977–78; Visiting Prof., Columbia University, 1984, 1985; Henry Luce Prof., Yale University, 1994. *Publications:* Romantic Image, 1957; John Donne, 1957; The Living Milton, 1960; Wallace Stevens, 1960; Puzzles & Epiphanies, 1962; The Sense of an Ending, 1967; Continuities, 1968; Shakespeare, Spenser, Donne, 1971; Modern Essays, 1971; D. H. Lawrence, 1973; Oxford Anthology of English Literature (ed. with John Hollander), 1973; The Classic, 1975; Selected Prose of T. S. Eliot (ed.), 1975; The Genesis of Secrecy, 1979; Essays on Fiction, 1971–82, 1983; Forms of Attention, 1985; The Literary Guide to the Bible (ed. with Robert Alter), 1987; History and Value, 1988; An Appetite for Poetry, 1989; Poetry, Narrative, History, 1990; Andrew Marvell (ed. with Keith Walker), 1990; The Uses of Error, 1991; The Oxford Book of Letters (ed. with Anita Kermode), 1995; Not Entitled (memoir), 1996; Shakespeare's Language, 2000; Pleasing Myself, 2001; Pieces of My Mind, 2003; The Age of Shakespeare 2004. Contributions: journals and periodicals, incl. London Review of Books. *Honours:* Officier, Ordre des Arts et des Sciences, 1973; Hon. Fellow, King's College, Cambridge, 1988, University College London, 1996; Knighted, 1991; Hon. doctorates; Hon. Foreign Mem., American Society of Arts and Letters; hon. mem. American Acad. of Arts and Sciences. *Literary Agent:* PFD, Drury House, 34–43 Russell Street, London, WC2B 5HA, England. *Address:* 9 The Oast House, Grange Road, Cambridge, CB3 9AP, England.

KERN, E. R. (see Kerner, Fred).

KERN, Gregory (see Tubb, Edwin Charles).

KERNAGHAN, Eileen (Shirley); Writer; b. 6 Jan. 1939, Enderby, BC, Canada; m. Patrick Walter Kernaghan, 22 Aug. 1959, two s. one d. *Education:* Elementary Teaching Certificate, University of British Columbia. *Career:* mem. Burnaby Writers Society; Federation of British Columbian Writers; Writers Union of Canada. *Publications:* The Upper Left-Hand Corner: A Writer's Guide for the Northwest (co-author), 1975; Journey to Aprilioth, 1980; Songs for the Drowned Lands, 1983; Sarsen Witch, 1988; Walking After Midnight, 1991. Contributions: journals and periodicals. *Honours:* Silver Porgy Award, West Coast Review of Books, 1981; Canadian Science Fiction and Fantasy Award, 1985.

KERNER, Fred, (F. R. Eady, Frohm Fredericks, Frederika Frohm, E. R. Kern, Frederick Kerr, D. F. Renrick, M. N. Thaler); Writer and Publisher; b. 15 Feb. 1921, Montréal, QC, Canada; m. Sally Dee Stouten 18 May 1959; two s. one d. *Education:* BA, Sir George Williams Univ. (Concordia Univ.), Montréal, 1942. *Career:* mem. World Intellectual Property Organization; Acad. of Canadian Writers; European Acad. of Arts, Sciences and Humanities; Organization of Canadian Authors and Publishers; Canadian Authors Asscn; Periodical Writers Asscn of Canada; Canadian Writers' Foundation; Asscn of American Publishers; MWA; Writers' Union of Canada; Authors' Guild; Authors' League of America; International PEN; National Speakers' Asscn; American Acad. of Politics and Social Sciences. *Publications:* Eat, Think and Be Slender (with L. Kotkin), 1954; The Magic Power of Your Mind (with W. Germain), 1956; Ten Days to a Successful Memory (with J. Brothers), 1957; Stress and Your Heart, 1961; Don't Count Calories (as Frederick Kerr), 1962; Secrets of Your Supraconscious (with W. Germain), 1965; What's Best For Your Child and You (with D. Goodman), 1966; Buy High, Sell Higher (with J. Reid), 1966; It's Fun to Fondue (as M. N. Thaler), 1968; Nadia (with I. Grumeza), 1977; Careers in Writing, 1985; Mad About Fondue, 1986; Prospering Through the Coming Depression (with A. Willman), 1988; Home Emergency Handbook and First Aid Guide, 1990; Fabulous Fondues, 2000. Editor: Love is a Man's Affair, 1958; Treasury of Lincoln Quotations, 1965; The Canadian Writers' Guide, various edns; Selling Your Short Fiction, 1992. Contributions: contributing writer to many books, magazines and journals. *Honours:* American Heritage Foundation Award, 1952; Queen's Silver Jubilee Medal, 1977; Allen Sangster Award, 1982; Air Canada Award, 1982; Canadian Book Publishers Council Award, 1984; International Mercury Award, 1990. *Address:* 1405–1555 Finch Ave E, Willowdale, ON M2J 4X9, Canada. *E-mail:* fkerner@pubproj.com.

KERR, Carole (see Carr, Margaret).

KERR, David; British author and academic; b. 1942, Carlisle, Cumbria. *Career:* f. and dir of theatre companies in UK, Malawi, Zambia and Botswana; Assoc. Prof. of English, Univ. of Botswana. *Publications:* non-fiction: African Popular Theatre 1996; poetry: Tangled Tongues 2003. *Address:* c/o Flambard Press, Stable Cottage, East Fourstones, Hexham, Northumberland NE47 5DX, England. *Telephone:* (1434) 674360. *Fax:* (1434) 674178. *Website:* www.flambardpress.co.uk.

KERR, (Anne) Judith; children's writer; b. 14 June 1923, Berlin, Germany; m. Nigel Kneale; one s. *Career:* sec., Red Cross, London, England 1941–45; teacher and textile designer 1948–53; script ed., scriptwriter, BBC TV, London 1953–58. *Publications:* The Tiger Who Came to Tea, 1968; Mog the Forgetful Cat, 1970; When Hitler Stole Pink Rabbit, 1971; When Willy Went to the Wedding, 1972; The Other Way Round, 1975, republished as Bombs on Aunt Dainty, 2002; Mog's Christmas, 1976; A Small Person Far Away, 1978; Mog and the Baby, 1980; Mog in the Dark, 1983; Mog and Me, 1984; Mog's Family of Cats, 1985; Mog's Amazing Birthday Caper, 1986; Mog and Bunny, 1988; Mog and Barnaby, 1990; How Mrs Monkey Missed the Ark, 1992; The Adventures of Mog, 1993; Mog on Fox Night, 1993; Mog in the Garden, 1994; Mog's Kittens, 1994; Mog and the Vee Ee Tee, 1996; The Big Mog Book, 1997; Birdie Halleluyah, 1998; Mog's Bad Thing, 2000; The Other Goose, 2001; Goodbye Mog, 2002. *Address:* c/o Harper Collins Publishers, 77–85 Fulham Palace Road, London W6 8JB, England.

KERR, Katharine; Novelist; b. 3 Oct. 1944, Cleveland, OH, USA; m. Howard Kerr, 1973. *Education:* Stanford University, 1962–63. *Publications:* Daggerspell, 1986; Darkspell, 1987; The Bristling Wood (UK edn as Dawnspell: The Bristling Wood), 1989; The Dragon Revenant (UK edn as Dragonspell: The Southern Sea), 1990; Polar City Blues, 1991; A Time of Exile: A Novel of the Westlands, 1991; A Time of Omens: A Novel of the Westlands, 1992; Resurrectiion, 1992; Days of Blood and Fire: A Novel of the Westlands (UK edn as A Time of War: Days of Blood and Fire), 1993; Days of Air and Darkness: A Novel of the Westlands (UK edn as A Time of Justice: Days of Air and Darkness), 1994; Freeze Frames (co-author), 1995; Snare, 2003. Contributions: anthologies. *Literary Agent:* Elizabeth Pomada, 1029 Jones St, San Francisco, CA 94109, USA. *Address:* 51 Sweeny, San Francisco, CA 94134, USA.

KERR, Philip Ballantyne; British writer; b. 22 Feb. 1956, Edinburgh, Scotland; m. Jane Thynne 1991; two s. one d. *Education:* Univ. of Birmingham. *Career:* film critic, New Statesman. *Publications:* March Violets 1989, The Pale Criminal 1990, The Penguin Book of Lies (ed.) 1990, A German Requiem 1991, A Philosophical Investigation 1992, The Penguin Book of Fights, Feuds, and Heartfelt Hatreds: An Anthology of Antipathy (ed.) 1992, Dead Meat 1993, Gridiron (aka The Grid) 1993, Esau 1996, A Five-Year Plan 1997, The Second Angel 1998, The Shot 1999, Dark Matter 2002; juvenile: Children of the Lamp: The Akhenaten Adventure 2004, Children of the Lamp: The Blue Djinn of Babylon 2005. *Literary Agent:* AP Watt Ltd, 20 John Street, London, WC1N 2DR, England. *Website:* www.apwatt.co.uk.

KERSHAW, Sir Ian; Prof. of Modern History and Author; b. 29 April 1943, Oldham, England; m. Dame Janet Elizabeth Murray Gammie 1966; two s. *Education:* BA, Univ. of Liverpool, 1965; DPhil, Merton College, Oxford, 1969. *Career:* Asst Lecturer in Medieval History, 1968–70, Lecturer, 1970–74, Lecturer in Modern History, 1974–79, Senior Lecturer, 1979–87, Reader Elect, 1987, Univ. of Manchester; Visiting Prof. of Contemporary History, Ruhr-Univ., Bochum, 1983–84; Prof. of Modern History, Univ. of Nottingham, 1987–89, Univ. of Sheffield, 1989–. *Publications:* Rentals and Ministers' Accounts of Bolton Priory, 1473–1539 (ed.), 1969; Bolton Priory: The Economy of a Northern Monastery, 1973; Der Hitler-Mythos: Volksmeinung und Propaganda im Dritten Reich, 1980, English trans., 1987; Popular Opinion and Political Dissent in the Third Reich: Bavaria, 1933–1945, 1983; The Nazi Dictatorship: Problems and Perspectives of Interpretation, 1985; Weimar: Why Did German Democracy Fail? (ed.), 1990; Hitler: A Profile in Power, 1991; Stalinism and Nazism (ed. with M. Lewin), 1997; Hitler, 1889–1936: Hubris, 1998; Hitler, 1936–1945: Nemesis, 2000; The Bolton Priory Compotus 1286–1325 (ed. with D. Smith), 2001. Contributions: scholarly journals. *Honours:* FRHistS, 1972–74, 1991, Alexander von Humboldt-Stiftung, 1976, Wissenschaftskolleg zu Berlin, 1989–90, British Acad., 1991; Bundesverdienstkreuz, Germany, 1994; Wolfson Literary Award, 2000; Bruno-Kreisley Prize, Austria, 2000; British Acad. Book Prize, 2001; knighted, 2002. *Address:* Room C7, 387 Glossop Rd, Dept of History, University of Sheffield, Sheffield S10 2TN, England.

KERSHAW, Peter (see Lucie-Smith, (John) Edward (Mckenzie)).

KERTÉSZ, Imre; Hungarian author and translator; b. 9 Nov. 1929, Budapest; m. 2nd Magda Kertész. *Career:* deported to Auschwitz, then Buchenwald during World War II 1944; worked for newspaper Világosság, Budapest 1948–51 (dismissed when it adopted CP line); mil. service 1951–53; ind. writer and trans. of German authors such as Nietzsche, Schnitzler, Freud, Roth, Wittgenstein and Canetti 1953–; has also written musicals for the theatre; his works have been translated into French, Swedish, German and English. *Publications include:* Sorstalanság (Fateless 1992) 1975, A nyomkeresö (The Pathfinder) 1977, A kudarc (Fiasco) 1988, Kaddis a meg nem születetett gyermekért (Kaddish for a Child not Born 1997) 1990, Az angol labogó (The English Flag) 1991, Gályanapló (Galley Diary) 1992, A Holocaust mint kultúra (The Holocaust as Culture) 1993, Jegyzökönyv 1993, Valaki más: a változás kró'nikája (I, Another: Chronicle of a Metamorphosis) 1997, A gondolatnyi csend, amig kivégzöoztag újratölt (Moment of Silence while the Execution Squad Reloads) 1998, A számüzött nyelv (The Exiled Language) 2001. *Honours:* Brandenburger Literaturpreis 1995, Leipzeiger Buchpreis zur Europäischen Verständigung 1997, WELT-Literaturpreis 2000, Ehrenpreis der Robert-Bosch-Stiftung 2001, Hans-Sahl-Preis 2002, Nobel Prize in Literature 2002. *Address:* c/o Magvetö Press, Balassi B.U. 7, 1055 Budapest, Hungary (Office); c/o Northwestern University Press, 625 Colfax Street, Evanston, IL 60208-4210, USA (Office).

KERTZER, David I.; Historian; b. 20 Feb. 1948, New York, NY, USA. *Education:* Brown Univ., Brandeis Univ. *Career:* Asst Prof. of Anthropology

Bowdoin Coll. 1973–79, Assoc. Prof. 1979–84, Prof. 1984–89, William R. Kenan Jr Prof. 1989–92, Chair. Dept of Sociology and Anthropology 1979–81, 1984–86, 1987–88, 1992; Paul Dupee Jr Univ. Prof. of Social Science, Brown Univ. 1992–, also Prof. of Anthropology 1992–, of History 1992–2001, of Italian Studies 2001–; Fulbright Sr Lecturer, Univ. of Catania 1978; Professore a contratto Univ. of Bologna 1987; Visiting Fellow Trinity Coll. Cambridge 1991; Visiting Scholar Posthumous Inst. and Univ. of Amsterdam 1994; Visiting Dir of Studies Ecole des Hautes Etudes en Sciences Sociales, Paris 1994; Prof. of Educ. American Acad. of Rome 1999; Fulbright Chair. Univ. of Bologna 2000; Visiting Prof. Ecole Normale Superieure, Paris 2002; guest lecturer at over 40 univs across the world; Co-Founder and Co-Ed. Journal of Modern Italian Studies 1994–; Ed. Book Series: New Perspectives in Anthropological and Social Demography 1996–; Pres. Soc. for the Anthropology of Europe 1994–96; mem. Ed. Bd Social Science History 1987–96, 2001–(04), Journal of Family History 1990–, Continuity and Change 1996–2000, Int. Studies Review 1998–2002; mem. Jury Lynton History Prize 2000–01; mem. Exec. Bd American Anthropological Asscn 1995–96, Nat. Inst. of Health Population Review Cttee 1996–99, Social Science History Asscn Publs Cttee 1998–, Nat. Research Council Cttee on Population 1999–, German Marshall Fund Advisory Bd 2000–02; contrib. to numerous nat. and state newspapers. *Publications:* Comrades and Christians: Religion and Political Struggle in Communist Italy 1980, Famiglia Contadina e Urbanizzazione 1981, Family Life in Central Italy 1880–1910: Sharecropping, Wage Labour and Coresidence (Marraro Prize, Soc. for Italian Historical Studies 1985) 1984, Ritual, Politics and Power 1988, Family, Political Economy and Demographic Change (Marraro 1990) 1989, Sacrificed for Honor: Italian Infant Abandonment and the Politics of Reproductive Control 1993, Politics and Symbols: The Italian Communist Party and the Fall of Communism, 1996, The Kidnapping of Edgardo Mortara (Nat. Jewish Book Award 1997, Best Book of the Year, Publishers Weekly, Toronto Globe and Mail 1997; stage version 'Edgard Mine' by Alfred Uhry premiered 2002) 1997, The Popes Against the Jews (UK edn The Unholy War 2002) 2001; contrib., ed. or co-ed. of numerous books; author of over 60 journal articles and 50 academic papers. *Honours:* Guggenheim Fellowship 1986, Nat. Endowment for the Humanities Fellowship 1995, Rockefeller Foundation Fellowship, Bellagio, Italy 2000. *Address:* Department of Anthropology, PO Box 1921, Brown University, Providence, RI 02912, USA. *E-mail:* David_Kertzer@Brown .edu. *Website:* www.davidkertzer.com.

KESSLER, Jascha Frederick, BA, MA, PhD; academic, poet, writer and dramatist; b. 27 Nov. 1929, New York, NY, USA; m. 1950; two s. one d. *Education:* University of Heights College of New York University, University of Michigan. *Career:* Faculty, University of Michigan, 1951–54, New York University, 1954–55, Hunter College, CUNY, 1955–56, Hamilton College, 1957–61; Prof. of English and Modern Literature, University of California at Los Angeles, 1961–; mem. Asscn of Literary Scholars and Critics; ASCAP. *Publications:* Poetry: Whatever Love Declares, 1969; After the Armies Have Passed, 1970; In Memory of the Future, 1976, revised edn as Collected Poems, 2000. Fiction: An Egyptian Bondage (short stories), 1967; Death Comes for the Behaviorist (short stories), 1983; Classical Illusions (short stories), 1985; Transmigrations: 18 Mythologems, 1985; Siren Songs and Classical Illusions (short stories), 1992; Rapid Transit 1948: An Unsentimental Education (novel), 1998. Plays: Selected Plays, 1998; Christmas Carols and Other Plays, 1998. Other: The Anniversary (opera libretto); Trans. *Honours:* National Endowment for the Arts Fellowship, 1974; Rockefeller Foundation Fellowship, 1979; Hungarian PEN Club Memorial Medal, 1979; George Soros Foundation Prize, 1989; California Arts Council Fellowship, 1993–94; many trans. prizes. *Address:* c/o Department of English, University of California at Los Angeles, Los Angeles, CA 90095, USA.

KESSLER, Lauren Jeanne; writer and academic; b. 4 April 1951, New York, NY, USA; m. Thomas Hager 1984; two s. one d. *Education:* BS, Northwestern University, 1971; MS, University of Oregon, 1975; PhD, University of Washington, 1980. *Career:* Dir, Graduate Program in Literary Nonfiction, School of Journalism and Communications, University of Oregon. *Publications:* The Dissident Press: Alternative Journalism in American History, 1984; When Worlds Collide, 1984; Aging Well, 1987; Mastering the Message, 1989; After All These Years: Sixties Ideals in a Different World, 1990; The Search, 1991; Stubborn Twig: A Japanese Family in America, 1993; Full Court Press, 1997; Happy Bottom Riding Club: The Life and Times of Pancho Barnes, 2000, Clever Girl: Elizabeth Bentley, the Spy Who Ushered in the McCarthy Era 2003. Contributions: scholarly journals. *Honours:* Excellence in Periodical Writing Award, Council for the Advancement of Secondary Education, 1987; Frances Fuller Victor Award for Literary Non-Fiction, 1994. *Address:* c/o School of Journalism and Communication, University of Oregon, Eugene, OR 97403, USA. *Website:* laurenkessler.uoregon.edu.

KEYES, Daniel; Author; b. 9 Aug. 1927, New York, NY, USA; m. Aurea Georgina Vazquez, 14 Oct. 1952, two d. *Education:* BA, 1950; MA, 1962. *Career:* Lecturer, Wayne State University, 1962–66; Prof., English, Ohio University, 1966–. *Publications:* Flowers for Algernon, 1966, filmed as Charly; The Touch, 1968; The Fifth Sally, 1980; The Minds of Billy Milligan (non-fiction), 1986; Daniel Keyes Short Stories, 1993; Daniel Keyes Reader, 1994; The Milligan Wars, 1995.

KHADRA, Yasmina; Algerian writer; b. (Mohamed Moulessehoul), 1956. *Education:* armed forces –2000; writer under female pseudonym. *Publications include:* novels: Morituri 1997, Double Blanc 1998, Les agneaux du seigneur 1999, A quoi revent les loups 1999, L'Automne aux Chimeres 2000, Les hirondelles de Kaboul (trans. as The Swallows of Kabul) 2002; other: L'écrivain (autobiog.) 2001. *Address:* c/o The Toby Press, PO Box 8531, New Milford, CT 06776-8531, USA. *Website:* www.tobypress.com.

KHARRAT, Edwar al-; Writer and Poet; b. 16 March 1926, Alexandria, Egypt; m., two s. *Education:* LLB, University of Alexandria, 1946. *Career:* mem. Egyptian Writers' Union; Egyptian PEN Club; High Council of Culture Committee on Fiction. *Publications:* High Walls, 1959; Hours of Pride, 1972; Ramah and the Dragon, 1980; Suffocations of Love and Mornings, 1983; The Other Time, 1985; City of Saffron, 1986; Girls of Alexandria, 1990; Waves of Nights, 1991; Bobello's Ruins, 1992; Penetrations of Love and Perdition, 1993; My Alexandria, 1993; The New Sensibility, 1994; From Silence to Rebellion, 1994; Transgeneric Writing, 1994; Ripples of Salt Dreams, 1994; Fire of Phantasies, 1995; Hymn to Density, 1995; 7 Interpretations, 1996; Wings of Your Bird Struck Me, 1996; Why?: Extracts of a Love Poem, 1996; Soaring Edifices, 1997; The Certitude of Thirst, 1998; Cry of the Unicorn, 1998; Throes of Facts and Madness, 1998; Beyond Reality, 1998; Voices of Modernity in Arabic Fiction, 1999; Seven Clouds, 2000; Boulders of Heaven, 2001; Way of the Eagle, 2002. Contributions: many Arab literary magazines. *Honours:* Arts and Letters Medal, 1972; Franco-Arab Friendship Award, 1989; Cavafy Prize, 1998; State Merit Award for Literature, 2000. *Address:* 45 Ahmed Hishmat St, Zamalak 11211, Cairo, Egypt.

KHATCHADOURIAN, Haig; Emeritus Prof. of Philosophy, Writer and Poet; b. 22 July 1925, Old City, Jerusalem, Palestine; m. Arpiné Yaghlian, 10 Sept. 1950, two s. one d. *Education:* BA, MA, American University of Beirut, Lebanon; PhD, Duke University, USA. *Career:* American University of Beirut, Lebanon, 1948–49, 1951–67; Andrew Mellon Postdoctoral Fellow Univ. of Pittsburgh 1963–64; Prof. of Philosophy, University of Southern California at Los Angeles, 1968–69; Prof. of Philosophy, 1969–94, Emeritus Prof., 1994–, University of Wisconsin at Milwaukee; Liberal Arts Fellow in Philosophy and Law Harvard Law School 1982–83; mem. Fellow, Royal Society for the Encouragement of Arts, Manufacture and Commerce; Foreign Mem., Armenian Acad. of Philosophy; Founding Mem., International Acad. of Philosophy. *Publications:* The Coherence Theory of Truth: A Critical Evaluation, 1961; Traffic with Time (co-author, poems), 1963; A Critical Study in Method, 1967; The Concept of Art, 1971; Shadows of Time (poems), 1983; Music, Film and Art, 1985; Philosophy of Language and Logical Theory: Collected Papers, 1996; The Morality of Terrorism, 1998; Community and Communitarianism, 1999; The Quest for Peace Between Israel and the Palestinians, 2000. Contributions: numerous professional and literary journals including Armenian Mind. *Address:* Dept of Philosophy, University of Wisconsin, Milwaukee, WI 53201, USA.

KHERDIAN, David; Author and Poet; b. 17 Dec. 1931, Racine, Wisconsin, USA; m. 1st Kato Rozeboom, 1968, divorced 1970; m. 2nd Nonny Hogrogian, 17 March 1971. *Education:* BS, University of Wisconsin, 1965. *Career:* Founder-Ed., Giligia Press, 1966–72, Press at Butterworth Creek, 1987–88, Fork Roads: Journal of Ethnic American Literature, 1995–96; Rare Book Consultant, 1968–69, Lecturer, 1969–70, Fresno State College; Poet-in-the-Schools, State of New Hampshire, 1971; Dir, Two Rivers Press, 1978–86; Founder, Ed., Stopinder: A Gurdjieff Journal for our Time, 2000; mem. PEN. *Publications:* On the Death of My Father and Other Poems, 1970; Homage to Adana, 1970; Looking Over Hills, 1972; The Nonny Poems, 1974; Any Day of Your Life, 1975; Country Cat, City Cat, 1978; I Remember Root River, 1978; The Road from Home: The Story of an Armenian Girl, 1979; The Farm, 1979; It Started With Old Man Bean, 1980; Finding Home, 1981; Taking the Soundings on Third Avenue, 1981; The Farm Book Two, 1981; Beyond Two Rivers, 1981; The Song of the Walnut Grove, 1982; Place of Birth, 1983; Right Now, 1983; The Mystery of the Diamond in the Wood, 1983; Root River Run, 1984; The Animal, 1984; Threads of Light: The Farm Poems Books III and IV, 1985; Bridger: The Story of a Mountain Man, 1987; Poems to an Essence Friend, 1987; A Song for Uncle Harry, 1989; The Cat's Midsummer Jamboree, 1990; The Dividing River/The Meeting Shore, 1990; On a Spaceship with Beelzebub: By a Grandson of Gurdjieff, 1990; The Great Fishing Contest, 1991; Junas's Journey, 1993; Asking the River, 1993; By Myself, 1993; Friends: A Memoir, 1993; My Racine, 1994; Lullaby for Emily, 1995. Editor: several books. Other: various trans. *Honours:* Jane Addams Peace Award, 1980; Banta Award, 1980; Boston Globe/Horn Book Award, 1980; Lewis Carroll Shelf Award, 1980; Newbery Honor Book Award, 1980; Friends of American Writers Award, 1982.

KHOURY, Elias; Novelist and Literary Critic; b. 1948, Ashrafiyyeh, nr Beirut, Lebanon. *Education:* History and sociology, in Beirut and Paris, France. *Career:* PLO Research Centre, 1973–79; Publisher, Su'un filastiniya (Palestinian Affairs) journal, 1976–79; Ed., culture section of journal As-Safir, –1991, culture section of daily newspaper, al-Nahar, 1992–; Dir, Masrah Beyrut theatre, 1993–98. *Publications:* Al-Jabal al-Saghir (The Little Mountain); Al-Wujuh al-bayda (The White Faces); Rahlat Gandhi al-Saghir (The Journey of Little Gandhi), 1991; Magma al-Asrar, 1992; Abwab al-Madinah (Gates of the City), 1993; Bab Al Shams, 1998; Mamlakat al-

Ghuraba (The Kingdom of Strangers), 1996; Yalo, 2002. *Honours:* Palestine Prize, 1998. *Address:* c/o University of Minnesota Press, Suite 290, 111 Third Ave S, Minneapolis, MN 55401, USA.

KHOURY-GHATA, Vénus; Lebanese novelist and poet; b. 1937, Béchаré, S Lebanon; m. 1st (divorced); three c.; m. 2nd Jean Ghata (died 1981); one d. *Career:* began career as journalist; moved to France 1972; fmr contributor and translator, Europe magazine; mem. selection cttee, Prix Mallarmé, Prix Max-Pol-Fouchet, Prix Max-Jacob; frequent radio broadcaster. *Publications:* poetry: (first collection) 1966, Les Ombres et leurs cris (Prix Guillaume-Apollinaire) 1980, Monologue du mort (Prix Mallarmé) 1987, Fable pour un peuple d'argile (Grand Prix de la Société des gens de lettres) 1992, Anthologie person-elle 1997, Elle dit 1999, Here There Was Once a Country (anthology in trans.) 2001, La Compassion des pierres 2001, Le Fleuve suivi de 'Du seul fait d'exister' 2001; novels: Vacarme pour une lune morte 1983, Les morts n'avaient pas d'ombres 1984, Mortmaison 1986, Bayarmine 1990, La Maestra (Prix Antigone) 1992, La maitresse du notable (Liberaturpreis) 1992, Les Fiancées du Cap Ténès 1995, Une maison au bord des larmes 1998, Privilège des morts 2001, Le Moine, l'ottoman et la femme du grand argentier 2003; contrib. to Ambit, Banipal: a Journal of Modern Arab Literature, Columbia, Field, Contemporary Poetry and Poetics, Jacket, Luna, Manhattan Review, Metre, New Yorker, Poetry, Shenandoah, Verse, Poetry London. *Honours:* Prix Supervielle 1997; Chevalier, Légion d'honneur 2000. *Address:* 16 avenue Raphael, 75016 Paris, France.

KHWAJA, Waqas Ahmad; Asst Prof. of English, Lawyer, Writer, Poet and Ed.; b. 14 Oct. 1952, Lahore, Pakistan; m. Maryam Khurshid, 6 Nov. 1978, four c. *Education:* BA, Government College, Lahore, 1971; LLB, 1974; MA, 1979; MA, PhD, Emory University, 1995. *Career:* Visiting Prof., Quaid-e-Azam Law College, 1988–91, Punjab Law College, 1988–92; Visiting Faculty, Lahore College for Arts and Sciences, 1989–90, Punjab University, 1990–91; Asst Prof. of English, Agnes Scott College, 1995–; mem. MLA of America; Writers Group, Lahore, Founder, 1984, convener and gen. ed., 1984–92. *Publications:* Cactus: An Anthology of Recent Pakistani Literature (ed. and trans.), 1984; Six Geese from a Tomb at Medum (poems), 1987; Mornings in the Wilderness (ed. and trans.), 1988; Writers and Landscapes (prose and poems), 1991; Miriam's Lament and Other Poems, 1992; Short Stories from Pakistan (ed. and trans.), 1992. Contributions: newspapers and magazines. *Honours:* Ansley Miller Scholar, Emory University, 1981; International Writing Fellowship, US Information Agency and University of Iowa, 1988; Hon. Fellow, University of Iowa, 1988; Commemorative Medal, Islamic Philosophic Society, Lahore, 1991. *Address:* 2923 Evans Wood Dr., Atlanta, GA 30040, USA.

KIBEDI VARGA, Aron, PhD; Dutch/Hungarian professor of French literature, interart studies and poet; b. 4 Feb. 1930, Szeged, Hungary; m. 1st T. Spreij 1954; m. 2nd K. Agh 1964; m. 3rd S. Bertho 1991; four s. one d. *Education:* Univs. of Amsterdam, Leiden, Sorbonne. *Career:* lecturer in French Literature, Free Univ. of Amsterdam 1954–66, Prof. 1971–; Prof. of French Literature, Univ. of Amsterdam 1966–71; Visiting Prof. Iowa Univ. 1971, Yale Univ. 1975, Princeton Univ. 1980, Rabat Univ. 1985, Coll. de France 1992; mem. Cttee Int. Soc. for the History of Rhetoric 1979–83; Pres. Int. Asscn Word and Image Studies 1987–93; mem. Royal Netherlands Acad. of Sciences 1981–; mem. Hungarian Acad. of Sciences 1990–. *Publications:* criticism: Les Constantes du Poème 1963, Rhétorique et Littérature 1970, Théorie de la Littérature (ed.) 1981, Discours récit, image 1989, Les Poétiques du classicisme (ed.) 1990, Le Classicisme 1998, Szavak, világok 1998, Noé könyvei 1999, Amszterdami krónika 2000, És felébred aminek neve van 2002, A jelen 2003; poetry (in Hungarian): Kint és Bent 1963, Téged 1975, Szépen 1991, Hántani, fosztani 2000, Oldás 2004. *Honours:* Dr. hc (Pécs) 1994. *Address:* Department of French, Vrije Universiteit, Amsterdam, Netherlands. *Telephone:* (20) 4446456 (Office). *Fax:* (20) 4446500 (Office).

KIBERD, Declan; Literary Critic and Educator; b. 24 May 1951, Dublin, Ireland. *Education:* Trinity College, Dublin; University of Oxford. *Career:* Lecturer in English, Prof. of Anglo-Irish Literature and Drama, University College, Dublin. *Publications:* Synge and the Irish Language, 1979; Men and Feminism in Modern Literature, 1985; Omrium Satlerum: Essays for Richard Ellmann (co-ed.), 1989; An Crann Faoi Bhlath-The Flowering Tree: Contemporary Irish Poems with Verse Translations (co-ed.), 1991; The Student's Annotated Ulysses (ed.), 1992; Idir Dhá Chultur, 1993; Inventing Ireland: The Literature of the Modern Nation, 1996; Irish Classics, 2000. *Address:* J203, Dept of English, University College, Dublin, Ireland.

KIDDER, Tracy; Writer; b. 12 Nov. 1945, New York, NY, USA; m. Frances T. Toland, 2 Jan. 1971, one s. one d. *Education:* AB, Harvard University, 1967; MFA, University of Iowa, 1974. *Career:* Contributing Ed., Atlantic Monthly, 1982–. *Publications:* The Road to Yuba City: A Journey into the Juan Corona Murders, 1974; The Soul of a New Machine, 1981; House, 1985; Among Schoolchildren, 1989; Old Friends, 1993; Home Town, 1999. Contributions: newspapers and magazines. *Honours:* Atlantic First Award, Atlantic Monthly, 1978; Sidney Hillman Foundation Prize, 1978; Pulitzer Prize in General Non-Fiction, 1982; American Book Award, 1982; Ambassador Book Award, 1990; Robert F. Kennedy Award, 1990; New England Book Award, 1994. *Address:* c/o George Borchardt Inc, 136 E 47th St, New York, NY 10019, USA.

KIDMAN, Dame Fiona (Judith); Writer and Poet; b. 26 March 1940, Hawera, New Zealand; m. Ernest Ian Kidman, 20 Aug. 1960, one s. one d. *Career:* mem. International PEN; New Zealand Book Council, pres., 1992–95; Patron, Cambodia Trust Aotearoa. *Publications:* Fiction: A Breed of Women, 1979; Mandarin Summer, 1981; Paddy's Puzzle, 1983, US edn as In the Clear Light, 1985; The Book of Secrets, 1987; True Stars, 1990; Ricochet Baby, 1996; The House Within, 1997; The Best of Fiona Kidman's Short Stories, 1998; A Needle in the Heart, 2002. Poetry: Honey and Bitters, 1975; On the Tightrope, 1978; Going to the Chathams, Poems: 1977–1984, 1985; Wakeful Nights: Poems Selected and New, 1991. Other: Search for Sister Blue (radio play), 1975; Gone North (with Jane Ussher), 1984; Wellington (with Grant Sheehan), 1989; Palm Prints, 1994. Contributions: periodicals. *Honours:* Scholarships in Letters, 1981, 1985, 1991, 1995; Mobil Short Story Award, 1987; Queen Elizabeth II Arts Council Award for Achievement, 1988; OBE, 1988; Victoria University Writing Fellowship, 1988; Pres. of Honour, New Zealand Book Council, 1997; Dame Commander of the New Zealand Order of Merit, 1998; A. W. Reed Award for Lifetime Achievement, 2001. *Address:* 28 Rakau Rd, Hataitai, Wellington 3, New Zealand. *E-mail:* fionakidman@compuserve.com.

KIELY, Benedict; Journalist and Writer; b. 15 Aug. 1919, Dromore, County Tyrone, Ireland. *Education:* National University of Ireland. *Career:* Journalist, Dublin, 1940–65; Visiting Prof. and Writer-in-Residence, several US universities. *Publications:* Land Without Stars, 1946; In a Harbour Green, 1949; Call for a Miracle, 1950; Honey Seems Bitter, 1952; The Cards of the Gambler: A Folktale, 1953; There Was an Ancient House, 1955; The Captain With the Whiskers, 1960; Dogs Enjoy the Morning, 1968; Proxopera: A Novella, 1977; Nothing Happens in Carmincross, 1985; Drink to the Bird (memoir), 1991; Selected Stories, 1993; As I Rode By Granard Moat: A Personal Anthology, 1997; Memoirs: The Waves Behind Us, 1999; 'A Raid into Dark Corners' and Other Essays, 1999; The Collected Stories of Benedict Kiely, 2001. *Honours:* American Irish Foundation Award, 1980; Irish Acad. of Letters Award, 1980; Irish Independent Literary Award, 1985; Hon. DLitt, National University of Ireland and Queen's University, Belfast. *Literary Agent:* AP Watt Ltd, 20 John St, London WC1N 2DR, England. *Address:* 119 Morehampton Rd, Donnybrook, Dublin 4, Ireland.

KILALEA, Rory; Zimbabwean short story writer and film producer. *Career:* Prod., own co. Rory Kilalea Films, producer of films and numerous advertisements. *Films produced:* A Dry White Season (also man.) 1989, Jit 1990. *Publications:* Whine of a Dog (short story in The New Writer) 1998, Zimbabwe Boy (short story in Asylum 98 and Other Stories) 2001. *Address:* Rory Kilalea Films, 7 Everett Close, Avondale, Harare, Zimbabwe.

KILLDEER, John (see Mayhar, Ardath).

KILLOUGH, (Karen) Lee; writer; b. 5 May 1942, Syracuse, KS, USA. *Career:* mem. SFWA, MWA, Sisters In Crime. *Publications:* A Voice Out of Ramah, 1979; The Doppelganger Gambit, 1979; The Monitor, the Miners, and the Shree, 1980; Aventine, 1981; Deadly Silents, 1982; Liberty's World, 1985; Spider Play, 1986; Blood Hunt, 1987; The Leopard's Daughter, 1987; Bloodlinks, 1988; Dragon's Teeth, 1990; Bloodwalk, 1997; Bridling Chaos, 1998; Blood Games, 2001; Wilding Nights, 2002. *Address:* PO Box 1167, Manhattan, KS 66505, USA. *E-mail:* klkillo@flinthills.com.

KILROY, Thomas; Writer, Dramatist and University Teacher; b. 23 Sept. 1934, Callan, Ireland; m. 1st three s.; m. 2nd Julia Lowell Carlson, 9 Dec. 1981, one d. *Education:* BA, 1956, MA, 1959, University College, Dublin. *Career:* Emeritus Prof. of Modern English, NUI Galway, 2002; mem. FRSL, 1971, Irish Acad. of Letters, 1973. *Publications:* Death and Resurrection of Mr Roche (play), 1968; The Oneill (play), 1969; The Big Chapel (novel), 1971; Talbots' Box (play), 1977; The Seagull (play adaptation), 1981; Double Cross (play), 1986; Ghosts, 1989; The Madame McAdam Travelling Theatre (play), 1990; Gold in the Streets (television), 1993; Six Characters in Search of An Author (adaptation), 1996; The Secret Fall of Constance Wilde (play), 1997: My Scandalous Life, 2001; The Shape of Metal (play), 2003. Contributions: Radio, television, journals, and magazines. *Honours:* Guardian Fiction Prize, 1971; Heinemann Award for Literature, 1971; Irish Acad. of Letters Prize, 1972; American-Irish Foundation Award for Literature, 1974. *Literary Agent:* Alan Brodie Representation, 211 Piccadilly, London W1J 9HF, England.

KILWORTH, Garry D(ouglas), (Garry Douglas); Writer; b. 5 July 1941, York, England; m. Annette Jill Bailey, 30 June 1962, one s. one d. *Education:* Business Studies, 1974; BA, English, 1985. *Career:* mem. PEN; Crimean War Society. *Publications:* In Solitary, 1977; The Night of Kadar, 1979; Split Second, 1979; Theatre of Timesmiths, 1984; Songbirds of Pain, 1984; Witchwater Country, 1986; Spiral Winds, 1987; The Wizard of Woodworld, 1987; Abandonati, 1988; Hunter's Moon, 1989; In the Hollow of the Deep-Sea Wave, 1989; The Foxes of First Dark, 1990; Standing on Samshan, 1992; Angel, 1993; In The Country of Tattooed Men, 1993; Hogfoot Right And Bird-Hands, 1993; Archangel, 1994; A Midsummer's Nightmare, 1996; The Roof of Voyaging, 1996; The Princely Flower, 1997; Land-of-Mists, 1998; Thunder Oak, 1998; Windjammer Run, 1998; Castle Storm, 1998; Shadow-Hawk, 1999; The Devil's Own, 2001; The Winter Soldiers, 2002. As Garry Douglas: Highlander, 1986; The Street, 1988. Other: Anthologies. Contributions: Magazines and newspapers. *Honours:*

Gollancz Short Story Award, Sunday Times, 1974; Carnegie Medal Commendation, Librarian Asscn, 1991; Lancashire Children's Book of the Year Award, 1995. *Address:* Wychwater, The Chase, Ashington, Essex, England.

KIM, Suji Kwock, BA, MFA; American writer and academic. *Education:* Yale Coll., Univ. of Iowa, Seoul Nat. Univ., Stanford Univ. *Career:* Asst. Prof. of English, Drew Univ., NJ. *Plays:* Private Property (co-author). *Publications:* Notes from the Divided Country 2003; contrib. to Poetry, Paris Review, The Nation, The New Republic, DoubleTake, Yale Review, Salmagundi, Threepenny Review, Ploughshares, New England Review, Southwest Review, Harvard Review, Michigan Quarterly Review, Asian-American Poetry. *Honours:* Nat. Endowment for the Arts Fellowship, Fine Arts Work Center Fellowship, New York Foundation for the Arts grant, California Arts Council grant, Washington State Artist Trust grant, Korea Foundation grant, Blakemore Foundation for Asian Studies grant; Walt Whitman Award 2002, The Nation/Discovery Award. *Address:* c/o Drew University, 36 Madison Avenue, Madison, NJ 07940, USA. *E-mail:* skkim@drew.edu. *Website:* www.drew.edu.

KIM HONG-IK; North Korean author. *Career:* lives in Seoul, Republic of Korea. *Publications:* He's Alive (in trans.). *Address:* c/o Korean PEN Centre, Room 1105, Oseong B/D, 13-5 Youido-dong, Yongdungpo-ku, Seoul, 150-010, Republic of Korea.

KINCAID, Jamaica, (Elaine Potter née Richardson Shawn); Writer; b. 25 May 1949, St John's, Antigua; m. Allen Shawn, 1979, one s. one d. *Education:* New School for Social Research; Franconia College. *Career:* Staff Writer, New Yorker, 1976–95. *Publications:* At the Bottom of the River, 1983; Annie John, 1985; A Small Place, 1988; Lucy, 1990; The Autobiography of My Mother, 1995; My Brother, 1997; My Favourite Plant: Writers and Gardeners on the Plants They Love, 1998; Poetics of Place (with Lynn Geesaman), 1998; My Garden (Book), 1999; Talk Stories, 2000; Mr Potter, 2002. Contributions: periodicals. *Honours:* Morton Dauwen Zabel Award, American Acad. and Institute of Arts and Letters, 1983; Lila Wallace-Reader's Digest Fund Annual Writer's Award, 1992. *Address:* PO Box 822, North Bennington, VT 05257, USA.

KING, Betty Alice; Novelist; b. 17 June 1919, Enfield, England; m. D. James King, 14 June 1941, two s. one d. *Education:* Queenswood School, Hertfordshire; Open University. *Career:* mem. Society of Authors; Samuel Pepys Asscn. *Publications:* The Lady Margaret, 1965; The Lord Jasper, 1967; The King's Mother, 1969; Margaret of Anjou, 1974; Emma Hamilton, 1976; Nell Gwyn, 1979; Claybourn, 1980; The French Countess, 1982; We Are Tomorrow's Past, 1984. Contributions: Hertfordshire Countryside; Enfield Gazette. *Address:* Crescent House, 31 North Rd, Hertford, Herts SG14 1LN, England.

KING, (David) Clive; novelist; b. 28 April 1924, Richmond, Surrey, England; m. 1st Jane Tuke 1948; one s. one d.; m. 2nd Penny Timmins 1974; one d. *Education:* Downing Coll. *Career:* mem. Soc. of Authors. *Publications:* The Town That Went South, 1959; Stig of the Dump, 1963; The Twenty-Two Letters, 1966; The Night the Water Came, 1973; Snakes and Snakes, 1975; Me and My Million, 1976; Ninny's Boat, 1980; The Sound of Propellers, 1986; The Seashore People, 1987; seven other books. *Honours:* Boston Globe-Horn Book Award, Honour Book 1980. *Address:* Pond Cottage, Low Road, Thurlton, Norwich NR14 6PZ, England.

KING, Cynthia; writer; b. 27 Aug. 1925, New York, NY, USA; m. Jonathan King 1944 (died 1997); three s. *Education:* Bryn Mawr Coll., Univ. of Chicago, New York Univ. Writers' Workshop. *Career:* Assoc. Ed., Hillman Periodicals 1945–50; Managing Ed., Fawcett Publications 1950–55; mem. Authors' Guild, Poets and Writers, Detroit Women Writers (pres. 1979–81). *Publications:* In the Morning of Time 1970, The Year of Mr Nobody 1978, Beggars and Choosers 1980, Sailing Home 1982; contrib. book reviews to New York Times Book Review, Detroit News, Houston Chronicle, LA Daily News, short fiction to Good Housekeeping, Texas Stories & Poems, Quartet. *Honours:* Michigan Council for the Arts Grant 1986, Detroit Women Writers Spring Readings Award 2002. *Address:* 228 River Street, Bethel, VT 05032, USA. *E-mail:* tonibking@adelphia.net.

KING, Francis Henry, (Frank Cauldwell), BA, MA, OBE, CBE, FRSL; British writer and drama and literary critic; b. 4 March 1923, Adelboden, Switzerland. *Education:* Balliol Coll., Oxford. *Career:* Drama Critic, Sunday Telegraph, 1978–88; mem. English PEN, pres., 1976–86; International PEN, pres., 1986–89, vice-pres., 1989–. *Publications:* Fiction: To the Dark Tower, 1946; Never Again, 1947; An Air That Kills, 1948; The Dividing Stream, 1951; The Dark Glasses, 1954; The Firewalkers, 1956; The Widow, 1957; The Man on the Rock, 1957; The Custom House, 1961; The Last of the Pleasure Gardens, 1965; The Waves Behind the Boat, 1967; A Domestic Animal, 1970; Flights, 1973; A Game of Patience, 1974; The Needle, 1975; Danny Hill, 1977; The Action, 1978; Act of Darkness, 1983; Voices in an Empty Room, 1984; Frozen Music, 1987; The Woman Who Was God, 1988; Punishments, 1989; Visiting Cards, 1990; The Ant Colony, 1991; Secret Lives (with Tom Wakefield and Patrick Gale), 1991; The One and Only, 1994; Ash on an Old Man's Sleeve, 1996; Dead Letters, 1997; Prodigies, 2001; The Nick of Time, 2003. Short Story Collections: So Hurt and Humiliated, 1959; The Japanese Umbrella, 1964; The Brighton Belle, 1968; Hard Feelings, 1976; Indirect Method, 1980; One is a Wanderer, 1985; A Hand at the Shutter, 1996. Other: E. M. Forster and His World, 1978; A Literary Companion to Florence, 1991; Autobiography: Yesterday Came Suddenly, 1993. *Honours:* Somerset Maugham Award, 1952; Katherine Mansfield Short Story Prize, 1965. *Literary Agent:* A. M. Heath & Co Ltd, 79 St Martin's Lane, London WC2N 4RE, England. *Address:* 19 Gordon Place, London W8 4JE, England. *E-mail:* fhk@dircon.co.uk.

KING, Janey (see Thomas, Rosie).

KING, Larry L.; Playwright, Author and Actor; b. 1 Jan. 1929, Putnam, TX, USA; m. Barbara S. Blaine, two s. three d. *Education:* Texas Technical University, 1949–50; Nieman Fellow, Harvard University, 1969–70; Duke Fellow of Communications, Duke University, 1975–76. *Career:* Visiting Ferris Prof. of Journalism and Political Science, Princeton University, 1973–74; Poet Laureate (life), Monahans (Texas) Sandhills Literary Society, 1977–. *Publications:* Plays: The Kingfish, 1979; The Best Little Whorehouse in Texas, 1978; Christmas: 1933, 1986; The Night Hank Williams Died, 1988; The Golden Shadows Old West Museum, 1989; The Best Little Whorehouse Goes Public, 1994; The Dead Presidents' Club, 1996. Other: The One-Eyed Man (novel), 1966; ...And Other Dirty Stories, 1968; Confessions of a White Racist, 1971; The Old Man and Lesser Mortals, 1974; Of Outlaws, Whores, Conmen, Politicians and Other Artists, 1980; Warning: Writer at Work, 1985; None But a Blockhead, 1986; Because of Lozo Brown, 1988. Contributions: Harper's; Atlantic Monthly; Life; New Republic; Texas Monthly; Texas Observer; New York; Playboy; Parade; Esquire; Saturday Evening Post; National Geographic. *Address:* 3025 Woodland Dr., NW, Washington, DC 20008, USA.

KING, Laurie R.; Writer; b. 19 Sept. 1952, Oakland, CA, USA; m. Noel Q. King, Nov. 1977, one s. one d. *Education:* BA, University of California, Santa Cruz, 1977; MA, Graduate Theological Union, Berkeley, 1984. *Career:* mem. MWA; Sisters in Crime; International Asscn of Crime Writers; CWA. *Publications:* A Grave Talent, 1993; The Beekeeper's Apprentice, 1994; To Play the Fool, 1995; A Monstrous Regiment of Women, 1995; With Child, 1996; A Letter of Mary, 1997; The Moor, 1998; A Darker Place, 1999; O Jerusalem, 1999; Night Work, 2000; Folly, 2001; Justice Hall, 2002; Keeping Watch, 2003; The Game, 2004. *Honours:* Edgar Award for Best First Novel, 1993; Creasey Award for Best First Novel, 1995; Nero Wolfe Award, Best Novel, 1996; Hon. Doctorate, Church Divinity School of the Pacific, 1997; Macavity Award, 2002. *Address:* PO Box 1152, Freedom, CA 95019, USA.

KING, Paul (see Drackett, Philip Arthur).

KING, Philip (see Levinson, Leonard).

KING, Stephen Edwin, (Richard Bachman), BS; American writer and screenwriter; b. 21 Sept. 1947, Portland, ME; m. Tabitha J. Spruce 1971; two s. one d. *Education:* Univ. of Maine. *Career:* teacher of English, Hampden Acad., ME 1971–73; writer-in-residence, Univ. of Maine at Orono 1978–79; mem. Authors' Guild of America, Screen Artists' Guild, Screen Writers of America, Writers' Guild. *Television:* Kingdom Hospital. *Publications:* novels: Carrie 1974, Salem's Lot 1975, The Shining 1976, The Stand 1978, The Dead Zone 1979, Firestarter 1980, Cujo 1981, Different Seasons 1982, The Dark Tower I: The Gunslinger 1982, Christine 1983, Pet Cemetery 1983, The Talisman (with Peter Straub) 1984, It 1986, The Eyes of the Dragon 1987, Misery 1987, The Dark Tower II: The Drawing of the Three 1987, Tommyknockers 1987, The Dark Half 1989, The Dark Tower III: The Waste Lands 1991, Needful Things 1991, Gerald's Game 1992, Dolores Claiborne 1992, Insomnia 1994, Rose Madder 1995, Desperation 1996, The Green Mile (serial novel) 1996, The Dark Tower IV: Wizard and Glass 1997, Bag of Bones 1997, The Girl Who Loved Tom Gordon 1999, Hearts in Atlantis 1999, Riding the Bullet 2000, The Plant (serial novel) 2000, Dreamcatcher 2001, Black House (with Peter Straub) 2001, From a Buick 8 2002, The Dark Tower V: Wolves of the Calla 2003, The Dark Tower VI: Song of Susannah 2004, The Dark Tower VII: The Dark Tower 2004; other: Night Shift (short stories) 1978, Danse Macabre (non-fiction) 1980, Different Seasons (short stories) 1982, Creepshow (comic book) 1982, Cycle of the Werewolf (illustrated novel) 1984, Skeleton Crew (short stories) 1985, Four Past Midnight (short stories) 1990, Nightmares and Dreamscapes (short stories) 1993, Head Down (story) 1993, Six Stories (short stories) 1997, Storm of the Century (screenplay) 1999, On Writing: A Memoir of the Craft (revised edn as Secret Windows) 2000, Everything's Eventual: 14 Dark Tales (short stories) 2002, numerous short stories, screenplays and television plays; as Richard Bachman: Rage 1977, The Long Walk 1979, Roadwork 1981, The Running Man 1982, Thinner 1984, The Regulators 1996. *Honours:* Medal for Distinguished Contribution to American Letters, Nat. Book Foundation 2003. *Address:* 49 Florida Avenue, Bangor, ME 04401, USA (Office). *Website:* www.stephenking.com (Office).

KING, Thomas; academic, writer, dramatist and poet; b. 24 April 1943, Sacramento, CA, USA; m. Kristine Adams 1970 (divorced 1980); two s. one d. *Education:* BA, English, 1970, MA, English, 1972, Chico State University; PhD, University of Utah, 1986. *Career:* Dir, Native Studies, 1971–73, Co-ordinator, History of the Indians of the Americas Program, 1977–79, University of Utah; Assoc. Dean, Student Services, Humboldt State University, 1973–77; Asst Prof. of Native Studies, 1978–89, Chair, Native Studies, 1985–87, University of Lethbridge; Assoc. Prof. of American Studies/Native Studies, 1989–95, Chair, Native Studies, 1991–93, University of Minnesota; Assoc. Prof. of English, University of Guelph, 1995–.

Publications: The Native in Literature: Canadian and Comparative Perspectives (ed. with Helen Hoy and Cheryl Calver), 1987; An Anthology of Short Fiction by Native Writers in Canada (ed.), 1988; All My Relations: An Anthology of Contemporary Canadian Native Fiction (ed.), 1990; Medicine River, 1990; A Coyote Columbus Story, 1992; Green Grass, Running Water, 1993; One Good Story, That One, 1993; Coyote Sings to the Moon, 1998; Truth and Bright Water, 1999; Coyote's Suit, 2002. Other: Films and radio and television dramas. Contributions: Reference works, books, anthologies, reviews, quarterlies and journals. *Honours:* Best Novel Award, Writers' Guild of Alberta, 1991; Josephine Miles Award, Oakland PEN, 1991; Canadian Authors Award for Fiction, 1994; American Library Asscn Notable Book Citation, 2001. *Address:* 7 Ardmay Crescent, Guelph, ON N1E 4L4, Canada.

KING-ARIBISALA, Karen; Nigerian writer; b. Guyana; m.; one s. *Career:* sr lecturer, Dept of English, Univ. of Lagos. *Publications:* Our Wife and Other Stories (short stories) (Commonwealth Writers Prize Best First Book, Africa Region) 1990, Kicking Tongues 1998. *Address:* c/o African Writers Series, Heinemann Educational Publishers, Halley Ctour, Jordan Hill, Oxford OX2 8EJ, England.

KING-HELE, Desmond George; Scientist, Author and Poet; b. 3 Nov. 1927, Seaford, Sussex, England; m. Marie Therese Newman, 1954, separated 1992, two d. *Education:* BA, Mathematics, 1948, MA, 1952, Trinity College, Cambridge. *Career:* Staff, 1948–68, Deputy Chief Scientific Officer, Space Dept, 1968–88, Royal Aircraft Establishment; Ed., Notes and Records of the Royal Society, 1989–96; various lectureships; mem. British National Committee for the History of Science, Medicine and Technology, chair., 1985–89; Institute of Mathematics and Its Applications, fellow; Royal Astronomical Society, fellow; Royal Society, fellow; Bakerian Lecturer, Royal Society, 1974. *Publications:* Shelley: His Thought and Work, 1960; Satellites and Scientific Research, 1960; Erasmus Darwin, 1963; Theory of Satellite Orbits in an Atmosphere, 1964; Space Research V (ed.), 1965; Observing Earth Satellites, 1966; Essential Writings of Erasmus Darwin (ed.), 1968; The End of the Twentieth Century?, 1970; Poems and Trixies, 1972; Doctor of Revolution, 1977; Letters of Erasmus Darwin (ed.), 1981; The RAE Table of Earth Satellites (ed.), 1981; Animal Spirits (poems), 1983; Erasmus Darwin and the Romantic Poets, 1986; Satellite Orbits in an Atmosphere: Theory and Applications, 1987; A Tapestry of Orbits, 1992; John Herschel (ed.), 1992; A Concordance to the Botanic Garden (ed.), 1994; Erasmus Darwin: A Life of Unequalled Achievement, 1999; Antic and Romantic (poems), 2000; Charles Darwin's Life of Erasmus Darwin (ed.), 2002. Contributions: numerous scientific and literary journals. *Honours:* Eddington Medal, Royal Astronomical Society, 1971; Charles Chree Medal, Institute of Physics, 1971; Lagrange Prize, Académie Royale de Belgique, 1972; Hon. Doctorates, Universities of Aston, 1979, and Surrey, 1986; Nordberg Medal, International Committee on Space Research, 1990; Society of Authors Medical History Prize, 1999. *Address:* 7 Hilltops Ct, 65 North Lane, Buriton, Hampshire GU31 5RS, England.

KING-SMITH, Dick; Writer; b. 27 March 1922, Bitton, Gloucestershire, England. *Education:* BEd, Bristol Univ., 1975. *Publications:* numerous include: The Fox Busters; Daggie Dogfoot; The Mouse Butcher; Magnus Powermouse; The Queen's Nose; The Sheep-Pig; Noah's Brother; Yob; E.S.P.; Friends and Brothers; Dodos are Forever; Sophie's Snail; The Trouble with Edward; Martin's Mice; The Water Horse; Paddy's Pot of Gold; Alpha Beasts; The Hodgeheg; Ace: The Very Important Pig; Harry's Mad; The Invisible Dog; The Merman; A Mouse Called Wolf; Mysterious Miss Slade; Smasher; Spider Sparrow; The Stray; Three Terrible Trins; Harriet's Hare; Dick King-Smith's Animal Friends; All Pigs are Beautiful; I Love Guinea Pigs; Blessu; Clever Duck; All Because of Jack; The Crownstarver; Charlie Muffin's Miracle Mouse; Funny Frank; Chewing the Cud; The Roundhill; Titus Rules!; Binnie Bone; The Golden Goose; Lady Lollypop; Aristotle; Jungle Jingles (poems), 2002. *Literary Agent:* AP Watt Ltd, 20 John St, London WC1N 2DR, England. *Address:* Diamond's Cottage, Queen Charlton, Near Keynsham, Somerset BS31 2SJ, England.

KINGDON, Robert McCune, AB, MA, PhD; Prof. of History and writer; b. 29 Dec. 1927, Chicago, IL, USA. *Education:* Oberlin College, Columbia University, University of Geneva. *Career:* Instructor to Asst Prof., University of Massachusetts, 1952–57; Visiting Instructor, Amherst College, 1953–54; Asst Prof. to Prof. of History, University of Iowa, 1957–65; Visiting Prof., Stanford University, 1964, 1980; Prof. of History, 1965–, Hilldale Prof. of History, 1988–98, University of Wisconsin at Madison; Ed., Sixteenth Century Journal, 1973–97; Mem., 1974–, Dir, 1975–87, Institute for Research in the Humanities; mem. American Society of Reformation Research, pres., 1971; International Federation of Societies and Institutions for the Study of the Renaissance; Renaissance Society of America, exec. board, 1972–92; American Society of Church History, pres., 1980. *Publications:* Geneva and the Coming of the Wars of Religion in France 1555–1563, 1956; Registres de la Compagnie des Pasteurs de Genévè au Temps de Calvin (ed. with J.-F. Bergier), 2 vols, 1962, 1964; William Cecil: Execution of Justice in England (ed.), 1965; William Allen: A True, Sincere and Modest Defence of English Catholics (ed.), 1965; Geneva and the Consolidation of the French Protestant Movement 1564–1572, 1967; Calvin and Calvinism: Sources of Democracy (co-ed. with R. D. Linder), 1970; Theodore de Béze: Du Droit des magistrats (ed.), 1971; Transition and Revolution: Problems and Issues of European Renaissance and Reformation History (ed.), 1974; The Political Thought of Peter Martyr Vermigli, 1980; Church and Society in Reformation Europe, 1985; Myths About the St Bartholomew's Day Massacres 1572–1576, 1988; A Bibliography of the Works of Peter Martyr Vermigli (ed. with J. P. Donnelly), 1990; Adultery and Divorce in Calvin's Geneva, 1995; Registres du Consistoire de Genève au temps de Calvin (co-ed.), Vol. I 1996, Vol. II 2001, Vol. III 2004; contrib. to scholarly journals. *Address:* 4 Rosewood Circle, Madison, WI 53711, USA. *E-mail:* rkingdon@wiscmail.wisc.edu.

KINGSOLVER, Barbara, BA, MS; American writer and poet; b. 8 April 1955, Annapolis, MD; m. 1st Joseph Hoffmann 1985 (divorced 1993); one d.; m. 2nd Steven Hopp 1995; one d. *Education:* DePauw University, University of Arizona. *Career:* Research Asst, Dept of Physiology, 1977–79, Technical Writer, Office of Arid Land Studies, 1981–85, University of Arizona, Tucson; Journalist, 1985–87; Author, 1987–; Founder, Bellwether Prize to recognize a first novel of social significance, 1997. *Publications:* The Bean Trees (novel), 1988; Homeland and Other Stories, 1989; Holding the Line: Women in the Great Arizona Mine Strike of 1983 (non-fiction), 1989; Animal Dreams (novel), 1990; Pigs in Heaven (novel), 1993; Another America (poems), 1994; High Tide in Tucson: Essays from Now or Never, 1995; The Poisonwood Bible (novel), 1998; Prodigal Summer (short stories), 2000; Small Wonder (essays), 2002. Contributions: many anthologies and periodicals. *Honours:* Feature-Writing Award, Arizona Press Club, 1986; American Library Asscn Awards, 1988, 1990; PEN Fiction Prize, 1991; Edward Abbey Ecofiction Award, 1991; Los Angeles Times Book Award for Fiction, 1993; PEN Faulkner Award, 1999; American Booksellers Book of the Year, 2000; National Humanities Medal, 2000. *Address:* c/o Frances Goldin, Suite 513, 57 E 11th Street, New York, NY 10003, USA.

KINGSTON, Maxine Hong, AB; writer and teacher; b. 27 Oct. 1940, Stockton, CA, USA; m. 1962; one s. *Education:* University of California, Berkeley. *Career:* teacher, University of California, Berkeley, 1990–2004; mem. American Acad. of Arts and Sciences; Authors' Guild; PEN American Centre; PEN West. *Publications:* The Woman Warrior, 1976; China Men, 1980; Hawai'i One Summer, 1987; Tripmaster Monkey: His Fake Book, 1989; To Be the Poet, 2002; The Fifth Book of Peace, 2003. Contributions: many publications. *Honours:* National Book Critics Circle Award 1977, Anisfield-Wolf Race Relations Book Award 1978, National Endowment for the Arts Fellowship 1980. Living Treasure of Hawai'i 1980, National Book Award 1981, Guggenheim Fellowship 1981, Hawai'i Award for Literature 1982, California Council for the Humanities Award 1985, Governor's Award for the Arts, CA 1989, PEN West Award in Fiction 1990, American Acad. and Institute of Arts and Letters Award 1990, Brandeis University National Women's Committee Major Book Collection Award 1992, National Humanities Medal 1997, Fred Cody Lifetime Achievement Award 1998, John Dos Passos Award 1998, hon. doctorates. *Address:* c/o Department of English, University of California at Berkeley, CA 94720, USA.

KINGTON, Miles (Beresford); Writer; b. 13 May 1941, Downpatrick, Northern Ireland; m. 1st Sarah Paine, 1964, divorced 1987, one s. one d.; m. 2nd Caroline Maynard, 1987, one s. *Education:* BA, Modern Languages, Trinity College, Oxford, 1963. *Career:* Jazz Reviewer, 1965, Columnist, 1980–87, The Times; Staff, 1967–73, Literary Ed., 1973–80, Columnist, 1980–87, Punch; Columnist, The Independent, 1987–. *Publications:* The World of Alphonse Allais, 1977, revised edn as A Wolf in Frog's Clothing, 1983; 4 Franglais books, 1979–82; Moreover, Too…, 1985; Welcome to Kington, 1985; The Franglais Lieutenant's Woman, 1986; Steaming Through Britain, 1990; Anthology of Jazz (ed.), 1992. *Address:* Lower Hayze, Limpley Stoke, Bath BA3 6HR, England.

KINLOCH, David; University Senior Lecturer, Poet and Ed.; b. 21 Nov. 1959, Glasgow, Scotland. *Education:* MA, University of Glasgow, 1982; DPhil, Balliol College, Oxford, 1986. *Career:* Junior Research Fellow, St Anne's College, Oxford, 1985–87; Research Fellow, University of Wales, 1987–89; Lecturer, University of Salford, 1989–90; Lecturer, 1990–94, Senior Lecturer, 1994–, University of Strathclyde; Ed., Southfields Magazine; Founder/Co-Ed., Verse Poetry Magazine. *Publications:* Other Tongues (co-author), 1990; Dustie-Fute, 1992; Paris-Forfar, 1994; Un Tour d'Ecosse, 2001. Contributions: Reviews, journals and magazines. *Address:* c/o Dept of English Studies, University of Strathclyde, Glasgow, Scotland.

KINNELL, Galway; Poet, Writer and Prof. of Creative Writing; b. 1 Feb. 1927, Providence, RI, USA; m. Inés Delgado de Torres, 1965, one s. two d. *Education:* MA, Princeton University. *Career:* Dir, Writing Program, 1981–84, Samuel F. B. Morse Prof. of Arts and Sciences, 1985–92, Erich Maria Remarque Prof. of Creative Writing, 1992–, New York University; Vermont State Poet, 1989–93; mem. PEN; Poetry Society of America; MLA; Acad. of Arts and Letters; Acad. of Arts and Sciences; Acad. of American Poets, board of chancellors, 2001–. *Publications:* Poetry: What a Kingdom It Was, 1960; Flower Herding on Mount Monadnock, 1963; Body Rags, 1966; The Book of Nightmares, 1971; The Avenue Bearing the Initial of Christ into the New World, 1974; Mortal Acts, Mortal Words, 1980; Selected Poems, 1982; The Past, 1985; When One Has Lived a Long Time Alone, 1990; Imperfect Thirst, 1994; The Essential Rilke, 1999; New Selected Poems, 2000. Other: The Poems of François Villon (trans.), 1965; Black Light (novel), 1966; On the Motion and Immobility of Douve, 1968; The Lackawanna Elegy, 1970; Interviews: Walking Down the Stairs, 1977; How the Alligator Missed Breakfast (children's story), 1982; The Essential

Whitman (ed.), 1987. *Honours:* National Institute of Arts and Letters Award, 1962; Cecil Hemley Poetry Prize, 1969; Medal of Merit, 1975; Pulitzer Prize in Poetry, 1983; National Book Award, 1983; John D. and Catherine T. MacArthur Foundation Fellowship, 1984. *Address:* RR 2 Box 138, Sheffield, VT 05866, USA.

KINNEY, Arthur F(rederick); Prof. of Literary History, Writer and Ed.; b. 5 Sept. 1933, Cortland, NY, USA. *Education:* BA, magna cum laude, Syracuse University, 1955; MA, Columbia University, 1956; PhD, University of Michigan, 1963. *Career:* Instructor, Yale University, 1963–66; Asst Prof., 1966–69, Assoc. Prof., 1969–73, Prof., 1973–85, Thomas W. Copeland Prof. of Literary History, 1985–, University of Massachusetts at Amherst; Founder-Ed., English Literary Renaissance journal, 1971–; Adjunct Prof., Clark University, 1973–, New York University, 1992–; Dir, Massachusetts Center for Renaissance Studies, 1996–; mem. MLA; Renaissance English Text Society, pres., 1985–; Renaissance Society of America; Shakespeare Asscn of America, trustee, 1995–; Sixteenth-Century Studies Conference Asscn. *Publications:* Rogues, Vagabonds, and Sturdy Beggars, 1973; Elizabethan Backgrounds, 1974; Humanist Poetics, 1986; John Skelton: Priest as Poet, 1987; Renaissance Historicism, 1987; Continental Humanist Poetics, 1989; Classical, Renaissance, and Postmodern Acts of the Imagination: Essays in Honor of O. B. Hardison Jr (ed.), 1994; Go Down, Moses: The Miscegenation of Time, 1997; Dorothy Parker Revisited, 1998; Shakespeare, Text and Theatre (ed.), 1999; Renaissance Drama: An Anthology of Plays and Performances Edited from Manuscript and Early Quartos (ed.), 1999; The Cambridge Companion to English Literature, 1500–1600, 2000; Tudor England: An Encyclopaedia, 2000; Blackwell Companion to Renaissance Drama (ed.), 2001; Lies Like Truth: Shakespeare, Macbeth and the Cultural Moment, 2001; New Essays on Hamlet, 2001; Shakespeare by Stages, 2003. Contributions: scholarly books and professional journals. *Honours:* Senior Huntington Library Fellow, 1973–74, 1978, 1983; Senior National Endowment for the Humanities Fellow, 1973–74, 1987–88; Senior Folger Shakespeare Library Fellow, 1974, 1990, 1992; Fulbright Fellow, Christ Church, Oxford, 1977–78; Chancellor's Medal, University of Massachusetts at Amherst, 1985. *Address:* c/o Dept of English, University of Massachusetts at Amherst, Amherst, MA 01003, USA. *E-mail:* afkinney@english.umass.edu.

KINNEY, Harrison Burton; Writer; b. 16 Aug. 1921, Mars Hill, ME, USA; m. Doris Getsinger, Feb. 1952, one s., three d. *Education:* BA, Washington and Lee University; MA, Columbia University. *Career:* mem. Authors' Guild. *Publications:* The Lonesome Bear, 1949; The Supper of Leonardo Da Vinci, 1953; Has Anybody Seen My Father?, 1960; The Kangaroo in the Attic, 1960; James Thurber: His Life and Times, 1993. Contributions: periodicals. *Address:* 551 Fifth Ave, New York, NY 10176-0187, USA.

KINSELLA, John; Australian poet, writer, editor and publisher; b. 1963, Perth, WA. *Education:* Univ. of Western Australia. *Career:* writer-in-Rresidence, Churchill Coll., Cambridge 1997; Ed., Salt literary journal; Publisher, Ed., Folio (Salt) Publishing. *Publications:* poetry: The Frozen Sea 1983, Night Parrots 1989, The Book of Two Faces 1989, Eschatologies 1991, Full Fathom Five 1993, Syzygy 1993, The Silo: A Pastoral Symphony 1995, Erratum/Frame(d) 1995, The Radnoti Poems 1996, Anathalamion 1996, The Undertow: New and Selected Poems 1996, Lightning Tree 1996, Poems: 1980–1994 1997, The Hunt and Other Poems 1998, Visitants 1999, Fenland Pastorals 1999, The Hierarchy of Sheep 2000, Auto 2001, Zoo (with Coral Hull) 2001, Outside the Panopticon 2002, Four Australian Poets (with others) 2003, Peripheral Light 2004; editor: The Bird Catcher's Song 1992, A Salt Reader 1995, Graphology 1997, The Benefaction 1997, Authenticities 1998, Directions in Contemporary Australian Poetry 1998, The May Anthologies 1999, Landbridge: An Anthology of Contempory Australian Poetry 1999, Vanishing Points Vol. 1 (with Rod Mengham) 2002; other: Genre (novel) 1997, Grappling Eros (short stories) 1998, Crop Circles (play in verse), From Poetry to Politics and Back Again 2000, Peter Porter in Conversation with John Kinsella (with Peter Porter) 2003; contrib. to newspapers and journals. *Honours:* Western Australian Premier's Award for Poetry 1993, Harri Jones Memorial Prize for Poetry, John Bray Poetry Award, Adelaide Festival 1996, Senior Fellowships, Literature Board of the Australia Council, Young Australian Creative Fellowship. *Address:* PO Box 202, Applecross, WA 6153, Australia.

KINSELLA, Thomas; Poet, Trans., Ed. and Prof. of English (retd); b. 4 May 1928, Dublin, Ireland; m. Eleanor Walsh, 27 Dec. 1955, one s. two d. *Career:* Irish Civil Service, 1946–65; Artist-in-Residence, 1965–67, Prof. of English, 1967–70, Southern Illinois University; Prof. of English, Temple University, Philadelphia, 1970–90; mem. Irish Acad. of Letters; American Acad. of Arts and Sciences. *Publications:* Poetry: Poems, 1956; Another September, 1958; Downstream, 1962; Nightwalker and Other Poems, 1968; Notes From the Land of the Dead, 1972; Butcher's Dozen, 1972; A Selected Life, 1972; Finistere, 1972; New Poems, 1973; Selected Poems, 1956–68, 1973; Song of the Night and Other Poems, 1978; The Messenger, 1978; Fifteen Dead, 1979; One and Other Poems, 1979; Poems, 1956–73, 1980; Peppercanister Poems, 1972–78, 1980; One Fond Embrace, 1981; Songs of the Psyche, 1985; Her Vertical Smile, 1985; St Catherine's Clock, 1987; Out of Ireland, 1987; Blood and Family, 1988; Personal Places, 1990; Poems From Centre City, 1990; Madonna, 1991; Open Court, 1991; From Centre City, 1994; Collected Poems, 1956–94, 1996; The Pen Shop, 1997; The Familiar, 1999; Godhead, 1999; Citizen of the World, 2000; Littlebody, 2000. Other: The Tain (trans. from Old Irish), 1970; Selected Poems of Austin Clarke (ed.), 1976; An Duanaire: Poems of the Dispossessed (trans.), 1981; The New Oxford Book of Irish Verse (ed. and trans.), 1986; The Dual Tradition: An Essay on Poetry and Politics in Ireland, 1995. *Honours:* Guinness Poetry Award, 1958; Denis Devlin Memorial Awards, 1966, 1969, 1988, 1994; Guggenheim Fellowships, 1968–69, 1971–72; Hon. PhD, National University of Ireland, 1984. *Address:* 639 Addison St, Philadelphia, PA 19147, USA.

KINSELLA, William Patrick, OC, BA, MFA; writer and poet; b. 25 May 1935, Edmonton, AB, Canada; m. 1st Myrna Salls 1957 (divorced 1963); three d.; m. 2nd Mildred Irene Clay-Heming 1965 (divorced 1978); m. 3rd Ann Ilene Knight 1978 (divorced); m. 4th Barbara L. Turner 1999. *Education:* University of Victoria, University of Iowa. *Publications:* Dance Me Outside, 1977; Scars, 1978; Shoeless Joe Jackson Comes to Iowa, 1980; Born Indian, 1981; Shoeless Joe, 1982; The Ballad of the Public Trustee, 1982; The Moccasin Telegraph, 1983; The Thrill of the Grass, 1984; The Alligator Report, 1985; The Iowa Baseball Confederacy, 1986; The Fencepost Chronicles, 1986; Five Stories, 1987; Red Wolf, Red Wolf, 1987; The Further Adventures of Slugger McBatt: Baseball Stories, 1987, revised edn as Go the Distance, 1995; The Miss Hobbema Pageant, 1988; The Rainbow Warehouse (poems with Ann Knight), 1989; Two Spirits Soar: The Art of Allen Sapp, 1990; Box Socials, 1991; A Series for the World, 1992; The Dixon Cornbelt League and Other Baseball Stories, 1993; Even at This Distance (poems with Ann Knight), 1994; Brother Frank's Gospel Hour, 1994; The Winter Helen Dropped By, 1995; If Wishes Were Horses, 1996; Magic Time, 1998; Japanese Baseball, 2000; The Secret of the Northern Lights, 2001. Contributions: many anthologies and periodicals. *Honours:* Houghton Mifflin Literary Fellowship, 1982; Books in Canada First Novel Award, 1982; Canadian Authors' Asscn Award for Fiction, 1982; Writers' Guild of Alberta Awards for Fiction, 1982, 1983; Vancouver Award for Writing, 1987; Stephen Leacock Medal for Humor, 1987; Canadian Booksellers' Asscn Author of the Year, 1987. *Address:* 9442 Nowell Street, Chilliwack, BC V2P 4X7, Canada. *E-mail:* buzzard2_99@yahoo.com.

KINZIE, Mary; Prof. of English, Poet, Critic and Ed.; b. 30 Sept. 1944, Montgomery, AL, USA. *Education:* BA, Northwestern University, 1967; Graduate Studies, Free University of Berlin, 1967–68; MA, 1970, MA, 1972, PhD, 1980, Johns Hopkins University. *Career:* Exec. Ed., TriQuarterly magazine, 1975–78; Instructor, 1975–78, Lecturer, 1978–85, Assoc. Prof., 1985–90, Martin J. and Patricia Koldyke Outstanding Teaching Prof., 1990–92, Prof. of English, 1990–, Dir of Creative Writing Program, 1979–, Northwestern University; mem. PEN; Poetry Society of America; Society of Midland Authors. *Publications:* Poetry: The Threshold of the Year, 1982; Summers of Vietnam, 1990; Masked Women, 1990; Autumn Eros and Other Poems, 1991; Ghost Ship, 1996; Drift, 2003. Non-Fiction: The Cure of Poetry in an Age of Prose: Moral Essays on the Poet's Calling, 1993; The Judge is Fury: Dislocation and Form in Poetry, 1994; A Poet's Guide to Poetry, 2000. Contributions: various books, anthologies, reviews, quarterlies, journals, and magazines. *Honours:* Illinois Arts Council Awards, 1977, 1978, 1980, 1982, 1984, 1988, 1990, 1993, and Artist Grant, 1983; DeWitt Wallace Fellow, MacDowell Colony, 1979; Devins Award for a First Vol. of Verse, 1982; Guggenheim Fellowship, 1986; Elizabeth Matchett Stover Memorial Award in Poetry, Southwest Review, 1987; Celia B. Wagner Award, Poetry Society of America, 1988; Pres.'s Fund for the Humanities Research Grant, 1990–91. *Address:* c/o College of Arts and Sciences, Dept of English, Northwestern University, University Hall 215, Evanston, IL 60208-2240, USA.

KIRALY, Sherwood; Writer and Ed.; b. 23 Oct. 1949, Chicago, IL, USA; m. 1st, one s. one d.; m. 2nd Patti J. Reynolds, 7 Feb. 1987. *Education:* Knox College. *Publications:* California Rush, 1990; Diminished Capacity, 1995; Big Babies, 1996. Contributions: newspapers and television. *Address:* c/o Berkley Books, 375 Hudson St, New York, NY 10014, USA.

KIRINO, Natsuo; Novelist; b. 1951, Kanazawa, Japan; m.; one c. *Publications:* numerous incl.: Hoho Ni Kakaru Ame (Rain Dropping on Cheeks), 1993; Out (in trans.), 1997; Yawarakana Hoho (Tender Cheeks), 1999; Gyokuran, 2002. *Honours:* Edogawa Ranpo Prize, 1993; Japanese Association Prize; Naoki Prize, 1999. *Address:* c/o Kodansha Europe Ltd, 95 Aldwych, London WC2B 4JF, England.

KIRK, Pauline Marguerite; Writer and Poet; b. 14 April 1942, Birmingham, England; m. Peter Kirk 4 April 1964; one s. one d. *Education:* Nottingham University, 1960–63; Sheffield University, 1963–64; Monash University, 1966–70; MA, Bretton Hall College, Leeds University, 1999. *Career:* Teacher, Methodist Ladies College, 1965–66; Teaching Fellow, Monash University, 1965–69; Tutor-Counsellor, Asst Senior Counsellor, Open University, 1971–88; Senior Officer, Leeds Dept of Social Service, 1988–95; Partner, Fighting Cock Press, 1996–; mem. Aireings, Partner, Fighting Cock Press, 1997–; Pennine Poets; Society of Authors. *Publications:* Fiction: Waters of Time, 1988; The Keepers, 1996. Poetry: Scorpion Days, 1982; Red Marl and Brick, 1985; Rights of Way, 1990; Travelling Solo, 1995; Return to Dreamtime, 1996; No Cure in Tears, 1997; Owlstone, 2002. Criticism: Brian Merrikin Hill: Poet and Mentor, 1999. Editor: A Survivor Myself: Experiences of Child Abuse, 1994; Local history booklets for Leeds City Council; Poetry Collections: Dunegrass, Brakken City, 1997; Chernobyl's Cloud, Natural Light, Kingfisher Days, 1998; The Imaginator, 2000; Imaginary Gates, 2001; Patterns in the Dark (second edn), 2001; Webbed Skylights of Tall Oaks (with Clare Chapman), 2002. Contributions: anthologies and other publications. *Honours:* Yorkshire and Humberside Arts New Beginnings Award, 1994. *Address:* 45 Middlethorpe Dr., York YO24 1NA, England.

KIRK-GREENE, Anthony (Hamilton Millard); University Lecturer, Fellow, Writer and Ed.; b. 16 May 1925, Tunbridge Wells, England; m. Helen Sellar, 1967. *Education:* BA, 1949, MA, 1954, Clare College, Cambridge; MA, University of Oxford, 1967. *Career:* Senior Lecturer in Government, Institute of Administration, Zaria, Nigeria, 1957–62; Prof. of Government, Ahmadu Bello University, Nigeria, 1962–65; University Lecturer and Fellow, St Antony's College, Oxford, 1967–92; Dir, Foreign Service Programme, University of Oxford, 1986–90; Asst Ed., New Dictionary of National Biography, 1996–2002; mem. African Studies Asscn, UK, pres., 1988–90; International African Institute; Royal African Society, vice-pres., 1992–. *Publications:* A Biographical Dictionary of the British Colonial Service, 1939–66, 1991; Diplomatic Initiative: A History of the Foreign Service Programme, 1994; On Crown Service, 1999; Britain's Imperial Administrators, 2000; The British Intellectual Engagement with Africa in the 20th Century (co-ed.), 2000. Contributions: various reference books and scholarly journals. *Honours:* Harkness Fellow, 1958–59; MBE, 1963; Hans Wolff Memorial Lecturer, 1973; FRHistS, 1985; Festschrift, 1993; Leverhulme Emeritus Fellowship, 1993; African Studies Asscn (USA) Best Text Prize, 1997; CMG, 2001. *Address:* c/o St Antony's College, Oxford OX2 6JF, England.

KIRKPATRICK, Clayton, AB; American newspaper editor; b. 8 Jan. 1915, Waterman, Ill.; m. Thelma Marie De Mott 1943 (died 1998); two s. two d. *Education:* Univ. of Ill. *Career:* reporter, City News Bureau, Chicago 1938; mem. staff, Chicago Tribune 1938–, Day City Ed. 1958–61, City Ed. 1961–63, Asst Man. Ed. 1963–65, Man. Ed. 1965–67, Exec. Ed. 1967–69, Ed. 1969–79; Vice-Pres. Chicago Tribune Co. 1967–77, Exec. Vice-Pres. 1977–79, Pres. 1979–81, Chair. 1981; Del. to 19th Gen. Conf., UNESCO, Nairobi 1976. *Honours:* Bronze Star Medal for service in World War II; Elijah Parish Lovejoy Award, Colby Coll. 1978; William Allen White Award, Univ. of Kansas 1977; Fourth Estate Award, Nat. Press Club 1979. *Address:* 471 Stagecoach Run, Glen Ellyn, IL 60137, USA (Home).

KIRKPATRICK, Sidney Dale; Writer and Film-maker; b. 4 Oct. 1955, New York, NY, USA; m. 26 Nov. 1983, two s. *Education:* BA, Hampshire College, Amherst, 1978; MFA, New York University, 1982. *Career:* Reader, Huntington Library, 1992; mem. PEN Center West, board of dirs, 1991–92. *Publications:* A Cast of Killers, 1986; Turning the Tide, 1991; Lords of Sipan, 1992. Contributions: Los Angeles Times; American Film. *Honours:* Winner, American Film Festival, 1982. *Address:* c/o Tim Seldes, Russell and Volkening, 50 W 29th St, New York, NY 10001, USA.

KIRKUP, James (Falconer); Poet, Author, Dramatist and Trans; b. 23 April 1923, South Shields, Tyne and Wear, England. *Education:* BA, Durham University. *Career:* Gregory Fellow in Poetry, University of Leeds, 1950–52; Visiting Poet and Head of the Dept of English, Bath Acad. of Art, Corsham, 1953–56; Prof. of English, University of Salamanca, 1957–58, Tohoku University of Malaya, Kuala Lumpur, 1961–62, Japan Women's University, Tokyo, 1963–70; Literary Ed., Orient/West Magazine, Tokyo, 1963–64; Prof. of English Literature, Nagoya University, 1969–72; Prof. of Comparative Literature, Kyoto University of Foreign Studies, 1976–88; mem. FRSL; British Haiku Society. *Publications:* Poetry: The Drowned Sailor and Other Poems, 1947; The Submerged Village and Other Poems, 1951; A Correct Compassion and Other Poems, 1952; The Spring Journey and Other Poems of 1952–53, 1954; the Descent Into the Cave and Other Poems, 1957; The Prodigal Son: Poems 1956–59, 1959; Refusal to Conform: Last and First Poems, 1963; Paper Windows: Poems from Japan, 1968; White Shadows, Black Shadows: Poems of Peace and War, 1970; A Bewick Bestiary, 1971; The Body Servant: Poems of Exile, 1971; Cold Mountain Poems, 1979; To the Ancestral North: Poems for an Autobiography, 1983; The Sense of the Visit: New Poems, 1984; Fellow Feelings, 1986; Throwback: Poems Towards the Autobiography, 1992; Shooting Stars, 1992; Strange Attractors, 1995; Counting to 9,999, 1995; Noems, Koans and a Navel Display, 1995; Collected Longer Poems, 2 vols, 1995, 1997; Selected Shorter Poems, 1995; Broad Daylight, 1996; Figures in a Setting, 1997; The Patient Obituarist, 1997; One-Man Band: Poems Without Words, 1998; Burning Giraffes, 1998; Tank Alphabet, 2000; Tokonoma, 2000; A Tiger in Your Tanka, 2000; Shields Sketches: Poems about Tyneside, 2002; An Island in the Sky: Poems for Andorra, 2002. Fiction: The Love of Others, 1962; Insect Summer, 1971; Gaijin on the Ginza, 1991; Queens Have Died Young and Fair, 1993. Non-Fiction: The Only Child: An Autobiography of Infancy, 1957; Sorrows, Passions, and Alarms: An Autobiography of Childhood, 1959; I, Of All People: An Autobiography of Youth, 1988; Object Lessons, 1990; A Poet Could Not But Be Gay: Some Legends of My Lost Youth, 1991; Me All Over: Memoirs of a Misfit, 1993; Child of the Tyne, 1997; Fumi Saito: In Thickets of Memory (trans.); Fumiko Miura: Pages from the Seasons (trans.). Other: travel books, essays, plays and trans. Contributions: various publications. *Honours:* many awards and prizes. *Literary Agent:* Curtis Brown Ltd, 10 Astor Pl., New York, NY 10003, USA. *Address:* c/o British Monomarks, Box 2780, London WC1N 3XX, England; Atic D, Edifici les Bons, Avinguda de Rouillac 7, Les Bons, Encamp, Andorra. *Telephone:* 831-065. *Fax:* 831-065.

KIRSCH, Jonathan; Novelist, Nonfiction Writer, Book Reviewer and Attorney; b. 19 Dec. 1949, Los Angeles, CA, USA; m. Ann Benjamin, 27 Dec. 1970, one s. one d. *Education:* BA, University of California, Santa Cruz, 1971; JD cum laude, Loyola University School of Law, 1976. *Career:* Book Reviewer, Los Angeles Times Book Review, 1968–; Ed., California magazine, formerly New West, 1977–83; Correspondent, Newsweek, 1979–80; Attorney, Kirsch and Mitchell, Los Angeles, 1988–. *Publications:* Bad Moon Rising (novel), 1977; Lovers in a Winter Circle (novel), 1978; Kirsch's Handbook of Publishing Law: For Authors, Publishers, Editors, and Agents, 1995; The Harlot by the Side of the Road: Forbidden Tales of the Bible, 1997; Moses: A Life, 1998. Contributions: More than 1,000 articles and book reviews to newspapers and magazines. *Literary Agent:* Laurie Fox, Linda Chester Literary Agency, Rockefeller Center, 630 Fifth Ave, New York, NY 10111, USA. *Address:* Kirsch and Mitchell, 2029 Century Park E, Suite 2750, Los Angeles, CA 90067, USA. *E-mail:* ursus@aol.com.

KIRSCH, Sarah; Author and Poet; b. 16 April 1935, Limlingerode, Germany; m. Rainer Kirsch, 1958, divorced 1968, one s. *Education:* Diploma, University of Halle, 1959; Johannes R. Becher Institute, Leipzig, 1963–65. *Publications:* Landaufenthalt, 1967; Die Vögel signen im Regen am Schönsten, 1968; Zaubersprüche, 1973; Es war der merkwürdigste Sommer, 1974; Musik auf dem Wasser, 1977; Rückenwind, 1977; Drachensteigen, 1979; Sieben Häute: Ausgewählte Gedichte 1962–79, 1979; La Pagerie, 1980; Erdreich, 1982; Katzenleben, 1984; Hundert Gedichte, 1985; Landwege: Eine Auswahl 1980–85, 1985; Irrstern, 1986; Allerlei-Rauh, 1988; Schneewärme, 1989; Die Flut, 1990; Spreu, 1991; Schwingrasen, 1991; Sic! natur!, 1992; Erlkönigs Tochter, 1992; Das simple Leben, 1994; Winternachtigall, 1995; Ich Crusoe, 1995; Nachtsonnen, 1995; Bodenlos, 1996. *Honours:* Petrarca Prize, 1976; Austrian State Prize for Literature, 1981; Austrian Critics Prize, 1981; Gandersheim Literary Prize, 1983; Hölderlin Prize, Bad Homburg, 1984; Art Prize, Schleswig-Holstein, 1987; Author-in-Residence, City of Mainz, 1988; Heinrich-Heine-Gesellschaft Award, Düsseldorf, 1992; Peter Huchel Prize, 1993; Konrad Adenauer Foundation Literature Prize, 1993; Büchner Prize, 1996. *Address:* Eiderdeich 22, 25794 Tielenhemme, Germany.

KISSINGER, Henry Alfred, AB, MA, PhD; American fmr government official, company executive and writer; b. 27 May 1923, Furth, Germany; m. 1st Ann Fleischer 1949 (divorced 1964); one s. one d.; m. 2nd Nancy Maginnes 1974. *Education:* Harvard University. *Career:* Exec. Dir, Harvard International Seminar, 1951–69; Faculty, Center for International Affairs, 1954–69, Assoc. Prof., 1959–62, Prof. of Government, 1962–69, Harvard University; Asst to the Pres. of the US for National Security Affairs, 1969–75; US Secretary of State, 1973–77; Founder-Chair., Kissinger Assocs Inc, New York City; Consultant, Adviser, and Mem. of various boards and commissions; mem. American Acad. of Arts and Sciences; American Political Science Asscn; Council on Foreign Relations. *Publications:* Nuclear Weapons and Foreign Policy, 1957; A World Restored: Castlereagh, Metternich and the Restoration of Peace 1812–1822, 1957; The Necessity for Choice: Prospects of American Foreign Policy, 1961; The Troubled Partnership: A Reappraisal of the Atlantic Alliance, 1965; Problems of National Strategy: A Book of Readings (ed.), 1965; American Foreign Policy: Three Essays, 1969; White House Years, 1979; For the Record: Selected Statements 1977–1980, 1981; Years of Upheaval, 1982; Observations: Selected Speeches and Essays 1982–1984, 1985; Diplomacy, 1994; Years of Renewal, 1999; Does America Need a Foreign Policy?: Toward a Diplomacy for the 21st Century, 2001. Contributions: Professional journals. *Honours:* Woodrow Wilson Prize, 1958; Guggenheim Fellowship, 1965–66; Nobel Prize for Peace, 1973; Distinguished Public Service Award, American Institute of Public Service, 1973; Presidential Medal of Freedom, 1977; Medal of Liberty, 1986. *Literary Agent:* International Creative Management, 40 W 57th Street, New York, NY 10019, USA.

KITANO, Takeshi; Japanese film director, actor, comedian and screenwriter; b. 18 Jan. 1947, Tokyo. *Education:* Meiji Univ. *Films:* Makoto-chan (actor) 1980, Danpu wataridori (actor) 1981, Manon (actor) 1981, Sukkari... sono ki de! (actor) 1981, Merry Christmas, Mr. Lawrence (actor) 1983, Jukkai no mosquito (actor) 1983, Kanashii kibun de joke (actor) 1985, Yasha (actor) 1985, Komikku zasshi nanka iranai! (actor) 1986, Anego (actor) 1988, Sono otoko, kyobo ni tsuki (writer, director, actor) 1989, Hoshi tsugu mono (actor) 1990, 3-4x jugatsu (writer, director, actor) 1990, Ano natsu, ichiban shizukana umi (writer, director) 1991, Sakana kara daiokishin! (actor) 1992, Erotikkuna kankei (actor) 1992, Sonatine (writer, director, actor) 1993, Kyôso tanjô (writer, actor) 1993, Minnâ-yatteruka! (writer, director, actor) 1995, Johnny Mnemonic (actor) 1995, Gonin (actor) 1995, Kidzu ritan (writer, director) 1996, Hana-bi (writer, director, actor) (Venice Film Festival Golden Lion) 1997, Tokyo Eyes (actor) 1998, Kikujiro no natsu (writer, director, actor) 1999, Gohatto (actor) 1999, Brother (writer, director, actor) 2000, Batoru rowaiaru (Battle Royale) (actor) 2000, Dolls (writer, director) 2002, Asakusa Kid (writer) 2002, Battle Royale II (actor) 2003, Zatôichi (writer, director, actor) (Venice Film Festival Silver Lion) 2003, Izô: Kaosu mataha fujôri no kijin (actor) 2004. *Address:* Office Kitano Inc., Tokyo, Japan. *E-mail:* office@office-kitano.co.jp. *Website:* www.office-kitano.co.jp.

KITCHEN, Martin, BA, PhD, FRHistS, FRSC; professor of history and writer; b. 21 Dec. 1936, Nottingham, England. *Education:* Magdalen Coll., Oxford and Univ. of London. *Career:* Faculty 1966–76, Prof. of History 1976–,

Simon Fraser Univ., Burnaby, BC. *Publications:* The German Officer Corps 1890–1914, 1968; A Military History of Germany, 1975; The Silent Dictatorship: The Politics of the German High Command Under Hindenburg and Ludendorff, 1976; Fascism, 1976; The Political Economy of Germany 1815–1914, 1978; The Coming of Austrian Fascism, 1980; Germany in the Age of Total War, 1981; British Policy Towards the Soviet Union During the Second World War, 1986; Europe Between the Wars, 1988; The Origins of the Cold War in Comparative Perspective: American, British and Canadian Relations with the Soviet Union, 1941–48, 1988; Nazi Germany at War, 1994; The British Empire and Commonwealth: A Short History, 1996; The Cambridge Illustrated History of Germany, 1996; Kasper Hauser, 2001; The German Offensives of 1918, 2001. Contributions: Professional journals. *Honours:* American Military Acad. Moncado Prize 1978. *Address:* c/o Dept of History, Simon Fraser University, Burnaby, BC V5A 1S6, Canada.

KITSIKIS, Dimitri, MA, PhD, FRSC; Canadian/French/Greek poet and university professor; b. 2 June 1935, Athens; m. 1st Anne Hubbard 1955 (divorced 1973); one s. one d.; m. 2nd Ada Nikolaros 1975; one s. one d. *Education:* American Coll. Athens, Ecole des Roches, Normandy, Lycée Lakanal and Lycée Carnot, Paris and Sorbonne, Paris. *Career:* Research Assoc. Grad. Inst. of Int. Studies, Geneva 1960–62, Centre for Int. Relations, Nat. Foundation of Political Science, Paris 1962–65, Nat. Centre for Scientific Research, Paris 1965–70; Assoc. Prof. of History of Int. Relations, Univ. of Ottawa 1970–83, Prof. 1983–96, Emer. Prof. 1996–; Sr Research Scholar, Nat. Centre of Social Research, Athens 1972–74; founder, Ed. Intermediate Region (journal) 1996–; adviser to govts of Greece and Turkey; numerous visiting professorships and other appts. *Publications:* author of 27 books, including Propaganda and Pressure in International Politics 1963, The Role of the Experts at the Paris Peace Conference of 1919 1972, A Comparative History of Greece and Turkey in the 20th Century 1978, History of the Greek-Turkish Area 1981, The Ottoman Empire 1985, The Third Ideology and Orthodoxy 1990, The Old Calendarists 1995, Turkish-Greek Empire 1996, The Byzantine Model of Government 2001; co-author of 33 other books; six vols of poetry; over 90 scholarly articles. *Honours:* First Prize in Poetry, Abdi Ipekçi Peace and Friendship Prize 1992. *Address:* Department of History, University of Ottawa, Ont. K1N 6N5, Canada (Office); 29 Travlantoni, Zographou, Athens 157.72, Greece. *Telephone:* (613) 562-5800 (Ottawa) (Office); (613) 834-4634 (Ottawa) (Home); (210) 777-6937 (Athens). *Fax:* (613) 562-5995 (Ottawa) (Office). *E-mail:* dkitsiki@uottawa.ca (Office); dkitsiki@rogers.com (Home). *Website:* members.rogers.com/dimitri-kitsikis (Office).

KITTREDGE, William Alfred, (Owen Rountree); academic and writer; b. 14 Aug. 1932, Portland, Oregon, USA; one s. one d. *Education:* BS, Agriculture, Oregon State University, 1954; MFA, University of Iowa, 1969. *Career:* Prof. Emeritus of English, University of Montana. *Publications:* We Are Not In This Together, 1982; Owning It All, 1984; Hole in the Sky, 1992; Who Owns the West?, 1996; Portable Western Reader (ed.), 1998; Balancing Water, 2000; The Nature of Generosity, 2000; Southwestern Homelands, 2002. Contributions: Time; Newsweek; New York Times; Wall Street Journal; Esquire; Outside; Paris Review. *Literary Agent:* Amanda Urban, ICM, 40 W 57th Street, New York, NY, USA. *Address:* 143 S Fifth Street E, Missoula, MT 59801, USA.

KIZAKI, Satoko (see Harada, Masako).

KIZER, Carolyn Ashley; poet and academic; b. 10 Dec. 1925, Spokane, Washington, USA. *Education:* BA, Sarah Lawrence College, 1945; Postgraduate studies, Columbia University, 1946–47; Studied poetry with Theodore Roethke, University of Washington, 1953–54. *Career:* Founder-Ed., Poetry North West, 1959–65; First Dir, Literature Programs, National Endowment for the Arts, 1966–70; Poet-in-Residence, University of North Carolina at Chapel Hill, 1970–74; Hurst Prof. of Literature, Washington University, St Louis, 1971; Lecturer, Barnard College, 1972; Acting Dir, Graduate Writing Program, 1972, Prof., School of Arts, 1982, Columbia University; Poet-in-Residence, Ohio University, 1974; Prof., University of Maryland, 1976–77; Poet-in-Residence, Distinguished Visiting Lecturer, Centre College, KY, 1979; Distinguished Visiting Poet, East Washington University, 1980; Elliston Prof. of Poetry, University of Cincinnati, 1981; Bingham Distinguished Prof., University of Louisville, 1982; Distinguished Visiting Poet, Bucknell University, 1982; Visiting Poet, SUNY at Albany, 1982; Prof. of Poetry, Stanford University, 1986; mem. American Civil Liberties Union; American Poets; Amnesty International; PEN; Acad. of American Poets, chancellor; Poetry Society of America; Associated Writing Programs, dir. *Publications:* Poetry: The Ungrateful Garden, 1961; Knock Upon Silence, 1965; Midnight Was My Cry, 1971; Mermaids in the Basement: Poems for Women, 1984; Yin: New Poems, 1984; Carrying Over, 1988; Harping On: Poems, 1985–1995, 1996. Prose: On Poems and Poets, 1993; Picking and Choosing: Prose on Prose, 1996. Contributions: poems and articles in various journals including The Paris Review; Antaeus; Michigan Quarterly. *Honours:* Governor's Awards, State of Washington, 1965, 1985, 1995, 1998; Pulitzer Prize in Poetry, 1985; American Acad. and Institute of Arts and Letters Award, 1985; San Francisco Arts Commission Award in Literature, 1986; Silver Medal, Commonwealth Club, 1998. *Address:* 19772 Eighth Street E, Sonoma, CA 95476, USA.

KLAM, Matthew; American writer; b. 1964. *Education:* Univ. of New Hampshire, Hollins Coll. *Career:* teacher of creative writing, St Albans School, American Univ., Stockholm Univ., Sweden. *Publications:* Sam the Cat and other stories 2000; contrib. to The New Yorker, Harpers, Allure, USA Weekend, Nerve, The Washington Post Magazine, New York Times Magazine. *Honours:* Robert Bingham/PEN Award, Nat. Endowment for the Arts grant, Whiting Writer's Award, O'Henry Award. *Address:* c/o Random House Inc, 1745 Broadway, New York, NY 10019, USA. *E-mail:* MattKlam@aol.com. *Website:* www.matthewklam.com.

KLAPPERT, Peter; Prof., Poet and Writer; b. 14 Nov. 1942, Rockville Center, New York, USA. *Education:* BA, Cornell University, 1964; MA, Renaissance English Literature, 1967, MFA, Poetry, 1968, University of Iowa. *Career:* Instructor, Rollins College, 1968–71; Briggs-Copeland Lecturer, Harvard University, 1971–74; Visiting Lecturer, New College, 1972; Writer-in-Residence, 1976–77, Asst Prof., 1977–78, College of William and Mary; Asst Prof., 1978–81, Dir, Graduate Writing Program, 1979–81, 1985–88, Assoc. Prof., 1981–91, Prof., 1991–, Dir, MFA Degree Program in Poetry, 1995–98, George Mason University; mem. Acad. of American Poets; Associated Writing Programs; Asscn of Literary Scholars and Critics; PEN; Poetry Society of America; Writers' Center, Bethesda, MD. *Publications:* On a Beach in Southern Connecticut, 1966; Lugging Vegetables to Nantucket, 1971; Circular Stairs, Distress in the Mirrors, 1975; Non Sequitur O'Connor, 1977; The Idiot Princess of the Last Dynasty, 1984; '52 Pick-Up: Scenes From the Conspiracy, A Documentary, 1984; Chokecherries: New and Selected Poems 1966–1999, 2000. Contributions: many anthologies, books, journals, and magazines. *Honours:* Yale Series of Younger Poets Prize, 1970; Yaddo Resident Fellowships, 1972, 1973, 1975, 1981; MacDowell Colony Resident Fellowships, 1973, 1975; National Endowment for the Arts Fellowships, 1973, 1979; Lucille Medwick Award, Poetry Society of America, 1977; Virginia Center for the Creative Arts Resident Fellowships, 1978, 1979, 1981, 1983, 1984, 1987, 1993, 1995; Millay Colony for the Arts Resident Fellowship, 1981; Ingram Merrill Foundation Grant, 1983; Klappert-Ai Poetry Award established in his honour by Gwendolyn Brooks, George Mason University, 1987; Poet-Scholar, American Library Asscn-National Endowment for the Humanities Voices and Visions Project, 1988. *Address:* 2003 Klingle Rd NW, Washington, DC 20010, USA. *E-mail:* petermail@earthlink.net.

KLASS, Perri Elizabeth; Pediatrician and Writer; b. 29 April 1958, Trinidad; two s. one d. *Education:* AB, magna cum laude, Biology, Radcliffe College, Harvard University, 1979; MD, Harvard Medical School, 1986. *Career:* mem. PEN New England, exec. board; American Acad. of Pediatrics; American Medical Women's Asscn; Massachusetts Medical Society; Tilling Society. *Publications:* Recombinations (novel), 1985; I Am Having An Adventure (short stories), 1986; A Not Entirely Benign Procedure (essays), 1987; Other Women's Children (novel), 1990; Baby Doctor (essays), 1992. Contributions: New York Times Magazine; Massachusetts Medicine; Discover; Vogue; Glamour; Esquire; Boston Globe Magazine; Mademoiselle; TriQuarterly; North American Review. *Honours:* O. Henry Awards, 1983, 1984, 1991, 1992, 1995; Honors Award, New England chapter, American Medical Writers Asscn, 1995. *Address:* c/o Maxine Groffskiy, 853 Broadway Suite, 708, New York, NY 10003, USA.

KLEIN, Joseph, (Joe Klein); Journalist and Writer; b. 7 Sept. 1946, New York, USA; m. Janet Eklund, 8 Feb. 1967, divorced 1975, two s. *Education:* AB, University of Pennsylvania, 1968. *Career:* Reporter, Beverly/Peabody Times, Beverly, Massachusetts, 1969–72, WGBH-TV, Boston, 1972; News Ed., Real Paper, Boston, 1972–74; Assoc. Ed., 1974–78, Washington Bureau Chief, 1976, Rolling Stone Magazine; Senior Ed., 1992–96, Contributing Ed., 1996–, Newsweek Magazine; Columnist, New Yorker Magazine, 1996–. *Publications:* Woody Guthrie: A Life, 1980; Payback: Five Marines After Vietnam, 1984; Primary Colors: A Novel of Politics (published anonymously), 1996; The Running Mate, 2000; The Natural (non-fiction), 2001. Contributions: newspapers and magazines. *Honours:* Robert Kennedy Journalism Award, 1973; Washington Monthly Journalism Award, 1989; Hon. DLitt, Franklin and Marshall College, Lancaster, Pennsylvania, 1990; National Headliner Award, 1994. *Address:* c/o Newsweek Magazine, 251 W 57th St, New York, NY 10019, USA.

KLEIN, Naomi; Writer, Journalist and Social Critic; b. 1970, Montréal, Canada; m. Avi Lewis. *Career:* columnist, The Globe and Mail, Canada, and The Guardian, UK; campaigner on issues of development economics, corporate accountability and consumer affairs; lectures and workshops world-wide on corporate branding and economic globalization, 1996–; frequent media commentator; guest lecturer, Harvard Univ., Yale Univ., McGill Univ. and New York Univ. *Publications:* No Logo: Taking Aim at the Brand Bullies, 2000; Fences and Windows: Dispatches from the Frontlines of the Globalization Debate, 2001; Battling Big Business: Countering Greenwash, Infiltration and Other Forms of Corporate Bullying, 2001. Contributions: The Nation, The Guardian, New Statesman, Newsweek International, New York Times, Village Voice, Ms Magazine. *Honours:* Canadian National Business Book Award, 2001; Prix Médiations, France, 2001; Ms Magazine's Women of the Year Award, 2001. *Address:* c/o Random House of Canada Ltd, 1 Toronto St, Unit 300, Toronto, ON M5C 2V6, Canada. *E-mail:* admin@nologo.org. *Website:* www.nologo.org.

KLEIN, Richard; Writer; b. 1941, USA. *Publications:* Cigarettes are Sublime, 1993; Eat Fat, 1996; Pop Surrealism (non-fiction, with Dominique Nahas), 1998; Jewelry Talks, 2001. *Address:* c/o Vintage USA, 1745 Broadway, New York, NY 10019, USA.

KLEIN, Theodore Eibon Donald; Writer and Ed.; b. 15 July 1947, New York, NY, USA. *Education:* AB, Brown University, 1969; MFA, Columbia University, 1972. *Career:* Ed.-in-Chief, Brown Daily Herald, 1968, Twilight Zone magazine, 1981–85, Crime Beat magazine, 1991–93; mem. Arthur Machen Society. *Publications:* The Ceremonies (novel), 1984; Dark Gods (story collection), 1985. Contributions: New York Times; New York Daily News; Washington Post Book World; Film column, Night Cry Magazine; Writer's Digest. *Honours:* Award for Best Novel, British Fantasy Society, 1985; Award for Best Novella, World Fantasy, 1986. *Address:* 210 W 89th St, New York, NY 10024, USA.

KLEIN, Zachary; Writer; b. 6 July 1948, New Brunswick, NJ, USA; two s. *Education:* Hillel Acad., Jewish Educational Centre, Mirrer Yeshia; University of Wisconsin. *Publications:* Still Among the Living, 1990; Two Way Toll, 1991; No Saving Grace, 1994. *Honours:* Notable Book of 1990, New York Times; Ed.'s Choice, Drood Review. *Address:* 5 Oakview Terace, Boston, MA 02130, USA.

KLEINZAHLER, August; American poet and writer; b. 10 Dec. 1949, Jersey City, NJ. *Education:* Univ. of Wisconsin at Madison, Univ. of Victoria. *Career:* Visiting Holloway Lecturer, Univ. of California at Berkeley 1987; mem. Poetry Soc. of America. *Publications:* A Calendar of Airs 1978, News and Weather: Seven Canadian Poets (ed.) 1982, Storm Over Hackensack 1985, On Johnny's Time 1988, Earthquake Weather 1989, Red Sauce, Whiskey and Snow 1995, Live from the Hong Kong Nile Club: Poems, 1975–1990 2000, The Strange Hours Travelers Keep (Griffin Int. Poetry Prize) 2004; contrib. to newspapers and magazines. *Honours:* Guggenheim Fellowship 1989, Lila Wallace-Reader's Digest Writers' Awards 1991–94. *Address:* PO Box 842, Fort Lee, NJ 07024, USA.

KLIKOVAC, Igor; poet and editor; b. 16 May 1970, Bosnia. *Education:* University of Sarajevo. *Career:* Ed., Literary Review, Sarajevo, 1991–92; Ed., Stone Soup Magazine, London, 1995–. *Publications:* Last Days of Peking (poems), 1996. Contributions: Literary Review; Echo; Bridge; Transitions; Stone Soup; New Iowa Review. *Address:* 37 Chesterfield Road, London W4 3HQ, England.

KLÍMA, Ivan, MA; Czech author and dramatist; b. 14 Sept. 1931, Prague; m. Helena Malá-Klímová 1958; one s. one d. *Education:* Charles Univ., Prague. *Career:* Ed. Československy spisovatel (publishing house) 1958–63; Ed. Literárni noviny 1963–67, Literárni Listy 1968, Listy 1968–69; Visiting Prof. Univ. of Mich. Ann Arbor 1969–70, Univ. of Calif. at Berkeley 1998; freelance author publishing abroad 1970–89; columnist Lidove Noviny newspaper; mem. Council, Czech Writers 1989–, Ed.'s Council, Lidové noviny 1996–97; Exec. Pres. Czech PEN Centre 1990–93, Deputy Pres. 1993–. *Publications:* Ship Named Hope 1968, A Summer Affair 1972, My Merry Mornings (short stories) 1979, My First Loves (short stories) 1985, Love and Garbage 1987, Judge on Trial 1987, My Golden Trades (short stories) 1992, The Island of Dead Kings 1992, The Spirit of Prague (essays, jtly) 1994, Waiting for the Dark, Waiting for the Light 1996, The Ultimate Intimacy (novel) 1997, No Saints or Angels 1999, Between Security and Insecurity: Prospects for Tomorrow 2000, Lovers for a Day: New and Collected Stories on Love 2000, Karel Capek: Life and Work 2002, The Premier and the Angel (in Czech) 2004; plays: The Castle 1964, The Master 1967, The Sweetshop Myriam 1968, President and the Angel, Klara and Two Men 1968, Bridegroom for Marcela 1968, The Games 1975, Kafka and Felice 1986; contribs to magazines. *Honours:* Hostovský Award, New York 1985, George Theiner Prize (UK) 1993, Franz Kafka Prize 2002, Medal for Outstanding Service to the Czech Repub. 2002. *Address:* České Centrum Mezinárodního, PEN Klubu, ul. 28, října 9, 11000 Prague 1, Czech Republic. *Telephone:* (2) 24221926 (Office).

KLINKOWITZ, Jerome, BA, MA, PhD; writer and academic; *Professor of English, University of Northern Iowa*; b. 24 Dec. 1943, Milwaukee, Wisconsin, USA; m. 1st Elaine Plaszynski 1966; m. 2nd Julie Huffman 1978; one s. one d. *Education:* Marquette University, University of Wisconsin. *Career:* Asst Prof., Northern Illinois University, 1969–70; Assoc. Prof., 1972–75, Prof. of English, 1975–, University Distinguished Scholar, 1985–, University of Northern Iowa; Fellow, University of Wisconsin 1968–69; mem. PEN American Center; MLA. *Publications:* Literary Disruptions, 1975; The Life of Fiction, 1977; The American 1960s, 1980; The Practice of Fiction in America, 1980; Kurt Vonnegut, 1982; Peter Handke and the Postmodern Transformation, 1983; The Self Apparent Word, 1984; Literary Subversions, 1985; The New American Novel of Manners, 1986; Rosenberg/Barthes/Hassan: The Postmodern Habit of Thought, 1988; Short Season and Other Stories, 1988; Their Finest Hours: Narratives of the RAF and Luftwaffe in World War II, 1989; Slaughterhouse-Five: Reinventing the Novel and the World, 1990; Listen: Gerry Mulligan/An Aural Narrative in Jazz, 1991; Donald Barthelme: An Exhibition, 1991; Writing Baseball, 1991; Structuring the Void, 1992; Basepaths, 1995; Yanks Over Europe, 1996; Here at Ogallala State U., 1997; Keeping Literary Company, 1998; Vonnegut in Fact, 1998; Owning a Piece of the Minors, 1999; With the Tigers Over China, 1999; You've Got To Be Carefully Taught: Relearning and Relearning Literature, 2001; The Vonnegut Effect, 2004; Pacific Skies 2004. Contributions: Over 250 essays to Partisan Review, New Republic, Nation, American Literature; Short stories to North American Review, Chicago Tribune, San Francisco Chronicle. *Honours:* PEN Syndicated Fiction Prizes, 1984, 1985. *Address:* Department of English, University of Northern Iowa, Cedar Falls, IA 50614-0502, USA.

KLJUSEV, Nikola, DEconSc; Macedonian politician, economist and poet; b. 2 Oct. 1927, Stip; m. 1956; one s. one d. *Education:* Belgrade Univ. *Career:* Asst Researcher Inst. for Industrial Scientific Research, Skopje 1953–60; Sr Researcher Inst. of Econs, Skopje 1960–67; Prof. Skopje Univ. 1968–91; mem. Macedonian Acad. of Arts and Sciences; Ed.-in-Chief, Economic Interview 1971–78, Dean Faculty of Econs Skopje Univ.; Prime Minister of Macedonia 1991–92; researcher 1992–98; Minister of Defence 1998–99; Pres. Council VMRO-DPMNE independent. *Publications:* economics titles: Period of Activization of Investment 1963, Criteria and Methods for Evaluation of Economic Efficiency of Investments 1965, Usage of Productive Capacity in Industry 1967, Policy and Economics of Investment in Companies 1968, Efficiency of Investment in Macedonian Industry 1969, Selected Problems of Theory and Policy of Economic Development 1978, Theory and Policy of Economic Development 1979, Investments (Theory, Economics, Policy) 1980; poetry: Stone Island 1994, Antithesis 1994, The Power of the Word 1994, Ode to the Word 1995, Non-germinated Seed 1996; Selected Works (six vols) 1997; essays: trilogy: I Faith and Delusion, II Unslept Nights, III Visions 1997–2000; Dictionary of the Heart 2001, Macedonian Economy in Transition 2002. *Honours:* Golden Wreath Award, 13 Nov. Prize, 11 Oktomvri Award for life's work. *Address:* Dimitar Mirasciev 19, Skopje, Macedonia. *Telephone:* (2) 773003.

KLUBACK, William; Prof. of Philosophy and Writer; b. 6 Nov. 1927, New York, NY, USA. *Education:* AB, George Washington University; AM, Columbia University; PhD, Hebrew University, Jerusalem. *Publications:* Paul Valéry, 6 vols, 1987–97; Juan Ramon Jiménez, 1995; Benjamin Fondane, 1996; Emil Cioran, 1997; Léopold Sédar Senghor, 1997. Contributions: Midstream; Shofar; Archives de Philosophie. *Address:* 65 Oriental Blvd, Apt 8D, New York, NY 11235, USA.

KLUGE, Paul Frederick, BA, MA, PhD; writer; b. 24 Jan. 1942, Berkeley Heights, NJ, USA; m. Pamela Hollie 1977. *Education:* Kenyon College, University of Chicago. *Career:* Visiting Prof., 1987–97, Writer-in-Residence, 1997–, Kenyon College. *Publications:* The Day That I Die, 1976; Eddie and the Cruisers, 1980; Season for War, 1984; MacArthur's Ghost, 1987; The Edge of Paradise: America in Micronesia, 1991; Alma Mater: A College Homecoming, 1993; Biggest Elvis, 1996. Contributions: periodicals. *Address:* c/o Department of English, Kenyon College, Gambler, OH 43022, USA.

KLUGER, Steve; Writer and Dramatist; b. 24 June 1952, Baltimore, MD, USA. *Education:* University of Southern California, 1971. *Publications:* Changing Pitches, 1984; Lawyers Say the Darndest Things, 1990; Last Days of Summer, 1998. Stage Plays: Cafe 50s, 1988–89; James Dean Slept Here, 1989; Pilots of the Purple Twilight, 1989; Jukebox Saturday Night, 1990; Yank: World War II From The Guys Who Brought You Victory, 1990; Bullpen, 1990; Bye Bye Brooklyn, 1997. Films: Once Upon a Crime, 1992; Yankee Doodle Boys, 1996; Bye Bye Brooklyn, 1997; Almost Like Being in Love, 1997. Contributions: Chicago Tribune; Los Angeles Times; Sports Illustrated; Inside Sports; Diversion; Playboy; Science Digest. *Literary Agent:* Brandt & Hochman Literary Agents Inc, 1501 Broadway, New York, NY 10036, USA.

KNAAK, Richard Allen; Author; b. 28 May 1961, Chicago, IL, USA. *Education:* BA, Rhetoric, University of Illinois. *Career:* mem. SFWA. *Publications:* The Legend of Huma, 1988; Firedrake, 1989; Ice Dragon, 1989; Kaz the Minotaur, 1990; Wolfhelm, 1990; Shadow Steed, 1990; The Shrouded Realm, 1991; Children of the Drake, 1991; Dragon Tome, 1992; The Crystal Dragon, 1993; King of the Grey, 1993; The Dragon Crown, 1994; Frostwing, 1995.

KNEALE, Matthew Nicholas Kerr, BA; writer; b. 24 Nov. 1960, London, England; m. Shannon Russell 2000. *Education:* Magdalen Coll., Oxford. *Publications:* Whore Banquets 1987, Inside Rose's Kingdom 1989, Sweet Thames 1992, English Passengers 2000, Small Crimes in an Age of Abundance (short stories) 2005. *Honours:* Somerset Maugham Award 1988, John Llewellyn Rhys Prize 1993, Whitbread Book of the Year 2000, Prix Relay du roman d'évasion 2002. *Literary Agent:* Rogers, Coleridge & White Ltd, 20 Powis Mews, London, W11 1JN, England.

KNECHT, Robert (Jean); Prof. of French History Emeritus and Writer; b. 20 Sept. 1926, London, England; m. 1st Sonia Hodge, 8 Aug. 1956, deceased 27 Dec. 1984; m. 2nd Maureen White, 28 Aug. 1986. *Education:* BA, 1948, MA, 1953, University of London. *Career:* Asst Lecturer, 1956–59, Lecturer, 1959–68, Senior Lecturer in Modern History, 1969–78, Reader, 1978–85, Prof. of French History, 1985–92, Prof. Emeritus and Hon. Senior Research Fellow, 1992–, University of Birmingham; Dir d'études associe, École des Hautes Études en Sciences Sociales, Paris, 1994; mem. FRHistS; Société de l'Histoire de France; Society for Renaissance Studies, chair, 1989–92; Society for the Study of French History, co-founder, 1987, chair., 1995–98. *Publications:* The Voyage of Sir Nicholas Carewe to the Emperor Charles V in the Year 1529 (ed.), 1959; Francis I and Absolute Monarchy, 1969; Renaissance and Reformation, 1969; The Fronde, 1975; Francis I, 1982, revised edn as Renaissance Warrior and Patron: The Reign of Francis I, 1994; French Renaissance Monarchy: Francis I and Henry II, 1984; The French Wars of Religion, 1559–1598, 1989; Richelieu, 1991; The Rise and Fall of Renaissance France, 1996; Catherine de'Medici, 1998; Un Prince de la Renaissance: François 1er et son royaume, 1998; The French Civil Wars, 2000; The French Religious Wars, 2002; Catherine de Médicis: pouvoir royal, amour maternel, 2003. Contributions: reference works, scholarly books and professional journals. *Honours:* Chevalier, Ordre des Palmes Académiques. *Address:* 79 Reddings Rd, Moseley, Birmingham B13 8LP, England.

KNIGHT, Andrew Stephen Bower; British editor and newspaper executive; *Director, News Corporation*; b. 1 Nov. 1939; m. 1st Victoria Catherine Brittain 1966 (divorced); one s.; m. 2nd Begum Sabiha Rumani Malik 1975 (divorced 1991); two d. *Career:* Ed. The Economist 1974–86; Chief Exec. Daily Telegraph 1986–89, Ed.-in-Chief 1987–89; Chair. News Int. PLC 1990–94; Chair. Ballet Rambert 1984–87; Chair. Times Newspaper Holdings 1990–94; Dir News Corpn 1991–, Rothschild Investment Trust CP 1996–; Chair. Shipston Home Nursing 1996–; Chair. Jerwood Charity 2003–; mem. Advisory Bd Center for Econ. Policy Research, Stanford Univ., USA 1981–; Gov. mem. Council of Man. Ditchley Foundation 1982–; now farms in Warwicks. and Dannevirke, NZ. *Address:* Compton Scorpion Manor, Shipston-on-Stour, Warwickshire, CV36 4PJ, England (Home).

KNIGHT, Arthur Winfield; Prof. of English, Writer, Poet and Film Critic; b. 29 Dec. 1937, San Francisco, CA, USA; m. Kit Duell, 25 Aug. 1976, one d. *Education:* AA, Santa Rosa Junior College, 1958; BA, English, 1960, MA, Creative Writing, 1962, San Francisco State University. *Career:* Prof. of English, California University of Pennsylvania, 1966–93; Film Critic, Russian River News, Guerneville, CA, 1991–92, Anderson Valley Advertiser, Boonville, CA, 1992–, Potpourri, Prairie Village, KS, 1993–95; Part-time Prof., University of San Francisco, 1995; mem. Western Writers of America. *Publications:* A Marriage of Poets (with Kit Knight), 1984; King of the Beatniks, 1986; The Beat Vision (co-ed.), 1987; Wanted!, 1988; Basically Tender, 1991; Cowboy Poems, 1993, retitled Outlaws, Lawmen and Bad Women; Tell Me An Erotic Story, 1993; The Darkness Starts Up Where You Stand, 1996; The Secret Life of Jesse James, 1996; The Cruelest Month, 1997; Johnnie D. (novel), 1999. Contributions: Reviews, quarterlies, and journals. *Honours:* First Place, Joycean Lively Arts Guild Poetry Competition, 1982. *Literary Agent:* Nat Sobel, Sobel Weber Assocs Inc, 146 E 19th St, New York, NY 10003-2404, USA. *Address:* 544 Citrus Heights, CA 956ll, USA.

KNIGHT, Bernard; Emeritus Prof. of Forensic Pathology and Writer; b. 3 May 1931, Cardiff, Wales. *Education:* MB, BCh, 1954, MD, 1966, Univ. of Wales; MRCP, FRCPath, 1976; Barrister of Gray's Inn, 1967; Diploma in Medical Jurisprudence, 1966. *Career:* Lecturer in Forensic Medicine, University of London, 1959–62; Medical Ed., Medicine, Science and the Law, 1960–63; Lecturer, 1962–65, Senior Lecturer, 1965–76, Reader to Prof. and Consultant in Forensic Pathology, College of Medicine, University of Wales, 1976–96; Senior Lecturer in Forensic Pathology, University of Newcastle, 1965–68; Managing Ed., 1992–96, Pathology Ed., 1980–92, Forensic Science International; mem. CWA. *Publications:* Fiction: The Lately Deceased, 1963; Thread of Evidence, 1965; Mistress Murder, 1968; Policeman's Progress, 1969; Tiger at Bay, 1970; Murder, Suicide or Accident, 1971; Deg Y Dragwyddoldeb, 1972; The Sanctuary Seeker, 1998; The Poisoned Chalice, 1998; Crowner's Quest, 1998; The Awful Secret, 1999; The Tinner's Corpse, 2000; The Grim Reaper, 2001; Fear in the Forest, 2003; Brennan, 2003. Non-Fiction: Legal Aspects of Medical Practice, 1972; Discovering the Human Body, 1980; Forensic Radiology, 1981; Lawyer's Guide to Forensic Medicine, 1982; Sudden Death in Infancy, 1983; Post-Modern Technicians Handbook, 1984; Pocket Guide to Forensic Medicine, 1985; Simpson's Forensic Medicine, 10th edn, 1991, 11th edn, 1996; Forensic Pathology, 1991; The Estimation of the Time Since Death (ed.), 1995. *Honours:* CBE, 1993; Hon. DSc, 1996; Hon. LLD, 1998; Hon. DM, 2000; Hon. PhD, 2001. *Address:* 26 Millwood, Cardiff CF14 0TL, Wales. *E-mail:* knight@whodunnit.freeserve.co.uk.

KNIGHT, David Marcus, BA, DPhil; academic and writer; b. 30 Nov. 1936, Exeter, England; m. Sarah Prideaux 1962; two s. four d. *Education:* University of Oxford. *Career:* Lecturer, 1964–75, Senior Lecturer, 1975–88, Reader, 1988–91, Prof. of History and Philosophy of Science, 1991–, University of Durham; General Ed., Cambridge Science Biographies, 1996–; mem. British Asscn; British Society for the History of Science, pres., 1995–96; Royal Institution. *Publications:* Atoms and Elements: A Study of Theories of Matter in England in the 19th Century, 1967; Natural Science Books in English 1600–1900, 1972; Sources for the History of Science 1660–1914, 1975; The Nature of Science: The History of Science in Western Culture since 1600, 1977; Zoological Illustration: An Essay Towards a History of Printed Zoological Pictures, 1977; The Transcendental Part of Chemistry, 1978; Ordering the World: A History of Classifying Man, 1981; The Age of Science: The Scientific World View in the 19th Century, 1986; A Companion to the Physical Sciences, 1989; Ideas in Chemistry: A History of the Science, 1992; Humphrey Davy: Science and Power, 1992; Science in the Romantic Era, 1998; The Making of the Chemist 1789–1914, 1998; Science and Spirituality: The Volatile Connection, 2003. Contributions: scholarly books and journals. *Address:* c/o Department of Philosophy, University of Durham, 50 Old Elvet, Durham DH1 3HN, England.

KNIGHT, Gareth (see Wilby, Basil Leslie).

KNIGHT, Kit; Writer and Poet; b. 21 Sept. 1952, North Kingston, RI, USA; m. Arthur Winfield Knight, 25 Aug. 1976, one d. *Education:* BA, Communications, California University of Pennsylvania, 1975. *Career:* Co-Ed., Unspeakable Views of the Individual, 1976–88; Poet and Columnist, Russian River News, Guerneville, CA, 1988–92; Poet/columnist, film critic, Russian River Times, Monte Rio, CA, 1997–99; Reviewer, Citizen's Echo, CA, 2000–; Film critic, City Times, Fair Oaks Times, Gold River News, Citrus Heights, CA, 2002–03; Film critic, columnist American River Sentinel Citrus Heights CA 2003–. *Publications:* A Marriage of Poets (with Arthur Winfield Knight), 1984; Women of Wanted Men, 1994. Contributions: periodicals. *Honours:* Perry Award for Best Achievement in Poetry, 1994. *Address:* PO Box 544, Citrus Heights, CA 95611, USA.

KNIGHT, William Edwards; Foreign Service Officer (retd), Publisher and Writer; b. 1 Feb. 1922, Tarrytown, New York, USA; m. Ruth L. Lee, 14 Aug. 1946, two s. *Education:* BA, Yale College, 1942; Pilot Training, US Army Air Force, 1943–44; MA, Yale University, 1946; Industrial College of the Armed Forces, 1961–62; State Dept Senior Seminar in Foreign Policy, 1971–72. *Career:* B-24 Co-Pilot, 1944–45; Foreign Service Officer, US Dept of State, 1946–75; Pres. and CEO, Araluen Press, 1982–; mem. Yale Club; Washington Independent Writers; Diplomatic and Consular Officers Retired; American Foreign Service Asscn; Army/Navy Country Club; Randolph Mountain Club. *Publications:* The Tiger Game, 1986; The Bamboo Game, 1993; Footprints in the Sand (light verse), 1995; Letter to the Twenty-Second Century: An American Family's Odyssey, 1998; The Devil's End Game, 2002. Contributions: journals. *Address:* Araluen Press, 5000 Park Pl., Suite 300, Bethesda, MD 20816, USA.

KNIGHTLEY, Phillip George; journalist and writer; b. 23 Jan. 1929, Sydney, NSW, Australia; m. Yvonne Fernandes 1964; one s. two d. *Career:* reporter, Northern Star, Lismore, 1948–49, Herald, Melbourne, 1952–54; reporter, 1954–56, Foreign Correspondent, 1956–60, Daily Mirror, Sydney; Ed., Imprint, Mumbai, 1960–62; Special Correspondent, Sunday Times, 1965–85; mem. Society of Authors; Royal Overseas League; The Queen's Club. *Publications:* Philby: The Spy Who Betrayed a Generation (with Bruce Page and David Leitch), 1968; The Games (with Hugh Atkinson), 1968; The Secret Lives of Lawrence of Arabia (with Colin Simpson), 1969; The First Casualty: The War Correspondent as Hero Propagandist and Myth-Maker, Crimea to Vietnam, 1975; Lawrence of Arabia, 1976; The Death of Venice (with Stephen Fay), 1976; Suffer the Children (ed.), 1979; The Vestey Affair, 1981; The Second Oldest Profession: The Spy as Bureaucrat, Patriot, Fantasist, and Whore, 1986; An Affair of State: The Profumo Case and the Framing of Stephen Ward (with Caroline Kennedy), 1987; Philby: KGB Masterspy, 1988; A Hack's Progress, 1997; Australia: A Biography of a Nation, 2000. *Honours:* British Journalist of the Year Awards, 1980, 1988. *Literary Agent:* The Sayle Literary Agency, Bickerton House, 25–27 Bickerton Road, London, N19 5JT, England. *Telephone:* (20) 7263-8681. *Fax:* (20) 7561-0529. *Address:* 4 Northumberland Place, London W2 5BS, England. *E-mail:* phillipgk@aol.com.

KNOPF, Alfred, Jr, AB; American publisher (retd); b. 17 June 1918, New York; m. Alice Laine 1952; one s. two d. *Education:* Union Coll. *Career:* with Atheneum Publishers 1959–88, Chair. 1964–88; fmr Vice-Chair. Scribner Book Cos; fmr Sr Vice-Pres. Macmillan Publishing Co. *Address:* 530 East 72nd Street, Apartment 18F, New York, NY 10021, USA (Home).

KNOPP, Lisa; Asst Prof., Writer and Poet; b. 4 Sept. 1956, Burlington, IA, USA; m. Colin Ramsay, 4 Sept. 1990, divorced 1996, one s. one d. *Education:* BA, Iowa Wesleyan College, 1981; MA, Western Illinois University, 1986; PhD, University of Nebraska, Lincoln, 1993. *Career:* Teaching Asst, 1988–93, Lecturer, 1994–95, University of Nebraska, Lincoln; Asst Prof., Southern Illinois University, 1995; mem. Associated Writing Programs; Asscn for the Study of Literature and the Environment; Western Literature Asscn. *Publications:* Field of Vision (essays), 1996. Contributions: anthologies, newspapers and periodicals. *Honours:* Frank Vogel Scholar in Non-Fiction, Bread Loaf Writers Conference, 1992; Second Place, Society of Midland Authors, 1996. *Address:* c/o Dept of English, Southern Illinois University, Carbondale, IL 62901-4503, USA.

KNOTT, William (Bill) Cecil, AA, BA, MA; writer; b. 7 Aug. 1927, Boston, MA, USA. *Education:* Boston University, SUNY at Oswego. *Career:* served US Air Force 1946–47; teacher, high schools in Connecticut, W Virginia, New Jersey and New York 1951–67; Prof. of English, SUNY at Potsdam 1967–82; mem. Western Writers of America (pres. 1980–81). *Publications:* Circus Catch 1963, Scatback 1964, Long Pass 1966, Night Pursuit 1966, Junk Pitcher 1967, Lefty's Long Throw 1967, High Fly to Center 1972, Fullback Fury 1974, The Craft of Fiction 1974, Taste of Vengeance 1975, Lyncher's Moon 1980, Longarm and the Railroaders 1980, Longarm on the Yellowstone 1980, The Golden Mountain 1980, Mission Code: King's Pawn 1981, The Trailsman Series (15 vols) 1984–86, The Golden Hawk Series (nine vols) 1986–88, Red Skies Over Wyoming 1986, The Texan 1987, Longarm and the Outlaws of Skull Canyon 1990, Longarm and the Tattoed Lady 1990. *Address:* c/o Western Writers of America, 209 E Iowa, Cheyenne, WY 82009, USA.

KNOX, Elizabeth; Novelist; b. 15 Feb. 1959, Wellington, New Zealand; m. Fergus Barrowman 1989; one s. *Education:* BA, Victoria University,

Wellington, 1986. *Career:* Lecturer, Film Studies, Victoria University, 1989; Writer-in-Residence, Victoria University of Wellington. *Publications:* After Z Hour, 1987; Paremata, 1989; Treasure, 1992; Pomare, 1994; Glamour and the Sea, 1996; Tawa, 1998; The Vinter's Luck, 1998; Black Oxen, 2000; The High Jump: A New Zealand Childhood, 2000; Billie's Kiss, 2001. Short Stories: The Sword, 1990; After Images, 1990; Post Mortem, 1990; Afraid, 1991; Take as Prescribed, 1991; The Black Disc, 1992; Heat, 1993; Where We Stopped, 1995; Depth Charge, 1995; Reuben Avenue, 1996; Getting Over It, 1997. Other: The Dig (short film script), 1994. *Honours:* ICI Bursary, 1988; PEN Award, 1988, Fellowship, 1991; New Zealand Book Council Lecture Award, 1998; Katherine Mansfield Memorial Fellowship, 1999. *Literary Agent:* AP Watt Ltd, 20 John St, London WC1N 2DR, England. *Address:* PO Box 11-806 Wellington, New Zealand.

KNOX-JOHNSTON, Sir Robin; Master Mariner and Author; b. 17 March 1939, Putney, London, England; m. 6 Jan. 1962, one d. *Education:* Master's Certificate, 1965. *Career:* mem. Younger Brother, Trinity House; Honourable Company of Master Mariners; Royal Institute of Navigation; National Maritime Museum, Cornwall. *Publications:* A World of My Own, 1969; Sailing, 1974; Twilight of Sail, 1978; Last But Not Least, 1978; Seamanship, 1986; The BOC Challenge 1986–87, 1987; The Cape of Good Hope, 1989; The History of Yachting, 1990; The Columbus Venture, 1991; Sea Ice Rock (with Chris Bonington), 1992; Cape Horn, 1994; Beyond Jules Verne, 1995. Contributions: Yachting World; Cruising World; Guardian. *Honours:* CBE, 1969; Hon. Doctor of Technology, Nottingham Trent University, 1993; Knighted, 1995. *Literary Agent:* Curtis Brown Ltd, Haymarket House, 28–29 Haymarket, London, SW1Y 4SP, England. *Telephone:* (20) 7393-4400. *Fax:* (20) 7393-4401. *E-mail:* info@curtisbrown.co.uk. *Website:* www.curtisbrown.co.uk. *Address:* St Francis Cottage, Torbryan, Newton Abbot, Devon TQ12 5UR, England.

KNOX-MAWER, June Ellis; Writer and Broadcaster; b. 10 May 1930, Wrexham, North Wales; m. Ronald Knox-Mawer, 30 June 1951, one s. one d. *Career:* Trained as Journalist, Chester Chronicle, 1948–50; Aden Correspondent, Daily Express, 1952–56; Presenter and Author, various literary and feature programmes, Womans Hour, BBC Radio 4, 1970–; mem. Royal Commonwealth Society; Commonwealth Trust. *Publications:* The Sultans Came to Tea, 1961; A Gift of Islands, 1965; A World of Islands, 1968; Marama, 1972; A South Sea Spell, 1975; Tales from Paradise, 1986; Marama of the Islands, 1986; Sandstorm, 1991; The Shadow of Wings, 1995; A Ram in the Well: A Welsh Homecoming, 2001. Contributions: Guardian; various women's magazines. *Honours:* Romantic Novel of the Year Award, 1992. *Literary Agent:* David Higham Associates, 5–8 Lower John St, Golden Sq., London W1F 9HA, England.

KNUDSON, Rozanne R.; writer; b. 1 June 1932, Washington, DC, USA. *Education:* BA, Brigham Young University, 1954; MA, University of Georgia, 1958; PhD, Stanford University, 1967. *Publications:* Selected Objectives in the English Language Arts (with Arnold Lazarus), 1967; Sports Poems (ed. with P. K. Ebert), 1971; Zanballer, 1972; Jesus Song, 1973; You Are the Rain, 1974; Fox Running, 1974; Zanbanger, 1977; Zanboomer, 1978; Weight Training for the Young Athlete (with F. Colombo), 1978; Starbodies (with F. Colombo), 1978; Rinehart Lifts, 1980; Just Another Love Story, 1982; Speed, 1982; Muscles, 1982; Punch, 1982; Zan Hagen's Marathon, 1984; Babe Didrikson, 1985; Frankenstein's 10 K, 1987; Martina Navratilova, 1986; Rinehart Shouts, 1986; Julie Brown, 1987; American Sports Poems (ed. with May Swenson), 1987; The Wonderful Pen of May Swenson, 1993; May Swenson: A Poet's Life in Photos, 1996. *Address:* 73 Blvd, Sea Cliff, NY 11579, USA.

KOCH, Christopher John; Author; b. 16 July 1932, Hobart, Tasmania, Australia; m. Irene Vilnonis, 23 April 1960, one s. *Education:* BA; DLitt, University of Tasmania. *Publications:* The Boys in the Island, 1958; Across the Sea Wall, 1965; The Doubleman, 1965; The Year of Living Dangerously, 1978; Crossing the Gap (essays), 1987; Highways to War, 1995; Out of Ireland, 1999. *Honours:* National Book Council Award for Australian Literature, 1979; Miles Franklin Prize, 1985, 1996; AO, 1995. *Literary Agent:* Margaret Connolly Assocs. *Address:* c/o 16 Winton St, Warrawee, Sydney, NSW 2074, Australia.

KOCH, Joanne Barbara, (Joanna Z. Adams), BA, MA, PhD; writer and dramatist; *Associate Professor of English, National-Louis University Chicago;* b. 28 March 1941, Chicago, IL, USA; m. Lewis Z. Koch 1964; one s. two d. *Education:* Cornell Univ., Columbia Univ., Southern Illinois Univ. *Career:* syndicated columnist, with Lewis Z. Koch, for Newspaper Enterprise Asscn 1971–75; Dir of Graduate Writing Program, Assoc. Prof. of English, National-Louis Univ., Chicago; Guest Lecturer on Women's Studies and Screenwriting, Northwestern Univ., Columbia Coll., Chicago; mem. Dramatists' Guild, Soc. of Midland Authors, Women in Film, Women in Theatre. *Plays:* Haymarket: Footnote to a Bombing (Piscator Foundation-SIU Int. Playwriting Award) 1985, Teeth (Illinois Arts Council grant) 1988, Hearts in the Wood (musical, with James Lucas) (Illinois Arts Council Playwriting Fellowship) 1992, Saul Bellow's Stories on Stage: A Silver Dish and The Old System (adaptations, with Sarah Cohen) (Streisand Festival Award) 1993, Nesting Dolls (PBS Broadcast, SIU Best New Play Award) 1994, Sophie, Totie & Belle (with Sarah Cohen) 1995, Safe Harbor 1999, A Leading Woman (Driehaus Foundation grant) 2002, Henrietta Szold: Woman of Valor (with Sarah Cohen) (Brandeis Univ. Hadassah Inst. Research grant) 2002, Courage Like a Wild Horse 2004, American Klezmer (musical, with Sarah Cohen, Owen Kalt, Ilya Levinson) 2004, Soul Sisters (with Sarah Cohen) 2005. *Publications:* The Marriage Savers (with Lewis Z. Koch) 1976, Readings in Psychology Today (contributor) 1978, Children: development through adolescence (with Allison Clarke-Stewart) 1983, Marriage and Family (with Diane Levande, Lewis Z. Koch) 1983, Child Psychology (with Clarke-Stewart) 1985, Good Parents for Hard Times (with Linda Freeman) 1991, Shared Stages: the Drama of Blacks and Jews (co-ed.) 2005; novels, as Joanna Z. Adams: Makeovers 1987, Rushes 1988, Intimate Connections 1989. *Honours:* American Psychoanalytic Asscn/Harris Media Award for Psychology Today article, Family Service Asscn award for writing. *Address:* 343 Dodge Avenue, Evanston, IL 60202, USA. *Telephone:* (847) 864-5357. *Fax:* (847) 864-2312. *E-mail:* jkoch@nl.edu.

KOEGLER, Hans Herbert, MA, PhD; academic and writer; b. 13 Jan. 1960, Darmstadt, Germany. *Education:* Johann Wolfgang von Goethe University, Frankfurt am Main. *Career:* Dissertation Fellow, German Fellowship Foundation, 1987–91; Research Fellow, Visiting Scholar, Northwestern University, New School for Social Research, University of California at Berkeley, 1989–90; Asst Prof., University of Illinois at Urbana-Champaign, 1991–97; Visiting Prof., University of Boston, 1997; Asst Prof., 1997–99, Assoc. Prof. of Philosophy, 1999–, University of North Florida. *Publications:* Die Macht des Dialogs: Kritische Hermeneutik nach Gadamer, 1992; Michel Foucault: Ein antihumanistischer Aufklarer, 1994, 2004; The Power of Dialogue: Critical Hermeneutics After Gadamer and Foucault, 1996, 1999; Empathy and Agency: The Problem of Understanding in the Human Sciences, 2000. Contributions: journals, reviews, periodicals and magazines. *Address:* c/o Department of Philosophy, University of North Florida, 4567 St Johns Bluff Road S, Jacksonville, FL 32224-2645, USA.

KOELB, Clayton; Prof. and Writer; b. 12 Nov. 1942, New York, NY, USA; m. Susan J. Noakes, 1 Jan. 1979, one s. one d. *Education:* BA, 1964, MA, 1966, PhD, 1970, Harvard University. *Career:* Asst Prof., Assoc. Prof., Prof. of German and Comparative Literature, 1969–91, Chair., Dept of Germanic Languages, 1978–82, University of Chicago; Visiting Prof., Purdue University, 1984–85, Princeton University, 1985–86; Visiting Eugene Falk Prof., 1990, Guy B. Johnson Prof., 1991–, Chair., Dept of Germanic Languages, 1997–, University of North Carolina, Chapel Hill; mem. MLA of America; International Asscn for Philosophy and Literature; Semiotics Society of America; Kafka Society of America. *Publications:* The Incredulous Reader, 1984; Thomas Mann's Goethe and Tolstoy, 1984; The Current in Criticism, 1987; Inventions of Reading, 1988; The Comparative Perspective on Literature, 1988; Kafka's Rhetoric, 1989; Nietzsche as Postmodernist, 1990; Thomas Mann's Death in Venice: A Critical Edition, 1994. Contributions: Professional journals. *Honours:* Germanistic Society of America Fellow, 1964–65; Woodrow Wilson Foundation Fellow, 1965; Danforth Foundation Fellow, 1965–69; Susan Anthony Potter Prize, Harvard University, 1970; Guggenheim Fellowship, 1993–94. *Address:* University of North Carolina, 414 Dey Hall, Chapel Hill, NC 27599, USA.

KOESTENBAUM, Wayne; Prof. of English, Poet, Writer and Critic; b. 20 Sept. 1958, San Jose, CA, USA. *Education:* BA, magna cum laude, English, Harvard College, 1980; MA, Creative Writing, Johns Hopkins University, 1981; PhD, English, Princeton University, 1988. *Career:* Assoc. Prof. of English, Yale University, 1988–97; Co-Ed., The Yale Journal of Criticism, 1991–96; Prof. of English, CUNY, 1997–. *Publications:* Double Talk: The Erotics of Male Literary Collaboration, 1989; Ode to Anna Moffo and Other Poems, 1990; The Queen's Throat: Opera, Homosexuality, and the Mystery of Desire, 1993; Rhapsodies of a Repeat Offender, 1994; Jackie Under My Skin: Interpreting an Icon, 1995; The Milk of Inquiry, 1999; Cleavage: Essays on Sex, Stars and Aesthetics, 2000; Andy Warhol, 2001. Other: Jackie O. (libretto for the opera by Michael Daugherty), 1997. Contributions: anthologies, books, newspapers, reviews, quarterlies, and journals. *Honours:* Whiting Fellowship in the Humanities, 1987–88; Twentieth Century Literature Prize in Literary Criticism, 1988; Co-Winner, Discovery/The Nation Poetry Contest, 1989; Morse Fellowship, Yale University, 1990–91; New York Times Book Review Notable Book, 1993; Whiting Writer's Award, 1994. *Address:* c/o English Program, Graduate School and University Center, City University of New York, 365 Fifth Ave, New York, NY 10016, USA.

KOGAN, Norman, BA, PhD; American academic and writer; b. 15 June 1919, Chicago, IL; m. Meryl Reich 1946; two s. *Education:* Univ. of Chicago. *Career:* Faculty 1949–88, Dir, Center for Italian Studies 1967–76, Univ. of Connecticut; Visiting Prof., Univ. of Rome 1973, 1979, 1987; Pres., Conference Group on Italian Politics 1975–77; Chair., Southern Europe Commission, Council for the Int. Exchange of Scholars 1976–80; mem. Soc. for Italian Historical Studies (exec. sec., treas. 1966–76), Connecticut State Chapter of the Fulbright Asscn (pres. 1990–95). *Publications:* Italy and the Allies 1956, The Government of Italy 1962, The Politics of Italian Foreign Policy 1963, A Political History of Postwar Italy 1966, Storia Politica dell' Italia Repubblicana 1982, A Political History of Italy: The Postwar Years 1983; contrib. to Yale Law Journal, Il Ponte, Western Political Quarterly, Journal of Politics, Comparative Politics, Indiana Law Journal. *Honours:* Knight, Order of Merit of the Italian Republic 1971. *Address:* 13 Westwood Road, Storrs Manfld, CT 06268-2403, USA.

KOGAWA, Joy (Nozomi); Writer and Poet; b. 6 June 1935, Vancouver, BC, Canada; m. David Kogawa 2 May 1957 (divorced 1968); one s. one d. *Education:* University of Alberta, 1954; Anglican Women's Training College, 1956; University of Saskatchewan, 1968. *Career:* Writer-in-Residence, University of Ottawa, 1978; mem. Canadian Civil Liberties Asscn, dir; Canadian Tribute to Human Rights, patron; League of Canadian Poets; PEN International; Writers Union of Canada. *Publications:* Poetry: The Splintered Moon, 1967; A Choice of Dreams, 1974; Jericho Road, 1977; Woman in the Woods, 1985. Fiction: Obasan, 1981; Naomi's Road, 1986; Itsuka, 1992; The Rain Ascends, 1995. Contributions: Canadian Forum; Chicago Review; Prism International; Quarry; Queen's Quarterly; West Coast Review; Others. *Honours:* First Novel Award, Books in Canada, 1982; Book of the Year Award, Canadian Authors Asscn, 1982; American Book Award, Before Columbus Foundation, 1982; Best Paperback Award, Periodical Distributors, 1982; Notable Book Citation, American Library Asscn, 1982; Mem. of the Order of Canada; Doctor of Laws, hc, 1991, 1993; Doctor of Letters, hc, 1992.

KOHUT, Thomas A(ugust); Prof. of History and Writer; b. 11 March 1950, Chicago, IL, USA; m. Susan Neeld Kohut, 21 June 1975, one s. one d. *Education:* BA, Oberlin College, 1972; MA, History, 1975, PhD, History, 1983, University of Minnesota; Graduate, Cincinnati Psychoanalytic Institute, 1984. *Career:* Asst Clinical Prof. of Psychiatry, University of Cincinnati, 1982–84; Asst Prof., 1984–90, Assoc. Prof., 1990–95, Sue and Edgar Wachenheim III Prof. of History, 1995–, Williams College; Guest Prof., University of Munich, 1988, University of Siegen, 1991–92, 1995–96; mem. American Historical Asscn; German Studies Asscn. *Publications:* Wilhelm II and the Germans: A Study in Leadership, 1991. Contributions: scholarly books, journals and anthologies. *Honours:* Deutscher Akademischer Austauschdienst Grant, 1978–79; International Research and Exchanges Board Grant, 1979; Fulbright Scholarship, 1987–88; Köhler Foundation Grant, 1996. *Address:* c/o Dept of History, Williams College, Williamstown, MA 01267, USA.

KOŁAKOWSKI, Leszek; Philosopher and Writer; b. 23 Oct. 1927, Radom, Poland; m. Tamara Dynenson, 19 Nov. 1949, one d. *Education:* MA, University of Łódź, 1950; PhD, University of Warsaw, 1953. *Career:* Asst in Philosophy, University of Łódź, 1947–49; Asst in Philosophy, 1950–59, Prof. and Chair., Section in the History of Philosophy, 1959–68, University of Warsaw; Visiting Prof., McGill University, 1968–69, University of California at Berkeley, 1969–70, Yale University, 1975, University of Chicago, 1981–94; Senior Research Fellow, All Souls College, Oxford, 1970–95; mem. American Acad. of Arts and Letters; Bayerische Akademie der Schönen Künste, Munich; International Institute of Philosophy; Polish Acad. of Sciences; Polish Philosophical Society; Polish Writers Asscn. *Publications:* Marxism and Beyond, 1968; Conversations with the Devil, 1972; Positivist Philosophy, 1972; Husserl and the Search for Certitude, 1975; Main Currents of Marxism, three vols, 1976–78; Religion If There Is No God, 1982; Bergson, 1985; Metaphysical Horror, 1988; Modernity on Endless Trial, 1990; God Owes Us Nothing, 1994; Freedom, Fame, Lying and Betrayal, 1999. Contributions: various publications. *Honours:* Jurzykowski Foundation Award, 1968; Friedenspreis des Deutschen Buchhandels, 1977; Fellow, British Acad., 1980; Charles Veillou Prix Européen d'Essai, Zürich, 1980; John D. and Catherine T. MacArthur Foundation Fellowship, 1983; Co-Winner, Erasmus Prize, 1984; Jefferson Award, 1986; Prix Tocqueville, 1993; White Eagle Order, 1997; Premio Nonino, 1998; Hon. doctorates. *Address:* 77 Hamilton Rd, Oxford OX2 7QA, England.

KOLLER, James; Writer, Poet and Artist; b. 30 May 1936, Oak Park, IL, USA; Divorced, two s. four d. *Education:* BA, North Central College, Naperville, IL, 1958. *Publications:* Poetry: Two Hands, 1965; Brainard and Washington Street Poems, 1965; The Dogs and Other Dark Woods, 1966; Some Cows, 1966; I Went To See My True Love, 1967; California Poems, 1971; Bureau Creek, 1975; Poems for the Blue Sky, 1976; Messages-Botschaften, 1977; Andiamo, 1978; O Didn't He Ramble-O ware er nicht unhergezogen, 1981; Back River, 1981; One Day at a Time, 1981; Great Things Are Happening-Grossartoge Dige passieren, 1984; Give the Dog a Bone, 1986; Graffiti Lyriques (with Franco Beltrametti), graphics and texts, 1987; Openings, 1987; Fortune, 1987; Roses Love Sunshine, 1989; This Is What He Said (graphics and texts), 1991; In the Wolf's Mouth, Poems 1972–88, 1995; The Bone Show, 1996; Iron Bells, 1999; Close to the Ground, 2000. Other: Messages, 1972; Working Notes 1960–82, 1985; Gebt dem alten Hund'nen Knochen (Essays, Gedichte and Prosa 1959–85), 1986; The Natural Order (essay and graphics), 1990; Like It Was (selected poems, prose and fiction), 2000. Fiction: If You Don't Like Me You Can Leave Me Alone, 1974; Shannon Who Was Lost Before, 1975; The Possible Movie, 1997. *Address:* PO Box 629, Brunswick, ME 04011, USA.

KOLM, Ronald Akerson; Writer, Ed. and Publisher; b. 21 May 1947, Pittsburgh, Pennsylvania, USA; m. Donna Sterling, 5 Sept. 1984, two s. *Education:* BA, Albright College, 1970. *Publications:* Plastic Factory, 1989; Welcome to the Barbecue, 1990; Suburban Ambush, 1991; Rank Cologne, 1991; The Unbearables (ed.), 1995; Crimes of the Beats (ed.), 1998; Help Yourself! (ed.), 2002. *Honours:* papers in the Fales Collection, New York Univ. Library. *Address:* 30–73 47th St, Long Island City, NY 11103, USA.

KOMRIJ, Gerrit; Dutch poet, novelist, essayist and playwright; b. 30 March 1944, Winterswijk. *Education:* Univ. of Amsterdam. *Career:* fmr Ed., literary magazine Maatstaf; founder of the Poetry Club and poetry magazine Awater; Ed. the Sandwich series of poetry anthologies; he has written under the pseudonyms Gerrit Andriesse, Joris Paridon, Mr Pennewip and Griet Rijmrok; Dutch Poet Laureate 2000–04. *Publications:* Maagdenburgse halve bollen 1968, Alle vlees is als gras of Het knekelhuis op de dodenakker (Poetry Prize of Amsterdam 1970) 1969, Ik heb Goddank twee goede longen 1971, Tutti-frutti 1972, Daar is het gat van de deur 1974, Fabeldieren 1975, Horen, zien en zwijgen. Vreugdetranen over de treurbuis 1977, Capriccio 1978, Dood aan de grutters 1978, Heremijntijd, exercities en ketelmuziek 1978, Papieren tijgers (Busken Huet Prize 1979) 1978, De Nederlandse poëzie van de negentiende en twintigste eeuw in duizend en enige gedichten 1979, De stankbel van de Nieuwezijds 1979, Het schip De Wanhoop 1979, Averechts 1980, Verwoest Arcadië 1980, De os op de klokketoren (Herman Gorter Prize 1982) 1981, Onherstelbaar verbeterd 1981, De phoenix spreekt 1982, Gesloten circuit 1982, Het chemisch huwelijk 1982, De paleizen van het geheugen 1983, Dit helse moeras 1983, Het boze oog 1983, Alles onecht 1984, Schrijfrecept 1984, De gelukkige schizo 1985, Verzonken boeken 1986, Lof der simpelheid 1988, Humeuren en temperamenten 1989, De pagode 1990, Over de bergen 1990, Met het bloed dat drukinkt heet 1991, Over de noodzaak van tuinieren 1991, De ondergang van het regenwoud 1993, Dubbelster 1993, Intimiteiten 1993, Alle gedichten tot gisteren 1994, De Nederlandse poëzie van de twaalfde tot en met de zestiende eeuw in duizend en enige bladzijden 1994, De buitenkant 1995, Een zakenlunch in Sintra en andere Portugese verhalen 1996, In liefde bloeyende: de Nederlandse poëzie van de 12de tot de 20ste eeuw in tien gedichten: een voorproefje 1996, Kijken is bekeken worden 1996, Niet te geloven 1997, Pek en zwavel 1997, In liefde bloeyende: de Nederlandse poëzie van de twaalfde tot en met de twintigste eeuw in honderd en enige gedichten (Gouden Uil prize 1999) 1998, Lood en hagel 1998, De Afrikaanse poëzie in duizend en enige gedichten 1999, De Afrikaanse poëzie: 10 gedichten en een lexicon 1999, 52 sonnetten bij het verglijden van de eeuw 2000, Poëzie is geluk 2000, De klopgeest 2001, Hutten en paleizen 2001, Luchtspiegelingen 2001, Trou moet blycken, of Opnieuw in liefde bloeyende: de Nederlandse poëzie van de twaalfde tot en met de eenentwintigste eeuw in honderd en enige gedichten 2001, Vreemd pakhuis 2001, Vreemde melodieën 2001; contrib. to Vrij Nederland magazine, NRC Handelsblad newspaper. *Honours:* hon. doctorate (Univ. of Leiden) 2000; Cestoda Prize 1975, Kluwer-prijs 1983, P. C. Hooft-prijs 1993. *Literary Agent:* Bas Pauw, Singel 464, 1017 Amsterdam, Netherlands. *Telephone:* (20) 620 62 61. *Fax:* (20) 620 71 79. *E-mail:* b.pauw@nlpvf.nl.

KOMUNYAKAA, Yusef, (James Willie Brown Jr); Prof. of Creative Writing and Poet; b. 29 April 1947, Bogalusa, LA, USA; m. Mandy Sayer, 1985. *Education:* BA, University of Colorado, 1975; MA, Colorado State University, 1978; MFA, University of California at Irvine, 1980. *Career:* Correspondent, then Ed., military newspaper, The Southern Cross; fmrly taught poetry, New Orleans schools, creative writing, Univ. of New Orleans; Visiting Prof., 1985, Assoc. Prof. of Afro-American Studies, 1987–96, Indiana Univ. at Bloomington; Prof. of Creative Writing, Princeton Univ., 1997–; Board of Chancellors, Acad. of American Poets, 1999; many poetry readings. *Publications:* Dedications and Other Darkhorses, 1977; Lost in the Bonewheel Factory, 1979; Copacetic, 1984; I Apologize for the Eyes in My Head, 1986; Toys in a Field, 1987; Dien Cai Dau, 1988; February in Sydney, 1989; The Jazz Poetry Anthology (ed. with Sascha Feinstein), 1991; Magic City, 1992; Neon Vernacular: New and Selected Poems, 1993; The Second Set: The Jazz Poetry Anthology Vol. 2 (ed. with Sascha Feinstein), 1996; Thieves of Paradise, 1998; Talking Dirty to the Gods, 2000; Pleasure Dome: New and Collected Poems 1975–1999, 2001. Contributions: anthologies and periodicals. *Honours:* two Creative Writing Fellowships, National Endowment for the Arts, 1981, 1987; San Francisco Poetry Center Award, 1986; Dark Room Poetry Prize, 1988; Pulitzer Prize in Poetry, 1994; Kingsley Tufts Poetry Award, 1994; William Faulkner Prize, Université de Rennes, 1994; Thomas Forcade Award; Hanes Poetry Prize; Union League Civic Arts and Poetry Prize, Chicago, 1998; Ruth Lilly Poetry Prize, 2001. *Address:* c/o Dept of English, Princeton University, Princeton, NJ 08544, USA.

KÖNIG, Hans; Writer; b. 30 Sept. 1925, Erlangen, Germany; m. 1 Jan. 1949, one s. *Career:* mem. Verband Fränkischer Schriftsteller; Pegnesischer Blumenorden. *Publications:* Der Pelzermärtl kummt, 1977; Woss wissd denn ihr, 1981; Anekdoten Erzählungen Originale aus Erlangen, 1981–84; Burschen, Knoten und Philister – Erlanger Studentenleben von 1843–1983, 1984; Erlangen vorwiegend heiter – ein unterhaltsamer Streifzug dürch die Stadt und ihre Geschichte, 1988; Wie es Lem so is, 1994. Contributions: anthologies, journals and periodicals. *Honours:* Verdienstmedaille und Verdienstkreuz der Bundesrepublik Deutschland, 1985–91; Kultureller Ehrenbrief der Stadt Erlangen, 1989; Ehrenkrenz des Pegnesischen Blumenordens, 1995; Frankenwurtel, 1999. *Address:* Tenneloher Str 26, 91058 Erlangen, Germany.

KONRÁD, György; Author; b. 2 April 1933, Debrecen, Hungary; m. Judit Lakner, three s., two d. *Education:* Eötvös Loránd University, Budapest. *Career:* mem. Akademie der Künste, Berlin; Bayerische Akademie der Schönen Künste, Munich; International PEN, pres., 1990–93. *Publications:* A látogató, 1969, English trans. as The Case Worker, 1974; A városalapító, 1977, English trans. as The City Builder, 1977; A cinkos, 1983, English trans. as The Loser, 1983; Kerti mulatságok, 1987, English trans. as A

Feast in the Garden, 1992; Köóra, 1994, English trans. as Stonedial, 2000. Other: Vols of essays. *Honours:* Herder Prize, Vienna and Hamburg, 1984; Charles Veillou Prix Europèen d'Essai, Zürich, 1986; Critics's Prize for Novel of the Year, Federal Republic of Germany, 1986; Kossuth Prize, Republic of Hungary, 1991; Friedenspreis des Deutschen Buchandels, 1991; Karlspreis, Aachen, 2001. *Address:* Torockó utca 3, 1026 Budapest, Hungary.

KOONTZ, Dean Ray, (David Axton, Brian Coffey, Deanna Dwyer, K. R. Dwyer, John Hill, Leigh Nichols, Anthony North, Richard Paige, Owen West), BS; American author; b. 9 July 1945, Everett, Pa; m. Gerda Ann Cerra 1966. *Education:* Shippensburg Univ. *Career:* fmr teacher of English; freelance author 1969–; work includes novels, short stories, science fiction/fantasy, social commentary/phenomena and journalism. *Publications:* (under various names) Star Quest 1968, The Fall of the Dream Machine 1969, Fear That Man 1969, Anti-Man 1970, Beastchild 1970, Dark of the Woods 1970, The Dark Symphony 1970, Hell's Gate 1970, The Crimson Witch 1971, A Darkness in My Soul 1972, The Flesh in the Furnace 1972, Starblood 1972, Time Thieves 1972, Warlock 1972, A Werewolf Among Us 1973, Hanging On 1973, The Haunted Earth 1973, Demon Seed 1973, Strike Deep 1974, After the Last Race 1974, Nightmare Journey 1975, The Long Sleep 1975, Night Chills 1976, The Voice of the Night 1980, Whispers 1980, The Funhouse 1980, The Eyes of Darkness 1981, The Mask 1981, House of Thunder 1982, Phantoms 1983, Darkness Comes 1984, Twilight 1984, The Door to December 1985, Strangers 1986, Shadow Fires 1987, Watchers 1987, Twilight Eyes 1987, Oddkins 1988, Servants of Twilight 1988, Lightning 1988, Midnight 1989, The Bad Place 1990, Cold Fire 1991, Hideaway 1992, Dragon Tears 1992, Winter Moon 1993, The House of Thunder 1993, Dark Rivers of the Heart 1994, Mr Murder 1994, Fun House 1994, Strange Highways 1994, Icebound 1995, Intensity 1995, The Key to Midnight 1995, Ticktock 1996, Santa's Twin 1996, Sole Survivor 1996, Fear Nothing 1997, Seize the Night 1998, False Memory 1999, From the Corner of His Eye 2001, One Door Away From Heaven 2001, By the Light of the Moon 2002, The Face 2003, Odd Thomas 2003. *Honours:* Hon. DLitt (Shippensburg) 1989. *Address:* POB 9529, Newport Beach, CA92658, USA.

KOOSER, Ted, (Theodore Kooser); Poet, Teacher and Company Vice-Pres; b. 25 April 1939, Ames, IA, USA; m. 1st Diana Tresslar 1962 (divorced 1969); one s.; m. 2nd Kathleen Rutledge 1977. *Education:* BS, Iowa State University, 1962; MA, University of Nebraska, 1968. *Career:* Underwriter, Bankers Life Nebraska, 1965–73; Part-Time Instructor in Creative Writing, 1970–, Senior Underwriter, 1973–84, Vice-Pres., 1984–98, Lincoln Benefit Life; Visiting Prof., University of Nebraska;. *Publications:* Poetry: Official Entry Blank, 1969; Grass County, 1971; Twenty Poems, 1973; A Local Habitation, and a Name, 1974; Shooting a Farmhouse: So This is Nebraska, 1975; Not Coming to be Barked At, 1976; Hatcher, 1978; Old Marriage and New, 1978; Cottonwood County (with William Kloefkorn), 1979; Sure Signs: New and Selected Poems, 1980; One World at a Time, 1985; The Blizzard Voices, 1986; Weather Central, 1994; Winter Morning Walks, 2000; 100 Postcards to Jim Harrison, 2000; Local Wonders, 2002; Seasons in the Bohemian Alps, 2002. Editor: The Windflower Home Almanac of Poetry, 1980; As Far as I Can See: Contemporary Writers of the Middle Plains, 1989. *Honours:* Prairie Schooner Prizes, 1975, 1978; National Endowment for the Arts Fellowships, 1976, 1984; Poetry Award, Society of Midland Authors, 1980; Stanley Kunitz Prize, 1984; Governor's Art Award, NE, 1988; Richard Hugo Prize, 1994. *Address:* 1820 Branched Oak Rd, Garland, NE 68360-9393, USA.

KOPIT, Arthur; Dramatist and Screenwriter; b. 10 May 1937, New York, NY, USA; m. Leslie Ann Garis, two s. one d. *Education:* AB, Harvard University, 1959. *Career:* Fellow, 1974–75, Playwright-in-Residence, 1975–76, Wesleyan University; CBS Fellow, 1976–77, Adjunct Prof. of Playwriting, 1977–80, Yale University; Adjunct Prof. of Playwriting, City College, CUNY, 1981–; mem. Dramatists Guild; Hasty Pudding Society; PEN; Signet Society; Writers Guild of America. *Publications:* Plays: Questioning of Nick, 1957; Gemini, 1957; Don Juan in Texas, 1957; On the Runway of Life You Never Know What's Coming Off Next, 1957; Across the River and Into the Jungle, 1958; Sing to Me Through Open Windows, 1959; To Dwell in a Place of Strangers, 1959; Aubade, 1959; Oh Dad, Poor Dad, Mamma's Hung You in the Closet and I'm Fellin' So Sad, 1960; Asylum, or What the Gentlemen Are Up To, and As For the Ladies, 1963; Mhil'daim, 1963; Chamber Music, 1965; Sing to Me Through Open Windows, 1965; The Day the Whores Came Out to Play Tennis, 1965; Indians, 1968; What's Happened to the Thorne's House, 1972; The Conquest of Everest, 1973; The Hero, 1973; Louisiana Territory, or Lewis and Clark Lost and Found, 1975; Secrets of the Rice, 1976; Wings, 1978; End of the World, 1984; Road to Nirvana, 1991. Contributions: Films and television. *Honours:* Vernon Rice Award, 1960; Outer Critics Circle Award, 1960; Guggenheim Fellowship, 1967; Rockefeller Foundation Grant, 1968; American Institute of Arts and Letters Award, 1971; National Endowment for the Humanities Grant, 1974; Prix Italia, 1978; Tony Award, 1982. *Address:* c/o The Tartleff Office, 375 Greenwich St, Suite 700, New York, NY 10013, USA.

KOPS, Bernard; poet, writer and dramatist; b. 28 Nov. 1926, London, England; m. Erica Gordon 1956; four c. *Career:* Lecturer, Spiro Institute, 1985–86, Surrey Education Authority, Ealing Education Authority, Inner London Education Authority, Arts Educational School/Acting Co, 1989–90, City Literary Institute, 1990–93. *Publications:* Poetry: Poems, 1955; Poems and Songs, 1958; Anemone for Antigone, 1959; Erica, I Want to Read You Something, 1967; For the Record, 1971; Barricades in West Hampstead, 1988; Grandchildren and Other Poems, 2000. Other: Awake for Mourning, 1958; Motorbike, 1962; Autobiography, The World is a Wedding, 1963; Yes From No Man's Land, 1965; By the Waters of Whitechapel, 1970; The Passionate Past of Gloria Gaye, 1971; Settle Down Simon Katz, 1973; Partners, 1975; On Margate Sands, 1978. Plays: The Hamlet of Stepney Green, 1958; Goodbye World, 1959; Change for the Angel, 1960; Stray Cats and Empty Bottles, 1961; Enter Solly Gold, 1962; The Boy Who Wouldn't Play Jesus, 1965; More Out Than In, 1980; Ezra, 1981; Simon at Midnight, 1982; Some of These Days, 1990; Sophie: Last of the Red Hot Mamas, 1990; Playing Sinatra, 1991; Androcles and the Lion, 1992; Dreams of Anne Frank, 1992; Who Shall I Be Tomorrow?, 1992; Call in the Night, 1995; Green Rabbi, 1997; Cafe Zeitgeist, 1998; Collected Plays, three vols, 1998, 2000, 2002; Shalom Bomb, 2000. *Honours:* Arts Council Bursaries, 1957, 1979, 1985, and Awards, 1991, 2003; C. Day-Lewis Fellowship, 1981–83; London Fringe Award, 1993; Writer's Guild of Great Britain Best Radio Play Award, 1995. *Literary Agent:* John Rush, Sheil Land Associates, 43 Doughty Street, London, England. *Address:* 41B Canfield Gardens, London, NW6 3JL, England.

KORDA, Michael (Vincent); Writer and Ed.; b. 8 Oct. 1933, London, England; m. 1st Carolyn Keese 16 April 1958 (divorced); one s.; m. 2nd Margaret Mogford. *Education:* BA, Magdalene College, Cambridge, 1958. *Career:* Editorial Asst to Ed.-in-Chief, Simon & Schuster Inc, New York City, 1958–. *Publications:* Male Chauvinism! How it Works, 1973; Power! How to Get It, How to Use It, 1975; Success!, 1977; Charmed Lives: A Family Romance, 1979; Worldly Goods, 1982; Queenie, 1985; The Fortune, 1988; Curtain, 1991; Another Life: A Memoir of Other People, 1999; Country Matters, 2001. Contributions: periodicals. *Address:* c/o Simon & Schuster Inc, 1230 Avenue of the Americas, New York, NY 10020, USA.

KORG, Jacob; Prof. of English Emeritus and Writer; b. 21 Nov. 1922, New York, NY, USA. *Education:* BA, City College, CUNY, 1943; MA, 1947, PhD, 1952, Columbia University. *Career:* Bard College, 1948–50; City College, CUNY, 1950–55; Asst to Assoc. Prof., 1955–65, Prof. of English, 1965–91, Prof. Emeritus, 1991–, University of Washington, Seattle; mem. International Asscn of University Profs of English; MLA; Asscn of Literary Scholars and Critics. *Publications:* Westward to Oregon (ed. with S. F. Anderson), 1958; Thought in Prose (ed. with R. S. Beal), 1958; An Introduction to Poetry, 1959; London in Dickens's Day (ed.), 1960; The Complete Reader (ed. with R. S. Beal), 1961; George Gissing's Commonplace Book (ed.), 1962; George Gissing: A Critical Biography, 1963; Dylan Thomas, 1965; The Force of Few Words, 1966; Twentieth Century Interpretations of Bleak House (ed.), 1968; The Poetry of Robert Browning (ed.), 1971; George Gissing: Thyrza (ed.), 1974; George Gissing: The Unclassed (ed.), 1978; Language in Modern Literature, 1979; Browning and Italy, 1983; Ritual and Experiment in Modern Poetry, 1995; Winter Love: Ezra Pound and H. D., 2003. Contributions: Professional journals. *Address:* 6530 51st Ave NE, Seattle, WA 98115, USA.

KORMONDY, Edward John, BA, MS, PhD; academic and writer; b. 10 June 1926, Beacon, New York, USA. *Education:* Tusculum College, University of Michigan. *Career:* Instructor in Zoology and Curator of Insects, Museum of Zoology, University of Michigan, 1955–57; Asst Prof. to Prof. of Biology, Oberlin College, 1957–68; Dir, Commission on Undergraduate Education in the Biological Sciences and the Office of Biological Education, American Institute of Biological Sciences, 1968–71; Faculty, 1971–79, Interim Acting Dean, 1972–73, Vice-Pres. and Provost, 1973–78, Evergreen State College, Olympia, Washington; Senior Professional Assoc., National Science Foundation, 1979; Provost and Prof. of Biology, University of Southern Maine, Portland, 1979–82; Vice-Pres. for Academic Affairs and Prof. of Biology, California State University, Los Angeles, 1982–86; Senior Vice-Pres., University of Hawaii, 1991–93; Chancellor and Prof. of Biology, University of Hawaii at Hilo and at West Oahu, 1986–93; Pres., University of West Los Angeles, 1995–97; Special Asst to the Pres., Pacific Oaks College, 2000. *Publications:* Introduction to Genetics, 1964; Readings in Ecology (ed.), 1965; Readings in General Biology (ed.), 2 vols, 1966; Concepts of Ecology, 1969; Population and Food (ed. with R. Leisner), 1971; Pollution (ed. with R. Leisner), 1971; Ecology (ed. with R. Leisner), 1971; Environmental Education: Academia's Response (with J. Aldrich), 1972; General Biology: The Natural History and Integrity of Organisms (with others), 1977; Handbook of Contemporary Developments in World Ecology (with F. McCormick), 1981; Environmental Sciences: The Way the World Works (with B. Nebel), 1981; Biology (with B. Essenfield), 1984; International Handbook of Pollution Control, 1989; Environmental Education: Academia's Response (with P. Corcoran), 1997; Fundamentals of Human Ecology (with D. Brown), 1998; University of Hawaii-Hilo: A College in the Making (with F. Inouye), 2001. Contributions: Professional journals. *Honours:* Hon. Doctor of Science, Tusculum College, 1997. *Address:* 1388 Lucile Avenue, Los Angeles, CA 90026-1520, USA.

KORNFELD, Robert Jonathan, BA; American dramatist, writer and poet; b. 3 March 1919, Newtonville, MA; m. Celia Seiferth 1945; one s. *Education:* Harvard Univ., Columbia Univ., Tulane Univ., New York Univ., New School for Social Research, Circle-in-the-Square School of Theatre, Playwrights' Horizons Theatre School and Laboratory. *Career:* visiting artist, American Acad., Rome 1996; playwright-in-residence, Univ. of Wisconsin

1998; mem. Authors' League, Dramatists' Guild, Nat. Arts Club, New York Drama League, PEN, Theater for the New City (bd mem. 2002), Bronx County Democratic Cttee. *Plays written:* Great Southern Mansions 1977, A Dream Within a Dream 1987, Landmarks of the Bronx 1990, Music For Saint Nicholas 1992, Hot Wind From the South 1995, The Hanged Man 1996. *Plays produced:* Father New Orleans 1997, The Queen of Carnival 1997, The Celestials 1998, Passage in Purgatory, Shanghai, China 2000, The Gates of Hell 2002. *Publications:* plays, fiction and poetry; contrib. to various publications. *Honours:* numerous awards and prizes. *Address:* The Withers Cottage, 5286 Sycamore Avenue, Riverdale, NY 10471, USA.

KOROTYCH, Vitaliy Alekseyevich; Russian/Ukrainian writer and poet; b. 26 May 1936, Kiev, Ukraine; m. Zinaida Korotych 1958; two s. *Education:* Kiev Medical Inst. *Career:* physician 1959–66; Ed. Ukrainian literary journal Ranok 1966–77; Ed.-in-Chief Vsesvit magazine 1978–86; Ed.-in-Chief Ogonyok weekly magazine 1986–91; USSR People's Deputy 1989–91; Prof. Boston Univ., USA 1991–98, returned to Moscow; ed. Boulevard magazine and others 1998–; mem. Ukrainian Writers' Union, sec., 1966–69. *Publications:* Golden Hands, 1961; The Smell of Heaven, 1962; Cornflower Street, 1963; O Canada!, 1966; Poetry, 1967; Metronome (novel), 1982; The Face of Enmity (novel), 1984; Memory, Bread and Love, 1986; Le Visage de la haine (travel essays), 1988; Glasnost und Perestroika, 1990; The Waiting Room (memoirs, Vol. I), 1991; On My Behalf (memoirs, Vol. II), 2000. Other: many translations from English into Ukrainian and other Slavonic languages. *Honours:* two State Prizes, USSR; A. Tolstoy Prize, 1982; Int. Julius Fuchik Prize, 1984; Wiental Prize, Georgetown Univ. (USA), 1987; Int. Ed. of the year, W P Revue (USA), 1989. *Address:* Trifonovskaya str. 11, Apt 156, 127018 Moscow, Russia.

KORZENIK, Diana; academic and writer; b. 15 March 1941, New York, NY, USA. *Education:* Oberlin College; BA, Vassar College; Master's Programme, Columbia University; DEd, Graduate School of Education, Harvard University. *Career:* Prof. Emerita, Massachusetts College of Art, Boston; mem. Friends of Longfellow House, founder, board mem.; American Antiquarian Society; Massachusetts Historical Society. *Publications:* Art and Cognition (ed. with Leondar & Perkins), 1977; Drawn to Art, 1986; Art Making and Education (with Maurice Brown), 1993; The Cultivation of American Artists (ed. with Sloat and Barnhill), 1997. Contributions: Professional journals and to magazines. *Honours:* Boston Globe L. L. Winship Literary Award, 1986; National Art Education Asscn Lowenfeld Award, 1998. *Address:* 7 Norman Road, Newton Highlands, MA 02461, USA.

KORZHAVIN, Naum; Russian writer and poet; b. (Mandel Emmanuel Moiseyevich Korzhavin), 14 Oct. 1925, Kiev, Ukraine. *Education:* Karaganda Mining Inst.; Gorky Inst. of Literature, Moscow, 1959. *Career:* first publication 1941; exiled to West (USA) 1974; revisited Moscow 1989; citizenship and membership of Writers' Union restored 1990. *Publications:* The Years, 1963; Where Are You?, 1964; Bread; Children in Auschwitz; Autumn in Karaganda; Verse, 1981; Selected Verse, 1983; Interlacements, 1987; Letter to Moscow, 1991; The Time is Given, 1992; To Myself, 1998. Contributions: émigré dissident journal, Kontinent. *Address:* 28c Colborne Road, Apt 2, Brighton, MA 02135, USA.

KOSTASH, Myrna Ann, BA, MA; Canadian writer; b. 2 Sept. 1944, Edmonton. *Education:* Univ. of Alberta, Univ. of Toronto. *Career:* writer-in-residence, Regina Public Library 1996–97; Lecturer, Univ. of Alberta 1998, 1999; mem. Writers' Union of Canada (chair. 1993–94), Writers' Guild of Alberta (pres. 1989–90), Canadian Conference of the Arts (bd of govs 1996–), PEN Canada. *Publications:* All of Baba's Children 1977, Long Way From Home 1980, No Kidding 1988, Bloodlines 1993, The Doomed Bridegroom: A Memoir 1998, The Next Canada: In Search of the Future Nation 2000; contrib. to Saturday Night, Canadian Forum, Brick, Border Crossings, Prairie Fire, Journal of Canadian Studies, mostovi, Literature na swiece. *Honours:* Canada Council Senior Artist Grants, Nat. Magazine Silver Prize. *Literary Agent:* Westwood Creative Artists, 94 Harbord Street, Toronto, ON M5S 1G6, Canada. *Address:* 10415 87th Avenue, Edmonton, AB T6E 2P4, Canada.

KOSTELANETZ, Richard (Cory); Writer, Poet, Critic, Artist and Composer; b. 14 May 1940, New York, NY, USA. *Education:* AB, Brown University, 1962; Graduate Studies, King's College, London, 1964–65; MA, Columbia University, 1966; Study in music and theatre, Morley College, London, and New School for Social Research, New York. *Career:* Literary Dir, Future Press, New York, 1976–; Sole Proprietor, Arcuae Editions, New York, 1978–; Contributing Ed. to various journals; Guest lecturer and reader at many colleges and universities; numerous exhibitions as an artist; mem. American PEN; American Society of Composers, Authors, and Publishers; International Asscn of Art Critics; Fellow, New Asscn of Sephardic/Mizrahi Artists and Writers International, 2000–02; others. *Publications:* Poetry: Visual Language, 1970; I Articulations/Short Fictions, 1974; Portraits From Memory, 1975; Numbers: Poems and Stories, 1976; Rain Rains Rain, 1976; Illuminations, 1977; Numbers Two, 1977; Richard Kostelanetz, 1980; Turfs/Arenas/Fields/Pitches, 1980; Arenas/Fields/Pitches/Turfs, 1982; Fields/Pitches/Turfs/Arenas, 1990; Solos, Duets, Trios, and Choruses, 1991; Wordworks: Poems Selected and New, 1993; Paritions, 1993; Repartitions, 1994; More Wordworks, 2002. Fiction: In the Beginning (novel), 1971; Constructs, 5 vols, 1975–91; One Night Stood (novel), 1977; Tabula Rasa: A Constructivist Novel, 1978; Exhaustive Parallel Intervals (novel), 1979; Fifty Untitled Constructivist Fictions, 1991; 3-Element Stories, 1998; many others. Non-Fiction: Recyclings: A Literary Autobiogrphy, 2 vols, 1974, 1984; The End of Intelligent Writing: Literary Politics in America, 1974; Metamorphosis in the Arts, 1980; The Old Poetries and the New, 1981; The Grants-Fix: Publicly Funded Literary Granting in America, 1987; The Old Fictions and the New, 1987; On Innovative Music(ian)s, 1989; Unfinished Business: An Intellectual Non-history, 1990; The New Poetries and Some Old, 1991; Published Encomia, 1967–91, 1991; On Innovative Art(ist)s, 1992; A Dictionary of the Avant-Gardes, 1993; On Innovative Performance(s), 1994; Fillmore East: 25 Years After: Recollections of Rock Theatre, 1995; An ABC of Contemporary Reading, 1995; Crimes of Culture, 1995; Radio Writings, 1995; John Cage (Ex)plain(ed), 1996; Thirty Years of Critical Engagement with John Cage, 1996; One Million Words of Booknotes, 1958–1993, 1996; Political Essays, 1999; Three Canadian Geniuses, 2001; Thirty-Five Years of Visible Writing, 2003. Plays: Vocal Shorts: Collected Performance Texts, 1998. Editor: many books. Other: Films; Videotapes; Radio Scripts; Recordings. Contributions: many anthologies; numerous poems, articles, essays, reviews in journals and other publications. *Honours:* Woodrow Wilson Fellowship, 1962–63; Fulbright Fellowship, 1964–65; Pulitzer Fellowship, 1965–66; Guggenheim Fellowship, 1967; One of Best Books, American Institute of Graphic Arts, 1976; Pushcart Prize, 1977; Deutscher Akademischer Austauschdienst Stipend, Berlin, 1981–83; American Society of Composers, Authors, and Publishers Awards, 1983–91. *Address:* PO Box 444, Prince St Station, New York, NY 10012-0008 USA. *Website:* www.richardkostelanetz.com.

KOTKER, (Mary) Zane, (Maggie Strong); writer; b. 2 Jan. 1934, Waterbury, CT, USA; m. Norman Kotker 1965; one s. one d. *Education:* MA, Columbia University 1959–60. *Publications:* novels: Bodies in Motion 1972, A Certain Man 1976, White Rising 1981, Mainstay (as Maggie Strong) 1988, Try to Remember 1997. *Honours:* National Endowment for the Arts Grant 1972.

KOTZWINKLE, William; Writer; b. 22 Nov. 1938, Scranton, Pennsylvania, USA; m. Elizabeth Gundy, 1970. *Education:* Rider College; Pennsylvania State University. *Publications:* Elephant Bangs Train, 1971; Hermes 3000, 1971; The Fat Man, 1974; Night-Book, 1974; Swimmer in the Secret Sea, 1975; Doctor Rat, 1976; Fata Morgana, 1977; Herr Nightingale and the Satin Woman, 1978; Jack in the Box, 1980; Christmas at Fontaine's, 1982; E.T., the Extra-Terrestrial: A Novel, 1982; Superman III, 1983; Queen of Swords, 1983; E.T., the Book of the Green Planet: A New Novel, 1985; Seduction in Berlin, 1985; Jewell of the Moon, 1985; The Exile, 1987; The Midnight Examiner, 1989; Hot Jazz Trio, 1989; The Game of Thirty, 1994. Other: many children's books. *Honours:* National Magazine Awards for Fiction, 1972, 1975; O. Henry Prize, 1975; World Fantasy Award for Best Novel, 1977; North Dakota Children's Choice Award, 1983, and Buckeye Award, 1984. *Address:* c/o Houghton Mifflin Co, 1 Beacon St, Boston, MA 02108, USA.

KOURVETARIS, George A.; Prof. of Sociology, Writer and Ed.; b. 21 Nov. 1933, Eleochorion, Arcadia, Greece; m. 1st Toula Savas 22 Nov. 1966 (divorced 1987); two s. one d.; m. 2nd Vassia Dumas Siapkaris 1998. *Education:* Assoc. Degree, Teacher's College, Tripolis, Greece, 1955; BS, Loyola University, Chicago, 1963; MA, Roosevelt University, Chicago, 1965; PhD, Northwestern University, Evanston, IL, 1969. *Career:* Asst Prof., Chicago City College, 1967; Fellow and Lecturer, Northwestern University, 1967–68; Asst Prof., 1969–73, Assoc. Prof., 1973–78, Prof. of Sociology, 1978–, Northern Illinois University, DeKalb; Founder-Ed., The Journal of Political and Military Sociology, 1973–; mem. American Sociological Asscn; European Community Studies Asscn; Modern Greek Studies Asscn; Southeast European Asscn. *Publications:* First and Second Generation Greeks in Chicago: An Inquiry Into Their Stratification and Mobility Patterns, 1971; Social Origins and Political Orientations of Officer Corps in a World Perspective (co-author), 1973; World Perspectives in the Sociology of the Military (co-ed.), 1977; Political Sociology: Readings in Research and Theory (co-ed.), 1980; Society and Politics: An Overview and Reappraisal of Political Sociology (co-author), 1980; A Profile of Modern Greece: In Search of Identity (co-author), 1987; Social Thought, 1994; The Impact of European Integration: Political, Sociological, and Economic Changes (co-ed.), 1996; Political Sociology: Structure and Process, 1997; Studies on Greek Americans, 1997; Studies in Modern Greek Society and Politics, 1999; The New Balkans: Disintegration and Reconstruction (co-ed.), 2002. Contributions: various scholarly books and journals, over 70 articles and over 35 book reviews; several poems in Greek and English in journals and newspapers. Other: TV series on the contributions of classical Greece to Western civilization, 2003–. *Honours:* various academic grants and awards; Heritage Award, Greek American Community Services, Chicago, 1987; Recognition Award, Hellenic Council on Education, Chicago, 1991; Dept Recognition Award for the Silver Anniversary of the Founding of the Journal of Political and Military Sociology, 1998. *Address:* 109 Andresen Ct, DeKalb, IL 60115, USA. *E-mail:* ykourvet@niu.edu.

KOZER, José; academic, poet and writer; b. 28 March 1940, Havana, Cuba; m. Guadalupe Kozer 1974; two d. *Education:* Law, Univ. of Havana; BA, New York Univ., 1965; MA, PhD equivalent, 1983, Queens College, CUNY. *Career:* Prof. of Spanish Literature and Language, Queens College, CUNY, 1960–97; fmr co-ed., Enlace magazine, New York. *Publications:* Poetry: 14

chapbooks, 29 books, incl.: Padres y otras profesiones, 1972; De Chepén a La Habana, 1973; Por la libre, 1973; Poemas de Guadalupe, 1974; Y así tomaron posesión en las ciudades, 1975; Este judío de números y letras, 1975; Nueve láminas, 1980; La rueca de los semblantes, 1980; Jarrón de las abreviaturas, 1980; Antología breve, 1981; The Ark Upon the Number, 1982; Bajo este cien, 1983; La garza sin sombras, 1985; Diptico de la restitucion, 1986; El carillón de los muertos, 1987; Carece de causa, 1988; Prójimos/Intimates, 1990; De donde oscilan los seres en sus proporciones, 1990; Una índole, 1993; Trazas del lirondo, 1993; A Caná, 1995; Et mutabile, 1995; La maquinaria ilimitada, 1996; AAA1144, 1997; No buscan reflejarse: Antología poética (1972–1980), 2000; Stet, 2003. Other: three books of prose, incl.: Medusario Muestra de Poesia Latinoamericana (ed. with Roberto Echavarren, Jacobo Sefamí), 1996. Contributions: numerous poetry magazines, literary journals, and newspapers in North and South America, and Spain. *Honours:* Gulbenkin Prize, Portugal, 1967; CINTAS Foundation Award, 1973; Julio Tovar Poetry Prize, 1974; CUNY/PSC Foundation Award, 1991. *Address:* 500 Three Islands Blvd, Apt 1209, Hallandale, FL 33009, USA. *E-mail:* josekozer@aol.com.

KOZIOŁ-PRZYBYLAK, Urszula; Writer, Playwright and Poet; b. 20 June 1931, Rakówka, Poland; m. Felikes Prybylak 1960. *Education:* BA, Univ. of Wroclaw. *Career:* High School teacher, 1954–71; Literary Ed., Poglady (Opinions), 1956, Odra, 1971–. *Publications:* Poetry: Gumowe klocki (Rubber Blocks), 1957; W. rytmie korzeni (In the Rhythm of the Roots), 1963; Smuga i promien (A Trace and a Ray), 1965; Lista obecnosci (Attendance Record), 1967; W. rytmie slonca (In the Rhythm of the Sun), 1974; Wybór wierszy (Select Poetry), 1976; Poezje wybrane (2nd edn), 1986; W. ptynnym slernie, 1998; Slany nieocsynislosci, 1999. Novels: Postoje pamieci (Stations of Memory, 3rd edn), 1977; Ptaki dla mysli (Birds for Thought, 2nd edn), 1983. Short stories: Z poczekalni (From the Waiting Room), 1978; Osobnego sny i prypowiesci (The Dreams and Parables of the Separate One), 1978; Noli me tangere, 1984. Plays: Król malowany (The Painted King), 1978; Trzy Swiaty (Three Worlds), 1981; Podwórkowcy (Yard Kids), 1982; Sportolino, 1982; Psujony (Spoilers), 1982; Zbieg z Babony (Escapee from Babona), 1983; Dziwna podróz Baczka do Gryslandii (Strange Voyage of Bug to Grysland), 1984; Magiczne imie (A Magic Name), 1985; O stolku (About a Chair), 1987; Zalmik (Laments), 1989; Zgaga, 1990; Postoje siowa (Stations of Words), 1995; Wielda Pawza (A Great Pause), 1996. Other: Osobnepo sny i pnypomisci, 1997. *Honours:* Literary Prize, Autumnal Encounters Festival of Gdańsk, 1963; Wladyslaw Broniewski Prize, Polish Students' Asscn, 1964; Literary Prize of Wroclaw, 1965; Koscielski Foundation of Geneva Prize, 1969; Polish Ministry of Culture Literary Prize, 1971; Kommandeur-Kreuz zum Orden der Wiedergelurf Polens, 1997; Kultur Preis Schlesien, Hanover, 1998; PEN-Club Award 1998. *Address:* Komandorska 37/6, 53-342 Wroclaw, Poland. *Telephone:* (71) 3673853. *Fax:* (71) 3435516.

KOZOL, Jonathan; Writer; b. 5 Sept. 1936, Boston, MA, USA. *Education:* BA, Harvard University, 1958; Graduate Studies, Magdalen College, Oxford, 1958–59. *Career:* Education activist; Visiting lecturer at innumerable colleges and universities, 1971–; mem. Asscn of American Rhodes Scholars; Fellowship of Reconciliation; National Coalition for the Homeless; National Coalition of Education Activists; PEN. *Publications:* Death at an Early Age: The Destruction of the Hearts and Minds of Negro Children in the Boston Public Schools, 1967; Free Schools, 1972, revised edn as Alternative Schools: A Guide for Educators and Parents, 1982; The Night is Dark and I am Far from Home, 1975; Children of the Revolution, 1978; Prisoners of Silence: Breaking the Bonds of Adult Illiteracy in the United States, 1979; On Being a Teacher, 1981; Illiterate America, 1985; Rachel and Her Children: Homeless Families in America, 1988; Savage Inequalities: Children in America's School, 1991; Amazing Grace: The Lives of Children and the Conscience of a Nation, 1995; Ordinary Resurrections: Children in the Years of Hope, 2000; Will Standards Save Public Education? (with Deborah Heier), 2000. Contributions: numerous periodicals. *Honours:* Rhodes Scholar, 1958–59; National Book Award, 1968; Guggenheim Fellowships, 1970, 1984; Field Foundation Fellow, 1972; Ford Foundation Fellow, 1976; Rockefeller Foundation Fellowships, 1978, 1983; Robert F. Kennedy Book Award, 1988; Conscience in Media Award, American Society of Journalists and Authors, 1988; Christopher Awards, 1988, 2000; New England Book Award, 1992; Anisfield-Wolf Book Award, 1995. *Address:* PO Box 145, Byfield, MA 01922, USA.

KRAMER, Aaron; Prof. of English Emeritus, Author, Poet and Trans; b. 13 Dec. 1921, New York, NY, USA; m. Katherine Kolodny, 10 March 1942, two d. *Education:* BA, 1941, MA, 1951, Brooklyn College, CUNY; PhD, New York University, 1966. *Career:* Instructor, 1961–63, Asst Prof., 1963–66, Adelphi University; Lecturer, Queens College, CUNY, 1966–68; Assoc. Prof., 1966–70, Prof. of English, 1970–91, Prof. Emeritus, 1991–, Dowling College, Oakdale, New York; mem. American Society of Composers, Authors and Publishers; Asscn for Poetry Therapy; Edna St Vincent Millay Society; e. e. cummings Society; International Acad. of Poets; PEN; Walt Whitman Birthplace Asscn, exec. board, 1969–85. *Publications:* The Glass Mountain, 1946; Poetry and Prose of Heine, 1948; Denmark Vesey, 1952; The Tinderbox, 1954; Serenade, 1957; Tune of the Calliope, 1958; Moses, 1962; Rumshinsky's Hat, 1964; Rilke: Visions of Christ, 1967; The Prophetic Tradition in American Poetry, 1968; Poetry Therapy (co-author), 1969; Melville's Poetry, 1972; On the Way to Palermo, 1973; Poetry the Healer (co-author), 1973; The Emperor of Atlantis, 1975; O Golden Land, 1976; Death Takes a Holiday, 1979; Carousel Parkway, 1980; The Burning Bush, 1983; In the Suburbs, 1986; A Century of Yiddish Poetry, 1989; Indigo, 1991; Life Guidance Through Literature (co-author), 1991; Dora Teitelboim: Selected Poems (ed. and trans.), 1995. Contributions: Professional journals. *Honours:* Hart Crane Memorial Award, 1969; Eugene O'Neill Theatre Center Prize, 1983; National Endowment for the Humanities Grant, 1993; Festschrift published in his honour, 1995. *Address:* 96 Van Bomel Blvd, Oakdale, NY 11769, USA.

KRAMER, Dale Vernon; academic and writer; b. 13 July 1936, Mitchell, SD, USA; m. Cheris Gamble Kramer 1960; two c. *Education:* BS, South Dakota State University, 1958; MA, 1960, PhD, 1963, Case Western Reserve University. *Career:* Instructor, 1962–63, Asst Prof., 1963–65, Ohio University; Asst Prof., 1965–67, Assoc. Prof., 1967–71, Prof. of English, 1971–96, Acting Head, Dept of English, 1982, 1986–87, Assoc. Dean, College of Arts and Sciences, 1992–95, University of Illinois; Assoc. Mem., Center for Advanced Study, Urbana, IL, 1971; Assoc. Vice-Provost, University of Oregon, 1990; mem. Asscn of American University Profs; Asscn for Documentary Editing; MLA; Society for Textual Scholarship; Victorian Periodicals Society. *Publications:* Charles Robert Maturin, 1973; Thomas Hardy: The Forms of Tragedy, 1975; Critical Approaches to the Fiction of Thomas Hardy (ed.), 1979; Thomas Hardy: The Woodlanders (ed.), 1981; Thomas Hardy: The Mayor of Casterbridge (ed.), 1987; Critical Essays on Thomas Hardy: The Novels (ed.), 1990; Thomas Hardy: Tess of the d'Urbervilles, 1991; The Cambridge Companion to Thomas Hardy, 1999. Contributions: Professional journals. *Honours:* American Philosophical Society Grants, 1969, 1986; National Endowment for the Humanities Grant, 1986; Boydston Prize, Asscn for Documentary Editing, 1997. *Address:* c/o Dept of English, University of Illinois at Urbana-Champaign, Champaign, IL 61801, USA.

KRAMER, Lawrence (Eliot); Prof. of English and Music, Writer and Ed.; b. 21 Aug. 1946, Philadelphia, PA, USA; m. Nancy S. Leonard, 3 March 1973. *Education:* BA, University of Pennsylvania, 1968; MPhil, 1970, PhD, 1972, Yale University. *Career:* Asst Prof. of English, University of Pennsylvania, 1972–78; Asst Prof., 1978–81, Assoc. Prof., 1981–87, Prof. of English and Comparative Literature, 1987–95, Prof. of English and Music, 1995–, Fordham University; Co-Ed., 19th Century Music; Visiting Prof., Yale University, 1994, Columbia University, 2001; mem. American Musicological Society; Society for Music Theory. *Publications:* Music and Poetry: The Nineteenth Century and After, 1985; Music as Cultural Practice, 1800–1900, 1990; Classical Music and Postmodern Knowledge, 1995; After the Lovedeath: Sexual Violence and the Making of Culture, 1997; Franz Schubert: Sexuality, Subjectivity, Song, 1998; Walt Whitman and Modern Music: War, Desire, and the Trials of Nationhood (ed.), 2000; Musical Meaning: Toward a Critical History, 2001, Opera and Modern Culture: Wagner and Strauss 2004. Contributions: scholarly books and journals. *Address:* 791 Slate Quarry Rd, Rhinebeck, NY 12572, USA.

KRAMER, Dame Leonie Judith, AC, BA, DPhil; Australian academic, writer and editor; b. 1 Oct. 1924, Melbourne, Vic.; m. Harold Kramer 1952 (deceased); two d. *Education:* University of Melbourne, University of Oxford. *Career:* Tutor, St Hugh's College, Oxford, 1949–52; Assoc. Prof., University of New South Wales, 1963–68; Prof. of Australian Literature, 1968–89, Deputy Chancellor, 1989–91, Prof. Emeritus, 1989–, Chancellor, 1991–2001, University of Sydney; Chair, Board of Dirs, National Institute of Dramatic Art, 1987–91; Deputy Chair. and Senior Fellow, Institute of Public Affairs, 1988–96; mem. Australian Acad. of Humanities, fellow; Pres., Order of Australia Asscn, 2001–04. *Publications:* Henry Handel Richardson and Some of Her Sources, 1954; Companion to Australia Felix, 1962; Coast to Coast, 1963–64, 1965; Myself When Laura: Fact and Fiction in Henry Handel Richardson's School Career, 1966; Henry Handel Richardson, 1967; Language and Literature: A Synthesis (with R. D. Eagleson), 1976; A. D. Hope (co-ed.), 1979; Oxford History of Australian Literature, 1981; Oxford Anthology of Australian Literature, 1985; My Country: Australian Poetry and Short Stories, 2 vols, 1985; James McAuley: Poetry, Essays and Personal Commentary (ed.), 1988; David Campbell: Collected Poems (ed.), 1989; Collected Poems of James McAuley (ed.), 1995. Contributions: numerous journals. *Honours:* hon. doctorates. *Address:* 12 Vaucluse Road, Vaucluse, NSW 2030, Australia.

KRAMER, Lotte Karoline; Poet and Painter; b. 22 Oct. 1923, Mainz, Germany; m. Frederic Kramer, 20 Feb. 1943, one s. *Education:* Art; History of Art. *Career:* mem. Decorative and Fine Arts Society; PEN; Peterborough Museum Society; Poetry Society; Ver Poets; Writers in Schools. *Publications:* Poetry: Scrolls, 1979; Ice Break, 1980; Family Arrivals, 1981; A Lifelong House, 1983; The Shoemaker's Wife, 1987; The Desecration of Trees, 1994; Earthquake and Other Poems, 1994; Selected and New Poems, 1980–1997; The Phantom Lane, 2000; Heimweh/Homesick, 1999. Contributions: anthologies, newspapers, reviews, quarterlies and journals. *Honours:* Second Prize, York Poetry Competition, 1972; Bursary, Eastern Arts Board, 1999; Second Prize, Manchester Cathedral Poetry Competition, 2002. *Address:* 4 Apsley Way, Longthorpe, Peterborough PE3 9NE, England.

KRANTZ, Judith (Tarcher); Writer; b. 9 Jan. 1928, New York, NY, USA; m. Stephen Falk Krantz, 19 Feb. 1954, two s. *Education:* BA, Wellesley

College, 1948. *Career:* Fashion Ed., Good Housekeeping, 1949–56; Contributor, McCalls, 1956–59, Ladies Home Journal, 1959–71; Contributing West Coast Ed., Cosmopolitan, 1971–79; mem. PEN. *Publications:* Scruples, 1978; Princess Daisy, 1980; Mistral's Daughter, 1982; I'll Take Manhattan, 1986; Till We Meet Again, 1989; Dazzle, 1990; Scruples Two, 1992; Lovers, 1994; Spring Collection, 1996; The Jewels of Tessa Kent, 1998; Sex and Shopping: Confessions of a Nice Jewish Girl, 2000. *Literary Agent:* Janklow & Nesbit Associates, 445 Park Ave, New York, NY 10022, USA.

KRAPF, Norbert; Prof. of English and Writer; b. 14 Nov. 1943, Jasper, IN, USA; m. 13 June 1970, one s. one d. *Education:* BA, English, St Joseph's College, IN, 1965; MA, English, 1966, PhD, English and American Literature, 1971, University of Notre Dame. *Career:* Faculty, 1970–84, Prof. of English, 1984–, Long Island University. *Publications:* Arriving on Paumanok, 1979; Lines Drawn from Durer, 1981; Circus Songs, 1983; A Dream of Plum Blossoms, 1985; Under Open Sky: Poets on William Cullen Bryant (ed.), 1986; Beneath the Cherry Sapling: Legends from Franconia (ed. and trans.), 1988; Shadows on the Sundial: Selected Early Poems of Rainer Maria Rilke (ed. and trans.), 1990; Somewhere in Southern Indiana: Poems of Midwestern Origins, 1993; Finding the Grain: Pioneer Journals and Letters from Dubois County, IN, 1996; Blue-eyed Grass: Poems of Germany, 1997: Bittersweet Along the Expressway: Poems of Long Island, 2000; The Country I Come From: Poems, 2002. Contributions: Professional journals. *Honours:* Lucille Medwick Memorial Award, Poetry Society of America, 1999. *Address:* c/o Dept of English, Long Island University, Brookville, NY 11548, USA.

KRATT, Mary; Writer and Poet; b. 7 June 1936, Beckley, West Virginia, USA; m. Emil F. Kratt, 29 Aug. 1959, one s. two d. *Education:* BA, Agnes Scott College, 1958; MA, University of North Carolina at Charlotte, 1992. *Career:* mem. North Carolina Writers Conference, chair., 1991–92; North Carolina Writers Network, board mem.; Poets and Writers. *Publications:* Southern Is, 1985; Legacy: The Myers Park Story, 1986; The Imaginative Spirit: Literary Heritage of Charlotte and Mecklenburg County, 1988; A Little Charlotte Scrapbook, 1990; A Bird in the House, 1991; The Only Thing I Fear is a Cow and a Drunken Man (poems and prose), 1991; Charlotte: Spirit of the New South, 1992; On the Steep Side (poems), 1993; Small Potatoes (poems), 1999; Valley (poems), 2000; Remembering Charlotte: Postcards from a New South City 1905–50, 2000; New South Women, 2001. Contributions: newspapers, reviews, and magazines. *Honours:* Lyricist Prize, 1982; Oscar Arnold Young Award for Best Original Poetry Book by a North Carolinian, 1983; Sidney Lanier Award, North Carolina Poetry Society, 1985; St Andrews Writer and Community Award, 1994; Distinguished Alumnae Writer Award, Agnes Scott College, 1994; MacDowell Colony Residency, 1996; Brockman Poetry Book Award, 2000. *Address:* 3328 Providence Plantation Lane, Charlotte, NC 28270, USA.

KRAUSS, Bruno (see Bulmer, Henry Kenneth).

KRAUSSER, Helmut; German novelist; b. 1964, Esslinger. *Education:* Univ. of Munich. *Career:* fmrly nightwatchman, pop singer, radio announcer, journalist. *Publications:* novels: Thanatos: Das schwarze Buch 1986, Könige über dem Ozean 1989, Fette Welt (Fat World) 1992, Der grosse Bagarozy (trans. as The Great Bagarozy) 1997, Schweine und Elefanten 1999. *Address:* c/o Dedalus Ltd, Langford Lodge, St Judith's Lane, Sawtry, Cambridgeshire PE28 5XE, England. *E-mail:* info@dedalusbooks.com. *Website:* www.dedalusbooks.com.

KRAUZER, Steven M(ark), (Terry Nelson Bonner); Writer; b. 9 June 1948, Jersey City, NJ, USA; m. Dorri T. Karasek, 2 Nov. 1992, two d. *Education:* BA, Yale University, 1970; MA, English Literature, University of New Hampshire, 1974. *Career:* mem. Writers Guild of America West; Authors' Guild; Authors League; MWA. *Publications:* The Cord Series, 1982–86; The Executioner Series, 1982–83; Blaze, 1983; The Diggers, 1983; The Dennison's War Series, 1984–86; Framework, 1989; Brainstorm, 1991; Rojak's Rule, 1992. Anthologies: Great Action Stories, 1977; The Great American Detective, 1978; Stories into Film, 1979; Triquarterly 48: Western Stories, 1980. Contributions: Magazines. *Address:* c/o Virginia Barber Literary Agency, 101 Fifth Ave, New York, NY 10003, USA.

KRAWIEC, Richard; Writer; b. 9 May 1952, Brockton, MA, USA; m. Mary Sturrock, 8 Aug. 1983, two s. *Education:* BS, Suffolk University, 1977; MA, University of New Hampshire, 1983. *Career:* mem. Associated Writing Programs; Authors' Guild; Poets and Writers. *Publications:* Time Sharing, 1986; Cardinal: A Contemporary Anthology from North Carolina (ed.), 1986; Faith in What?, 1996; And Fools of God, 2000. Contributions: newspapers and magazines. *Honours:* National Endowment for the Arts Fellowship, 1992; North Carolina Arts Council Fellowship, 1999. *Address:* 319 Wilmot Dr., Raleigh, NC 27606, USA.

KRESS, Nancy; Teacher and Writer; b. 20 Jan. 1948, Buffalo, NY, USA; m. 1st Michael Kress (divorced); two s.; m. 2nd Mark P. Donnelly 19 Aug. 1988. *Education:* BS, SUNY at Plattsburgh, 1969; MS, Education, 1978, MA, English, 1979, SUNY at Brockport. *Career:* Elementary School Teacher, Penn Yan, 1970–73; Adjunct Instructor, SUNY at Brockport, 1980–; Senior Copywriter, Stanton and Hucko, Rochester, 1984–; mem. SFWA. *Publications:* The Prince of Morning Bells, 1981; The Golden Grove, 1984; The White Pipes, 1985; Trinity and Other Stories, 1985; An Alien Light, 1988; Brain Rose, 1990; Maximum Light, 1998. Contributions: anthologies and periodicals. *Honours:* Nebula Award, SFWA, 1985.

KRIEGER, Murray; University Research Prof. and Writer; b. 27 Nov. 1923, Newark, NJ, USA; m. Joan Alice Stone, 15 June 1947, one s. one d. *Education:* Rutgers University, 1940–42; MA, University of Chicago, 1948; PhD, Ohio State University, 1952. *Career:* Prof. of English and Dir of the Program in Criticism, University of California at Irvine, 1966–85; Prof. of English, University of California at Los Angeles, 1972–83; University Prof., 1974–94, Co-Dir, 1975–77, Dir, 1977–81, School of Criticism and Theory, Hon. Senior Fellow, 1981–, Dir, Humanities Research Institute, 1987–89, University Research Prof., 1994–, University of California; mem. Acad. of Literary Studies; American Acad. of Arts and Sciences, fellow; International Asscn of University Profs of English; MLA. *Publications:* The Problems of Aesthetics (ed. with Eliseo Vivas), 1953; The New Apologists for Poetry, 1956; The Tragic Vision, 1960; A Window to Criticism: Shakespeare's Sonnets and Modern Poetics, 1964; Northrop Frye in Modern Criticism (ed.), 1966; The Play and Place of Criticism, 1967; the Classic Vision, 1971; Theory of Criticism: A Tradition and Its System, 1976; Directions for Criticism: Structuralism and Its Alternatives (ed. with L. S. Dembo), 1977; Poetic Presence and Illusion, 1979; Arts on the Level, 1981; The Aims of Representation: Subject/Text/History (ed.), 1987; Words About Words About Words: Theory, Criticism and the Literary Text, 1988; A Reopening of Closure: Organicism Against Itself, 1989; Ekphrasis: The Illusion of the Natural Sign, 1992; The Ideological Imperative: Repression and Resistance in Recent American Theory, 1993; The Institution of Theory, 1994. Contributions: scholarly publications. *Honours:* several Research Fellowships; Humboldt Foundation Research Prize, Federal Republic of Germany, 1986–87; Medal, University of California at Irvine, 1990. *Address:* 407 Pinecrest Dr., Laguna Beach, CA 92651, USA.

KRIPKE, Saul (Aaron); Philosopher, University Educator and Writer; b. 13 Nov. 1940, Bay Shore, NY, USA; m. Margaret P. Gilbert, 1976. *Education:* BA, Harvard University, 1962. *Career:* Fellow, 1963–66, Lecturer, 1966–68, Harvard University; Lecturer-Asst Prof., Princeton University, 1965–66; Assoc. Prof., 1968–72, Prof., 1972–76, Rockefeller University, New York; Visiting Fellow, All Souls College, Oxford, 1977–78, 1989–90; Prof. of Philosophy, Princeton University, 1977–98; Visiting Prof., Hebrew University, Jerusalem, 1998–; mem. American Acad. of Arts and Sciences, fellow; Asscn for Symbolic Logic, exec. committee, 1997–99; British Acad., corresponding fellow. *Publications:* Naming and Necessity, 1980; Wittgenstein on Rules and Private Language, 1982. Contributions: scholarly books and professional journals. *Honours:* Fulbright Fellowship, 1962–63; Guggenheim Fellowships, 1968–69, 1977–78; Hon. doctorates, University of Nebraska, 1977, Johns Hopkins University, 1997, University of Haifa, 1998; National Endowment for the Humanities Grant, 1998. *Address:* c/o Dept of Philosophy, Hebrew University, Jerusalem, Israel.

KRIST, Gary Michael; Writer; b. 23 May 1957, New Jersey, USA; m. Elizabeth Cheng, 2 Oct. 1983, one d. *Education:* AB, Comparative Literature, Princeton University, 1979; Fulbright Scholar, Universität Konstanz, 1980. *Career:* mem. PEN; National Book Critics Circle. *Publications:* The Garden State (short stories), 1988; Bone by Bone (short stories), 1994; Bad Chemistry (novel), 1998; Chaos Theory (novel), 1999; Extravagance (novel), 2002. Contributions: New York Times Book Review; Salon Internet; Washington Post; Hudson Review; New Republic. *Honours:* Sue Kaufman Prize, American Acad. of Arts and Letters, 1989. *Literary Agent:* Eric Simonoff, Janklow & Nesbit Associates, 445 Park Ave, New York, NY 10022, USA. *Address:* 22 W 23rd St, New York, NY 10010, USA. *E-mail:* gary@garykrist.com. *Website:* www.garykrist.com.

KRISTEVA, Julia; French academic, linguist, psychoanalyst and writer; b. 24 June 1941, Silven, Bulgaria; m.; one s. *Education:* Diploma, University of Sofia, 1963; Preparation for Doctorate, Acad. of Sciences and Comparative Literature, Sofia; École pratique des Hautes-Études, Paris; Doctorate, French Literature, 1968; Doctorat d'Etat es Lettres, University of Paris VII, 1973. *Career:* Researcher in Linguistics and French Literature, Laboratory of Social Anthropology, l'École des Hautes Études en Sciences Sociales, 1967–73; Prof. of Linguistics, 1973–99, Prof. classe exceptionelle, 1999–, University of Paris VII; Permanent Visiting Prof., Dept of French Literature, Columbia University, New York, 1974; Private Psychoanalytic Practice, Paris, 1978–; Permanent Visiting Prof., Dept of Comparative Literature, University of Toronto, Canada, 1992; mem. Editorial Board, Tel quel, 1970–82; Société psychanalytique de Paris. *Publications:* Séméiotike: Recherches pour une sémanalyse (trans. as Desire in Language: A Semiotic Approach to Literature and Art) 1969, Le Langage, cet inconnu, Une initiation a la linguistique (trans. as Language: The Unknown: An Initiation into Linguistics) 1969, Le Texte du roman 1970, La Révolution du langage poétique (trans. as Revolution in Poetic Language) 1974, Des Chinoises (trans. as About Chinese Women) 1974, La Traversée des signes (with others) 1975, Polylogue 1977, Folle Vérité (with Jean Michel Ribettes) 1979, Pouvoirs de l'horreur, Essai sur l'abjection (trans. as Powers of Horror: An Essay on Abjection) 1980, Histoires d'amour (trans. as Tales of Love) 1983, Au commencement était l'amour: Psychanalyse et foi (trans. as In the Beginning Was Love: Psychoanalysis and Faith) 1985, Soleil noir: Depression et melancolie (trans. as Black Sun: Depression and Melancholia) 1987, Etrangers à nous-mêmes (trans. as Strangers to Ourselves)

1988, Lettre ouverte à Harlem Désir (trans. as Nations Without Nationalism) 1990, Les Samouraïs (trans. as The Samurai) 1990, Le Veil Homme et les loups (trans. as The Old Man and the Wolves) 1991, Les Nouvelles Maladies de l'âmé (trans. as New Maladies of the Soul) 1993, Le Temps sensible: Proust et l'Expérience littéraire (trans. as Time and Sense: Proust and the Experience of Literature) 1994, Possessions 1994, La révolte intime: Pouvoirs et limites de la psychanalyse II 1997, Contre la dépression nationale: Conversation avec Philippe Petit 1997, L'avenir d'une révolte 1998, La génie féminin, vol. I Hannah Arendt 1999, vol. II Melanie Klein 2000, vol. III Colette 2002, Meurtre à Byzance 2004; contrib. to books, professional journals and periodicals. *Honours:* Chevalier, Ordre des Arts et des Lettres, 1987; Prix Henri Hertz, Chancellerie des universités de Paris, 1989; Chevalier, Ordre nat. du Mérite, 1991; Chevalier, Légion d'honneur, 1997. *Address:* c/o University of Paris VII-Denis Diderot, UFR de Sciences des Textes et Documents, 34–44, 2e étage, 2 pl. Jussieu, 75005 Paris, France.

KRISTOF, Agota; Writer; b. 30 Oct. 1935, Csikvand, Hungary; one s. two d. *Education:* BS, Neuchâtel, Switzerland. *Career:* mem. Swiss Authors Asscn. *Publications:* Le grand cahier, 1986, English trans. as The Notebook, 1988; Le preuve, 1988, English trans. as The Proof, 1991; Le troisième mensonge, 1991, English trans. as The Third Lie, 1996; Hier, 1995. *Honours:* European Prize for French-Speaking Authors, 1986; Canada-Switzerland Prize, 1988; Schiller Prize, Switzerland, 1988.

KRISTOL, Irving; editor, writer and academic; *Co-Editor, The Public Interest*; b. 22 Jan. 1920, New York, NY, USA; m. Gertrude Himmelfarb 1942; one s. one d. *Education:* City College, CUNY. *Career:* Managing Ed., Commentary Magazine, 1947–52; Co-Founder and Co-Ed., Encounter magazine, 1953–58; Ed., The Reporter magazine, 1959–60; Exec. Vice-Pres., Basic Books Inc, 1961–69; Co-Ed., The Public Interest magazine, 1965–; Faculty, New York University, 1969–88; John M. Olin Senior Fellow, American Enterprise Institute, 1987–; mem. American Acad. of Arts and Sciences, fellow; Council on Foreign Relations. *Publications:* On the Democratic Idea in America, 1972; Two Cheers for Capitalism, 1978; Reflections of a Neoconservative, 1983; Neoconservatism: The Autobiography of an Idea, 1995. Editor: Encounters (with Stephen Spender and Melvin Lasky), 1963; Confrontation: The Student Rebellion and the University (with Daniel Bell), 1969; Capitalism Today, 1971; The American Commonwealth (with Nathan Glazer), 1976; The Americans (with Paul Weaver), 1976; The Crisis in Economic Theory, 1981; Third World Instability (with others), 1985. Contributions: various publications. *Address:* The Public Interest, 1112 16th Street NW, Suite 140, Washington, DC 20036, USA (Office).

KROETSCH, Robert; Prof. of English and Writer; b. 26 June 1927, Heisler, AB, Canada. *Education:* BA, University of Alberta, 1948; MA, Middlebury College, Vermont, 1956; PhD, University of Iowa, 1961. *Career:* Asst Prof., 1961–65, Assoc. Prof., 1965–68, Prof. of English, 1968–78, SUNY at Binghamton; Prof. of English, 1978–85, Distinguished Prof., 1985–, University of Manitoba. *Publications:* The Studhorse Man, 1969; Badlands, 1975; What the Cow Said, 1978; Alibi, 1983; Completed Field Notes (poems), 1989; The Lovely Treachery of Words, 1989; The Puppeteer, 1992; The Hornbooks of Rita K., 2001. *Address:* 4081 Cedar Hill Rd, Victoria, BC V8N 3C2, Canada.

KROKER, Arthur W.; professor, writer and editor; b. 27 Aug. 1945, Winnipeg, Manitoba, Canada; m. Marilouise DiRusso, 9 Aug. 1975, one c. *Education:* BA, University of Windsor, 1967; MS, Purdue University, 1971; PhD, Political Science, McMaster University, 1975. *Career:* Asst Prof., 1975–80, Dir, Canadian Studies, 1979–80, Assoc. Prof. of Political Science, 1980–81, University of Winnipeg; Founding Ed., Canadian Journal of Political and Social Theory, 1975–93, renamed CTHEORY: Theory, Technology, and Culture, 1993–; Assoc. Prof., 1981–87, Prof. of Political Science, 1987–, Concordia University, Montréal; Guest Lecturer, colleges, universities, art museums; mem. Canadian Political Science Asscn; Canadian Communication Asscn; Asscn for Canadian Studies; Conference for the Study of Political Thought. *Publications:* Technology and the Canadian Mind: Innis, McLuhan and Grant, 1984; Panic Encyclopedia: The Definitive Guide to the Postmodern Scene, 1989; The Possessed Individual: Technology and the French Postmodern, 1992; Spasm: Virtual Reality, Android Music, and Electric Flesh, 1993; Data Trash: The Theory of the Virtual Class (co-author), 1994; Hacking the Future: Stories for the Flesh-Eating 90s (co-author), 1996; Digital Delirium (co-ed.), 1997. Contributions: anthologies; Articles and reviews to periodicals. *Honours:* Grants, Social Sciences and Humanities Research Council of Canada; Invited Distinguished Fellow, Society of the Humanities, Cornell University, 1999.

KRONENFELD, Judy Z., BA, MA, PhD; poet and writer; *Lecturer, Creative Writing Department, University of California, Riverside*; b. 17 July 1943, New York, NY, USA; m. David Brian Kronenfeld 1964; one s. one d. *Education:* Smith Coll., Stanford Univ., Univ. of Oxford. *Career:* Lecturer 1971, 1984–, Visiting Scholar 1977–78, 1981–83, Instructor 1978, Visiting Asst Prof. 1980–81, 1988–89, Univ. of California at Riverside; Lecturer 1972–73, 1978–79, Visiting Lecturer 1984, 1985–86, Visiting Assoc. Prof. 1987, Univ. of California at Irvine; Asst Prof., Purdue Univ. 1976–77. *Publications:* Shadow of Wings (poems) 1991, King Lear and the Naked Truth: Rethinking the Language of Religion and Resistance 1998; contrib. articles in scholarly books and journals, poems in anthologies, reviews, quarterlies and magazines. *Honours:* Leverhulme Trust Fund Fellowship 1968–69, Squaw Valley Community of Writers Scholarship 1983, Non-Senate Academic Distinguished Researcher Award, Univ. of California at Riverside 1996–97. *Address:* 3314 Celeste Drive, Riverside, CA 92507, USA. *Website:* pages.sbcglobal.net/david-judy/judy.html.

KROSS, Jaan; Estonian author and translator; b. 19 Feb. 1920, Tallinn; m. 3rd Ellen Niit-Kross 1958; two s. two d.(one from previous marriage). *Education:* Tartu Univ. *Career:* involved in nat. resistance under the Nazi occupation 1943–44; arrested by Nazis Sept. 1944; Lecturer Tartu Univ. 1945–46; arrested by Soviet authorities in 1946 and imprisoned in Intalager (Gulag), Komi Autonomous Repub. 1946–50; deported to Krasnoyarsk region 1950–54; fully exonerated 1960; Sec. Estonian Writers' Union 1976–81, Deputy Chair. 1981–; published prose and poetry 1970–; mem. Riigikogu (Estonian Parl.) 1992–93. *Publications:* poems: The Coal Enricher 1958; travel books: Earth and Marble 1968, The Gulag Archipelago, Four Monologues on St George 1970; fiction: Between Three Plagues 1970–80, Professor Marten's Departure 1984, The Czar's Madman 1985, The Conspiracy and Other Stories 1995, Tahtamaa Farm 2001, Treading Air 2003; also literary and cultural reviews, opera librettos; works translated into more than 20 languages. *Honours:* Dr hc (Tartu Univ.) 1989, (Helsinki Univ.) 1990; Prix du Meilleur Livre Etranger 1989, Amnesty Int. Golden Flame Prize for Literature 1990, Baltic Ass. Literature Prize 1999. *Address:* Harju Street 1, Apt. 6, 10146 Tallinn, Estonia (Home). *Telephone:* (2) 441-697 (Home).

KRUGMAN, Paul Robin, PhD; American professor of economics; *Professor of Economics and International Affairs, Princeton University*; b. 28 Feb. 1953, Albany, New York; m. Robin Leslie Bergman 1983. *Education:* Yale Univ., Massachusetts Inst. of Tech. *Career:* Asst Prof., Yale Univ. 1977–79; Asst Prof. MIT 1979–80, Assoc. Prof. 1980–82, Prof. 1983–2000; Sr Staff Economist, Council of Econ. Advisers 1982–83; Columnist, New York Times 1999–; Prof. of Econs and Int. Affairs, Princeton Univ. 2000–. *Publications:* Market Structure and Foreign Trade (with E. Helpman) 1985, International Economics, Theory and Policy (with M. Obsfeld) 1988, The Age of Diminished Expectations 1990, Rethinking International Trade 1990, Geography and Trade 1991, Currencies and Crises 1992, Peddling Prosperity 1994, The Great Unravelling: From Boom to Bust in Three Short Years 2003. *Honours:* John Bates Clark Medal 1991. *Address:* Princeton University, Princeton, NJ 08544, USA.

KRUKOWSKI, Lucian Wladyslaw; Prof. of Philosophy, Artist and Writer; b. 22 Nov. 1929, New York, NY, USA; m. Marilyn Denmark, 17 Jan. 1955, one d. *Education:* BA, Brooklyn College, CUNY, 1952; BFA, Yale University, 1955; MS, Pratt Institute, 1958; PhD, Washington University, St Louis, 1977. *Career:* Faculty, Pratt Institute, 1955–69; Dean, School of Fine Arts, 1969–77, Prof. of Philosophy, 1977–96, Chair., Dept of Philosophy, 1986–89, Prof. Emeritus of Philosophy, 1996–, Washington University, St Louis; mem. American Philosophical Asscn; Society for Aesthetics. *Publications:* Art and Concept, 1987; Aesthetic Legacies, 1992. Anthologies: The Arts, Society, and Literature, 1984; The Reasons of Art, 1985; Cultural Literacy and Arts Education, 1990; Ethics and Architecture, 1990; The Future of Art, 1990; Schopenhauer, Philosophy and the Arts, 1996. Contributions: Professional journals. *Address:* 6003 Kingsbury, St Louis, MO 63112, USA.

KRUPAT, Arnold; Prof., Writer and Ed.; b. 22 Oct. 1941, New York, NY, USA; one s. one d. *Education:* BA, New York University, 1962; MA, 1965, PhD, 1967, Columbia University. *Career:* Prof., Sarah Lawrence College. *Publications:* For Those Who Come After, 1985; I Tell You Now (ed. with Brian Swann), 1987; Recovering the Word (ed. with Brian Swann), 1987; The Voice in the Margin, 1989; Ethnocriticism: Ethnography, History, Literature, 1992; New Voices: Essays on Native American Literature (ed.), 1993; Native American Autobiography (ed.), 1993; The Turn to the Native: Studies in Culture and Criticism, 1996; Everything Matters: Autobiographical Essays by Native American Writers (ed. with Brian Swann), 1997; Red Matters: Native American Studies, 2002. Contributions: numerous critical journals. *Address:* Sarah Lawrence College, Bronxville, NY 10708, USA.

KUHN, Laura (Diane); Musicologist and Ed.; b. 19 Jan. 1953, San Francisco, CA, USA. *Education:* Vocal and piano training, San Francisco, 1975–82; BA, Dominican College, San Rafael, CA, 1981; MA, 1986, PhD, 1992, University of California at Los Angeles. *Career:* Mem., San Francisco Symphony Chorus, 1980, Oakland Symphony Chorus, 1980–82; Music Critic, Independent Journal, Marin County, CA, 1980–82; Reviewer, Los Angeles Times, 1982–87, New York Times, 1986–89; Vocalist, Daniel Lentz Group, 1983–85; Editorial Assoc., Nicolas Slonimsky, 1984–95; Assoc., John Cage, 1986–92; Asst Prof., Arizona State University West, Phoenix, 1991–96; Founder-Dir, John Cage Trust, New York City, 1993–; Secretary, American Music Center, New York City, 1995–2000. *Publications:* Baker's Biographical Dictionary of Musicians (contributing ed.), seventh edn, 1984, eighth edn, 1992, (classical ed.), ninth edn, 2001; A Pronouncing Pocket Manual of Musical Terms (ed.), fifth edn, 1995; Baker's Biographical Dictionary of 20th Century Classical Musicians (ed.), 1997; Baker's Dictionary of Opera (ed.), 2000. Contributions: Supplement to Music Since 1900, 1986; Music Since 1900, fifth edn, 1994, sixth edn, 2001; Music Today;

Musical Quarterly; Perspectives of New Music. *Honours:* Outstanding Reference Source Citation, American Library Asscn, 1998. *Address:* 341 Furnace Dock Rd, No. 12, Cortland Manor, NY 10567, USA.

KULTERMANN, Udo; American academic and writer; b. 14 Oct. 1927, Stettin, Germany. *Education:* University of Greifswald, 1946–50; PhD, University of Münster, 1953. *Career:* Dir, City Art Museum, Leverkusen, 1959–64; Prof. of Architecture 1967–94, Prof. Emeritus, 1994–, Washington University, St Louis; International Correspondent, MIMAR, Singapore/London, 1981–92; mem. National Faculty of Humanities, Arts, and Sciences, Atlanta, 1986–; Croatian Acad. of Sciences and Arts, Zagreb, corresponding mem., 1997–. *Publications:* Architecture of Today, 1958; Hans und Wassili Luckhardt: Bauten und Projekte, 1958; Dynamische Architektur, 1959; New Japanese Architecture, 1960; Junge deutsche Bildhauer, 1963; Der Schlüssel zur Architektur von heute, 1963; New Architecture in Africa, 1963; New Architecture in the World, 1965; Geschichte der Kunstgeschichte: Der Weg einer Wissenschaft, 1966; Architektur der Gegenwart, 1967; The New Sculpture, 1967; The New Painting, 1969; New Directions in African Architecture, 1969; Kenzo Tange: Architecture and Urban Design, 1970; Modern Architecture in Color (with Werner Hofmann), 1970; Art and Life: The Function of Intermedia, 1970; New Realism, 1972; Ernest Trova, 1977; Die Architektur im 20. Jahrhundert, 1977; I Contemporanei: Storia della scultura nel mondo, 1979; Architecture in the Seventies, 1980; Architekten der Dritten Welt, 1980; Contemporary Architecture in Eastern Europe, 1985; Kleine Geschichte der Kunsttheorie, 1987; Visible Cities-Invisible Cities: Urban Symbolism and Historical Continuity, 1988; Art and Reality: From Fiedler to Derrida: Ten Approaches, 1991; Architecture in the 20th Century, 1993; Die Maxentius Basilika: Ein Schlüsselwerk spätantiker Architektur, 1996; Architektur der Welt (ed.), 1996–; St James Modern Masterpieces: The Best of Art, Architecture, Photography and Design Since 1945 (ed.), 1998; Contemporary Architecture in the Arab States: Renaissance of a Region, 1999; Architecture in South and Central Africa in World Architecture: A Critical Mosaic 1900–2000 (ed.), 2000; Thirty Years After: The Future of the Past, 2002. Contributions: books, encyclopedias and periodicals. *Honours:* Distinguished Faculty Award, Washington University, St Louis, 1985. *Address:* 300 Mercer Street, 17B, New York, NY 10003, USA. *E-mail:* ukulter@rcn.rom.

KUMAR, Shiv K(umar); Prof. of English (retd) and Poet; b. 16 Aug. 1921, Lahore, Punjab, India. *Education:* PhD, Fitzwilliam College, Cambridge, 1956. *Career:* Prof. of English, Osmania University, 1959–86. *Publications:* Articulate Silences, 1970; Cobwebs in the Sun, 1974; Subterfuges, 1976; Woodpeckers, 1979; Trapfalls in the Sky, 1986. Editor: British Romantic Poets: Recent Revelations, 1966; Indian Verse in English, 1970, 1971. *Honours:* FRSL, 1978. *Address:* 2-F/Kakatiya Nagar, PO Jamia Osmania, Hyderabad 500 007, India.

KUMIN, Maxine Winokur; Poet, Writer and Teacher; b. 6 June 1925, Philadelphia, Pennsylvania, USA; m. Victor M. Kumin, 29 June 1946, one s. two d. *Education:* AB, 1946, MA, 1948, Radcliffe College. *Career:* Instructor, 1958–61, Lecturer in English, 1965–68, Tufts University; Lecturer, Newton College of the Sacred Heart, Massachusetts, 1971; Visiting Lecturer, Prof., and Writer, University of Massachusetts, Amherst, 1972, Columbia University, 1975, Brandeis University, 1975, Washington University, St Louis, 1977, Princeton University, 1977, 1979, 1982, Randolph-Macon Women's College, Lynchburg, Virginia, 1978, Bucknell University, 1983, Atlantic Center for the Arts, New Smyrna Beach, FL, 1984, University of Miami, 1995; mem. PEN; Poetry Society of America; Writers Union. *Publications:* Poetry: Halfway, 1961; The Privilege, 1965; The Nightmare Factory, 1970; Up Country: Poems of New England, New and Selected, 1972; House, Bridge, Fountain, Gate, 1975; The Retrieval System, 1978; Our Ground Time Here Will Be Brief, 1982; Closing the Ring, 1984; The Long Approach, 1985; Nurture, 1989; Looking for Luck, 1992; Connecting the Dots, 1996; Selected Poems 1960–1990, 1997; The Long Marriage, 2001; Bringing Together: Uncollected Early Poems, 2003. Fiction: Through Dooms of Love, 1965; The Passions of Uxport, 1968; The Abduction, 1971; The Designated Heir, 1974; Why Can't We Live Together Like Civilized Human Beings?, 1982. Other: In Deep: Country Essays, 1987; To Make a Prairie: Essays on Poets, Poetry, and Country Living, 1989; Women, Animals, and Vegetables: Essays and Stories, 1994; Quit Monks or Die!, 1999; Inside the Halo and Beyond (memoir), 2000; Always Beginning (essays), 2000. For Children: various books. Contributions: numerous magazines and journals. *Honours:* Lowell Mason Palmer Award, 1960; National Endowment for the Arts Grant, 1966; National Council on the Arts Fellowship, 1967; William Marion Reedy Award, 1968; Eunice Tietjens Memorial Prize, 1972; Pulitzer Prize in Poetry, 1973; American Acad. of Arts and Letters Award, 1980; Acad. of American Poets Fellowship, 1985; Levinson Award, 1987; Poet Laureate, State of New Hampshire, 1989; Sarah Josepha Hale Award, 1992; Poet's Prize, 1994; Aiken Taylor Poetry Award, 1995; Centennial Award, Harvard Graduate School, 1996; Ruth Lilly Poetry Prize, 1999; various hon. doctorates. *Literary Agent:* Giles Anderson Agency, New York, USA. *Address:* 40 Harriman Lane, Warner, NH 03278, USA.

KUMMINGS, Donald D.; Prof. of English, Poet and Writer; b. 28 July 1940, Lafayette, IN, USA; Divorced 18 Aug. 1978, m. 21 March 1987, two s. *Education:* BA, 1962, MA, 1964, Purdue University; PhD, English and American Studies, Indiana University, 1971. *Career:* Instructor, Adrian College, Michigan, 1964–66; Assoc. Instructor, Indiana University, 1966–70; Asst Prof., 1970–75, Chair, Dept of English, 1974–76, 1991–94, Assoc. Prof., 1975–85, Prof. of English, 1985–, University of Wisconsin, Parkside; Book Review Ed., The Mickle Street Review, 1983–90. *Publications:* Walt Whitman, 1940–1975: A Reference Guide, 1982; The Open Road Trip: Poems, 1989; Approaches to Teaching Whitman's Leaves of Grass, 1990; The Walt Whitman Encyclopedia (ed. with J. R. LeMaster), 1998. Contributions: anthologies, reviews, quarterlies, and journals. *Honours:* Acad. of American Poets Prize, 1969; Posner Poetry Prize, Council for Wisconsin Writers, 1990; Wisconsin Prof. of the Year, Carnegie Foundation for the Advancement of Teaching, 1997. *Address:* c/o Dept of English, University of Wisconsin, Parkside, Kenosha, WI 53141, USA.

KUNDERA, Milan; Czech/French writer; b. 1 April 1929, Brno; m. Věra Hrabánková 1967. *Education:* Film Faculty, Acad. of Music and Dramatic Arts, Prague. *Career:* Asst, later Asst Prof., Film Faculty, Acad. of Music and Dramatic Arts, Prague 1958–69; Prof., Univ. of Rennes 1975–80; Prof. Ecole des hautes études en sciences sociales, Paris 1980–; mem. Union of Czechoslovak Writers 1963–69; mem. Editorial Bd Literární noviny 1963–67, 1968. *Publications:* drama: The Owner of the Keys 1962, Two Ears, Two Weddings (Slowness) 1968, The Blunder 1969, Jacques et son maître 1971–81; short stories: Laughable Loves 1970; novels: The Joke 1967, Life is Elsewhere 1973, La Valse aux adieux (The Farewell Waltz) 1976, Livre du rire et de l'oubli (The Book of Laughter and Forgetting) 1979, The Unbearable Lightness of Being 1984, L'Identità (Identity) 1997, La Ignorancia (Ignorance 2002) 2000; poetry: Man: A Broad Garden 1953, The Last May 1954–55 1961, Monologues 1957–64 1965; essays: About the Disputes of Inheritance 1955, The Czech Deal 1968, Radicalism and Exhibitionism 1969, The Stolen West or the Tragedy of Central Europe 1983, The Art of the Novel 1987, Les Testaments trahis (Testaments Betrayed: An Essay in Nine Parts) 1993, Immortality 1990, Slowness 1995. *Honours:* Officier Légion d'honneur 1990; Hon. doctorate (Michigan) 1983; Union of Czechoslovak Writers' Prize (for The Joke) 1968, Czechoslovak Writers' Publishing House Prize (for Laughable Loves) 1969, Prix Médicis (for Life is Elsewhere) 1973, Premio letterario Mondello (for The Farewell Party) 1978, Commonwealth Award (for all his work) 1981, Prix Europa-Littérature 1982, Los Angeles Times Prize (for Unbearable Lightness of Being) 1984, Jerusalem Prize (for all his work) 1985, Prix de la critique de l'Acad. Française 1987, Nelly Sachs Preis (for all his work) 1987, Österreichische Staatspreis für Europäische Literatur 1988, The Independent (newspaper) Prize, London 1991, Aujourd'hui Prize (France) 1993, Jaroslav-Seifert Prize 1994, Medal of Merit (Czech Repub.) 1995, J. G. Herder Prize (Austria) 2000, Grand Prize Acad. Française 2001. *Address:* c/o Gallimard, 5 rue Sébastien-Bottin, 75007 Paris; c/o Ecole des hautes études en sciences sociales, 54 blvd Raspail, Paris 75006, France.

KUNENE, Mazisi Raymond, MA; South African poet, political activist and lecturer; b. 1930, Durban; m. Mabowe Mathabo Kunene; four c. *Education:* Univs of Natal and London. *Career:* European and US African Nat. Congress (ANC) Rep. 1959; co-f. Int. Anti-Apartheid Movt; exiled, during which lectured, Stanford Univ., Univ. of Calif., LA; returned to South Africa, Prof. in the School of Languages and Literature, Univ. of Kwazulu-Natal 1993–; Africa's Poet Laureate in UNESCO 1993–. *Publications include:* 13 vols of work, 38 individual poems, two film scripts and a play; Zulu Poems 1970, Emperor Shaka the Great (16,400 verses) 1979, Anthem of the Decades 1981, The Ancestor and the Sacred Mountain 1982. *Honours:* Hon. DLitt (Univ. of Kwazulu-Natal) 2000. *Address:* c/o School of Languages and Literature, University of Kwazulu-Natal, University Road Westville, Private Bag X 54001, Durban 4000, South Africa.

KUNERT, Günter; Poet, Author and Dramatist; b. 6 March 1929, Berlin, Germany; m. Marianne Todten. *Education:* Hochschule für angewandte Kunst, Berlin-Weissensee. *Career:* mem. Deutsche Akademie für Sprache und Dichtung eV, Darmstadt. *Publications:* Poetry: Wegschilder und Mauerinschriften, 1950; Erinnerung an einen Planeten: Gedichte aus Fünfzehn Jahren, 1963; Der ungebetene Gast, 1965; Verkündigung des Wetters, 1966; Warnung vor Spiegeln, 1970; Im weiteren Fortgang, 1974; Unterwegs nach Utopia, 1977; Abtötungsverfahren, 1980; Stilleben, 1983; Berlin beizeiten, 1987; Fremd daheim, 1990; Mein Golem, 1996; Nachtvorstellung, 1999. Novel: Im Namen der Hüte, 1967. Other: Der ewige Detektiv und andere Geschichten, 1954; Kramen in Fächen: Geschichten, Parabeln, Merkmale, 1968; Die Beerdigung findet in aller Stille statt, 1968; Tagträume in Berlin und andernorts, 1972; Gast aus England, 1973; Der andere Planet: Ansichten von Amerika, 1974; Warum schreiben?: Notizen ins Paradies, 1978; Ziellose Umtriebe: Nachrichten von Reisen und Daheimsein, 1979; Verspätete Monologe, 1981; Leben und Schreiben, 1983; Vor der Sintflut: Das Gedicht als Arche Noah, 1985; Die letzten Indianer Europas, 1991; Erwachsenenspiele (autobiog.), 1997. *Honours:* Heinrich Mann Prize, 1962; Heinrich Heine Prize, Düsseldorf, 1985; Hölderlin Prize, 1991; Georg-Trakl Prize, Austria, 1997. *Address:* Schulstrasse 7, 25560 Kaisborstel, Germany.

KÜNG, Dinah Lee; American journalist and author; b. Detroit, MI; m.; three c. *Career:* reporter, Washington Post, National Public Radio, International Herald Tribune, The Economist; Hong Kong bureau chief, Business Week. *Publications:* novels: Left in the Care of 1998, A Visit from Voltaire 2003. *Honours:* Overseas Press Club Award for Best Human Rights Coverage 1992. *Address:* c/o Peter Halban Publishers Ltd, 22 Golden Square, London,

W1F 9JW, England. *Telephone:* (20) 7437-9300. *Fax:* (20) 7437-9512. *E-mail:* books@halbanpublishers.com. *Website:* www.halbanpublishers.com.

KÜNG, Hans; Prof. of Ecumenical Theology Emeritus and Author; b. 19 March 1928, Lucerne, Switzerland. *Education:* Philosophy, Theology, Pontifical Gregorian University, Rome; Institut Catholique, Paris; Sorbonne, University of Paris. *Career:* Ordained Roman Catholic Priest, 1954; Practical Ministry, Lucerne Cathedral, 1957–59; Asst for Dogmatic Catholic Theology, University of Münster/Westphalia, 1959–60; Prof. of Fundamental Theology, 1960–63, Prof. of Dogmatic and Ecumenical Theology, 1963–80, Dir, Institute of Ecumenical Research, 1963–96, Prof. of Ecumenical Theology, 1980–96, Prof. Emeritus, 1996–, University of Tübingen; Pres., Foundation for a Global Ethic, Germany, 1995–, Switzerland, 1997–; various guest professorships and lectureships throughout the world; mem. Exec. Editorial Committee of 'Concilium'; PEN American Center; PEN Centre of West Germany. *Publications:* The Council: Reform and Reunion, 1961; That the World May Believe, 1963; The Council in Action, 1963; Justification: The Doctrine of Karl Barth and a Catholic Reflection, 1964; Structures of the Church, 1964; Freedom Today, 1966; The Church, 1967; Truthfulness, 1968; Infallible?: An Inquiry, 1971; Why Priests?, 1972; On Being a Christian, 1976; Signposts for the Future, 1978; The Christian Challenge, 1979; Freud and the Problem of God, 1979; Does God Exist?, 1980; The Church: Maintained in Truth, 1980; Eternal Life?, 1984; Christianity and the World Religions: Paths to Dialogue with Islam, Hindus and Buddhism (with others), 1986; The Incarnation of God, 1986; Church and Change: The Irish Experience, 1986; Why I Am Still A Christian, 1987; Theology for a Third Millennium: An Ecumenical View, 1988; Christianity and Chinese Religions (with Julia Ching), 1989; Paradigm Change in Theology: A Symposium for the Future, 1989; Reforming the Church Today, 1990; Global Responsibility: In Search of a New World Ethic, 1991; Judaism, 1992; Mozart: Traces of Transcendence, 1992; Credo: The Apostles' Creed Explained for Today, 1993; Great Christian Thinkers, 1994; A Dignified Dying (with Walter Jens), 1995; Christianity, 1995; A Global Ethic for Global Politics and Economics, 1997; The Catholic Church: A Short History, 2001; Tracing the Way: Spiritual Dimensions of the World Religions, 2002; My Struggle for Freedom (memoir), 2004. Other: Ed. and co-ed. of many publications. *Honours:* Oskar Pfister Award, American Psychiatric Asscn, 1986; Interfaith Gold Medallion, International Council of Christians and Jews, 1998; Theodor Heuss Prize, Theodor Heuss Foundation, Stuttgart, 1998; Hon. Citizen of the City of Sursee, Switzerland, 1998; Ernst Robert Curtius Literary Award, Bonn, 2001; Göttingen Peace Award, 2002; Hon. Citizen of the City of Syracuse, Italy, 2002; Hon. Citizen of the City of Tübingen, Germany, 2002; Order of Merit of the Federal Republic, 2003; many hon. doctorates. *Address:* Waldhäuserstr 23, 72076 Tübingen, Germany.

KUNITZ, Stanley (Jasspon); Poet, Ed., Essayist and Educator; b. 29 July 1905, Worcester, Massachusetts, USA; m. 1st Helen Pearce 1930 (divorced 1937); m. 2nd Eleanor Evans 21 Nov. 1939 (divorced 1958); one d.; m. 3rd Elise Asher 21 June 1958. *Education:* AB, summa cum laude, 1926, MA, 1927, Harvard University. *Career:* Ed., Wilson Library Bulletin, 1928–43; Teacher, Bennington College, 1946–49; Prof. of English, Potsdam State Teachers College, New York, 1949–50; Lecturer, New School for Social Research, New York City, 1950–57; Visiting Prof. of Poetry, University of Washington, Seattle, 1955–56, Yale University, 1970, Rutgers University at Camden, NJ, 1974; Visiting Prof. of English, Queens College, CUNY, 1956–57, Brandeis University, 1958–59; Lecturer, 1963–66, Adjunct Prof. in Writing, Graduate School of the Arts, 1967–85, Columbia University; Consultant on Poetry, 1974–76, Hon. Consultant in American Letters, 1979–83, Library of Congress, Washington, DC; Visiting Prof. and Senior Fellow in Humanities, Princeton University, 1978, Vassar College, 1981; Poet Laureate of the USA, 2000–01; numerous poetry readings and lectures; mem. American Acad. and Institute of Arts and Letters, 1968–; Acad. of American Poets, chancellor, 1970–95; Founding Mem., Board of Dirs, Fine Arts Work Center, Provincetown, 1968–; Poets House, New York, founding pres., 1985–90. *Publications:* Poetry: Intellectual Things, 1930; Passport to the War: A Selection of Poems, 1944; Selected Poems, 1928–1958, 1958; The Testing Tree: Poems, 1971; The Terrible Threshold: Selected Poems, 1940–70, 1974; The Coat Without a Seam: Sixty Poems, 1930–72, 1974; The Lincoln Relics, 1978; Poems of Stanley Kunitz: 1928–78, 1979; The Wellfleet Whale and Companion Poems, 1983; Next-to-Last Things: New Poems and Essays, 1985; Passing Through: The Later Poems, 1995; The Collected Poems, 2000. Non-Fiction: Robert Lowell: Poet of Terribilità, 1974; A Kind of Order, a Kind of Folly: Essays and Conversations, 1975; Interviews and Encounters, 1993. Editor: British Authors of the Nineteenth Century (with Howard Haycraft), 1936; American Authors, 1600–1900: A Biographical Dictionary of American Literature (with Howard Haycraft), 1938; Twentieth Century Authors: A Biographical Dictionary (with Howard Haycraft), 1942, first supplement, 1955; British Authors before 1800: A Biographical Dictionary (with Howard Haycraft), 1952; European Authors, 1000–1900: A Biographical Dictionary of European Literature (with Vineta Colby), 1967; The Essential Blake, 1987; The Wild Card, Selected Poems of Karl Shapiro (with David Ignatow), 1998. Contributions: many anthologies, books and periodicals. *Honours:* Garrison Medal for Poetry, Harvard University, 1926; Oscar Blumenthal Prize, 1941; Guggenheim Fellowship, 1945–46; Amy Lowell Travelling Fellowship for Poetry, 1953–54; Levinson Prize for Poetry, 1956; Harriet Monroe Award, University of Chicago, 1958; Ford Foundation Grant, 1958–59; National Institute of Arts and Letters Grant, 1959; Pulitzer Prize in Poetry, 1959; Brandeis University Creative Arts Award, 1964; Lenore Marshall Award for Poetry, 1980; National Endowment for the Arts Senior Fellow, 1984; Bollingen Prize, 1987; Walt Whitman Award, 1987; State Poet of New York, 1987–88; Montgomery Fellow, Dartmouth College, 1991; Centennial Medal, Harvard University, 1992; National Medal of Arts, 1993; Shelley Memorial Award, 1995; National Book Award for Poetry, 1995; Medal for Distinguished Service in the Arts, Fine Arts Work Center, Provincetown, 1997–; Robert Frost Medal, 1998. *Address:* 37 W 12th St, New York, NY 10011, USA.

KUNKEL, Thor; German novelist; b. 1963, Frankfurt. *Publications:* The Black Light Terranium 2000, Ein Brief an Hanny Porter 2001, Final Stage 2004. *Honours:* Ernst-Willner Award. *Literary Agent:* c/o Eichborn Berlin AG, Kaiserstr 66, 60329 Frankfurt am Main, Germany. *Telephone:* (49) 69 2560 0358. *Fax:* (49) 69 2560 030. *Website:* www.eichborn.de.

KUNSTLER, James Howard; Author; b. 19 Oct. 1948, New York, NY, USA; m. 15 June 1996. *Education:* BS, Brockport State College, 1971. *Publications:* The Wampanaki Tales, 1979; A Clown in the Moonlight, 1981; The Life of Byron Jaynes, 1983; An Embarrassment of Riches, 1985; Blood Solstice, 1986; The Halloween Ball, 1987; The Geography of Nowhere, 1993; Home From Nowhere, 1996. Contributions: Atlantic Monthly; New York Times Sunday Magazine. *Honours:* Humanities Prize, 1995. *Address:* PO Box 193, Saratoga Springs, NY 12866, USA.

KUNZE, Reiner; Poet and Author; b. 16 Aug. 1933, Oelsnitz, Germany; m. Elisabeth Mifka, one s. one d. *Education:* University of Leipzig, 1951–55. *Career:* mem. Bavarian Acad. of Fine Arts, Munich; Deutsche Akademie für Sprache und Dichtung, Darmstadt. *Publications:* Poetry: Vögel über dem Tau, 1959; Widmungen, 1963; Sensible wege, 1969; Zimmerlautstärke, 1972; Auf eigene hoffnung, 1981; Gespräch mit der amsel, 1984; Eines jeden einziges leben, 1986; Wohin der Schlaf sich schlafen legt, 1991; Ein tag auf dieser erde, 1998; Gedichte, 2000. Other: Der Löwe Leopold, 1970; Die wunderbaren Jahre, 1976; Das weisse Gedicht, 1989; Mensch ohne Macht, 1991; Am Sonnenhang, 1992; wo Freiheit ist, 1994; Steine und Lieder, 1996; Bindewort deutsch, 1997. *Honours:* German Children's Book Prize, 1971; Literary Prize, Bavarian Acad. of Fine Arts, Munich, 1973; Georg Trakl Prize, Salzburg, 1977; Georg Büchner Prize, 1977; Bavarian Film Prize, 1979; Eichendorff Literature Prize, 1984; Federal Cross of Merit, First Class, Germany, 1984; Upper Bavarian Cultural Prize, 1988; Freemasons' Prize for Culture, Chemnitz, 1993; Europapreis für Poesie, Serbien, 1998; Friedrich-Hölderlin-Preis, 1999; Christian Ferber Ehrengabe, 2000; Hans-Sahl-Literaturpreis, 2001; Bayerischer Maximiliansorden für Kunst und Wissenschaft, 2001; Kunstpreis zur deutsch-tschechischen Verständigung, 2002. *Address:* Am Sonnenhang 19, 94130 Obernzell, Germany.

KUNZRU, Hari Mohan Nath; British writer and journalist; b. 1969, Woodford Green, Essex, England. *Education:* Wadham Coll., Oxford and Warwick Univ. *Career:* fmr journalist, Music Ed. Wallpaper magazine, Assoc. Ed. Wired magazine, Contrib. Ed. Mute magazine. *Publications:* novels: The Impressionist (Observer Young Travel Writer of the Year 1999, Betty Trask Prize) 2002, Transmission 2004; other: short stories, journalism; contrib. to Wired, The Economist, London Review of Books. *Literary Agent:* Curtis Brown, Haymarket House, 28–29 Haymarket, London, SW1 4SP, England. *Telephone:* (20) 7396-6600. *Website:* www.harikunzru.com.

KUPPNER, Frank; Writer and Poet; b. 1951, Glasgow, Scotland. *Education:* University of Glasgow. *Publications:* Fiction: Ridiculous! Disgusting!, 1989; A Very Quiet Street, 1989; A Concussed History of Scotland, 1990; Something Very Like Murder, 1994. Poetry: A Bad Day for the Sung Dynasty, 1984; The Intelligent Observation of Naked Women, 1987; Everything is Strange, 1994. *Address:* c/o Polygon, 22 George Sq., Edinburgh EH8 9LF, Scotland.

KUREISHI, Hanif, BA; British author and dramatist; b. 5 Dec. 1954, Bromley; m. Tracey Scoffield, three c. *Education:* King's Coll. London. *Career:* worked as typist at Riverside Studios; writer-in-residence, Royal Court Theatre, London 1981, 1985–86. *Stage plays:* Soaking the Heat 1976, The Mother Country (Thames TV Playwright Award) 1980, The King and Me 1980, Outskirts (RSC) 1981, Cinders (after the play by Janusz Glowacki) 1981, Borderline (Royal Court) 1981, Artists and Admirers (after a play by Ostrovsky, with David Leveaux) 1981, Birds of Passage (Hampstead Theatre) 1983, Mother Courage (adaptation of a play by Brecht, RSC) 1984, Sleep With Me (Nat. Theatre) 1999, When the Night Begins (Hampstead Theatre) 2004. *Screenplays:* My Beautiful Laundrette (Evening Standard Best Film Award 1986, New York Critics' Best Screenplay Award 1987) 1986, Sammy and Rosie Get Laid 1988, London Kills Me (also directed) 1991, My Son The Fanatic 1997, The Mother 2002. *TV film:* The Buddha of Suburbia (BBC) 1993. *Publications:* fiction: The Buddha of Suburbia (Whitbread Award for Best First Novel) 1990, The Black Album 1995, Love in a Blue Time (short stories) 1997, Intimacy 1998, Midnight All Day (short stories) 1999, Gabriel's Gift 2000, The Body 2002; non-fiction: The Rainbow Sign (autobiography) 1986, Eight Arms to Hold You (essay) 1991, Dreaming and Scheming: Reflections on Writing and Politics (essays) 2002, My Ear at his Heart (autobiog.) 2004; editor: The Faber Book of Pop (jtly) 1995; stories in Granta, Harpers (USA), London Review of Books and The

Atlantic; regular contrib. to New Statesman and Society. *Honours:* George Devine Award 1981, Chevalier, Ordre des Arts et des Lettres 2002. *Literary Agent:* Rogers, Coleridge & White Ltd, 20 Powis Mews, London, W11 1JN, England.

KURKOV, Andrey; Ukrainian author and screenwriter; b. 1961, St Petersburg, USSR. *Education:* Foreign Language Inst., Kiev. *Career:* fmr journalist, film cameraman. *Publications:* novels in trans.: Death and the Penguin 1996, The Case of the General's Thumb 2003, Penguin Lost 2003; other: four children's books, various screenplays. *Address:* c/o The Harvill Press, Random House, 20 Vauxhall Bridge Road, London, SW1V 2SA, England. *Website:* www.randomhouse.co.uk.

KURTZ, Katherine (Irene); Author; b. 18 Oct. 1944, Coral Gables, FL, USA; m. Scott Roderick MacMillan, 9 April 1983, one s. *Education:* BS, University of Miami, 1966; MA, University of California, Los Angeles, 1971. *Career:* mem. Authors' Guild; SFWA. *Publications:* Deryni Rising, 1970; Deryni Checkmate, 1972; High Deryni, 1973; Camber of Culdi, 1976; Saint Camber, 1978; Camber the Heretic, 1981; Lammas Night, 1983; The Bishop's Heir, 1984; The King's Justice, 1985; The Quest for Saint Camber, 1986; The Legacy of Lehr, 1986; The Deryni Archives, 1986; The Harrowing of Gwynedd, 1989; Deryni Magic: A Grimoire, 1990; King Javan's Year, 1992; The Bastard Prince, 1994; Two Crowns for America, 1996; King Kelson's Bride, 2000; St Patrick's Gargoyle, 2001; In the King's Service, 2003. With Deborah Turner Harris: The Adept, 1991; Lodge of the Lynx, 1992; The Templar Treasure, 1993; Dagger Magic, 1994; Death of an Adept, 1996; The Temple and the Stone, 1998; The Temple and the Crown, 2001. With Robert Reginald: Codex Derynianus, 1998. Editor: Tales of the Knights Templar, 1995; On Crusade, 1998; Deryni Tales, 2002; Crusade of Fire, 2002. various short stories. *Honours:* Edmund Hamilton Memorial Award, 1977; Balrog Award, 1982. *Address:* Holybrooke Hall, Kilmacanogue, Bray, County Wicklow, Ireland. *E-mail:* kkurtz@iol.ie. *Website:* www.deryni.com.

KURZMAN, Dan; Writer; b. 27 March 1929, San Francisco, CA, USA; m. Florence Knopf. *Education:* BA, University of California at Berkeley, 1946; Certificate, Sorbonne, University of Paris, 1947. *Career:* Correspondent, International News Service, 1948, NBC, Middle East, 1950–53, Washington Post, 1962–69; Feature Writer, Marshall Plan Information Office, Paris, 1948–49; Bureau Chief, McGraw Hill World News Service, Tokyo, 1954–59; Contributor, Washington Star, 1975–80, Independent News Alliance, 1979–84, San Francisco Chronicle, 1991–92. *Publications:* Kishi and Japan: The Search for the Sun, 1960; Subversion of the Innocents, 1963; Santo Domingo: Revolt of the Damned, 1965; Genesis 1948: The First Arab-Israeli War, 1970; The Race for Rome, 1975; The Bravest Battle: The Twenty-Eight Days of the Warsaw Ghetto Uprising, 1976; Miracle of November: Madrid's Epic Stand 1936, 1980; Ben-Gurion: Prophet of Fire, 1983; Day of the Bomb: Countdown to Hiroshima, 1985; A Killing Wind: Inside Union Carbide and the Bhopal Catastrophe, 1987; Fatal Voyage: The Sinking of the USS Indianapolis, 1990; Left to Die: The Tragedy of the USS Juneau, 1994; Blood and Water: Sabotaging Hitler's Bomb, 1995; Soldier of Peace: The Life of Yitzhak Rabin, 1922–1995, 1998; Disaster: The Great San Francisco Earthquake and Fire of 1906, 2001. Contributions: New York Times Op-Ed Page, 1988–; Washington Post, book reviewer, 1988–; Los Angeles Times, book reviewer, 1988–. *Address:* The Parker Imperial, 7855 Blvd E, North Bergen, NJ 07047, USA.

KUSHNER, Tony, BA, MFA; dramatist; b. 16 July 1956, New York, NY, USA. *Education:* Columbia Univ., New York Univ. *Career:* playwright-in-residence, Juilliard School, New York 1990–92. *Publications:* Yes, Yes, No, No, 1985; Stella, 1987; A Bright Room Called Day, 1987; Hydriotaphia, 1987; The Illusion, 1988, revised version, 1990; The Persistence of Prejudice, 1989; Widows (with Ariel Dorfman), 1991; Angels in America: A Gay Fantasia on National Themes, Part One: Millennium Approaches, 1991, and Part Two: Perestroika, 1992; Holocaust and the Liberal Imagination, 1994; Thinking About the Longstanding Problems of Virtue and Happiness, 1995; Homebody/Kabul, 2001. *Honours:* National Endowment for the Arts Grants, 1985, 1987, 1993; Princess Grace Award, 1986; New York State Council for the Arts Fellowship, 1987; John Whiting Award, Arts Council of Great Britain, 1990; Kennedy Center/American Express Fund for New American Plays Awards, 1990, 1992; Kesserling Award, National Arts Club, 1992; Will Glickman Prize, 1992; Evening Standard Award, 1992; Pulitzer Prize in Drama, 1993; Antoinette Perry Award, 1993; American Acad. of Arts and Letters Award, 1994; PEN/Nabokov Award, 2002. *Literary Agent:* Steven Barclay Agency, 12 Western Avenue, Petaluma, CA 94952, USA. *Telephone:* (707) 773-0654. *Fax:* (707) 778-1868. *Website:* www.barclayagency.com.

KUSKIN, Karla Seidman, (Nicholas J. Charles); children's writer and illustrator; b. 17 July 1932, New York, NY, USA; m. 1st Charles M. Kuskin 1955 (divorced 1987); one s. one d.; m. 2nd William L. Bell 1989. *Education:* Antioch College, 1950–53; BFA, Yale University, 1955. *Career:* Illustrator for several publishers; Conductor of poetry and writing workshops. *Publications:* Roar and More, 1956; James and the Rain, 1957; In the Middle of the Trees, 1958; The Animals and the Ark, 1958; Just Like Everyone Else, 1959; Which Horse is William?, 1959; Square As a House, 1960; The Bear Who Saw the Spring, 1961; All Sizes of Noises, 1962; Alexander Soames: His Poems, 1962; How Do You Get From Here to There?, 1962; ABCDEFGHIJKLMNOPQRSTUVWXYZ, 1963; The Rose on My Cake, 1964; Sand and Snow, 1965; Jane Anne June Spoon and Her Very Adventurous Search for the Moon, 1966; The Walk the Mouse Girls Took, 1967; Watson, the Smartest Dog in the USA, 1968; In the Flaky Frosty Morning, 1969; Any Me I Want To Be: Poems, 1972; What Did You Bring Me?, 1973; Near the Window Tree: Poems and Notes, 1975; A Boy Had a Mother Who Brought Him a Hat, 1976; A Space Story, 1978; Herbert Hated Being Small, 1979; Dogs and Dragons, Trees and Dreams: A Collection of Poems, 1980; Night Again, 1981; The Philharmonic Gets Dressed, 1982; Something Sleeping in the Hall, 1985; The Dallas Titans Get Ready for Bed, 1986; Jerusalem, Shining Still, 1987; Soap Soup, 1992; A Great Miracle Happened Here: A Chanukah Story, 1993; Patchwork Island, 1994; City Dog, 1994; City Noise, 1994; Paul, 1994; James and the Rain, 1995; Thoughts, Pictures and Words (autobiog. for children) 1995, The Upstairs Cat 1997, The Sky is Always in the Sky (poems) 1998, I Am Me 2000, The Animals and the Ark 2002, Moon Have You Met My Mother (poetry collection) 2003. Contributions: magazines and periodicals. *Honours:* Book Show Awards, American Institute of Graphic Arts, 1955–60; Children's Book Award, International Reading Asscn, 1976; Children's Book Council Showcase Selections, 1976–77; National Council of Teachers of English Award for Poetry, 1979; Children's Science Book Award, New York Acad. of Sciences, 1980; American Library Asscn Awards, 1980, 1982, 1993; School Library Journal Best Book, 1987; John S. Burrough Science Award, 1992. *Address:* 96 Joralemon Street, New York, NY 11201, USA.

KUTTNER, Paul; Publicity Dir and Author; b. 20 Sept. 1922, Berlin, Germany; m. Ursula Timmermann 1963 (divorced 1972); one s. *Education:* Bryanston College, 1939–40. *Career:* US Publicity Dir, Guinness Book of World Records, 1964–89; Publicity Dir, Sterling Publishing Co Inc, 1989–96. *Publications:* The Man Who Lost Everything, 1976; Condemned, 1983; Absolute Proof, 1984; The Iron Virgin, 1985; History's Trickiest Questions, 1990; Arts & Entertainment's Trickiest Questions, 1993; Science's Trickiest Questions, 1994; The Holocaust: Hoax or History? – The Book of Answers to Those Who Would Deny the Holocaust, 1997. Other: Trans. Contributions: Der Weg; London Week. *Address:* 37–26 87th St, Apt 5C, Jackson Heights, NY 11372, USA.

KWEI-ARMAH, Kwame; British actor, playwright and singer; b. (Ian Roberts), 1967, London; three c. *Education:* Barbara Speake Stage School. *Career:* writer-in-residence, Bristol Old Vic 1999–01; currently writer on attachment to the Nat. Theatre Studio; took part in Celebrity Fame Acad. (BBC) 2003. *Plays as writer:* Big Nose (adaptation of Rostand's Cyrano De Bergerac, Belgrade Theatre, Coventry) 1999, Blues Brother Soul Sister (musical, Bristol Old Vic) 2000, A Bitter Herb (Peggy Ramsey Bursary, Bristol Old Vic) 2001, Hold On (Durham Theatre Royal) 2002, Elmina's Kitchen (Royal Nat. Theatre, Charles Wintour Award for Most Promising Playwright, Evening Standard Theatre Awards 2004) 2003, Fix Up (Royal Nat. Theatre) 2004. *Plays as actor:* Mozart and Salieri (Crucible, Sheffield). *Films:* Cutthroat Island 1995. *Television:* Between The Lines 1994, Casualty 1999–2004, Holby City 2000, Pride 2004. *Recordings:* album: Kwame 2003. *Honours:* Evening Standard Charles Wintour Award for Most Promising Playwright 2003. *Address:* c/o Methuen Publishing Head Office, 215 Vauxhall Bridge Road, London, SW1V 1EJ, England. *Website:* www.methuen.co.uk.

KYLE, Duncan (see Broxholme, John Franklin).

KYLE, Susan (Eloise Spaeth), (Diana Blayne, Diana Palmer); Author; b. 12 Dec. 1946, Cuthbert, GA, USA; m. James Edward Kyle, 9 Oct. 1972, one s. *Education:* BA, Piedmont College, 1995. *Career:* mem. Authors' Guild. *Publications:* Heather's Song, 1982; Diamond Spur, 1988; Amelia, 1993; Nora, 1994; All That Glitters, 1995; many other books. Contributions: journals and magazines. *Address:* PO Box 844, Cornelia, GA 30531, USA.

L

LA PLANTE, Lynda; British television dramatist and novelist; b. 15 March 1946, Formby; m. Richard La Plante (divorced). *Education:* Royal Coll. of Dramatic Art. *Career:* fmr actress; appeared in The Gentle Touch, Out, Minder; founder and Chair. La Plante Productions 1994–. *Television includes:* Prime Suspect 1991, 1993, 1995, Civvies, Framed, Seekers, Widows (series), Comics (two-part drama) 1993, Cold Shoulder 2 1996, Cold Blood, Bella Mafia 1997, Trial and Retribution 1997–, Killer Net 1998, Mind Games 2000, The Warden 2001, Framed 2002, Widows (mini-series) 2002, The Commander 2003. *Publications include:* The Widows 1983, The Widows II 1985, The Talisman 1987, Bella Mafia 1991, Framed 1992, Civvies 1992, Prime Suspect 1992, Seekers 1993, Entwined 1993, Prime Suspect 2 1993, Lifeboat 1994, Cold Shoulder 1994, Prime Suspect 3 1994, She's Out 1995, The Governor 1996, Cold Blood 1996, Trial and Retribution 1997, Cold Heart 1998, Trial and Retribution 2 1998, Trial and Retribution 3 1999, Trial and Retribution 4 2000, Sleeping Cruelty 2000, Trial and Retribution 5 2002, Trial and Retribution 6 2002, Royal Flush 2002, Like a Charm (short stories) 2004, Above Suspicion (novel) 2004. *Address:* La Plante Productions Ltd, Paramount House, 162–170 Wardour Street, London, W1F 8ZX, England (Office). *Telephone:* (20) 7734-6767. *Fax:* (20) 7734-7878. *Website:* www.laplanteproductions.com.

LA TOURETTE, Jacqueline; Writer; b. 5 May 1926, Denver, CO, USA. *Education:* San Jose State College, 1948–51. *Publications:* The Joseph Stone, 1971; A Matter of Sixpence, 1972; The Madonna Creek Witch, 1973; The Previous Lady, 1974; The Pompeii Scroll, 1975; Shadows in Umbria, 1979; The Wild Harp, 1981; Patarran, 1983; The House on Octavia Street, 1984; The Incense Tree, 1986. *Address:* c/o Raines and Raines, 71 Park Ave, New York, NY 10016, USA.

LABERGE, Marie; Dramatist, Author, Poet and Ed.; b. 29 Nov. 1950, Québec, Canada. *Education:* Université Laval, 1970–72; Conservatoire d'art dramatique de Québec, 1972–75. *Career:* Pres., Centre d'essai des auteurs dramatiques, 1987–89; Theatre Ed., Editions du Boréal, 1991–. *Publications:* Avec l'hiver qui s'en vient, 1981; Ils étaient venus pour…, 1981; C'était avant la guerre à l'Anse à Gilles, 1981, English trans. as Before the War, Down at l'Anse à Gilles, 1986; Jocelyne Trudelle trouvée morte dans ses larmes, 1983; Deux tangos pour toute une vie, 1985; L'homme gris, 1986, English trans. as Night, 1988; Le Night Cap Bar, 1987; Oublier, 1987, English trans. as Forgetting, 1988; Aurélie, ma soeur, 1988, English trans. as Aurélie, My Sister, 1989; Le Blanc, 1989; Juillet, 1989; Quelques adieux, 1992; Pierre, ou, La consolation, 1992; Annabelle, 1996; Le gout du bonheur, 2000. Contributions: Film, radio, television and various publications. *Honours:* Gov.-Gen.'s Award for Drama, 1982; Chevalier, Ordre des Arts et des Lettres, 1989; Prix des Lectrices de Elle-Québec, 1992. *Address:* c/o Editions du Boréal, 447 rue Saint-Denis, Montréal, QC H2J 2L2, Canada.

LaBUTE, Neil; American playwright and film writer and director; b. 19 March 1963, Detroit, MI; m.; two c. *Education:* Brigham Young Univ., Univ. of Kansas, New York Univ. *Films:* In the Company of Men (writer, dir) (Sundance Film Festival Filmmakers' Trophy, Soc. of Texas Film Critics Best Original Screenplay award, New York Film Critics Circle Best First Film) 1997, Your Friends and Neighbors (writer, dir) 1998, Tumble (writer) 2000, Nurse Betty (dir) 2000, Possession (screenplay writer, dir) 2002, The Shape of Things (writer, dir) 2003. *Theatre productions:* Woyzeck, Dracula, Sangguinarians & Sycophants, Ravages, Rounder, Lepers, Filthy Talk For Troubled Times, In the Company of Men (Asscn for Mormon Letters Award for Drama 1993) 1992, Bash: Latterday Plays 2000, The Shape of Things 2001, The Distance From Here (Almeida, London) 2002, The Mercy Seat 2002, Merge 2003. *Publications:* In the Company of Men 1998, Your Friends and Neighbors 1999, Bash: Latterday Plays 2000, The Shape of Things 2001, The Distance from Here 2003, The Mercy Seat 2003, Seconds of Pleasure (short stories) 2004. *Literary Agent:* Sanford-Gross Agency, 1015 Gayley Avenue, Suite 301, Los Angeles, CA 90024, USA.

LACEY, Robert; Author; b. 3 Jan. 1944, Guildford, Surrey, England. *Education:* BA, 1966, Diploma in Education, 1967, MA, 1970, Selwyn College, Cambridge. *Career:* Asst Ed., Sunday Times Magazine, 1969–73; Ed., Look! pages, Sunday Times, 1973–74. *Publications:* The French Revolution, 2 vols, 1968; The Rise of Napoleon, 1969; The Peninsular War, 1969; 1812: The Retreat From Moscow, 1969; Robert, Earl of Essex: An Elizabethan Icarus, 1971; The Life and Times of Henry Vlll, 1972; The Queens of the North Atlantic, 1973; Sir Walter Raleigh, 1973; Sir Francis Drake and the Golden Hinde, 1975; Heritage of Britain (ed., contributor), 1975; Majesty: Elizabeth ll and the House of Windsor, 1977; The Kingdom: Arabia and the House of Saud, 1981; Princess, 1982; Aristocrats, 1983; Ford: The Men and the Machine, 1986; God Bless Her: Her Majesty Queen Elizabeth the Queen Mother, 1987; Little Man: Meyer Lansky and the Gangster Life, 1991; Grace, 1994; Royal: Her Majesty Queen Elizabeth II, 2002.

LACKEY, Mercedes; Writer; b. 24 June 1950, Chicago, IL, USA; m. 1st Anthony Lackey 10 June 1972 (divorced); m. 2nd Larry Dixon 14 Dec. 1990. *Education:* BS, Purdue University, 1972. *Career:* mem. SFWA. *Publications:* Arrow's Flight, 1987; Arrows of the Queen, 1987; Arrow's Fall, 1988; Oathbound, 1988; Magic's Pawn, 1989; Oathbreakers, 1989; Reap the Whirlwind (with C. J. Cherryh), 1989; Children of the Night, 1990; Knight of Ghosts and Shadows (with Ellen Guon), 1990; Magic's Price, 1990; Magic's Promise, 1990; By the Sword, 1991; The Elvenbane (with Andre Norton), 1991; Jinx High, 1991; Winds of Fate, 1991; Born to Run (with Larry Dixon), 1992; Castle of Deception (with Joshua Sherman), 1992; The Lark and the Wren, 1992; The Last Herald Mage, 1992; Summoned to Tourney (with Ellen Guon), 1992; The Ship Who Searched (with Anne McCaffrey), 1992; Wheels of Fire (with Mark Shepherd), 1992; Winds of Change, 1992; Wing Commander: Freedom Flight (with Ellen Guon), 1992; Burning Water, 1993; Fortress of Frost and Fire (with Ru Emerson), 1993; If I Pay Thee Not in Gold (with Piers Anthony), 1993; Prison of Souls (with Mark Shepherd), 1993; Rediscovery: A Novel of Darkover (with Marion Zimmer Bradley), 1993; The Robin and the Kestrel, 1993; When the Bough Breaks (with Holly Lisle), 1993; Winds of Fury, 1993; The Black Gryphon (with Larry Dixon), 1994; A Cast of Corbies (with Joshua Sherman), 1994; Chrome Circle (with Larry Dixon), 1994; Sacred Ground, 1994; Storm Warning, 1994; The Eagle and the Nightingales, 1995; Elvenblood (with Andre Norton), 1995; The Fire Rose, 1995; Storm Rising, 1995; Tiger Burning Bright (with Andre Norton and Marion Zimmer Bradley), 1995; The White Gryphon (with Larry Dixon), 1995; Firebird, 1996; Lammas Night, 1996; The Silver Gryphon (with Larry Dixon), 1996; Storm Breaking, 1996; Four and Twenty Blackbirds, 1997; Owlflight (with Larry Dixon), 1997; Owlsight (with Larry Dixon), 1998; The Black Swan, 1999; The Chrome Bone (with Larry Dixon), 1999; Owlknight (with Larry Dixon), 1999; The River's Gift, 1999; Werehunter, 1999; Brightly Burning, 2000; Beyond the World's End, 2001; The Serpent's Shadow, 2001. Contributions: many anthologies and periodicals. *Address:* c/o Russell Galen, 845 Third Ave, New York, NY 10022, USA.

LACOUTURE, Jean Marie-Gérard, DenSoc; French writer; b. 9 June 1921, Bordeaux; m. Simonne Grésillon; one d. *Career:* journalist 1946–72; Press Attaché, Résidence-Générale of France, Morocco 1947–49; Diplomatic Ed. Combat 1950–51; reporter, Le Monde 1951–72; corresp., France-Soir, Egypt 1954–56; Research Fellow, Harvard Univ. 1966; Dir of Collections, Editions du Seuil 1962–80. *Publications include:* Cinq Hommes et la France 1961, De Gaulle 1965, Le Vietnam entre deux paix 1965, Hô Chi Minh 1967, Nasser 1971, André Malraux, une vie dans le siècle 1973, Un sang d'encre 1974, Léon Blum 1977, Survive le peuple cambodgien! 1978, Signes du Taureau 1979, François Mauriac (two vols) 1980, Pierre Mendès France 1981, Le Piéton de Bordeaux 1981, Profils perdus 1983, De Gaulle (three vols) 1984–86, Algérie: la guerre est finie 1985, Champollion: Une vie de lumières 1989, Enquête sur l'auteur 1989, Jésuites (two vols) 1991–92, Voyous et gentlemen: une histoire du rugby 1993, le Désempire (jtly) 1993, Une adolescence du siècle 1994, Mes héros et nos monstres 1995, Montaigne à cheval 1996, Histoire de France en cent tableaux 1997, Mitterrand (two vols) 1998, Greta Garbo: la dame aux caméras 1999, Stendhal – Le bonheur vagabond 2004; several works in collaboration with Simonne Lacouture and others. *Honours:* Officer, Légion d'honneur, Commdr des Arts et Lettres; Prix Sola Cabiati de la Ville de Paris 1996. *Address:* 37 quai des Grands Augustins, 75006 Paris, France.

LAFFIN, John (Alfred Charles); Author, Journalist and Lecturer; b. 21 Sept. 1922, Sydney, NSW, Australia; m. Hazelle Stonham, 6 Oct. 1943, deceased 13 March 1997, one s. two d. *Education:* MA; DLitt. *Career:* Battlefield Archaeologist; Adviser/Consultant, War, Military History and Islam; Founder, John Laffin Australian Battlefield Museum, 1988; mem. Society of Authors, UK; Australian Society of Authors; Pres., Families and Friends of the First A I F. *Publications:* Return to Glory, 1953; Digger: Story of the Australian Soldier, 1959; Codes and Ciphers, 1964; Anzacs at War, 1965; Jackboot: Story of the German Soldier, 1965; The Hunger to Come, 1966; Women in Battle, 1967; Devil's Goad, 1970; Americans in Battle, 1972; The Arab Mind, 1974; Dagger of Islam, 1979; Damn the Dardanelles!, 1980; Fight for the Falklands, 1982; The PLO Connections, 1982; Australian Army at War 1899–1975, 1982; The Man the Nazis Couldn't Catch, 1984; On the Western Front, 1985; Know the Middle East, 1985; Brassey's Battles, 1986; War Annual 1, 1986; War Annual 2, 1987; Battlefield Archaeology, 1987; War Annual 3, 1987; Western Front, 1916–17: The Price of Honour, 1988; Western Front, 1917–18: The Cost of Victory, 1988; Holy War – Islam Fights, 1988; War Annual 4, 1988; British Butchers and Bunglers of World War I, 1989; War Annual 5, 1991; The Western Front Illustrated, 1991; Dictionary of Africa Since 1960, 1991; Guidebook to Australian Battlefields of France and Flanders 1916–18, 1992; Digging up the Diggers, War, 1993; Panorama of the Western Front, 1993; A Western Front Companion, 1994; Forever Forward, 1994; War Annual 6, 1994; Aussie Guide to Britain, 1995; Hitler Warned Us, 1995; War Annual 7, 1995; Brassey's Book of Espionage 1996; War Annual 8, 1997; British VCs of World War II, 1997; The Spirit and the Source (poems), 1997; Gallipoli, 1999; The Somme, 1999; Raiders: Great Exploits of the Second World War, 1999; The Battle of Hamel: Australians' Finest Victory, 1999; Combat Surgeons, 1999; A Kind of Immortality (autobiog.), Vol. 1, 2000. Contributions: newspapers, magazines and journals. *Address:* 37 Horizon Ave, Sundown Village, Narrabundah, ACT 2604, Australia.

LAFFONT, Robert Raoul, LenD; French publishing executive; b. 30 Nov. 1916, Marseille; m. Hélène Furterer 1987; three s. two d. (from previous marriages). *Education:* Lycée Pérrier, Marseille and Ecole des Hautes Etudes Commerciales, Paris. *Career:* Lt 94th Regt of Artillery, Montagne; f. Editions Robert Laffont, Marseille 1941, transferred to Paris 1945, Pres. 1959–86; Fondateur du Pont-Royal. *Publication:* Robert Laffont, éditeur 1974, Léger étonnement avant le saut 1995. *Honours:* Chevalier, Légion d'Honneur, Officier, Ordre Nat. du Mérite. *Address:* Editions Robert Laffont, 24 avenue Marceau, 75008 Paris (Office); 11 rue Pierre Nicole, Paris 75005, France (Home). *Telephone:* 43-29-12-33 (Office); 43-26-02-41 (Home).

LAGZDINS, Viktors; Writer; b. 28 Aug. 1926, Riga, Latvia; m. Dzidra Reita, 6 June 1952, one d. *Education:* Pedagogic School, Liepaja, 1947; Diploma of Education, Faculty of Philology, Riga Pedagogic Institute, 1958. *Career:* Teacher, 1947–58; Journalist, Liepaja newspaper, 1958–63, Riga magazine, 1963–82; mem. Writers' Union of Latvia, 1959–, chair. of the prose section, 1979–80. *Publications:* Parbaude, English trans. as The Test, 1959; Indianu Virsaitis Drossirdigais Kikakis, 1963; Kedes Loks, 1972; Nakts Mezazos, English trans. as A Night at Elk Farm, 1976; Zili Zala, English trans. as The Blue and The Green, 1986. *Address:* Agenskalna iela 22-48, Riga 1046, Latvia.

LAHIRI, Jhumpa, BA, MA, PhD; British/American novelist and teacher; b. 1967, London, England; m.; one s. *Education:* Barnard Coll., Boston Univ. *Career:* tutor in Creative Writing, Boston Univ., Rhode Island School of Design. *Publications:* novels: Interpreter of Maladies 1999, The Namesake 2003; short story contribs to The New Yorker 1998. *Honours:* Pulitzer Prize for Fiction 2000, New Yorker Debut of the Year Award, Guggenheim Fellowship 2002. *Address:* c/o Houghton Mifflin Co., 222 Berkeley Street, Boston, MA 02116, USA. *Telephone:* (617) 351-5000. *Website:* www.hmco .com.

LAI, Jimmy; Hong Kong business executive, journalist and publisher. *Career:* Propr Giordano (retail clothing chain) 1980–, Chair. 1980–94; Publr Next Magazine 1990–, Apple Daily 1995–. *Address:* Apple Daily, 6/F Garment Centre, 576–586 Castle Peak Road, Cheung Sha Wan; Next Magazine, Westlands Centre, 10/F, 20 Westlands Road, Quarry Bay, Hong Kong, Special Administrative Region, People's Republic of China. *Telephone:* 29908685 (Apple Daily); 28119686 (Next Magazine). *Fax:* 23708908 (Apple Daily); 28113862 (Next Magazine).

LAI, Larissa; Writer and Poet; b. 13 Sept. 1967, La Jolla, CA, USA. *Education:* BA, Sociology, University of British Columbia, 1990. *Career:* Asst Curator, Yellow Peril: Reconsidered, 1990; Co-ordinator, Saw Video Co-op, 1991; Television and Video Assoc., Banff Centre for the Arts, 1994; Ed., Front Magazine, 1994–95; Gallery Animateur, Vancouver Art Gallery, 1996–97; Writer-in-Residence, University of Calgary, 1997–98; mem. Writers Union of Canada; Asian Canadian Writers Workshop. *Publications:* Fiction: New Reeboks, 1994; The Home Body, 1994; Water, and Other Measures of Distance, 1996; The Voice of the Blind Concubine, 1996; The Peacock Hen, 1996. Poetry: The Birdwoman, 1990; Lullabye for the Insect Catcher, 1990; Eighty Years Bathing, 1991; Where, 1991; Trap I, 1991; Trap II, 1991; Bone China, 1991; Nora, 1991; Glory, 1991; Arrangements, 1991; Shade, 1991; Nostalgia, 1992; Calling Home, 1992; The Escape, 1992; Tell: Longing and Belonging, 1994. *Honours:* Astraea Foundation Emerging Writers Award, 1995. *Address:* 78 Albany Avenue, Toronto, ON M5R 3C3, Canada.

LAIRD, Elizabeth Mary Risk, BA, MLitt; writer; b. 21 Oct. 1943, Wellington, New Zealand; m. David Buchanan McDowall 1975; two s. *Education:* Bristol Univ., Edinburgh Univ. *Publications:* Red Sky in the Morning 1988, Arcadia 1990, Kiss the Dust 1991, Hiding Out 1993, Secret Friends 1996, Jay 1997, The Wild Things Series 1999–2000, Jake's Tower 2001, The Garbage King 2003, A Little Piece of Ground 2003, Paradise End 2004. *Honours:* Children's Book Award 1992, Glass Globe Award Dutch Royal Geographical Soc. 1992, Smarties Young Judges Award 1994, Lancashire Book Award 1997. *Address:* 31 Cambrian Road, Richmond, Surrey TW10 6JQ, England.

LAKE, David John; University Prof. and Writer; b. 26 March 1929, Bangalore, India; m. Marguerite Ivy Ferris 30 Dec. 1964; one d. three step-c. *Education:* BA, MA, DipEd, Trinity College, Cambridge, 1949–53; Diploma of Linguistics, University of Wales, Bangor, 1964–65; PhD, University of Queensland, Australia, 1974. *Publications:* Hornpipes and Funerals (poems), 1973; The Canon of Thomas Middleton's Plays, 1975; Walkers on the Sky, 1976; The Right Hand of Dextra, 1977; The Wildings of Westron, 1977; The Gods of Xuma, 1978; The Man who Loved Morlocks, 1981; The Changelings of Chaan, 1985. Contributions: Extrapolation; Science Fiction Studies; Foundation; Notes and Queries; Explicator; Ring Bearer; Wellsian. *Honours:* Ditmar Awards for Best Australian Science Fiction Novel, 1977, 1982, and for Short Fiction, 1999. *Address:* 7 Eighth Ave, St Lucia, Qld 4067, Australia.

LAL, Deepak (Kumar); Prof. of International Devt Studies and Writer; b. 3 Jan. 1940, Lahore, India; m. Barbara Ballis, 1971, one s. one d. *Education:* BA, St Stephen's College, Delhi, 1959; MA, 1962, BPhil, 1965, Jesus College, Oxford. *Career:* Indian Foreign Service, 1963–65; Lecturer, Christ Church, Oxford, 1966–68; Research Fellow, Nuffield College, Oxford, 1968–70; Lecturer, 1970–79, Reader, 1979–84, Prof. of Political Economy, 1984–93, Prof. Emeritus, 1993–, University College London; Research Administrator, World Bank, Washington, DC, 1983–87; James S. Coleman Prof. of International Devt, University of California at Los Angeles, 1991–. *Publications:* Wells and Welfare, 1972; New Economic Policies of India, 1973; Methods of Project Analysis: A Review, 1974; Appraising Foreign Investment in Developing Countries (co-author), 1975; Unemployment and Wage Inflation in Industrial Economies, 1977; Men or Machines: A Study of Labour-Capital Substitution in Road Construction in the Philippines (with others), 1978; Poverty, Power, and Prejudice, 1978; Market Access for Semi-Manufactures from Developing Countries, 1979; Poverty and Growth in Kenya (with Paul Collier), 1980; Prices for Planning: Towards the Reform of Indian Planning, 1980; A Liberal International Economic Order: The International Monetary System and Economic Development, 1980; The Poverty of 'Development Economics', 1983; The Real Effects of Stabilization and Structural Adjustment Policies: An Extension of the Australian Adjustment Model, 1984; Labour and Poverty in Kenya: 1900–1980 (with Paul Collier), 1986; Stagflation, Savings, and the State: Perspectives on the Global Economy (ed. with Martin Wolf), 1986; The Hindu Equilibrium, two vols, 1988–89; Aspects of Indian Labour, 1989; Impediments to Trade Liberalization in Sri Lanka (with Sarath Rajapatirana), 1989; Nationalised Universities: Paradox of the Privatisation Age, 1989; Public Policy and Economic Development: Essays in Honour of Ian Little (ed. with Maurice Scott), 1990; The Limits of International Co-operation, 1990; Political Economy and Public Policy, 1990; Development Economics (ed.), four vols, 1991; The Repressed Economy, 1993; Against Dirigisme: The Case for Unshackling Economic Markets, 1994; From Closed to Open Economy Macroeconomics: The Real Exchange Rate and Capital Inflows, India: 1981–1994 (with D. K. Joshi), 1994; The Political Economy of Poverty, Equity, and Growth: A Comparative Study (with H. Myint), 1996; Unintended Consequences: The Impact of Factor Endowments, Culture, and Politics on Long-Run Economic Performance, 1998; Unfinished Business, 1999; Trade, Development and Political Economy (ed. with R. Snape), 2001. Contributions: Professional journals. *Address:* c/o Dept of Economics, University of California at Los Angeles, 405 Hilgard Ave, Los Angeles, CA 90024, USA.

LAMB, Andrew (Martin); Writer on Music; b. 23 Sept. 1942, Oldham, Lancashire, England; m. Wendy Ann Davies, 1 April 1970, one s. two d. *Education:* Corpus Christi College, Oxford, 1960–63; MA, University of Oxford. *Career:* mem. Fellow, Institute of Actuaries; Lancashire County Cricket Club. *Publications:* Jerome Kern in Edwardian London, 1985; Ganzl's Book of the Musical Theatre (with Kurt Ganzl), 1988; Skaters' Waltz: The Story of the Waldteufels, 1995; An Offenbach Family Album, 1997; Shirley House to Trinity School, 1999; 150 Years of Popular Musical Theatre, 2000; Leslie Stuart: Composer of Florodora, 2002. Editor: The Moulin Rouge, 1990; Light Music from Austria, 1992; Leslie Stuart: My Bohemian Life, 2003. Contributions: The New Grove Dictionary of Music and Musicians; The New Grove Dictionary of American Music; The New Grove Dictionary of Opera; Gramophone; Musical Times; Classic CD; American Music; Music and Letters; Wisden Cricket Monthly; Cricketer; Listener; Notes. *Address:* 12 Fullers Wood, Croydon CR0 8HZ, England. *E-mail:* andrew-lamb@fullerswood.fsnet.co.uk.

LAMB, Elizabeth Searle; Poet, Writer and Ed.; b. 22 Jan. 1917, Topeka, KS, USA; m. F. Bruce Lamb, 11 Dec. 1941, deceased 1992, one d. *Education:* BA, 1939, BMus, 1940, University of Kansas. *Career:* Ed., Frogpond, 1984–90, 1994; Co-Ed., Haiku Southwest, 1993–94; mem. Haiku Society of America; Haiku International, Japan; Assen of International Renku, Japan; Haiku Canada; Poetry Society of America. *Publications:* Pelican Tree and Other Panama Adventures (co-author), 1953; Today and Every Day, 1970; Inside Me, Outside Me, 1974; In This Blaze of Sun, 1975; Picasso's Bust of Sylvette, 1977; 39 Blossoms, 1982; Casting Into a Cloud, 1985; Lines for My Mother, Dying, 1988; The Light of Elizabeth Lamb: 100 American Haiku, 1993; Ripples Spreading Out, 1997; Platek Irysa (Petals of Iris), 1998; Across the Windharp, 1999. Contributions: many anthologies, journals, and magazines. *Honours:* Cicada Awards Canada 1977, 1980, Henderson Awards 1978, 1981, 1982, 1991, 1993, Dellbrook Poetry Award 1979, HSA Merit Book Awards 1979, 1983, 1987, Yuki Teikei 1981, 1982, 1989, 1994, Certificate of Achievement Haiku Society of America 1995, Hon. Curator American Haiku Archive, California State Library, Sacramento 1996–97, 55th Basho Festival English Haiku Special Award Japan, Sora Award Haiku Soc. of America 2003. *Address:* 970 Acequia Madre, Sante Fe, NM 87505, USA. *Telephone:* (505) 982-8890. *E-mail:* eslamb@earthlink.net.

LAMBDIN, Dewey Whitley, II, BS; writer; b. 21 Jan. 1945, San Diego, CA, USA; m. 1st Melinda Alice Phillips 1971; m. 2nd Julie Dawn Pascoe 1984. *Education:* Montana State Univ. *Career:* mem. Sisters in Crime. *Publications:* The King's Coat, 1989; The French Admiral, 1990; King's Commission, 1991; King's Privateer, 1992; The Gun Ketch, 1993; For King and Country, 1994; HMS Cockerel, 1995; King's Commander, 1997. Contributions: newspapers and periodicals. *Honours:* Theme Vault, University of Tennessee 1963. *Address:* c/o Wieser & Wieser Inc, 118 E 25th Street, New York, NY 10010, USA.

LAMBERT, Angela Maria; Writer and Journalist; b. 14 April 1940, Beckenham, Kent, England; m. Martin Lambert 10 Dec. 1962 (divorced Aug. 1966); one s. two d. *Education:* St Hilda's College, Oxford, 1959–61; Degree, Philosophy, Politics and Economics. *Career:* Publishing, 1961–62; Journalism, 1962–63; Politics, 1964–67; Newspaper Journalism, 1967–72; Television Reporter, 1972–88; Newspaper Feature Writer and Columnist, The Independent, 1988–95, Daily Mail, 1995–2000, The Sunday Telegraph, 2001–; mem. Exec. Committee, English PEN, 1991–96. *Publications:* Non-Fiction: Unquiet Souls, 1984; 1939: The Last Season of Peace, 1989. Fiction: Love Among the Single Classes, 1986; No Talking after Lights, 1989; A Rather English Marriage, 1991; The Constant Mistress, 1994; Kiss and Kin, 1997; Golden Lads and Girls, 1998; The Property of Rain, 2001. Contributions: several, 1965–. *Honours:* Romantic Novel of the Year, 1988. *Literary Agent:* Caradoc King, AP Watt Ltd, 20 John St, London WC1N 2DR, England.

LAMBERT, Derek (William), (Richard Falkirk); Journalist and Author; b. 10 Oct. 1929, London, England. *Career:* Journalist, Devon, Norfolk, Yorkshire and National newspapers, 1950–68. *Publications:* Fiction: For Infamous Conduct, 1970; Grans Slam, 1971; The Great Land, 1977; The Lottery, 1983. Mystery Fiction: Angels in the Snow, 1969; The Kites of War, 1970; The Red House, 1972; The Yermakov Transfer, 1974; Touch the Lion's Paw, 1975; The Saint Peter's Plot, 1978; The Memory Man, 1979; I, Said the Spy, 1980; Trance, 1981; The Red Dove, 1982; The Judas Code, 1983; The Golden Express, 1984; The Man Who Was Saturday, 1985; Chase, 1987; Triad, 1988. Mystery Novels as Richard Falkirk: The Chill Factor, 1971; The Twisted Wire, 1971; Blackstone, 1972; Beau Blackstone, 1973; Blackstone's Fancy, 1973; Blackstone and the Scourge of Europe, 1974; Blackstone Underground, 1976; Blackstone on Broadway, 1977. Other: The Sheltered Days: Growing Up in the War, 1965; Don't Quote Me – But, 1979; And I Quote, 1980; Unquote, 1981; Just Like the Blitz: A Reporter's Notebook, 1987; The Night and the City, 1989; The Gate of the Sun, 1990. *Address:* 350 Hudson St, New York, NY 10014, USA.

LAMBERT, Gavin; writer; b. 23 July 1924, East Grinstead, England. *Education:* Magdalen Coll., Oxford. *Career:* Co-Ed., Sequence magazine 1947–50; Ed., Sight and Sound 1950–56; writer, reviewer 1956–; mem. Acad. of Motion Pictures, Arts and Sciences. *Publications:* fiction: The Slide Area 1959, Inside Daisy Clover 1963, The Goodbye People 1971, In the Night all Cats are Grey 1976, Running Time 1983; non-fiction: On Cukor 1973, The Dangerous Edge 1975, Norma Shearer 1990, Nazimova 1997, Mainly About Lindsay Anderson 2000, Natalie Wood: a Life 2004. *Honours:* Thomas R. Coward Memorial Award for Fiction 1966, William K. Everson Award, Nat. Board of Review 1997. *Literary Agent:* Joy Harris Literary Agency Inc, 156 Fifth Avenue, Suite 617, New York, NY 10010, USA. *Address:* 1338 N Laurel Avenue, Apt 102, West Hollywood, CA 90046, USA. *E-mail:* gavinlambert@adelphia.net.

LAMBOT, Isobel Mary, (Daniel Ingham, Mary Turner); Novelist; b. 21 July 1926, Birmingham, England; m. Maurice Edouard Lambot, 19 Dec. 1959, deceased. *Education:* BA, Liverpool University; Teaching Certificate, Birmingham University. *Career:* Tutor in Creative Writing, Lichfield Evening Institute, 1973–80; mem. CWA; Society of Authors; Writers' Guild of Great Britain; MWA. *Publications:* As Isobel Lambot: Taste of Murder, 1966; Deadly Return, 1966; Shroud of Canvas, 1967; Dangerous Refuge, 1967; Danger Merchant, 1968; The Queen Dies First, 1968; Killer's Laughter, 1968; Let the Witness Die, 1969; Point of Death, 1969; Watcher on the Shore, 1971; Come Back and Die, 1972; Grip of Fear, 1974; The Identity Trap, 1978; Past Tense, 1979; Rooney's Gold, 1984; Still Waters Run Deadly, 1987; Blood Ties, 1987; Bloody Festival, 1991; The Flower of Violence, 1992; The Craft of Writing Crime Novels, 1992. As Daniel Ingham: Contract for Death, 1972. As Mary Turner: The Justice Hunt, 1975; So Bright a Lady, 1977; Runaway Lady, 1980. Contributions: Women's journals.

LAMBRAKIS, Christos; Greek newspaper proprietor and journalist; b. 24 Feb. 1934. *Education:* London School of Econs, UK. *Career:* Publr and Ed. weekly Tachydromos (Courier) 1955–; succeeded father as propr of dailies To Vima (Tribune), Ta Nea (News) and the weeklies Economicos Tachydromos (Economic Courier) 1957, Omada (The Team) 1958; Publr monthly Epoches 1963; Pres. Greek Section, Int. Press Inst.; imprisoned (Folegandros Prison Island) Nov. 1967. *Address:* c/o Lambrakis Press, Odos Christou Lada 3, 102 37 Athens, Greece. *Telephone:* 3230-221.

LAMBRON, Marc; French journalist and writer; b. 4 Feb. 1957, Lyon; m. Sophie Missoffe 1983; one s. two d. *Education:* Ecole normale supérieure, Institut d'etudes politiques, Ecole nationale d'admin. *Career:* columnist, Point 1986–, Madame Figaro; mem. Conseil d'Etat 1985–. *Publications:* L'Impromptu de Madrid 1988, La nuit des masques 1990, Carnet de bal 1992, L'oeil du silence 1993, 1941 1997, Etrangers dans la nuit 2001, Carnet de bal II 2003, Les Menteurs 2004. *Honours:* Chevalier, Ordre des Arts et des Lettres, Chevalier, Légion d'honneur 2004; Prix des Deux Magots 1989, Prix Colette 1991, Prix Fémina 1993. *Address:* 17 rue Lagrange, 75005 Paris, France. *Telephone:* 1-40-51-02-12. *Fax:* 1-46-33-43-18.

LAMM, Donald Stephen, BA; American publisher; *Literary Agent, Carlisle & Company*; b. 31 May 1931, New York; m. Jean S. Nicol 1958; two s. one d. *Education:* Fieldston School, Yale Univ. and Univs of Oxford, UK. *Career:* Counter-intelligence Corps, US Army 1953–55; joined W. W. Norton & Co. Inc. 1956, college rep. 1956–59, Ed. 1959–2000, Dir 1964–2000, Vice-Pres. 1968–76, Chair. 1984–2000; currently Literary Agent, Carlisle & Co.; Regents Lecturer, Univ. of Calif., Berkeley 1997–99; Pres. Yale Univ. Press; mem. Advisory Council Inst. of Early American History and Culture 1979–82; mem. Council on Foreign Relations 1978–; mem. Council, Woodrow Wilson Center, Int. Advisory Bd, Logos; Guest Fellow, Yale Univ. 1980, 1985; Trustee, The Roper Center 1984–; Fellow, Branford Coll. Yale Univ. 1985–2000, Center for Advanced Study in Behavioral Sciences 1998–99; Guest Fellow Woodrow Wilson Center 1996; Pres. Bd of Govs Yale Univ. 1986–; Ida H. Beam Distinguished Visiting Prof. Univ. of Iowa 1987–88; mem. American Acad. of Arts and Sciences (first book publisher elected in AAAS history). *Publications:* Economics and the Common Reader 1989, Beyond Literacy 1990, Book Publishing in the United States Today 1997, Perception, Cognition and Language 2000. *Address:* Carlisle & Co., 24 East 64th Street, New York, NY 10021 (Office); 741 Calle Picacho, Santa Fe, NM 87301, USA (Home).

LAMMING, George (Eric); Novelist; b. 8 June 1927, Carrington Village, Barbados. *Career:* Writer-in-Residence, University of the West Indies, Jamaica, 1967–68. *Publications:* In the Castle of My Skin, 1953; The Emigrants, 1955; Of Age and Innocence, 1958; Water with Berries, 1971; Natives of My Person, 1972. Short Stories: David's Walk, 1948; A Wedding in Spring, 1960; Birthday Weather, 1966; Birds of a Feather, 1970. *Honours:* Guggenheim Fellowship, 1954; Maugham Award, 1957; Canada Council Fellowship, 1962; DLitt, University of the West Indies, 1980.

LAMMON, Martin; Prof. of English and Poet; b. 19 June 1958, Wilmington, OH, USA; m. Frances Elizabeth Davis, 17 Aug. 1996. *Education:* BA, Wittenberg University, 1980; MA, 1982, PhD, 1991, Ohio University. *Career:* Visiting Instructor in English, Juniata College, Huntingdon, Pennsylvania, 1988–91; Asst Prof., then Assoc. Prof. of English, Fairmont State College, West Virginia, 1991–97; Co-Founder and Co-Ed., Kestrel: A Journal of Literature and Art, 1992–97; Prof. of English and Fuller E. Callaway Endowed Flannery O'Connor Chair in Creative Writing, Georgia College and State University, Milledgeville, 1997–; mem. Associated Writing Programs. *Publications:* Written in Water, Written in Stone: Twenty Years of Poets on Poetry (ed.), 1996; News From Where I Live: Poems, 1998. Contributions: periodicals. *Honours:* Fellow, West Virginia Commission on the Arts, 1994; Arkansas Poetry Award, University of Arkansas Press, 1997; Neruda Prize for Poetry, Nimrod International Journal, 1997. *Address:* 103 Cambridge Dr. S, Milledgeville, GA 31061-9047, USA. *E-mail:* mlammon@mail.gac.peachnet.edu.

LAMONT-BROWN, Raymond, MA, AMIET; writer, broadcaster and JP; b. 20 Sept. 1939, Horsforth, England; m. 2nd Dr Elizabeth Moira McGregor 1985. *Career:* Managing Ed., Writers Monthly 1984–86; mem. Soc. of Authors, Scotland, Rotary Int. (pres. St Andrews Branch 1984–85); Fellow, Soc. of Antiquaries of Scotland. *Publications include:* Discovering Fife 1988, The Life and Times of Berwick-upon-Tweed 1988, The Life and Times of St Andrews 1989, Royal Murder Mysteries 1990, Scottish Epitaphs 1990, Scottish Superstitions 1990, Scottish Witchcraft 1994, Scottish Folklore 1996, St Andrews 1996, Kamikaze: Japan's Suicide Samurai 1997, Scotland of One Hundred Years Ago 1998, Kempeitai: Japan's Dreaded Military Police 1998, Edward VII's Last Loves 1998, Tutor to the Dragon Emperor 1999, John Brown: Queen Victoria's Highland Servant 2000, Royal Poxes and Potions 2001, Ships from Hell 2002, Fife in History and Legend 2003, Villagers of Fife 2003, Humphry Davy 2004, Andrew Carnegie 2005; contrib. to magazines and newspapers, TV and radio scripts. *Address:* 11 Seabourne Gardens, Broughty Ferry, Dundee, DD5 2RT, Scotland.

LAMPARD, Dulcie Irene; Writer; b. 30 May 1923, Albany, WA, Australia. *Publications:* Ride!, 1985; Saddle Up!, 1994. *Honours:* Bookshop of the Year Awards, 1980, 1984, 1988. *Address:* 1045 Mayo Rd, Wooroloo, WA 6558, Australia.

LAMPITT, Dinah; Author; b. 6 March 1937, Essex, England; m. L. F. Lampitt 28 Nov. 1959 (deceased); one s. one d. *Education:* Regent Street Polytechnic, London. *Career:* mem. Society of Authors; CWA. *Publications:* Sutton Place, 1983; The Silver Swan, 1984; Fortune's Soldier, 1985; To Sleep No More, 1987; Pour the Dark Wine, 1989; The King's Women, 1992; As Shadows Haunting, 1993; Banishment, 1994; Death in the Dark Walk, 1995; Death at the Beggar's Opera, 1996; Death at the Devil's Tavern, 1997; Death on the Romney Marsh, 1998. Serials: The Moonlit Door; The Gemini Syndrome; The Staircase; The Anklets; The Wardrobe. Contributions: numerous short stories to women's magazines. *Address:* c/o Darley Anderson, Estelle House, 11 Eustace Rd, London SW6 1JB, England.

LAMPLUGH, Lois Violet, BA; writer; b. 9 June 1921, Barnstaple, Devon, England; m. Lawrence Carlile Davis 1955; one s. one d. *Education:* Open University. *Career:* Editorial Staff, Jonathan Cape Publishers, 1946–56; mem. West Country Writers' Asscn. *Publications:* The Pigeongram Puzzle, 1955; Nine Bright Shiners, 1955; Vagabond's Castle, 1957; Rockets in the Dunes, 1958; Sixpenny Runner, 1960; Midsummer Mountains, 1961; Rifle House Friends, 1965; Linhay on Hunter's Hill, 1966; Fur Princess and Fir Prince, 1969; Mandog, 1972; Sean's Leap, 1979; Winter Donkey, 1980; Falcon's Tor, 1984; Barnstaple: Town on the Taw, 1983; History of Ilfracombe, 1984; Minehead and Dunster, 1987; A Shadowed Man: Henry Williamson, 1990; Take Off From Chivenor, 1990; Sandrabbit, 1991; Lundy: Island Without Equal, 1993; A Book of Georgeham and the North West Corner of Devon, 1995; Ilfracombe in Old Photographs, 1996; Two Rivers Meeting, 1998; Four Centuries of Devon Dialect, forthcomming. Contributions: Western Morning News.

LAN, David Mark; Writer, Dramatist, Dir and Social Anthropologist; b. 1 June 1952, Cape Town, South Africa. *Education:* BA, University of Cape Town, 1972; BSc, 1976, PhD, 1983, LSE; Writer-in-Residence, Royal Court Theatre, 1996–97; Artistic Dir, Young Vic Theatre, 2000. *Publications:* Guns and Rain, Guerrillas and Spirit Mediums in Zimbabwe, 1985. Plays: Painting a Wall, 1974; Bird Child, 1974; Homage to Been Soup, 1975; Paradise, 1975; The Winter Dancers, 1977; Not in Norwich, 1977; Red Earth, 1978; Sergeant Ola and His Followers, 1979; Flight, 1986; A Mouthful of Birds (with Caryl Churchill), 1986; Desire, 1990; The Ends of the Earth, 1996. Television Films: The Sunday Judge, 1985; The Crossing, 1988; Welcome Home Comrades, 1990; Dark City, 1990. Radio Plays: Charley Tango, 1995. Television: Artist Unknown (writer, dir), 1996; Royal Court Diaries (writer, dir), 1997. Adaptations: Ghetto, 1989; Hippolytos, 1991; Ion, 1993; The She Wolf, 1996; Uncle Vanya, 1998; The Cherry Orchard, 2000. *Honours:* John Whiting Award, 1977; George Orwell Memorial Award, 1983; Zürich International Television Prize, 1990. *Address:* c/o Judy Daish Assocs, 2 St Charles Mews, London W10 6EG, England.

LANCASTER, David (see Heald, Timothy Villiers).

LANCASTER-BROWN, Peter; Author; b. 13 April 1927, Cue, WA, Australia; m. Johanne Nyrerod, 15 Aug. 1953, one s. *Education:* Astronomy; Surveying; Mining Engineering; Civil Engineering. *Career:* mem. Society of Authors. *Publications:* Twelve Came Back, 1957; Call of the Outback, 1970; What Star is That?, 1971; Astronomy in Colour, 1972; Australia's Coast of Coral and Pearl, 1972; Comets, Meteorites, and Men, 1973; Megaliths, Myths, and Men, 1976; Planet Earth in Colour, 1976; Megaliths and Masterminds, 1979; Fjord of Silent Men, 1983; Astronomy, 1984; Halley and His Comet, 1985; Halley's Comet and the Principia, 1986; Skywatch, 1993. Contributions: Blackwood's Nature; New Scientist; Sky and Telescope. *Address:* 10A St Peter's Rd, Aldeburgh, Suffolk IP1 5BG, England.

LANCHESTER, John; British novelist and journalist; b. 1962, Hamburg, Germany; m. *Education:* football writer, obituary writer, book ed., restaurant critic; editorial bd, London Review of Books. *Publications:* novels: The Debt to Pleasure 1996, Mr Phillips 2000, Fragrant Harbour 2002; contrib. to Granta, New York Times Book Review, New York Times Magazine, The New Yorker. *Honours:* Whitbread First Novel Award, Hawthornden Prize. *Address:* c/o London Review of Books, 28 Little Russell Street, London, WC1A 2HN, England.

LANDESMAN, Jay (Irving); Author, Dramatist, Producer and Publisher; b. 15 July 1919, St Louis, MO, USA; m. Frances Deitsch, 15 July 1950, two s. *Education:* University of Missouri, 1938–40; Rice Institute, Houston, 1940–42. *Career:* mem. American Federation of Television and Radio Artists; Dramatists Guild. *Publications:* The Nervous Set (novel), 1954, as a musical, 1959; A Walk on the Wild Side (musical), 1960; Molly Darling (musical), 1963; The Babies (play), 1969; Bad Nipple (novel), 1970; Rebel Without Applause (memoir), 1987; Small Day Tomorrow (screenplay), 1990; Jaywalking (memoir), 1992. *Address:* 8 Duncan Terrace, London N1 8BZ, England.

LANDIS, James David, BA; publisher and writer; b. 30 June 1942, Springfield, MA, USA; m. 1st Patricia Lawrence Straus 1964 (divorced); one d.; m. 2nd Denise Evelyn Tillar 1982; two s. *Education:* Yale College. *Career:* Asst Ed., Abelard Schuman, 1966–67; Ed. to Senior Ed., 1967–80, Senior Vice-Pres., 1985–91, Publisher and Ed.-in-Chief, 1988–91, William Morrow & Co; Editorial Dir, Senior Vice-Pres. and Publisher, Quill Trade paperbacks, 1980–85; mem. PEN. *Publications:* The Sisters Impossible, 1979; Love's Detective, 1984; Daddy's Girl, 1984; Joey and the Girls, 1987; The Band Never Dances, 1989; Looks Aren't Everything, 1990; Lying in Bed, 1995. Contributions: periodicals. *Honours:* Roger Klein Award for Editing, 1973; Advocate Humanitarian Award, 1977; Morton Dauwen Zabel Award for Fiction, American Acad. of Arts and Letters, 1996. *Literary Agent:* Henry Dunow Literary Agency, 22 West 23rd Street, Fifth Floor, New York, NY 10010, USA. *Telephone:* (212) 645-7606.

LANDIS, Jill Marie; Writer and Teacher; b. 8 Nov. 1948, Clinton, IN, USA; m. Sephen Landis, 15 May 1971. *Education:* BA, History, California State University, Long Beach; California Life Teaching Credential. *Career:* Teacher, various writing workshops and seminars; mem. Romance Writers of America; Novelists Inc; Authors' Guild. *Publications:* Sunflower, 1988; Wildflower, 1989; Rose, 1990; Jade, 1991; Come Spring, 1992; Past Promises, 1993; Until Tomorrow, 1994; After All, 1995; Last Chance, 1995; Day Dreamer, 1996; Just Once, 1997; Glass Beach, 1998. Contributions: anthologies, including: Loving Hearts, 1992; Sweet Hearts, 1993; Three Mothers and a Cradle, 1995; Heartbreak Ranch, 1997; Summer Love, 1997. *Honours:* various awards. *Address:* c/o Penguin Group (USA) Inc, 375 Hudson St, New York, NY 10014, USA.

LANDON, Howard Chandler Robbins, BMus; musicologist and writer; b. 6 March 1926, Boston, MA, USA; m. 1st Christa Landon; m. 2nd Else Radant. *Education:* Swarthmore College, Boston University. *Career:* Guest Lecturer, various US and European colleges and universities; many radio and television talks; mem. Musicological societies. *Publications:* The Symphonies of Joseph Haydn, 1955; The Mozart Companion (ed. with Donald Mitchell), 1956; The Collected Correspondence and London Notebooks of Joseph Haydn, 1959; Beethoven: A Documentary Study, 1970; Essays on the Viennese Classical Style: Gluck, Haydn, Mozart, Beethoven, 1970; Haydn: Chronicle and Works, 5 vols, 1976–80; Haydn: A Documentary Study, 1981; Mozart and the Masons, 1983; Handel and His World, 1984; 1791: Mozart's Last Year, 1988; Haydn: His Life and Music (with D. Jones), 1988; Mozart: The Golden Years, 1989; The Mozart Compendium (ed.), 1990; Mozart and Vienna, 1991; Five Centuries of Music in Venice, 1991; Une Journée Particulière de Mozart, 1993; Vivaldi: Voice of the Baroque, 1993; The Mozart Essays, 1995; Horns in High C (memoir), 1999. Other: Ed. of complete edns of Haydn's symphonies, 1965–68, string quartets (co-ed.), 1968–83, and piano trios, 1970–78. Contributions: scholarly books and professional journals. *Address:* Chateau de Foncoussières, 81800 Rabastens, Tarn, France.

LANE, Helen, (Helen Hudson); Writer; b. 31 Jan. 1920, New York, NY, USA; m. Robert Lane 15 Nov. 1944; two s. *Education:* BA, Bryn Mawr College, 1941; MA, 1943, PhD, 1950, Columbia University. *Career:* mem. Authors' Guild; Authors League; American PEN. *Publications:* Tell the Time to None, 1966; Meyer Meyer, 1967; The Listener, 1968; Farnsbee South, 1971; Criminal Trespass, 1986; A Temporary Residence, 1987; Dinner at Six: Voices from the Soup Kitchen, 2002. Contributions: Antioch Review; Sewannee Review; Virginia Quarterly; Northwest Review; Mademoiselle; Quarterly Review of Literature; Red Book; Ellery Queen; Mid-Stream; Best American Short Stories; O. Henry Prize Stories; Ploughshares; Mediterranean Review. *Honours:* Virginia Quarterly Prize Story, 1963. *Address:* 200 Leeden Hill Dr., No. 600B, Hamden, CT 06517, USA.

LANE, Millicent Elizabeth Travis, BA, MA, PhD; Canadian poet and writer; b. (Millicent Elizabeth Travis), 23 Sept. 1934, San Antonio, TX, USA; m. Lauriat Lane 1957; one s. one d. *Education:* Vassar Coll., Cornell Univ. *Career:* assistantships, Cornell Univ., Univ. of New Brunswick; poetry reviewer, Fiddlehead Magazine; mem. League of Canadian Poets (life mem. 2003–), Writers' Federation of New Brunswick. *Publications:* Five Poets: Cornell 1960, An Inch or So of Garden 1969, Poems 1969–72 1973, Homecomings 1977, Divinations and Shorter Poems, 1973–78 1980, Walking Under the Nebulae 1981, Reckonings: Poems 1979–83 1988, Solid Things: Poems New and Selected 1993, Temporary Shelter 1993, Night Physics 1994, Keeping Afloat 2001, Touch Earth 2004; contrib. to reviews, quarterlies and journals. *Honours:* Hon. Research Assoc., Univ. of New Brunswick, Pat Lowther Prize, League of Canadian Poets 1980, Atlantic Poetry Prize 2002, Alden Nowlan Prize for Literary Excellence 2003. *Address:* 807 Windsor Street, Fredericton, NB E3B 4G7, Canada.

LANE, Patrick; Writer and Poet; b. 26 March 1939, Nelson, BC, Canada; four s., one d. *Education:* University of British Columbia. *Career:* Ed., Very Stone House, Publishers, Vancouver, 1966–72; Writer-in-Residence, University of Manitoba, Winnepeg, 1978–79, University of Ottawa, 1980, University of Alberta, Edmonton, 1981–82, Saskatoon Public Library, 1982–83, Concordia University, 1985, Globe Theatre Co, Regina, Saskatchewan, 1985–; mem. League of Canadian Poets; Writer's Union of Canada; PEN, Canada. *Publications:* Letters From the Savage Mind, 1966; For Rita: In Asylum, 1969; Calgary City Jail, 1969; Separations, 1969; Sunflower Seeds, 1969; On the Street, 1970; Mountain Oysters, 1971; Hiway 401 Rhapsody, 1972; The Sun Has Begun to Eat the Mountain, 1972; Passing into Storm, 1973; Beware the Months of Fire, 1974; Certs, 1974; Unborn Things: South American Poems, 1975; For Riel in That Gawdam Prison, 1975; Albino Pheasants, 1977; If, 1977; Poems, New and Selected, 1978; No Longer Two People (with Lorna Uher), 1979; The Measure, 1980; Old Mother, 1982; Woman in the Dust, 1983; A Linen Crow, a Caftan Magpie, 1985; Milford and Me, 1989; Winter, 1990; Mortal Remains, 1992; Too Spare, Too Fierce, 1995; Selected Poems, 1978–1997, 1997; The Bare Plum of Winter Rain, 2000. Contributions: Most major Canadian magazines, American and English journals. *Honours:* Governor-General's Award for Poetry, 1979; Canadian Authors' Asscn Award, 1985; British Columbia Book Award, 1997.

LANE, Roumelia; Writer; b. 31 Dec. 1927, Bradford, West Yorkshire, England; m. Gavin Green, 1 Oct. 1949, one s. one d. *Career:* mem. Society of Authors of Great Britain; Writers Guild of Great Britain; Writers Guild of America (East and West). *Publications:* Sea of Zanj; Rose of the Desert; Cafe Mimosa; Harbour of Deceit; Desert Haven; Bamboo Wedding; Night of the Beguine; The Chasm; The Nawindi Flier. Television and film scripts: Stardust; The Chasm; Tender Saboteur; Chantico; Turn of the Tide; Gilligan's Last Gamble; Where Are the Clowns?; Death From the Past. Contributions: various journals and magazines. *Address:* Casa Mimosa, Santa Eugenia, Majorca, Beleares, Spain.

LANG, King (see Tubb, Edwin Charles).

LANG, Grace (see Floren, Lee).

LANGE, Hartmut; German author and dramatist; b. 31 March 1937, Berlin; m. Ulrike Ritter 1971. *Education:* Babelsberg Film School. *Career:* playwright at Deutsches Theater, Berlin 1961–65; freelance writer, W Berlin 1965–. *Publications:* Die Selbstverbrennung 1982, Deutsche Empfindungen 1983, Die Waldsteinsonate 1984, Das Konzert 1986, Die Ermüdung 1988, Vom Werden der Vernunft 1988, Gesammelte Theaterstücke (Collected Plays) 1988, Die Wattwanderung 1990, Die Reise nach Triest 1991, Die Stechpalme 1993, Schnitzlers Würgeengel 1995, Der Herr im Café 1996, Italienische Novellen 1998, Eine andere Form des Glücks 1999, Die Bildungsreise 2000, Das Streichquartett 2001, Irrtum als Erkenntnis 2002.

Honours: Gerhart-Hauptmann-Preis 1968, Literatur Preis der Adenauer Stiftung 1998, Ehrengabe der Schiller-Stiftung von 1859 2000, Stato Svevo Preis 2003. *Address:* Hohenzollerndamm 197, 10717 Berlin, Germany; 06010 Niccone, Perugia, Italy.

LANGE, John (see Crichton, (John) Michael).

LANGER, Lawrence Lee; academic and writer; b. 20 June 1929, New York, NY, USA; m. Sondra Weinstein 1951; one s. one d. *Education:* BA, City College, CUNY, 1951; MA, 1952, PhD, 1961, Harvard University. *Career:* Instructor, 1956–61, Asst Prof., 1961–66, Assoc. Prof., 1966–72, Prof., 1972–76, Alumnae Chair Prof., 1976–92, Prof. Emeritus, 1992–, Simmons College; mem. PEN. *Publications:* The Holocaust and the Literary Imagination, 1975; The Age of Artocity: Death in Modern Literature, 1978; Versions of Survival: The Holocaust and the Human Spirit, 1982; Holocaust Testimonies: The Ruins of Memory, 1991; Admitting the Holocaust: Collected Essays, 1994; Art from the Ashes: A Holocaust Anthology, 1994. Contributions: journals. *Honours:* National Book Critics Circle Award 1991. *Address:* 249 Adams Avenue, West Newton, MA 02165, USA.

LANGFORD, Gary (Raymond); Writer, Dramatist, Poet and Senior Lecturer; b. 21 Aug. 1947, Christchuch, New Zealand; one d. *Education:* BA, 1969, MA, History, 1971, MA, English, 1973, University of Canterbury; Diploma of Teaching Drama, Christchurch Secondary Teachers College, 1973. *Career:* Senior Lecturer in Creative Writing, University of Western Sydney, 1986; Writer-in-Residence, University of Canterbury, 1989. *Publications:* Over 20 books, including novels and poetry. Other: Plays and scripts for stage, radio, and television. Contributions: anthologies and other publications. *Honours:* Australia Council Young Writers Fellowship, 1976; Alan Marshall Award, 1983. *Literary Agent:* Curtis Brown Pty, PO Box 19, Paddington, NSW 2021, Australia.

LANGFORD GINIBI, Ruby; Author and Poet; b. 26 Jan. 1934, Box Ridge Mission, Coraki, NSW, Australia; (Divorced); four s. five d. (three deceased). *Career:* mem. Australian Society of Authors. *Publications:* Don't take your love to town, 1988; Real Deadly, 1992; My Bundjalung People, 1994; Haunted By The Past, 1998. Contributions: Women's Weekly; HQ; Sun Herald; Meanjin; Best of Independent, monthly, 1990; A to Z Authorship by Ken Methold; Aboriginal English, 1996; Australian Literary Studies; Canonozities by Southerlys, 1997. *Honours:* Human Rights Literature, 1988; Hon. Fellowship, 1995. *Literary Agent:* Rose Crestwell, Cameron & Crestwell Agency, Suite 5, Edgecliff Court, 2 New McLean Street, NSW 2027, Australia.

LANGHOLM, Neil (see Bulmer, Henry Kenneth).

LANGLAND, Joseph Thomas; academic and writer; b. 16 Feb. 1917, Spring Grove, Minnesota, USA; m. Judith Gail Wood 1943; two s. one d. *Education:* AA, Santa Ana College, 1936; BA, 1940, MA, 1941, Graduate Studies, 1946–48, University of Iowa; Harvard University, Columbia University, 1953–54. *Career:* Instructor, Dana College, 1941–42, University of Iowa, 1946–48; Asst, then Assoc. Prof., University of Wyoming, 1948–49; Assoc. Prof. to Prof., 1959–80, Prof. Emeritus, 1980–, University of Massachusetts. *Publications:* A Dream of Love, 1986; Twelve Poems, 1991; Selected Poems, 1992. Contributions: Reviews, quarterlies, journals, and magazines. *Honours:* Ford Foundation Faculty Fellowship; Amy Lowell Poetry Fellowship; New England Living Legend; Chancellor's Prize. *Address:* 18 Morgan Circle, Amherst, MA 01002, USA.

LANGTON, Jane (Gillson); Writer; b. 30 Dec. 1922, Boston, Massachusetts, USA; m. William Langton, 10 June 1943, deceased 1997, three s. *Education:* BA, 1944, MA, 1945, University of Michigan; MA, Radcliffe College, 1948. *Publications:* For Adults: The Transcendental Murder, 1964; Dark Nantucket Noon, 1975; The Memorial Hall Murder, 1978; Natural Enemy, 1982; Emily Dickinson is Dead, 1984; Good and Dead, 1986; Murder at the Gardner, 1988; The Dante Game, 1991; God in Concord, 1992; Divine Inspiration, 1993; The Shortest Day, 1995; Dead as a Dodo, 1996; The Face on the Wall, 1998; The Thief of Venice, 1999; Murder at Monticello, 2001; The Escher Twist, 2002; The Deserter, Murder at Gettysburg, 2003. Children's Books: Her Majesty, Grace Jones, 1961; Diamond in the Window, 1962; The Swing in the Summerhouse, 1967; The Astonishing Stereoscope, 1971; The Boyhood of Grace Jones, 1972; Paper Chains, 1977; The Fledgling, 1980; The Fragile Flag, 1984; The Time Bike, 2000. *Honours:* Newbery Honor Book, 1981; Nero Wolfe Award, 1984. *Literary Agent:* Meg Ruley, Jane Rotrosen Agency, New York. *Address:* 9 Baker Farm Rd, Lincoln, MA 01773, USA. *E-mail:* janelangton@earthlink.net. *Website:* www.janelangton.com.

LANIER, Sterling E(dmund); Writer and Sculptor; b. 18 Dec. 1927, New York, NY, USA. *Career:* Research Historian, Winterthur Museum, Switzerland, 1958–60; Ed., John C. Winston Co, 1961, Chilton Books, 1961–62, 1965–67, Macrae-Smith Co, 1963–64; Full-time Writer and Sculptor, 1967–. *Publications:* The War for the Lot (children's), 1969; The Peculiar Exploits of Brigadier Ffellowes (short stories), 1972; Hiero's Journey, 1973; The Unforsaken Hiero, 1983; Menace Under Marwood, 1983; The Curious Quest of Brig Ffellowes, 1986. *Literary Agent:* Curtis Brown Ltd, 10 Astor Pl., New York, NY 10003, USA.

LANSDALE, Joe R(ichard); Writer; b. 28 Oct. 1951, Gladwater, TX, USA; m. 1st Cassie Ellis 25 June 1970 (divorced 1972); m. 2nd Karen Ann Morton 25 Aug. 1973; one s. one d. *Education:* Tyler Junior College, 1970–71; University of Texas at Austin, 1971–72; Stephen F. Austin State University, 1973, 1975, 1976. *Career:* mem. Horror Writers of America, vice-pres., 1987–88; Western Writers of America, treas., 1987. *Publications:* Act of Love, 1981; Best of the West (ed.), 1986; Dead in the West, 1986; The Magic Wagon, 1986; The Nightrunners, 1987; The Drive In: A 'B' Movie with Blood and Popcorn Made in Texas, 1988; By Bizarre Hands, 1989; Cold in July, 1989; The New Frontier: The Best of Today's Western Fiction (ed.), 1989; Razored Saddles (ed. with Pat Lo Brutto), 1989; The Drive In 2: Not Just One of Them Sequels, 1990; Savage Season, 1990; Batman: Captured by the Engines, 1991; On the Far Side of the Cadillac Desert with Dead Folks, 1991; Stories by Mama Lansdale's Youngest Boy, 1991, revised edn as Best Sellers Guaranteed, 1993; The Steel Valentine, 1991; Dark at Heart: All New Tales of Dark Suspense (ed. with Karen Lansdale), 1992; Steppin' Out, Summer '68, 1992; Tight Little Stitches on a Dead Man's Back, 1992; Drive-By (with Andrew H. Vachss), 1993; Electric Gumbo, 1994; Jonah Hex: Two-Gun Mo, 1994; Mucho Mojo, 1994; The West That Was (ed. with Thomas W. Knowles), 1994; Wild West Show (ed. with Thomas W. Knowles), 1994; Writer of the Purple Rage, 1994; The Two-Bear Mambo, 1995; Weird Business (ed. with Richard Klaw), 1995; Bad Chili, 1997; A Fistful of Stories, 1997; Rumble Tumble, 1998; The Bottoms, 2000; Zeppelins West, 2000; Captains Outrageous, 2001; A Fine Dark Line, 2003. *Honours:* several awards. *Address:* 199 CR 508, Nacogdoches, TX 75961, USA.

LANTRY, Mike (see Tubb, Edwin Charles).

LAPHAM, Lewis H.; Writer; b. 8 Jan. 1935, San Francisco, CA, USA; m., three c. *Education:* BA, Yale University, 1956; University of Cambridge. *Career:* Reporter, San Francisco Examiner, 1957–59, New York Herald Tribune, 1960–62; Ed., Harper's Magazine, 1976–81, 1983–; Syndicated newspaper columnist, 1981–87; University Lecturer; Appearances on American and British television, National Public Radio and Canadian Public Radio. *Publications:* Fortune's Child (essays), 1980; Money and Class in America, 1988; Imperial Masquerade, 1990; Hotel America: Scenes in the Lobby of the Fin-de-Siècle, 1995; Waiting for the Barbarians, 1997; The Agony of Mammon, 1999; Lapham's Rules of Influence, 1999; Theater of War, 2002. Contributions: Monthly essay for Harper's magazine as 'Notebook'; Commentary; National Review; Yale Literary Magazine; Elle; Fortune; Forbes; American Spectator; Vanity Fair; Parade; Channels; Maclean's; London Observer; New York Times; Wall Street Journal. *Honours:* National Magazine Award for Essays, 1995; Thomas Paine Journalism Award, 2002. *Address:* c/o Harper's Magazine, 666 Broadway, New York, NY 10012, USA.

LAPID, Haim; Israeli writer and critic; b. 1967, nr Tel-Aviv. *Education:* Tel-Aviv Univ. *Career:* served in the Israeli army as paratrooper; fmrly taught Social and Behavioural Psychology; Lecturer on Negotiation Theory, organizational consultant for hi-tech industries. *Publications include:* novels: Reshimotav Ha-Nistarot (trans. as The Secret Notes of my Deputy) 1983, Breznitz 1992, Pesha Ha-Ketivah (trans. as The Crime of Writing) 1998, Ha-Mehila (trans. as The Burrow) 2002; short story collections: Meshicha Negdit (trans. as Opposite Attraction) 1995; non-fiction: Ahavot Rishonot (trans. as First Loves) 1993. *Address:* c/o The Toby Press, PO Box 8531, New Milford, CT 06776-8531, USA. *Website:* www.tobypress.com.

LAPINE, James (Elliot); Dramatist and Dir; b. 10 Jan. 1949, Mansfield, Ohio, USA; m. Sarah Marshall Kernochan, 24 Feb. 1985, one d. *Education:* BA, Franklin and Marshall College; MFA, California Institute of the Arts. *Career:* Dir of several plays and films; Lecturer on drama; mem. Dramatists Guild. *Publications:* Photographs, 1977; Table Settings, 1980; Twelve Dreams, 1983; Sunday in the Park with George, 1984; Into the Woods, 1987; Falsettoland, 1990; Luck, Pluck and Virtue, 1993; Passion, 1994. *Honours:* Obie Award, 1977; George Oppenheimer/Newsday Award, 1983; Pulitzer Prize for Drama, 1984; New York Critic's Circle Awards, 1984, 1988; Tony Awards, 1988, 1992, 1994. *Address:* c/o International Creative Management, 40 W 57th St, New York, NY 10019, USA.

LAPPING, Brian (Michael); Television Producer, Journalist and Ed.; b. 13 Sept. 1937, London, England. *Education:* BA, Pembroke College, Cambridge, 1959. *Career:* Reporter, Daily Mirror, London, 1959–61; Reporter and Deputy Commonwealth Correspondent, The Guardian, London, 1961–67; Ed., Venture, Fabian Society monthly journal, 1965–69; Feature Writer, Financial Times, London, 1967–68; Deputy Ed., New Society, London, 1968–70; Television Producer, Granada Television Ltd, 1970–88; Exec. Producer, World in Action 1976–78, The State of the Nation 1978–80, End of Empire 1980–85; Chief Exec., Brian Lapping Assocs, 1988–; Exec. Producer, Countdown to War, 1989; Hypotheticals (three programmes annually for BBC2); The Second Russian Revolution (8 programmes for BBC2), 1991; Question Time (weekly for BBC1), 1991–94; The Washington Version (for BBC2), 1992; Watergate (for BBC2), 1994; Fall of the Wall (for BBC2), 1994; The Death of Yugoslavia, 1995; The 50 Years War: Israel and the Arabs, 1998; Hostage, 1999; Endgame in Ireland, 2002; Tackling Terror, 2002. *Publications:* More Power to the People (co-ed.), 1968; The Labour Government 1964–70, 1970; The State of the Nation: Parliament (ed.), 1973; The State of the Nation: The Bounds of Freedom, 1980; End of

Empire, 1985; Apartheid: A History, 1986. *Honours:* RTS Award, Broadcasting Press Guild Award, 1991; Emmy Award, DuPont Award; 12 international awards, 1995. *Address:* 61 Eton Ave, London NW3, England.

LAPTEV, Ivan Dmitrievich; Editor and Journalist; b. 15 Oct. 1934, Sladkoye, Omsk District, USSR; m. Tatyana Kareva 1966; one d. *Education:* Siberian Road Transport Inst.; Acad. of Social Sciences. *Career:* worked for CPSU Cen. Cttee; mem. CPSU 1960–91; worked at Omsk River Port 1952–60; teacher 1960–61; instructor, Soviet Army Sports Club 1961–64, literary collaborator and special corresp. Sovietskaya Rossiya 1964–67; Consultant for Kommunist (later named Free Thought) 1967–73; work with CPSU Cen. Cttee 1973–78; Section Ed. Pravda 1978–82, Deputy Ed. 1982–84; Chief Ed. Izvestiya 1984–90; mem. USSR Supreme Soviet 1989–91; People's Deputy of the USSR 1989–91; Chair. Council of Union 1990–91; Gen. Man. Izvestiya Publrs 1991–94; Deputy Chair. Fed. Press Cttee 1994–95, Chair. 1995–99; Head of Sector Professional Acad. of State Service to Russian Presidency 1995–; mem. Int. Acad. of Information 1993; Pres. Asscn of Chief Eds and Publrs 1993–. *Publications:* Ecological Problems, 1978; The World of People in the World of Nature, 1986. Contributions: over 100 scientific articles on ecological problems. *Address:* Academy of State Service, Vernadskogo prosp. 84, 117606 Moscow, Russia.

LAQUEUR, Walter; American historian, writer and editor; b. 26 May 1921, Breslau, Germany; m. 1st Barbara Koch 1941 (deceased); two d.; m. 2nd Christa Susi Wichmann 1996. *Education:* Hebrew University, Jerusalem. *Career:* Founder-Ed., Survey, London, 1955–67; Visiting Prof., Johns Hopkins University, 1957, University of Chicago, 1958, Harvard University, 1977; Dir, Institute of Contemporary History, Wiener Library, London, 1964–92; Co-Founder and Ed., Journal of Contemporary History, 1966–; Prof. of the History of Ideas and Politics, Brandeis University, 1967–72; Prof. of History, University of Tel-Aviv, 1970–80; Chair., International Research Council, Center for Strategic and International Studies, Washington, DC, 1973–; Ed., Washington Papers, 1973–, Washington Quarterly, 1978–; University Prof. of Government, Georgetown University, 1977–91. *Publications:* Communism and Nationalism in the Middle East, 1956; The Soviet Union and the Middle East, 1959; Young Germany, 1962; Russia and Germany, 1966; The Fate of the Revolution, 1967; The Road to War, 1967; The Struggle for the Middle East, 1969; Europe Since Hitler, 1970; Out of the Ruins of Europe, 1971; A History of Zionism, 1972; Confrontation: The Middle East and World Politics, 1974; Weimar, 1975; Guerrilla, 1976; Terrorism, 1977; Guerrilla Reader, 1977; Terrorism Reader, 1978; A Continent Astray, 1979; The Missing Years, 1980; Political Psychology of Appeasement, 1980; Farewell to Europe, 1981; The Terrible Secret, 1981; America, Europe, and the Soviet Union, 1983; Germany Today, 1985; A World of Secrets, 1985; The Age of Terrorism, 1987; The Long Road to Freedom: Russia and Glasnost, 1989; Stalin, 1991; Thursday's Child Has Far to Go (autobiog.), 1992; Black Hundred, 1993; The Dream That Failed, 1994; Fascism, 1997; The New Terrorism, 1999; Generation Exodus, 2001; Yale Encyclopedia of the Holocaust (ed.), 2001; No End to War: Terrorism in the 21st Century, 2003. Contributions: scholarly books and journals. *Honours:* First Distinguished Writer's Award, Center for Strategic and International Studies, 1969; Grand Cross of Merit, Federal Republic of Germany, 1987; Hon. doctorates, Hebrew Union College, 1988, Adelphi University, 1993, Brandeis University, 1994. *Address:* c/o International Research Council, Center for Strategic and International Studies, 1800 K Street NW, Washington, DC 20006, USA.

LARA BOSCH, José Manuel; Spanish media executive; *President and CEO, Grupo Planeta;* m.; four c. *Career:* CEO Grupo Planeta (owns TV and radio stations, publishing imprints, chain of bookshops, newspapers and real estate firms) 1998–2003, Pres. and CEO 2003–; Pres. Antena 3, Quiero TV; Chair. Inst. of Family Businesses 2001–, Fundación José Manuel Lara; fmr Vice-Pres. Círculo de Economía; mem. admin. council of Fira de Barcelona. *Address:* Editorial Planeta SA, Edifici Planeta, Diagonal 662–664, 08034 Barcelona, Spain (Office). *Telephone:* (93) 2285800. *Fax:* (93) 2177140.

LARSEN, Eric Everett; Prof. of English and Writer; b. 29 Nov. 1941, Northfield, Minnesota, USA; m. Anne Schnare, 5 June 1965, two d. *Education:* BA, Carleton College, 1963; MA, 1964, PhD, 1971, University of Iowa. *Career:* Prof. of English, John Jay College of Criminal Justice, CUNY, 1971–; mem. National Asscn of Scholars; Asscn of Literary Scholars and Critics; National Book Critics Circle. *Publications:* Fiction: An American Memory, 1988; I Am Zoe Handke, 1992. Contributions: Harper's; New Republic; Nation; Los Angeles Times Book Review; North American Review; New England Review. *Honours:* Heartland Prize, Chicago Tribune, 1988. *Address:* c/o Dept of English, John Jay College of Criminal Justice, City University of New York, 445 W 59th St, New York, NY 10019, USA.

LARSEN, Jeanne (Louise); Prof. of English, Writer, Poet and Trans; b. 9 Aug. 1950, Washington, DC, USA; m. Thomas Hugh Mesner 13 Aug. 1977; one step-s. one step-d. *Education:* BA, Oberlin College, 1971; MA, Hollins College, 1972; Graduate Research Certificate, Nagasaki University, 1980; PhD, University of Iowa, 1983. *Career:* Lecturer, Tunghai University, 1972–74; Asst Prof., 1975, 1980–86, Assoc. Prof., 1986–92, Prof. of English, 1992–98, Hollins College; Prof. of English, Hollins University, 1998–; mem. Asscn for Asian Studies; Authors' Guild; International Asscn for the Fantastic in the Arts; PEN; Poets and Writers. *Publications:* Fiction: Silk Road, 1989; Bronze Mirror, 1991; Manchu Palaces, 1996. Poetry: James Cook in Search of Terra Incognita: A Book of Poems, 1979. Other: Brocade River Poems: Selected Works of the Tang Dynasty Courtesan Xue Tao (trans. and ed.), 1987; Engendering the Word: Feminist Essays in Psychosexual Poetics (ed. with others), 1989. Contributions: scholarly books, anthologies, learned journals and periodicals. *Honours:* First Selection, Associated Writing Programs' Annual Poetry Book Competition, 1979; Resident Fellowships, Virginia Center for the Creative Arts, 1982, 1986, 1987, 1989, 1990, 1995; John Gardner Fellowship in Fiction, Bread Loaf Writers' Conference, 1990; William L. Crawford Award for Year's Best New Novelist, International Asscn for the Fantastic in the Arts, 1990; National Endowment for the Arts Fellowship in Trans., 1995. *Address:* c/o Dept of English, Hollins University, Roanoke, VA 24020, USA.

LARUE, Monique; Author and College Teacher; b. 1948, Montréal, QC, Canada. *Education:* BPh, Univ. of Montréal, 1970; MA, Philosophy, 1971, Doctorat de 3éme cycle en lettres, 1976, Sorbonne, Univ. of Paris. *Career:* Teacher, Dept of French, Collège Edouard Montpetit, Montréal, 1974–; mem. Académie des Lettres du Québec. *Publications:* La cohorte fictive, 1979; Les faux fuyants, 1982; Copies conformes (trans. as True Copies), 1989; Promenades littéraires dans Montréal (with Jean-Francois Chassay), 1989; La démarche du crabe, 1995; La Gloire de cassiodore, 2002. *Honours:* Grand Prix du livre de Montréal, 1990, 1996; Prix du roman du Gouverneur Général du Canada, 2002. *Address:* c/o Union des écrivaines et des écrivains québécois, La Maison des écrivains, 3492 Ave Laval, Montréal, QC H2X 3C8, Canada.

LASKA, Vera; Prof. of History, Lecturer, Columnist and Author; b. 21 July 1928, Košice, Czechoslovakia; m. Andrew J. Laska, 5 Nov. 1949, two s. *Education:* MA, History, 1946, MA, Philosophy, 1946, Charles University, Prague; PhD, History, University of Chicago, 1959. *Career:* Prof. of History, Regis College, Weston, Massachusetts, 1966–; Fulbright Prof., Charles University, Prague, 1993. *Publications:* Remember the Ladies: Outstanding Women of the American Revolution, 1976; Franklin and Women, 1978; Czechs in America 1633–1977, 1978; Benjamin Franklin the Diplomat, 1982; Women in the Resistance and in the Holocaust, 1983; Nazism, Resistance and Holocaust: A Bibliography, 1985; Two Loves of Benjamin Franklin (in Czech), 1994. Contributions: Over 350 articles and book reviews in newspapers and professional journals. *Honours:* Outstanding Educator of America, 1972; Kidger Award for Excellence in History, 1984; George Washington Honor Medal in Communication, 1990; Fulbright Prof., Prague, 1992–93. *Address:* 50 Woodchester Dr., Weston, MA 02493, USA.

LASKOWSKI, Jacek Andrzej; Dramatist and Trans; b. 4 June 1946, Edinburgh, Scotland; m. Anne Grant Howieson, 8 July 1978, two d. *Education:* MagPhil, Jagiellonian Universiy, Kraków, Poland, 1973. *Career:* Literary Man., Haymarket Theatre, Leicester, 1984–87; mem. Society of Authors, vice-chair., Broadcasting Committee, 1983–83; Writers' Guild of Great Britain. *Publications:* Plays produced: Dreams to Damnation, BBC Radio 3, 1977; Pawn Takes Pawn, BBC Radio 4, 1978; The Secret Agent, BBC Radio 4, 1980; Nostromo, BBC Radio 4, 1985; Phoney Physician (after Molière), 1986; Orestes/Electra (with Nancy Meckler), 1987; Wiseguy Scapino (after Molière), 1993. *Address:* 52 Holme Rd, West Bridgford, Nottingham NG2 5AD, England. *E-mail:* jaceklaskowski@yahoo.com.

LAU, Evelyn (Yee-Fun); Poet and Writer; b. 2 July 1971, Vancouver, Canada. *Publications:* Poetry: You Are Not Who You Claim, 1990; Oedipal Dreams, 1992; In the House of the Slaves, 1994. Fiction: Fresh Girls and Other Stories, 1993; Other Women (novel), 1995; Choose Me (short stories). Non-Fiction: Runaway: Diary of a Street Kid, 1989; Inside Out: Reflections on a Life So Far (autobiog.), 2001. Contributions: periodicals. *Honours:* Air Canada Award, 1989. *Address:* c/o Northwest Passages, 628 Penzer St, Kamloops, BC V2C 3G5, Canada.

LAURENS, Joanna, BA; British playwright; b. 1978. *Education:* Queen's Univ., Belfast. *Career:* writer on attachment at the Nat. Theatre, London; currently writer-in-residence, RSC. *Plays:* The Three Birds (Critics' Circle Most Promising Playwright Award, Time Out Award for Most Outstanding New Talent) 2000, Five Gold Rings (Almeida, London) 2003, Poor Beck (RSC) 2004. *Literary Agent:* c/o Royal Shakespeare Company, Royal Shakespeare Theatre, Waterside, Stratford-upon-Avon, Warwickshire CV37 6BB, England. *Fax:* (1789) 262341. *E-mail:* info@rsc.org.uk. *Website:* www.rsc.org.uk.

LAURENTS, Arthur; Dramatist, Writer and Dir; b. 14 July 1917, New York, NY, USA. *Education:* BA, Cornell University, 1937. *Career:* mem. Acad. of Motion Picture Arts and Sciences; Authors League; Dramatists Guild; PEN; Screenwriters Guild; Theatre Hall of Fame. *Publications:* Plays: Home of the Brave, 1946; The Bird Cage, 1950; The Time of the Cuckoo, 1952; A Clearing in the Woods, 1956; Invitation to a March, 1960; The Enclave, 1973; Scream, Houston, 1978; The Hunting Season, 1995; The Radical Mystique, 1995; My Good Name, 1997. Musical Plays: West Side Story, 1957; Gypsy, 1959; Do I Hear a Waltz?, 1964; Hallelujah Baby, 1967; Nick and Nora, 1991. Screenplays: The Snake Pit, 1948; Rope, 1948; Caught, 1948; Anna Lucasta, 1949; Anastasia, 1956; Bonjour Tristesse, 1958; The Way We Were, 1973; The Turning Point, 1977. Fiction: The Way We Were, 1972; The Turning Point, 1977. Other: Original Story By (memoir), 2000. *Honours:* Tony Awards, 1967, 1984; Drama Desk Awards, 1974, 1978;

Golden Glove Award, 1977; Writers Guild of America, 1977; Best Dir Award, 1985. *Literary Agent:* William Morris Agency, 1325 Avenue of the Americas, New York, NY 10019, USA.

LAURO, Shirley (Shapiro); Actress, Playwright and Teacher; b. 18 Nov. 1933, Des Moines, IA, USA; m. 1st Norton Mezvinsky (divorced); m. 2nd Louis Paul Lauro 18 Aug. 1973. *Education:* BS, Northwestern University, 1955; MS, University of Wisconsin at Madison, 1957. *Career:* Actress, stage, films, and television; Instructor, City College, CUNY, 1967–71, Yeshiva University, 1971–76, Manhattan Community College, 1978, Marymount Manhattan College, 1978–79; Literary Consultant, 1975–80, Resident Playwright, 1976–, Ensemble Studio Theatre, New York City; Resident Playwright, Alley Theatre, Houston, 1987; Adjunct Prof. of Playwrighting, Tisch School of the Arts, New York University, 1989–; mem. Authors' Guild; Authors League; Dramatists Guild; League of Professional Theatre Women; PEN; Writers Guild of America. *Publications:* The Edge, 1965; The Contest, 1975; Margaret and Kit, 1979; In the Garden of Eden, 1982; Sunday Go to Meetin', 1986; Pearls on the Moon, 1987; A Piece of My Heart, 1992; A Moment in Time, 1994; The Last Trial of Clarence Darrow, 1997; Railing it Uptown, 1997. Contributions: periodicals. *Address:* 275 Central Park W, New York, NY 10024, USA.

LAVEN, Mary; British academic and writer. *Career:* Lecturer in History, Univ. of Cambridge; Fellow, Jesus Coll., Cambridge. *Publications:* Virgins of Venice: Enclosed Lives and Broken Vows in the Renaissance Convent 2002. *Honours:* Mail on Sunday/John Llewellyn Rhys Prize. *Address:* c/o Jesus College, Cambridge, CB5 8BL, England.

LAVENTHOL, David, MA; American publisher; *Chairman and Editorial Director, Columbia Journalism Review;* b. 15 July 1933, Philadelphia; m. Esther Coons 1958; one s. one d. *Education:* Yale Univ. and Univ. of Minnesota. *Career:* reporter, later News Ed., St Petersburg Times 1957–63; City Ed. New York Herald Tribune 1963–66; Asst Man. Ed. The Washington Post 1966–69; Assoc. Ed. Newsday 1969, Exec. Ed. 1969–70, Ed. 1970–78, Publr and CEO 1978–86, Chair. 1986–87; Group Vice-Pres. Times Mirror 1981–86, Sr Vice-Pres. 1986, Pres. 1987–93; CEO and Publr LA Times 1989–93; Ed.-at-Large Times Mirror Co., LA 1994–98, Consultant Ed. 1998–99; Ed. and Publr Columbia Journalism Review 1999–; Chair. Pulitzer Prize Bd 1988–89; Vice-Chair. Int. Press Inst. 1985–92, Chair. 1992–95; Chair. Museum of Contemporary Art, LA 1993–97; Dir Newspaper Advertising Bureau, American Press Inst. 1988–, LA Times Washington Post/News Service, Times Mirror Foundation, United Negro Coll. Fund; mem. Bd Dirs Assoc. Press 1993–96, Columbia Journalism School 1995–, Nat. Parkinson Foundation 1995–, Saratoga Performing Arts Center 1993–96; mem. American Soc. of Newspaper Eds Writing Awards Bd, American Newspaper Publr Asscn, Century Asscn, Council on Foreign Relations. *Address:* Columbia Journalism Review, Columbia University, 2950 Broadway, New York, NY 10027, USA (Office). *E-mail:* malibunal@aol.com (Office).

LAVERS, Norman; Teacher and Writer; b. 21 April 1935, Berkeley, CA, USA; m. Cheryl Dicks, 20 July 1967, one s. *Education:* BA, 1960, MA, 1963, San Francisco State University; PhD, University of Iowa, 1969. *Publications:* Mark Harris (criticism) 1978; Selected Short Stories, 1979; Jerzy Kosinski (criticism) 1982; The Northwest Passage (novel), 1984; Pop Culture Into Art: The Novels of Manuel Puig (criticism), 1988; Growing up in Berkeley with the Bomb (autobiog.), 1998. Contributions: Ed., Arkansas Review; Contributing Ed., Bird Watcher's Digest. *Honours:* National Endowment for the Arts Fellowships, 1982, 1991; Ed.'s Choice Award, 1986; Hohenberg Award, 1986; O. Henry Award, 1987; Pushcart Award, 1992; William Peden Prize, 1992; Porter Fund Award, 1995. *Address:* 3068 CR 901, Jonesboro, AR 72401, USA.

LAVIN, S. R.; Poet and Writer; b. 2 April 1945, Springfield, Massachusetts, USA; two s., four d. *Education:* AIC, BA, 1967; MA, Literature, Trinity College, 1970. *Career:* Poet-in-Residence, Clark University, Worcester, Massachusetts, 1972; Prof. of English, Castleton State College, Vermont, 1987–99. *Publications:* Poetry: The Stonecutters at War with the Cliff Dwellers, 1972; Cambodian Spring, 1973; Let Myself Shine, 1979. Fiction: Metacomet. Translation: I and You, by Martin Buber. Contributions: Cold Drill; Hiram; I.P.R.; Mandrake; Stand; Vermont Literary Magazine; Chinese Poetry International. *Address:* c/o Parchment Press, 52 S River St, Coxsackie, NY 12051, USA.

LAW, Michael; Dramatist, Writer and Trans; b. 17 April 1925, Kerman, Iran; m. Dorothea V. Schön 15 Aug. 1954; four s. *Education:* BA, Modern Languages Tripos, Univ. of Cambridge, 1951. *Career:* Lecturer in Education, Univ. of Leeds, 1969–83; mem. Society of Authors; Writers' Guild. *Publications:* The Vienna Opera House (trans.), 1955; Caricature from Leonard to Picasso (trans.), 1957; Seven German Readers for Schools, 1960–75; How to Read German (textbook), 1963; Brecht's Man is Man (trans.), 1983; Tankred Dorst's The Great Diatribe Outside the City Wall (trans.), 1998. Plays: Two or Three Ghosts, 1997; Come and Get Me, 1997, A Companion for Claire, 1997; Helen of Rhodes, 1997; Aquarium, 1997; The Magic Man, 1997; Just Us, 1998; The Nurse's Tale, 1998; The Wench is Dead, 1998. Contributions: numerous educational journals. *Honours:* many drama prizes. *Address:* 90A Upper Tollington Park, London N4 4NB, England. *E-mail:* mlaw@blueyonder.co.uk.

LAWRENCE, Clifford Hugh; Prof. of Medieval History Emeritus and Writer; b. 28 Dec. 1921, London, England; m. Helen Maud Curran 11 July 1953; one s. five d. *Education:* BA, 1948, MA, 1953, DPhil, 1956, Univ. of Oxford. *Career:* Asst Lecturer, 1951, Lecturer, 1953–63, Reader in Medieval History, 1963–70, Bedford College, London; External Examiner, Univ. of Newcastle upon Tyne, 1972–74, Univ. of Bristol, 1975–77, Univ. of Reading, 1977–79; Prof. of Medieval History, 1970–87, Prof. Emeritus, 1987–, Univ. of London; mem. FRHistS; Society of Antiquaries. *Publications:* St Edmund of Abingdon: A Study in Hagiography and History, 1960; The English Church and the Papacy in the Middle Ages, 1965; The University in State and Church, Vol. 1 of The History of the University of Oxford, 1984; Medieval Monasticism: Forms of Religious Life in Western Europe in the Middle Ages, 1984; The Friars: The Impact of the Early Mendicant Movement on Western Society, 1994; The Life of St Edmund, by Matthew Paris (trans. and biographer), 1996. Contributions: reference works, scholarly books and journals. *Address:* 11 Durham Rd, London SW20 0QH, England.

LAWRENCE, Karen Ann; Writer; b. 5 Feb. 1951, Windsor, Ontario, Canada; m. Robert Gabhart, 18 Dec. 1982, one s. *Education:* BA, University of Windsor, 1973; MA, University of Alberta, 1977. *Career:* mem. Writers' Union of Canada; Asscn of Canadian Radio and Television Artists. *Publications:* Nekuia: The Inanna Poems, 1980; The Life of Helen Alone, 1986; Springs of Living Water, 1990. *Honours:* WHSmith/Books in Canada First Novel Award, 1987; Best First Novel Award, PEN, Los Angeles Center, 1987. *Address:* 2153 Pine St, San Diego, CA 92103, USA. *E-mail:* karenannlawrence@cox.net.

LAWRENCE, Louise; Novelist; b. 5 June 1943, Surrey, England; m. Graham Mace, 28 Aug. 1987, one s. two d. *Publications:* Andra, 1971; Power of Stars, 1972; Wyndcliffe, 1974; Sing and Scatter Daisies, 1977; Star Lord, 1978; Cat Call, 1980; Earth Witch, 1981; Calling B for Butterfly, 1982; Dram Road, 1983; Children of the Dust, 1985; Moonwind, 1986; Warriors of Taan, 1986; Extinction is Forever, 1990; Ben-Harran's Castle, 1992; The Disinherited, 1994. *Address:* 22 Church Rd, Cinderford, Gloucestershire GL14 2EA, England.

LAWRENCE, P. (see Tubb, Edwin Charles).

LAWS, Stephen; Local Council Administrator and Writer; b. 13 July 1952, Newcastle upon Tyne, England; m. Lyn Hunter 1980 (divorced 1989); one d. *Education:* Ordinary National Certificate, Higher National Certificate, Public Administration, College of Arts and Technology. *Career:* County and Borough Council administrative positions; Senior Committee Administrator for Central Administration, Newcastle City Council, Newcastle upon Tyne, 1982–; mem. British Fantasy Society; National Asscn of Local Government Officers. *Publications:* Ghost Train, 1985; Spectre, 1985; The Wyrm, 1987; The Frighteners, 1990; Darkfall, 1992; Voyages into Darkness (co-author), 1993; Macabre, 1994; Annabel Says, 1997. Contributions: articles and short stories to periodicals. *Honours:* Three Sunday Sun Awards, for short stories; Radio Newcastle Award, for short story. *Literary Agent:* AP Watt Ltd, 20 John St, London WC1N 2DR, England. *Address:* c/o Publicity Dir, Souvenir Press Ltd, 43 Great Russell St, London WC1B 3PA, England.

LAWSON, Chet (see Tubb, Edwin Charles).

LAWSON, Hon. Dominic Ralph Campden, BA, FRSA; journalist and editor; b. 17 Dec. 1956, London, England; m. 1st Jane Fiona Wastell Whytehead 1982 (divorced 1991); m. 2nd Hon. Rosamond Monckton 1991; two d. *Education:* Westminster School, Christchurch College, Oxford. *Career:* mem. staff World Tonight and The Financial World Tonight (BBC) 1979–81; mem. staff Financial Times (Energy Corresp. and Lex column) 1981–87; Deputy Ed. The Spectator 1987–90, Ed. 1990–95; Ed. The Sunday Telegraph 1995–; Columnist, Sunday Corresp. 1990, The Financial Times 1991–94, Daily Telegraph 1994–95. *Publications:* Korchnoi, Kasparov, 1983; Britain in the Eighties (co-author), 1989; The Spectator Annual (ed.), 1992, 1993, 1994; The Inner Game, 1993. *Honours:* Harold Wincott Prize for Financial Journalism; Ed. of the Year; Society of Magazine Eds, 1990. *Address:* c/o The Sunday Telegraph, 1 Canada Square, Canary Wharf, London E14 5DT, England.

LAWSON, Sarah (Anne); Writer, Poet and Trans; b. 4 Nov. 1943, Indianapolis, IN, USA; m. Alastair Pettigrew, 8 April 1969, deceased 20 Sept. 1992. *Education:* BA, Indiana University, 1965; MA, University of Pennsylvania, 1966; PhD, University of Glasgow, 1971. *Career:* mem. English PEN; Poetry Society; RSL; Society of Authors; Trans' Asscn. *Publications:* New Writers and Writing 16, 1979; The Treasure of the City of Ladies, by Christine de Pisan (trans.), 1985; Dutch Interiors (poems), 1985; Poetry Introduction 6 (with others), 1986; A Foothold in Florida, by René de Laudonniere (trans.), 1992; Down Where the Willow is Washing Her Hair (poems), 1995; A Fado for My Mother, 1996; Below the Surface (poems), 1996; The Girls' Consent, by Leandro Fernandez de Moratín (trans.), 1998; Twelve Scenes of Malta, 2000; Jacques Prévert, Selected Poems (trans.), 2002; The Dialogue of the Dogs, by Miguel de Cervantes (trans.), 2003. Contributions: anthologies, reviews, quarterlies and journals. *Honours:* C. Day-Lewis Fellowship, 1979–80. *Address:* 186 Albyn Rd, London SE8 4JQ, England.

LAYTON, Irving (Peter); Poet and Author; b. 12 March 1912, Neamt, Romania; m. 1st Faye Lynch 13 Sept. 1938 (divorced 1946); m. 2nd Betty Frances Sutherland; one s. one d.; m. 3rd Aviva Cantor; one s.; m. 4th Harriet Bernstein (divorced 1983); one d.; m. 5th Anna Pottier. *Education:* BSc, Macdonald College, 1939; MA, McGill University, 1946. *Career:* Poet-in-Residence, University of Guelph, 1969; Visiting Prof., 1978, Adjunct Prof., 1988, 1989, Writer-in-Residence, 1989, Concordia University; Writer-in-Residence, University of Toronto, 1981. *Publications:* Poetry: numerous vols, including: The Collected Poems of Irving Layton, 1971; The Darkening Fire: Selected Poems, 1945–68, 1975; The Unwavering Eye: Selected Poems, 1969–75; Uncollected Poems, 1935–59, 1976; A Wild Peculiar Joy: Selected Poems, 1945–82, 1982; Final Reckoning: Poems 1982–86, 1987; Fornalux: Selected Poems, 1928–90, 1992. Other: Engagements: The Prose of Irving Layton, 1972; Taking Sides: The Collected Social and Political Writings, 1977; Waiting for the Messiah: A Memoir, 1985; Wild Gooseberries: The Selected Letters of Irving Layton, 1989; Irving Layton and Robert Creeley: The Complete Correspondence, 1953–78, 1990. Editor: various anthologies. Contributions: many publications. *Honours:* Governor-General's Award for Poetry, 1959; First Prize, Prix Litteraire de Québec, 1963; Centennial Medal, 1967; Doctor of Civil Laws, Bishop's University, 1970; Officer of the Order of Canada, 1976; DLitt, Concordia University, 1976, York University, Toronto, 1976; Canada Council Arts Award, 1979–81; Petrarch Award for Poetry, Italy, 1993. *Address:* c/o McClelland & Stewart, 481 University Ave, Toronto, Ontario M5G 2E9, Canada.

LAZARUS, Arnold (Leslie); Writer and Poet; b. 20 Feb. 1914, Revere, Massachusetts, USA; m. Keo Felker, 24 July 1938, two s. two d. *Education:* BA, University of Michigan, 1935; BS, Middlesex Medical School, 1937; MA, 1939, PhD, 1957, University of California, Los Angeles. *Career:* mem. Acad. of American Poets; American Society for Theatre Research; Comparative Literature Asscn; MLA; Poetry Society of America. *Publications:* Entertainments and Valedictions, 1970; Harbrace Adventures in Literature (ed. with R. Lowell and E. Hardwick), 1970; Modern English (ed. with others), 1970; A Suit of Four, 1973; The Indiana Experience, 1977; Beyond Graustark (with Victor H. Jones), 1981; Glossary of Literature and Composition (ed. with H. Wendell Smith), 1983; Best of George Ade (ed.), 1985; Some Light: New and Selected Verse, 1988; A George Jean Nathan Reader (ed.), 1990. Contributions: numerous periodicals. *Honours:* Ford Foundation Fellow, 1954; Kemper McComb Award, 1976. *Address:* 709 Chopin Dr., Sunnyvale, CA 94087, USA.

LAZARUS, Henry (see Slavitt, David Rytman).

LAZARUS, Marguerite, (Marguerite Gascoigne, Anna Gilbert); Author; b. 1 May 1916, Durham, England; m. Jack Lazarus, 3 April 1956. *Education:* BA, English Language and Literature, 1937, MA, 1945, Durham University. *Career:* mem. Society of Authors. *Publications:* Images of Rose, 1973; The Look of Innocence, 1975; A Family Likeness, 1977; Remembering Louise, 1978; The Leavetaking, 1979; Flowers for Lilian, 1980; Miss Bede is Staying, 1982; The Long Shadow, 1984; A Walk in the Wood, 1989; The Wedding Guest, 1993; The Treachery of Time, 1995; A Hint of Witchcraft, 2000; A Morning in Eden, 2002. Contributions: Magazines and BBC. *Honours:* Romantic Novelists' Major Award, 1976; Catherine Cookson Award, 1994. *Address:* c/o Watson Little Ltd, Capo di Monte, Windmill Hill, London NW3 6RJ, England.

LAZENBY, John Francis; British academic and writer; b. 14 April 1934, Tiruchirapalli, Tamil Nadu, India; m. Elizabeth Mary Leithead 1967; one s. one d. *Education:* MA, Oxon; Scholar, Keble College, Oxford, 1952–56; Senior Demy, Magdalen College, Oxford, 1957–59. *Career:* Lecturer in Ancient History, King's College, Newcastle upon Tyne, University of Durham, 1959–62; Lecturer, 1962–71, Senior Lecturer, 1971–79, Reader, 1979–94, Prof., 1994–99, of Ancient History, Prof. Emeritus, 1999–, University of Newcastle upon Tyne. *Publications:* The Catalogue of the Ships in Homer's Iliad, 1970; Hannibal's War, 1978; The Spartan Army, 1985; The Defence of Greece, 490–479 BC, 1993; The First Punic War, 1996. Contributions: scholarly journals. *Address:* 15 Rectory Terrace, Gosforth, Newcastle upon Tyne NE3 1YB, England.

LE CARRÉ, John (see Cornwell, David John Moore).

LE CLÉZIO, Jean Marie Gustave; Author; b. 13 April 1940, Nice, France; m. 1st Rosalie Piquemal, 1961, one d.; m. 2nd Jemia Jean, 1975. *Education:* University of Nice; University of Bristol; University of London. *Publications:* Le procès-verbal, 1963; La fièvre, 1965; Le procès, 1965; Le déluge, 1966; L'extase matérielle, 1967; Terra amata, 1967; Le livre des fruites, 1969; La guerre, 1970; Haï, 1971; Conversations, 1971; Les géants, 1973; Mydriase, 1973; Voyages de l'autre côté, 1975; Les prophéties du Chylam Balam, 1976; Mondo et autres histoires, L'inconnu sur la terre, 1978; Désert, 1980; Trois villes saintes, 1980; Le ronde et autres faits divers, 1982; Journal du chercheur d'or, 1985; Voyage à Rodrigues, 1986; Le rêve mexicain, 1988; Printemps et autre saisons, 1989; Sirandanes, Suivi de petit lexique de la langue créole et des oiseaux (co-author), 1990; Onitsha, 1991; Etoile errante, 1992; Diego et Frida, 1993; La Quarantaine, 1995; Le poisson d'or, 1997; La fête chantée, 1997; Hasard et Angoli Mala, 1999. *Honours:* Chevalier, Ordre des Arts et des Lettres; Chevalier, Légion d'honneur; Prix Renaudot, 1963; Grand Prix Paul Morand, Académie Française, 1980; Grand Prix Jean Giono, 1997; Prix Prince de Monaco, 1998. *Address:* c/o Editions Gallimard, 5 rue Sebastien-Bottin, 75007 Paris, France.

LE GOFF, Jacques (Louis); Historian and Writer; b. 1 Jan. 1924, Toulon, France; m. Anna Dunin-Wasowicz, 1962, one s. one d. *Career:* Fellow, Lincoln College, Oxford, 1951–52; Asst, University of Lille, 1954–59; Prof., later Pres., École des hautes études en sciences, Paris, 1960–77; Co-Ed., Annales. *Publications:* Marchands et banquiers du moyen âge, 1956; Les intellectuels au moyen âge, 1957; Le moyen âge, 1962; La civilisation de l'occident médiéval, 1964; Pour un autre moyen âge, 1978, English trans. as Time, Work and Culture in the Middle Ages, 1980; La naissance du purgatoire, 1981; L'apogée de la chrétienté, 1982; L'imaginaire médiéval, 1985, English trans. as The Medieval Imagination, 1988; La bourse et la vie, 1986; Histoire de la France religeuse (co-author), 1988; L'homme médiéval, 1989, English trans. as Medieval Callings, 1990; L'etat et les pouvoirs, 1989; St Louis, 1996; Une vie pour l'histoire, 1996; L'Europe racontée aux jeunes, 1996; Un autre moyen âge, 1999. Contributions: scholarly books and journals. *Honours:* Grand Prix Nationale, 1987; Gold Medal, CNRS, 1991; Grand Prix Gobert, 1996; Grand Prix d'Histoire, 1997.

LE GUIN, Ursula Kroeber, BA, MA; American writer and poet; b. 21 Oct. 1929, Berkeley, CA, USA; m. Charles A. Le Guin 1953; three c. *Education:* Radcliffe College, Columbia Univ. *Career:* Lecturer or Writer-in-Residence, Clarion West, Portland State Univ., Pacific Univ., Reading Univ., UK, First Australian Workshop in Speculative Fiction, Indiana Univ. Writers Conference, Revelle Coll. of the Univ. of California, San Diego, Kenyon Coll., Tulane Univ. Mellon Lecturer, Bennington Coll. Writing Program, Beloit Coll., Haystack Summer Program of Portland State Univ., Flight of the Mind Writing Workshop, Stanford Univ., San José State Univ., Malheur Field Station Summer Writing Workshop. *Publications:* Fiction: Rocannon's World, 1966; Planet of Exile, 1966; City of Illusion, 1967; A Wizard of Earthsea (Earthsea series), 1968; The Left Hand of Darkness, 1969; The Tombs of Atuan (Earthsea series), 1970; The Lathe of Heaven, 1971; The Farthest Shore (Earthsea series), 1972; The Dispossessed: An Ambiguous Utopia, 1974; The Wind's Twelve Quarters (short stories), 1975; The Word for World is Forest, 1976; Very Far away from Anywhere Else, 1976; Orsinian Tales (short stories), 1976; Malafrena, 1979; The Beginning Place, 1980; The Compass Rose (short stories), 1982; The Eye of the Heron, 1983; Always Coming Home, 1985; Buffalo Gals (short stories), 1987; Tehanu (Earthsea series), 1990; Searoad (short stories), 1991; A Fisherman of the Inland Sea (short stories), 1994; Four Ways to Forgiveness (short stories), 1995; Unlocking the Air (short stories), 1996; The Telling, 2000; Tales from Earthsea (Earthsea series), 2001; The Other Wind (Earthsea series), 2001; The Birthday of the World (short stories), 2002. Children's Books: Leese Webster, 1979; Cobbler's Rune, 1983; Solomon Leviathan, 1988; Catwings, 1988; A Visit from Dr Katz, 1988; Fire and Stone, 1989; Catwings Return, 1989; Fish Soup, 1992; A Ride on the Red Mare's Back, 1992; Wonderful Alexander and the Catwings, 1994; Jane on her Own, 1999; Tom Mouse, 2002. Poetry: Wild Angels, 1974; Walking in Cornwall (chapbook), 1976; Tillai and Tylissos (chapbook, with Theodora Kroeber), 1979; Hard Words, 1981; In the Red Zone (chapbook, with Henk Pander) 1983; Wild Oats and Fireweed, 1988; No Boats (chapbook), 1992; Blue Moon over Thurman Street (with Roger Dorband) 1993; Going out with Peacocks, 1994; Sixty Odd, 1999. Non-Fiction: Dancing at the Edge of the World (criticism), 1989; The Language of the Night (criticism), 1992; A Winter Solstice Ritual for the Pacific Northwest (chapbook, with Vonda N. McIntyre), 1991; Findings (chapbook), 1992; The Art of Bunditsu (chapbook), 1993; Lao Tzu: Tao Te Ching: A Book About The Way And The Power Of The Way (trans.), 1997; The Twins, The Dream/Las Gemelas, El Sueño (trans. with Diana Bellessi), 1997; Steering the Craft (criticism), 1998. Contributions: periodicals incl. New Yorker, Omni, Redbook, Fantasy and Science Fiction, Fantastic, Amazing, Playboy, Playgirl, Tri-Quarterly, Kenyon Review, Calyx, Milkweed, Mr Cogito, Seattle Review, NW Review, Open Places, Backbone, Orion, Parabola, Paradoxa, Yale Review, Antaeus Foundation, SF Studies, Critical Inquiry. *Honours:* Columbia University Fellow, 1952; Fulbright Fellow, 1953; Boston Globe-Horn Book Award, 1968; Hugo Awards, 1969, 1973, 1974, 1975, 1988; Nebula Awards, 1969, 1975 (two), 1990, 1996; Newbery Silver Medal, 1972; National Book Award for Children's Books, 1972; Locus Awards, 1973, 1984, 1995, 1996, 2001, 2002 (two); Jupiter Awards, 1975, 1976; Lewis Carroll Shelf Award, 1979; Gandalf Award, 1979; Janet Heidinger Kafka Prize, 1986; Prix Lectures-Jeunesse, 1987; International Fantasy Award, 1988; Pushcart Prize, 1991; Harold D. Vursell Memorial Award, American Acad. of Arts and Letters, 1991; H. L. Davis Fiction Award, 1992; Hubbub annual poetry award, 1995; Asimov's Readers Award, 1995; Theodore Sturgeon Award, 1995; James Triptree Jr Awards, 1995, 1996, 1997; Bumbershoot Arts Award, Seattle, 1998; Robert Kirsch Lifetime Achievement Award, Los Angeles Times, 2000; 2001 Lifetime Achievement Award, Pacific NW Booksellers Asscn, 2001; Endeavor Award, 2001; Willamette Writers Lifetime Achievement Award, 2002; PEN/Malamud Award for Short Fiction, 2002; Hon. degrees, Bucknell Univ., Lawrence Univ., Univ. of Oregon, Western Oregon State Coll., Lewis & Clark Coll., Occidental Coll., Emory Univ., Kenyon Coll., Portland State Univ. *Literary Agent:* Virginia Kidd Agency, PO Box 278, Milford, PA 18337, USA. *Address:* PO Box 10541, Portland, OR 97296-0541, USA. *Website:* www.ursulakleguin.com.

LE MAR, Angie; British writer and performer. *Education:* Univ. of Cambridge. *Television:* The Real McCoy (BBC2), Get Up Stand Up (Channel 4). *Radio:* The Ladies' Room (Choice FM London). *Plays:* Funny Black Women on the Edge (writer, dir and performer) 2003, Live at the Palladium (performer) 2003, Sisters Under the Skin (writer) 2004. *Honours:* BECA Best Stand-Up Female 2000, BECA Most Original Material 2001, Men & Women of Merit 2002, European Federation of Black Women (EFBWO) in Business 2002. *Address:* c/o Choice FM Radio, 291–299 Borough High Street, London, SE1 1JG, England. *Website:* www.angielemar.com.

LE MINH KHUE; Vietnamese writer and editor. *Career:* war correspondent, Tien Phong (Vanguard), Giaia Phong (Liberation); Chief Fiction Ed., Vietnam Writers' Asscn. *Publications:* The Stars, The Earth, The River 1997; as co-editor: The Other Side of Heaven: Post-War Fiction by Vietnamese and American Writers 1995. *Address:* c/o Vietnam Writers' Association, Nguyen Dinh Chieu Str., Hanoi, Viet Nam. *E-mail:* nhavan.bdn@fpt.vn.

LE PLASTRIER, Robert (see Warner, Francis).

LEAKEY, Richard (Erskine Frere); Paleontologist, Public Servant and Writer; b. 19 Dec. 1944, Nairobi, Kenya; m. Maeve Gillian Epps, 1970, three d. *Education:* Duke of York School, Nairobi. *Career:* Administrative Dir, 1968–74, Dir, 1974–89, Mem., Board of Dirs, 1999–, National Museums of Kenya; Leader, East Rudolf, later East Turkana Research Project, Rift Valley, Kenya, 1968–; Dir, Wildlife and Conservation Management Service, Kenya, 1989–90; Chair., 1989–93, Dir, 1993–94, 1998–99, Kenya Wildlife Service; Man. Dir, Richard Leakey and Assocs, 1994–98; Sec.-Gen., SAFINA, 1995–98; MP, Kenya, 1998; Permanent Sec., Sec. to the Cabinet and Head of the Public Service, Kenya, 1999–; mem. East African Wild Life Society, chair., 1984–89; Foundation for Research into the Origin of Man, chair., 1974–81; Wildlife Clubs of Kenya, trustee, 1980–. *Publications:* Origins (with R. Lewin), 1978; People of the Lake (with R. Lewin), 1979; Koobi Fora Research Project, Vol. I (with M. G. Leakey), 1979; The Making of Mankind, 1981; Human Origins, 1982; One Life, 1984; Origins Reconsidered (with R. Lewin), 1992; The Origins of Humankind (with R. Lewin), 1995; The Sixth Extinction: Biodiversity and its Survival (with R. Lewin), 1996. Contributions: General History of Africa, Vol. I, 1976, scholarly journals and television. *Honours:* various hon. doctorates; Golden Ark Medal for Conservation, 1989. *Address:* PO Box 24926, Nairobi, Kenya.

LEALE, Barry Cavendish; poet; b. 1 Sept. 1930, Ashford, Middlesex, England. *Publications:* Under a Glass Sky 1975, Preludes 1977, Leviathan and Other Poems 1984, The Colours of Ancient Dreams 1984; contrib. to anthologies and periodicals. *Address:* Flat E10, Peabody Estate, Wild Street, London, WC2B 4AH, England.

LEAPMAN, Michael Henry; Writer and Journalist; b. 24 April 1938, London, England; m. Olga Mason, 15 July 1965, one s. *Career:* Journalist, The Times, 1969–81; mem. RSA; Society of Authors; National Union of Journalists; Garden Writers' Guild. *Publications:* One Man and His Plot, 1976; Yankee Doodles, 1982; Companion Guide to New York, 1983; Barefaced Cheek, 1983; Treachery, 1984; The Last Days of the Beeb, 1986; Kinnock, 1987; The Book of London (ed.), 1989; London's River, 1991; Treacherous Estate, 1992; Eyewitness Guide to London, 1993; Master Race (with Catrine Clay), 1995; Witnesses to War, 1998; The Ingenious Mr Fairchild, 2000; The World for a Shilling, 2001; Inigo: The Troubled Life of Inigo Jones, Architect of the English Renaissance, 2003. Contributions: numerous magazines and journals. *Honours:* Campaigning Journalist of the Year, British Press Award, 1968; Thomas Cook Travel Book Award, Best Guide Book of 1983; Garden Writers Guild Award, 1995; Times Education Supplement Senior Book Award, 1999. *Literary Agent:* Felicity Bryan, 2A North Parade, Oxford OX2 6PE, England. *Address:* 13 Aldebert Terrace, London SW8 1BH, England. *E-mail:* mhleapman@msn.com.

LEAR, Peter (see Lovesey, Peter).

LEASOR, (Thomas) James; author; b. 20 Dec. 1923, Erith, Kent, England; m. Joan Margaret Bevan 1951; three s. *Education:* City of London School; BA, 1948, MA, 1952, Oriel College, Oxford. *Career:* Feature Writer, Foreign Correspondent, Daily Express, London, 1948–55; Editorial Adviser, Newnes and Pearson, later IPC, publishing, 1955–69; Dir, Elm Tree Books, 1970–73. *Publications:* Novels and non-fiction books. *Honours:* Order of St John; FRSA. *Address:* Swallowcliffe Manor, Salisbury, Wiltshire SP3 5PB, England.

LEAVITT, David; Writer; b. 23 June 1961, Pittsburgh, PA, USA. *Education:* BA, Yale University, 1983. *Career:* Prof. of English, University of Florida, 2000–; mem. PEN; Authors' Guild. *Publications:* Family Dancing, 1984; The Lost Language of Cranes, 1986; Equal Affections, 1989; A Place I've Never Been, 1990; While England Sleeps, 1993; The Penguin Book of Gay Short Stories (ed. with Mark Mitchell), 1994; Arkansas, 1997; The Page Turner, 1998; Martin Bauman, 2000; Florence: A Delicate Case, 2002. Contributions: periodicals. *Honours:* O. Henry Award, 1984; National Endowment for the Arts Grant, 1985; Guggenheim Fellowship, 1990; New York Public Library Literary Lion, 1995. *Literary Agent:* The Wylie Agency, 250 W 57th St, Suite 2114, New York, NY 10107, USA.

LEBOW, Jeanne; Writer, Poet, Teacher and Photographer; b. 29 Jan. 1951, Richmond, Virginia, USA; m. 1st Howard Lebow 1975 (divorced 1981); m. 2nd Steve Shepard 1985. *Education:* AB, English, College of William and Mary, 1973; MA, Liberal Arts, Hollins College, 1982; PhD, English, University of Southern Mississippi, 1989; Master Naturalist Program, 1998–. *Career:* Instructor, Memphis State University, 1982–84; Teaching Asst, University of Southern Mississippi, 1984–87; Fulbright Lecturer in American Studies, University of Ouagadougou, Burkina Faso, 1987–88; Asst Prof., Northeast Missouri State University, 1988–92; Freelance Nature Columnist, 1991–; Adjunct Prof., 1992–93, 1994–95, Visiting Prof., 1993–94, University of Southern Mississippi. *Publications:* The Outlaw James Copeland and the Champion-Belted Empress (poems), 1991. Contributions: anthologies, books, reviews, and journals. *Honours:* National Award, Georgia State Poetry Society, 1983; Mississippi Humanities Council Grants, 1994, 1995. *Address:* PO Box 1295, Gautier, MS 39553, USA. *E-mail:* shepart@datasync.com.

LEBRECHT, Norman; Writer; b. 11 July 1948, London, England; m. Elbie Spivack 1977; three d. *Career:* fmr columnist, Daily Telegraph; Asst Ed., London Evening Standard; mem. Society of Authors. *Publications:* Discord, 1982; Book of Musical Anecdotes, 1985; Mahler Remembered, 1987; Music in London, 1991; The Maestro Myth, 1991; The Companion to 20th Century Music, 1992; Who Killed Classical Music?, 1997; Covent Garden: Dispatches from the English Culture War, 1945–2000, 2000; The Song of Names, 2002. *Honours:* Whitbread First Novel Award, 2002. *Literary Agent:* Curtis Brown Ltd, Haymarket House, 28–29 Haymarket, London, SW1Y 4SP, England. *Telephone:* (20) 7393-4400. *Fax:* (20) 7393-4401. *E-mail:* info@curtisbrown.co.uk. *Website:* www.curtisbrown.co.uk.

LEBRUN HOLMES, Sandra; Writer, Film-maker and Researcher; b. 24 April 1924, Bulcoomatta Station, NSW, Australia; m. Cecil William Holmes, 1956, two s. one d. *Education:* Anthropology, Sydney University, 2 years. *Career:* mem. Australian Society of Authors; Film Dirs Guild. *Publications:* Yirawala: Artist and Man, 1972; Yirawala: Painter of the Dreaming, 1992. Contributions: various publications. *Address:* Box 439 PO, Potts Pt, NSW 2011, Australia.

LECKIE, Ross; Journalist, Writer and Investment Man; b. 5 June 1957, Scotland; m. Vera Wolfing (divorced 1992); two s. two d. *Education:* Corpus Christi College, Oxford; MA, Classics, University of Oxford, 1980; Royal Agricultural College, Cirencester, 1980–81. *Career:* Reviewer, Times, London, 1993–; Head of Corporate Communications, Martin Currie Investment Management, Edinburgh, 1996–; mem. Fellow, Society of Antiquaries of Scotland; Hellenic Society; Speculative Society, pres., 1985–87. *Publications:* Bluff Your Way in the Classics, 1989; Grampian, 1991; The Gourmet's Companion, 1994; Hannibal, 1995; Scipio, 1997; Carthage, 1998. *Address:* c/o Shiel Land, 43 Doughty St, London WC1N 2LF, England.

LEE, Chang-rae, BA, MFA; American novelist; b. 29 July 1965, Seoul, Republic of Korea; m. Michelle Branca 1993. *Education:* Phillips Exeter, Yale Univ., Univ. of Oregon. *Career:* moved to USA 1968; Asst Prof., Univ. of Oregon; Prof. and Dir, MFA program, Hunter Coll., CUNY. *Publications:* Native Speaker 1995 (PEN/Hemingway Award for First Fiction), A Gesture Life 1999 (screenplay 2000), Aloft 2004; contribs to The New York Times Magazine. *Honours:* American Book Award, Before Columbus Foundation 1995, American Library Asscn Notable Book of the Year Award 1995, Barnes & Noble Discover Great New Writers Award 1995, one of New Yorker magazine's best fiction writers under 40. *Address:* c/o Creative Writing Program, Hunter College, City University of New York, 695 Park Avenue, New York, NY 10021, USA.

LEE, (William) David; poet and academic; b. 13 Aug. 1944, Matador, TX, USA; m. Jan M. Lee 1971; one s. one d. *Education:* BA, Colorado State University, 1967; Idaho State University, 1970; PhD, University of Utah, 1973. *Career:* Prof. of English, 1971–, Chair, 1973–82, Acting Chair, 1984–85, Dept of English, Head, 1987–, Dept of Language and Literature, Southern Utah University; Poetry Ed., Weber Studies, 1986–; John Neihardt Distinguished Lectureships, State of Nebraska, 1990, 1996; First Poet Laureate, State of Utah, 1997; mem. National Foundation for Advancement of the Arts, board of dirs, 1996–; Western States Foundation; Writers at Work, board of advisers, 1993–. *Publications:* The Porcine Legacy, 1978; Driving and Drinking, 1979; Shadow Weaver, 1984; The Porcine Canticles, 1984; Paragonah Canyon, Autumn, 1990; Day's Work, 1990; My Town, 1995; Covenants, 1996; The Fish, 1997; The Wayburne Pig, 1998; A Legacy of Shadows: Poems 1979–1999, 1999. Contributions: many anthologies, reviews, quarterlies, journals, and magazines. *Honours:* National Endowment for the Arts Fellowship, 1985; First Place, Poetry, Creative Writing Competition, 1988, Publication Prize, 1989, Utah Arts Council; Outstanding Utah Writer, Utah Endowment for the Humanities and National Council of Teachers of English, 1990; Governor's Award for Lifetime Achievement, Utah, 1994; Western States Book Award, 1995; Mountain and Plain Booksellers Award, 1995; Gov.'s Award in the Humanities, 2001; Bronze Minuteman Award for Lifetime Service to State and Nation, 2000. *Address:* c/o Department of Language and Literature, Southern Utah University, Cedar City, UT 84720, USA.

LEE, Dennis Beynon; Poet and Writer; b. 31 Aug. 1939, Toronto, Ontario, Canada; m. 1st, one s. one d.; m. 2nd Susan Perly, 1985. *Education:* BA, 1962, MA, 1965, University of Toronto. *Career:* Lecturer, University of Toronto, 1963–67; Ed., House of Anasi Press, 1967–72; Consulting Ed., Macmillan of Canada, 1972–78; Poetry Ed., McClelland and Stewart,

1981–84; mem. PEN, Canada; Writers' Union of Canada. *Publications:* Poetry: Kingdom of Absence, 1967; Civil Elegies, 1972; The Gods, 1979; The Difficulty of Living on Other Planets, 1998; Riffs, 1993; Nightwatch: New and Selected Poems, 1968–96, 1996. Children's Poetry: Wiggle to the Laundromat, 1970; Alligator Pie, 1974; Nicholas Knock, 1974; Garbage Delight, 1977; Jelly Belly, 1983; Lizzy's Lion, 1984; The Ice Cream Store, 1991. Non-Fiction: Savage Fields, 1977. Contributions: journals and magazines. *Honours:* Governor-General's Award for Poetry, 1972; Mem. of the Order of Canada, 1994. *Address:* c/o Westwood Creative Artists, 10 St Mary St, No. 510, Toronto, Ontario M4Y 1P9, Canada.

LEE, Hamilton; academic, poet and writer; b. 10 Oct. 1921, Zhouxian, Shandong, China; m. Jean C. Chang 1945; one s. three d. *Education:* BS, Beijing Normal University, 1948; MA, University of Minnesota, 1958; DEd, Wayne State University, Detroit, 1964. *Career:* Teacher of English, High Schools, Taiwan, 1948–56; Research Assoc., Wayne State University, Detroit, 1958–64; Visiting Prof. of Chinese Literature, Seton Hall University, summer, 1964; Asst Prof., Moorhead State University, 1964–65; Visiting Scholar, Harvard University, 1965 and Summer 1966; Assoc. Prof., University of Wisconsin at La Crosse, 1965–66; Prof., 1966–84, Prof. Emeritus, 1984–, East Stroudsburg University, Pennsylvania; Visiting Fellow, Princeton University, 1976–78; mem. Acad. of American Poets; Distinguished Mem., Mem. of Advisory Panel, International Society of Poets; Poetry Society of America; Pennsylvania Poetry Society; World Literary Acad., fellow; World Future Society. *Publications:* Readings in Instructional Technology, 1970; Relection (poems), 1989; Revelation (poems), 1991. Contributions: numerous anthologies, journals, and literary magazines. *Honours:* many poetry contest awards; Ed.'s Choice, National Library of Poetry, 1994.

LEE, (Nelle) Harper; writer; b. 28 April 1926, Monroeville, AL, USA. *Education:* Huntington Coll., Univ. of Alabama. *Career:* mem. National Council on the Arts 1966–71. *Publications:* To Kill a Mockingbird, 1960. Other: Love—In Other Words (essay in Vogue), 1961; Christmas to Me (essay in McCalls), 1961; When Children Discover America (essay in McCalls), 1965; High Romance and Adventure (essay, part of the Alabama History and Heritage Festival), 1983. Contributions: numerous magazines. *Honours:* Alabama Library Assen Award, 1961; Brotherhood Award, National Conference of Christians and Jews, 1961; Pulitzer Prize for Fiction, 1961; Best Sellers' Paperback of the Year Award, 1962; hon. doctorates. *Address:* c/o J. B. Lippincott Co, 227 E Washington Square, Philadelphia, PA 19106, USA.

LEE, John Darrell; writer and fmr academic; b. 12 March 1931, Indiahoma, Oklahoma, USA. *Education:* BA, Texas Technological College, 1952; MSJ, West Virginia University, 1965. *Career:* Former Prof. of Journalism. *Publications:* Caught in the Act, 1968; Diplomatic Persuaders, 1968; Assignation in Algeria, 1971; The Ninth Man, 1976; The Thirteenth Hour, 1978; Lago, 1980; Stalag Texas, 1990. *Literary Agent:* Don Congdon Associates Inc, 156 Fifth Avenue, Suite 625, New York, NY 10010, USA.

LEE, Lance (Wilds); Dramatist, Poet, Writer and Ed.; b. 25 Aug. 1942, New York, NY, USA; m. Jeanne Barbara Hutchings, 30 Aug. 1962, two d. *Education:* Boston University; BA, Brandeis University, 1964; MFA, Playwriting and Dramatic Literature, Yale School of Drama, 1967. *Career:* Lecturer, University of Bridgeport, 1967–68; Asst Prof., University of California at Los Angeles, 1971–73, California State University at Northridge, 1981–; Instructor, Southern Connecticut State College, 1968; Senior Lecturer, Asst Prof., University of Southern California at Los Angeles, 1968–71; mem. Acad. of American Poets; Poetry Society of America; PEN. *Publications:* Fox, Hound and Huntress (play), 1973; Time's Up (play), 1979; The Understructure of Screenwriting (with Ben Brady), 1988; Wrestling with The Angel (poems), 1990; A Poetics for Screenwriters, 2001; Second Chances (novel), 2001; Time's Up and Other Plays, 2001; Becoming Human (poems), 2001; with others: On the Waterfront 2003. Contributions: Reviews, quarterlies, journals, and periodicals, in England and the US. *Honours:* Arts of the Theatre Foundation Fellowship, 1967; University of Southern California Research and Publication Grants, 1970, 1971; Rockefeller Foundation Grant, Office for Advanced Drama Research, 1971; Theatre Development Fund Grant, 1976; National Endowment for the Arts Fellowship, 1976; Squaw Valley Scholarships in Poetry, 1982, 1983; Port Townsend Writers Conference Scholarship in Poetry, 1985. *Address:* c/o Reece Halsey Agency, 8733 Sunset Blvd, Los Angeles, CA 90069, USA.

LEE, Tanith; British writer and playwright; b. 19 Sept. 1947, London; m. John Kaiine 1992. *Education:* Prendergast Grammar School. *Television and radio writing:* two episodes of Blake's Seven (BBC TV), several radio plays. *Publications:* The Betrothed (short stories) 1968, The Dragon Hoard (juvenile) 1971, Princess Hynchatti and Some Other Surprises (juvenile) 1972, Animal Castle (juvenile) 1972, Companions on the Road (juvenile) 1975, The Birthgrave 1975, Don't Bite the Sun 1976, The Storm Lord 1976, The Winter Players (juvenile) 1976, East of Midnight (juvenile) 1977, Drinking Sapphire Wine 1977, Volkhavaar 1977, Vazkor, Son of Vazkor 1978, Quest for the White Witch 1978, Night's Master 1978, The Castle of Dark (juvenile) 1978, Shon the Taken (juvenile) 1979, Death's Master 1979, Electric Forest 1979, Sabella (aka The Blood Stone) 1980, Kill the Dead 1980, Day by Night 1980, Delusion's Master 1981, The Silver Metal Lover 1982, Cyrion (short stories) 1982, Prince on a White Horse (juvenile) 1982, Sung in Shadow 1983, Anackire 1983, Red as Blood, or Tales from the Sisters Grimmer 1983, The Dragon Hoard 1984, The Beautiful Biting Machine (short stories) 1984, Tamastara, or the Indian Nights (short stories) 1984, Days of Grass 1985, The Gorgon and Other Beastly Tales 1985, Dreams of Dark and Light 1986, Women as Demons: The Male Perception of Women Through Space and Time 1989, Blood of Roses 1990, Black Unicorn 1995, The Book of the Mad 1998, The Book of the Dead 1998, White as Snow 2000, East of Midnight 2001, Queen of the Wolves 2001, Faces Under Water 2002, Wolf Wing 2002, Piratica (juvenile) 2004, Fatal Woman (short stories) 2004, Thirty-Four (novel) 2004, Death of the Day 2004, Cast a Bright Shadow (book I of Lionwolf trilogy) 2004. *Honours:* August Derleth Award 1985, World Fantasy Award. *Address:* c/o Hodder Headline, 338 Euston Road, London, NW1 3BH, England. *Website:* www.tanithlee.com.

LEE, Warner (see Battin, B. W).

LEE, Wayne C., (Lee Sheldon); Author; b. 2 July 1917, Lamar, NE, USA. *Career:* mem. Western Writers of America, pres., 1970–71; Nebraska Writers Guild, pres., 1974–76. *Publications:* Prairie Vengeance, 1954; Broken Wheel Ranch, 1956; Slugging Backstop, 1957; His Brother's Guns, 1958; Killer's Range, 1958; Bat Masterson, 1960; Gun Brand, 1961; Blood on the Prairie, 1962; Thunder in the Backfield, 1962; Stranger in Stirrup, 1962; The Gun Tamer, 1963; Devil Wire, 1963; The Hostile Land, 1964; Gun in His Hand, 1964; Warpath West, 1965; Fast Gun, 1965; Brand of a Man, 1966; Mystery of Scorpion Creek, 1966; Trail of the Skulls, 1966; Showdown at Julesburg Station, 1967; Return to Gunpoint, 1967; Only the Brave, 1967; Doomed Planet (as Lee Sheldon), 1967; Sudden Guns, 1968; Trouble at Flying H, 1969; Stage to Lonesome Butte, 1969; Showdown at Sunrise, 1971; The Buffalo Hunters, 1972; Suicide Trail, 1972; Wind Over Rimfire, 1973; Son of a Gunman, 1973; Scotty Philip: The Man Who Saved the Buffalo (non-fiction), 1975; Law of the Prairie, 1975; Die Hard, 1975; Law of the Lawless, 1977; Skirmish at Fort Phil Kearney, 1977; Gun Country, 1978; Petticoat Wagon Train, 1978; The Violent Man, 1978; Ghost of a Gunfighter, 1980; McQuaid's Gun, 1980; Trails of the Smoky Hill (non-fiction), 1980; Shadow of the Gun, 1981; Guns at Genesis, 1981; Putnam's Ranch War, 1982; Barbed Wire War, 1983; The Violent Trail, 1984; White Butte Guns, 1984; War at Nugget Creek, 1985; Massacre Creek, 1985; The Waiting Gun, 1986; Hawks of Autumn, 1986; Wild Towns of Nebraska (non-fiction), 1988; Arikaree War Cry, 1992; Bad Men and Bad Towns (non-fiction), 1993; Deadly Days in Kansas (non-fiction), 1997. *Address:* PO Box 906, Imperial, NE 69033, USA.

LEE KUEI-SHIEN; poet, essayist, translator, chemical engineer and patent agent; b. 19 June 1937, Taipei, Taiwan; m. Wang Huei-uei 1965; one s. one d. *Education:* Taipei Institute of Technology, European Language Center, Ministry of Education. *Career:* mem. International Acad. of Poets, founder-fellow; Li Poetry Society; Rilke Gesellschaft; Taiwan PEN, pres., 1995. *Publications:* (in Chinese): poetry: 14 works 1963–2001; essays: 20 works 1971–2002; translator: 25 works 1969–2001; contrib. to anthologies and other publications. *Honours:* Hon. PhD, Chemical Engineering, Marquis Giuseppe Scicluna International University Foundation, 1985; Albert Einstein International Acad. Foundation Alfred Nobel Medal for Peace, 1991; Poetic Creation Award, Le Poetry Society, 1994; Secretary General, Asian Poets Conference, 1995; Best World Poet of the Year, 1997, 1998; Poet of the Millennium Award, 2000; New Millennium Michael Madhusudan Award, 2002; Taiwan Premier Culture Award, 2002. *Address:* Room 705, Asia Enterprise Center, No. 142 Minchuan E Road, Sec 3, Taipei 105, Taiwan.

LEE, Stewart Graham, BA; British writer, comedian and director; b. 5 April 1968, Solihull, West Midlands. *Education:* Univ. of Oxford. *Career:* writer-performer, The Oxford Revue 1987–89; solo stand-up work 1989–; writer-performer with Richard Herring in double act Lee & Herring 1991–99; rock music critic, The Sunday Times 1995–. *Radio:* On The Hour (writer, BBC Radio 4) 1991–92, Lionel Nimrod's Inexplicable World (BBC Radio 4) 1992–93, Lee & Herring's Fist Of Fun (BBC Radio 1) 1993, Lee & Herring (BBC Radio 1) 1994–95, patron and regular presenter for Resonance FM London 2002–. *Television:* Fist Of Fun (BBC2) 1995–96, Harry Hill (script ed., Avalon TV/Channel 4) 1997–2000, This Morning with Richard Not Judy (BBC2) 1998–99, Attention Scum (writer and dir, BBC2) 2000. *Theatre:* Jerry Springer: The Opera (co-writer and dir) 2002, writer-performer for Edinburgh Festival shows, including Cluub Zarathustra, Pea Green Boat, King Dong Vs Moby Dick. *Publications:* Lee & Herring's Fist Of Fun (with Richard Herring) 1995, The Perfect Fool 2001; contrib. to Vox, Q, The Guardian. *Honours:* Writer's Guild Award 1992, Sony Gold Award 1992, Evening Standard Theatre Awards 2003, Critics Circle Theatre Awards 2003. *Literary Agent:* Avalon Management, 4a Exmoor Street, London, W10 6BD, England. *Telephone:* (20) 7598-5000. *Website:* www.stewartlee.co.uk; www.jerryspringertheopera.com.

LEECH, Geoffrey Neil, BA, MA, DLitt, PhD, FBA; academic and writer; b. 16 Jan. 1936, Gloucester, England; m. Frances Anne Berman 1961; one s. one d. *Education:* University College London, Lancaster Univ. *Career:* Asst Lecturer, 1962–64, Lecturer, 1965–69, University College London; Reader, 1969–74, Prof. of Linguistics and Modern English, 1974–1996, Emer. Prof. 1996–, University of Lancaster; Visiting Prof., Brown University, 1972, Kobe University, 1984, Kyoto University, 1991, Meikai Univ. 1999; mem. Academia Europea. *Publications:* English in Advertising, 1966; A Linguistic Guide to English Poetry, 1969; Towards a Semantic Description of English, 1969; Meaning and the English Verb, 1971; A Grammar of Contemporary English (with R. Quirk, S. Greenbaum, and J. Svartvik), 1972; Semantics, 1974; A Communicative Grammar of English (with J. Svartvik), 1975; Explorations in Semantics and Pragmatics, 1980; Style in Fiction (with Michael H. Short), 1981; English Grammar for Today (with R. Hoogenraad and M. Deuchar), 1982; Principles of Pragmatics, 1983; A Comprehensive Grammar of the English Language (with R. Quirk, S. Greenbaum, and J. Svartvik), 1985; Computers in English Language Teaching and Research (ed. with C. N. Candlin), 1986; The Computational Analysis of English (ed. with R. Garside and G. Sampson), 1987; An A-Z of English Grammar and Usage, 1989; Introducing English Grammar, 1992; Statistically-driven Computer Grammars in English (ed. with E. Black and R. Garside), 1993; Spoken English on Computer (ed. with G. Myers and J. Thomas), 1995; Corpus Annotation (ed. with R. Garside and T. McEnery), 1997, Longman Grammar of Spoken and Written English (with D. Biber, S. Johansson, S. Conrad and E. Finegan) 1999, Longman Student Grammar of Spoken and Written English (with D. Biber and S. Conrad) 2002. Contributions: A Review of English Literature, Int. Journal of Corpus Linguistics, Language Learning, Lingua, New Society, Linguistics, Dutch Quarterly Review of Anglo-American Letters, TLS; Prose Studies, The Rising Generation, Transactions of the Philological Society. *Honours:* FilDr, University of Lund, 1987. *Address:* Dept of Linguistics and Modern English Language, Lancaster University, Lancaster LA1 4YT, England.

LEEDOM-ACKERMAN, Joanne, BA, MA; writer; b. 7 Feb. 1947, Dallas, TX, USA; m. Peter Ackerman 1972; two s. *Education:* Principia College, Johns Hopkins University, Brown University. *Career:* mem. International PEN (vice-pres.), Writers in Prison Cttee 1993–97. *Publications:* No Marble Angels, 1985; The Dark Path to the River, 1988; Women for All Seasons (ed.), 1989. Contributions: anthologies, newspapers, and magazines. *Address:* 3229 R Street NW, Washington, DC 20007, USA.

LEES-MILNE, James; Author; b. 6 Aug. 1908, Worcestershire, England. *Education:* Eton College, 1921–26; Grenoble University, 1927–28; MA, Magdalen College, Oxford, 1931. *Career:* Private Secretary to Baron Lloyd, 1931–35; Staff Mem., Reuters, 1935–36. *Publications:* The National Trust (ed.), 1945; The Age of Adam, 1947; National Trust Guide: Buildings, 1948; Tudor Renaissance, 1951; The Age of Inigo Jones, 1953; Roman Mornings, 1956; Baroque in Italy, 1959; Baroque in Spain and Portugal, 1960; Earls of Creation, 1962; Worcestershire: A Shell Guide, 1964; St Peter's, 1967; English Country Houses: Baroque, 1970; Another Self, 1970; Heretics in Love (novel), 1973; Ancestral Voices, 1975; William Beckford, 1976; Prophesying Peace, 1977; Round the Clock (novel), 1978; Harold Nicolson, 2 vols, 1980–81; The Country House (anthology), 1982; The Last Stuarts, 1983; Enigmatic Edwardian, 1986; Some Cotswold Country Houses, 1987; The Fool of Love, 1987; Venetian Evenings, 1988; Bachelor Duke, 1991; People and Places, 1992; A Mingled Measure, 1994; Fourteen Friends, 1996; Holy Dread: Diaries 1982–1984, 2002. *Honours:* FRSL; Society of Arts, fellow.

LEESON, Robert Arthur; journalist and writer; b. 31 March 1928, Barnton, Cheshire, England; m. Gunvor Hagen 1954; one s. one d. *Education:* University of London. *Career:* Literary Ed., Morning Star, London, 1960–80; mem. International Board of Books for Young People, British Section, treasurer, 1972–91; Writers' Guild of Great Britain, chair., 1985–86. *Publications:* Third Class Genie, 1975; Silver's Revenge, 1978; Travelling Brothers, 1979; It's My Life, 1980; Candy for King, 1983; Reading and Righting, 1985; Slambash Wangs of a Compo Gormer, 1987; Coming Home, 1991; Zarnia Experiment 1–6, 1993; Robin Hood, 1994; Red, White and Blue, 1996; Liar, 1999; The Song of Arthur, 2000; My Sister Shahrazad, 2001; Onda Wind Rider, 2003; Partners in Crime, 2003. Contributions: newspapers and journals. *Honours:* Eleanor Farjeon Award for Services to Children and Literature, 1985. *Address:* 18 McKenzie Road, Broxbourne, Hertfordshire EN10 7JH, England.

LEFFLAND, Ella Julia; Writer; b. 25 Nov. 1931, Martinez, CA, USA. *Education:* BA, Fine Arts, San Jose State College, 1953. *Publications:* Mrs Munck, 1970; Love out of Season, 1974; Last Courtesies, 1979; Rumors of Peace, 1980; The Knight, Death and the Devil, 1990. Contributions: New Yorker; Harper's; Atlantic Monthly; Mademoiselle; New York Magazine; New York Times. *Honours:* Gold Medals for Fiction, 1974, 1979, Silver Medal, 1991, Commonwealth Club of California; O. Henry First Prize, 1977; Bay Area Book Reviewers Award for Fiction, 1990. *Address:* Wallace Literary Agency, 177 E 70th St, New York, NY 10021, USA.

LEGGATT, Alexander Maxwell; Prof. of English and Writer; b. 18 Aug. 1940, Oakville, Ontario, Canada; m. Anna Thomas, 31 March 1964, four d. *Education:* BA, University of Toronto, 1962; MA, 1963, PhD, 1965, Shakespeare Institute, Stratford-on-Avon, affiliated with University of Birmingham. *Career:* Lecturer, 1965–67, Asst Prof., 1967–71, Assoc. Prof., 1971–75, Prof. of English, 1975–, University College, University of Toronto; Assoc. Ed., Modern Drama, 1972–75; Editorial Board, English Studies in Canada, 1984–91, University of Toronto Quarterly, 1996–, Studies in Theatre and Performance, 1999–, Renaissance and Reformation, 2000, Modern Drama, 2000–; mem. Amnesty International; Anglican Church of Canada, lay reader, 1979–; Asscn of Canadian College and University Teachers of English; International Asscn of University Profs of English; International Shakespeare Asscn, exec. committee, 1987–96; PEN Canada; Shakespeare Asscn of America, trustee, 1986–89; Arts and Letters Club of Toronto. *Publications:* Citizen Comedy in the Age of Shakespeare, 1973; Shakespeare's Comedy of Love, 1974; Ben Jonson: His Vision and His Art, 1981; English Drama: Shakespeare to the Restoration, 1988; Shakespeare's Political Drama, 1988; Harvester-Twayne New Critical Introductions to Shakespeare: King Lear, 1988; Coriolanus: An Annotated Bibliography (co-author), 1989; Craft and Tradition: Essays in Honour of William Blissett (co-ed.), 1990; Shakespeare in Performance: King Lear, 1991; Jacobean Public Theatre, 1992; English Stage Comedy 1490–1990, 1998; Introduction to English Renaissance Comedy, 1999; Cambridge Companion to Shakespearean Comedy (ed.), 2002; Approaches to Teaching English Renaissance Drama (co-ed.), 2002. Contributions: many scholarly journals. *Honours:* Guggenheim Fellowship, 1985–86; Killam Research Fellowship, 1995; Outstanding Teaching Award, University of Toronto, 1995; Faculty Award, University of Toronto, Alumni Awards of Excellence, 1998. *Address:* c/o University College, University of Toronto, Toronto, ON M5S 3H7, Canada.

LEHANE, Dennis; American novelist; b. 1966, Dorchester, Boston, MA. *Publications:* A Drink Before the War 1994, Darkness Take My Hand 1996, Sacred 1997, Gone Baby Gone 1998, Prayers for Rain 1999, Mystic River 2001, Shutter Island 2003. *Honours:* Anthony Award, Barry Award for Best Novel, Massachusetts Book Award in Fiction. *Address:* c/o Bantam, 61–63 Uxbridge Road, London, W5 5SA, England. *Website:* www .dennislehanebooks.com.

LEHMAN, David (Cary); Writer, Poet and Ed.; b. 11 June 1948, New York, NY, USA; m. Stefanie Green, 2 Dec. 1978, one s. *Education:* BA, 1970, PhD, 1978, Columbia University; BA, MA, 1972, University of Cambridge. *Career:* Instructor, Brooklyn College, CUNY, 1975–76; Asst Prof., Hamilton College, Clinton, New York, 1976–80; Fellow, Society for the Humanities, Cornell University, 1980–81; Lecturer, Wells College, Aurora, New York, 1981–82; Book Critic and Writer, Newsweek, 1983–89; Series Ed., The Best American Poetry, 1988–, Poets on Poetry, 1994–; Editorial Adviser in Poetry, W. W. Norton & Co, 1990–93. *Publications:* Some Nerve, 1973; Day One, 1979; Beyond Amazement: New Essays on John Ashbery (ed.), 1980; James Merrill: Essays in Criticism (ed.), 1983; An Alternative to Speech, 1986; Ecstatic Occasions, Expedient Forms: 65 Leading Contemporary Poets Select and Comment on Their Poems (ed.), 1987; Twenty Questions, 1988; The Perfect Murder: A Study in Detection, 1989; Operation Memory, 1990; The Line Forms Here, 1992; Signs of the Times: Deconstruction and the Fall of Paul de Man, 1992; The Best American Poetry (ed. with Charles Simic), 1992; The Best American Poetry (ed. with Louise Glück), 1993; The Big Question, 1995; Valentine Place, 1996. Contributions: anthologies, newspapers, reviews and journals. *Honours:* Acad. of American Poets Prize, 1974; Ingram Merrill Foundation Grants, 1976, 1982, 1984; National Endowment for the Humanities Grant, 1979; National Endowment for the Arts Fellowship, 1987; American Acad. of Arts and Letters Fellowship, 1990; Lila Wallace-Reader's Digest Fund Writers Award, 1991–94.

LEHRER, Keith (Edward); Philosopher, Prof., Writer and Artist; b. 10 Jan. 1936, Minneapolis, MN, USA; m.; two s. *Education:* BA, University of Minnesota, 1957; AM, 1959, PhD, 1960, Brown University. *Career:* Instructor and Asst Prof., Wayne State University, 1960–63; Asst Prof. to Prof., University of Rochester, 1963–73; Visiting Assoc. Prof., University of Calgary, 1966; Prof., 1974–90, Regents Prof., 1990–, University of Arizona; Hon. Prof., Karl-Franzens-University, Graz, 1985–; Assoc., CREA, École Polytechnique, Paris, 1993–94; mem. American Philosophical Asscn, pres., 1989, chair, national board of officers, 1992–95; Council for Philosophical Studies; Institute International de Philosophie, Paris and Lund; Vereinigung für Wissenschaftliche Grundlagen-forschung, Austria, hon. mem. *Publications:* Philosophical Problems and Arguments: An Introduction (with James Cornman), 1968; Knowledge, 1978; Rational Consensus in Science and Society: A Philosophical and Mathematical Study (with Carl Wagner), 1981; Thomas Reid, 1989; Metamind, 1990; Theory of Knowledge, 1990; Self-Trust: A Study of Reason, Knowledge and Autonomy, 1997. Editor: several books. Contributions: numerous books and journals. *Honours:* ACLS Fellowship, 1973–74; National Endowment for the Humanities Fellowship, 1980; Guggenheim Fellowship, 1983–84; Visiting Fellow, University of London, 1996, and Australian National University, 1997; Citation for Distinguished Achievement, Brown University, 1988; Hon. doctorate, University of Graz, 1997. *Address:* 65 Sierra Vista Dr., Tucson, AZ 85719, USA. *E-mail:* lehrer@email.arizona.edu. *Website:* w3.arizona.edu/~phil/faculty/klehrer.htm.

LEICHUK, Alan; writer and teacher; b. 15 Sept. 1938, New York, NY, USA; m. Barbara 1981; two s. *Education:* BA, Brooklyn College, CUNY, 1960; MA, 1963, PhD, 1965, Stanford University. *Career:* Brandeis University, 1966–81; Amherst College, 1982–84; Dartmouth College, 1985–; Visiting Writer, Prof., Haifa University, 1986–87, CUNY, 1993; Visiting Writer, University of Rome II, 1996; Salgo Prof. in American Literature, ELTE University, Budapest, 1999–2000. *Publications:* Fiction: American Mischief, 1973; Shrinking, 1978; Miriam in Her Forties, 1985; Brooklyn Roy, 1990; Playing the Game, 1995. For Young Adults: On Home Ground, 1987; Eight Great Hebrew Short Novels (co-ed.), 1982. Contributions: New York Times Book Review; New Republic; Dissent; Atlantic Monthly; New York

Review of Books. *Honours:* Guggenheim Fellowship, 1976–77; Fulbright Award, 1986–87. *Address:* c/o Georges Borchardt, 136 E 57th Street, New York, NY 10022, USA.

LEIGH, Meredith (see Kenyon, Bruce (Guy)).

LEIGH, Mike; Dramatist and Film and Theatre Dir; b. 20 Feb. 1943, Salford, Lancashire, England; m. Alison Steadman 1973 (divorced 2001); two s. *Education:* RADA; Camberwell School of Arts and Crafts; Central School of Art and Design; London Film School. *Publications:* Plays: The Box Play, 1965; My Parents Have Gone to Carlisle, 1966; The Last Crusade of the Five Little Nuns, 1966; Nenaa, 1967; Individual Fruit Pies, 1968; Down Here And Up There, 1968; Big Basil, 1968; Epilogue, 1969; Glum Victoria and the Lad with Specs, 1969; Bleak Moments, 1970; A Rancid Pong, 1971; Wholesome Glory, The Jaws of Death, 1973; Dick Whittington and His Cat, 1973; Babies Grow Old, 1974; The Silent Majority, 1974; Abigail's Party, 1977 (also TV play); Ecstasy, 1979; Goose-Pimples, 1981; Smelling a Rat, 1988; Greek Tragedy, 1989; It's a Great Big Shame!, 1993. TV Films: A Mug's Game, 1973; Hard Labour, 1973; The Permissive Society, The Birth of the 2001 FA Cup Final Goalie, Old Chums, Probation, A Light Snack, Afternoon, all 1975; Nuts in May, 1976; Knock for Knock, 1976; The Kiss of Death, 1977; Who's Who, 1978; Grown Ups, 1980; Home Sweet Home, 1981; Meantime, 1983; Four Days in July, 1984. Feature Films: Bleak Moments, 1971; The Short and Curlies, 1987; High Hopes, 1988; Life is Sweet, 1990; Naked, 1993; Secrets and Lies, 1996; Career Girls, 1997; Topsy-Turvy, 1999; All or Nothing, 2002. Radio Play: Too Much of a Good Thing, 1979. *Honours:* Golden Leopard, Locarno Film Festival, 1972; Golden Hugo, Chicago Film Festival, 1972; George Devine Award, 1973; Evening Standard Award, 1981; Drama Critics Choice, London, 1981; Critics Prize, Venice Film Festival, 1988; Hon. MA, Salford University, 1991, Northampton University, 2000; Hon. DLitt, Staffordshire University, 2000; Hon. doctorate, Essex Univ., 2002; OBE, 1993; Best Dir Award, 1993, Palme D'Or, 1996, Cannes Film Festival. *Literary Agent:* PFD, Drury House, 34–43 Russell St, London WC2B 5HA, England.

LEIGH FERMOR, Patrick (Michael); Author; b. 11 Feb. 1915, London, England. *Education:* King's School, Canterbury. *Career:* mem. Athens Acad., visiting mem. *Publications:* The Traveller's Tree, 1950; Julie de Carneilhan and Chance Acquaintances, by Colette (trans.), 1951; A Time to Keep Silence, 1953; The Violins of Saint-Jacques, 1953; Mani, 1958; Roumeli, 1966; A Time of Gifts, 1977; Between the Woods and the Water, 1986; Three Letters from the Andes, 1991. *Honours:* DSO; OBE; CLitt; DLitt; Chevalier, Ordre des Arts et des Lettres. *Address:* Messrs John Murray Ltd, 50 Albemarle St, London W1, England.

LEITH, Linda; Writer and Ed.; b. 13 Dec. 1949, Belfast, Northern Ireland; m. András Barnabás Göllner, 19 July 1974, three s. *Education:* BA, Philosophy, McGill University, 1970; PhD, Queen Mary College, London, 1976. *Publications:* Telling Differences: New English Fiction From Quebec (anthology), 1989; Introducing Hugh MacLennan's 'Two Solitudes' (essay), 1990; Birds of Passage (novel), 1993; The Tragedy Queen (novel), 1995. Contributions: many magazines and journals.

LEITHAUSER, Brad; Poet and Writer; b. 27 Feb. 1953, Detroit, Michigan, USA; m Mary Jo Salter, 1980, one d. *Education:* BA, 1975, JD, 1980, Harvard University. *Career:* Research Fellow, Kyoto Comparative Law Center, 1980–83; Visiting Writer, Amherst College, 1984–85; Lecturer, Mount Holyoke College, 1987–88. *Publications:* Poetry: Hundreds of Fireflies, 1982; A Seaside Mountain: Eight Poems from Japan, 1985; Cats of the Temple, 1986; Between Leaps: Poems 1972–1985, 1987; The Mail from Anywhere: Poems, 1990. Fiction: The Line of Ladies, 1975; Equal Distance, 1985; Hence, 1989; Seaward, 1993. Non-Fiction: Penchants & Places: Essays and Criticism, 1995. Editor: The Norton Book of Ghost Stories, 1994; No Other Book, 1999. *Honours:* Harvard University-Acad. of American Poets Prizes, 1973, 1975; Harvard University McKim Garrison Prizes, 1974, 1975; Amy Lowell Traveling Scholarship, 1981–82; Guggenheim Fellowship, 1982–83; Lavan Younger Poets Award, 1983; John D. and Catherine T. MacArthur Foundation Fellowship, 1983–87. *Address:* c/o Alfred A. Knopf Inc, 299 Park Ave, New York, NY 10171, USA.

LELAND, Christopher Towne, BA, MA, PhD; writer and academic; b. 17 Oct. 1951, Tulsa, Oklahoma, USA. *Education:* Pomona College, University of California at San Diego. *Career:* Prof. of English, Wayne State University, 1990–; mem. Poets and Writers; MLA. *Publications:* Mean Time, 1982; The Last Happy Men: The Generation of 1922, Fiction and the Argentine Reality, 1986; Mrs Randall, 1987; The Book of Marvels, 1990; The Prof. of Aesthetics, 1994; Letting Loose, 1996; The Art of Compelling Fiction, 1998. Contributions: Principal Translator, Open Door by Luise Valenzvela 1988. *Honours:* Fellow, Massachusetts Artists Foundation, 1985. *Address:* c/o Dept of English, Wayne State University, Detroit, MI 48202, USA.

LELCHUK, Alan; Writer; b. 15 Sept. 1938, New York, NY, USA; m. Barbara Kreiger, 7 Oct. 1979, two s. *Education:* BA, Brooklyn College, CUNY, 1960; MA, 1963, PhD, English Literature, 1965, Stanford University. *Career:* Brandeis University, 1966–81; Assoc. Ed., Modern Occasions, 1980–82; Amherst College, 1982–84; Dartmouth College, 1985–; Fulbright Writer-in-Residence, Haifa University, Israel, 1986–87; Visiting Writer, City College, CUNY, 1991; Ed., Publisher, Steerforth Press, South Royalton, Vermont, 1993–; Salgo Prof. of American Literature and Writing, ELTE University, Budapest, 1999–2000; Fulbright Prof., International Univ. of Moscow, 2003–04; mem. PEN; Authors' Guild. *Publications:* American Mischief, 1973; Miriam at Thirty-Four, 1974; Shrinking: The Beginning of My Own Ending, 1978; 8 Great Hebrew Short Novels (co-ed.), 1983; Miriam in Her Forties, 1985; On Home Ground, 1987; Brooklyn Boy, 1989; Playing the Game, 1995; Ziff: A Life?, 2003. Contributions: New York Times Book Review; Sewanee Review; Atlantic; New Republic; Dissent; New York Review of Books. *Honours:* Guggenheim Fellowship, 1976–77; Mishkenot Sha'Ananim Resident Fellow, 1976–77; Fulbright Awards, 1986–87, (Russia), 2003–04; Manuscript Collection, Mugar Memorial Library, Boston University. *Address:* RFD 2, Canaan, NH 03741, USA. *E-mail:* alan.lelchuk@dartmouth.edu.

LELYVELD, Joseph (Salem); Journalist and Ed.; b. 5 April 1937, Cincinnati, Ohio, USA; m. Carolyn Fox, 14 June 1958, two d. *Education:* BA, 1958, MA, 1959, Harvard University; MS, Columbia University, 1960. *Career:* Staff, 1963–, Foreign Correspondent, 1965–86, Foreign Ed., 1987–89, Managing Ed., 1990–94, Exec. Ed., 1994–, New York Times; mem. Century Asscn. *Publications:* Move Your Shadow: South Africa Black and White, 1985. Contributions: periodicals. *Honours:* George Polk Memorial Awards, 1972, 1984; Guggenheim Fellowship, 1984; Pulitzer Prize in General Non-Fiction, 1986; Los Angeles Times Book Prize, 1986; Sidney Hillman Award, 1986; Cornelius P. Ryan Award, 1986. *Address:* c/o The New York Times, 229 W 43rd St, New York, NY 10036, USA.

LEM, Stanisław; Author; b. 12 Sept. 1921, Lvov, Russia; m. Barbara Lesnik, 11 Aug. 1953, one s. *Education:* Studied Medicine in Lvov, 1939–41, and Kraków, Poland, 1944–45. *Career:* Lecturer, University of Kraków, part-time, 1973–; mem. International Asscn of Poets, Playwrights, Eds, Essayists and Authors. *Publications:* Czlowiek z Marsa (trans. as Man From Mars), 1946; Astronauci (trans. as The Astronauts), 1954; Oblok Magellana (trans. as The Magellan Nebula), 1955; Szpital Przemienienia (trans. as Hospital of the Transfiguration), 1955; Dialogs, 1957; Dzienniki gwiazdowe (trans. as The Star Diaries), 1957; Eden, 1959; Sledztwo (trans. as The Investigation), 1959; Powrot z gwiazd (trans. as Return from the Stars), 1961; Pamietnik znaleziony w wannie (trans. as Memoir Found in a Bathtub), 1961; Solaris, 1961; Summa technologiae, 1964; Bajki robotow (trans. as Mortal Engines), 1964; Niezwyciezony (trans. as The Invincible), 1964; Cyberiada (trans. as The Cyberiad), 1965; Wysoki Zamek (trans. as Highcastle a Remembrance), 1966; Opowiesci o pilocie Pirxie (trans. as Tales of Pirx the Pilot), 1968; Filozofia przypadku (trans. as The Philosophy of Chance), 1968; Glos Pana (trans. as His Master's Voice), 1968; Fantastyka i futurologia (trans. as Science Fiction and Futurology), 1970; Doskonala Proznia (trans. as A Perfect Vacuum), 1971; Wielkosć urojona (trans. as Imaginary Magnitude), 1973; Katar (trans. as The Chain of Chance), 1976; Golem XIV, 1981; Wizja lokalna (trans. as Eyewitness Account), 1982; Kongres futurologiczny (trans. as The Fururological Congress), 1983; Fiasko (trans. as Fiasco), 1987; Pokoj na Ziemi (trans. as Peace on Earth), 1987; Tajemnica chinskiego pokoju (trans. as The Mystery of the Chinese Room), 1996. Contributions: New Yorker; Encounter; Penthouse; Omni. *Honours:* Polish Ministry of Culture Awards, 1965, 1973; Polish State Prize for Literature, 1976; Austrian State Award for European Literature, 1985; Alfred Jurzykowski Foundation for Literature Prize, 1987; Hon. PhD, University of Wrocław. *Address:* c/o Franz Rottensteiner, Marchettigasse 9 17, 1060 Vienna, Austria. *E-mail:* solaris@lem.pl. *Website:* www.cyberiad.info.

LEMASTER, Jimmie Ray, BS, MA, PhD; academic, poet, writer and editor; b. 29 March 1934, Pike County, OH, USA; m. Wanda May Ohnesorge 1966; one s. two d. *Education:* Defiance College, Bowling Green State University, Ohio. *Career:* Faculty, Defiance College, 1962–77; Prof. of English and Dir of American Studies, Baylor University, 1977–; Assoc. Ed., 1988–90, Ed., 1992–96, JASAT (Journal of the American Studies Asscn of Texas); mem. American Studies Asscn; Conference of College Teachers of English; Jesse Stuart Foundation, board of dirs, 1989–99; Mark Twain Circle of America; MLA. *Publications:* Poetry: The Heart is a Gypsy, 1967; Children of Adam, 1971; Weeds and Wildflowers, 1975; First Person, Second, 1983; Purple Bamboo, 1986; Journey to Beijing, 1992. Other: Jesse Stuart: A Reference Guide, 1979; Jesse Stuart: Kentucky's Chronicler-Poet, 1980; The New Mark Twain Handbook (with E. Hudson Long), 1985. Editor: Poets of the Midwest, 1966; The World of Jesse Stuart: Selected Poems, 1975; Jesse Stuart: Essays on His Work (with Mary Washington Clarke), 1977; Jesse Stuart: Selected Criticism, 1978; Jesse Stuart on Education, 1992; The Mark Twain Encyclopedia (with James D. Wilson), 1993; Walt Whitman: An Encyclopedia (with Donald D. Kummings), 1998. *Honours:* South and West Inc Publishers Award, 1970; Ohio Poet of the Year, 1976; Hon. Doctor of Letters, Defiance College, 1988; Outstanding Reference Source Citation, American Library Asscn, 1993. *Address:* 4408 Westchester Drive, Waco, TX 76710, USA.

LENKIEWICZ, Rebecca; British playwright and actress; b. 1969, Plymouth. *Education:* Central School, London. *Plays as actress:* Tales from Ovid, Bollocks, A Midsummer Night's Dream, Flight, Half Moon, King Lear, Twelfth Night, Two Gentlemen of Verona, Soho. *Television as actress:* State of Play, Casualty, Doctors, Down to Earth, The Inspector Lynley Mysteries. *Film as actress:* Wonderland 1999. *Plays as writer:* Soho 2000, The Night Season 2004. *Radio as writer:* Fighting for Words (BBC Radio 4) 2004. *Honours:* Fringe First, Edinburgh Festival 2000. *Literary Agent:* Georgina

Ruffhead, David Higham Associates, 5–8 Lower John Street, Golden Square, London, W1F 9HA, England. *Telephone:* (20) 7434-5900. *Fax:* (20) 7437-1072. *E-mail:* dha@davidhigham.co.uk. *Website:* www.davidhigham .co.uk.

LENTRICCHIA, Frank; Prof. and Writer; b. 23 May 1940, Utica, New York, USA; m. 1st Karen Young 24 June 1967 (divorced 1973); two c.; m. 2nd Melissa Christensen 1973 (divorced 1992); m. 3rd Johanna McAuliffe 1994; one c. *Education:* BA, Utica College of Syracuse University, 1962; MA, 1963, PhD, 1966, Duke University. *Career:* Asst Prof., University of California at Los Angeles, 1966–68; Asst Prof., 1968–70, Assoc. Prof., 1970–76, Prof., 1976–82, University of California at Irvine; Autrey Prof. of Humanities, Rice University, 1982–84; Gilbert Prof. of Literature, Duke University, 1984–; mem. MLA; PEN. *Publications:* The Gaiety of Language: An Essay on the Radical Poetics of W. B. Yeats and Wallace Stevens, 1968; Robert Frost: Modern Poetics and the Landscapes of Self, 1975; Robert Frost: A Bibliography, 1913–1974 (ed. with Melissa Christensen Lentricchia), 1976; After the New Criticism, 1980; Criticism and Social Change, 1983; Ariel and the Police, 1988; Critical Terms for Literary Study, 1990; New Essays on White Noise, 1991; Introducing Don DeLillo, 1991; The Edge of Night: A Confession, 1994; Johnny Critelli and The Knifemen: Two Novels, 1996; The Music of the Inferno: A Novel, 1999; Lucchesi and The Whale, 2001; Dissent from the Homeland (with Stanley Hauerwas), 2002, Close Reading: The Reader (with Andrew DuBois) 2003, Modernist Lyric in the Culture of Capital (with Andrew DuBois) 2003, Crimes of Art and Terror (with Jody McAuliffe) 2003. Contributions: Professional journals. *Address:* c/o Program in Literature, Duke University, Durham, NC 27708, USA.

LENZ, Siegfried; Author and Dramatist; b. 17 March 1926, Lyck, Germany; m. Liseselotte Lenz. *Education:* Philosophy, English Philology, and History of Literature, Hamburg. *Career:* mem. Berlin Acad. of Arts; Deutsche Akademie für Sprache und Dichtung eV, Darmstadt; Free Acad. of Arts, Hamburg; PEN. *Publications:* Es waren Habichte in der Luft, 1951; Duell mit dem Schatten, 1953; So zärtlich war Suleyken, 1955; Der Mann im Strom, 1957; Der Jäger des spotts, 1958; Brot und Spiele, 1959; Das Feuerschiff, 1960; Der Zeit der Schuldlosen, 1961; Stimmungen der See, 1962; Lehmanns Erzählungen oder so schön war mein Markt, 1964; Der Spielverderber, 1965; Haussuchung, 1967; Deutschstunde, 1968; Das Vorbild, 1973; Der Geist der Mirabella: Geschichten aus Bollerup, 1974; Einstein überquert die Elbe bei Hamburg, 1975; Heimatmuseum, 1978; Ein Kriegsende, 1984; Exerzierplatz, 1985; Das serbische Mädchen, 1987; Die Klangprobe, 1990; Die Auflehnung, 1994; Ludmilla, 1996. *Honours:* Lessing Prize, Hamburg, 1953; Gerhart Hauptmann Prize, 1961; Hon. Doctorates, University of Hamburg, 1976, Ben Gurion University, Beer Sheva, 1993; Literary Prize, Freemasons of Germany, 1979; Thomas Mann Prize, 1984; Peace Prize, Federal Book Trade Asscn, 1988; Bavarian Literature Prize, 1995. *Address:* Preusserstrasse 4, 22605, Hamburg, Germany.

LEONARD, Elmore, PhB; American novelist and screenwriter; b. 11 Oct. 1925, New Orleans, LA; m. 1st Beverly Claire Cline 1949 (divorced 1977); three s. two d.; m. 2nd Joan Leanne Lancaster 1979 (died 1993); m. 3rd Christine Kent 1993. *Education:* Univ. of Detroit. *Career:* mem. Writers' Guild of America, Authors' Guild, MWA, Western Writers of America, PEN. *Publications:* novels: The Bounty Hunters 1953, The Law at Randado 1954, Escape from Five Shadows 1956, Last Stand at Saber River 1959, Hombre 1961, The Big Bounce 1969, The Moonshine War 1969, Valdez is Coming 1970, Forty Lashes Less One 1972, Mr Majestyk 1974, Fifty-Two Pickup 1974, Swag 1976, Unknown Man # 89 1977, The Hunted 1977, The Switch 1978, Gold Coast 1979, Gun Sights 1979, City Primeval 1980, Split Images 1981, Cat Chaser 1982, Stick 1983, La Brava 1983, Glitz 1985, Bandits 1986, Touch 1987, Freaky Deaky 1988, Killshot 1989, Get Shorty 1990, Maximum Bob 1991, Rum Punch 1992, Pronto 1993, Riding the Rap 1995, Out of Sight 1996, Jackie Brown 1997, Cuba Libre (also film screenplay) 1998, Be Cool (also film screenplay) 1999, Pagan Babies 2000, Tishomingo Blues 2002, When the Women Come Out to Dance 2002, A Coyote's in the House (juvenile) 2004, Mr Paradise 2004; short story collections: Dutch Treat 1985, Double Dutch Treat 1986, The Tonto Woman and Other Stories 1998. *Honours:* Hon. DLitt (Florida Atlantic Univ.) 1995, (Univ. of Detroit Mercy) 1997; MWA Edgar Allan Poe Award 1984, MWA Grand Master Award 1992, Michigan Foundation for the Arts Award for Literature 1985. *Address:* c/o Random House Inc., 201 East 50th Street, New York, NY 10022 (Office); c/o Michael Siegel, 9150 Wilshire Blvd, Suite 350, Beverly Hills, CA 90212, USA. *Website:* www.elmoreleonard.com.

LEONARD, Hugh, (John Keyes Byrne); Playwright; b. 9 Nov. 1926, Dublin, Ireland; m. Paule Jacquet, 1955, deceased 2000, one d. *Education:* Presentation College, Dún Laoghaire. *Publications:* Plays: The Big Birthday, 1957; A Leap in the Dark, 1957; Madigan's Lock, 1958; A Walk on the Water, 1960; The Passion of Peter Ginty, 1961; Stephen D, 1962; The Poker Session, 1963; Dublin 1, 1963; The Saints Go Cycling In, 1965; Mick and Mick, 1966; The Quick and the Dead, 1967; The Au Pair Man, 1968; The Barracks, 1969; The Patrick Pearse Motel, 1971; Da, 1973; Thieves, 1973; Summer, 1974; Times of Wolves and Tigers, 1974; Irishmen, 1975; Time Was, 1976; A Life, 1977; Moving Days, 1981; The Mask of Moriarty, 1984; Moving, 1991; Senna for Sonny, 1994; The Lily Lally Show, 1994; Chamber Music, 1994; Magic, 1997; Love in the Title, 1998. Television: Silent Song, 1967; Nicholas Nickleby, 1977; London Belongs to Me, 1977; The Last Campaign, 1978; The Ring and the Rose, 1978; Strumpet City, 1979; The Little World of Don Camillo, 1980; Kill, 1982; Good Behaviour, 1982; O'Neill, 1983; Beyond the Pale, 1984; The Irish RM, 1985; A Life, 1986; Troubles, 1987; Parnell and the Englishwoman, 1988; A Wild People, 2001. Films: Herself Surprised, 1977; Da, 1984; Widows' Peak, 1984; Troubles, 1984; Banjaxed, 1995. Autobiography: Home Before Night, 1979; Out After Dark, 1988. *Honours:* Hon. Writers Guild Award, 1966; Tony Award; Critics Circle Award; Drama Desk Award; Outer Critics Award, 1978; Doctor of Literature, Trinity College, Dublin, 1988. *Address:* 6 Rossaun Pilot View, Dalkey, County Dublin, Ireland.

LEONARD, Richard (Dick) Lawrence, MA; journalist, editor, broadcaster and writer; b. 12 Dec. 1930, Ealing, Middlesex, England; m. Irene Heidelberger 1963; one s. one d. *Education:* Institute of Education, London, Essex University. *Career:* Senior Research Fellow, Essex University, 1968–70; MP, Labour Party, Romford, 1970–74; Asst Ed., The Economist, 1974–85; Visiting Prof., Free University of Brussels, 1988–96; Brussels and European Union Correspondent, The Observer, 1989–96; Senior Adviser, Center for European Policy Studies, 1994–; mem. Fabian Society, chair., 1977–78; Reform Club. *Publications:* Elections in Britain, 1968; The Backbencher and Parliament (co-ed.), 1972; Paying for Party Politics, 1975; The Socialist Agenda (co-ed.), 1981; World Atlas of Elections (co-author), 1986; Pocket Guide to the EEC, 1988; Elections in Britain Today, 1991; The Economist Guide to the European Community, 1992, ninth edn as The Economist Guide to the European Union, 2005; Replacing the Lords, 1995; Eminent Europeans (co-author), 1996; Crosland and New Labour (ed.), 1998; The Pro-European Reader (co-ed.), 2001; A Century of Premier: Salisbury to Blair 2004. Contributions: newspapers and periodicals worldwide. *Address:* 32 rue des Bégonias, 1170 Brussels, Belgium.

LEONARD, Thomas (Tom) Anthony, MA; writer and poet; *Professor of Creative Writing, Glasgow University*; b. 22 Aug. 1944, Glasgow, Scotland; m. Sonya Maria O'Brien 1971; two s. *Education:* Glasgow Univ. *Career:* writer-in-residence, Renfrew District Libraries 1986–89, Glasgow Univ./Strathclyde Univ. 1991–92, Bell Coll. of Technology 1993–94; Prof. of Creative Writing, Glasgow Univ. 2001–. *Publications:* Intimate Voices (writing), 1965–83 1984, Situations Theoretical and Contemporary 1986, Radical Renfrew (ed.) 1990, Nora's Place 1990, Places of the Mind: The Life and Work of James Thomson 'BV' Cafe 1993, Reports From the Present: Selected Works 1982–94 1995, access to the silence 2004; contrib. to Edinburgh Review. *Honours:* jt winner, Saltire Scottish Book of the Year Award 1984. *Address:* 56 Eldon Street, Glasgow, G3 6NJ, Scotland.

LEONG, Russell Charles, (Wallace Lin), BA, MFA; writer, poet and editor; *Adjunct Full Professor of English, University of California at Los Angeles*; b. 7 Sept. 1950, San Francisco, CA, USA. *Education:* San Francisco State Coll., Nat. Taiwan Univ., Univ. of California at Los Angeles. *Career:* Adjunct Full Prof. of English, Dept of English, and Ed. Amerasia Journal, Asian American Studies Center, Univ. of California at Los Angeles. *Publications:* fiction: Phoenix Eyes and Other Stories (American Book Award 2001) 2000; poetry: The Country of Dreams and Dust (PEN Josephine Miles Literature Award) 1993; non-fiction: A History Reclaimed: An Annotated Bibliography of Chinese Language Materials on the Chinese of America (ed. with Jean Pang Yip) 1986, Frontiers of Asian American Studies: Writing, Research, and Criticism (ed. with G. Nomura, R. Endo and S. Sumida) 1989, Moving the Image: Independent Asian Pacific American Media Arts 1970–1990 (ed.) 1991, Los Angeles—Struggle toward Multiethnic Community: Asian America, African America, and Latino Perspectives (ed. with Edward T. Chang) 1995, Asian American Sexuality: Dimensions of the Gay and Lesbian Experience 1996; contrib. to anthologies and periodicals. *Address:* c/o Asian American Studies Center, 3230 Campbell Hall, University of California at Los Angeles, Los Angeles, CA 90095-1546, USA. *E-mail:* rleong@ucla.edu.

LEOTTA, Guido; Writer, Poet and Publisher; b. 2 May 1957, Faenza, Italy. *Education:* Accountant's Diploma. *Career:* Pres., Tratti/Mobydick Cultural Co-operative and Publishing House, 1987; Author and Co-ordinator, Tratti Folk Festival, 1989–2000. *Publications:* Sacsaphone (collected novels), 1981; Anatre (short stories), 1989; Strategie di Viaggio Nel Non Amore (poems), 1992; Il Bambino Ulisse (children's stories), 1995; Passo Narrabile (novel), 1997; Leviatamo (poems), 1999; Doppio Diesis (novel), 2000. Contributions: anthologies and magazines. *Honours:* Premio Leonforte for Children's Stories, 1991; Laoghaire Poetry Prize, Ireland, 1994; Premio Selezione Bancarellino, 1996. *Address:* Corso Mazzini, 85 48018 Faenza RA, Italy.

LEPSCHY, Anna Laura; Prof. of Italian and Writer; b. 30 Nov. 1933, Turin, Italy; m. 20 Dec. 1962. *Education:* BLitt, MA, Somerville College, Oxford, 1952–57. *Career:* Prof. of Italian, University College London; Hon. Research Fellow, Univ. of Cambridge; mem. Pirandello Society, pres., 1988–92; Society for Italian Studies, chair, 1988–95; Asscn for the Study of Modern Italy; Associazione Internazionale di Lingua e Letteratura Italiana, Vice-Pres., 1998–. *Publications:* Viaggio in Terrasanta 1480, 1966; The Italian Language Today (co-author), 1977; Tintoretto Observed, 1983; Narrativa e Teatro fra due Secoli, 1984; Varietà linguistiche e pluralità di codici nel Rinascimento, 1996; Davanti a Tintoretto, 1998; L'amanuense analfabeta e altri saggi (co-author), 1999; Ufficiale al Merito della Repubblica Italiana, 1994. Contributions: Italian Studies; Romance Studies; Studi Francesi;

Studi sul Boccaccio; Studi Novecenteschi; Yearbook of the Pirandello Society; Modern Languages Notes; Lettere Italiane. *Address:* Dept of Italian, University College, Gower St, London WC1E 6BT, England. *E-mail:* a.lepschy@ucl.ac.uk.

LERMAN, Rhoda; Writer; b. 18 Jan. 1936, Far Rockaway, NY, USA; m. Robert Lerman, 15 Sept. 1957, one s. two d. *Education:* BA, University of Miami, 1957. *Career:* National Endowment for the Arts Distinguished Prof. of Creative Writing, Hartwick College, Oneonta, New York, 1985; Visiting Prof. of Creative Writing, 1988, 1990, Chair, English Literature, 1990, SUNY at Buffalo. *Publications:* Call Me Ishtar, 1973; Girl That He Marries, 1976; Eleanor, a Novel, 1979; Book of the Night, 1984; God's Ear, 1989; Animal Acts, 1994.

LERNER, Laurence David, BA, MA; British retd academic, writer and poet; b. 12 Dec. 1925, Cape Town, South Africa; m. Natalie Winch 1948; four s. *Education:* University of Cape Town, Pembroke Coll., Cambridge. *Career:* Lecturer, University College of the Gold Coast, 1949–53, Queen's University, 1953–62; Lecturer to Prof., University of Sussex, 1962–84; Kenan Prof., Vanderbilt University, Nashville, Tennessee, 1985–95; several visiting professorships. *Publications:* Poems, 1955; Domestic Interior and Other Poems, 1959; The Directions of Memory: Poems 1958–63, 1964; Selves, 1969; A.R.T.H.U.R.: The Life and Opinions of a Digital Computer, 1974; The Man I Killed, 1980; A.R.T.H.U.R. and M.A.R.T.H.A., or, The Loves of the Computer, 1980; Chapter and Verse: Bible Poems, 1984; Selected Poems, 1984; Rembrandt's Mirror, 1987. Fiction: The Englishmen, 1959; A Free Man, 1968; My Grandfather's Grandfather, 1985. Play: The Experiment, 1980. Non-Fiction: The Truest Poetry, 1960; The Truthtellers: Jane Austen, George Eliot, Lawrence, 1967; The Uses of Nostalgia, 1973; An Introduction to English Poetry, 1975; Love and Marriage: Literature in its Social Context, 1979; The Frontiers of Literature, 1988; Angels and Absences, 1997; Wandering Prof., 1999. Contributions: newspapers, reviews, journals, and magazines. *Honours:* South-East Arts Literature Prize, 1979; FRSL, 1986. *Address:* Abinger, 1-B Gundreda Road, Lewes, East Sussex BN7 1PT, England.

LERNER, Michael P(hillip); Writer; b. 7 Feb. 1943, Newark, NJ, USA. *Education:* AB, Columbia University, 1964; MA, 1968, PhD, 1972, University of California at Berkeley. *Publications:* Surplus Powerlessness, 1986; Jewish Renewal, 1994; Blacks and Jews, 1995; The Politics of Meaning, 1995; Best Contemporary Jewish Writing (ed.), 2001. Contributions: newspapers and magazines. *Address:* c/o Tikkun Magazine, 26 Fell St, San Francisco, CA 94102, USA.

LERNER, Robert E(arl); Prof. of History and Writer; b. 8 Feb. 1940, New York, NY, USA; m. Erdmut Krumnack, 25 Oct. 1963, two d. *Education:* BA, University of Chicago, 1960; MA, 1962, PhD, 1964, Princeton University; University of Münster, 1962–63. *Career:* Instructor, Princeton University, 1963–64; Asst Prof., Western Reserve University, 1964–67; Asst Prof., 1967–71, Assoc. Prof., 1971–76, Prof., 1976–, Peter B. Ritzma Prof. in the Humanities, 1993–, Northwestern University. *Publications:* The Age of Adversity: The Fourteenth Century, 1968; The Heresy of the Free Spirit in the Later Middle Ages, 1972; Western Civilizations (co-author), ninth edn, 1980, to 13th edn, 1998; World Civilizations (co-author), sixth edn, 1982, to ninth edn, 1997; The Powers of Prophecy: The Cedar of Lebanon Vision from the Mongol Onslaught to the Dawn of the Enlightenment, 1983; Weissagungen über die Päpste (with Robert Moynihan), 1985; Johannes de Rupescissa, Liber secretorum eventuum: Edition critique, traduction et introduction historique (with C. Morerod-Fattebert), 1994; Propaganda Miniata: Le origini delle profezie papali 'Ascende Calve' (with Orit Schwartz), 1994; Neue Richtungen in der hoch – und spätmittelalterlichen Bibelexegese (ed.), 1995; The Feast of Saint Abraham, 2000. Contributions: Professional journals; TLS. *Honours:* Fulbright Senior Fellowship, 1967–68; National Endowment for the Humanities Research Grant, 1972–73; American Acad. in Rome Fellowship, 1983–84; Guggenheim Fellowship, 1984–85; Rockefeller Foundation Study Center Residency, Bellagio, Italy, 1989; Historisches Kolleg, Munich, Forschungspreis, 1992, Stipendiat, 1992–93; Woodrow Wilson Center for Scholars Fellow, 1996–97; Max-Planck-Gesellschaft Prize for International Co-operation, 1998. *Address:* c/o Dept of History, Northwestern University, Evanston, IL 60208, USA.

LEROI, Armand Marie, BSc, PhD; Dutch evolutionary biologist; *Reader in Evolutionary Developmental Biology, Imperial College London*; b. 16 July 1964, Wellington, New Zealand. *Education:* Dalhousie Univ., Halifax, Canada, Univ. of California at Irvine, USA. *Career:* postdoctoral work at the Albert Einstein Coll. of Medicine, New York; Lecturer, Imperial Coll. London 1996–2001, Reader in Evolutionary Developmental Biology 2001–. *Television:* Mutants (three-part series, Channel 4) 2004. *Publications:* Mutants: On the Form, Errors and Varieties of the Human Body 2003; contrib. to London Review of Books; numerous research papers. *Address:* Department of Biological Sciences, Silwood Park Campus, Imperial College London, Ascot, Berkshire SL5 7PY, England. *Telephone:* (20) 7594-2396. *Fax:* (20) 7594-2339. *E-mail:* a.leroi@imperial.ac.uk. *Website:* www.armandleroi.com.

LEROY, Gilles; Writer; b. 28 Dec. 1958, Paris, France. *Publications:* Habibi, novel, 1987; Maman est morte, 1990; Les Derniers seront les premiers, 1991; Madame X (novel), 1992; Les Jardins publics (novel), 1994; Les Mâitres du monde (novel), 1996; Machines à sous (novel), 1998; Soleil noir (novel), 2000; L'amant russe (novel), 2002. *Honours:* Prix de la Nouvelle, Nanterre, 1992; Prix Valery-Larbaud, 1999. *Address:* c/o Mercure de France SA, Subsidiary of Editions Gallimard, 26 rue de Conde, 75006 Paris, France.

LESCHAK, Peter; writer; b. 11 May 1951, Chisholm, MN, USA; m. Pamela Cope May 1974. *Career:* Contributing Ed., Twin Cities magazine 1984–86, Minnesota Monthly 1984–89; mem. Authors' Guild. *Publications:* Letters from Side Lake 1987, The Bear Guardian 1990, Bumming with the Furies 1993, Seeing the Raven 1994, Hellroaring 1994, The Snow Lotus 1996, Rogues and Toads 1999, Trials by Wildfire 2000, Ghosts of the Fireground 2002. *Honours:* Minnesota Book Award 1991. *Address:* PO Box 51, Side Lake, MN 55781, USA.

LESOURNE, Jacques François; French newspaper editor and academic; *President, Futuribles International*; b. 26 Dec. 1928, La Rochelle; m. Odile Melin, 1961; one s. two d. *Education:* Lycée Montaigne, Bordeaux, École Polytechnique, École Nationale Supérieure des Mines de Paris. *Career:* Head Econ. Service of French Collieries 1954–57; Dir Gen., later Pres. METRA Int. and SEMA 1958–75; Prof. of Econs École des Mines de Saint-Étienne 1958–61; Prof. of Industrial Econs École Nationale Supérieure de la Statistique 1960–63; Pres. Asscn Française d'Informatique et de Recherche Operationnelle 1966–67; mem. Council Int. Inst. of Applied Systems Analysis, Vienna 1973–79, Inst. of Man. Science 1976–79; Prof. Conservatoire Nat. des Arts et Métiers 1974–; Dir Projet Interfuturs OECD 1976–79; Dir of Studies, Inst. Auguste Comte 1979–81; Pres. Comm. on Employment and Social Relations of 8th Plan 1979–81; mem. Comm. du Bilan 1981, Council European Econ. Asscn 1984–89; Pres. Asscn Française de Science Économique 1981–83, Int. Federation of Operational Research Socs 1986–89; Dir and Man. Ed. Le Monde 1991–94; Pres. Futuribles Int. 1993–, Centre for Study and Research on Qualifications 1996–; mem. Acad. des Technologies. *Publications:* Economic Technique and Industrial Management 1958, Du bon usage de l'étude économique dans l'entreprise 1966, Les systèmes du destin 1976, L'entreprise et ses futurs 1985, Éducation et société, L'après-Communisme, de l'Atlantique à l'Oural 1990, The Economics of Order and Disorder 1991, Vérités et mensonges sur le chômage 1995, Le Modèle français: Grandeur et Décadence 1998, Un Homme de notre Siècle 2000, Ces Avenirs qui n'ont pas eu lieu 2001, Leçons de Microéconomie évolutionniste (with A. Orléan and B. Wallises) 2002. *Honours:* Officier, Légion d'honneur, Commdr, Ordre nat. du Mérite, Officier des Palmes Académiques. *Address:* 52 rue de Vaugirard, 75006 Paris, France (Home). *Telephone:* 1-43-25-66-05 (Home). *Fax:* 1-56-24-47-98. *E-mail:* jolesourne@wanadoo.fr (Home).

LESSARD, Suzannah; Writer; b. 12 Jan. 1944, Islip, New York, USA; one s. *Education:* BA, Columbia School of General Studies, 1969. *Career:* Ed., Contributor, Washington Monthly, 1969–73; Staff Writer, New Yorker, 1975–95; mem. PEN. *Publications:* The Architect of Desire: Beauty and Danger in the Stanford White Family. *Honours:* Whiting Award, 1995; Woodrow Wilson International Center for Scholars Fellow, 2001–02; Jenny Moore Writer's Fellowship, George Washington University, 2002–03. *Literary Agent:* The Wylie Agency, 4–8 Rodney St, London N1 9JH, England. *Address:* c/o The Dial Press, 1540 Broadway, NY 10036, USA.

LESSER, Milton (see Marlowe, Stephen).

LESSER, Rika; Poet and Trans; b. 21 July 1953, New York, NY, USA. *Education:* BA, Yale University, 1974; University of Göteborg, 1974–75; MFA, Columbia University, 1977. *Career:* Visiting Lecturer, Yale University, 1976, 1978, 1987–88, Baruch College, CUNY, 1979; Poetry Workshop Instructor, Young Men's and Young Women's Hebrew Asscn, New York, 1982–85, 2002–; Jenny McKean Moore Visiting Lecturer in English, George Washington University, 1985–86; Master Artist-in-Residence, Atlantic Center for the Arts, New Smyrna Beach, FL, 1998; Adjunct Assoc. Prof. of Trans., Columbia University, 1998–; featured poet at the Geraldine R. Dodge Poetry Festival, 2000; poetry trans. workshop instructor, 92nd Street Y, New York, 2002–; mem. Acad. of American Poets; American PEN; ASCAP; Associated Writing Programs; Poets and Writers. *Publications:* Poetry: Etruscan Things, 1983; All We Need of Hell, 1995; Growing Back: Poems, 1972–1992, 1997. Translations: 11 books, 1975–96. *Honours:* Ingram Merrill Foundation Award, 1978–79; Harold Morton Landon Trans. Prize for Poetry, Acad. of American Poets, 1982; Batchelder Award, 1990; American-Scandinavian Foundation Trans. Prize, 1992; George Bogin Memorial Award, Poetry Society of America, 1992; Swedish Writers' Foundation Award, 1995; Swedish Acad. Poetry Trans. Prize, 1996; Fulbright-Hays Senior Scholar Award, Stockholm Univ. English Dept, 1999; National Endowment for the Arts Fellowship, 2001. *Address:* 133 Henry St, Apt 5, New York, NY 11201, USA.

LESSING, Doris May, CH, CLit; British writer; b. 22 Oct. 1919, Kermanshah, Persia; m. 1st F. A. C. Wisdom 1939–43; m. 2nd Gottfried Anton Nicolai Lessing 1944 (divorced 1949); two s. (one deceased) one d. *Education:* Roman Catholic Convent and Girls' High School, Salisbury, Southern Rhodesia. *Career:* Assoc. mem. American Acad. of Arts and Letters 1974; Nat. Inst. of Arts and Letters (USA) 1974; mem. Inst. for Cultural Research 1974; Pres. Book Trust 1996–. *Publications:* novels: The Grass is Singing 1950, Children of Violence (Martha Quest 1952, A Proper Marriage 1954, A Ripple from the Storm 1965, The Four-Gated City 1969), Retreat to Innocence

1956, The Golden Notebook (Prix Médicis for French trans., Carnet d'Or 1976) 1962, Landlocked 1965, Briefing for a Descent into Hell 1971, The Summer Before the Dark 1973, The Memoirs of a Survivor 1974, Canopus in Argos series (Re: Colonised Planet 5, Shikasta 1979, The Marriages between Zones Three, Four and Five 1980, The Sirian Experiments 1981, The Making of the Representative for Planet 8 1982, The Sentimental Agents in the Volyen Empire 1983), The Diary of a Good Neighbour (as Jane Somers) 1983, If the Old Could (as Jane Somers) 1984, The Diaries of Jane Somers 1984, The Good Terrorist 1985 (WHSmith Literary Award 1986, Palermo Prize and Premio Internazionale Mondello 1987), The Fifth Child 1988, Love, Again 1996, Playing the Game 1996, Mara and Dann 1999, Ben, in the World 2000, The Old Age of El Magnifico 2000, The Sweetest Dream 2001; short stories: Collected African Stories: Vol. 1, This Was the Old Chief's Country 1951, Vol. 2, The Sun Between Their Feet 1973, Five 1953, The Habit of Loving 1957, A Man and Two Women 1963, African Stories 1964, Winter in July 1966, The Black Madonna 1966, The Story of a Non-Marrying Man and Other Stories 1972, A Sunrise on the Veld 1975, A Mild Attack of the Locusts 1977, Collected Stories: Vol. 1, To Room Nineteen 1978, Vol. 2, The Temptation of Jack Orkney 1978, London Observed: Stories and Sketches 1992, The Grandmothers 2003; non-fiction includes: Going Home 1957 (revised edn 1968), In Pursuit of the English 1960, Particularly Cats 1967, Particularly Cats and More Cats 1989, African Laughter: Four Visits to Zimbabwe 1992, Under My Skin: Volume One of My Autobiography to 1949 (Los Angeles Times Book Prize 1995, James Tait Memorial Prize 1995) 1994, Walking in the Shade: Volume Two of My Autobiography 1949–62 1997; plays: Each His Own Wilderness 1958, Play with a Tiger 1962, The Singing Door 1973; other: Fourteen Poems 1959, A Small Personal Voice 1974, Doris Lessing Reader 1990. *Honours:* Hon. Fellow MLA (US) 1974; D.Fellow in Literature (East Anglia) 1991; Hon. DLitt (Princeton) 1989, Durham (1990), (Warwick) 1994, (Bard Coll. New York State) 1994, (Harvard) 1995, (Oxford) 1996; five Somerset Maugham Awards, Soc. of Authors 1954–, Austrian State Prize for European Literature 1981, Shakespeare Prize, Hamburg 1982, Grinzane Cavour Award, Italy 1989, Woman of the Year, Norway 1995, Premio Internacional Cataluña, Spain 1999, David Cohen Literary Prize 2001, Príncipe de Asturias Prize, Spain 2001, PEN Award 2002. *Address:* c/o Jonathan Clowes Ltd, 10 Iron Bridge House, Bridge Approach, London, NW1 8BD, England.

LESTARI, Dewi, (Dee); Indonesian novelist and singer; b. 20 Jan. 1976. *Career:* grad. of political and social sciences; f. singing trio RSD (Rida, Sita, Dewi); f. Truedee Books to publish her first novel 2001. *Publication:* Supernova (novel) 2001, Supernova 2.1: Akar 2003. *Website:* www.truedee .net.

LETHEM, Jonathan Allen; American novelist and editor; b. 19 Feb. 1964, New York, NY. *Education:* High School for Music and Art, New York; Bennington Coll., Vermont. *Publications:* novels: Gun, with Occasional Music 1994, Amnesia Moon 1995, The Wall of the Sky, The Wall of the Eye (short stories) 1996, As She Climbed Across the Table 1997, Girl in Landscape 1998, Motherless Brooklyn 1999, This Shape We're In 2000, The Vintage Book of America (ed.) 2000, Da Capo Best Music Writing (ed. with Paul Bresnick) 2002, The Fortress of Solitude 2003, Thirsty People 2005. *Honours:* CWA Silver Dagger Award, The Salon Book Award, National Book Critics' Circle Award. *Address:* c/o Faber and Faber Ltd, 3 Queen Square, London, WC1N 3AU, England. *Website:* www.faber.co.uk.

LETTE, Kathy; Australian author and playwright; *Writer in Residence, Savoy Hotel, London*; b. 11 Nov. 1958, Sydney; m. Geoffrey Robertson 1990; one s. one d. *Career:* fmr columnist, Sydney and NY; fmr satirical news writer and presenter Willasee Show, Channel 9; fmr TV sitcom writer Columbia Pictures, LA; fmr guest presenter This Morning with Richard and Judy, ITV; writer-in-residence, The Savoy, London 2003–. *Plays include:* Wet Dreams 1985, Perfect Mismatch 1985, Grommits 1986, I'm So Happy For You, I Really Am 1991. *Films:* Puberty Blues 1982, Mad Cow 2001. *Publications:* Puberty Blues (with G. Carey) 1979, Hit and Ms 1984, Girls' Night Out 1987, The Llama Parlour 1991, Foetal Attraction 1993, Mad Cows 1996, She Done Him Wrong (essays), The Constant Sinner by Mae West (introduction) 1995, Altar Ego 1998, Nip 'n Tuck 2001, Dead Sexy 2003; contribs to Sydney Morning Herald, The Bulletin, Cleo Magazine. *Honours:* Australian Literature Board Grant 1982. *Address:* c/o Pan Macmillan, 25 Eccleston Place, London, SW1W 9NF (Office); c/o Ed Victor, 6 Bayley Street, London, WC1B 3HB, England. *Telephone:* (20) 7304-4100 (Office). *Fax:* (20) 7304-4111 (Office). *E-mail:* kathy.lette@virgin.net (Office). *Website:* www.kathylette.com (Office).

LEVENSON, Christopher; Canadian poet, editor, translator and educator; b. 13 Feb. 1934, London, England. *Education:* University of Cambridge; University of Bristol; MA, University of Iowa, 1970. *Career:* Teacher, University of Münster, 1958–61, Carleton University, Ottawa, 1968–99; Ed.-in-Chief, ARC magazine, 1978–88; Founder-Dir, ARC Reading Series, Ottawa, 1981–91; Series Ed., Harbinger Poetry Series, 1995–99; Poetry Ed., Literary Review of Canada, 1997; mem. League of Canadian Poets. *Publications:* Poetry: In Transit, 1959; Cairns, 1969; Stills, 1972; Into the Open, 1977; The Journey Back, 1978; Arriving at Night, 1986; The Return, 1986; Half Truths, 1990; Duplicities: New and Selected Poems, 1993; The Bridge, 2000; Belvédère (trans.), 2002. Other: Seeking Heart's Solace (trans.), 1981; Light of the World (trans.), 1982; Reconcilable Differences: The Changing Face of Poetry by Canadian Men Since 1970 (ed.), 1994. Other: Requiem 53 (contributed texts to requiem for 50th anniversary of Dutch floods of 1953), 2003. Contributions: various anthologies, reviews, quarterlies, and journals. *Honours:* Eric Gregory Award, 1960; Archibald Lampman Award, 1987. *Address:* 333 St Andrew Street, Ottawa, ON K1N 5G9, Canada. *E-mail:* clevenson@rogers.com.

LEVER, Sir (Tresham) Christopher Arthur Lindsay, Bt, BA, MA, FRGS; naturalist and writer; b. 9 Jan. 1932, London, England; m. 1st 1970; m. 2nd Linda Weightman McDowell Goulden 1975. *Education:* Eton, Trinity Coll., Cambridge. *Career:* consultant, various conservation and animal welfare organizations. *Publications:* Goldsmiths and Silversmiths of England, 1975; The Naturalized Animals of the British Isles, 1977; Naturalized Mammals of the World, 1985; Naturalized Birds of the World, 1987; The Mandarin Duck, 1990; They Dined on Eland: The Story of the Acclimatisation Societies, 1992; Naturalized Animals: The Ecology of Successfully Introduced Species, 1994; Naturalized Fishes of the World, 1996; The Cane Toad: The History and Ecology of a Successful Colonist, 2001; Naturalized Reptiles and Amphibians of the World, 2003. Contributions: many books, professional journals and general publications. *Honours:* hon. life mem., Brontë Society 1988, FLS. *Address:* Newell House, Winkfield, Berkshire SL4 4SE, England.

LÉVESQUE, Anne-Michèle; Writer; b. 29 May 1939, Val d'Or, QC, Canada; Widow, two d. *Education:* BS, University of Montréal, 1957; Outremont Business College, 1958. *Career:* mem. Regroupement des Écrivains de l'Abitibi-TemisCamingue; Union des écrivaines et des écrivains québécois; Conseil de la Culture de l'Abitibi-Térniscamingue; Aventuriers de la Plume, Conseil de la Culture de l'Abitibi-Témiscamingue, Cercle des Écrivains. *Publications:* Persil Frisé 1992, A La Recherche d'un Salaud 1994, Fleurs de Corail 1994, La Maison du Puits Sacré 1997, Quartiers divers 1997, Meurtres à la sauce tomate 1999, Rapt 2000, Abitibissimo 2000, Fleur Invitait au Troisième 2002, Rumeurs et Marées 2002. Contributions: Lumière d'Encre, Arcade magazines. *Honours:* First Prize, Concours Littéraire, 1991, Arthur Ellis Award for Best Mystery Novel in French Canada 2002. *Literary Agent:* 184 Williston Street, Val-d'Or, QC J9P 4S7, Canada. *Address:* 184 Williston St, Val d'Or, QC J9P 4S7, Canada. *E-mail:* aml@cablevision.qc.ca. *Website:* www.cablevision.qc.ca/aml.

LEVEY, Sir Michael (Vincent); Art Historian and Writer; b. 8 June 1927, London, England; m. Brigid Brophy, 1954, deceased 1995, one d. *Education:* Exeter College, Oxford. *Career:* Asst Keeper, 1951–66, Deputy Keeper, 1966–68, Keeper, 1968–73, Deputy Dir, 1970–73, Dir, 1973–87, National Gallery, London; Slade Prof. of Fine Art, Cambridge, 1963–64, Oxford, 1994–95; mem. Ateneo Veneto, foreign mem.; British Acad., fellow; FRSL. *Publications:* Six Great Painters, 1956; National Gallery Catalogues: 18th Century Italian Schools, 1956; The German School, 1959; Painting in 18th Century Venice, 1959; From Giotto to Cézanne, 1962; Dürer, 1964; The Later Italian Paintings in the Collection of HM The Queen, 1964; Canaletto Paintings in the Royal Collection, 1964; Tiepolo's Banquet of Cleopatra, 1966; Rococo to Revolution, 1966; Bronzino, 1967; Early Renaissance, 1967; Fifty Works of English Literature We Could Do Without (co-author), 1967; Holbein's Christina of Denmark, Duchess of Milan, 1968; A History of Western Art, 1968; Painting at Court, 1971; The Life and Death of Mozart, 1971; The Nude: Themes and Painters in the National Gallery, 1972; Art and Architecture in 18th Century France (co-author), 1972; The Venetian Scene, 1973; Botticelli, 1974; High Renaissance, 1975; The World of the Ottoman Art, 1976; Jacob van Ruisdael, 1977; The Case of Walter Pater, 1978; The Painter Depicted, 1981; Tempting Fate, 1982; An Affair on the Appian Way, 1984; Pater's Marius the Epicurean (ed.), 1985; Giambattista Tiepolo, 1986; The National Gallery Collection: A Selection, 1987; Men at Work, 1989; The Soul of the Eye: Anthology of Painters and Painting (ed.), 1990; Painting and Sculpture in France 1700–1789, 1992; Florence: A Portrait, 1996; The Chapel is on Fire (memoir), 2000; The Burlington Magazine Anthology (ed.), 2003. Contributions: periodicals. *Honours:* Hawthornden Prize, 1968; Knighted, 1981; Hon. Fellow, Royal Acad., 1986; Banister Fletcher Prize, 1987; Lieutenant, Royal Victorian Order, 1995. *Address:* 36 Little Lane, Louth, Lincolnshire LN11 9DU, England.

LÉVI-STRAUSS, Claude; French academic and writer; b. 28 Nov. 1908, Brussels, Belgium; m. 1st Dina Dreyfus 1932; m. 2nd Rose Marie Ullmo 1946; one s.; m. 3rd Monique Roman 1954; one s. *Education:* Sorbonne, University of Paris. *Career:* Prof., University of São Paulo, 1935–39; Visiting Prof., New School for Social Research, New York, 1942–45; Assoc. Dir, Musée de l'Homme, Paris, 1949–50; Dir of Studies, École Pratique des Hautes Études, Paris, 1950–74; Prof., 1959–82, Hon. Prof., 1983–, College de France, Paris; mem. Académie Française; American Acad. of Arts and Letters, foreign mem.; American Acad. of Arts and Sciences, foreign mem.; American Philosophical Society, hon. mem.; British Acad., foreign mem.; National Acad. of Sciences, foreign mem. *Publications:* La vie familiale et sociale des indiens Nambikwara, 1948; Les structures élémentaires de la parenté, 1949; Tristes tropiques, 1955; Anthropologie structurale, 1958; Le totémisme aujourd'hui, 1962; La pensée sauvage, 1962; Le cru et le cuit, 1964; Du miel aux cendres, 1966; L'origine des manières de table, 1968; L'homme nu, 1971; Anthropologie structurale deux, 1973; La voie des masques, 1975, 1979; Le regard éloigné, 1983; Paroles données, 1984; La potière jalouse, 1985; De près et de loin (with Didier Eribon), 1988; Histoire de Lynx, 1991; Regarder, écouter, lire, 1993; Saudaldes do Brasil, 1994.

Honours: Grand Croix, Légion d'honneur; Commdr, Ordre nat. du Mérite; Commdr, Palmes académiques, Ordre des Arts et des Lettres; various hon. doctorates; Prix Paul Pelliot, 1949; Huxley Memorial Medal, 1965; Gold Medal, Centre National de la Recherche Scientifique, 1967; Erasmus Prize, 1973; Aby M. Warburg Prize, 1996; Meister Eckhart Prize 2003. *Address:* 2 rue des Marronniers, 75016 Paris, France.

LEVIN, (Henry) Bernard, CBE, BSc; journalist, broadcaster and writer; b. 19 Aug. 1928, England. *Education:* LSE. *Career:* writer, broadcaster, radio and television 1952–; writer, numerous domestic and foreign newspapers and journals, 1953–; mem. English Asscn, pres., 1984–85. *Publications:* The Pendulum Years, 1971; Taking Sides, 1979; Conducted Tour, 1981; Speaking Up, 1982; Enthusiasms, 1983; The Way We Live Now, 1984; A Shakespeare Mystery, 1985; Hannibal's Footsteps, 1985; In These Times, 1986; To the End of the Rhine, 1987; All Things Considered, 1988; A Walk Up Fifth Avenue, 1989; Now Read On, 1990; If You Want My Opinion, 1992; A World Elsewhere, 1994; I Should Say So, 1995; Enough Said, 1998. *Honours:* various journalistic awards; Order of Polonia Restituta, 1976; Hon. Fellow, LSE, 1977. *Address:* c/o The Times, 1 Pennington Street, London E1 9XN, England.

LEVIN, Gabriel; poet, translator and editor; b. Israel. *Career:* editorial bd mem., Ibis Editions, Jerusalem. *Publications include:* poetry: Sleepers of Beulah 1992, Ostraca 1999; prose: Hezekiah's Tunnel 1997; translations: Poems from the Diwan by Yehuda Halevi 2002; editor: Found in Translation: A Hundred Years of Modern Hebrew Poetry 1999; contrib. to TLS, American Poetry Review, American Book Review, Boston Review. *Address:* Ibis Editions, PO Box 8074, German Colony, Jerusalem, Israel. *E-mail:* ibis@netvision.net.il. *Website:* www.ibiseditions.com.

LEVIN, Gerald Manuel, BA, LLB; American publishing executive; b. 6 May 1939, Philadelphia; m. 1st Carol S. Needlemam 1959 (divorced 1970), two s. (one s. deceased), one d.; m. 2nd Barbara Riley 1970, one s. one d. *Education:* Haverford Coll. and Univ. of Pa. *Career:* Assoc. Simpson, Thatcher & Bartlett, New York 1963–67; Gen. Man., COO Devt and Resources Corpn New York 1967–71; Rep. Int. Basic Economy Corpn Tehran 1971–72; Vice-Pres. Programming, Home Box Office, New York 1972–73, Pres., CEO 1973–76, Chair., CEO 1976–79; Group Vice-Pres. (Video), Time Inc. New York 1979–84, Exec. Vice-Pres. 1984–88, Vice-Chair., Dir 1988–90; Vice-Chair., Dir Time-Warner Inc. (to merge with Turner Broadcasting Systems) New York 1990–92, COO 1991, Chair. 1990–95; Pres. 1992–95, Jt CEO 1992–93, CEO and Chair. 1992–2001, CEO AOL Time Warner 2001–02 (created after merger of Time Warner and American Online 2000); Dir NY Stock Exchange; Treas. NY Philharmonic Orchestra; mem. Bd of Dirs Whittle Communications Partnership, New York, Ronald H. Brown Foundation, Living Memorial to the Holocaust (Museum of Jewish Heritage). *Honours:* Hon. LLD (Texas Coll.) 1985, (Middlebury Coll.) 1994, Hon. LHD (Univ. of Denver) 1995; Media Person of the Year Award, Cannes Lions Int. Advertising Festival 2001. *Address:* c/o AOL Time Warner, 75 Rockfeller Plaza, # 2919, New York, NY 10019, U.S.A.

LEVIN, Ira, AB; American writer and dramatist; b. 27 Aug. 1929, New York, NY; m. 1st Gabrielle Aronsohn 1960 (divorced 1968); three s.; m. 2nd Phyllis Finkel 1979 (divorced 1982). *Education:* Horace Mann School, Drake Univ., Iowa, New York Univ. *Career:* US Army 1953–55, wrote training films for the troops and a service comedy No Time for Sergeants (film version released 1958); mem. Authors' Guild, Authors' League of America, ASCAP, Dramatists Guild (mem. Council 1980–). *Plays:* No Time for Sergeants 1956, Interlock 1958, Critic's Choice 1960, General Seeger 1962, Drat! The Cat! 1965, Dr Cook's Garden 1967, Veronica's Room 1973, Deathtrap 1978, Break a Leg 1981, Cantorial 1982, Footsteps 2003. *Television:* Lights Out (series, episode 'Leda's Portrait') 1951, General Electric Theater (series, episode 'The Devil You Say') 1953, The United States Steel Hour (series, episodes 'No Time for Sergeants', 'The Notebook Warrior') 1953. *Publications:* A Kiss Before Dying 1953, Rosemary's Baby 1967, This Perfect Day 1970, The Stepford Wives 1972, The Boys from Brazil 1976, Sliver 1991, Son of Rosemary 1997. *Honours:* MWA Edgar Allan Poe Awards 1953, 1980, MWA Grand Master Award 2003. *Literary Agent:* Harold Ober Associates, 425 Madison Avenue, New York, NY 10017, USA.

LEVINE, Norman; Writer; b. 22 Oct. 1923, Ottawa, Ontario, Canada; m. 1st Margaret Emily Payne, 2 Jan. 1952, deceased 1978, three d.; m. 2nd Anne Sarginson, 10 Aug. 1983. *Education:* BA, 1948, MA, 1949, McGill University, Montréal; Trinity College, Cambridge, 1945; King's College, London, 1949–50. *Publications:* Canada Made Me (travel), 1958; From a Seaside Town (novel), 1970; I Don't Want to Know Anyone Too Well (short stories), 1971; Champagne Barn, 1984; Something Happened Here (short stories), 1991–92; Pourquoi habitez-vous si loin?, 1997. Contributions: Atlantic Monthly; Sunday Times; New Statesman; Spectator; Vogue; Harper's Bazaar; Encounter; TLS; Saturday Night. *Address:* c/o Liepman AG, Maienburgweg, 8044 Zürich, Switzerland.

LEVINE, Paul; Writer and Lawyer; b. 9 Jan. 1948, Williamsport, Pennsylvania, USA; m. Alice Holmstrom 22 Aug. 1975 (divorced 27 July 1992); one s. one d. *Education:* BA, Pennsylvania State University, 1969; JD, University of Miami, 1973. *Career:* Admitted to the Bar, State of Florida, 1973, US Supreme Court, 1977, District of Columbia, 1978, Commonwealth of Pennsylvania, 1989; Attorney and/or Partner, various law firms, 1973–91; mem. American Bar Asscn; American Trial Lawyers Asscn; Authors' Guild. *Publications:* What's Your Verdict?, 1980; To Speak for the Dead, 1990; Night Vision, 1992; False Dawn, 1994; Mortal Sin, 1994; Slashback, 1995; Fool Me Twice, 1996. *Address:* c/o International Creative Management, 40 W 57th St, New York, NY 10019, USA.

LEVINE, Philip; Poet, Writer and Prof. of English (retd); b. 10 Jan. 1928, Detroit, Michigan, USA; m. Frances Artley, 12 July 1954, three s. *Education:* BA, 1950, AM, 1955, Wayne State University; MFA, University of Iowa, 1957; Studies with John Berryman, 1954. *Career:* Instructor, 1958–69, Prof. of English, 1969–92, California State University at Fresno; Elliston Prof. of Poetry, University of Cincinnati, 1976; Poet-in-Residence, National University of Australia, Canberra, 1978; Visiting Prof. of Poetry, Columbia University, 1978, 1981, 1984, New York University, 1984, 1991, Brown University, 1985; Chair., Literature Panel, National Endowment for the Arts, 1985; various poetry readings; mem. American Acad. of Arts and Letters; Acad. of American Poets, chancellor, 2000–. *Publications:* Poetry: On the Edge, 1961; Silent in America: Vivas for Those Who Failed, 1965; Not This Pig, 1968; 5 Detroits, 1970; Thistles: A Poem of Sequence, 1970; Pili's Wall, 1971; Red Dust, 1971; They Feed, They Lion, 1972; 1933, 1974; New Season, 1975; On the Edge and Over: Poems Old, Lost, and New, 1976; The Names of the Lost, 1976; 7 Years from Somewhere, 1979; Ashes: Poems New and Old, 1979; One for the Rose, 1981; Selected Poems, 1984; Sweet Will, 1985; A Walk with Tom Jefferson, 1988; New Selected Poems, 1991; What Work Is, 1991; The Simple Truth: Poems, 1994; The Mercy, 1995. Non-Fiction: Don't Ask (interviews), 1979; Earth, Stars, and Writers (with others), lectures, 1992; The Bread of Time: Toward an Autobiography, 1994. Contributions: many anthologies and reviews. *Honours:* Joseph Henry Jackson Award, San Francisco Foundation, 1961; National Endowment for the Arts Grants, 1969, 1976, 1981, 1987; Frank O'Hara Prizes, 1973, 1974; Award of Merit, American Acad. of Arts and Letters, 1974; Levinson Prize, 1974; Guggenheim Fellowships, 1974, 1981; Harriet Monroe Memorial Prize for Poetry, University of Chicago, 1976; Leonore Marshall Award for Best American Book of Poems, 1976; American Book Award for Poetry, 1979; National Book Critics Circle Prize, 1979; Notable Book Award, American Library Asscn, 1979; Golden Rose Award, New England Poetry Society, 1985; Ruth Lilly Award, 1987; Elmer Holmes Bobst Award, New York University, 1990; National Book Award for Poetry, 1991; Silver Medal in Poetry, Commonwealth Club of California, 1992, 2000; Pulitzer Prize in Poetry, 1995. *Address:* 4549 N Van Ness Blvd, Fresno, CA 93704, USA.

LEVINE, Stuart George; academic, writer and musician; b. 25 May 1932, New York, NY, USA; m. Susan Fleming Matthews 1963; two s. one d. *Education:* AB, magna cum laude, Harvard University; MA, 1956, PhD, 1958, Brown University. *Career:* Instructor, 1958–61, Asst Prof., 1961–65, Assoc. Prof., 1965–69, Chair., Dept of American Studies, 1965–70, Prof., 1969–92, Prof. Emeritus, 1992–, University of Kansas; Visiting Prof., Kansas State University, 1964, University of Missouri at Kansas City, 1966, 1974, California State University at Los Angeles, 1969, 1971; Fulbright Distinguished Lecturer, Naples, Italy, 1995; Fulbright Professorships, Argentina, Mexico, Costa Rica, Chile; Guest Professorship, University of the West Indies, Mona; Founder-ed., American Studies, 1959–90; many engagements as a professional French horn player. *Publications:* Materials for Technical Writing, 1963; The American Indian Today (with Nancy O. Lurie), 1968; Edgar Poe, Seer and Craftsman, 1972; The Short Fiction of Edgar Allan Poe: An Annotated Edition (with Susan F. Levine), 1976; The Monday-Wednesday-Friday Girl and Other Stories, 1994; Eureka: Edgar Allan Poe (with Susan F. Levine), 2003; Poe's Critical Theory: The Major Documents (ed. with Susan F. Levine), 2003. Contributions: various scholarly reviews, quarterlies, and journals. *Honours:* Anisfield-Wolf Award in Race Relations, 1968; Theodore Blegen Award, 1975; Citation for 30-year editorship of American Studies, 1989; Gross Award for Short Fiction, 1994. *Address:* 1644 University Drive, Lawrence, KS 66044, USA.

LEVINSON, Jerrold; Prof. and Writer; b. 11 July 1948, New York, NY, USA; m. Karla Hoff, 14 July 1985, one d. *Education:* BS, Chemistry, Philosophy, MIT, 1969; PhD, Philosophy, University of Michigan, 1974. *Career:* Asst Prof., SUNY at Albany, 1974–75; Asst Prof., 1976–81, Assoc. Prof., 1981–91, Prof., 1991–, University of Maryland at College Park; Visiting Prof., University of London, 1991, Johns Hopkins University, 1993, University of Rennes, 1998, Columbia University, 2000; mem. American Society for Aesthetics, pres., 2001–03. *Publications:* Music, Art, and Metaphysics, 1990; The Pleasures of Aesthetics, 1996; Apprehending Music, 1998; Aesthetics and Ethics (ed.), 1998; Oxford Handbook of Aesthetics (ed.), 2002. *Honours:* National Endowment for the Humanities Fellowship, 1980. *Address:* 4209 Underwood St, University Park, MD 20782, USA. *E-mail:* jl32@umail.umd.edu.

LEVINSON, Leonard, (Nicholas Brady, Clay Dawson, Josh Edwards, J. Farragut Jones, Leonard Jordan, Philip King, John Mackie, Bruno Rossi, Cynthia Wilkerson), BA; American writer; b. 1935, New Bedford, MA. *Education:* Michigan State Univ. *Career:* other pseudonyms include Michael Bodren, Frank Burleson, Lee Chang, Glen Chase, Richard Hale Curtis, Gordon Davis, Richard Gallagher, March Hastings, Robert Novak, Philip Rawls, Jonathon Scofield, Jonathon Trask. *Publications:* as Bruno Rossi: Worst Way To Die 1974, Headcrusher 1974; as Nicholas Brady: Shark Fighter 1975; as Leonard Jordan: Operation Perfida 1975, Without

Mercy 1981; as Cynthia Wilkerson: Sweeter Than Candy 1978, The Fast Life 1979; as Philip King: Hydra Conspiracy 1979; as Gordon Davis: The Battle of the Bulge 1981; as John Mackie: Hit the Beach 1983, Nightmare Alley 1985; as Clay Dawson: Gold Town 1989; as J. Farragut Jones: 40 Fathoms Down 1990; as Josh Edwards: Searcher 1990, Warpath 1991. *Literary Agent:* Lowenstein-Yost Associates Inc, Suite 601, 121 W 27th Street, New York NY 10001, USA. *Telephone:* (212) 206-1630. *Fax:* (212) 727-0280.

LEVY, Alan; Journalist, Ed. and Author; b. 10 Feb. 1932, New York, NY, USA. *Education:* AB, Brown University, 1952; MS, Columbia University, 1953. *Career:* Reporter, Courier-Journal, Louisville, 1953–60; Foreign Correspondent, Life Magazine and Good Housekeeping Magazine, Prague, 1967–71, New York Times and International Herald Tribune, Vienna, 1971–91; Dramaturg, English Theatre Ltd, Vienna, 1977–82; Founding Ed.-in-Chief, Prague Post, 1991–; mem. American PEN; American Society of Journalists and Authors; Authors' Guild; Czech Union of Journalists; Dramatists Guild; Foreign Correspondents Asscn of Prague; Foreign Press Asscn of Vienna; Overseas Press Club. *Publications:* Draftee Confidential Guide (with B. Krisher and J. Cox), 1957, revised edn (with R. Flaste), 1966; Operation Elvis, 1960; The Elizabeth Taylor Story, 1961; Wanted: Nazi Criminals at Large, 1962; Interpret Your Dreams, 1962; Kind-Hearted Tiger (with G. Stuart), 1964; The Culture Vultures, 1968; God Bless You Real Good: My Crusade with Billy Graham, 1969; Rowboat to Prague, 1972; Good Men Still Live, 1974; The Bluebird of Happiness, 1976; Forever, Sophia, 1979; So Many Heroes, 1980; The World of Ruth Draper (play), 1982; Just an Accident (libretto for requiem), 1983; Ezra Pound: The Voice of Silence, 1983; W. H. Auden: In the Autumn of the Age of Anxiety, 1983; Treasures of the Vatican Collections, 1983; Vladimir Nabokov: The Velvet Butterfly, 1984; Ezra Pound: A Jewish View, 1988; The Wiesenthal File, 1993. Contributions: newspapers and magazines. *Honours:* Bernard De Voto Fellowship, 1963; Golden Johann Strauss Medal, Vienna, 1981; Ernst Krenek Prize, Vienna, 1986. *Address:* c/o Serafina Clarke, 96 Tunis Rd, London W12 7EY, England.

LEVY, Andrea, BA; British writer; b. 7 March 1956, London; m. Bill Mayblin; two step-d. *Education:* Highbury Hill High School, London and Middlesex Polytechnic. *Career:* fmrly worked in the costume depts of the BBC and Royal Opera House. *Publications:* Every Light in the House Burnin' 1994, Never Far from Nowhere 1996, Fruit of the Lemon 1999, Small Island (Orange Prize) 2004. *Honours:* Arts Council Award 1998. *Literary Agent:* David Grossman Literary Agency, 118B Holland Park Avenue, London, W11 4VA, England. *Telephone:* (20) 7221-2770. *Fax:* (20) 7221-1445. *Address:* c/o Review Press, Hodder Headline, 338 Euston Road, London, NW1, England.

LEVY, Bernard-Henri; French writer; b. 5 Nov. 1948, Beni-Saf, Algeria; m. 1st Sylvie Bouscasse 1980; one s. one d.; m. 2nd Arielle Sonnery 1993. *Education:* Ecole Normale Supérieure (rue d'Ulm), Paris. *Career:* War Corresp. for Combat 1971–72; Lecturer in Epistemology, Univ. of Strasbourg, in Philosophy, Ecole Normale Supérieure 1973; mem. François Mitterrand's Group of Experts 1973–76; joined Editions Grasset as Ed. 'nouvelle philosophie' series 1973; Ed. Idées section, Quotidien de Paris; Contrib. to Nouvel Observateur and Temps Modernes 1974; Co-Founder Action Int. contre la Faim 1980, Radio Free Kabul 1981, SOS Racisme; f. and Dir Règle du jeu 1990–; Pres. Supervisory Council Sept-Arte 1993–; seconded by French Govt to Kabul, Afghanistan 2002. *Film directed:* Le Jour la Nuit 1997. *Publications:* Bangladesh: Nationalisme dans la révolution 1973, Les Indes rouges 1973, La barbarie à visage humain 1977 (Prix d'honneur 1977), Le testament de Dieu 1979, L'idéologie française 1981, Questions de principe 1983, Le diable en tête (Prix Médicis) 1984, Impressions d'Asie 1985, Questions de principe II 1986, Eloge des intellectuels 1987, Les derniers jours de Charles Baudelaire (Prix Interallié) 1988, Questions de principe III 1990, Frank Stella: Les années 80 1990, Les bronzes de César 1991, Les aventures de la liberté 1991, Piet Mondrian 1992, Piero Della Francesca 1992, Le jugement dernier (play) 1992, Questions de principe IV 1992, Les hommes et les femmes (jtly) 1993, Un jour dans la mort de Sarajevo (screenplay, jtly) 1993, Bosna! (screenplay, jtly) 1994, La pureté dangereuse 1995, Questions de principe V 1995, Le lys et la cendre 1996, Comédie 1997, The Rules of the Game 1998 (revised edn What Good Are Intellectuals?: 44 Writers Share Their Thoughts 2000), Le siècle de Sartre 2000, Réflexion sur la guerre, Le mal et la fin de l'histoire 2001, Mémoire vive 2001, Qui a tué Daniel Pearl? 2003. *Address:* Editions Grasset et Fasquelle, 61 rue des Saint-Pères, 75006 Paris, France. *Telephone:* 1-44-39-22-00. *Fax:* 1-42-22-64-18.

LEVY, Peter B.; Historian; b. 11 May 1956, Burlingame, CA, USA; m. Diane Krejsa, 19 Aug. 1984, one s. one d. *Education:* BA, University of California, Berkeley, 1978; MA, 1980, PhD, 1986, Columbia University. *Career:* Visiting Assisitant Prof. of History, Rutgers University, Newark Campus, NJ, 1986–88; Assoc. Prof. of History, York College, Pennsylvania, 1989–; mem. American Historical Asscn; Organization of American Historians. *Publications:* Let Freedom Ring: A Documentary History of the Modern Civil Rights Movement (co-ed.), 1992; The New Left and Labor in the 1960s, 1994; Encyclopedia of the Reagan-Bush Years, 1996; The Civil Rights Movement, 1998; America in the Sixties: Right, Left, and Center, 1999. *Address:* 1214 Temfield Rd, Towson, MD 21286, USA. *E-mail:* plevy@ycp.edu.

LEWIN, Hugh; South African writer; b. 1939, Eastern Transvaal. *Career:* joined African Resistance Movement 1964; imprisoned 1965–72; on release, moved to London, later Zimbabwe; returned to South Africa 1990; fmr Dir, Inst. for the Advancement of Journalism; mem. Truth Commission Human Rights Violations Cttee; currently a media trainer. *Publications include:* Bandiet: Seven Years in a South African Jail 1974, Jafta 1989, The Picture That Came Alive 1993, Bandiet Out of Jail 2001. *Honours:* Olive Schreiner Prize 2001–02. *Address:* c/o Random House Inc, 1745 Broadway, New York, NY 10019, USA. *Website:* www.randomhouse.com.

LEWIN, Michael Zinn; Writer and Dramatist; b. 21 July 1942, Cambridge, Massachusetts, USA; one s. one d. *Education:* AB, Harvard University, 1964; Churchill College, Cambridge. *Career:* Co-Ed., CWA Annual Anthology, 1992–94; mem. Detection Club; CWA; MWA; Private Eye Writers Asscn; Authors' Guild. *Publications:* Author of 16 novels including: Called by a Panther, 1991; Underdog, 1993; Family Business, 1995; Rover's Tales, 1998; Cutting Loose, 1999; Family Planning, 1999; The Reluctant Detective, 2001. Other: various radio plays, stage plays and short stories. *Honours:* Maltese Falcon Society Best Novel, 1987; Raymond Chandler Society of Germany Best Novel, 1992; Mystery Masters Award, 1994. *Address:* Garden Flat, 15 Bladud Buildings, Bath BA1 5LS, England. *Website:* www.michaelzlewin.com.

LEWIN, Roger A.; Psychiatrist, Teacher, Writer and Poet; b. 22 Jan. 1946, Cleveland, OH, USA; m. 1st Julia Vandivort 11 June 1977 (died 1988); one d.; m. 2nd Joan Lilienthal 3 May 1990. *Education:* BA, magna cum laude, Harvard University; MD, Wright State University, 1981. *Career:* Resident, 1981–85, Psychiatrist, 1985–91, Teacher, Supervisor, 1991–, Sheppard and Enoch Pratt Hospital, Towson, MD; Private Practice of Psychiatry, 1981–. *Publications:* Losing and Fusing (co-author), 1992; Compassion, 1996; New Wrinkles (poems), 1996; Creative Collaboration in Psychotherapy, 1997; Spring Fed Pond, 2003. *Honours:* Ford Foundation Grant, 1965; Ginsburg Fellow, Group for the Advancement of Psychiatry, 1981–85. *Address:* 504 Club Lane, Towson, MD 21286, USA. *E-mail:* oaktree@comcast.net.

LEWING, Anthony Charles, (Mark Bannerman); Author; b. 12 July 1933, Colchester, England; m. Françoise Faury, 2 July 1966, one s. one d. *Career:* Royal Army Pay Corps, 1951–89; Civil Service, 1989–95. *Publications:* Grand Valley Feud, 1995; The Beckoning Noose, 1996; Escape to Purgatory, 1996; The Early Lynching, 1997; Renegade Rose, 1997; Ride into Destiny, 1997; Goose Pimples, 1997; Man Without a Yesterday, 1998; Trail to Redemption, 1998; Bridges to Cross, 1998; Short Story World, 1999; Comanchero Rendezvous, 1999; The Cornish Woman, 1999; Frank Riddle – Frontiersman, 1999; Pinkerton Man, 2000; Galvanized Yankee, 2001; Railroaded, 2001; Lust to Kill, 2003, Blind Trail 2004, Bender's Boot 2004. Contributions: over 300 short stories in magazines, newspapers and anthologies. *Address:* Greenmantle, Horseshoe Lane, Ash Vale, Surrey GU12 5LJ, England. *E-mail:* Anthony.lewing@ntlworld.com.

LEWIS, Anthony, AB; journalist and academic; b. 27 March 1927, New York, NY, USA; m. 1st Linda Rannells 1951 (divorced); one s. two d.; m. 2nd Margaret H. Marshall 1984. *Education:* Harvard Univ. *Career:* deskman, Sunday Dept, 1948–52, Reporter, Washington Bureau, 1955–64, Chief, London Bureau, 1965–72, Editorial Columnist, 1969–2001, New York Times; Reporter, Washington Daily News, 1952–55; Lecturer on Law, Harvard University, 1974–89; James Madison Visiting Prof., Columbia University, 1983–; mem. American Acad. of Arts and Sciences. *Publications:* Gideon's Trumpet, 1964; Portrait of a Decade: The Second American Revolution, 1964; Make No Law: The Sullivan Case and the First Amendment, 1991; Written into History: Pulitzer Prize Reporting of the Twentieth Century from the New York Times (ed.), 2001. Contributions: Professional journals. *Honours:* Heywood Broun Award, 1955; Pulitzer Prizes for National Reporting, 1955, 1963; Nieman Fellow, 1956–57; Best Fact-Crime Book Award, MWA, 1964; Hon. DLitt, Adelphi University, 1964, Rutgers University, 1973, Williams College, 1978, Clark University, 1982; Hon. LLD, Syracuse University, 1979, Colby College, 1983, Northeastern University, 1987. *Address:* 1010 Memorial Drive, Cambridge, MA 02138, USA.

LEWIS, Arnold; architectural historian, art historian and academic; b. 13 Jan. 1930, New Castle, Pennsylvania, USA; m. Beth Irwin 1958; two s. one d. *Education:* BA, Allegheny College, 1952; MA, 1954, PhD, 1962, University of Wisconsin; University of Bonn, 1959–60; University of Munich, 1960. *Career:* Wells College, Aurora, New York, 1962–64; College of Wooster, Ohio, 1964–96; mem. College Art Asscn; Society of Architectural Historians, dir, 1979–82. *Publications:* American Victorian Architecture, 1975; Wooster in 1876, 1976; American Country Houses of the Gilded Age, 1983; American Interiors of the Gilded Age (with James Turner and Steven McQuillin), 1987; An Early Encounter with Tomorrow: Europeans, Chicago's Loop, and the World's Columbian Exposition, 1997. Contributions: Journal of the Society of Architectural Historians. *Honours:* Founder's Award, Journal of the Society of Architectural Historians, 1974; Western Reserve Book Award, Society of Architectural Historians, 1977; Barzun Prize in Cultural History, American Philosophical Society, 1998. *Address:* c/o Dept of Art, College of Wooster, Wooster, OH 44691, USA.

LEWIS, Bernard; American academic and writer; b. 31 May 1916, London, England; m. Ruth Helene Oppenhejm 1947 (divorced 1974); one s. one d. *Education:* BA, 1936, PhD, 1939, University of London; Diplome des études semitiques, University of Paris, 1937. *Career:* Prof. of History of the Near and Middle East, University of London, 1949–74; Visiting Prof., University of California at Los Angeles, 1955–56, Columbia University, 1960, Indiana University, 1963, University of California at Berkeley, 1965, Collège de France, 1980, École des Hautes Études en Sciences Sociales, Paris, 1983, University of Chicago, 1985; Class of 1932 Lecturer, 1964, Cleveland E. Dodge Prof. of Near Eastern Studies, 1974–86, Prof. Emeritus, 1986–, Princeton University; Visiting Mem., 1969, Mem., 1974–86, Institute for Advanced Study, Princeton, NJ; Dir, Annenberg Research Institute, Philadelphia, 1986–90; Tanner Lecturer, Brasenose College, Oxford, 1990; Merle Curti Lecturer, University of Wisconsin, 1993; mem. American Acad. of Arts and Sciences; American Historical Society; American Oriental Society; American Philosophical Society; British Acad., fellow; Council on Foreign Relations; Royal Asiatic Society; Royal Historical Society; Royal Institute of International Affairs. *Publications:* The Origins of Ismailism: A Study of the Historical Background of the Fatimid Caliphate, 1940; The Arabs in History, 1950; Notes and Documents from the Turkish Archives: A Contribution to the History of the Jews in the Ottoman Empire, 1952; Encyclopedia of Islam (co-ed.), 1956–86; The Emergence of Modern Turkey, 1961; Istanbul and the Civilization of the Ottoman Empire, 1963; The Assassins: A Radical Sect in Islam, 1967; The Cambridge History of Islam (ed. with P. M. Holt and Ann K. S. Lambton), 2 vols, 1970; Islam in History: Ideas, Men and Events in the Middle East, 1973; Islam, from the Prophet Muhammad to the Capture of Constantinople (ed. and trans.), 2 vols, 1974; History: Remembered, Recovered, Invented, 1975; Studies in Classical and Ottoman Islam: Seventh to Sixteenth Centuries, 1976; The World of Islam: Faith, People, Culture, 1976; The Muslim Discovery of Europe, 1982; Christians and Jews in the Ottoman Empire, 2 vols, 1982; The Jews of Islam, 1985; Semites and Anti-Semites: An Inquiry into Conflict and Prejudice, 1986; The Political Language of Islam, 1988; Race and Slavery in the Middle East: A Historical Enquiry, 1990; Islam and the West, 1993; The Shaping of the Modern Middle East, 1994; Cultures in Conflict: Christians, Muslims, and Jews in the Age of Discovery, 1995; The Middle East: Two Thousand Years of History from the Rise of Christianity to the Present Day, 1995; The Future of the Middle East, 1997; The Multiple Identities of the Middle East, 1998; A Middle East Mosaic: Fragments of Life, Letters and History, 2000; What Went Wrong?: The Clash Between Islam and Modernity in the Middle East, 2002; The Crisis of Islam: Holy War and Unholy Terror, 2003; From Babel to Dragomans: Interpreting the Middle East 2004. Contributions: Professional journals. *Honours:* Citation of Honour, Turkish Ministry of Culture, 1973; Fellow, University College London, 1976; Harvey Prize, Technion-Israel Institute of Technology, 1978; Atatürk Peace Prize, 1998; 11 hon. doctorates. *Address:* c/o Department of Near Eastern Studies, 110 Jones Hall, Princeton University, Princeton, NJ 08544, USA.

LEWIS, Bill (see Lewis, William Edward).

LEWIS, Charles (see Dixon, Roger).

LEWIS, David L(evering); Prof. of History and Writer; b. 25 May 1936, Little Rock, AR, USA; m. 1st Sharon Siskind 15 April 1966 (divorced Oct. 1988); two s. one d.; m. 2nd Ruth Ann Stewart 15 April 1994; one d. *Education:* BA, Fisk University, 1956; MA, Columbia University, 1958; PhD, LSE, 1962. *Career:* Lecturer, University of Ghana, 1963–64, Howard University, Washington, DC, 1964–65; Asst Prof., University of Notre Dame, 1965–66; Assoc. Prof., Morgan State College, Baltimore, 1966–70, Federal City College, Washington, DC, 1970–74; Prof. of History, University of the District of Columbia, 1974–80, University of California at San Diego, La Jolla, 1981–85; Martin Luther King Jr Prof. of History, Rutgers University, 1985–; mem. African Studies Asscn; American Asscn of University Profs; American Historical Asscn; Authors' Guild; Organization of American Historians; Society for French Historical Studies; Southern Historical Asscn; American Acad. of Arts and Sciences, 2002; American Philosophical Society, 2002. *Publications:* Martin Luther King: A Critical Biography, 1971; Prisoners of Honor: The Dreyfus Affair, 1973; District of Columbia: A Bicentennial History, 1977; When Harlem Was in Vogue: The Politics of the Arts in the Twenties and the Thirties, 1981; Harlem Renaissance: Art of Black America (with others), 1987; The Race to Fashoda: European Colonialism and African Resistance in the Scramble for Africa, 1988; W. E. B. Du Bois: Biography of a Race, 1868–1919, 1994; The Portable Harlem Renaissance Reader (ed.), 1994; W. E. B. Du Bois: A Reader (ed.), 1995; W. E. B. Du Bois: The Fight for Equality and the American Century, 2001; The Man Who Invented Hitler, 2003. *Honours:* American Philosophical Society Grant, 1967; Social Science Research Council Grant, 1971; National Endowment for the Humanities Grant, 1975; Woodrow Wilson International Center for Scholars Fellow, 1977–78; Guggenheim Fellowship, 1986; Bancroft Prize, 1994; Ralph Waldo Emerson Prize, 1994; Pulitzer Prizes for Biography, 1994, 2001; Francis Parkman Prize, 1994; Fellow, John D. and Catherine T. MacArthur Foundation, 1999. *Address:* c/o Dept of History, Van Dyck Hall, Rutgers University, New Brunswick, NJ 08903, USA.

LEWIS, Desmond Francis, BA; poet and writer; b. 18 Jan. 1948, Colchester, Essex, England; m. Denise Jean Woolgar 1970; one s. one d. *Education:* Lancaster University. *Publications:* contrib. hundreds of prose poems and stories to various UK and US publications.

LEWIS, F(rances) R.; Writer; b. 30 April 1939, USA; m. Howard D. Lewis, 16 April 1961, two s. one d. *Education:* BA, SUNY at Albany, 1960. *Career:* mem. Associated Writing Programs; International Women's Writing Guild; Poets and Writers. *Publications:* various short stories. Contributions: anthologies and periodicals. *Honours:* PEN-National Endowment for the Arts Syndicated Fiction Project Awards, 1986, 1988; Millay Colony Fellow, 1991; MacDowell Colony Fellow, 1993. *Address:* PO Box 12093, Albany, NY 12212, USA.

LEWIS, Jeremy Morley, BA, MA, FRSL; British writer; b. 15 March 1942, Salisbury, Wiltshire, England; m. Petra Lewis 1968, two d. *Education:* Trinity Coll., Dublin and Sussex Univ. *Career:* Ed., Andre Deutsch Ltd 1969–70, OUP 1977–79; Literary Agent, AP Watt Ltd 1970–76; Dir, Chatto and Windus 1979–89; Deputy Ed., London Magazine 1991–94; Editorial Consultant, Peters, Fraser & Dunlop Group Ltd 1994–2002; Commissioning Ed., The Oldie 1997–; mem. R. S. Surtees Soc. (sec.). *Publications:* Playing for Time, 1987; Chatto Book of Office Life, 1992; Kindred Spirits, 1995; Cyril Connolly: A Life, 1997; Tobias Smollett, 2003. *Literary Agent:* Gillon Aitken Associates Ltd, 18–21 Cavaye Place, London, SW10 9PT, England. *Telephone:* (20) 7373-8672. *Fax:* (20) 7373-6002. *Address:* c/o The Oldie, 65 Newman Street, London, W1T 3EG, England.

LEWIS, Mervyn (see Frewer, Glyn Mervyn Louis).

LEWIS, Russell T.; American newspaper executive; *President and CEO, The New York Times Company*; b. 1948. *Career:* Pres., Gen. Man. The New York Times, New York 1993–97, Pres., CEO 1997–. *Address:* The New York Times, 229 West 43rd Street, New York, NY 10036, USA (Office). *Telephone:* (212) 556-1234. *Fax:* (212) 556-7389. *Website:* www.nytco.com.

LEWIS, Warn B., Jr; Prof. of German and Writer; b. 8 May 1938, Minneapolis, Minnesota, USA; m. Erika Cornehl, 19 Sept. 1961, three d. *Education:* BA cum laude, Amherst College, 1960; MA, University of Minnesota at Twin Cities, 1965; PhD, University of Pennsylvania, 1968. *Career:* Asst Prof. of German, University of Iowa, Iowa City, 1968–71; Asst Prof., 1971–73, Assoc. Prof. of German, 1973–99, Prof. of German, 1999–, University of Georgia, Athens; mem. International Brecht Society; Modern Language Asscn of America; German Studies Asscn; Society for Exile Studies; Eugene O'Neill Society; Northeast MLA, Chair., German-American Literary Relations, 1985–86, 1989–90; South Atlantic MLA. *Publications:* Poetry and Exile: An Annotated Bibliography of the Works and Criticism of Paul Zech, 1975; Eugene O'Neill: The German Reception of America's First Dramatist, 1984; German and International Perspectives on the Spanish Civil War: The Aesthetics of Partisanship (contributor), 1992; Paul Zech's The Bird in Langfoot's Belfry (ed.), 1993; The Ironic Dissident: Frank Wedekind in the View of His Critics, 1997. Contributions: Comparative Literature Studies; Modern Language Studies; German Quarterly; German Life and Letters; Modern Drama. *Honours:* Fellow, Alexander von Humboldt Foundation, 1979–80. *Address:* 490 S Milledge Ave, Athens, GA 30605, USA. *E-mail:* wlewis@arches.uga.edu.

LEWIS, William Edward, (Bill Lewis); Poet, Writer, Ed., Storyteller and Mythographer; b. 1 Aug. 1953, Maidstone, Kent, England; m. Ann Frances Morris, 17 Oct. 1981. *Career:* Writer-in-Residence, Brighton Festival, 1985; mem. Medway Poets, founder mem.; Stuckist Group, founder mem. *Publications:* Poems, 1975–83, 1983; Night Clinic, 1984; Communion, 1986; Rage Without Anger, 1987; Skyclad Christ, 1992; Paradigm Shift (ed.), 1992; Coyote Cosmos (short stories), 1994; Translation Women, 1996; The Book of North Kent Writers (co-ed.), 1996; The Wine of Connecting (poems), 1996; Intellect of the Heart, 1997; Shattered English: Complete North Kent Poems, 1998; Leaving the Autoroute (short stories), 1999; Beauty is the Beast (poems), 2000. Contributions: Best Horror and Fantasy, 1997, 1998; Jungewelt; Anthologies, review, and journals. *Address:* 66 Glencoe Rd, Chatham, Kent ME4 5QE, England.

LEWIS-SMITH, Anne Elizabeth, (Emily Devereaux, A. McCormick, Quilla Slade); poet, writer, editor and publisher; b. 14 April 1925, London, England; m. Peter Lewis-Smith 1944; one s. two d. *Career:* Asst Ed., 1967–83, Ed., 1983–91, Envoi; Ed., Aerostat, 1973–78, British Asscn of Friends of Museums Yearbook, 1985–91; Publisher, Envoi Poets Publications, 1986–; mem. PEN. *Publications:* Seventh Bridge, 1963; The Beginning, 1964; Flesh and Flowers, 1967; Dandelion Flavour, 1971; Dinas Head, 1980; Places and Passions, 1986; In the Dawn, 1987; Circling Sound, 1996; Feathers, Fancies and Feelings, 2000. Contributions: newspapers and magazines. *Honours:* Tissadier Diploma for Services to International Aviation; Debbie Warley Award for Services to International Aviation; Dorothy Tutin Award for Services to Poetry. *Address:* Pen Ffordd, Newport, Pembrokeshire SA42 0QT, Wales.

LEY, Alice Chetwynd; Novelist and Teacher; b. 12 Oct. 1913, Halifax, Yorkshire, England; m. Kenneth James Ley, 3 Feb. 1945, two s. *Education:* Diploma in Sociology, University of London; Gilchrist Award of 1962 for work in connection with Diploma in Sociology. *Career:* Tutor in Creative Writing, 1962–84, Lecturer in Sociology and Social History, 1968–71, Harrow College of Further Education; mem. Jane Austen Society; Romantic Novelists Asscn, chair., 1970, hon. life mem., 1987–; Society of Women Writers and Journalists. *Publications:* 19 novels. Contributions: numerous journals.

LEYS, Simon (see Ryckmans, Pierre).

LEYTON, Sophie (see Walsh, Sheila).

L'HEUREUX, John (Clarke); Prof. of English and Writer; b. 26 Oct. 1934, South Hadley, Massachusetts, USA; m. Joan Ann Polston, 26 June 1971. *Education:* AB, 1959, Licentiate in Philosophy, 1960, Weston College; MA, Boston College, 1963; Licentiate in Sacred Theology, Woodstock College, 1967; Postgraduate Studies, Harvard University, 1967–68. *Career:* Writer-in-Residence, Georgetown University, 1964–65, Regis College, 1968–69; Ordained Roman Catholic Priest, 1966, laicized, 1971; Staff Ed., 1968–69, Contributing Ed., 1969–83, The Atlantic; Visiting Prof., Hamline University, 1971, Tufts College, 1971–72; Visiting Asst Prof., Harvard University, 1973; Asst Prof., 1973–79, Dir, Creative Writing Programme, 1976–89, Assoc. Prof., 1979–81, Prof., 1981–, Lane Prof. of the Humanities, 1985–90, Stanford University. *Publications:* Quick as Dandelions, 1964; Rubrics for a Revolution, 1967; Picnic in Babylon, 1967; One Eye and a Measuring Rod, 1968; No Place for Hiding, 1971; Tight White Collar, 1972; The Clang Birds, 1972; Family Affairs, 1974; Jessica Fayer, 1976; Desires, 1981; A Woman Run Mad, 1988; Comedians, 1990; An Honorable Profession, 1991; The Shrine at Altamira, 1992; The Handmaid of Desire, 1996; Having Everything, 1999; The Miracle, 2002. *Address:* c/o Dept of English, Stanford University, Stanford, CA 94305, USA.

LI, Bihua; Taiwanese novelist and screenwriter. *Publications:* Her Pao chu yen hua 1983, The Last Princess of Manchuria 1992, Farewell my Concubine (also co-writer of screenplay) 1993. *Address:* c/o HarperCollins Publishing, 10 E 53rd Street, New York, NY 10022, USA. *Website:* www.harpercollins.com.

LIBBY, Ronald T(heodore); Prof. of Political Science and Writer; b. 20 Nov. 1941, Los Angeles, CA, USA; two d. *Education:* BA, Washington State University, Pullman, 1965; MA, 1966, PhD, 1975, University of Washington, Seattle. *Career:* Lecturer, University of Botswana, Lesotho, and Swaziland, 1973–75, Malawi, 1975–76, and Zambia, 1976–79; Visiting Asst Prof., University of Notre Dame, 1981–83; Senior Lecturer, University of the West Indies, Jamaica, 1983–85, Victoria University of Wellington, New Zealand, 1987–89; Visiting Assoc. Prof., Northwestern University, 1985–86; Senior Research Fellow, Australian National University, 1986–87; Prof. and Chair, Dept of Political Science, Southwest State University, Marshall, Minnesota, 1989–96, Saint Joseph's University, Philadelphia, 1996–2000; Prof., Dept of Political Science, University of North Florida, Jacksonville, 2000–. *Publications:* Towards an Africanized US Policy for Southern Africa, 1980; The Politics of Economic Power in Southern Africa, 1987; Hawke's Law: The Politics of Mining and Aboriginal Land Rights in Australia, 1989; Protecting Markets: US Policy and the World Grain Trade, 1992; Eco-Wars: Political Campaigns and Social Movements, 1999. Contributions: scholarly books and journals. *Honours:* Grants; Visiting Research Scholar, University of California at Irvine, 1972; Outstanding Academic Book, Choice magazine, 1990. *Address:* c/o Dept of Political Science and Public Administration, University of North Florida, 4567 St Johns Bluff Rd, South Jacksonville, FL 32224-2645, USA. *E-mail:* rtl2129@aol.com.

LICHTENSTEIN, Nelson; Historian; b. 15 Nov. 1944, Frederick, MD, USA; m. Eileen Boris, 26 Jan. 1979, one s. *Education:* PhD, History, University of California at Berkeley, 1974. *Career:* Asst Prof., Assoc. Prof., Catholic University of America, 1981–89; Prof., University of Virginia, 1989–; mem. American Historical Asscn; Organization of American Historians. *Publications:* Political Profiles: The Kennedy Years (ed.), 1976; Political Profiles: The Johnson Years (ed.), 1976; Labor's War at Home: The CIO in World War II, 1982; On the Line: Essays in the History of Auto Work (co-ed.), 1989; Major Problems in the History of American Workers: Documents and Essays (ed.), 1991; Industrial Democracy in America: The Ambiguous Promise (co-ed.), 1993; The Most Dangerous Man in Detroit: Walter Reuther and the Fate of American Labor, 1995; The United States, 1940–2000, 2000.

LICKONA, Thomas (Edward); Developmental Psychologist, Prof. of Education, Writer, Consultant and Lecturer; b. 4 April 1943, Poughkeepsie, New York, USA; m. Judith Barker, 10 Sept. 1966, two s. *Education:* BA, English, Siena College, 1964; MA, English, Ohio University, 1965; PhD, Psychology, SUNY at Albany, 1971. *Career:* Instructor, SUNY at Albany, 1968–70; Asst Prof., 1970–75, Assoc. Prof., 1975–82, Prof. of Education, 1982–, SUNY at Cortland; Visiting Prof., Harvard University, 1978–79, Boston University, 1979–80; numerous radio and television talk show appearances; mem. Asscn for Moral Education; Character Counts Coalition, advisory board; Character Education Partnership, board of dirs; Medical Institute for Sexual Health, advisory board. *Publications:* Open Education: Increasing Alternatives for Teachers and Children (ed. with Jessie Adams, Ruth Nickse, and David Young), 1973; Moral Development and Behavior: Theory, Research, and Social Issues (ed.), 1976; Raising Good Children: Helping Your Child Through the Stages of Moral Development, 1983; Educating for Character: How Our Schools Can Teach Respect and Responsibility, 1991; Sex, Love and You (with Judith Lickona and William Boudreau), 1994. Contributions: journals and magazines. *Honours:* Distinguished Alumni Award, SUNY at Albany; Christopher Award, 1992. *Address:* c/o State University of New York at Cortland, PO Box 2000, Cortland, NY 13045, USA.

LIDDLE, Peter (Hammond); Senior Lecturer in History and Writer; b. 26 Dec. 1934, Sunderland, England. *Education:* BA, Univ. of Sheffield, 1956; Teacher's Certificate, Univ. of Nottingham, 1957; Diploma in Physical Education, Loughborough College of Physical Education, 1957. *Career:* History Teacher, Havelock School, Sunderland, 1957; Head, History Dept, Gateacre Comprehensive School, Liverpool, 1958–67; Lecturer, Notre Dame College of Education, 1967; Lecturer, 1967–70, Senior Lecturer in History, 1970–, Sunderland Polytechnic; Keeper of the Liddle Collection, Univ. of Leeds, 1988–99; Dir, The Second World War Experience Centre, Leeds, 1999–; mem. British Audio Visual Trust; FRHistS. *Publications:* Men of Gallipoli, 1976; World War One: Personal Experience Material for Use in Schools, 1977; Testimony of War 1914–18, 1979; The Sailor's War 1914–18, 1985; Gallipoli: Pens, Pencils and Cameras at War, 1985; 1916: Aspects of Conflict, 1985; Home Fires and Foreign Fields, 1985; The Airman's War 1914–18, 1987; The Soldier's War 1914–18, 1988; Voices of War, 1988; The Battle of the Somme, 1992; The Worst Ordeal: Britons at Home and Abroad 1914–18, 1994; Facing Armageddon: The First World War Experienced (co-ed. and contributor), 1996; Passchendaele in Perspective: The Third Battle of Ypres (ed. and contributor), 1997; At the Eleventh Hour (co-ed. and contributor), 1998; For Five Shillings a Day (ed. and contributor), 2000; The Great World War, 1914–45 (co-ed. and contributor), two vols, 2000–01. Contributions: journals and books. *Honours:* MLitt, Univ. of Newcastle, 1975; PhD, Univ. of Leeds, 1997; Distinguished Lecturer, Sam Houston State Univ., Huntsville, TX, 2003. *Address:* Prospect House, 39 Leeds Rd, Rawdon, Leeds LS19 6NW, England.

LIDDY, James, (Daniel Reeves); Prof. of English, Poet and Writer; b. 1 July 1934, Dublin, Ireland. *Education:* BA, 1956, MA, 1959, English Language and Literature, National University of Ireland; Barrister-at-Law, King's Inns, Dublin, 1961. *Career:* Visiting Lecturer, San Francisco State College, 1967–68; Visiting Asst Prof., SUNY at Binghamton, 1969, University of Wisconsin at Parkside, 1972–73; Visiting Lecturer, Lewis and Clark College, Portland, Oregon, 1970, University College, Galway, 1973–74; Asst Prof., Denison University, Ohio, 1970–71; Lecturer, Delgado Community College, New Orleans, 1975; Visiting Asst Prof., 1976, Lecturer and Poet-in-Residence, 1976–80, Asst Prof., 1981–82, Assoc. Prof., 1982–88, Prof. of English, 1988–, University of Wisconsin at Milwaukee; mem. Aosdána, Irish Acad. of Arts and Letters. *Publications:* Poetry: In a Blue Smoke, 1964; Blue Mountain, 1968; A Life of Stephen Dedalus, 1968; A Munster Song of Love and War, 1969; Orpheus in the Ice Cream Parlour, 1975; Corca Bascin, 1977; Comyn's Lay, 1979; Moon and Starr Moments, 1982; At the Grave of Father Sweetman, 1984; A White Thought in a White Shade, 1987; In the Slovak Bowling Alley, 1990; Art is Not for Grownups, 1990; Trees Warmer Than Green: Notes Towards a Video of Avondale House, 1991; Collected Poems, 1994; Epitaphery, 1997; Gold Set Dancing, 2000. Other: Esau My Kingdom for a Drink, 1962; Patrick Kavanagh: An Introduction to His Work, 1971; Baudelaire's Bar Flowers (trans.), 1975; You Can't Jog for Jesus: Jack Kerouac as a Religious Writer, 1985; Young Men Go Walking (novella), 1986. Contributions: books and journals. *Honours:* University of Wisconsin at Parkside Teaching Award, 1973; Council of Wisconsin Writers Prize for Poetry, 1995. *Address:* c/o Dept of English and Comparative Literature, University of Wisconsin at Milwaukee, PO Box 413, Milwaukee, WI 53201, USA.

LIDMAN, Sara; Writer; b. 30 Dec. 1923, Sweden. *Education:* Uppsala Univ. *Career:* first four books deal with life in sparsely populated northern Sweden; in South Africa 1960, in Kenya 1962–64, in North Viet Nam 1965. *Publications:* Tjärdalen, 1953; Hjortronlandet, 1955; Aina, 1956; Regnspiran, 1958; Bära mistel, 1960; Jag o min son, 1961; Med fem diamanter, 1964; Samtal i Hanoi, 1966; Gruva, 1968; Vänner o uvänner, 1969; Marta, Marta, 1970; Fåglarna i Nam Dinh, 1973; Libretto till två baletter, Inga träd skall väcka dig, 1974; Balansen, 1975; Din tjänare hör, 1977.

LIEBER, Robert James, BA, PhD; American writer; *Professor of Government, Georgetown University*; b. Chicago, IL. *Education:* Univ. of Wisconsin, Univ. of Chicago, Harvard Univ. *Career:* Asst Prof. 1968–72, Assoc. Prof. 1972–77, Chair., Dept of Political Science 1975–76, 1977–80; Prof. 1977–81, Univ. of California at Davis; Visiting Prof. Fudan Univ., Shanghai 1988; Postdoctoral Fellow, St Antony's Coll., Oxford 1969–70; Research Assoc., Center for Int. Affairs, Harvard Univ. 1974–75; Fellow, Woodrow Wilson International Center for Scholars, Washington, DC 1980–81, 1999–2000; Prof. of Government 1982–, Chair., Dept of Government 1990–96, Acting Chair., Dept of Psychology 1997–99, Georgetown Univ.; mem. American Political Science Asscn, Council on Foreign Relations, Int. Inst. for Strategic Studies. *Publications:* British Politics and European Unity: Parties, Elites, and Pressure Groups, 1970; Theory and World Politics, 1972; Contemporary Politics: Europe (co-author), 1976; Oil and the Middle East War, 1976; Eagle Entangled: US Foreign Policy in a Complex World (co-ed. and contributor), 1979; Will Europe Fight for Oil? (ed.), 1983; Eagle Defiant: US Foreign Policy in the 1980s (co-ed. and contributor), 1983; The Oil Decade: Conflict and Cooperation in the West, 1986; Eagle Resurgent?: The Reagan Era in American Foreign Policy (co-ed. and contributor), 1987; Eagle in a New World: American Grand Strategy in the Post-Cold War Era (co-ed. and contributor) 1992, Eagle Adrift: American Foreign Policy at the End of the Century (ed. and contributor) 1997, No Common Power: Understanding International Relations 4th edn 2001,

Eage Rules? Foreign Policy and American Primacy in the 21st Century (ed. and contributor) 2002. Contributions: scholarly books, professional journals and general periodicals. *Honours:* Guggenheim Fellowship 1973–74, Rockefeller International Relations Fellowship 1978–79, Ford Foundation Grant 1981. *Address:* c/o Department of Government, Georgetown University, Washington, DC 20057-1034, USA. *E-mail:* lieberr@georgetown.edu.

LIEBERMAN, Herbert Henry; Novelist, Playwright and Ed.; b. 22 Sept. 1933, New Rochelle, New York, USA; m. Judith Barsky, 9 June 1963, one d. *Education:* AB, City College, CUNY, 1955; AM, Columbia University, 1957. *Career:* mem. MWA; International Asscn of Crime Writers. *Publications:* The Adventures of Dolphin Green, 1967; Crawlspace, 1971; The Eighth Square, 1973; Brilliant Kids, 1975; City of the Dead, 1976; The Climate of Hell, 1978; Nightcall from a Distant Time Zone, 1982; Night Bloom, 1984; The Green Train, 1986; Shadow Dancers, 1989; Sandman Sleep, 1993; The Girl with the Botticelli Eyes, 1996; The Vagabond of Holmby Park, 2003. *Honours:* First Prize for Playwriting, University of Chicago, 1963; Guggenheim Fellowship, 1964; Grand Prix de Littérature Policière, Paris, 1978. *Address:* c/o Georges Borchardt, 136 E 57th St, New York, NY 10022, USA.

LIEBERMAN, Laurence; Prof. of English and Creative Writing, Poet, Writer and Ed.; b. 16 Feb. 1935, Detroit, Michigan, USA; m. Bernice Braun, 17 June 1956, one s. two d. *Education:* BA, 1956, MA, 1958, University of Michigan; Doctoral Program, University of California, 1958–60. *Career:* Assoc. Prof. of English, College of the Virgin Islands, 1964–68; Assoc. Prof. of English, 1968–70, Prof. of English and Creative Writing, 1970–, University of Illinois at Urbana-Champaign; Poetry Ed., University of Illinois Press, 1971–; mem. Acad. of American Poets; Associated Writing Programs; Poetry Society of America. *Publications:* The Unblinding (poems), 1968; The Achievement of James Dickey, 1968; The Osprey Suicides (poems), 1973; Unassigned Frequencies: American Poetry in Review, 1964–77, 1977; God's Measurements, 1980; Eros at the World Kite Pageant: Poems, 1979–83, 1983; The Mural of Wakeful Sleep (poems), 1985; The Creole Mephistopheles (poems), 1990; New and Selected Poems: 1962–92, 1993; The St Kitts Monkey Feuds (poem), 1995; Beyond the Muse of Memory: Essays on Contemporary American Poets, 1995; Dark Songs: Slave House and Synagogue, 1996; Compass of the Dying (poems), 1998; The Regatta in the Skies: Selected Long Poems, 1999; Flight from the Mother Stone, 2000. Contributions: anthologies, reviews, journals, and magazines. *Honours:* Yaddo Foundation Fellowship, 1964; Illinois Arts Council Fellowship, 1981; National Endowment for the Arts Fellowship, 1986–87; Jerome J. Shestack Poetry Prize, American Poetry Review, 1986–87. *Address:* 1304 Eliot Dr., Urbana, IL 61801, USA.

LIEBERTHAL, Kenneth Guy; Prof. of Political Science and Writer; b. 9 Sept. 1943, Asheville, NC, USA; m. Jane Lindsay, 15 June 1968, two s. *Education:* BA, Dartmouth College, 1965; MA, 1968, Certificate for East Asian Institute, 1968, PhD, Political Science, 1972, Columbia University. *Career:* Instructor, 1972, Asst Prof., 1972–75, Assoc. Prof., 1976–82, Prof., 1982–83, Political Science Dept, Swarthmore College; Visiting Prof., 1983, Prof., 1983–, Political Science Dept, William Davidson Prof. of Business Administration, University of Michigan Business School, 1995–, Arthur Thurnau Prof. of Political Science, 1995–98, University of Michigan, Ann Arbor; Special Asst to the Pres. and Senior Dir for Asia, National Security Council, White House, 1998–2000; Editorial Boards, China Economic Review, China Quarterly, Journal of Contemporary China. *Publications:* Policy Making in China: Leaders, Structures and Processes (with Michel Oksenberg), 1988; Research Guide to Central Party and Government Meetings in China 1949–86 (with Bruce Dixon), 1989; Perspectives on Modern China: Four Anniversaries (co-ed.), 1991; Bureaucracy, Politics and Policy Making in Post-Mao China (co-ed.), 1991; Governing China, 1995. Contributions: Foreign Affairs, China Quarterly; Book reviews to American Political Science Review; China Economic Review; China Quarterly. *Address:* 701 Tappan St, Room D3224, Ann Arbor, MI 48104-1234, USA.

LIEBESCHUETZ, John Hugo Wolfgang Gideon, BA, PhD; British retd academic and writer; b. 22 June 1927, Hamburg, Germany; m. Margaret Rosa Taylor 1955; one s. three d. *Education:* University of London. *Career:* Prof. and Head of Dept of Classical and Archaeological Studies, University of Nottingham, 1979–92. *Publications:* Antioch, 1972; Continuity and Change in Roman Religion, 1979; Barbarians and Bishops, 1992; From Diocletian to the Arab Conquest, 1992; Decline and Fall of the Roman City, 2001. *Honours:* Fellow, British Acad., 1992; Corresponding Fellow, German Archaeological Institute, 1994; Fellow, University College London, 1997; Fellow, Society of Antiquaries. *Address:* 1 Clare Valley, The Park, Nottingham NG7 1BU, England. *E-mail:* wolf@liebeschuetz5472.fsnet.co.uk.

LIEBLER, Michael Lynn, BA, MA; lecturer and poet; b. 24 Aug. 1953, Detroit, MI, USA; m. Pamela Mary Liebler 1976; one s. one d. *Education:* Oakland University, Rochester, MI. *Career:* part-time Instructor, Henry Ford Community College, 1980–86; Lecturer, 1981–92, Senior Lecturer, 1992–, Wayne State University; Detroit Dir, National Writers' Voice Project, 1995–; Arts and Humanities Dir, YMCA of Metro Detroit; mem. American Asscn of University Profs; Associated Writing Programs; MLA; National Council of Teachers of English; National Writers Voice Project; National Writers Corp Program; Poetry Resource Center of Michigan, pres., 1987–93; Popular Culture Asscn. *Publications:* Measuring Darkness, 1980; Breaking the Voodoo: Selected Poems, 1990; Deliver Me, 1991; Stripping the Adult Century Bare, 1995; Brooding the Heartlands, 1998. Contributions: Rattle; Exquisite Corpse; Cottonwood Review; Relix Magazine; Christian Science Monitor; Detroit Sunday Journal; Review of Contemporary Fiction; American Book Review. *Address:* PO Box 120, Roseville, MI 48066, USA.

LIFSHIN, Lyn (Diane); Poet and Teacher; b. 12 July 1944, Burlington, Vermont, USA. *Education:* BA, Syracuse University, 1960; MA, University of Vermont, 1963. *Career:* Instructor, SUNY at Cobleskill, 1968, 1970; Writing Consultant, New York State Mental Health Dept, Albany, 1969, Empire State College of SUNY at Saratoga Springs, 1973; Poet-in-Residence, Mansfield State College, Pennsylvania, 1974, University of Rochester, New York, 1986, Antioch's Writers' Conference, Ohio, 1987. *Publications:* Poetry: Over 75 collections, including: Upstate Madonna: Poems, 1970–74, 1975; Shaker House Poems, 1976; Some Madonna Poems, 1976; Leaning South, 1977; Madonna Who Shifts for Herself, 1983; Kiss the Skin Off, 1985; Many Madonnas, 1988; The Doctor Poems, 1990; Apple Blossoms, 1993; Blue Tattoo, 1995; The Mad Girl Drives in a Daze, 1995. Editor: Tangled Vines: A Collection of Mother and Daughter Poems, 1978; Ariadne's Thread: A Collection of Contemporary Women's Journals, 1982; Unsealed Lips, 1988. Contributions: many books and numerous other publications, including journals. *Honours:* Hart Crane Award; Bread Loaf Scholarship; Yaddo Fellowships, 1970, 1971, 1975, 1979, 1980; MacDowell Fellowship, 1973; Millay Colony Fellowships, 1975, 1979; Jack Kerouac Award, 1984; Centennial Review Poetry Prize, 1985; Madeline Sadin Award, New York Quarterly, 1986; Footwork Award, 1987; Esterscefller Award, 1987. *Address:* 2142 Appletree Lane, Niskayuna, NY 12309, USA.

LIFTON, Robert Jay; Psychiatrist, Prof. and Writer; *Visiting Professor of Psychiatry, Cambridge Health Alliance/Harvard Medical School;* b. 16 May 1926, New York, NY, USA; m. Betty Kirschner, 1 March 1952, two d. *Education:* Cornell University, 1942–44; MD, New York Medical College, 1948. *Career:* Intern, Jewish Hospital, New York, 1948–49; Resident, SUNY Downstate Medical Center, 1949–51; Faculty, Washington School of Psychiatry, 1954–55; Research Assoc. in Psychiatry, Harvard University, 1955–61; Foundation's Fund for Research Psychiatry Assoc. Prof. of Psychiatry and Psychology, 1961–67, Research Prof., 1967–, Yale Medical School; Distinguished Prof. of Psychiatry and Psychology, Dir, Center on Violence and Human Survival, John Jay College of Criminal Justice, Graduate School and University Center, and Mount Sinai School of Medicine, CUNY, 1985–2003; Visiting Prof. of Psychiatry Cambridge Health Alliance/Harvard Medical School 2003–; several guest lectureships; mem. American Acad. of Arts and Sciences, fellow; American Psychiatric Asscn; Asscn of Asian Studies; Federation of American Scientists; Society for Psychological Study of Social Issues. *Publications:* Thought Reform and the Psychology of Totalism: A Study of Brainwashing in China, 1961; Revolutionary Immorality: Mao Tse-Tung and the Chinese Cultural Revolution, 1968; Death in Life: Survivors of Hiroshima, 1969; History and Human Survival, 1970; Boundaries: Psychological Man in Revolution, 1970; Home from the War: Vietnam Veterans–Neither Victims Nor Executioners, 1973; Living and Dying (with Eric Olson), 1974; The Life of the Self, 1976; Six Lives, Six Deaths: Portraits from Modern Japan (with Shuichi Kato and Michael Reich), 1979; The Broken Connection: On Death and the Continuity of Life, 1979; Indefensible Weapons: The Political and Psychological Case Against Nuclearism (with Richard A Falk), 1982; In a Dark Time, 1984; The Nazi Doctors: Medical Killing and Psychology of Genocide, 1986; The Future of Immortality and Other Essays for a Nuclear Age, 1987; The Genocidal Mentality: Nazi Holocaust and Nuclear Threat (with Eric Markusen), 1990; The Protean Self: Human Resilience in an Age of Fragmentation, 1993; Hiroshima in America: Fifty Years of Denial, 1995; Destroying the World to Save It: Aum Shinrikyo, Apocalyptic Violence and the New Global Terrorism, 1999; Who Owns Death?: Capital Punishment, the American Conscience and the End of Executions (with Greg Mitchell), 2000, Superpower Syndrome: America' Apocalyptic Confrontation with the World 2003. Contributions: Professional journals. *Honours:* National Book Award, 1970; Van Wyck Brooks Award, 1971; Hiroshima Gold Medal, 1975; Gandhi Peace Award, 1984; Bertrand Russell Society Award, 1985; Holocaust Memorial Award, 1986; National Jewish Book Award, 1987; Los Angeles Times Book Prize for History, 1987; Lisl and Leo Eitinger Award, Oslo, 1988; Max A Hayman Award, American Orthopsychiatrists Asscn, 1992; National Living Treasure Award, Psychiatric Institute, 1994; Outstanding Achievement Award, Armenian-American Society for Studies on Stress and Genocide, 1996. *Address:* Dept of Psychiatry, 1493 Cambridge Street, Cambridge,MA 02139, USA.

LIGHTMAN, Alan Paige, AB, PhD; American physicist, writer and teacher; b. 28 Nov. 1948, Memphis, TN; m. Jean Greenblatt 1976; two d. *Education:* Princeton Univ., California Inst. of Technology. *Career:* Postdoctoral Fellow, Cornell Univ. 1974–76; Asst Prof., Harvard Univ. 1976–79; staff scientist, Smithsonian Astrophysical Observatory, Cambridge 1979–88; Prof. of Science and Writing 1988–, John E. Burchard Chair 1995–2001, MIT; Fellow, American Acad. of Arts and Sciences; mem. American Astronomical Soc.; Fellow, American Physical Soc. *Publications:* fiction: Einstein's Dreams 1993, Good Benito 1994, The Diagnosis 2000, Reunion 2003; non-fiction: Problem Book in Relativity and Gravitation 1974, Radiative

Process in Astrophysics (with George B. Rybicki) 1976, Time Travel and Papa Joe's Pipe 1984, A Modern Day Yankee in a Connecticut Court and Other Essays on Science 1986, Origins: The Lives and Worlds of Modern Cosmologists (with Roberta Brawer) 1990, Ancient Light: Our Changing View of the Universe (adapted from Origins) 1991, Great Ideas in Physics 1992, Time for the Stars: Astronomy in the 1990s 1992, The World is Too Much with Me: Finding Private Space in the Wired World 1992, Dance for Two: Selected Essays 1996; editor: Revealing the Universe: Prediction and Proof in Astronomy (with James Cornell) 1982, The Best American Essays 2000; contrib. to professional journals and literary magazines. *Honours:* Most Outstanding Science Book in the Physical Sciences Award, Asscn of American Publishers 1990, Boston Globe Winship Book Prize 1993, American Inst. of Physics Andrew Gemant Award 1996, Nat. Public Radio Book of the Month 1998. *Address:* Massachusetts Institute of Technology, 77 Massachusetts Avenue, Cambridge, MA 02139, USA. *Telephone:* (617) 253-1000. *Website:* web.mit.edu.

LILIENTHAL, Alfred M(orton); Author, Historian, Attorney and Lecturer; b. 25 Dec. 1913, New York, NY, USA. *Education:* BA, Cornell University, 1934; LLD, Columbia University School of Law, 1938. *Career:* Ed., Middle East Perspective, 1968–85; mem. University Club; Cornell Club; National Press Club; Capital Hill Club. *Publications:* What Price Israel?, 1953; There Goes the Middle East, 1958; The Other Side of the Coin, 1965; The Zionist Connection I, 1978; The Zionist Connection II, 1982. Contributions: numerous journals. *Honours:* National Press Club Book Hons, 1982. *Address:* 800 25 NW, Washington, DC 20037, USA.

LILLINGTON, Kenneth (James); Author, Dramatist and Lecturer in English Literature (retd); b. 7 Sept. 1916, London, England. *Education:* St Dunstan's College; Wandsworth Training College. *Career:* Lecturer in English Literature, Brooklands Technical College, Weybridge, Surrey. *Publications:* The Devil's Grandson, 1954; Soapy and the Pharoah's Curse, 1957; Conjuror's Alibi, 1960; The Secret Arrow, 1960; Blue Murder, 1960; A Man Called Hughes, 1962; My Proud Beauty, 1963; First (and Second) Book of Classroom Plays, 1967–68; Fourth (and Seventh) Windmill Book of One-Act Plays, 1967–72; Cantaloup Crescent, 1970; Olaf and the Ogre, 1972; Nine Lives (ed.), 1977; For Better for Worse, 1979; Young Map of Morning, 1979; What Beckoning Ghost, 1983; Selkie, 1985; Full Moon, 1986. *Address:* 90 Wodeland Ave, Guildford, Surrey GU2 5LD, England.

LIM, Catherine; Singaporean writer, poet and educator; b. 23 March 1942, Kedah, Malaysia; m. 1964 (divorced 1980); one s. one d. *Education:* BA, English, University of Malaysia, 1963; MA, Applied Linguistics, 1979, PhD, 1987, National University of Singapore. *Career:* Education Officer, 1965–78; Deputy Dir of Curriculum Development, Institute of Singapore, Singapore, 1979–85; Lecturer in Sociolinguistics, Seameo Regional Centre, Singapore, 1989–90; Writer of English instructional texts, Singapore. *Publications:* Little Ironies: Stories of Singapore, 1978; Or Else, the Lightning God and Other Stories, 1980; The Serpent's Tooth (novel), 1982; They Do Return (short stories), 1983; Three Gifts from the Green Dragon and Other Stories from Chinese Literature, 1986; The Shadow of a Shadow of a Dream: Love Stories of Singapore, 1987; O Singapore!: Stories in Celebration, 1989; Deadline for Love and Other Stories, 1992; Love's Lonely Impulses (poems), 1992; The Woman's Book of Superlatives (short stories), 1993; The Best of Catherine Lim (short stories), 1993; The Bondmaid (novel), 1995; The Song of Silver Frond (novel), 2003. *Address:* 18 Leedon Heights, Suite 07-05, Farrer Road, 1026, Singapore.

LIM, Shirley Geok-lin; Prof. of English and Women's Studies, Author and Poet; b. 27 Dec. 1944, Malacca, Malaya; m. Dr Charles Bazerman, 27 Nov. 1972, one s. *Education:* BA, English Literature, 1967, MA Studies, 1967–69, University of Malaya; MA, 1971, PhD, 1973, English and American Literature, Brandeis University. *Career:* Lecturer and Teaching Asst, University of Malaya, 1967–69; Teaching Fellow, Queens College, CUNY, 1972–73; Asst Prof., Hostos Community College, CUNY, 1973–76; Lecturer, Universiti Sains, Penang, Malaysia, 1974; Assoc. Prof., SUNY at Westchester, 1976–90; Writer-in-Residence, University of Singapore, 1985, East West Center, Honolulu, 1988; Prof. of Asian American Studies, 1990–93, Prof. of English and Women's Studies, 1993–, University of California at Santa Barbara; Fulbright Distinguished Lecturer, Nanyang Technological University, 1996; Chair, Prof. of English, University of Hong Kong, 1999–; mem. American Studies; Asscn for Asian American Studies; Asscn for Commonwealth Languages and Literatures; MLA; Multi-Ethnic Literatures of the United States; National Women's Studies Asscn. *Publications:* Crossing the Peninsula and Other Poems, 1980; Another Country and Other Stories, 1982; No Man's Grove and Other Poems, 1985; Modern Secrets: New and Selected Poems, 1989; Nationalism and Literature: Literature in English from the Philippines and Singapore, 1993; Monsoon History: Selected Poems, 1994; Writing Southeast/Asia in English: Against the Grain, 1994; Life's Mysteries: The Best of Shirley Lim, 1995; Among the White Moon Faces: An Asian-American Memoir of Homelands, 1996; Two Dreams: Short Stories, 1997; What the Fortune Teller Didn't Say, 1998; Joss and Gold, 2001. Editor: The Forbidden Stitch: An Asian American Women's Anthology, 1989; Reading the Literatures of Asian America, 1992; One World of Literature, 1993; Asian American Literature: An Anthology, 2000. Contributions: anthologies, books, reviews, quarterlies, and journals. *Honours:* numerous grants and fellowships; Fulbright Scholarship, 1969–72; Commonwealth Poetry Prize, 1980; American Book Awards, 1990, 1997. *Address:* c/o English Dept, University of California at Santa Barbara, Santa Barbara, CA 93106, USA.

LIM, Suchen Christine; Teacher, Writer and Dramatist; b. 15 July 1948, Malaysia; two s. *Education:* National University of Singapore, 1970–73, 1984. *Publications:* Ricebowl, 1984; The Amah: A Portrait in Black and White (play), 1986; Gift From the Gods, 1990; Fistful of Colours, 1993; A Bit of Earth, 2000. Contributions: anthologies and journals. *Honours:* Shell Short Play Award, National University of Singapore, 1986; Singapore Literature Prize, 1992; Fulbright Award, 1996. *E-mail:* suchenchristinelim@hotmail.com.

LIMA, Robert; academic, writer, poet, dramatist, translator and editor; b. 7 Nov. 1935, Havana, Cuba; m. Sally Murphy 1964; two s. two d. *Education:* BA, English, Philosophy, and History, 1957, MA, Theatre and Drama, 1961, Villanova University; PhD, Romance Languages and Literatures, New York University, 1968. *Career:* Lecturer, Hunter College, CUNY, 1962–65; Asst Prof., 1965–69, Assoc. Prof., 1969–73, Prof. of Spanish and Comparative Literature, 1973–, Pennsylvania State University; mem. Poetry Society of America; International PEN, American Center; Institute for the Arts and Humanistic Studies, fellow emeritus; Academia Norteamericana de la Lengua Española, academician; Real Academia Española, corresponding mem. *Publications:* Reader's Encyclopedia of American Literature (co-ed.), revised edn, 1962; The Theatre of García Lorca, 1963; Borges the Labyrinth Maker (ed. and trans.), 1965; Ramón del Valle-Inclán, 1972; An Annotated Bibliography of Ramón del Valle-Inclán, 1972; Dos ensayos sobre teatro español de los veinte (co-author), 1984; Valle-Inclán: The Theatre of His Life, 1988; Savage Acts: Four Plays (ed. and trans.), 1993; Borges and the Esoteric (ed. and contributor), 1993; Valle-Inclán: El teatro de su vida, 1995; Dark Prisms: Occultism in Hispanic Drama, 1995; Homenaje a/Tribute to Martha T. Halsey (co-ed. and contributor), 1995; Ramón del Valle-Inclán, An Annotated Bibliography, Vol. I: The Works, 1999; The Alchemical Art of Leonora Carrington, Special Issue of Cauda Pavonis, Studies in Hermeticism (ed. and contributor), 2001; Tracking the Minotaur (criticism), 2003; The Dramatic World of Valle-Inclán, 2003. Poetry: Fathoms, 1981; The Olde Ground, 1985; Mayaland, 1992; Sardinia/Sardegna, 2001. Contributions: many books, reference works, anthologies, newspapers, reviews, quarterlies, and journals. *Honours:* Fellowships; Awards; Enxebre Ordre da Vieira, 2002; Distinguished Alumnus Medal, College of Arts and Sciences, Villanova University, 1999. *Address:* c/o Dept of Spanish, Italian, and Portuguese, Pennsylvania State University, N346 Burrowes Bldg, University Park, PA 16802, USA.

LIMONOV, Eduard; Russian writer and poet; b. (Eduard Veniaminovich Savenko), 22 Feb. 1943, Dzerzhinsk, Gorky Dist; m. 1st Yelena Limonova Shchapova 1971 (divorced); m. 2nd Natalia Medvedeva (divorced). *Career:* first wrote poetry at age of 15; in Kharkov 1965–67, moved to Moscow in 1967, worked as a tailor; left USSR 1974; settled in NY 1975; moved to Paris 1982; participant in Russian nationalist movt 1990–; returned to Russia 1991; Chair. Nat. Radical Party 1992–93; Chair. Nat. Bolshevik Party 1994–; arrested on terrorism and conspiracy charges 2001, sentenced by Saratov Oblast Court to four years' imprisonment for illegal acquisition and possession of arms April 2003, released June 2003; f. Russia without Putin movement Jan. 2004. *Publications include:* verse and prose in Kontinent, Ekho, Kovcheg, Apollon –1977 (in trans. in England, USA, Austria and Switzerland), It's Me – Eddie (novel) 1979, Russian (Russkoye) (verse) 1979, Diary of a Failure 1982, Teenager Savenko: Memoir of a Russian Punk 1983, The Young Scoundrel (memoir) 1986, The Death of Contemporary Heroes 1993, The Murder of the Sentry 1993, Selected Works (3 vols) 1999, The Exile (with Mark Ames and Matt Taibbi) 2000, My Political Biography; articles in Russian Communist and Nationalist newspapers 1989–.

LIN, Wallace (see Leong, Russell Charles).

LIN, Yanni; Hong Kong writer. *Publications include:* Ming yue 1985, Song jun he chu 1989, Qing chun zhi zang 1990, Wei wo er sheng 1990, Xue si gu ren ren si xue 1991.

LINACRE, Sir (John) Gordon Seymour, Kt, CBE, AFC, DFM, CCMI, FRSA; British newspaper executive; b. 23 Sept. 1920, Sheffield; m. Irene A. Gordon 1943; two d. *Education:* Firth Park Grammar School, Sheffield. *Career:* served RAF, rank of Squadron Leader 1939–46; journalistic appointments Sheffield Telegraph/Star 1937–47; Kemsley News Service 1947–50; Deputy Ed. Newcastle Journal 1950–56, Newcastle Evening Chronicle 1956–57; Ed. Sheffield Star 1958–61; Asst Gen. Man. Sheffield Newspapers Ltd 1961–63; Exec. Dir Thomson Regional Newspapers Ltd, London 1963–65; Man. Dir Yorkshire Post Newspapers Ltd 1965–83, Deputy Chair. 1981–83, Chair. 1983–90, Pres. 1990–; Dir United Newspapers PLC 1969–91, Deputy Chair. 1981–91, Chief Exec. 1983–88; Deputy Chair. Express Newspapers PLC 1985–88; also fmr Chair. United Provincial Newspapers Ltd, Sheffield Newspapers Ltd, Lancashire Evening Post Ltd, Northampton Mercury Co. Ltd, East Yorkshire Printers Ltd etc.; Dir Yorkshire TV 1969–90; Chair. Leeds Univ. Foundation 1989–2000; Chair. Chameleon TV Ltd 1994–; Chair. Opera North Ltd 1978–98, Pres. 1998–; many other professional and public appointments. *Honours:* Commendatore, Ordine al Merito della Repubblica Italiana 1973, Grand Ufficiale 1987; Kt Order of the White Rose, Finland 1987; Hon. LLD (Leeds) 1991. *Address:* White Windows, Staircase Lane, Bramhope, Leeds, LS16 9JD, England. *Telephone:* (113) 284-2751.

LINCOLN, Bruce (Kenneth); Prof. and Writer; b. 5 March 1948, Philadelphia, Pennsylvania, USA; m. Louise Gibson Hassett, 17 April 1971, two d. *Education:* BA, Haverford College, 1970; PhD, University of Chicago, 1976. *Career:* Asst Prof., 1976–79, Assoc. Prof., 1979–84, Prof. of Humanities, Religious Studies and South Asian Studies, and Chair, Religious Studies Programme, 1979–86, Prof. of Comparative Studies in Discourse and Society, 1986–93, University of Minnesota; Visiting Prof., Università degli Studi di Siena, 1984–85, University of Uppsala, 1985, Novosibirsk State Pedagogical Institute, 1991, University of Copenhagen 1998, Collège de France, 2003; Prof. of the History of Religions, Anthropology, Classics and Middle Eastern Studies, 1993–2000, Caroline E. Haskell Prof. of the History of Religions, 2000–, University of Chicago. *Publications:* Priests, Warriors, and Cattle: A Study in the Ecology of Religions, 1981; Emerging from the Chrysalis: Studies in Rituals of Women's Initiation, 1981; Religion, Rebellion, Revolution: An Interdisciplinary and Crosscultural Collection of Essays (ed.), 1985; Myth, Cosmos, and Society: Indo-European Themes of Creation and Destruction, 1986; Discourse and the Construction of Society: Comparative Studies of Myth, Ritual, and Classification, 1989; Death, War, and Sacrifice: Studies in Ideology and Practice, 1991; Authority: Construction and Corrosion, 1994; Theorizing Myth: Narrative, Ideology and Scholarship, 1999; Holy Terrors: Thinking about Religion after September 11, 2002. Contributions: Professional journals. *Honours:* ACLS Grant, 1979; Rockefeller Foundation Grant, 1981; Best New Book in History of Religion Citation, ACLS, 1981; Guggenheim Fellowship, 1982–83; National Endowment for the Humanities Grant, 1986; Outstanding Academic Book Citation, Choice, 1989; Scholar of the College, University of Minnesota, 1990–93; Excellence in the Study of Religion (Analytical-Descriptive Studies), American Acad. of Religion, 2000; Gordon J. Laing Prize, Univ. of Chicago Press, 2003. *Address:* 5735 S Dorchester Ave, Chicago, IL 60637, USA. *E-mail:* blincoln@midway.uchicago.edu.

LINDBLOM, Charles Edward; Prof. and Writer; b. 21 March 1917, Turlock, CA, USA; m. Rose K. Winther, 4 June 1942, two s. one d. *Education:* BA, Stanford University, 1937; PhD, University of Chicago, 1945. *Career:* Instructor, University of Minnesota, 1939–46; Asst Prof. to Prof., Yale University, 1946–; mem. American Political Science Asscn. *Publications:* Unions and Capitalism, 1949; Politics, Economics and Welfare, 1953; The Intelligence of Democracy, 1965; The Policy Making Process, 1968; Politics and Markets, 1977; Usable Knowledge, 1979; Democracy and the Market System, 1988; Inquiry and Change, 1990; The Market System, 2001. Contributions: professional journals. *Address:* 1230 Seville Rd, Santa Fe, NM 87505, USA.

LINDE, Nancy; College Lecturer, Writer and Poet; b. 21 Dec. 1949, New York, NY, USA; m. Stephan A. Khinoy 1980 (divorced 1990). *Education:* BA, 1971, MA, 1972, CUNY. *Career:* Lecturer, College of Staten Island, CUNY, 1978–85, 1988–; Mem., Board of Dirs, Woodstock Writers Worskhop, 1980–; mem. American Aikido Federation. *Publications:* The Orange Cat Bistro (novel), 1996. Other: Arabesque (screenplay), 1969. Contributions: periodicals. *Honours:* Poetry Prize, CUNY, 1970.

LINDEMAN, Jack; academic, poet and writer; b. 31 Dec. 1924, Philadelphia, Pennsylvania, USA. *Education:* West Chester State College, Pennsylvania, 1949; University of Pennsylvania, 1949; University of Mississippi, 1949–50; Villanova University, 1973. *Career:* Ed., Whetstone, 1955–61; Faculty, Lincoln University, Pennsylvania, 1963–64, Temple University, 1964–65; Faculty, 1969–85, Prof. Emeritus, 1985–, Kutztown University, Pennsylvania; Poetry Ed., Time Capsule, 1981–83; mem. Poets and Writers. *Publications:* Twenty-One Poems; The Conflict of Convictions; Appleseed Hollow, 2001. Contributions: anthologies, quarterlies, reviews, journals and magazines, including: Apocalypse; Bellowing Ark; Beloit Poetry Journal; Blueline; Blue Unicorn; California Poetry Quarterly; California Quarterly; Christian Science Monitor; Colorado Quarterly; Commonweal; Dickinson Review; Eureka Literary Magazine; Harper's Bazaar; High Plains Review; Hollins Critic; Kansas Quarterly; Massachusetts Review; Nation; New World Writing; Oregon East; Poetry; Prairie Schooner; Rocky Mountain Review; Slant; South Carolina Review; Southern Poetry Review; Southwest Review; Calapooya, Chiron Review, Poetry Motel, The Poet's Page, San Fernando Poetry Journal. *Address:* 133 S Franklin Street, Fleetwood, PA 19522-1810, USA.

LINDEY, Christine; Art Historian; b. 26 Aug. 1947, France. *Education:* BA, History of European Art, Courtauld Institute, University of London, 1973. *Publications:* Superrealist Painting and Sculpture, 1980; 20th Century Painting: Bonnard to Rothko, 1981; Art in the Cold War, 1990. *Address:* c/o West Herts College, Hempstead Rd, Watford WD1 3EZ, England.

LINDHOLM, Megan (see Ogden, Margaret (Astrid) Lindholm).

LINDNER, Carl Martin; Prof. of English and Poet; b. 31 Aug. 1940, New York, NY, USA; one s. one d. *Education:* BS, 1962, MA, 1965, City College, CUNY; PhD, University of Wisconsin at Madison, 1970. *Career:* Asst Prof., 1969–74, Assoc. Prof., 1974–87, Prof. of English, 1987–, University of Wisconsin at Parkside. *Publications:* Vampire, 1977; The Only Game, 1981; Shooting Baskets in a Dark Gymnasium, 1984; Angling into Light, 2001; Eat and Remember, 2001. Contributions: Reviews, journals, and periodicals. *Honours:* Wisconsin Arts Board Creative Writing Fellowship for Poetry, 1981; Stella C. Gray Teaching Excellence Awards, 1990–91, 2000–01; University of Wisconsin at Parkside Award for Excellence in Research and Creative Activity, 1996. *Address:* c/o Dept of English, University of Wisconsin at Parkside, PO Box 2000, Wood Rd, Kenosha, WI 53141, USA.

LINDOP, Grevel Charles Garrett; academic, poet, writer and editor; b. 6 Oct. 1948, Liverpool, England; m. Amanda Therese Marian Cox 1981; one s. two d. *Education:* Liverpool College; MA, BLitt, Wadham College, Oxford; PhD, Univ. of Manchester. *Career:* Lecturer, 1971–84, Senior Lecturer, 1984–93, Reader in English Literature, 1993–96, Prof. of Romantic and Early Victorian Studies, 1996–2001, Univ. of Manchester; Dir, Temenos Acad., and Ed., Temenos Acad. Review, 2000–03; mem. Temenos Acad., fellow; Buddhist; Wordsworth Trust, fellow. *Publications:* Poetry: Against the Sea, 1970; Fools' Paradise, 1977; Moon's Palette, 1984; Tourists, 1987; A Prismatic Toy, 1991; Selected Poems, 2000; Touching the Earth: Books I–IV, 2001. Prose: British Poetry Since 1960 (with Michael Schmidt), 1971; The Opium-Eater: A Life of Thomas De Quincey, 1981; A Literary Guide to the Lake District, 1993; The Path and the Palace: Reflections on the Nature of Poetry, 1996. Editor: Selected Poems, by Thomas Chatterton, 1971; Confessions of an English Opium-Eater and Other Writings, by Thomas De Quincey, 1985; The White Goddess, by Robert Graves, 1997; The Works of Thomas De Quincey, 21 vols, 2000–2003. Contributions: Poetry Nation Review; TLS; others. *Honours:* Lake District Book of the Year Award, 1993. *Address:* 216 Oswald Road, Chorton-cum-Hardy, Manchester, M21 9GW, England.

LINDQVIST, Sven, PhD; Swedish writer; b. 1932, Stockholm; m. Agneta Stark 1986; one s. one d. *Education:* Stockholm Univ. *Publications include:* China in Crisis 1965, The Shadow: Latin America Faces the Seventies 1972, Dig Where You Stand: How to Research a Job 1978, The Myth of Wu Tao-tzu 1979, Land and Power in South America 1979, Exterminate All the Brutes 1996, The Skull Measurer's Mistake 1997, Desert Divers 2000, A History of Bombing 2001, Bench Press 2003. *Honours:* Dr hc (Uppsala Univ.), Hon. Professorship from Swedish government. *Address:* c/o Granta Books, 2–3 Hanover Yard, Noel Road, London, N1 8BE, England. *Website:* www.svenlindqvist.net.

LINDSAY, (John) Maurice; poet, writer and editor; b. 21 July 1918, Glasgow, Scotland; m. 1946; one s. three d. *Education:* Glasgow Acad., 1928–36; Scottish National Acad. of Music, 1936–39. *Career:* Programme Controller, Border Television, 1959–62, Chief Interviewer, 1962–67; Dir, The Scottish Civic Trust, 1967–83; Ed., Scottish Review, 1975–85; Pres., Asscn for Scottish Literary Studies, 1982–83; Hon. Sec.-Gen., Europa Nostra, 1983–90; mem. Asscn of Scottish Literary Studies; Hon. Fellow, Royal Incorporation of Architects in Scotland. *Publications:* The Advancing Day, 1940; Predicament, 1942; No Crown for Laughter, 1943; The Enemies of Love: Poems, 1941–45, 1946; Selected Poems, 1947; At the Wood's Edge, 1950; Ode for St Andrew's Night and Other Poems, 1951; The Exiled Heart: Poems, 1941–56, 1957; Snow Warning and Other Poems, 1962; One Later Day and Other Poems, 1964; This Business of Living, 1971; Comings and Goings, 1971; Selected Poems, 1942–72, 1973; The Run from Life: More Poems, 1942–72, 1975; Walking Without an Overcoat: Poems, 1972–76, 1977; Collected Poems, two vols, 1979, 1993; A Net to Catch the Wind and Other Poems, 1981; The French Mosquitoe's Woman and Other Diversions, 1985; Requiem for a Sexual Athlete and Other Poems and Diversions, 1988; The Scottish Dog (with Joyce Lindsay), 1989; The Theatre and Opera Lover's Quotation Book (with Joyce Lindsay), 1993; News of the World: Last Poems, 1995; Speaking Likenesses, 1997; The Burns Quotation Book (with Joyce Lindsay), 1999; Worlds Apart (poems), 2000; Glasgow: Fabric of a City, 2000. Other: edns of poetry, plays, etc. *Honours:* Territorial Decoration; CBE, 1979; DLitt, Univ. of Glasgow, 1982. *Address:* Park House, 104 Dumbarton Road, Bowling, G60 5BB, Scotland.

LINDSEY, David L., BA; writer and editor; b. 6 Nov. 1944, Kingsville, Texas, USA; m. Joyce Lindsey. *Education:* University of North Texas. *Career:* freelance ed. 1972–80; founder, Heidelberg Publishers; Acquisitions Ed. for the Humanities, University of Texas Press. *Publications:* Mysteries: Black Gold, Red Death, 1983; A Cold Mind, 1983; Heat from Another Sun, 1984; Spiral, 1986; In the Lake of the Moon, 1988; Mercy, 1990; Body of Truth, 1992; An Absence of Light, 1994; Requiem for a Glass Heart, 1996; The Color of Night, 1999; Animosity, 2001. *Honours:* Bochumer Krimi Archiv Award, Best Suspense Novel of the Year, Germany, 1992. *Literary Agent:* Aaron Priest Literary Agency, 708 Third Avenue, 23rd Floor, New York, NY 10017, USA. *E-mail:* dlindsey1@austin.rr.com.

LINE, David (see Davidson, Lionel).

LINETT, Deena; Prof. of English and Writer; b. 30 Aug. 1938, Boston, Massachusetts, USA; two s. one d. *Education:* DEd, Rutgers University, 1982. *Career:* Prof. of English, Montclair State University; mem. PEN American Center; Poets and Writers; Acad. of American Poets; Poetry Society of America. *Publications:* On Common Ground, 1983; The Translator's Wife, 1986; Rare Earths: Poems, 2001. Contributions: journals. *Honours:* Yaddo Fellowships, 1981, 1985; PEN-Syndicated Fiction Project, 1990; Residency, Hawthornden Castle International Retreats for Writers, 1996, 2001. *Address:* c/o Dept of English, Montclair State University, Upper Montclair, NJ 07043, USA.

LINGARD, Joan Amelia; Author; b. 8 April 1932, Edinburgh, Scotland; three d. *Education:* General Teaching Diploma, Moray House Training

College, Edinburgh. *Career:* mem. Society of Authors in Scotland, chair., 1982–86; Scottish PEN, hon. vice-pres.; Dir, Edinburgh Book Festival. *Publications:* Children's Books: The Twelfth Day of July, 1970; Frying as Usual, 1971; Across the Barricades, 1972; Into Exile, 1973; The Clearance, 1974; A Proper Place, 1975; The Resettling, 1975; Hostages to Fortune, 1976; The Pilgrimage, 1976; The Reunion, 1977; The Gooseberry, 1978; The File on Fraulein Berg, 1980; Strangers in the House, 1981; The Winter Visitor, 1983; The Freedom Machine, 1986; The Guilty Party, 1987; Rags and Riches, 1988; Tug of War, 1989; Glad Rags, 1990; Between Two Worlds, 1991; Hands Off Our School!, 1992; Night Fires, 1993; Lizzie's Leaving, 1995; Dark Shadows, 1998; A Secret Place, 1998; Tom and the Tree House, 1998; The Egg Thieves, 1999; River Eyes, 2000; Natasha's Will, 2000; Me and My Shadow, 2001; Tortoise Trouble, 2002; Tell the Moon to Come Out, 2003. Fiction: Liam's Daughter, 1963; The Prevailing Wind, 1964; The Tide Comes In, 1966; The Headmaster, 1967; A Sort of Freedom, 1968; The Lord on Our Side, 1970; The Second Flowering of Emily Mountjoy, 1979; Greenyards, 1981; Sisters by Rite, 1984; Reasonable Doubts, 1986; The Women's House, 1989; After Colette, 1993; Lizzie's Leaving, 1995; Dreams of Love and Modest Glory, 1995; The Kiss, 2002. *Honours:* Scottish Arts Council Bursary, 1967–68; Preis der Leseratten ZDF, Germany, 1986; Buxtehuder Bulle, Germany, 1987; Scottish Arts Council Award, 1994; MBE, 1998. *Literary Agent:* David Higham Associates, 5–8 Lower John St, Golden Sq., London W1F 9HA, England.

LINGEMAN, Richard Roberts, BA; editor and writer; b. 2 Jan. 1931, Crawfordsville, IN, USA; m. Anthea Judy Nicholson 1965; one d. *Education:* Haverford College, Yale Law School, Columbia University Graduate School. *Career:* Exec. Ed., Monocle magazine, 1960–69, The Nation, 1978–; Assoc. Ed., Columnist, The New York Times Book Review, 1969–78; mem. Authors' Guild; National Book Critics Circle; New York Historical Society; PEN; Society of American Historians. *Publications:* Drugs from A to Z, 1969; Don't You Know There's a War On?, 1971; Small Town America, 1980; Theodore Dreiser: At the Gates of the City, 1871–1907, 1986; Theodore Dreiser: An American Journey, 1908–1945, 1990. *Honours:* Chicago Sun-Times Book of the Year Award, 1990.

LINKLATER, Magnus (Duncan); Journalist, Broadcaster and Writer; b. 21 Feb. 1942, Orkney, Scotland; m. Veronica Lyle, 1967, two s. one d. *Education:* University of Freiburg; Sorbonne, University of Paris; BA, Modern Languages, Trinity Hall, Cambridge. *Career:* Reporter, Daily Express, Manchester, 1965–66, London Evening Standard, 1966–67; Editorial positions, Evening Standard, 1967–69, Sunday Times, 1969–72, 1975–83, Sunday Times Colour Magazine, 1972–75; Managing Ed., News, The Observer, 1983–86; Ed., London Daily News, 1987, The Scotsman, 1988–94; Columnist, The Times, 1994–; Broadcaster, Radio Scotland, 1994–; Chair., Scottish Arts Council, 1996–. *Publications:* Hoax: The Inside Story of the Howard Hughes/Clifford Irving Affair (with Stephen Fay and Lewis Chester), 1972; Jeremy Thorpe: A Secret Life (with Lewis Chester and David May), 1979; Massacre: The Story of Glencoe, 1982; The Falklands War (with others), 1982; The Fourth Reich: Klaus Barbie and the Neo-Fascist Connection (with Isabel Hilton and Neal Ascherson), 1984; Not With Honour: Inside Story of the Westland Scandal (with David Leigh), 1986; For King and Conscience: The Life of John Graham of Claverhouse, Viscount Dundee (with Christian Hesketh), 1989; Anatomy of Scotland (co-ed.), 1992; Highland Wilderness (with Colin Prior), 1993; People in a Landscape, 1997. *Honours:* Hon. DArts, Napier University, 1994; Hon. LLD, University of Aberdeen, 1997; Hon. DLitt, Glasgow University, 2001; Fellow, Royal Society of Edinburgh. *Address:* 5 Drummond Pl., Edinburgh EH3 6PH, Scotland. *E-mail:* magnus.linklater@blueyonder.co.uk.

LINNEY, Romulus; Dramatist and Writer; b. 21 Sept. 1930, Philadelphia, Pennsylvania, USA; m. 1st Ann Leggett Sims 14 April 1963 (divorced 1966); one d.; m. 2nd Jane Andrews 14 Sept. 1967; one d. *Education:* AB, Oberlin College, 1953; MFA, Yale School of Drama, 1958; New School for Social Research, New York City, 1960. *Career:* Visiting Assoc. Prof. of Dramatic Arts, University of North Carolina at Chapel Hill, 1961; Dir of Fine Arts, North Carolina State College, Raleigh, 1962–64; Faculty, Manhattan School of Music, New York City, 1964–72; Visiting Prof., Columbia University, 1972–74, Connecticut College, 1979, University of Pennsylvania, 1979–86, Princeton University, 1982–85; mem. Actor's Equity Asscn; Authors' Guild; Authors League of America; Dirs Guild; PEN. *Publications:* Plays: The Sorrows of Frederick, 1966; Democracy and Esther, 1973; The Love Suicide at Schofield Barracks, 1973; Holy Ghosts, 1977; Old Man Joseph and His Family, 1978; El Hermano, 1981; The Captivity of Pixie Shedman, 1981; Childe Byron, 1981; F.M., 1984; The Death of King Philip, 1984; Sand Mountain, 1985; A Woman Without a Name, 1986; Pops, 1987; Heathen Valley, 1990; Three Poets, 1990; Unchanging Love, 1990; Juliet–Yancey–April Snow, 1990; Spain, 1993. Fiction: Heathen Valley, 1962; Slowly, by Thy Hand Unfurled, 1965; Jesus Tales, 1980. *Honours:* National Endowment for the Arts Grant, 1974; Guggenheim Fellowship, 1980; Obie Awards, 1980, 1990; Mishma Prize, 1981; American Acad. and Institute of Arts and Letters Award, 1984; Rockefeller Foundation Fellowship, 1986. *Address:* 35 Claremont Ave, 9N, New York, NY 10027, USA.

LINSCOTT, Gillian; Journalist and Writer; b. 27 Sept. 1944, Windsor, England; m. Tony Geraghty, 18 June 1988. *Education:* Somerville College, Oxford, 1963–66; Degree, English Language and Literature, University of Oxford, 1966. *Career:* mem. Society of Authors; CWA. *Publications:* A Healthy Body, 1984; Murder Makes Tracks, 1985; Knightfall, 1986; A Whiff of Sulphur, 1987; Unknown Hand, 1988; Murder, I Presume, 1990; Sister Beneath the Sheet, 1991; Hanging on the Wire, 1992; Stage Fright, 1993; Widow's Peak, 1994; Crown Witness, 1995; Dead Man's Music, 1996; Dance on Blood, 1998; Absent Friends, 1999; The Perfect Daughter, 2000; Dead Man Riding, 2002; Blood on the Wood, 2003. *Honours:* Ellis Peters Historical Dagger, CWA, 2000; Herodotus Award, Historical Mystery Appreciation Society. *Address:* Wood View, Hope Under Dinmore, Leominster, Herefordshire HR6 0PP, England.

LIPMAN, Elinor; Writer; b. 16 Oct. 1950, Lowell, Massachusetts, USA; m. Robert M. Austin, 29 July 1975, one s. *Education:* AB, Simmons College, Boston, 1972. *Career:* Lecturer, Smith College, 1997–; mem. Authors' Guild. *Publications:* Into Love and Out Again (short stories), 1987; Then She Found Me, 1990; The Way Men Act, 1992; Isabel's Bed, 1995; The Inn at Lake Devine, 1999; The Ladies' Man, 1999; The Dearly Departed, 2001; The Pursuit of Alice Thrift, 2003. Contributions: Yankee; Playgirl; Ascent; Ladies Home Journal; Cosmopolitan; Self; New England; Living; Redstart; Wigwag. *Honours:* Distinguished Story Citations, Best American Short Stories, 1984, 1985. *Address:* 67 Winterberry Lane, Northampton, MA 01060, USA.

LIPPY, Charles (Howard); Distinguished Prof. of Religious Studies, Writer and Ed.; b. 2 Dec. 1943, Binghamton, NY, USA. *Education:* BA, Dickinson College, 1965; MDiv, Union Theological Seminary, 1968; MA, 1970, PhD, 1972, Princeton Univ. *Career:* Asst Prof., Oberlin College, 1972–74, West Virginia Wesleyan College, 1975–76; Visiting Assoc. Prof., Miami Univ., 1974–75; Asst Prof., 1976–80, Assoc. Prof., 1980–85, Prof. of History and Religion, 1985–88, Prof. of Religion, 1988–94, Clemson Univ.; Visiting Scholar, Univ. of North Carolina at Chapel Hill, 1984; Visiting Prof. of Religion, 1990–91, Visiting Research Scholar, 2000–01, Emory Univ.; LeRoy A Martin Distinguished Prof. of Religion Studies, Univ. of Tennessee at Chattanooga, 1994–; mem. American Acad. of Religion; American Catholic Historical Asscn; American Society of Church History; American Studies Asscn; Organization of American Historians; Society for the Scientific Study of Religion; South Carolina Acad. of Religion, pres., 1981–82; United Methodist Historical Society. *Publications:* Seasonable Revolutionary: The Mind of Charles Chauncy, 1981; A Bibliography of Religion in the South, 1985; Religious Periodicals of the United States: Academic and Scholarly Journals (ed.), 1986; Encyclopedia of the American Religious Experience (ed. with Peter W. Williams), three vols, 1988; Twentieth-Century Shapers of American Popular Religion (ed.), 1989; The Christadelphians in North America, 1989; Christianity Comes to the Americas, 1492–1776 (with Robert Choquette and Stafford Poole), 1992; Religion in South Carolina (ed.), 1993; Being Religious, American Style: A History of Popular Religiosity in the United States, 1994; Popular Religious Magazines of the United States (ed. with P. Mark Fackler), 1995; Modern American Popular Religion: A Critical Assessment and Annotated Bibliography, 1996; The Evangelicals: A Historical, Thematic, and Biographical Guide (with Robert H. Krapohl), 1999; Pluralism Comes of Age: American Religion in the Twentieth Century, 2000; Where Rivers Run and Mountains Rise (ed. with John L. Topolewski and Nancy Topolewski), 2002. Contributions: reference works, scholarly books and journals. *Honours:* several grants; Outstanding Academic Book Citations, Choice, 1987, 1989, 2001; Outstanding Reference Work Citation, American Library Asscn, 1988. *Address:* 711 Hurricane Creek Rd, Chattanooga, TN 37421, USA.

LIPSET, Seymour Martin; Sociologist, Political Scientist, Prof., Writer and Ed.; b. 18 March 1922, New York, NY, USA; m. 1st Elsie Braun, 26 Dec. 1944, deceased Feb. 1987, two s. one d.; m. 2nd Sydnee Guyer, 29 July 1990. *Education:* BS, City College, CUNY, 1943; PhD, Columbia University, 1949. *Career:* Asst Prof., 1948–50, Prof. of Sociology, 1956–66, Dir, Institute of International Studies, 1962–66, University of California at Berkeley; Henry Ford Visiting Research Prof., Yale University, 1960–61; Visiting Prof. of Social Relations and Government, 1965–66, Prof. of Government and Sociology, 1966–75, Harvard University; Senior Fellow, Hoover Institution, 1975–; Prof. of Political Science and Sociology, 1975–92, Caroline S. G. Munro Prof., 1981–92, Stanford University; Co-Ed., Public Opinion magazine, 1977–89, International Journal of Public Opinion Research, 1989–; Fulbright 40th Anniversary Distinguished Lecturer, 1987; Visiting Scholar, Russell Sage Foundation, 1988–89; Hazel Prof. of Public Policy, George Mason University, 1990–; mem. American Acad. of Arts and Sciences; American Philosophical Society; American Political Science Asscn, pres., 1981–82; American Sociological Asscn, pres., 1992–93; International Political Science Asscn; International Sociological Asscn; National Acad. of Sciences; Sociological Research Asscn, pres., 1985; World Asscn of Public Opinion Research, pres., 1984–86. *Publications:* Social Mobility in Industrial Society (with R. Bendix), 1959; Political Man, 1960; The First New Nation, 1963; Revolution and Counter Revolution, 1968; The Politics of Unreason (with Earl Raab), 1970; Rebellion in the University, 1972; The Divided Academy, 1975; Education and Politics at Harvard (with David Riesman), 1975; Dialogues on American Politics (with I. L. Horowitz), 1978; The Confidence Gap (with William Schneider), 1983; Consensus and Confilct, 1987; American Pluralism and the Jewish Community, 1990; Continental Divide: The Institutions and Values of the United States and Canada, 1990; The Educational Background of American Jews, 1994; Jews and the New American Scene (with Earl Raab), 1995; The Encyclopedia of

Democracy (ed.), 4 vols, 1995; American Exceptionalism: A Double-Edged Sword, 1996; Democracy in Asia and Africa, 1998; Democracy in Europe and the Americas, 1998. Contributions: many scholarly books and journals. *Honours:* 125th Anniversary Alumni Medal, City College, CUNY, 1963; Gunnar Myrdal Prize, 1970; Tod Harris Medal, 1971; Center for Advanced Study in Behavioral Sciences Fellow, 1971–72; M. B. Rawson Award, 1986; Leon Epstein Prize, American Political Science Asscn, 1989; Marshall Sklare Award, 1993; Woodrow Wilson Center for International Scholars Fellow, 1995–96; various hon. doctorates. *Address:* c/o Hoover Institution, Stanford University, Stanford, CA 94305, USA.

LIPSEY, David Lawrence; Journalist and Writer; b. 21 April 1948, Cheltenham, Gloucestershire, England; m. Margaret Robson, 1982, one d. *Education:* Magdalen College, Oxford. *Career:* Research Asst, General and Municipal Workers' Union, 1970–72; Special Adviser to Anthony Crossland, MP, 1972–77; Staff, Prime Minister, 1977–79; Journalist, 1979–80, Ed., 1986–88, New Society; Political Staff, 1980–82, Economics Ed., 1982–86, The Sunday Times; Co-Founder and Deputy Ed., The Sunday Correspondent, 1988–90; Assoc. Ed., The Times, 1990–92; Journalist, 1992–, Political Ed., 1994–, The Economist; mem. Fabian Society, chair., 1981–82. *Publications:* Labour and Land, 1972; The Socialist Agenda: Crosland's Legacy (ed. with Dick Leonard), 1981; Making Government Work, 1982; The Name of the Rose, 1992. *Address:* 44 Drakefield Rd, London SW17 8RP, England.

LIPSKEROV, Dmitry; writer and playwright; b. USSR. *Career:* co-f., Debut Prize 2001. *Publications:* Gotlib's Space; The Forty Years of Chanchzhoe (novel), 2001; Relatives (novel), 2001. *Address:* c/o EKSMO Publishing House, Klari Tsetkin ul., d.18/5, Moscow 127299, Russia. *E-mail:* info@eksmo.ru.

LISLE, Holly; Writer; b. Oct. 1960, Salem, Ohio, USA. *Education:* Assoc. Degree in Nursing, Richmond Community College, 1982. *Career:* mem. SFWA. *Publications:* Arhel series: Fire in the Mist, 1992, Bones of the Past, 1993, Mind of the Magic, 1995. Minerva Wakes, 1993; When the Bough Breaks (co-author), 1993; The Rose Sea (co-author), 1994; Mall, Mayhem and Magic, 1995; Glenraven (co-author), 1996. Devil's Point series: Sympathy for the Devil, 1996, The Devil and Dan Cooley (co-author), 1996, Hell on High (co-author), 1997; Hunting the Corrigan's Blood, 1997. Bard's Tale series: Thunder of the Captains (co-author), 1996, Wrath of the Princes (co-author), 1997, Curse of the Black Heron, in press; Glenraven: In the Shadow of the Rift (co-author), in press. Contributions: Short stories to anthologies including Women of War; The Enchanter Reborn; Chicks in Chainmail. *Honours:* Compton Crook Award for Best First Novel, 1993. *Literary Agent:* Scovil, Chichak, Galen Literary Agency, New York, USA. *Address:* c/o Russell Galen, Scovil, Chichak, Galen Literary Agency, 381 Park Ave S, Suite 1020, New York, NY 10016, USA.

LISNYANSKAYA, Inna Lvovna; Russian writer and poet; b. 24 June 1928, Baku; m. Semen I. Lipkin; one d. *Career:* began writing poetry at age 10; first works published 1948; poems published in Moscow literary journal Novyi mir (New World) and Iunost (Youth) 1957–; in internal exile 1979–89, following contribs to literary almanac Metropole; resgnd from Union of Writers 1980 (membership restored 1989). *Publications include:* This Happened to Me 1957, Faithfulness 1958, Not Simply Love 1963, At First Hand 1966, Grape Light 1978, Rains and Mirrors 1983, Verse 1970–83, 1984, On the Edge of Sleep 1984, The Circle 1985, Airy Layer 1990, Poetry 1991, The Music of Akhmatova's 'Poem without a Hero' 1991, After Everything 1994, The Lonely Gift 1995, The Box with a Triple Bottom (Study on Akhmatova's Poem Without the Hero) 1995, Selected Poetry 2000; contribsto literary journals including Novyi mir, Oktiabr, Znamia. *Address:* Usievicha Street 8, Apt 16, 125315 Moscow, Russia. *Telephone:* (095) 155-75-98.

LISTER, Richard Percival; Author, Poet and Painter; b. 23 Nov. 1914, Nottingham, England; m. Ione Mary Wynniatt-Husey 24 June 1985. *Education:* BSc, Manchester Univ. *Publications:* Fiction: The Way Backwards, 1950; The Oyster and the Torpedo, 1951; Rebecca Redfern, 1953; The Rhyme and the Reason, 1963; The Questing Beast, 1965; One Short Summer, 1974. Poetry: The Idle Demon, 1958; The Albatross, 1986. Travel: A Journey in Lapland, 1965; Turkey Observed, 1967; Glimpses of a Planet, 1997. Biography: The Secret History of Genghis Khan, 1969; Marco Polo's Travels, 1976; The Travels of Herodotus, 1979. Short Story Collections: Nine Legends, 1991; Two Northern Stories, 1996. Contributions: Punch; New Yorker; Atlantic Monthly. *Honours:* FRSL, 1970. *Address:* Flat I, 42 St James Gdns, London W11 4RQ, England.

LITT, Toby; British writer; b. 1968, Ampthill, Bedfordshire, England. *Education:* Worcester Coll., Oxford, Univ. of East Anglia. *Career:* lived in Prague 1990–93; mem. English PEN. *Publications:* Adventures in Capitalism (short stories) 1996, Beatniks (novel) 1997, Corpsing (novel) 2000, Deadkidsongs (novel) 2001, Exhibitionism (short stories) 2002, Finding Myself (novel) 2003, Ghost Story 2004; contrib. to anthologies, including Class Work 1995, Neonlit 1998, Fortune Hotel 1998, Girlboy 1999, New Writing 8 1999, All Hail the New Puritans 2000, The Mammoth Book of Best New Erotica 2000, New English Book of Internet Stories 2000, Time Out Book of London Stories 2 2000, New Writing 9 2000; contrib. to The Idler, The Erotic Review, Interzone, Ambit, Concrete, Passport, The Guardian, Big Issue, Modern Painters, Art Quarterly. *Honours:* Curtis Brown Fellowship 1995. *Literary Agent:* The Marsh Agency, 11 Dover Street, London, W1S 4LJ, England. *Telephone:* (20) 7399-2800. *Fax:* (20) 7399-2801. *Website:* www.marsh-agency.co.uk. *Address:* c/o Hamish Hamilton, Penguin Books Ltd, 80 Strand, London, WC2R 0RL, England. *Website:* www.tobylitt.com.

LITTELL, Robert; writer; b. 1935, New York, NY, USA. *Career:* journalist Newsweek 1964. *Publications:* Read America First 1968, If Israel Lost the War (with Richard Z. Cheznoff and Edward Klein) 1969, The Czech Black Book 1969, The Defection of A. J. Lewinter 1973, Sweet Reason 1974, The October Circle 1976, Mother Russia 1978, The Debriefing 1979, The Amateur 1981, The Sisters 1985, The Revolutionist 1988, The Once and Future Spy 1990, An Agent in Place 1991, The Visiting Professor 1994, Walking Back the Cat 1996, For the Future of Israel (with Shimon Peres) 1998, The Company 2002. *Address:* c/o The Overlook Press, One Overlook Drive, Woodstock, NY 12498, USA.

LITTLE, Charles Eugene; Writer; b. 1 March 1931, Los Angeles, CA, USA; m. Ila Dawson. *Education:* BA, Creative Writing, Wesleyan University, 1955. *Career:* Editorial Dir, Open Space Action Magazine, 1968–69; Ed.-in-Chief, American Land Forum, 1980–86; Books Ed., Wilderness Magazine, 1987–97; Consulting Ed., Johns Hopkins University Press, 1989–. *Publications:* Challenge of the Land, 1969; Space for Survival (with J. G. Mitchell), 1971; A Town is Saved... (with photos by M. Mort), 1973; The American Cropland Crisis (with W. Fletcher), 1980; Green Fields Forever, 1987; Louis Bromfield at Malabar (ed.), 1988; Greenways for America, 1990; Hope for the Land, 1992; Discover America: The Smithsonian Book of the National Parks, 1995; The Dying of the Trees, 1995. Contributions: Magazines and journals. *Address:* 33 Calle del Norte, Placitas, NM 87043, USA.

LITTLE, Geraldine Clinton; Poet and Writer; b. 20 Sept. 1925, Portstewart, Ireland; m. Robert Knox Little, 26 Sept. 1953, three s. *Education:* BA, Goddard College, 1971; MA, Trenton State College, 1976. *Career:* Adjunct Prof. of English; mem. Haiku Society of America; PEN; Poetry Society of America. *Publications:* Hakugai: Poem from a Concentration Camp, 1983; Seasons in Space, 1983; A Well-Tuned Harp, 1988; Beyond the Boxwood Comb, 1988; Heloise and Abelard: A Verse Play, 1989; Star-Mapped, 1989. Contributions: journals. *Honours:* Associated Writing Programs' Anniversary Award, 1986; Pablo Neruda Award, 1989; Grants. *Address:* 1200 Campus Dr., Mt Holly, NJ 08060, USA.

LITVINOFF, Emanuel; Writer and Dramatist; b. 30 June 1915, London, England. *Career:* Dir, Contemporary Jewish Library, London, 1958–88; Founder, Jews in Eastern Europe, journal, London. *Publications:* Conscripts: A Symphonic Declaration, 1941; The Untried Soldier, 1942; A Crown for Cain, 1948; The Lost Europeans, 1959; The Man Next Door, 1968; Journey Through a Small Planet, 1972; Notes for a Survivor, 1973; A Death Out of Season, 1974; Soviet Anti-Semitism: The Paris Trial (ed.), 1974; Blood on the Snow, 1975; The Face of Terror, 1978; The Penguin Book of Jewish Short Stories (ed.), 1979; Falls the Shadow, 1983. *Literary Agent:* David Higham Associates, 5–8 Lower John St, Golden Sq., London W1F 9HA, England.

LIU, Timothy; poet, writer and academic; b. 2 Oct. 1965, San Jose, CA, USA. *Education:* BA, Brigham Young University, 1989; MA, University of Houston, 1991. *Career:* Asst Prof., Cornell College, 1994–98, William Paterson University, 1998–; mem. Associated Writing Programs; PEN American Center. *Publications:* A Zipper of Haze, 1988; Vox Angelica: Poems, 1992; Burnt Offerings, 1995; Say Goodnight, 1998; Word of Mouth: An Anthology of Gay American Poets, 2000; Hard Evidence, 2001. Contributions: Reviews, quarterlies and journals. *Honours:* Norma Farber First Book Award, Poetry Society of America, 1992; John Ciardi Fellowship, Bread Loaf Writers' Conference, 1993; Holloway Lecturer, University of California at Berkeley, 1997; Judge's Choice Award, Bumbershoot Festival, 1998. *Address:* c/o William Paterson University, 300 Pompton Road, Wayne, NJ 07470, USA.

LIU XINWU; Chinese writer; b. 4 June 1942, Chengdu, Sichuan Prov.; m. Lu Xiaoge 1970; one s. *Education:* Beijing Teachers' Coll. *Career:* school teacher 1961–76; with Beijing Publishing House 1976–80; lived in Beijing 1950–; Ed.-in-Chief People's Literature 1987–89; professional writer 1980–; mem. Standing Cttee, China All Nation Youth Fed. –1992; mem. Council, Chinese Writers' Asscn. *Publications:* short stories: Class Counsellor (Nationwide Short Story Prize) 1977, The Position of Love 1978, I Love Every Piece of Green Leaves (Nationwide Short Story Prize) 1979, Black Walls 1982, A Scanning over the May 19th Accident 1985; novels: Ruyi (As You Wish) 1980, Overpass 1981, Drum Tower (Mao Dun Literature Prize) 1984; Liu Xinwu Collected Works (eight vols) 1993. *Address:* 8 Building No. 1404, Anding Menwai Dongheyan, Beijing 100011, People's Republic of China. *Telephone:* 4213965 (Home).

LIVELY, Penelope Margaret, OBE, CBE, FRSL; British writer; b. 17 March 1933, Cairo, Egypt; m. Jack Lively 1957; one s. one d. *Education:* St Anne's Coll. Oxford. *Career:* mem. Bd British Library 1993–99, Bd British Council 1998–; mem. Soc. of Authors, PEN. *Publications:* juvenile fiction: Astercote 1970, The Whispering Knights 1971, The Wild Hunt of Hagworthy 1971, The Driftway 1972, Going Back 1973, The Ghost of Thomas Kempe (Carnegie Medal) 1973, The House in Norham Gardens 1974, Boy Without a Name 1975, Fanny's Sister 1976, The Stained Glass Window 1976, A

Stitch in Time (Whitbread Award) 1976, Fanny and the Monsters 1978, The Voyage of QV66 1978, Fanny and the Battle of Potter's Piece 1980, The Revenge of Samuel Stokes 1981, Uninvited Ghosts and Other Stories 1984, Dragon Trouble, Debbie and the Little Devil 1984, A House Inside Out 1987, The Cat, the Crow and the Banyan Tree 1994, Heatwave 1996, Beyond the Blue Mountains: Stories 1997, Spiderweb 1998, In Search of a Homeland: The Story of the Aeneid 2001; fiction: The Road to Lichfield 1977, Nothing Missing but the Samovar and Other Stories (Southern Arts Literature Prize) 1978, Treasures of Time (Nat. Book Award) 1979, Judgement Day 1980, Next to Nature, Art 1982, Perfect Happiness 1983, Corruption and Other Stories 1984, According to Mark 1984, Moon Tiger (Booker-McConnell Prize) 1986, Pack of Cards: Stories 1978–86 1986, Passing On 1989, City of the Mind 1991, Cleopatra's Sister 1993, The Photograph 2003; non-fiction: The Presence of the Past: An Introduction to Landscape History 1976, Oleander, Jacaranda (autobiog.) 1994, A House Unlocked (memoir) 2001; other: television and radio scripts; contrib. to numerous journals and magazines. *Honours:* Hon. Fellow Swansea Univ. 2002; Hon. DLitt (Tufts Univ.) 1993, (Warwick) 1998.

LIVINGS, Henry; Writer and Playwright; b. 20 Sept. 1929, Prestwich, Lancashire, England. *Education:* Liverpool University, 1945–47. *Publications:* Stop it Whoever You Are, 1961; Nil Caborundum, 1963; Kelly's Eye and Other Plays, 1965; Eh?, 1965; The Little Mrs Foster Show, 1967; Good Grief!, 1968; Honour and Offer, 1969; The Ffinest Ffamily in the Land, 1970; Pongo Plays 1–6, 1971; The Jockey Drives Late Nights, 1972; Six More Pongo Plays, 1974; Jonah, 1975; That the Medals and the Baton Be Put in View: The Story of a Village Band 1875–1975, 1975; Cinderella, 1976; Pennine Tales, 1983; Flying Eggs and Things: More Pennine Tales, 1986; The Rough Side of the Boards, 1994. *Address:* 49 Grains Rd, Delph, Oldham OL3 5DS, England.

LJUNGGREN, Olof, LLBMDhc; Swedish publisher and business executive; b. 5 Jan. 1933, Eskilstuna; m. 1st Lena Carlsöö; m. 2nd Margreth Bäcklund; three s. *Education:* Univ. of Stockholm. *Career:* Sec. Tidningarnas Arbetsgivareförening (Swedish Newspaper Employers' Asscn) 1959–62, Pres. and CEO 1962–66; Deputy Pres. and CEO Allers Förlag AB 1967–72, Pres. and CEO 1972–74; Pres. and CEO Svenska Dagbladet 1974–78; Pres. and CEO Svenska Arbetsgivareföreningen (Swedish Employers' Confed.) 1978–89; Chair. of Bd Askild & Kärnekull Förlag AB 1971–74, Nord Artel AB 1971–78, Centralförbundet Folk och Försvar (Vice-Chair. 1978–83) 1983–86, Richard Hägglöf Fondkommission AB 1984–87, Svenska Dagbladet 1989–91, Liber AB 1990–98 (Vice-Chair. 1998–), Intentia AB 1994–, AMF 1995–, AFA 1995–2001, Addum AB 1996–99, Consolis AB Oy 1997–; mem. Bd, SPP 1978–93, Investor 1989–92, Providentia 1989–92, Alfa Laval 1989–92, Trygg Hansa 1990–95, and numerous other bds. *Honours:* Kt Commdr Order of the White Rose of Finland 1982, The King's Medal of the 12th Dimension with the Ribbon of the Order of the Seraphim 1987, Kommendörskorset av Den Kgl. Norske Fortjenstorden; Hon. MD. *Address:* Skeppargatan 7, 114 52 Stockholm, Sweden. *Telephone:* (707) 472346 (Office); (8) 6678785 (Home). *Fax:* (8) 6678785 (Home). *E-mail:* olof.ljunggren2@comhem.se (Home).

LLEWELLYN, Sam; Author; b. 2 Aug. 1948, Isles of Scilly; m. Karen Wallace, 15 Feb. 1975, two s. *Education:* BA, 1970, MA, 1973, St Catherine's College, Oxford. *Career:* Ed., Picador, 1973–76; Senior Ed., McClelland and Stewart, 1976–79; Pres., Publisher, Arch Books, 1982–; Captain, SY Lucille, 1993–; mem. Society of Authors; CPRE; British Acad.; Cruising Asscn. *Publications:* Hell Bay, 1980; The Worst Journey in the Midlands, 1983; Dead Reckoning, 1987; Blood Orange, 1988; Death Roll, 1989; Pig in the Middle, 1989; Deadeye, 1990; Blood Knot, 1991; Riptide, 1992; Clawhammer, 1993; Maelstrom, 1994; The Rope School, 1994; The Magic Boathouse, 1994; The Iron Hotel, 1996; Storm Force from Navarone, 1996; The Polecat Cafe, 1998; The Shadow in the Sands, 1998; Thunderbolt from Navarone, 1998; The Sea Garden, 2000; Wonderdog, 2000; The Malpas Legacy, 2001. Contributions: The Times; The Telegraph. *Honours:* Premio di Letteratura per l'Infanzia, 1992. *Literary Agent:* Curtis Brown Ltd, Haymarket House, 28–29 Haymarket, London, SW1Y 4SP, England. *Telephone:* (20) 7393-4400. *Fax:* (20) 7393-4401. *E-mail:* info@curtisbrown.co.uk. *Website:* www.curtisbrown.co.uk.

LLOYD, Sir Geoffrey Ernest Richard, BA, MA, PhD; academic and writer; b. 25 Jan. 1933, London, England; m. Janet Elizabeth Lloyd 1956; three s. *Education:* King's College, Cambridge. *Career:* Fellow, 1957, Senior Tutor, 1969–73, King's College, Cambridge; Asst Lecturer in Classics, 1965–67, Lecturer in Classics, 1967–74, Reader in Ancient Philosophy and Science, 1974–83, Prof. of Ancient Philosophy and Science, 1983–2000, University of Cambridge; Bonsall Prof., Stanford University, 1981; Sather Prof., University of California at Berkeley, 1984; Visiting Prof., Beijing University and Acad. of Sciences, 1987; Master, Darwin College, 1989–2000; Prof. at Large, Cornell University, 1990–96; mem. British Acad., fellow; East Asian History of Science Trust, chair., 1992–2002; International Acad. of the History of Science, 1997. *Publications:* Polarity and Analogy, 1966; Early Greek Science: Thales to Aristotle, 1970; Greek Science After Aristotle, 1973; Magic, Reason and Experience, 1979; Science, Folklore and Ideology, 1983; Science and Morality in Greco-Roman Antiquity, 1985; The Revolution of Wisdom, 1987; Demystifying Mentalities, 1990; Methods and Problems in Greek Science, 1991; Adversaries and Authorities, 1996; Aristotelian Explorations, 1996; The Way and the Word (with N. Sivin), 2002, The Ambitions of Curiosity 2002, In the Grip of Disease, Studies in the Greek Imagination 2003. Editor: Hippocratic Writings, 1978; Aristotle on Mind and Senses (with G. E. L. Owen), 1978; Le Savoir Grec (with Jacques Brunschwig), 1996; Greek Thought, 2000. Contributions: books and journals. *Honours:* Hon. Fellow King's College Cambridge 1990, Darwin College Cambridge 2000; Hon. Foreign Mem. American Acad. of Arts and Sciences 1995Hon. LittD (Athens) 2003Knighted 1997Sarton Medal 1987. *Address:* 2 Prospect Row, Cambridge CB1 1DU, England.

LLOYD, Kathleen Annie, (Kathleen Conlon, Kate North); Writer; b. 4 Jan. 1943, Southport, England; m. Frank Lloyd 3 Aug. 1962 (divorced); one s. *Education:* BA, King's College, Durham Univ. *Career:* mem. Society of Authors. *Publications:* Apollo's Summer Look, 1968; Tomorrow's Fortune, 1971; My Father's House, 1972; A Twisted Skein, 1975; A Move in the Game, 1979; A Forgotten Season, 1980; Consequences, 1981; The Best of Friends, 1984; Face Values, 1985; Distant Relations, 1989; Unfinished Business, 1990. As Kate North: Land of My Dreams, 1997; Gollancz, 1997. Contributions: Atlantic Review; Cosmopolitan; Woman's Journal; Woman; Woman's Own. *Address:* 26A Brighton Rd, Birkdale, Southport PR8 4DD, England.

LLOYD, Trevor Owen; Emeritus Prof. of History and Writer; b. 30 July 1934, London, England. *Education:* BA, Merton College, Oxford, 1956; MA, DPhil, Nuffield College, Oxford, 1959. *Career:* Lecturer, 1959–63, Asst Prof., 1963–67, Assoc. Prof., 1967–73, Prof., 1973–97, Dept of History, University of Toronto; mem. William Morris Society; Victorian Studies Asscn of Ontario; Royal Historical Society. *Publications:* Canada in World Affairs 1957–59, 1968; The General Election of 1880, 1968; Suffragettes International, 1971; The Growth of Parliamentary Democracy in Britain, 1973; Empire, Welfare State, Europe: English History 1906–1992, 1993, revised edn as Empire, Welfare State, Europe: The United Kingdom 1906–2001, 2002; The British Empire 1558–1995, 1996; Empire: The History of the British Empire, 2001. Contributions: various journals. *Honours:* Guggenheim Fellowship, 1978–79. *Address:* Dept of History, University of Toronto, Toronto M5S 1A1, Canada.

LLOYD-JONES, Sir (Peter) Hugh Jefferd, MA (Oxon); classical scholar and writer; b. 21 Sept. 1922, St Peter Port, Jersey, Channel Islands; m. 1st Frances Hedley 1953 (divorced 1981); two s. one d.; m. 2nd Mary R. Lefkowitz 1982. *Education:* Christ Church, Oxford. *Career:* mem. British Acad., fellow; Acad. of Athens, corresponding mem.; American Acad. of Arts and Sciences; American Philosophical Society; Rheinisch-Westfälische Akademie; Bayerische Akademie der Wissenschaften; Accademia di Lettere, Archeologia e Belle Arti, Naples. *Publications:* The Justice of Zeus, 1971; Blood for the Ghosts, 1982; Supplementum Hellenisticum (with P. J. Parsons), 1983; Sophoclis Fabulae (with N. G. Wilson), 1990; Sophoclea (with N. G. Wilson), 1990; Academic Papers, 2 vols, 1990; Greek in a Cold Climate, 1991; Sophocles (ed. and trans.), 3 vols, 1994–96; Sophocles: Second Thoughts (with N. G. Wilson), 1997. Contributions: numerous periodicals. *Honours:* Hon. DHL, University of Chicago, 1970; Hon. PhD, University of Tel-Aviv, 1984; Knighted, 1989; Hon. DPhil, University of Thessalonica, 1999. *Address:* 15 West Riding, Wellesley, MA 02482, USA.

LO LIYONG, Taban, BA, MFA; novelist, poet and essayist; b. 1939, Kajokaji, Sudan. *Education:* Nat. Teachers' Coll., Kampala, Uganda, Howard Univ., Washington, DC and Univ. of Iowa, USA. *Career:* taught at univs in Kenya, Tanzania, Papua New Guinea, Sudan, Japan and Australia; currently Prof. of Literature, Univ. of Venda, South Africa. *Publications:* poetry: Frantz Fanon's Uneven Ribs: With Poems More and More 1971, Another Nigger Dead 1972, Ballads of Underdevelopment: Poems and Thoughts 1974, To Still a Passion 1977, The Cows of Shambat 1992, Carrying Knowledge up a Palm Tree 1997, Homage to Onyame 1998; prose: Fixions 1969, Eating Chiefs: Lwo Culture from Lolwe to Malkal 1970, Uniformed Man: Essays 1977, Thirteen Offensives Against our Enemies: Essays 1977, Meditations 1978, Images of Women in Folktales and Short Stories of Africa, Another Last Word 1990. *Address:* University of Venda, Private bag X5050, Thohoyandou 0950, Northern Province, South Africa.

LO MONACO, Sheryl (Virginia); Writer; b. 30 Aug. 1949, California, USA; one s. two d. *Education:* AA, Orange Coast College, Costa Mesa, CA, 1969–73; BA, California State University, Fullerton, 1973–76. *Career:* mem. National Writers' Asscn; International Women's Writing Guild; International Writers' Union; Sisters in Crime. *Publications:* Contributions: Futures Magazine (short stories). *Address:* Casella Postale 111, 90041 Balestrate (PA), Italy. *E-mail:* lomonacov@usa.net.

LOADES, David Michael; Prof. of History (retd) and Writer; b. 19 Jan. 1934, Cambridge, England; m. Judith Anne Atkins, 18 April 1987. *Education:* BA, 1958, MA, PhD, 1961, DLitt, 1981, Emmanuel College, Cambridge. *Career:* Lecturer in Political Science, University of St Andrews, 1961–63; Lecturer in History, University of Durham, 1963–70; Senior Lecturer, 1970–77, Reader, 1977–80, Prof. of History, 1980–96, University College of North Wales, Bangor; Dir, British Acad. John Foxe Project, 1993; mem. FRHistS; Society of Antiquaries of London, fellow. *Publications:* Two Tudor Conspiracies, 1965; The Oxford Martyrs, 1970; The Reign of Mary Tudor, 1979; The Tudor Court, 1986; Mary Tudor: A Life, 1989; The Tudor Navy, 1992; John Dudley: Duke of Northumberland, 1996; Tudor Government, 1997; England's Maritime Empire, 2000; Elizabeth: The Golden Reign of Gloriana, 2003; Elizabeth I, 2003. Editor: The Papers of George Wyatt, 1968;

The End of Strife, 1984; Faith and Identity, 1990; John Foxe and the English Reformation, 1997; John Foxe: An Historical Perspective, 1999; The Anthony Roll of Henry VIII (with C. S. Knighton), 2000; Letters from the Mary Rose (with C. S. Knighton), 2002; The Chronicles of the Tudor Queens, 2002. Contributions: journals. *Address:* The Cottage, Priory Lane, Burford, Oxon OX18 4SG, England.

LOBO, Tatiana; Chilean writer; b. 1939, Puerto Montt. *Publications:* novels: Asalto al paraiso (trans. as Assault on Paradise) 1993, Calypso 1996; short stories: Tiempo de Claveles 1989; non-fiction: Entre Dios y el Diablo: Mujeres de la colonia: crónicas 1993, Negros y Blancos: Todo Mezclado (with Mauricio Meléndez) 1997. *Address:* c/o Curbstone Press, 321 Jackson Street, Willimantic, CT 06226-1738, USA. *E-mail:* info@curbstone.org. *Website:* www.curbstone.org.

LOCHHEAD, Douglas (Grant); Poet, Writer and Prof. of Canadian Studies Emeritus; b. 25 March 1922, Guelph, Ontario, Canada; m. Jean St Clair 17 Sept. 1949 (deceased); two d. *Education:* BA, 1943, BLS, 1951, McGill University; MA, University of Toronto, 1947. *Career:* Librarian, Victoria College, BC, 1951–52, Cornell University, Ithaca, New York, 1952–53, Dalhousie University, Halifax, NS, 1953–60, York University, Toronto, 1960–63; Librarian and Fellow, Massey College, 1963–75; Prof. of English, University College, University of Toronto, 1963–75; Davidson Prof. of Canadian Studies and Dir of the Centre for Canadian Studies, 1975–87, Prof. Emeritus, 1987–, Mount Allison University, Sackville, New Brunswick; Visiting Prof., University of Edinburgh, 1983–84; mem. League of Canadian Poets, life mem.; Bibliographical Society of Canada. *Publications:* The Heart is Fire, 1959; It is all Around, 1960; Millwood Road Poems, 1970; The Full Furnace: Collected Poems, 1975; A & E, 1980; Battle Sequence, 1980; High Marsh Road, 1980; The Panic Field, 1984; Tiger in the Skull: New and Selected Poems, 1959–85, 1986; Dykelands, 1989; Upper Cape Poems, 1989; Black Festival: A Long Poem, 1991; Homage to Henry Alline & Other Poems, 1992; Breakfast at Mel's and Other Poems of Love and Places, 1997; All Things Do Continue (poems), 1997; Cape Enragé: Poems on a Raised Beach, 2000; Weathers: New and Selected Poems, 2002; Orkney: October Diary, 2002: Midgic: A Place, A Poem, 2003. Contributions: various publications. *Honours:* Golden Dog Award, 1974; Fellow, Royal Society of Canada, 1976; Hon. DLitt, St Mary's University, 1987; Hon. LLD, Dalhousie University, 1987. *Address:* 9 Quarry Lane, Sackville, NB E4L 4G3, Canada.

LOCHHEAD, Liz; Poet, Playwright, Screenwriter and Teacher; b. 26 Dec. 1947, Motherwell, Scotland. *Education:* Diploma, Glasgow School of Art, 1970. *Career:* Art teacher in Glasgow and Bristol schools; Lecturer, Univ. of Glasgow. *Publications:* Poetry: Memo for Spring, 1972; The Grimm Sisters, 1981; Dreaming of Frankenstein and Collected Poems, 1984; True Confessions and New Clichés, 1985; Bagpipe Muzak, 1991; Cuba/Dog House (with Gina Moxley), 2000; The Colour of Black and White: Poems 1984–2003, 2003. Plays: Blood and Ice, 1982; Silver Service, 1984; Dracula (adaptation), 1989; Mary Queen of Scots Got Her Head Chopped Off, 1989; Moliere's Tartuffe (Scots trans. in rhyming couplets); Perfect Days, 1998; Medea (adaptation), 2000; Misery Guts (adaptation), 2002. Unpublished Plays: Disgusting Objects; Rosaleen's Baby; Red Hot Shoes; Same Difference; Shanghaied; Fancy You Minding That; Sweet Nothings; True Confessions; Complete Alternative of the World, Part One. Other: Now and Then (screenplay), 1972; Damages (BBC TV drama). Contributions: anthologies, incl.: Penguin Modern Poets Vols 3 and 4; Shouting It Out, 1995. *Honours:* BBC Scotland Prize, 1971; Scottish Arts Council Award, 1972. *Address:* c/o Nick Hern Books Ltd, The Glasshouse, 49a Goldhawk Rd, London W12 8QP, England.

LOCKE, Hubert Gaylord; Prof. of Public Service and Writer; b. 30 April 1934, Detroit, Michigan, USA; two d. *Education:* BA, Latin and Greek, Wayne State University, 1955; BD, New Testament Studies, University of Chicago, 1959; MA, Comparative Literature, University of Michigan, 1961. *Career:* Asst Dir, 1957–62, Dir, 1967–70, Office of Religious Affairs, Adjunct Asst Prof. of Urban Education, 1970–72, Wayne State University; Assoc. Prof. of Urban Studies and Dean, College of Public Affairs and Community Service, University of Nebraska, 1972–75; Prof., 1976–, Assoc. Dean, College of Arts and Sciences, 1976–77, Vice-Provost for Academic Affairs, 1977–82, Dean, Graduate School of Public Affairs, 1982–87, John and Marguerite Corbally Prof. of Public Service, 1996–, University of Washington, Seattle; mem. Commission on State Trial Courts, State of Washington; Institute of European/Asian Studies, board of governors; Interfaith Housing Inc, board of dirs; National Acad. of Public Administration, board of trustees. *Publications:* The Detroit Riot of 1967, 1969; The Care and Feeding of White Liberals, 1970; The German Church Struggle and the Holocaust (ed. with Franklin H. Littell), 1974; The Church Confronts the Nazis (ed.), 1984; Exile in the Fatherland: The Prison Letters of Martin Niemöller (ed.), 1986; The Barmen Confession: Papers from the Seattle Assembly (ed.), 1986; The Black Antisemitism Controversy: Views of Black Protestants (ed.), 1992; Learning From History, 2000; Groping for God in God-Forsaken Places 2003. Contributions: books and professional journals. *Honours:* Michigan Bar Asscn Liberty Bell Award, 1967; Hon. Doctor of Divinity, Payne Theological Seminary, 1968, Chicago Theological Seminary, 1971; Hon. Doctor of Humane Letters, University of Akron, 1971, University of Nebraska, 1992, University of Bridgeport, 1997; Distinguished Alumni Award, Wayne State University, 1979. *Address:* c/o 2801 First Avenue 609, Seattle, WA 98121, USA.

LOCKE, Ralph P(aul); Musicologist, Teacher and Writer; b. 9 March 1949, Boston, Massachusetts, USA; m. Lona M. Farhi, 26 May 1979, two d. *Education:* BA, cum laude, Music, Harvard University, 1970; MA, 1974, PhD, 1980, History and Theory of Music, University of Chicago. *Career:* Faculty, Eastman School of Music, Rochester, New York, 1975–; Senior Ed., Eastman Studies in Music; Editorial Board Mem., Univ. of Rochester Press, Journal of Musicological Research, H-mus TXT, Ad Parnassum; mem. American Musicological Society; International Musicological Society; Sonneck Society for American Music. *Publications:* Music, Musicians, and the Saint-Simonians, 1986; Cultivating Music in America: Women Patrons and Activists since 1860, 1997. Contributions: reference books and professional journals. *Honours:* Best Article Citation, Music Library Asscn, 1980; Galler Dissertation Prize, 1981; ASCAP-Deems Taylor Awards, 1992, 1996, 1999. *Address:* c/o Dept of Musicology, Eastman School of Music, 26 Gibbs St, Rochester, NY 14604, USA.

LOCKE, Robert Howard, (Clayton Bess); Librarian, Playwright and Author; b. 30 Dec. 1944, Vallejo, CA, USA. *Education:* BA, Speech Arts, California State University, Chico, 1965; MA, Drama, San Francisco State University, 1967; MS, Library Science, Simmons College, Boston, 1973. *Publications:* As Clayton Bess: Story for a Black Night, 1982; The Truth About the Moon, 1984; Big Man and the Burn-Out, 1985; Tracks, 1986; The Mayday Rampage, 1993. Plays: The Dolly; Play; Rose Jewel and Harmony; On Daddy's Birthday; Murder and Edna Redrum; Premiere. *Honours:* Best First Novel, Commonwealth Club of California, 1982; Best Book for Young Adults, American Library Asscn, 1987.

LOCKERBIE, D(onald) Bruce; Scholar and Writer; b. 25 Aug. 1935, Capreol, Ontario, Canada. *Education:* AB, 1956, MA, 1963, New York University. *Career:* Scholar-in-Residence, Stony Brook School, New York, 1957–91; Visiting Consultant at American Schools in Asia and Africa, 1974; Visiting Lecturer/Consultant to American universities. *Publications:* Billy Sunday, 1965; Patriarchs and Prophets, 1969; Hawthorne, 1970; Melville, 1970; Twain, 1970; Major American Authors, 1970; Success in Writing (with L. Westdahl), 1970; Purposeful Writing, 1972; The Way They Should Go, 1972; The Liberating Word, 1974; The Cosmic Center: The Apostles' Creed, 1977; A Man under Orders: Lt Gen William K. Harrison, 1979; Who Educates Your Child?, 1980; The Timeless Moment, 1980; Asking Questions, 1980; Fatherlove, 1981; In Peril on the Sea, 1984; The Christian, the Arts and Truth, 1985; Thinking and Acting Like a Christian, 1989; Take Heart (with L. Lockerbie), 1990; College: Getting In and Staying In (with D. Fonseca), 1990; A Passion for Learning, 1994; From Candy Sales to Committed Donors, 1996; Dismissing God, 1998. *Honours:* DHL, Eastern College, 1985, Taylor University 1993. *Address:* PO Box 26, Stony Brook, NY 11790, USA.

LOCKLEY, John; GP and Writer; b. 10 Feb. 1948, Sale, Cheshire, England; m. Mavis June Watt, 5 Aug. 1972, two s. one d. *Education:* Gonville and Caius Colleges, Cambridge, 1966–69; MA, 1975; MB BChir (Cantab), 1973. *Career:* House Surgeon, Royal London Hospital, 1972; Vocational Training Course for General Practice, Colchester, 1973; General Practitioner, Ampthill, Bedfordshire, England, 1976–; Ed., Torus, 2000; mem. Society of Authors. *Publications:* The Complete BBC Computer User Handbook, 1988; Acorn to PC: Changing from DFS and ADFS to DOS, 1990; A Practical Workbook for the Depressed Christian, 1991; Headaches – A Comprehensive Guide to Relieving Headaches and Migraine, 1993; After the Fire, 1994; After the Fire II – A Still Small Voice, 1996; After the Fire III – Chronicles, 1998. Contributions: many articles to General Practitioner, Daily Telegraph, Daily Mail and Guardian; Doctor Magazine. *Honours:* Medeconomics GP Writer of the Year, 1989. *Address:* 107 Flitwick Rd, Ampthill, Bedfordshire MK45 2NT, England.

LOCKLIN, Gerald (Ivan); Author, Poet, Dramatist, Literary Critic and Prof. of English; b. 17 Feb. 1941, Rochester, NY, USA; m. 1st Mary Alice Keefe; one s. two d.; m. 2nd Maureen McNicholas; one s. one d.; m. 3rd Barbara Curry; one s. one d. *Education:* BA, St John Fisher College, 1961; MA, 1963, PhD, 1964, University of Arizona. *Career:* Instructor in English, California State College at Los Angeles, 1964–65; Asst Prof. to Prof. of English, California State University at Long Beach, 1965–; mem. Associated Writing Programs; e. e. cummings Society; Hemingway Society; PEN; Western Literature Asscn. *Publications:* Sunset Beach, 1967; The Toad Poems, 1970; Poop and Other Poems, 1973; Toad's Europe, 1973; Locked In, 1973; Son of Poop, 1974; Tarzan and Shane Meet the Toad (with others), 1975; The Chase: A Novel, 1976; The Criminal Mentality, 1976; The Four-Day Week and Other Stories, 1977; Pronouncing Borges, 1977; A Weekend on Canada, 1979; The Cure: A Novel for Speed Readers, 1979; Two Summer Sequences, 1979; Two Weeks on Mr Stanford's Farm, 1980; The Last of Toad, 1980; Two for the Seesaw and One for the Road, 1980; Scenes from a Second Adolescence, 1981; A Clear and Present Danger to Society, 1981; By Land, Sea, and Air, 1982; Why Turn a Perfectly Good Toad into a Prince?, 1983; Fear and Paternity in the Pauma Valley, 1984; The Ensenada Poems (with Ray Zepada), 1984; The Case of the Missing Blue Volkswagen, 1984; The Phantom of the Johnny Carson Show, 1984; We Lose L.A. (with Ray Zepeda), 1985; The English Mini-Tour, 1987; Gringo and Other Poems, 1987; Gerald Haslam, 1987; A Constituency of Dunces, 1988; Children of a Lesser Demagogue, 1988; On the Rack, 1988; Lost and found, 1989; The Treasure of the Sierra Faulkner, 1989; The Gold Rush and Other Stories, 1989; The Rochester Trip, 1990; The Conference, 1990; The Illegitimate Son of Mr Madman, 1991; The Firebird Poems, 1992; A New Geography of Poets (ed. with Edward Field and Charles Stetler), 1992; The Old Mongoose and Other Poems, 1994; Big Man on Canvas, 1994; The Cabo Conference, 1995; Charles Bukowski: A Sure Bet, 1996; The Pittsburgh Poems, 1996; The Macao/Hong Kong Trip, 1996; The Hospital Poems, 1998; Two Novellas (with Donna Hilbert), 1998; Down and Out: A Novel for Adults, 1999; Hemingway Colloquium: The Poet Goes to Cuba, 1999; Candy Bars, 2000; A Simpler Time, a Simpler Place: Three Mid-Century Stories, 2000; The Iceberg Theory, 2000; Four Jazz Women, 2000; Art and Life, 2000; The Sixth Jazz Chapbook, 2001; Familiarities, 2001; The Life Force Poems, 2002; The Mystical Exercycle, 2002; The Pocket Book, 2003; Henry's Gift, 2003; Takes on Bill Evans, 2003; More Takes on Bill Evans, 2003; The Dorset Poems, 2003. Contributions: periodicals. *Address:* c/o Dept of English, California State University at Long Beach, Long Beach, CA 90840, USA.

LOCKRIDGE, Ernest Hugh; Prof. and Novelist; b. 28 Nov. 1938, Bloomington, IN, USA; m. Laurel Richardson, 12 Dec. 1981, two s. three d. *Education:* BA, Indiana University, 1960; MA, 1961, PhD, 1964, Yale University. *Career:* Prof., Yale University, 1963–71, Ohio State University, 1971–. *Publications:* Fiction: Hartspring Blows His Mind, 1968; Prince Elmo's Fire, 1974; Flying Elbows, 1975. Non-Fiction: 20th Century Studies of the Great Gatsby, 1968. Contributions: Professional journals. *Honours:* Book-of-the-Month Club Selection, 1974; Distinguished Teaching Award, Ohio State University, 1985. *Address:* 143 W South St, Worthington, OH 43085, USA.

LOCKWOOD, Lewis (Henry); Musicologist, Prof. of Music, Writer and Ed.; b. 16 Dec. 1930, New York, NY, USA. *Education:* BA, Queens College, CUNY, 1952; MFA, 1955, PhD, 1960, Princeton University. *Career:* Faculty, 1958–65, Assoc. Prof., 1965–68, Prof., 1968–80, Chair., Dept of Music, 1970–73, Princeton University; Ed., Journal of the American Musicological Society, 1963–66, Beethoven Forum, 1991–; Prof. of Music, 1980–2002, Chair., Dept of Music, 1988–90, Harvard University; Gen. Ed., Studies in Musical Genesis and Structure, 1984–98; mem. American Acad. of Arts and Sciences; American Musicological Society, pres., 1987–88, hon. mem., 1993–. *Publications:* Music in Renaissance Ferrara, 1400–1505, 1984; Beethoven Essays: Studies in Honor of Elliot Forbes (co-ed.), 1984; Essays in Musicology: A Tribute to Alvin Johnson (co-ed.), 1990; Beethoven: Studies in the Creative Process, 1992; Beethoven: The Music and the Life, 2003. Contributions: scholarly books and journals. *Honours:* National Endowment for the Humanities Senior Fellowships, 1973–74, 1984–85; Guggenheim Fellowship, 1977–78; Hon. Doctorates, Università degli Studi, Ferrara, 1991, New England Conservatory of Music, 1998; ASCAP–Deems Taylor Award, 1993; Festschrift published in his honour, 1997. *Address:* c/o Dept of Music, Harvard University, Cambridge, MA 02138, USA. *E-mail:* llockw@fas.harvard.edu.

LODGE, David John, CBE, BA, MA, PhD; writer and academic; b. 28 Jan. 1935, London, England; m. Mary Frances Jacob 1959; two s. one d. *Education:* University College London, University of Birmingham. *Career:* Asst, British Council, London, 1959–60; Asst Lecturer, 1960–62, Lecturer, 1963–71, Senior Lecturer, 1971–73, Reader, 1973–76, Prof. of Modern English Literature, 1976–87, Hon. Prof. of Modern English Literature, 1987–2000, University of Birmingham; Visiting Assoc. Prof., University of California at Berkeley, 1969; Henfield Writing Fellow, University of East Anglia, 1977; Fellow, University College London, 1982; Hon. Prof., Goldsmiths College, London, 1992. *Publications:* Fiction: The Picturegoers, 1960; Ginger, You're Barmy, 1962; The British Museum is Falling Down, 1965; Out of the Shelter, 1970; Changing Places: A Tale of Two Campuses, 1975; How Far Can You Go?, 1980, US edn as Souls and Bodies, 1982; Small World: An Academic Romance, 1984; Nice Work, 1988; Paradise News, 1991; Therapy, 1995; Home Truths: A Novella, 1999; Thinks..., 2001; Author, Author 2004. Non-Fiction: Language of Fiction, 1966; Graham Greene, 1966; The Novelist at the Crossroads and Other Essays on Fiction and Criticism, 1971; Evelyn Waugh, 1971; The Modes of Modern Writing: Metaphor, Metonymy and the Typology of Modern Literature, 1977; Modernism, Antimodernism, and Postmodernism, 1977; Working with Structuralism: Essays and Reviews on Nineteenth- and Twentieth-Century Literature, 1981; Write On: Occasional Essays, 1986; After Bakhtin: Essays on Fiction and Criticism, 1990; The Art of Fiction: Illustrated from Classic and Modern Texts, 1992; The Practice of Writing: Essays, Lectures, Reviews, and a Diary, 1996; Consciousness and the Novel, 2002. Editor: Twentieth-Century Literary Criticism: A Reader, 1972; Modern Criticism and Theory: A Reader, 1988. Contributions: periodicals and television. *Honours:* Yorkshire Post Fiction Prize, 1975; Hawthornden Prize, 1976; Whitbread Award for the Novel and for Book of the Year, 1980; Sunday Express Book of the Year, 1988; RTS Award for Best Drama Serial, 1990; Chevalier, Ordre des Arts et des Lettres, 1997. *Address:* c/o Department of English, University of Birmingham, Birmingham B15 2TT, England.

LOEWE, Michael (Arthur Nathan); Lecturer in Chinese Studies (retd) and Writer; b. 2 Nov. 1922, Oxford, England. *Education:* Magdalen College, Oxford, 1941; BA, 1951, PhD, 1962, University of London; MA, University of Cambridge, 1963. *Career:* Lecturer in History of the Far East, University of London, 1956–63; Lecturer in Chinese Studies, University of Cambridge, 1963–90. *Publications:* Imperial China: The Historical Background to the Modern Age, 1966; Records of Han Administration, 2 vols, 1967; Everyday Life in Early Imperial China During the Han Period, 202 BC–AD 220, 1968; Crisis and Conflict in Han China, 104 B.C. to A.D. 9, 1974; Ancient Cosmologies (ed. with Carmen Blacker), 1975; Ways to Paradise: The Chinese Quest for Immortality, 1979; Divination and Oracles (ed. with Carmen Blacker), 1981; Chinese Ideas of Life and Death: Faith, Myth, and Reason in the Han Period (202 B.C.-A.D. 220), 1982; The Ch'in and Han Empires, 221 B.C.-A.D. 220, Vol. 1 of The Cambridge History of China (ed. with Denis Twichett), 1986; The Pride That Was China, 1990; Early Chinese Texts: A Bibliographical Guide, 1993; Divination, Mythology and Monarchy in Han China, 1994; The Cambridge History of Ancient China (ed. with E. Shaughnessy), 1999; A Biographical Dictionary of the Qin, Former Han and Xin Periods, 2000. Contributions: scholarly publications. *Honours:* Fellow, Society of Antiquaries, 1972; Fellow, Clare Hall, 1968–90; Foreign Hon. Mem., American Acad. of Arts and Sciences, 2002. *Address:* Willow House, Grantchester, Cambridge CB3 9NF, England.

LÖFGREN, Lars, PhD; Swedish theatre, film and television director, playwright and poet; b. 6 Sept. 1935, The Arctic Circle; m. Anna-Karin Gillberg 1963; one s. two d. *Education:* Gustavus Adolphus Coll., USA, Stanford Univ., USA, Sorbonne, France, Uppsala Univ., Sweden. *Career:* Dir Royal Dramatic Theatre of Sweden 1985–97, Nordic Museum 1997–2001. *Publications:* various plays, filmscripts, TV scripts, poetry, novels, svensk teater — Artistry of the Swedish Theater 2003. *Honours:* Royal Prize of Swedish Acad. 1996. *Address:* The Office of the Marshal of the Court of the Royal Palace, 11130 Stockholm (Office); sjötullsbacken 27, 11525 Stockholm Sweden. *Telephone:* (8) 402–6000 (Office); (8) 855822 (Home). *E-mail:* lars.lofgren@po7.se (Home).

LOGAN, Mark (see Nicole, Christopher (Robin)).

LOGUE, Christopher John; British writer and poet; b. 23 Nov. 1926, Southsea; m. Rosemary Hill 1985. *Education:* Prior Park Coll., Bath and Portsmouth Grammar School. *Screenplays:* The End of Arthur's Marriage 1965, Savage Messiah 1972, Crusoe (based on Defoe's novel, with Walon Green) 1989. *Recordings:* Red Bird (poetry and jazz, with Tony Kinsey and Bill Le Sage) 1960, Songs from the Establishment 1962, The Death of Patroclus 1963, Audiologue (recordings 1958–98) 2001. *Film roles:* Swinburne in Ken Russell's Dante's Inferno 1966, John Ball in John Irvin's The Peasant's Revolt 1969, Cardinal Richelieu in Ken Russell's The Devils 1970; also TV and stage roles. *Publications:* poetry: Wand & Quadrant 1953, Devil, Maggot & Son 1954, The Weakdream Sonnets 1955, The Man Who Told His Love: 20 Poems Based on P. Neruda's 'Los Cantos d'amores' 1958, Songs 1959, Songs from 'The Lily-White Boys' 1960, Patrocleia 1962, Pax 1967, The Establishment Songs 1966, The Girls 1969, New Numbers 1969, Abecedary 1977, Ode to the Dodo 1981, War Music 1981, Fluff 1984, Kings 1991, The Husbands 1994, Selected Poems 1996, Prince Charming: A Memoir 1999, Logue's Homer: War Music 2001, All Day Permanent Red 2003; plays: The Trial of Cob & Leach 1959, The Lily-White Boys (with Harry Cookson) 1959, Antigone 1961, The Seven Deadly Sins 1986; other: Lust, by Count Plamiro Vicarion (ed.) 1955, Count Palmiro Vicarion's Book of Limericks (ed.) 1959, The Arrival of the Poet in the City: A Treatment for a Film 1964, True Stories 1966, The Children's Book of Comic Verse (ed.) 1979, The Bumper Book of True Stories 1980, London in Verse (ed.) 1982, Sweet & Sour: An Anthology of Comic Verse (ed.) 1983, The Oxford Book of Pseuds (ed.) 1983, The Children's Book of Children's Rhymes (ed.) 1986; contrib. to Private Eye, The Times, Sunday Times. *Honours:* First Wilfred Owen Award for Poetry 1998, Civil List Pension for Services to Literature 2002. *Address:* 41 Camberwell Grove, London, SE5 8JA, England.

LOMAS, Herbert; Poet, Critic and Trans; b. 7 Feb. 1924, Yorkshire, England; m. Mary Marshall Phelps, 29 June 1968, one s. one d. *Education:* BA, 1949, MA, 1952, University of Liverpool. *Career:* Teacher, Spetsai, Greece, 1950–51; Lecturer, Senior Lecturer, University of Helsinki, 1952–65; Senior Lecturer, 1966–72, Principal Lecturer, 1972–82, Borough Road College; mem. Society of Authors; Finnish Acad.; Finnish Literary Society; Pres., Suffolk Poetry Society, 1999–. *Publications:* Chimpanzees are Blameless Creatures, 1969; Who Needs Money?, 1972; Private and Confidential, 1974; Public Footpath, 1981; Fire in the Garden, 1984; Letters in the Dark, 1986; Trouble, 1992; Selected Poems, 1995; A Useless Passion, 1998; The Vale of Todmorden, 2003. Translations: Territorial Song, 1991; Contemporary Finnish Poetry, 1991; Fugue, 1992; Wings of Hope and Daring, 1992; The Eyes of the Fingertips are Opening, 1993; Black and Red, 1993; Narcissus in Winter, 1994; The Year of the Hare, 1994; Two Sequences for Kuhmo, 1994; In Wandering Hall, 1995; Selected Poems, Eeva-Lisa Manner, 1997; Three Finnish Poets, 1999; A Tenant Here, 1999; Not Before Sundown, 2003. Contributions: Reviews, journals, and magazines. *Honours:* Prize, Guinness Poetry Competition; Cholmondeley Award; Poetry Book Society Biennial Trans. Award; Knight First Class, Order of the White Rose of Finland, 1991: Finnish State Prize for Trans., 1991. *Address:* North Gable, 30 Crag Path, Aldeburgh, Suffolk IP15 5BS, England. *E-mail:* herbert@hlomas.freeserve.co.uk.

LOMAX, Marion (see Bolam, Robyn).

LOMBINO, Salvatore (see Hunter, Evan).

LOMPERIS, Timothy John; American academic and writer; b. 6 March 1947, Guntur, India; m. Ana Maria Turner 1976; one s. one d. *Education:* AB, magna cum laude, History and Political Science, Augustana College, 1969; MA, School of Advanced International Studies, Johns Hopkins University, 1975; MA, Political Science, 1978, PhD, Political Science, 1981, Duke University. *Career:* Instructor and Asst Prof., Louisiana State University, 1980–84; Visiting Asst Prof., 1983–84, Asst Prof. of Political Science, 1984–94, Duke University; John M. Olin Postdoctoral Fellow, Harvard University, 1985–86; Fellow, Woodrow Wilson International Center for Scholars, Washington, DC, 1988–89; Assoc. Prof. of Political Science, United States Military Acad., West Point, New York, 1994–96; Prof. of Political Science and Chair., Dept of Political Science, St Louis University, 1996–. *Publications:* The War Everyone Lost–and Won: America's Intervention in Viet Nam's Twin Struggles, 1984; Hindu Influence on Greek Philosophy: The Odyssey of the Soul from the Upanishads to Plato, 1984; 'Reading the Wind': The Literature of the Vietnam War, 1987; From People's War to People's Rule: Insurgency, Intervention, and the Lessons of Vietnam, 1996. Contributions: scholarly journals. *Honours:* United States Army Bronze Star, 1973; Vietnamese Army Staff Medal First Class, 1973; Presidential Outstanding Community Achievement Award for Vietnam Era Veterans, Chapel Hill, NC, 1979; Helen Dwight Reid Award, American Political Science Asscn, 1982; Civilian Superior Service Award, United States Military Acad., West Point, New York, 1996. *Address:* c/o Department of Political Science, St Louis University, St Louis, MO 63103, USA.

LONDON, Joan; Australian writer; b. 1948, Perth, WA. *Publications:* Sister Ships (short stories) (Age Book of the Year, Western Australia Week Literary Award) 1986, Letter to Constantine (short stories) (Steele Rudd Award, West Australian Premier's Award for Fiction) 1994, Gilgamesh (novel) (Age Book of the Year for Fiction 2002) 2001, The New Dark Age (short stories) 2004. *Address:* c/o Pan Macmillan Australia, Level 18, St Martin's Tower, 31 Market Street, Sydney, NSW 2000, Australia.

LONG, Robert Emmet, BA, MA, PhD; literary critic and writer; b. 7 June 1934, Oswego, NY, USA. *Education:* Columbia Univ., Syracuse Univ. *Career:* Instructor, SUNY 1962–64; Asst Prof., Queens Coll., CUNY 1968–71. *Publications:* The Achieving of the Great Gatsby: F. Scott Fitzgerald 1920–25, 1979; The Great Succession: Henry James and the Legacy of Hawthorne, 1979; Henry James: The Early Novels, 1983; John O'Hara, 1983; Nathanael West, 1985; Barbara Pym, 1986; James Thurber, 1988; James Fenimore Cooper, 1990; The Films of Merchant Ivory, 1991; Ingmar Bergman: Film and Stage, 1994; Broadway, the Golden Years: Jerome Robbins and the Great Choreographers and Dirs, 1940 to the Present, 2001; John Huston: Interviews, 2001; George Cukor; Interviews, 2001. Editor: American Education, 1985; Drugs and American Society, 1985; Vietnam, Ten Years After, 1986; Mexico, 1986; The Farm Crisis, 1987; The Problem of Waste Disposal, 1988; AIDS, 1989; The Welfare Debate, 1989; Energy and Conservation, 1989; Japan and the USA, 1990; Censorship, 1990; The Crisis in Health Care, 1991; The State of US Education, 1991; The Reunification of Germany, 1992; Immigration to the United States, 1992; Drugs in America, 1993; Banking Scandals: The S&L and BCCI, 1993; Religious Cults in America, 1994; Criminal Sentencing, 1995; Suicide, 1995; Immigration, 1996; Affirmative Action, 1996; Multiculturalism, 1997; Right to Privacy, 1997. Contributions: several hundred articles in magazines, journals and newspapers. *Address:* 254 S Third Street, Fulton, NY 13069, USA.

LONG, Robert Hill; Senior Lecturer in Creative Writing, Poet and Writer; b. 23 Nov. 1952, Raleigh, NC, USA; m. Sandra Morgen, 22 March 1980, one s. one d. *Education:* BA, Comparative Literature, Davidson College, 1975; MFA, Program for Writers, Warren Wilson College, 1983. *Career:* Visiting Lecturer, Clark University, University of Hartford, Smith College, University of Connecticut at Torrington, 1987–91; Senior Lecturer in Creative Writing, University of Oregon, 1991–; mem. Associated Writing Programs. *Publications:* The Power to Die (poems), 1987; The Work of the Bow (poems), 1997; The Effigies (fiction), 1998. Contributions: various anthologies and journals. *Honours:* Aspen Writers' Conference Poetry Fellowship, 1981; First Prize, North Carolina Poetry Award, 1986; Grand Prize, A Living Culture in Durham Anthology, 1986; North Carolina Arts Council Literary Fellowship, 1986; National Endowment for the Arts Fellowship, 1988; Cleveland State University Poetry Center Prize, 1995; Oregon Arts Commission Literary Fellowship, 1997. *Address:* c/o Program in Creative Writing, University of Oregon, Eugene, OR 97403, USA.

LONGLEY, Edna; British poet, academic and critic; *Emerita Professor, Queen's University*; m. Michael Longley. *Education:* Trinity Coll., Dublin. *Career:* Lecturer 1964–76, Sr Lecturer 1976–87, Reader 1987–91, Prof. 1991–2002, Emerita Prof. 2002–, School of English, Queen's Univ., Belfast; editorial bd mem., Fortnight and Yeats Annual. *Publications:* poetry: Poetry in the Wars 1986, Alice in Wormland: Selected Poems 1990, From Kathleen to Anorexia 1990, The Living Stream: Literature and Revisionism in Ireland 1994; editor: Language Not to Be Betrayed (with others) 1985, The Biggest Egg in the World 1987, Yeats Annual: That Accusing Eye, Yeats and his Irish Readers (with others) 1996, The Bloodaxe Book of 20th Century Poetry from Britain and Ireland (with others) 2000; contrib. reviews to TLS, The Irish Times, Poetry Review, Thumbscrew, Metre, BBC Radio. *Address:* c/o Bloodaxe Books Ltd, Highgreen, Tarset, Northumberland NE48 1RP, England. *Website:* www.bloodaxebooks.com.

LONGMATE, Norman Richard, BA, MA, FRHistS; writer; b. 15 Dec. 1925, Newbury, Berkshire, England. *Education:* Worcester Coll., Oxford. *Career:* Leader Writer, Evening Standard, 1952; Feature Writer, Daily Mirror, 1953–56; Schools Radio Producer, 1963–65, Senior, subsequently Chief Asst, BBC Secretariat, 1965–83; mem. Oxford Society; Society of Authors; Fortress Study Group; United Kingdom Fortification Club; Historical Asscn; Ramblers Asscn; Society of Sussex Downsmen; Prayer Book Society. *Publications:* A Socialist Anthology (ed.), 1953; Oxford Triumphant, 1955; King Cholera, 1966; The Waterdrinkers, 1968; Alive and Well, 1970; How We Lived Then, 1971; If Britain had Fallen, 1972; The Workhouse, 1974; The Real Dad's Army, 1974; The GI's, 1975; Milestones in Working Class History, 1975; Air Raid, 1976; When We Won the War, 1977; The Hungry Mills, 1978; The Doodlebugs, 1981; The Bombers, 1982; The Breadstealers, 1984; Hitler's Rockets, 1985; Defending the Island from Caesar to the Armada, 1989.

LONGWORTH, Philip; Historian and Writer; b. 17 Feb. 1933, London, England. *Education:* BA, 1956, MA, 1960, Balliol College, Oxford. *Career:* Prof. of History, McGill University, Montréal, 1984–. *Publications:* A Hero of Our Time, by Lermontov (trans.), 1962; The Art of Victory, 1965; The Unending Vigil, 1967; The Cossacks, 1969; The Three Empresses, 1971; The Rise and Fall of Venice, 1974; Alexis, Tsar of All the Russias, 1984; The Making of Eastern Europe, 1992. Contributions: periodicals. *Address:* c/o Dept of History, McGill University, 845 Sherbrooke St W, Montréal, QC H3A 2T5, Canada.

LONGYEAR, Barry B.; Writer; b. 12 May 1942, Harrisburg, Pennsylvania, USA. *Publications:* City of Baraboo, 1980; Manifest Destiny (short stories), 1980; Circus World (short stories), 1980; Elephant Song, 1981; The Tomorrow Testament, 1983; It Came from Schenectady, 1984; Sea of Glass, 1986; Enemy Mine, 1988; Saint MaryBlue, 1988; Naked Came the Robot, 1988; The God Box, 1989; Infinity Hold, 1989; The Homecoming, 1989; Slag Like Me, 1994; The Change, 1994; Yesterday's Tomorrow, 1997; The Enemy Papers, 1998. *Address:* PO Box 100, Vienna Rd, Rt 41, New Shanon, ME 04955, USA.

LOPATE, Phillip; Prof. of English, Writer, Poet and Ed.; b. 16 Nov. 1943, New York, NY, USA; m. Cheryl Cipriani 31 Dec. 1990; one c. *Education:* BA, Columbia College, 1964; PhD, Union Institute, 1979. *Career:* Assoc. Prof. of English, University of Houston, 1980–88; Assoc. Prof. of Creative Writing, Columbia University, 1988–90; Prof. of English, Bennington College, 1990, Hofstra University, 1991–; Ed., The Anchor Essay Annual, 1997–99. *Publications:* Fiction: Confessions of Summer, 1979; The Rug Merchant, 1987. Poetry: The Eyes Don't Always Want to Stay Open, 1972; The Daily Round, 1976. Other: Being with Children (memoir), 1975; Bachelorhood (essays), 1981; Against Joie de Vivre (essays), 1989; Portrait of My Body (essays), 1996; Totally, Tenderly, Tragically (film criticism), 1998; Getting Personal, 2003; Waterfront, 2003; Rudy Burckhardt (biog.), 2003. Editor: Journal of a Living Experiment, 1979; The Art of the Personal Essay, 1994; Writing New York, 1998. Contributions: anthologies, newspapers, reviews, quarterlies, journals and magazines. *Honours:* Guggenheim Fellowship; National Endowment for the Arts Grants; New York Foundation for the Arts Grants; Christopher Medallion; Texas Institute of Letters Award; New York Public Library Center for Scholars and Writers Fellowship. *Address:* 402 Sackett St, New York, NY 11231, USA.

LOPES, Henri (Marie-Joseph); Novelist; b. 12 Sept. 1937, Leopoldville, Belgian Congo; m. Nirva Pasbeau, 13 May 1961, one s., three d. *Education:* Licence es Lettres, 1962, Diplome d'Études Supérieures, History, 1963, Sorbonne, University of Paris. *Publications:* Tribaliques, 1971, English trans. as Tribaliks, 1989; La Nouvelle Romance, 1976; Sans Tam-Tam, 1977; The Laughing Cry, 1988; Le Chercheur d'Afriques, 1990; Sur L'Autre Rive, 1992; Le Lys et le Flamboyant, 1997. *Honours:* Grand Prix de la Littérature d'Afrique Noire, 1972; Prix Jules Verne, 1990; Dr hc, University Paris-Val de Marne, France; Grand Prix de Littérature de La Francophonie de L'Académie Française, 1993; Homme de Lettres 1993, 1994.

LOPEZ, Barry Holstun, BA, MA; writer; b. 6 Jan. 1945, Port Chester, NY, USA; m. Sandra Jean Landers 1967. *Education:* University of Notre Dame. *Career:* mem. PEN American Center. *Publications:* Desert Notes, 1976; Giving Birth to Thunder, 1978; River Notes, 1978; Of Wolves and Men, 1978; Winter Count, 1981; Arctic Dreams, 1986; Crossing Open Ground, 1988; The Rediscovery of North America, 1991; Field Notes, 1994; About this Life: Journeys on the Threshold of Memory, 1998. Contributions: periodicals. *Honours:* John Burroughs Medal, 1979; Christopher Medals, 1979, 1987; American Acad. of Arts and Letters Award, 1986; Guggenheim Fellowship, 1987; National Book Award, 1987; Hon. LDH, Whittier College, 1988; Lannan Foundation Award, 1990. *Literary Agent:* Steven Barclay Agency, 12 Western Avenue, Petaluma, CA 94952, USA. *Telephone:* (707) 773-0654. *Fax:* (707) 778-1868. *Website:* www.barclayagency.com.

LOPEZ, Tony; University Reader in Poetry, Poet and Writer; b. 5 Nov. 1950, London, England; m. Sara Louise Banham, 19 Oct. 1985, one s. one d. *Education:* BA, Literature, University of Essex, 1980; PhD, English, Gonville & Caius College, Cambridge. *Career:* Lecturer in English, University of Leicester, 1986–87, University of Edinburgh, 1987–89; Lecturer to Reader in Poetry, University of Plymouth, 1989–. *Publications:* Snapshots, 1976; Change, 1978; The English Disease, 1979; A Handbook of British Birds, 1982; Abstract and Delicious, 1983; The Poetry of W. S. Graham, 1989; A Theory of Surplus Labour, 1990; Stress Management, 1994; Negative Equity, 1995; False Memory, 1996. Contributions: anthologies and periodicals. *Honours:* Blundel Award, 1990; Wingate Scholarship, 1996. *Literary Agent:* MBA Literary Agents Ltd, 62 Grafton Way, London W1T 5DW, England.

LORD, Graham John; Author; b. 16 Feb. 1943, Umtali, Southern Rhodesia; m. Jane Carruthers, 12 Sept. 1962, deceased 2000, two d., Partner, Juliet Lewis. *Education:* BA, University of Cambridge, 1965. *Career:* Literary Ed., Sunday Express, London, 1969–92; Originator, 1987, Judge, 1987–92, Sunday Express Book of the Year Award; Ed., Raconteur, short story magazine, 1994–95. *Publications:* Marshmallow Pie, 1970; A Roof Under Your Feet, 1973; The Spider and the Fly, 1974; God and All His Angels, 1976; The Nostradamus Horoscope, 1981; Time Out of Mind, 1986; Ghosts of King Solomon's Mines, 1991; Just the One: The Wives and Times of Jeffrey Bernard, 1992; A Party to Die For, 1997; James Herriot: The Life of a Country Vet, 1997; Sorry, We're Going to have to Let You Go, 1999; Dick Francis: A Racing Life, 1999; Arthur Lowe, 2002; Niv: The Authorised Biography of David Niven, 2003. Contributions: newspapers. *Literary Agent:* Curtis Brown Ltd, 7 Queensferry St, Edinburgh EH2 4QS, Scotland.

LORENZ, Sarah E. (see Winston, Sarah).

LORIGA, Ray; Spanish writer, screenwriter and film director; b. 1967, Madrid. *Films include:* Live Flesh (writer, with Pedro Almodóvar) 1997, La pistola de mi hermano (dir) 1997, Todos los aviones del mundo (writer) 2001, El Séptimo día (writer) 2004. *Publications include:* Lo Peor de todo 1993, Heroes 1994, My Brother's Gun: A Novel of Disposable Lives, Immediate Fame and a Big Black Automatic 1997, Tokyo Doesn't Love Us Anymore 2004; contrib. to Crime Hamper. *Address:* c/o Canongate Books, 14 High Street, Edinburgh, EH1 1TE, Scotland.

LORRIMER, Claire (see Clark, Patricia Denise).

LOTT, Bret; Asst Prof. of English and Writer; b. 8 Oct. 1958, Los Angeles, CA, USA; m. Melanie Kai Swank, 28 June 1980, two s. *Education:* BA, California State University at Long Beach, 1981; MFA, University of Massachusetts, 1984. *Career:* Reporter, Daily Commercial News, Los Angeles, 1980–81; Instructor in Remedial English, Ohio State University, Columbus, 1984–86; Asst Prof. of English, College of Charleston, 1986–; mem. Associated Writing Programs; Poets and Writers. *Publications:* The Man Who Owned Vermont, 1987; A Stranger's House, 1988; A Dream of Old Leaves, 1989; The Hunt Club, 1997. Contributions: anthologies and periodicals. *Honours:* Awards and fellowships. *Address:* c/o Dept of English, College of Charleston, Charleston, SC 29424, USA.

LOTT, Tim; British writer and broadcaster; b. 1956, London. *Education:* Harlow Coll. and LSE. *Career:* journalist, Sounds magazine, City Limits magazine; television producer; panellist, Newsnight Review (BBC2) 2001–. *Publications:* The Scent of Dried Roses (memoir) 1996, White City Blue (novel) 1999, Rumours of a Hurricane (novel) 2002, The Love Secrets of Don Juan (novel) 2003; contrib. 'What Young Men Do', Granta 62 1998. *Honours:* J.R. Ackerley Prize for Autobiography, Whitbread First Novel Award. *Address:* c/o Viking, Penguin Books Ltd, 80 Strand, London, WC2R 0RL, England. *Website:* www.penguin.co.uk.

LOUW, Raymond; Publisher and Editor; b. 13 Oct. 1926, Cape Town, South Africa; m. Jean Ramsay Byres 1950; two s. one d. *Education:* Parktown High School, Johannesburg. *Career:* reporter on Rand Daily Mail 1946–50, Worthing Herald 1951–52, North-Western Evening Mail 1953–54, Westminster Press Provincial Newspapers (London) 1955–56; Night News Ed. Rand Daily Mail 1958–59, News Ed. 1960–65, Ed. 1966–77; News Ed. Sunday Times 1959–60; Chair. SA Morning Newspaper Group 1975–77; Gen. Man. SA Associated Newspapers 1977–82; Ed. and Publr Southern Africa Report 1982–; Chair. Media Defence Fund 1989–94, Campaign for Open Media 1985–94 (now merged as Freedom of Expression Inst., Chair. 1994–96); New Era Schools Trust; mem. Task Group on Govt Communications 1996; chosen by Int. Press Inst. to travel to Cameroon to make plea for release from jail of Pius Njawe (Ed. of Le Messager) 1998; mem. Exec. Board, Int. Press Inst., London, 1979–87, Fellow 1994; Independent Media Comm., 1994. *Publications:* Four Days in Lusaka – Whites from 'Home' in talks with the ANC, 1989; Report on the media situation in South Africa (for UNESCO), 1994. Contributions: narrative for Nelson Mandela Pictorial Biography by Peter Magubane; numerous papers and articles on the media and press freedom. *Honours:* Pringle Medals for services to journalism, 1976, 1992. *Address:* 23 Duncombe Rd, Forest Town, Johannesburg 2193, South Africa. *E-mail:* rlouw@sn.apc.org. *Website:* www.sareport.co.za.

LOVE, William F., BA, MBA; writer; b. 20 Dec. 1932, Oklahoma City, OK, USA; m. Joyce Mary Athman 1970; two d. *Education:* St John's Univ., Collegeville, Minnesota, Univ. of Chicago. *Career:* mem. Authors' Guild, Int. Assen of Crime Writers, MWA, PEN Midwest, Private Eye Writers of America, Soc. of Midland Authors. *Publications:* The Chartreuse Clue 1990, The Fundamentals of Murder 1991, Bloody Ten 1992.

LØVEID, Cecilie Meyer; Playwright and Poet; b. 21 Aug. 1951, Mysen, Norway; m. Bjørn H. Ianke 1978; one s. two d. *Education:* arts and crafts school in Bergen and studies in graphic design, theatre history and drama. *Career:* mem. editorial staff, Profil (magazine) 1969; Sec. Norsk Forfattersentrum, Vestlandsardelingen 1974; Teacher, Writing Arts Centre, Bergen 1986; mem. Literary Council, Den norske Fordatterforening 1987. *Publications:* Most (novel), 1972; Sug (novel), 1979; Måkespisere (radio play), 1982; Balansedame (play), 1986; Maria Q. (play), 1991; Rhindøtrene (play), 1996. *Honours:* Prix Italia, 1982; Aschehons Prize; Donblans Prize. *Address:* Huitfeldtsgt. 36, 0253 Oslo, Norway.

LOVELACE, Merline A., BA, MS; writer and fmr Air Force Officer; b. 9 Sept. 1946, Northampton, Massachusetts, USA; m. Cary A. Lovelace 1970. *Education:* Ripon College, Troy State University, Middlebury College, Princeton University, Air War College, Kennedy School of Government, Harvard University. *Career:* served to Colonel, US Air Force, 1968–91; novelist, mainly romances, 1991–; mem. Romance Writers of America, pres., Oklahoma Chapter. *Publications:* Bits and Pieces, 1993; Maggie and Her Colonel, 1994; Alena, 1994; Sweet Song of Love, 1994; Dreams and Schemes, 1994; Siren's Call, 1994; Somewhere in Time, 1994; His Lady's Ransom, 1995; Night of the Jaguar, 1995, Cowboy and the Cossack, 1995, Undercover Man, 1996, Perfect Double, 1996; Lady of the Upper Kingdom, 1996; Line of Duty, 1996; Beauty and the Bodyguard, 1996; Halloween Honeymoon, 1996; Thanksgiving Honeymoon, 1996; Valentine's Honeymoon, 1997; Duty and Dishonor, 1997; Above and Beyond, 1997; Countess in Buckskin, 1997; White Tiger/Green Dragon, 1997. Contributions: anthologies. *Honours:* Southwest Writers Workshop Prize for Best Historical Novel, 1992; Best Kismet Romance, Romantic Times, 1993. *Address:* 2325 Tuttington, Oklahoma City, OK 73170, USA.

LOVELL, Sir (Alfred Charles) Bernard; academic and writer; b. 31 Aug. 1913, Oldland Common, Gloucestershire, England; m. Mary Joyce Chesterman 1937 (died 1993); two s. three d. *Education:* University of Bristol. *Career:* Prof. of Radio Astronomy, 1951–80, Prof. Emeritus, 1980–, University of Manchester; Dir, Jodrell Bank Experimental Station, later Nuffield Radio Astronomy Laboratories, 1951–81; various visiting lectureships; mem. American Acad. of Arts and Sciences, hon. foreign mem.; American Philosophical Society; International Astronomical Union, vice-pres., 1970–76; New York Acad.; Royal Astronomical Society, pres., 1969–71; Royal Society, fellow; Royal Swedish Acad., hon. mem. *Publications:* Science and Civilisation, 1939; World Power Resources and Social Development, 1945; Radio Astronomy, 1951; Meteor Astronomy, 1954; The Exploration of Space by Radio, 1957; The Individual and the Universe, 1958; The Exploration of Outer Space, 1961; Discovering the Universe, 1963; Our Present Knowledge of the Universe, 1967; The Explosion of Science: The Physical Universe (ed. with T. Margerison), 1967; The Story of Jodrell Bank, 1968; The Origins and International Economics of Space Exploration, 1973; Out of the Zenith, 1973; Man's Relation to the Universe, 1975; P. M. S. Blackett: A Biographical Memoir, 1976; In the Centre of Immensities, 1978; Emerging Cosmology, 1981; The Jodrell Bank Telescopes, 1985; Voice of the Universe, 1987; Pathways to the Universe (with Sir Francis Graham Smith), 1988; Astronomer By Chance (autobiog.), 1990; Echoes of War, 1991. Contributions: Professional journals. *Honours:* OBE, 1946; Duddell Medal, 1954; Royal Medal, 1960; Knighted, 1961; Ordre du Mérite pour la Recherche et l'Invention, 1962; Churchill Gold Medal, 1964; Gold Medal, Royal Astronomical Society, 1981; many hon. doctorates. *Address:* The Quinta, Swettenham, Cheshire CW12 2LD, England.

LOVELL, Mary S(ybilla); Writer; b. 23 Oct. 1941, Prestatyn, North Wales, Wales; m. 2nd Geoffrey A. H. Watts 11 July 1991; one s. two step-s. two step-d. *Career:* mem. Society of Authors; R. S. Surtees Society, vice-pres., 1980–; FRGS. *Publications:* Hunting Pageant, 1980; Cats as Pets, 1982; Boys Book of Boats, 1983; Straight on Till Morning, 1987; The Splendid Outcast, 1988; The Sound of Wings, 1989; Cast No Shadow, 1991; A Scandalous Life, 1995; The Rebel Heart, 1996; A Rage to Live, 1998; The Mitford Girls, 2001; Bound to a Star, 2003. *Address:* Stroat House, Stroat, Gloucestershire NP6 7LR, England. *E-mail:* sybil@stroat24.fsnet.co.uk. *Website:* www.marylovell.com.

LOVELOCK, Yann Rufus; Writer, Poet and Trans; b. 11 Feb. 1939, Birmingham, England; m. Ann Riddell, 28 Sept. 1961. *Education:* BA, English Literature, St Edmund Hall, Oxford, 1963. *Career:* various Writer-in-Residencies; mem. Freundkreis Poesie Europe, asst dir; La Société de Langue et de la Littérature Wallonnes, corresponding mem. *Publications:* The Vegetable Book, 1972; The Colour of the Weather (ed. and trans.), 1980; The Line Forward, 1984; A Vanishing Emptiness (ed. and part trans.), 1989; A Townscape of Flanders, Versions of Grace by Anton von Wilderode (trans.), 1990; Landscape with Voices, Poems 1980–95, 1995; In the Pupil's Mirror (ed. and trans.), 1997; Some 25 other books of poems, experimental prose, anthologies and trans. Contributions: periodicals and anthologies. *Honours:* Silver Medal, Haute Académie d'Art et de Littérature de France, 1986. *Address:* 80 Doris Rd, Birmingham, West Midlands B11 4NF, England.

LOVESEY, Peter, (Peter Lear); Writer; b. 10 Sept. 1936, Whitton, Middlesex, England; m. Jacqueline Ruth Lewis, 30 May 1959, one s. one d. *Education:* BA, English, University of Reading, 1958. *Career:* mem. CWA, chair., 1991–92; Detection Club; Society of Authors. *Publications:* The

Kings of Distance, 1968; Wobble to Death, 1970; The Detective Wore Silk Drawers, 1971; Abracadaver, 1972; Mad Hatters Holiday, 1973; Invitation to a Dynamite Party, 1974; A Case of Spirits, 1975; Swing, Swing Together, 1976; Goldengirl, 1977; Waxwork, 1978; Official Centenary History of the Amateur Athletic Asscn, 1979; Spider Girl, 1980; The False Inspector Dew, 1982; Keystone, 1983; Butchers (short stories), 1985; The Secret of Spandau, 1986; Rough Cider, 1986; Bertie and the Tinman, 1987; On the Edge, 1989; Bertie and the Seven Bodies, 1990; The Last Detective, 1991; Diamond Solitaire, 1992; Bertie and the Crime of Passion, 1993; The Crime of Miss Oyster Brown (short stories), 1994; The Summons, 1995; Bloodhounds, 1996; Upon a Dark Night, 1997; Do Not Exceed the Stated Dose (short stories), 1998; The Vault, 1999; The Reaper, 2000; Diamond Dust, 2002; The Sedgemoor Strangler and Other Stories of Crime, 2002; The House Sitter, 2003. *Honours:* Macmillan/Panther First Crime Novel Award, 1970; CWA Silver Dagger, 1978, 1995, 1996 and Gold Dagger, 1982 and Cartier Diamond Dagger, 2000; Grand Prix de Littérature Policière, 1985; Prix du Roman D'Aventures, 1987; Anthony Award, 1992; Macavity Award 1997. *Literary Agent:* Vanessa Holt Ltd, 59 Crescent Rd, Leigh-on-Sea, Essex SS9 2PF, England.

LOW, Lois Dorothea, (Zoe Cass, Dorothy Mackie Low, Lois Paxton); Writer; b. 15 July 1916, Edinburgh, Scotland. *Education:* Edinburgh Ladies' College. *Career:* mem. CWA; Romantic Novelists Asscn, chair., 1969–71; Society of Authors. *Publications:* Isle for a Stranger, 1962; Dear Liar, 1963; A Ripple on the Water, 1964; The Intruder, 1965; A House in the Country, 1968; The Man Who Died Twice, 1969; To Burgundy and Back, 1970; The Quiet Sound of Fear, 1971; Who Goes There?, 1972; Island of the Seven Hills, 1974; The Silver Leopard, 1976; A Twist in the Silk, 1980; The Man in the Shadows, 1983.

LOW, Rachael, BSc, PhD; film historian; b. 6 July 1923, London, England. *Education:* LSE. *Career:* researcher, British Film Inst., London 1945–48; Gulbenkian Research Fellow 1968–71, Fellow Commoner 1983, Lucy Cavendish Coll., Cambridge. *Publications:* History of the British Film 1896–1906 1948, Films of Comment and Persuasion of the 1930s 1979, Documentary and Educational Films of the 1930s 1979, History of the British Film (with Roger Manvell) 1906–1914 1949, 1914–1918 1950, 1918–1929 1971, 1929–1939 Vols I and II 1979, Vol. III 1985. *Address:* c/o Routledge (Media and Cultural Studies), Building 4, Park Square, Milton Park, Abingdon, OX14 4RN, England.

LOW, Robert Nicholas; Journalist and Writer; b. 15 Aug. 1948, Addlestone, Surrey, England; m. Angela Levin, 6 Oct. 1983, one s. *Education:* BA, Fitzwilliam College, Cambridge. *Career:* Teacher, University of Chile, La Serena, 1970–72; Journalist, Birmingham Post & Mail, 1973–77, The Observer, 1977–93; Senior Ed.-Deputy Ed., British Edition, 1994–98, European Bureau Chief, 1998–, Reader's Digest. *Publications:* The Kidnap Business (with Mark Bles), 1987; The Observer Book of Profiles (ed.), 1991; La Pasionaria, The Spanish Firebrand, 1992; W. G.: A Life of W. G. Grace, 1997. *Literary Agent:* Curtis Brown Ltd, Haymarket House, 28–29 Haymarket, London, SW1Y 4SP, England. *Telephone:* (20) 7393-4400. *Fax:* (20) 7393-4401. *E-mail:* info@curtisbrown.co.uk. *Website:* www.curtisbrown.co.uk. *Address:* 33 Canfield Gardens, London NW6 3JP, England. *E-mail:* bob.low@readersdigest.co.uk.

LOW(-WESO), Denise; Poet, Writer and University Instructor of Humanities; b. 9 May 1949, Emporia, KS, USA; m. Thomas F. Weso, two s. *Education:* BA, English, 1971, MA, English, 1974, PhD, English, 1997, University of Kansas; MFA, Creative Writing, Wichita State University, 1984. *Career:* Asst Instructor, 1970–72, Lecturer, 1977–84, Visiting Lecturer, 1988, University of Kansas; Temporary Instructor, Kansas State University, 1975–77; Part-time Instructor, Washburn University, Topeka, 1982–84; Instructor of Humanities, Haskell Indian Nations University, Lawrence, KS, 1984–; mem. Associated Writing Programs; MLA; Poets and Writers. *Publications:* Dragon Kite, 1981; Quilting, 1984; Spring Geese and Other Poems, 1984; Learning the Language of Rivers, 1987; Starwater, 1988; Selective Amnesia: Stiletto I, 1988; Vanishing Point, 1991; Tulip Elegies: An Alchemy of Writing, 1993; Touching the Sky: Essays, 1994; New and Selected Poems: 1980-99, 1999; Thailand Journal, 2003. Contributions: anthologies, books, reviews, quarterlies, journals, and magazines. *Honours:* several grants and fellowships. *Address:* c/o Haskell Indian Nations University, Lawrence, KS 66046, USA. *E-mail:* deniselow9@hotmail.com.

LOWBURY, Edward (Joseph Lister); Physician, Poet and Writer; b. 6 Dec. 1913, London, England; m. Alison Young, 12 June 1954 (died 2001); three d. *Education:* BA, 1936, BM and BCh, 1939, University College, Oxford; MA; London Hospital Medical College, 1940; DM, University of Oxford, 1957. *Career:* Bacteriologist, Medical Research Council Burns Research Unit, Birmingham Accident Hospital, 1949–79; Founder-Hon. Dir, Hospital Infection Research Laboratory, Birmingham, 1966–79; mem. British Medical Asscn; Fellow, Royal College of Pathologists; RSL; Founder Mem. and First Pres. of Hospital Infection Society; Hon. Fellow, Royal College of Physicians; Royal College of Surgeons. *Publications:* Poetry: Over 20 collections, including: Time for Sale, 1961; Daylight Astronomy, 1968; The Night Watchman, 1974; Poetry and Paradox: Poems and an Essay, 1976; Selected Poems, 1978; Selected and New Poems, 1990; Collected Poems 1993; Mystic Bridge 1997, Blind Man's Buff 2001. Non-Fiction: Thomas Campion: Poet, Composer, Physician (with Alison Young and Timothy Salter), 1970; Drug Resistance in Antimicrobial Therapy (with G. A. Ayliffe), 1974; Hallmarks of Poetry (essays), 1994; To Shirk No Idleness: A Critical Biography of the Poet Andrew Young (with Alison Young), 1998. Editor: Control of Hospital Infection: A Practical Handbook (with others), 1975; The Poetical Works of Andrew Young (with Alison Young), 1985. Contributions: numerous medical, scientific, and literary publications, including reference works and journals. *Honours:* Newdigate Prize, 1934; Hon. Research Fellow, Birmingham University; John Keats Memorial Lecturer Award, 1973; Everett Evans Memorial Lecturer Award, 1977; DSc, Aston University, 1977; A. B. Wallace Memorial Lecturer and Medal, 1978; Hon. Prof. of Medical Microbiology, Aston University, 1979; LL D, Birmingham University, 1980; OBE, 1980. *Address:* c/o 25 Churston Gardens, London N11 2NJ, England.

LOWDEN, Desmond Scott; Writer; b. 27 Sept. 1937, Winchester, Hampshire, England; m. 14 July 1962, one s. one d. *Career:* mem. CWA. *Publications:* Bandersnatch, 1969; The Boondocks, 1972; Bellman and True, 1975; Boudapesti 3, 1979; Sunspot, 1981; Cry Havoc, 1984; The Shadow Run, 1989; Chain, 1990. *Honours:* Silver Dagger Award, CWA, 1989. *Literary Agent:* Rogers, Coleridge & White Ltd, 20 Powis Mews, London W11 1JN, England.

LOWE, Barry; Playwright, Writer and Scriptwriter; b. 16 May 1947, Sydney, NSW, Australia; Partner: Walter Figallo, 24 Dec. 1972. *Career:* mem. Australian Writers Guild; Australian Society of Authors. *Publications:* Plays: Writers Camp, first performed, 1982; Tokyo Rose, 1989; The Death of Peter Pan, 1989; Seeing Things, 1994; Relative Merits, 1994; The Extraordinary Annual General Meeting of the Size-Queen Club, 1996. Contributions: various publications. *Literary Agent:* Kevin Palmer, 258 Bulwara Road, Ultimo, NSW 2007, Australia.

LOWE, John Evelyn; Writer; b. 23 April 1928, London, England; m. 1st Susan Sanderson 1956; two s. one d.; m. 2nd Yuki Nomura 1989; one d. *Education:* English Literature, New College, Oxford, 1950–52. *Career:* Assoc. Ed., Collins Crime Club, 1953–54; Ed., Faber Furniture Series, 1954–56; Deputy Story Ed., Pinewood Studios, 1956–57; Visiting Prof., British Cultural Studies Doshisha Univ., Kyoto, Japan, 1979–81; Literary Ed., Kansai Time Out Magazine, 1985–89; Visiting Prof., International Research Centre for Japanese Studies, Kyoto, 2001–02; mem. Society of Antiquaries, fellow; FRSA. *Publications:* Thomas Chippendale, 1955; Cream Coloured Earthenware, 1958; Japanese Crafts, 1983; Into Japan, 1985; Into China, 1986; Corsica – A Traveller's Guide, 1988; A Surrealist Life – Edward James, 1991; A Short Guide to the Kyoto Museum of Archaeology, 1991; Glimpses of Kyoto Life, 1996; The Warden – A Portrait of John Sparrow, 1998; Old Kyoto, A Short Social History, 2000. Contributions: Encyclopaedia Britannica; Oxford Junior Encyclopaedia; New Dictionary of National Biography; American Scholar; Country Life; Listener; Connoisseur; Apollo; Others. *Honours:* Hon. Fellow, Royal College of Art. *Address:* 2 rue Jean Guiton, 47300 Villeneuve sur Lot, France. *Telephone:* (5) 53 41 72 53.

LOWE, Stephen; Playwright; b. 1 Dec. 1947, Nottingham, England; m. 1st Tina Barclay; one s.; m. 2nd Tanya Myers; two d. *Education:* BA, English and Drama, 1969; Postgraduate Research, 1969–70. *Career:* Senior Tutor in Writing for Performance, Dartington College of Arts Performance, 1978–82; Resident Playwright, Riverside Studios, London, 1982–84; Senior Tutor, Birmingham University, 1987–88; Nottingham Trent University Advisory Board to Theatre Design Degree, 1987–; Chair., East Midlands Arts, 2001–02; Trustee, Arts Council England, Chair. Arts Council England, East Midlands, 2002–; mem. Theatre Writers Union; Writers Guild; PEN. *Publications:* Touched, 1981; Cards, 1983; Moving Pictures and Other Plays, 1985; Body and Soul in Peace Plays, 2 vols, 1985, 1990; Divine Gossip/Tibetan Inroads, 1988; Ragged Trousered Philanthropists, 1991. Contributions: books and journals. *Honours:* George Devine Award for Playwriting, 1977. *Literary Agent:* Judy Daish Assocs. *Address:* c/o Sara Stroud, Judy Daish Assocs, 2 St Charles Pl., London W10 6EG, England. *E-mail:* steplowe.1@ntlworld.com.

LOWELL, Susan Deborah; Writer; b. 27 Oct. 1950, Chihuahua, Mexico; m. William Ross Humphreys, 21 March 1975, two d. *Education:* BA, 1972, MA, 1974, Stanford University; MA, PhD, 1979, Princeton University. *Career:* mem. Southern Arizona Society of Authors. *Publications:* Ganado Red: A Novella and Stories, 1988; I am Lavinia Cumming, 1993. *Honours:* Milkweed Editions National Fiction Prize, 1988; Mountain and Plains Booksellers Asscn Regional Book Award, Children's Writing, 1994. *Address:* c/o Milkweed Editions, Open Book Bldg, 1011 Washington Ave S, Suite 300, Minneapolis, MN 55415, USA.

LOWERY, Joanne; English Educator, Writer and Ed.; b. 30 July 1945, Cleveland, Ohio, USA; m. Stephen Paul Lowery 15 June 1968 (divorced 1988); one s. one d. *Education:* AB, University of Michigan, 1967; MA, University of Wisconsin, 1968. *Career:* Part-time Instructor of English, Elgin College, 1986–91, College of DuPage, Glen Ellyn, 1991–96, St Mary's College, Notre Dame, 1997–98; Poetry Ed., Black Dirt, literary magazine, 1994–99. *Publications:* Coming to This, 1990; Corinth, 1990; Heroics, 1996; Double Feature, 2000. Contributions: Magazines. *Honours:* New Letters Literary Award, 1993. Address 412 Evelyn Ave, Kalamazoo, MI 49001, USA.

LOWNIE, Andrew (James Hamilton); Literary Agent, Writer and Ed.; b. 11 Nov. 1961, Kenya; m. Angela Doyle 2 May 1998; one s. one d. *Education:* Magdalene College, Cambridge, 1981–84; BA, Cantab; MA, Cantab; MSc, Univ. of Edinburgh, 1989. *Career:* Mem., 1985–86, Dir, 1986–88, John Farquharson Literary Agents; Dir, Andrew Lownie Assocs, 1988–; Partner, Denniston and Lownie, 1991–93; Dir, Thistle Publishing, 1996–; mem. Asscn of Authors' Agents; Society of Authors; The Biographer's Club, sec., 1998–; PEN, exec. cttee, 2000. *Publications:* North American Spies, 1992; Edinburgh Literary Guide, 1992; John Buchan: The Presbyterian Cavalier, 1995; John Buchan's Collected Poems (ed.), 1996; The Complete Short Stories of John Buchan, Vols 1–3 (ed.), 1997–98; The Literary Companion to Edinburgh, 2000. Contributions: books and periodicals. *Honours:* English Speaking Union Scholarship, 1979–80. *Address:* 17 Sutherland St, London SW1V 4JU, England.

LOWRY, Beverly (Fey); Writer; b. 10 Aug. 1938, Memphis, Tennessee, USA; m. Glenn Lowry, 3 June 1960, two s. *Education:* University of Mississippi, 1956–58; BA, Memphis State University, 1960. *Publications:* Come Back, Lolly Ray, 1977; Emma Blue, 1978; Daddy's Girl, 1981; The Perfect Sonya, 1987; Breaking Gentle, 1988; Crossed Over: The True Story of the Houston Pickax Murders, 1992; The Track of Real Desire, 1994. Contributions: newspapers and magazines. *Address:* c/o Penguin Books, 375 Hudson St, New York, NY 10014, USA.

LOWRY, Lois; Writer; b. 20 March 1937, Honolulu, HI, USA; m. Donald Grey Lowry 11 June 1956 (divorced 1977); two s. two d. *Education:* Brown University, 1954–56; BA, University of Southern Maine, 1972. *Publications:* Children's Books: A Summer to Die, 1977; Find a Stranger, Say Goodbye, 1978; Anastasia Krupnik, 1979; Autumn Street, 1979; Anastasia Again!, 1981; Anastasia at Your Service, 1982; Taking Care of Terrific, 1983; Anastasia Ask Your Analyst, 1984; Us and Uncle Fraud, 1984; One Hundredth Thing About Caroline, 1985; Anastasia on Her Own, 1985; Switcharound, 1985; Anastasia Has the Answers, 1986; Rabble Starkey, 1987; Anastasia's Chosen Career, 1987; All About Sam, 1988; Number the Stars, 1989; Your Move J. P.!, 1990; Anastasia at This Address, 1991; Attaboy Sam!. 1992; The Giver, 1993; Anastasia Absolutely, 1995; See You Around, Sam, 1996; Stay! Keeper's Story, 1997; Looking Back, 1998; Zooman Sam, 1999; Gathering Blue, 2000. *Honours:* Children's Literature Award, International Reading Asscn, 1978; American Library Asscn Notable Book Citation, 1980; Boston Globe-Horn Book Award, 1987; National Jewish Book Award, 1990; Newbery Medals, 1990, 1994. *Literary Agent:* Phyllis Westberg, Harold Ober Assocs. *Address:* 205 Brattle St, Cambridge, MA 02138, USA.

LUCAS, Celia; Writer; b. 23 Oct. 1938, Bristol, England; m. Ian Skidmore, 20 Oct. 1971. *Education:* BA, Modern History, St Hilda's College, Oxford, 1961. *Career:* mem. Welsh Acad., 1989–. *Publications:* Prisoners of Santo Tomas, 1975; Steel Town Cats, 1987; Glyndwr Country (with Ian Skidmore), 1988; Anglesey Rambles (with Ian Skidmore), 1989; The Adventures of Marmaduke Purr Cat, 1990; The Terrible Tale of Tiggy Two, 1995; Madoc's Prickly Problem, 2000. Contributions: numerous journals and magazines. *Honours:* TIR NA N-OG Award for Junior Fiction, 1988; Irma Chilton Award for Junior Fiction, 1995.

LUCAS, Craig; Dramatist and Screenwriter; b. 30 April 1951, Atlanta, GA, USA. *Education:* BFA, Boston University, 1973. *Career:* mem. Dramatists' Guild; PEN; Writers' Guild. *Publications:* Plays: Missing Persons, 1980; Reckless, 1983; Blue Window, 1984; Prelude to a Kiss, 1987; The Scare, 1989; Anti-Naturalism, 1989; Reckless [and] Blue Window: Two Plays by Craig Lucas, 1989; God's Heart, 1994; The Dying Gaul, 1996; Savage Light (with David Schulner), 1996. Musicals: Marry Me a Little (with Stephen Sondheim), 1981; Three Postcards (with Craig Carnelia), 1987. Screenplays: Blue Window, 1987; Longtime Companion, 1990; Prelude to a Kiss, 1991; Reckless, 1995. *Honours:* Guggenheim Fellowship, 1984; Los Angeles Drama Critics Award, 1985; Rockefeller Grant, 1988, and Fellowship, 1988; Outer Critics' Circle Award, 1990; Obie Award, 1990; Audience Award, Sundance Film Festival, 1990; Yaddo Colony Fellowship, 1994. *Literary Agent:* William Morris Agency, One William Morris Pl., Beverly Hills, CA 90212, USA.

LUCAS, John; Prof. of English, Poet, Writer and Publisher; b. 26 June 1937, Exeter, Devon, England; m. 30 Sept. 1961, one s. one d. *Education:* BA, Philosophy and English Literature, 1959, PhD, 1965, University of Reading. *Career:* Asst Lecturer, University of Reading, 1961–64; Lecturer, Senior Lecturer, Reader, University of Nottingham, 1964–77; Visiting Prof., University of Maryland and Indiana University, 1967–68; Prof. of English, Loughborough University, 1977–; Reasearch prof., Nottingham Trent University, 1996–; Lord Byron Visiting Prof., University of Athens, 1984–85; Publisher, Shoestring Press, 1994–; mem. John Clare Society; Poetry Book Society, chair., 1988–92; FRSA; William Morris Society. *Publications:* About Nottingham, 1971; A Brief Bestiary, 1972; Egils Saga: Versions of the Poems, 1975; The Days of the Week, 1983; Studying Grosz on the Bus, 1989; Flying to Romania, 1992; One for the Piano, 1997; The Radical Twenties, 1997; On the Track: Poems, 2000; A World Perhaps: New and Selected Poems, 2002; Starting to Explain: Essays on 20th-Century British and Irish Poetry, 2003. Contributions: anthologies, newspapers, reviews; BBC Radio 3 and 4. *Honours:* Poetry Prize for Best First Full Vol. of Poetry, Aldeburgh Festival, 1990. *Address:* 19 Devonshire Ave, Beeston, Nottingham NG9 1BS, England.

LUCAS, John (Randolph); Reader in Philosophy (retd) and Writer; b. 18 June 1929, England; m. Morar Portal, 1961, two s. two d. *Education:* St Mary's College, Winchester; MA, Balliol College, Oxford, 1952. *Career:* Junior Research Fellow, 1953–56, Fellow and Tutor, 1960–96, Merton College, Oxford; Fellow and Asst Tutor, Corpus Christi College, Cambridge, 1956–59; Jane Eliza Procter Visiting Fellow, Princeton University, 1957–58; Leverhulme Research Fellow, Leeds University, 1959–60; Gifford Lecturer, University of Edinburgh, 1971–73; Margaret Harris Lecturer, University of Dundee, 1981; Harry Jelema Lecturer, Calvin College, Grand Rapids, 1987; Reader in Philosophy, University of Oxford, 1990–96; mem. British Acad., fellow; British Society for the Philosophy of Science, pres., 1991–93. *Publications:* Principles of Politics, 1966; The Concept of Probability, 1970; The Freedom of the Will, 1970; The Nature of Mind, 1972; The Development of Mind, 1973; A Treatise on Time and Space, 1973; Essays on Freedom and Grace, 1976; Democracy and Participation, 1976; On Justice, 1980; Space, Time and Causality, 1985; The Future, 1989; Spacetime and Electromagnetism, 1990; Responsibility, 1993; Ethical Economics, 1996; The Conceptual Roots of Mathematics, 1999. Contributions: scholarly journals. *Address:* Lambrook House, East Lambrook, Somerset TA13 5HW, England.

LUCAS, Stephen E.; Prof. and Writer; b. 5 Oct. 1946, White Plains, New York, USA; m. Patricia Vore, 14 June 1969, two s. *Education:* BA, University of California at Santa Barbara, 1968; MA, 1971, PhD, 1973, Pennsylvania State University. *Career:* Asst Prof., 1972–76, Assoc. Prof., 1976–82, Prof., 1982–, University of Wisconsin at Madison; Visiting Assoc. Prof., University of Virginia, 1979; mem. International Society for the History of Rhetoric; Organization of American Historians; National Communication Asscn. *Publications:* Portents of Rebellion: Rhetoric and Revolution in Philadelphia, 1765–1776, 1976; The Art of Public Speaking, 1983; George Washington: The Wisdom of an American Patriot, 1998. Contributions: scholarly books and journals. *Honours:* National Communication Asscn Golden Anniversary Book Award, 1977; J. Jeffrey Auer Lecturer, Indiana University, 1988; Wisconsin Teaching Acad., 1997; National Communication Asscn Golden Anniversary Monograph Award, 1999; Donald H. Ecroyd Award for Outstanding Teaching in Higher Education, National Communication Asscn, 2001; Hon. Prof., University of International Business and Economics, Beijing, 2001. *Address:* c/o Dept of Communication Arts, University of Wisconsin at Madison, Madison, WI 53706, USA.

LUCE, Henry, III, BA; American publisher, journalist and foundation administrator; *Chairman Emeritus, The Henry Luce Foundation*; b. 28 April 1925, New York; m. 1st Patricia Potter 1947 (divorced 1954); one s. one d.; m. 2nd Claire McGill 1960 (died 1971); three step-s.; m. 3rd Nancy Bryan Cassiday 1975 (died 1987); two step-s. (one deceased); m. 4th Leila Elliott Burton Hadley 1990; two step-s. two step-d. *Education:* Brooks School and Yale Univ. *Career:* served USNR 1943–46; Commdr's Asst, Hoover Comm. on Org. Exec. Branch of Govt 1948–49; Reporter, Cleveland Press 1949–51; Washington Corresp. Time Inc. 1951–53, Time writer 1953–55, Head New Bldg Dept 1956–60, Asst to Publr 1960–61, Circulation Dir Fortune and Architectural Forum 1961–64, House and Home 1962–64, Vice-Pres. 1964–80, Chief London Bureau 1966–68, Publr Fortune 1968–69, Publr Time 1969–72; Vice-Pres. for Corporate Planning and Dir Time Inc. 1967–89; Dir Time Warner Inc. 1989–96; Pres. and CEO Henry Luce Foundation 1958–90, Chair. and CEO 1990–2002, Chair. Emer. 2002–; Pres. Asscn of American Corresps in London 1968; Pres. The New Museum of Contemporary Art 1977–98; Chair. American Security Systems Inc.; mem. American Council for UN Univ., Foreign Policy Asscn (Gov., Medal 1997); Trustee, Eisenhower Exchange Fellowships, Princeton Theological Seminary, Center of Theological Inquiry, Coll. of Wooster, China Inst. in America, A Christian Ministry in the Nat. Parks, New York Historical Soc.; Pres. The Pilgrims; Chair. American Russian Youth Orchestra; Dir Nat. Cttee on US–China Relations, Fishers Island Devt Co. *Honours:* Hon. LHD (St Michael's Coll., Long Island Univ., Pratt Inst.); Hon. LLD (Coll. of Wooster); Hon. DLitt (Cen. Philippine Univ.); Dr hc (Mapuce Inst. of Tech.); American Asscn of Museums Medal for Distinguished Philanthropy 1994, Cen. Park Conservancy Frederick Law Olmstead Award 1996, St Nicholas Soc. Medal 1998, Augustine Graham Medal, Brooklyn Museum of Art 2000, Conrado Benitez Medal, Philippine Univ. for Women 2000. *Address:* Suite 1500, 720 Fifth Avenue, New York, NY 10019 (Office); Mill Hill Road, Mill Neck, NY 11765, USA (Home); 4 Sutton Place, New York, NY 10022. *Telephone:* (212) 582-5531 (Office); (516) 922-0356 (Home); (212) 759-8640. *Fax:* (212) 246-1867 (Office); (212) 759-6831 (Home). *E-mail:* hl@hluce.org (Office).

LUCIE-SMITH, (John) Edward McKenzie, (Peter Kershaw); art critic, poet, journalist and broadcaster; b. 27 Feb. 1933, Kingston, Jamaica. *Education:* MA, Modern History, Merton College, Oxford. *Career:* mem. FRSL. *Publications:* A Tropical Childhood, 1961; Confessions and Histories, 1964; Penguin Modern Poets 6 (with Jack Clemo and George MacBeth), 1964; Penguin Book of Elizabethan Verse (ed.), 1965; What is a Painting?, 1966; The Liverpool Scene (ed.), 1967; A Choice of Browning's Verse (ed.), 1967; Penguin Book of Satirical Verse (ed.), 1967; Thinking About Art, 1968; Towards Silence, 1968; Movements in Art Since 1945,

1969; British Poetry Since 1945 (ed.), 1970; A Primer of Experimental Verse (ed.), 1971; French Poetry: The Last Fifteen Years (ed. with S. W. Taylor), 1971; A Concise History of French Painting, 1971; Symbolist Art, 1972; Eroticism in Western Art, 1972; The First London Catalogue, 1974; The Well Wishers, 1974; The Burnt Child (autobiog.), 1975; The Invented Eye, 1975; World of the Makers, 1975; How the Rich Lived (with Celestine Dars), 1976; Joan of Arc, 1976; Work and Struggle (with Celestine Dars), 1977; Fantin-Latour, 1977; The Dark Pageant (novel), 1977; Art Today, 1977; A Concise History of Furniture, 1979; Super Realism, 1979; Cultural Calendar of the Twentieth Century, 1979; Art in the Seventies, 1980; The Story of Craft, 1981; The Body, 1981; A History of Industrial Design, 1983; Art Terms: An Illustrated Dictionary, 1984; Art in the Thirties, 1985; American Art Now, 1985; Lives of the Great Twentieth Century Artists, 1986; Sculpture Since 1945, 1987; The New British Painting (with Carolyn Cohen and Judith Higgins), 1988; Art in the Eighties, 1990; Art Deco Painting, 1990; Fletcher Benton, 1990; Jean Rustin, 1991; Harry Holland, 1992; Art and Civilization, 1992; The Faber Book of Art Anecdotes (ed.), 1992; Andres Nagel, 1992; Wendy Taylor, 1992; Alexander, 1992; British Art Now, 1993; Race, Sex and Gender: Issues in Contemporary Art, 1994; Elisabeth Frink: A Portrait (with Elisabeth Frink), 1994; American Realism, 1994; Art Today, 1995; Visual Arts in the Twentieth Century, 1996; As Erotica, 1997; Lyn Chadwick, 1997; Adam, 1998; Zoo, 1998; Women and Art (with Judy Chicago), 1999; Judy Chicago, 2000; Flesh and Stone (photographs), 2000; Changing Shape: New and Selected Poems, 2002. Contributions: many newspapers and journals. *Literary Agent:* Rogers, Coleridge & White Ltd, 20 Powis Mews, London W11 1JN, England.

LUCIUS, Wulf D. von, Dr rer. pol; German scientific publisher; b. 29 Nov. 1938, Jena; m. Akka Achelis 1967; three s. *Education:* Heidelberg, Berlin and Freiburg. *Career:* mil. service 1958–60; Asst Inst. of Econometrics, Freiburg 1965–66; worked in several publishing houses and as public accountant 1966–69; partner and Man. Dir Gustav Fischer Verlag 1969–95; mem. Bd of Exec. Officers, German Publrs. Asscn (Börsenverein) 1976–86; mem. Bd C. Hanser Verlag 1984–; Publr and Pres. Lucius & Lucius Verlag, Stuttgart 1996–; Chair. Int. Publishers Copyright Council 1995–98, Asscn of Scientific Publrs in Germany 1994–2001; mem. Exec. Cttee Int. Publrs Asscn Geneva 1996–; Bd of the German Nat. Library 1981–. *Publications:* Bücherlust-Vom Sammeln 2000; numerous articles on publishing, copyright and book history. *Honours:* Friedrich-Perthes-Medaille 1999, Antiquaria Preis 2001. *Address:* Gerokstr. 51, 70184 Stuttgart (Office); Ameisenbergstrasse 22, 7000 Stuttgart 1, Germany. *Telephone:* (711) 242060 (Office); (711) 264386 (Home). *Fax:* (711) 242088 (Office). *E-mail:* lucius@luciusverlag.com (Office). *Website:* luciusverlag.com (Office).

LUCKLESS, John (see Irving, Clifford (Michael)).

LUDWIKOWSKI, Rett R(yszard); Prof. of Law and Writer; b. 6 Nov. 1943, Skawina-Kraków, Poland; m. Anna Ludwikowski, 19 Jan. 1995, one s. one d. *Education:* LLM, Law, 1966, PhD Law, 1971, Habilitation, Law, 1976, Jagiellonian University, Kraków. *Career:* Senior Lecturer, 1967–71, Adjunct Prof., 1971–76, Asst Prof., 1976–81, Assoc. Prof. of Law 1981, Senior Fulbright Scholar 1997, Jagiellonian University, Kraków; Visiting Prof., Elizabethtown College, Pennsylvania, 1982–83, Alfred University, 1983; Visiting Scholar, Hoover Institution, Stanford University, 1983, Max Planck Institute, Hamburg, 1990; Visiting Prof. of Politics, 1984, Visiting Prof. of Law, 1985, Prof. of Law, 1986–, Dir, Comparative and International Law Institute, 1987–, Catholic University of America, Washington, DC, Co-Dir School of American Law Kraków 2000–. *Publications:* The Crisis of Communism: Its Meaning, Origins and Phases, 1986; Continuity and Change in Poland, 1991; Constitutionalism and Human Rights (ed. with Kenneth Thompson), 1991; The Beginning of the Constitutional Era: A Comparative Study of the First American and European Constitution (with William Fox Jr), 1993; Constitution Making in the Countries of Former Soviet Dominance, 1996; Regulations of International Trade and Business, 2 vols, 1996, 1998; Comparative Constitutional Law, 2000, Comparative Rights and Fundamental Freedoms Vol. I (Man.Ed.) 2002. Contributions: scholarly books and journals. *Honours:* various grants. *Address:* Columbus School of Law, Catholic University of America, Washington, DC 20064, USA.

LUEBKE, Frederick (Carl); Prof. of History Emeritus and Writer; b. 26 Jan. 1927, Reedsburg, Wisconsin, USA. *Education:* BS, Concordia University, River Forest, IL, 1950; MA, Claremont Graduate University, 1958; PhD, University of Nebraska, 1966. *Career:* Assoc. Prof., 1968–72, Prof., 1972–87, Charles Mach Distinguished Prof. of History, 1987–94, Prof. Emeritus, 1994–, University of Nebraska; Ed., Great Plains Quarterly, 1980–84; Dir, Center for Great Plains Studies, 1983–88. *Publications:* Immigrants and Politics, 1969; Ethnic Voters and the Election of Lincoln (ed.), 1971; Bonds of Loyalty: German-Americans and World War I, 1974; The Great Plains: Environment and Culture (ed.), 1979; Ethnicity on the Great Plains (ed.), 1980; Vision and Refuge: Essays on the Literature of the Great Plains (co-ed.), 1981; Mapping the North American Plains (co-ed.), 1987; Germans in Brazil: A Comparative History of Cultural Conflict During World War I, 1987; Germans in the New World: Essays in the History of Immigration, 1990; A Harmony of the Arts: The Nebraska State Capital (ed.), 1990; Nebraska: An Illustrated History, 1995; European Immigration in the American West: Community Histories (ed.), 1998. Contributions: Professional journals. *Address:* 3117 Woodsdale Blvd, Lincoln, NE 68502, USA.

LUELLEN, Valentina (see Polley, Judith Anne).

LUHRMANN, Bazmark (Baz) Anthony; Australian film and theatre director; b. 17 Sept. 1962, NSW; m. Catherine Martin 1997. *Education:* Narrabeen High School, Sydney. *Career:* theatre work with Peter Brook; owns Bazmark production co., Sydney; acting roles in films The Winter of Our Dreams 1982, The Dark Room 1984. *Films:* Strictly Ballroom 1992, La Bohème (TV) 1993, Romeo + Juliet 1996, Moulin Rouge 2001. *Plays:* Strictly Ballroom, Haircut. *Operas directed:* La Bohème, Sydney 1990, New York 2002–03, San Francisco 2002, A Midsummer Night's Dream, Sydney 1993. *Screenplays written:* Strictly Ballroom 1992, Romeo + Juliet 1996, Moulin Rouge (also story) 2001. *Literary Agent:* Hilary Linstead & Associates Pty Ltd, PO Box 1536, Strawberry Hills, NSW 2012, Australia.

LUHRMANN, Tanya Marie; Prof. of Anthropology and Writer; b. 24 Feb. 1959, Dayton, Ohio, USA. *Education:* BA summa cum laude, Harvard University, 1981; MPhil, Social Anthropology, 1982, PhD, Social Anthropology, 1986, University of Cambridge. *Career:* Research Fellow, Christ's College, Cambridge, 1985–89; Assoc. Prof. of Anthropology, 1989–98, Prof. of Anthropology, 1998–, University of California at San Diego; Prof., Cttee on Human Development, Univ. of Chicago, 2000–; mem. American Anthropology Asscn; Society for Psychological Anthropology; Royal Anthropological Institute. *Publications:* Persuasions of the Witch's Craft, 1989; The Good Parsi, 1996; Of Two Minds: The Growing Disorder in American Society, 2000. Contributions: Professional journals. *Honours:* Bowdoin Prize, 1981; National Science Foundation Graduate Fellow, 1982–85; Emanuel Miller Prize, 1983; Partingdon Prize, 1985; Stirling Prize, 1986; Fulbright Award, 1990; Turner Prize, 2000. *Address:* c/o Committee on Human Development, University of Chicago, 5730 South Woodlawn, Chicago, IL 60637, USA.

LUKACS, John Adalbert; American retd academic and writer; b. 31 Jan. 1924, Budapest, Hungary; m. 1st Helen Schofield 1953 (deceased 1970); one s. one d.; m. 2nd Stephanie Harvey 1974 (died 2003). *Education:* PhD, Palatine Joseph University, Budapest, 1946. *Career:* Prof. of History, 1947–94, Chair., Dept of History, 1947–93, Chestnut Hill College, Philadelphia; Visiting Prof., La Salle College, 1949–82, Columbia University, 1954–55, University of Toulouse, 1964–65, University of Pennsylvania, 1964, 1967, 1968, 1995–97, Johns Hopkins University, 1970–71, Fletcher School of Law and Diplomacy, 1971–72, Princeton University, 1988, University of Budapest, 1991; mem. American Catholic History Asscn, pres., 1977; Society of American Historians, fellow; American Philosophical Society. *Publications:* The Great Powers and Eastern Europe, 1953; A History of the Cold War, 1961; The Decline and Rise of Europe, 1965; Historical Consciousness, 1968; The Passing of the Modern Age, 1970; The Last European War, 1939–41, 1976; 1945: Year Zero, 1978; Philadelphia: Patricians and Philistines, 1900–1950, 1981; Outgrowing Democracy: A Historical Interpretation of the US in the 20th Century, 1984; Budapest 1900, 1988; Confessions of an Original Sinner, 1990; The Duel: Hitler vs. Churchill, 10 May–31 August 1940, 1991; The End of the 20th Century and the End of the Modern Age, 1993; Destinations Past, 1994; George P. Kennan and the Origins of Containment: The Kennan/Lukacs Correspondence, 1997; The Hitler of History, 1997; A Thread of Years, 1998; Five Days in London, 1999; At the End of an Age, 2002; Churchill: Visionary, Statesman, Historian, 2002. Contributions: many scholarly journals. *Honours:* Ingersoll Prize, 1991; Order of Merit, Republic of Hungary, 1994. *Address:* Valley Park Road, Phoenixville, PA 19460, USA.

LUKAS, Richard Conrad, BA, MA, PhD; historian and academic; b. 29 Aug. 1937, Lynn, Massachusetts, USA. *Education:* Florida State University. *Career:* Research Consultant, US Air Force Historical Archives, 1957–58; Asst Prof., 1963–66, Assoc. Prof., 1966–69, Prof., 1969–83, University Prof. of History, 1983–89, Tennessee Technological University, Cookeville; Prof., Wright State University, Lake Campus, 1989–92; Adjunct Prof., University of South Florida, Fort Myers, 1993–96; Consultant, Documentary Films, Zegota: A Time to Remember, 1997; Burning Questions, 1998. *Publications:* Eagles East: The Army Air Forces and the Soviet Union, 1941–45, 1970; From Metternich to the Beatles (ed.), 1973; The Strange Allies: The United States and Poland 1941–45, 1978; Bitter Legacy: Polish-American Relations in the Wake of World War II, 1982; Forgotten Holocaust: The Poles under German Occupation, 1986; Out of the Inferno: Poles Remember the Holocaust, 1989; Did the Children Cry?: Hitler's War Against Jewish and Polish Children, 1994. *Honours:* Doctor of Humane Letters, 1987; Polonia Restituta, 1988; Janusz Korczak Literary Award, 1996; Waclaw Jedrzejewicz History Award, 2000; Kosciuszko Foundation's Joseph Slotkowski Achievement Award, 2001. *Address:* 4460 Winston Lane N, Sarasota, FL 34235, USA.

LUKER, Nicholas (John Lydgate); University Senior Lecturer in Russian, Writer, Ed. and Trans; b. 26 Jan. 1945, Leeds, England; one s. *Education:* MA, French, Russian, Hertford College, Oxford, 1968; Lecteur d'Anglais, University of Grenoble, 1967; Postgraduate Scholar, Slavonic Studies, 1968–70, PhD, 1971, University of Nottingham. *Career:* Lecturer, 1970–88, Senior Lecturer in Russian, 1988–, University of Nottingham; various visiting lectureships and fellowships in New Zealand and USA; mem.

British Asscn of Slavists. *Publications:* Alexander Grin, 1973; The Seeker of Adventure, by Alexander Grin (trans. with B. Scherr), 1978; A I Kuprin, 1978; The Forgotten Visionary, 1982; An Anthology of Russian Neo-Realism: The 'Znanie' School of Maxim Gorky (ed. and trans.), 1982; Fifty Years On: Gorky and His Time (ed.), 1987; Alexander Grin: Selected Short Stories (ed. and trans.), 1987; From Furmanov to Sholokhov: An Anthology of the Classics of Socialist Realism (ed. and trans.), 1988; In Defence of a Reputation: Essays on the Early Prose of Mikhail Artsybashev, 1990; The Russian Short Story, 1900–1917 (ed.), 1991; Urban Romances, by Yuri Miloslavsky (ed. and co-trans.), 1994; After the Watershed: Russian Prose, 1917–1927 (ed.), 1996. Contributions: numerous scholarly journals. *Address:* c/o Dept of Slavonic Studies, University of Nottingham, Nottingham NG7 2RD, England.

LUMSDEN, Lynne Ann; American publishing executive; b. 30 July 1947, Battle Creek, Mich.; m. Jon Harden 1986; one d. *Education:* Univ. of Paris, Sarah Lawrence Coll., City Grad. Center and New York Univ. *Career:* copy ed., Harcourt, Brace, Jovanovich, New York 1970–71; ed., Appleton-Century Crofts, New York 1971–73; Coll. Div. Prentice Hall 1974–78, Sr Ed. Coll. Div. 1978–81; Asst Vice-Pres. and Ed.-in-Chief, Spectrum Books 1981–82, Vice-Pres. and Editorial Dir, Gen. Publishing Div. 1982–85; Exec. Vice-Pres., Publr and Co-owner, Dodd, Mead & Co., Inc. New York 1985–89; Owner, Chair. JBH Communications Inc. Hartford, Conn. 1989–; Publr Hartford News and Southside Media 1989–. *Address:* 11 Hammer Street, Hartford, CT 06114, USA (Office).

LUND, Gerald N(iels); Educator (retd) and Writer; b. 12 Sept. 1939, Fountain Green, UT, USA; m. Lynn Stanard, 5 June 1963, three s., four d. *Education:* BA, Sociology, 1965, MS, Sociology, 1969, Brigham Young University; Pepperdine College; University of Judaism. *Career:* Educator, 1965–99; mem. Asscn of Mormon Letters, hon. lifetime mem., 1997. *Publications:* The Coming of the Lord, 1971; This is Your World, 1973; One in Thine Hand, 1981; The Alliance, 1983; Leverage Point, 1986; The Freedom Factor, 1987; The Work and the Glory, nine vols, 1990–2000; The Kingdom and the Crown, two vols, 2000, 2002. Contributions: Monographs and periodicals. *Honours:* Best Novel Awards, Asscn of Mormon Letters, 1991, 1993; Frankie and John K. Orton, 1994; LDS Independent Booksellers Asscn Awards, 1994, 1997, 2000, 2001. *Address:* PO Box 30178, Salt Lake City, UT 84130, USA.

LUNN, Janet Louise; Writer; b. 28 Dec. 1928, Dallas, Texas, USA; m. Richard Lunn, 1 March 1950, four s., one d. *Education:* Queen's University, Kingston, Ontario. *Career:* Writer-in-Residence, Regina Public Library, Saskatchewan, 1982–83, Kitchener Public Library, Ontario, 1987, Ottawa University, Ontario, 1993; mem. Writers' Union of Canada, chair, 1984–85; Canadian Children's Book Center; PEN Canada. *Publications:* The Country, 1967; Double Spell, 1968; Larger Than Life, 1979; The Twelve Dancing Princesses, 1979; The Root Cellar, 1981; Shadow in Hawthorn Bay, 1986; Amos's Sweater, 1988; Duck Cakes for Sale, 1989; One Hundred Shining Candles, 1990; The Story of Canada, 1992; Ghost Stories for Children (ed.), 1994; The Hollow Tree, 1997; The Umbrella Party, 1998; Charlotte, 1998. Contributions: periodicals. *Honours:* Hon. LLD, Queen's University, 1992; Order of Ontario, 1996; Order of Canada, 1997.

LUPOFF, Richard Allen; Author; b. 21 Feb. 1935, New York, NY, USA; m. Patricia Enid Loring, 27 Aug. 1958, two s. one d. *Education:* BA, University of Miami at Coral Gables, 1956. *Career:* Ed., Canaveral Press, 1963–70; Contributing Ed., Crawdaddy Magazine, 1968–71, Science Fiction Eye, 1988–90; Ed., Canyon Press, 1986–. *Publications:* Edgar Rice Burroughs: Master of Adventure, 1965; All in Color for a Dime, 1971; Sword of the Demon, 1977; Space War Blues, 1978; Sun's End, 1984; Circumpolar!, 1984; Lovecrafts Book, 1985; The Forever City, 1987; The Comic Book Killer, 1988; The Classic Car Killer, 1992; The Bessie Blue Killer, 1994; The Sepia Siren Killer, 1994; The Cover Girl Killer, 1995. Contributions: Ramparts; Los Angeles Times; Washington Post; San Francisco Chronicle; New York Times; Magazine of Fantasy and Science Fiction. *Honours:* Hugo Award, 1963. *Address:* 3208 Claremont Ave, Berkeley, CA 94705, USA.

LURAGHI, Raimondo; academic and writer; b. 16 Aug. 1921, Milan, Italy; m. 1950; one s. one d. *Education:* MD, University of Turin, 1946; PhD, University of Rome, 1958. *Career:* Prof. of History, Junior College, 1954–64; Prof. of American History, 1964–95, Emeritus Prof., 1995–, University of Genoa; mem. Italian Asscn for Military History, pres. *Publications:* Storia della Guerra Civile Americana, 1966; Gli Stati Uniti, 1972; The Rise and Fall of the Plantation South, 1975; Marinai del Sud, 1993; A History of the Confederate Navy 1861–1865, 1995. Contributions: Italian, French, American and Chinese historical magazines. *Address:* Corso Regina Margherita 155, 10122 Turin, Italy.

LURIE, Alison, AB; American novelist and professor of English; *Whiton Professor of American Literature, Cornell University*; b. 3 Sept. 1926, Chicago, IL; m. 1st Jonathon Peale Bishop 1948 (divorced 1985); three s.; m. 2nd Edward Hower 1996. *Education:* Radcliffe Coll., Mass. *Career:* Editorial Asst Oxford University Press 1946; worked as receptionist and secretary; Lecturer in English, Cornell Univ. 1969–73, Adjunct Assoc. Prof. 1973–76, Assoc. Prof. 1976–79, Whiton Prof. of American Literature 1979–; Yaddo Foundation Fellow 1963, 1964, 1966, 1984, Guggenheim Fellow 1965, Rockefeller Foundation Fellow 1967. *Publications:* V. R. Lang: a Memoir 1959, Love and Friendship 1962, The Nowhere City 1965, Imaginary Friends 1967, Real People 1969, The War Between the Tates 1974, Only Children 1979, Clever Gretchen and Other Forgotten Folktales (juvenile) 1980, The The Heavenly Zoo (juvenile) 1980, Fabulous Beasts (juvenile) 1981, Foreign Affairs 1984 (Pulitzer Prize in Fiction 1985), The Man with a Shattered World 1987, The Truth about Lorin Jones 1988, Women and Ghosts 1994, The Last Resort 1998, Familiar Spirits 2001; non-fiction: The Language of Clothes 1981, Don't Tell the Grown Ups, Subversive Children's Literature (essays) 1990, Boys and Girls Forever: Reflections on Children's Classics (essays) 2003. *Honours:* New York State Cultural Council Foundation Grant 1972; American Acad. of Arts and Letters Literature Award 1978, Prix Femina Étranger 1989, Parents' Choice Foundation Award 1996. *Literary Agent:* AP Watt Ltd, 20 John Street, London, WC1N 2DR, England. *Address:* Department of English, Cornell University, Ithaca, New York, NY 14853, USA. *E-mail:* al28@cornell.edu (Office).

LURIE, Morris; writer; b. 30 Oct. 1938, Melbourne, Vic., Australia. *Career:* Writer-in-Residence, Latrobe University, 1984, Holmesglen Tafe, 1992. *Publications:* novels: Rappaport 1966, The London Jungle Adventures of Charlie Hope 1968, Rappaport's Revenge 1973, Flying Home 1978, Seven Books for Grossman 1983, Madness 1991; short stories: Happy Times 1969, Inside the Wardrobe 1975, Running Nicely 1979, Dirty Friends 1981, Outrageous Behaviour 1984, The Night We Ate the Sparrow 1985, Two Brothers Running 1990, The String 1995, Welcome to Tangier 1997, The Secret Strength of Children 2001; children's books: The Twenty-Seventh Annual African Hippopotamus Race 1969, Arlo the Dandy Lion 1971, The Story of Imelda Who Was Small 1984, Night-Night! 1986, What's That Noise? What's That Sound? 1991, Racing the Moon 1993, Zeeks Alive! 1997, Boy in a Storm at Sea 1997; autobiography: Whole Life 1987; contributions to Virginia Quarterly Review, The New Yorker, The New York Yimes, Antaeus, The Times, Punch, Telegraph Magazine, The Age (Australia); stories broadcast and plays telecast. *Honours:* State of Victoria Short Story Award 1973, National Book Council Selection 1980, Children's Book Council Honour Book 1983, Bicentennial Banjo Award 1988. *Address:* 141 Woodhouse Grove, Box Hill North, Victoria 3129, Australia.

LUSTBADER, Eric Van; Writer; b. 24 Dec. 1946, New York, NY, USA; m. Victoria Lustbader. *Education:* BA, Columbia University, 1968. *Publications:* The Sunset Warrior, 1977; Shallows of Night, 1978; Dai-San, 1978; Beneath an Opal Moon, 1980; The Ninja, 1980; Sirens, 1981; Black Heart, 1982; The Miko, 1984; Jian, 1985; Shan, 1987; Zero, 1988; French Kiss, 1988; White Ninja, 1989; Angel Eyes, 1991; Black Blade, 1993; The Keishe, 1993; Batman: The Last Angel, 1994; The Floating City, 1994. Contributions: Magazines. *Address:* c/o Henry Morrison Inc, Box 235, Bedford Hills, NY 10507, USA.

LUSTIG, Arnošt; Writer, Screenwriter and Educator; b. 21 Dec. 1926, Prague, Czechoslovakia; m. Vera Weislitz, 24 July 1949, one s. one d. *Education:* MA, College of Political and Social Science, Prague, 1951. *Career:* Arab-Israeli War Correspondent, Radio Prague, 1948–49; Correspondent, Czechoslovak Radio, 1950–68; Screenwriter, Barrandov Film Studies, Prague, 1960–68, Jadran Film Studio, Zagreb, 1969–70; Visiting Lecturer, English, 1971–72, Visiting Prof., English, 1972–73, Drake University; Prof., Literature and Film, American University, Washington, DC, 1973–; mem. Franz Kafka Society, Prague, hon. pres. *Publications:* Night and Hope, 1958; Diamonds of the Night, 1958; Street of Lost Brothers, 1959; Dita Saxova, 1962; My Acquaintance Vili Feld, 1962; A Prayer for Katarina Horovitzova, 1964; Nobody Will be Humiliated, 1964; Bitter Smells of Almonds, 1968; Darling, 1969; The Unloved (From the Diary of a Seventeen Year Old), 1986; Indecent Dreams, 1988; Jewish Trilogy, 1999–2001; Essays, 2001; Lovely Green Eyes, 2002. Films/Screenplays: Transport from Paradise, 1963; Diamonds of the Night, 1964; Dita Saxova, 1968; The Triumph of Memory, 1989; Precious Legacy, 1995; A Prayer for Katerina Horovitzova. Biographical Documentary: Fighter, 2000. Other: Trans. *Honours:* State Prize, 1965; National Jewish Book Awards, 1980, 1986; Doctor of Hebrew Letters, Spertus College, 1986; Karel Čopek Prize, 1996. *Address:* 4000 Tunlaw Rd NW, Apt 825, Washington, DC 20007, USA.

LUTTWAK, Edward Nicolae; American political scientist and writer; b. 4 Nov. 1942, Arad, Romania; m. Dalya Iaari 1970; one s. one d. *Education:* Carmel College, England; BSc, LSE, 1964; PhD, Johns Hopkins University, 1975. *Career:* Assoc. Dir, Washington Center of Foreign Policy Research, DC, 1972–75; Visiting Prof. of Political Science, Johns Hopkins University, 1973–78; Senior Fellow, 1976–87, Research Prof. in International Security Affairs, 1978–82, Arleigh Burke Chair in Strategy, 1987–, Dir, Geo-Economics, 1991–, Center for Strategic and International Studies, Washington, DC; Nimitz Lecturer, University of California, Berkeley, 1987; Tanner Lecturer, Yale University, 1989. *Publications:* A Dictionary of Modern War, 1971, new edn (with Stuart Koehl), 1991; The Grand Strategy of the Roman Empire: From the First Century A.D. to the Third, 1976; The Economic and Military Balance Between East and West 1951–1978 (ed. with Herbert Block), 1978; Sea Power in the Mediterranean (with R. G. Weinland), 1979; Strategy and Politics: Collected Essays, 1980; The Grand Strategy of the Soviet Union, 1983; The Pentagon and the Art of War: The Question of Military Reform, 1985; Strategy and History, 1985; On the Meaning of Victory: Essays on Strategy, 1986; Global Security: A Review of Strategic and Economic Issues (ed. with Barry M. Blechman), 1987; Strategy: The Logic of War and Peace, 1987; The Endangered American

Dream: How to Stop the United States from Becoming a Third World Country and How to Win the Geo-Economic Struggle for Industrial Supremacy, 1993; Turbo-Capitalism: Winners and Losers in the Global Economy, 1999; La renaissance de la puissance aerienne stategique, 1999; Che cos'é davvero la democrazia (with Susanna Creperio Verratti), 2000; Il Libro delle Liberta, 2000; Strategy Now (ed.), 2000, revised edn as Strategy, 2002. Contributions: numerous books and periodicals. *Address:* c/o Center for Strategic and International Studies, Georgetown University, 1800 K Street NW, Washington, DC 20006, USA.

LUTZ, John Thomas; Writer; b. 11 Sept. 1939, Dallas, Texas, USA; m. Barbara Jean Bradley, 15 March 1958, one s. two d. *Education:* Meramac Community College. *Career:* mem. MWA; Private Eye Writers of America, board of dirs. *Publications:* The Truth of the Matter, 1971; Buyer Beware, 1976; Bonegrinder, 1977; Lazarus Man, 1979; Jericho Man, 1980; The Shadow Man, 1981; Exiled (with Steven Greene), 1982; Nightlines, 1985; The Right to Sing the Blues, 1986; Tropical Heat, 1986; Ride the Lightning, 1987; Scorcher, 1987; Kiss, 1988; Shadowtown, 1988; Time Exposure, 1989; Flame, 1990; Diamond Eyes, 1990; SWF Seeks Same, 1990; Bloodfire, 1991; Hot, 1992; Dancing with the Dead, 1992; Spark, 1993; Shadows Everywhere (short stories), 1994; Thicker Than Blood, 1994; Death by Jury, 1995; Torch, 1995; Burn, 1996; Lightning, 1996; Final Seconds (with David August), 1998, Oops!, 1998; Until You are Dead (short stories) 1998, The Nudger Dilemmas (short stories) 2001, The Night Caller 2001, The Night Watcher 2002. Contributions: anthologies and magazines. *Honours:* Scroll, 1981, Edgar Award, 1983, MWA; Shamus Awards, 1982, 1988; Private Eye Writers of America Life Achievement Award, 1995. *Address:* 880 Providence Ave, Webster Groves, MO 63119, USA.

LUX, Thomas; Poet and Teacher; b. 10 Dec. 1946, Northampton, Massachusetts, USA; m. Jean Kilbourne, 1983, one d. *Education:* BA, Emerson College, Boston, 1970; University of Iowa, 1971. *Career:* Managing Ed., Iowa Review, 1971–72, Ploughshares, 1973; Poet-in-Residence, Emerson College, 1972–75; Faculty, Sarah Lawrence College, 1975, Warren Wilson College, 1980–, Columbia University, 1980–. *Publications:* The Land Sighted, 1970; Memory's Handgrenade, 1972; The Glassblower's Breath, 1976; Sunday, 1979; Like a Wide Anvil From the Moon the Light, 1980; Massachusetts, 1981; Tarantulas on the Lifebuoy, 1983; Half Promised Land, 1986; Sunday: Poems, 1989; The Drowned River, 1990; A Boat in the Forest, 1992; Pecked to Death by Swans, 1993; Split Horizon, 1994; The Sanity of Earth and Grass (ed. with Jane Cooper and Sylvia Winner), 1994. *Honours:* Bread Loaf Scholarship, 1970; MacDowell Colony Fellowships, 1973, 1974, 1976, 1978, 1980, 1982; National Endowment for the Arts Grants, 1976, 1981, 1988; Guggenheim Fellowship, 1988; Kingsley Tufts Poetry Award, 1995.

LUXON, Thomas H.; University Educator and Writer; b. 26 April 1954, Darby, Pennsylvania, USA; m. 1st Nancy Ellen Gray 15 June 1980 (divorced 1985); m. 2nd Ivy Schweitzer 15 July 1988; one s. one d. *Education:* BA, Brown University, 1977; AM, 1978, PhD, 1984, University of Chicago. *Career:* William Rainey Harper Instructor, University of Chicago, 1984–85; Visiting Asst Prof. of English, St Lawrence University, Canton, New York, 1985–86; Asst Prof. of English, Franklin and Marshall College, Lancaster, Pennsylvania, 1987–88; Assoc. Prof. of English, 1988–, Dept Vice-Chair, 1994–96, Dartmouth College, Hanover, NH; mem. John Bunyan Society of North America; MLA of America; Milton Society of America. *Publications:* Literal Figures: Puritan Allegory and the Reformation, 1995; Milton and Manliness: Friends and Lovers, 1999. Contributions: Prose Studies: Literature, History, Theory. *Honours:* Fellow, National Endowment for the Humanities, 1985–86.

LYKIARD, Alexis Constantine, BA, MA; poet, writer and translator; b. 2 Jan. 1940, Athens, Greece. *Education:* King's Coll., Cambridge. *Career:* Creative Writing Tutor, Arvon Foundation 1974–; writer-in-residence, Sutton Central Library 1976–77, Loughborough Art College 1982–83, Tavistock, Devon Libraries 1983–85, HMP Channings Wood 1988–89, HMP Haslar 1993–94; mem. Soc. of Authors. *Publications:* Lobsters 1961, Journey of the Alchemist 1963, The Summer Ghosts 1964, Wholly Communion (ed.) 1965, Zones 1966, Paros Poems 1967, A Sleeping Partner 1967, Robe of Skin 1969, Strange Alphabet 1970, Best Horror Stories of J. Sheridan Le Fanu (ed.) 1970, Eight Lovesongs 1972, The Stump 1973, Greek Images 1973, Lifelines 1973, Instrument of Pleasure 1974, Last Throes 1976, Milesian Fables 1976, A Morden Tower Reading 1976, The Drive North 1977, New Stories 2 (ed.) 1977, Scrubbers 1983, Cat Kin 1985, Out of Exile 1986, Safe Levels 1990, Living Jazz 1991, Beautiful is Enough 1992, Omnibus Occasions 1995, Selected Poems 1956–96 1997, Jean Rhys Revisited 2000, Skeleton Keys 2003; many French translations. *Address:* 77 Latimer Road, Exeter, Devon EX4 7JP, England.

LYNCH, Frances (see Compton, David Guy).

LYNCH, John, MA, PhD, FRHistS; academic and historian; b. 11 Jan. 1927, Boldon, England. *Education:* University of Edinburgh, University of London. *Career:* Lecturer in History, University of Liverpool, 1954–61; Lecturer, Reader and Prof. of Latin American History, University College London, 1961–74; Prof. of Latin American History and Dir of Institute of Latin American Studies, University of London, 1974–87. *Publications:* Spanish Colonial Administration 1782–1810: The Intendant System in the Viceroyalty of the Río de la Plata, 1958; Spain Under the Habsburgs, 2 vols, 1964, 1967; The Origins of the Latin American Revolutions 1808–1826 (with R. A. Humphreys), 1965; The Spanish American Revolutions 1808–1826, 1973; Argentine Dictator: Juan Manuel de Rosas 1829–1852, 1981; The Cambridge History of Latin America (with others), Vol. 3, 1985, Vol. 4, 1986; Bourbon Spain 1700–1808, 1989; Caudillos in Spanish America 1800–1850, 1992; Latin American Revolutions 1808–1826: Old and New World Origins, 1994; Massacre in the Pampas, 1872: Britain and Argentina in the Age of Migration, 1998; Latin America Between Colony and Nation, 2001. *Honours:* Encomienda Isabel La Católica, Spain, 1988; Dr hc, University of Seville, 1990; Order of Andrés Bello, First Class, Venezuela, 1995. *Address:* 8 Templars Crescent, London N3 3QS, England. *E-mail:* johnlynch53@msn.com.

LYNCH, Thomas; Writer, Poet and Funeral Dir; b. 16 Oct. 1948, Detroit, MI, USA; four c. *Publications:* Skating with Heather Grace (poems), 1986; Grimalkin and Other Poems, 1994; The Undertaking: Life Studies from the Dismal Trade (non-fiction), 1997; Still Life in Milford (poems), 1998; Bodies in Motion and at Rest (poems), 2000. *Address:* 404 E Liberty, Milford, MI 48381, USA. *E-mail:* thoslynch@aol.com.

LYNDS, Dennis, (William Arden, Nick Carter, Michael Collins, John Crowe, Carl Dekker, Maxwell Grant, Mark Sadler); Writer; b. 15 Jan. 1924, St Louis, MO, USA; m. 1st Doris Flood 1949 (divorced 1956); m. 2nd Sheila McErlean 1961 (divorced 1985); two d.; m. 3rd Gayle Hallenbeck Stone 1986. *Education:* BA, Hofstra College, 1949; MA, Syracuse University, 1951. *Publications:* Combat Soldier, 1962; Uptown Downtown, 1963; Why Girls Ride Sidesaddle (short stories), 1980; Freak, 1983; Minnesota Strip, 1987; Red Rosa, 1988; Castrato, 1989; Chasing Eights, 1990; The Irishman's Horse, 1991; Cassandra in Red, 1992; Crime, Punishment and Resurrection, 1992; Talking to the World, 1995; The Cadillac Cowboy, 1995; Fortune's World, 2000; Spies and Thieves, Cops and Killers, etc., 2002; Lost Souls, 2003. *Honours:* Edgar of MWA, 1968; Lifetime Achievement Award, Private Eye Writers of America, 1988; Marlowe Lifetime Achievement Award, MWA SoCal, 2002. *Address:* 12 St Anne Dr., Santa Barbara, CA 93109, USA. *E-mail:* dennislynds@cox.net. *Website:* dennislynds.com.

LYNN, Jonathan; Theatre and Film Dir, Actor and Writer; b. 3 April 1943, Bath, England. *Education:* MA, Pembroke College, Cambridge, 1964. *Career:* Artistic Dir, Cambridge Theatre Co, 1976–81; Company Dir, National Theatre, 1987. *Publications:* A Proper Man, 1976; The Complete Yes Minister, 1984; Yes Prime Minister, Vol. I, 1986; Yes Prime Minister, Vol. II, 1987; Mayday, 1993. Other: various screenplays and television series. *Literary Agent:* PFD, Drury House, 34–43 Russell St, London WC2B 5HA, England.

LYNTON, Ann (see Rayner, Claire Berenice).

LYNTON, Harriet Ronken; Writer; b. 22 May 1920, Rochester, Minnesota, USA; m. Rolf P. Lynton, 16 April 1955, one s. two d. *Education:* AB, Radcliffe College. *Career:* Faculty, Harvard Business School, 1945–54; mem. North Carolina Writers Network. *Publications:* Administering Changes, 1952; Training for Human Relations, 1954; The Days of the Beloved, 1974; My Dear Nawab Sahib, 1991; Born to Dance, 1995. Contributions: The Homesteaders; Potpourri; The Literary Arts. *Address:* 458 Fearrington Post, Pittsboro, NC 27312, USA.

LYONS, Arthur; Writer; b. 5 Jan. 1946, Los Angeles, CA, USA; m. Marie Lyons. *Education:* BA, University of California, Santa Barbara, 1967. *Publications:* The Second Coming: Satanism in America, 1970; The Dead Are Discreet, 1974; All God's Children, 1975; The Killing Floor, 1976; Dead Ringer, 1977; Castles Burning, 1979; Hard Trade, 1981; At the Hands of Another, 1983; Three With a Bullet, 1985; Fast Fade, 1987; Unnatural Causes (with Thomas Noguchi), 1988; Satan Wants You, 1988; Other Poeple's Money, 1989; Physical Evidence (with Thomas Noguchi), 1990; The Blue Sense (with Marcello Truzzi), 1991; False Pretences, 1993. *Address:* c/o Penguin Putnam, 375 Hudson St, New York, NY 10014, USA.

LYONS, Elena (see Fairburn, Eleanor M.).

LYONS, Garry Fairfax, BA, MA; dramatist; b. 5 July 1956, Kingston-upon-Thames, England; m. Ruth Caroline Willis 1985; one s. one d. *Education:* Univ. of York, Univ. of Leeds. *Career:* playwright-in-residence, Major Road Theatre Co 1983; Fellow in Theatre, Univ. of Bradford 1984–88; mem. Theatre Writers' Union. *Productions include:* Echoes from the Valley 1983, Mohicans 1984, St Vitus' Boogie 1985, Urban Jungle 1985, The Green Violinist 1986, Irish Night 1987, Divided Kingdoms 1989, The People Museum 1989, Dream Kitchen 1992, Frankie and Tommy 1992, Wicked Year 1994. *Literary Agent:* International Creative Management, 4–6 Soho Square, London, W1D 3PZ, England.

M

NOTE: All names beginning Mc and Mac are treated as if they began Mac.

MA FEI (see Marr, William Wei-Yi).

MA VAN KHANG; Vietnamese writer; b. (Dinh Trong Doan), 1 Dec. 1936, Kim Lien, nr Hanoi. *Education:* Hanoi Pedagogical Univ. *Career:* fmr headmaster in Lao Cai Province; Deputy Ed.-in-Chief, Lao Cai newspaper; Ed.-in-Chief, Labor Publishing House 1976; Ed.-in-Chief, Foreign Literary Review section, Exec. Cttee mem. 1995–2000, Viet Nam Writers' Asscn. *Publications in translation:* novels: The French Silver Coin 1979, Summer Rain 1982, The Athlete in his Arena 1982, Border Area 1983, Young Moon 1984, The Garden in the Season of Falling Leaves 1986, The Lonely Orphan 1989, A Marriage Without Certificate 1989, Bi, The Wandering Dog 1992, Against the Flood 1999; short story collections: A Beautiful Day 1986, Ripe Fruits in Autumn 1988, The Strong Breeze 1992, Moonlight on the Small Yard 1995, Suburb 1996, The Classical Circle 1997, Lotus Marsh 1997, A Windy Afternoon 1998. *Honours:* Viet Nam Writers' Asscn Best Novel 1986, Best Short Story Collection 1995, ASEAN Literary Prize 1998. *Address:* c/o Curbstone Press, 321 Jackson Street, Willimantic, CT 06226-1738, USA. *E-mail:* info@curbstone.org. *Website:* www.curbstone.org.

MAALOUF, Amin; Writer; b. 25 Feb. 1949, Beirut, Lebanon; m. Andrée Abouchdid, 24 April 1971, three c. *Education:* Université Saint-Joseph, Beirut; Université de Lyon. *Career:* Journalist, An-Nahar, 1971–76, Economia, 1976–77; Ed., Jeune Afrique, 1978–79, 1982–84. *Publications:* Les Croisades vues par les Arabes, 1983; Léon l'Africain, 1986; Samarcande, 1988; Les Jardins de lumière, 1991; Le Premier siècle après Béatrice, 1992; Le Rocher de Tanios, 1993; Les Echelles du Levant, 1996; Les Identités meurtrières, 1998; Le Périple de Baldassare, 2000; L'Amour de Loin, 2001. *Honours:* Grand prix de la Méditerranée; Prix France-Liban; Grand prix de l'Unicef; Prix Paul Flat, l'Académie française; Prix Goncourt, 1993. *Address:* c/o Editions Grasset, 61 rue des Saints-Pères, 75006 Paris, France.

MABBETT, Ian William, BA, MA, DPhil; historian and university lecturer; *Emeritus Professor, Aichi Bunkyo University*; b. 27 April 1939, London, England; m. Jacqueline Diana June Towns 1971; two d. *Education:* University of Oxford. *Career:* Faculty, Monash University; Prof., Aichi Bunkyo University, 2000–02, Emer. Prof. 2002–; mem. Federation of Australian Writers. *Publications:* A Short History of India, 1968; Modern China, The Mirage of Modernity, 1985; Kings and Emperors of Asia, 1985; Patterns of Kingship and Authority in Traditional Asia (ed.), 1985; The Khmers (co-author), 1995, Sociology of Early Buddhism (co-author) 2003. Contributions: Hemisphere, Canberra; Asian Pacific Quarterly, Seoul; History Today, London; The Cambridge History of Southeast Asia. *Honours:* Pres., IXth World Sanskrit Conference 1994; Gold Medal Asiatic Society 1999. *Address:* c/o School of Historical Studies, Monash University, Clayton, Vic. 3800, Australia. *E-mail:* ian.mabbett@arts.monash.edu.au.

MABEY, Richard Thomas; Writer and Broadcaster; b. 20 Feb. 1941, Berkhamsted, Hertfordshire, England. *Education:* BA, 1966, MA, 1971, St Catherine's College, Oxford. *Career:* Senior Ed., Penguin Books, 1966–73; mem. Botanical Society of British Isles, council, 1981–83; Nature Conservancy, council, 1982–86; London Wildlife Trust, pres., 1982–92; Plantlife, advisory council, 1990–; Open Spaces Society, vice-pres., 2003–; Richard Jefferies Society, pres., 1996–98. *Publications:* The Pop Process, 1969; Food for Free, 1972; Unofficial Countryside, 1973; Street Flowers, 1976; Plants with a Purpose, 1977; The Common Ground, 1980; The Flowering of Britain, 1980; In a Green Shade, 1983; Oak and Company, 1983; Frampton Flora, 1985; Gilbert White, 1986; The Flowering of Kew, 1988; Home Country, 1990; Whistling in the Dark, 1993; Oxford Book of Nature Writing (ed.), 1995; Flora Britannica, 1996. Contributions: Times; Telegraph; Sunday Times; Observer; The Guardian; Nature; Modern Painters; Independent. *Honours:* Information Book Award, Times Educational Supplement, 1977; Children's Book Award, New York Acad. of Sciences, 1984; Whitbread Biography Award, 1986; National Book Awards, 1997; Hon. DSc, University of St Andrews, 1997. *Address:* c/o Sheil Land Assocs, 43 Doughty St, London WC1N 2LF, England.

MAC AVOY, Roberta Ann; Writer; b. 13 Dec. 1949, Cleveland, Ohio, USA. *Education:* BA, Case Western Reserve University, 1971. *Publications:* Tea with the Black Dragon, Damiano, 1983; Damiano's Lute, Raphael, 1984; The Book of Kells (co-author), 1985; Twisting the Rope, 1986; The Grey Horse, 1987; The Third Eagle, 1989; Lens of the World, 1990. *Address:* Underhill at Nelson Farm, 1669 Nelson Rd, Scotts Valley, CA 95066, USA.

MAC LOW, Jackson; Poet, Composer, Painter and Multimedia Performance Artist; b. 12 Sept. 1922, Chicago, IL, USA; m. Anne Tardos. *Education:* Chicago Musical College, 1927–32; Northwestern University School of Music, 1932–36; AA, University of Chicago, 1941; BA, Brooklyn College, CUNY, 1958. *Career:* Teacher, New York University, 1966–73, Mannes College of Music, 1966, Naropa University, 1975, 1991, 1994, 1999, SUNY at Albany, 1984, at Binghamton, 1989, and at Buffalo, 1990, 1997, Temple University, 1989, Schule für Dichtung, Vienna, 1992, 1993, Bard College, 1994, Brown University, 1994; Regents Lecturer, University of California at San Diego, 1990; Distinguished Visiting Writer, Saint Mary's College, Moraga, CA, 2000; mem. PEN American Centre; Poetry Society of America; Poets Advisory Committee, New York. *Publications:* 26 books, incl.: The Twin Plays: Port-au-Prince and Adams County Illinois, 1963; The Pronouns: A Collection of 40 Dances – For the Dancers, 1964; August Light Poems, 1967; 22 Light Poems, 1968; Stanzas for Iris Lezak, 1972; 21 Matched Asymmetries, 1978; A Dozen Douzains for Eve Rosenthal, 1978; Asymmetries 1-260, 1980; From Pearl Harbor Day to FDR's Birthday, 1982; French Sonnets, 1984; The Virginia Woolf Poems, 1985; Representative Works, 1938–1985, 1986; Words and Ends from Ez, 1989; Twenties: 100 Poems, 1991; Pieces o' Six: Thirty-Three Poems in Prose, 1992; 42 Merzgedichte in Memorian Kurt Schwitters, 1994; Barnesbook, 1996; 20 Forties, 1999; Struggle Through, 2001; Les Quarantains (extracts), 2001; Doings: An Assortment of Performance Pieces, 1955–2002, 2002. Contributions: various publications. *Honours:* Creative Artists Public Service Fellowship in Multimedia, 1973–74, and in Poetry, 1976–77; National Endowment for the Arts Fellowship, 1978; Guggenheim Fellowship, 1985; New York Foundation for the Arts Fellowship, 1988; Wallace Stevens Award, Acad. of American Poets, 1999. *Address:* 42 N Moore St, New York, NY 10013, USA.

McADAM, Douglas John, BA, MA, PhD; academic and writer; b. 31 Aug. 1951, Pasadena, CA, USA; m. Tracy Lynn Stevens 1988. *Education:* Occidental College, Los Angeles, SUNY at Stony Brook. *Career:* Instructor, Occidental College, Los Angeles, 1975, SUNY at Stony Brook, 1977–79; Asst Prof., George Mason University, Fairfax, Virginia, 1979–82; Asst Prof., 1983–86, Assoc. Prof., 1986–90, Prof. of Sociology, 1990–98, University of Arizona; Fellow, Center for Advanced Study in the Behavioral Sciences, 1991–92, 1997–98, Udall Center for Studies in Public Policy, 1994–95; Hollingshead Lecturer, Yale University, 1997; Prof. of Sociology, 1998–, Dir, Center for Advanced Study in the Behavioral Sciences, 2001–, Stanford University; mem. American Sociological Asscn; Sociological Research Asscn. *Publications:* The Politics of Privacy (with James Rule, Linda Stearns, and David Uglow), 1980; Political Process and the Development of Black Insurgency, 1930–1970, 1982; Freedom Summer, 1988; Collective Behavior and Social Movements (with Gary Marx), 1994; Comparative Perspectives on Social Movements: Political Opportunities, Mobilizing Structures, and Cultural Framings (ed. with John McCarthy and Mayer Zald), 1996; Social Movements: Readings on Their Emergence, Mobilization and Dynamics (with David Snow), 1996; How Movements Matter: Theoretical and Comparative Studies on the Consequences of Social Movements (ed. with Marco Giugni and Charles Tilly), 1998; From Contention to Democracy (ed. with Marco Guigni and Charles Tilly), 1999; Dynamics of Contention (with Sydney Tarrow and Charles Tilly), 2001; Silence and Voice in the Study of Contentious Politics (with others), 2001. Contributions: scholarly books and professional journals. *Honours:* Guggenheim Fellowship, 1984–85; Gustavus Myers Center Outstanding Book, 1988; C. Wright Mills Award, 1990; elected to American Acad. of Arts and Sciences, 2003. *Address:* c/o Department of Sociology, Stanford University, Stanford, CA 94305, USA.

MacALAN, Peter (see Ellis, Peter Berresford).

McALLISTER, Casey (see Battin, B. W.).

MacAULAY, David Alexander, BArch; writer and illustrator; b. 2 Dec. 1946, Burton-on-Trent, England; m. 1st Janice Elizabeth Michel 1970 (divorced); one d.; m. 2nd Ruth Marris 1978 (divorced); m. 3rd Charlotte Valerie. *Education:* Rhode Island School of Design. *Publications:* Cathedral: The Story of Its Construction, 1973; City: A Story of Roman Planning and Construction, 1974; Pyramid, 1975; Underground, 1976; Castle, 1977; Great Movements in Architecture, 1978; Motel of the Mysteries, 1979; Unbuilding, 1980; Electricity, 1983; Mill, 1983; BAAA, 1985; Why the Chicken Crossed the Road, 1987; The Way Things Work, 1988; Black and White, 1990; Ship, 1993; Shortcut, 1995. *Honours:* Caldecott Honor Books, 1973, 1977; Christopher Medal, 1991. *Address:* c/o Houghton Mifflin Co, 222 Berkeley Street, Boston, MA 02116, USA.

McAULEY, James John; academic and poet; b. 8 Jan. 1936, Dublin, Ireland; m. Deirdre O'Sullivan 1982. *Education:* University College Dublin, University of Arkansas, Fayetteville. *Career:* Ed., Dolmen Press, Dublin, 1960–66; Prof., Eastern Washington University, Cheney, 1978–; Dir, Eastern Washington University Press, 1993. *Publications:* Observations, 1960; A New Address, 1965; Draft Balance Sheet, 1970; Home and Away, 1974; After the Blizzard, 1975; The Exile's Recurring Nightmare, 1975; Recital, Poems, 1975–80, 1982; The Exile's Book of Hours, 1982; Coming and Going: New and Selected Poems, 1968–88, 1989. Play: The Revolution, 1966. Libretto: Praise, 1981. *Honours:* National Endowment for the Arts Grant, 1972; Washington Governor's Award, 1976. *Address:* Eastern Washington University Press, MS No. 14, Eastern Washington University, Cheney, WA 99004, USA.

McAULEY, Paul J., BSc, PhD; British biologist and writer; b. 23 April 1955, Stroud, Gloucestershire, England. *Education:* Univ. of Bristol. *Publications:* Four Hundred Billion Stars 1988, Secret Harmonies 1989, Eternal

Light 1991, The King of the Hill and Other Stories 1991, In Dreams (ed. with Kim Newman) 1992, Red Dust 1993, Pasquale's Angel 1994, Fairyland 1995, The Invisible Country 1996, Child of the River 1997, Ancients of Days 1998, Shrine of Stars 1999, The Secret of Life 2001, Whole Wide World 2001, While Devils 2004; contrib. to magazines. *Honours:* Philip K. Dick Memorial Award for Best New Novel 1989, Arthur C. Clarke Award for Best British Novel 1995, Sidewise Award 1995, British Fantasy Society Short Story Award 1995, John W. Campbell Award 1996. *Literary Agent:* Antony Harwood Ltd, Office 109, Riverbank House, 1 Putney Bridge Approach, London, SW6 3JD, England.

McBAIN, Ed (see Hunter, Evan).

McBRIDE, James; American writer, journalist and musician; b. New York, NY; m.; two c. *Education:* Oberlin Conservatory of Music, OH, Columbia Univ., NY. *Career:* fmr staff writer, Washington Post, People magazine, Boston Globe; songwriter for artists, including Anita Baker, Grover Washington Jr, Gary Burton; mem. Nat. Council on the Arts. *Publications:* The Color of Water: A Black Man's Tribute to his White Mother 1996, Autobiography of Quincy Jones (with Quincy Jones) 2001, Miracle at St Anna 2002; contrib. to Essence, Rolling Stone, New York Times. *Honours:* Dr hc (Whitman Coll., Coll. of New Jersey) ; Ansfield-Wolf Book Award for Literary Excellence 1997. *Address:* c/o Bloomsbury Publishing PLC, 38 Soho Square, London, W1V 5DF, England. *Website:* www.jamesmcbride.com.

McBRIDE, Jule, BA, MFA; writer; b. 27 Oct. 1959, Charleston, West Virginia, USA. *Education:* West Virginia State College, University of Pittsburgh. *Publications:* Wild Card Wedding, 1993; Baby Trap, 1993; The Wrong Wife, 1994; The Baby and the Bodyguard, 1994; Bride of the Badlands, 1995; The Baby Maker, 1995; The Bounty Hunter's Baby, 1996; Baby Romeo, 1996; Cole in My Stocking, 1996; Mission: Motherhood, 1997; Verdict: Parenthood, 1997; Wed to a Stranger, 1997; Who's Been Sleeping in My Bed?, 1997; Diagnosis: Daddy, 1998; How the West Was Wed, 1998; AKA: Marriage, 1998; Smoochin' Santas, 1998; Santa Slept Over, 1999; The Strong Silent Type, 1999. Contributions: anthologies. *Honours:* Reviewer's Choice Award for Best Series Romance, Romantic Times, 1993. *Literary Agent:* Karen Solem, Writers House Inc, 21 W 26th Street, New York, NY 10010, USA.

McBRIEN, Richard Peter, AA, BA, MA, STD; academic and writer; b. 19 Aug. 1936, Hartford, CT, USA. *Education:* St Thomas Seminary, Bloomfield, CT, St John Seminary, Brighton, Pontifical Gregorian University, Rome. *Career:* Assoc. Pastor, Our Lady of Victory, West Haven, CT, 1962–63; Prof. and Dean of Studies, Pope John XXIII National Seminary, Weston, MA, 1965–70; Prof. of Theology, 1970–80, Dir of Religious Education and Pastoral Ministry, 1975–80, Boston College, Newton, MA; Visiting Fellow, John J. Kennedy School of Government, Harvard University, 1976–77; Prof. of Theology, 1980–, Chair., Dept of Theology, 1980–91, University of Notre Dame, IN; mem. American Acad. of Religion; Catholic Theological Society of America, pres., 1973–74; College Theology Society. *Publications:* Do We Need Church?, 1969; Catholicism, two vols, 1980; Caesar's Coin: Religion and Politics in America, 1987; Encyclopedia of Religion (ed.), 1987; Report on the Church: Catholicism After Vatican II, 1992; The HarperCollins Encyclopedia of Catholicism (ed.), 1995; Responses to 101 Questions on the Chuch, 1996; Inside Catholicism, 1996; Lives of the Popes: The Pontiffs from St Peter to John Paul II (ed.), 1997; Lives of the Saints: From Mary and St Francis of Assisi to John XXIII and Mother Teresa (ed.), 2001. Contributions: various publications. *Honours:* Best Syndicated Weekly Column Awards, Catholic Press Asscn of the USA and Canada, 1975, 1977, 1978, 1984; John Courtney Murray Award, Catholic Theological Society of America, 1976; Christopher Award, 1981. *Address:* c/o Department of Theology, University of Notre Dame, 327 O'Shaughnessy Hall, Notre Dame, IN 46556, USA.

McCABE, Patrick; writer and dramatist; b. 27 March 1955, Clones, Co Monoghan, Ireland; m. Margot Quinn 1981; two d. *Education:* St Patrick's Teacher Training Coll., Dublin. *Publications:* The Adventures of Shay Mouse, 1985; Music on Clinton Street, 1986; Carn, 1989; The Butcher Boy, 1992; Frank Pig Says Hello (play based on The Butcher Boy), 1992; The Dead School, 1995; Breakfast on Pluto, 1998; Mondo Desperado, 1999; Emerald Germs of Ireland, 2001; Call Me the Breeze, 2003. Contributions: anthologies, periodicals and BBC Radio. *Honours:* Hennessy Award, Irish Press, 1979; Irish Times/Aer Lingus Award, 1992. *Address:* c/o Picador, Macmillan Books, 25 Eccleston Place, London SW1W 9NF, England.

McCAFFREY, Anne Inez, BA; writer; b. 1 April 1926, Cambridge, MA, USA; m. Wright Johnson 1950 (divorced 1970); two s. one d. *Education:* Radcliffe Coll., Univ. of Dublin. *Career:* mem. Authors' Guild; MWA; Novelists' Ink; PEN, Ireland; SFWA. *Publications:* Restoree, 1967; Dragonflight (graphic novel), 1968; The Ship Who Sang, 1969; Decision at Doona, 1969; Alchemy and Academe (ed.), 1970; Dragonquest: Being the Further Adventures of the Dragonriders of Pern, 1971; Mark of Merlin, 1971; Ring of Fear, 1971; To Ride Pegasus (short stories), 1973; Cooking Out of This World (ed.), 1973; Kilternan Legacy, 1975; A Time When, 1975; Dragonsong, 1976; Dragonsinger, 1977; Get Off the Unicorn (short stories), 1977; The White Dragon, 1978; Dinosaur Planet, 1979; Dragondrums, 1979; The Worlds of Anne McCaffrey, 1981; Crystal Singer, 1982; The Coelura, 1983; Moreta: Dragonlady of Pern, 1983; Dinosaur Planet Survivors, 1984; Habit is an Old Horse (short stories), 1984; Stitch in Snow, 1984; The Girl Who Heard Dragons (short stories), 1985; Killashandra, 1985; Nerilka's Story, 1986; The Year of the Lucy, 1986; The Lady (UK edn as The Carradyne Touch), 1987; Dragonsdawn, 1988; People of Pern, 1988; The Renegades of Pern, 1989; The Dragonlover's Guide to Pern (with Jody-Lynn Nye), 1989; Pegasus in Flight, 1990; Sassinak (with Elizabeth Moon), 1990; The Death of Sleep (with Jody-Lynn Nye), 1990; The Rowan, 1990; Crisis on Doona (with Jody Lynn Nye), 1991; Generation Warriors, 1991; Rescue Run, 1991; All The Weyrs of Pern, 1991; Three Women, 1992; Crystal Line, 1992; The Partnership (with Margaret Ball), 1992; The Ship Who Searched (with Mercedes Lackey), 1992; Damia, 1992; The Planet Pirates (with Elizabeth Moon and Jody Lynn Nye), 1993; The City Who Fought (with S. M. Stirling), 1993; Powers That Be (with Elizabeth Ann Scarborough), 1993; Damia's Children, 1993; The Dolphin's Bell: A Tale of Pern, 1993; The Chronicles of Pern: First Fall (short stories), 1993; Power Lines (with Elizabeth Ann Scarborough), 1994; The Ship Who Won (with Jody-Lynn Nye), 1994; Treaty Planet, 1994; Lyon's Pride, 1994; The Dolphins of Pern, 1994; Treaty at Doona, 1994; Dragons, 1994; An Exchange of Gifts, 1995; Power Play (with Elizabeth Ann Scarborough), 1995; Freedom's Landing, 1995; A Diversity of Dragons (children's fiction with Richard Woods), 1995; Serve It Forth: Cooking with Anne McCaffrey (ed. with John Betancourt), 1996; No One Noticed the Cat, 1996; Space Opera (ed. with Elizabeth Ann Scarborough), 1996; Black Horses for the King, 1996; Acorna: The Unicorn Girl (with Margaret Ball), 1997; Red Star Rising (short stories), 1997; Freedom's Choice, 1997; The Ship Avenged (with S. M. Stirling), 1997; Freedom's Challenge, 1998; If Wishes Were Horses, 1998; Dragonseye, 1998; Masterharper of Pern, 1998; Acorna's People (with Elizabeth Ann Scarborough), 1999; Acorna's Quest (with Margaret Ball), 1999; Nimisha's Ship, 1999; The Tower and the Hive, 1999; Pegasus in Space, 2000; Acorna's World (with Elizabeth Ann Scarborough), 2000; The Skies of Pern, 2001; Freedom's Ransom, 2002; Dragon's Kin (with Todd McCaffrey), 2003. Contributions: anthologies and periodicals. *Honours:* Hugo Award, World Science Fiction Society, 1967; Nebula Award, SFWA, 1968; E. E. Smith Award, 1975; Ditmar Award, 1979; Eurocon/Streso Award, 1979; Gandalf Award, 1979; Barlog Award, 1980; Golden PEN Award, 1981; Science Fiction Book Club Awards, 1986, 1989, 1991, 1992, 1993; Margaret A. Edwards Lifetime Achievement Award for Outstanding Literature for Young Adults, School Library Journal, 1999; Cthulu Award, BSFA, 2000. *Address:* Dragonhold Underhill, Timmore Lane, Newcastle, Co Wicklow, Ireland.

McCALL, Christina, BA; writer and editor; b. 29 Jan. 1935, Toronto, ON, Canada; m. 1st Peter Charles Newman 1959 (divorced 1977); m. 2nd Stephen Clarkson 1978; three d. *Education:* Jarvis College Institute, Toronto, Victoria College, University of Toronto. *Career:* Staff, 1956–58, Assoc. Ed., 1971–74, Maclean's; Assoc. Ed., then Ottawa Ed., Chatelaine, 1958–62; Ottawa Ed., 1967–70, Exec. Ed., 1976, Contributing Ed., 1980–88, 1994–, Saturday Night; National Reporter, Globe and Mail, 1974–76. *Publications:* The Man from Oxbow, 1967; Grits: An Intimate Portrait of the Liberal Party, 1982; Trudeau and Our Times (co-author), Vol. 1, The Magnificent Obsession, 1990, Vol. 2, The Heroic Delusion, 1994; Pearson: The Unlikely Gladiator, 1999. *Honours:* Southam Fellowship in Journalism, University of Toronto, 1977; National Magazine Award Gold Medal, 1981; Canadian Authors' Asscn Book of the Year Award, 1983; Governor-General's Award for Non-Fiction, 1990; John W. Dafoe Prize, 1995. *Address:* 59 Lowther Avenue, Toronto, ON M5R 1C5, Canada. *Telephone:* (416) 925-3596. *Fax:* (416) 925-9171. *E-mail:* cmccall@interlog.com.

McCALL SMITH, Alexander; writer; *Professor of Medical Law, University of Edinburgh*; b. 1948, Southern Rhodesia (now Zimbabwe); m. Elizabeth; two d. *Career:* Prof. of Medical Law, Univ. of Edinburgh; mem. Human Genetics Commission (vice-chair.), UNESCO International Bioethics Commission, British Medical Journal Ethics Cttee (chair.), Roslin Institute Ethics Cttee (chair.). *Publications:* fiction: The No. 1 Ladies' Detective Agency 1998, Tears of the Giraffe 2000, Morality for Beautiful Girls 2001, The Kalihari Typing Schools for Men 2002, The Full Cupboard of Life (Saga Award for Wit) 2003, At the Villa of Reduced Circumstances 2003, Portuguese Irregular Verbs 2003, Crushed Strawberry 2004, 44 Scotland Street (serialised in The Scotsman) 2004, The Sunday Philosophy Club 2004; non-fiction: Law and Medical Ethics (with J. K. Mason) 1983, The Duty to Rescue: The Jurisprudence of Aid (with Michael A. Menlowe) 1993, Forensic Aspects of Sleep (with C. Shapiro) 1997, Justice and the Prosecution of Old Crimes: Balancing Legal, Psychological, and Moral Concerns (with Daniel W. Shuman) 2000, The Criminal Law of Botswana; children's fiction includes: White Hippo 1980, The Perfect Hamburger 1982, Jeffrey's Joke Machine 1990, The Five Lost Aunts of Harriet Bean 1990, Marzipan Max 1991, Uncle Gangster 1991, The Spaghetti Tangle 1992, Harriet Bean and the League of Cheats 1991, The Ice-Cream Bicycle 1992, Akimbo and the Lions 1992, The Doughnut Ring 1992, Springy Jane 1992, The Princess Trick 1992, The Cowgirl Aunt of Harriet Bean 1993, My Chameleon Uncle 1993, The Muscle Machine 1993, Paddy and the Ratcatcher 1994, The Banana Machine 1994, Akimbo and the Crocodile Man 1995, Billy Rubbish 1995, The Watermelon Boys 1996, Calculator Annie 1996, The Bubblegum Tree 1996, Bursting Balloons Mystery 1997, The Popcorn Pirates 1999, Chocolate Money Mystery 1999; short story collections: Heavenly Date and Other Stories 1995, revised edn as Heavenly Date: And Other Flirtations 2003, Children of Wax: African Folk Tales 1991. *Honours:* British Books Awards Author of the Year 2004, Booksellers Asscn Author of the Year

2004, Waterstones Author of the Year 2004. *Literary Agent:* David Higham Associates, 5–8 Lower John Street, Golden Square, London, W1F 9HA, England. *Website:* www.no1ladiesdetective.com.

McCANN, Colum; writer; b. 1965, Ireland; m. Allison Hawke. *Education:* Clonkeen College; Dublin Institute of Technology; University of Texas at Austin. *Publications:* Fishing the Sloe-Black River, 1993; Songdogs, 1995; This Side of Brightness, 1998; Everything in This Country Must, 2000; Dancer, 2003. Contributions: books and newspapers. *Honours:* Hennessy/Sunday Tribune Award for Best First Fiction 1991 and Best New Writer 1991, Rooney Prize for Irish Literature 1994, Irish Book of the Year 2000, Princess Grace Memorial Literary Award 2002, Esquire Magazine Writer of the Year 2003. *Address:* c/o Henry Holt & Co Inc, 115 W 18th Street, New York, NY 10011, USA.

McCARRY, Charles; journalist, editor and writer; b. 14 June 1930, Pittsfield, Massachusetts, USA; m. Nancy Neill 1953; four s. *Career:* reporter and Ed., Lisbon Evening Journal, Ohio, 1952–55; reporter and columnist, Youngstown Vindicator, Ohio, 1955–56; Asst to US Secretary of Labor, Washington, DC, 1956–57; employee, CIA 1958–67; Ed.-at-Large, National Geographic magazine, 1983–90. *Publications:* The Miernik Dossier, 1973; The Tears of Autumn, 1975; The Secret Lovers, 1977; The Better Angels, 1979; The Last Supper, 1983; The Bride of the Wilderness, 1988; Second Sight, 1991. Non-Fiction: Citizen Nader, 1972; Double Eagle (with Ben Abruzzo, Maxie Anderson and Larry Newman), 1979; Isles of the Caribbean (co-author), 1979; The Great Southwest, 1980; Caveat, 1983; For the Record (with Donald Y. Regan), 1988; Inner Circles: How America Changed the World (with Alexander M. Haig Jr), 1992; Shelley's Heart, 1995; Lucky Bastard, 1998; Old Boys 2004; contrib. to periodicals. *Address:* c/o Weidenfeld and Nicholson, 5 Upper St Martin's Lane, London WC2H 9EA, England.

McCARTHY, Cormac, (Charles McCarthy Jr); writer and dramatist; b. 20 July 1933, Providence, RI, USA; m. Lee Holleman 1961 (divorced); one c.; m. 2nd Anne deLisle 1967 (divorced). *Publications:* Fiction: The Orchard Keeper, 1965; Outer Dark, 1968; Child of God, 1974; Suttree, 1979; Blood Meridian, or The Evening Redness in the West, 1985; All the Pretty Horses, 1992; The Crossing, 1994; Cities of the Plain, 1998. Plays: The Gardner's Son, 1977; The Stonemason, 1994. *Honours:* Ingram Merrill Foundation Grant, 1960; William Faulkner Foundation Award, 1965; American Acad. of Arts and Letters Travelling Fellowship, 1965–66; Rockefeller Foundation Grant, 1966; Guggenheim Fellowship, 1976; John D. and Catherine T. MacArthur Foundation Fellowship, 1981; National Book Award, 1992; National Book Critics Circle Award, 1993. *Address:* c/o Alfred A. Knopf Inc, 299 Park Avenue, New York, NY 10171, USA.

MacCARTHY, Fiona, MA, FRSL; biographer and cultural historian; b. 23 Jan. 1940, London, England; m. David Mellor 1966; one s. one d. *Education:* University of Oxford. *Career:* reviewer, The Times, 1981–91, The Observer, 1991–2000; mem. PEN Club; RSL. *Publications:* The Simple Life: C. R. Ashbee in the Cotswolds, 1981; The Omega Workshops: Decorative Arts of Bloomsbury, 1984; Eric Gill, 1989; William Morris: A Life for our Time, 1994; Stanley Spencer, 1997; Byron: Life and Legend, 2002. Contributions: Guardian; TLS; New York Review of Books. *Honours:* RSA Bicentenary Medal, 1987; Hon. Fellowship, Royal College of Art, 1989; Wolfson History Prize, 1995; Hon. DLitt, University of Sheffield, 1996; Hon. Doctorate, Sheffield Hallam University, 2001; Senior Fellowship, Royal College of Art, 1997. *Address:* The Round Building, Hathersage, Sheffield S32 1BA, England.

McCARTHY, Gary, BS, MS; writer; b. 23 Jan. 1943, South Gate, CA, USA; m. Virginia Kurzwell 1969; one s. three d. *Education:* California State University, University of Nevada. *Career:* Labour Economist, State of Nevada, Carson City, 1970–77; Economist, Copley International Corp, La Jolla, CA, 1977–79. *Publications:* The Derby Man, 1976; Showdown at Snakegrass Junction, 1978; The First Sheriff, 1979; Mustang Fever, 1980; The Pony Express War, 1980; Winds of Gold, 1980; Silver Shot, 1981; Explosion at Donner Pass, 1981; The Legend of the Lone Ranger, 1981; North Chase, 1982; Rebel of Bodie, 1982; The Rail Warriors, 1983; Silver Winds, 1983; Wind River, 1984; Powder River, 1985; The Last Buffalo Hunt, 1985; Mando, 1986; The Mustangers, 1987; Transcontinental, 1987; Sodbuster, 1988; Blood Brothers, 1989; Gringo Amigo, 1990; Whiskey Creek, 1992; The American River, 1992; Comstock Camels, 1993; The Gila River, 1993; Yosemite, 1995; Grand Canyon, 1996; Mesa Verde, 1997.

McCARTHY, Patrick A., BA, MA, PhD; American academic and writer; *Professor of English, University of Miami at Coral Gables*; b. 12 July 1945, Charlottesville, VA; m. 1st; three c.; m. 2nd Yolanda A. Armstrong 1997. *Education:* Univ. of Virginia, Univ. of Wisconsin at Milwaukee. *Career:* Instructor in English, Murray State Univ., KY 1968–69, William Paterson Coll. of New Jersey 1973–74, Broome Community Coll., Binghamton, NY 1975–76; Visiting Prof. of English, SUNY at Binghamton 1974–75; Asst Prof. 1976–81, Assoc. Prof. 1981–84, Prof. of English 1984–, Univ. of Miami at Coral Gables. *Publications:* The Riddles of 'Finnegans Wake' 1980, Olaf Stapledon 1982, Critical Essays on Samuel Beckett (ed.) 1986, The Legacy of Olaf Stapledon: Critical Essays and an Unpublished Manuscript (ed. with Charles Elkins and Martin H. Greenberg) 1989, 'Ulysses': Portals of Discovery 1990, Critical Essays on James Joyce's 'Finnegans Wake' (ed.) 1992, Forests of Symbols: World, Text and Self in Malcolm Lowry's Fiction 1994, Malcolm Lowry's La Mordida: A Scholarly Edition (ed.) 1996, Joyce/Lowry: Critical Perspectives (ed. with Paul Tiessen) 1997, Star Maker (ed.) 2004. *Address:* c/o Department of English, University of Miami at Coral Gables, Coral Gables, FL 33124, USA. *E-mail:* p.mccarthy@miami.edu.

McCARTHY, Wil, BS; engineer and writer; b. 16 Sept. 1966, Princeton, NJ, USA; m. 1st Kumiko McCarthy (divorced 1990); m. 2nd Cathy Polk; one s. *Education:* University of Colorado, Boulder. *Career:* Space Launch Systems Engineer, 1988–97, Flight Systems Engineer, 1997–, Lockheed-Martin Corporation, Denver, CO; Creative Writing Instructor, Colorado Free University and Jefferson Adult and Continuing Education Programme; mem. SFWA; North Colorado Writers Workshop, former Pres. *Publications:* Aggressor Six, 1994; A Midnight Clear (co-author), 1994; Flies from the Amber, 1995; Murder in the Solid State, 1996; The Fall of Sirius, 1996; Bloom, 1998. Contributions: anthologies; Periodicals including: Colorado Engineer; Aboriginal SF; Interzone; Analog; Isaac Asimov's Science Fiction Magazine; ComputerEdge; SF Age; SFWA Bulletin. *Address:* c/o Lockheed-Martin Astronautics, PO Box 179, Denver, CO 80201, USA.

McCARTHY, William Edward John, BA, PhD; writer; b. 30 July 1925, London, England. *Education:* Ruskin College, Merton College, Oxford, Nuffield College, Oxford. *Career:* Research Fellow, Nuffield College, 1959–63; Staff Lecturer, Tutor, Industrial Relations, 1964–65, Fellow, Nuffield College and Centre for Management Studies, 1968–, University of Oxford; Dir of Research, Royal Commission on Trade and Unions and Employers Asscn, London, 1965–68; Senior Economic Adviser, Dept of Employment, 1968–70; Special Adviser, European Economic Commission, 1974–75. *Publications:* The Future of the Unions, 1962; The Closed Shop in Britain, 1964; The Role of Shop Stewards in British Industrial Relations: A Survey of Existing Information and Research, 1966; Disputes Procedures in Britain (with Arthur Ivor Marsh), 1966; Employers' Associations: The Results of Two Studies (with V. G. Munns), 1967; The Role of Government in Industrial Relations, Shop Stewards and Workshop Relations: The Results of a Study, 1968; Industrial Relations in Britain: A Guide for Management and Unions (ed.), 1969; The Reform of Collective Bargaining: A Series of Case Studies, 1971; Trade Unions, 1972; Coming to Terms with Trade Unions (with A. J. Collier), 1972; Management by Agreement (with N. D. Ellis), 1973; Wage Inflation and Wage Leadership (with J. F. O'Brien and V. C. Dowd), 1975; Making Whitley Work, 1977; Change in Trade Unions (co-author), 1981; Strikes in Post War Britain (with J. W. Durcun), 1985; Freedom at Work, 1985; The Future of Industrial Democracy, 1988; Employee Relations Audits (co-author), 1992; Legal Intervention in Industrial Relations (ed.), 1992; New Labour at Work, 1997; Fairness at Work and Trade Union Recognition, 1998. *Address:* 4 William Orchard Close, Old Headington, Oxford, England.

McCAULEY, Martin, BA, PhD; academic and writer; b. 18 Oct. 1934, Omagh, Northern Ireland. *Education:* University of London. *Career:* Senior Lecturer in Soviet and East European Studies, 1968–91, Senior Lecturer in Politics, 1991–98, Chair., Dept of Social Sciences, 1993–96, School of Slavonic and East European Studies, University College London; mem. Economic and Social Research Council; Politics and Society Group. *Publications:* The Russian Revolution and the Soviet State 1917–1921 (ed.), 1975; Khruschev and the Development of Soviet Agriculture: The Virgin Land Programme, 1953–64, 1976; Communist Power in Europe 1944–1949 (ed. and contributor), 1977; Marxism-Leninism in the German Democratic Republic: The Socialist Unity Party (SED), 1978; The Stalin File, 1979; The Soviet Union Since 1917, 1981; Stalin and Stalinism, 1983; Origins of the Cold War, 1983; The Soviet Union Since Brezhnev (ed. and contributor), 1983; The German Democratic Republic Since 1945, 1984; Octobrists to Bolsheviks: Imperial Russia 1905–1917, 1984; Leadership and Succession in the Soviet Union, East Europe and China (ed. and contributor), 1985; The Origins of the Modern Russian State 1855–1881 (with Peter Waldron), 1986; The Soviet Union under Gorbachev (ed.), 1987; Gorbachev and Perestroika (ed.), 1990; Khrushchev, 1991; The Soviet Union 1917–1991, 1991; Directory of Russian MPs (ed.), 1993; Longman Biographical Directory of Decision Makers in Russia and the Successor States (ed.), 1994; Who's Who in Russia and the Soviet Union, 1997; Russia 1917–1941, 1997; Longman Companion to Russia since 1914, 1997; Gorbachev, 1998; America, Russia and the Cold War 1949–1991, 1998; Afghanistan and Central Asia, 2001. Contributions: Professional journals. *Address:* c/o School of Slavonic and East European Studies, University College London, Senate House, Malet Street, London WC1E 7HU, England. *E-mail:* andermccauley@hotmail.com.

McCLANE, Kenneth Anderson, Jr, AB, MA, MFA; academic, poet and eriter; b. 19 Feb. 1951, New York, NY, USA; m. Rochelle Evette Woods 1983. *Education:* Cornell University. *Career:* Instructor, Colby College, 1974–75; Luce Visiting Prof., Williams College, 1983; Assoc. Prof., 1983–89, Prof., 1989–93, W. E. B. DuBois Prof., 1993–, Cornell University; Visiting Prof., Wayne State University, 1987, University of Michigan, 1989, Washington University, 1991; mem. Associated Writing Programs; Poets and Writers. *Publications:* Take Five: Collected Poems, 1988; Walls: Essays 1985–90, 1991. Contributions: journals. *Honours:* George Harmon Coxe Award, 1973; Corson Morrison Poetry Prize, 1973. *Address:* c/o Department of English, Cornell University, Rockefeller Hall, Ithaca, NY 14853, USA.

McCLARY, Susan Kaye, BMus, MA, PhD; academic and writer; *Professor of Musicology, University of California at Los Angeles*; b. 2 Oct. 1946, St Louis, MO, USA. *Education:* Southern Illinois Univ., Harvard Univ. *Career:* Lecturer, Trinity Coll., Hartford, CT 1977; Asst Prof. 1977–83, Assoc. Prof. 1983–90, Prof. of Musicology 1990–92, Univ. of Minnesota; Prof. of Musicology, McGill Univ. 1992–94, Univ. of California at Los Angeles 1994–; Ernest Bloch Visiting Prof., Univ. of California at Berkeley 1993; mem. American Musicological Soc. *Publications:* The Transition from Modal to Tonal Organization in the Works of Monteverdi 1976, Music and Society: The Politics of Composition, Performance and Reception (ed. with R. Leppert) 1987, Feminine Endings: Music, Gender, and Sexuality 1991, Georges Bizet: Carmen 1992, Conventional Wisdom: The Content of Musical Form 2000; contrib. to scholarly books and journals. *Honours:* John D. and Catherine T. MacArthur Foundation Fellowship 1995. *Address:* c/o Department of Musicology, University of California at Los Angeles, Los Angeles, CA 90095, USA.

McCLATCHY, Joseph Donald, Jr, AB, PhD; poet, writer and editor; b. 12 Aug. 1945, Bryn Mawr, Pennsylvania, USA. *Education:* Georgetown University, Yale University. *Career:* Instructor, LaSalle College, Philadelphia, 1968–71; Assoc. Ed., Four Quarters, 1968–72; Asst Prof., Yale University, 1974–81; Poetry Ed., 1980–91, Ed., 1991–, The Yale Review; Lecturer in Creative Writing, Princeton University, 1981–93; Prof. of English, Yale Univ., 2002–; mem. American Acad. of Arts and Letters; American Acad. of Arts and Sciences; International PEN; Acad. of American Poets, chancellor, 1996–2003. *Publications:* Anne Sexton: The Artist and Her Critics, 1978; Scenes from Another Life (poems), 1981; Stars Principal (poems), 1986; James Merrill: Recitative: Prose (ed.), 1986; Kilim (poems), 1987; Poets on Painters: Essays on the Art of Painting by Twentieth-Century Poets (ed.), 1988; White Paper: On Contemporary American Poetry, 1989; The Rest of the Way (poems), 1990; The Vintage Book of Contemporary American Poetry (ed.), 1990; Woman in White: Selected Poems of Emily Dickinson (ed.), 1991; The Vintage Book of Contemporary World Poetry (ed.), 1996; Ten Commandments (poems), 1998; Twenty Questions (essays), 1998; Hazmat (poems), 2002; Selected Poems of Edna St Vincent Millay, 2003; Division of Spoils (poems), 2003. Contributions: anthologies and magazines. *Honours:* Woodrow Wilson Fellowship, 1967–68; O. Henry Award, 1972; Ingram Merrill Foundation Grant, 1979; Michener Award, 1982; Gordon Barber Memorial Award, 1984, Melville Cane Award, 1991, Poetry Society of America; Eunice Tietjens Memorial Prize, 1985, Oscar Blumenthal Prize, 1988, Levinson Prize, 1990, Poetry Magazine; Witter Bynner Poetry Prize, 1985, Award in Literature, 1991, American Acad. of Arts and Letters; National Endowment for the Arts Fellowship, 1986; Guggenheim Fellowship, 1988; Acad. of American Poets Fellowship, 1991. *Address:* 15 Grand Street, Stonington, CT 06378, USA.

McCLURE, Gillian Mary, BA; British children's writer and illustrator; b. (Gillian Mary Coltman), 29 Oct. 1948, Bradford, England; three s. *Education:* Horsham High School for Girls, Bristol University, Moray House. *Career:* mem. CWIG Soc. of Authors (cttee mem. 1989–95), PLR Advisory Cttee 1992. *Publications:* The Emperor's Singing Bird 1974, Prickly Pig 1976, Fly Home McDoo 1979, What's The Time Rory Wolf? 1982, Tog The Ribber (illustrator, by Paul Coltman) 1985, What Happened To The Picnic? 1986, Witch Watch (illustrator, by Paul Coltman) 1989, Cat Flap 1990, Tinker Jim (illustrator, by Paul Coltman) 1992, The Christmas Donkey 1993, Norse Myths (illustrator, by Kevin Crossley-Holland) 1993, Poems That Go Bump In The Night 1994, The Little White Hen (illustrator, by Philippa Pearce) 1995, Selkie (Parent's Guide to Children's Media Award, USA 2000) 1999, Tom Finger 2001, Bruna (illustrator, by Anne Cottringer) 2003. *Literary Agent:* Curtis Brown Ltd, Haymarket House, 28–29 Haymarket, London, SW1Y 4SP, England. *Telephone:* (20) 7393-4400. *Fax:* (20) 7393-4401. *E-mail:* info@curtisbrown.co.uk. *Website:* www.curtisbrown.co.uk. *Address:* 9 Trafalgar Street, Cambridge, CB4 1ET, England. *E-mail:* gillianmcclure@ntlworld.com. *Website:* www.geocities.com/gillianmarymcclure.

McCLURE, James Howe; managing director and writer; b. 9 Oct. 1939, Johannesburg, South Africa. *Career:* journalist, Natal, Edinburgh, Oxford, 1963–69; Deputy Ed., Oxford Times Group, 1971–74; Managing Dir, Sabensa Gakula Ltd, Oxford, 1975–. *Publications:* The Steam Pig, 1971; The Caterpillar Cop, 1972; Four and Twenty Virgins, 1973; The Gooseberry Fool, 1974; Snake, 1975; Killers, 1976; Rogue Eagle, 1976; The Sunday Hangman, 1977; The Blood of an Englishman, 1980; Spike Island: Portrait of a British Police Division, 1980; The Artful Egg, 1984; Copworld, 1985; Imago: A Modern Comedy of Manners, 1988; The Song Dog, 1991. *Honours:* Gold Dagger Award, 1971, Silver Dagger Award, 1976, CWA. *Address:* 14 York Road, Headington, Oxford OX3 8NW, England.

McCLURE, Michael Thomas, BA; academic, poet, dramatist and writer; b. 20 Oct. 1932, Marysville, KS, USA; m. Joanna Kinnison 1954; one d. *Education:* University of Wichita, University of Arizona, San Francisco State College. *Career:* Asst Prof., 1962–77, Assoc. Prof., 1977–78, Prof., 1978–, California College of Arts and Crafts, Oakland; Playwright-in-Residence, American Conservatory Theatre, San Francisco, 1975; Assoc. Fellow, Pierson College, Yale University, 1982. *Publications:* Poetry: Passage, 1956; For Artaud, 1959; Hymns to St Geryon and Other Poems, 1959; The New Book: A Book of Torture, 1961; Dark Brown, 1961; Ghost Tantras, 1964; 13 Mad Sonnets, 1964; Hail Thee Who Play, 1968; The Sermons of Jean Harlow and the Curses of Billy the Kid, 1969; Star, 1971; The Book of Joanna, 1973; Rare Angel (writ with raven's blood), 1974; September Blackberries, 1974; Jaguar Skies, 1975; Antechamber and Other Poems, 1978; The Book of Benjamin, 1982; Fragments of Perseus, 1983; Selected Poems, 1986; Rebel Lions, 1991; Simple Eyes and Other Poems, 1994. Plays: The Growl, in Four in Hand, 1964; The Blossom, or, Billy the Kid, 1967; The Beard, 1967; The Shell, 1968; The Cherub, 1970; Gargoyle Cartoons (11 plays), 1971; The Mammals, 1972; The Grabbing of the Fairy, 1973; Gorf, 1976; General Gorgeous, 1975; Goethe: Ein Fragment, 1978; The Velvet Edge, 1982; The Beard and VKTMs: Two Plays, 1985. Fiction: The Mad Club, 1970; The Adept, 1971. Other: Meat Science Essays, 1963; Freewheelin' Frank, Secretary of the Angels, as Told to Michael McClure by Frank Reynolds, 1967; Scratching the Beat Surface, 1982; Specks, 1985; Lighting the Corners: On Art, Nature, and the Visionary: Essays and Interviews, 1993. *Honours:* National Endowment for the Arts Grants, 1967, 1974; Guggenheim Fellowship, 1971; Magic Theatre Alfred Jarry Award, 1974; Rockefeller Foundation Fellowship, 1975; Obie Award, 1978. *Address:* 264 Downey Street, San Francisco, CA 94117, USA.

MacCOBY, Michael, BA, PhD; consultant and writer; b. 5 March 1933, Mt Vernon, NY, USA; m. Sandylee Weille 1959; one s. three d. *Education:* Harvard University; New College, Oxford, University of Chicago, Mexican Institute of Psychoanalysis. *Career:* mem. PEN; Signet Society; Cosmos; American Psychological Asscn; American Anthropological Asscn; National Acad. of Public Administration. *Publications:* Social Change and Character in Mexico and the United States, 1970; Social Character in a Mexican Village (with E. Fromm), 1970; The Gamesman, 1977; The Leader, 1981; Why Work, 1988; Sweden at the Edge, 1991; A Prophetic Analyst (with M. Cortina), 1996; Agents of Change (with C. Heckscher, R. Ramirez, P. E. Tixier), 2003; The Productive Narcissist, 2003. *Honours:* McKinsey Award. *Address:* 4825 Linnean Avenue NW, Washington, DC 20008, USA. *E-mail:* michael@maccoby.com. *Website:* www.maccoby.com.

McCOLLEY, Diane Kelsey, AB, PhD; academic and writer; b. 9 Feb. 1934, Riverside, CA, USA; m. Robert M. McColley 1958; one s. five d. *Education:* Univ. of California at Berkeley, Univ. of Illinois at Urbana-Champaign. *Career:* Teaching Asst, 1966–74, Visiting Lecturer, 1975–78, Univ. of Illinois at Urbana-Champaign; Asst Prof., 1979–84, Assoc. Prof., 1984–93, Prof. of English, 1993–, Camden College of Arts and Sciences, Rutgers Univ.; Visiting Fellow, Lucy Cavendish College, Univ. of Cambridge, 1990; mem. Asscn for the Study of Literature and the Environment; Asscn of Literary Scholars and Critics; Milton Society of America, pres., 1990; MLA; Renaissance Society of America. *Publications:* Milton's Eve, 1983; A Gust for Paradise: Milton's Eden and the Visual Arts, 1993; Poetry and Music in Seventeenth-Century England, 1997. Contributions: scholarly books and journals. *Honours:* National Endowment for the Humanities Fellowship, 1989–90; American Philosophical Society Research Grant, 1990; James Holly Hanford Award, Milton Society of America, 1993. *Address:* c/o Camden College of Arts and Sciences, Rutgers University, Camden, NJ 08102, USA.

McCONCHIE, Lyn, (Jan Bishop, Elizabeth Underwood); writer; b. 3 April 1946, Auckland, New Zealand. *Career:* Justice Dept, Agriculture and Fisheries Dept, Probation Dept; mem. SFWA; CWA; FAW; NZSA. *Publications:* Farming Daze (as Elizabeth Underwood), 1993; The Key of the Kelian, 1995; The Lonely Troll (also as) The Troll's New Jersey, 1997; Tales From the Marrigan Trade House, 1998; Ciara's Song, 1998; The Troll and the Taniwha, 1998. Contributions: New Zealand Cat Fancy Yearbook; Disinformation. *Honours:* Australasion Medal, 1992; New York Public Library Best Books for Teenagers Listing, 1995; Music Medallion, 1996, 1997. *Literary Agent:* Sternig and Bryne, USA. *Address:* Farside Farm, R. D. Norsewood 5491, New Zealand.

McCONICA, James Kelsey, BA, MA, DPhil, FRHistS; academic and writer; b. 24 April 1930, Luseland, Saskatchewan, Canada. *Education:* University of Saskatchewan, University of Oxford, University of Toronto. *Career:* Instructor, 1956–57, Asst Prof., 1957–62, University of Saskatchewan; Assoc. Prof., 1967–70, Prof. of History, 1971–, later Prof. Emeritus, Pontifical Institute of Mediaeval Studies, Toronto, Pres. 1996–; Ordained Roman Catholic Priest, 1968; Visiting Fellow, 1969–71, 1977, Special Ford Lecturer, 1977, Research Fellow, 1978–84, Academic Dean, 1990–92, All Souls College, Oxford; Fellow, Davis Center for Historical Studies, Princeton University, 1971; Prof., University of Toronto, 1972–; Pres., University of St Michael's College, Toronto, 1984–90; Research Fellow All Souls Coll. Oxford 1990–97; mem. American Society for Reformation Research; Canadian Society for Renaissance Studies; Oxford Historical Society; Renaissance Society of America; Royal Society of Canada, fellow; British Acad., Corresponding Fellow; Royal Belgian Acad., Foreign Mem. *Publications:* English Humanists and Reformation Politics under Henry VIII and Edward VI, 1965; The Correspondence of Erasmus (ed.), Vol. III, 1976, Vol. IV, 1977; Thomas More: A Short Biography, 1977; The History of the University of Oxford (ed.), Vol. III, 1986; Erasmus, 1991. Contributions: books and professional journals. *Honours:* Hon. Fellow Exeter Coll. Oxford 2003Hon. LLD (Saskatchewan 1986, St Francis Xavier 1999, Regina 1999); Hon. DLitt (Windsor 1989), DUniv (St Paul 2002)Rhodes Scholar 1951, Guggenheim Fellowship 1969–70, Killiam Senior Research Scholar 1976–77. *Address:* Pontifical Institute of Mediaeval Studies, 59 Queen's Park Crescent East, Toronto, Ontario M5S 2C4, Canada.

McCONKEY, James Rodney, BA, MA, PhD; academic and writer; *Professor Emeritus, Cornell University*; b. 2 Sept. 1921, Lakewood, OH, USA; m. Gladys Jean Voorhees 1944; three s. *Education:* Cleveland Coll., Western Reserve Univ., Univ. of Iowa. *Career:* Asst Prof. to Assoc. Prof., Morehead State Coll., KY 1950–56; Dir, Morehead Writer's Workshop 1951–56, Antioch Seminar in Writing and Publishing, Yellow Springs, OH 1957–60; Asst Prof. to Assoc. Prof. 1956–62, Prof. of English 1962–87, Goldwin Smith Prof. of English Literature 1987–92, Prof. Emeritus 1992–, Cornell Univ.; mem. PEN. *Publications:* The Novels of E. M. Forster 1957, The Structure of Prose (ed.) 1963, Night Stand 1965, Crossroads: An Autobiographical Novel 1968, A Journal to Sahalin (novel) 1971, The Tree House Confessions (novel) 1979, Court of Memory 1983, To a Distant Island (novel) 1984, Chekhov and Our Age: Responses to Chekhov by American Writers and Scholars (ed.) 1984, Kayo: The Authentic and Annotated Autobiographical Novel from Outer Space 1987, Rowan's Progress 1992, Stories from My Life with the Other Animals 1993, The Anatomy of Memory (ed.) 1996, The Telescope in the Parlor (essays) 2004; contrib. to magazines. *Honours:* Eugene Saxton Literary Fellow 1962–63, Nat. Endowment for the Arts Essay Award 1967, Ohioana Book Award 1969, Guggenheim Fellowship 1969–70, American Acad. of Arts and Letters Award 1979. *Address:* 402 Aiken Road, Trumansburg, NY 14886, USA.

McCONNELL, Will (see Snodgrass, W. D.).

McCORMICK, A. (see Lewis-Smith, Anne Elizabeth).

McCORMICK, John Owen, BA, MA, PhD; writer; *Professor of Comparative Literature Emeritus, Rutgers University*; b. 20 Sept. 1918, Thief River Falls, MN, USA; m. Mairi MacInnes 1954; three s. one d. *Education:* Univ. of Minnesota, Harvard Univ. *Career:* Senior Tutor and Teaching Asst, Harvard University, 1946–51; Lecturer, Salzburg Seminar in American Studies, Austria, 1951–52; Lecturer of American Studies, Free University of Berlin, 1952–53, 1954–59; Prof. of Comparative Literature, 1959–, now Emeritus, Rutgers University, New Brunswick, NJ. *Publications:* Catastrophe and Imagination, 1957; Versions of Censorship (with Mairi MacInnes), 1962; The Complete Aficionado, 1967; The Middle Distance: A Comparative History of American Imaginative Literature, 1919–1932, 1971; Fiction as Knowledge: The Modern Post-Romantic Novel, 1975; George Santayana: A Biography, 1987; Sallies of the Mind: Essays of Francis Fergusson (ed. with G. Core), 1997; Seagoing: Memoir, 2000; Santayana, 2003. Contributions: numerous magazines, journals and reviews. *Honours:* Longview Award for Non-Fiction, 1960; Guggenheim Fellowships, 1964–65, 1980–81; National Endowment for the Humanities Senior Fellow, 1983–84; American Acad. and Institute of Arts and Letters Prize, 1988. *Address:* 31 Huntington Road, York YO31 8RL, England.

McCOURT, Frank; Irish writer; b. 19 Aug. 1930, New York, NY, USA. *Education:* New York Univ. *Career:* taught in New York City public schools for 27 years; moved to Ireland 1935; with brother Malachy performed a two-person musical review based on their life as young men in Ireland. *Publications:* Angela's Ashes (autobiog.) (National Book Critics Circle Award 1997, Los Angeles Times Book Award 1997, Pulitzer Prize in Biography 1997) 1996, 'Tis: A Memoir (autobiog.) 1999. *Address:* c/o Author Mail, Seventh Floor, HarperCollins Publishers Inc, 10 E 53rd Street, New York, NY 10022, USA.

McCOURT, James, BA; writer; b. 4 July 1941, New York, NY, USA. *Education:* Manhattan College, New York University, Yale University. *Publications:* Mawrdew Czgowchuz, 1975; Kaye Wayfaring, 1984; Time Remaining, 1993; Delancey's Way, 2000. Contributions: anthologies and magazines. *Literary Agent:* Elaine Markson, 44 Greenwich Avenue, New York, NY 10011, USA.

McCRACKEN, Elizabeth, BA, MA, MFA, MS; writer and teacher; b. 1966, USA. *Education:* Boston University, University of Iowa. *Career:* Adjunct Asst Lecturer, Drexel University and Evening College, Philadelphia, 1991–92; Mem., Writing Committee, 1993–, Instructor, Summer Program, 1996–98, Fine Arts Work Center, Provincetown; Community Writing Instructor, Sommerville Arts Council, 1995, 1996; Writing Instructor, Iowa Summer Writing Festival, 1997, 1998; Writer-in-Residence, Western Michigan University, 1998. *Publications:* Here's Your Hat What's Your Hurry?, 1993; The Giant's House, 1996; Niagara Falls All Over Again, 2001. Contributions: anthologies and periodicals. *Honours:* James Michener Grant, 1990; Fine Arts Work Centre Fellowships, Provincetown, 1990–91, 1992–93; National Endowment for the Arts Fellowship, 1992; MacDowell Colony Fellowship, 1993; Notable Book of the Year, American Library Asscn, 1996; Discovery Award, Barnes and Noble, 1997; Harold D. Vursell Memorial Award, American Acad. of Arts and Letters, 1997; Guggenheim Fellowship, 1998. *Address:* PO Box 441702, Somerville, MA 02144, USA. *E-mail:* mccrake@world.std.com.

McCRACKEN, Kathleen Luanne, PhD; Canadian poet and literary critic; b. 26 Oct. 1960, Dundalk, Ont. *Education:* York Univ. and Univ. of Toronto, Ont. *Career:* Teaching Asst, Course Dir and Lecturer Univ. of Toronto and Ryerson Polytechnic Inst. 1985–89; Course Dir Dept of English, York Univ. 1988–89; Postdoctoral Fellowship, Social Sciences and Humanities Research Council, Univ. Coll. Dublin, Ireland 1989–91; Lecturer in American Studies Univ. of Ulster at Jordanstown, Belfast, NI 1992–; has presented papers at confs in Canada, Ireland and USA; Ontario Arts Council Writers' Grantee (four times); Univ. of Toronto Open Fellowship; Ontario Grad. Scholarships; mem. League of Canadian Poets, Modern Language Asscn, Anglo-Irish Literature. *Publications include:* Reflections 1978, Into Celebration 1980, The Constancy of Objects 1980, Reflections: A Creative History of the One-Room Schoolhouse in Proton Township (jtly) 1978, A Geography of Souls 2002; poetry and literary criticism published in various Canadian, American, Irish and British journals. *Address:* Faculty of Humanities, University of Ulster at Jordanstown, Shore Road, Newtownabbey, Co. Antrim, BT37 0QB, Northern Ireland (Office). *Telephone:* (2890) 366192 (Office). *Fax:* (2090) 852611 (Office). *E-mail:* kl.mccracken@ulst.ac.uk.

McCRAW, Thomas Kincaid, BA, MA, PhD; academic, writer and editor; b. 11 Sept. 1940, Corinth, Mississippi, USA; m. Susan Morehead 1962; one s. one d. *Education:* University of Mississippi, University of Wisconsin. *Career:* Asst Prof., 1970–74, Assoc. Prof., 1974–78, University of Texas at Austin; Newcomen Fellow, 1973–74, Visiting Assoc. Prof., 1976–78, Prof., 1978–89, Isidor Straus Prof. of Business History, 1989–, Harvard University; Ed., Business History Review, 1994–; mem. American Economic Asscn; Business History Conference, trustee, 1986–95, pres., 1989; Economic History Asscn; Massachusetts Historical Society; Organization of American Historians. *Publications:* Morgan Versus Lilienthal: The Feud Within the TVA, 1970; TVA and the Power Fight, 1933–39, 1971; Regulation in Perspective: Historical Essays (ed.), 1981; Prophets of Regulation, 1984; America Versus Japan (ed.), 1986; The Essential Alfred Chandler (ed.), 1988; Management Past and Present (co-author), 1996; Creating Modern Capitalism (ed.), 1997; The Intellectual Venture Capitalist: John H. McArthur and the Work of the Harvard Business School, 1980–1995 (co-ed.), 1999; American Business, 1920–2000: How It Worked, 2000. Contributions: scholarly books and journals. *Honours:* Woodrow Wilson Fellow, 1966–67; William P. Lyons Master's Essays Award, Loyola University, Chicago, 1969; Younger Humanist Award, National Endowment for the Humanities, 1975; Pulitzer Prize in History, 1985; Thomas Newcomen Book Award, 1986; Inducted, Alumni Hall of Fame, University of Mississippi, 1986. *Address:* c/o Harvard University Business School, Soldiers Field, Boston, MA 02163, USA.

McCREADY, Jack (see Powell, Talmage).

McCRORIE, Edward Pollitt, PhD; professor of English, poet and translator; b. 19 Nov. 1936, Central Falls, RI, USA; m. 1995. *Education:* Brown Univ. *Career:* Prof. of English, Providence College, RI. *Publications:* After a Cremation (poems), 1974; The Aeneid of Virgil (trans.), 1995. Contributions: journals. *Address:* c/o Department of English, Providence College, Providence, RI 02918, USA.

McCRUM, (John) Robert, MA; British writer and newspaper editor; b. 7 July 1953; m. 1st Olivia Timbs (divorced 1984); m. 2nd Sarah Lyall 1995; two d. *Education:* Sherborne School, Corpus Christi Coll., Cambridge and Univ. of Pennsylvania. *Career:* house reader Chatto & Windus 1977–79; Editorial Dir Faber and Faber Ltd 1979–89, Ed.-in-Chief 1990–96; Literary Ed. Observer newspaper 1996–; scriptwriter and co-producer The Story of English TV series 1980–86. *Publications:* In the Secret State 1980, A Loss of Heart 1982, The Fabulous Englishman 1984, The Story of English 1986, The World is a Banana 1988, Mainland 1991, The Psychological Moment 1993, Suspicion 1996, My Year Off 1998, Wodehouse: A Life (biog.) 2004. *Honours:* Tony Godwin Prize 1979, Peabody Award 1986, Emmy Award 1987. *Address:* The Observer, 119 Farringdon Road, London, EC1R 3ER, England.

McCRYSTAL, Cahal (Cal); journalist, writer, critic and broadcaster; b. 20 Dec. 1935, Belfast, Northern Ireland; m. Stella Doyle 1958; three s. *Education:* St Mary's College, Dundalk, St Malachy's College, Belfast. *Career:* reporter, Northern Herald; labour correspondent, Belfast Telegraph; crime reporter, chief reporter, foreign correspondent, New York Bureau Chief, News Ed., Foreign Features Ed. and columnist, Sunday Times, London; sr writer and columnist, Independent on Sunday; sr writer, The Observer; literary critic, Financial Times, Independent on Sunday; mem. editorial bd, British Journalism Review. *Publications:* Watergate: The Full Inside Story (co-author), 1973; Reflections on a Quiet Rebel, 1997. Contributions: Vanity Fair, British Magazines, Poetry Ireland Review, and British Journalism Review. *Honours:* various journalism awards, Belfast Arts Council Literary Award 1998. *Literary Agent:* Greene & Heaton Ltd, 37 Goldhawk Road, London W12 8QQ, England.

McCULLAGH, Sheila Kathleen, MBE, MA; writer; b. 3 Dec. 1920, Surrey, England. *Education:* Bedford Froebel College, Univ. of Leeds. *Career:* Lecturer, Univ. of Leeds Institute of Education, 1949–57; mem. Society of Authors. *Publications:* Pirate Books, 1957–64; Tales and Adventures, 1961; Dragon Books, 1963–70; One, Two, Three and Away, 1964–92; Tim Books, 1974–83; Into New Worlds, 1974; Hummingbirds, 1976–92; Whizzbang Adventurers, 1980; Buccaneers, 1980; New Buccaneers, 1984; Where Wild Geese Fly, 1981; Puddle Lane, 1985–88; The Sea Shore (and other information books), 1992. *Literary Agent:* AP Watt Ltd, 20 John Street, London WC1N 2DR, England. *Address:* 27 Royal Crescent, Bath, NE Somerset BA1 2LT, England.

MacCULLOCH, Diarmaid, MA, DipTheol, DD, PhD, FRHistS, FSA; academic, writer and editor; *Professor of the History of the Church, St Cross College, Oxford*; b. 31 Oct. 1951, Folkestone, England. *Education:* University of

Cambridge, University of Liverpool, University of Oxford. *Career:* Junior Research Fellow, Churchill College, Cambridge, 1976–78; Tutor in History, Wesley College, Bristol, 1978–90; Lecturer in Theology, University of Bristol, 1978–95; Lecturer in Theology, 1995–97, Senior Tutor, 1996–2000, Prof. of the History of the Church, 1997–, St Cross College, Oxford; Ed., Journal of Ecclesiastical History, 1995–. *Publications:* The Chorography of Suffolk (ed.), 1976; Suffolk and the Tudors: Politics and Religion in an English County, 1500–1600, 1986; Groundwork of Christian History, 1987; How to Read Church History, Vol. II (with J. Comby), 1988; The Later Reformation in England, 1547–1603, 1990; The Reign of Henry VIII: Politics, Policy, and Piety (ed.), 1995; Thomas Cranmer: A Life, 1996; Tudor Rebellions (with Anthony Fletcher), fourth edn, 1997; Tudor Church Militant: Edward VI and the Protestant Reformation, 2000; Reformation: Europe's House Divided 1490–1700, 2003. Contributions: learned books and journals. *Honours:* Whitfield Prize, Royal Historical Society, 1986; Duff Cooper Prize, 1996; Whitbread Biography Prize, 1996; James Tait Black Memorial Prize, 1996. *Address:* c/o St Cross College, Oxford OX1 3LW, England.

McCULLOUGH, Colleen; Australian author; b. 1 June 1937, Wellington, NSW; m. Ric Robinson 1984. *Education:* Holy Cross Coll., Woollahra, Sydney Univ., Inst. of Child Health, London Univ. *Career:* trained as neuroscientist and worked in Sydney and English hospitals; researcher lecturer Dept of Neurology, Yale Univ. Medical School, USA 1967–77; moved to Norfolk Island, S Pacific 1979; mem. New York Acad. of Sciences, Bd of Visitors Int. Programs Center Dept of Political Science, Univ. of Oklahoma; Fellow American Asscn for the Advancement of Science; Patron Gerontology Foundation of Australia. *Publications:* novels: Tim 1974, The Thorn Birds 1977, An Indecent Obsession 1981, A Creed for the Third Millennium 1985, The Ladies of Missalonghi 1987, The First Man in Rome 1990, The Grass Crown 1991, Fortune's Favourites 1993, Caesar's Women 1996, Caesar 1997, The Song of Troy 1998, The Courage and the Will 1999, Morgan's Run 2000, The October Horse 2002; non-fiction: Cooking with Colleen McCullough and Jean Easthope 1982, Roden Cutler, VC – The Biography 1998. *Honours:* Hon. Founding Gov. Prince of Wales Medical Research Inst.; Hon. DLitt (Macquarie) 1993; designated one of Australia's Living National Treasures. *Address:* 'Out Yenna', Norfolk Island, Oceania (via Australia). *Fax:* (6723) 23313.

McCULLOUGH, David Gaub, BA; historian and writer; b. 7 July 1933, Pittsburgh, Pennsylvania, USA; m. Rosalee Ingram Barnes 1954; three s. two d. *Education:* Yale Univ. *Career:* Ed., Time Inc, New York City, 1956–61, United States Information Agency, Washington, DC, 1961–64, American Heritage Publishing Co, New York City, 1964–70; Scholar-in-Residence, University of New Mexico, 1979, Wesleyan University, 1982, 1983; Host, Smithsonian World, 1984–88, The American Experience, 1988–, PBS-TV; Visiting Prof., Cornell University, 1989; mem. Jefferson Legacy Foundation; National Trust for Historic Preservation; Society of American Historians; Harry S. Truman Library Institute. *Publications:* The Great Bridge, 1972; The Path Between the Seas, 1977; The Johnstown Flood, 1978; Mornings on Horseback, 1981; Brave Companions, 1991; Truman, 1992; John Adams, 2001. *Honours:* National Book Award for History, 1978; Samuel Eliot Morison Award, 1978; Cornelius Ryan Award, 1978; Francis Parkman Prizes, 1978, 1993; Los Angeles Times Prize for Biography, 1981; American Book Award for Biography, 1982; Pulitzer Prizes in Biography, 1993, 2002; Harry S. Truman Public Service Award, 1993; Pennsylvania Governor's Award for Excellence, 1993; St Louis Literary Award, 1993; Pennsylvania Society Gold Medal Award, 1994; National Book Foundation Medal for Distinguished Contributions to American Letters, 1995; Marian McFadden Memorial Lecturer, Indianapolis-Marion County Public Library, 2002; various hon. doctorates. *Literary Agent:* Janklow & Nesbit Associates, 445 Park Avenue, New York, NY 10022, USA.

McCULLOUGH, Kenneth (Ken), BA, MFA; poet, writer and teacher; b. 18 July 1943, Staten Island, NY, USA. *Education:* University of Delaware, University of Iowa. *Career:* Teacher, Montana State University, 1970–75, University of Iowa, 1983–95, Kirkwood Community College, Cedar Rapids, 1987, St Mary's University, Winona, Minnesota, 1996; Writer-in-Residence, South Carolina ETV Network, 1975–78; Participant, Artist-in-the-Schools Program, Iowa Arts Council, 1981–96; mem. Associated Writing Programs; Asscn of American University Profs; National Asscn of College Academic Advisers; Renaissance Artists and Writers Asscn and Renaissance International; Rocky Mountain MLA; SFWA. *Publications:* Poetry: The Easy Wreckage, 1971; Migrations, 1972; Creosote, 1976; Elegy for Old Anna, 1985; Travelling Light, 1987; Sycamore Oriole, 1991; Walking Backwards, 1997. Contributions: numerous publications. *Honours:* Acad. of American Poets Award, 1966; Second Place, Ark River Awards, 1972; Helene Wurlitzer Foundation of New Mexico Residencies, 1973, 1994; National Endowment for the Arts Fellowship, 1974; Second Prize, Sri Chinmoy Poetry Awards, 1980; Writers' Voice Capricorn Book Award, 1985; Second Place, Pablo Neruda Award, Nimrod magazine 1990; Third Prize, Kudzu Poetry Contest, 1990; Ucross Foundation Residency, WY, 1991; Witter Bynner Foundation for Poetry Grant, 1993; Iowa Arts Council Grants, 1994, 1996.

McCULLY, Emily Arnold, (Emily Arnold), BA, MA; writer and illustrator; b. 7 Jan. 1939, Galesburg, IL, USA; two s. *Education:* Brown University, Columbia University. *Career:* mem. PEN Society; Authors' Guild. *Publications:* A Craving, 1982; Picnic, 1985; Life Drawing, 1986; Mirette on the High Wire, 1992; The Amazing Felix, 1993; Little Kit, or, the Industrious Flea Circus Girl, 1995; The Pirate Queen, 1995. *Honours:* O. Henry Award Collection, 1977; Caldecott Award, 1993. *Literary Agent:* Harriet Wasserman, 137 E 36th Street, New York, NY 10026, USA.

McCUNN, Ruthanne Lum, BA, DipEd; writer; b. 21 Feb. 1946, San Francisco, CA, USA; m. Donald H. McCunn 1965. *Education:* Univ. of Texas at Austin, San Francisco State Coll. *Career:* Guest Lecturer, Univ. of California at Santa Cruz 1988, Cornell Univ. 1989, Univ. of San Francisco 1993, 1996; mem. American Civil Liberties Union, Amnesty Int., Chinese for Affirmative Action, Chinese Historical Soc., Int. Inst. of San Francisco. *Publications:* An Illustrated History of the Chinese in America, 1979; Thousand Pieces of Gold, 1981; Pie-Biter, 1983; Sole Survivor, 1985; Chinese American Portraits: Personal Histories, 1828–1888, 1988; Chinese Proverbs, 1991; Wooden Fish Songs, 1995; The Moon Pearl, 2000. Contributions: journals. *Honours:* American Book Award, Before Columbus Foundation, 1984; Best Non-Fiction Adventure Book, Southwestern Booksellers Asscn, 1985; Best Non-Fiction Book Citation, Choice, 1989; Distinguished Achievement Award, National Women's Political Caucus, 1991; Jeanne Fair McDonnell Best Fiction Award, Women's Heritage Museums, 1997. *Address:* 1007 Castro, San Francisco, CA 94114, USA. *Website:* www.mccunn.com.

McDERMOTT, Alice, BA, MA; writer; b. 27 June 1953, New York, NY, USA; m. David M. Armstrong. *Education:* SUNY, University of New Hampshire. *Career:* mem. Associated Writing Programs; PEN; Poets and Writers; Writer's Guild. *Publications:* A Bigamist's Daughter, 1982; That Night, 1987; At Weddings and Wakes, 1991; Charming Billy, 1998; Child of My Heart, 2002. Contributions: Magazines. *Honours:* Whiting Writers Award, 1987; National Book Award, 1998. *Address:* 8674-3 Villa La Jolla Drive, La Jolla, CA 92037, USA.

McDEVITT, Jack, BA, MA; writer; b. 14 April 1935, Philadelphia, PA, USA; m. Maureen McAdams 1967; two s. one d. *Education:* La Salle College, Wesleyan University. *Career:* mem. SFWA. *Publications:* The Hercules Text, 1986; A Talent for War, 1989; The Engines of God, 1994; Ancient Shores, 1996; Standard Candles, 1996; Eternity Road, 1997; Moonfall, 1998; Infinity Beach, 2000; Deepsix, 2001; Chindi, 2002. Contributions: various publications. *Honours:* Philip K. Dick Special Award, 1986; UPC Grand Prize, 1992. *Address:* 57 Sunset Blvd, Brunswick, GA 31525, USA.

McDONAGH, Martin; Irish playwright; b. 1970, London, England. *Career:* fmr resident playwright, Royal Nat. Theatre, London. *Plays:* The Beauty Queen of Leenane 1996, The Cripple of Inishmaan 1997, The Lonesome West 1997, A Skull In Connwemara 1997, The Lieutenant of Inishmore 2001, The Mamturk Rifleman, The Pillowman 2003. *Publications:* Plays One 1999, Plays Two 2004. *Honours:* Evening Standard Award for Most Promising Playwright, Tony Awards, USA. *Address:* The Rod Hall Agency Ltd, 3 Charlotte Mews, London, W1T 4DZ, England. *Telephone:* (20) 7637-0706. *Fax:* (20) 7637-0807. *E-mail:* office@rodhallagency.com. *Website:* www.rodhallagency.com.

MacDONALD, Alastair A., BLitt, MA, PhD; academic, poet and writer; *Professor of English Emeritus, Memorial University*; b. 24 Oct. 1920, Aberlour, Scotland. *Education:* University of Aberdeen, Christ Church, Oxford, University of Manchester. *Career:* Temporary Senior English Master, King William's College, Isle of Man, 1953; Prof. of English, 1955–87, Prof. Emeritus, 1992–, Memorial University, NF, Canada; various poetry readings; mem. League of Canadian Poets; Scottish Poetry Library Asscn; Writers' Alliance of Newfoundland and Labrador. *Publications:* Poetry: Between Something and Something, 1970; Shape Enduring Mind, 1974; A Different Lens, 1981; Towards the Mystery, 1985; A Figure on the Move, 1991; Landscapes of Time: New, Uncollected, and Selected Poems, 1994; If More Winters, Or This the Last 2003. Novel: Flavian's Fortune, 1985. Other: Prose and criticism. Contributions: various anthologies, reviews, journals and magazines. *Honours:* Best Poem, Canadian Author and Bookman, 1972; New Voices in American Poetry, 1973; First Prize for Poetry, 1976, Hon. Mention, 1978, Second Prize for Poetry, 1982, Newfoundland Government Arts and Letters Competition. *Address:* c/o Department of English, Arts and Administration Bldg, Memorial University, St John's, NL A1C 5S7, Canada.

MacDONALD, Cynthia, BA, MA; poet and lecturer; b. 2 Feb. 1928, New York, NY, USA; m. E. C. Macdonald 1954 (divorced 1975); one s. one d. *Education:* Bennington College, Vermont, Mannes College of Music, New York, Sarah Lawrence College. *Career:* Asst Prof., 1970–74, Assoc. Prof. and Acting Dean of Studies, 1974–75, Sarah Lawrence College; Prof., Johns Hopkins University, 1975–79; Consultant, 1977–78, Co-Dir, Writing Program, 1979–, University of Houston; Guest Lecturer at various universities, colleges, seminars, etc; mem. American Society of Composers, Authors, and Publishers; Associated Writing Programs. *Publications:* Amputations, 1972; Transplants, 1976; Pruning the Annuals, 1976; (W)holes, 1980; Alternate Means of Transport, 1985; Living Wills: New and Selected Poems, 1991; I Can't Remember, 1997. Contributions: anthologies and other publications. *Honours:* MacDowell Colony Grant, 1970; National Endowment for the Arts Grants, 1973, 1979; Yaddo Foundation Grants, 1974, 1976, 1979; CAPS Grant, 1976; American Acad. and Institute of Arts and

Letters Award, 1977; Rockefeller Foundation Fellow, 1978. *Address:* c/o Alfred A. Knopf Inc, 1745 Broadway, Suite 81, New York, NY 10019–4305, USA.

McDONALD, Forrest, BA, MA, PhD; academic, historian and writer; b. 7 Jan. 1927, Orange, TX, USA; m. 1st; three s. two d.; m. 2nd Ellen Shapiro 1963. *Education:* University of Texas. *Career:* Exec. Secretary, American History Research Centre, Madison, Wisconsin, 1953–58; Assoc. Prof., 1959–63, Prof. of History, 1963–67, Brown University; Prof., Wayne State University, 1967–76; Prof., 1976–87, Distinguished University Research Prof., 1987–, University of Alabama, Tuscaloosa; Presidential Appointee, Board of Foreign Scholarships, Washington, DC, 1985–87; Adviser, Centre of Judicial Studies, Cumberland, Virginia, 1985–92; James Pinckney Harrison Prof., College of William and Mary, 1986–87; Jefferson Lecturer, National Endowment for the Humanities, 1987; mem. American Antiquarian Society; Philadelphia Society; The Historical Society. *Publications:* We the People: The Economic Origins of the Constitution, 1958; Insull, 1962; E Pluribus Unum, 1965; The Presidency of George Washington, 1974; The Phaeton Ride, 1974; The Presidency of Thomas Jefferson, 1976; Alexander Hamilton: A Biography, 1979; Novus Ordo Seclorum, 1985; Requiem, 1988; The American Presidency: An Intellectual History, 1994; States' Rights and the Union 1776–1876, 2000. Contributions: Professional journals. *Honours:* Guggenheim Fellowship, 1962–63; George Washington Medal, Freedom's Foundation, 1980; Frances Tavern Book Award, 1980; Best Book Award, American Revolution Round Table, 1986; Richard M. Weaver Award, Ingersoll Foundation, 1990; First Salvatori Award, Intercollegiate Studies Institute, 1992; Salvatori Book Award, Intercollegiate Studies Institute, 1994; Mount Vernon Society Choice, One of the Ten Great Books on George Washington, 1998. *Address:* PO Box 155, Coker, AL 35452, USA.

McDONALD, Gregory Christopher, BA; writer; b. 15 Feb. 1937, Shrewsbury, MA, USA; m. 1st Susan Aiken 1963 (divorced 1990); two s.; m. 2nd Cheryle Higgins 2001. *Education:* Harvard Univ. *Career:* Critic, Boston Globe, 1966–73; mem. Authors' Guild; CWA; Dramatists Guild; MWA, pres., 1985–86; Writers Guild of America. *Publications:* Fiction: Running Scared, 1964; Fletch, 1974; Confess, Fletch, 1976; Flynn, 1977; Love Among the Mashed Potatoes, 1978; Fletch's Fortune, 1978; Fletch Forever, 1978; Who Took Tony Rinaldi?, 1980; Fletch and the Widow Bradley, 1981; The Buck Passes Flynn, 1981; Fletch's Moxie, 1982; Fletch and the Man Who, 1983; Carioca Fletch, 1984; Flynn's In, 1984; Fletch Won, 1985; Safekeeping, 1985; Fletch, Too, 1986; Fletch Chronicle, 3 vols, 1986–88; A World Too Wide, 1987; Exits and Entrances, 1988; Merely Players, 1988; The Brave, 1991; Son of Fletch, 1993; Fletch Reflected, 1994; Skylar, 1995; Skylar in Yankeeland, 1997; Flynn's World, 2003. Non-Fiction: The Education of Gregory McDonald, 1985. Editor: Last Laughs, 1986. *Honours:* Edgar Allan Poe Awards, MWA, 1975, 1977; Humanitarian of the Year Award, Tennessee Asscn of Federal Executives, 1989; Citizen of the Year Award, National Asscn of Social Workers, 1990; Roger William Straus Award, 1990; Alex Haley Award, 1992. *Literary Agent:* Arthur Greene Esquire, 101 Park Avenue, New York, NY 10178, USA.

MacDONALD, Hugh John, BA, MA, PhD; musicologist and academic; b. 31 Jan. 1940, Newbury, Berkshire, England; m. 1st Naomi Butterworth 1963; one s. three d.; m. 2nd Elizabeth Babb 1979; one s. *Education:* University of Cambridge. *Career:* Lecturer in Music, University of Cambridge, 1966–71, University of Oxford, 1971–80; Gardiner Prof. of Music, University of Glasgow, 1980–87; Avis Blewett Prof. of Music, Washington University, St Louis, 1987–. *Publications:* Berlioz Orchestral Music, 1969; Skryabin, 1978; Berlioz, 1982; Berlioz: Correspondance générale, Vol. 4, 1984, Vol. 5, 1989, Vol. 6, 1995, Vol. 7, 2001, Vol. 8, 2002; Selected Letters of Berlioz, 1995; Berlioz's Orchestration Treatise, 2002. Contributions: The New Grove Dictionary of Music and Musicians; The New Grove Dictionary of Opera; many journals. *Honours:* Grand Prix de Littérature Musicale Charles Cros, 1985, 1996. *Address:* c/o Department of Music, Washington University, St Louis, MO 63130, USA.

McDONALD, Ian A., FRSL; poet, writer, dramatist and editor; b. 18 April 1933, St Augustine, Trinidad; m. Mary Angela Callender 1984; three s. *Education:* Queen's Royal Coll., Trinidad, Univ. of Cambridge. *Career:* CEO, Sugar Asscn of the Caribbean; Dir, Theatre Co of Guyana, Georgetown 1981–; Ed., Kyk-Over-Al West Indian literary journal 1984–; Chair., Demerana Publishers 1988–. *Publications:* The Tramping Man (play), 1969; The Humming Bird Tree (novel), 1969; Selected Poems, 1983; Mercy Ward, 1988; Essequibo, 1992; Jaffo the Calypsonian (poems), 1994; The Heinemann Book of Caribbean Poetry (co-ed.), 1994; The Collected Poems of A. J. Seymour (co-ed.). *Honours:* Hon. DLitt (Univ. of the West Indies) 1997; Guyana Nat. Award 1987. *Address:* c/o Demerara Sugar Terminal, River View, Ruimveldt, Georgetown, Guyana. *Fax:* 2266104. *E-mail:* dstisc@guyana.net.gy.

MacDONALD, Malcolm (see Ross-MacDonald, Malcolm John).

MacDONALD, Marianne, BA, BLitt, PhD; writer; b. 9 July 1934, Kenora, ON, Canada; m. Erik Korn 1958 (divorced 1998); two s. *Education:* McGill University, University of Oxford, University of Keele. *Career:* Lecturer in English, University of Toronto, 1960–62; Lecturer in American Studies, University of Keele, 1964–69; Principal Lecturer in English, Middlesex Polytechnic, 1972–86; mem. CWA; Crime Writers of Canada; Sisters in Crime. *Publications:* Fiction: Death's Autograph, 1996; Ghost Walk, 1997; Smoke Screen, 1999; Road Kill, 2000; Blood Lies, 2001; Die Once, 2002. Children's Books: Black Bass Rock, 1952; Smugglers Cove, 1955; The Treasure of Ur, 1958; The Pirate Queen, 1991; The Eighty-Nine Pennies of Emma Jones, 1992; The Witch Repair, 1995. Other: The State of Literary Theory Today (ed.), 1982; Ezra Pound: purpose/form/meaning, 1983; Ezra Pound and History (ed.), 1985. *Honours:* Woodrow Wilson Fellowship 1954–55. *Literary Agent:* David Higham Associates, 5–8 Lower John Street, Golden Square, London W1F 9HA, England.

McDONALD, Walter Robert, BA, MA, PhD; academic, poet and writer; b. 18 July 1934, Lubbock, TX, USA; m. Carol Ham 1959; two s. one d. *Education:* Texas Technological College, University of Iowa. *Career:* Faculties, US Air Force Acad., University of Colorado, Texas Tech University; Paul W. Horn Prof. of English and Poet-in-Residence, Texas Tech University, Lubbock; mem. Texas Asscn of Creative Writing Teachers; PEN; Poetry Society of America; Assoc. Writing Programs; Texas Institute of Letters, councillor; Conference of College Teachers of English of Texas. *Publications:* Poetry: Caliban in Blue, 1976; One Thing Leads to Another, 1978; Anything, Anything, 1980; Working Against Time, 1981; Burning the Fence, 1981; Witching on Hardscrabble, 1985; Flying Dutchman, 1987; After the Noise of Saigon, 1988; Rafting the Brazos, 1988. Fiction: A Band of Brothers: Stories of Vietnam, 1989; Night Landings, 1989; The Digs in Escondido Canyon, 1991; All That Matters: The Texas Plains in Photographs and Poems, 1992; Where Skies Are Not Cloudy, 1993; Counting Survivors, 1995. Contributions: numerous journals and magazines. *Honours:* Poetry Awards, Texas Institute of Letters, 1976, 1985, 1987; George Elliston Poetry Prize, 1987; Juniper Prize, 1988; Western Heritage Awards for Poetry, National Cowboy Hall of Fame, 1990, 1992; 1993. *Address:* Department of English, Texas Tech University, Lubbock, TX 79409, USA.

MacDONOGH, Giles Malachy Maximilian, BA, MA; writer and journalist; b. 6 April 1955, London, England. *Education:* Balliol College, Oxford, University of Oxford, École des Hautes Études Pratiques, France. *Career:* freelance journalist, 1983–; Ed., Made in France, 1984; columnist, Financial Times, 1989–; mem. International PEN; Octagon of Wine Writers. *Publications:* A Palate in Revolution: Grimod de La Reynière and the Almanach des Gourmands, 1987; A Good German: Adam von Trott zu Solz, 1990; The Wine and Food of Austria, 1992; Brillat Savarin: The Judge and his Stomach, 1992; Syrah Grenache, Mourvèdre, 1992; Prussia, the Perversion of an Idea, 1994; Berlin, 1997; The Last Kaiser: The Life of Wilhelm II, 2001. Contributions: Reference works, books, and periodicals. *Honours:* Glenfiddich Special Award, 1988. *Literary Agent:* Curtis Brown Ltd, Haymarket House, 28–29 Haymarket, London, SW1Y 4SP, England. *Telephone:* (20) 7393-4400. *Fax:* (20) 7393-4401. *E-mail:* info@curtisbrown.co.uk. *Website:* www.curtisbrown.co.uk.

MacDOUGALL, Ruth Doan, BEd; writer; b. 19 March 1939, Laconia, NH, USA; m. Donald K. MacDougall 1957. *Education:* Bennington College, Keene State College. *Career:* mem. National Writers' Union. *Publications:* The Lilting House, 1965; The Cost of Living, 1971; One Minus One, 1971; The Cheerleader, 1973; Wife and Mother, 1976; Aunt Pleasantine, 1978; The Flowers of the Forest, 1981; A Lovely Time Was Had By All, 1982; Snowy, 1993; Fifty Hikes in the White Mountains, 1997; Fifty More Hikes in New Hampshire, 1998; The Cheerleader: 25th Anniversary Edition, 1998; A Woman Who Loved Lindbergh, 2001; Henrietta Snow, 2004. Contributions: book reviewer: New York Times Book Review; Newsday; Others. *Honours:* Winner, PEN Syndicated Fiction Project, 1983, 1984, 1985. *Address:* 285 Range Road, Center Sandwich, NH 03227, USA. *Website:* www.ruthdoanmacdougall.com.

McDOUGALL, Walter Allan, BA, MA, PhD; academic and writer; b. 3 Dec. 1946, Washington, DC, USA; m. 2nd Jonna van Zanten 1988; two c. *Education:* Amherst College, University of Chicago. *Career:* US Army, Viet Nam, 1968–70; Asst Prof., 1975–83, Assoc. Prof., 1983–87, Prof. of History, 1987–, University of California, Berkeley; Prof. of History and Alloy-Ansin Chair in International Relations, 1988–, University of Pennsylvania; Senior Fellow, Dir of Center for America and the West, Foreign Policy Research Institute, Philadelphia, 1991–; Ed., Orbis, 1999–2001; mem. American Church Union; Pumpkin Papers Irregulars. *Publications:* France's Rhineland Diplomacy 1914–1924: The Last Bid for a Balance of Power in Europe, 1978; The Grenada Papers (ed. with Paul Seabury), 1984; Social Sciences and Space Exploration: New Directions for University Instruction (contributor), 1984; ...The Heavens and the Earth: A Political History of the Space Age, 1985; Let the Sea Make a Noise, 1993; Promised Land, Crusader State: The American Encounter with the World Since 1776, 1997. Contributions: numerous articles and reviews to periodicals. *Honours:* Pulitzer Prize for History, 1986; Visiting Scholar, Hoover Institution, 1986; One of America's Ten Best College Profs, Insight, 1987; Dexter Prize for Best Book, Society for the History of Technology, 1987. *Address:* 208 College Hall, University of Pennsylvania, Philadelphia, PA 19104–6379, USA.

MacDOWELL, Douglas Maurice, BA, MA, DLitt, FRSE, FBA; academic and writer; *Professor of Greek Emeritus, University of Glasgow*; b. 8 March 1931, London, England. *Education:* Balliol College, Oxford. *Career:* Asst Lecturer, Lecturer, Sr Lecturer, Reader in Greek and Latin, Univ. of Manchester 1958–71; Prof. of Greek 1971–2001, Prof. Emeritus 2001–, Univ. of Glasgow. *Publications:* Andokides: On the Mysteries (ed.), 1962; Athenian

Homicide Law, 1963; Aristophanes: Wasps (ed.), 1971; The Law in Classical Athens, 1978; Spartan Law, 1986; Demosthenes: Against Meidias (ed.), 1990; Aristophanes and Athens, 1995; Antiphon and Andocides (with M. Gagarin), 1998; Demosthenes: On the False Embassy (ed.), 2000. *Address:* Department of Classics, University of Glasgow, Glasgow, G12 8QQ, Scotland.

McDOWELL, Edwin Stewart, BS; journalist and writer; b. 13 May 1935, Somers Point, NJ, USA; m. Sathie Akimoto 1973; one s. two d. *Education:* Temple Univ. *Career:* Staff, New York Times; mem. Authors' Guild. *Publications:* Three Cheers and a Tiger, 1966; To Keep Our Honor Clean, 1980; The Lost World, 1988. *Address:* c/o New York Times, 229 W 43rd Street, New York, NY 10036, USA.

MacDOWELL, John (see Parks, Timothy Harold).

McDOWELL, John Henry, BA, MA; academic and writer; b. 7 March 1942, Boksburg, South Africa; m. Andrea Lehrke 1977. *Education:* St John's College, Johannesburg, University College of Rhodesia and Nyasaland, New College, Oxford. *Career:* Fellow and Praelector in Philosophy, 1966–86, Emeritus Fellow, 1988, University College, Oxford; University Lecturer, 1967–86, John Locke Lecturer, 1991, University of Oxford; James C. Loeb Fellow in Classical Philosophy, Harvard University, 1969; Visiting Prof., University of Michigan, 1975, University of California at Los Angeles, 1977, University of Minnesota, 1982, Jadavpur University, Kolkata, 1983; Senior Fellow, Princeton University, 1984; Prof. of Philosophy, 1986–88, University Prof. of Philosophy, 1988–, University of Pittsburgh; mem. Fellow, British Acad., 1983; Fellow, American Acad. of Arts and Sciences. *Publications:* Theaetetus by Plato (trans.), 1973; Truth and Meaning (ed. with Gareth Evans), 1976; The Varieties of Reference, by Gareth Evans (ed.), 1982; Subject, Thought, and Context (ed. with Philip Pettit), 1986; Mind and World, 1994; Mind, Value, and Reality, 1998; Meaning, Knowledge, and Reality, 1998. Contributions: scholarly books and journals. *Address:* c/o Department of Philosophy, University of Pittsburgh, Pittsburgh, PA 15260, USA.

McELDOWNEY, Eugene, BA; writer and journalist; b. 27 June 1943, Belfast, Northern Ireland; m. Maura Magill 1970; one s. one d. *Education:* Queen's University, Belfast. *Career:* Journalist, Night Ed., Irish Times, Dublin, Ireland, 1972–; mem. National Union of Journalists. *Publications:* A Kind of Homecoming, 1994; A Stone of the Heart, 1995; The Sad Case of Harpo Higgins, 1996; Murder at Piper's Gut, 1997; The Faloorie Man, 1999; Stella's Story, 2002. *Address:* c/o Imrie and Dervis, 7 Carlton Mansions, Holmleigh Road, London N16 5PX, England.

McELROY, Colleen Johnson, BS, MS, PhD; academic, poet and writer; b. 30 Oct. 1935, St Louis, MO, USA; m. (divorced); one s. one d. *Education:* Kansas State University, University of Washington, Seattle. *Career:* Ed., Dark Waters, 1973–79; Prof., University of Washington, Seattle, 1973–. *Publications:* Music From Home, 1976; The Halls of Montezuma, 1979; The New Voice, 1979; Winters Without Snow, 1979; Lie and Say You Love Me, 1981; Queen of the Ebony Isles, 1984; Jesus and Fat Tuesday, 1987; What Madness Brought Me Here, 1990. Contributions: various journals. *Address:* c/o Creative Writing Program, Department of English, University of Washington, Seattle, WA 98195, USA.

McELROY, Joseph Prince, BA, MA, PhD; writer; b. 21 Aug. 1930, New York, NY, USA. *Education:* Williams College, Columbia University. *Publications:* A Smuggler's Bible, 1966; Hind's Kidnap, 1969; Ancient History, 1971; Lookout Cartridge, 1974; Plus, 1977; Ship Rock, 1980; Women and Men, 1987; Actress in the House, 2003. *Address:* c/o Georges Borchardt, 136 E 57th Street, New York, NY 10022, USA.

McELROY, Lee (see Kelton, Elmer Stephen).

MACER-STORY, Eugenia; Writer, Dramatist and Poet; b. 20 Jan. 1945, Minneapolis, MN, USA; m. Leon A. Story 1970 (divorced 1975); one s. *Education:* BS, Speech, Northwestern University, 1965; MFA, Playwriting, Columbia University, 1968. *Career:* mem. Dramatists' Guild; US Psychotronics Asscn; Poet's House, New York; American Society for Psychical Research. *Publications:* Congratulations: The UFO Reality, 1978; Angels of Time: Astrological Magic, 1981; Du Fu Man Chu Meets the Lonesome Cowboy: Sorcery and the UFO Experience, 1991; Legacy of Daedalus, 1995; Cattle Bones and Coke Machines (anthology), 1995; The Dark Frontier, 1997; Crossing Jungle River (poems), 1998; Troll: Other Interdimensional Invasions (short stories), 2000; Vanishing Questions (poems), 2000; Carrying Thunder, 2002; Doing Business in the Adrondocks (metaphysical travelogue), 2002. Plays: Meister Hemmelin, 1994; Double or Nothing, 1994; Radish, 1995; Conquest of the Asteroids, 1996; Mister Shooting Star, 1997; Wild Dog Casino, 1998; Holy Dragonet, 1998–99; Old Gaffer from Boise, 2000; Redecoration According to Currier, 2000; Ars Chronicon Sylvestre, 2002. Contributions: numerous publications. *Honours:* Shubert Fellowship, 1968. *Address:* Magick Mirror Communications, PO Box 741, JAF Bldg, New York, NY 10116, USA.

McEVEDY, Colin Peter, BA, BM, BCH, DM, DPM; writer; b. 6 June 1930, Stratford, England. *Education:* Magdalen College, Oxford, University of London. *Publications:* The Penguin Atlas of Medieval History, 1961; The Penguin Atlas of Ancient History, 1967; The Atlas World History (with Sarah McEvedy), 3 vols, 1970–73; The Penguin Atlas of Modern History, 1972; Atlas of World Population History (with Richard Jones), 1980; The Penguin Atlas of African History, 1980; The Penguin Atlas of Recent History (Europe since 1815), 1982; The Century World History FactFinder, 1984; The Penguin Atlas of North American History, 1988; The New Penguin Atlas of Medieval History, 1992. Contributions: Bubonic Plague; Scientific American. *Address:* 7 Caithness Road, London W14, England.

McEWAN, Ian Russell, CBE, BA, MA, FRSL; British writer; b. 21 June 1948, Aldershot, Hampshire, England; m. 1st Penny Allen 1982 (divorced 1995); two s. two d.; m. 2nd Annalena McAfee. *Education:* University of Sussex, University of East Anglia. *Publications:* First Love, Last Rites, 1975; In Between the Sheets, 1978; The Cement Garden, 1978; The Imitation Game, 1981; The Comfort of Strangers, 1981; The Child in Time, 1987; The Innocent, 1990; Black Dogs, 1992; The Daydreamer, 1994; The Short Stories, 1995; Enduring Love, 1997; Amsterdam, 1998; Atonement, 2001. Other: Or Shall We Die? (libretto for the oratorio by Michael Berkeley), 1982; The Imitation Game (film script); The Ploughman's Lunch (film script). *Honours:* Somerset Maugham Award, 1975; Whitbread Award, 1987; Hon. DLitt, University of Sussex, 1989, University of East Anglia, 1993, University of London, 2000; Prix Fémina, 1993; Fellow, American Acad. of Arts and Sciences, 1995; Booker Prize, 1998; Shakespeare Prize, 1999; National Book Critics Circle Award for Fiction, 2002. *Address:* c/o Jonathon Cape, Random Century House, 20 Vauxhall Bridge Road, London SW1V 2SA, England.

McFARLAND, Ronald Earl, AA, BA, MA, PhD; professor of English, poet and writer; b. 22 Sept. 1942, Bellaire, OH, USA; m. Elsie Roseland Watson 1966; one s. two d. *Education:* Brevard Junior College, Florida State University, University of Illinois. *Career:* Teaching Asst, Florida State University, 1964–65, University of Illinois, 1967–70; Instructor, Sam Houston State College, 1965–67; Asst Prof., Assoc. Prof., 1970–79, Prof. of English, 1979–, University of Idaho; Idaho State Writer-in-Residence, 1984–85; Exchange Prof., Ohio University, 1985–86; mem. Acad. of American Poets; Hemingway Society; Pacific Northwest American Studies Asscn. *Publications:* Poetry: Certain Women, 1977; Composting at Forty, 1984; The Haunting Familiarity of Things, 1993; Stranger in Town, 2000; The Hemingway Poems, 2000; The Mad Waitress Poems, 2000; Ballygloves, 2000. Fiction: Catching First Light (short stories), 2001. Non-Fiction: The Villanelle: Evolution of a Poetic Form, 1988; David Wagoner, 1989; Norman Maclean, 1993; Tess Gallagher, 1995; The World of David Wagoner, 1997; Understanding James Welch, 2000. Editor: Eight Idaho Poets, 1979; James Welch, 1987; Norman Maclean (with Hugh Nichols), 1988; Idaho's Poetry: A Centennial Anthology (with William Studebaker), 1988; Deep Down Things: Poems of the Inland Pacific Northwest (with Franz Schneider and Kornel Skovajsa), 1990. Contributions: scholarly books and journals, poetry anthologies, reviews, quarterlies, and periodicals. *Honours:* National Endowment for the Arts Grant, 1978; Asscn for the Humanities in Idaho Grant, 1983; Burlington-Northern Faculty Achievement Award, 1990; Alumni Award for Faculty Excellence, 1991; Distinguished Alumnus, Brevard Community College, 1996; University of Idaho Faculty Award for Creative Excellence, 2002.

MacFARLANE, Robert; British writer and academic; b. 1976, Nottingham. *Education:* Nottingham High School, Emmanuel Coll., Cambridge. *Career:* Fellow, Emmanuel Coll., Cambridge. *Publications:* Mountains of the Mind: A History of a Fascination (Guardian First Book Award, Somerset Maugham Award 2004) 2003, Wild Eyed 2005; contrib. to The Sunday Times, The Observer, TLS, The Spectator, Evening Standard. *Literary Agent:* Toby Eady Associates Ltd, Third Floor, 9 Orme Court, London, W2 4RL, England. *Telephone:* (20) 7792-0092. *Fax:* (20) 7792-0879. *E-mail:* toby@tobyeady.demon.co.uk. *Website:* www.tobyeadyassociates.co.uk. *Address:* c/o Emmanuel College, University of Cambridge, St Andrew's Street, Cambridge, CB2 3AP, England.

McFEELY, William Shield, BA, MA, PhD; academic and writer; b. 25 Sept. 1930, New York, NY, USA; m. Mary Drake 1952; one s. two d. *Education:* Amherst College, Yale University. *Career:* Asst Prof., 1966–69, Assoc. Prof., 1969–70, Yale University; Prof. of History, 1970–80, Rodman Prof. of History, 1980–82, Andrew W. Mellon Prof. in the Humanities, 1982–86, Mount Holyoke College; Visiting Prof., University College London, 1978–79, Amherst College, 1980–81; Visiting Prof., 1984–85, John J. McCloy Prof., 1988–89, University of Massachusetts; Richard B. Russell Prof. of American History, 1986–94, Abraham Baldwin Prof. of the Humanities, 1994–, University of Georgia; mem. American Historical Asscn; Authors' Guild; Century Asscn; Organization of American Historians; PEN; Southern Historical Asscn. *Publications:* Yankee Stepfather: General O. O. Howard and the Freedmen, 1968; The Black Man in the Land of Equality (with Thomas J. Ladenburg), 1969; Grant: A Biography, 1981; Ulysses S. Grant: Memoirs and Selected Letters 1839–1865 (ed. with Mary Drake McFeely), 1990; Frederick Douglass, 1991; Sapelo's People: A Long Walk into Freedom, 1994. *Honours:* Morse Fellow, 1968–69; Fellow, ACLS, 1974–75; Pulitzer Prize in Biography, 1982; Francis Parkman Prize, 1982; Guggenheim Fellowship, 1982–83; National Endowment for the Humanities Grant, 1986–87; Avery O. Craven Award, 1992; Lincoln Prize, 1992.

McGAHERN, John; writer; b. 12 Nov. 1934, Leitrim, Ireland; m. Madeline Green 1973. *Education:* University College, Dublin. *Career:* Research Fellow, University of Reading, 1968–71; O'Connor Prof., Colgate University, 1969, 1972, 1977, 1979, 1983, 1992; Visiting Fellow, Trinity College, 1988. *Publications:* The Barracks, 1963; The Dark, 1965; Nightlines, 1970; The Leavetaking, 1975; Getting Through, 1978; The Pornographer, 1979; High Ground, 1985; The Rockingham Shoot, BBC 2, 1987; Amongst Women, 1990; The Collected Stories, 1992; That They May Face the Rising Sun (US edn as By the Lake), 2001. *Address:* c/o Faber and Faber, 3 Queen Square, London WC1N 3AU, England.

McGARRY, Jean, BA, MA; writer and teacher; b. 18 June 1952, Providence, RI, USA. *Education:* Harvard University, Johns Hopkins University. *Career:* teacher, Johns Hopkins University; mem. Associated Writing Programs. *Publications:* Airs of Providence, 1985; The Very Rich Hours, 1987; The Courage of Girls, 1992. Contributions: Antioch Review; Southern Review; Southwest Review; Sulfur; New Orleans Review. *Honours:* Short Fiction Prize, Southern Review-Louisiana State University, 1985.

McGINN, Bernard John, BA, STL, PhD; academic, writer, translator and editor; b. 19 Aug. 1937, Yonkers, NY, USA; m. Patricia Ferris 1971; two s. *Education:* St Joseph's Seminary and College, Yonkers, NY, Pontifical Gregorian University, Rome, Columbia University, University of Munich, Brandeis University. *Career:* Lecturer, Regis College, Weston, Massachusetts, 1966–67; Instructor, Catholic University of America, Washington, DC, 1968–69; Instructor, 1969–70, Asst Prof., 1970–75, Assoc. Prof., 1975–78, Prof. of Historical Theology and the History of Christianity, 1978–, Naomi Shenstone Donnelley Prof., 1992–, Divinity School, University of Chicago; mem. American Society of Church History, pres., 1995–; Eckhart Society; International Society for the Promotion of Eriugenean Studies, pres.; Medieval Acad. of America, fellow, 1994–; National Humanities Centre, USA, fellow, 1999–2000. *Publications:* The Golden Chain: A Study in the Theological Anthropology of Isaac of Stella, 1972; The Crusades, 1973; Visions of the End: Apocalyptic Traditions in the Middle Ages, 1979; The Calabrian Abbot: Joachim of Fiore in the History of Western Thought, 1985; The Presence of God: A History of Christian Mysticism, 3 vols, 1991, 1994, 1998; Apocalypticism in the Western Tradition, 1994; Antichrist: Two Thousand Years of the Human Fascination with Evil, 1994. Translator: Apocalyptic Spirituality, 1979; Meister Eckhart: The Essential Sermons, Commentaries, Treatises and Defense (with Edmund Colledge), 1981; Meister Eckhart: Teacher and Preacher (with Frank Tobin and Elvira Borgstadt), 1986. Editor: Three Treatises on Man: A Cistercian Anthropology, 1977; Christian Spirituality: Origins to the Twelfth Century (with John Meyendorff and Jean Leclercq), 1985; Christian Spirituality: High Middle Ages and Reformation (with Jill Raitt and John Meyendorff), 1987; Mystical Union and Monotheistic Faith: An Ecumenical Doctrine (with Moshe Idel), 1989; God and Creation: An Ecumenical Symposium (with David B. Burrell), 1990; The Apocalypse in the Middle Ages (with Richard K. Emmerson), 1992; Meister Eckhart and the Beguine Mystics: Hadewijch of Brabant, Mechthild of Magdeburg, and Marguerite Porete, 1994; Eriugena: East and West: Papers of the Eighth International Colloquium of the Society for the Promotion of Eriugenean Studies: Chicago and Notre Dame, 18–20 October 1991 (with Willemiem Otten), 1994; The Encyclopedia of Apocalypticism, Vol. 2: Apocalypticism in Western History and Cultures, 1998. Contributions: articles in many books and journals. *Honours:* Fulbright-Hays Research Fellowship, 1967–68; Research Fellow, Institute for Advanced Studies, Hebrew University, Jerusalem, 1988–89, and Institute for Ecumenical and Cultural Research, St John's University, 1992. *Address:* 5701 S Kenwood, Chicago, IL 60637, USA.

McGINNISS, Joe, BS; writer; b. 9 Dec. 1942, New York, NY, USA. *Education:* Holy Cross College. *Career:* newspaper reporter 1964–68. *Publications:* The Selling of the President, 1968; The Dream Team, 1972; Heroes, 1976; Going to Extremes, 1980; Fatal Vision, 1983; Blind Faith, 1989; Cruel Doubt, 1991; Last Brother, 1993; The Miracle of Castel di Sangro, 1999. *Address:* c/o Elaine Koster, 55 Central Park W, Suite 6, New York, NY 10023, USA.

McGONIGAL, James, MA, MPhil, PhD; educator and poet; b. 20 May 1947, Dumfries, Scotland; m. Mary Alexander 1970; one s. three d. *Education:* University of Glasgow. *Career:* High School English Teacher, 1971–84; College Lecturer, 1985–91; Head, Dept of English, 1991–92, Dept of Language and Literature, 1992–, St Andrew's College of Education, Glasgow; mem. Council, Asscn for Scottish Literary Studies. *Publications:* A Sort of Hot Scotland: New Writing Scotland 12 (with A. L. Kennedy), 1994; Last Things First: New Writing Scotland 13 (with A. L. Kennedy), 1995; Sons of Ezra: British Poets and Ezra Pound (with M. Alexander), 1995; Full Strength Angels: New Writing Scotland 14 (with K. Jamie), 1996; Driven Home: Selected Poems, 1998; Across the Water: 'Irishness' in Contemporary Scottish Literature (co-ed.), 2000; Scottish Religious Poems: From Columba to the Present (co-ed.), 2000; The Star You Steer By: Basil Bunting and British Modernism (co-ed.), 2000. Contributions: Aquarius; The Dark Horse; New Blackfriars; New Edinburgh Review; Temenos; various others. *Address:* c/o Department of Curriculum Studies, Faculty of Education, University of Glasgow, Duntocher Road, Bearsden, Glasgow G61 4QA, Scotland.

McGOUGH, Roger Joseph, CBE, OBE, MA, DLitt; British poet and children's writer; b. 9 Nov. 1937, Liverpool; m. 1st Thelma Monaghan 1970 (divorced 1980); m. 2nd Hilary Clough 1986; three s. one d. *Education:* St Mary's Coll., Liverpool, Hull Univ. *Career:* Poetry Fellow Univ. of Loughborough 1973–75; writer-in-residence Western Australia Coll. of Educ., Perth 1986, Univ. of Hamburg 1994; Vice-Pres. The Poetry Society 1996– (mem. Exec. Council 1989–93); Fellow John Moores Univ. 1999; Trustee Chelsea Arts Club 1987–, fmr Chair.; Freeman City of Liverpool 2001. *Music:* wrote and performed Top Twenty hits Lily the Pink and Thank U Very Much 1968–69. *Plays include:* The Sound Collector and My Dad's a Fire-eater (for children); wrote lyrics for Broadway production of The Wind in the Willows 1984. *Plays for radio include:* Summer with Monika, FX, Walking the Dog. *Television:* Kurt, Mungo, B. P. and me (Thames Television) 1985, The Elements (Channel 4) (Royal Television Soc. Award) 1993. *Publications:* The Mersey Sound (with Brian Patten and Adrian Henri) 1967, Watchwords 1969, After the Merrymaking 1971, Out of Sequence 1972, Gig 1972, Sporting Relations 1974, In the Glassroom 1976, Summer with Monika 1978, Holiday on Death Row 1979, Unlucky for Some 1981, Waving at Trains 1982, Melting into the Foreground 1986, Blazing Fruit: Selected Poems 1967–1987 1989, You at the Back 1991, Defying Gravity 1992, The Spotted Unicorn 1998, The Way Things Are 1999, Everyday Eclipses 2002, Collected Poems of Roger McGough 2003; for children: Mr Noselighter 1977, The Great Smile Robbery 1982, Sky in the Pie 1983, The Stowaways 1986, Noah's Ark 1986, Nailing the Shadow 1987, An Imaginary Menagerie 1988, Helen Highwater 1989, Counting by Numbers 1989, Pillow Talk 1990, The Lighthouse That Ran Away 1991, My Dad's a Fire-eater 1992, Another Custard Pie 1993, Lucky 1993, Stinkers Ahoy! 1995, The Magic Fountain 1995, The Kite and Caitlin 1996, Bad Bad Cats 1997, Until I Met Dudley 1998, Good Enough to Eat 2002, Moonthief 2002, The Bees' Knees 2002, Dotty Inventions 2002, What On Earth Can It Be? 2003; ed: Strictly Private 1981, The Kingfisher Book of Comic Verse 1986, The Kingfisher Books of Poems About Love 1997, The Ring of Words (anthology) 1998, Wicked Poems 2002, All the Best 2002. *Honours:* Hon. Prof. Thames Valley Univ. 1993; Hon. MA (Nene Coll.) 1998; Signal Award 1984, 1998, BAFTA Awards 1984, 1992, Cholmondeley Award 1998. *Literary Agent:* PFD, Drury House, 34–43 Russell Street, London, WC2B 5HA, England. *Telephone:* (20) 7344-1000. *Fax:* (20) 7836-9539. *E-mail:* personal@rogermcgough.org.uk. *Website:* www.rogermcgough.org.uk.

McGOVERN, Ann, BA; writer; b. 25 May 1930, New York, NY, USA; m. Martin L. Scheiner 1970; three s. one d. *Education:* University of New Mexico. *Career:* publisher, The Privileged Traveler, 1986–90; mem. Explorers Club; PEN; Authors' Guild; Society of Children's Book Writers; Women's Forum. *Publications:* Over 50 books including: If You Lived in Colonial Times, 1964; Too Much Noise, 1967; Stone Soup, 1968; The Secret Soldier, 1975; Sharks, 1976; Shark Lady, The Adventures of Eugenie Clark, 1978; Playing with Penguins amd Other Adventures in Antarctica, 1994; Lady in the Box, 1997; Adventures of the Shark Lady Eugenie Clark Around the World, 1998. Contributions: Signature; Saturday Review. *Honours:* Outstanding Science Books, National Science Teachers Asscn, 1976, 1979, 1984, 1993; Author of the Year, Scholastic Publishing Inc, 1978; Cuffie Award, 1998. *Address:* 30 E 62nd Street, New York, NY 10021, USA.

MacGOWAN, Christopher John, BA, MA, PhD; academic, writer and editor; *Professor of English, College of William and Mary, Williamsburg*; b. 6 Aug. 1948, London, England; m. Catherine Levesque 1988. *Education:* King's College, Cambridge, Princeton University, USA. *Career:* Research Asst, The Writings of Henry D. Thoreau, 1981–83; Asst Prof., 1984–90, Assoc. Prof., 1990–96, Prof., 1996–, College of William and Mary, Williamsburg, Virginia; mem. MLA, William Carlos Williams Soc. (pres. 1989–91). *Publications:* William Carlos Williams' Early Poetry: The Visual Arts Background, 1984; The Collected Poems of William Carlos Williams, Vol. I, 1909–1939 (co-ed.), 1986, Vol. II, 1939–1962 (ed.), 1988; William Carlos Williams' Paterson (ed.), 1992; The Letters of Denise Levertov and William Carlos Williams (ed.), 1998. Contributions: Reference works and journals. *Honours:* James Prize, King's College, Cambridge, 1976, 1977; Teaching Assistantship, Pennsylvania State University, 1976–77; Graduate Fellowship, Princeton University, 1977–81; Summer Grants, College of William and Mary, 1985, 1987, 1989; Summer Stipend, 1986, Fellowship 1990–91, National Endowment for the Humanities. *Address:* Department of English, College of William and Mary, Williamsburg, VA 23187, USA.

McGRATH, Alister Edgar, BA, BD, MA, DD, DPhil; academic and writer; b. 23 Jan. 1953, Belfast, Northern Ireland; m. Joanna Ruth Collicutt 1980; one s. one d. *Education:* University of Oxford. *Career:* Curate, St Leonards Parish Church, Wollaton, Nottingham, 1980–83; Lecturer in Historical and Systematic Theology, 1983–95, Principal, 1995–, Wycliffe Hall, Oxford; Mem., Faculty of Theology, 1983–, University Research Lecturer in Theology, 1993–99, Prof. of Historical Theology, 1999–, University of Oxford; Research Prof. of Systematic Theology, Regent College, Vancouver, BC, 1993–97. *Publications:* Luther's Theology of the Cross, 1985; Iustitia Dei: A History of the Christian Doctrine of Justification, 1986; The Intellectual Origins of the European Reformation, 1987; Reformation Thought: An Introduction, 1988; Explaining Your Faith Without Losing Your Friends, 1989, revised edn as Explaining Your Faith, 1996; A Life of John Calvin, 1990; The Genesis of Doctrine, 1990; Making Sense of the Cross, 1992; What Was God Doing on the Cross?, 1992; The Dilemna of Self-Esteem: The Cross and Christian Confidence, 1992; Suffering, 1992; Understanding Doctrine: Its Relevance and Purpose for Today, 1992; The Blackwell Encyclopedia of Modern Christian Thought (ed.), 1993; The Renewal of Anglicanism, 1993; Intellectuals Don't Need God and Other Modern Myths: Building Bridges to Faith Through Apologetics, 1993; The Making of Modern German Christology, 1750–1990, 1994; Spirituality in an Age of Change: Rediscovering the Spirit of the Reformers, 1994; Christian Theology: An Introduction, 1994; How Shall We Reach Them? (with Michael Green), 1995; Evangelicalism and the Future of Christianity, 1995; Beyond the Quiet Time: Practical Evangelical Spirituality, 1995; Suffering and God, 1995; The Christian Theology Reader (ed.), 1995; A Passion for Truth: The Intellectual Coherence of Evangelicalism, 1996; An Introduction to Christianity, 1997; The NIV Bible Companion: A Basic Commentary on the Old and New Testaments, 1997; J. I. Packer: A Biography (UK edn as To Know and Serve God), 1997; The Foundations of Dialogue in Science and Religion, 1998; Historical Theology: An Introduction to the History of Christian Thought, 1998; 'I Believe': Exploring the Apostles' Creed, 1998; Christian Spirituality: An Introduction, 1999; The Unknown God: Searching for Spiritual Fulfilment, 1999; Science and Religion: An Introduction, 1999; The Hodder Dictionary of Bible Themes (gen. ed.), 1999; The NIV Thematic Reference Bible (gen. ed.), 1999; Christian Literature: An Anthology (ed.), 2000; The J. I. Packer Collection (ed.), 2000; The Journey: A Pilgrim in the Lands of the Spirit, 2000; In the Beginning: The Story of the King James Bible, 2001; The Re-enchantment of Nature: Science, Religion and the Human Sense of Wonder, 2003. *Address:* c/o Wycliffe Hall, 54 Banbury Road, Oxford OX2 6PW, England.

McGRATH, Patrick, BA; British writer; b. 7 Feb. 1950, London, England. *Education:* University of London and Simon Fraser University, Burnaby, BC. *Career:* Managing Ed., Speech Technology magazine 1982–87. *Publications:* The Lewis and Clark Expedition 1985, Blood and Water and Other Tales 1988, The Grotesque 1989, New York Life or, Friends and Others 1990, Spider 1990, Dr Haggard's Disease 1993, Asylum 1996, Martha Peake: A Novel of the Revolution 2000, Port Mungo 2004; contrib. to periodicals. *Address:* 21 E Second Street, No. 10, New York, NY 10003, USA.

MacGREGOR, David Roy, BA, MA, ARIBA, FRHistS; writer; b. 26 Aug. 1925, London, England; m. Patricia Margaret Aline Purcell-Gilpin 1962. *Education:* Trinity College, Cambridge, Hammersmith School of Building. *Career:* mem. Soc. of Nautical Research (council mem. 1959–63, 1965–69, 1974–77, 1980–85, hon. vice-pres. 1985), Maritime Trust. *Publications:* The Tea Clippers, 1952; The China Bird, 1961; Fast Sailing Ships 1775–1875, 1973; Clipper Ships, 1977; Merchant Sailing Ships 1775–1815, 1980; Merchant Sailing Ships 1815–1850, 1984; Merchant Sailing Ships 1858–1875, 1984. Contributions: Mariner's Mirror; Journal of Nautical Archaeology. *Honours:* Gold Medal, Daily Express 1973. *Address:* 99 Lonsdale Road, London SW13 9DA, England.

McGREGOR, Iona, BA; writer; b. 7 Feb. 1929, Aldershot, England. *Education:* University of Bristol. *Career:* mem. Scottish PEN. *Publications:* Fiction: Death Wore a Diadem, 1989; Alice in Shadowtime, 1992. Children's Fiction: An Edinburgh Reel, 1968; The Popinjay, 1969; The Burning Hill, 1970; The Tree of Liberty, 1972; The Snake and the Olive, 1974. Non-Fiction: Edinburgh and Eastern Lowlands, 1979; Wallace and Bruce, 1986; Importance of Being Earnest, 1987; Huckleberry Finn, 1988. *Honours:* Writer's Bursary, Scottish Arts Council, 1989.

McGUANE, Thomas Francis, III, BA, MFA; writer; b. 11 Dec. 1939, Wyandotte, Michigan, USA; m. 1st Portia Rebecca Crockett 1962 (divorced 1975); one s.; m. 2nd Margot Kidder 1976 (divorced 1977); one d.; m. 3rd Laurie Buffett 1977; one step-d. one d. *Education:* University of Michigan, Olivet College, Michigan State University, Yale University, Stanford University. *Publications:* The Sporting Club, 1969; The Bushwacked Piano, 1971; Ninety-Two in the Shade, 1973; Panama, 1977; An Outside Chance: Essays on Sports, 1980, revised edn as An Outside Chance: Classic and New Essays on Sports, 1990; Nobody's Angel, 1982; In the Crazies: Book and Portfolio, 1984; Something to Be Desired, 1984; To Skin a Cat, 1986; Silent Seasons: Twenty-One Fishing Stories, 1988; Keep the Change, 1989; Nothing But Blue Skies, 1992; Some Horses, 1999; The Cadence of Grass, 2002. *Honours:* Wallace Stegner Fellowship, Stanford University, 1966–67; Richard and Hinda Rosenthal Foundation Award, American Acad. of Arts and Letters, 1971; Hon. doctorates, Montana State University, 1993, Rocky Mountain College, 1995. *Address:* PO Box 25, McLeod, MT 59052, USA.

McGUCKIAN, Medbh, BA, MA; poet and teacher; b. 12 Aug. 1950, Belfast, Northern Ireland; m. John McGuckian 1977; three s. one d. *Education:* Queen's University, Belfast. *Career:* Teacher, Dominican Convent, Fortwilliam Park, Belfast, 1974; Instructor, St Patrick's College, Knock, Belfast, 1975–; Writer-in-Residence, Queen's University, Belfast, 1986–88. *Publications:* Poetry: Single Ladies: Sixteen Poems, 1980; Portrait of Joanna, 1980; Trio Poetry (with Damian Gorman and Douglas Marshall), 1981; The Flower Master, 1982; The Greenhouse, 1983; Venus and the Rain, 1984; On Ballycastle Beach, 1988; Two Women, Two Shores, 1989; Marconi's Cottage, 1991; The Flower Master and Other Poems, 1993; Captain Lavender, 1994; Drawing Ballerinas, 2001. Editor: The Big Striped Golfing Umbrella: Poems by Young People from Northern Ireland, 1985. *Honours:* National Poetry Competition Prize, 1979; Eric Gregory Award, 1980; Rooney Prize, 1982; Ireland Arts Council Award, 1982; Alice Hunt Bartlett Award, 1983; Cheltenham Literature Festival Poetry Competition Prize, 1989. *Address:* c/o Gallery Press, Oldcastle, County Meath, Ireland.

McGUINNESS, Frank, BA, MPh; Irish dramatist, writer, poet and academic; b. 29 July 1953, Buncrana, Donegal. *Education:* University College, Dublin. *Career:* Lecturer in English, University of Ulster, Coleraine, 1977–79, University College, Dublin, 1979–80, 1997–, St Patrick's College, Maynooth, 1984–97; Dir, Abbey Theatre, Dublin, 1992–96; mem. Aosdána. *Publications:* Plays: The Factory Girls, 1982; Borderlands, 1984; Observe the Sons of Ulster Marching Towards the Somme, 1985; Baglady, 1985; Innocence 1986; Carthaginians, 1988; Peer Gynt (adaptation of Ibsen's play), 1988; Mary and Lizzie, 1989; Three Sisters (adaptation of Chekhov's play), 1990; Someone Who'll Watch Over Me, 1992; The Bird Sanctuary 1994; Plays One, 1996; A Doll's House (adaptation of Ibsen's play), 1997; Mutabilitie 1997, Electra (adaptation of Sophocles's play) 1997, The Storm (adaptation of Ostrousky's play) 1998, Miss Julie (adaptation of Strindberg's play) 2000, Gates of Gold 2002, Selected Plays Vol. 2 2002. Other: In Loving Memory (poems), 1989; Booterstown (poems), 1994; The Dazzling Dark: New Irish Places, 1996; Dancing at Lughnasa (screenplay), 1998; Dolly West's Kitchen, 1999; The Sea With No Ships (poems), 1999, The Stone Jug (poems) 2003; Hecuba 2004. *Honours:* Rooney Prize, 1985; Harvey's Award, 1985; Most Promising Playwright Award, Evening Standard, 1986; Plays and Players Award, 1986; Cheltenham Prize, 1986; Charrington Award, 1987; Ewart-Biggs Peace Prize, 1987; Edinburgh Fringe First Award, 1988; Prix des Journalists, Prague, 1989; Irish-American Literary Prize, 1992; Best Play, Independent on Sunday, 1992; New York Drama Critics' Award, 1993; Writers' Guild Award, 1993; Tony Award for Best Revival, 1997; Officier, Ordre des Arts et des Lettres. *Address:* 32 Booterstown Avenue, Dublin, Ireland.

McGURN, Barrett, AB; writer; b. 6 Aug. 1914, New York, NY, USA; m. Janice Ann McLaughlin 1962; five s. one d. *Education:* Fordham University, New York. *Career:* reporter, New York and Paris Herald Tribune, 1935–66; Bureau Chief, Herald Tribune, Rome, Paris, Moscow, 1946–62; mem. Overseas Press Club of America, pres., 1963–65; Foreign Press Asscn in Italy, pres., 1961, 1962; National Press Club, Washington, DC. *Publications:* Decade in Europe, 1958; A Reporter Looks at the Vatican, 1960; A Reporter Looks at American Catholicism, 1966; America's Court, The Supreme Court and the People, 1997; Pilgrim's Guide to Rome, 1999. Contributions: Reader's Digest; Catholic Digest; Commonweal; Colliers; Yank. *Honours:* Long Island University Polk Award, 1956; Overseas Press Club Award, 1957; Hon. DLitt, Fordham University, 1958. *Address:* 5229 Duvall Drive, Bethesda, MD 20816-1875, USA. *E-mail:* jmcgurn@erols.com.

MCCGWIRE, Michael Kane, OBE, BSc; fmr Royal Navy Commander, fmr professor, foreign policy analyst and writer; b. 9 Dec. 1924, Madras (now Chennai), India; m. Helen Jean Scott 1952, two s. three d. *Education:* Royal Naval Coll., Dartmouth and Univ. of Wales. *Career:* officer, Royal Navy 1942–67; Prof., Dalhousie Univ. 1971–79; Senior Fellow, Brookings Institution, Washington, DC 1979–90; Visiting Prof., Univ. of Cambridge 1990–93; Hon. Prof. of International Politics, Univ. of Wales 1997–. *Publications:* Military Objectives and Soviet Foreign Policy 1987, Perestroika and Soviet National Security 1991, NATO Expansion and European Security 1997; editor: Soviet Naval Developments 1973, Soviet Naval Policy 1975, Soviet Naval Influence 1977; contrib. to 40 books and numerous journals. *Address:* Hayes, Durlston, Swanage, Dorset BH19 2JF, England.

McHUGH, Heather, BA, MA; American professor of English, poet, writer and translator; b. 20 Aug. 1948, San Diego, CA; m. Nikolai Popov. *Education:* Radcliffe Coll., Harvard Univ., Univ. of Denver. *Career:* Assoc. Prof., SUNY at Binghamton 1974–83; Core Faculty, MFA Program for Writers, Goddard Coll., later Warren Wilson Coll. 1976–; Milliman Distinguished Writer-in-Residence and Prof. of English, Univ. of Washington 1984–; Holloway Lecturer in Poetry, Univ. of California at Berkeley 1987; Visiting Prof., Univ. of Iowa 1991–92, 1995, Univ. of California at Los Angeles 1994, Univ. of California at Irvine 1994; Coal-Royalty Chair in Poetry, Univ. of Alabama, Tuscaloosa 1992; Elliston Prof. of Poetry, Univ. of Cincinnati 1993; Visiting Lecturer, Univ. of Bergen, Norway 1994; mem. Acad. of American Poets (bd of chancellors 1999–), American Acad. of Arts and Sciences. *Publications:* poetry: Dangers 1977, A World of Difference 1981, To the Quick 1987, Shades 1988, Hinge & Sign: Poems 1968–1993 1994, The Father of the Predicaments (Poems 1993–1998) 1999; essays: Broken English: Poetry and Partiality 1993; translator: D'Apres Tout: Poems by Jean Follain 1981, Because the Sea is Black: Poems by Blaga Dimitrova (with Niko Boris) 1989; other: Where Are They Now? (with Tom Phillips) 1990, Glottal Sytop: 101 Poems by Paul Celan (with Nikolai Popov); contrib. to many anthologies and journals. *Honours:* National Endowment for the Arts Grants 1974, 1979, 1981, Pushcart Prizes 1978 et seq, Guggenheim Fellowship 1989, Woodrow Wilson Nat. Poetry Fellow 1992–93, Daniel A. Pollack Prize, Harvard Univ. and Harvard Coll. Library 1995, Bingham Prize, Boston Book Review 1995, TLS Int. Book of the Year List 1995, Lila Wallace/Reader's Digest Writing Award 1996–99, O. D. Hardison Award 1998, PEN Voelker Prize 2000. *Address:* c/o Department of English, Box 354330, University of Washington, Seattle, WA 98195, USA.

McILVANNEY, William, MA; writer and poet; b. 25 Nov. 1936, Kilmarnock, Ayrshire, Scotland. *Education:* University of Glasgow. *Publications:* Fiction: Remedy is None, 1966; A Gift from Nessus, 1968; Docherty, 1975;

Laidlaw, 1977; The Papers of Tony Veitch, 1983; The Big Man, 1985; Walking Wounded (short stories), 1989. Poetry: The Long Ships in Harbour, 1970; Landscapes and Figures, 1973; Weddings and After, 1984.

McINERNEY, Jay, BA; writer; b. 13 Jan. 1955, Hartford, CT, USA; m. 1st Mary Reymond 1984; m. 2nd Helen Bransford 1991. *Education:* Williams College, Syracuse University. *Career:* mem. Authors' Guild; Authors League of America; PEN; Writers Guild. *Publications:* Bright Lights, 1984; Ransom, 1985; Story of My Life, 1988; Brightness Falls, 1992; Savage and Son, 1995; The Last of the Savages, 1996; Model Behavior, 1998; How It Ended, 2000; Bacchus and Me, 2001. Contributions: anthologies and magazines. *Literary Agent:* International Creative Management, 40 W 57th Street, New York, NY 10019, USA.

MacINNES, Patricia, BA, MFA; writer; b. 7 April 1954, Quantico, Virginia, USA. *Education:* San Diego State University, University of Montana, Missoula. *Publications:* The Last Night on Bikini, 1995. Contributions: journals. *Honours:* Wallace Stegner Writing Fellowship, Stanford University, 1984; Nelson Algren Award for Short Fiction, 1987; Writing Fellowship, Provincetown Fine Arts Work Center, 1988–89; Ludwig Vogelstein Grant, 1989. *Address:* c/o Mary Jack Wald Associates, 111 E 14th Street, PMB 113, New York, NY 10003, USA.

McINNIS, (Harry) Donald, AB; writer and dramatist; b. 18 April 1916, Worcester, MA, USA; m. Marjorie E. Graber 1948; two s. two d. *Education:* Clark University, American University, Johns Hopkins University. *Career:* mem. Australian Writers Guild; US Dramatists Guild. *Publications:* The Running Years, 1986; Cobwebs and Twigs, 1990; Will – Man from Stratford (play), 1992; New Work No Lines (play), 1994. *Honours:* special awards, US Government, Government of Guatemala, Republic of Korea. *Address:* 22 Chauvel Circle, Chapman, ACT 2611, Australia.

MacINTYRE, Alasdair, BA, MA; philosopher, academic and writer; b. 12 Jan. 1929, Glasgow, Scotland. *Education:* Queen Mary College, London, Manchester University, University of Oxford. *Career:* Lecturer, Manchester University, 1951–57, Leeds University, 1957–61; Research Fellow, Nuffield College, Oxford, 1961–62; Senior Fellow, Princeton University, 1962–63; Fellow, University College, Oxford, 1963–66; Riddell Lecturer, University of Newcastle upon Tyne, 1964; Bampton Lecturer, Columbia University, 1966; Prof. of the History of Ideas, Brandeis University, 1969–72; Dean, College of Liberal Arts, 1972–73, Prof. of Philosophy and Political Science, 1972–80, Boston University; Henry Luce Prof., Wellesley College, 1980–82; W. Alton Jones Prof., Vanderbilt University, 1982–88; Gifford Lecturer, University of Edinburgh, 1988; Henry Luce Scholar, Yale University, 1988–89; McMahon/Hank Prof., 1988–94, Research Prof. of Philosophy, 2000–, University of Notre Dame, IN; Prof. of Arts and Sciences, Duke University, 1995–2000; mem. American Acad. of Arts and Sciences; British Acad., corresponding mem.; Hon. Mem., Royal Irish Acad. *Publications:* Marxism and Christianity, 1953; The Unconscious, 1957; Short History of Ethics, 1966; Against the Self-Images of the Age, 1971; After Virtue: A Study in Moral Theory, 1981; Whose Justice? Which Rationality?, 1988; Three Rival Versions of Moral Enquiry, 1990; First Principles, Final Ends and Contemporary Philosophy, 1990; Dependent-Rational Animals, 1999. *Address:* c/o Philosophy Department, University of Notre Dame, Notre Dame, IN 46556, USA.

McINTYRE, Ian James, BA, MA; writer and broadcaster; b. 9 Dec. 1931, Banchory, Kincardineshire, Scotland; m. Leik Sommerfelt Vogt 1954; two s. two d. *Education:* St John's College, Cambridge, College of Europe, Bruges, Belgium. *Career:* Ed., At Home and Abroad, 1959; Programme Services Officer, Independent Television Authority, 1961; Writer, Broadcaster, 1970–76, Controller, Radio 4, 1976–78, Controller, Radio 3, 1978–87, BBC; Assoc. Ed., The Times, London, 1989–90. *Publications:* The Proud Doers: Israel After Twenty Years, 1968; Words: Reflections on the Uses of Language (ed. and contributor), 1975; Dogfight: The Transatlantic Battle over Airbus, 1992; The Expense of Glory: A Life of John Reith, 1993; Dirt and Deity: A Life of Robert Burns, 1996; Garrick, 1999; Joshua Reynolds: The Life and Times of the First President of the Royal Academy, 2003; Contributions: The Listener; The Times; The Independent. *Honours:* Theatre Book Prize 1999. *Address:* Spylaw House, Newlands Avenue, Radlett, Hertfordshire WD7 8EL, England. *E-mail:* mcintyre@dircon.co.uk.

MacINTYRE, Stuart Forbes, BA, MA, PhD; academic and writer; b. 21 April 1947, Melbourne, Vic., Australia; m. 1st Margaret Joan Geddes 1970; m. 2nd Martha Adele Bruton 1976; two d. *Education:* University of Melbourne, Monash University, University of Cambridge. *Career:* Tutor in History, 1976, Lecturer in History, 1979, Murdoch University, Perth; Research Fellow, St John's College, Cambridge, 1977–78; Lecturer, 1980–84, Senior Lecturer, 1984–86, Reader in History, 1987–90, Ernest Scott Prof., 1990–, University of Melbourne; mem. Acad. of the Social Sciences in Australia. *Publications:* A Proletarian Science: Marxism in Britain 1917–1933, 1980; Little Moscows, 1980; Militant: The Life and Times of Paddy Troy, 1983; Ormond College Centenary Essays (ed.), 1983; Making History (ed.), 1984; Winners and Losers: The Pursuit of Social Justice in Australian History, 1985; The Oxford History of Australia, Vol. IV, 1986; The Labour Experiment, 1989; A Colonial Liberalism: The Lost World of Three Victorian Visionaries, 1990; A History for a Nation, 1995; The Reds: The Communist Party of Australia, from Origins to Illegality, 1998. Contributions: Professional journals. *Address:* c/o Department of History, University of Melbourne, Parkville, Vic. 3052, Australia.

MACK, William P.; Naval Officer (retd) and Writer; b. 6 Aug. 1915, Hillsboro, IL, USA; m. Ruth McMillian, 11 Nov. 1939, one s. one d. *Education:* BS, US Naval Acad.; National War College; George Washington University. *Career:* US Naval Officer, 1935–75; Deputy Asst Secretary of Defense, 1968–71. *Publications:* Non-Fiction: Naval Officers Guide, 1958; Naval Customs, Traditions and Usage, 1978; Command at Sea, 1980. Fiction: South to Java, 1988; Pursuit of the Sea Wolf, 1991; Checkfire, 1992; New Guinea, 1993; Straits of Messina, 1994; Lieutenant Christopher Captain Kulburnie. Contributions: various publications. *Honours:* Alfred Thayer Mahan Award for Literary Excellence, Navy League, 1982. *Address:* 3607 Rundelac Rd, Annapolis, MD 21403, USA.

McKAY, Donald Fleming, BA, MA, PhD; poet, writer and editor; b. 25 June 1942, Owen Sound, ON, Canada; m. (divorced); one s. one d. *Education:* Bishop's University, University of Ontario, University College, Swansea, Wales. *Career:* teacher, University of New Brunswick, 1990–96; Ed., The Fiddlehead; mem. League of Canadian Poets; PEN; Writers' Union of Canada. *Publications:* Air Occupies Space, 1973; Long Sault, 1975; Lependu, 1978; Lightning Ball Bait, 1980; Birding, or Desire, 1983; Sanding Down This Rocking Chair on a Windy Night, 1987; Night Field, 1991; Apparatus, 1997; Another Gravity, 2000. Contributions: periodicals. *Honours:* Canadian Authors' Asscn Award for Poetry, 1983; Governor-General's Award for Poetry, 1991; National Magazine Award for Poetry, 1991. *Address:* 434 Richmond Avenue, Victoria, BC V8S 3Y4, Canada.

MACKAY, James Alexander, (Ian Angus, William Finlay, Bruce Garden, Alex Matheson, Peter Whittington); Author and Journalist; b. 21 Nov. 1936, Inverness, Scotland; m. 1st Mary Patricia Jackson 24 Sept. 1960 (divorced 1972); one s. one d.; m. 2nd Renate Finlay-Freundlich 11 Dec. 1992. *Education:* MA, History, 1958, DLitt, 1993, Glasgow University. *Career:* Philatelic Columnist, The New Daily, 1962–67; Columnist, Financial Times, 1967–85; Ed.-in-Chief, IPC Stamp Encyclopaedia, 1968–72; Antiques Advisory Ed., Ward Lock, 1972–79; Ed., The Burns Chronicle, 1977–91, The Postal Annual, 1978–90, The Burnsian, 1986–89, Seaby Coin and Medal Bulletin, 1990–92, Coin Yearbook, 1994–, Medal Yearbook, 1995–, Stamp Yearbook, 1996–, Banknotes Yearbook, 2001–; Consultant Ed., Antiques Today, 1992–94, Stamp and Coin Mart, 1993–, Coin News, 1994–, International Stamp and Exhibition News, 1996–; General Ed., Encyclopedia of World Facts, 1999–2001; mem. Burns Federation, exec. council, 1977–95; Glasgow Philatelic Society, pres., 2001–02; West of Scotland Numismatic Society, sec., 1992–, vice-pres., 2003–(05). *Publications:* The Tapling Collection, 1964; Glass Paperweights, 1973; The Dictionary of Stamps in Colour, 1973; The Dictionary of Western Sculptors in Bronze, 1977; The Guinness Book of Stamps Facts and Feats, 1982; Complete Works of Robert Burns, 1986; Complete Letters of Burns, 1987; Burns A–Z: The Complete Word Finder, 1990; Burns: A Biography, 1992; Vagabond of Verse: A Life of Robert W. Service, 1993; William Wallace: Brave Heart, 1994; The Eye Who Never Slept: A Life of Allan Pinkerton, 1995; Michael Collins: A Life, 1996; Sounds Out of Silence: A Life of Alexander Graham Bell, 1997; Thomas Lipton, 1998; John Paul Jones, 1998; Clans and Tartans of Scotland, 2000; Fans, 2000; Scotland's Posts, 2001; Glasgow's Other River, 2001; Antiques at a Glance, four vols, 2002; Soldiering on St Kilda, 2002. Contributions: numerous publications. *Honours:* Silver Medal Amphilex, Amsterdam, 1965; Vermeil Medals, Spellman Foundation, USA, 1982, 1987, 1990; Thomas Field Award for Services to Irish Philatelic Literature, 1983; Saltire Book of the Year, 1993; Gold Medal, American Philatelic Society, 1998. *Address:* 67 Braidpark Dr., Glasgow G46 6LY, Scotland. *E-mail:* james.mackay2@ntlworld.com.

MACKAY, Shena; Writer; b. 6 June 1944, Edinburgh, Scotland; m. Robin Brown 1964 (divorced 1982); three d. *Education:* Tonbridge Girls' Grammar School, Kent; Kidbrooke Comprehensive, London. *Publications:* Dust Falls on Eugene Schlumberger, 1964; Toddler on the Run, 1964; Music Upstairs, 1965; Old Crow, 1967; An Advent Calendar, 1971; Babies in Rhinestones, 1983; A Bowl of Cherries, 1984; Redhill Rococo, 1986; Dreams of Dead Women's Handbags, 1987; Dunedin, 1992; The Laughing Academy, 1993; Such Devoted Sisters (ed.), 1993; Collected Stories, 1994; The Orchard on Fire, 1996; Friendship (ed.), 1997; The Artist's Widow, 1998; The World's Smallest Unicorn, 1999; Heligoland, 2003. *Honours:* Fawcett Prize, 1987. *Address:* c/o Vintage Books, Random House, 20 Vauxhall Bridge Rd, London SW1V 2SA, England.

MACKAY, Simon (see Nicole, Christopher Robin).

McKEAN, John Maule Laurie, BArch, MA; academic and writer; b. 7 Nov. 1943, Glasgow, Scotland; two s. one d. *Education:* University of Strathclyde, University of Essex. *Career:* Architect in practice, 1966–67, 1969–71; Teacher of Architectural Design, University of Ceylon, 1968–69, University of East London, 1976–80, University of North London, 1980–90; Teacher of Design and Architectural History, UNL, 1983–88, Middlesex University 1984–88; Dir of Interior Architecture, 1990–95, Prof. of Architecture, 1995–, University of Brighton. *Publications:* Architecture of the Western World (co-author), 1980; Learning from Segal, 1989; Royal Festival Hall, 1991; Crystal Palace, 1994; Leicester Engineering Building, 1994; Alexander Thomson (co-author), 1995; The Parthenon, 1996; C. R. Mackintosh (co-author), 1996; Charles Rennie Mackintosh, 2000; Giancarlo De Carlo; Layered Places, 2004. Contributions: Architects' Journal; Building Design; Spazio e Societa, Milan; Architectural History; Journal of Architecture. *Honours:* two AIA International Book Awards; elected mem., Critics Circle of International Asscn of Architects, 1990; Architects' Journal Books of the Year, 2001. *Address:* c/o University of Brighton, Brighton BN2 4AT, England. *E-mail:* john.mckean@brighton.ac.uk.

McKEE, Louis, BA; poet, writer and editor; b. 31 July 1951, Philadelphia, PA, USA; m. Christine Caruso 1978 (divorced 1982). *Education:* LaSalle Coll., Temple Univ. *Career:* Ed., Painted Bride Quarterly, 1984–88, One Trick Pony, 1997–; Co-Ed., Axe Factory Review, 1984–; mem. Acad. of American Poets; PEN; Poetry Society of America; Poets and Writers. *Publications:* Schuylkill Country, 1982; The True Speed of Things, 1984; Safe Water, 1986; No Matter, 1987; Oranges, 1989; Angelus, 1990; Three Poems, 1993; River Architecture: Poems from Here and There: Selected Poems, 1973–1993, 1999; Right as Rain, 2000; Near Occasions of Sin, 2000. Contributions: anthologies, reviews, quarterlies and journals. *Address:* 8460 Frankford Avenue, Philadelphia, PA 19136, USA.

McKENNA, Patricia Ann (see Goedicke, Patricia).

MacKENNEY, Richard, BA, PhD, FRHistS; historian and educator; b. 2 April 1953, Aylesbury, Buckinghamshire, England. *Education:* Queens' College, Cambridge, University of Edinburgh. *Career:* Sr Lecturer in History, University of Edinburgh. *Publications:* Tradesmen and Traders: The World of the Guilds in Venice and Europe, c. 1250–c. 1650, 1987; The City-State, 1500–1700: Republican Liberty in an Age of Princely Power, 1989; Sixteenth-Century Europe: Expansion and Conflict, 1993; Renaissance Italians, 1300–1600, 1997. Contributions: various specialised articles to journals and periodicals. *Honours:* Graduate Fellow, Rotary Foundation, Rotary International, 1975–76. *Literary Agent:* David Higham Associates, 5–8 Lower John Street, Golden Square, London W1F 9HA, England. *Address:* Department of History, University of Edinburgh, William Robertson Building, George Square, Edinburgh EH8 9JY, Scotland.

MacKENZIE, David, AB, MA, PhD; academic; *Professor of History Emeritus, University of North Carolina at Greensboro*; b. 10 June 1927, Rochester, NY, USA; m. Patricia Williams 1953; three s. *Education:* University of Rochester, Columbia University. *Career:* Prof. of History, US Merchant Marine Acad., 1953–58, Princeton Univ., 1959–61, Wells College, 1961–68, Univ. of North Carolina, Greensboro, 1969–2000; Prof. Emeritus, Univ. of North Carolina, Greensboro, 2000–. *Publications:* The Serbs and Russian Pan-Slavism 1875–1878, 1967; The Lion of Tashkent: The Career of General M. G. Cherniaev, 1974; Ilija Garasanin: The Balkan Bismarck, 1985; Ilija Garasanin Drzavnik i Diplomata, 1987; Apis: The Congenial Conspirator, 1989; Imperial Dreams/Harsh Realities: Tsarist Russian Foreign Policy, 1815–1917, 1993; From Messianism to Collapse: Soviet Foreign Policy 1917–1991, 1994; The Black Hand on Trial: Salonika 1917, 1995; Violent Solutions: Revolutions, Nationalism, and Secret Societies in Europe to 1918, 1996; Serbs and Russians, 1996; Solunski proces, 1997; Exonerating the Black Hand 1917–1953, 1999; Obnova Solunshog procesa, 2001; Count N. P. Ignat'ev: Father of Lies?, 2002; A History of Russia, the Soviet Union and Beyond, sixth edn, 2002; Russia and the USSR in the Twentieth Century, fourth edn, 2002; One Foot in Russia, the Other in Yugoslavia, a Memoir, 2003. Contributions: books and professional journals. *Address:* 1000 Fairmont Street, Greensboro, NC 27401, USA.

MacKENZIE, Norman Hugh, BA, MA, DipEd, PhD, FRSC; academic and writer; *Professor of English Emeritus, Queen's University, Kingston*; b. 8 March 1915, Salisbury, Rhodesia; m. Rita Mavis Hofmann 1948; one s. one d. *Education:* Rhodes University, South Africa, University of London. *Career:* Prof. of English 1966–80, Emeritus Prof. 1980–, Queen's University, Kingston, ON, Canada. *Publications:* South African Travel Literature in the 17th Century, 1955; The Outlook for English in Central Africa, 1960; Hopkins, 1968; A Reader's Guide to G. M. Hopkins, 1981. Editor: The Poems of Gerard Manley Hopkins (with W. H. Gardner), 1967; Poems by Hopkins, 1974; The Early Poetic Manuscripts and Notebooks of Gerard Manley Hopkins in Facsimile, 1989; The Poetical Works of Gerard Manley Hopkins, 1990; The Later Poetic Manuscripts of Gerard Manley Hopkins in Facsimile, 1991. Contributions: books and journals, including: International Review of Education; Bulletin of the Institute for Historical Research; TLS; Modern Language Quarterly; Queen's Quarterly. *Honours:* Hon. DLitt, 1989. *Address:* 416 Windward Place, Kingston, ON K7M 4E4, Canada.

McKEOWN, Tom S., BA, MA, MFA; poet and writing consultant; b. 29 Sept. 1937, Evanston, IL, USA; m. Patricia Haebig 1989; one s. one d. *Education:* University of Michigan, Vermont College. *Career:* Writer-in-Residence, Stephens College, 1968–74; Poet-in-Residence, Savannah College of Art and Design, 1982–83, University of Wisconsin, Oshkosh, 1983–87, University of Wisconsin at Madison, 1989–94. *Publications:* The Luminous Revolver, 1973; The House of Water, 1974; Driving to New Mexico, 1974; Certain Minutes, 1978; Circle of the Eye, 1982; Three Hundred Tigers, 1994. Contributions: newspapers, reviews, and magazines. *Honours:* Avery Hopwood Award, 1968; Wisconsin Arts Fellowship, 1980. *Address:* 1220 N Gammon Road, Middleton, WI 53562, USA.

McKERNAN, Llewellyn McKinnie, BA, MA; poet and children's writer; b. 12 July 1941, Hampton, AR, USA; m. John Joseph McKernan 1967; one d. *Education:* Hendrix College, University of Arkansas, Brown University. *Career:* Instructor of English, Georgia Southern College, 1966–67; Adjunct Prof. of English, Marshall University, 1980–86, 1991; Prof. of English, St Mary's College, 1989; mem. West Virginia Writers; Poetry Society of West Virginia; Society of Children's Book Writers and Illustrators. *Publications:* Short and Simple Annals, 1979; More Songs of Gladness, 1987; Bird Alphabet, 1988; Many Waters, 1993; This is the Day and This is the Night, 1994. Contributions: Reviews and journals. *Honours:* Third Prize, Chester H. Jones National Poetry Competition, 1982; West Virginia Humanities Artist Grant, 1983; Second Prize, National Founders Award Contest, NFSPS, 1994. *Address:* Route 10, PO Box 4639B, Barboursville, WV 25504, USA.

MacKERRAS, Colin Patrick, BA, MLitt, PhD; academic, writer and editor; b. 26 Aug. 1939, Sydney, NSW, Australia; m. Alyce Barbara Brazier 1963; two s. three d. *Education:* University of Melbourne, Australian National University, University of Cambridge. *Career:* Foreign Expert, Beijing Institute of Foreign Languages, 1964–66, 1986; Research Scholar, 1966–69, Research Fellow, 1969–73, Senior Research Fellow, 1973, Australian National University; Prof., 1974–, Chair., 1979–85, Head, 1988–89, 1996–2000, School of Modern Asian Studies, Griffith University; mem. Asian Studies Asscn of Australia, pres., 1992–95; Chinese Studies Asscn, pres., 1991–93; Queensland History Teachers Asscn; Fellow, Australian Acad. of the Humanities, 1999. *Publications:* From Fear to Friendship: Australia's Policies Towards the People's Republic of China 1966–1982 (with Edmund S. K. Fung), 1985; Western Images of China, 1989; Portaits of China, 1989; Dragon's Tongue: Communicating in Chinese (with Peter Chang, Yu Hsiu-ching, and Alyce Mackerras), 2 vols, 1990–91; Chinese Drama: A Historical Survey, 1990; The Cambridge Handbook of Contemporary China (with Amanda Yorke), 1991; Unlocking Australia's Language Potential: Profiles of Nine Key Languages in Australia, Vol. 2: Chinese (with Doug Smith, Ng Bee Chin, and Kam Louie), 1993; China Since 1978: Reform, Modernisation, and 'Socialism with Chinese Characteristics' (with Pradeep Taneja and Graham Young), 1994; China's Minorities: Integration and Modernization in the Twentieth Century, 1994; China's Minority Cultures: Identities and Integration Since 1912, 1995; Peking Opera, 1997; China in Transformation 1900–1949 1998, The New Cambridge Handbook of Contemporary China 2001, China's Ethnic Minorities and Globalisation 2003. Editor: Essays on the Sources for Chinese History (with Donald Leslie and Wang Gungwu), 1973; China: The Impact of Revolution, A Survey of Twentieth Century China, 1976; Chinese Theater from Its Origins to the Present Day, 1983; Marxism in Asia (with Nick Knight), 1985; Drama in the People's Republic of China (with Constantine Tung), 1987; Chinese Language Teaching and Its Application (with Hugh Dunn), 1987; Contemporary Vietnam: Perspectives from Australia (with Robert Cribb and Allan Healy), 1988; Eastern Asia: An Introductory History, 1992; Asia Since 1945: History Through Documents, 1992; China in Revolution: History Through Documents, 1993; Imperialism, Colonialism and Nationalism in East Asia: History Through Documents, 1994; Australia and China: Partners in Asia, 1996; Dictionary of the Politics of the People's Republic of China (with Donald H. McMillen and Andrew Watson) 1998, Culture and Society in the Asia-Pacific (with Richard Maidment) 1998, Sinophiles and Sinophones, Western Views of China, An Anthology 2000, Ethnicity in Asia 2003. Contributions: various scholarly books and journals. *Honours:* Co-Recipient, Gold Citation for the Media Peace Prize, United Nations Asscn of Australia 1981, Albert Einstein International Acad. Foundation Cross of Merit Award 1993, Medal, Outstanding Contributions to Australia-China Cultural Relations 1999, Centenary Medal Australia 2003. *Address:* c/o School of International Business and Asian Studies, Griffith University, Nathan, Qld, 4111, Australia.

MACKESY, Piers Gerald; Historian and Writer; b. 15 Sept. 1924, Cults, Aberdeenshire, Scotland. *Education:* BA, Christ Church, Oxford, 1950; DPhil, Oriel College, Oxford, 1953; DLitt, Oxford, 1978. *Career:* Harkness Fellow, Harvard University, 1953–54; Fellow, 1954–87, Emeritus, 1988–, Pembroke College, Oxford; Visiting Fellow, Institute for Advanced Study, Princeton, NJ, 1961–62; Visiting Prof., California Institute of Technology, 1966; mem. National Army Museum, council mem., 1983–92; Society for Army Historical Research, council mem., 1985–94; British Acad., fellow, 1988. *Publications:* The War in the Mediterranean 1803–1810, 1957; The War for America 1775–1783, 1964; Statesmen at War: The Strategy of Overthrow 1798–1799, 1974; The Coward of Minden: The Affair of Lord George Sackville, 1979; War without Victory: The Downfall of Pitt 1799–1802, 1984; British Victory in Egypt, 1801: The End of Napoleon's Conquest, 1995. *Honours:* Templer Medal, 1995. *Address:* Westerton Farmhouse, Dess, by Aboyne, Aberdeenshire AB34 5AY, Scotland.

MACKEY, James Patrick; Prof. of Theology Emeritus and Writer; *Professor Emeritus, University of Edinburgh*; b. 9 Feb. 1934, Waterford, Ireland; m. Hanorah Noelle Quinlan, 1973, one s. one d. *Education:* BA, National University of Ireland, 1954; LPh, 1955, BD, 1957, STL, 1959, DD, 1960, Pontifical University, Maynooth; PhD, Queen's University, Belfast, 1965. *Career:* Ordained Priest, 1958; Lecturer in Philosophy, Queen's University, Belfast, 1960–66; Lecturer in Theology, St John's College, Waterford, 1966–69; Assoc. Prof., 1969–73, Prof. of Philosophical and Systematic Theology, 1973–79, Visiting Prof., 1990, University of San Francisco; Visiting Prof., University of California at Berkeley, 1974–75, Dartmouth

College, 1989, Trinity College, University of Dublin, 1999–; Thomas Chalmers Prof. of Theology, 1979–99, Dean, Faculty of Divinity, 1984–88, Dir, Graduate School and Assoc. Dean, 1995–99, Prof. Emeritus, 1999–, University of Edinburgh; Dir Derry City Conf. on the Cultures of Europe 1992; Ed., Studies in World Christianity, 1995–2001. *Television:* series scriptwriter/presenter: The Hall of Mirrors 1984, The Gods of War 1986. *Publications:* The Modern Theology of Tradition, 1962; Life and Grace, 1966; Tradition and Change in the Church, 1968; Contemporary Philosophy of Religion, 1968; Morals, Law and Authority (ed.), 1969; The Church: Its Credibility Today, 1970; The Problems of Religious Faith, 1972; Jesus: The Man and the Myth, 1979; The Christian Experience of God as Trinity, 1983; Religious Imagination (ed.), 1986; Modern Theology: A Sense of Direction, 1987; New Testament Theology in Dialogue (with J. D. G. Dunn), 1987; Introduction to Celtic Christianity (ed.) 1989, Power and Christian Ethics 1993, The Cultures of Europe (ed.) 1994, The Critique of Theological Reason 2000, Religion and Politics in Ireland (ed.). Contributions: Professional journals. *Honours:* Hon. Fellow, Faculty of Divinity, University of Edinburgh, 1999. *Address:* 15 Glenville Park, Dunmore Rd, Waterford, Ireland. *E-mail:* jpmackey_ie@yahoo.co.uk.

MACKEY, Mary, (Kate Clemens); Author, Poet and Prof. of English; b. 21 Jan. 1945, Indianapolis, IN, USA; Pnr Angus Wright. *Education:* BA, Radcliffe College, 1966; MA, 1967, PhD, Comparative Literature, 1970, University of Michigan. *Career:* Asst Prof., 1972–76, Assoc. Prof., 1976–80, Prof. of English, 1980–, California State University at Sacramento; mem. Feminist Writers' Guild; National Book Critics Circle; PEN American Center West, pres., 1989–92; Writers' Guild of America. *Publications:* Fiction: Immersion, 1972; McCarthy's List, 1979; The Last Warrior Queen, 1983; A Grand Passion, 1986; The Kindness of Strangers, 1988; Season of Shadows, 1991; The Year the Horses Came, 1993; The Horses at the Gate, 1996; The Fires of Spring, 1998; The Stand In (as Kate Clemens), 2003; Sweet Revenge (as Kate Clemens), 2004. Poetry: Split Ends, 1974; One Night Stand, 1977; Skin Deep, 1978; The Dear Dance of Eros, 1987. Other: Chance Music (ed. with Mary MacArthur), 1977. Contributions: periodicals. *Honours:* Woodrow Wilson Fellowship, 1966–67; Virginia Center for the Creative Arts Fellowship, 1999, 2002. *Address:* c/o Dept of English, California State University at Sacramento, Sacramento, CA 95819, USA. *E-mail:* mackeym@mindspring.com. *Website:* csus.edu/indiv/m/mackeym.

MACKEY, Nathaniel, AB, PhD; academic, poet, writer and editor; *Professor, University of California at Santa Cruz*; b. 25 Oct. 1947, Miami, FL, USA; m. Pascale Gaitet 1991; one d. one step-s. *Education:* Princeton University, Stanford University. *Career:* Asst Prof., University of Wisconsin at Madison 1974–76; Ed., Hambone literary magazine 1974–; Asst Prof. and Dir of Black Studies, University of Southern California at Los Angeles 1976–79; Visiting Prof., Occidental College 1979; Asst Prof. 1979–81, Assoc. Prof. 1981–87, Prof. 1987–, Board of Studies in Literature and American Studies Program, University of California at Santa Cruz; Writer-in-Residence, Washington, DC, Project for the Arts, 1986, Institute of American Indian Arts, Santa Fe, New Mexico, 1987, 1988, Brown University, 1990, Intersection for the Arts, San Francisco, 1991; Faculty, Naropa Institute, Boulder, summers 1991, 1993; Visiting Foreign Artist, Kootenay School of Writing, Vancouver, BC, 1994; mem. Acad. of American Poets, board of chancellors, 2001–. *Publications:* Poetry: Four for Trane, 1978; Septet for the End of Time, 1983; Eroding Witness, 1985; Outlandish, 1992; School of Udhra, 1993; Song of the Andoumboulou: 18–20, 1994; Whatsaid Serif, 1998. Fiction: From a Broken Bottle Traces of Perfume Still Emanate, Vol. I, Bedouin Hornbook, 1986, Vol. II, Djbot Baghostus's Run, 1993. Non-Fiction: Discrepant Engagement: Dissonance, Cross-Culturality and Experimental Writing, 1993. Other: Moment's Notice: Jazz in Poetry and Prose (ed. with Art Lange), 1993. Other: Strick: Song of the Andoumboulou 16–25 (poems with musical accompaniment), 1995. Contributions: anthologies, scholarly journals and magazines. *Honours:* Co-ordinating Council of Literary Magazines Ed.'s Grant, 1985; Whiting Writer's Award, 1993.

MACKIE, John (see Levinson, Leonard).

MacKINNON, Catharine Alice, BA, JD, PhD; academic and writer; *Professor of Law, University of Michigan at Ann Arbor*; b. 7 Oct. 1946, USA. *Education:* Smith College, Yale University. *Career:* Asst Prof. of Law, University of Minnesota, 1982–84; Prof. of Law, York University, Toronto, 1988–90, University of Michigan at Ann Arbor, 1989–; Visiting Prof., University of Chicago, 1997–. *Publications:* Sexual Harrassment of Working Women: A Case of Sex Discrimination, 1979; Feminism Unmodified: Discourses on Life and Law, 1987; Pornography and Civil Rights: A New Day for Women's Equality (with Andrea Dworkin), 1988; Toward a Feminist Theory of the State, 1989; Only Words, 1993; In Harm's Way: The Pornography Civil Rights Hearings (with Andrea Dworkin), 1998; Sex Equality, 2001. Contributions: journals. *Address:* c/o School of Law, University of Michigan, Ann Arbor, MI 48109, USA.

McKISSACK, Frederick Lemuel, BS; American writer; b. 12 Aug. 1939, Nashville, TN; m. Patricia McKissack 1964; three s. *Education:* Tennessee Agricultural and Industrial State Univ. *Career:* fmrly civil engineer. *Publications:* with Patricia McKissack: Abram, Abram, Where Are We Going? 1984, A Long Hard Journey: The Story of the Pullman Porter (Coretta Scott King Award) 1990, Martin Luther King, Jr: Man of Peace 1991, Carter G. Woodson: The Father of Black History 1991, Sojourner Truth: Ain't I a Woman (Boston Globe Horn Book Award for Non-Fiction 1993, Coretta Scott King Award 1993) 1992, Jesse Owens: Olympic Star 1992, Paul Robeson: A Voice to Remember 1992, Langston Hughes: Great American Poet 1992, African-American Inventors 1994, Black Diamond (Coretta Scott King Award) 1994, Christmas in the Big House, Christmas in the Quarters (Coretta Scott King Award 1995, ABC Children's Booksellers Choices Award 1995) 1994, George Washington Carver: The Peanut Scientist 1994, Red-Tail Angels: The Story of the Tuskegee Airmen of World War II (Carter G. Woodson Outstanding Merit Book 1996) 1995, Rebels Against Slavery: American Slave Revolts (Coretta Scott King Award 1997) 1996, Let My People Go (with illustrations by James E. Ransome) 1998, Young, Black and Determined: a biography of Lorraine Hansberry 1998, Black Hands, White Sails: The Story of African-American Whalers (Carter G. Woodson Book Award 2000, Coretta Scott King Award 2000, Soc. of Midland Authors Book Award for Juvenile Non-fiction 2000) 1999, Bugs! 2000, Nzingha: Warrior Queen of Matamba 2000, Ida B. Wells-Barnett: A Voice Against Violence (Soc. of School Librarians Int. Book Award) 2001, Messy Bessey's Garden (with illustrations by Dana Regan) 2002, Ralph J. Bunche: Peacemaker 2002, Satchel Paige: The Best Arm in Baseball 2002, Zora Neale Hurston, Writer and Storyteller 2002, Hard Labor: The First African Americans 1619 2004. *Honours:* Jane Addams Children's Book Award, 1990; Boston Globe/Horn Book Award, 1993. *Address:* c/o Scholastic, 557 Broadway, New York, NY 10012, USA.

McKISSACK, Patricia L'Ann Carwell, BA, MA; American writer; b. 9 Aug. 1944, Smyrna, TN; m. Frederick Lemuel McKissack 1964; three s. *Education:* Tennessee Agricultural and Industrial State Univ., Webster Univ. *Career:* fmrly teacher and children's book ed. *Publications:* The Inca 1985, Flossie & the Fox 1986, A Picture of Freedom: The Diary of Clotee, a Slave Girl, Belmont Plantation, Virginia, 1859, The Dark Thirty: Southern Tales of the Supernatural (Coretta Scott King Award 1993, John Newbery Medal 1993) 1992, Run Away Home 1997, Ma Dear's Aprons (with illustrations by Floyd Cooper) 1997, Can You Imagine (with photographs by Myles Pinkney) 1997, Color Me Dark 2000, The Honest-to-Goodness Truth (with illustrations by Giselle Potter) (Soc. of School Librarians Int. Book Award 2000, Storytelling World Award 2001) 2000, Nzingha: Warrior Queen of Matamba 2000, Goin' Someplace Special (with illustrations by Jerry Pinkney) (Coretta Scott King Award 2002, ABC Children's Booksellers Choices Award 2002) 2001; with Frederick McKissack: Abram, Abram, Where Are We Going? 1984, A Long Hard Journey: The Story of the Pullman Porter (Coretta Scott King Award) 1990, Martin Luther King, Jr: Man of Peace 1991, Carter G. Woodson: The Father of Black History 1991, Sojourner Truth: Ain't I a Woman (Boston Globe Horn Book Award for Non-Fiction 1993, Coretta Scott King Award 1993) 1992, Jesse Owens: Olympic Star 1992, Paul Robeson: A Voice to Remember 1992, Langston Hughes: Great American Poet 1992, African-American Inventors 1994, Black Diamond (Coretta Scott King Award) 1994, Christmas in the Big House, Christmas in the Quarters (Coretta Scott King Award 1995, ABC Children's Booksellers Choices Award 1995) 1994, George Washington Carver: The Peanut Scientist 1994, Red-Tail Angels: The Story of the Tuskegee Airmen of World War II (Carter G. Woodson Outstanding Merit Book 1996) 1995, Rebels Against Slavery: American Slave Revolts (Coretta Scott King Award 1997) 1996, Let My People Go (with illustrations by James E. Ransome) 1998, Young, Black and Determined: a biography of Lorraine Hansberry 1998, Black Hands, White Sails: The Story of African-American Whalers (Carter G. Woodson Book Award 2000, Coretta Scott King Award 2000, Soc. of Midland Authors Book Award for Juvenile Non-fiction 2000) 1999, Bugs! 2000, Nzingha: Warrior Queen of Matamba 2000, Ida B. Wells-Barnett: A Voice Against Violence (Soc. of School Librarians Int. Book Award) 2001, Messy Bessey's Garden (with illustrations by Dana Regan) 2002, Ralph J. Bunche: Peacemaker 2002, Satchel Paige: The Best Arm in Baseball 2002, Zora Neale Hurston, Writer and Storyteller 2002, Hard Labor: The First African Americans 1619 2004. *Honours:* Jane Addams Children's Book Award 1990, Boston Globe/Horn Book Award 1993. *Address:* c/o Scholastic, 557 Broadway, New York, NY 10012, USA.

MACKSEY, Kenneth John; army officer (retd) and historian; b. 1 July 1923, Epsom, Surrey, England. *Education:* Royal Military Coll., Sandhurst, British Army Staff Coll. *Career:* Officer, Royal Tank Regiment, British Army 1941–68, until retirement with rank of Major 1968; Deputy Ed., History of the Second World War, History of the First World War 1968–70. *Publications:* The Shadow of Vimy Ridge 1965, To the Green Fields Beyond 1965, Armoured Crusader: General Sir Percy Hobart 1967, Africa Korps, Panzer Division 1968, Crucible of Power: The Fight for Tunisia 1969, Tank Force 1970, Tank: A History of AFVs 1970, Tank Warfare, Beda Fomm 1971, The Guinness History of Land (Sea, Air) Warfare (three vols) 1973–76, Battle (aka Anatomy of a Battle) 1974, The Partisans of Europe in the Second World War 1975, The Guinness Guide to Feminine Achievements 1975, Guderian: Panzer General 1975, The Guinness Book 1952, 1953, 1954 (three vols) 1977–79, Kesselring 1978, Rommel's Campaigns and Battles 1979, The Tanks, Vol. III of the History of the Royal Tank Regiment 1979, Invasion: The German Invasion of England, July 1940 1980, The Tank Pioneers 1981, History of the Royal Armoured Corps 1914–1975 1983, Commando Strike 1985, First Clash 1985, Technology in War 1986, Godwin's Saga 1987, Military Errors of World War II 1987, Tank Versus Tank 1988, For Want of a Nail 1989, The Penguin Encyclopedia of Modern Warfare 1991, The Penguin Encyclopedia of Technology 1993, The

Hitler Options 1994, From Triumph to Disaster: The Fatal Flaws of German Generalship from Moltke to Guderian 1996, Turning Points (memoirs) 1997, Why the Germans Lose at War: The Myth of German Military Superiority 1999, Without Enigma 2000, The Searchers: How Radio Interception Changed the Course of Both World Wars 2003. *Address:* Whatley Mill, Beaminster, Dorset DT8 3EN, England.

McKUEN, Rod; poet, composer and writer; b. 29 April 1933, Oakland, CA, USA. *Career:* many concert, film, and television appearances. *Publications:* Poetry: And Autumn Came, 1954; Stanyan Street and Other Sorrows, 1966; Listen to the Warm, 1967; Lonesome Cities, 1968; Twelve Years of Christmas, 1968; In Someone's Shadow, 1969; A Man Alone, 1969; With Love, 1970; Caught in the Quiet, 1970; New Ballads, 1970; Fields of Wonder, 1971; The Carols of Christmas, 1971; And to Each Season, 1972; Pastorale, 1972; Grand Tour, 1972; Come to Me in Silence, 1973; America: An Affirmation, 1974; Seasons in the Sun, 1974; Moment to Moment, 1974; Beyond the Boardwalk, 1975; The Rod McKuen Omnibus, 1975; Alone, 1975; Celebrations of the Heart, 1975; The Sea Around Me, 1977; Hand in Hand, 1977; Coming Close to Earth, 1978; We Touch the Sky, 1979; Love's Been Good To Me, 1979; Looking for a Friend, 1980; The Power Bright and Shining, 1980; Too Many Midnights, 1981; Rod McKuen's Book of Days, 1981; The Beautiful Strangers, 1981; The Works of Rod McKuen, Vol. 1 (poems), 1950–82, 1982; Watch for the Wind..., 1982; Rod McKuen: 1984 Book of Days, 1983; The Sound of Solitude, 1986; Intervals, 1987. Prose: Finding My Father: One Man's Search for Identity, 1976; An Outstretched Hand, 1980. Other: various classical, film, and television scores. *Honours:* 41 Gold and Platinum Records Awards; Grand Prix du Disque, Paris, 1966, 1974, 1975, 1982; Grammy Award, 1969. *Address:* PO Box 2783, Los Angeles, CA 90078, USA.

McLANATHAN, Richard, AB, PhD; writer and art historian; b. 12 March 1916, Methuen, Massachusetts, USA; m. Jane Fuller 1942. *Education:* Harvard University. *Career:* Visiting Prof., US and European Universities; Museum Curator, Dir, Trustee. *Publications:* Images of the Universe, 1966; The Pageant of Medieval Art and Life, 1966; The American Tradition in the Arts, 1968; The Brandywine Heritage, 1971; Art in America, 1973; The Art of Marguerite Stix, 1977; East Building, A Profile, National Gallery of Art, 1978; World Art in American Museums, 1983; Gilbert Stuart, 1986; Michelangelo, 1993. Contributions: numerous journals and magazines. *Honours:* Prix de Rome, 1948; Distinguished Service Award, United States Information Agency, 1959; Rockefeller Senior Fellowship, 1975.

McLAREN, Colin Andrew, BA, MPhil, DipArch; writer; b. 14 Dec. 1940, Middlesex, England; one s. one d. *Education:* University of London. *Career:* Librarian, Univ. of Aberdeen –1999; mem. Society of Authors. *Publications:* Rattus Rex, 1978; Crows in a Winter Landscape, 1979; Mother of the Free, 1980; A Twister over the Thames, 1981; The Warriors under the Stone, 1983; Crown and Gown: An Illustrated History of the University of Aberdeen (with J. J. Carter), 1994; Rare and Fair: A Visitor's History of Aberdeen University Library, 1995. Contributions: BBC Radio 3 and 4. *Honours:* Society of Authors Award for Best Adaptation, 1986.

McLAREN, John David, BA, BEd, MA, PhD; academic, writer and editor; b. 7 Nov. 1932, Melbourne, Vic., Australia. *Education:* University of Melbourne, Monash University. *Career:* Assoc. Ed., 1966–93, Ed., 1993–97, Consulting Ed., 1997–, Overland; Head, Dept of General Studies, 1972–75, and Humanities, 1975–76, Foundation Chair., School of the Arts, 1973–76, Darling Downs Institute of Advanced Education; Head, Dept of Humanities, Footscray Institute of Technology, 1976–89; Ed., Australian Book Review, 1978–86; Principal Lecturer, Footscray Institute of Technology/Victoria University of Technology, 1989–91; Prof. of Humanities, 1991–97, Hon. Prof., 1997–2001, Emeritus Prof., 2001–, Victoria University of Technology; mem. Asscn for the Study of Australian Literature; Australian Studies Asscn for South Asia, vice-pres., 1997–; International Australian Studies Asscn, hon. life mem.; South Pacific Asscn for Commonwealth Language and Literature Studies. *Publications:* Our Troubled Schools, 1968; Dictionary of Australian Education, 1974; Australian Literature: An Historical Introduction, 1989; The New Pacific Literatures: Culture and Environment in the European Pacific, 1993; Prophet from the Desert: Critical Essays on Patrick White (ed.), 1995; Writing in Hope and in Fear: Postwar Australian Literature as Politics, 1945–72, 1996; States of Imagination, 2001; Free Radicals, 2003. Contributions: scholarly books and journals. *Honours:* Fulbright Senior Scholar, 1990; Australian Research Council Research Grants, 1991, 1993, 1996; Humanities Research Centre Scholar, Australian National University, 1994. *Address:* c/o Victoria University of Technology, PO Box 14428, MCMC, Melbourne, Vic. 8001, Australia. *E-mail:* john.mclaren@vu.edu.au.

MacLAVERTY, Bernard, BA; Irish writer and dramatist; b. 14 Sept. 1942, Belfast; m. Madeline McGuckin 1967; one s. three d. *Education:* Queen's Univ., Belfast. *Career:* fmrly medical lab. technician, English teacher; fmr writer-in-residence Univ. of Aberdeen; mem. Aosdána. *Television:* plays: My Dear Palestrina 1980, Phonefun Limited 1982, The Daily Woman 1986, Sometime in August 1989; documentary: Hostages 1992; adaptation: The Real Charlotte, by Somerville and Ross 1989. *Screenplays:* Cal 1984, Lamb 1985, Bye-Child (short film, also dir) 2003. *Radio plays:* My Dear Palestrina 1980, Secrets 1981, No Joke 1983, The Break 1988, Some Surrender 1988, Lamb 1992. *Publications:* novels: Lamb 1980, Cal 1983, Grace Notes 1997, The Anatomy School 2001; short story collections: Secrets and Other Stories 1977, A Time to Dance and Other Stories 1982, The Great Profundo and Other Stories 1987, Walking the Dog and Other Stories 1994; juvenile fiction: A Man in Search of a Pet 1978, Andrew McAndrew 1988. *Honours:* Northern Ireland and Scottish Arts Councils Awards, Irish Sunday Independent Award 1983, London Evening Standard Award for Screenplay 1984, jt winner Scottish Writer of the Year 1988, Soc. of Authors Travelling Scholarship 1994, Saltire Scottish Book of the Year Award 1997, Stakis Scottish Writer of the Year, Whitbread Novel of the Year, Creative Scotland Award 2003. *Literary Agent:* Gill Coleridge, Rogers, Coleridge & White, 20 Powis Mews, London, W11 1JN, England. *Address:* 26 Roxburgh Street, Hillhead, Glasgow, G12 9AP, Scotland. *Website:* www.bernardmaclaverty.com.

MacLEAN, Arthur (see Tubb, Edwin Charles).

MacLEAN, Rory, BA; writer and film-maker; b. 5 Nov. 1954, Vancouver, BC, Canada; m. Katrin Latta 1992. *Education:* Ryerson Polytechnic Inst. *Publications:* A Dead Czech 1989, Stalin's Nose: Across the Face of Europe 1993, The Oatmeal Ark: Across Canada by Water 1996, Under the Dragon: Travels in a Betrayed Land 1998, Next Exit Magic Kingdom: Florida Accidentally 2000, Falling for Icarus 2004; contrib. to newspapers and periodicals. *Honours:* The Independent Travel Writing Award, Yorkshire Post Best First Book Award, Publishing Marketing Asscn Award, Arts Council of England Writers Award 1998. *Literary Agent:* Sayle Literary Agency, Bickerton House, 25–27 Bickerton Road, London, N19 5JT, England.

McLELLAN, David Thorburn, MA, DPhil; British academic and writer; *Professor of Political Theory, University of Kent*; b. 10 Feb. 1940, Hertford, England; m. Annie Brassart 1967; two d. *Education:* St John's Coll., Oxford. *Career:* Prof. of Political Theory, Univ. of Kent. *Publications:* The Young Hegelians and Karl Marx 1969, Karl Marx: His Life and Thought 1974, Engels 1977, Marxism After Marx 1980, Ideology 1986, Marxism and Religion 1987, Simone Weil: Utopian Pessimist 1989, Unto Caesar: The Political Importance of Christianity 1993, Political Christianity 1997; contrib. to professional journals. *Address:* c/o Department of Politics and International Relations, Rutherford College, University of Kent, Canterbury, Kent CT2 7NX, England.

MacLEOD, Alison; writer; b. 12 April 1920, Hendon, Middlesex, England. *Publications:* The Heretics (aka The Heretic), 1965; The Hireling (in UK as The Trusted Servant), 1968; City of Light (in UK as No Need of the Sun), 1969; The Muscovite, 1971; The Jesuit (in US as Prisoner of the Queen), 1972; The Portingale, 1976; The Death of Uncle Joe, 1997. *Address:* 63 Muswell Hill Place, London N10 3RP, England.

MacLEOD, Alistair, BA, BEd, MA, PhD; writer and academic; *Professor of English Emeritus, University of Windsor*; b. 20 July 1936, North Battleford, SK, Canada; m. Anita MacLellan 1971; six s. *Education:* Nova Scotia Teachers College, St Francis Xavier University, University of New Brunswick, University of Notre Dame. *Career:* Prof. of English, Nova Scotia Teachers College, 1961–63; Faculty, Indiana University at Fort Wayne, 1966–69; Prof. of English, 1969–2000, Prof. Emeritus, 2000–, University of Windsor. *Publications:* The Lost Salt Gift of Blood, 1976; As Birds Bring Forth the Sun and Other Stories, 1986; No Great Mischief, 2000; Island, 2000. Contributions: anthologies and periodicals. *Honours:* Hon. doctorates, St Francis Xavier University, 1987, University College, Cape Breton, 1991; Best Book of the Year, Publisher's Weekly, 1988; International IMPAC Dublin Literary Award, 2001. *Address:* c/o Department of English, University of Windsor, Windsor, ON N9B 3P4, Canada.

MacLEOD, Charlotte, (Alisa Craig, Matilda Hughes); American writer; b. 12 Nov. 1922, Bath, England. *Publications:* as Charlotte MacLeod: Mystery of the White Knight 1964, Next Door to Danger 1965, The Fat Lady's Ghost 1968, Mouse's Vineyard (children's) 1968, Ask Me No Questions 1971, Brass Pounder (children's) 1971, Astrology for Sceptics (non-fiction) 1972, King Devil 1978, Rest You Merry 1978, The Family Vault 1979, The Luck Runs Out 1979, The Withdrawing Room 1980, We Dare Not Go a Hunting 1980, The Palace Guard 1981, Wrack and Rune 1982, Cirak's Daughter (children's) 1982, The Bilbao Looking Glass 1983, Something the Cat Dragged In 1983, Maid of Honour (children's) 1984, The Convival Codfish 1984, The Curse of the Giant Hogweed 1985, The Plain Old Man 1985, Grab Bag 1987, The Corpse in Oozak's Pond 1987, The Recycled Citizen 1988, The Silver Ghost 1988, Vane Pursuit 1989, The Gladstone Bag 1990; as Matilda Hughes: The Food of Love 1965, Headlines for Caroline 1967; as Alisa Craig: A Pint of Murder 1980, The Grub-and-Stakers Move a Mountain 1981, Murder Goes Mumming 1981, The Terrible Tide 1983, The Grub-and-Stakers Quilt a Bee 1985, The Grub-and-Stakers Pinch a Poke 1988, Trouble in the Brasses 1989, The Grub-and-Stakers Spin and Yarn 1990, An Owl Too Many, Something in the Water. *Literary Agent:* Jed Mattes, 175 W 73rd Street, New York, NY 10023, USA.

McLEOD, Joseph Bertram, BA; poet, dramatist, teacher, artistic director and farmer; b. 21 Oct. 1929, Hamilton, ON, Canada; m. Susan Maslak; one s. one d. *Education:* McMaster University, University of Toronto. *Career:* Artistic Dir, Peterborough Summer Theatre and Minkler Theatre, Seneca College; mem. League of Canadian Poets; PEN International; Writers Union of Canada. *Publications:* Poetry: Conversations with Maria, 1974;

Collected Citizen, 1976; And the Rivers Our Blood, 1977; Cleaning the Bones, 1977; Protect My House, 1977; Greendream: Collected and New Poems, 1982; Shorter Chinese Lyrics, 1984; Rim Poems, 1990; From the Fringe of China. Plays: Sam Slick, 1985. Contributions: anthologies; Periodicals, including: Canadian Forum; Cardinal; Bitterroot; Fiddlehead; Four Quarters; Inscape; North; Poet and Critic; Poetry Australia; Poetry Florida; Quixote; Trace. *Honours:* Canada Council Award; Ontario Arts Council Award. *Address:* c/o League of Canadian Poets, 24 Ryerson Avenue, Toronto, ON M5T 2P3, Canada.

McLEOD, Wallace Edmond, BA, AM, PhD; academic and writer; *Professor of Classics Emeritus, Victoria College, University of Toronto*; b. 30 May 1931, East York, ON, Canada; m. Elizabeth Marion Staples 1957; three s. one d. *Education:* University of Toronto, Harvard University. *Career:* instructor, Trinity College, Hartford, CT, 1955–56, University of British Columbia, 1959–61; Lecturer, University of Western Ontario, 1961–62; Special Lecturer, 1962–63, Asst Prof., 1963–66, Assoc. Prof., 1966–74, Anson Jones Lecturer, 1984, Prof. of Classics, 1974–96, Prof. Emeritus, 1996–, ANZMRC Lecturer, 1997, Inaugural Sam Houston Lecturer, 1998, Walter Calloway Lecturer, 2002, Victoria College, University of Toronto; mem. Freemason; Philalethes Society, pres., 1992; Society of Blue Friars, Grand Abbot, 1991; Classical Asscn of Canada; American Philological Asscn; Archaeological Institute of America. *Publications:* Composite Bows from the Tomb of Tut'ankhamun, 1970; Beyond the Pillars: More Light on Freemasony (ed. and contributor), 1973; Meeting the Challenge: The Lodge Officer at Work (ed. and contributor), 1976; The Sufferings of John Coustos (ed.), 1979; Whence Come We?: Freemasonry in Ontario 1764–1980 (ed. and contributor), 1980; Self Bows and Other Archery Tackle from the Tomb of Tut'ankhamun, 1982; The Old Gothic Constitutions (ed.), 1985; The Old Charges, 1986; A Candid Disquisition (ed.), 1989; For the Cause of Good, 1990; The Grand Design: Selected Masonic Addresses and Papers, 1991; The Quest for Light: Selected Masonic Addresses, 1997; Freemasonry on Both Sides of the Atlantic: Essays Concerning the Craft in the British Isles, Europe, the United States, and Mexico (assoc. ed.), 2002; A Daily Advancement in Masonic Knowledge: The Collected Blue Friar Lectures (ed. and contributor) 2003; contrib. to numerous books and journals. *Honours:* Philalethes Certificate of Literature 1984. *Address:* c/o Victoria College, University of Toronto, 73 Queen's Park, Toronto, ON M5S 1K7, Canada. *E-mail:* w.mcleod@utoronto.ca.

McLERRAN, Alice, BA, MS, MPH, PhD; writer; b. 24 June 1933, West Point, NY, USA; m. Larry Dean McLerran 1976; two s. one d. *Education:* University of California, Harvard School of Public Health. *Career:* mem. Authors' Guild; Society of Children's Book Writers and Illustrators. *Publications:* The Mountain that Loved a Bird, 1985; Secrets, 1990; Roxaboxen, 1991; I Want to go Home, 1992; Dreamsong, 1992; Hugs, 1993; Kisses, 1993; The Ghost Dance, 1995; The Year of the Ranch, 1996; The Legacy of Roxaboxen: A Collection of Voices, 1998; Dragonfly, 2000. *Honours:* Southwest Book Award, 1991; Notable Children's Trade Book in Field of Social Studies, 1996, 1997. *Address:* 70 S Country Road, Bellport, NY 11713, USA.

McMANUS, (I.) Chris; British author and academic. *Career:* fmrly at Univ. Coll. London, Imperial Coll. School of Medicine; Prof. of Psychology and Medical Education, Dept of Psychology, Univ. of London 1997; Assoc. Ed. of Laterality 1995–2000; Assoc. Ed., British Journal of Psychology; editorial bd mem., Journal of Health Psychology, Psychology – Health and Medicine, Developmental Neuropsychology, Perception, Medical Education. *Publications:* Psychology in Medicine 1992, Right Hand Left Hand (Aventis Prize 2003) 2002; contrib. to British Journal of Psychology, British Medical Journal, Journal of Hygiene, The Lancet, Nature, New Scientist, Perception, Times Higher Education Supplement, TLS. *Honours:* Wellcome Trust Prize 2002. *Address:* Royal Free & University College Medical School, University College London, Centre for Health Informatics & Multiprofessional Education, Fourth Floor, Holborn Union Building, The Archway Campus, Highgate Hill, London, N19 3UA, England. *Telephone:* (20) 7288-3378. *Fax:* (20) 7288-3322. *E-mail:* i.mcmanus@chime.ucl.ac.uk. *Website:* www.chime.ucl.ac.uk/~rmhiicm; www.righthandlefthand.com.

McMANUS, James, BA, MA; poet, writer and teacher; b. 22 March 1951, New York, NY, USA; m. Jennifer Arra 1992; one s. one d. *Education:* University of Illinois at Chicago. *Career:* Faculty, School of the Art Institute, Chicago, 1981–; mem. Associated Writing Programs; PEN. *Publications:* several works. Contributions: many publications. *Honours:* Guggenheim Fellowship, 1994–95. *Address:* c/o School of the Art Institute, 37 S Wabash, Chicago, IL 60603, USA.

McMASTER, Juliet Sylvia, BA, MA, PhD; academic and writer; *University Professor of English, University of Alberta*; b. 2 Aug. 1937, Kisumu, Kenya; m. Rowland McMaster 1968; one s. one d. *Education:* St Anne's College, Oxford, University of Alberta. *Career:* Asst Prof., 1965–70, Assoc. Prof., 1970–76, Prof., 1976–86, University Prof., 1986–, University of Alberta; General Ed., Juvenilia Press, 1994–; mem. Jane Austen Society of North America; Asscn of Canadian University Teachers of English. *Publications:* Thackeray: The Major Novels, 1971; Jane Austen's Achievement, 1976; Trollope's Palliser Novels, 1978; Jane Austen on Love, 1978; The Novel from Sterne to James, 1981; Dickens the Designer, 1987; The Beautifull Cassandra, 1993; Jane Austen the Novelist, 1995; Cambridge Companion to Jane Austen (co-ed.), 1997. Contributions: 19th-Century Fiction; Victorian Studies; Modern Language Quarterly; English Studies in Canada. *Honours:* Canada Council Post-Doctoral Fellowship, 1969–70; Guggenheim Fellowship, 1976–77; McCalla Professorship, 1982–83; University of Alberta Research Prize, 1986; Killam Research Fellowship, 1987–88; Molson Prize Winner, 1994. *Address:* Department of English, University of Alberta, AB T6G 2E5, Canada.

McMASTER, Susan, (S. M. Page), BA, PGCE; poet and editor; b. 11 Aug. 1950, Toronto, ON, Canada; m. Ian McMaster 1969; two d. *Education:* Carleton Univ., Ottawa Teachers' College. *Career:* Founding Ed., Branching Out Magazine, 1973–75; Senior Book Ed., National Gallery of Canada, 1989–98, 2002–; Ed.-in-Chief, Vernissage, 1999–2002; mem. League of Canadian Poets; PEN. *Publications:* Pass This Way Again (co-author), 1983; Dark Galaxies, 1986; North/South (co-author), 1987; Dangerous Graces (ed.), 1987; Women and Language (ed.), 1990; Two Women Talking, Erin Mouré and Bronwen Wallace, 1991; Illegitimate Positions (ed.), 1991; The Hummingbird Murders, 1992; Learning to Ride, 1994; Dangerous Times, 1996; Uncommon Prayer, 1997; Siolence: Poets on Violence and Silence (ed.), 1998; Waging Peace: Poetry and Political Action (ed.), 2002; La Deriva del Pianeta/World Shift (in English with Italian trans.), 2003; Courage, 2004. Other: Wordmusic (with First Draft), 1987; Audio tape (with Sugarbeat), 1997; Sugar Beat music and poetry (CD), 1999; Geode music and poetry (CD), 2000. Contributions: Magazines, journals and anthologies. *Honours:* various awards from Canada Council for the Arts, Ontario Arts Council, Regional Municipality of Ottawa Carleton. *Address:* 43 Belmont Avenue, Ottawa, ON K1S 0T9, Canada.

McMILLAN, James Coriolanus, MA; journalist; b. 30 Oct. 1925, England; m. Doreen Smith 1953; three s. one d. *Education:* University of Glasgow. *Publications:* The Glass Lie, 1964; American Take-Over, 1967; Anatomy of Scotland, 1969; The Honours Game, 1970; Roots of Corruption, 1971; British Genius (with Peter Grosvenor), 1972; The Way We Were 1900–1950 (trilogy), 1977–80; Five Men at Nuremberg, 1984; The Dunlop Story, 1989; From Finchley to the World – Margaret Thatcher, 1990. *Address:* Thurleston, Fairmile Park Road, Cobham, Surrey KT11 2PL, England.

MacMILLAN, Margaret Olwen, BA, PhD; Canadian historian and writer; b. 1943, Toronto, ON. *Education:* Univ. of Toronto, St Antony's Coll., Oxford, England. *Career:* Prof. of History, Ryerson Univ. Toronto 1975–2002; Provost, Trinity Coll., Univ. of Toronto 2002–. *Publications:* non-fiction: Women of the Raj 1988, Canada and NATO: Uneasy Past, Uncertain Future 1990, Peacemakers: Six Months that Changed the World 2001, Paris 1919 2002, Parties Long Estranged: Canada and Australia in the 20th Century (co-ed.) 2003. *Honours:* Gov.-Gen.'s Literary Award 2003, BBC4 Samuel Johnson Prize for Non-Fiction, Duff Cooper Award, Hessell-Tiltman Prize. *Address:* Department of History, University of Toronto, Sidney Smith Hall, 100 St George Street, Room 2074, Toronto, ON M5S 3G3, Canada.

McMILLAN, Terry, BA; writer; b. 18 Oct. 1951, Port Huron, MI, USA; one s. *Education:* University of California at Berkeley, Columbia University. *Career:* instructor, University of Wyoming, 1987–88; Prof., University of Arizona at Tucson, 1990–92; mem. Authors' League; PEN. *Publications:* Mama, 1987; Disappearing Acts, 1989; Breaking Ice: An Anthology of Contemporary African-American Fiction (ed.), 1990; Waiting to Exhale, 1992; How Stella Got Her Groove Back, 1996; A Day Late and a Dollar Short, 2001. *Honours:* National Endowment for the Arts Fellowship, 1988. *Address:* c/o Speakers Worldwide, 5301 Wisconsin Avenue NW, Suite 330, Washington, DC 20015, USA.

McMILLEN, Neil Raymond, BA, MA, PhD; American academic and writer; *Professor of History, University of Southern Mississippi, Hattiesburg*; b. 2 Jan. 1939, Lake Odessa, MI. *Education:* University of Southern Mississippi, Vanderbilt University. *Career:* Asst Prof. of History, Ball State University, Muncie, 1967–69; Asst Prof., 1969–70, Assoc. Prof., 1970–78, Prof. of History, 1978–, University of Southern Mississippi, Hattiesburg. *Publications:* The Citizens' Council: Organized Resistance to the Second Reconstruction, 1971; Thomas Jefferson: Philosopher of Freedom, 1973; Dark Journey: Black Mississippians in the Age of Jim Crow, 1989; A Synopsis of American History (with Charles Bolton), eighth edn, 1997. *Honours:* Bancroft Prize 1990. *Address:* Department of History, University of Southern Mississippi, Hattiesburg, MS 39401, USA.

McMULLEN, Christopher, BA, MA; writer; b. 21 Dec. 1948, Sale, Vic., Australia. *Education:* University of Melbourne, Canberra College of Adult Education, Latrobe University, Deakin University. *Career:* computer systems analyst, Bureau of Meteorology 1981–; speaker to various groups; mem. SFWA. *Publications:* Call to the Edge, 1992; Voices in the Light, 1994; Mirror Sun Rising, 1995; The Centurion's Empire, 1998; Souls in the Great Machine, 1999; The Miocene Arrow, 2000; Eyes of the Calculor, 2001; Voyage of the Shadowmoon, 2002. Non-Fiction: Strange Constellations: A History of Australian Science Fiction (with Russell Blackford and Van Ikin), 1999. Contributions: anthologies, including: Australian Science Fiction and Fantasy, 1985–91; Periodicals, including: Eidolon; Sirius; Aurealis; Analog Science Fiction and Fact; Magazine of Fantasy and Science Fiction. *Honours:* Writing Prize, World Science Fiction Convention, 1985; Ditmar Awards, 1991, 1992, 1996; William Atheling Awards, 1992, 1993, 1996, 1998, 2000; Aurealis Awards, 1998, 2000, 2003; Analog Readers

Award, 2002. *Literary Agent:* Chris Lotts, Ralph M. Vicinaga Ltd, 303 W 18th Street, New York, NY 10010, USA. *Address:* PO Box 2653x, Melbourne, Vic. 3001, Australia.

MacMULLEN, Ramsay, AB, AM, PhD; retd academic, writer and publisher; b. 3 March 1928, New York, NY, USA; m. 1st Edith Merriman Nye 1954 (divorced 1991); two s. two d.; m. 2nd Margaret McNeill 1992. *Education:* Harvard University. *Career:* Instructor to Asst Prof., University of Oregon, 1956–61; Assoc. Prof. to Prof., 1961–67, Chair., Dept of Classics, 1965–66, Brandeis University; Fellow, Institute for Advanced Study, Princeton, NJ, 1964–65; Prof., 1967–93, Chair., Dept of History, 1970–72, Dunham Prof. of History and Classics, 1979–93, Master, Calhoun College, 1984–90, Yale University; mem. Asscn of Ancient Historians, pres., 1978–81; Friends of Ancient History; Society for the Promotion of Roman Studies. *Publications:* Soldier and Civilian in the Later Roman Empire, 1963; Enemies of the Roman Order, 1966; Constantine, 1969; Roman Social Relations, 1974; Roman Government's Response to Crisis, 1976; Paganism in the Roman Empire, 1981; Christianizing the Roman Empire, 1984; Corruption and the Decline of Rome, 1988; Changes in the Roman Empire, 1990; Paganism and Christianity (with E. N. Lane), 1992; Christianity and Paganism, 1997; Sisters of the Brush, 1997; Romanisation in the Time of Augustus, 2001; Sarah's Choice, 1828–32, 2001; Feeling in History, Ancient and Modern, 2003. Contributions: professional journals. *Honours:* Fulbright Fellowship, 1960–61; Porter Prize, College Art Asscn, 1964; Guggenheim Fellowship, 1964; Senior Fellow, National Endowment for the Humanities, 1974–75; Lifetime Award for Scholarly Distinction, American Historical Asscn, 2000. *Address:* 25 Temple Court, New Haven, CT 06511, USA. *E-mail:* ramsay.macmullen@yale.edu.

McMURTRY, Larry Jeff, BA, MA; writer; b. 3 June 1936, Wichita Falls, TX, USA; m. Josephine Ballard 1959 (divorced 1966); one s. *Education:* North Texas State College, Rice University. *Career:* instructor, Texas Christian University, Ft Worth, 1961–62; Lecturer in English and Creative Writing, Rice University, 1963–69; Visiting Prof., George Mason College, 1970, American University, 1970–71; mem. Texas Institute of Letters. *Publications:* Fiction: Horseman, Pass By, 1961; Leaving Cheyenne, 1963; The Last Picture Show, 1966; Moving On, 1970; All My Friends Are Going to be Strangers, 1972; Terms of Endearment, 1975; Somebody's Darling, 1978; Cadillac Jack, 1982; The Desert Rose, 1983; Lonesome Dove, 1985; Texasville, 1987; Anything for Billy, 1988; Some Can Whistle, 1989; Buffalo Girls, 1990; The Evening Star, 1992; Streets of Laredo, 1993; Pretty Boy Floyd (with Diana Ossana), 1994; The Late Child, 1995; Dead Man's Walk, 1995; Zeke and Ned (with Diana Ossana), 1997; Comanche Moon, 1997; Duane's Depressed, 1999; Walter Benjamin at the Dairy Queen, 1999; Boone's Lick, 2000; Sin Killer: The Berrybender Narratives, Book One, 2002, Book Two, 2003. Non-Fiction: In a Narrow Grave: Essays on Texas, 1968; It's Always We Rambled: An Essay on Rodeo, 1974; Film Flam: Essays on Hollywood, 1987; Sacagawea's Nickname: Essays on the American West, 2002. Screenplays: The Last Picture Show (with Peter Bogdanovich), 1971; Texasville, 1990; Montana, 1990; Falling From Grace, 1992; Memphis (with Cybill Shepherd), 1992. Editor: Still Wild: Short Fiction of the American West, 1950 to the Present, 2000; Roads, 2000. Contributions: newspapers and periodicals. *Honours:* Wallace Stegner Fellow, 1960; Jesse H. Jones Award, 1962, Barbara McCombs/Lon Tinkle Award, 1986, Texas Institute of Letters; Guggenheim Fellowship, 1964; Pulitzer Prize for Fiction, 1986. *Address:* c/o Saria Co Inc, 2509 N Campbell, No. 95, Tucson, AZ 85719, USA.

McNab, Andy; British writer. *Career:* joined the infantry 1976, mem. 22 SAS Regiment, B Squadron 1984–93; Dir, security co. running a specialist training course for individuals working in hostile environments. *Publications:* fiction: Remote Control 1997, Crisis Four 2000, Fire Wall 2001, Last Light 2002, Liberation Day 2002, Dark Winter 2003, Deep Black 2004; non-fiction: Bravo Two Zero (autobiog.) 1993, Immediate Action (autobiog.) 1995. *Honours:* DCM, MM. *Address:* c/o Transworld, 61–63 Uxbridge Road, London, W5 5SA, England. *Website:* www.booksattransworld.co.uk/andymcnab/home.htm.

MacNAB, Roy Martin, MA, DLitt; writer, poet and retd diplomat; b. 17 Sept. 1923, Durban, South Africa; m. Rachel Heron-Maxwell 1947; one s. one d. *Education:* Hilton College, Natal, South Africa, Jesus College, Oxford, University of South Africa. *Publications:* The Man of Grass and Other Poems, 1960; The French Colonel, 1975; Gold Their Touchstone, 1987; For Honour Alone, 1988. Co-Editor: Oxford Poetry, 1947; Poets in South Africa, 1958; Journey Into Yesterday, 1962. Editor: George Seferis: South African Diary, 1990; The Cherbourg Circles, 1994. Contributions: TLS; Spectator; Poetry Review; History, Today. *Honours:* Silver Medal, RSA, 1958. *Address:* 9/18 Elm Park Gardens, London SW10 9PD, England.

McNAIR, Wesley, BA, MA, MLitt; academic and poet; b. 19 June 1941, Newport, NH, USA; m. Diane Reed McNair 1962; three s. one d. *Education:* Keene State College, Middlebury College. *Career:* Assoc. Prof., Colby Sawyer College, 1968–87; Senior Fulbright Prof., Catholic University of Chile, 1977–78; Visiting Prof., Dartmouth College, 1984, Colby College, 2000–01; Assoc. Prof. to Prof., University of Maine at Farmington, 1987–98. *Publications:* The Town of No, 1989; Twelve Journeys in Maine, 1992; My Brother Running, 1993; Talking in the Dark, 1998; Mapping the Heart: Reflections on Place and Poetry, 2002; Fire: Poems, 2002. Contributions: anthologies, reviews, quarterlies, and journals. *Honours:* National Endowment for the Humanities Fellowship in Literature, 1970–71; National Endowment for the Arts Fellowships, 1980, 1990; Devins Award, 1984; Eunice Tietjens Prize, 1984; Guggenheim Fellowship, 1986; Pushcart Prize, 1986; New England Emmy Award, 1991; Rockefeller Residency, Bellagio, Italy, 1993; Theodore Roethke Prize, 1993; Yankee Magazine Poetry Prize, 1995; Sarah Josepha Hale Medal, 1997. *Address:* c/o Department of Humanities, University of Maine at Farmington, Farmington, ME 04938, USA.

McNALLY, Terrence; playwright; b. 3 Nov. 1939, St Petersburg, FL, USA. *Career:* Stage Man., Actors Studio, New York 1961; tutor 1961–62; film critic, The Seventh Art 1963–65; Asst Ed., Columbia Coll. Today 1965–66. *Publications:* Apple Pie, Sweet Eros Next and Other Plays 1969, Three Plays: Cuba Si!, Bringing It All Back Home, Last Gasps 1970, Where Has Tommy Flowers Gone? 1972, Bad Habits: Ravenswood and Dunelawn 1974, The Ritz and Other Plays 1976, The Rink 1985, And Things That Go Bump in the Night 1990, Frankie and Jonny in the Clair de Lune 1990, Kiss of the Spider Woman (with John Kander and Fred Ebb) 1992, Lips Together, Teeth Apart 1992, Until Your Heart Stops 1993, Love! Valour! Compassion! 1994, Masterclass 1995, Ragtime (with Stephen Flaherty and Lynn Ahrens) 1997, Corpus Christi 1998, Dead Man Walking (libretto) 2000, The Stendhal Syndrome 2003. *Honours:* Stanley Award 1962, Obie Award 1974, American Acad. of Arts and Letters Citation, Nat. Inst. of Arts and Letters Citation, Four Tony Awards, Pulitzer Award, two Guggenheim Awards. *Address:* 218 W 10th Street, New York, NY 10014, USA.

McNAMARA, Eugene Joseph, BA, MA, PhD; academic, editor, poet and writer; b. 18 March 1930, Oak Park, IL, USA; m. Margaret Lindstrom 1952; four s. one d. *Education:* DePaul University, Northwestern University. *Career:* Ed., University of Windsor Review, 1965–, Mainline, 1967–72, Sesame Press, 1973–80; Prof. of English, University of Windsor. *Publications:* Poetry: For the Mean Time, 1965; Outerings, 1970; Dillinger Poems, 1970; Love Scenes, 1971; Passages, 1972; Screens, 1977; Forcing the Field, 1980; Call it a Day, 1984. Short Stories: Salt, 1977; Search for Sarah Grace, 1978; Spectral Evidence, 1985; The Moving Light, 1986. Contributions: Queens Quarterly; Saturday Night; Chicago; Quarry; Denver Quarterly. *Address:* 166 Randolph Place, Windsor, ON N9B 2T3, Canada.

McNAMARA, Robert James, BA, MA, PhD; academic and poet; *Senior Lecturer in English, University of Washington, Seattle*; b. 28 March 1950, New York, NY, USA; one d. *Education:* Amherst College, Colorado State University, University of Washington, Seattle. *Career:* Founder-Ed., L'Epervier Press, 1977; Senior Lecturer in English, University of Washington, Seattle, 1985–; mem. Acad. of American Poets; PEN West. *Publications:* Second Messengers, 1990. Contributions: anthologies, reviews, quarterlies, and journals. *Honours:* National Endowment for the Arts Fellowship, 1987–88; Fulbright Grant, Jadavpur University, Kolkata, 1993. *Address:* c/o Department of English, Box 354330, University of Washington, Seattle, WA 98195, USA.

MacNEACAIL, Aonghas; writer and poet; b. 7 June 1942, Uig, Isle of Skye, Scotland; m. Gerda Stevenson 1980; one s. *Education:* University of Glasgow. *Career:* Writing Fellowships, The Gaelic College, Isle of Skye, 1977–79, An Comunn Gaidhealachm Oban, 1979–81, Ross-Cromarty District Council, 1988–90; mem. Scottish Poetry Library Asscn, council mem., 1984–. *Publications:* Poetry Quintet, 1976; Imaginary Wounds, 1980; Sireadh Bradain Sicir/Seeking Wise Salmon, 1983; An Cathadh Mor/The Great Snowbattle, 1984; An Seachnadh/The Avoiding, 1986; Rocker and Water, 1990. Contributions: many publications. *Honours:* Grampian TV Gaelic Poetry Award; Diamond Jubilee Award, Scottish Asscn for the Speaking of Verse, 1985; An Comunn Gaidhealach Literary Award, 1985.

McNEILL, Daniel Richard, AB, JD; writer; b. 1 June 1947, San Francisco, CA, USA; m. Rosalind Gold 1984. *Education:* University of California at Berkeley, Harvard Law School. *Career:* mem. Authors' Guild. *Publications:* Fuzzy Logic, 1993; The Face, 1998. *Honours:* Los Angeles Times Book Prize in Science and Technology 1993.

McNEISH, James, BA; writer; b. 23 Oct. 1931, Auckland, New Zealand. *Education:* University of Auckland. *Career:* Writer-in-Residence, Berlin Kunstler-program 1983; Research Fellow Nat. Library of New Zealand 1999. *Publications:* Tavern in the Town, 1957; Fire Under the Ashes, 1965; Mackenzie, 1970; The Mackenzie Affair, 1972; Larks in a Paradise (co-author), 1974; The Glass Zoo, 1976; As for the Godwits, 1977; Art of the Pacific (with Brian Brake), 1980; Belonging: Conversations in Israel, 1980; Joy, 1982; Walking on My Feet, 1983; The Man from Nowhere: A Berlin Diary, 1985; Lovelock, 1986; Penelope's Island, 1990; The Man from Nowhere and Other Prose, 1991; My Name is Paradiso 1995, Mr Halliday and the Circus Master 1996, The Mask of Sanity: the Bain Murders 1997, An Albatross Too Many 1998, Dance of the Peacocks: New Zealanders in Exile in the Time of Hitler and Mao Tse-tung 2003. *Address:* c/o Michael Gifkins, POB 6496, Auckland, New Zealand. *E-mail:* michael.gifkins@xtra.co.nz.

McNICHOLAS, Conor; British; *Editor, New Musical Express*; b. 1974, Bradford, West Yorkshire, England. *Career:* fmr News Ed., Ministry, Mixmag 2000–01; Ed., Muzik 2001–02, New Musical Express (NME) 2002–.

Address: New Musical Express, IPC Specialist Group, 25th Floor, King's Reach Tower, Stamford Street, London, SE1 9LS, England (Office). *Website:* www.nme.com.

McPHEE, John Angus, AB; academic and writer; *Professor of Journalism, Princeton University*; b. 8 March 1931, Princeton, NJ, USA; m. 1st Pryde Brown 1957; four d.; m. 2nd Yolanda Whitman 1972; two step-s. two step-d. *Education:* Princeton University, University of Cambridge. *Career:* Dramatist, Robert Montgomery Presents Television Programme, 1955–57; Assoc. Ed., Time magazine, New York City, 1957–64; Staff Writer, The New Yorker magazine, 1965–; Ferris Prof. of Journalism, Princeton University, 1975–; mem. American Acad. of Arts and Letters; Geological Society of America, fellow. *Publications:* A Sense of Where You Are, 1965; The Headmaster, 1966; Oranges, 1967; The Pine Barrens, 1968; A Roomful of Hovings, 1969; The Crofter and the Laird, 1969; Levels of the Game, 1970; Encounters with the Archdruid, 1972; Wimbledon: A Celebration, 1972; The Deltoid Pumpkin Seed, 1973; The Curve of Binding Energy, 1974; Pieces of the Frame, 1975; The Survival of the Bark Canoe, 1975; The John McPhee Reader, 1977; Coming into the Country, 1977; Giving Good Weight, 1979; Alaska: Images of the Country (with Galen Rowell), 1981; Basin and Range, 1981; In Suspect Terrain, 1983; La Place de la Concorde Suisse, 1984; Table of Contents, 1985; Rising from the Plains, 1986; Outcroppings, 1988; The Control of Nature, 1989; Looking for a Ship, 1990; Assembling California, 1993; The Ransom of Russian Art, 1994; Irons in the Fire, 1997; Annals of the Former World, 1998; The Founding Fish, 2002. *Honours:* American Acad. and Institute of Arts and Letters Award, 1977; Woodrow Wilson Award, Princeton University, 1982; American Asscn of Petroleum Geologists Journalism Awards, 1982, 1986; John Wesley Powell Award, United States Geological Survey, 1988; Walter Sullivan Award, American Geophysical Union, 1993; Pulitzer Prize for Non-Fiction, 1999; Public Service Award, Geological Society of America, 2002; various hon. doctorates. *Address:* 475 Drake's Corner Road, Princeton, NJ 08540, USA.

McPHERSON, Conor; dramatist; b. 1971, Dublin, Ireland. *Education:* Univ. Coll., Dublin. *Career:* writer-in-residence, Bush Theatre, London 1996; co-f., Fly by Night Theatre Co. Dublin. *Publications:* plays: Rum and Vodka 1992, The Good Thief 1994, This Lime Tree Bower 1995, The Weir 1997, Port Authority, Come on Over, St Nicholas 1997, A Dublin Carol 2000, The Stars Lose Their Glory, A Light in the Window of Industry, Shining City 2004; screenplays: I Went Down 1997, Saltwater (adaptation of This Lime Tree Bower) 2000, The Actors 2003,. *Honours:* Two Olivier Awards, incl. for Best New Play; Evening Standard Most Promising Playwright Award, 1997; Stewart Parker Trust Award, 1995; Guiness/National Theatre Ingenuity Award; Outer Critics Circle Award for Best Play; George Devine Award for Best New Play in London; San Sebastian Film Festival Best Screenplay Award.

McPHERSON, James A., BA, LLB, MFA; academic and writer; *Professor of English, University of Iowa*; b. 16 Sept. 1943, Savannah, GA, USA; m. (divorced); one d. *Education:* Morris Brown College, Harvard Law School, University of Iowa. *Career:* Rhetoric Program and Law School, University of Iowa, 1968–69; Lecturer, University of California at Santa Cruz, 1969–72; Asst Prof., Morgan State University, 1975–76; Assoc. Prof., University of Virginia, Charlottesville, 1976–81; Visiting Scholar, Yale Law School, New Haven, 1978; Prof. of English, Writers' Workshop, University of Iowa, 1981–; Lecturer, Meiji University, Tsuda College, Chiba University, 1989–90, Japan; mem. American Civil Liberties Union; PEN; Writers Guild; National Asscn for the Advancement of Colored People; American Acad. of Arts and Sciences. *Publications:* Hue and Cry, 1969; Railroad, 1976; Elbow Room, 1977; Crabcakes, 1998; A Region Not Home, 1999. Contributions: Atlantic; Harvard Advocate; Ploughshares; Nimrod; New York Times; Esquire; Reader's Digest; Washington Post; World Literature Today; Doubletake; Harper's. *Honours:* Guggenheim Fellowship, 1973; Pulitzer Prize for Fiction, 1978; MacArthur Prize Fellows Award, 1981; Award for Excellence in Teaching, University of Iowa, 1990; Green Eyeshades Award for Excellence in Print Commentary, Society of Southern Journalists, 1994; Fellow, Center for Advanced Studies, Stanford University, 1997–98, 2002–03. *Address:* 711 Rundell Street, Iowa City, IA 52240, USA.

McPHERSON, James Munro, BA, PhD; academic, writer and editor; *Professor of American History, Princeton University*; b. 11 Oct. 1936, Valley City, ND, USA; m. Patricia Rasche 1957; one d. *Education:* Gustavus Adolphus College, Johns Hopkins University. *Career:* instructor, 1962–65, Asst Prof., 1965–66, Assoc. Prof., 1966–72, Prof., 1972–82, of History, Edwards Prof. of American History, 1982–91, George Henry Davis '86 Prof. of American History, 1991–, Princeton University; Commonwealth Fund Lecturer in American History, University College London, 1982; mem. American Historical Asscn, pres., 2003–04; American Philosophical Society; Society of American Historians, pres., 2000–01; Southern Historical Asscn. *Publications:* The Struggle for Equality: Abolitionists and the Negro in the Civil War and Reconstruction, 1964; The Negro's Civil War: How American Negroes Felt and Acted During the War for the Union (ed.), 1965; Marching Toward Freedom: The Negro in the Civil War, 1968; The Anti-Slavery Crusade in America (co-ed.), 59 vols, 1969; Blacks in America: Bibliographical Essays (with others), 1971; The Abolitionist Legacy: From Reconstruction to the NAACP, 1975; Ordeal by Fire: The Civil War and Reconstruction, 1981; Religion, Race and Reconstruction: Essays in Honor of C. Vann Woodward (co-ed.), 1982; Battle Cry of Freedom, 1988; Battle Chronicles of the Civil War (ed.), six vols, 1989; Abraham Lincoln and the Second American Revolution, 1991; Images of the Civil War, 1992; Gettysburg, 1993; The Atlas of the Civil War (ed.), 1994; What They Fought For, 1861–1865, 1994; 'We Cannot Escape History': Lincoln and the Last Best Hope of Earth (ed.), 1995; Drawn with the Sword: Reflections on the American Civil War, 1996; The American Heritage New History of the Civil War (ed.), 1996; For Cause and Comrades: Why Men Fought in the Civil War, 1997; Lamson of the Gettysburg: The Civil War Letters of Lieutenant Roswell H. Lamson (co-ed.), 1997; Writing the Civil War: The Quest to Understand (co-ed.), 1998; Is Blood Thicker Than Water?: Crises of Nationalism in the Modern World, 1998; The Encyclopedia of Civil War Biographies (ed.), three vols, 1999; To the Best of My Ability: The American Presidents (ed.), 2000; Crossroads of Freedom: Antietam, 2002; Hallowed Ground: A Walk at Gettysburg, 2003. Contributions: Reference works, scholarly books and professional journals. *Honours:* Woodrow Wilson Fellow, 1958–62; Danforth Fellow, 1958–62; Anisfield-Wolf Award, 1965; Guggenheim Fellowship, 1967–68; Huntingdon Library-National Endowment for the Humanities Fellowship, 1977–78; Center for Advanced Study in the Behavioural Sciences Fellowship, 1982–83; Hunting-Seaver Institute Fellow, 1987–88; Pulitzer Prize in History, 1989; Christopher Award, 1989; Best Book Award, American Military Institute, 1989; R. Stanton Avery Fellow, Huntingdon Library, 1995–96; Lincoln Prize, 1998; Theodore and Franklin D. Roosevelt Prize in Naval History, 1998. *Address:* c/o Department of History, 129 Dickinson Hall, Princeton University, Princeton, NJ 08544, USA. *E-mail:* jmcpherson@princeton.edu.

McPHERSON, Sandra Jean, BA; academic and poet; *Professor of English, University of California at Davis*; b. 2 Aug. 1943, San Jose, CA, USA; m. 1st Henry D. Carlile 1966 (divorced 1985); one d.; m. 2nd Walter D. Pavlich 1995. *Education:* San Jose State University, University of Washington. *Career:* Visiting Lecturer, University of Iowa, 1974–76, 1978–80; Holloway Lecturer, University of California, Berkeley, 1981; Teacher, Oregon Writers Workshop, Portland, 1981–85; Prof. of English, University of California, Davis, 1985–; Ed. and publisher, Swan Scythe Press, 1999–. *Publications:* Elegies for the Hot Season, 1970; Radiation, 1973; The Year of Our Birth, 1978; Patron Happiness, 1983; Streamers, 1988; The God of Indeterminacy, 1993; Edge Effect, 1996; The Spaces Between Birds, 1996; A Visit to Civilisation, 2002. Contributions: periodicals. *Honours:* Ingram Merrill Foundation Grants, 1972, 1984; National Endowment for the Arts Grants, 1974, 1980, 1985; Guggenheim Fellowship, 1976; Oregon Arts Commission Fellowship, 1984; American Acad. and Institute of Art and Letters Award, 1987. *Address:* c/o Department of English, University of California at Davis, CA 95616, USA.

McQUAIN, Jeffrey Hunter, AA, BA, MA, PhD; writer, researcher and word historian; b. 23 Nov. 1955, Frederick, MD, USA. *Education:* Montgomery College, University of Maryland, American University. *Career:* researcher to William Safire, New York Times 1983–; mem. MLA. *Publications:* The Elements of English, 1986; Guide to Good Word Usage, 1989; Power Language, 1996; Coined by Shakespeare, 1998; Never Enough Words, 1999; Homegrown English, 2002; Coined by God, 2003; The Bard on the Brain, 2003. Contributions: New York Times Magazine. *Honours:* Words From Home Award 1996. *Address:* PO Box 4008, Rockville, MD 20849, USA.

McQUEEN, Priscilla (Cilla) Muriel, MA; poet and artist; b. 22 Jan. 1949, Birmingham, England; m. Ralph Hotere 1974 (divorced 1986); one d. *Education:* Otago University, Dunedin, New Zealand. *Career:* mem. Australasian Performing Rights Asscn; PEN. *Publications:* Homing In, 1982; Anti Gravity, 1984; Wild Sweets, 1986; Benzina, 1988; Berlin Diary, 1990; Crikey, 1994. Contributions: various publications. *Honours:* New Zealand Book Awards for Poetry, 1983, 1989, 1991; Fulbright Visiting Writers Fellowship, 1985; Robert Burns Fellowships, 1985, 1986; Australia-New Zealand Exchange Writers' Fellowship, 1987; Goethe Institute Scholarship, Berlin, 1988. *Address:* 33 Skibo Street, Kew, Dunedin, New Zealand.

McRAE, Hamish Malcolm Donald, BSc; journalist and writer; b. 20 Oct. 1943, Barnstaple, Devon, England; m. Frances Annes Cairncross 1971; two d. *Education:* Fettes College, Edinburgh, Trinity College, Dublin. *Career:* Ed., Euromoney, 1972, Business and City, The Independent, 1989; Financial Ed., The Guardian, 1975; Assoc. Ed., The Independent, 1991. *Publications:* Capital City – London as a Financial Centre (with Frances Cairncross), 1973; The Second Great Crash (with Frances Cairncross), 1975; Japan's Role in the Emerging Global Securities Market, 1985; The World in 2020, 1994. Contributions: numerous magazines and journals. *Honours:* Financial Journalist of the Year, Wincott Foundation, 1979; Special Merit Award, Amex Bank Review Essays, 1987; Columnist of the Year, Periodical Publishers Asscn Awards, 1996. *Address:* 6 Canonbury Lane, London N1 2AP, England.

MACSOVSZKY, Peter; Teacher and Writer; b. 4 Nov. 1966, Slovakia. *Education:* Graduate, Teachers Training College, Mitra; Master Degree, University of Constantine the Philosopher. *Career:* mem. Obec Slovensky Spisovatelov. *Publications:* Strach z Utopie, English trans. as Fear of Utopia, 1994; Ambit, 1995; Somrak Cudnosti, English trans. as The Dusk of Chastity, 1996; Cvicna Pitva, English trans. as Training Autopsy, 1997; A'lbonctan, English trans. as False Pathology, 1998.

MacTHÒMAIS, Ruaraidh (see Thomson, Derick Smith).

McTRUSTRY, Christifor John; screenwriter and novelist; b. 29 Oct. 1960, Wellington, NSW, Australia; m. Patricia Rose Dravine 1986; one s. one d. *Education:* Bachelor of Creative Arts, 1989, Master of Creative Arts, 1990, University of Wollongong. *Career:* mem. Australian Writers Guild; Australian National Playwrights Centre; Australian Society of Authors; MWA; Crime Writers Asscn of Australia. *Publications:* The Cat Burglar, 1995; The Card Shark, 1996; Axeman!, 1997; Frankenkid, 1997; George and the Dragon, 1997; Susie Smelly-Feet, 1997. Other: Television and radio series. *Address:* 22 Stanleigh Crescent, West Wollongong, NSW 2500, Australia.

MacVEY, John Wishart, BA; writer; b. 19 Jan. 1923, Kelso, Scotland. *Education:* diploma in applied chemistry, University of Strathclyde, Open University, Milton Keynes. *Career:* fmr technical information officer. *Publications:* Speaking of Space (with C. P. Snow, B. Lovell and P. Moore), 1962; Alone in the Universe?, 1963; Journey to Alpha Centauri, 1965; How We Will Reach the Stars, 1969; Whispers from Space, 1973; Interstellar Travel: Past, Present and Future, 1977; Space Weapons/Space War, 1979; Where We Will Go When the Sun Dies?, 1980; Colonizing Other Worlds, 1984; Time Travel, 1987. *Address:* Mellendean, 15 Adair Avenue, Saltcoats, Ayrshire KA21 5QS, Scotland.

McWHIRTER, George, BA, MA; writer, poet, translator and academic; b. 26 Sept. 1939, Belfast, Northern Ireland; m. Angela Mairead Coid 1963; one s. one d. *Education:* Queen's University, University of British Columbia. *Career:* Co-Ed.-in-Chief, 1977, Advisory Ed., 1978–, Prism International Magazine; Prof., 1970–, Head of Creative Writing, 1983–93, University of British Columbia; mem. League of Canadian Poets; Writers' Union of Canada; PEN; Literary Trans Asscn of Canada. *Publications:* Catalan Poems, 1971; Bodyworks, 1974; Queen of the Sea, 1976; God's Eye, 1981; Coming to Grips with Lucy, 1982; Fire Before Dark, 1983; Paula Lake, 1984; Cage, 1987; The Selected Poems of José Emilio Pacheco (ed. and trans.), 1987; The Listeners, 1991; A Bad Day to be Winning, 1992; A Staircase for All Souls, 1993; Incubus: The Dark Side of the Light, 1995; Musical Dogs, 1996; Fab, 1997; Where Words Like Monarchs Fly (ed. and trans.), 1998; Ovid in Saskatchewan, 1998; Eyes to See Otherwise: The Selected Poems of Homero Aridjis, 1960–2000 (co-ed. and trans.), 2001; The Book of Contradictions (poems), 2002. Contributions: numerous magazines and journals. *Honours:* McMillan Prize, 1969; Commonwealth Poetry Prize, 1972; F. R. Scott Prize, 1988; Ethel Wilson Fiction Prize, 1988; Killan Prize for Teaching, University of British Columbia, 1998. *Address:* 4637 W 13th Avenue, Vancouver, BC V6R 2V6, Canada.

McWILLIAM, Candia Frances Juliet, BA, FRSL; writer; b. 1 July 1955, Edinburgh, Scotland; m. 1st Earl of Portsmouth 1981; m. 2nd F. E. Dinshaw 1986; two s. one d. *Education:* Sherborne School for Girls, Girton College, Cambridge. *Career:* mem. Society of Authors, PEN. *Publications:* A Case of Knives, 1988; A Little Stranger, 1989; Debatable Land, 1994; Wait Till I Tell You, 1997. *Honours:* Betty Trask Prize; Scottish Arts Council Prize; Guardian Fiction Prize; Pumio Grinzane Cavour, Italy; Forderpreis, Germany. *Address:* c/o Bloomsbury Publishing, 38 Soho Square, London W1V 5DE, England.

MADDEN, David; Educator, Writer, Critic, Ed., Poet and Dramatist; b. 25 July 1933, Knowville, Tennessee, USA; m. Roberta Margaret Young, 6 Sept. 1956, one s. *Education:* BS, University of Tennessee, 1957; MA, San Francisco State College, 1958; Postgraduate Studies, Yale Drama School, 1959–60. *Career:* Faculty, Appalachian State Teachers College, Boone, NC, 1957–58, Centre College, 1964–66, Ohio University, 1966–68; Asst Ed., Kenyon Review, 1964–66; Writer-in-Residence, 1968–92, Dir, Creative Writing Program, 1992–94, and US Civil War Center, 1992–99, Alumni Prof., 1994, Louisiana State University; Donald and Veliva Crunbley Prof. of Creative Writing, 2000; mem. Associated Writing Programs; Authors League. *Publications:* Fiction: The Beautiful Greed, 1961; Cassandra Singing, 1969; The Shadow Knows, 1970; Brothers in Confidence, 1972; Bijou, 1974; The Suicide's Wife, 1978; Pleasure-Dome, 1979; On the Big Wind, 1980; The New Orleans of Possibilities, 1982; Sharpshooter, 1995. Non-Fiction: Wright Morris, 1964; The Poetic Image in 6 Genres, 1969; James M. Cain, 1970; Creative Choices: A Spectrum of Quality and Technique in Fiction, 1975; Harlequin's Stick: Charlie's Cane: A Comparative Study of Commedia dell' arte and Silent Slapstick Comedy, 1975; A Primer of the Novel: For Readers & Writers, 1980; Writer's Revisions (with Richard Powers), 1981; Cain's Craft, 1986; Revising Fiction, 1988; The World of Fiction, 1990; The Fiction Tutor, 1990; Eight Classic American Novels, 1990; A Pocketful of Prose: Vintage, 1992; A Pocketful of Prose: Contemporary, 1992. Editor: Proletarian Writers of the Thirties, 1968; Tough Guy Writers of the Thirties, 1968; American Dreams, American Nightmares, 1970; Rediscoveries, 1971; The Popular Culture Explosion (with Ray B. Browne), 1972; The Contemporary Literary Scene (assoc. ed.), 1973; Nathanael West: The Cheaters and the Cheated, 1973; Remembering James Agee, 1974; Studies in the Short Story, fourth–sixth edns, 1975–84; Rediscoveries II (with Peggy Bach), 1988; Classics of Civil War Fiction, 1991; Beyond the Battlefield (ed.). Contributions: poems, essays and short stories in various publications. *Honours:* John Golden Fellow in Playwriting, 1959; Rockefeller Foundation Grant in Fiction, 1969; National Council on the Arts Award, 1970. *Address:* 614 Park Blvd, Baton Rouge, LA 70806, USA.

MADDOX, Carl (see Tubb, Edwin Charles).

MADDOX, Sir John Royden, Kt; British writer and publishing editor; b. 27 Nov. 1925; m. 1st Nancy Fanning (died 1960); one s. one d.; m. 2nd Brenda Power Murphy 1960; one s. one d. *Education:* Christ Church, Oxford, King's Coll., London. *Career:* asst lecturer, then lecturer in Theoretical Physics, Manchester Univ. 1949–55; science corresp. The Guardian 1955–64; Affiliate, Rockefeller Inst., New York 1962–63; Asst Dir Nuffield Foundation and Co-ordinator Nuffield Foundation Science Teaching Project 1964–66; Man. Dir Macmillan Journals Ltd 1970–72; Dir Macmillan & Co. Ltd 1968–73; Chair. Maddox Editorial Ltd 1972–74; Dir Nuffield Foundation 1975–80; Ed. Nature 1966–73, 1980–96; mem. Crickadarn and Gwendwr Community Council 1981–. *Publications:* The Spread of Nuclear Weapons (jtly) 1962, Revolution in Biology 1964, The Doomsday Syndrome 1972, Beyond the Energy Crisis 1975, What Remains to be Discovered 1987. *Honours:* Hon. Fellow Royal Soc. 2000; Hon. DTech (Surrey) 1982, Hon. DSc (Univ. of E Anglia) 1992, (Liverpool) 1994. *Address:* 9 Pitt Street, London, W8 4NX, England (Home). *Telephone:* (20) 7937-9750 (Home).

MADELEY, John; Writer and Broadcaster; b. 14 July 1934, Salford, England; m. Alison Madeley, 10 March 1962, one s. one d. *Education:* BA, Economics, 1972. *Career:* Broadcaster, BBC and Deutsche Welle. *Publications:* Human Rights Begin with Breakfast, 1981; Diego Garcia: Contrast to the Falklands, 1982; When Aid is No Help, 1991; Trade and the Poor, 1992; Big Business, Poor People: The Impact of Transnational Corporations on the World Poor, 1999; Hungry for Trade: How the poor pay for free trade, 2000; Food for All: The Need for a New Agriculture, 2001; A People's World: Alternatives to Economic Globalization, 2003. Contributions: newspapers and magazines. *Address:* 19 Woodford Close, Caversham, Reading, Berkshire RG4 7HN, England.

MADGETT, Naomi Long; Poet, Publisher and Prof. of English Emeritus; b. 5 July 1923, Norfolk, Virginia, USA; m. Leonard P. Andrews Sr. *Education:* BA, Virginia State College, 1945; MEd, English, Wayne State University; PhD, International Institute for Advanced Studies, 1980. *Career:* Research Assoc., Oakland University; Lecturer in English, University of Michigan; Assoc. Prof. to Prof. of English Emeritus, Eastern Michigan University; Publisher; Ed., Lotus Press. *Publications:* Songs to a Phantom Nightingale, 1941; One and the Many, 1956; Star by Star, 1965; Pink Ladies in the Afternoon, 1972; Exits and Entrances, 1978; Phantom Nightingale, 1981; A Student's Guide to Creative Writing, 1990. Contributions: numerous anthologies and journals. *Address:* 16886 Inverness Ave, Detroit, MI 48221, USA.

MADSEN, Richard Paul; Prof. of Sociology and Writer; b. 2 April 1941, Alameda, CA, USA; m. Judith Rosselli, 12 Jan. 1974. *Education:* BA, Maryknoll College, Glen Ellyn, IL, 1963; BD, 1967, MTh, 1968, Maryknoll Seminary, Ossining, New York; MA, 1972, PhD, 1977, Harvard University. *Career:* Ordained, Roman Catholic Priest, 1968; Maryknoll missioner, Taiwan, 1968–71; Left priesthood, 1974; Lecturer in Sociology, Harvard University, 1977–78; Asst Prof., 1978–83, Assoc. Prof., 1983–85, Prof. of Sociology, 1985–, University of California at San Diego, La Jolla; mem. American Sociological Asscn; Asscn of Asian Studies, governing council for China and Inner Asia, 1989–91. *Publications:* Chen Village: The Recent History of a Peasant Community in Mao's China (with Anita Chan and Jonathan Unger), 1984, revised edn as Chen Village Under Mao and Deng, 1992; Morality and Power in a Chinese Village, 1984; Habits of the Heart: Individualism in American Life (with Robert N. Bellah, William M. Sullivan, Ann Swidler and Steven M. Tipton), 1985; Individualism and Commitment in American Life: A Habits of the Heart Reader (with Robert N. Bellah, William M. Sullivan, Ann Swidler and Steven M. Tipton), 1987; Unofficial China (ed. with Perry Link and Paul Pickowicz), 1989; The Good Society (with Robert N. Bellah, William M. Sullivan, Ann Swidler and Steven M. Tipton), 1991; China and the American Dream: A Moral Inquiry, 1995; China's Catholics: Tragedy and Hope in a Emerging Civil Society, 1998; Meaning and Modernity: Religion, Polity and Self (with William M. Sullivan, Ann Swidler and Steven M. Tipton), 2002; Popular China: Unofficial Culture in a Globalising Society (with Perry Link and Paul Pickowicz), 2002; The Many and the One: Religious and Secular Perspectives in Ethical Pluralism in the Modern World (with Tracy B. Strong), 2003. Contributions: journals. *Honours:* C. Wright Mills Award, Society for the Study of Social Problems, 1985; Current Interest Book Award, Los Angeles Times, 1985; Book Award, Asscn of Logos Bookstores, 1986. *Address:* c/o Dept of Sociology, University of California at San Diego, La Jolla, CA 92093, USA.

MAGDALEN, I. I. (see Botsford, Keith).

MAGEE, Bryan, MA; British author and broadcaster; b. 12 April 1930, London; m. Ingrid Söderlund 1954 (died 1986); one d. *Education:* Christ's Hosp., Lycée Hôche, Versailles, Keble Coll. Oxford and Yale Univ. *Career:* Army Intelligence Corps 1948–49; TV reporter This Week; music and theatre critic Musical Times and The Listener; Lecturer in Philosophy, Balliol Coll. Oxford 1970–71; Visiting Fellow, All Souls Coll. Oxford 1973–74; MP for Leyton 1974–83; Pres. Critics Circle of GB 1983–84; Hon. Sr Research Fellow, King's Coll. London 1984–94, Visiting Prof. 1994–2000; Hon. Fellow, Queen Mary Coll. London 1988–; Fellow, Queen Mary and Westfield Coll. London 1989–; Visiting Fellow Wolfson Coll. Oxford 1991–94, New Coll. Oxford 1995, Merton Coll. Oxford 1998, St. Catherine's Coll. Oxford 2000, Peterhouse Cambridge 2001, Clare Hall Cambridge

2004; also at Yale, Harvard, Sydney, LSE; newspaper columnist; mem. Arts Council of GB and Chair. Music Panel 1993–94; mem. Soc. of Authors. *Television:* Men of Ideas 1978. *Publications:* Crucifixion and Other Poems 1951, Go West Young Man 1958, The New Radicalism 1962, The Democratic Revolution 1964, Towards 2000 1965, One in Twenty 1966, The Television Interviewer 1966, Aspects of Wagner 1968 (revised edn 1988), Modern British Philosophy 1971 (re-issued as Talking Philosophy 2001), Popper 1973, Facing Death 1977, Men of Ideas 1978, The Philosophy of Schopenhauer 1983, 1997, The Great Philosophers 1987, On Blindness 1995 (re-issued as Sight Unseen 1998), Confessions of a Philosopher 1997, The Story of Philosophy 1998, Wagner and Philosophy 2000, Clouds of Glory: A Childhood in Hoxton 2003. *Honours:* Hon. Fellow Keble Coll. Oxford 1994–; Silver Medal, Royal TV Soc. 1978. *Literary Agent:* A. P. Watt Ltd, 20 John Street, London, WC1N 2DR. *Address:* Wolfson College, Oxford, OX2 6UD, England.

MAGEE, Wes(ley Leonard Johnston); Poet and Writer; b. 20 July 1939, Greenock, Scotland; m. Janet Elizabeth Parkhouse, 10 Aug. 1967, one s. one d. *Education:* Teaching Certificate, Goldsmiths College, University of London, 1967; Advanced Certificate in Education, University of Bristol, 1972. *Career:* mem. Poetry Society of Great Britain; Philip Larkin Society. *Publications:* Over 40 books for children, 1972–98. Contributions: Reviews and journals. *Honours:* New Poets Award, 1972; Poetry Book Society Recommendation, 1978; Cole Scholar, FL, 1985. *Address:* Crag View Cottage, Thorgill, Rosedale, North Yorkshire YO18 8SG, England.

MAGER, Donald Northrop; academic, poet and writer; b. 24 Aug. 1942, Santa Rita, NM, USA; m. Barbara Feldman (divorced); two s.; pnr William McDowell. *Education:* BA, Drake University, 1964; MA, Creative Writing, Syracuse University, 1966; PhD, English Literature, Wayne State University, 1986. *Career:* Instructor, Syracuse University; Assoc. Prof., Johnson C. Smith University; mem. MLA. *Publications:* Poetry: To Track the Wounded One: A Journal, 1988; Glosses: Twenty-four Preludes and Etudes, 1995; That Which is Owed to Death, 1998; Borderings, 1998; Good Turns, 2001; Akhmatova (opera libretto), 2002; Elegance of the Ungraspable, 2003. Contributions: anthologies, books, reviews, quarterlies, journals, and magazines. *Honours:* First Prize, Hallmark Competition, 1965; Approach Magazines Award, 1978; Tompkings Award First Prize for Poetry, Wayne State University, 1986; First Prize, The Lyricist Statewide Poetry Competition, Campbell University, 1992; Assoc. Artist Residency, Atlantic Center for the Arts, New Smyrna Beach, FL, 1994; Winner, Union County Writers Club Chapbook Contest, 1998. *Address:* c/o Johnson C. Smith University, UPO 2441, Charlotte, NC 28216, USA.

MAGNUSSON, Magnus; Writer, Trans. and Broadcaster; b. 12 Oct. 1929, Reykjavík, Iceland; m. Mamie Baird, 1954, two s. one deceased, three d. *Education:* MA, Jesus College, Oxford, 1951. *Career:* mem. Society of Antiquaries of London, fellow, 1991; Royal Scottish Geographical Society, fellow, 1991. *Publications:* Introducing Archaeology, 1972; Viking Expansion Westwards, 1973; The Clacken and the Slate, 1974; Hammer of the North, 1976, second edn as Viking Hammer of the North, 1980; BC: The Archaeology of the Bible Lands, 1977; Landlord or Tenant?: A View of Irish History, 1978; Iceland, 1979; Vikings!, 1980; Magnus on the Move, 1980; Treasures of Scotland, 1981; Lindisfarne: The Cradle Island, 1984; Iceland Saga, 1987; I've Started, So I'll Finish, 1997; Rum: Nature's Island, 1997; Magnus Magnusson's Quiz Book, 2000; Scotland: The Story of a Nation, 2000. Translator: (with Hermann Palsson) Njal's Saga, 1960; The Vinland Sagas, 1965; King Herald's Saga, 1966; Laxaela Saga, 1969; (all by Halldor Laxness): The Atom Station, 1961; Paradise Reclaimed, 1962; The Fish Can Sing, 1966; World Light, 1969; Christianity under Glacier, 1973; (by Samivel) Golden Iceland, 1967. Editor: Echoes in Stone, 1983; Reader's Digest Book of Facts, 1985; Chambers Biographical Dictionary, 1990; The Nature of Scotland, 1994. Contributions: many books. *Honours:* Knight of the Order of the Falcon, 1975, Knight Commander, 1986, Iceland; Silver Jubilee Medal, 1977; Iceland Media Award, 1985; Hon. Knighthood, Great Britain, 1989; Hon. Fellow, Jesus College, Oxford, 1990; Hon. degrees, and many other hons and awards. *Literary Agent:* Rogers, Coleridge & White Ltd, 20 Powis Mews, London W11 1JN, England. *Address:* Blairskaith House, Balmore-Torrance, Glasgow G64 4AX, Scotland.

MAGNUSSON, Sigurdur A.; Writer and Poet; b. 31 March 1928, Reykjavík, Iceland; m. 1st (divorced); m. 2nd (divorced); two s. three d. *Education:* University of Iceland, 1948–50; University of Copenhagen, 1950–51; University of Athens, 1951–52; University of Stockholm, 1952–53; BA, New School for Social Research, New York, 1955. *Career:* Literary and Drama Critic, Morgunbladid, 1956–67; Ed.-in-Chief, Samvinnan, 1967–74; Mem., International Writing Programme, University of Iowa, 1976, 1977; Mem., International Artists' Programme, West Berlin, 1979–80; Mem., Jury, Nordic Council Prize for Literature, 1990–98; mem. Amnesty International, chair., 1988–89, 1993–95; Greek-Icelandic Society, chair., 1985–88; Society of Icelandic Drama Critics, chair., 1963–71; Writers' Union of Iceland, chair., 1971–78. *Publications:* In English: Northern Sphinx: Iceland and the Icelanders from the Settlement to the Present, 1977; Iceland: Country and People, 1978; The Iceland Horse, 1978; The Postwar Poetry of Iceland, 1982; Icelandic Writing Today, 1982; Iceland Crucible: A Modern Artistic Renaissance, 1985; The Icelanders, 1990; Iceland: Isle of Light, 1995. Other: 31 books in Icelandic; 28 trans into Icelandic from English, Danish, German and Greek. Contributions: Professional journals. *Honours:* Golden Cross of Phoenix, Greece, 1955; Cultural Council Prize for Best Play, 1961, and Best Novel, 1980; European Jean Monnet Prize for Literature, 1995. *Address:* Barónsstíg 49, 101 Reykjavík, Iceland.

MAGORIAN, James, BS, MS; poet and writer; b. 24 April 1942, Palisade, NE, USA. *Education:* University of Nebraska, Illinois State University, University of Oxford, Harvard University. *Publications:* Poetry: Hitchhiker in Hall County, 1968; The Garden of Epicurus, 1971; Safe Passage, 1977; Phases of the Moon, 1978; Tap Dancing on a Tightrope, 1981; Taxidermy Lessons, 1982; The Walden Pond Caper, 1983; The Emily Dickinson Jogging Book, 1984; Weighing the Sun's Light, 1985; The Hideout of the Sigmund Freud Gang, 1987; Borderlands, 1992; The Yellowstone Meditations, 1996; Haymarket Square, 1998. Fiction: America First, 1992; The Man Who Wore Layers of Clothing in the Winter, 1994; Hearts of Gold, 1996; Souvenir Pillows From Mars, 1996. Other: Children's books. Contributions: Reviews, quarterlies, and journals. *Address:* 1225 N 46th Street, Lincoln, NE 68503, USA.

MAGORIAN, Michelle Jane; Writer and Actress; b. 6 Nov. 1947, Southsea, Portsmouth, Hampshire, England; m. Peter Keith Venner Aug. 1987 (divorced 1998); two s. *Education:* Diploma, Speech and Drama, Rose Bruford College of Speech and Drama, Kent, 1969; École Internationale de Mime Marcel Marceau, Paris, 1969–70. *Career:* mem. Society of Authors; PEN; British Actors Equity. *Publications:* Fiction: Goodnight Mister Tom, 1981 (also libretto for musical, 2001); Back Home, 1984; A Little Love Song, 1991; Cuckoo in the Nest, 1994. Poetry: Waiting for My Shorts to Dry 1989, Orange Paw Marks 1991. Short Stories: In Deep Water 1992, A Spoonful of Jam 1998, Be Yourself 2003. Librettos: Hello Life! 2004, Tinsel 2004. Contributions: Puffin Post. *Honours:* Guardian Award for Children's Fiction, UK, 1981; Children's Award, International Reading Asscn, USA, 1982; Notable Children's Books, 1982, Best Book of Young Adults, 1982, Young Adult Reviewers Choice, 1982, American Library Asscn; Western Australia Young Readers Book Award, 1983; Western Australia Young Readers Book Award, 1987; BAFTA, 1999. *Literary Agent:* Rogers, Coleridge & White Ltd, 20 Powis Mews, London W11 1JN, England. *E-mail:* michelle.magorian@virgin.net.

MAGRIS, Claudio; Italian journalist, writer and university professor; b. 10 April 1939, Trieste; m. Marisa Madieri 1964; two s. *Education:* Univ. of Turin. *Career:* Lecturer in German Language and Literature, Univ. of Trieste 1968–70, Turin 1970–78, Trieste 1978–; mem. Deutsche Akad. für Sprache und Dichtung (Darmstadt), Österreichische Akad. der Wissenschaften, Accad. delle Scienze di Torino, Ateneo Veneto, Akad. der Wissenschaften (Göttingen). *Publications:* Il Mito absburgico nella letteratura austriaca moderna 1963, 1988, Wilhelm Heinse 1968, Lontano da dove. Joseph Roth e la tradizione ebraico-orientale 1971, Dietro le parole 1978, Itaca e oltre 1982, Trieste. Un'identità di frontiera 1982, 1987, L'anello di Clarisse 1984, Illazioni su una sciabola 1984, Danubio 1986 (trans. in numerous languages), Stadelmann 1988, Microcosmi 1997, Utopia e disincanto 1999; numerous essays and book reviews in Corriere della Sera and other European newspapers and periodicals; trans. Ibsen, Kleist, Schnitzler, Büchner. *Honours:* Debenedetti 1972, Val di Comino 1978, Goethe Medaille 1980, Aquileia 1983, Premiolino 1983, San Giusto d'Oro 1984, Musil Medaille der Stadt Klagenfurt 1984, Bagutta 1987, Accad. dei Lincei 1987, Marotta 1987, Città di Modena 1987, Antico Fattore 1988, Juan Carlos I 1989, Premio Strega 1997, Premio Chiara alla Carriera 1999, Premio Würth per la Cultura Europea 1999, Premio Grinzane Piemonte 1999, Medaglia d'Oro della Cultura della Scuola e dell' Arte 1999, Premio Sikken 2000, Premio Nietsche 2000, Premium Erasmianum 2001, Leipziger Buchpreis zur Europäischen Verständigung 2001, Osterreichisches Ehrenkreuz für Wissenschaft und Kunst (First Class), Prince of Asturias Prize for Letters 2004. *Address:* Università degli Studi Trieste, Piazzale Europa 1, 34127 Trieste; Via Carpaccio 2, Trieste, Italy. *Telephone:* (040) 6767111 (Office); (040) 305428. *Fax:* (040) 6763093 (Office); (040) 314455.

MAGRS, Paul, BA, MA, PhD; British writer and lecturer; b. 12 Nov. 1969, Jarrow, Tyne and Wear, England. *Education:* Lancaster Univ. *Career:* Lecturer and creative writing organizer, Univ. of East Anglia, Norwich 1997–. *Publications:* fiction: Marked for Life 1995, Does it Show? 1997, Playing Out 1997, Could it be Magic? 1998, Modern Love 2000, All the Rage 2001, Strange Boy 2002, Aisles 2003, Hands Up 2003, The Good, the Bat and the Ugly 2004, To the Devil a Diva 2004; Dr Who books: The Scarlet Empress 1998, The Blue Angel 1999, Verdigris 2000, Mad Dogs and Englishmen 2002; contrib. to New Writing. *Address:* c/o Simon and Schuster UK Ltd, Africa House, 64–78 Kingsway, London, WC2B 6AH, England. *E-mail:* enquiries@simonandschuster.co.uk. *Website:* www.simonsays.co.uk.

MAHAPATRA, Jayanta; Poet, Writer and Ed.; b. 22 Oct. 1928, Cuttack, Orissa, India; Trans. m. Jyotsna Rani Das, 16 Jan. 1951, one s. *Education:* University of Cambridge, 1941; BSc, Utkal University, 1946; MSc, Patna University, 1949. *Career:* Lecturer, Reader, 1950–86; Poet-in-Residence, Rockefeller Foundation Conference Center, Bellagio, Italy, 1986; Poetry Ed., The Telegraph, Kolkata, 1994–98; Ed., Lipi, 1998. *Publications:* Close the Sky, 1971; Svayamvara and Other Poems, 1971; A Rain of Rites, 1976; Waiting, 1979; Relationship, 1980; The False Start, 1980; Life Signs, 1983; Dispossessed Nests, 1984; Selected Poems, 1987; Burden of Waves and Fruit, 1988; Temple, 1989; A Whiteness of Bone, 1992; The Best of Jayanta

Mahapatra, 1995; Shadow Space, 1997; The Green Gardener, 1997; Bare Face, 2001. Other: various children's stories and trans; Ed., Chandrabhaga magazine, 2000–. Contributions: Reviews, quarterlies, and journals. *Honours:* Jacob Glatstein Memorial Award, Chicago, 1975; National Acad. of Letters Award, New Delhi, 1981; El consejo nacional para la cultura y las artes, Mexico, 1994; Gangadhar National Award for Poetry, 1994; Jaidayal Harmony Award, 1994. *Address:* Tinkonia Bagicha, Cuttack 753 001, Orissa, India. *Telephone:* (671) 2617434.

MAHARIDGE, Dale (Dimitro); University Lecturer and Writer; b. 24 Oct. 1956, Cleveland, Ohio, USA. *Education:* Cleveland State University, 1974–76; Cuyahoga Community College, 1976. *Career:* Staff, Gazette, Medina, Ohio, 1977–78; Journalist, Sacramento Bee, CA, 1980–91; Asst Prof., Columbia University, 1991–92; Lecturer, Stanford University, 1992–; mem. Sierra Club. *Publications:* Journey to Nowhere: The Saga of the New Underclass, 1985; And Their Children After Them: The Legacy of 'Let Us Now Praise Famous Men', James Agee, Walker Evans, and the Rise and Fall of Cotton in the South, 1989; Yosemite: A Landscape of Life, 1990; The Last Great American Hobo, 1993; The Coming White Minority: California, Multiculturalism, and the Nation's Future, 1999. Contributions: periodicals. *Honours:* World Hunger Award, New York City, 1987; Lucius W. Nieman Fellowship, Harvard University, 1988; Pulitzer Prize for General Non-Fiction, 1990; Pope Foundation Award, 1994; Freedom Forum Profs' Publishing Program Grant, 1995; Social Justice Journalism Award, Hunter College, CUNY, 2001. *Address:* c/o Dept of Communications, Stanford University, Stanford, CA 94305, USA.

MAHER, Terence Anthony; British bookseller and publisher; *Chairman, Maher Booksellers Ltd.*; b. 5 Dec. 1935, Manchester; m. Barbara Grunbaum 1960; three s. *Education:* Xaverian Coll., Manchester. *Career:* Controller, Carborundum Co. Ltd 1961–69; Dir Corp. Finance, First Nat. Finance Corpn 1969–72; f. Pentos PLC 1972, Chair., CEO –1993; Chair. and CEO Dillons Bookstores 1977–93; Athena Int. 1980–93, Ryman 1987–93; Chair. The Chalford Publishing Co. Ltd 1994–98, Maher Booksellers Ltd 1995–, Race Dynamics Ltd 1998–; Founder Trustee of Liberal Democrats 1988; mem. Advisory Council on Libraries 1997–98; Fellow of the Chartered Asscn of Certified Accountants. *Publications:* (jtly) Counterblast 1965, Effective Politics 1966, Against My Better Judgement (autobiog.) 1994, Unfinished Business (fiction) 2003. *Address:* 33 Clarence Terrace, Regent's Park, London, NW1 4RD; The Old House, Whichford, nr Shipston on Stour, Warwicks., CV36 5PG, England. *Telephone:* (20) 7723-4254 (London); (1608) 684-614 (Whichford).

MAHFOUZ, Naguib; Egyptian author; b. 11 Dec. 1911, Gamaliya, Cairo; m. Attiyat Allah 1954; two d. *Education:* Univ. of Cairo. *Career:* civil servant 1934; successively with Univ. of Cairo, Ministry of Waqfs, Dept of Arts and Censorship Bd 1936–59; Dir Foundation for Support of Cinema, State Cinema Org. 1959–69; contrib. to Al Ahram. *Films based on his works include:* The Beginning and the End, Midaq Alley, Respected Sir; numerous films in Arabic. *Television based on his works includes:* Palace Walk, Palace of Desire; numerous others in Arabic. *Publications in English include:* fiction: Midaq Alley 1966, Mirrors 1977, Miramar 1978, Children of Gebelawi 1981 (retitled Children of our Alley 1996), The Thief and the Dogs 1984, Wedding Song 1984, The Beginning and the End 1985, Autumn Quail 1985, The Beggar 1986, Respected Sir 1986, The Search 1987, God's World 1988, Fountain and Tomb 1988, Palace Walk 1989 (Egyptian State Prize 1956 for Arabic Edn), Palace of Desire 1991, Sugar Street 1992, The Journey of Ibn Fattouma 1992, Adrift on the Nile 1993, Al-Harafish 1994, Arabian Nights and Days 1995, The Day The Leader was Killed 1997, Echoes of an Autobiography 1997, Akhenaton: Dweller in Truth 1998, The Cairo Trilogy 2000; Naguib Mahfouz at Sidi Gabere: Conversations with the Nobel Laureate 2001, The Complete Naguib Mahfouz Library: The Twenty Fiction Vols of the Nobel Laureate in English 2001; Voices from the Other World: Ancient Egyptian Tales 2002; publications in Arabic include: over 40 novels and 16 short story collections. *Honours:* Hon. mem. American Acad. of Arts and Letters, American Acad. of Arts and Sciences 2002; Nat. Prize for Letters 1970; Nobel Prize for Literature 1988; Collar of the Repub. 1972, Order of the Repub. *Address:* American University in Cairo Press, 113 Sharia Kasr El Aini, Cairo, Egypt (Office). *Telephone:* (2) 797-6398 (Office). *Fax:* (2) 794-1440 (Office). *E-mail:* aleya@aucegypt.edu (Office). *Website:* www.aucpress.com (Office).

MAHJOUB, Jamal; British/Sudanese novelist; b. 1960, London. *Education:* Comboni Coll., Sudan, Atlantic Coll., S Wales, Univ. of Sheffield, England. *Publications:* Navigation of a Rainmaker 1989, The Cartographer's Angel 1993, Wings of Dust 1994, In the Hour of Signs 1996, The Carrier 1998, Travelling with Djinns 2003. *Honours:* The Guardian/Heinemann African Novel Competition. *Address:* c/o Vintage, Random House UK Ltd, 20 Vauxhall Bridge Road, London, SW1V 2SA, England. *Website:* www.randomhouse.co.uk.

MAHON, Derek; Critic, Ed. and Poet; b. 23 Nov. 1941, Belfast, Northern Ireland. *Education:* BA, Belfast Institute; BA, Trinity College, Dublin, 1965. *Career:* Drama Critic, Ed., Poetry Ed., New Statesman, 1981–; Poet-in-Residencies. *Publications:* Twelve Poems, 1965; Night-Crossing, 1968; Lives, 1972; The Man Who Built His City in Snow, 1972; The Snow Party, 1975; Light Music, 1977; The Sea in Winter, 1979; Poems 1962–1978, 1979; Courtyards in Delft, 1981; The Hunt by Night, 1982; A Kensington Notebook, 1984; Antarctica, 1986; Selected Poems, 1991. Editor: Modern Irish Poetry, 1972; The Penquin Book of Contemporary Irish Poetry, 1990. *Literary Agent:* Rogers, Coleridge & White Ltd, 20 Powis Mews, London W11 1JN, England.

MAIDEN, Jennifer Margaret, BA; poet and writer; b. 7 April 1949, Penrith, NSW, Australia. *Education:* Macquarie Univ. *Publications:* Tactics 1974, The Occupying Forces 1975, The Problem of Evil 1975, Birthstones 1978, The Border Loss 1979, For the Left Hand 1981, The Terms 1982, The Trust 1988, Play with Knives 1990, Selected Poems of Jennifer Maiden 1990, Acoustic Shadow 1993, Mines 1999; contrib. to numerous newspapers and magazines. *Honours:* several Australia Council Fellowships and grants, Grenfell Henry Lawson Award 1979, New South Wales Premier's Prizes 1991, 2000, Victorian Premier's Prize 1991, Christopher Brennan Award for Lifetime Achivement 1999. *Address:* PO Box 4, Penrith, NSW 2751, Australia.

MAIER, Paul Luther; Prof. of Ancient History; b. 31 May 1930, St Louis, MO, USA; m. Joan M. Ludtke 1967; four d. *Education:* MA, Harvard University, 1954; MDiv, Concordia Seminary, St Louis, 1955; Postgraduate Studies, Heidelberg; PhD, University of Basel, 1957. *Career:* Campus Chaplain, 1958–99, Prof. of Ancient History, 1961–, Western Michigan University. *Publications:* A Man Spoke, A World Listened: The Story of Walter A Maier, 1963; Pontius Pilate, 1968; First Christmas, 1971; First Easter, 1973; First Christians, 1976; The Flames of Rome, 1981; In the Fullness of Time, 1991; A Skeleton in God's Closet, 1994; More Than a Skeleton, 2003. Editor: The Best of Walter A Maier, 1980; Josephus: The Jewish War, 1982. Ed. and Translator: Josephus: The Essential Writings, 1988; Josephus: The Essential Works, 1995; Eusebius: The Church History, 1999. Children's Books: The Very First Christmas, 1998; The Very First Easter, 2000; The Very First Christians, 2001. Contributions: many professional journals. *Honours:* Alumni Award for Teaching Excellence, 1974, Distinguished Faculty Scholar, 1981, Western Michigan University; Outstanding Educator in America, 1974–75; Prof. of the Year, Council for the Advancement and Support of Education, 1984; Citation, Michigan Acad. of Sciences, Arts and Letters, 1985; Gold Medallion Book Award, ECPA, 1989, 1999; Christus in Mundo Award, Concordia University, 2001. *Address:* c/o Dept of History, Western Michigan University, Kalamazoo, MI 49008, USA.

MAILER, Norman (Kingsley); Writer; b. 31 Jan. 1923, Long Beach, CA, USA; m. 1st Beatrice Silverman 1944 (divorced 1951); one d.; m. 2nd Adele Morales 1954 (divorced 1962); two d.; m. 3rd Lady Jeanne Campbell 1962 (divorced 1963); one d.; m. 4th Beverly Rentz Bentley 1963 (divorced 1980); two s. one d.; m. 5th Carol Stevens (divorced); one d.; m. 6th Norris Church 1980; one s. *Education:* BS, Harvard University. *Career:* mem. PEN, pres., 1984–86; American Acad. of Arts and Letters. *Publications:* The Naked and the Dead, 1948; Barbary Shore, 1951; The Deer Park, 1955 (dramatised 1967); Advertisements for Myself, 1959; Deaths for the Ladies (poems), 1962; The Presidential Papers, 1963; An American Dream, 1964; Cannibals and Christians, 1966; Why are We in Vietnam?, 1967; The Armies of the Night, 1968; Miami and the Siege of Chicago, 1968; Moonshot, 1969; A Fire on the Moon, 1970; The Prisoner of Sex, 1971; Existential Errands, 1972; St George and the Godfather, 1972; Marilyn, 1973; The Faith of Graffiti, 1974; The Fight, 1975; Some Honourable Men, 1976; Genius and Lust: A Journey Through the Writings of Henry Miller, 1976; A Transit to Narcissus, 1978; The Executioner's Song, 1979; Of Women and Their Elegance, 1980; The Essential Mailer, 1982; Pieces and Pontifications, 1982; Ancient Evenings, 1983; Tough Guys Don't Dance, 1983; Harlot's Ghost, 1991; How the Wimp Won the War, 1991; Oswald's Tale, 1995; Portrait of Picasso as a Young Man, 1995; The Gospel According to the Son, 1997; The Time of Our Time, 1998; The Spooky Art, 2003. Contributions: numerous journals and magazines. *Honours:* National Book Award for Arts and Letters, 1969; Pulitzer Prize for Non-Fiction, 1969; Award for Outstanding Service to the Arts, McDowell Colony, 1973. *Address:* c/o Rembar, 19th W 44th St, New York, NY 10036, USA.

MAILLARD, Keith; Canadian writer, poet and academic; b. 28 Feb. 1942, Wheeling, WV, USA; m.; two d. *Education:* West Virginia Univ.; Vancouver Community College. *Career:* Instructor, 1980–89, Asst Prof., 1989–94, Assoc. Prof. of Creative Writing, 1994–, Univ. of British Columbia; mem. Federation of British Columbia Writers. *Publications:* Novels: Two Strand River, 1976; Alex Driving South, 1980; The Knife in My Hands, 1981; Cutting Through, 1982; Motet, 1989; Light in the Company of Women, 1993; Hazard Zones, 1995; Gloria, 1999; The Clarinet Polka, 2003. Poetry: Dementia Americana, 1994. Contributions: newspapers, reviews and journals; Expansive Poetry (anthology). *Honours:* Ethel Wilson Fiction Prize, 1990; Gerald Lampert Prize for Best First Book of Poetry, League of Canadian Poets, 1995. *Address:* c/o UBC Creative Writing Program, Buchanan Room E462, 1866 Main Mall, University of British Columbia, Vancouver, BC V6T 1Z1, Canada. *E-mail:* maillard@interchange.ubc.ca.

MAILLET, Antonine; Author and Dramatist; b. 10 May 1929, Bouctouche, NB, Canada. *Education:* Collège de Notre-Dame d'Acadie, Moncton, 1950; MA, University of Moncton, 1959; Licence es Lettres, University of Montréal, 1962; Doctorat ès Lettres, Université Laval, 1970. *Career:* Teacher, University of Moncton, 1965–67, Collège des Jesuites, Québec, 1968–69, Université Laval, 1971–74, University of Montréal, 1974–75; Visiting Prof., University of California at Berkeley, 1983, SUNY at Albany, 1985; mem.

Académie canadienne-française; Asscn des Écrivains de Langue Française; PEN; Queen's Privy Council for Canada; Royal Society of Canada; Société des Gens de Lettres de France. *Publications:* Pointe-aux-Coques, 1958; On a mangé la dune, 1962; La Sagouine, 1971; Don l'Original, 1972, English trans. as The Tale of Don l'Original, 1978; Par derrière chez mon père, 1972; Mariaagélas, 1973; Emmanuel a Joseph a Davit, 1975; La Cordes-de-bois, 1977; Pélagie-la-Charrette, 1979, English trans. as Pélagie: The Return to a Homeland, 1982; Cent ans dans les bois, 1981; La Gribouille, 1982; Crache-a-Pic, 1984, English trans. as The Devil is Loose, 1986; Le huitième jour, 1986, English trans. as On the Eighth Day, 1989; L'Oursiade, 1990; Les Confessions de Jeanne de Valois, 1992; Le Foire de la Saint-Barthélmy, trans. from Ben Jonson, 1994; L'Ile-sux-Puces, 1996; Le Chemin St-Jacques (novel), 1996; Chronique d'une sorcière de vent (novel), 1999; Madame Perfecta, 2001. Other: many plays. *Honours:* Governor-General's Award for Fiction, 1972; Prix France-Canada, 1975; Prix Goncourt, France, 1979; Officer des Palmes académiques françaises, 1980; Companion of the Order of Canada, 1982; Officer des Arts et des Lettres de France, 1985; Officer, Ordre nat. du Québec, 1990; Commdr, Ordre du mérite culturel de Monaco, 1993; several hon. doctorates. *Address:* 735 Antonine Maillet Ave, Montréal, QC H2V 2Y4, Canada.

MAINE, David (see Avice, Claude (Pierre Marie)).

MAIR, (Alexander) Craig, BA; educator and writer; b. 3 May 1948, Glasgow, Scotland; m. Anne Olizar 1970; two s. one d. *Education:* Stirling Univ. *Career:* mem. Scottish Society of Antiquaries, fellow; Educational Institute of Scotland; various local history groups. *Publications:* A Time in Turkey, 1973; A Star for Seamen, 1978; The Lighthouse Boy, 1981; Britain at War 1914–18, 1982; Mercat Cross and Tolbooth, 1988; David Angus, 1989; Stirling, The Royal Burgh, 1990; The Incorporation of Glasgow Maltmen: A History, 1990.

MAIRS, Nancy Pedrick, AB, MFA, PhD; writer; b. 23 July 1943, Long Beach, CA, USA; m. George Anthony Mairs 1963; one s. one d. *Education:* Wheaton College, Massachusetts, University of Arizona. *Career:* mem. Authors' Guild; Poets and Writers; National Women's Studies Asscn. *Publications:* Instead it is Winter, 1977; In All the Rooms of the Yellow House, 1984; Plaintext, 1986; Remembering the Bone House, 1989; Carnal Acts, 1990; Ordinary Time, 1993; Voice Lessons, 1994; Waist High in the World, 1996; A Troubled Guest, 2001. Contributions: American Voice; MSS; Tri Quarterly. *Honours:* Western States Book Award, 1984; National Endowment for the Arts Fellowship, 1991. *Address:* 579 S Third Avenue, Tucson, AZ 85701, USA. *Website:* www.nancymairs.com.

MAJA-PEARCE, Adewale; Researcher, Consultant, Writer and Poet; b. 3 June 1953, London, England. *Education:* BA, University of Wales, Swansea, 1975; MA, School of Oriental and African Studies, London, 1986. *Career:* Researcher, Index on Censorship, London, 1986–; Consultant, Heinemann International, Oxford, 1986–94; mem. PEN; Society of Authors. *Publications:* Christopher Okigbo: Collected Poems (ed.), 1986; In My Father's Country: A Nigerian Journey (non-fiction), 1987; Loyalties (short stories), 1987; How Many Miles to Babylon? (non-fiction), 1990; The Heinemann Book of African Poetry in English (ed.), 1990; Who's Afraid of Wole Soyinka?: Essays on Censorship, 1991; A Mask Dancing: Nigerian Novelists of the Eighties, 1992. Contributions: various periodicals. *Address:* 33 St George's Rd, Hastings, East Sussex TN34 3NH, England.

MAJOR, André; Writer and Poet; b. 22 April 1942, Montréal, QC, Canada; m. Ginette Lepage, June 1970, one s. one d. *Education:* Collège de Montréal; Collège des Eudistes. *Publications:* Fiction: Nouvelles, 1963; Le Cabochon, 1964; La chair de poule, 1965; Le Vent du diable, 1968; L'Épouvantail, 1974, English trans. as The Scarecrows of Saint-Emmanuel, 1977; L'Épidéme, 1975, English trans. as Inspector Therrien, 1980; Les Rescapés, 1976, English trans. as Man on the Run, 1984; La folle d'Elvis, English trans. as Hooked on Elvis, 1983; L'hiver au coeur, 1987, English trans. as The Winter of the Heart, 1989; La vie provisoire, 1995, English trans. as A Provisional Life, 1997. Poetry: Le froid se meurt, 1961; Holocauste à 2 voix, 1961; Poèmes pour durer, 1969. Other: Journal: Le Sourire d'Anton ou l'adieu au roman (1975–92), 2001. *Honours:* Gov.-Gen.'s Literary Award, 1977; Prix Canada-Communauté française de Belgique, 1991; Prix Études françaises, 2001. *Address:* 10595 Rue Tanguay, Montréal, QC H3L 3G9, Canada.

MAJOR, Clarence; poet, writer, artist and academic; b. 31 Dec. 1936, Atlanta, GA, USA; m. 1st Joyce Sparrow 1958 (divorced 1964); m. 2nd Pamela Ritter. *Education:* BS, SUNY at Albany, 1976; PhD, Union Graduate School, 1978. *Career:* Ed., Coercion Review, 1958–66, Writer-in-Residence, Center for Urban Education, New York, 1967–68, Teachers and Writers Collaborative-Teachers College, Columbia University, 1967–71, Aurora College, IL, 1974, Albany State College, GA, 1984, Clayton College, Denver, 1986, 1987; Assoc. Ed., Caw, 1967–70, Journal of Black Poetry, 1967–70; Lecturer, Brooklyn College, CUNY, 1968–69, 1973, 1974–75, Cazenovia College, New York, 1969, Wisconsin State University, 1969, Queens College, CUNY, 1972, 1973, 1975, Sarah Lawrence College, 1972–75, School of Continuing Education, New York University, 1975; Columnist, 1973–76, Contributing Ed., 1976–86, American Poetry Review; Asst Prof., Howard University, 1974–76, University of Washington, 1976–77; Visiting Asst Prof., University of Maryland at College Park, 1976, SUNY at Buffalo, 1976; Assoc. Prof., 1977–81, Prof., 1981–89, University of Colorado at Boulder; Ed., 1977–78, Assoc. Ed., 1978–, American Book Review; Prof., 1989–, Dir, Creative Writing, 1991–, University of California at Davis. *Publications:* Poetry: The Fires That Burn in Heaven, 1954; Love Poems of a Black Man, 1965; Human Juices, 1965; Swallow the Lake, 1970; Symptons and Madness, 1971; Private Line, 1971; The Cotton Club: New Poems, 1972; The Syncopated Cakewalk, 1974; Inside Diameter: The France Poems, 1985; Surfaces and Masks, 1988; Some Observations of a Stranger in the Latter Part of the Century, 1989; Parking Lots, 1992; Configurations: New and Selected Poems 1958–1998, 1998; Waiting for Sweet Betty, 2002. Fiction: All-Night Visitors, 1969; NO, 1973; Reflex and Bone Structure, 1975; Emergency Exit, 1979; My Amputations, 1986; Such Was the Season, 1987; Painted Turtle: Woman with Guitar, 1988; Fun and Games, 1990; Dirty Bird Blues, 1996. Non-Fiction: Come By Here: My Mother's Life, 2002. Other: Dictionary of Afro-American Slang, 1970; The Dark and Feeling: Black American Writers and Their Work, 1974; Juba to Jive: A Dictionary of African-American Slang, 1994; Necessary Distance, 2001. Editor: Writers Workshop Anthology, 1967; Man is Like a Child: An Anthology of Creative Writing by Students, 1968; The New Black Poetry, 1969; Calling the Wind: Twentieth Century African-American Short Stories, 1993; The Garden Thrives: Twentieth Century African-American Poetry, 1995. *Honours:* Fulbright-Hays Exchange Award, 1981–83; Western States Book Award, 1986; Pushcart Prize, 1989. *Address:* c/o Dept of English, University of California at Davis, Davis, CA 95616, USA.

MAJOR, Devorah; American poet, novelist, performer, lecturer and editor; b. San Francisco, CA. *Career:* poet-in-residence, San Francisco Fine Arts Museum; Mediator, California Lawyer for the Arts; Poet Laureate of San Francisco; composer (with Guillermo Galindo), Trade Routes 2005. *Publications:* novels: An Open Weave 1995, Brown Glass Windows 2002; poetry: Travelling Women (with Opal Palmer Adisa) 1989, Street Smarts 1996; other: Where River Meets Ocean 2003, With More Than Tongue 2003. *Honours:* inducted into San Francisco State Univ. Hall of Fame ; PEN Oakland/Josephine Miles Award, First Novelist Award from American Library Asscn Black Caucus. *Address:* c/o Curbstone Press, 321 Jackson Street, Willimantic, CT 06226-1738, USA. *E-mail:* info@curbstone.org. *Website:* www.curbstone.org.

MAJOR, Kevin (Gerald); Writer; b. 12 Sept. 1949, Stephenville, NF, Canada; m. Anne Crawford, 3 July 1982, two s. *Education:* BSc, Memorial University, St John's, NF, 1972. *Career:* mem. Writers' Union of Canada. *Publications:* Far from Shore 1980, Thirty-Six Exposures 1984, Dear Bruce Springsteen 1987, Blood Red Ochre 1989, Eating Between the Lines 1991, Diana: My Autobiography 1993, No Man's Land 1995, Gaffer: A Novel of Newfoundland 1997, The House of Wooden Santas 1997, Eh? to Zed: A Canadian Abecedarium 2000, As Near to Heaven by Sea: A History of Newfoundland and Labrador 2001, Ann and Seamus 2003. *Honours:* Book of the Year Award, Canadian Asscn of Children's Librarians 1978, Canada Council Award for Children's Literature 1978, Canadian Young Adult Book Award 1980, Book of the Year Award for Children, Canadian Library Asscn 1991, Vicky Metcalf Award 1992, Mr Christie Award 1998. *Address:* 27 Poplar Ave, St John's, NF A1B 1C7, Canada.

MAKANIN, Vladimir Semenovich; Writer; b. 13 March 1937, Orsk, Orenburg Region, USSR. *Education:* Moscow Univ., Higher Workshop for Scenario Writers and Film Dirs. *Publications:* Straight Line, 1965; Air-Vent, Portrait and Around (novel), 1976; Story About an Old Settlement (short stories), 1974; Voices, 1982; River with a Fast Current, 1983; Where the Skies Meet the Hills, 1987; One and One, 1987; Subject of Averaging, 1992; The Loss: A Novella and Two Stories (Writings from an Unbound Europe); Baize-Covered Table with Decanter, 1993; Quasi, 1993; Captives, 1996; Escape Hatch and The Long Road Ahead: Two Novellas, 1998; Underground, or a Hero of Our Time, 1998; Letter 'A', 2000; A Good Love Story, 2000. *Honours:* Russian Booker Prize, 1993; Pushkin Prize, 1998; Penne Prize, Italy, 1999; Russian State Prize, 2000. *Address:* Novinski Blvd 16, Apt 14, 121069 Moscow, Russia. *Telephone:* (095) 291-92-53. *Fax:* (095) 781-01-82. *E-mail:* vmakanin@hotmail.com.

MAKINE, Andreï; writer; b. 1957, Siberia, Russia. *Career:* lives in Paris, France, writes in French. *Publications:* A Hero's Daughter (in trans.), Au Temps du Fleuve Amour (trans. as Once Upon the River Love) 1994, Le Testament Français (trans. as Dreams of My Russian Summers) (Prix Goncourt, Prix Médicis Étranger) 1995, The Crime of Olga Arbelina (in trans.) 1999, Requiem for a Lost Empire (in trans.) 2001, A Life's Music (in trans.) 2002. *Address:* c/o Arcade Publishing, 141 Fifth Avenue, Eighth Floor, New York, NY 10010, USA.

MALA'IKA, Nazik al-; Poet and Critic; b. 1922, Baghdad, Iraq; m. Abdel-Hadi Mahbouba 1961. *Education:* Higher Teachers' Training College, Baghdad; Fine Arts Institute; scholarship, Princeton Univ., NJ, USA; MA, Literature, Univ. of Wisconsin. *Career:* Lecturer, Arabic Dept, Education College, Baghdad, Univ. of Kuwait. *Publications:* A'shiqat Al-Layl, 1947; Shazaya wa ramad (Ashes and Shrapnel), 1949; Al-mar'a baina 'ltarafain, al-salbiyya wa 'l-akh-laq (essay, Woman Between Passivity and Positive Morality), 1953; Al-tajzi'iyya fi 'l-mujtama' al-Arabi (essay, Fragmentation in Arab Society), 1954; Qarárat al-mawya, 1958; Qadaya 'l-shi'r al-mu'asir (essays), 1962; Shaýarat al-qamar, 1968; Ma'sát al-hayát wa ugniya li-l-insán, 1970; Al-taýzi'iyya fi-l-muýtama' al-'arabi, 1974; Yugayyir alwána-hu l-bahr, 1977; Li-l-salat wa-l-tawra, 1978; Youghiyar Alouanah Al-Bahr, 1999.

MALLET-JONES, Françoise; French novelist; b. 6 July 1930, Antwerp, Belgium. *Education:* Bryn Mawr Coll., Pennsylvania, Sorbonne, University of Paris. *Career:* reader, Grasset Publishers 1965–. *Publications:* Into the Labyrinth, 1951; The Red Room, 1955; Cordelia and Other Stories, 1956; House of Lies, 1956; Café Celeste, 1958; The Favourite, 1961; Signs and Wonders, 1966; The Witches: Three Tales of Sorcery, 1968; The Underground Game, 1973; Allegra, 1976; Le Rire de Laura, 1985; La Tristesse du cerf-volant, 1988; Adriana Sposa, 1989; Divine, 1991. Other: French version of Shelagh Delaney's play A Taste of Honey, 1960; A Letter to Myself, 1964; The Paper House, 1970; Juliette Greco, 1975; Marie-Paule Belle, 1987. *Honours:* Ordre National du Mérite 1986.

MALLON, Maurus Edward; Teacher, Writer and Dramatist; b. 10 July 1932, Greenock, Scotland. *Education:* MA, University of Glasgow, 1956; BEd, University of Manitoba, Winnipeg, 1966. *Career:* mem. Living Authors' Society; National Writers' Asscn, USA; PEN, Canada. *Publications:* Basileus, 1971; The Opal, 1973; Pegaso, 1975; Way of the Magus, 1978; Anogia, 1980; Bammer McPhie, 1984; Treasure Mountain, 1986; Postcards, 1991; Ex Novo Mundo (short stories), 1992; Compendulum, 1993; A Matter of Conscience (play), 1994. *Address:* Box 331, Deep River, Ontario K0J 1P0, Canada.

MALLON, Thomas, MA, PhD; American writer and academic; b. 2 Nov. 1951. *Education:* Brown Univ., Harvard Univ. *Career:* fmr Literary Ed., GQ; fmr Prof. of English, Vassar Coll.; Visiting Scholar, St Edmund's Coll., Cambridge, England. *Publications:* Edmund Blunden 1983, A Book of One's Own: People and Their Diaries 1984, Arts and Sciences: A Seventies Seduction 1988, Stolen Words: Forays into the Origins and Ravages of Plagarism 1989, Aurora 7 1991, Rockets and Rodeos and Other American Spectacles 1993, Henry and Clara 1994, Dewey Defeats Truman 1997, Two Moons 2001, Bandbox 2004; contrib. to GQ, Harper's, The New Yorker, American Scholar, Yale Review Architectural Digest, New York Times Book Review, The Washington Post Book World. *Honours:* Rockefeller Fellowship 1986; Ingram Merrill Award 1994. *Address:* c/o Pantheon, Random House Inc, 1745 Broadway, New York, NY 10019, USA. *Website:* www.randomhouse.com.

MALOUF, (George Joseph) David; poet and novelist; b. 20 March 1934, Brisbane, Qld, Australia. *Education:* BA, University of Queensland, 1954. *Career:* Asst Lecturer in English, University of Queensland, 1955–57; Supply Teacher, London, 1959–61; Teacher of Latin and English, Holland Park Comprehensive, 1962; Teacher, St Anselm's Grammar School, 1962–68; Senior Tutor and Lecturer in English, University of Sydney, 1968–77. *Publications:* Poetry: Bicycle and Other Poems, 1970; Neighbours in a Thicket: Poems, 1974; Poems, 1975–1976, 1976; Wild Lemons, 1980; First Things Last, 1981; Selected Poems, 1981; Selected Poems, 1959–1989, 1994. Fiction: Johnno (novel), 1975; An Imaginary Life (novel), 1978; Child's Play (novella), 1981; The Bread of Time to Come (novella), 1981, republished as Fly Away Peter, 1982; Eustace (short story), 1982; The Prowler (short story), 1982; Harland's Half Acre (novel), 1984; Antipodes (short stories), 1985; The Great World (novel), 1990; Remembering Babylon (novel), 1993: The Conversations at Curlow Creek (novel), 1996; Dream Stuff (short stories), 2000. Play: Blood Relations, 1988. Opera Libretti: Voss, 1986; Mer de Glace; Baa Baa Black Sheep, 1993. Memoir: Twelve Edmondstone Street, 1985. Editor: We Took Their Orders and Are Dead: An Anti-War Anthology, 1971; Gesture of a Hand (anthology), 1975. Contributions: Four Poets: David Malouf, Don Maynard, Judith Green, Rodney Hall, 1962; Australian; New York Review of Books; Poetry Australia; Southerly; Sydney Morning Herald. *Honours:* Grace Leven Prize for Poetry, 1974; Gold Medals, Australian Literature Society, 1975, 1982; Australian Council Fellowship, 1978; New South Wales Premier's Award for Fiction, 1979; Victorian Premier's Award for Fiction, 1985; New South Wales Premier's Award for Drama, 1987; Commonwealth Writer's Prize, 1991; Miles Franklin Award, 1991; Prix Femina Étranger, 1991; Inaugural International IMPAC Dublin Literary Award, 1996; Newstadt Laureat, 2000. *Address:* 53 Myrtle Street, Chippendale, NSW 2008, Australia.

MALZBERG, Barry, (Mike Barry, Francine de Natale, Claudine Dumas, Mel Johnson, Lew W. Mason, K. M. O'Donnell, Gerrold Watkins); Writer; b. 24 July 1939, New York, NY, USA. *Education:* AB, 1960, Graduate Studies, 1964–65, Syracuse University. *Publications:* Author or ed. of over 30 books under various pseudonyns. *Address:* Box 61, Teaneck, NJ 07666, USA.

MAMONOVA, Tatyana; Russian author, academic, poet and activist. *Career:* literary journalist, critic for Aurora Publications; post-doctoral fellow at the Bunting Inst. at Harvard Univ.; founder, Woman & Russia 1979 (now Woman & Earth and Woman & Earth Almanac). *Publications:* non-fiction: Women and Russia 1984, Russian Women's Studies: Essays on Sexism in Soviet Culture 1989, Women's Glasnost versus Glasnost: Stopping Russian Backlash 1994. *Honours:* Diamond Homer Trophy for Famous Poet 1998, Living Legacy Award by Int. Women's Centre of San Diego 2002. *Address:* Woman & Earth, 467 Central Park W, Suite 7F, New York, NY 10025, USA. *Telephone:* (212) 866-8130. *Website:* www.dorsai.org/~womearth.

MAMET, David (Alan); Dramatist, Dir and Writer; b. 30 Nov. 1947, Chicago, IL, USA; m. 1st Lindsay Crouse Dec. 1977 (divorced); m. 2nd Rebecca Pidgeon 22 Sept. 1991. *Education:* BA, Goddard College, Plainfield, Vermont, 1969. *Career:* Artist-in-Residence, Goddard College, 1971–73; Artistic Dir, St Nicholas Theatre Co, Chicago, 1973–75; Guest Lecturer, University of Chicago, 1975, 1979, New York University, 1981; Assoc. Artistic Dir, Goodman Theater, Chicago, 1978; Assoc. Prof. of Film, Columbia University, 1988; Chair. of the Board, Atlantic Theater Co. *Publications:* Plays: The Duck Variations, 1971; Sexual Perversity in Chicago, 1973; Reunion, 1973; Squirrels, 1974; American Buffalo, 1976; A Life in the Theatre, 1976; The Water Engine, 1976; The Woods, 1977; Lone Canoe, 1978; Praire du Chien, 1978; Lakeboat, 1980; Donny March, 1981; Edmond, 1982; The Disappearance of the Jews, 1983; Glengarry Glen Ross, 1984; The Shawl, 1985; Speed-the-Plow, 1987; Bobby Gould in Hell, 1989; The Old Neighborhood, 1991; Oleanna, 1992; The Cryptogram, 1994; Death Defying Acts, 1995; Boston Marriage, 1999. Screenplays: The Postman Always Rings Twice, 1979; The Verdict, 1980; The Untouchables, 1986; House of Games, 1986; Things Change (with Shel Silverstein), 1987; We're No Angels, 1987; Homicide, 1991; Hoffa, 1991; Oleanna, 1994; The Edge, 1997; Wag the Dog, 1997; Spanish Prisoner, 1998; The Winslow Boy, 1999; State and Main, 2001. Fiction: The Village, 1994; The Old Religion, 1997. Poetry: The Hero Pony, 1990. Essays: Writing in Restaurants, 1986; Some Freaks, 1989; On Directing Film, 1990; The Cabin, 1992; True and False: Heresy and Common Sense for the Actor, 1997. *Honours:* CBS Creative Writing Fellowship, Yale University Drama School, 1976–77; Obie Awards, 1976, 1983; New York Drama Critics Circle Awards, 1976, 1987; Rockefeller Foundation Grant, 1977; Outer Critics Circle Award, 1978; Pulitzer Prize for Drama, 1987. *Literary Agent:* Rosenstone/Wender Agency, 38 E 29th St, 10th Floor, New York, NY 10016, USA.

MAMLEYEV, Yuri; writer, playwright, poet and philosopher; b. 11 Dec. 1931, Moscow, Russia; m. Farida Mamleyev 1973. *Education:* Forestry Inst., Moscow. *Career:* mem. French PEN Centre, Russian PEN Centre, Russian Union of Writers, Russian Union of Playwrights. *Publications:* The Sky Above Hell 1980, Iznanka Gogena 1982, Chatouny 1986, Zhivaja Smert 1986, Derniere Comedie 1988, Golos iz Nichto 1990, Utopi Moyu Golovu 1990, Vechnyi dom 1991, Der Murder aus dem Nichts 1992, Izbzannoe 1993, Die Letzte Komödie 1994, Shatuny 1996, Union Mistice 1997, Chernoe zerkalo 1998, J. M. Chatouny 1998, Der Tod des Erotomanen 1999, Moskovski Gambit 1999, Bluzhdajusheje Vremia 2001, Chernoe zerkalo 2001, Bunt luny 2001, Mir i khokhot 2003; contrib. to periodicals. *Honours:* Int. Pushkin Award of Alfred Töpfer, Hamburg, Germany 2000, Andrei Belyi Prize 2001. *Address:* 142 rue Legendre, 75017 Paris, France; Apt 132, Michuzinski Prospect 37, Poccus Mockba, Moscow 117607, Russia.

MANA, Samira Al; Writer and Ed.; b. 25 Dec. 1935, Basra, Iraq; m. Salah Niazi, July 1959, two d. *Education:* BA, University of Baghdad, 1958; Postgraduate Diploma in Librarianship, Ealing Technical College, 1976. *Career:* Asst Ed., Alightrab Al-Adabi (Literature of the Exiled), 1985–; mem. PEN Club. *Publications:* The Forerunners and the Newcomers, 1972; The Song, 1976; A London Sequel, 1979; Only a Half, 1979; The Umbilical Cord, 1990; The Oppressers (novel), 1997; The Soul and Other Stories, 1999; Look at Me... Look at Me (novel), 2002. Contributions: Alightrab Al-Adabi; many short stories in Arabic magazines; Trans in Dutch and English periodicals. *Address:* 46 Tudor Dr., Kingston-Upon-Thames, Surrey KT2 5PZ, England. *E-mail:* almananiazi@supanet.com. *Website:* alightirab.cjb.net.

MANCHESTER, Rt Rev Seán; author and Catholic prelate; b. 15 July 1944, Nottingham, England. *Education:* Doctor of Pastoral Ministry, St David's College, 1990; ordained priest 15 July 1990, consecrated Bishop 4 Oct. 1991. *Career:* Pres. Vampire Research Society 1970; Founder and Superior General Ordo Sancti Graal 1973; Exec. Dir Holy Grail Outreach Ministry to those in Cults and the Occult 1988; Chair. Society of St George 1990; Primate Ecclesia Apostolica Jesu Christi 1991; Bishop of Glastonbury 1993; Presiding Bishop, British Old Catholic Church 2000; Founder and Presiding Bishop Sacerdotal Soc. of the Precious Blood 2002; mem. Pax Christi; Patron Guardians Against Satanic Pollution 1990. *Publications:* From Satan to Christ: A Story of Salvation 1988, The Highgate Vampire: The Infernal World of the Undead Unearthed at London's Highgate Cemetery 1991, Mad, Bad and Dangerous to Know: The Life of Lady Caroline Lamb 1992, The Grail Church: Its Ancient Tradition and Renewed Flowering 1995, The Vampire Hunter's Handbook: A Concise Vampirological Guide 1997, Carmel: A Vampire Tale 2000, Stray Ghosts: A Fragment of a Memoir 2003. *Honours:* Companion, Order of the Sangreal, Companion, Holy Order of St Michael and St George, Knight Commander, Order of St George. *Address:* 5 John Street, Penmachno, Betwys-y-Coed, Gwynedd LL24 0UH, N Wales. *E-mail:* bishopmanchester@holygrail-church.fsnet.co.uk.

MANDELA, Nelson Rolihlahla; Politician and Lawyer; b. 18 July 1918, Umtata, Transkei, South Africa; m. 1st Evelyn Mandela 1944 (divorced 1957); four c. (two deceased); m. 2nd Winnie Mandela 1958 (divorced 1996); two d.; m. 3rd Graca Machel 18 July 1998. *Education:* University College, Fort Hare; Univ. of the Witwatersrand. *Career:* legal practice, Johannesburg 1952; Nat. organizer African Nat. Congress (ANC); on trial for treason 1956–61 (acquitted 1961); arrested 1962, sentenced to five years' imprisonment Nov. 1962; on trial for further charges 1963–64, sentenced to life imprisonment June 1964; released Feb. 1990; Deputy Pres. ANC 1990–91, Pres. 1991–97, mem. Nat. Exec. Cttee 1991–; Pres. of South Africa 1994–99; Chancellor Univ. of the North 1992–; Jt Pres. United World Colls. 1995–. *Publications:* No Easy Walk to Freedom, 1965; How Far We Slaves Have

Come: South Africa and Cuba in Today's World (with Fidel Castro), 1991; Nelson Mandela Speaks: Forging a Non-Racial Democratic South Africa, 1993; Long Walk to Freedom, 1994. *Honours:* Hon. LLD (Nat. Univ. of Lesotho) 1979, (City Coll. of City Univ. of New York) 1983, (Lancaster) 1984, (Strathclyde) 1985, (Calcutta) 1986, (Harare) 1987, (Kent) 1992, Hon. DLitt (Texas Southern Univ.) 1991; Dr hc (Complutense) 1991; Hon. DCL (Oxford) 1996, Cambridge (1996), Hon. LLD (London) 1996, Bristol (1996), (Nottingham) 1996, (Warwick) 1996, (De Montfort) 1996, (Glasgow Caledonian) 1996; Hon. Fellow Magdalene Coll., Cambridge 2001; Hon. Freeman of London; Jawaharlal Nehru Award (India) 1979, Bruno Kreisky Prize for Human Rights 1981, Freedom of City of Glasgow 1981, Hon. Citizen of Rome 1983, Simon Bolivar Int. Prize (UNESCO) 1983; Third World Prize 1985, Sakharov Prize 1988, Gaddafi Human Rights Prize 1989, Freeman of Dublin 1988, Bharat Ratna (India) 1990, Order of the Niger 1990, Jt winner Houphouët Prize (UNESCO) 1991, Nishan-e-Pakistan 1992, Premio Príncipe de Asturias 1992, Liberty Medal (USA) 1993; shared Nobel Prize for Peace 1993; Mandela-Fulbright Prize 1993; Hon. Bencher Lincoln's Inn 1994; Tun Abdul Razak Award 1994; Anne Frank Medal 1994, Int. Freedom Award 2000; Hon. QC 2000. *Address:* c/o ANC, 51 Plein St, Johannesburg 2001, South Africa. *E-mail:* info@anc.org.za.

MANDLER, Peter, BA, PhD; historian; b. 29 Jan. 1958, Boston, Massachusetts, USA; m. Ruth Ehrlich 1987; one s. one d. *Education:* Magdalen College, Oxford, Harvard University. *Career:* Asst Prof., Princeton University, 1984–91; Senior Lecturer, 1991–95, Reader, 1995–97, Prof., 1997–, London Guildhall University; mem. Royal Historical Society, hon. sec., 1998–. *Publications:* Aristocratic Government in the Age of Reform, 1990; The Uses of Charity (ed.), 1990; After the Victorians (co-ed.), 1994; The Fall and Rise of the Stately Home, 1997. Contributions: journals, magazines and newspapers.

MANEA, Norman; Author and Prof. of European Culture; b. 19 July 1936, Suceava, Romania; m. Josette-Cella Boiangiu, 28 June 1969. *Education:* MS, Institute of Construction, Faculty of Hydrotechnology, Bucharest, 1959. *Career:* International Acad. Fellow, 1989–92, Frances Flournoy Prof. of European Culture, 1992–, Bard College; numerous lectures. *Publications:* Fiction: Noaptea pe latura lunga, 1969; Captivi, 1970; Atrium, 1974; Primele porti, 1975; Cartea fiului, 1976; Zilele si jocul, 1977; Octombrie, ora opt, 1981, English trans. as October, Eight O'Clock, 1992; Plicul Negru, 1986, English trans. as The Black Envelope, 1995; Compulsory Happiness, 1993. Other: Anii de ucenicie ai lui August Prostul, 1979; Pe contur, 1984; On Clowns: The Dictator and the Artist, 1992; Casa melcului, 1999; The Hooligan's Return, 2003. Contributions: anthologies, periodicals and television. *Honours:* Literary Prize, Asscn of Bucharest Writers, 1979; Deutscher Akademischer Austauschdienst Grant, Berlin, 1987; Fulbright Scholarship, 1988; International Acad. for Scholarship and the Arts Fellowship, Bard College, 1989–92; Guggenheim Fellowship, 1992; John D. and Catherine T. MacArthur Foundation Fellowship, 1992; National Jewish Book Award, Jewish Book Council/Jewish Welfare Board, 1993; Literary Lion Award, New York Public Library, 1993; International Nomino Prize for Literature, 2001. *Address:* c/o Bard College, Annandale-on-Hudson, NY, 12504, USA.

MANES, Christopher; Writer; b. 24 May 1957, Chicago, IL, USA; one d. *Education:* BA, 1979, JD, 1992, University of California; MA, University of Wisconsin, 1981. *Career:* mem. California State Bar Asscn; Writers Guild. *Publications:* Place of the Wild, 1994; Post Modernism and Environmental Philosophy, 1994. Contributions: Reference works, books, journals and magazines. *Address:* 69853 Fatima Way, Cathedral City, CA 92234-2519, USA.

MANHIRE, William (Bill), BA, MPhil; New Zealand poet, writer and academic; b. 27 Dec. 1946, Invercargill; m. Barbara Marion McLeod 1970; one s. one d. *Education:* S Otago Dist High School, Otago Boys' High School, Univ. of Otago at Dunedin, Univ. Coll., London, UK. *Career:* Lecturer in English, Vic. Univ., Wellington 1973, f. influential creative writing programme 1976, Prof. of Creative Writing and English Literature 1997–; Dir Int. Inst. of Modern Letters 2001–; Fiction Ed. Victoria Univ. Press 1976–96; Fulbright Visiting Prof. in NZ Studies, Georgetown Univ., USA Jan.–June 1999; inaugural Te Mata Estate New Zealand Poet Laureate 1997–99; Nuffield Fellowship 1981. *Publications:* Malady 1970, The Elaboration 1972, Song Cycle 1975, How to Take Your Clothes Off at the Picnic 1977, Dawn/Water 1980, Good Looks 1982, Locating the Beloved and Other Stories 1983, Zoetropes: Poems 1972–82 1984, Maurice Gee 1986, The Brain of Katherine Mansfield 1988, The New Land: A Picture Book 1990, The Old Man's Example 1990, Milky Way Bar 1991, An Amazing Week in New Zealand 1993, Fault 1994, South Pacific 1994, Hoosh 1995, My Sunshine 1996, Songs of My Life 1996, Sheet Music: Poems 1967–1982 1996, Mutes and Earthquakes 1997, What to Call Your Child 1999, Doubtful Sounds: Essays and Interviews 2000, Collected Poems 2001, Collected Poems 2001, Under the Influence 2003; editor: New Zealand Listener Short Stories Vol.1 1977, Vol. 2 1978, Some Other Country: New Zealand's Best Short Stories (with Marion McLeod) 1984, Six by Six 1989, Soho Square 1991, 100 New Zealand Poems 1994, Denis Glover: Selected Poems 1995, Spectacular Babies (with Karen Anderson) 2001. *Honours:* NZ Book Award 1977, 1984, 1992, 1996; Montana Book Award 1994. *Address:* Creative Writing Programme, International Institute of Modern Letters, Victoria University of Wellington, PO Box 600, Wellington, New Zealand. *Telephone:* (4) 463-6808. *Fax:* (4) 463-6865 (Office). *E-mail:* bill.manhire@vuw.ac.nz (Office).

MANKELL, Henning; Swedish playwright and writer; b. 3 Feb. 1948, Stockholm; m. 3rd Eva Bergman 1998; four sons. *Career:* merchant seaman 1964–66; Dir Teatro Avenida, Maputo, Mozambique 1987–. *Plays include:* The Amusement Park 1068, Tale on the Beach of Time 1997. *Publications include:* fiction: The Stone-Blaster 1972, Fångvårdskolonin som försvann 1979, En seglares död 1981, Mördare utan ansikte 1991, Skyggerne 1995, Comédia infantil 1995, Ildspor 1996, Berättelse på tidens strand 1998, Pyramiden 1999; Kurt Wallander series: Mördare utan ansikte (Faceless Killers) 1991, Hundarna i Riga (The Dogs of Riga) 1992, Den vita lejoninnan (The White Lioness) 1993, Mannen som log 1994, Villospår (Sidetracked) 1995, Den femte kvinnan (The Fifth Woman) 1996, Steget efter (One Step Behind) 1997, Brandvägg (Firewall) 1998, Danslärarens återkomst (The Return of the Dancing Master) 1999, Innan Frosten (Before the Frost) 2002; juvenile: Secrets of the Fire 1995, Playing with Fire 2001; non-fiction: I Die, But the Memory Lives On: The World's Aids Crisis and the Memory Book Project 2004. *Honours:* Swedish Mystery Acad. Prize 1991, German Crime Prize 1999, Macallan CWA Golden Dagger Award 2001, Author of the Year, Germany 2002. *Address:* c/o The Harvill Press, Random House, 20 Vauxhall Bridge Road, London, SW1V 2SA, England. *Website:* www.harvill.com.

MANLOW, James; British poet and novelist; b. 1978, Hertfordshire, England. *Publications:* Attraction 2004. *Literary Agent:* c/o John Murray Ltd, 50 Albemarle Street, London, W1S 4BD, England. *Website:* www.johnmurray.co.uk.

MANN, Anthony Phillip; Writer and Theatre Dir; b. 7 Aug. 1942, North Allerton, Yorkshire, England. *Education:* BA, English and Drama, Manchester University, 1966; MA, Design and Directing, Humboldt State University, CA, 1969. *Career:* Trustee, New Zealand Players, 1992; mem. PEN, New Zealand; British Society of Dowsers; New Zealand Asscn for Drama in Education. *Publications:* Eye of the Queen, 1982; Master of Paxwax, 1986; Fall of the Families, 1987; Pioneers, 1988; Wulfsyarn – A Mosaic, 1990; A Land Fit For Heroes, Vol. 1, Into the Wild Wood, 1993, Vol. 2, Stand Alone Stan, 1994, Vol. 3, The Dragon Wakes, 1995, Vol. 4, The Burning Forest, 1996. Contributions: books. *Honours:* Personal Chair in Drama, Victoria University of Wellington, 1997. *Address:* 22 Bruce Ave, Brooklyn, Wellington, New Zealand.

MANN, Christopher Michael, (Zithulele); Poet, Writer and Dramatist; b. 6 April 1948, Port Elizabeth, South Africa; m. Julia Georgina Skeen 10 Dec. 1981, one s. one d. *Education:* BA, University of the Witwatersrand, 1969; MA, University of Oxford, 1973; MA, University of London, 1974. *Publications:* First Poems, 1977; A New Book of South African Verse (ed. with Guy Butler), 1979; New Shades, 1982; Kites, 1990; Mann Alive (video and book), 1992; South Africans: A Series of Portrait Poems, 1995; Heartlands: A Series of Place Poems, 2002. Plays: The Sand Labyrinth, 2001; Mahoon's Testimony, 1995; The Horn of Plenty: A Series of Painting-Poems, with Julia Skeen (artist), 1997; Frail Care: A Play in Verse, 1997; The Roman Centurion's Good Friday, Cathedral of St Michael and St George, 1999. Contributions: numerous journals and magazines. *Honours:* Newdigate Prize; Olive Schreiner Award; South African Performing Arts Council Playwright Award; Hon. DLitt, University of Durban-Westville, 1993. *Address:* 19 Frances St, Grahamstown, 6140, South Africa.

MANN, Emily Betsy, BA, MFA; American writer, theatre director and playwright; b. 12 April 1952, Boston, MA; m. Gary Mailman; one s. from previous m. *Education:* Harvard Univ., Univ. of Minn. *Career:* Resident Dir Guthrie Theatre, Minneapolis 1976–79; Dir Brooklyn Acad. of Music (BAM) Theatre Co., Brooklyn, NY 1980–81; freelance writer and dir, New York 1981–90; Artistic Dir McCarter Theatre, Princeton, NJ 1990–; mem. Soc. of Stage Dirs and Choreographers, Theatre Communications Group, New Dramatists, PEN, Writer's Guild; mem. Exec. Bd Dramatists' Guild. *Plays:* Annulla Allen: The Autobiography of a Survivor 1977, Still Life (six Obie Awards 1981, Fringe First Award 1985) 1982, Execution of Justice (Helen Hayes Award, Bay Area Theatre Critics Circle Award, HBO/USA Award, Playwriting Award Women's Cttee Dramatists Guild for Dramatizing Issues of Conscience) 1986, Having Our Say: The Delaney Sisters' First 100 Years (LA Nat. Asscn for the Advancement of Colored People – NAACP Award for Best Play) 1994, Greensboro: A Requiem 1996, Betsey Brown: A Rhythm and Blues Musical (musical, with Ntozake Shange). *Plays translated or adapted:* Nights and Days (Les nuits et les jours, Pierre Laville) 1985, Miss Julie 1992, The House of Bernarda Alba 1997, Meshugah 1998, Uncle Vanya 2003, The Tempest, The Cherry Orchard. *Screenplays:* Fanny Kelly 1981, You Strike a Woman, You Strike a Rock: The Story of Winnie Mandela 1988, The Greensboro Massacre 1992, Having Our Say (Christopher Award, Peabody Award) 1999. *Publication:* Testimony: 4 Plays by Emily Mann 1997, Political Stages (co-ed.) 2002. *Honours:* Alumnae Recognition Award, Harvard Univ. 1999; BUSH Fellowship 1975–76; Rosamond Gilder Award, New Drama Forum Asscn 1983; NEA Asscns Grant 1984; Tony Award for Outstanding Regional Theatre 1984; Guggenheim Fellowship 1985; McKnight Fellowship 1985; CAPS Award 1985; NEA Playwrights Fellowship 1986; Women of Achievement Award, Brandeis Univ. 1995; Woman of Achievement Award, Douglass Coll. of NJ 1996;

Outstanding Achievement in the Theatre, Rosamond Gilder Award 1999. *Address:* McCarter Theatre, 91 University Place, Princeton, NJ 08540-5121, USA. *E-mail:* emann@mccarter.org. *Website:* www.mccarter.org.

MANNING, Ned; Australian playwright and actor. *Television appearances:* Young Ramsay 1980, Prisoner: Cell Block H 1981, A Country Practice 1990, The Brides of Christ 1991, Heartbreak High 1994. *Plays as writer:* Us or Them 1984, Close to the Bone 1994, Kingaroy (with Martin Buzacott) 1996, Luck of the Draw 2000. *Address:* c/o Currency Press Pty Ltd, PO Box 2287, Strawberry Hills, NSW 2012, Australia. *E-mail:* enquiries@currency.com.au. *Website:* www.currency.com.au.

MANNING, Paul; Author; b. 22 Nov. 1912, Pasadena, CA, USA; m. Louise Margaret Windels, 22 March 1947, four s. *Education:* Occidental College, Los Angeles. *Career:* Ed., Time-Life, New York City, 1937–38, Everyweek, 1939; Chief European Correspondent in London, Newspaper Enterprise Asscn and Scripps Howard Newspaper Group, 1939–42; Joined Edward R. Murrow as CBS News Commentator from London, England, 1942; Only journalist to witness and broadcast both German surrender ceremonies, Reims, France, and Japanese surrender aboard USS Missouri, Tokyo Bay; mem. Eighth Air Force Historical Society. *Publications:* Mr England: Biography of Winston Churchill, 1941; Martin Bormann: Nazi in Exile, 1986; Hirohito: The War Years, 1986; The Silent War: KGB Against the West, 1987; Years of War, 1988. Contributions: New York Times; Reader's Digest; Saturday Evening Post; Articles to numerous journals including 8th Air Force News. *Honours:* Special Citations, Secretary of War Robert Patterson and Secretary of Navy James Forrestal.

MANNING, Phillip; Science Writer; b. 8 July 1936, Atlanta, GA, USA; m. Diane Karraker, 26 Nov. 1960, one s. one d. *Education:* BS, The Citadel, 1958; PhD, University of North Carolina at Chapel Hill, 1963. *Career:* mem. National Asscn of Science Writers. *Publications:* Afoot in the South, 1993; Palmetto Journal, 1995; Orange Blossom Trails, 1997; Islands of Hope, 1999. Contributions: Over 100 articles published in Backpacker, Field & Stream. *Honours:* National Outdoor Book Award, 1999. *Address:* 315 E Rosemary St, Chapel Hill, NC 27514, USA.

MANNING, Robert Joseph; American journalist; b. 25 Dec. 1919, Binghamton, NY; m. 1st Margaret Marinda Raymond 1944 (died 1984); three s.; m. 2nd Theresa Slomkowski 1987. *Career:* US Army service 1942–43; Nieman Fellow, Harvard Univ. 1945–46; State Dept and White House Corresp. United Press. 1944–46, Chief UN Corresp. United Press. 1946–49; Writer, Time magazine 1949–55, Senior Ed. 1955–58, Chief, London Bureau, Time, Life, Fortune, Sports Illustrated magazines 1958–61; Sunday Ed., New York Herald Tribune 1961–62; Asst Sec. of State for Public Affairs, US Dept of State 1962–64; Exec. Ed. Atlantic Monthly 1964–66, Ed.-in-Chief 1966–80; Vice-Pres. Atlantic Monthly Co. 1966–80; Ed.-in-Chief Boston Publishing Co. 1981–87; Pres., Ed.-in-Chief Bobcat Books Inc., Boston 1987–; Fellow, Kennedy Inst. of Politics, Harvard Univ. 1980; mem. AAAS. *Publications include:* Who We Are 1976, The Swamp Root Chronicle 1992, The Vietnam Experience (25 vols). *Address:* 1200 Washington Street, Apt 507, Boston, MA 02118, USA (Office and Home). *E-mail:* bobcat1225@rcn.com (Office).

MANOR, Jason (see Hall, Oakley Maxwell).

MANSEL, Philip Robert Rhys; Writer; b. 19 Oct. 1951, London, England. *Education:* MA, Balliol College, Oxford, 1974; PhD, University College London, 1978. *Career:* Ed., The Court Historian, Newsletter of the Society for Court Studies, 1995; mem. Society for Court Studies. *Publications:* Louis XVIII 1981, Pillars of Monarchy 1984, Sultans in Splendour: The Last Years of the Ottoman World 1988, The Court of France 1789–1830 1989, Charles Joseph de Ligne 1992, Constantinople 1995, The French Emigrés in Europe 1789–1814 1999, Paris Between Empires 1814–1852 2001; Prince of Europe: The Life of Charles-Joseph de Ligne 1735–1814 2003. Contributions: Apollo, History Today, International Herald Tribune, Spectator, Times Literary Supplement. *Address:* 13 Prince of Wales Terrace, London W8 5PG, England.

MANSELL, Chris; Poet and Writer; b. 1 March 1953, Sydney, NSW, Australia; m. Steven G. Sturgess Dec. 1986; one s. one d. *Education:* BEc, Univ. of Sydney. *Career:* Residencies incl.: Curtin Univ., 1985, Univ. of Southern Queensland, 1990, K. S. Prichard Centre, 1992, Bundanon, 1996; Lecturer, Univ. of Wollongong, 1987–89, Univ. of Western Sydney, 1989–91; mem. Australian Society of Authors; Poets Union. *Publications:* Delta, 1978; Head, Heart and Stone, 1982; Redshift/Blueshift, 1988; Shining Like a Jinx, 1992; Day Easy Sunlight Fine, 1995; Fickle Brat, 2002; Stalking the Rainbow, 2002. Contributions: many reviews, quarterlies and magazines. *Honours:* Amelia Chapbook Award, 1987; Queensland Premier's Prize for Poetry, 1993. *Literary Agent:* Rachel Skinner, Raftos Management. *Address:* PO Box 94, Berry, NSW 2535, Australia. *E-mail:* writerslink@ozemail.com.au. *Website:* www.chris.mansell.name.

MANSER, Martin Hugh; Reference Book Ed.; b. 11 Jan. 1952, Bromley, England; m. Yusandra Tun 1979; one s. one d. *Education:* BA, Univ. of York, 1974; MPhil, C.N.A.A., 1977. *Publications:* Concise Book of Bible Quotations, 1982; A Dictionary of Everyday Idioms, 1983; Listening to God, 1984; Pocket Thesaurus of English Words, 1984; Children's Dictionary, 1984; Macmillan Student's Dictionary, 1985; Penguin Wordmaster Dictionary, 1987; Guinness Book of Words, 1988; Dictionary of Eponyms, 1988; Visual Dictionary, Bloomsbury Good Word Guide, 1988; Printing and Publishing Terms, 1988; Marketing Terms, 1988; Guinness Book of Words, 1988; Bible Promises: Outlines for Christian Living, 1989; Oxford Learner's Pocket Dictionary; Get To the Roots: A Dictionary of Words and Phrase Origins, 1992; The Lion Book of Bible Quotations, 1992; Oxford Learner's Pocket Dictionary with Illustrations, 1992; Guide to Better English, 1994; Chambers Compact Thesaurus, 1994; Bloomsbury Key to English Usage, 1994; Collins Gem Daily Guidance, 1995; NIV Thematic Study Bible, 1996; Chambers English Thesaurus, 1997; Dictionary of Bible Themes, 1997; NIV Shorter Concordance, 1997; Guide to English Grammar, 1998; Crash Course in Christian Teaching, 1998; Dictionary of the Bible, 1998; Christian Prayer, 1998; Bible Stories, 1999; Millennium Quiz Book (ed.), 1999; I Never Knew That Was in the Bible, 1999; Pub Quiz Book, 1999; Trivia Quiz Book, 1999; Children's Dictionary, 1999; Lion Bible Quotation Collection, 1999; New Penguin English Thesaurus (joint ed.), 2000; The Westminster Collection of Christian Quotations (compiler), 2001; Heinemann English Dictionary (man. ed.), fifth edn, 2001; NIV Comprehensive Concordance (consultant ed.), 2001; Writer's Manual (joint ed.), 2002; Dictionary of Foreign Words and Phrases, 2002; Dictionary of Proverbs, 2002; Eagle Handbook of Bible Prayers (joint ed.), 2002; Holy Bible: NRSV Cross-Reference Edition (man. ed.), 2003. *Address:* 102 Northern Rd, Aylesbury, Bucks HP19 9QY, England.

MANSFIELD, Sir Peter, Kt, BSc, PhD, FRS; British professor of physics; *Professor Emeritus in Residence, University of Nottingham*; b. 9 Oct. 1933, London; m. Jean M. Kibble 1962; two d. *Education:* William Penn School, Peckham and Queen Mary Coll., London, Univ. of London. *Career:* Research Assoc. Dept of Physics, Univ. of Ill. 1962; lecturer, Univ. of Nottingham 1964, Sr Lecturer 1967, Reader 1970, Prof. of Physics 1979–94, Prof. Emer. in Residence 1995–; MRC Professorial Fellow 1983–88; Sr Visitor, Max Planck Inst. for Medical Research, Heidelberg 1972–73; Fellow, Queen Mary Coll. 1985; Pres. Soc. of Magnetic Resonance in Medicine 1987–88. *Publications:* NMR Imaging in Biomedicine 1982, NMR Imaging (co-ed.) 1990, MRI in Medicine 1995; some 200 scientific publs in learned journals. *Honours:* Hon. FRCR 1992; Hon. FInstP 1996; Hon. mem. British Inst. of Radiology (BIR) 1993; Hon. DrMed (Strasbourg) 1995; Hon. DSc (Univ. of Kent at Canterbury) 1996; Royal Soc. Wellcome Foundation Gold Medal and Prize 1985, Duddell Medal, Inst. of Physics 1988, Royal Soc. Mullard Medal 1990, ISMAR Prize 1992, Barclay Medal, BJR 1993, Gold Medal, European Asscn of Radiology 1995, Garmisch-Partenkirchen Prize for MRI 1995, Rank Prize 1997, Nobel Prize for Medicine (jtly) 2003; several other awards. *Address:* Magnetic Resonance Centre, Department of Physics and Astronomy, University of Nottingham, NG7 2RD, England. *Telephone:* (115) 9514740 (Office). *Fax:* (115) 9515166 (Office).

MANTEL, Hilary (Mary); Author; b. 6 July 1952, Derbyshire, England; m. Gerald McEwen, 23 Sept. 1972. *Education:* LSE; Sheffield University; Bachelor of Jurisprudence, 1973. *Career:* mem. FRSL; Society of Authors. *Publications:* Every Day is Mother's Day, 1985; Vacant Possession, 1986; Eight Months on Ghazzah Street, 1988; Fludd, 1989; A Place of Greater Safety, 1992; A Change of Climate, 1994; An Experiment in Love, 1995; The Giant, O'Brien, 1998; Giving Up the Ghost: A Memoir, 2003; Learning to Talk (short stories), 2003. Contributions: Film column, Spectator, 1987–91; Book reviews to range of papers. *Honours:* Shiva Naipaul Prize, 1987; Winifred Holtby Prize, 1990; Cheltenham Festival Prize, 1990; Southern Arts Literature Prize, 1990; Sunday Express Book of the Year Award, 1992; Hawthornden Prize, 1996. *Literary Agent:* A. M. Heath & Co Ltd, 79 St Martin's Lane, London WC2N 4RE, England.

MANWARING, Randle (Gilbert); Poet and Writer; b. 3 May 1912, London, England; m. Betty Violet Rout, 9 Aug. 1941, three s., one d. *Education:* Private schools; MA, University of Keele, 1982. *Career:* mem. Downland Poets, chair., 1981–83; Kent and Sussex Poetry Society; Society of Authors; Society of Sussex Authors. *Publications:* The Heart of This People, 1954; Satires and Salvation, 1960; Christian Guide to Daily Work, 1963; Under the Magnolia Tree, 1965; Slave to No Sect and Other Poems, 1966; Crossroads of the Year, 1975; Insurance, 1976; From the Four Winds, 1976; In a Time of Unbelief, 1977; The Swifts of Maggiore, 1981; The Run of the Downs, 1984; Collected Poems, 1986; A Study of Hymn Writing and Hymn-singing in the Christian Church, 1990; Some Late Lark Singing, 1992; Love So Amazing, 1995; The Swallow, The Fox and the Cuckoo, 1997; Trade Winds, 2001; From Controversy to Co-Existence, 2002. Contributions: Reviews, quarterlies, and magazines. *Address:* Marbles Barn, Newick, East Sussex BN8 4LG, England.

MAPLE, Gordon Extra; Writer and Dramatist; b. 6 Aug. 1932, Jersey, Channel Islands; m. Mabel Atkinson-Frayn, 29 Jan. 1953, one s. one d. *Career:* mem. BPM, Oxford Yec; FRSL. *Publications:* Limeade, 1963; Here's a Funny Thing, 1964; Dog, 1967; Elephant, 1968; Tortoise, 1974; Singo, 1975; Napoleon Has Feet, 1977; Pink Circle, 1984; Chateau Schloss, 1985; Popeye, 1985; Keeping in Front (memoirs), 1986; Sour Grapes (with Miles Whittier), 1986; Yet Another Falklands Film, 1987. *Honours:* Evening Standard Awards, 1964, 1973; SWEAT Award, 1986. *Address:* The Manor, Milton, nr Banbury, Oxfordshire, England.

MARAS, Karl (see Bulmer, Henry Kenneth).

MARBER, Patrick; Dramatist and Dir; b. 19 Sept. 1964, London, England. *Education:* BA, English Langage and Literature, Wadham College, Oxford,

1986. *Publications:* Dealer's Choice, 1995; After Miss Julie, 1996; Closer, 1997; Howard Katz, 2001. Contributions: Theatre and television. *Honours:* Evening Standard Awards for Best Comedy, 1995, 1997; Writers' Guild Award for Best West End Play, 1995; Critics' Circle Award for Best Play, 1997; Olivier Award, 1998; New York Drama Critics' Award, 1999. *Address:* c/o Judy Daish Assocs Ltd, 2 St Charles Pl., London W10 6EG, England.

MARCEAU, Felicien; Author and Playwright; b. 16 Sept. 1913, Cortenberg, Belgium. *Career:* mem. Académie Française. *Publications:* Plays: L'Oeuf, 1956; La Bonne Soupe, 1958; La Preuve par Quatre, 1964; Madame Princesse, 1965; Le Babour, 1968; L'Homme en Question, 1973; A Nous de Jouer, 1979. Fiction: L'Homme du Roi, 1952; Bergere Legere, 1953; Les Elans du Coeur, 1955; Creezy, 1969; Le Corps de Mon Ennemi, 1975; Appelez-moi Mademoiselle, 1984; La Carriole du Pere Juniet, 1985; Les Passions Partagees, 1987; Un Oiseau Dans Le Ciel, 1989; La Terrasse de Lucrezia, 1993; La Grande Fille, 1997. Memoirs: Les Années Courtes, 1968; Une insolente Liberte ou Les Aventures de Casanova, 1983; Les Ingenus, 1992; Le Voyage de Noce de Figaro, 1994; L'Affiche, 2000. *Honours:* Prix Pellman du Théâtre, 1954; Prix Interallie, 1955; Prix Goncourt, 1969; Grand Prix Prince Pierre de Monaco, 1974; Grand Prix de Théâtre, 1975; Prix Jean Giono, 1993; Prix Jacques Audibezzti, 1994. *Address:* c/o Editions Gallimard, 5 Rue Sebastien-Bottin, Paris 75007, France.

MARCH, Jessica (see Africano, Lillian).

MARCHANT, Anyda, (Sarah Aldridge), AB, MA, LLB; writer; b. 27 Jan. 1911, Rio de Janeiro, Brazil. *Education:* Nat. Univ., Washington, DC. *Career:* admitted to the bars of Virginia, District of Columbia, and US Supreme Court; staff, Law Library, Library of Congress, Washington, DC 1940–45, Bureau of Foreign and Domestic Commerce, US Dept of Commerce, Washington, DC 1951–53, Int. Bank for Reconstruction and Development, Washington, DC 1954–73; co-founder, Naiad Press 1974, A & M Books 1995. *Publications:* The Latecomer 1974, Tottie: A Tale of the Sixties 1975, Cytherea's Breath 1976, All True Lovers 1978, The Nesting Place 1982, Madame Aurora 1983, Misfortune's Friend 1985, Magdalena 1987, Keep to Me Stranger 1989, A Flight of Angels 1992, Michaela 1994, Amantha 1995, Nina in the Wilderness 1997, O, Mistress Mine 2003; contrib. to books and journals. *Honours:* Jeanine Rae Award, Nat. Women's Music Festival, Bloomington, IN 1992. *Address:* 212 Laurel Street, Rehoboth Beach, DE 19971, USA. *Website:* home.switchboard.com/sarahaldridge.

MARCINKEVIČIUS, Justinas; Poet, Playwright and Trans; b. 10 March 1930, Vazhatkiemis, Lithuania; m. Genovaite Kalvaityte 1955; two d. *Education:* Univ. of Vilnius. *Career:* began literary career 1953; mem. CPSU 1957–90; USSR People's Deputy 1989–91; mem. Lithuanian Acad. of Science, 1990; Lithuanian Council of Culture and Art, 1991. *Publications:* I Ask to Speak, 1955; The Twentieth Spring, 1955; The Pine that Laughed, 1961; Blood and Ashes, 1961; Hands that Share out the Bread, 1963; The Wall, 1965; Mindaugas, 1968; The Cathedral, 1971; Mazhvidas, 1977; The Tender Touch of Life, 1978; The Only Land, 1984; For the Living and the Dead, 1988; Lullaby to the Homeland and the Mother, 1992; By the Rye and by the Hearth, 1993; Poems from the Diary, 1993; The Harmony of the Flowing River, 1995. *Honours:* State Prizes (twice), People's Poet of Lithuania; J. G. Horder Award, 1997; Polish PEN Centre Award, 1997; Santarvé Award, 1999; Grand Duke Gediminas Order. *Address:* Mildos gve. 33, Apt 6, 2055 Vilnius, Lithuania.

MARCUS, Emilie, BA, PhD; American; *Editor, Cell*; b. 1960. *Education:* Wesleyan Univ., Univ. of Yale, Salk Inst., CA. *Career:* fmr Ed., Neuron; Ed., Cell 2003–. *Address:* Cell, Cell Press, 1100 Massachusetts Avenue, Third Floor, Cambridge, MA 02138, USA (Office). *Website:* www.cell.com.

MARCUS, Ruth (Barcan); Prof. of Philosophy and Writer; b. 2 Aug. 1921, New York, NY, USA; Divorced, two s. two d. *Education:* BA, New York University, 1941; MA, 1942, PhD 1946, Yale University. *Career:* Research Assoc., Institute for Human Relations, 1945–47, Reuben Post Halleck Prof. of Philosophy, 1973–, Yale University; Visiting Prof., 1950–57, Prof. of Philosophy, 1970–73, Northwestern University; Asst Prof. to Assoc. Prof., Roosevelt University, Chicago, 1957–63; Prof. of Philosophy, Head, Dept of Philosophy, University of Illinois, Chicago, 1964–70; Fellow, Center for Advanced Study, University of Illinois, 1968–69, Center for Advanced Study in the Behavioral Sciences, Stanford, CA, 1979; Visiting Fellow, Institute for Advanced Study, University of Edinburgh, 1983, Wolfson College, Oxford, 1985, 1986, Clare Hall, Cambridge, 1988; Mellon Senior Fellow, National Humanities Center, 1992–93; Visiting Distinguished Prof., University of California, Irvine, 1994–; mem. American Acad. of Arts and Sciences; Board of Officers, Chair., 1977–83, American Philosophical Asscn; Asscn for Symbolic Logic, pres., 1981–83; Council on Philosophical Studies, pres., 1985–; Institut International de Philosophie, pres., 1990–93; Philosophy of Science Asscn. *Publications:* The Logical Enterprise (ed.), 1975; Logic, Methodology, and Philosophy of Science, VII (ed.), 1986; Modalities: Philosophical Essays, 1993. Contributions: scholarly books and journals. *Honours:* Guggenheim Fellowship, 1953–54; Medal, Collège de France, 1986; Hon. LHD, University of Illinois, 1995; Wilbur Cross Medal, Yale University, 2000. *Address:* c/o Dept of Philosophy, Yale University, PO Box 208306, New Haven, CT 06525, USA.

MARCUS, Steven; Prof. of English, College Dean and Writer; b. 13 Dec. 1928, New York, NY, USA; m. Gertrud Lenzer, 20 Jan. 1966, one s. *Education:* AB, 1948, PhD, 1961, Columbia University. *Career:* Prof. of English, 1966–, George Delacorte Prof. of Humanities, 1976–, Chair., Dept of English and Comparative Literature, 1977–80, 1985–90, Vice-Pres., School of Arts and Sciences, 1993–95, Dean, Columbia College, 1993–95, Columbia University; Fellow, Center for Advanced Studies in the Behavioural Sciences, 1972–73; Dir of Planning, 1974–76, Chair. of the Exec. Committee, Board of Dirs, 1976–80, National Humanities Center; Chair., Lionel Trilling Seminars, 1976–80; mem. Acad. of Literary Studies, fellow; American Acad. of Arts and Sciences, fellow; American Acad. of Psychoanalysis; American Psychoanalytic Asscn; Institute for Psychoanalytic Teaching and Research. *Publications:* Dickens: From Pickwick to Dombey, 1965; Other Victorians, 1966; Engels, Manchester and the Working Class, 1974; Representations: Essays on Literature and Society, 1976; Doing Good (with others), 1978; Freud and the Culture of Psychoanalysis, 1984. Editor: The Life and Work of Sigmund Freud (with Lionel Trilling), 1960; The World of Modern Fiction, 2 vols, 1968; The Continental Op, 1974; Medicine and Western Civilization (with David Rothman), 1995. Contributions: Professional journals and to general periodicals. *Honours:* Guggenheim Fellowship, 1967–68; Rockefeller Foundation Fellowship, 1980–81; National Humanities Center Fellowship, 1980–82; Fulbright Fellowship, 1982–84; Hon. DHL, Clark University, 1985. *Address:* c/o Dept of English and Comparative Literature, Columbia University, New York, NY 10027, USA.

MARFEY, Anne; Writer and Adjunct Lecturer in Danish; b. 19 Feb. 1927, Copenhagen, Denmark; m. Dr Peter Marfey 6 Jan. 1964 (deceased); one s. one d. *Education:* Teachers' Certificate, Danish Teachers' College, Copenhagen, 1950; Postgraduate studies, Columbia University, 1961–62; PhD, Pacific Western University, HI, 1998. *Career:* Adjunct Lecturer in Danish, SUNY at Albany; Representative for Danes Worldwide, Albany Area; mem. Danish Writers Guild; Board Mem., UN Albany; US-China Friendship Asscn, Albany; New York Acad. of Sciences, 1997; American Asscn of University Women, 1998. *Publications:* Learning to Write, 1961; Vejen til hurtigere Laesning, 1962; Svante, 1965; Las Bedre, 1966; Amerikanere, 1967; Telefontraden, 1968; Skal Skal ikke, 1969; How Parents Can Help Their Child with Reading, 1976; Rose's Adventure, 1989; Moderne Dansk, 1989; The Duckboat, The Pump, The Pine Tree, 1994; The Chipmunk, 1994; The Miracle of Learning, 1997; The Ugly Carrot, 2002. *Address:* 9 Tudor Rd, Albany, NY 12203, USA.

MARGOLIN, Phillip (Michael); Lawyer and Writer; b. 20 April 1944, New York, NY, USA; m. Doreen Stamm, 22 Dec. 1968, one s. one d. *Education:* BA, American University, 1965; JD, New York University, 1970. *Career:* Law Clerk to the Chief Judge, Oregon Court of Appeals, 1970–71; Deputy District Attorney and Special Agent for Multnomah County, OR, 1971–72; Partner, Nash & Margolin, 1974–80, Margolin & Margolin, 1986–96, Portland, OR; mem. MWA; National Asscn of Criminal Defense Lawyers; Oregon Criminal Defense Lawyers Asscn; Oregon State Bar Asscn. *Publications:* Heartstone, 1978; The Last Innocent Man, 1981; Gone, but Not Forgotten, 1993; After Dark, 1995; The Burning Man, 1996; The Undertaker's Widow, 1998; Wild Justice, 2000. Contributions: Professional journals, anthologies and periodicals. *Address:* c/o Margolin & Margolin, 621 SW Morrison St, Portland, OR 97205, USA.

MARGOSHES, Dave, BA, MFA; writer and poet; b. 8 July 1941, New Brunswick, NJ, USA; m. Ilya Silbar 1963. *Education:* Univ. of Iowa. *Career:* instructor, numerous writers' workshops and creative writing courses; writer-in-residence, Univ. of Winnipeg 1995–96, Saskatoon Public Library 2001–02. *Publications:* Third Impressions (short stories with Barry Dempster and Don Dickinson) 1982, Small Regrets (short stories) 1986, Walking at Brighton (poems) 1988, Northwest Passage (poems) 1990, Nine Lives (short stories) 1991, Saskatchewan 1992, Long Distance Calls (short stories) 1996, Fables of Creation (short stories) 1997, Tommy Douglas: Building the New Society (biog.) 1999, We Who Seek: A Love Story (novella) 1999, I'm Frankie Sterne (novel) 2000, Purity of Absence (poems) 2001, Drowning Man (novel) 2003; contrib. to numerous anthologies, journals and magazines. *Honours:* Canadian Author and Bookman Poem of the Year Award 1980, Saskatchewan Writers' Guild Long Manuscript Award 1990, Second Prize, League of Canadian Poets' Nat. Poetry Contest 1991, Stephen Leacock Award for Poetry 1996, John V. Hicks Award for Fiction 2001, City of Regina Writing Award 2004. *Address:* 2922 19th Avenue, Regina, SK S4T 1X5, Canada. *E-mail:* dmargos@sasktel.net.

MARIANI, Paul (Louis); Prof., Writer and Poet; b. 29 Feb. 1940, New York, NY, USA; m. Eileen Spinosa, 24 Aug. 1963, three s. *Education:* BA, Manhattan College, 1962; MA, Colgate University, 1964; PhD, Graduate School and Univ. Center, CUNY, 1968. *Career:* Asst Prof., John Jay College of Criminal Justice, CUNY, 1967–68; Asst Prof., 1968–71, Assoc. Prof., 1971–75, Prof., 1975–, Distinguished University Prof., 1985, University of Massachusetts, Amherst; Robert Frost Fellow, 1980, Faculty, 1982, 1983, 1984, Robert Frost Prof., 1983, Visiting Lecturer, 1986, School of English, Poetry Staff, 1985–96, Bread Loaf Writers' Conference; Dir, The Glen, Colorado Springs, 1995, 1996, 1998; Chair in English, Boston College, 2000–; Poetry Ed., America Magazine, 2000–; mem. Acad. of American Poets; Poetry Society of America. *Publications:* Poetry: Timing Devices, 1979; Crossing Cocytus, 1982; Prime Mover, 1985; Salvage Operations: New and Selected Poems, 1990; The Great Wheel, 1996. Other: William Carlos Williams: A New World Naked, 1981; Dream Song: The Life of John

Berryman, 1990; Lost Puritan: A Life of Robert Lowell, 1994; The Broken Tower: A Life of Hart Crane, 1999; Thirty Days: On Retreat with the Exercises of St Ignatius, 2002; God and the Imagination: On Poets, Poetry and the Ineffable, 2002. Contributions: books and journals. *Honours:* National Endowment for the Humanities Fellowships, 1972–73, 1981–82; New Jersey Writers' Award, 1982; New York Times Notable Books, 1982, 1994, 1999; Chancellor's Medal, University of Massachusetts, 1984; National Endowment for the Arts Fellowship, 1984; Choice Awards, Prairie Schooner, 1989, 1995; Ohioana Award, 2000; Catholic Press Asscn Award for Popular Presentation of the Catholic Faith, 2003; Hon. DHL, Manhattan College, 1998; Hon. DHL, The Elms College, 2001. *Address:* Box M, Montague, MA 01351, USA.

MARÍAS FRANCO, Javier; Spanish writer and translator; b. 20 Sept. 1951, Madrid. *Education:* Universidad Complutense de Madrid. *Career:* translator and writer of film screenplays 1969; editor at Alfaguara 1974; lecturer at various univs world-wide; mem. Int Parliament of Writers (exec. council 2001–). *Publications:* novels: Los dominios del lobo 1971, Travesía del horizonte 1972, El Monarca del tiempo 1978, El hombre sentimental (Premio Herralde de Novela, Premio Ennio Flaiano 2000) 1986, El Siglo 1982, Todas las almas (Premio Ciudad de Barcelona) 1989, Corazón tan blanco (Premio de la Crítica 1993, Prix L'Oeil et la Lettre 1993, Int. IMPAC Prize 1997) 1992, Mañana en la batalla piensa en mí (Premio Fastenrath de la Real Academia Española de la Lengua 1995, Premio Internacional de Novela Rómulo Gallegos 1995, Prix Fémina Étranger, France 1996, Premio Arzobispo Juan de San Clemente 1995, Premio Letterario Internazionale Mondello-Cittá di Palermo 1998) 1994, Negra espalda del tiempo 1998, Tu rostro mañana (Premio Salambó 2003) 2002; other fiction: Gospel (screenplay) 1969, Mientras ellas duermen (short stories) 1990, Cuando fui mortal (short stories) 1996, Mala índole (short story) 1998; non-fiction: Pasiones pasadas (articles and essays) 1991, Vidas escritas (articles) 1992, Literatura y fantasma (articles and essays) 1993, Vida del fantasma (articles) 1995, Si yo amaneciera otra vez (articles and poems) 1997, Miramientos (articles) 1997, Mano de sombra (articles) 1997, Desde que te vi morir (articles and poems) 1999, Seré amado cuando falte (articles) 1999, Salvajes y sentimentales (articles) 2000, A veces un caballero (articles) 2001; numerous translations; contrib. to anthologies, including Cuentos únicos 1989, El hombre que parecia no querer nada 1996; contrib. to journals and newspapers, including El País, El Diario de Barcelona, Hiperión, Revista de Occidente. *Honours:* Chevalier, Ordre des Arts et des Lettres, Premio Comunidad de Madrid 1998; Premio Nacional de Traducción for translation of Tristram Shandy 1979, Alberto Moravia Int. Prize, Rome 2000, Grinzane Cavour prize, Turin 2000. *Literary Agent:* Mercedes Casanovas Agencia Literaria, Iradier 24, 08017 Barcelona, Spain. *E-mail:* webmaster@javiermarias.es. *Website:* www.javiermarias.es.

MARINEAU, Michele; Writer and Trans; b. 12 Aug. 1955, Montréal, QC, Canada; Divorced, one s. one d. *Education:* BA, Traduction et Histoire de l'art, University of Montréal, 1988. *Career:* mem. Union des écrivaines et des écrivains québécois; Corporation Professionnelle des Traducteurs et Interprétes Agréés du Québec; Asscn des Traducteurs Litteraires du Canada; Communication-Jeunesse. *Publications:* Cassiopée ou L'été Polonais, 1988; L'été des Baleines, 1989; L'Homme du Cheshire, 1990; Pourquoi pas Istambul?, 1991; La Route de Chlifa, 1992. *Honours:* Prix du Gouverneur Général, 1988, 1993; Prix, Brive-Montréal, 1993; Prix, Alvine-Bélisle, 1993. *Literary Agent:* Editions Québec/Amérique, 425 St Jean Baptiste, Montréal, QC, Canada. *Address:* 4405 rue de Brebeuf, Montréal, QC H2J 3K8, Canada.

MARIZ, Linda Catherine French, (Linda French); Mystery Novelist; b. 27 Nov. 1948, New Orleans, LA, USA; m. George Eric Mariz, 22 Aug. 1970, one s. one d. *Education:* BA, History, University of Missouri, Columbia, 1970; MA, History, Western Washington University, 1973. *Career:* Creative Writing Instructor, Western Washington University, 1994; mem. Sisters in Crime; International Asscn of Crime Writers; Washington Commission for the Humanities. *Publications:* As Linda Mariz: Body English, 1992; Snake Dance, 1992. As Linda French: Talking Rain, 1998; Coffee to Die For, 1998; Steeped in Murder, 1999. Contributions: Cash Buyer (story) in Reader, I Murdered Him Too (anthology), 1995. *Literary Agent:* Jane Chelius, 548 Second St, New York, NY, USA. *Address:* 708 17th St, Bellingham, WA 98225, USA.

MARK, Janet (Jan) Marjorie, NDD; writer and dramatist; b. 22 June 1943, Welwyn, Hertfordshire, England; m. Neil Mark 1969 (divorced 1989); one s. one d. *Education:* Canterbury College of Art. *Career:* teacher, Southfields School, Gravesend, Kent 1965–71; Arts Council Writer-Fellow, Oxford Polytechnic 1982–84. *Publications:* fiction: Two Stories 1984, Zeno was Here 1987, God's Story 1997, The Eclipse of the Century 1999, Heathrow Nights 2000; plays: Izzy 1985, Interference 1987, Captain Courage and the Rose Street Gang (with Stephen Cockett) 1987, Time and the Hour, and, Nothing to Be Afraid Of 1990; other: over 30 children's novels 1976–, including Useful Idiots 2004; over 10 children's story collections 1980–99, including The Oxford Book of Children's Stories (ed.) 1993; nine picture books 1986–95; contrib. to anthologies, periodicals, radio and television. *Honours:* Penguin/Guardian Award 1975, Carnegie Medals 1976, 1983, Rank Observer Prize 1982, Angel Literary Awards 1983, 1988. *Literary Agent:* David Higham Associates, 5–8 Lower John Street, Golden Square, London, W1F 9HA, England. *Address:* 98 Howard Street, Oxford, OX4 3BG, England.

MARKHAM, Edward Archibald; British editor, poet, writer, dramatist and academic; b. 1 Oct. 1939, Montserrat. *Education:* University of Wales, University of East Anglia, University of London. *Career:* Lecturer, Abraham Moss Centre, Manchester, 1976–78; Asst Ed., Ambit Magazine, London, 1980–85; Ed., Artrage, 1985–87, Sheffield Thursday, 1992–2000; Writer-in-Residence, University of Ulster, Coleraine, 1988–91; Prof., Sheffield Hallam University, 1991–97. *Publications:* Poetry: Crossfire, 1972; Lambchops, 1976; Love Poems, 1978; Games and Penalities, 1980; Love, Politics and Food, 1982; Human Rites: Selected Poems, 1970–82, 1983; Lambchops in Papua New Guinea, 1985; Living in Disguise, 1986; Towards the End of a Century, 1989; Letter from Ulster and the Hugo Poems, 1993; Misapprehensions, 1995; A Rough Climate, 2002; John Lewis & Co, 2003. Plays: The Masterpiece, 1964; The Private Life of the Public Man, 1970; Dropping Out is Violence, 1971; Dreamers, 2001. Short Stories: Something Unusual, 1986; Ten Stories, 1994; Taking the Drawing Room Through Customs: Selected Stories, 2002. Other: A Papua New Guinea Sojourn: More Pleasures of Exile (memoir), 1998; Marking Time (novel) 1999. Editor: Hinterland, 1989; The Penguin Book of Caribbean Short Stories, 1996. *Honours:* C. Day-Lewis Fellowship, 1980–81; Certificate of Honour, Government of Montserrat, 1997. *Address:* c/o Anvil Press Poetry Ltd, Neptune House, 70 Royal Hill, London SE10 8RF, England.

MARKHAM, Marion Margaret; Writer; b. 12 June 1929, Chicago, IL, USA; m. Robert Bailey Markham, 30 Dec. 1955, two d. *Education:* BS, Northwestern University. *Career:* mem. Society of Midland Authors; MWA; Authors' Guild of America; Society of Children's Book Writers. *Publications:* Escape from Velos, 1981; The Halloween Candy Mystery, 1982; The Christmas Present Mystery, 1984; The Thanksgiving Day Parade Mystery, 1986; The Birthday Party Mystery, 1989; The April Fool's Day Mystery, 1991; The Valentine's Day Mystery, 1992. *Address:* 2415 Newport Rd, Northbrook, IL 60062, USA.

MARKISH, David; Author; b. 24 Sept. 1938, Moscow, Russia; m. 6 June 1990, Nathalie Laskina, two s. *Education:* Gorky Literary Institute, Moscow; Higher Courses for Screenwriters and Cinema Dirs, Moscow. *Publications:* Five Close to the Sky, 1966; A New World for Simon Ashkenazy, 1976; The Cock, 1980; Forward, 1980; Jesters, 1983; The Dog, 1984; In the Shadow of a Big Stone, 1986; The Field, 1989; The Garnet Shaft, 1990; My Enemy Cat, 1991; To Be Like Others, 2000; To Become Lutov, 2001. *Honours:* 7 Israeli Literary Awards; British Book League Award; International Literary Award of Ukraine; Machabeli Literary Award of Georgia. *Literary Agent:* Ruth Lippman Agency, Zürich. *Address:* Erez 65, Or-Ehuda, Israel. *E-mail:* markishd@inter.net.il.

MARKOVIĆ, Predrag; Serbia and Montenegro (Serbian) politician and publisher; b. 7 Dec. 1955, Cepure. *Education:* Univ. of Belgrade. *Career:* Ed. Student, Vreme (newspapers), Vidici (magazine); owner Stubovi Culture publishing house 1993–; Pres. G17 PLUS Man. Bd 2000–01, Pres. Political Council, mem. Exec. Bd 2001–02, Vice-Pres. G17 PLUS party 2003–; Pres. Nat. Ass. of Serbia 2004–; Acting Pres. of Serbia 2004; Pres. Asscn of Publrs of Serbia and Montenegro; mem. PEN, Serbian Literary Soc. *Publications:* Morali su doći nasmejani lavovi 1983, Otemenost duše 1989. *Address:* c/o Office of the President, Andrićev venac 1, 11000 Belgrade, Serbia and Montenegro (Office).

MARKS, Stanley; Writer and Dramatist; b. 1929, London, England; m. Eve Mass, one s. one d. deceased. *Education:* University of Melbourne. *Career:* Journalist and Foreign Correspondent, Australia, UK, USA, Canada; Originator-Writer, MS cartoon series, Australian and New Zealand newspapers, 1975–80; Ed., journal of Melbourne Holocaust Centre; mem. Australian Society of Authors. *Publications:* God Gave You One Face, 1964; Graham is an Aboriginal Boy, 1968; Fifty Years of Achievement, 1972; Animal Olympics, 1972; Rarua Lives in Papua New Guinea, 1974; Ketut Lives in Bali, 1976; St Kilda Sketchbook, 1980; Malvern Sketchbook, 1981; Welcome to Australia, 1981; Out and About in Melbourne, 1988; St Kilda Heritage Sketchbook, 1995. Contributions: newspapers and journals. *Address:* 348 Bambra Rd, South Caulfield, Melbourne, Vic. 3162, Australia.

MARKWORT, Helmut; German journalist, publisher, editor and presenter; *Editor-in-Chief and CEO, Focus Magazine*; b. 8 Dec. 1936, Darmstadt. *Career:* started in journalism 1956, various posts in local media –1966; founder Ed.-in-Chief of several magazines and radio stations; Ed.-in-Chief and CEO Focus Magazine 1993–; Man. Focus TV 1996–; Publr Focus Money 2000–; Head of Bd Tomorrow Focus AG 2001–, Playboy Publishing Deutschland AG 2002–; presenter Bookmark 2004. *Honours:* Horizont 'Mann der Medien' Award 1983, 1993, Advertising Age 'Marketing Superstar' 1994, Hildegard von Bingen Award for Journalism, BDS Mittelstandspreis Award, Bavarian's Merit Medal 1996, Nat. Merit Cross (1st Class) 1999. *Address:* Focus Magazine, Arabella str. 23, 81925, Munich, Germany (Office). *Fax:* (89) 92502026 (Office). *Website:* www.focus.de (Office).

MARLATT, Daphne Shirley; poet and writer; b. 11 July 1942, Melbourne, Vic., Australia; m. Gordon Alan Marlatt 1963 (divorced 1970); one s. *Education:* BA, English and Creative Writing, University of British Columbia, 1964; MA, Comparative Literature, Indiana University, 1968.

Career: Co-Ed., Tessera (Journal), 1983–91; Special Lecturer in Creative Writing, University of Saskatchewan, 1998–99; mem. Writers' Union of Canada. *Publications:* Frames of a Story, 1968; Leaf/Leaf/s, 1969; Rings, 1971; Vancouver Poems, 1972; Steveston, 1974; Our Lives, 1975; Steveston Recollected: A Japanese-Canadian History (with M. Koizumi), 1975; Zócalo, 1977; Opening Doors: Vancouver's East End (with Carole Itter), 1979; What Matters, 1980; Selected Writing: Net Work, 1980; How Hug a Stone, 1983; Touch to My Tongue, 1984; Double Negative (with Betsy Warland), 1988; Ana Historic, 1988; Salvage, 1991; Ghost Works, 1993; Taken, 1996; Readings from the Labyrinth, 1998; This Tremor Love Is, 2001. *Address:* c/o Writers' Union of Canada, 24 Ryerson Avenue, Toronto, ON M5T 2P3, Canada.

MARLIN, Henry (see Giggal, Kenneth).

MARLOW, Joyce; Writer; b. 27 Dec. 1929, Manchester, England. *Career:* Professional Actress, 1950–65. *Publications:* The Man with the Glove, 1964; A Time to Die, 1966; Billy Goes to War, 1967; The House on the Cliffs, 1968; The Peterloo Massacre, 1969; The Tolpuddle Martyrs, 1971; Captain Boycott and the Irish, 1973; The Life and Times of George I, 1973; The Uncrowned Queen of Ireland, 1975; Mr and Mrs Gladstone, 1977; Kings and Queens of Britain, 1977; Kessie, 1985; Sarah, 1987; Anne, 1989; Tribunals and Appeals, 1991; Virago Book of Women of the Great War, 1998; Virago Book of Votes for Women, 2000. *Address:* 3 Spring Bank, New Mills, High Peak SK22 4AS, England. *E-mail:* joycem@cbits.net.

MARLOWE, Hugh (see Patterson, Henry (Harry)).

MARLOWE, Stephen, (Andrew Frazer, Milton Lesser, Jason Ridgway, C. H. Thames); Author; b. 7 Aug. 1928, New York, NY, USA; m. 1st Leigh Lang, 1950; m. 2nd Ann Humbert, 1964, two d. *Education:* AB, College of William and Mary, 1949. *Career:* Writer-in-Residence, College of William and Mary, 1974–75, 1980–81. *Publications:* Over 50 novels, including: The Shining, 1963; Colossus, 1972; The Valkyrie Encounter, 1978; The Memoirs of Christopher Columbus, 1987; The Death and Life of Miguel de Cervantes, 1991; The Lighthouse at the End of the World, 1995. *Honours:* Prix Gutenberg du Livre, 1988; Life Achievement Award, Private Eye Writers of America, 1997. *Address:* c/o Mildred Marmur Assocs, 2005 Palmer Ave, PMB 127, Larchmont, NY 10538, USA.

MARNY, Dominique Antoinette Nicole; Novelist, Screenwriter and Journalist; b. 21 Feb. 1948, Neuilly, France; m. Michel Marny 5 Oct. 1970 (divorced); one d. *Career:* mem. PEN Club. *Publications:* Crystal Palace, 1985; Les orages desirés, 1988; Les fous de lumière, 1991; Les desirs et les jours, 1993; Les courtisanes, 1994; Les belles de Cocteau, 1995. Contributions: Madame Figaro; Vogue; Marie France. *Honours:* Prix Madame Europe, 1993. *Address:* 4 Ave de New York, 75016 Paris, France.

MAROWITZ, Charles; Writer; b. 26 Jan. 1934, New York, USA; m. Jane Elizabeth Allsop, 14 Dec. 1980. *Career:* Artistic Dir, Malibu Stage Co, Texas Stage Co; West Coast Correspondent, Theatre Week Magazine; Senior Ed., Matzoh Ball Gazette; Theatre Critic, Los Angeles Village View; Guest Artist-in-Residence, California State University, Long Beach, CA, 1997; mem. Dramatists Guild; Writers Guild; Asscn of Literary Scholars and Critics. *Publications:* The Method as Means, 1961; The Marowitz Hamlet, 1966; The Shrew, 1972; Artaud at Rodez, 1975; Confessions of a Counterfeit Critic, 1976; The Marowitz Shakespeare, 1980; Act of Being, 1980; Sex Wars, 1983; Sherlock's Last Case, 1984; Prospero's Staff, 1986; Potboilers, 1986; Recycling Shakespeare, 1990; Burnt Bridges, 1991; Directing the Action, 1992; Cyrano de Bergerac (trans.), 1995; Alarums and Excursions, 1996; The Other Way: An Alternative Approach to Acting and Directing, 1998; Boulevard Comedies, 2000; Stage Dust, 2001; Roar of the Canon; Kott and Marowitz on Shakespeare (with Jan Kott), 2002. Contributions: newspapers, journals and magazines. *Honours:* Order of Purple Sash, 1965; Whitbread Award, 1967; First Prize, Louis B. Mayer Award, 1984. *Literary Agent:* Elaine Rogers, Kneerim and Williams, Boston, USA. *Address:* 3058 Sequit Dr., Malibu, CA 90265, USA.

MARQUAND, David Ian, FBA, FRHistS, FRSA; British professor of politics; *Principal, Mansfield College, Oxford*; b. 20 Sept. 1934, Cardiff; m. Judith M. Reed 1959; one s. one d. *Education:* Emanuel School, Magdalen Coll. Oxford. *Career:* Sr scholar, St Antony's Coll. Oxford 1957–58; teaching Asst Univ. of Calif. 1958–59; editorial writer, The Guardian 1959–61; Research Fellow, St Antony's Coll. Oxford 1962–64; lecturer in politics, Univ. of Sussex 1964–66; mem. Parl. (Labour) for Ashfield, Notts. 1966–77; del. to Council of Europe and W.E.U. assemblies 1970–73; Opposition spokesman on treasury affairs 1971–72; Chief Adviser, Sec.-Gen. European Comm. 1977–78; Prof. of Contemporary History and Politics, Salford Univ. 1978–91; Prof. of Politics, Univ. of Sheffield 1991–96, Dir Political Economy Research Centre 1993–96, Hon. Prof. 1997–; Prin. Mansfield Coll., Univ. of Oxford 1996–; Jt Ed. The Political Quarterly 1987–96. *Publications:* Ramsay Macdonald 1973, Parliament for Europe 1979, The Unprincipled Society 1988, The Progressive Dilemma 1991, The New Reckoning 1997, Religion and Democracy 2000, Decline of the Public 2004. *Honours:* George Orwell Memorial Prize 1979. *Address:* Mansfield College, Oxford, OX1 3TF, England. *Telephone:* (1865) 270980.

MÁRQUEZ, Gabriel García (see García Márquez, Gabriel).

MARR, David; Australian journalist, writer and television producer. *Career:* worked on TV programme, Four Corners (ABC); feature writer, Sydney Morning Herald. *Publications:* Barwick, 1981; The Ivanov Trail; Patrick White—A Life, 1991; Patrick White—Letters, 1994; The High Price of Heaven (essays), 1999; Dark Victory: The Story of The Tampa (with Marian Wilkinson), 2002. *Honours:* NSW Premier's Literary Award, 1981; numerous literary awards. *Literary Agent:* Australian Literary Management, 2A Booth Street, Balmain, NSW 2041, Australia. *Address:* c/o Allen & Unwin, PO Box 8500, St Leonards, NSW 1590, Australia.

MARR, William Wei-Yi, (Ma Fei); Engineer (retd), Poet and Ed.; b. 3 Sept. 1936, China; m. Jane Jy Chyun Liu 22 Sept. 1962; two s. *Education:* Taipei Institute of Technology, 1957; MS, Marquette Univ., 1963; PhD, Univ. of Wisconsin, 1969. *Career:* Editorial Adviser, The Chinese Poetry International, New World Poetry; Adviser, Chinese Writers Asscn of Greater Chicago, Asscn of Modern Chinese Literature and Arts of North America; mem. Chinese Artists Asscn of North America; Illinois State Poetry Society, pres., 1993–95; Li Poetry Society; New Poetry, Beijing, vice-pres., 1994–; Poets Club of Chicago. *Publications:* In the Windy City, 1975; Selected Poems, 1983; White Horse, 1984; Selected Poems of Fei Ma, 1985; The Galloping Hoofs, 1986; Road, 1987; Selected Short Poems, 1991; Fly Spirit, 1992; Selected Poems, 1994; Autumn Window, 1995; A Microscopic World, 1998; Not All Flowers Need to Bear Fruit, 2000; The Collected Poems of Fei Ma, 2000; Selected Poems of William Marr, 2003. Contributions: periodicals and magazines. *Honours:* Wu Cho Liu Poetry Award, 1982; Li Poetry Trans. Award, 1982, and Poetry Award, 1984. *Address:* 737 Ridgeview St, Downers Grove, IL 60516, USA. *E-mail:* marrfei@aol.com. *Website:* hometown.aol.com/marrfei/bmz.htm.

MARRECO, Anne (see Wignall, Anne).

MARRODAN, Mario Angel, LicenDer, LicenFil; lawyer, critic, writer, poet and editor; b. 7 June 1932, Portugalete, Vizcaya, Spain; m. Mercedes Gómez Estíbaliz 1961; two s. *Career:* mem. Asociación Española de Críticos de Arte, Asociación Española de Críticos Literarios, Asociación Colegial de Escritores de España, Int. Asscn of Art Critics, Soc. of Basque Studies, Fraternity of the Béret. *Publications:* over 300 books, incl. vols of essays, art criticism and poetry; 300 poetas cantan a Bilbao 2000; contrib. to magazines and journals. *Honours:* Golden Seagull, Royal Basque Soc. of Friends of the Nation. *Address:* Apdo de Correos 16, 48920 Portugalete, Vizcaya, Spain.

MARS-JONES, Adam; Author; b. 1954, England. *Education:* Westminster School; Trinity Hall, Cambridge; Univ. of Virginia. *Career:* film critic, The Independent, 1989–97; film critic, The Times, 1999–2001. *Publications:* Lantern Lecture (short stories), 1981; Fabrications (novel), 1981; Mae West is Dead, 1983; The Darker Proof (with Edmund White), 1987; Venus Envy: On Masculinity and Its Discontents (essays), 1990; Monopolies of Loss, 1992; The Waters of Thirst (novel), 1993; Fulfilment, 1993; Hypo Vanilla (novel), 1996; Blind Bitter Happiness (essays), 1997. *Honours:* Somerset Maugham Award, 1982. *Address:* 42B Calabria Rd, Highbury, London N5 1HU, England.

MARSDEN, George M., BA, BD, MA, PhD; academic and writer; *Francis A. McAnaney Professor of History, University of Notre Dame*; b. 25 Feb. 1939, Harrisburg, Pennyslvania, USA; m. Lucie Commeret, 30 March 1969, one s. one d. *Education:* Haverford Coll., Westminster Theological Seminary, Yale Univ. *Career:* instructor, Asst, and Assoc. Prof. 1965–74, Prof. 1974–86, Calvin Coll., Grand Rapids; Assoc. Ed., Christian Scholar's Review 1970–77; Visiting Prof. of Church History, Trinity Evangelical Divinty School, Deerfield, IL 1976–77; Ed., The Reformed Journal 1980–90; Visiting Prof. of History, Univ. of California at Berkeley 1986, 1990; Prof. of the History of Christianity in America, Divinity School, Duke Univ. 1986–92; Francis A. McAnaney Prof. of History, Univ. of Notre Dame 1992–; mem. American Soc. of Church History (pres. 1992), Inst. for the Study of American Evangelicals (advisory council). *Publications:* The Evangelical Mind and the New School Presbyterian Experience 1970, A Christian View of History? (ed. with Frank Roberts) 1975, Fundamentalism and American Culture: The Shaping of Twentieth-Century Evangelicalism, 1870–1925 1980, Eerdman's Handbook to the History of Christianity in America (co-ed.) 1983, The Search for Christian America (with Mark A. Noll and Nathan O. Hatch) 1983, Evangelicalism and Modern America (ed.) 1984, Reforming Fundamentalism: Fuller Seminary and the New Evangelicalism 1987, Religion and American Culture 1990, Understanding Fundamentalism and Evangelicalism 1991, The Secularization of the Academy (ed. with Bradley J. Longfield) 1992, The Soul of the American University 1994, The Outrageous Idea of Christian Scholarship 1997, Jonathan Edwards: A Life (Soc. for Eighteenth Century Studies Annibel Jenkins Prize 2002–04, Bancroft Prize 2004, Org. of American Historians Merle Curti Award 2004, Historical Soc. Eugene Genovese Prize 2004, John Pollock Award for Christian Biography 2004, Christianity Today Book Award for History and Biography 2004) 2003; contrib. to many scholarly books and journals. *Honours:* Younger Humanists Fellowship, Nat. Endowment for the Humanities 1971–72, Fellow, Calvin Center for Christian Scholarship 1979–80, Book of the Year Citations, Eternity magazine 1981, 1988, Calvin Research Fellowship 1982–83, J. Howard Pew Freedom Trust Grant 1988–92, Guggenheim Fellowship 1995. *Address:* c/o Department of History, University of Notre Dame, Notre Dame, IN 46556, USA.

MARSDEN, Peter Richard Valentine; Archaeologist and Writer; b. 29 April 1940, Twickenham, Middlesex, England; m. Frances Elizabeth Mager, 7 April 1979, two s. one d. *Education:* Kilburn Polytechnic; University of Oxford. *Career:* mem. Society of Antiquaries, fellow; Institute of Field Archaeologists. *Publications:* Londinium, 1971; The Wreck of the Amsterdam, 1974; Roman London, 1980; The Marsden Family of Paythorne and Nelson, 1981; The Roman Forum Site in London, 1987; The Historic Shipwrecks of South-East England, 1987. Contributions: Geographical Magazine; Independent; TLS; Illustrated London News; Telegraph Colour Magazine; various academic journals. *Address:* 21 Meadow Lane, Lindfield, West Sussex RH16 2RJ, England.

MARSDEN, Simon Neville Llewelyn; Writer and Photographer; b. 1 Dec. 1948, Lincoln, England; m. Caroline Stanton, 30 Aug. 1984, one s. one d. *Education:* Ampleforth College, Yorkshire; Sorbonne, University of Paris. *Career:* mem. Chelsea Arts Club; Arthur Machen Society. *Publications:* In Ruins, 1980; The Haunted Realm, 1986; Visions of Poe, 1988; Phantoms of the Isles, 1990; The Journal of a Ghost Hunter, 1994; Beyond the Wall: The Lost World of East Germany, 1999; Venice, City of Haunting Dreams, 2001; The Twilight Hour, 2003. *Honours:* Arts Council of Great Britain Awards, 1975, 1976. *Address:* The Presbytery, Hainton, Market Rasen, Lincolnshire LN8 6LR, England.

MARSÉ, Juan Faneca Roca; Spanish writer; b. 8 Jan. 1933, Barcelona. *Publications:* Encerrados con un solo juguete 1961, Esta cara de la luna 1962, Ultimatas tardes con Teresa 1966, La oscura historia de la prima Montse 1970, Si te dicen que caí 1973, Confidencias de un chorizo 1977, La muchacha de las bragas de oro 1978, Un día volveré (trans. as One Day I Will Return) 1982, La ronda de Guinardó 1984, La fuga del Rio Lobo (trans. as The Flight of Wolf River) 1985, Teniente Bravo 1987, El amante bilingue 1990, El embrujo de Shangai (trans. as The Bewitchment of Shanghai) 1993, Las mujeres de Juanito Marés 1997, Rabos de Lagartija (trans. as Lizard Tails) 2000; contrib. to Dietario de Posguerra 1998. *Honours:* Planeta Prize 1978, European Literature Prize 1994. *Address:* c/o Random House UK Ltd, 20 Vauxhall Bridge Road, London, SW1V 2SA, England. *Website:* www.randomhouse.co.uk.

MARSHALL, Jack; Writer and Poet; b. 25 Feb. 1937, New York, NY, USA. *Education:* Brooklyn Public Schools. *Publications:* The Darkest Continent, 1967; Bearings, 1970; Floats, 1972; Bits of Thirst, 1974; Bits of Thirst and Other Poems and Translations, 1976; Arriving on the Playing Fields of Paradise, 1983; Arabian Nights, 1986; Sesame, 1993. *Address:* 1056 Treat Ave, San Francisco, CA 94110, USA.

MARSHALL, Owen, (Owen Marshall Jones); Writer; b. 17 Aug. 1941, Te Kuiti, New Zealand; m. Jacqueline Hill Dec. 1965; two d. *Education:* MA, Univ. of Canterbury, 1964; Diploma in Teaching, Christchurch Teachers College, 1965. *Publications:* Supper Waltz Wilson, 1979; The Master of Big Jingles, 1982; The Day Hemingway Died, 1984; The Lynx Hunter, 1987; The Divided World, 1989; Tomorrow We Save the Orphans, 1991; A Many Coated Man, 1995; Coming Home in the Dark, 1995; The Best of Owen Marshall, 1997; Harlequin Rex, 1999; When Gravity Snaps, 2002; Essential New Zealand Short Stories (ed.), 2002. Contributions: numerous magazines and journals. *Honours:* New Zealand Literary Fund Scholarship in Letters, 1988; Robert Burns Fellowship, 1992; ONZM, 2000; Hon. DLitt, Univ. of Canterbury, 2002; Creative New Zealand Arts Fellowship. *Address:* 10 Morgans Rd, Timaru, New Zealand.

MARSHALL, Paule; Writer; b. 9 April 1929, New York, NY, USA; m. 1st Kenneth E. Marshall 1957 (divorced 1963); one s.; m. 2nd Nourry Menard 1970. *Education:* BA, English Literature, Brooklyn College, CUNY, 1953. *Career:* Staff, Our World magazine, 1953–56. *Publications:* Brown Girl, Brownstones, 1959; Soul Clap Hands and Sing, 1962; The Chosen Place, The Timeless People, 1969; Praisesong for the Widows, 1983; Reena and Other Stories, 1983; Daughters, 1991; The Fisher King, 2000. Contributions: anthologies and periodicals. *Honours:* Guggenheim Fellowship, 1961; John D. and Catherine T. MacArthur Foundation Fellowship, 1992.

MARSTEN, Richard (see Hunter, Evan).

MARTEL, Yann; Canadian writer; b. 1963, Spain. *Education:* Trent Univ. *Career:* grew up in Alaska, BC, Costa Rica, France, Ont. and Mexico; fmr tree planter, dishwasher, security guard; became professional writer 1990. *Publications:* Facts Behind the Helsinki Roccamatios (short stories) (Journey Prize) 1993, Self (novel) 1996, Life of Pi (novel) (Hugh MacLennan Prize for Fiction 2001, Man Booker Prize 2002) 2001, We Ate the Children Last (short stories) 2004. *Address:* c/o Knopf Canada, Random House of Canada Ltd, One Toronto Street, Unit 300, Toronto, ON M5C 2VC, Canada (Office). *Telephone:* (416) 364-4449 (Office). *Fax:* (416) 364-6863 (Office). *Website:* www.randomhouse.ca (Office).

MARTELLA, Maureen; writer; b. 28 Jan. 1947, Dublin, Ireland; m. Antonio Martella; three s. one d. *Education:* St Brigids Coll., Co. Dublin. *Publications:* Are You the Other Listener? (poems), Bugger Bucharest (novel) 1995, Maddy Goes to Holywood (novel) 1999, Annie's New Life (novel) 2000, A Perfect Partnership (novel) 2004; contrib. to Woman's Way (Dublin), radio documentaries (RTE Radio), Sunday Miscellany (RTE Radio). *Address:* Nunsland, Naas, Co Kildare, Ireland. *Website:* www.maureenmartella.com.

MARTI, René; Author and Poet; b. 7 Nov. 1926, Frauenfeld, Switzerland; m. Elizabeth Wahrenberger, 13 Oct. 1955, one s. two d. *Education:* Commercial School, Lausanne; Cambridge Proficiency Class, Polytechnic School, London; Diploma in French and English; Science of Literature and Philosophy, University of Konstanz. *Career:* mem. PEN and other literary organizations; Regensburger Shcriftstellergruppe intern., Turmbund Innsbruck, Verband Kath. Schriftsteller Oesterreichs. *Publications:* Das unauslöschliche Licht, 1954; Dom des Herzens, 1967; Die fünf Unbekannten (with others), 1970; Der unsichtbare Kreis, 1975; Weg an Weg, 1979; Besuche dich in der Natur (with Lili Keller), 1983; Gedichte zum Verschenken (with Lili Keller), 1984; Stationen, 1986; Die verbrannten Schreie, 1989; Gib allem ein bisschen Zeit (with Brigitta Weiss), 1993; Rückblicke, 1996; Spatenstich für die Rose (with Magdalena Obergfell), 2001. Contributions: numerous anthologies, newspapers, magazines, and radio. *Honours:* several publishing grants; AWMM Lyric Poetry Prize, Luxemburg, 1985. *Address:* Haus am Herterberg, Haldenstrasse 5, 8500 Frauenfeld, Switzerland.

MARTIN, Alexander George; Writer; b. 8 Nov. 1953, Baltimore, MD, USA; m. 28 July 1979, two s. *Education:* MA, English, University of Cambridge, 1975; Diploma, Theatre, University College, Cardiff, 1976. *Career:* mem. Society of Authors. *Publications:* Boris the Tomato, 1984; Snow on the Stinker, 1988; The General Interruptor, 1989; Modern Poetry, 1990; Modern Short Stories, 1991. *Honours:* Betty Trask Award, 1988. *Literary Agent:* David Higham Associates, 5–8 Lower John St, Golden Sq., London W1F 9HA, England.

MARTIN, David (Alfred); Prof. of Sociology Emeritus, Priest, International Fellow and Writer; b. 30 June 1929, London, England; m. 1st Daphne Sylvia Treherne, 1953, one s.; m. 2nd Bernice Thompson, 30 June 1962, two s. one d. *Education:* DipEd, Westminster College, 1952; External BSc, 1959, PhD, 1964, University of London; Postgraduate Scholar, LSE, 1959–61. *Career:* Asst Lecturer, Sheffield University, 1961–62; Lecturer, 1962–67, Reader, 1967–71, Prof. of Sociology, 1971–89, Prof. Emeritus, 1989–, LSE; Ordained Deacon, 1983, Priest, 1984; Scurlock Prof. of Human Values, Southern Methodist University, Dallas, 1986–90; Senior Professorial Fellow, later International Fellow, Institute for the Study of Economic Culture, Boston University, 1990–; various visiting lectureships; mem. International Conference of the Sociology of Religion, pres., 1975–83. *Publications:* Pacifism, 1965; A Sociology of English Religion, 1967; The Religious and the Secular, 1969; Tracts Against the Times, 1973; A General Theory of Secularisation, 1978; Dilemmas of Contemporary Religion, 1978; Crisis for Cranmer and King James (ed.), 1978; The Breaking of the Image, 1980; Theology and Sociology (co-ed.), 1980; No Alternative (co-ed.), 1981; Unholy Warfare (co-ed.), 1983; Divinity in a Grain of Bread, 1989; Tongues of Fire, 1990; The Forbidden Revolution, 1996; Reflections on Sociology and Theology, 1997; Does Christianity Cause Wars?, 1997; Pentecostalism, 2000; The World Their Parish, 2001; Christian Language in the Secular City, 2002; Christian Language and Its Mutations, 2002; Christian Language in the Secular City, 2002. Contributions: journals. *Honours:* Hon. Asst Priest, Guildford Cathedral, 1983–; Hon. Prof., Lancaster University, 1993–.; Hon. Doctor of Theology, University of Helsinki, 2000. *Address:* Cripplegate Cottage, 174 St John's Rd, Woking, Surrey GU21 7PQ, England.

MARTIN, George Whitney, BA, LLB; writer; b. 25 Jan. 1926, New York, USA. *Education:* Harvard Coll., Trinity Coll., Cambridge, Univ. of Virginia Law School. *Career:* practised law 1955–59; writer 1959–. *Publications:* The Damrosch Dynasty, America's First Family of Music 1983, Verdi, His Music, Life and Times (fourth edn) 1992, Aspects of Verdi (second edn) 1993, Verdi at The Golden Gate, Opera and San Francisco in the Gold Rush Years 1993, The Opera Companion (fifth edn) 1997, Twentieth Century Opera, A Guide 1999; contrib. numerous articles on Verdi and his operas in The Opera Quarterly. *Address:* 53 Crosslands Drive, Kennett Square, PA 19348, USA.

MARTIN, Jay (Herbert); Psychoanalyst, Prof., Author and Ed.; b. 30 Oct. 1935, Newark, NJ, USA; m. Helen Bernadette Saldini, 9 June 1956, one s. two d. *Education:* BA, Columbia University, 1956; MA, 1957, PhD, 1960, Ohio State University; PhD, Psychoanalysis, Southern California Psychoanalytic Institute, 1983. *Career:* Instructor in English, Pennsylvania State University, 1957–58; Instructor in English and American Studies, 1960–64, Asst Prof., 1964–67, Assoc. Prof., 1967–68, Yale University; Prof. of English, American Studies and Comparative Culture, 1968–79, Lecturer and Clinical Supervisor in Psychiatry and Human Behaviour, University of California at Irvine, 1978–95; Leo S. Bing Prof. of English and American Literature, University of Southern California at Los Angeles, 1979–96; Prof., Claremount McKenna College, CA, 1996–; Dai Ho Chun Distinguished Visiting Prof. Univ. of Hawaii (Honolulu); mem. American Psychoanalytic Asscn; Authors' Guild; International Psychoanalytic Asscn; MLA. *Publications:* Winfield Townley Scott (ed) 1961, Conrad Aiken: A Life of His Art 1962, Harvests of Change: American Literature 1865–1914 1967, A Collection of Critical Essays on 'The Waste Land' (ed.) 1968, Nathanael West: The Art of His Life 1970, Robert Lowell 1970, Twentieth-Century Views of Nathanael West: A Collection of Critical Essays (ed.) 1972, A Singer in the Dawn: Reinterpretations of Paul Laurance Dunbar 1975, A Dunbar Reader (ed. with Gossie H. Hudson) 1975, Always Merry and Bright: The Life of Henry Miller: An Unauthorized Biography 1978, Winter Dreams: An American in Moscow 1979, Economic Depression and American

Humor (ed.) 1984, Who Am I This Time?: Uncovering the Fictive Personality 1988, A Corresponding Leap of Love: Henry Miller, Lying and Dying 1996, Henry Miller's Dream Song 1996, Swallowing Tigers Whole: Conceptions of the Desirable in American Life and Education 1997, Journey to Heavenly Mountain 2002, The Education of John Dewey 2003. Contributions: scholarly books, professional journals and literary periodicals. *Honours:* American Philosophical Society Fellowship 1966, Guggenheim Fellowship 1966–67, Rockefeller Foundation Senior Fellowship in the Humanities 1977–78, National Endowment for the Humanities Senior Research Grant 1983–84, Research Fellow Rockefeller Study Center Bellagio Italy 1985–86, Burlington Northern Foundation Award for Outstanding Scholarship 1989, Durfee Fellowship to China 2000, University of Southern California at Los Angeles Distinguished Emeritus Prof. Award 2001. *Address:* c/o Claremont McKenna College, 850 N Columbia Ave, Claremont, CA 91711, USA.

MARTIN, Sir Laurence (Woodward); Emeritus Prof., Research Assoc. and Writer; b. 30 July 1928, Saint Austell, England; m. Betty Parnall, 19 Aug. 1951, one s. one d. *Education:* BA, History, 1948, MA, 1952, Christ's College, Cambridge; MA, International Politics, 1951, PhD, 1955, Yale University. *Career:* Instructor, Yale University, 1955–56; Asst Prof., MIT, 1956–61; Assoc. Prof., Johns Hopkins University 1961–64; Wilson Prof. of International Politics, 1964–68, Visiting Prof., 1985–, University of Wales; Research Assoc., Washington Center of Foreign Policy Research, 1964–76, 1979–; Prof. of War Studies, 1968–77, Fellow, 1983–, King's College, University of London; Vice-Chancellor, 1978–90, Emeritus Prof., 1991, University of Newcastle upon Tyne; BBC Reith Lecturer, 1981; Dir, Royal Institute of International Affairs, 1991–96; Burke Chair in Strategy, 1998–2000, Senior Adviser, 2000, Center for Strategic and International Studies, Washington, DC; mem. Center of International and Strategic Studies; Royal Institute of International Affairs. *Publications:* 60 including: The Anglo-American Tradition in Foreign Affairs (with Arnold Wolfers), 1956; Peace without Victory, 1958; Neutralism and Non-Alignment, 1962; The Sea in Modern Strategy, 1967; America in World Affairs (co-authors), 1970; Arms and Strategy, 1973; Retreat from Empire? (co-author), 1973; Strategic Thought in the Nuclear Age (co-author), 1979; The Two-Edged Sword, 1982; Before the Day After, 1985; The Changing Face of Nuclear Warfare, 1987; British Foreign Policy (co-author), 1997. *Honours:* Hon. DCL, University of Newcastle upon Tyne, 1991; Knighted, 1994. *Address:* 35 Witley Ct, Coram St, London WC1N 1HD, England. *E-mail:* lw.martin@virgin.net.

MARTIN, (Roy) Peter, (James Melville), MBE, BA, MA; British writer; b. 5 Jan. 1931, London, England; two s. *Education:* Birkbeck Coll., London, Tübingen Univ., Germany. *Career:* crime fiction reviewer, Hampstead, Highgate Express 1983–2000; mem. CWA, Detection Club. *Publications:* 13 Superintendent Otani mysteries, The Imperial Way 1986, A Tarnished Phoenix 1990, The Chrysanthemum Throne 1997. *Literary Agent:* Curtis Brown Ltd, Haymarket House, 28–29 Haymarket, London, SW1Y 4SP, England. *Telephone:* (20) 7393-4400. *Fax:* (20) 7393-4401. *E-mail:* info@curtisbrown.co.uk. *Website:* www.curtisbrown.co.uk.

MARTIN, Philip John Talbot, BA; retd lecturer and poet; b. 28 March 1931, Melbourne, Vic., Australia. *Education:* University of Melbourne. *Career:* Tutor to Senior Tutor in English, University of Melbourne, 1960–62; Lecturer in English, Australian National University, 1963; Lecturer to Senior Lecturer, Monash University, 1964–88. *Publications:* Poetry: Voice Unaccompanied, 1970; A Bone Flute, 1974; From Sweden, 1979; A Flag for the Wind, 1982; New and Selected Poems, 1988. Other: Shakespeare's Sonnets: Self Love and Art (criticism), 1972; Lars Gustafsson: The Stillness of the World Before Bach (trans.), 1988. Contributions: 7 anthologies, 1986–98; Age; Australian; Carleton Miscellany; Helix; Meanjin; New Hungarian Quarterly; Poetry USA; Quadrant; Southerly; TLS. *Address:* 25/9 Nicholson Street, Balmain 2041, NSW, Australia.

MARTIN, Ralph G(uy); Writer; b. 4 March 1920, Chicago, IL, USA; m. Marjorie Jean Pastel, 17 June 1944, one s. two d. *Education:* BJ, University of Missouri, 1941. *Career:* Managing Ed., Box Elder News Journal, Brigham, Utah, 1941; Assoc. Ed., The New Republic, New York City, 1945–48, Newsweek magazine, New York City, 1953–55; Exec. Ed., House Beautiful, New York City, 1955–57; mem. Authors' Guild; Century Asscn; Dramatists Guild; Overseas Press Club. *Publications:* Boy from Nebraska, 1946; The Best is None too Good, 1948; Eleanor Roosevelt: Her Life in Pictures (with Richard Harrity), 1958; The Human Side of FDR (with Richard Harrity), 1959; Front Runner, Dark Horse (with Ed Plaut), 1960; Money, Money, Money (with Morton Stone), 1961; Man of Destiny: Charles de Gaulle (with Richard Harrity), 1962; World War II: From D-Day to VE-Day (with Richard Harrity), 1962; The Three Lives of Helen Keller (with Richard Harrity), 1962; Ballots and Bandwagons, 1964; The Bosses, 1964; President from Missouri, 1964; Skin Deep, 1964; World War II: Pearl Harbor to VJ-Day, 1965; Wizard of Wall Street, 1965; The GI War: 1941–1945, 1967; A Man for All People: Hubert H. Humphrey, 1968; Jennie: The Life of Lady Randolph Churchill, 2 vols, 1969, 1971; Lincoln Center for the Performing Arts, 1971; The Woman He Loved: The Story of the Duke and Duchess of Windsor, 1973; Cissy: The Life of Elenor Medill Patterson, 1979; A Hero of Our Time: An Intimate Study of the Kennedy Years, 1983; Charles and Diana, 1985; Golda: Golda Meir, the Romantic Years, 1988; Henry and Clare: An Intimate Portrait of the Luces, 1991; Seeds of Destruction: Joe Kennedy and His Sons, 1995. Contributions: books and periodicals. *Address:* 235 Harbor Rd, Westport, CT 06880, USA.

MARTIN, Rhona (Madeline); Writer and Artist; b. 3 June 1922, London, England; m. 1st Peter Wilfrid Alcock 9 May 1941 (divorced); two d.; m. 2nd Thomas Edward Neighbour. *Career:* Part-time Tutor, Creative Writing, University of Sussex, 1986–91; mem. Romantic Novelists Asscn; Society of Authors; PEN; Friends of the Arvon Foundation; Society of Limners. *Publications:* Gallows Wedding, 1978; Mango Walk, 1981; The Unicorn Summer, 1984; Goodbye Sally, 1987; Writing Historical Fiction, 1988. Contributions: London Evening News; South East Arts Review; Cosmopolitan; Prima. *Honours:* Georgette Heyer Historical Novel Award, 1978. *Address:* 25 Henwood Crescent, Pembury, Kent TN2 4LJ, England.

MARTIN, Robert Bernard, (Robert Bernard); academic and writer; b. 11 Sept. 1918, La Harpe, IL, USA. *Education:* AB, University of Iowa, 1943; AM, Harvard University, 1947; BLitt, University of Oxford, 1950. *Career:* Prof. of English, 1950–75, Prof. Emeritus, 1975, Princeton University; Citizens Prof. of English, 1980–81, 1984–88, Prof. Emeritus, 1988–, University of Hawaii; mem. FRSL; Tennyson Society, hon. vice-pres. *Publications:* The Dust of Combat: A Life of Charles Kingsley, 1959; Enter Rumour: Four Early Victorian Scandals, 1962; The Accents of Persuasion: Charlotte Brontë's Novels, 1966; The Triumph of Wit: Victorian Comic Theory, 1974; Tennyson: The Unquiet Heart, 1980; With Friends Possessed: A Life of Edward FitzGerald, 1985; Gerard Manley Hopkins: A Very Private Life, 1991; 3 other critical books and 4 novels. Contributions: numerous magazines and journals. *Honours:* Guggenheim Fellowships, 1971–72, 1983–84; Senior Fellow, National Endowment for the Humanities, 1976–77; Fellow, Rockefeller Research Center, 1979; Duff Cooper Award, 1981; James Tait Black Memorial Prize, 1981; Christian Gauss Award, 1981; DLitt, University of Oxford, 1987; Fellow, National Humanities Center, 1988–89.

MARTIN, Ruth (see Rayner, Claire Berenice).

MARTIN, Valerie; American writer; b. 1948, Missouri. *Publications:* novels: Set in Motion 1978, Alexandra 1980, A Recent Martyr 1987, Mary Reilly 1990, The Great Divorce 1994, Italian Fever 1999, Property (Orange Prize for Fiction) 2003; other: Love: Short Stories 1976, The Consolation of Nature and Other Stories 1988, Salvation: Scenes from the Life of St Francis (biog.) 2001. *Address:* c/o Alfred A. Knopf, 299 Park Avenue, Fourth Floor, New York, NY 10171, USA (Office).

MARTIN, Victoria Carolyn; Writer; b. 22 May 1945, Windsor, Berkshire, England; m. Tom Storey, 28 July 1969, four d. *Education:* Winkfield Place, Berks, 1961–62; Byam Shaw School of Art, 1963–66. *Publications:* September Song, 1970; Windmill Years, 1975; Seeds of the Sun, 1980; Opposite House, 1984; Tigers of the Night, 1985; Obey the Moon, 1987. Contributions: Woman; Woman's Own; Woman's Realm; Woman's Journal; Good Housekeeping; Woman's Weekly; Redbook; Honey, 1967–87. *Address:* Newells Farm House, Lower Beeding, Horsham, Sussex RH13 6LN, England.

MARTINAC, Paula; Writer and Ed.; b. 30 July 1954, Pittsburgh, Pennsylvania, USA; Companion of Katie Hogan. *Education:* BA, Chatham College, Pittsburgh, 1976; MA, College of William and Mary, 1979. *Career:* Asst Curator, West Virginia State Museum, Charleston, 1979–82; Production Ed., Prentice-Hall Inc, Englewood Cliffs, NJ, 1982–85; Mem., Editorial Collective, Womanews, 1982–85; Production Dir, Feminist Press, CUNY, 1985–94; Ed., 1988–90, Mem., Editorial Board, 1990–92, Conditions magazine, New York; Curator, In Our Own Write reading series, New York City Lesbian and Gay Community Services Center, 1988–90; Panelist, Cultural Council Foundation, New York City, 1991. *Publications:* The One You Call Sister: New Women's Fiction (ed., contributor), 1989; Out of Time (novel), 1990; Home Movies, 1993; k d lang, 1996; Chicken (novel), 1997; The Queerest Places: A National Guide to Gay and Lesbian Historic Sites, 1997; The Lesbian and Gay Book of Love and Marriage: Creating the Stories of Our Lives, 1998. Contributions: books and periodicals including: Focus: A Journal for Lesbians; Conditions; Binnewater Tides; Sinister Wisdom; Queer City; Art and Understanding; Blithe House Quarterly. *Honours:* Lambda Literary Award for Lesbian Fiction, 1990; Puffin Foundation Grant, 1990; Best Book for Teens Citation, New York Public Library, 1997. *Literary Agent:* Curtis Brown Ltd, 10 Astor Pl., New York, NY 10003, USA.

MARTÍNEZ, Tomás Eloy, MA; Argentine novelist, essayist and journalist; b. 1934, Tucumán. *Education:* Univ. of Tucumán, Univ. of Paris VII. *Career:* film critic, La Nación, Buenos Aires 1957–61; production chief, Primera Plana, Buenos Aires 1962–69; European correspondent based in Paris, Abril 1969–70; Ed., Panorama 1970–72, cultural supplement of La Opinión 1972–75; Literary Ed. 1975–77, Consultant Ed. 1977–78, El Nacional, Caracas; f., production chief, El Diario de Caracas 1979; jt f., Siglo 21, Guadalajara 1991; f., Ed., literary supplement Primer Plano for Página/12, Buenos Aires 1991–95; columnist, La Nación, Buenos Aires 1996–, New York Times Syndicate 1996–; numerous conferences, courses in univs throughout Europe and America; Prof., Univ. of Maryland 1984–87; Distinguished Prof. and Dir of Latin American Studies programme, Rutgers Univ., NJ; Fellow, Woodrow Wilson Center for Int. Scholars, Washington, DC, Guggenheim Foundation, Kellogg Inst., Univ. of Notre-Dame, IN.

Screenplays include: (with Augusto Roa Bastos) El último piso 1962, El terrorista 1962, El demonio en la sangre 1964, La Madre María 1974. *Publications:* Estructuras del cine argentino (essay) 1961, Sagrado (novel) 1969, La pasión según Trelew (non-fiction) 1974, Los testigos de afuera (essay) 1978, Lugar común la muerte (short stories) 1979, El retrato del artista enmascarado (essay) 1982, La novela de Perón 1985, La mano del amo 1991, Santa Evita 1995, Las memorias del General (novel) 1996, El suelo argentino (non-fiction) 1999, Ficciones verdaderas (short stories) 2000, El vuelo de la reina 2002; numerous essays. *Honours:* Dr hc (John F. Kennedy Univ., Buenos Aires), (Univ. of Tucumán); Premio Alfaguara de Novela 2002. *Address:* Rutgers University, Spanish & Portuguese Department, 105 George Street, New Brunswick, NJ 08901, USA. *E-mail:* eloy@rci.rutgers.edu.

MARTONE, Michael; Prof., Writer and Poet; b. 22 Aug. 1955, Fort Wayne, IN, USA; m. Theresa Pappas, 3 April 1984. *Education:* Butler University, Indianapolis, 1973–76; AB, English, Indiana University, 1977; MA, Fiction Writing, Johns Hopkins University, 1979. *Career:* Asst Prof., 1980–83, Assoc. Prof., 1983–87, Iowa State University; Ed., Poet and Critic magazine, 1981–86; Contributing Ed., North American Review, 1984–; Briggs-Copeland Lecturer on Fiction, 1987–89, Briggs-Copeland Asst Prof. on Fiction, 1989–91, Harvard University; Assoc. Prof. of English, 1991–96, Syracuse University; Prof., Dir, Program for Creative Writing, 1996–, University of Alabama; mem. Associated Writing Programs; National Writers Union; PEN. *Publications:* Fiction: Alive and Dead in Indiana, 1984; Safety Patrol, 1988; Fort Wayne is Seventh on Hitler's List, 1990; Pensees: The Thoughts of Dan Quayle, 1994; Seeing Eye, 1995; The Blue Guide to Indiana, 2001. Prose Poems: At a Loss, 1977; Return to Powers, 1985; The Sex Lives of the Fantastic Four. Other: The Flatness and Other Landscapes (essays), 1999. Editor: A Place of Sense: Essays in Search of the Midwest, 1988; Townships: Pieces of the Midwest, 1992; The Scribner Anthology of Contemporary Short Fiction, 1999. Contributions: various books and journals. *Honours:* National Endowment for the Arts Fellowships, 1983, 1988; Margaret Jones Fiction Prize, Black Ice magazine, 1987; Ingram Merrill Foundation Award, 1989; Pushcart Prize, 1990; Second Place, Thin Air Fiction Contest, 1998; Honorable Mention, 32 Pages Chapbook Contest, 1998; Associated Writing Programs Award for Non-Fiction, 1998. *Address:* PO Box 21179, Tuscaloosa, AL 35402, USA.

MARTY, Martin Emil; academic, writer and editor; b. 5 Feb. 1928, West Point, NE, USA; m. 1st Elsa Schumacher 1952 (died 1981); seven c.; m. 2nd Harriet Lindemann 1982. *Education:* AB, 1949, MDiv, 1952, Concordia Seminary, St Louis; STM, Lutheran School of Theology, Chicago, 1954; PhD, American Religious and Intellectual History, University of Chicago, 1956. *Career:* Ordained Lutheran Pastor, 1952; Pastor, 1950–63; Assoc. Ed., 1956–85, Senior Ed., 1985–98, Christian Century magazine; Co-Ed., Church History magazine, 1963–97; Prof. of the History of Modern Christianity, 1963–, Assoc. Dean, Divinity School, 1970–75, Fairfax M. Cone Distinguished Service Prof., 1978–98, Prof. Emeritus, 1998–, University of Chicago; Ed., Context, 1969–; Dir, The Public Religion Project, 1996–99; Chair., Board of Regents, 1996–2001, Senior Regents, 2002–, St Olaf College; mem. American Acad. of Arts and Sciences, fellow; American Acad. of Religion, pres., 1987–88; American Catholic Historical Asscn, pres., 1981; American Philosophical Society; American Society of Church History, pres., 1971; Society of American Historians, fellow. *Publications:* A Short History of Christianity, 1959; The New Shape of American Religion, 1959; The Improper Opinion, 1961; The Infidel: Freethought and American Religion, 1961; Baptism, 1962; The Hidden Discipline, 1963; Second Chance for American Protestants, 1963; The Religious Press in America (co-author), 1963; Babylon by Choice, 1964; Church Unity and Church Mission, 1964; Varieties of Unbelief, 1964; What Do We Believe?: The Stance of Religion in America (with Stuart E. Rosenberg and Andrew Greeley), 1968; The Search for a Usable Future, 1969; The Modern Schism: Three Paths to the Secular, 1969; Righteous Empire: The Protestant Experience in America, 1970, revised second edn as Protestantism in the United States, 1986; Protestantism, 1972; You Are Promise, 1973; The Fire We Can Light, 1973; The Lutheran People, 1973; What a Catholic Believes as Seen by a Non-Catholic, 1974; The Pro and Con Book of Religious America, 1975; A Nation of Behavers, 1976; Good News in the Early Church, 1976; Religion, Awakening and Revolution, 1977; Religion in America, 1950 to the Present (with Douglas W. Johnson and Jackson W. Carroll), 1979; Friendship, 1980; The Lord's Supper, 1980; Religious Crises in Modern America, 1980; By Way of Response, 1981; The Public Church: Mainline, Evangelical, Catholic, 1981; Health/Medicine and the Faith Traditions: An Inquiry into Religion and Medicine (with Kenneth L. Vaux), 1982; A Cry of Absence: Reflections for the Winter of the Heart, 1983; Health and Medicine in the Lutheran Tradition: Being Well, 1983; Faith and Ferment: An Interdisciplinary Study of Christian Beliefs and Practices (with Joan D. Chittister), 1983; Christian Churches in the United States, 1800–1983, 1984; Christianity in the New World, 1984; Pilgrims in Their Own Land: Five Hundred Years of Religion in America, 1984; Modern American Religion, Vol. I, The Irony of it All, 1986, Vol. II, The Noise of Conflict, 1991, Vol. III, Under God, Indivisible, 1996; An Invitation to American Catholic History, 1986; Religion and Republic: The American Circumstance, 1987; The Glory and the Power: The Fundamentalist Challenge to the Modern World (with R. Scott Appleby), 1992; Places Along the Way: Meditation on the Journey of Faith (with Micah Marty), 1994; A Short History of American Catholicism, 1995; Our Hope for Years to Come (with Micah Marty), 1995; The One and the Many, 1997; The Promise of Winter: Quickening the Spirit on Ordinary Days and in Fallow Seasons (with Micah Marty), 1997; When True Simplicity is Gained: Finding Spiritual Clarity in a Complex World (with Micah Marty), 1998; Politics, Religion and the Common Good, 2000; Education, Religion and the Common Good, 2001. Editor: many books, including: The Fundamentalism Project (with R. Scott Appleby), five vols, 1991–95; Civil Religion, Church and State, 1992; Varieties of Protestantism, 1992; The Writing of American Religious History, 1992; Fundamentalism and Evangelicalism, 1993; Varieties of Religious Expression, 1993; Native American Religion and Black Protestantism, 1993; The Unrelieved Paradox: Studies in the Theology of Franz Bibfeldt (with Jerald C. Brauer), 1994. Contributions: numerous publications. *Honours:* Over 65 hon. doctorates; Brotherhood Award, 1960; National Book Award, 1971; Christopher Award, 1985; National Humanities Medal, 1997; Alumni Medal, University of Chicago, 1998. *Address:* 239 Scottswood Road, Riverside, IL 60546, USA. *E-mail:* memarty@aol.com.

MARWICK, Arthur; Prof. of History and Writer; b. 29 Feb. 1936, Edinburgh, Scotland; one d. *Education:* MA, University of Edinburgh, 1957; BLitt, Balliol College, Oxford, 1960. *Career:* Asst Lecturer, University of Aberdeen, 1959–60; Lecturer, University of Edinburgh, 1960–69; Visiting Prof. of History, SUNY at Buffalo, 1966–67, Rhodes College, Memphis, 1991, University of Perugia, 1991; Prof. of History, 1969–, Dean of Arts, 1978–84, The Open University; Visiting Scholar, Hoover Institution, and Visiting Prof., Stanford University, 1984–85; Directeur d'études invité, L'École des hautes études en sciences sociales, Paris, 1985. *Publications:* The Explosion of British Society 1914–1962, 1963; Clifford Allen: The Open Conspirator, 1964; The Deluge: British Society and the First World War, 1965; Britain in the Century of Total War: War, Peace and Social Change 1900–1967, 1968; The Nature of History, 1970; War and Social Change in the Twentieth Century, 1974; The Home Front: The British and the Second World War, 1976; Women at War 1914–1918, 1977; Class: Image and Reality in Britain, France and the USA Since 1930, 1980; The Thames and Hudson Illustrated Dictionary of British History (ed.), 1980; British Society Since 1945, 1982; Britain in Our Century: Images and Controversies, 1984; Class in the Twentieth Century (ed.), 1986; Beauty in History: Society, Politics and Personal Appearance, c1500 to the Present, 1988; The Arts, Literature and Society (ed.), 1990; Culture in Britain Since 1945, 1991; The Sixties: Cultural Revolution in Britain, France, Italy and the United States 1958–74, 1998; A Modern History of the British Isles, 1914–1999: Circumstances, Events and Outcomes, 2000; Windows on the Sixties: Exploring Key Texts of Media and Culture (co-ed.), 2000; The New Nature of History: Knowledge, Evidence, Language, 2001; The Arts in the West Since 1945, 2002. Contributions: Professional journals. *Honours:* DLitt, Edinburgh, 1980; FRHistS; FRSA. *Address:* 67 Fitzjohn's Ave, Flat 5, Hampstead, London NW3 6PE, England.

MARX, Arthur; Film Writer, Television Writer, Playwright, Dir and Author; b. 21 July 1921, New York, NY, USA. *Education:* University of Southern California, Los Angeles, 1939–40. *Career:* mem. Authors' Guild; Dramatists Guild; International Asscn of Crime Writers; Writers Guild of America. *Publications:* The Ordeal of Willie Brown, 1951; Life with Groucho (biog.), 1954; Not as a Crocodile (short stories), 1958; The Impossible Years (play), 1965; Minnie's Boys (play), 1970; Son of Groucho (autobiog.), 1972; Everybody Loves Somebody Sometime, Especially Himself (biog.), 1974; Sugar and Spice (play), 1974; My Daughter's Rated X (play), 1975; Goldwyn, 1976; Red Skelton (biog.), 1979; Groucho: A Life in Revue (play), 1986; The Nine Lives of Mickey Rooney (biog.), 1986; The Ghost and Mrs Muir (play), 1987; My Life with Groucho (biog.), 1988; Set to Kill (mystery novel), 1993; The Secret Life of Bob Hope (biog.), 1993. Contributions: Los Angeles Magazine; Cigar Aficionado. *Address:* c/o Scovil, Chichak & Galen, 381 Park Ave S, New York, NY 10016, USA.

MARX, Michael William; Writer, Publisher and Teacher; b. 11 Jan. 1951, Philadelphia, PA, USA; m. Ilsun Kang, one s. two d. *Education:* BA, Hobart and William Smith Colleges, New York, 1973; MFA, New York University, 1976; MA, English, Indiana State University. *Career:* Teacher, Indiana State University, 1999–, Lake Land College, Danville, IL, 2000–, Ivy Tech State College, Terre Haute, Indiana, 2001–. *Publications:* A War Ends, 1985; Eric Greenfield – Middle American, 1987; Justus – A Upopia, 1999. Contributions: newspapers, magazines and journals. *E-mail:* michael@michaelmarx.com.

MASCHLER, Thomas Michael; British publisher; b. 16 Aug. 1933; m. 1st Fay Coventry 1970 (divorced 1987); one s. two d.; m. 2nd Regina Kulinicz 1988. *Education:* Leighton Park School. *Career:* Production Asst, André Deutsch 1955–56; Editor, MacGibbon and Kee 1956–58; Fiction Editor, Penguin Books 1958–60; Editorial Dir, Jonathan Cape Ltd 1960–70, Dir 1960–, Chair. 1970–91, Publr 1991–; Dir Random House 1987; Assoc. Producer The French Lieutenant's Woman (film) 1981. *Publications:* Ed. Declarations 1957, New English Dramatists Series 1959–63. *Address:* c/o Random Century House, 20 Vauxhall Bridge Road, London, SW1V 2SA, England.

MASLOW, Jonathan Evan; Writer; b. 4 Aug. 1948, Long Branch, NJ, USA; m. Liliya Khobotkova, 1992. *Education:* BA, American Literature, Marlboro College, Vermont; MS, Columbia University Graduate School of

Journalism. *Career:* Staff Reporter, Cape May County Herald, 1997–2002; Asst City Ed., Herald, 2002–; mem. Authors' Guild. *Publications:* The Owl Papers, 1983; Bird of Life, Bird of Death: A Political Ornithology of Central America, 1986; Sacred Horses: Memoirs of a Turkmen Cowboy, 1994; Torrid Zone: Six Stories of the Gulf Coast, 1995; Footsteps in the Jungle, 1996; Skulls (poems written to accompany Leonard Baskin woodcuts), 2002. Other: A Tramp in the Darien (screenplay), 1990; Geldi: Horsemen of the Turkmen Steppes (screenplay), 1993. Contributions: Magazines and reviews. *Honours:* George Varsell Award, American Acad. of Arts and Letters, 1988; Guggenheim Fellowship, 1989–90; John Heinz Fellowship in Environmental Journalism, 1999; Knight International Press Fund Fellowship, 2001. *Address:* 6636 Petersburg Rd, Woodbine, NJ 08270, USA.

MASON, Bobbie Ann; Writer; b. 1 May 1940, Mayfield, KY, USA; m. Roger B. Rawlings, 12 April 1969. *Education:* BA, University of Kentucky, 1962; MA, SUNY at Binghamton, 1966; PhD, University of Connecticut, 1972. *Career:* Asst Prof. of English, Mansfield State College, PA, 1972–79; Writer-in-Residence, Univ. of Kentucky, 2001–; mem. Authors' Guild; PEN; Southern Fellowship of Writers. *Publications:* Nabokov's Garden, 1974; The Girl Sleuth: A Feminist Guide to the Bobbsey Twins, Nancy Drew and Their Sisters, 1976; Shiloh and Other Stories, 1982; In Country, 1985; Spence + Lila, 1988; Love Life, 1989; Feather Crowns, 1993; Midnight Magic, 1998; Clear Springs, 1999; Zigzagging Down a Wild Trail, 2001; Elvis Presley, 2003. Contributions: anthologies and magazines. *Honours:* Ernest Hemingway Award, 1982; National Endowment for the Arts Grant, 1983; Pennsylvania Arts Council Grants, 1983, 1989; American Acad. and Institute of Arts and Letters Award, 1984; Guggenheim Fellowship, 1984; O. Henry Anthology Awards, 1986, 1988; Southern Book Awards, 1993, 2002. *Address:* c/o Amanda Urban, International Creative Management, 40 W 57th St, New York, NY 10019, USA.

MASON, Connie; Writer; b. 22 April 1930, Niles, MI, USA; m. Lewis G. Mason, 1 July 1950, one s. two d. *Publications:* Tender Fury, 1984; Caress and Conquer, 1985; For Honor's Sake, 1985; Promised Splendour, 1986; My Lady Vixen, 1986; Desert Ecstasy, 1987; Wild is my Heart, 1987; Bold Land, Bold Love, 1988; Tempt the Devil, 1988; Beyond the Horizon, 1989; Love me with Fury, 1989; Wild Love, Wild Land, 1989; Promise Me Forever, 1990; Brave Land, Brave Love, 1990; Surrender to the Fury, 1990; A Frontier Christmas, 1990; Ice and Rapture, 1991; A Promise of Thunder, 1991; Lord of the Night, 1991; Treasures of the Heart, 1992; Wilderness Christmas, 1992; Tears Like Rain, 1993; Wind Rider, 1993; Their First Noel, 1993; Sierra, 1994; Christmas Miracle, 1994; The Lion's Bride, 1994; Taken by You, 1996; Pure Temptation, 1996; A Love to Cherish, 1996; Flame, 1997; Shadow Walker, 1997; To Love a Stranger, 1997; Sheik, 1998; Viking, 1998; Swept Away, 1998; To Tame a Renegade, 1998; Pirate, 1998; Gunslinger, 1999; To Tempt a Rogue, 1999; The Outlaws: Rafe, 2000; A Taste of Sin, 2000; The Outlaws: Jess, 2000; A Breath of Scandal, 2001; The Outlaws: Sam, 2001; The Dragon Lord, 2001; A Touch so Wicked, 2002; The Rogue and the Hellion, 2002; Lionheart, 2002. *Honours:* Storyteller of the Year, Career, 1992; Achievement Award, Romantic Times, 1994. *Address:* PO Box 2908, Portland, OR 97208-2908, USA.

MASON, David James; academic, poet, critic and writer; b. 11 Dec. 1954, Bellingham, WA, USA; m. Anne Lennox 1988; one step-d. *Education:* BA, magna cum laude, English, Colorado College, 1978; MA, English, 1986, PhD, English, 1989, University of Rochester. *Career:* Visiting Instructor, 1983, 1987, Visiting Prof., 1986, 1987, 1988, 1994, Asst Prof., 1998–, Assoc. Prof., 2000–, Colorado College; Instructor, University of Rochester, 1986–88; Asst Prof., 1989–93, Assoc. Prof., 1993–98, Moorhead State University. *Publications:* Blackened Peaches, 1989; Small Elegies, 1990; The Buried Houses, 1991; Questions at Christmas, 1994; Three Characters from a Lost Home, 1995; The Country I Remember, 1996; Land Without Grief, 1996; Rebel Angeles: 25 Poets of the New Formalism (ed. with Mark Jarman), 1996; Kalamitsi, 1997; The Poetry of Life and the Life of Poetry (essays), 2000; Western Wind: An Introduction to Poetry (co-ed.), 2000; Twentieth Century American Poetry (co-ed.), 2003; Twentieth Century American Poetics (co-ed.), 2003; Arrivals (poems), 2004. Contributions: books, reviews, quarterlies, and journals. *Honours:* Nicholas Roerich Poetry Prize, 1991; Alice Fay Di Castagnola Award, Poetry Society of America, 1993; Minnesota Prof. of the Year, Carnegie Foundation for the Advancement of Teaching and Council for Advancement and Support of Education, 1994; Hon. DHL, Colorado College, 1996; Fulbright Artist-in-Residence Fellowship, Greece, 1997. *Address:* 1131 Paradise Valley Drive, Woodland Park, CO 80863, USA.

MASON, Francis Kenneth, FRHistS; editor, writer, archivist and researcher; b. 4 Sept. 1928, London, England. *Education:* Royal Air Force Coll., Cranwell. *Career:* Ed., Flying Review Int. 1963–64; Managing Dir, Profile Publications Ltd 1964–67, Alban Book Services Ltd, Watton, Norfolk; Managing Ed., Guiness Superlatives Ltd, Enfield, Middlesex 1968–71. *Publications:* author 91 books and ed. of numerous others 1961–96; contrib. to radio and television. *Honours:* Int. History Diploma, Aero Club of France, Paris 1973, Founder Fellowship, Canadian Guild of Authors 1988. *Address:* 68 Hunter's Oak, Watton, Thetford, Norfolk IP25 6HL, England.

MASON, Haydn Trevor; academic and writer; b. 12 Jan. 1929, Saundersfoot, Pembrokeshire, Wales. *Education:* BA, University College of Wales, 1949; AM, Middlebury College, Vermont, 1951; DPhil, Jesus College, Oxford, 1960. *Career:* Instructor, Princeton University, 1954–57; Lecturer, 1964–65, Reader, 1965–67, University of Reading; Prof. of European Literature, University of East Anglia, 1967–79; Ed., Studies on Voltaire and the Eighteenth Century, 1977–95; Prof. of French Literature, University of Paris III, 1979–81; Prof. of French, 1981–94, Prof. Emeritus and Senior Research Fellow, 1994–, University of Bristol; Scholar-in-Residence, University of Maryland, 1986; General Ed., Complete Works of Voltaire, 1998–2001; Pres., MHRA, 1999; mem. Asscn of University Profs of French, chair., 1981–82; Society for French Studies, pres., 1982–84; British Society for Eighteenth-Century Studies, pres., 1984–86; International Society for Eighteenth-Century Studies, pres., 1991–95; Voltaire Foundation, dir, 1977–97, chair., board of dirs, 1989–93. *Publications:* Pierre Bayle and Voltaire, 1963; Marivaux: Les Fausses Confidences (ed.), 1964; Leibniz-Arnauld Correspondence (trans. and ed.), 1967; Voltaire: Zadig and Other Stories (ed.), 1971; Voltaire, 1974; Voltaire: A Life, 1981; French Writers and Their Society 1715–1800, 1982; Cyrano de Bergerac: L'Autre Monde, 1984; Voltaire: Discours en vers sur l'homme (ed.), 1991; Candide: Optimism Demolished, 1992; Candide (ed.), 1995; Voltaire: Micromégas and Other Short Fictions, 2002; Le Mondain (ed.), 2003. *Honours:* Officier, Ordre des Palmes Académiques, 1985; Médaille d'Argent de la Ville de Paris, 1989; Prize Winner (with A. Mason), Philosophical Dialogue Competition, European Humanities Research Centre, 1998. *Address:* c/o Dept of French, University of Bristol, Bristol BS8 1TE, England. *E-mail:* haydn .mason@ukgateway.net.

MASON, Lee W. (see Malzberg, Barry).

MASON, Sarah J., (Hamilton Crane), MA; novelist; b. 18 Dec. 1949, Bishop's Stortford, Hertfordshire, England; m. William G. Welland 1976. *Education:* St Andrews Univ., Scotland. *Career:* mem. CWA, Soc. of Authors. *Publications:* Let's Talk of Wills 1985, Murder in the Maze (Trewley and Stone series) 1993, Frozen Stiff (Trewley and Stone series) 1993, Corpse in the Kitchen (Trewley and Stone series) 1993, Dying Breath (Trewley and Stone series) 1994, Sew Easy to Kill (Trewley and Stone series) 1996, Seeing is Deceiving (Trewley and Stone series) 1997, Death on her Doorstep 2003; as Hamilton Crane: Miss Seeton Cracks the Case 1991, Miss Seeton Paints the Town 1991, Hands Up, Miss Seeton 1992, Miss Seeton by Moonlight 1992, Miss Seeton Rocks the Cradle 1992, Miss Seeton Goes to Bat 1993, Miss Seeton Plants Suspicion 1993, Miss Seeton Rules 1994, Starring Miss Seeton 1994, Miss Seeton Undercover 1994, Sold to Miss Seeton 1995, Sweet Miss Seeton 1996, Bonjour Miss Seeton 1997, Miss Seeton's Finest Hour 1999. *Literary Agent:* Curtis Brown Ltd, Haymarket House, 28–29 Haymarket, London, SW1Y 4SP, England. *Telephone:* (20) 7393-4400. *Fax:* (20) 7393-4401. *E-mail:* info@curtisbrown.co.uk. *Website:* www .curtisbrown.co.uk. *E-mail:* 101336.2336@compuserve.com.

MASON, Stanley Allen, MA; editor, translator, poet and dramatist; b. 16 April 1917, Blairmore, AB, Canada; m. Cloris Ielmini 1944; one d. *Education:* Oriel College, Oxford. *Career:* Technical Trans., 1943–63; Literary Ed., Graphis Magazine, 1963–83; Ed., Elements, Dow Chemical Europe house organ, 1969–75. *Publications:* Modern English Structures (with Ronald Ridout), four vols, 1968–72; A Necklace of Words (poems), 1975; A Reef of Honours (poems), 1983; Send Out the Dove (play), 1986; The Alps, by Albrecht von Haller (trans.), 1987; The Everlasting Snow (poems), 1993; Collected Poems, 1993; A German Treasury (anthology, trans.), 1993–95. Contributions: many publications. *Honours:* Borestone Mountain Poetry Award; Living Playwright Award.

MASSIE, Allan (Johnstone); Author; b. 19 Oct. 1938, Singapore; m. Alison Agnes Graham Langlands 1973; two s. one d. *Education:* Trinity Coll., Glenalmond; BA, Trinity Coll., Cambridge. *Career:* Fiction Reviewer, The Scotsman, 1976–; Creative Writing Fellow, Univ. of Edinburgh, 1982–84, Univ. of Glasgow and Univ. of Strathclyde, 1985–86; Columnist, Glasgow Herald, 1985–88, Sunday Times Scotland, 1987–, Daily Telegraph, 1991–; mem. FRSL; Scottish Arts Council. *Publications:* Fiction: Change and Decay in All Around I See, 1978; The Last Peacock, 1980; The Death of Men, 1981; One Night in Winter, 1984; Augustus: The Memoirs of the Emperor, 1986; A Question of Loyalties, 1989; The Hanging Tree, 1990; Tiberius: The Memoirs of an Emperor, 1991; The Sins of the Father, 1991; These Enchanted Woods, 1993; Caesar, 1993; The Ragged Lion, 1994; King David, 1995; Arthur the King, 2003; Caligula, 2003. Other: Muriel Spark, 1979; Ill Met by Gaslight: Five Edinburgh Murders, 1980; The Caesars, 1983; Edinburgh and the Borders: In Verse (ed.), 1983; A Portrait of Scottish Rugby, 1984; Eisenstadt: Aberdeen, Portrait of a City, 1984; Colette: The Woman, the Writer and the Myth, 1986; 101 Great Scots, 1987; PEN New Fiction: Thirty-Two Short Stories (ed.), 1987; How Should Health Services be Financed? A Patient's View, 1988; The Novelist's View of the Market Economy, 1988; Byron's Travels, 1988; Glasgow: Portraits of a City, 1989; The Novel Today: A Critical Guide to the British Novel, 1970–1989, 1990; Edinburgh, 1994. Contributions: periodicals. *Honours:* Niven Award, 1981; Scottish Arts Council Award, 1982. *Address:* Thirladean House, Selkirk TD7 5LU, Scotland.

MASSIE, Robert Kinloch, BA; American writer; b. 5 Jan. 1929, Lexington, KY; m. 1st Suzanne L. Rohrbach 1954 (divorced 1990); one s. two d.; m. 2nd Deborah L. Karl 1992; one s. two d. *Education:* Yale Univ., Univ. of Oxford. *Career:* reporter, Collier's magazine, New York 1955–56; writer, Newsweek magazine, New York 1956–62, USA-1 magazine, New York 1962, Saturday

Evening Post, New York 1962–65; Ferris Prof. of Journalism, Princeton Univ. 1977, 1985; Mellon Prof. in the Humanities, Tulane Univ. 1981; mem. Authors' Guild of America, PEN, Soc. of American Historians. *Publications:* Nicholas and Alexandra 1967, Journey 1976, Peter the Great: His Life and World 1980, Dreadnought: Britain, Germany and the Coming of the Great War 1991, The Romanovs: The Final Chapter 1995, Castles of Steel: Britain, Germany and the Winning of the Great War at Sea 2004; contrib. to periodicals. *Honours:* Christopher Award 1976, Pulitzer Prize for Biography 1981. *Address:* 60 W Clinton Avenue, Irvington, NY 10533, USA.

MASSON, Jeffrey Moussaieff, BA, PhD; writer, editor and translator; b. (Jeffrey Lloyd Masson), 28 March 1941, Chicago, IL, USA; m. Leila Siller; one d. two s. *Education:* Harvard Univ. *Career:* Instructor in Religious Studies, Brown Univ., 1967–68; Asst Prof. of Sanskrit and Indian Studies, 1969–70, Assoc. Prof., 1970–75, Prof., 1976–80, Univ. of Toronto; Visiting Prof. of Sanskrit, 1978–79, Research Assoc., Dept of South and Southeast Asian Studies, 1981–92, Visiting Lecturer, Graduate School of Journalism, 1994, Univ. of California at Berkeley; Projects Dir, Sigmund Freud Archives, New York, 1980–81; Visiting Part-time Lecturer in Journalism, Univ. of Michigan, 1993. *Publications:* Santarasa and Abhinavagupta's Philosophy of Aesthetics (with M. V. Patwardhan), 1969; Avimaraka: Love's Enchanted World (with D. D. Kosambi), 1970; Aesthetic Rapture: The Rasadhyaya of the Natyasastra (with M. V. Patwardhan), two vols, 1970; The Oceanic Feeling: The Origins of Religious Sentiment in Ancient India, 1980; Love Poems from the Ancient Sanskrit (with W. S. Merwin), 1981, revised edn as The Peacock's Egg, 1983; The Assault on Truth: Freud's Suppression of the Seduction Theory, 1984; Complete Letters of Sigmund Freud to Wilhelm Fuess, 1887–1904 (ed. and trans.), 1985; A Dark Science: Women, Sexuality and Psychiatry in the Nineteenth Century, 1987; Against Therapy: Emotional Tyranny and the Myth of Psychological Healing, 1988; The Dhvanyaloka of Anandavardhana with the Locana of Abhinavagupta (co-ed. and co-trans.), 1990; Final Analysis: The Making and Unmaking of a Psychoanalyst, 1991; My Father's Guru: A Journey Through Spirituality and Disillusion, 1992; When Elephants Weep: The Emotional Lives of Animals (with Susan McCarthy), 1994; Lost Prince: The Unsolved Mystery of Kaspar Hauser, 1996; Dogs Never Lie About Love: The Emotional World of Dogs, 1997; The Emperor's Embrace: The Evolution of Fatherhood, 1999; Dogs Have the Strangest Friends and Other True Stories of Animal Feelings, 1999; The Nine Emotional Lives of Cats, 2002; The Pig Who Sang to the Moon: The Emotional World of Farm Animals, 2003; The Pig Who Sang to the Moon 2004; contrib. articles to Atlantic Monthly, International Journal of Psycho-Analysis, New York Times. *Honours:* Hon. Fellow, Dept of Philosophy, Univ. of Auckland. *Literary Agent:* Elaine Markson Literary Agency, 44 Greenwich Avenue, New York, NY 10011, USA. *Address:* PO Box 25930, St Heliers, Auckland, New Zealand.

MASTER, Simon Harcourt; British publisher; b. 10 April 1944, Caterham; m. Georgina M. C. Batsford 1969; two s. *Education:* Ardingly Coll. Sussex. *Career:* Publishing Dir Pan Books Ltd 1973–80, Man. Dir 1980–87; Chief Exec. Random House UK and Exec. Vice-Pres. Random House Int. Group 1987–89, Group Man. Dir Random Century Group 1989–90, Group Deputy Chair. 1989–, Chair., CEO Gen. Books Div., Random House UK 1992–; Chair., Arrow Books 1990–92; Dir (non-exec.) HMSO 1990–95; mem. Council Publrs Asscn 1989–95 (Vice-Pres. 1995–96, 2000–2001, Pres. 1996–97, 2001–02). *Address:* Flat 1, St George's Mansions, Causton Street, London, SW1P 4RZ, England (Home). *Telephone:* (20) 7630-7121 (Home).

MASTERS, Hilary (Thomas); Author and Prof. of English and Creative Writing; b. 3 Feb. 1928, Kansas City, MO, USA; m. 1st Polly Jo McCulloch 5 March 1955 (divorced 1986); one s. two d.; m. 2nd Kathleen E. George 7 June 1994. *Education:* Davidson College, 1944–46; AB, Brown University, 1952. *Career:* Ed.-Publisher, Hyde Park Record newspaper, New York, 1956–59; Prof. of English and Creative Writing, Carnegie Mellon University, 1983–; several visiting university positions; mem. Associated Writing Programs; Authors' Guild; Authors' League of America; PEN Center, New York. *Publications:* The Common Pasture, 1967; An American Marriage, 1969; Palace of Strangers, 1971; Last Stands: Notes from Memory, 1982; Clemmons, 1985; Hammertown Tales, 1986; Cooper, 1987; Manuscript for Murder, 1987; Strickland, 1989; Success: New and Selected Stories, 1992; Home Is the Exile, 1996; In Montaigne's Tower, 2000. Contributions: anthologies and periodicals. *Honours:* Yaddo Fellowships, 1980, 1982, 2000; Fulbright Lecturer to Finland, 1983; Ed.'s Choice, Time magazine, 1984; Los Angeles Times Notable Novel, 1990; Monroe Spears Prize, Sewanee Review, 1997; Balch Prize for Fiction, 1998. *Address:* c/o Dept of English, Carnegie Mellon University, Pittsburgh, PA 15213, USA.

MATAS, Carol; Writer; b. 14 Nov. 1949, Winnipeg, Manitoba, Canada; m. Per K. Brask, 19 Feb. 1977, one s. one d. *Education:* BA, English, University of Western Ontario, 1969; Graduate, Actors' Lab, London England, 1972. *Career:* mem. International PEN; Manitoba Writers Guild; Society of Children's Book Writers and Illustrators; Writers Guild of Canada; Writer's Union of Canada. *Publications:* The D.N.A Dimension, 1982; The Fusion Factor, 1986; Zanu, 1986; Me, Myself and I, 1987; Lisa, 1987, US edn as Lisa's War, 1989; Jesper, 1989, US edn as Code Name Kris, 1990; Adventure in Legoland, 1991; The Race, 1991; Sworn Enemies, 1993; Safari Adventure in Legoland, 1993; Daniel's Story, 1993; The Lost Locket, 1994; The Burning Tree, 1994; Of Two Minds (with Perry Nodelman), 1994; The Primrose Path, 1995; After the War, 1996; More Minds (with Perry Nodelman), 1996; The Freak, 1997; The Garden, 1997; Greater Than Angels, 1998; Telling, 1998. *Honours:* many awards and citations for young people's literature. *Address:* c/o Ashley Grayson Literary Agency, 1342 18th St, San Pedro, CA 90732, USA.

MATHESON, Alex (see Mackay, James Alexander).

MATHESON, Richard (Burton); Writer and Dramatist; b. 20 Feb. 1926, Allendale, NJ, USA; m. Ruth Ann Woodson, 1 July 1952, two s. two d. *Education:* BA, University of Missouri, 1949. *Career:* mem. Dramatists' Guild; Writers' Guild. *Publications:* Novels: Someone is Bleeding, 1953; Fury on Sunday, 1953; I Am Legend, 1954; The Shrinking Man, 1956; A Stir of Echoes, 1958; Ride the Nightmare, 1959; The Beardless Warriors, 1960; Hell House, 1971; Bid Time Return, 1975; What Dreams May Come, 1978; Earthbound, 1982; Through Channels, 1989; Journal of the Gun Years, 1991; The Gunfight, 1993; 7 Steps to Midnight, 1993; Shadow on the Sun, 1994; The Memoirs of Wild Bill Hickock, 1995; Now You See It..., 1995; Passion Play, 2000; Hunger and Thirst, 2000. Other: Born of Man and Woman: Tales of Science Fiction and Fantasy, 1954; The Shores of Space, 1957; Shock: Thirteen Tales to Thrill and Terrify, 1961; Shock II, 1964; Shock III, 1966; Shock Waves, 1970; By the Gun: Six from Richard Matheson, 1993; Shadow on the Sun, 1993; The Path, 1993; The Memoirs of Wild Bill Harris, 1996; The Twilight Zone Scripts of Richard Matheson, 1998; Hunger and Thirst, 2000; Camp Pleasant, 2001; ABU and the 7 Marvels, 2002; Hunted Past Reason, 2002; A Primer of Reality, 2002. Non-Fiction: The Path: Metaphysics for the '90s, 1993; Robert Bloch: Appreciations of the Master (ed. with Ricia Mainhardt), 1995; Mediums Rare, 2000. Other: many screenplays. *Honours:* Hugo Award, World Science Fiction Convention, 1958; Writers' Guild Awards, 1960, 1974; World Fantasy Award, 1976, and Life Achievement Award, 1984; Bram Stoker Award, 1990. *Address:* PO Box 81, Woodland Hills, CA 91365, USA.

MATHEWS, Harry; writer, poet, editor and translator; b. 14 Feb. 1930, New York, NY, USA. *Education:* Princeton Univ., Harvard Univ., L'École Normale de Musique, Paris. *Publications:* prose: The Conversions 1962, The Tlooth 1966, The Sinking of the Odradek Stadium and Other Novels 1975, Selected Declarations of Dependence 1977, Country Cooking and Other Stories 1980, Cigarettes 1987, The Orchard (memoirs) 1988, Twenty Lines a Day 1988, Singular Pleasures 1988, The American Experience 1991, Immeasurable Distances (criticism) 1991, The Journalist 1994, Oulipo Compendium (co-ed.) 1998, Sainte Catherine 2000, The Human Country 2002, The Case of the Persevering Maltese: Collected Essays 2003; poetry: The Planisphere 1974, Trial Impressions 1977, Armenian Papers 1987, Out of Bounds 1989, A Mid-Season Sky 1992; contrib. to numerous anthologies, reviews, quarterlies and journals. *Honours:* Nat. Endowment for the Arts grant 1982, American Acad. and Inst. of Arts and Letters Award 1991. *Literary Agent:* Maxine Groffsky, 2 Fifth Avenue, New York, NY 10011, USA. *E-mail:* hmathews2@cs.com.

MATHEWS, Nieves Hayat, (Nieves de Madariaga), BA; writer and poet; b. 3 Dec. 1917, Glasgow, Scotland; m. Paul William Mathews 1939; one s. one d. *Education:* King's College, London. *Publications:* She Died Without a Light, 1956; Francis Bacon: The History of a Character Assassination, 1996. Contributions: Reviews and journals. *Address:* Tecognano, 52040, Montanare di Cortona, Arezzo, Italy.

MATHIAS, Roland Glyn; Poet and Writer; b. 4 Sept. 1915, Talybont-on-Usk, Breconshire, Wales; m. Mary (Molly) Hawes, 4 April 1944, one s. two d. *Education:* BA, Modern History, 1936, BLitt (by thesis), 1939, MA, 1944, Jesus College, Oxford. *Career:* Schoolmaster; Ed., The Anglo-Welsh Review, 1961–76; Extra-Mural Lecturer, University College, Cardiff, 1970–77; Visiting Prof., University of Alabama at Birmingham, 1971; mem. Welsh Arts Council, chair., literature committee, 1976–79. *Publications:* Poetry: Break in Harvest, 1946; The Roses of Tretower, 1952; The Flooded Valley, 1960; Absalom in the Tree, 1971; Snipe's Castle, 1979; Burning Brambles, 1983; A Field at Vallorcines, 1996; The Collected Poems of Roland Mathias, 2002. Short Stories: The Eleven Men of Eppynt, 1956. Non-Fiction: Whitsun Riot, 1963; Vernon Watkins, 1974; John Cowper Powys as Poet, 1979; A Ride Through the Wood, 1985; Anglo-Welsh Literature: An Illustrated History, 1987; The Collected Short Stories of Roland Mathias, 2001. Contributions: many literary journals and periodicals. *Honours:* Hon. DHL, Georgetown University, Washington, DC, 1985. *Address:* Deffrobani, 5 Maescelyn, Brecon, Powys LD3 7NL, Wales.

MATHIEU, André, (Andrew Matthew, Andrew Matthews); Novelist; b. 10 April 1942, Beauce, France; m. B. Perron, 20 July 1963, one d. *Education:* BA, Laval University. *Publications:* Nathalie, 1982; La Sauvage, 1985; Aurore, 1990; Donald and Marion, 1990; Arnold's Treasure, 1994; 20 Others.

MATRAY, James Irving, BA, MA, PhD; academic and writer; *Professor of History, California State University, Chico*; b. 6 Dec. 1948, Chicago, IL, USA; m. Mary Karin Heine 1971; one s. one d. *Education:* Lake Forest Coll., Univ. of Virginia. *Career:* Visiting Asst Prof. 1980–82, Asst Prof. 1982–87, Assoc. Prof. 1987–92, Prof. of History 1992–2002, New Mexico State Univ.; Visiting Assoc. Prof. of History, Univ. of Southern California 1988–89; Distinguished Visiting Scholar, Hyung Hee Univ., Seoul 1990; Dept Chair, Prof. of History, California State Univ., Chico 2002–; mem. American Historical Asscn, Soc. for Historians of American Foreign Relations. *Pub-*

lications: The Reluctant Crusade: American Foreign Policy in Korea 1941–1950 1985, Historical Dictionary of the Korean War 1991, Korea and the Cold War: Division, Destruction, and Disarmament (ed. with Kim Chull-Baum) 1993, Japan's Emergence as a Global Power 2000, East Asia and the United States: An Encyclopedia of Relations Since 1784, Korea Divided: The 38th Parallel and the DMZ; contrib. to many scholarly books and journals. *Honours:* several research grants, Soc. for Historians of American Relations Stuart L. Bernath Article Award (co-recipient) 1980, Best Reference Book Award, Library Journal 1992, Outstanding Academic Book Award, Choice 1992. *Address:* 246 Eagle Nest Drive, Chico, CA 95928, USA.

MATSON, Clive; Poet, Playwright and Teacher; b. 13 March 1941, Los Angeles, CA, USA. *Education:* Undergraduate work, University of Chicago, 1958–59; MFA, Poetry, School of the Arts, Columbia University. *Publications:* Mainline to the Heart, 1966; Space Age, 1969; Heroin, 1972; On the Inside, 1982; Equal in Desire, 1983; Hourglass, 1987; Breath of Inspiration (essay), 1987; Let the Crazy Child Write, 1998. Contributions: anthologies and journals. *Honours:* Graduate Writing Fellowship, Columbia University, 1987–88. *Address:* 472 44th St, Oakland, CA 94609, USA.

MATTESON, Stefanie (Newton); Writer; b. 9 Oct. 1946, Hackensack, NJ, USA; m. 1st David Bruce Matteson 1971 (divorced 1994); one s. one d.; m. 2nd Richard Leon Grocholski 31 Dec. 1994 (divorced 2002). *Education:* BA, Chemistry, Skidmore College, Saratoga Springs, New York, 1968; Boston University, 1969; School of Public Communications. *Career:* mem. MWA, Dir, New York Chapter, 1996–97; Sisters in Crime. *Publications:* Murder at the Spa, 1990; Murder at Teatime, 1991; Murder on the Cliff, 1991; Murder on the Silk Road, 1992; Murder at the Falls, 1993; Murder on High, 1994; Murder among the Angels, 1996; Murder under the Palms, 1997. *Literary Agent:* Dominick Abel Literary Agency, 146 W 82nd St, No. 1B, New York, NY 10024, USA. *Address:* 610 Old Chester Rd, Far Hills, NJ 07931, USA.

MATTHEW, Andrew (see Mathieu, André).

MATTHEW, Christopher Charles Forrest; Novelist, Journalist and Broadcaster; b. 8 May 1939, London, England; m. Wendy Mary Matthew, 19 Oct. 1979, two s. one d. *Education:* BA, MA, St Peter's College, Oxford. *Career:* Ed., Times Travel Guide, 1972–73; Columnist, Punch, 1983–88; Restaurant Critic, Vogue (UK), 1983–86; Book and Television Reviewer, Daily Mail; mem. Society of Authors. *Publications:* A Different World: Stories of Great Hotels, 1976; Diary of a Somebody, 1978; Loosely Engaged, 1980; The Long Haired Boy, 1980; The Crisp Report, 1981; Three Men in a Boat (with Benny Green), 1982; The Junket Man, 1983; How to Survive Middle Age, 1983; Family Matters, 1987; The Amber Room, 1995; A Nightingale Sang in Fernhurst Road, 1998; Now We Are Sixty, 1999; Knocking On, 2001; Now We Are Sixty (and a bit), 2003. Contributions: newspapers, magazines and television. *Address:* 35 Drayton Gardens, London SW10 9RY, England. *E-mail:* cmatt@onetel.net.uk.

MATTHEWS, Andrew (see Mathieu, André).

MATTHEWS, Patricia Anne, (P. A. Brisco, Patty Brisco, Laura Wylie); Author; b. 1 July 1927, San Fernando, CA, USA; m. 1st Marvin Owen Brisco 1946 (divorced 1961); two s.; m. 2nd Clayton Hartly Matthews 1971. *Education:* California State University, Los Angeles. *Career:* mem. Romantic Writers Asscn; MWA; Sisters in Crime; Novelists Ink. *Publications:* Merry's Treasure, 1969; The Other People, 1970; The House of Candles, 1973; Mist of Evil, 1976; Love, Forever More, 1977; Raging Rapids, 1978; Love's Daring Dream, 1978; Love's Golden Destiny, 1979; Love's Many Faces (poems), 1979; The Night Visitor, 1979; Love's Raging Tide, 1980; Love's Sweet Agony, 1980; Love's Bold Journey, 1980; Tides of Love, 1981; Embers of Dawn, 1982; Flames of Glory, 1983; Dancer of Dreams, 1984; Gambler in Love, 1985; Tame the Restless Heart, 1986; Destruction at Dawn, 1986; Twister, 1986; Enchanted, 1987; Thursday and the Lady, 1987; Mirrors, 1988; The Dreaming Tree, 1989; Sapphire, 1989; Oasis, 1989; The Death of Love, 1990; The Unquiet, 1991. With Clayton Matthews: Midnight Whispers, 1981; Empire, 1982; Midnight Lavender, 1985; The Scent of Fear, 1992; Taste of Evil, 1993; Vision of Death, 1993; The Sound of Murder, 1994. Contributions: anthologies and magazines. *Honours:* Porgie Award, 1979, Silver Medal, 1983, Bronze Medal, 1983, West Coast Review of Books; Team Writing Award (with Clayton Hartly Matthews), 1983, Reviewers Choice Awards for Best Historical Gothic, 1986–87, Affaire de Coeur Silver Pen Readers Award, 1989, Romantic Times. *Address:* c/o Jay Garon, 415 Central Park W, New York, NY 10025, USA.

MATTHIAS, John (Edward); Prof., Poet, Writer and Trans; b. 5 Sept. 1941, Columbus, Ohio, USA; m. Diana Clare Jocelyn, 27 Dec. 1967, two c. *Education:* BA, Ohio State University, 1963; MA, Stanford University, 1966; Postgraduate Studies, University of London, 1966–67. *Career:* Asst Prof., 1967–73, Assoc. Prof., 1973–80, Prof., 1980–, University of Notre Dame; Visiting Fellow in Poetry, 1976–77, Assoc., 1977–, Clare Hall, Cambridge; Visiting Prof., Skidmore College, 1978, University of Chicago, 1980; mem. American Literary Trans Asscn; PEN American Center; Poetry Society of America. *Publications:* Bucyrus, 1971; 23 Modern Poets (ed.), 1971; Turns, 1975; Crossing, 1979; Five American Poets (ed.), 1979; Contemporary Swedish Poetry (trans. with Goran Printz-Pahlson), 1979; Barthory and Lermontov, 1980; Northern Summer: New and Selected Poems, 1984; David Jones: Man and Poet, 1989; Tva Dikter, 1989; A Gathering of Ways, 1991; Reading Old Friends, 1992; Selected Works of David Jones, 1993; Swimming at Midnight: Selected Shorter Poems, 1995; Beltane at Aphelion: Collected Longer Poems, 1995. Contributions: numerous anthologies, reviews, quarterlies, and journals. *Honours:* Fulbright Grant, 1966; Swedish Institute Trans. Award, 1977–78; Columbia University Trans. Award, 1978; Ingram Merrill Foundation Awards, 1984, 1990; Society of Midland Authors Poetry Award, 1986; Society for the Study of Midwestern Literature Poetry Prize, 1986; Slobodan Janovic Literary Prize, 1989; George Bogin Memorial Award, Poetry Society of America, 1990; Lilly Endowment Grant, 1991–92; Ohio Library Asscn Poetry Award, 1996. *Address:* c/o Dept of English, University of Notre Dame, Notre Dame, IN 46556, USA.

MATTHIESSEN, Peter, BA; American writer; b. 22 May 1927, New York; m. 1st Patricia Southgate 1951 (divorced); m. 2nd Deborah Love 1963 (died 1972); three s. one d.; m. 3rd Maria Eckhart 1980. *Education:* Sorbonne, Paris, Yale Univ. *Career:* co-founder and Ed. The Paris Review 1953–; ordained a Zen Monk 1981; fmr corresp., New Yorker; Trustee New York Zoological Soc. 1965–78; mem. American Acad. of Arts and Letters 1974–, Nat. Inst. of Arts and Science 1986–. *Publications:* Race Rock 1954, Partisans 1955, Raditzer 1960, Wildlife in America 1959, The Cloud Forest 1961, Under the Mountain Wall 1963, At Play in the Fields of the Lord 1965, The Shore Birds of North America 1967, Oomingmak: The Expedition to the Musk Ox Island in the Bering Sea 1967, Sal si puedes 1969, Blue Meridian 1971, The Tree Where Man Was Born 1972, The Wind Birds 1973, Far Tortuga 1975, The Snow Leopard 1978, Sand Rivers 1981, In the Spirit of the Crazy Horse 1983, Indian Country 1984, Midnight Turning Grey 1984, Nine-Headed Dragon River 1986, Men's Lives 1986, Partisans 1987, On the River Styx 1989, Killing Mr Watson 1990, African Silences 1991, Baikal 1992, African Silences 1992, Baikal 1992, Shadows of Africa 1992, East of Lo Monthang: In the Land of Mustang 1995, Lost Man's River 1997, Bone by Bone (novel) 1999, Tigers in the Snow 2000, Peter Matthiessen Reader: Non Fiction 1959-1991 2000, An African Trilogy 2000, Sal si Puedes – Cesar Chávez and the New American Revolution 2000, Birds of Heaven: Travels with Cranes 2001, Ends of the Earth: Voyages to Antarctica 2003. *Honours:* Atlantic Prize 1950, American Acad. of Arts and Letters Award 1963, National Book Award 1978, John Burroughs Medal 1981, African Wildlife Leadership Foundation Award 1982, Gold Medal for Distinction in Natural History 1985, Orion-John Hay Award 1999, Soc. of Conservation Biologists Award 1999, Heinz Award for Arts and Humanities 2000, Lannan Lifetime Achievement Award 2002, Harvard Nat. History Museum Roger Tory Peterson Medal 2003. *Address:* The Paris Review, 541 East 72 Street, New York, NY 10021, USA.

MATTINGLEY, Christobel Rosemary; Writer; b. 26 Oct. 1931, Adelaide, SA, Australia; m. Cecil David Mattingley, 17 Dec. 1953, two s. one d. *Education:* BA, German, 1951; Registration Certificate and Assoc. of the Library Asscn of Australia, 1971. *Publications:* Windmill at Magpie Creek, 1971; The Great Ballagundi Damper Bake, 1975; Rummage, 1981; The Angel with a Mouth Organ, 1984; The Miracle Tree, 1985; Survival in Our Own Land: Aboriginal Experiences in South Australia since 1836, 1988; The Butcher, the Beagle and the Dog Catcher, 1990; Tucker's Mob, 1992; The Sack, 1993; No Gun for Asmir, 1993; The Race, 1995; Asmir in Vienna, 1995; Escape from Sarajevo, 1996; Ginger, 1997; Daniel's Secret, 1997; Work Wanted, 1998; Hurry up Alice, 1998; Cockawun and Cockatoo, 1999; First Friend, 2000; King of the Wilderness, 2001, Ruby of Trowulta. Contributions: Australian Library Journal; New Zealand Libraries; Landfall; Reading Time; Classroom; Magpies; Something About the Author Autobiography Series. *Honours:* Advance Australia Award, 1990; Hon. Doctorate, University of South Australia, 1995; AM, 1996; Patron, Society of Women Writers, 1998–; Pheme Tanner Award, La Trobe University, 1999. *Literary Agent:* Curtis Brown, 2 Boundary Street, Paddington, NSW 2021, Australia. *Address:* 10 Rosebank Terrace, Stonyfell, SA 5066, Australia.

MATURA, Thaddee; Franciscan Monk, Theologian and Scholar; b. 24 Oct. 1922, Zalesie Wielkie, Poland. *Education:* LicTh, Pontificio Ateneo Antoniano, Rome, 1953; LicBiblical Studies, Studio Biblico Francescano, Jerusalem, 1955. *Career:* Entered Franciscan Order, 1940; Mem., Tantur Ecumenical Institute, Jerusalem, 1973–75; Religious Counselor, all cloistered monasteries, France, 1981–90. *Publications:* Célibat et communauté: Les Fondements évangéliques de la vie religieuse, 1967, English trans. as Celibacy and Community: The Gospel Foundation for Religious Life, 1968; La Vie religieuse au tournant, 1971, English trans. as The Crisis of Religious Life, 1973; Readings in Franciscanism (ed. with Dacian Francis Bluma), 1972; La Naissance d'un charisme, 1973, English trans. as The Birth of a Movement, 1975; Le Projet évangélique de François d'Assise aujourd-hui, 1977, English trans. as The Gospel Life of Francis of Assisi Today, 1980; Le Radicalisme évangélique, 1978, English trans. as Gospel Radicalism, 1984; Franz von Assisi (with Anton Rotzetter), 1981; François d'Assise, Ecrits (with Theophile Desbonnets), 1981; Suivre Jésus, 1983; Claire d'Assise, Ecrits (with Marie-France Becker), 1985; Une absence ardente, 1988; Dieu le Père trés saint, 1990; Chants de terre étrangere, 1991; Prier 15 jours avec François d'Assise, 1994, English trans. as A Dwelling Place fo the Most High, 1999; François d'Assise 'auteur spirituel',

1996, English trans. as Francis of Assisi: The Message in his Writings, 1997; François d'Assise, maître de vie spirituelle, 2000. *Address:* 33 rue de la Porte-Evèque, 84000 Avignon, France. *E-mail:* thaddee.matura@wanadoo .fr.

MATVEJEVIC, Predrag; Writer; b. 1932, Mostar, Yugoslavia. *Career:* frmly Prof. of French Literature, Zagreb Univ., Prof. of Comparative Literatures, Sorbonne, Paris; emigrated to France, 1991–94, Italy, 1994–; currently teaches at New Sorbonne, Paris, and Slavic Studies, La Sapienza Univ., Rome; Vice-Pres., International PEN, London; Pres., Foundation Laboratori Mediterraneo, Naples; mem. f. mem., Sarajevo Asscn, Paris and Rome. *Publications:* Pour une poétique de l'événement, 1979; Breviario Mediterraneo, 1987; Epistolario dell'altra Europa, 1992; Sarajevo Motta, 1995; Ex Jugoslavia. Diario di una guerra, 1995; Golfo di Venezia; Mondo Ex - Confessioni, 1996; Tra asilo ed esilio, 1998; Il Mediterraneo e l'Europa lezioni al College de France, 1998; I signori della guerra, 1999; Isolario mediterraneo, 2000. *Honours:* European Essay Prize, 1992; French European Book Prize, 1993; Légion d'honneur. *Address:* c/o International PEN, 9–10 Charterhouse Bldgs, Goswell Rd, London EC1M 7AT, England. *E-mail:* matvejevic@mclink.it. *Website:* www.giardini.sm/matvejevic/.

MAUPIN, Armistead Jones, Jr, BA; writer; b. 13 May 1944, Washington, DC, USA. *Education:* University of North Carolina at Chapel Hill. *Career:* reporter, News and Courier, Charleston, 1970–71, Associated Press, 1971–72; Columnist, Pacific Sun, San Francisco, 1974, San Francisco Chronicle, 1976–77. *Publications:* Tales of the City, 1978; More Tales of the City, 1980; Further Tales of the City, 1982; Babycakes, 1984; Significant Others, 1987; Sure of You, 1989; Maybe the Moon, 1992; The Night Listener, 2000. Other: Libretto for the musical Heart's Desire, 1990. Television Programme: Armistead Maupin's Tales of the City, 1993. Contributions: periodicals. *Honours:* Best Dramatic Serial Award, RTS, 1994; George Foster Peabody Award, 1994. *Literary Agent:* Steven Barclay Agency, 12 Western Avenue, Petaluma, CA 94952, USA. *Telephone:* (707) 773-0654. *Fax:* (707) 778-1868. *Website:* www.barclayagency.com. *Address:* 584 Castro Street, No. 528, San Francisco, CA 94114, USA.

MAVOR, Elizabeth Osborne; Author; b. 17 Dec. 1927, Glasgow, Scotland. *Education:* St Andrews, 1940–45; St Leonard's and St Anne's Colleges, Oxford, 1947–50. *Publications:* Summer in the Greenhouse, 1959; The Temple of Flora, 1961; The Virgin Mistress: A Biography of the Duchess of Kingston, 1964, US edn as The Virgin Mistress: A Study in Survival: The Life of the Duchess of Kingston; The Redoubt, 1967; The Ladies of Llangollen: A Study in Romantic Friendship, 1971; A Green Equinox, 1973; Life with the Ladies of Llangollen, 1984; The Grand Tour of William Beckford, 1986; The White Solitaire, 1988; The American Journals of Fanny Kemble, 1990; The Grand Tours of Katherine Wilmot, France 1801–3 and Russia 1805–7, 1992; The Captain's Wife, The South American Journals of Maria Graham 1821–23, 1993. *Literary Agent:* Curtis Brown Ltd, Haymarket House, 28–29 Haymarket, London, SW1Y 4SP, England. *Telephone:* (20) 7393-4400. *Fax:* (20) 7393-4401. *E-mail:* info@curtisbrown.co .uk. *Website:* www.curtisbrown.co.uk.

MAXWELL, Catherine Fern, (Cathy Maxwell); Writer; b. 17 July 1953, Memphis, Tennessee, USA; m. Kevin M. Maxwell, 27 May 1979, one s. two d. *Education:* BA, Washington University, 1975. *Publications:* All Things Beautiful, 1994; Treasured Vows, 1996; You and No Other, 1996; Falling in Love Again, 1997; When Dreams Come True, in press. *Honours:* Corecipient, First Place Award, Best Read of 1994, Reader's Voice; Award, Best Historical Love and Laughter, Romantic Times, 1996. *Literary Agent:* Rowland-Axelrod, 510 E 23rd St, Suite 8-G, New York, NY 10010-5020, USA. *Address:* PO Box 1532, Midlothian, VA 23113, USA. *E-mail:* CathyMaxwell@msn.com.

MAXWELL, Douglas; British playwright; b. 1974. *Plays:* The Chameleon's Play 1997, The Crusader 1998, Helmet 1999, Our Bad Magnet 2000, Decky Does a Bronco 2001, Variety 2002. *Honours:* Fringe First, Edinburgh Festival. *Literary Agent:* PFD, Drury House, 34–43 Russell Street, London, WC2B 5HA, England. *Telephone:* (20) 7344-1000. *Fax:* (20) 7836-9543. *Website:* www.pfd.co.uk.

MAXWELL, Glyn (Meurig); Poet, Writer, Reviewer and Ed.; b. 7 Nov. 1962, Welwyn Garden City, Hertfordshire, England. *Education:* BA, English, Worcester College, Oxford, 1985; MA, Creative Writing, Boston University, Massachusetts, 1988. *Career:* mem. PEN; Poetry Society. *Publications:* Tale of the Mayor's Son (poems), 1990; Out of the Rain (poems), 1992; Gnyss the Magnificent: Three Verse Plays, 1993; Blue Burneau (novel), 1994; Rest for the Wicked (poems), 1995; The Breakage, 1998; Time's Fool, 2001. Contributions: Reviews, journals, and magazines. *Honours:* Poetry Book Society Choice, 1990, and Recommendation, 1992; Eric Gregory Award, 1991; Somerset Maugham Award, 1993. *Address:* c/o Bloodaxe Books Ltd, Highgreen, Tarset, Northumberland NE48 1RP, England.

MAXWELL, Gordon Stirling; Archaeologist; b. 21 March 1938, Edinburgh, Scotland; m. Kathleen Mary King, 29 July 1961, two d. *Education:* MA, University of St Andrews. *Career:* Curatorial Officer, Royal Commission for Ancient and Historical Monuments, Scotland, 1964–; mem. FRSA; Society of Antiquaries of London, fellow; Society of Antiquaries of Scotland, fellow. *Publications:* The Impact of Aerial Reconnaissance on Archaeology (ed.), 1983; Rome's Northwest Frontier: The Antonine Wall, 1983; The Romans in Scotland, 1989; A Battle Lost: Romans and Caledonians at Mons Graupius, 1990. Contributions: Britannia; Proceedings of the Society of Antiquaries of Scotland; Glasgow Archaeological Journal. *Address:* Micklegarth, 72a High St, Aberdour, Fife KY3 0SW, Scotland.

MAXWELL, Ian, MA; British/French publisher; b. 15 June 1956, Maisons-Laffitte, France; brother of Kevin Maxwell ; m.1st Laura Plumb 1991 (divorced 1998); m. 2nd Tara Dudley Smith 1999. *Education:* Marlborough Coll. and Balliol Coll., Oxford. *Career:* Man. Dir Pergamon Press France 1980–81; Jt Man. Dir Pergamon Pres. GmbH 1980; Marketing Dir Pergamon Press Inc. 1982–83; Dir Sales Devt BPCC PLC 1985–86; Dir Group Marketing BPCC PLC (now Maxwell Communication Corpn PLC) 1986; Chair. Agence Centrale de Presse, Paris 1986–89; Dir TFI TV station, Paris 1987–89; CEO Maxwell Pergamon Publrs 1988–89; Jt Man. Dir Maxwell Communication Corpn 1988–91; Acting Chair. Mirror Group Newspapers 1991; Dir New York Daily News –1991, Telemonde Holdings 1997–; publishing consultant Westbourne Communications Ltd 1993; Publr Maximov Publs Ltd. 1995–; Chair. Derby Co. Football Club 1984–87, Vice-Chair. 1987–91; mem. Nat. Theatre Devt Council 1986; Pres. Club d'Investissement Media 1988.

MAXWELL, John (see Freemantle, Brian (Harry)).

MAXWELL, Patricia Anne, (Jennifer Blake, Maxine Patrick, Patricia Ponder, Elizabeth Trehearne); writer and poet; b. 9 March 1942, Winn Parish, LA, USA; m. Jerry R. Maxwell 1957; two s. two d. *Career:* writer-in-residence, Univ. of Northeastern Louisiana; mem. Nat. League of American Pen Women, Romance Writers of America. *Publications include:* Love's Wild Desire, 1977; Tender Betrayal, 1979; The Storm and the Splendor, 1979; Golden Fancy, 1980; Embrace and Conquer, 1981; Royal Seduction, 1983; Surrender in Moonlight, 1984; Midnight Waltz, 1985; Fierce Eden, 1985; Royal Passion, 1986; Prisoner of Desire, 1986; Southern Rapture, 1987; Louisiana Dawn, 1987; Perfume of Paradise, 1988; Love and Smoke, 1989; Spanish Serenade, 1990; Joy and Anger, 1991; Wildest Dreams, 1992; Arrow to the Heart, 1993; Shameless, 1994; Silver-Tongued Devil, 1996; Tigress, 1996; Garden of Scandal, 1997. Contributions: anthologies and periodicals. *Honours:* Best Historical Romance Novelist of the Year, 1985; Reviewer's Choices, 1984, 1995, Romantic Times; Golden Treasure Award, Romance Writers of America, 1987; Romance Hall of Fame, Affaire de Coeur, 1995; Frank Waters Award for Writing Excellence, 1997. *Literary Agent:* Richard Curtis Associates Inc., 171 E 74th Street, Second Floor, New York, NY 10021, USA. *Website:* www.curtisagency.com.

MAY, Beatrice (see Astley, Thea).

MAY, Derwent (James); Author and Journalist; b. 29 April 1930, Eastbourne, Sussex, England; m. Yolanta Izabella Sypniewska, one s. one d. *Education:* MA, Lincoln College, Oxford, 1952. *Career:* Theatre and Film Critic, Continental Daily Mail, Paris, 1952–53; Lecturer in English, University of Indonesia, 1955–58; Senior Lecturer in English, Universities of Łódź and Warsaw, 1959–63; Chief Leader Writer, TLS, 1963–65; Literary Ed., The Listener, 1965–86; Literary and Arts Ed., Sunday Telegraph, 1986–90, The European, 1990–91; European Arts Ed., The Times, 1992–; mem. Beefsteak Club; Garrick Club. *Publications:* Fiction: The Professionals, 1964; Dear Parson, 1969; The Laughter in Djakarta, 1973; A Revenger's Comedy, 1979. Non-Fiction: Proust, 1983; The Times Nature Diary, 1983; Hannah Arendt, 1986; The New Times Nature Diary, 1993; Feather Reports, 1996; Critical Times: The History of the Times Literary Supplement 2001; How To Attract Birds to Your Garden, 2001. Contributions: Encounter; Hudson Review. *Honours:* Mem., Booker Prize Jury, 1978; Hawthornden Prize Committee, 1987–. *Address:* 201 Albany St, London NW1 4AB, England.

MAY, Gita; Prof. of French and Writer; b. 16 Sept. 1929, Brussels, Belgium; m. Irving May, 21 Dec. 1947. *Education:* Hunter College, CUNY, 1953; MA, 1954, PhD, 1957, Columbia University. *Career:* Prof. of French and Chair., Dept of French, Columbia University; Gen. Ed., The Age of Revolution and Romanticism, 1990–; mem. Société Française d'Étude du 18e Siècle; Société Diderot; North American Society for the Study of Rousseau. *Publications:* Diderot Studies III (ed. with O. Fellows), 1961; Madame Roland and the Age of Revolution, 1970; Stendhal and the Age of Napoleon, 1977; Diderot: Essais sur la peinture, Vol. XIV of his complete works (ed.), 1984; Pensées détachées sur la peinture, 1995; Rebecca West, 1996, Anita Brookner, 1997; Graham Swift, 1999. Contributions: Dictionary of Literary Biography, 2003; books and professional journals. *Honours:* Guggenheim Fellowship, 1964; Officier, Ordre des Palmes Académiques, 1981; National Endowment for the Humanities Senior Fellow, 1971; Van Amringe Distinguished Book Award, Columbia University, 1971. Memberships American Society of 18th Century Studies, pres., 1985–86; MLA, exec. council, 1980–83. *Address:* c/o Dept of French, Columbia University, 516 Philosophy Hall, New York, NY 10027, USA. *E-mail:* gm9@columbia.edu.

MAY, Julian; Writer; b. 10 July 1931, Chicago, IL, USA; m. Thaddeus E. Dikty, 1953, two s. one d. *Publications:* Over 250 books including: The Many Colored Land, 1981; The Golden Torc, 1982; The Nonborn King, 1983; The Adversary, 1984; Intervention, 1987; Black Trillium, 1990; Jack the Bodiless, 1991; Blood Trillium, 1992; Diamond Mask, 1994; Magnificat, 1996; Sky Trillium, 1997; Perseus Spur, 1998. *Address:* Box 851 Mercer Island, WA 98040, USA.

MAY, Naomi Young; Novelist, Journalist and Painter; b. 27 March 1934, Glasgow, Scotland; m. Nigel May, 3 Oct. 1964, two s. one d. *Education:* Slade School of Fine Art, London, 1953–56; Diploma, Fine Art, University of London. *Career:* mem. PEN. *Publications:* At Home, 1969, radio adaptation, 1987; The Adventurer, 1970; Troubles, 1976. Contributions: anthologies, newspapers, and magazines. *Honours:* History of Art Prize, Slade School of Fine Art. *Address:* 6 Lion Gate Gardens, Richmond, Surrey TW9 2DF, England.

MAY, Sarah; British author; b. 1972, Northumberland. *Education:* Univ. of London, Univ. of Lancaster. *Publications:* novels: The Nudist Colony 1999, Spanish City 2002, The Internationals 2003. *Honours:* Amazon.co.uk Writers' Bursary 2001. *Literary Agent:* c/o Chatto & Windus, 20 Vauxhall Bridge Road, London, SW1V 2SA, England. *Telephone:* (20) 7840-8400. *Fax:* (20) 7233-6117. *Website:* www.randomhouse.co.uk.

MAY, Stephen James, (Julian Poole); American writer; b. 10 Sept. 1946, Toronto, ON, Canada; m. Caroline Casteel 1972; one s. *Education:* AA, El Camino College, 1970; BA, 1975, MA, 1977, California State University at Carson; DLitt, International University, Mumbai, 1992. *Career:* Instructor in English, Colorado Northwestern College, 1992–98; Visiting Prof. of English, University of Northern Colorado, 1999–; mem. Colorado Authors' League; James Michener Society; Society of Southwestern Authors; Western Writers of America; World Literary Acad.; Zane Grey Society. *Publications:* Pilgrimage: A Journey Through Colorado's History and Culture, 1987; Intruders in the Dust, 1988; Fire from the Skies, 1990; Footloose on the Santa Fe Trail, 1992; A Land Observed, 1993; Zane Grey: Romancing the West, 1997; Maverick Heart: The Further Adventures of Zane Grey, 2000; Rascals, 2001. Contributions: Denver Post; Frontier Rocky Mountain News; Southwest Art; Artists of the Rockies; National Geographic. *Honours:* Non-Fiction Award, Western Writers of America, 2001; Non-Fiction Award, Colorado Authors' League, 2001. *Address:* 731 Peregrine Run, Fort Collins, CO 80524, USA. *E-mail:* stepkm@msn.com.

MAYER, Bernadette; Poet and Writer; b. 12 May 1945, New York, NY, USA; one s. two d. *Education:* New School for Social Research, New York City. *Career:* Resident Dir, St Mark's Poetry Project, Greenwich Village, 1980–84; various workshops. *Publications:* Ceremony Latin, 1964; Story, 1968; Moving, 1971; The Basketball Article (with Anne Waldman), 1975; Memory, 1975; Studying Hunger, 1975; Poetry, 1976; Eruditio Ex Memoria, 1977; The Golden Book of Words, 1978; Midwinter Day, 1982; Incidents Reports Sonnets, 1984; Utopia, 1984; Mutual Aid, 1985; The Art of Science Writing (with Dales Worsley), 1989; Sonnets, 1989; The Formal Field of Kissing, 1990; A Bernadette Mayer Reader, 1992; The Desires of Mothers to Please Others in Letters, 1994. Contributions: anthologies. *Address:* c/o Hard Press Inc, PO Box 184, West Stockbridge, MA 01266, USA.

MAYER, Peter, MA; American publisher; b. Hampstead, London. *Education:* Columbia Univ., Christ Church, Oxford. *Career:* Grad. Fellow Indiana Univ.; Fulbright Fellow, Freie Universität Berlin 1959; worked with Orion Press before joining Avon books for 14 years; Publr and Pres. Pocketbooks 1976–78; Chief. Exec. Penguin Books Ltd, London 1978–96, later Chair. Penguin USA; exec. positions with The Overlook Press (co-f. with his father 1970) 1996–, acquired Duckworth Publrs 2003; Fellow Ind. Univ. *Publication:* The Pacifist Conscience (ed.) 1966. *Address:* c/o Penguin USA, 375 Hudson Street, New York, NY 10014, USA.

MAYER, Robert; Writer; b. 24 Feb. 1939, New York, NY, USA; m. La Donna Cocilovo 24 Feb. 1989; one step-d. *Education:* BA, City College, CUNY, 1959; MS, Journalism, Columbia University, 1960. *Career:* Reporter, Columnist, Newsday, 1961–71; Managing Ed., Santa Fe Reporter, 1988–90. *Publications:* Superfolks, 1977; The Execution, 1979; Midge and Decker, 1982; Sweet Salt, 1984; The Grace of Shortstops, 1984; The Search, 1986; The Dreams of Ada, 1987; I, JFK, 1989. Contributions: Vanity Fair; New York Magazine; Travel and Leisure; Rocky Mountain Magazine; New Mexico Magazine; Santa Fe Reporter; Newsday. *Honours:* National Headliner Award, 1968; Mike Berger Awards, 1969, 1971.

MAYER-KOENIG, Wolfgang; Poet, Writer, Ed., University Prof. and Industrial Dir; b. 28 March 1946, Vienna, Austria. *Education:* Universities of Vienna, Saarbrücken, and Los Angeles. *Career:* mem. Acad. Tiberina; Acad. Burckhardt St Gallen; Acad. Consentina; Acad. Europa; Board mem., Austrian Writers' Asscn; PEN; Vice-pres., Robert-Musil Archive Asscn, 1975–. *Publications:* Sichtbare Pavilions, 1969; Stichmarken, 1970; Texte und Bilder, 1972; Sprache-Politik-Aggression, 1975; Texte und Zeichnungen, 1975; Psychologie und Literatursprache, 1976; Language-Politics-Agression, 1977; Italienreisen Goethes, 1978; Robert Musils Moglichkeitsstil, 1979; In den Armen unseres Waerters, 1980; Chagrin non dechiffré, 1986; A Hatalom bonyolult Angyala, 1988; Underestimated Deep, 1989; A Complicated Angel, 1989; Responsibility of Writing: Contributions to a Modern Grammar, 1990; Risks of Writing, 1991; Verzögerung des Vertrauens, 1995; Colloquios nel Cuarto, 1996; Fire and Ice, 1996; Mirror Wading, 1996; Verkannte Tiefe, 1996; Grammatik der Modernen Poesie, 1996; Behind Desires Deficits, 1997; Confessions of an Angry Loving European, 1999. Contributions: various publications. *Honours:* Theodor Körner Prize for Poetry, 1974; officer Order of Merit, Egypt, 1974; Austrian Cross of Honour for Science and Arts, 1976; Cross of Honour, Lower Austria, 1982; Commander Order of St Agatha, San Marino, 1982; Golden medal of merit, International ARC, 1983; Ordre du Mérite Africain, 1983; Chevalier, Ordre des Arts et des Lettres, 1987; Golden cross Order of Eagle of Tyrol, 1988; Papal Lateran Cross, first class; Grand Cross of Honour, Government of Carinthia, 1993; Cross of merit first class of Lilienfeld, 1984; Cross of Merit of Greek Orthodox Papal Patriarch of Alexandria, Egypt; Star of Peace, Rome, Italy; Premio Prometeo Aureo Lazio, Vienna Art Foundation prize; New Century Award. *Address:* Hernalser Guertel 41, 1170 Vienna, Austria.

MAYHAR, Ardath, (Frank Cannon, Frances Hurst, John Killdeer); Writer and Poet; b. 20 Feb. 1930, Timpson, Texas, USA; m. Joe E. Mayhar, June 1958. *Education:* Self-educated. *Career:* mem. SFWA; Western Writers of America. *Publications:* Over 40 books, including: How the Gods Wove in Kyrannon, 1979; Soul Singer of Tyrnos, 1981; Runes of the Lyre, 1982; Lords of the Triple Moons, 1983; The World Ends in Hickory Hollow, 1985; A Place of Silver Silence, 1987; Texas Gunsmoke, 1988; Far Horizons, 1994; Island in the Swamp, 1994; Hunters of the Plains, 1995; High Mountain Winter, 1996; Riddles and Dreams Images, 2003. Contributions: Quarterlies and magazines. *Honours:* Awards and prizes for fiction and poetry. *Address:* 533 CR 486, Chireno, TX 75937, USA. *E-mail:* ardathm@netdot.com. *Website:* netdot.com/ardathm/.

MAYNE, Richard (John); Writer and Broadcaster; b. 2 April 1926, London, England; m. Jocelyn Mudie Ferguson, two d. *Education:* MA, PhD, Trinity College, Cambridge, 1947–53. *Career:* Rome Correspondent, New Statesman, 1953–54; Official of the European Community, Luxembourg and Brussels, 1956–63; Personal Asst to Jean Monnet, Paris, 1963–66; Paris Correspondent, 1963–73, Co-Ed., 1990–94, Encounter; Visiting Prof., University of Chicago, 1970; Dir, Federal Trust, London, 1971–73; Head, UK Offices of the European Commission, London, 1973–79; Film Critic, Sunday Telegraph, London, 1987–89, The European, 1990–98; mem. Society of Authors; Royal Institute of International Affairs; Federal Trust for Education and Research. *Publications:* The Community of Europe, 1962; The Institutions of the European Community, 1968; The Recovery of Europe, 1970; The Europeans, 1972; Europe Tomorrow (ed.), 1972; The New Atlantic Challenge (ed.), 1975; The Memoirs of Jean Monnet (trans.), 1978; Postwar: The Dawn of Today's Europe, 1983; Western Europe: A Handbook (ed.), 1987; Federal Union: The Pioneers (with John Pinder), 1990; Europe: A History of its Peoples (trans.), 1990; History of Europe (trans.), 1993; A History of Civilizations (trans.), 1994; The Language of Sailing, 2000. Contributions: newspapers and magazines. *Honours:* Scott-Moncrieff Prize for Trans. from French, 1978; Officier, Ordre des Arts et des Lettres, 2002. *Address:* Albany Cottage, 24 Park Village E, Regent's Park, London NW1 7PZ, England.

MAYNE, Seymour; Prof. of English, Poet, Writer, Ed. and Trans; b. 18 May 1944, Montréal, QC, Canada. *Education:* BA, English, McGill University, 1965; MA, English and Creative Writing, 1966, PhD, 1972, University of British Columbia. *Career:* Lecturer, University of British Columbia, 1972; Lecturer, 1973, Asst Prof., 1973–78, Assoc. Prof., 1978–85, Prof. of English, 1985–, University of Ottawa; Visiting Prof., 1979–80, Visiting Prof. and Scholar, 1983–84, 1992, Writer-in-Residence, 1987–88, Hebrew University of Jerusalem; Visiting Prof., Concordia University, Montréal, 1982–83, University of La Laguna, Spain, 1993; Adjunct Research Prof., Carleton University, 2002–; Contributing Ed., 1982–90, Poetry Ed., 1990–95, Viewpoints; Contributing Ed., Tel-Aviv Review, 1989–96, Poet Lore, 1992–, Jerusalem Review, 1997–2001; Founder-Consulting Ed., Bywords, 1990–, Graffito, 1994–. *Publications:* That Monocycle the Moon, 1964; Tiptoeing on the Mount, 1965; From the Portals of Mouseholes, 1966; Manimals, 1969; Mouth, 1970; For Stems of Light, 1971; Face, 1971; Name, 1975; Diasporas, 1977; The Impossible Promised Land: Poems New and Selected, 1981; Children of Abel, 1986; Diversions, 1987; Six Ottawa Poets (with others), 1990; Killing Time, 1992; The Song of Moses and Other Poems, 1995; Five-O'Clock Shadows (with others), 1996; Dragon Trees, 1997; City of the Hidden, 1998; Carbon Filter, 1999; Light Industry, 2000; Hail: Word Sonnets, 2002. Other: Ed. or co-ed. of 13 books, 1968–97; Trans. or co-trans. of eight books, 1974–98. Contributions: anthologies, books, journals, reviews, and quarterlies. *Honours:* numerous grants and fellowships; Chester Macnaghten First Prize in Creative Writing, 1962; J. I. Segal Prize in English-French Literature, 1974; York Poetry Workshop Award, 1975; American Literary Trans Asscn Poetry Trans. Award, 1990; Jewish Book Committee Prize, 1994; Louis L. Lockshin Memorial Award, 1997; Fuerstenberg-Aaron Prize, 2000; Capital Educators' Award, 2003. *Address:* c/o Dept of English, Faculty of Arts, University of Ottawa, PO Box 450, Station A, Ottawa, Ontario K1N 6N5, Canada.

MAYO, Wendell; academic, writer and poet; b. 16 Aug. 1953, Corpus Christi, TX, USA; m. Deborah Masonis 1982. *Education:* BS, 1975, PhD, 1991, Ohio State University; BA, University of Toledo, 1980; University of Houston, 1984–85; MFA, Vermont College, 1988. *Career:* Asst Prof. of English, Indiana University-Purdue University, Fort Wayne, 1991–94; Asst Prof., then Assoc. Prof. of Creative Writing and Literature, University of Southwestern Louisiana, Lafayette, 1994–96; Asst Prof. of Creative Writing and Literature, Bowling Green State University, Ohio, 1996–; mem. Associated Writing Programs; Society for the Study of Midwestern Literature. *Publications:* Centaur of the North (short stories), 1996; In Lithuanian Wood (novel); B Horror and Other Stories, 1999; Giesmininkas (short stories). Contributions: various reviews, quarterlies and magazines, including: Harvard Review; Prairie Schooner; Western Humanities Review; Missouri

Review; New Letters; The Yale Review; North American Review; Threepenny Review; Anthologies, including: City Wilds; 100% Pure Florida Fiction. *Honours:* Fellow, Millay Colony for the Arts, 1992; Master Fellow, Indiana Arts Commission, 1992; Yado Fellow, 1992, 1994, 1996; Fellow, Edward F. Albee Foundation, 1993; First Prize for Fiction, Mississippi Valley Review, 1995, New Delta Review, 1996; Premio Aztlan, University of New Mexico, 1997; National Endowment for the Arts, 2001; Fulbright Grant, 2002. *Address:* 210 Liberty Hi Street, PO Box 153, Haskins, OH 43525, USA. *E-mail:* wmayo@bgnet.bgsu.edu.

MAYRÖCKER, Friederike; Author, Poet and Dramatist; b. 20 Dec. 1924, Vienna, Austria. *Education:* Teacher of English training. *Career:* Teacher of English, 1946–69; mem. several Austrian and German literary asscns. *Publications:* Larifari: Ein konfuses Buch, 1956; Tod durch Musen: Poetische Texte, 1966; Minimonsters Traumlexikon: Texte in Prosa, 1968; Fantom Fan, 1971; Je ein umwölkter gipfel: Erzählung, 1973; Das Licht in der Landschaft, 1976; Fast ein Frühling des Markus M., 1976; Heiligenanstalt, 1978; Die Abschiede, 1980; Magische Blätter, Vols I–IV, 1983–87, Vol. V, 1999; Reise durch die Nacht, 1984; Das Herzzerreiszende der Dinge, 1985; Winterglück: Gedichte, 1982–85, 1986; Mein Herz mein Zimmer mein Name, 1988; Stilleben, 1991; Lection, 1994; Notizen auf einem Kamel, 1996; Das zu Sehende, das zu Hörende, 1997; Brütt oder die Seufzenden Gärten, 1998; Benachbarte Metalle, 1998; Mein Arbeitstirol (poems); Die kommunizierenden Gefäsze, 2003. Contributions: journals and magazines. *Honours:* Great Austrian State Prize, 1982; Friedrich-Hölderlin Prize, 1993; Great Literature Prize, Bavarian Acad. of Fine Arts, Munich, 1996; Else-Lasker-Schüler Prize, 1996; Meersburger Droste Prize, 1997; Georg Buchner Prize, 2001; Internationaler Buchpreis: Premio Internazionale, 2003. *Address:* Zentagasse 16/40, 1050 Vienna, Austria. *Telephone:* (1) 545-6660.

MAYSON, Marina (see Rogers, Rosemary).

MAZER, Norma Fox; Writer; b. 15 May 1931, New York, NY, USA; m. Harry Mazer, 12 Feb. 1950, one s., three d. *Education:* Antioch College; Syracuse University. *Publications:* I Trissy, 1971; A Figure of Speech, 1973; Saturday, The Twelfth of October, 1975; Dear Bill, Remember Me, 1976; The Solid Gold Kid, 1977; Up in Seth's Room, 1979; Mrs Fish, Ape and Me and the Dump Queen, 1980; Taking Terri Mueller, 1981; When We First Met, 1982; Summer Girls, Love Boys, and Other Stories, 1982; Someone To Love, 1983; Supergirl, 1984; Downtown, 1984; A, My Name is Ami, 1986; Three Sisters, 1986; B, My Name is Bunny, 1987; After the Rain, 1987; Silver, 1988; Heartbeat, 1989; Babyface, 1989; C, My Name is Cal, 1990; D, My Name is Danita, 1991; Bright Days, Stupid Nights, 1992; E, My Name is Emily, 1991; Out of Control, 1993. Contributions: English Journal; Alan Review; The Writer; Signal; Writing; Redbook; Playgirl; Voice; Ingenue. *Literary Agent:* Elaine Markson Literary Agency, 44 Greenwich Ave, New York, NY 10011, USA. *Address:* Brown Gulf Rd, Jamesville, NY 13078, USA.

MAZLISH, Bruce; Prof. of History and Writer; b. 15 Sept. 1923, New York, NY, USA; m. 1st, three s., one d.; m. 2nd Neva Goodwin, 22 Nov. 1988. *Education:* BA, 1944, MA, 1947, PhD, 1955, Columbia University. *Career:* Instructor, University of Maine, 1946–48, Columbia University, 1949–50; Instructor, 1950–53, Faculty, 1955–, Prof. of History, 1965–, Chair., History Section, 1965–70, Head, Dept of Humanities, 1974–79, MIT; Dir, American School, Madrid, 1953–55; mem. American Acad. of Arts and Sciences, fellow; Rockefeller Family Fund, board of dirs; Toynbee Prize Foundation, board of dirs. *Publications:* The Western Intellectual Tradition (with J. Bronowski), 1960; The Riddle of History, 1966; In Search of Nixon, 1972; James and John Stuart Mill: Father and Son in the 19th Century, 1975; The Revolutionary Ascetic, 1976; Kissinger: The European Mind in American Policy, 1976; The Meaning of Karl Marx, 1984; A New Science: The Breakdown of Connections and the Birth of Sociology, 1989; The Leader, the Led and the Psyche, 1990; The Fourth Discontinuity: The Co-Evolution of Humans and Machines, 1993; Progress: Fact or Illusion? (with Les Marx), 1996; The Uncertain Sciences, 1998. Editor: Psychoanalysis and History, 1963; The Railroad and the Space Program: An Exploration in Historical Analogy, 1965; Conceptualizing Global History (with Ralph Bultjens), 1993. Contributions: Professional journals. *Honours:* Clement Staff Essay Award, 1968; Toynbee Prize, 1986–87. *Address:* 11 Lowell St, Cambridge, MA 02138, USA.

MAZUR, Grace Dane; Writer; b. 22 April 1944, Boston, MA, USA; m. Barry C. Mazur, one s. *Education:* BA, Harvard College, 1971; PhD, Harvard University, 1981; MFA, Warren Wilson College, 1993. *Career:* Teacher, Harvard University Extension School, 1996–. *Publications:* Silk (short stories), 1996; Trespass (novel), 1998. Contributions: Reviews and journals. *Honours:* Bread Loaf Literary Fellowship. *Address:* c/o Writers House, 21 W 26th St, New York, NY 10010, USA.

MAZZARELLA, David; Newspaper Editor; b. 1938, USA. *Career:* with Assoc. Press, Lisbon, New York, Rome 1962–70; with Daily American, Rome 1971–75, Gannett News, Washington, DC 1976–77, The Bridgewater, Bridgewater, NJ 1977–83; Ed., Sr Vice-Pres. USA Today –1999; Ombudsman Stars and Stripes newspaper 2000–01, Ed. Dir 2001–. *Address:* c/o Stars and Stripes, 529 14th St NW, Suite 350, Washington DC 20450, USA. *Website:* www.stripes.com.

MAZZARO, Jerome Louis; academic, poet, writer and editor; b. 25 Nov. 1934, Detroit, Michigan, USA. *Education:* AB, Wayne University, 1954; MA, University of Iowa, 1956; PhD, Wayne State University, 1963. *Career:* Instructor, University of Detroit, 1958–61; Ed., Fresco, 1960–61, Modern Poetry Studies, 1970–79; Asst Prof., SUNY at Cortland, 1962–64; Asst Ed., North American Review, 1963–65, Noetics, 1964–65; Prof. of English and Comparative Literature, SUNY at Buffalo, 1964–96; Contributing Ed., Salmagundi, 1967–97, American Poetry Review, 1972–, Italian-American, 1974–88; Poetry Ed., Helios, 1977–79; mem. Dante Society of America; Mark Twain Society. *Publications:* The Achievement of Robert Lowell, 1939–1959, 1960; Juvenal: Satires (trans.), 1965; The Poetic Themes of Robert Lowell, 1965; Changing the Windows (poems), 1966; Modern American Poetry (ed.), 1970; Transformation in the Renaissance English Lyric, 1970; Profile of Robert Lowell (ed.), 1971; Profile of William Carlos Williams (ed.), 1971; William Carlos Williams: The Later Poetry, 1973; Postmodern American Poetry, 1980; The Figure of Dante: An Essay on the 'Vita Nuova', 1981; The Caves of Love (poems), 1985; Rubbings (poems), 1985; John Logan: The Collected Poems (ed. with Al Poulin), 1989; John Logan: The Collected Fiction (ed.), 1991; Mind Plays: Luigi Pirandello's Theatre, 2000; Robert Lowell and Ovid, 2001; War Games (fiction), 2001; Robert Lowell and America, 2002; Weathering the Changes (poems), 2002; Memory and Making, 2003. Contributions: Reference works, books and journals. *Honours:* Guggenheim Fellowship, 1964–65; Hadley Fellowship, 1979–80. *Address:* 392 Central Park W, Apartment 11J, New York, NY 10025, USA.

MEAD, Matthew; poet and translator; b. 12 Sept. 1924, Buckinghamshire, England. *Career:* Ed., Satis Magazine, Edinburgh 1960–62. *Publications:* A Poem in Nine Parts 1960, Identities 1964, Kleinigkeiten 1966, Identities and Other Poems 1967, Penguin Modern Poets 16 (with Harry Guest and J. Beeching) 1970, In the Eyes of the People 1973, Minusland 1977, The Midday Muse 1979, A Roman in Cologne 1986, A Sestina at the End of Socialism 1996, A Dozen Villanelles 1999, The Sentences of Death 2000, Walking Out of the World 2003; also numerous trans. from German (with Ruth Mead). *Address:* c/o Anvil Press, Neptune House, 70 Royal Hill, London, SE10 8RF, England.

MEADES, Jonathan Turner; journalist, writer and broadcaster; b. 21 Jan. 1947, Salisbury, Wiltshire, England; m. 1st Sally Dorothee Renee Brown 1980 (divorced); two d.; m. 2nd Frances Anne Bentley 1988 (divorced); two d.; m. 3rd Colette Claudine Forder 2003. *Education:* King's Coll., Taunton, RADA, Univ. of Bordeaux. *Career:* Ed., Event 1981–82; Features Ed., Tatler 1982–85; restaurant critic 1986–2001, columnist 2002–, The Times. *Television:* The Victorian House, Abroad in Britain, Further Abroad, Jerry Building, Even Further Abroad, Meades Eats, Heart Bypass, Victoria Died in 1901 and is Still Alive Today, tvSSFBM. *Publications:* This is Their Life 1979, An Illustrated Atlas of the World's Great Buildings 1980, Filthy English 1984, Peter Knows What Dick Likes 1989, Pompey 1993, The Fowler Family Business 2001, Incest and Morris Dancing 2002; contrib. to Times, Sunday Times, Observer, Independent. *Honours:* Essay Prize, Paris Int. Art Film Festival 1994, Glenfiddich Awards 1986, 1990, 1996. *Literary Agent:* Capel and Land, 24 Wardour Street, London, W1D 6PS, England.

MEARS, Gillian; Author; b. 21 July 1964, Lismore, NSW, Australia. *Education:* BA, 1985. *Career:* mem. Australian Society of Authors. *Publications:* Ride a Cock Horse (short stories), 1989; Fineflour (short stories), 1990; The Mint Lawn, 1991; The Grass Sister, 1995; Collected Stories, 1997; Paradise Is a Place (essay), 1997; A Map of the Gardens (short stories), 2002. Contributions: periodicals. *Honours:* Commonwealth Writers Regional First Book Prize, 1989, and Regional Best Book Prize, 1996; Australian/Vogel Award, 1991. *Literary Agent:* Barbara Mobbs, PO Box 126, Edgecliff, NSW 2027, Australia. *E-mail:* bmobbs@pogo.com.au.

MEASHAM, Donald Charles; Teacher of Higher Education (retd), Writer and Ed.; b. 19 Jan. 1932, Birmingham, England; m. Joan Doreen Barry, 15 Dec. 1954, one s. one d. *Education:* BA, Birmingham University, 1953; MPhil, Nottingham University, 1971. *Career:* Founding Ed. 1983, Company Secretary, Co-Ed., 1988–2001, Staple New Writing. *Publications:* Leaving, 1965; Fourteen, 1965; English Now and Then, 1965; Larger Than Life, 1967; Quattordicenni, 1967; The Personal Element, 1967; Lawrence and the Real England, 1985; Ruskin: The Last Chapter, 1989; Twenty Years of Twentieth Century Poetry, 2001. Contributions: periodicals. *Address:* Tor Cottage, 81 Cavendish Rd, Matlock, Derbyshire DE4 3HD, England.

MECKEL, Christoph; Author, Poet and Graphic Artist; b. 12 June 1935, Berlin, Germany. *Education:* Studied Graphic Art, Freiburg, Paris, Munich. *Career:* mem. Acad. of Science and Literature, Mainz; Akademie für Sprache und Dichtung eV, Darmstadt; PEN. *Publications:* Manifest der Toten, 1960; Im Land der Umbramauten, 1961; Wildnisse, 1962; Die Drummheit liefert uns ans Messer: Zeitgespräch in zehn Sonetten (with Volker von Törne), 1967; Bockshorn, 1973; Wen es angeht, 1974; Komödie der Hölle, 3 vols, 1979, 1984, 1987; Suchbild: Über meinen Vater, 1980; Ein roter Faden, 1983; Das Buch Jubal, 1987; Das Buch Shiralee, 1989; Von den Luftgeschäften der Poesie, 1989; Die Messingstadt, 1991; Gesang vom unterbrochenen Satz, 1995. *Honours:* Rainer Maria Rilke Prize, 1979; Georg Trakl Prize, 1982; Literature Prize, Kassel, 1993. *Address:* Kulmbacherstr 3, 10777 Berlin, Germany.

MEDEIROS, Teresa, AA; American writer; b. 26 Oct. 1962, Heidelberg, Germany; m. Michael Medeiros 1984. *Education:* Madisonville Community

Coll. *Career:* mem. Kentucky Romance Writers, Novelists Inc, Romance Writers of America. *Publications:* Lady of Conquest, 1989; Shadows and Lace, 1990; Heather and Velvet, 1991; Once an Angel, 1993; A Whisper of Roses, 1993; Thief of Hearts, 1994; Fairest of Them All, 1995; Breath of Magic, 1996; Touch of Enchantment, 1997; Nobody's Darling, 1998; Charming the Prince, 1999; The Bride and the Beast, 2000. *Address:* 239 Crossbar Court, Hopkinsville, KY 42240, USA.

MEDOFF, Mark (Howard); Dramatist and Screenwriter; b. 18 March 1940, Mount Carmel, IL, USA; m. Stephanie Thorne, three d. *Education:* BA, University of Miami, Coral Gables, 1962; MA, Stanford University, 1966. *Career:* mem. Actors Equity Asscn; Screen Actors Guild; Writers Guild of America. *Publications:* Plays: When You Comin' Back, Red Ryder?, 1973; Children of a Lesser God, 1979; The Majestic Kid, 1981; The Hands of Its Enemy, 1984; The Heart Outright, 1986; Big Mary, 1989; Stumps, 1989; Stephanie Hero, 1990; Kringle's Window, 1991. Film Scripts: Good Guys Wear Black, 1977; When You Comin' Back, Red Ryder?, 1978; Off Beat, 1985; Apology, 1986; Children of a Lesser God, 1987; Clara's Heart, 1988; City of Joy, 1992. Contributions: periodicals. *Honours:* Obie Award, 1974; Drama Desk Awards, 1974, 1980; New York Outer Critics Circle Awards, 1974, 1980; Guggenheim Fellowship, 1974–75; Antoinette Perry Award, 1980; Governor's Award for Excellence in the Arts, State of New Mexico, 1980; Distinguished Alumnus, University of Miami, 1987; California Media Access Award, 1988.

MEDVED, Michael; Film Critic, Writer and Radio Talk Show Host; b. 3 Oct. 1948, Philadelphia, Pennsylvania, USA; m. 1st Nancy Harris Herman 5 Aug. 1972 (divorced 1983); m. 2nd Diane Elvenstar 27 Jan. 1985; one s. two d. *Education:* BA, Yale University, 1969; MFA, California State University at San Francisco, 1974. *Career:* Political Speech Writer, 1970–73; Creative Dir, Advertising, Anrick Inc, Oakland, CA, 1973–74; Co-Founder and Pres., Pacific Jewish Center, Venice, CA, 1977–94; On-Air Film Critic, People Now, Cable News Network, 1980–83; Pres., Emanuel Streisand School, Venice, CA, 1980–85; On-Air Film Critic and Co-Host, Sneak Previews, PBS-TV, 1985–96; Chief Film Critic, New York Post, 1993–98; Radio Talk Show Host, Seattle, Washington, 1996–; Nationally Syndicated Radio Host, SRN Radio Network, 1998–; mem. American Federation of Television and Radio Artists; Writers Guild of America. *Publications:* What Really Happened to the Class of '65?, 1976; The 50 Worst Films of All Time (with Harry Medved), 1978; The Shadow Presidents, 1979; The Golden Turkey Awards (with Harry Medved), 1980; Hospital, 1983; The Hollywood Hall of Shame (with Harry Medved), 1984; Son of Golden Turkey Awards (with Harry Medved), 1986; Hollywood vs America, 1992; Saving Childhood (with Diane Medved), 1998. Contributions: periodicals. *Address:* c/o KV1, 1809 Seventh Ave, Suite 200, Seattle, WA 98101, USA.

MEDVEDEV, Roy (Alexandrovich); Historian, Sociologist and Author; b. 14 Nov. 1925, Tbilisi, Russia; m. Galina A Gaidina, 1956, one s. *Education:* University of Leningrad; Russian Acad. of Pedagogical Sciences. *Career:* Deputy to Ed.-in-Chief, Publishing House of Pedagogical Literature, Moscow, 1957–59; Head of Dept, Research Institute of Vocational Education, 1960–70, Senior Scientist, 1970–71, Russian Acad. of Pedagogical Sciences; People's Deputy, Supreme Soviet of the USSR, 1989–91; Mem., Central Committee, Communist Party of Russia, 1990–91; Co-Chair., Socialist Party of Labour, 1991–. *Publications:* A Question of Madness (with Zhores Medvedev), 1971; Let History Judge, 1972; On Socialist Democracy, 1975; Khrushchev: The Years in Power (with Zhores Medvedev), 1976; Political Essays, 1976; Problems in the Literary Biography of Mikhail Sholokhov, 1977; Samizdat Register, 2 vols (ed.), 1977, 1980; Philip Mironov and the Russian Civil War (with S. Starikov), 1978; The October Revolution, 1979; On Stalin and Stalinism, 1979; On Soviet Dissent, 1980; Nikolai Bukharin: The Last Years, 1980; Leninism and Western Socialism, 1981; An End to Silence, 1982; Khrushchev, 1983; All Stalin's Men, 1984; China and the Superpowers, 1986; Time of Change (with G. Chiesa), 1990; Brezhnev: A Political Biography, 1991; Gensek s Lybianki (political biog. of Andropov), 1994; Capitalism in Russia?, 1998; Post Soviet Russia, 2000; The Unknown Stalin (with Zhores Medvedev), 2001; The Time of Putin, 2002. Contributions: Professional journals and general publications. *Address:* Abonement Post Box 258, Moscow A-475, 125475, Russia.

MEDVEDEV, Zhores (Alexandrovich); Biologist and Writer; b. 14 Nov. 1925, Tbilisi, USSR; m. Margarita Nikolayevna Buzina, 1951, two s. *Education:* Timiriazev Acad. of Agricultural Sciences, Moscow; Institute of Plant Physiology, Soviet Acad. of Sciences. *Career:* Scientist to Senior Scientist, Dept of Agrochemistry and Biochemistry, Timiriazev Acad. of Agricultural Sciences, Moscow, 1951–62; Head of Laboratory, Molecular Radiobiology, Institute of Medical Radiology, Obninsk, 1963–69; Senior Scientist, All-Union Scientific Research Institute of Physiology and Biochemistry of Farm Animals, Borovsk, 1970–72, National Institute for Medical Research, London, 1973–92; mem. American Gerontological Society; Biochemical Society. *Publications:* Protein Biosynthesis and Problems of Heredity, Development, and Ageing, 1963; Molecular-Genetic Mechanisms of Development, 1968; The Rise and Fall of T. D. Lysenko, 1969; The Medvedev Papers, 1970; A Question of Madness (with Roy Medvedev), 1971; Ten Years After, 1973; Khrushchev: The Years in Power (with Roy Medvedev), 1976; Soviet Science, 1978; The Nuclear Disaster in the Urals, 1979; Andropov, 1983; Gorbachev, 1986; Soviet Agriculture, 1987; The Legacy of Chernobyl, 1990; The Unknown Stalin (with Roy Medvedev), 2001. Contributions: many professional journals. *Honours:* René Schubert Prize in Gerontology, 1985. *Address:* 4 Osborn Gardens, London NW7 1DY, England. *Telephone:* (20) 8346-4158.

MEEK, Jay; Prof. and Poet; b. 23 Aug. 1937, Grand Rapids, Michigan, USA; m. Martha George, 29 Aug. 1966, one d. *Education:* BA, University of Michigan, 1959; MA, Syracuse University, 1965. *Career:* Faculty, Wake Forest University, 1977–80, Sarah Lawrence College, 1980–82; Assoc. Prof., MIT, 1982–83; Writer-in-Residence, Memphis State University, 1984; Prof., University of North Dakota, 1985–. *Publications:* The Week the Dirigible Came, 1976; Drawing on the Walls, 1980; Earthly Purposes, 1984; Stations, 1989; Windows, 1994; Headlands: New and Selected Poems, 1997. Contributions: journals and magazines. *Honours:* National Endowment for the Arts Award, 1972–73; Guggenheim Fellowship, 1985–86; Bush Artist Fellowship, 1989. *Address:* c/o Dept of English, University of North Dakota, Box 7209, University Station, Grand Forks, ND 58202, USA.

MEGGED, Aharon; Writer; b. 10 Aug. 1920, Wloclawek, Poland; m. Eda Zoritte 1946; two s. *Career:* Ed., MASSA, 1953–55; Literary Ed., Lamerchav Daily, 1955–68; Cultural Attaché, Israel Embassy, London, England, 1968–71; Columnist, Davar Daily, 1971–85; mem. Israel PEN Centre, pres., 1980–87; Hebrew Acad., 1982–. *Publications:* Hedva and I, 1953; Fortunes of a Fool, 1960; Living on the Dead, 1965; The Short Life, 1971; The Bat, 1975; Asahel, 1978; Heinz, His Son and the Evil Spirit, 1979; Journey in the Month of Av, 1980; The Flying Camel and the Golden Hump, 1982; The Turbulent Zone (essays), 1985; Foiglmann, 1987; The Writing Desk (literary essays), 1988; Anat's Day of Illumination, 1992; Longing for Olga, 1994; Iniquity, 1996; Love-Flowers from the Holy Land, 1998; Persephone Remembers, 2000; Until Evening, 2001; Beautiful Milisinda, 2002; Yolam's Vengeance, 2003. Plays: Hedva and I, 1955; Hannah Senesh, 1963; Genesis, 1965; The High Season, 1968. Contributions: Atlantic Monthly; Encounter; Midstream; Listener; Moment; Present Tense; Partisan Review; Ariel. *Honours:* Brenner Prize, 1960; Bialik Prize, 1973; Present Tense, New York, 1983; Agnon Prize, 1997; Wizo-Paris Prize, 1998; Prime Minister's Prize, 1998; Pres.'s Prize, 2001; Israel Prize for Literature, 2003. *Literary Agent:* Lipman Ag, Marienberg St 23, POB 572, 8044 Zürich, Switzerland. *Address:* 8 Pa'amoni St., Tel-Aviv 62918, Israel. *Telephone:* (3) 6021680. *Fax:* (3) 6022408. *E-mail:* meged1@zahav.net.il.

MEHROTRA, Sri Ram; Author and Educator; b. 23 June 1931, Anantram, Etawah, Uttar Pradesh, India; m. Eva Mehrotra, 24 July 1957. *Education:* MA, History, University of Allahabad, 1950; PhD, History, University of London, 1960. *Career:* Lecturer, University of London, 1962; Prof., Himachal Pradesh University, 1972; Visiting Prof., University of Wisconsin, 1974; Visiting Fellow, St John's College, Cambridge, 1983–84; Nehru Prof., MD University, 1992–96. *Publications:* India and the Commonwealth, 1885–1929, 1965; The Emergence of the Indian National Congress, 1971; The Commonwealth and the Nation, 1978; Towards India's Freedom and Partition, 1979; A History of the Indian National Congress, Vol. 1, 1885–1918, 1995. Contributions: scholarly journals. *Address:* Seva, Kenfield Estate, Ambedkar Chowk, Shimla, HP 171004, India.

MEHTA, Gita; writer; b. 1943, Delhi, India; m. Ajai Singh 'Sonny' Mehta; one s. *Education:* Univ. of Cambridge. *Career:* Dir, documentaries about India for BBC, NBC. *Publications:* Karma Cola: Marketing The Mystic East 1979, Raj (novel) 1989, A River Sutra (novel) 1993, Snakes and Ladders: Glimpses of Modern India (essays) 1997, Mountain Sutra 1999; contrib. essay 'Unborn', in Clemente 1999. *Address:* c/o Random House, 1745 Broadway, 15-3, New York, NY 10019, USA.

MEHTA, Ajai Singh (Sonny); publishing company executive; *President and Editor-in-Chief, Knopf Publishing Group*; b. 1942, India; m. Gita Mehta; one s. *Education:* Lawrence School, Sanawar, and Univ. of Cambridge. *Career:* fmrly with Pan and Picador Publs, UK; Pres. Alfred A. Knopf Div. of Random House, New York 1987–, now also Ed.-in-Chief; Pres., Ed.-in-Chief Knopf Publishing Group. *Address:* Alfred A. Knopf Inc., 299 Park Avenue, New York, NY 10171, USA.

MEHTA, Ved (Parkash); Writer and Teacher; b. 21 March 1934, Lahore, India; m. Linn Fenimore Cooper Cary, 1983, two d. *Education:* BA, Pomona College, 1956; BA, 1959, MA, 1962, University of Oxford; MA, Harvard University, 1961; Hon. Fellow, Balliol College, 1999. *Career:* Residential Fellow, Eliot House, Harvard University, 1959–61; Staff Writer, The New Yorker magazine, 1961–94; Visiting Scholar, Case Western Reserve University, 1974; Beatty Lecturer, McGill University, 1979; Visiting Prof., Bard College, 1985, 1986, Sarah Lawrence College, 1988, New York University, 1989–90; Visiting Fellow, Balliol College, Oxford, 1988–89; Visiting Prof., Yale University, 1990–93, Williams College, 1994, Vassar College, 1994–96; Senior Fellow, Freedom Forum, Media Studies Center, Visiting Scholar, Columbia University, 1996–97; Fellow, Center for Advanced Studies in the Behavioural Sciences, 1997–98; mem. Council on Foreign Relations. *Publications:* Face to Face, 1957; Walking the Indian Streets, 1960; Fly and the Fly-Bottle, 1963; The New Theologian, 1966; Delinquent Chacha, 1967; Portrait of India, 1970; John is Easy to Please, 1971; Mahatma Gandhi and His Apostles, 1977; The New India, 1978; Photographs of Chachaji, 1980; A Family Affair: India Under Three Prime Ministers, 1982; Three Stories of the Raj, 1986; Rajiv Gandhi and Rama's Kingdom, 1994; A Ved Mehta Reader: The Craft of the Essay, 1998. Continents of Exile autobiographical series: Daddyji, 1972; Mamaji, 1979;

Vedi, 1982; The Ledge Between the Streams, 1984; Sound-Shadows of the New World, 1986; The Stolen Light, 1989; Up At Oxford, 1993; Remembering Mr Shawn's New Yorker, 1998; All for Love, 2001; Dark Harbor, 2003; The Red Letters, 2004. Contributions: PBS-TV and BBC-TV. *Honours:* Guggenheim Fellowships, 1971–72, 1977–78; Ford Foundation Grant, 1971–76; Asscn of Indians in America Award, 1978; Ford Foundation Public Policy Grant, 1979–82; John D. and Catherine T. MacArthur Foundation Fellowship, 1982–87; Distinguished Service Award, Asian/Pacific American Library Asscn, 1986; New York City Mayor's Liberty Medal, 1986; New York Institute for the Humanities Fellowship, 1988–92; Literary Lion Medal, New York Public Library, 1990; Literary Lion Centennial Medal, 1996; Hon. doctorates. *Address:* 139 E 79th St, New York, NY 10021, USA. *Website:* www.vedmehta.com.

MEIGHAN, Roland, FRSA; Writer, Publisher and Consultant; b. 29 May 1937, Sutton Coldfield, England; m. Janet Meighan; one s. two step-s. *Education:* DSocSc; PhD; BSc; LCP. *Career:* various school teacher positions; Lecturer, Senior Lecturer in Education, University of Birmingham; Special Prof. of Education, University of Nottingham; Independent Writer and Consultant; Founder Dir Educational Heretics Press. *Publications:* Flexischooling 1988, Theory and Practice of Regressive Education 1993, The Freethinkers' Guide to the Educational Universe 1994, John Holt: Personalised Education and the Reconstruction of Schooling 1995, The Next Learning System 1997, The Next Learning System: Pieces of the Jigsaw 2000, Learning Unlimited 2001, Natural Learning and the Natural Curriculum 2001, John Holt: Personalised Learning Instead of Uninvited Teaching 2002, A Sociology of Educating (4th edn) 2003. Contributions: Natural Parent Magazine; Observer; Yorkshire Post; Times Educational Supplement. *Address:* 113 Arundel Dr., Bramcote Hills, Nottingham NG9 3FO, England.

MEINER, Richard; German publisher; b. 8 April 1918, Dresden; m. Ursula Ehlert 1947; one s. one d. *Career:* mil. service 1937–45; f. Richard Meiner Verlag, Hamburg 1948–64; Dir Verlage Felix Meiner 1964–81, Felix Meiner Verlag GmbH, Hamburg 1981–98. *Publications:* Verlegerische Betreuung der Philosophischen Bibliothek, Corpus Philosophorum Teutonicorum Medii Aevi, G.W.F. Hegel, Gesammelte Werke. Krit. Ausgabe, G.W.F. Hegel, Vorlesungen, Kant-Forschungen, Nicolai de Cusa Opera omnia. Krit. Ausgabe, Handbuch PRAGMATIK, Studien zum achtzehnten Jahrhundert und weitere philosophische Reihen und Einzelmonographien. *Honours:* Mil. Medal; Gold Medal of Union of German Booksellers 1983; Medal of Honour of German Bücherei Leipzig 1987, Hon. Fellow German Soc. for Philosophy in Germany 1988, Bundesverdienstkreuz I. Klasse 1989. *Address:* c/o Felix Meiner Verlag GmbH, Richardstrasse 47, 22081 Hamburg, Germany.

MEINKE, Peter; Prof. of Literature (retd), Poet and Writer; b. 29 Dec. 1932, New York, NY, USA; m. Jeanne Clark, 14 Dec. 1957, two s. two d. *Education:* AB, Hamilton College, 1955; MA, University of Michigan, 1961; PhD, University of Minnesota, 1965. *Career:* Asst Prof., Hamline University, St Paul, Minnesota, 1961–66; Prof. of Literature and Dir of the Writing Workshop, Eckerd College, St Petersburg, FL, 1966–93; Fulbright Senior Lecturer, University of Warsaw, 1978–79; Visiting Distinguished Writer, University of Hawaii, 1993, University of North Carolina, Greensboro, 1996; Fellow, Le Château de Lavigny, Switzerland, 1998; Darden Chair in Creative Writing, Old Dominion Univ., Norfolk, VA, 2003–; several writer-in-residencies; mem. Acad. of American Poets; Poetry Society of America. *Publications:* Lines from Neuchâtel, 1974; The Night Train and the Golden Bird, 1977; The Rat Poems, 1978; Trying to Surprise God, 1981; The Piano Tuner, 1986; Underneath the Lantern, 1987; Night Watch on the Chesapeake, 1987; Far from Home, 1988; Liquid Paper: New and Selected Poems, 1991; Scars, 1996; Campocorto, 1996; The Shape of Poetry, 1999; Zinc Fingers, 2000; Greatest Hits, 2001. Contributions: periodicals. *Honours:* First Prize, Olivet Sonnet Competition, 1966; National Endowment for the Arts Fellowships, 1974, 1989; Gustav Davidson Memorial Award, 1976, Lucille Medwick Memorial Award, 1984, Emily Dickinson Award, 1992, Poetry Society of America; Flannery O'Connor Award, 1986; Paumanok Poetry Award, 1993; Master Artist's Fellowship, Fine Arts Work Center, Provincetown, 1995. *Address:* 147 Wildwood Lane SE, St Petersburg, FL 33705, USA. *E-mail:* meinkep@eckerd.edu.

MELCHETT, Sonia (see Sinclair, Sonia Elizabeth).

MELCHIOR, Ib Jorgen; writer, dramatist and director; b. 17 Sept. 1917, Copenhagen, Denmark. *Education:* Stenhus Coll., Univ. of Copenhagen. *Career:* writer, dir, over 500 live and filmed TV episodes, 12 feature films, 60 documentary films, 1959–76; mem. Authors' Guild; Dirs Guild of America; Manuscript Society; Writers Guild of America. *Films include:* Where There's Smoke... (dir) 1957, Live Fast, Die Young (writer) 1958, The Angry Red Planet (writer and dir) 1960, Reptilicus (writer) 1961, Journey to the Seventh Planet (writer) 1962, Robinson Crusoe on Mars (writer) 1964, The Time Travelers (writer and dir) 1964, Terrore nello spazio (writer) 1965, Ambush Bay (writer) 1966, Keep Off the Grass (dir) 1970, Death Race 2000 (writer) 1975. *Television includes:* The Perry Como Show (series dir) 1948, The March of Medicine (series dir) 1958, Men Into Space (series writer) 1959, The Outer Limits (series writer) 1963. *Publications:* Order of Battle 1972, Sleeper Agent 1975, The Haigerloch Project 1977, The Watchdogs of Abaddon 1979, The Marcus Device 1980, Hour of Vengeance 1982, Eva 1984, V-3 1985, Code Name: Grand Guignol 1987, Steps and Stairways 1989, Quest 1990, Hitler's Werewolves 1991, Case by Case 1993, Reflections on the Pool 1997, Lauritz Melchior: The Golden Years of Bayreuth 2003. *Honours:* Golden Scroll 1976, Hamlet Award 1982, Outstanding American-Scandinavian 1995. *Address:* 8228 Marmont Lane, Los Angeles, CA 90069, USA.

MELDRUM, James (see Broxholme, John Franklin).

MELEAGROU, Evie; Author and Poet; b. 28 May 1930, Nicosia, Cyprus; m. Dr John Meleagrou, MD, 26 Nov. 1952, one s. two d. *Education:* Diplome de la Literature Française, Athenaeum Institute, Athens; BA, University of London. *Career:* Producer, Literary Programmes, CBC, 1952–55; Ed., Cyprus Chronicles, 1960–72; Secretary, Cyprus Chronicles Cultural Centre, 1960–74; Cyprus Representative, World Writers Conference, 1965; mem. Cyprus Chronicles Cultural Centre, general secretary; Cyprus Cultural Asscn of Women, general secretary; First Cypriot Writers Asscn, secretary, 1961–70; Asscn of Greek Writers, Athens; Cyprus State Literary Awards Committee, 1969–79. *Publications:* Solomon's Family, 1957; Anonymous City, 1963; Eastern Mediterranean, 1969; Conversations with Che, 1970; Penultimate Era, 1981; Persona is the Unknown Cypriot Woman (literary essays and poetry), 1993; The Virgin Plunge in the Ocean Depths (short stories and novels), 1993; Cyprus Chronaca (historical essays), 1974–1992, 1993; Other: Trans. *Honours:* Severian Literary Prize, 1945; First Pancyprian Prize Short Story Competition, 1952; Pancyprian Novella Competition, 1957; Cyprus National Novel Awards, 1970, 1982; Panhellenic National Novel Award, 1982. *Literary Agent:* Dodoni Publishing House, 3 Asklipios St, Athens, 10679, Greece. *Address:* 22 Messolongi St, Nicosia, Cyprus.

MELECKI, Maciej; Poet and Screenwriter; b. 1969, Poland. *Career:* works at the Mikolów Institute; Co-ed., Arcadia journal. *Publications:* Poetry: Zachodzenie za siebie (Behind the Self), 1993; Te sprawy (Such Things), 1995; Niebezpiecznie blisko (Dangerously Close), 1996; Dalsze zajecia (Further Goings Behind), 1998; Zimni ogrodnicy (Mid-May Cold Spell), 1999; Przypadki i odmiany (Cases and Declensions), 2001. Screenplays: Wojaczek (co-writer), 1997; Autsajder, 2000; Dzien Oszusta, 2000. Contributions: Chicago Review; anthologies: Inny Swit, 1994; Macie swoich poetów, 1995, 1997; Dlugie pozegnanie, 1997; Antologia wspólczesnej poezji polskiej, 2000; 14, 44, 2000. *Address:* c/o Polish Cultural Institute, 34 Portland Pl., London W1B 1HQ, England.

MELFI, Mary; Author, Poet and Dramatist; b. 10 June 1951, near Rome, Italy; m. George Nemeth, 17 May 1975, two s. *Education:* BA, Loyola College, Concordia University, 1973; MLS, McGill University, 1977. *Publications:* The Dance, the Cage and the Horse (poems), 1976; A Queen Is Holding a Mummified Cat (poems), 1982; A Bride in Three Acts (poems), 1983; A Dialogue with Masks (novella), 1985; The O Canada Poems, 1986; A Season in Beware (poems), 1989; Infertility Rites (novel), 1991; Ubu: The Witch Who Would Be Rich (children's novel), 1994; Sex Therapy (play), 1996; Painting Moments, Art, AIDS and Nick Palazzo (ed.), 1998; Stages: Selected Poems, 1998; Office Politics (poems), 1999. Contributions: many reviews, quarterlies and journals. *Honours:* Canada Council Arts Grants, 1981–82, 1982–83; Québec Arts Council Grants, 1993–94, 1996–97; Canadian Heritage Grant, 1995. *Address:* 5040 Grand Blvd, Montréal, QC H3X 3S2, Canada.

MELLERS, Wilfrid (Howard); Emeritus Prof. of Music, Composer and Author; b. 26 April 1914, Leamington, Warwickshire, England; m. 1st Vera M. Hobbs; m. 2nd Pauline P. Lewis, three d.; m. 3rd Robin S. Hildyard. *Education:* Leamington College, 1933; BA, 1936, MA, 1938, University of Cambridge; DMus, University of Birmingham, 1960. *Career:* Staff Tutor in Music, University of Birmingham, 1948–60; Andrew Mellon Prof. of Music, University of Pittsburgh, 1960–63; Prof. of Music, University of York, 1964–81; Visiting Prof., City University, 1984–; mem. Sonneck Society, hon. mem. *Publications:* Music and Society: England and the European Tradition, 1946; Studies in Contemporary Music, 1947; François Couperin and the French Classical Tradition, 1950; Music in the Making, 1952; Romanticism and the 20th Century, 1957; The Sonata Principle, 1957; Music in a New Found Land: Themes and Developments in the History of American Music, 1964; Harmonious Meeting: A Study of the Relationship between English Music, Poetry, and Theatre, c. 1600–1900, 1965; Caliban Reborn: Renewal in Twentieth-Century Music, 1967; Twilight of the Gods: The Music of the Beatles, 1973; Bach and the Dance of God, 1980; Beethoven and the Voice of God, 1983; A Darker Shade of Pale: A Backdrop to Bob Dylan, 1984; Angels of the Night: Popular Female Singers of Our Time, 1986; The Masks of Orpheus: Seven Stages in the Story of European Music, 1987; Le Jardin Retrouvé: Homage to Federico Mompou, 1989; Vaughan Williams and the Vision of Albion, 1989; The Music of Percy Grainger, 1992; Francis Poulenc, 1994; Between Old Worlds and New: Occasional Writings on Music by Wilfrid Mellers, 1998; Singing in the Wilderness, 2001; Celestial Music: The Voice of God Perhaps, 2001; Celestial Music: Some Masterpieces of Religious Music, 2002. Contributions: Reference works and journals. *Honours:* Hon. DPhil, City University, 1981; OBE, 1982. *Address:* Oliver Sheldon House, 17 Aldwark, York YO1 7BX, England.

MELLING, John Kennedy; Drama Critic, Ed., Writer, Lecturer, Broadcaster and Chartered Accountant; b. 11 Jan. 1927, Westcliff-on-Sea, Essex, England. *Education:* Thirsk School, 1932–38; Westcliff High School for

Boys, 1938–42. *Career:* Drama Critic, The Stage, 1957–90, Fur Weekly News, 1968–73; Ed., The Liveryman Magazine, 1970–75, Chivers Black Dagger Series of Crime Classics, 1986–91; Radio Crime Book Critic, BBC London, 1984–85, BBC Essex, 1987; mem. BAFTA; Institute of Taxation, fellow; FRSA; CWA, committee mem., 1985–88; Cookery and Food Asscn; Edinburgh Press Club; Marylebone Rifle and Pistol Club; American Federation of Police, international life vice-pres.; Fellow, Faculty of Building. *Publications:* Discovering Lost Theatres, 1969; Southend Playhouses from 1793, 1969; Discovering Theatre Ephemera, 1973; Discovering London's Guilds and Liveries, 1973; She Shall Have Murder, 1987; Murder in the Library (ed.), 1987; Crime Writers' Handbook of Practical Information (ed.), 1989; Gwendoline Butler: Inventor of the Women's Police Procedural, 1993; Alchemy of Murder, 1993; Murder Done to Death, 1996; Scaling the High C's (with John L. Brecknock), 1996. Plays: George... From Caroline, 1971; Diarists' Pleasures, 1982; Murder at St Dunstan's, 1983. Contributions: newspapers and journals; regular columnist, Crime Time; 1996–2002. *Honours:* Knight Grand Cross; Order of St Michael; Knight, Order of St Basil, 1984; CWA Award for Outstanding Services, 1989; Medal of Honor, American Law Enforcement Officers Asscn. *Address:* 44A Tranquil Vale, Blackheath, London SE3 0BD; 85 Chalkwell Ave, Westcliff-on-Sea, Essex SS0 8NL, England.

MELLOR, David Hugh, BA, ScD, MEng, MSc, PhD; academic and writer; b. 10 July 1938, England. *Education:* University of Cambridge, University of Minnesota. *Career:* Research Student in Philosophy, 1963–68, Fellow, 1965–70, Pembroke College, University Asst Lecturer in Philosophy, 1965–70, University Lecturer in Philosophy, 1970–83, Fellow, 1971–, and Vice-Master, 1983–87, Darwin College, University Reader in Metaphysics, 1983–85, Prof. of Philosophy, 1986–99, Prof. Emeritus, 1999–, Pro-Vice-Chancellor, 2000–01, University of Cambridge; Visiting Fellow in Philosophy, Australian National University, Canberra, 1975; Hon. Prof. of Philosophy, University of Keele, 1989–92; mem. Aristotelian Society, pres., 1992–93; British Acad., fellow, 1983–; British Society for the Philosophy of Science, pres., 1985–87; Analysis Trust, chair., 2001–. *Publications:* The Matter of Chance, 1971; Real Time, 1981; Cambridge Studies in Philosophy, (ed.), 1978–82; Matters of Metaphysics, 1991; The Facts of Causation, 1995; Real Time II, 1998. Contributions: scholarly journals. *Honours:* Hon. PhD, Lund University, 1997. *Address:* 25 Orchard Street, Cambridge CB1 1JS, England.

MELTZER, David; Poet, Writer, Teacher, Ed. and Musician; b. 17 Feb. 1937, Rochester, NY, USA; m. Christina Meyer, 1958, one s., three d. *Education:* Los Angeles City College, 1955–56; University of California at Los Angeles, 1956–57. *Career:* Ed., Maya, 1966–71, Tree magazine and Tree Books, 1970–; Faculty, Graduate Poetics Program, 1980–, Chair, Undergraduate Writing and Literature Program, Humanities, 1988–, New College of California, San Francisco. *Publications:* Poetry: Poems (with Donald Schenker), 1957; Ragas, 1959; The Clown, 1960; Station, 1964; The Blackest Rose, 1964; Oyez!, 1965; The Process, 1965; In Hope I Offer a Fire Wheel, 1965; The Dark Continent, 1967; Nature Poem, 1967; Santamaya (with Jack Shoemaker), 1968; Round the Poem Box: Rustic and Domestic Home Movies for Stan and Jane Brakhage, 1969; Yesod, 1969; From Eden Book, 1969; Abulafia Song, 1969; Greenspeech, 1970; Luna, 1970; Letters and Numbers, 1970; Bronx Lil/Head of Lilian S.A.C., 1970; 32 Beams of Light, 1970; Knots, 1971; Bark: A Polemic, 1973; Hero/Lil, 1973; Tens: Selected Poems 1961–1971, 1973; The Eyes, the Blood, 1973; French Broom, 1973; Blue Rags, 1974; Harps, 1975; Six, 1976; Bolero, 1976; The Art, the Veil, 1981; The Name: Selected Poetry 1973–1983, 1984; Arrows: Selected Poetry 1957–1992, 1994; No Eyes: Lester Young, 2001. Fiction: Orf, 1968; The Agency, 1968; The Agent, 1968; How Many Blocks in the Pile?, 1968; Lovely, 1969; Healer, 1969; Out, 1969; Glue Factory, 1969; The Martyr, 1969; Star, 1970; The Agency Trilogy, 1994; Under, 2000. Other: We All Have Something to Say to Each Other: Being an Essay Entitled 'Patchen' and Four Poems, 1962; Introduction to the Outsiders, 1962; Bazascope Mother, 1964; Journal of the Birth, 1967; Isla Vista Notes: Fragmentary, Apocalyptic, Didactic Contradictions, 1970; Two-way Mirror: A Poetry Note-Book, 1977; San Francisco Beat: Talking With the Poets, 2002. Editor: Journal for the Protection of All Beings 1 and 3 (with Lawrence Ferlinghetti and Michael McClure), 2 vols, 1961, 1969; The San Francisco Poets, 1971, revised as Golden Gate, 1976; Birth: An Anthology, 1973; The Secret Garden: An Anthology in the Kabbalah, 1976; Death, 1984; Reading Jazz: The White Invention of Jazz, 1993; Writing Jazz, 1997. *Honours:* Council of Literary Magazine Grants, 1972, 1981; National Endowment for the Arts Grants, 1974, 1975; Tombstone Award for Poetry, James Ryan Morris Memorial Foundation, 1992. *Address:* Box 9005, Berkeley, CA 94709, USA.

MELVILLE, James (see Martin, (Roy) Peter).

MELVILLE, Jennie (see Butler, Gwendoline (Williams)).

MEMMI, Albert; French writer; b. 15 Dec. 1920, Tunis; m. Germaine Dubach 1946; three c. *Education:* Lycée Carnot, Tunis, Univ. of Algiers and Univ. de Paris à la Sorbonne. *Career:* Teacher of Philosophy, Tunis 1955; Dir Psychological Centre, Tunis 1956; moved to France 1956; Researcher, CNRS, Paris 1959–; Asst Prof. Ecole pratique des hautes études 1959–66, Prof. 1966–70; Prof., Inst. de Psychanalyse, Paris 1968–; Prof. Univ. of Paris 1970–, Dir Social Sciences Dept 1973–76, Dir Anthropological Lab.; mem. Acad. des Sciences d'Outre-mer; Vice-Pres. Pen Club 1977-80, Comité nat. Laïcité-République 1991. *Publications include:* Le Statue de Sel (trans. as The Pillar of Salt) 1953, Strangers 1955, Portrait du colonisé (non-fiction, trans. as Colonized, Colonizer) 1957, Portrait of a Jew 1962, Anthologie des écrivains nord-africains 1965, Les français et le racisme 1965, The Liberation of the Jew 1966, Dominated Man 1968, Le Scorpion (trans. as The Scorpion) 1969, Decolonisation 1970, Jews and Arabs 1974, Entretien 1975, La terre intérieure 1976, Le Désert 1977, The Dependence 1979, Le racisme 1982, Ce que je crois 1985, L'Écriture colorée 1986, Les écrivains francophones du Maghreb 1987, Le Pharaon 1988, Le Mirliton du ciel (poems) 1990, Bonheurs 1992, A contre-courants 1993, Ah, quel bonheur 1995, Le Juif et l'autre 1995, Le Buveur et l'amoureux 1998, Le nomade immobile 2000, Dictionnaire à l'usage des incrédules. *Honours:* Officier Légion d'honneur; Commdr Ordre de Nichan Iftikhar; Officier Palmes académiques, Officier Arts et Lettres, Officier Ordre République Tunisienne; Chevalier des affaires culturelles du Burkina Faso; Dr hc (Ben Gurion) 1999; Prix de Carthage 1953, Prix Fénéon 1953, Prix Simba 1978, Prix de l'Union Rationaliste, Grand Prix Littéraire de l'Afrique du Nord, Grand Prix de la ville de Bari. *Address:* 5 rue Saint Merri, 75004 Paris, France. *Telephone:* 1-40-29-08-31. *Fax:* 1-42-74-25-22.

MEMMOTT, David R., BA; editor, writer and poet; b. 10 Dec. 1948, Grand Rapids, MI, USA; m. Susan A. Memmott 1974; one d. *Education:* Eastern Oregon State University. *Career:* Man. Ed., 1986–90, Contributing Ed., 1990, 1997, Ice River: Magazine of Speculative Writing; mem. Council for Literature of the Fantastic; Institute for Noetic Sciences. *Publications:* Alpha Gallery: Selections from the Fantastic Small Press (poetry ed.), 1991; House on Fire: Poetry and Collage, 1992; The Larger Earth: Descending Notes of a Grounded Astronaut (poems), 1996; Within the Walls of Jericho (poems), 1998; Shadow Bones (short stories), 1999. *Honours:* Co-ordinating Council of Literary Magazines Grant, 1988; Oregon Arts Commission Grants, 1988, 1989; Fishtrap Fellow, 1990; Rhysling Award, 1990; Literary Arts Inc Fellowships, 1995, 2000. *Address:* 1003 Y Avenue, PO Box 3235, La Grande, OR 97850, USA.

MENDES, David, (Bob Mendes); Writer and Poet; b. 15 May 1928, Antwerp, Belgium. *Career:* mem. Flemish Writers' Guild; PEN Club. *Publications:* Two collections of poetry, two plays, four short story collections and 11 novels, including: Day of Shame, 1988; The Chunnel Syndrome, 1989; The Fourth Sura, 1990; The Fraud Hunters, 1991; Vengeance, 1992; Races/ Riots, 1993; Link, 1994; Merciless, 1995; The Power of Fire, 1996; The Power of Ice, 1998; Taste of Freedom, 1999; Dirty Dancing, 2000; Blood Feud, 2001. *Honours:* Golden Noose Awards, 1993, 1997; Dutch Award for Best Thriller (twice); Cultural Award, Schoten, 2000. *Literary Agent:* Dan Wright, Ann Wright Literary Agency, 136 E 56th Street, New York, NY 10022, USA. *Address:* Wezelsebaan 191, 2900 Schoten, Belgium. *E-mail:* bob.mendes@pandora.be. *Website:* www.mendes.be.

MENDOZA, Mario; Novelist; b. 1964, Bogotá, Colombia. *Education:* BA, Literature, Univ. of Bogotá; MA, Latin American Literature, Fundación José Ortega y Gasset, Toledo, Spain. *Publications:* La ciudad de los umbrales, 1992; La travesía del vidente (short stories), 1995; Scorpio City, 1998; Relato de un asesino, 2001; Satanás, 2003. *Honours:* Premio Nacional de Literatura, Instituto Distrital de Cultura y Turismo, 1995. *Address:* c/o Seix Barral, Avda Diagonal 662–664, 7°, Barcelona 08034, Spain.

MERCHANT, Carolyn; Prof. and Environmental Historian; b. 12 July 1936, Rochester, New York, USA. *Education:* AB, Vassar College, 1958; MA, History of Science, 1962, PhD, History of Science, 1967, University of Wisconsin. *Career:* fmr Chair. Dept of Conservation and Resource Studies, now Prof. of Environmental History, Philosophy, and Ethics, University of California at Berkeley; Fellowships including MacArthur Fellow in Ecological Humanities Nat. Humanities Center 2001; Consultantships; Lectureships; Pres. American Soc. for Environmental History 2001–03. *Publications:* The Death of Nature: Women, Ecology and the Scientific Revolution, 1980; Ecological Revolutions: Nature, Gender, and Science in New England, 1989; Radical Ecology: The Search for a Livable World, 1992; Major Problems in American Environmental History: Documents and Essays (ed.), 1993; Key Concepts in Critical Theory: Ecology (ed.), 1994; Earthcare: Women and the Environment, 1996; Green Versus Gold: Sources in California's Environmental History (ed.), 1998, Columbia Guide to American Environmental History 2002, Reinventing Eden: The Fate of Nature in Western Culture 2003, Encyclopedia of World Environmental History (co-ed with John McNeill and Shepard Krech III) 2003. Contributions: scholarly journals. *Honours:* National Science Foundation Grants, 1976–78; National Endowment for the Humanities Grants, 1977, 1981–83; Center for Advanced Study in the Behavioural Sciences, fellow, 1978; ACLS Fellowship, 1978; Fulbright Senior Scholar, Umeå, Sweden, 1984; Guggenheim Fellowship, 1995; Hon. Doctorate, Umeå University, Sweden, 1995. *Address:* c/o Dept of Environmental Science Policy and Management, University of California, 135 Giannini Hall, Berkeley, CA 94720–3312, USA.

MEREDITH, Christopher (Laurence); Writer, Poet and Senior Lecturer; b. 15 Dec. 1954, Tredegar, Wales; m. V. Smythe, 1 Aug. 1981, two s. *Education:* BA, Philosophy and English, University College Wales, Aberystwyth, 1976. *Career:* Senior Lecturer, University of Glamorgan; mem. Yr Academi Gymreig, English language section. *Publications:* Poetry: This,

1984; Snaring Heaven, 1990. Fiction: Shifts, 1988; Griffri, 1991. Contributions: Literary magazines in Wales, England and USA. *Honours:* Eric Gregory Award, 1984; Welsh Arts Council Young Writer's Prize, 1985 and Fiction Prize, 1989. *Address:* c/o Seren Books, Wyndham St, Bridgend, Mid Glamorgan, Wales.

MEREDITH, William Morris, AB; American poet and retd academic; b. 9 Jan. 1919, New York, NY. *Education:* Princeton Univ. *Career:* Instructor in English and Woodrow Wilson Fellow in Writing, Princeton University, 1946–50; Assoc. Prof. in English, University of Hawaii, 1950–51; Assoc. Prof., 1955–65, Prof. in English, 1965–83, Connecticut College, New London; Instructor, Bread Loaf School of English, Middlebury College, Vermont, 1958–62; Consultant in Poetry, Library of Congress, Washington, DC, 1978–80; mem. Acad. of American Poets, chancellor; National Institute of Arts and Letters. *Publications:* Poetry: Love Letters from an Impossible Land, 1944; Ships and Other Figures, 1948; The Open Sea and Other Poems, 1958; The Wreck of the Thresher and Other Poems, 1964; Winter Verse, 1964; Year End Accounts, 1965; Two Pages from a Colorado Journal, 1967; Earth Walk: New and Selected Poems, 1970; Hazard, the Painter, 1975; The Cheer, 1980; Partial Accounts: New and Selected Poems, 1987. Non-Fiction: Reasons for Poetry and the Reason for Criticism, 1982; Poems Are Hard to Read, 1991. Editor: Shelley: Poems, 1962; University and College Poetry Prizes, 1960–66, 1966; Eighteenth-Century Minor Poets (with Mackie L. Jarrell), 1968; Poets of Bulgaria (with others), 1985. Translator: Guillaume Apollinaire: Alcools: Poems, 1898–1913, 1964. *Honours:* Yale Series of Younger Poets Award, 1943; Harriet Monroe Memorial Prize, 1944; Rockefeller Foundation Grants, 1948, 1968; Oscar Blumenthal Prize, 1953; National Institute of Arts and Letters Grant, 1958, and Loines Prize, 1966; Ford Foundation Fellowship, 1959–60; Van Wyck Brooks Award, 1971; National Endowment for the Arts Grant, 1972, and Fellowship, 1984; Guggenheim Fellowship, 1975–76; International Vaptsarov Prize for Literature, Bulgaria, 1979; Los Angeles Times Prize, 1987; Pulitzer Prize in Poetry, 1988. *Address:* 6300 Bradley Avenue, Bethseda, MD 20817, USA.

MERI, Lennart; Writer, Politician and Film Dir; b. 29 March 1929, Tallinn, Estonia; m. 1st Regina Ojavere 1953 (divorced); m. 2nd Helle Pihlak; two s. one d. *Education:* Tartu Univ. *Career:* deported to Siberia with family, 1941–46; forbidden to practise history, took part in scientific expeditions to Middle Asia; Head of Manuscript Section, Vanemuine Theatre; worked for Estonian Radio; Scriptwriter and Dir, Tallinnfilm; Sec., Estonian Writers' Asscn; Founder, Dir, Estonian Institute, 1989–90; active in Movement for Independence, 1980s; Minister of Foreign Affairs, 1990–92; Ambassador to Finland, April–Oct. 1992; Pres. of Estonia, 1992–2001; Documentary films: Veelinnunrahva, 1970; Linnutee Tuuled, 1977; Kaleva Hääled, 1986; Toorumi Pojad, 1989; Šamaan, 1997. *Publications:* Kobrade Ja Karakurtide Jälgedes, 1959; Laevapoisid Rohelisel Ookeanil, 1961; Tulemägede Maale, 1964; Virmaliste Väraval, 1974; Hõbevalge, 1976; Lähenevad Rannad, 1977; 1940 Eestis. Dokumente Ja Materjale (with others), 1989; Tulen maasta, jonka nimi on Viro (collection of speeches), 1995; Presidendkõned, 1996; 'Tacituse tahtel' (in Mare Nostrum - Mare Balticum), 2000. *Honours:* Dr hc, Helsinki Univ., 1976; several decorations including from Mexico, Sweden, Finland, Denmark, Jordan, Latvia. *Address:* Pilviku str. 3, Tallin, Estonia.

MERRILL, Christopher Lyall, BA, MA; poet, writer, editor, translator and academic; *Director of the International Writing Program, University of Iowa*; b. 24 Feb. 1957, Northampton, MA, USA; m. Lisa Ellen Gowdy 1983; two d. *Education:* Middlebury Coll., Univ. of Washington at Seattle. *Career:* Teaching Fellow, Univ. of Utah 1983–87; Dir, Santa Fe Writers' Conference 1987–90; Founder-Dir, Taos Conference on Writing and the Natural World 1987–92, Santa Fe Literary Center 1988–92; General Ed., Peregrine Smith Poetry Series 1987–; Poetry Ed., Orion Magazine 1993–; Adjunct Prof., Santa Fe Community Coll. 1988–90; Adjunct Faculty, Northwest Writing Inst., Lewis and Clark Coll. 1993–95; Faculty, Open Society Inst., Univ. of Sarajevo 1995; William H. Jenks Chair in Contemporary Letters, Coll. of the Holy Cross 1995–2000; Visiting Lecturer, Chatham Coll. 1999–2000; Prof. of English 2000–, Dir, Int. Writing Program 2000–, Univ. of Iowa; Literary Critic, The World (Public Radio Int.) 2000–; mem. Acad. of American Poets, Authors' Guild, PEN American Center. *Publications:* Workbook (poems) 1988, Fevers and Tides (poems) 1989, The Forgotten Language: Contemporary Poets and Nature (ed.) 1991, From the Faraway Nearby: Georgia O'Keefe as Icon (ed. with Ellen Bradbury) 1992, The Grass of Another Country: A Journey Through the World of Soccer 1993, Watch Fire (poems) 1994, Anxious Moments, by Aleš Debeljak (trans.) 1994, The Old Bridge: The Third Balkan War and the Age of the Refugee 1995, What Will Suffice: Contemporary American Poets on the Art of Poetry (ed. with Christopher Buckley) 1995, The Forest of Speaking Trees: An Essay on Poetry 1996, Your Final Pleasure: An Esssay on Reading 1996, The Four Questions of Melancholy: New and Selected Poems of Tomaz Šalamun (ed.) 1996, The Way to the Salt Marsh: A John Hay Reader (ed.) 1998, Only the Nails Remain: Scenes from the Balkan Wars 1999, Brilliant Water (poems) 2001, The City and the Child, by Aleš Debeljak (trans.) 2003, Things of the Hidden God: Journey to the Holy Mountain 2005; contrib. to many periodicals. *Honours:* Sherman Brown Neff Fellowship, Univ. of Utah 1986–87, John Ciardi Fellow in Poetry, Bread Loaf Writers' Conference 1989, Pushcart Prize in Poetry 1990, Ingram Merrill Foundation Award in Poetry 1991, Readers' Choice Award in Poetry, Prairie Schooner 1992, Peter I. B. Lavan Younger Poets Award, Acad. of American Poets 1993, Trans. Award, Slovenian Ministry of Culture 1997, Writers Asscn of Bosnia-Herzegovina Annual Literary Award, The Bosnian Stecak 2001. *Address:* 216 McLean Street, Iowa City, IA 52242 (Home); International Writing Program, Shambaugh House, University of Iowa, 430 N Clinton Street, Iowa City, IA 52242-2020, USA (Office). *Telephone:* (319) 335-2609 (Office). *Fax:* (319) 335-3843 (Office). *Website:* www.christophermerrillbooks.com.

MERRIN, Jeredith; Prof. of English, Writer and Poet; b. 9 April 1944, California, USA; one d. *Education:* BS, Iowa State University, 1968; MA, San Jose State University, 1978; PhD, University of California at Berkeley, 1987. *Career:* Instructor, Gifted Program, University of California at Berkeley, 1983–85; Asst Prof., 1987–93, Assoc. Prof., 1993–97, Prof. of English, 1997–, Ohio State University, Columbus; Presenter, workshops and poetry readings. *Publications:* An Enabling Humility: Marianne Moore, Elizabeth Bishop, and the Uses of Tradition, 1990; Shift (poems), 1996; Bat Ode (poems), 2001. Contributions: books, anthologies, reviews, quarterlies and journals. *Honours:* Lilly Foundation Fellow, 1988–89; Regdale Artists Colony Residencies, 1990, 1991, 1996; Fellow, Skidmore College, 1993; Elizabeth Gee Award for Research on Women, 1993; National Endowment for the Humanities Grants, 1995, 1997. *Address:* c/o Dept of English, Ohio State University, 164 W 17th Ave, Columbus, OH 43210, USA.

MERTZ, Barbara Louise Gross, (Barbara Michaels, Elizabeth Peters); Writer; b. 29 Sept. 1927, Canton, IL, USA; Divorced, one s. one d. *Education:* PhD, University of Chicago, 1952. *Career:* mem. ACWL, Pres., 1991–94; Advisory Board, KMT: A Modern Journal of Ancient Egypt; Advisory Board, The Writer. *Publications:* Temples, Tombs & Hieroglyphs, 1964; Red Land, Black Land, 1966; The Master of Blacktower, 1966; Sons of the Wolf, 1967; The Jackal's Head, 1968; Ammie Come Home, 1968; Prince of Darkness, 1969; The Camelot Caper, 1969; The Dark on the Other Side, 1970; The Crying Child, 1971; The Night of 400 Rabbits, 1971; Greygallows, 1972; The Seventh Sinner, 1972; Witch, 1973; Borrower of the Night, 1973; House of Many Shadows, 1974; Murders of Richard III, 1974; Sea King's Daughter, 1975; Crocodile on the Sandbank, 1975; Patriot's Dream, 1976; Legend in Green Velvet, 1976; Wings of the Falcon, 1977; Devil-May-Care, 1977; Wait For What Will Come, 1978; Street of the Five Moons, 1978; The Walker in the Shadows, 1979; Summer of the Dragon, 1979; The Wizard's Daughter, 1980; The Love Talker, 1980; The Curse of the Pharaohs, 1981; Someone in the House, 1981; The Copenhagen Connection, 1982; Black Rainbow, 1982; Silhouette in Scarlet, 1983; Here I Stay, 1983; Die for Love, 1984; The Grey Beginning, 1984; The Mummy Case, 1985; Be Buried in the Rain, 1985; Lion in the Valley, 1986; Shattered Silk, 1986; Trojan Gold, 1987; Search the Shadows, 1987; Deeds of the Disturber, 1988; Naked Once More, 1989; Smoke and Mirrors, 1989; Into the Darkness, 1990; The Last Camel Died at Noon, 1991; Vanish with the Rose, 1992; Houses of Stone, 1993; The Snake, the Crocodile, and the Dog, 1992; Night Train to Memphis, 1994; Stitches in Time, 1995; The Hippopotamus Pool, 1996; The Dancing Floor, 1997; Seeing a Large Cat, 1997; The Ape Who Guards the Balance, 1998; Other Worlds, 1999; The Falcon at the Portal, 1999; He Shall Thunder in the Sky, 2000; Lord of the Silent, 2001; The Golden One, 2002; Children of the Storm, 2003. Contributions: reference works and periodicals. *Honours:* Lifetime Achievement Award, Bouchercon, 1986; Agatha Best Novel, Malice Domestic, 1992; Doctor of Humane Letters, Hood College, 1992; Grand Master Award, MWA, 1998. *Address:* c/o Dominick Abel, 146 W 82nd St, No. 1B, New York, NY 10024, USA.

MERVILLON, Pol-Jean (see Nadaus, Roland).

MERWIN, William Stanley, AB; American poet, dramatist, writer and translator; b. 30 Sept. 1927, New York, NY; m. Diane Whalley 1954. *Education:* Princeton Univ. *Career:* Playwright-in-Residence, Poet's Theatre, Cambridge, Massachusetts, 1956–57; Poetry Ed., The Nation, 1962; Assoc., Theatre de la Citié, Lyons, 1964–65; Special Consultant in Poetry, Library of Congress, Washington, DC, 1999; mem. Acad. of American Poets; American Acad. of Arts and Letters. *Publications:* poetry: A Mask for Janus 1952, The Dancing Bears 1954, Green with Beasts 1956, The Drunk in the Furnace 1960, The Moving Target 1963, The Lice 1967, Three Poems 1968, Animae 1969, The Carrier of Ladders 1970, Signs 1971, Writings to an Unfinished Accompaniment 1973, The First Four Books of Poems 1975, Three Poems 1975, The Compass Flower 1977, Feathers from the Hill 1978, Finding the Islands 1982, Opening the Hand 1983, The Rain in the Trees 1988, Selected Poems 1988, Travels 1993, The Vixen 1996, The Folding Cliffs 1998; plays: Darkling Child (with Dido Milroy) 1956, Favor Island 1957, The Gilded West 1961, adaptations of five other plays; other: A New Right Arm, West Wind: Supplement of American Poetry (ed.) 1961, The Miner's Pale Children 1970, Houses and Travellers 1977, Unframed Originals: Recollections 1982, Regions of Memory: Uncollected Prose 1949–1982 1987, The Essential Wyatt (ed.) 1989, The Lost Upland 1993; translator: Selected Translations 1948–1968 1968, Selected Translations 1968–1978 1979, Sir Gawain and the Green Knight: A New Verse Translation 2004. *Honours:* Yale Series of Younger Poets Award, 1952; Bess Hokin Prize, 1962; Ford Foundation Grant, 1964; Harriet Monroe Memorial Prize, 1967; PEN Trans. Prize, 1969; Rockefeller Foundation Grant, 1969; Pulitzer Prize in Poetry, 1971; Acad. of American Poets Fellowship, 1973; Shelley Memorial Award, 1974; National Endowment for the Arts Grant, 1978; Bollingen Prize, 1979; Aiken Taylor Award, 1990; Maurice English Award,

1990; Dorothea Tanning Prize, 1994; Lenore Marshall Award, 1994; Ruth Lilly Poetry Prize, 1998. *Literary Agent:* Steven Barclay Agency, 12 Western Avenue, Petaluma, CA 94952, USA. *Telephone:* (707) 773-0654. *Fax:* (707) 778-1868. *Website:* www.barclayagency.com. *Address:* c/o Georges Borchardt Inc, 136 E 57th Street, New York, NY 10022. USA.

MESERVE, Walter Joseph; academic, editor and writer; b. 10 March 1923, Portland, Maine, USA; m. 1st; two s. two d.; m. 2nd Mollie Ann Lacey 1981. *Education:* Portland Junior College, 1941–42; AB, Bates College, Lewiston, Maine, 1947; MA, Boston University, 1948; PhD, University of Washington, 1952. *Career:* Instructor to Prof., University of Kansas, 1951–68; Prof. of Dramatic Literature and Theory, 1968–88, Dir, Institute for American Theatre Studies, 1983–88, Indiana University; Vice-Pres., Feedback Services, New York City, Brooklin, Maine, 1983–; Ed.-in-Chief, Feedback Theatrebooks, 1985–; Distinguished Prof., 1988–93, Distinguished Prof. Emeritus, 1993–, Graduate School and Univ. Center, PhD Programs in Theatre and English, CUNY; Co-Ed., American Drama and Theatre journal, 1989–93; mem. Cosmos Club. *Publications:* The Complete Plays of W. D. Howells (ed.), 1960; Outline History of American Drama, 1965; American Satiric Comedies (co-ed.), 1969; Robert E. Sherwood, 1970; Modern Drama from Communist China (co-ed.), 1970; Studies in Death of a Salesman (ed.), 1972; Modern Literature from China (co-ed.), 1974; An Emerging Entertainment: The Drama of the American People to 1828, 1977; The Revels History of Drama in English, Vol. VIII: American Drama (co-author), 1977; Cry Woolf (co-author), 1982; Heralds of Promise: The Drama of the American People During the Age of Jackson 1829–1849, 1986; Who's Where in the American Theatre (co-ed.), 1990; A Chronological Outline of World Theatre (co-author), 1992; The Theatre Lover's Cookbook (co-ed.), 1992; Musical Theatre Cookbook (co-ed.), 1993. *Honours:* National Endowment for the Humanities Fellowships, 1974–75, 1983–84, 1988–89; Rockefeller Foundation Fellowship, 1979; Guggenheim Fellowship, 1984–85. *Address:* PO Box 174, Brooklin, ME 04616, USA.

MESSENT, Peter Browning; Prof. of Modern American Literature; b. 24 Oct. 1946, Wimbledon, England; m. 1st Brenda 10 July 1972 (divorced); one s. one d.; m. 2nd Carin 9 July 1994. *Education:* BA, American Studies, 1969, MA, 1972, University of Manchester; PhD, University of Nottingham, 1991. *Career:* Temporary Lecturer, University of Manchester, 1972–73; Lecturer, 1973–94, Senior Lecturer in American and Canadian Studies, 1994–95, Reader, 1995–99, Prof., 1999–, Modern American Literature, University of Nottingham; mem. British Asscn for American Studies; Mark Twain Circle. *Publications:* Twentieth Century Views: Literature of the Occult (ed.), 1981; New Readings of the American Novel, 1990; Ernest Hemingway, 1992; Henry James: Selected Tales (ed.), 1992; Mark Twain, 1997; Criminal Proceedings (ed.), 1997; The Short Works of Mark Twain: A Critical Study, 2001. Contributions: books, journals, and magazines. *Address:* c/o School of American and Canadian Studies, University of Nottingham, Nottingham NG7 2RD, England.

MESSER, Thomas Maria; American museum director and writer; b. 9 Feb. 1920, Bratislava, Czechoslovakia; m. Remedios Garcia Villa 1948. *Education:* Institute of International Education, 1939; Thiel College, Greenville, Pennsylvania, 1939–41; BA, Boston University, 1942; Degree, Sorbonne, University of Paris, 1947; MA, Harvard University, 1951. *Career:* Dir, Roswell Museum, New Mexico, 1949–52, Institute of Contemporary Art, Boston, 1957–61; Asst Dir, 1952–53, Dir of Exhibitions, 1953–55, Dir, 1955–56, American Federation of Arts, New York City; Adjunct Prof., Harvard University, 1960, Barnard College, 1966, 1971; Dir, 1961–88, Dir Emeritus, 1988–, Solomon R. Guggenheim Museum, New York City; Pres., MacDowell Colony, 1977–78, 1993–94; Prof., Hochschule für Angewandte Kunst, Vienna, 1984, Goethe University, Frankfurt am Main, 1991–92, 1993–; Chief Curator, Schinn Kunsthalle, Frankfurt am Main, 1994–2002; mem. Trustee, Fontana Foundation, Milan, 1988–; Trustee, Institute of International Education, 1991–2000, Hon. Trustee 2000–. *Publications:* Edvard Munch, 1973; Vasily Randinsky, 1997. Contributions: various museum catalogues and art journals. *Honours:* Officier, Légion d'honneur, 1989; Göthe Medal, Germany. *Address:* 35 Sutton Place, New York, NY 10022, USA.

MESTAS, Jean-Paul; Poet, Writer and Trans; b. 15 Nov. 1925, Paris, France; m. Christiane Schoubrenner, 23 Dec. 1977, two s. one d. *Education:* BA, 1947, LLB, 1947, Institute of Political Studies, Paris. *Career:* mem. International Acad., Chennai, fellow; International Poetry, Republic of Korea; International Writers and Artists, board of research. *Publications:* various poems, essays, and trans, 1965–95. Contributions: many anthologies and periodicals. *Honours:* Excellence in Poetry, International Poet, New York, 1982; Premio de la Cultura, Palermo, 1991; Prix Marcel Beguey, Bergerac, 1992.

MESTROVIC, Stjepan; American academic, writer and editor; b. 12 March 1955, Croatia; two d. *Education:* BA, 1976, EdM, 1977, MTS, 1979, Harvard University; PhD, Syracuse University, 1982. *Career:* Prof. of Sociology, Texas A & M University, College Station, USA, 1990–; Series Ed., Postmodern Social Futures; Series Ed., Eastern Europe; mem. American Sociological Asscn; Schopenhauer Society. *Publications:* Emile Durkheim and the Reformation of Sociology, 1988; The Coming Fin de Siècle: An Application of Durkheim's Sociology to Modernity and Postmodernity, 1991; Durkheim and Postmodern Culture, 1992; The Road from Paradise,: The Possibility of Democracy in Eastern Europe, 1993; Habits of the Balkan Heart: Social Character and the Fall of Communism, 1993; The Barbarian Temperament: Towards a Postmodern Critical Theory, 1993; The Balkanization of the West: The Confluence of Postmodernism with Postcommunism, 1994; Genocide after Emotion: The Postemotional Balkan War, 1996; This Time We Knew: Western Responses to Genocide in Bosnia (co-ed.), 1996; The Conceit of Innocence: How the Conscience of the West Was Lost in the War against Bosnia, 1997; Postemotional Society, 1997; Anthony Giddens: The Last Modernist, 1998. *Honours:* Fellow, National Endowment for the Humanities, 1986–87; Fulbright Fellow in Croatia, 1992–93. *Address:* Department of Sociology, Texas A & M University, College Station, TX 77843-4351, USA. *E-mail:* mestrovic@tmu.edu.

METCALF, John Wesley, BA; Canadian writer and editor; b. 12 Nov. 1938, Carlisle, England; m. Myrna Teitelbaum 1975; three s. three d. *Education:* University of Bristol. *Career:* Writer-in-Residence, University of New Brunswick, 1972–73, Loyola of Montréal, 1976, University of Ottawa, 1977, Concordia University, Montréal, 1980–81, University of Bologna, 1985; Senior Ed., Porcupine's Quill Press, 1989–; Ed., Canadian Notes and Queries, 1997–. *Publications:* The Lady Who Sold Furniture, 1970; The Teeth of My Father, 1975; Girl in Gingham, 1978; Selected Stories, 1982; Kicking Against the Pricks, 1982; Adult Entertainment, 1986; What is a Canadian Literature?, 1988; Volleys, 1990; How Stories Mean, 1992; Shooting the Stars, 1993; Freedom from Culture: Selected Essays, 1982–92, 1994; Acts of Kindness and of Love (co-author), 1995; Forde Abroad, 2003; An Aesthetic Underground: A Literary Memoir, 2003; Standing Stones: the Best Stories of John Metcalf 2004; contrib. to many publications. *Honours:* various Canada Council Arts Awards. *Address:* 128 Lewis Street, Ottawa, ON K2P 0S7, Canada.

METZGER, Deena; Writer, Poet, Playwright, Teacher and Healer; b. 17 Sept. 1936, New York, NY, USA; m. 1st H. Reed Metzger, 26 Oct. 1957; m. 2nd Michael Ortiz Hill, 20 Dec. 1987, two s. *Education:* BA, Brooklyn College, CUNY; MA, University of California; PhD, International College, Los Angeles. *Career:* Prof., Los Angeles Valley College, 1966–69, 1973–74, 1975–79; Faculty, California Institute of the Arts, 1970–75; International Lecturer, Teacher of Writing, Supervision and Training of Healers in the Ethical, Creative and Spiritual Aspects of Healing, 1997–. *Publications:* Skin Shadows/Silence, 1976; Dark Milk, 1978; The Book of Hags, 1978; The Axis Mundi Poems, 1981; What Dinah Thought, 1989; Looking for the Face of God, 1989; A Sabbath Among the Ruins, 1992; Writing for Your Life: A Guide and Companion to the Inner Worlds, 1992; Tree: Essays and Pieces (co-ed.), 1997; Intimate Nature: Women's Bond with Animals (co-ed.), 1998. *Address:* PO Box 186, Topanga, CA 90290, USA.

METZGER, Henry, AB, MD, FAAS; American (b. German) scientific researcher; b. 23 March 1932, Mainz, Germany; m. Deborah Stashower 1957; two s. one d. *Education:* Univ. of Rochester, Columbia Univ. *Career:* emigrated to USA 1938; Intern, then Asst Resident, Col-Presbyterian Medical Center 1957–59; Research Assoc., NIAMD, NIH 1959–61, Medical Officer, Arthritis and Rheumatism Branch, Bethesda, MD 1963–73, Chief, Section on Chemical Immunology 1973–, Chief, Arthritis and Rheumatism Branch, Nat. Inst. of Arthritis and Musculoskeletal and Skin Diseases 1983–94, Dir Intramural Research Program 1987–98; Fellow Helen Hay Whitney Foundation, Dept of Biology, Univ. of Calif., San Diego 1961–63; Pres. American Asscn of Immunologists 1991–92; Pres. Int. Union of Immunological Socs 1992–95; mem. Health Research Council BMFT, German Govt 1994–97; mem. NAS. *Publications:* over 200 scientific papers and contribs to scientific journals. *Honours:* Hon. mem. Chilean and French Socs of Immunology; several awards. *Address:* 3410 Taylor Street, Chevy Chase, MD 20815, USA (Home).

MEWSHAW, Michael; Author and Poet; b. 19 Feb. 1943, Washington, DC, USA; m. Linda Kirby, 17 June 1967, two s. *Education:* MA, 1966, PhD, 1970, University of Virginia. *Career:* Instructor, 1970, Visiting Writer, 1989–91, University of Virginia; Asst Prof. of English, University of Massachusetts, 1970–71; Asst Prof. to Assoc. Prof. of English, University of Texas, Austin, 1973–83; Visiting Artist, 1975–76, Writer-in-Residence, 1977–78, American Acad., Rome; mem. PEN; Society of Fellows of the American Acad. in Rome; Texas Institute of Letters; US Tennis Writers Asscn. *Publications:* Fiction: Man in Motion, 1970; Waking Slow, 1972; The Troll, 1974; Earthly Bread, 1976; Land Without Shadow, 1979; Year of the Gun, 1984; Blackballed, 1986; True Crime, 1991. Non-Fiction: Life for Death, 1980; Short Circuit, 1983; Money to Burn: The True Story of the Benson Family Murders, 1987; Playing Away: Roman Holidays and Other Mediterranean Encounters, 1988; Ladies of the Court: Grace and Disgrace on the Women's Tennis Tour, 1993. Contributions: newspapers and magazines. *Honours:* Fulbright Fellowship, 1968–69; William Rainey Fellowship, 1970; National Endowment for the Arts Fellowship, 1974–75; Carr Collins Awards for Best Book of Non-Fiction, 1980, 1983; Guggenheim Fellowship, 1981–82; Book of the Year Award, Tennis Week, 1993. *Literary Agent:* William Morris Agency, 1325 Avenue of the Americas, New York, NY 10019, USA.

MEYER, Ben F(ranklin); Prof. of Religious Studies and Writer; b. 5 Nov. 1927, Chicago, IL, USA; m. Denise Oppliger, 27 March 1969. *Education:* BA, 1952, MA, 1953; STM, University of Santa Clara, 1958; SSL, Biblical Institute, Rome, 1961; STD, Gregorian University, Rome, 1965. *Career:* Asst Prof. of Religion, Graduate Theological Union, Berkeley, 1965–68;

Assoc. Prof., 1969–74, Prof. of Religious Studies, 1974–, McMaster University, Hamilton, Ontario; mem. Canadian Society of Biblical Studies, pres., 1988–89; Society of Biblical Literature; Studiorum Novi Testament Societas. *Publications:* The Man for Others, 1970; The Church in Three Tenses, 1971; The Aims of Jesus, 1979; The Early Christians, 1986; Critical Realism and the New Testament, 1989; Lonergan's Hermenuetics (ed. with S. E. McEvenue), 1989; Christus Faber: The Master Builder and the House of God, 1992; One Loaf, One Cup, 1993; Five Speeches That Changed the World, 1994; Reality and Illusion in New Testament Scholarship, 1995. Contributions: Professional journals. *Address:* c/o Dept of Religious Studies, McMaster University, Hamilton, Ontario L8S 4K1, Canada.

MEYER, Lynn (see Slavitt, David Rytman).

MEYERS, Carol; Prof., Archaeologist and Writer; b. 26 Nov. 1942, Wilkes-Barre, PA, USA; m. Eric Meyers, 25 June 1964, two d. *Education:* AB, Biblical History, Literature, and Interpretation, Wellesley College, 1964; Hebrew Union College Biblical and Archaeological School, Jerusalem, 1964; Hebrew University, Jerusalem, 1964–65; MA, 1966, PhD, 1975, Near Eastern and Judaic Studies, Brandeis University. *Career:* Lecturer, 1975, Part-time Lecturer, 1976–77, Visiting Asst Prof., 1979, University of North Carolina at Chapel Hill; Asst Prof., 1977–84, Assoc. Prof., 1984–90, Prof., 1990–, Mary Grace Wilson Prof. of Religion, 2002–, Duke University; Assoc. Ed., Semeia, 1990–96, Bulletin of the American Schools of Oriental Research, 1997–; Mem., Center of Theological Inquiry, Princeton, 1991–; Visiting Faculty, MA Program in Judaic Studies, University of Connecticut, 1994–; mem. American Acad. of Religion; American Schools of Oriental Research; Archaeological Institute of America; Archaeology Society of Jordan; Asscn for Jewish Studies; British School of Archaeology in Jerusalem; Catholic Biblical Asscn; Center for Cross-Cultural Research on Women, Oxford; Israel Exploration Society; Palestine Exploration Society; Society for Values in Higher Education; Society of Biblical Literature; Wellesley College Center for Research on Women; Women's Asscn of Ancient Near Eastern Studies. *Publications:* The Tabernacle Menorah: A Synthetic Study of a Symbol from the Biblical Cult, 1976; Excavations at Ancient Meiron: Upper Galilee, Israel, 1971–72, 1974–75, 1977 (with E. M. Meyers and J. F. Strange), 1981; The Word of the Lord Shall Go Forth (ed. with M. O'Connor), 1983; Haggai, Zechariah 1–8 (with E. Meyers), 1987; Discovering Eve: Ancient Israelite Women in Context, 1988; Excavations at the Ancient Synagogue of Gush Halav (with E. Meyers), 1990; Sepphoris (with E. Netzer and E. Meyers), 1992; Zechariah 9–14 (with E. Meyers), 1993; Ethics and Politics in the Hebrew Bible (ed. with D. A. Knight), 1995; Community, Identity, and Ideology: Social Science Approaches to the Hebrew Bible (ed. with C. W. Carter), 1996; Sepphoris in Galilee: Cross-Currents of Culture (ed. with R. Nagy, E. M. Meyers, and Z. Weiss), 1996; Families in Ancient Israel (with L. G. Perdue, J. Blenkinsopp, and J. J. Collins), 1997; Women in Scripture: A Dictionary of Named and Unnamed Women in the Hebrew Bible, the Apocryphal/Deuterocanonical Books, and the New Testament (ed. with T. Craven and R. S. Kraemer), 2000. Contributions: scholarly books and professional journals. *Honours:* various grants; National Endowment for the Humanities Fellowships, 1982–83, 1990–91; Howard Foundation Fellowship, 1985–86; International Corresponding Fellow, Ingeborg Rennert Center for Jerusalem Studies, Bar Ilan University, Israel, 1998–; Education Endowment Award, Women's Institute for Continuing Jewish Education, 2001. *Address:* c/o Dept of Religion, Duke University, Box 90964, Durham, NC 27708, USA. *Telephone:* (919) 660-3530. *E-mail:* carol@duke.edu.

MEYERS, Jeffrey, BA, MA, PhD, FRSL; writer; b. 1 April 1939, New York, NY, USA. *Education:* Univ. of Michigan, Univ. of California at Berkeley. *Publications:* Fiction and the Colonial Experience 1973, The Wounded Spirit: A Study of Seven Pillars of Wisdom 1973, T. E. Lawrence: A Bibliography 1975, A Reader's Guide to George Orwell 1975, George Orwell: The Critical Heritage 1975, Painting and the Novel 1975, A Fever at the Core 1976, George Orwell: An Annotated Bibliography of Criticism 1977, Married to Genius 1977, Homosexuality and Literature, 1890–1930 1977, Katherine Mansfield: A Biography 1978, The Enemy: A Biography of Wyndham Lewis 1980, Wyndham Lewis: A Revaluation 1980, D. H. Lawrence and the Experience of Italy 1982, Hemingway: The Critical Heritage 1982, Disease and the Novel, 1860–1960 1984, Hemingway: A Biography 1985, D. H. Lawrence and Tradition 1985, The Craft of Literary Biography 1985, The Legacy of D. H. Lawrence 1987, Manic Power: Robert Lowell and his Circle 1987, Robert Lowell: Interviews and Memoirs 1988, The Biographer's Art 1989, The Spirit of Biography 1989, T. E. Lawrence: Soldier, Writer, Legend 1989, Graham Greene: A Revaluation 1989, D. H. Lawrence: A Biography 1990, Joseph Conrad: A Biography 1991, Edgar Allan Poe: His Life and Legacy 1992, Scott Fitzgerald: A Biography 1994, Edmund Wilson: A Biography 1995, Robert Frost: A Biography 1996, Bogart: A Life in Hollywood 1997, Gary Cooper: American Hero 1998, Orwell: Wintry Conscience of a Generation 2000, Privileged Moments: Encounters with Writers 2000, Hemingway: Life into Art 2000, The Sir Arthur Conan Doyle Reader 2002, Inherited Risk: Errol and Sean Flynn in Hollywood and Vietnam 2002, Somerset Maugham: A Life 2004, The Somerset Maugham Reader 2004, Impressionist Quartet: The Intimate Genius of Manet and Morisot, Degas and Cassatt 2005. *Address:* 84 Stratford Road, Kensington, CA 94707, USA. *E-mail:* vjmeyers@nothingbutnet.net.

MEYNELL, Hugo Anthony, BA, PhD; academic and writer; *Professor of Religious Studies, University of Calgary*; b. 23 March 1936, Derbyshire, England; m. Jennifer Routledge 1969; three d. one adopted s. *Education:* King's College, Cambridge. *Career:* Lecturer, University of Leeds, 1961–81; Visiting Prof., Emory University, 1978; Prof. of Religious Studies, University of Calgary, 1981–; mem. Canadian Philosophical Asscn; Canadian Society for Religious Studies; Royal Society of Canada. *Publications:* Sense, Nonsense and Christianity, 1964; Grace versus Nature, 1966; The New Theology and Modern Theologians, 1967; God and the World, 1971; An Introduction to the Philosophy of Bernard Lonergan, 1976; Freud, Marx and Morals, 1981; The Intelligible Universe: A Cosmological Argument, 1982; The Nature of Aesthetic Value, 1986; The Theology of Bernard Lonergan, 1986; The Art of Handel's Operas, 1986; Is Christianity True?, 1994. Contributions: scholarly journals. *Address:* c/o Department of Religious Studies, Social Sciences 1301, 2500 University Drive NW, Calgary, AB T2N 1N4, Canada.

MIALL, Robert (see Burke, John Frederick).

MICHAELS, Anne, BA; Canadian poet, novelist, writer and teacher; b. 15 April 1958, Toronto, ON. *Education:* Univ. of Toronto. *Career:* many workshops and guest residencies; teacher of creative writing, Univ. of Toronto 1988–; mem. League of Canadian Poets, Writers' Union of Canada. *Publications:* poetry: The Weight of Oranges 1986, Miner's Pond 1991, Skin Divers 1999; fiction: Fugitive Pieces 1996; contrib. to numerous anthologies, reviews and magazines. *Honours:* Epstein Award for Poetry 1980, Commonwealth Poetry Prize for the Americas 1986, Canadian Authors' Asscn Award for Poetry 1991, Nat. Magazine Award for Poetry 1991, Chapter/Books in Canada First Novel Award 1997, Trillium Award 1997, Lannan Prize 1997, Guardian Fiction Award 1997, H. H. Wingate Award 1997, Orange Prize for Fiction 1997, Harry Ribalow Award 1998, Acerbi Prize 2001. *Literary Agent:* McClelland and Stewart Inc, 481 University Avenue, Suite 900, Toronto, ON M5G 2E9, Canada.

MICHAELS, Barbara (see Mertz, Barbara Louise Gross).

MICHAELS, Kristin (see Williams, Jeanne R.).

MICHEL, Sandra Seaton; Writer, Poet and Ed.; b. 30 Jan. 1935, Hancock, MI, USA; m. Philip R. Michel, 28 July 1956, three s., one d. *Education:* BA, Stanford University, 1980. *Career:* Delaware State Arts Council and National Endowment for the Arts Residency Artist in Creative Writing, 1974–79, 1984–; Ed., Highland Publishing House, 1996–; mem. Society of Children's Book Writers and Illustrators; National League of Pen Women, state pres., 1996–98. *Publications:* My Name is Jaybird, 1972; No More Someday, 1973; From the Peninsula South, 1980; Thomas, My Brother, 1981; Visions to Keep, 1990. *Honours:* Distinguished Service Award, Lutheran Community Services Board, Wilmington, 1994–95; First State Writers Poetry Award, 1998. *Address:* 3 Lanark Dr., Wilmington, DE 19803, USA. *E-mail:* sandramichel@att.net.

MIDDLEBROOK, Diane Wood, AB, MA, PhD; American academic, writer, poet and biographer; b. 16 April 1939, Pocatello, ID; m. 1st Jonathan Middlebrook 1963 (annulled 1972); one d.; m. 2nd Carl Djerassi 1985. *Education:* Whitman Coll., Walla Walla, WA, Univ. of Washington, Yale Univ. *Career:* Asst Prof., 1966–73, Assoc. Prof., 1974–83, Dir, Center for Research on Women, 1977–79, Assoc. Dean, Undergraduate Studies, 1979–82, Prof. of English, 1983–2002, Chair, Program in Feminist Studies, 1985–88, Howard H. and Jessie T. Watkins University Prof., 1985–90, Stanford University; Visiting Assoc. Prof., Rutgers University, 1973; mem. Chadwyck-Healey LION (Literature Online), editorial board, 1997–; Djerassi Resident Artists Program, trustee, 1980–96, chair, board, 1994; Humanities West, advisory board, 1997–; Investigative Reporters and Eds, 1995–; MLA, 1966–; Biographers' Club, London, 1999–; California Classical Asscn, 1999–; International Asscn of University Profs of English, 1999–; Royal Soc. for the Encouragement of the Arts, Manufacturing & Commerce 2003. *Publications:* Walt Whitman and Wallace Stevens, 1974; Worlds Into Words: Understanding Modern Poems, 1980; Gin Considered as a Demon (poems), 1983; Coming to Light: American Women Poets (ed. with Marilyn Yalom), 1985; Selected Poems of Anne Sexton (ed. with Diana Hume George), 1988; Anne Sexton: A Biography, 1991; Suits Me: The Double Life of Billy Tipton, 1998, Her Husband: Hughes & Plath, a Marriage 2003. Contributions: books, anthologies and journals, including poems, articles and reviews. *Honours:* Woodrow Wilson Fellowship, 1961; Albert S. Cook Memorial Prize for Poetry, 1962, Theron Rockwell Field Prize for Doctoral Dissertation, 1968, Yale University; Acad. of American Poets Prize, 1965; Dean's Award for Distinguished Teaching, 1977, Walter J. Gores Award for Excellence in Teaching, 1987, Stanford University; National Endowment for the Humanities Fellowship, 1982–83; Fellow, Bunting Institute, Radcliffe College, 1982–83, Stanford Humanities Center, 1983–84, Rockefeller Study Center, Bellagio, Italy, 1990; Guggenheim Fellowship, 1988–89; Commonwealth Club of California Gold Medal for Non-Fiction, 1992; Hon. DLitt, Kenyon College, 1999. *Address:* 1101 Green Street, No. 1501, San Francisco, CA 94109, USA.

MIDDLETON, (John) Christopher; academic, poet, writer and translator; b. 10 June 1926, Truro, Cornwall, England; one s. two d. *Education:* BA, Merton College, Oxford, 1951; MA, DPhil, 1954, University of Oxford. *Career:* Lecturer, University of Zürich, 1952–55; Lecturer, 1955–65, Senior

Lecturer, 1965–66, King's College, University of London; Visiting Assoc. Prof., 1961–62, Prof. of Germanic Languages and Literatures, 1966–98, Prof. Emeritus, 1998–, University of Texas at Austin; Judith E. Wilson Lecturer, University of Cambridge, 1992; Poet-in-Residence, W. B. Yeats Poetry Summer School, Sligo, Ireland, 1993; various poetry readings. *Publications:* Poetry: Torse 3: Poems 1949–61, 1962; Nonsequences/ Selfpoems, 1965; Our Flowers and Nice Bones, 1969; The Lonely Suppers of W. V. Balloon, 1975; Carminalenia, 1980; 111 Poems, 1983; Two Horse Wagon Going By, 1986; The Balcony Tree, 1992; Some Dogs, 1993; Intimate Chronicles, 1996; The Swallow Diver, 1997; Twenty Tropes for Doctor Dark, 2000; The World Pavilion and Selected Poems, 2001. Prose: Pataxanadu and Other Prose, 1977; Serpentine, 1985; In the Mirror of the Eighth King, 1999; Crypto-Topographia, 2002. Other: 'Bolshevism in Art' and Other Expository Writings, 1978; The Pursuit of the Kingfisher, 1983; Jackdaw Jiving: Selected Essays on Poetry and Translation, 1998. Translator: Ohne Hass und Fahne (with W. Deppe and H. Schönherr), 1958; Modern German Poetry, 1910–60 (with Michael Hamburger), 1962; German Writing Today, 1967; Selected Poems, by Georg Trakl, 1968; Selected Letters, by Friedrich Nietzsche, 1969; Selected Poems, by Friedrich Hölderlin and Eduard Mörike, 1972; Selected Poems of Goethe, 1983; Selected Stories, by Robert Walser, 1983; Andalusian Poems (with Leticia Garza-Falcón), 1993; Faint Harps and Silver Voices: Selected Translations, 1999. *Honours:* Sir Geoffrey Faber Poetry Prize, 1964; Guggenheim Fellowship, 1974–75; Deutscher Akademischer Austauschdienst Fellowships, 1975, 1978; National Endowment for the Arts Fellowship, 1980; Schlegel-Tieck Trans. Prize, 1985; Max Geilinger-Stiftung Prize in Anglo-Swiss Cultural Relations, 1987; Soeurette Diehl Fraser Award for Trans., Texas Institute of Letters, 1993: Camargo Foundation Fellow, 1999. *Address:* 1112 W 11th Street, No. 201, Austin, TX 78703, USA.

MIDDLETON, Osman Edward; Author; b. 25 March 1925, Christchurch, New Zealand; m. 1949 (divorced); one s. one d. *Education:* Auckland University College, 1946, 1948; University of Paris, 1955–56. *Career:* Robert Burns Fellow, University of Otago, 1970–71; Visiting Lecturer, Universities of Canterbury, 1971, Zürich, Frankfurt, Giessen, Kiel, Erlangen, Regensburg, Turin, Bologna, Pisa, Venice, Rome, 1983; Writer-in-Residence, Michael Karolyi Memorial Foundation, Vence, France, 1983; mem. New Zealand Asscn of the Blind and Partially Blind, committee, 1970–95. *Publications:* 10 Stories, 1953; The Stone and Other Stories, 1959; From the River to the Tide (children's), 1962; A Walk on the Beach, 1964; The Loners, 1972; Selected Stories, 1976; Confessions of an Ocelot, 1979; The Big Room and Other Stories, 1998. Contributions: anthologies worldwide; numerous magazines and journals. *Honours:* Achievement Award, 1959, Scholarship in Letters, 1965, New Zealand Literary Fund; Second New Zealand Katherine Mansfield Award, 1960; Hubert Church Prose Award, 1964; Joint Winner, New Zealand Prose Fiction Award, 1976; Joint Winner, John Cowie Reid Short Story Award, 1989. *Address:* 20 Clifford St, Dalmore, Dunedin, New Zealand.

MIDDLETON, Stanley; Novelist; b. 1 Aug. 1919, Bulwell, Nottingham, England; m. Margaret Shirley Charnley, 22 Dec. 1951, two d. *Education:* University College, Nottingham; BA, University of London; Cert Ed, University of Cambridge; MEd, Nottingham University. *Career:* Head of English, High Pavement College, Nottingham; Judith E. Wilson Visiting Fellow, Emmanuel College, Cambridge; mem. PEN. *Publications:* A Short Answer, 1958; Harris's Requiem, 1960; A Serious Woman, 1961; The Just Exchange, 1962; Two's Company, 1963; Him They Compelled, 1964; The Golden Evening, 1968; Wages of Virtue, 1969; Brazen Prison, 1971; Holiday, 1974; Still Waters, 1976; Two Brothers, 1978; In a Strange Land, 1979; The Other Side, 1980; Blind Understanding, 1982; Entry into Jerusalem, 1983; Daysman, 1984; Valley of Decision, 1985; An After Dinner's Sleep, 1986; After a Fashion, 1987; Recovery, 1988; Vacant Places, 1989; Changes & Chances, 1990; Beginning to End, 1991; A Place to Stand, 1992; Married Past Redemption, 1993; Catalysts, 1994; Toward the Sea, 1995; Live and Learn, 1996; Brief Hours, 1997; Against the Dark, 1997; Necessary Ends, 1999; Small Change, 2000; Love in the Provinces, 2002. Contributions: various. *Honours:* FRSL; Hon. degrees; Co-Recipient, Booker Prize, 1974. *Address:* 42 Caledon Rd, Sherwood, Nottingham NG5 2NG, England.

MIHAILOVICH, Vasa D.; American retd academic, writer and poet; b. 12 Aug. 1926, Prokuplje, Yugoslavia; m. Branka 1957; two s. *Education:* BA, 1956, MA, 1957, Wayne State University; PhD, University of California at Berkeley, 1966. *Career:* Instructor, 1961–63, Asst Prof., 1963–68, Assoc. Prof., 1968–75, Prof. of Slavic Languages and Literatures, 1975–95, University of North Carolina at Chapel Hill; mem. Asscn of Writers of Serbia. *Publications:* Library of Literary Criticism: Modern Slavic Literatures, 2 vols, 1972, 1976; Introduction to Yugoslav Literature, 1973; A Comprehensive Bibliography of Yugoslav Literature in English, 1976; Contemporary Yugoslav Poetry, 1977; Stari i Novi Vilajet, 1977; Bdenja, 1980; Emigranti i Druge Price, 1980; Krugovi na Vodi, 1982; U Tudjem Pristanistu, 1988; Serbian Poetry From the Beginnings to the Present, 1988; Litija Malih Praznika, 1990; Na Brisanom Prostoru, 1994; Bozic u Starom Kraju, 1994; Dictionary of Literary Biography: South Slavic Writers, 2 vols, 1994, 1997; Songs of the Serbian People: From the Collections of Vuk St Karadzic, 1997; Rasejano Slovo/The Scattered Word, 1997; Braca i Druge Price, 1997; Sesta Rukovet, 2002; Elze i Druge Price, 2002. Contributions: Books Abroad/World Literature Today; Saturday Review; Serbian Studies; Slavic and East European Journal; Slavic Review. *Honours:* Serbian PEN Center, 1988; Zlatni Prsten, 1994; Vukova Zaduzbina, 1997; Povelja Rastko Petrovic, 1998; In a Foreign Harbor: Essays in Honour of Vasa D. Mihailovich, 2000. *Address:* 821 Emory Drive, Chapel Hill, NC 27514, USA. *E-mail:* vamih@aol.com.

MIKHAIL, Edward Halim; academic and writer; b. 29 June 1926, Cairo, Egypt. *Education:* BA, 1947, BEd, 1949, University of Cairo; DES, Trinity College, Dublin, 1959; PhD, University of Sheffield, 1966. *Career:* Lecturer to Asst Prof., University of Cairo, 1949–66; Assoc. Prof., 1966–72, Prof. of English Literature, 1972–, University of Lethbridge. *Publications:* The Social and Cultural Setting of the 1890s, 1969; John Galsworthy the Dramatist, 1971; Comedy and Tragedy: A Bibliography of Criticism, 1972; Sean O'Casey: A Bibliography of Criticism, 1972; A Bibliography of Modern Irish Drama 1899–1970, 1972; Dissertations on Anglo-Irish Drama, 1973; The Sting and the Twinkle: Conversations with Sean O'Casey (co-ed.), 1974; J. M. Synge: A Bibliography of Criticism, 1975; Contemporary British Drama 1950–1976: An Annotated Critical Bibliography, 1976; W. B. Yeats: Interviews and Recollections, 1977; J. M. Synge: Interviews and Recollections, 1977; English Drama 1900–1950, 1977; Lady Gregory: Interviews and Recollections, 1977; Oscar Wilde: An Annotated Bibliography of Criticism, 1978; A Research Guide to Modern Irish Dramatists, 1979; Oscar Wilde: Interviews and Recollections, 1979; The Art of Brendan Behan, 1979; Brendan Behan: An Annotated Bibliography of Criticism, 1980; An Annotated Bibliography of Modern Anglo-Irish Drama, 1982; Brendan Behan: Interviews and Recollections, 1982; Lady Gregory: An Annotated Bibliography of Criticism, 1982; Sean O'Casey and His Critics, 1985; The Abbey Theatre, 1987; Sheridan: Interviews and Recollections, 1989; James Joyce: Interviews and Recollections, 1990; The Letters of Brendan Behan, 1991; Goldsmith: Interviews and Recollections, 1993; Dictionary of Appropriate Adjectives, 1994. Contributions: journals. *Address:* No. 115, 100-2 Avenue S, Lethbridge, AB T1J OB5, Canada.

MIKLOWITZ, Gloria, BA; writer; b. 18 May 1927, New York, NY, USA; m. Julius Miklowitz 1948; two s. *Education:* Hunter College, CUNY, University of Michigan, New York University. *Career:* Instructor, Pasadena City College, 1970–80; mem. Society of Children's Book Writers and Illustrators. *Publications:* some 60 books for children 1964–; contrib. to newspapers, journals and magazines. *Honours:* Western Australia Young Book Award, 1984; Bucks Herald for Teens Publishers Award, 1990; Wyoming Soaring Eagle Award, 1993; Sugarman Family Award for Best Book for Children on a Jewish Theme 1999. *Address:* 5255 Vista Miguel Drive, La Canada, CA 91011, USA.

MILES, Jack, (John Russiano Miles); Journalist, Critic and Educational Administrator; b. 30 July 1942, Chicago, IL, USA; m. Jacqueline Russiano, 23 Aug. 1980, one d. *Education:* LittB, Xavier University, Cincinnati, 1964; PhB, Pontifical Gregorian University, Rome, 1966; Hebrew University, Jerusalem, 1966–67; PhD, Harvard University, 1971. *Career:* Asst Prof., Loyola University, Chicago, 1970–74; Asst Dir, Scholars Press, Missoula, Montana, 1974–75; Postdoctoral Fellow, University of Chicago, 1975–76; Ed., Doubleday & Co, New York City, 1976–78; Exec. Ed., University of California Press at Berkeley, 1978–85; Book Ed., 1985–91, Mem., Editorial Board, 1991–95, Los Angeles Times; Dir, Humanities Center, Claremont Graduate School, CA, 1995–; mem. American Acad. of Religion; Amnesty International; National Books Critics Circle, pres., 1990–92; PEN. *Publications:* Retroversion and Text Criticism, 1984; God: A Biography, 1995; Christ: A Crisis in the Life of God, 2001. Contributions: many periodicals. *Honours:* Guggenheim Fellowship, 1990–91; Pulitzer Prize in Biography, 1996. *Address:* Graduate Center, Claremont Graduate School, Claremont, CA 91711, USA.

MILLAR, Sir Ronald (Graeme); Dramatist, Screenwriter and Author; b. 12 Nov. 1919, Reading, England. *Education:* King's College, Cambridge. *Career:* Actor; Screenwriter, Hollywood, 1948–54. *Publications:* Plays: Frieda, 1946; Champagne for Delilah, 1948; Waiting for Gillian, 1954; The Bride and the Bachelor, 1956; The More the Merrier, 1960; The Bride Comes Back, 1960; The Affair (after C. P. Snow), 1961; The New Men (after C. P. Snow), 1962; The Masters (after C. P. Snow), 1963; Number 10, 1967; Abelard and Heloise, 1970; The Case in Question (after C. P. Snow), 1975; A Coat of Varnish (after C. P. Snow), 1982. Musicals: Robert and Elizabeth, 1964; On the Level, 1966. Autobiography: A View from the Wings, 1993. *Honours:* Knighted, 1980. *Address:* 7 Sheffield Terrace, London W8 7NG, England.

MILLER, Alexander (Alex) McPhee, BA, DipEd; author; b. 27 Dec. 1936, London, England; m. 1st Anne Roslyn Neil 1962 (divorced 1983); one s. one d.; m. 2nd Stephanie Ann Pullin 1983. *Education:* Univ. of Melbourne, Hawthorn Inst. *Career:* Visiting Fellow, La Trobe Univ. 1994–; mem. Australian Soc. of Authors, Fellowship of Australian Writers. *Publications:* Watching the Climbers on the Mountain 1988, The Tivington Nott 1989, The Ancestor Game (Miles Franklin Award, Commonwealth Writers Prize 1993) 1992, The Sitters 1995, Conditions of Faith 2000, Journey to the Stone Country (Miles Franklin Award 2003) 2002; plays: Kitty Howard 1978, The Exiles 1981; contrib. to newspapers, journals and periodicals. *Honours:* Braille Book of the Year Award 1990, Barbara Ramsden Award, Fellowship of Australian Writers 1993. *Address:* c/o Hodder & Stoughton, 338 Euston Road, London, NW1 3BH, England.

MILLER, Andrew; Writer; b. 29 April 1960, Bristol, England. *Publications:* Ingenious Pain, 1997; Casanova, 1998; Oxygen, 2001. *Honours:* James Tait Black Memorial Prize for Fiction, 1997; International IMPAC Dublin Literary Award, 1999; Grinzane Cavour Prize, Italy. *Address:* c/o Sheil Land Assocs, 43 Doughty St, London WC1N 2LF, England.

MILLER, Anesa, (Anesa Miller-Pogacar); Writer, Poet, Ed., Trans. and Educator; b. 8 June 1954, Wichita, KS, USA; m. 1st Timothy Pogacar 1980 (divorced 1990); m. 2nd Jack Panksepp 1 May 1991; two d. *Education:* BA, Occidental College, 1976; MA, PhD, University of Kansas, 1992. *Career:* Instructor in Russian Language and Literature, University of Kansas, 1979–83, Bowling Green State University, Ohio, 1986–94; Ed., Memorial Foundation for Lost Children, 1994–. *Publications:* After the Future: Paradoxes of Postmodernism and Contemporary Russian Culture (trans. and ed.), 1995; Re-Entering the Sign: Articulating New Russian Culture (co-ed.), 1995; A Road Beyond Loss: Three Cycles of Poems and an Epilogue, 1995. Contributions: periodicals. *Address:* c/o Memorial Foundation for Lost Children, 708 E Wooster, Bowling Green, OH 43402, USA. *E-mail:* jpankse@bgnet.bgsu.edu.

MILLER, Arthur; Dramatist and Writer; b. 17 Oct. 1915, New York, NY, USA; m. 1st Mary G. Slattery 5 Aug. 1940 (divorced 1956); one s. one d.; m. 2nd Marilyn Monroe June 1956 (divorced 1961); m. 3rd Ingeborg Morath Feb. 1962; one s. one d. *Education:* AB, University of Michigan, 1938. *Career:* Prof. of Contemporary Theatre, University of Oxford, 1995–; mem. American Acad. of Arts and Letters; International PEN, pres., 1965–69. *Publications:* Plays: Honors at Dawn, 1936; No Villain: They Too Arise, 1937; The Man Who Had All the Luck, 1944; That They May Win, 1944; All My Sons, 1947; Death of a Salesman, 1949; The Crucible, 1953; A View from the Bridge, 1955; A Memory of Two Mondays, 1955; After the Fall, 1964; Incident at Vichy, 1964; The Price, 1968; Fame, 1970; The Reason Why, 1970; The Creation of the World and Other Business, 1972; Up From Paradise, 1974; The Archbishop's Ceiling, 1976; The American Clock, 1983; Some Kind of Love Story, 1983; Elegy for a Lady, 1983; Playing for Time, 1986; Danger Memory!, 1986; The Last Yankee, 1990; The Ride Down Mt Morgan, 1991; Broken Glass, 1994; Mr Peters' Connections, 2000; Finishing the Picture, 2003. Screenplays: The Story of G.I. Joe, 1945; The Witches of Salem, 1958; The Misfits, 1961; The Hook, 1975; Everybody Wins, 1990. Other: Situation Normal, 1944; Focus, 1945; Jane's Blanket, 1963; I Don't Need You Anymore, 1967; In Russia, 1969; In the Country, 1977; The Theatre Essays of Arthur Miller, 1978; Chinese Encounters, 1979; Salesman in Beijing, 1987; Timebends: A Life, 1987; The Misfits and Other Stories, 1987; Homely Girl, 1994; Echoes Down the Corridor (essays), 2000; Resurrection Blues, 2003; Finishing the Picture, 2003. *Honours:* New York Drama Critics Circle Awards, 1947, 1949; Tony Awards, 1947, 1949, 1953; Donaldson Awards, 1947, 1949, 1953; Pulitzer Prize in Drama, 1949; Obie Award, 1958; National Institute of Arts and Letters Gold Medal, 1959; Brandeis University Creative Arts Award, 1970; George Foster Peabody Award, 1981; Emmy Awards, 1981, 1985; Literary Lion Award, New York Public Library, 1983; John F. Kennedy Lifetime Achievement Award, 1984; Algur Meadows Award, Southern Methodist University, 1991; National Medal of Arts, 1993; Berlin Prize Fellowship, 1998; PEN/Laura Pels Foundation Award, 1998; Dorothy and Lilian Gish Prize, 1999; Antoinette Perry Lifetime Achievement Award, 1999; Prix Molière, 1999; National Book Awards, Medal for Distinguished Contribution to American Letters, 2001; Premio Príncipe de Asturias, 2002; Jerusalem Prize, 2003. *Address:* Tophet Rd, Roxbury, CT 06783, USA.

MILLER, Edmund; Prof., Poet and Writer; b. 18 July 1943, New York, NY, USA. *Education:* BA, summa cum laude, C. W. Post Campus, Long Island University, 1965; MA, Ohio State University, 1969; PhD, SUNY at Stony Brook, 1975. *Career:* Lecturer, Ohio State University, 1968–69; Instructor, Rockhurst College, 1969–71; Asst Prof., Temple University, 1977–78, Illinois State University, 1979–80; Assoc. Prof., Hofstra University, 1980–81; Asst Prof., 1981–86, Assoc. Prof., 1986–90, Prof., 1990–, Chair., Dept of English, 1993, C. W. Post Campus, Long Island University; mem. Conference on Christianity and Literature; Lewis Carroll Society of North America; Milton Society of America, life mem.; MLA, life mem. *Publications:* Poetry: Fucking Animals: A Book of Poems, 1973; The Nadine Poems, 1973; Winter, 1975; A Rider of Currents, 1986; The Happiness Cure, and Other Poems, 1993; Leavings, 1995. Non-Fiction: Drudgerie Divine: The Rhetoric of God and Man in George Herbert, 1979; Exercises in Style, 1980; Like Season'd Timber: New Essays on George Herbert (ed. with Robert DiYanni), 1987; George Herbert's Kinships: An Ahnentafel with Annotations, 1993. Fiction: Night Times, 2000. Contributions: books and journals. *Address:* c/o Dept of English, C. W. Post Campus, Long Island University, Brookville, NY 11548, USA. *E-mail:* edmund.miller@liw.edu.

MILLER, Hugh; Writer; b. 27 April 1937, Wishaw, Lanarkshire, Scotland. *Education:* University of Glasgow; Stow College; London Polytechnic. *Publications:* A Pocketful of Miracles, 1969; Secrets of Gambling, 1970; Professional Presentations, 1971; The Open City, 1973; Levels, 1973; Drop Out, 1973; Short Circuit, 1973; Koran's Legacy, 1973; Kingpin, 1974; Double Deal, 1974; Feedback, 1974; Ambulance, 1975; The Dissector, 1976; A Soft Breeze from Hell, 1976; The Saviour, 1977; The Rejuvenators, Terminal 3, 1978; Olympic Bronze, 1979; Head of State, 1979; District Nurse, 1984; Honour a Physician, 1985; Eastenders, 1986; Teen Eastenders, 1986; Snow on the Wind, 1987; Silent Witnesses, 1988; The Paradise Club, 1989; An Echo of Justice, 1990; Home Ground, 1990; Skin Deep, 1992; Scotland Yard (co-author), 1993; Unquiet Minds, 1994; Proclaimed in Blood, 1995; Prime Target, 1996; Ballykissangel, 1997; Borrowed Time, 1997; Forensic Fingerprints, 1998; Charlie's Case Notes, 1999; Secrets of the Dead, 2000; Crimewatch Solved, 2001; What the Corpse Revealed, 2002, Mindset 2003. *Address:* c/o Lucas Alexander Whitley Ltd, 14 Vernon St, London W14 0RJ, England.

MILLER, Ian (see Milne, John Frederick).

MILLER, Sir Jonathan (Wolfe); Theatre, Film and Television Dir and Writer; b. 21 July 1934, London, England; m. Helen Rachel Collet, 1956, two s. one d. *Education:* MB, BCh, St John's College, Cambridge, 1959. *Career:* Resident Fellow in the History of Medicine, 1970–73, Fellow, 1981–, University College London; Assoc. Dir, National Theatre, 1973–75; Visiting Prof. in Drama, Westfield College, London, 1977–; Artistic Dir, Old Vic, 1988–90; Research Fellow in Neuropsychology, University of Sussex; mem. Royal Acad., fellow; American Acad. of Arts and Sciences. *Publications:* McLuhan, 1971; Freud: The Man, His World, His Influence (ed.), 1972; The Body in Question, 1978; Subsequent Performances, 1986; The Don Giovanni Book: Myths of Seduction and Betrayal (ed.), 1990; On Reflection, 1998. *Honours:* Silver Medal, RTS, 1981; CBE, 1983; Albert Medal, RSA, 1990; Hon. DLitt, University of Cambridge, 1996; KBE, 2002. *Address:* c/o IMG Artists, 616 Chiswick High Rd, London W4 5RX, England. *E-mail:* jford@imgworld.com. *Website:* www.imgartists.com.

MILLER, Karl (Fergus Connor); Prof. of Modern English Literature (retd), Writer and Ed.; b. 2 Aug. 1931, England; m. Jane Elisabeth Collet; two s. one d. *Education:* Downing College, Cambridge. *Career:* Asst Principal, HM Treasury, 1956–57; Producer, BBC TV, 1957–58; Literary Ed., The Spectator, 1958–61, The New Statesman, 1961–67; Ed., The Listener, 1967–73; Lord Northcliffe Prof. of Modern Literature, Univ. Coll. London, 1974–92; Ed., 1979–89, Co-Ed., 1989–92, London Review of Books; mem. FRSL. *Publications:* Poetry from Cambridge, 1952–54 (ed.), 1955; Writing in England Today: The Last Fifteen Years (ed.), 1968; Memoirs of a Modern Scotland (ed.), 1970; A Listener Anthology, August 1967–June 1970 (ed.), 1970; A Second Listener Anthology (ed.), 1973; Cockburn's Millennium, 1975; Robert Burns (ed.), 1981; Doubles: Studies in Literary History, 1985; Authors, 1989; Rebecca's Vest (autobiog.), 1993; Boswell and Hyde, 1995; Dark Horses, 1998; Electric Shepherd: A Likeness of James Hogg, 2003. *Honours:* James Tait Black Memorial Prize; Scottish Arts Council Book Award. *Address:* 26 Limerston St, London SW10 0HH, England.

MILLER, Leslie Adrienne, BA, MA, MFA, PhD; poet and academic; b. 22 Oct. 1956, Medina, OH, USA. *Education:* Stephens College, University of Missouri, University of Iowa, University of Houston. *Career:* Dir, Creative Writing Program, Stephens College, 1983–87; Visiting Writer, University of Oregon, 1990; Assoc. Prof. of English, University of St Thomas, 1991–; mem. Associated Writing Programs; MLA; Poetry Society of America; Poets and Writers. *Publications:* Hanging on the Sunburned Arm of Some Homeboy (with Matthew Graham), 1982; No River, 1987; Staying Up for Love, 1990 Ungodliness, 1994; Yesterday Had a Man In It, 1998. Contributions: anthologies, reviews, quarterlies, and journals. *Honours:* National Endowment for the Arts Fellowship, 1989; John and Becky Moores Fellowship, University of Houston, 1990; Goethe-Institut Cultural Exchange Fellowship, Berlin, 1992; Loft-McKnight Award in Poetry, 1993, and Award of Distinction, 1998.

MILLER, Marc William; Writer; b. 29 Aug. 1947, Annapolis, MD, USA; m. Darlene File, 24 Sept. 1981, one s. one d. *Education:* BS, Sociology, University of Illinois, 1969. *Career:* Contributing Ed., Fire and Movement Magazine, 1977–84; Staff, Grenadier Magazine, 1977–79, Journal of the Traveller's Aid Society, 1979–85, Challenge Magazine, 1986–92; mem. Acad. of Adventure Gaming Arts and Sciences; Game Designer's Guild; SFWA. *Publications:* Traveller, 1977; Imperium, 1977; 2300 AD, 1986; Mega Traveller, 1988; Mega Traveller II, Quest for the Ancients, 1991; Spellbound, 1992. Contributions: journals. *Honours:* several awards.

MILLER, Sue, BA, MA; writer; b. 29 Nov. 1943, USA; m. 1st (divorced); one s.; m. 2nd Doug Bauer (divorced 2001). *Education:* Radcliffe College, Harvard Univ., Boston Univ., Wesleyan Univ. *Career:* mem. PEN; Chair, PEN New England, 1999–2003. *Publications:* The Good Mother 1986, Inventing the Abbotts and Other Stories 1987, Family Pictures: A Novel 1990, For Love 1993, The Distinguished Guest 1995, While I Was Gone: A Novel 1999, The World Below 2001, The Story of My Father 2003. *Honours:* MacDowell Colony Fellowship; Guggenheim Fellowship. *Literary Agent:* Maxine Groffsky Literary Agency, 2 Fifth Avenue, New York, NY 10011, USA. *Address:* c/o Bloomsbury, 38 Soho Square, London, W1D 3HB, England.

MILLETT, Kate, (Katherine Murray Millett); Feminist, Writer, Sculptor, Painter and Photographer; b. 14 Sept. 1934, St Paul, Minnesota, USA; m. Fumio Yoshimura 1965 (divorced 1985). *Education:* BA, University of Minnesota, 1956; MA, St Hilda's College, Oxford, 1958; PhD, Columbia University, 1970. *Career:* Instructor of English, University of North Carolina, Greensboro, 1958; Teacher of English, Waseda University, Tokyo, 1961–63; Instructor of English and Philosophy, Barnard College, 1964–69; Instructor of Sociology, Bryn Mawr College, 1971; Distinguished Visiting Prof., State College of Sacramento, 1972–73; mem. Congress of Racial

Equality; National Organization of Women. *Publications:* Sexual Politics, 1970; Prostitution Papers, 1971; Flying, 1974; Sita, 1977; The Basement, 1980; Going to Iran, 1981; The Loony-Bin Trip, 1990; The Politics of Cruelty, 1994; A.D., 1996. Contributions: periodicals. *Address:* c/o Georges Borchardt Inc, 136 E 57th St, New York, NY 10022, USA.

MILLHAUSER, Steven; Author; b. 3 Aug. 1943, New York, NY, USA; m. Cathy Allis, 16 June 1986, one s. one d. *Education:* BA, Columbia College, 1965; Brown University, 1968–71. *Publications:* Edwin Mullhouse: The Life and Death of an American Writer, 1972; Portrait of a Romantic, 1976; In the Penny Arcade, 1986; From the Realm of Morpheus, 1986; The Barnum Museum, 1990; Little Kingdoms, 1993; The Knife Thrower and Other Stories, 1998. *Honours:* Prix Médicis Étranger, 1975; Award in Literature, 1987.

MILLHISER, Marlys (Joy); Writer; b. 27 May 1938, Charles City, IA, USA; m. David Millhiser, 25 June 1960, one s. one d. *Education:* BA, University of Iowa, 1960; MA, University of Colorado, 1963. *Career:* mem. Authors' Guild; Colorado Authors League; MWA; Sisters in Crime; Western Writers of America. *Publications:* Michael's Wife, 1972; Nella Waits, 1974; Willing Hostage, 1976; The Mirror, 1978; Nightmare Country, 1981; The Threshold, 1984; Murder at Moot Point, 1992; Death of the Office Witch, 1993; Murder in a Hot Flash, 1995. Contributions: Magazines. *Honours:* Top Hand Awards, 1975, 1985.

MILLINGTON, Barry (John); Music Journalist and Writer; b. 1 Nov. 1951, Essex, England; m. Deborah Jane Calland 1996. *Education:* BA, University of Cambridge, 1974. *Career:* Chief Music Critic, Evening Standard; Artistic Dir, Hampstead and Highgate Festival, 1999–2003; mem. Critics' Circle; Royal Musical Asscn. *Publications:* Wagner, 1984; Selected Letters of Richard Wagner (trans. and ed. with S. Spencer), 1987; The Wagner Compendium: A Guide to Wagner's Life and Music (ed.), 1992; Wagner in Performance (ed. with S. Spencer), 1992; Wagner's Ring of the Nibelung: A Companion (ed. with S. Spencer), 1993. Contributions: The New Grove Dictionary of Opera, 1992; The New Grove Dictionary of Music and Musicians, revised edn, 2001; Newspapers and magazines. *Address:* 50 Denman Dr. S, London NW11 6RH, England. *E-mail:* bmillin397@aol.com.

MILLS, Kyle; Novelist; b. 1966, USA. *Publications:* Rising Phoenix, 1997; Storming Heaven, 1998; Free Fall, 2000; Burn Factor, 2001; Sphere of Influence, 2002; Smoke Screen, 2003. *Address:* c/o Hodder & Stoughton, 338 Euston Rd, London NW1 3BH, England.

MILLS, Magnus; British writer; b. 1954, Birmingham. *Education:* Wolverhampton Polytechnic. *Publications:* novels: The Restraint of Beasts 1998, All Quiet on the Orient Express 1999, Three to See the King 2001, The Scheme for Full Employment 2003; short story collections: Only When the Sun Shines Brightly 1999; contrib. to The Independent, The Verb (BBC Radio 3), Front Row (BBC Radio 4). *Address:* c/o Flamingo, 77–85 Fulham Palace Road, London, W6 8JB, England. *Website:* www.harpercollins.co.uk.

MILLS, Ralph Joseph, Jr; Prof. of English Emeritus, Poet and Writer; b. 16 Dec. 1931, Chicago, IL, USA; m. Helen Daggett Harvey, 25 Nov. 1959, one s. two d. *Education:* BA, Lake Forest College, 1954; MA, 1956, PhD, 1963, Northwestern University; University of Oxford, 1956–57. *Career:* Instructor, 1959–61, Asst Prof., 1962–65, University of Chicago; Assoc. Prof., 1965–67, Prof. of English, 1967–97, Prof. Emeritus, 1997–, University of Illinois at Chicago. *Publications:* Poetry: Door to the Sun, 1974; A Man to His Shadow, 1975; Night Road, 1978; Living with Distance, 1979; With No Answer, 1980; March Light, 1983; For a Day, 1985; Each Branch: Poems 1976–1985, 1986; A While, 1989; A Window in Air, 1993; In Wind's Edge, 1997; Grasses Standing: Selected Poems, 2000. Other: Contemporary American Poetry, 1965; On the Poet and His Craft: Selected Prose of Theodore Roethke (ed.), 1965; Edith Sitwell: A Critical Essay, 1966; Kathleen Raine: A Critical Essay, 1967; Creation's Very Self: On the Personal Element in Recent American Poetry, 1969; Cry of the Human: Essays on Contemporary American Poetry, 1975. Contributions: books and journals. *Honours:* English-Speaking Union Fellowship, 1956–57; Illinois Arts Council Awards for Poetry, 1979, 1983, 1984; Society of Midland Authors Prize for Poetry, 1980; Carl Sandburg Prize for Poetry, 1984; William Carlos Williams Prize, Poetry Society of America, 2002. *Address:* 1451 N Astor St, Chicago, IL 60610, USA.

MILNE, John Frederick, (Ian Miller); Author and Scriptwriter; b. 20 Sept. 1952, Bermondsey, England; m. Sarah Laetitia Beresford Verity, 1983, two s. *Education:* St Joseph's Academy, Blackheath; Chelsea School of Art; BA, Fine Arts, Ravensborne School of Art, 1979. *Career:* mem. Writers' Guild. *Publications:* Tyro, 1981; London Fields, 1982; Wet Wickets and Dusty Balls, 1982; Dead Birds, 1984; Out of the Blue, 1985; Shadow Play, 1986; Daddy's Girl, 1988; Alive and Kicking, 1998. Contributions: Television and periodicals. *Honours:* John Llewelyn Rhys Prize, 1986; Writers' Guild Award, 1991; Edgar, MWA, 1998. *Literary Agent:* The Agency, 24 Pottery Lane, Holland Park, London W11 4LZ, England. *E-mail:* john.milne@orange.net.

MIŁOSZ, Czesław, MJuris; Polish/American poet, novelist, critic, essayist, translator and academic; b. 30 June 1911, Szetejnie, Lithuania. *Education:* University of Wilno. *Career:* Programmer, Polish National Radio, Warsaw, 1934–39; Diplomatic Service, Polish Ministry of Foreign Affairs, 1945–50; Visiting Lecturer, 1960–61, Prof. of Slavic Languages and Literatures, 1961–78, Prof. Emeritus, 1978–, University of California at Berkeley; mem. American Acad. and Institute of Arts and Letters; American Acad. of Arts and Sciences; American Asscn for the Advancement of Slavic Studies; Polish Institute of Letters and Sciences in America. *Publications:* Poetry: Poems, 1940; Poems, 1969; Selected Poems, 1973; Selected Poems, 1976; The Bells in Winter, 1978; The Separate Notebooks, 1984; Collected Poems, 1990; Provinces: Poems 1987–1991, 1991; Facing the River: New Poems, 1995; Roadside Dog, 1998; New and Collected Poems, 1931–2001, 2001. Fiction: The Seizure of Power, 1955; The Issa Valley, 1981. Non-Fiction: The Captive Mind (essays), 1953; Native Realm: A Search for Self-Definition (essays), 1968; The History of Polish Literature, 1969; Emperor of the Earth: Modes of Eccentric Vision, 1977; Nobel Lecture, 1981; Visions From San Francisco Bay, 1982; The Witness of Poetry (lectures), 1983; The Land of Ulro, 1984; The Rising of the Sun, 1985; Unattainable Earth, 1986; Beginning With My Streets: Essays and Recollections, 1992; Striving Towards Being (correspondence), 1997; To Begin Where I Am: Selected Essays, 2001. Editor and Translator: Postwar Polish Poetry: An Anthology, 1965. *Honours:* Prix Littéraire Européen, Les Guildes du Livre, Geneva, 1953; Marian Kister Literary Award, 1967; Guggenheim Fellowship, 1976; Neustadt International Literary Prize, 1978; Nobel Prize for Literature, 1980; National Medal of Arts, 1990; several hon. doctorates. *Address:* c/o Dept of Slavic Languages and Literatures, University of California at Berkeley, Berkeley, CA 94720, USA.

MILTNER, Robert F.; Writer, Poet and Educator; b. 25 Feb. 1949, Cleveland, Ohio, USA; m. 1st Linda Smith 1975 (divorced 1996); m. 2nd Mari Artzner Wolf 12 Oct. 1996 (divorced 2002); one s. one d. *Education:* BA, Xavier University, 1971; MEd, John Carroll University, 1987; PhD, Kent State University, 1998. *Career:* English Teacher, private religious high schools, Denver, CO, 1975–77, including Dept Head, Parma, Ohio, 1977–87; Co-ordinator for Developmental Education, 1987–93, 1993–95, Instructor in English, 1987–95, Dir, Writing Center, 1990–92, 1995–97, Asst Prof. of English, 1998–, Kent State University, Stark Campus, Canton, Ohio; Instructor in English, Walsh University, Canton, 1993–94; mem. Associated Writing Programs; American Asscn of University Profs. *Publications:* The Seamless Serial Hour (poems), 1993; Against the Simple (poems), 1995; On the Off Ramp (poems), 1996; Ghost of a Chance (poems), 2002; Four Crows on a Phone Line (poems), 2002; A Box of Light (prose poems), 2002; Curriculum materials. Contributions: New York Quarterly; English Journal; Chiron Review; Ohioana Quarterly; Mid-American Review; Birmingham Poetry Review. *Honours:* Wick Poetry Chapbook Award, 1994. *E-mail:* rmiltner@stark.kent.edu.

MINARIK, John Paul, BS, BA; poet, writer and engineer; b. 6 Nov. 1947, McKeesport, PA, USA; m. Susan Kay Minarik 1988; one s. *Education:* Carnegie Mellon Univ., Univ. of Pittsburgh. *Career:* engineer, United Steel Corpn 1966–71; Instructor, Community Coll. of Allegheny County 1977–83; teaching consultant, Univ. of Pittsburgh 1978–96; Poet-in-the-Schools, Pennsylvania Council on the Arts 1979–83; project engineer-consultant, Economy Industrial Corpn 1981–82; Chief Engineer, New Directions 1989–96; founder-Ed., Acad. of Prison Arts; Advisory Ed., Greenfield Review Press; poetry readings; mem. American Soc. of Mechanical Engineers. *Publications:* (book) 1974, Patterns in the Dusk 1978, Past the Unknown, Remembered Gate 1981, Kicking Their Heels with Freedom (ed.) 1982; contrib. to over 100 newspapers in the USA, journals including American Ethnic, Backspace, Caprice, Carnegie Mellon Magazine, Confrontation, Gravida, Greenfield Review, Happiness Holding Tank, Hyacinths and Biscuits, Interstate, Joint Conference, Journal of Popular Culture, Mill Hunk Herald, New Orleans Review, Nitty-Gritty, Old Main, Painted Bride Quarterly, Pittsburgh and Tri-State Area Poets, Prison Writing Review, Poetry Society of America Bulletin, Small Pond, Sunday Clothes; poems read on Monitoradio, Voice of America, WQED-FM and WYEP, and at Three Rivers Arts Festival and American Wind Symphony. *Honours:* hon. mention PEN Writing Award 1976–77, Carnegie Magazine Best Book of the Year Citation 1982, poetry and prose writing contest winner, Pennsylvania Dept of Corrections 1985, 1988. *Address:* 1600 Walters Mill Road, Somerset, PA 15510, USA.

MINATOYA, Lydia; Writer; b. 8 Nov. 1950, New York, NY, USA; one s. *Education:* BA, Saint Lawrence University, 1972; MA, George Washington University, 1976; PhD, University of Maryland, 1981. *Publications:* Talking to High Monks in the Snow, 1992; The Strangeness of Beauty, 1999. *Honours:* PEN Jerard Fund Award, 1991; American Library Asscn Notable Book, 1992; New York Public Library Notable Book, 1992; Pacific Northwest Booksellers Award, 1993. *Address:* Harper Collins, 10 E 53rd St, New York, NY 10022-5299, USA.

MINEAR, Richard H(offman); Prof. of History and Writer; b. 31 Dec. 1938, Evanston, IL, USA; m. Edith Christian, 1962, two s. *Education:* BA, Yale University, 1960; MA, 1962, PhD, 1968, Harvard University. *Career:* Asst Prof., Ohio State University, 1967–70; Assoc. Prof., 1970–75, Prof. of History, 1975–, University of Massachusetts; mem. Asscn for Asian Studies. *Publications:* Japanese Tradition and Western Law, 1970; Victors' Justice, 1971; Through Japanese Eyes, 1974; Requiem for Battleship Yamato by Yoshida Mitsuru (ed. and trans.), 1985; Hiroshima: Three Witnesses, 1990; Black Eggs by Kurihara Sadako (ed. and trans.), 1994; When we say 'Hiroshima', 1999; Dr Seuss Goes to War, 1999; Japan's Past, Japan's Future: One Historian's Odyssey by Ienaga Saburo (ed. and trans.),

2000. Contributions: Professional journals and general magazines. *Address:* c/o Dept of History, University of Massachusetts, Amherst, MA 01003, USA.

MINER, Earl (Roy); Prof. and Writer; b. 21 Feb. 1927, Marshfield, Wisconsin, USA; m. Virginia Lane, 15 July 1950, one s. one d. *Education:* BA, 1949, MA, 1951, PhD, 1955, University of Minnesota. *Career:* Prof., Princeton University; mem. American Comparative Literature Asscn; American Society for 18th Century Studies; Asscn for Asian Studies; International Comparative Literature Asscn; Milton Society of America; Renaissance Society of America. *Publications:* The Japanese Tradition in British and American Literature, 1958; Japanese Court Poetry, 1961; Dryden's Poetry, 1967; Comparative Poetics, 1992; Naming Properties, 1996. Contributions: Professional journals. *Honours:* Fulbright Lectureships, 1960–61, 1966–67, 1985; ACLS Fellowship, 1963; Guggenheim Fellowship, 1977–78; Yamagato Banto Prize, 1988; Koizumi Yakumo Prize, 1991; Howard T. Behrman Prize, 1993; Order of the Rising Sun with Gold Rays and Neck Ribbon, Government of Japan, 1994. *Address:* Princeton University, Princeton, NJ 08544, USA.

MINGAY, Gordon Edmund, BA, PhD, FRHistS; academic and writer; b. 20 June 1923, Long Eaton, Derbyshire, England; m. Mavis Tippen 1945. *Education:* University of Nottingham. *Career:* Lecturer, Woolwich Polytechnic, London, 1953–56, LSE, 1957–65; Reader in Economic History, 1965–68, Prof. of Agrarian History, 1968–85, Prof. Emeritus, 1985–, University of Kent, Canterbury; Ed., Agricultural History Review, 1972–84; mem. British Agricultural History Society, pres., 1987–89. *Publications:* English Landed Society in the Eighteenth Century, 1963; The Agricultural Revolution 1750–1880 (with J. D. Chambers), 1966; Land, Labour, and Population in the Industrial Revolution (ed. with E. L. Jones), 1967; Enclosure and the Small Farmer in the Age of the Industrial Revolution, 1968; Britain and America: A Study of Economic Change 1850–1939 (with Philip S. Bagwell), 1970; Fifteen Years On: The B.E.T. Group 1956–1971, 1973; The Gentry, 1975; Arthur Young and His Times, 1975; Georgian London, 1975; Rural Life in Victorian England, 1976; The Agricultural Revolution, 1977; Mrs Hurst Dancing, 1981; The Victorian Countryside (ed.), 1981; An Epic of Progress: A History of British Friesian Cattle, 1982; The Transformation of Britain 1830–1939, 1986; The Agrarian History of England and Wales, Vol. VI, 1750–1850 (ed.), 1989; The Rural Idyll, 1989; The Unquiet Countryside (ed.), 1989; A Social History of the English Countryside, 1990; Land and Society in England 1750–1980, 1994; Parliamentary Enclosure in England 1750–1850, 1997. Contributions: Professional journals. *Address:* Mill Field House, Selling Court, Selling, Faversham, Kent ME13 9RJ, England.

MINOGUE, Valerie Pearson; academic, writer and editor; b. 26 April 1931, Llanelli, South Wales; m. Kenneth Robert Minogue 1954 (divorced 2000); one s. one d. *Education:* BA, 1952, MLitt, 1956, Girton College, Cambridge. *Career:* Asst Lecturer, University College, Cardiff, Wales, 1952–53; Contributor, Cambridge Italian Dictionary, 1956–61; Lecturer, 1963–74, Senior Lecturer, 1975–81, Queen Mary College, London, England; Prof., 1981–88, Research Prof., 1988–96, Prof. Emeritus, 1996–, University of Wales Swansea; Founding Ed., 1982–98, General Ed., 1998–2003, Romance Studies; mem. MHRA; Society for French Studies; Romance Studies Institute; Émile Zola Society; Asscn internationale des études françaises; Amis de Cerisy-Pontigny; Société Marguerite Duras du Royaume Uni. *Publications:* Proust: Du Côté de chez Swann, 1973; Nathalie Sarraute: The War of the Words, 1981; Zola: L'Assommoir, 1991; Eight texts, Pléiade Oeuvres complètes of Nathalie Sarraute (ed., with notes and critical essays), 1996. Contributions: Quadrant; Literary Review; Modern Language Review; French Studies; Romance Studies; Forum for Modern Language Studies; New Novel Review; Revue des Sciences Humaines; TLS; Esprit Créateur; Theatre Research International; Critique; numerous chapters in books. *Honours:* Mary Elizabeth Ponsonby Prize for French Literature. *Address:* 23 Richford Street, London W6 7HJ, England. *E-mail:* v_minogue@ukonline.co.uk.

MINOT, Susan Anderson; Writer; b. 7 Dec. 1956, Boston, Massachusetts, USA; m. Davis McHenry, 30 April 1988, divorced. *Education:* BA, Brown University, 1978; MFA, Columbia University, 1983. *Publications:* Monkeys, 1986; Lost & Other Stories, 1989; Folly, 1992; Evening, 1998; Rapture, 2002. Contributions: New Yorker; Grand Street; Paris Review; Mademoiselle; Harper's; GQ; New England Monthly; Conde Nasts Traveler; Esquire; New York Times Magazine; Atlantic Monthly. *Honours:* Prix Fémina Étranger, 1987.

MINTER, David (Lee); Prof. of English and Writer; b. 20 March 1935, Midland, Texas, USA. *Education:* BA, 1957, MA, 1959, North Texas State University; BD, 1961, PhD, 1965, Yale University. *Career:* Lecturer, University of Hamburg, 1965–66, Yale University, 1966–67; Asst Prof., 1967–69, Assoc. Prof. 1969–74, Prof., 1974–80, 1991–, Rice University; Prof., Dean of Emory College, Vice-Pres. for Arts and Sciences, Emory University, 1981–90. *Publications:* The Interpreted Design as a Structural Principle in American Prose, 1969; William Faulkner: His Life and Work, 1980; The Harper American Literature, 1986; The Norton Critical Edn of The Sound and the Fury, 1987; A Cultural History of the American Novel: Henry James to William Faulkner, 1994; Faulkner's Questioning Narratives: Fiction of His Major Phase 1929–1942, 2001. Contributions: Professional journals. *Address:* 6100 Main St, Houston, TX 77005, USA.

MIRABELLI, Eugene; writer and academic; b. 3 Feb. 1931, Arlington, Massachusetts, USA; m. Margaret Anne Black 1959; one s. two d. *Education:* BA, 1952, PhD, 1964, Harvard University; MA, Johns Hopkins University, 1955. *Career:* Faculty, Williams College, 1960–64, SUNY at Albany, 1965–95; mem. Authors' Guild; PEN American Center; Board Mem., Officer, Non-Profit Alternative Literary Programs (ALPS). *Publications:* The Burning Air, 1959; The Way In, 1968; No Resting Place, 1972; The World at Noon, 1994; The Language Nobody Speaks, 1999. Contributions: numerous fiction and non-fiction book reviews in various publications. *Honours:* Rockefeller Foundation Grant, 1969. *Address:* 29 Bennett Terrace, Delmar, NY 12054, USA.

MIRI, Yu; Essayist and Author; b. 22 June 1968, Yokohama, Japan; one s. *Publications:* Family Cinema; Fish Swimming in Stone; Life; Soul; Happiness; Voice; Death; Rouge; Gold Rush; Fullhouse; Specimen of Family; Encyclopedia of My Private Talk (short stories). *Honours:* Kishida Kunio Drama Prize; Akutagawa Prize, 1997; Izumi Kyoka Prize; Noma Bungei Newcomer Literature Prize.

MISTRY, Rohinton, BA; Canadian author; b. 3 July 1952, Bombay (now Mumbai), India; m. Freny Elavia 1975. *Education:* St Xavier's High School, Bombay, Univ. of Bombay, Univ. of Toronto, Canada. *Career:* took lessons in music theory and composition; mem. folk-singing band; moved to Canada 1975; clerk and accountant Canadian Imperial Bank of Commerce, Toronto 1975–85; began writing short stories 1982; novels have been translated into German, Swedish, Norwegian, Danish and Japanese. *Publications include:* Coming Attraction (short stories) 1986, Tales from Firozsha Baag 1987, Swimming Lessons and Other Stories from Firozsha Baag (short stories) 1989, Such a Long Journey (novel) 1991, A Fine Balance (novel) 1995, Family Matters (novel) 2002. *Honours:* Hon. PhD (Ottawa) 1996; Hart House Literary Prizes (two) 1985, Contributor's Prize, Canadian Fiction Magazine 1985, Gov.-Gen.'s Award 1991, Commonwealth Writers' Prize for Best Book 1991, First Novel Award, W.H. Smith/Books in Canada 1991, Giller Prize 1995, Winifred Holtby Prize, RSL 1995, Los Angeles Times Award for Fiction 1996. *Literary Agent:* Bruce Westwood, Westwood Creative Artists Ltd, 94 Harbord Street, Toronto, Ont. M5S 1G6, Canada.

MITCHARD, Jacquelyn; Writer; b. 10 Dec. 1953, Chicago, IL, USA; m. Dan Allegretti, 1981, deceased 1993, five c. *Education:* BA, English Literature, Rockford College, 1973. *Career:* Reporter, Man. Ed., Pioneer Press, Chicago, 1976–79; Metro Reporter, Columnist, Milwaukee Journal, 1984–88; Syndicated columnist. *Publications:* Mother Less Child: The Love Story of a Family, 1985; Jane Addams: Pioneer in Social Reform and Activist for World Peace, 1991; Jane Addams: Peace Activist (co-author), 1992; The Deep End of the Ocean (fiction), 1996; A Theory of Relitivity (fiction), 2001. Other: Screenplays. *Honours:* Maggie Awards for Public Service Magazine Journalism, 1993, 1994; Parenting Network Public Awareness Award, 1997; Milwaukee Press Club Headliner Award, 1997; Anne Powers Award for Fiction, Council of Wisconsin Writers, 1997.

MITCHELL, Adrian, (Volcano Jones, Apeman Mudgeon, Gerald Stimpson); Poet, Writer, Dramatist and Lyricist; b. 24 Oct. 1932, London, England; two s. three d. *Education:* Christ Church, Oxford, 1953–55. *Career:* Granada Fellow, University of Lancaster, 1968–70; Fellow, Wesleyan University, 1972; Resident Writer, Sherman Theatre, 1974–75, Unicorn Theatre for Children, 1982–83; Judith Wilson Fellow, University of Cambridge, 1980–81; Fellow in Drama, Nanyang University, Singapore, 1995; Dylan Thomas Fellow, UK Festival of Literature, Swansea, 1995; mem. RSL; Society of Authors; Writers Guild. *Publications:* Plays with Songs, 1995; The Siege, 1996; The Lion, the Witch and the Wardrobe, 1998; Who Killed Dylan Thomas, 1998. Contributions: newspapers, magazines, and television. *Honours:* Eric Gregory Award; PEN Trans. Prize; Tokyo Festival Television Film Award; Hon. Doctorate, North London University, 1997. *Literary Agent:* PFD, Drury House, 34–43 Russell St, London WC2B 5HA, England.

MITCHELL, David; British writer; b. Jan. 1969, Lancashire, England; m. Keiko Mitchell; one d. *Education:* Univ. of Kent. *Career:* taught English in Japan early 1990s–2003. *Publications:* Ghostwritten 1999, number9dream 2001, Cloud Atlas 2004. *Honours:* Betty Trask Award 1999, Mail on Sunday/John Llewellyn Rhys Prize 1999. *Address:* c/o Sceptre, Hodder Headline Ltd, 338 Euston Road, London, NW1 3BH, England.

MITCHELL, David John; Writer; b. 24 Jan. 1924, London, England; m. 1955, one s. *Education:* Bradfield College, Berkshire; MA, Modern History, Trinity College, Oxford, 1947. *Career:* Staff Writer, Picture Post, 1947–52; mem. Society of Authors. *Publications:* Women on the Warpath, 1966; The Fighting Pankhursts, 1967; 1919 Red Mirage, 1970; Pirates, 1976; Queen Christabel, 1977; The Jesuits: A History, 1980; The Spanish Civil War, 1982; Travellers in Spain, 1990. Contributions: newspapers and magazines. *Address:* 20 Mountacre Close, Sydenham Hill, London SE26 6SX, England.

MITCHELL, Jerome; academic and writer; b. 7 Oct. 1935, Chattanooga, Tennessee, USA. *Education:* BA, Emory University, 1957; MA, 1959, PhD, 1965, Duke University. *Career:* Asst Prof., University of Illinois, 1965–67; Assoc. Prof., 1967–72, Prof., 1972–97, University of Georgia; Fulbright

Guest Prof., University of Bonn, 1972–73; Visiting Exchange Prof., University of Erlangen, 1975; Richard Merton Guest Prof., University of Regensburg, 1978–79. *Publications:* Thomas Hoccleve: A Study in Early 15th Century English Poetic, 1968; Hoccleve's Works: The Minor Poems, 1970; Chaucer: The Love Poet, 1973; The Walter Scott Operas, 1977; Scott, Chaucer and Medieval Romance, 1987; Old and Middle English Literature, 1994; More Scott Operas, 1996. Contributions: various scholarly journals. *Address:* PO Box 1268, Athens, GA 30603, USA.

MITCHELL, Julian; Author and Dramatist; b. 1 May 1935, Epping, Essex, England. *Education:* BA, Wadham College, Oxford, 1958. *Publications:* Imaginary Toys, 1961; A Disturbing Influence, 1962; As Far as You Can Go, 1963; The White Father, 1964; A Heritage and Its History (play), 1965; A Family and a Fortune (play), 1966; A Circle of Friends, 1966; The Undiscovered Country, 1968; Jennie Lady Randolph Churchill: A Portrait with Letters (with Peregrine Churchill), 1974; Half-Life (play), 1977; Another Country (play), 1982, (film), 1984; Francis (play), 1983; After Aida (play), 1985; Falling Over England (play), 1994; August (adaptation of Uncle Vanya) (play), 1994, (film), 1995; Wilde (film script), 1997. Contributions: Welsh History Review; Monmouthshire Antiquary; Modern Painters. *Address:* 47 Draycott Pl., London SW3 3DB, England.

MITCHELL, Kenneth (Ronald); Prof., Writer and Dramatist; b. 13 Dec. 1940, Moose Jaw, Saskatchewan, Canada; m. Jeanne Shami, 23 Aug. 1983, four s., one d. *Education:* BA, 1965, MA, 1967, University of Saskatchewan. *Career:* Instructor, 1967–70, Prof., 1984–, University of Regina; Visiting Prof., University of Beijing, 1980–81, Foreign Affairs College, Beijing, 1986–87; mem. Canadian Asscn of University Teachers; Playwrights Union of Canada. *Publications:* Wandering Rafferty, 1972; The Meadowlark Connection, 1975; Everybody Gets Something Here, 1977; Cruel Tears (co-author), 1977; Horizon: Writings of the Canadian Prairie (ed.), 1977; The Con Man, 1979; Davin, 1979; Sinclair Ross, 1981; Ken Mitchell Country, 1984; Gone the Burning Sun, 1985; Through the Nan Da Gate, 1986; Witches and Idiots, 1990; The Plainsman, 1992; Stones of the Dalai Lama, 1993. *Honours:* Ottawa Little Theatre Prize, 1971; Canadian Authors Asscn Award for Best Canadian Play, 1985; Order of Canada, 1999. *Address:* c/o Dept of English, University of Regina, Regina, SK S4S 0A2, Canada.

MITCHELL, Roger (Sherman); Poet and Teacher; b. 8 Feb. 1935, Boston, Massachusetts, USA; two d. *Education:* AB, Harvard College, 1957; MA, University of Colorado, 1961; PhD, Manchester University, 1963. *Career:* Ed., Minnesota Review, 1973–81; Dir, Writers Conferences, 1975–85, Creative Writing Program, 1978–96, Indiana University; mem. Associated Writing Programs. *Publications:* Letters from Siberia, 1971; Moving, 1976; A Clear Space on a Cold Day, 1986; Adirondack, 1988; Clear Pond, 1991; The Word for Everything, 1996; Braid, 1997; Savage Baggage, 2001. Contributions: periodicals. *Honours:* Abby M. Copps Award, 1971; Midland Poetry Award, 1972; Borestone Mountain Award, 1973; PEN Award, 1977; Arvon Foundation Awards, 1985, 1987; National Endowment for the Arts Fellowships, 1986, 2001; Chester H. Jones Award, 1987. *Address:* 1010 E First St, Bloomington, IN 47401, USA.

MITCHELL, Susanna Ryland; Writer; b. 8 April 1941, Newry, Northern Ireland; m. Charles Donald Mitchell, 1965, two d. *Education:* Graduate, University of Cambridge. *Publications:* The Token, 1984; The Christening, 1986; The Colour of His Hair, 1994. *Literary Agent:* Curtis Brown Ltd, Haymarket House, 28–29 Haymarket, London, SW1Y 4SP, England. *Telephone:* (20) 7393-4400. *Fax:* (20) 7393-4401. *E-mail:* info@curtisbrown.co.uk. *Website:* www.curtisbrown.co.uk. *Address:* 63 Cloudesley Road, London N1 0EL, England.

MITCHELL, William John Thomas; Prof., Ed. and Writer; b. 24 March 1942, Anaheim, CA, USA; m. Janice Misurell, 11 Aug. 1968, one s. one d. *Education:* BA, Michigan State University, 1963; MA, PhD, 1968, Johns Hopkins University. *Career:* Ed., Critical Inquiry, 1979–; Prof. of English and Art History, Chair, Dept of English, 1989–92, University of Chicago; Fairchild Distinguished Scholar, Cal Tech, 1994; Berg Prof., New York University, 1998, 2000; Maclean Visiting Prof., Colorado College, 2001; Hawke Prof., University of South Australia, 2001; mem. Acad. of Literary Studies; MLA; PEN. *Publications:* Blake's Composite Art, 1977; The Language of Images, 1980; The Politics of Interpretation, 1983; Against Theory, 1983; Iconology, 1986; Art and the Public Sphere, 1993; Landscape and Power, 1993; Picture Theory, 1994; The Last Dinosaur Book: The Life and Times of a Cultural Icon, 1998. Contributions: Professional journals and general periodicals. *Honours:* American Philosophical Society Essay Prize, 1968; National Endowment for the Humanities Fellowships, 1978, 1986; Guggenheim Fellowship, 1983; Gaylord Donnelley Distinguished Service Professorship, 1989; College Art Asscn's Charles Rufus Morey Prize for Distinguished Book in Art History, 1996; Laing Prize for Picture Theory, University of Chicago Press, 1997; Berlin Prize Fellow, American Acad. in Berlin, 2002. *Address:* c/o Dept of English and Art History, University of Chicago, 1050 E 59th St, Chicago, IL 60637, USA.

MITSON, Eileen Nora; Author; b. 22 Sept. 1930, Langley, Essex, England; m. Arthur Samuel Mitson 22 Sept. 1951; two d. (one deceased). *Education:* Cambridge Technical College and School of Art, 1946–47. *Career:* Columnist, Christian Woman magazine, later Woman Alive Magazine, 1982–94. *Publications:* Beyond the Shadows, 1968; Amazon Adventure, 1969; The Inside Room, 1973; A Kind of Freedom, 1976; Reaching for God, 1978; Creativity (co-author), 1985. *Address:* 39 Oaklands, Hamilton Rd, Reading, Berkshire RG1 5RN, England.

MITTMAN, Stephanie; Writer and Artist; b. 15 April 1950, New York, NY, USA; m. Alan Mittman, 30 Aug. 1969, one s. one d. *Education:* BA, Ithaca College, 1971. *Career:* mem. Authors' Guild; Novelists Inc; Romance Writers of America. *Publications:* Bridge to Yesterday, 1995; A Taste of Honey, 1995; The Marriage Bed, 1996; Sweeter than Wine, 1997; The Courtship, 1997; A Kiss to Dream On, 1998; Head Over Heels, 1999; A Heart Full of Miracles, 2000. Contributions: anthologies. *Honours:* Best Sweet Historical Award, American Online Romance Reader Awards, 1995; Reviewer's Choice Certificate of Excellence, Romantic Times, 1996; Best Americana Historical Romance Award, Romantic Times, 1997; Career Achievement Award, Romantic Times, 1997. *Literary Agent:* Irene Goodman Literary Agency, 521 Fifth Ave, New York, NY 10175, USA. *Address:* c/o MLGW, 190 Willis Ave, Mineola, NY 11501, USA. *E-mail:* smittman@tweny.rr.com.

MIZUMURA, Minae; Japanese novelist; b. 1951, Tokyo; m. *Education:* Yale Coll., Yale Univ. *Career:* teacher at Princeton Univ., Univ. of Michigan, Stanford Univ.; mem. Int. Writing Program at Univ. of Iowa 2003. *Publications:* Zoku Meian (trans. Light and Darkness Continued) 1990, Shishosetsu from Left to Right (trans. An I-Novel from Left to Right) 1995, Tegami - Shiori wo Suete 1998, Honkaku Shosetsu (trans. An Orthodox Novel) 2002. *Honours:* Japan Foundation Fellowship 1983 ; Geijutsu Sensho Award 1991, Noma Award 1995, Yomiuri Literary Award 2002. *Address:* International Writing Program, University of Iowa, 100 Shambaugh House, 430 N Clinton Street, Iowa City, IA 52242, USA. *Telephone:* (319) 335-0128. *E-mail:* iwp@uiowa.edu. *Website:* wwwuiowa.edu/~iwp.

MLECHIN, Leonid M.; Russian journalist and writer; b. 12 June 1957; m.; one s. *Education:* Moscow State Univ. *Career:* staff, head of division, Deputy Ed.-in-Chief weekly Novoye Vremya 1979–93; Deputy Ed.-in-Chief newspaper Izvestia 1993–96; political reviewer All-Russian State Cttee on Radio and Television 1996–97; writer and narrator Particular Dossier (TV-Tsentr) 1997–. *Publications include:* more than 20 books, including detective stories, novels, historical non-fiction, and biographies of Yevgeny Primakov and the chairmen of the KGB. *Address:* TV-Tsentr, ul. B. Tatarskaya 33/1, Moscow 113184, Russia (Office). *Telephone:* (095) 215-18-12 (Office); (095) 217-75-50 (Office).

MNATSAKANOVA, Elizaveta Arkad'evna; Russian poet and teacher; b. 1922, Baku, Azerbaijan. *Education:* Moscow Conservatory, Moscow State Univ. *Career:* teacher of literature, Universität Wien, Austria. *Publications include:* Shagi i vzdokhi: Chetyre knigi stikhov 1982, Perm': Izdatel'stvo Permskogo gosudarstvennogo universiteta 1994, Velikoe tikhoe more (The Great Quiet Sea: 10 poems in memory of Anne N. Segodnia) 1996, Vita breve. *Honours:* Oden Literary Prize. *Address:* c/o Universität Wien, Dr Karl Lueger-ring 1, 1010 Vienna, Austria.

MO, Timothy (Peter); Writer; b. 30 Dec. 1950, Hong Kong. *Education:* Convent of the Precious Blood, Hong Kong; Mill Hill School, London; BA, St John's College, Oxford. *Publications:* The Monkey King, 1978; Sour Sweet, 1982; An Insular Possession, 1986; The Redundancy of Courage, 1991; Brownout on Breadfruit Boulevard, 1995; Renegade or Halo2, 1999. Contributions: periodicals. *Honours:* Gibbs Prize, 1971; Geoffrey Faber Memorial Prize, 1979; Hawthornden Prize, 1983; E. M. Forster Award, American Acad. of Arts and Letters, 1992; James Tait Black Memorial Prize, 1999. *Address:* c/o Paddleless Press, BCM Paddleless, London WC1N 3XX, England.

MO YAN; Chinese novelist; b. (Guan Moyan), 1955, Gaomi, Shandong Prov. *Education:* PLA Acad. of Arts, Beijing Normal Univ. *Career:* joined PLA 1976. *Publications:* Red Sorghum Family, The Song of Heaven's Garlic Shoots, Thirteen Steps, The Herbivora Family, Jiuguo.

MOAT, John; Author and Poet; b. 11 Sept. 1936, India; m. 1962, one s. one d. *Education:* MA, University of Oxford, 1960. *Publications:* 6d per Annum, 1966; Heorot (novel), 1968; A Standard of Verse, 1969; Thunder of Grass, 1970; The Tugen and the Toot (novel), 1973; The Ballad of the Leat, 1974; Bartonwood (children's), 1978; Fiesta and the Fox Reviews and His Prophecy, 1979; The Way to Write (with John Fairfax), 1981; Skeleton Key, 1982; Mai's Wedding (novel), 1983; Welcombe Overtunes, 1987; The Missing Moon, 1988; Firewater and the Miraculous Mandarin, 1990; Practice, 1994; The Valley (poems and drawings), 1998; 100 Poems, 1998; Rain (short stories), 2000. *Address:* Crenham Mill, Hartland, North Devon EX39 6HN, England.

MODIANO, Patrick (Jean); Author; b. 30 July 1945, Boulogne-Billancourt, France; m. Dominique Zehrfuss, 1970, two d. *Publications:* La Place de l'Etoile, 1968; La Ronde de nuit, 1969; Les Boulevards de ceinture, 1972; Lacombe Lucien (screenplay), 1974; Villa triste, 1975; Livret de famille, 1977; Rue des boutiques obscures, 1978; Une jeunesse, 1981; De si braves garcons, 1982; Quartier perdu, 1984; Voyage de Noces, 1990; Chien de Printemps, 1993; Du plus loin de l'oubli, 1996; Dora Bruder, 1997; Des inconnues, 1999; La Petite Bijou, 2001. *Honours:* Prix Roger Nimier, 1968; Prix Goncourt, 1978; Chevalier, Ordre des Arts et des Lettres. *Address:* c/o Editions Gallimard, 5 rue Sebatien Bottin, 75007 Paris, France.

MOFFAT, Gwen; Author; b. 3 July 1924, Brighton, Sussex, England; m. Gordon Moffat, 1948, one d. *Career:* mem. CWA; Society of Authors. *Publications:* Space Below My Feet, 1961; Two Star Red, 1964; On My Home Ground, 1968; Survival Count, 1972; Lady With a Cool Eye, 1973; Deviant Death, 1973; The Corpse Road, 1974; Hard Option, 1975; Miss Pink at the Edge of the World, 1975; Over the Sea to Death, 1976; A Short Time to Live, 1976; Persons Unknown, 1978; Hard Road West, 1981; The Buckskin Girl, 1982; Die Like a Dog, 1982; Last Chance Country, 1983; Grizzly Tail, 1984; Snare, 1987; The Stone Hawk, 1989; The Storm Seekers, 1989; Rage, 1990; The Raptor Zone, 1990; Pit Bull, 1991; Veronica's Sisters, 1992; The Outside Edge, 1993; Cue the Battered Wife, 1994; The Lost Girls, 1998; A Wreath of Dead Moths, 1998; Running Dogs, 1999; Private Sins, 1999; Quicksand, 2001; Retribution, 2002; Man Trap, 2003. Contributions: newspapers and magazines. *Address:* c/o Juliet Burton, 2 Clifton Ave, London W12 9DR, England. *Telephone:* (20) 8762-0148. *Fax:* (20) 8743-8765. *E-mail:* juliet .burton@virgin.net. *Website:* www.twbooks.co.uk/authors/gmoffat.html.

MOFFEIT, Tony A.; Librarian and Poet; b. 14 March 1942, Claremont, Oklahoma, USA. *Education:* BSc, Psychology, Oklahoma State University, 1964; MLS, University of Oklahoma, 1965. *Career:* Asst Dir, Library, 1980–, Poet-in-Residence, 1986–95, University of Southern Colorado; Dir, Pueblo Poetry Project, 1980–; mem. American Library Asscn. *Publications:* La Nortenita, 1983; Outlaw Blues, 1983; Shooting Chant, 1984; Coyote Blues, 1985; Hank Williams Blues, 1985; The Spider Who Walked Underground, 1985; Black Cat Bone, 1986; Dancing With the Ghosts of the Dead, 1986; Pueblo Blues, 1986; Boogie Alley, 1989; Luminous Animal, 1989; Poetry is Dangerous, the Poet is an Outlaw, 1995. Contributions: journals and magazines. *Honours:* Jack Kerouac Award, 1986; National Endowment for the Arts Fellowship, 1992. *Address:* 1501 E Seventh, Pueblo, CO 81001, USA.

MOFFETT, Judith; Poet, Writer and Teacher; b. 30 Aug. 1942, Louisville, KY, USA; m. Edward B. Irving, 1983. *Education:* BA, Hanover College, IN, 1964; MA, Colorado State University, 1966; University of Wisconsin at Madison, 1966–67; MA, 1970, PhD, 1971, University of Pennsylvania. *Career:* Fulbright Lecturer, University of Lund, Sweden, 1967–68; Asst Prof., Behrend College, Pennsylvania State University, 1971–75; Visiting Lecturer, University of Iowa, 1977–78; Visiting Lecturer, 1978–79, Asst Prof., 1979–86, Adjunct Asst Prof., 1986–88, Adjunct Assoc. Prof., 1988–93, Adjunct Prof. of English, 1993–94, University of Pennsylvania. *Publications:* Poetry: Keeping Time, 1976; Whinny Moor Crossing, 1984. Fiction: Pennterra, 1987; The Ragged World, 1991; Time, Like an Ever-Rolling Stream, 1992; Two That Came True, 1992. Other: James Merrill: An Introduction to the Poetry, 1984; Homestead Year: Back to the Land in Suburbia, 1995. *Honours:* Fulbright Grants, 1967, 1973; American Philosophical Society Grant, 1973; Eunice Tiejens Memorial Prize, 1973; Borestone Mountain Poetry Prize, 1976; Levinson Prize, 1976; Ingram Merrill Foundation Grants, 1977, 1980, 1989; Columbia University Trans. Prize, 1978; Bread Loaf Writers Conference Tennessee Williams Fellowship, 1978; Swedish Acad. Trans. Prize, 1982; National Endowment for the Humanities Trans. Fellowship, 1983; National Endowment for the Arts Fellowship, 1984; Swedish Acad. Trans. Grant, 1993.

MOGGACH, Deborah, BA, DipEd, FRSL; British writer; b. 28 June 1948, London; m. Anthony Moggach 1971 (divorced); one s. one d. *Education:* Camden School for Girls, Univ. of Bristol, Univ. of London. *Career:* Chair. Soc. of Authors 1999–2001; mem. PEN. *Television:* (dramas) To Have and To Hold 1986, Stolen 1990, Goggle-Eyes (adaptation) 1993 (Writers' Guild Award for Best Adapted TV Serial), Seesaw 1998, Close Relations 1998, Love in a Cold Climate (adaptation) 2001, Final Demand 2003. *Play:* Double Take. *Publications:* novels: You Must Be Sisters 1978, Close to Home 1979, A Quiet Drink 1980, Hot Water Man 1982, Porky 1983, To Have and To Hold 1986, Driving in the Dark 1988, Stolen 1990, The Stand-in 1991, The Ex-Wives 1993, Seesaw 1996, Close Relations 1997, Tulip Fever 1999, Final Demand 2001, These Foolish Things 2004; short stories: Smile 1987, Changing Babies 1995. *Literary Agent:* Curtis Brown, 28–29 Haymarket, London, SW1Y 4SP, England. *Telephone:* (20) 7396-6600. *Fax:* (20) 7396-0110.

MOHRT, Michel; Writer and Ed.; b. 28 April 1914, Morlaix, France; m. Françoise Jarrier, 1955, one s. *Education:* Law School, Rennes. *Career:* Lawyer, Marseilles Bar until 1942; Prof., Yale University, 1947–52; Ed., Head of English Trans, Les Editions Gallimard, 1952–; mem. Académie Française, 1985; Garrick Club. *Publications:* Fiction: Le repit: Mon royaume pour un cheval, 1949; La prison martitime, 1961; La campagne d'Italie, 1965; L'ours des Adirondacks, 1969; Deux Americaines à Paris, 1974; Les moyens du bord, 1975; La guerre civile, 1986; Le Telesieje, 1989; Un soir a Londres, 1991; Jessica, 2002. Essays: Montherlant, homme libre, 1943; Le nouveau Roman American, 1956; L'air du large, 1969; La maison du père, 1979; Vers l'Ouest, 1988; Benjamin ou Lettes sur l'Inconstance, 1989. Plays: Une jeu d'enfer, 1970; On Liquide et on s'en va Sotie, 1992; Tombeau de la Rouërie, 2000. *Honours:* Officier, Légion d'honneur; Croix de guerre; Grand Prix du roman de l'Académie Française, 1962; Grand Prix de la Critique Littéraire, 1970; Grand prix du Littérature de l'Académie Française, 1983. *Address:* Editions Gallimard, 5 rue Sebastien-Bottin, Paris 75007, France.

MOJTABAI, Ann Grace; Author and Educator; b. 8 June 1937, Brooklyn, NY, USA; m. Fathollah Motabai, 27 April 1960, divorced 1966, one s. one d. *Education:* BA, Philosophy, Antioch College, 1958; MA, Philosophy, 1968, MS, Library Science, 1970, Columbia University. *Career:* Lecturer in Philosophy, Hunter College, CUNY, 1966–68; Briggs-Copeland Lecturer on English, Harvard University, 1978–83; Writer-in-Residence, University of Tulsa, 1983–; mem. Mark Twain Society; PEN; Texas Institute of Letters. *Publications:* Mundome, 1974; The 400 Eels of Sigmund Freud, 1976; A Stopping Place, 1979; Autumn, 1982; Blessed Assurance, 1986; Ordinary Time, 1989; Called Out, 1994; Soon, 1998. Contributions: New York Times Book Review; New Republic; Philosophy Today; Philosophical Journal. *Honours:* Radcliffe Institute Fellow, 1976–78; Guggenheim Fellowship, 1981–82; Richard and Hinda Rosenthal Award, American Acad. and Institute of Arts and Letters, 1983; Lillian Smith Award, Southern Regional Council, 1986; Award in Literature, American Acad. of Arts and Letters, 1993. *Address:* 2329 Woodside, Amarillo, TX 79124-1036, USA. *E-mail:* agmojtabai@aol.com.

MOKYR, Joel; Prof. and Writer; b. 26 July 1946, Leyden, the Netherlands; m. Margalit B. Mokyr, 29 Sept. 1969, two d. *Education:* BA, Hebrew University, 1968; PhD, Yale University, 1974. *Career:* mem. Fellow, American Acad. of Arts and Sciences, 1996; Economic History Asscn, pres., 2003–04. *Publications:* Industrialization in the Low Countries, 1976; Why Ireland Starved, 1983; The Lever of Riches, 1990; The British Industrial Revolution, 1993; The Gifts of Athena, 2002. *Address:* Dept of Economics, Northwestern University, Evanston, IL 60208, USA.

MOLE, John Douglas; Poet and Critic; b. 12 Oct. 1941, Taunton, Somerset, England; m. Mary Norman, 22 Aug. 1968, two s. *Education:* MA, Magdalene College, Cambridge, 1964. *Career:* Teacher, Haberdashers' School, Elstree, 1964–73; Exchange Teacher, Riverdale School, New York, 1969–70; Head, Dept of English, Verulam School, 1973–81, St Albans School, 1981–98; Poet-in-Residence, Magdalene College, Cambridge, 1996; Visiting Poet, University of Hertfordshire, 1998–; Poet to the City of London, 1999–; mem. Society of Authors; Ver Poets, pres.; Toddington Poetry Society, pres. *Publications:* Poetry: Feeding the Lake, 1981; In and Out of the Apple, 1984; Homing, 1987; Boo to a Goose, 1987; The Mad Parrot's Countdown, 1989; Catching the Spider, 1990; The Conjuror's Rabbit, 1992; Depending on the Light, 1993; Selected Poems, 1995; Hot Air, 1996; Copy Cat (for children), 1997; The Dummy's Dilemma, 1999; For the Moment, 2000; The Wonder Dish, 2002. Other: Passing Judgements: Poetry in the Eighties, 1989; Poetry (ed.), 1945–80; Figures of Speech (ed.), 2000. Contributions: newspapers, reviews, and magazines. *Honours:* Eric Gregory Award, 1970; Signal Award for Outstanding Contribution to Children's Poetry, 1988; Cholmondeley Award, 1994. *Address:* 11 Hill St, St Albans, Hertfordshire AL3 4QS, England. *E-mail:* john_mole@bigfoot.com.

MOLINA, Silvia; Mexican novelist; b. 11 Oct. 1946, México, DF. *Publications:* La mañana debe seguir gris (Gray Skies Tomorrow) 1977, La familia vino del norte 1987, Imagen de Héctor 1990, Un hombre cerca 1993, El amor que me juraste (The Love You Promised Me) 1999. *Honours:* Xavier Villarrutia Prize 1977. *Address:* c/o Curbstone Press, 321 Jackson Street, Willimantic, CT 06226-1738, USA. *E-mail:* info@curbstone.org. *Website:* www.curbstone.org.

MOLLENKOTT, Virginia (Ramey); Prof. of English Emeritus, Writer and Lecturer; b. 28 Jan. 1932, Philadelphia, Pennsylvania, USA; m. Friedrich H. Mollenkott, 17 June 1954, divorced 1973, one s. *Education:* BA, Bob Jones University, 1953; MA, Temple University, 1955; PhD, New York University, 1964. *Career:* Chair, Dept of English, Shelton College, 1955–63, Nyack College, 1963–67; Assoc. Prof., 1967–74, Prof. of English, 1974–97, Chair, Dept of English, 1972–76, Prof. Emeritus, 1997–, William Paterson University; mem. Milton Society of America, life mem.; MLA, life mem. *Publications:* Adamant and Stone Chips: A Christian Humanist Approach to Knowledge, 1967; In Search of Balance, 1969; Adam Among the Television Trees: An Anthology of Verse by Contemporary Christian Poets (ed.), 1971; Women, Men and the Bible, 1976; Speech, Silence, Action, 1980; Is the Homosexual My Neighbor? (with L. D. Scanzoni), 1978; The Divine Feminine: Biblical Imagery of God as Female, 1983; Views from the Intersection (with Catherine Barry), 1984; Women of Faith in Dialogue (ed.), 1987; Sensuous Spirituality: Out from Fundamentalism, 1992; Omnigender: A Trans-Religious Approach, 2001. Contributions: numerous journals and reviews; The Witness (contributing ed.), 1994. *Honours:* Penfield Fellow, 1973, Andiron Award, 1964, Founders Day Award, 1964, New York University; Hon. DMin, Samaritan College, 1989; New Jersey Lesbian and Gay Coalition Achievement Award, 1992; SAGE (Senior Action in a Gay Enrironment) Lifetime Achievement Award, 1999; Lambda Literary Award, 2002. *Address:* 11 Yearling Trail, Hewitt, NJ 07421, USA.

MOLLOY, Michael (John); Journalist, Ed. and Writer; b. 22 Dec. 1940, England; m. Sandra June Foley, 1964, three d. *Education:* Ealing School of Art. *Career:* Staff, 1962–70, Asst Ed., 1970–75, Deputy Ed., 1975, Ed., 1975–85, Daily Mirror; Dir, 1976–90, Ed.-in-Chief, 1985–90, Mirror Group Newspapers; Ed., Sunday Mirror, 1986–88. *Publications:* The Black Dwarf, 1985; The Kid from Riga, 1987; The Harlot of Jericho, 1989; The Century, 1990; The Gallery, 1991; Sweet Sixteen, 1992; Cat's Paw, 1993; Home Before Dark, 1994; Dogsbody, 1995. *Address:* 62 Culmington Rd, London W13 9NH, England.

MOLONEY, Tom; British publishing executive; *CEO, Emap;* b. 1959. *Career:* joined Emap PLC (radio and magazines outfit) 1981, apptd Group Man. Dir Emap Metro and Elan 1989, Chief Exec. Consumer Magazines UK 1995–99, has overseen launch of magazines Heat, More, Q and Empire, mem. Exec. Bd 1995–, COO then Pres. and CEO Emap USA 1999–2001, Group COO 2001–03, CEO 2003–. *Address:* Emap PLC, 40 Bernard Street, London, WC1N 1LW, England (Office). *Telephone:* (20) 7278-1452 (Office). *Website:* www.emap.com (Office).

MOLTMANN, Jürgen, DTh, DThH; German academic and writer; *Professor of Systematic Theology Emeritus, University of Tübingen;* b. 8 April 1926, Hamburg; m. Elisabeth Wendel 1952; four d. *Education:* University of Göttingen. *Career:* Ordained Minister; Prof., Kirchliche Hochschule, Wuppertal, 1958–63; Prof. of Systematic Theology and Social Ethics, University of Bonn, 1963–67; Prof. of Systematic Theology, 1967–94, Prof. Emeritus, 1994–, Faculty of Protestant Theology, University of Tübingen. *Publications in translation:* The Theology of Hope, 1967; Hope and Planning, 1971; Man: Christian Anthropology in the Conflicts of the Present, 1971; The Gospel of Liberation, 1973; Theology and Joy, 1973; The Crucified God, 1975; The Experiment Hope, 1975; The Church in the Power of the Spirit, 1977; The Open Church: Invitation to a Messianic Life-Style, 1978; The Future of Creation, 1979; Trinity and the Kingdom of God, 1981; God in Creation, 1986; The Way of Jesus Christ, 1990; The Spirit of Life, 1992; The Coming of God, 1996; God for a Secular Society, 1999. Contributions: scholarly books and journals. *Honours:* Premio letterario d'isola d'elba, 1971; Amos-Comenius Medal, 1992; Ernst Bloch Prize, Ludwigshafen, 1995; Grawemeyer Award, 2000; Verdienstorden, Baden-Württemberg, 2001; many hon. doctorates. *Address:* c/o Faculty of Protestant Theology, Eberhard-Karls Universität Tübingen, Liebermeisterstr. 12, 72076 Tübingen, Germany.

MOMADAY, Navarre Scott; writer, painter and academic; b. 27 Feb. 1934, Lawton, Oklahoma, USA; m. Regina Heitzer 1978; four d. *Education:* BA, University of New Mexico, 1958; MA, 1960, PhD, 1963, Stanford University. *Career:* Visiting Prof., Columbia University, Princeton University, 1979; Writer-in-Residence, Southeastern University, 1985, Aspen Writers Conference, 1986; mem. PEN. *Publications:* House Made of Dawn, 1968; The Way to Rainy Mountain, 1969; The Names, 1976; The Gourd Dancer, 1976; The Ancient Child, 1989; In the Presence of the Sun, 1992; Enchanted Circle, 1993; The Native Americans (with Linda Hozan), 1993; The Man Made of Words, 1997. *Honours:* Pulitzer Prize in Fiction, 1969; Premio Mondello, Italy, 1979; Hon. Degrees, various universities. *Literary Agent:* Julian Bach Literary Agency, 22 East 71st Street, New York, NY 10021, USA.

MOMI, Balbir Singh; Teacher and Education Officer (retd), Writer, Dramatist, Ed. and Trans; b. 20 Nov. 1935, Amagarh, India; m. Baldev Kaur, 28 Oct. 1954, four d. *Education:* Honours in Punjabi, 1953, MA, Punjabi, 1970, Persian, 1974, PhD registration, 1977, Panjab University, Chandigarh. *Career:* Lecturer and Research Asst, GND University, Amritsar, 1974–76; Literary Ed., Perdesi Canafi Ajit Punjab, Toronto, 1982–97; mem. International Cultural Forum, India and Canada, senior international vice-pres., 1993–. *Publications:* Novels, short stories, plays and trans. Contributions: many publications. *Honours:* various literary awards. *Address:* 17 Donaldson Dr., Brampton, ON L6Y 3H1, Canada.

MOMPLE, Lilia, BA; Mozambique writer; b. 1935; m. *Education:* studied social work in Portugal. *Career:* Sec.-Gen., Mozambique Writers' Asscn, 1995–2001, Pres., 1997–99; mem., UNESCO Exec. Council. *Publications:* No One Killed Suhara 1988, The Eyes of the Green Cobra 1997, Muhupitit Alima (screenplay) 1988, Neighbours: The Story of a Murder 1995, Celina's Banquet (novel) 2001. *Address:* c/o African Writers Series, Heinemann Educational Publishers, Halley Court, Jordan Hill, Oxford OX2 8EJ, England.

MONACO, James Frederick, BA, MA; writer and publisher; b. 15 Nov. 1942, New York, NY, USA; m. Susan R. Schenker 1976; two s. one d. *Education:* Muhlenberg College, Columbia University. *Career:* mem. Bd of Dirs, Copyright Clearance Center Inc 2002–; mem. Authors' Guild, Writers Guild. *Publications:* How to Read a Film 1977 (multimedia edn) 2000, American Film Now 1979, The New Wave 1976, Media Culture 1977, Celebrity 1977, Connoisseur's Guide to the Movies 1985, The International Encyclopedia of Film 1991, The Movie Guide 1992, Cinemania: Interactive Movie Guide 1992, Dictionary of New Media 1999; contrib. to numerous publications. *Address:* UNET 2 Corporation, 80 E 11th Street, New York, NY 10003, USA.

MONETTE, Madeleine; Author; b. 3 Oct. 1951, Montréal, QC, Canada; m. William R. Leggio, 27 Dec. 1979. *Education:* MA, Literature, University of Québec. *Career:* mem. Québec Writers Union; PEN. *Publications:* Le Double Suspect, 1980, English trans. as Doubly Suspect, 2000; Petites Violences, 1982; Fuites et Poursuites, 1982; Plages, 1986; L'Aventure, la Mesaventure, 1987; Amandes et melon, 1991; Nouvelles de Montréal, 1992; La Femme furieuse, 1997; Nouvelles d'Amérique, 1998; Ligne de métro, 2002. Contributions: periodicals. *Honours:* Robert-Cliche Award, 1980; Grants, Canadian Council of Arts, the Conseil des Arts et des Lettres du Québec, Fonds Gabrielle-Roy. *Address:* 2 Charlton St, 11K, New York, NY 10014, USA. *E-mail:* mmonet@aol.com.

MONEY, David Charles; Teacher (retd) and Writer; b. 5 Oct. 1918, Oxford, England; m. Madge Matthews, 30 Nov. 1945, one s. *Education:* Honours Degree, Chemistry, 1940, Geography, 1947, St John's College, Oxford. *Career:* mem. Farmer's Club; FRGS. *Publications:* Human Geography, 1954; Climate, Soils and Vegetation, 1965; The Earth's Surface, 1970; Patterns of Settlement, 1972; Environmental Systems (series), 1978–82; Foundations of Geography, 1987; Climate and Environmental Systems, 1988; China – The Land and the People, 1984; China Today, 1987; Australia Today, 1988; Environmental Issues – The Global Consequences, 1994; China in Change, 1996; The Vocation of Bachan Singh, 1997; Weather and Climate, 2000. *Honours:* Geographical Asscn, hon. mem. *Address:* 52 Park Ave, Bedford MK40 2NE, England.

MONEY, Keith; Author, Artist and Photographer; b. 1934, Auckland, New Zealand. *Publications:* Salute the Horse, 1960; The Horseman in Our Midst, 1963; The Equestrian World, 1963; The Art of the Royal Ballet, 1964; The Art of Margot Fonteyn, 1965; The Royal Ballet Today, 1968; Fonteyn: The Making of a Legend, 1973; John Curry, 1978; Anna Pavlova: Her Life and Art, 1982; The Bedside Book of Old Fashioned Roses, 1985; Some Other Sea: The Life of Rupert Brooke, 1988–89; Margot, assoluta, 1993; Fonteyn and Nureyev: The Great Years, 1994. Other: Screenplays. Contributions: anthologies, journals, and magazines. *Address:* Carbrooke Hall Farm, Thetford, Norfolk, England.

MONGRAIN, Serg; Writer, Poet and Photographer; b. 15 Jan. 1948, Trois Rivières, QC, Canada. *Education:* Mathematical Université du Québec, 1972. *Career:* mem. Union des écrivaines et des écrivains québécois. *Publications:* L'Oeil du l'idée, 1988; Le calcul des heures, 1993; L'objet des sens, 1996; Brouillard, 1999; Le Poème déshabillé, 2000; Gladys, 2001. As Photographer: Lis: écris, 1981; L'image titre, 1981; Agrestes, 1988; Québec Kerouak Blues, 1998. Other: many exhibition catalogues in art. Contributions: periodicals. *Address:* 994 rue Sainte Cécile, Trois Rivières, QC G9A 1L3, Canada.

MONTAG, Tom, BA; poet, writer, editor and publisher; b. 31 Aug. 1947, Fort Dodge, IA, USA. *Education:* Dominican Coll. of Racine. *Career:* Ed., publisher, Monday Morning Press, Milwaukee 1971–, Margins Books 1974–. *Publications:* Wooden Nickel 1972, Twelve Poems 1972, Measurers 1972, To Leave This Place 1972, Making Hay 1973, The Urban Ecosystem: A Holistic Approach (ed. with F. Stearns) 1974, Making Hay and Other Poems 1975, Ninety Notes Toward Partial Images and Lover Prints 1976, Concerns: Essays and Reviews 1977, Letters Home 1978, The Essential Ben Zen 1992. *Address:* c/o Sparrow Press, 193 Waldron Street, West Lafayette, IN 47906, USA.

MONTAGUE, John (Patrick); Poet, Writer and Lecturer; b. 28 Feb. 1929, New York, NY, USA. *Education:* BA, 1949, MA, 1953, University College, Dublin; Postgraduate Studies, Yale University, 1953–54; MFA, University of Iowa, 1955. *Career:* Lecturer in Poetry, University College, Cork. *Publications:* Forms of Exile, 1958; The Old People, 1960; Poisoned Lands and Other Poems, 1961; The Dolmen Miscellany of Irish Writing (ed.), 1962; Death of a Chieftain and Other Stories, 1964; All Legendary Obstacles, 1966; Patriotic Suite, 1966; A Tribute to Austin Clarke on His Seventieth Birthday, 9th May 1966 (ed. with Liam Miller), 1966; Home Again, 1967; A Chosen Light, 1967; Hymn to the New Omagh Road, 1968; The Bread God: A Lecture, with illustrations in Verse, 1968; A New Siege, 1969; The Planter and the Gael (with J. Hewitt), 1970; Tides, 1970; Small Secrets, 1972; The Rough Field (play), 1972; The Cave of Night, 1974; O'Riada's Farewell, 1974; The Faber Book of Irish Verse (ed.), 1974; A Slow Dance, 1975; The Great Cloak, 1978; Selected Poems, 1982; The Dead Kingdom, 1984; Mount Eagle, 1989. *Address:* Dept of English, University College, Cork, Ireland.

MONTAZAM, Mir Ali Asghar, BA, MA, PhD; Iranian academic, historian and writer; b. 25 Sept. 1935, Tabnz. *Education:* Middle East Coll., Beirut, American Univ. of Beirut, Lebanon and Univ. of Tehran. *Career:* diplomat, historian, univ. lecturer. *Publications include:* non-fiction: The Politics of Religion in the Middle East 1988, The Life and Times of Ayatollah Khomeini 1994, Iran and Ayatollah Khomeini 1997, Islam and Mullahcracy in Iran 2000, Islam in Iran: The Background to the Rule of Anarchy and Despotism in the Country's Islamic Past and Present 2003; novel: The Strange Death of a Dream 1998. *Address:* c/o Eurasia Press Ltd, 5 Elsie Lane Court, Westbourne Park Villas, London, W2 5EF, England.

MONTEFIORE, Simon Sebag; British writer and historian; b. 1965, London; m. Santa Montefiore; two c. *Education:* Gonville and Caius Coll., Univ. of Cambridge. *Career:* presenter of BBC documentaries. *Publications:* novel: King's Parade 1991; non-fiction: My Affair with Stalin 1997, Prince of Princes: The Life of Potemkin 2000, Stalin: The Court of the Red Tsar 2003, A History of Caucasus 2005, Elizaveta: The Life and Times of the Empress of Russia 2006; contrib. to The Sunday Times, New York Times, The Guardian, New Republic, The Spectator. *Literary Agent:* Georgina Capel, Capel & Land, 29 Wardour Street, London, W1V 3HB, England.

MONTEJO, Eugenio; Venezuelan poet and writer; b. 1938, Caracas. *Education:* Univ. of Harvard, USA. *Film appearance:* 21 Grams 2003. *Publications:* poetry: Elegos 1967, Muerte y memoria 1972, Algunas palabras 1976, Terredad 1978, Trópico absoluto 1982, Alfabeto del mundo 1986, Adiós al siglo XX 1992, El azul de la tierra 1997, Partitura de la cigarra

1999, Tiempo transfigurado 2001, The Trees: Selected Poems 1967–2004 (in trans.) 2004; essays: La ventana oblicua 1974. *Honours:* Nat. Prize for Literature 1998. *Address:* c/o Salt Publishing, PO Box 937, Great Wilbraham, Cambridge, CB1 5JX, England. *E-mail:* info@saltpublishing.com. *Website:* www.saltpublishing.com.

MONTEJO, Victor; Guatemalan writer and lecturer; b. 1951. *Career:* Prof. of Anthropology, Univ. of California at Davis. *Publications include:* El Q'Amil: El Hombre Rayo (trans. as Man of Lightning) 1984, Testimony: Death of a Guatemalan Village 1987, The Bird Who Cleans the World 1992, Voices from Exile: Violence and Survival in Modern Maya History 1999. *Literary Agent:* c/o Curbstone Press, 321 Jackson Street, Willimantic, CT 06226-1738, USA. *E-mail:* info@curbstone.org. *Website:* www.curbstone.org.

MONTELEONE, Thomas Francis; Writer and Dramatist; b. 14 April 1946, Baltimore, MD, USA; m. Elizabeth, two s. one d. *Education:* BS, Psychology, 1964, MA, English Literature, 1973, University of Maryland. *Career:* mem. SFWA; Horror Writers of America. *Publications:* The Time Swept City, 1977; The Secret Sea, 1979; Night Things, 1980; Dark Stars and Other Illuminations, 1981; Guardian, 1981; Night Train, 1984; Lyrica, 1987; The Magnificent Gallery, 1987; Crooked House, 1988; Fantasma, 1989; Borderlands, 1990; Borderlands 2, 1991; Borderlands 3, 1992; The Blood of the Lamb, 1992; Borderlands 4, 1993. Contributions: anthologies and magazines. *Honours:* Nebula Awards, 1976, 1977; Gabriel Award, 1984; Bronze Award, International Film and TV Festival, New York, 1984; Bram Stoker Award for Superior Achievement in the Novel, 1993. *Literary Agent:* Howard Morhaim Literary Agency, 841 Broadway, Suite 604, New York, NY 10003, USA.

MONTGOMERY, David John, BA; British newspaper executive; b. 6 Nov. 1948, Bangor, Northern Ireland; m. 1st Susan Frances Buchanan Russell 1971 (divorced 1987); m. 2nd Heidi Kingstone 1989 (divorced 1997); m. 3rd Sophie, Countess of Woolton 1997. *Education:* Queen's Univ., Belfast. *Career:* Sub-Ed., Daily Mirror London, Manchester 1973–76, Asst Chief Sub-Ed. 1976–80; Chief Sub-Ed. The Sun 1980; Asst Ed. Sunday People 1982; Asst Ed. News of the World 1984, Ed. 1985–87; Ed. Today 1987–91 (Newspaper of the Year 1988); Man. Dir News UK 1987–91; Chief Exec. London Live TV 1991–92, Dir 1991–; Chief Exec. Mirror Group 1992–99; Dir Satellite Television PLC 1986–91, News Group Newspapers 1986–91, Donohue Inc. 1992–95, Newspaper Publishing 1994–98, Scottish Media Group 1995–99, Press Asscn 1996–99; Chair. Tri-Mex Group PLC 1999–, Mecom 2000–, Yava 2000–, Africa Lakes PLC 2000–, Integrated Educ. Fund Devt Bd, NI 2000–, Espresso 2001–. *Address:* ALC, 7–10 Chandos Street, London, W1G 9DQ; 15 Collingham Gardens, London, SW5 0HS, England. *Telephone:* (20) 7323-5440 (Office); (20) 7373-1982 (Home). *E-mail:* dmontgomery@tri-mex.com (Office).

MONTGOMERY, Marion H., Jr; Prof. of English, Writer and Poet; b. 16 April 1925, Thomaston, GA, USA; m. Dorothy Carlisle, 20 Jan. 1952, one s., four d. *Education:* AB, 1950, MA, 1953, University of Georgia; Creative Writing Workshop, University of Iowa, 1956–58. *Career:* Asst Dir, University of Georgia Press, 1950–52; Business Man., Georgia Review, 1951–53; Instructor, Darlington School for Boys, 1953–54; Instructor, 1954–60, Asst Prof., 1960–67, Assoc. Prof., 1967–70, Prof. of English, 1970–, University of Georgia; Writer-in-Residence, Converse College, 1963. *Publications:* Fiction: The Wandering of Desire, 1962; Darrell, 1964; Ye Olde Bluebird, 1967; Fugitive, 1974. Poetry: Dry Lightening, 1960; Stones from the Rubble, 1965; The Gull and Other Georgia Scenes, 1969. Non-Fiction: Ezra Pound: A Critical Essay, 1970; T. S. Eliot: An Essay on the American Magus, 1970; The Reflective Journey Toward Order: Essays on Dante, Wordsworth, Eliot and Others, 1973; Eliot's Reflective Journey to the Garden, 1978; The Prophetic Poet and the Spirit of the Age, Vol. 1, Why Flannery O'Connor Stayed Home, 1980, Vol. II, Why Poe Drank Liquor, 1983, Vol. III, Why Hawthorne Was Melancholy, 1984; Possum, and Other Receipts for the Recovery of 'Southern' Being, 1987; The Trouble with You Innerleckchuls, 1988; The Men I Have Chosen for Fathers: Literary and Philosophical Passages, 1990; Liberal Arts and Community: The Feeding of the Larger Body, 1990; Virtue and Modern Shadows of Turning: Preliminary Agitations, 1990; Romantic Confusions of the Good: Beauty as Truth, Truth Beauty, 1997; Concerning Intellectual Philandering: Poets and Philosophers, Priests and Politicians, 1998; Making: The Proper Habit of Our Being, 1999; The Truth of Things: Liberal Arts and the Recovery of Reality, 1999; Romancing Reality: Homo Viator and the Scandal of Beauty, 2000; John Crowe Ransom and Allen Tate: At Odds About the Ends of History and the Mystery of Nature, 2003; Eudora Welty and Walker Percy: The Concept of Home in Their Lives and Literature, 2003. Contributions: anthologies and magazines. *Honours:* Eugene Saxton Memorial Award, 1960; Georgia Writers' Asscn Literary Achievement Award in Poetry, 1970; Earhart Foundation Fellowship, 1973–74; Stanley W. Lindberg Award, 2001. *Address:* PO Box 115, Crawford, GA 30630, USA.

MOODY, Rick, BA, MFA; American writer and editor; b. (Hiram F. Moody III), 18 Oct. 1961, New York, NY. *Education:* Brown Univ., Columbia Univ. *Publications:* Garden State: A Novel 1991, The Ice Storm 1994, The Ring of Brightest Angels Around Heaven (short stories) 1995, Demonology 2001, The Black Veil 2002; contrib. to various periodicals. *Honours:* Ed.'s Book Award, Pushcart Press 1991. *Address:* c/o Little, Brown & Co, 1271 Avenue of the Americas, New York, NY 10020, USA.

MOONEY, Bel; Writer and Broadcaster; b. 8 Oct. 1946, Liverpool, England; m. Jonathan Dimbleby, 23 Feb. 1968, one s. one d. *Education:* BA, English Language and Literature, University College London, 1969. *Career:* Columnist, Daily Mirror, 1979–80, Sunday Times, 1982–83, The Listener, 1984–86; Television interview series, television films and radio programmes; Governor, Bristol Polytechnic, 1989–91. *Publications:* Fiction: The Windsurf Boy, 1983; The Anderson Question, 1985; The Fourth of July, 1988; Lost Footsteps, 1993; Intimate Letters, 1997. Children's Books: Liza's Yellow Boat, 1980; I Don't Want To!, 1985; The Stove Haunting, 1986; I Can't Find It!, 1988; It's Not Fair!, 1989; A Flower of Jet, 1990; But You Promised!, 1990; Why Not?, 1990; I Know!, 1991; The Voices of Silence, 1994; I'm Scared!, 1994; I Wish!, 1995; The Mouse with Many Rooms, 1995; Why Me?, 1996; I'm Bored!, 1997; Joining the Rainbow, 1997; The Green Man, 1997; It's not my Fault, 1999; So What!, 2002; Kitty's Friends, 2003. Other: The Year of the Child, 1979; Differences of Opinion, 1984; Father Kissmass and Mother Claws (with Gerald Scarfe), 1985; Bel Mooney's Somerset, 1989; From this Day Forward, 1989; Perspectives for Living, 1992; Devout Sceptics, 2003. *Honours:* Fellow, University College London, 1994, Liverpool John Moores University, 2002; Hon. DLitt, Bath University, 1998. *Literary Agent:* David Higham Associates, 5–8 Lower John St, Golden Sq., London W1F 9HA, England.

MOORCOCK, Michael (John), (Edward P. Bradbury, Desmond Read); Writer; b. 18 Dec. 1939, Mitcham, Surrey, England. *Career:* Ed., Tarzan Adventures, 1956–58, Sexton Blake Library, 1959–61, New Worlds, London, 1964–79. *Publications:* The Stealer of Souls and Other Stories (with James Cawthorn), 1961; Caribbean Crisis, 1962; The Fireclown, 1965, as The Winds of Limbo, 1969; The Sundered World, 1965, as The Blood Red Game, 1970; Stormbringer, 1965; Warriors of Mars, 1965, as The City of the Beast, 1970; The Distant Suns (with Philip James), 1975; The Quest for Tanelorn, 1975; The Adventures of Una Persson and Catherine Cornelius in the Twentieth Century, 1976; The End of All Songs, 1976; Moorcock's Book of Martyrs, 1976; The Lives and Times of Jerry Cornelius, 1976; Legends from the End of Time, 1976; The Sailor on the Seas of Fate, 1976; The Transformation of Miss Mavis Ming, 1977, as Messiah at the End of Time, 1978; The Weird of the White Wolf, 1977; The Bane of the Black Sword, 1977; Sojan (for children), 1977; Condition of Muzak, 1977; Glorianna, 1978; Dying for Tomorrow, 1978; The Golden Barge, 1979; My Experiences in the Third World War, 1980; The Russian Intelligence, 1980; The Great Rock'n'Roll Swindle, 1980; Byzantium Endures, 1981; The Entropy Tanga, 1981; The Warhound and the World's Pain, 1981; The Brothel in Rosenstrasse, 1982; The Dancers at the End of Time (omnibus), 1983; The Retreat from Liberty, 1983; The Language of Carthage, 1984; The Opium General and Other Stories, 1984; The Chronicles of Castle Brass, 1985; Letters from Hollywood, 1986; The City in the Autumn Stars, 1986; The Dragon in the Sword, 1986; Death is No Obstacle, 1992; Blood, 1994; The War Amongst Angels, 1996; Tales from the Texas Woods, 1997; King of the City, 2001. Editor: The Best of New Worlds, 1965; England Invaded, 1977; New Worlds: An Anthology, 1983. *Address:* c/o Anthony Sheil Assocs, 43 Doughty St, London WC1N 2LF, England.

MOORE, Ann S., BSc, MBA; American publisher and media executive; *Chair and CEO, Time Inc.*; b. 1950, McLean, Va; m. Donovan Moore; one s. *Education:* Vanderbilt Univ., Nashville, Harvard Univ. Business School. *Career:* financial analyst, Time Inc. 1978, served in various exec. positions including Publr and Pres. People magazine (est. spin-offs Teen People, Instyle, Real Simple, People en Español 2001), cr. Sports Illustrated for Kids 1989, Exec. Vice-Pres. Time Inc. 2001–02, Chair. and CEO 2002–, responsible for Time magazine, People, Fortune, Money, Entertainment Weekly and 135 other titles (first woman in position). *Address:* Time Inc., Rockefeller Plaza, New York, NY 10019, USA (Office). *Telephone:* (212) 484-8000 (Office). *Website:* www.aoltimewarner.com (Office).

MOORE, Charles Hilary, MA; British journalist; *Group Consulting Editor, The Daily Telegraph*; b. 31 Oct. 1956, Hastings; m. Caroline Baxter 1981; twin s. and d. *Education:* Eton Coll. and Trinity Coll. Cambridge. *Career:* editorial staff, Daily Telegraph 1979–81, leader writer 1981–83; Asst Ed. and Political Columnist, The Spectator 1983–84, Ed. 1984–90, fortnightly columnist ('Another Voice') 1990–95; weekly columnist, Daily Express 1987–90; Deputy Ed. Daily Telegraph 1990–92; Ed. Sunday Telegraph 1992–95, Daily Telegraph 1995–2003, Group Consulting Ed. Daily Telegraph 2003–; Trustee T. E. Utley Memorial Fund, Benenden Council, ShareGift. *Publications:* 1936 (ed. with C. Hawtree) 1986, The Church in Crisis (with A. N. Wilson and G. Stamp) 1986, A Tory Seer: The Selected Journalism of T. E. Utley (ed. with S. Heffer) 1986. *Address:* c/o Daily Telegraph, 1 Canada Square, Canary Wharf, London, E14 5DT, England.

MOORE, Christopher Hugh; Historian and Writer; b. 9 June 1950, Stoke-on-Trent, England; m. Louise Brophy, 7 May 1977. *Education:* BA, University of British Columbia, 1971; MA, University of Ottawa, 1977. *Career:* mem. Writers Union of Canada; Canadian Historical Asscn; Ontario Historical Society; Heritage Canada Foundation. *Publications:* Louisbourg Portraits, 1982; The Loyalists, 1984; The Illustrated History of Canada (co-author), 1987. Other: School texts, historical guidebooks, educational software programmes, and radio documentaries. Contributions: numerous scholarly journals and magazines. *Honours:* Governor-General's Award for Non-Fiction, 1982; Canadian Historical Asscn Award of Merit, 1984; Secretary of State's Prize for Excellence in Canadian Studies, 1985. *Address:* 620 Runnymede Rd, Toronto, Ontario M6S 3A2, Canada.

MOORE, Eric (see Bruton, Eric).

MOORE, John Evelyn; Naval Officer (retd), Ed. and Writer; b. 1 Nov. 1921, Sant Illario, Italy; m. 1st Joan Pardoe, 1945, one s. two d.; m. 2nd Barbara Kerry. *Career:* Royal Navy, 1939–72; Ed., Jane's Fighting Ships, 1972–87, Jane's Naval Review, 1982–87; Hon. Prof., University of Aberdeen, 1987–90, St Andrews University, 1990–92; mem. FRGS. *Publications:* Jane's Major Warships, 1973; The Soviet Navy Today, 1975; Submarine Development, 1976; Soviet War Machine (co-author), 1976; Encyclopaedia of World's Warships (co-ed.), 1978; World War 3 (co-author), 1978; Seapower and Politics, 1979; Warships of the Royal Navy, 1979; Warships of the Soviet Navy, 1981; Submarine Warfare: Today and Tomorrow (co-author), 1986; The Impact of Polaris, 1999. *Address:* 1 Ridgelands Close, Eastbourne, East Sussex BN20 8EP, England.

MOORE, Lorrie, (Marie Lorena Moore); Prof. of English and Writer; b. 13 Jan. 1957, Glens Falls, New York, USA. *Education:* BA, St Lawrence University, 1978; MFA, Cornell University, 1982. *Career:* Lecturer in English, Cornell University, 1982–84; Asst Prof., 1984–87, Assoc. Prof., 1987–91, Prof. of English, 1991–, University of Wisconsin at Madison; mem. Associated Writing Programs; Authors' Guild; Authors League. *Publications:* Self-Help, 1985; Anagrams, 1986; The Forgotten Helper, 1987; Like Life, 1990; I Know Some Things: Stories About Childhood by Contemporary Writers (ed.), 1992; Birds of America, 1998. Contributions: periodicals. *Honours:* several fiction prizes; various fellowships. *Address:* c/o Dept of English, University of Wisconsin at Madison, Madison, WI 53706, USA.

MOORE, Michael; American author, filmmaker and political commentator; b. 1954, Davison, MI. *Career:* elected to local school bd aged 18; active in student politics; began career as journalist with The Flint Voice, later Ed., expanded into The Michigan Voice; Ed. Mother Jones magazine, San Francisco 1986–88. *Television includes:* Pets or Meat: The Return to Flint 1992, TV Nation (NBC) 1994, The Awful Truth (Channel 4) 1999. *Films:* Talion (dir) 1966, Paradise Hawaiian Style (dir) 1966, An Eye for an Eye (dir) 1966, The Fastest Guitar Alive (dir) 1968, Buckskin (dir) 1968, Roger and Me (writer, dir, producer) 1989, Canadian Bacon (dir) 1994, The Big One (dir) 1997, And Justice for All (dir) 1998, Bowling for Columbine (screenwriter, dir, producer; Jury Award, Cannes Film Festival 2003, Acad. Award for Best Documentary 2003) 2002, Fahrenheit (dir; Palme d'Or, Cannes Film Festival) 9/11 2004. *Film appearances:* Pony Express 1953, Lucky Number 1999, EdTV 1999. *Publications:* Downsize This!: Random Threats from an Unarmed America 1996, Stupid White Men (Book of the Year, British Book Awards 2003) 2001, Adventures in a TV Nation (with Kathleen Glynn) 2002, Dude, Where's My Country? 2003. *Address:* c/o Random House Inc., 299 Park Avenue, New York, NY 10170, USA (Office). *E-mail:* mike@michaelmoore.com. *Website:* www.michaelmoore.com.

MOORE, Sir Patrick Alfred Caldwell-; Astronomer, Writer and Ed.; b. 4 March 1923, Pinner, Middlesex, England. *Education:* Private. *Career:* The Sky at Night, BBC TV series, 1957–; Ed., Year Book of Astronomy, 1962–; Dir, Armagh Planetarium, 1965–68; mem. British Astronomical Asscn, pres., 1982–84; Royal Astronomical Society of Canada; Royal Astronomical Society of New Zealand. *Publications:* Over 60 books, including: The Amateur Astronomer, 1970; Atlas of the Universe, 1970; Guide to the Planets, 1976; Guide to the Moon, 1976; Guide to the Stars, 1977; Guide to Mars, 1977; Out of the Darkness: The Planet Pluto (co-author), 1980; The Unfolding Universe, 1982; Travellers in Space and time, 1983; The Return of Halley's Comet (co-author), 1984; Stargazing, 1985; Exploring the Night Sky with Binoculars, 1986; The A-Z of Astronomy, 1986; TV Astronomer, 1987; The Planet Uranos (co-author), 1988; The Planet Neptune, 1989; Mission to the Planets, 1990; A Passion for Astronomy, 1991; Fireside Astronomy, 1992; The Starry Sky, 1994; The Great Astronomical Revolution, 1994; Stars of the Southern Skies, 1994; Guinness Book of Astronomy, 1995; Teach Yourself Astronomy, 1995; Eyes on the Universe, 1997; Patrick Moore on Mars, 1999; Astronomy Data Book, 2000. *Honours:* Lorimer Gold Medal, 1962; Goodacre Gold Medal, 1968; OBE, 1968; CBE, 1988; Hon. DSc, University of Lancaster, 1974, Hatfield Polytechnic, 1989, University of Birmingham, 1990; Jackson-Gwilt Medal, Royal Astronomical Society, 1977; Roberts-Klumpke Medal, Astronomical Society of the Pacific, 1979; Minor Planet No. 2602 named 'Moore' in his honour; Royal Astronomical Society Millennium Award, 2000; Knighted, 2001. *Address:* Farthings, 39 West St, Selsey, West Sussex PO20 9AD, England.

MOORE, Susanna; American writer; b. 9 Dec. 1948, Bryn Mawr, PA; m., one d. *Publications:* My Old Sweetheart 1982, The Whiteness of Bones 1989, Sleeping Beauties 1993, In the Cut 1995, One Last Look 2003. *Honours:* PEN/Ernest Hemingway Citation, American Acad. of Arts and Letters Sue Kaufman Prize 1983. *Literary Agent:* International Creative Management, 40 W 57th Street, New York, NY 10019, USA.

MOOREHEAD, Caroline, BA; journalist and writer; b. 28 Oct. 1944, London, England. *Education:* University of London. *Career:* reporter, Time magazine, Rome, 1968–69; feature writer, Telegraph Magazine, London, 1969–70, The Times, London, 1973–88; Features Ed., Times Educational Supplement, 1970–73; human rights columnist, The Independent, 1988–93. *Publications:* Myths and Legends of Britain (ed. and trans.), 1968; Helping: A Guide to Voluntary Work, 1975; Fortune's Hostages, 1980; Sidney Bernstein: A Biography, 1983; Freya Stark: A Biography, 1985; Troublesome People: Enemies of War 1916–1986, 1987; Over the Rim of the World: The Letters of Freya Stark (ed.), 1988; Betrayed: Children in the Modern World, 1988; Bertrand Russell: A Life, 1992; The Lost Treasures of Troy, 1996; 6 Dunant's Dream: War, Switzerland and the Red Crown, 1998; Iris Onigo: A Life, 1999; Martha Gellhorn: A Life, 2003. Contributions: newspapers and magazines. *Address:* 89 Gloucester Avenue, London NW1, England.

MOORHOUSE, Frank; Writer; b. 21 Dec. 1938, Nowra, Qld, Australia. *Education:* University of Queensland; WEA. *Career:* Pres., Australian Society of Authors, 1979–82; Chair., Copyright Council of Australia, 1985; mem. Groucho Club, London; AM. *Publications:* Futility and Other Animals, 1969; The Americans, Baby, 1972; The Electrical Experience, 1974; Conference-Ville, 1976; Tales of Mystery and Romance, 1977; Days of Wine and Rage, 1980; Room Service, 1986; Forty-Seventeen, 1988; Lateshows, 1990; Dark Palace, 2000. Contributions: Bulletin. *Honours:* Henry Lawson Short Story Prize, 1970; National Award for Fiction, 1975; Awgie Award, 1976; Gold Medal for Literature, Australian Literary, 1989; Miles Franklin Award, 2001.

MOORHOUSE, Geoffrey, FRSL; Author; b. 29 Nov. 1931, Bolton, Lancashire, England; m. 1st Janet Marion Murray 1956; two s. two d. (one deceased); m. 2nd Barbara Jane Woodward 1974 (divorced 1978); m. 3rd Marilyn Isobel Edwards 1983 (divorced 1996). *Education:* Bury Grammar School. *Career:* Editorial Staff, Bolton Evening News, 1952–54, Grey River Argus, New Zealand, Auckland Star, and Christchurch Star-Sun, 1954–56, News Chronicle, 1957, Guardian, Manchester, 1958–70. *Publications:* The Other England, 1964; The Press, 1964; Against All Reason, 1969; Calcutta, 1971; The Missionaries, 1973; The Fearful Void, 1974; The Diplomats, 1977; The Boat and the Town, 1979; The Best-Loved Game (Cricket Society Award) 1979; India Britannica, 1983; Lord's, 1983; To the Frontier (Thomas Cook Award) 1984; Imperial City: The Rise and Rise of New York, 1988; At the George, 1989; Apples in the Snow, 1990; Hell's Foundations: A Town, Its Myths and Gallipoli, 1992; Om: An Indian Pilgrimage, 1993; A People's Game: The Centenary History of Rugby League Football 1895–1995, 1995; Sun Dancing: A Medieval Vision, 1997; Sydney: The Story of a City, 1999; The Pilgrimage of Grace: The Rebellion That Shook Henry VIII's Throne, 2002. Contributions: newspapers and magazines. *Honours:* , 1979; Thomas Cook Award, 1984. *Address:* Park House, Gayle, near Hawes, North Yorkshire DL8 3RT, England. *Telephone:* (1969) 667456.

MORENCY, Pierre; Poet, Writer, Dramatist and Broadcaster; b. 8 May 1942, Lauzon, QC, Canada. *Education:* BA, Collège de Lévis, 1963; Licence ès Lettres, Université Laval, Québec, 1966. *Career:* Broadcaster; Co-Founder, Estuaire poetry journal; mem. PEN Club; Union des écrivaines et des écrivains québécois. *Publications:* L'ossature, 1972; Lieu de naissance, 1973; Le temps des oiseaux, 1975; Torrentiel, 1978; Effets personnels, 1987; L'oeil américain: Histories naturelles du Nouveau Monde, 1989; Lumière des oiseaux: Histoires naturelles du Nouveau Monde, 1992; Les paroles qui marchent dans la nuit, 1994; La vie entière, 1996. *Honours:* Prix Alain Grandbois, 1987; Prix Québec-Paris, 1988; Prix Ludger Duvernay, 1991; Prix France Québec, 1992; Chevalier, Ordre des Arts et des Lettres. *Address:* 155 Ave Laurier, QC G1R 2K8, Canada.

MORETON, John (see Cohen, Morton Norton).

MORGAN, Abi; British playwright; b. 1969, Cardiff, S Glamorgan, Wales. *Plays:* Skinned 1998, Splendour 2000, Tender 2001, Tiny Dynamite 2002. *Address:* c/o Faber and Faber Ltd, 3 Queen Square, London, WC1N 3AU, England. *Website:* www.faber.co.uk.

MORGAN, Edwin George, OBE, MA; Scottish poet, writer and translator; b. 27 April 1920, Glasgow. *Education:* Rutherglen Acad., High School of Glasgow, Univ. of Glasgow. *Career:* RAMC 1940–46; Asst Lecturer, Univ. of Glasgow 1947–50, Lecturer 1950–65, Senior Lecturer 1965–71, Reader 1971–75, Titular Prof. of English 1975–80, Prof. Emeritus 1980–; Visiting Prof., Univ. of Strathclyde 1987–90; Hon. Prof., Univ. Coll., Wales 1991–95; Poet Laureate of Glasgow 1997–; The Scots Makar (Scottish nat. poet) 2004–(07); has trans poetry from Hungarian, Italian, French, German, Russian, Spanish and Anglo-Saxon. *Publications:* poetry: The Vision of Cathkin Braes 1952, The Cape of Good Hope 1955, Starryveldt 1965, Scotch Mist 1965, Sealwear 1966, Emergent Poems 1967, The Second Life 1968, Gnomes 1968, Proverbfolder 1969, Penguin Modern Poets 15 (with Alan Bold and Edward Brathwaite) 1969, The Horseman's Word: A Sequence of Concrete Poems 1970, Twelve Songs 1970, The Dolphin's Song 1971, Glasgow Sonnets 1972, Instamatic Poems 1972, The Whittrick: A Poem in Eight Dialogues 1973, From Glasgow to Saturn 1973, The New Divan 1977, Colour Poems 1978, Star Gate: Science Fiction Poems 1979, Poems of Thirty Years 1982, Grafts/Takes 1983, Sonnets from Scotland 1984, Selected Poems 1985, From the Video Box 1986, Newspoems 1987, Themes on a Variation 1988, Tales from Limerick Zoo 1988, Collected Poems 1990, Hold Hands Among the Atoms 1991, Sweeping Out the Dark 1994, Virtual and Other Realities 1997, Demon 1999, New Selected Poems 2000, Cathures 2002, Love and a Life 2003; other: Collins Albatross Book of Longer Poems:

English and American Poetry from the Fourteenth Century to the Present Day (ed.) 1963, Scottish Poetry 1–6 (co-ed.) 1966–72, New English Dramatists 14 (ed.) 1970, Essays 1974, East European Poets 1976, Hugh MacDiarmid 1976, Scottish Satirical Verse (ed.) 1980, Twentieth Century Scottish Classics 1987, Nothing Not Giving Messages (interviews) 1990, Crossing the Border: Essays in Scottish Literature 1990, Language, Poetry and Language Poetry 1990, Collected Translations 1996, Evening Will Come They Will Sew the Blue Sail 1991, James Thomson: The City of Dreadful Night (ed.) 1993. *Honours:* Cholmondeley Award for Poetry 1968, Scottish Arts Council Book Awards 1968, 1973, 1975, 1977, 1978, 1983, 1984, 1991, 1992, Hungarian PEN Memorial Medal 1972, Soros Translation Award 1985, Queen's Gold Medal for Poetry 2000, Saltire Soc. and Scottish Arts Council Lifetime Achievement Award 2003. *Address:* 19 Whittingehame Court, Glasgow, G12 0BG, Scotland. *Website:* www.edwinmorgan.com.

MORGAN, Mihangel (see Morgan-Finch, Mihangel Ioan).

MORGAN, (Colin) Peter; poet and dramatist; b. 7 June 1939, Leigh, Lancashire, England. *Career:* Creative Writing for Northern Arts, Loughborough University, 1975–77. *Publications:* A Big Hat or What, 1968; Loss of Two Anchors, 1970; Poems for Shortie, 1973; The Grey Mare Being the Better Steed, 1973; I See You on My Arm, 1975; Ring Song, 1977; The Poet's Deaths, 1977; Alpha Beta, 1979; The Spring Collection, 1979; One Greek Alphabet, 1980; Reporting Back, 1983; A Winter Visitor, 1984; The Pete Morgan Poetry Pack, 1984. Plays: Still the Same Old Harry, 1972; All the Voices Going Away, 1979. Television Documentaries. *Honours:* Arts Council of Great Britain Award, 1973. *Address:* c/o Fordon Fraser Publications, Eastcotts Road, Bedford MK4Z 0JX, England.

MORGAN, Piers Stefan; British journalist; b. 30 March 1965, Guildford; m. Marion E. Shalloe 1991; three s. *Education:* Cumnor House Preparatory School, Chailey School, Sussex, Lewes Priory Sixth Form Coll. and Harlow Journalism Coll. *Career:* reporter, Surrey and S London newspapers 1987–89; Showbusiness Ed. The Sun 1989–94; Ed. The News of the World 1994–95, Daily Mirror (now The Mirror) 1995–2004. *Television:* presenter, The Importance of Being Famous (Channel 4) 2004. *Publications:* Private Lives of the Stars 1990, Secret Lives of the Stars 1991, Phillip Schofield, To Dream a Dream 1992, Take That, Our Story 1993, Take That: On the Road 1994. *Honours:* Atex Award for Nat. Newspaper Ed. of Year 1994, Newspaper of the Year Award, What the Papers Say 2001, GQ Ed. of the Year 2002, Newspaper of the Year, British Press Awards 2002. *Literary Agent:* William Morris Agency Inc., 52–53 Poland Street, London, W1F 7LX, England. *Telephone:* (20) 7534-6800. *Fax:* (20) 7534-6900.

MORGAN, Robert; Prof. of English, Poet and Writer; b. 3 Oct. 1944, Hendersonville, NC, USA; m. Nancy K. Bullock, 1965, one s. two d. *Education:* Emory College, Oxford, 1961–62; North Carolina State University, Raleigh, 1962–63; BA, University of North Carolina at Chapel Hill, 1965; MFA, University of North Carolina at Greensboro, 1968. *Career:* Instructor, Salem College, Winston-Salem, NC, 1968–69; Lecturer, 1971–73, Asst Prof., 1973–78, Assoc. Prof., 1978–84, Prof., 1984–92, Kappa Alpha Prof. of English, 1992–, Cornell University. *Publications:* Poetry: Zirconia Poems, 1969; The Voice in the Crosshairs, 1971; Red Owl, 1972; Land Diving, 1976; Trunk & Thicket, 1978; Groundwork, 1979; Bronze Age, 1981; At the Edge of the Orchard Country, 1987; Sigodlin, 1990; Green River: New and Selected Poems, 1991. Fiction: The Blue Valleys: A Collection of Stories, 1989; The Mountains Won't Remember Us and Other Stories, 1992; The Hinterlands: A Mountain Tale in Three Parts, 1994; The Truest Pleasure, 1995; Gap Creek, 1999; Topsoil Road, 2000; This Rock, 2001; Brave Enemies: A Novel of the American Revolution, 2003; New and Selected Poems, 2004. Non-Fiction: Good Measure: Essays, Interviews and Notes on Poetry, 1993. *Honours:* National Endowment for the Arts Fellowships, 1968, 1974, 1981, 1987; Southern Poetry Review Prize, 1975; Eunice Tietjins Award, 1979; Jacaranda Review Fiction Prize, 1988; Guggenheim Fellowship, 1988–89; Amon Liner Prize, 1989; James G. Hanes Poetry Prize, 1991; North Carolina Award in Literature, 1991; Southern Book Award, 2000. *Address:* c/o Dept of English, Goldwin Smith Hall, Cornell University, Ithaca, NY 14853, USA.

MORGAN, Robin (Evonne); Journalist, Ed., Writer and Poet; b. 29 Jan. 1941, Lake Worth, FL, USA; one c. *Education:* Columbia University. *Career:* Ed., Grove Press, 1967–70; Visiting Chair and Guest Prof., New College, Sarasota, FL, 1973; Ed. and Columnist, 1974–87, Ed.-in-Chief, 1989–93, Ms Magazine; Distinguished Visiting Scholar and Lecturer, Rutgers University, 1987; mem. Feminist Writers' Guild; Media Women; North American Feminist Coalition; Sisterhood is Global Institute, co-founder. *Publications:* Sisterhood is Powerful: An Anthology of Writings from the Women's Liberation Movement (ed.), 1970; Going Too Far: The Personal Chronicle of a Feminist, 1978; The Anatomy of Freedom: Feminism, Physics and Global Politics, 1982; Sisterhood is Global: The International Women's Movement Anthology (ed.), 1984; The Demon Lover: On the Sexuality of Terrorism, 1989; The Word of a Woman: Feminist Dispatches 1968–91, 1992. Fiction: Dry Your Smile: A Novel, 1987; The Mer-Child: A New Legend, 1991. Poetry: Monster, 1972; Lady of the Beasts, 1976; Death Benefits, 1981; Depth Perception: New Poems and a Masque, 1982; Upstairs in the Garden: Selected and New Poems, 1968–88, 1990. Plays: In Another Country, 1960; The Duel, 1979. Contributions: Magazines and periodicals. *Honours:* National Endowment for the Arts Grant, 1979–80; Yaddo Grant, 1980; Ford Foundation Grants, 1982, 1983, 1984; Feminist of the Year Award, Fund for a Feminist Majority, 1990.

MORGAN, Robin Richard; Journalist, Ed. and Writer; b. 16 Sept. 1953, Stourbridge, England; two s. one d. *Career:* Ed., Sunday Times Magazine, 1995–. *Publications:* The Falklands War (co-author), 1982; Bullion (co-author), 1983; Rainbow Warrior (co-author), 1986; Manpower (ed.), 1986; Ambush (co-author), 1988; Book of Movie Biographies (co-ed.), 1997. *Honours:* Campaigning Journalist of the Year, 1982, 1983. *Address:* c/o Sunday Times Magazine, 1 Pennington St, London E1 9XW, England.

MORGAN, Rozanne (see Gentle, Mary Rosalyn).

MORGAN-FINCH, Mihangel Ioan, (Mihangel Morgan); University Lecturer, Writer and Poet; b. 7 Dec. 1959, Aberdare, Wales. *Education:* BA, 1990, PhD, 1995, University of Wales. *Career:* mem. Gorsedd Beirdd; Ynys Prydain. *Publications:* Diflaniad Fy Fi, 1988; Beth Yw Rhif Ffon Duw, 1991; Hen Lwybr A Storiau Eraill, 1992; Saith Pechod Marwol, 1993; Dirgel Ddyn, 1993; Te Gyda'r Frenhines, 1994; Tair Ochr Geiniog, 1996. Contributions: several publications. *Honours:* Prose Medal, Eisteddfod, 1993. *Address:* Porth Ceri, Talybont, Aberystwyth, Dyfed, Wales.

MORIARTY, J. (see Kelly, Tim).

MORIARTY, Marilyn Frances, BA, MA, PhD; academic, writer and poet; b. 6 Jan. 1953, Fort Jackson, SC, USA. *Education:* University of Edinburgh, University of Florida, University of California at Irvine. *Career:* Instructor in Rhetoric and Composition, Saddleback Community College, Mission Viejo, CA, 1985–86; Fellow, University of California at Irvine, 1991, National Humanities Center, 1994; Asst Prof., 1992–98, Assoc. Prof. of English, 1998–, Hollins University, Roanoke, VA. *Publications:* Critical Architecture and Contemporary Culture (co-ed.), 1994; Writing Science Through Critical Thinking, 1997; Moses Unchained, 1998. Contributions: periodicals. *Honours:* First Place Award, University of Utah Novella Contest, 1987; Katherine Anne Porter Prize for Fiction, Arts and Humanities Council, Tulsa, 1990; Creative Non-Fiction Prize, Associated Writing Programs, 1996; Peregrine Prize for Short Fiction, Amberst Writers and Artists Press, 1997. *Address:* PO Box 9535, Hollins University, Roanoke, VA 24020, USA. *E-mail:* moriarty@hollins.edu.

MÖRING, Marcel; Novelist; b. 1957, Enschede, Holland. *Publications:* Mendels erfenis, 1990; Betaaldag, 1991; Het grote verlangen (The Great Longing), 1992; De Kotzker, 1993; Bederf is de weg van alle vlees (Decay is the Way of All Flesh, novella), 1994; Het derde testament, 1995; In Babylon, 1997; Nachtzwemmen, 1998; Modelvliegen, 2001. *Honours:* Geertjan Lubberhuizen Prize for Best Debut, 1990; AKO Prize, 1992; two Golden Owl awards, 1998. *Literary Agent:* AP Watt Ltd, 20 John St, London WC1N 2DR, England. *Website:* www.marcelmoring.com.

MORITZ, Albert Frank, BA, MA, PhD; poet and writer; b. 15 April 1947, Niles, OH, USA; m. Theresa Carrothers; one s. *Education:* Marquette University. *Career:* Northrop Frye Visiting Lecturer in Poetry, University of Toronto, 1993–94. *Publications:* Here, 1975; Signs and Certainties, 1979; Music and Exile, 1980; Black Orchid, 1981; The Pocket Canada (with Theresa Moritz), 1982; Canada Illustrated: The Art of Nineteenth-Century Engraving, 1982; Between the Root and the Flower, 1982; The Visitation, 1983; America the Picturesque: The Art of Nineteenth-Century Engraving, 1983; Stephen Leacock: A Biography (with Theresa Moritz), 1987; Song of Fear, 1992; The Ruined Cottage, 1993; Mahoning, 1994; Phantoms in the Ark, 1994. Contributions: periodicals. *Honours:* American Acad. of Arts and Letters Award, 1991; Guggenheim Fellowship, 1993; Ingram Merrill Foundation Fellowship, 1993–94.

MORLAND, Dick (see Hill, Reginald (Charles)).

MORLEY, Patricia Marlow; Writer and Educator; b. 25 May 1929, Toronto, Ontario, Canada; m. Lawrence W. Morley, divorced, three s., one d. *Education:* BA, English Language and Literature, University of Toronto, 1951; MA, English, Carleton University, 1967; PhD, English Literature, University of Ottawa, 1970. *Career:* Asst Prof. of English, 1972–75, Assoc. Prof., 1975–80, Fellow, 1979–89, Prof. of English and Canadian Studies, 1980–89, Lifetime Hon. Fellow, 1989–, Simone de Beauvoir Institute, Concordia University, Montréal; mem. Writer's Union of Canada. *Publications:* The Mystery of Unity: Theme and Technique in the Novels of Patrick White, 1972; The Immoral Moralists: Hugh MacLennan and Leonard Cohen, 1972; Robertson Davies: Profiles in Canadian Drama, 1977; The Comedians: Hugh Hood and Rudy Wiebe, 1977; Morley Callaghan, 1978; Kurelek: A Biography, 1986; Margaret Laurence: The Long Journey Home, 1991; As Though Life Mattered: Leo Kennedy's Story, 1994; The Mountain is Moving: Japanese Women's Lives, 1999. Contributions: Professional and mainstream journals. *Honours:* Ottawa-Carleton Literary Award, 1988; Hon. Doctor of Sacred Letters, Thorneloe College, Laurentian University, 1992.

MORLEY, Sheridan Robert; Journalist, Broadcaster and Writer; b. 5 Dec. 1941, Ascot, Berkshire, England; m. 1st Margaret Gudekjo, 18 July 1965, divorced 1990, one s. two d.; m. 2nd Ruth Leon, 1995. *Education:* MA, Merton College, Oxford, 1964. *Career:* Staff, ITN, 1964–67; Interviewer, Late Night Up, BBC2, 1967–73; Deputy Features Ed., 1973–75, Arts Diarist and Television Critic, 1989–90, The Times; Arts Ed., 1975–88,

Drama Critic, 1975–89, Punch; London Drama Critic, International Herald Tribune, 1979–; Drama Critic, Spectator, 1990–; Film Critic, Sunday Express, 1992–95; Arts presenter, BBC Radio 2; Regular radio and television appearances; Dir, Noel and Gertie, 1997, A Song at Twilight, 1999, Noel Coward Tonight, 2001, The Lodger, 2002; Deviser and dir, The Jermyn Street Revue, 2000; Co-host, The Coward Centenary Gala, Carnegie Hall, 1999; Host, New York Tribute to Sir John Gielgud, 2000; mem. Critics Circle. *Publications:* A Talent to Amuse: The Life of Noël Coward, 1969; Review Copies, 1975; Oscar Wilde, 1976; Sybil Thorndike, 1977; Marlene Dietrich, 1977; Gladys Cooper, 1979; Noel Coward and His Friends (with Cole Lesley and Graham Payn), 1979; The Stephen Sondheim Songbook, 1979; Gertrude Lawrence, 1981; The Noel Coward Diaries (ed. with Graham Payn), 1982; Tales from the Hollywood Raj, 1983; Shooting Stars, 1983; The Theatregoers' Quiz Book, 1983; Katharine Hepburn, 1984; The Other Side of the Moon, 1985; Bull's Eyes (ed.), 1985; Ingrid Bergman, 1985; The Great Stage Stars, 1986; Spread a Little Happiness, 1986; Out in the Midday Sun, 1988; Elizabeth Taylor, 1988; Odd Man Out: The Life of James Mason, 1989; Our Theatres in the Eighties, 1990; Methuen Book of Theatrical Short Stories (ed.), 1992; Robert My Father, 1993; Methuen Book of Movie Stories (ed.), 1993; Audrey Hepburn, 1993; Ginger Rogers, 1995; Faces of the 90s, 1995; Dirk Bogarde: Rank Outsider, 1996; Gene Kelly (with Ruth Leon), 1996; Marilyn Monroe (with Ruth Leon), 1997; Hey Mr Producer, The Musicals of Cameron Mackintosh (with Ruth Leon), 1998; Beyond the Rainbow: Judy Garland, 1999; Oberon Theatre Chronicle, 1999; A Century of Theatre, 2001; The Coward Companion, 2001; John Gielgud, 2001; Asking for Trouble, 2002. Stage: Spread a Little Happiness, London, 1996; Noel and Gertie, 1997. Contributions: newspapers and journals. *Honours:* BP Arts Journalist of the Year, 1990. *Address:* 7 Ivory Sq., Plantation Wharf, London SW11 3UF, England.

MORPURGO, Michael, MBE; British children's author; b. 5 Oct. 1943, St Albans, Hertfordshire; m. Clare Morpurgo. *Career:* co-f., Farms for City Children project; Children's Laureate 2003–05. *Publications include:* Beyond the Rainbow Warrior, Billy the Kid, Black Queen, Colly's Barn, Conker, Dear Olly, Escape from Shangri-La, Farm Boy, Friend or Foe, From Hearabout Hill, Grania O'Malley, Joan of Arc, Kensuke's Kingdom, King of the Cloud Forests, Long Way Home, Marble Crusher, Mr Nobody's Eyes, My Friend Walter, Out of the Ashes, Red Eyes at Night, Sam's Duck, Snakes and Ladders, The Butterfly Lion, The Nine Lives of Montezuma, The Rainbow Bear, The Sleeping Sword, The War of Jenkins' Ear, The White Horse of Zennor, The Wreck of the Zanzibar, Toro! Toro!, Twist of Gold, Waiting for Anya, War Horse, Wartman, Who's a Big Bully Then?, Why the Whales Came, Wombat Goes Walkabout, The Last Wolf 2002, Private Peaceful 2003. *Honours:* Whitbread Children's Book Award 1995, Smarties Book Prize 1996, Bronze Prize in 6–8 years group 2003, Children's Book Awards 1996, 2000, 2002. *Address:* Farms for City Children, Nethercott House, Iddesleigh, Winkleigh, Devon EX19 8BG, England.

MORRALL, Clare; writer and music teacher; b. 1952, Exeter, England; two c. *Publications:* Astonishing Splashes of Colour 2003. *Literary Agent:* The Marsh Agency, 11 Dover Street, London, W1S 4LJ, England. *Telephone:* (20) 7399-2800. *Fax:* (20) 7399-2801. *Website:* www.marsh-agency.co.uk. *Address:* c/o Tindal Street Press, 217 The Custard Factory, Gibb Street, Birmingham B9 4AA, England.

MORRELL, David; Author; b. 24 April 1943, Kitchener, Ontario, Canada; m. Donna Maziarz 10 Oct. 1965; one s. (deceased) one d. *Education:* BA, University of Waterloo, 1966; MA, 1967, PhD, 1970, Pennsylvania State University. *Career:* Asst Prof., 1970–74, Assoc. Prof., 1974–77, Prof. of American Literature, 1977–86, University of Iowa; mem. Horror Writers of America; Writers Guild of America. *Publications:* Fiction: First Blood, 1972; Testament, 1975; Last Reveille, 1977; The Totem, 1979; Blood Oath, 1982; The Hundred-Year Christmas, 1983; The Brotherhood of the Rose, 1984; Rambo: First Blood, Part II, 1985; The Fraternity of the Stone, 1985; The League of Night and Fog, 1987; Rambo III, 1988; The Fifth Profession, 1990; The Covenant of the Flame, 1991; Assumed Identity, 1993; Desperate Measures, 1994; Extreme Denial, 1996; Double Image, 1998. Non-Fiction: John Barth: An Introduction, 1976; Fireflies, 1988. Contributions: journals and magazines. *Honours:* Distinguished Recognition Award, Friends of American Writers, 1972; Best Novella Awards, Horror Writers of America, 1989, 1991. *Address:* c/o Henry Morrison, PO Box 235, Beford Hills, NY 10507, USA.

MORRILL, John Stephen; Prof. of British and Irish History and Writer; b. 12 June 1946, Manchester, England; m. Frances Mead, 1968, four d. *Education:* BA, 1967, MA, DPhil, 1971, Trinity College, Oxford. *Career:* Keasby Lecturer in History, 1970–71, Junior Research Fellow, 1971–74, Trinity College, Oxford; College Lecturer in History, St Catherine's College, Oxford, 1973–74; Lecturer in Modern History, University of Stirling, 1974–75; Dir of Studies in History, 1975–91, Fellow, 1975–, Tutor, 1979–91, Admissions Tutor, 1983–87, Senior Tutor, 1987–91, Vice-Master, 1994–, Selwyn College, Cambridge; Asst Lecturer and Lecturer, 1975–92, Reader in Early Modern History, 1992–98, Prof. of British and Modern Irish History, 1998–, University of Cambridge; Ordained Permanent Deacon, Roman Catholic Church, 1996; mem. Fellow, British Acad., 1995; FRHistS, 1977. *Publications:* Cheshire 1630–1660, 1974; The Revolt of the Provinces 1630–1650, 1976; The Cheshire Grand Jury 1625–1659, 1976; The Civil Wars and Interregnum: Sources for Local Historians (with G. E. Aylmer), 1979; Seventeenth-Century Britain, 1980; Reactions to the English Civil War (ed.), 1982; Land Men and Beliefs (ed.), 1985; Charles I, 1989; Oliver Cromwell and the English Revolution, 1990; The National Covenant in its British Context (ed.), 1990; The Impact of the English Civil War (ed.), 1991; Revolution and Restoration (ed.), 1992; The Nature of the English Revolution, 1993; Public Men and Private Conscience in Seventeenth-Century England (with P. Slack and D. Woolf), 1993; The Oxford Illustrated History of Tudor and Stuart Britain (ed.), 1996; The British Problem 1534–1707: State Formation in the Atlantic Archipelago (with B. Bradshaw), 1996; Revolt in the Provinces: The English People and the Tragedies of War, 1998; Soldiers and Statesmen of the English Revolution (co-author), 1998. Contributions: scholarly books and journals. *Address:* c/o Selwyn College, Cambridge CB3 9DQ England.

MORRIS, Desmond John; Zoologist; b. 24 Jan. 1928, Purton, Wiltshire, England; m. Ramona Baulch, 30 July 1952, one s. *Education:* BSc, Birmingham University, 1951; DPhil, University of Oxford, 1954. *Career:* mem. Scientific Fellow, Zoological Society of London. *Publications:* The Biology of Art, 1962; The Big Cats, 1965; Zootime, 1966; The Naked Ape, 1967; The Human Zoo, 1969; Patterns of Reproductive Behaviour, 1970; Intimate Behaviour, 1971; Manwatching, 1977; Animal Days, 1979; The Soccer Tribe, 1981; Bodywatching: A Field Guide to the Human Species, 1985; Catwatching, 1986; Dogwatching, 1986; Catlore, 1987; The Human Nestbuilders, 1988; The Animal Contract, 1990; Animal-Watching, 1990; Babywatching, 1991; Christmas Watching, 1992; The World of Animals, 1993; The Naked Ape Trilogy, 1994; The Human Animal, 1994; The World Guide to Gestures, 1994; Bodytalk: A World Guide to Gestures, 1994; Catworld: A Feline Encyclopedia, 1996; The Human Sexes: A Natural History of Man and Woman, 1997; Illustrated Horsewatching, 1998; Cool Cats: The 100 Cat Breeds of the World, 1999; Body Guards: Protective Amulets and Charms, 1999; The Naked Ape and Cosmetic Behaviour (with Kaori Ishida), 1999; The Naked Eye, 2000; Dogs: A Dictionary of Dog Breeds, 2001; Peoplewatching, 2002. Contributions: many journals and magazines. *Honours:* Hon. DSc, Reading University, 1998. *Address:* c/o Jonathan Cape, Random Century House, 20 Vauxhall Bridge Rd, London SW1V 2SA, England. *Website:* www.desmond-morris.com.

MORRIS, Edmund; American writer; b. 27 May 1940, Nairobi, Kenya. *Education:* Rhodes Univ. *Publications:* The Rise of Theodore Roosevelt (Pulitzer Prize in Biography 1980) 1979, Dutch: A Memoir of Ronald Reagan 1999, Theodore Rex 2001. *Address:* 222 Central Park S, New York, NY 10019, USA.

MORRIS, Jan, (James Morris), BA, MA, FRSL; Welsh writer; b. 2 Oct. 1926, Clevedon, Somerset, England. *Education:* Christ Church Coll., Oxford. *Career:* mem. Yr Academi Gymreig. *Publications:* as James Morris: Coast to Coast (US edn as I Saw the USA), 1956; The Market of Seleukia (US edn as Islam Inflamed: A Middle East Picture), 1957; Sultan in Oman, 1957; Coronation Everest, 1958; South African Winter, 1958; The Hashemite Kings, 1959; Venice, 1960; South America, 1961; The World Bank: A Prospect (US edn as The Road to Huddersfield: A Journey to Five Continents), 1963; Cities, 1963; The Outriders: A Liberal View of Britain, 1963; The Presence of Spain, 1964; Oxford, 1965; Pax Britannica: The Climax of an Empire, 1968; The Great Port: A Passage through New York, 1969; Places, 1972; Heaven's Command: An Imperial Progress, 1973; Farewell the Trumpets: An Imperial Retreat, 1978. As Jan Morris: Conundrum (autobiog.), 1974; Travels, 1976; The Oxford Book of Oxford (ed.), 1978; Destinations: Essays from 'Rolling Stone', 1980; The Venetian Empire: A Sea Voyage, 1980; The Spectacle of Empire, 1982; A Venetian Bestiary, 1982; Stones of Empire: The Buildings of the Raj, 1984; Among the Cities, 1985; Journeys, 1985; Last Letters from Hav: Notes from a Lost City, 1985; The Matter of Wales: Epic Views of a Small Country, 1985; Scotland: The Place of Visions, 1986; Manhattan, '45, 1987; Hong Kong: Xianggang, 1988; Pleasures of a Tangled Life (autobiog.), 1989; Ireland: Your Only Place, 1990; City to City, 1990; Sydney, 1992; Locations, 1993; A Machynlleth Triad, 1994; Fisher's Face, 1995; The Princeship of Wales, 1995; The World of Venice, 1995; 50 Years of Europe, 1997; Hong Kong: Epilogue to an Empire, 1997; Lincoln: A Foreigner's Quest, 2000; A Writer's World: Travels 1950–2000, 2003. *Honours:* Commonwealth Fund Fellow, 1953; Cafe Royal Prize, 1957; George Polk Memorial Award, 1960; Heinemann Award, RSL, 1961; Hon. Fellow, Royal Institute of British Architects, 1998; Hon. doctorates, University of Wales, University of Glamorgan. *Literary Agent:* AP Watt Ltd, 20 John Street, London, WC1N 2DR, England. *Address:* Trefan Morys, Llanystumdwy, Cricieth, Gwynedd LL52 0LP, Wales.

MORRIS, Janet Ellen, (Casey Prescott, Daniel Stryker); Writer; b. 25 May 1946, Boston, Massachusetts, USA; m. 31 Oct. 1970. *Career:* mem. SFWA; MWA; New York Acad. of Science; National Intelligence Study Center; Asscn of Old Crows. *Publications:* Silistra Quartet, 1976–78, 1983–84; Dream Dance Trilogy, 1980–83; I the Sun, 1984; Heroes in Hell, 10 vols, 1984–88; Beyond Sanctuary, 3 vols, 1985–86; Warlord, 1986; The Little Helliad, 1986; Outpassage, 1987; Kill Ratio, 1987; City at the Edge of Time, 1988; Tempus Vabound, 1989; Target (with David Drake), 1989; Warrior's Edge, 1990; Threshold, 1991; Trust Territory, 1992; American Warrior, 1992; The Stalk, 1994. Contributions: various publications. *Honours:* Hellva Award for Best Novel, 1985. *Literary Agent:* Curtis Brown Ltd, 10 Astor Pl., New York, NY 10003, USA.

MORRIS, Mark, BA; British writer; b. 15 June 1963, Bolsover, Derbyshire, England; m. Nel Whatmore 1990; one s. one d. *Education:* Trinity and All Saints Coll., Horsforth, Leeds. *Career:* mem. British Fantasy Soc. *Publications:* fiction: Toady 1989, Stitch 1991, The Immaculate 1992, The Secret of Anatomy 1994, Close to the Bone (short stories) 1995, Mr Bad Face 1996, Longbarrow 1997, Doctor Who: The Bodysnatchers 1997, Genesis 1999, Doctor Who: Deep Blue 1999, Fiddleback (as J. M. Morris) 2002; contrib. to Fear, Interzone, Million, SFX, The Third Alternative, The Dark Side, Me, Skeleton Crew, Beyond. *Literary Agent:* PFD, Drury House, 34–43 Russell Street, London, WC2B 5HA, England.

MORRIS, Mary, BA, MA, MPhil; American writer; b. 14 May 1947, Chicago, IL; m. Larry O'Connor 1989, one d. *Education:* Tufts College, Columbia Univ. *Career:* teacher, Princeton Univ. 1980–87, 1991–94, New York Univ. 1988–94, Sarah Lawrence Coll. 1994; mem. American PEN, Authors' Guild, Friends of the American Acad. in Rome. *Publications:* Nothing to Declare: Memoirs of a Woman Travelling Alone 1989, Wall to Wall: From Beijing to Berlin by Rail 1992, A Mother's Love 1993, Maiden Voyages 1993, House Arrest 1996, The Lifeguard 1997, Angels and Aliens 1998, Acts of God 2000; contrib. to periodicals. *Honours:* Rome Prize, Guggenheim Fellowship. *Literary Agent:* Ellen Levine, Trident Media Group, 41 Madison Avenue, New York, NY 10010, USA. *E-mail:* mmorris348@yahoo.com. *Website:* www .marymorris.net.

MORRIS, Mary (Joan) McGarry; Writer; b. 1943, Meriden, CT, USA; m. Michael Morris, 1962, one s., four d. *Education:* University of Vermont, 1960–62; University of Massachusetts, 1962–63. *Publications:* Vanished, 1988; A Dangerous Woman, 1991; Songs in Ordinary Time, 1995; Fiona Range, 2000. Contributions: periodicals. *Address:* c/o Naggar Literary Agency, 216 E 75th St, New York, NY 10021, USA.

MORRIS, Sara (see Burke, John Frederick).

MORRIS, Stephen; Artist, Poet and Writer; b. 14 Aug. 1935, Smethwick, England; m. 31 Aug. 1963, divorced 1 Jan. 1989, one s. two d. *Education:* Moseley Art School, 1950–53; Fircroft College, 1958–59; Marie Borgs Folk High School, 1959–60; Cardiff University, 1960–63; Leicester University, 1965–66. *Career:* Asst Lecturer, 1967–69, Lecturer, 1969–72, Senior Lecturer, 1972–86, Wolverhampton University; 50 one-man painting exhibitions. *Publications:* Poetry: The Revolutionary, 1972; The Kingfisher Catcher, 1974; Death of a Clown, 1976; The Moment of Truth, 1978; Too Long at the Circus, 1980; Rolling Dice, 1986; To Forgive the Unforgivable, 1997; Twelve, 1998. Other: Lord of Death (play), 1963. Contributions: Guardian; Observer; Peace News; Rolling Stone; Sunday Times; Tribune. *Honours:* elected to be a Companion of the Guild of St George, 2001. *Address:* 4 Rue Las Cours, Aspiran, L'Herault 34800, France.

MORRIS, Vera (see Kelly, Tim).

MORRISON, Anthony James, (Tony Morrison); Television Producer and Writer; b. 5 July 1936, Gosport, England; m. Elizabeth Marion Davies, 30 July 1965, one s. one d. *Education:* BSc, University of Bristol, 1959. *Career:* Partner, South American Pictures; Dir, Nonesuch Expeditions Ltd. *Publications:* Steps to a Fortune (co-author), 1967; Animal Migration, 1973; Land Above the Clouds, 1974; The Andes, 1976; Pathways to the Gods, 1978; Lizzie: A Victorian Lady's Amazon Adventure (co-ed.), 1985; The Mystery of the Nasca Lines, 1987; Margaret Mee: In Search of Flowers of the Amazon (ed.), 1988; QOSQO: Navel of the World, 1995. *Address:* 48 Station Rd, Woodbridge, Suffolk IP12 4AT, England.

MORRISON, Bill; Playwright and Theatre Dir; b. 22 Jan. 1940, Ballymoney, Northern Ireland; Divorced, one s. one d. *Education:* LLB, Queen's University, Belfast, 1962. *Career:* Resident Playwright, Victoria Theatre, Stoke-on-Trent, 1968–71, Everyman Theatre, Liverpool, 1976–79; Assoc. Dir, 1981–83, Artistic Dir, 1983–85, Liverpool Playhouse. *Publications:* Stage Plays: Patrick's Day, 1971; Flying Blind, 1979; Scrap, 1982; Cavern of Dreams (with Carol Ann Duffy), 1984; Be Bop a Lula, 1988; A Love Song for Ulster, 1993; Drive On, 1996. Radio and Stage Plays: Sam Slade is Missing, 1971; The Love of Lady Margaret, 1972; Ellen Cassidy, 1975; The Emperor of Ice Cream, 1977; Blues in a Flat, 1989; The Little Sister, 1990. Radio Plays: The Great Gun-Running Episode, 1973; Simpson and Son, 1977; Maguire, 1978; The Spring of Memory, 1981; Affair, 1991; Three Steps to Heaven, 1992; Waiting for Lefty, 1994; Murder at the Cameo, 1996. Television Plays: McKinley and Sarah, 1974; Joggers, 1979; Potatohead Blues, 1980; Shergar, 1986; A Safe House, 1990; Force of Duty, 1992; C'mon Everybody, 1996; A Love Song for Ulster, 1999. *Honours:* Best Programme, Rye Radio Awards, 1981. *Literary Agent:* Alan Brodie Representation, 211 Piccadilly, London W1J 9HF, England.

MORRISON, (Philip) Blake, BA, MA, PhD, FRSL; British author, poet and dramatist; b. 8 Oct. 1950, Burnley, Lancashire, England; m. Katherine Ann Drake 1976; two s. one d. *Education:* Univ. of Nottingham, McMaster Univ., Univ. Coll. London. *Career:* Poetry and Fiction Ed. TLS 1978–81; Deputy Literary Ed. 1981–86, Literary Ed. 1987–89, The Observer; Literary Ed., The Independent on Sunday 1990–94; Prof. of Creative Writing, Goldsmiths Coll., London 2003–. *Publications:* The Movement: English Poetry and Fiction of the 1950s 1980, Seamus Heaney 1982, Penguin Book of Contemporary British Poetry (ed. with Andrew Motion) 1982, Dark Glasses (poems) 1984, The Ballad of the Yorkshire Ripper and Other Poems 1987, The Yellow House (juvenile) 1987, And When Did You Last See Your Father? (memoir) 1993, The Cracked Pot: A Play, after Heinrich von Kleist 1996, As If: A Crime, a Trial, a Question of Childhood 1997, Too True (essays and stories) 1998, Dr Ox's Experiment (libretto) 1998, Selected Poems 1999, The Justification of Johann Gutenberg (novel) 2000, Things My Mother Never Told Me (memoir) 2002. *Honours:* Eric Gregory Award 1980, Somerset Maugham Award 1984, Dylan Thomas Prize 1985, E. M. Forster Award 1988, J. R. Ackerley Prize 1994. *Address:* 54 Blackheath Park, London, SE3 9SJ, England.

MORRISON, Dorothy Jean Allison; Author and Lecturer; b. 17 Feb. 1933, Glasgow, Scotland; m. James F. T. Morrison, 12 April 1955, one s. one d. *Education:* MA, University of Glasgow. *Career:* Principal Teacher of History, Montrose Acad., 1968–73; Lecturer in History, Dundee College of Education, 1973–83; Adviser to Scottish History series, History at Hand series, Scotland's War series, Scottish TV; mem. Church and Nation Committee, Church of Scotland, 1996–; Netherbow Council for the Arts, Church of Scotland, 2000. *Publications:* Old Age, 1972; Young People, 1973; Health and Hospitals, 1973; The Civilian War (with M. Cuthbert), 1975; Travelling in China, 1977; The Romans in Britain, 1978; Billy Leaves Home, 1979; Story of Scotland (with J. Halliday), I, 1979, 1980, II, 1982; The Great War, 1914–18, 1981; Historical Sources for Schools, I Agriculture, 1982; History Around You, 1983; People of Scotland, I, 1983, II, 1985; Ancient Greeks (with John Morrison), 1984; Handbook on Money Management, 1985; Modern China, 1987; The Rise of Modern China, 1988; Montrose Old Church – A History, 1991; Scotland's War, 1992; A Sense of History – Castles, 1994; Ancient Scotland, 1996; The Wars of Independence, 1996; Changed Days in Montrose (with Isobel Reynolds), 1999; The Lifeboat: 200 Years of Service, 2000; Rural Schools in Angus (with Isobel Reynolds), 2003. *Address:* Craigview House, Usan, Montrose, Angus DD10 9SD, Scotland.

MORRISON, Robert Hay; Poet, Writer and Trans; b. 11 May 1915, South Yarra, Melbourne, Australia; m. Anna Dorothea Booth, 20 Sept. 1939, one s. one d. *Publications:* Lyrics from Pushkin, 1951; Lyric Images, 1954; A Book of South Australian Verse, 1957; Opus 4, 1971; Australia's Russian Poets, 1971; Some Poems of Verlaine, 1972; Australia's Ukrainian Poets, 1973; Leaf-fall, 1974; America's Russian Poets, 1975; Australia's Italian Poets, 1976; In the Ear of Dusk, 1977; The Secret Greenness and Other Poems, 1978; One Hundred Russian Poems, 1979; Ancient Chinese Odes, 1979; Sonnets from the Spanish, 1980; For the Weeks of the Year, 1981; Poems for an Exhibition, 1985; Poems from My Eight Lives, 1989; Poems from Mandelstam, 1990; All I Have is a Fountain, 1995; The Voice of the Hands, 1997. Contributions: newspapers, reviews, and journals. *Honours:* Prize, International Haiku Contest, 1990; Roberts Memorial Prize, USA, 1994. *Address:* 6 Bradfield St, Burnside, SA 5066, Australia.

MORRISON, Sally; Writer; b. 29 June 1946, Sydney, NSW, Australia; one s. *Education:* BSc, Australian National University, 1970. *Career:* mem. Fellowship of Australian Writers; Australian Society of Authors; Victorian Writers Centre. *Publications:* Who's Taking You to the Dance? (novel), 1979; I Am a Boat (short stories), 1989; Mad Meg (novel), 1994. Contributions: Bulletin; Australian Literary Supplement; Overland; Quadrant; Island; Sydney Morning Herald; Age Monthly Review. *Honours:* Project Assistance Grants, Victorian Ministry of the Arts, 1988, 1993, 1994; Writer's Grants, Australia Council Literary Board, 1990, 1991, 1992; National Book Council Banjo Award for Fiction, 1995. *Address:* c/o Margaret Connolly and Assocs, PO Box 495, Wahroonga, NSW 2021, Australia.

MORRISON, Toni (Chloe Anthony Wofford), MA; American novelist; b. 18 Feb. 1931, Lorain, Ohio; m. Harold Morrison 1958 (divorced 1964); two c. *Education:* Lorain High School, Howard Univ., Cornell Univ. *Career:* taught English and Humanities, Tex. Southern Univ. 1955–57, Howard Univ. 1957–64; Ed., then Sr Ed.Random House, New York 1965–85; Assoc. Prof. of English, State Univ. of New York 1971–72, Schweitzer Prof. of the Humanities 1984–89; Robert F. Goheen Prof. of the Humanities, Princeton Univ. 1989–; Visiting Lecturer Yale Univ. 1976–77, Bard Coll. 1986–88; Clark Lecturer Trinity Cambridge 1990; Massey Lecturer Harvard Univ. 1990; mem. Council, Authors Guild, American Acad. of Arts and Sciences, American Acad. of Arts and Letters, Authors League of America, Nat. Council on the Arts. *Publications:* The Bluest Eye 1970, Sula 1974, The Black Book (ed) 1974, Song of Solomon 1977, Tar Baby 1983, Dreaming Emmett (play) 1986, Beloved 1987 (Pulitzer Prize and Robert F. Kennedy Book Award 1988), Jazz 1992, Playing in the Dark: Whiteness and the Literary Imagination (lectures) 1992, Race-ing Justice, En-gendering Power (ed, essays) 1992, Honey and Rue (song cycle) 1993, Nobel Prize Speech 1994, Birth of a Nation'hood: Gaze, Script and Spectacle in the O. J. Simpson Trial 1997, Paradise 1998, Collected Essays of James Baldwin (ed) 1998, Love 2003; co-author, for children: The Big Box (poems) 1999, The Book of Mean People 2002, The Ant or the Grasshopper, The Lion or the Mouse 2003. *Honours:* Commdr Ordre des Arts et des Lettres; Ohioana Book Award 1975, American Acad. and Inst. of Arts and Letters Award 1977, Nat. Book Critics Circle Awards 1977, 1997, NY State Gov.'s Arts Award 1987, Nobel Prize for Literature 1993, Nat. Book Foundation Medal 1995, Nat. Medal of Arts 2000. *Literary Agent:* Suzanne Gluck, International Creative Management, 40 57th Street West, New York, NY 10019, USA. *Address:* Princeton University, Writing Program, 185 Nassau Street, Princeton, NJ 08544, USA.

MORRISON, Tony (see Morrison, Anthony James).

MORTIMER, Sir John Clifford; barrister, playwright and novelist; b. 21 April 1923, London, England; m. 1st Penelope Ruth Fletcher; one s. one d.; m. 2nd Penelope Gollop; two d. *Education:* Brasenose Coll., Oxford. *Career:* called to the Bar, 1948; Queen's Council, 1966; Master of the Bench, Inner Temple, 1975; mem. Howard League for Penal Reform, pres., 1991–; Royal Court Theatre, chair., 1990–2002; RSL, chair., 1989–97. *Publications:* Charade, 1947; Rumming Park, 1948; Answer Yes or No, 1950; Like Men Betrayed, 1953; Three Winters, 1956; The Narrowing Stream, 1958; Will Shakespeare, 1977; Rumpole of the Bailey, 1978; The Trials of Rumpole, 1979; Rumpole's Return, 1981; Clinging to the Wreckage (autobiog.), 1982; In Character, 1983; Rumpole and the Golden Thread, 1983; Rumpole's Last Case, 1986; Paradise Postponed, 1986; Character Parts (interviews), 1986; Summer's Lease, 1988; Rumpole and the Age of Miracles, 1988; Titmuss Regained, 1989; Rumpole à la Carte, 1990; Rumpole on Trial, 1992; Dunster, 1992; Murders and Other Friends (autobiog.), 1993; Rumpole and the Angel of Death, 1996; Felix in the Underworld, 1997; The Sound of Trumpets, 1998; The Summer of a Doormouse (autobiog.), 2000; Rumpole and the Primrose Path (short stories), 2002; Where There's a Will, 2003; Rumpole and the Penge Bungalow Murders 2004. Plays: The Dock Brief and Other Plays, 1959; The Wrong Side of the Park, 1960; Two Stars for Comfort, 1962; The Judge, 1967; Come As You Are, 1970; A Voyage Round My Father, 1972; The Bells of Hell, 1977; Naked Justice, 2001. Film Scripts: John and Mary, 1970; Edwin, 1984. Television Series: Rumpole of the Bailey, 9 series; Brideshead Revisited, 1981; Unity Mitford, 1981; The Ebony Tower, 1984; Paradise Postponed, 1986; Summer Lease, 1989; Titmus Regained, 1991; Under the Hammer, 1993. Contributions: various periodicals. *Honours:* Italia Prize, 1958; British Acad. Writers Award, 1979; Writer of the Year, BAFTA, 1980; Book of the Year, Yorkshire Post, 1982; Hon. doctorates. *Literary Agent:* PFD, Drury House, 34–43 Russell Street, London, WC2B 5HA, England.

MORTON, Colin Todd; Novelist, Poet and Ed.; b. 26 July 1948, Toronto, ON, Canada; m. Mary Lee Bragg, 30 Aug. 1969, one s. *Education:* BA, Univ. of Calgary, 1970; MA, English, Univ. of Alberta, 1979. *Career:* Creative Writing Instructor, Algonquin College, 1993–94; Writer-in-Residence, Concordia College, 1995–96, Connecticut College, 1997; mem. League of Canadian Poets, Vice-Pres., 2000–01. *Publications:* Poetry: In Transit, 1981; This Won't Last Forever, 1985; Word/Music (cassette with First Draft), 1986; North/South (with A. McClure and S. McMaster), 1987; The Merzbook: Kurt Schwitters Poems, 1987; Two Decades: From A Century of Inventions, 1987; Primiti Too Taa (poetry film), 1987; How to Be Born Again, 1992; Coastlines of the Archipelago, 2000. Novel: Oceans Apart, 1995. Contributions: reviews and journals; anthologies incl.: Capital Poets, 1989; In the Clear, 1998; Vintage '94, 1995. *Honours:* CBC Radio Literary Competition, third prize, 1984; Archibald Lampman Award, 1986; ASIFA East Film Festival, New York, best soundtrack, 1988; National Educational Film and Video Festival, bronze apple, 1988; Short Grain Contest, second prizes, prose poem, 1989, postcard fiction, 1990; Jane Jordan Poetry Contest, third prize, 1991; Nepean Library Short Story Contest, second prize, 1993; Archibald Lampman Award for Poetry, 2001. *Address:* 40 Grove Ave, Ottawa, ON K1S 3A6, Canada. *E-mail:* cmorton@sympatico.ca. *Website:* www3.sympatico.ca/cmorton.

MORTON, Frederic; Author; b. 5 Oct. 1924, Vienna, Austria; m. Marcia Colman, 28 March 1957, one d. *Education:* BS, College of the City of New York, 1947; MA, New School for Social Research, New York City. *Career:* mem. Authors' Guild; PEN Club. *Publications:* The Rothschilds, 1962; A Nervous Splendour, 1978; The Forever Street, 1987; Thunder at Twilight, 1991. Contributions: newspapers and journals. *Literary Agent:* Lantz Office Ltd, 200 W 57th St, Suite 503, New York, NY 10019, USA.

MORTON, G. L. (see Fryer, Jonathan).

MORTON, Henry Albert, (Harry Morton); retd academic and writer; b. 20 July 1925, Gladstone, MB, Canada. *Education:* BA, BEd, University of Manitoba; MA, University of Cambridge; PhD, University of Otago, New Zealand. *Career:* mem. Blenheim Club; New Zealand Society of Authors; Royal New Zealand Airforce Asscn. *Publications:* And Now New Zealand, 1969; The Wind Commands, 1975; Which Way New Zealand, 1975; Why Not Together?, 1978; The Whale's Wake, 1982; The Farthest Corner, 1988. *Honours:* Sir James Wattie Award, Book of the Year, 1976. *Address:* 55B Brooklyn Drive, Blenheim, Marlborough, New Zealand.

MOSEROVÁ, Jaroslava, MD, PhD, DSc; Czech politician, international organization official, plastic surgeon (burns specialist) and writer; *Senator*; b. 17 Jan. 1930, Prague; m. Milan David; one s. *Education:* Warren Coll., Swannanoe, NC, Arts Students League, NY, Charles Univ., Prague. *Career:* house surgeon Surgical Dept, Duchcov 1955–60; specialist Burns Centre, Charles Univ. 1960–65, Head of Research 1965–90; mem. Czech Nat. Council 1990–91; Amb. to Australia and New Zealand 1991–93; Sec.-Gen. Czech Comm. for UNESCO 1993–95, mem. UNESCO Exec. 1995–99, Pres. Gen. Conf. 1999–2001; elected mem. Parl. Senate of Czech Repub. 1996–, Vice-Pres. 1997; first woman candidate for Pres. 2003; has also written films and plays, illustrated children's books and translated English literature texts; mem. PEN Int., Rotary Int., Czech Writers' Asscn, Czech Translators' Asscn, Czech Fine Arts Asscn, Olga Havel's Good Will Foundation, Prague School of Fine Arts. *Films:* (screenplays) Killing with Kindness, Double Role. *Radio Plays:* Such a Nice Boy, A Letter to Wollongong. *Publications:* The Atlas of Plastic Surgery, The Healing and Treatment of Skin Defects; Historky (short stories) 2003; translations of over 50 works, including novels by Dick Francis, Jacob Bronowski and John Mortimer. *Honours:* Europe Integration Prize, Hungary, Med. Acad. Medal, Poland, Charles Univ. Med. School Gold Medal, UNESCO Gold Medal. *Address:* Parliamentary Senate of the Czech Republic, Valdštejnské nám. Č. 4, 118 01 Prague 1 (Office); Pošta Làzně Bohdaneč, 53341 Prague 43, Czech Republic (Home). *Telephone:* (2) 57072375 (Office). *Fax:* (2) 57534500 (Office). *E-mail:* moserovaj@senat.cz (Office). *Website:* www.moserova.cz (Office).

MOSES, Daniel (David); Writer, Dramatist and Poet; b. 18 Feb. 1952, Ohsweken, Ontario, Canada. *Education:* BA, York University, 1975; MFA, University of British Columbia, 1977. *Career:* Instructor in Creative Writing, University of British Columbia, 1990; Instructor in Playwrighting, Graduate Drama Centre, University of Toronto, 1992; Resident Artist, Banff Centre for the Arts, 1993; Writer-in-Residence, University of Western Ontario, 1994, University of Windsor, 1995–96; mem. League of Canadian Poets; Playwrights Union of Canada; Writers' Guild of Canada; Writers' Union of Canada. *Publications:* Plays: The Dreaming Beauty, 1989; Coyote City, 1991; Almighty Voice and His Wife, 1992; The Indian Medicine Shows, 1995. Poetry: Delicate Bodies, 1980; The White Line. Other: An Anthology of Canadian Native Literature in English (co-ed.), 1992. *Honours:* First Prize, Theatre Canada National Playwrighting Competition, 1990; Winner, New Play Centre Playwrighting Competition, 1994. *Address:* 1 Browning Ave, No. 4, Toronto, ON M4K 1V6, Canada.

MOSLEY, Nicholas, (Lord Ravensdale); Author; b. 25 June 1923, London, England; m., five c. *Education:* Balliol College, Oxford, 1946–47. *Publications:* Spaces of the Dark, 1951; The Rainbearers, 1955; Corruption, 1957; African Switchback, 1958; The Life of Raymond Raynes, 1961; Meeting Place, 1962; Accident, 1965; Experience and Religion: A Lay Essay in Theology, 1965; Assassins, 1966; Impossible Object, 1968, screenplay, 1975; Natalie, Natalia, 1971; The Assassination of Trotsky, 1972, screenplay, 1973; Julian Grenfell: His Life and the Times of His Death 1988–1915, 1976; Catastrophe Practice, 1979; Imago Bird, 1980; Serpent, 1981; Rules of the Game: Sir Oswald and Lady Cynthia Mosley 1896–1933, 1982; Beyond the Pale: Sir Oswald Mosley and Family 1933–1980, 1983; Judith, 1986; Hopeful Monsters, 1990; Efforts at Truth, 1994; Children of Darkness and Light, 1996; The Hesperides Tree, 2001; Inventing God, 2003. *Honours:* Whitbread Prize, 1990. *Address:* 2 Gloucester Crescent, London NW1 7DS, England.

MOSLEY, Walter; American writer; b. 1952, Los Angeles; m. Joy Kellman 1987 (divorced). *Education:* Goddard Coll., Johnson State Coll., City Coll. CUNY. *Career:* Artist-in-Residence Africana Studies Inst., NY Univ. 1996; mem. Bd of Dirs Nat. Book Awards, Poetry Soc. of America; past Pres. MWA. *Publications include:* Devil in a Blue Dress (Shamus Award) 1990, A Red Death 1991, White Butterfly 1992, Black Betty 1994, RL's Dream 1995, A Little Yellow Dog 1996, Gone Fishin' 1997, Always Outnumbered, Always Outgunned 1997, Blue Light 1998, Walkin' the Dog 1999, Fearless Jones 2001, Futureland: Nine Stories of an Imminent Future 2001, Bad Boy Brawly Brown 2002, Fear Itself 2003, Six Easy Pieces (short stories) 2003, What Next: An African American Initiative Toward World Peace 2003, The Man in My Basement 2004; contribs to New York Times, Library of Contemporary Thought, New Yorker, GQ, Esquire, USA Weekend, Los Angeles Times Magazine, Savoy. *Honours:* American Library Asscn Literary Award 1996, O. Henry Award 1996, Anisfield Wolf Award 1996, TransAfrica Int. Literary Prize 1998. *Literary Agent:* W. W. Norton, 500 Fifth Avenue, Floor 6, New York, NY 10110, USA. *Website:* www.waltermosley.com.

MOSS, Norman Bernard; Journalist and Writer; b. 30 Sept. 1928, London, England; m. Hilary Sesta, 21 July 1963, two s. *Education:* Hamilton College, New York, 1946–47. *Career:* Staff Journalist with newspapers, news agencies and radio networks; mem. International Institute of Strategic Studies; Society of Authors. *Publications:* Men Who Play God – The Story of the Hydrogen Bomb, 1968; A British-American Dictionary, 1972; The Pleasures of Deception, 1976; The Politics of Uranium, 1982; Klaus Fuchs: The Man Who Stole the Atom Bomb, 1987; Managing the Planet, 2000; 19 Weeks: America, Britain and the Fateful Summer of 1940, 2003. *Honours:* Magazine Writer of the Year, Periodical Publishers Asscn, 1982. *Address:* 21 Rylett Crescent, London W12 9RP, England.

MOTION, Andrew Peter, MLitt, FRSA; British biographer and poet; *Poet Laureate*; b. 26 Oct. 1952, London, England; m. 1st Joanna J. Powell 1973 (divorced 1983); m. 2nd Janet Elisabeth Dalley 1985; two s. one d. *Education:* Radley Coll. and Univ. Coll., Oxford. *Career:* Lecturer in English, Univ. of Hull 1977–81; Ed. Poetry Review 1981–83; Poetry Ed. Chatto & Windus 1983–89, Editorial Dir 1985–87; Prof. of Creative Writing Univ. of E Anglia, Norwich 1995–2003; Chair. Literature Advisory Panel Arts Council of England 1996–98; Poet Laureate 1999–; Chair of Creative Writing, Royal Holloway Coll., University Coll. London 2003–; mem. Poetry Soc. (vice-pres.). *Publications:* poetry collections: The Pleasure Steamers 1978, Independence 1981, The Penguin Book of Contemporary British Poetry (ed., anthology) 1982, Secret Narratives 1983, Dangerous Play (Rhys Memorial Prize) 1984, Natural Causes 1987, Love in a Life 1991, The Price of

Everything 1994, Salt Water 1997, Selected Poems 1996–97 1998, Public Property 2001, Here to Eternity: An Anthology of Poetry (ed.) 2001; poems as Poet Laureate: Remember This: An Elegy on the Death of HM Queen Elizabeth The Queen Mother 2002, A Hymn for the Golden Jubilee 2002, On the Record (for Prince William's 21st birthday) 2003; non-fiction: The Poetry of Edward Thomas 1981, Philip Larkin 1982, The Lamberts (Somerset Maugham Award 1987) 1986, Philip Larkin: A Writer's Life 1993, William Barnes Selected Poems (ed.) 1994, Keats 1997, Wainewright the Poisoner 2000; fiction: The Pale Companion 1989, Famous for the Creatures 1991, The Invention of Dr Cake 2003; other: additional texts for a performance of Haydn's Seven Last Words of Our Saviour on the Cross 2003. *Honours:* Hon. DLitt (Hull) 1996, (Exeter) 1999, (Brunel) 2000, (A.P.U.) 2001, (Open Univ.) 2002; Arvon/Observer Prize 1982, Dylan Thomas Award 1987, Whitbread Biography Award 1993. *Address:* c/o Faber & Faber, 3 Queen Square, London, WC1N 3AU, England.

MOTT, Michael (Charles Alston); Prof. of English Emeritus, Writer and Poet; b. 8 Dec. 1930, London, England; m. 1st Margaret Ann Watt, 6 May 1961, deceased 1990, two d.; m. 2nd Emma Lou Powers, 16 Nov. 1992. *Education:* Diploma, Central School of Arts and Crafts, London; Intermediate Law Degree, Law Society, London; BA, History of Art, University of London, Courtauld and Warburg Institutes, London. *Career:* Ed., Air Freight, 1954–59, Thames and Hudson publishers, 1961–64; Asst Ed., Adam International Review, 1956–66, The Geographical Magazine, 1964–66; Poetry Ed., The Kenyon Review, 1966–70; Visiting Prof. and Writer-in-Residence, Kenyon College, 1966–70, SUNY at Buffalo, 1968, Concordia University, Montréal, QC, 1970, 1974, Emory University, 1970–77, College of William and Mary, 1978–79, 1985–86; Prof. of English, 1980–92, Prof. Emeritus, 1992–, Bowling Green State University; mem. Amnesty International; British Lichen Society; RGS. *Publications:* Fiction: The Notebooks of Susan Berry, 1962; Master Entrick, 1964; Helmet and Wasps, 1964; The Blind Cross, 1968. Poetry: Absence of Unicorns, Presence of Lions, 1977; Counting the Grasses, 1980; Corday, 1986; Piero di Cosimo: The World of Infinite Possibility, 1990; Taino, 1992; Woman and the Sea: Selected Poems, 1999. Non-Fiction: The Seven Mountains of Thomas Merton, 1984. Contributions: journals and newspapers. *Honours:* Governor's Award in Fine Arts, State of Georgia, 1974; Guggenheim Fellowship, 1979–80; Hon. DLitt, St Mary's College, Notre Dame, 1983; Christopher Award, 1984; Ohioana Book Award, 1985; Olscamp Research Award, 1985; Nancy Dasher Book Award, 1985; Fortsam Award, 1999, Allen Tate Award in Poetry 2002. *Address:* 122 The Colony, Williamsburg, VA 23185, USA.

MOTTRAM, Eric; Professor and Poet; b. 1920, England. *Education:* Univ. of Cambridge. *Career:* Prof., King's Coll., London 1983; other univ. appointments in USA, India, Europe. *Publications:* Inside the Whale, 1970; The He Expression, 1973; Local Movement, 1973; Two Elegies, 1974; Against Tyranny, 1975; 1922 Earth Raids and Other Poems, 1973–75, 1976; Homage to Braque, 1976; Spring Ford, 1977; Tunis, 1977; Elegy 15: Neruda, 1978; Precipe of Fishes, 1979; 1980 Mediate; Elegies, 1981; A Book of Herne, 1975–81; Interrogation Rooms: Poems, 1980–81; Address, 1983; Three Letters, 1984; The Legal Poems, 1984; Selected Poems, 1989; Peace Projects and Brief Novels, 1989. Other: Studies and edns of American Literature. *Address:* Dept of English, King's College, University of London, The Strand, London WC2R 2LS, England.

MOUNT, (William Robert) Ferdinand, BA, FRSL; British writer and journalist; b. 2 July 1939, London; m. Julia Margaret Lucas 1968; two s. (one deceased), one d. *Education:* Eton Coll., Christ Church, Oxford. *Career:* Political Ed. The Spectator 1977–82, 1985, Literary Ed. 1984–85; Head Prime Minister's Policy Unit 1982–84; Political Columnist The Standard 1980–82, The Times 1984–85, Daily Telegraph 1985–90, Sunday Times 1997–; Ed. Times Literary Supplement 1991–2002; Sr Columnist The Sunday Times 2002–; mem. RSL (mem. of Council 2002–). *Publications:* Very Like a Whale 1967, The Theatre of Politics 1972, The Man Who Rode Ampersand 1975, The Clique 1978, The Subversive Family 1982, The Selkirk Strip 1987, Of Love and Asthma 1991 (Hawthornden Prize 1992), The British Constitution Now 1992, Communism 1992, Umbrella 1994, The Liquidator 1995, Jem (and Sam) 1998, Fairness 2001, Heads You Win 2004. *Honours:* Hon. Fellow (Univ. of Wales, Lampeter) 2002. *Address:* 17 Ripplevale Grove, London, N1 1HS, England. *Telephone:* (20) 7607-5398.

MOUNTFIELD, David (see Grant, Neil).

MOYERS, Bill; Journalist, Broadcaster and Writer; b. 5 June 1934, Hugo, Oklahoma, USA; m. Judith Davidson, 18 Dec. 1954, two s. one d. *Education:* BJ, University of Texas, 1956; Graduate Studies, University of Edinburgh, 1956–57; MTh, Southwestern Baptist Theological Seminary, 1959. *Career:* Personal Asst, Senator Lyndon B. Johnson, 1960; Assoc. Dir, 1961–62, Deputy Dir, 1963, Peace Corps; Special Asst, 1963–67, Press Secretary, 1965–67, Pres. Lyndon B. Johnson; Publisher, Newsday, Garden City, New York, 1967–70; Ed.-in-Chief, Bill Moyers Journal, Public-TV, 1971–76, 1978–81; Chief Correspondent, CBS Reports, CBS-TV, 1976–78; Senior News Analyst, CBS News, CBS-TV, 1981–86; Founder and Exec. Dir, Public Affairs TV Inc, 1987–; various special series, PBS-TV; mem. American Acad. of Arts and Sciences, fellow; Society of American Historians; American Philosophical Society, fellow. *Publications:* Listening to America, 1971; Report from Philadelphia, 1987; The Secret Government, 1988; Joseph Campbell and the Power of the Myth, 1988; A World of Ideas, 1989; Healing and the Mind, 1993; Genesis, 1996; Fooling With Words, 1999. *Honours:* George Foster Peabody Awards, 1976, 1980, 1985, 1986, 1988, 1989, 1990; George Polk Awards, 1981, 1986; Communicator of the Decade Award, Religious Communications Congress, 1990; TV Hall of Fame, 1995; Religious Liberty Award, American Jewish Committee, 1995; Charles Frankel Prize in the Humanities, 1995; Nelson Mandela Award for Health and Human Rights, 1996; numerous Emmy Awards.

MOYES, Jojo; British writer and journalist; b. 1969, London; m.; two c. *Career:* fmr arts and media correspondent, The Independent newspaper; contrib. to Woman's Hour (BBC Radio 4). *Publications:* Sheltering Rain 2002, Foreign Fruit (aka Windfallen) 2003, The Peacock Emporium 2004. *Honours:* Parker Romantic Novelist of the Year 2004. *Literary Agent:* AP Watt Ltd, 20 John Street, London, WC1N 2DR, England. *Telephone:* (20) 7405-6774. *Fax:* (20) 7831-2154. *E-mail:* apw@apwatt.co.uk. *Website:* www.apwatt.co.uk.

MOYNIHAN, Daniel Patrick; US Senator (retd) and Writer; b. 16 March 1927, Tulsa, Oklahoma, USA; m. Elizabeth Therese Brennan, 29 May 1955, two s. one d. *Education:* City College, CUNY, 1943; BA, Tufts University, 1948; MA, 1949, PhD, 1961, Fletcher School of Law and Diplomacy. *Career:* Special Asst, 1961–62, Exec. Asst, 1962–63, to the US Secretary of Labor; Asst Secretary of Labor, 1963–65; Fellow, Center for Advanced Studies, Wesleyan University, 1965–66; Prof. of Education and Urban Politics, 1966–73, Senior Mem., 1966–77, Prof. of Government, 1973–77, Kennedy School of Government, Harvard University; Asst for Urban Affairs, 1969–70, Counsellor, 1969–70, Consultant, 1971–73, to the Pres. of the USA; US Ambassador to India, 1973–75; US Permanent Representative to the United Nations, 1975–76; US Senator (Democrat) from the State of New York, 1977–2001. *Publications:* Beyond the Melting Pot (with Nathan Glazer), 1963; The Defenses of Freedom: The Public Papers of Arthur J. Goldberg (ed.), 1966; Equal Educational Opportunity (co-author), 1969; On Understanding Poverty: Perspectives for the Social Sciences (ed.), 1969; The Politics of a Guaranteed Income, 1973; Coping: On the Practice of Government, 1974; Ethnicity: Theory and Experience (ed. with Nathan Glazer), 1975; A Dangerous Place (with S. Weaver), 1978; Counting Our Blessings: Reflections on the Future of America, 1980; Loyalties, 1984; Family and Nation, 1986; Came the Revolution: Argument in the Reagan Era, 1988; On the Law of Nations, 1990; Pandaemonium: Ethnicity in International Politics, 1993; Miles to Go: A Personal History of Social Policy, 1996; Secrecy: The American Experience, 1999. Contributions: Professional journals. *Honours:* Meritorious Service Award, US Dept of Labor, 1965; Centennial Medal, Syracuse University, 1969; International League for Human Rights Award, 1975; John LaFarge Award for Interracial Justice, 1980; Medallion, SUNY at Albany, 1984; Henry Medal, Smithsonian Institution, 1985; SEAL Medallion, Central Intelligence Agency, 1986; Laetare Medal, University of Notre Dame, 1992; Thomas Jefferson Award, 1993; numerous hon. doctorates.

MPHAHLELE, Ezekiel, (Es'kia Mphahlele); Author and Prof. of African Literature; b. 17 Dec. 1919, Pretoria, South Africa. *Education:* MA, University of South Africa, Pretoria, 1956. *Career:* Teacher of English and Afrikaans, Orlando High School, Johannesburg, 1942–52; Fiction Ed., Drum magazine, Johannesburg, 1955–57; Lecturer in English Literature, University of Ibadan, Nigeria, 1957–61; Dir of African Programmes, International Asscn for Cultural Freedom, Paris, 1961–63; Dir, Chem-chemi Creative Centre, Nairobi, Kenya, 1963–65; Lecturer, University College, Nairobi, 1965–66, University of Denver, 1966–74, University of Pennsylvania, 1974–77; Prof. of African Literature, University of the Witwatersrand, Johannesburg, 1979–. *Publications:* Man Must Live and Other Stories, 1947; Down Second Avenue (autobiog.), 1959; The Living Dead and Other Stories, 1961; The African Image (essays), 1962; Modern African Stories (ed. with E. Komey), 1964; African Writing Today (ed.), 1967; In Corner B and Other Stories, 1967; The Wanderers (novel), 1971; Voices in the Whirlwind and Other Essays, 1972; Chirundu (novel), 1979; The Unbroken Song, 1981; Bury Me at the Marketplace, 1984; Father Come Home, 1984; Afrika My Music: An Autobiography 1957–1983, 1986. *Honours:* Hon. doctorates. *Address:* African Studies Institute, University of the Witwatersrand, Johannesburg 2001, South Africa.

MUAMBA, Muepu; Journalist, Writer and Poet; b. 23 Nov. 1946, Tshilundu, Belgian Congo. *Education:* Institut St Ferdinand, Jernappes, Belgium. *Career:* mem. Maison Africaine de la Poesie Internationale, Dakar; Royal African Society, London; Société Française des Gens de Lettres, Paris; Union Internale des Journalistes et de la Presse de la Langue Française, Paris. *Publications:* Afrika in eigener Sache (essays with Jochen Klicker and Klaus Paysan), 1980; Devoir d'ingerence, 1988; Moi Qui T'Amour, 1997; Ma Terre d'O, 1999. Contributions: various anthologies and periodicals. *Address:* c/o M. Kohlert-Nemeth, Schaumainkal 99, 6000 Frankfurt am Main 70, Germany.

MUDGEON, Apeman (see Mitchell, Adrian).

MUDIMBE, Valentin Yves, DèsL; Congolese writer, academic, poet and philosopher; *Research Professor, Duke University*; b. 1941, Zaire. *Education:* Univ. of Louvain. *Career:* Teaching Asst in Indo-European Languages, Romance Philology and Gen. Linguistics, Dept of Romance Languages, Lovanium Univ., Kinshasa 1966–68; Lecturer in French Civilization, École Nationale de Droit et d'Administration, Kinshasa 1967–68; Teaching and

Research Asst in Indo-European Languages, Philology and African Literature, Louvain Univ., Belgium 1968–70; Lecturer in Socio-linguistics, Laboratory of Comparative Ethnology and Sociology, Univ. of Paris-Nanterre 1969–71; Asst Prof. of Indo-European Languages and Historical Linguistics of French, Dept of Romance Languages, Lovanium Univ. of Kinshasa, Lubumbashi 1970–71; Dean of the Faculty of Philosophy and Letters, Nat. Univ. of Zaïre 1972–74, Assoc. Professor of Indo-European Languages, Comparative Philology and Gen. Linguistics, Dept of Romance Languages 1971–74, Prof. of Classics, Indo-European Languages and Comparative Philology, Dept of Classics and Dept of Romance Languages 1974–80; Margaret Gest Prof. of Comparative Religions, Haverford Coll., Haverford, Pennsylvania 1981–82, Ira Reid Prof. of History and Sociology 1982–83, Prof. of General Programs 1984–87; Prof. of Romance Studies and Comparative Literature, Duke Univ., Durham, NC 1988–90, Ruth F. DeVarney Prof. of Romance Studies, Prof. of Comparative Literature, Prof. of Cultural Anthropology 1991–94, Research Prof., The Literature Program 1995–; William R. Kenan Jr. Prof., Depts of French and Italian, Comparative Literature, and Classics, Program in Modern Thought and Literature and Center for African Studies, Stanford Univ., California 1995–; numerous visiting lecturing positions; has served on the editorial boards of numerous journals and periodicals; Fellow, Academia de la Investigación Científica, Mexico 1996; mem. African Studies Asscn (USA), World Phenomenology Inst., Soc. for Phenomenology and Existential Philosophy, Académie Royale des Sciences d'Outre-Mer, Brussels, Belgium (corresponding mem.), Société Américaine de Philosophie de Langue Française (life mem.). *Publications include:* Déchirures (poems) 1971, Initiation au Français (two vols) 1971, Réflexions sur la vie quotidienne 1972, Autour de la Nation 1972, Français: les structures fondamentales, Vol. I 1972, Vol. II 1972, Vol. III (with P. Detienne) 1973, Vol. IV (with A. Tashdjian, M. Le Boul and M. Pierre) 1974, Entretailles (poems) 1973, Entre les eaux (novel) (Int. Catholic Literature Grand Prize 1975) 1973, L'Autre face du royaume: une introduction à la critique des languages en folie 1973, Les Fuseaux parfois 1974, Le Prix du Péché: Essai de Psychanalyse Existentielle des Traditions Européennes et Africaines (with J. L. Vincke) 1974, Le bel immonde (novel) 1976, Contributions à l'etude des variations du genre grammatical des mots français d'origine latine 1976, Le Vocabulaire Politique Zaïrois: une étude de sociolinguistique (with Eloko a N.O., Losso Gazi, Matumele M. and N.Y. Rubango) 1976, Procédés d'enrichissement et création de termes nouveaux dans un groupe de langues de l'Afrique Centrale (with Mombo Lutete, Kilanga M., Lupukisa Wasamba) 1976, L'Ecart 1979, Air: Etude Sémantique 1979, Du Congo au Zaïre 1960–1980: Essai de Bilan (with A. Huybrechts, L. Peeters, J. Vanderlinden, D. Van Der Steen and B. Verhaegen) 1980, La Culture et la Science au Zaïre 1960–1975 (essay) 1980, Visage de la Philosophie et de la Théologie Contemporaines au Zaïre (essay) 1981, L'Odeur du père 1982, The Invention of Africa: Gnosis, Philosophy and the Order of Knowledge (US African Studies Asscn Herskovits Award 1989) 1988, Shaba Deux (novel) 1989, Fables and Parables 1991, The Idea of Africa 1994, Les corps glorieux des mots et des êtres 1994, Tales of Faith 1997; ed. of numerous books and journals; contrib. articles and conference papers. *Honours:* Dr hc (Université Paris-Denis Diderot, Paris VII) 1997; French-language Writers' Asscn Senghor Grand Prize 1977; Chevalier de la Pléiade, Ordre de la Francophonie et du Dialogue des Cultures, Paris 1977, Gold Medal of Scientific and Civil Merit, Republic of Zaïre 1980. *Address:* The Literature Program, Duke University, 115 Art Museum, PO Box 90673, Durham, NC 27708, USA. *E-mail:* vmudimbe@duke.edu. *Website:* www.duke.edu.

MUEHL, Lois Baker, BA, MA; retd academic, writer and poet; b. 29 April 1920, Oak Park, IL, USA; m. Siegmar Muehl 1944; two s. two d. *Education:* Oberlin College, University of Iowa. *Career:* fmr Assoc. Prof. of Rhetoric; mem. Iowa Poetry Asscn; National League of American Pen Women; University Women's Writers Group. *Publications:* My Name is..., 1959; Worst Room in the School, 1961; The Hidden Year of Devlin Bates, 1967; Winter Holiday Brainteasers, 1979; A Reading Approach to Rhetoric, 1983; Trading Cultures in the Classroom (with Siegmar Muehl), 1993; Talkable Tales, 1993. Other: Poems. Contributions: scholarly journals and to general magazines. *Honours:* Old Gold Creative Fellowship, 1970; Community Service Commendation, Merced, California, 1984; Grand Prize, Poetry Guild Contest, 1997. *Address:* 701 Oaknoll Drive, Iowa City, IA 52246, USA.

MUELLER, Lisel, BA; American poet, writer and translator; b. 8 Feb. 1924, Hamburg, Germany; m. Paul E. Mueller 1943; two d. *Education:* Univ. of Evansville, Indiana Univ. *Career:* instructor in poetry, Elmhurst Coll. 1969–72; associated with poets in the schools programme 1972–77; Visiting Prof., Goddard Coll. and Warren Wilson Coll. 1977–86. *Publications:* poetry: Dependencies 1965, Life of a Queen 1970, The Private Life 1976, Voices from the Forest 1977, The Need to Hold Still 1980, Second Language 1986, Waving from Shore 1989, Learning to Play by Ear (essays and poetry) 1990, Alive Together 1996; contrib. to anthologies and journals. *Honours:* Friends of Literature Robert M. Ferguson Memorial Award 1966, Helen Bullis Awards 1974, 1977, Lamont Poetry Selection 1975, Emily Clark Balch Award 1976, Nat. Book Award 1981, Hon. doctorate (Lake Forest Coll.) 1985, NEA Fellowship 1990, Carl Sandburg Award 1990, Pulitzer Prize for Poetry 1997, Ruth Lilly Poetry Prize 2002. *Address:* c/o Louisiana State University Press, PO Box 25053, Baton Rouge, LA 70894-5053, USA.

MUGGESON, Margaret Elizabeth, (Margaret Dickinson, Everatt Jackson); Writer; b. 30 April 1942, Gainsborough, Lincolnshire, England; m. Dennis Muggeson, 19 Sept. 1964, two d. *Education:* Lincoln College of Technology, 1960–61. *Career:* mem. Romantic Novelists Asscn. *Publications:* Pride of the Courtneys, 1968; Brackenbeck, 1969; Portrait of Jonathan, 1970; The Road to Hell (as Everatt Jackson), 1975; Abbeyford Trilogy, 1981; Lifeboat!, 1983; Beloved Enemy, 1984; Plough the Furrow, 1994; Sow the Seed, 1995; Reap the Harvest, 1996; The Miller's Daughter, 1997; Chaff Upon the Wind, 1998; The Fisher Lass, 1999; The Tulip Girl, 2000; The River Folk, 2001; Tangled Threads, 2002. *Address:* 17 Seacroft Dr., Skegness, Lincolnshire PE 25 3AP, England.

MÜHRINGER, Doris Agathe Annemarie; Poet and Writer; b. 18 Sept. 1920, Graz, Austria. *Career:* mem. Asscn of Austrian Writers; Kogge; PEN; Poium. *Publications:* Gedichte I, 1957, II, 1969, III, 1976, IV, 1984; Tag, mein Jahr (with H. Valencak), 1983; Das hatten die Ratten vom Schatten: Ein Lachbuch, 1989; Reisen wir (poems), 1995; Aber ietzt zögerst etu Späte Gedichte, 1999. Contributions: numerous literary magazines, domestic and foreign. *Honours:* Georg Trakl Prize, 1954; Award of Achievement, Vienna, 1961; Lyric Prize of Steiermark, 1973; Austrian State Scholarship, 1976; Award of Achievement, Board of Austrian Litera-Mechana, 1984; Grosser Literturpreis des Landes Steiermark, 1985. *Address:* Goldeggasse 1, 1040 Vienna, Austria.

MUIR, Richard; Author, Photographer, Lecturer, Ed. and Researcher; b. 18 June 1943, Yorkshire, England; m., one s. *Education:* BA, Geography, 1967, PhD, 1970, University of Aberdeen. *Career:* Ed., National Trust Regional Histories and Countryside Commission National Park Series; Co-founder and Ed., LANDSCAPES Journal, 2000–; Hon. Research Fellow, University of Aberdeen, 2001–. *Publications:* Over 40 books, including: Modern Political Geography, 1975; Hedgerows: Their History and Wildlife (with N. Muir), 1987; Old Yorkshire, 1987; The Countryside Encyclopaedia, 1988; Fields (with Nina Muir), 1989; Portraits of the Past, 1989; The Dales of Yorkshire, 1991; The Villages of England, 1992; The Coastlines of Britain, 1993; Political Geography: A New Introduction, 1997; The Yorkshire Countryside: A Landscape History, 1997; Approaches to Landscape, 1999; The New Reading the Landscape, 2000; Landscape Detective, 2001. Contributions: Academic journals and general periodicals. *Honours:* Yorkshire Arts Literary Prize, 1982–83. *Address:* 20 Stray Walk, Harrogate, Yorkshire HG2 8HU, England. *E-mail:* richard.muir1@btinternet.com. *Website:* www.richardmuir.net.

MUJICA, Barbara, AB, MA, PhD; academic and writer; *Professor of Spanish, Georgetown University*; b. 25 Dec. 1943, Los Angeles, CA, USA; m. Mauro E. Mujica 1966; one s. two d. *Education:* University of California at Los Angeles, Middlebury Graduate School, Paris, New York University. *Career:* Teacher of French, University of California at Los Angeles Extension Division, 1963–64; Assoc. Ed. of Modern Languages, Harcourt Brace Jovanovich, New York City, 1966–73; Instructor, 1973–74, Asst Prof. of Romance Languages, 1974, Baruch College, CUNY; Asst Prof., 1974–79, Assoc. Prof., 1979–91, Prof. of Spanish, 1991–, Georgetown University; Ed. Comedia Performance; mem. American Asscn of Teachers of Spanish and Portuguese; American Asscn of University Profs; American Council on the Teaching of Foreign Languages; Asscn for Hispanic Classical Theater, Board of Dirs; Feministas Unidas; MLA; Washington Independent Writers; Writer's Center; South Atlantic MLA; Golden Age Division, Secretary, 1999, Pres., 2000, PEN International; National Writers Union; Asociación de Escritoras de España y las Américas. *Publications:* scholarly: Readings in Spanish Literature (ed. with Anthony Zahareas), 1975; Calderón's Characters: An Existential Point of View, 1983; Expanding the Curriculum in Foreign Language Classes: Spanish and Contemporary Affairs (with William Cressey and Mark Goldin), 1983; Iberian Pastoral Characters, 1986; Texto y espectáculo: Selected Proceedings of the Symposium on Spanish Golden Age Theater, March, 1987, 1989; Texto y vida: Introducción a la literatura española, 1990; Antología de literatura española, Vol. I, La Edad Media (with Amanda Curry), 1991, Vol. II, Renacimiento y Siglo de Oro, 1991, Vol. III, Siglos XVIII y XIX (with Eva Florensa), 1999; Et in Arcadia Ego: Essays on Death in the Pastoral Novel (with Bruno Damiani), 1990; Texto y vida: Introducción a la literatura hispanoamericana, 1992; Looking at the Comedia in the Year of the Quincentennial (ed. with Sharon Voros), 1993; Premio Nóbel: Once grandes escritores del mundo hispánico (ed.), 1997; Books of the Americas: Reviews and Interviews from Americas Magazine, 1990–1991, 1997; El texto puesto en escena (ed. with Anita Stoll), 2000; Hispanomundo, 2001; Early Modern Spanish Women Writers 2004. Other: The Deaths of Don Bernardo (novel), 1990; Sanchez across the Street (short stories), 1997; Far from My Mother's Home (short stories), 1999; Frida (novel), 2001; Affirmative Actions (novel) 2004. Contributions: anthologies, scholarly publications and the popular press. *Honours:* Poets and Writers Recognition for Fiction, New York, 1984; One of Best Fifty Op Ed Pieces of the Decade, New York Times, 1990; Winner, E. L. Doctorow International Fiction Contest, 1992; Pangolin Prize for Best Short Story of 1998. *Address:* c/o Department of Spanish and Portuguese, Georgetown University, Box 571039, Washington, DC 20057, USA.

MUKHERJEE, Bharati; American (b. Indian) writer and academic; b. 27 July 1940, Kolkata, India; m. Clarke Blaise 1963; two s. *Education:* BA, Univ. of Calcutta, 1959; MA, Univ. of Baroda; MA, PhD, Univ. of Iowa. *Career:* Lecturer, Skidmore Coll., Queens Coll., CUNY; Assoc. Prof., McGill

Univ.; Prof., Univ. of California at Berkeley, 1990. *Publications:* The Tiger's Daughter, 1971; The Tiger's Daughter and Wife, 1975; Days and Nights in Calcutta (with Clark Blaise), 1977; Darkness, 1985; The Sorrow and the Terror (with Clark Blaise), 1987; The Middleman and Other Stories, 1988; Jasmine, 1989; The Holder of the World, 1993; Leave it to Me, 1996; Desirable Daughters, 2002. *Honours:* National Book Critics Circle Award, USA, 1988. *Literary Agent:* Janklow & Nesbit Associates, 445 Park Avenue, New York, NY 10022, USA.

MUKUNDAN, M.; Short Story Writer and Novelist; b. 10 Sept. 1942, Mayyazhi, Mahe, Kerala, India. *Career:* Malayalam writer; Deputy Cultural Attaché, French Embassy in New Delhi, India. *Publications:* novels and collections of short stories incl.: Delhi (novel), 1969; Mayyazhi Puzhayude Theerangalil (On the Banks of the Mayyazhi); Daivathinte Vikrithikal (God's Mischief); Appam Chudunna Kunkiyamma; Lesli Achante Kadangal; Ee Lokam Athiloru Manushyan; Nrittam (Dance); Adithyanum Radhayum Mattu Chilarum; Oru Dalit Yuvathiyude Kadanakatha; Nirtham; Haridwaril Manikal Muzhangunnu (The Bells are Tolling in Haridwar); Kesavante Vilapanghal. Contributions: Mathrubhumi; various periodicals. *Honours:* NV Prize; Crossword Award; Kerala State Award; Kendra Sahitya Academi Awards, 1989, 1994; Chevalier, Ordre des Arts et des Lettres, 1998; Katha Award, 2003. *Address:* c/o Penguin Books India Pvt Ltd, #11 Community Centre, Panchsheel Park, New Delhi, India.

MULDOON, Paul Benedict, BA, FRSL; Irish poet and university professor; b. 20 June 1951, Portadown, NI; m. Jean Hanff Korelitz 1987; one s. one d. *Education:* St Patrick's Coll., Armagh, Queen's Univ., Belfast. *Career:* radio and TV producer, BBC NI 1973–86; has taught at Cambridge Univ., Univ. of E Anglia, Columbia Univ., Univ. of Calif. at Berkeley, Univ. of Mass. 1986–; Lecturer, Princeton Univ. 1987–88, 1990–95, Dir Creative Writing Program 1993, Prof. 1995–, Howard G. B. Clark Prof. in the Humanities 1998–; Visiting Prof. Univ. of Mass 1989–90, Bread Loaf School of English 1997–; elected Hon. Prof. of Poetry Oxford Univ. 1999–2004; mem. Aosdána, Poetry Soc. of GB (pres. 1996–), American Acad. of Arts and Sciences 2000. *Publications:* poetry: Knowing My Place 1971, New Weather 1973, Spirit of Dawn 1975, Mules 1977, Names and Addresses 1978, Immram 1980, Why Brownlee Left 1980, Out of Siberia 1982, Quoof 1983, The Wishbone 1984, Selected Poems 1968–83 1986, Meeting the British 1987, Madoc: A Mystery 1990, Incantata 1994, The Prince of the Quotidian 1994, The Annals of Chile (T. S. Eliot Prize) 1995; Kerry Slides 1996, New Selected Poems 1968–1994 1996, Hopewell Haiku 1997, The Bangle (Slight Return) 1998, Hay (poems) 1999, Poems 1968–1998 2001; for children: The O-O's Party 1981, The Last Thesaurus 1995, The Noctuary of Narcissus Batt 1997; other: Monkeys (TV play) 1989, Shining Brow (opera libretto) 1993, Six Honest Serving Men (play) 1995, Bandanna (opera libretto) 1999, To Ireland, I (essays) 2000; ed.: The Scrake of Dawn 1979, The Faber Book of Contemporary Irish Poetry 1986, The Essential Byron 1989, The Faber Book of Beasts 1997, Moy Sand and Gravel (Pulitzer Prize for Poetry) 2002; trans.: The Astrakhan Cloak, by Nuala Ni Dhomhnaill 1993, The Birds, by Aristophanes (with Richard Martin) 1999. *Honours:* Eric Gregory Award 1972, Sir Geoffrey Faber Memorial Awards 1980, 1991, Guggenheim Fellowship 1990, American Acad. of Arts and Letters Award for Literature 1996, Irish Times Poetry Prize 1997, Pulitzer Prize for Poetry 2003, Griffin Prize 2003. *Address:* Creative Writing Program, Princeton University, Princeton, NJ 08544, USA. *Website:* www.paulmuldoon.net (Home).

MULLER, Marcia; Writer and Ed.; b. 28 Sept. 1944, Detroit, MI, USA; m. 1st Frederick T. Guilson Jr 12 Aug. 1967 (divorced 1981); m. 2nd Bill Pronzini 1992. *Education:* BA, English, 1966, MA, Journalism, 1971, Univ. of Michigan. *Publications:* Edwin of the Iron Shoes, 1977; Ask the Cards a Question, 1982; The Cheshire Cat's Eye, 1983; The Tree of Death, 1983; Games to Keep the Dark Away, 1984; Leave a Message for Willie, 1984; Double (with Bill Pronzini), 1984; The Legend of Slain Soldiers, 1985; There's Nothing to Be Afraid of, 1985; Beyond the Grave (with Bill Pronzini), 1986; The Cavalier in White, 1986; The Lighthouse (with Bill Pronzini), 1987; Eye of the Storm (with Bill Prozini), 1988; There Hangs the Knife, 1988; Dark Star, 1989; The Shape of Dread, 1989; There's Something in a Sunday, 1989; Trophies and Dead Things, 1990; Deceptions, 1991; Where Echoes Live, 1991; Pennies on a Dead Woman's Eyes, 1992; The Wall, 1993; Wolf in the Shadows, 1993; Till the Butchers Cut Him Down, 1994; A Wild and Lonely Place, 1995; The McCone Files: The Complete Sharon McCone Stories, 1995; The Broken Promise Land, 1996; Both Ends of the Night, 1997; While Other People Sleep, 1998; Duo (with Bill Pronzini), 1998; A Walk Through the Fire, 1999; Listen to the Silence, 2000; McCone and Friends, 2000; Point Deception, 2001; Dead Midnight, 2002. Editor: several anthologies. *Honours:* American Mystery Award, 1989; Shamus Award, 1991, Life Achievement Award, 1993, Private Eye Writers of America; Anthony Boucher Awards, 1994, 1996; Lifetime Achievement in Suspense Award, Romantic Times, 1999. *Literary Agent:* Aaron M. Priest Literary Agency Inc, 708 Third Ave, New York, NY 10017, USA.

MULLIN, Chris(topher John); MP and Writer; b. 12 Dec. 1947, Chelmsford, Essex, England; m. Nguyen Thi Ngoc, 14 April 1987, two d. *Education:* LLB, University of Hull. *Career:* Sub-Ed., BBC World Service, 1974–78; Ed., Tribune, 1982–84; MP, Labour Party, Sunderland South, 1987–; Chair., Home Affairs Select Committee, 1997–99, 2001–03; Under Sec., Dept of Environment, 1999–2001, Dept of International Development, 2001, Foreign Office, 2003–. *Publications:* Fiction: A Very British Coup, 1982; The Last Man Out of Saigon, 1986; The Year of the Fire Monkey, 1991. Non-Fiction: Error of Judgement: The Truth About the Birmingham Bombings, 1986. *Literary Agent:* PFD, Drury House, 34–43 Russell St, London WC2B 5HA, England. *Address:* c/o House of Commons, London SW1A 0AA, England.

MUNGOSHI, Charles Muzuva; Author, Poet and Dramatist; b. 2 Dec. 1947, Chivhu, Southern Rhodesia; m. Jesesi Jaboon, 1976, four s., one d. *Career:* Writer-in-Residence, University of Zimbabwe, 1985–87; Visiting Arts Fellow, University of Durham, 1990. *Publications:* Fiction: Makunun'unu Maodzamwoyo, 1970; Coming of the Dry Season, 1972; Waiting for the Rain, 1975; Ndiko Kupindana Kwanazuva, 1975; Some Kinds of Wounds, 1980; Kunyarara Hakusi Kutaura?, 1983; Setting Sun and the Rolling World, 1987; One Day Long Ago: Tales from a Shona Childhood, 1991; Walking Still, 1997. Poetry: The Milkman Doesn't Only Deliver Milk, 1981. Other: The Axe (film), 1999. *Honours:* several literary awards. *Address:* PO Box 1688, Harare, Zimbabwe.

MUNIF, Abdelrahman; Novelist; b. 1933, Amman, Jordan; m. *Education:* Law, Baghdad; PhD, Petroleum Economics, Univ. of Belgrade. *Career:* oil economist, Baghdad, and for OPEC; Ed., periodical, al-Naft wa al-Tanmiyya (Oil and Development), 1975; moved to Boulogne, France, and later Damascus, Syria; full-time writer, 1981–. *Publications:* Al-Ashjar wa-ightiyal Marzuq, 1973; Qissat hubb majusiyyah, 1974; Sharq al-Mutawasit, 1975; Al-Nihayat (Endings), 1978; Sibaq al-masafat al-tawilah, 1979; Alam bi-la khara' it (with Jabra Ibrahim Jabra), 1982; Mudun al-milh: Vol. 1: Al-tih (Cities of Salt), 1984, Vol. 2: Al-ukhdul (The Trench), 1985, Vol. 3: Taqasim al-layl wa-al-nahar (Variations on Night and Day), 1989, Vol. 4: Al-Munbatt, 1989, Vol. 5: Badiyat al-zulumat, 1989; Hina tarakna al-jisr, 1990; Al-an huna, 1991; Al-dimuqratiyyah awalan, al dimuqratiyyah daiman, 1992; Sirat Madinah (Story of a City), 1994; Urwat al-Zaman al-bahi, 1997. *Address:* c/o Random House UK Ltd, Random House, 20 Vauxhall Bridge Rd, London SW1V 2SA, England.

MUNONYE, John (Okechukwu); Novelist; b. 22 April 1929, Akokwa, Nigeria; m. Regina Nwokeji, 1957, one s. one d. *Education:* Cert Ed, University of London, 1953. *Career:* Chief Inspector of Education, East Central State, 1973–76, Imo State, 1976–77. *Publications:* The Only Son, 1966; Obi, 1969; Oil Man of Obange, 1971; A Wreath for Maidens, 1973; A Dancer of Fortune, 1974; Bridge to a Wedding, 1978. Short Stories: Silent Child, 1973; Pack Pack Pack, 1977; Man of Wealth, 1981; On a Sunday Morning, 1982; Rogues, 1985. *Honours:* Mem., Order of the Niger, 1980. *Address:* PO Box 436 Orlu, Imo State, Nigeria.

MUNRO, Alice, BA; Canadian writer; b. 10 July 1931, Wingham, Ont.; m. 1st James A. Munro 1951 (divorced 1976); three d.; m. 2nd Gerald Fremlin 1976. *Education:* Univ. of Western Ont. *Publications:* Dance of the Happy Shades 1968 (Gov.-Gen.'s Award for Literature 1968), A Place for Everything 1970, Lives of Girls and Women 1971, Something I've Been Meaning to Tell You 1974, Who Do You Think You Are? (aka The Beggar Maid) 1978, The Moons of Jupiter 1982, The Progress of Love 1986, Friend of My Youth 1990, Open Secrets 1994, Selected Stories 1996, The Love of A Good Woman 1998, Hateship, Friendship, Courtship, Loveship, Marriage 2001. *Honours:* Gov.-Gen.'s Award for Literature 1978, 1986, Canadian Booksellers' Award 1972, Marian Engel Award 1986, Canada-Australia Literary Prize 1994, Lannan Literary Award 1995, WH Smith Literary Award 1996, Fiction Prize, Nat. Book Critics Circle 1999, Giller Prize 1999, O. Henry Award 2001. *Address:* The Writers Shop, 1325 Avenue of the Americas, Floor 16, New York, NY 10019, USA (Office); PO Box 1133, Clinton, ON, N0M 1L0, Canada (Home).

MUNRO, David Mackenzie; Geographer, Ed. and Writer; b. 28 May 1950, Glasgow, Scotland. *Education:* BSc, 1973, PhD, 1983, University of Edinburgh. *Career:* Research Assoc., then Research Fellow, University of Edinburgh, 1979–96; Dir and Secretary, Royal Scottish Geographical Society, 1996–; Consultant, Times Atlas of the World, 2000; mem. Michael Bruce Trust, chair.; National Trust for Scotland, council mem.; Permanent Committee on Geographical Names for British Official Use, chair.; FRGS; FRSA; Society of Antiquaries, Scotland, fellow. *Publications:* Chambers World Gazetteer (ed.), 1988; Ecology and Environment in Belize (ed.), 1989; A World Record of Major Conflict Areas (with Alan J. Day), 1990; The Hutchinson Guide to the World (assoc. ed.), 1990; Loch Leven and the River Leven: A Landscape Transformed, 1994; The Oxford Dictionary of the World (ed.), 1995. Contributions: Reference works and journals. *Address:* c/o Royal Scottish Geographical Society, 40 George St, Glasgow G1 1QE, Scotland.

MUNRO, J. Richard, BA; American publishing executive; b. 1931; m. *Education:* Colgate, Columbia and New York Univs. *Career:* joined Time Inc. 1957; Pres. Pioneer Press Inc. (Time subsidiary) 1969; Publr Sports Illustrated 1969–71; Vice-Pres. Time Inc. 1971–75, Group Vice-Pres. for Video 1975–79, Exec. Vice-Pres. 1979–80, Pres. 1980–86, CEO 1980–90, Chair. 1986–90, Chair. Exec. Comm. 1990, also Dir; Chair. Genentech Inc. 1997–; Dir IBM Corpn. *Honours:* Hon. LittD (Richmond Univ.) 1983; Purple Heart with two Clusters. *Address:* Time Inc., Time & Life Building, 75 Rockefeller Plaza, New York, NY 10019, USA.

MUNRO, John Murchison; University Administrator and Writer; b. 29 Aug. 1932, Wallasey, Cheshire, England; m. Hertha Ingrid Bertha Lipp, 12

Aug. 1956, two s. two d. *Education:* BA, English Literature, University of Durham, 1955; PhD, English Literature, Washington University, St Louis, 1960. *Career:* Part-time Instructor of English, Washington University, St Louis, 1956–60; Instructor, University of North Carolina, 1960–63; Asst Prof., University of Toronto, Canada, 1963–65; Prof., American University of Beirut, Lebanon, 1965–87; Dir, Outreach Services, Prof. of Mass Communications, 1987–, Assoc. Dean for External Affairs, 1990–97, American University, Cairo, Egypt; Contributing Ed., Cairo Times, 1997–; Media Consultant, NSCE, Cairo, 1998–. *Publications:* English Poetry in Transition, 1968; Arthur Symons, 1969; The Decadent Poets of the 1890s, 1970; Selected Poems of Theo Marzials, 1974; James Elroy Flecker, 1976; A Mutual Concern: The Story of the American University of Beirut, 1977; Cyprus: Between Venus and Mars (with Z. Khuri), 1984; Selected Letters of Arthur Symons (with Karl Beckson), 1988; Theatre of the Absurd: Lebanon, 1982–88, 1989. Contributions: scholarly journals and general periodicals. *Honours:* Fulbright Research Award, University of California, Los Angeles, 1987. *Address:* MEDA Team, Egypt, 29 Ismail Mohammed St, Zamalek, Cairo, Egypt.

MUNRO, Rona; Playwright; b. 7 Sept. 1959, Aberdeen, Scotland. *Education:* MA, University of Edinburgh, 1980. *Career:* Literary Assoc., Hampstead Theatre, London, 1996–. *Publications:* Fugue, 1983; Piper's Cave, 1985; Saturday at the Commodore, 1989; Bold Girls, 1990; Your Turn to Clear the Stair, 1992; The Maiden Stone, 1995; Iron, 2003. Other: Plays for Stage, Radio and Film. *Honours:* Evening Standard Award, 1991. *Address:* I.C.M., Oxford St, London W1D 1BS, England.

MURA, David Alan, BA, MFA; poet, writer and teacher; b. 17 June 1952, Great Lakes, IL, USA; m. Susan Sencer 1983; one d. *Education:* Grinnell Coll., Univ. of Minnesota, Vermont Coll. *Career:* Instructor 1979–85, Assoc. Dir of the Literature Program 1982–84, Writers and Artists-in-the-Schools, St Paul, Minnesota; faculty mem., The Loft, St Paul, Minnesota 1984–; Instructor, St Olaf Coll. 1990–91; Visiting Prof., Univ. of Oregon 1991; various poetry readings; mem. Asian-American Renaissance Conference, Center for Arts Criticism (pres. 1991–92), Jerome Foundation, Playwrights' Center. *Publications:* A Male Grief: Notes on Pornography and Addiction 1987, After We Lost Our Way (poems) 1989, Turning Japanese 1991, The Colors of Desire (poems) 1995, Where the Body Meets Memory 1996; contrib. to anthologies and magazines. *Honours:* Fanny Fay Wood Memorial Prize, Acad. of American Poets 1977, US/Japan Creative Artist Fellow 1984, Nat. Endowment for the Arts Fellowships 1985, 1993, Discovery/Nation Award 1987, Nat. Poetry Series Contest 1988, Pushcart Prize 1990, Minnesota State Arts Board Grant and Fellowship 1991, New York Times Notable Book of the Year 1991, Loft McKnight Award of Distinction 1992, Lila Wallace Reader's Digest Writers' Award 1995, Hon. DHumLitt (Cornell Coll.) 1997. *Address:* 1920 E River Terrace, Minneapolis, MN 55414, USA.

MURAKAMI, Haruki, BA; Japanese writer; b. 12 Jan. 1949, Kyoto; m. Yoko Takahashi 1971. *Education:* Kobe High School, Waseda Univ. *Career:* owner Peter Cat jazz club, Tokyo 1974–81; began writing in 1978l lived in Europe 1991–95, USA 1991–95; Visiting Scholar Princeton Univ. 1991–93; Una's Lecturer in the Humanities, Univ. of Calif. Berkeley 1992; writer-in-residence Tufts Univ. 1993–95; returned to Japan 1995. *Publications:* fiction: Pinball 1973, Hear the Wind Sing 1979 (Gunzo New Writer Award 1979), A Wild Sheep Chase 1982 (Noma Shinjin Literary Award for New Writers 1982), A Slow Boat to China 1983, A Day in the Life 1983, Hard Boiled Wonderland and The End of the World 1985 (Junichi Tanizaki Award 1985), Norwegian Wood 1987, Dance Dance Dance 1988, South of the Border, West of the Sun 1992, The Wind-Up Bird Chronicle (Yomiuri Literary Award 1996) 1994–95, All the Children of God Dance 2000, Sputnik Sweetheart 2001, Kafka on the Shore 2004; short stories: The Elephant Vanishes 1986, Dead Heat on the Merry-Go-Round 1985, Kureta Kanô 1989, After the Quake 2002, Birthday Stories (ed.) 2004; non-fiction: Underground 1997, Underground II (Kuwahara Takeo Award) 1998; essays: Murakami's House of the Rising Sun 1984, A Young Reader's Guide to Short Fiction 1997; has translated works by F. Scott Fitzgerald, Raymond Carver, Truman Capote, Paul Theroux, John Irving, J. D. Salinger etc. *Literary Agent:* International Creative Management, 40 West 57th Street, New York, NY 10019, USA.

MURDOCH, (Keith) Rupert, AC; American (b. Australian) publisher, broadcaster and media business developer; *Chairman and CEO, The News Corporation Ltd. and Fox Entertainment Group*; b. 11 March 1931, Melbourne, Victoria; m. 1st Patricia Booker (divorced); one d.; m. 2nd Anna Maria Torv 1967 (divorced); two s. one d.; m. 3rd Wendi Deng 1999; one d. *Education:* Geelong Grammar School, Victoria and Worcester Coll., Oxford. *Career:* inherited Adelaide News 1954; has since built up Cruden Investments, a Murdoch family co. which owns 30 per cent of News Corpn (Group CEO 1979–, Chair. 1991–); has acquired newspapers, broadcasting and other interests in Australia, UK, USA, Latin America, Europe and Asia, including: Australia – newspapers: The Australian (national), Daily Telegraph, Sunday Telegraph, Daily Mirror (Sydney), Sunday Sun (Brisbane), The News and Sunday Mail (Adelaide), The Sunday Times (Perth); USA – New York Post; UK – newspapers: Sun, News of the World (national, acquired 1969); acquired Times Newspapers Ltd 1981, group includes The Times, The Sunday Times, The Times Literary Supplement, The Times Educational Supplement, The Times Higher Education Supplement; Dir Times Newspapers Holdings 1981–, Chair. 1982–90, 1994–; magazines: Weekly Standard (US politics); television: British Sky Broadcasting (UK), STAR (Asia), Fox Entertainment (owning Fox Broadcasting, Fox Cable Networks, Fox Sport Networks), owns 34% of satellite DIRECTV Group (all US; other interests include book publisher HarperCollins and ownership of 35 US television stations; Chair., CEO Fox Entertainment Group USA 1992–. *Honours:* Commdr of the White Rose (First Class) 1985; Kt Order of St Gregory the Great 1998. *Address:* 1 Virginia Street, London, E98 1EX, England; News Ltd, 2 Holt Street, Surry Hills, Sydney, NSW 2010, Australia; News Corporation, 1211 Avenue of the Americas, New York, NY 10036, USA.

MURNANE, Gerald; writer; b. 1939, Melbourne, Vic., Australia; m.; three s. *Education:* BA, University of Melbourne, 1969. *Career:* Lecturer, Victoria College, Melbourne; Senior Lecturer, Deakin University, Melbourne. *Publications:* Tamarisk Row, 1974; A Lifetime on Clouds, 1976; The Plains, 1982; Landscape with Landscape, 1985; Inland, 1988; Velvet Waters (short stories), 1990; Emerald Blue (short stories), 1995. *Honours:* Patrick White Literary Award, 1999. *Literary Agent:* Golvan Arts, PO Box 766, Kew Victoria 3101, Australia. *Address:* 2 Falcon Street, Macleod, Vic. 3085, Australia.

MURPHEY, Rhoads; Prof. of Asian Studies and History and Writer; b. 13 Aug. 1919, Philadelphia, Pennsylvania, USA; m. 1st Katherine Elizabeth Quinn, 26 Nov. 1942, deceased July 1950, one s. one d.; m. 2nd Eleanor Taylor Albertson, 12 Jan. 1952, one s. one d. *Education:* AB, 1941, MA, 1942, PhD, 1950, Harvard University. *Career:* Asst Prof. of Geography, Ohio State University, 1950–51; Asst Prof. to Prof. of Geography, University of Washington, 1952–64; Prof. of Asian Studies and History, University of Michigan, Ann Arbor, 1964–; mem. Asscn of American Geographers; Asscn for Asian Studies, pres., 1987–88; American Historical Asscn. *Publications:* Shanghai: Key to Modern China, 1953; A New China Policy (with others), 1967; An Introduction to Geography, 1969; The Scope of Geography, 1969; The Treaty Ports and China's Modernization, 1970; China Meets the West, 1975; The Mozartian Historian (with others), 1976; The Outsiders, 1977; The Fading of the Maoist Vision, 1980; Civilizations of the World (with others), 1990; A History of Asia, 1992; East Asia: A New History, 1996. Contributions: scholarly books and journals. *Honours:* Ford Foundation Fellowship, 1955–56; Guggenheim Fellowship, 1966–67; National Endowment for the Humanities Fellowship, 1972–73; Hons Award, Asscn of American Geographers, 1980. *Address:* 2012 Washtenaw Ave, Ann Arbor, MI 48104, USA.

MURPHY, Clive; Writer, Poet, Compiler and Ed.; b. 28 Nov. 1935, Liverpool, England. *Education:* BA, LLB, Trinity College, Dublin, 1958; Solicitor, Incorporated Law Society of Ireland, 1958. *Career:* mem. PEN; RSL, assoc.; Society of Authors. *Publications:* Novels: Summer Overtures, 1972; Freedom for Mr Mildew, 1975; Nigel Someone, 1975. Poetry: Sour Grapes, 2000; Cave Canem, 2002; Orts and All, 2003. Other: compiler or ed., 10 autobiographies, 1978–94. Contributions: anthologies and magazines. *Honours:* Co-Winner, Adam International Review First Novel Competition, 1968. *Address:* 132 Brick Lane, London E1 6RU, England.

MURPHY, Dervla Mary; Author and Critic; b. 28 Nov. 1931, Cappoquin, Ireland; one d. *Education:* Ursuline Convent, Waterford. *Publications:* Full Tilt, 1965; Tibetan Foothold, 1966; The Waiting Land, 1967; In Ethiopia With a Mule, 1968; On a Shoestring to Coorg, 1976; Where the Indus is Young, 1977; A Place Apart, 1978; Wheels Within Wheels, 1979; Race to the Finish?, 1981; Eight Feet in the Andes, 1983; Muddling Through in Madagascar, 1985; Ireland, 1985; Tales From Two Cities, 1987; Cameroon with Egbert, 1989; Transylvania and Beyond, 1992; The Ukimwi Road, 1993; South From the Limpopo, 1997; Visiting Rwanda, 1998; One Foot in Laos, 1999; Through the Embers of Chaos, 2002; Stymied in the BAM Zone, 2004. *Honours:* Ewart-Biggs Memorial Prize, 1978; Irish American Cultural Institute Literary Award, 1985. *Address:* Lismore, County Waterford, Ireland.

MURPHY, Jill; British writer and illustrator; b. 1949, Wimbledon, London; one s. *Education:* Chelsea Coll. of Art, Croydon and Camberwell Schools of Art. *Career:* fmr nanny, now writer of jr fiction and illustrator. *Publications include:* My Teddy 1973, The Worst Witch 1975, Peace at Last 1980, The Worst Witch Strikes Again 1981, A Bad Spell for the Worst Witch 1982, On the Way Home 1982, Whatever Next! 1983, Geoffrey Strangeways 1985, Baby Bear's Press-out Book 1985, Five Minutes' Peace 1986, All in One Piece 1987, Worlds Apart 1989, A Piece of Cake 1989, The Christmas Babies 1992, The Worst Witch All at Sea 1993, A Quiet Night In 1993, The Last Noo-noo 1995, All For One 2002. *Address:* c/o Puffin Books, 80 Strand, London, WC2R 0RL, England.

MURPHY, Richard; Poet and Author; b. 6 Aug. 1927, Co Galway, Ireland. *Education:* BA, MA, 1948, Magdalen College, Oxford; Sorbonne, University of Paris, 1955. *Career:* various visiting positions, including University of Virginia, 1965, University of Reading, 1968, Bard College, Annandale-on-Hudson, New York, 1972–74, Princeton University, 1974–75, University of Iowa, 1976–77, Syracuse University, 1977–78, Catholic University of America, Washington, DC, 1983, Pacific Lutheran University, Tacoma, Washington, 1985, Wichita State University, 1987; Compton Lecturer in Poetry, University of Hull, 1969; O'Connor Prof. of Literature, Colgate University, 1971; Distinguished Visiting Prof., University of Tulsa,

1992–95; mem. FRSL. *Publications:* The Archaeology of Love, 1955; The Woman of the House, 1959; The Last Galway Hooker, 1961; Sailing to an Island, 1963; The Battle of Aughrim, 1968; High Island, 1974; Selected Poems, 1979; The Price of Stone, 1985; The Mirror Wall, 1989; New Selected Poems, 1989; The Kick: A Memoir, 2002. Contributions: various periodicals. *Honours:* several poetry awards. *Address:* c/o Granta Books, 2–3 Hanover Yard, Noel Rd, London N1 8BE, England.

MURPHY, Tom, (Thomas Murphy); Dramatist, Writer and Dir; b. 23 Feb. 1935, Tuam, Co Galway, Ireland; m. Mary Lindisfarne Hamilton-Hippisley, 1966, two s. one d. *Education:* Tuam Vocational School; Voational Teachers' Training College, Dublin. *Plays:* Tom Murphy at the Abbey (six-play celebration Irish Nat. Theatre) 2001. *Publications:* The Seduction of Morality (novel), 1994; Plays, four vols, 1998. Other: Stage Plays: On the Outside, 1959; A Whistle in the Dark, 1961; A Crucial Week in the Life of a Grocer's Assistant, 1966; The Orphans, 1968; Famine, 1968; The Morning After Optimism, 1971; The White House, 1972; On the Inside, 1974; The Sanctuary Lamp, 1975; The J. Arthur Maginnis Story, 1976; The Blue Macushla, 1980; The Gigli Concert, 1983; Conversations on a Homecoming, 1985; Bailegangaire, 1985; A Thief of a Christmas, 1986; Too Late for Logic, 1989; The Patriot Game, 1991; The Wake, 1997, The House 2000, The Drunkard 2003, The Cherry Orchard 2004. *Honours:* Hon. DLitt (Dublin 1998, NUI Galway 2000)Irish Acad. of Letters Award, 1972; Harveys Awards, 1983, 1985; Independent Newspapers Awards, 1983, 1989; Drama-Logue Critics' Award, 1995; Irish Times ESB Theatre Awards Special Tribute 1997, Best Play 2000. *Address:* 4 Garville Rd, Dublin 6, Ireland.

MURPHY, Walter Francis; McCormick Prof. of Jurisprudence Emeritus and Writer; b. 21 Nov. 1929, Charleston, South Carolina, USA; m. Mary Therese Dolan, 28 June 1952, two d. *Education:* AB, University of Notre Dame, 1950; AM, George Washington University, 1954; PhD, University of Chicago, 1957. *Career:* Research Fellow, Brookings Institution, Washington, DC, 1957–58; Asst Prof., 1958–61, Assoc. Prof., 1961–65, Prof. of Politics, 1965–95, McCormick Prof. of Jurisprudence, 1968–95, Prof. Emeritus, 1995–, Princeton University; mem. American Acad. of Arts and Sciences, fellow; American Political Science Assen. *Publications:* Courts, Judges and Politics (ed. with C. Herman Pritchett and Lee Epstein), 1961; Congress and the Court, 1962; American Democracy (co-author), fourth–10th edns, 1963–83; Elements of Judicial Strategy, 1964; Wiretapping on Trial, 1965; Modern American Democracy (with M. N. Danielson), 1969; The Study of Public Law (with Joseph Tanenaus), 1972; Public Evaluations of Constitutional Courts (co-author), 1974; Comparative Constitutional Law (co-author), 1977; The Vicar of Christ (fiction), 1979; Basic Cases in Constitutional Law (ed. with W. D. Lockard), 1980; The Roman Enigma (fiction), 1981; Upon This Rock (fiction), 1986; American Constitutional Interpretation (with J. Fleming, S. A. Barber and S. Macedo), third edn, 2003. Contributions: professional journals. *Honours:* Distinguished Service Cross; Purple Heart; Birkhead Award, 1958; Merriam-Cobb-Hughes Award, 1963; Guggenheim Fellowship, 1973–74; National Endowment for the Humanities Fellowship, 1978–79; Chicago Foundation for Literature Award, 1980; Lifetime Achievement Award, Law and Courts Section, American Political Science Assen, 1995. *Address:* 1533 Eagle Ridge Dr. NE, Albuquerque, NM 87122, USA. *E-mail:* wmurphy37@comcast.net.

MURRAY, Douglas; British journalist and biographer; b. 1979. *Education:* Eton Public School, Magdalen Coll., Oxford. *Publications:* Bosie: A Biography of Lord Alfred Douglas 2000. *Literary Agent:* c/o Hodder and Stoughton General, 338 Euston Road, London, NW1 3BH, England. *Website:* www.hodderheadline.co.uk.

MURRAY, Frances (see Booth, Rosemary).

MURRAY, John; British novelist; b. 1950, Cumbria; m.; one d. *Career:* founder and co-ed., Panurge 1984. *Publications:* novels: Samarkand 1985, Kin 1986, Radio Activity 1993, Riever Blues 1996, John Dory 2001, Jazz Etc. 2003; short story collection: Pleasure 1987. *Honours:* Dylan Thomas Award 1988, winner of creative category, Lakeland Book of the Year 2002. *Literary Agent:* c/o Independent Northern Publishers, Flambard Press, PO Box 990, Newcastle upon Tyne, NE99 2US, England. *Telephone:* (191) 212-0354. *E-mail:* info@northernpublishers.co.uk. *Website:* www.flambardpress.co.uk.

MURRAY, John R.; British publisher and author; *Chairman, John Murray (Publishers) Limited. Education:* Univ. of Oxford. *Career:* currently Chair. John Murray (Publrs) Ltd (bought by Hodder Headline 2002). *Publications include:* Old Chestnuts Warmed Up (ed.) 2002. *Address:* Hodder Headline, 338 Euston Road, London, NW1 3BH, England (Office). *Website:* www.johnmurray.co.uk (Office); www.hodderheadline.co.uk (Office).

MURRAY, Leslie (Les) Allan, BA; Australian poet, writer and translator; b. 17 Oct. 1938, Nabiac, NSW; m. 1962; three s. two d. *Education:* University of Sydney. *Career:* Co-Ed., Poetry Australia, 1973–80; Poetry Reader, Angus and Robertson Publishers, 1976–91; Literary Ed., Quadrant, 1990–; mem. Poetry Society of Great Britain, hon. vice-pres. *Publications:* Poetry: The Ilex Tree (with Geoffrey Lehmann), 1965; The Weatherboard Cathedral, 1969; Poems Against Economics, 1972; Lunch and Counter Lunch, 1974; Selected Poems: The Vernacular Republic, 1976; Ethnic Radio, 1978; The Boys Who Stole the Funeral, 1980; Equanimities, 1982; The People's Otherworld, 1983; Persistence in Folly, 1984; The Australian Year (with Peter Solness), 1986; The Daylight Moon, 1986; Dog Fox Field, 1990; Collected Poems, 1991; The Rabbiter's Bounty, 1992; Translations from the Natural World, 1991; Subhuman Redneck Poems, 1997; Fredy Neptune: A Novel in Verse, 1998; Learning Human: New Selected Poems, 2001. Prose: The Peasant Mandarin, 1978; Blocks and Tackles, 1991; The Paperbark Tree: Selected Prose, 1992; A Working Forest, 1997. Editor: The New Oxford Book of Australian Verse, 1986; Collins Dove Anthology of Australian Religious Verse, 1986; Fivefathers: Five Australian Poets of the Pre-Academic Era, 1994. Contributions: many publications. *Honours:* Grace Leven Prizes, 1965, 1980, 1990; Cook Bicentennial Prize, 1970; National Book Awards, 1974, 1984, 1985, 1991, 1993; C. J. Dennis Memorial Prize, 1976; Gold Medal, Australian Literary Society, 1984; New South Wales Premier's Prize, 1984, 1993; Canada-Australia Award, 1985; Australian Broadcasting Corporation Bicentennial Prize, 1988; National Poetry Award, 1988; AM, 1989; Victorian Premier's Prize, 1993; Petrarca Preis, Germany, 1995; T. S. Eliot Prize, 1997; Queen's Gold Medal for Poetry, 1999; Hon. doctorates. *Literary Agent:* Margaret Connolly and Assocs, 16 Winton Street, Warrawee, NSW 2074, Australia.

MURRELL, John; Canadian dramatist and translator; b. 15 Oct. 1945, Lubbock, TX, USA. *Education:* BFA, Southwestern University, Georgetown, Texas, 1966; BEd, University of Calgary, 1969. *Career:* Playwright-in-Residence, Alberta Theatre Project, 1975–76; Assoc. Dir, Stratford Festival, 1977–78; Dramaturg, Theatre Calgary, 1981–82; Head, Playwright's Colony, Banff Centre School of Fine Art, 1986, Theatre Section, Canada Council, 1988–92. *Publications:* Haydn's Head, 1973; Power in the Blood, 1975; Teaser (with Kenneth Dyba), 1975; Arena, 1975; A Great Noise, a Great Light, 1976; Memoir, 1977; Waiting for the Parade, 1980; Farther West, 1986; New World, 1986; October, 1988; Democracy, 1992; Faraway Nearby, 1995. *Honours:* Clifford E. Lee Playwrighting Award, 1975. *Address:* c/o Talonbooks, No. 104-3100 Production Way, Burnaby, BC V5A 4R4, Canada.

MUSCHG, Adolf, PhD; writer, dramatist and academic; b. 13 May 1934, Zollikon, Switzerland. *Education:* Zürich, Cambridge, England. *Career:* Prof., Eidgenössische Technische Hochschule, Zürich 1970–. *Publications:* Im Sommer des Hasen, 1965; Fremdkörper, 1968; Das Kerbelgericht, 1969; Die Aufgeregten von Goethe, 1971; Liebesgeschichten, 1972; Albissers Grund, 1974; Kellers Abend, 1975; Gottfried Keller, 1977; Baiyun oder die Freundschaftsgesellschaft, 1980; Literatur als Therapie?, 1981; Das Licht und der Schlüssel, 1984; Der rote Ritter, 1993; Nur ausziehen wollte sie sich nicht, 1995. *Honours:* Hermann Hesse Prize, 1974; Literature Prize, Zürich, 1984; Carl Zuckmayer Medal, 1990; Georg Büchner Prize, 1994. *Address:* Hasenackerstrasse 24, 8708 Männedorf, Switzerland.

MUSGRAVE, Susan; Canadian poet and writer; b. 12 March 1951, Santa Cruz, CA, USA; m. 3rd Stephen Reid 1986; two d. *Career:* Instructor and Writer-in-Residence, University of Waterloo, Ontario, 1983–85; Instructor, Kootenay School of Writing, BC, 1986, Camosun College, Victoria, 1988–; Writer-in-Residence, University of New Brunswick, 1985, University of Western Ontario, 1992–93, University of Toronto, 1995, Victoria School of Writing, 1996, 1998; Writer-in-Electronic-Residence, York University and Writers' Development Trust, 1991–; mem. British Columbia Federation of Writers; Writer's Union of Canada, chair, 1997–98. *Publications:* Poetry: Songs of the Sea-Witch, 1970; Entrance of the Celebrant, 1972; Grave-Dirt and Selected Strawberries, 1973, revised edn as Selected Strawberries and Other Poems, 1977; The Impstone, 1976; Becky Swan's Book, 1978; A Man to Marry, A Man to Bury, 1979; Tarts and Muggers: Poems New and Selected, 1982; Cocktails at the Mausoleum, 1985; The Embalmer's Art: Poems New and Selected, 1991; In the Small Hours of the Rain, 1991; Forcing the Narcissus, 1994; Things That Keep and Do Not Change, 1999; What the Small Day Cannot Hold: Collected Poems, 1970–1985, 2000. Fiction: The Charcoal Burners, 1980; The Dancing Chicken, 1987; Cargo of Orchids, 2000. Other: Great Musgrave, 1989; Clear Cut Words: Writers for Clayoquot (ed.), 1993; Musgrave Landing: Musings on the Writing Life, 1994; Because You Loved Being a Stranger: 55 Poets Celebrate Patrick Lane (ed.), 1994. Children's Books: Gullband (poems), 1974; Hag Head (fiction), 1980; Kestrel and Leonardo (poems), 1990; Dreams Are More Real than Bathtubs (fiction), 1998. Contributions: many anthologies, reviews, quarterlies, and journals. *Honours:* many grants; Second Prize, National Magazine Award, 1981; First Prize, B. P. Nichol Poetry Chapbook Award, 1991; Readers' Choice Award, Prairie Schooner, 1993; Vicky Metcalf Short Story Ed.'s Award, 1996. *Address:* PO Box 2421, Station Main, Sidney, BC V8L 3Y3, Canada.

MUSGROVE, Frank; Prof. of Education Emeritus and Writer; b. 16 Dec. 1922, Nottingham, England; m. Dorothy Ellen Nicholls, one d. *Education:* BA, Magdalen College, Oxford, 1947; PhD, University of Nottingham, 1958. *Career:* Lecturer, University of Leicester, 1957–62; Senior Lecturer, University of Leeds, 1963–65; Prof. of Research in Education, University of Bradford, 1965–70; Sarah Fielden Prof. of Education, 1970–82, Prof. Emeritus, 1982–, University of Manchester; Co-Ed., Research in Education, 1971–76; Hon. Prof., University of Hull, 1985–88; various guest lectureships; mem. Royal Anthropological Institute; FRSA. *Publications:* The Migratory Elite, 1963; Youth and the Social Order, 1964; The Family, Education and Society, 1966; Society and the Teacher's Role (with P. H. Taylor), 1969; Patterns of Power and Authority in English Education, 1971;

Ecstasy and Holiness, 1974; Margins of the Mind, 1977; School and the Social Order, 1979; Education and Anthropology, 1982; The North of England: A History from Roman Times to the Present, 1990. Contributions: Professional journals. *Honours:* Doctor of Letters, Open University, 1982. *Address:* Dib Scar, the Cedar Grove, Beverley, East Yorkshire HU17 7EP, England.

MUSICANT, Ivan Martin; Naval Historian; b. 18 Dec. 1943, New York, NY, USA; m. Gretchen Granlund Musicant, 17 July 1982, one s. *Education:* BA, History, Bemidji State University. *Publications:* United States Armored Cruisers: A Design and Operational History, 1985; Battleship At War: The Epic Story of the USS Washington, 1986; The Banana Wars: United States Military Intervention in Latin America, 1990; Divided Waters: The Naval History of the Civil War, 1995; Empire by Default: The Spanish-American War, 1998. Contributions: journals, reviews, periodicals and quarterlies. *Honours:* Samuel Eliot Morison Awards for Naval Literature, 1987, 1998. *Address:* 3701 Glendale Terrace, Minneapolis, MN 55410, USA.

MUSKE-DUKES, Carol Anne; poet, writer and academic; b. 17 Dec. 1945, St Paul, Minnesota, USA; m. David Dukes 1983 (died 2000); one step-s. one d. *Education:* BA, English, Creighton University, Omaha, 1967; MA, English, California State University, San Francisco, 1970. *Career:* Founder-Writing Program Dir, Art Without Walls, New York, 1971–84; Lecturer, New School for Social Research, New York City, 1975; Asst Prof., University of New Hampshire, 1978–79; Visiting Writer, 1978, Visiting Poet, 1983, 1993, University of California at Irvine; Adjunct Prof., Columbia University, 1979–81; Visiting Poet, Iowa Writers' Workshop, 1980; Jenny McKean Moore Lecturer, George Washington University, 1980–81; Writer-in-Residence, University of Virginia, 1981; Lecturer, 1984–88, Asst Prof., 1989–91, Assoc. Prof., 1991–93, Prof., 1993–, Founder-Dir, PhD Program in Creative Writing and Literature, 1999–, University of Southern California, Los Angeles; Visiting Fiction Writer, University of California, Los Angeles, 1989; mem. Poetry Society of America, West, program dir and pres., 1992–94. *Publications:* Poetry: Camouflage, 1975; Skylight, 1981; Wyndmere, 1985; Applause, 1989; Red Trousseau, 1993; An Octave Above Thunder: Selected and New Poems, 1997. Fiction: Dear Digby, 1989; Saving St Germ, 1993; Life After Death, 2001; Married to the Icepick Killer: A Poet in Hollywood, 2002. Non-Fiction: Women and Poetry (essays), 1997. Contributions: numerous anthologies and journals. *Honours:* Dylan Thomas Poetry Award, 1973; Pushcart Prizes, 1978, 1988–89, 1992–93, 1998; Alice Fay di Castagnola Award, Poetry Society of America, 1979; Guggenheim Fellowship, 1981; National Endowment for the Arts Grant, 1984; Ingram Merrill Foundation Fellowship, 1988; New York Times Most Notable Book Citation, 1993; Alumni Achievement Award, Creighton University, 1996; Witter Bynner Award, Library of Congress, Washington, DC, 1997–98. *Literary Agent:* Aaron Priest Literary Agency, 708 Third Avenue, 23rd Floor, New York, NY 10017, USA. *Address:* c/o Dept of English, University of Southern California, Los Angeles, CA 90095, USA.

MUTIS, Alvaro; Poet and Novelist; b. 25 Aug. 1923, Bogotá, Colombia; m. Mireya Durán; three s. *Publications:* Poetry: La balanza, 1948; Los elementos del desastre, 1953; Reseñas de los Hospitales de Ultramar, 1955; Los Trabajos Perdidos, 1965; Summa de Maqroll el Gaviero, 1973; Caravansary, 1981; Los emisarios, 1984; Crónica regia y alabanza del reino, 1985; Un homenaje y siete nocturnos, 1986. Novels: Diario de Lecumberri, 1960; La mansión de Araucaíma, 1973; La verdadera historia del flautista de Hammelin, 1982; La Nieve del Almirante; Ilona llega con la lluvia, 1987; Un bel morir, 1989; La última escala del Tramp Steamer, 1989; La muerte del estratega, 1990; Amirbar, 1990; Abdul Bashur, soñador de navíos, 1991; Tríptico de mar y tierra, 1993. Essays: Contextos para Maqroll, 1997; De lecturas y algo del mundo, 1999; Caminos y encuentros de Maqroll el Gaviero, 2001. *Honours:* Premio Nacional de Letras, 1974; Premio Nacional de Poesía, 1983; Premio de la Crítica 'Los Abriles', 1985; Comendador de la Orden del Águila Azteca, Mexico, 1988; Premio Xavier Villaurrutia, Mexico, 1988; Dr hc, Universidad del Valle, Colombia, 1988; Commdr., Ordre des Arts et des Lettres, France, 1989; Prix Médicis Étranger, France, 1989; Nonino Prize, Italy, 1990; Ordre nat. du Mérite, France, 1993; Roger Caillois Prize, France, 1993; Gran Cruz de la Orden de Boyacá, 1993; Gran Cruz de la Orden de Alfonso X el Sabio, Spain, 1996; Grinzane-Cavour Prize, Italy, 1997; Premio Príncipe de Asturias de las Letras, Spain, 1997; Premio Reina Sofía de Poesía Iberoamericana, Spain, 1997; Rossone d'Oro Prize, Italy, 1997; Trieste Poetry Prize, Italy, 2000; Premio Cervantes, Spain, 2001; Neustadt Prize, 2002. *Address:* c/o Picador, Pan Macmillan, 20 New Wharf Rd, London N1 9RR, England.

MWANGI, Meja; Novelist; b. 1948, Nanyuki, Kenya. *Education:* Kenyatta College. *Career:* soundman, TV ORTF, 1972–73; film librarian, British Council, 1974–75; Fellow in Writing, Iowa Univ., 1975–76; also film dir, casting agent and location man. *Publications:* Kill Me Quick, 1973; Carcase for Hounds, 1974; Going Down River Road, 1976; The Cockroach Dance, 1979; The Bushtrackers, 1980; Bread of Sorrow, 1987; Weapon for Hunger, 1989; The Return of Shaka, 1990; Striving for the Wind, 1990. Other: children's books, plays. *Honours:* Jomo Kenyatta Prize, 1974. *Address:* c/o African Writers Series, Heinemann Educational Publishers, Halley Ct, Jordan Hill, Oxford OX2 8EJ, England.

MYERS, Jack (Elliot); Prof. of English, Poet and Writer; b. 29 Nov. 1941, Lynn, Massachusetts, USA; m. 1st Nancy, 1967; m. 2nd Willa, 1981; m. 3rd Thea, 1993, three s., one d. *Education:* BA, English Literature, University of Massachusetts, Boston, 1970; MFA, Poetry Writing, University of Iowa, 1972. *Career:* Asst Prof., 1975–81, Assoc. Prof., 1982–88, Prof. of English, 1988–, Dir, Creative Writing Program, 1990–94, Southern Methodist University, Dallas; Poetry Ed., Fiction International, 1978–80, Cimarron Review, 1989–91; Faculty, MFA Program in Writing, Vermont College, 1981–; Distinguished Poet-in-Residence, Wichita State University, 1992; Distinguished Visiting Writer, University of Idaho, 1993; Distinguished Writer-in-Residence, Northeast Louisiana University, 1995; mem. Associated Writing Programs; PEN; Texas Asscn of Creative Writing Teachers; Texas Institute of Letters. *Publications:* Poetry: Black Sun Abraxas, 1970; Will It Burn, 1974; The Family War, 1977; I'm Amazed That You're Still Singing, 1981; Coming to the Surface, 1984; As Long as You're Happy, 1986; Blindsided, 1993; Human Being, 1997. Other: A Trout in the Milk: A Composite Portrait of Richard Hugo, 1980; New American Poets of the 80s (ed. with Roger Weingarten), 1984; The Longman Dictionary of Poetic Terms, 1985; A Profile of Twentieth-Century American Poetry (ed. with David Wojahn), 1991; New American Poets of the 90s (ed. with Roger Weingarten), 1991; Leaning House Poets, Vol. 1 (ed. with Mark Elliott), 1996; One On One, 1999. Contributions: anthologies, reviews, quarterlies, journals, and magazines. *Honours:* Acad. of American Poets Award, 1972; Texas Institute of Letters Poetry Awards, 1978, 1993; Yaddo Fellowship, 1978; National Endowment for the Arts Fellowships, 1982–83, 1986–87; Winner, National Poetry Series Open Competition, 1985; Southern Methodist University Author's Award, 1987.

MYERSON, Julie, BA; British writer and journalist; b. 1960, Nottingham; m. Jonathan Myerson; three c. *Education:* Univ. of Bristol. *Career:* staff mem., Royal Nat. Theatre, London; publicist, columnist, broadcaster, panellist on Newsnight Review (BBC2). *Publications include:* novels: Sleepwalking 1994, The Touch 1996, Me and the Fatman 1998, Laura Blundy 2000, Something Might Happen 2003; non-fiction: Home: The Story of Everyone Who Ever Lived in Our House 2004. *Honours:* Elle talent contest 1993. *Address:* Jonathan Cape Ltd, 20 Vauxhall Bridge Road, London, SW1V 2SA, England. *Website:* www.randomhouse.co.uk.

MYNERS, Paul, FRSA; British publishing executive; *Chairman, Guardian Media Group*; b. 1 April 1948; m.; five c. *Education:* Univ. of London. *Career:* finance writer, Daily Telegraph –1974; N. M. Rothschild 1974–85; CEO Gartmore Investment Man. 1985–87, Chair. 1987–2001; Deputy Chair. Powergen 1999–2001; Exec. Dir Nat. Westminster Bank 1999–2000; Dir City Disputes Panel, Financial Reporting Council, Lloyds of London Investment Cttee; Chair. Guardian Media Group 2001–; Dir (non-exec.) mmO; $_2$ 2001–, Bank of NY, Marks & Spencer 2002, interim Chair. June 2004–; Chair. Tate St Ives; mem. Royal Acad. Trust, United Response. *Address:* Guardian Media Group, 75 Farringdon Road, London, EC1M 3JX (Office); Gartmore House, 8 Fenchurch Place, London, EC3M 4PH, England. *Telephone:* (20) 7278-2332 (Guardian) (Office); (20) 7782-2000. *Fax:* (20) 7242-0679 (Guardian) (Office). *Website:* www.gmgplc.co.uk.

MYRDAL, Jan; Writer and Columnist; b. 19 July 1927, Stockholm, Sweden; m. 1st Nadja Wiking, 1948; m. 2nd Maj Liedberg, 1953; m. 3rd Gun Kessle, 1956, one s. one d. *Publications:* (in English trans.) Report from a Chinese Village, 1965; Chinese Journey, 1965; Confessions of a Disloyal European, 1968; Angkor: An Essay on Art and Imperialism, 1970; China: The Revolution Continued, 1971; Gates to Asia, 1971; Albania Defiant, 1976; The Silk Road, 1979; China Notebook, 1975–78, 1979; Return to a Chinese Village, 1984; India Waits, 1984; Childhood, 1991; Another World, 1993; 12 Going on 13, 1995. Contributions: newspapers and journals. *Honours:* Hon. doctorates; Chevalier, Ordre des Arts et des Lettres, 1990. *Address:* Kalvängen 70 D, 73991 Skinnskatteberg, Sweden. *E-mail:* myrdal@myrdal.pp.se.

N

NÁDAS, Péter; Novelist, Essayist and Playwright; b. 1942, Budapest, Hungary. *Publications:* A biblia (short stories), 1967; Kulcskereso játék (short stories), 1969; Egy családregény vége (The End of a Family Story, novel), 1977; Takarítás (play), 1977; Találkozás (play), 1979; Leírás, 1980; Temetés, 1980; Nézotér, 1983; Emlékiratok kónyve (A Book of Memories), 1986; Játéktér, 1988; Égi és földi szerelem, 1991; Találtcetli, 1992; A Lovely Tale of Photography (in trans.), 1999; Valamennyi fény, 2000; Love (in trans.), 2001. *Honours:* Prize for Hungarian Art, 1989; Austrian State Prize for European Literature, 1991; Vilenica International Prize for Literature, 1998. *Address:* c/o Jonathan Cape, 20 Vauxhall Bridge Rd, London SW1V 2SA, England.

NADAUS, Roland, (Pol-Jean Mervillon); Writer and Poet; b. 28 Nov. 1945, Paris, France; m. Simone Moris, 9 Sept. 1967, one d. *Career:* mem. PEN Club of France. *Publications:* Maison de Paroles, 1969; Journal: Vrac, 1981; Je ne Tutoie que Dieu et ma femme (poems), 1992; Dictionnaire initiatique de l'orant, 1993; L'homme que tuèrent les mouches, 1996. Contributions: journals. *Honours:* Prix Gustave Gasser, 1993.

NADER, Ralph; Consumer Advocate, Lecturer, Writer and Lawyer; b. 27 Feb. 1934, Winsted, CT, USA. *Education:* BA, magna cum laude, Princeton University, 1955; LLB, Harvard University, 1958. *Career:* Admitted to the Bar, CT, 1958, MA, 1959, US Supreme Court, 1959; Lecturer in History and Government, University of Hartford, 1961–63; Founder-Dir, various consumer advocacy groups; Lecturer, many colleges and universities; Candidate for Pres. of the USA, 1996, 2000, 2004; mem. American Acad. of Arts and Sciences; American Bar Asscn. *Publications:* Unsafe at Any Speed, 1965; Action for a Change (co-author), 1972; Who Runs Congress?, 1972; Whistle Blowing: The Report on the Conference on Professional Responsibility (ed.), 1972; You and Your Pension (co-author), 1973; The Consumer and Corporate Accountability (ed.), 1973; Corporate Power in America (co-ed.), 1973; Taming the Giant Corporation (co-author), 1976; Verdicts on Lawyers (co-ed.), 1976; The Menace of Atomic Energy (co-author), 1977; The Lemon Book, 1980; Who's Poisoning America? (co-ed.), 1981; The Big Boys, 1986; Winning the Insurance Game (co-author), 1990; Good Works, 1993; No Contest: Corporate Lawyers and the Perversion of Justice in America, 1996; The Ralph Nader Reader, 2000; Crashing the Party, 2002. Contributions: periodicals. *Address:* c/o Consumer Advocate Center, PO Box 19367, Washington, DC 20036, USA.

NADICH, Judah; Rabbi and Writer; b. 13 May 1912, Baltimore, MD, USA; m. Martha Hadassah Ribalow, 26 Jan. 1947, three d. *Education:* AB, College of New York, 1932; Jewish Theological Seminary of America, 1932–36; MA, Columbia University, 1936; Rabbi, Master of Arts, Doctor of Hebrew Literature, 1953. *Career:* mem. Jewish Book Council of America, pres., 1970–72; Rabbinical Assembly, pres., 1972–74. *Publications:* Eisenhower and the Jews, 1953; Menachem Ribalow: The Flowering of Modern Hebrew Literature (trans.), 1957; Louis Ginzberg: Al Halakhah Ve-Aggadah (ed.), 1960; Jewish Legends of the Second Commonwealth, 1983; Legends of the Rabbis, 1994; Rabbi Akiba and His Contemporaries, 1998. Contributions: Reference works, books, and journals. *Honours:* Croix de Guerre, 1945; Aleh, Israel, 1985. *Address:* 1040 Park Ave, 4D, New York, NY 10128, USA.

NADOLNY, Sten, DPhil; German writer; b. 29 July 1942, Zehdenick/Havel. *Publications:* Netzkarte 1981, Die Entdeckung der Langsamkeit 1983, Selim oder die Gabe der Rede 1990, Das Erzählen und die guten Absichten 1990, Ein Gott der Frechheit 1994, Er oder ich 1999, Ullsteinroman 2003. *Honours:* Ingeborg Bachmann Prize 1980, Hans Fallada Prize 1985, Vallombrosa Prize, Florence 1986, Ernst Hoferichter Prize 1995. *Literary Agent:* Agence Hoffman, Bechsteinstrasse 2, 80804 Munich, Germany. *Telephone:* (89) 308 48 07. *Fax:* (89) 308 21 08.

NAFISI, Azar, PhD; Iranian writer and academic; b. 1962; m.; one d. *Education:* Oklahoma Univ., USA. *Career:* fmrly teacher, Tehran Univ., Allemeh Tabatabai Univ.; fmrly visiting fellow, Oxford Univ.; currently Dir of the Dialogue Project, School of Advanced Int. Studies, Johns Hopkins Univ., Washington, DC, USA. *Publications:* Anti-Terra: A Study of Vladimir Nabokov's Novels 1994, Reading Lolita in Tehran: A Memoir in Books 2003; contrib. numerous chapters and articles on promotion of democracy, human rights in Muslim societies, women's rights, literature, culture. *Address:* The Paul H. Nitze School of Advanced International Studies, Johns Hopkins University, The Nitze Building, 1740 Massachusetts Avenue, Washington, DC 20036, USA.

NAFTALI, Ben (see Offen, Yehuda).

NAGATSUKA, Ryuji; Prof. and Writer; b. 20 April 1924, Nagoya, Japan; m. 20 July 1949. *Education:* Graduated, French Literature, University of Tokyo, 1948. *Career:* Prof., Nihon University, 1968–; mem. Asscn Internationale des Critiques Littéraires, Paris. *Publications:* Napoleon tel qu'il était, 1969; J'étais un kamikaze, 1972; George Sand, sa vie et ses oeuvres, 1977; Napoleon, 2 vols, 1986; Talleyrand, 1990. Contributions: Yomiuri Shimbun. *Honours:* Prix Pierre Mille, 1972; Prix Senghor, 1973. *Address:* 7-6-37 Oizumigakuen-cho, Nerima-ku, Tokyo, Japan.

NAGEL, Paul Chester, BA, MA, PhD; historian and writer; b. 14 Aug. 1926, Independence, MO, USA; m. Joan Peterson 1948; three s. *Education:* Univ. of Minnesota. *Career:* historian, Strategic Air Command, US Air Force, Omaha, 1951–53; Asst Prof., Augustana Coll., Sioux Falls, SD 1953–54; Asst Prof. to Assoc. Prof., Eastern Kentucky Univ., Richmond 1954–61; Visiting Prof., Amherst Coll. 1957–58, Vanderbilt Univ. 1959, Univ. of Minnesota 1964; Faculty 1961–65, Prof. of History 1965–69, Dean, Coll. of Arts and Sciences 1965–69, Univ. of Kentucky; Special Asst to the Pres. for Academic Affairs 1969–71, Prof. of History 1969–78, Vice-Pres. for Academic Affairs 1971–74, Univ. of Missouri; Prof. of History and Head of Dept of History, Univ. of Georgia 1978–80; Dir, Virginia Historical Soc., Richmond 1981–85; Distinguished Lee Scholar, Lee Memorial Foundation 1986–90; Visiting Scholar, Duke Univ. 1991–92, Univ. of Minnesota 1992–, Carleton Coll. 1993–; mem. Colonial Williamsburg Foundation (trustee 1983–95), Massachusetts Historical Soc., Pilgrim Soc., Soc. of American Historians, Southern Historical Asscn (pres. 1984–85). *Publications:* One Nation Indivisible: The Union in American Thought 1776–1861 1964, This Sacred Trust: American Nationality 1798–1898 1971, Missouri: A History 1977, Descent from Glory: Four Generations of the John Adams Family 1983, Extraordinary Lives: The Art and Craft of American Biography (co-author) 1986, The Adams Women: Abigail and Louisa Adams, Their Sisters and Daughters 1987, George Caleb Bingham (co-author) 1989, The Lees of Virginia: Seven Generations of an American Family 1990, Massachusetts and the New Nation (co-author) 1992, John Quincy Adams: A Public Life, A Private Life 1997, The German Migration to Missouri 2002, George Caleb Bingham: Missouri's Famed Painter and Forgotten Politician 2004; contrib. to professional journals and general publications. *Honours:* Best Book Award 1977, Book of the Month Club Main Selection 1983, Laureate of Virginia 1988, American Soc. of Colonial Dames Book Award 1998. *Address:* 1425 10th Avenue S, Apt 655, Minneapolis, MN 55404, USA.

NAGEL, Thomas; American academic and writer; b. 4 July 1937, Belgrade, Yugoslavia; m. 1st Doris Blum 1958 (divorced 1973); m. 2nd Anne Hollander 1979. *Education:* BA, Cornell University, 1958; BPhil, Corpus Christi College, Oxford, 1960; PhD, Harvard University, 1963. *Career:* Asst Prof. of Philosophy, University of California at Berkeley, 1963–66; Asst Prof., 1966–69, Assoc. Prof., 1969–72, Prof., 1972–80, Princeton University; Tanner Lecturer, Stanford University, 1977; Tanner Lecturer, 1979, John Locke Lecturer, 1990, University of Oxford; Prof. of Philosophy, 1980–, Chair., Dept of Philosophy, 1981–86, Prof. of Philosophy and Law, 1986–, New York University; Howison Lecturer, University of California at Berkeley, 1987; Thalheimer Lecturer, Johns Hopkins University, 1989; Hempel Lecturer, Princeton University, 1995; Whitehead Lecturer, Harvard University, 1995; Immanuel Kant Lecturer, Stanford University, 1995; mem. American Acad. of Arts and Sciences, fellow; British Acad., fellow. *Publications:* The Possibility of Altruism, 1970; Mortal Questions, 1979; The View from Nowhere, 1986; What Does It All Mean?, 1987; Equality and Partiality, 1991; Other Minds: Critical Essays, 1969–94, 1995; The Last Word, 1997. Contributions: scholarly journals. *Honours:* Guggenheim Fellowship, 1966–67; National Endowment for the Humanities Fellowships, 1978–79, 1984–85; Hon. Fellow, Corpus Christi College, Oxford, 1992–. *Address:* c/o School of Law, New York University, 40 Washington Square S, New York, NY 10012, USA.

NAGY, Gáspár; Hungarian poet, writer and editor; b. 4 May 1949, Bérbaltavár; m. Márta Szabó 1974; one s. two d. *Education:* teacher training coll., Szombathely. *Career:* mem. Hungarian Writers' Asscn (sec. 1981–85), Hungarian Art Acad. (sec. 2001–). *Publications:* poems: Koronatűz 1975, Halántékdob 1978, Földi pörök 1982, Kibiztosított beszéd 1987, Áron mondja 1986, Múlik a Jövőnk 1989, Mosolyelágazás 1993, Fölös ébrenlétem 1994, Tudom, nagy nyári délután lesz 1998, Szabadrabok 1999, Húsz év a kétezerből 2000, Amíg fölragyog a jászol 2001, Nem szabad feledni 2002, Ezredváltó sűrű évek 2003; fiction: Augusztusban Ludvík Jahn nyomában 1995, Kanizsa(vár) vissza 1999; essays: Zónaidő 1995, Szavak a rengetegből 2004; contrib. to journals, magazines, periodicals and newspapers. *Honours:* Radnóti 1977, József Attila 1990, Greve 1993, Getz Award 1995, Balassi Prize 1999, Kossuth Prize 2000, András Görömbei: Nagy Gáspár (monograph) 2004. *Address:* Felkeszi v 17, 2092 Budakeszi, Hungary. *E-mail:* gasparn@hu.inter.net.

NAGY, Paul; Writer; b. 23 Aug. 1934, Hungary. *Education:* BA, Hungary, 1953; Diploma, French Language and Literature, Sorbonne, University of Paris, 1962. *Career:* Co-Founder, Atelier Hongrois, 1962, p'ART video review, 1987; mem. Union des écrivains français; Union des écrivains hongrois. *Publications:* Les faineants de Hampstead, 1969; SadisfactionS, 1977; Journal in-time, I, 1984, II, 1994; Points de Repères 'Postmodernes': Lyotard, Habermas, Derrida, 1993; Les genres nouveaux de la littérature, 1995; Sacrés Grecs!, 1998; Le texte inaccessible, 1999. Contributions: several publications. *Honours:* Prix Attila József, Budapest, 2000. *Address:* 141 Ave Jean Jaures, 92120 Montrouge, France.

NAHAL, Chaman; Writer; b. 2 Aug. 1927, Sialkot, India. *Education:* MA, Delhi University, 1948; PhD, University of Nottingham, 1961. *Career:*

Mem., Dept of English, Delhi University, 1963–; Columnist, Talking About Books, The Indian Express newspaper, 1966–73; Assoc. Prof. of English, Long Island University, New York, USA, 1968–70. *Publications:* The Weird Dances (short stories), 1965; A Conversation with J. Kristnamurti, 1965; D. H. Lawrence: An Eastern View, 1970; Drugs and the Other Self (ed.), 1971; The Narrative Pattern in Ernest Hemingway's Fiction, 1971; The New Literatures in English, 1985; The Bhagavad-Gita: A New Rendering, 1987. Fiction: My True Faces, 1973; Azadi, 1975; Into Another Dawn, 1977; The English Queens, 1979; The Crown and the Loincloth, 1982; Sunrise in Fiji, 1988; The Salt of Life, 1990. *Address:* 2/1 Kalkaji Extension, New Delhi 110019, India.

NAIFEH, Steven (Woodward); Writer; b. 19 June 1952, Tehran, Iran. *Education:* AB, Princeton University, 1974; JD, 1977, MA, 1978, Harvard University. *Publications:* Culture Making: Money, Success, and the New York Art World, 1976; Moving Up in Style (with Gregory White Smith), 1980; Gene Davis, 1981; How to Make Love to a Woman, 1982; What Every Client Needs to Know About Using a Lawyer, 1982; The Bargain Hunter's Guide to Art Collecting, 1982; Why Can't Men Open Up?: Overcoming Men's Fear of Intimacy, 1984; The Mormon Murders: A True Story of Greed, Forgery, Deceit, and Death, 1988; Jackson Pollack: An American Saga, 1989; The Best Lawyers in America (ed. with Gregory White Smith), 1990; The Best Doctors in America (ed. with Gregory White Smith), 1992; Final Justice: The True Story of the Richest Man Ever Tried for Murder, 1993; A Stranger in the Family: A True Story of Murder, Madness, and Unconditional Love, 1995; On a Street Called Easy, In a Cottage Called Joye, 1996; Making Miracles Happen, 1997. *Honours:* Pulitzer Prize for Biography, 1991. *Address:* 1359 Silver Bluff Rd, Suite F2, Aiken, SC 29803, USA.

NAIPAUL, Sir Vidiadhar Surajprasad, Kt, CLit, BA, FRSL; Trinidadian-born writer; b. 17 Aug. 1932, Chaguanas; m. 1st Patricia Ann Hale 1955 (died 1996); m. 2nd Nadira Khannum Alvi 1996. *Education:* Queen's Royal Coll., Port-of-Spain and Univ. Coll. Oxford. *Career:* for two years freelance broadcaster with the BBC, producing programmes for the Caribbean area; fiction reviewer on New Statesman 1958–61; grant from Trinidad Govt to travel in Caribbean and S America 1961; in India 1962–63, 1975, 1988–89, in Uganda 1965–66, in USA 1969, 1978–79, 1987–88, in Argentina 1972, 1973–74, 1977, 1991, in Venezuela 1977, 1985, in Iran, Pakistan, Malaysia and Indonesia 1979–80, 1995; mem. Soc. of Authors. *Publications:* The Mystic Masseur 1957, The Suffrage of Elvira 1958, Miguel Street 1959, A House for Mr Biswas 1961, The Middle Passage 1962, Mr Stone and the Knights Companion 1963, An Area of Darkness 1964, The Mimic Men 1967, A Flag on the Island 1967 (collection of short stories), The Loss of El Dorado 1969, In a Free State 1971, The Overcrowded Barracoon (essays) 1972, Guerrillas 1975, India: A Wounded Civilization 1977, A Bend in the River 1979, A Congo Diary 1980, The Return of Eva Perón 1980, Among the Believers 1981, Finding the Centre 1984, The Enigma of Arrival 1987, A Turn In The South 1989, India: A Million Mutinies Now 1990, A Way in the World 1994, Beyond Belief 1998, Letters Between a Father and Son 1999, Reading and Writing: a Personal Account 2000, Half a Life 2001, Literary Occasions 2004, Magic Seeds 2004. *Honours:* Hon. DLitt (Univ. of the W Indies, St Augustine) 1975, (St Andrews) 1979, (Columbia) 1981, (Cambridge) 1983, (London) 1988, (Oxford) 1992; John Llewelyn Rhys Memorial Prize 1958, Somerset Maugham Award 1961, Phoenix Trust Award 1962, Hawthornden Prize 1964, W. H. Smith Award 1968, Booker Prize 1971, Jerusalem Prize 1983, Ingersoll Prize 1986, David Cohen British Literature Prize 1993, Nobel Prize for Literature 2001. *Address:* Gillon Aitken Associates Ltd, 18–21 Cavaye Place, London, SW10 9PT, England. *Telephone:* (20) 7373-8672. *Fax:* (20) 7373-6002.

NANDA, Bal Ram; Historian and Writer; b. 11 Oct. 1917, Rawalpindi, India; m. Janak Khosla, 24 May 1946, two s. *Education:* MA, History, University of Punjab, Lahore, 1939. *Career:* Dir, Nehru Memorial Museum and Library, New Delhi, 1965–79; mem. Institute for Defence Studies and Analyses, New Delhi; Authors' Guild of India; Indian International Centre. *Publications:* Mahatma Gandhi: A Biography, 1958; The Nehrus, Motilal and Jawaharlal, 1962; Gandhi: A Pictorial Biography, 1972; Gokhale: The Indian Moderates and the British Raj, 1977; Jawaharlal Nehru: A Pictorial Biography, 1980; Gandhi and His Critics, 1986; Gandhi, Pan-Islamism, Imperialism and Nationalism in India, 1989; In Gandhi's Footsteps: Life and Times of Jamnalal Bajaj, 1990; Jawaharal Nehru: Rebel and Statesman, 1996; The Making of a Nation: India's Road to Independence, 1998, In Search of Gandhi 2002, Witness to Partition 2003. Editor: Socialism in India, 1972; Indian Foreign Policy: The Nehru Years, 1975; Science and Technology in India, 1977; Essays in Modern Indian History, 1980; Selected Works of Gobind Ballabh Pant, Vols 1–18, 1993–2002; Mahatma Gandhi: 125 Years, 1995. Contributions: numerous newspapers, magazines and journals. *Honours:* Rockefeller Fellowship, 1964; National Fellowship, Indian Council of Social Science Research, New Delhi, 1979; Dadabhai Naoroji Memorial Prize, 1981; Padma Vibhushan 2003. *Address:* S-174 Panchshila Park, New Delhi 110017, India.

NAOMI, French Wallace, BA, MFA; dramatist and poet; b. 17 Aug. 1960, USA. *Education:* Hampshire College, University of Iowa. *Career:* teacher of play writing, University of Iowa 1990–93; playwright-in-residence, Illinois State University 1994. *Publications:* Slaughter City (play); In the Heart of America (play); To Dance a Stony Field (poems). Contributions: Reviews, journals, and magazines. *Honours:* The Nation/Discovery Award; Kentucky Arts Council Fellowship; Mobil Playwriting Award; Susan Smith Blackburn Playwriting Award.

NAPELS, Stella (see Van De Laar, Waltherus Antonius Bernardinus).

NAPIER, William McDonald, (Bill Napier); Astronomer and Writer; b. 29 June 1940, Perth, Scotland; m. Nancy Miller Baillie, 7 July 1965, one s. one d. *Education:* BSc, 1963; PhD, 1966. *Career:* mem. Royal Astronomical Society, fellow; International Astronomical Union; Spaceguard UK; Committee on Space Research; European Astronomical Society. *Publications:* The Cosmic Serpent, 1982; The Cosmic Winter, 1990; The Origin of Comets, 1990; Nemesis (novel), 1998; Revelation (novel), 2000; The Lure (novel), 2002. Contributions: New Scientist; Astronomy Today. *Honours:* Joint recipient, Arthur Beer Memorial Prize, 1986–87; Hon. Prof., University of Wales, Cardiff. *Address:* Armagh Observatory, College Hill, Armagh BT61 9DG, Northern Ireland.

NARAYAMA, Fujio; Writer and Poet; b. 13 June 1948, Iwate, Japan. *Education:* Graduate in Drama, Toho Gakuen Junior College, Tokyo, 1970. *Career:* mem. Japan Writers Asscn; MWA; Mystery Writers of Japan; Sino-Japanese Cultural Exchange Society. *Publications:* Manhattan Ballad, 1977; Sanctuary of Evil, 1979; Lay Traps in the Winter, 1981; The Scarred Bullet, 1989; Neverending Night, 1992. *Honours:* Iwate Arts Festival Awards, 1967, 1969; All Yomimono New Writer's Award, 1975.

NASAW, David, PhD; American writer and historian; *Distinguished Professor of History, City University of New York. Education:* Columbia Univ. *Career:* Distinguished Prof. of History, Graduate Center, City Univ. of New York; historical consultant for television documentaries. *Publications:* Schooled to Order: A Social History of Public Schooling in United States 1979, Children of the City: At Work and at Play 1985, Going Out: The Rise and Fall of Public Amusements 1993, The Chief: The Life of William Randolph Hearst 2000; articles include: Learning to go to the Movies, in American Heritage (Nov. 1993), Teaching Cultural History to Graduate Students, in Radical History Review (Fall 1996), Cities of Light, Landscapes of Pleasure, in Landscapes of Modernity (ed. by Oliver Zunz and David Ward) 1992; contrib. to New Yorker, The Nation, Traveler and other periodicals. *Address:* The Graduate Center, The City University of New York, 365 Fifth Avenue, New York, NY 10016-4309, USA (Office). *Telephone:* (212) 817-8431 (Office). *E-mail:* dnasaw@gc.cuny.edu (Office).

NASH, Gary Baring; Prof. of History and Writer; b. 27 July 1933, Philadelphia, Pennsylvania, USA; m. 1st Mary Workum, 20 Dec. 1955, divorced, one s., three d.; m. 2nd Cynthia Shelton, 24 Oct. 1981. *Education:* BA, 1955, PhD, 1964, Princeton University. *Career:* Asst to the Dean, Graduate School, 1959–61, Instructor, 1964–65, Asst Prof., 1965–66, Princeton University; Asst Prof., 1966–68, Assoc. Prof., 1969–72, Prof. of History, 1972–, Dean, Undergraduate Curriculum Development, 1984–91, University of California at Los Angeles; Assoc. Dir, 1988–94, Dir, 1994–, National Center for History in the Schools; Co-Chair., National History Studies Project, 1992–95; mem. American Antiquarian Society; American Historical Asscn; Institute of Early American History and Culture; Organization of American Historians, pres., 1994–95; Society of American Historians. *Publications:* Quakers and Politics: Pennsylvania, 1681–1726, 1968; Class and Society in Early America, 1970; The Great Fear: Race in the Mind of America (ed. with Richard Weiss), 1970; Red, White, and Black; The Peoples of Early America, 1974; The Urban Crucible: Social Change, Political Consciousness, and the Origins of the American Revolution, 1979; Struggle and Survival in Colonial America (ed. with David Sweet), 1980; The Private Side of American History (co-ed.), 2 vols, 1983, 1987; The American People: Creating a Nation and a Society (with J. R. Jeffrey), 2 vols, 1985, 1989; Retracing the Past, 2 vols, 1985, 1989; Race, Class and Politics: Essays on American Colonial and Revolutionary Society, 1986; Forging Freedom: The Formation of Philadelphia's Black Community, 1720–1840, 1988; Race and Revolution, 1990; Freedom by Degrees: Emancipation and Its Aftermath in Pennsylvania (with Jean R. Soderlund), 1991; American Odyssey: The United States in the 20th Century, 1991; History on Trial: Culture Wars and the Teaching of the Past (with Charlotte Crabtree and Ross Dunn), 1997; Forbidden Love: The Secret History of Mixed-Race America, 1999; First City: Philadelphia and the Forging of Historical Memory, 2001. Contributions: Professional journals. *Honours:* Guggenheim Fellowship, 1969–70; ACLS Fellowship, 1973–74. *Address:* 16174 Alcima Ave, Pacific Palisades, CA 90272, USA.

NASIRI, Buthaina al; Iraqi short story writer and publisher; b. 1947. *Education:* Univ. of Baghdad Coll. of Arts. *Career:* moved to Cairo, Egypt 1979, where she runs a publishing house specializing in the works of Iraqi writers under UN sanctions. *Publications:* five short story collections in Arabic; Final Night (in trans.) 2003. *Address:* c/o The American University in Cairo Press, 113 Sharia Kasr el Aini Street, Cairo, Egypt. *E-mail:* aucpress@aucegypt.edu. *Website:* www.aucpress.com.

NASRALLAH, Emily, BA; Lebanese novelist, journalist and feminist; b. 6 July 1931, Kfeir; m. Philip Nasrallah 1957; two s. two d. *Education:* Shoueifat Nat. Coll., Beirut Univ. Coll., American Univ. of Beirut. *Career:* mem. writing staff, Al-Sayyad magazine and Al-Anwar newspaper 1955–70; Cultural and Public Relations Consultant, Beirut Univ. Coll. 1973–75; feature writer and Ed., Fayruz Magazine 1981–87; ECWA Deligate to UN Women's Forum on Population and Devt, New York, USA 1974; writer and feminist, one of the Beirut Decentrist women writers; participated in Olympics Authors' Festival, Calgary, Canada 1988; panellist and guest reader, PEN Int. Congress, Toronto and Montréal, Canada 1989. *Publications:* (in Arabic): novels: Birds of September 1962, The Oleander Tree 1968, The Bondaged 1974, Those Memories 1980, Flight Against Time 1981, Sleeping Ember 1995; short story collections: The Source 1978, The Woman in Seventeen Stories 1983, The Lost Mill 1984, Our Daily Bread 1990, Stations of Departure 1996, Days Recounted 1997, Gypsy Nights 1998, Forgotten Papers, Black and White; children's books: Island of Illusion (short stories) 1973, The Resplendent Flower 1975, Little Shadi 1977, A Cat's Diary 1997, On a Snow Carpet, Anda the Fool; non-fiction: Pioneer Women, from East and West (vols 1–6) 1986. *Honours:* Laureate Best Novel 1962, Poet Said Akl Prizes 1962, 2002, Friends of the Book Prize 1962, Fayruz Magazine Prize for Outstanding Literary Works 1983, Khalil Gibran Prize, Arab Heritage Union in Australia 1991, LIBBY Children's Book Prize 1998, IBBY Honour List for Children's Novel 1998. *Address:* Osman Bldg, Ain-el-Tineh, Verdun Street, POB 11-6245, Beirut, Lebanon. *Website:* www.emilynasrallah.com.

NASREEN, Taslima; Bangladeshi feminist, author and doctor; b. 25 Aug. 1962, Mymensingh, E Pakistan (now Bangladesh); m. 3rd (divorced). *Education:* Mymensingh Medical Coll., Dhaka Univ. *Career:* practised as a gynaecologist 1986–93; columnist Ajker Kagoj 1989; books banned in Bangladesh and Indian state of W Bengal, fatwa (death threat) pronounced against her 1993; left Bangladesh to live in self-imposed exile in Sweden 1994, later in Germany, USA and France; conducting research into women's rights in Islamic countries Harvard Univ. 2003–04; has published 16 books. *Publications include:* Laija (Shame) (novel) 1993, Nirbachito Kolam, Nosto meyer nosto goddo, choto choto dukkho kotha (selected columns), Opoppokkho, Bhromor koio gia, Sodh, Fera (Return), Nirbachito Kobita, Amar Meyebela, Utal Hawa 2002, Dwihkandita (Split in Two, autobiog.) 2003. *Honours:* Dr hc (Ghent Univ., Belgium) 1995; Ananda Puroshkar, India 1992, Kurt Tukholsky Prize, Sweden 1994, Feminist of the Year, USA 1994, Human Rights Award, French Govt 1994, Edit de Nantes Award, France 1994, Monismanien Prize, Sweden 1995, Sakharov Prize, European Parl. 1995, Int. Humanist Award, Int. Humanist and Ethical Union 1996. *Address:* c/o Penguin Books India Pvt. Ltd, #11 Community Centre, Panchsheel Park, New Delhi 110 017, India.

NASSAR, Eugene Paul; Prof. of English, Writer and Poet; b. 20 June 1935, Utica, New York, USA; m. Karen Nocian, 30 Dec. 1969, one s. two d. *Education:* BA, Kenyon College, 1957; Rhodes Scholarship, 1958; MA, Worcester College, Oxford, 1960; PhD, Cornell University, 1962. *Career:* Instructor in English, Hamilton College, 1962–64; Asst Prof., 1964–66, Assoc. Prof., 1966–71, Prof. of English, 1971–, Utica College, Syracuse University; Dir, Ethnic Heritage Studies Center. *Publications:* Wallace Stevens: An Anatomy of Figuration, 1965; The Rape of Cinderella: Essays in Literary Continuity, 1970; Selections from a Prose Poem: East Utica, 1971; The Cantos of Ezra Pound: The Lyric Mode, 1975; Wind of the Land: Two Prose Poems, 1979; Essays: Critical and Metacritical, 1983; Illustrations to Dante's Inferno, 1994; A Walk Around the Block: Literary Texts and Social Contexts, 1999. Editor: several books. Contributions: various publications. *Honours:* NEH Fellowship, 1972. *Address:* 918 Arthur St, Utica, NY 13501, USA.

NASSAUER, Rudolf; Writer and Poet; b. 8 Nov. 1924, Frankfurt am Main, Germany. *Education:* University of Reading, 1943–45. *Publications:* Poems, 1947; The Holigan, 1959; The Cuckoo, 1962; The Examination, 1973; The Unveiling, 1975; The Agents of Love, 1976; Midlife Feasts, 1977; Reparations, 1981; Kramer's Goats, 1986.

NATHAN, Leonard Edward; academic, poet, writer and translator; b. 8 Nov. 1924, Los Angeles, CA, USA; m. Carol G. Nash 1949; one s. two d. *Education:* BA, 1950, MA, 1951, PhD, 1961, University of California at Berkeley. *Career:* Instructor, Modesto Junior College, CA, 1954–60; Prof., 1961–91, Chair., Dept of Rhetoric, 1968–72, Prof. Emeritus, 1991–, University of California at Berkeley. *Publications:* Poetry: Glad and Sorry Seasons, 1963; The Matchmaker's Lament, 1967; The Day the Perfect Speakers Left, 1969; Flight Plan, 1971; Without Wishing, 1973; Coup and Other Poems, 1975; The Likeness: Poems Out of India, 1975; Returning Your Call, 1975; Teachings of Grandfather Fox, 1976; Lost Distance, 1978; Dear Blood, 1980; Holding Patterns, 1982; Carrying On: New and Selected Poems, 1985; The Potato Eaters, 1999; Tears of the Old Magician, 2003. Prose: The Tragic Drama of W. B. Yeats: Figures in Dance, 1963; The Poet's Work: An Introduction to Czesław Miłosz (with Arthur Quinn), 1991; Diary of a Left-Handed Bird Watcher, 1996. Translator: First Person, Second Person, by 'Agyeya', 1971; Grace and Mercy in Her Wild Hair, by Ramprasad Sen (with Clinton Seely), 1982; Songs of Something Else, by Gunnar Ekelof (with James Larson), 1985; Happy as a Dog's Tail, by Anna Swir (with Czesław Miłosz), 1985; With the Skin, by Aleksander Wat (with Czesław Miłosz), 1989; Talking to My Body, by Anna Swir (with Czesław Miłosz), 1996. Contributions: Reviews, journals, and magazines. *Honours:* Phalen Award for Narrative Poetry, 1955; Longview Foundation Award for Poetry, 1962; Creative Arts Fellowships, University of California, 1963–64, 1973–74; American Institute of Indian Studies Fellowship, 1967–68; National Institute of Arts and Letters Award, 1971; Guggenheim Fellowship, 1976–77; Commonwealth Club of California, Medals for Poetry, 1976, 1980, 1999. *Address:* 40 Beverly Road, Kensington, CA 94707, USA.

NATHAN, Robert S(tuart); Writer; b. 13 Aug. 1948, Johnstown, Pennsylvania, USA. *Education:* BA, Amherst College, 1970. *Career:* Producer, Law and Order series, NBC-TV. *Publications:* Amusement Park, 1977; Rising Higher, 1981; The Religion, 1982; The Legend, 1986; The White Tiger, 1988; In the Deep Woods, 1989. Other: In the Deep Woods (television film), 1992. Contributions: periodicals and national public radio.

NATUSCH, Sheila (Ellen); Writer and Illustrator; b. 14 Feb. 1926, Invercargill, New Zealand; m. Gilbert G. Natusch, 28 Nov. 1950. *Education:* MA, Otago University, 1948. *Publications:* Stewart Island (with N. S. Seaward), 1951; Native Plants, 1956; Native Rock, 1959; Animals of New Zealand, 1967, new edtion, 1999; A Bunch of Wild Orchids, 1968; New Zealand Mosses, 1969; Brother Wohlers: A Biography, 1969; On the Edge of the Bush: Women in Early Southland, 1976; Hell and High Water: A German Occupation of the Chatham Islands 1843–1910, 1977; The Cruise of the Acheron: Her Majesty's Steam Vessel on Survey in New Zealand Waters 1848–1851, 1978; The Roaring Forties, 1978; Fortnight in Iceland, 1979; Wild Fare for Wilderness Foragers, 1979; A Pocket Full of Pebbles, 1983; Southward Ho!: The Search for a Southern Edinburgh, 1844, 1985; Granny Gurton's Garden (with Lois Chambers), 1987; William Swainson: The Anatomy of a Nineteenth-Century Naturalist, 1987; Roy Traill of Stewart Island, 1991; An Island Called Home, 1992; The Natural World of the Traills: An Investigation into Some of the 19th Century Naturalists of a Particular Family in Scotland and the Colonies, 1996; Ruapuke Visited, 1998; My Dear Friend Tuckett, Vol. I, 1998; Wellington Awash, 2000; Pop Kelp, 2000. Contributions: books and periodicals. *Honours:* Hubert Church Award, PEN New Zealand, 1969. *Address:* 46 Owhiro Bay Parade, Wellington 6002, New Zealand.

NAUMANN, Michael, DPhil; German publisher; *Editor-in-Chief, Die Zeit*; b. 8 Dec. 1941, Köthen; m. Christa Wessel 1969 (divorced); one s. one d. *Education:* Univ. of Munich and Queen's Coll., Oxford, UK. *Career:* Asst Prof., Univ. of Bochum 1971–76; Florey Scholar, Queen's Coll. Oxford 1976–78; Ed., Foreign Corresp. Die Zeit, Hamburg 1978–82; Sr Foreign Ed. Der Spiegel, Hamburg 1982–84; Publr Rowohlt Verlag, Reinbek 1984–95; Pres. and CEO Henry Holt and Co., New York 1996–; Minister of State for Culture 1998–2000; Ed.-in-Chief Die Zeit 2001–. *Publications:* Der Abbau einer Verkehrten Welt 1969, Amerika liegt in Kalifornien 1983, Strukturwandel des Heroismus 1984, Die Geschichte ist offen 1990, Die schönste Form der Freiheit 2001. *Honours:* Commdr Légion d'honneur. *Address:* Die Zeit, Pressehaus, Speersort 1, 20095 Hamburg, Germany (Office). *Telephone:* (40) 32800 (Office); (40) 327111. *Website:* www.zeit.de (Office).

NAUMOFF, Lawrence Jay; Author; b. 23 July 1946, Charlotte, NC, USA; Divorced, one s. *Education:* BA, University of North Carolina, Chapel Hill, 1969. *Career:* mem. PEN. *Publications:* The Night of the Weeping Women, 1988; Rootie Kazootie, 1990; Taller Women, 1992; Silk Hope, NC, 1994; A Plan for Women, 1997. Contributions: various literary magazines, short stories. *Honours:* Thomas Wolfe Memorial Award, 1969; National Endowment for the Arts Grant, 1970; Whiting Foundation Writers Award, 1990. *Address:* 1240 Epps Clark Rd, Siler City, NC 27344, USA.

NAVON, Robert, BA, MS, MA, PhD; editor, poet, writer and philosopher; b. 18 May 1954, New York, NY, USA. *Education:* Lehman College, CUNY, SUNY at Geneseo, New School for Social Research, New York City, University of New Mexico. *Career:* mem. Society of Ancient Greek Philosophy; American Philosophical Assn. *Publications:* Patterns of the Universe, 1977; Autumn Songs: Poems, 1983; The Pythagorean Writings, 1986; Healing of Man and Woman, 1989; Harmony of the Spheres, 1991; Cosmic Patterns, Vol. I, 1993; Great Works of Philosophy, 7 vols (ed.). *Honours:* New York State Regents Scholar, 1971; Intern, Platform Assn, 1980.

NAYLOR, Gloria; Author; b. 25 Jan. 1950, New York, NY, USA. *Education:* BA, Brooklyn College, CUNY, 1981; MA, Yale University, 1983. *Career:* Writer-in-Residence, Cummington Community of the Arts, 1983; Visiting Prof., George Washington University, 1983–84, Princeton University, 1986–87, Boston University, 1987; United States Information Agency Cultural Exchange Lecturer, India, 1985; Visiting Writer, New York University, 1986; Fannie Hurst Visiting Prof., Brandeis University, 1988; Senior Fellow, Society for the Humanities, Cornell University, 1988; Pres., One Way Productions films, New York City, 1990–. *Publications:* The Women of Brewster Place: A Novel in Seven Stories, 1982; Lindin Hills, 1985; Mama Day, 1988; Bailey's Cafe, 1992; Children of the Night: The Best Short Stories by Black Writers, 1967 to the Present (ed.), 1995; The Men of Brewster Place, 1998. Contributions: Magazines. *Honours:* National Book Award for Best First Novel, 1983; Distinguished Writer Award, Mid-Atlantic Writers Assn, 1983; National Endowment for the Arts Fellowship, 1985; Candace Award, National Coalition of 100 Black Women, 1986; Guggenheiim Fellowship, 1988; Lillian Smith Award, 1989. *Address:* c/o One Way Productions, 638 Second St, New York, NY 11215, USA.

NAYLOR, Phyllis; Writer; b. 4 Jan. 1933, Anderson, IN, USA. *Education:* Diploma, Joliet Junior College, 1953; BA, American University, 1963.

Publications: over 118 books for adults or children, 1965–. *Honours:* Newbery Medal, American Library Asscn, 1992. *Address:* 9910 Holmhurst Rd, Bethesda, MD 20817, USA.

NAYLOR, Thomas (Herbert); Prof. of Economics Emeritus and Writer; b. 30 May 1936, Jackson, Mississippi, USA; m. Magdalena Raczkowska, 14 Dec. 1985, one s. one d. *Education:* BS, Mathematics, Millsaps College, 1958; BS, Industrial Engineering, Columbia University, 1959; MBA, Quantitative Business Analysis, Indiana University, 1961; PhD, Economics, Tulane University, 1964. *Career:* Instructor, Tulane University, 1961–63; Asst Prof., 1964–66, Assoc. Prof., 1966–68, Prof. of Economics, 1968–93, Prof. Emeritus, 1994–, Duke University; Visiting Prof., University of Wisconsin, 1969–70, Middlebury College, 1993–94, University of Vermont, 1994–96; Pres., Social Systems Inc, 1971–80; Managing Dir, Naylor Group, 1980. *Publications:* Linear Programming (with Eugene Byrne), 1963; Computer Simulation Techniques (with Joseph L. Balintfy, Donald S. Burdick and King Chu), 1966; Microeconomics and Decision Models of the Firm (with John Vernon), 1969; Computer Simulation Experiments with Models of Economic Systems, 1971; Corporate Planning Models, 1979; Strategic Planning Management, 1980; Managerial Economics: Corporate Economics and Strategy (with John M. Vernon and Kenneth Wertz), 1983; The Corporate Strategy Matrix, 1986; The Gorbachev Strategy, 1988; The Cold War Legacy, 1991; The Search for Meaning, 1994; The Abandoned Generation: Rethinking Higher Education (with William H. Willimon), 1995; The Search for Meaning in the Workplace (with Rolf Osterberg and William H. Willimon), 1996; Downsizing the USA, 1997; Affluenza, 2001; The Vermont Manifesto, 2003. Contributions: various scholarly books and journals. *Address:* 202 Stockbridge Rd, Charlotte, VT 05445, USA.

NDEBELE, Njabulo Simakahle, PhD; South African academic and writer; b. 4 July 1948, Johannesburg; m. Kathleen Mpho; one s. two d. *Education:* Univs of Botswana, Lesotho and Swaziland, Cambridge Univ., UK. *Career:* Head of Dept, Nat. Univ. of Lesotho, Dean of Humanities Faculty 1987, Pro-Vice-Chancellor 1988; Chair. and Head of Dept of African Literature, Wits Univ.; Vice-Rector, Univ. of the Western Cape; Vice-Chancellor and Prin., Univ. of the North, Scholar in Residence, Ford Foundation; Vice-Chancellor, Univ. of Cape Town July 2000–; Chair. S African Broadcasting Policy Project, Ministry of Post, Telecommunications and Broadcasting, S African Univs Vice-Chancellors' Asscn –2000; mem. Exec. Bd AA4, AC4. *Publications:* Fools and Other Stories 1983, Bonolo and the Peach Tree 1991, Rediscovery of the Ordinary 1991, The Prophetess 1992, Sarah, Rings and I 1993, South African Literature and Culture: Rediscovery of the Ordinary 1994, Death of a Son 1996, The Cry of Winnie Mandela (novel) 2004. *Honours:* Dr hc (Natal Univ., Chicago State Univ., Vrije Univ. Amsterdam, Soka Univ. Japan); President's Award, Lincoln Univ.; Fiftieth Anniversary Distinguished Service Award, Nat. Univ. of Lesotho; NOMA Award for Publishing in Africa; Sanlam Award for Outstanding Fiction; Pringle Prize for Outstanding Criticism. *Address:* University of Cape Town, Private Bag, Rondebosch 7701, Cape Town (Office); Glenara, Burg Road, Rondebosch 7700, Cape Town, South Africa (Home). *Telephone:* (21) 6502105, (21) 6502106 (Office). *Fax:* (21) 6892440 (Office). *E-mail:* vc@bremner.uct.ac.za (Office). *Website:* www.uct.ac.za (Office).

NDIBE, Okey A.; Poet and Writer; b. 1960, Yola, Nigeria; m. Sheri Fafunwa-Ndibe; three c. *Career:* fmr magazine ed.; moved to USA, 1988; f. ed., African Commentary magazine; Visiting Writer-in-Residence, Asst Prof. of English, Connecticut College; weekly column, Nigerian newspaper, Guardian. *Publications:* Arrows of Rain, 2000. Contributions: An Anthology of New West African Poets; essays in numerous magazines. *Address:* c/o African Writers Series, Heinemann Educational Publishers, Halley Ct, Jordan Hill, Oxford OX2 8EJ, England.

NEAL, Patricia (see Flagg, Fannie).

NEATE, Patrick; writer and journalist; b. London, England. *Publications:* Musungu Jim and the Great Chief Tuloko, 2000; Twelve Bar Blues, 2001; The London Pigeon Wars, 2003. Contributions: Q, The Face, Mixmag, Sky. *Honours:* Whitbread Novel Award 2001. *Address:* c/o Penguin Books Ltd, 80 Strand, London WC2R 0RL, England.

NEEDLE, Jan; Writer; b. 8 Feb. 1943, Holybourne, England. *Education:* Drama Degree, Victoria University of Manchester, 1971. *Publications:* Albeson and the Germans, 1977; My Mate Shofiq, 1978; A Fine Boy for Killing, 1979; The Size Spies, 1979; Rottenteeth, 1980; The Bee Rustlers, 1980; A Sense of Shame, 1980; Wild Wood, 1981; Losers Weepers, 1981; Another Fine Mess, 1981; Brecht (with Peter Thomson), 1981; Piggy in the Middle, 1982; Going Out, 1983; A Pitiful Place, 1984; Great Days at Grange Hill, 1984; Tucker's Luck, 1984; Behind the Bike Sheds, 1985; A Game of Soldiers, 1985; Tucker in Control, 1985; Wagstaffe, The Wind-Up Boy, 1987; Uncle in the Attic, 1987; Skeleton at School, 1987; In the Doghouse, 1988; The Sleeping Party, 1988; Mad Scramble, 1989; As Seen on TV, 1989; The Thief, 1990; The Bully, 1992; Wagstaff and the Life of Crime, 1992; The Wicked Trade, 1998; The Bully (with Viv Gardner), 2000; Dracula (with Viv Gardner), 2001. Television Plays and Serials: A Game of Soldiers, 1985; Truckers, 1987; Soft Soap, 1987; The Thief, 1989; The Bill, 1992. *Literary Agent:* David Higham Associates, 5–8 Lower John St, Golden Sq., London W1F 9HA, England. *Address:* Rye Top, Knowl Top Lane, Uppermill, Oldham OL3 6LQ, England.

NEEDLEMAN, Jacob; Prof. of Philosophy and Writer; b. 6 Oct. 1934, Philadelphia, PA, USA; m. 1st Carla Satzman 30 Aug. 1959 (divorced 1989); one s. one d.; m. 2nd Gail Anderson Dec. 1990. *Education:* BA, Harvard University, 1956; University of Freiburg im Breisgau, 1957–58; PhD, Yale University, 1961. *Career:* Research Assoc., Rockefeller Institute, New York, 1961–62; Asst Prof. to Assoc. Prof. of Philosophy, 1962–66, Prof. of Philosophy, 1967–, Chair., Dept of Philosophy, 1968–69, San Francisco State University; Visiting Scholar, Union Theological Seminary, 1967–68; Dir, Center for the Study of New Religions, Graduate Theological Union, Berkeley, 1977–83. *Publications:* Being-in-the-World, 1963; The New Religions, 1970; Religion for a New Generation, 1973; The Sword of Gnosis (ed.), 1973; Sacred Tradition and Present Need (ed.), 1974; A Sense of the Cosmos, 1975; On the Way to Self-Knowledge: Sacred Tradition and Psychotherapy, 1976; Understanding the New Religions (ed.), 1978; Speaking of My Life: The Art of Living in the Cultural Revolution, 1979; Lost Christianity, 1980; Consciousness and Tradition, 1982; The Heart of Philosophy, 1982; Sorcerers, 1986; Sin and Scientism, 1986; Money and the Meaning of Life, 1991; Real Philosophy: An Anthology of the Universal Search for Meaning (ed.), 1991; Modern Esoteric Sprituality, 1992; The Way of the Physician, 1993; The Indestructible Question, 1994; A Little Book on Love, 1996; Time and the Soul, 1998; The American Soul, 2002. Contributions: books and journals. *Address:* c/o Dept of Philosophy, San Francisco State University, 1600 Holloway Ave, San Francisco, CA 94132, USA.

NEELY, Mark Edward, Jr, BA, PhD; writer, editor and academic; b. 10 Nov. 1944, Amarillo, TX, USA; m. Sylvia Eakes 1966. *Education:* Yale University. *Career:* Dir, Louis A Warren Lincoln Library and Museum, Fort Wayne, Indiana; Visiting Instructor, Iowa State University, 1971–72; Ed., Lincoln Lore, 1973–; Prof., St Louis University; mem. Abraham Lincoln Asscn; Indiana Asscn of Historians, pres., 1987–88; Society of Indiana Archivists, pres., 1980–81. *Publications:* The Abraham Lincoln Encyclopedia, 1981; The Lincoln Image: Abraham Lincoln and the Popular Print (with Harold Holzer and Gabor S. Boritt), 1984; The Insanity File: The Case of Mary Todd Lincoln (with R. Gerald McMurty), 1986; The Confederate Image: Prints of the Lost Cause, 1987; The Lincoln Family Album: Photographs from the Personal Collection of a Historic American Family, 1990; The Fate of Liberty: Abraham Lincoln and Civil Liberties, 1991; The Last Best Hope on Earth: Abraham Lincoln and the Promise of America, 1993; Mine Eyes Have Seen the Glory: The Civil War in American Art (with Harold Holzer), 1993. *Honours:* Pulitzer Prize for History, 1992. *Address:* c/o Dept of History, St Louis University, 221 N Grand Avenue, St Louis, MO 63103, USA.

NEHAMAS, Alexander, BA, PhD; Spanish academic and writer; b. 22 March 1946, Athens, Greece; m. Susan Glimcher 1983; one s. *Education:* Swarthmore Coll., Princeton Univ. *Career:* Asst Prof. 1971–76, Assoc. Prof. 1976–81, Prof. of Philosophy 1981–86, Univ. of Pittsburgh; Visiting Fellow 1978–79, Prof. of Philosophy 1988, 1990–, Edmund N. Carpenter II Class of 1943 Prof. in the Humanities 1989–, Prof. of Comparative Literature 1990–, Princeton Univ.; Mills Prof. of Philosophy 1983, Sather Prof. of Classical Literature 1993, Univ. of California at Berkeley; Visiting Scholar 1983–84, Prof. of Philosophy 1986–90, Univ. of Pennsylvania; mem. American Acad. of Arts and Sciences, American Soc. for Aesthetics, Modern Greek Studies Asscn, North American Nietzsche Soc., American Philosophical Asscn, British Soc. for Aesthetics. *Publications:* Nietzsche: Life as Literature, 1985; Plato's 'Symposium' (trans. and ed. with Paul Woodruff), 1989; Aristotle's 'Rhetoric': Philosophical Essays (co-ed. with D. J. Furley), 1994; Plato's 'Phaedrus' (trans. and ed. with Paul Woodruff), 1995; The Art of Living: Socratic Reflections from Plato to Foucault, 1998; Virtues of Authenticity: Essays on Plato and Socrates, 1999. Contributions: books and professional journals. *Honours:* National Endowment for the Humanities Fellowship, 1978–79; Guggenheim Fellowship, 1983–84; Romanell-Phi Beta Kappa Prof. in Philosophy, 1990–91; Hon. DPhil, University of Athens, 1993; Phi Beta Kappa Visiting Scholar, 1995; Howard T. Behrman Award for Distinguished Achievement in the Humanities, Princeton University, 1999; Award for Distinguished Achievement, Acad. of Athens, 2000; International Nietzshe Prize, 2001, Mellon Distinguished Achievement in the Humanities Award 2001. *Address:* 692 Pretty Brook Road, Princeton, NJ 08540, USA.

NEIL, Andrew Ferguson, MA, FRSA; British editor, writer, broadcaster and publisher; *Publisher, Press Holdings*; b. 21 May 1949, Scotland. *Education:* Paisley Grammar School, Univ. of Glasgow. *Career:* with Conservative Party Research Dept 1971–73; with The Economist 1973–83, Ulster Political then Industrial Corresp. 1973–79, American Corresp. 1979–82, UK Ed. 1982–83; Ed. The Sunday Times 1983–94; Exec. Ed. Fox TV News, USA 1994; Exec. Chair. Sky TV 1988–90; Publr Press Holdings, including The Business, The Scotsman, Scotland on Sunday, Edinburgh Evening News 1996–; Chair. Business Europe.com. 1999–; regular anchorman and TV commentator UK and USA; anchorman, The Daily Politics (BBC2) and This Week (BBC1), Contrib. Ed. Vanity Fair, New York 1994–; writer, speaker and broadcaster 1994–; Lord Rector Univ. of St Andrews 1999–2002. *Publications:* The Cable Revolution 1982, Britain's Free Press: Does It Have One? 1989, Full Disclosure 1996, British Excellence 1999, 2000, 2001. *Honours:* Hon. DLit (Napier Univ.) 1998; Hon. DUniv (Paisley) 2001; Hon.

LLD (St Andrews) 2002. *Address:* Glenburn Enterprises, PO Box 584, London, SW7 3QY, England. *Telephone:* (20) 7240-9968. *E-mail:* afneil@aol.com (Office).

NEILL, William, (Uilleam Neill); Teacher (retd), Poet and Writer; b. 22 Feb. 1922, Prestwick, Ayrshire, Scotland; m. 1st, two d.; m. 2nd Doris Marie Walker, 2 April 1970. *Education:* MA, University of Edinburgh, 1971; Teacher's Certificate, 1972. *Career:* mem. PEN International, Scottish Branch. *Publications:* Scotland's Castle, 1970; Poems, 1970; Four Points of a Saltire (co-author), 1970; Despatches Home, 1972; Galloway Landscape, 1981; Cnù a Mogail, 1983; Wild Places, 1985; Blossom, Berry, Fall, 1986; Making Tracks, 1991; Straight Lines, 1922; Tales from the Odyssey, 1992; Selected Poems 1969–92, 1994; Caledonian Cramboclink, 2001. Contributions: various publications, BBC Scotland, and BBC Radio 4. *Honours:* Bardic Crown, National Gaelic MOD, 1969; Sloan Verse Prize, 1970; Grierson Prize, 1970; Scottish Arts Council Book Award, 1985. *Address:* Burnside, Crossmichael, Castle Douglas, Kirkcudbrightshire DG7 3AP, Scotland.

NELSON, Antonya; writer and academic; b. 6 Jan. 1961, Wichita, KS, USA; m. Robert L. Boswell 1984; two s. *Education:* BA, University of Kansas, 1983; MFA, University of Arizona, 1986. *Career:* Asst Prof., 1989–95, Assoc. Prof. of English, 1995–, New Mexico State University. *Publications:* The Expendables, 1990; In the Land of Men, 1992; Family Terrorists: A Novella and Seven Stories, 1994; Talking in Bed, 1996; Nobody's Girl: A Novel, 1998; Living to Tell: A Novel, 2000. Contributions: anthologies and periodicals. *Honours:* Nelson Algren Award, 1988, Heartland Award, 1996, Chicago Tribune; Flannery O'Connor Award, 1990; American Library Asscn Award, 2000; Guggenheim Fellowship, 2000–01. *Address:* c/o Department of English, New Mexico State University, Las Cruces, NM 88003, USA.

NELSON, Marguerite (see Floren, Lee).

NELSON, Marilyn, (Marilyn Nelson Waniek), BA, MA, PhD; American professor of English, poet and translator; b. 26 April 1946, Cleveland, OH; one s. one d. *Education:* Univ. of California at Davis, Univ. of Pennsylvania, Univ. of Minnesota. *Career:* Visiting Asst Prof., Reed Coll., Portland, OR 1971–72; Asst Prof., St Olaf Coll., Northfield, MN 1973–78; instructor, Univ. of Hamburg 1977; Asst Prof. to Prof. of English, Univ. of Connecticut at Storrs 1978–; faculty, MFA Program, New York Univ. 1988, 1994, Vermont Coll. 1991; Elliston poet-in-residence, Univ. of Cincinnati 1994; writer-in-residence, Vanderbilt Univ. 1999; Visiting Prof., US Military Acad., West Point 2000; Connecticut Poet Laureate 2001–; mem. Associated Writing Programs, Poetry Soc. of America, Soc. for the Study of Multi-Ethnic Literature of the USA, Soc. for Values in Higher Education. *Publications:* For the Body 1978, The Cat Walked Through the Casserole (with Pamela Espeland) 1984, Mama's Promises 1985, The Homeplace (Annisfield-Wolf Award 1992) 1990, Partial Truth 1992, Magnificat 1995, The Fields of Praise: New and Selected Poems (The Poets Prize 1998) 1997, Carver: A Life in Poems 2001, Triolets for Triolet (chapbook); contrib. to books and journals. *Honours:* Kent Fellowship, 1976; National Endowment for the Arts Fellowships, 1981, 1990; Danish Ministry of Culture Grant, 1984; Connecticut Arts Award, 1990; Individual Artist Grant, Connecticut Commission for the Arts, 1990; Fulbright Teaching Fellow, 1995; Contemplative Practices Fellowship, 1999; Boston Globe/Horn Book Award, 2001; Newbery Honor Book, 2002; Coretta Scott King Honor Book, 2002; Flora Stieglitz Strauss Award, 2002; Guggenheim Fellowship, 2001; Poet Laureate, State of Connecticut, 2001–. *Address:* Department of English, University of Connecticut, Storrs, CT 06269, USA.

NELSON, Richard; Dramatist and Screenwriter; b. 17 Oct. 1950, Chicago, IL, USA. *Education:* BA, Hamilton College, 1972. *Career:* Literary Man., BAM Theatre Co, Brooklyn, 1979–81; Assoc. Dir, Goodman Theatre, Chicago, 1980–83; Dramaturg, Guthrie Theatre, Minneapolis, 1981–82. *Publications:* The Vienna Notes (in Word Plays I), 1980; II Campiello (adaptation), 1981; An American Comedy and Other Plays, 1984; Between East and West (in New Plays USA 3), 1986; Principia Scriptoriae, 1986; Strictly Dishonorable and Other Lost American Plays (ed.), 1986; Rip Van Winkle, 1986; Jungle Coup (in Plays from Playwrights Horizons), 1987; Accidental Death of an Anarchist (adaptation), 1987. *Address:* 32 South St, Rhinebeck, NY 12572, USA.

NETTL, Bruno; Prof. of Music and Anthropology Emeritus, Writer and Ed.; b. 14 March 1930, Prague, Czechoslovakia; m. Wanda Maria White, 15 Sept. 1952, two d. *Education:* BA, 1950, MA, 1951, PhD, 1953, Indiana University; MA, Library Science, University of Michigan, 1960. *Career:* Instructor in Music, 1953–54, Asst Prof. of Music, 1954–56, 1959–64, Music Librarian, 1958–64, Wayne State University; Ed., Ethnomusicology, 1961–65, 1988–2002, Yearbook of the International Folk Music Council, 1975–77; Assoc. Prof. of Music, 1965–67, Prof. of Music and Anthropology, 1967–92, Prof. Emeritus, 1992–, Chair., Division of Musicology, 1967–72, 1975–77, 1982–85, University of Illinois; numerous visiting lectureships and professorships; mem. American Acad. of Arts and Sciences; American Musicological Society, hon. mem., 1995–; College Music Society; International Council for Traditional Music; International Musicological Society; Society of Ethnomusicology, pres., 1969–71, hon. mem., 2001. *Publications:* North American Indian Musical Styles, 1954; Music in Primitive Culture, 1956; An Introduction to Folk Music in the United States, 1960, third edn, revised by H. Myers, as Folk Music in the United States: An Introduction, 1976; Cheremis Musical Styles, 1960; Reference Materials in Ethnomusicology, 1961; Theory and Method in Ethnomusicology, 1964; Folk and Traditional Music of the Western Continents, 1965; Daramad of Chahargah: A Study in the Performance Practice of Persian Music (with B. Foltin Jr), 1972; Contemporary Music and Music Cultures (with C. Hamm and R. Byrnside), 1975; Eight Urban Musical Cultures: Tradition and Change (ed.), 1978; The Study of Ethnomusicology: 29 Issues and Concepts, 1983; The Western Impact on World Music: Change, Adaptation, and Survival, 1985; The Radif of Persian Music: Studies of Structure and Cultural Context, 1987; Blackfoot Musical Thought: Comparative Perspectives, 1989; Comparative Musicology and Anthropology in Music: Essays on the History of Ethnomusicology (ed. with P. Bohlman), 1991; Excursions in World Music (with others), 1992; Community of Music: An Ethnographical Seminar in Champaign-Urbana (ed. with others), 1993; Heartland Excursions: Ethnomusicological Reflections on Schools of Music, 1995; In the Course of Performance: Studies in the World of Musical Improvisation (ed. with M. Russell), 1998; Encounters in Ethnomusicology, 2002. Contributions: scholarly books and journals. *Honours:* Hon. LHD, University of Chicago, 1993, University of Illinois, 1996, Carleton College, 2000, Kenyon College, 2002; Koizumi Prize in Ethnomusicology, Tokyo, 1994. *Address:* 1423 Cambridge Dr., Champaign, IL 61821, USA.

NEUBERGER, Julia Babette Sarah; Rabbi, Author and Broadcaster; b. 27 Feb. 1950, London, England; m. Anthony John Neuberger, 17 Sept. 1973, one s. one d. *Education:* Newnham College, Cambridge, 1969–73; BA, Assyriology, Hebrew, MA, 1975, University of Cambridge; Rabbinic Ordination, Leo Baeck College, 1977. *Career:* Chief Exec., The King's Fund, London, 1997–; Judge, Irish Times International Fiction Prize, 1997, Irish Times Irish Literature Prizes, 1999. *Publications:* Judaism, 1986; Caring for Dying People of Different Faiths, 1987; Days of Decision, 4 vols (ed.), 1987; Whatever's Happening to Women?, 1991; A Necessary End (ed. with John White), 1991; Ethics and Healthcare: Research Ethics Committees in the UK, 1992; The Things that Matter, 1993; On Being Jewish, 1995; Dying Well: A Guide to Enabling a Good Death, 1999. Contributions: Jewish Chronicle; Times; Irish Times; Irish Sunday Tribune; Vogue; Cosmopolitan; Sunday Times; Telegraph; Sunday Express; Mail on Sunday; Evening Standard. *Honours:* Hon. Fellow, Mansfield College, Oxford; Hon. Fellow, City and Guilds Institute; Hon. Doctorates from the Universities of Humberside, Ulster, City, Nottingham, Open, Stirling, Oxford Brookes, Teesside, Queen's University, Belfast; Trustee, Imperial War Museum. *Address:* The King's Fund, 11–13 Cavendish Sq., London W1M 0AN, England.

NEUGEBOREN, Jay Michael; writer and academic; b. 30 May 1938, New York, NY, USA; m. 1st Betsey Bendorf 1964 (divorced); two s. one d.; m. 2nd Judy Karasik 1985 (divorced 1987). *Education:* BA, Columbia University, 1959; MA, Indiana University, 1963. *Career:* Preceptor in English, Columbia University, 1964–66; Visiting Writer, Stanford University, 1966–67; Asst Prof., SUNY at Albany, 1969–70; Prof. and Writer-in-Residence, University of Massachusetts at Amherst, 1971–2001; mem. Authors' Guild; PEN; Writers' Guild. *Publications:* Big Man, 1966; Listen Ruben Fontanez, 1968; Corky's Brother, 1969; Parentheses: An Autobiographical Journey, 1970; Sam's Legacy, 1974; An Orphan's Tale, 1976; The Stolen Jew, 1981; Before My Life Began, 1985; Poli: A Mexican Boy in Early Texas, 1989; Don't Worry About the Kids: Stories, 1997; Imagining Robert: My Brother, Madness, and Survival: A Memoir, 1997; Transforming Madness: New Lives for People Living With Mental Illness, 1999; News from the New American Diaspora and Other Tales of Exile, 2001. Contributions: many anthologies and periodicals. *Honours:* Transatlantic Review Novella Award, 1967; National Endowment for the Arts Fellowships, 1972–73, 1989–90; Guggenheim Fellowship, 1978–79; Kenneth B. Smilen/Present Tense Award for Best Novel, 1982; Edward Lewis Wallant Prize for Best Novel, 1985; Ken Book Award, National Alliance for the Mentally Ill, 2000. *Literary Agent:* Richard Parks, 138 E 16th Street, New York, NY 10003, USA. *Address:* 35 Harrison Avenue, Northampton, MA 01060, USA. *E-mail:* jneug@earthlink.net.

NEUMEYER, Peter F(lorian); Prof. and Writer; b. 4 Aug. 1929, Munich, Germany; m. Helen Wight Snell 28 Dec. 1952; three s. *Education:* BA, 1951, MA, 1955, PhD, 1963, Univ. of California at Berkeley. *Career:* Asst Prof., Harvard Univ., 1963–69; Assoc. Prof., State Univ. of New York at Stony Brook, 1969–75; Prof. and Chair., Dept of English, West Virginia Univ., 1975–78; Prof., 1978–95, Prof. Emeritus, 1995–, San Diego State Univ. *Publications:* Kafka's The Castle, 1969; Donald and the..., 1969; Donald Has a Difficulty, 1970; The Faithful Fish, 1971; Elements of Fiction (co-ed.), 1974; Homage to John Clare, 1980; Image and Makers (co-ed.), 1984; The Phantom of the Opera (adaptation), 1988; The Annotated Charlotte's Web, 1994. Contributions: journals. *Address:* 45 Marguerita Rd, Kensington, CA 94707, USA.

NEUSTADT, Richard Elliott; academic and writer; b. 26 June 1919, Philadelphia, Pennsylvania, USA; m. 1st Bertha Frances Cummings 1945 (died 1984); one s. one d.; m. 2nd Shirley Williams 1987. *Education:* AB, University of California at Berkeley, 1939; MA, 1941, PhD, 1951, Harvard University. *Career:* Economist, US Office of Price Administration, 1942, US Bureau of the Budget, 1946–50, White House, Washington, DC, 1950–53; Prof. of Public Administration, Cornell University, 1953–54; Prof. of Government, Columbia University, 1954–64; Visiting Prof., Princeton University, 1957, University of California at Berkeley, 1986, Cornell University, 1992, University of Essex, 1994–95; Visiting Lecturer, 1961–62, Assoc. Mem., 1965–67, 1990–92, Nuffield College, Oxford; Consultant to Pres. John F. Kennedy, 1961–63, Pres. Lyndon B. Johnson, 1964–66; Prof. of Government, 1965–78, Lucius N. Littauer Prof. of Public Administration, 1978–87, Douglas Dillon Prof., 1987–89, Prof. Emeritus, 1989–, Harvard University; Fellow, Center for Advanced Study in the Behavioral Sciences, 1978–79; mem. American Acad. of Arts and Sciences, fellow; American Philosophical Society; American Political Science Asscn; Council on Foreign Relations; Institute for Strategic Studies; National Acad. of Public Administration. *Publications:* Presidential Power, 1960; Alliance Politics, 1970; The Swine Flu Affair (with Harvey V. Fineberg), 1978, republished as The Epidemic That Never Was, 1982; Thinking in Time (with Ernest R. May), 1986; Report to JFK, 1999; Preparing to be President, 2000. Contributions: Professional journals. *Address:* 79 JFK Street, Cambridge, MA 02138, USA.

NEUSTATTER, Angela Lindsay; Journalist; b. 24 Sept. 1943, Buckinghamshire, England; Author. two s. *Education:* Regent Street Polytechnic, London; Diploma in Journalism. *Publications:* Twiggy: Health and Beauty, 1985; Mixed Feelings, 1986; Hyenas in Petticoats: A Look at 20 Years of Feminism, 1989; Look the Demon in the Eye, 1996, revised edn as This is Our Time, 1998. Contributions: Guardian; Times; Observer; Sunday Telegraph; Daily Telegraph. *Honours:* Feminist Top Twenty List, 1986; Institute for the Study of Drug Dependency Award, 1994. *Address:* 32 Highbury Pl., London N5, England.

NEVILLE, Robert Cummings; Prof. of Philosophy and Religion and Author; b. 1 May 1939, St Louis, MO, USA; m. Elizabeth E. Neville, 1963, three d. *Education:* BA, 1960, MA, 1962, PhD, 1963, Yale University. *Career:* Instructor, Yale University, 1963–65; Visiting Lecturer and Instructor, Wesleyan University, 1964–65; Asst Prof., 1965–68, Assoc. Prof., 1968–73, Fordham University; Assoc. for the Behavioral Sciences, Institute of Society, Ethics, and the Life Sciences, Hastings-on-Hudson, New York, 1971–73; Assoc. Prof., 1971–74, Prof. of Philosophy, 1974–77, SUNY at Purchase; Adjunct Prof. of Religious Studies and Research Prof., 1977–78, Prof. of Philosophy and Prof. of Religious Studies, 1978–87, SUNY at Stony Brook; Prof., Depts of Religion and Philosophy, and School of Theology, 1987–, Dean, School of Theology, 1988–, Boston University; mem. American Acad. of Religion, pres., 1992; American Philosophical Asscn; American Theological Society; Boston Theological Society; Institute of Society, Ethics, and the Life Sciences; Society for Studies of Process Philosophies; Society of Philosophers in America; International Society for Chinese Philosophy, pres., 1993; Metaphysical Society of America, pres., 1989. *Publications:* God the Creator: On the Transendence and Prescence of God, 1968; The Cosmology of Freedom, 1974; Soldier, Sage, Saint, 1978; Creativity and God: A Challenge to Process Theology, 1980; Reconstruction of Thinking, 1981; The Tao and the Daimon: Segments of a Religious Enquiry, 1982; The Puritan Smile, 1987; Recovery of the Measure, 1989; Behind the Masks of God, 1991; A Theology Primer, 1991; The Highroad Around Modernism, 1992; Eternity's and Time's Flow, 1993; Normative Cultures, 1995; The Truth of Broken Symbols, 1996; The God Who Beckons, 1999; Boston Confucianism, 2000; Symbols of Jesus, 2002; Religion in Late Modernity, 2002. Editor: Operating on the Mind: The Psychosurgery Conflict (with Willard Gaylin and Joel Meister), 1975; Encyclopedia of Bioethics (assoc. ed.), 1978; New Essays in Metaphysics, 1987; The Recovery of Philosophy in America (with Thomas Kasulis), 1997; The Human Condition, 2001; Ultimate Realities, 2001; Religious Truth, 2001. Contributions: books, professional journals, and periodicals. *Address:* 5 Cliff Rd, Milton, MA 02186, USA.

NEVINS, Francis Michael, Jr, AB, JD; academic and writer; *Professor of Law, St Louis University School of Law*; b. 6 Jan. 1943, Bayonne, NJ, USA; m. 1st Muriel Walter 1966 (divorced 1978); m. 2nd Patricia Brooks 1982. *Education:* St Peter's Coll., New York Univ. *Career:* admitted to the New Jersey Bar 1967; Asst Prof. 1971–75, Assoc. Prof. 1975–78, Prof. 1978–, St Louis Univ. School of Law. *Publications:* fiction: Publish and Perish 1975, Corrupt and Ensnare 1978, The 120-Hour Clock 1986, The Ninety Million Dollar Mouse 1987, Into the Same River Twice 1996, Beneficiaries' Requiem 2000, Night of Silken Snow and Other Stories 2001, Leap Day and Other Stories 2003; non-fiction: Detectionary (co-author) 1971, Royal Bloodline: Ellery Queen, Author and Detective 1974, Missouri Probate: Intestacy, Wills and Basic Administration 1983, The Films of Hopalong Cassidy 1988, Cornell Woolrich: First You Dream, Then You Die 1988, Bar-20: The Life of Clarence E. Mulford, Creator of Hopalong Cassidy 1993, Joseph H. Lewis: Overview, Interview and Filmography 1998, The Films of the Cisco Kid 1998, Paul Landres: A Director's Stories 2000, The Sound of Detection 2001; editor/co-editor (fiction): Nightwebs 1971, The Good Old Stuff 1983, Exeunt Murderers 1983, Buffet for Unwelcome Guests 1983, More Good Old Stuff 1985, Carnival of Crime 1985, Hitchcock in Prime Time 1985, The Best of Ellery Queen 1985, Leopold's Way 1985, The Adventures of Henry Turnbuckle 1987, Better Mousetraps 1988, Mr President – Private Eye 1988, Death on Television 1989, Little Boxes of Bewilderment 1989, The Night My Friend 1991, Night and Fear 2003; editor/co-editor (non-fiction): The Mystery Writer's Art 1970, Mutiplying Villainies 1973, The Anthony Boucher Chronicles (three vols) 2001–02. *Honours:* MWA Edgar Awards 1975, 1988. *Address:* 7045 Cornell, University City, MO 63130, USA.

NEWBERY, Linda; British writer and children's writer; b. 12 Aug. 1952, Romford, Essex, England; m. *Publications include:* Run with the Hare 1988, Hard and Fast 1990, Some Other War 1990, The Kind Ghosts 1991, The Wearing of the Green 1992, Riddle Me This 1993, Smoke Cat 1995, The Shouting Wind 1995, A Fear of Heights 1996, The Cliff Path 1996, Whistling Jack 1997, The Big Animal Ghost Book 1999, The Nowhere Girl 1999, Flightsend 1999, The Cat with Two Names 2000, The Little Mermaid 2001, The Damage Done 2001, Windfall 2002, Break Time 2002, The Shell House 2002, Sisterland 2003, Polly's March 2004, At the Firefly Gate 2004. *Literary Agent:* Maggie Noach Literary Agency, 22 Danville Crescent, London, W6 0HJ, England. *Telephone:* (20) 8748-8057. *Fax:* (20) 8748-2926. *E-mail:* m-noach@dircon.co.uk. *E-mail:* linda@lindanewbery.co.uk. *Website:* www.lindanewbery.co.uk.

NEWBOULD, Brian (Raby); Emer. Prof. of Music and Writer; b. 26 Feb. 1936, Kettering, England; m. 1st Anne Leicester, 1960, one s., one d.; m. 2nd Ann Airton, 1976, one d. *Education:* BA, General Arts, 1957, BMus, 1958, MA, 1961, University of Bristol. *Career:* Lecturer, Royal Scottish Acad. of Music, Glasgow, 1960–65, University of Leeds, 1965–79; Prof. of Music, University of Hull, 1979–2001, Emer. Prof. 2001–; talks/discussions on national radio, lectures with live illustrations by Allegri String Quartet, Chilingirian String Quartet, the Lindsays, London Mozart Trio, Jyväskylä Sinfonia. *Publications:* Schubert and the Symphony: A New Perspective, 1992; Schubert: The Music and the Man, 1997; Schubert Studies (ed.), 1998, Schubert the Progressive (ed.) 2003, Music to an Unpurged Ear 1981, Musical Analysis in the Sixth Form. Other: Realisations, completions, transcriptions and orchestrations of works by Schubert including realisation of fragmentary Symphony No.7 in E 1979, fragmentary Symphony No.10 in D 1981, completion of Symphony No.8 in B minor ('Unfinished') 1982, transcription for clarinet and string quartet of Arpeggione Sonata 1996, completion of fragmentary Klavierstück 1995, String Trio in B flat 2000, fragmentary Piano Sonata in C ('Reliquie') 2003. Contributions: Musical Times, Music & Letters, 19th-Century Music, Current Musicology Music Review, Musiktheorie, Schubert-Jahrbuch, Schubert durch die Brille, The Schubertian, BBC Music Magazine, The Guardian, The Scotsman, Glasgow Herald, Daily Telegraph, Radio Times, Jewish Echo, Classic CD, Classical Music, Ovation, Journal of the Conductors' Guild, the Beethoven Newsletter, Nieuwsbrief Franz-Schubert Stichting, Meddelelse Franz Schubert Selskabet Danmark, Music Teacher. *Honours:* Hon. Vice-Pres. Schubert Inst. (UK), Hon. Pres. Sheffield Gramophone Soc. *Address:* c/o Dept of Music, University of Hull, Hull HU6 7RX, England. *E-mail:* B .R.Newbould@hull.ac.uk. *Website:* www.briannewbould.co.uk.

NEWBY, (George) Eric; writer; b. 6 Dec. 1919, England; m. Wanda Skof 1946; one s. one d. *Education:* St Paul's School. *Career:* Travel Ed., The Observer, and General Ed., Time Off Books, 1964–73; mem. Asscn of Cape Horners; FRGS; FRSL; Garrick Club. *Publications:* The Last Grain Race, 1956; A Short Walk in the Hindu Kush, 1958; Something Wholesale, 1962; Slowly Down the Ganges, 1966; Time Off in Southern Italy, 1966; Grain Race: Pictures of Life Before the Mast in a Windjammer, 1968; The Wonders of Britain (co-author), 1968; The Wonders of Ireland (co-author), 1969; Love and War in the Apennines, 1971; The World of Evelyn Waugh (co-author), 1973; Ganga, 1973; World Atlas of Exploration, 1975; Great Ascents, 1977; The Big Red Train Ride, 1978; A Traveller's Life, 1982; On the Shores of the Mediterranean, 1984; A Book of Travellers' Tales, 1985; Round Ireland in Low Gear, 1987; What the Traveller Saw, 1989; A Small Place in Italy, 1994; A Merry Dance Around the World, 1995; Departures and Arrivals, 1999; Learning the Ropes, 1999; Around the World in 80 Years, 2000. *Honours:* Military Cross, 1945; CBE, 1994; Hon. DLitt, University of Bournemouth, 1994; Hon. Doctorate, Open University, 1997. *Address:* Pine View House, 4 Pine View Close, Chilworth, Surrey GU4 8RS, England.

NEWCOMER, James William; academic, writer and poet; b. 14 March 1912, Gibsonburg, OH, USA; m. 1946; one s. two d. *Education:* PhB, Kenyon College; MA, University of Michigan; PhD, University of Iowa. *Publications:* Non-Fiction: Maria Edgeworth the Novelist, 1967; Maria Edgeworth, 1973; The Grand Duchy of Luxembourg, 1984; Lady Morgan the Novelist, 1990; Luxembourg, 1995; The Nationhood of Luxembourg, 1996. Poetry: The Merton Barn Poems, 1979; The Resonance of Grace, 1984. Contributions: journals and periodicals. *Honours:* Commander, Order of Merit, Hon. Mem., L'Institut Grand-Ducal, Grand Duchy of Luxembourg. *Address:* 1100 Elizabeth Blvd, Fort Worth, TX 76110, USA.

NEWHOUSE, Samuel I., Jr; American publishing executive; *Chairman and CEO, Advance Publications, Inc.*; b. 1928; m. Victoria Newhouse. *Career:* took over father's Staten Island Advance co. 1922 and built newspaper and magazine chain; Chair. Condé Nast Publs Inc., New York and Chair., CEO Advance Publs Inc., New York; fmr mem. Bd NY Museum of Modern Art. *Honours:* Henry Johnson Fisher Award, Magazine Publishers' Asscn 1985. *Address:* Advance Publications, Inc. 950 Fingerboard Road, Staten Island, NY 10305, USA. *Telephone:* (212) 286-2860. *Fax:* (212) 981-1456. *Website:* www.advance.net.

NEWLAND, Courttia; British writer, playwright and theatre director; b. 1973, London. *Career:* resident playwright, Post Office Theatre 2000–. *Plays:* Euripides' Women of Troy 1999, The Far Side 2000, Mother's Day 2002, B Is For Black 2003. *Publications:* novels: The Scholar 1997, Society Within 1999, IC3 (co-ed.) 2001, Snakeskin 2002; contrib. to Disco 2000, New Writers 8, Afrobeat. *Address:* c/o Abacus, Brettenham House, Lancaster Place, London, WC2E 7EN, England.

NEWLAND, Martin, MA(Theol); British newspaper editor; *Editor, The Daily Telegraph*; b. 1961, Nigeria; m.; four c. *Education:* Univ. of London. *Career:* reporter, The Catholic Herald 1986–89; night reporter, The Daily Telegraph 1989, News Ed. mid-1990s, Ed. 2003–; Deputy Ed. The National Post, Canada 1998–2003. *Address:* The Daily Telegraph, Telegraph Group Ltd, 1 Canada Square, Canary Wharf, London, E14 5DT, England (Office). *Telephone:* (20) 7538-5000 (Office). *Website:* www.telegraph.co.uk (Office).

NEWMAN, Andrea; Writer; b. 7 Feb. 1938, Dover, England; (divorced). *Education:* BA, English, 1960, MA, 1972, University of London. *Career:* mem. PEN; Writers' Guild. *Publications:* A Share of the World, 1964; Mirage, 1965; The Cage, 1966; Three Into Two Won't Go, 1967; Alexa, 1968; A Bouquet of Barbed Wire, 1969; Another Bouquet, 1977; An Evil Streak, 1977; Mackenzie, 1980; A Sense of Guilt, 1988; Triangles, 1990; A Gift of Poison, 1991; Imogen's Face (TV script), 1998; Pretending to be Judith (TV script), 2001. Contributions: Magazines and television. *Address:* c/o Rod Hall, 7 Goodge Pl., London W1, England.

NEWMAN, Aubrey N(orris); Prof. of History and Writer; b. 14 Dec. 1927, London, England. *Education:* MA, University of Glasgow, 1949; BA, 1953, MA, DPhil, 1957, Wadham College, Oxford. *Career:* Research Fellow, Bedford College, University of London, 1954–55; Prof. of History, University of Leicester; mem. Jewish Historical Society of England, pres., 1977–79. *Publications:* The Parliamentary Diary of Sir Edward Knatchbull, 1722–1730, 1963; The Stanhopes of Chevening: A Family Biography, 1969; The United Synagogue, 1870–1970, 1977; The Jewish East End, 1840–1939, 1981; The Board of Deputin, 1760–1985: A Brief Survey, 1987; The World Turned Inside Out: New Views on George II, 1988. *Address:* c/o Dept of History, University of Leicester, Leicester LE1 7RH, England.

NEWMAN, G(ordon) F.; Writer and Dramatist; b. 22 May 1947, England; two s. *Career:* mem. Writers' Guild. *Publications:* Sir, You Bastard, 1970; You Nice Bastard, 1972; The Abduction, 1972; The Player and the Guest, 1972; Billy: A Family Tragedy, 1972; The Split, 1973; Three Professional Ladies, 1973; The Price, 1974; The Streetfighter, 1975; The Guvnor, 1977; The List, 1980; The Obsession, 1980; Charlie and Joanna, 1981; The Men With the Guns, 1982; Law and Order, 1983; Set a Thief, 1986; The Testing Ground, 1987; Trading the Future, 1992; Circle of Poison, 1995. Plays: Operation Bad Apple, 1982; An Honourable Trade, 1986; The Testing Ground, 1989. Screenplay: Number One, 1984. Television Plays: Law and Order, 1978; Billy, 1979; The Nation's Health, 1983; Here Is the News, 1989; Black and Blue, 1992; The Healer, 1994; Judge John Deed (series), 2000–02. *Honours:* Writer's Awards, BAFTA, 1992, Best Drama, 1995; Golden Knight, 1999. *Literary Agent:* Talent Media Group, Oxford House, 76 Oxford St, London W1D 1BS, England. *Address:* Broad Heath House, Broad Heath, Radnorshire LD8 2HG, England.

NEWMAN, Jay; Canadian/American academic and writer; b. 28 Feb. 1948, New York, NY, USA. *Education:* BA, Brooklyn College, CUNY, 1968; MA, Brown University, 1969; PhD, York University, 1971. *Career:* Lecturer, 1971–72, Asst Prof., 1972–77, Assoc. Prof., 1977–82, Prof. of Philosophy, 1982–, University of Guelph; mem. Royal Society of Canada, fellow; Canadian Theological Society, pres., 1990–91. *Publications:* Foundations of Religious Tolerance, 1982; The Mental Philosophy of John Henry Newman, 1986; Fanatics and Hypocrites, 1986; The Journalist in Plato's Cave, 1989; Competition in Religious Life, 1989; On Religious Freedom, 1991; Religion vs Television: Competitors in Cultural Context, 1996; Religion and Technology: A Study in the Philosophy of Culture, 1997; Inauthentic Culture and Its Philosophical Critics, 1997; Biblical Religion and Family Values: A Problem in the Philosophy of Culture, 2001. *Honours:* several grants; Distinguished Alumnus Award, Brooklyn College, CUNY, 1988. *Address:* 313-19 Woodlawn Road E, Guelph, ON N1H 7B1, Canada.

NEWMAN, John Kevin; Prof. of Classics and Writer; b. 17 Aug. 1928, Bradford, Yorkshire, England; m. Frances M. Stickney, 8 Sept. 1970, one s. two d. *Education:* BA, Lit Humaniores, 1950, BA, Russian, 1952, MA, 1953, University of Oxford; PhD, University of Bristol, 1967. *Career:* Classics Master, St Francis Xavier College, Liverpool, 1952–54, Downside School, Somerset, 1955–69; Faculty, 1969–, Prof. of Classics, 1980–, University of Illinois, Urbana; Ed., Illinois Classical Studies, 1982–87. *Publications:* Augustus and the New Poetry, 1967; The Concept of Vates in Augustan Poetry, 1967; Latin Compositions, 1976; Golden Violence, 1976; Dislocated: An American Carnival, 1977; Pindar's Art, 1984; The Classical Epic Tradition, 1986; Roman Catullus, 1990; Lelio Guidiccioni, Latin Poems, 1992; Horace-Bénédict de Saussure (with A. V. Carozzi), 1995; Augustan Propertius, 1997; de Saussure on Geography (with A. V. Carozzi), 2003. *Honours:* Silver Medals, Vatican, Rome, 1960, 1962, 1965, 1997. *Address:* 703 W Delaware Ave, Urbana, IL 61801, USA.

NEWMAN, Lesléa; Writer, Poet and Teacher; b. 5 Nov. 1955, New York, NY, USA. *Education:* BS, Education, University of Vermont, 1977; Certificate in Poetics, Naropa Institute, 1980. *Career:* Teacher, women's writing workshops; mem. Authors' Guild; Authors League of America; Poets and Writers. *Publications:* Good Enough to Eat, 1986; Love Me Like You Mean It, 1987; A Letter to Harvey Milk, 1988; Heather Has Two Mommies, 1989; Bubbe Meisehs by Shayneh Maidelehs, 1989; Secrets, 1990; In Every Laugh a Tear, 1992; Writing from the Heart, 1992; Every Woman's Dream, 1994; Fat Chance, 1994; Too Far Away to Touch, 1995; A Loving Testimony: Remembering Loved Ones Lost to AIDS, 1995; The Femme Mystique, 1995; Remember That, 1996; My Lover is a Woman: Contemporary Lesbian Love Poems, 1996; Out of the Closet and Nothing to Wear, 1997; Matzo Ball Moon, 1998; Still Life With Buddy, 1998; Girls Will Be Girls, 2000; Signs of Love, 2000; Cats, Cats, Cats!, 2001; She Loves Me, She Loves Me Not (short stories), 2002; Dogs, Dogs, Dogs!, 2002; Runaway Dreidel, 2002; Felicia's Favourite Story, 2002. Contributions: Magazines. *Honours:* Massachusetts Artists Fellowship in Poetry, 1989; National Endowment for the Arts Fellowship, 1997. *Literary Agent:* Curtis Brown Ltd, 10 Astor Pl., New York, NY 10003, USA. *Address:* PO Box 815, Northampton, MA 01061, USA.

NEWMAN, Paul Nigel; Author, Poet and Ed.; b. 12 Oct. 1945, Bristol, England. *Education:* Weston Super-Mare Technical College, 1960–64; St Paul's College, Cheltenham, 1966–71. *Career:* Founder and Ed., Abraxas: A Journal of Literature, Philosophy and Ideas, 1991–. *Publications:* Channel Passage, 1975; The Hill of the Dragon, 1979; Channel Portraits, 1980; Grandeur and Decay, 1981; Somerset Villages, 1986; Bath, 1986; Bristol, 1987; Gods and Graven Images, 1987; Spiders and Outsiders, 1989; The Meads of Love, 1994; Murder as an Antidote for Boredom, 1996; In Many Ways Frogs (poems with A. R. Lamb,), 1997; Lost Gods of Albion, 1998; A History of Terror, 2000. Contributions: Writers Monthly; Third Stone; British Archaeology; South West Arts; Westwords; Cornish Review; Psychopoetica; Ramraid Extraordinaire; Story Cellar; Dreams from a Strangers Café. *Address:* 57 Eastbourne Rd, St Austell, Cornwall, England.

NEWMAN, Peter C(harles); Journalist and Writer; b. 10 May 1929, Vienna, Austria; m. 1st Christina McCall, divorced; m. 2nd Camilla Jane Turner, divorced; m. 3rd Alvie Björklund, two d. *Education:* Upper Canada College, Toronto; BA, 1950, MCom, 1954, University of Toronto. *Career:* Asst Ed., 1951–54, Montréal Ed., 1954–55, Production Ed., 1955–56, Financial Post; Asst Ed., 1956–60, Ottawa Ed., 1960–63, National Affairs Ed., 1963–64, Ed., 1971–82, Senior Contributing Ed., 1982–, Maclean's magazine; Ottawa Ed., 1964–69, Ed.-in-Chief, 1969–71, Toronto Daily Star; Visiting Prof. of Political Science, McMaster University, 1969–71, York University, 1979–80; Prof. of Creative Writing, University of Victoria, 1985–90. *Publications:* Flame of Power: Intimate Profiles of Canada's Greatest Businessmen, 1959; Renegade in Power: The Diefenbaker Years, 1963; The Distemper of Our Times, 1968; Home Country: People, Places and Power Politics, 1973; The Canadian Establishment, Vol. 1, The Great Business Dynasties, 1975; Bronfman Dynasty: The Rothschilds of the New World, 1978; The Acquistors: The Canadian Establishment, Vol. 2, 1981; The Establishment Man: Portrait of Power, 1982; True North, Not Strong and Free: Defending the Peaceable Kingdom in the Nuclear Age, 1983; Debrett's Illustrated Guide to the Canadian Establishment (general ed.), 1983; Company of Adventurers: An Unauthorized History of the Hudson's Bay Company, 1985; Caesars of the Wilderness, 1985; Sometimes a Great Nation: Will Canada Belong to the 21st Century?, 1988; Empire of Bay, 1989; Merchant Princes, 1991; Canada 1892: Portraits of a Promised Land, 1992; The Canadian Revolution From Deference to Defiance, 1995; Defining Moments, 1996; Titans: How the New Canadian Establishment Seized Power, 1998. Contributions: newspapers, journals, and television. *Honours:* National Newspaper Award for Journalism, 1971; Quill Award for Excellence in Canadian Journalism, 1977; Officer, 1979, Companion, 1990, Order of Canada; Knight Commander, Order of St Lazarus, 1980; Canadian Authors Asscn Literary Award for Non-Fiction, 1986. *Address:* 777 Bay St, Toronto, Ontario M5W 1A7, Canada.

NEYREY, Jerome H(enry); Roman Catholic Priest, Prof., Writer and Ed.; b. 5 Jan. 1940, New Orleans, LA, USA. *Education:* BA, magna cum laude, 1963, MA, 1964, PhL, 1964, St Louis University; MDiv, 1970, MTh, 1972, Regis College, Toronto; PhD, Yale University, 1977; STL, Weston School of Theology, 1987. *Career:* Ordained Roman Catholic Priest, 1970; Faculty, Weston School of Theology, 1977–92; Assoc. Ed., New Testament Abstracts, 1977–81, Catholic Biblical Quarterly, 1983–91, 1994–, Biblical Theology Bulletin, 1986–, Hervormde Teologiese Studies, 1995–, Journal for the Study of the New Testament, 1997–; Visiting Prof., Pontifical Biblical Institute, Rome, 1989; Prof., University of Notre Dame, IN, 1992–; mem. Catholic Biblical Asscn; Society of Biblical Literature; The Context Group: Project on the Bible in Its Cultural Environment, charter mem., 1989–. *Publications:* First Timothy, Second Timothy, Titus, James, First Peter, Second Peter, Jude, Vol. Nine, Collegeville Bible Commentary, 1983; Christ is Community, 1985; The Passion Narrative in St Luke, 1985; The Resurrection Stories, 1988; Calling Jesus Names (with Bruce Malina), 1988; An Ideology of Revolt: John's Christology in Social-Science Perspective, 1988; Paul, In Other Words: A Cultural Reading of His Letters, 1990; The Social World of Luke–Acts: Models for Interpretation (ed.), 1991; Peter and Jude, Anchor Bible Commentary, 1993; Portraits of Paul: An Archaeology of Ancient Personality (with Bruce Malina), 1996; Honor and Shame in the Gospel of Matthew, 1998. Contributions: Catholic Biblical Quarterly;

Journal of Biblical Literature; Biblica; Novum Testamentum; New Testament Studies; Journal for the Study of the New Testament; Journal for the Study of Judaism. *Honours:* Bannan Fellowship, Santa Clara University, 1984–85; Young Scholars Grant, 1984; ATS Grant, 1989; Lilly Foundation, 1989; Plowshares, 1990. *Address:* c/o Dept of Theology, University of Notre Dame, Notre Dame, IN 46556, USA. *E-mail:* neyrey.1@nd.edu. *Website:* www.nd.edu/~jneyreyl.

NGEMA, Mbongeni; South African writer, producer and composer; b. 1955, Hlabisa. *Career:* mem. Gibson Kente's acting co., f. Cttee Artists; est. S African struggle theatre on London and New York stages 1981. *Plays:* Woza Albert! (with Percy Mtwa and Barney Simon) 1981, Asinamali 1983, Township Fever 1989, Sarafina! 1992, The Zulu 2000. *Publications:* Voices of Sarafina! Songs of Hope and Freedom 1988; contrib. to Woza Afrika!: A Collection of South African Plays 1986, Where is the Way: Song and Struggle in South Africa 1990. *Address:* c/o Skotaville Publishers, African Books Collective Ltd, The Jam Factory, 27 Park End Street, Oxford, OXI IHU, England.

NGUYEN DUY; Vietnamese poet, writer and dramatist; b. 12 Dec. 1948, Dong Ve, Thanh Hoa. *Education:* Univ. of Hanoi. *Career:* served as militia squad leader defending Ham Rong-Thanh Hoa 1965–67; staff mem., Van Nghe Giai Phong (Liberation Literature and Arts) newspaper 1967–77; representative of Van Nghe (Literature and Arts) in the South 1977–. *Publications:* ten poetry collections incl.: Anh trang (Moonlight), Qua Tang (The Gift), Ve (Returning), Distant Road: Selected Poems 1999; also three memoir collections, one novel. *Honours:* Van Nghe Poetry Prize 1973, Viet Nam Writers' Association Poetry Prize 1985. *Address:* c/o Van Nghe, 17 Tran Quoc Toan, Hanoi, Viet Nam.

NI CHUILLEANAIN, Eilean; Lecturer, Writer and Poet; b. 28 Nov. 1942, Ireland; m. Macdara Woods, 27 June 1978, one s. *Education:* BA, 1962, MA, 1964, University College, Cork; BLitt, Lady Margaret Hall, Oxford, 1969. *Career:* Lecturer in Mediaeval and Renaissance English, Trinity College, Dublin, 1966–; Prof. of American History and Institutions, University of Oxford, 1969–78; mem. Aosdána; Irish Writers Union. *Publications:* Acts and Monuments, 1972; Site of Ambush, 1975; Cork, 1977; The Second Voyage, 1977; The Rose-Geranium, 1981; Irish Women: Image and Achievement (ed.), 1985; The Magdalene Sermon, 1989; The Brazen Serpent, 1994. Contributions: Cyphers Literary Magazine; Journal of Ecclesiastical History; Poems in many magazines. *Honours:* Irish Times Poetry Prize, 1966; Patrick Kavanagh Pize, 1972; O'Shaughnessy Poetry Award, 1992. *Address:* 2 Quarry Hollow, Headington, Oxford OX3 8JR, England.

NÍ DHOMHNAILL, Nuala (Maire); Poet and Dramatist; b. 16 Feb. 1952, St Helens, Lancashire, England; m. Dogan Leflef, 16 Dec. 1973, one s., three d. *Education:* BA, English and Irish, 1972, HDipEd, 1973, University College, Cork. *Career:* Instructor, Middle East Technical University, Ankara, 1975–80; Writer-in-Residence, University College, Cork, 1992–93; Visiting Prof., New York University, 1998, Villanova University, 2001; John J. Burns Library Visiting Scholar, Boston College, 1998–99; mem. Aosdána; Irish Writers' Union; Poetry Ireland. *Publications:* An Dealg Droighinn, 1981; Feár Suaithinseach, 1984; Raven Introductions (with others), 1984; Selected Poems/Rogha Danta, 1986; Pharoah's Daughter, 1990; Feís, 1991; The Astrakhan Cloak, 1992; Jumping Off Shadows: Selected Contemporary Irish Poets (ed. with Greg Delanty), 1995; Cead Aighnis, 1998; In the Heart of Europe: Poems for Bosnia, 1998; The Water Horse, 1999. Contributions: many anthologies and magazines. *Honours:* Oireachtas Poetry Awards, 1982, 1989, 1990, 1998; Irish Arts Council Awards, 1985, 1988; O'Shaughnessy Poetry Award, Irish-American Foundation, 1988; Ireland Fund Literature Prize, 1991; Gulbenkian Foundation New Horizons Bursary, 1995; Hon. Doctorate, Dublin City University, 1995. *Address:* 2 Little Meadow, Pottery Rd, Dun Laoghaire, Co Dublin, Ireland.

NICHOLLS, Christine Stephanie, BA, MA, DPhil; editor and writer; b. 23 Jan. 1943, Bury, Lancashire, England; m. Anthony James Nicholls 1966; one s. two d. *Education:* Lady Margaret Hall, Oxford, St Antony's College, Oxford. *Career:* Henry Charles Chapman Research Fellow, Institute of Commonwealth Studies, University of London, 1968–69; Joint Ed., 1977–89, Ed., 1989–95, Dictionary of National Biography; Ed., Sutton Pocket Biographies, 1996–. *Publications:* The Swahili Coast, 1971; Cataract (with Philip Awdry), 1985; Power: A Political History of the 20th Century, 1990; Missing Persons, 1993; 1986–90, 1996; The Hutchinson Encyclopedia of Biography, 1996; David Livingstone, 1998; The History of St Antony's College, Oxford, 1950–2000, 2000; Elspeth Huxley: A Biography, 2002. *Address:* 27 Davenant Road, Oxford OX2 8BU, England.

NICHOLS, Grace; Guyanese writer and poet; b. 18 Jan. 1950; pnr John Agard; two d. *Education:* Univ. of Guyana, Georgetown. *Career:* moved to UK 1976. *Publications:* Trust You, Wriggly 1980, I is a Long Memoried Woman (Commonwealth Poetry Prize 1983) 1983, Leslyn in London 1984, The Fat Black Woman's Poems 1984, The Discovery 1986, Whole of a Morning Sky 1986, Come on into my Tropical Garden 1988, Black Poetry (ed.) 1988, Lazy Thoughts of a Lazy Woman and Other Poems 1989, Can I Buy a Slice of Sky? (ed.) 1991, No Hickory Dickory Dock (with John Agard) 1991, Give Yourself a Hug 1994, A Caribbean Dozen (ed.) 1994, Sunris 1996, Asana and the Animals 1997, The Poet Cat (children's book) 2000. *Honours:* Arts Council Bursary 1988, Guyana Prize for Poetry 1996. *Address:* Curtis Brown Ltd, Haymarket House, 28–29 Haymarket, London, SW1Y 4SP, England; .

NICHOLS, John (Treadwell); Writer; b. 23 July 1940, Berkeley, CA, USA; Divorced, one s. one d. *Education:* BA, Hamilton College, 1962. *Career:* Visiting Prof., University of New Mexico, 1992, 1993. *Publications:* The Sterile Cuckoo, 1965; The Wizard of Loneliness, 1966; The Milagro Beanfield War, 1974; The Magic Journey, 1978; If Mountains Die, 1979; A Ghost in the Music, 1979; The Nirvana Blues, 1981; The Last Beautiful Days of Autumn, 1982; In Praise of Mountain Lions (with Edward Abbey), 1984; On the Mesa, 1986; American Blood, 1987; A Fragile Beauty: John Nichol's Milagro Country, 1987; The Sky's the Limit: A Defense of the Earth, 1990; An Elegy for September, 1992; Keep It Simple: A Defense of the Earth, 1992; Conjugal Bliss: A Comedy of Marital Arts, 1994; Dancing on the Stones: Selected Essays, 2000; An American Child Supreme: The Education of a Liberation Ecologist, 2001; The Voice of the Butterfly: A Novel, 2001. Contributions: periodicals. *Honours:* Hon. doctorates; New Mexico Gov.'s Award, 1981. *Address:* PO Box 1165, Taos, NM 87571, USA.

NICHOLS, Leigh (see Koontz, Dean Ray).

NICHOLS, Peter Richard, FRSL; British playwright; b. 31 July 1927, Bristol; m. Thelma Reed 1960; one s. two d. (and one d. deceased). *Education:* Bristol Grammar School, Bristol Old Vic School and Trent Park Training Coll. *Career:* actor, mostly in repertory 1950–55; schoolteacher 1958–60; mem. Arts Council Drama Panel 1973–75; playwright-in-residence, Guthrie Theatre, Minneapolis; Visiting Writer, Nanyang Coll., Singapore 1994; directed revivals of Joe Egg and Forget-me-not Lane (Greenwich), National Health (Guthrie, Minneapolis) and first productions of Born in the Gardens (Bristol), A Piece of My Mind (Southampton), Blue Murder (Bristol), Nicholodeon (Bristol). *Plays:* A Day in the Death of Joe Egg 1967, The National Health 1969, Forget-me-Not Lane 1971, Chez Nous 1973, The Freeway 1974, Privates on Parade 1977, Born in the Gardens 1979, Passion Play 1980, Poppy (musical) 1982, A Piece of My Mind 1986, Blue Murder 1995, So Long Life 2000, Nicholodeon 2000. *Films:* Catch Us If You Can 1965, Georgy Girl 1967, Joe Egg 1971, The National Health 1973, Privates on Parade 1983. *Television:* plays include Walk on the Grass 1959, Promenade 1960, Ben Spray 1961, The Reception 1961, The Big Boys 1961, Continuity Man 1963, Ben Again 1963, The Heart of the Country 1963, The Hooded Terror 1963, When the Wind Blows 1964, The Brick Umbrella 1968, Daddy Kiss It Better 1968, The Gorge 1968, Hearts and Flowers 1971, The Common 1973 and Greeks Bearing Gifts (in the Inspector Morse series). *Publications:* Feeling You're Behind (memoirs) 1984, Nichols: Plays One and Two 1991, Diary 1969–71, Diary Selection 2000; all listed plays published separately; archive now available in Manuscripts Dept, British Library. *Honours:* Tony Award, New York 1985; recipient of several SWET and four Evening Standard Drama Awards; Ivor Novello Award for Best Musical 1977. *Literary Agent:* Alan Brodie Representation, 211 Piccadilly, London, W1V 9LD, England. *Address:* 22 Belsize Park Gardens, London, NW3 4LH, England.

NICHOLS, Roger (David Edward); Writer and Broadcaster; b. 6 April 1939, Ely, Cambridgeshire, England; m. Sarah Edwards 11 April 1964; two s. one d. *Education:* MA, Worcester College, Oxford. *Career:* Master, St Michael's College, Tenbury, 1966–73; Lecturer, Open University, 1974–80, University of Birmingham, 1974–80. *Publications:* Debussy, 1973; Through Greek Eyes (with Kenneth McLeish), 1974; Messiaen, 1975; Through Roman Eyes (with Kenneth McLeish), 1976; Ravel, 1977; Greek Everyday Life (with Sarah Nichols), 1978; Ravel Remembered, 1987; Debussy: Letters (ed. and trans.), 1987; Claude Debussy: Pelléas et Mélisande (with Richard Langham Smith), 1989; Debussy Remembered, 1992; The Life of Debussy, 1998; The Harlequin Years: Music in Paris 1917–1929, 2002. *Address:* The School House, The Square, Kington, Herefordshire HR5 3BA, England. *E-mail:* roger.nichols@iname.com.

NICHOLS, (Joanna) Ruth; theologian and writer; b. 4 March 1948, Toronto, ON, Canada; m. W. N. Houston 1974. *Education:* BA, University of British Columbia; MA, Religious Studies, 1972, PhD, Theology, 1977, McMaster University. *Publications:* Ceremony of Innocence, 1969; A Walk Out of the World, 1969; The Marrow of the World, 1972; Song of the Pearl, 1976; The Left-handed Spirit, 1978; The Burning of the Rose, 1989; What Dangers Deep: A Story of Philip Sidney, 1992. *Honours:* Shankar International Literary Contest Awards, 1963, 1965; Woodrow Wilson Fellowship, 1968; Fellow, 1971–72, Research Fellow, 1978, Canada Council; Gold Medal, Canadian Asscn of Children's Librarians, 1972.

NICHOLSON, Christina (see Nicole, Christopher (Robin)).

NICHOLSON, Geoffrey Joseph; Writer; b. 4 March 1953, Sheffield, England. *Education:* MA, English, Gonville and Caius College, Cambridge, 1975; MA, Drama, University of Essex, Colchester, 1978. *Publications:* Street Sleeper, 1987; The Knot Garden, 1989; What We Did On Our Holidays, 1990; Hunters and Gatherers, 1991; Big Noises, 1991; The Food Chain, 1992; Day Trips to the Desert, 1992; The Errol Flynn Novel, 1993; Still Life with Volkswagens, 1994; Everything and More, 1994; Footsucker, 1995; Bleeding London, 1997; Flesh Guitar, 1998; Female Ruins, 1999; Bedlam Burning, 2000; Frank Lloyd Wright, A Beginner's Guide, 2002; Andy Warhol, A Beginner's Guide, 2002. Contributions: Ambit magazine;

Grand Street; Tiger Dreams; Night; Twenty Under 35; A Book of Two Halves; The Guardian; Independent; Village Voice; New York Times Book Review; Salon.Com. *Literary Agent:* AP Watt Ltd, 20 John Street, London WC1N 2DR, England.

NICHOLSON, Margaret Beda (see Yorke, Margaret).

NICHOLSON, Michael Thomas; Foreign Correspondent and Writer; b. 9 Jan. 1937, Romford, Essex, England; m. Diana Margaret Slater, 16 Dec. 1968, two s. two d. *Education:* MA, Univ. of Leicester. *Publications:* Partridge Kite, 1978; Red Joker, 1979; December Ultimatum, 1981; Across the Limpoto, 1985; Pilgrims Rest, 1987; Measure of Danger, 1991; Natasha's Story, 1993. *Honours:* OBE, 1991. *Address:* Grayswood House, Grayswood, Surrey GU27 2DR, England.

NICHOLSON, Robin (see Nicole, Christopher (Robin)).

NICHOLSON, William; British author and screenwriter; b. 1948; m.; three c. *Education:* Univ. of Cambridge. *Career:* documentary maker and producer, BBC Television, mid-1970s to mid-1980s; screenwriter for television and film. *Television screenplays:* Shadowlands 1985, Sweet as You Are 1987, Life Story 1987, A Private Matter 1992, Crime of the Century 1996. *Film screenplays:* The Vision 1987, Sarafina! 1992, Shadowlands 1993, Nell 1994, First Knight 1995, Firelight 1997, Gladiator 2000. *Publications:* novels: The Seventh Level 1979, The Society of Others 2004; juvenile novels: The Wind Singer (Wind on Fire trilogy, book one) (Nestlé Smarties Book Prize) 2000, Slaves of the Mastery (Wind on Fire trilogy, book two) 2001, Firesong (Wind on Fire trilogy, book three) 2002, Seeker (Noble Warriors trilogy, book one) 2005. *Literary Agent:* PFD, Drury House, 34–43 Russell Street, London, WC2B 5HA, England. *Telephone:* (20) 7344-1000. *Fax:* (20) 7836-9543. *Website:* www.pfd.co.uk.

NICKLAM, Jimmy; Ni-Vanuatu politician; *Minister of Finance*. *Career:* mem. Vanua'aku Pati (VP); MP for Tanna; Minister of Finance 2004–. *Address:* Ministry of Finance, PMB 058, Port Vila, Vanuatu (Office). *Telephone:* 23032 (Office). *Fax:* 279337 (Office).

NICOL, Michael George; Writer, Poet and Journalist; b. 17 Nov. 1951, Cape Town, South Africa; one s. one d. *Education:* BA, University of South Africa, 1993. *Career:* Reporter, To The Point, Johannesburg, 1974–76, The Star, Johannesburg, 1976–79; Ed., African Wildlife, Johannesburg, 1979–81; Freelance Journalist, 1981–85; Asst to the Ed., Leadership, Cape Town, 1986–88; Writer, Journalist, 1989–. *Publications:* Among the Souvenirs (poems), 1979; The Powers That Be (novel), 1989; A Good-Looking Corpse (history), 1991; This Day and Age (novel), 1992; This Sad Place (poems), 1993; Horseman (novel), 1994; The Waiting Country (memoir), 1995; The Ibis Tapestry (novel), 1998; Bra Henry (novella for young adults), 1998; The Invisible Line: The Life and Photography of Ken Oosterbroek (biog.), 1998. Contributions: The Guardian; New Statesman; London Magazine. *Honours:* Ingrid Jonker Award, 1980.

NICOLE, Christopher (Robin), (Daniel Adams, Leslie Arlen, Robin Cade, Peter Grange, Nicholas Grant, Caroline Gray, Mark Logan, Simon Mackay, Christina Nicholson, Robin Nicholson, Alan Savage, Alison York, Andrew York); Novelist; b. 7 Dec. 1930, Georgetown, Guyana; m. Diana Bachmann, 8 May 1982, four s., three d. *Education:* Harrison College, Barbados; Queen's College, Guyana; Fellow, Canadian Bankers Asscn. *Career:* mem. Society of Authors; Literary Guild of America; Mark Twain Society. *Publications:* As Christopher Nicole: The Seeds of Power, 1995; The Masters, 1995; The Red Tide, 1995; The Red Gods, 1996; The Scarlet Generation, 1997; Death of a Tyrant, 1997; The Trade, 1997; Shadows in the Sun, 1998; Guns in the Desert, 1998; Prelude to War, 1999; To All Eternity, 1999; The Quest, 1999; Be Not Afraid, 2000; Ransom Island, 2001; The Search, 2002; The Pursuit, 2002. As Nicholas Grant: Khan, 1993; Siblings, 1995. As Alan Savage: Eleanor of Aquitaine, 1995; Queen of Love, 1995; The Sword and the Scalpel, 1996; The Sword and the Jungle, 1996; The Sword and the Prison, 1997; Stop Rommel, 1998; The Afrika Crops, 1998; The Traitor Within, 1999; Commando, 1999; The Cause, 2000; The Tiger, 2000; Partisan, 2001; Murder's Art, 2002; Battleground, 2002. As Caroline Gray: Masquerade, 1997; The Promised Lane, 1997; The Phoenix, 1998; The Torrent, 1999; The Inheritance, 1999. Jointly with Diana Bachmann: Her Name will be Faith, 1988; The Red Death, 1989; Meltdown, 1990; Arctic Peril, 1993; Growth, 1993; Where the River Rises, 1994; Shadow at Evening, 1994; The Burning Rocks, 1995; Children of Hell, 1996; Dry, 1996; The Trench, 1998. Contributions: numerous journals and magazines. *Address:* Marlow House, St Jacques, St Peter Port, Guernsey GY1 1SW, Channel Islands. *E-mail:* christopher.nicole@cwcom.

NICOLOPULOS, Thania; Brazilian poet and writer; b. 12 Jan. 1924, Pernambuco; m. Ricardo Farias Rosas 1942; one s. one d. *Education:* La Prensa, Mexico. *Career:* freelance writer 1960–; founder and Ed. Centro Editorial Mexicano Osiris 1974; Fellow Altrusas, Red Cross, Fed. of Int. Volunteers; mem. Asscn Escritores Poetas Mexicanos, Soc. Autores Compositores, Anthropology Museum of Mexico. *Publications:* Interpretación de los Sueños 1965, El Mágico Lenguaje de los Sueños 1967, Antologí del Pensamiento 1973, Tlaltelolco Presente 1974, El Despertar de los Sentidos 1975, Metáforas y Paradijas 1975, Un album de poesie musicale 1979, Interpretación de las Manos 1980, Sebàstiana la Medium 1981, El Verano de la Vida 1982, La Ofrenda 1983, Remonicencias 1983, Poesía Haiku en español 1990. *Address:* Sierra Ventana 545, 11000 México, DF, Mexico.

NICOLSON, Nigel; British writer; b. 19 Jan. 1917, London, England; m. Philippa Tennyson d'Eyncourt 1953; one s. two d. *Education:* Eton Coll., Balliol Coll., Oxford. *Career:* co-founder-Dir, Weidenfeld & Nicolson publishers 1949–; MP 1952–59; mem. RSL, Jane Austen Soc., Trollope Soc. *Publications:* People and Parliament 1958, Lord of the Isles 1960, Alex, Biography of Field Marshal Alexander 1973, Portrait of a Marriage 1973, Mary Curzon 1977, Napoleon 1812 1985, The World of Jane Austen 1991, Long Life (memoirs) 1997; editor: Letters and Diaries of Harold Nicolson (three vols), Letters of Virginia Woolf (six vols), The Queen and Us 2003. *Honours:* Whitbread Prize. *Address:* Sissinghurst Castle, Cranbrook, Kent TN17 2AB, England.

NIEMI, Mikael; Swedish writer and poet; b. 1959. *Plays:* Man måste kunna försvara sig (Radioteater) 1988, Ulosveisu (Tornedalsteatern) 1991, Specialaren (Lule Stassteater) 1992, Ska hon vara snygg eller oneurotisk (Radioteater) 1993, Kuppari (Tornedalsteatern) 1994, Innan det rasar (Teater Normlösa) 1994, Ulkojärvi cabaré (Radioteater) 1995–96, Elsa Laula (Sydsamisk Teater) 1996, Bondånger (comedy series for SvT) 1997, Samerevy (Dolgi Teater, Kiruna) 1997, Konsten att begrava en kärring (Upsala Stadsteater) 1998, Kalla tjejer och varma killar (Tornedalsteatern) 2000, Hej Hitler (Lule Stassteater) 2000, Min pappa är knivjonglör (ToTe, Kiruna) 2000, Dansa din djävul (Tornedalsteatern) 2001, En ö i Valhall (S. Ölands Musikteater) 2001, Tahto rautanen on (Tornedalsteatern) 2002. *Publications:* Näsblod under högmässan (poems) 1988, Mitt i skallen! (non-fiction) 1988, Änglar med mausergevär (poems) 1989, Med rötter häruppe (non-fiction) 1989, Kyrkdjävulen (juvenile fiction) 1994, Blodsugarna (juvenile fiction) 1997, Populärmusik från Vittula (novel, Popular Music from Vittula, aka Popular Music) (Augustpriset) 2000. *Honours:* Tidningen Vis litteraturpris 2000, Årets Norrbottning 2000, Din bok - vårt val 2000, Årets Bok, Månadens boks pris 2002, Piratenpriset 2002. *Address:* c/o Norstedts, Manus, PO Box 2052, 103 12 Stockholm, Denmark.

NIFFENEGGER, Audrey, BFA, MFA; American novelist and visual artist; b. 13 June 1963, South Haven, MI. *Education:* School of the Art Inst. of Chicago, Northwestern Univ. *Career:* Prof., Columbia Coll., Chicago Centre (Interdisciplinary Book Arts, MFA program). *Publications:* The Time Traveller's Wife (novel) 2003. *Honours:* Ragdale Foundation Fellowship 1996–2003, Illinois Art Council Fellowship in Prose 2000. *Literary Agent:* c/o MacAdam/Cage Publishing, 1900 Wazee Street, Suite 210, Denver, CO 80202, USA. *Telephone:* (303) 753-7565. *Fax:* (303) 753-7566. *Website:* www.macadamcage.com.

NIGG, Joseph Eugene, BA, MFA, PhD; editor and writer; b. 27 Oct. 1938, Davenport, IA, USA; m. 1st Gayle Madsen 1960 (divorced 1979); two s.; m. 2nd Esther Muzzillo 1989. *Education:* Kent State University, University of Iowa, University of Denver. *Career:* Asst Ed., Essays in Literature, 1974–75; Assoc. Ed., Liniger's Real Estate, 1979–85; Fiction Ed., Wayland Press, 1985–92; mem. Colorado Authors League. *Publications:* The Book of Gryphons, 1982; The Strength of Lions and the Flight of Eagles, 1982; A Guide to the Imaginary Birds of the World, 1984; Winegold, 1985; The Great Balloon Festival, 1989; Wonder Beasts, 1995; The Book of Fabulous Beasts, 1998; The Book of Dragons and Other Mythical Beasts, 2002. Contributions: various journals and magazines. *Honours:* Non-Fiction Book of the Year Awards, Colorado Authors League, 1983, 1985, 1989, 1996, 2003; Mary Chase Author of the Year, Rocky Mountain Writers Guild, 1984. *Address:* 1114 Clayton Street, Denver, CO 80206, USA.

NIGHTINGALE, (William) Benedict Herbert; theatre critic and writer; b. 14 May 1939, London, England; m. Anne Bryan Redmon 1964; two s. one d. *Education:* BA, Magdalene College, Cambridge; University of Pennsylvania. *Career:* Gen. writer and Northern Drama Critic, The Guardian, 1963–66; Literary Ed., New Society, 1966–68; Theatre Critic, New Statesman, 1968–86, The Times, 1990–; Sunday Theatre Critic, New York Times, 1983–84; Prof. of English, Theatre and Drama, University of Michigan, 1986–89. *Publications:* Charities, 1973; Fifty Modern British Plays, 1981; Fifth Row Center, 1985; The Future of the Theatre, 1998. Contributions: numerous periodicals and journals. *Address:* 40 Broomhouse Road, London SW6 3QX, England.

NIKLANDER, Hannu; Poet, Writer and Critic; b. 1951, Helsinki, Finland; m. Kirsti Salmi-Niklander. *Education:* MA, Univ. of Helsinki, 1983. *Publications:* Poetry: Kotiinpäin, 1974; Maakuntalaulu, 1979; Kauniisti Niiaava Tytär, 1983; Suksien Surujuhla, 1985; Muodonmuutoksia, 1987; Vackert Nigande Dotter, 1989. Fiction: Kenkää enolle (short stories, with Anja Kauranen and Kosti Sironen), 1983; Öinen Kävely (short stories), 1989; Sairaskertomuksia (short stories), 1994; Aurinko Katsoo Taakseen (novel), 1999; Leskimiehen Kevät (short stories), 2000. Non-Fiction: Kössi Kaatran Elämää Ja Lohjalaisvaiheita (essays), 1982; Kahvilavieraan Muistiinpanot (essays), 1987; Tuokiokuvia Euroopasta (essays), 1990; Vaahteranlehti Ja Vaakunalilja, 1996. Contributions: Länsi-Uusimaa, Porvoon Seutu, Helsingin Sanomat, Etelä-Suomen Sanomat, Suomenmaa, Kirjastolehti, Suomen Luonto, Parnasso, Kanava, Kaltio. *Honours:* State award for literature, 1999. *Address:* c/o Atena Kustannus Oy, Pl 436, 40101 Jyväskylä, Finland.

NIKOSI, Lewis; Writer and Dramatist; b. 5 Dec. 1936, Natal, South Africa. *Education:* M. C. Sultan Technical College, 1954–55; Harvard University, 1961–62; Diploma in Literature, University of London, 1974; University of Sussex, 1977. *Career:* Staff, Ilange Lae Natal (Zulu newspaper), Durban, 1955–56, Drum magazine and Golden City Post, Johannesburg, 1956–60, South African Information Bulletin, Paris, 1962–68; Radio Producer, BBC Transcription Centre, London, 1962–64; Literary Ed., New African magazine, London, 1965–68. *Publications:* The Rhythm of Violence, 1964; Home and Exile (essays), 1965; The Transplanted Heart: Essays on South Africa, 1975; Tasks and Masks: Themes and Styles of African Literature, 1981; Mating Birds (novel), 1986.

NIMIER, Marie; French writer; b. 1957, Paris. *Publications:* novels: Sirène 1985, La Girafe 1987, L'Hypnotisme à la portée de tous (trans. as Hypnotism Made Easy) 1992, La caresse 1994, Celui qui court derrière loiseau 1996, Sabine Weiss: Des enfants 1997, La Nouvelle pornographie 2000; contrib. to Fictions contemporaines au féminin 2002. *Address:* c/o Éditions Gallimard, 5 rue Sébastien-Bottin, 75328, Paris, France.

NISBET, Jim; Writer and Poet; b. 20 Jan. 1947, USA. *Publications:* Poems for a Lady, 1978; Gnachos for Bishop Berkeley, 1980; The Gourmet (novel), 1980; Morpho (with Alaistair Johnston), 1982; The Visitor, 1984; Lethal Injection (novel), 1987; Death Puppet (novel), 1989; Laminating the Conic Frustum, 1991; Small Apt, 1992; Ulysses' Dog, 1993; Sous le Signe de la Razoir, 1994.

NISH, Ian Hill, CBE; academic and writer; b. 3 June 1926, Edinburgh, Scotland; m. Rona Margaret Speirs 1965; two d. *Education:* University of Edinburgh, 1943–51; University of London, 1951–56. *Career:* University of Sydney, NSW, Australia, 1957–62, LSE, England, 1962–91; mem. European Asscn of Japanese Studies, pres., 1985–88; British Asscn of Japanese Studies, pres., 1978. *Publications:* Anglo-Japanese Alliance, 1966; The Story of Japan, 1968; Alliance in Decline, 1972; Japanese Foreign Policy, 1978; Anglo-Japanese Alienation 1919–52, 1982; Origins of the Russo-Japanese War, 1986; Contemporary European Writing on Japan, 1988; Japan's Struggle with Internationalism, 1931–33, 1993; The Iwakura Mission in America and Europe, 1998; Collected Writings, Part I, 2001, Part II, 2002. *Honours:* Order of the Rising Sun, Japan 1991. *Address:* Oakdene, 33 Charlwood Drive, Oxshott, Surrey KT22 0HB, England.

NITCHIE, George Wilson; Prof. of English Emeritus, Writer and Poet; b. 19 May 1921, Chicago, IL, USA; m. Laura Margaret Woodard 19 Jan. 1947; three d. *Education:* BA, Middlebury College, 1943; MA, 1947, PhD, 1958, Columbia University. *Career:* Instructor, 1947–50, Asst Prof., 1950–59, Assoc. Prof., 1959–66, Prof. of English, 1966–86, Chair., Dept of English, 1972–79, Prof. Emeritus, 1986–, Simmons College; mem. American Asscn of University Profs. *Publications:* Human Values in the Poetry of Robert Frost, 1960; Marianne Moore: An Introduction to the Poetry, 1969. Contributions: various critical essays in scholarly journals and poems in many publications. *Address:* 50 Pleansantview Ave, Weymouth, MA 02188, USA.

NIVEN, Larry, (Laurence Van Cott Niven); Writer; b. 30 April 1938, Los Angeles, CA, USA; m. Marilyn Joyce Wisowaty, 6 Sept. 1969. *Education:* California Institute of Technology, 1956–58; BA, Mathematics, Washburn University, KS, 1962. *Publications:* Neutron Star, 1966; Ringworld, 1970; Inconstant Moon, 1971; The Hole Man, 1974; Protector, 1974; The Borderland of Sol, 1975; Dream Park (with Steven Barnes), 1981; Football (with Jerry Pournelle), 1985; Playgrounds, 1991; The Gripping Hand (with Jerry Pournelle), 1993; Ringworld's Children, 2004. Contributions: books and magazines. *Honours:* Science Fiction Achievement Awards, 1966, 1970, 1971, 1974, 1975; Nebula Best Novel, 1970; Australian Best International Science Fiction, 1972, 1974; Inkpot Award, San Diego Comic Convention, 1979; Hon. DLitt, Washburn University, 1984. *Address:* c/o Spectrum Literary Agency, 111 Eighth Vanalden Ave, Tarzana, CA 91356, USA.

NIXON, Colin Harry; Poet and Writer; b. 9 March 1939, London, England; m. Betty Morgan, 2 Sept. 1967, three d. *Education:* Diploma, Sociology, University of London, 1968. *Career:* Civil Servant, 1960–99; Disablement Resettlement Officer, 1974–83; ACAS Conciliation Officer, 1983–99. *Publications:* Roads, 1975; Geography of Love, 1977; With All Angles Equal, 1980; The Bright Idea, 1983. Contributions: anthologies, including: Spongers, 1984; Affirming Flame, 1989; Poetry Street 3, 1991; Red Candle Treasury, 1948–1998, 1998; The Art of Haiku 2000, 2000; Periodicals, including: Outposts; Tribune; Countryman; Cricketer. *Honours:* George Camp Memorial Poetry Prizes, 1975, 1983. *Address:* 72 Barmouth Rd, Wandsworth Common, London SW18 2DS, England.

NOAKES, Vivien; Writer; b. 16 Feb. 1937, Twickenham, England; m. Michael Noakes, 9 July 1960, two s. one d. *Education:* MA, DPhil, English, Senior Scholar, Somerville College, Oxford. *Career:* Judge RSL W.H. Heinemann Award 1999–2004, Winifred Holtby Prize 1999–2004; mem. FRSL; Society of Authors; PEN. *Publications:* Edward Lear: The Life of a Wanderer, 1968; For Lovers of Edward Lear, 1978; Scenes from Victorian Life, 1979; Edward Lear 1812–1888, The Catalogue of the Royal Acad. Exhibition, 1985; The Selected Letters of Edward Lear, 1988; The Painter Edward Lear, 1991; The Imperial War Museum Catalogue of Isaac Rosenberg, 1998; The Daily Life of the Queen: An Artist's Diary, 2000; Edward Lear: The Complete Verse and Other Nonsense (ed.), 2001, revised edn as Edward Lear: The Complete Nonsense and Other Verse, 2002. Contributions: Times; TLS; Daily Telegraph; New Scientist; Punch; Harvard Magazine; Tennyson Research Bulletin. *Literary Agent:* Watson, Little Ltd, Capo di Monte, Windmill Hill, London NW3 6RJ, England. *Address:* 146 Hamilton Terrace, London NW8 9UX, England. *E-mail:* mail@vivien-noakes.co.uk. *Website:* www.vivien-noakes.co.uk.

NOBBS, David Gordon, BA; writer; b. 13 March 1935, Orpington, Kent, England; m. 1st Mary Jane Goddard 1968 (divorced 1998); two step-s. one step-d.; m. 2nd Susan Sutcliffe 1998; one step-d. *Education:* Marlborough College, St John's College, Cambridge. *Publications:* The Itinerant Lodger, 1965; Ostrich Country, 1967; A Piece of the Sky is Missing, 1968; The Fall and Rise of Reginald Perrin, 1975; The Return of Reginald Perrin, 1977; The Better World of Reginald Perrin, 1978; Second From Last in the Sack Race, 1983; A Bit of a Do, 1986; Pratt of the Argus, 1988; Fair Dos, 1990; The Cucumber Man, 1994; The Legacy of Reginald Perrin, 1995; Going Gently, 2000; I Didn't Get Where I Am Today (autobiog.), 2003; Sex and Other Changes 2004. *Address:* 10 Iron Bridge House, Bridge Approach, London NW1 8BD, England.

NOEL, Lise; Writer and Columnist; b. 19 April 1944, Montréal, QC, Canada. *Education:* BA, 1965, Licence in Letters, 1970, MA, History, 1975, PhD, History, 1982, University of Montréal; University of Aix-en-Provence, France. *Publications:* Intolerance: The Parameters of Oppression, 1994. Contributions: Critère; Liberté; Possibles; Service Social; Le Devoir. *Honours:* Hachette-Larousse, 1967; Governor-General's Award for Non-Fiction, 1989; Myers Centre Award for the Study of Human Rights in North America, 1994. *Address:* 2608 Chemin Cote Sainte Catherine, Montréal, QC H3T 1B4, Canada.

NOËL-HUME, Ivor; Archaeologist and Writer; b. 1927, London, England. *Education:* St Lawrence College, Kent, 1942–44. *Career:* Archaeologist, Guildhall Museum Corp, London, 1949–57; Chief Archaeologist, 1957–64, Dir, Dept of Archaeology, 1964–72, Resident Archaeologist, 1972–87, Colonial Williamsburg; Research Assoc., Smithsonian Institution, Washington, DC, 1959–; Guest Curator, Steuben Glass Co, 1990; Dir, Roanoke Project, 1991–93; Chair., Jamestown Rediscovery Advisory Board, 1994–95; mem. American Antiquarian Society; Society of Antiquaries, London, fellow; Society of Historical Archaeology; Society for Post-Medieval Archaeology; Virginia Archeological Society. *Publications:* Archaeology in Britain, 1953; Tortoises, Terrapins and Turtles (with Audrey Noël-Hume), 1954; Treasure in the Thames, 1956; Great Moments in Archaeology, 1957; Here Lies Virginia, 1963; 1775: Another Part of the Field, 1966; Historical Archaeology, 1969; Artifacts of Early America, 1970; All the Best Rubbish, 1974; Early English Delftware, 1977; Martin's Hundred, 1982; The Virginia Adventure, 1994; Shipwreck: History from the Bermuda Reeds, 1995; In Search of This and That, 1995; If These Pots Could Talk, 2001. Films: Doorway to the Past, 1968; The Williamsburg File, 1976; Search for a Century, 1981. Contributions: Professional journals. *Honours:* Award for Historical Archaeology, University of South Carolina, 1975; Hon. Doctor of Humane Letters, University of Pennsylvania, 1976, College of William and Mary, Williamsberg, VA, 1983; Achievement Award, National Society of the Daughters of the Founders and Patriots of America, 1989, National Society of the Daughters of the American Colonists, 1990; OBE, 1992. *Address:* 2 W Circle, Williamsburg, VA 23185, USA. *E-mail:* thamesis@widomaker.com.

NOLAN, Patrick; Prof., Writer and Dramatist; b. 2 Jan. 1933, New York, NY, USA; three s. *Education:* MA, University of Detroit; PhD, English Literature, Bryn Mawr College. *Career:* Instructor, University of Detroit; Prof., Villanova University; mem. Writers Guild of America, West; Dramatists Guild. *Publications:* Films: Hourglass Moment, 1969; Jericho Mile, 1978. Plays: Chameleons, 1981; Midnight Rainbows, 1991. *Honours:* Emmy Award, 1979; Citation, Teaching Excellence, Philadelphia Magazine, 1980. *Address:* c/o Dept of English, Villanova University, Villanova, PA 19085, USA.

NOLAN, William F(rancis), (Frank Anmar, Mike Cahill, F. E. Edwards, Michael Phillips); Writer and Poet; b. 6 March 1928, Kansas City, MO, USA. *Education:* Kansas City Art Institute, 1946–47; San Diego State College, 1947–48; Los Angeles City College, 1953. *Publications:* Barney Oldfield, 1961; Phil Hall: Yankee Champion, 1962; Impact 20 (short stories), 1963; John Huston: King Rebel, 1965; Sinners and Superman, 1965; Death is for Losers, 1968; Dashiell Hammett: A Casebook, 1969; Alien Horizons (short stories), 1974; Hemingway: Last Days of the Lion, 1974; Wonderworlds (short stories), 1977; Hammett: A Life on the Edge, 1983; Things Beyond Midnight (short stories), 1984; Dark Encounters (poems), 1986; Logan: A Trilogy, 1986; How to Write Horror Fiction, 1990; Six in Darkness (short stories), 1993; Night Shapes (short stories), 1993. *Address:* c/o Loni Perkins Assocs Literary Agency, 301 W 53rd St, New York, NY 10019, USA.

NONHEBEL, Clare; Writer; b. 7 Nov. 1953, London, England; m. Robin Nonhebel, 30 Aug. 1975. *Education:* BA, French Studies, University of Warwick. *Career:* mem. MENSA. *Publications:* Cold Showers, 1985; The Partisan, 1986; Incentives, 1988; Healed and Souled, 1988; Child's Play, 1991; Eldred Jones, Lulubelle and the Most High (novel), 1998; Don't Ask Me to Believe (non-fiction), 1998; Far From Home, (non-fiction), 1999; Healing for Life (non-fiction), 2000. Contributions: newspapers, journals, and magazines. *Honours:* Joint Winner, Betty Trask Award, 1984. *Literary*

Agent: Curtis Brown Ltd, Haymarket House, 28–29 Haymarket, London, SW1Y 4SP, England. *Telephone:* (20) 7393-4400. *Fax:* (20) 7393-4401. *E-mail:* info@curtisbrown.co.uk. *Website:* www.curtisbrown.co.uk.

NORFOLK, Lawrence; Writer; b. 1963, London, England. *Publications:* Novels: Lemprière's Dictionary, 1991; The Pope's Rhinoceros, 1997; In the Shape of a Boar, 2000. Other: ed. of anthologies. *Address:* c/o Orion, Orion House, 5 Upper St Martin's Lane, London WC2H 9EA, England.

NORFOLK, Mark; British playwright; b. Croydon, Surrey. *Career:* co-founder, Prussia Lane Productions. *Plays:* Fear as the Dark Get 1998, Buy Your Leave 1998, Knock Down Ginger 2000, Wrong Place 2003, Fess Up 2003. *Screenplay:* Love Is Not Enough 2001. *Literary Agent:* Prussia Lane Productions, 1a Upper Brockley Road, London, SE4 1SY, England. *Telephone:* (20) 8692-6618. *Fax:* (20) 8692-6618. *Website:* www.prussialane.com.

NORLING, Bernard; Prof. of History (retd) and Writer; b. 23 Feb. 1924, Hunters, Washington, USA; m. Mary Pupo, 30 Jan. 1948. *Education:* BA, Gonzaga University, 1948; MA, 1949, PhD, 1955, University of Notre Dame. *Career:* Instructor, 1952–55, Asst Prof., 1955–61, Assoc. Prof., 1961–71, Prof. of History, 1971–86, University of Notre Dame; mem. Indiana Asscn of Historians; Michiana Historians, pres., 1972. *Publications:* Towards a Better Understanding of History, 1960; Timeless Problems in History, 1970; Understanding History Through the American Experience, 1976; Return to Freedom, 1983; Behind Japanese Lines, 1986; The Nazi Impact on a German Village, 1993; Lapham's Raiders, 1996; The Intrepid Guerrillas of North Luzon, 1999. Contributions: Magazines and journals. *Honours:* Best Teacher of Freshman, University of Notre Dame, 1968. *Address:* 504 E Pokagon St, South Bend, IN 46617-1326, USA.

NORMAN, Barry Leslie, CBE; British writer and broadcaster; b. 21 Aug. 1933, London; m. Diana Narracott 1957; two d. *Education:* Highgate School, London. *Career:* Entertainment Ed. Daily Mail, London 1969–71; weekly columnist The Guardian 1971–80; Writer and Presenter of BBC 1 Film 1973–81, 1983–98, The Hollywood Greats 1977–79, 1984, The British Greats 1980, Omnibus 1982, Film Greats 1985, Talking Pictures 1988, Barry Norman's Film Night, BSkyB 1998–2001; Radio 4 Today 1974–76, Going Places 1977–81, Breakaway 1979–80. *Publications:* Novels: The Matter of Mandrake 1967, The Hounds of Sparta 1968, End Product 1975, A Series of Defeats 1977, To Nick a Good Body 1978, Have a Nice Day 1981, Sticky Wicket 1984, The Birddog Tape 1992, The Mickey Mouse Affair 1995, Death on Sunset 1998; non-fiction: Tales of the Redundance Kid 1975, The Hollywood Greats 1979, The Movie Greats 1981, The Film Greats 1985, Talking Pictures 1987, The Good Night In Guide 1992, 100 Best Films of the Century 1992, And Why Not? (autobiog.) 2002. *Honours:* Hon. DLitt (E Anglia) 1991, (Herts.) 1996; Richard Dimbleby Award, BAFTA 1981, Columnist of the Year Award 1990. *Address:* c/o Curtis Brown Ltd, Haymarket House, 28–29 Haymarket, London, SW1Y 4SP, England. *Telephone:* (20) 7396-6600.

NORMAN, Geraldine (Lucia), (Geraldine Keen, Florence Place); Journalist and Writer; b. 13 May 1940, Wales; m. Frank Norman, July 1971. *Education:* MA, Mathematics, St Anne's College, Oxford, 1961; University of California at Los Angeles, USA, 1961–62. *Career:* UK Representative, State Hermitage Museum, St Petersburg. *Publications:* The Sale of Works of Art (as Geraldine Keen), 1971; 19th Century Painters and Paintings: A Dictionary, 1977; The Fake's Progress (co-author), 1977; The Tom Keating Catalogue (ed.), 1977; Mrs Harper's Niece (as Florence Place), 1982; Biedermeier Painting, 1987; Top Collectors of the World (co-author), 1993; The Hermitage: The Biography of a Great Museum, 1997. Contributions: newspapers. *Honours:* News Reporter of the Year, 1976. *Address:* 5 Seaford Ct, 220 Great Portland St, London W1, England.

NORMAN, John; academic, writer and poet; b. 20 July 1912, Syracuse, NY, USA; m. Mary Lynott 1948; four d. *Education:* BA, 1935, MA, 1938, Syracuse University; PhD, Clark University, 1942. *Publications:* Edward Gibbon Wakefield: A Political Reappraisal, 1963; Labor and Politics in Libya and Arab Africa, 1965; Life Lines: A Volume of Verse, 1997. Contributions: anthologies, reference books, and journals. *Honours:* World Poetry Prize, 1991. *Address:* 94 Cooper Road, John's Pond, Ridgefield, CT 06877, USA.

NORMAN, Marsha, BA, MAT; American playwright and writer; b. 21 Sept. 1947, Louisville, KY; m. 1st Michael Norman (divorced 1974); m. 2nd Dann C. Byck Jr 1978 (divorced); m. 3rd Timothy Dykman; one s. one d. *Education:* Agnes Scott Coll. and Univ. of Louisville. *Career:* Rockefeller playwright-in-residence grantee 1979–80; American Acad. and Inst. for Arts and Letters grantee. *Plays:* Getting Out 1977, Third and Oak 1978, Circus Valentine 1979, The Holdup 1980, 'Night, Mother 1982, Traveler in the Dark 1984, Sarah and Abraham 1987, The Secret Garden (musical) 1991, Loving Daniel Boone 1992, The Red Shoes 1993, Trudy Blue 1995. *Television plays:* It's the Willingness 1978, In Trouble at Fifteen 1980, The Laundromat 1985, The Pool Hall 1989, Face of a Stranger 1991. *Publications:* The Fortune Teller (novel) 1987; books of lyrics; plays. *Honours:* Pulitzer Prize for Drama 1983; Tony Award 1991; many other awards and prizes.

NORRELL, Gregory T.; Writer, Poet and Publisher; b. 24 Nov. 1960, Tallahassee, FL, USA; m. Karen Norrell, 1980, divorced 1995, one s. one d. *Education:* BS, State University of West Georgia, 1985; PhD, SUNY at Albany, 1989. *Career:* Publisher, Dandelion Press and Dandelion Media, Idaho Falls, 1955–; Owner, Dandelion Studios, Dandelion Multimedia Recording Division; mem. Acad. of American Poets; Web Poets Society, founder. *Publications:* 'Til Death Do Us Part (short stories), 1997; 95 Windows: An Unofficial Poetry Collection from the Microsoft Network, 1997; Amongst the Shadows (poems), 1997; The River of No Return (novel), 1998; Impact (novel), 1999. *Address:* 1935 E 113 South St, Idaho Falls, ID 83404, USA. *E-mail:* dandelion@dandelion-multimedia.com.

NORRIS, Kathleen, BA; poet and writer; b. 27 July 1947, Washington, DC, USA; m. David J. Dwyer. *Education:* Bennington Coll. *Career:* Poet-in-Residence, North Dakota Arts Council, 1979–92; Oblate, Benedictine Order, 1986–; mem. National Book Critics Circle; Poetry Society of America. *Publications:* Poetry: Falling Off, 1971; From South Dakota: Four Poems, 1978; The Middle of the World, 1981; How I Came to Drink My Grandmother's Piano: Some Benedictine Poems, 1989; The Year of Common Things, 1990; The Astronomy of Love, 1994; Little Girls in Church, 1995. Other: Dakota: A Spiritual Geography, 1993; The Cloister Walk, 1996; Amazing Grace: A Vocabulary of Faith, 1998; The Quotidian Mysteries, 1998. Editor: Leaving New York: Writers Look Back, 1995. Contributions: anthologies and periodicals. *Honours:* Big Table Poetry Series Younger Poets Award, 1971; Creative Artists Public Service Programme Grant, New York State, 1972; Fine Arts Work Centre Fellowship, Provincetown, Massachusetts, 1972; Bush Foundation Grant, 1993; Guggenheim Foundation Grant, 1994; Western Libraries Asscn Award, 1995. *Literary Agent:* Steven Barclay Agency, 12 Western Avenue, Petaluma, CA 94952, USA. *Telephone:* (707) 773-0654. *Fax:* (707) 778-1868. *Website:* www.barclayagency.com. *Address:* PO Box 570, Lemmon, SD 57638, USA.

NORRIS, Ken; Prof. of Canadian Literature and Poet; b. 3 April 1951, New York, NY, USA; two d. *Education:* BA, SUNY at Stony Brook, 1972; MA, Concordia University, 1975; PhD, McGill University, 1980. *Career:* Prof. of Canadian Literature, University of Maine, 1985–; mem. League of Canadian Poets; Writers' Union of Canada. *Publications:* Vegetables, 1975; The Perfect Accident, 1978; Autokinesis, 1980; Whirlwinds, 1983; The Better Part of Heaven, 1984; Islands, 1986; Report: Books 1–4, 1988, 8–11, 1993; In the House of No, 1991; Full Sun: Selected Poems, 1992; The Music, 1995; Odes, 1997; Limbo Road, 1998. Contributions: various reviews, journals, and periodicals. *Honours:* Third Prize, CBC Literary Competition, 1986. *Address:* c/o Dept of English, University of Maine, 5752 Neville Hall, Room 304, Orono, ME 04469, USA.

NORRIS, Leslie; Prof., Poet and Writer; b. 21 May 1921, Merthyr Tydfil, Wales; m. Catherine Mary Morgan, 1948. *Education:* MPhil, University of Southampton, 1958. *Career:* Principal Lecturer, West Sussex Institute of Education, 1956–74; Prof., Brigham Young University, Provo, Utah, 1981–; mem. FRSL; Welsh Acad., fellow. *Publications:* Tongue of Beauty, 1941; Poems, 1944; The Loud Winter, 1960; Finding Gold, 1964; Ransoms, 1970; Mountains, Polecats, Pheasants and Other Hegies, 1973; Selected Poems, 1986; Collected Poems, 1996. Contributions: various publications. *Honours:* British Arts Council Award, 1964; Alice Hunt Bartlett Prize, 1969; Cholmondeley Poetry Prize, 1979; Katherine Mansfield Award, 1981. *Address:* 849 S Carterville Rd, Orem, UT 84058, USA.

NORSE, Harold George; Prof., Writer and Poet; b. 6 July 1916, New York, NY, USA. *Education:* BA, Brooklyn College, CUNY, 1938; MA, New York University, 1951. *Career:* Instructor, Cooper Union College, New York, 1949–52, Lion School of English, Rome, Italy, 1956–57, United States Information Service School, Naples, Italy, 1958–59; Instructor in Creative Writing, San Jose State University, CA, 1973–75; Prof. in Creative Writing, New College of California, 1994–95; mem. PEN. *Publications:* The Roman Sonnets of Giuseppe Gioacchino Belli (trans.), 1960; Karma Circuit (poems), 1967; Hotel Nirvana (poems), 1974; Carnivorous Saint (poems), 1977; Mysteries of Magritte (poems), 1984; Love Poems, 1986; Memoirs of a Bastard Angel (autobiog.), 1989; Seismic Events (poems), 1993. Contributions: journals and magazines. *Honours:* National Endowment for the Arts Fellowship, 1974; R. H. de Young Museum Grant, 1974; Lifetime Achievement Award in Poetry, National Poetry Asscn, 1991. *Address:* 157 Albion St, San Francisco, CA 94110, USA.

NORTH, Anthony (see Koontz, Dean Ray).

NORTH, Elizabeth (Stewart); Author and Teacher of Creative Writing; b. 20 Aug. 1932, Hampshire, England. *Education:* BA, University of Leeds, 1973. *Career:* Writer-in-Residence, Bretton Hall College of Higher Education, 1984–85. *Publications:* Make Thee an Ark (radio play), 1969; Wife Swopping (radio play), 1969; The Least and Vilest Things (novel), 1971; Pelican Rising (novel), 1975; Enough Blue Sky (novel), 1977; Everything in the Garden (novel), 1978; Florence Avenue (novel), 1980; Dames (novel), 1981; Ancient Enemies (novel), 1982; The Real Tess (radio feature), 1984; Jude the Obscure (adaptation for radio), 1985.

NORTH, Kate (see Lloyd, Kathleen Annie).

NORTHCUTT, Wayne; Prof. of History and Writer; b. 5 July 1944, New Orleans, LA, USA. *Education:* BA, History, 1966, MA, History, 1968, California State University, Long Beach; PhD, Modern European History, University of California, Irvine, 1974. *Career:* Teaching Asst, 1969–72,

Teaching Assoc., 1973–74, 1979–80, University of California, Irvine; Lecturer, 1972–73, Asst Prof., 1975–78, Monterey Institute of International Studies, California; Lecturer, Schiller College, Paris, 1978; Asst Prof., 1980–83, Assoc. Prof., 1983–88, Prof. of History, 1988–, Niagara University; Foreign Expert, Chinese People's University, Beijing, 1983; Adjunct Prof. of History, SUNY at Buffalo, 1993–. *Publications:* The French Socialist and Communist Party Under the Fifth Republic, 1958–1981: From Opposition to Power, 1985; Historical Dictionary of the French Fourth and Fifth Republics, 1946–1991 (ed.-in-chief), 1992; Mitterrand: A Political Biography, 1992; The Regions of France: A Reference Guide to History and Culture, 1996. Contributions: scholarly books and journals. *Honours:* numerous research grants and fellowships. *Address:* c/o Dept of History, Niagara University, PO Box 1932, Niagara University, NY 14109, USA.

NORTON, Augustus Richard; academic and writer; b. 2 Sept. 1946, New York, NY, USA; m. Deanna J. Lampros 1969; one s. *Education:* BA, magna cum laude, Political Science, 1974, MA, Political Science, 1974, University of Miami; Certification in Modern Standard Arabic and Cairene Dialect, Defense Language Institute, Monterey, CA, 1979; PhD, Political Science, University of Chicago, 1984. *Career:* Asst Prof. of Military Science, 1974–78, Adjunct Asst Prof. of Political Science, 1975–77, University of Illinois-Chicago Circle Campus; Adjunct Asst Prof. of Political Science, Old Dominion University, 1979–80; Asst Prof., 1981–84, Assoc. Prof. of International Studies, 1984, Permanent Assoc. Prof. of Comparative Politics, 1984–90, Prof. of Political Science, 1990–93, US Military Acad., West Point, NY; Visiting Assoc. Prof. of Political Science, University of Texas at Austin, 1986; Visiting Research Prof., New York University, 1992–95; Prof. of International Relations and Anthropology, Boston University, 1993–; Distinguished Visiting Fellow, Oxford Centre for Islamic Studies, 2000; mem. American Political Science Asscn; Asscn for Middle East Women's Studies; Council on Foreign Relations; Middle East Studies Asscn. *Publications:* Studies in Nuclear Terrorism (senior ed. and contributor), 1979; International Terrorism: An Annotated Bibliography and Research Guide (senior ed.), 1980; The Emergence of a New Lebanon: Fantasy or Reality? (co-author), 1984; NATO: A Bibliography and Resource Guide (senior ed.), 1985; Touring Nam: The Vietnam War Reader (co-ed. and contributor), 1985; Amal and the Shi'a: Struggle for the Soul of Lebanon, 1987; The International Relations of the Palestine Liberation Organization (senior ed. and contributor), 1989; UN Peacekeepers: Soldiers with a Difference, 1990; Political Tides in the Arab World, 1992; Civil Society in the Middle East (ed.), 2 vols, 1995–96; Al-Amn fi al-sharq al-awsat: Tujahat jdida (ed. and contributor), 1999; Hizballah: Extremist Ideals vs Mundane Politics, 2000. Contributions: Reference works, scholarly books, professionsl journals and non-specialist publications, including: Survival; Foreign Policy; Current History; New Outlook; New Leader; Middle East Journal. *Honours:* various grants and fellowships; Outstanding Academic Book Citation, Choice, 1980. *Address:* c/o Dept of International Relations, Boston University, 152 Bay State Road, Boston, MA 02215, USA.

NORTON, Rictor, BA, MA, PhD; editor and writer; b. 25 June 1945, Friendship, NY, USA. *Education:* Florida Southern College, Florida State University. *Career:* Instructor, Florida State University, 1970–72; Research Ed., Gay News, London, 1974–78; Foreign Rights Man., Western Publishing Co, London, 1979–90; mem. International William Beckford Society; National Trust; Royal Horticultural Society; Alpine Garden Society; London Natural History Society; RSPB. *Publications:* The Homosexual Literary Tradition: An Interpretation, 1974; College English 36 (co-ed.), 1974; Mother Clap's Molly House: The Gay Subculture in England, 1700–1830, 1992; The Myth of the Modern Homosexual: Queer History and the Search for Cultural Unity, 1997; My Dear Boy: Gay Love Letters Through the Centuries (ed.), 1998; The Mistress of Udolpho: The Life of Ann Radcliffe, 1999; Gothic Readings, 2000; Eighteenth-Century British Erotica (ed.), 2002. Contributions: The Male Homosexual in Literature: A Bibliography; New Dictionary of National Biography; Essays to Gay Roots, vols one and two; Articles to scholarly journals and periodicals, including: American Imago; Renascence; Yearbook of Comparative and General Literature; Gay News; Gay Sunshine; Advocate; Columns and book reviews to periodicals. *Address:* 29 Huddleston Road, Tufnell Park, London N7 0AD, England. *E-mail:* norton@infopt.demon.co.uk.

NORWICH, John Julius Cooper, (2nd Viscount of Aldwick); Writer and Broadcaster; b. 15 Sept. 1929, London, England; m. 1st Anne Frances May Clifford 5 Aug. 1952 (divorced 1985); one s. one d.; m. 2nd Mollie Philipps 14 June 1989. *Education:* Univ. of Strasbourg, 1947; New College, Oxford, 1949–52. *Career:* Entered Foreign Office, 1952; Third Sec., British Embassy, Belgrade, 1955–57; Second Sec., British Embassy, Beirut, 1957–60; Mem., British Delegation to Disarmament Conference, Geneva, 1960–64; First Sec., Foreign Office, 1961–64; Chair., British Theatre Museum, 1966–71, Venice in Peril Fund, 1970–99, World Monuments Fund in Britain, 1994–; Ed., New Shell Guides to Britain, 1987–91; Dir, Robclif Productions Ltd, 1991–94; Has made some 30 documentary films for television, mainly on history and architecture; mem. FRSL; FRGS; Society of Authors, fellow. *Publications:* Mount Athos (with Reresby Sitwell), 1966; The Normans in the South, 1016–1130 (US edn as The Other Conquest), 1967; Sahara, 1968; The Kingdom in the Sun, 1130–1194, 1970; Great Architecture of the World (ed.), 1975; A History of Venice, Vol. I: Venice: The Rise to Empire, 1977; Christmas Crackers: Ten Commonplace Selections, 1970–79, 1980; A History of Venice, Vol. II: Venice: The Greatness and the Fall, 1981; Britain's Heritage (ed.), 1982; The Italian World: History, Art, and the Genius of a People (ed.) 1983, revised edn as The Italians: History, Art, and the Genius of a People, 1989; The Architecture of Southern England, 1985; Fifty Years of Glyndebourne: An Illustrated History, 1985; A Taste for Travel: An Anthology (ed.), 1985; Byzantium, Vol. I, 1988, Vol. II: The Apogee, 1991, Vol. III: Decline and Fall, 1995, abridged edn as A Short History of Byzantium, 1997; Venice: A Traveller's Companion, 1990; More Christmas Crackers: Ten Commonplace Selections, 1980–89, 1990; The Oxford Illustrated Encyclopaedia of the Arts, Vol. Five (ed.), 1990; Five Centuries of Music in Venice (with H. C. Robbins Landon), 1991; Sovereign II: A Celebration of Forty Years of Service, 1992; Venice in Old Photographs, 1870–1920 (with Dorothea Ritter), 1994; Love in the Ancient World (with Christopher Miles), 1997; The Twelve Days of Christmas, 1998; Shakespeare's Kings: The Great Plays and the History of England in the Middle Ages, 1337–1485, 2000; Still More Christmas Crackers: Ten Commonplace Selections, 1990–1999, 2000; Paradise of Cities: Venice and its Nineteenth-Century Visitors, 2003. Contributions: numerous magazines and journals. *Honours:* Succeeded father as 2nd Viscount Norwich of Aldwick, 1954; CVO, 1993; Commendatore, Ordine al Merito della Repubblica Italiana. *Literary Agent:* Felicity Bryan, 2A North Parade, Oxford, England. *Address:* 24 Blomfield Rd, London W9 1AD, England. *Telephone:* (20) 7286-5050. *Fax:* (20) 7266-2561. *E-mail:* jjnorwich@dial.pipex.com.

NORWICH, William; Columnist and Novelist; b. 18 July 1954, Norwich, CT, USA. *Education:* BA, Hampshire College, 1976; MFA, Columbia University. *Career:* Columnist, New York Daily News, 1985–, Harper's and Queen, 1989–, New York Observer; Ed.-at-Large, US Vogue. *Publications:* Learning to Drive (novel), 1996. Contributions: periodicals, including: House and Garden; Interview; Premiere; Redbook; Vanity Fair. *Address:* c/o New York Observer, 54 E 64th St, New York, NY 10021, USA.

NOTHOMB, Amélie; Belgian writer; b. 13 Aug. 1967, Kobe, Japan. *Education:* Université Libre de Bruxelles. *Publications include:* Hygiène de l'assassin 1992, Le Sabotage amoureux 1993, Les Combustibles 1994, Les Catallinaires 1995, Péplum 1996, Attentat 1997, Mercure 1998, Stupeur et tremblements (Grand Prix du Roman, Acad. française) 1999, Métaphysique des tubes 2000, Cosmétique de l'ennemi 2001, Robert des noms propres 2002. *Honours:* Prix Rene-Fallet, Prix Alain Fournier (two times).

NOTLEY, Alice; Poet and Writer; b. 8 Nov. 1945, Bisbee, AZ, USA; m. 1st Ted Berrigan, 1972, deceased 1983, two s.; m. 2nd Douglas Oliver, 10 Feb. 1988. *Education:* BA, Barnard College, 1967; MFA, University of Iowa, 1969. *Publications:* Poetry: 165 Meeting House Lane, 1971; Phoebe Light, 1973; Incidentals in the Days World, 1973; For Frank O'Hara's Birthday, 1976; Alice Ordered Me to be Made: Poems 1975, 1976; A Diamond Necklace, 1977; Songs for the Unborn Second Baby, 1979; When I Was Alive, 1980; Waltzing Matilda, 1981; How Spring Comes, 1981; Three Zero, Turning Thirty (with Andrei Codrescu), 1982; Sorrento, 1984; Margaret and Dusty, 1985; Parts of a Wedding, 1986; At Night the States, 1988; Selected Poems of Alice Notely, 1993. Other: Doctor Williams' Heiresses: A Lecture, 1980; Tell Me Again, 1981; Homer's 'Art', 1990; The Scarlet Cabinet: A Compendium of Books (with Douglas Oliver), 1992. Contributions: various publications. *Honours:* National Endowment for the Arts Grant, 1979; Poetry Center Award, 1981; General Electric Foundation Award, 1983; Fund for Poetry Awards, 1987, 1989. *Address:* 101 St Mark's Pl., No. 12A, New York, NY 10009, USA.

NOURISSIER, François; Author, Journalist, Critic and Ed.; b. 18 May 1927, Paris, France; m. 1st Marie-Thérèse Sobesky, 1949, two s.; m. 2nd Cécile Muhlstein, 1962, one d. *Education:* École libre des sciences politiques, Paris; Faculté de Droit, Paris. *Career:* Sec.-Gen., Editions Denoël, 1952–56; Ed.-in-Chief, La Parisienne, 1956–58; Literary Adviser, Editions Grasset, 1958–95; Literary Critic, Les Nouvelles littéraires, 1963–72, Le Point, 1972–, Le Figaro, 1975–, Le Figaro Magazine, 1978–; Literary Dir, Vogue, French edn, 1964–66; Contributing Ed., Vogue, American edn, 1964–; Film Critic, L'Express, 1970–72; mem. Académie Goncourt, 1977–, sec.-gen., 1983–96, pres., 1996–. *Publications:* L'eau grise, 1951; Lorca, 1955; Les orphelins d'Auteuil, 1956; Le corps de Diane, 1957; Portrait d'un indifférent, 1957; Bleu comme la nuit, 1958; Un petit bourgeois, 1964; Une histoire française, 1966; Les Français, 1967, English trans. as The French, 1970; Le maître de maison, 1968; La crève, 1970; Cartier-Bresson's France, 1971; Allemande, 1973; Lettre à mon chien, 1975; Lettre ouverte à Jacques Chirac, 1977; Le musée de l'homme, 1979; L'empire des nuages, 1981; La fête des pères, 1986; En avant, calme et droit, 1987; Bratislava, 1990; Autos graphie, 1990; Le gardien des ruines, 1992; Mauvais genre, 1994; Le bar de l'escadrille, 1997; A défaut de génie (autobiog.), 2000; Prince des berlingots, 2003. *Honours:* Commdr, Ordre des Arts et des Lettres: Commdr, Légion d'honneur; Commdr, Ordre nat. du Mérite; Prix Félix Fénéon, 1952; Grand Prix de la Guilde du Livre, Switzerland, 1965; Grand Prix du Roman, Académie Française, 1965; Prix Fémina, 1970; Prix Prince Pierre de Monaco, 1975; Grand Prix de la Ville de Paris, 1987; Prix Mondial Cino del Duca, 2002. *Address:* c/o Editions Grasset, 61 rue des Saints-Pères, 75006 Paris, France.

NOVA, Craig; Writer; b. 5 July 1945, Los Angeles, CA, USA; m. Christina Barnes, 2 July 1977, two c. *Education:* BA, University of California at Berkeley, 1967; MFA, Columbia University, 1969. *Publications:* Turkey

Hash, 1972; The Geek, 1975; Incandescence, 1978; The Good Son, 1982; The Congressman's Daughter, 1986; Tornado Alley, 1989; Trombone, 1992; The Book of Dreams, 1994; The Universal Door, 1997. *Honours:* National Endowment for the Arts Fellowships, 1973, 1975, 1985; Guggenheim Fellowship, 1977. *Address:* c/o Stanford J. Greenburger Assocs Inc, 825 Third Ave, New York, NY 10022, USA.

NOVAK, Maximillian Erwin; Prof. of English Emeritus, Writer and Ed.; b. 26 March 1930, New York, NY, USA; m. Estelle Gershgoren, 21 Aug. 1966, two s. one d. *Education:* PhD, University of California at Los Angeles, 1958; DPhil, St John's College, Oxford, 1961. *Career:* Asst Prof. of English, University of Michigan, 1958–62; Prof. of English, 1962–2001, Prof. Emeritus, 2001–, University of California at Los Angeles; mem. American Society of 18th Century Studies; MLA. *Publications:* Economics and the Fiction of Daniel Defoe, 1962; Defoe and the Nature of Man, 1963; Congreve, 1970; Realism, Myth and History in the Fiction of Daniel Defoe, 1983; Eighteenth-Century English Literature, 1983; Stoke Newington Defoe, Vol. 1, 1999, Vol. 2, 2000; Daniel Defoe, Master of Fictions, 2001. Editor: The Works of John Dryden, Vol. X, 1971, Vol. XIII, 1984; The Wild Man Within, 1972; English Literature in the Age of Disguise, 1977; The Collected Writings of Daniel Defoe, 1999–; Passionate Encounters, 2000. Contributions: scholarly books and journals. *Honours:* Fulbright Fellowship, 1955–57; Guggenheim Fellowships, 1965–66, 1985–86; American Philosophical Society Fellowship, 1979; National Endowment for the Humanities Fellowship, 1980–81; Beinecke Library Fellow, 1991; Pres.'s Fellow, University of California, 1991–; Huntingdon Library Fellow, 1991–. *Address:* 451 S El Camino Dr., Beverly Hills, CA 90212, USA. *E-mail:* novak@humnet.ucla.edu.

NOVAK, Michael (John); Prof., Author and Ed.; b. 9 Sept. 1933, Johnstown, PA, USA; m. Karen Ruth Laub 29 June 1963; one s. two d. *Education:* AB, Stonehill College, North Easton, Massachusetts, 1956; BT, Gregorian Univ., Rome, 1958; MA, Harvard Univ., 1966. *Career:* Assoc. Prof. of Philosophy and Religious Studies, State Univ. of New York at Old Westbury, 1968–71; Provost, Disciplines College, State Univ. of New York at Old Westbury, 1969–71; Assoc. Dir for Humanities, Rockefeller Foundation, New York, 1973–75; Resident Scholar in Religion and Public Policy, 1978–, George Frederick Jewett Chair in Public Policy Research, 1983–, Dir, Social and Political Studies, 1987–, American Enterprise Institute, Washington, DC; Head (with rank of Ambassador), US Delegation, UN Human Rights Commission, Geneva, 1981, 1982, Conference on Security and Co-operation in Europe, 1986; Founder-Publisher, 1982–96, Ed.-in-Chief, 1993–96, Crisis; Faculty, Univ. of Notre Dame, 1986–87; various lectureships; mem. American Acad. of Religion; Catholic Theological Society; Council on Foreign Relations; Institute for Religion and Democracy, dir, 1981–; National Center of Urban and Ethnic Affairs, dir, 1982–86; Society of Christian Ethics; Society of Religion in Higher Education. *Publications:* The Tiber was Silver (novel), 1961; A New Generation, 1964; The Experience of Marriage, 1964; The Open Church, 1964; Belief and Unbelief, 1965; A Time to Build, 1967; Vietnam: Crisis of Conscience (with Brown and Herschel), 1967; American Philosophy and the Future, 1968; A Theology for Radical Politics, 1969; Naked I Leave (novel), 1970; The Experience of Nothingness, 1970; Story in Politics, 1970; All the Catholic People, 1971; Ascent of the Mountain, Flight of the Dove, 1971; Politics: Realism and Imagination, 1971; A Book of Elements, 1972; The Rise of the Unmeltable Ethnics, 1972; Choosing Our King, 1974; The Joy of Sports, 1976; The Guns of Lattimer, 1978; The American Vision, 1978; Rethinking Human Rights I, 1981, II, 1982; The Spirit of Democratic Capitalism, 1982; Confession of a Catholic, 1983; Moral Clarity in the Nuclear Age, 1983; Freedom with Justice, 1984; Human Rights and the New Realism, 1986; Will It Liberate?: Questions About Liberation Theology, 1986; Character and Crime, 1986; The New Consensus on Family and Welfare, 1987; Taking Glasnost Seriously: Toward an Open Soviet Union, 1988; Free Persons and the Common Good, 1989; This Hemisphere of Liberty, 1990; The Spirit of Democratic Capitalism, 1991; Choosing Presidents, 1992; The Catholic Ethic and the Spirit of Capitalism, 1993; To Empower People: From State to Civil Society, 1996; Business as a Calling, 1996; The Fire of Invention, 1997; Tell Me Why, 1998; On Cultivating Liberty, 1999; A Free Society Reader (ed.), 2000; Three in One: Essays on Democratic Capitalism, 1976–2000, 2001; On Two Wings: Humble Faith and Common Sense at the American Founding, 2001. Contributions: numerous publications. *Honours:* Freedom Award, Coalition for a Democratic Majority, 1979; George Washington Honor Medal, Freedom Foundation, 1984; Award of Excellence, Religion in Media, 1985; Ellis Island Medal of Honor, 1986; Anthony Fisher Prize, 1992; Templeton Prize for Progress in Religion, 1994; International Award, Institution for World Capitalism, Jacksonville University, FL, 1994; Gold Medal, Slovak Acad. of Sciences, 2000; Masaryk Award, Czech Republic, 2000; many hon. doctorates. *Address:* c/o American Enterprise Institute, 1150 17th St NW, Washington, DC 20036, USA.

NOWRA, Louis; playwright and writer; b. 12 Dec. 1950, Melbourne, Vic., Australia. *Education:* La Trobe Univ., Victoria. *Career:* co-Artistic Dir, Lighthouse Co, Sydney 1983. *Publications:* Albert Names Edward, 1975; Inner Voices, 1977; Visions, 1978; Inside the Island, 1980; The Precious Woman, 1980; The Song Room, 1981; Royal Show, 1982; The Golden Age, 1985; Whitsunday Opera Libretto, 1988; Byzantine Flowers, 1989; Summer of the Aliens, 1989; Cosi, 1992; Radiance, 1993; Crow, 1994. Fiction: The Misery of Beauty, 1976; Palu, 1987; Red Nights, 1997. Other: radio, television and screenplays. *Honours:* Prix Italia 1990, Australia-Canada Award 1993. *Literary Agent:* Hilary Linstead & Associates, PO Box 1536, Strawberry Hills, NSW 2012, Australia.

NOYES, Stanley Tinning; Writer and Poet; b. 7 April 1924, San Francisco, CA, USA; m. Nancy Black, 12 March 1949, two s. one d. *Education:* BA, English, 1950, MA, English, 1951, University of California, Berkeley. *Career:* mem. PEN American Center. *Publications:* No Flowers for a Clown (novel), 1961; Shadowbox (novel), 1970; Faces and Spirits (poems), 1974; Beyond the Mountains (poems), 1979; The Commander of Dead Leaves (poems), 1984; Los Comanches: The Horse People, 1751–1845, 1993; Comanches in the New West: Historic Photographs, 1895–1908, 1999, Annus Mirabilis: A Peripatetic Calendar (poems) 2003. Contributions: Reviews and quarterlies. *Honours:* MacDowell Fellow, 1967. *Address:* 634 E Garcia, Santa Fe, NM 87505, USA.

NUDELSTEJER, Sergio; Journalist and Writer; b. 24 Feb. 1924, Warsaw, Poland; m. Tosia Malamud. *Education:* National University of Mexico. *Publications:* Theodor Herzl: Prophet of Our Times, 1961; The Rebellion of Silence, 1971; Albert Einstein: A Man in His Time, 1980; Franz Kafka: Conscience of an Era, 1983; Rosario Castellanos: The Voice, the Word, the Memory (anthology), 1984; Borges: Getting Near to His Literary Work, 1987; Elias Canetti: The Language of Passion, 1990; Spies of God: Authors at the End of the Century, 1992; Stefan Zweig: The Conscience of Man, 1992; Everlasting Voices: Latin American Writers, 1996; Jerusalem: 3000 Years of History, 1997. Contributions: periodicals. *Address:* Heraclito 331, Apt 601, Polanco 11560, México, DF, Mexico.

NUMMI, Lassi; writer, poet, journalist and literary editor; b. 9 Oct. 1928, Helsinki, Finland; m. Pirkko Aho 1959; two s. *Education:* University of Helsinki. *Career:* mem. Finnish Writers' Union, pres., 1969–72, hon. mem., 1982–; PEN Centre Finland, pres., 1983–88. *Publications:* 30 books 1949–2004, including Collected Poems 1978 1998, Requiem 1990, Grandfather's Poems 1999, Mediterranean 2000; contrib. to Uusi Suomi newspaper, Nykypäivä newspaper. *Honours:* State Literary Prizes, 1950, 1964, 1968, 1978, 1983; Pro Finlandia Medal, 1972; Hon. PhD, 1986; Savonia Prize, 1990; Suometar Journalist Prize, 1990; State Prof. of Art, 1990–95; Hon. DTh, 2000. *Address:* Ulvilantie 11 BA, 00350 Helsinki, Finland. *Fax:* (9) 506 2905.

NUNN, Frederick McKinley; Prof. of History and Writer; b. 29 Oct. 1937, Portland, Oregon, USA; m. 1st Tey Diana Rebolledo, 10 Sept. 1960, divorced 1973, one d.; m. 2nd Susan Karant Boles, 8 Feb. 1974, one d. *Education:* BA, University of Oregon, 1959; MA, 1963, PhD, 1963, University of New Mexico. *Career:* Asst Prof., 1965–67, Assoc. Prof., 1967–72, Prof. of History, 1972–, Portland State University, Oregon. *Publications:* Chilean Politics, 1920–31: The Honorable Mission of the Armed Forces, 1970; The Military in Chilean History: Essays on Civil-Military Relations, 1810–1973, 1976; Yesterday's Soldiers: European Military Professionalism in South America, 1890–1940, 1983; The Time of the Generals: Latin American Professional Militarism in World Perspective, 1992. Contributions: Professional journals. *Address:* c/o Dept of History, Portland State University, PO Box 751, Portland, OR 92707, USA.

NUSSBAUM, Martha Craven, BA, MA, PhD; American philosopher, classicist, academic and writer; b. 6 May 1947, New York, NY; m. Alan Jeffrey Nussbaum 1968 (divorced 1987); one d. *Education:* New York University, Harvard University. *Career:* Asst Prof. of Philosophy and Classics, 1975–80, Assoc. Prof., 1980–83, Harvard University; Visiting Prof., Wellesley College, 1983–84; Assoc. Prof. of Philosophy and Classics, 1984–85, Prof. of Philosophy, Classics, and Comparative Literature, 1985–87, David Benedict Prof. of Philosophy, Classics, and Comparative Literature, 1987–89, Prof., 1989–95, Brown University; Visiting Fellow, All Souls College, Oxford, 1986–87; Gifford Lecturer, University of Edinburgh, 1993; Visiting Prof. of Law, 1994, Prof. of Law and Ethics, 1995–96, Prof. of Philosophy, 1995–, Ernst Freund Prof. of Law and Ethics, 1996–99, University of Chicago; mem. American Acad. of Arts and Sciences, fellow; American Philological Asscn; American Philosophical Asscn; American Philosophical Society; PEN. *Publications:* Aristotle's De Motu Animalium, 1978; Language and Logic (ed.), 1983; The Fragility of Goodness, 1986; Love's Knowledge, 1990; Essays on Aristotle's De Anima (ed. with A Rorty), 1992; The Quality of Life (ed. with A Sen), 1993; Passions and Perceptions (ed. with J. Brunschwig), 1993; The Therapy of Desire, 1994; Women, Culture, and Development (ed.), 1995; Poetic Justice, 1996; Cultivating Humanity, 1997; Sex and Social Justice, 1998; Hiding From Humanity: Disgust, Shame and the Law 2004. *Honours:* Guggenheim Fellowship, 1983; Creative Arts Award, Brandeis University, 1990; Spielvogel-Diamondstein Award, 1991. *Address:* c/o Department of Philosophy, University of Chicago, 1111 E 60th Street, Chicago, IL 60637, USA.

NWAPA, Flora; Author; b. 1931, Nigeria. *Education:* Univ. College Ibadan; Edinburgh Univ. *Career:* fmrly, Women's Education Officer, Calabar, teacher of English and geography, Queen's School, Enugu, Asst Registrar, Univ. of Lagos; fmr mem., East Central State Exec. Council, Commissioner for Lands, Survey and Urban Development; first Nigerian woman to be published. *Publications:* Efuru, 1966; Idu, 1970; Emeka: Driver's Guard, 1972; Wives at War and Other Stories, 1992; One is Enough, 1992; This is

Lagos and Other Stories, 1992; Never Again, 1992; Women Are Different, 1995. *Address:* c/o African Writers Series, Heinemann Educational Publishers, Halley Ct, Jordan Hill, Oxford OX2 8EJ, England.

NYE, Robert; Poet, Novelist, Playwright, Critic and Trans; b. 15 March 1939, London, England; m. 1st Judith Pratt 1959 (divorced 1967); three s.; m. 2nd Aileen Campbell 1968; one d. one step-s. one step-d. *Education:* Southend High School, Essex. *Career:* Poetry Critic, The Times, 1971–96; mem. FRSL, 1977–. *Publications:* Poetry: Juvenilia 1, 1961; Juvenilia 2, 1963; Darker Ends, 1969; Agnus Dei, 1973; Two Prayers, 1974; Five Dreams, 1974; Divisions on a Ground, 1976; A Collection of Poems, 1955–1988, 1989; 14 Poems, 1994; Henry James and Other Poems, 1995; Collected Poems, 1995; New and Selected Poems, 2004. Fiction: Doubtfire, 1967; Tales I Told My Mother, 1969; Falstaff, 1976; Merlin, 1978; Faust, 1980; The Voyage of the Destiny, 1982; The Facts of Life and Other Fictions, 1983; The Memoirs of Lord Byron, 1989; The Life and Death of My Lord Gilles de Rais, 1990; Mrs Shakespeare: The Complete Works, 1993; The Late Mr Shakespeare, 1998. Plays: Sawney Bean (with William Watson), 1970; The Seven Deadly Sins: A Mask, 1974; Three Plays: Penthesilia, Fugue, and Sisters, 1976. Editor: A Choice of Sir Walter Ralegh's Verse, 1972; William Barnes of Dorset: A Selection of His Poems, 1973; A Choice of Swinburne's Verse, 1973; The English Sermon, 1750–1850, 1976; The Faber Book of Sonnets, 1976; PEN New Poetry 1, 1986; First Awakenings: The Early Poems of Laura Riding (co-ed.), 1992; A Selection of the Poems of Laura Riding, 1994. Other: Trans and children's books. Contributions: The Times; The Scotsman; Periodicals, magazines and journals in the UK and USA. *Honours:* Eric Gregory Award, 1963; Arts Council Bursaries, 1970, 1973; James Kennaway Memorial Award, 1970; Guardian Fiction Prize, 1976; Hawthornden Prize, 1977; Society of Authors travel scholarship, 1991. *Literary Agent:* Curtis Brown Ltd, 7 Queensferry St, Edinburgh EH2 4QS, Scotland.

NYSTROM, Debra; poet, writer and university professor; b. 12 July 1954, Pierre, SD, USA. *Education:* BA, English, University of South Dakota, 1976; Boston University, 1978–79; MFA, Creative Writing, Goddard College, 1980; Postgraduate Fellowship in Poetry, University of Virginia, 1982–83. *Career:* Faculty in Creative Writing, University of Virginia, 1984–; mem. Associated Writing Programs; Poetry Society of America. *Publications:* A Quarter Turn, 1991; Torn Sky, 2003. Contributions: various anthologies, reviews, quarterlies, and journals. *Honours:* Virginia Commission for the Arts Prizes for Poetry, 1987, 1997; Balch Prize for Poetry, Virginia Quarterly Review, 1991; James Boatwight Prizes for Poetry, Shenandoah, 1994, 2000; Borders Books/HEART Prize, 2002. *Address:* University of Virginia, Dept of English, 219 Bryan Hall, PO Box 400121, Charlottesville, VA 22904-4121, USA.

O

OAKES, Philip; Author and Poet; b. 31 Jan. 1928, Burslem, Staffordshire, England; m. 1st Stella Fleming (divorced 1988); one s. one d.; m. 2nd Gillian Chapman 1989. *Career:* Scriptwriter, Granada TV and BBC, London, 1958–62; Film Critic, The Sunday Telegraph, London, 1963–65; Asst Ed., Sunday Times Magazine, 1965–67; Arts Columnist, Sunday Times, London, 1969–80; Columnist, Independent on Sunday, London, 1990, Guardian Weekend, London, 1991–. *Publications:* Unlucky Jonah: Twenty Poems, 1954; The Punch and Judy Man (screenplay, with Tony Hancock), 1962; Exactly What We Want (novel), 1962; In the Affirmative (poems), 1968; The God Botherers (US edn as Miracles: Genuine Cases Contact Box 340, novel), 1969; Married/Singular (poems), 1973; Experiment at Proto (novel), 1973; Tony Hancock: A Biography, 1975; The Entertainers (ed.), 1975; A Cast of Thousands (novel), 1976; The Film Addict's Archive, 1977; From Middle England (memoirs), 1980; Dwellers All in Time and Space (memoirs), 1982; Selected Poems, 1982; At the Jazz Band Ball (memoirs); Shopping for Women (novel), 1994. *Address:* Fairfax Cottage, North Owersby, Lincolnshire LN8 3PX, England.

OAKLEY, Ann (Rosamund); Prof. of Sociology and Social Policy and Writer; b. 17 Jan. 1944, London, England; one s. two d. *Education:* MA, Somerville College, Oxford, 1965; PhD, Bedford College, London, 1974. *Career:* Research Officer, Social Research Unit, Bedford College, London, 1974–79; Wellcome Research Fellow, Radcliffe Infirmary, National Perinatal Epidemiology Unit, Oxford, 1980–83; Deputy Dir, Thomas Coram Research Unit, 1985–90, Dir, Social Science Research Unit, 1990–, Prof. of Sociology and Social Policy, 1991–, University of London. *Publications:* Sex, Gender and Society, 1972; The Sociology of Housework, 1974; Housewife, 1974, US edn as Women's Work: A History of the Housewife, 1975; The Rights and Wrongs of Women (ed. with Juliet Mitchell), 1976; Becoming a Mother, 1980; Women Confined, 1980; Subject Women, 1981; Miscarriage (with A McPherson and H. Roberts), 1984; Taking It Like a Woman, 1984; The Captured Womb: A History of the Medical Care of Pregnant Women, 1984; Telling the Truth about Jerusalem, 1986; What Is Feminism (ed. with Juliet Mitchell), 1986; The Men's Room, 1988; Only Angels Forget, 1990; Matilda's Mistake, 1990; Helpers in Childbirth: Midwifery Today (with S. Houd), 1990; The Secret Lives of Eleanor Jenkinson, 1992; Social Support and Motherhood: The Natural History of a Research Project, 1992; Essays on Women, Medicine and Health, 1992; Scenes Originating in the Garden of Eden, 1993; Young People, Health and Family Life (with J. Brannen, K. Dodd and P. Storey), 1994; The Politics of the Welfare State (ed. with S. Williams), 1994; Man and Wife, 1996; A Proper Holiday, 1996; The Gift Relationship by Richard Titmuss (with John Ashton), 1997; Overheads, 1999; Experiments in Knowing: Gender and Method in the Social Sciences, 2000; Gender on Planet Earth, 2002. Contributions: scholarly books and journals. *Address:* c/o The Sayle Agency, Bickerton House, 25–27 Bickerton Rd, London N19 5 JT, England.

OANDASAN, William Cortes; Poet and Ed.; b. 17 Jan. 1947, Santa Rosa, CA, USA; m. 28 Oct. 1973, two d. *Education:* BA, 1974; MA, 1981; MFA, 1984; Instructor's Credential, 1989. *Career:* Ed., A Publications, 1976–; Senior Ed., American Indian Culture and Research Journal, 1981–86; Instructor, English Dept, University of Orleans, Louisiana State University, 1988–90; mem. Associated Writing Programs; MLA; Society for the Study of Multi-Ethnic Literatures; Asscn for the Study of American Indian Literatures; National Asscn of Ethnic Studies; Philological Society of the Pacific Coast. *Publications:* Moving Inland, 1983; Round Valley Songs, 1984; Summer Night, 1989. Contributions: anthologies, reviews and journals, including: Colorado Review; Southern California Anthology; California Courier; American Indian Culture and Research Journal; Approaches to Teaching World Literature; Harper's Anthology of 20th Century Native American Poetry. *Honours:* Publishing Grant, National Endowment for the Arts, 1977; American Book Award, 1985; Summer Scholar Award for Writers, 1989; Research Council Grant, 1989. *Address:* 3832 W Ave 43, No. 13, Los Angeles, CA 90041, USA.

OATES, Joyce Carol, (Rosamond Smith), MA; American writer, poet and publisher; b. 16 June 1938, Lockport, NY; m. Raymond J. Smith 1961. *Education:* Syracuse Univ. and Univ. of Wisconsin at Madison. *Career:* instructor 1961–65, Univ. of Detroit, Asst Prof. of English 1965–67; faculty mem. Dept of English, Univ. of Windsor, ON 1967–78; publisher (with Raymond Joseph Smith), Ontario Review 1974–; writer-in-residence, Princeton Univ. 1978–81, Prof. 1987–; mem. American Acad., Inst. of Arts and Letters; Guggenheim Fellow 1967–68. *Plays:* Three Plays: Ontological Proof of My Existence, Miracle Play, The Triumph of the Spider Monkey 1980, Twelve Plays 1991, The Perfectionist and Other Plays 1995. *Publications:* novels: With Shuddering Fall 1964, A Garden of Earthly Delights 1967, Expensive People 1968, Them 1969, Wonderland 1971, Do With Me What You Will 1973, The Assassins: A Book of Hours 1975, Childworld 1976, Son of the Morning 1978, Unholy Loves 1979, Cybele 1979, Bellefleur 1980, A Sentimental Education 1981, Angel of Light 1981, A Bloodsmoor Romance 1982, Mysteries of Winterthurn 1984, Solstice 1985, Marya: A Life 1986, You Must Remember This 1987, American Appetites 1989, Because it is Bitter and Because it is my Heart 1990, Black Water 1992, Foxfire 1993, What I Lived For 1994, Zombie 1995, First Love: A Gothic Tale 1996, We Were the Mulvaneys 1996, Man Crazy 1997, My Heart Laid Bare 1998, Come Meet Muffin 1998, The Collector of Hearts 1999, Broke Heart Blues 1999, Blonde: A Novel 2000, Middle Age: A Romance 2002, I'll Take You There 2002, Big Mouth and Ugly Girl 2002, The Tattooed Girl 2004, Rape: A Love Story 2004, I Am No One You Know 2004, The Falls 2004; short story collections: By the North Gate 1963, Upon the Sweeping Flood and Other Stories 1966, The Wheel of Love 1970, Cupid and Psyche 1970, Marriages and Infidelities 1972, A Posthumous Sketch 1973, The Girl 1974, Plagiarized Material 1974, The Goddess and Other Women 1974, Where Are You Going, Where Have You Been?: Stories of Young America 1974, The Hungry Ghosts: Seven Allusive Comedies 1974, The Seduction and Other Stories 1975, The Poisoned Kiss and Other Stories from the Portuguese 1975, The Triumph of the Spider Monkey 1976, Crossing the Border 1976, Night-Side 1977, The Step-Father 1978, All the Good People I've Left Behind 1979, Queen of the Night 1979, The Lamb of Abyssalia 1979, A Middle-Class Education 1980, A Sentimental Education 1980, Last Day 1984, Wild Saturday and Other Stories 1984, Wild Nights 1985, Raven's Wing 1986, The Assignation 1988, Heat and Other Stories 1991, Where Is Here? 1992, Haunted Tales of the Grotesque 1994, Faithless: Tales of Transgression 2001; poetry: Women in Love and Other Poems 1968, Anonymous Sins and Other Poems 1969, Them (Nat. Book Award 1970) 1969, Love and its Derangements 1970, Wooded Forms 1972, Angel Fire 1973, Dreaming America and Other Poems 1973, The Fabulous Beasts 1975, Seasons of Peril 1977, Women Whose Lives are Food, Men Whose Lives are Money 1978, Celestial Timepiece 1980, Nightless Nights: Nine Poems 1981, Invisible Women: New and Selected Poems 1970–1982 1982, Luxury of Sin 1984, The Time Traveller: Poems 1983–1989 1989; non-fiction: The Edge of Impossibility: Tragic Forms in Literature 1972, The Hostile Sun: The Poetry of D. H. Lawrence 1973, New Heaven, New Earth: The Visionary Experience in Literature 1974, The Stone Orchard 1980, Contraries: Essays 1981, The Profane Art: Essays and Reviews 1983, Funland 1983, On Boxing 1987, (Woman) Writer: Occasions and Opportunities 1988, George Bellows: American Artist (biog.) 1995, The Faith of a Writer: Life, Craft, Art 2004; editor: Scenes from American Life: Contemporary Short Fiction 1973, The Best American Short Stories 1979 (with Shannon Ravenel) 1979, Night Walks: A Bedside Companion 1982, First Person Singular: Writers on Their Craft 1983, Story: Fictions Past and Present (with Boyd Litzinger) 1985, Reading the Fights (with Daniel Halpern) 1988, The Oxford Book of American Short Stories 1993; as Rosamond Smith: The Lives of the Twins 1987, Kindred Passions 1988, Soul-Mate 1989, Nemesis 1990, Snake Eyes 1992, You Can't Catch Me 1995, Double Delight 1997, Starr Bright Will Be With You Soon 1999, The Barrens 2001, Beasts 2003; fiction in nat. magazines. *Honours:* O. Henry Prize Story Award 1967, 1968, Rea Award for Short Story 1990, Elmer Holmes Bukst Award 1990. *Address:* Department of Creative Writing, Princeton University, 117/185 Nassau Street, Princeton, NJ 08544 (Office); c/o John Hawkins, 71 W 23rd Street, Suite 1600, New York, NY 10010, USA.

OATES, Stephen B(aery); Prof. and Writer; b. 5 Jan. 1936, Pampa, Texas, USA; m. 1st, one s. one d.; m. 2nd Marie Philips. *Education:* BA, 1958, MA, 1960, PhD, 1969, University of Texas at Austin. *Career:* Instructor, 1964–67, Asst Prof., 1967–68, Arlington State College; Asst Prof., 1968–70, Assoc. Prof., 1970–71, Prof. of History, 1971–80, Adjunct Prof. of English, 1980–85, Paul Murray Kendall Prof. of Biography, 1985–, University of Massachusetts at Amherst; various guest lectureships; mem. American Antiquarian Society; Society of American Historians; Texas Institute of Letters. *Publications:* Confederate Cavalry West of the River, 1961; John Salmon Ford: Rip Ford's Texas (ed.), 1963; The Republic of Texas (general ed.), 1968; Visions of Glory, Texas on the Southwestern Frontier, 1970; To Purge This Land with Blood: A Biography of John Brown, 1970; Portrait of America (ed.): Vol. I, From the European Discovery to the End of Reconstruction, Vol. II, From Reconstruction to the Present, 1973; The Fires of Jubilee: Nat Turner's Fierce Rebellion, 1975; With Malice Toward None: The Life of Abraham Lincoln, 1977; Our Fiery Trial: Abraham Lincoln, John Brown, and the Civil War Era, 1979; Let the Trumpet Sound: The Life of Martin Luther King Jr, 1982; Abraham Lincoln: The Man Behind the Myths, 1984; Biography as High Adventure: Life-Writers Speak on Their Art (ed.), 1986; William Faulkner: The Man and the Artist, a Biography, 1987; A Woman of Valor: Clara Barton and the Civil War, 1994; The Approaching Fury: Voices of the Storm, 1820–1861, 1997; The Whirlwind of War: Voices of the Storm, 1861–1865, 1998. Contributions: Professional journals. *Honours:* Texas State Historical Asscn Fellow, 1968; Texas Institute of Letters Fellow, 1969; Guggenheim Fellowship, 1972; Christopher Awards, 1977, 1982; Barondess/Lincoln Award, New York Civil War Round Table, 1978; National Endowment for the Humanities Fellow, 1978; Robert F. Kennedy Memorial Book Award, 1983; Institute for Advanced Studies in the Humanities Fellow, 1984; Kidger Award, New England History Teachers Asscn, 1992; Nevins-Freeman Award, Chicago Civil War Round Table, 1993. *Address:* 10 Bridle Path, Amherst, MA 01002, USA.

O'BALANCE, Edgar; Writer; b. 17 July 1918, Dalkey, County Dublin, Ireland; m. 1st Mary Edington-Gee, 1949, deceased 1969, two s. one d.; m. 2nd Kathleen Barbara Tanner, 1972. *Education:* Private studies, Ireland.

Career: mem. Military Commentators Circle. *Publications:* The Arab-Israeli War, 1956; The Sinai Campaign, 1956; The Story of the French Foreign Legion, 1961; The Red Army of China, 1962; The Indo-China War 1945–1954, 1964; The Red Army of Russia, 1964; The Greek Civil War 1948–1960, 1966; The Algerian Insurrection 1954–1962, 1967; The Third Arab-Israeli War 1967, 1972; The Kurdish Revolt 1961–1970, 1973; Arab Guerrilla Power, 1974; The Electronic War in the Middle East 1968–1970, 1974; The Wars in Vietnam 1954–1972, 1975; The Secret War in the Sudan 1955–1972, 1977; No Victor, No Vanquished, 1978; The Language of Violence, 1979; Terror in Ireland, 1979; The Tracks of the Bear, 1982; The Gulf War, 1988; The Cyanide War, 1989; Terrorism in the 1980s, 1989; Wars in Afghanistan: 1839–1990, 1991; Civil War in Bosnia: 1992–1994; The Kurdish Struggle: 1920–94, 1995; Islamic Fundamentalist Terrorism, 1996; Wars in the Caucasus: 1990–95, 1996. *Address:* Wakebridge Cottage, Wakebridge, Matlock, Derbyshire, England.

OBERMAN, Sheldon Arnold; Writer and Educator; b. 20 May 1949, Winnipeg, MB, Canada; m. 1st Lee Anne Block, 8 Sept. 1973, divorced 1990, one s. one d.; m. 2nd Lisa Ann Dveris, 2 Sept. 1990, one c. *Education:* BA, English, University of Winnipeg, 1972; BA, English, University of Jerusalem, 1973; Teaching Certificate, University of Manitoba, 1974. *Career:* Teacher, W. C. Miller Collegiate, Altona, 1975–76, Joseph Wolinsky Collegiate, Winnipeg, 1976–95. *Publications:* The Folk Festival Book, 1983; Lion in the Lake: A French-English Alphabet Book, 1988; Julie Gerond and the Polka Dot Pony, 1988; TV Sal and the Game Show from Outer Space, 1993; This Business with Elijah, 1993; The Always Prayer Shawl, 1994; The White Stone in the Castle Wall, 1995; Always Adam, 1995; By the Hanukkah Light, 1997; The Shaman's Nephew, 1999; The Wisdom Bird: A Tale of Solomon and Sheba, 2000. *Honours:* International Silver Medal, Leipzig Germany International Book Fair, 1991; National Jewish Book Award, Jewish Book Council, 1994; Sydney Taylor Award, 1995, 2000; Best Book of the Year, Child's magazine, 1995; Reading Rainbow Feature Book, 1996; McMally Book of the Year, 1997; Notable Social Studies Trade Book, Children's Book Council, 1999; Parents' Choice Silver Honor Book, 1999; Norma Fleck Award for Children's Non-Fiction, 2000; Outstanding Book Award, Parent Council, 2001. *Address:* c/o Joseph Wolinsky Collegiate, 123 Doncaster Ave, Winnipeg, MB R2W 0E1, Canada. *E-mail:* soberman@mts.net. *Website:* www.sheldonoberman.com/index.shtml.

O'BRIEN, Alison D., AB, PhD; American scientist and writer; *Professor, Uniformed Services University of the Health Sciences. Education:* Univ. of California at Davis, Ohio State Univ. *Career:* Prof. and Chair of Dept of Microbiology and Immunology, Uniformed Services Univ. of the Health Sciences. *Publications include:* co-author: Bacterial Toxins: Friends or Foes? 1999, Microbiology: A Centenary Perspective 1999; co-editor: Escherichia coli and Other Shiga Toxins Producing E.coli 1998, Comparative Pathogenicity of E.coli 2003. *Address:* Department of Microbiology and Immunology, Uniformed Services University of the Health Sciences, 4301 Jones Bridge Road, Bethesda, MD 20814, USA. *E-mail:* aobrien@usuhs.mil. *Website:* www.usuhs.mil.

O'BRIEN, Conor Cruise, (Donat O'Donnell); Writer and Ed.; b. 3 Nov. 1917, Dublin, Ireland; m. 1st Christine Foster 1939 (divorced 1962); one s. one d.; m. 2nd Máire MacEntee 1962; one adopted s. one adopted d. *Education:* BA, 1940, PhD, 1953, Trinity College, Dublin. *Career:* Mem., Irish diplomatic service, 1944–61; Vice-Chancellor, University of Ghana, 1962–65; Albert Schweitzer Prof. of Humanities, New York University, 1965–69; Mem., Labour Party, Dublin North-east, Dail, 1969–77, Senate, Republic of Ireland, 1977–79; Visiting Fellow, Nuffield College, Oxford, 1973–75; Minister for Posts and Telegraphs, 1973–77; Pro-Chancellor, University of Dublin, 1973–; Fellow, St Catherine's College, Oxford, 1978–81; Ed.-in-Chief, The Observer, 1979–81; Visiting Prof. and Montgomery Fellow, Dartmouth College, NH, 1984–85; Senior Resident Fellow, National Humanities Center, NC, 1993–94; mem. Royal Irish Acad.; RSL. *Publications:* Maria Cross, 1952; Parnell and His Party, 1957; The Shaping of Modern Ireland (ed.), 1959; To Katanga and Back, 1962; Conflicting Concepts of the UN, 1964; Writers and Politics, 1965; The United Nations: Sacred Drama, 1967; Murderous Angels (play), 1968; Power and Consciousness, 1969; Conor Cruise O'Brien Introduces Ireland, 1969; Albert Camus, 1969; The Suspecting Glance (with Máire Cruise O'Brien), 1970; A Concise History of Ireland, 1971; States of Ireland, 1972; King Herod Advises (play), 1973; Neighbours: The Ewart-Biggs Memorial Lectures 1978–79, 1980; The Siege: The Saga of Israel and Zionism, 1986; Passion and Cunning, 1988; God Land: Reflections on Religion and Nationalism, 1988; The Great Melody: A Thematic Biography and Commented Anthology of Edmund Burke, 1992; Ancestral Voices, 1994; On the Eve of the Millennium, 1996; The Long Affair: Thomas Jefferson and the French Revolution, 1996; My Life and Themes (memoir), 1998. *Honours:* Valiant for Truth Media Award, 1979; Hon. doctorates. *Address:* Whitewater, Howth Summit, Dublin, Ireland.

O'BRIEN, Edna; Author, Dramatist and Poet; b. 15 Dec. 1936, Tuamgraney, County Clare, Ireland; m. 1954, divorced 1964, two s. *Education:* Convents; Pharmaceutical College of Ireland. *Publications:* The Country Girls, 1960; The Lonely Girl, 1962; Girls in Their Married Bliss, 1963; August is a Wicked Month, 1964; Casulaties of Peace, 1966; The Love Object, 1968; A Pagan Place, 1970; Night, 1972; A Scandalous Woman, 1974; Mother Ireland, 1976; Johnnie I Hardly Knew You, 1977; Mrs Reinhardt and Other Stories, 1978; Virginia (play), 1979; The Dazzle, 1981; Returning, 1982; A Christmas Treat, 1982; A Fanatic Heart, 1985; Tales for Telling, 1986; Flesh and Blood (play), 1987; Madame Bovary (play), 1987; The High Road, 1988; On the Bone (poems), 1989; Lantern Slides, 1990; Time and Tide, 1992; House of Splendid Isolation, 1994; Down by the River, 1997; James Joyce: A Biography, 1999; In the Forest, 2001. *Honours:* Yorkshire Post Novel Award, 1971; Los Angeles Times Award, 1990; Writers' Guild Award, 1993; European Prize for Literature, 1995. *Literary Agent:* David Godwin Associates, 55 Monmouth St, London WC2H 9DG, England.

O'BRIEN, Sean Patrick, BA, MA, PGCE; writer and poet; b. 19 Dec. 1952, London, England. *Education:* Selwyn Coll., Cambridge, University of Birmingham, University of Hull, University of Leeds. *Career:* Fellow in Creative Writing, University of Dundee, 1989–91; Northern Arts Literary Fellow, 1992–94; Visiting Writer, University of Odense, Denmark, 1996, Hokudai University, Sapporo, Japan, 1997; Lecturer in Writing, Sheffield Hallam University, 1998–; Writer-in-Residence, University of Leeds, 1999. *Publications:* The Indoor Park, 1983; The Frighteners, 1987; Boundary Beach, 1989; HMS Glasshouse, 1991; Ghost Train, 1995; The Deregulated Muse: Essays on Contemporary Poetry in Britain and Ireland, 1998; The Firebox: Poetry in Britain and Ireland after 1945 (ed.), 1998; Downriver, 2001. Plays: Laughter When We're Dead; My Last Barmaid. Contributions: anthologies, newspapers, reviews, and radio. *Honours:* Eric Gregory Award, 1979; Somerset Maugham Award, 1984; Cholmondeley Award, 1988; Arts Council Writer's Bursary, 1992; E. M. Forster Award, 1993; Forward Prizes, 1995, 2001. *Literary Agent:* Gillon Aitken Associates Ltd, 18–21 Cavaye Place, London, SW10 9PT, England. *Telephone:* (20) 7373-8672. *Fax:* (20) 7373-6002.

O'BRIEN, (William) Timothy; writer; b. 1 Oct. 1946, Austin, MN, USA; m. Anne O'Brien. *Education:* BA, Macalester College, 1968; Graduate Studies, Harvard University. *Publications:* If I Die in a Combat Zone, Box Me Up and Ship Me Home, 1973; Northern Lights, 1975; Going After Cacciato, 1978; The Nuclear Age, 1981; The Things They Carried: A Work of Fiction, 1990; In the Lake of Woods, 1994; Tomcat in Love, 1998; July July, 2002. Contributions: Magazines. *Honours:* O. Henry Memorial Awards, 1976, 1978; National Book Award, 1979; Vietnam Veterans of America Award, 1987; Heartland Prize, Chicago Tribune, 1990. *Literary Agent:* International Creative Managment, 40 W 57th Street, New York, NY 10019, USA.

OBSTFELD, Raymond, (Pike Bishop, Jason Frost, Don Pendleton, Carl Stevens); Asst Prof. of English, Wrier, Poet, Dramatist and Screenwriter; b. 22 Jan. 1952, Williamsport, Pennsylvania, USA. *Education:* BA, Johnston College, University of Redlands, 1972; MA, University of California at Davis, 1976. *Career:* Lecturer to Asst Prof. of English, Orange Coast College, 1976–; mem. MWA. *Publications:* Fiction: The Golden Fleece, 1979; Dead-End Option, 1980; Dead Heat, 1981; Dead Bolt, 1982; The Remington Factor, 1985; Masked Dog, 1986; Redtooth, 1987; Brainchild, 1987; The Whippin Boy, 1988. As Pike Bishop: Diamondback, 1983; Judgement at Poisoned Well, 1983. As Jason Frost: Warlord series, 1983–85; Invasion USA, 1985. As Don Pendleton: Bloodsport, 1982; Flesh Wounds, 1983; Savannah Swingsaw, 1985; The Fire Eaters, 1986. As Carl Stevens: The Centaur Conspiracy, 1983; Ride of the Razorback, 1984. Poetry: The Cat With Half a Face, 1978. Contributions: anthologies and other publications.

O'CASEY, Brenda (see Haycraft, Anna (Margaret)).

O'CONNELL, Richard James; academic, poet and translator; b. 25 Oct. 1928, New York, NY, USA. *Education:* BS, Temple University, 1956; MA, Johns Hopkins University, 1957. *Career:* Instructor, 1957–61, Asst Prof., 1961–69, Assoc. Prof., 1969–86, Senior Assoc. Prof., 1986–93, Prof. Emeritus, 1993–, Temple University; Fulbright Lecturer, University of Brazil, Rio de Janeiro, 1960, University of Navarre, Pamplona, Spain, 1962–63; Guest Lecturer, Johns Hopkins University, 1961–74; Poet-in-the-Schools, Pennsylvania Council for the Arts, 1971–73; mem. Associated Writing Programs; MLA; PEN. *Publications:* From an Interior Silence, 1961; Cries of Flesh and Stone, 1962; New Poems and Translations, 1963; Brazilian Happenings, 1966; Terrane, 1967; Thirty Epigrams, 1971; Hudson's Fourth Voyage, 1978; Temple Poems, 1985; Hanging Tough, 1986; Battle Poems, 1987; Selected Epigrams, 1990; Lives of the Poets, 1990; The Caliban Poems, 1992; RetroWorlds, 1993; Simulations, 1993; Voyages, 1995; The Bright Tower, 1997. Translator: various works, including: Irish Monastic Poems, 1975; Middle English Poems, 1976; More Irish Poems, 1976; Epigrams from Martial, 1976; The Epigrams of Luxorius, 1984; New Epigrams from Martial, 1991. *Honours:* Contemporary Poetry Press Prize, 1972. *Address:* 1147 Hillsboro Mile, Suite 510, Hillsboro Beach, FL 33062, USA. *Telephone:* (954) 426-8906.

O'CONNOR, Joseph, BA, MA; Irish writer, playwright and critic; b. 20 Sept. 1963, Glenageary, Co. Dublin. *Education:* Univ. Coll., Dublin, Univ. of Oxford, Univ. of Leeds. *Plays:* Red Roses and Petrol 1995. *Publications:* novels: Cowboys and Indians 1991, Desperadoes 1995, The Salesman 1998, Inishowen 2000, The Last of the Irish Males 2001, Star of the Sea 2002; biography: Even the Olives are Bleeding: The Life and Times of Charles Donnelly 1992; contrib. and columnist for The Sunday Tribune. *Honours:* Hennessy Award. *Literary Agent:* c/o Random House UK Ltd, 20 Vauxhall Bridge Road, London, SW1V 2SA, England. *Website:* www.randomhouse.co.uk.

Ó'CURRAOIN, Seán, BA, MA, LLB; poet; b. Connemara, County Galway, Ireland. *Career:* fmr chief translator, Irish Parliament; linguistic researcher and Asst Ed. on Ó Dónaill's Irish-English Dictionary; mem. Irish Trans Asscn, Folklore of Ireland Soc. *Publications:* Soilse ar na Dumhchannaí 1985, Beairtle 1985, Tinte Sionnaigh (short stories) 1985, De Ghlaschloch an Oileáin (biog. of Máirtín O'Cadhain) 1987, Iascairín Chloch na Cora 2000, Cloch na Cainte (poems) 2003, Boscaí (short stories) 2003; contrib. to Comhar, Feasta, Innti, Cyphers. *Address:* 18 Ascaill Verbena, Br. Chill Bharróg, Baile Átha Cliath 13, Ireland.

ODA, Makoto; Author; b. 2 June 1932, Osaka, Japan; m. Hyon Sune Dec. 1982; one d. *Education:* University of Tokyo, 1957; Harvard University, 1958–59. *Career:* mem. Japanese PEN. *Publications:* Japanese Intellectuals (essay), 1964; HIROSHIMA (novel), 1981; Far From Vietnam (novel), 1992; Thought on the Earthquake and War (critical essay), 1996; Demokratia (critical essay), 1997; Osaka Symphony (novel), 1997; Stomping on Aboji (short story), 1998; Gyokusai (novel), 1998; Deep Sound (novel), 2002; Children's War (short stories), 2003. *Honours:* Lotus Prize, Afro-Asian Writers Asscn, 1987; Kawabata Yasunari Literary Prize, 1997. *Address:* 1-41-801 Ohama-cho, Nishinomiya, Japan.

ØDEGÅRD, Knut; Poet, Writer and Critic; b. 6 Nov. 1945, Molde, Norway; m. Thorgerdur Ingólfsdóttir, 2 Aug. 1981, two d. *Education:* Theology and Philosophy, University of Oslo; LittD, 1999. *Career:* Poetry Critic, Aftenposten newspaper, 1968–; Man. Dir, Scandinavian Centre, Nordens Hus, Reykjavík, 1984–89; Pres., Norwegian Festival of International Literature, 1992–; Consul, Republic of Slovakia, 1995–97; Consul Gen., Republic of Macedonia, 1997–; mem. Acad. of Norwegian Language; Icelandic Society of Authors; Literary Acad. of Romania; Norwegian Literary Council; Norwegian Society of Authors. *Publications:* 24 poetry books, 1967–98, including: Bee-buzz, Salmon Leap, 1968; Cinema Operator, 1991; Ventriloquy, 1994; Selected Poems, 1995; Missa, 1998. Other: Books of prose and essays; Play; Two non-fiction books about Iceland, 1992, 1998. *Honours:* Knighted by Pres. of Iceland, 1987; Norwegian State Scholar for Life, 1989–; Grand Knight Commander, Order of the Icelandic Falcon, 1993; International Order of Merit, 1993; Knight, Norwegian Order of Literature, 1995; Knighted by the King of Norway, 1998. *Literary Agent:* J. W. Cappelen, Oslo, Norway. *Address:* Chateau Parkv 42, 6400 Molde, Norway. *E-mail:* knut.odegard@moldenett.no.

ODELL, Peter Randon, BA, MA, PhD, FRSA, FRGS; academic and writer; b. 1 July 1930, Coalville, England; m. Jean Mary McKintosh 1957; two s. two d. *Education:* Univ. of Birmingham, Fletcher School of Law and Diplomacy, Cambridge. *Career:* Economist, Shell International Petroleum Co 1958–61; Lecturer 1961–65, Senior Lecturer 1965–68, Visiting Prof. 1983–2001, LSE; Prof. of Economic Geography 1968–81, Dir, Centre for Int. Energy Studies 1981–91, Prof. Emeritus 1991–, Erasmus Univ., Rotterdam; Stamp Memorial Lecturer, Univ. of London 1975; Prof., Coll. of Europe, Bruges 1983–90; Scholar-in-Residence, Rockefeller Centre, Bellagio, Italy 1984; European Ed., Energy Journal 1988–90; Killam Visiting Scholar, Univ. of Calgary 1989; Visiting Scholar, Univ. of Plymouth 1996–2003; Fellow, Inst. of Energy. *Publications:* An Economic Geography of Oil, 1963; Oil: The New Commanding Height, 1966; Natural Gas in Western Europe: A Case Study in the Economic Geography of Energy Resources, 1969; Oil and World Power: A Geographical Interpretation, 1970; Economies and Societies in Latin America (with D. A. Preston), 1973; Energy: Needs and Resources, 1974; The North Sea Oil Province (with K. E. Rosing), 1975; The West European Energy Economy: The Case for Self-Sufficiency, 1976; The Optimal Development of the North Sea Oilfields (with K. E. Rosing), 1976; The Pressures of Oil: A Strategy for Economic Revival (with L. Vallenilla), 1978; British Offshore Oil Policy: A Radical Alternative, 1980; The Future of Oil, 1980–2080 (with K. E. Rosing), 1980; Energie: Geen Probleem? (with J. A. van Reijn), 1981; The International Oil Industry: An Interdisciplinary Perspective (ed. with J. Rees), 1986; Global and Regional Energy Supplies: Recent Fictions and Fallacies Revisited, 1991; Energy in Europe: Resources and Choices, 1990; The New Europe: Energy Resources and Choices, 1998; Fossil Fuel Reserves in the 21st Century, 1999; Oil and Gas: Crises and Controversies 1961–2000, Vol. 1: Global Issues, 2001, Vol. 2: Europe's Entanglement, 2002. *Honours:* Canadian Council Fellow 1978, Int. Asscn for Energy Economics Prize 1991, Royal Scottish Geographical Soc. Centenary Medal 1993. *Address:* 22A Compton Road, London, N1 2PB, England. *Telephone:* (20) 7359-8199. *E-mail:* peter@odell.u-net.com.

ODELL, Robin Ian; Writer; b. 19 Dec. 1935, Totton, Hampshire, England; m. Joan Bartholomew, 19 Sept. 1959. *Career:* mem. Paternosters; Our Society. *Publications:* Jack the Ripper in Fact and Fiction, 1965; Exhumation of a Murder, 1975; Jack the Ripper: Summing-up and Verdict (with Colin Wilson), 1977; The Murderers' Who's Who (with J. H. H. Gaute), 1979; Lady Killers, 1980; Murder Whatdunit, 1982; Murder Whereabouts, 1986; Dad Help Me Please (with Christopher Berry-Dee), 1990; A Question of Evidence, 1992; The Long Drop, 1993; Landmarks in Twentieth Century Murder, 1995; The International Murderer's Who's Who, 1996. Contributions: Crimes and Punishment; The Criminologist. *Honours:* FCC Watts Memorial Prize, 1957; Edgar Award, MWA, 1980. *Address:* 11 Red House Dr., Sonning Common, Reading RG4 9NT, England. *E-mail:* bobodell@compuserve.com.

O'DONNELL, Donat (see O'Brien, Conor Cruise).

O'DONNELL, K. M. (see Malzberg, Barry).

O'DONNELL, M. R. (see Ross-Macdonald, Malcolm John).

O'DONNELL, Mary (Elizabeth Eugenie); Writer, Poet and Critic; b. 3 April 1954, Monaghan, Ireland; m. Martin Nugent, 18 June 1977; one d. *Education:* BA, German and Philosophy, 1977, Diploma, Higher Education, 1983, Maynooth College. *Career:* Writer-in-Residence, University College, Dublin, and County Laois, 1995; Teacher of Creative Writing, University of Iowa, Summer Writing Programme, Trinity College, Dublin, 1998–2000; mem. Poetry Ireland, Aosdana. *Publications:* Reading the Sunflowers in September (poems), 1990; Strong Pagans and Other Stories, 1991; The Light-Makers (novel), 1992; Spiderwoman's Third Avenue Rhapsody (poems), 1993; Virgin and the Boy (novel), 1996; Unlegendary Heroes (poems), 1998; The Elysium Testament (novel), 1999, September Elegies (poems) 2003. Contributions: anthologies, reviews, quarterlies, and periodicals. *Honours:* Second Prize, Patrick Kavanagh Poetry Award, 1986; Allingham Poetry Award, 1988, Jameson Short Story Award Listowel 1990, 2nd Prize V. S. Pritchett Short Story Award 2000. *Address:* Rook Hollow, Newtownmacabe, Maynooth, Co Kildare, Ireland. *E-mail:* maryelizabeth@eircom.net. *Website:* www.maryodonnell.com.

O'DONNELL, Peter, (Madeleine Brent); Author; b. 11 April 1920, London, England. *Education:* Catford Central School, London. *Career:* Writer of Strip Cartoons, Garth, 1953–66, Tug Transom, 1954–66, Romeo Brown, 1956–62, Modesty Blaise, 1963–2001. *Publications:* Modesty Blaise, 1965; Sabre-Tooth, 1966; I, Lucifer, 1967; A Taste for Death, 1969; The Impossible Virgin, 1971; Pieces of Modesty (short stories), 1972; The Silver Mistress, 1973; Murder Most Logical (play), 1974; Last Day in Limbo, 1976; Dragon's Claw, 1978; The Xanadu Talisman, 1981; The Night of Morningstar, 1982; Dead Man's Handle, 1985; Cobra Trap, 1996. As Madeleine Brent: Tregaron's Daughter, 1971; Moonraker's Bride, 1973; Kirkby's Changeling, 1975; Merlin's Keep, 1977; The Capricorn Stone, 1979; The Long Masquerade, 1981; A Heritage of Shadows, 1983; Stormswift, 1984; Golden Urchin, 1986. *Address:* 49 Sussex Sq., Brighton BN2 1GE, England.

O'DONOGHUE, (James) Bernard; academic and poet; b. 14 Dec. 1945, Cullen, Co. Cork, Ireland; m. Heather MacKinnon 1977; one s. two d. *Education:* MA in English, 1968, BPhil in Medieval English, 1971, Lincoln College, Oxford. *Career:* Lecturer and Tutor in English, Magdalen College, Oxford, 1971–95; Fellow in English, Wadham College, Oxford, 1995–; mem. Poetry Society, London, 1984–; FRSL, 1999; Fellow, English Society, 1999. *Publications:* Razorblades and Pencils, 1984; Poaching Rights, 1987; The Weakness, 1991; Gunpowder, 1995; Here Nor There, 1999; Outliving, 2003. Contributions: Norton Anthology of Poetry; Poetry Ireland Review; Poetry Review; TLS. *Honours:* Southern Arts Literature Prize, 1991; Whitbread Poetry Award, 1995. *Address:* Wadham College, Oxford OX1 3PN, England.

O'DONOHOE, Nick; writer and academic; b. 31 Oct. 1952, Charles City, IA, USA; m. Lynn Anne Evans 1978. *Education:* BA, Carleton College, 1975; PhD, Syracuse University, 1983. *Career:* Instructor, 1981–83, Asst Prof., 1983–, Virginia Polytechnic Institute and State University, Blacksburg; mem. MWA. *Publications:* April Snow, 1984; Wind Chill, 1985; Open Season, 1986; Too, Too Solid Flesh, 1989; The Magic and the Healing, 1994; Under the Healing Sign, 1995; The Healing of Crossroads, 1996. *Address:* c/o Ace Books, 375 Hudson Street, New York, NY 10014, USA.

O'DRISCOLL, Dennis; editor and poet; b. 1 Jan. 1954, Thurles, County Tipperary, Ireland; m. Julie O'Callaghan 1985. *Education:* University College, Dublin. *Career:* Literary Organiser, Dublin Arts Festival, 1977–79; Ed., Poetry Ireland Review, 1986–87. *Publications:* Kist, 1982; Hidden Extras, 1987. Co-Editor: The First Ten Years: Dublin Arts Festival Poetry, 1979. *Honours:* Irish Arts Council Bursary.

ŌE, Kenzaburō; Author; b. 31 Jan. 1935, Ehime, Shikoku, Japan; m. Yukari Kenzaburō; two c. *Education:* French Literature, Univ. of Tokyo, 1959. *Publications:* Fiction: Shisha no ogori (trans. as The Catch), 1958; Memushiri kouchi (trans. as Nip the Buds, Shoot the Kids), 1958; Miru mae ni tobe, 1958; Nichijo seikatsu no boken, 1963; Kojinteki na taiken (trans. as A Personal Matter), 1964; Hiroshima noto, 1965; Man'en gannen no futtoburu (trans. as The Silent Cry), 1967; Pinchi ranna chosho (trans. as The Pinch Runner Memorandum), 1976; Warera no kyoki o iki nobiru michi o, 1969; Okinawa noto, 1970; Shosetsu no hoho, 1978; Natsukashii toshi e no tegami, 1986; M/T to mori no fushigi no monogatari, 1986; Chiryo no to, 1990; A Healing Family (in trans.), 1996; A Quiet Life (in trans.), 1998; Rouse Up, O Young Men of the New Age (in trans.), 2002; Somersault (in trans.), 2003. Non-Fiction: Hiroshima Notes, 1963; Japan, the Ambiguous, and Myself: The Nobel Prize Speech and Other Lectures, 1995. *Honours:* Akutagawa Prize, Japanese Society for the Promotion of Literature, 1958; Shinchosha Literary Prize, 1964; Tanizaki Prize, 1967; Europelia Arts Festival Literary Prize, 1989; Nobel Prize for Literature, 1994. *Address:* 585 Seijo-machi, Setagaya-Ku, Tokyo, Japan.

O'FAOLAIN, Julia; Irish writer; b. 6 June 1932, London, England; m. Lauro Rene Martines 1957; one s. *Education:* BA, 1952, MA, 1953, University College, Dublin; Univ. of Rome, 1952–53; Sorbonne, Paris, 1953–55. *Career:* mem. Aosdána; Society of Authors; FRSL; Dir, Susan Smith Blackburn Prize. *Publications:* We Might See Sights! and Other Stories, 1968; Godded and Codded, 1970; Not in God's Image: Women in History from the Greeks to the Victorians (ed. with Lauro Rene Martines), 1973; Man in the Cellar,

1974; Women in the Wall, 1975; No Country for Young Men, 1980; Daughters of Passion, 1982; The Obedient Wife, 1982; The Irish Signorina, 1984; The Judas Cloth, 1992; Ercoli e il Guardiano notturno, 1999. Contributions: newspapers and magazines. *Literary Agent:* Rogers, Coleridge and White Ltd, 20 Powis Mews, London W11 1JN, England.

O'FARRELL, John; British scriptwriter and writer; b. 27 March 1962, Maidenhead, Berkshire, England; m.; two c. *Education:* Univ. of Exeter. *Career:* newspaper columnist, The Independent, The Guardian. *Writing for radio:* Week Ending (BBC Radio 4) 1987–92, Peter Dickson's Nightcap (BBC Radio 2) 1987–89, A Look Back at the Nineties (BBC Radio 4) 1992–93. *Radio:* as performer: The News Quiz (BBC Radio 4), We've Been Here Before (BBC Radio 4). *Writing for television:* Spitting Image (ITV) 1989–95, Brian Conley: This Way Up (ITV) 1990, Smith and Jones (TalkBack/BBC1) 1990–93, Clive Anderson Talks Back (Hat Trick/Channel 4) 1993–95, Room 101 (Hat Trick/BBC2) 1994–97, Have I Got News For You (Hat Trick/BBC2) 1994–99, The Peter Principle (Hat Trick/BBC1) 1995–2000, Never Mind The Horrocks (Hat Trick/Channel 4) 1996, The Best Show in the World... Probably (BBC1) 1998. *Television appearances:* The 11 O'Clock Show (TalkBack/Channel 4) 2000, Grumpy Old Men (BBC2) 2003. *Publications:* non-fiction: Things Can Only Get Better 1998, Global Village Idiot 2001, I Blame the Scapegoats 2003; fiction: The Best A Man Can Get 2000, This is Your Life 2002. *Address:* c/o Random House UK Ltd, 20 Vauxhall Bridge Road, London, SW1V 2SA, England. *Website:* www.randomhouse.co.uk.

O'FARRELL, Maggie, BA; Northern Irish novelist; b. 1972; pnr William Sutcliffe; one s. *Education:* Univ. of Cambridge. *Career:* fmr journalist. *Publications:* After You'd Gone (Betty Trask Prize 2001) 2000, My Lover's Lover 2002, The Distance Between Us 2004. *Address:* c/o Hodder Headline Ltd, 338 Euston Road, London, NW1 3BH, England.

OFFEN, Yehuda, (Huri Halim, Ben Naftali); Writer and Poet; b. 4 April 1922, Altona, Germany; m. Tova Arbisser, 28 March 1946, one d. *Education:* BA, University of London, 1975; MA, Comparative Literature, Hebrew University of Jerusalem, 1978. *Career:* Senior Ed., Al Hamishmar, Daily Guardian, 1960–80; mem. ACUM (Society of Authors, Composers and Eds in Israel); Hebrew Writers Asscn, Israel; International Acad. of Poets, USA; International Federation of Journalists, Brussels; National Federation of Israeli Journalists; PEN Centre, Israel. *Publications:* L'Lo L'An, 1961; Har Vakhol, 1963; Lo Agadat Khoref, 1969; Nofim P'nima, 1979; B'Magal Sagur (short stories), 1979; N'Vilat Vered, 1983; Shirim Bir'hov Ayaif, 1984; P'Gishot Me'ever Lazman, 1986; Massekhet Av, 1986; Stoning on the Cross Road (short stories), 1988; Who Once Begot a Star, 1990; Silly Soil, 1992; Back to Germany, 1994. Contributions: various publications. *Honours:* ACUM (Society of Authors, Composers and Eds in Israel) Prizes for Literature, 1961, 1979, 1984; Talpir Prize for Literature, 1979; Efrat Prize for Poetry, 1989. *Address:* 8 Gazit St, Tel-Aviv 69417, Israel.

O'FIANNACHTA, Pádraig, BA, MA, PhD; academic, poet, writer and editor; b. 20 Feb. 1927, County Kerry, Ireland. *Education:* St Patrick's College, Maynooth, National University of Ireland, University College, Cork, Pontifical University, Maynooth. *Career:* Lecturer, 1959–60, Prof. of Early Irish and Lecturer in Welsh, 1960–81, Prof. of Modern Irish, 1981–92, St Patrick's College, Maynooth; mem. Cumann na Sagart; Oireachtas, pres., 1985; Poetry Ireland; Royal Irish Acad. *Publications:* Ponc, 1966; Ruin, 1969; Feoirlingi Fileata, 1972; Donn Bo, 1976; An Bíobla Naofa (ed. and trans.), 1981; Spaisteoireacht, 1982; Deora De, 1987; Léim An Dá Míle, 1999. Contributions: various publications. *Honours:* Hon. DPh (Maynooth) 1995, DLittHum (SHU) 2004; Douglas Hyde Prize for Literature 1969, Monsignor 1998. *Address:* Dingle, Tralee, County Kerry, Ireland.

O'FLAHERTY, Patrick Augustine; academic and writer; b. 6 Oct. 1939, Long Beach, NF, Canada. *Education:* BA, 1959, MA, 1960, Memorial University, St John's, NF; PhD, University of London, 1963. *Career:* Prof., 1965–95, Head, Dept of English, 1981–86, Prof. Emeritus, 1997–, Memorial University; mem. Writers' Union of Canada. *Publications:* The Rock Observed, 1979; Part of the Main: An Illustrated History of Newfoundland and Labrador (with Peter Neary), 1983; Summer of the Greater Yellowlags, 1987; Priest of God, 1989; A Small Place in the Sun, 1989; Come Near at Your Peril: A Visitor's Guide to the Island of Newfoundland, 1992; Benny's Island, 1994; Reminiscences of J. P. Howley: Selected Years (co-ed.), 1997; Old Newfoundland: A History to 1843, 1999. Contributions: numerous publications. *Address:* PO Box 2676, St John's, NF A1C 6K1, Canada.

OGDEN, Hugh; Prof., Poet and Writer; b. 11 March 1937, Erie, Pennsylvania, USA; m. Ruth Simpson, 3 March 1960, one s. two d. *Education:* BA, Haverford College, 1959; MA, New York University, 1961; PhD, University of Michigan, 1967. *Career:* Teaching Asst, 1961–65, Instructor, 1965–67, University of Michigan; Asst Prof., 1967–75, Assoc. Prof., 1975–91, Prof., 1991–, Trinity College, Hartford, CT; mem. Associated Writing Programs; Poetry Society of America; Poets and Writers. *Publications:* Looking for History, 1991; Two Road and this Spring, 1993; Windfalls, 1996; Gift, 1998; Natural Things, 1998. Contributions: Reviews, quarterlies, and journals. *Honours:* Connecticut Commission on the Arts Poetry Project Grant, 1990; National Endowment for the Arts Grant, 1993. *Address:* c/o Dept of English, Trinity College, Hartford, CT 06106, USA.

OGDEN, Margaret (Astrid) Lindholm, (Megan Lindholm, Robin Hobb); Writer; b. 1952, Oakland, CA, USA; m.; four c. *Education:* Univ. of Denver. *Publications:* As Megan Lindholm: Harpy's Flight, 1983; The Windsingers, 1984; The Limbreth Gate, 1984; The Wizard of the Pigeons, 1986; The Reindeer People, 1988; Wolf's Brother, 1988; Luck of the Wheels, 1989; Cloven Hooves, 1991; Gypsy (with Steven Brust), 1992; Alien Earth, 1992. As Robin Hobb: The Assassin's Apprentice, 1995; Royal Assassin, 1996; Assassin's Quest, 1997; Ship of Magic, 1998; The Mad Ship, 1999; Ship of Destiny, 2000; Fool's Fate, 2003. Contributions: anthologies and periodicals. *Address:* c/o Bantam Books, 1540 Broadway, New York, NY 10036, USA.

OGG, Wilson Reid; Social Scientist, Philosopher, Lawyer, Poet, Lyricist and Educator; b. 26 Feb. 1928, Alhambra, CA, USA. *Education:* AB, 1949; JD, 1952, University of California. *Career:* Psychology Instructor, US Armed Forces Institute, Daegu, Republic of Korea, 1953–54; English Instructor, Daegu English Language Institute, 1954; Trustee Sec., First Unitarian Church of Berkeley, 1957–58; Research Attorney, Continuing Education of the Bar, University of California, 1958–63; Vice-Pres., International House Asscn, 1961–62; Pres., Board Chair., California Society for Physics Study, 1963–65; Private Law Practice, 1955–; Dir of Admissions, International Society for Philosophical Enquiry, 1981–84; mem. American Mensa; ASCAP; International Acad. of Law and Sciences; New York Acad. of Sciences; San Francisco Bar Asscn. *Publications:* Contributions: various anthologies and journals. *Honours:* Commendation Ribbon W. Medal Pendant; Cultural Doctorate, World University; Hon. DD, University of Life Church, 1969; Hon. Doctorate, Religious Humanities, 1970. *Address:* Pinebrook at Bret Harte Way, 8 Bret Harte Way, Berkeley, CA 94708, USA. *E-mail:* wilsonogg@cal.berkeley.edu.

O'GRADY, Desmond James Bernard; Poet, Writer and Trans; b. 27 Aug. 1935, Limerick, Ireland; one s. two d. *Education:* MA, 1964, PhD, 1982, Harvard University. *Career:* Secondary School Teacher, University Prof., 1955–82; mem. Aosdána. *Publications:* Chords and Orchestrations, 1956; Reilly, 1961; Prof. Kelleher and the Charles River, 1964; Separazioni, 1965; The Dark Edge of Europe, 1967; The Dying Gaul, 1968; Off Licence (trans.), 1968; Hellas, 1971; Separations, 1973; Stations, 1976; Sing Me Creation, 1977; The Gododdin (trans.), 1977; A Limerick Rake (trans.), 1978; The Headgear of the Tribe, 1979; His Skaldcrane's Nest, 1979; Grecian Glances (trans.), 1981; Alexandria Notebook, 1989; The Seven Arab Odes (trans.), 1990; Tipperary, 1991; Ten Modern Arab Poets (trans.), 1992; My Fields This Springtime, 1993; Alternative Manners (trans.), 1993; Trawling Tradition: Collected Translations, 1954–1994, 1994; Il Galata Morente, 1996; The Road Taken: Poems, 1956–1996, 1996; The Golden Odes of Love (trans.), 1997; C. P. Cavafy: Selected Poems (trans.), 1998; The Wandering Celt, 2001; The Battle of Kinsale, 1601, 2002; The Song of Songs (trans.), 2002, The Wide World (a casebook) 2003. Prose Memoirs: Ezra Pound, Patrick Kavanagh, Samuel Beckett, Olga Rudge, Anna Akhmatova. Essays: On poetry, poets, translating poetry. Contributions: anthologies and magazines. *Address:* Ardback, Kinsale, County Cork, Ireland.

O'GRADY, Tom; Poet, Writer, Dramatist, Trans., Ed. and Vintner; b. 26 Aug. 1943, Baltimore, MD, USA; m. Bronwyn Southworth, two s. *Education:* BA, English, University of Baltimore, 1966; MA, English, Johns Hopkins University, 1967; Graduate Studies, English and American Literature, University of Delaware, 1972–74. *Career:* Teacher of writing and literature, various colleges and universities, 1966–96; Founder-Ed., The Hampden-Sydney Poetry Review, 1975–; numerous lectures and poetry readings. *Publications:* Poetry: Unicorn Evils, 1973; Establishing a Vineyard, 1977; Photo-Graphs, 1980; The Farmville Elegies, 1981; In the Room of the Just Born, 1989; Carvings of the Moon, 1992; Sun, Moon, and Stars, 1996. Prose: Shaking the Tree: A Book of Works and Days, 1993; The Same Earth, The Same Sky: New and Selected Poems and Translations, 2002. Editor: The Hampden-Sydney Poetry Anthology, 1990. Other: Trans; Stage and television plays. Contributions: anthologies, newspapers, journals, and magazines. *Honours:* Leache Prize for Poetry, 1975; Ed.'s Award, Co-ordinating Council of Literary Magazine, 1977; Merit Award, 1977, Mettauer Research Award, 1984, Trustees Award, 1986, Hampden-Sydney College; Virginia Prize for Poetry, 1989; Teacher of the Arts Award, National Foundation for Advancement in the Arts, 1989–90; Virginia Center for the Arts Fellowship Residency, 1995; Henrico Theater Co Prize, 1997. *Address:* c/o Rose Bower Vineyard and Winery, PO Box 126, Hampden-Sydney, VA 23943, USA.

O'HAGAN, Andrew; writer, editor and journalist; b. 1968, Glasgow, Scotland. *Education:* Univ. of Strathclyde. *Career:* fmrly film critic, Daily Telegraph; contributing ed., London Review of Books, Granta. *Publications:* The Missing: A Social History of Glasgow and Gloucester (non-fiction) 1995, Calling Bible John (radio adaptation of an excerpt from The Missing) 1996, Our Fathers (novel) 1999, The End of British Farming (non-fiction) 2001, New Writing 11 (ed.) 2002, Personality (novel) (James Tait Black Memorial Prize for Fiction) 2003; contrib. to London Review of Books, Granta, New York Review of Books, The Weekenders (anthology) 2001. *Honours:* Winifred Holtby Memorial Prize 1999, BAFTA Award 1996, E.M. Forster Award, American Acad. of Arts and Letters. *Literary Agent:* AP Watt Ltd, 20 John Street, London, WC1N 2DR, England.

OHNEMUS, Günter; German writer, translator and critic; b. 1946. *Publications include:* Siebenundsechzig Ansichten einer Frau 1995, Der Tiger auf deiner Schulter (trans. as The Tiger on your Shoulder) 1998, Reise in die Angst 2002, The Russian Passenger 2004. *Honours:* Tukan-Award, Alfred Kerr Award. *Address:* c/o Bitter Lemon Press, 37 Arundel Gardens, London, W11 2LW, England. *E-mail:* fvh@bitterlemonpress.com. *Website:* www.bitterlemonpress.com.

OJAIDE, Tanure; Poet, Writer and Prof. of African-American and African Studies; b. 24 April 1948, Okpara Island, Nigeria; m. Anne Numuoja, 1976, five c. *Education:* Certificate, Federal Government College, Warri, 1967; BA, English, University of Ibadan, 1971; MA, Creative Writing, 1979, PhD, English, 1981, Syracuse University. *Career:* Teacher of English, Federal Government College, Warri, 1973–75; Lecturer in English and Communication, Petroleum Training Institute, Effurun, 1975–77; Lecturer, 1977–85, Senior Lecturer, 1985–87, Reader, 1987–89, University of Maiduguri; Visiting Johnston Prof. of Third World Literatures, Whitman College, Walla Walla, WA, 1989–90; Asst Prof., 1990–93, Assoc. Prof., 1993–98, Prof. of African-American and African Studies, 1998–, University of North Carolina at Charlotte; National Endowment for the Humanities Prof., Albright College, Reading, PA, 1996–97; mem. African Literature Asscn; African Studies Asscn; Associated Writing Programs; Asscn of Nigerian Authors; International Asscn of University Profs of English; International Black Writers, Charlotte, NC; MLA of America; North Carolina Writers' Network. *Publications:* Poetry: Children of Iroko and Other Poems, 1973; Labyrinths of the Delta, 1986; The Eagle's Vision, 1987; Poems, 1988; The Endless Song, 1989; The Fate of Vultures and Other Poems, 1990; The Blood of Peace, 1991; Daydream of Ants, 1997; Delta Blues and Home Songs, 1998; Invoking the Warrior Spirit: New and Selected Poems, 1999; Cannons for the Brave, 1999; When It No Longer Matters Where You Live, 1999; In the Kingdom of Songs: A Trilogy of Poems, 1995–2000, 2001. Other: Yono Urhobo: Obe Rerha (with S. S. Ugheteni), 1981; The Poetry of Wole Soyinka, 1994; Poetic Imagination in Black Africa: Essays on African Poetry, 1996; Great Boys: An African Childhood, 1998; The New African Poetry: An Anthology (ed. with Tijan M. Sallah), 1999; Texts and Contexts: Culture, Society, and Politics in Modern African Literature (with Joseph Obi), 2001; God and his Medicine Men: Short Stories, 2002. Contributions: books, anthologies, magazines and journals. *Honours:* Africa Regional Winner, Commonwealth Poetry Prize, 1987; Overall Winner, BBC Arts and Africa Poetry Award, 1988; Asscn of Nigerian Authors' Portey Prizes, 1988, 1994; All-Africa Okigbo Prizes for Poetry, 1988, 1997; Fellow, Headlands Center for the Arts, Sausalito, CA, 1994; National Endowment for the Humanities Fellowship, 1999–2000; Residency, Bellagio Center for Scholars and Artists, 2001. *Address:* c/o African-American and African Studies Dept, University of North Carolina at Charlotte, Charlotte, NC 28223, USA. *E-mail:* tojadie@email.uncc.edu.

OKAI, Atukwei; Ghanian poet and academic; b. 1941, Accra; m.; one d. *Education:* Gorky Literary Inst. Moscow, Univ. of London. *Career:* teacher in Russian literature, Univ. of Ghana; faculty mem., Inst. of African Studies, Legon; exec., Pan-African Writers' Asscn (PAWA). *Publications:* poetry: Flowerfall 1969, The Oath of the Fontomfrom and Other Poems 1971, Lorgorligi Logarithms 1974, The Anthill in the Sea 1988. *Literary Agent:* c/o Pan-African Writers' Association, PAWA House, Roman Ridge, POB C456, Accra, Ghana. *Telephone:* (21) 773 062. *Fax:* (21) 773 042. *E-mail:* pawa@ghana.com.

OKRI, Ben, OBE, FRSL, FRSA; Nigerian/British author and poet; b. 15 March 1959, Minna. *Education:* John Donne's School, Peckham, London, Children's Home School, Sapele, Nigeria, Christ High School, Ibadan, Urhobo Coll. Warri and Univ. of Essex, UK. *Career:* staff writer and librarian, Afriscope magazine 1978; poetry ed. West Africa magazine 1983–86; broadcaster with BBC 1983–85; Fellow Commoner in Creative Arts, Trinity Coll. Cambridge 1991–93; mem. Int. PEN, a Vice-Pres. English Centre of Int. PEN 1997–; mem. Bd Royal Nat. Theatre of GB 1999–; mem. Soc. of Authors; mem. RSL (mem. of Council). *Play:* In Exilus (The Studio, Royal Nat. Theatre of GB) 2001. *Television:* Great Railway Journey: London to Arcadia 1996. *Publications:* Flowers and Shadows 1980, The Landscapes Within 1982, Incidents at the Shrine 1986, Stars of the New Curfew 1988, The Famished Road (Booker Prize) 1991, An African Elegy (vol. of poems) 1992, Songs of Enchantment 1993, Astonishing the Gods 1995, Birds of Heaven (essays) 1996, Dangerous Love (novel) 1996, A Way of Being Free (non-fiction) 1997, Infinite Riches (novel) 1998, Mental Fight (epic poem) 1999, In Arcadia (novel) 2002; poems, essays, short stories. *Honours:* Hon. DLitt (Westminster) 1997, (Essex) 2002; Commonwealth Prize for Africa 1987, Paris Review Aga Khan Prize for Fiction 1987, Premio Letterario Internazionale, Chianti Ruffino-Antico Fattore 1992, Premio Grinzane Cavour 1994, The Crystal Award (World Econ. Forum, Switzerland) 1995, Premio Palmi 2000. *Address:* c/o Orion Books, Orion House, 5 Upper St Martin's Lane, London, WC2H 9EA, England.

OLASKY, Marvin; Prof. of Journalism, Writer and Ed.; b. 12 June 1950, Malden, MA, USA; m. Susan Northway, 27 June 1976, four s. *Education:* BA, Yale University, 1971; MA, 1974, PhD, 1976, University of Michigan. *Career:* Reporter and correspondent, Boston Globe, 1970–71, 1973; Reporter, Bulletin, Bend, OR, 1971–72; Lecturer, San Diego State University, 1976–77; Academic Affairs Co-ordinator and Speechwriter, Du Pont Co, Wilmington, DE, 1978–83; Asst Prof., 1983–88, Assoc. Prof., 1988–93, Prof. of Journalism, 1993–, University of Texas at Austin; Bradley Resident Scholar, Heritage Foundation, 1989–90; Resident Scholar, Americans United for Life, 1990–91; Ed., Philanthropy, Culture and Society, 1991–94; Ed.-at-Large, World, 1991–94, Ed. 1994–2001, Ed.-in-Chief 2001–; Sr Fellow Acton Inst. 1999; mem. National Asscn of Scholars. *Publications:* Corporate Public Relations: A New Historical Perspective, 1987; Patterns of Corporate Philanthropy: Public Affairs and the Forbes 100, 1987; Turning Point: A Christian Worldview Declaration (with Herbert Schlossberg), 1987; Prodigal Press: The Anti-Christian Bias of the News Media, 1988; The Press and Abortion, 1838–1988, 1988; More Than Kindness: A Compassionate Approach to Childbearing (with Susan Olasky), 1990; Central Ideas in the Development of American Journalism, 1991; The Tragedy of American Compassion, 1992; Abortion Rites: A Social History of Abortion in America, 1992; Philanthropically Correct: The Story of the Council on Foundations, 1993; Loving Your Neighbor: A Principled Guide to Charity, 1995; Fighting for Liberty and Virtue: Political and Cultural Wars in Eighteenth-Century America, 1995; Renewing American Compassion, 1996; Telling the Truth: How to Revitalize Christian Journalism, 1996; Whirled Views: Tracking Today's Culture Storms (with Joel Belz), 1997; The American Leadership Tradition: Moral Vision from Washington to Clinton, 1999, revised edn as The American Leadership Tradition: The Inevitable Impact of a Leader's Faith on a Nation's Destiny, 2000; Compassionate Conservatism: What It Is, What It Does, and How It Can Transform America, 2000, Standing for Christ in a Modern Babylon 2003. Contributions: periodicals. *Address:* c/o Dept of Journalism, University of Texas at Austin, Austin, TX 78712, USA.

OLDKNOW, Antony, BA, PhD; poet, writer, literary translator and academic; *Professor of Literature, Eastern New Mexico University*; b. 15 Aug. 1939, Peterborough, England. *Education:* Univ. of Leeds, Univ. of Edinburgh, Univ. of North Dakota, USA. *Career:* Ed., Publisher, Scopcraeft Press Inc 1966–; travelling writer, The Plains Book Bus 1979–81; writer-in-residence, Wisconsin Arts Board 1980–83; poetry staff, Cottonwood 1984–87; Prof. of Literature, Eastern New Mexico Univ. 1987–; Assoc. Ed., Blackwater Quarterly 1993. *Publications:* Lost Allegory 1967, Tomcats and Tigertails 1968, The Road of the Lord 1969, Anthem for Rusty Saw and Blue Sky 1975, Consolations for Beggars 1978, Miniature Clouds 1982, Ten Small Songs 1985, Clara d'Ellébeuse (trans.) 1992, The Villages and Other Poems (trans.) 1993; contrib. short stories and articles to anthologies, reviews, journals and magazines. *Address:* Department of Languages and Literature, Eastern New Mexico University, Portales, NM 88130, USA.

OLDS, Sharon; poet and academic; b. 19 Nov. 1942, San Francisco, CA, USA. *Education:* BA, Stanford University, 1964; PhD, Columbia University, 1972. *Career:* Lecturer-in-Residence on Poetry, Theodor Herzl Institute, New York, 1976–80; Adjunct Prof., 1983–90, Dir, 1988–91, Assoc. Prof., 1990–, Graduate Program in Creative Writing, New York University; Fanny Hurst Chair in Literature, Brandeis University, 1986–87; New York State Poet, 1998–2000. *Publications:* Satan Says, 1980; The Dead and the Living, 1984; The Gold Cell, 1987; The Matter of This World: New and Selected Poems, 1987; The Sign of Saturn, 1991; The Father, 1992; The Wellspring, 1996; Blood, Tin, Straw, 1999; The Unswept Room, 2002. *Honours:* Creative Arts Public Service Award, 1978; Madeline Sadin Award, 1978; Guggenheim Fellowship, 1981–82; National Endowment for the Arts Fellowship, 1982–83; Lamont Prize, 1984; National Book Critics Circle Award, 1985; Lila Wallace-Reader's Digest Fellowship, 1993–96. *Address:* c/o Department of English, New York University, 19 University Place, New York, NY 10003, USA.

OLDSEY, Bernard Stanley, BA, MA, PhD; retd academic, editor and writer; b. 18 Feb. 1923, Wilkes-Barre, PA, USA; m. Ann Marie Re 1946; one s. one d. *Education:* Pennsylvania State University. *Career:* Instructor to Assoc. Prof. of English, Pennsylvania State University, 1951–69; Senior Fulbright Prof. of American Literature, Universidad de Zaragoza, Spain, 1964–65; Prof. of English, West Chester University of Pennsylvania, 1969–90; Ed., College Literature, 1974–90; Prof., University of Innsbruck, Austria, 1986; mem. Authors' Guild. *Publications:* From Fact to Judgment, 1957; The Art of William Golding, 1967; The Spanish Season (novel), 1970; Hemingway's Hidden Craft, 1979; Ernest Hemingway: Papers of a Writer (ed.), 1981; British Novelists, 1930–1960, 1983; Critical Essays on George Orwell, 1985; The Mayfield Story, 1999; The Snows of Yesteryear (novel), 2001. *Address:* 520 William Ebbs Lane, West Chester, PA 19380, USA.

O'LEARY, Patsy B(aker); Writer, Poet and Teacher; b. 23 Sept. 1937, NC, USA; m. Denis L. O'Leary, 1962, divorced 1979, one d. *Education:* BS, East Carolina College, 1959; MA, California State University at Northridge, 1979. *Career:* Instructor in Creative Writing, Pitt Community College, 1980–; Lecturer in English, 1980–81, and Communications, 1990–95, East Carolina University; mem. National Writers' Union; Poets and Writers; North Carolina Writers Network; Southeastern Writers Asscn. *Publications:* With Wings as Eagles (novel), 1997; Phoenix (poem); A Voice Heard in Ramah (short story). *Honours:* First Place Awards for article, 1981, 1982, for novel-in-progress, 1981, 1982, for inspirational poem, 1983, Council of Authors and Journalists; First Place Award for short story, Tar Heel Writer's Roundtable, 1984; Award established in her honour, Pitt Community College, 1989. *Literary Agent:* Barrie Van Dyck Agency Inc, 217 Spruce St, Philadelphia, PA 19106, USA. *Address:* 310 Baytree Dr., Greenville, NC 27858, USA.

OLIVER, (Symmes) Chadwick; writer; b. 30 March 1928, Cincinnati, OH, USA; m. Betty Jane Jenkins 1952; one s. one d. *Publications:* Shadows in the Sun, 1954; Another Kind (short stories), 1955; The Winds of Time, 1957; Unearthly Neighbors, 1960; Ecology and Cultural Continuity as Contributing Factors in the Social Organization of the Plains Indians, 1962; The Wolf is My Brother (western novel), 1967; The Shores of Another Sea, 1971; The Edge of Forever (short stories), 1971; Giants in the Dust, 1976; Cultural Anthropology: The Discovery of Humanity, 1980; Broken Eagle, 1989. *Honours:* Western Heritage Award for Best Novel, 1989. *Address:* 301 Eanes Road, Austin, TX 78746, USA.

OLIVER, Douglas Dunlop; Poet, Novelist and Prosodist; b. 14 Sept. 1937, Southampton, England; m. 1st Janet Hughes July 1962; m. 2nd Alice Notley Feb. 1988; two d. two step-s. *Education:* BA, Literature, 1975, MA, Applied Linguistics, 1982, University of Essex. *Career:* Journalist, newspapers in England, Agence France-Presse, Paris, 1959–72; University Lecturer, Literature, English, various, 1975–; Editorial Board, Franco-British Studies; Co-Ed., Gare du Nord Magazine. *Publications:* Oppo Hectic, 1969; The Harmless Building, 1973; In the Cave of Succession, 1974; The Diagram Poems, 1979; The Infant and the Pearl, 1985; Kind, 1987; Poetry and Narrative in Performance, 1989; Three Variations on the Theme of Harm, 1990; Penniless Politics, 1991; The Scarlet Cabinet (with Alice Notley), 1992; Selected Poems, 1996; Penguin Modern Poets 10, 1996. Contributions: anthologies including: A Various Art, 1987; The New British Poetry 1968–1988, 1988; numerous poems, articles, fiction, to magazines and journals. *Honours:* Eastern Arts Grant, 1977; South-East Arts Grant, 1987; Fund for Poetry Grants, 1990, 1991; Judith E. Wilson Lecturer, University of Cambridge, 1995. *Address:* c/o British Institute in Paris, 11 Rue de Constantine, 75007 Paris, France.

OLIVER, Mary; Poet and Educator; b. 10 Sept. 1935, Cleveland, Ohio, USA. *Education:* Ohio State University; Vassar College. *Career:* Mather Visiting Prof., Case Western Reserve University, 1980, 1982; Poet-in-Residence, Bucknell University, 1986; Elliston Visiting Prof., University of Cincinnati, 1986; Margaret Banister Writer-in-Residence, Sweet Briar College, 1991–95; William Blackburn Visiting Prof. of Creative Writing, Duke University, 1995; Catharine Osgood Foster Prof., Bennington College, 1996–; mem. PEN. *Publications:* No Voyage, and Other Poems, 1963; The River Styx, Ohio, and Other Poems, 1972; The Night Traveler, 1978; Twelve Moons, 1978; Sleeping in the Forest, 1979; American Primitive, 1983; Dream Work, 1986; Provincetown, 1987; House of Light, 1990; New and Selected Poems, 1992; A Poetry Handbook, 1994; White Pine: Poems and Prose Poems, 1994; Blue Pastures, 1995; West Wind, 1997; Rules for the Dance, 1998; Winter Hours, 1999; The Leaf and the Cloud, 2000; What Do We Know, 2002. Contributions: periodicals in the US and England. *Honours:* Poetry Society of America First Prize, 1962; Devil's Advocate Award, 1968; Shelley Memorial Award, 1972; National Endowment for the Arts Fellowship, 1972–73; Alice Fay di Castagnola Award, 1973; Guggenheim Fellowship, 1980–81; American Acad. and Institute of Arts and Letters Award, 1983; Pulitzer Prize in Poetry, 1984; Christopher Award, 1991; L. L. Winship Award, 1991; National Book Award for Poetry, 1992; Lannan Literary Award, 1998. *Address:* c/o Molly Malone Cook Literary Agency, Box 619, Provincetown, MA 02657, USA.

OLIVER, Roland Anthony; Prof. of the History of Africa and Author; b. 30 March 1923, Srinagar, Kashmir; m. 1st Caroline Florence, 1947, deceased 1983, one d.; m. 2nd Suzanne Miers, 1990. *Education:* MA, PhD, King's College, Cambridge. *Career:* Foreign Office, 1942–45; R. J. Smith Research Studentship, King's College, Cambridge, 1946–48; Lecturer, School of Oriental and African Studies, 1948–58; Reader in African History, 1958–63, Prof. of the History of Africa, 1963–86, University of London; Ed. (with J. D. Fage), Journal of African History, 1960–73; Francqui Prof., University of Brussels, 1961; Visiting Prof., Northwestern University, 1962, Harvard University, 1967; mem. Académie Royale des Sciences d'Outremer, Brussels, corresponding mem.; African Studies Asscn, pres., 1967–68; British Acad., fellow; British Institute in Eastern Africa, pres., 1981–93; International Congress of Africanists; Royal African Society, vice-pres., 1965–2000. *Publications:* The Missionary Factor in East Africa, 1952; Sir Harry Johnston and the Scramble for Africa, 1957; The Dawn of African History (ed.), 1961; A Short History of Africa (with J. D. Fage), 1962; A History of East Africa (ed. with Gervase Mathew), 1963; Africa since 1800 (with A. E. Atmore), 1967; The Middle Age of African History (ed.), 1967; Papers in African Prehistory (with J. D. Fage), 1970; Africa in the Iron Age (with B. M. Fagan), 1975; The Cambridge History of Africa (general ed. with J. D. Fage), 8 vols, 1975–86; The African Middle Ages, 1400–1800 (with A. E. Atmore), 1981; The African Experience, 1991; In the Realms of Gold: Pioneering in African History, 1997; Medieval Africa (with A. E. Atmore), 2001. Contributions: scholarly journals. *Honours:* Haile Selassie Prize Trust Award, 1966; Distinguished Africanist Award, American African Studies Asscn, 1989; Hon. Fellow, School of Oriental and African Studies, 1992. *Address:* Frilsham Woodhouse, Thatcham, Berkshire RG18 9XB, England.

OLLARD, Richard Laurence; Historian and Writer; b. 9 Nov. 1923, Bainton, Yorkshire, England. *Education:* MA, New College, Oxford, 1952. *Career:* Lecturer, 1948–52, Senior Lecturer in History and English, 1952–59, Royal Naval College, Greenwich; Senior Ed., William Collins and Sons, London, 1960–83; mem. FRSL; Society of Antiquaries, fellow. *Publications:* Historical Essays 1600–1750 (ed. with H. E. Bell), 1963; The Escape of Charles II, 1967; Man of War: Sir Robert Holmes and the Restoration Navy, 1969; Pepys, 1974; War Without an Enemy: A History of the English Civil Wars, 1976; The Image of the King: Charles I and Charles II, 1979; An English Education: A Perspective of Eton, 1982; For Veronica Wedgwood These: Studies on 17th Century History (ed. with Pamela Tudor Craig), 1986; Clarendon and His Friends, 1987; Fisher and Cunningham: A Study in the Personalities of the Churchill Era, 1991; Cromwell's Earl: A Life of Edward Montagu, First Earl of Sandwich, 1994; Dorset: A Pimlico County History Guide, 1995; The Sayings of Samuel Pepys, 1996; The Diaries of A. L. Rowse (ed.), 2003. *Literary Agent:* Curtis Brown Ltd, Haymarket House, 28–29 Haymarket, London, SW1Y 4SP, England. *Telephone:* (20) 7393-4400. *Fax:* (20) 7393-4401. *E-mail:* info@curtisbrown.co.uk. *Website:* www.curtisbrown.co.uk.

OLMSTEAD, Andrea Louise, BM, MA; musicologist; b. 5 Sept. 1948, Dayton, Ohio, USA; m. Larry Thomas Bell 1982. *Education:* Hartt Coll. of Music, New York Univ. *Career:* faculty, The Juilliard School 1972–80, Boston Conservatory 1981–; mem. Sonneck Soc. *Publications:* Roger Sessions and His Music 1985, Conversations with Roger Sessions 1987, The New Grove 20th Century American Masters 1987, The Correspondence of Roger Sessions 1992, Juilliard: A History 1999; contrib. to Journal of the Arnold Schoenberg Institute, American Music, Musical Quarterly, Tempo, Musical America, Perspectives of New Music, Music Library Asscn Notes. *Honours:* Nat. Endowment for the Humanities grants, Outstanding Academic Book, Choice 1986. *Address:* 73 Hemenway Street, Apt 501, Boston, MA 02115, USA. *E-mail:* LBell10276@aol.com. *Website:* www.AndreaOlmstead.com.

OLSEN, Lance; Writer, Poet and Critic; b. 14 Oct. 1956, USA; m. Andrea Hirsch, 3 Jan. 1981. *Education:* BA, University of Wisconsin, 1978; MFA, University of Iowa, 1980; MA, 1982, PhD, 1985, University of Virginia. *Career:* Prof. of Creative Writing and Contemporary Fiction, University of Idaho, 1996–2001; Writer-in-Residence, State of Idaho, 1996–98; Fulbright Scholar, Turku, Finland, 2000. *Publications:* Ellipse of Uncertainty, 1987; Circus of the Mind in Motion, 1990; Live From Earth, 1991; William Gibson, 1992; My Dates With Franz, 1993; Natural Selections (poems with Jeff Worley), 1993; Scherzi, I Believe, 1994; Tonguing the Zeitgeist, 1994; Lolita, 1995; Burnt, 1996; Time Famine, 1996; Rebel Yell: A Short Guide to Fiction Writing, 1998; Sewing Shut My Eyes, 2000; Freaknest, 2000; Girl Imagined By Chance, 2002; Hideous Beauties, 2003. Contributions: journals and magazines. *Address:* PO Box 306, New Meadows, ID 83654, USA.

OLSEN, Theodore Victor, (Joshua Stark, Christopher Storm, Cass Willoughby); Writer; b. 25 April 1932, Rhinelander, Wisconsin, USA; m. Beverly Butler, 25 Sept. 1976. *Education:* BSc, English, University of Wisconsin, 1955. *Career:* mem. Western Writers of America. *Publications:* Haven of the Hunted, 1956; The Rhinelander Story, 1957; The Man from Nowhere, 1959; McGivern, 1960; High Lawless, 1960; Gunswift, 1960; Ramrod Rider, 1960; Brand of the Star, 1961; Brothers of the Sword, 1962; Savage Sierra, 1962; The Young Duke, 1963; Break the Young Land, 1964; The Sex Rebels, 1964; A Man Called Brazos, 1964; Canyon of the Gun, 1965; Campus Motel, 1965; The Stalking Moon, 1965; The Hard Men, 1966; Autumn Passion, 1966; Bitter Grass, 1967; The Lockhart Breed, 1967; Blizzard Pass, 1968; Arrow in the Sun, 1969; Keno, 1970; A Man Named Yuma, 1971; Eye of the Wolf, 1971; There Was a Season, 1973; Mission to the West, 1973; Run to the Mountain, 1974; Track the Man Down, 1975; Day of the Buzzard, 1976; Westward They Rode, 1976; Bonner's Stallion, 1977; Rattlesnake, 1979; Roots of the North, 1979; Allegories for One Man's Moods, 1979; Our First Hundred Years, 1981; Blood of the Breed, 1982; Birth of a City, 1983; Red is the River, 1983; Lazlo's Strike, 1983; Lonesome Gun, 1985; Blood Rage, 1987; A Killer is Waiting, 1988; Under the Gun, 1989; The Burning Sky, 1991; The Golden Chance, 1992. Contributions: 20 short stories in Ranch Romances, 1956–57. *Honours:* Award of Merit, State Historical Society of Wisconsin, 1983; Western Writers of America Spur Award for Best Western Paperback Novel, 1992. *Address:* PO Box 856, Rhinelander, WI 54501, USA.

OLSON, Peter; Publisher; b. 1 May 1950, Chicago, IL, USA; m. 1st 1874; three c.; m. 2nd Candice Carpenter. *Education:* AB, magna cum laude, History, Harvard Univ.; JD, cum laude, Harvard Law School; MBA, Harvard Business School. *Career:* Assoc. Attorney, Baker & Botts, Washington, DC, 1976, Hamada & Matsumoto, Tokyo, Japan, 1977–79; Officer, International Division, Dresdner Bank, Frankfurt, Germany, 1979–81, Deputy Man., Corporate Business Dept, Tokyo, Japan, 1981–84, Man., Credit Dept, Tokyo, 1984–87, Vice-Pres., Planning Dept, Treasury Division, Frankfurt, 1987–88; Man., Bertelsmann AG Corporate Office, Gütersloh, Germany, 1988, Sr Vice-Pres., Doubleday Book and Music Clubs, Inc, Garden City, NY, USA, 1989, Pres., Bertelsmann, Inc, New York, 1990, Exec. Vice-Pres. and Chief Financial Officer, then Chief Administrative Officer, Bantam Doubleday Dell Publishing Group, New York, 1992–94, Chair. and CEO, Bertelsmann Book Group North America, New York, 1994–98, and mem. of Bertelsmann Book AG Exec. Board, 1994–, Chair. and CEO, Random House, Inc, New York, 1998–. *Address:* Random House, 1745 Broadway, New York, NY 10019, USA.

OLSON, Toby, (Merle Theodore Olson); Prof. of English, Writer and Poet; b. 17 Aug. 1937, Berwyn, IL, USA. *Education:* BA, English and Philosophy, Occidental College, Los Angeles, 1965; MA, English, Long Island University, 1968. *Career:* Assoc. Dir, Aspen Writers' Workshop, 1964–67; Asst Prof., Long Island University, 1966–74; Faculty, New School for Social Research, New York City, 1967–75; Prof. of English, Temple University, Philadelphia, 1975–2000. *Publications:* Fiction: The Life of Jesus, 1976; Seaview, 1982; The Woman Who Escaped From Shame, 1986; Utah, 1987; Dorit in Lesbos, 1990; The Pool, 1991; Reading, 1992; At Sea, 1993; Write Letter to Billy, 2000. Poetry: Maps, 1969; Worms Into Nails, 1969; The Hawk-Foot Poems, 1969; The Brand, 1969; Pig's Book, 1970; Vectors, 1972; Fishing, 1973; The Wrestler and Other Poems, 1974; City, 1974; Changing Appearances: Poems 1965–1975, 1975; Home, 1976; Three and One, 1976; Doctor Miriam, 1977; Aesthetics, 1978; The Florence Poems, 1978; Birdsongs, 1980; Two Standards, 1982; Still/Quiet, 1982; Sitting in Gusevik, 1983; We Are the Fire, 1984; Unfinished Building, 1993; Human Nature, 2000. Editor: Writing Talks: Views on Teaching Writing from Across the Professions (with Muffy E. A. Siegel), 1983. Opera Libretti: Dorit, 1994; Chihuahua, 1999. Contributions: numerous anthologies, newspapers, and magazines. *Honours:* CAPS Award in Poetry, New York State, 1974; Pennsylvania Council on the Arts Fellowship, 1983; PEN/Faulkner Award for Fiction, 1983; Guggenheim Fellowship, 1985; National Endowment for the Arts Fellowship, 1985; Yaddo Fellowships, 1985, 1986; Rockefeller Foundation Fellowship, Bellagio, Italy, 1987; Creative Achievement Award, Temple University, 1990; PENN/Book Philadelphia Award for Fiction, 1990. *Address:* 275 S 19th St, Philadelphia, PA 19103, USA.

OLUDHE-MacGOYE, Marjorie Phyllis; Kenyan writer and poet; b. 21 Oct. 1928, Southampton, England; m. D. G. W. Oludhe-Macgoye 1960 (died 1990); three s. one d. *Education:* BA, English, 1948, MA, 1953, University of London. *Publications:* Growing Up at Lina School (children's), 1971; Murder in Majengo (novel), 1972; Song of Nyarloka and Other Poems, 1977; Coming to Birth (novel), 1986; The Story of Kenya (history), 1986; The Present Moment (novel), 1987; Street Life (novella), 1988; Victoria and Murder in Majengo, 1993; Homing In (novel), 1994; Moral Issues in Kenya, 1996; Chira (novel), 1997; The Black Hand Gang (children's), 1997; Make It Sing and Other Poems, 1998; Further Adventures of the Black Hand Gang (children's), 2003. Contributions: anthologies, reviews, and journals. *Honours:* BBC Arts in Africa Poetry Award, 1982; Sinclair Prize for Fiction, 1986. *Address:* PO Box 70344, Nairobi 00400, Kenya.

O'MALLEY, Mary; Playwright; b. 19 March 1941, Bushey, Hertfordshire, England. *Career:* Writer-in-Residence, Royal Court Theatre, 1977. *Publications:* Superscum, 1972; A 'Nevolent Society, 1974; Oh If Ever a Man Suffered, 1975; Once a Catholic, 1977; Look out, Here Comes Trouble, 1978; Talk of the Devil, 1986. *Honours:* Evening Standard Award, 1978. *Address:* Knockeven, Cliffs of Moher, County Clare, Ireland.

OMAN, Julia Trevelyan; Designer and Writer; b. 11 July 1930, London, England; m. Roy Colin Strong, 10 Sept. 1971. *Education:* Royal Scholar, 1953, Silver Medal, 1955, Royal College of Art, London. *Career:* Designer for television, opera, film, theatre and ballet; mem. Chartered Society of Designers, fellow. *Publications:* Street Children (with B. S. Johnson), 1964; Elizabeth R (with Roy Strong), 1971; Mary Queen of Scots (with Roy Strong), 1972; The English Year (with Roy Strong), 1982; A Celebration of Gardens (with Roy Strong), 1991; A Country Life (with Roy Strong), 1994; Vanitas (with Gianni Versale), 1994; On Happiness (with Roy Strong), 1997; Garden Party (with Roy Strong), 2000. Contributions: periodicals. *Honours:* Royal Designer for Industry, RSA, 1977; CBE, 1986; Hon. DLitt, University of Bristol, 1987. *Address:* c/o Oman Productions Ltd, The Laskett, Much Birch, Herefordshire HR2 8HZ, England.

OMOTOSO, Kole, BA, PhD; writer; b. Nigeria. *Education:* Univ. of Ibadau, Univ. of Edinburgh, Scotland. *Career:* Lecturer, Dept of Arabic and Islamic Studies, Univ. of Ibadau, 1972–76; Senior Lecturer, Head of Dept of Dramatic Arts, Dir of the Univ. of Ife Theatre, Univ. of Ife, Ile-Ife, 1976–88; Visiting Prof., Dept of English Studies, Univ. of Stirling, Scotland, 1989–90; Visiting Prof., Dept of English, National Univ. of Lesotho Roma, Lesotho, Aug.–Dec. 1990; worked with Tawala Theatre, London, England, 1991; Prof. of English, Univ. of the Western Cape, Cape Town, 1991–2000; Second Prof. and Researcher of Drama, Univ. of Stellenbosch, 2001–. *Publications:* Fiction: The Edifice, 1972; The Combat, 1972; Just Before Dawn, 1988. Non-Fiction: The Theatrical into Theatre: A Study of Drama in the English-speaking Caribbean, 1982; Achebe or Soyinka?: A Re-interpretation and a Study in Contrasts, 1995. Other: Short story collection, plays, historical narratives. Contributions: numerous articles. *Address:* University of Stellenbosch, Private Bag XI, Matieland 7602, South Africa. *E-mail:* bankole@yebo.co.za.

ONDAATJE, (Philip) Michael, BA, MA; Canadian poet, novelist, dramatist, teacher and film director; b. 12 Sept. 1943, Colombo, Sri Lanka. *Education:* St Thomas' Coll., Colombo, Dulwich Coll., London, Bishop's Univ., Lennoxville, QC, Univ. of Toronto, Queen's Univ., Kingston, ON. *Career:* teacher, University of Western Ontario, 1969–71, Glendon College, York University, Toronto, 1971–; Visiting Prof., University of Hawaii, 1979, Brown University, Providence, RI, 1990; Film Dir. *Publications:* Poetry: The Dainty Monsters, 1967; The Man With Seven Toes, 1969; Left Handed Poems, 1970; Rat Jelly, 1973; Elimination Dance, 1978; There's a Trick with a Knife I'm Learning to Do: Poems, 1963–1978, 1979; Claude Glass, 1979; Tin Roof, 1982; Secular Love, 1984; All Along the Mazinaw: Two Poems, 1986; The Cinnamon Peeler: Selected Poems, 1989; Handwriting, 1998. Fiction: The Collected Works of Billy the Kid, 1970; Coming Through Slaughter, 1976; In the Skin of a Lion, 1987; The English Patient, 1992; Anil's Ghost, 2000. Criticism: Leonard Cohen, 1970. Non-Fiction: Running in the Family, 1982. Editor: The Broken Ark, verse, 1971, revised edn as A Book of Beasts, 1979; Personal Fictions: Stories by Monroe, Wiebe, Thomas, and Blaise, 1977; The Long Poem Anthology, 1979; Brushes With Greatness: An Anthology of Chance Encounters with Greatness (with Russell Banks and David Young), 1989; The Brick Anthology (with Linda Spalding), 1989; From Ink Lake: An Anthology of Canadian Short Stories, 1990; The Faber Book of Contemporary Canadian Short Stories, 1990. *Honours:* Ralph Gustafson Award, 1965; Epstein Award, 1966; E. J. Pratt Medal, 1966; Canadian Governor-General's Awards for Literature, 1971, 1980, 1992; WHSmith/Books in Canada First Novel Award, 1977; Canada-Australia Prize, 1980; City of Toronto Arts Award, 1987; Trillium Book Awards, 1987, 1992; Booker McConnell Prize, British Book Council, 1992; Canadian Authors Asscn Author of the Year Award, 1993; Chianti Ruffino-Antonio Fattore International Literary Prize, 1994; Nelly Sachs Award, 1995; Premio Grinzane Cavour, 1996; Irish Times International Literature Prize, 2001. *Literary Agent:* Steven Barclay Agency, 12 Western Avenue, Petaluma, CA 94952, USA. *Telephone:* (707) 773-0654. *Fax:* (707) 778-1868. *Website:* www.barclayagency.com.

ONDERDONK, Andrew B., PhD; American academic; *Editor-in-Chief, Journal of Clinical Microbiology. Career:* Prof. of Pathology, Harvard Medical School; Dir of Clinical Microbiology, Channing Laboratory at Brigham and Women's Hospital; Pres. of the Int. Soc. for Anaerobic Bacteria; Ed.-in-Chief, Journal of Clinical Microbiology. *Address:* Journal of Clinical Microbiology, American Society for Microbiology, 1752 N Street NW, Washington, DC 20036-2904, USA (Office). *E-mail:* aonderdonk@channing.harvard.edu. *Website:* jcm.asm.org.

O'NEILL, Gilda, BA, MA; British writer and historian; b. 1951, Bethnal Green, London; m. *Education:* Open Univ., North East London Polytechnic, Univ. of Kent. *Publications:* novels: The Cockney Girl 1992, Whitechapel Girl 1993, The Bells of Bow 1994, Just Around the Corner 1995, Cissie Flowers 1996, Dream On 1997, The Lights of London 1998, Playing Around 2000, Getting There 2001, Sins of their Fathers 2002, Make Us Traitors 2004, Of Woman Born 2004; non-fiction: Pull No More Bines: Hop-Picking Memories of a Vanished Way of Life 1990, A Night Out with the Girls: Women Having a Good Time 1993, My East End: Memories of Life in Cockney London 1999, Our Street: East End Life in the Second World War 2003. *Honours:* Dr hc (East London Univ.). *Address:* c/o William Heinemann, 20 Vauxhall Bridge Road, London, SW1V 2SA, England. *Website:* www.randomhouse.co.uk.

O'NEILL, Joseph; Writer and Barrister; b. 23 Feb. 1964, Cork, Ireland; m. Sally Singer, 30 Dec. 1994. *Education:* BA, Law, Girton College, Cambridge, 1985. *Career:* Barrister, 1990–. *Publications:* This is the Life, 1991; The Breezes, 1995; Bood-Dark Track, 2001. Contributions: Reviews and articles in: TLS; Spectator; Literary Review. *Literary Agent:* Rogers, Coleridge & White Ltd, 20 Powis Mews, London W11 1JN, England.

O'NEILL, Michael Stephen Charles, BA, DPhil; academic, writer, poet and editor; *Professor of English, University of Durham*; b. 2 Sept. 1953, Aldershot, Hampshire, England; m. Rosemary Ann McKendrick 1977; one s. one d. *Education:* Exeter College, Oxford. *Career:* Faculty 1979–91, Sr Lecturer 1991–93, Reader 1993–95, Prof. of English 1995–, Univ. of Durham; co-founder and Ed., Poetry Durham 1982–94; Fellow, English Asscn 2000–. *Publications:* The Human Mind's Imaginings: Conflict and Achievement in Shelley's Poetry, 1989; Percy Bysshe Shelley: A Literary Life, 1989; The Stripped Bed (poems), 1990; Auden, MacNeice, Spender: The Thirties Poetry (with Gareth Reeves), 1992; Percy Bysshe Shelley (ed.), 1993; The 'Defence of Poetry' Fair Copies (ed.), 1994; Keats: Bicentenary Readings (ed.), 1997; Fair-Copy Manuscripts of Shelley's Poems in American and European Libraries (ed. with Donald H. Reiman), 1997; Romanticism and the Self-Conscious Poem, 1997; Literature of the Romantic Period: A Bibliographical Guide (ed.), 1998; Shelley: The Major Works (ed. with Zachary Leader), 2003; A Routledge Literary Sourcebook on the Poems of W. B. Yeats (ed.), 2003. Contributions: books and journals. *Honours:* Eric Gregory Award 1983, Cholmondeley Award 1990. *Address:* c/o Department of English Studies, University of Durham, Hallgarth House, 77 Hallgarth Street, Durham DH1 3AY, England.

O'NEILL, Paul; Author; b. 26 Oct. 1928, St John's, NF, Canada. *Education:* National Acad. of Theatre Arts, New York. *Career:* mem. Canadian Authors Asscn; Canadian Radio Producers Asscn; Newfoundland and Labrador Arts Council, chair., 1988–89; Newfoundland Writers Guild; Writers Union of Canada. *Publications:* Spindrift and Morning Light, 1968; The City in Your Pocket, 1974; The Oldest City, 1975; Seaport Legacy, 1976; Legends of a Lost Tribe, 1976; Breakers, 1982; The Seat Imperial, 1983; A Sound of Seagulls, 1984; Upon This Rock, 1984. Other: Radio and stage plays; Television and film scripts. Contributions: many periodicals. *Honours:* Literary Heritage Award, Newfoundland Historical Society; Robert Weaver Award, National Radio Producers Asscn of Canada, 1986; Hon. Doctor of Laws, Memorial University of Newfoundland, 1988; Order of Canada, 1990; Newfoundland and Labrador Arts Hall of Honour, 1991; Canada Commemorative Medal, 1992. *Address:* 115 Rennies Mill Rd, St John's, NF A18 2P2, Canada.

O'NEILL, Robert John; historian, editor and writer; b. 5 Nov. 1936, Melbourne, Vic., Australia; m. Sally Margaret Burnard 1965; two d. *Education:* BE, University of Melbourne, 1960; BA, 1963, MA, 1965, DPhil, 1965, University of Oxford. *Career:* Served in the Australian Army, 1955–68; Senior Lecturer in History, Royal Military College of Australia, 1968–69; Senior Fellow in International Relations, 1969–77, Professorial Fellow, 1977–82, Australian National University; Official Australian Historian for the Korean War, 1969–82; Dir, 1982–87, Chair., Council, 1996–2000, International Institute for Strategic Studies, London; Chichele Prof. of the History of War, 1987–2001, Dir of Graduate Studies, Modern History Faculty, 1990–92, University of Oxford; Fellow, All Souls College, Oxford, 1987–2001; Trustee Imperial War Museum 1990–98, Chair. of Trustees 1998–2001; Chair. of Council Australian Strategic Policy Inst. 2000–; Chair. of Council Univ. of Sydney Graduate School of Govt 2003–; mem. Fellow, Acad. of the Social Sciences of Australia, 1978; FRHistS, 1990. *Publications:* The German Army and the Nazi Party, 1933–1939, 1966; Vietnam Task, 1968; General Giap: Politician and Stategist, 1969; The Strategic Nuclear Balance (ed.), 1975; The Defence of Australia: Fundamental New Aspects (ed.), 1977; Insecurity: The Spread of Weapons in the Indian and Pacific Oceans (ed.), 1978; Australian Dictionary of Biography (co-ed.), Vols 7–14, 1979–97; New Directions in Strategic Thinking (ed. with David Horner), 1981; Australia in the Korean War, 1950–1953, Vol. 1, Strategy and Diplomacy, 1981, Vol. 2, Combat Operations, 1985; Australian Defence Policy for the 1980s (ed. with David Horner), 1982; Security in East Asia (ed.), 1984; The Conduct of East-West Relations in the 1980s (ed.), 1985; New Technology and Western Security Policy (ed.), 1985; Doctrine, the Alliance and Arms Control (ed.), 1986; East Asia, the West and International Security (ed.), 1987; Security in the Mediterranean (ed.), 1989; The West and the Third World (ed. with R. J. Vincent), 1990; Securing Peace in Europe, 1945–1962 (ed. with Beatrice Heuser), 1992; War, Strategy and International Politics (co-ed.), 1992; Alternative Nuclear Futures (ed. with John Bayliss), 1999. Contributions: Professional journals. *Honours:* Rhodes Scholar, 1961; AM, 1988; Hon. Fellow, Brasenose College, Oxford, 1990. *Address:* c/o All Souls College, Oxford OX1 4AL, England.

ONWUEME, Osonye Tess, (Tess Akaeke Onwueme, Tess Osonye Onwueme); dramatist, novelist and academic; b. 8 Sept. 1955, Nigeria; m. Obika Gray 1998; two s. three d. *Education:* BA, Education, 1979, MA, Literature, 1982, University of Ife; PhD, African Drama, University of Benin, 1988. *Career:* Lecturer, University of Ife, 1980–82; Asst Prof., Federal University of Technology, Owerri, 1982–87; Assoc. Prof. and Head, Performing Arts Dept, Imo State University, 1986–88; Assoc. Prof., Montclair State University, NJ, 1990–92, Wayne State University, Detroit, 1990–98; Prof. of English and Africana Studies, Vassar College, 1992–93; Distinguished Prof. of Cultural Diversity and Prof. of English, University of Wisconsin at Eau Claire, 1994–; mem. African Literature Asscn; African Studies Asscn; Asscn of Nigerian Authors; International Women Playwrights Asscn; Organization of Women Writers of African Descent; PEN International. *Publications:* A Hen Too Soon, 1983; The Broken Calabash, 1984; The Desert Encroaches, 1985; Ban Empty Barn, 1986; A Scent of Onions, 1986; Mirror for Campus, 1987; The Reign of Wazobia, 1988; Legacies, 1989; Riot in Heaven, 1996; The Missing Face, 1997; Tell it to Women, 1997; Shakara: Dance Hall Queen, 2000; Why the Elephant Has No Butt, 2000; Then She Said It: An Epic Drama, 2002; What Mama Said, 2003. Contributions: periodicals. *Honours:* Drama Prizes, Asscn of Nigerian Authors, 1985, 1995, 2001; Distinguished Authors Award, Ife International Bookfair, 1988; Ford Foundation Award, 2000. *Literary Agent:* Kimberly Crank, 1019 Huebsh Street, Eau Claire, WI 54701, USA. *Address:* c/o Dept of English, University of Wisconsin at Eau Claire, Eau Claire, WI 54701, USA.

ONYEAMA, Charles Dillibe Ejiofor; Publisher, Author and Journalist; b. 6 Jan. 1951, Enugu, Nigeria; m. Ethel Ekwueme, 15 Dec. 1984, four s. *Education:* Premier School of Journalism, Fleet Street, London, England. *Career:* Board of Dirs, Star Printing and Publishing Co Ltd, 1992–94; Managing Dir, Delta Publications (Nigeria) Ltd. *Publications:* Nigger at Eton, 1972; John Bull's Nigger, 1974; Sex is a Nigger's Game, 1975; The Book of Black Man's Humour, 1975; I'm the Greatest, 1975; Juju, 1976; Secret Society, 1977; Revenge of the Medicine Man, 1978; The Return, 1978; Night Demon, 1979; Female Target, 1980; The Rules of the Game, 1980; The Story of an African God, 1982; Modern Messiah, 1983; Godfathers of Voodoo, 1985; African Legend, 1985; Correct English, 1986; Notes of a So-Called Afro-Saxon, 1988. Contributions: Books and Bookmen; Spectator; Times; Daily Express; Sunday Express; Drum; West Africa; Roots; Guardian; Evening News. *Address:* 8B Byron Onyeama Close, New Haven, PO Box 1171, Enugu, Enugu State, Nigeria.

ONYEFULU, Ifeoma; Author and Photographer; b. 30 March 1959, Onitsha, Nigeria; m. Roger Malbert, 18 Nov. 1988, two s. *Education:* Higher National Diploma in Business Management, Seven Sisters College, London 1982. *Publications:* A is for Africa, 1993; Emeka's Gift, 1994; Chidi Only Likes Blue, 1997; One Big Family, 1996; My Grandfather is a Magician, 1998, Ebele's Favourite, 1999; A Triangle for Adaora, 2000; And Saying Goodbye, 2001. *Honours:* Notable Book Award, USA. *Address:* 15 Bickerton Rd, London N19 5JU, England.

OOKA, Makoto; Poet and Author; b. 16 Feb. 1931, Mishima City, Japan; m. Kaneko Aizawa, 1957, one s. one d. *Education:* Degree in Literature, Tokyo National University, 1953. *Career:* Asst Prof., 1965–70, Prof., 1970–87, Meiji University, Tokyo; Prof., National University of Fine Arts and Music, Tokyo, 1988–93; Soshitsu Sen XV Distinguished Lecturer in Japanese Culture and Visiting Fellow, Donald Keene Center of Japanese Culture, Columbia University, 2000; mem. Japan Art Acad.; Japanese PEN, pres., 1989–93; Poetry International, Rotterdam; Poet's Asscn, Japan, pres., 1979–81. *Publications:* (in English trans.) A String Around Autumn: Selected Poems, 1952–1980, 1982; A Play of Mirrors: Eight Major Poets of Modern Japan (ed. with Thomas Fitzsimmons), 1987; The Colors of Poetry: Essays in Classic Japanese Verse, 1991; Elegy and Benediction: Selected Poems, 1947–1989, 1991; A Poet's Anthology: The Range of Japanese Poetry, 1994; What the Kite Thinks: A Linked Poem (with others), 1994; Taiga (with Taiga Ike and Tadashi Kobayashi), 1994; Beneath the Sleepless Tossing of the Planets: Selected Poems, 1972–1989, 1995; The Poetry and Poetics of Ancient Japan (ed.), 1997; Love Songs from the Man'yoshu: Selections from a Japanese Classic, 2000. *Honours:* Officier, Ordre des Arts et des Lettres, 1993; Asahi Prize, 1996; Imperial Award, Japanese Art Acad., 1996; Designated 'Person of Cultural Merit', Japanese government, 1997. *Address:* 2-18-1-2606, Chiyoda-Ku, Lidabashi, Tokyo 102-0072, Japan.

OPIE, Iona; Writer; b. 13 Oct. 1923, Colchester, England; m. Peter Opie 2 Sept. 1943 (deceased); two s. one d. *Publications:* A Dictionary of Superstitions (with Moira Tatem), 1989; The People in the Playground, 1993. With Peter Opie: The Oxford Dictionary of Nursery Rhymes, 1951; The Oxford Nursery Rhyme Book, 1955; The Lore and Language of Schoolchildren, 1959; Puffin Book of Nursery Rhymes, 1963; A Family Book of Nursery Rhymes, 1964; Children's Games in Street and Playground, 1969; The Oxford Book of Children's Verse, 1973; Three Centuries of Nursery Rhymes and Poetry for Children, 1973; The Classic Fairy Tales, 1974; A Nursery Companion, 1980; The Oxford Book of Narrative Verse, 1983; The Singing Game, 1985; Babies: an unsentimental anthology, 1990; Children's Games with Things, 1997. *Honours:* Hon. MA, Oxon, 1962, Open University, 1987; Hon. DLitt, University of Southampton, 1987, University of Nottingham, 1991; Hon. Doctorate, University of Surrey, 1997, CBE, 1999. *Address:* Mells House, Liss, Hampshire GU33 6JQ, England.

O'REILLY, Kenneth; Historian and Writer; b. 24 Oct. 1951, New York, NY, USA; m. Maureen Alice Moore, 7 Aug. 1976, three s. *Education:* BA, University of Detroit, 1973; MA, Central Michigan University, 1975; PhD, Marquette University, 1981. *Career:* Prof. of History, University of Alaska, Anchorage, 1983–; Writer. *Publications:* Hoover and the Un-Americans: The FBI, HUAC, and the Red Menace, 1983; 'Racial Matters': The FBI's Secret File on Black America, 1960–1972, 1989; Black Americans: The FBI Files, 1994; Nixon's Piano: Presidents and Racial Politics from Washington to Clinton, 1995. *Literary Agent:* c/o Free Press, 1230 Avenue of the Americas, New York, NY 10020, USA. *Address:* 18728 Snowy Plover, Anchorage, AK 99516, USA.

ORFALEA, Gregory Michael; Writer and Ed.; b. 9 Aug. 1949, Los Angeles, CA, USA; m. Eileen Rogers, 4 Aug. 1984, three s. *Education:* AB, English, Georgetown University; MFA, Creative Writing, University of Alaska. *Career:* Reporter, Northern Virginia Sun, 1971–72; Prof., Santa Barbara City College, CA, 1974–76; Ed., Political Focus, 1979–81, Small Business Administration, 1985–91, Resolution Trust Corporation, 1991–95, Federal Deposit Insurance Corporation, 1995–96, Comptroller of the Currency, 1996–97, Freddie Mac, 1997–; mem. American PEN. *Publications:* Before the Flames, 1988; The Capital of Solitude, 1988; Grape Leaves, 1988; Imagining America: Stories of the Promised Land, 1991; Messengers of the Lost Battalion, 1997. Contributions: Washington Post; TriQuarterly; Cleveland Plain-Dealer; Christian Science Monitor. *Honours:* California Arts Council Award, 1976; American Middle East Peace Research Award, 1983; District of Columbia Commission on the Arts and Humanities Awards, 1991, 1993. *Address:* 3220 Patterson St NW, Washington, DC 20015, USA.

ORGEL, Doris, (Doris Adelberg); Writer; b. 15 Feb. 1929, Vienna, Austria; m. Shelley Orgel, 25 June 1949, two s. one d. *Education:* BA, Barnard College, 1960. *Career:* Senior Staff Writer, Ed., Publications and Media Group, Bank Sheer College of Education, 1961–. *Publications:* Sarah's Room, 1963; The Devil in Vienna, 1978; My War with Mrs Galloway, 1985; Whiskers Once and Always, 1986; Midnight Soup and a Witch's Hat, 1987; Starring Becky Suslow, 1989; Nobodies and Somebodies, 1991; Next Time I Will, 1993; The Mouse Who Wanted To Marry, 1993; Ariadne, Awake, 1994. Young Adult Fiction: Risking Love, 1985; Crack in the Heart, 1989. Other: Some 30 works. Contributions: Cricket magazine. *Address:* c/o Writers House, 21 W 26th St, New York, NY 10010, USA.

ORLANDERSMITH, Dael; American playwright and performer; b. Harlem, NY. *Stage appearances:* Macbeth, Romeo and Juliet, Raisin in the Sun, Goin' for Dolo, US, European and Australian tours with the Nuyorican Poets' Cafe, Leftover Life to Kill (solo show). *Plays written:* Beauty's Daughter 1993, Liar Liar 1994, Monster, The Gimmick 1997, Yellowman 2002. *Publications:* Lone Dancer Underground (novel). *Honours:* OBIE Award 1994, New York Foundation for the Arts Fellowship, Helen Merrill Award for Emerging Playwrights. *Address:* c/o Random House Inc, 1745 Broadway, Third Floor, New York, NY 10019, USA. *Website:* www .randomhouse.com.

ORLEDGE, Robert Francis Nicholas; Prof. of Music and Author; b. 5 Jan. 1948, Bath, Somerset, England. *Education:* Assoc., Royal College of Organists, 1964; Clare College, Cambridge; BA, Music, 1968, MA, 1972, PhD, 1973, University of Cambridge. *Career:* Prof. of Music, University of Liverpool; mem. Royal Musical Asscn; Centre de Documentation Claude Debussy; Asscn des Amis de Charles Koechlin; Fondation Erik Satie. *Publications:* Gabriel Fauré, 1979; Debussy and the Theatre, 1982; Charles Koechlin (1867–1950): His Life and Works, 1989; Satie the Composer, 1990; Satie Remembered, 1995. Contributions: Music and Letters; Musical Quarterly; Musical Times; Music Review; Current Musicology; Journal of the Royal Musical Asscn. *Address:* Windermere House, Windermere Terrace, Liverpool L8 3SB, England.

ORMEROD, Roger; Author; b. 17 April 1920, Wolverhampton, Staffordshire, England. *Publications:* Time to Kill, 1974; The Silence of the Night, 1974; Full Fury, 1975; A Spoonful of Luger, 1975; Sealed with a Loving Kill, 1976; The Colour of Fear, 1976; A Glimpse of Death, 1976; Too Late for the Funeral, 1977; The Murder Come to Mind, 1977; A Dip into Murder, 1978; The Weight of Evidence, 1978; The Bright Face of Danger, 1979; The Amnesia Trap, 1979; Cart Before the Hearse, 1979; More Dead than Alive, 1980; Double Take, 1980; One Breathless Hour, 1981; Face Value, 1983; Seeing Red, 1984; The Hanging Doll Murder, 1984; Dead Ringer, 1985; Still Life with Pistol, 1986; A Death to Remember, 1986; An Alibi Too Soon, 1987; The Second Jeopardy, 1987; An Open Window, 1988; By Death Possessed, 1988; Guilt on the Lily, 1989; Death of an Innocent, 1989; No Sign of Life, 1990; Hung in the Blance, 1990; Farewell Gesture, 1990. *Address:* c/o Constable, 10 Orange St, London WC2H 7EG, England.

ORMSBY, Frank; Poet, Writer and Ed.; b. 30 Oct. 1947, Enniskillen, Co Fermanagh, Northern Ireland. *Education:* BA, English, 1970, MA, 1971, Queen's University, Belfast. *Career:* Ed., The Honest Ulsterman, 1969–89. *Publications:* A Store of Candles, 1977; Poets from the North of Ireland (ed.), 1979; A Northern Spring, 1986; Northern Windows: An Anthology of Ulster Autobiography (ed.), 1987; The Long Embrace: Twentieth Century Irish Love Poems (ed.), 1987; Thine in Storm and Calm: An Amanda McKittrick Ros Reader (ed.), 1988; The Collected Poems of John Hewitt (ed.), 1991; A Rage for Order: Poetry of the Northern Ireland Troubles (ed.), 1992; The Ghost Train, 1995; The Hip Flask: Short Poems from Ireland (ed.), 2000. *Address:* 33 North Circular Rd, Belfast BT15 5HD, Northern Ireland.

O'ROURKE, Patrick Jake, BA, MA; writer and editor; b. 14 Nov. 1947, Toledo, OH, USA; m. 1st Amy Lumet 1990 (divorced 1992); m. 2nd Christina Mallon 1995; two c. *Education:* Miami University, Oxford, OH, Johns Hopkins University. *Career:* writer, 1972–81, Ed.-in-Chief, 1978–81, National Lampoon; Correspondent, Rolling Stone, 1985–2001, Atlantic Monthly, 2001–. *Publications:* Modern Manners, 1983; The Bachelor Home Companion, 1987; Republican Party Reptile, 1987; Holidays in Hell, 1989; Parliament of Whores, 1991; Give War a Chance, 1992; All the Trouble in the World, 1994; Age and Guile, 1995; Eat the Rich, 1998; The CEO of the Sofa, 2001. Contributions: periodicals. *Address:* c/o Atlantic Monthly, 77 N Washington Street, Boston, MA 02114, USA.

ORR, Gregory (Simpson); Prof. of English, Poet and Writer; b. 3 Feb. 1947, Albany, New York, USA; m. Trisha Winer, 1973, two d. *Education:* BA, Antioch College, 1969; MFA, Columbia University, 1972. *Career:* Asst Prof., 1975–80, Assoc. Prof., 1980–88, Prof. of English, 1988–, University of Virginia; Poetry Consultant, Virginia Quarterly Review, 1976–; Visiting Writer, University of Hawaii at Manoa, 1982. *Publications:* Poetry: Burning the Empty Nests, 1973; Gathering the Bones Together, 1975; Salt Wings, 1980; The Red House, 1980; We Must Make a Kingdom of It, 1986; New and Selected Poems, 1988; City of Salt, 1995. Non-Fiction: Stanley Kunitz: An Introduction to the Poetry, 1985; Richer Entanglements: Essays and Notes on Poetry and Poems, 1993. *Honours:* Acad. of American Poets Prize, 1970; YM-YWHA Discovery Award, 1970; Bread Loaf Writers Conference Transatlantic Review Award, 1976; Guggenheim Fellowship, 1977; National Endowment for the Arts Fellowships, 1978, 1989; Fulbright Grant, 1983. *Address:* c/o Dept of English, University of Virginia, Charlottesville, VA 22903, USA.

ORSENNA, Erik, (Erik Arnoult); Author and Academic; b. 22 March 1947, Paris, France; m. 2nd Catherine Clavier; one s. one d. *Education:* Ecole Saint-Jean de Béthune, Versailles; Univ. de Sciences Économiques; Inst. des Sciences Politiques, Paris. *Career:* lecturer, Inst. d'Etudes Politiques, Paris, 1975–80, Ecole Normale Supérieure, 1977–81; Sr Lecturer, Univ. de Paris, 1978–81; Tech. Adviser to Ministry of Co-operation and Devt, 1981–83, Cultural Adviser to Presidency, 1983–85, Personal Adviser to Minister of Foreign Affairs, 1990–92; Literary Ed., Editions Ramsay, 1977–81; Counsel, Conseil d'Etat, 1985–, Sr mem., 2000–; Pres. Centre, Int. de la Mer, 1991–, Ecole Nat. Supérieure du Paysage, 1995–; Vice-Pres., Cytale Soc., 2000–; mem. Acad. Française, 1998. *Publications:* Espace national et déséquilibre monétaire, 1977; La Vie comme à Lausanne, 1997; Une comédie française, 1980; L'Exposition coloniale, 1988; Grand Amour, 1993; Histoire du monde en neuf guitares, 1996; Longtemps, 1998; Portrait d'un homme heureux, André Le Nôtre 1613–1700, 2000; La Grammaire est une chanson donce, 2001. *Honours:* Prix Goncourt, 1988. *Address:* Conseil d'Etat, Place du Palais Royal, 75001 Paris, France; Institut de France, 23 quai Conti, 75006 Paris, France.

ORSZAG-LAND, Thomas; Writer, Poet and Trans; b. 12 Jan. 1938, Budapest, Hungary. *Career:* mem. Foreign Press Asscn; International PEN, fellow; Royal Institute of International Affairs; Society of Authors. *Publications:* Berlin Proposal, 1990; Free Women, 1991; Tales of Matriarchy, 1998. Translator: Bluebeard's Castle, by Bartok, 1988; Splendid Stags, by Bartok, 1992; 33 Poems by Radnoti, 1992; Poems by Mezei, 1995. Contributions: newspapers and reviews. *Address:* PO Box 1213, London, N6 6HZ, England.

ORTIZ, Simon J(oseph); Poet and Writer; b. 27 May 1941, Albuquerque, New Mexico, USA; m. Marlene Foster, Dec. 1981, divorced Sept. 1984, three c. *Education:* Fort Lewis College, 1961–62; University of New Mexico, 1966–68; University of Iowa, 1968–69. *Career:* Instructor, San Diego State University, 1974, Institute of American Arts, Santa Fe, New Mexico, 1974, Navajo Community College, Tsaile, AZ, 1975–77, College of Marin, Kentfield, CA, 1976–79, University of New Mexico, Albuquerque, 1979–81, Sinte Gleska College, Mission, SD, 1985–86, Lewis and Clark College, Portland, Oregon, 1990; Consulting Ed., Navajo Comunity College Press, Tsaile, 1982–83, Pueblo of Acoma Press, Acoma, New Mexico, 1982–84; Arts Coordinator, Metropolitan Arts Commission, Portland, Oregon, 1990. *Publications:* Naked in the Wind (poems), 1971; Going for the Rain (poems), 1976; A Good Journey (poems), 1977; Howbah Indians (short stories), 1978; Song, Poetry, Language (essays), 1978; Fight Back: For the Sake of the People, For the Sake of the Land (poems and prose), 1980; From Sand Creek: Rising in This Heart Which is Our America (poems), 1981; A Poem is a Journey, 1981; The Importance of Childhood, 1982; Fightin': New and Collected Stories, 1983; Woven Stone: A 3-in-1 Volume of Poetry and Prose, 1991; After and Before the Lightning (poems), 1994. Editor: Califa: The California Poetry (co-ed.), 1978; A Ceremony of Brotherhood (co-ed.), 1980; Earth Power Coming (anthology of Native American short fiction), 1983. Contributions: various anthologies and textbooks. *Honours:* National Endowment for the Arts Discovery Award, 1969, and Fellowship, 1981; Honored Poet, White House Salute to Poetry and American Poets, 1980; New Mexico Humanities Council Humanitarian Award for Literary Achievement, 1989.

OSBORN, Karen; Novelist and Poet; b. 26 April 1954, Chicago, IL, USA; m. Michael Jenkins 21 May 1983; two d. *Education:* BA, cum laude, Hollins College, 1979; MFA, University of Arkansas at Fayetteville, 1983. *Career:* Poet, 1979–83, Dir, 1982–83, Arkansas Poetry in the Schools; Instructor of English, Clemson University, 1983–87; Part-time Instructor of English, University of Kentucky, 1988–93; various workshops and readings. *Publications:* Patchwork, 1991; Between Earth and Sky, 1996; The River Road, 2003. Contributions: numerous anthologies, including: Jumping Pond: Poems and Stories from the Ozarks; Cardinal: A Contemporary Anthology; Hollins Anthology; Poems to numerous periodicals, including: Artemis; Mid American Review; Seattle Review; Tar River Poetry; Embers; Southern Review; Kansas Quarterly; Poet Lore; Passages North; Montana Review; Centennial Review; Wisconsin Review. *Honours:* Hollins Literary Festival Awards for Poetry, for Fiction, 1979; Nancy Thorp Prize for Poetry, 1979; Mary Vincent Long Award, Distinguished Literary Achievement, 1979; Kentucky Foundation for Women Grant, 1991; Al Smith Artists Fellowship Award for Fiction, Kentucky Arts Council, 1991; New York Times Notable Book, 1991. *Address:* c/o Gelfman Shneider, 250 W 57th St, New York, NY 10107, USA. *Website:* www.karenosborn.com.

OSBORNE, Charles (Thomas); Writer, Critic and Poet; b. 24 Nov. 1927, Brisbane, Qld, Australia. *Education:* Griffith University, 1944. *Career:* Asst Ed., London Magazine, 1968–66; Asst Literary Dir, 1966–71, Dir, 1971–86, Arts Council of Great Britain; Opera Critic, Jewish Chronicle, 1985–; Chief Theatre Critic, Daily Telegraph, 1986–92; mem. Critics' Circle; PEN; FRSL. *Publications:* The Gentle Planet, 1957; Swansong, 1968; The Complete Operas of Verdi, 1969; W. H. Auden: The Life of a Poet, 1980; Letter to W. H. Auden and Other Poems, 1984; Giving It Way, 1986; The Bel Canto Operas, 1994; The Pink Danube, 1998. Contributions: anthologies, newspapers and journals. *Honours:* Gold Medal, 1993. *Address:* 125 St George's Rd, London SE1 6HY, England.

OSBORNE, Maggie, (Margaret Ellen Osborne); Writer; b. 10 June 1941, Los Angeles, CA, USA; m. George M. Osborne II, 27 April 1972, one s. *Publications:* Alexa, 1980; Salem's Daughter, 1981; Portrait in Passion, 1981; Yankee Princess, 1982; Rage to Love, 1983; Flight of Fancy, 1984; Castles and Fairy Tales, 1986; Winter Magic, 1986; The Heart Club, 1987; Where There's Smoke, 1987; Chase the Heart, 1987; Heart's Desire, 1988; Dear Santa, 1989; Partners (with Carolyn Bransford), 1989; Jigsaw, 1990; American Pie, 1990; Lady Reluctant, 1991; Emerald Rain, 1991; Happy New Year Darling, 1992; Murder By the Book, 1992; The Pirate and His Lady, 1992; Cache Poor, 1993; A Wish and a Kiss, 1993; The Accidental Princess, 1994; The Drop in Bride, 1994; The Wives of Bowie Stone, 1994; Silver Lining, 2000; I Do, I Do, I Do, 2000. *Address:* Box 868, Dillon, CO 80435, USA.

OSBORNE, Mary Pope; Writer; b. 20 May 1949, Fort Sill, Oklahoma, USA; m. Will Osborne, 16 May 1976. *Education:* BA, University of North Carolina. *Career:* mem. Pres., Authors' Guild Inc., 1993–97. *Publications:* Run, Run, As Fast As You Can, 1982; Love Always, Blue, 1983; Best Wishes, Joe Brady, 1984; Mo to the Rescue, 1985; Last One Home, 1986; Beauty and the Beast, 1987; Christopher Columbus, Admiral of the Ocean Sea, 1987;

Pandora's Box, 1987; Jason and the Argonauts, 1988; The Deadly Power of Medusa (with Will Osborne), 1988; Favorite Greek Myths, 1989; A Visit to Sleep's House, 1989; Mo and His Friends, 1989; American Tall Tales, 1990; Moonhorse, 1991; Spider Kane Series, 1992; Magic Tree House Series 1993–2004; Mermaid Tales, 1993; Molly and the Prince, 1994; Haunted Waters, 1994; Favourite Norse Myths, 1996; One World, Many Religions, 1996; Rockinghorse Christmas, 1997; Favourite Medieval Tales, 1998; Standing in the Light, 1998; The Life of Jesus, 1998, Adaline Falling Star 2000, My Secret War 2001, My Brother's Keeper 2001, After the Rain 2001, Kate and the Beanstalk 2001, The Brave Little Seamstress 2002, New York's Bravest 2002, Happy Birthday, America 2003, Tales from the Odyssey Series 2002–2005. *Honours:* Distinguished Alumnus Award, University of North Carolina, 1994. *Literary Agent:* Brandt & Hochman Literary Agents Inc, 1501 Broadway, New York, NY 10036, USA.

OSERS, Ewald; Poet, Writer and Trans; b. 13 May 1917, Prague, Czechoslovakia; m. Mary Harman 3 June 1942; one s. one d. *Education:* University of Prague; BA, University of London. *Career:* Editorial Dir, Babel, 1979–87; mem. International PEN, English Centre, fellow; Poetry Society; FRSL; Society of Authors. *Publications:* Poetry: Wish You Were Here, 1976; Arrive Where We Started, 1995. Translator: over 140 books, incl. 42 vols of poetry. Contributions: magazines. *Honours:* Cyril and Methodius Order, First Class, Bulgaria, 1987; European Poetry Trans. Prize, 1987; Vitezlaw Nezval Medal, Czechoslovakia, 1987; Golden Pen, Macedonia, 1988; Hon. DPhil hc, Palacky Univ., Olomouc, 1990; Officer's Cross of Merit, Germany, 1991; Order of Merit, Czech Republic, 1997; San Masaryk Award, 2001; Premma Bohemica, 2001. *Address:* 33 Reades Lane, Sonning Common, Reading, Berkshire RG4 9LL, England.

O'SIADHAIL, Micheal, BA, MLitt; poet and writer; b. 12 Jan. 1947, Dublin, Ireland; m. Brid Carroll 1970. *Education:* Trinity Coll., Dublin, Univ. of Oslo. *Career:* Lecturer, Trinity College, Dublin, 1969–73; Prof., Dublin Institute for Advanced Studies, 1974–87; Visiting Prof., University of Iceland, 1982; Ed., Poetry Ireland Review, 1989–91; Ireland's Advisory Committee on Cultural Relations 1990–97; mem. Aosdána, founder-mem., 1982–; Arts Council of the Republic of Ireland, 1988–93; Dublin International Writers' Festival, board mem.; Ireland Literary Exchange, founder-chair., 1992–99. *Publications:* Poetry: Springnight, 1983; The Image Wheel, 1985; The Chosen Garden, 1990; Hail! Madam Jazz: New and Selected Poems, 1992; A Fragile City, 1995; Our Double Time, 1998; Poems 1975–1995, 1999; The Gossamer Wall: Poems in Witness to the Holocaust, 2002. Other: Learning Irish, 1980; Modern Irish, 1989. *Honours:* Irish-American Cultural Prize for Poetry, 1982; Poetry Book of the Year, Sunday Tribune, 1992; Marten Toonder Prize for Literature, 1998. *Address:* 5 Trimleston Avenue, Booterstown, Co Dublin, Ireland. *Website:* www .osiadhail.com.

OSTRIKER, Alicia Suskin; Prof. of English and Creative Writing, Poet and Writer; b. 11 Nov. 1937, New York, NY, USA; m. Jeremiah P. Ostriker, 2 Dec. 1958, one s. two d. *Education:* BA, Brandeis University, 1959; MA, 1960, PhD, 1964, University of Wisconsin. *Career:* Asst Prof., 1965–68, Assoc. Prof., 1968–72, Prof. of English and Creative Writing, 1972–, Rutgers University; mem. MLA; PEN; Poetry Society of America, board of governors, 1988–91. *Publications:* Poetry: Songs, 1969; Once More Out of Darkness and Other Poems, 1974; A Dream of Springtime: Poems, 1970–77, 1978; The Mother-Child Papers, 1980; A Woman Under the Surface, 1983; The Imaginary Lover, 1986; Green Age, 1989; The Crack in Everything, 1996; The Little Space: Poems Selected and New 1968–1998, 1998. Criticism: Vision and Verse in William Blake, 1965; Writing Like a Woman, 1982; Stealing the Language, 1986; Feminist Revision and the Bible, 1993; The Nakedness of the Fathers: Biblical Visions and Revisions, 1994; Dancing at the Devil's Party: Essays of Poetry, Politics and the Erotic, 2000. Contributions: Professional journals and general publications. *Honours:* National Endowment for the Arts Fellowship, 1977; Guggenheim Fellowship, 1984–85; William Carlos Williams Prize, Poetry Society of America, 1986; Strousse Poetry Prize, Prairie Schooner, 1987; Anna Rosenberg Poetry Award, 1994; Paterson Poetry Prize, 1996; San Francisco State Poetry Center Award, 1997; Bookman News Book of the Year, 1998. *Address:* 33 Philip Dr., Princeton, NJ 08540, USA.

OSTROM, Hans (Ansgar); Prof. of English, Writer and Poet; b. 29 Jan. 1954, Grass Valley, CA, USA; m. Jacquelyn Bacon, 18 July 1983, one s. *Education:* BA, English, 1975, MA, English, 1979, PhD, English, 1982, University of California at Davis. *Career:* Faculty, University of California at Davis, 1977–80, 1981–83; Visiting Lecturer in American Studies, Johannes Gutenberg University, Mainz, 1980–81; Prof. of English, University of Puget Sound, Tacoma, Washington, 1983–; Fulbright Senior Lecturer, University of Uppsala, 1994; mem. American Asscn of University Profs; Conference on College Composition and Communication; MLA; National Book Critics Circle; National Council of Teachers of English. *Publications:* The Living Language: A Reader (co-ed.), 1984; Leigh Hunt: A Reference Guide (with Tim Lulofs), 1985; Spectrum: A Reader (co-ed.), 1987; Lives and Moments: An Introduction to Short Fiction, 1991; Three to Get Ready (novel), 1991; Langston Hughes: A Study of the Short Fiction, 1993; Colors of a Different Horse (ed. with Wendy Bishop), 1994; Water's Night (poems with Wendy Bishop), 1994; Genres of Writing: Mapping the Territories of Discourse (ed. with Wendy Bishop), 1997; The Coast Starlight (poems), 1998. Contributions: books, journals, reviews, and magazines. *Honours:* First Prize, Harvest Awards, University of Houston, 1978; Grand Prize, Ina Coolbrith Memorial Award, 1979; First Prize, Warren Eyster Competition, New Delta Review, 1985; Second Prize, Redbook Magazine Annual Fiction Contest, 1985; John Lantz Fellowship, University of Puget Sound, 1996–97. *Address:* c/o Dept of English, University of Puget Sound, Tacoma, WA 98416, USA.

O'SULLIVAN, Vincent (Gerard); Poet, Writer, Dramatist and Ed.; b. 28 Sept. 1937, Auckland, New Zealand. *Education:* MA, University of Auckland, 1959; BLitt, Lincoln College, Oxford, 1962. *Publications:* In Quiet, 1956; Opinions: Chapters on Gissing, Rolfe, Wilde, Unicorn, 1959; Our Burning Time, 1965; Revenants, 1969; An Anthology of Twentieth Century New Zealand Poetry (ed.), 1970; Bearings, 1973; New Zealand Poetry in the Sixties, 1973; Katherine Mansfield's New Zealand, 1975; New Zealand Short Stories (ed.), 1975; From the Indian Funeral, 1976; James K. Baxter, 1976; Miracle: A Romance, 1976; Butcher & Co, 1977; The Boy, the Bridge, the River, 1978; Brother Jonathan, Brother Kafka, 1980; Dandy Edison for Lunch and Other Stories, 1981; The Rose Ballroom and Other Poems, 1982; The Butcher Papers, 1982; The Oxford Book of New Zealand Writing Since 1945 (ed. with MacDonald P. Jackson), 1983; The Collected Letters of Katherine Mansfield (ed. with Margaret Scott), three vols, 1984–96; Shuriken (play), 1985; Survivals, 1986; The Pilate Tapes, 1986; Poems of Katherine Mansfield (ed.), 1988; Jones and Jones (play), 1989; Billy, 1990; The Snow in Spain, 1990; Palms and Minarets: Selected Stories, 1992; Selected Poems, 1992; The Oxford Book of New Zealand Short Stories (ed.), 1994; Believers to the Bright Coast, 1998. *Honours:* Jessie Mackay Award, 1965; Farmers Poetry Prize, 1967; New Zealand Book Award, 1981. *Address:* Pukeroro, RD 3, Hamilton, New Zealand.

OSWALD, Debra; Australian playwright and writer; two s. *Education:* Australian Nat. Univ., Australian Film and Television School. *Plays:* Going Under 1983, Dags 1986, Lumps 1993, Gary's House 1996, Sweet Road 2000, Mr Bailey's Minder 2004. *Writing for television:* Police Rescue, Palace of Dreams, Bananas in Pyjamas, Sweet and Sour, Dancing Daze, The Secret Life of Us. *Publications include:* juvenile fiction: The Return of the Baked Bean 1990, Nathan and the Ice Rockets 1998, Frank and the Emergency Joke 2000, The Redback Leftovers 2000, The Fifth Quest 2002. *Literary Agent:* RGM Associates, PO Box 128, Surry Hills, NSW 2010, Australia. *Telephone:* (2) 9281-3911. *Fax:* (2) 9281-4705. *E-mail:* info@rgm.com.au. *Website:* www.rgm.com.au.

OTCHAKOVSKY-LAURENS, Paul, LenD; French publisher; b. 10 Oct. 1944, Valreas, Vaucluse; adopted s. of Berthe Laurens; m. Monique Pierret 1970; one s. one d. *Education:* Coll. and Lycée de Sablé sur Sarthe, Coll. Montalembert de Courbevoie, Coll. St Croix de Neuilly and Faculté de Droit, Paris. *Career:* Reader, Editions Christian Bourgois 1969–70; Dir of Collection, Editions Flammarion 1970–77; Dir of Collections, then Dir of Dept Editions Hachette 1977–82; Pres. Dir-Gen. Editions P.O.L. 1983–. *Honours:* Commdr Ordre des Arts et des Lettres, Chevalier Légion d'honneur. *Address:* Editions P.O.L., 33 rue Saint-André-des-Arts, 75006 Paris, France. *Telephone:* 1-43-54-21-20. *E-mail:* otchakov@pol-editeur.fr (Office).

OTTEN, Charlotte F(ennema); Prof. of English (retd), Poet and Writer; b. 1 March 1926, Chicago, IL, USA; m. Robert T. Otten, 21 Dec. 1948, two s. *Education:* AB, English and American Language and Literature, Calvin College, Grand Rapids, 1949; MA, English and American Language and Literature, 1969, PhD, English Literature and Language, 1971, Michigan State University. *Career:* Assoc. Prof. of English, Grand Valley State University, Allendale, Michigan, 1971–77; Lecturer on Women and Literature, University of Michigan Extension Center, 1972; Prof. of English, Calvin College, Grand Rapids, 1977–91; mem. Milton Society of America; MLA; Shakespeare Asscn of America; Society for Literature and Science; Society for Textual Scholarship; Society of Children's Book Writers and Illustrators. *Publications:* Environ'd with Eternity: God, Poems, and Plants in Sixteenth and Seventeenth Century England, 1985; A Lycanthropy Reader: Werewolves in Western Culture, 1986; The Voice of the Narrator in Children's Literature (ed. with Gary D. Schmidt), 1989; English Women's Voices, 1540–1700, 1992; The Virago Book of Birth Poetry, 1993; The Book of Birth Poetry, 1995; January Rides the Wind, 1997; The Literary Werewolf: An Anthology, 2002; Something Sweeter than Honey, 2002. Contributions: scholarly books and journals and poetry journals. *Honours:* several grants and fellowships; Eds' Choice, Booklist, 1997. *Address:* c/o Dept of English, Calvin College, 3201 Burton St SE, Grand Rapids, MI 49546, USA.

OUELLETTE, (Marie Léonne) Francine, DFA; writer; b. 11 March 1947, Montréal, QC, Canada; one d. *Career:* mem. Union des écrivaines et des écrivains québécois. *Publications:* Au Nom du Père et du Fils, 1984; Le Sorcier, 1985; Sire Gaby du Lac, 1989; Les Ailes du Destin, 1992; Le Grand Blanc, 1993; L'Oiseau Invisible, 1994; BIP, 1995. *Honours:* France-Québec, Jean Hamelin, 1986; Prix, Du Grand Public, 1993. *Address:* PO Box 30, 1044 ch Presquîle, Lac des Iles, QC J0W 1J0, Canada.

OUOLOGUEM, Yambo, (Utto Rodolph); Writer and Poet; b. 1940, Bandiagary, Dogon, French Sudan (now Mali). *Education:* Doctorate in sociology. *Career:* Teacher, Lycée de Charenton, Paris, 1964–66. *Publications:* Le Devoir de violence (Bound to Violence), 1968; Lettre ouverte à la France-nègre, 1969; Les Milles et un bibles du sexe (as Utto Rodolph), 1969; Terres du Soleil (with others), 1971. Contributions: Nouvelle somme. *Honours:* Prix Théophraste-Renaudot, 1968.

OUTERS, Jean-Luc; writer; b. 5 March 1949, Belgium. *Publications:* L'ordre du jour (novel) 1987, Avec le temps (essay) 1993, Corps de métier (novel) 1993, La place du mort (novel) 1995, La compagnie des eaux (novel) 2001, Le bureau de l'heure (novel) 2004; contrib. numerous articles in Le Soir, La Libre Belgique, Libération. *Honours:* Prix Rossel 1993, Prix AT&T 1995. *Address:* c/o Actes Sud, BP 38, 13633 Arles Cedex, France.

OUTRAM, Richard Daley, BA; poet and publisher; b. 9 April 1930, Oshawa, ON, Canada; m. Barbara Howard 1957. *Education:* Victoria Coll., Univ. of Toronto. *Career:* co-founder (with Barbara Howard), The Gauntlet Press 1959; reading and exhibition of published work, Nat. Library of Canada 1986; mem. PEN Canada, Arts and Letters Club of Toronto. *Publications:* Eight Poems, 1959; Exsulate, Jubilate, 1966; Creatures, 1972; Seer, 1973; Thresholds, 1974; Locus, 1974; Turns and Other Poems, 1975; Arbor, 1976; The Promise of Light, 1979; Selected Poems 1960–1980, 1984; Man in Love, 1985; Benedict Abroad, 1988; Hiram and Jenny, 1989; Mogul Recollected, 1993; Around and About the Toronto Islands, 1993; Peripatetics, 1994; Tradecraft, 1994; Eros Descending, 1995. *Honours:* City of Toronto Book Award 1999. *Address:* 226 Roslin Avenue, Toronto, ON M4N 1Z6, Canada.

OVADIA, Moni; Playwright and Musician; b. 1946, Plovdiv, Bulgaria. *Publications:* Perché no?, 1996; Oylem Goylem, 1998; L'ebreo che ride, 1998; La porta di sion, 1999; Ballata di fine millennio, 1999; Speriamo che tenga, 2001; Le Baladin du monde yiddish, 2002; Vai a te stesso, 2002. *Address:* c/o Giulio Einaudi Editore, Via Biancamano 2, 10121 Turin, Italy. *Website:* www.moniovadia.it.

OVENDEN, Graham Stuart, MA, ARCA, ARCM; British art historian, artist and poet; b. 11 Feb. 1943, Alresford, Hants.; m. Ann. D. Gilmore 1969; one s. one d. *Education:* Alresford Dames School, Itchen Grammar School, Southampton, Southampton Coll. of Art, Royal Coll. of Music and Royal Coll. of Art. *Career:* corresp. and critic, Architecture Design Magazine; Founder mem. South West Acad. of Fine and Applied Art. *Publications:* Illustrators of Alice 1971, Victorian Children 1972, Clementina, Lady Harwarden 1973, Pre-Raphaelite Photography 1972, Victorian Erotic Photography 1973, Aspects of Lolita 1975, A Victorian Album (with Lord David Cecil) 1976, Satirical Poems and Others 1983, The Marble Mirror (poems) 1984, Lewis Carroll Photographer 1984; Graham Ovenden... A Monograph with Essays by Laurie Lee, etc. 1987, Sold With All Faults (poems) 1991; photographs: Alphonse Mucha 1973, Hill & Adamson 1973, Graham Ovenden – Childhood Streets (Photographs 1956–64) 1998; contribs on art to numerous journals. *Address:* Barley Splatt, Panters Bridge, Mount, nr Bodmin, Cornwall, England.

OVERY, Paul (Vivian); Art Critic and Historian and Writer; b. 14 Feb. 1940, Dorchester, England; m. Tag Gronberg 1992. *Education:* BA, 1962, MA, 1966, King's College, Cambridge. *Career:* Art Critic, The Listener, London, 1966–68, The Financial Times, London, 1968–70; Literary Ed., New Society, London, 1970–71; Chief Art Critic, The Times, London, 1973–78; Freelance critic and writer, 1978–; Reader in the History and Theory of Moderism, Middlesex University, 1997–; mem. National Union of Journalists; Society of Authors; International Asscn of Art Critics. *Publications:* Edouard Manet, 1967; De Stijl, 1969; Kandinsky: The Language of the Eye, 1969; Paul Neagu: A Generative Context, 1981; The Rietveld Schroder House (co-author), 1988; The Complete Rietveld Furniture (with Peter Vöge), 1993; The Cell in the City (essay), in Cubism and Architecture, 1997; Norman Foster: 30 Colours (co-author), 1998. Contributions: periodicals and journals. *Honours:* Leverhulme Research Fellowship, 1984–85. *Literary Agent:* Johnson & Alcock Ltd, Clerkenwell House, 45–47 Clerkenwell Green, London EC1R 0HT, England. *Address:* 92 South Hill Park, London NW3 2SN, England.

OVERY, Richard James, BA, MA, PhD, FRHistS, FBA; academic and writer; *Professor of Modern History, King's College London*; b. 23 Dec. 1947, London, England; m. 1st Tessa Coles 1969 (divorced 1976); m. 2nd Jane Giddens 1979 (divorced 1992); m. 3rd Kim Turner 1992; one s. four d. *Education:* Gonville and Caius Coll., Cambridge. *Career:* Research Fellow, Churchill Coll., Cambridge 1972–73; Fellow and Coll. Lecturer, Queens' Coll., Cambridge 1973–79; Asst Univ. Lecturer, Univ. of Cambridge 1976–79; Lecturer 1980–88, Reader 1988–92, Prof. of Modern History 1992–, King's Coll. London. *Publications:* William Morris, Viscount Nuffield 1976, The Air War 1939–1945 1980, The Nazi Economic Recovery 1982, Goering: The Iron Man 1984, The Origins of the Second World War 1987, The Road to War 1989, War and Economy in the Third Reich 1994, The Interwar Crisis 1919–1939 1994, Why the Allies Won 1995, The Penguin Atlas of the Third Reich 1996, The Times Atlas of the Twentieth Century 1996, Bomber Command 1939–1945 1997, Russia's War 1998, The Times History of the World (gen. ed.) 1999, The Battle 2000, The Times History of the Twentieth Century 2003, The Dictators: Hitler's Germany and Stalin's Russia 2004; contrib. to scholarly books and professional journals. *Honours:* T. S. Ashton Prize 1983, Cass Prize for Business Economy 1987. *Address:* c/o Department of History, King's College, University of London, Strand, London, WC2R 2LS, England.

OVESEN, Ellis; Poet, Writer, Artist and Composer; b. 18 July 1923, New Effington, SD, USA; m. Thor Lowe Smith, 27 Aug. 1949, two s. *Education:* MA, cum laude, University of Wisconsin, 1948; California Teacher's Credential, San Jose State University, 1962; Extra classes in poetry writing. *Career:* Teacher of English, University of Wisconsin, 1946–48, San Jose State University, 1962–63; Teaching Poetry, 1963–90; mem. National Writers Club; California Writers Club; Poetry Society of America; California State Poetry Society. *Publications:* Gloried Grass, 1970; Haloed Paths, 1973; To Those Who Love, 1974; The Last Hour: Lives Touch, 1975; A Time for Singing, 1977; A Book of Praises, 1977; Beloved I, 1980, II, 1990; The Green Madonna, 1984; The Flowers of God, 1985; The Keeper of the Word, 1985; The Wing Brush, 1986; The Year of the Snake, 1989; The Year of the Horse, 1990. Contributions: Poet India; Los Altos Town Crier; Paisley Moon; Fresh Hot Bread; Samvedana; Plowman. *Honours:* Los Altos Hills Poet, 1976–90; Hon. Doctorate, World Acad. of Arts and Culture, 1986; Dame of Merit, Knights of Malta, 1988; Golden Poet Awards, 1988, 1989, 1991; Research Fellow, 1992.

OWEN, Deborah; American/British literary agent; b. 8 July 1942, NY; m. David Anthony Llewellyn Owen (now Lord Owen) 1968; two s. one d. *Career:* Founder and Literary Agent Deborah Owen Ltd 1971; Vice-Pres. Cttee Asscn of Authors' Agents 1991–94; mem. Bd of Dirs Viva radio 1993, Advisory Bd London Symphony Orchestra, Fulbright Comm. *Address:* 78 Narrow Street, Limehouse, London, E14 8BP, England. *Telephone:* (20) 7987-5119.

OWEN, Eileen; Poet and Writer; b. 27 Feb. 1949, Concord, NH, USA; m. John D. Owen, 19 June 1971. *Education:* BA, Spanish, University of New Hampshire, 1971; BA, English, 1979, MA, Creative Writing, 1981, University of Washington. *Career:* Artist-in-Residence, Ucross Foundation, WY, 1984. *Publications:* Facing the Weather Side, 1985. Contributions: Reviews and journals. *Honours:* Honourable Mention, Washington Poets Asscn. *Address:* 18508 90th Ave W, Edmonds, WA 98020, USA.

OWEN, Sir Geoffrey David, Kt, MA; British newspaper editor; b. 16 April 1934; m. 1st Dorothy J. Owen 1961 (died 1991); two s. one d.; m. 2nd Miriam Marianna Gross 1993. *Education:* Rugby School and Balliol Coll., Oxford. *Career:* joined Financial Times as feature writer and Industrial Corresp. 1958, US Corresp. 1961, industrial 1967; Exec. Industrial Reorganization Corpn 1967–69; Dir of Admin, Overseas Div. of British Leyland Int. 1969, Dir of Personnel and Admin 1972; Deputy Ed. Financial Times 1974–80, Ed. 1981–90; Dir Business Policy Programme, Centre for Econ. Performance, LSE 1991–98, Sr Fellow Inter-disciplinary Inst. of Man. 1998–; mem. Council Foundation for Mfg and Industries 1993–; Chair. Wincott Foundation 1998–; Dir Laird Group 2000–. *Publications:* Industry in the USA 1966, From Empire to Europe 1999. *Address:* London School of Economics and Political Science, Houghton Street, London, WC2A 2AE, England. *Telephone:* (20) 7405-7686. *Fax:* (20) 7242-0392. *Website:* www.lse.ac.uk (Office).

OWEN, Jan Jarrold; Poet and Writer; b. 18 Aug. 1940, Adelaide, SA, Australia; two s. one d. *Education:* BA, 1963, University of Adelaide; ALAA, 1970. *Career:* Writer-in-Residence, Venice Studio of the Literature Board of the Australian Council, 1989, Tasmanian State Institute of Technology, 1990, Brisbane Grammar School, 1993, Tasmanian Writers Union, 1993, B. R. Whiting Library, Rome, 1994, Rimbun Dahan, Kuala Lumpur, 1997–98; mem. South Australian Writers' Centre. *Publications:* Boy With a Telescope, 1986; Fingerprints on Light, 1990; Blackberry Season, 1993; Night Rainbows, 1994. Contributions: newspapers and magazines. *Honours:* Ian Mudie Prize, 1982; Jessie Litchfield Prize, 1984; Grenfell Henry Lawson Prize, 1985; Harri Jones Memorial Prize, 1986; Anne Elder Award, 1987; Mary Gilmore Prize, 1987; Wesley Michel Wright Poetry Prize, 1992.

OWENS, Agnes; Writer; b. 24 May 1926, Milngavie, Scotland; m. Patrick Owens, 30 Aug. 1964, three s., four d. *Career:* mem. Scottish PEN Centre. *Publications:* Gentlemen of the West, 1985; Lean Tales, 1985; Like Birds in the Wildnerness, 1986; A Working Mother, 1994; People Like That, 1996; For the Love of Willie, 1998; Bad Attitudes, 2003. *Address:* 21 Roy Young Ave, Balloch, Dunbartonshire G83 8ER, Scotland.

OWENS, John Edwin; Political Scientist; b. 13 June 1948, Widnes, Cheshire, England; m. Margaret Owens 1 Oct. 1971; one s. one d. *Education:* BA, Univ. of Reading, 1973; Univ. of Warwick, 1973–75; PhD, Univ. of Essex, 1982. *Career:* Lecturer, Central London Polytechnic, 1978–85, Univ. of Essex, 1985–86; Senior Lecturer, 1986–98, Reader, 1998–2002, Prof. of United States Govt and Politics, 2002–, Univ. of Westminster, London; mem., Editorial Boards, Presidential Studies Quarterly, Journal of Legislative Studies, Politics and Policy; mem. Political Studies Asscn, UK; Legislative Studies Section, American Political Science Asscn; International Political Science Asscn; British Asscn of American Studies. *Publications:* After Full Employment (with John Kearne), 1986; Congress and the Presidency: Institutional Politics in a Separated System (with Michael Foley), 1996; The Republican Takeover of Congress (with Dean McSweeney), 1998; Political Leadership in Context (with Erwin C. Hargrove), 2003. Contributions: American Review of Politics; British Journal of Political Science; Journal of Legislative Studies; Political Studies; Politics and Policy; Roll Call; Times Higher Educational Supplement. *Address:* Centre for the Study of Democracy, University of Westminster, 100 Park Village E, London NW1 3SR, England.

OWENS, Rochelle; Poet, Dramatist, Critic, Prof. and Trans; b. 2 April 1936, New York, NY, USA; m. 1st David Owens, 30 March 1956, divorced 1959; m. 2nd George Economou, 17 June 1962. *Education:* Theatre Arts, New School for Social Research, New York City; University of Montréal, Alliance Française, Paris, New York. *Career:* Visiting Lecturer, University of California at San Diego, 1982; Writer-in-Residence, Brown University, 1989; Adjunct Prof., University of Oklahoma at Norman, 1993–; Poet- and Playwright-in-Residence, Deep South Writers Conference, University of Southwestern Louisiana, 1997; mem. American Society of Composers, Authors, and Publishers; Dramatists' Guild. *Publications:* Poetry: Not Be Essence That Cannot Be, 1961; Four Young Lady Poets (with others), 1962; Salt and Core, 1968; I Am the Babe of Joseph Stalin's Daughter: Poems 1961–1971, 1972; Poems From Joe's Garage, 1973; The Joe 82 Creation Poems, 1974; The Joe Chronicles, Part 2, 1979; Shemuel, 1979; French Light, 1984; Constructs, 1985; W. C. Fields in French Light, 1986; How Much Paint Does the Painting Need, 1988; Black Chalk, 1992; Rubbed Stones and Other Poems, 1994; New and Selected Poems, 1961–1996, 1997; Luca: Discourse on Life and Death, 2001. Plays: Futz and What Came After, 1968; The Karl Marx Play and Others, 1974; Emma Instigated Me, 1976; The Widow and the Colonel, 1977; Mountain Rites, 1978; Chucky's Hunch, 1982; The Passers by Liliane Atlan (trans.), 1993; Plays by Rochelle Owens: Collection of 4 Plays, 2000. Editor: Spontaneous Combustion: Eight New American Plays, 1972. Contributions: anthologies and journals. *Honours:* Rockefeller Grants, 1965, 1976; Obie Awards, 1965, 1967, 1982; Yale School of Drama Fellowship, 1968; American Broadcasting Corporation Fellowship, 1968; Guggenheim Fellowship, 1971; National Endowment for the Arts Award, 1976; Villager Award, 1982; Franco-Anglais Festival de Poésie, Paris, 1991; Rockefeller Foundation Resident Scholar, Bellagio, Italy, 1993; Oklahoma Centre for the Book Award, 1998. *Address:* 1401 Magnolia, Norman, OK 73072, USA.

OXLEY, William; Poet, Writer and Trans; b. 29 April 1939, Manchester, England; m. Patricia Holmes, 13 April 1963, two d. *Education:* Manchester College of Commerce, 1953–55. *Publications:* The Dark Structures, 1967; New Workings, 1969; Passages from Time: Poems from a Life, 1971; The Icon Poems, 1972; Sixteen Days in Autumn (travel), 1972; Opera Vetera, 1973; Mirrors of the Sea, 1973; Eve Free, 1974; Mundane Shell, 1975; Superficies, 1976; The Exile, 1979; The Notebook of Hephaestus and Other Poems, 1981; Poems of a Black Orpheus, 1981; The Synopthegms of a Prophet, 1981; The Idea and Its Imminence, 1982; Of Human Consciousness, 1982; The Cauldron of Inspiration, 1983; A Map of Time, 1984; The Triviad and Other Satires, 1984; The Inner Tapestry, 1985; Vitalism and Celebration, 1987; The Mansands Trilogy, 1988; Mad Tom on Tower Hill, 1988; The Patient Reconstruction of Paradise, 1991; Forest Sequence, 1991; In the Drift of Words, 1992; The Playboy, 1992; Cardboard Troy, 1993; The Hallsands Tragedy, 1993; Collected Longer Poems, 1994; Completing the Picture (ed.), 1995; The Green Crayon Man, 1997; No Accounting for Paradise (autobiog.), 1999; Firework Planet (children's), 2000; Reclaiming the Lyre: New and Selected Poems, 2001. Contributions: anthologies and periodicals. *Address:* 6 The Mount, Furzeham, Brixham, South Devon TQ5 8QY, England.

OZ, Amos, BA; Israeli writer and academic; b. 4 May 1939, Jerusalem, Palestine; m. Nily Zuckerman 1960; one s. two d. *Education:* Hebrew University, Jerusalem. *Career:* Teacher of Literature and Philosophy, Hulda High School, Givat Brenner Regional High School, 1963–86; Visiting Fellow, St Cross College, Oxford, 1969–70; Writer-in-Residence, Hebrew University, Jerusalem, 1975, 1990, University of Tel-Aviv, 1996; Visiting Prof., University of California at Berkeley, 1980; Writer-in-Residence and Prof. of Literature, Colorado College, Colorado Springs, 1984–85; Writer-in-Residence and Visiting Prof. of Literature, Boston University, 1987, Princeton University, 1997; Prof. of Hebrew Literature, 1987–, Agnon Chair in Modern Hebrew, 1990–, Ben-Gurion University of the Negev; Weidenfeld Visiting Prof. of European Comparative Literature, St Anne's College, Oxford, 1998. *Publications:* Where the Jackals Howl, 1965; Elsewhere Perhaps (novel), 1966; My Michael, 1968; Unto Death (two novellas), 1971; Touch the Water, Touch the Wind (novel), 1973; Different People, 1974; The Hill of Evil Counsel (novel), 1976; Soumchi (novel), 1978; Under This Blazing Light, 1979; A Perfect Peace, 1982 (novel); In the Land of Israel (essays), 1983; Black Box, 1987; The Slopes of Lebanon (essays), 1987; To Know a Woman (novel), 1988; Fima (novel), 1991; Don't Pronounce it Night, 1994; Israel, Palestine and Peace (essays), 1994; Panther in the Basement, 1995 (novel); The Story Begins (essays), 1996; All Our Hopes, 1998; The Same Sea, 1999; A Tale of Love and Darkness (memoir), 2002. *Honours:* Officier, Ordre des Arts et des Lettres; Holon Prize, 1965; Brenner Prize, 1976; Bernstein Prize, 1983; Bialik Prize, 1986; Wingate Prize, London, 1988; Prix Fémina, Paris, 1989; Hon. Doctorate, University of Tel-Aviv, 1992; German Publishers' International Peace Prize, 1992; German Friedenspreis, 1992; Hamore Prize, 1993; Israeli Prize for Literature, 1998; Norwegian Authors' Union Freedom of Expression Prize, 2002. *Literary Agent:* Deborah Owen Ltd, 78 Narrow Street, London E14, England.

OZICK, Cynthia; Author, Poet, Dramatist, Critic and Trans; b. 17 April 1928, New York, NY, USA; m. Bernard Hallote, 7 Sept. 1952, one d. *Education:* BA, cum laude, English, New York University, 1949; MA, Ohio State University, 1950. *Career:* mem. American Acad. of Arts and Letters; American Acad. of Arts and Sciences; Authors' League; Dramatists' Guild; PEN. *Publications:* Trust, 1966; The Pagan Rabbi and Other Stories, 1971; Bloodshed and Three Novellas, 1976; Levitation: Five Fictions, 1982; Art and Ardor: Essays, 1983; The Cannibal Galaxy, 1983; The Messiah of Stockholm, 1987; Metaphor and Memory: Essays, 1989; The Shawl, 1989; Epodes: First Poems, 1992; What Henry James Knew, and Other Essays on Writers, 1994; Portrait of the Artist as a Bad Character, 1996; The Cynthia Ozick Reader, 1996; Fame and Folly, 1996; The Puttermesser Papers, 1997; Quarrel and Quandary (essays), 2000. Contributions: many anthologies, reviews, quarterlies, journals, and periodicals. *Honours:* Guggenheim Fellowship, 1982; Mildred and Harold Strauss Living Award, American Acad. of Arts and Letters, 1983; Lucy Martin Donnelly Fellow, Bryn Mawr College, 1992; PEN/Spiegel-Diamonstein Award for the Art of the Essay, 1997; Harold Washington Literary Award, City of Chicago, 1997; John Cheever Award, 1999; Lannan Foundation Award, 2000; many hon. doctorates. *Address:* 34 Southview St, New Rochelle, NY 10805, USA.

P

PACK, Robert; Prof., Poet and Writer; b. 29 May 1929, New York, NY, USA; m. 1st Isabelle Miller, 1950; m. 2nd Patricia Powell, 1961, two s. one d. *Education:* BA, Dartmouth College, 1951; MA, Columbia University, 1953. *Career:* Teacher, Barnard College, 1957–64; Abernathy Prof., Middlebury College, Vermont, 1970–; Dir, Bread Loaf Writers Conferences, 1973–. *Publications:* Poetry: The Irony of Joy, 1955; A Stranger's Privilege, 1959; Guarded by Women, 1963; Selected Poems, 1964; Home from the Cemetery, 1969; Nothing But Light, 1972; Keeping Watch, 1976; Waking to My Name: New and Selected Poems, 1980; Faces in a Single Tree: A Cycle of Monologues, 1984; Clayfield Rejoices, Clayfield Laments: A Sequence of Poems, 1987; Before It Vanishes: A Packet for Prof. Pagels, 1989; Fathering the Map: New and Selected Later Poems, 1993. Other: Wallace Stevens: An Approach to His Poetry and Thought, 1958; Affirming Limits: Essays on Morality, Choice and Poetic Form, 1985; The Long View: Essays on the Discipline of Hope and Poetic Craft, 1991. Editor: The New Poets of England and America (with Donald Hall and Louis Simpson), 1957; Poems of Doubt and Belief: An Anthology of Modern Religious Poetry (with Tom Driver), 1964; Literature for Composition on the Theme of Innocence and Experience (with Marcus Klein), 1966; Short Stories: Classic, Modern, Contemporary (with Marcus Klein), 1967; Keats: Selected Letters, 1974; The Bread Loaf Anthology of Contemporary American Poetry (with Sydney Lea and Jay Parini), 1985; The Bread Loaf Anthology of Contemporary American Short Stories (with Jay Parini), 2 vols, 1987, 1989; Poems for a Small Planet: An Anthology of Nature Poetry (with Jay Parini), 1993. *Honours:* Fulbright Fellowship, 1956; American Acad. of Arts and Letters Grant, 1957; Borestone Mountain Poetry Award, 1964; National Endowment for the Arts Grant, 1968. *Address:* c/o Middlebury College, Middlebury, VT 05742, USA.

PACKER, Zuwena Z., BA, MA, MFA; American writer; b. 12 Jan. 1973, Chicago, IL. *Education:* Yale Univ., John Hopkins Univ. *Career:* teacher of English and Creative Writing in Baltimore; Stegner Fellow, Stanford Univ. *Publications:* Drinking Coffee Elsewhere (short stories) 2003. *Honours:* Whiting Writer's Award, Rona Jaffe Foundation Writers Award, Ms Giles Whiting Award, Billingham Review Award. *Address:* c/o Canongate Books, 14 High Street, Edinburgh, EH1 1TE, Scotland. *Telephone:* (131) 557-5111. *Fax:* (131) 557-5211. *E-mail:* info@canongate.co.uk. *Website:* www.canongate.co.uk.

PADEL, Ruth, BA, PhD, FRSL; British poet, writer and journalist; b. 8 May 1946, London, England; one d. *Education:* University of Oxford. *Career:* mem. PEN, Royal Zoological Soc., Soc. of Authors. *Publications:* poetry: Alibi 1985, Summer Snow 1990, Angel 1993, Fusewire 1996, Rembrandt Would Have Loved You 1998, Voodoo Shop 2002; non-fiction: In and Out of the Mind 1992, Whom Gods Destroy 1995, I'm a Man 2000, 52 Ways of Looking at a Poem 2002. *Honours:* Nat. Poetry Competition First Prize 1996, Poetry Book Soc. Recommendation 1993, 2002, Choice 1998, Cholmondley Award 2004. *Literary Agent:* Colville and Walsh, 2 Ganton Street, London, W1F 7GL, England.

PADFIELD, Peter Lawrence Notton; Author; b. 3 April 1932, Kolkata, India; m. Dorothy Jean Yarwood, 23 April 1960, one s. two d. *Career:* mem. Society for Nautical Research. *Publications:* The Sea is a Magic Carpet, 1960; The Titanic and the Californian, 1965; An Agony of Collisions, 1966; Aim Straight: A Biography of Admiral Sir Percy Scott, 1966; Broke and the Shannon: A Biography of Admiral Sir Philip Broke, 1968; The Battleship Era, 1972; Guns at Sea: A History of Naval Gunnery, 1973; The Great Naval Race: Anglo-German Naval Rivalry 1900–1914, 1974; Nelson's War, 1978; Tide of Empires: Decisive Naval Campaigns in the Rise of the West, Vol. I 1481–1654, 1979, Vol. II 1654–1763, 1982; Rule Britannia: The Victorian and Edwardian Navy, 1981; Beneath the Houseflag of the P & O, 1982; Dönitz, The Last Führer, 1984; Armada, 1988; Himmler, Reichsführer SS, 1990; Hess: Flight for the Führer, 1991, revised edn as Hess: The Führer's Disciple, 1993; War Beneath the Sea: Submarine Conflict 1939–1945, 1995; Maritime Supremacy and the Opening of the Western Mind: Naval Campaigns that Shaped the Modern World 1588–1782, 1999. Fiction: The Lion's Claw, 1978; The Unquiet Gods, 1980; Gold Chains of Empire, 1982; Salt and Steel, 1986.

PADGAONKAR, Dileep, PhD; Indian journalist; *Editor, The Times of India*; b. 1 May 1944, Pune; m. Latika Tawadey 1968; two s. *Education:* Fergusson Coll., Pune, Institut des Hautes Etudes Cinématographiques, Paris, Sorbonne, Paris. *Career:* Paris Corresp. of The Times of India 1968–73, Asst Ed., Bombay and Delhi 1973–78, Assoc. Ed. 1986–88, Ed. 1988–; Information Chief for Asia and Pacific, UNESCO 1978–81; Deputy Dir Office of Public Information, Paris 1981–85, Acting Dir 1985–86, Acting Dir Communication Sector 1986. *Publication:* When Bombay Burned (Ed.) 1993. *Address:* The Times of India, Times House, 7 Bahadur Shah Zafar Marg, New Delhi 110002 (Office); C-313, Defence Colony, New Delhi 110024, India (Home). *Telephone:* (11) 3312277 (Office); (11) 4697949 (Home). *Fax:* (11) 3323346. *Website:* www.timesofindia.com (Office).

PADOVANO, Anthony Thomas; academic and writer; b. 18 Sept. 1934, Harrison, NJ, USA; m. Theresa P. Lackamp 1974; three s. one d. *Education:* BA, magna cum laude, Seton Hall Univ., 1956; STB, magna cum laude, 1958, STL, magna cum laude, 1960, STD, magna cum laude, 1962, Pontifical Gregorian Univ., Rome; PhL, St Thomas Pontifical International Univ., Rome, 1962; MA, New York Univ., 1971; PhD, Fordham Univ., 1980. *Career:* Prof. of Systematic Theology, Darlington School of Theology, Mahwah, NJ, 1962–74; Prof. of American Literature, Ramapo Coll. of New Jersey, 1971–; various visiting professorships; mem. Catholic Theological Society of America; International Federation of Married Priests; International Thomas Merton Society; Priests for Equality. *Publications:* The Cross of Christ, The Measure of the World, 1962; The Estranged God, 1966; Who Is Christ?, 1967; Belief in Human Life, 1969; American Culture and the Quest for Christ, 1970; Dawn Without Darkness, 1971; Free to Be Faithful, 1972; Eden and Easter, 1974; A Case for Worship, 1975; Presence and Structure, 1975; America: Its People, Its Promise, 1975; The Human Journey: Thomas Merton, Symbol of a Century, 1982; Contemplation and Compassion, 1984; Winter Rain: A Play in One Act and Six Scenes, 1985; His Name is John: A Play in Four Acts, 1986; Christmas to Calvary, 1987; Love and Destiny, 1987; Summer Lightning: A Play in Four Acts and Four Seasons, 1988; Conscience and Conflict, 1989; Reform and Renewal: Essays on Authority, Ministry and Social Justice, 1990; A Celebration of Life, 1990; The Church Today: Belonging and Believing, 1990; Scripture in the Street, 1992; A Retreat with Thomas Merton: Biography as Spiritual Journey, 1995; Hope is a Dialogue, 1998; Resistance and Renewal, 2002. Contributions: books and periodicals. *Honours:* awards and citations; all professional and personal papers retained in the archives of the Univ. of Notre Dame, IN. *Address:* c/o School of American and International Studies, Ramapo College of New Jersey, Mahwah, NJ 07430, USA.

PAGE, Bruce; British journalist and publisher; b. 1 Dec. 1936, London; m. 1st Anne Gillison 1964 (divorced 1969); m. 2nd Anne L. Darnborough 1969; one s. one d. *Education:* Melbourne High School and Melbourne Univ. *Career:* trained as journalist, Melbourne Herald 1956–60; Evening Standard, London 1960–62; Daily Herald, London 1962–64; various exec. posts, Sunday Times, London 1964–76; Assoc. Ed. Daily Express 1977; Ed. New Statesman 1978–82; Dir Direct Image Systems and Communications 1992–95; various awards for journalism. *Publications:* co-author: Philby, the Spy who Betrayed a Generation, An American Melodrama, Do You Sincerely Want to be Rich?, Destination Disaster, Ulster (contrib.), The Yom Kippur War, The British Press. *Address:* 32 Lauderdale Tower, Barbican, London, EC2Y 8BY; Beach House, Shingle Streeet, Shottisham, Suffolk, IP12 3BE, England. *Telephone:* (20) 7628-3847; (1394) 411427. *E-mail:* bruce@pages.dircon.co.uk (Home).

PAGE, Clarence; Journalist and Columnist; b. 2 June 1947, Dayton, Ohio, USA; m. Lisa Johnson Cole, 3 May 1987. *Education:* BS in Journalism, Ohio University, 1969. *Career:* Reporter and Asst City Ed., 1969–80, Columnist and Editorial Board Mem., 1984–, Chicago Tribune; Dir, Dept of Community Affairs, WBBM-TV, 1980–82; Syndicated Columnist; many television appearances. *Publications:* Contributions: various periodicals. *Honours:* James P. McGuire Award, 1987; Pulitzer Prize for Commentary, 1989. *Address:* c/o Tribune Media Services, 435 N Michigan Ave, Suite 600, Chicago, IL 60611, USA.

PAGE, Geoffrey Donald, BA, DipEd; poet, writer and educator; b. 7 July 1940, Grafton, NSW, Australia; one s. *Education:* University of New England, Armidale, NSW. *Career:* Head, Dept of English, Narrabundah College, Canberra, 1974–2001; Writer-in-Residence, University of Wollongong, NSW, 1982, Curtin University, 1990, Edith Cowan University, 1993; mem. Australian Society of Authors. *Publications:* The Question, 1971; Smalltown Memorials, 1975; Collecting the Weather, 1978; Cassandra Paddocks, 1980; Clairvoyant in Autumn, 1983; Shadows from Wire: Poems and Photographs of Australians in the Great War Australian War Memorial (ed.), 1983; Benton's Conviction, 1985; Century of Clouds: Selected Poems of Guillaume Apollinaire (trans. with Wendy Coutts), 1985; Collected Lives, 1986; Smiling in English, Smoking in French, 1987; Footwork, 1988; Winter Vision, 1989; Invisible Histories, 1990; Selected Poems, 1991; Gravel Corners, 1992; On the Move (ed.), 1992; Human Interest, 1994; Reader's Guide to Contemporary Australian Poetry, 1995; The Great Forgetting, 1996; The Secret, 1997; Bernie McGann: A Life in Jazz, 1998; Collateral Damage, 1999; The Scarring, 1999; Darker and Lighter, 2001; Day after Day: Selected Poems of Salvatore Quasimodo (trans. with R. F. Brissenden and Loredana Nardi-Ford), 2002; Drumming on Water, 2003; The Indigo Book of Modern Australian Sonnets, 2003; My Mother's God 2003, Cartes Postales 2004. Contributions: newspapers and magazines. *Honours:* Australia Council Literature Board Grants, 1974, 1983, 1987, 1989, 1992, 1997, 2000; Queensland Premier's Prize, 1990; Patrick White Literary Award, 2001. *Address:* 8/40 Leahy Close, Narrabundah, ACT 2604, Australia.

PAGE, Jeremy Neil; Educator, Poet and Ed.; b. 23 Feb. 1958, Folkestone, Kent, England. *Education:* BA, French and Theatre Studies, University of Warwick, 1980; French Drama and Theatre History, University of Bristol, 1983; DipRSA, Teaching English as a Foreign Language; Certificates in Counselling. *Career:* Ed., The Frogmore Papers, 1983–; Teacher and Trainer, 1984–, Dir of Studies, 1995–, International House, London; Founder, Frogmore Poetry Prize, 1987; Teacher, Academia Britannica,

Arezzo, Italy, 1987–88; Series Ed., Crabflower Pamphlets, 1990–. *Publications:* Bliss, 1989; Frogmore Poetry (co-ed.), 1989; Secret Dormitories, 1993. Contributions: various anthologies and journals. *Honours:* Grand Transcendent Knight Salamander, Acad. of Paraphysical Science, 1992. *Address:* 6 Vernon Rd, Hornsey, London N8 0QD, England.

PAGE, Katherine Hall; Writer; b. 9 July 1947, New Jersey, USA; m. Alan Hein, 5 Dec. 1975, one s. *Education:* AB, Wellesley College, 1969; EdM, Tufts University, 1974; DEd, Harvard University, 1985. *Career:* mem. Mystery Readers International; MWA; Authors' Guild; Sisters in Crime; American Crime Writers League; Society of Children's Bookwriters and Illustrators; International Asscn of Crime Writers; Boston Author's Club; Brontë Society; Agatha Christie Society. *Publications:* The Body in the Belfry, 1990; The Body in the Bouillon, 1991; The Body in the Kelp, 1991; The Body in the Vestibule, 1992; The Body in the Cast, 1993; The Body in the Basement, 1994; The Body in the Bog, 1996; The Body in the Fjord, 1997; The Body in the Bookcase, 1998; The Body in the Big Apple, 1999; The Body in the Moonlight, 2001. Children's Fiction: Christie and Company, 1996; Christie and Company Down East, 1997; Christie and Company in the Year of the Dragon, 1998; Bon Voyage Christie and Company, 1999. *Honours:* Agatha for Best First Domestic Mystery, 1991. *Literary Agent:* Faith Hamlin, Sanford J. Greenburger Associates Inc, 55 Fifth Ave, New York, NY 10003, USA.

PAGE, Louise; Playwright; b. 7 March 1955, London, England. *Education:* BA, University of Birmingham, 1976. *Career:* Resident Playwright, Royal Court Theatre, 1982–83. *Publications:* Want Ad, 1977; Glasshouse, 1977; Tissue, 1978; Lucy, 1979; Hearing, 1979; Flaws, 1980; House Wives, 1981; Salonika, 1982; Real Estate, 1984; Golden Girls, 1984; Beauty and the Beast, 1985; Diplomatic Wives, 1989; Adam Wasxa Gardener, 1991; Like to Live, 1992; Hawks and Doves, 1992. Other: Radio and television plays. *Honours:* George Devine Award, 1982.

PAGE, Norman; academic and writer; b. 8 May 1930, Kettering, Northamptonshire, England; m. Jean Hampton 1958; three s. one d. *Education:* BA, 1951, MA, 1955, Emmanuel College, Cambridge; PhD, University of Leeds, 1968. *Career:* Principal Lecturer in English, Ripon College of Education, Yorkshire, 1960–69; Asst Prof., 1969–70, Assoc. Prof., 1970–75, Prof. of English, 1975–85, University of Alberta; Prof. of Modern English Literature, University of Nottingham, 1985–; mem. Royal Society of Canada, fellow; Thomas Hardy Society; Vice-Pres., Newstead Abbey Byron Society; Vice-Pres., Tennyson Society. *Publications:* The Language of Jane Austen, 1972; Speech in the English Novel, 1973; Thomas Hardy, 1977; A. E. Housman: A Critical Biography, 1983; A Kipling Companion, 1984; E. M. Forster, 1988; Tennyson: An Illustrated Life, 1992; Auden and Isherwood: The Berlin Years, 1998; Oxford Reader's Companion to Hardy, 2000. Contributions: London Magazine; London Review of Books; Literary Review. *Honours:* Guggenheim Fellowship, 1979; University of Alberta Research Prize, 1983. *Address:* 23 Braunston Road, Oakham, Rutland LE15 6LD, England.

PAGE, Patricia Kathleen; Canadian writer, poet and painter; b. 23 Nov. 1916, Swanage, Dorset, England; m. W. Arthur Irwin 1950; one step-s. two step-d. *Education:* studied art with Frank Schaeffer, Brazil, Charles Seliger, New York; Art Students League, New York; Pratt Graphics, New York. *Career:* scriptwriter, National Film Board, Canada, 1946–50; Conducted writing workshops, Toronto, 1974–77; Teacher, University of Victoria, BC, 1977–78; mem. PEN International; Writers' Union of Canada; League of Canadian Poets. *Publications:* The Sun and the Moon (novel), 1944; As Ten as Twenty, 1946; The Metal and the Flower, 1954; Cry Ararat: Poems New and Selected, 1967; The Sun and the Moon and Other Fictions, 1973; Poems Selected and New, 1974; To Say the Least (ed.), 1979; Evening Dance of the Grey Flies, 1981; The Glass Air (poems, essays, and drawings), 1985; Brazilian Journal (prose), 1988; I-Sphinx: A Poem for Two Voices, 1988; A Flask of Sea Water (fairy story), 1989; The Glass Air: Poems Selected and New, 1991; The Travelling Musicians (children's book), 1991; Unless the Eye Catch Fire (short story), 1994; The Goat That Flew (fairy story), 1994; Hologram: A Book of Glosas, 1994; A Children's Hymn for the United Nations, 1995; The Hidden Room, Collected Poems, 2 vols, 1997; Alphabetical (poem), 1998; Compass Rose (Italian trans. of selected poems), 1998; And Once More Saw the Stars: Four Poems for Two Voices (with Philip Stretford), 2001; A Kind of Fiction (short stories), 2001. Contributions: journals and magazines. *Honours:* Governor-General's Award for Poetry, 1954; Oscar Blumenthal Award for Poetry, 1974; Officer of the Order of Canada, 1977; National Magazines Gold Award, 1986, and Silver Award, 1990, for Poetry; British Columbia Book Awards, Hubert Evans Prize, 1988; Banff Centre School of Fine Arts National Award, 1989; Subject of National Film Board film Still Waters, 1991; Readers' Choice Award, Prairie Schooner, 1994; Subject of two-part sound feature The White Glass, CBC, 1996; Subject of special issue of Malahat Review, 1997; b p Nichol Chapbook Award, 1998; Companion of the Order of Canada, 1999; Hon. doctorates including: DLitt University of Toronto, 1998. *Literary Agent:* Kathryn Mulders Literary Agency, 185–911 Yates Street, Victoria, BC V8V 4Y9, Canada. *Website:* www.kmla.ca. *Address:* 3260 Exeter Road, Victoria, BC V8R 6A6, Canada. *Website:* www.winchestergalleriesltd.com.

PAGE, Robin; Writer; b. 3 May 1943, Cambridgeshire, England. *Publications:* Down with the Poor, 1971; The Benefits Racket, 1972; Down Among the Dossers, 1973; The Decline of an English Village, 1974; The Hunter and the Hunted, 1977; Weather Forecasting: The Country Way, 1977; Cures and Remedies: The Country, 1978; Weeds: The Country Way, 1979; Animal Cures: The Country Way, 1979; The Journal of a Country Parish, 1980; Journeys into Britain, 1982; The Country Way of Love, 1983; The Wildlife of the Royal Estates, 1984; Count One to Ten, 1986; The Fox's Tale, 1986; The Duchy of Cornwall, 1987; The Fox and the Orchid, 1987; The Twitcher's Guide to British Birds, 1989. *Address:* Bird's Farm, Barton, Cambridgeshire, England.

PAGE, S. M. (see McMaster, Susan).

PAGE, Stephen; British publisher. *Career:* CEO, Faber & Faber Ltd 2001–. *Literary Agent:* Faber and Faber Ltd, 3 Queen Square, London, WC1N 3AU, England. *Telephone:* (20) 7465-0045. *Fax:* (20) 7465-0034. *E-mail:* contact@faber.co.uk. *Website:* www.faber.co.uk.

PAGELS, Elaine Hiesey, PhD; American writer and professor of religion; b. 13 Feb. 1943, Palo Alto, CA; m 1st Heinz R. Pagels 1969 (died 1988); two s. (one died 1987) one d.; m. 2nd Kent Greenawalt 1995. *Education:* Stanford and Harvard Univs. *Career:* Asst Prof., Barnard Coll., Columbia Univ. 1970–74, then Assoc. Prof., later Prof. of Religion and Head of Dept of Religion 1974–82; Harrington Spear Paine Prof. of Religion, Princeton Univ. 1982–; mem. American Acad. of Religion, Biblical Theologians Club, Soc. of Biblical Literature; Aspen Inst. of Humanistic Studies Mellon Fellow 1974, Hazen Fellow 1975, Rockefeller Foundation Fellowship 1978, Guggenheim Fellowship 1979, John D. and Catherine T. MacArthur Foundation Fellowship 1981. *Publications:* The Johannine Gospel in Gnostic Exegesis: Heracleon's Commentary on John 1973, The Gnostic Paul: Gnostic Exegesis of the Pauline Letters 1975, The Gnostic Gospels (Nat. Book Critics' Circle Award, Nat. Book Award 1980) 1979, The Gnostic Jesus and Early Christian Politics 1981, Adam, Eve and the Serpent 1988, The Origin of Satan: The New Testament Origins of Christianity's Demonization of Jews, Pagans and Heretics 1995, Beyond Belief: The Secret Gospel of Thomas 2003; contrib. to various scholarly books and journals. *Honours:* National Endowment for the Humanities grant 1972. *Address:* University of Princeton, Department of Religion, Princeton, NJ 08544, USA (Office).

PAGLIA, Camille (Anna); Prof. of Humanities and Media Studies and Writer; b. 2 April 1947, Endicott, New York, USA. *Education:* BA, SUNY at Binghamton, 1968; MPhil, 1971, PhD, 1974, Yale University. *Career:* Faculty, Bennington College, Vermont, 1972–80; Visiting Lecturer, Wesleyan University, 1980; Visiting Lecturer, Yale University, 1980–84; Asst Prof., 1984–87, Assoc. Prof., 1987–91, Prof. of Humanities, 1991–2000, University Prof. and Prof. of Humanities and Media Studies, 2000–, Philadelphia College of the Performing Arts, later the University of the Arts, Philadelphia. *Publications:* Sexual Personae: Art and Decadence from Nefertiti to Emily Dickinson, 1990; Sex, Art, and American Culture: Essays, 1992; Vamps and Tramps: New Essays, 1994; Alfred Hitchcock's 'The Birds', 1998. Contributions: journals, periodicals and websites. *Address:* University of the Arts, 320 S Broad St, Philadelphia, PA 19102, USA.

PAIGE, Richard (see Koontz, Dean Ray).

PAIGE, Robin (see Albert, Susan Wittig).

PAIN, Margaret; Poet and Ed.; b. 27 March 1922, Woking, Surrey, England. *Education:* Business college. *Career:* Co-Ed., Weyfarers Magazine, 1978–97; mem. Surrey Poetry Centre; Wey Poets, chair., 1987–94. *Publications:* Walking to Eleusis, 1967; No Dark Legend, 1977; A Fox in the Garden, 1979; Shadow Swordsman, 1988. Contributions: various anthologies, 1972–2000, and other publications. *Honours:* Third Prize, 1977, Eleanor B. North Award, First Prize, 1981, Surrey Poetry Centre Open Competition; Joint Third Prize, Lake Aske Memorial Award, 1977; First Prize, New Poetry Competition, 1978; Special Commendation, South East Arts Group Literary Prize, 1985. *Address:* Hilltop Cottage, 9 White Rose Lane, Woking, Surrey GU22 7JA, England.

PAINTER, John, ThL, THSchol, BD, PhD; academic and writer; *Professor of Theology, Charles Sturt University*; b. 22 Sept. 1935, Bellingen, NSW, Australia; m. Gillian Gray 1963; two d. *Education:* Australian Coll. of Theology, Univ. of London, Durham Univ. *Career:* Tutor, St John's Coll., Durham, England 1965–68; Assoc. Prof., Univ. of Cape Town, South Africa 1971–76; Assoc. Prof., Reader, Latrobe Univ., Melbourne 1977–97; Prof. of Theology, St Mark's School of Theology, Charles Sturt Univ., Canberra 1997–; Fellow, Australian Acad. of the Humanities 1991–. *Publications:* John: Witness and Theologian 1975, Theology and Hermeneutics: Rudolf Bultmann's Interpretation of the History of Jesus 1987, The Quest for the Messiah 1991, Worlds in Conflict 1997, Just James, The Brother of Jesus in History and Tradition 1997, 1, 2, and 3 John 2002; contrib. to New Testament Studies, Journal for the Study of the New Testament, Scottish Journal of Theology. *Honours:* Centenary Medal 2003. *Address:* PO Box 321, Jamison Centre, Macquarie, ACT 2614, Australia.

PAKENHAM, Thomas Francis Dermot, BA; British historian and writer; b. 14 Aug. 1933; m. Valerie 1964; two s. two d. *Education:* Dragon School, Oxford, Belvedere Coll., Dublin, Ampleforth Coll., York, Magdalen Coll., Oxford. *Career:* travelled in Nr East and Ethiopia 1955–56; freelance writer

1956–58; editorial staff mem., Times Educational Supplement 1958–60, Sunday Telegraph 1961, The Observer 1961–64; Chair. Ladbroke Asscn 1988–91; mem., Victorian Soc. (co-founder 1958–, cttee mem. 1958–64) Historic Irish Tourist Houses and Gardens Asscn (co-founder, cttee mem. 1968–72), British-Irish Asscn (treas. 1972–2002, chair. 2002–), Christopher Ewart-Biggs Memorial Trust (sec., co-founder 1976–), Irish Tree Soc. (founder and chair. 1990–); sr assoc. mem. St Antony's Coll., Oxford 1979–81. *Publications:* non-fiction: The Mountains of Rasselas: an Ethiopian Adventure 1959, The Year of Liberty: History of the Great Irish Rebellion of 1798 1969, The Boer War (Cheltenham Prize 1980) 1979, Dublin: A Traveller's Companion (with Valerie Pakenham) 1988, The Scramble for Africa (Alan Paton Memorial Prize 1992, WHSmith Award 1992) 1991, Meetings with Remarkable Trees 1996, Remarkable Trees of the World 2002, Mythic Woods: The World's Most Remarkable Forests 2004, Remarkable Baobab 2004. *Honours:* Hon. DLitt (Ulster) 1992. *Address:* 111 Elgin Crescent, London, W11 2JF, England; Tullynally, Castlepollard, Westmeath, Ireland.

PALAHNIUK, Chuck; American novelist and essayist; b. 21 Feb. 1962, Pasco, WA. *Education:* Univ. of Oregon. *Publications:* novels: Fight Club 1996, Invisible Monsters 1999, Survivor 2000, Lullaby 2002, Nana 2003, Diary 2003; short story collections: Choke 2001, Fugitives and Refugees: A Walk through Portland, Oregon 2003, Stranger than Fiction: True Stories 2004, Nonfiction 2004; contrib. to Bikini, Black Book, Gear, The Guardian, The Stranger. *Literary Agent:* c/o Doubleday Publishing, Random House, 1745 Broadway, New York, NY 10019, USA. *E-mail:* ddaypub@randomhouse.com. *Website:* www.randomhouse.com/doubleday.

PALEI, Marina Anatolevna; Russian writer; b. (Marina Anatolevna Spivak), 1955, Leningrad; m. (divorced); one s. *Education:* Inst. of Medicine, Mechnikov Hospital, Leningrad, Gorky Inst. of Literature, Moscow. *Career:* model at the Mukhina Fine Arts Inst., Leningrad; joined amateur theatre group; lecturer and speaker across Europe 1992–; writer-in-residence, Bellagio Centre, Italy; mem. Russian Soc. of Authors, Russian PEN, Netherlands Soc. of Authors. *Publications include:* Pominovenie (trans. as Remembrance of the Devil) 1990, Evgesha i Annushka (trans. as Evgesha and Annushka) 1990, Kabiriia s Obvodnogo kanala (trans. as Kabiria from the Obvodnyi Canal) 1991; short story collections: Otdelenie propashchikh (trans. as The Lost Souls' Division) 1991, Iz zhizni avtoovetchikov (trans. as From the Life of Answering Machines) 1993. *Honours:* Rockefeller Foundation grant. *Literary Agent:* Bettina Nibbe, Nibbe & Wiedling Literary Agency, Rumfordstrasse 10, 80469, Munich, Germany. *Telephone:* (89) 290 840 12. *Fax:* (89) 290 840 50. *E-mail:* nibbe@nibbe-wiedling.de. *Website:* www.nibbe-wiedling.de.

PALEY, Grace; Author, Poet and University Teacher (retd); b. 11 Dec. 1922, New York, NY, USA; m. 1st Jess Paley 20 June 1942 (divorced); one s. one d.; m. 2nd Robert Nichols 1972. *Education:* Hunter College, CUNY, 1938–39; New York University. *Career:* Teacher, Columbia University, Syracuse University, Sarah Lawrence College, City College, CUNY; Poet Laureate, State of Vermont, 2003–; mem. American Acad. of Arts and Letters. *Publications:* Fiction: The Little Disturbances of Man: Stories of Women and Men at Love, 1959; Enormous Changes at the Last Minute, 1974; Later the Same Day, 1985; The Collected Stories, 1994. Poetry: Long Walks and Intimate Talks (includes stories), 1991; New and Collected Poems, 1992; Begin Again, 2000. Contributions: books, anthologies and magazines. *Honours:* Guggenheim Fellowship, 1961; National Institute of Arts and Letters Award, 1970; Edith Wharton Citation of Merit as the first State Author of New York, New York State Writers Institute, 1986; National Endowment for the Arts Senior Fellowship, 1987; Vermont Governor's Award for Excellence in the Arts, 1993. *Address:* Box 620, Thetford Hill, VT 05074, USA.

PALIN, Michael Edward, CBE, BA; British actor, writer and traveller; b. 5 May 1943, Sheffield, Yorks.; m. Helen M. Gibbins 1966; two s. one d. *Education:* Birkdale School, Sheffield, Shrewsbury School, Brasenose Coll. Oxford. *Career:* Pres. Transport 2000; actor and writer: Monty Python's Flying Circus, BBC TV 1969–74, Ripping Yarns, BBC TV 1976–80; actor: Three Men in a Boat, BBC 1975: writer: East of Ipswich, BBC TV 1987, Number 27, BBC TV, The Weekend (play for stage) 1994; actor and co-author, films: And Now for Something Completely Different 1970, Monty Python and the Holy Grail 1974, Monty Python's Life of Brian 1979, Time Bandits 1980, Monty Python's 'The Meaning of Life' 1982; actor, writer and co-producer The Missionary 1982; actor, co-scriptwriter American Friends 1991; actor in: Jabberwocky 1976, A Private Function 1984, Brazil 1985, A Fish Called Wanda 1988 (Best Supporting Film Actor, BAFTA Award 1988), GBH (Channel 4 TV) 1991, Fierce Creatures 1997; TV series: contrib. to Great Railway Journeys of the World, BBC TV 1980, 1993, presenter Around the World in 80 Days 1989, Pole to Pole 1992, Palin's Column 1994, Full Circle 1997, Michael Palin's Hemingway Adventure 1999, Sahara 2002. *Television:* art documentaries (presenter); Palin on Redpath 1997, The Bright Side of Life 2000, The Ladies Who Loved Matisse 2003. *Publications include:* Monty Python's Big Red Book 1970, Monty Python's Brand New Book 1973, Montypythonscrapbook 1979, Dr Fegg's Encyclopaedia of All World Knowledge 1984, Limericks 1985, Around the World in 80 Days 1989, Pole to Pole 1992, Hemingway's Chair 1995, Full Circle 1997, Michael Palin's Hemingway Adventure 1999, Sahara 2002, The Pythons Autobiography (co-author) 2003; for children: Small Harry and the Toothache Pills 1981, The Mirrorstone 1986, The Cyril Stories 1986. *Honours:* Dr hc (Sheffield) 1992, (Queen's, Belfast) 2000, (with Monty Python) Michael Balcon Award for outstanding contribution to cinema, BAFTA 1987, Travel Writer of the Year, British Book Awards 1993, Lifetime Achievement Award, British Comedy Awards 2002, BCA Illustrated Book of the Year Award 2002. *Literary Agent:* Mayday Management, 34 Tavistock Street, London, WC2E 7PB, England. *Telephone:* (20) 7497-1100. *Fax:* (20) 7497-1133.

PALING, Chris; Writer and Radio Producer; b. 7 Dec. 1956, Derby, England; m. Julie Fiona 18 Aug. 1979; one s. one d. *Education:* BA, Economic History, Sussex Univ., 1975–78. *Publications:* After the Raid; Deserters; Morning All Day; The Silent Sentry; Newton's Swing, 2000; The Repentant Morning, 2003. Contributions: Literary Review; Punch; Independent Magazine; Spectator. *Literary Agent:* Rogers, Coleridge & White Ltd, 20 Powis Mews, London W11 1JN, England.

PALLEY, Julian; Prof. of Spanish Literature, Poet and Trans; b. 16 Sept. 1925, Atlantic City, NJ, USA; m. Shirley Wilson, 17 Sept. 1950, four s. *Education:* BA, Mexico City College, 1950; MA, Spanish, University of Arizona, 1952; PhD, Romance Languages, University of New Mexico, 1958. *Career:* Instructor, Rutgers University, 1956–59; Assoc. Prof., Arizona State University, 1959–62, University of Oregon, 1962–66; Prof. of Spanish Literature, University of California at Irvine, 1966–; mem. California State Poetry Society. *Publications:* Spinoza's Stone, 1976; Bestiary, 1987; Pictures at an Exhibition, 1989; Family Portraits, 1994. Other: several trans. Contributions: Reviews, quarterlies, and journals. *Honours:* Arizona Quarterly Poetry Prize, 1956; Jefferson Poetry Prize, 1976. *Address:* c/o Dept of Spanish and Portuguese, University of California at Irvine, Irvine, CA 92697, USA.

PALMER, Alan Warwick; Writer; b. 28 Sept. 1926, Ilford, Essex, England; m. Veronica Mary Cordell, 1 Sept. 1951. *Education:* MA, 1950, MLitt, 1954, Oriel College, Oxford. *Career:* Asst Master, 1951–53, Senior History Master, 1953–69, Highgate School, London; mem. FRSL. *Publications:* A Dictionary of Modern History, 1789–1945, 1962; Independent Eastern Europe: A History (with C. A. Macartney), 1962; Yugoslavia, 1964; The Gardeners of Salonika, 1965; Napoleon in Russia, 1967; The Lands Between: A History of East Central Europe Since the Congress of Vienna, 1970; Metternich, 1972; The Life and Times of George VI, 1972; Russia in War and Peace, 1972; Alexander I: Tsar of War and Peace, 1974; Age of Optimism, 1974; Nations and Empires (ed.), 1974; Frederick the Great, 1974; Bismark, 1976; Kings and Queens of England, 1976; Quotations in History: A Dictionary of Historical Quotations, c. 800 AD to the Present (with Victoria Palmer), 1976; The Kaiser: Warlord of the Second Reich, 1978; Princes of Wales, 1979; The Facts on File Dictionary of 20th Century History, 1979; The Penguin Dictionary of Twentieth-Century History, 1979; Who's Who in Modern History, 1980; Who's Who in Shakespeare's England (with Veronica Palmer), 1981; The Chancelleries of Europe, 1983; Royal England: A Historical Gazetteer (with Veronica Palmer), 1983; An Encyclopedia of Napoleon's Europe, 1984; Crowned Cousins: The Anglo-German Royal Connection, 1985; The Banner of Battle: The Story of the Crimean War, 1987; Who's Who in Bloomsbury (with Veronica Palmer), 1987; The East End: Four Centuries of London Life, 1989; The Chronology of British History (with Veronica Palmer), 1992; The Decline and Fall of the Ottoman Empire, 1992; Twilight of the Habsburgs: The Life and Times of Emperor Francis Joseph, 1995; Dictionary of the British Empire and Commonwealth, 1996; The Pimlico Chronology of British History: From 250,000 BC to the Present (with Victoria Palmer), 1996; Who's Who in World Politics: From 1860 to the Present Day, 1996; Victory 1918, 2000. Contributions: journals. *Address:* 4 Farm End, Woodstock, Oxford OX20 1XN, England.

PALMER, Diana (see Kyle, Susan (Eloise Spaeth)).

PALMER, Frank Robert; academic, linguist and writer; b. 9 April 1922, Westerleigh, Gloucestershire, England; m. Jean Elisabeth Moore 1948; three s. two d. *Education:* MA, New College, Oxford, 1948; Graduate Studies, Merton College, Oxford, 1948–49. *Career:* Lecturer in Linguistics, School of Oriental and African Studies, University of London, 1950–52, 1953–60; Prof. of Linguistics, University College of North Wales, Bangor, 1960–65; Prof. and Head, Dept of Linguistic Science, 1965–87, Dean, Faculty of Letters and Social Sciences, 1969–72, University of Reading; mem. Academia Europaea; British Acad., fellow; Linguistic Society of America; Philological Society. *Publications:* The Morphology of the Tigre Noun, 1962; A Linguistic Study of the English Verb, 1965; Selected Papers of J. R. Firth, 1951–1958 (ed.), 1968; Prosodic Analysis (ed.), 1970; Grammar, 1971; The English Verb, 1974; Semantics, 1976; Modality and the English Modals, 1979; Mood and Modality, 1986; Studies in the History of Western Linguistics (co-ed.), 1986; Grammatical Roles and Relations, 1994; Grammar and Meaning (ed.), 1995; Modality in Contemporary English (co-ed.), 2003. Contributions: Professional journals. *Address:* Whitethorns, Roundabout Lane, Winnersh, Wokingham, Berkshire RG41 5AD, England.

PALMER, John, BA; playwright and director; b. 13 May 1943, Sydney, NS, Canada. *Education:* Carleton Univ., Ottawa. *Career:* dramaturg, Assoc., Factory Theatre Lab, Toronto 1970–73; co-founder, Co-Artistic Dir, Literary Man., Toronto Free Theatre 1972–76; resident playwright, Canadian

Repertory Theatre, Toronto 1983–87, Nat. Theatre School of Canada 1993–94; Course Dir, Final Year Playwrighting, York Univ., Toronto 1991–93. *Films:* Sugar (writer, dir) (Best Feature, Toronto Lesbian and Gay Film Festival) 2004. *Publications:* 2 Plays: The End, and A Day at the Beach 1991, Before the Guns, Memories for my Brother, Part I, Dangerous Traditions: Four Passe-Muraille Plays 1992, Henrik Ibsen On the Necessity of Producing Norwegian Drama 1992–93, Singapore 2001; contrib. to various publications. *Address:* 32 Monteith Street, Toronto, ON M4Y 1K7, Canada. *Telephone:* (416) 967-7455. *E-mail:* jp@darsmedia.com.

PALMER, Leslie (Howard); Prof. of Literature, Poet and Writer; b. 25 Jan. 1941, Memphis, Tennessee, USA; m. 27 Aug. 1965, one s. one d. *Education:* BA, University of Memphis, 1962; MA, 1963, PhD, 1966, University of Tennessee, Knoxville. *Career:* Instructor, University of Tennessee, 1966–67; Prof. of Literature, University of North Texas, Denton, 1967–; mem. Coda; MHRA; MLA; PEN. *Publications:* Ten Poems, 1980; A Red Sox Flag, 1983; Ode to a Frozen Dog, and Other Poems, 1992; Artemis' Bow, 1993; The Devil Sells Ice Cream, 1994; The Jim Tom Poems, 1996; The Bryn Mawr Poems, 1998; Swollen Foot, 1999; Disgraceland, 2000; Last Bite, 2001. Contributions: numerous anthologies, reviews, quarterlies, journals, and magazines. *Honours:* Beaudoin Gemstone Awards, 1962, 1963; Mid-south Poetry Award, 1963; Cape Rock Poetry Award, 1990. *Address:* 1905 W Oak, Denton, TX 76201, USA.

PALMER, (George) Michael, BA, MA; poet, writer and translator; b. 11 May 1943, New York, NY, USA; m. Cathy Simon 1972; one d. *Education:* Harvard Univ. *Publications:* Plan of the City of O, 1971; Blake's Newton, 1972; C's Songs, 1973; The Circular Gates, 1974; Without Music, 1977; Alogon, 1980; Notes for Echo Lake, 1981; Code of Signals: Recent Writings in Poetics (ed.), 1983; First Figure, 1984; Sun, 1988; An Alphabet Underground, 1993; At Passages, 1995; The Lion Bridge, 1998; The Danish Notebook, 1999; The Promises of Glass, 2000; Codes Appearing: Poems 1979–1988, 2001; Fatal 2003. Other: trans; ed. of books. Contributions: many anthologies, books and journals. *Address:* 265 Jersey Street, San Francisco, CA 94114, USA.

PAMUK, Orhan; Turkish novelist; b. 7 June 1952, Istanbul; m. Aylin Turegen 1982 (divorced 2001); one d. *Education:* Robert Coll., Istanbul Technical Univ., Inst. of Journalism at Istanbul Univ. *Publications:* Cevdet Bey ve Ogullari (Cevdet Bey and His Sons) 1983, Sessiz Ev (The Quiet House) 1983, Beyaz Kale (trans. as The White Castle) 1985, Kara Kitap (trans. as The Black Book) 1990, Gizli Yuz (screenplay of Kara Kitap) 1992, Yeni Hayat (trans. as The New Life) 1995, My Name is Red (trans.) (IMPAC Dublin Literary Award 2003) 2000, Istanbul 2003, Snow (trans.) 2004; contrib. to various newspapers and magazines. *Honours:* Milliyet Press Novel Contest, first prize 1979, Orhan Kemal Novel Prize 1983, Madarali Novel Prize 1984, Prix de la Découverte Européenne 1991. *Address:* c/o Faber and Faber Ltd, 3 Queen Square, London, WC1N 3AU, England.

PANICHAS, George Andrew; Educator, Literary Critic and Scholar; b. 21 May 1930, Springfield, Massachusetts, USA. *Education:* BA, American International College, 1951; MA, Trinity College, Hartford, CT, 1952; PhD, University of Nottingham, 1962. *Career:* Instructor, 1962–63, Asst Prof., 1963–66, Assoc. Prof., 1966–68, Prof. of English, 1968–92, University of Maryland; Editorial Adviser, 1972–77, Assoc. Ed., 1978–83, Ed., 1984–, Modern Age: A Quarterly Review. *Publications:* Adventure in Consciousness: The Meaning of D. H. Lawrence's Religious Quest, 1964; Renaissance and Modern Essays (co-ed.), 1966; Epicurus, 1967; The Reverent Discipline: Essays in Literary Criticism and Culture, 1974; The Burden of Vision: Dostoevsky's Spiritual Art, 1977; The Courage of Judgement: Essays in Literary Criticism, Culture and Society, 1983; The Critic as Conservator: Essays in Literature, Society and Culture, 1992; The Critical Legacy of Irving Babbitt: An Appreciation, 1999; Growing Wings to Overcome Gravity: Criticism as the Pursuit of Virtue, 1999. Other: Ed. of various books. Contributions: books and journals. *Honours:* FRSA, 1971–; Grant, Earhart Foundation, 1982. *Address:* Dept of English, University of Maryland, College Park, MD 20742, USA.

PANIKER, Ayyappa; Prof. of English (retd), Poet, Writer, Ed. and Trans; b. 12 Sept. 1930, Kavalam, India; m. Sreeparvathy Paniker, 1961, two d. *Education:* BA, Travancore University, 1951; MA, Kerala University, 1959; CTE, Hyderabad, 1966; MA, PhD, 1971, Indiana University. *Career:* Lecturer, 1951–73, Reader, 1973–80, Prof. of English and Head, Dept of English, 1980–90, University of Kerala; Chief Ed., Medieval Indian Literature, 1990–94; Birla Fellowship, 1994–96; UNESCO Subcommission for Culture; mem. National Book Trust; National Literacy Mission; Sahitya Akademi; MLA, hon. mem. *Publications:* numerous books, incl.: Ayyappa Panikerude Kritikal I, 1974, II, 1982, III, 1990, IV, 2000; Ayyappa Panikerude Lekhanangal I, 1982, II, 1990; Selected Poems, 1985; Mayakovskiyude Kavitakal, 1987; Gotrayanam, 1989; Avatarikakal, 1993; Medieval Indian Literature (ed.), 1998; Madhyakala Malayala Karuta, 1998; Indian Narratology. Contributions: many anthologies, books, reviews, quarterlies, journals, and magazines. *Honours:* Kerala Sahitya Akademi Award, 1975, and Fellowship, 2003; Kalyani Krishna Menon Prize, 1977; Central Sahitya Akademi Award, 1984; Asan Prize, 1991; Muscat Award, Kerala Cultural Centre, 1992; Sahitya Parishad Award, 1993; Rockefeller Fellowship, 1996; Kabir Prize, 1997; Indira Gandhi Fellowship, 1997–99; Gandadhar Meher Award, 1998; Fulbright ACLS Fellowship; Pandalam Prize, 2002. *Address:* 111 Gandhi Nagar, Trivandrum 695014, India. *E-mail:* tvm_ayyappa@sancharnet.in.

PANNENBERG, Wolfhart (Ulrich); Prof. of Systematic Theology (retd) and Author; b. 2 Oct. 1928, Stettin, Germany; m. Hilke Sabine Schütte, 3 May 1954. *Education:* ThD, University of Heidelberg, 1953. *Career:* Ordained Lutheran Minister, 1955; Privatdozent, University of Heidelberg, 1955–58; Prof. of Systematic Theology, University of Wuppertal, 1958–61, University of Mainz, 1961–67; Prof. of Systematic Theology and Head of the Institute of Ecumenical Theology, University of Munich, 1967–94; several visiting professorships; mem. Bavarian Acad. of Sciences; British Acad., fellow. *Publications:* Offenbarung als Geschichte, 1961, English trans. as Revelation as History, 1969; Was ist der Mensch?: Die Anthropologie der Gegenwart im Lichte der Theologie, 1962, English trans. as What is Man?, 1970; Grundzüge der Christologie, 1964, English trans. as Jesus: God and Man, 1968; Grundfragen systematischer Theologie, 2 vols, 1967, 1980, English trans. as Basic Questions in Theology, 2 vols, 1970–71; Theology and the Kingdom of God, 1969; Spirit, Faith and Church (with Carl E. Braaten and Avery Dulles), 1970; Thesen zur Theologie der Kirche, 1970; Das Glaubensbekenntnis, 1972, English trans. as The Apostles' Creed in the Light of Today's Questions, 1972; Gottesgedanke und menschliche Freiheit, 1972, English trans. as The Idea of God and Human Freedom, 1973; Wissenschaftstheorie und Theologie, 1973, English trans. as Theology and the Philosophy of Science, 1976; Glaube und Wirklichkeit, 1975, English trans. as Faith and Reality, 1977; Ethik und Ekklesiologie, 1977, English trans., 1983; Human Nature, Election and History, 1977; Anthropologie in Theologischer Perspektive, 1983, English trans. as Anthropology in Theological Perspective, 1985; Christian Spirituality, 1983; Christenum in Einer Säkularisierten Welt, 1988, English trans. as Christianity in a Secularized World, 1989; Systematische Theologie, 3 vols, 1988–93, English trans. as Systematic Theology, 3 vols, 1991–98; Metaphysik und Gottesgedanke, 1988, English trans. as Metaphysics and the Idea of God, 1990; An Introduction to Systematic Theology, 1991; Toward a Theology of Nature: Essays on Science and Faith, 1993; Grundlagen der Ethik, 1996; Theologie und Philosophie, 1996; Problemgeschichte der neueren Evangelischen Theologie in Deutschland, 1997; Beiträge zur systematischen Theologie, 3 vols, 1999–2000. Contributions: scholarly books and journals. *Honours:* Hon. doctorates, University of Glasgow, 1972, University of Manchester, 1977, Trinity College, Dublin, 1979, University of St Andrews, Scotland, 1993, University of Cambridge, 1997, University Comillas, Madrid, 1999. *Address:* Sudetenstrasse 8, 82166 Gräfelfing, Germany.

PANYCH, Morris (Stephen); Dramatist, Writer, Actor and Dir; b. 30 June 1952, Calgary, AB, Canada. *Education:* Radio and Television Arts, NAIT, Edmonton, 1971–73; BFA, University of British Columbia, 1977. *Publications:* Last Call, 1983; 7 Stories, 1990; The Ends of the Earth, 1993; Other Schools of Thought, 1994; Vigil, 1995. *Honours:* 6 Jessie Awards, Vancouver Theatre; Governor-General's Award for English Drama, 1994. *Address:* c/o Christopher Banks and Assocs, 6 Adelaide St E, Suite 610, Toronto, ON M5C 1H6, Canada.

PAOLINI, Christopher; American children's writer; b. Montana. *Career:* self-published first book. *Publications:* Inheritance Trilogy: Book I: Eragon 2002, Book II: Eldest 2005. *Literary Agent:* Simon Lipskar, Writers' House, 21 W 26th Street, New York, NY 10010, USA. *Website:* www.alagaesia.com.

PAOLUCCI, Anne Attura, BA, MA, PhD; retd academic, poet, writer, dramatist and editor; b. Rome, Italy; m. Henry Paolucci. *Education:* Barnard College, Columbia University. *Career:* Instructor, 1959–61, Asst Prof., 1961–69, City College, CUNY; Fulbright Lecturer, University of Naples, 1965–67; Research Prof., 1969–75, Prof. of English, 1969–97, Chair, Dept of English, 1974–75, 1982–91, Dir, Doctor of Arts Degree Program in English, 1982–96, St John's University, Jamaica, New York; Founder, Publisher, and Ed.-in-Chief, Review of National Literatures, 1970–; Founder-Pres., Council on National Literatures, 1974–; mem. American Comparative Literature Asscn; CUNY, board of trustees, 1996–, chair., 1997–; Dante Society of America; Dramatists Guild; Hegel Society of America; International Comparative Literature Asscn; MLA; PEN American Center; Pirandello Society of America, pres., 1972–95; Renaissance Asscn of America; Renaissance Institute of America; Shakespeare Asscn of America; World Centre for Shakespeare Studies. *Publications:* Poetry: Poems Written for Sbek's Mummies, Marie Menken, and Other Important People, Places, and Things 1977, Riding the Mast Where It Swings 1980, Gorbachev in Concert (and Other Poems) 1991, Queensboro Bridge (and Other Poems) 1995. Fiction: Eight Short Stories 1977, Sepia Tones: Seven Short Stories 1985, Terminal Degrees 1997, Do Me A Favor (and Other Stories) 2002, In Wolf's Clothing 2003. Non-Fiction: Hegel on Tragedy (with Henry Paolucci) 1962, A Short History of American Drama 1966, Eugene O'Neill, Arthur Miller, Edward Albee 1967, From Tension to Tonic: The Plays of Edward Albee 1972, Pirandello's Theater: The Recovery of the Stage for Dramatic Art 1974, Dante and the 'Quest for Eloquence' in the Vernacular Languages of India (with Henry Paolucci) 1984. Plays: Minions of the Race 1978 (video 2002), Cipango! 1986. Editor: Dante's Influence on American Writers 1977. Contributions: numerous books, reviews, and journals. *Honours:* Fulbright Scholarship, Italy, 1951–52; Woodbridge Hon. Fellowship, Columbia University, 1961–62; Writer-in-Residence, Yaddo, 1965; ACLS Grant, 1978; Cavaliere, 1986, Commendatore, 1992, Order of

Merit, Italy; Gold Medal, Canada, 1991; Hon. Degree in Humane Letters, Lehman College, CUNY, 1995. *Address:* 166 25 Powells Cove Blvd, Beechhurst, NY 11357, USA.

PAPALEO, Joseph; Prof. of Literature and Writing and Writer; b. 13 Jan. 1926, New York, NY, USA; m., four s. *Education:* BA, Sarah Lawrence College, 1949; Diploma di Profitto, University of Florence, Italy, 1951; MA, Columbia University, 1952. *Career:* Teacher, Fieldston Prep School, 1952–60; Prof. of Literature and Writing, Sarah Lawrence College, 1960–68, 1969–92; Guest Prof., Laboratorio de Cibernetica, Naples, Italy, 1968–69; mem. Authors' Guild; Italian American Writers Asscn; American Asscn of University Profs. *Publications:* All the Comforts (novel), 1968; Out of Place (novel), 1971; Picasso at Ninety One, 1988. Other: several short stories. Contributions: journals and magazines. *Honours:* Guggenheim Fellowship, 1974; Ramapo College Poetry Prize, 1986.

PAPAS, William; Author; b. 1927, South Africa. *Education:* South Africa; Beckham, England. *Career:* Formerly Cartoonist, The Guardian, The Sunday Times Newspapers, Punch Magazine; Book Illustrator, Painter, Print Maker; mem. Savage Club, London. *Publications:* The Press, 1964; The Story of Mr Nero, 1965; The Church, 1965; Parliament, 1966; Freddy the Fell-Engine, 1966; The Law, 1967; Tasso, 1967; No Mules, 1967; Taresh, the Tea Planter, 1968; A Letter from India, 1968; A Letter from Israel, 1968; Theodore, or, The Mouse Who Wanted to Fly, 1969; Elias the Fisherman, 1970; The Monk and the Goat, 1971; The Long-Haired Donkey, 1972; The Most Beautiful Child, 1973; The Zoo, 1974; People of Old Jerusalem, 1980; Papas' America, 1986; Papas' Portland, 1994.

PAPINEAU, David Calder; Philosopher, Prof. and Writer; b. 30 Sept. 1947, Como, Italy; m. Rose Wild, 6 July 1986, one s. one d. *Education:* BSc, University of Natal, 1967; BA, 1970, PhD, 1974, University of Cambridge. *Career:* Prof., King's College, London, 1990–; mem. British Society for the Philosophy of Science, Pres., 1993–95. *Publications:* For Science in the Social Sciences, 1978; Theory and Meaning, 1979; Reality and Representation, 1987; Philosophical Naturalism, 1993; Introducing Consciousness, 2000; Thinking About Consciousness, 2002. *Address:* Dept of Philosophy, King's College, London WC2R 2LS, England.

PARES, Marion, (Judith Campbell, Anthony Grant); Writer; b. 7 Nov. 1914, West Farleigh, Kent, England; m. Humphrey Pares, 5 June 1937, four d. *Publications:* Family Pony, 1962; The Queen Rides, 1965; Horses in the Sun, 1966; Police Horse, 1967; World of Horses, 1969; World of Ponies, 1970; Anne: Portrait of a Princess, 1970; Family on Horseback (with N. Toyne), 1971; Princess Anne and Her Horses, 1971; Elizabeth and Philip, 1972; The Campions, 1973; Royalty on Horseback, 1974; The World of Horses, 1975; Anne and Mark, 1976; Queen Elizabeth II, 1979; The Mutant, 1980; Charles: A Prince of His Time, 1980; The Royal Partners, 1982; Royal Horses, 1983. *Literary Agent:* A. M. Heath & Co Ltd, 79 St Martin's Lane, London WC2N 4RE, England.

PARETSKY, Sara; Novelist; b. 8 June 1947, Ames, IA, USA; m.; three steps. *Education:* PhD, History, Univ. of Chicago, 1977; MBA, Univ. of Chicago. *Publications:* Indemnity Only, 1982; Deadlock, 1984; Killing Orders, 1985; Bitter Medicine, 1987; Blood Shot (aka Toxic Shock), 1988; Burn Marks, 1990; A Woman's Eye (ed.), 1991; Guardian Angel, 1992; Tunnel Vision, 1994; Windy City Blues (short stories), 1995; Women on the Case (ed.), 1996; Ghost Country, 1998; Hard Time, 1999; Total Recall, 2001; Blacklist, 2003. Contributions: New York Times; Illinois Issues; Law, Text, and Culture; Women's Review of Books; Mary Higgins Clark Mystery Magazine; anthologies: Family Portraits; 1st Culprit; 2nd Culprit. *Honours:* CWA Silver Dagger Award, 1988; Marlowe Award, German Crime Writers Asscn, 1993; Hon. Doctor of Letters, MacMurray College, IL, 1993; Mark Twain Award for Distinguished Contribution to Midwest Literature, 1996; Visiting Fellow, Wolfson College Oxford, 1997; Hon. Doctor of Letters, Columbia College, Chicago, 1999; CWA Diamond Dagger Award, 2002. *Literary Agent:* Dominick Abel Literary Agency Inc, 146 W 82nd St, Suite 1B, New York, NY 10024, USA. *Telephone:* (212) 877-0710. *Fax:* (212) 595-3133. *E-mail:* dominickabelagency@att.net. *Website:* www.saraparetsky.com.

PARINI, Jay (Lee); Prof. of English, Author, Poet and Literary Critic; b. 2 April 1948, Pittston, Pennsylvania, USA; m. Devon Stacey Jersild, 21 June 1981, three s. *Education:* AB, Lafayette College, 1970; PhD, University of St Andrews, Scotland, 1975. *Career:* Faculty, Dartmouth College, 1975–82; Co-Founder, New England Review, 1976; Prof. of English, Middlebury College, 1982–. *Publications:* Fiction: The Love Run, 1980; The Patch Boys, 1986; The Last Station, 1990; Bay of Arrows, 1992; Benjamin's Crossing, 1997; The Apprentice Lover, 2002. Poetry: Singing in Time, 1972; Anthracite Country, 1982; Town Life, 1988; House of Days, 1988. Other: Theodore Roethke: An American Romantic, 1979; An Invitation to Poetry, 1988; John Steinbeck: A Biography, 1995; Some Necessary Angels (essays), 1998; Robert Frost, 1999. Editor: Gore Vidal: Writer Against the Grain, 1992; The Columbia History of American Poetry, 1993; The Columbia Anthology of American Poetry, 1995; The Norton Book of American Autobiography, 1999. *Address:* Route 1, Box 195, Middlebury, VT 05753, USA.

PARIS, Bernard Jay; Prof. of English (retd) and Writer; b. 19 Aug. 1931, Baltimore, MD, USA; m. Shirley Helen Freedman, 1 April 1949, one s. one d. *Education:* AB, 1952, PhD, 1959, Johns Hopkins University. *Career:* Instructor, Lehigh University, 1956–60; Asst Prof., 1960–64, Assoc. Prof., 1964–67, Prof., 1967–81, Michigan State University; Prof. of English, University of Florida, 1981–96; Dir, Institute for Psychological Study of the Arts, 1985–92, International Karen Horney Society, 1991–; mem. MLA of America; Hon. Mem., Asscn for the Advancement of Psychoanalysis; Scientific Assoc., American Acad. of Psychoanalysis; Hon. Mem., American Institute for Psychoanalysis. *Publications:* Experiments in Life: George Eliot's Quest for Values, 1965; A Psychological Approach to Fiction: Studies in Thackeray, Stendhal, George Eliot, Dostoevsky and Conrad, 1974; Character and Conflict in Jane Austen's Novels, 1978; Third Force Psychology and the Study of Literature (ed.), 1986; Shakespeare's Personality (co-ed.), 1989; Bargains with Fate: Psychological Crises and Conflicts in Shakespeare and His Plays, 1991; Character as a Subversive Force in Shakespeare: The History and the Roman Plays, 1991; Karen Horney: A Psychoanalyst's Search for Self-Understanding, 1994; Imagined Human Beings: A Psychological Approach to Character and Conflict in Literature, 1997; The Therapeutic Process, by Karen Horney (ed.), 1999; The Unknown Karen Horney, by Karen Horney (ed.), 2000; Rereading George Eliot: Changing Responses to Her Experiments in Life, 2003. Contributions: numerous scholarly and literary journals. *Honours:* National Endowment for the Humanities Fellow, 1969; Guggenheim Fellowship, 1974. *Address:* 1430 NW 94th St, Gainesville, FL 32606, USA. *E-mail:* bjparis@ufl.edu.

PARISI, Joseph Anthony, BA, MA, PhD; editor, writer, poet and consultant; b. 18 Nov. 1944, Duluth, Minnesota, USA. *Education:* College of St Thomas, St Paul, Minnesota, University of Chicago. *Career:* Instructor to Asst Prof. of English, Roosevelt University, Chicago, 1969–78; Assoc. Ed., 1976–83, Acting Ed., 1983–85, Ed., 1985–, Poetry Magazine, Chicago; Visiting and Adjunct Asst Prof. of English, University of Illinois at Chicago, 1978–87; Consultant, American Library Asscn, 1980–; Chair, Ruth Lilly Poetry Prize, 1986–, and Fellowships, 1989–; Producer, Writer, and Host, Poets in Person, National Public Radio, 1991; Exec. Dir, Modern Poetry Asscn, 1996–. *Publications:* The Poetry Anthology, 1912–1977: Sixty-five Years of America's Most Distinguished Verse Magazine (ed. with Daryl Hine), 1978; Voices & Visions: Viewer's Guide, 1987; Marianne Moore: The Art of a Modernist (ed.), 1989; Poets in Person: Listener's Guide, 1992. Contributions: Reference books, scholarly journals, and literary publications. *Honours:* Everett Helm Travelling Fellowship, 1999; Guggenheim Fellowship, 2000. *Address:* 3440 N Lake Shore Drive, Chicago, IL 60657, USA.

PARKER, D(avid) C.; Theologian and Educator; b. 4 July 1953, Boston, Lincolnshire, England; m. Karen Parker, two s. two d. *Education:* MTheol, University of St Andrews, 1975; Diploma in Theology, University of Cambridge, 1976; DTheol, University of Leiden, 1990. *Career:* Curate, Christian churches, London, 1977–80, Oxfordshire, 1980–85; Theological College Tutor, Birmingham, 1985–93; Lecturer, Reader, Prof. in Theology, University of Birmingham; Co-Ed., International Greek New Testament Project; mem. Studiorum Novi Testamenti Societas, Co-chair. of Textual Criticism Seminar; Society of Biblical Literature. *Publications:* Codex Bezae: An Early Christian Manuscript and Its Text, 1992; The Living Text of the Gospels, 1997. *Address:* Centre for the Editing of Texts in Religion, Graduate Institute in Theology, University of Birmingham, Elmfield House, Bristol Rd, Birmingham B29 6LQ, England. *E-mail:* d.c.parker@bham.ac.uk.

PARKER, Gordon; Author and Playwright; b. 28 Feb. 1940, Newcastle upon Tyne, England. *Education:* Newcastle Polytechnic, 1965–68. *Career:* Book Reviewer, BBC Radio and ITV. *Publications:* The Darkness of the Morning, 1975; Lightning in May, 1976; The Pool, 1978; Action of the Tiger, 1981. Radio plays: The Seance, 1978; God Protect the Lonely Widow, 1982. *Address:* 14 Thornhill Close, Seaton Delaval, Northumberland, England.

PARKER, Gwendolyn M(cDougald); Writer; b. 9 June 1950, Durham, NC, USA. *Education:* BA, Radcliffe College; JD, LLM, New York University School of Law. *Publications:* These Same Long Bones, 1994; Trespassing, My Sojourn in the Halls of Privilege, 1997. *Honours:* Notable Book of the Year Citation, New York Times, 1994. *Address:* Marie Brown Assocs, 625 Broadway, Room 902, New York, NY 10012, USA.

PARKER, Peter Robert Nevill, BA, FRSL; British writer; b. 2 June 1954, Hereford, England. *Education:* Univ. Coll. London. *Career:* exec. cttee mem., English PEN 1994–97; trustee 1994–, Chair. 1998–2000, PEN Literary Foundation; Assoc. Ed., New Dictionary of National Biography 1996–; cttee mem. London Library 1998–. *Publications:* The Old Lie 1987, Ackerley 1989, The Reader's Companion to the Twentieth-Century Novel (ed.) 1994, The Reader's Companion to Twentieth-Century Writers (ed.) 1995, Isherwood 2004; contrib. to Daily Telegraph, Independent, Sunday Times, Hortus. *Literary Agent:* David Higham Associates, 5–8 Lower John Street, Golden Square, London, W1F 9HA, England.

PARKER, Robert B(rown); Author; b. 17 Sept. 1932, Springfield, MA, USA; m. Joan Hall 26 Aug. 1956; two s. *Education:* BA, Colby College, 1954; MA, 1957, PhD, 1971, Boston Univ. *Career:* Lecturer, Boston Univ., 1962–64; Faculty, Lowell State College, 1964–66, Bridgwater State College, 1966–68; Asst Prof., 1968–73, Assoc. Prof., 1973–76, Prof. of English, 1976–79, Northeastern Univ. *Publications:* Fiction: The Godwulf Manuscript, 1973; God Save the Child, 1974; Mortal Stakes, 1975; Promised Land, 1976; The Judas Goat, 1978; Wilderness, 1979; Looking for Rachel Wallace, 1980; Early Autumn, 1981; A Savage Place, 1981; Surrogate, 1982; Ceremony,

1982; The Widening Gyre, 1983; Love and Glory, 1983; Valediction, 1984; A Catskill Eagle, 1985; Taming a Sea Horse, 1986; Pale Kings and Princes, 1987; Crimson Joy, 1988; Playmates, 1989; Poodle Springs (completion of unfinished novel by R. Chandler), 1989; Stardust, 1990; Perchance to Dream, 1991; Pastime, 1991; Double Deuce, 1992; Paper Doll, 1993; All Our Yesterdays, 1994; Walking Shadow, 1994; Thin Air, 1995; Chance, 1996; Small Vices, 1997; Night Passage, 1997; Sudden Mischief, 1998; Trouble in Paradise, 1998; Hush Money, 1999; Family Honor, 1999; Perish Twice, 2000; Hugger Mugger, 2001; Potshot, 2001; Gunman's Rhapsody, 2001; Death in Paradise, 2001; Widow's Walk, 2002; Shrink Rap, 2002. Other: The Personal Response to Literature, 1971; Order and Diversity, 1973; Three Weeks in Spring (with Joan Parker), 1978. *Literary Agent:* Helen Brann Agency Inc, 94 Curtis Rd, Bridgewater, CT 06752, USA.

PARKES, Roger Graham; Novelist and Scriptwriter; b. 15 Oct. 1933, Chingford, Essex, England; m. Tessa Isabella McLean, 5 Feb. 1964, one s. one d. *Education:* National Diploma of Agriculture. *Career:* Staff Writer, Farming Express, Scottish Daily Express, 1959–63; Ed., Farming Express, 1963; Staff Script Ed., Drama, BBC TV, London, 1964–70; mem. Writers Guild of Great Britain; Magistrates Asscn. *Publications:* Death Mask, 1970; Line of Fire, 1971; The Guardians, 1973; The Dark Number, 1973; The Fourth Monkey, 1978; Alice Ray Morton's Cookham, 1981; Them and Us, 1985; Riot, 1986; Y-E-S, 1986; An Abuse of Justice, 1988; Troublemakers, 1990; Gamelord, 1991; The Wages of Sin, 1992. Contributions: Daily Express; Sunday Express. *Honours:* Grand Prix de Littérature, Paris, 1974. *Address:* Cartlands Cottage, Kings Lane, Cookham Dean, Berkshire SL6 9AY, England.

PARKIN, Andrew Terence Leonard, (Jiang An Dao); Poet and Critic; b. 30 June 1937, Birmingham, England; m. 1st Christine George, 14 June 1959, one s.; m. 2nd Françoise Lentsch, 28 April 1990. *Education:* BA, 1961, MA, 1965, Pembroke College, Cambridge; PhD, University of Bristol, 1969. *Career:* Ed., Canadian Journal of Irish Studies, 1974–89; Prof. of English, University of British Columbia, Chinese University of Hong Kong; mem. Canadian Asscn for Irish Studies, hon. life mem.; League of Canadian Poets; Cambridge Club of Paris; Writers' Union of Canada. *Publications:* Stage One: A Canadian Scenebook, 1973; The Dramatic Imagination of W. B. Yeats, 1978; Shaw's Caesar and Cleopatra, 1980; Dion Boucicault: Selected Plays, 1987; Dancers in a Web, 1987; Yeats's Herne's Egg, 1991; Yokohama Days, Kyoto Nights, 1991; File on Nichols, 1993; Hong Kong Poems, 1997; The Humanities (ed.), 2001; Shakespeare Global/Local: The Hong Kong Imaginary in Transcultural Production (ed. with K. K. Tam and Terry Yip), 2002; The Rendez-Vous: Poems of Multicultural Experience, 2003. Contributions: Over 100 essays and reviews in scholarly journals; Over 30 radio broadcasts; Two television interviews; 200 poems. *Honours:* Most Distinguished Ed. of a Learned Journal, 1989; Hon. Adviser, Chinese Acad. of Social Sciences, Beijing, 2000–; Prof. Emeritus, Hon. Senior Tutor, Shaw College, Chinese University of Hong Kong, 2001–. *Address:* 52 rue du Rendez-vous, Paris 75012, France.

PARKS, Timothy Harold, (John MacDowell); Educator, Translator and Author; b. 19 Dec. 1954, Manchester, England. *Education:* BA, University of Cambridge, 1977; MA, Harvard University, 1979. *Career:* mem. Authors Society. *Publications:* Tongues of Flame, 1985; Loving Roger, 1986; Home Thoughts, 1987; Family Planning, 1989; Cara Massimina, 1990; Goodness, 1991; Italian Neighbours, 1992; Juggling the Stars, 1993; Shear, 1993; Mimi's Ghost, 1995; An Italian Education, 1996; Europa, 1997; Adultery and Other Diversions, 1999; Destiny, 2000; A Season With Verona, 2002; Judge Savage, 2003. Short Stories: Keeping Distance, 1988; The Room, 1992. Other: Translating Style: The English and their Italian Translations, 1999; Hell and Back: Reflections on Writers and Writing from Dante to Rushdie, 2001; numerous translations from Italian. Contributions: numerous articles, reviews and talks for BBC Radio 3. *Honours:* Somerset Maugham Award, 1986; Betty Trask Prize, 1986; Rhys Prize, 1986; John Floria Prize for Best Trans. from Italian. *Literary Agent:* Curtis Brown Ltd, Haymarket House, 28–29 Haymarket, London, SW1Y 4SP, England. *Telephone:* (20) 7393-4400. *Fax:* (20) 7393-4401. *E-mail:* info@curtisbrown.co.uk. *Website:* www.curtisbrown.co.uk.

PARMET, Herbert Samuel; Prof. of History Emeritus and Writer; b. 28 Sept. 1929, New York, NY, USA; m. Joan Kronish, 12 Sept. 1948, one d. *Education:* BS, SUNY at Oswego, 1951; MA, Queens College, CUNY, 1957; Postgraduate Studies, Columbia University, 1958–62. *Career:* Prof. of History, 1968–83, Distinguished Prof. of History, 1983–95, Prof. Emeritus, 1995–, Graduate School and University Center, CUNY; Consultant, ABC-TV, New York City, 1983, KERA-TV, Dallas, 1986–91, WGBH-TV, Boston, 1988–91; mem. American Historical Asscn; Authors' Guild; Authors League; Organization of American Historians; Society of American Historians, fellow. *Publications:* Aaron Burr: Portrait of an Ambitious Man, 1967; Never Again: A President Runs for a Third Term, 1968; Eisenhower and the American Crusades, 1972; The Democrats: The Years after FDR, 1976; Jack: The Struggles of John F. Kennedy, 1980; JFK: The Presidency of John F. Kennedy, 1983; Richard Nixon and His America, 1990; George Bush: The Life of a Lone Star Yankee, 1997; Presidential Power: From the New Deal to the New Right, 2002. Contributions: Professional journals. *Honours:* National Endowment for the Humanities Grant, 1987. *Address:* 36 Marsten Lane, Hillsdale, NY 12529, USA.

PARQUE, Richard (Anthony); Writer, Poet and Teacher; b. 8 Oct. 1935, Los Angeles, CA, USA; m. Vo Thi Lan, 1 May 1975, three s. *Education:* BA, 1958, MA, 1961, California State University, Los Angeles; California State Teaching Credential, 1961; Postgraduate studies, University of Redlands. *Career:* mem. Authors' Guild; Acad. of American Poets. *Publications:* Sweet Vietnam, 1984; Hellbound, 1986; Firefight, 1987; Flight of the Phantom, 1988; A Distant Thunder, 1989. Contributions: journals, magazines and newspapers. *Honours:* Bay Area Poets Award, 1989; Viet Nam novels have been placed in the Colorado State University Vietnam War Collection. *Address:* PO Box 327, Verdugo City, CA 91046, USA.

PARRINDER, (John) Patrick, MA, PhD; academic and literary critic; b. 11 Oct. 1944, Wadebridge, Cornwall, England; two d. *Education:* Christ's Coll., Darwin Coll., Cambridge. *Career:* Fellow, King's College, Cambridge, 1967–74; Lecturer, 1974–80, Reader, 1980–86, Prof. of English, 1986–, University of Reading; mem. H. G. Wells Society; Science Fiction Foundation; Society of Authors. *Publications:* H. G. Wells, 1970; Authors and Authority, 1977; Science Fiction: Its Criticism and Teaching, 1980; James Joyce, 1984; The Failure of Theory, 1987; Shadows of the Future, 1995. Editor: H. G. Wells: The Critical Heritage, 1972; Science Fiction: A Critical Guide, 1979; Learning from Other Worlds, 2000. Contributions: London Review of Books; many academic journals. *Honours:* Pres.'s Award, World Science Fiction, 1987; Leverhulme Major Research Fellowship, 2001–04; Fellow, English Asscn, 2001. *Address:* School of English and American Literature, University of Reading, PO Box 218, Reading, Berkshire RG6 6AA, England. *E-mail:* j.p.parrinder@reading.ac.uk.

PARROTT, Jasper William, BA; British impresario and agent; b. 8 Sept. 1944, Stockholm, Sweden; m. Cristina Ortiz; two d. *Education:* Tonbridge School, Peterhouse Cambridge. *Career:* joined Ibbs and Tillett Ltd 1965–69; f. Harrison Parrott Ltd 1969, Chair. and Man. Dir 1987–; Dir Japan Festival 1991, Swiss Festival in UK 1991; Dir Rambert Dance Co. 1993–98; Hon. Trustee Kew Foundation, Royal Botanical Gardens 1991–. *Publication:* Beyond Frontiers: Vladimir Ashkenazy. *Address:* Harrison Parrott, 12 Penzance Place, London, W11 4PA, England (Office). *Telephone:* (20) 7229-9166 (Office). *Fax:* (20) 7221-5042 (Office). *E-mail:* info@harrisonparrott.co.uk (Office). *Website:* www.harrisonparrott.com (Office).

PARRY, Graham; Prof. of English and Author; b. 5 Jan. 1940, Sutton Coldfield, England; m. Barbara Henry, 4 Nov. 1967. *Education:* BA, 1961, MA, 1965, Pembroke College, Cambridge; PhD, Columbia University, 1965. *Career:* Preceptor, Columbia University, USA, 1962–65; Asst Prof., University of British Columbia, Canada, 1965–67; Lecturer in English, University of Leeds, England, 1967–76; Visiting Prof., Université de Toulouse, France, 1972–73, City College, CUNY, 1975–76, Doshisha University, Japan, 1981–82; Lecturer in English, 1977, then Prof. of Renaissance Literature, University of York. *Publications:* Lady Mary Wroth's Urania 1975, The Pre-Raphaelite Image: Style and Subject 1848–56 1978, Hollar's England: A Mid-Seventeenth Century View 1980, The Golden Age Restor'd: The Culture of the Stuart Court 1603–1642 1981, Seventeenth-Century Poetry: The Social Context 1985, The Seventeenth Century: The Intellectual and Cultural Context of English Literature 1603–1700 1989, The Trophies of Time: English Antiquarians of the Seventeenth Century 1995, The Life and Letters of John Talman 1997, Milton and the Terms of Liberty (Ed. with J. Raymond) 2002. *Address:* 28 Micklefield Lane, Rawdon, Leeds, England.

PARSONS, Tony; British writer; b. 1955, Essex, England; m. 1st Julie Burchill (divorced); one s.; m. 2nd. *Career:* fmr journalist, NME; columnist, The Mirror; regular guest, Newsnight Review, The Late Show (BBC TV). *Publications:* Man and Boy 1999, One for My Baby 2001, Man and Wife 2002, The Family Way 2004; contrib. to Arena, Daily Mail, Daily Telegraph, Elle, The Face, GQ, Guardian, Marie Claire, Red, Spectator, Sunday Times. *Honours:* Butler and Tanner Book of the Year 2001, Nielsen BookScan and the Times Platinum Book Award, British Book Awards 2002. *Literary Agent:* AP Watt Ltd, 20 John Street, London, WC1N 2DR, England.

PASCHEN, Elise Maria; Arts Administrator and Poet; b. 4 Jan. 1959, Chicago, IL, USA. *Education:* BA, Harvard University, 1982; MPhil, 1984, DPhil, 1988, University of Oxford. *Career:* Exec. Dir, Poetry Society of America; mem. National Arts Club. *Publications:* Houses: Coasts, 1985; Infidelities, 1996. Contributions: Reviews, journals, and magazines. *Honours:* Lloyd McKim Garrison Medal for Poetry, Harvard University, 1982; Joan Grey Untermyer Poetry Prize, Harvard University/Radcliffe College, 1982; Richard Selig Prize for Poetry, Magdalen College, Oxford, 1984; Nicholas Roerich Poetry Prize, 1996. *Address:* c/o Poetry Society of America, 15 Gramercy Park, New York, NY 10003, USA.

PATCHETT, Ann; Writer; b. 2 Dec. 1963, Los Angeles, CA, USA. *Education:* BA, Sarah Lawrence Coll., 1984; MFA, Univ. of Iowa, 1987. *Career:* Writer-in-Residence, Allegheny Coll., 1989–90; Visiting Asst Prof., Murray State Univ., 1992. *Publications:* The Patron Saint of Liars, 1992; Taft, 1994; The Magician's Assistant, 1997; Bel Canto, 2001; Patron Saint of Liars, 2003. Contributions: anthologies; periodicals, incl.: New York Times Sunday Magazine; Chicago Tribune; Boston Globe; Vogue; GQ; Elle; Gourmet. *Honours:* James A. Michener/Copernicus Award, Univ. of Iowa, 1989; Yaddo Fellow, 1990; Millay Fellow, 1990; Resident Fellow, Fine Arts Work Center, Provincetown, MA, 1990–91; Notable Book, American Library Asscn, 1992; Bunting Fellowship, Mary Ingram Bunting Institute, Radcliffe Coll., 1993; Janet Heidinger Kafka Prize, 1994; National Banner Tennessee Writer of the Year Award, 1994; Orange Prize, 2002; Guggenheim Fellowship, 1994; PEN/Faulkner Award, 2002. *Address:* c/o Carol Fass Ivy Publishing, 201 E 50th St, New York, NY 10022, USA. *Website:* www.annpatchett.com.

PATERSON, Alistair (Ian), (Ian Hughes); Poet, Writer and Educational Consultant; b. 28 Feb. 1929, Nelson, New Zealand; m. Dec. 1984, two s. three d. *Education:* BA, University of New Zealand, 1961; Diploma in Education, University of Auckland, 1972. *Career:* Royal New Zealand Navy, 1954–74; Dean of General Studies, New Zealand Police, 1974–78; Tertiary Inspector, New Zealand Dept of Education, 1979–89; Educational Consultant, 1990–; mem. PEN; Wellington Poetry Society. *Publications:* Caves in the Hills, 1965; Birds Flying, 1973; Cities and Strangers, 1976; The Toledo Room: A Poem for Voices, 1978; 15 Contemporary New Zealand Poets (ed.), 1980; Qu'appelle, 1982; The New Poetry, 1982; Incantations for Warriors, 1982; Oedipus Rex, 1986; Short Stories from New Zealand (ed.), 1988; How to be a Millionaire by Next Wednesday (novel), 1994. Contributions: various publications. *Honours:* Fulbright Fellowship, 1977; John Cowie Reid Award, University of Auckland, 1982; Katherine Mansfield Award for Fiction, 1993; New Zealand Creative Writing Grant, 1995.

PATERSON, Donald (Don); poet, editor and musician; b. 30 Oct. 1963, Dundee, Scotland. *Career:* writer-in-residence, Dundee Univ. 1993–95; Poetry Ed. Picador Ltd. *Publications:* Nil Nil 1993, God's Gift to Women (T. S. Eliot Prize) 1997, The Eyes 1999, The White Lie: New and Selected Poetry 2001, Landing Light (T. S. Eliot Prize, Whitbread Award for Poetry) 2003; other: ed. of numerous anthologies and collections. *Honours:* Eric Gregory Trust Fund Award 1990, Arvon/Observer International Poetry Competition 1993, Forward Poetry Prize 1993, Scottish Arts Council Book Awards 1993, 1997, 1999, Geoffrey Faber Memorial Prize 1998. *Address:* c/o Faber and Faber, 3 Queen Square, London, WC1N 3AU, England.

PATERSON, Stuart A.; Writer, Poet and Ed.; b. 31 Jan. 1966, Truro, Cornwall, England. *Education:* Stirling University, 1988–92. *Career:* Founder-Ed., Spectrum review, 1990–96; Scottish Arts Council Writer-in-Residence, Dumfries and Galloway Region, 1996–98; mem. Kilmarnock North West Writers Group, founder; Artists for Independence; Scottish Poetry Library; Scottish National Party. *Publications:* Mulaney of Larne and Other Poems, 1991; Saving Graces, 1997. Contributions: anthologies, reviews, newspapers and journals. *Honours:* Eric Gregory Award, 1992; Scottish Arts Council Writer's Bursary, 1993. *Address:* c/o 2A Leslie Rd, New Farm Loch, Kilmarnock, Ayrshire KA3 7RR, Scotland.

PATON WALSH, Jill; Writer; b. 29 April 1937, London, England; m. Anthony Paton Walsh, one s. two d. *Education:* Diploma in Education, 1959, MA, St Anne's College, Oxford. *Career:* Permanent Visiting Faculty Mem., Centre for Children's Literature, Simmons College, Boston, MA, 1978–86; Gertrude Clarke Whittall Lecturer, Library of Congress, 1978; Whitbread Prize Judge, 1984; Co-owner, Green Bay Publications; mem. Chair., Cambridge Book Assen, 1987–89; Society of Authors, mem., management committee; Children's Literature New England, adjunct British board mem. *Publications:* Lapsing, 1986; A School for Lovers, 1989; The Wyndham Case, 1993; Knowledge of Angels, 1994; A Piece of Justice, 1995; Goldengrove Unleaving, 1997; The Serpentine Cave, 1997; Thrones, Dominations, 1998; A Desert in Bohemia, 2000. Children's Fiction: The Dolphin Crossing, 1967; Fireweed, 1970; Goldengrove, 1972; Unleaving, 1976; A Chance Child, 1978; The Green Book, 1981; A Parcel of Patterns, 1984; Gaffer Samson's Luck, 1985; Torch, 1987; Birdy and the Ghosties, 1989; Matthew and the Sea Singer, 1992; When Grandma Came, 1992; Pepi and the Secret Names, 1994; Connie Came to Play, 1995; Thomas and the Tinners, 1995; When I was Little Like You, 1997. Contributions: articles and reviews to many journals. *Honours:* Book World Festival Award, 1970; Whitbread Prize (children's novel), 1974; Boston Globe-Horn Book Award, 1976; Arts Council Creative Writing Fellowship, 1976–78; The Universe Prize, 1984; Smarties Grand Prix, 1984; CBE, 1996; FRSL, 1996. *Literary Agent:* David Higham Associates, 5–8 Lower John St, Golden Sq., London W1F 9HA, England. *Website:* www.greenbay.co.uk/jpw.html.

PATRICK, Maxine (see Maxwell, Patricia Anne).

PATRICK, Susan (see Clark, Patricia Denise).

PATRICK, William (see Haining, Peter (Alexander)).

PATTEN, Brian; Poet and Writer; b. 7 Feb. 1946, Liverpool, England. *Career:* Regents Lecturer, University of California at San Diego; mem. Chelsea Arts Club. *Publications:* Poetry: The Mersey Sound: Penguin Modern Poets 10, 1967; Little Johnny's Confession, 1967; The Home Coming, 1969; Notes to the Hurrying Man: Poems, Winter '66–Summer '68, 1969; The Irrelevant Song, 1970; At Four O'Clock in the Morning, 1971; Walking Out: The Early Poems of Brian Patten, 1971; The Eminent Professors and the Nature of Poetry as Enacted Out by Members of the Poetry Seminar One Rainy Evening, 1972; The Unreliable Nightingale, 1973; Vanishing Trick, 1976; Grave Gossip, 1979; Love Poems, 1981; New Volume, 1983; Storm Damage, 1988; Grinning Jack: Selected Poems, 1990; Armada, 1996; The Utterly Brilliant Book of Poetry (ed.), 1998. Editor: Clare's Countryside: A Book of John Clare, 1981. Children's Books: Prose: The Jumping Mouse, 1972; Mr Moon's Last Case, 1975; Emma's Doll, 1976; Jimmy Tag-along, 1988; Grizzelda Frizzle, 1992; Impossible Parents, 1994; Beowulf, a version, 1999; The Story Giant, 2002. Poetry: Gargling With Jelly, 1985; Thawing Frozen Frogs, 1990; The Puffin Book of 20th Century Children's Verse, 1991; The Magic Bicycle, 1993; The Utter Nutters, 1994; The Blue and Green Ark, 1999; Juggling with Gerbils, 2000; Ben's Magic Telescope, 2003. Contributions: journals and newspapers. *Honours:* Special Award, MWA, 1977; Arts Council of England Writers Award, 1998; Freedom of the City of Liverpool, 2001; Hon. Fellowship, John Moore's Univerisity, 2002; FRSL, 2003. *Literary Agent:* Rogers, Coleridge & White Ltd, 20 Powis Mews, London W11 1JN, England.

PATTERSON, Glenn, BA, MA; Northern Irish writer; b. 9 Aug. 1961, Belfast; m. Ali Fitzgibbon 1995. *Education:* Univ. of East Anglia. *Career:* Writer-in-the-Community, Arts Council, Northern Ireland 1989–91; Creative Writing Fellow, Univ. of East Anglia 1992; Writer-in-Residence, Univ. Coll., Cork 1993–94, Queen's Univ., Belfast 1994–97; mem. Arts Council Northern Ireland (bd mem. 1996–2000), Soc. of Authors. *Publications:* Burning Your Own 1988, Fat Lad 1992, Black Night at Big Thunder Mountain 1995, The International 1999, Number 5 2003, That Which Was 2004. *Honours:* Betty Trask Prize 1988, Rooney Prize for Irish Literature 1988. *Literary Agent:* Antony Harwood Ltd, 103 Walton Street, Oxford, OX2 6EB, England.

PATTERSON, Glenn, MA; Irish novelist; b. 1961, Belfast. *Education:* Univ. of East Anglia. *Career:* community writer for Lisburn and Craigavon 1989–91; writer-in-residence, Univ. of East Anglia, Univ. of Cork, Queen's Univ., Belfast. *Publications:* novels: Burning Your Own 1988, Fat Lad 1992, Black Night at Big Thunder Mountain 1995, The International 1999, Number 5 2003, That Which Was 2004. *Honours:* Rooney Award for Irish Literature 1988, Betty Trask Award 1988. *Literary Agent:* c/o Hamish Hamilton, Penguin Books Ltd, 80 Strand, London, WC2R 0RL, England. *Website:* www.penguin.co.uk.

PATTERSON, Henry (Harry), (Martin Fallon, James Graham, Jack Higgins, Hugh Marlowe); Author; b. 27 July 1929, Newcastle upon Tyne, England; m. 1st Amy Margaret Hewitt, 1958, divorced, 1984, one s., three d.; m. 2nd Denise Lesley Anne Palmer, 1985. *Education:* Certificate in Education, Carnegie College, 1958; BSc, LSE, 1962. *Career:* NCO, The Blues, 1947–50, 1950–58. *Publications:* Sad Wind from the Sea, 1959; Cry of the Hunter, 1960; The Thousand Faces of Night, 1961; Comes the Dark Stranger, 1962; Wrath of the Lion, 1963; Pay the Devil, 1963; The Dark Side of the Island, 1963; A Phoenix in Blood, 1964; Thunder at Noon, 1964, re-released as Dillinger, 1983; The Graveyard Shift, 1965; Iron Tiger, 1966; Brought in Dead, 1967; Hell is Always Today, 1968; Toll for the Brave, 1971; To Catch a King (aka The Judas Gate), 1979. As Martin Fallon: The Testament of Caspar Schultz, 1962; Year of the Tiger, 1963; The Keys to Hell, 1965; Mignight Never Comes, 1966; Dark Side of the Street, 1967; A Fine Night for Dying, 1969; Day of Judgement, 1979. As James Graham: A Game for Heroes, 1970; The Wrath of God, 1971; The Khufra Run, 1972; The Run to Morning, 1974. As Jack Higgins: East of Desolation, 1968; In the Hour Before Midnight, 1969; Night Judgement at Sinos, 1970; The Last Place God Made, 1971; The Savage Day, 1972; The Eagle Has Landed, 1975; Storm Warning, 1976; The Valhalla Exchange, 1976; A Prayer for the Dying, 1977; Solo (aka The Creatan Lover), 1980; Lucianos Luck, 1981; Touch the Devil, 1982; Exocet, 1983; Confessional, 1985; Night of the Fox, 1986; Memoirs of a Dance Hall Romeo, 1989; A Season in Hell, 1989; The Eagle Has Flown, 1990; Cold Harbour, 1990; Eye of the Storm (aka Midnight Man), 1992; Thunder Point, 1993; On Dangerous Ground, 1994; Angel of Death, 1995; Sheba, 1995; Drink With the Devil, 1996; The President's Daughter, 1997; The Violent Enemy, 1997; Flight of Eagles, 1998; The White House Connection, 1999; Day of Reckoning, 2000; Edge of Danger, 2001; The Keys of Hell, 2002; Bad Company, 2003. As Hugh Marlowe: Seven Pillars to Hell, 1963; Passage by Night, 1964; A Candle for the Dead (aka The Violent Enemy), 1966. *Literary Agent:* Ed Victor Ltd, 6 Bayley St, Bedford Sq., London WC1B 3HB, England.

PATTERSON, James, BA, MA; American writer and fmr advertising executive; b. 22 March 1947, Newburgh, NY; m.; one s. *Education:* Manhattan Coll., Vanderbilt Univ. *Career:* wrote first novel 1976; joined J. Walter Thompson as jr copywriter 1971, subsequently Exec. Creative Dir, CEO, Chair. 1990–96. *Publications:* The Thomas Berryman Number (MWA Edgar Award) 1976, The Season of the Machete 1977, The Jericho Commandment (aka See How They Run) 1979, Virgin 1980, Black Market 1986, The Midnight Club 1989, The Day America Told the Truth: What People Really Believe About Everything that Matters (non-fiction, with Peter Kim) 1991, Along Came a Spider 1993, The Second American Revolution 1994, Kiss the Girls 1995, Hide & Seek 1996, Jack & Jill 1996, Miracle on the 17th Green (with Peter de Jonge) 1996, Cat & Mouse 1997, When the Wind Blows 1998, Pop Goes the Weasel 1999, Cradle and All (revised version of Virgin) 2000, Roses are Red 2000, Suzanne's Diary for Nicholas 2001, 1st to Die 2001, Violets are Blue 2001, 2nd Chance (with Andrew Gross) 2002, Four Blind Mice 2002, The Beach House (with Peter de Jonge) 2002, The Jester 2003, The Lake House 2003, The Big Bad Wolf 2003, 3rd Degree 2003, Sam's Letters to Jennifer 2004, London Bridges 2004. *Address:* c/o Little, Brown and Company, 1271 Avenue of the Americas, New York, NY 10020, USA (Office). *Website:* www.jamespatterson.com.

PATTERSON, (Horace) Orlando Lloyd; academic and writer; b. 5 June 1940, Jamaica. *Education:* BSc, University of the West Indies, 1962; PhD, LSE, 1965. *Career:* Prof. of Sociology, 1971–, John Cowles Prof. of Sociology,

1993, Harvard University; Assoc. Ed., American Sociological Review, 1989–92; mem. American Acad. of Arts and Sciences, fellow; American Sociological Asscn. *Publications:* Fiction: The Children of Sisyphus, 1964; An Absence of Ruins, 1967; Die the Long Day, 1972. Non-Fiction: The Sociology of Slavery: Jamaica 1655–1838, 1967; Ethnic Chauvinism: The Reactionary Impulse, 1977; Slavery and Social Death: A Comparative Study, 1982; Freedom, 1991; The Ordeal of Integration: Progress and Resentment in America's 'Racial' Crisis, 1997; Rituals of Blood: The Consequences of Slavery in Two American Centuries, 1999. Contributions: books and professional journals. *Honours:* Best Novel in English Award, Dakar Festival of Negro Arts, 1965; Co-Winner, Ralph Bunche Award, American Political Science Asscn, 1983; Distinguished Contribution to Scholarship Award, American Sociological Asscn, 1983; Walter Channing Cabot Faculty Prizes, Harvard University, 1983, 1997; National Book Award for Non-Fiction, 1991; University of California at Los Angeles Medal, 1992; Order of Distinction, Government of Jamaica, 1999; Hon. Doctor of Humane Letters, New School University, 2000. *Address:* c/o Department of Sociology, Harvard University, Cambridge, MA 02138, USA.

PATTERSON, Richard North, BA, JD; novelist; b. 22 Feb. 1947, Berkeley, CA, USA; m. Laurie Anderson Patterson 1993; four s. two d. *Education:* Ohio Wesleyan Univ., Case Western Reserve Law School. *Career:* mem. PEN (bd of dirs). *Publications:* The Lasko Tangent, 1979; The Outside Man, 1981; Escape the Night, 1983; Private Screening, 1985; Degree of Guilt, 1993; Eyes of a Child, 1995; The Final Judgement, 1995; Silent Witness, 1997; When the Wind Blows, 1998; Protect and Defend, 2000; Balance of Power, 2003. Contributions: Magazines, journals and newspapers. *Honours:* Edgar Allan Poe Award, 1979; French Grand Prix de Littérature Policière, 1995; Pres.'s Award to Distinguished Alumni, Case Western Reserve University, 1997. *Address:* c/o PEN American Center, 568 Broadway, New York, NY 10012, USA.

PATTISON, Robert; Prof. of English and Writer; b. 28 Oct. 1945, Orange, NJ, USA. *Education:* AB, Yale University; MA, University of Sussex, 1968; PhD, Columbia University, 1974. *Career:* Adjunct Lecturer, Richmond College, CUNY, 1974; Adjunct Instructor, Queensborough Community College, CUNY, 1974–75; Instructor of English, St Vincent's College, St John's University, New York, 1975–77; Prof. of English, Southampton College, Long Island University, New York, 1978–. *Publications:* The Child Figure in English Literature, 1978; Tennyson and Tradition, 1980; On Literacy, 1982; The Triumph of Vulgarity, 1987; The Great Dissent: John Henry Newman and the Liberal Heresy, 1991. Contributions: Nation; ADE Bulletin; University of Toronto Quarterly; Mosaic; New York Times; Dickens Studies Newsletter; various edited vols. *Honours:* Long Island University Trustees Awards for Scholarship, 1979, 1985; Rockefeller Foundation Fellowship, 1980–81; Guggenheim Fellowship, 1988–87. *Address:* PO Box 2106, Southampton, NY 11969, USA.

PAUL, Jeremy; Writer; b. 29 July 1939, Bexhill, Sussex, England; m. Patricia Garwood, 26 Nov. 1960, four d. *Education:* King's, Canterbury and St Edmund Hall, Oxford. *Career:* mem. Writers Guild of Great Britain. *Publications:* Books: Sing Willow, 2002. Other: numerous TV plays, series and adaptations, 1960–, incl.: Upstairs, Downstairs, 1971–75; Country Matters, 1972; The Duchess of Duke Street, 1976; Danger, UXB, 1977; A Walk in the Forest, 1980; The Flipside of Dominick Hide (with Alan Gibson), 1980; Sorrell and Son, 1983; By the Sword Divided, 1985; The Adventures, Return and Memoirs of Sherlock Holmes, 1984–94; Lovejoy, 1991–94; Hetty Wainthropp Investigates, 1996–98; Midsomer Murders, 2001. Theatre: David Going Out, 1971; Manoeuvres, 1971; The Little Match Girl (with Strachan and Stewart), 1976; Visitors (with Carey Harrison), 1980; The Secret of Sherlock Holmes, 1988; The Watcher, 1989. Film: Countess Dracula, 1970. *Address:* 4 Seymer Pl., Swanage, Dorset BH19 2AJ, England.

PAULIN, Tom, (Thomas Neilson Paulin); Poet, Critic and Lecturer in English Literature; b. 25 Jan. 1949, Leeds, Yorkshire, England; m. Munjiet Kaut Khosa, 1973, two s. *Education:* BA, University of Hull; BLitt, Lincoln College, Oxford. *Career:* Lecturer, 1972–89, Reader in Poetry, 1989–94, University of Nottingham; G. M. Young Lecturer in English Literature, University of Oxford, 1994–; Fellow, Hertford College, Oxford, 1994–. *Publications:* Poetry: Theoretical Locations, 1975; A State of Justice, 1977; Personal Column, 1978; The Strange Museum, 1980; The Book of Juniper, 1981; Liberty Tree, 1983; The Argument at Great Tew, 1985; Fivemiletown, 1987; Selected Poems 1972–90, 1993; Walking a Line, 1994; The Wind Dog, 1999; The Invasion Handbook, 2002. Other: Thomas Hardy: The Poetry of Perception, 1975; Ireland and the English Crisis, 1984; The Faber Book of Political Verse (ed.), 1986; Hard Lines 3 (co-ed.), 1987; Minotaur: Poetry and the Nation State, 1992; Writing to the Moment: Selected Critical Essays, 1996; The Day Star of Liberty: William Hazlitt's Radical Style (biog.), 1998. *Honours:* Eric Gregory Award, 1978; Somerset Maugham Award, 1978; Faber Memorial Prize, 1982; Fulbright Scholarship, 1983–84. *Address:* c/o Faber and Faber, 3 Queen Sq., London WC1N 3AU, England.

PAULSON, Ronald (Howard); Prof. of Humanities and Writer; b. 27 May 1930, Bottineau, ND, USA; m. Barbara Lee Appleton, 25 May 1957, divorced 1982, one s. one d. *Education:* BA, 1952, PhD, 1958, Yale University. *Career:* Instructor, 1958–59, Asst Prof., 1959–62, Assoc. Prof., 1962–63, University of Illinois; Prof. of English, 1967–75, Chair., Dept of English, 1968–75, Andrew W. Mellon Prof. of Humanities, 1973–75, Mayer Prof. of Humanities, 1984–, Chair., Dept of Humanities, 1985–91, Johns Hopkins University; Prof. of English, Yale University, 1975–84; mem. American Acad. of Arts and Sciences, fellow; American Society of 18th Century Studies, pres., 1986–87. *Publications:* Theme and Structure in Swift's Tale of a Tub, 1960; Fielding: The Critical Heritage (ed. with Thomas Lockwood), 1962; Fielding: 20th Century Views (ed.), 1962; Hogarth's Graphic Works, 1965; The Fictions of Satire, 1967; Satire and the Novel, 1967; Satire: Modern Essays in Criticism, 1971; Hogart: His Life, Art and Times, 1971; Rowlandson: A New Interpretation, 1972; Emblem and Expression: Meaning in Eighteenth Century English Art, 1975; The Art of Hogarth, 1975; Popular and Polite Art in the Age of Hogarth and Fielding, 1979; Literary Landscape: Turner and Constable, 1982; Book and Painting: Shakespeare, Milton and the Bible, 1983; Representations of Revolution, 1983; Breaking and Remaking, 1989; Figure and Abstraction in Contemporary Painting, 1990; Hogarth: Vol. I, The Making of the Modern Moral Subject, 1991, Vol. II, High Art and Low, 1992, Vol. III, Art and Politics, 1993; The Beautiful, Novel and Strange: Aesthetics and Heterodoxy, 1996; The Analysis of Beauty (ed.), 1997; Don Quixote in England: The Aesthetics of Laughter, 1998; The Life of Henry Fielding: A Critical Biography, 2000. Contributions: Professional journals. *Honours:* Guggenheim Fellowships, 1965–66, 1986–87; National Endowment for the Humanities Fellow, 1977–78. *Address:* 2722 St Paul St, Baltimore, MD 21218, USA.

PAVIĆ, Milorad; Poet, Novelist and Historian; b. 15 Oct. 1929, Belgrade, Yugoslavia; m. 1st Branka Pavic; one s. one d.; m. 2nd Jasmina Mihailovic. *Education:* Belgrade Univ.; DPhil, literary history, Univ. of Zagreb. *Career:* journalist, Radio Belgrade, 1958–63, Prosveta Publrs, 1963–74; Prof., Dean, Faculty of Philosophy, Novy Sad Univ., 1974–82; Prof., Belgrade Univ., 1982–94; lecturer, Univ. of Paris (Sorbonne); mem., Serbian Academy of Sciences and Arts, 1991–. *Publications:* Vojislav Ilic (1860–1894), 1961; Vojislav Ilic, njegovo vreme i delo (non-fiction), 1962; Palimpsesti (poems), 1967; Istorija srpske knjizevnosti baroknog doba (non-fiction), 1970; Mesecev kamen (poems), 1971; Vojislav Ilic i evropsko pesnistvo, 1971; Gavril Stefanovic Venclovic, 1972; Gvozdena zavesa (short stories), 1973; Jezicko pamcenje i pesnicki oblik, 1976; Konji svetoga Marka (short stories), 1976; Istorija srpske knjizevnosti klasicizma i predromantizma, 1979; Ruski hrt/Borzoi, 1979; Nove beogradske price, 1981; Duse se kupaju poslednji put, 1982; Radjanje nove srpske knjizevnosti (non-fiction), 1983; Hazarski recnik (novel, trans. as Dictionary of the Khazars), 1984; Istorija, stalez i stil, 1985; Izabrana dela, 1985; Predeo slikan cajem (novel, trans. as Landscape Painted with Tea), 1988; Izvrnuta rukavica, 1989; Kratka istorija Beograda, 1990; Unutrasnja strana vetra ili roman o Heri i Leandru (novel, trans. as The Inner Side of the Wind), 1991; Istorija srpske knjizevnosti, 1991; Pozorisni jelovnik za uvek i dan vise (Forever and a Day, screenplay), 1993; Poslednja ljubav u Carigradu (novel, trans. as Last Love in Constantinople), 1994; Sesir od riblje koze, 1996; Stakleni puz, 1998; Milorad Pavic, Jasmina Mihajlovic, 1998; Glinena armija, 1999; Kutija za pisanje, 1999. Contributions: numerous articles and essays. *Address:* Brace Baruh 2, Belgrade, Serbia and Montenegro. *E-mail:* mpavic@eunet.yu. *Website:* www.khazars.com.

PAXMAN, Jeremy Dickson, MA; British journalist and author; b. 11 May 1950, Leeds; one s. two d. *Education:* Malvern Coll., St Catharine's Coll., Cambridge. *Career:* journalist, Northern Ireland 1973–77; reporter, BBC TV Tonight and Panorama programmes 1977–85, presenter BBC TV Breakfast Time 1986–89, Newsnight 1989–, Univ. Challenge 1994–, Start the Week, Radio 4, 1998–2002; Fellow St Edmund Hall, Oxford, St Catharine's Coll. Cambridge 2001; Vice-Pres. The Wild Trout Trust (WTT) 2004–. *Publications:* A Higher Form of Killing (co-author) 1982, Through the Volcanoes 1985, Friends in High Places 1990, Fish, Fishing and the Meaning of Life 1994, The Compleat Angler 1996, The English 1998, The Political Animal 2002; numerous articles in newspapers and magazines. *Honours:* Dr hc (Leeds, Bradford) 1999; Royal TV Soc. Award for Int. Reporting, Richard Dimbleby Award, BAFTA 1996, 2000, Interview of the Year, Royal TV Soc. 1997, 1998, 2001, Voice of the Viewer and Listener Presenter of the Year 1994, 1997, Variety Club Media Personality of the Year 1999. *Address:* c/o BBC TV, London, W12 7RJ, England.

PAXSON, Diana L(ucile); Writer and Ed.; b. 20 Feb. 1943, Detroit, MI, USA; m. Donald C. Studebaker, 1968, two s. *Education:* BA, Mills College, 1964; MA, University of California at Berkeley, 1968. *Career:* Ordained Minister, Fellowship of the Spiral Path, 1982; Ed., Idunna journal, 1996–; mem. Equinox; SFWA. *Publications:* Lady of Light, 1982; Lady of Darkness, 1983; Brisingamen, 1984; Silverhaird the Wanderer, 1986; White Mare, Red Stallion, 1986; The Earthstone, 1987; The Paradise Tree, 1987; The Sea Star, 1988; The White Raven, 1988; The Wind Crystal, 1990; Lady of Darkness, 1990; The Serpent's Tooth, 1991; The Wolf and the Raven, 1993; Master of Earth and Water, 1993; The Shield Between the Worlds, 1994; Sword of Fire and Shadow, 1995; The Dragons of the Rhine, 1995; The Lord of Horses, 1996. Contributions: Short stories to various publications. *Address:* PO Box 472, Berkeley, CA 94701, USA.

PAXTON, Lois (see Low, Lois Dorothea).

PAYNE, (William) David; writer; b. 13 April 1955, Henderson, NC, USA. *Publications:* Confessions of a Taoist on Wall Street: A Chinese American Romance, 1984; Early from the Dance, 1989; Ruin Creek, 1993; Gravesend

Light, 2000. *Honours:* Houghton Mifflin Company Fellowship 1984. *Literary Agent:* Janklow & Nesbit Associates, 445 Park Avenue, New York, NY 10022, USA.

PEACOCK, Molly; Writer and Poet; b. 30 June 1947, Buffalo, NY, USA; m. Michael Groden, 19 Aug. 1992. *Education:* BA, magna cum laude, Harpur College, SUNY at Binghamton, 1969; MA, Johns Hopkins University, 1977. *Career:* Lecturer, SUNY at Binghamton, 1975–76, University of Delaware, 1978–79; Writer-in-Residence, Delaware State Arts Council, 1978–81, University of Western Ontario, 1995–96; English Faculty, Friends Seminary, New York City, 1981–87; Visiting Poet, Hofstra University, 1986, Columbia University, 1986, 1992, Carlow College, 1993; Poet-in-Residence, Bucknell University, 1993, Bennington College, 2001; Contributing Writer, House & Garden, 1996–2001; Regents Lecturer, University of California at Riverside, 1998; mem. Acad. of American Poets; Associated Writing Programs; PEN; Poetry Society of America, pres., 1989–95. *Publications:* Poetry: And Live Apart, 1980; Raw Heaven, 1984; Take Heart, 1989; Original Love, 1995; Cornucopia, 2002. Other: Paradise, Piece by Piece (literary memoir), 1998; How to Read a Poem... and Start a Poetry Circle, 1999. Editor: Poetry in Motion: 100 Poems from the Subways and Buses (with Elise Paschen and Neil Neches), 1996; The Private I: Privacy in a Public Age (essays). Contributions: anthologies, reviews, quarterlies, journals, and magazines. *Honours:* MacDowell Colony Fellowships, 1975–76, 1979, 1982, 1985, 1989; Danforth Foundation Fellowships, 1976–77; Yaddo Fellowships, 1980, 1982; Ingram Merrill Foundation Awards, 1981, 1986; New Virginia Review Fellowship, 1983; PEN/National Endowment for the Arts Fiction Award, 1984; New York Foundation for the Arts Grant, 1985, 1989; National Endowment for the Arts Grant, 1990. *Address:* 505 E 14th St, No. 3G, New York, NY 10009, USA; 109 Front St E, No. 1041, Toronto, ON M5A 4P7, Canada.

PEARCE, Brian Louis; Poet, Author, Dramatist and Lecturer; b. 4 June 1933, London, England; m. Margaret Wood, 2 Aug. 1969, one d. *Education:* MA, University College London. *Career:* Examiner in English Literature, Library Asscn, 1964–70; College Librarian-Senior Lecturer, Richmond upon Thames College, 1977–88; Occasional Lecturer, National Portrait Gallery, London, 1990–; Hon. Librarian, Theological College of Zimbabwe, Bulawayo, 1997–98; mem. Browning, David Jones, De la Mare, Hopkins, Masefield, Palgrave Societies; PEN; FRSA; RSL. *Publications:* Poetry: Selected Poems 1951–1973 1978, Dutch Comfort 1985, Gwen John Talking 1985, Jack O'Lent 1991, Leaving the Corner: Selected Poems 1973–1985 1992, Coeli et terra 1993, Thames Listener: Poems 1949–89 1993, The Proper Fuss 1996, 'City Whiskers' sequence in The Playing of the Easter Music (with Caws and Caseley) 1996. Fiction: Victoria Hammersmith 1987, London Clay 1991, The Bust of Minerva 1992, A Man in his Room 1992, Battersea Pete 1994, The Servant of his Country 1994, The Tufnell Triptych 1997, Tribal Customs 1997, The Goldhawk Variations 1999, Willesden Paper 2002, St Zacchs 2003. Plays: The Eagle and the Swan, 1966; Shrine Rites, 1990; The Damien Offices, 2000; The Widow of Gozo, 2002. Other: Palgrave: Selected Poems (ed.), 1985; Thomas Twining of Twickenham, 1988; The Fashioned Reed: The Poets of Twickenham from 1500, 1992; Varieties of Fervour: Portraits of Victorian and Edwardian Poets, 1996; Dame Ethel Walker: An Essay in Reassessment, 1997; The Palgraves and John Murray: Letters (ed.), 1997; The Idea of Nicodemus: Sermons and Prayers, 2000; Clemo the Poet, 2002. Contributions: various publications. *Honours:* First Place, Christian Poetry Competition, 1989. *Address:* The Marish, 72 Heathfield S, Twickenham, Middlesex TW2 7SS, England.

PEARCE, Mary Emily; Writer; b. 7 Dec. 1932, London, England. *Career:* mem. Society of Authors. *Publications:* Apple Tree Lean Down, 1973; Jack Mercybright, 1974; The Sorrowing Wind, 1975; Cast a Long Shadow, 1977; The Land Endures, 1978; Seedtime and Harvest, 1980; Polsinney Harbour, 1983; The Two Farms, 1985; The Old House at Railes, 1993. *Address:* Owls End, Shuthonger, Tewkesbury, Gloucestershire, England.

PEARCE, (Ann) Philippa, OBE, MA, FRSL; British children's writer; b. 1920, Great Shelford; m. Martin James Graham Christie 1963 (deceased); one d. *Education:* Perse Girls' School, Cambridge and Girton Coll., Cambridge. *Career:* civil servant 1942–45; producer and scriptwriter for BBC Radio School Broadcasting Dept 1945–58; Ed. Educ. Dept Clarendon Press 1958–60; part-time Children's Ed. André Deutsch Ltd 1960–67; freelance writer 1967–73; lectures in field; reviews for TLS and The Guardian newspapers. *Publications:* novels: Minnow on the Say (aka The Minnow Leads to Treasure) 1954, Tom's Midnight Garden (Carnegie Medal) 1958, A Dog So Small 1962, The Children of the House (with Sir Brian Fairfax-Lucy, aka The Children of Charlecote: The Battle of Bubble and Squeak) (Whitbread Prize 1978) 1968, The Way to Sattin Shore 1983, The Little Gentleman 2004; short story collections (older children): What the Neighbours Did and other stories (British Honour Book for the Hans Christian Andersen Award) 1972, The Shadow-Cage and Other Tales of the Supernatural 1977, The Elm Street Lot (originally on BBC TV) 1979, Who's Afraid? and other strange stories 1986, The Rope and other stories 2000, Familiar and Haunting 2002; short story collections (younger children): Lion at School and other stories 1985, Here Comes Tod! 1992; short stories/picture books: Mrs Cockle's Cat 1961, The Squirrel Wife 1971, Beauty and the Beast (re-telling) 1972, Inside her Head (in Puffin Post, 14:3) 1980, Face to Face (in anthology, A Sporting Chance) 1985, Emily's Own Elephant 1987, The Toothball 1987, Freddy 1988, Old Belle's Summer Holiday 1989, The Odd Glove (in anthology, The Sea-Baby and other magical stories to read aloud) 1996, The Little White Hen 1996, The Ghost in Annie's Room 2001, The Pedlar of Swaffham (re-telling) 2001, Motorway Dog (in anthology, BBC Children in Need Story Collection) 2002, Amy's Three Best Things 2003; other: The Sins of Miss Halliday (adult short story) 1977, Wings of Courage (trans. of Les Ailes de Courage, by George Sands) 1982, Dread and Delight: A Century of Children's Ghost Stories (ed.) 1995; contrib. criticism, autobiographical work, etc. to books, journals and periodicals. *Honours:* Hon. DLitt (Hull) 1995. *Literary Agent:* Laura Cecil Literary Agency, 17 Alwyne Villas, London, N1 2HG, England. *E-mail:* lauracecil@mac.com.

PEARLMAN, Daniel D.; Prof. and Writer; b. 22 July 1935, New York, NY, USA; one d. *Education:* BA, Brooklyn College, CUNY, 1957; MA, 1958, PhD, 1968, Columbia University. *Career:* Dept Chair, University of Idaho, 1976–80; Prof., 1980–, Dept Chair, 1980–83, University of Rhode Island. *Publications:* The Barb of Time: On the Unity of Ezra Pound's Cantos, 1969; Guide to Rapid Revision, eighth edn, 2002; Letter Perfect: An ABC for Business Writers, 1985; The Final Dream and Other Fictions, 1995; Black Flames (novel), 1997; The Best Known Man in the World (short stories), 2001; Memini (novel), 2003. Contributions: science fiction magazines and anthologies, incl.: Amazing Stories; Synergy; Semiotext SF; Simulations: 15 Tales of Virtual Reality; Imaginings: An Anthology of Long Short Fiction; short stories to literary journals, incl.: Florida Review; New England Review/Bread Loaf Quarterly; Quarterly West. *Address:* c/o Dept of English, University of Rhode Island, Kingston, RI 02881, USA. *E-mail:* dpearl@uri.edu.

PEARSALL, Derek Albert; Prof. of English Emeritus and Writer; b. 28 Aug. 1931, Birmingham, England; m. Rosemary Elvidge, 30 Aug. 1952, two s. three d. *Education:* BA, 1951, MA, 1952, University of Birmingham. *Career:* Asst Lecturer, Lecturer, King's College, University of London, 1959–65; Lecturer, Senior Lecturer, Reader, 1965–76, Prof., 1976–87, University of York; Visiting Prof., 1985–87, Gurney Prof. of English, 1987–2000, Prof. Emeritus, 2000–, Harvard University; mem. Early English Text Society, council mem.; Medieval Acad. of America, fellow; New Chaucer Society, pres., 1988–90; American Acad. of Arts and Sciences, fellow. *Publications:* John Lydgate, 1970; Landscapes and Seasons of the Medieval World (with Elizabeth Salter), 1973; Old English and Middle English Poetry, 1977; Langland's Piers Plowman: An Edition of the C-Text, 1978; The Canterbury Tales: A Critical Study, 1985; The Life of Geoffrey Chaucer: A Critical Biography, 1992; John Lydgate (1371–1449): A Bio-bibliography, 1997; Chaucer to Spenser: An Anthology of Writings in English 1375–1575, 1999; Gothic Europe 1200–1450, 2001; Arthurian Romance: A Short Introduction, 2003. *Address:* 4 Clifton Dale, York YO30 6LJ, England.

PEARSALL, Ronald; Author; b. 20 Oct. 1927, Birmingham, England. *Education:* Birmingham College of Art, 1952–54. *Publications:* Is That My Hook in Your Ear?, 1966; Worm in the Bud, 1969; The Table-Rappers, 1972; The Possessed, 1972; The Exorcism, 1972; Diary of Vicar Veitch, 1972; A Day at the Big Top, 1973; The Wizard and Elidog, 1973; Victorian Sheet Music Covers, 1973; Victorian Popular Music, 1973; Edwardian Life and Leisure, 1973; Collecting Mechanical Antiques, 1973; Collecting Scientific Instruments, 1974; Inside the Antique Trade (with Graham Webb), 1974; Edwardian Popular Music, 1975; Night's Black Angels, 1975; Collapse of Stout Party, 1975; Popular Music of the 1920s, 1976; Public Purity Private Shame, 1976; The Alchemists, 1976; The Belvedere, 1976; Conan Doyle, 1977; Antique Hunter's Handbook, 1978; Tides of War, 1978; Thomas en Olihond, 1979; The Iron Sleep, 1979; Making and Managing an Antique Shop, 1979; Tell Me Pretty Maiden, 1981; Practical Painting, 1983, 4 vols, 1990; Joy of Antiques, 1988; The Murder in Euston Square, 1989; Antique Furniture for Pleasure and Profit, 1990; Lifesaving, 1991; Painting Abstract Pictures, 1991; Encyclopedia of Everyday Antiques, 1992; Antique Furniture Almanac, 1992. *Address:* Sherwell, St Teath, Bodmin, Cornwall PL30 3JB, England.

PEARSE, Lesley Margaret; Novelist; b. 24 Feb. 1945, Rochester, Kent, England; three d. *Education:* Northbrook School Lee, London. *Career:* mem. Romantic Writers Asscn; RNA, West Country Writers Asscn. *Publications:* Georgia, 1992; Tara, 1993; Clarity, 1994; Father Unknown, 2001; Till We Meet Again, 2002; Remember Me, 2003. Contributions: periodicals. *Address:* 16 Withleigh Rd, Knowle, Bristol BS4 2LQ, England.

PEARSON, Ridley; Author; b. 13 March 1953, Glen Cove, New York, USA. *Education:* University of Kansas, 1972; Brown University, 1974. *Career:* mem. Writers Guild of America; MWA; Authors' Guild; International Asscn of Crime Writers. *Publications:* Never Look Back, 1985; Blood of the Albatross, 1986; The Seizing of Yankee Green Mall, 1987; Undercurrents, 1988; Probable Cause, 1990; Hard Fall, 1992; The Angel Maker, 1993; No Witnesses, 1994; Chain of Evidence, 1995; Beyond Recognition, 1997; The Pied Piper, 1998; The First Victim, 1999; Middle of Nowhere, 2000; Parallel Lies, 2001; The Art of Deception, 2002. *Honours:* Fulbright Fellow, 1990–91. *Address:* PO Box 715, Boise, ID 83701, USA.

PEARSON, Thomas Reid, BA, MA; writer; b. 27 March 1956, Winston-Salem, NC, USA. *Education:* North Carolina State Univ., Pennsylvania State Univ. *Publications:* A Short History of a Small Place 1985, Off for the Sweet Hereafter 1986, The Last of How It Was 1987, Call and Response

1989, Gospel Hour 1991, Cry Me a River 1993, Blue Ridge 2000, True Cross 2004. *Literary Agent:* Young Agency, 156 Fifth Avenue, New York, NY 10010, USA.

PEARSON, William Harrison, (Bill Pearson); Writer and University Teacher (retd); b. 18 Jan. 1922, Greymouth, New Zealand. *Education:* Greymouth Technical High School, 1934–38; MA, Canterbury University College, Christchurch, 1948; PhD, King's College, University of London, England, 1952. *Publications:* Coal Flat, 1963; Henry Lawson Among Maoris, 1968; Fretful Sleepers and Other Essays, 1974; Rifled Sanctuaries, 1984; Six Stories, 1991. *Honours:* Co-Recipient, Landfall Readers Award, 1960; New Zealand Book Award for Non-Fiction, 1975. *Address:* 49 Lawrence St, Herne Bay, Auckland, New Zealand.

PECK, Dale; American writer and critic; b. 1967, Long Island, NY. *Education:* Drew Univ., NJ and Columbia Univ. *Career:* book reviewer, Village Voice Literary Supplement, London Book Review, New York Times. *Publications:* Fucking Martin (novel, aka Martin and John) 1993, The Law of Enclosures (novel) 1996, Now It's Time to Say Goodbye (novel) 1998, What We Lost (memoir) 2003, Hatchet Jobs (criticism) 2004. *Honours:* Guggenheim Fellowship. *Address:* c/o Houghton Mifflin Publishing, 222 Berkeley Street, Boston, MA 02116, USA.

PECK, Morgan Scott, AB, MD; psychiatrist and writer; b. 22 May 1936, New York, NY, USA; m. Lily Ho 1959; one s. two d. *Education:* Middlebury College, Harvard University, Case Western Reserve University. *Career:* US Army, 1963–72; Psychiatric practice, New Preston, CT, 1972–84; Medical Dir, New Milford Hospital Mental Health Clinic, 1973–81; Co-Founder and Board Mem., Foundation for Community Encouragement, Ridgefield, CT, 1984–93. *Publications:* The Road Less Traveled: A New Psychology of Love, Traditional Values and Spiritual Growth 1978, People of the Lie: The Hope for Healing Human Evil 1983, What Return Can I Make?: The Dimensions of the Christian Experience (with Marilyn von Waldener and Patricia Kay) 1985, The Different Drum: Community Building and Peace 1987, A Bed by the Window: A Novel of Mystery and Redemption 1990, The Friendly Snowflake: A Fable of Faith, Love and Family 1992, Further Along the Road Less Traveled: The Unending Journey toward Spiritual Growth 1993, A World Waiting to Be Born: Civility Rediscovered 1993, Meditations from the Road: Daily Reflections from the Road Less Traveled and the Different Drum 1993, In Search of Stones: A Pilgrimage of Faith, Reason and Discovery 1995, In Heaven as on Earth 1996, The Road Less Traveled and Beyond: Spiritual Growth in an Age of Anxiety 1997, Denial of the Soul: Spiritual and Medical Perspectives on Euthanasia and Mortality 1997. *Address:* Bliss Road, New Preston, CT 06777, USA.

PECKER, David J., CPA; American publishing executive; *Chairman, President and CEO, American Media, Inc.*; b. 24 Sept. 1951; m. Karen Balan 1987. *Education:* Pace and New York Univs. *Career:* fmrly Sr Auditor Price Waterhouse & Co.; fmrly Man. Financial Reporting Diamandis Communications Inc., also Dir Financial Reporting, Dir Accounting, Asst Controller; Exec. Vice-Pres. Hachette Magazines Inc. 1990–91, Pres. 1991–92, Pres., CEO 1992–99; Chair., Pres. CEO American Media Inc. 1999–; mem. Fashion Group's Int. Advisory Bd, NY City Partnership Cttee, American Man. Asscn; mem. Bd Dirs Pace Univ., Drug Enforcement Agents Foundation 1995–. *Address:* American Media Inc., 4950 Communications Avenue, T-Rex Technology Center, Boca Raton, FL 33431, USA (Office). *Telephone:* (561) 997-7733 (Office). *Fax:* (561) 272-8411 (Office). *Website:* www.nationalenquirer.com (Office).

PECKHAM, Morse; academic, writer and editor; b. 17 Aug. 1914, Yonkers, NY, USA. *Education:* BA, University of Rochester, 1935; MA, 1938, PhD, 1947, Princeton University. *Career:* Instructor, 1946–47, Asst Prof. 1948–49, Rutgers University; Asst Prof., 1949–52, Assoc. Prof., 1952–61, Dir, Institute for Humanistic Education for Business Executives, 1953–54, University Press, 1953–55, Prof., 1961–67, University of Pennsylvania, Philadelphia; Distinguished Prof. of English and Comparative Literature, 1967–80, Distinguished Prof. Emeritus, 1980–, University of South Carolina, Columbia. *Publications:* On the Origin of Species: A Variorum Text, by Charles Darwin (ed.), 1959; Humanistic Education for Business Executives: An Essay in General Education, 1960; Word, Meaning, Poem: An Anthology of Poetry (ed. with Seymour Chapman), 1961; Beyond the Tragic Vision: The Quest for Identity in the Nineteenth Century, 1962; Man's Rage for Chaos: Biology, Behaviour and the Arts, 1965; Romanticism: The Culture of the Nineteenth Century (ed.), 1965; Paracelsus, by Robert Browning (ed.), 1969; Art and Pornography: An Experiment in Explanation, 1969; The Triumph of Romanticism: Speculation on Some Heroes of a Culture Crisis, 1970; Pippa Passes, by Robert Browning (ed.), 1971; Luria, by Robert Browning (ed.), 1973; Romanticism and Behaviour: Collected Essays II, 1976; Sordello, by Robert Browning (ed.), 1977; Explanation and Power: The Control of Human Behavior, 1979; Romanticism and Ideology, 1985; The Birth of Romanticism, 1986.

PEDEN, W(illiam) Creighton; Fuller E; b. 25 July 1935, Concord, NC, USA; Callaway Prof. Emeritus of Philosophy; Writer; Editor. m. 2nd Harriet McKnight Peden 6 Oct. 1978; two d. one step-s. *Education:* BA, Davidson College, NC, 1957; MA, 1960, BD, 1962, University of Chicago; PhD, St Andrews University, Scotland, 1965. *Career:* Founding Faculty, Florida Presbyterian College, 1960–61; Asst Prof., St Andrews College, 1964–65; Prof., Radford College, Virginia, 1965–68; Chair, Dept of Philosophy, Millikin University, Decatur, IL, 1968–69; Visiting Prof., Iliff School of Theology, 1969, 1973, 1978, University of Glasgow, 1982–83, Vrije University, Amsterdam, 1991; Fuller E. Callaway Prof. of Philosophy, 1969–93, Prof. Emeritus, 1993–, Augusta College, later Augusta State University, GA; Founding Ed., Journal of Social Philosophy, 1970–83; Founding Co-Ed., American Journal of Theology and Philosophy, 1980–91; Exec. Dir, 1987–92, Pres., 1992–98, Highlands Institute for American Religious Thought; Scholar-in-Residence, University of Copenhagen, 1988; Pres., Highlands Institute for American Religious and Philosophical Thought, 1998–; mem. American Acad. of Religion; American Philosophical Asscn; North American Society for Social Philosophy; Social Philosophy Research Institute; Society for the Advancement of American Philosophy; Society of Religious Humanism. *Publications:* Wieman's Empirical Process Philosophy, 1977; Whitehead's View of Reality (with Charles Hartshorne), 1981; The Chicago School: Voices of Liberal Religious Thought, 1987; The Philosopher of Free Religion: Francis Ellingwood Abbot, 1836–1903, 1992; Civil War Pulpit to World's Parliament of Religion: The Thought of William James Potter, 1829–1893, 1996. Editor: Philosophical Reflections on Education and Society (with Donald Chapman), 1978; Critical Issues in Philosophy of Education (with Donald Chapman), 1979; Philosophy for a Changing Society, 1983; Philosophical Essays on Ideas of a Good Society, 1988; Freedom, Equality and Social Change, 1989; God, Values and Empiricism, 1989; Revolution, Violence, and Equality, 1990; Terrorism, Justice and Social Values, 1990; The American Constitutional Experiment, 1991; Communitarianism, Liberalism, and Social Responsibility, 1991; Rights, Justice, and Community, 1992; The Bill of Rights: Bicentennial Reflections, 1993; Freedom, Dharma, and Rights, 1993; New Essays in Religious Naturalism (with Larry E. Axel), 1993; The Chicago School of Theology: Pioneers in Religious Inquiry (with J. Stone), 2 vols, 1996; The Collected Essays of Francis Ellingwood Abbot (1836–1903): American Philosopher and Free Religionist (with Everett J. Tarbox Jr), 4 vols, 1996. Contributions: scholarly Books and journals. *Honours:* Awards; Grants; Fellow, Society of Philosophers in America. *Address:* PO Box 2009, Bonnie Dr., Highlands, NC 28741, USA.

PEDRAM, Abdul Latif; Poet, Writer and Journalist; b. 1963, Badakhstan, Afghanistan. *Career:* Taught journalism, 1989–91; Deputy Ed.-in-Chief, Haghighat-e Enghelab-e Sor, Ed.-in-Chief, Theoretical supplement, 1982–85; f. and Ed.-in-Chief, Shora journal, 1988–89; Deputy dir, Hakim Nasser Khosrow Balki Foundation Library, Baghlan (Ed.-in-Chief, Hojjat foundation journal, f., foundation newletter, Kian), 1996–98; Lecturer of literary critique, thought and poetry, Univ. of Baghlan, Pol-i Khomri, 1996–98; moved to France, 1998–; mem., board of eds, Peyvand journal; mem. International Parliament of Writers (hon. mem.); Asscn of the Persian Speakers of the World Peyvand (hon. mem.). *Publications:* Poetry: Naqshi dar abgineh va baran (A figure in Crystal and Rain), 1979; Lahzehay-e massloub (Crucified Moments), 1983; She'rhay-e enzeva (Poems of Solitude), 1984; Khatabeh az sakouyeh hendo-koush (A letter from the Hend and Koush), 1988; Mo'aleghe-ye hashtom (The Eighth Moalegheh), 1988; Ta'reef-e talkh-e mandan, 1999. Prose: Delavaraneh kuhestan (The Bravemen from the Mountains), 1979; Safarnomeyeh Czechoslovaqui (My Travels in Czechoslovakia), 1980; Chand nokteh beh sheeveyeh tarh (A Few Points Told in Rough), 1983; Darssyahey journalism (Lessons in Journalism, two vols), 1988; Chahar magholeyeh falsafi (Four Philosophical Essays), 1990; Afateh ideology (The Evil of Ideology), 1996; Dar zarurateh jodayee deen az siasat (About the Necessity of Separation of Religion from Politics), 1996. Contributions: numerous articles in newspapers and journals, incl. Erfan; Avaz; Jowandun; Iness; Hevad. *Honours:* Reporters sans Frontières grant, 1998; Hellman-Helmet Prize, Human Rights Watch, 1999.

PEERY, Janet; Writer, Book Reviewer and Teacher of Fiction; b. 18 July 1948, Wichita, KS, USA; m. 1st William Peery, 23 Jan. 1976, divorced 1988, three d.; m. 2nd Cy Bolton, 5 Nov. 1994. *Education:* BA, Speech Pathology, Audiology, 1975, MFA, Fiction, 1992, Wichita State University. *Career:* Teacher of Fiction, Warren Wilson College, Sweet Briar College, Old Dominion University. *Publications:* Alligator Dance (short stories), 1993; The River Beyond the World (novel), 1996. Contributions: Reviews, quarterlies and journals, including: New Virginia Review; Shenandoah; Black Warrior Review; Chattahoochee Review; Kansas Quarterly; Southwest Review; Quarterly West; Los Angeles Times; Washington Post Book World. *Honours:* Writers at Work Fellowship, 1990; National Endowment for the Arts Fellowship, 1990; Goodheart Prizes, Washington and Lee University, 1991, 1992; Seaton Award, Kansas Quarterly, 1992; Whiting Writers' Award, 1992; Rosenthal Award, American Acad. of Arts and Letters, 1993. *Address:* c/o Darhansoff and Verrill Literary Agency, 179 Franklin St, New York, NY 10013, USA.

PELECANOS, George Peter; American journalist, writer and screenwriter; b. 18 Feb. 1957, Washington, DC; m.; three c. *Career:* Los Angeles Times Book Award 2003, Int. Crime Novel of the Year in France, Germany and Japan. *Television:* The Wire (writer and story ed., HBO). *Publications:* novels: A Firing Offense 1992, Nick's Trip 1993, Shoedog 1994, Down by the River 1995, The Big Blowdown 1996, The Sweet Forever 1999, King Suckerman 2000, Shame the Devil 2000, Right as Rain 2001, Hard Revolution 2002, Hell to Pay 2002, Soul Circus 2003, Drama City 2005;

contrib. to Esquire, GQ, The Washington Post. *Address:* c/o The Orion Publishing Group Ltd, 5 Upper St Martin's Lane, London, WC2H 9EA, England. *Website:* www.orionbooks.co.uk.

PELEVIN, Viktor Olegovich; Russian writer; b. 27 Nov. 1962, Moscow. *Education:* Moscow Power Engineering Inst., Gorky Inst. of Literature, Moscow. *Career:* army service; corresp. Face-to-Face journal 1989–90; journal Science and Religion; author of numerous novels and stories. *Publications include:* (most in trans.) Omon Ra (novel), Vera Pavlovna's Ninth Dream, Reconstructor, Prince of Gosplan, The Life of Insects, The Yellow Arrow (novella), Ivan Kublakhanov, Generation, Babylon, The Blue Lantern (short stories) (Russian Booker Prize 1994), Crystal World, A Werewolf Problem in Central Russia (short stories), Chapayev and Pustota (Buddha's Little Finger) 1996, The Clay Machine-Gun (novel), Generation P 1999, Homo Zapiens (with others) 2002, Transition Period Dialectics: Out of Nowhere to Nowhere, Pt One: Numbers, Pt Two: Life 2003. *Honours:* Wanderer Prize 1995. *Literary Agent:* Aragi, 143 West 27th Street, Suite 4F, New York, NY 10001, USA. *Address:* c/o Vagrius Publishing House, Tikhvinskaya str. 7/1, 129090 Moscow, Russia; c/o Faber and Faber Ltd, 3 Queen Square, London, WC1N 3AU, England.

PELIKAN, Jaroslav Jan; Prof. of History and Writer; b. 17 Dec. 1923, Akron, Ohio, USA; m. Sylvia Burica, 9 June 1946, two s. one d. *Education:* Graduated, Concordia Junior College, Ft Wayne, IN, 1942; BD, Concordia Theological Seminary, St Louis, 1946; PhD, University of Chicago, 1946. *Career:* Faculty, Valparaiso University, 1946–49, Concordia Seminary, St Louis, 1949–53, University of Chicago, 1953–62; Titus Street Prof. of Ecclesiastical History, 1967–72, Sterling Prof. of History, 1972–96, Dean, Graduate School, 1973–78, Dir, Division of Humanities, 1974–75, Chair., Medieval Studies, 1974–75, 1978–80, William Clyde DeVane Lecturer, 1984–86, Yale University; Visiting Prof., Annenberg School of Communications, University of Pennsylvania, 1998–2001; various guest lectureships; mem. American Acad. of Arts and Sciences, pres., 1994–97; American Historical Asscn; American Philosophical Society; American Society of Church History, pres., 1965; International Congress of Luther Research, pres., 1971; Medieval Acad. of America, fellow. *Publications:* From Luther to Kierkegaard, 1950; Fools for Christ, 1955; The Riddle of Roman Catholicism, 1959; Luther the Expositor, 1959; The Shape of Death, 1961; The Light of the World, 1962; Obedient Rebels, 1964; The Finality of Jesus Christ in an Age of Universal History, 1965; The Christian Intellectual, 1966; Spirit Versus Structure, 1968; Development of Doctrine, 1969; Historical Theology, 1971; The Christian Tradition, 5 vols, 1971–89; Scholarship and Its Survival, 1983; The Vindication of Tradition, 1984; Jesus Through the Centuries, 1985; The Mystery of Continuity, 1986; Bach Among the Theologians, 1986; The Excellent Empire, 1987; The Melody of Theology, 1988; Confessor Between East and West, 1990; Imago Dei, 1990; Eternal Feminines, 1990; The Idea of the University: A Reexamination, 1992; Christianity and Classical Culture, 1993; Faust the Theologian, 1995; The Reformation of the Bible/The Bible of the Reformation, 1996; Mary Through the Centuries, 1996. Editor: Makers of Modern Theology, 5 vols, 1966–68; The Preaching of Chrysostom, 1967; Interpreters of Luther, 1968; Twentieth-Century Theology in the Making, 3 vols, 1969–70; The Preaching of Augustine, 1973; The World Treasury of Modern Religious Thought, 1991; Sacred Writings, 7 vols, 1992. Contributions: many books and professional journals. *Honours:* Abingdon Award, 1959; John Gilmary Shea Prize, American Catholic Historical Asscn, 1971; National Award, Slovak World Congress, 1973; Religious Book Award, Catholic Press Asscn, 1974; Christian Unity Award, Atonement Friars, 1975; Senior Fellow, Carnegie Foundation for the Advancement of Teaching, 1982–83; Festschrifts published in his honour, 1984, 1996; Haskins Medal, Medieval Acad. of America, 1985; Award for Excellence, American Acad. of Religion, 1989; Umanita Award, Newbery Library, 1990; Joseph A Sittler Award, 1993; various hon. doctorates and other hons. *Address:* 156 Chestnut Lane, Hamden, CT 06518, USA.

PELLETIER, Chantal; French writer and screenwriter; b. 1949, Lyon. *Writing for television:* En cas de bonheur (TF1) 1989, Divisé par deux (adaptation, Antenne 2) 1990, Carré d'as (FR2) 1992, Le prix d'une femme (FR3) 1994, Danger d'aimer (FR3) 1998. *Publications include:* novels: Supermarché rayon bonheur 1990, Le fils d'Ariadne 1992, Le squatt 1996, La vande tuera 1997, Éros et Thalasso 1998, Le Chant du bouc 2000, Troubles fêtes 2001, More is Less (in trans.) 2002, La visite 2003, Eddy Mitchell. *Address:* c/o Éditions Gallimard, 5 rue Sébastien-Bottin, 75328 Paris, France. *Website:* www.gallimard.fr.

PEMBERTON, Margaret; Writer; b. 10 April 1943, Bradford, England; m., one s., four d. *Career:* mem. CWA; Romantic Novelists Asscn; PEN; Society of Authors. *Publications:* Harlot 1981, Lion of Languedoc 1981, The Flower Garden 1982, Silver Shadows, Golden Dreams 1985, Never Leave Me 1986, Multitude of Sins 1988, White Christmas in Saigon 1990, An Embarrassment of Riches 1992, Zadruga 1993, Moonflower Madness 1993, Tapestry of Fear 1994, The Londoners 1995, Magnolia Square 1996, Yorkshire Rose 1996, Coronation Summer 1997, A Many Splendoured Thing 2002; as Maggie Hudson: Tell Me No Secrets 1998, Fast Women 1999, Looking for Mr Big 2000, Nowhere to Run 2001. *Address:* 13 Manor Lane, London SE13, England.

PENDLETON, Don (see Obstfeld, Raymond).

PENHALL, Joe; British playwright; b. 1968. *Plays:* Some Voices 1994, Love and Understanding 1997 (also film adaptation), Blue/Orange 2000, Pale Horse 2003. *Film:* Enduring Love (screen adaptation). *Address:* c/o Methuen Publishing Ltd, 215 Vauxhall Bridge Road, London, SW1V 1EL, England. *Website:* www.methuen.co.uk.

PENROSE, Sir Roger, Kt, OM, PhD, FRS; British mathematician; *Professor Emeritus of Mathematics, University of Oxford*; b. 8 Aug. 1931, Colchester; m. 1st Joan Wedge 1959 (divorced 1981), three s.; m. 2nd Vanessa Thomas 1988. *Education:* Univ. Coll. School, Univ. Coll. London and St John's Coll. Cambridge. *Career:* Asst Lecturer, Bedford Coll. London 1956–57; Research Fellow, St John's Coll. Cambridge 1957–60; NATO Research Fellow, Princeton and Syracuse Univs 1959–61; Research Assoc. King's Coll. London 1961–63; Visiting Assoc. Prof. Univ. of Tex. Austin 1963–64; Reader, Birkbeck Coll. London 1964–66, Prof. of Applied Math. 1966–73; Rouse Ball Prof. of Math. Univ. of Oxford 1973–98, Prof. Emer. 1998–; Gresham Prof. of Geometry, Gresham Coll. 1998; Fellow, Univ. Coll. London 1975; Hon. Fellow, St John's Coll. Cambridge 1987; Visiting Prof. Yeshiva, Princeton and Cornell Univs 1966–67, 1969; Lovett Prof. Rice Univ. Houston 1983–87; Distinguished Prof. of Physics and Math. Syracuse Univ. 1987–93, Francis and Helen Pentz Distinguished Prof. of Physics and Math., Pa State Univ. 1993–; mem. London Math. Soc., Cambridge Philosophical Soc., Inst. for Math. and its Applications, Int. Soc. for Gen. Relativity and Gravitation; Fellow Birkbeck Coll. 1998, Inst. of Physics 1999; Foreign Assoc. Nat. Acad. of Sciences, USA 1998. *Publications:* Techniques of Differential Topology in Relativity 1973, Spinors and Space-time (with W. Rindler), (Vol. I) 1984, (Vol. II) 1986, The Emperor's New Mind 1989, The Nature of Space and Time (with S. W. Hawking) 1996, The Large, the Small and the Human Mind 1997, White Mars (with B. Aldiss) 1999, The Road to Reality: A Complete Guide to the Laws of the Universe 2004; articles in scientific journals. *Honours:* Dr hc, (New Brunswick) 1992, (Surrey) 1993, (Bath) 1994, (London) 1995, (Glasgow) 1996, (Essex) 1996, (St Andrew's) 1997, (Santiniketon) 1998, Hon. DUniv (Open Univ.) 1998; Adams Prize (Cambridge Univ.) 1966–67, Dannie Heinemann Prize (American Physics Soc. and American Inst. of Physics) 1971, Eddington Medal (with S. W. Hawking) (Royal Astronomical Soc.) 1975, Royal Medal (Royal Soc.) 1985, Wolf Foundation Prize for Physics (with S. W. Hawking) 1988, Dirac Medal and Prize, Inst. of Physics 1989, Einstein Medal 1990, Science Book Prize 1990, Naylor Prize, London Math. Soc. 1991. *Address:* Mathematical Institute, 24–29 St Giles, Oxford, OX1 3LB, England. *Telephone:* (1865) 273578. *Fax:* (1865) 273583. *E-mail:* rouse@maths.ox.ac.uk (Office).

PEPETELA; novelist; b. (Artur Carlos Mauricio Pestana), 1941, Benguela, Angola. *Career:* co-f., Centre of Angolan Studies, Algeria; fmr Deputy Minister of Education, Angola; mem. Angolan Writers' Union. *Publications:* A revolta da casa dos ídolos, As aventuras de Ngunga, Muana Puó 1978, Mayombe 1980, O cão e os calús 1985, Yaka 1984, Lueji, o nascimento dum império 1990, A geração da utopia 1992, O desejo de Kianda (trans. as The Return of the Water Spirit) 1995, Parábola do cágado velho 1996, A gloriosa família 1997, Jaime Bunda, agente secreto 2001, Jaime Bunda e a morte do agente americano 2003. *Honours:* National Literature Prize 1986, Camões Prize 1997, Rio Branco Order 2002. *Literary Agent:* Dr Ray-Güde Mertin Literarische Agentur, Friedrichstrasse 1, 61348 Bad Homburg, Germany. *Telephone:* 6172-29842. *Fax:* 6172-29771. *E-mail:* info@mertin-litag.de.

PEPPE, Rodney Darrell; Author and Artist; b. 24 June 1934, Eastbourne, East Sussex, England; m. Tatjana Tekkel, 16 July 1960, two s. *Education:* Eastbourne School of Art, 1951–53, 1955–57; London County Council Central School of Art, 1957–59; NDD, Illustration (special subject) and Central School Diploma. *Career:* mem. Society of Authors. *Publications:* The Alphabet Book, 1968; The House That Jack Built, 1970; Odd One Out, 1974; Henry series, 1975–84; The Mice Who Lived in a Shoe, 1981; Run Rabbit, Run!, 1982; The Kettleship Pirates, 1983; The Mice and the Flying Basket, 1985; The Mice and the Clockwork Bus, 1986; Huxley Pig series, 1989; The Mice on the Moon, 1992; The Mice and the Travel Machine, 1993; The Magic Toybox, 1996; Gus and Nipper, 1996; Hippo Plays Hide and Seek, 1997; Angelmouse series, 2000; Automata and Mechanical Toys, 2002. Contributions: periodicals. *Address:* Stoneleigh House, 6 Stoneleigh Dr., Livermead, Torquay, Devon TQ2 6TR, England.

PEPPERCORN, Lisa Margot; Brazilian musicologist; b. 2 Oct. 1913, Frankfurt am Main, Germany; m. Lothar Bauer 1938. *Education:* Royal Conservatory, Brussels. *Career:* music correspondent based in Brazil, New York Times 1939–46, Musical America 1940–47; musicological research 1946–52. *Publications:* H. Villa-Lobos, Leben und Werk des brasilianischen Komponisten 1972, Villa-Lobos: The Music 1991, Villa-Lobos: Collected Studies 1992, Letters 1994, The World of Villa-Lobos in Pictures and Documents 1996; contrib. to numerous international publications. *Honours:* Choice Magazine Outstanding Academic Book Citation 1992. *Address:* Schulhaus Strasse 53, 8002 Zürich, Switzerland. *Telephone:* (1) 202-0339.

PERELMAN, Robert (Bob); poet, writer and academic; b. 2 Dec. 1947, Youngstown, OH, USA; m. Francie Shaw 1975; two s. *Education:* MA, University of Michigan, 1969; MFA, University of Iowa, 1970; PhD, University of California, 1990. *Career:* Ed., Hills magazine, 1973–80; Asst Prof., 1990–95, Assoc. Prof., 1995–, University of Pennsylvania. *Publications:* Braille, 1975; Seven Works, 1978; aka, 1979; Primer, 1981; To the Reader, 1984; The First World, 1986; Writing/Talks (ed.), 1985; Face Value, 1988;

Captive Audience, 1988; Virtual Reality, 1993; The Trouble with Genius: Reading Pound, Joyce, Stein, and Zukovsky, 1994; The Marginalization of Poetry: Language Writings and Literary History, 1996; The Future of Memory, 1998. *Address:* c/o Department of English, University of Pennsylvania, Philadelphia, PA 19104, USA.

PERES DA COSTA, Suneeta, BA, MFA; Australian playwright; b. 1976, Sydney, NSW. *Education:* Univ. of Technology, Sydney, Sarah Lawrence Coll., New York, USA, Univ. of Sydney. *Radio plays:* Watermark (ABC Radio), Angelina's Song (ABC Radio), Children See Everything (ABC Radio), Fire and Water (ABC Radio). *Plays:* I am an Island 1995, Free Men 1996, Blood is Blue 1996, The Art of Straying 1998, Klactoveesedstene 2001. *Honours:* Sydney Theatre Company-ICI Young Playwrights' Award 1995, 1996; New South Wales Ministry for the Arts Philip Parsons Young Playwrights' Award 1996, Ian Reed Foundation Prize for Radio Drama 1998. *Literary Agent:* RGM Associates, PO Box 128, Surry Hills, NSW 2010, Australia. *Telephone:* (2) 9281-3911. *Fax:* (2) 9281-4705. *E-mail:* info@rgm.com.au. *Website:* www.rgm.com.au.

PÉREZ-REVERTE, Arturo; Spanish journalist and writer; b. 24 Nov. 1951, Cartagena. *Career:* journalist, war correspondent, Pueblo; war correspondent, Spanish nat. television. *Publications:* El Husar 1986, El maestro de esgrima (trans. as The Fencing Master) 1988, La tabla de Flandes (trans. as The Flanders Panel) 1990, El club Dumas (trans. as The Dumas Club) 1993, La sombra del Aguila 1993, Territorio comanche 1994, Cachito: un asunto de honor 1995, La piel del tambor (trans. as The Seville Communion) 1995, El capitán Alatriste 1996, Limpieza de sangre 1997, El sol de Breda 1998, Patente de corso 1998, La carta esférica (trans. as The Nautical Chart) 2000, El oro del rey 2000, Con ánimo de ofender 2001, La reina del sur (trans. as The Queen of the South) 2002, El caballero del jubón amarillo 2003; contrib. to Spanish periodicals. *Literary Agent:* c/o Ana Lyons, RDC Agencia Literaria, Fernando VI 13–15, 3° derecha, 2804 Madrid, Spain. *Telephone:* (91) 308 55 85. *Fax:* (91) 308 56 00. *E-mail:* rdc@club.idecnet.com.

PERKINS, Emily; New Zealand novelist; b. 1970, Christchurch. *Education:* New Zealand Drama School, Victoria Univ. *Career:* fmrly TV actor. *Publications:* Not Her Real Name (short stories) (Geoffrey Faber Memorial Prize for Fiction) 1996, Leave Before You Go (novel) 1998, The Picnic Virgin (ed.) 2000, The New Girl (novel) 2001. *Address:* c/o Pan Macmillan, 20 New Wharf Road, London, N1 9RR, England.

PERKINS, George Burton, AB, MA, PhD; editor and writer; b. 16 Aug. 1930, Lowell, Massachusetts, USA; m. Barbara Miller 1964; three d. *Education:* Tufts College, Duke University, Cornell University. *Career:* Teaching Asst, Cornell University, 1957–60; Asst Prof., Farleigh Dickinson University, 1963–66; Lecturer, American Literature, University of Edinburgh, 1966–67; Prof., Eastern Michigan University, 1967–2001; General Ed., Journal of Narrative Technique, 1970–92; mem. various professional organizations. *Publications:* Writing Clear Prose, 1964; The Theory of the American Novel, 1970; Realistic American Short Fiction, 1972; American Poetic Theory, 1972; The American Tradition in Literature (with B. Perkins), ninth edn, 1988; The Practical Imagination (with Frye and Baker), 1985; Contemporary American Literature (with B. Perkins), 1991; Harper Collins Reader's Encyclopedia of American Literature (with Perkins and Leininger), 2002; Kaleidoscope (with B. Perkins), 1993; Women's Work (with Perkins and Warhol), 1994; The Harper Handbook to Literature (with Frye, Baker and Perkins), 1997; A Season in New South Wales, 1998. Contributions: Professional journals. *Honours:* Duke University Fellow, 1953–54; Cornell University Fellow, 1954–55; Distinguished Faculty Award, Eastern Michigan University, 1978; Fellow, Institute for Advanced Studies in the Humanities, University of Edinburgh, 1981; Senior Fulbright Scholar, University of Newcastle, Australia, 1989. *Address:* 1316 King George Blvd, Ann Arbor, MI 48108, USA. *E-mail:* george.perkins@emich.edu.

PERKINS, Michael; Writer and Ed.; b. 3 Nov. 1942, Lansing, Michigan, USA; m. Renie (Shoemaker) McCune, 20 June 1960, one s. two d. *Education:* New School for Social Research, New York City, 1962; Ohio University, Athens, 1963; City College, CUNY, 1966. *Career:* Ed., Tompkins Square Press, 1966–68, Croton Press Ltd, 1969–72, Ulster Arts Magazine, 1978–79; Program Dir, Woodstock Guild, 1985–95, Woodstock Library, 1985–; Senior Ed., Masquerade Books, New York City, 1992–98; mem. Authors' Guild; National Book Critics Circle. *Publications:* Evil Companions 1968, Down Here 1969, The Secret Record 1977, The Persistence of Desire 1977, The Good Parts 1994, Gift of Choice 1994, Dark Matter 1996, Coming Up (ed.) 1996, Burn 2002, I Could Walk All Day 2002. Contributions: Reviews and periodicals. *Address:* 750 Ohayo Mt Rd, Glenford, NY 12433, USA.

PERLIS, Vivian; Musicologist, Musician and Writer; b. 26 April 1928, New York, NY, USA. *Education:* BMus, 1949, MMus, 1952, University of Michigan; Postgraduate studies in harp, Philadelphia Acad. of Music, 1953–54, and in musicology, Columbia University, 1962–64. *Career:* Reference Librarian, Music Library, 1967–72, Senior Research Assoc. and Founder, Oral History, American Music Project, 1972–, School of Music, Yale University; Lecturer, University of Southern California at Los Angeles, 1974–75; Visiting Senior Research Fellow, Brooklyn College, CUNY, 1976–77; Visiting Lecturer, Wesleyan University, 1992–93. *Publications:* Charles Ives Remembered: An Oral History, 1974; An Ives Celebration: Papers and Panels of the Charles Ives Centennial Festival-Conference (with H. Wiley Hitchcock), 1977; Two Men for Modern Music, 1978; The Charles Ives Papers, 1983; Copland: 1900 through 1942 (with Aaron Copland), 1984; Copland: Since 1943 (with Aaron Copland), 1989. Contributions: many publications and television documentaries. *Honours:* Charles Ives Award, National Institute of Arts and Letters, 1971; Otto Kinkeldey Award, American Musicological Society, 1975; ASCAP-Deems Taylor Award, 1985; Guggenheim Fellowship, 1987; Irving Lowens Award, Sonneck Society, 1991. *Address:* 139 Goodill Rd, Weston, CT 06883, USA. *E-mail:* vperlis@optonline.net.

PERREIN, Michèle Marie-Claude; Writer and Dramatist; b. 30 Oct. 1929, La Réole, France; m. Jacques Laurent, divorced. *Education:* University of Bordeaux. *Publications:* La sensitive, 1956; Le soleil dans l'oeil, 1957; Barbastre, 1960; La flemme, 1961; Le cercle, 1962; Le petit jules, 1965; M'oiselle S, la Chineuse, 1970; La partie de plaisir, 1971; Le buveur de Garonne, 1973; Le mâle aimant, 1975; Gemma Lapidaire, 1976; Entre chienne et louve, 1978; Comme une fourmi cavalière, 1980; Ave Caesar, 1982; Les cotonniers de Bassalane, 1984; La Margagne, 1989. Other: several plays. Contributions: periodicals. *Address:* c/o Grassett et Fasqualle, 61 rue des Saints-pères, 75006 Paris, France.

PERRETT, Bryan; Author and Military Historian; b. 9 July 1934, Liverpool, England; m. Anne Catherine Trench, 13 Aug. 1966. *Education:* Liverpool College. *Career:* Defence Correspondent to Liverpool Echo, during Falklands War and Gulf War; mem. Rotary Club of Ormskirk; Army Records Society; Society for Army Historical Research. *Publications:* The Czar's British Squadron (with A. Lord), 1981; A History of Blitzkrieg, 1983; Knights of the Black Cross: Hitler's Panzerwaffe and its Leaders, 1986; Desert Warfare, 1988; Encyclopaedia of the Second World War (with Ian Hogg), 1989; Canopy of War, 1990; Liverpool: A City at War, 1990; Last Stand: Famous Battles Against the Odds, 1991; The Battle Book: Crucial Conflicts in History from 1469 BC to the Present, 1992; At All Costs: Stories of Impossible Victories, 1993; Seize and Hold: Master Strokes of the Battlefield, 1994; Iron Fist: Crucial Armoured Engagements, 1995; Against All Odds! More Dramatic Last Stand Actions, 1995; Impossible Victories: Ten Unlikely Battlefield Successes, 1996; The Real Hornblower: The Life and Times of Admiral Sir James Gordon, GCB, 1998; The Taste of Battle, 2000; The Changing Face of Battle, 2000; Gunboat!, 2000; Last Convoy, 2000; Beach Assault, 2000; Heroes of the Hour, 2001; My Story: Trafalgar, 2002; My Story: The Crimea, 2002; My Story: Waterloo, 2003; For Valour: Victoria Cross and Medal of Honour Battles, 2003. Contributions: War Monthly; Military History; World War Investigator; War in Peace (partwork); The Elite (partwork). *Literary Agent:* Watson Little Ltd, Capo di Monte, Windmill Hill, London NW3 6RJ, England. *Address:* 7 Maple Ave, Burscough, Nr Ormskirk, Lancashire L40 5SL, England. *E-mail:* bryan@perrett3.fsnet.co.uk.

PERRIAM, Wendy Angela; Writer and Poet; b. 23 Feb. 1940, London, England; m. 1st 22 Aug. 1964, one d.; m. 2nd John Alan Perriam, 29 July 1974. *Education:* St Anne's College, Oxford, 1958–61; BA, History, 1961, MA, 1972, University of Oxford; LSE, 1963–64. *Career:* mem. British Actors Equity Asscn; PEN; Society of Authors. *Publications:* Absinthe for Elevenses, 1980; Cuckoo, 1981; After Purple, 1982; Born of Woman, 1983; The Stillness, The Dancing, 1985; Sin City, 1987; Devils, for a Change, 1989; Fifty-Minute Hour, 1990; Bird Inside, 1992; Michael, Michael, 1993; Breaking and Entering, 1994; Coupling, 1996; Second Skin, 1998; Lying, 2000; Dreams, Demons and Desire, 2001; Tread Softly, 2002; Virgin in the Gym and Other Stories, 2004. Contributions: anthologies, newspapers and magazines. *Literary Agent:* Curtis Brown Ltd, Haymarket House, 28–29 Haymarket, London, SW1Y 4SP, England. *Telephone:* (20) 7393-4400. *Fax:* (20) 7393-4401. *E-mail:* info@curtisbrown.co.uk. *Website:* www.curtisbrown.co.uk. *Website:* www.perriam.demon.co.uk.

PERRICK, Penny; Novelist and Critic; b. 30 June 1941, London, England; m. Clive Labovitch, 26 June 1962, divorced 1973, one s. one d. *Education:* Alliance Française, Paris. *Career:* Feature Writer, Vogue magazine, 1959–62; Columnist, The Sun, 1974–79; Columnist, The Times, 1983–89; Fiction Ed., Sunday Times, 1989–95; mem. Society of Authors; RSL. *Publications:* Malina, 1993; Impossible Things, 1995; Evermore, 1997. Contributions: Times; Sunday Times; Country Homes and Interiors; You Magazine; The Irish Times; The Irish Tatler; Gardens Illustrated. *Address:* Parnells, The Quay, Roundstone, Connemara, Co Galway, Ireland.

PERRIE, Walter; Poet, Author and Critic; b. 5 June 1949, Lanarkshire, Scotland. *Education:* MA, Mental Philosophy, Univ. of Edinburgh, 1975; MPhil, English Studies, Univ. of Stirling, 1989. *Career:* Ed., Chapman, 1970–75; Scottish-Canadian Exchange Fellow, Univ. of British Columbia, Canada, 1984–85; Managing Ed., Margin: International Arts Quarterly, 1985–90; Stirling Writing Fellow, Univ. of Stirling, 1991. *Publications:* Metaphysics and Poetry (with Hugh MacDiarmid), 1974; Poem on a Winter Night, 1976; A Lamentation for the Children, 1977; By Moon and Sun, 1980; Out of Conflict, 1982; Concerning the Dragon, 1984; Roads that Move: A Journey Through Eastern Europe, 1991; Thirteen Lucky Poems, 1991; From Milady's Wood and Other Poems, 1997; The Light in Strathearn (poems), 2000. Contributions: journals and periodicals. *Honours:* Scottish Arts Council Bursaries, 1976, 1983, 1994, and Book Awards, 1976, 1983;

Eric Gregory Award, 1978; Ingram Merrill Foundation Award, 1987; Scottish Arts Council Writers Bursary, 1999; Society of Authors Travelling Scholarship, 2000. *Address:* 10 Croft Pl., Dunning, Perthshire PH2 0SB, Scotland.

PERRY, John Curtis; Prof. of History and Writer; b. 18 July 1930, Orange, NJ, USA; m. Sarah Hollis French, 14 Sept. 1957, five c. *Education:* BA, Chinese, 1952, MA, History and Regional Studies, 1953, Yale University; PhD, History, Harvard University, 1962. *Career:* Instructor, 1962–64, Asst Prof. of History, 1964–66, Connecticut College; Asst Prof., 1966–68, Assoc. Prof., 1968–74, Prof. of History, 1974–80, Acting Dir, College Library, 1975–76, Carleton College; Visiting Research Assoc., Fairbank Center, 1976–79, Japan Institute, 1979–80, Assoc. in Research, 1980–, Harvard University; Henry Willard Denison Prof. of History, 1981–, Organizer-Dir, Fletcher North Pacific Seminars, 1985–97, Fletcher School of Law and Diplomacy, Tufts University; mem. American Historical Asscn; Asscn for Asian Studies; Japan Society. *Publications:* Beneath the Eagle's Wings: Americans in Occupied Japan, 1980; Sentimental Imperialists: The American East Asian Experience (with James C. Thomson Jr and Peter W. Stanley), 1981; Facing West: Americans and the Opening of the Pacific, 1994; The Flight of the Romanovs: A Family Saga (with Constantine Pleshakov), 1999. Contributions: scholarly books, journals, newspapers, radio and television. *Honours:* Research Grants, NIRA, 1986–87, Nippon Foundation, 1998–2001, Japan Economic Foundation, 2000–; Order of the Sacred Treasure, Japan, 1991. *Address:* c/o Fletcher School of Law and Diplomacy, Tufts University, Medford, MA 02155, USA.

PERRY, Ritchie, (John Allen); Teacher and Author; b. 7 Jan. 1942, King's Lynn, Norfolk, England. *Education:* BA, St John's College, Oxford, 1964. *Publications:* The Fall Guy, 1972; Nowhere Man, US edn as A Hard Man to Kill, 1973; Ticket to Ride, 1973; Holiday with a Vengeance, 1974; Your Money and Your Wife, 1975; One Good Death Deserves Another, 1976; Dead End, 1977; Brazil: The Land and Its People, 1977; Copacabana Stud (as John Allen), 1977; Dutch Courage, 1978; Bishop's Pawn, 1979; Up Tight (as John Allen), 1979; Grand Slam, 1980; Fool's Mate, 1981; Foul Up, 1982; MacAllister, 1984; Kolwezi, 1985; Presumed Dead, 1988; Comeback, 1991. Children's Books: George H. Ghastly, 1982; George H. Ghastly to the Rescue, 1982; George H. Ghastly and the Little Horror, 1985; Fenella Fang, 1986; Fenella Fang and the Great Escape, 1987; Fenella Fang and the Wicked Witch, 1989; The Creepy Tale, 1989; Fenalla Fang and the Time Machine, 1991; The Runton Werewolf, 1994. *Address:* The Linhay, Water Lane, West Runton, Norfolk NR27 9QP, England.

PERUTZ, Kathrin; Author and Exec; b. 1 July 1939, New York, NY, USA. *Education:* BA, Barnard College, 1960; MA, New York University, 1966. *Career:* Exec. Dir, Contact Program Inc; mem. PEN; Authors' Guild. *Publications:* The Garden, 1962; A House on the Sound, 1964; The Ghosts, 1966; Mother is a Country: A Popular Fantasy, 1968; Beyond the Looking Glass: America's Beauty Culture, 1970; Marriage is Hell: The Marriage Fallacy, 1972; Reigning Passions, 1978; Writing for Love and Money, 1991. Also as Johanna Kingsley: Scents, 1985; Faces, 1987. *Address:* 16 Avalon Rd, Great Neck, NY 10021, USA.

PESETSKY, Bette, BA, MFA; American writer; b. 16 Nov. 1932, Milwaukee, WI; m. Irwin Pesetsky 1956; one s. *Education:* Washington Univ., Univ. of Iowa. *Career:* mem. PEN. *Publications:* Stories Up to a Point, 1982; Author from a Savage People, 1983; Midnight Sweets, 1988; Digs, 1988; Confessions of a Bad Girl, 1989; Late Night Muse, 1991; Cast a Spell, 1993. Contributions: New Yorker; Vanity Fair; Ms; Vogue; Paris Review; Ontario Review; Stand. *Honours:* Creative Writing Fellowship, National Endowment for the Arts, 1979–80; Creative Writing Public Service Award, New York Council for the Arts, 1980–81. *Address:* Hilltop Park, Dobbs Ferry, NY 10522, USA.

PETERFREUND, Stuart (Samuel); Prof. of English and Poet; b. 30 June 1945, New York, NY, USA; m. 1st Carol Jean Litzler, 12 Sept. 1981, divorced 17 Dec. 1997, one d.; m. 2nd Christina Sieber, 6 May 2001. *Education:* BA, English, Cornell University, 1966; MFA, Creative Writing, University of California at Irvine, 1968; English Literature and German Language, Columbia University, 1970–71; PhD, English, University of Washington, 1974. *Career:* Lecturer, University of Puget Sound, 1975; Asst Prof., University of Arkansas at Little Rock, 1975–78; Asst Prof., 1978–82, Assoc. Prof., 1982–91, Prof. of English and Chair, 1991–99, Prof. of English, 1999–, Dept of English, Northeastern Univ.; mem. American Society for Eighteenth-Century Studies; British Society for History of Science; Byron Society; History of Science Society; Interdisciplinary Nineteenth-Century Studies; International Asscn for Philosophy and Literature; Keats-Shelley Asscn of America; MLA; Poets and Writers; Society for Literature and Science, pres., 1995–97; Wordsworth-Coleridge Asscn. *Publications:* Poetry: The Hanged Knife and Other Poems, 1970; Harder than Rain, 1977; Interstatements, 1986. Other: William Blake in the Age of Newton: Essays on Literature as Art and Science, 1998; Shelley Among Others: The Play of the Intertext and the Idea of Language, 2002. Editor: Critical Theory and the Teaching of Literature, 1985; Culture/Criticism/Ideology, 1986; Literature and Science: Theory and Practice, 1990. Contributions: scholarly books, professional journals, poetry anthologies, and reviews. *Honours:* Grants; Fellowships; First Prize in Poetry, Writers' Digest Competition, 1970; Poet-in-Residence, Southern Literary Festival, 1977; First Prize, Worcester County Poetry Asscn Contest, 1989; Third Prize, Abiko Journal Poetry Contest, 1994; Third Prize, Anna Davidson Rosenberg Award for Poems on the Jewish Experience, 1996. *Address:* c/o Dept of English, Northeastern University, 406 Holmes Hall, 360 Huntington Ave, Boston, MA 02115, USA.

PETERKIEWICZ, Jerzy, MA, PhD; academic, poet, writer and dramatist; b. 29 Sept. 1916, Fabianki, Poland. *Education:* University of Warsaw, University of St Andrews, Scotland, King's College, London. *Career:* Lecturer, then Reader, 1952–72, Head, Dept of East European Languages and Literature, 1972–77, Prof. of Polish Language and Literature, 1972–79, University of London. *Publications:* Prowincja 1936, Wiersze i poematy 1938, Pogrzeb Europy 1946, The Knotted Cord 1953, Loot and Loyalty 1955, Polish Prose and Verse 1956, Antologia liryki angielskiej 1958, Future to Let 1958, Isolation 1959, Five Centuries of Polish Poetry (with Burns Singer) 1960, revised edn (also with Jon Stallworthy) 1970, The Quick and the Dead 1961, That Angel Burning at My Left Side 1963, Poematy Londynskie 1965, Inner Circle 1966, Green Flows the Bile 1969, The Other Side of Silence: The Poet at the Limits of Language 1970, The Third Adam 1975, Easter Vigil and Other Poems, by Karol Wojtyla (Pope John Paul II) (ed. and trans.) 1979, Kula magiczna 1980; Collected Poems, by Karol Wojtyla (Pope John Paul II) (ed. and trans.) 1982, Poezje Wybrane 1986, Literatura polska w perspektywie europejskiej (essays trans. from English) 1986, Modlitwy intelektu 1988, Messianic Prophecy: a case for reappraisal 1991, In the Scales of Fate (autobiog.) 1993, Wiersze dobrzynskie 1994, The Place Within: The Poetry of Pope John Paul II (ed. and trans.) 1994, Metropolitan Idyll (bilingual Edn) 1998, Poezje-poems by Karel Wojtyla (Pope John Paul II) (trans.) 1998, Slowa sa bez Poreczy (Poems 1935–56) 1998, Cyprian Norwid: Poems, Letters, Drawings (ed. and trans. with Christine Brooke-Rose) 2000, John Paul II: Roman Triptych (ed. and trans.) 2003. Contributions: numerous periodicals and BBC3. *Honours:* Commander, Cross, Order of Polonia Restituta, 1995.

PETERS, Andrew Fusek; British/Czech poet and children's writer; b. Prague, Czechoslovakia. *Career:* grew up in London; vocalist, didgeridu player and collaborator with Tim Juckes in the band Colour People; composer with Ben Rodway; radio work includes features for Talking Poetry (BBC Radio 4), children's poetry for BBC Radio 5, Poetry Please (BBC Radio 4); television work includes Wham Bam Strawberry Jam (BBC1), Carlton Country (Carlton Central), Heart of the Country (Carlton); mem. Nat. Asscn of Writers in Education, Poetry Soc., Poetry Soc. Poetryclass Team. *Plays:* with Polly Peters: Twisted, Much Ado About Clubbing, Angelcake, Dragon Chaser. *Publications include:* juvenile fiction: When I Come to the Dark Country 1997, The Moon is on the Microphone 1997, The Barefoot Book of Strange and Spooky Stories 1997, May the Angels be With Us: Poems of Life, Love, AIDS and Death 1999, Sadderday and Funday (with Polly Peters) 2001, Plays with Attitude (collection of plays, with Polly Peters) 2001, Poems with Attitude: Uncensored 2002, Ed and the Witchblood 2003, Dragon and Mousie 2003, Hubble Bubble 2003, Monkey's Clever Tale 2003, The Tiger and the Wise Man 2004; editor: Sheep Don't Go To School 1999, The Upside Down Frown 1999, The Unidentified Frying Omelette 2000, Out of Order 2002, The Dog Ate My Bus Pass (co-ed.) 2004, Love, Hate and My Best Mate (co-ed.) 2004; contrib. to Poems About Festivals 2000, Poems About Seasons 2000. *Address:* The Old Chapel, Lydbury North, Shropshire SY7 8AU, England; c/o Bloodaxe Books Ltd, Highgreen, Tarset, Northumberland NE48 1RP, England (Office). *E-mail:* andrew@tallpoet.com. *Website:* www.tallpoet.com.

PETERS, Catherine Lisette; Lecturer and Writer; b. 30 Sept. 1930, London, England; m. 1st John Glyn Barton, 14 Jan. 1952, three s.; m. 2nd Anthony Storr, 9 Oct. 1970. *Education:* BA, 1980, MA, 1984, University of Oxford. *Career:* Ed., Jonathan Cape, 1960–74; Lecturer in English, Somerville College, Oxford, 1981–92; mem. Wilkie Collins Society; Society of Authors; FRSL; International PEN. *Publications:* Thackeray's Universe, 1987; The King of Inventors: A Life of Wilkie Collins, 1991; Charles Dickens, 1998; Byron, 2000. Contributions: books and journals. *Literary Agent:* PFD, Drury House, 34–43 Russell St, London WC2B 5HA, England. *Address:* 45 Chalfont Rd, Oxford OX2 6TJ, England.

PETERS, Elizabeth (see Mertz, Barbara Louise Gross).

PETERS, Janis; Latvian diplomatist, writer and poet; b. 30 June 1939, Liepāja Region, Latvia; m. Baiba Kalniņa 1969; one s. *Career:* started as journalist in Latvian newspapers, later freelance; Chair. Bd of Latvian Writers' Union 1985–89; participant democratic movt for independence; Chair. Org. Cttee People's Front of Latvia 1988; USSR People's Deputy 1989–90; Perm. Rep. of Council of Ministers of Latvia to Russia 1990–91, then Amb. to Russian Fed. 1991–97; mem. govt del. to negotiations with Russia 1992–. *Publications:* more than 30 books of poetry, prose and essays in Latvian, Russian and English. *Honours:* Hon. mem. Latvian Acad. of Sciences 1990–, Latvian Univ. 1991–; Cavaliere di San Marco 1993. *Address:* Vesetas str. 8, Apt 12, 1013 Riga, Latvia. *Telephone:* (2) 370-774. *Address:* Latvijas vestnieciba (Embassy of Latvia in Russia), Ul. Chapligina 3, Moscow 103062, Russia.

PETERS, Lance; Author, Dramatist and Screenwriter; b. 8 May 1934, Auckland, New Zealand; m. Laura Chiang, 25 Feb. 1981, two s. two d. *Career:* mem. Hon. Life Mem., Australian Writers Guild, pres., 1970–72; Australian Society of Authors; Writers Guild of Great Britain; BAFTA.

Publications: Carry On Emmannuelle, 1978; The Dirty Half Mile, 1981; Cut-Throat Alley, 1982; Enemy Territory, 1988; God's Executioner, 1988; The Civilian War Zone, 1989; The Red Collar Gang, 1989; The Dirty Half Mile (Again), 1989; Gross Misconduct, 1993; Savior in the Grave, 1994. Other: Assault with a Deadly Weapon (play); 5 screenplays; many television comedies, documentaries. Contributions: numerous popular magazines. *Address:* 291 Fitzwilliam Rd, Vaucluse, Sydney, NSW 2030, Australia.

PETERS, Margot McCullough; Prof. of English Emerita and Author; b. 13 May 1933, Wausau, Wisconsin, USA; m. Peter Ridgway Jordan, 5 Nov. 1981, one s. one d. *Education:* BA, 1961, MA, 1965, PhD, 1969, University of Wisconsin at Madison. *Career:* Asst Prof. of English, Northland College, Ashland, Wisconsin, 1963–66; Asst Prof., 1969–74, Assoc. Prof., 1974–77, Prof. of English, 1977–91, Prof. Emerita, 1991–, University of Wisconsin at Whitewater; Kathe Tappe Vernon Prof. of Biography, Dartmouth College, 1978; mem. Authors' Guild; Brontë Society; Mark Twain Society; Bernard Shaw Society; Wisconsin Center for the Book. *Publications:* Charlotte Brontë: Style in the Novel, 1973; Unquiet Soul: A Biography of Charlotte Brontë, 1975; Bernard Shaw and the Actresses, 1980; Mrs Pat: The Life of Mrs Patrick Campbell, 1984; The House of Barrymore, 1990; Wild Justice (as Margret Pierce), 1995; May Sarton: A Biography, 1997; Design for Living: Lunt and Fontanne, 2003. Contributions: Professional journals, newspapers, reviews, and periodicals. *Honours:* Friends of American Writers Award for Best Prose Work, 1975; ACLS Fellow, 1976–77; George R. Freedley Memorial Awards, 1980, 1984; Banta Awards, 1981, 1985; Guggenheim Fellowship, 1988–89; Wisconsin Institute for Research in the Humanities Grant, 1988–89; English-Speaking Union Ambassador Award, 1991; Wisconsin Library Assen Distinguished Achievement Awards, 1991, 1998; Triangle Book Publishers Judy Gran Award, 1998. *Address:* 511 College St, Lake Mills, WI 53551, USA. *E-mail:* margot@gdinet.com.

PETERS, Michael Adrian; Prof. and Writer; b. 4 Sept. 1948, Wellington, New Zealand; m. Christine Athlone Besley 23 Nov. 1996; two s. *Education:* BA, Geography, Victoria University of Wellington, 1971; Diploma of Teaching, Christchurch College of Education, 1972; MA, Philosophy, PhD, Education, University of Auckland, 1979–84. *Career:* Secondary Teacher, Linwood High School, 1973–78; Head of Geography, Longbay High School, 1979–80; Private Consultant, 1981–89; Lecturer in Education, University of Canterbury, 1990–92; Senior Lecturer, 1993–95, Assoc. Prof., 1996–2000, Prof., 2000–, University of Auckland; Research Prof., University of Glasgow, 2000–; Adjunct Prof., Communication Studies, Auckland University of Technology, 2001–; Ed., Educational, Philosophy and Theory journals, Policy Futures in Education, E-Learning online journals; mem. Council Mem., Humanities Society of New Zealand, 1997–98. *Publications:* Education and the Postmodern Condition, 1995; Poststructuralism, Politics and Education, 1996; Critical Theory, Poststructuralism and the Social Context, 1996; Cultural Politics and the University, 1997; Virtual Technologies and Tertiary Education, 1998; Naming the Multiple: Poststructuralism and Education, 1998; Wittgenstein: Philosophy, Postmodernism, Pedagogy (with James Marshall), 1999; Individualism and Community: Education and Social Policy in the Postmodern Condition (with James Marshall), 1999; University Futures and the Politics of Reform (with Peter Roberts), 1999; Nietzsche's Legacy for Education: Past and Present Values (with James Marshall and Paul S. Meyers), 2001; Postructuralism, Marxism and Neoliberalism: Between Politics and Theory, 2001; Richard Rorty: Education, Philosophy and Politics (with Paulo Ghiraldelli); Heidegger, Education and Modernity, 2002; Critical Theory and the Human Condition: Founders and Praxis (with Colin Lankshear and Mark Olssen), 2003. Contributions: journals. *Honours:* Postgraduate Scholarship, University of Auckland, 1981; Macmillan Brown Lectures, University of Canterbury, 2000. *Address:* c/o Faculty of Education, University of Glasgow, St Andrews Bldg, 11 Eldon St, Glasgow G3 6NH, Scotland. *Website:* www.gla.ac.uk/~map6p/index.html.

PETERS, Richard (see Haining, Peter (Alexander)).

PETERS, Richard Stanley; academic and writer; b. 31 Oct. 1919, Missouri, India; m. Margaret Lee Duncan 1943; one s. two d. *Education:* Clifton College, Bristol; Queen's College, Oxford; Birkbeck College, London; BA, Oxon; BA, London; PhD, London, 1949. *Career:* Part-time Lecturer, 1946–49, Full-time Lecturer, 1949–58, Reader in Philosophy, 1958–62, Birkbeck College, London; Visiting Prof., Harvard University, 1961, University of Auckland, 1975; Prof. of the Philosophy of Education, 1962–82, Prof. Emeritus, 1982–, University of London; Part-time Lecturer, Bedford College, London, and LSE, 1966; Visiting Fellow, Australian National University, Canberra, 1969. *Publications:* Ethics and Education, 1945; Brett's History of Psychology, revised edn, 1953; Hobbes, 1956; The Concept of Motivation, 1958; Social Principles and the Democratic State (with S. I. Benn), 1959; Authority, Responsibility and Education, 1960; Ethics and Education, 1966; The Concept of Education (ed.), 1967; Perspectives on Plowden (ed.), 1969; The Logic of Education (with P. H. Hirst), 1970; Hobbes and Rousseau (ed. with M. Cranston), 1971; Education and the Development of Reason (ed. with R. F. Dearden and P. H. Hirst), 1972; Reason and Compassion, 1973; The Philosophy of Education (ed.), 1973; Psychology and Ethical Development, 1974; Nature and Conduct (ed.), 1975; The Role of the Head (ed.), 1976; Education and the Education of Teachers, 1977; John Dewey Reconsidered (ed.), 1977; Essays on Education, 1981; Moral Development and Moral Education, 1981. *Address:* Flat 3, 16 Shepherd's Hill, Highgate, London N6 5AQ, England.

PETERS, Robert Louis; Prof. of English, Poet and Writer; b. 20 Oct. 1924, Eagle River, Wisconsin, USA; Divorced, three s., one d. *Education:* BA, 1948, MA, 1949, PhD, 1952, University of Wisconsin at Madison. *Career:* Instructor, University of Idaho, 1952–53, Boston University, 1953–55; Asst Prof., Ohio Wesleyan University, 1955–58; Assoc. Prof., Wayne State University, 1958–63; Prof. of English, University of California at Riverside, 1963–68, and Irvine, 1968–94; mem. American Society for Aesthetics; PEN; Writer's Guild. *Publications:* The Drowned Man to the Fish, 1978; Picnic in the Snow: Ludwig of Bavaria, 1982; What Dillinger Meant to Me, 1983; Hawker, 1984; Kane, 1985; Ludwig of Bavaria: Poems and a Play, 1986; The Blood Countess: Poems and a Play, 1987; Haydon, 1988; Brueghel's Pigs, 1989; Poems: Selected and New, 1992; Goodnight Paul: Poems, 1992; Snapshots for a Serial Killer: A Fiction and Play, 1992; Zapped: 3 Novellas, 1993; Nell: A Woman from Eagle River, 1994; Lili Marlene: A Memoir of World War II, 1995; Familial Love: Poems, 2001. Other: Victorians in Literature and Art, 1961; The Crowns of Apollo: Swinburne's Principles of Literature and Art, 1965; The Letters of John Addington Symonds (co-ed.), 3 vols, 1967–69; Letter to a Tutor: The Tennyson Family Letters to Henry Graham Dakyns (ed.), 1988. Contributions: Professional journals. *Honours:* Guggenheim Fellowship, 1966–67; Yaddo, MacDowell Colony, and Ossabaw Island Project Fellowships, 1973–74; National Endowment for the Arts Grant, 1974. *Address:* 9431 Krepp Dr., Huntington Beach, CA 92646, USA.

PETERSEN, Peter James; Writer and Teacher; b. 23 Oct. 1941, Santa Rosa, CA, USA; m. Marian Braun, 6 July 1964, two d. *Education:* AB, Stanford University; MA, San Francisco State University; PhD, University of New Mexico. *Career:* English Instructor, Shasta College; mem. Society of Children's Bookwriters and Illustrators. *Publications:* Would You Settle for Improbable 1981, Nobody Else Can Walk It for You 1982, Going for the Big One 1986, Good-bye to Good Ol'Charlie 1987, The Freshman Detective Blues 1987, I Hate Camping 1991, Liars 1992, The Sub 1993, I Hate Company 1994, White Water 1997, Can You Keep A Secret 1997, My Worst Friend 1998, I Hate Weddings 2000, Rising Water 2002. *Honours:* National Endowment for the Humanities Fellowship 1976–77, William Allen White Award, Children's Crown Award. *Address:* 1243 Pueblo Ct, Redding, CA 96001, USA. *E-mail:* pjpetersen@charter.net.

PETERSON, Donald Macandrew; Lecturer in Cognitive Science and Writer; b. 23 June 1956, Dumfries, Scotland. *Education:* MA, Philosophy and Psychology, Edinburgh University, 1978; PhD, Philosophy, University College London, 1985; MSc, DIc, in Foundations of Advanced Information Technology, Imperial College, London, 1986. *Career:* mem. Society of Artificial Intelligence and the Simulation of Behaviour. *Publications:* Wittgenstein's Early Philosophy – Three Sides of the Mirror, 1990. Contributions: Professional journals and magazines. *Address:* Dept of Computer Science, University of Birmingham, Birmingham B15 2TT, England.

PETERSON, Robert; Writer and Poet; b. 2 June 1924, Denver, CO, USA; one d. *Education:* BA, University of California, Berkeley, 1947; MA, San Francisco State College, 1956. *Career:* Writer-in-Residence, Reed College, Portland, Oregon, 1969–71; mem. Marin Poetry Society. *Publications:* Home for the Night, 1962; The Binnacle, 1967; Wondering Where You Are, 1969; Lone Rider, 1976; Under Sealed Orders, 1976; Leaving Taos, 1981; The Only Piano Player in La Paz, 1985; Waiting for Garbo: 44 Ghazals, 1987; All The Time in the World, 1996. *Honours:* National Endowment for the Arts Grant, 1967; Amy Lowell Travelling Fellowship, 1972–73. *Address:* PO Box 417, Fairfax, CA 94978, USA.

PETRAKIS, Harry Mark; writer; b. 5 June 1923, St Louis, MO, USA; m. Diane Perparos 1945; three s. *Education:* University of Illinois. *Career:* teacher, writing workshops; McGuffey Visiting Lecturer, Ohio University, 1971; Writer-in-Residence, Chicago Public Library, 1976–77, Chicago Board of Education, 1978–79; Kazantzakis Prof., San Francisco State University, 1992; mem. Authors' Guild; PEN; Writers Guild of America, West. *Publications:* Lion at My Heart, 1959; The Odyssey of Kostas Volakis, 1963; Pericles on 31st Street, 1965; The Founder's Touch, 1965; A Dream of Kings, 1966; The Waves of Night, 1969; Stelmark: A Family Recollection, 1970; In the Land of Morning, 1973; The Hour of the Bell, 1976; A Petrakis Reader: 28 Stories, 1978; Nick the Greek, 1979; Days of Vengeance, 1983; Reflections on a Writer's Life and Work, 1983; Collected Stories, 1986; Ghost of the Sun, 1990; Tales of the Heart, 1999; Twilight of the Ice, 2002. Contributions: various magazines. *Honours:* Carl Sandburg Award; Ellis Island Medal of Honour, 1995. *Address:* 80 East Road, Dune Acres, Chesterton, IN 46304, USA.

PETRIE, Paul James; Prof. of English (retd) and Poet; b. 1 July 1928, Detroit, Michigan, USA; m. Sylvia Spencer, 21 Aug. 1954, one s. two d. *Education:* BA, 1950, MA, 1951, Wayne State University; PhD, University of Iowa, 1957. *Career:* Assoc. Prof., Peru State University, 1958–59; Instructor to Prof. of English, University of Rhode Island, 1959–90. *Publications:* Confessions of a Non-Conformist, 1963; The Race With Time and the Devil, 1965; From Under the Hill of Night, 1969; The Academy of Goodbye, 1974; Light From the Furnace Rising, 1978; Not Seeing is Believing, 1983; Strange Gravity, 1985; The Runners, 1988. Contributions:

newspapers, reviews, quarterlies, journals, and magazines. *Honours:* Scholarly Achievement Award, University of Rhode Island, 1983; Catholic Press Award, 1985; Arts Achievement Award, Wayne State University, 1990. *Address:* 200 Dendron Rd, Peace Dale, RI 02879, USA.

PETROBELLI, Pierluigi, BLitt, MFA; Italian musicologist and writer; *Professor of Music History, University of Rome 'La Sapienza'*; b. 18 Oct. 1932, Padua. *Education:* Univ. of Rome, Princeton Univ., Harvard Univ. Summer School, Univ. of California at Berkeley. *Career:* Ed., Rivista Italiana di Musicologia 1968–71, Studi verdiani 1981–; teaching asst 1968–70, Assoc. Prof. of Music History 1970–72, Univ. of Parma; librarian and teacher of music history, Rossini Conservatory, Pesaro 1970–73; Lecturer in Music, King's Coll., London 1973–77; Reader in Musicology, Univ. of London 1978–80; Dir, Istituto di Studi Verdiani, Parma 1980–89, Istituto Nazionale di Studi Verdiani, Parma 1989–; Prof. of Music History, Univ. of Perugia 1981–83, Univ. of Rome 'La Sapienza' 1983–; Chair of Italian Culture, Univ. of California at Berkeley 1988; Lauro de Bosis Lecturer in the History of Italian Civilization, Harvard Univ. 1996; mem. Academia Europaea, American Musicological Soc. (corresponding mem.), Royal Musical Asscn, United Kingdom (foreign hon. mem.), Accademia dei Lincei. *Publications:* Thematic Catalog of an 18th-Century Collection of Italian Instrumental Music (held in the Music Library, Univ. of California at Berkeley, with V. Duckles and M. Elmer) 1963, Giuseppe Tartini: le fonti biografiche 1968, Mozart's Il re pastore (critical edn, with Wolfgang Rehm) 1984, Carteggio Verdi-Ricordi 1880–1881 (co-ed.) 1988, Tartini, le sue idee e il suo tempo 1992, Music in the Theater: Essays on Verdi and Other Composers 1994; contrib. to scholarly books and professional journals. *Address:* 34 via di San Anselmo, 00153 Rome, Italy. *E-mail:* petrobel@rmcisadu.let.uniromat.it.

PETROSKI, Catherine (Ann); Writer; b. 1939, St Louis, MO, USA; m. Henry Petroski, 15 July 1966, one s. one d. *Education:* BA, MacMurray College, 1961; MA, University of Illinois, 1962. *Career:* mem. Authors' Guild; National Book Critics Circle. *Publications:* Gravity and Other Stories, 1981; Beautiful My Mane is the Wind, 1983; The Summer That Lasted Forever, 1984; A Bride's Passage: Susan Hathorn's Year Under Sail, 1997. Contributions: Reviews, quarterlies, and periodicals. *Honours:* Berlin Prize, 1960; Texas Institute of Letters Prize, 1976; National Endowment for the Arts Fellowships, 1978–79, 1983–84; PEN Syndicated Fiction Prizes, 1983–85, 1988; Hon. DLitt, MacMurray College, 1984; O. Henry Award, 1989; John Lyman Book Award, 1997. *Address:* 3910 Plymouth Rd, Durham, NC 27707, USA.

PETROSKI, Henry; Engineer, Prof. of History and Writer; b. 6 Feb. 1942, New York, NY, USA; m. Catherine Ann Groom, 15 July 1966, one s. one d. *Education:* BME, Manhattan College, 1963; MS, 1964, PhD, 1968, University of Illinois. *Career:* Instructor, University of Illinois, 1965–68; Asst Prof., University of Texas at Austin, 1968–74; Engineer, Argonne National Laboratory, 1975–80; Assoc. Prof. of Civil Engineering, 1980–87, Dir, Graduate Studies, 1981–86, Prof. 1987–93, Chair, Dept of Civil and Environmental Engineering, 1991–2000, Aleksandar S. Vesic Prof., 1993–, Prof. of History, 1995–, Duke University; mem. American Society of Civil Engineers; American Society of Mechanical Engineers; National Acad. of Engineering; American Acad. of Arts and Sciences. *Publications:* To Engineer is Human, 1985; Beyond Engineering, 1986; The Pencil, 1990; The Evolution of Useful Things, 1992; Design Paradigms, 1994; Engineers of Dreams, 1995; Invention by Design, 1996; Remaking the World, 1997; The Book on the Bookshelf, 1999; Paperboy: Confessions of a Future Engineer (memoir), 2002; Small Things Considered, 2003. Contributions: Professional journals, including American Scientist; television. *Honours:* Hon. doctorates, Clarkson University, 1990, Trinity College, 1997, Valparaiso University, 1999, Manhattan College, 2003; National Endowment for the Humanities Fellowship, 1987–88; Guggenheim Fellowship, 1990–91; Best Book Award in Engineering, American Asscn of University Presses, 1994. *Address:* c/o School of Engineering, Duke University, PO Box 90287, Durham, NC 27708, USA.

PETRUSHEVSKAYA, Liudmila Stefanovna; Russian author, playwright and poet; b. 26 May 1938, Moscow; m. 1st Evgenij Kharatian; one s.; m. 2nd Boris Pavlov; one s. one d. *Education:* Moscow Univ. *Career:* newspaper and radio journalist 1957–73; started writing short stories 1968, plays and folk tales 1971; stage productions and publ. of works were forbidden for many years; first underground performance 1975, first official performance, Tallinn 1979; mem. Bayerische Akad. der Schönen Kunste 1997. *Plays include:* Two Windows 1971, Music Lessons 1973, Cinzano 1973, Love 1974, The Landing 1974, Andante 1975, The Execution, A Glass of Water, Smirnova's Birthday 1977–78, Three Girls in Blue 1980, Colombina's Flat 1981, Moscow Choir 1984, The Golden Goddess 1986, The Wedding Night 1990, The Men's Quarters 1992; co-author of screenplay Tale of Tales (prize for best animated film of all time, Los Angeles 1980). *Publications:* Immortal Love 1988, Songs of the 20th Century 1988, On the Way to the God Eros 1993, The Mystery of the House 1993; (children's books) Vasilli's Treatment 1991, Once Upon a Time There Was a Trrrr! 1994, Real Fairy Tales 1997, The Alphabet's Tale 1997; Complete Works (5 vols) 1996, The Girl's House 1998, Find Me, My Dream 2000. *Honours:* Int. A. Pushkin Prize (Germany) 1991, prizes for the best short story of the year from Ogoniok 1988, 1989 and Oktiabr 1993, 1996, Grand Prize for play The Time: Night, Annual All-Russian Theatre Festival of Solo Theatre, Perm 1995, Moscow-Penne Prize (Russia/Italy) 1996. *Address:* Staroslobodsky per. 2A, Apt 20, 107113 Moscow, Russia. *Telephone:* 269-74-48. *Fax:* 269-74-48.

PETTERSON, Per; Norwegian writer; b. 18 July 1952, Hemnes. *Career:* fmr librarian, bookseller. *Publications:* Aske i munnen, sand i skoa (short stories) 1987, Ekkoland (novel) 1989, Det er griet for meg (novel) 1992, Til Sibir (novel, trans. as To Siberia) 1996, I kjølvannet (novel) 2000, Ut å stjæle hester (novel) 2003. *Address:* c/o Harvill Press, 20 Vauxhall Bridge Road, London, SW1V 2SA, England. *Website:* www.randomhouse.co.uk.

PETTIFER, Julian; Writer and Broadcaster; b. 21 July 1935, Malmesbury, England. *Education:* St John's College, Cambridge, 1955–58. *Career:* TV Reporter, Writer, Presenter, Southern TV, 1958–62; Tonight, 1962–64, 24 Hours, 1964–69, Panorama, 1969–75, BBC; Presenter, Cuba – 25 Years of Revolution, series, 1984, Host, Busman's Holiday, 1985–86, ITV; numerous TV documentaries including: Vietnam War Without End, 1970; The World About Us, 1976; The Spirit of 76, 1976; Diamonds in the Sky, 1979; Nature Watch, 5 series, 1981–90; Automania, 1984; The Living Isles, 1986; Africawatch, 1989; Missionaries, 1990; BBC Assignment, 1993–94; BBC Correspondent, 1994–95; mem. Royal Society for Nature Conservation, vice-pres., 1992–; RSPB, pres., 1994–2000. *Publications:* Diamonds in the Sky: A Social History of Air Travel (co-author), 1979; Nature Watch (co-author), 1981; Automania (co-author), 1984; The Nature Watchers (co-author), 1985; Missionaries (co-author), 1990; Nature Watch (co-author), 1994. *Honours:* Reporter of the Year Award, Guild of Television Dirs and Producers, 1968; Royal Geographical Society Cherry Kearton Award for Wildlife Films, 1990; Royal Scottish Geographical Society Mungo Park Award, 1995. *Literary Agent:* Curtis Brown Ltd, Haymarket House, 28–29 Haymarket, London, SW1Y 4SP, England. *Telephone:* (20) 7393-4400. *Fax:* (20) 7393-4401. *E-mail:* info@curtisbrown.co.uk. *Website:* www.curtisbrown.co.uk.

PETTIT, Philip Noel, PhD; Irish/Australian professor of social and political theory; *Professor of Politics, Princeton University*; b. 20 Dec. 1945, Ballinasloe, Ireland; m. Eileen McNally 1978; two s. *Education:* Maynooth Coll., Nat. Univ. of Ireland, Queen's Univ. Belfast, Northern Ireland. *Career:* lecturer, Univ. Coll. Dublin 1968–72, 1975–77; Research Fellow, Trinity Hall Cambridge, UK 1972–75; Prof. of Philosophy, Univ. of Bradford, UK 1977–83; Professorial Fellow, Research School of Social Sciences, ANU, Canberra 1983–89, Prof. of Social and Political Theory 1989–2002; Visiting Prof. of Philosophy, Columbia Univ., New York 1997–2001; Prof. of Politics, Princeton Univ. 2002–; Fellow Acad. of Social Sciences, Australia, Australian Acad. of Humanities. *Publications:* Concept of Structuralism 1975, Judging Justice 1980, Semantics and Social Science (with G. Macdonald) 1981, Not Just Deserts: A Republican Theory of Criminal Justice (with J. Braithwaite) 1990, The Common Mind: An Essay on Psychology, Society and Politics 1992, Republicanism: A Theory of Freedom and Government 1997, A Theory of Freedom: From the Psychology to the Politics of Agency 2001, Rules, Reasons and Norms: Selected Essays 2002. *Honours:* Hon. mem. Italian Soc. for Analytical Philosophy; Hon. DLitt (Nat. Univ. of Ireland) 2000; Univ. Medal, Univ. of Helsinki 1992. *Address:* Department of Politics, Corwin Hall, Princeton University, Princeton, NJ 08544-1012, USA (Office); 605/2 Marcus Clarke St, Canberra, ACT, Australia (Home). *Telephone:* (2) 6262-7092 (Home).

PETTY, William Henry; Educator (retd) and Poet; b. 7 Sept. 1921, Bradford, Yorkshire, England; m. Margaret Elaine Bastow, 31 May 1948, one s. two d. *Education:* Peterhouse, Cambridge, 1940–41, 1945; MA, Cantab, 1950; BSc, London, 1953; DLitt, Kent, 1983. *Career:* Administrative, Teaching and Lecturing posts, London, Doncaster, North and West Ridings of Yorkshire, Kent, 1945–73; Chief Education Officer, Kent, 1973–84; Chair. of Govs, Christ Church University College, Canterbury, 1992–94; mem. Poetry Society; English Asscn. *Publications:* No Bold Comfort, 1957; Conquest, 1967; Educational Administration (co-author), 1980; Executive Summaries (booklets), 1984–90; Springfield: Pieces of the Past, 1994; Genius Loci (with Robert Roberts), 1995; The Louvre Imperial, 1997; Interpretations of History, 2000; No-one Listening, 2002; Breaking Time, 2003. Contributions: various anthologies, reviews, quarterlies and journals. *Honours:* Cheltenham Festival of Literature Prize, 1968; Camden Festival of Music and the Arts Prize, 1969; Greenwood Prize, Poetry Society, 1978; Lake Aske Memorial Award, 1980; CBE, 1981; Swanage Festival of Literature Prize, 1995; Ali Competition Prize, 1995; Kent Federation of Writers Prize, 1995; White Cliffs Prize, 2000. *Address:* Willow Bank, Moat Rd, Headcorn, Kent TN27 9NT, England.

PEYSER, Joan Gilbert, BA, MA; American musicologist and writer; b. 12 June 1931, New York, NY. *Education:* Barnard Coll., Columbia Univ. *Career:* Ed., The Musical Quarterly 1977–84; mem. American Musicological Soc., Music Critics Asscn, PEN. *Publications:* The New Music: The Sense Behind the Sound 1971, revised second edn as Twentieth Century Music: The Sense Behind the Sound 1981, Boulez: Composer, Conductor, Enigma 1976, The Orchestra: Origins and Transformations 1986, Bernstein: A Biography 1987, The Memory of All That: The Life of George Gershwin 1993, To Boulez and Beyond: Music in Europe Since the Rite of Spring 1999; contrib. to periodicals and journals. *Honours:* six ASCAP/Deems Taylor Awards, first prize in the humanities Asscn of American Publishers 1986. *Address:* 19 Charlton Street, New York, NY 10014, USA.

PEYTON, Kathleen Wendy, (Kathleen Herald, K. M. Peyton); Writer; b. 2 Aug. 1929, Birmingham, England; m. Michael Peyton, 1950, two d. *Education:* ATD, Manchester School of Art. *Publications:* As Kathleen Herald: Sabre, the Horse from the Sea, 1947; The Mandrake, 1949; Crab the Roan, 1953. As K. M. Peyton: North to Adventure, 1959; Stormcock Meets Trouble, 1961; The Hard Way Home, 1962; Windfall, 1963; Brownsea Silver, 1964; The Maplin Bird, 1964; The Plan for Birdsmarsh, 1965; Thunder in the Sky, 1966; Flambards Trilogy, 1969–71; The Beethoven Medal, 1971; The Pattern of Roses, 1972; Pennington's Heir, 1973; The Team, 1975; The Right-Hand Man, 1977; Prove Yourself a Hero, 1977; A Midsummer Night's Death, 1978; Marion's Angels, 1979; Flambards Divided, 1981; Dear Fred, 1981; Going Home, 1983; The Last Ditch, 1984; Froggett's Revenge, 1985; The Sound of Distant Cheering, 1986; Downhill All the Way, 1988; Darkling, 1989; Skylark, 1989; No Roses Round the Door, 1990; Poor Badger, 1991; Late to Smile, 1992; The Boy Who Wasn't There, 1992; The Wild Boy and Queen Moon, 1993; Snowfall, 1994; The Swallow Tale, 1995; Swallow Summer, 1995; Unquiet Spirits, 1997; Firehead, 1998; Swallow the Star, 1998; Blind Beauty, 1999; Small Gains, 2003. *Honours:* New York Herald Tribune Award, 1965; Carnegie Medal, 1969; Guardian Award, 1970. *Address:* Rookery Cottage, North Fambridge, Chelmsford, Essex CM3 6LP, England.

PEYTON, Richard (see Haining, Peter (Alexander)).

PHELAN, Tom, (Thomas J. Phelan); Writer; b. 5 Nov. 1940, Mountmellick, Co Laois, Ireland; m. Patricia Mansfield, 14 Sept. 1991, two s. *Education:* BA, Philosophy, St Patrick's Seminary, Carlow, 1965; MA, University of Seattle, 1977. *Career:* Priest; Asst Prof. of English, Harriman College, New York; mem. Authors' Guild; Irish Writers' Union; Poets and Writers. *Publications:* In the Season of the Daisies, 1993; Iscariot, 1995; Derrycloney, 1999. Other: Saying Goodbye (short story), 1995; In the Vatican Museum (short story), 1998. *Address:* c/o Brandon Book Publishers, Cooleen, Dingle, Co Kerry, Ireland.

PHILANDERSON, Flavian Titus, (Johnny Goad, Flavian P. Stimulus, John Stimulus); Journalist and Writer; b. 3 March 1933, Penang, British Malaya; m. Martha Bernadette Pillai, 29 Dec. 1956, two s. two d. *Education:* Overseas School Certificate A, University of Cambridge, 1951; Teacher Training, Ministry of Education, British Administration, Malaya; Fiction Writing, Premier School of Journalism, Fleet Street, London. *Career:* mem. Australian Society of Authors; Royal Australian Historical Society; Fellowship of Australian Writers. *Publications:* A Course in Primary English (co-author), 1969; Window in the Sky (novel), 1982; Diary of a Sydney Girl, 1992; All Flesh Is Grass, 1995. Contributions: various publications. *Address:* 'San Antone', 32 Hillcrest Ave, Winston Hills, Sydney, NSW 2153, Australia.

PHILIP, Marlene Nourbese; Poet, Writer and Lawyer; b. 3 Feb. 1947, Tobago; m. Paul Chamberlain, 1978, three c. *Education:* BSc, University of the West Indies, 1968; MA, 1970, LLB, 1973, University of Western Ontario. *Publications:* Thorns, 1980; Salmon Courage, 1983; Harriet's Daughter, 1988; She Tries Her Tongue, Her Silence Softly Breaks, 1989; Looking for Livingstone: An Odyssey of Silence, 1991; Frontiers: Essays and Writings on Racism and Culture, 1992; Showing Grit: Showboating North of the 44th Parallel, 1993. *Honours:* Casa de las Americas Prize for Poetry, 1988; Toronto Book Award for Fiction, 1990; Max and Greta Abel Award for Multicultural Literature, 1990; Guggenheim Fellowship, 1990; Toronto Arts Award, 1995. *Address:* c/o Women's Press, 517 College St, Suite 233, Toronto, ON M6G 4A2, Canada.

PHILLIPS, Adam; British psychoanalyst and writer. *Career:* fmr Principal Child Psychotherapist, Charing Cross Hospital, London; Series Ed., Penguin translations of Sigmund Freud's work. *Publications:* On Kissing, Tickling and Being Bored: Psychoanalytic Essays on the Unexamined Life 1993, On Flirtation 1994, Terrors and Experts 1995, Monogamy 1996, The Beast in the Nursery 1998, Darwin's Worms: On Life Stories and Death Stories 2000, Promises Promises: Essays on Psychoanalysis and Literature 2000, Houdini's Box: The Art of Escape 2001, Psychoanalysis 2001, Equals 2002, On Sanity 2005. *Address:* c/o Faber and Faber Ltd, 3 Queen Square, London, WC1N 3AU, England. *Website:* www.faber.co.uk.

PHILLIPS, Carl; Prof., Poet and Writer; b. 23 July 1959, Everett, WA, USA. *Education:* BA, magna cum laude, Greek and Latin, Harvard University, 1981; MAT, Latin and Classical Humanities, University of Massachusetts at Amherst, 1983; MA, Creative Writing, Boston University, 1993. *Career:* Poet-in-Residence, 1993–94, Asst Prof., 1994–96, Assoc. Prof., 1996–2000, Dir, Writing Program, 1996–98, 2000–, Prof., 2000–, Washington University, St Louis; Visiting Asst Prof., Harvard University, 1995–96; Faculty, Warren Wilson College, 1997–; Visiting Writer-in-Residence, University of Iowa, 1998; mem. Acad. of American Poets; Associated Writing Programs; MLA; PEN American Center; Poetry Society of America. *Publications:* In the Blood, 1992; Cortège, 1995; From the Devotions, 1998; Pastoral, 2000; The Tether, 2001; Rock Harbor, 2002. Contributions: many anthologies, reviews, quarterlies and journals. *Honours:* Samuel French Morse Poetry Prize, 1992; Acad. of American Poets Prize, 1993; Guggenheim Fellowship, 1997–98; Witter Bynner Fellowship, 1997–98; Pushcart Prizes, 1998, 2001; Lambda Literary Award in Poetry, 2001; American Acad. of Arts and Letters Award in Literature, 2001; Kingsley Tufts Poetry Prize, 2002. *Address:* 1026 Fairmount Ave, St Louis, MO 63139, USA.

PHILLIPS, Caryl, BA, FRSL; British/Saint Christopher and Nevis writer and academic; *Professor of English and Henry R. Luce Professor of Migration and Social Order, Barnard College*; b. 13 March 1958, St Kitts, West Indies. *Education:* The Queen's Coll. Oxford. *Career:* Writer-in-Residence, The Factory Arts Centre, London 1980–82, Univ. of Mysore, India 1987, Univ. of Stockholm 1989; visiting writer, Amherst Coll., Mass., USA 1990–92, Writer-in-Residence and Co-Dir Creative Writing Center 1992–94, Prof. of English 1994–97, Prof. of English and Writer-in-Residence 1997–98; Prof. of English and Henry R. Luce Prof. of Migration and Social Order, Barnard Coll., Columbia Univ., New York 1998–; writing instructor, Arvon Foundation, UK 1983–; Visiting Prof. of Humanities, Univ. of W Indies, Barbados 1999–2000; Consultant Ed. Faber Inc., Boston 1992–94; Contributing Ed. Bomb Magazine, New York 1993–; Consultant Ed. Graywolf Press, Minneapolis 1994–; Dir Heartland Productions Ltd 1994–2000; Advisory Ed. Wasifiri Magazine, London 1995–; Series Ed. Faber and Faber, London 1996–2000; mem. Arts Council of GB Drama Panel 1982–85, British Film Inst. Production Bd 1985–88, Bd, The Bush Theatre, London 1985–89; mem. English PEN 1997, Writers' Guild (UK) 1997, American PEN, council mem. 1998; Hon. Sr mem. Univ. of Kent 1988–; Fellow New York Public Library 2002–03. *Films:* Playing Away 1986, The Mystic Masseur 2001. *Plays:* Strange Fruit 1980, Where There is Darkness 1982, The Shelter 1983. *Radio:* plays: The Wasted Years (BBC Giles Cooper Award for Best Radio Play of the Year) 1984, Crossing the River 1985, The Prince of Africa 1987, Writing Fiction 1991; several documentaries. *Television:* The Final Passage (Channel 4) 1996. *Publications:* fiction: The Final Passage (Malcolm X Prize for Literature) 1985, A State of Independence 1986, Higher Ground 1989, Cambridge (Sunday Times Young Writer of the Year Award) 1991, Crossing the River (James Tait Black Memorial Prize) 1993, The Nature of Blood 1997; non-fiction: The European Tribe (Martin Luther King Memorial Prize) 1987, The Atlantic Sound 2000, A New World Order: Selected Essays 2001, A Distant Shore (Commonwealth Writers Prize Eurasia Region Best Book Award 2004, Commonwealth Writers Prize 2004) 2003; editor: Extravagant Strangers 1997, The Right Set: A Tennis Anthology 1999. *Honours:* Hon. AM (Amherst Coll.) 1995, Hon. DUniv (Leeds Metropolitan) 1997, York (2003), Hon. DLitt (Leeds) 2003; British Council 50th Anniversary Fellowship 1984, Guggenheim Fellowship 1992; Lannan Literary Award 1994. *Literary Agent:* Georgia Garrett, A. P. Watt Ltd, 20 John Street, London, WC1N 2DR, England. *Telephone:* (20) 7405-6774. *Fax:* (20) 7831-2145. *E-mail:* apw@apwatt.co.uk. *Website:* www.carylphillips.com.

PHILLIPS, Edward O.; Teacher and Writer; b. 26 Nov. 1931, Montréal, QC, Canada. *Education:* BA, McGill University, 1953; LL.L, University of Montréal, 1956; AMT, Harvard University, 1957; MA, Boston University, 1962. *Career:* mem. Canadian Writers Union; PEN. *Publications:* Sunday's Child, 1981; Where There's a Will, 1984; Buried on Sunday, 1986; Hope Springs Eternal, 1988; Sunday Best, 1990; The Landlady's Niece, 1992; The Mice Will Play, 1996; Working on Sunday, 1998; No Early Birds, 2001. Contributions: Short stories to various Canadian journals. *Honours:* Arthur Ellis Award, 1986. *Address:* 425 Wood Ave, Westmount, QC H3Y 3J3, Canada.

PHILLIPS, Jayne Anne; Writer; b. 19 July 1952, Buckhannon, West Virginia, USA; m. Mark Brian Stockman 26 May 1985; one s. two step-s. *Education:* BA, West Virginia University, 1974; MFA, University of Iowa, 1978. *Career:* Adjunct Assoc. Prof. of English, Boston University, 1982–; Fanny Howe Chair of Letters, Brandeis University, 1986–87; mem. Authors' Guild; Authors League of America; PEN. *Publications:* Sweethearts, 1976; Counting, 1978; Black Tickets, 1979; How Mickey Made It, 1981; Machine Dreams, 1984; Fast Lanes, 1984; Shelter, 1994; Motherkind, 2000. *Honours:* Pushcart Prizes, 1977, 1979, 1983; Fels Award in Fiction, Co-ordinating Council of Literary Magazines, 1978; National Endowment for the Arts Fellowships, 1978, 1985; St Lawrence Award for Fiction, 1979; Sue Kaufman Award for Fiction, American Acad. and Institute of Arts and Letters, 1980; O. Henry Award, 1980; Bunting Institute Fellowship, Radcliffe College, 1981; Notable Book Citation, American Library Asscn, 1984; Best Book Citation, New York Times, 1984. *Address:* c/o International Creative Management, 40 W 57th St, New York, NY 10019, USA.

PHILLIPS, Kate; Writer; b. 30 July 1966, Pomona, CA, USA; m., two c. *Education:* BA summa cum laude, Dartmouth College, 1988; MA, English, 1992, PhD, History of American Civilization, 1997, Harvard University. *Career:* Teacher, Beijing Normal University, People's Republic of China, 1988–89; Grant Writer, Newsletter Ed., Irish Immigration Center, Boston, 1992–95. *Publications:* White Rabbit, 1996; Helen Hunt Jackson: A Literary Life, 2003. *Address:* c/o Ann Borchardt, Georges Borchardt Literary Agency, 136 E 57th St, New York, NY 10022, USA.

PHILLIPS, Louis; Prof. of Humanities, Writer, Dramatist and Poet; b. 15 June 1942, Lowell, MA, USA; m. Patricia L. Ranard, 26 Aug. 1971, two s. *Education:* BA, Stetson University, 1964; MA, University of North Carolina at Chapel Hill, 1965; MA, CUNY, 1967. *Career:* Prof. of Humanities, School of Visual Arts, New York, 1977–. *Publications:* The Man Who Stole the Atlantic Ocean, 1971; Theodore Jonathon Wainwright is Going to Bomb the Pentagon, 1973; The Time, the Hour, the Solitariness of the Place, 1986; A Dream of Countries Where No One Dare Live, 1994; The Hot Corner, 1997. Contributions: The Georgia Review; Massachusetts Review; Chicago

Review; Regular Columnist for The Armchair Detective; Shakespeare Bulletin. *Literary Agent:* Fifi Oscard Agency. *Address:* 375 Riverside Dr., Apt 14C, New York, NY 10025, USA.

PHILLIPS, Michael (see Nolan, William Francis).

PHILLIPS, Robert (Schaeffer); Prof. of English, Poet and Writer; b. 2 Feb. 1938, Milford, DE, USA; m. Judith Anne Bloomingdale, 16 June 1962, one s. *Education:* BA, English, 1960, BA, Communications, 1960, MA, American Literature, 1962, Syracuse University. *Career:* Instructor, New School for Social Research, New York City, 1966–68, Belle Levine Arts Center, 1968–69; Poetry Review Ed., Modern Poetry Studies, 1969–73; Prof. of English, 1991–, Dir, Creative Writing Program, 1991–96, John and Rebecca Moores University Scholar, 1998–2003, University of Houston; Poetry Reviewer, Houston Post, 1992–95, Houston Chronicle, 1995–; mem. Acad. of American Poets; American PEN Center, board of dirs; Asscn of Literary Scholars and Critics; English-Speaking Union; Friends of Poets and Writers; National Book Critics Circle; Poetry Society of America; South Central MLA; Texas Institute of Letters, councillor; The Poets' Prize, chair. *Publications:* Poetry: Inner Weather, 1966; The Pregnant Man, 1978; Running on Empty, 1981; Personal Accounts: New and Selected Poems, 1966–1986, 1986; The Wounded Angel, 1987; Face to Face, 1993; Breakdown Lane, 1994; Spinach Days, 2000; Interviews: The Madness of Art, 2003. Fiction: The Land of the Lost Content, 1970; Public Landing Revisited, 1992; News About People You Know, 2002. Criticism: Aspects of Alice (ed.), 1971; The Confessional Poets, 1973; Denton Welch, 1974; William Goyen, 1978. Contributions: many anthologies, reviews, quarterlies, and journals. *Honours:* American Acad. and Institute of Arts and Letters Award, 1987; Arents Pioneer Medal, Syracuse University, 1988; Greenwood Award, 1993; New York Times Notable Book of the Year Citations, 1994, 2000; Fort Concho Literary Festival Fiction Prize, 1994. *Address:* c/o Creative Writing Program, Dept of English, University of Houston, Houston, TX 77204, USA.

PHILLIPS, Warren Henry, BA; American publisher and newspaper executive; b. 28 June 1926, New York City; m. Barbara Anne Thomas 1951; three d. *Education:* Queens Coll. *Career:* Copyreader Wall Street Journal 1947–48, Foreign Corresp., Germany 1949–50, Chief, London Bureau 1950–51, Foreign Ed. 1951–53, News Ed. 1953–54, Man. Ed. Midwest Edition 1954–57, Man. Ed. Wall Street Journal 1957–65, Publr 1975–88; Exec. Ed. Dow Jones & Co. 1965–70; Vice-Pres. and Gen. Man. Dow Jones & Co. Inc. 1970–71, Editorial Dir 1971–88, Exec. Vice-Pres. 1972, Pres. 1972–79, CEO 1975–90, Chair. 1978–91, mem. Bd of Dirs 1972–97, Dir Emer. 1997–; Pres. American Council on Educ. for Journalism 1971–73; Co-Publr Bridge Works Publishing Co. 1992–; mem. Bd of Dirs Public Broadcasting Service 1991–97; Pres. American Soc. of Newspaper Eds 1975–76; mem. Pulitzer Prizes Bd 1977–87; Trustee, Columbia Univ. 1980–93, Trustee Emer. 1993–; mem. Visitors' Cttee Kennedy School of Govt, Harvard Univ. 1984–90, 1992–97; mem. Corp. Advisory Bd Queens Coll. 1986–90, Foundation Bd of Trustees 1990–97. *Publication:* China: Behind the Mask (with Robert Keatley) 1973. *Honours:* Hon. LHD (Pace) 1982, (Queens Coll.) 1987, (Long Island) 1987; Hon. JD (Portland) 1973. *Address:* Bridge Works Publishing, PO Box 1798, Bridgehampton, NY 11932, USA. *Telephone:* (631) 537-3418. *Fax:* (631) 537-5092.

PHILLIPS, Will (see Williamson, Philip G.).

PHILLIS, Sir Robert Weston, Kt, BA, FRSA, FRTS; British media executive; *Chief Executive, Guardian Media Group;* b. 3 Dec. 1945, Croydon; m. Jean Derham 1966; three s. *Education:* John Ruskin Grammar School and Univ. of Nottingham. *Career:* apprentice, printing industry 1961–65; Thomson Regional Newspapers Ltd 1968–69; British Printing Corpn Ltd 1969–71; lecturer in industrial relations, Univ. of Edin. and Scottish Business School 1971–75; Visiting Fellow, Univ. of Nairobi 1974; Personnel Dir, later Man. Dir Sun Printers Ltd 1976–79; Man. Dir Independent TV Publs Ltd 1979–82; Man. Dir Cen. Independent TV PLC 1981–87, Dir Non-Exec. 1987–91; Group Man. Dir Carlton Communications PLC 1987–91; Chief Exec. Independent TV News (ITN) 1991–93; Man. Dir BBC World Service 1993–94, Deputy Dir-Gen. BBC 1993–97, Chair. BBC Worldwide 1994–97; Chief Exec. Guardian Media Group 1997–; Chair. ITV Network Programming Cttee 1984–86, ITV Film Purchase Group 1985–87, Zenith Productions 1984–91, Trader Media Group Ltd 2001–; Dir (non-exec.) ITN Ltd 1982–87; Dir and Trustee TV Trust for the Environment, Teaching Awards Trust 2001–; Vice-Chair. (Int.), Int. Council, Nat. Acad. of TV Arts and Sciences 1994–97 (Life Fellow), (Dir 1985–93); Vice-Pres. European Broadcasting Union 1996–97; Hon. Prof. Univ. of Stirling 1997; Fellow, Royal TV Soc. 1993 (Chair. 1989–92, Vice-Pres. 1994); Trustee Nat. Film and TV School Foundation. *Honours:* Hon. DLitt (Salford Univ.) 1999; Hon. DLit (City Univ.) 2000; Hon. DLitt (Nottingham Univ.) 2003. *Address:* Guardian Media Group, 75 Farringdon Road, London, England (Office). *Telephone:* (20) 7239-9711 (Office). *Fax:* (20) 7713-4709 (Office). *E-mail:* bob.phillis@gmgplc.co.uk (Office). *Website:* www.gmgplc.co.uk (Office).

PHILP, Peter; Writer; b. 10 Nov. 1920, Cardiff, Wales; m. 25 Sept. 1940, two s. *Career:* mem. Society of Authors. *Publications:* Beyond Tomorrow, 1947; The Castle of Deception, 1952; Love and Lunacy, 1955; Antiques Today, 1960; Antique Furniture for the Smaller Home, 1962; Furniture of the World, 1974; The Real Sir John (play), 1995. Contributions: Times; Antique Dealer and Collectors Guide; Antique Collecting; Antique Furniture Expert (with Gillian Walkling), 1991; Antiques Trade Gazette, regular feature, 1992–. *Honours:* Arts Council Award, 1951; C. H. Foyle Award, 1951. *Address:* 77 Kimberley Rd, Cardiff CF23 5DP, Wales.

PHIPPS, Constantine (Edmund), (Marquis of Normanby); Company Dir and Author; b. 24 Feb. 1954, Whitby, North Yorkshire, England; m. Nicola St Aubyn, 21 July 1990, two s. one d. *Education:* MA, Politics, Philosophy, Economics, Worcester College, Oxford. *Publications:* Careful With the Sharks, 1985; Among the Thin Ghosts, 1989. Other: The Day's Work by Rudyard Kipling (ed.), 1988. *Address:* Mulgrave Castle, Whitby YO21 3RJ, England.

PICANO, Felice; Writer and Poet; b. 22 Feb. 1944, New York, NY, USA. *Education:* BA, cum laude, Queens College, CUNY, 1960. *Career:* mem. PEN Club; Writers Guild of America; Authors' Guild; Publishing Triangle. *Publications:* Smart as the Devil, 1975; Eyes, 1976; Deformity Lover and Other Poems, 1977; The Lure, 1979; Late in the Season, 1980; An Asian Minor, 1981; Slashed to Ribbons in Defense of Love and Other Stories, 1982; House of Cards, 1984; Ambidextrous, 1985; Men Who Loved Me, 1989; To the Seventh Power, 1989; The New Joy of Gay Sex, 1992; Dryland's End, 1995; Like People in History, 1995. Contributions: Men on Men; Violet Quill Reader; numerous magazines and journals. *Honours:* PEN Syndicated Short Fiction Award; Chapbook Award, Poetry Society of America.

PICARD, Barbara Leonie; Author; b. 4 Dec. 1917, Richmond, Surrey, England. *Publications:* Ransom for a Knight, 1956; Lost John, 1962; One is One, 1965; The Young Pretenders, 1966; Twice Seven Tales, 1968; Three Ancient Kings, 1972; Tales of Ancient Persia, revised edn, 1993; The Iliad, 1991; The Odyssey, 1991; French Legends, Tales and Fairy Stories, 1992; German Hero-sagas and Folk-tales, 1993; Tales of the Norse Gods, 1994; Selected Fairy Tales, 1994; The Deceivers, 1996; The Midsummer Bride, 1999. *Address:* c/o Oxford University Press, Great Clarendon St, Oxford OX2 6DP, England.

PICARD, Robert George; Writer; b. 15 July 1951, Pasadena, CA, USA; m. Elizabeth Carpelan, 15 Sept. 1979, two d., one s. *Education:* BA, Loma Linda University, 1974; MA, California State University, Fullerton, 1980; PhD, University of Missouri, 1983. *Career:* Ed., Journal of Media Economics, 1988–97; Assoc. Ed., Political Communication and Persuasion, 1989–91. *Publications:* The Press and the Decline of Democracy, 1985; Press Concentration and Monopoly, 1988; The Ravens of Odin: The Press in the Nordic Nations, 1988; In the Camera's Eye: News Coverage of Terrorist Events, 1991; Media Portrayals of Terrorism: Functions and Meaning of News Coverage, 1993; The Cable Networks Handbook, 1993; Joint Operating Agreements: The Newspaper Preservation Act and its Application, 1993; The Newspaper Publishing Industry, 1997. *Address:* 2806 Gertrude St, Riverside, CA 92506, USA.

PICHASKE, David Richard, BA, MA, PhD; academic, poet, writer and editor; *Professor of English, Southwest State University;* b. 2 Sept. 1943, Kenmore, NY, USA; m. 1st Elaine Ezekian 1968 (divorced 1988); one s. one d.; m. 2nd Michelle Payne 1991. *Education:* Wittenberg University, Ohio University. *Career:* Assoc. Prof. of English, Bradley Polytechnical Institute, Peoria, IL, 1970–80; Ed., Spoon River Quarterly, 1977–; Prof. of English, Southwest State University, Marshall, MN, 1980–; Senior Fulbright Lecturer, Łódź, Poland, 1989–91, Rīga, Latvia, 1997–98, Ulaanbaatar, Mongolia 2003; mem. Asscn for the Study of Literature and the Environment; Society for the Study of Midwest Literature. *Publications:* Beowulf to Beatles: Approaches to Poetry, 1972; Writing Sense: A Handbook of Composition, 1975; Chaucer's Literary Pilgrimage: Movement in the Canterbury Tales, 1978; A Generation in Motion: Popular Music and Culture in the 1960s, 1979; Beowulf to Beatles and Beyond: The Varieties of Poetry, 1980; The Poetry of Rock, 1981; The Jubilee Diary: April 10 1980–April 19 1981, 1982; Salem/Peoria, 1883–1982, 1982; Bringing the Humanities to the Countryside: Access to the Humanities in Western Minnesota (ed. with Gerrit Groen), 1985; Tales from Two Rivers (ed. with John E. Halwas), Vol. 4, 1987; Visiting the Father and Other Poems, 1987; Late Harvest: Rural American Writing (ed.), 1991; Poland in Transition, 1989–1991, 1994; Exercises Against Retirement (poems), 1995; Southwest Minnesota: The Land and the People, 2000; UB03 2003, A Place Called Home 2003, Harassment: A Novel of Ideas 2003, Hallelujah Anyway 2004; contrib. to reviews, quarterlies and journals. *Address:* c/o Department of English, Southwest State University, Marshall, MN 56258, USA.

PICKARD, Tom, (Thomas Marriner Pickard); writer, poet and documentary film-maker; b. 7 Jan. 1946, Newcastle upon Tyne, England; m. Svava Barker 1999; two s. one d. *Career:* Arts Council writer-in-residence, Univ. of Warwick 1979–80. *Publications:* High on the Walls, 1967; New Human Unisphere, 1969; The Order of Chance, 1971; Guttersnipe, 1972; Dancing Under Fire, 1973; Hero Dust: New and Selected Poems, 1979; OK Tree, 1980; The Jarrow March, 1982; Custom and Exile, 1985; We Make Ships, 1989; Tiepin Eros: New and Selected Poems, 1994; Fuckwind: New Poems and Songs, 1999; Hole in the Wall: New and Selected Poems, 2001. Other: Television plays and documentaries. Contributions: Chicago Review; London Magazine; Northern Review; Sniper Logic; David Jones Journal. *Literary Agent:* Judy Daish Associates, 2 St Charles Place, London, W10 6EG, England.

PICKERING, Paul Granville; Novelist and Playwright; b. 9 May 1952, Rotherham, England; m. Alison Beckett, 11 Dec. 1983, one d. *Education:* BA, Psychology, Leicester University. *Career:* mem. Society of Authors. *Publications:* Wild About Harry, 1985; Perfect English, 1986; The Blue Gate of Babylon, 1989; Charlie Peace, 1991. Plays: After Hamlet, 1994; Walk Her Home. 1999. Contributions: Times; Sunday Times; Independent; Anthologies. *Address:* c/o Mic Cheetham, 11–12 Dover St, London W1X 3PH, England. *E-mail:* ryetrip@aol.com.

PICOULT, Jodi; American writer; b. 1967, Long Island, NY; m. Tim Van Leer; three c. *Education:* Univ. of Princeton. *Publications:* novels: Songs of the Humpback Whale: A Novel in Five Voices 1992, Harvesting the Heart 1993, Picture Perfect 1995, Mercy 1996, Keeping Faith 1999, Pact: A Love Story 1999, Plain Truth 2000, Salem Falls 2001, Second Glance 2003, Falling to Earth 2004, My Sister's Keeper 2004, Vanishing Acts 2005. *Honours:* New England Bookseller Award for Fiction 2003. *Address:* c/o Simon & Schuster UK Ltd, Africa House, 64–78 Kingsway, London, WC2B 6AH, England. *E-mail:* www.jodipicoult.com.

PIEL, Gerard, AB; American editor and publisher; b. 1 March 1915, New York; m. 1st Mary Tapp Bird 1938 (divorced 1955); two s. (one deceased); m. 2nd Eleanor Virden Jackson 1955; one d. *Education:* Phillips Acad., Andover, Mass. and Harvard Coll. *Career:* Editorial Assoc., Science Ed., Life 1938–45; Asst to Pres., Henry J. Kaiser Co. and associated enterprises 1945–46; Organizer, Pres. Scientific American Inc., Publr Scientific American 1947–84, Chair of Bd 1984–87, Chair. Emer. 1987; Chair. Comm. Delivery Personal Health Services, New York 1966–68, Trustees, Foundation for Child Devt; mem. Bd Overseers Harvard Univ. 1966–68, 1973–79; Trustee American Museum of Natural History, Radcliffe Coll. 1962–80, Phillips Acad., New York Botanical Garden, Henry J. Kaiser Family Foundation, Mayo Foundation, American Bd of Medical Specialities, René Dubos Center for Human Environment; mem. Council on Foreign Relations, American Philosophical Soc., Inst. of Medicine; Fellow American Acad. of Arts and Sciences, AAAS (Pres. 1985, Chair. 1986). *Publications:* Science in the Cause of Man 1962, The Acceleration of History 1972, Only One World 1992, The Age of Science 2001. *Honours:* numerous hon. doctorates; George Polk Award 1961, Kalinga Prize 1962, Bradford Washburn Award 1966, Arches of Science Award 1969, Rosenberger Medal, Univ. of Chicago 1973, A. I. Djavakhishvili Medal (Univ. of Tbilisi), Publr of the Year, Magazine Publrs Asscn 1980. *Address:* 1115 Fifth Avenue, New York, NY 10128, USA (Home).

PIELMEIER, John; Dramatist and Actor; b. 3 Feb. 1949, Altoona, Pennsylvania, USA; m. Irene O'Brian, 9 Oct. 1982. *Education:* BA, Catholic University of America; MFA, Pennsylvania State University. *Career:* mem. Writers Guild of America; Dramatists Guild; American Federation of Television and Radio Artists; Actors Equity Asscn. *Publications:* Agnes of God, 1983; Haunted Lives (A Witches Brew, A Ghost Story, A Gothic Tale), 1984. *Honours:* Christopher Award, 1984; Humanitas Award, 1984. *Address:* c/o Artists Agency, 230 W 55th St, New York, NY 10019, USA.

PIERARD, Richard Victor, BA, MA, PhD; academic and writer; b. 29 May 1934, Chicago, IL, USA; m. Charlene Burdett 1957; one s. one d. *Education:* California State Univ., Los Angeles, Univ. of Hamburg, Univ. of Iowa. *Career:* instructor, Univ. of Iowa 1964; Asst Prof. 1964–67, Assoc. Prof. 1967–72, Prof. of History 1972–2000, Indiana State Univ., Terre Haute; Research Fellow, Univ. of Aberdeen 1978; Fulbright Prof., Univ. of Frankfurt 1984–85, Univ. of Halle 1989–90; mem. American Historical Soc., American Soc. of Church History, American Soc. of Missiology, Baptist World Alliance (Baptist Heritage study cttee 1990–2000), Evangelical Theological Soc. (pres. 1985), Greater Terre Haute Church Federation (pres. 1987–88), Int. Asscn of Mission Studies, American Baptist Historical Soc. (bd of mans). *Publications:* Protest and Politics: Christianity and Contemporary Affairs (with Robert G. Clouse and Robert D. Linder), 1968; The Unequal Yoke: Evangelical Christianity and Political Conservatism, 1970; The Cross and the Flag (ed. with Robert G. Clouse and Robert D. Linder), 1972; Politics: A Case for Christian Action (with Robert D. Linder), 1973; The Twilight of the Saints: Christianity and Civil Religion in Modern America (with Robert D. Linder), 1977; Streams of Civilization, Vol. II (with Robert G. Clouse), 1980; Bibliography on the Religious Right in America, 1986; Civil Religion and the Presidency (with Robert D. Linder), 1988; Two Kingdoms: The Church and Culture Through the Ages (with Robert G. Clouse and E. M. Yamauchi), 1993; The Revolution of the Candles (with Joerg Swoboda), 1996; The New Millennium Manual (with Robert G. Clouse and Robert N. Hosdck), 1999. Contributions: many books, reference works, and professional journals. *Honours:* Research and Creativity Award, Indiana State Univ. 1994.

PIERCE, Meredith Ann; Writer; b. 5 July 1958, Seattle, Washington, USA. *Education:* AA, Liberal Arts, 1976, BA, English, 1978, MA, English, 1980, University of Florida. *Career:* mem. Authors' Guild; SFWA. *Publications:* The Darkangel, 1982; A Gathering of Gargoyles, 1984; The Woman Who Loved Reindeer, 1985; Birth of the Firebringer, 1985; Where the Wild Geese Go, 1988; Rampion, 1989; The Pearl of the Soul of the World, 1990. Contributions: Magazines. *Honours:* several citations and awards for children's and young adult literature. *Address:* 703 NW 19th St, Gainesville, FL 32603, USA.

PIERCY, Marge, BA, MA; American poet, writer and editor; b. 31 March 1936, Detroit, MI; m. 3rd Ira Wood 1982. *Education:* Univ. of Michigan, Northwestern Univ. *Career:* poet-in-residence, Univ. of Kansas 1971; Distinguished Visiting Lecturer, Thomas Jefferson Coll. and Grand Valley State Coll. 1975; staff, Fine Arts Work Center, Provincetown, Massachusetts 1976–77; fiction writer-in-residence, Coll. of the Holy Cross, Worcester, Massachusetts 1976, Ohio State Univ. 1985; Butler Chair of Letters, SUNY at Buffalo 1977; Elliston Poet-in-Residence, Univ. of Cincinnati 1986; Poetry Ed., Tikkun 1988–96, Lilith 2000–; DeRoy Distinguished Visiting Prof., Univ. of Michigan 1992; Ed., Leapfrog Press 1997–; Bilgray Scholar-in-Residence, Univ. of Arizona 2001; residencies, Temple Island, MN 2002, Trinity Coll., TX 2003; numerous readings, workshops and lectures; mem. Authors' Guild, Authors' League, Nat. Writers' Union, New England Poetry Club, Poetry Soc. of America. *Publications:* poetry: Breaking Camp 1968, Hard Loving 1969, 4-Telling (with Bob Hershon, Emmett Jarrett and Dick Lourie) 1971, To Be of Use 1973, Living in the Open 1976, The Twelve-Spoked Wheel Flashing 1978, The Moon is Always Female 1980, Circles on the Water (selected poems) 1982, Stone, Paper, Knife 1983, My Mother's Body 1985, Available Light 1988, Mars and Her Children 1992, What are Big Girls Made Of? 1997, The Art of Blessing the Day 1999, Early Grrrl 1999, Colors Passing Through Us 2003; fiction: Going Down Fast 1969, Dance the Eagles to Sleep 1970, Small Changes 1973, Woman on the Edge of Time 1976, The High Cost of Living 1978, Via 1980, Braided Lives 1982, Fly Away Home 1984, Gone to Soldiers 1987, Summer People 1989, He, She and It 1991, The Longings of Women 1994, City of Darkness, City of Light 1996, Storm Tide (with Ira Wood) 1998, Three Women 1999; non-fiction: Parti-Colored Blocks for a Quilt (essays) 1982, So You Want to Write: How to Master the Craft of Writing Fiction and the Personal Narrative (with Ira Wood) 2001, Sleeping with Cats (memoir) 2002; contrib. to numerous anthologies and periodicals. *Honours:* Borestone Mountain Poetry Awards 1968, 1974, Nat. Endowment for the Arts Award 1978, Carolyn Kizer Poetry Prizes 1986, 1990, Sheaffer-PEN/New England Award for Literary Excellence 1989, Brit ha-Dorot Award, The Shalom Center 1992, Arthur C. Clarke Award for Best Science Fiction Novel 1993, American Library Asscn Notable Book Award 1997, Paterson Poetry Prize 2000, Peterson Award for Literary Achievement 2004, Hon. DHumLitt (Hebrew Union Coll.) 2004. *Address:* c/o Middlemarsh Inc, PO Box 1473, Wellfleet, MA 02667, USA. *E-mail:* hagolem@c4.net.

PIERPOINT, Katherine Mary; Writer and Poet; b. 1961, Northampton, England. *Education:* BA, Modern Languages, University of Exeter, 1984. *Publications:* Truffle Beds, 1995. *Honours:* Somerset Maugham Award, 1996; Sunday Times Young Writer of the Year, 1996; Royal Literary Fund Fellowship, 2003–04. *Address:* c/o 18 King St, Canterbury, Kent CT1 2AJ, England.

PIERRE, D. B. C. (Dirty But Clean); Mexican/Australian novelist; b. (Peter Finlay), 1961, Australia. *Publication:* Vernon God Little (Man Booker Prize, Bollinger Everyman Woodhouse Award, Whitbread Prize for first novel) 2003. *Address:* c/o Faber and Faber, 3 Queen Square, London, WC1 3AU, England.

PIGLIA, Ricardo; Argentinian writer and journalist; b. 1941, Adrogué, Buenos Aires. *Career:* Prof. of Romance Literatures, Princeton Univ., USA. *Publications:* Artificial Respiration 1994, Assumed Name 1996, Absent City 2000, Money to Burn 2003. *Address:* c/o Granta, 2–3 Hanover Yard, Noel Road, London, N1 8DE, England. *Website:* www.granta.com.

PIGOTT, Mark, (David Riggs), BA, PhD; American biographer and academic; m. *Education:* Univ. of Harvard. *Career:* Asst Prof., Stanford Univ. 1970–85; Prof., School of Humanities and Sciences, Stanford Univ. 1985–. *Publications:* as David Riggs: Ben Jonson: A Life 1989, The World of Christopher Marlowe 2004. *Honours:* Frank Knox Fellowship 1963–64, Nat. Endowment for the Humanities and Stanford Humanities Centre Fellowships, Guggenheim Foundation Fellowship. *Address:* School of Humanities and Sciences, Stanford University, Stanford, CA 94305, USA.

PIGUET-CUENDET, Suzanne (see Deriex, Suzanne).

PIKE, Charles R. (see Bulmer, Henry Kenneth).

PIKE, Charles R. (see Harknett, Terry).

PILCHER, Rosamunde, (Jane Fraser), OBE; British writer; b. 22 Sept. 1924, Lelant, Cornwall; m. Graham Pilcher 1946; four c. *Publications:* A Secret to Tell 1955, April 1957, On My Own 1965, Sleeping Tiger 1967, Another View 1969, The End of the Summer 1971, Snow in April 1972, The Empty House 1973, The Day of the Storm 1975, Under Gemini 1976, Wild Mountain Thyme 1979, The Carousel 1982, Voices in Summer 1984, The Blue Bedroom and Other Stories 1985, The Shell Seekers 1987, September 1990, Blackberry Days 1991, Flowers in the Rain and Other Stories 1991, Coming Home (Romantic Novelists Asscn Novelist of the Year 1996) 1995, Winter Solstice 2000; as Jane Fraser: Halfway to the Moon 1949, The Brown Fields 1951, Dangerous Intruder 1951, Young Bar 1952, A Day Like Spring 1953, Dear Tom 1954, Bridge of Corvie 1956, A Family Affair 1958, A Long Way from Home 1963, The Keeper's House 1963; contrib. to Woman and Home, Good Housekeeping. *Honours:* Deutscher Videopreis 1996, Bunte magazine Bambi Award 1997, Goldene Kamera Award, Hörzu 1998. *Address:* Penrowan, Longforgan, Dundee DD2 5ET, Scotland.

PILGER, John (Richard); Journalist, Writer and Film-maker; b. Sydney, NSW, Australia; one s. one d. *Education:* Sydney High School, Journalism Cadet Training, Australian Consolidated Press. *Career:* Journalist, Sydney Daily/Sunday Telegraph, 1958–62, Reuters, London, 1962, Daily Mirror, London, 1963–86; Documentary Film-maker, Granada TV, United Kingdom, 1969–71, Associated Television, 1972–80, Central Television, United Kingdom, 1980–; Columnist, New Statesman, London, 1991–; Visiting Fellow Deakin Univ. 1995. *Publications:* The Last Day, 1975; Aftermath: The Struggle of Cambodia and Vietnam, 1981; The Outsiders, 1983; Heroes, 1986; A Secret Country, 1989; Distant Voices, 1992; Hidden Agendas, 1998; Reporting the World, John Pilger's Great Eyewitness Photographers, 2001; The New Rulers of the World, 2002. Other: 57 documentary films. Contributions: The Guardian; Independent; New Statesman, UK; New York Times; The Age, Melbourne. *Honours:* Descriptive Writer of the Year, UK, 1966; Journalist of the Year, UK, 1967, 1979; International Reporter of the Year, UK, 1970; Reporter of the Year, UK, 1974; Richard Dimbleby Award, BAFTA, 1991; Emmy Award, USA, 1991; George Foster Peabody Award, USA, 1992; Hon. DLitt, Staffordshire University, Kingston University; Hon. DPhil, Dublin City University, Ireland; Hon. PhD, Oxford Brookes University; Hon. LLD, St Andrews University, Hon. DUniv, The Open Univ.; Frank H. T. Rhodes Professorship Cornell Univ., USA2003. *Address:* 57 Hambalt Rd, London SWX 9EQ, England. *E-mail:* jpilger2003@yahoo.co.uk.

PILLING, Christopher (Robert); Writer, Poet, Trans. and Playwright; b. 20 April 1936, Birmingham, England; m. Sylvia Hill 6 Aug. 1960; one s. two d. *Education:* Diplôme d'Études françaises, University of Poitiers; BA, University of Leeds, 1957; Certificate of Education, Loughborough College, 1959. *Career:* English Asst, École Normale, Moulins, France, 1957–58; Teacher of French and PE, Wirral Grammar School, Cheshire, 1959–61, King Edward's School for Boys, Birmingham, 1961–62; Teacher of French and Athletics, and House Master, Ackworth School, Yorkshire, 1962–73; Reviewer, TLS, 1973–74; Head of Modern Languages and Housemaster, Knottingley High School, West Yorkshire, 1973–78; Tutor, Dept of Adult Education, University of Newcastle upon Tyne, 1978–80; Head of French, Keswick School, Cumbria, 1980–88; mem. Cumbrian Poets, co-founder, sec.; Society of Authors; Trans Asscn; Cercle Édouard et Tristan Corbière; North Cumbria Playwrights; Les Amis de Max Jacob; SLATE (New Writing Cumbria); Cumbria Cultural Skills Partnership. *Publications:* Snakes and Girls, 1970; In All the Spaces on All the Lines, 1971; Foreign Bodies, 1992; Cross Your Legs and Wish, 1994; These Jaundiced Loves, by Tristan Corbière (trans.), 1995; The Lobster Can Wait, 1998; In the Pink, 1999; The Dice Cup, by Max Jacob (trans. with David Kennedy), 2000; The Ghosts of Greta Hall (with Colin Fleming), 2001; Tree Time, 2003; Emperor on a Lady's Bicycle, 2003; Love at the Full, by Lucien Becker (trans.), 2003. Contributions: books, anthologies, reviews, quarterlies, journals and newspapers. *Honours:* New Poets Award, 1970; Arts Council Grants, 1971, 1977; Kate Collingwood Award, 1983; Northern Arts Writers Award, 1985, and Tyrone Guthrie Centre Residency, 1994; Lauréat du Concours Européen de Création Littéraire, Centre Culturel du Brabant Wallon, Belgium, 1992; European Poetry Trans. Network Residencies, 1995, 1998; European Commission Residency, Collège International des Traducteurs Littéraires, Arles, 1996; Hawthornden Fellowship, 1998; Trans. Residency at the British Centre for Literary Trans., University of East Anglia, 2000. *Address:* 25 High Hill, Keswick, Cumbria CA12 5NY, England.

PILON, Jean-Guy; Poet and Writer; b. 12 Nov. 1930, St Polycarpe, QC, Canada; m. Denise Viens, two s. *Education:* BA, 1951, LLL, 1954, University of Montréal. *Career:* Co-Founder and Dir, Liberté, 1959–79; mem. Académie des lettres du Québec; Royal Society of Canada. *Publications:* Poetry: La Fiancée du Matin, 1953; Les Cloitres de l'Eté, 1955; L'Homme et le Jour, 1957; La Mouette et le Large, 1960; Recours au pays, 1961; Pour saluer une ville, 1963; Comme eau retenue, 1969; Saisons pour la Continuelle, 1969; Silences pour une souveraine, 1972. Novel: Solange, 1966. Contributions: various publications. *Honours:* David Prize, 1957; Louise Labé Prize, 1969; France-Canada Prize, 1969; Governor-General's Award for Poetry, 1970; Athanase David Prize, 1984; Officer of the Order of Canada, 1987; Chevalier, Ordre nat. du Québec, 1987; Officer, Ordre des Arts et des Lettres, 1992. *Address:* 5724 Cote St-Antoine, Montréal, QC H4A 1R9, Canada.

PINCHER, (Henry) Chapman, BSc; writer; b. 29 March 1914, Ambala, India; m. 1st; one d. one s.; m. 2nd Constance Wolstenholme 1965. *Career:* Defence, Science and Medical Ed., Daily Express, 1946–73; Chief Defence Correspondent, Beaverbrook Newspapers, 1972–79. *Publications:* Breeding of Farm Animals, 1946; A Study of Fishes, 1947; Into the Atomic Age, 1947; Spotlight on Animals, 1950; Evolution, 1950; It's Fun Finding Out (with Bernard Wicksteed), 1950; Sleep and How to Get More of It, 1954; Sex in Our Time, 1973; Inside Story, 1978; Their Trade is Treachery, 1981; Too Secret Too Long, 1984; The Secret Offensive, 1985; Traitors: The Labyrinth of Treason, 1987; A Web of Deception, 1987; The Truth about Dirty Tricks, 1991; One Dog and Her Man, 1991; Pastoral Symphony, 1993; A Box of Chocolates, 1993; Life's a Bitch!, 1996; Tight Lines!, 1997. Fiction: Not with a Bang, 1965; The Giantkiller, 1967; The Penthouse Comspirators, 1970; The Skeleton at the Villa Wolkonsky, 1975; The Eye of the Tornado, 1976; The Four Horses, 1978; Dirty Tricks, 1980; The Private World of St John Terrapin, 1982; Contamination, 1989. *Honours:* Granada Award, Journalist of the Year, 1964; Reporter of the Decade, 1966; Hon. DLitt, University of Newcastle upon Tyne, 1979; Fellow, King's College, London, 1979. *Address:* The Church House, 16 Church Street, Kintbury, Near Hungerford, Berkshire RG15 0TR, England.

PINCIO, Tommaso; Italian writer; b. 1963, Rome. *Publications:* novels: M 1999, Lo Spazio Sfinito 2000, Un amore dell'Altro Mondo (trans. as Love Shaped Story) 2002; contrib. to Il Manifesto, Nuovi Argomenti. *Address:* c/o Flamingo, 77–85 Fulham Palace Road, London, W6 8JB, England. *Website:* www.harpercollins.co.uk.

PINEAU, Gisèle; Writer and Psychiatric Nurse; b. 1956, Paris, France. *Education:* Université de Nanterre; Centre Hospitalier de Villejuif. *Publications:* Un papillon dans la cité, 1992; La grande drive des esprits, 1993; L'espérance-macadam, 1995–96; L'exil selon Julia, 1996; L'âme prètée aux oiseaux, 1998. Other: many essays and short stories. Contributions: various publications. *Honours:* Prix Écritures d'Iles, 1987; Prix Carbet de la Caraïbe, 1993; Grand Prix des Lectrices de Elle, 1994; Oscar Littérature du Conseil de la Guadeloupe, 1996; Prix RFO Radio Télévision Française, 1996; Grande Prix du Livre de Jeunesse de la Martinique, 1996.

PINGEL, Martha (see Taylor, Velande Pingel).

PINKER, Steven, BA, PhD; American psychologist, scientist, writer and academic; *Johnstone Family Professor of Psychology, Harvard University*; b. 18 Sept. 1954, Montreal, Canada; m. Ilavenil Subbiah 1995. *Education:* McGill Univ., Canada, Harvard Univ. *Career:* Asst Prof. Harvard Univ. 1980–81, Stanford Univ. 1981–82, MIT 1982–85; Assoc. Prof. Dept of Brain and Cognitive Sciences, MIT 1985–89, Prof. 1989–, Peter de Florez Prof. 2000–03, Margaret MacVicar Fellow 2000–; Co-Dir Center for Cognitive Science MIT 1985–94, Dir McDonnell-Pew Center for Cognitive Neuroscience 1994–99; Johnstone Family Prof. of Psychology Harvard Univ. 2003–; Assoc. Ed. Cognition. *Publications include:* Language Learnability and Language Development 1984, Visual Cognition (ed.) 1985, Connections and Symbols (ed. with J.Mehler) 1988, Learnability and Cognition: The Acquisition of Argument Structure 1989, The Language Instinct 1994 (William James Book Prize, American Psychological Asscn 1995), How the Mind Works 1997 (William James Book Prize, American Psychological Asscn 1999), Words and Rules: The Ingredients of Language 1999, The Blank Slate: The Modern Denial of Human Nature 2002; contribs to Animal Learning and Behavior, Annals of the New York Academy of Sciences, Behavioral and Brain Sciences, Canadian Journal of Psychology, Child Development, Cognition, Cognitive Psychology, Cognitive Science, Communication and Cognition, Journal of Child Language, Journal of Cognitive Neuroscience, Journal of Experimental Psychology, Journal of Mental Imagery, Journal of Psycholinguistic Research, Journal of Verbal Learning and Verbal Behavior, Language and Cognitive Processes, Language, Lingua, Memory and Cognition, Monographs of the Society for Research in Child Development, Nature, New York Times, The New Yorker, Papers and Reports in Child Language, Psychological Science, Science, Slate, Time, Trends in Cognitive Science, Trends in Neurosciences, Visual Cognition. *Honours:* Hon. DSc (McGill) 1999, Hon. DPhil (Tel-Aviv) 2003, Hon. DUniv (Surrey) 2003; Distinguished Scientific Award for Early Career Contribution to Psychology, American Psychological Asscn 1984, Boyd R. McCandless Young Scientist Award, Div. of Developmental Psychology, American Psychological Asscn 1986, Troland Research Award NAS 1993, Linguistics, Language and the Public Interest Award, Linguistics Soc. of America 1997, Los Angeles Times Book Prize in Science and Technology 1998, Golden Plate Award, American Acad. of Achievement 1999, Humanist Laureate Int. Acad. of Humanism 2001. *Address:* Department of Brain and Cognitive Sciences NEW20-413, Massachusetts Institute of Technology, Cambridge, MA 02139, USA (Office). *Telephone:* (617) 253-8946 (Office). *Fax:* (617) 258-8654 (Office). *E-mail:* steve@psyche.mit.edu (Office). *Website:* www.mit.edu/~pinker (Office).

PINNER, David John; Writer and Dramatist; b. 6 Oct. 1940, Peterborough, England; m. Catherine, 23 Oct. 1965, one s. one d. *Education:* RADA, 1959–60. *Publications:* Plays: Dickon, 1965; Fanghorn, 1966; The Drums of Snow, 1969; Corgi, 1969; The Potsdam Quartet, 1973; An Evening with the GLC, 1974; The Last Englishman, 1975; Lucifer's Fair, 1979; Screwball, 1985; The Teddy Bears' Picnic, 1988; Cartoon; Hereward the Wake; Shakebag; Revelations; The Sins of the Mother; Lenin in Love, 2000. Television Plays: Juliet and Romeo, 1975; 2 Crown Courts, 1978; The Potsdam Quartet, 1980; The Sea Horse. Novels: Ritual, 1967; With My Body, 1968; There'll Always Be an England, 1984. Non-Fiction: Newton's Darkness: Two Dramatic Views (with Carl Djerassi), 2003. *Address:* c/o Oberon Books Ltd, 521 Caledonian Rd, London N7 9RH, England.

PINNEY, Lucy Catherine, BA; writer and journalist; b. 25 July 1952, London, England; m. Charles Pinney 1975; two s. one d. *Education:* York Univ. *Career:* columnist, The Times. *Publications:* The Pink Stallion 1988, Tender Moth 1994, A Country Wife 2004; contrib. to Sunday Times, Observer, Daily Mail, Telegraph, Company, Cosmopolitan, Country Living, Country Homes and Interiors, She. *Address:* Egremont Farm, Payhembury, Honiton, Devon EX14 0JA, England. *E-mail:* lucy@egremont.eurobell.co.uk.

PINNOCK, Winsome, BA, MA; British playwright; b. 1961, London, England. *Education:* Goldsmiths Coll. London, Birkbeck Coll. London. *Career:* playwright-in-residence, Tricycle Theatre, Kilburn 1990, Royal Court Theatre, London 1991, Clean Break Theatre Co. 1994. *Plays:* The Wind of Change 1987, Leave Taking (Liverpool Playhouse) 1988, Picture Palace 1988, A Rock in Water 1989, A Hero's Welcome 1989, Talking in Tongues 1991. *Television plays:* episodes in South of the Border and Chalkface Series. *Film screenplay:* Bitter Harvest. *Honours:* Thames TV Award 1991, George Devine Award 1991. *Literary Agent:* Lemon, Unna and Durbridge, 24 Pottery Lane, Holland Park, London, W11 4LZ, England.

PINSKER, Sanford, BA, PhD; academic, writer and poet; *Shadek Professor of Humanities, Franklin and Marshall College*; b. 28 Sept. 1941, Washington, Pennsylvania, USA; m. Ann Getson 1968; one s. one d. *Education:* Washington and Jefferson Coll., Univ. of Washington. *Career:* Asst Prof. 1967–74, Assoc. Prof. 1974–84, Prof. 1984–88, Shadek Prof. of Humanities 1988–, Franklin and Marshall Coll.; Visiting Prof., Univ. of California at Riverside 1973, 1975; Fulbright Sr Lecturer, Belgium 1984–85, Spain 1990–91; Pennsylvania Humanist 1985–87, 1990–91, 1996–97; Ed., Academic Questions 1995–; mem. Nat. Book Critics Circle. *Publications:* The Schlemiel as Metaphor: Studies in the Yiddish and American-Jewish Novel, 1971; The Comedy That 'Hoits': An Essay on the Fiction of Philip Roth, 1975; Still Life and Other Poems, 1975; The Languages of Joseph Conrad, 1978; Between Two Worlds: The American Novel in the 1960s, 1978; Philip Roth: Critical Essays, 1982; Memory Breaks Off and Other Poems, 1984; Conversations with Contemporary American Writers, 1985; Whales at Play and Other Poems of Travel, 1986; Three Pacific Northwest Poets: Stafford, Hugo, and Wagoner, 1987; The Uncompromising Fictions of Cynthia Ozick, 1987; Bearing the Bad News: Contemporary American Literature and Culture, 1990; Understanding Joseph Heller, 1991; Jewish-American Literature and Culture: An Encyclopedia (ed. with Jack Fischel), 1992; Jewish-American Fiction, 1917–1987, 1992; Sketches of Spain (poems), 1992; The Catcher in the Rye: Innocence Under Pressure, 1993; Oedipus Meets the Press and Other Tragi-Comedies of Our Time, 1996. Contributions: Articles, stories, poems, and reviews in numerous publications. *Address:* 700 N Pine Street, Lancaster, PA 17603, USA.

PINSKY, Robert Neal, BA, MA, PhD; American academic, poet, writer, editor and translator; b. 20 Oct. 1940, Long Branch, NJ; m. Ellen Jane Bailey 1961; three d. *Education:* Rutgers University, Stanford University. *Career:* Asst Prof. of English, University of Chicago, 1966–67; Prof. of English, Wellesley College, 1967–80, University of California at Berkeley, 1980–89, Boston University, 1988–; Poetry Ed., The New Republic, 1978–87, Slate, 1996–; Visiting Lecturer in English, Harvard University, 1980; Poet Laureate of the USA 1997–2000; mem. Acad. of American Poets; American Acad. of Arts and Letters; American Acad. of Arts and Sciences. *Publications:* Landor's Poetry, 1968; Sadness and Happiness, 1975; The Situation of Poetry, 1977; An Explanation of America, 1980; The Separate Notebooks, by Czesław Miłosz (co-trans.), 1984; History of My Heart, 1984; Poetry and the World, 1988; The Want Bone, 1990; The Inferno of Dante, 1995; The Figured Wheel: New and Collected Poems 1966–1996, 1996; The Sounds of Poetry, 1998; The Handbook of Heartbreak, 1998; Jersey Rain, 2000; Americans' Favourite Poems: The Favourite Poem Anthology (ed. with Maggie Dietz), 2000. Contributions: anthologies and journals. *Honours:* Fulbright Fellowship, 1965; Stegner Fellowship in Creative Writing, 1965; National Endowment for the Humanities Fellowship, 1974; Massachusetts Council for the Arts Award, 1976; Oscar Blumenthal Prize, 1979; American Acad. and Institute of Arts and Letters Award, 1980; Saxifrage Prize, 1980; Guggenheim Fellowship, 1980; Eunice B. Tietjens Prize, 1983; National Endowment for the Arts Fellowship, 1984; William Carlos Williams Prize, 1985; Landon Prize in Trans., 1995; Los Angeles Times Book Award, 1995; Shelley Memorial Award, 1996; Ambassador Book Award in Poetry, 1997. *Literary Agent:* Steven Barclay Agency, 12 Western Avenue, Petaluma, CA 94952, USA. *Telephone:* (707) 773-0654. *Fax:* (707) 778-1868. *Website:* www.barclayagency.com. *Address:* c/o Creative Writing Program, Boston University, 236 Bay State Road, Boston, MA 02215, USA.

PINTER, Frances Mercedes Judith, PhD; American publisher; b. 13 June 1949, Venezuela; m. David Percy 1985. *Career:* Research Officer, Centre for Criminological Research, Oxford Univ., UK 1976–79; Man. Dir Pinter Publrs 1979–94; Chair. Independent Publrs Guild 1979–82, Publrs Assn E European Task Force 1990–; Man. Dir Cen. European Univ. Press 1994–96; Chair. Bd of Trustees, Int. House 2001; Deputy Chair. Book Devt Council 1985–89; mem. Bd UK Publrs Assn 1987–92, IBIS Information Services 1988–90, Libra Books 1991–; Exec. Dir Centre for Publishing Devt 1994–, Open Soc. Inst. 1994–99; Visiting Fellow, LSE 2000–01. *Address:* 25 Belsize Park, London, NW3 4DU, England (Home). *E-mail:* frances@pinter.org.uk (Office).

PINTER, Harold, CH, CBE, CLit, FRSL; British playwright, writer and poet; b. 10 Oct. 1930, London; m. 1st Vivien Merchant 1956 (divorced 1980, died 1982); one s.; m. 2nd Lady Antonia Fraser 1980. *Education:* Hackney Downs Grammar School, London. *Career:* actor mainly in English and Irish prov. repertory 1949–58; playwright 1957–; Assoc. Dir Nat. Theatre 1973–83; Dir United British Artists 1983–85; Jt Ed. Publr Greville Press 1988–; bd mem. Cricket World 1989–; BAFTA Fellowship 1997. *Film:* Mansfield Park 1999. *Plays:* The Room 1957, The Dumb Waiter 1957, The Birthday Party 1957, A Slight Ache 1958, The Hothouse 1958, The Caretaker 1959, A Night Out 1959, Night School 1960, The Dwarfs 1960, The Collection 1961, The Lover 1962, Tea Party (TV play) 1965, The Homecoming 1964, The Basement (TV play) 1966, Landscape 1967, Silence 1968, Night (one act play) 1969, Old Times 1970, Monologue (one act play) 1972, No Man's Land 1974, Betrayal 1978, Family Voices 1980, Other Places 1982, A Kind of Alaska 1982, Victoria Station 1982, One for the Road 1984, Mountain Language 1988, The New World Order 1991, Party Time 1991, Moonlight 1993, Ashes to Ashes 1996, Celebration 2000, Remembrance of Things Past 2000, Press Conference (sketch) 2002. *Screenplays:* The Caretaker 1962, The Servant 1962, The Pumpkin Eater 1963, The Quiller Memorandum 1965, Accident 1966, The Birthday Party 1967, The Go-Between 1969, Langrishe Go Down 1970, A la Recherche du Temps Perdu 1972, The Last Tycoon 1974, The French Lieutenant's Woman 1980, Betrayal 1981, Victory 1982, Turtle Diary 1984, The Handmaid's Tale 1987, Reunion 1988, The Heat of the Day 1988, The Comfort of Strangers 1989, The Trial 1989. *Plays directed:* The Man in the Glass Booth, London 1967, NY 1968, Exiles 1970, 1971, Butley 1971, (film) 1973, Next of Kin 1974, Otherwise Engaged 1975, The Rear Column 1978, Close of Play 1979, Quartermaine's Terms 1981, Incident at Tulse Hill 1982, The Trojan War Will Not Take Place 1983, The Common Pursuit 1984, Sweet Bird of Youth 1985, Circe and Bravo 1986, Vanilla 1990, The New World Order 1991, Party Time 1991, Party Time (TV) 1992, Oleanna 1993, Ashes to Ashes 1996, Twelve Angry Men 1996, The Late Middle Classes 1999, Celebration 2000, The Room 2000, No Man's Land 2001. *Television:* A Night Out 1960, Huis Clos 1965, The Basement 1967, Rogue Male 1976, Lanerishe, Go Down 1978, The Birthday Party 1987, Breaking the Code 1997, Catastrophe 2000, Wit 2000. *Publications:* Poems and Prose 1949–77 1978, The Proust Screenplay (with Joseph Losey and Barbara Bray) 1978, Collected Poems and Prose 1986, 100 Poems by 100 Poets (co-ed.) 1986, The Dwarfs (novel) 1990, Various Voices: prose, poetry, politics 1948–1998 1999, Politics 1948–1998 1999, Cancer Cells (poem) 2002. *Honours:* Hon. Fellow (Queen Mary Coll.) 1987; Hon. DLitt (Reading) 1970, (Birmingham) 1971, (Glasgow) 1974, (East Anglia) 1974, (Stirling) 1979, (Brown) 1982, (Hull) 1986, (Sussex) 1990, (Bristol) 1998, Hon. Degree (Turin) 2002; Shakespeare Prize, Hamburg 1973, Austrian Prize for European Literature 1973, Pirandello Prize 1980, Commonwealth Award for Dramatic Arts, Washington, DC 1981, Donatello Prize 1982, Chilean Order of Merit 1992, David Cohen British Literature Prize 1995, Special Olivier Award 1995, Molière d'Honneur, Paris 1997, Sunday Times Award for Literary Excellence 1997, RSL Companion of Literature 1998, Critics' Circle Award for Distinguished Service to the Arts 2000, Brianza Poetry Prize, Italy 2000, South Bank Show Award for Outstanding Achievement in the Arts 2001, S. T. Dupont Golden Pen Award 2001, Premio Fiesole ai Maestri del Cinema, Italy 2001, Laurea ad honorem, Univ. of Florence 2001, World Leaders Award Toronto 2001, Hermann Kesten Medallion, German PEN, Berlin 2001. *Literary Agent:* Judy Daish Associates, 2 St Charles Place, London, W10 6EG, England. *Website:* www.haroldpinter.org.

PIONTEK, Heinz; Poet and Author; b. 15 Nov. 1925, Kreuzburg, Silesia, Germany; m. Gisela Dallman, 1951. *Education:* Theologisch-Philosophische Hochschule, Dillingen. *Career:* mem. Bavarian Acad. of Fine Arts, Munich. *Publications:* Poetry: Die Furt, 1952; Die Rauchfahne, 1953; Wassermarken, 1957; Mit einer Kranichfeder, 1962; Klartext, 1966; Tot oder lebendig, 1971; Die Zeit der anderen Auslegung, 1976; Früh im September, 1982; Helldunkel, 1987. Fiction: Dichterleben, 1976; Juttas Neffe, 1979; Zeit meines Lebens, 1984; Stunde der Uberlebenden, 1989; Goethe unterwegs in Schlesien: Fast ein Roman, 1993. Collections: Die Erzählungen 1950–1970, 1971; Träumen, Wachen, Widerstehen: Aufzeichnungen aus diesen Jahren, 1978; Das Handwerk des Lesens: Erfahrungen mit Buchern und Autoren, 1979; Farbige Schatten, Die Aufzeichnungen, Die Reisepresa, 1984; Feuer im Wind, Die Erzählungen, Die Hörspiele, Eine Komödie, 1985; Werkauswahl: Indianersommer (selected poems), 1990, and Anhalten um eine Hand (selected stories), 1990. *Honours:* Tukan Prize, 1971; Georg Büchner Prize, 1976; Werner Egk Prize, 1981. *Address:* Duffer Strasse 97, 8000 Munich 50, Germany.

PIPES, Richard, BA, MA, PhD; American academic and writer; *Frank B. Baird Jr Professor of History Emeritus, Harvard University*; b. 11 July 1923, Cieszyn, Poland; m. Irene Eugenia Roth 1946; two s. *Education:* Muskingum Coll., Cornell Univ., Harvard Univ. *Career:* faculty, Russian Research Center, Harvard Univ. 1950–, Prof. of History 1958–, Assoc. Dir 1962–64, Dir 1968–73, Frank B. Baird Jr Prof. of History 1975–96, Frank B. Baird Jr Prof. of History Emeritus 1996–; Visiting Asst Prof. of History, Univ. of California at Berkeley 1955–56; Fellow, Center for Advanced Study in the Behavioural Sciences, Stanford, CA 1969–70; Sr Consultant, Stanford Research Inst. 1973–78; Dir, East European and Soviet Affairs, Nat. Security Council 1981–82; Fellow, American Acad. of Arts and Sciences 1965–; mem. Council on Foreign Relations; foreign mem. Polish Acad. of Arts and Sciences (PAU) 1996–. *Publications:* Formation of the Soviet Union, 1954; Karamzin's Memoir on Ancient and Modern Russia, 1959; The Russian Intelligentsia (ed.), 1961; Social Democracy and the St Petersburg Labor Movement, 1963; Of the Russe Commonwealth (1591), by Giles Fletcher (ed. with John Fine), 1966; Revolutionary Russia (ed.), 1968; Europe Since 1815, 1970; Struve: Liberal on the Left, 1870–1905, 1970; P. B. Struve: Collected Works in Fifteen Vols (ed.), 1973; Russia Under the Old Regime, 1974; Soviet Strategy in Europe (ed.), 1976; Struve: Liberal on the Right, 1905–1944, 1980; U.S.–Soviet Relations in the Era of Détente, 1981; Survival is Not Enough, 1984; Russia Observed, 1989; The Russian Revolution, 1990; Communism: The Vanished Specter, 1993; Russia Under the Bolshevik Regime, 1994; A Concise History of the Russian Revolution, 1995;

The Unknown Lenin: From the Secret Archive (ed.), 1996; Three 'Whys' of the Russian Revolution, 1996; Property & Freedom, 1999; Land-Tenure in Pre-Roman Antiquity and its Political Consequences, 2001; Communism: A History, 2001; The Degaev Affair, 2003; Vixi: The Memoirs of a Non-Belonger, 2003. Contributions: scholarly books and journals. *Honours:* George Louis Beer Prize, American Historical Asscn, 1955; Guggenheim Fellowships, 1956, 1965; Fellow, ACLS, 1965; Hon. doctorates, Adelphi College, 1991, Muskingum College, 1998, University of Silesia, 1994; Walter Channing Cabot Fellow, Harvard University, 1990–91; Commander's Cross of Merit, Poland, 1996; Hon. Citizen, 1997, Hon. Consul, 1997–, Republic of Georgia. *Address:* 17 Berkeley Street, Cambridge, MA 02138, USA.

PIRIE, David (Tarbat); Dramatist and Writer; b. 4 Dec. 1946, Dundee, Scotland; m. Judith Harris, 21 June 1983, one s. one d. *Education:* University of York; University of London. *Career:* Tutor; Film Critic, Ed., Time Out Magazine, 1980–84; mem. Soho House, London 1990. *Publications:* Heritage of Horror, 1974; Mystery Story, 1980; Anatomy of the Movies, 1981; The Patient's Eyes, 2001; The Night Calls, 2002. Films: Rainy Day Women, 1984; Wild Things, 1988; Black Easter, 1993; Element of Doubt, 1996. Television: Never Come Back, BBC serial, 1989; Ashenden, BBC serial, 1990; Natural Lies, serial, 1991; The Woman in White, 1997; Murder Rooms: The Dark Beginnings of Sherlock Holmes, 2000; Murder Rooms 2: The Safe House, 2002. Contributions: various journals. *Honours:* Drama Prize, New York Festival, 1985; Best TV Network Series Prize, 1990, Best TV Feature Film Prize, 1996, Chicago Film Festival; Best TV Detective Series, Crimescene/Sherlock Holmes Magazine/NFT Awards, 2002. *Literary Agent:* The Agency, 24 Pottery Lane, Holland Park, London W11 4LZ, England.

PIRSIG, Robert M(aynard); Author; b. 6 Sept. 1928, Minneapolis, Minnesota, USA; m. 1st Nancy Ann James, 10 May 1954, divorced Aug. 1978, two s.; m. 2nd Wendy Kimball, 28 Dec. 1978, one d. *Education:* BA, 1950, MA, 1958, University of Minnesota. *Publications:* Zen and the Art of Motorcycle Maintenance, 1974; Lila, 1991. *Honours:* Guggenheim Fellowship, 1974; AAAL Award, 1979. *Address:* c/o Bantam Books, 1540 Broadway, New York, NY 10036, USA.

PITCHER, Harvey John; Writer; b. 26 Aug. 1936, London, England. *Education:* BA, Russian, University of Oxford. *Publications:* Understanding the Russians, 1964; The Chekhov Play: A New Interpretation, 1973; When Miss Emmie was in Russia, 1977; Chekhov's Leading Lady, 1979; Chekhov: The Early Stories, 1883–1888 (with Patrick Miles), 1982; The Smiths of Moscow, 1984; Lily: An Anglo-Russian Romance, 1987; Muir and Mirrielees: The Scottish Partnership that became a Household Name in Russia, 1994; Witnesses of the Russian Revolution, 1994; Chekhov: The Comic Stories, 1998; If Only We Could Know: An Interpretation of Chekhov, by Vladimir Kataev (ed. and trans.), 2002. Contributions: TLS. *Address:* 37 Bernard Rd, Cromer, Norfolk NR27 9AW, England.

PITT, Barrie William Edward; Historian; b. 7 July 1918, Galway, Ireland; m. 1st Phyllis Kate Edwards, one s., deceased; m. 2nd Sonia Deidre Hoskins, 1953, divorced 1971; m. 3rd Frances Mary Moore, 1983. *Career:* Historical Consultant to the BBC series, The Great War, 1963. *Publications:* The Edge of Battle, 1958; Zeebrugge, St George's Day, 1918, 1958; Coronel and Falkland, 1960; The Last Act, 1962; Purnell's History of the Second World War (ed.), 1964; Ballantine's Illustrated History of World War I (ed.-in-chief), 1967; Purnell's History of the First World War (ed.), 1969; Ballantine's Illustrated History of the Violent Century (ed.-in-chief), 1971; British History Illustrated (ed.), 1974–78; The Battle of the Atlantic, 1977; The Crucible of War: Western Desert, 1941, 1980; The Crucible of War: Year of Alamein, 1942, 1982; Special Boat Squadron, 1983. Contributions: Encyclopaedia Britannica; Sunday Times. *Address:* 10 Wellington Rd, Taunton, Somerset TA1 4EG, England.

PITT, David George; Prof. of English Literature (retd) and Writer; b. 12 Dec. 1921, Musgravetown, NF, Canada; m. Marion Woolfrey, 5 June 1946, one s. one d. *Education:* BA, English, Mt Allison University, 1946; MA, 1948, PhD, 1960, University of Toronto. *Career:* Prof. of English Literature, Memorial University of Newfoundland, 1949–83; mem. Asscn of Canadian University Teachers of English; Humanities Asscn of Canada. *Publications:* Elements of Literacy, 1964; Windows of Agates, 1966; Critical Views on Canadian Writers: E. J. Pratt, 1969; Toward the First Spike: The Evolution of a Poet, 1982; Goodly Heritage, 1984; E. J. Pratt: The Truant Years, 1984; E. J. Pratt: The Master Years, 1987; Tales From the Outer Fringe, 1990. *Honours:* Medal for Biography, University of British Columbia, 1984; Artist of the Year, Newfoundland Arts Council, 1988; Hon. LLD, Mt Allison University, 1989. *Address:* 7 Chestnut Pl., St John's, NF A1B 2T1, Canada.

PITT-KETHLEY, (Helen) Fiona, BA; writer and poet; b. 21 Nov. 1954, Edgware, Middlesex, England; m. James Plaskett; one s. *Education:* Chelsea School of Art. *Publications:* London, 1984; Rome, 1985; The Tower of Glass, 1985; Gesta, 1986; Sky Ray Lolly, 1986; Private Parts, 1987; Journeys to the Underworld, 1988; The Perfect Man, 1989; The Misfortunes of Nigel, 1991; The Literary Companion to Sex, 1992; The Maiden's Progress, 1992; Too Hot to Handle, 1992; Dogs, 1993; The Pan Principle, 1994; The Literary Companion to Low Life, 1995; Double Act, 1996; Memo from a Muse, 1999; Red Light Districts of the World, 2000; Baker's Dozen, 2000; My Schooling (autobiog.), 2000. Contributions: numerous newspapers and magazines. *Honours:* Calouste Gulbenkian Award 1995.

PITTOCK, Murray George Hornby; academic, writer and editor; b. 5 Jan. 1962, Nantwich, England; m. Anne Grace Thornton Martin 1989; two d. *Education:* MA, English Language and Literature, University of Glasgow, 1983; DPhil, University of Oxford, 1986. *Career:* British Acad. Postdoctoral Fellow, 1988–89, University of Aberdeen; Lecturer and Reader, Dept of English Literature, 1994–96, University of Edinburgh; Co-Ed., Scottish Studies Review, 2000–; Prof. in Literature, 1996–2003, Head, Dept of Literature, 1997–2000, University of Strathclyde; Prof. of Scottish and Romantic Literature, Univ. of Manchester 2003–; Assoc. Ed., New Dictionary of National Biography; mem. Fellow, Society of Antiquaries, Scotland; Royal Historical Society; English Asscn; RSA. *Publications:* The Invention of Scotland 1991, Spectrum of Decadence: The Literature of the 1890s 1993, Poetry and Jacobite Politics in Eighteenth-Century Britain and Ireland 1994, The Myth of the Jacobite Clans 1995, Inventing and Resisting Britain 1997, Jacobitism 1998, Celtic Identity and the British Image 1999, Scottish Nationality 2001, The Jacobite Relics of Scotland 2002, 2003, A New History of Scotland 2003. Contributions: scholarly books and journals. *Honours:* various research grants; Royal Society of Edinburgh BP Humanities Research Prize, 1992–93; British Acad., Chatterton Lecturer, 2002. *Address:* Dept of English and American Studies, University of Manchester, Manchester, M13 9VZ, England. *E-mail:* murray.g..pittock@man.ac.uk.

PLACE, Florence (see Norman, Geraldine (Lucia)).

PLAICE, Stephen James; writer, poet and librettist; b. 9 Sept. 1951, Watford, Hertfordshire, England; m. Marcia Bellamy, two c. *Education:* BA Hons, German, 1973, MPhil, Comparative Literature, 1979, University of Sussex; University of Marburg, 1972; University of Zürich, 1975. *Career:* Writer-in-Residence HM Prison, Lewes 1987–94; Artistic Dir Alarmist Theatre 1987–2002; Ed. Printer's Devil 1990–2002. *Publications:* Rumours of Cousins 1983, Over the Rollers 1992, Misper (libretto) 2000, Zoë (libretto) 2004. *Address:* 83 Stanford Rd, Brighton, East Sussex BN1 5PR, England. *Telephone:* (1273) 700849. *E-mail:* cultureshock@ntlworld.com.

PLAIN, Belva; Writer; b. 9 Oct. 1919, New York, NY, USA; m. Irving Plain, 14 June 1941, deceased 1982, three c. *Education:* Barnard College. *Publications:* Evergreen, 1978; Random Winds, 1980; Eden Burning, 1982; Crescent City, 1984; The Golden Cup, 1987; Tapestry, 1988; Blessings, 1989; Harvest, 1990; Treasures, 1992; Whispers, 1993; Daybreak, 1994; The Carousel, 1995; Promises, 1996; Secrecy, 1997; Homecoming, 1997; Legacy of Silence, 1998; Fortune's Hand, 1999; After the Fire, 2000; Looking Back, 2001; Her Father's House, 2002. *Literary Agent:* Janklow & Nesbit Associates, 445 Park Ave, New York, NY 10022, USA. *Address:* c/o Delacourte Press, 1540 Broadway, New York, NY 10036, USA.

PLANTE, David (Robert); Writer; b. 4 March 1940, Providence, RI, USA. *Education:* University of Louvain, Belgium, 1959–60; BA, Boston College, 1961. *Career:* Writer-in-Residence, University of Tulsa, 1979–82; Visiting Fellow, University of Cambridge, 1984–85; L'Université de Québec à Montréal, 1990; Gorky Institute of Literature, Moscow, 1991; Prof., Columbia University, 1998–. *Publications:* Fiction: The Ghost of Henry James, 1970; Slides, 1971; Relatives, 1974; The Darkness of the Body, 1974; Figures in Bright Air, 1976; The Family, 1978; The Country, 1981; The Woods, 1982; The Foreigner, 1984; The Catholic, 1986; The Native, 1988; The Accident, 1991; Annunciation, 1994; The Age of Terror, 1999. Non-Fiction: Difficult Women: A Memoir of Three, 1983. Contributions: anthologies and magazines. *Honours:* Henfield Fellow, University of East Anglia, 1975; British Arts Council Grant, 1977; Guggenheim Fellowship, 1983; American Acad. and Institute of Arts and Letters Award, 1983; Senior Mem., King's College, Cambridge; FRSL. *Address:* 38 Montagu Sq., London W1, England.

PLANTINGA, Alvin; Prof. of Philosophy and Writer; b. 15 Nov. 1932, Ann Arbor, Michigan, USA; m. Kathleen Ann DeBoer, 16 June 1955, two s. two d. *Education:* AB, Calvin College, Grand Rapids, 1954; MA, University of Michigan, 1955; PhD, Yale University, 1958. *Career:* Instructor, Yale University, 1957–58; Assoc. Prof., Wayne State University, 1958–63; Prof., Calvin College, 1963–82; Fellow, Center for Advanced Study in the Behavioral Sciences, 1968–69; Visiting Fellow, Balliol College, Oxford, 1975–76; John A O'Brien Prof. of Philosophy, 1982–, Dir, Center for Philosophy of Religion, 1983–, University of Notre Dame, IN; Gifford Lecturer, Aberdeen University, 1987; mem. Fellow, American Acad. of Arts and Sciences, 1975; American Philosophical Asscn; Society of Christian Philosophers, pres., 1983–86. *Publications:* God and Other Minds, 1967; The Nature of Necessity, 1974; God, Freedom, and Evil, 1974; Does God Have a Nature?, 1980; Faith and Rationality, 1983; Warrant: The Current Debate, 1993; Warrant and Proper Function, 1993; Warranted Christian Belief, 2000. *Honours:* Guggenheim Fellowship, 1971–72; National Endowment for the Humanities Fellowships, 1975–76, 1987, 1995–96; Hon. doctorates. *Address:* c/o Dept of Philosophy, University of Notre Dame, Notre Dame, IN 46556, USA.

PLANTINGA, Leon B(rooks); Musicologist, Prof. and Writer; b. 25 March 1935, Ann Arbor, MI, USA. *Education:* BA, Calvin College, 1957; MMus, Michigan State University, 1959; PhD, Yale University, 1964. *Career:* Faculty, 1963–74, Prof., 1974–, Acting Chair., 1978–79, Chair., 1979–86,

Dept of Music, Dir, Division of Humanities, 1991–97, Yale University; mem. American Musicological Society. *Publications:* Schumann as Critic, 1967; Muzio Clementi: His Life and Music, 1977; Romantic Music: A History of Musical Style in Nineteenth-Century Europe, 1984; Anthology of Romantic Music, 1984; Beethoven's Concertos: History, Style, Performance, 1999. Contributions: scholarly books and journals. *Honours:* ASCAP-Deems Taylor Award, 1985. *Address:* c/o Dept of Music, Yale University, PO Box 208310, New Haven, CT 06520, USA. *E-mail:* leon.plantinga@yale.edu.

PLATELL, Amanda, BA; Australian newspaper executive. *Career:* fmr mem. staff Perth Daily News; moved to London 1986; joined Today newspaper, later Features Production Ed., then Deputy Ed.; fmr mem. staff London Daily News; Group Man. Dir Mirror Group Newspapers (MGN) 1995–96, Head of Promotions for MGN Titles, mem. subsidiary MGN Bd, Group Man. Dir and Acting Ed. Sunday Mirror 1996–97; Ed. Sunday Express 1998–99; Head of Media, Conservative Party 1999–2001. *Publication:* Scandal 1999. *Address:* c/o Conservative Central Office, 32 Smith Square, Westminster London, SW1P 3HH, England.

PLATER, Alan Frederick, FRSL, FRSA; British writer; b. 15 April 1935, Jarrow-on-Tyne; m. 1st Shirley Johnson 1958 (divorced 1985); two s. one d.; m. 2nd Shirley Rubinstein 1986; three step-s. *Education:* Kingston High School and King's Coll. Newcastle-upon-Tyne. *Career:* trained as architect; full-time writer 1960–; has written extensively for radio, TV, films and theatre, also for The Guardian, Listener, New Statesman, etc.; Co.-Chair. Writers' Guild of GB 1986–87, Pres. 1991–95; Visiting Prof., Univ. of Bournemouth 2001–. *Plays include:* A Smashing Day, Close the Coalhouse Door, And a Little Love Besides, Swallows on the Water, Trinity Tales, The Fosdyke Saga, Fosdyke Two, On Your Way, Riley!, Skyhooks, A Foot on the Earth, Prez, Rent Party (musical), Sweet Sorrow, Going Home, I Thought I Heard a Rustling, Shooting the Legend, All Credit to the Lads, Peggy for You, Tales From the Backyard, Only a Matter of Time, Barriers. *Films include:* The Virgin and the Gypsy, It Shouldn't Happen to a Vet, Priest of Love, Keep the Aspidistra Flying. *Radio includes:* Only a Matter of Time, Time Added on for Injuries, The Devil's Music. *Television includes:* series: Z Cars, Softly Softly, The Beiderbecke Trilogy; adaptations: Barchester Chronicles, The Fortunes of War, A Very British Coup, Campion, A Day in Summer, A Few Selected Exits, Oliver's Travels, Dalziel and Pascoe; recent plays: Doggin' Around, The Last of the Blonde Bombshells. *Publications:* The Beiderbecke Affair 1985, The Beiderbecke Tapes 1986, Misterioso 1987, The Beiderbecke Connection 1992, Oliver's Travels 1994; plays and shorter pieces in various anthologies. *Honours:* Hon. Fellow, Humberside Coll. of Educ. 1983; Hon. DLitt (Hull) 1985; Hon. DCL (Northumbria) 1997; Royal TV Soc. Writers' Award 1988, BAFTA Writers' Award 1988 and many other awards. *Literary Agent:* Alexandra Cann Representation, 12 Abingdon Road, London, W8 6AF, England. *Telephone:* (20) 7938-4002.

PLATH, James Walter, BA, MA, PhD; writer, editor and educator; b. 29 Oct. 1950, Chicago, IL, USA; three s. three d. *Education:* California State University at Chico, University of Wisconsin-Milwaukee. *Career:* Prof. of English, Illinois Wesleyan University; mem. Acad. of American Poets; Fitzgerald Society; Fulbright Asscn; Hemingway Society; Illinois College Press Asscn; Society of Midland Authors. *Publications:* Conversations With John Updike, 1994; Courbet, On the Rocks, 1994; Remembering Ernest Hemingway, 1999. Contributions: anthologies, reviews, periodicals, journals, quarterlies, magazines and newspapers. *Honours:* Fulbright Scholar; Ed.'s Award, Council of Literary Magazines and Presses, 1990; Pantagraph Award for Teaching Excellence 2004. *Address:* c/o Department of English, Illinois Wesleyan University, Bloomington, IL 61702-2900, USA.

PLATT, Charles; Writer and Poet; b. 26 April 1945, London, England; one d. *Education:* University of Cambridge; London College of Printing. *Publications:* Fiction: The Garbage World, 1967; The City Dwellers, 1970, US edn as Twilight of the City, 1977; Planet of the Voles, 1971; New Worlds 6 (ed. with M. Moorcock), 1973, US edn as New Worlds 5, 1974; New Worlds 7 (ed. with H. Bailey), 1974, US edn as New Worlds 6, 1975; Sweet Evil, 1977; Free Zone, 1989; Soma, 1989; The Silicon Man, 1991. Non-Fiction: Dream Makers: The Uncommon People Who Write Science Fiction, 1980; When You Can Live Twice as Long, What Will You Do?, 1989. Poetry: Highway Sandwiches (with T. M. Disch and M. Hacker), 1970; The Gas, 1970. *Address:* c/o Gollancz, 14 Henrietta St, London WC2E 8QJ, England.

PLATTHY, Jeno; Poet, Writer, Ed. and Publisher; b. 13 Aug. 1920, Hungary; m. Carol Louise Abell, 25 Sept. 1976. *Education:* Peter Pazmany University, Budapest, 1939–42; Jozsef Ferencz University, 1943–44; Catholic University of America, 1963–65. *Career:* Ed.-in-Chief, Monumenta Classical Perennia, 1967–84; Exec. Dir, Federation of International Poetry Asscns of UNESCO, 1976–96; Publisher, New Muses, 1976–; mem. Acad. of American Poets; American Society of Composers, Authors and Publishers; Asscn of Literary Critics and Scholars; International PEN Club; International Poetry Society; Literarische Union, Germany. *Publications:* Poetry: numerous vols, 1976–99, including: Odes Europénnes, 1986; Asian Elegies, 1987; Nova Comoedia, 3 parts, 1988, 1990, 1991; Elegies Asiatiques, 1991; Paeans, 1993; Prosodia, 1994; Songs of the Soul, 1996; Ultimacy, 1999. Other: Sources on the Earliest Greek Libraries with the Testimonia, 1968; Ch'u Yuan, 1975; The Mythical Poets of Greece, 1985; Bartók: A Critical Biography, 1988; Plato: A Critical Biography, 1990; Near-Death Experiences in Antiquity, 1992; The Duino Elegies of Rilke (trans. and commentary), 1999. Contributions: various publications. *Honours:* Poet Laureate, World Congress of Poets, 1973; Confucius Award, 1974; Poet Laureate and Pres., International Congress of Poets, 1976; Officier, Ordre des Arts et des Lettres, 1992. *Address:* 961 W Sled Circle, Santa Claus, IN 47579, USA.

PLENEL, Edwy; Journalist; b. 31 Aug. 1952, Nantes, France; m. Nicole Lapierre; one d. *Education:* Institut d'études politiques, Paris. *Career:* journalist Rouge 1976–78, Matin de Paris 1980; joined Le Monde 1980, Educ. Ed. 1980–82, Legal columnist 1982–90, Reporter 1991, Head Legal Dept 1992–94, Chief Ed. 1994–95, Asst Editorial Dir 1995–96, Ed. 1996–2000, Ed.-in-Chief 2000–. *Publications:* L'Effet Le Pen 1984, La République inachevée: l'État et l'école en France 1985, Mourir a Ouvéa: le tournant calédonien 1988, Voyage avec Colomb 1991, La République menacée: dix ans d'effet Le Pen 1992, La Part d'ombre 1992, Un temps de chien 1994, Les Mots volés 1997, L'Epreuve 1999. *Address:* Le Monde, 21 bis rue Claude Bernard, 75242 Paris Cedex, France. *E-mail:* plenel@lemonde.fr. *Website:* www.lemonde.fr.

PLUMLY, Stanley (Ross); Poet and Prof. of English; b. 23 May 1939, Barnesville, Ohio, USA. *Education:* BA, Wilmington College, 1961; MA, Ohio University, 1968. *Career:* Instructor in Creative Writing, Louisiana State University, 1968–70; Ed., Ohio Review, 1970–75, Iowa Review, 1976–78; Prof. of English, Ohio University, 1970–74, University of Houston, 1979–; Visiting lecturer at several universities. *Publications:* In the Outer Dark, 1970; How the Plains Indians Got Horses, 1973; Giraffe, 1973; Out-of-the-Body Travel, 1977; Summer Celestial, 1983; Boy on the Step, 1989; The Marriage in the Trees, 1997; The New Bread Loaf Anthology of Contemporary American Poetry (ed. with Michael Collier), 1999; Now That My Father Lies Down Beside Me: New and Selected Poems, 1970–2000, 2000. Contributions: periodicals. *Honours:* Delmore Schwartz Memorial Award, 1973; Guggenheim Fellowhip, 1973; National Endowment for the Arts Grant, 1977. *Address:* c/o Dept of English and Creative Writing, University of Houston, 4800 Calhoun, Houston, TX 77004, USA.

POCOCK, Tom, (Guy Allcot); Author and Journalist; b. 18 Aug. 1925, London, England; m. Penelope Casson 26 April 1969; two d. *Career:* mem. Society of Authors. *Publications:* Nelson and His World, 1968; Chelsea Reach, 1970; Fighting General, 1973; Remember Nelson, 1977; The Young Nelson in the Americas, 1980; 1945: The Dawn Came Up Like Thunder, 1983; East and West of Suez, 1986; Horatio Nelson, 1987; Alan Moorehead, 1990; The Essential Venice, 1990; Sailor King, 1991; Rider Haggard and the Lost Empire, 1993; Norfolk, 1995; A Thirst for Glory, 1996; Battle for Empire, 1998; Nelson's Women, 1999; Captain Marryat, 2000; The Terror Before Trafalgar, 2002. Contributions: numerous newspapers and magazines. *Honours:* Anderson Medal, Society for Nautical Research, 2002. *Address:* 22 Lawrence St, London SW3 5NF, England.

PODHORETZ, Norman, AB, BHL, BA, MA; editor and writer; b. 16 Jan. 1930, New York, NY, USA; m. Midge Rosenthal Decter 1956; one s. three d. *Education:* Columbia University, Jewish Theological Seminary, University of Cambridge. *Career:* Assoc. Ed., 1956–58, Ed.-in-Chief, 1960–95, Ed.-at-Large, 1995–, Commentary Magazine; Mem., University Seminar on American Civilization, Columbia University, 1958; Ed.-in-Chief, Looking Glass Library, 1959–60; Chair., New Directions Advisory Committee, United States Information Agency, 1981–87; Senior Fellow, Hudson Institute, 1995–; mem. Council on Foreign Relations. *Publications:* Doings and Undoings: The Fifties and After in American Writing, 1964; The Commentary Reader (ed.), 1966; Making It, 1968; Breaking Ranks, 1979; The Present Danger, 1980; Why We Were in Vietnam, 1982; The Bloody Crossroads, 1986; Ex-Friends, 1999; My Love Afffair with America, 2000; The Prophets, 2002. Contributions: periodicals. *Honours:* Fulbright Fellowship, 1950–51; Kellet Fellow, University of Cambridge, 1950–52; Hon. LHD, Hamilton College, 1969, Yeshiva University, 1991, Boston University, 1995, Adelphi University, 1996; Hon. LLD, Jewish Theological Seminary, 1980. *Address:* c/o Commentary Magazine, American Jewish Committee, 165 E 56th Street, New York, NY 10022, USA.

POHL, Frederik (James MacCreigh); Writer and Ed.; b. 26 Nov. 1919, New York, NY, USA. *Career:* Book Ed. and Assoc. Circulation Man., Popular Science Co, New York City, 1946–49; Literary Agent, New York City, 1949–53; Ed., Galaxy Publishing Co, New York City, 1960–69; Exec. Ed., Ace Books, New York City, 1971–72; Science Fiction Ed., Bantam Books, New York City, 1973–79; mem. Authors' Guild; SFWA, pres., 1974–76; World Science Fiction, pres., 1980–82. *Publications:* Author or ed. of over 45 books, 1953–98. *Address:* c/o World, 855 S Harvard Dr., Palatine, IL 60067, USA.

POIRIER, Richard; Literary Critic; b. 9 Sept. 1925, Gloucester, Massachusetts, USA. *Education:* University of Paris, 1946; BA, Amherst College, 1949; MA, Yale University, 1950; Fulbright Scholar, University of Cambridge, 1952; PhD, Harvard University, 1960. *Career:* Williams College, 1950–52; Harvard University, 1955–62; Rutgers University, 1962–; Ed., Partisan Review, 1963–71, Raritan Quarterly, 1980–; Vice-Pres., Founder, Library of America, 1980–; mem. Poets, Playwrights, Editors, Essayists and Novelists; American Acad. of Arts and Letters; American Acad. of Arts and Sciences; Century Club. *Publications:* Comic Sense of Henry James, 1960; In Defense of Reading (co-ed.), 1962; A World Elsewhere, 1966; The Performing Self, 1971; Norman Mailer, 1976; Robert Frost: The Work of

Knowing, 1977; The Renewal of Literature, 1987; Poetry and Pragmatism, 1992; Trying It Out in America: Literary and Other Performances, 1999. Contributions: Daedalus; New Republic; Partisan Review; New York Review; London Review of Books; TLS. *Honours:* Fulbright Fellow, 1952; Bollingen Fellow, 1963; Guggenheim Fellowship, 1967; National Endowment for the Humanities Fellow, 1972; HHD, Amherst College, 1978; Award, American Acad. of Arts and Letters, 1980; Literary Lion, New York Public Library, 1992. *Address:* 104 W 70th St, 9B, New York, NY 10023, USA.

POLAND, Dorothy Elizabeth Hayward, (Alison Farely, Jane Hammond); Author; b. 3 May 1937, Barry, Wales. *Publications:* As Alison Farely: The Shadows of Evil, 1963; Plunder Island, 1964; High Treason, 1966; Throne of Wrath, 1967; Crown of Splendour, 1968; The Lion and the Wolf, 1969; Last Roar of the Lion, 1969; Leopard From Anjou, 1970; King Wolf, 1974; Kingdom under Tyranny, 1974; Last Howl of the Wolf, 1975; The Cardinal's Nieces, 1976; The Tempestuous Countess, 1976; Archduchess Arrogance, 1980; Scheming Spanish Queen, 1981; Spain for Mariana, 1982. As Jane Hammond: The Hell Raisers of Wycombe, 1970; Fire and the Sword, 1971; The Golden Courtesan, 1975; Shadow of the Headsman, 1975; The Doomtower, 1975; Witch of the White House, 1976; Gunpowder Treason, 1976; The Red Queen, 1976; The Queen's Assassin, 1977; The Silver Madonna, 1977; Conspirator's Moonlight, 1977; Woman of Vengeance, 1977; The Admiral's Lady, 1978; The Secret of Petherick, 1982; The Massingham Topaz, 1983; Beware the King's Enchantress, 1983; Moon in Aries, 1984; Eagle's Talon, 1984; Death in the New Forest, 1984; One Voyage Too Far, 2003. *Address:* Horizons, 99 Dock View Rd, Barry, Glamorgan, Wales. *E-mail:* polandandangelcake@aol.com.

POLE, Jack Richon, BA, MA Cantab., PhD, FRHistS; historian and writer; b. 14 March 1922, London, England; m. Marilyn Louise Mitchell 1952 (divorced 1988); one s. two d. *Education:* University of Oxford, Princeton University. *Career:* Instructor, Princeton University, 1952–53; Asst Lecturer to Lecturer in American History, University College London, 1953–63; Reader in American History and Government, University of Cambridge; Fellow, 1963–79, Vice-Master, 1975–78, Churchill College, Cambridge; Fellow, Center for Advanced Study in the Behavioral Sciences, USA, 1969–70; Guest Scholar, Woodrow Wilson International Center, Washington, DC, 1978–79; Rhodes Prof. of American History and Institutions, University of Oxford, 1979–89; Fellow, St Catherine's College, Oxford, 1979–; Senior Research Fellow, College of William and Mary, Virginia, 1991; Leverhulme Trust Emeritus Fellow, 1991–93; mem. British Acad., fellow; Selden Society; International Commission for the History of Representative and Parliamentary Institutions, vice-pres., 1990–; British Nineteenth Century American Historians, hon. vice-pres.; American Historical Asscn, hon. foreign mem., 2003. *Publications:* Abraham Lincoln and the Working Classes of Britain, 1959; Abraham Lincoln, 1964; Political Representation in England and the Origins of the American Republic, 1966; The Advance of Democracy (ed.), 1967; The Seventeenth Century: The Origins of Legislative Power, 1969; The Revolution in America: Documents of the Internal Development of America in the Revolutionary Era (ed.), 1971; The Meanings of American History (co-ed.), 1971; Foundations of American Independence, 1763–1815, 1972; American Historical Documents (general ed.), 1975; The Decision for American Independence, 1975; The Idea of Union, 1977; The Pursuit of Equality in American History, 1978; Paths to the American Past, 1979; The Gift of Government: Political Responsibility from the English Restoration to American Independence, 1983; Colonial British America: Essays in the New History of the Early Modern Era (co-ed.), 1983; The American Constitution: For and Against: The Federalist and Anti-Federalist Papers (ed.), 1987; The Blackwell Encyclopedia of the American Revolution (co-ed.), 1991, revised edn as Companion to the American Revolution, 1999; Freedom of Speech: Right or Privilege?, 1998. Contributions: Reference works and professional journals. *Address:* 20 Divinity Road, Oxford OX4 1LJ, England.

POLIAKOFF, Stephen; British playwright and film director; b. 1952, London; m. Sandy Welch 1983; one d. one s. *Education:* Westminster School and Univ. of Cambridge. *Films:* Hidden City, Close My Eyes 1992 (Best British Film Award, Evening Standard), Century 1995, The Tribe 1998, Food of Love 1998. *Theatre:* Clever Soldiers 1974, The Carnation Gang 1974, Hitting Town 1975, City Sugar 1976, Strawberry Fields (Nat. Theatre) 1978, Shout Across the River (RSC) 1978, The Summer Party 1980, Favourite Nights 1981, Breaking the Silence (RSC) 1984, Coming in to Land (Nat. Theatre) 1987, Playing with Trains (RSC) 1989, Siena Red 1992, Sweet Panic (Hampstead) 1996, Blinded by the Sun (Nat. Theatre) 1996 (Critics' Circle Best Play Award), Talk of the City (RSC) 1998, Remember This (Nat. Theatre) 1999. *Television:* plays: Caught on a Train 1980 (BAFTA Award), She's Been Away (Venice Film Festival Prize), Shooting the Past 1999 (Prix Italia), Perfect Strangers 2001; drama: The Lost Prince 2003. *Publications:* Plays One 1989, Plays Two 1994, Plays Three 1998, Sweet Panic and Blinded by the Sun, Talk of the City, Shooting the Past, Remember This. *Address:* 33 Devonia Road, London, N1 8JQ, England. *Telephone:* (20) 7354-2695.

POLING-KEMPES, Lesley Ann; Writer; b. 9 March 1954, Batavia, New York, USA; m. James Kempes, 31 May 1976, one s. one d. *Education:* BA, cum laude, University of New Mexico, 1976. *Publications:* Harvey Girls: Women Who Opened the West, 1989; Canyon of Remembering, 1996; Valley of Shining Stone: The Story of Abiquiu, 1997. Contributions: Puerta del Sol; Writer's Forum 16; Best of the West 3; Higher Elevations; New Mexico Magazine. *Honours:* Zia Award for Excellence, New Mexico Press Women, 1991. *Address:* PO Box 36, Abiquiu, NM 87510, USA.

POLITO, Robert; Writer and Poet; b. 27 Oct. 1951, Boston, Massachusetts, USA; m. Kristine M. Harris, 27 June 1987. *Education:* BA, Boston College, 1973; PhD, Harvard University, 1981. *Career:* Faculty, Harvard University, 1976–81, Wellesley College, 1981–89, New York University, 1990–92, New School for Social Research, New York City, 1992–. *Publications:* Fireworks: The Lost Writings of Jim Thompson (ed.), 1988; A Reader's Guide to James Morrill's The Changing Light at Sandover, 1994; Doubles (poems), 1995; Savage Art: A Biography of Jim Thompson, 1995. Contributions: newspapers and magazines. *Honours:* National Book Critics Circle Award, 1995. *Address:* c/o Writing Program, New School for Social Research, 66 W 12th St, No. 507, New York, NY 10021, USA.

POLKINGHORNE, Rev. Canon John Charlton, Kt, KBE, MA, PhD, ScD, FRS; British ecclesiastic and physicist; b. 16 Oct. 1930, Weston-super-Mare; m. Ruth I. Martin 1955; two s. one d. *Education:* Perse School, Cambridge, Trinity Coll. Cambridge and Westcott House, Cambridge. *Career:* Commonwealth Fund Fellow Calif. Inst. of Tech. 1955–56; Lecturer, Univ. of Edin. 1956–58; Lecturer, Univ. of Cambridge 1958–65, Reader 1965–68, Prof. of Math. Physics 1968–79; Fellow, Trinity Coll. Cambridge 1954–86; ordained deacon 1981, priest 1982; Curate, St Andrew's, Chesterton 1981–82, St Michael & All Angels, Bedminster 1982–84; Vicar of St Cosmus and St Damian in the Blean 1984–86; Fellow and Dean, Trinity Hall, Cambridge 1986–89, Hon. Fellow 1989–; Pres. Queens' Coll. Cambridge 1989–96, Fellow 1989–, Hon. Fellow 1996–; Canon Theologian, Liverpool Cathedral 1994–; Six Preacher, Canterbury Cathedral 1996–; mem. Church of England Doctrine Comm. 1989–95, Human Genetics Advisory Comm. 1996–99, General Synod 1999–2000, Human Genetics Comm. 2000–02. *Publications:* The Analytic S-Matrix (jointly) 1966, The Particle Play 1979, Models of High Energy Processes 1980, The Way the World Is 1983, The Quantum World 1984, One World 1986, Science and Creation 1988, Science and Providence 1989, Rochester Roundabout 1989, Reason and Reality 1991, Science and Christian Belief 1994, Quarks, Chaos and Christianity 1994, Serious Talk 1995, Scientists as Theologians 1996, Beyond Science 1996, Searching for Truth 1996, Belief in God in an Age of Science 1998, Science and Theology 1998, Faith, Science and Understanding 2000, The End of the World and the Ends of God (ed with M. Welker) 2000, Faith in the Living God (with M. Welker) 2001, The Work of Love (ed.) 2001, The God of Hope and the End of the World 2002, Quantum Theory: A Very Short Introduction 2002, Living with Hope 2003. *Honours:* Hon. Prof. of Theoretical Physics, Univ. of Kent 1984–89, Hon. Fellow St Edmund's Coll., Cambridge 2002; Hon. DD (Kent) 1994, (Durham) 1999; Hon. DSc (Exeter) 1994, (Leicester) 1995, (Marquette) 2003; Templeton Prize 2002. *Address:* Queens' College, Cambridge, CB3 9ET, England.

POLKINHORN, Harry; Writer, Poet, Ed. and Trans; b. 3 March 1945, Calexico, CA, USA; m. Armida Romero, 1 March 1986, divorced 1991, one d. *Education:* BA, University of California at Berkeley, 1967; MA, English, MA, Art, 1982, San Diego State University; PhD, New York University, 1975. *Publications:* Excisions (poems), 1976; Radix Zero (poems), 1981; Volvox (poems), 1981; El Libro de Calo: Pachuco Slang Dictionary, 1983, revised edn as El Libro de Calo: Chicano Slang Dictionary (co-author), 1986; Travelling with Women (fiction), 1983; Anaesthesia (poems), 1985; Bridges of Skin Money (visual poems), 1986; Summary Dissolution (visual poems), 1988; Jerome Rothenberg: A Descriptive Bibliography, 1988; Lorenia La Rosa: A Travelogue (fiction), 1989; Begging for Remission (poems), 1989; Teraphim (visual poems), 1995; Mount Soledad (poems), 1996; Throat Shadow (poems), 1997; Blueshift (poems), 1998. Other: Ed. or co-ed. of several publications; Trans. Contributions: periodicals, including: American Book Review; Afterimage; Poetics Journal; Photostatic; Moody Street Irregulars; Smile; Uno Más Uno; Score; Tempus Fugit; La Poire d'Angoisse; Sink; Kaldron. *Address:* PO Box 927428, San Diego, CA 92192, USA. *E-mail:* hpolkinh@mail.sdsu.edu.

POLLAND, Madelaine Angela, (Frances Adrian); Writer; b. 31 May 1918, Kinsale, County Cork, Ireland. *Publications:* Children of the Red King, 1961; Beorn the Proud, 1962; The White Twilight, 1962; Chuiraquimba and the Black Robes, 1962; City of the Golden House, 1963; The Queen's Blessing, 1963; Flame over Tara, 1964; Thicker Than Water, 1964; Mission to Cathay, 1965; Queen Without Crown, 1965; Deirdre, 1967; The Little Spot of Bother, 1967, US edn as Minutes of a Murder; To Tell My People, 1968; Stranger in the Hills, 1968; Random Army, 1969, US edn as Shattered Summer; To Kill a King, 1970; Alhambra, 1970; A Family Affair, 1971; Package to Spain, 1971; Daughter to Poseidon, 1972, US edn as Daughter of the Sea; Prince of the Double Axe, 1976; Double Shadow (as Francis Adrian), 1977; Sabrina, 1979; All Their Kingdoms, 1981; The Heart Speaks Many Ways, 1982; No Price Too High, 1984; As It Was in the Beginning, 1987; Rich Man's Flowers, 1990; The Pomegranate House, 1992. *Address:* Edificio Hercules 634, Avenida Gamonal, Arroyo de La Miel, Malaga, Spain.

POLLARD, Eve; British newspaper editor; b. 25 Dec. 1945; m. 1st Barry L. D. Winkleman 1968 (divorced 1978); one d.; m. 2nd Sir Nicholas M. Lloyd 1978; one s. *Career:* Fashion Ed. Honey 1967–68; Fashion Ed. Daily Mirror Magazine 1968–69, top feature writer 1969–70, Women's Ed. Sunday

Mirror 1971–81, Ed. (and responsible for launch of Sunday Mirror Magazine) 1988–91; Women's Ed. Observer Magazine 1970–71; Asst Ed. Sunday People 1981–83; Features Ed., Presenter TV-AM 1983–85; Ed. Elle USA (and launched magazine, New York) 1985–86, Sunday magazine News of the World 1986, You magazine Mail on Sunday 1986–88, Sunday Express and Sunday Express Magazine 1991–94; f. Wedding Magazine 1999; TV Presenter The Truth About Women; Founder and Chair. Women in Journalism 1995–; mem. English Tourism Council (fmrly English Tourist Bd) 1993–2000, Competition Comm. 1999–; Ed. of the Year, Focus Awards 1991. *Publications:* Jackie: Biography of Mrs J. K. Onassis 1971, Splash! 1995, Best of Enemies 1996, Double Trouble 1997, Unfinished Business 1998. *Address:* c/o Simpson–Fox Associates, 52 Shaftesbury Avenue, London, W1V 7DE, England.

POLLARD, Jane, (Jane Jackson, Dana James); Author; b. 22 Nov. 1944, Goole, Yorkshire, England; m. 3rd Michael Pollard 2 June 1992; two s. one d. *Career:* mem. Romantic Novelists Asscn; Society of Authors; Historical Novel Society. *Publications:* Harlyn Tremayne, 1984; Doctor in The Andes, 1984; Desert Flower, 1986; Doctor in New Guinea, 1986; Rough Waters, 1986; The Marati Legacy, 1986; The Eagle and the Sun, 1986; The Consul's Daughter, 1986; Heart of Glass, 1987; Tarik's Mountain, 1988; Snowfire, 1988; Pool of Dreaming, 1988; Dark Moon Rising, 1989; Love's Ransom, 1989; A Tempting Shore, 1992; Bay of Rainbows, 1993; Deadly Feast, 1997; A Place of Birds, 1997; The Iron Road, 1999; Eye of the Wind, 2001; Tide of Fortune, 2004. Contributions: periodicals, radio and television. *Literary Agent:* Dorian Literary Agency, Upper Thornehill, 27 Church Rd, St Marychurch, Torquay TQ1 4QY, England. *Address:* 32 Cogos Park, Comfort Rd, Mylor, Falmouth, Cornwall TR11 5SF, England.

POLLARD, John Richard Thornhill, BA, MA, MLitt; fmr sr lecturer in classics and writer; b. 5 April 1914, Exeter, Devon, England; m. Shirley Holt 1952; one s. three d. *Education:* University College, Exeter, University of Oxford. *Career:* Captain, Devonshire Regiment and King's African Rifles 1939–45; Sr Lecturer in Classics, University College of North Wales, Bangor. *Publications:* Journey to the Styx 1955, Adventure Begins in Kenya 1957, Africa for Adventure 1961, African Zoo Man 1963, Wolves and Werewolves 1964, Helen of Troy 1965, Seers, Shrines and Sirens 1965, The Long Safari 1967, Virgil: The Aeneid Appreciation (with C. Day-Lewis) 1969, Birds in Greek Life and Myth 1977, Divination and Oracles: Greece, Civilization of the Ancient Mediterranean 1986, No County to Compare 1994. *Address:* The Yard, Red Wharf Bay, Anglesey, LL75 8RX, Wales.

POLLEY, Jacob, MA; British poet and screenwriter; b. 1975, Carlisle, Cumbria. *Education:* Univ. of Lancaster. *Career:* writer-in-residence, The Wordsworth Trust 2002. *Film:* Flickerman and the Ivory-Skinned Woman (co-author). *Publications:* poetry: Salvage 2000, The Brink 2003. *Honours:* Arts Council of England/BBC Radio 4 First Verse Award 2002, Soc. of Authors Eric Gregory Award 2002. *Address:* c/o Picador Publishing, 20 New Wharf Road, London, N1 9RR, England.

POLLEY, Judith Anne, (Helen Kent, Valentina Luellen, Judith Stewart); Author; b. 15 Sept. 1938, London, England; m. Roy Edward Polley, 28 March 1959, one s. *Education:* High School, Belgravia and Maida Vale, London. *Career:* mem. Founding Mem., English Romantic Novelists Asscn. *Publications:* About 50 books, including: To Touch the Stars, 1980; Beloved Enemy, 1980; Don't Run From Love, 1981; Moonshadow, 1981; Prince of Deception, 1981; Beloved Adversary, 1981; Shadow of the Eagle, 1982; Silver Salamander, 1982; The Wind of Change, 1982; The Measure of Love, 1983; The Peaceful Homecoming, 1983; The Valley of Tears, 1984; Moonflower, 1984; Elusive Flame of Love, 1984; Mistress of Tanglewood, 1984; Black Ravenswood, 1985; The Lord of Darkness, 1985; Devil of Talland, 1985; Passionate Pirate, 1986; Where the Heart Leads, 1986; Love the Avenger, 1986; The Devil's Touch, 1987; My Lady Melisande, 1987; Dark Star, 1988; Love and Pride (Book 1), 1988; The Web of Love (Book 2), 1989; Winter Embers, Summer Fire, 1991; To Please a Lady, 1992; One Love, 1993; Hostage of Love, 1994; many foreign edns and trans. Contributions: Woman's Weekly Library; Woman's Realm; Woman's Weekly Fiction series; Museum of Peace and Solidarity, Samarkand, Uzbekistan. *Address:* Calcada, 8150 São Braz de Alportel, Algarve, Portugal.

POLLITT, Katha; Writer, Poet and Ed.; b. 14 Oct. 1949, New York, NY, USA; Divorced, one c. *Education:* BA, Harvard University, 1972; MFA, Columbia University, 1975. *Career:* Literary Ed., 1982–84, Contributing Ed., 1986–92, Assoc. Ed., 1992–, The Nation; Junior Fellow, Council of Humanities, Princeton University, 1984; Lecturer, New School for Social Research, New York City, 1986–90, Poetry Center, 92nd Street YMHA and WYHA, New York City, 1986–95. *Publications:* Antarctic Traveller, 1982; Reasonable Creatures: Essays on Women and Feminism, 1994. Contributions: journals and periodicals. *Honours:* National Book Critics Circle Award, 1983; I B. Lavan Younger Poet's Award, Acad. of American Poets, 1984; National Endowment for the Arts Grant, 1984; Guggenheim Fellowship, 1987; Whiting Fellowship, 1993. *Address:* 317 W 93rd St, New York, NY 10025, USA.

POLLOCK, John (Charles); Clergyman and Writer; b. 9 Oct. 1923, London, England; m. Anne Barrett-Lennard, 4 May 1949. *Education:* BA 1946, MA 1948, Trinity College, Cambridge. *Career:* Asst Master, Wellington College, Berkshire, 1947–49; Ordained Anglican Deacon, 1951, Priest, 1952; Curate, St Paul's Church, Portman Square, London, 1951–53; Rector, Horsington, Somerset, 1953–58; Ed., The Churchman (quarterly), 1953–58; mem. English Speaking Union Club. *Publications:* Candidate for Truth, 1950; A Cambridge Movement, 1953; The Cambridge Seven, 1955; Way to Glory: The Life of Havelock of Lucknow, 1957; Shadows Fall Apart, 1958; The Good Seed, 1959; Earth's Remotest End, 1960; Hudson Taylor and Maria, 1962; Moody Without Sankey, 1963; The Keswick Story, 1964; The Christians from Siberia, 1964; Billy Graham, 1966; The Apostle: A Life of Paul, 1969, revised edn as Paul the Apostle, 1999; Victims of the Long March, 1970; A Foreign Devil in China: The Life of Nelson Bell, 1971; George Whitefield and the Great Awakening, 1972, revised edn as Whitfield: The Evangelist, 2000; Wilberforce, 1977, revised edn as Wilberforce: God's Statesman, 2001; Billy Graham: Evangelist to the World, 1979; The Siberian Seven, 1979; Amazing Grace: John Newton's Story, 1981, revised edn as Newton: The Liberator, 2000; The Master: A Life of Jesus, 1984, revised edn as Jesus: The Master, 1999; Billy Graham: Highlights of the Story, 1984; Shaftesbury: The Poor Man's Earl, 1985, revised edn as Shaftesbury: The Reformer, 2000; A Fistful of Heroes: Great Reformers and Evangelists, 1988; John Wesley 1989, revised edn as Wesley: The Preacher, 2000; On Fire for God: Great Missionary Pioneers, 1990; Fear No Foe: A Brother's Story, 1992; Gordon: The Man Behind the Legend, 1993; Kitchener: The Road to Omdurman, 1998; Kitchener: Saviour of the Nation, 2000; Kitchener (comprising The Road to Omdurman and Saviour of the Nation), 2001, The Billy Graham Story 2003. Contributions: Reference works and religious periodicals. *Honours:* The John Pollock Award for Christian Biography created in his name, Samford Univ. 1999; Hon. DLitt, Samford University, USA, 2002. *Address:* Rose Ash House, South Molton, Devonshire EX36 4RB, England.

POLOMÉ, Edgar Ghislain Charles; American academic and writer; b. 31 July 1920, Brussels, Belgium; m. 1st Julia Joséphine Schwindt 1944 (died 1975); one s. one d.; m. 2nd Barbara Baker Harris 1980 (divorced 1991); m. 3rd Sharon Looper Rankin 1991. *Education:* BA, 1940, PhD, 1949, Free University of Brussels; MA, Catholic University of Louvain, 1943. *Career:* Prof. of Germanic Languages, Athénée Adolphe Max, Brussels, 1942–56; Prof. of Linguistics, University of the Belgian Congo, 1956–61; Visiting Assoc. Prof., 1961–62, Prof. of Germanic, Oriental and African Languages and Literatures, 1961–90, Dir, Center for Asian Studies, 1962–72, Christie and Stanley Adams Jr Centennial Prof. of Liberal Arts, 1984–98, Prof. Emeritus, 1998–, University of Texas at Austin; Co-Ed., 1973–, Managing Ed., 1987–, Journal of Indo-European Studies; Co-Ed., Mankind Quarterly, 1980–; mem. American Anthropological Asscn; American Institute of Indian Studies; American Oriental Society; Indogermanische Gesellschaft; Linguistics Society of America; MLA; Societas Linguistica Europea; Société de Linguistique de Paris; Hon. Mem., Belgian Asscn for Celtic Studies. *Publications:* Swahili Language Handbook, 1967; Language Surveys in the Developing Nations (ed. with Sirarpi Ohannessian and Charles Ferguson), 1974; Linguistics and Literary Studies in Honor of Archibald A. Hill (ed. with M. A. Jazayery and Werner Winter), 1976; Language in Tanzania (ed. with C. P. Hill), 1980; Man and the Ultimate: A Symposium (ed.), 1980; The Indo-Europeans in the Fourth and Third Millennia (ed.), 1982; Language, Society and Paleoculture, 1982; Essays on Germanic Religion, 1989; Guide to Language Change (ed.), 1990; Reconstructing Languages and Cultures (ed.), 1992; Indo-European Religion after Dumézil (co-ed.), 1996; Festschrift J. Puhvel (co-ed.). 1997. Contributions: scholarly books and professional journals. *Honours:* Fulbright-Hays Scholar, University of Kiel, 1968; First Sociolinguistic Prize, University of Umeå, Sweden, 1988. *Address:* 2701 Rock Terrace Drive, Austin, TX 78704, USA.

POLONSKY, Antony (Barry); Lecturer in International History and Writer; b. 23 Sept. 1940, Johannesburg, South Africa. *Education:* BA, University of the Witwatersrand, 1960; MA, DPhil, University of Oxford, 1967. *Career:* Lecturer in East European History, University of Glasgow, 1968–70; Lecturer in International History, LSE, 1970–, University of London, 1981–. *Publications:* Politics in Independent Poland, 1972; The Little Dictator, 1975; The Great Powers and the Polish Question, 1976; The Beginnings of Communist Rule in Poland (with B. Druckier), 1978; The History of Poland since 1863 (co-author), 1981; My Brother's Keeper?: Recent Polish Debates on the Holocaust, 1990; Jews in Eastern Poland and the USSR (ed. with Norman Davies), 1991; From Shtetl to Socialism: Studies from Polin, 1994. Contributions: Professional journals.

PONDER, Patricia (see Maxwell, Patricia Anne).

PONIATOWSKA, Elena; Mexican writer and journalist; b. 19 May 1932, Paris, France. *Career:* mem. exec. bd, Int. Center for Writing and Translation, Univ. of California at Irvine. *Publications include:* Hasta no verte Jesús mío 1969, Ay vida, no me mereces de noche vienes 1974, Quendo Diego te Abreza Quiela 1978, Fuerte es el silencio 1982, Lilus Kikus 1982, Domingo siete 1983, Dear Diego 1986, Nada, nadie: Las voces del temblor 1988, Compañeros de México: Women Photograph Women 1990, Todo México 1990, Frida Kahlo: The Camera Seduced 1992, Luz y luna, las lunitas 1996, Tinisima 1996, Guerrero vieja 1997, Todo empezó el domingo 1998, Octavio Paz, las palabras del árbol 1998, Paseo de la Reforma 1998, El Niño: Children of the Streets, Mexico City 1999, La casa en Mango Street 1999, Cuentos Méxicanos 1999, La noche de Tlatelolco 1999, Las soldaderas 2000, La piel del cielo 2001, Here's To You Jesusa 2001, Cartas de Alvaro Mutis a Elena Poniatowska 2002, Tlapaleria 2003. *Honours:* Nat. Mexican

Award for Journalism 1979. *Address:* International Center for Writing and Translation, School of Humanities, 172 Humanities Instruction Building, University of California, Irvine, CA 92697-3380, USA.

POOLE, Josephine (see Helyar, Jane Penelope Josephine).

POOLE, Julian (see May, Stephen James).

POOLE, Margaret Barbara, (Peggy Poole, Terry Roche, Margaret Thornton); Broadcaster, Poet and Writer; b. 8 March 1925, Petham, Kent, England; m. Reginald Poole, 10 Aug. 1949, three d. *Career:* Co-Organiser, Jabberwocky 1968–86; Producer-Presenter, First Heard poetry programme, BBC Radio Merseyside, 1976–88; Poetry Consultant, BBC Network Northwest, 1988–96; ran five-day poetry course Swanwick Summer School; Tutor Writers' News Home Study Course for Poetrymem. Poetry Society; Society of Women Writers and Journalists. *Publications:* Never a Put-up Job 1970, Cherry Stones and Other Poems 1983, No Wilderness in Them 1984, Midnight Walk 1986, Hesitations 1990, Trusting the Rainbow 1994, From the Tide's Edge 1999, Polishing Pans, Transported, Selected Poems. Editor (anthologies): Windfall 1994; Poet's England: Cumbria 1995; Marigolds Grow Wild on Platforms 1996; Perceptions 2000. *Honours:* First Prize, Waltham Forest Competition, 1987; Prizewinner, Lancaster Literature Festival, 1987, 1991; First Prize, Southport Competition, 1989; Prizewinner, LACE Competition, 1992; Sandburg-Livesey Award, 1999. *Address:* 36 Hilbre Ct, West Kirby, Wirral, Merseyside L48 3JU, England. *E-mail:* peggypoole@hilbrecourt.fsnet.co.uk.

POOLE, Richard Arthur; Tutor in English Literature and Poet; b. 1 Jan. 1945, Yorkshire, England; m. Sandra Pauline Smart 18 July 1970; one s. *Education:* BA, 1966, MA, 1968, University College of North Wales. *Career:* Tutor in English Literature, Coleg Harlech, 1970–2001; Ed., Poetry Wales, 1992–96; mem. Welsh Acad. *Publications:* Goings and Other Poems, 1978; Words Before Midnight, 1981; Natural Histories, 1989; Autobiographies and Explorations, 1994; That Fool July, 2003. Contributions: many reviews and journals. *Address:* Glan-y-Werydd, Llandanwg, Gwynedd LL46 2SD, Wales.

POPE, Pamela Mary Alison; writer; b. 26 April 1931, Lowestoft, Suffolk, England; m. Ronald Pope 1954; two d. *Career:* mem. Romantic Novelists Asscn; Society of Women Writers and Journalists. *Publications:* The Magnolia Seige, 1982; The Candleberry Tree, 1982; Eden's Law, 1983; The Wind in the East, 1989; The Rich Pass By, 1990; Neither Angels Nor Demons, 1992; A Collar of Jewels, 1994. Contributions: Good Housekeeping; Woman; Woman's Realm; Vanity Fair; True; Loving; Hampshire Magazine; Hampshire Life; London Evening News.

POPESCU, Christine, (Christine Pullein-Thompson); Children's Writer; b. 30 Oct. 1930, London, England; m. Julian Popescu, 6 Oct. 1954, two s. two d. *Career:* mem. British House Society; PEN; Society of Authors. *Publications:* 103 children's books, 1956–93. Contributions: Magazines. *Address:* The Old Parsonage, Mellis, Eye, Suffolk IP23 8EE, England.

PORAD, Francine Joy; Poet and Painter; b. 3 Sept. 1929, Seattle, Washington, USA; m. Bernard L. Porad, 12 June 1949, three s., three d. *Education:* BFA, University of Washington, 1976. *Career:* Ed., Brussels Sprout haiku journal, 1988–95, Red Moon Anthologies, 1996; mem. Asscn of International Renku; Haiku Society of America, pres., 1993–95; National League of American Pen Women. *Publications:* many poetry books, including: Pen and Inklings, 1986; After Autumn Rain, 1987; Free of Clouds, 1989; Round Renga Round, 1990; A Mural of Leaves, 1991; Joy is My Middle Name, 1993; Waterways, 1995; Extended Wings, 1996; Fog Lifting, 1997; Let's Count the Trees (edited by Le Roy Gorman), 1998; Cur*rent, Linked Haiku, 1998; Other Rens, 2000; The Perfect Worry-stone, 2000; Other Rens, Book 2 plus Book 3, 2000; Trio of Wrens, 2000; To Find the Words (anthology, co-ed.). Contributions: Haiku journals world-wide. *Honours:* Cicada Chapbook Award, 1990; International Tanka Awards, 1991, 1992, 1993; First Prize, Poetry Society of Japan International Tanka Competition, 1993; Haiku Society of America Merit Book Awards, 1994, 2000; Haiku Oregon Pen Women Award, 1995. *Address:* 6944 SE 33rd, Mercer Island, WA 98040, USA. *E-mail:* poradf@aol.com.

PORTER, Andrew (Brian); Music Critic, Writer, Ed. and Trans; b. 26 Aug. 1928, Cape Town, South Africa. *Education:* Diocesan College, Cape Town; MA, University College, Oxford. *Career:* Music Critic, Financial Times, 1952–72, New Yorker, 1972–73, 1974–92, Observer, 1992–97, TLS, 1997–; Assoc. Ed., Opera, 1953–56; Ed., Musical Times, 1960–67; Visiting Fellow, All Souls College, Oxford, 1972–73; Ernest Bloch Prof., University of California at Berkeley, 1980–81; mem. American Musicological Society, corresponding mem., 1993–; Royal Musical Asscn. *Publications:* A Musical Season, 1974; A Music of Three Seasons, 1974–1977, 1978; Music of Three More Seasons, 1977–1980, 1981; Verdi's Macbeth: A Sourcebook (ed. with D. Rosen), 1984; Musical Events: A Chronicle, 1980–1983, 1987; Musical Events: A Chronicle, 1983–1986, 1989. Other: Trans of opera librettos by Handel, Haydn, Mozart, Rossini, Verdi, Wagner, Strauss and others into English; Librettos for contemporary operas. Contributions: books, reviews, quarterlies and journals. *Honours:* ASCAP–Deems Taylor Awards, 1975, 1978, 1981; National Music Theatre Award, 1985. *Address:* 9 Pembroke Walk, London W8 6PQ, England.

PORTER, Bernard (John); Prof. of Modern History and Writer; b. 5 June 1941, Essex, England; m. Deidre O'Hara, 29 July 1972, one s. two d. *Education:* BA, 1963, MA, PhD, 1967, Corpus Christi College, Cambridge. *Career:* Fellow, Corpus Christi College, Cambridge, 1966–68; Lecturer, 1968–78, Senior Lecturer, 1978–87, Reader, 1987–92, University of Hull; Prof. of Modern History, University of Newcastle, 1992–. *Publications:* Critics of Empire: British Radical Attitudes to Colonialism in Africa 1896–1914, 1968; The Lion's Share: A Short History of British Imperialism 1850–1970, 1976; The Refugee Question in Mid-Victorian Politics, 1979; Britain, Europe and the World 1850–1982: Delusions of Grandeur, 1983; The Origins of the Vigilant State: The London Metropolitan Police Special Branch Before the First World War, 1987; Plots and Paranoia: A History of Political Espionage in Britain 1790–1988, 1989; Britannia's Burden: The Political Development of Britain 1857–1990, 1994. Contributions: Professional journals. *Address:* c/o Dept of History, University of Newcastle, Newcastle upon Tyne, NE 7RU, England.

PORTER, Brian (Ernest); Lecturer and Writer; b. 5 Feb. 1928, Seasalter, Kent, England. *Education:* BSc, 1954, PhD, 1962, LSE. *Career:* Lecturer in Political Science, University of Khartoum, 1963–65; Lecturer, 1965–71, Senior Lecturer in International Politics, 1971–85, University College, Aberystwyth; Acting Vice-Counsel, Muscat, 1967; Hon. Lecturer in International Relations, University of Kent, Canterbury, 1984–; mem. FRHistS; Royal Institute of International Affairs. *Publications:* Britain and the Rise of Communist China, 1967; The Aberystwyth Papers: International Politics 1919–1969 (ed.), 1972; The Reason of States (co-author), 1982; Home Fires and Foreign Fields: British Social and Military Experience in the First World War (co-author), 1985; The Condition of States (co-author), 1991; Martin Wight's International Theory: The Three Traditions (co-ed.), 1991. *Honours:* Gladstone Memorial Essay Prize, 1956; Mrs Foster Watson Memorial Prize, 1962–67.

PORTER, Burton (Frederick); Prof. of Philosophy, Academic Dean and Writer; b. 22 June 1936, New York, NY, USA; m. 1st Susan Jane Porter 10 May 1966 (divorced 1974); one d.; m. 2nd Barbara Taylor Metcalf 31 Dec. 1980; one s. one step-d. *Education:* BA, University of Maryland, 1959; Postgraduate Studies, University of Oxford, 1962; PhD, St Andrews University, Scotland, 1969. *Career:* Asst Prof., University of Maryland Overseas Division, London, 1966–69; Assoc. Prof., King's College, Wilkes-Barre, Pennsylvania, 1969–71; Dept Chair and Prof. of Philosophy, Russell Sage College, Troy, New York, 1971–87; Head, Humanities and Communications Dept, Drexel University, 1987–91; Dean of Arts and Sciences, 1991–99, Prof. of Philosophy, 1999–, Western New England College, Springfield, Massachusetts; mem. American Philosophical Asscn. *Publications:* Deity and Morality, 1968; Philosophy: A Literary and Conceptual Approach, 1974; Personal Philosophy: Perspectives on Living, 1976; The Good Life: Alternatives in Ethics, 1980; Reasons for Living: A Basic Ethics, 1988; Religion and Reason, 1993; The Voice of Reason, 2001; Philosophy Through Fiction and Film, 2003. Contributions: Professional journals. *Honours:* Outstanding Educator of America, 1973. *Address:* c/o Dept of Communications and Humanities, Western New England College, Springfield, MA 01119, USA.

PORTER, Joshua Roy; Theologian and Writer; b. 1921, England. *Career:* Fellow, Chaplain and Tutor, Oriel College, Oxford and University Lecturer in Theology, University of Oxford, 1949–62; Canon and Prebendary of Wightring, Chichester Cathedral and Theological Lecturer, 1965–88; Dean, Faculty of Arts 1968–71, Dept Head and Prof. of Theology 1962–86, University of Exeter; mem. Wiccamical Canon and Prebendary of Exceit, Chichester Cathedral, 1988–2001; Society for Old Testament Study, Pres., 1983; Society of Biblical Literature; Folklore Society, Pres., 1976–79; Prayer Book Society, Vice-Chair., 1987–96. *Publications:* Eight Oxford Poets (with J. Heath-Stubbs and S. Keyes), 1941; Poetry from Oxford in War-Time (with W. Bell) 1944; World in the Heart, 1944; Promise and Fulfilment (with F. F. Bruce), 1963; Moses and Monarchy, 1963; The Extended Family in the Old Testament, 1967; A Source Book of the Bible for Teachers (with R. C. Walton), 1970; Proclamation and Presence (ed. with J. I. Durham), 1970; The Non-Juring Bishops, 1973; The Journey to the Other World (with H. R. E. Davidson), 1975; The Book of Leviticus, 1976; Animals in Folklore (ed. with W. D. M. Russell), 1978; The Monarchy, the Crown and the Church, 1978; Tradition and Interpretation (with G. W. Anderson), 1979; A Basic Introduction to the Old Testament (with R. C. Walton), 1980; Folklore Studies in the Twentieth Century (co-ed.), 1980; Divination and Oracles (with M. Loewe and C. Blacker), 1981; The Folklore of Ghosts (with H. R. E. Davidson), 1981; Israel's Prophetic Tradition (co-author), 1982; Tracts for Our Times (co-author), 1983; The Hero in Tradition and Folklore (with C. Blacker), 1984; Arabia and the Gulf: From Traditional Society to Modern States (with I. Netton), 1986; Schöpfung und Befreiung (co-author), 1989; Synodical Government in the Church of England, 1990; Christianity and Conservatism (co-author), 1990; Oil of Gladness, 1993; Boundaries and Thresholds (with H. R. E. Davidson), 1993; World Mythology, 1993; The Illustrated Guide to the Bible, 1995; Jesus Christ: The Jesus of History, the Christ of Faith, 1999; The First and Second Prayer Books of Edward VI (ed.), 1999; The Lost Bible, 2001; Supernatural Enemies (with H. R. E. Davidson), 2001; The New Illustrated Companion to the Bible, 2003. *Address:* 36 Theberton St, Barnsbury, London N1 OQX, England.

PORTER, Peter Neville Frederick, FRSL; Australian poet, writer and broadcaster; b. 16 Feb. 1929, Brisbane, Qld; m. 1st Jannice Henry 1961 (died 1974); two d.; m. 2nd Christine Berg 1991. *Education:* Church of England Grammar School Brisbane and Toowoomba Grammar School. *Career:* fmr journalist in Brisbane; came to UK 1951; worked as clerk, bookseller and advertising writer; full-time writer and broadcaster 1968–. *Publications:* Once Bitten, Twice Bitten 1961, Penguin Modern Poets, No. 2 1962, Poems, Ancient and Modern 1964, A Porter Folio 1969, The Last of England 1970, Preaching to the Converted 1972, After Martial (trans.) 1972, Jonah (with A. Boyd) 1973, The Lady and the Unicorn (with A. Boyd) 1975, Living in a Calm Country 1975, New Poetry I (co-ed.) 1975, The Cost of Seriousness 1978, English Subtitles 1981, Collected Poems (Duff Cooper Prize) 1983, Fast Forward 1984, Narcissus (with A. Boyd) 1985, The Automatic Oracle (Whitbread Poetry Award) 1987, Mars (with A. Boyd) 1988, A Porter Selected 1989, Possible Worlds 1989, The Chair of Babel 1992, Millennial Fables 1995, New Writing (ed. with A. S. Byatt) 1997, The Oxford Book of Modern Verse (ed.) 1997, The Shared Heritage: Australian and English Literature 1997, The Oxford Book of Modern Australian Verse (ed.) 1997, Dragons in Their Pleasant Places 1997, Collected Poems 1961–1999 (two vols) 1999, Max is Missing (Forward Poetry Prize 2002) 2001, Saving from the Wreck: Essays on Poetry 2001, Rivers 2002; contrib. to various publications. *Honours:* Hon. DLitt (Melbourne) 1985, (Loughborough) 1987, (Sydney) 1999, (Queensland) 2001, Queen's Gold Medal for Poetry 2002. *Address:* 42 Cleveland Square, London, W2 6DA, England (Home). *Telephone:* (20) 7262-4289 (Home). *Fax:* (20) 7262-4289 (Home). *E-mail:* peter.porter3@btopenworld.com (Home).

PORTIS, Charles McColl; Writer; b. 28 Dec. 1933, El Dorado, AR, USA. *Education:* BA, University of Arkansas, 1958. *Publications:* Fiction: Norwood, 1966; True Grit, 1968; The Dog of the South, 1979; Masters of Atlantis, 1985; Gringos, 1991. *Address:* 7417 Kingwood, Little Rock, AR 72207, USA.

PORTWAY, Christopher (John); Writer; b. 30 Oct. 1923, Halstead, Essex, England; m. Jaroslava Krupickova, 4 April 1957, one s. one d. *Career:* mem. FRGS. *Publications:* Journey to Dana, 1955; The Pregnant Unicorn, 1969; All Exits Barred, 1971; Corner Seat, 1972; Lost Vengeance, 1973; Double Circuit, 1974; The Tirana Assignment, 1974; The Anarchy Pedlars, 1976; The Great Railway Adventure, 1983; Journey Along the Spine of the Andes, 1984; The Great Travelling Adventure, 1985; Czechmate, 1987; Indian Odyssey, 1993; A Kenyan Adventure, 1993; Pedal for Your Life, 1996; A Good Pair of Legs, 1999; The World Commuter, 2001. Contributions: periodicals. *Honours:* Winston Churchill Fellow, 1993. *Address:* 22 Tower Rd, Brighton BN2 0GF, England.

POSNER, Gerald; Attorney and Writer; b. 20 May 1954, San Francisco, CA, USA; m. Trisha D. Levene, April 1984. *Education:* BA, University of California, 1975; JD, Hastings College of Law, 1978. *Career:* mem. National Writers Union; Authors' Guild; PEN. *Publications:* Mengele: The Complete Story, 1986; Warlords of Crime, 1988; Bio-Assassins, 1989; Hitler's Children, 1991; Case Closed, 1993; Citizen Perot, 1996; Killing the Dream, 1998. Contributions: New York Times; New Yorker; Chicago Tribune; US News & World Report; Talk Magazine.

POSTE, George, CBE, PhD, FRS, FRCVS, FRCPath, BVSC; British research scientist and industry executive; *CEO, Health Technology Networks*; b. 30 April 1944, Polegate, Sussex; m. Linda Suhler 1992; one s. two d. *Education:* Bristol Univ. *Career:* lecturer Royal Postgrad. Medical School, Univ. of London 1969–72; Prof. of Experimental Pathology, State Univ. of New York (SUNY) 1973–80; Vice-Pres. Research and Devt SmithKline Beecham 1980–88, Research and Devt Technologies 1989–92, Chair., Pres. Research and Devt 1992–97, Chief Science and Tech. Officer 1997–99; CEO Health Tech. Networks 2000–; partner Care Capital, Princeton 2000–; Research Prof. Univ. of Pa 1981–, Univ. of Tex. Medical Center 1986–; Fleming Fellow Lincoln Coll. Oxford 1995, Pitt Fellow Pembroke Coll. Cambridge 1996, Fellow, Hoover Inst., Stanford Univ. 2000–; mem. Human Genetics Advisory Cttee 1996–; mem. Bd Govs Center for Molecular Medicine and Genetics, Stanford Univ. 1992–; mem. Alliance for Ageing 1992–97; Jt Ed. Cell Surface Reviews 1976–83, New Horizons in Therapeutics 1984–. *Publications:* numerous reviews and papers in learned journals. *Honours:* Hon. FRCP 1993; Hon. Fellow Univ. Coll. London 1993; Hon. DSc 1987, (Sussex) 1999; Hon. LLD (Bristol) 1995, (Dundee) 1998. *Address:* Health Technology Networks, PO Box 647, Gilbertsville, PA 19525, USA (Office). *Telephone:* (610) 705-0828 (Office). *Fax:* (610) 705-0810 (Office). *E-mail:* gposte@healthtechnetwork.com (Office).

POSTER, Jem; British poet and critic. *Career:* fmr archaeologist; Dir of the creative writing diploma, Oxford Univ. Dept for Continuing Education. *Publications:* poetry: By Some Other Route 1994, Brought to Light 2001; novel: Courting Shadows 2002; criticism: Thirties Poets 1993, A Preface to Virginia Woolf 2001. *Honours:* Fellow, Kellogg Coll. *Address:* c/o Bloodaxe Books Ltd, Highgreen, Tarset, Northumberland NE48 1RP, England. *E-mail:* jem.poster@conted.ox.ac.uk.

POTTER, Jeremy (Ronald); Writer and Publisher; b. 25 April 1922, London, England; m. 11 Feb. 1950, one s. one d. *Education:* MA, Queen's College, Oxford. *Publications:* Good King Richard?, 1983; Pretenders, 1986; Independent Television in Britain, Vol. 3: Politics and Control 1968–80, 1989 and Vol. 4: Companies and Programmes 1968–80, 1990; Tennis and Oxford, 1994. Fiction: Hazard Chase, 1964; Death in Office, 1965; Foul Play, 1967; The Dance of Death, 1968; A Trail of Blood, 1970; Going West, 1972; Disgrace and Favour, 1975; Death in the Forest, 1977; The Primrose Hill Murder, 1992; The Mystery of the Campden Wonder, 1995. *Address:* The Old Pottery, Larkins Lane, Headington, Oxford OX3 9DW, England.

POTTS, Robert; British writer; *Editor, Poetry Review*. *Education:* Univ. of Oxford. *Career:* fmrly Politics Ed., TLS; poetry critic, The Guardian; judge, Geoffrey Faber Memorial Prize 1998; Jt Ed., Poetry Review 2002–. *Publications:* contrib. to The Times, The Observer, Atlantic Monthly, London Magazine, Literary Review, Scribners' British Writers' Series, BBC Radio London. *Address:* Poetry Review, The Poetry Society, 22 Betterton Street, London, WC2H 9BX, England. *Website:* www.poetrysociety.org.uk.

POULIN, Gabrielle; Writer and Poet; b. 21 June 1929, St Prosper, QC, Canada. *Education:* MA, University of Montréal; DLitt, University of Sherbrooke. *Career:* Writer-in-Residence, Ottawa Public Library, 1988; mem. Union des écrivaines et des écrivains québécois. *Publications:* Les Miroirs d'un poète: Image et reflets de Paul Éluard, 1969; Cogne la caboche, 1979, English trans. as All the Way Home, 1984; L'age de l'interrogation, 1937–52, 1980; Un cri trop grand (novel), 1980; Les Mensonges d'Isabelle (novel), 1983; La couronne d'oubli (novel), 1990; Petites fugues pour une saison sèche (poems), 1991; Le livre de déraison (novel), 1994; Mon père aussi était horloger (poems), 1996; Qu'est-ce qui passe ici si tard? (novel), 1998; La vie l'écriture (memoir), 2000. Contributions: periodicals. *Honours:* Swiss Embassy Prize, 1967; II Arts Council of Canada Grants, 1968–83, 1985; Champlain Literary Prize, 1979; Carleton Literary Prize, Ottawa, 1983; Alliance Française Literary Prize, 1984; Salon du Livre de Toronto Literary Prize, 1994. *Address:* 1997 Ave Quincy, Ottawa, ON K1J 6B4, Canada.

POULIN, Jacques; Writer; b. 23 Sept. 1937, Saint-Gédéon-de-Beauce, QC, Canada. *Education:* Licence en orientation professionnelle, Université Laval, 1960. *Career:* mem. Union des écrivaines et des écrivains québécois. *Publications:* Mon cheval pour un royaume, 1967, English trans. as My Horse for a Kingdom, 1979; Jimmy, 1969, English trans., 1979; La coeur de la baleine bleue, 1970, English trans. as The Heart of the Blue Whale, 1979; Faites de beaux rêves, 1974; Les Grandes marées, 1978, English trans. as Spring Tides, 1986; La tournée d'automne, 1993. *Honours:* Prix de La Presse, 1974; Gov.-Gen.'s Literary Award, 1978; Prix David, 1995. *Address:* c/o Union des écrivaines et des écrivains québécois, La Maison des écrivains, 3492 ave Laval, Montréal, QC H2X 3C8, Canada.

POURER, Aleksandr Mikhailovich (see Galin, Aleksandr).

POURNELLE, Jerry Eugene, (Wade Curtis); Writer, Lecturer and Consultant; b. 7 Aug. 1933, Shreveport, LA, USA. *Education:* University of Iowa, 1953–54; BS, 1955, MS, 1957, PhD, Psychology, 1960, PhD, Political Science, 1964, University of Washington. *Career:* mem. Operations Research Society of America, fellow; American Asscn for the Advancement of Science, fellow; SFWA, pres., 1974. *Publications:* Red Heroin (as Wade Curtis), 1969; The Strategy of Technology: Winning the Decisive War (with Stefan Possony), 1970; Red Dragon (as Wade Curtis), 1971; A Spaceship for the King, 1973; Escape From the Planet of the Apes (novelization of screenplay), 1973; The Mote in God's Eye (with Larry Niven), 1974; 20/20 Vision (ed.), 1974; Birth of Fire, 1976; Inferno (with Larry Niven), 1976; West of Honor, 1976; High Justice (short stories), 1977; The Mercenary, 1977; Lucifer's Hammer (with Larry Niven), 1977; Exiles to Glory, 1978; Black Holes (ed.), 1979; A Step Further Out (non-fiction), 1980; Janisseries, 1980; Oath of Fealty (with Larry Niven), 1981; Clan and Crown (with Roland Green), 1982; There Will Be War (co-ed.), 1983; Mutual Assured Survival (with Dean Ing), 1984; Men of War (co-ed.), 1984; Blood and Iron (co-ed.), 1984; Day of the Tyrant (co-ed.), 1985; Footfall (with Larry Niven), 1985; Warriors (co-ed.), 1986; Imperial Stars: The Stars at War, Republic and Empire (co-ed.), 2 vols, 1986–87; Guns of Darkness (co-ed.), 1987; Storms of Victory (with Roland Green), 1987; Legacy of Hereot (with Larry Niven), 1987; Prince of Mercenaries, 1989; The Gripping Hand (with Larry Niven), 1993. Contributions: Magazines.

POWELL, Geoffrey Stewart, (Tom Angus); Soldier, Bookseller and Writer; b. 25 Dec. 1914, Scarborough, Yorkshire, England; m. Felicity Wadsworth, 15 July 1944, one s. one d. *Education:* Scarborough College, 1923–31; Army Staff College, 1945–46; United States Command and General Staff College, 1950–51; Joint Services Staff College, 1953–54; BA, Open University, 1981. *Publications:* The Green Howards, 1968; The Kandyan Wars, 1973; Men at Arnhem, 1978; Suez: The Double War (with Roy Fullick), 1979; The Book of Campden, 1982; The Devil's Birthday: The Bridges to Arnhem, 1984; Plumer: The Soldier's General, 1990; The Green Howards: 300 Years of Service, 1992; Buller: A Scapegoat: A Life of General Sir Redvers Buller, VC, 1994. Contributions: journals and magazines. *Honours:* FRHistS, 1989. *Address:* Chipping Campden, Goucestershire GL55 6AE, England.

POWELL, Neil Ashton, BA, MPhil; British writer and poet; b. 11 Feb. 1948, London, England. *Education:* Univ. of Warwick. *Career:* mem. Soc. of Authors. *Publications:* Suffolk Poems, 1975; At the Edge, 1977; Carpenters of Light, 1979; Out of Time, 1979; A Season of Calm Weather, 1982; Selected Poems of Fulke Greville (ed.), 1990; True Colours: New and Selected Poems, 1991; Unreal City, 1992; The Stones on Thorpeness Beach, 1994; Roy Fuller: Writer and Society, 1995; Gay Love Poetry (ed.), 1997; The Language of Jazz, 1997; Selected Poems, 1998; George Crabbe: An English Life, 2004; A Halfway House, 2004. Contributions: anthologies, newspapers, reviews, and journals. *Honours:* Eric Gregory Award 1969. *Address:* c/o Carcanet Press, Fourth Floor, Alliance House, Cross Street, Manchester M2 7AP, England.

POWELL, Padgett; Prof. of Creative Writing and Writer; b. 25 April 1952, Gainesville, FL, USA; m. Sidney Wade, 22 May 1984, two d. *Education:* BA, College of Charleston 1975; MA, University of Houston, 1982. *Career:* Prof. of Creative Writing, University of Florida, Gainesville, 1984–; mem. PEN; Authors' Guild; Writers Guild of America, East. *Publications:* Edisto (novel), 1984; A Woman Named Drown (novel), 1987; Typical (short stories), 1991; Edisto Revisited (novel), 1996; Aliens of Affection (short stories), 1998; Mrs Hollingsworth's Men (novel), 2000. Contributions: periodicals including: Harper's Magazine; New Yorker; Paris Review; Travel and Leisure. *Honours:* Best Book Citation, Time Magazine, 1984; Whiting Foundation Writers' Award, 1986; American Acad. and Institute of Arts and Letters Rome Fellowship in Literature 1987. *Literary Agent:* Cynthia Cannell, 833 Madison Ave, Suite 3-C, New York, NY 10021, USA. *Address:* Dept of English, University of Florida, Gainesville, FL 32611, USA.

POWELL, Talmage, (Jack McCready); Writer; b. 4 Oct. 1920, Hendersonville, NC, USA. *Education:* University of North Carolina. *Publications:* Cabins & Castles, 1981; Western Ghosts, 1990; New England Ghosts, 1990; Murder for Halloween, 1994; Encyclopedia Mysteriosa, 1994; Wild Game, 1994; Six-Gun Ladies: Stories of Women on the American Western Frontier, 1996. Contributions: anthologies, films, and television. *Address:* 33 Caledonia Rd, Kenilworth, Asheville, NC 28803, USA.

POWER, Susan; Writer; b. 12 Oct. 1961, Chicago, IL, USA. *Education:* Radcliffe College; JD, Harvard University Law School; MFA, University of Iowa Writers Workshop. *Career:* mem. Standing Rock Sioux Reservation. *Publications:* Fiction: The Grass Dancer, 1994; Strong Heart Society, 1997. Contributions: journals including: Atlantic Monthly; Paris Review; Ploughshares; Story; Short stories to anthologies. *Honours:* Award for First Fiction, Ernest Hemingway Foundation, 1995; Iowa Arts Fellowship; James Michener Fellowship; Bunting Institute Fellowship; Alfred Hodder Fellowship; Other fellowships. *Address:* c/o Penguin Putnam, 375 Hudson St, New York, NY 10014, USA.

POWERS, M. L. (see Tubb, Edwin Charles).

POWERS, Richard; American author; b. 1957; m. Jane Powers. *Career:* teacher of creative writing, Univ. of Illinois. *Publications:* Three Farmers on Their Way to a Dance (Richard and Hinda Rosenthal Foundation Award, American Acad. and Institute of Arts and Letters, PEN/Hemingway Foundation special citation) 1985, Prisoner's Dilemma 1988, The Gold Bug Variations 1991, Operation Wandering Soul 1993, Galatea 2.2 1995, Gain (American Soc. of Historians James Fenimore Cooper Prize 1999) 1998, Plowing the Dark (American Academy and Institute of Arts and Letters Vursell Prize) 2000, The Time of Our Singing (WHSmith Literary Award 2004) 2003; contrib. to journals and magazines. *Honours:* John D. and Catherine T. MacArthur Foundation Grant 1989. *Literary Agent:* Gunther Stuhlmann, Box 276, Beckett, MA 01223, USA.

POWERS, Thomas (Moore); Writer and Ed.; b. 12 Dec. 1940, New York, NY, USA; m. Candace Molloy 21 Aug. 1965; three d. *Education:* BA, Yale University, 1964. *Career:* Reporter, Rome Daily American, 1965–67, United Press International, 1967–70; Ed.-Founding Partner, Steerforth Press, South Royalton, Vermont, 1993–; mem. Council on Foreign Relations; PEN American Center. *Publications:* Diana: The Making of a Terrorist, 1971; The War at Home, 1973; The Man Who Kept the Secrets: Richard Helms and the CIA, 1979; Thinking About the Next War, 1982; Total War: What It Is, How It Got That Way, 1988; Heisenberg's War: The Secret History of the German Bomb, 1993; The Confirmation, 2000; Intelligence Wars: American Secret History from Hitler to Al Qaeda, 2003. Contributions: New York Review of Books; London Review of Books. *Honours:* Pulitzer Prize for National Reporting, 1971. *Literary Agent:* Janklow & Nesbit Associates, 445 Park Ave, New York, NY 10022, USA. *Address:* 106 Chelsea St, South Royalton, VT 05068, USA.

POWNALL, David; Author and Dramatist; b. 19 May 1938, Liverpool, England; m. 1st Glenys Elsie Jones, 1961, divorced, one s.; m. 2nd Mary Ellen Ray, 1981, one s.; m. 3rd Alex Sutton, 1993, one s. *Education:* BA, University of Keele, 1960. *Career:* Resident Writer, Century Theatre, 1970–72; Resident Playwright, Duke's Playhouse, Lancaster, 1972–75; Founder-Resident Writer, Paines Plough Theatre, London, 1975–80; mem. FRSL. *Publications:* Fiction: The Raining Tree War, 1974; African Horse, 1975; The Dream of Chief Crazy Horse, 1975; God Perkins, 1977; Light on a Honeycomb, 1978; Beloved Latitudes, 1981; The White Cutter, 1989; The Gardener, 1990; Stagg and His Mother, 1991; The Sphinx and the Sybarites, 1994; The Catalogue of Men. Plays: Over 40 stage plays, 1969–98; Radio and television plays. *Honours:* Edinburgh Festival Fringe Awards, 1976, 1977; Giles Cooper Awards, 1981, 1985; John Whiting Award, Arts Council of Great Britain, 1982; Sony Gold and Silver Awards for Original Radio Drama, 1994, 1995, 1996; Hon. DLitt, Keele University, 2001. *Literary Agent:* Johnson & Alcock Ltd, Clerkenwell House, 45–47 Clerkenwell Green, London EC1R 0HT, England.

POYER, Joseph (Joe) John, BA; writer, editor and publisher; b. 30 Nov. 1939, Battle Creek, Michigan, USA; m. Bonnie Prichard 1987. *Education:* Michigan State University. *Career:* Publisher/Ed., Safe and Secure Living, International Military Review, International Naval Review. *Publications:* Fiction: North Cape, 1968; Balkan Assignment, 1971; Chinese Agenda, 1972; Shooting of the Green, 1973; The Contract, 1978; Tunnel War, 1979; Vengeance 10, 1980; Devoted Friends, 1982; Time of War, 2 vols, 1983, 1985. Non-Fiction: The 45–70 Springfield, 1991; US Winchester Trench and Riot Guns, 1993; Pocket Guide 45–70 Springfield, 1994; The M1 Garand, 1936 to 1957, 1995; The SKS Carbine, 1997; The M14-type Rifles, 1997; The SAFN Battle Rifle, 1998; The Swedish Mauser Rifles, 1999; The M16/AR15 Rifles, 2000, The Model 1903 Springfield Rifle and its Variations 2001, The American Krag Rifle and Carbine 2002, Swiss Magazine Loading Rifles 1869–1958 2003, The AK-47 and AK-74 Rifles and Their Variations 2004; contrib. to journals. *Address:* PO Box 1027, Tustin, CA 92681, USA.

PRABHU, Avatar (see Crasta, Richard).

PRALL, Stuart Edward; academic and writer; b. 2 June 1929, Saginaw, Michigan, USA; m. Naomi Shafer 1958; one s. one d. *Education:* BA, Michigan State University, 1951; MA, University of Rhode Island, 1953; University of Manchester, England, 1953–54; PhD, Columbia University, 1960. *Career:* Queens College and Graduate School and University Center, CUNY, 1955–58, 1960–2001; Newark State College, NJ, 1958–60; Exec. Officer, PhD Program in History, Graduate School and University Center, CUNY, 1988–94; mem. North American Conference on British Studies. *Publications:* The Agitation for Law Reform during the Puritan Revolution, 1640–1660, 1966; The Puritan Revolution: A Documentary History, 1968; The Bloodless Revolution: England, 1688, 1972; A History of England, 1991; Church and State in Tudor and Stuart England, 1993; The Puritan Revolution and the English Civil War, 2002. Contributions: The Development of Equity in Tudor England; American Journal of Legal History. *Honours:* Fulbright Scholar, University of Manchester, 1953–54; FRHistS, 1978. *Address:* 7050 Owl's Nest Terrace, Bradenton, FL 34203, USA; 2791 Rte 760, Bethel, NB E5C 1T2, Canada.

PRAMOEDYA ANANTA TOER; novelist, essayist and critic; b. 20 Feb. 1925, Blora, East Java, Indonesia; m. *Career:* worked with Domei Japanese news agency, –1945; manuscript of first book, Sepulah Kepala Nika (Ten Chiefs of Nika), written in 1945, lost before printing; 2nd Lieut., Indonesian revolution, Bekasi, east of Jakarta; with Voice of Free Indonesia producing Indonesian language magazine; arrested by Dutch, July 1947; wrote first major works in Bukit Duri gaol; ed., Indonesian Library of Congress, –1951; ed., Modern Indonesian Literature dept, Balai Pustaka publishing house, ed. magazines, Indonesia and Kunang-kunang, 1951–; leading figure in Lekkra, Indonesian Communist Party cultural asscn, 1958–; arrested on order of Gen. A. H. Nasution in connection with book on overseas Chinese, 1960–61; ed., Lentera section of newspaper Bintang Timur, 1962–65; lecturer, Indonesian language and literature, Univ. of Res Publika; teacher at Dr Abdul Rivai Academy for Journalism; co-f., Multatuli Literature Academy; arrested and imprisoned without trial, Buni island, 1966–80; novels banned, May 1981. *Publications:* Krandji-Bekasi Djatuh, 1947; Perburuan (The Fugitive), 1950; Keluarga Gerilya, 1950; Subuh: Tjerita-Tjerita Pendek Revolusi (short stories), 1950; Percikan Revolusi (short stories), 1950; Mereka Jang Dilumpuhkan, 1951; Bukan Pasar Malam (A Heap of Ashes), 1951; Di Tepi Kali Bekasi, 1951; Dia Yang Menyerah, 1951; Cerita dari Blora (short stories), 1952; Gulat di Djakarta, 1953; Midah–Si Manis Bergigi Emas (novel), 1954; Korupsi (novel), 1954; Cerita dari Djakarta (short stories), 1957; Cerita Tjalon Arang, 1957; Suatu Peristiwa di Banten Selatan, 1958; Sekali Peristawa di Bengen Selatan, 1958; Hoa Kiau di Indonesia, 1960; Panggil Aku Kartini Saja I & II, 1962; Realisme Sosialis & Sastra Indonesia, 1963; Bumi Manusia (This Earth of Mankind), 1980; Anak Semua Bangsa (Child of All Nations), 1980; Sikap dan Peran Kaum Intelektual di Dunia Ketiga, 1982; Tempo Doeloe (ed.), 1982; Gadis Pantai (The Girl from the Coast), 1982; Jejak Langkah (Footsteps), 1985; Hikayat Siti Mariah (ed.), 1987; Rumah Kaca (House of Glass), 1988; Memoar Oei Tjoe Tat (ed.), 1995; Nyanyi Sunyi Seorang Bisu I, 1995; Arus Balik, 1995; Nyanyi Sunyi Seorang Bisu II, 1997; Tales from Djakarta: Caricatures of Circumstances and Their Human Beings, 1999; The Mute's Soliloquy: A Memoir, 2000. *Honours:* Balai Putaska literary prize; Ramon Magsaysay Award for Journalism, 1995. *Address:* c/o Penguin Books Ltd, 80 Strand, London WC2R 0RL, England.

PRANTERA, Amanda; Author; b. 23 April 1942, England. *Publications:* Strange Loop, 1984; The Cabalist, 1985; Conversations with Lord Byron on Perversion, 163 Years After His Lordship's Death, 1987; The Side of the Moon, 1991; Pronto-Zoe, 1992; The Young Italians, 1993; Spoiler, 2003. *Address:* Jane Conway Gordon, 1 Old Compton St, London, W1V 5PH, England.

PRASHAD, Vijay, PhD; writer and journalist; b. Kolkata, India. *Education:* Univ. of Chicago, USA. *Career:* Assoc. Prof. and Dir, International Studies Program, Trinity College, Hartford, CT, USA; Ed., Amerasia Journal; mem. Center for Third World Organizing (board mem.); Forum of Indian Leftists (co-founder). *Publications:* The Karma of Brown Folk, 2000; Untouchable Freedom: A Social History of a Dalit Community, 2000; Everybody was Kung Fu Fighting: Afro-Asian Connections and the Myth of Cultural Purity, 2002; The American Scheme: Three Essays, 2002; War Against the

Planet: The Fifth Afghan War, Imperialism and Other Assorted Fundamentalism, 2002; Fat Cats and Running Dogs: The Enron Stage of Capitalism, 2002; Keeping Up with the Dow Joneses: Stocks, Jails, Welfare, 2003. Contributions: Colorlines; Himal South Asia; Frontline; www.truthindia.com; Little India; ZNET. *Address:* c/o Trinity College, Hartford, CT 06106, USA. *Telephone:* (870) 297-2518. *E-mail:* vijay .prashad@trincoll.edu.

PRATCHETT, Terence (Terry) David John, OBE; British writer; b. 28 April 1948, Beaconsfield, Bucks.; m. Lyn Marian Purves 1968; one d. *Career:* journalist 1965–80; Press Officer Cen. Electricity Generating Bd 1980–87; Chair. Soc. of Authors 1994–95. *Publications:* Discworld series: The Dark Side of the Sun 1976, Strata 1981, The Colour of Magic 1983, The Light Fantastic 1986, Equal Rites 1987, Mort 1987, Sourcery 1989, Wyrd Sisters 1988, Pyramids (BSFA Award for best novel) 1989, Eric 1989, Guards! Guards! 1989, Moving Pictures 1990, Reaper Man 1991, Witches Abroad 1991, Small Gods 1992, Lords and Ladies 1993, Men at Arms 1993, The Streets of Ankh-Morpork (with Stephen Briggs) 1993, Soul Music 1994, Interesting Times 1994, The Discworld Companion (with Stephen Briggs) 1994, Maskerade 1995, Discworld Map (with Stephen Briggs) 1995, Feet of Clay 1996, Hogfather 1996, The Pratchett Portfolio (with Paul Kidby) 1996, Jingo 1997, The Last Continent 1998, Carpe Jugulum 1998, A Tourist Guide to Lancre (with Stephen Briggs and Paul Kidby) 1998, The Fifth Elephant 1999, Death's Domain (with Paul Kidby) 1999, The Truth 2000, Nanny Ogg's Cookbook (with Stephen Briggs, Tina Hannan and Paul Kidby) 2000, The Last Hero 2001, Thief of Time 2001, Night Watch 2002, The Science of the Discworld I, II, III (with others) 2002, Monstrous Regiment 2003, The Wee Free Men 2003, A Hat Full of Sky 2004, Going Postal 2004; other fiction: The Carpet People 1971, The Unadulterated Cat (with Gray Jolliffe) 1989, Truckers 1989, Diggers 1990, Wings 1990, Good Omens: The Nice and Accurate Predictions of Agnes Nutter, Witch (with Neil Gaiman) 1990, Only You Can Save Mankind 1992, Johnny and the Dead 1993, Johnny and the Bomb 1996, The Amazing Maurice and his Educated Rodents (Carnegie Medal) 2001; other: short stories. *Honours:* Hon. DLitt (Warwick Univ.) 1999. *Literary Agent:* Colin Smythe, PO Box 6, Gerrards Cross, Buckinghamshire SL9 8XA, England. *Telephone:* (1753) 886000. *Website:* www.terrypratchettbooks.com.

PRATLEY, Gerald Arthur, OC; Writer and Teacher; b. 3 Sept. 1923, London, England; three d. *Education:* Diploma in the Teaching of Film, Queen's University, 1949. *Career:* Co-founder and Pres., Toronto Film Society, 1948–55; Film Critic, Commentator and Broadcaster, CBC Network Radio, Toronto, 1948–75; Chair., Toronto and District Film Council, 1952–57; Dir., Canadian Film Institute, Ottawa, 1958–60; Film Time, CFRB Radio, 1965–70; Dir, Film Programming, Centennial Commission, Ottawa, 1966–67; Dir, Programmer, Little Cinema, Toronto, 1968–69; Chair., International Jury, Canadian Film Awards, 1968–78; Founder, Dir, Ontario Film Institute, 1968–90; University teaching positions, 1968–99; Film Critic, Canada AM, 1970–75; Dir, Stratford International Film Festival, Stratford, Ontario, 1970–76; Programmer, Moderator, International Film Week, Bowling Green State University, Ohio, 1992–99; Ministry of Citizenship, Judge, Ceremonial, 1996–2002; Assoc. Ed., Kinema, University of Waterloo, 1993–; mem. Arts and Letters Club; St Georges Society; Royal Commonwealth Society; Churchill Society; Canadian Motion Picture Pioneers; Writers' Guild of Canada; Toronto Press Club; Acad. of Canadian Cinema and Television. *Publications:* The Cinema of John Frankenheimer, 1970; The Cinema of Otto Preminger, 1972; The Cinema of David Lean, 1973; The Cinema of John Huston, 1975; Torn Sprockets: The Uncertain Projection of the Canadian Film, 1987; The Films of John Frankenheimer, 1998. Contributions: periodicals. *Honours:* Order of Canada, 1984; ACTRA Writers' Guild, The Writers' Block, 'A Friend of Canadian Screenwriters Through the Years', Toronto, 1987; Hon. DLitt, York University, Toronto, 1991; Canada 125th Anniversary Commemorative Medal, 1992; Canadian Film Celebration Achievement Award, Calgary, 1992; Hon. Doctorates of Letters, University of Waterloo, 1993, Bowling Green State University, 1994; Toronto Film Critics' Asscn Award for 'Outstanding Contribution to the Advancement of Cinema', 1998; Canadian Acad. of Cinema and Television, Special Genie Award, 2001. *Address:* 350 Front Street, Apt 606, Belleville, ON K8N 5M5, Canada.

PRAWER, Siegbert Salomon; academic and writer; b. 15 Feb. 1925, Cologne, Germany; m. Helga Alice Schaefer 1949; two s. (one deceased) two d. *Education:* Jesus College, Cambridge; Christ's College, Cambridge; Charles Oldham Shakespeare Scholar, 1945, MA, 1950, LittD, 1962, Cantab; PhD, University of Birmingham, 1953; MA, 1969, DLitt, 1969, Oxon. *Career:* Asst Lecturer to Senior Lecturer, University of Birmingham, 1948–63; Prof. of German, Westfield College, University of London, 1964–69; Taylor Prof. of German Language and Literature, 1969–86, Prof. Emeritus, University of Oxford; Professorial Fellow, 1969–86, Dean of Degrees, 1978–93, Supernumerary Fellow, 1986–90, Hon. Fellow, 1990, Queen's College, Oxford; Fulbright Exchange Scholar, 1956–57; various visiting professorships and fellowships; mem. British Acad., fellow; British Comparative Literature Asscn, pres., 1984–87, hon. fellow, 1989; Hon. fellow, Jesus College, Cambridge; Deutsche Akademie für Sprache und Dichtung, corresponding fellow; English Goethe Society, pres., 1990–94; MLA of America, hon. mem. *Publications:* German Lyric Poetry, 1952; Mörike und seine Leser, 1960; Heine's Buch der Lieder: A Critical Study, 1960; Heine: The Tragic Satirist, 1962; The Penguin Book of Lieder (ed.), 1964; Essays in German Language, Culture and Society (ed. with L. W. Forster), 1969; The Romantic Period in Germany (ed.), 1970; Seventeen Modern German Poets (ed.), 1971; Comparative Literary Studies: An Introduction, 1973; Karl Marx and World Literature, 1976; Caligari's Children: The Film as Tale of Terror, 1980; Heine's Jewish Comedy: A Study of His Portraits of Jews and Judaism, 1983; Frankenstein's Island: England and the English in the Writings of Heinrich Heine, 1986; Israel at Vanity Fair: Jews and Judaism in the Writings of W. M. Thackeray, 1992; The Cabinet of Dr Caligari (co-ed. of German screenplay), 1996; Breeches and Metaphysics: Thackeray's German Discourse, 1997; W. M. Thackeray's European Sketch Books: A Study of Literary and Graphic Portraiture, 2000; Sternberg's The Blue Angel, 2002; Herzog's Nosferatu, 2004. Contributions: scholarly publications; TLS. *Honours:* Goethe Medal, 1973; Isaac Deutscher Memorial Prize, 1977; Hon. DPhil, University of Cologne, 1984; Friendrich Gundolf Prize, 1986; Hon. DLitt, University of Birmingham, 1988; Gold Medal, German Goethe Society, 1995. *Address:* 9 Hawkswell Gardens, Oxford OX2 7EX, England.

PRESCOTT, Casey (see Morris, Janet Ellen).

PRESCOTT, Richard Chambers; Poet and Writer; b. 1 April 1952, Houston, Texas, USA; m. Sarah Elisabeth Grace, 13 Oct. 1981. *Publications:* The Sage, 1975; Moonstar, 1975; Neuf Songes (Nine Dreams), 1976; The Carouse of Soma, 1977; Lions and Kings, 1977; Allah Wake Up, 1978; Night Reaper, 1979; Dragon Tales, 1983; Dragon Dreams, 1986; Dragon Prayers, 1988; Dragon Songs, 1988; Dragon Maker, 1989; Dragon Thoughts, 1990; Tales of Recognition, 1991; Kings and Sages, 1991; Dragon Sight: A Cremation Poem, 1992; Three Waves, 1992; Years of Wonder, 1992; Dream Appearances, 1992; Remembrance, Recognition and Return, 1992; Spare Advice, 1992; The Imperishable, 1993; The Dark Deitess, 1993; Disturbing Delights: Waves of the Great Goddess, 1993; The Immortal: Racopa and the Rooms of Light, 1993; Hanging Baskets, 1993; Writer's Block and Other Gray Matters, 1993; The Resurrection of Quantum Joe, 1993; The Horse and the Carriage, 1993; Kalee Bhava: The Goddess and Her Moods, 1995; Because of Atma, 1995; The Skills of Kalee, 1995; Measuring Sky without Ground, 1996; Kalee: The Allayer of Sorrows, 1996; The Goddess and the God Man, 1996; Living Sakti: Attempting Quick Knowing in Perpertual Perception and Continuous Becoming, 1997; The Mirage and the Mirror, 1998; Inherent Solutions to Spiritual Obscurations, 1999; The Ancient Method, 1999; Quantum Kamakala, 2000. Contributions: articles and essays to professional publications. *Address:* 8617 188th St SW, Edmonds, WA 98026, USA.

PRESNYAKOV, Oleg; playwright; b. Sverdlovsk, Siberia, USSR. *Career:* taught literary theory and psychology, Ekaterinburg; co-f., Gorky Urals State Univ. youth theatre; writes and produces plays with brother, Vladimir Presnyakov; connected with New Writing Project, Russia. *Publications:* with Vladimir Presnyakov: Set-2, We Shall Overcome 2002, Terrorism 2002, Plenniye Dukhi (Captive Spirits) 2003, Playing the Victim 2003. *Literary Agent:* Judy Daish Associates Ltd, 2 St Charles Place, London, W10 6EG, England. *Telephone:* (20) 8964-8811. *Fax:* (20) 8964-8966.

PRESNYAKOV, Vladimir; playwright; b. Sverdlovsk, Siberia, USSR. *Career:* taught literary theory and psychology, Ekaterinburg; co-f., Gorky Urals State Univ. youth theatre; writes and produces plays with brother, Oleg Presnyakov; connected with New Writing Project, Russia. *Publications:* with Oleg Presnyakov: Set-2, We Shall Overcome 2002, Terrorism 2002, Plenniye Dukhi (Captive Spirits) 2003, Playing the Victim 2003. *Literary Agent:* Judy Daish Associates Ltd, 2 St Charles Place, London, W10 6EG, England. *Telephone:* (20) 8964-8811. *Fax:* (20) 8964-8966.

PRESS, John Bryant; Poet and Writer; b. 11 Jan. 1920, Norwich, England; m. Janet Crompton, 20 Dec. 1947, one s. one d. *Education:* Corpus Christi College, Cambridge. *Career:* mem. FRSL. *Publications:* The Fire and the Fountain, 1955; The Chequer'd Shade, 1958; A Map of Modern English Verse, 1969; The Lengthening Shadows, 1971; John Betjeman, 1974; Poets of World War ll, 1984; A Girl with Beehive Hair, 1986. Contributions: Encounter; Southern Review; Art International. *Honours:* RSL Heinemann Award, 1959; First Prize, Cheltenham Poetry Festival, 1959. *Address:* 5 S Parade, Frome, Somerset BA11 1EJ, England.

PRESTON, Ivy Alice Kinross; Writer; b. 11 Nov. 1913, Timaru, Canterbury, New Zealand; m. Percival Edward James Preston, 14 Oct. 1937, two s. two d. *Career:* mem. South Canterbury Writers Guild; New Zealand Women Writers Society; South Island Writers Asscn; Romance Writers of America; Romantic Novelists Asscn, London. *Publications:* The Silver Stream (autobiog.), 1958; Hospital on the Hill, 1967; Voyage of Destiny, 1974; The House Above the Bay, 1976; Fair Accuser, 1985; Stranger From the Sea, 1987. Other: 40 romance novels. Contributions: many publications. *Address:* 95 Church St, Timaru, South Canterbury, New Zealand.

PRESTON, Paul, CBE, MA, DPhil, FRHistS; British acdemic; *Professor of International History, London School of Economics*; b. 21 July 1946, Liverpool; m. Gabrielle P. Ashford-Hodges 1983; two s. *Education:* St Edward's Coll. Liverpool, Oriel Coll. Oxford and Univ. of Reading. *Career:* Research Fellow, Centre for Mediterranean Studies, Rome 1973–74; Lecturer in History, Univ. of Reading 1974–75; Lecturer in Modern History,

Queen Mary Coll. London 1975–79, Reader 1979–85, Prof. of History 1985–91; Prof. of Int. History, LSE 1991–; regular contrib. to Times Literary Supplement; columnist in ABC, Diario 16 and El País, Madrid. *Publications:* The Coming of the Spanish Civil War 1978, The Triumph of Democracy in Spain 1986, The Spanish Civil War 1986, The Politics of Revenge 1990, Franco: A Biography 1993, Las tres Españas del 36 1998, Comrades: Portraits from the Spanish Civil War 1999, Juan Carlos: A People's King 2004. *Honours:* Comendador, Orden del Mérito Civil (Spain) 1987. *Address:* Department of International History, London School of Economics, Houghton Street, London, WC2A 2AE (Office); 10 Woodland Gardens, Muswell Hill, London, N10 3UA, England (Home). *Telephone:* (20) 7955-7107 (Office); (20) 8883-4058 (Home). *Fax:* (20) 7955-7107 (Office); (20) 8482-9865 (Home). *Website:* www.lse.ac.uk (Office).

PRESTON, Peter John; Journalist, Ed. and Newspaper Exec; b. 23 May 1938, England; m. Jean Mary Burrell, 1962, two s. two d. *Education:* MA, English Literature, St John's College, Oxford. *Career:* Political Reporter, 1963–64, Education Correspondent, 1965–66, Diary Ed., 1966–68, Features Ed., 1968–72, Production Ed., 1972–75, Ed., 1975–95, The Guardian; British Exec. Chair., International Press Institute, 1988–; Ed.-in-Chief and Chair., The Guardian and The Observer, 1995–96; Non-Exec. Dir, Guardian Media Group, 1996–98; Dir, Guardian Foundation, 1997–. *Publications:* 51st State (novel), 1998. Contributions: newspapers and journals. *Honours:* Hon. DLitt, Loughborough University, 1982; Hon. Doctorate, University of Essex, 1994. *Address:* c/o The Guardian and The Observer, 119 Farringdon Rd, London EC1R 3ER, England.

PRESTON, Richard McCann; Writer; b. 5 Aug. 1954, Cambridge, Massachusetts, USA; m. 11 May 1985. *Education:* BA, summa cum laude, Pomona College, 1977; PhD, English and American Literature, Princeton University, 1983. *Career:* Lecturer in English, Princeton University, 1983; Visiting Fellow, Princeton University Council of the Humanities, 1994–95; mem. Authors' Guild. *Publications:* First Light, 1987; American Steel, 1991; The Hot Zone, 1994; Cobra's Eye, 1997. Contributions: newspapers and magazines. *Honours:* American Institute of Physics Science Writing Award, 1988; Asteroid 3686 named 'Preston', 1989; AAAS, Westinghouse Award, 1992; MIT McDermott Award, 1993. *Literary Agent:* Janklow & Nesbit Associates, 445 Park Ave, New York, NY 10022, USA.

PREUSS, Paul F.; Writer; b. 7 March 1942, Albany, GA, USA; m. 1st Marsha May Pettit, 1963, one d.; m. 2nd Karen Reiser, 1973; m. 3rd Debra Turner, 1993. *Education:* BA, cum laude, Yale University, 1966. *Career:* mem. Northern California Science Writers Asscn; SFWA; Bay Area Book Reviewers' Asscn. *Publications:* The Gates of Heaven, 1980; Re-entry, 1981; Broken Symmetries, 1983; Human Error, 1985; Venus Prime series (with Arthur C. Clarke), 1987–91; Starfire, 1988; The Ultimate Dinosaur, 1992; Core, 1993; Secret Passages, 1997. Contributions: books and newspapers; New York Review of Science Fiction. *Address:* 304 Donahue St, Sausalito, CA 94965, USA.

PRICE, (Alan) Anthony, MA; writer, journalist and editor; b. 16 Aug. 1928, Hertfordshire, England; m. Yvonne Ann Stone 1953; two s. one d. *Education:* Merton College, Oxford. *Career:* Ed., The Oxford Times, 1972–88. *Publications:* The Labryinth Makers, 1970; The Alamut Ambush, 1971; Colonel Butler's Wolf, 1972; October Men, 1973; Other Paths to Glory, 1974; Our Man in Camelot, 1975; War Game, 1976; The '44 Vintage, 1978; Tomorrow's Ghost, 1979; The Hour of the Donkey, 1980; Soldier No More, 1981; The Old Vengeful, 1982; Gunner Kelly, 1983; Sion Crossing, 1984; Here Be Monsters, 1985; For the Good of the State, 1986; A New Kind of War, 1987; A Prospect of Vengeance, 1988; The Memory Trap, 1989; The Eyes of the Fleet, 1990. *Honours:* CWA Silver Dagger 1970, Gold Dagger 1974, Swedish Acad. of Detection Prize 1978. *Address:* Wayside Cottage, Horton cum Studley, Oxford OX33 1AW, England.

PRICE, Glanville; academic and writer; b. 16 June 1928, Rhaeadr, Wales; m. Christine Winifred Thurston 1954; three s. one d. *Education:* BA, 1949, MA, 1952, University of Wales Bangor; Dr de l'Université de Paris, 1956. *Career:* Prof. of French, University of Stirling, 1967–72; Prof. of French, 1972–92, Research Prof., 1992–95, Prof. Emeritus, 1995–, University of Wales Aberystwyth; mem. MHRA, chair., 1979–90; Philological Society. *Publications:* The Present Position of Minority Languages in Western Europe, 1969; The French Language, Present and Past, 1971; The Year's Work in Modern Language Studies (co-ed.), 1972–92; William, Count of Orange: Four Old French Epics (ed.), 1975; Romance Linguistics and the Romance Languages (with Kathryn F. Bach), 1977; The Languages of Britain, 1984; Ireland and the Celtic Connection, 1987; An Introduction to French Pronunciation, 1991; A Comprehensive French Grammar, 1992; The Celtic Connection (ed.), 1992; Hommages offerts à Maria Manoliu (ed. with Coman Lupu), 1994; Encyclopedia of the Languages of Europe (ed.), 1998; Languages in Britain and Ireland, 2000. Contributions: Professional journals. *Address:* c/o Dept of European Languages, University of Wales Aberystwyth, Ceredigion SY23 3DY, Wales.

PRICE, (Edward) Reynolds; academic, writer, poet and dramatist; b. 1 Feb. 1933, Macon, NC, USA. *Education:* AB, Duke University, 1955; BLitt, Merton College, Oxford, 1958. *Career:* Faculty, 1958–61, Asst Prof., 1961–68, Assoc. Prof., 1968–72, Prof., 1972–77, James B. Duke Prof., 1977–, Duke University; Writer-in-Residence, University of North Carolina at Chapel Hill, 1965, University of Kansas, 1967, 1969, 1980, University of North Carolina at Greensboro, 1971; Glasgow Prof., Washington and Lee University, 1971; Faculty, Salzburg Seminar, 1977; mem. American Acad. of Arts and Letters. *Publications:* A Long and Happy Life, 1962; The Names and Faces of Heroes, 1963; A Generous Man, 1966; Love and Work, 1968; Permanent Errors, 1970; Things Themselves, 1972; The Surface of Earth, 1975; Early Dark, 1977; A Palpable God, 1978; The Source of Light, 1981; Vital Provisions, 1982; Private Contentment, 1984; Kate Vaiden, 1986; The Laws of Ice, 1986; A Common Room, 1987; Good Hearts, 1988; Clear Pictures, 1989; The Tongues of Angels, 1990; The Use of Fire, 1990; New Music, 1990; The Foreseeable Future, 1991; Conversations with Reynolds Price, 1991; Blue Calhoun, 1993; Full Moon, 1993; The Collected Stories, 1993; A Whole New Life, 1994; The Promise of Rest, 1995; Three Gospels, 1996; Roxanne Slade, 1998. *Honours:* William Faulkner Foundation Award for Notable First Novel, 1962; Sir Walter Raleigh Awards, 1962, 1976, 1981, 1984, 1986; Guggenheim Fellowship, 1964–65; National Endowment for the Arts Fellowship, 1967–68; National Institute of Arts and Letters Award, 1971; Bellamann Foundation Award, 1972; North Carolina Award, 1977; National Book Critics Circle Award, 1986; Elmer H. Bobst Award, 1988; R. Hunt Parker Award, North Carolina Literary and Historical Society, 1991. *Address:* PO Box 99014, Durham, NC 27708, USA.

PRICE, Richard, BA, PhD; poet, librarian, editor and writer; b. 15 Aug. 1966, Reading, England; m. Jacqueline Canning 1990; two d. *Education:* University of Strathclyde, Glasgow. *Career:* Curator, Modern British Collections, British Library, London, 1992–; mem. Asscn of Scottish Literary Studies; Poetry Society, council, 1998–2002. *Publications:* Poetry: Sense and a Minor Fever, 1993; Tube Shelter Perspective, 1993; Marks & Sparks, 1995; Hand Held, 1997; Perfume and Petrol Fumes, 1999; Frosted, Melted, 2002. Other: The Fabulous Matter of Fact: The Poetics of Neil M. Gunn, 1991; César Vallejo: Translations, Transformations, Tributes (ed. with Stephen Watts), 1998; La nouvelle alliance: Influences francophones sur la littérature ecossaise (ed. with David Kinloch), 2000; The Star You Steer By: Basil Bunting and 'British' Modernism (ed. with James McGonigal), 2000; A Boy in Summer (short stories), 2002. Contributions: Comparative Criticism; Independent; Scotland on Sunday; Verse; Poetry Review; PN Review; Edinburgh Review; Object Permanence. *Address:* c/o Modern British Collections, British Library, 96 Euston Road, London NW1 2DB, England.

PRICE, Richard; American writer and screenwriter; b. 12 Oct. 1949, New York, NY. *Screenplays include:* The Wanderers 1979, The Color of Money 1986, New York Stories 1989, Sea of Love 1989, Night and the City 1992, Mad Dog and Glory 1993, Kiss of Death 1995, Clockers 1995, Ransom 1996, Shaft 2000, Freedomland 2004. *Television:* The Wire (series writer) 2002. *Publications:* novels: The Wanderers 1975, Bloodbrothers 1978, The Breaks 1983, Clockers 1992, Freedomland 1998, Samaritan 2003. *Address:* c/o Bloomsbury Publishing PLC, 38 Soho Square, London, W1V 5DF, England. *Website:* www.bloomsbury.com.

PRICE, Roger (David); Prof. of Modern History and Writer; b. 7 Jan. 1944, Port Talbot, Wales. *Education:* BA, University of Wales, University College of Swansea, 1965. *Career:* Lecturer, 1968–82, Senior Lecturer, 1982–83, Reader in Social History, 1984–91, Prof. of European History, 1991–94, University of East Anglia; Prof. of Modern History, University of Wales, Aberystwyth, 1993–; mem. FRHistS, 1983. *Publications:* The French Second Republic: A Social History, 1972; The Economic Modernization of France, 1975; Revolution and Reaction: 1848 and the Second French Republic (ed. and contributor), 1975; 1848 in France, 1975; An Economic History of Modern France, 1981; The Modernization of Rural France: Communications Networks and Agricultural Market Structures in 19th Century France, 1983; A Social History of 19th Century France, 1987; The Revolutions of 1848, 1989; A Concise History of France, 1993; Documents on the French Revolution of 1848, 1996; Napoleon III and the French Second Empire, 1997; The French Second Empire: An Anatomy of Political Power, 2001. Contributions: numerous magazines and journals. *Honours:* DLitt, University of East Anglia, 1985. *Address:* Dept of History and Welsh History, University of Wales, Aberystwyth, Ceredigion SY23 3DY, Wales. *E-mail:* rdp@aber.ac.uk.

PRICE, Stanley; Writer and Dramatist; b. 12 Aug. 1931, London, England; m. Judy Fenton, 5 July 1957, one s. *Education:* MA, University of Cambridge. *Career:* mem. Writer's Guild; Dramatists Club. *Publications:* Fiction: Crusading for Kronk, 1960; A World of Difference, 1961; Just for the Record, 1962; The Biggest Picture, 1964. Stage Plays: Horizontal Hold, 1967; The Starving Rich, 1972; The Two of Me, 1975; Moving, 1980; Why Me?, 1985. Screenplays: Arabesque, 1968; Gold, 1974; Shout at the Devil, 1975. Television Plays: All Things Being Equal, 1970; Exit Laughing, 1971; Minder, 1980; The Kindness of Mrs Radcliffe, 1981; Moving, 1985; Star Quality, series, 1986; Close Relations, 1986–87; The Bretts, 1990. Contributions: Observer; Sunday Telegraph; New York Times; Los Angeles Times; Punch; Plays and Players; New Statesman; Independent; Town. *Address:* Douglas Rae, 28 Charing Cross Rd, London WC2, England.

PRICE, Susan; children's author; b. 8 July 1955, Brades Row, England. *Career:* mem. Soc. of Authors. *Publications:* Devil's Piper, 1973; Twopence a Tub, 1975; Sticks and Stones, 1976; Home from Home, 1977; Christopher Uptake, 1981; The Carpenter (short stories), 1981; In a Nutshell, 1983; From Where I Stand, 1984; Ghosts at Large, 1984; Odin's Monster, 1986;

The Ghost Drum, 1987; The Bone Dog, 1989; Forbidden Doors, 1990; The Sterkarm Handshake, 1998; A Sterkarm Kiss 2004. *Honours:* The Other Award, 1975; Carnegie Medal, 1987; The Guardian Children's Fiction Award, 1999. *Address:* c/o Faber and Faber Ltd, 3 Queen Square, London WC1N 3AU, England.

PRICE, Victor; Writer and Poet; b. 10 April 1930, Newcastle, County Down, Northern Ireland. *Education:* BA, Modern Languages (French and German), Queen's University, Belfast, 1947–51. *Career:* With the BBC, 1956–90, ending as Head of German Language Service. *Publications:* The Death of Achilles, 1963; The Other Kingdom, 1964; Caliban's Wooing, 1966; The Plays of Georg Büchner, 1971; Two Parts Water (poems), 1980. Contributions: Financial Times; Scotsman; BBC World Service; Deutschland Rundfunk; Channel Four.

PRIEST, Christopher McKenzie; Author; b. 14 July 1943, Cheadle, Cheshire, England; m. Laura; one s. one d. *Publications:* Indoctrinaire, 1970; Fugue for a Darkening Island, 1972; Real-Time World (short stories), 1974; Inverted World, 1974; The Space Machine, 1976; A Dream of Wessex, 1977; An Infinite Summer, 1979; The Affirmation, 1981; The Glamour, 1984; The Book on the Edge of Forever (non-fiction), 1984; The Quiet Woman, 1990; The Prestige, 1995; The Extremes, 1998; The Dream Archipelago, 1999; The Separation, 2002; short stories, television plays. Contributions: Impulse, New Worlds, New Writings in SF; various anthologies. *Honours:* John W. Campbell Jr Memorial Award for Outstanding British Novel, 1972; BSFA Awards, for Best Novel, 1974, 1999, 2003, for Best Short Story, 1979; Ditmar Awards for Best International Novel, 1977, 1982; Kurd Lasswitz Award for Best Foreign Novel, 1988; James Tait Black Memorial Prize for Fiction, 1995; World Fantasy Award, 1996; Prix Utopia Lifetime Achievement Award, 2001; Grand Prix de l'Imaginaire, 2001; Arthur C. Clarke Award, 2003. *Literary Agent:* PFD, Drury House, 34–43 Russell St, London WC2B 5HA, England. *Telephone:* (20) 7344-1000. *Fax:* (20) 7836-9539. *E-mail:* ChrPr997@aol.com. *Website:* www.christopher-priest.co.uk.

PRIGOV, Dmitri Aleksandrovich; Russian poet, writer and artist; b. 5 Nov. 1940, Moscow; m. Nadezhda Georgiyevna Bourova; one s. *Education:* Moscow Higher School of Arts. *Career:* worker Likhachev Automobile Factory 1957–59, 1964; architect Main Dept of Architecture of Moscow 1967–72; freelance 1972–; mem. Russian Painters' Union, Russian Writers' Union, Russian PEN Club. *Exhibitions:* has taken part in art exhbns in Russia, Israel, Germany, Italy, USA, South Korea, France, UK, Spain, Denmark, Netherlands, Hungary, Czech Repub.; Metropolis, Berlin 1990, 100 Möglichkeiten, InterArt, Berlin, 1991, Russian Museum, St Petersburg 1994, Dmitri Prigov 1975–1995, France, Germany, Hungary. *Publications include:* Black Poodle (play), Tears of Heraldic Soul 1990, Poet Ohne Personlichkeit 1991, Der Militioner und die Andere 1992, Sixty Drops of Blood 1993, The Place of God (play) 1995, The Appearance of the Verse after its Death (poems) 1996; Collected Poems 1975–1988 1997, Soviet Texts 1997, Poems 1990–1994 1998, Texts of Our Life 1995, Katharsis (play) 1998, Collected Poems Vols I and II 1997, Live in Moscow (novel) 2000. *Honours:* Pushkin Prize for Literature. *Address:* Volgina str. 25, korp. 2, Apt 207, 117437 Moscow, Russia (Home); 26 Abbey Drive, London, SW17 9PN, England (Home). *Telephone:* (095) 330-49-50 (Russia); (20) 8767-7386 (England). *Fax:* (095) 330-49-50 (Russia); (20) 8767-7386 (England). *E-mail:* bokrovan@aol.com (Home).

PRINCE, Alison Mary; British writer and poet; b. 26 March 1931, Kent, England; m. Goronwy Siriol Parry 1957; two s. one d. *Education:* Beckenham Grammar School, Univ. of London, Goldsmiths Coll. *Career:* fmrly farmer, art teacher and TV scriptwriter; Fellow in Creative Writing, Jordanhill Coll., Glasgow 1988–90; currently writer and illustrator of children's fiction; organizes creative writing workshops in schools in Scotland, sponsored by Scottish Arts Council; columnist The Arran Banner; mem. Scottish PEN, Soc. of Authors. *Publications:* juvenile: The Doubting Kind 1974, How's Business 1985, The Ghost Within 1987, The Blue Moon Day 1989, Having Been in the City (poems) 1994, The Witching Tree 1996, The Sherwood Hero (Guardian Children's Fiction Award) 1996, Magic Dad 1997, Fergus, Fabulous Ferret 1997, Screw Loose 1998, Cat Number Three 1999, Dear Del 1999, Second Chance 2000, A Nation Again 2000, Bird Boy 2000, Bumble 2001, Oranges and Murder 2001, The Fortune Teller 2001, My Tudor Queen 2001, Boojer 2002, Turnaround 2002, Dora Saves the Prince 2002; other: The Necessary Goat (essays) 1992, Kenneth Grahame: An Innocent in the Wild Wood (biog.) 1994, Hans Christian Andersen: The Fan Dancer (biog.) 1998. *Honours:* Literary Review Grand Poetry Prize, Scottish Arts Council Awards for Children's Literature 2001, 2002. *Address:* Burnfoot, Whiting Bay, Isle of Arran KA27 8QL, Scotland.

PRINCE, Mona; Egyptian novelist. *Publications:* Three Suitcases for Departure (in Arabic) 2003. *Address:* c/o American University in Cairo, POB 2511, 113 Sharia Kasr El-Aini, Cairo, Egypt.

PRINCE, Peter (Alan); Writer; b. 10 May 1942, Bromley, England. *Education:* BA, University of Pennsylvania, 1964; MA, Columbia University, 1966. *Publications:* Play Things, 1972; Dogcatcher, 1974; Agents of a Foreign Power, 1977; The Good Father, 1983; Death of a Soap Queen, 1990; The Great Circle, 1997; Waterloo Story, 1999. Other: several television plays, including Oppenheimer, 1980. Contributions: periodicals. *Honours:* Somerset Maugham Award, Society of Authors, 1973; BAFTA Award, 1980. *Address:* 31 Meteor St, London SW11, England.

PRINGLE, Heather Anne; Writer; b. 8 Dec. 1952, Edmonton, AB, Canada; m. 11 March 1978. *Education:* BA, University of Alberta, 1973; MA, University of British Columbia, 1976. *Publications:* In Search of Ancient North America, 1996; The Mummy Congress, 2001. Contributions: Science; Discover; Stern; Geo; New Scientist; National Geographic Traveler; Islands; Saturday Night; Canadian Geographic. *Honours:* Excellence in Science Journalism Award for Magazines, American Asscn for the Advancement of Science, 2001; National Magazine Award, 1988; Authors Award, 1992. *Literary Agent:* Anne McDermid and Assocs, 78 Albany Ave, Toronto, ON M5R 3C3, Canada. *Address:* 825 Granville St, Suite 202, Vancouver, BC V6Z 1K9, Canada. *Website:* www.heatherpringle.com.

PRIOR, Allan; Author; b. 13 Jan. 1922, Newcastle upon Tyne, England. *Education:* Newcastle upon Tyne; Blackpool. *Publications:* A Flame in the Air, 1951; The Joy Ride, 1952; The One-Eyed Monster, 1958; One Away, 1961; The Interrogators, 1965; The Operators, 1966; The Loving Cup, 1968; The Contract, 1970; Paradiso, 1972; Affair, 1976; Never Been Kissed in the Same Place Twice, 1978; Theatre, 1981; A Cast of Stars, 1983; The Big March, 1983; Her Majesty's Hit Man, 1986; Führer: The Novel, 1991; The Old Man and Me, 1994; The Old Man and Me Again, 1996. *Address:* 11 Cokers Lane, Croxted Rd, London SE21 8NF, England.

PRITCHARD, R(obert) John; Historian; b. 30 Nov. 1945, Los Angeles, CA, USA; m. 1st Sonia Magbanna Zaide, 15 Aug. 1969, divorced 1984, one s. one d.; m. 2nd Lady Selina Elaine Antonia FitzAlan-Howard Lodge, 20 Dec. 1989. *Education:* AB, University of California, 1967; MA, 1968, PhD, 1980, LSE; LLB, University of Kent at Canterbury, 1996; Bar Vocational Course, Inns of Court School of Law, 1996–97, London. *Career:* Lecturer in History, University of Kent, 1990–93; Fellow in War Studies, King's College, London, 1990–93; Simon Senior Research Fellow in History, University of Manchester, 1993–94; Dir, Historical Enterprises, 1993–; Dir, Robert M. Kempner Collegium, 1996–2000; Lecturer in Law, Business Studies and History, Stafford House College, Canterbury 2001–; mem. Middle Temple, 1995–; FRHistS, 1987–. *Publications:* Reichstag Fire: Ashes of Democracy 1972, Cry Sabotage (co-author) 1972, The Tokyo War Crimes Trial: An International Symposium (co-author) 1984, General History of the Philippines Vol. 1: The American Half-Century 1898–1946 (co-author) 1984, Far Eastern Influences on British Strategy Towards the Great Powers 1937–39 1987, Overview of the Historical Importance of the Tokyo War Trial 1987, Total War: Causes & Courses of the Second World War (co-author) 1989, 1995, Japan and the Second World War (with Lady Toskiko Marks) 1989, Unit 731: The Japanese Army's Secret of Secrets (co-author) 1989, From Pearl Harbour to Hiroshima (co-author), 1993, The Cambridge Encyclopedia of Japan (co-author) 1993, La Déportation: La Système Concentrationnaire Nazi (co-author) 1995, Wada umi no Koe wo Kiku: senso sekinin to Ningen no Tsumi; to no Ma (Harken to the Cries at Our Birth: The Intervals Separating War Responsibility and Crimes of Humanity) (co-author) 1996, The Tokyo Major War Crimes Trial: The Records of the International Military Tribunal for the Far East with an Authoritative Commentary and Comprehensive Guide 1998–, World War II in Asia and the Pacific and the War's Aftermath, with General Themes: A Handbook of Literature and Research (co-author) 1998, Showa Japan: Political, Economic and Social History 1926–1989, II: 1941–1952, Section I: Politics & Economics (co-author) 1999, 1945: War and Peace in the Pacific, Selected Essays (co-author) 1999, The Penguin History of the Second World War 1999, International Criminal Law, III: Enforcement (co-author) 1999, A History of Anglo-Japanese Relations, III: The Military Dimension (co-author) 2003, International Humanitarian Law: Origins, Challenges, Prospects (with John N. Carey and William V. Dunlap), 3 vols, 2003, Encyclopedia of Genocide and Crimes against Humanity (co-author) 2004. *Honours:* many grants and fellowships. *Address:* 11 Charlotte Sq., Margate, Kent, CT9 1LR, England.

PRITCHARD, William H(arrison); Prof. of English and Author; b. 12 Nov. 1932, Binghamton, New York, USA; m. Marietta Pritchard, 24 Aug. 1957, three s. *Education:* BA, Amherst College, 1953; Columbia University, 1953–54; MA, English, 1956, PhD, English, 1960, Harvard University. *Career:* Instructor, 1958–61, Asst Prof., 1961–65, Assoc. Prof., 1965–70, Prof., 1970–, later Henry Clay Folger Prof. of English, Amherst College; Mem., Editorial Board, Hudson Review; mem. Asscn of Literary Scholars and Critics. *Publications:* Wyndham Lewis, 1968; Wyndham Lewis: Profiles in Literature, 1972; W. B. Yeats (ed.), 1972; Seeing Through Everything: English Writers 1918–1940, 1977; Lives of the Modern Poets, 1980; Frost: A Literary Life Reconsidered, 1984; Randall Jarrell: A Literary Life, 1990; Selected Poems of Randall Jarrell (ed.), 1990; Playing It By Ear: Literary Essays and Reviews, 1994; English Papers: A Teaching Life, 1995; Talking Back to Emily Dickinson and Other Essays, 1998; Updike: America's Man of Letters, 2000; Shelf Life: Literary Essays and Reviews, 2003. Contributions: Boston Sunday Globe; Hudson Review; New York Times Book Review; numerous others. *Honours:* ACLS Junior Fellowship, 1963–64, and Fellowship, 1977–78; Guggenheim Fellowship, 1973–74; National Endowment for the Humanities Fellowships, 1977–78, 1986; Book of essays, Under Criticism, published in his honour, 1998. *Address:* 62 Orchard St, Amherst, MA 01002, USA.

PROKHANOV, Aleksandr Andreevich; Writer, Journalist and Publisher; b. 1938, Moscow, USSR. *Education:* Moscow Institute of Aviation. *Career:* fmr correspondent, various Moscow newspapers, publisher, newspaper, Den; Ed., nationalist newspaper, Zavtra. *Publications:* Idu v moi put (I'm Entering My Way, prose), 1971; Kochuiushchaia roza (A Wandering Rose, novel), 1976; Vremia polden (The Time is Noon, novel), 1977; Mesto deistviia (A Place of Action, novel), 1980; Vechnyi gorod (Eternal Town, novel), 1981; Derevo v tsentre Kabula (The Tree in Kabul Downtown, novel), 1982; Risunki batalista (The Sketches of the Battle-pieces Painter, novel), 1985; Angel proletel (An Angel Has Flown, novel), 1991; Poslednii soldat imperii (The Last Soldier of the Empire, novel), 1992; Dvorets (The Palace, novel), 1994; Mr Hexagon, 2001. Contributions: various journals and magazines incl.: Znamia, Lunost, Oktiabr, Nash sovremennik. *Honours:* National Bestseller Prize, 2002.

PROSE, Francine; Author and College Teacher; b. 1 April 1947, New York, NY, USA; m. Howard Michels, 24 Sept. 1976, two s. *Education:* BA, Radcliffe College, 1968; MA, Harvard University, 1969. *Career:* Teacher of Creative Writing, Harvard University, 1971–72; Visiting Lecturer in Fiction, University of Arizona at Tucson, 1982–84; Instructor, Bread Loaf Writers' Conference, 1984; Faculty, MFA Program, Warren Wilson College, 1984–; mem. Associated Writing Programs; PEN. *Publications:* Judah the Pious, 1973; The Glorious Ones, 1974; Stories From Our Living Past, 1974; Marie Laveau, 1977; Animal Magnetism, 1978; Household Saints, 1981; Hungry Hearts, 1983; Bigfoot Dreams, 1986; Women and Children First and Other Stories, 1988; Primitive People, 1992; A Peaceable Kingdom, 1993; Hunters and Gatherers, 1995; The Demon's Mistake: A Story from Chelm, 2000; Blue Angel: A Novel, 2000; On Writing Short Stories (with others), 2000. Contributions: periodicals. *Honours:* Jewish Book Council Award, 1973; MLLE Award, Mademoiselle, 1975; Edgar Lewis Wallant Memorial Award, Hartford Jewish Community Center, 1984. *Address:* c/o Master of Fine Arts Program, Warren Wilson College, Swannanoa, NC 28778, USA.

PROUD, Linda Helena; Writer; b. 9 July 1949, Broxbourne, England; m. David Smith. *Education:* Diploma, Design and Exhibition, College of Distributive Trades, London. *Career:* mem. Writers in Oxford, newsletter ed., 1996–98. *Publications:* Consider England, 1994; Knights of the Grail, 1995; Tabernacle for the Sun, 1997; 2000 Years, 1999; Icons: A Sacred Art, 2000; Angels, 2001. *Honours:* Southern Arts Bursary Fund, 1995; Hawthornden Fellowship, 1998. *Literary Agent:* Johnson & Alcock Ltd, Clerkenwell House, 45–47 Clerkenwell Green, London EC1R 0HT, England.

PROULX, Edna Annie, MA; American writer; b. 22 Aug. 1935, Norwich, Conn.; m. 3rd James Hamilton Lang 1969 (divorced 1990); three s. one d. *Education:* Univ. of Vermont and Sir George Williams (now Concordia) Univ., Montréal. *Career:* freelance journalist, Vt 1975–87; f. Vershire Behind the Times newspaper, Vershire, Vt; short stories appeared in Blair & Ketchums Country Journal, Esquire, etc.; Vt Council Arts Fellowship 1989, Ucross Foundation Residency, Wyo. 1990, 1992; mem. PEN; Guggenheim Fellow 1993; active anti-illiteracy campaigner. *Publications:* Heart Songs and Other Stories 1988, Postcards 1992 (PEN/Faulkner Award for Fiction 1993), The Shipping News 1993 (Chicago Tribune's Heartland Prize for Fiction, Irish Times Int. Fiction Prize, Nat. Book Award for Fiction (all 1993), Pulitzer Prize for Fiction 1994), Accordion Crimes 1996, Best American Short Stories of 1997 (ed.), Brokeback Mountain 1998, Close Range: Wyoming Stories 1998, That Old Ace in the Hole 2002; numerous articles. *Honours:* Hon. DHumLitt (Maine) 1994; stories listed in Best American Short Stories 1983, 1987; Alumni Achievement Award, Univ. of Vt 1994, New York Public Library Literary Lion 1994, Dos Passos Prize for Literature 1996, American Acad. of Achievement Award 1998, Book Award, The New Yorker 2000, Amb. Book Award, English Speaking Union 2000. *Address:* c/o Simon Schuster Inc., 1230 Avenue of the Americas, New York, NY 10020. *Address:* PO Box 230, Centennial, WY 82055, USA. *Fax:* (307) 742-6159.

PRUNTY, (Eugene) Wyatt; academic, poet, writer and editor; b. 15 May 1947, Humbolt, TN, USA; m. Barbara Heather Svell 1973; one s. one d. *Education:* BA, University of the South, 1969; MA, Johns Hopkins University, 1973; PhD, Louisiana State University, 1979. *Career:* Instructor in English, Louisiana State University, 1978–79; Asst Prof. to Prof. of English, Virginia Polytechnic Institute and State University, 1978–89; Visiting Writer, Washington and Lee University, 1982–83; Visiting Assoc. and Prof. Johns Hopkins University 1987–89, Elliot Coleman Prof. 1988; Carlton Prof. of English University of the South 1989–; f. Dir Sewanee Writers' Conf.; f. and ed Sewanee Writers' Series; mem. Associated Writing Programs; College English Asscn; English Institute; MLA of America. *Publications:* Poetry: Domestic of the Outer Banks, 1980; The Times Between, 1982; What Women Know, What Men Believe, 1986; Balance as Belief, 1989; The Run of the House, 1993; Since the Noon Mail Stopped, 1997; Unarmed and Dangerous: New and Selected Poems, 1999. Other: Fallen from the Symboled World: Precedents for the New Formalism, 1990; Sewanee Writers on Writing (ed.), 2001. Contributions: anthologies, reviews, quarterlies and journals. *Honours:* Poetry Prize, Sewanee Review 1969; Fellow, Bread Loaf Writers' Conference 1982, Guggenheim Fellowship 2001–02, Rockefeller Foundation residency 2002. *Address:* c/o Department of English, University of the South, Sewanee, TN 37383, USA.

PRUTKOV, Kozma (see Snodgrass, W. D.).

PRYCE-JONES, David; Writer; b. 15 Feb. 1936, Vienna, Austria; m. 29 July 1959, one s. two d. *Education:* BA, MA, Magdalen College, Oxford, 1956–59. *Career:* Literary Ed., Time & Tide, 1961, Spectator, 1964; Senior Ed., National Review, New York, 1999; mem. RSL. *Publications:* Owls & Satyrs, 1961; The Sands of Summer, 1963; Next Generation, 1964; Quondam, 1965; The Stranger's View, 1967; The Hungarian Revolution, 1969; Running Away, 1969; The Face of Defeat, 1971; The England Commune, 1973; Unity Mitford, 1976; Vienna, 1978; Shirley's Guild, 1981; Paris in the Third Reich, 1983; Cyril Connolly, 1984; The Afternoon Sun, 1986; The Closed Circle, 1989; Inheritance, 1992; You Can't Be Too Careful, 1993; The War That Never Was, 1995. Contributions: numerous journals and magazines. *Honours:* Wingate Prize, 1986; Sunlight Literary Prize, 1989. *Address:* Lower Pentwyn, Gwenddwr, Powys LD2 3LQ, Wales.

PRYOR, Boori Monty; Writer; b. 12 July 1950, Australia. *Publications:* Maybe Tomorrow (with Meme McDonald), 1998; My Girragundji (with Meme McDonald), 1998; The Binna Binna Man (with Meme McDonald), 1999; Reconcilliation, 2000. Contributions: Australian Bookseller and Publisher, 1999; The Bulletin, 2000. *Honours:* Children's Book Council of Australia Book of the Year Award for Younger Readers, 1999; NSW State Literary Award for Younger Readers, 2000, and Book of the Year, 2000, and Ethnic Affairs Commission Award, 2000; Australian Audio Book Awards, Author/Narrator Category winner and Overall Narration Book Winner. *Address:* c/o Jenny Darling and Assocs, PO Box 413, Toorak, 3142 Vic., Australia.

PULLEIN-THOMPSON, Christine (see Popescu, Christine).

PULLMAN, Philip, CBE, BA, FRSL; British author; b. 19 Oct. 1946, Norwich, England; m. Jude Speller 1970; two s. *Education:* Exeter Coll., Oxford. *Career:* teacher in Oxford 1972–86; part-time lecturer Westminster Coll., Oxford 1986–96. *Publications:* One More River 1973, Count Karlstein 1982, The Ruby in the Smoke (Sally Lockhart series) 1985, The Shadow in the Plate 1986, The Shadow in the North (Sally Lockhart series) 1987, Spring-Heeled Jack 1989, The Tiger in the Well (Sally Lockhart series) 1990, The Broken Bridge 1990, The White Mercedes 1992, The Tin Princess (Sally Lockhart series) 1994, The New Cut Gang: Thunderbolt's Waxwork 1994, The New Cut Gang: The Gas-fitter's Ball 1995, The Wonderful Story of Aladdin and the Enchanted Lamp 1995, The Firework-Maker's Daughter 1995, Northern Lights (aka The Golden Compass, vol. I, His Dark Materials trilogy) (Carnegie Medal 1996, Guardian Children's Fiction Prize 1996, British Book Awards Children's Book of the Year 1996) 1995, Clockwork 1996, The Subtle Knife (vol. II, His Dark Materials trilogy) 1997, The Butterfly Tattoo 1998, Mossycoat 1998, Detective Stories (ed.) 1998, I Was a Rat! 1999, The Amber Spyglass (vol. III, His Dark Materials trilogy) (British Book Awards WHSmith Children's Book of the Year, Whitbread Children's Book of the Year Prize 2001, Whitbread Book of the Year Award 2001) 2000, Puss-in-Boots 2000, Sherlock Holmes and the Limehouse Horror 2001, Lyra's Oxford 2003; contrib. reviews to Times Educational Supplement, The Guardian. *Honours:* New English Library First Novel Competition 1969, BA/Book Data Author of the Year Award 2001, Booksellers' Asscn Author of the Year 2001, 2002, British Book Awards Author of the Year Award 2002, Whitbread Book of the Year Award 2002. *Literary Agent:* Caradoc King, A. P. Watt Ltd, 20 John Street, London, WC1N 2DR, England. *Telephone:* (20) 7405-6774. *Fax:* (20) 7831-2154. *Website:* www.philip-pullman.com.

PUNTER, David Godfrey; Prof. of English, Writer and Poet; b. 19 Nov. 1949, London, England; m. Caroline Case, 5 Dec. 1988, one s. two d. *Education:* BA, 1970, MA, 1974, PhD, 1984, University of Cambridge. *Career:* Lecturer in English, University of East Anglia, 1973–86; Prof. and Head of Dept, Chinese University of Hong Kong, 1986–88; Prof. of English, University of Stirling, 1988–2000; Prof. of English, University of Bristol, 2000–. *Publications:* The Literature of Terror, 1980; Blake, Hegel and Dialectic, 1981; Romanticism and Ideology, 1982; China and Class, 1985; The Hidden Script, 1985; Introduction to Contemporary Cultural Studies (ed.), 1986; Lost in the Supermarket, 1987; Blake: Selected Poetry and Prose (ed.), 1988; The Romantic Unconscious, 1989; Selected Poems of Philip Larkin (ed.), 1991; Asleep at the Wheel, 1997; Gothic Pathologies, 1998; Spectral Readings (ed.), 1999; Selected Short Stories, 1999; Companion to the Gothic (ed.), 2000; Writing the Passions, 2000; Postcolonial Imaginings, 2000. Contributions: Hundreds of articles, essays, and poems in various publications. *Honours:* FRSA; Fellow, Society of Antiquaries (Scotland); Scottish Arts Council Award; Founding Fellow, Institute of Contemporary Scotland; DLitt, University of Stirling. *Address:* The Coach House, Church Lane, Backwell, Bristol BS48 3JJ, England.

PURDY, James (Amos); Author, Poet and Dramatist; b. 17 July 1923, Ohio, USA. *Education:* University of Chicago; University of Puebla, Mexico. *Publications:* Fiction: Dream Palace, 1956; Malcolm, 1959; The Nephew, 1961; Cabot Wright Begins, 1964; Eustace Chisholm and the Works, 1967; Jeremy's Version, 1970; I Am Elijah Thrush, 1972; The House of the Solitary Maggot, 1974; Color of Darkness, 1974; In a Shallow Grave, 1976; Narrow Rooms, 1978; Mourners Below, 1981; On Glory's Course, 1984; In the Hollow of His Hand, 1986; Candles of Your Eyes, 1986; Garments the Living Wear, 1989; Collected Stories, 1956–1986, 1991; Out with the Stars, 1992; Gertrude of Stony Island Avenue, 1998. Poetry: The Running Sun,

1971; Sunshine Is an Only Child, 1973; Lessons and Complaints, 1978; Sleep Tight, 1979; The Brooklyn Branding Parlors, 1985; Collected Poems, 1990. Plays: Cracks, 1963; Wedding Finger, 1974; Two Plays, 1979; Scrap of Paper, 1981; The Berrypicker, 1981; Proud Flesh, 1981; Gertrude of Stony Island Avenue (novel), 1997. *Honours:* National Institute of Arts and Letters Grant, 1958; Guggenheim Fellowships, 1958, 1962; Ford Foundation Grant, 1961; Morton Dauwen Zabel Fiction Award, American Acad. of Arts and Letters, 1993; Oscar Williams and Gene Durwood Poetry Award, 1995. *Address:* 236 Henry St, New York, NY 11201, USA.

PURPURA, Lia; Poet and Teacher; b. 22 Feb. 1964, Long Island, New York, USA; m. Jed Gaylin, 1992, one s. *Education:* BA, English, Oberlin College, 1986; MFA, Poetry, Iowa Writers Workshop, 1990. *Career:* Dept of Writing and Media, Loyola College, Baltimore, MD, 1990. *Publications:* The Brighter the Veil, 1996; Taste of Ash and Berliner Tagebuch-Poems of Grzegorz Musial, in press; Trans., poems by Katarzyna Borun-Jagodzinska and Krzysztof Piechowicz. Contributions: poems to numerous journals including: American Poetry Review; Antioch Review; Denver Quarterly; Ploughshares; Essays and reviews to several journals including: Willow Springs; Verse. *Honours:* Acad. of American Poets Award, 1986; Teaching and Writing Fellowship, University of Iowa Writers Workshop, 1988–90; Fulbright Fellowship, 1991–92; Blue Mountain Center Residency, 1995; First Prize, Visions International Trans. Prize, 1996; Millay Colony Resident Fellow, 1996.

PURSER, Philip John; Journalist and Author; b. 28 Aug. 1925, Letchworth, England; m. Ann Elizabeth Goodman, 18 May 1957, one s. two d. *Education:* MA, St Andrews University, 1950. *Career:* Staff, Daily Mail, 1951–57; Television Critic, Sunday Telegraph, 1961–87; mem. Writers Guild of Great Britain; BAFTA. *Publications:* Peregrination 22, 1962; Four Days to the Fireworks, 1964; The Twentymen, 1967; Night of Glass, 1968; The Holy Father's Navy, 1971; The Last Great Tram Race, 1974; Where is He Now?, 1978; A Small Explosion, 1979; The One and Only Phyllis Dixey, 1978; Halliwell's Television Companion (with Leslie Halliwell), 1982; Shooting the Hero, 1990; Poeted: The Final Quest of Edward James, 1991; Done Viewing, 1992. Contributions: numerous magazines and journals. *Address:* 10 The Green, Blakesley, Towcester, Northamptonshire NN12 8RD, England.

PURVES, Elizabeth (Libby) Mary, OBE, BA; British journalist, broadcaster and writer; b. 2 Feb. 1950, London, England; m. Paul Heiney 1980; one s. one d. *Education:* Univ. of Oxford. *Career:* presenter-writer, BBC 1975–; Ed., Tatler 1983. *Publications:* Adventures Under Sail (ed.) 1982, Britain at Play 1982, The Sailing Weekend Book 1984, How Not to Be a Perfect Mother 1987, One Summer's Grace 1989, How Not to Raise a Perfect Child 1991, Casting Off 1995, A Long Walk in Wintertime 1996, Home Leave 1997, More Lives Than One 1998, Holy Smoke 1998, Regatta 1999, Passing Go 2000, A Free Woman 2001, Mother Country 2002, Continental Drift 2003, Radio 2003, Acting Up (novel) 2004; contrib. to newspapers and magazines. *Honours:* Best Book of the Sea 1984, Columnist of the Year 1999, Desmond Wettern Award 1999. *Literary Agent:* Rogers, Coleridge & White, 20 Powis Mews, London, W11 15N, England.

PUTNAM, Hilary; Philosopher, Prof. and Writer; b. 31 July 1926, Chicago, IL, USA; m. 1st Erna Diesendruck 1 Nov. 1948 (divorced 1962); m. 2nd Ruth Anna Hall 11 Aug. 1962; two s. two d. *Education:* BA, Philosophy, Univ. of Pennsylvania, 1948; PhD, Philosophy, Univ. of California at Los Angeles, 1951. *Career:* Instructor in Philosophy, Northwestern Univ., 1952–53; Asst Prof., 1953–60, Assoc. Prof., 1960–61, of Philosophy, Princeton Univ.; Prof. of the Philosophy of Science, MIT, 1961–65; Prof. of Philosophy, 1965–, Walter Beverly Pearson Prof. of Modern Mathematics and Mathematical Logic, 1976–95, Cogan Univ. Prof., 1995–2000, Cogan Univ. Prof. Emeritus, 2000–, Harvard Univ.; mem. American Acad. of Arts and Sciences, fellow; American Philosophical Asscn; Asscn for Symbolic Logic; British Acad., corresponding fellow; Institut de France, correspondant; American Philosophical Society; Philosophy of Science Asscn. *Publications:* Philosophy of Logic, 1971; Philosophical Papers: Vol. 1, Mathematics, Matter and Method, 1975, Vol. 2, Mind, Language and Reality, 1975, Vol. 3, Realism and Reason, 1983; Meaning and the Moral Sciences, 1978; Reason, Truth and History, 1981; Philosophy of Mathematics (ed. with Paul Benacerraf), revised edn, 1983; Epistemology, Methodology and Philosophy of Science: Essays in Honor of Carl G. Hempel on the Occasion of his 80th Birthday (ed. with W. K. Essler and W. Stegmüller), 1985; The Many Faces of Realism, 1987; Realism with a Human Face, 1990; Renewing Philosophy, 1992; Pursuits of Reason: Essays Presented to Stanley Cavell (ed. with T. Cohen and P. Guyer), 1992; Definitions, 1993; Pragmatism: An Open Question, 1994; Words and Life, 1994; The Threefold Cord: Mind, Body and World, 1999; The Collapse of the Fact/Value Dichotomy, 2002. *Honours:* Guggenheim Fellowship; National Endowment for the Humanities Fellowship; National Science Foundation Fellowship; Rockefeller Foundation Fellowship. *Address:* 116 Winchester Rd, Arlington, MA 02174, USA. *E-mail:* hputnam@fas.harvard.edu.

PYBUS, Rodney; Writer and Poet; b. 5 June 1938, Newcastle upon Tyne, England; m. Ellen Johnson, 24 June 1961, two s. *Education:* BA, Classics, English, MA, 1965, Gonville and Caius College, Cambridge. *Career:* Lecturer, Macquarie University, Australia, 1976–79; Literature Officer, Cumbria, 1979–81; mem. Poetry Society; Society of Authors. *Publications:* In Memoriam Milena, 1973; Bridging Loans, 1976; At the Stone Junction, 1978; The Loveless Letters, 1981; Talitha Cumi, 1985; Cicadas in Their Summers: New and Selected Poems, 1988; Flying Blues, 1994; In Memoriam Milena, 1995. Contributions: numerous publications. *Honours:* Alice Hunt Bartlett Award, Poetry Society, 1974; Arts Council Writer's Fellowships, 1982–85; National Poetry Competition Awards, 1984, 1985, 1988; Hawthornden Fellowship, 1988; First Prize, Peterloo Poetry Competition, 1989. *Address:* 21 Plough Lane, Sudbury, Suffolk CO10 2AU, England. *E-mail:* rodneypybus@ntlworld.com.

PYNCHON, Thomas Ruggles, Jr; Author; b. 8 May 1937, Glen Cove, Long Island, New York, USA. *Education:* BA, Cornell University, 1958. *Publications:* V, 1963; The Crying of Lot 49, 1965; Gravity's Rainbow, 1973; Mortality and Mercy in Vienna, 1976; Low-lands, 1978; Slow Learner (short stories), 1984; In the Rocket's Red Glare, 1986; Vineland, 1990; Mason and Dixon, 1997. Contributions: periodicals. *Honours:* Rosenthal Foundation Award, National Institute of Arts and Letters, 1967; Howells Medal, American Acad. of Arts and Letters, 1975; John D. and Catherine T. MacArthur Foundation Fellowship, 1988. *Address:* c/o Melanie Jackson Agency, 250 W 57th St, Suite 1119, New York, NY 10107, USA.

Q

QUANDT, William B(auer); Prof. of Politics and Writer; b. 23 Nov. 1941, Los Angeles, CA, USA; m. 1st Anna Spitzer, 21 June 1964, divorced 1980; m. 2nd Helena Cobban, 21 April 1984, one d. *Education:* BA, Stanford University, 1963; PhD, MIT, 1968. *Career:* Researcher, Rand Corpn, Santa Monica, CA, 1967–72; Staff Mem., 1972–74, Senior Staff Mem., 1977–79, National Security Council, Washington, DC; Assoc. Prof., University of Pennsylvania, 1974–76; Senior Fellow, Brookings Institution, Washington, DC, 1979–94; Senior Assoc., Cambridge Energy Research Assocs, Massachusetts, 1983–90; Prof. of Government and Foreign Affairs, University of Virginia, 1994–; mem. Council on Foreign Relations; Middle East Institute; Middle East Studies Asscn, pres., 1987–88. *Publications:* Revolution and Political Leadership: Algeria 1954–68, 1969; The Politics of Palestinian Nationalism, 1973; Decade of Decisions, 1977; Saudi Arabia in the 1980s, 1981; Camp David: Peacemaking and Politics, 1986; The Middle East: Ten Years After Camp David, 1988; The United States and Egypt, 1990; Peace Process: American Diplomacy and the Arab–Israeli Conflict Since 1967, 1994; The Algerian Crisis (with Andrew Preire), 1996; Between Ballots and Bullets: Algeria's Transition from Authoritarianism, 1998. Contributions: Professional journals. *Honours:* NDEA Fellow, 1963; Social Science Research Council Fellow, 1966; Council on Foreign Relations Fellow, 1972. *Address:* c/o Dept of Politics, University of Virginia, PO Box 400787, Charlottesville, VA 22904-4787, USA.

QUARTON, Marjorie; Farmer (retd) and Writer; b. 25 Oct. 1930, Nenagh, Co Tipperary, Ireland; m. John Quarton, one d. *Career:* mem. Irish PEN; Writers' Union. *Publications:* Corporal Jack, 1987; No Harp Like My Own, 1988; Breakfast The Night Before, 1989; Renegade, 1991; Saturday's Child, 1993; One Dog, His Man and His Trials, 1994; The Working Border Collie, 1998. Contributions: newspapers and journals. *Address:* 1 Casement Terrace, Dublin Rd, Nenagh, Co Tipperary, Ireland. *E-mail:* mquarton@eircom .net.

QUERRY, Ron(ald Burns); Novelist; b. 22 March 1943, Washington, DC, USA; m. Elaine Stribling Querry, one d. *Education:* BA, Central State University, Oklahoma, 1969; MA, New Mexico Highlands University, 1970; PhD, University of New Mexico, 1975. *Career:* Asst Prof., New Mexico Highlands University, 1975–77; Assoc. Prof., Lake Erie College, 1979–83; Instructor, University of Oklahoma, 1979–83; Visiting Assoc. Prof., Writer-in-Residence, University of Oklahoma, 1993–; mem. PEN. *Publications:* Growing Old at Willie Nelson's Picnic, 1983; I See By My Get-Up, 1987; Native Americans Struggle for Equality, 1992; The Death of Bernadette Lefthand, 1993; Bad Medicine, 1998. Contributions: journals, anthologies, periodicals and quarterlies. *Honours:* Literary Award, 1994.

QUICK, Barbara; Writer; b. 28 May 1954, Los Angeles, CA, USA; m. John Quick, 1 Aug. 1988. *Education:* BA, Literature, University of California, Santa Cruz. *Publications:* Northern Edge (novel), 1990; The Stolen Child (novel), 1997. Contributions: New York Times Book Review. *Honours:* Second Place, Ina Coolbrith Poetry Prize, 1977; Citation, B. Dalton Bookseller, 1990. *Literary Agent:* Wales Literary Agency, PO Box 9428, Seattle, WA 98109-0428, USA.

QUIGNARD, Pascal Charles Edmond; Writer; b. 23 April 1948, Verneuil-sur-Avre, France; one s. *Education:* Faculté des Lettres de Nanterre. *Career:* lecturer, 1969–77; mem., Cttee of Lecturing, 1977–94; Sec.-Gen. for Editorial Devt, Editions Gallimard; Pres., Int. Festival of Opera and Baroque Theatre, Château de Versailles, 1990–94; Pres., Concert des Nations, 1990–93. *Publications:* L'être du balbutiement, 1969; Alexandra de Lycophron, 1971; La parole de la Délie, 1974; Michel Deguy, 1975; Echo, 1975; Sang, 1976; Le lecteur, 1976; Hiems, 1977; Sarx, 1977; Inter aerias fagos, 1977; Sur le défaut de terre, 1979; Carus, 1979; Le secret du domaine, 1980; Petits traités (vols I–VIII), 1990; Les tablettes de buis d'Apronenia Avitia, 1984; Le vœu de silence (essay), 1985; Une gêne technique à l'égard des fragments, 1986; Ethelrude et Wolframm, 1986; Le salon de Wurtemberg, 1986; La leçon de musique, 1987; Les escaliers de Chambord, 1989; La raison, 1990; Albucius, 1990; Tous les matins du monde, 1991; Georges de La Tour, 1991; La Frontière, 1992; Le nom sur le bout de la langue, 1993; Le sexe et l'effroi, 1994; L'occupation américaine, 1994; Rhétorique spéculative, 1995; L'amour conjugal, 1995; Les septante, 1995; La haine de la musique, 1996; Vie secrète, 1998; Terrasse à Rome, 2000; Les ombres errantes, 2002. *Honours:* Chevalier, Légion d'honneur; Prix de la Société des gens de lettres, 1998; Grand prix du roman de la Ville de Paris, 1998; Prix de la fondation Prince Pierre de Monaco, 2000; Grand Prix du roman de l'Acad. française, 2000; Prix Goncourt, 2002. *Address:* c/o Editions Calmann-Lévy, 3 rue Auber, 75009 Paris, France.

QUILLER, Andrew (see Bulmer, Henry Kenneth).

QUINNEY, Richard; Prof. of Sociology Emeritus and Writer; b. 16 May 1934, Elkhorn, WI, USA. *Education:* BS, Carroll College, 1956; MA, Sociology, Northwestern University, 1957; PhD, Sociology, University of Wisconsin, 1962. *Career:* Instructor, St Lawrence University, 1960–62; Asst Prof., University of Kentucky, 1962–65; Assoc. Prof., 1965–70, Prof., 1970–73, New York University; Visiting Prof., CUNY, 1974–75, Boston University, 1975; Visiting Prof., 1975–78, Adjunct Prof., 1978–83, Brown University; Assoc. Ed., Victimology, 1976–82, Contemporary Crises, 1977–90, California Sociologist, 1977–, Critical Sociology, 1978–, Western Sociological Review, 1982–, Journal of Political and Military Sociology, 1984–, Visual Sociology, 1991–, Contemporary Justice Review, 1997–; Distinguished Visiting Prof., 1978–79, Adjunct Prof., 1980–83, Boston College; Prof., University of Wisconsin at Milwaukee, 1980; Prof. of Sociology, 1983–97, Prof. Emeritus, 1998–, Northern Illinois University; mem. American Society of Criminology; American Sociological Asscn. *Publications:* Criminal Behavior Systems: A Typology (with Marshall B. Clinard), 1967, third edn (with Marshall B. Clinard and John Wildeman), 1994; The Problem of Crime, 1970, third edn (with John Wildeman), 1991; The Social Reality of Crime, 1970; Criminal Justice in America: A Critical Understanding (ed.), 1974; Critique of Legal Order: Crime Control in Capitalist Society, 1974; Criminology: Analysis and Critique of Crime in America, 1975; Class, State, and Crime: On the Theory and Practice of Criminal Justice, 1977; Capitalist Society: Readings for a Critical Sociology (ed.), 1979; Providence: The Reconstruction of Social and Moral Order, 1980; Marxism and Law (ed. with Piers Beirne), 1982; Social Existence: Metaphysics, Marxism and the Social Sciences, 1982; Criminology as Peacemaking (ed. with Harold E. Pepinsky), 1991; Journey to a Far Place: Autobiographical Reflections, 1991; For the Time Being: Ethnography of Everyday Life, 1998. Contributions: Professional journals. *Honours:* Edwin Sutherland Award, American Society of Criminology, 1984; Fulbright Lecture and Research Award, University College, Galway, Ireland, 1986; Pres.'s Award, Western Society of Criminology, 1992; Canterbury Visiting Fellowship, University of Canterbury, New Zealand, 1993; Fellow, American Society of Criminology, 1995.

QUINTANA, Leroy V., BA, MA; American poet and writer; *Professor of English, San Diego Mesa College*; b. 1944, Alberquerque, NM. *Education:* Univ. of New Mexico, Univ. of Denver, New Mexico State Univ. *Career:* served in Viet Nam war 1967–68; Prof. of English, San Diego Mesa Coll. *Publications include:* Hijo del Pueblo 1976, Sangre 1981, Interrogations 1990, The History of Home 1993, My Hair Turning Gray Among Strangers 1996, The Great Whirl of Exile 1999, La Promesa and other stories 2002. *Honours:* American Book Awards 1981, 1992, Southwest Book Award 1981. *Address:* c/o Curbstone Press, 321 Jackson Street, Willimantic, CT 06226-1738, USA. *E-mail:* info@curbstone.org. *Website:* www.curbstone.org.

QUINTAVALLE, Uberto Paolo; Writer; b. 1 Nov. 1926, Milan, Italy; m. Josephine Hawke, 1970, five s. *Education:* DLitt, University of Milan, 1949; Playwriting, Yale Drama School, 1950. *Career:* mem. PEN Club, Italy, sec.-gen. *Publications:* La festa, 1953; Segnati a dito, 1956; Capitale Mancata, 1959; Tutti compromessi, 1961; Rito Romano, rito ambrosiano, 1964; Carolinda, 1974; Il Dio riciclato, 1989; Le Diecimila Canzoni di Putai, 1992; Fastoso Degrado, 1993; Il Memoriale di Pinocchio, 1993; Filottete, 1994; Milano Perduta, 1994; Incerca di Upamanyu, 1995; Le Erinni, 1996. Contributions: Il Corriere Della Sera; Il Ciornale.

QUIRK, Baron (Life Peer), cr. 1994, of Bloomsbury; **Charles Randolph Quirk;** academic and writer; b. 12 July 1920, Isle of Man, England; m. 1st Jean Williams 1946 (divorced 1979); two s.; m. 2nd Gabriele Stein 1984. *Education:* BA, 1947, MA, 1949, PhD, 1951, DLitt, 1961, University College London. *Career:* Lecturer in English, 1947–54, Prof. of English Language, 1960–68, Quain Prof. of English Language and Literature, 1968–81, University College London; Commonwealth Fund Fellow, Yale Univ. and Univ. of Michigan, 1951–52; Reader in English Language and Literature, 1954–58, Prof. of English Language, 1958–60, Univ. of Durham; Vice-Chancellor, Univ. of London, 1981–85; mem. Academia Europaea; American Acad. of Sciences; British Acad., pres., 1985–89. *Publications:* The Concessive Relation in Old English Poetry, 1954; Studies in Communication (with A. J. Ayer and others), 1955; An Old English Grammar (with C. L. Wrenn), 1955, revised edn (with S. E. Deskis), 1994; Charles Dickens and Appropriate Language, 1959; The Teaching of English (with A. H. Smith), 1959; The Study of the Mother-Tongue, 1961; The Use of English, 1962; Prosodic and Paralinguistic Features in English (with D. Crystal), 1964; A Common Language (with A. H. Marckwardt), 1964; Investigating Linguistic Acceptability (with J. Svartvik), 1966; Essays on the English Language: Mediaeval and Modern, 1968; Elicitation Experiments in English (with S. Greenbaum), 1970; A Grammar of Contemporary English (with S. Greenbaum, G. Leech, and J. Svartvik), 1972; The English Language and Images of Matter, 1972; A University Grammar in English (with S. Greenbaum), 1973; The Linguist and the English Language, 1974; Old English Literature: A Practical Introduction (with V. Adams and D. Davy), 1975; A Corpus of English Conversation (with J. Svartvik), 1980; Style and Communication in the English Language, 1982; A Comprehensive

Grammar of the English Language (with S. Greenbaum, G. Leech and J. Svartvik), 1985; English in the World (with H. Widdowson), 1985; Words at Work: Lectures on Textual Structure, 1986; English in Use (with G. Stein), 1990; A Student's Grammar of the English Language (with S. Greenbaum), 1990; An Introduction to Standard English (with G. Stein), 1993; Grammatical and Lexical Variance in English, 1995. Contributions: scholarly books and journals. *Honours:* numerous hon. doctorates; various fellowships. *Address:* University College London, Gower Street, London WC1E 6BT, England.

QUOIREZ, Françoise (see Sagan, Françoise).

R

RAAB, Lawrence (Edward); Prof. of English, Poet and Writer; b. 8 May 1946, Pittsfield, Massachusetts, USA; m. Judith Ann Michaels, 29 Dec. 1968, one d. *Education:* BA, Middlebury College, 1968; MA, Syracuse University, 1972. *Career:* Instructor, American University, 1970–71; Lecturer, University of Michigan, 1974; Prof. of English, Williams College, 1976–; Staff, Bread Loaf School of English, 1979–81, Bennington Writer's Conference, 1988, Bread Loaf Writer's Conference, 1994. *Publications:* Poetry: Mysteries of the Horizon, 1972; The Collector of Cold Weather, 1976; Other Children, 1986; What We Don't Know About Each Other, 1993; The Probable World, 2000; Visible Signs: New and Selected Poems, 2003. Contributions: many anthologies, scholarly journals, and periodicals. *Honours:* Acad. of American Poets Prize, 1972; National Endowment for the Arts Fellowships, 1972, 1984; Robert Frost Fellowship, Bread Loaf Writer's Conference, 1973; Yaddo Residencies, 1979–80, 1982, 1984, 1986–90, 1994, 1996, 1998; Bess Hokin Prize, Poetry Magazine, 1983; National Poetry Series Winner, 1992; MacDowell Colony Residencies, 1993, 1995, 1997, 2000. *Address:* 139 Bulkley St, Williamstown, MA 01267, USA.

RABAN, Jonathan, BA, FRSL; British author and critic; b. 14 June 1942, Fakenham, Norfolk; m. 1st Bridget Johnson (divorced 1970s); m. 2nd Caroline Cuthbert 1985 (divorced 1992); m. 3rd Jean Cara Lenihan 1992 (divorced 1997); one d. *Education:* King's School, Worcester, Peter Symonds School, Winchester, Brockenhurst Grammar and Univ. of Hull. *Career:* Asst Lecturer Univ. Coll. of Wales, Aberystwyth 1965–67; Lecturer in English and American Literature, Univ. of E Anglia 1967–69; professional writer 1969–; emigrated to USA 1990; mem. Soc. of Authors. *Publications:* The Technique of Modern Fiction 1969, Mark Twain: Huckleberry Finn 1969, The Society of the Poem 1971, Soft City 1973, Robert Lowell's Poems (ed.) 1974, Arabia Through the Looking Glass 1979, Old Glory 1981 (RSL Heinemann Award and Thomas Cook Award 1982), Foreign Land (novel) 1985, Coasting 1986, For Love and Money 1987, God, Man & Mrs Thatcher 1989, Hunting Mister Heartbreak 1990 (Thomas Cook Award 1991), The Oxford Book of the Sea (Ed.) 1992, Bad Land: An American Romance 1996 (Nat. Book Critics Circle Award and PEN/West Creative Nonfiction Award 1997), Passage to Juneau 1999, Waxwings (novel) 2003; contribs to Harper's, Esquire, New Republic, New York Review of Books, Outside, Granta, New York Times Book Review, Vogue. *Literary Agent:* Gillon Aitken Associates Ltd, 18–21 Cavaye Place, London, SW10 9PT, England. *Telephone:* (20) 7373-8672. *Fax:* (20) 7373-6002.

RABE, Berniece; Author; b. 11 Jan. 1928, Parma, MO, USA; m. 30 July 1946, three s., one d. *Education:* BSEd, National College; Graduate work in Psychology and Administration, Northern Illinois University and Roosevelt University; MA, Columbia College, Chicago. *Career:* Writing Instructor, Columbia College, Chicago; Consultant, Missouri Council of the Arts; mem. Society of Midland Authors; Off Campus Writers; Fox Valley Writers. *Publications:* Rass, 1973; Naomi, 1975; The Girl Who Had No Name, 1977; The Orphans, 1978; Who's Afraid, 1980; Margaret's Moves, 1987; A Smooth Move, 1987; Rehearsal for the Bigtime, 1988; Where's Chimpy, 1988; Tall Enough to Own the World, 1988; Magic Comes In It's Time, 1993; The Legend of the First Candy Cares, 1994. Other: Two film scripts; Picture books for children. Contributions: Short stories and articles. *Honours:* Honor Book, 1975, Golden Kite Award, 1977, National Society of Children's Book Writers; Midland Author's Award, 1978; Notable Book of the Year, American Library Asscn, 1982; National Children's Choice Award, 1987.

RABE, David (William); Dramatist, Screenwriter and Author; b. 10 March 1940, Dubuque, IA, USA; m. 1st Elizabeth Pan, 1969, divorced, one c.; m. 2nd Jill Clayburgh, March 1979. *Education:* BA in English, Loras College, 1962; MA, Villanova University, 1968. *Career:* Feature Writer, Register, New Haven, 1969–70; Asst Prof., Villanova University, 1970–72. *Publications:* Plays: The Basic Training of Pavlo Hummel, 1971; Sticks and Bones, 1971; The Orphan, 1973; In the Boom Boom Room, 1973; Burning, 1974; Streamers, 1976; Goose and Tomtom, 1976; Hurlyburly, 1984; Those the River Keeps, 1990; Crossing Guard, 1994. Screenplays: I'm Dancing as Fast as I Can, 1982; Streamers, 1983; Casualties of War, 1989; State of Grace, 1990; The Firm, 1993. Novel: Recital of the Dog, 1992. *Honours:* Rockefeller Foundation Grant, 1969; Associated Press Award, 1970; Drama Desk Award, 1971; Drama Guild Award, 1971; Elizabeth Hull-Kate Warriner Award, Dramatists Guild, 1971; Obie Award, 1971; Outer Critics' Circle Award, 1972; Tony Award, 1972; American Acad. of Arts and Letters Awards, 1974, 1976; Guggenheim Fellowship, 1976; New York Drama Critics' Circle Award, 1976. *Address:* c/o Grove-Atlantic, 841 Broadway, Fourth Floor, New York, NY 10003, USA.

RACHLIN, Nahid; Writer and Instructor; b. 6 June 1944, Abadan, Iran; m. Howard Rachlin, one d. *Education:* BA, Psychology, Lindenwood College, St Charles, Missouri; Creative Writing, Columbia University. *Career:* New York University, School of Continuing Education, 1978–90; Marymount Manhattan College, 1986–87; Hofstra University, 1988–90; Yale University, 1989–90; Hunter College, CUNY, 1990; Barnard College, 1991–; mem. PEN. *Publications:* Foreigner, 1978; John Murray, 1978; Married to a Stranger, 1983; Veils, 1992. Contributions: Reviews, journals and magazines. *Honours:* Doubleday-Columbia Fellowship; Stegner Fellowship, Stanford University; National Endowment for the Arts Grant; Bennet Certificate Award; PEN Syndicated Fiction Project.

RACIONERO GRAU, Luis; Spanish librarian, professor of economics and writer; b. 1940, Seu d'Urgell, Lleida. *Education:* Univ. of Calif. at Berkeley, USA, Churchill Coll., Cambridge, UK. *Career:* industrial engineer, Barcelona 1965; Prof. of MicroEcons, Faculty of Econ. Sciences and Urban Studies, School of Architecture, Barcelona; fmr Dir Spanish Coll., Paris; Dir-Gen. Biblioteca Nacional, Madrid 2001–04. *Publications include:* Taoista textos de estética 1991, Atenas de Pericles 1993, El arte de escribir 1995, La sonrisa de la Gioconda: Memorias de Leonardo 1999, Filosofias del Underground 2000, El pecado original 2001, Oriente y Occidente 2001, El progreso decadente (Espasa de Ensayo Prize) 2001, El alquimista trouador 2003. *Address:* c/o Editorial Planeta, Córcega 273-277, 08008 Barcelona, Spain.

RADDEN, Jennifer H.; academic and writer; b. 10 Sept. 1943, Melbourne, Vic., Australia. *Education:* BA, University of Melbourne, 1968; BPhil, 1971, DPhil, 1976, University of Oxford. *Career:* Psychiatric Social Worker, Melbourne, 1966–67, Greenfield, MA, USA, 1971–72; Lecturer in Philosophy, Tufts University, Medford, Massachusetts, 1972–74; Lecturer, 1975–84, Asst Prof., 1984–89, Assoc. Prof., 1990–97, Prof. of Philosophy, 1997–, Chair., 2002–, University of Massachusetts at Boston; Guest Lecturer, Bentley College, 1988, La Trobe University, Australia, 1995, 1996, University of Warwick, England, 1995, Linköping University, Sweden, 1996, University of Oregon, USA, 1997, University of Copenhagen, Denmark, 1997, University of Texas Southwestern Medical Center, USA, 1997; Mem., Forensic Psychiatry Group, 1992–99, Human Rights Committee, 1996–2000, Massachusetts Mental Health Center and Harvard Medical School; Mem., Ethics Committee, 1996–, McLean Hospital; mem. American Philosophical Asscn; Society for Women in Philosophy; Asscn for the Advancement of Philosophy and Psychiatry, Exec. Board, 1992–2002, Pres., 1997–; Society for Practical and Professional Ethics. *Publications:* Madness and Reason, 1985; Pathologies of the Modern Self: Post Modern Studies in Narcissism, Schizophrenia and Depression (contributor), 1987; Divided Minds and Successive Selves: Ethical Issues in Disorders of Identity and Personality, 1996; The Nature of Melancholy. Contributions: Philosophical Studies; Current Opinion in Psychiatry; Philosophy and Phenomenological Research; Journal of Social Theory and Practice; Dialogue. *Honours:* Fellow, Harvard University, 1991. *Address:* Department of Philosophy, University of Massachusetts at Boston, MA 02125, USA. *E-mail:* jennifer .radden@umb.edu.

RADLEY, Sheila (see Robinson, Sheila (Mary)).

RAE, Hugh Crauford, (James Albany, Robert Crawford, R. B. Houston, Stuart Stern, Jessica Stirling); Novelist; b. 22 Nov. 1935, Glasgow, Scotland; m. Elizabeth Dunn, 3 Sept. 1960, one d. *Career:* mem. Scottish Asscn of Writers. *Publications:* Skinner, 1965; Night Pillow, 1966; A Few Small Bones, 1968; The Saturday Epic, 1970; Harkfast, 1976; Sullivan, 1978; Haunting at Waverley Falls, 1980; Privileged Strangers, 1982. As Jessica Stirling: The Spoiled Earth, 1974; The Hiring Fair, 1976; The Dark Pasture, 1978; The Deep Well at Noon, 1980; The Blue Evening Gone, 1982; The Gates at Midnight, 1983; Treasures on Earth, 1985; Creature Comforts, 1986; Hearts of Gold, 1987; The Good Provider, 1988; The Asking Price, 1989; The Wise Child, 1990; The Welcome Light, 1991; Lantern for the Dark, 1992; Shadows on the Shore, 1993; The Penny Wedding, 1994; The Marrying Kind, 1995; The Workhouse Girl, 1996; The Island Wife, 1997; Prized Possessions, 2001. As James Albany: Warrior Caste, 1982; Mailed Fist, 1982; Deacon's Dagger, 1982; Close Combat, 1983; Matching Fire, 1983; Last Bastion, 1984; Borneo Story, 1984. *Address:* Drumore Farm Cottage, Balfron Station, Stirlingshire, Scotland.

RAE, John Malcolm; Writer; b. 20 March 1931, London, England. *Education:* MA, Sidney Sussex College, Cambridge, 1955; PhD, King's College, London. *Publications:* The Custard Boys, 1960; Conscience and Politics, 1970; The Golden Crucifix, 1974; The Treasure of Westminster Abbey, 1975; Christmas is Coming, 1976; Return to the Winter Place, 1979; The Third Twin: A Ghost Story, 1980; The Public School Revolution, 1981; Letters from School, 1987; Too Little, Too Late?, 1989; Delusions of Grandeur, 1993; Letters to Parents, 1998; Sister Genevieve, 2001. Contributions: Encounter; TLS; Times Educational Supplement; Times; Sunday Telegraph. *Honours:* United Nations Award for Film Script, 1962. *Address:* 25 Cedar Lodge, Lythe Hill Park, Haslemere, Surrey GU27 3TD, England.

RAE, Simon; British poet, biographer, broadcaster and playwright; b. 1952. *Career:* poet-in-residence, Warwickshire County Cricket Club/Midlands Arts Centre 1999; founder mem., Top Edge Theatre Productions. *Radio:* Poetry Please (presenter, BBC Radio 4), 20,000 Frenchmen under the Sea (writer) 1993, A Memory Lost (writer) 1994, Who Shall Bind the Infinite? (writer) 1995, Not at Dorking (writer) 1996. *Plays:* A Quiet Night In 1999, Grass 2001, Rose 2003. *Publications:* poetry: Faber Introduction 5 1982, Great Tew 1989, Seren Poets 2 1990, Calendar 1990, Soft Targets 1991,

Thatcher's Inferno 1992, Listening to the Lake 1993, Allotment 1996, Rapid Response: Poems from The Guardian 1991–1996, The Face of War 1999, Empires 2001, Caught On Paper: Cricket Poems 2002; biography: W.G. Grace: A Life 1998, It's Not Cricket: A History of Skulduggery, Sharp Practice and Downright Cheating in the Noble Game 2001; editor: The Orange Dove of Fiji: Poems for the World Wide Fund for Nature 1989, The Faber Book of Drink, Drinkers and Drinking 1991, The Faber Book of Murder 1994, The Faber Book of Christmas 1996, News That Stays News: The Twentieth Century in Poems 1999; contrib. poetry to anthologies, including Give Me Shelter 1991, Klaonica: Poems for Bosnia 1993, Bearing Witness 1995, The Gift: New Writing for the NHS 2002; contrib. to The Guardian, TLS, The Observer, New Statesman, Poetry Review, London Magazine, Leviathan. *Honours:* Royal Literary Fund Fellow, Warwick Univ. 1999–2001, Oxford Brookes Univ. 2003; Nat. Poetry Competition winner 1999, Southern Arts Literature Bursary, Gregory Award. *Address:* Faber and Faber Ltd, 3 Queen Square, London, WC1N 3AU, England. *Website:* www.faber.co.uk.

RAE-ELLIS, Vivienne, (Antonia Bell); Writer; b. 23 July 1930, Tasmania, Australia; m. W. F. Ellis, 31 May 1952, one s. one d. *Career:* mem. Australian Society of Authors; FRGS; RSL; Society of Authors, London. *Publications:* Lively Libraries, 1975; Trucanini: Queen or Traitor?, 1976; Queen Trucanini (with Nancy Cato), 1976; Menace at Oyster Bay, 1978; The Tribe With No Feet, 1978; Louisa Anne Meredith: A Tigress in Exile, 1979; The Cavendish Affair, 1980; Black Robinson, 1988; True Ghost Stories, 1990. Contributions: books, newspapers, journals, radio and television. *Address:* Gainsborough's House, 17 The Circus, Bath BA1 2ET, England. *E-mail:* vraellis@gifford.co.uk.

RAFFEL, Burton Nathan; academic, lawyer, writer, poet, editor and translator; b. 27 April 1928, New York, NY, USA; m. Elizabeth Clare Wilson 1974; three s. three d. *Education:* BA, Brooklyn College, CUNY, 1948; MA, Ohio State Univ., 1949; JD, Yale Univ., 1958. *Career:* Lecturer, Brooklyn College, CUNY, 1950–51; Ed., Foundation News, 1960–63; Instructor, 1964–65, Asst Prof., 1965–66, State Univ. of New York at Stony Brook; Assoc. Prof., State Univ. of New York at Buffalo, 1966–68; Visiting Prof., Haifa Univ., 1968–69, York Univ., Toronto, 1972–75, Emory Univ., 1974; Prof. of English and Classics, Univ. of Texas at Austin, 1969–71; Sr Tutor (Dean), Ontario College of Art, Toronto, 1971–72; Prof. of English, 1975–87, Lecturer in Law, 1986–87, Univ. of Denver; Ed.-in-Chief, Denver Quarterly, 1976–77; Contributing Ed., Humanities Education, 1983–87; Dir, Adirondack Mountain Foundation, 1987–89; Advisory Ed., The Literary Review, 1987–2003; Distinguished Prof. of Humanities and Prof. of English, Univ. of Louisiana at Lafayette, 1989–2003; mem. National Faculty. *Publications:* Non-Fiction: The Development of Modern Indonesian Poetry, 1967; The Forked Tongue: A Study of the Translation Process, 1971; Introduction to Poetry, 1971; Why Re-Create?, 1973; Robert Lowell, 1981; T. S. Eliot, 1982; American Victorians: Explorations in Emotional History, 1984; How to Read a Poem, 1984; Ezra Pound: The Prime Minister of Poetry, 1985; Politicians, Poets and Con Men, 1986; The Art of Translating Poetry, 1988; Artists All: Creativity, the University, and the World, 1991; From Stress to Stress: An Autobiography of English Prosody, 1992; The Art of Translating Prose, 1994; The Annotated Milton, 1999. Fiction: After Such Ignorance, 1986; Founder's Fury (with Elizabeth Raffel), 1988; Founder's Fortune (with Elizabeth Raffel), 1989. Poetry: Mia Poems, 1968; Four Humours, 1979; Changing the Angle of the Sun-Dial, 1984; Grice, 1985; Evenly Distributed Rubble, 1985; Man as a Social Animal, 1986; Beethoven in Denver, and other poems, 1999. Other: numerous trans.; annotated version of Hamlet, 2003. Contributions: professional journals. *Honours:* Frances Steloff Prize for Fiction, 1978; American-French Foundation Trans. Prize, 1991; several grants. *Address:* 203 S Mannering Avenue, Lafayette, LA 70508, USA. *E-mail:* bnraffel@cox-internet.com.

RAGAN, James; poet, dramatist and academic; b. 19 Dec. 1944, Pennsylvania, USA; m. Debora Ann Skovranko 1982; one s. two d. *Education:* BA, Vincent College, 1966; PhD, Ohio University, 1971. *Career:* Prof. and Dir, Professional Writing Program, University of Southern California, 1981–; Visiting Prof., CALTECH, 1989–; Poet-in-Residence, Charles University, Prague, 1993–; mem. Associated Writing Programs; MLA; Modern Poetry Asscn; PEN; Poetry Society of America; Writers Guild of America, West. *Publications:* In the Talking Hours, 1979; Womb-Weary, 1990; Yevgeny Yevtushenko: The Collected Poems (ed.), 1991; The Hunger Wall, 1995; Lusions, 1996. Contributions: anthologies, reviews, quarterlies, journals, and magazines. *Honours:* Humanitarian Award, Swan Foundation, Pittsburgh, 1972; National Endowment for the Arts Grant, 1972; Fulbright Fellow, 1985, 1988; Co-Winner, Gertrude Claytor Award, Poetry Society of America, 1987; Hon. Doctorate of Humane Letters, St Vincent College, 1990, Richmond University, London, 2001; Medal of Merit for Poetry, Ohio University, 1990; Telly Award, Poet's Corner, BHTV, 1996; Hon. Mem., Russian Acad. of Arts and Sciences, 1997. *Address:* 1516 Beverwil Drive, Los Angeles, CA 90035, USA.

RAHIMI, Atiq, PhD; novelist and film-maker; b. 1962, Kabul, Afghanistan; m. *Education:* Univ. of Kabul, Sorbonne, France. *Career:* political asylum in France 1985–. *Publications:* Earth and Ashes (in English trans.) 2001, Les Mille maisons du reve et de la terreur (in French trans.) 2002. *Address:* c/o Chatto & Windus, Random House, 20 Vauxhall Bridge Road, London, SW1V 2SA, England.

RAINE, Craig (Anthony); Poet and Writer; b. 3 Dec. 1944, Shildon, County Durham, England; m. Ann Pasternak Slater, 27 April 1972, three s., one d. *Education:* Honours Degree in English Language and Literature, 1966, BPhil, 1968, Exeter College, Oxford. *Career:* Lecturer, Exeter College, Oxford, 1971–72, Lincoln College, Oxford, 1974–75, Christ Church, Oxford, 1976–79; Books Ed., New Review, London, 1977–78; Ed., Quarto, London, 1979–80; Poetry Ed., New Statesman, London, 1981, Faber and Faber, London, 1981–91; Fellow, New College, Oxford, 1991–; Ed., Areté, 1999–; mem. PEN; RSL. *Publications:* Poetry: The Onion, Memory, 1978; A Journey to Greece, 1979; A Martian Sends a Postcard Home, 1979; A Free Translation, 1981; Rich, 1984; '1953': A Version of Racine's Andromaque, 1990; History: The Home Movie, 1994; Clay: Whereabouts Unknown, 1996; A la recherche du temps perdu, 2000; Collected Poems, 2000. Other: The Electrification of the Soviet Union (libretto), 1986; A Choice of Kipling's Prose (ed.), 1987; Haydn and the Valve Trumpet (essays), 1990; In Defence of T. S. Eliot (essays), 2000. Contributions: periodicals. *Honours:* First Prizes, Cheltenham Festival Poetry Competition, 1977, 1978; Prudence Farmer Awards, New Statesman, 1979, 1980; Cholmondeley Award, 1983; Sunday Times Award for Literary Distinction, 1999. *Literary Agent:* David Godwin Associates, 55 Monmouth St, London WC2H 9DG, England. *Address:* c/o New College, Oxford OX1 3BN, England.

RAJAN, Tilottama, BA, MA, PhD, FRSC; academic, writer and poet; *Canada Research Chair in English and Theory, University of Western Ontario*; b. 1 Feb. 1951, New York, NY, USA. *Education:* Trinity Coll., Toronto, Univ. of Toronto. *Career:* Asst Prof., Huron Coll., Univ. of Western Ontario 1977–80; Asst Prof. 1980–83, Assoc. Prof. 1983–85, Queen's Univ.; Prof., Univ. of Wisconsin at Madison 1985–90; Prof. 1990–, Dir Centre for the Study of Theory and Criticism 1995–2001, Canada Research Chair in English and Theory 2001–, Univ. of Western Ontario; mem. Canadian Comparative Literature Asscn, Univ. of Teachers of English, Keats-Shelley Asscn, MLA of America, North American Soc. for the Study of Romanticism, Wordsworth-Coleridge Asscn. *Publications:* Myth in a Metal Mirror 1967, Dark Interpreter: The Discourse of Romanticism 1980, The Supplement of Reading 1990, Intersections: Nineteenth Century Philosophy and Contemporary Theory 1995, Romanticism, History and the Possibilities of Genre 1998, Deconstruction and the Remainders of Phenomenology: Sartre, Derrida, Foucault, Baudrillard 2002, After Poststructuralism: Writing the Intellectual History of Theory 2002, Idealism Without Absolutes: Philosophy and Romantic Culture (with Arkady Plotnitsky) 2004; contrib. to professional journals. *Honours:* Guggenheim Fellowship 1987–88. *Address:* 870 Wellington Street, London, ON N6A 5S7, Canada. *E-mail:* trajan@uwo.ca.

RAJIC, Négovan, BEng, DipEng; Canadian writer; b. 24 June 1923, Belgrade, Yugoslavia; m. Mirjana Knezevic 1970; one s. one d. *Education:* Gymnasium of Belgrade, Univ. of Belgrade, Conservatoire des Arts et Metiers, France. *Career:* fought with Resistance during World War II; settled in France 1947; research engineer, physics laboratory, École Polytechnique de Paris 1956–63; electronics teacher, France 1963–69; settled in Canada 1969; Prof. of Mathematics, Collège de Trois-Rivières –1987; mem. Int. PEN, Asscn of Writers of Québec. *Publications:* Les Hommes-Taupes (trans. as The Mole Men) 1978, Propos d'un vieux radoteur (trans. as The Master of Srappado) 1982, Sept Roses pour une boulangère (trans. as Seven Roses for a Baker) 1987, Service pénitentiaire national (trans. as The Shady Business) 1988, Vers l'autre rive: Adieu Belgrade (novel) (Grand prix culturel de Trois-Rivières 2001) 2000, Le Puits ou histoire sans queue ni tête (play); contrib. numerous articles and short stories to publications. *Honours:* hon. mem. Asscn of Serbian Writers, Belgrade; Prix Esso du Cercle du Livre de France 1978, Prix Air Canada for best short story 1980, Prix Slobodan Yovanovitch, Asscn des écrivains et artistes serbes en éxil 1984, Prix littéraire de Trois-Rivières 1988, Franz Kafka Medal, European Circle, Prague 2000. *Address:* 300 rue Dunant, Trois-Rivières, QC G8Y 2W9, Canada.

RAMA RAU, Santha, (Rama Rau Wattles); Writer; b. 24 Jan. 1923, Chennai, India; m. 1st Faubion Bowers, 24 Oct. 1951, divorced 1966, one s.; m. 2nd Gurdon W. Wattles, 1970. *Education:* BA, Wellesley College, USA, 1945. *Publications:* Home to India, 1945; East of Home, 1950; This India, 1953; Remember the House, 1955; View to the South-East, 1957; My Russian Journey, 1959; A Passage to India (dramatisation of E. M. Forster's novel), 1962; Gifts of Passage, 1962; The Cooking of India, 1970; The Adventuress, 1970; A Princess Remembers, 1976; An Inheritance, 1977. Contributions: numerous journals and magazines. *Honours:* Hon. Degrees, Bates College, 1960, Roosevelt University, 1962, Brandeis University, 1962, Russell Sage College, 1965; Mlle Mag Merit Award, 1965; Asscn of Indians in America Award, 1977. *Literary Agent:* William Morris Agency, 1325 Avenue of the Americas, New York, NY 10019, USA.

RAMBAUD, Patrick; Author; b. 21 April 1946, Paris, France; m. Phamthi Tieu Hong, 1988. *Publications:* La saignée, 1970; Les aventures communautaires de Wao-le-Laid (with Michel-Antoine Burnier), 1973; Les complots de la liberté: 1832 (with Michel-Antoine Burnier), 1976; Parodies (with Michel-Antoine Burnier), 1977; 1848 (with Michel-Antoine Burnier), 1977; Le Roland Barthes sans peine (with Michel-Antoine Burnier), 1978; Comme des rats, 1980; La farce des choses et autres parodies (with Michel-Antoine Burnier), 1982; Fric-Frac, 1984; La mort d'un ministre, 1985; Frontière suisse (with Jean-Marie Stoerkel), 1986; Comment se tuer sans en avoir l'air, 1987; Virginie Q, 1988; Le visage parle (with Bernard Haller), 1988; Bernard Pivot reçoit..., 1989; Le dernier voyage de San Marco, 1990; Ubu Président ou l'imposteur, 1990; Les carnets secrets d'Elena Ceaucescu (with Francis Szpiner), 1990; Les mirobolantes aventures de Fregoli, 1991; Mururoa mon amour, 1996; Le gros secret, 1996; Oraison funèbres des dignitaires politiques qui ont fait leur temps et feignent de l'ignorer (with André Balland), 1996; La bataille, 1997; Le journalisme sans peine (with Michel-Antoine Burnier), 1997; Les aventures de Mai, 1998; Il neigeait, 2000. *Honours:* Prix Alexandre Dumas, 1976; Prix Lamartine, 1981; Prix de l'Insolent, 1988; Grand Prix du Roman, Académie Française, 1997; Prix Goncourt, 1997. *Address:* c/o Editions Grasset, 61 rue des Saints-Pères, 75006 Paris, France.

RAMDIN, Ronald Andrew; Historian, Biographer, Novelist and Lecturer; b. 20 June 1942, Marabella, Trinidad; m. Irma de Freitas, 20 Dec. 1969, one s. *Education:* Diploma in Speech and Drama, New Era Acad. of Drama and Music, 1963; Diploma in Industrial Relations and Trade Union Studies, University of Middlesex, 1977; BSc, Economics, LSE, 1982; DLitt, University of London, 1995. *Career:* First Sec., Whitley Council, British Library, 1973–75; Section Exec. Mem., Museums and Galleries Commission; mem. Society of Authors; FRHistS; FRSA. *Publications:* From Chattel Slave to Wage Earner, 1982; Introductory Text: The Black Triangle, 1984; The Making of the Black Working Class in Britain, 1987; Paul Robeson: The Man and His Mission, 1987; World in View: The West Indies, 1990; Reimaging Britain: 500 Years of Black and Asian History; Arising From Bondage: A History of East Indians in the Caribbean 1838–1991, 1992; The Other Middle Passage, 1995. Essays: 'Multicultural Britain' in Fragments of British Culture, 1998; 'The English Test: Post-War Immigration' in England 1945–2000, 2000. Contributions: Anglo-British Review; City Limits; Dragon's Teeth; Race Today; Caribbean Times; West Indian Digest; History Workshop Journal; Wasafiri; Dalit Voice; The Hindu. *Honours:* Scarlet Ibis Medal, Gold Award, Trinidad and Tobago High Commission, 1990; Hansib, Caribbean Times Community Award, 1990. *Address:* c/o The British Library, Oriental and India Office Collections, 96 Euston Rd, London NW1 2DB, England.

RAMÍREZ MERCADO, Sergio; Nicaraguan politician and author; *President, Movimiento de Renovación Sandinista (MRS)*; b. 5 Aug. 1942, Masatepe, Masaya; m. Gertrudis Guerrero Mayorga 1964; one s. two d. *Education:* Univ. Autónoma de Nicaragua. *Career:* was active in revolutionary student movt and founding mem. of Frente Estudiantil Revolucionario 1962; mem. Cen. American Univ. Supreme Council (CSUCA), Costa Rica 1964, Pres. 1968; mem. Int. Comm. of FSLN (Sandinista Liberation Front) 1975; undertook tasks on diplomatic front, propaganda and int. work on behalf of FSLN leading to overthrow of regime 1979; mem. Junta of Nat. Reconstruction Govt 1979–; Vice-Pres. of Nicaragua 1984–90; minority leader, Speaker, Nat. Ass. 1990–94; Pres. Movimiento de Renovación Sandinista (MRS) 1994–; MRS pre-cand. for presidency 1996; co-founder literary journal Ventana. *Publications include:* Cuentos 1963, El cuento centroamericano 1974, Charles Atlas también muere 1976, El cuento nicaragüense 1976, Castigo divino 1988, Confesión de amor 1991, Clave de sol 1992, Cuentos 1994, Oficios compartidos 1994, Un baile de máscaras 1995, Margarita, Está Linda la Mar. *Honours:* Dr hc (Cen. Univ. of Ecuador); Bruno Kreisky Prize 1988, Alfaguara Prize (Madrid) 1998; Chevalier des Arts et des Lettres 1993. *Address:* MRS, Tienda Katty lc. Abajo, Apdo. 24, Managua, Nicaragua. *Telephone:* (2) 78-0279. *Fax:* (2) 78-0268. *Website:* www.sergioramirez.org.ni (Office).

RAMKE, Bin; Prof. of English, Ed. and Poet; b. 19 Feb. 1947, Port Neches, Texas, USA; m. 31 May 1967, one s. *Education:* Louisiana State University, 1970; MA, University of New Orleans, 1971; PhD, Ohio University, 1975. *Career:* Prof. of English, Columbus University, GA, 1976–85, University of Denver, 1985–; Ed., Contemporary Poetry Series, University of Georgia Press, 1984–; Poetry Ed., 1985–, Ed., 1994–, The Denver Quarterly; mem. Associated Writing Programs; National Book Critics Circle; PEN, American Centre. *Publications:* The Difference Between Night and Day, 1978; White Monkeys, 1981; The Language Student, 1987; The Erotic Light of Gardens, 1989; Massacre of the Innocents, 1995. Contributions: Reviews, quarterlies, and journals. *Honours:* Yale Younger Poets Award, 1977; Texas Institute of Arts and Letters Award for Poetry, 1978; Iowa Poetry Award, 1995. *Address:* c/o Dept of English, University of Denver, Denver, CO 80208, USA.

RAMPERSAD, Arnold; Prof. of English and Writer; b. 13 Nov. 1941, Trinidad; m. 1985, one c. *Education:* BA, MA, Bowling Green State University; MA, PhD, Harvard University. *Publications:* Melville's Israel Potter: A Pilgrimage and Progress, 1969; The Art and Imagination of W. E. B. Dubois, 1976; Life of Langston Hughes, Vol. I, 1902–1941: I Too Sing America, 1986, Vol. II, 1941–1967: I Dream a World, 1988; Slavery and the Literary Imagination (co-ed.), 1989; Days of Grace: A Memoir (with Arthur Ashe), 1993. *Honours:* Ansfield Wolf Book Award in Race Relations, Cleveland Foundation, 1987; Clarence L. Hotte Prize, Phelps Stoke Fund, 1988; American Book Award, 1990. *Address:* Dept of English, Princeton University, Princeton, NJ 08544, USA.

RAMPLING, Anne (see Rice, Anne).

RAMSAY-BROWN, John Andrew, (Jay Ramsay); Poet, Writer, Ed. and Trans; b. 20 April 1958, Guildford, Surrey, England. *Education:* BA, English Language and Literature, Pembroke College, Oxford, 1980; Foundation Year Diploma in Psycho-synthesis, London Institute, 1987. *Career:* mem. College of Psychic Studies, London; Poetry Society; Psychosynthesis Education and Trust, London. *Publications:* Psychic Poetry: A Manifesto, 1985; Angels of Fire (co-ed.), 1986; New Spiritual: Selected Poems, 1986; Trwyn Meditations, 1987; The White Poem, 1988; Transformation: The Poetry of Spiritual Consciousness (ed.), 1988; The Great Return, books 1 to 5, 2 vols, 1988; Transmissions, 1989; Strange Days, 1990; Journey to Eden (with Jenny Davis), 1991; For Now (with Geoffrey Godbert), 1991; The Rain, the Rain, 1992; St Patrick's Breastplate, 1992; Tao Te Ching: A New Translation, 1993; I Ching, 1995; Kuan Yin, 1995; Chuang Tzu (with Martin Palmer), 1996; Alchemy: The Art of Transformation, 1996; Earth Ascending: An Anthology of New and Living Poetry (ed.), 1996; Kingdom of the Edge: New and Selected Poems 1980–1998, 1998. Contributions: periodicals. *Address:* c/o Susan Mears, The Old Church, Monkton Deverill, near Warminster, Wiltshire BA12 7EX, England.

RAMSEY, Jarold William; academic, poet, writer and dramatist; b. 1 Sept. 1937, Bend, Oregon, USA; m. Dorothy Ann Quinn 1959; one s. two d. *Education:* BA, English, University of Oregon, 1959; PhD, English Literature, University of Washington, 1966. *Career:* Acting Instructor, University of Washington, 1962–65; Asst Prof., 1965–70, Assoc. Prof., 1970–80, Prof. 1980–97, Prof. Emeritus, 1997–, University of Rochester; Visiting Prof. of English, University of Victoria, BC, 1974, 1975–76; mem. MLA. *Publications:* Poetry: The Space Between Us, 1970; Love in an Earthquake, 1973; Dermographia, 1983; Hand-Shadows, 1989. Plays and Libretti: Coyote Goes Upriver (play), 1981; The Lodge of Shadows (cantata with Samuel Adler), 1974. Non-Fiction: Coyote Was Going There: Indian Literature of the Oregon Country, 1977; Reading the Fire: Essays in the Traditional Indian Literature of the Far West, 1983. Editor: Elizabeth and Melville Jacobs, Nehalem Tillamook Tales, 1990; The Stories We Tell: Anthology of Oregon Folk Literature (with Suzi Jones), 1994. Contributions: anthologies, reviews, quarterlies, and journals. *Honours:* National Endowment for the Arts Grant, 1974, and Fellowship, 1975; Ingram Merrill Foundation Grant, 1975; Don Walker Award for Best Essay on Western Literature, 1978; Helen Bullis Award for Poetry, 1984; Quarterly Review International Poetry Prize, 1989. *Address:* 5884 NW Highway, No. 26, Madras, OR 97741, USA.

RAND, Peter; Writer; b. 23 Feb. 1942, San Francisco, CA, USA; m. Bliss Inui, 19 Dec. 1976, one s. *Education:* MA, Johns Hopkins University, 1975. *Career:* Fiction Ed., Antaeus, 1970–72; Ed., Washington Monthly, 1973–74; Teaching Fellow, Johns Hopkins University, 1975; Lecturer in English, Columbia University, 1976–91; mem. PEN; Authors' Guild; Poets and Writers; East Asian Institute, Columbia University; Research Assoc., Fairbank Center, Harvard University. *Publications:* Firestorm, 1969; The Time of the Emergency, 1977; The Private Rich, 1984; Gold From Heaven, 1988; Deng Xiaoping: Chronicle of an Empire, by Ruth Ming (ed. and trans. with Nancy Liu and Lawrence R. Sullivan), 1994; China Hands, 1995. Contributions: periodicals. *Honours:* CAPS, 1977.

RANDALL, Margaret; Writer, Poet, Photographer, Teacher and Activist; b. 6 Dec. 1936, New York, NY, USA; one s., three d. *Career:* Managing Ed., Frontiers: A Journal of Women's Studies, 1990–91; Distinguished Visiting Prof., University of Delaware, 1991; Visiting Prof., Trinity College, Hartford, CT, 1992. *Publications:* Giant of Tears, 1959; Ecstasy is a Number, 1961; Poems of the Glass, 1964; Small Sounds from the Brass Fiddle, 1964; October, 1965; Twenty-Five Stages of My Spine, 1967; Getting Rid of Blue Plastic, 1967; So Many Rooms Has a House But One Roof, 1967; Part of the Solution, 1972; Day's Coming, 1973; With These Hands, 1973; All My Used Parts, Shackles, Fuel, Tenderness and Stars, 1977; Carlota: Poems and Prose from Havana, 1978; We, 1978; A Poetry of Resistance, 1983; The Coming Home Poems, 1986; Albuquerque: Coming Back to the USA, 1986; This is About Incest, 1987; Memory Says Yes, 1988; The Old Cedar Bar, 1992; Dancing with the Doe, 1992; Hunger's Table: The Recipe Poems, 1997. Oral History: Cuban Women Now, 1974; Sandino's Daughters, 1981. Photography: Women Brave in the Face of Danger, 1985; Nicaragua Libre!, 1985. Contributions: anthologies, reviews, journals, and magazines. *Honours:* First Prizes, Photography, Nicaraguan Children's Asscn, 1983; Creating Ourselves National Art Exhibition, 1992. *Address:* 50 Cedar Hill Rd NE, Albuquerque, NM 87122, USA.

RANDALL, William Lowell; Educator and Writer; b. 1 Dec. 1950, Black's Harbour, NB, Canada. *Education:* AB, Harvard University, 1972; MDiv, Emmanuel College, Victoria University, 1976; University of Cambridge, 1976–77; ThM, Princeton Theological Seminary, 1979; DEd, University of Toronto, 1992. *Career:* Minister, United Church of Canada, 1979–90; English Instructor, Seneca College of Applied Arts and Technology, North York, Ontario, 1991–95; Adjunct Lecturer, Saint Bonaventure University, 1992–94; Part-time Instructor, University of Toronto, 1993; Seminar Facilitator, Site Leader, Brock University, 1993–95; Visiting Chair, 1995, Research Assoc., 1996–, Programme in Gerontology, St Thomas University, Fredericton, NB; Mem., Editorial Board, Interchange, journal on philosophy of education; mem. Canadian Asscn for the Study of Adult Education: Harvard Club of Toronto; International Society for Educational Biography; Canadian Asscn on Gerontology. *Publications:* Who Has Seen the Wind: Sermons from St Paul's, 1988; Restorying Our Lives: Personal Growth through Autobiographical Reflection (co-author), 1991; The Stories We Are: An Essay on Self-Creation, 1995. Contributions: articles to Aging and

Biography: Explorations in Adult Development, and to Interchange. *Honours:* Harvard Regular Scholarship, Harvard University, 1968–72; Wallace, Mitchell, and Billes Postgraduate Scholarships, Emmanuel College, Victoria University, 1973–76; McLeod Scholarship, United Church of Canada, 1989–91.

RANKIN, Ian James, (Jack Harvey), BA; writer; b. 1960, Cardenden, Fife, Scotland; m. Miranda; two s. *Education:* Edinburgh Univ. *Career:* mem. CWA, Int. Asscn of Crime Writers. *Publications:* The Flood 1986, Watchman 1988, Death is Not the End 1998, Beggars Banquet (short stories) 2002, Inspector Rebus series: Knots and Crosses 1987, Hide and Seek 1991, Tooth and Nail (aka Wolfjack) 1992, A Good Hanging and Other Stories (short stories) 1992, Strip Jack 1992, The Black Book 1993, Mortal Causes 1994, Let it Bleed 1996, Black and Blue 1997, The Hanging Garden 1998, Dead Souls 1999, Set in Darkness 2000, The Falls 2000, Resurrection Men 2001, A Question of Blood 2003, Fleshmarket Close 2004; as Jack Harvey: Witch Hunt 1993, Bleeding Hearts 1994, Blood Hunt 1995; contrib. to anthologies. *Honours:* CWA Golden Dagger 1997, Hawthornden Fellow, Chandler-Fulbright Award in Detective Fiction, CWA Dagger for best short story 1994. *Address:* Orion House, 5 Upper St Martin's Lane, London, WC2H 9EA, England. *Website:* www.ianrankin.net.

RANSFORD, Tessa; Poet, Writer and Ed.; b. 8 July 1938, Mumbai, India; m. 1st Iain Kay Stiven, 29 Aug. 1959, divorced 1986, one s., three d.; m. 2nd Callum Macdonald, 7 Dec. 1989, deceased. *Education:* MA, University of Edinburgh, 1958; Teacher Training, Craiglockhart College of Education, 1980. *Career:* Founder, School of Poets, Edinburgh, 1981–; Dir, Scottish Poetry Library, 1984–99; Ed., Lines Review, 1988–99; Freelance Poetry Practitioner and Adviser, 1999–; mem. Fellow, Institute for Contemporary Scotland, 2000, Centre for Human Ecology, 2003; Saltire Society, hon. mem., 1993; Scottish International PEN; Scottish Library Asscn, hon. mem., 1999; Scottish Poetry Library, ex-officio hon. mem., 1999; Society of Authors. *Publications:* Light of the Mind, 1980; Fools and Angels, 1984; Shadows from the Greater Hill, 1987; A Dancing Innocence, 1988; Seven Valleys, 1991; Medusa Dozen and Other Poems, 1994; Scottish Selection, 1998; When it Works it Feels Like Play, 1998; Indian Selection, 2000; Natural Selection, 2001; Noteworthy Selection, 2002. Contributions: anthologies, reviews, and journals. *Honours:* Scottish Arts Council Book Award, 1980; Howard Sergeant Award for Services to Poetry, 1989; Heritage Society of Scotland Annual Award, 1996; OBE, 2000; Society of Authors Travelling Scholarship, 2001; Royal Literary Fund Writing Fellowship, 2001–03; Hon. DUniv, Univ. of Paisley, 2003. *Address:* 31 Royal Park Terrace, Edinburgh EH8 8JA, Scotland. *Website:* www.scottish-pamphlet-poetry.com/tessa.

RANSOM, Bill; Writer and Poet; b. 6 June 1945, Puyallup, Washington, USA; one d. *Education:* BA, University of Washington, 1970. *Career:* Poetry-in-the-Schools Master Poet, National Endowment for the Arts, 1974–77; mem. International Asscn of Machinists and Aerospace Workers; Poetry Society of America; Poets and Writers; Poets, Essayists, and Novelists; SFWA. *Publications:* Fiction: The Jesus Incident, 1979; The Lazarus Effect, 1983; The Ascension Factor, 1988; Jaguar, 1990; Viravax, 1993; Burn, 1995. Poetry: Finding True North, 1974; Waving Arms at the Blind, 1975; Last Rites, 1979; The Single Man Looks at Winter, 1983; Last Call, 1984; Semaphore, 1993. Other: Learning the Ropes (poems, essays, and short fiction), 1995. Contributions: numerous publications. *Honours:* National Endowment for the Arts Discovery Award, 1977. *Address:* PO Box 284, Grayland, WA 98547, USA.

RANSOM, Jane Reavill; Poet and Writer; b. 28 June 1958, Boulder, CO, USA. *Education:* BA, Indiana University, 1980; MA, English, MA, Comparative Literature, New York University. *Career:* Asst Ed., San Juan Star, 1981–84; National and International News Ed., New York Daily News, 1984–89; Adjunct Prof., New York University, 1991; Guest lecturer in creative writing. *Publications:* Without Asking (poems), 1989; Bye-Bye (novel), 1997; Scene of the Crime: Poems, 1997; Missed (essay), 1997. *Honours:* Nicholas Roerich Poetry Prize, Story Line Press, 1989; New York University Press Award, 1997; Fellowships and residencies. *Literary Agent:* Linda Chester Literary Agency, Rockefeller Center, 630 Fifth Avenue, New York, NY 10103, USA.

RAO, Raja; Author; b. 21 Nov. 1909, Hassan, Mysore, India; m. 1st Camille Mouly 1931; m. 2nd Katherine Jones, April 1966, one s.; m. 3rd Susan Vaught, 1986. *Education:* Aligarh Muslim University, 1926–27; BA, Nizam College, Hyderabad, University of Chennai, 1929; University of Montpellier, 1929–30; Sorbonne, University of Paris, 1930–33. *Career:* Prof. of Philosophy, University of Texas at Austin, 1966–80. *Publications:* Kanthapura, 1938; The Cow of the Barricades and Other Stories, 1947; The Serpent and the Rope, 1960; The Cat and Shakespeare: A Tale of India, 1965; Comrade Kirillov, 1976; The Chessmaster and His Moves, 1978; The Policeman and the Rose, 1978; On Ganga Ghat, 1989. *Honours:* Sahitya Acad. Award, 1964; Padma Bhushan, Government of India, 1970; Neustadt International Prize for Literature, 1988. *Address:* 1806 Pearl, Austin, TX 78701, USA.

RAPHAEL, Frederic (Michael); Author, Dramatist and Trans; b. 14 Aug. 1931, Chicago, IL, USA; m. Sylvia Betty Glatt 17 Jan. 1955; two s. one d. (deceased). *Education:* Charterhouse; MA, St John's College, Cambridge. *Career:* mem. FRSL. *Publications:* Obbligato, 1956; The Earlsdon Way, 1958; The Limit of Love, 1960; A Wild Surmise, 1961; The Trouble With England, 1962; The Graduate Wife, 1962; Lindmann, 1963; Orchestra and Beginners, 1967; Like Men Betrayed, 1970; Who Were You With Last Night?, 1972; April, June and November, 1972; Richard's Things, 1973; Bookmarks (ed.), 1975; California Time, 1975; The Glittering Prizes, 1976; The Poems of Catallus (trans. with Kenneth McLeish), 1976; Somerset Maugham and His World, 1977; Sleeps Six, 1979; Cracks in the Ice: Views and Reviews, 1979; Oxbridge Blues, 1980; Byron (biog.), 1982; Heaven and Earth, 1985; Think of England, 1986; After the War, 1988; The Hidden I, 1990; The Complete Plays of Aeschyulus (trans. with Kenneth McLeish), two vols, 1991; Of Gods and Men, 1992; A Double Life, 1993; France, the Four Seasons, 1994; The Latin Lover and Other Stories, 1994; Old Scores, 1995; The Necessity of Anti-Semitism, 1997; Coast to Coast, 1998; Historicism and Its Poverty, 1998; Karl Popper, 1999; All His Sons, 1999; Eyes Wide Open: A Memoir of Stanley Kubrick and Eyes Wide Shut, 1999; The Benefits of Doubt, 2000; Personal Terms: The 1950s to 1960s (memoir), 2001; A Spoilt Boy (autobiog.), 2003. Screenplays: Nothing But the Best, 1964; Darling, 1965; Two for the Road, 1967; Far From the Madding Crowd, 1967; A Severed Head, 1972; Daisy Miller, 1974; The Glittering Prizes, 1976; Rogue Male, 1976; Something's Wrong, 1978; School Play, 1979; The Best of Friends, 1979; Richard's Things, 1981; After the War, 1989; The Man in the Brooks Brothers Shirt, 1991; Eyes Wide Shut, 1999. Plays: From the Greek, 1979; The Daedalus Dimension, 1982; The Thought of Lydia, 1988; The Empty Jew, 1993. Contributions: various publications. *Honours:* Lippincott Prize, 1961; Academy Award, 1966; RTS Award, 1976; ACE Awards, US Cable Television, 1985, 1991; Prix Genevois, 2000. *Literary Agent:* Rogers, Coleridge & White Ltd, 20 Powis Mews, London W11 1JN, England.

RAPOPORT, Janis; Poet, Writer and Dramatist; b. 22 June 1946, Toronto, Ontario, Canada; m. 1st, one s. two d.; m. 2nd Douglas Donegani, 20 May 1980, one d. *Education:* BA, University of Toronto, 1967. *Career:* Assoc. Ed., Tamarack Review, 1970–82; Playwright-in-Residence, Tarragon Theatre, 1974–75; Dir, Ethos Cultural Development Foundation, 1981–; Ed., Ethos magazine, 1983–87; Part-time Instructor, Sheridan College, 1984–86; Writer-in-Residence, St Thomas Public Library, 1987, Beeton Public Library, 1988, Dundas Public Library, 1990, North York Public Library, 1991; Instructor, School of Continuing Studies, University of Toronto, 1988–; mem. League of Canadian Poets; Playwrights' Union of Canada; Writers' Guild of Canada; Writers' Union of Canada. *Publications:* Within the Whirling Moment, 1967; Foothills, 1973; Jeremy's Dream, 1974; Landscape (co-ed.), 1977; Dreamgirls, 1979; Imaginings (co-author), 1982; Upon Her Fluent Route, 1992; After Paradise, 1996. Contributions: anthologies, newspapers, magazines, and radio. *Honours:* Canadian Council Arts Award, 1981–82; AIGA Certificate of Excellence, 1983; New York Dirs Club Award, 1983; Outstanding Achievement Award, American Poetry Asscn, 1986; Toronto Arts Council Research and Development Awards, 1990, 1992; Excellence in Teaching Award for Creative Writing, School of Continuing Studies, University of Toronto, 1998.

RASHID, Ahmed; Pakistani journalist and author; *Correspondent, The Daily Telegraph*; b. 1948, Rawalpindi; m.; three c. *Education:* Univ. of Cambridge, UK. *Career:* currently Pakistan, Afghanistan and Cen. Asia Corresp. The Daily Telegraph, Far Eastern Economic Review; writes regularly for several Pakistani newspapers and magazines; broadcaster on TV and radio stations around the world, including BBC World Service, ABC Australia, Radio France Int. and German Radio. *Publications include:* The Resurgence of Central Asia: Islam or Nationalism, Fundamentalism Reborn: Afghanistan and the Taliban, Jihad: The Rise of Militant Islam in Central Asia, Taliban: Islam, Oil and the New Great Game in Central Asia. *Honours:* Nisar Osmani Award for Courage in Journalism, Human Rights Soc. of Pakistan. *Address:* The Daily Telegraph, 1 Canada Square, Canary Wharf, London, E14 5DT, England (Office). *Telephone:* (20) 7538-5000 (Office). *Fax:* (20) 7513-2506 (Office). *E-mail:* dtnews@telegraph.co.uk (Office). *Website:* www.telegraph.co.uk (Office).

RATCLIFFE, Eric Hallam; poet, writer, editor, retd physicist and retd information scientist; b. 8 Aug. 1918, Teddington, Middlesex, England. *Career:* Founder-Ed., Ore 1955–95. *Publications:* Over 30, including: The Visitation, 1952; The Chronicle of the Green Man, 1960; Gleanings for a Daughter of Aeolus, 1968; Leo Poems, 1972; Commius, 1976; Nightguard of the Quaternary, 1979; Ballet Class, 1986; The Runner of the Seven Valleys, 1990; The Ballad of Polly McPoo, 1991; Advent, 1992; The Golden Heart Man, 1993; Fire in the Bush: Poems, 1955–1992, 1993; William Ernest Henley (1849–1903): An Introduction, 1993; The Caxton of Her Age: The Career and Family Background of Emily Faithfull (1835–1895), 1993; Winstanley's Walton, 1649: Events in the Civil War at Walton-on-Thames, 1994; Ratcliffe's Megathesaurus, 1995; Anthropos, 1995; Odette, 1995; Sholen, 1996; The Millennium of the Magician, 1996; The Brussels Griffon, 1996; Strange Furlongs, 1996; Wellington—A Broad Front, 1998; Capabilities of the Alchemical Mind, 1999; Cosmologia, 2000; Loyal Women, 2000; The Ghost with Nine Fathers, 2001; No Jam in the Astral, 2002; On Baker's Level, 2002; The Divine Peter, 2002; Desert Voices: A Tribute to Abu'l-Ala, 2003. Contributions: anthologies and journals. *Honours:* Baron, Royal Order of the Bohemian Crown, 1995. *Address:* 7 The Towers, Stevenage, Hertfordshire SG1 1HE, England. *E-mail:* chessmaster@ntlworld.com.

RATHBONE, Julian, BA; British writer and poet; b. 10 Feb. 1935, London. *Education:* Clayesmore School, Magdalene Coll., Cambridge. *Career:* teacher of English, Ankara, London, W Sussex 1959–73; full-time writer 1973–; contrib. The Times, The New Statesman, Literary Review, The Guardian, The Independent, The Sunday Telegraph, TLS. *Publications include:* With My Knives I Know I'm Good 1969, Trip Trap 1972, Kill Cure 1975, Bloody Marvellous 1975, Carnival 1976, King Fisher Lives 1976, Raving Monarchist 1977, Joseph 1979, Euro-killers 1979, Last Resort 1980, Base Case 1981, Spy of the Old School 1982, Watching the Detectives 1983, Wellington's War 1984, Nasty, Very 1984, Lying in State 1985, Greenfinger 1987, The Crystal Contract 1988, The Pandora Option 1990, Dangerous Games 1991, Intimacy 1995, Blame Hitler 1997, The Last English King 1997, Trajectories 1998, Brandenburg Concerto 1998, Sand Blind 2000, Kings of Albion 2000, Accidents Will Happen 2000, Beyond Reasonable Doubt 2000, Homage 2001, A Very English Agent 2002, As Bad as it Gets 2003, Birth of a Nation 2004; screenplays, poetry. *Honours:* Swanage Int. Poetry Prize, Crime Writers Short Story Silver Dagger, Deutsche Krimi Preis. *Address:* Sea View, School Road, Thorney Hill, near Christchurch, Dorset, BH23 8DS, England. *Telephone:* (1425) 673313. *Fax:* (1425) 673313. *E-mail:* julianrathbone@btinternet.com (Home).

RATNER, Rochelle; Poet, Writer and Ed.; b. 2 Dec. 1948, Atlantic City, NJ, USA; m. Kenneth Thorp 30 March 1990. *Career:* Poetry Columnist, Soho Weekly News, 1975–82; Co-Ed., Hand Book, 1976–82; Exec. Ed., American Book Review, 1978–; Small Press Columnist, Library Journey, 1985; Poetry Consultant, Israel Horizons, 1988–97; Ed., New Jersey Online: Reading Room, 1995–96; NBCC Board of Dirs, 1995–; mem. Authors' Guild; Hudson Valley Writers Guild; National Book Critics Circle; National Writers Union; PEN; Poetry Society of America; Poets and Writers. *Publications:* Poetry: A Birthday of Waters, 1971; False Trees, 1973; The Mysteries, 1976; Pirate's Song, 1976; The Tightrope Walker, 1977; Quarry, 1978; Combing the Waves, 1979; Sea Air in a Grave Ground Hog Turns Toward, 1980; Hide and Seek, 1980; Practicing to be a Woman: New and Selected Poems, 1982; Someday Songs, 1992; Zodiac Arrest, 1995; Tellings, 2003; House and Home, 2003. Fiction: Bobby's Girl, 1986; The Lion's Share, 1991. Other: Trying to Understand What It Means to be a Feminist: Essays on Women Writers, 1984; Bearing Life: Women's Writings on Childlessness (ed.), 2000. *Honours:* Susan Koppelman Award, 2000. *Address:* 609 Columbus Ave, Apt 16F, New York, NY 10024, USA. *E-mail:* rochelleratner@mindspring.com. *Website:* www.rochelleratner.com.

RATUSHINSKAYA, Irina Borisovna; Poet and Writer; b. 4 March 1954, Odessa, Russia; m. Igor Geraschenko, 17 Nov. 1979, two s. *Education:* Diploma in Physics, University of Odessa. *Career:* Visiting Scholar, Northwestern University, Evanston, IL, 1987–88; mem. PEN International, London. *Publications:* No I'm Not Afraid, 1986; A Tale of Three Heads, 1986; Beyond the Limit, 1987; Grey is the Colour of Hope, 1988; Pencil Letter, 1988; In the Beginning, 1990; The Odessans, 1996. Contributions: various anthologies, 1989–95. *Honours:* Poetry International Rotterdam Award, 1986; Ross McWhirter Foundation, 1987; Christopher Award, USA, 1988; Individual Templeton Award, UK, 1993.

RAVITCH, Diane Silvers; Research Prof. and Writer; b. 1 July 1938, Houston, TX, USA; m. Richard Ravitch 26 June 1960 (divorced 1986); three s. (one deceased). *Education:* BA, Wellesley College, 1960; PhD, Columbia University, 1975. *Career:* Adjunct Asst Prof., 1975–78, Assoc. Prof., 1978–83, Adjunct Prof., 1983–91, Teachers College, Columbia University; Asst Sec., Office of Research and Improvements, US Dept of Education, Washington, DC, 1991–93; Visiting Fellow, 1993–94, Non-Resident Senior Fellow, 1994–, Brown Chair in Education Policy, 1997–, Brookings Institution, Washington, DC; Senior Research Scholar, 1994–98, Research Prof., 1998–, New York University; mem. American Acad. of Arts and Sciences; National Acad. of Education; New York Historical Society; PEN International; Society of American Historians. *Publications:* The Great School Wars: New York City, 1805–1973, 1974; The Revisionists Revised, 1977; Educating and Urban People (co-author), 1981; The Troubled Crusade: American Education, 1945–1980, 1983; The School and the City (co-author), 1983; Against Mediocrity (co-author), 1984; The Schools We Deserve, 1985; Challenges to the Humanities (co-author), 1985; What Do Our 17-Year-Olds Know? (co-author), 1987; The American Reader (co-ed.), 1990; The Democracy Reader (co-ed.), 1992; National Standards in American Education, 1995; Learning from the Past (ed.), 1995; Debating the Future of American Education (ed.), 1995; New Schools for a New Century (co-ed.), 1997; Left Back, 2000; City Schools (ed.), 2000. Contributions: scholarly books and professional journals. *Honours:* several hon. doctorates; Guggenheim Fellowship, 1977–78; Wellesley College Alumnae Achievement Award, 1989; Award for Distinguished Service, New York Acad. of Public Education, 1994. *Address:* New York University, 26 Washington Sq., New York, NY 10003, USA.

RAVVIN, Norman; Novelist and University Instructor; b. 26 Aug. 1963, Calgary, AB, Canada. *Education:* BA, 1986, MA, English, 1988, University of British Columbia; PhD, University of Toronto, 1994. *Career:* Instructor, Concordia University; General Ed., Hungry I Books, 2000–; mem. Writers Guild of Alberta; Asscn of Canadian College and University Teachers of English; MLA of America. *Publications:* Café des Westens (novel) 1991, Sex, Skyscrapers and Standard Yiddish (short stories) 1997, A House of Words: Jewish Writing, Identity and Memory (essays) 1997, Great Stories of the Sea (ed.) 1999, Hidden Canada: An Intimate Travelogue 2001, Not Quite Mainstream: Canadian Jewish Short Stories (ed.) 2001, Lola by Night (novel) 2003. Contributions: anthologies: Fresh Blood: New Canadian Gothic Fiction, The Nelson Introduction to Literature; journals: Canadian Jewish Studies, Canadian Literature, English Studies in Canada, Malcolm Lowry Review, Prairie Fire, Prism International, Studies in Canadian Literature, Wascana Review, West Coast Review, Western Living. *Honours:* K. M. Hunter Emerging Artist Award, Alberta Culture and Multiculturalism New Fiction Award 1990, PhD Fellowship, Social Sciences and Humanities Research Council of Canada. *Address:* c/o Concordia University, Dept of Religion, Montréal, QC H3G 1M8, Canada.

RAWN, Melanie (Robin); Writer; b. 12 June 1954, Santa Monica, CA, USA. *Education:* BA, History, Scripps College, 1975; Graduate School, University of Denver, 1975–76; Teacher Credentials, California State University at Fullerton, 1980. *Career:* mem. SFWA. *Publications:* Dragon Prince, 1988, The Star Scroll, 1989, Sunrunner's Fire, 1990; Stronghold, 1990, The Dragon Token, 1992, Skybowl, 1993; The Ruins of Ambrai, 1994; The Golden Key (co-author), 1996; The Mageborn Traitor, 1997. *Address:* c/o Scovil Chichak Galen Inc, 381 Park Ave S, New York, NY 10016, USA. *Website:* www.melanierawn.com.

RAWNSLEY, Andrew Nicholas James; Journalist, Broadcaster and Author; b. 5 Jan. 1962, Leeds, England; m. Jane Hall, 1990, three d. *Education:* Sidney Sussex College, Cambridge; MA, History, Cambridge. *Career:* BBC, 1983–85; Reporter, Feature Writer, 1985–87, Political Columnist, 1987–93, The Guardian; Writer, Presenter, A Week in Politics, 1989–97, Bye Bye Blues, 1997, Blair's Year, 1998, Channel 4 series; Assoc. Ed., Chief Political Commentator, The Observer, 1993–; Writer, Presenter, The Agenda, ITV series, 1996, The Westminster Hour, Radio 4 series, 1998–; The Unauthorised Biography of the United Kingdom, 1999. *Publications:* Servants of the People: The Inside Story of New Labour, 2000. *Honours:* Student Journalist of the Year, 1983; Young Journalist of the Year, 1987; Columnist of the Year, What the Papers Say Awards, 2000; Book of the Year, Channel 4/House Magazine Political Awards, 2001; Journalist of the Year, Channel 4 Political Awards, 2003; FRSA. *Literary Agent:* Rogers, Coleridge & White Ltd, 20 Powis Mews, London W11 1JN, England. *Address:* The Observer, 119 Farringdon Rd, London EC1R 3ER, England. *E-mail:* andrew.rawnsley@observer.co.uk.

RAWORTH, Thomas Moore; Poet and Writer; b. 19 July 1938, London, England; m. Valerie Murphy, four s., one d. *Education:* MA, University of Essex, 1970. *Career:* Poet-in-Residence, University of Essex, 1969, Northeastern University, Chicago, 1973–74, King's College, Cambridge, 1977–78; Lecturer, Bowling Green State University, Ohio, 1972–73; Visiting Lecturer, University of Texas, 1974–75, University of Cape Town, 1991, University of San Diego, 1996; mem. PEN. *Publications:* The Relation Ship, 1967; The Big Green Day, 1968; A Serial Biography, 1969; Lion, Lion, 1970; Moving, 1971; Act, 1973; Ace, 1974; Common Sense, 1976; Logbook, 1977; Sky Tails, 1978; Nicht Wahr, Rosie?, 1979; Writing, 1982; Levre de Poche, 1983; Heavy Light, 1984; Tottering State: Selected Poems, 1963–83, 1984; Lazy Left Hand, 1986; Visible Shivers, 1987; All Fours, 1991; Catacoustics, 1991; Eternal Sections, 1991; Survival, 1991; Clean and Well Lit: Selected Poems 1987–1995, 1996; Collected Poems, 2003. Contributions: periodicals. *Honours:* Alice Hunt Bartlett Prize, 1969; Cholmondeley Award, 1971; International Committee on Poetry Award, New York, 1988. *Address:* 3 St Philip's Rd, Cambridge CB1 3AQ, England.

RAWSON, Claude Julien, BA, BLitt, MA; academic, writer and editor; b. 8 Feb. 1935, Shanghai, China; m. Judith Ann Hammond 1959; three s. two d. *Education:* Magdalen College, Oxford. *Career:* Lecturer in English, University of Newcastle, 1957–65; Lecturer, then Prof., 1965–85, Hon. Prof., 1985–, University of Warwick; George Sherburn Prof. of English, University of Illinois, 1985–86; George M. Bodman Prof. of English, 1986–96, Maynard Mack Prof. of English, 1996–, Yale University; Ed., Modern Language Review, Yearbook of English Studies, 1974–88; Gen. Ed., Unwin Critical Library, 1975–, Blackwell Critical Biographies, 1985–; Exec. Ed., Cambridge History of Literary Criticism, 1983–; Chair. and General Ed., Yale edn of the Private Papers of James Boswell, 1990–2000; Gen. Ed., Cambridge edn of the Works of Jonathan Swift, 2001–; Gen. Ed. The Works of Jonathan Swift (Cambridge edn) 2001; General Editor Cambridge Edition of the Works of Jonathan Swift, 2001; mem. Fellow, American Acad. of Arts and Sciences; British Society for 18th Century Studies, pres., 1974–75; American Society for 18th Century Studies, 1970–; MHRA, committee mem., 1974–88; Fellow of American Academy of Arts and Sciences. *Publications:* Henry Fielding, 1968; Focus Swift, 1971; Henry Fielding and the Augustan Ideal Under Stress, 1972; Gulliver and the Gentle Reader, 1973; Fielding: A Critical Anthology, 1973; The Character of Swift's Satire, 1983; English Satire and the Satiric Tradition, 1984; Order from Confusion Sprung: Studies in 18th Century Literature, 1985; Thomas Parnell's Collected Poems (ed. with F. P. Lock), 1989; Satire and Sentiment 1660–1800, 1994; Jonathan Swift: A Collection of Critical Essays (ed.), 1995; Cambridge History of Literary Criticism, Vol. 4: The Eighteenth Century (ed. with H. B. Nisbet), 1997; God, Gulliver and Genocide: Barbarism and the European Imagination, 1492–1945, 2001; Basic Writings of Jonathan Swift (ed. with Ian Higgins), 2002. *Address:* 50 Malthouse Lane, Kenilworth, Warwickshire CV8 1AD, England.

RAY, David (Eugene); Prof. of English Emeritus, Poet and Writer; b. 20 May 1932, Sapulpa, OK, USA; m. Suzanne Judy Morrish, 21 Feb. 1970, one s., three d. *Education:* BA, 1952, MA, 1957, University of Chicago. *Career:* Instructor, Wright Junior College, 1957–58, Northern Illinois University, 1958–60; Instructor, Cornell Univ., 1960–64; Asst Prof., Reed College, Portland, OR, 1964–66; Lecturer, University of Iowa, 1969–70; Visiting Assoc. Prof., Bowling Green State University, 1970–71; Ed., New Letters Magazine, 1971–85; Prof. of English, 1971–95, Prof. Emeritus, 1995–, University of Missouri, Kansas City; Visiting Prof., Syracuse University, 1978–79, University of Rajasthan, India, 1981–82; Exchange Prof., University of Otago, New Zealand, 1987; Visiting Fellow, University of Western Australia, 1991; Senior Acad. Prof., University of Arizona, 1996–; mem. Acad. of American Poets; PEN; Poetry Society of America. *Publications:* X-Rays, 1965; Dragging the Main and Other Poems, 1968; A Hill in Oklahoma, 1972; Gathering Firewood: New Poems and Selected, 1974; Enough of Flying: Poems Inspired by the Ghazals of Ghalib, 1977; The Tramp's Cup, 1978; The Farm in Calabria and Other Poems, 1979; The Touched Life, 1982; On Wednesday I Cleaned Out My Wallet, 1985; Elysium in the Halls of Hell, 1986; Sam's Book, 1987; The Maharani's New Wall, 1989; Not Far From the River, 1990; Wool Highways, 1993; Kangaroo Paws, 1995; Heartstones: New and Selected Poems, 1998; Demons in the Diner, 1999; The Endless Search: A Memoir, 2003; One Thousand Years, 2003. Short Stories: The Mulberries of Mingo, 1978. Contributions: journals and newspapers. *Honours:* William Carlos Williams Awards, 1979, 1993; PEN Syndicated Fiction Awards, 1982–86; Bernice Jennings Award for Traditional Poetry, Amelia Magazine, 1987; Maurice English Poetry Award, 1988; National Poetry Award, Passaic Community College, 1989; First Prize, Stanley Hanks Memorial Contest, St Louis Poetry Centre, 1990; New England Poetry Club Daniel Varoujan Award, 1996; New Millennium Poetry Award, 1997; Allen Ginsberg Poetry Award, Poetry Centre, Paterson, 1997; Explorations magazine Poetry Award, 1997; Amelia Magazine Long Poem Award, 1998; Richard Snyder Memorial Prize, 1999; Flyway Magazine Poetry Award, 2000; Nuclear Age Peace Foundation Poetry Award, 2001. *Address:* 2033 E 10th St, Tucson, AZ 85719, USA. *E-mail:* djray@gci-net.com. *Website:* www.davidraypoet.com.

RAY, Robert Henry; Prof. of English and Writer; b. 29 April 1940, San Saba, Texas, USA; m. Lynette Elizabeth Dittmar, 1 Sept. 1962, two d. *Education:* BA, 1963, PhD, 1967, University of Texas at Austin. *Career:* Asst Prof. of English, 1967–75, Assoc. Prof. of English, 1975–85, Prof. of English, 1985–, Graduate Program Dir, Baylor University; mem. MLA of America; John Donne Society. *Publications:* The Herbert Allusion Book, 1986; Approaches to Teaching Shakespeare's King Lear, 1986; A John Donne Companion, 1990; A George Herbert Companion, 1995; An Andrew Marvell Companion, 1998. Contributions: various publications. *Address:* Dept of English, PO Box 97406, Baylor University, Waco, TX 76798, USA. *E-mail:* Robert_Ray@baylor.edu.

RAY, Robert J., BA, MA, PhD; teacher and writer; b. 15 May 1935, Amarillo, TX, USA; m. 1st Ann Allen (divorced); m. 2nd Margot M. Waale 1983. *Education:* University of Texas, Austin. *Career:* Instructor, 1963–65, Asst Prof., 1965–68, Assoc. Prof., 1968–75, Prof., 1976, Beloit College, Wisconsin; Writing Teacher, Valley College, 1984–88, University of California, Irvine, 1985–88; Adjunct Prof., Chapman College, 1988–; mem. MWA. *Publications:* The Art of Reading: A Handbook on Writing (with Ann Ray), 1968; The Heart of the Game (novel), 1975; Cage of Mirrors (novel), 1980; Small Business: An Entrepreneur's Plan (with L. A. Eckert and J. D. Ryan), 1985; Bloody Murdock (novel), 1987; Murdock for Hire (novel), 1987; The Hitman Cometh (novel), 1988; Dial M for Murder (novel), 1988; Murdock in Xanadu (novel), 1989. *Address:* c/o Ben Kamsler, H. N. Swanson Inc, 8523 Sunset Blvd, Los Angeles, CA 90069, USA.

RAYBAN, Chlöe (see Bear, Carolyn Ann).

RAYMOND, Diana Joan; Novelist; b. 25 April 1916, London, England; m. Ernest Raymond, Aug. 1940, one s. *Education:* Cheltenham Ladies' College. *Career:* mem. Society of Authors. *Publications:* The Small Rain, 1954; Guest of Honour, 1960; The Climb, 1962; People in the House, 1964; Incident on a Summer's Day, 1974; Emma Pride, 1981; Lily's Daughter, 1974; Roundabout, 1994; The Sea Family, 1997. *Address:* 22 The Pryors, E Heath Rd, London NW3 1BS, England.

RAYMOND, Mary (see Keegan, Mary Constance).

RAYMOND, Patrick Ernest; Royal Air Force Officer (retd) and Writer; b. 25 Sept. 1924, Cuckfield, Sussex, England; m. Lola Pilpel, 27 May 1950, one s. *Education:* Art School, Cape Town, South Africa. *Career:* Royal Air Force, rising to Group Captain, 1942–77. *Publications:* A City of Scarlet and Gold, 1963; The Lordly Ones, 1965; The Sea Garden, 1970; The Last Soldier, 1974; A Matter of Assassination, 1977; The White War, 1978; The Grand Admiral, 1980; Daniel and Esther, 1989. *Address:* 24 Chilton Rd, Chesham, Buckinghamshire HP5 2AU, England.

RAYNER, Claire Berenice, (Sheila Brandon, Ann Lynton, Ruth Martin), OBE; British writer and broadcaster; b. 22 Jan. 1931, London; m. Desmond Rayner 1957; two s. one d. *Education:* Royal Northern and Guy's Hosps, London. *Career:* nurse and midwife until 1960; writer advice columns in Petticoat, The Sun, The Sunday Mirror 1980–88, Today newspaper, Woman's Own 1966–88, Woman magazine 1988–92; has made numerous radio broadcasts for BBC, LBC radio and Capital Radio, London; many TV appearances including Pebble Mill at One, Kitchen Garden (co-presenter), Claire Rayner's Casebook 1980, 1983, 1984, BBC Breakfast TV, TV-AM Advice Spot 1985, A Problem Shared (British Sky Broadcasting TV), The David Frost Programme; has produced In Company with Claire Rayner, women's health and family life videos; Pres. Gingerbread, The Patient's Asscn, British Humanist Asscn 1999–; fmr mem. Royal Coll. of Nursing Cttee on Ethics; mem. Video Appeals Cttee British Bd of Film Classification, Council Charter 88, Royal Comm. on Funding of Care of the Elderly 1998–99; Assoc. Non-Exec. Dir Royal London Hosps Trust (Barts and the London); Fellow Soc. of Authors; Patron the Terrence Higgins Trust. *Publications include:* fiction: The Hive 1967, The Meddlers 1970, A Time to Heal 1972, The Performers (12 Vol. saga) 1973–1986, Reprise 1980, Family Chorus 1984, The Virus Man 1985, Maddie 1988, The Poppy Chronicles (six vols) 1987–, Omnibus of Three Hospital Novels (reprint, as Sheila Brandon) 1989, Postscripts 1991, Dangerous Things 1992, The Barnabus crime novels 1993, 1994, 1995, 1996, 1997; non-fiction: For Children 1967, Mothercraft (as Ann Lynton) 1967, Woman's Medical Dictionary 1971, People in Love: Modern Guide to Sex in Marriage, Kitchen Garden (jtly) 1976, Related to Sex 1979, Claire Rayner's Lifeguide 1980, Baby and Young Child Care 1981, The Body Book, Growing Pains 1984, The Getting Better Book 1985, Safe Sex 1987, The Don't Spoil Your Body Book 1989, How Did I Get Here From There? (autobiog.) 2003; books published in many countries; contribs to Design magazine (journal of the Design Council), nat. newspapers, professional medical journals. *Honours:* Hon. Fellow Univ. of N London 1988; Freeman, City of London 1981; Hon. DUniv (Oxford Brookes) 2000, (Middlesex) 2002; Medical Journalist of the Year 1987, Best Specialist Consumer Columnist of the Year, Publisher Magazine 1988. *Address:* Holly Wood House, Roxborough Avenue, Harrow-on-the-Hill, Middx, HA1 3BU, England. *Telephone:* (20) 8864-9898. *Fax:* (20) 8422-3710. *E-mail:* clairerayner@harrowhill.demon.co.uk.

RAYSON, Hannie; playwright; b. 31 March 1957, Brighton, Melbourne, Vic., Australia. *Education:* BA, University of Melbourne, 1977; Dip Art in Dramatic Arts, Victoria College of Arts, 1980. *Career:* Writer-in-Residence, various institutions; Literature Board, Australia Council, 1992–95. *Publications:* Please Return to Sender, 1980; Mary, 1981; Leave it Till Monday, 1984; Room to Move, 1985; Hotel Sorrento, 1990; SLOTH (television play), 1992; Falling From Grace, 1994; After George (play), 2001. *Honours:* Australian Writers Guild Awards, 1986, 1991; New South Wales Premier's Literary Award; Sidney Myer Performing Arts Award, 1996. *Literary Agent:* Hilary Linstead & Associates, PO Box 1536, Strawberry Hills, NSW 2012, Australia.

RAZ, Joseph; Prof. of the Philosophy of Law and Writer; b. 21 March 1939, Haifa, Palestine. *Education:* Magister Juris, Hebrew University, Jerusalem, 1963; DPhil, University of Oxford, 1967. *Career:* Lecturer, Hebrew University, Jerusalem, 1967–70; Research Fellow, Nuffield College, Oxford, 1970–72; Tutorial Fellow, 1972–85, Prof. of the Philosophy of Law, 1985–, Balliol College, Oxford; Visiting Prof., 1995–2002, Prof., 2002–, Columbia Univ., New York; mem. American Acad. of Arts and Sciences, hon. foreign mem.; British Acad., fellow. *Publications:* The Concept of a Legal System, 1970; Practical Reason and Norms, 1975; The Authority of Law, 1979; The Morality of Freedom, 1986; Ethics in the Public Domain, 1994; Engaging Reason, 2000; Value, Respect and Attachment, 2001; The Practice of Value, 2003. Contributions: Professional journals and other publications. *Honours:* W. J. M. Mackenzie Book Prize, Political Studies Asscn, UK, 1987; Elaine and David Spitz Book Prize, Conference for the Study of Political Thought, New York, 1987; Hon. Doctorate, Katolieke University, Brussels, 1993. *Address:* c/o Balliol College, Oxford OX1 3BJ, England.

READ, Anthony; Writer and Dramatist; b. 21 April 1935, Staffordshire, England; m. Rosemary E. Kirby, 29 March 1958, two d. *Education:* Central School of Speech and Drama, London, 1952–54. *Career:* mem. Trustee, Past Chair., Writers Guild of Great Britain. *Publications:* The Theatre, 1964; Operation Lucy (with David Fisher), 1980; Colonel Z (with David Fisher), 1984; The Deadly Embrace (with David Fisher), 1988; Kristallnacht (with David Fisher), 1989; Conspirator (with Ray Bearse), 1991; The Fall of Berlin (with David Fisher), 1992; Berlin: The Biography of a City (with David Fisher), 1994; The Proudest Day: India's Long Road to Independence (with David Fisher), 1997; The Devil's Disciples: The Lives and Times of Hitler's Inner Circle, 2003. Other: over 200 television films, plays, series and serials. *Honours:* Pye Colour TV Award, 1983; Wingate Literary Prize, 1989. *Address:* 7 Cedar Chase, Taplow, Buckinghamshire, England. *E-mail:* readwrites@msn.com.

READ, Desmond (see Moorcock, Michael (John)).

READ, Miss (see Saint, Dora Jessie).

READ, Piers Paul, MA, FRSL; British writer; b. 7 March 1941, Beaconsfield; m. Emily Albertine Boothby 1967; two s. two d. *Education:* Ampleforth Coll., York and St John's Coll., Cambridge. *Career:* Artist-in-Residence, Ford Foundation, W Berlin 1964; Sub-Ed. Times Literary Supplement, London 1965; Harkness Fellow Commonwealth Fund, New York 1967–68; Council mem. Inst. of Contemporary Arts (ICA), London 1971–75; Cttee of Man. Soc. of Authors, London 1973–76; mem. Literature Panel Arts Council, London 1975–77; Adjunct Prof. of Writing, Columbia Univ., New York 1980; Chair.

Catholic Writers' Guild 1992–97; Bd mem. Aid to the Church in Need 1991–; Trustee Catholic Library 1997–; mem. RSL (mem. of Council 2001–). *Publications:* Game in Heaven with Tussy Marx 1966, The Junkers 1968, Monk Dawson 1969, The Professor's Daughter 1971, The Upstart 1973, Alive: The Story of the Andes Survivors 1974, Polonaise 1976, The Train Robbers 1978, A Married Man 1979, The Villa Golitsyn 1981, The Free Frenchman 1986, A Season in the West 1988, On the Third Day 1990, Quo Vadis? The Subversion of the Catholic Church 1991, Ablaze: The Story of Chernobyl 1993, A Patriot in Berlin 1995, Knights of The Cross 1997, The Templars 1999, Alice in Exile 2001, Alec Guinness: The Authorised Biography 2003. *Honours:* Sir Geoffrey Faber Memorial Prize 1968, Somerset Maugham Award 1969, Hawthornden Prize 1969, Thomas More Award (USA) 1976, James Tait Black Memorial Prize 1988. *Address:* 50 Portland Road, London, W11 4LG, England. *Telephone:* (20) 7727-5719. *Fax:* (20) 7460-2499. *E-mail:* piersread@dial.pipex.com.

READE, Hamish (see Gray, Simon James Holliday).

REANEY, James (Crerar); Prof., Poet and Dramatist; b. 1 Sept. 1926, South Easthope, Ontario, Canada; m. 29 Dec. 1951, two s. one d. *Education:* BA, 1948, MA, 1949, University of Toronto. *Career:* Faculty, University of Manitoba, Winnipeg, 1948–60; Prof., Middlesex College, University of Western Ontario, 1960–; mem. Asscn of Canadian University Teachers, pres., 1959–60; Playwright's Union of Canada; League of Canadian Poets. *Publications:* Poetry: The Red Heart, 1949; A Suit of Nettles, 1958; Twelve Letters to a Small Town, 1962; The Dance of Death at London, 1963; Poems, 1972; Selected Shorter and Longer Poems, 1975–76; Performance Poems, 1990. Plays: Night Blooming Cereus, 1959; The Killdeer, 1960; One Masque, 1960; The Sun and the Moon, 1965; Listen to the Wind, 1966; The Canada Tree, 1967; Genesis, 1968; Masque, 1972; The Donnellys: A Trilogy, 1973–75; Baldoon, 1976; King Whistle, 1979; Antler River, 1980; Gyroscope, 1981; I, the Parade, 1982; The Canadian Brothers, 1983; Alice Through the Looking Glass (adaptation of Lewis Carroll's book), 1994. Opera Libretti: The Shivaree (music by John Beckwith), 1982; Crazy to Kill (music by John Beckwith). Other: The Box Social and Other Stories, 1996. Contributions: books, journals and periodicals. *Honours:* Governor-General's Awards, 1949, 1958, 1963; University of Alberta Award for Letters, 1974; Order of Canada, 1975. *Literary Agent:* David Johnston, 932 Logan Ave, Toronto, ON M4K 3E4, Canada. *Address:* 276 Huron St, London, ON N6A 2J9, Canada.

REBUCK, Gail Ruth, CBE, BA, FRSA; British publishing executive; *Chairman and CEO, Random House Group Ltd*; b. 10 Feb. 1952, London; m. Philip Gould 1985; two d. *Education:* Lycée Français de Londres, Univ. of Sussex. *Career:* Production Asst, Grisewood & Dempsey (children's book packager) 1975–76; Ed., later Publr Robert Nicholson Publs London Guidebooks 1976–79; Publr Hamlyn Paperbacks 1979–82; Founder Partner Century Publishing Co. Ltd, Publishing Dir Non-Fiction 1982–85, Publr Century Hutchinson 1985–89, Chair. Random House Div., Random Century 1989–91, Chair. and Chief Exec. Random House UK Ltd (now Random House Group) 1991–; mem. COPUS 1995–97, Creative Industries Task Force 1997–2000; Non-Exec. Dir, Work Foundation 2001–; Trustee Inst. for Public Policy Research (IPPR) 1993–; mem. Court Univ. of Sussex 1997–; Council RCA 1999–. *Address:* The Random House Group Ltd, 20 Vauxhall Bridge Road, London, SW1V 2SA, England (Office). *Telephone:* (20) 7840-8886. *Fax:* (20) 7233-6120. *E-mail:* grebuck@randomhouse.co.uk (Office). *Website:* www.randomhouse.co.uk.

REDDY, T. Vasudeva; Lecturer in English, Writer and Poet; b. 21 Dec. 1943, Mittapalem, India; m. 5 Nov. 1970, two s. one d. *Education:* BSc, 1963; MA, English, 1966; PGDTE, 1983; PhD, English, 1985. *Career:* mem. International Poets Acad., Chennai; World Poetry Society, CA. *Publications:* When Grief Rains (poems), 1982; The Vultures (novel), 1983; The Broken Rhythms (poems), 1987; Jane Austen, 1987; Jane Austen: Matrix of Matrimony, 1987; The Fleeting (poems), 1989. Contributions: journals and magazines. *Address:* Narasingapuram Post, Via Chandragiri, Pin 517 102, AP, India.

REECE, Henry Michael, BA, DPhil; British; *CEO, Oxford University Press*; b. 10 Aug. 1953; m. Allison Jane King 1993. *Education:* Univ. of Bristol, Univ. of Oxford. *Career:* Tutor in History, Univ. of Exeter 1977–78; Field Sales Ed., Prentice Hall Int. 1979–82; Academic Sales Man. 1982–84, UK Sales Man. 1984–85, Asst Vice-Pres. 1985–88, Simon and Schuster Int.; Exec. Ed., Allyn & Bacon, USA 1988–91; Man. Dir, Pitman Publishing 1991–94; Exec. Dir, Longman Group Ltd 1994–95; Exec. Dir, Pearson Professional 1995–97; Man. Dir, Financial Times Professional 1997–98; CEO, Oxford Univ. Press (Sec. to the Delegates, and Chair. Group Strategy Cttee) 1998–; Non-Exec. Dir, Knowledge Pool 2000–01; mem. Publishers' Asscn (mem. of council 1999–2004, pres. 2004–). *Honours:* Fellow, Jesus Coll., Oxford 1998–. *Address:* Oxford University Press, Great Clarendon Street, Oxford, OX2 6DP, England. *E-mail:* enquiry@oup.co.uk. *Website:* www.oup.co.uk.

REED, Ishmael (Scott); Writer, Poet, Publisher, Ed. and Teacher; b. 22 Feb. 1938, Chattanooga, Tennessee, USA; m. 1st Priscilla Rose, 1960, divorced 1970, one d.; m. 2nd Carla Blank-Reed, 1970, one d. *Education:* University of Buffalo, 1956–60. *Career:* Lecturer, University of California at Berkeley, 1967–, University of Washington, 1969–70, SUNY at Buffalo, 1975, 1979, University of Arkansas, 1982, Columbia University, 1983, Harvard University, 1987, University of California at Santa Barbara, 1988; Chair. and Pres., Yardbird Publishing Company, 1971–; Dir, Reed Cannon and Johnson Communications, 1973–; Visiting Prof., 1979, Assoc. Fellow, 1983–, Calhoun House, Yale University; Visiting Prof., Dartmouth College, 1980; Co-Founder (with Al Young) and Ed., Quilt Magazine, 1981–; Assoc. Fellow, Harvard University Signet Society, 1987–; mem. Before Columbus Foundation, pres., 1976–. *Publications:* Fiction: The Free-Lance Pallbearers, 1967; Yellow Black Radio Broke-Down, 1969; Mumbo-Jumbo, 1972; The Last Days of Louisiana Red, 1974; Flight to Canada, 1976; The Terrible Twos, 1982; Reckless Eyeballing, 1986; The Terrible Threes, 1989; Japanese by Spring, 1993. Poetry: Catechism of a Neoamerican Hoodoo Church, 1970; Conjure: Selected Poems 1963–1970, 1972; Chattanooga, 1973; A Secretary to the Spirits, 1978; New and Collected Poems, 1988. Other: The Rise, Fall and...? of Adam Clayton Powell (with others), 1967; Shrovetide in Old New Orleans, 1978; God Made Alaska for the Indians, 1982; Cab Calloway Stands in for the Moon, 1986; Ishmael Reed: An Interview, 1990; Airin' Dirty Laundry, 1993; Multi-America, 1996. Editor: 19 Necromancers from Now, 1970; Yardbird Reader, 5 vols, 1971–77; Yardbird Lives! (with Al Young), 1978; Calafia: The California Poetry, 1979; Quilt 2-3 (with Al Young), 2 vols, 1981–82; Writin' is Fightin': Thirty-Seven Years of Boxing on Paper, 1988; The Before Columbus Foundation Fiction Anthology: Selections from the American Book Awards, 1980–1990 (with Kathryn Trueblood and Shawn Wong), 1992; The Reed Reader, 2000. *Honours:* National Endowment for the Arts Grant, 1974; Rosenthal Foundation Award, 1975; Guggenheim Fellowship, 1975; American Acad. of Arts and Letters Award, 1975; Michaux Award, 1978. *Address:* c/o Ellis J. Freedman, 415 Madison Ave, New York, NY 10017, USA.

REED, Jane Barbara, CBE, FRSA; British publishing executive; b. 31 March 1940, Letchworth, Herts. *Education:* Royal Masonic School. *Career:* Ed. Woman's Own 1969–79; Publr IPC Magazines Ltd Women's Monthly Magazines Group 1979–81; Ed.-in-Chief Woman magazine 1981–83; Asst Man. Dir IPC Specialist Educ. and Leisure Group 1983; Man. Dir IPC Holborn Publishing Group 1983–85; Man. Ed. Features Section Today newspaper 1985–86, Man. Ed. 1985–89; Dir of Corp. Affairs, News Int. PLC 1989–2000; Dir Nat. Acad. of Writing 2001–; fmr Pres. Media Soc.; mem. Council Nat. Literacy Trust; Dir (non-Exec.) Media Trust; Trustee St Katharine & Shadwell Trust. *Publications:* Girl About Town 1965, Kitchen Sink—or Swim? (jtly) 1981. *Honours:* Ed. of the Year 1975, 1981, Mark Boxer Award for Lifetime Achievement 2002. *Address:* News International PLC, POB 495, 1 Virginia Street, London, EC1 9XY (Office); 41 Chipstead Street, London, SW6 3SR, England (Home). *Telephone:* (20) 7782-6090 (Office). *Fax:* (20) 7782-6097 (Office).

REED, Jeremy, BA; poet and writer; b. 1951, Jersey, Channel Islands. *Education:* Univ. of Essex, Colchester. *Publications:* poetry: Target 1972, Saints and Psychotics: Poems 1973–74 1974, Vicissitudes 1974, Diseased Near Deceased 1975, Emerald Cat 1975, Ruby Onocentaur 1975, Blue Talaria 1976, Count Bluebeard 1976, Jack's in His Corset 1978, Walk on Through 1980, Bleecker Street 1980, No Refuge Here 1981, A Long Shot to Heaven 1982, A Man Afraid 1982, By the Fisheries 1984, Elegy for Senta 1985, Skies 1985, Border Pass 1986, Selected Poems 1987, Engaging Form 1988, The Escaped Image 1988, Nineties 1990, Diving for Pearls 1990, Red-Haired Android 1992; fiction: The Lipstick Boys 1984, Blue Rock 1987, Madness: The Price of Poetry 1990. *Honours:* Somerset Maugham Award 1985. *Address:* c/o Jonathan Cape Ltd, 20 Vauxhall Bridge Road, London, SW1V 2SA, England.

REEDER, Carolyn; Writer; b. 16 Nov. 1937, Washington, DC, USA; m. Jack Reeder, 15 Aug. 1959, one s. one d. *Education:* BA, 1959, MEd, 1971, American University. *Career:* mem. Children's Book Guild of Washington, DC, former treasurer; Authors' Guild. *Publications:* Non-Fiction: Shenandoah Heritage (with Jack Reeder), 1978; Shenandoah Vestiges (with Jack Reeder), 1980; Shenandoah Secrets (with Jack Reeder), 1991. Children's Fiction: Shades of Gray, 1989; Grandpa's Mountain, 1991; Moonshiner's Son, 1993; Across the Lines, 1997; Foster's War, 1998; Captain Kate, 1999; Before the Creeks Ran Red, 2003. *Honours:* Scott O'Dell Award for Historical Fiction, 1989; Child Study Asscn Award, 1989; American Library Asscn Notable Book, 1989; Honour Book for the Jane Addam's Children's Book Award, 1989; Notable Trade Book in the Language Arts, 1989; Jefferson Cup Award, 1990; International Reading Asscn Young Adult Choice, 1991; Joan G. Sugarman Children's Book Award, 1992–93; Hedda Seisler Mason Honor Award, 1995. *Address:* 7314 University Ave, Glen Echo, MD 20812, USA. *Website:* www.reederbooks.com.

REEMAN, Douglas Edward, (Alexander Kent); British writer; b. 15 Oct. 1924, Thames Ditton, Surrey, England; m. Kimberley June Jordan 1985. *Publications:* A Prayer for the Ship 1958, High Water 1959, Send a Gunboat 1960, Dive in the Sun 1961, The Hostile Shore 1962, The Last Raider 1963, With Blood and Iron 1964, HMS Saracen 1965, Path of the Storm 1966, The Deep Silence 1967, The Pride and the Anguish 1968, To Risks Unknown 1969, The Greatest Enemy 1970, Against the Sea 1971, Rendezvous – South Atlantic 1972, Go In and Sink! 1973, The Destroyers 1974, Winged Escort 1975, Surface with Daring 1976, Strike from the Sea 1978, A Ship Must Die 1979, Torpedo Run 1981, Badge of Glory 1982, The First to Land 1984, D-Day: A Personal Reminiscence 1984, The Volunteers 1985, The Iron Pirate 1986, In Danger's Hour 1988, The White Guns 1989, Killing Ground 1991, The Horizon 1993, Sunset 1994, A Dawn Like Thunder 1996, Battlecruiser

1997, Dust on the Sea 1999, For Valour 2000, Twelve Seconds to Live 2002, Knife Edge 2004; as Alexander Kent: To Glory We Steer 1968, Form Line of Battle 1969, Enemy in Sight! 1970, The Flag Captain 1971, Sloop of War 1972, Command a King's Ship 1974, Signal – Close Action! 1974, Richard Bolitho – Midshipman 1975, Passage to Mutiny 1976, In Gallant Company 1977, Midshipman Bolitho and the 'Avenger' 1978, Captain Richard Bolitho, RN 1978, The Inshore Squadron 1978, Stand Into Danger 1980, A Tradition of Victory 1981, Success to the Brave 1983, Colours Aloft! 1986, Honour This Day 1987, With All Despatch 1988, The Only Victor 1990, Beyond the Reef 1992, The Darkening Sea 1993, For My Country's Freedom 1995, Cross of St George 1996, Sword of Honour 1998, Second to None 1999, Relentless Pursuit 2001, Man of War 2003; contrib. to various journals and magazines. *Literary Agent:* PFD, Drury House, 34–43 Russell Street, London, WC2B 5HA, England.

REES, David Benjamin; Minister of Religion, Writer and Ed.; b. 1 Aug. 1937, Wales; m. 31 July 1963, two s. *Education:* BA, BD, MSc, University of Wales; MA, University of Liverpool; PhD, University of Salford. *Career:* Minister, Presbyterian Church of Wales, Cynon Valley, 1962–68, Heathfield Road, Liverpool, 1968–; Founder Sec. Modern Welsh Publications 1963–; Part-time Lecturer, University of Liverpool, 1970–2001; Prof. of Theology, 1998–; Ed., Peace and Reconciliation Magazine, 2000, Y Bont/ Bridge, 1997–; mem. Cymmrodorion Society; Welsh Acad. *Publications:* Wales: A Cultural History 1980, Preparation for a Crisis: Adult Education in England and Wales 1945–1980 1981, Liverpool, Welsh and Their Religion 1984, Owen Thomas: A Welsh Preacher in Liverpool 1991, The Welsh of Merseyside 1997, Local and Parliamentary Politics in Liverpool from 1800 to 1911 1999, The Welsh of Merseyside in the Twentieth Century 2001, Vehicles of Hope and Grace (ed) 2003. Contributions: magazines and newspapers. *Honours:* Ellis Griffith Prize, 1979. *Address:* 32 Garth Dr., Liverpool L18 6HW, England. *E-mail:* ben@garthdrive.co.uk. *Website:* www .welshpublications.co.uk; www.lordsdaywales.co.uk.

REES, Sir Martin John; Astronomer Royal, Prof. and Author; b. 23 June 1942, UK; m. Caroline Humphrey 1986. *Education:* Shrewsbury School; Trinity Coll., Cambridge. *Career:* Fellow, Jesus Coll., Cambridge 1967–69; Research Assoc. Calif. Inst. of Tech. 1967–68, 1971; mem. Inst. for Advanced Study, Princeton 1969–70, Prof. 1982–96; Visiting Prof. Harvard Univ. 1972, 1986–87; Prof. Univ. of Sussex 1972–73; Plumian Prof. of Astronomy and Experimental Philosophy, Univ. of Cambridge 1973–91, Royal Soc. Research Prof. 1992–; Astronomer Royal 1995–; Fellow, King's Coll., Cambridge 1969–72, 1973–; Visting Prof. Imperial Coll., London 2001–, Leicester Univ. 2001–; Dir Inst. of Astronomy 1977–82, 1987–91; Regents Fellow, Smithsonian Inst. 1984–88; mem. Council Royal Soc. 1983–85, 1993–95; Pres. Royal Astronomical Soc. 1992–94, British Asscn for the Advancement of Science 1994–95; Trustee British Museum 1996–2002, Inst. for Advanced Study, Princeton, USA 1998–2001, Nat. Endowment for Sciences, Tech. and Arts 1998, Kennedy Memorial Trust 1999, Inst. for Public Policy Research 2001; Foreign Assoc. NAS; mem. Academia Europaea 1989, Pontifical Acad. of Sciences 1990; Foreign mem. American Philosophical Soc., Royal Swedish Acad. of Science, Russian Acad. of Sciences, Norwegian Acad. of Arts and Science, Accad. Lincei (Rome), Royal Netherlands Acad. *Publications:* Perspectives in Astrophysical Cosmology, 1995; Gravity's Fatal Attraction (with M. Begelman), 1995; Before the Beginning, 1997; Just Six Numbers, 1999; Our Cosmic Habitat, 2001; Our Final Century?, 2003. Other: ed., numerous books. Contributions: articles and reviews in scientific journals and numerous general articles. *Honours:* FRS; Hon. Fellow Trinity Coll. and Jesus Coll., Cambridge, Indian Acad. of Sciences, Univ. of Wales, Cardiff 1998, Inst. of Physics 2001; Foreign Hon. mem. American Acad. of Arts and Sciences; Officier, Ordre des Arts et des Lettres; Hon. DSc (Sussex) 1990, (Leicester) 1993, (Copenhagen, Keele, Uppsala, Newcastle) 1995, (Toronto) 1997, (Durham) 1999, (Oxford) 2000; Heinemann Prize, American Inst. of Physics 1984, Gold Medal (Royal Astronomical Soc.) 1987, Guthrie Medal, Inst. of Physics 1989, Balzan Prize 1989, Robinson Prize for Cosmology 1990, Bruce Medal, Astronomical Soc. of Pacific 1993, Science Writing Award, American Inst. of Physics 1996, Bower Award (Franklin Inst.) 1998, Rossi Prize, American Astronomical Soc. 2000, Cosmology Prize of Gruber Foundation 2001. *Address:* King's College, Cambridge, CB2 1ST, England.

REES, Paul; British journalist; *Editor, Q. Career:* contributor, Brum Beat; News Ed., Raw –1995; News Ed., freelance writer, Ed., Kerrang! 1995–2002; Ed., Q magazine 2002–. *Address:* Q, EMAP Publishing, Mappin House, 4 Winsley Street, London, W1W 8HF, England. *E-mail:* Editor@Q4music.com. *Website:* www.q4music.com.

REES-MOGG, Baron (Life Peer), cr. 1988, of Hinton Blewett in the County of Avon; **William Rees-Mogg,** Kt; British journalist and publisher; *Chairman, Pickering and Chatto Publishers*; b. 14 July 1928, Bristol; m. Gillian Shakespeare Morris 1962; two s. three d. *Education:* Charterhouse and Balliol Coll., Oxford. *Career:* Pres. Oxford Union 1951; Financial Times 1952–60, Chief Leader Writer 1955–60, Asst Ed. 1957–60; City Ed. Sunday Times 1960–61, Political and Econ. Ed. 1961–63, Deputy Ed. 1964–67; Ed. of The Times 1967–81, Dir The Times Ltd 1968–81; Vice-Chair. BBC 1981–86; Chair. Arts Council 1982–89; Chair. Broadcasting Standards Council 1988–93; mem. Exec. Bd Times Newspapers Ltd 1968–81, Dir 1978–81; Dir Gen. Electric Co. 1981–97; Chair. and Propr Pickering and Chatto Publishers Ltd 1983–; Chair. Sidgwick and Jackson 1985–89, Int. Business Communications PLC 1994–98, Fleet Street Publications 1995–; Dir M & G Group 1987, EFG Pvt. Bank and Trust Co. 1993–, Value Realization Trust PLC 1996–98, Newsmax Media, Inc., USA; columnist The Times 1992–; mem. Int. Cttee Pontifical Council for Culture 1983–87. *Publications:* The Reigning Error: the Crisis of World Inflation 1974, An Humbler Heaven 1977, How to Buy Rare Books 1985, Blood in the Streets (with James Dale Davidson) 1987, The Great Reckoning (with James Dale Davidson) 1992, Picnics on Vesuvius 1992, The Sovereign Individual (with James Dale Davidson) 1997. *Honours:* Hon. LLD (Bath) 1977, (Leeds) 1992. *Address:* 17 Pall Mall, London, SW1Y 5LU, England. *Telephone:* (20) 7242-2241. *Fax:* (20) 7405-6216.

REEVE, Franklin Dolier, PhD; academic, writer, poet, translator and editor; b. 18 Sept. 1928, Philadelphia, Pennsylvania, USA; m. Laura C. Stevenson; seven c. *Education:* Columbia University. *Career:* Lecturer, Columbia University, 1952–61; Prof. of Letters, Wesleyan University, 1962–2002; Visiting Prof., University of Oxford, 1964, Columbia University, 1988; Visiting Lecturer, Yale University, 1972–86; Ed., Poetry Review, 1982–84; mem. Pettee Memorial Library, trustee; Marlboro Review, advisory board; New England Poetry Society, board dir. *Publications:* Five Short Novels by Turgenev (trans.), 1961; Anthology of Russian Plays (trans.), 1961, 1963; Aleksandr Blok: Between Image and Idea, 1962; Robert Frost in Russia, 1964; The Russian Novel, 1966; In the Silent Stones, 1968; The Red Machines, 1968; Just Over the Border, 1969; The Brother, 1971; The Blue Cat, 1972; White Colors, 1973; Nightway, 1987; The White Monk, 1989; The Garden (trans.), 1990; Concrete Music, 1992; The Trouble with Reason (trans.), 1993; A Few Rounds of Old Maid and Other Stories, 1995; The Blue Boat on the St Anne, 1999; The Moon and Other Failures, 1999; A World You Haven't Seen, 2001; The Urban Stampede and Other Poems, 2002. Contributions: journals and periodicals. *Honours:* American Acad. of Arts and Letters Award, 1970; PEN Syndicated Fiction Awards, 1985, 1986; Golden Rose, New England Poetry Society, 1994. *Address:* PO 14, Wilmington, VT 05363, USA.

REGÀS, Rosa, BPhil; Spanish writer and journalist; *General Director, Biblioteca Nacional*; b. 1933, Barcelona; m.; five c. *Education:* Barcelona Univ. *Career:* editorial staff with Seix Barral 1964–70, with Edhasa; f. and Publisher, La Gaya Ciencia 1970–, journals Arquitectura Vis, Cuadernos de la Gaya Ciencia 1976–; trans. for UN 1983–94; Head of Culture Dept of Casa de América, part of Foreign Affairs Ministry 1994–98; Gen. Dir Biblioteca Nacional de España 2004–. *Publications include:* fiction: Memoria de Almator (novel) 1991, Azul (novel) (Premio Nadal) 1994, Pobre corazón (short stories) 1996, Barcelona, un día (short stories) 1998, Luna Lunera (novel) (Premio Ciudad de Barcelona) 1999, La canción de Dorotea (novel) (Premio Planeta) 2001, contrib. short stories to anthologies, including Relatos para un fin de milenio 1998, Cuentos solidarios 1999, Mujeres al alba 1999, La paz y la palabra 2003; non-fiction: La cuina de l'ampurdanet (leaflet) 1985, Ginebra (leaflet) 1988, Canciones de amor y de batalla: 1993–1995 (articles) 1995, Viaje a la luz del Cham 1995, Una revolución personal 1997, Desde el mar 1997, España: una nueva mirada (leaflet) 1997, Más canciones 1995–1998 (articles) 1998, La creación, la fantasía y la vida (essay) 1998, Sangre de mi sangre (essay) 1999, Diario de una abuela de verano (biog.) 2004, El valor de la protesta (articles) 2004; contrib. essays to collections, including Retratos literarios 1997, Ser mujer 2000, and to numerous journals and periodicals. *Address:* Biblioteca Nacional, Paseo de Recoletos 20, 28071 Madrid, Spain (Office). *E-mail:* directorgeneral@bne.es (Office). *Website:* www.bne.es (Office).

REICH, Robert Bernard, MA, JD; American political economist, academic and fmr government official; *Professor, Brandeis University Graduate School for Advanced Studies in Social Welfare*; b. 24 June 1946, Scranton, Pa; m. Clare Dalton 1973; two s. *Education:* Dartmouth Coll., Oxford Univ. (UK), Yale Univ. *Career:* Asst Solicitor-Gen., US Dept of Justice, Washington 1974–76; Dir of Policy Planning FTC, Washington 1976–81; mem. Faculty John F. Kennedy School of Govt, Harvard Univ. 1981–92; fmr Econ. Adviser to Pres. Bill Clinton; Sec. of Labor 1993–97; Prof. Brandeis Univ. Grad. School for Advanced Studies in Social Welfare 1997–; Chair. Biotechnology Section US Office Tech. Assessment, Washington 1990–91; Chair. Editorial Bd The American Prospect 1990–; mem. Bd of Dirs, Econ. Policy Inst., Washington; Contributing Ed. The New Republic, Washington 1982–93; Rhodes Scholar 1968. *Publications:* The Next American Frontier 1983, Tales of a New America 1987, The Power of Public Ideas (co-author) 1987, The Work of Nations 1991, Putting People First 1997, Locked in the Cabinet 1997, The Future of Success 2001, Reason: Why Liberals Will Win the Battle for America 2004. *Address:* Brandeis University, 415 South Street, Waltham, MA 022454. *Telephone:* (781) 736-2000. *Fax:* (781) 736-8699. *Website:* www.brandeis.edu (Office).

REICHS, Kathleen (Kathy), PhD; American writer and forensic anthropologist; b. Chicago; m. Paul Reichs; two d. one s. *Education:* Northwestern Univ. *Career:* forensic anthropologist, Office of the Chief Medical Examiner, Carolina, USA, Laboratoires des Sciences Judiciaires et de Médecine Légale, Canada; mem. bd of dirs American Acad. of Forensic Sciences; Prof. of Anthropology, Univ. of North Carolina at Charlotte. *Publications:* Déjà Dead (Ellis Award for Best First Novel) 1997, Death Du Jour 1999, Deadly Decisions 2000, Fatal Voyage 2001, Grave Secrets 2002, Bare Bones 2003,

Monday Mourning 2004. *Address:* c/o Random House, 20 Vauxhall Bridge Road, London, SW1V 2SA, England (Office). *Website:* www.kathyreichs.com (Office).

REID, Alastair; Writer, Trans. and Poet; b. 22 March 1926, Whithorn, Wigtonshire, Scotland. *Education:* MA, University of St Andrews, Scotland, 1949. *Career:* Visiting Lecturer at universities in the UK and USA; Staff Writer, Correspondent, New Yorker, 1959–. *Publications:* To Lighten my House, 1953; Oddments, Inklings, Omens, Moments, 1959; Passwords: Places, Poems, Preoccupations, 1963; Mother Goose in Spanish, 1967; Corgi Modern Poets in Focus 3, 1971; Weathering: Poems and Translations, 1978; Whereabouts: Notes on Being a Foreigner, 1987; An Alastair Reid Reader, 1995. Other: Stories for children and trans. from Spanish of Pablo Neruda, Jorge Luis Borges and other writers. *Honours:* Scottish Arts Council Award, 1979. *Address:* c/o The New Yorker, 4 Times Sq., New York, NY 10036-6592, USA.

REID, Christina; Playwright; b. 12 March 1942, Belfast, Northern Ireland. *Education:* Queen's University, Belfast, 1982–83. *Career:* Writer-in-Residence, Lyric Theatre, Belfast, 1983–84, Young Vic Theatre, London, 1988–89. *Publications:* Did You Hear the One About the Irishman?, 1980; Tea in a China Cup, 1983; Joyriders, 1986; The Last of a Dyin' Race, 1986; The Belle of The Belfast City, 1986; My Name? Shall I Tell You My Name?, 1987; Les Miserables (after Hugo), 1992; Clowns, 1996; Christina Reid: Plays One, 1997; The King of the Castle, 1999. Other: Plays produced in England, Ireland, Europe (in trans.) and the USA. *Honours:* Ulster TV Drama Award, 1980; Giles Cooper Award, 1986; George Devine Award, 1986. *Literary Agent:* Alan Brodie Representation, 211 Piccadilly, London W1J 9HF, England.

REID, Philip (see Ingrams, Richard Reid).

REIDY, Carolyn Kroll, PhD; American publishing executive; *President, Adult Publishing Division, Simon and Schuster*; b. (Carolyn Judith Kroll), 2 May 1949, Washington, DC; m. Stephen Kroll Reidy 1974. *Education:* Middlebury Coll. Vt and Indiana Univ. *Career:* various positions, Random House, New York 1975–83; Dir of Subsidiary Rights, William Morrow & Co., New York 1983–85; Vice-Pres. Assoc. Publr, Vintage Books, Random House, New York 1985–87; Assoc. Publr, Random House (concurrent with Assoc. Publr and Publr of Vintage Books) 1987–88; Publr, Vintage Books 1987–88, Anchor Books, Doubleday, New York 1988; Pres. and Publr, Avon Books, New York 1988–92; Pres. and Publr, Simon and Schuster Trade Div. 1992–2001, Pres. Adult Publishing Div., Simon and Schuster 2001–; Dir NAMES Project 1994–98, New York Univ. Center for Publishing 1997–, Literacy Partners, Inc. 1999–. *Honours:* Matrix Award 2002. *Address:* Simon and Schuster, 1230 Avenue of the Americas, New York, NY 10020, USA (Office). *Telephone:* (212) 698-7323 (Office). *Fax:* (212) 698-7035 (Office). *E-mail:* carolyn.reidy@simonandschuster.com (Office). *Website:* simonsays.com (Office).

REIF, Stefan Clive; Prof. and Writer; b. 21 Jan. 1944, Edinburgh, Scotland; m. Shulamit Stekel 19 Sept. 1967; one s. one d. *Education:* BA, 1964, PhD, 1969, University of London; MA, 1976, LittD, 2002, University of Cambridge. *Career:* Ed., University of Cambridge Library's Genizah Series, 1978–; Prof. of Medieval Hebrew Studies and Dir of Genizah Research, Univ. of Cambridge; mem. Fellow, Royal Asiatic Society; Council, Jewish Historical Society of England; Fellow, Mekize Nirdamim Society, Jerusalem; British Asscn for Jewish Studies; Society for Old Testament Study. *Publications:* Shabbethai Sofer and his Prayer-book, 1979; Interpreting the Hebrew Bible, 1981; Published Material from the Cambridge Genizah Collections, 1988; Genizah Research after Ninety Years, 1992; Judaism and Hebrew Prayer, 1993; Hebrew Manuscripts at University of Cambridge Library, 1997; A Jewish Archive from Old Cairo, 2000; Why Medieval Hebrew Studies, 2001; The Cambridge Genizah Collections: Their Contexts and Significance, 2002. Contributions: Over 250 articles in Hebrew and Jewish studies. *Address:* Taylor-Schechter Genizah Research Unit, University of Cambridge Library, West Rd, Cambridge CB3 9DR, England.

REINEROVÁ, Lenka; writer and journalist; b. 17 May 1916, Prague, Czechoslovakia. *Publications:* Hranice uzavreny, 1956; Grenze Geschlossen, 1958; Ein für allemal, 1962; Barva slunce a noci, 1969; Der Ausflug zum Schwanensee, 1983; Es began in der Melantrichgasse, 1985; Die Premiere, 1989; Sklo a porcelan, 1991; Das Traumcafe einer Pragerin, 1991; Mandelduft, 1998; Zu Hause in Prag, 2000; Alle Farben der Sonne und der Nacht 2003, Ehrenbürgerin der Stadt Prag seit 2003. *Honours:* Schillerring 1999, Goethe Medal 2003. *Address:* c/o Aufbau-Verlag GmbH, Postfach 193, 10105 Berlin, Germany.

REISMAN, Heather; Canadian publishing executive; *CEO, Indigo & Chapters Incorporated*; b. Montreal; m. Gerald Schwartz; four c. *Education:* McGill Univ. *Career:* Co-Founder and Man. Dir Paradigm Consulting 1979–95; Pres. Cott Corpn 1995–96; Founder, Pres. and CEO Indigo Books, Music and Café, Inc. 1996–2001, Pres. and CEO Indigo & Chapters Inc. (following merger with Chapters Inc. 2001) 2001–; mem. Bd Rogers Cable, Williams-Sonoma Inc.; Dir and Officer Mt Sinai Hosp.; fmr Gov. McGill Univ., Toronto Stock Exchange. *Publications include:* numerous articles on media, communications, manufacturing and retailing. *Address:* Indigo & Chapters Inc., 90 Ronson Drive, Toronto, Ont., M9W 1C1, Canada (Office). *Fax:* (416) 243-5420 (Office).

REISS, James; Prof. of English, Poet, Writer and Ed.; b. 11 July 1941, New York, NY, USA; m. Barbara Eve Klevs, 21 June 1964, divorced 1995, two d. *Education:* BA, English, 1963, MA, English, 1964, University of Chicago. *Career:* Instructor, 1965–69, Asst Prof., 1969–73, Assoc. Prof., 1973–81, Prof., 1981–, of English, Miami University, Oxford, Ohio; Visiting Poet and Assoc. Prof. of English, Queens College, CUNY, 1975–76; Ed., Miami University Press, 1992–; numerous poetry readings; mem. Acad. of American Poets; Poetry Society of America. *Publications:* Self-Interviews: James Dickey (co-ed.), 1970; The Breathers (poems), 1974; Express (poems), 1983; The Parable of Fire (poems), 1996; Ten Thousand Good Mornings (poems), 2001. Contributions: many anthologies and periodicals. *Honours:* First Prizes, Acad. of American Poets, 1960, 1962; MacDowell Colony Fellowships, 1970, 1974, 1976, 1977; Two Borestone Mountain Poetry Awards, 1974; Consuelo Ford Award, 1974, Lucille Medwick Award, 1989, Poetry Society of America; National Endowment for the Arts Fellowship, 1974–75; Bread Loaf Fellowship, 1975; Creative Artists Public Service Awards, New York State Council on the Arts, 1975–76; Ohio Arts Council Grants, 1980, 1981; Nancy Dasher Book Award, College English Asscn of Ohio, 1984; Dorland Mountain Arts Colony Fellow, 1991, 1993, 1999; James Laughlin Award, Acad. of American Poets, 1995; Pushcart Prize, 1996. *Address:* c/o Dept of English, 326 Bachelor Hall, Miami University, Oxford, OH 45056, USA.

REITER, David Philip; Publisher and Writer; b. 30 Jan. 1947, Cleveland, Ohio, USA; m. Cherie Lorraine Reiter, 26 April 1992. *Education:* BA, Independent Study, University of Oregon; MA, American Literature, University of Alberta, Canada; PhD, Creative Writing, University of Denver, 1982. *Career:* Lecturer, Cariboo University College, Canada, 1975–84, University of British Columbia, 1984, British Columbia Institute of Technology, 1984, University of Canberra, Australia, 1986–90. *Publications:* The Snow in Us, 1989; Changing House, 1991; The Cave After Saltwater Tide, 1992. Contributions: Australian, Canadian, US and UK journals. *Honours:* Queensland Premier's Poetry Award, 1989; Imago-QUT Short Story Competition, 1990. *Address:* 15 Gavan St, Ashgrove, Qld 4060, Australia.

REMINI, Robert V(incent); Prof. of History Emeritus, Research Prof. of Humanities Emeritus and Writer; b. 17 July 1921, USA; m. Ruth T. Kuhner, 1948, one s. two d. *Education:* BS, Fordham University, 1943; MA, 1947, PhD, 1951, Columbia University. *Career:* Instructor, 1947–51, Asst Prof., 1951–59, Assoc. Prof. of American History, 1959–65, Fordham University; Prof. of History, 1965–91, Research Prof. of Humanities, 1985–91, Prof. of History Emeritus and Research Prof. of Humanities Emeritus, 1991–, University Historian, 1997–, University of Illinois at Chicago; mem. American Historical Asscn; Society of Amerian Historians. *Publications:* Martin Van Buren and the Making of the Democratic Party, 1959; The Election of Andrew Jackson, 1963; Andrew Jackson, 1966; Andrew Jackson and the Bank War, 1967; Freedom's Frontiers: The Story of the American People (with James I. Clark), 1975; We the People: A History of the United States (with James I. Clark), 1975; The Revolutionary Age of Jackson, 1976; Andrew Jackson and the Course of American Empire, 1767–1821, 1977; The Era of Good Feelings and the Age of Jackson, 1816–1841 (with Edwin A. Miles), 1979; The American People: A History (with Arthur S. Link, Stanley Coben, Douglas Greenberg and Robert McMath), 1981; Andrew Jackson and the Course of American Freedom, 1822–1833, 1981; Andrew Jackson and the Course of American Democracy, 1833–1845, 1984; The Legacy of Andrew Jackson: Essays on Democracy, Indian Removal and Slavery, 1988; The Life of Andrew Jackson, 1988; The Jacksonian Era, 1989; Andrew Jackson: A Bibliography (with Robert O. Rupp), 1991; Henry Clay: Statesman for the Union, 1991; Daniel Webster: The Man and His Time, 1997; The Battle of New Orleans, 1999; The University of Illinois at Chicago: A Pictorial History (with Fred W. Beuttler and Melvin G. Holly), 2000; Andrew Jackson and His Indian Wars, 2001, John Quincy Adams 2002, Joseph Smith 2002. Contributions: scholarly books and journals. *Honours:* Hon. doctorates; Guggenheim Fellowship, 1978–79; Rockefeller Foundation Fellowships, Bellagio, Italy, 1979, 1989; George Washington Medal of Honor, Freedom Foundation, 1982; National Book Award, 1984; Carl Sandburg Award, 1989; Society of Midland Authors Award for Biography, 1992; American Historical Asscn Award for Scholarly Distinction, 2001; Western Writers of America Award, 2002, Chicago Historical Soc. Award for Distinguished Scholarship 2003. *Address:* c/o Dept of History, University of Illinois, PO Box 4348, Chicago, IL 60680, USA.

REMNICK, David J., AB; American journalist, editor and writer; *Editor-in-Chief, The New Yorker*; b. 29 Oct. 1958, Hackensack, NJ; m. Esther B. Fein; two s. one d. *Education:* Princeton Univ. *Career:* reporter, The Washington Post 1982–91; staff writer, The New Yorker 1992–, Ed.-in-Chief 1998–. *Publications:* Lenin's Tomb: The Last Days of the Soviet Empire 1993, The Devil Problem (and other true stories) 1996, Resurrection: The Struggle for a New Russia 1997, King of the World: Muhammad Ali and the Rise of an American Hero 1998, Life Stories: Profiles from The New Yorker (ed.) 1999, Wonderful Town: Stories from The New Yorker (ed.) 1999; contrib. to newspapers and periodicals. *Honours:* Livingston Award 1991, Pulitzer Prize for General Non-fiction 1994, George Polk Award 1994, Helen Bernstein Award 1994. *Address:* The New Yorker, Four Times Square, New York, NY 10036, USA (Office).

RÉMY, Pierre-Jean (see Angremy, Jean-Pierre).

RENAS, Y. (see Elberg, Yehuda).

RENAUD, (Ernest) Hamilton Jacques; writer, poet and translator; b. 10 Nov. 1943, Montréal, QC, Canada; two s. one d. *Career:* critic and researcher, Radio Canada 1965–67; reporter, Metro-Express, Montréal 1966; critic, Le Devoir, Montréal 1975–78; teacher, creative writing workshop, University of Québec 1980–89; spokesman, Equality Party 1989; researcher, Senator Jacques Hebert 1990. *Publications include:* Electrodes (poems), 1962; Le Casse (short stories), 1964; Clandestines (novel), 1980; L'espace du Diable (short stories), 1989; Les Cycles du Scorpion (poems), 1989; La Constellation du Bouc Emissaire (non-fiction), 1993. Contributions: various publications. *Address:* 205 Ivy Crescent 3, Ottawa, ON K1M 1X9, Canada.

RENAUT, Alain; Philosopher, Prof. and Writer; b. 25 Feb. 1948, Paris, France; m. Sylvie Mesure, 1984. *Education:* École Normale Supérieure, Paris. *Career:* Researcher, Institut Raymond Aron, Écoles des Hautes Études en Sciences Sociales, Paris, 1984–; Prof., University of Caen, 1986–. *Publications:* La Pensée 68: Essais sur l'individualisme contemporain (co-author), 1985; Itinéraires de l'individu, 1987; Heidegger et les modernes, 1988; L'Ere de l'individu: Contribution à une histoire de la subjectivité, 1989; Philosophie du droit (co-author), 1991; Sartre: Le Dernier Philosophe, 1995. Contributions: scholarly books and journals. *Address:* 135 ave Flouquet, 94290 L'Hay-les-Roses, France.

RENDELL OF BABERGH, Baroness (Life Peer), cr. 1997, of Aldeburgh in the County of Suffolk; **Ruth Barbara Rendell,** (Barbara Vine), CBE, FRSL; British crime novelist; *Life Peer, House of Lords*; b. 17 Feb. 1930; m. Donald Rendell 1950 (divorced 1975), remarried 1977 (died 1999); one s. *Education:* Loughton County High School. *Publications include:* From Doon with Death 1964, To Fear a Painted Devil 1965, Vanity Dies Hard 1965, A New Lease of Death (aka Sins of the Father) 1967, Wolf to the Slaughter 1967, The Secret House of Death 1968, The Best Man to Die 1969, A Guilty Thing Surprised 1970, No More Dying Then 1971, One Across, Two Down 1971, Murder Being Once Done 1972, Some Lie and Some Die 1973, The Face of Trespass 1974, Shake Hands Forever 1975, A Demon in My View 1976, A Judgement in Stone 1976, A Sleeping Life 1978, Make Death Love Me 1979, The Lake of Darkness 1980, Put on by Cunning (aka Death Notes) 1981, Master of the Moor 1982, The Speaker of Mandarin 1983, The Killing Doll 1984, The Tree of Hands 1984, An Unkindness of Ravens 1985, Live Flesh 1986, Heartstones 1987, Talking to Strange Men 1987, The Veiled One 1988, The Bridesmaid 1989, Mysterious 1990, Going Wrong 1990, The Strawberry Tree 1990, Walking on Water 1991, Kissing the Gunner's Daughter 1992, The Crocodile Bird 1993, Simisola 1994, Blood Lines 1996, The Keys to the Street 1997, Road Rage 1997, A Sight for Sore Eyes 1998, Harm Done 1999, Babes in the Wood 2002, The Rottweiler 2003, Thirteen Steps Down 2004; as Barbara Vine: A Dark-Adapted Eye 1986, A Fatal Inversion 1987, The House of Stairs 1988, Gallowglass 1990, King Solomon's Carpet 1991, Asta's Book 1993, The Children of Men 1994, No Night is Too Long 1994, The Keys to the Street 1996, The Brimstone Wedding 1996, The Chimney Sweeper's Boy 1998, Grasshopper 2000, The Blood Doctor 2002; short story collections: The Fallen Curtain 1976, Means of Evil 1979, The Fever Tree 1982, The New Girlfriend 1985, Collected Short Stories 1987, Undermining the Central Line (with Colin Ward) 1989, The Copper Peacock 1991, Blood Lines 1995, Piranha to Scurfy and Other Stories 2001; other: A Warning to the Curious: The Ghost Stories of M. R. James (ed.) 1987, Ruth Rendell's Suffolk 1989, The Reason Why: An Anthology of the Murderous Mind (ed.) 1995, Harm Done (ed.) 2000. *Honours:* Dr hc (Essex) 1990; Arts Council Nat. Book Award for Genre Fiction 1981, Sunday Times Award for Literary Excellence 1990 and other awards. *Address:* 26 Cornwall Terrace Mews, London, NW1 5LL; House of Lords, London, SW1A 0PW, England.

RENÉE, BA; playwright and writer; b. (Renée Gertrude Taylor), 19 July 1929, Napier, New Zealand. *Education:* University of Auckland. *Career:* Robert Burns Fellowship, University of Otago, 1989; Writers Fellowship, University of Waikato, New Zealand, 1995. *Publications:* Secrets: Two One-Woman Plays, 1982; Breaking Out, 1982; Setting the Table, 1982; What Did You Do in the War, Mummy?, 1982; Asking For It, 1983; Dancing, 1984; Wednesday to Come, 1984; Groundwork, 1985; Pass It On, 1986; Born to Clean, 1987; Jeannie Once, 1990; Touch of the Sun, 1991; Missionary Position, 1991; The Glass Box, 1992; Tiggy Tiggy Touchwood, 1992; Willy Nilly (novel), 1990; Daisy and Lily, 1993; Does This Make Sense To You?, 1995; The Snowball Waltz (novel), 1997; Let's Write Plays (textbook for schools), 1998; Yin and Tonic (humour), 1998; The Skeleton Woman (novel), 2002. Other: Television plays and short stories. *Honours:* Project Grant, 1991; Queen Elizabeth II Arts Council Scholarship in Letters, 1993. *Address:* PO Box 31033, Lower Hutt, New Zealand.

RENFREW OF KAIMSTHORN, Baron (Life Peer), cr. 1991, of Hurlet in the District of Renfrew; **Andrew Colin Renfrew,** PhD, ScD, FBA, FSA; British archaeologist; *Fellow, McDonald Institute for Archaeological Research, University of Cambridge*; b. 25 July 1937, Stockton-on-Tees; m. Jane M. Ewbank 1965; two s. one d. *Education:* St Albans School, St John's Coll., Cambridge and British School of Archaeology, Athens. *Career:* Lecturer in Prehistory and Archaeology, Univ. of Sheffield 1965–70, Sr Lecturer 1970–72, Reader in Prehistory and Archaeology 1972; Prof. of Archaeology and Head of Dept, Univ. of Southampton 1972–81; Disney Prof. of Archaeology, Univ. of Cambridge 1981–2004, Dir McDonald Inst. for Archaeological Research 1990–2004, Fellow 2004–; Fellow St John's Coll., Cambridge 1981–86; Master Jesus Coll., Cambridge 1986–97, Prof. Fellow 1997–2004, Emer. Fellow 2004–; Hon. FSA (Scotland); Foreign Assoc. Nat. Acad. of Sciences, USA; Visiting Lecturer, Univ. of Calif. at Los Angeles 1967; mem. Ancient Monuments Bd for England 1974–84, Royal Comm. on Historical Monuments 1977–87, Historic Buildings and Monuments Comm. for England 1984–86, Ancient Monuments Advisory Cttee 1984–2002, British Nat. Comm. for UNESCO 1984–86; Trustee British Museum 1991–2001. *Publications:* The Emergence of Civilization 1972, Before Civilization 1973, The Explanation of Culture Change (ed.) 1973, British Prehistory (ed.) 1974, Transformations: Mathematical Approaches to Culture Change 1979, Problems in European Prehistory 1979, An Island Polity 1982, Theory and Explanation in Archaeology (ed.) 1982, Approaches to Social Archaeology 1984, The Archaeology of Cult 1985, Peer, Polity Interaction and Socio-Political Change (ed.) 1986, Archaeology and Language: The Puzzle of Indo-European Origins 1987, The Idea of Prehistory (co-author) 1988, Archaeology: Theories, Methods and Practice (co-author) 1991, The Cycladic Spirit 1991, The Archaeology of Mind (co-ed. with E. Zubrow) 1994, Loot, Legitimacy and Ownership 2000, Archaeogenetics (ed.) 2000, Figuring It Out 2003; contribs to Archaeology, Scientific American. *Honours:* Hon. Fellow Royal Soc. of Edinburgh 2001Hon. LittD (Sheffield) 1990, (Southampton) 1995, (Edinburgh) 2004, (Liverpool) 2004; Dr hc (Faculty of Letters, Univ. of Athens) 1991 Rivers Memorial Medal, British Anthropological Inst. 1979, Sir Joseph Larmor Award 1981, Huxley Memorial Medal, Royal Anthropological Inst. 1991, Prix Int. Fyssen, Fondation Fyssen, Paris 1997, Language and Culture Prize, Univ. of Umeå, Sweden 1998, Rivers Memorial Medal, European Science Foundation Latsis Prize 2003. *Literary Agent:* Curtis Brown Ltd, Haymarket House, 28–29 Haymarket, London, SW1Y 4SP. *Telephone:* (20) 7393-4400. *Fax:* (20) 7393-4401. *E-mail:* info@curtisbrown.co.uk. *Website:* www.curtisbrown.co.uk. *Address:* c/o McDonald Institute for Archaeological Research, Downing Street, Cambridge, CB2 3ER, England. *Telephone:* (1223) 333521. *Fax:* (1223) 333536.

RENRICK, D. F. (see Kerner, Fred).

RESCHER, Nicholas; American academic and writer; b. 15 July 1928, Hagen, Westphalia, Germany; m. 1st Frances Short 1951; one d.; m. 2nd Dorothy Henle 1968; two s. one d. *Education:* BS, Queens College, CUNY, 1949; PhD, Princeton University, 1951. *Career:* Instructor in Philosophy, Princeton University, 1951–52; Assoc. Prof. of Philosophy, Lehigh University, Bethlehem, Pennsylvania, 1957–61; University Prof. of Philosophy, 1961–, University of Pittsburgh; Secretary General, International Union of the History and Philosophy of Science, United Nations Educational, Scientific, and Cultural Organization, 1969–75; Hon. Mem., Corpus Christi College, Oxford, 1977–; Founder-Ed., American Philosophical Quarterly, History of Philosophy Quarterly, and Public Affairs Quarterly; mem. Academia Europea; Institut International de Philosphie; Royal Asiatic Society; Académie Internationale de Philosophie des Sciences; American Philosophical Assn, Pres.; American Catholic Philosophical Assn, Pres.; G. W. Leibniz Society of America, pres. *Publications:* The Coherence Theory of Truth 1973, Scientific Progress 1978, The Limits of Science 1985, A System of Pragmatic Idealism, 3 vols, 1992–93, Predicting the Future 1997, Complexity 1998, Paradoxes 2001, Philosophical Reasoning 2001. Contributions: various scholarly journals. *Honours:* Hon. doctorates, Loyola University, Chicago, 1970, University of Córdoba, Argentina, 1992, Lehigh University, 1993, University of Konstanz, Germany, 1995, Fern-Universitaet Hagen, Germany, 2002; Alexander von Humboldt Prize, Germany, 1983. *Address:* c/o Department of Philosophy, University of Pittsburgh, 1012 Cathedral, Pittsburgh, PA 15260, USA.

RESTAK, Richard Martin; Physician and Author; b. 4 Feb. 1942, Wilmington, DE, USA; m. Carolyn Serbent, 18 Oct. 1968, three d. *Education:* MD, Georgetown Medical School, 1966; Trained in Neurology and Psychiatry. *Career:* Consultant, Encyclopedia of Bioethics, 1978; Special Contributing Ed., Science Digest, 1981–85; Editorial Board, Integrative Psychiatry: An International Journal for the Synthesis of Medicine and Psychiatry, 1986; mem. American Acad. of Neurology; American Acad. of Psychiatry and the Law; American Psychiatric Assn; Behavioral Neurology Society; New York Acad. of Sciences; International Neuropsychological Society; National Book Critics Circle; International Brotherhood of Magicians; Philosophical Society of Washington. *Publications:* Premeditated Man: Bioethics and the Control of Future Human Life, 1975; The Brain: The Last Frontier: Explorations of the Human Mind and Our Future, 1979; The Self Seekers, 1982; The Brain, 1984; The Infant Mind, 1986; The Mind, 1988; The Brain Has a Mind of Its Own, 1991; Receptors, 1994; Modular Brain, 1994; Brainscopes, 1995; Older and Wiser, 1997; The Secret Life of the Brain, 2001; Mozart's Brain and the Fighter Pilot, 2001; The New Brain, 2003. Contributions: anthologies, journals, and periodicals. *Honours:* National Endowment for the Humanities Fellowship, 1976; Claude Bernard Science Journalism Award, National Society for Medical Research, 1976; Distinguished Alumni Award, Gettysburg College, 1985. *Address:* 1800 R St NW, Suite C-3, Washington, DC 20009, USA.

RESTON, James Barrett, Jr; Writer; b. 8 March 1941, New York, NY, USA; m. Denise Brender Leary, 12 June 1971. *Education:* University of Oxford, 1961–62; BA, University of North Carolina at Chapel Hill, 1963. *Career:*

Reporter, Chicago Daily News, 1964–65; Lecturer in Creative Writing, University of North Carolina at Chapel Hill, 1971–81; mem. Authors' Guild; Dramatists Guild; PEN. *Publications:* Fiction: To Defend, To Destroy, 1971; The Knock at Midnight, 1975. Non-Fiction: The Amnesty of John David Herndon, 1973; Perfectly Clear: Nixon from Whittier to Watergate (with Frank Mankiewicz), 1973; The Innocence of Joan Little: A Southern Mystery, 1977; Our Father Who Art in Hell: The Life and Death of Jim Jones, 1981; Sherman's March and Vietnam, 1985; The Lone Star: The Life of John Connally, 1989; Collision at Home Plate: The Lives of Peter Rose and Bart Giamatti, 1991; Galileo: A Life, 1994; The Last Apocalypse: Europe at the Year 1000 AD, 1998; Warriors of God: Richard the Lionheart and Saladin in the Third Crusade, 2002. Other: Radio and television documentaries and plays. Contributions: various periodicals. *Honours:* Dupont-Columbia Award, 1982; Prix Italia, Venice, 1982; National Endowment for the Arts Grant, 1982; Valley Forge Award, 1985. *Address:* 4714 Hunt Ave, Chevy Chase, MD 20815, USA.

REVERE, Michael Rigsby; Writer, Poet, Musician and Music Teacher; b. 26 July 1951, East Point, GA, USA; Partner, Judy Revere, one s. one d. *Education:* Southwestern Community College, Sylva, NC. *Career:* Guest lectures, poetry readings and workshops. *Publications:* Spirit Happy (poems), 1974; The Milky Way Poems, 1976; Shotgun Vision (poems), 1977; Fire and Rain (poems), 1998; Lizard Man: Collected Poems 1969–2002 (with original music soundscapes CD), 2002. Contributions: journals and periodicals. *Address:* PO Box 1328, Cullowhee, NC 28723, USA.

REYES, Carlos; Poet and Teacher; b. 2 June 1935, Marshfield, MO, USA; m. 1st Barbara Ann Hollingsworth, 13 Sept. 1958, divorced 1973, one s., three d.; m. 2nd Karen Ann Stoner, 21 May 1979, divorced 1992; m. 3rd Elizabeth Atly, 27 Dec. 1993, divorced 2003. *Education:* BA, University of Oregon, 1961; MA, ABD, University of Arizona, 1965. *Career:* Governor's Advisory Committee on the Arts, Oregon, 1973; Poet to the City of Portland, 1978; Poet-in-Residence, various public schools in Oregon and Washington; Ed., Hubbub, 1982–90, Ar Mhuin Na Muicea (journal of Irish literature, music, current events), 1995; mem. Portland Poetry Festival Inc, board, 1974–84; PEN Northwest, co-chair, 1992–93; Mountain Writers Series, board, 1996–2000. *Publications:* The Prisoner, 1973; The Shingle Weaver's Journal, 1980; At Doolin Quay, 1982; Nightmarks, 1990; A Suitcase Full of Crows, 1995; Poemas de la Isla (trans. of Josefina de la Torre), 2000; Puertas Abiertas/Open Doors (bilingual edn of poems by Edwin Madrid), 2000; Obra Poética Completa de Jorge Carrera Andrade/Complete Poetic Works of Jorge Carrera Andrade (bilingual edn) 2003. Contributions: various journals and magazines. *Honours:* Oregon Arts Commission Individual Artist Fellowship, 1982; Yaddo Fellowship, 1984; Fundación Valparaíso, Mojácar, Spain, fellow, 1998. *Address:* 2210 NE Weidler, Portland, OR 97232, USA.

REYN, Evgeny Borisovich; Russian poet and writer; b. 29 Dec. 1935, Leningrad; m. Nadejda Reyn 1989; one s. *Education:* Leningrad Technical Inst. *Career:* freelance poet published in samizdat magazine Sintaksis and émigré press abroad in magazines Grani, Kovcheg; participated in publication of almanac Metropol; literary debut in Russia 1984; Prof., Moscow M. Gorky Inst. of Lit.; mem. Writers' Union, Union of Moscow Writers, Russian PEN Centre. *Television:* Kuprin 1967, The Thcukokkala 1969, The Tenth Chapter 1970, Journeys with Josef Brodsky 1993, Josef Brodsky: The Hatchings to Portrait 1996. *Publications:* The Names of Bridges 1984, Shore Line 1989, The Darkness of Mirrors 1989, Breda 1995, Irretrievable Day 1991, Counter-Clockwise 1992, Nezhnosmo 1993, Selected Poems 1993, The Prognostication 1994, The Top-booty 1995, The Others 1996, The News Stages of the Life of The Moscow Beau Monde 1997, Balkony 1998, Arch over Water 2000, The Remarks of Marathonman: Inconclusive memoirs 2003, The Overground Transition 2004. *Honours:* Peterburg Prize of Arts 'Tsarskoye Selo' 1995, State Prize of Russia in Literature and Art 1996, Independent Alexander Block Literature Award 1999, Alfred Tepfer Foundation Pushkin Prize (Gamburg, Germany) 2003, State Pushkin Prize in Literature and Art 2004, Grinzane Cavour Prize (Turin, Italy) 2004. *Address:* Leningradsky Prospect, 75, Apt 167, 125057 Moscow (Home). *Telephone:* (095) 157 20 14. *E-mail:* Reyne@cnt.ru.

REYNOLDS, David James, BA, MA, PhD, FRHistS; academic and writer; *Professor of International History, University of Cambridge*; b. 17 Feb. 1952, Orpington, Kent, England; m. Margaret Philpott Ray 1977; one s. *Education:* University of Cambridge. *Career:* Choate Fellow, 1973–74, Warren Fellow, 1980–81, Harvard University; Research Fellow, Gonville and Caius College, Cambridge, 1978–80, 1981–83; Fellow, Christ's College, Cambridge, 1983–; Asst Lecturer in History, 1984–88, Lecturer, 1988–97, Reader in International History, 1997–2002, Prof. of International History, 2002–, University of Cambridge. *Publications:* The Creation of the Anglo-American Alliance, 1937–1941: A Study in Competitive Co-operation, 1981; Lord Lothian and Anglo-American Relations, 1939–1940, 1983; An Ocean Apart: The Relationship Between Britain and America in the Twentieth Century (with David Dimbleby), 1988; Britannia Overruled: British Policy and World Power in the Twentieth Century, 1991; Allies at War: The Soviet, American, and British Experience, 1939–1945 (ed. with Warren F. Kimball and A. O. Chubarian), 1994; Rich Relations: The American Occupation of Britain, 1942–1945, 1995; One World Divisible: A Global History Since 1945, 2000; From Munich to Pearl Harbor: Roosevelt's America and the Origins of the Second World War, 2001. Contributions: scholarly books and journals. *Honours:* Bernath Prize, Society for Historians of American Foreign Relations, 1982; Distinguished Book Award, Society for Military History, 1996. *Address:* c/o Christ's College, Cambridge CB2 3BU, England.

REYNOLDS, Graham; Writer and Art Historian; b. 10 Jan. 1914, London, England. *Education:* BA, Queens' College, Cambridge. *Publications:* Nicholas Hilliard and Isaac Oliver, 1947; English Portrait Miniatures, 1952; Painters of the Victorian Scene, 1953; Catalogue of the Constable Collection, Victoria and Albert Museum, 1960; Constable, The Natural Painter, 1965; Victorian Painting, 1966; Turner, 1969; Concise History of Watercolour Painting, 1972; Catalogue of Portrait Miniatures, Wallace Collection, 1980; The Later Paintings and Drawings of John Constable, 2 vols, 1984; English Watercolours, 1988; The Earlier Paintings of John Constable, 2 vols, 1996; Catalogue of European Portrait Minatures, Metropolitan Museum of Art, New York, 1996; The Miniatures in the Collection of HM the Queen, The Sixteenth and Seventeenth Centuries, 1999. Contributions: TLS; Burlington Magazine; Apollo; New Departures. *Honours:* Mitchell Prize, 1984; OBE, 1984; British Acad., fellow, 1993; Hon. Keeper of Minatures, Fitzwilliam Museum, Cambridge, 1994; CVO, 2000. *Address:* The Old Manse, Bradfield St George, Bury St Edmunds, Suffolk IP30 0AZ, England.

REYNOLDS, Keith Ronald, (Kev Reynolds); Author, Photojournalist and Lecturer; b. 7 Dec. 1943, Ingatestone, Essex, England; m. Linda Sylvia Dodsworth, 23 Sept. 1967, two d. *Career:* mem. Outdoor Writers' Guild. *Publications:* Walks and Climbs in the Pyrenees, 1978; Mountains of the Pyrenees, 1982; The Weald Way and Vanguard Way, 1987; Walks in the Engadine, 1988; The Valais, 1988; Walking in Kent, 1988; Classic Walks in the Pyrenees, 1989; Classic Walks in Southern England, 1989; The Jura, 1989; South Downs Way, 1989; Eye on the Hurricane, 1989; The Mountains of Europe, 1990; Visitors Guide to Kent, 1990; The Cotswold Way, 1990; Alpine Pass Route, 1990; Classic Walks in the Alps, 1991; Chamonix to Zermatt, 1991; The Bernese Alps, 1992; Walking in Ticino, 1992; Central Switzerland, 1993; Annapurna, A Trekkers' Guide, 1993; Walking in Kent, Vol. II, 1994; Everest, A Trekkers' Guide, 1995; Langtang: A Trekkers Guide, 1996; Tour of the Vanoise, 1996; Walking in the Alps, 1998; Kangchenjunga: A Trekkers' Guide, 1999; Walking in Sussex, 2000; 100 Hut Walks in the Alps, 2000; Manaslu: A Trekkers' Guide, 2000; The South Downs Way, 2001; The North Downs Way, 2001. Contributions: The Great Outdoors; Climber and Hill Walker; Environment Now; Trail Walker; Country Walking; High. *Address:* Little Ct Cottage, Froghole, Crockham Hill, Edenbridge, Kent TN8 6TD, England. *E-mail:* kev.reynolds@virgin.net. *Website:* www.kevreynolds.co.uk.

REYNOLDS, Sheri; Writer; b. 29 Aug. 1967, Conway, South Carolina, USA. *Education:* AB, Davidson College, 1989; MFA, Virginia Commonwealth University, 1992. *Career:* Part-time Instructor of English, Virginia Commonwealth University; mem. Authors' Guild. *Publications:* Bitterroot Landing, 1994; A Gracious Plenty, 1997. *Address:* 700 Albermarle St, Richmond, VA 23220, USA.

REYNOLDS, Vernon; University Teacher and Writer; b. 14 Dec. 1935, Berlin, Germany; m. Frances Glover, 5 Nov. 1960, one s. one d. *Education:* BA, PhD, University of London; MA, University of Oxford. *Publications:* Budongo: A Forest and its Chimpanzees, 1965; The Apes, 1967; The Biology of Human Action, 1976; The Biology of Religion (with R. Tanner), 1983; Primate Behaviour: Information, Social Knowledge and the Evolution of Culture (with D. Quiatt), 1993. *Honours:* Prof. Emeritus, Univ. of Oxford; Fellow Emeritus, Magdalen College, Oxford. *Address:* Orchard House, West St, Alfriston, East Sussex BN26 5UX, England.

REZVANI, Serge; Russian writer and artist; b. 1928, Tehran, Iran. *Publications include:* Light Years 1971, La Loi humaine 1983, Le Testament amoureux 1984, La Folie tintoretto 1994, Les Années Lula 1998, Enigma 1998, La Cité potemkine 1998, L'Origine du monde 2000. *Literary Agent:* c/o Dedalus Ltd, Langford Lodge, St Judith's Lane, Sawtry, Cambridgeshire PE28 5XE, England. *E-mail:* info@dedalusbooks.com. *Website:* www.dedalusbooks.com.

RHEINSBERG, Anna Rose Anette; German poet and essayist; b. 24 Sept. 1956, Berlin; m. 1st Matthias Hoffbauer 1975 (divorced 1979); m. 2nd Mischka Krahl Rheinsberg 1980; one s. *Education:* Friedrichs Gymnasium (Kassel) and Philipps Univ. (Marburg). *Career:* mem. feminist movt 1975–; writer and ed.; acted in Anna experimental film, Austria 1980. *Publications:* Bella Donna 1981, Hannah 1982, Alles trutschen (2nd edn) 1989, Wolfskuss 1984, Annakonda 1985, 1986, Marthe und Ruth 1987, Fée 1987, Herzlos 1988, Kriegs/Läufe 1989, Narcisse noir 1990. *Address:* Wehrdaer Weg 43a, 3550 Marburg/Lahn 1, Germany. *Telephone:* (6421) 64375.

RHODES, Anthony (Richard Edward); Writer and Trans; b. 24 Sept. 1916, Plymouth, Devon, England; m. Rosaleen Forbes, 9 April 1956. *Education:* Royal Military Acad., Woolwich; MA, Trinity College, Cambridge; Licence et Lettres, University of Geneva. *Career:* mem. Society of Authors; PEN; Bucks Club; Beefsteak Club. *Publications:* Sword of Bone, 1942; The Uniform, 1949; A Sabine Journey, 1952; A Ball in Venice, 1953; The General's Summer House, 1954; The Dalmation Coast, 1955; Where the Turk Trod, 1956; The Poet as Superman: A Life of Gabriele D'Annunzio, 1959; Rise and Fall of Louis Renault, 1966; The Prophet's Carpet, 1969; Princes of the Grape, 1970; Art Treasures of Eastern Europe, 1971; The

Vatican in the Age of the Dictator, 1922–45, 1973; Propaganda in the Second World War, 1976; The Vatican in the Age of the Liberal Democracies, 1983; The Vatican in the Age of the Cold War, 1992. Other: 15 book-length trans from French, Italian and German. Contributions: Encounter; Sunday Telegraph. *Honours:* Cavaliere Commendatore del'Ordine di San Gregorio Magno (Papal Title). *Address:* 46 Fitzjames Ave, London W14, England.

RHODES, Richard (Lee); Writer; b. 4 July 1937, Kansas City, KS, USA; m. 1st; three c.; m. 2nd Ginger Untrif 1993. *Education:* BA, Yale University, 1959. *Career:* mem. Authors' Guild. *Publications:* The Inland Ground: An Evocation of the American Middle West, 1970; The Ungodly (fiction), 1973; The Ozarks, 1974; Holy Secrets (fiction), 1978; Looking for America: A Writer's Odyssey, 1979; The Last Safari (fiction), 1980; Sons of Earth (fiction), 1981; The Making of the Atomic Bomb, 1987; Farm: A Year in the Life of an American Farmer, 1989; A Hole in the World: An American Boyhood, 1990; Making Love: An Erotic Odyssey, 1992; Nuclear Renewal: Common Sense About Energy, 1993; Dark Sun: The Making of the Hydrogen Bomb, 1995; How to Write, 1995; Trying to Get Some Dignity: Stories of Triumph Over Childhood Abuse (with Ginger Rhodes), 1996; Deadly Feasts: Tracking the Secrets of a Terrifying New Plague, 1997; Visions of Technology, 1999; Why They Kill, 1999; Masters of Death, 2002. Contributions: numerous magazines and journals. *Honours:* Guggenheim Fellowship, 1974–75; National Endowment for the Arts Fellowship, 1978; Ford Foundation Fellowship, 1981–83; Alfred P. Sloan Foundation Fellowships, 1985, 1993, 1995, 2002; National Book Award in Non-Fiction, 1987; National Book Critics Circle Award for General Non-Fiction, 1987; Pulitzer Prize for General Non-Fiction, 1988; Hon. Doctorate, Westminster College, Fulton, Missouri, 1988; MacArthur Foundation Program on Peace and International Co-operation, 1990–91. *Literary Agent:* Janklow & Nesbit Associates, 445 Park Ave, New York, NY 10022, USA.

RHONE, Trevor Dave; playwright, director and screenwriter; b. 24 March 1940, Kingston, Jamaica; m. Camella King 1974; two s. one d. *Education:* Rose Bruford Coll. of Speech and Drama. *Career:* resident playwright, Barn Theatre, Kingston 1968–75. *Publications:* Old Time Story 1981, Two Can Play 1984. *Honours:* Inst. of Jamaica Silver Musgrave Medal 1972, Gold Musgrave Medal 1988, Commander of the Order of Distinction, Nat. Honour, Jamaica 1980, Acad. Award, Film Canada 1989. *Address:* 1 Haining Mews, Kingston 5, Jamaica.

RHOTEN, Kenneth; Writer, Composer, Inventor and Artist; b. 28 Dec. 1950, Hammond, IN, USA; m. 1st Virginia Haynie 1974 (divorced 1977); m. 2nd Robin Damron 1984 (divorced 1985); m. 3rd Josephine Meese 1986 (deceased 2000). *Publications:* Dark Twist of Fate (novel), 1995; Dark Twist of Fate and Other Works, 1999. Other: Stories and songs. *Address:* PO Box 225, 9981 Firebaugh, Stoy, IL 62464, USA.

RIBMAN, Ronald (Burt); Dramatist; b. 28 May 1932, New York, NY, USA; m. Alice Rosen, 27 Aug. 1967, one s. one d. *Education:* Brooklyn College, CUNY, 1950–51; BBA, 1954, MLitt, 1958, PhD, 1962, University of Pittsburgh. *Career:* Asst Prof. of English, Otterbein College, 1962–63; Rockefeller Playwright-in-Residence, Public Theater, 1975; mem. Dramatists Guild. *Publications:* Harry, Noon and Night, 1965; The Journey of the Fifth Horse, 1966; The Ceremony of Innocence, 1967; Passing Through from Exotic Places, 1969; Fingernails Blue as Flowers, 1971; A Break in the Skin, 1972; The Poison Tree, 1976; Cold Storage, 1977; Buck, 1982; Seize the Day, 1985; The Cannibal Masque, 1988; The Rug Merchants of Chaos, 1991; Dream of the Red Spider, 1993. Contributions: Films and television. *Honours:* Obie Award, 1966; Rockefeller Foundation Grants, 1966, 1968; Guggenheim Fellowship, 1970; National Endowment for the Arts Fellowship, 1973; Straw Hat Award, 1973; Elizabeth Hull-Kate Warriner Award, 1977; Drama Critics Award, 1977; Playwrights USA Award, 1984. *Address:* c/o Dramatists Play Service Inc, 440 Park Ave S, New York, NY 10016, USA.

RICCI, Nino (Pio); Author; b. 23 Aug. 1959, Leamington, Ontario, Canada. *Education:* BA, English, York University, 1981; MA, Creative Writing, Concordia University, 1987; Italian Literature, University of Florence. *Career:* Teacher of Creative Writing and Canadian Literature, Concordia University, 1987–88; Mem., Board of Dirs, 1990–97, Pres., 1995–96, Canadian Centre, International PEN. *Publications:* Lives of the Saints, 1990; In a Glass House, 1993; Where She Has Gone, 1997. *Honours:* F. G. Bressani Prize for Fiction, 1990; Governor-General's Award for Fiction, 1990; WHSmith/Books in Canada First Novel Award, 1990; Betty Trask Award, 1991; Winifred Holtby Prize for Best Regional Novel, 1991. *Literary Agent:* Anne McDermid & Assocs, 92 Wilcocks St, Toronto M5S 1C8, Canada.

RICE, Anne, (Anne Rampling, A. N. Roquelaure), BA, MA; American writer; b. 4 Oct. 1941, New Orleans, LA; m. Stan Rice 1961; one s. one d. (deceased). *Education:* Texas Women's Univ., San Francisco State Coll., Univ. of California at Berkeley. *Career:* mem. Authors' Guild. *Publications:* Interview with the Vampire 1976, The Feast of All Saints 1979, Cry to Heaven 1982, The Claiming of Sleeping Beauty (as A. N. Roquelaure) 1983, Beauty's Punishment (as A. N. Roquelaure) 1984, The Vampire Lestat 1985, Exit to Eden (as Anne Rampling) 1985, Beauty's Release (as A. N. Roquelaure) 1985, Belinda (as Anne Rampling) 1986, The Queen of the Damned 1988, The Mummy, or Ramses the Damned 1989, The Witching Hour 1990, The Tale of the Body Thief 1992, Lasher 1993, Taltos 1994, Memnoch the Devil 1995, Servant of the Bones 1996, Violin 1997, Pandora 1998, Armand 1998, Vittorio the Vampire 1999, Merrick 2000, Blood and Gold 2001, The Master of Rampling Gate (short story) 2002, Blackwood Farm 2002, Blood Canticle 2003. *Address:* c/o Alfred A. Knopf Inc, 299 Park Avenue, New York, NY 10171, USA. *Website:* www.annerice.com.

RICE, Earle Wilmont, Jr; writer; b. 21 Oct. 1928, Lynn, Massachusetts, USA; m. Georgia Joy Black Wood 1958; one s. one d. *Education:* San Jose City Coll., Foothill Coll., Los Altos. *Career:* mem. Soc. of Children's Book Writers and Illustrators, League of World War I Aviation Historians, Cross and Cockade Int., US Naval Inst., Air Force Asscn. *Publications:* fiction: Tiger, Lion, Hawk 1977, The Animals 1979, Fear on Ice 1981, More Than Macho 1981, Death Angel 1981, The Gringo Dies at Dawn 1993; non-fiction: The Cuban Revolution 1995, The Battle of Britain 1996, The Battle of Midway 1996, The Inchon Invasion 1996, The Battle of Belleau Wood 1996, The Attack on Pearl Harbor 1996, The Tet Offensive 1996, The Nuremberg Trials 1996, The Salem Witch Trials 1996, The O. J. Simpson Trial 1996, The Final Solution 1997, Nazi War Criminals 1997, The Battle of the Little Bighorn 1997, Life Among the Great Plains Indians 1997, Life During the Crusades 1997, Life During the Middle Ages 1997, The Kamikazes 1999, Strategic Battles of the Pacific 2000, Strategic Battles in Europe 2000, The Bombing of Pearl Harbor 2000, The Third Reich: Demise of the Nazi Dream 2000, The Cold War: Collapse of Communism 2000, Sir Francis Drake: Navigator and Pirate 2002, Normandy 2002, First Battle of the Marne 2002, The Battle of Gettysburg 2002; adaptations: Dracula 1995, All Quiet on the Western Front 1995, The Grapes of Wrath 1996, Claire Chennault, Flying Tiger 2003, Manfred von Richthofen The Red Baron 2003, George S. Paton 2003, Erwin J. E. Rommel 2003, Douglas MacArthur 2004, Korea 1950: Pusan to Chosin 2004, Point of No Return: Tonkin Gulf and the Vietnam War 2004, Alexandra David-Néel: Explorer at the Roof of the World 2004, Great Military Leaders (series ed.) 2004; contrib. to California Today, Calliope, PSA Magazine, Pro/Am Hockey Review. *Honours:* Children's Book Chapters Category, Second Place 1993, Third Place 1994, Ninth Hon. Mention, Novel Chapter 1994, Florida State Writing Competition, Florida Freelance Writers' Asscn. *Address:* PO Box 2131, Julian, CA 92036-2131, USA. *E-mail:* ericejr@julian-ca.com.

RICH, Adrienne Cecile, AB; American poet and writer; b. 16 May 1929, Baltimore, MD; m. Alfred H. Conrad 1953 (died 1970); three s. *Education:* Radcliffe Coll. *Career:* Visiting Poet, Swarthmore College, 1966–68; Adjunct Prof., Columbia University, 1967–69; Lecturer, 1968–70, Instructor, 1970–71, Asst Prof., 1971–72, Prof., 1974–75, City College, CUNY; Fannie Hurst Visiting Prof., Brandeis University, 1972–73; Prof. of English, Douglass College, New Brunswick, NJ, 1976–78; A. D. White Prof.-at-Large, Cornell University, 1981–85; Clark Lecturer and Distinguished Visiting Prof., Scripps College, Claremont, CA, 1983; Visiting Prof., San Jose State University, CA, 1985–86; Burgess Lecturer, Pacific Oaks College, Pasadena, CA, 1986; Prof. of English and Feminist Studies, Stanford University, 1986–93; Board of Chancellors, Acad. of American Poets, 1999–2002. *Publications:* poetry: A Change of World 1951, (Poems) 1952, The Diamond Cutters and Other Poems 1955, Snapshots of a Daughter-in-Law: Poems 1954–1962 1963, Necessities of Life: Poems 1962–1965 1966, Selected Poems 1967, Leaflets: Poems 1965–1968 1969, The Will to Change: Poems 1968–1970 1971, Diving into the Wreck: Poems 1971–1972 (National Book Award 1974) 1973, Poems Selected and New 1975, Twenty-One Love Poems 1976, The Dream of a Common Language: Poems 1974–1977 1978, A Wild Patience Has Taken Me This Far: Poems 1978–1981 1981, Sources 1983, The Fact of a Doorframe: Poems Selected and New 1950–1984 1984, Your Native Land, Your Life 1986, Time's Power: Poems 1985–1988 1989, An Atlas of the Difficult World: Poems 1988–1991 1991, Collected Early Poems 1950–1970 1993, Dark Fields of the Republic: Poems 1991–1995 1995, Midnight Salvage: Poems 1995–1998 1999, Fox: Poems 1998–2000 2001, The Fact of a Doorframe: Poems 1950–2000 2002; other: Of Woman Born: Motherhood as Experience and Institution 1976, On Lies, Secrets and Silence: Selected Prose 1966–1978 1979, Blood, Bread and Poetry: Selected Prose 1979–1985 1986, What is Found There: Notebooks on Poetry and Politics 1993, Arts of the Possible: Essays and Conversations 2001. *Honours:* Yale Series of Younger Poets Award, 1951; Guggenheim Fellowships, 1952, 1961; American Acad. of Arts and Letters Award, 1961; Bess Hokin Prize, 1963; Eunice Tietjens Memorial Prize, 1968; National Endowment for the Arts Grant, 1970; Shelley Memorial Award, 1971; Ingram Merrill Foundation Grant, 1973; Fund for Human Dignity Award, 1981; Ruth Lilly Prize, 1986; Brandeis University Creative Arts Award, 1987; Elmer Holmes Bobst Award, 1989; Commonwealth Award in Literature, 1991; Frost Silver Medal, Poetry Society of America, 1992; Los Angeles Times Book Award, 1992; Lenore Marshall/Nation Award, 1992; William Whitehead Award, 1992; Lambda Book Award, 1992; Harriet Monroe Prize, 1994; John D. and Catherine T. MacArthur Foundation Fellowship, 1994; Tanning Prize, 1996; Lannan Foundation Lifetime Achievement Award, 1999; Bollingen Prize for Poetry, 2003; hon. doctorates. *Literary Agent:* Steven Barclay Agency, 12 Western Avenue, Petaluma, CA 94952, USA. *Telephone:* (707) 773-0654. *Fax:* (707) 778-1868. *Website:* www.barclayagency.com. *Address:* c/o W. W. Norton & Co, 500 Fifth Avenue, New York, NY 10110, USA.

RICH, Elaine Sommers, BA, MA; writer and poet; b. 8 Feb. 1926, Plevna, IN, USA; m. Ronald L. Rich 1953; three s. one d. *Education:* Goshen Coll., Michigan State Univ. *Career:* instructor, Goshen Coll. 1947–49, 1950–53, Bethel Coll., North Newton, KS 1953–66; Lecturer, Int. Christian Univ.,

Tokyo 1971–78; columnist, Mennonite Weekly Review 1973–; Adviser to Int. Students, Bluffton Coll., OH 1979–89; Adjunct Prof. of English, Univ. of Findlay, OH 1990–95, Owens Community Coll. 1995–97; mem. Fellowship of Reconciliation, Int. League for Peace and Freedom. *Publications:* Breaking Bread Together (ed.) 1958, Hannah Elizabeth 1964, Tomorrow, Tomorrow, Tomorrow 1966, Am I This Countryside? 1981, Mennonite Women 1683–1983: A Story of God's Faithfulness 1983, Spiritual Elegance: A Biography of Pauline Krehbiel Raid 1987, Prayers for Everyday 1990, Walking Together in Faith (ed.) 1993, Pondered in Her Heart 1998; contrib. to books and journals. *Address:* 112 S Spring Street, Bluffton, OH 45817, USA.

RICH, Frank Hart, BA; critic; b. 2 June 1949, Washington, DC, USA; m. 1st Gail Winston 1976; two s.; m. 2nd Alexandra Rachelle Witchel 1991. *Education:* Harvard Univ. *Career:* Co-Ed., Richmond Mercury, Virginia, 1972–73; Senior Ed. and Film Critic, New York Times Magazine, 1973–75; Film Critic, New York Post, 1975–77; Film and Television Critic, Time Magazine, 1977–80; Chief Drama Critic, 1980–93, Op-Ed Columnist, 1994–, New York Times; Assoc. Fellow, Jonathan Edwards College, Yale University, 1998–. *Publications:* The Theatre Art of Boris Aronson (with others), 1987; Hot Seat: Theater Criticism for the New York Times, 1980–1993, 1998; Ghost Light, 2000. Contributions: newspapers and periodicals. *Literary Agent:* Steven Barclay Agency, 12 Western Avenue, Petaluma, CA 94952, USA. *Telephone:* (707) 773-0654. *Fax:* (707) 778-1868. *Website:* www.barclayagency.com. *Address:* c/o The New York Times, 229 W 43rd Street, New York, NY 10036, USA.

RICH, Robert R., BA, MD; American microbiologist, immunologist and writer; *Editor-in-Chief, Journal of Immunology*. *Education:* Oberlin Coll. OH, Univ. of Kansas School of Medicine, Univ. of Washington School of Medicine, Seattle, Nat. Insts of Health, Harvard Medical School. *Career:* Asst Prof, then Assoc. Prof. 1973–78, Head of Immunology section 1977–98, Prof. 1978–95, Vice-Pres. and Dean of Research 1990–98, Distinguished Service Prof. 1995–98, Microbiology and Immunology and Medicine, Baylor Coll. of Medicine; mem. of Immunobiology Study Section, Nat. Insts of Health 1977–81; Investigator, Howard Hughes Medical Inst. 1977–91; Advisory Ed., The Journal of Experimental Medicine 1981–84; mem., Transplantation Biology and Immunology Sub-cttee 1982–86, chair. 1984–86 NIAID; Assoc. Ed., The Journal of Infectious Diseases 1983–88; mem. 1984–88, chair. 1986–88, Nat. Research Cttee for Arthritis Foundation; mem. of bd of dirs 1988–93, chair. 1991, American Board of Allergy and Immunology; editiorial bd mem., The Journal of Clinical Immunology 1989–96; mem. 1989–94, chair. 1993–94, Nat. Multiple Sclerosis Soc. Research Programs Advisory Cttee; mem. of bd of dirs, American Board of Internal Medicine 1990–93; Section Ed. and Deputy Ed. 1991–2002, Ed.-in-Chief 2003–, The Journal of Immunology; mem. of cttee on public affairs 1993–2000, chair. 1994–2000, American Assen of Immunologists; pres., Clinical Immunology Soc. 1995; mem. of bd of dirs 1998–, pres. and chair. 2001–02, FASEB; Exec. Assoc., Dean/Research and Strategic Initiatives 1998–, Prof. of Medicine, Microbiology and Immunology 1998–, Emory Univ. School of Medicine; Vice-Pres., American Acad. of Allergy, Asthma and Immunology. *Publications:* over 200 publications (some collaborative). *Address:* Journal of Immunology, 9650 Rockville Pike, Bethesda, MD 20814-3998, USA. *Website:* www.jimmunol.org.

RICHARDS, Cyndi (see Richeson, Cena Golder).

RICHARDS, David Adams; Canadian writer; b. 17 Oct. 1950, Newcastle, NB. *Education:* St Thomas University, NB. *Publications:* The Coming of Winter 1974, Blood Ties 1976, Dancers at Night 1978, Lives of Short Duration 1981, Road to the Stilt House 1985, Nights Below Station Street 1988, Evening Snow Will Bring Such Peace 1990, For Those Who Hunt the Wounded Down 1993, Mercy Among the Children 2000, The Bay of Love and Sorrows 2003, River of the Brokenhearted 2004. *Honours:* Governor-General's Award 1988, Canada Authors Assen Literary Award 1991, Canada-Australian Literary Award 1992. *Address:* c/o Canada Council, 350 Albert Street, PO Box 1047, Ottawa, ON K1P 5V8, Canada.

RICHARDS, Denis George; Writer; b. 10 Sept. 1910, London, England; m. Barbara Smethurst, 6 Jan. 1940, four d. *Education:* BA, 1931, MA, 1935, Trinity Hall, Cambridge. *Career:* mem. Arts Club; Society of Authors; Garrick Club; RAF Club. *Publications:* An Illustrated History of Modern Europe, 1938; An Illustrated History of Modern Britain, 1951; Royal Air Force, 1939–45 (with H. St G. Saunders), 3 vols, 1953, 1954; Offspring of the Vic: A History of Morley College, 1958; Britain Under the Tudors and Stuarts, 1958; The Battle of Britain: The Jubilee History (with Richard Hough), 1989; The Few and the Many, 1990; The Hardest Victory: RAF Bomber Command in the Second World War, 1994; Recalling the Flavour: Reflections 1910–1941, 1999; It Might Have Been Worse: Reflections 1941–1996, 1999. Contributions: Books and Bookmen; Daily Telegraph Supplement; Financial Times; Dictionary of National Biography. *Honours:* C. P. Robertson Memorial Trophy, 1956; OBE, 1990. *Address:* 14 Garden Wing, Kekewich House, London N6 4DL, England.

RICHARDS, Hubert John; Lecturer and Writer; b. 25 Dec. 1921, Weilderstadt, Germany; m. 22 Dec. 1975, one s. one d. *Education:* STL (Licence in Theology), Gregorian University, Rome; LSS (Licence in Scripture), Biblical Institute, Rome. *Career:* mem. Norfolk Theological Society. *Publications:* The First Christmas: What Really Happened?, 1973; The Miracles of Jesus: What Really Happened?, 1975; The First Easter: What Really Happened?, 1977; Death and After: What Will Really Happen?, 1979; What Happens When You Pray?, 1980; Pilgrim to the Holy Land, 1985; Focus on the Bible, 1990; The Gospel According to St Paul, 1990; God's Diary, 1991; Pilgrim to Rome, 1994; Quips and Quotes, 1997; Anthology for the Church Year, 1998; Philosophy of Religion, 1998; The Bible: What Does It Really Say?, 1999; Who's Who and What's What in the Bible, 1999; More Quips and Quotes, 2000; Jesus: Who Did He Think He Was?, 2000; The Bible: 150 Readings, 2001; 1,600 Quips and Quotes, 2003. Contributions: Regular articles and reviews in various publications. *Address:* 59 Park Lane, Norwich, Norfolk NR2 3EF, England.

RICHARDS, Sean (see Haining, Peter (Alexander)).

RICHARDSON, Joanna, MA, FRSL; British author; b. London. *Education:* The Downs School, Seaford, Sussex, St Anne's Coll., Oxford. *Career:* mem. Council, RSL 1961–86. *Radio:* numerous interviews, trans. of plays and novels, and feature programmes for Third Programme (now BBC Radio 3) and Home Service (now BBC Radio 4). *Publications:* Fanny Brawne: a biography 1952, Théophile Gautier: his Life and Times 1958, Edward FitzGerald 1960, The Pre-Eminent Victorian: A Study of Tennyson 1962, The Everlasting Spell: A Study of Keats and his Friends 1963, Introduction to Victor Hugo: Choses Vues 1964, Edward Lear 1965, George IV: A Portrait 1966, Creevey and Greville 1967, Princess Mathilde 1969, Verlaine 1971, Enid Starkie 1973, Stendhal: A Critical Biography 1974, Victor Hugo 1976, Zola 1978, Keats and his Circle: An Album of Portraits 1980, The Life and Letters of John Keats 1981, Letters from Lambeth: the Correspondence of the Reynolds Family with John Freeman Milward Dovaston 1808–1815, 1981, Paris Under Siege 1982, Colette 1983, The Brownings 1986, Judith Gautier (first non-French winner Prix Goncourt de la Biographie 1989) 1987, Portrait of a Bonaparte: The Life and Times of Joseph-Napoleon Primoli 1851–1927 1987, Baudelaire 1994; editor: FitzGerald: Selected Works 1962, Essays by Divers Hands 1964, Verlaine Poems (and trans.) 1974, Baudelaire Poems (and trans.) 1975, Gautier, Mademoiselle de Maupin (and trans.) 1981; has contributed to The Times, The Times Literary Supplement, Sunday Times, Spectator, New Statesman, New York Times Book Review, The Washington Post, French Studies, French Studies Bulletin, Modern Language Review, Keats-Shelley Memorial Bulletin, etc. *Honours:* Chevalier, Ordre des Arts et des Lettres. *Literary Agent:* Curtis Brown Group, Haymarket House, 28–29 Haymarket, London, SW1Y 4SP, England. *Telephone:* (20) 7396-6600.

RICHARDSON, Robert Dale, Jr; Former Prof. of English, Independent Scholar and Writer; b. 14 June 1934, Milwaukee, Wisconsin, USA; m. 1st Elizabeth Hall, 7 Nov. 1959, divorced 1987; m. 2nd Annie Dillard, 10 Dec. 1988, three d. *Education:* AB, 1956, PhD in English and American Literature, 1961, Harvard University. *Career:* Instructor, Harvard University, 1961–63; Asst Prof., 1963–68, Assoc. Prof., 1968–72, Chair., Dept of English, 1968–73, Prof. of English, 1972–87, Assoc. Dean for Graduate Studies, 1975–76, University of Denver; Assoc. Ed., 1967–76, 1983–87, Book Review Ed., 1976–83, Denver Quarterly; Visiting Fellow, Huntington Library, 1973–74; Visiting Prof., Queens College and Graduate School and Univ. Center, CUNY, 1978, Sichuan University, People's Republic of China, 1983; Prof. of English, University of Colorado, 1987; Visiting Lecturer, Yale University, 1989; Visiting Prof. of Letters, 1990, Adjunct Prof. of Letters, 1993–94, Wesleyan University; Assoc. Fellow, Calhoun College, Yale University, 1997–; mem. American Studies Assen; Assen of Literary Scholars and Critics; Authors' Guild; Emerson Society; Melville Society; Society of American Historians; Society for Eighteenth Century Studies; Thoreau Society. *Publications:* Literature and Film, 1969; The Rise of Modern Mythology, 1680–1860 (with B. Feldman), 1972; Myth and Literature in the American Renaissance, 1978; Henry Thoreau: A Life of the Mind, 1986; Ralph Waldo Emerson: Selected Essays, Lectures and Poems (ed.), 1990; Emerson: The Mind on Fire, 1995; Three Centuries of American Poetry (with Allen Mandelbaum), 1999. Contributions: scholarly books and journals. *Honours:* Melcher Prizes, 1986, 1995; Guggenheim Fellowship, 1990; Francis Parkman Prize, 1995; Washington Irving Award for Literary Excellence, 1995; Dictionary of Literary Biography Award for a Distinguished Literary Biography, 1995; New York Times Book Review Notable Book Citation, 1995; Special Award in Literature, American Acad. of Arts and Letters, 1998; Emerson Society Prize, 2001; Thoreau Society Distinguished Achievement Award, 2001; Hon. Doctor of Humane Letters, Meadville Lombard Theological School, 2003. *Literary Agent:* Russell & Volkening. *Address:* 143 W Margaret Lane, Hillsborough NC 27278, USA. *E-mail:* rrichardson@aol.com.

RICHESON, Cena Golder, (Velma Chamberlain, Jessica Jains, Cyndi Richards), AA, BA; writer and poet; b. 11 April 1941, Oregon, USA; m. Jerry Dale Richeson 1961; two s. *Education:* Diablo Valley College, California State University. *Career:* Instructor, Shasta College, CA, 1974–76, Liberty Union High School, Brentwood, CA, 1984–85; Columnist, Anderson Press Weekly Newspaper, CA, 1976–78; Frontier Correspondent, National Tombstone Epitaph, Tucson, 1986–; Book Reviewer, Publishers Weekly, 1994–95; mem. California Writers Club, pres., 1991–92; Society of Children's Book Writers; Zane Grey's West Society. *Publications:* contrib. to anthologies and periodicals. *Address:* PO Box 268, Knightsen, CA 94548, USA.

RICHIE, Donald (Steiner); Critic and Writer; b. 17 April 1924, Lima, Ohio, USA; m. Mary Evans, Nov. 1961, divorced 1965. *Education:* Antioch College, 1942; US Maritime Acad., 1943; BS, Columbia University, 1953. *Career:* Film Critic, Pacific Stars and Stripes, Tokyo, 1947–49; Arts Critic, Saturday Review of Literature, New York City, 1950–51, The Nation, New York, 1959–61, Newsweek Magazine, New York, 1973–76, Time Magazine, 1997; Film Critic, 1953–69, Literary Critic, 1972–03, Japan Times, Tokyo; Lecturer in American Literature, Waseda University, Tokyo, 1954–59; Curator of Film, Museum of Modern Art, New York City, 1968–73; Toyoda Chair, University of Michigan, 1993; Lecturer, Film, Temple University, 1996–03. *Publications:* Where Are the Victors? (novel), 1956; The Japanese Film: Art and Industry (with Joseph L. Anderson), 1959; The Japanese Movie: An Illustrated History, 1965; The Films of Akira Kurosawa, 1965; Companions of the Holiday (novel), 1968; George Stevens: An American Romantic, 1970; The Inland Sea, 1971; Japanese Cinema, 1971; Three Modern Kyogen, 1972; Ozu: The Man and His Films, 1974; Ji: Signs and Symbols of Japan (with Mana Maeda), 1975; The Japanese Tatoo, 1980; Zen Inklings: Some Stories, Fables, Parables, Sermons and Prints with Notes and Commentaries, 1982; A Taste of Japan: Food Fact and Fable, What the People Eat, Customs and Etiquette, 1985; Viewing Film, 1986; Introducing Tokyo, 1987; A Lateral View, 1987; Different People: Pictures of Some Japanese, 1987; Tokyo Nights, 1988; Japanese Cinema: An Introduction, 1990; The Honorable Visitors, 1994; Partial Views, 1995; The Temples of Kyoto, 1995; Lafcadio Hearn's Japan: An Anthology of His Writings on the Country and its People (ed.), 1997; The Memoirs of the Warrior Kumagai, 1999; Tokyo: A View of the City, 1999; A Hundred Years of Japanese Film: A Short History and a Selective Guide to Videos and DVDs, 2001; The Donald Richie Reader: Fifty Years of Writing on Japan (ed. by Arturo Silva), 2001; The Image Factory: Fads and Fashions in Japan, 2003; Japanese Literature Reviewed, 2003; Tokyo Story: The Script, 2003. *Honours:* Citations, Government of Japan, 1963, 1970, 1983; Citation, US National Society of Film Critics, 1970; Kawakita Memorial Foundation Award, 1983; Presidential Citation, New York University, 1989; Novikoff Award, San Francisco Film Festival, 1990; Tokyo Metropolitan Government Cultural Award, 1993; John D. Rockefeller III Award, 1994; Japan Foundation Prize, 1995; Hon. doctorate, University of Maryland, 1999; Japan Society Award, New York, 2001. *Address:* Ueno 2, 12.18 (804), Taito-ku, Tokyo 110 0005, Japan.

RICHTER, Harvena; University Lecturer (retd), Writer and Poet; b. 13 March 1919, Reading, Pennsylvania, USA. *Education:* BA, University of New Mexico, 1938; MA, 1955, PhD, 1966, New York University. *Career:* Lecturer, New York University, 1955–66, University of New Mexico, 1969–89; mem. Authors' Guild. *Publications:* The Human Shore, 1959; Virginia Woolf: The Inward Voyage, 1970; Writing to Survive: The Private Notebooks of Conrad Richter, 1988; The Yaddo Elegies and Other Poems, 1995; Green Girls: Poems Early and Late, 1996; The Innocent Island, 1999; Frozen Light: The Crystal Poems, 2002; The Golden Fountains: Sources of Energy and Life, 2002. Contributions: Magazines and newspapers. *Honours:* Grants and fellowships. *Address:* 1932 Candelaria Rd NW, Albuquerque, NM 87107, USA.

RICKS, Christopher Bruce, BA, BLitt, MA, FBA; British academic and writer; *Warren Professor of the Humanities, Boston University*; b. 18 Sept. 1933, London; m. 1st Kirsten Jensen 1956 (divorced 1975); two s. two d.; m. 2nd Judith Aronson 1977; one s. two d. *Education:* King Alfred's School, Wantage, Oxon., Balliol Coll., Oxford. *Career:* 2nd Lt Green Howards 1952; Andrew Bradley Jr Research Fellow Balliol Coll. Univ. of Oxford 1957, Fellow Worcester Coll. 1958–68; Prof. of English Bristol Univ. 1968–75; Fellow Christ's Coll., Prof. of English Univ. of Cambridge 1975–86, King Edward VII Prof. of English Literature 1982–86; Prof. of English Boston Univ. 1986–98, Warren Prof. of the Humanities 1998–, Co-Dir Editorial Inst. 1999–; elected Prof. of Poetry, Univ. of Oxford 2004–(09); Visiting Prof. at Univs of Berkeley and Stanford 1965, Smith Coll. 1967, Harvard Univ. 1971, Wesleyan 1974, Brandeis 1977, 1981, 1984, USA; Vice-Pres. Tennyson Soc.; Fellow American Acad. of Arts and Sciences 1991. *Publications:* Milton's Grand Style 1963, Tennyson 1972, Keats and Embarrassment 1974, The Force of Poetry 1984, T. S. Eliot and Prejudice 1988, Beckett's Dying Words 1993, Essays in Appreciation 1996, Reviewery 2002, Allusion to the Poets 2002, Dylan's Visions of Sin 2003; editor: Poems and Critics: An Anthology of Poetry and Criticism from Shakespeare to Hardy 1966, A. E. Housman: A Collection of Critical Essays 1968, Alfred Tennyson: Poems 1842 1968, John Milton: Paradise Lost and Paradise Regained 1968, The Poems of Tennyson 1969, The Brownings: Letters and Poetry 1970, English Poetry and Prose 1540–1674 1970, English Drama to 1710 1971, Selected Criticism of Matthew Arnold 1972, The State of the Language (with Leonard Michaels) 1980, The New Oxford Book of Victorian Verse 1987, Collected Poems and Selected Prose of A. E. Housman 1988, The Faber Book of America (with William Vance) 1992, Inventions of the March Hare: Poems 1909–1917 by T. S. Eliot 1996, The Oxford Book of English Verse 1999, Selected Poems of James Henry 2002; contrib. to professional journals. *Honours:* Hon. Fellow, Balliol Coll. 1989, Worcester Coll. 1990, Christ's Coll. Cambridge 1993; Hon. DLitt (Oxford) 1998; George Orwell Memorial Prize 1979; Beefeater Club Prize for Literature 1980, Distinguished Achievement Award Andrew W. Mellon Foundation 2004. *Address:* University of Oxford, University Offices, Wellington Square, Oxford, OX1 2JD, England; 39 Martin Street, Cambridge, MA 02138, USA; Lasborough Park, near Tetbury, Glos., GL8 8UF, England. *Telephone:* (617) 354-7887 (USA); (1666) 890252 (England).

RIDGWAY, Jason (see Marlowe, Stephen).

RIDLEY, Matt, BA, DPhil; British journalist and writer; b. 1958, Newcastle upon Tyne, England; m. Anya Hurlbert; two c. *Education:* Univ. of Oxford. *Career:* Science Ed. and American Ed., The Economist 1983–92; columnist, Sunday Telegraph, Daily Telegraph 1993–2000; Chair., Int. Centre for Life, Newcastle upon Tyne 2000–; Deputy Chair., Northern Rock plc; Chair., Northern 2 VCT; Dir, Northern Investors Co plc. *Publications:* The Red Queen: Sex and the Evolution of Human Nature 1993, The Origins of Virtue: Human Instincts and the Evolution of Co-operation 1996, Genome: The Autobiography of a Species in 23 Chapters 1999, Nature via Nurture: Genes, Experience and What Makes us Human 2003; contrib. articles and book reviews in The Times, Guardian, TLS, New Statesman, TIME, Newsweek, New York Times, Wall Street Journal, Atlantic Monthly, Discover, Natural History. *Address:* c/o Fourth Estate, 77–85 Fulham Palace Road, London, W6 8JB, England.

RIDPATH, Ian (William); Writer and Broadcaster; b. 1 May 1947, Ilford, Essex, England. *Career:* mem. Fellow, Royal Astronomical Society. *Publications:* Over 30 books, including: Worlds Beyond, 1975; Encyclopedia of Astronomy and Space (ed.), 1976; Messages From the Stars, 1978; Stars and Planets, 1978; Young Astronomer's Handbook, 1981; Hamlyn Encyclopedia of Space, 1981; Life Off Earth, 1983; Collins Guide to Stars and Planets, 1984; Gem Guide to the Night Sky, 1985; Secrets of the Sky, 1985; A Comet Called Halley, 1985; Longman Illustrated Dictionary of Astronomy and Astronautics, 1987; Monthly Sky Guide, 1987; Star Tales, 1989; Norton's Star Atlas (ed.), 1989; Book of the Universe, 1991; Atlas of Stars and Planets, 1992; Oxford Dictionary of Astronomy (ed.), 1997; Eyewitness Handbook of Stars and Planets, 1998; Gem Stars, 1999; Collins Encyclopedia of the Universe (gen. ed.), 2001; The Times Space, 2002. *Address:* 48 Otho Ct, Brentford Dock, Brentford, Middlesex TW8 8PY, England. *Website:* www.ianridpath.tk.

RIDPATH, Michael William Gerrans; Author; b. 7 March 1961, Exeter, England; m. Barbara Nunemaker 1 Oct. 1994; one s. two d. *Education:* History, Merton Coll., Oxford, 1979–82. *Career:* mem. Society of Authors, Managing Cttee; CWA; People of Today. *Publications:* Free to Trade, 1995; Trading Reality, 1996; The Market Maker, 1998; Fatal Error, 2003. *Address:* c/o Blake Friedmann, 37–41 Gower St, London WC1E 6HH, England.

RIFAAT, Alifa; Short Story Writer; b. 1930, Cairo, Egypt; m. (deceased); three c. *Publications:* Bahiyaa's Eyes; Distant View of a Minaret (in trans.), 1983; The Long Night of Winter. *Address:* c/o African Writers Series, Heinemann Educational Publishers, Halley Ct, Jordan Hill, Oxford OX2 8EJ, England.

RIFBJERG, Klaus (Thorvald); Author, Poet and Dramatist; b. 15 Dec. 1931, Copenhagen, Denmark; m. Inge Merete Gerner, 28 May 1955, one s. two d. *Education:* Princeton University, 1950–51; University of Copenhagen, 1951–56. *Career:* Literary Critic, Information, Copenhagen, 1955–57, Politiken, Copenhagen, 1959–65; Ed.-in-Chief, Vindrosen, 1959–63; Literary Dir, Gyldendal Publishers, Copenhagen, 1984–92; mem. Danish Acad. *Publications:* Over 40 novels, 1958–2000, including: Anna (jeg) Anna, 1969, English trans. as Anna (I) Anna, 1982; De hellige aber, 1981, English trans. as Witness to the Future, 1987. Poetry: numerous poems, including: Selected Poems, 1976; Three Poems, 1982; Krigen, 1992, English trans. as War, 1995. Other: Plays, short stories, children's books, etc. *Honours:* Aarestrup Medal, 1964; Danish Critics' Award, 1965; Grant of Honour, Danish Dramatists, 1966; Danish Acad. Award, 1966; Golden Laurels, 1967; Søren Gyldendal Award, 1969; Nordic Council Award, 1970; Grant of Honour, Danish Writers' Guild, 1973; P. H. Prize, 1979; Holberg Medal, 1979; H. C. Andersen Prize, 1988; Nordic Prize, Swedish Acad., 1999; Hon. doctorates, University of Lund, 1991, University of Odense, 1996. *Address:* c/o Gyldendal Publishers, 3 Klareboderne, 1001 Copenhagen, Denmark.

RIGGS, David (see Pigott, Mark).

RILEY, Denise; Poet, Philosopher and Trans; b. 1948, England. *Education:* PhD, Philosophy, University of Sussex. *Publications:* Marxism for Infants, 1977; No Fee: A Line or Two for Free, 1979; Some Poems: 1968–1978 (with Wendy Mulford), 1982; War in the Nursery: Theories of the Child and Mother, 1983; Dry Air, 1985; 'Am I That Name?': Feminism and the Category of 'Women' in History, 1988; Poets on Writing: Britain, 1970–1991 (ed.), 1992; Mop Mop Georgette: New and Selected Poems, 1993; Selected Poems, 2001; The Words of Selves: Identification, Solidarity, Irony, 2001. Contributions: several publications. *Address:* c/o Cambridge University Press, The Edinburgh Bldg, Shaftesbury Rd, Cambridge CB2 2RU, England.

RIMINGTON, Dame Stella, DCB, MA; British civil servant; b. 1935; m. John Rimington 1963; two d. *Education:* Nottingham High School for Girls, Edinburgh Univ. *Career:* Dir-Gen. Security Service 1992–96; Dir (non-exec.) Marks and Spencer 1997–, BG PLC 1997–2000, BG Group 2000–, GKR. Group (now Whitehead Mann GKR) 1997–2001; Chair. Inst. of

Cancer Research 1997–2001. *Publications:* Open Secret 2001, At Risk (novel) 2004. *Honours:* Hon. Air Commodore 7006 (VR) Squadron Royal Auxiliary Air Force 1997–2001; Hon. LLB (Nottingham) 1995, (Exeter) 1996. *Address:* PO Box 1604, London, SW1P 1XB, England.

RINALDI, Nicholas Michael, AB, MA, PhD; American academic, writer and poet; *Professor, Fairfield University*; b. 2 April 1934, New York, NY; m. Jacqueline Tellier 1959; three s. one d. *Education:* Shrub Oak Coll., Fordham Univ. *Career:* Instructor to Asst Prof., St John's Univ. 1960–65; Lecturer, CUNY 1966; Assoc. Prof., Columbia Univ. 1966; Asst Prof. to Prof., Prof., Fairfield Univ. 1966–; Prof., Univ. of Connecticut 1972; mem. Associated Writing Programs; Poetry Society of America. *Publications:* novels: Bridge Fall Down 1985, The Jukebox Queen of Malta 1999, Between Two Rivers 2004; poetry: The Resurrection of the Snails 1977, We Have Lost Our Fathers 1982, The Luftwaffe in Chaos 1985; contrib. to periodicals and journals, including Virginia Quarterly Review. *Honours:* Joseph P. Slomovich Memorial Award for Poetry, 1979; All Nations Poetry Awards, 1981, 1983; New York Poetry Forum Award, 1983; Eve of St Agnes Poetry Award, 1984; Charles Angoff Literary Award, 1984. *Address:* c/o English Department, Fairfield University, 1073 N Benson Road, Fairfield, CT 06824, USA.

RINDO, Ronald J.; academic and writer; b. 21 March 1959, Milwaukee, WI, USA; m. Ellen S. Meyer, 13 Oct. 1984, one s. one d. *Education:* BA, Carroll College, 1981; MA, 1984, PhD, 1989, University of Wisconsin, Milwaukee. *Career:* Asst Prof. of English, Birmingham Southern College, AL, 1989–92, University of Wisconsin, Oshkosh, 1992–; mem. MLA; Society for the Study of Midwestern Literature; Wisconsin Council of Teachers of English. *Publications:* Suburban Metaphysics and Other Stories, 1990; Secrets Men Keep (short stories), 1995. Contributions: anthologies, books, reviews and periodicals. *Honours:* Milwaukee Small Press Award, 1989, Wisconsin Writer's Award, Wisconsin Library Asscn, 1990; Bell South Foundation Grant, 1990; Wye Fellow, Aspen Institute, 1991; Wisconsin Humanities Council Grant, 1995.

RIPLEY, Michael David, (Mike Ripley); Critic and Writer; b. 29 Sept. 1952, Huddersfield, England; m. Alyson Jane White, 8 July 1978, two d. *Education:* BA, Economic History, University of East Anglia. *Career:* Crime Fiction Critic, Sunday Telegraph, 1989–91; Crime Critic, The Daily Telegraph, 1991–; mem. CWA; Sisters in Crime, USA; Dorothy L. Sayers Society. *Publications:* Just Another Angel, 1988; Angel Touch, 1989; Angel Hunt, 1990; Angel Eyes, 1992; Angel City, 1993; Angel in Arms, 1994; Angel Confidential, 1995; Family of Angels, 1996; That Angel Look, 1997; Bootlegged Angel, 2000; Family of Angels, 2001; Lights, Camara, Angel, 2001; Double Take, 2001; Angels in Arms, 2001; Angel Underground, 2002. Short stories: The Body of the Beer, 1989; Smeltdown, 1990; Gold Sword, 1990. Contributions: Fresh Blood anthology series (ed.); 'Britcrit' Column Mystery Scene, USA. *Honours:* Last Laugh Awards, CWA, 1989, 1991; Angel Literary Award for Fiction, 1990. *Literary Agent:* David Higham Associates, 5–8 Lower John St, Golden Sq., London W1F 9HA, England.

RITTER, Erika; Dramatist and Writer; b. 1948, Regina, Saskatchewan, Canada. *Education:* McGill University, Montréal, 1968; MA, University of Toronto, 1970. *Career:* Writer-in-Residence, Concordia University, 1984; Playwright-in-Residence, Smith College, 1985, Stratford Festival, 1985. *Publications:* Plays: A Visitor from Charleston, 1975; The Splits, 1978; Winter, 1671, 1979; Automatic Pilot, 1980; The Passing Scene, 1982; Murder at McQueen, 1986; The Road to Hell, 1992. Other: Urban Scrawl, 1984; Ritter in Residence, 1987; The Hidden Life in Humans, 1997. *Honours:* Chalmers Award, 1980; ACTRA Award, 1982. *Address:* c/o Shain Jaffe, Great North Artists, 350 Dupont St, Toronto, Ontario M5R 1V9, Canada.

RIVARD, David; Writer, Poet and Ed.; b. 2 Dec. 1953, Fall River, MA, USA; m. Michaela Sullivan, 17 Dec. 1982, one d. *Education:* BA, Southeastern Massachusetts University, 1975; MFA, University of Arizona, 1982. *Career:* Faculty, Dept of English, Tufts University; Poetry Ed., Harvard Review. *Publications:* Torque, 1988; Wise Poison, 1996; Bewitched Playground, 2000. Contributions: periodicals. *Honours:* Fine Arts Work Center Fellowships, Provincetown, Massachusetts, 1984–85, 1986–87; National Endowment for the Arts Fellowships, 1986, 1991; Agnes Lynch Starrett Poetry Prize, University of Pittsburgh, 1987; Pushcart Prize, 1994; Massachusetts Cultural Council Fellow, 1994; James Laughlin Award, Acad. of American Poets, 1996; Guggenheim Fellowship, 2001. *Address:* 72 Inman St, Apt A, Cambridge, MA 02139, USA.

RIVAS, Manuel; Spanish journalist, novelist and poet; b. 1957, A Coruña. *Career:* contributor to Galician literature, co-establishing a number of Galician- and Spanish-language journals. *Publications:* poetry: Libro de Entroido 1979, Balada nas praias do Oeste 1985, Mohicania 1987, Ningún cisne 1989; novels: Todo ben 1985, Un millón de vacas (Premio de la Crítica) 1989, Os comedores de patatas 1991, Qué me queres, amor? (Premio Nacional de Narrativa) 1996, El pueblo de la noche 1997, O lapis do carpinteiro 1998, Ella, maldita alma 1999, A man dos paíños 2000; numerous short stories; contrib. to El País, El Ideal Gallego, Diario de Galicia, La voz de Galicia. *Address:* c/o Harvill Press, 2 Aztec Row, Berners Road, London, N1 0PW, England.

RIVERA-GARZA, Cristina, PhD; Mexican writer, poet and historian; b. 1964, Matamoros, Tamaulipas. *Education:* Nat. Autonomous Univ. of Mexico, Mexico City, Univ. of Houston, TX, USA. *Career:* Assoc. Prof. of Mexican History, San Diego State Univ.; Head of Creative Writing Narrative Program, Centro Cultural Tijuana. *Publications:* La guerra no importa 1991, La más mia 1998, Nadie me verá llorar (trans. as No One Will See Me Cry) 2000, La cresta de Ilion 2002, Ningún reloj cuenta esto 2002, Hombres frágiles 2005; contrib. to Hispanic American Historical Review, Journal of the History of Medicine. *Literary Agent:* c/o Curbstone Press, 321 Jackson Street, Willimantic, CT 06226-1738, USA. *E-mail:* info@curbstone.org. *Website:* www.curbstone.org.

RIX, Timothy John, CBE, BA, CIMgt, FRSA, F.INST.D.; British publisher; b. 4 Jan. 1934, Maidenhead, Berks.; m. 1st Wendy E. Wright 1960 (dissolved 1967); m. 2nd Gillian Greenwood 1968; one s. two d. *Education:* Radley Coll., Clare Coll., Cambridge and Yale Univ. *Career:* joined Longmans Green & Co. Ltd 1958, Overseas Educ. Publr 1958–61, Publishing Man. Far East and SE Asia 1961–63, Head, English Language Teaching Publishing 1964–68, Div. Man. Dir 1968–72, Jt Man. Dir 1972–76, Chief Exec. Longman Group Ltd 1976–90, Chair. 1984–90; Chair. Addison-Wesley-Longman Group Ltd 1988–89; Chair. Pitman Examinations Inst. 1987–90; Dir Pearson Longman Ltd (now Pearson PLC) 1979–83, Goldcrest Television 1981–83, Yale Univ. Press Ltd, London 1984–, ECIC (Man.) Ltd 1990–92, Blackie & Son Ltd 1990–93, B.H. Blackwell Ltd 1991–95, Geddes and Grosset Ltd 1996–98, Jessica Kingsley Publrs Ltd 1997–, Frances Lincoln Ltd 1997–, Meditech Media Ltd 1997–2003, Scottish Book Source 1999–, Central European Univ. Press 1999–; Pres. Publrs' Asscn 1981–83; mem. British Library Bd 1986–96, British Council Bd 1988–97, Health Educ. Authority Bd 1995–99; Chair. Book Trust 1986–88, British Library Centre for the Book 1989–95, Book Marketing Ltd 1990–2003, Soc. of Bookmen 1990–92, British Library Publishing 1992–2003, Book Aid Int. 1994–, Bell Educational Trust 1994–2001, Nat. Book Cttee 1997–2003, Edin. Univ. Press 2001–; mem. Oxford Brookes Univ. Devt Cttee 1991–96, Finance Cttee, Oxford Univ. Press 1992–2002, Council, Ranfurly Library Service 1992–94, Advisory Council, Inst. of English Studies, London Univ. 2000–; Hon. Pres. Independent Publishers' Guild 1993–; Gov. English-Speaking Union 1998–. *Publications:* articles on publishing in trade journals. *Address:* Top Flat, 27 Wolseley Road, London, N8 8RS, England. *Telephone:* (20) 8341-4160. *Fax:* (20) 8341-4160. *E-mail:* tim@rixpublishing.co.uk (Home).

ROBB, Graham Macdonald, BA, PGCE, PhD, FRSL; British writer; b. 2 June 1958, Manchester, England; m. Margaret Hambrick 1986. *Education:* University of Oxford, Goldsmiths College, London, Vanderbilt University, Nashville, TN. *Career:* mem. Society of Authors. *Publications:* Le Corsaire – Satan en Silhouette, 1985; Baudelaire Lecteur de Balzac, 1988; Scenes de La Vie de Bohème (ed.), 1988; Baudelaire (trans.), 1989; La Poésie de Baudelaire et La Poésie Française, 1993; Balzac, 1994; Unlocking Mallarmé, 1996; Victor Hugo: A Biography, 1998; Rimbaud, 2000; Strangers: Homosexual Love in the Nineteenth Century, 2003. Contributions: TLS; London Review of Books; New York Times; New York Review of Books. *Honours:* Postdoctoral Research Fellow; British Acad. Fellowship, 1987–90; Whitbread Biography of the Year Award, 1997; RSL Heinemann Award, 1998. *Address:* 139 Hollow Way, Oxford OX4 2NE, England.

ROBB, J. D. (see Roberts, Nora).

ROBBE-GRILLET, Alain; Writer, Film-maker and Agronomist; b. 18 Aug. 1922, Brest, France; m. Catherine Rstakian 1957. *Education:* Institute Nat. Agronomique. *Career:* Chargé de Mission, Inst. Nat. de la Statistique 1945–48; Engineer Inst. des Fruits Tropicaux (Guinea, Morocco, Martinique and Guadeloupe) 1949–51; Literary Adviser Editions de Minuit 1955–85; teacher, New York Univ. 1972–97; Dir Centre for the Sociology of Literature, Univ. of Brussels 1980–88. Films directed: L'immortelle, 1963; Trans-Europ-Express, 1967; L'homme qui ment, 1968; L'Eden et après, 1970; Glissements progressifs du plaisir, 1974; Le jeu avec le feu, 1975; La belle captive, 1983; Un bruit qui rend fou, 1995; mem. various professional organizations. *Publications:* Fiction: Les gommes, 1953; Le voyeur, 1955; La jalousie, 1957; Dans le labyrinthe, 1959; La maison de rendez-vous, 1965; Projet pour une révolution à New York, 1970; Topologie d'une cité fantôme, 1976; La belle captive, 1977; Un régicide, 1978; Souvenirs du triangle d'or, 1978; Djinn, 1981; Le miroir qui revient, 1984; Angélique ou l'enchantment, 1988; Les derniers jours de Corinthe, 1994; La reprise, 2001. Short Story Collection: Instantanés, 1962. Essay: Pour un nouveau roman, 1964; Le voyageur: textes, causeries et entretiens (1947–2001), 2001. Screenplay: L'année dernière à Marienbad, 1961. *Honours:* Chevalier, Légion d'honneur; Officier, Ordre nat. du Mérite; Prix Louis Delluc, 1963; Premio Vittorio de Sica, 2001. *Address:* 18 blvd Maillot, 92200 Neuilly-sur-Seine, France.

ROBBINS, Kenneth Randall; academic, writer and dramatist; b. 7 Jan. 1944, Douglasville, GA, USA; m. Dorothy Dodge 1988; one s. one d. *Education:* AA, Young Harris College, 1964; BSEd, Georgia Southern University, 1966; MFA, University of Georgia, 1969; PhD, Southern Illinois University at Carbondale, 1982. *Career:* Asst Prof., Jacksonville University, FL, 1974–79; Assoc. Prof., Newberry College, South Carolina, 1977–85, University of South Dakota, 1985–; Presenter, Black Hills Writers Conference, 1986–90; Ed., Wayne S. Knutson Dakota Playwriting Series; mem. American College Theatre Festival; Asscn of Theatre in Higher Education; Dramatists Guild; The Loft, Minneapolis; Playwright's Centre,

Minneapolis; Society for Humanities and Technology; Southeastern Theatre Conference. *Publications:* The Dallas File (play), 1982; Buttermilk Bottoms (novel), 1987. Contributions: journals and radio. *Honours:* Toni Morrison Prize for Fiction, 1986; Associated Writing Programs Novel Award, 1986; Festival of Southern Theatre Awards, 1987, 1990. *Address:* c/o University of South Dakota, Vermillion, SD 57069-2390, USA.

ROBBINS, Richard (Leroy); Prof., Poet, Writer and Ed.; b. 27 Aug. 1953, Los Angeles, CA, USA; m. Candace L. Black, 8 Sept. 1979, two s. *Education:* AB, English, San Diego State University, 1975; MFA, Creative Writing, University of Montana, 1979. *Career:* Co-Ed., Cafeteria, 1971–81, CutBank and SmokeRoot Press, 1977–79, Montana Arts Council anthologies, 1979–81; Writer-in-Residence, Poet-in-the-Schools, Montana Arts Council, 1979–81; Instructor, Moorhead State University, 1981–82, Oregon State University, 1982–84; Prof., Minnesota State University, Mankato, 1984–; Asst Ed., Mankato Poetry Review, 1984–; mem. Associated Writing Programs; The Loft; Poetry Society of America; Western Literature Asscn. *Publications:* Where We Are: The Montana Poets Anthology (ed. with Lex Runciman), 1978; Toward New Weather, 1979; The Invisible Wedding, 1984; Famous Persons We Have Known, 2000. Contributions: 20 anthologies, 1978–, reviews, quarterlies, and journals. *Honours:* First Prize in Poetry, Branford P. Millar Award, Portland Review, 1978; Frontier Award, University of Montana, 1978; Individual Artist Fellowships, Minnesota State Arts Board, 1986, 1999; Robert H. Winner Memorial Award, Poetry Society of America, 1988; National Endowment for the Arts Fellowship, 1992; McKnight Individual Artist Grants, 1993, 1996, and Fellowship, 1997; Hawthornden Fellowship, 1998; Loft Award of Distinction in Poetry, 2000. *Address:* c/o Dept of English, Minnesota State University, 230 Armstrong Hall, Mankato, MN 56001, USA.

ROBBINS, Tom, (Thomas Eugene Robbins); Writer; b. 1936, Blowing Rock, NC, USA; m. 1st; m. 2nd Terrie Robbins, divorced, one s.; m. 3rd Alexa D'Avalon, two s. *Education:* Washington and Lee University, 1954–56; Degree in Social Science, Richmond Professional Institute, Virginia, 1959; University of Washington, 1963. *Publications:* Guy Anderson, 1965; Another Roadside Attraction, 1971; Even Cowgirls Get the Blues, 1976; Still Life with Woodpecker, 1980; Jitterbug Perfume, 1984; Skinny Legs and All, 1990; Half Asleep in Frog Pajamas, 1994; Fierce Invalids Home From Hot Climates, 2000; Villa Incognito, 2003. *Address:* PO Box 338, La Conner, WA 98257, USA.

ROBERSON, John Royster, BA, MA; editor and writer; b. 7 March 1930, Roanoke, VA, USA; m. Charlene Grace Hale 1966; one s. one d. *Education:* University of Virginia, University of Grenoble, France, US Army Language School, Monterey, CA. *Career:* Asst to Senior Ed., Holiday, 1959–70; Copywriter, N. W. Ayer Advertising, 1971–76; Assoc. to Senior Staff Ed., Reader's Digest Condensed Books, 1976–95; mem. International House of Japan; US China People's Friendship Asscn; Science Education Centre, Fairfield County, CT, pres. of board of dirs. *Publications:* China from Manchu to Mao 1699–1976, 1980; Japan from Shogun to Sony 1543–1984, 1985; Transforming Russia 1692–1991, 1992; Japan Meets the West, 1998. Contributions: Atlantic; Holiday; Reader's Digest; Studies in Bibliography; Virginia Magazine of History and Biography. *Honours:* Raven Society, University of Virginia, 1950; Rotary International Fellowship, University of Grenoble, 1951–52. *Address:* 16 Hassake Road, Old Greenwich, CT 06870, USA.

ROBERTS, Andrew, MA, FRSL; British author; b. 13 Jan. 1963, London, England. *Education:* Gonville and Caius Coll., Cambridge. *Career:* mem. Beefsteak Club, University Pitt Club, Cambridge, Brooks's. *Publications:* The Holy Fox: A Biography of Lord Halifax 1991, Eminent Churchillians 1994, The Aachen Memorandum 1995, Salibury: Victorian Titan 1999, Napoleon and Wellington 2001, Hitler and Churchill: Secrets of Leadership 2003, What Might Have Been: Leading Historians on Twelve 'What Ifs' of History (ed.) 2004; contrib. to Sunday Telegraph, Literary Review. *Honours:* Hon. Doctor of Humane Letters, Univ. of Westminster, Fulton, MO, 2000. *Literary Agent:* Capel & Land Ltd, 29 Wardour Street, London, W1D 6PS, England. *Address:* 11 Ovington Square, London, SW3 1LH, England. *Website:* www.andrew-roberts.net.

ROBERTS, Brian; Writer; b. 19 March 1930, London, England. *Education:* Teacher's Certificate, St Mary's College, Twickenham, 1955; Diploma in Sociology, University of London, 1958. *Career:* Teacher of English and History, 1955–65. *Publications:* Ladies in the Veld, 1965; Cecil Rhodes and the Princess, 1969; Churchills in Africa, 1970; The Diamond Magnates, 1972; The Zulu Kings, 1974; Kimberley: Turbulent City, 1976; The Mad Bad Line: The Family of Lord Alfred Douglas, 1981; Randolph: A Study of Churchill's Son, 1984; Cecil Rhodes: Flawed Colossus, 1987; Those Bloody Women: Three Heroines of the Boer War, 1991. *Literary Agent:* Andrew Lownie, 17 Sutherland St, London SW1V 4JU, England. *Address:* 7 The Blue House, Market Place, Frome BA11 1AP, England.

ROBERTS, Gregory David; Australian writer; b. 1952, Melbourne, Vic. *Publications:* Shantaram 2003. *Address:* c/o Scribe Publishing, 313 Rathdowne Street, Carlton, Vic. 3053, Australia. *E-mail:* scribe@bigpond.net.au. *Website:* www.scribepub.com.au.

ROBERTS, Irene, (Roberta Carr, Elizabeth Harle, I. M. Roberts, Ivor Roberts, Iris Rowland, Irene Shaw); Writer; b. 27 Sept. 1925, London, England. *Career:* Woman's Page Ed., South Hams Review, 1977–79; Tutor, Creative Writing, Kingsbridge Community College, 1978–; mem. Romantic Novelists Asscn, founder-mem. *Publications:* Shadows on the Moon, 1968; Thunder Heights, 1969; Surgeon in Tibet, 1970; Birds Without Bars, 1970; The Shrine of Fire, 1970; Sister at Sea, 1971; Gull Haven, 1971; Moon Over the Temple, 1972; The Golden Pagoda, 1972; Desert Nurse, 1976; Nurse in Nepal, 1976; Stars Above Raffael, 1977; Hawks Burton, 1979; Symphony of Bells, 1980; Nurse Moonlight, 1980; Weave Me a Moonbeam, 1982; Jasmine for a Nurse, 1982; Sister on Leave, 1982; Nurse in the Wilderness, 1983; Moonpearl, 1986; Sea Jade, 1987; Kingdom of the Sun, 1987; Song of the Nile, 1987. Children's Books: Holiday's for Hanbury, 1964; Laughing is for Fun, 1964. As Ivor Roberts: Jump into Hell, 1960; Trial by Water, 1961; Green Hell, 1961. As Iris Rowland: Blue Feathers, 1967; Moon Over Moncrieff, 1969; Star Drift, 1970; Rainbow River, 1970; The Wild Summer, 1970; Orange Blossom for Tara, 1971; Blossoms in the Snow, 1971; Sister Julia, 1972; Golden Bubbles, 1976; Hunter's Dawn, 1977; Golden Triangle, 1978; Forgotten Dreams, 1978; Temptation, 1983; Theresa, 1985. As Roberta Carr: Sea Maiden, 1965; Fire Dragon, 1967; Golden Interlude, 1970. As Elizabeth Harle: Golden Rain, 1964; Gay Rowan, 1965; Sandy, 1967; Spray of Red Roses, 1971; The Silver Summer, 1971; The Burning Flame, 1979; Come to Me Darling, 1983. As Irene Shaw: Moonstone Manor, 1968, US edn as Murder Mansion 1976; The Olive Branch, 1968. As I. M. Roberts: The Throne of the Pharoahs, 1974; Hatsheput, Queeen of the Nile, 1976; Hour of the Tiger, 1985; Jezebel Street, 1994; Limehouse Lady, 1995; More Laughter Than Tears, 1996; London's Pride in Progress, 1997. *Address:* Alpha House, Higher Town, Marlborough, Kingsbridge, South Devon TQ7 3RL, England.

ROBERTS, Ivor (see Roberts, Irene).

ROBERTS, Leonard, (Len Roberts); Prof. of English, Poet and Trans; b. 13 March 1947, Cohoes, New York, USA; m. 31 Dec. 1981, two s. one d. *Education:* BA, English, Siena College, 1970; MA, English, University of Dayton, 1972; PhD, English, Lehigh University, 1976. *Career:* Prof. of English, Northampton College, 1974–83, 1986–87, 1989–93, 1995–; Visiting Asst Prof., Lafayette College, 1983–85; Visiting Prof., University of Pittsburgh, 1984–; Fulbright Scholar, Janus Pannonius University, Pécs, Hungary, 1988–89, University of Turku, Finland, 1994; mem. MLA; Pennsylvania Council on the Arts, advisory board, 1990–; Poetry Society of America; Poets and Writers. *Publications:* Poetry: Cohoes Theater, 1980; From the Dark, 1984; Sweet Ones, 1988; Black Wings, 1989; Learning About the Heart, 1992; Dangerous Angels, 1993; The Million Branches: Selected Poems and Interview, 1993; Counting the Black Angels, 1994; The Trouble-Making Finch, 1998; The Silent Singer: New and Selected Poems, 2001. Translator: The Selected Poems of Sándor Csoóri, 1992. Contributions: anthologies and journals. *Honours:* Pennsylvania Council on the Arts Writing Awards in Poetry, 1981, 1986, 1987, 1991; National Endowment for the Arts Awards, 1984, 1989; Great Lakes and Prairies Award, 1988; National Poetry Series Award, 1988; Soros Foundation Poetry Trans. Awards, 1989, 1990, 1992, 1997; Guggenheim Fellowship, 1990–91; Pushcart Prize, 1991; Witter Bynner Poetry Trans. Award, 1991–92; Winner, Silverfish Review Chapbook Competition, 1992; First Prize, Wildwood Poetry Contest, 1993; National Endowment for the Humanities Trans. Award, 1999; Pennsylvania Council on the Arts Poetry Award, 2000. *Address:* 2443 Wassergass Rd, Hellertown, PA 18055, USA.

ROBERTS, Michèle Brigitte, MA (Oxon), ALA, FRSL; British novelist and poet; b. 20 May 1949, Herts.; m.1st Howard Burns 1984 (divorced 1987); m. 2nd Jim Latter 1991 (divorced 2004); two step-s. *Education:* Convent Grammar School, Somerville Coll., Oxford and University Coll. London. *Career:* British Council Librarian, Bangkok 1973–74; Poetry Ed. Spare Rib 1974, City Limits 1981–83; Visiting Fellow Univ. of E Anglia 1992, Univ. of Nottingham Trent 1994; Visiting Prof. Univ. of Nottingham Trent 1996–2001; Prof. of Creative Writing, Univ. of E Anglia 2002–; Chair. Literary Cttee British Council 1998–2002; Judge Booker Prize 2001; mem. Soc. of Authors. *Plays:* The Journeywoman 1988, Child-Lover 1995. *Television film:* The Heavenly Twins (Channel 4) 1993. *Publications include:* novels: A Piece of the Night 1978, The Visitation 1983, The Wild Girl 1984, The Book of Mrs Noah 1987, In the Red Kitchen 1990, Daughters of the House 1992, Flesh and Blood 1994, Impossible Saints 1997, Fair Exchange 1999, The Looking-Glass 2000, The Mistressclass 2003; (ed. jtly) Mind Readings 1996; short stories: During Mother's Absence 1993, Playing Sardines 2001; essays: Food, Sex and God 1998; poetry: The Mirror of the Mother 1986; plays: Psyche and the Hurricane 1991, Child Lover 1993, All the Selves I Was 1995. *Honours:* Chevalier des Arts et des Lettres 2001; Hon. MA (Nene) 1999; WHSmith Literary Award 1993. *Literary Agent:* Gillon Aitken Associates Ltd, 18–21 Cavaye Place, London, SW10 9PT, England. *Telephone:* (20) 7373-8672. *Fax:* (20) 7373-6002. *Address:* School of English and American Studies, University of East Anglia, Norwich, Norfolk NR4 7TJ, England.

ROBERTS, Nora, (J. D. Robb); American writer; b. 10 Oct. 1950, Silver Spring, MD. *Career:* mem. Romance Writers of America, Novelists Inc. *Publications:* Irish Thoroughbred 1981, Blithe Images 1982, Song of the West 1982, Search for Love 1982, Island of Flowers 1982, The Heart's Victory 1982, From This Day 1983, Her Mother's Keeper 1983, Reflections 1983, Once More with Feeling 1983, Untamed 1983, Dance of Dreams 1983, Tonight and Always 1983, This Magic Moment 1983, Endings and Beginnings 1984, Storm Warning 1984, Sullivan's Woman 1984, Rules of the Game 1984, Less of a Stranger 1984, A Matter of Choice 1984, The Law is a Lady 1984, First Impressions 1984, Opposites Attract 1984, Promise Me Tomorrow 1984, Partners 1985, The Right Path 1985, Boundary Lines 1985, Summer Desserts 1985, Dual Images 1985, Night Moves 1985, Playing the Odds 1985, Tempting Fate 1985, All the Possibilities 1985, One Man's Art 1985, The Art of Deception 1986, One Summer 1986, Treasures Lost, Treasures Found 1986, Risky Business 1986, Lessons Learned 1986, Second Nature 1986, A Will and a Way 1986, Home for Christmas 1986, Affaire Royale 1986, Mind Over Matter 1987, Temptation 1987, Hot Ice 1987, Sacred Sins 1987, For Now, Forever 1987, Command Performance 1987, The Playboy Prince 1987, Brazen Virtue 1988, Local Hero 1988, Irish Rose 1988, The Name of the Game 1988, Rebellion 1988, The Last Honest Woman 1988, Dance to the Piper 1988, Skin Deep 1988, Sweet Revenge 1989, Loving Jack 1989, Best Laid Plans 1989, Gabriel's Angel 1989, Lawless 1989, Public Secrets 1990, Taming Natasha 1990, Night Shadow 1991, Genuine Lies 1991, With This Ring 1991, Night Shift 1991, Without a Trace 1991, Luring a Lady 1991, Courting Catherine 1991, A Man for Amanda 1991, For the Love of Lilah 1991, Suzannah's Surrender 1991, Carnal Innocence 1992, Unfinished Business 1992, The Welcoming 1992, Honest Illusions 1992, Divine Evil 1992, Captivated 1992, Entranced 1992, Charmed 1992, Second Nature 1993, Private Scandals 1993, Falling for Rachel 1993, Time Was 1993, Times Change 1993, Boundary Lines 1994, Hidden Riches 1994, Nightshade 1994, The Best Mistake 1994, Night Smoke 1994, Born in Fire 1994, Born in Ice 1995, True Betrayals 1995, Born in Shame 1996, Montana Sky 1996, From the Heart 1997, Sanctuary 1997, Holding the Dream 1997, Daring to Dream 1997, Finding the Dream 1997, The Reef 1998, The Winning Hand 1998, Sea Swept 1998, Homeport 1999, The Perfect Neighbor 1999, Megan's Mate 1999, Enchanted 1999, Rising Tides 1999, Inner Harbor 1999, Carolina Moon 2000, The Villa 2001, Heaven and Earth 2001, Three Fates 2002, Chesapeake Blue 2002, Key of Knowledge 2003, Key of Light 2003, Once Upon a Midnight 2003, Birthright 2003, Remember When 2003, Blue Dahlia 2004, Northern Lights 2004, Key of Valor 2004; as J. D. Robb: Only Survivors Tell Tales 1990, Naked in Death 1995, Glory in Death 1995, Rapture in Death 1996, Ceremony in Death 1997, Vengeance in Death 1997, Holiday in Death 1998, Immortal in Death 1998, Silent Night 1998, Loyalty in Death 1999, Conspiracy in Death 1999, Witness in Death 2000, Judgment in Death 2000, Seduction in Death 2001, Out of this World 2001, Betrayal in Death 2001, Reunion in Death 2002, Purity in Death 2002, Imitation in Death 2003, Remember When 2003, Portrait in Death 2003, Once Upon a Midnight 2003, Divided in Death 2004, Visions in Death 2004. *Honours:* various Romance Writers of America Awards. *Literary Agent:* Writers House Inc., 21 W 26th Street, New York, NY 10010, USA. *Telephone:* (212) 685-2400. *Fax:* (212) 685-1781. *E-mail:* write2nora@msn.com. *Website:* www.noraroberts.com.

ROBERTS, Willo Davis; Writer; b. 29 May 1928, Grand Rapids, Michigan, USA; m. David Roberts, 20 May 1949, two s. two d. *Career:* mem. MWA, Society of Children's Book Writers, Seattle Freelancers, Pacific Northwest Writers Conference, Sisters In Crime. *Publications:* 99 books including: Murder at Grand Bay, 1955; The Girl Who Wasn't There, 1957; Nurse Kay's Conquest, 1966; The Tarot Spell, 1970; King's Pawn, 1971; White Jade, 1975; The Black Pearl series, eight vols, 1978–80; The Search for Willie, 1980; A Long Time To Hate, 1982; Keating's Landing, 1984; The Annalise Experiment, 1985; To Share a Dream, 1986; Madawaska, 1988. Children's Books: The View from the Cherry Tree, 1975; Don't Hurt Laurie, 1977; The Girl with the Silver Eyes, 1980; Pet Sitting Peril, 1983; Eddie and the Fairy God Puppy, 1984; Baby Sitting is a Dangerous Job, 1985; The Magic Book, 1986; Sugar Isn't Everything, 1987; Megan's Island, 1988; Nightmare, 1989; Scared Stiff, 1991; Dark Secrets, 1991; Jo and the Bandit 1992, What Are We Going To Do About David? 1993, Caught! 1995, The Absolutely True Story 1995, Twisted Summer 1996 (Young Hoosier Award 2000), Secrets at Hidden Valley 1998, The Kidnappers 1998, Pawns 1998, Hostage 2000 (Nevada Young Readers' Award), Buddy is a Stupid Name for a Girl 2001, Undercurrents 2002, Rebel 2003, Blood on his Hands 2004. *Honours:* Mark Twain Award, 1980, Pacific Northwest Writers Achievement Award, 1986, Edgar Allan Poe Awards, 1988, 1995, 1997, Washington State Governor's Award for contributions to the field of children's books 1990, Florida Sunshine State Award 1994. *Address:* 12020 W Engebretsen Rd, Granite Falls, WA 98252, USA.

ROBERTSON, Barbara; Writer; b. 20 July 1931, Toronto, Ontario, Canada. *Education:* BA, University of Toronto, 1953; MA, Queen's University, Kingston, 1957. *Publications:* The Wind Has Wings (ed. with M. A. Downie), 1968, revised edn as The New Wind Has Wings, 1984; Wilfrid Laurier: The Great Conciliator, 1971; The Well-Filled Cupboard (with M. A. Downie), 1987, revised edn as The Canadian Treasury of Cooking and Gardening, 1997; Doctor Dwarf and Other Poems for Children (ed. with M. A. Downie), 1990; Ottawa at War: The Grant Dexter Memoranda 1939–1945 (ed. with F. W. Gibson), 1994. Contributions: periodicals. *Address:* 52 Florence St, Kingston, Ontario K7M 1Y6, Canada.

ROBERTSON, Denise; Writer and Broadcaster; b. 9 June 1933, Sunderland, England; m. 1st Alexander Robertson, 19 March 1960; m. 2nd John Tomlin, 3 Nov. 1973, five s. *Publications:* Year of Winter, 1986; Land of Lost Content, 1987; Blue Remembered Hills, 1987; Second Wife, 1988; None to Make You Cry, 1989; Remember the Moment, 1990. Contributions: numerous publications. *Honours:* Constable Fiction Trophy, 1985. *Address:* 9 Springfield Crescent, Seaham, County Durham, England.

ROBERTSON, Geoffrey Ronald; Queen's Counsel, Barrister and Writer; b. 30 Sept. 1946, Sydney, NSW, Australia; m. Kathy Lette, 1990, one s. one d. *Education:* BA, 1966, LLB, 1970, University of Sydney; BCL, University College, 1972. *Career:* Barrister, 1973; Queen's Counsel, 1988; Pres., UN Special Court for war crimes in Sierra Leone; Visiting Prof., Birkbeck and Queen Mary Colleges, London. *Publications:* Reluctant Judas, 1976; Obscenity, 1979; People Against the Press, 1983; Does Dracula Have Aids?, 1986; Geoffrey Robertson's Hypotheticals, 1986; Freedom, the Individual and the Law, 1989; The Trials of Oz, 1992; Media Law (with A. Nicol), 1992; The Justice Game, 1998; Crimes Against Humanity: The Struggle for Global Justice, 2000. *Address:* Doughty Street Chambers, 11 Doughty St, London WC1N 2PL, England.

ROBERTSON, James Irvin, Jr; Prof. of History; b. 18 July 1930, Danville, Virginia, USA; m. Elizabeth Green, 1 June 1952, two s. one d. *Education:* BA, Randolph-Macon College, 1954; MA, 1955, PhD, 1959, Emory University; LittD, Randolph-Macon College, 1980. *Career:* Assoc. Prof. of History, University of Montana, 1965–67; Prof. of History, 1967–75, C. P. Miles Prof. of History, 1976–92, Alumni Distinguished Prof. of History, 1992–, Virginia Polytechnic Institute and State University; mem. Virginia Historical Society; Organization of American Historians; Southern Historical Asscn; Confederate Memorial Society. *Publications:* The Stonewall Brigade, 1963; The Civil War Letters of General Robert McAllister, 1965; Recollections of a Maryland Confederate Soldier, 1975; Four Years in the Stonewall Brigade, 1978; The 4th Virginia Infantry, 1980; Civil War Sites in Virginia: A Tour-Guide, 1982; The 18th Virginia Infantry, 1983; Tenting Tonight: The Soldiers' View, 1984; General A. P. Hill, 1987; Soldiers Blue and Gray, 1988; Civil War: America Becomes One Nation, 1992; Jackson and Lee: Legends in Gray (with Mort Kunstler), 1995; Stonewall Jackson: The Man, The Soldier, The Legend, 1997. Contributions: More than 150 articles in historical journals and history magazines; Regular appearances in Civil War programmes on television and radio. *Honours:* Freeman-Nevins Award, 1981; Bruce Catton Award, 1983; William E. Wine Award for Teaching Excellence, 1983; A. P. Andrews Memorial Award, 1985; James Robertson Award of Achievement, 1985. *Address:* Dept of History, Virginia Polytechnic Institute and State University, Blacksburg, VA 24061, USA.

ROBINETTE, Joseph Allen; College Prof. and Playwright; b. 8 Feb. 1939, Rockwood, Tennessee, USA; m. Helen M. Seitz, 27 Aug. 1965, four s., one d. *Education:* BA, Carson-Newman College, 1960; MA, 1966, PhD, 1972, Southern Illinois University. *Career:* mem. American Society of Composers, Authors and Publishers; American Asscn for Theatre in Education; Opera for Youth. *Publications:* The Fabulous Fable Factory, 1975; Once Upon a Shoe (play), 1979; Legend of the Sun Child (musical), 1982; Charlotte's Web (dramatization), 1983; Charlotte's Web (musical with Charles Strouse), 1989; Anne of Green Gables (dramatization), 1989; The Lion, the Witch and the Wardrobe (dramatization), 1989; The Trial of Goldilocks (operetta), 1990; Dorothy Meets Alice (musical), 1991; Stuart Little (dramatization), 1992; The Trumpet of the Swan (dramatization), 1993; The Adventures of Beatrix Potter and Her Friends (musical), 1994; The Littlest Angel (musical), 1994; The Jungle Book (dramatization), 1995. Contributions: Children's Theatre News; Opera For Youth News. *Honours:* Charlotte Chorpenning Cup, National Children's Playwriting Award, 1976. *Address:* Dept of Theatre and Dance, Rowan College, Glassboro, NJ 08028, USA.

ROBINS, Patricia (see Clark, Patricia Denise).

ROBINSON, David Bradford, AA, BA, BS, MA, MS, DSc, PhD, JD; poet and writer; b. 14 April 1937, Richmond, Virginia, USA. *Career:* mem. Int. Soc. of Poets. *Publications:* Characteristics of Cesium 1978, Lyric Treasure One 1978, Collected Poems 1987, Praise the Wilderness: Nineteen Original New Poems to Survival 1990; contrib. to anthologies and reviews. *Honours:* Golden Poet Award 1987, Pegasus Time Capsule Award 1991, Albert Einstein Medal 1994, World Lifetime Achivement Award 1996. *Address:* PO Box 1414, Miami Shores, FL 33153, USA.

ROBINSON, David Julien; Film Critic, Festival Dir and Writer; b. 6 Aug. 1930, England. *Education:* BA, King's College, Cambridge. *Career:* Assoc. Ed., Sight and Sound, and Ed., Monthly Film Bulletin, 1956–58; Programme Dir, National Film Theatre, 1959; Film Critic, Financial Times, 1959–74, The Times, 1974–92; Dir, Garrett Robinson Co, 1987–88, The Davids Film Co, 1988–, Channel 4 Young Film-maker of the Year Competition, Edinburgh Film Festival, 1992–95, Pordenone Silent Film Festival, Italy, 1997–; Guest Dir, Edinburgh Film Festival, 1989–91. *Publications:* Hollywood in the Twenties, 1969; Buster Keaton, 1969; The Great Funnies, 1972; World Cinema, 1973, US edn as The History of World Cinema, 1974; Chaplin: The Mirror of Opinion, 1983; Chaplin: His Life and Art, 1985; The Illustrated History of the Cinema (co-ed.), 1986; Music of the Shadows, 1990; Masterpieces of Animation 1833–1908, 1991; Richard Attenborough, 1992; Georges Méliès, 1993; Lantern Images: Iconography of the Magic Lantern 1440–1880, 1993; Sight and Sound Chronology of the Cinema, 1994–95; Musique et cinema muet, 1995; Charlot: Entre rires et larmes, 1995; Peepshow to Palace, 1995; Light and Image: Incunabula of the Motion Picture (co-author), 1996. Contributions: newspapers and periodicals. *Honours:* several prizes. *Address:* 96–100 New Cavendish St, London W1M 7FA, England, and 1 Winifreds Dale, Cavendish Rd, Bath BA1 2UD, England.

ROBINSON, Derek, (Dirk Robson), MA; writer; b. 12 April 1932, Bristol, England; m. Sheila Collins 1968. *Education:* Downing College, Cambridge. *Publications:* Goshawk Squadron, 1971; Rotten With Honour, 1973; Kramer's War, 1977; The Eldorado Network, 1979; Piece of Cake, 1983; War Story, 1987; Artillery of Lies, 1991; A Good Clean Fight, 1993; Hornet's Sting, 1999; Kentucky Blues, 2002; Damned Good Show, 2002. *Literary Agent:* David Higham Associates, 5–8 Lower John Street, Golden Square, London W1F 9HA, England; T. C. Wallace Ltd, Suite 1001, 425 Madison Avenue, New York, NY 10017, USA. *Address:* Shapland House, Somerset Street, Kingsdown, Bristol BS2 8LZ, England.

ROBINSON, Jeffrey, BS; writer; b. 19 Oct. 1945, New York, NY, USA; m. Aline Benayoun 1985; one s. one d. *Education:* Temple Univ., Philadelphia. *Career:* mem. PEN. *Television, radio and screenplays:* The Laundrymen 1996, Same Time Next Week 2000, Tightrope 2002, Rossum's Cyber Café 2003, Sister Banjo 2003, The Real Amos 'n' Andy 2004. *Publications:* Bette Davis – Her Stage and Film Career 1983, Teamwork 1984, The Risk Takers 1985, Pietrov and Other Games (fiction) 1985, Minus Millionaires 1986, The Ginger Jar (fiction) 1986, Yamani – The Inside Story 1988, Rainier and Grace 1989, The Risk Takers – Five Years On 1990, The End of the American Century 1992, The Laundrymen 1994, Bardot – Two Lives 1994, The Margin of the Bulls (fiction) 1995, The Hotel 1996, The Monk's Disciples (fiction) 1996, The Manipulators 1997, A True and Perfect Knight (fiction) 1998, The Merger 2000, Prescription Games 2001, The Sink 2003, Standing Next to History (with Joseph Petro) 2005; contrib. more than 700 articles and short stories to major magazines and journals world-wide. *Honours:* Overseas Press Club 1984, Benedictine After Dinner Speaker of the Year 1990. *Literary Agent:* Bell-Lomax Agency, James House, 1 Babmaes Street, London, SW1 6HF, England.

ROBINSON, Kim Stanley, BA, MA, PhD; American author; b. 23 March 1952, Waukegan, IL. *Education:* Univ. of California at San Diego, Boston Univ. *Career:* Visiting Lecturer, Univ. of California at San Diego 1982, 1985, Univ. of California at Davis 1982–84, 1985. *Publications:* Icehenge 1984, The Wild Shore 1984, The Memory of Whiteness 1985, The Planet on the Table (short stories) 1986, Escape from Kathmandu (short stories) 1987, The Gold Coast 1988, Pacific Edge 1990, A Short, Sharp Shock 1990, Remaking History (short stories) 1991, Red Mars 1992, Green Mars 1993, Blue Mars 1996, Antarctica 1997, Martians 1999, Vinland the Dream 2002, The Years of Rice and Salt 2002, Forty Signs of Rain 2004; other: Future Primitive (ed.) 1982, The Novels of Philip K. Dick 1984, Nebula Awards Showcase (ed.) 2002; contrib. to periodicals and anthologies. *Address:* 17811 Romelle Avenue, Santa Ana, CA 92705, USA.

ROBINSON, Robert Henry; Writer and Broadcaster; b. 17 Dec. 1927, Liverpool, England; m. Josephine Mary Richard, 1958, one s. two d. *Education:* MA, Exeter College, Oxford. *Publications:* Landscape With Dead Dons, 1956; Inside Robert Robinson, 1965; The Conspiracy, 1968; The Dog Chairman, 1982; Everyman Book of Light Verse (ed.), 1984; Bad Dreams, 1989; Prescriptions of a Pox Doctor's Clerk, 1991; Skip All That: Memoirs, 1996; The Club, 2000. Contributions: newspapers, radio and television. *Literary Agent:* Curtis Brown Ltd, Haymarket House, 28–29 Haymarket, London, SW1Y 4SP, England. *Telephone:* (20) 7393-4400. *Fax:* (20) 7393-4401. *E-mail:* info@curtisbrown.co.uk. *Website:* www.curtisbrown.co.uk. *Address:* 16 Cheyne Row, London SW3, England.

ROBINSON, Sheila (Mary), (Sheila Radley, Hester Rowan); Writer; b. 18 Nov. 1928, Cogenhoe, Northamptonshire, England. *Education:* BA, University of London. *Publications:* Overture in Venice, 1976; The Linden Tree, 1977; Death and the Maiden, 1978; Snowfall, 1978; The Chief Inspector's Daughter, 1981; A Talent for Destruction, 1982; Blood on the Happy Highway, 1983; Fate Worse Than Death, 1985; Who Saw Him Die?, 1987; This Way Out, 1989; Cross My Heart and Hope to Die, 1992; Fair Game, 1994; New Blood from Old Bones, 1998.

ROBINSON, Spider; Writer; b. 24 Nov. 1948, New York, NY, USA. *Education:* BA, SUNY at Stony Brook, 1972. *Publications:* Telempath, 1976; Callahan's Crossing Saloon, 1977; Stardance (with Jeanne Robinson), 1979; Antinomy, 1980; Time Travelers Strictly Cash, 1981; Mindkiller, 1982; Melancholy Elephants, 1984; Night of Power, 1985; Callahan's Secret, 1986; Time Pressure, 1987; Callahan and Company, 1987; Starseed, 1991; Lady Slings the Booze, 1993; Off the Wall at Callahan's, 1994; Starmind, 1994; Callahan's Legacy, 1996; God is an Iron and Other Stories, 2002. *Address:* c/o Ace Books, 375 Hudson St, New York, NY 10014, USA.

ROBSON, Dirk (see Robinson, Derek).

ROCHE, Billy, (William Michael Roche); Playwright and Author; b. 11 Jan. 1949, Wexford, Ireland. *Career:* Singer, the Roach Band, 1975–80; Playwright-in-Residence, Bush Theatre, London, 1988; Writer in Asscn with Druid Theatre, Galway, 1997, The Abbey Theatre, Dublin, 2000. *Publications:* Plays: A Handful of Stars, 1987; Amphibians, 1987; Poor Beast in the Rain, 1989; Belfry, 1991; The Cavalcaders, 1993; On Such As We, 2001. Novel: Tumbling Down, 1986. Film Script: Trojan Eddie, 1997. *Honours:* London Theatre Fringe Award, 1992; Time Out Award, 1992; San Sebastian Film Festival Prize for Trojan Eddie, 1997. *Address:* 44 Pineridge, Clonard, Wexford, Ireland.

ROCHE, Terry (see Poole, Margaret Barbara).

RODDY, Lee; Writer; b. 22 Aug. 1921, Marion County, IL, USA; m. Cicely Price, 17 Oct. 1947, one s. one d. *Education:* AA, Los Angeles City College, 1945. *Career:* mem. Authors' Guild of America; Authors League; National Society of Children's Book Writers. *Publications:* The Life and Times of Grizzly Adams, 1977; The Lincoln Conspiracy, 1977; Jesus, 1979; Ghost Dog of Stoney Ridge, 1985; Dooger, Grasshopper Hound, 1985; The City Bear's Adventures, 1985; The Hair Pulling Bear Dog, 1985; Secret of the Shark Pit, 1988; Secret of the Sunken Sub, 1989; The Overland Escape, 1989; The Desperate Search, 1989; Danger on Thunder Mountain, 1990; Secret of the Howland Cave, 1990; The Flaming Trap, 1990; Mystery of the Phantom Gold, 1991; The Gold Train Bandits, 1992. Other: several books made into films and television programmes. *Honours:* various awards and book club selections. *Address:* PO Box 700, Penn Valley, CA 95946, USA.

RODGERS, Carolyn Marie; Prof., Writer, Poet and Ed.; b. 14 Dec. 1942, Chicago, IL, USA. *Education:* BA, Roosevelt University, 1981; MA, University of Chicago, 1983. *Career:* Prof. of Afro-American Literature, 1969, Lecturer in English and Co-ordinator of Poetry Workshop, 1970, Columbia College; Poet-in-Residence, University of Washington, 1970, Indiana University, 1974, Roosevelt University, 1983; Founder-Ed., Eden Press, 1991, Rare Form newsletter, 1994–; mem. Gwendolyn Brooks Writing Workshop; Organization of Black American Culture. *Publications:* Paper Soul, 1968; Songs of a Blackbird, 1970; How I Got Ovah, 1976; The Heart as Evergreen, 1978; Translation, 1980; A Little Lower Than the Angels, 1984; Morning Glory, 1989; The Religious Poetry of Carolyn M. Rodgers, 1993; Daughters of Africa, 1993; We're Only Human, 1994; A Train Called Judah, 1996; Chosen to Believe, 1996; Salt: The Salt of the Earth, 1999. Contributions: journals and magazines. *Honours:* National Endowment for the Arts Award, 1970; Conrad Kent Rivers Award, 1970; Society of Midland Authors Award, 1970; Carnegie Writer's Grant, 1980; Television Gospel Tribute, 1982; PEN Grant, 1987. *Address:* PO Box 804271, Chicago, IL 60680, USA.

RODOLPH, Utto (see Ouologuem, Yambo).

RODRIGUES, Louis Jerome; Writer, Poet and Trans; b. 20 July 1938, Chennai, India; m. 1st Malinda Weaving (deceased); one s.; m. 2nd Josefina Bernet Soler 6 Oct. 1984; one s. *Education:* BA, English, 1960; MA, Intermediate Histories and Logic, 1962, University of Chennai; MA, MPhil, Anglo-Saxon, 1965–67, University of London; MA, Law and English Tripos, 1971–73, 1977; PhD, University of Barcelona, 1990. *Career:* Asst Dir, Benedict, Mannheim, 1977; Dir of Studies, Inlingua, Barcelona, 1978–82; Dir, Phoenix, Barcelona, 1982–87; mem. International Asscn of Anglo-Saxonists; RSL; Society of Authors, exec. committee mem., 1988–91; Trans. Asscn; American Literary Trans. Asscn. *Publications:* A Long Time Waiting, 1979; Anglo-Saxon Riddles, 1990; Seven Anglo-Saxon Elegies, 1991; Chiaroscuro, 1991; The Battles of Maldon and Brunanburh, 1991; Anglo-Saxon Verse Runes, 1992; Anglo-Saxon Verse Charms, Maxims and Heroic Legends, 1993; Anglo-Saxon Elegiac Verse, 1994; Anglo-Saxon Didactic Verse, 1995; Three Anglo-Saxon Battle Poems, 1995; Salvador Espriu: Selected Poems (trans.), 1997; Beowulf and the Fight at Finnsburh. Contributions: various publications. *Honours:* Poetry Trans. Prize, Catholic University of America, Washington, DC, 1993. *Address:* 132 Wisbech Rd, Littleport, Ely, Cambridgeshire CB6 1JJ, England.

RODRIGUEZ, Judith Catherine, BA, MA; poet, dramatist, librettist, editor and lecturer; b. 13 Feb. 1936, Perth, WA, Australia; m. 1st Fabio Rodriguez 1964 (divorced 1981); four c.; m. 2nd Thomas Shapcott 1982. *Education:* University of Queensland, Brisbane, Girton College, Cambridge, University of London. *Career:* Lecturer in External Studies, University of Queensland, Brisbane, 1959–60; Lecturer in English, Philippa Fawcett College of Education, London, 1962–63, University of the West Indies, Jamaica, 1963–65, St Mary's College of Education, Twickenham, 1966–68, Macarthur Institute of Higher Education, Milperra, Sydney, 1987–88, Royal Melbourne Institute of Technology, 1988–89, Victoria College, 1989–92; Teacher of English as a Foreign Language, St Giles School of English, London, 1965–66; Lecturer, 1969–75, Senior Lecturer in English, 1977–85, La Trobe University, Bundoora, Australia; Writer-in-Residence, Rollins College, FL, 1986; Senior Lecturer, Deakin University, 1993–2003; Visiting Fellow, Univ. of Madras, 2000–04; mem. Australian Society of Authors; Melbourne PEN Centre; Victorian Writer's Centre. *Publications:* Poetry: Four Poets, 1962; Nu-Plastik Fanfare Red, 1973; Water Life, 1976; Shadow on Glass, 1978; Mudcrab at Gambaro's, 1980; Witch Heart, 1982; Floridian Poems, 1986; The House By Water: New and Selected Poems, 1988; The Cold, 1992; Terror: Poems 2002. Play: Poor Johanna (with Robyn Archer), 1994. Opera Libretto: Lindy, 1994. Editor: Mrs Noah and the Minoan Queen, 1982; Poems Selected from the Australian's 20th Anniversary Competition (with Andrew Taylor), 1985; Modern Swedish Poetry (with Thomas Shapcott), 1985; Collected Poems of Jennifer Rankin, 1990. Contributions: numerous publications. *Honours:* Arts Council of Australia Fellowships, 1974, 1978, 1983; Government of South Australia Biennial Prize for Literature, 1978; International PEN Peter Stuyvesant Prize for

Poetry, 1981; AM, 1994; Christopher Brennan Award, Fellowship of Australian Writers, 1994. *Address:* PO Box 231, Mont Albert, Vic. 3127, Australia. *E-mail:* rodju@tpg.com.au.

RODRIGUEZ, Luis J.; American poet and writer; b. 1954, El Paso, TX. *Career:* regular speaker and poet at nat. conferences and cultural centres; founder, Tia Chucha Press. *Publications include:* poetry: The Concrete River 1991, Poems Across the Pavement 1993, Trochemoche 1998; How to Make Sure Your Child Behaves 2000, Music of the Mill 2004; short story collections: The Republic of East L.A. 2003; juvenile: La llaman América (trans. as America is her Name) 1998, It Doesn't Have to be This Way 1999; memoirs: Always Running: La Vida Loca: Gang Days in L.A. 1995; contrib. to The Nation, Los Angeles Weekly, America's Review. *Honours:* Carl Sandburg Award for Non-Fiction, Poetry Center Book Award from San Francisco State Univ., PEN Oakland/Josephine Miles Award for Poetry 1991, Skiping Stones Award, Paterson Prize for Books for Young People, Hispanic Heritage Award for Excellence in Literature 1998. *Literary Agent:* Steven Barclay Agency, 12 Western Avenue, Petaluma, CA 94952, USA. *Telephone:* (707) 773-0654. *Fax:* (707) 778-1868. *Website:* www.barclayagency.com.

ROEBUCK, Derek; Lawyer and Writer; b. 22 Jan. 1935, Stalybridge, England; m. Susanna Leonie Hoe, 18 Aug. 1981, two s. one d. *Education:* MA, Oxon, 1960; MCom, Victoria University of Wellington, 1965. *Career:* mem. Selden Society. *Publications:* Author or co-author of 40 books on law and history, including: Credit and Security in Asia, 10 vols (with D. E. Allan and M. E. Hiscock), 1973–80; Whores of War: Mercenaries Today (with Wilfred Burchett), 1976; The Background of the Common Law, second edn, 1990; Hong Kong Digest of Contract, 1995; Hong Kong Digest of Criminal Law, 3 vols, 1995–96; Hong Kong Digest of Criminal Procedure, 3 vols, 1996–97; The Taking of Hong Kong: Charles and Clara Elliot in China Waters (with Susanna Hoe), 1999; A Miscellany of Disputes, 2000; Ancient Greek Arbitration, 2001; The Charitable Arbitrator: How to Mediate and Arbitrate in Louis XIV's France, 2002. Contributions: Over 40 articles on law, history and language. *Address:* 20A Plantation Rd, Oxford OX2 6JD, England.

ROGERS, Evelyn, (Keller Graves); Writer and Teacher; b. 30 Aug. 1935, Mobile, AL, USA; m. Jay Rogers, 22 March 1957, two c. *Education:* BA, English, Journalism, North Texas State University, 1957; MA, Library Science, Our Lady of the Lake University, 1975. *Career:* mem. Romance Writers of America; National Society of Arts and Letters; Novelists Inc; San Antonio Romance Authors; Opera Guild of San Antonio. *Publications:* Brazen Embrace (co-author), 1987; Rapture's Gamble (co-author), 1987; Desire's Fury (co-author), 1988; Velvet Vixen (co-author), 1988; Lawman's Lady (co-author), 1988; Midnight Sins, 1989; Texas Kiss, 1989; Wanton Slave, 1990; A Love So Wild, 1991; Surrender to the Night, 1991; Sweet Texas Magic, 1992; Desert Fire, 1992; Desert Heat, 1993; Flame, 1994; Raven, 1995; Angel, 1995; Wicked, 1996; The Forever Bride, 1997; Betrayal, 1997; Hot Temper, 1997; Texas Empires: Crown of Glory, 1998; Golden Man, 1999; Lone Star, 1999; Second Opinion, 1999; Longhorn, 2000; Devil in the Dark, 2001; The Loner, 2001; The Grotto, 2002; The Ghost of Carnal Cove, 2002, Dark of the Moon 2003. Novellas: Cactus and Thistle, 1991; A Christmas Wagon, 1993; Always Paradise, 1994; Gentle Rain, 1995; The Gold Digger, 1997; Something Borrowed, 2000. *Honours:* Prism Award for Best Light Paranormal Novel, Romance Writers of America, Fantasy, Futuristic and Paranormal Chapter, 1997; Texas Gold Award, East Texas Romance Writers of America. *Literary Agent:* Evan Marshall Agency, 6 Tristan Pl., Pine Brook, NJ 07058-9445, USA. *Address:* 2722 Belvoir Dr., San Antonio, TX 78230, USA.

ROGERS, Floyd (see Spence, William (John Duncan)).

ROGERS, Sir Frank Jarvis, Kt; British newspaper publisher; b. 24 Feb. 1920, Lawton, Cheshire; m. 1st Esma Sophia Holland 1949 (died 1998); two d.; m. 2nd Sheena Phillip 2001. *Education:* Wolstanton Grammar School. *Career:* journalist 1937–49; mil. service 1940–46; Gen. Man. Nigerian Daily Times 1949–52; Man. Argus, Melbourne 1952–55; Man. Dir Overseas Newspapers 1958–60; Dir Daily Mirror 1960–65; Man. Dir IPC 1965–70; Vice-Chair. Newspaper Publrs Asscn 1968–69, Dir 1971–73, Chair. 1990–98; Chair. Nat. Newspapers Steering Group 1970–72; Dir EMAP (fmrly East Midland Allied Press) 1971–91, Chair. 1973–90; Adviser on Corp. Affairs The Plessey Co. Ltd 1973–81; Deputy Chair. Argyll Investments Ltd 1982–90; Exec. Dir 1986–, Deputy Chair. Daily Telegraph PLC 1986–95; Trustee Reuters Founders Share Co. 1989–, Chair. 1998–99. *Address:* Greensleeves, Loudwater Drive, Loudwater, Rickmansworth, Herts., WD3 4HJ, England.

ROGERS, Ingrid; Pastor, Teacher and Writer; b. 3 May 1951, Rinteln, Germany; m. H. Kendall Rogers, 9 June 1972, one s. one d. *Education:* DUEL, Sorbonne Nouvelle, Paris, 1971; University of Oxford, 1972–73; Staatsexamen, 1974, PhD, 1976, Philipps University, Marburg; Doctor of Ministry Degree, Bethany Theological Seminary, 1988. *Publications:* Tennessee Williams: A Moralist's Answer to the Perils of Life, 1976; Peace Be Unto You, 1983; Swords into Plowshares, 1983; In Search of Refuge, 1984; Glimpses of Clima, 1989; Recollections of East Germany, 1996. *Honours:* Christopher Book Award, 1985; Angel Award of Excellence, 1985. *Address:* Manchester College, Box 131, North Manchester, IN 46962, USA.

ROGERS, Jane Rosalind, BA, PGCE, FRSL; British writer; b. 21 July 1952, London, England; m. Michael Harris 1981; one s. one d. *Education:* New Hall, Cambridge, Leicester Univ. *Career:* writer-in-residence, Northern Coll., Barnsley, South Yorkshire 1985–86, Sheffield Polytechnic 1987–88; Judith E. Wilson Fellow, Cambridge 1991; tutor for MA in writing, Sheffield Hallam Univ. 1994–; mem. Soc. of Authors. *Radio:* Shirley (BBC Radio 4, drama serial) 2002, Island (radio play) 2002. *Publications:* novels: Separate Tracks 1983, Her Living Image 1984, The Ice is Singing 1987, Mr Wroe's Virgins (also scripted BBC TV serial) 1991, Promised Lands 1995, Island 1999, The Voyage Home 2004; other: Dawn and the Candidate (screenplay) 1989, Good Fiction Guide (ed.) 2001; contrib. to magazines. *Honours:* North West Arts Writers Bursary 1985, Somerset Maugham Award 1985, Samuel Beckett Award 1990, Writers' Guild Award for Best Fiction Book 1996, Arts Council Writers Bursary 1996. *Literary Agent:* PFD, Drury House, 34–43 Russell Street, London, WC2B 5HA, England. *E-mail:* jane.rogers@btinternet.com.

ROGERS, Linda (Hall); Poet, Writer and Lecturer; b. 10 Oct. 1944, Port Alice, BC, Canada; m. Rick Van Krugel, three s. *Education:* MA, English Literature, University of British Columbia. *Career:* Lecturer, University of British Columbia, University of Victoria, Camosum College, Malaspina College; mem. Federation of British Columbia Writers, pres.; League of Canadian Poets; Society of Canadian Composers; Writers Union of Canada. *Publications:* Some Breath, 1978; Queens of the Next Hot Star, 1981; I Like to Make a Mess, 1985; Witness, 1985; Singing Rib, 1987; Worm Sandwich, 1989; The Magic Flute, 1990; Brown Bag Blues, 1991; Letters from the Doll Hospital, 1992; Hard Candy, 1994; The Half Life of Radium, 1994; Frankie Zapper and the Disappearing Teacher, 1994; Molly Brown is Not a Clown, 1996; Love in the Rainforest (selected poetry), 1996; Heaven Cake, 1997; The Saning, 1999; The Broad Canvas: Portraits of Women Artists (non-fiction), 1999; Say My Name (novel), 2000; Rehearsing the Miracle (poems), 2001; P. K. Page: Essays on Her Work (ed.), 2001; Al Purdy: Essays on His Work (ed.), 2002; Bill Bissett: Essays on His Work (ed.), 2002; The Bursting Test (poems). Contributions: journals, magazines, and newspapers. *Honours:* Aya Poetry Prize, 1983; Canada Council Arts Awards, 1987, 1990; British Columbia Writers Poetry Prize, 1989; Cultural Services Award, 1990; Alcuin Awards, 1991, 2002; Gov.-Gen.'s Centennial Medal for Poetry and Performance, 1993; Stephen Leacock Awards for Poetry, 1994, 1996; Dorothy Livesay Award for Poetry, 1995; Voices Israel Poetry Award, 1995; Peoples Poetry Award, 1996; Acorn Rukeyser Award, 1999; Cardiff Poetry Prizes, 1999, 2001; Canada's Peoples Poet, 2000; Bridport Poetry Prize, England, 2000; Millennium Award, 2000; Prix Anglais (France), 2000; Petra Kenny Award, 2001. *Address:* 1235 Styles St, Victoria, BC V9A 3Z6, Canada. *E-mail:* lrogers@pacificoast.net.

ROGERS, Michael Alan; Journalist, Ed. and Writer; b. 29 Nov. 1950, Santa Monica, CA, USA; m. Donna Rini, 9 Oct. 2000. *Education:* BA, Creative Writing, Stanford University, 1972. *Career:* Assoc. Ed., Rolling Stone Magazine, San Francisco, 1972–76; Ed.-at-Large, Outside magazine, San Francisco, 1976–78; Visiting Lecturer in Fiction, University of California at Davis, 1980; Senior Writer, Newsweek magazine, 1983–; Man. Ed., Newsweek InterActive, 1993–97; Exec. Prod., Broadband Division, Washington Post Co, 1995–96; Vice-Pres., Washingtonpost.Newsweek Interactive, 1996–; Ed. and Gen. Man., Newsweek.MSNBC.com, 1998–; mem. Authors' Guild; Sierra Club. *Publications:* Mindfogger, 1973; Biohazard, 1977; Do Not Worry About the Bear, 1979; Silicon Valley, 1982; Forbidden Sequence, 1988. Contributions: newspapers and magazines. *Honours:* Distinguished Science Writing Award, American Asscn for the Advancement of Science, 1976; Best Feature Articles Award, Computer Press Asscn, 1987. *Address:* c/o Newsweek, 251 W 57th St, New York, NY 10019, USA.

ROGERS, Pat; Prof. and Writer; b. 17 March 1938, Beverley, Yorkshire, England. *Education:* BA, 1961, MA, 1965, PhD, 1968, Fitzwilliam College, Cambridge. *Career:* Fellow, Sidney Sussex College, Cambridge, 1964–69; Lecturer, King's College, University of London, 1969–73; Prof. of English, University College of North Wales, Bangor, 1973–76, University of Bristol, 1977–86; DeBartolo Prof. of Liberal Arts, University of South Florida, Tampa, 1986–. *Publications:* Daniel Defoe: A Tour Through Great Britain, 1971; Grub Street: Studies on a Sub-culture, 1972, revised edn as Hacks and Dunces, 1980; Daniel Defoe: The Critical Heritage (ed.), 1972; The Augustan Vision: An Introduction to Pope, 1976; The Eighteenth Century (ed.), 1978; Henry Fielding: A Biography, 1979; Swift: Complete Poems, Literature and Popular Culture in the Eighteenth Century (ed.), 1983; Eighteenth-Century Encounters, 1985; The Oxford Illustrated History of English Literature (ed.), 1987; The Economy of Arts in the 18th Century, 1989; An Outline of English Literature, 1992; Essays on Pope, 1993; Johnson and Boswell in Scotland, 1993. *Address:* Dept of English, University of South Florida, Tampa, FL 33620, USA.

ROGERS, Rosemary, (Marina Mayson); Writer; b. 7 Dec. 1932, Sri Lanka; m. 1st Summa Navaratnam, 16 Jan. 1953, divorced, two s. two d.; m. 2nd Leroy Rogers, 1957, divorced 1964; m. 3rd Christopher M. Kadison, 1984. *Education:* BA, English, 1952. *Career:* mem. Writers Guild of America; Authors' Guild. *Publications:* Sweet Savage Love, 1974; Wildest Heart, 1974; Dark Fires, 1975; Wicked Loving Lies, 1976; The Crowd Pleasers, 1978; The Insiders, 1979; Lost Love, Last Love, 1980; Love Play, 1981; Surrender to Love, 1982; The Wanton, 1984; Bound by Desire, 1988. Contributions: Star Magazine; Good Housekeeping.

ROHAN, Michael Scott, (Mike Scott Rohan, Michael Scot); Writer and Ed.; b. 22 Jan. 1951, Edinburgh, Scotland; m. Deborah Rohan. *Education:* MA, University of Oxford, 1973. *Publications:* The Hammer and the Cross (co-author), 1980; Fantastic People (co-author), 1982; First Byte: Choosing and Using a Home Computer, 1983; Run to the Stars, 1983; The BBC Micro Add-On-Guide (co-author), 1985; The Ice King (co-author), 1986, US edn as Burial Rites, 1987; The Anvil of Ice, 1986, The Forge in the Forest, 1987, The Hammer of the Sun, 1988; Chase the Morning, 1990, The Gates of Noon, 1992, The Horns of Tartarus (co-author), 1992; Cloud Castles, 1993; The Lord of the Middle Air, 1994; The Classical Video Guide (ed.), 1994; Maxie's Little Demon, 1997. Contributions: anthologies and periodicals. *Honours:* All Time Great Fantasy Short Story, Gamemaster International, 1991; William F. Crawford Award for Best First Fantasy Novel, International Asscn for the Fantastic Arts, 1991. *Address:* Maggie Noach Literary Agency, 21 Redan St, London W14 0AB, England.

ROHEN, Edward, (Bruton Connors); Poet, Writer and Artist; b. 10 Feb. 1931, Dowlais, South Wales; m. Elizabeth Jarrett, 4 April 1961, one d. *Education:* ATD, Cardiff College of Art, 1952. *Career:* Art Teacher, Ladysmith High, BC, Canada, 1956–57; Head of Art, St Bonaventures, London, 1958–73, Ilford County High for Boys, Essex, 1973–82; mem. Academician, Centro Cultural Literario e Artistico de o Jornal de Felgeiras, Portugal; Korean War Veterans Writers and Arts Society; Welsh Acad. *Publications:* Nightpriest, 1965; Bruised Concourse, 1973; Old Drunk Eyes Haiku, 1974; Scorpio Broadside 15, 1975; Poems/Poemas, 1976; 109 Haiku and One Seppuku for Maria, 1987; Sonnets for Maria Marriage, 1988; Sonnets: Second Sequence for Maria, 1989. Contributions: anthologies and magazines. *Address:* 57 Kinfauns Rd, Goodmayes, Ilford, Essex IG3 9QH, England.

ROHRBACH, Peter Thomas, (James Cody); Writer; b. 27 Feb. 1926, New York, NY, USA; m. Sheila Sheehan, 21 Sept. 1970, one d. *Education:* BA, MA, Catholic University of America. *Career:* mem. Authors' Guild of America; Poets, Playwrights, Editors, Essayists and Novelists; Washington Independent Writers. *Publications:* 17 books, including: Conversation with Christ, 1981; Stagecoach East, 1983; American Issue, 1985; The Largest Event: World War II, 1993; National Issue, 1994. Contributions: Encyclopedias and periodicals. *Address:* 9609 Barkston Ct, Potomac, MD 20850, USA.

ROLAND, Alex; Prof. of History and Writer; b. 7 April 1944, Providence, RI, USA; m. 29 June 1979, four c. *Education:* BS, Engineering, US Naval Acad., 1966; MA, American History, University of Hawaii, 1970; PhD, Military History, Duke University, 1974. *Career:* Historian, National Aeronautics and Space Administration, 1973–81; Assoc. Prof., 1981–87, Prof. of History, 1987–, Chair, Dept of History, 1996–99, Duke University; Harold K. Johnson Visiting Prof. of Military History, US Army War College, 1988–89; Senior Fellow, MIT, 1994–95; mem. Society for Military History; Society for the History of Technology, pres., 1995–96. *Publications:* Underwater Warfare in the Age of Sail, 1978; Model Research: The National Advisory Committee for Aeronautics, 1915–1958, 2 vols, 1985; A Spacefaring People: Perspectives on Early Spaceflight (ed.), 1985; Men in Arms: A History of Warfare and Its Interrelationships with Western Society (with Richard A Preston and Sydney F. Wise), fifth edn, 1991; Atmospheric Flight (ed. with Peter Galison), 2000; The Military – Industrial Complex, 2001. Contributions: scholarly books and journals. *Honours:* Grants and fellowships; Fellow, Dibner Institute, MIT, 1993–94. *Address:* c/o Dept of History, Duke University, Durham, NC 27708, USA.

ROLIN, Jean; Novelist, Journalist and Essayist; b. 1949, France. *Publications:* La ligne de front, 1988; Cyrille et Méthode, 1994; Joséphine, 1994; Journal de Gand aux Aléoutiennes, 1995; Zones, 1995; L'Organisatión, 1996; Chemins d'eau, 1998; Campagnes, 2000; La Clôture, 2001; La Frontière belge, 2001; Dingos—Cherbourg-est/Cherbourg-ouest, 2002; Traverses. Contributions: numerous newspapers and magazines, incl. Libération, Le Figaro, Géo. *Honours:* Albert Londres Prize, 1988; Prix Médicis Étranger, 1996. *Address:* c/o Éditions Gallimard, 5 rue Sébastien-Bottin, 75328 Paris, Cedex 07, France.

ROLLS, Eric Charles; Writer and Poet; b. 25 April 1923, Grenfell, NSW, Australia; m. 1st Joan Stephenson, 27 Feb. 1954, deceased 1985, two s. one d.; m. 2nd Elaine van Kempen, 1988. *Career:* mem. Australian Society of Authors; National Book Council. *Publications:* Sheaf Tosser, 1967; They All Ran Wild, 1969; Running Wild, 1973; The River, 1974; The Green Mosaic, 1977; Miss Strawberry Verses, 1978; A Million Wild Acres, 1981; Celebration of the Senses, 1984; Doorways: A Year of the Cumberdeen Diaries, 1989; Selected Poetry, 1990; Sojourners, 1993; From Forest to Sea, 1993; Citizens, 1996; A Celebration of Food and Wine (three vols), 1997; Australia: A Biography, Vol. 1, 2000; Visions of Australia, 2002. Contributions: Bulletin; Overland; National Times; Age; Sydney Morning Herald; Independent Monthly; Sun Herald; various others. *Honours:* David Myer Trust Award for Poetry, 1968; Captain Cook Bicentennial Award for Non-Fiction, 1970; John Franklin Award for Children's Books, 1974; Braille Book of the Year, 1975; The Age Book of the Year, 1981; Talking Book of the Year, 1982; Fellow, Australian Acad. of the Humanities, 1985; Australian Creative Fellow, 1991; AM, 1991; Hon. Doctorate, University of Canberra, 1995; Centenary Medal, 2003. *Address:* PO Box 2038, North Haven, NSW 2443, Australia. *E-mail:* rollsvk@kooee.com.au.

ROLOFF, Michael, BA, MA; American playwright, poet and writer; b. (translator), 19 Dec. 1937, Berlin, Germany. *Education:* Haverford Coll., Pennsylvania, Stanford Univ. *Film screenplays:* Feelings 1982, Darlings and Monsters 1983, Graduation Party 1984. *Plays:* Wolves of Wyoming 1985, Palombe Blue 1985, Schizzohawk 1986. *Publications:* poetry: Headshots 1984, It Won't Grow Back 1985; fiction: Darlings and Monsters Quartet (four vols) 1986; other: numerous trans from German. *Address:* c/o Picador USA, 175 Fifth Avenue, New York, NY 10010, USA.

ROMER, Stephen Charles Mark; University Lecturer and Poet; b. 20 Aug. 1957, Bishops Stortford, Hertfordshire, England; m. Bridget Stevens, 17 July 1982, one s. *Education:* Radley College, 1970–74; English Tripos, Double First, Trinity Hall, Cambridge, 1975–78; Harvard University, 1978–79; British Institute, Paris, 1980–81; PhD, Cantab, 1985. *Publications:* The Growing Dark, 1981; Firebird 3, 1985; Idols, 1986; Plato's Ladder, 1992. Contributions: anthologies, journals, and periodicals. *Honours:* Gregory Award for Poetry, 1985. *Address:* 6 rue de Vemeuil, 75007 Paris, France.

ROMERIL, John; playwright; b. 26 Oct. 1945, Melbourne, Vic., Australia. *Education:* BA, Monash University, Clayton, 1970. *Career:* Writer-In-Residence, various Australian groups and National University, Singapore, 1974–87. *Publications:* A Nameless Concern, 1968; The Kitchen Table, 1968; The Man from Chicago, 1969; In a Place Like Somewhere Else, 1969; Chicago, Chicago, 1970; Marvellous Melbourne, 1970; Dr Karl's Kure, 1970; Whatever Happened to Realism?, 1971; Rearguard Action, 1971; Hackett Gets Ahead, 1972; Bastardy, 1972; Waltzing Matilda, 1974; The Floating World, 1974; The Golden Holden Show, 1975; The Accidental Poke, 1977; Mickey's Moomba, 1979; Centenary Dance, 1984; The Kelly Dance, 1984; Definitely Not the Last, 1985; Koori Radio, 1987; Top End, and History of Australia (co-author), 1989; Lost Weekend, 1989; Black Cargo, 1991; The Reading Boy, 1991; Working Out, 1991. Other: Television plays. *Honours:* Victorian Government Drama Fellowship, 1988. *Literary Agent:* Almost Managing, PO Box 1034, Carlton, Vic. 3053, Australia.

ROMTVEDT, David William; Writer and Poet; b. 7 June 1950, Portland, Oregon, USA; m. Margo Brown, 30 May 1987. *Education:* BA, Reed College, 1972. *Career:* State Literature Consultant, WY, 1987; Assoc. Prof. of English, Adjunt Assoc. Prof. of American Studies, University of Wyoming. *Publications:* Free and Compulsory for All, 1984; Moon, 1984; Letters from Mexico, 1987; Black Beauty and Kiev the Ukraine, 1987; Crossing the River: Poets of the Western US, 1987; How Many Horses, 1988; A Flower Whose Name I Do Not Know, 1992; Crossing Wyoming, 1992; Certainty, 1996; Windmill: Essays from Four Mile Ranch. Contributions: Paris Review; Canadian Forum; American Poetry Review; Poets and Writers Magazine. *Honours:* Residency Award, 1979, Fellowship, 1987, Tri-National Exchange Fellowship, 1996, National Endowment for the Arts; Pushcart Prize, 1991; National Poetry Series Award, 1991; Wyoming Gov.'s Arts Award, 2000. *Address:* 457 N Main, Buffalo, WY 82834, USA.

RONAN, Frank; novelist; b. 6 May 1963, New Ross, Ireland. *Publications:* The Men Who Loved Evelyn Cotton, 1989; A Picnic in Eden, 1991; The Better Angel, 1992; Dixie Chicken, 1994; Handsome Men are Slightly Sunburnt (short stories), 1996; Lovely, 1996; Home, 2002. *Honours:* Irish Times/Aer Lingus Irish Literature Prize 1989. *Literary Agent:* Rogers, Coleridge & White Ltd, 20 Powis Mews, London W11 1JN, England.

RONAY, Egon, LLD; British publisher and journalist; b. Pozsony, Hungary; m. 2nd Barbara Greenslade 1967; one s. (and two d. by previous marriage). *Education:* School of Piarist Order, Budapest, Univ. of Budapest and Acad. of Commerce, Budapest. *Career:* trained in kitchens of family catering firm and abroad; managed 5 restaurants within family firm; emigrated from Hungary 1946; Gen. Man. 2 restaurant complexes in London before opening own restaurant The Marquee 1952–55; gastronomic and good living columnist, Sunday Times 1986–91 and Sunday Express 1991, weekly columnist on eating out, food, wine and tourism, Daily Telegraph and later Sunday Telegraph 1954–60; weekly column, The Evening News 1968–74; Ed. Egon Ronay's Guide to Eating at the Airport 1992–94; mem. Acad. des Gastronomes (France) 1979; Founder Int. Acad. of Gastronomy; Founder and Pres. British Acad. of Gastronomes; Founder and Ed. the Egon Ronay Guides 1957, Publr and Ed. 1957–85. *Publications:* Egon Ronay's Guides 1957–84 annually, The Unforgettable Dishes of My Life 1989. *Honours:* Médaille de la Ville de Paris 1983, Chevalier de l'Ordre du Mérite Agricole 1987. *Telephone:* (20) 7584-1384 (Office). *E-mail:* egon@egonronay.com (Office).

ROOKE, Daphne Marie; Writer; b. 6 March 1914, Boksburg, South Africa; m. 1 June 1937, one d. *Publications:* A Grove of Fever Trees, 1950; Mittee, 1951; Ratoons, 1953; Wizards Country, 1957; Beti, 1959; A Lover for Estelle, 1961; The Greyling, 1962; Diamond Jo, 1965; Boy on the Mountain, 1969; Margaretha de la Porte, 1976; Three Rivers: A Memoir, 2003. Contributions: journals. *Honours:* First Prize, APB Novel Competition, 1946; Doctor of Literature, hc, University of Natal, 1997. *Address:* 54 Regatta Ct, Oyster Row, Cambridge CB5 8NS, England.

ROOKE, Leon; Author; b. 11 Sept. 1934, Roanoke Rapids, NC, USA. *Education:* Mars Hill College, NC, 1953–55; University of North Carolina at Chapel Hill, 1955–57, 1961. *Career:* Writer-in-Residence, University of North Carolina, 1965–66, University of Victoria, 1972–73, University of Southwest Minnesota, 1974–75, University of Toronto, 1984–85, University of Western Ontario, 1990–91; Visiting Prof., University of Victoria, 1980–81; mem. PEN; Writers' Union of Canada. *Publications:* Fiction: Last One Home Sleeps in the Yellow Bed, 1968; Vault, 1974; The Broad Back of the Angel, 1977; The Love Parlour, 1977; Fat Woman, 1980; The Magician in Love, 1980; Death Suite, 1982; The Birth Control King of the Upper Volta, 1983; Shakespeare's Dog, 1983; Sing Me No Love Songs I'll Say You No Prayers, 1984; A Bolt of White Cloth, 1984; How I Saved the Province, 1990; The Happiness of Others, 1991; A Good Baby, 1991; Who Do You Love?, 1992; Muffins, 1995. Stage Plays: A Good Baby, 1991; The Coming, 1991; 4 others. Contributions: About 300 short stories in leading North American journals. *Honours:* Canada and Australia Literary Prize, 1981; Best Paperback Novel of the Year, 1981; Governor-General's Award, 1984; North Carolina Award for Literature, 1990. *Address:* 209 Main St, Eden Mills, Ontario N0B 1P0, Canada.

ROOM, Adrian Richard West; Writer; b. 27 Sept. 1933, Melksham, England. *Education:* Honours Degree, Russian, 1957, Diploma, Education, 1958, University of Oxford. *Career:* mem. FRGS; English Place-Name Society; American Name Society. *Publications:* Place-Names of the World, 1974; Great Britain: A Background Studies English-Russian Dictionary, 1978; Room's Dictionary of Confusibles, 1979; Place-Name Changes since 1900, 1980; Naming Names, 1981; Room's Dictionary of Distinguishables, 1981; Dictionary of Trade Name Origins, 1982; Room's Classical Dictionary, 1983; Dictionary of Cryptic Crossword Clues, 1983; A Concise Dictionary of Modern Place-Names in Great Britain and Ireland, 1983; Dictionary of Changes in Meaning, 1986; Dictionary of Coin Names, 1988; Dictionary of Dedications, 1990; A Name for Your Baby, 1992; The Street Names of England, 1992; Brewer's Dictionary of Names, 1992; Corporate Eponymy, 1992; Place-Name Changes 1900–91, 1993; The Naming of Animals, 1993; African Place-Names, 1994; Cassell Dictionary of Proper Names, 1994; A Dictionary of Irish Place-Names, 1994; Cassell Dictionary of First Names, 1995; Brewer's Dictionary of Phrase and Fable, revised edn, 1995; Literally Entitled, 1996; An Alphabetical Guide to the Language of Name Studies, 1996; Placenames of Russia and the Former Soviet Union, 1996; Placenames of the World, 1997; Dictionary of Pseudonyms, 1998; Cassell Dictionary of Word Histories, 1999: Cassell's Foreign Words and Phrases, 2000; Dictionary of Art Titles, 2000; Dictionary of Music Titles, 2000; Brewer's Dictionary of Modern Phrase and Fable, 2000; Encyclopedia of Corporate Names Worldwide, 2002; Penguin Dictionary of British Place Names, 2003. *Address:* 12 High St, St Martin's, Stamford, Lincolnshire PE9 2LF, England.

ROORBACH, Bill; academic and writer; b. 18 Aug. 1953, Chicago, IL, USA; m. Juliet Brigitte Karelsen 1990; one d. *Education:* BA, Ithaca College, 1976; MFA, Columbia University, 1990. *Career:* Asst Prof. of English, University of Maine at Farmington, 1991–95; Asst Prof., 1995–98, Assoc. Prof. of English, 1998–, Ohio State University; mem. Associated Writing Programs; Authors' Guild; MLA of America. *Publications:* Summers with Juliet, 1992; Writing Life Stories: How to Make Memories into Memoirs, Ideas into Essays, and Life into Literature, 1998; The Art of Truth: A Contemporary Creative Nonfiction Reader (ed.), 2000; Big Bend: Stories, 2001; The Smallest Color, 2001. Contributions: anthologies, magazines, reviews, quarterlies and journals. *Honours:* Ohio Arts Council Grants; Flannery O'Connor Award, 2001. *Address:* c/o Department of English, Ohio State University, Columbus, OH 43210, USA.

ROOT, William Pitt; Prof. and Poet; b. 28 Dec. 1941, Austin, Texas, USA; m. Pamela Uschuk, 6 Nov. 1988, one d. *Education:* BA, University of Washington, 1964; MFA, University of North Carolina at Greensboro, 1966. *Career:* Stegman Fellow, Stanford University, 1967–68; Asst Prof., Michigan State University, 1967–68; Visiting Writer-in-Residence, Amherst College, 1971, University of Southwest Louisiana, 1976, Wichita State University, 1976, University of Montana, 1978, 1980, 1982–85, Pacific Lutheran University, 1990; Prof., Hunter College, CUNY, 1986–; Poet Laureate of Tuscon, AZ, 1997–. *Publications:* The Storm and Other Poems, 1969; Striking the Dark Air for Music, 1973; A Journey South, 1977; Reasons for Going It on Foot, 1981; In the World's Common Grasses, 1981; Invisible Guests, 1984; Faultdancing, 1986; Trace Elements from a Recurring Kingdom, 1994. Contributions: Magazines and periodicals. *Honours:* Acad. of American Poetry Prize, 1967; Rockefeller Foundation Grant, 1969–70; Guggenheim Fellowship, 1970–71; National Endowment for the Arts Grant, 1973–74; Pushcart Awards, 1977, 1980, 1985; US-UK Exchange Artist, 1978–79; Stanley Kunitz Poetry Award, 1981; Guy Owen Poetry Award, 1984. *Address:* c/o Dept of English, Hunter College, City University of New York, 695 Park Ave, New York, NY 10021, USA.

ROQUELAURE, A. N. (see Rice, Anne).

RORTY, Richard (McKay); Philosopher, Prof. and Writer; b. 4 Oct. 1931, New York, NY, USA; m. 1st Amelie Sarah Oksenberg, 15 June 1954, divorced 1972, one s.; m. 2nd Mary R. Varney, 4 Nov. 1972, one s. one d. *Education:* BA, 1949, MA, 1952, University of Chicago; PhD, Yale University, 1956. *Career:* Instructor, Yale University, 1955–57; Instructor, 1958–60, Asst Prof., 1960–61, Wellesley College; Faculty, 1961–70, Prof. of Philosophy, 1970–81, Stuart Prof. of Philosophy, 1981–82, University Prof. of Humanities, 1982–, University of Virginia; mem. American Acad. of Arts and Sciences; American Philosophical Asscn. *Publications:* Philosophy and the Mirror of Nature, 1979; Consequences of Pragmatism, 1982; Contingency, Irony, and Solidarity, 1989; Objectivity, Relativism, and Truth, 1991; Essays on Heidegger and Others, 1991; Essays on Aristotle's De Anima (ed. with Martha Nussbaum), 1992; Achieving Our Country: Leftist Thought in 20th-Century America, 1998. *Honours:* Guggenheim Fellowship, 1973–74; MacArthur Foundation Fellow, 1981–86.

ROSE, Andrew Wyness; Barrister and Writer; b. 11 Feb. 1944, England. *Education:* Trinity College, Cambridge, 1963–67; MA; LLM; Called to Bar, Grays Inn, London, 1968. *Career:* Barrister, 1968–; mem. Crimes Club, 1996. *Publications:* Stinie: Murder on the Common, 1985; Scandal at the Savoy, 1991. *Address:* c/o Society of Authors, 84 Drayton Gardens, London SW10 GSB, England.

ROSE, Daniel Asa; Writer, Essayist, Poet and Ed.; b. 20 Nov. 1949, New York, NY, USA; m. 1st Laura Love 30 Nov. 1974 (divorced); two s.; m. 2nd Shelley Roth 5 Sept. 1993; two s. *Education:* AB, English, Brown Univ., 1971. *Career:* Arts and Culture Ed., The Forward; Travel Columnist, Esquire; Book Reviewer, Vanity Fair; Travel Ed., Madison. *Publications:* Flipping For It, 1987; Small Family with Rooster, 1988; Hiding Places: A Father and His Sons Retrace their Family's Escape from the Holocaust, 2000. Other: screenplays, poems, stories, reviews and literary essays. Contributions: The New Yorker; The New York Times Magazine; GQ; Esquire; Playboy. *Honours:* O. Henry Prize, 1980; PEN Literary Awards, 1987, 1988; Massachusetts Cultural Council Award, 1992. *Address:* 138 Bay State Rd, Rehoboth, MA 02769, USA.

ROSE, Joel Steven, BA, MFA; writer; b. 1 March 1948, Los Angeles, CA, USA; m. Catherine Texier; two d. *Education:* Hobart College, Columbia University. *Career:* mem. Co-ordinating Council of Literary Magazines; Poets and Writers; Writers Guild of America. *Publications:* Kill the Poor (novel), 1988; Between C and D (co-ed.), 1988; Love is Strange (co-ed.), 1993. Contributions: newspapers and magazines. *Honours:* National Endowment for the Arts Award, 1986; New York State Council on the Arts Award, 1986–87.

ROSE, Kenneth Vivian; Writer; b. 15 Nov. 1924, Bradford, Yorkshire, England. *Education:* Repton School; Scholar, MA, New College, Oxford, 1948. *Career:* Asst Master, Eton College, 1948; Editorial Staff, Daily Telegraph, 1952–60; Founder, Writer, Albany Column, Sunday Telegraph, 1961–97. *Publications:* Superior Person: A Portrait of Curzon and his Circle in Late Victorian England, 1969; The Later Cecils, 1975; William Harvey: A Monograph, 1978; King George V, 1983; Kings, Queens and Courtiers: Intimate Portraits of the Royal House of Windsor, 1985; Harold Nicolson, 1992; Elusive Rothschild: The Life of Victor, 3rd Baron, 2003. Contributions: Dictionary of National Biography. *Honours:* FRSL, 1976; Wolfson Award for History, 1983; Whitbread Award for Biography, 1983; Yorkshire Post Biography of the Year Award, 1984; CBE, 1996. *Address:* 38 Brunswick Gardens, London W8 4 AL, England.

ROSE, Marion (see Harris, Marion Rose).

ROSE, Mark Allen, AB, BLitt, PhD; academic and writer; *Professor of English, University of California at Santa Barbara*; b. 4 Aug. 1939, New York, NY, USA; m. Anne Benningham; one s. *Education:* Princeton Univ., Merton Coll., Harvard Univ. *Career:* Instructor to Assoc. Prof. of English, Yale Univ. 1967–74; Prof. of English, Univ. of Illinois 1974–77; Prof. of English, Univ. of California at Santa Barbara 1977–, Assoc. Vice-Chancellor 2001–; Dir, Univ. of California Humanities Research Inst. 1989–94; mem. MLA, Renaissance Soc. of America, Shakespeare Soc. of America. *Publications:* Heroic Love 1968, Golding's Tale 1972, Shakespearean Design 1972, Spenser's Art 1975, Alien Encounters 1981, Authors and Owners 1993; editor: Twentieth Century Views of Science Fiction 1976, Twentieth Century Interpretations of Antony and Cleopatra 1977, Bridges to Science Fiction (with others) 1980, Shakespeare's Early Tragedies 1994, Norton Shakespere Workshop 1997. *Honours:* Woodrow Wilson Fellow 1961, Henry Fellow 1961–62, Dexter Fellow 1966, Morse Fellow 1970–71, Nat. Endowment for the Humanities Fellowships 1979–80, 1990–91. *Address:* 1135 Oriole Road, Montecito, CA 93108, USA. *E-mail:* mrose@english.ucsb.edu.

ROSE, Richard; Prof. of Public Policy and Writer; b. 9 April 1933, St Louis, MO, USA; m. Rosemary J. Kenny, 14 April 1956, two s. one d. *Education:* BA, Comparative Drama, Johns Hopkins University, 1953; Postgraduate Studies, LSE, 1954; DPhil, Social Studies, University of Oxford, 1960. *Career:* Political public relations, Mississippi River Road, 1954–55; Reporter, St Louis Post-Dispatch, 1955–57; Lecturer in Government, University of Manchester, 1961–66; Visiting Lecturer, Political Science, University of Illinois, Urbana, 1962; Prof. of Politics, 1966–76, Founder-Dir and Prof. of Public Policy, Centre for the Study of Public Policy, 1976–, University of Strathclyde; Visiting Lecturer in Political Sociology, University of Cambridge, 1967, European University Institute, Florence, 1977, 1978; Hinkley Distinguished Prof., Johns Hopkins University, 1987; Visiting Prof, Wissenschaftszentrum Berlin, 1988–90, Instituto Ortega y Gasset, Madrid, 2000; Sr Fellow, Oxford Internal Institute, 2003–; mem. American Acad. of Arts and Sciences, hon. foreign mem.; Finnish Acad. of Science and Letters, hon. foreign mem.; International Political Science Asscn, council mem., 1976–82; UK Political Studies Asscn. *Publications:* The British General Election of 1959 (with D. E. Butler), 1960; Must Labour Lose? (with M. Abrams), 1960; Politics in England, 1964; Influencing Voters: A Study in Campaign Rationality, 1967; People in Politics: Observations across the Atlantic, 1970; Governing Without Consensus: An Irish Perspective, 1971; International Almanack of Electoral History (with T. T. Mackie), 1974; The Problem of Party Government, 1974; Northern Ireland: A Time of Choice, 1976; Managing Presidential Objectives, 1976; What is Governing? Purpose and Policy in Washington, 1978; Can Government Go Bankrupt? (with G. Peters), 1978; Do Parties Make a Difference?, 1984; United Kingdom Facts (with I. McAllister), 1982; Understanding the United Kingdom: The Territorial Dimension in Government, 1982; The Nationwide Competition for Votes: The 1983 British Election (with I. McAllister), 1984; Understanding Big Government: The Programme Approach, 1984;Public Employment in Western Nations (with others), 1985; Voters Begin to Choose: From Closed Class to Open Elections in Britain (with I. McAllister), 1986; Patterns of Parliamentary Legislation (with D. Van Mechelen), 1986; Ministers and Ministries: A Functional Analysis, 1987; Taxation by Political Inertia (with T. Karran), 1987; The Postmodern President: The White House Meets the World, 1988; Ordinary People in Public Policy: A Behavioural Analysis, 1989; Training Without Trainers? How Germany Avoids Britain's Supply-side Bottleneck (with G. Wignanek), 1990; The Loyalties of Voters: A Lifetime Learning Model (with I. McAllister), 1990; Lesson-Drawing in Public Policy: A Guide to Learning Across Time and Space, 1993; Inheritance in Public Policy: Change Without Choice in Britain (with P. L. Davies), 1994; What is Europe? A Dynamic Perspective, 1996; How Russia Votes (with S. White and I. McAllister), 1997; Democracy and its Alternatives: Understanding Post-Communist Societies (with W. Mishler and C. Haerpfer), 1998; International Encyclopedia of Elections (with others), 2000; The Prime Minister in a Shrinking World, 2001; Elections Without Order: Russia's Challenge to Vladimir Putin (with Neil Munro), 2002; Elections and Parties in New European Democracies, 2003. Other: ed. of several books; seminar and conference papers; trans; designed websites. Contributions: periodicals and newspapers including: The Times; Sunday Times; Financial Times; Daily Telegraph; New Society; Economist; Professional journals and books; Broadcasts for radio and television. *Honours:* Guggenheim Fellowship, 1974; Fellow, British Acad., 1992; Amex Prize in International Economics, 1992; Lasswell Award for Lifetime Achievement in Public Policy of the Policy Studies Organization, 1999; Fellow, Acad. of the Learned Societies for the Social Sciences, 2000; Lifetime Achievement Award of the Political Studies Asscn of the UK, 2000; various fellowships, research grants. *Address:* c/o Centre for the Study of Public Policy, University of Strathclyde, Livingstone Tower, Glasgow G1 1XH, Scotland. *Website:* www.cspp.strath.ac.uk.

ROSEN, Charles, PhD; American pianist and writer; b. 5 May 1927, New York, NY. *Education:* Juilliard School of Music, Princeton Univ., Univ. of S. California. *Career:* studied piano with Moriz Rosenthal and Hedwig Kanner-Rosenthal 1938–45; recital début, New York 1951; first complete recording of Debussy Etudes 1951; première of Double Concerto by Elliott Carter, New York 1961; has played recitals and as soloist with orchestras throughout America and Europe; has made over 35 recordings including Stravinsky: Movements with composer conducting 1962, Bach: Art of Fugue, Two Ricercares, Goldberg Variations 1971, Beethoven: Last Six Sonatas 1972, Boulez: Piano Music, Vol. I, Diabelli Variations, Beethoven Concerto No. 4, 1979, Schumann: The Revolutionary Masterpieces, Chopin: 24 Mazurkas 1991; Prof. of Music, State Univ. of NY 1972–90; Guggenheim Fellowship 1974; Messenger Lectures, Cornell Univ. 1975, Bloch Lectures, Univ. of Calif., Berkeley 1977, Gauss Seminars, Princeton Univ. 1978; Norton Prof. of Poetry, Harvard Univ. 1980–81; George Eastman Prof., Balliol Coll., Oxford 1987–88, Prof. of Music and Social Thought, Univ. of Chicago 1988–96. *Publications:* The Classical Style: Haydn, Mozart, Beethoven 1971, Beethoven's Last Six Sonatas 1972, Schoenberg 1975, Sonata Forms 1980, Romanticism and Realism: The Mythology of Nineteenth-Century Art (with Henri Zerner) 1984, The Musical Language of Elliott Carter 1984, Paisir de jouer, plaiser de penser 1993, The Frontiers of Meaning: Three Informal Lectures on Music 1994, The Romantic Generation 1995, Romantic Poets, Critics and Other Madmen 1998, Critical Entertainment: Music Old and New 2000, Beethoven's Piano Sonatas: A Short Companion 2001, Piano Notes 2003; contrib. to books, newspapers and journals. *Honours:* Hon. DMus (Trinity Coll., Dublin 1976, Leeds Univ. 1976, Durham Univ.); Dr hc (Cambridge) 1992; Nat. Book Award 1972, Edison Prize, Netherlands 1974. *Literary Agent:* John Gingrich Management Inc, PO Box 1515, New York, NY 10023, USA.

ROSEN, Michael, MA; British children's writer, poet, broadcaster and critic; b. 7 May 1946, Harrow, Middlesex, England. *Education:* Wadham Coll., Oxford, Reading Univ. *Career:* worked for BBC television, on Play School and other children's programmes, BBC radio as presenter, Treasure Islands (Radio 4), Best Worlds (Radio 3), Meridian (World Service), Word of Mouth (Radio 4); mem. Poetry Soc. (vice-pres.). *Publications:* Backbone (play), 1969; Mind Your Own Business (poems), 1974; Wouldn't You Like to Know (poems), 1977; You Can't Catch Me, 1981; Everybody Here, 1982; A Cat and Mouse Story, 1982; Nasty!, 1984; Quick, Let's Get Out of Here (poems), 1985; Under the Bed, 1986; Smelly Jelly, Smelly Fish, 1986; A Spider Bought a Bicycle and Other Poems, 1987; Hard-boiled Legs, 1988; Down at the Doctor's, 1988; The Deadman Tapes, 1989; Here Come the Horribles, 1989; Rude Rhymes, 1989; Dirty Ditties, 1990; Inky Pinky Ponky, 1990; Sinbad the Sailor, 1990; Freckly Feet and Itchy Knees, 1990; The Royal Huddle and the Royal Muddle, 1990; Culture Shock, 1990; Norma and the Washing Machine, 1990; Vulgar Verses, 1991; Goodies and Daddies, 1991; Clever Cakes, 1991; Nuts About Nuts, 1993; Songbird Story, 1993; Bumping Bertha, 1993; Arabian Frights, 1994; Michael Rosen's Horribly Silly Stories, 1994; A Different Story: Poems from the Past, 1994; Moving, 1995; Just Kids: How to Survive the Twos to Twelves, 1995; Even Stevens FC, 1995; Crow and Hawk, 1995; Michael Rosen's Book of Very Silly Poems, 1996; Don't Put the Mustard in the Custard (poems), 1996; Smacking My Lips, 1996; Tea in the Sugar Bowl, 1997; You Wait Till I'm Older Than You!, 1997; The Hypnotiser, 1997; The Wicked Tricks of Till Owlyglass, 1997; This is Our House, 1998; Michael Rosen's Book of Nonsense, 1997; Little Rabbit Foo Foo, 1999; Snore!, 1999; My Bug, 1999; Lunch Boxes Don't Fly, 1999; The Man Who Sold His Shadow, 1999; Rover, 1999; Mission Ziffoid, 1999; You're Thinking About Doughnuts, 1999; Night-night, Knight, 1999; Centrally Heated Knickers, 2000; We're Going on a Bear Hunt, 2001; Uncle Billy Being Silly, 2001; Shakespeare: His Work and His World, 2001; Even More Nonsense from Michael Rosen, 2001; Carrying the Elephant: A Memoir of Love and Loss (adult poems), 2002; Lovely Old Roly, 2002; No Breathing in Class, 2003; Oww!, 2003; Howler, 2003; Romeo and Juliet, 2003; This Is Not My Nose (poems) 2004. Contributions: anthologies, magazines. *Honours:* Signal Prize 1982. *Address:* c/o Bloomsbury Publishing PLC, 38 Soho Square, London, W1D 3HB, England. *E-mail:* rosenmichael@hotmail.com. *Website:* www.bloomsbury.com/childrens/.

ROSEN, Norma; Writer and Teacher; b. 11 Aug. 1925, New York, NY, USA; m. Robert S. Rosen, 1960, one s. one d. *Education:* BA, Mt Holyoke College, 1946; MA, Columbia University, 1953. *Career:* Teacher of Creative Writing, New School for Social Research, New York City, 1965–69, University of Pennsylvania, 1969, Harvard University, 1971, Yale University, 1984, New York University, 1987–95; mem. PEN; Authors' Guild. *Publications:* Joy to Levine!, 1962; Green, 1967; Touching Evil, 1969; At the Center, 1982; John and Anzia: An American Romance, 1989; Accidents of Influence: Writing as a Woman and a Jew in America (essays), 1992; Biblical Women Unbound: Counter-Tales (narratives), 1996. Contributions: anthologies and other publications.

ROSENBERG, Bruce Alan; Teacher and Writer; b. 27 July 1934, New York, NY, USA; m. Ann Harleman, 20 June 1981, three s. *Education:* BA, Hofstra University, 1955; MA, Pennsylvania State University, 1960; PhD, Ohio State University, 1965. *Career:* mem. Folklore Fellows International. *Publications:* The Art of the American Folk Preacher, 1970; Custer and the Epic of Defeat, 1975; The Code of the West, 1982; The Spy Story, 1987; Can These Bones Live?, 1988; Ian Fleming, 1989; The Neutral Ground, 1995. Contributions: Over 60 professional journals. *Honours:* James Russell Lowell Prize, 1970; Chicago Folklore Prizes, 1970, 1975.

ROSENBERG, Liz; academic, poet and writer; b. 3 Feb. 1956, Glen Cove, NY, USA; m. David Bosnick 1996; one s. *Education:* BA, Bennington College, 1976; MA, Johns Hopkins University, 1978; PhD, Comparative Literature, SUNY at Binghamton, 1997. *Career:* Assoc. Prof. of English, SUNY at Binghamton; Guest Teacher-Poet, various venues; many poetry readings; mem. Associated Writing Programs; PEN. *Publications:* The Fire Music (poems), 1987; A Book of Days (poems), 1992; Children of Paradise (poems), 1994; Heart and Soul (novel), 1996; The Invisible Ladder (ed.), 1997; Earth-Shattering Poems (ed.), 1998; These Happy Eyes (prose poems), 1999. Contributions: many newspapers, reviews, and journals. *Honours:* Kelloggs Fellow, 1980–82; Pennsylvania Council of the Arts Poetry Grant, 1982; Agnes Starrett Poetry Prize, 1987; Claudia Lewis Poetry Prize, 1997; Best Book for Teens Citation, New York Public Library, 1997; Paterson Prizes for Children's Literature, 1997, 1998. *Address:* c/o Department of English, General Literature, and Rhetoric, State University of New York at Binghamton, PO Box 6000, Binghamton, NY 13902, USA.

ROSENBERG, Nancy Taylor; Writer; b. 9 July 1946, Dallas, Texas, USA; m. 1st Calvin S. Kyrme, divorced, two s. one d.; m. 2nd Jerry Rosenberg, two d. *Education:* Gulf Park College; University of California at Los Angeles. *Publications:* Mitigating Circumstances, 1993; Interest of Justice, 1993; The Eyewitness, 1994; First Offense, 1994; California Angel, 1995; Conflict of Interest, 2002. *Address:* c/o Dytton Publicity, 375 Hudson St, New York, NY 10014, USA.

ROSENBERG, Peter Michael; Writer; b. 11 July 1958, London, England. *Education:* BSc, University of Sussex, 1979. *Publications:* The Usurper (co-author), 1988; Kissing Through a Pane of Glass, 1993; Touched By a God or Something, 1994; Because It Makes My Heart Beat Faster, 1995; Daniel's Dream, 1996. Contributions: journals and magazines. *Honours:* Second Prize, Betty Trask Award, 1992. *Literary Agent:* Christopher Little Literary Agency, 10 Eel Brook Studios, 125 Moore Park Rd, London SW6 4PS, England. *Address:* 430 St Ann's Rd, London N15 3JJ, England. *E-mail:* peter.rosenberg@virgin.net.

ROSENBLATT, Joseph (Joe); poet, writer and artist; b. 26 Dec. 1933, Toronto, ON, Canada; m. Faye Smith 1970; one s. *Education:* Central Technical School, Toronto, George Brown Coll., Toronto. *Career:* Ed., Jewish Dialog magazine 1969–83; writer-in-residence, Univ. of Western Ontario, London 1979–80, Univ. of Victoria, BC 1980–81, Saskatoon Public Library, Saskatchewan 1985–86; Visiting Lecturer, Univ. of Rome 1987, Univ. of Bologna 1987. *Publications:* The Voyage of the Mood 1960, The LSD Leacock 1963, The Winter of the Luna Moth 1968, Greenbaum 1970, The

Bumblebee Dithyramb 1972, Blind Photographer: Poems and Sketches 1973, Dream Craters 1974, Virgins and Vampires 1975, Top Soil 1976, Doctor Anaconda's Solar Fun Club: A Book of Drawings 1977, Loosely Tied Hands: An Experiment in Punk 1978, Snake Oil 1978, The Sleeping Lady 1979, Brides of the Stream 1984, Escape from the Glue Factory: A Memoir of a Paranormal Toronto Childhood in the Late Forties 1985, Poetry Hotel: Selected Poems 1963–1985 1985, The Kissing Goldfish of Siam: A Memoir of Adolescence in the Fifties 1989, Gridi nel Buio 1990, Beds and Consenting Dreamers 1994, The Joe Rosenblatt Reader 1995, The Voluptuos Gardener: The Collected Art and Writing of Joe Rosenblatt 1973–1996 1996; contrib. to many publications. *Honours:* Canada Council Senior Arts Awards 1973, 1976, 1980, 1987, Ontario Arts Council Poetry Award 1970, Gov.-Gen.'s Award for Poetry 1976, British Columbia Book Award for Poetry 1986. *Address:* 221 Elizabeth Avenue, Qualicum Beach, BC V9K IG8, Canada.

ROSENDORFER, Herbert; German novelist and academic; b. 19 Feb. 1934, Bolzano. *Career:* fmr attorney and judge (retd), Prof. of German Literature, Univ. of Munich. *Publications:* novels: Der Ruinenbaumeister (trans. as The Architect of Ruins) 1969, Stephanie und das vorige Leben (trans. as Stephanie or a Previous Existence) 1977, Briefe in die chinesische Vergangenheit (trans. as Letters Back to Ancient China) 1983, Die Nacht der Amazonen 1989, Ein Liebhaber ungerader Zahlen 1994, Die grosse Umwendung: neue Briefe in die chinesische Vergangenheit 1997, Kadon, Ehemaliger Gott 2001. *Honours:* Jean-Paul Prize 1999. *Literary Agent:* c/o Dedalus Ltd, Langford Lodge, St Judith's Lane, Sawtry, Cambridgeshire PE28 5XE, England. *E-mail:* info@dedalusbooks.com. *Website:* www.dedalusbooks.com.

ROSENGARTEN, Theodore; Writer; b. 17 Dec. 1944, New York, NY, USA; m. 1974, one s. *Education:* AB, Amherst College, 1966; PhD, Harvard University, 1975. *Publications:* All God's Dangers: The Life of Nate Shaw, 1974. *Honours:* National Book Award, 1975. *Address:* PO Box 8, McClellanville, SC 29458, USA.

ROSENTHAL, Barbara Ann; Writer, Artist, Photographer and Video Artist; b. 17 Aug. 1948, New York, NY, USA; two d. *Education:* BFA, Carnegie-Mellon University, 1970; MFA, Queens College, CUNY, 1975. *Career:* Ed.-in-Chief, Patterns, 1967–70; Adjunct Lecturer in English, College of Staten Island, CUNY, 1990–. *Publications:* Clues to Myself, 1982; Sensations, 1984; Old Address Book, 1985; Homo Futurus, 1986; In the West of Ireland, 1992; Children's Shoes, 1993; Soul and Psyche, 1999. Contributions: anthologies and journals. *Honours:* various awards and residencies. *Address:* 727 Avenue of the Americas, New York, NY 10010, USA.

ROSENTHAL, Thomas Gabriel, MA; British publisher, critic and broadcaster; b. 16 July 1935; m. Ann Judith Warnford-Davis; two s. *Education:* Perse School, Cambridge and Pembroke Coll., Cambridge. *Career:* served RA 1954–56; joined Thames and Hudson Ltd 1959, Man. Dir Thames and Hudson Int. 1966; joined Martin Secker and Warburg Ltd as Man. Dir 1971, Dir Heinemann Group of Publrs 1972–84, Man. Dir William Heinemann Int. Ltd 1979–84, Chair. World's Work Ltd 1979–84, Heinemann Zsolnay Ltd 1979–84, Kaye and Ward Ltd 1980–84, William Heinemann, Australia and SA 1981–82, Pres. Heinemann Inc. 1981–84; Jt Man. Dir and Jt Chair. André Deutsch Ltd 1984, CEO 1987–96, Sole Man. Dir and Chair. 1987, Chair. 1984–98; Chair. Frew McKenzie (Antiquarian Booksellers) 1985–93, Bridgewater Press 1997–; Art Critic The Listener 1963–66; Chair. Soc. of Young Publrs 1961–62; mem. Cambridge Univ. Appointments Bd 1967–71, Exec. Cttee Nat. Book League 1971–74, Cttee of Man. Amateur Dramatic Club, Cambridge (also Trustee), Council RCA 1982–87, Exec. Council Inst. of Contemporary Arts 1987–99 (Chair. 1996–99); Trustee Phoenix Trust; mem. Editorial Bd Logos 1989–93. *Publications:* Monograph on Jack B. Yeats 1964, Monograph on Ivon Hitchens (with Alan Bowness) 1973; A Reader's Guide to European Art History 1962, A Reader's Guide to Modern American Fiction 1963, Monograph on Arthur Boyd (with Ursula Hoff) 1986, The Art of Jack B. Yeats 1993, Sidney Nolan 2002; articles in journals and newspapers. *Address:* Flat 7, Huguenot House, 19 Oxendon Street, London, SW1Y 4EH, England. *Telephone:* (20) 7839-3589. *Fax:* (20) 7839-0651.

ROSS, Angus (see Giggal, Kenneth).

ROSS, Helaine (see Daniels, Dorothy).

ROSS, Jonathan (see Rossiter, John).

ROSS, Malcolm (see Ross-Macdonald, Malcolm John).

ROSS-MacDONALD, Malcolm John, (Malcolm MacDonald, M. R. O'Donnell, Malcolm Ross); writer, editor and designer; b. 29 Feb. 1932, Chipping, Sodbury, Gloucestershire, England; m. Ingrid Giehr; two d. *Education:* Falmouth School of Art, 1950–54; Diploma, University College London, 1958. *Career:* Lektor, Folk University, Sweden, 1959–61; Exec. Ed., Aldus Books, 1962–65; Visiting Lecturer, Hornsey College of Art, 1965–69; mem. Authors' Guild; Society of Authors. *Publications:* The Big Waves, 1962; Macdonald Illustrated Encyclopaedia (exec. ed.), 10 vols, 1962–65; Spare Part Surgery (co-author), 1968; Machines in Medicine, 1969; The Human Heart, 1970; World Wildlife Guide, 1971; Beyond the Horizon, 1971; Every Living Thing, 1973; World from Rough Stones, 1974; Origin of Johnny, 1975; Life in the Future, 1976; The Rich Are With You Always, 1976; Sons of Fortune, 1978; Abigail, 1979; Goldeneye, 1981; The Dukes, 1982; Tessa'd'Arblay, 1983; In Love and War, 1984; Mistress of Pallas, 1986; Silver Highways, 1987; The Sky with Diamonds, 1988; A Notorious Woman, 1988; His Father's Son, 1989; An Innocent Woman, 1989; Hell Hath No Fury, 1990; A Woman Alone, 1990; The Captain's Wives, 1991; A Woman Scorned, 1991; A Woman Possessed, 1992; All Desires Known, 1993; To the End of Her Days, 1993; Dancing on Snowflakes, 1994; For I Have Sinned, 1994; Kernow and Daughter, 1994; Crissy's Family, 1995; Tomorrow's Tide, 1996; The Carringtons of Helston, 1997; Like a Diamond, 1998; Tamsin Harte, 2000; Rose of Nancemellin, 2001. Contributions: Sunday Times; New Scientist; Science Journal; Month; Jefferson Encyclopaedia. *E-mail:* mirossmac2@eircom.net. *Website:* www.malcolmmacdonald.org.

ROSSI, Bruno (see Levinson, Leonard).

ROSSITER, John, (Jonathan Ross); Writer; b. 2 March 1916, Devonshire, England. *Education:* Preparatory and military schools, Woolwich and Bulford, 1924–32. *Career:* Detective Chief Superintendent, Wiltshire Constabulary, 1939–69; Flight Lieutenant, RAF/VR, 1943–46; Columnist, Wiltshire Courior, Swindon, 1963–64; mem. CWA. *Publications:* As Jonathan Ross: The Blood Running Cold, 1968; Diminished by Death, 1968; Dead at First Hand, 1969; The Deadest Thing You Ever Saw, 1969; Death's Head, 1982; Dead Eye, 1983; Dropped Dead, 1984; Fate Accomplished, 1987; Sudden Departures, 1988; A Time for Dying, 1989; Daphne Dead and Done For, 1990; Murder be Hanged, 1992; The Body of a Woman, 1994; Murder! Murder! Burning Bright, 1996; This Too Too Sullied Flesh, 1997. As John Rossiter: The Victims, 1971; A Rope for General Dietz, 1972; The Manipulators, 1973; The Villains, 1974; The Golden Virgin, 1975; The Man Who Came Back, 1978; Dark Flight, 1981. Contributions: Police Review. *Literary Agent:* David Higham Associates, 5–8 Lower John St, Golden Sq., London W1F 9HA, England. *Address:* 3 Leighton Home Farm Ct, Wellhead Lane, Westbury, Wilts BA13 3PT, England.

ROSSITER, John (see Crozier, Brian Rossiter).

ROSSNER, Judith (Perelman); Writer; b. 1 March 1935, New York, NY, USA; m. 1st Robert Rossner, 13 June 1954, divorced; m. 2nd Mort Persky, 9 Jan. 1979, divorced, one s. one d. *Education:* City College, CUNY, 1952–55. *Career:* mem. Authors' Guild; PEN. *Publications:* To the Precipice, 1966; Nine Months in the Life of an Old Maid, 1969; Any Minute I Can Split, 1972; Looking for Mr Goodbar, 1975; Attachments, 1977; Emmeline, 1980; August, 1983; His Little Women, 1990; Olivia or the Weight of the Past, 1994; Perfidia, 1997. Contributions: Magazines and journals.

ROSTON, Murray, MA, PhD; academic and writer; *Professor of English, Bar-Ilan University*; b. 10 Dec. 1928, London, England. *Education:* Queens' Coll., Cambridge, Queen Mary Coll., London. *Career:* Prof. of English, Bar-Ilan Univ., Ramat Gan, Israel 1956–; Permanent Adjunct Prof., Univ. of California, Los Angeles 1999–. *Publications:* Prophet and Poet: The Bible and the Growth of Romanticism 1965, Biblical Drama in England from the Middle Ages to the Present Day 1968, The Soul of Wit: A Study of John Donne 1974, Milton and the Baroque 1980, Sixteenth-Century English Literature 1982, Renaissance Perspectives in Literature and the Visual Arts 1987, Changing Perspectives in Literature and the Visual Arts, 1650–1820 1990, Victorian Contexts in Literature and the Visual Arts 1995, Modernist Patterns in Literature and the Visual Arts 1999, The Search for Selfhood in Modern Literature 2001; contrib. to professional journals. *Address:* 51 Katznelson Street, Kiryat Ono, Israel.

ROTBLAT, Sir Joseph; Prof. of Physics Emeritus and Writer; b. 4 Nov. 1908, Warsaw, Poland. *Education:* MA, University of Warsaw; PhD, University of Liverpool. *Career:* Prof. of Physics, 1950–76, Prof. Emeritus, 1976–, Medical College of St Batholomew's Hospital, University of London; Sec.-Gen., 1957–73, Pres., 1988–97, Pres. Emeritus, 1997–, Pugwash Conferences. *Publications:* Radioactivity and Radioactive Substances (with Sir James Chadwick), 1961; Science and World Affairs, 1962; The Uses and Effects of Nuclear Energy (co-author), 1964; Aspects of Medical Physics (ed.), 1966; Pugwash: The First Ten Years, 1967; Scientists in the Quest for Peace: A History of the Pugwash Conferences, 1972; Nuclear Reactors: To Breed or Not to Breed, 1977; Nuclear Energy and Nuclear Weapon Proliferation, 1979; Nuclear Radiation in Warfare, 1981; Scientists, the Arms Race and Disarmament, 1982; The Arms Race at a Time of Decision, 1984; Nuclear Strategy and World Security, 1985; World Peace and the Developing Countries, 1986; Strategic Defence and the Future of the Arms Race, 1987; Co-existence, Co-operation and Common Security, 1988; Verification of Arms Reductions, 1989; Global Problems and Common Security, 1989; Nuclear Proliferation: Technical and Economic Aspects, 1990; Global Security Through Co-Operation, 1990; Towards a Secure World in the 21st Century, 1991; Striving for Peace, Security and Development in the World, 1992; A Nuclear-Weapon-Free World: Desirable? Feasible?, 1993; World Citizenship: Allegiance to Humanity, 1997; Nuclear Weapons: The Road to Zero, 1998. *Honours:* CBE, 1965; Albert Einstein Peace Prize, 1992; Fellow, Royal Society, 1995; Nobel Prize for Peace, 1995; Knight Commander of the Order of St. Michael and St. George, 1998. *Address:* 8 Asmara Rd, London NW2 3ST, England.

ROTH, Andrew; Political Correspondent and Writer; b. 23 April 1919, New York, NY, USA; m. Mathilda Anna Friederich, 1949, divorced 1984, one s. one d. *Education:* BSS, City College, CUNY, 1939; MA, Columbia University, 1940; Harvard University. *Career:* Reader, City College, CUNY, 1939; Research Assoc., Institute of Pacific Relations, 1940; Editorial Writer, The Nation, 1945–46; Foreign Correspondent, Toronto Star Weekly, 1946–50; London Correspondent, France Observateur, Sekai, Singapore Standard, 1950–60; Dir, Parliamentary Profiles, 1955–; Political Correspondent, Manchester Evening News, 1972–84, New Statesman, 1984–96. *Publications:* Japan Strikes South, 1941; French Interests and Policies in the Far East, 1942; Dilemma in Japan, 1945; The Business Background of MPs, 1959; The MPs Chart, 1967; Enoch Powell: Tory Tribune, 1970; Can Parliament Decide..., 1971; Heath and the Heathmen, 1972; Lord on the Board, 1972; Sir Harold Wilson: Yorkshire Walter Mitty, 1977; Parliamentary Profiles, Vols I–IV, 1984–85; New MPs of '92, 1992; Mr Nice Guy and His Chums, 1993; New MPs of '97, 1997; New MPs of '01, 2001. *Address:* 34 Somali Rd, London NW2 3RL, England.

ROTH, Gerhard (Jürgen); Writer and Photographer; b. 24 June 1942, Graz, Austria; m. 1st Erika Wolfgruber, 16 Sept. 1963, divorced 1986; m. 2nd Senta Thonhauser, 1995, one s. two d. *Education:* University of Graz Medical School, 1961–67. *Publications:* Die Autobiographie des Albert Einstein, 1972; Der Ausbruch des Ersten Weltkriegs und andere Romane, 1972; Der Wille zur Krankheit, 1973; Der grosse Horizont, 1974; Ein Neuer Morgen, 1976; Winterreise, 1978; Der stille Ozean, 1980, English trans. as The Calm Ocean, 1993; Circus Saluti, 1981; Die schönen Bilder beim Trabrennen, 1982; Das Töten des Bussards, 1982; Dorfchronik zum Landläufiger Tod, 1984; Die Vergessenen, 1986; Am Abgrund, 1986; Der Untersuchungsrichter: Die Geschichte eines Entwurfs, 1988; Die Geschichte der Dunkelheit: Ein Bericht 1991; Eine Reise in das Innere von Wien, 1991; Das doppelköpfige Österreich, 1995; Der See, 1995, English trans. as The Lake, 2000; Der Plan, 1998; Der Berg, 2000. Other: various plays, essays, etc. *Honours:* Literature Prizes, State of Styria, 1972, 1973, 1976; Critic's Prize, South West German Radio, 1978; Fellowship, City of Hamburg, 1979–80; Alfrid Döblin Prize, 1983; Marie Luise Kaschnitz Prize, 1992; Vienna Literary Prize, 1992; Peter-Rossegger Prize, 1994; Hon. Prize, Austrian Booksellers, 1994. *Address:* Am Heumarkt 7437, N030 Vienna, Austria.

ROTH, Philip Milton, BA, MA; American writer; b. 19 March 1933, Newark, NJ; m. 1st Margaret Martinson 1959 (died 1968); m. 2nd Claire Bloom 1990 (divorced 1994). *Education:* Newark College of Rutgers University, Bucknell University, University of Chicago. *Career:* Teacher of English, University of Chicago, 1956–58; Writer-in-Residence, Princeton University, 1962–64; Adjunct Prof., University of Pennsylvania, 1976–77; Distinguished Prof., Hunter College, CUNY, 1989–92; mem. American Acad. of Arts and Letters. *Publications:* Goodbye, Columbus, 1959; Letting Go, 1962; When She Was Good, 1967; Portnoy's Complaint, 1969; Our Gang, 1971; The Breast, 1972; The Great American Novel, 1973; My Life as a Man, 1974; Reading Myself and Others, 1975; The Prof. of Desire, 1977; The Ghost Writer, 1979; Zuckerman Unbound, 1981; The Anatomy Lesson, 1983; The Prague Orgy, 1985; Zuckerman Bound, 1985; The Counterlife, 1987; The Facts, 1988; Deception, 1990; Patrimony, 1991; Operation Shylock, 1993; Sabbath's Theater, 1995; American Pastoral, 1997; I Married a Communist, 1998; The Human Stain, 2000; The Dying Animal, 2001; The Plot Against America 2004. Contributions: periodicals. *Honours:* Guggenheim Fellowship, 1959–60; National Institute of Arts and Letters Award, 1960; National Book Awards, 1962, 1995; National Book Critics Circle Awards, 1988, 1992; PEN-Faulkner Awards, 1993, 2001; Pulitzer Prize in Fiction, 1998; Prix Médicis Étranger, 2002. *Literary Agent:* The Wylie Agency, 250 W 57th Street, Suite 2114, New York, NY 10107, USA.

ROTHE-VALLBONA, Rima Gretel; writer and academic; b. 15 March 1931, San José, Costa Rica; m. Carlos Vallbona 1956; one s. three d. *Education:* BA, BS Colegio Superior de Señoritas, San José, Costa Rica, 1948; Diploma, Prof. of French in a Foreign Country, University of Paris, Sorbonne, 1953; Diploma in Spanish Philology, University of Salamanca, Spain, 1954; MA, University of Costa Rica, 1962; DML, Doctor in Modern Languages, Middlebury College, USA, 1981. *Career:* faculty mem. University of St Thomas, Texas 1964–95, Visiting Prof. Summer Program in Argentina 1972, Prof. of Spanish 1978–95, Emer. Prof. 1995–; Visiting Prof. Rice University 1980–83, Summer Program in Spain 1974; Cullen Foundation Prof. of Spanish 1989–95, Prof. Emeritus 1995–. *Publications:* Noche en vela (novel), 1968; Polvo del camino (short stories), 1971; Yolanda Oreamuno (literary essay), 1972; La Salamandra Rosada (short stories), 1979; La Obra en prosa de Eunice Odio (literary essay), 1981; Mujeres y agonias (short stories), 1982; Las sombras que perseguimos (novel), 1983; Baraja de soledades (short stories), 1983; Cosecha de pecadores (short stories), 1988; El arcangel del perdon (short stories), 1990; Mundo, demonio y mujer (novel), 1991; Los infiernos de la mujer y algo mas (short stories), 1992; Vida y sucesos de la Monja Alferez, 1992; Flowering Inferno: Tales of Sinking Hearts (short stories), 1993; Tormy, la gata prodigiosa de Donaldito (children's short story), 1997. *Honours:* Jorge Luis Borges Short Stories Prize 1977, Ancora Award for Best Book in Costa Rica 1983–84, Medal of Civil Service (Spain) 1989. *Address:* 3706 Lake Street, Houston, TX 77098, USA. *E-mail:* rvallbona@aol.com.

ROTHENBERG, Jerome (Dennis); Prof. of Visual Arts and Literature, Poet and Writer; b. 11 Dec. 1931, New York, NY, USA; m. Diane Brodatz, 25 Dec. 1952, one s. *Education:* BA, City College, CUNY, 1952; MA, University of Michigan, 1953. *Career:* Prof. of English and Comparative Literature, SUNY at Binghamton, 1986–88; Prof. of Visual Arts and Literature, University of California at San Diego, 1988–; mem. New Wilderness Foundation; PEN International. *Publications:* New Young German Poets, 1959; White Sun Black Sun, 1960; Technicians of the Sacred, 1968; Poems for the Game of Silence: Selected Poems, 1971; Shaking the Pumpkin, 1972; America Prophecy, 1973; Poland/1931, 1974; Revolution of the Word, 1974; A Big Jewish Book, 1977; A Seneca Journal, 1978; Numbers and Letters, 1980; Vienna Blood, 1980; Pre-Faces, 1981; That Dada Strain, 1983; Symposium of the Whole, 1983; 15 Flower World Variations, 1984; A Merz Sonata, 1985; New Selected Poems, 1970–85, 1986; Exiled in the Word, 1989; Khurbn and Other Poems, 1989; Further Sightings and Conversations, 1989; The Lorca Variations, 1994; Gematria, 1994; An Oracle for Delfi, 1995; Poems for the Millennium, two vols, 1995, 1998; Pictures of the Crucifixion, 1996; Seedings and Other Poems, 1996; The Book Spiritual Instrument, 1996; A Paradise of Poets, 1999; A Book of the Book, 2000; The Case for Memory, 2001; A Book of Witness: Spells and Gris-Gris (poems), 2003; María Sabina Selections, 2003. Contributions: various publications. *Honours:* National Endowment for the Arts Fellowship, 1975; Guggenheim Fellowship, 1976; American Book Award, 1982; Trans. Award, PEN Center, USA West, 1994, 2002; Josephine Miles Literary Awards, PEN Oakland, 1994, 1996. *Address:* c/o Dept of Visual Arts, University of California at San Diego, La Jolla, CA 92093, USA. *E-mail:* jrothenb@vesd.edu.

ROTHERMERE, 4th Viscount, cr. 1919, of Hemsted; **Jonathan Harold Esmond Vere Harmsworth,** BA; British newspaper publisher; *Chairman, Daily Mail and General Trust PLC;* b. 3 Dec. 1967, London; m. Claudia Clemence 1993; one s. three d. *Education:* Gordonstoun School, Scotland, Kent School, Conn., USA, Duke Univ., USA. *Career:* joined Mirror Group 1993; joined Northcliffe Newspapers Group Ltd 1995; Deputy Man. Dir, then Man. Dir Evening Standard 1997; Chair. Assoc. Newspapers Ltd 1998–; Chair. Assoc. New Media 1998, Daily Mail and Gen. Trust PLC 1998–; Pres. Newspaper Press Fund 1999–. *Address:* Daily Mail and General Trust PLC, Room 602, Northcliffe House, 2 Derry Street, London, W8 5TT, England (Office). *Telephone:* (20) 7938-6613. *Fax:* (20) 7937-0043. *E-mail:* chairman@chairman.dmgt.co.uk (Office).

ROUDINESCO, Elisabeth; Historian and Writer; b. 10 Sept. 1944, Paris, France. *Education:* State Doctor of Letters Degree, History and Human Science, University of Paris; École Pratique des Hautes Études, Paris. *Career:* mem. Société International d'histoire de la Psychiatrie et de la Psychanalyse, Paris. *Publications:* Histoire de la Psychanalyse en France, 1885–1985, 2 vols, 1982, 1986; Madness and Revolution, 1991; Jacques Lacan: Esquisse d'une vie Histoire d'une Systéme de Pensée, 1993; Pourquoi la psychanalyse?, 1999; De Quoi demain dialogue (with Jacques Derrida), 2001; La Famille endèsordre, 2002. Contributions: various publications. *Address:* 89 ave Denfert-Rochereau, 75014 Paris, France.

ROUNTREE, Owen (see Kittredge, William Alfred).

ROUSE, Anne Barrett; Poet and Writer; b. 26 Sept. 1954, Washington, DC, USA. *Education:* BA, History, University of London, 1977. *Career:* Dir, Islington Mind, 1992–95; Visiting Writing Fellow, University of Glasgow, 2000–02; mem. Poetry Society; Writers' Guild. *Publications:* Sunset Grill, 1993; Timing, 1997. Contributions: periodicals. *Honours:* Poetry Book Society Recommendations, 1993, 1997. *Address:* c/o Bloodaxe Books Ltd, Highgreen, Tarset, Northumberland NE48 1RP, England.

ROUSSEAU, George (Sebastian); Prof. of English Literature and Writer; b. 23 Feb. 1941, New York, NY, USA. *Education:* BA, Amherst College, 1962; MA, 1964, PhD, 1966, Princeton University. *Career:* Osgood Fellow in English Literature, 1965–66, Woodrow Wilson Dissertation Fellow, 1966, Princeton University; Book Reviewer, The New York Times, 1967–; Instructor, Harvard University, 1966–68; Asst Prof., 1968–69, Assoc. Prof., 1969–76, Prof. of English, 1976–94, University of California at Los Angeles; Fulbright Resident Prof., West Germany, 1970; Hon. Fellow, Wolfson College, Cambridge, 1974–75; Overseas Fellow, University of Cambridge, 1979; Visiting Fellow Commoner, Trinity College, Cambridge, 1982; Senior Fulbright Resident Scholar, Sir Thomas Browne Institute, Netherlands, 1983; Visiting Exchange Prof., King's College, Cambridge, 1984; Senior Fellow, National Endowment for the Humanities, 1986–87; Visiting Fellow and Waynflete Lecturer, Magdalen College, Oxford, 1993–94; Regius Prof. of English Literature, King's College, University of Aberdeen, 1994–98; Research Prof. of Humanities, De Montfort University, 1999–2002; mem., Faculty of Modern History, Univ. of Oxford, 2003–; mem. many professional organizations. *Publications:* This Long Disease My Life: Alexander Pope and the Sciences (ed. with Marjorie Hope Nicolson), 1968; John Hill's Hypochondriasis, 1969; English Poetic Satire: Wyatt to Byron (with N. Rudenstine), 1969; The Augustan Milieu: Essays Presented to Louis A Landa (ed. with Eric Rothstein), 1970; Tobias Smollett: Bicentennial Essays Presented to Lewis M. Knapp (co-ed.), 1971; Organic Form: The Life of an Idea (ed.), 1972; Goldsmith: The Critical Heritage, 1974; The Renaissance Man in the 18th Century, 1978; The Ferment of Knowledge: Studies in the Historiography of Eighteenth Century Science (ed. with Roy Porter), 1980; The Letters and Private Papers of Sir John Hill, 1981; Tobias Smollett: Essays of Two Decades, 1982; Literature and Science (ed.), 1985; Science and the Imagination: The Berkeley Conference (ed.), 1985; Sexual Underworlds of the Enlightenment (ed. with Roy Porter), 1987; The Enduring Legacy: Alexander Pope Tercentenary Essays (ed. with P.

Rogers), 1988; Exoticism in the Enlightenment (with Roy Porter), 1990; Perilous Enlightenment: Pre- and Post-Modern Discourses: Sexual, Historical, 1991; Enlightenment Crossings: Pre- and Post-Modern Discourses: Anthropological, 1991; Enlightenment Borders: Pre- and Post-Modern Discources: Medical, Scientific, 1991; Hysteria Before Freud (co-author), 1993; Gout: The Patrician Malady, 1998; Framing and Imagining Disease (ed.), 2003; Marguerite Yourcenar: A Biography, 2003. Contributions: Professional journals and general publications. *Honours:* Clifford Prize, 1987; Leverhulme Trust Awardee, 1999–2001. *Address:* Osterley House, Wellshead, Harwell Village, Oxfordshire OX11 0HD, England. *E-mail:* george.rousseau@magdalen.oxford.ac.uk.

ROUX, Jean-Louis; Actor, Theatre Administrator, Writer and Senator; b. 18 May 1923, Montréal, QC, Canada; m. Monique Oligny, 28 Oct. 1950, one s. *Education:* Collège Ste Marie; BA, cum laude, 1943, Medical Studies, 1943–46, University of Montréal. *Career:* Actor in numerous stage, radio and television productions; Founder, Le Théâtre d'Essai de Montréal, 1950; Founder, 1951, Secretary-General, 1953–63, Artistic Dir, 1966–82, Théâtre du Nouveau Monde; Senator of Canada, 1993–96; Lieutenant-Governor, Province of Québec, 1996–97; Chair., Canada Council for the Arts, 1998–; mem. National Theatre School of Canada, life governor; Royal Society of Canada. *Publications:* En Grève (co-author), 1963; Bois-Brulés, 1967; La Tragédie du Roi Lear, 1996; Nous sommes tous des acteurs, 1997. Other: various radio and television scripts. *Honours:* Best Actor, Congrès du Spectacle, 1960; Centenary of Confederation Medal, 1967; Société St-Jean Baptiste Victor-Morin Prize, 1969; Officer, 1971, Companion, 1987, of the Order of Canada; Molson Prize, 1977; World Theatre Award, 1985; Hon. doctorates. *Address:* 4145 Blueridge Crescent, No. 2, Montréal, QC H3H 1S7, Canada.

ROWAN, Deidre (see Williams, Jeanne R.).

ROWAN, Hester (see Robinson, Sheila (Mary)).

ROWBOTHAM, David Harold, AM, BA; poet, writer and journalist; b. 27 Aug. 1924, Toowoomba, Qld, Australia; m. Ethel Jessie Matthews 1952; two d. *Education:* Univ. of Queensland. *Career:* Commonwealth Literary Fund Lecturer in Australian Literature 1956, 1961, 1964; Arts Ed. 1970–80, Literary Ed. 1980–87, Brisbane Courier-Mail; mem. Australian Soc. of Authors, Fellowship of Australian Writers. *Publications:* poetry: Ploughman and Poet 1954, Inland 1958, All the Room 1964, Bungalow and Hurricane 1967, The Makers of the Ark 1970, The Pen of Feathers 1971, Mighty Like a Harp 1974, Selected Poems 1975, Maydays 1980, New and Selected Poems, 1945–93 1994, The Ebony Gates: New & Wayside Poems 1996, Poems for America 2002; fiction: Town and City 1956, The Man in the Jungle 1964; contrib. to numerous magazines and journals, to numerous anthologies world-wide. *Honours:* Grace Leven Prize 1964, Second Prize for Poetry, New South Wales Captain Cook Bi-Centenary Celebrations Literary Competition 1970, Emeritus Fellowship in Australian Literature, Literature Bd, Australia Council 1989. *Address:* 28 Percival Terrace, Holland Park, Brisbane, Qld 4121, Australia. *Website:* www.qct.com.au/rowbotham/.

ROWE, Bridget; British newspaper editor; b. 16 March 1950; m. James Anthony Nolan; one s. *Education:* St Michael's School (Limpsfield). *Career:* Ed Look Now 1971–76, Women's World 1976–81; Asst Ed. The Sun 1981–82; launched News of the World Sunday magazine 1981–86; Ed. Woman's Own 1986–90, TV Times 1990–91, Sunday Mirror 1991–92, The People 1992–96, Man. Dir 1995–98; Man. Dir Sunday Mirror 1995–98, Ed. 1997–98; Dir of Communications National Magazines 1998–99; Content Dir Yava 2000–. *Address:* c/o The People, 1 Canada Sq, Canary Wharf, London E14 5AP, England.

ROWLAND, Iris (see Roberts, Irene).

ROWLAND, Peter Kenneth; Writer; b. 26 July 1938, London, England. *Education:* Graduate, University of Bristol, 1960. *Publications:* The Last Liberal Governments: The Promised Land 1905–1910, 1968; The Last Liberal Governments: Unfinished Business 1911–1914, 1971; Lloyd George, 1975; Macaulay's History of England in the 18th Century (ed.), 1980; Macaulay's History of England from 1485 to 1685 (ed.), 1985; Autobiography of Charles Dickens (ed.), 1988; The Disappearance of Edwin Drood, 1991; Thomas Day 1748–1789: Virtue Almost Personified, 1996; Just Stylish, 1998; Raffles and His Creator, 1999; What's Where in the Saturday Books, 2002. *Address:* 18 Corbett Rd, Wanstead, London E11 2LD, England.

ROWLAND-ENTWISTLE, (Arthur) Theodore Henry, BA, BSc, FRGS; writer; b. 30 July 1925, Clayton-le-Moors, Lancashire, England. *Education:* Open University. *Career:* fellow, Zoological Soc. *Publications:* Famous Composers (with J. Cooke), 1974; Animal Worlds (with J. Cooke), 1975; Famous Explorers (with J. Cooke), 1975; Facts and Records Book of Animals, 1975; Famous Kings and Emperors (with J. Cooke), 1977; The World You Never See: Insect Life, 1977; Our Earth, 1977; The Restless Earth, 1977; Exploring Animal Homes, 1978; Seashore Life (as T. E. Henry), 1983; Fishes (as James Hall-Clarke), 1983; Fact Book of British History (with J. Cooke), 1984; Heraldry, 1984; Houses, 1985; World of Speed, 1985; Confucius, 1986; Stamps, 1986; Nebuchadnezzar, 1986; Rivers and Lakes, 1986; Focus on Rubber, 1986; Great British Architects, 1986; Great British Inventors, 1986; Great British Kings and Queens, 1986; Great British Reformers, 1986; Focus on Coal, 1987; The Royal Marines, 1987; The Secret Service, 1987; The Special Air Service, 1987; Jungles and Rainforests, 1987; Three-Dimensional Atlas of the World, 1988; Flags, 1988; Guns, 1988; Focus on Silk, 1989; Weather and Climate, 1991; Funfax History of Britain, 1993; Question and Answer Quiz Book (with A. Kramer), 1995; World Events and Dates, 1995; Paras, 1997. Contributions: various encyclopaedias and periodicals. *Literary Agent:* Rupert Crew Ltd, 1A King's Mews, London, WC1N 2JA, England. *Address:* W Dene, Stonestile Lane, Hastings, Sussex TN35 4PE, England.

ROWLANDS, John, MA, DPhil; British novelist, critic and editor. *Education:* Univ. of Wales, Univ. of Oxford. *Career:* fmr Prof. of Welsh, Univ. of Wales, Aberystwyth –2003. *Publications include:* T. Rowland Hughes (criticism) 1975, Y Meddwl a'r Dychmyg Cymraeg Llyfrau and Taliesin (general series ed.), The Bloodaxe Book of Modern Welsh Poetry (ed. with Menna Elfyn) 2003. *Address:* c/o Bloodaxe Books Ltd, Highgreen, Tarset, Northumberland NE48 1RP, England. *Website:* www.bloodaxebooks.com.

ROWLING, Joanne Kathleen (J. K.), OBE, BA; British writer; b. 31 July 1965, Chipping Sodbury, England; m. 1st (divorced); one d.; m. 2nd Neil Murray 2001; one s. *Education:* Wyedean Comprehensive School, Exeter Univ., Moray House Teacher Training Coll. *Publications:* Harry Potter and the Philosopher's Stone (aka Harry Potter and the Sorcerer's Stone) (Smarties Prize, British Book Awards Children's Book of the Year) 1997, Harry Potter and the Chamber of Secrets (Smarties Prize, British Book Awards Children's Book of the Year) 1998, Harry Potter and the Prisoner of Azkaban (Smarties Prize) 1999, Harry Potter and the Goblet of Fire 2000, Quidditch Through the Ages by Kennilworthy Whisp 2001, Fantastic Beasts and Where to Find Them by Newt Scamander 2001, Harry Potter and the Order of the Phoenix (WHSmith People's Choice fiction prize 2004) 2003. *Honours:* Premio Príncipe de Asturias 2003. *Literary Agent:* Christopher Little Literary Agency, Ten Eel Brook Studios, 125 Moore Park Road, London, SW6 4PS, England. *Telephone:* (20) 7736-4455. *Fax:* (20) 7736-4490. *Website:* www.jkrowling.com.

ROY, Arundhati; Writer, Artist, Actress and Activist; b. 1960, Bengal, India; m. 1st Gerard Da Cunha (divorced); m. 2nd Pradeep Krishen. *Education:* Delhi School of Architecture. *Publications:* The God of Small Things, 1997; The End of Imagination (essay), 1998; The Cost of Living (essays), 1998; The Great Common Good (essay), 1999; War Is Peace, 2000; The Algebra of Infinite Justice (essays), 2001; Power Politics, 2002. Screenplays: In Which Annie Gives It Those Ones; Electric Moon. Contributions: periodicals. *Honours:* Booker Prize, 1997; Lannan Prize for Cultural Freedom, 2002. *Address:* c/o HarperCollins Publishers, 77–85 Fulham Palace Rd, Hammersmith, London W6 8JB, England.

ROYLE, Nicholas John, BA; British writer; b. 20 March 1963; m. Kate Ryan 1996; one s. one d. *Education:* Queen Mary Coll., London. *Career:* mem. Soc. of Authors. *Publications:* fiction: Counterparts 1993, Saxophone Dreams 1996, The Matter of the Heart 1997, The Director's Cut 2000, Antwerp 2004; editor: Darklands 1991, Darklands 2 1992, A Book of Two Halves 1996, The Tiger Garden: A Book of Writers' Dreams 1996, The Time Out Book of New York Short Stories 1997, The Agony and the Ecstasy 1998, The Ex Files 1998, Neonlit: The Time Out Book of New Writing 1998, The Time Out Book of Paris Short Stories 1999, Neonlit: The Time Out Book of New Writing Vol. 2 1999, The Time Out Book of London Short Stories Vol. 2 2000; contrib. to Independent, Guardian, Time Out, New Statesman, Literary Review. *Literary Agent:* John Saddler, Curtis Brown Ltd, Haymarket House, 28–29 Haymarket, London, SW1Y 4SP, England. *Telephone:* (20) 7393-4400. *Fax:* (20) 7393-4401. *E-mail:* info@curtisbrown.co.uk. *Website:* www.curtisbrown.co.uk. *Address:* 11 Atwood Road, Manchester, M20 6TA, England.

RÓZEWICZ, Tadeusz; Poet and Playwright; b. 9 Oct. 1921, Radomsko, Poland. *Education:* Jagiellonian Univ., Kraków. *Career:* fmr factory worker and teacher; mem. Art Acad. of Leipzig; Corresp. mem., Bavarian Acad. of Fine Arts, 1982–; Acad. of Arts (GDR). *Publications:* Poetry: 15 vols of poetry, incl. Niepokój (Faces of Anxiety); Czerwona rekawiczka (The Red Glove); Czas, który idzie (The Time Which Goes On); Równina (The Plain); Srebrny klos (The Silver Ear); Rozmowa z ksieciem (Conversation with the Prince); Zielona róza (The Green Rose); Nic w plaszczu Prospera (Nothing in Prosper's Overcoat); Twarz (The Face); Duszyczka (A Little Soul); Poezje (Poetry), 1987; Slowo po slowie (Word by Word), 1994; Zawsze fragment (Always the Fragment), 1996; Zawsze fragment: Recycling (Always the Fragment: Recycling), 1999; Matka odchodzi (The Mother Goes), 2000; Nozyk profesora (The Professor's Knife), 2001; Szara strefa, 2002. Plays: Kartoteka (The Card Index); Grupa Laokoona (Laocoön's Group); Swiadkowie albo nasza mala stabilizacja (The Witnesses); Akt przerywany (The Interrupted Act); Smieszny staruszek (The Funny Man); Wyszedl z domu (Gone Out); Spaghetti i miecz (Spaghetti and the Sword); Maja córeczka (My Little Daughter); Stara kobieta wysiaduje (The Old Woman Broods); Na czworakach (On All Fours); Do piachu (Down to Sand); Biale malzenstwo (White Marriage); Odejscie Glodomora (Starveling's Departure); Na powierzchni poematu i w srodku: nowy wybór wierszy; Pulapka (The Trap); Próba rekonstrukcji (Spread Card Index); Kartoteka rozrzucona (The Card Index Scattered). Prose: Tarcza z pajeczyny; Opowiadania wybrane (Selected Stories); Na powierzchni poematu (They Came to See a Poet), 1991; Plaskorzezba (Bas-Relief), 1991; Nasz starszy brat, 1992;

Historia pieciu wierszy, 1993. *Honours:* State Prize for Poetry, 1955, 1956; Home Army Cross, London, 1956; Literary Prize, City of Kraków, 1959; Prize of Minister of Culture and Art, 1962; State Prize 1st Class, 1966; Alfred Jurzykowski Foundation Award, New York, 1966; Medal of 30th Anniversary of People's Poland, 1974; Order of Banner of Labour (2nd class), 1977; Austrian National Prize for European Literature, 1982; Prize of Minister of Foreign Affairs, 1974, 1987; Golden Wreath Prize for Poetry, Yugoslavia, 1987; Dr hc, Wroclaw, 1991, Silesian Univ., Katowice, 1999, Jagiellonian Univ., 2000, Kraków, 2000, Warsaw, 2001; Great Cross of Polonia Restituta Order, 1996; Wladyslaw Reymont Literary Prize, 1999; Nike Literary Prize, 2000. *Address:* ul. Januszowicka 13m 14, 53-135 Wroclaw, Poland. *Telephone:* (71) 3677138.

RUBENS, Bernice Ruth; Author; b. 26 July 1923, Cardiff, Wales; m. Rudi Nassauer, 1947, two d. *Education:* BA, University of Wales, 1944. *Career:* Author, Dir, documentary films on Third World subjects; mem. Fellow, University College, Cardiff. *Publications:* Fiction: Set on Edge, 1960; Madame Sontsatzka, 1962; Mate in Three, 1964; The Elected Member, 1968; Sunday Best, 1970; Go Tell the Lemming, 1972; I Sent a Letter to My Love, 1974; Ponsonby Post, 1976; A Five-year Sentence, 1978; Spring Sonata, 1979; Birds of Passage, 1980; Brothers, 1982; Mr Wakefield's Crusade, 1985; Our Father, 1987; Kingdom Come: A Solitary Grief, 1991; Mother Russia, 1992; Autobiopsy, 1993; Yesterday in the Back Lane, 1995; The Waiting Game, 1997; I, Dreyfus, 1999; Milwaukee, 2001; Nine Lives, 2002; The Sergeant's Tale, 2003. *Honours:* Booker Prize, 1970; American Blue Ribbon for Documentary Film, 1972; Hon. DLitt, University of Wales. *Address:* 213A Goldhurst Terrace, London NW6 3ER, England.

RUBIN, Diana Kwiatkowski; Poet and Writer; b. 30 Dec. 1958, New York, NY, USA; m. Paul Rubin, 4 Jan. 1986, one s. two d. *Education:* BA, Marymount Manhattan College, 1988; MA, New York University, 1994. *Career:* mem. Acad. of American Poets. *Publications:* Spirits in Exile, 1990; Visions of Enchantment, 1991; Dinosauria, 1995. Contributions: Poet; Amelia; Wind; Quest; Fox Cry; Voices International. *Honours:* First Prize, Sparrowgrass Poetry Forum Awards, 1998. *Address:* PO Box 398, Piscataway, NJ 08855, USA.

RUBIN, Larry Jerome; Prof. of English and Poet; b. 14 Feb. 1930, Bayonne, NJ, USA. *Education:* BA, 1951, MA, 1952, PhD, 1956, Emory University. *Career:* Instructor, 1956–58, Asst Prof., 1958–65, Assoc. Prof., 1965–73, Prof., 1973–99, English, Georgia Tech University; mem. Poetry Society of America; Poetry Society of Georgia. *Publications:* The World's Old Way, 1963; Lanced in Light, 1967; All My Mirrors Lie, 1975; Unanswered Calls, 1997. Contributions: New Yorker; Harper's Magazine; The Nation; Poetry; Sewanee Review; London Magazine. *Honours:* Reynolds Lyric Award, Poetry Society of America; Annual Award, Poetry Society of America; Smith-Mundt Award; Fulbright Awards; several grants. *Address:* Box 15014, Druid Hills Branch, Atlanta, GA 30333, USA.

RUBIN, Louis Decimus, Jr; Prof. of English (retd), Publisher (retd), Writer and Ed.; b. 19 Nov. 1923, Charleston, SC, USA; m. Eva Redfield, 2 June 1951, two s. *Education:* College of Charleston, 1940–42; Yale University, 1943–44; BA, University of Richmond, 1946; MA, 1949, PhD, 1954, Johns Hopkins University. *Career:* Instructor in English, Johns Hopkins University, 1948–54; Ed., Hopkins Review, 1949–53, Provincial, 1956–57, Hollins Critic, 1963–69, Louisiana State University Press Southern Literary Studies, 1964–73, 1975–93, Southern Literary Journal, 1969–89; Assoc. Ed., News Leader, Richmond, Virginia, 1956–57; Assoc. Prof., 1957–59, Prof., 1960–67, Hollins College; Prof. of English, 1967–72, University Distinguished Prof. of English, 1972–89, University of North Carolina at Chapel Hill; Founder-Pres., 1982–88, Editorial Dir, 1989–91, Algonquin Books of Chapel Hill; mem. Fellowship of Southern Writers, chancellor, 1991–93; Society for the Study of Southern Literature, pres., 1974–76; South Atlantic MLA; South Carolina Acad. of Authors. *Publications:* Thomas Wolfe: The Weather of His Youth, 1955; No Place on Earth: Ellen Glasgow, James Branch Cabell, and Richmond-in-Virginia, 1959; The Golden Weather, 1961; The Faraway Country: Writers of the Modern South, 1963; The Curious Death of the Novel: Essays in American Literature, 1967; The Teller in the Tale, 1967; George W. Cable: The Life and Times of a Southern Heretic, 1969; The Writer in the South, 1972; Black Poetry in America: Two Essays in Interpretation (with Blyden Jackson), 1974; William Elliott Shoots a Bear: Essays on the Southern Literary Imagination, 1976; Virginia: A Bicentennial History, 1977; The Wary Fugitives: Four Poets and the South, 1978; The Boll Weevil and the Triple Play, 1979; Surfaces of a Diamond, 1981; A Gallery of Southerners, 1982; Before the Game, 1988; The Edge of the Swamp: A Study in the Literature and Society of the Old South, 1989; Small Craft Advisory: A Book About the Building of a Boat, 1991; The Mockingbird in the Gum Tree: A Literary Gallimaufry, 1991; The Heat of the Sun, 1995; Babe Ruth's Ghost: And Other Historical and Literary Speculations, 1996; Seaports of the South: A Journey, 1998; A Memory of Trains: The Boll Weevil and Others, 2000; An Honorable Estate: My Time in the Working Press, 2001. Editor: Over 20 books, including: Southern Renascence: The Literature of the Modern South (with R. D. Jacobs), 1953; The Lasting South (with J. J. Kilpatrick), 1957; South: Modern Southern Literature in its Cultural Settings (with R. D. Jacobs), 1961; The Idea of an American Novel (with J. R. Moore), 1961; The Hollins Poets, 1967; Southern Writing, 1585–1920 (with R. B. Davis and C. H. Holman), 1970; The Comic Imagination in American Literature, 1973; The Literary South, 1979; Southern Writers: A Biographical Dictionary (with Robert Bain and Joseph N. Flora), 1979; The American South: Portrait of a Culture, 1979; The History of Southern Literature (with others), 1985; A Writer's Companion, 1996. Contributions: numerous scholarly journals and periodicals. *Honours:* Guggenheim Fellowship, 1956; Fulbright Professorship to France, 1960; ACLS Fellowship, 1964; Distinguished Virginian Award, 1972; Mayflower Society Award, 1978; Jules F. Landry Award, Louisiana State University Press, 1978; North Carolina Award, 1992; several hon. doctorates. *Address:* 702 Gimghoul Rd, Chapel Hill, NC 27514, USA.

RUBINA, Dina Ilyinichna; Uzbekistan writer; b. 19 Sept. 1953, Tashkent. *Education:* Tashkent State Conservatory. *Career:* music teacher Tashkent Inst. of Culture 1977–90; literary debut in Yunost magazine 1971; emigrated to Israel 1990; book publications, theatrical stagings, film, newspaper editing (Pyatnitza and others); Head Dept of Public and Cultural Relations, The Jewish Agency in Russia 1999–2003. *Films:* Zavtra, kak obychno 1984, Na Verhney Maslovke 2004. *Publications:* The Double-Barrelled Name (short stories) 1990, In Thy Gates 1994, An Intellectual Sat Down on the Road 1995, Here Comes the Messiah 1997, The Escort Angel 1998, The Last Wild Boar from Pontevedra Forest 1998, High Water in Venice 1999, Several Hurried Words of Love (short stories) 2003. *Honours:* Ministry of Culture Award 1982, Arye Dulchin Award (Israel) 1991, Israel Writers' Union Award 1995, Best Book of literary season, France 1996. *Address:* Et Ha'zmir, 11/8, 98491 Maale-Adumim, Israel (Home). *Telephone:* 2-5352435 (Home). *Fax:* 2-5352435 (Home). *E-mail:* d.rubina@mail.ru (Home). *Website:* www.dinarubina.com (Home).

RUDKIN, James David; Dramatist; b. 29 June 1936, London, England; m. Alexandra Margaret Thompson, 3 May 1967, two s. one deceased, two d. *Education:* MA, St Catherine's College, Oxford, 1957–61. *Career:* Judith E. Wilson Fellow, University of Cambridge, 1984; mem. Hellenic Society. *Publications:* Afore Night Come (stage play), 1964; Schoenberg's Moses und Aron (trans. for Royal Opera), 1965; Ashes (stage play), 1974; Cries From Casement as His Bones are Brought to Dublin (radio play), 1974; Penda's Fen (TV film), 1975; Hippolytus (trans. from Euripides), 1980; The Sons of Light (stage play), 1981; The Triumph of Death (stage play), 1981; Peer Gynt (trans. from Ibsen), 1983; The Saxon Shore (stage play), 1986; Rosmersholm (trans. from Ibsen), 1990; When We Dead Waken (trans. from Ibsen), 1990. Opera Libretti: The Grace of Todd, music by Gordon Crosse, 1969; Inquest of Love, music by Jonathan Harvey, 1993; Broken Strings, music by Param Vir, 1994. Contributions: Drama; Tempo; Encounter; Theatre Research Journal. *Honours:* Evening Standard Most Promising Dramatist Award, 1962; John Whiting Drama Award, 1974; Obie Award, New York, 1977; New York Film Festival Gold Medal for Screenplay, 1987; European Film Festival Special Award, 1989; Sony Silver Radio Drama Award, 1994. *Address:* c/o Casarotto Ramsay Ltd, National House, 60–66 Wardour St, London W1V 4ND, England. *Website:* www.davidrudkin.com.

RUDMAN, Mark; poet, critic, editor, translator and academic; b. 11 Dec. 1948, New York, NY, USA; m. Madelaine Bates; one s. *Education:* BA, New School for Social Research, 1971; MFA, Columbia University, 1974. *Career:* Poetry and Criticism Ed., 1975–, Ed.-in-Chief, 1984–, Pequod Journal; Writer-in-Residence, University of Hawaii, 1978, SUNY at Buffalo, 1979, Wabash College, 1979; Adjunct Lecturer, Queens College, CUNY, 1980–81; Lecturer, Parsons School of Design, 1983; Poet-in-Residence and Assoc. Prof., York College, CUNY, 1984–88; Asst Dir and Adjunct Prof., Graduate Creative Writing Program, New York University, 1986–; Adjunct Prof., Columbia University, 1988–91, 1992–; Poet-in-Residence, SUNY at Purchase, 1991; Walt Whitman Poet, 1998; mem. PEN; Poetry Society of America, board of governors, 1984–88. *Publications:* In the Neighboring Cell (poems), 1982; The Mystery in the Garden (chapbook), 1985; By Contraries and Other Poems: 1970–1984, Selected and New, 1986; The Ruin Revived (chapbook), 1986; The Nowhere Steps (poems), 1990; Literature and the Visual Arts (ed.), 1990; Diverse Voices: Essays on Poetry, 1993; Rider (poems), 1994; Realm of Unknowing: Meditations on Art, Suicide, Uncertainty, and Other Transformations, 1995; The Millennium Hotel (poems), 1996; Provoked in Venice (poems), 1999; The Killers (poems), 2000; The Couple, 2001. Translator: Square of Angels, by B. Antonych, 1976; My Sister – Life, by Pasternak, 1983. Contributions: poems and essays in many anthologies and other publications. *Honours:* Acad. of American Poets Award, 1971; PEN Trans. Fellowship, 1976; Yaddo Residencies, 1977, 1983; Ed.'s Award, Co-ordinating Council for Literary Magazines, 1981; Ingram Merrill Foundation Fellowship, 1983–84; Max Hagward Award for Trans., 1984; New York Foundation of the Arts Fellowship, 1988; National Book Critics Circle Award in Poetry, 1994; National Endowment for the Arts Fellowship, 1995; Guggenheim Fellowship, 1996–97. *Address:* 817 West End Avenue, New York, NY 10025, USA.

RUDMAN, Michael P.; American publishing executive; b. 1950, New York. *Education:* Univ of Michigan and New York Univ. *Career:* Pres. Nat. Learning Corpn, also CEO, Dir; Pres. Delaney Books Inc., also CEO, Dir; Pres. Frank Merriwell Inc., also CEO, Dir; mem. Asscn of American Publishers. *Address:* National Learning Corporation, 212 Michael Drive, Syosset, NY 11791, USA.

RUDOLF, Anthony, BA, ; poet, writer and translator; b. 6 Sept. 1942, London, England; m. (divorced); one s. one d. *Education:* Trinity Coll.,

Cambridge, British Inst., Paris. *Career:* co-founder and Ed., Menard Press, London 1969; Advisory Ed., Modern Poetry in Translation 1973–; Adam Lecturer, King's Coll., London 1990; Pierre Rouve Memorial Lecturer, Sofia 2001; Visiting Lecturer, Faculty of Arts and Humanities, London Metropolitan Univ. 2001–03; Royal Literary Fund Fellow, Univ. of Hertfordshire 2003–(05). *Publications:* The Same River Twice 1976, After the Dream: Poems 1964–79 1980, Primo Levi's War Against Oblivion 1990, Mandorla 1999, The Arithmetic of Memory 1999; translations of poetry; contrib. to periodicals and newspapers. *Address:* 8 The Oaks, Woodside Avenue, London, N12 8AR, England. *E-mail:* anthony.rudolf@virgin.net.

RUELL, Patrick (see Hill, Reginald (Charles)).

RUFIN, Jean-Christophe, MD; French writer and doctor; b. 28 June 1952, Bourges; one s. two d. *Education:* Lycées Janson-de-Sailly and Claude Bernard, Paris, Pitié-Salpêtrière School of Medicine, Paris. *Career:* Hosp. Intern, Paris 1975–81, Dir of Clinic 1981–83; Medical Dir Action Int. Contre la Faim (ACF) 1983–85; Chief of Mission of Sec. of State for Human Rights 1986–88; Cultural Attaché French Embassy in Brazil 1989–90; Vice-Pres. Médécins sans Frontières (MSF) 1991–93; Adviser to Minister of Defence 1993–95; Hospital Dr, Nanterre Hosp. 1994–95; Conference Dir Univ. de Paris-Nord 1993–95; Admin. French Red Cross 1995; Dir of Research Inst. des Relations Int. et Stratégiques (Iris) 1996, later Deputy Dir. *Publications:* Le Piège humanitaire 1986, L'Empire et les nouveaux barbares 1992, La Dictature libérale (Prix Jean-Jacques Rousseau) 1994, L'Aventure humanitaire 1994, L'Abyssin (Prix Goncourt, Prix Méditerranée) 1997, Sauver Ispahan 1998, Les Causes perdues (Prix Bergot, Prix Interallié) 1999, Rouge Brésil (Prix Goncourt) 2001. *Honours:* Chevalier des Arts et des Lettres. *Address:* 73 rue du Cherche-Midi, 75006 Paris, France (Home). *E-mail:* jchrufin@club-internet.fr (Home).

RÚFUS, Milan; Slovak poet, literary historian and essayist; b. 10 Dec. 1928, Závazná Poruba; m.; one d. *Education:* Comenius Univ., Bratislava. *Career:* at Inst. of Slovak Language and Literature Faculty of Philosophy Comenius Univ. 1952–89; Assoc. Prof., Lecturer in Slovak Language and Literature Inst. Universitario, Naples 1971–72; mem. Club of Ind. Writers of Slovakia. *Publications:* Until We Have Matured 1956, Bells 1968, A Triptych 1969, People of the Mountains 1969, The Table of the Poor 1972, The Cradle 1972, A Boy is Drawing a Rainbow 1974, Music of Forms (accompanied by paintings by L. Fulla) 1977, Forest (accompanied by photographs by M. Martincek) 1978, Ode to Joy 1981, Severe Bread 1987, A Late Self-Portrait 1993, Reading from Destiny 1996, Dragonfly 1998, Simple One Until the Little Roots of its Hair 2000; children's: Book of Fairy Tales 1975, Saturday Evenings 1979, A Small Well 1985, Silent Fern 1990, Small Prayers 1990, Small Prayers for a Child 1995; essays: Man, Time and Work 1968, Four Epistles to People 1969, On Literature 1974, And What is a Poem 1978, Epistles Old and New 1997, Time of Shy Questions 2001. *Honours:* Hon. LittD (Bratislava); State Prize 1970, Slovak Nat. Prize 1982, World Congress of Slovaks Nat. Prize, Nat. Literature Prize 1996; Tomáš Garrigue Masaryk Order 1990, L'udovít Štúr Order (1st Class) 1993. *Address:* Fialkové údolie 31, 811 01 Bratislava, Slovakia. *Telephone:* (7) 5441-2948.

RUHM, Gerhard; Writer, Poet, Dramatist, Composer and Graphic Artist; b. 12 Feb. 1930, Vienna, Austria. *Education:* Acad. of Music, Vienna, 1945–51. *Career:* mem. Acad. of Fine Arts, Hamburg. *Publications:* Literarisches Cabaret (with H. Artmann and K. Bayer), 1958–59; hosn rosn baa (with H. Artmann and F. Achleitner), 1959; Kinderoper (with H. Artmann and K. Bayer), 1964; Gesammelte Gedichte, 1970; Gesammelte Theaterstücke 1954–1971, 1972; Erste Folger Kurzer Hörstücker, 1973; Zweite Folge kurzer Hörstücke, 1975, 1975; wald: ein deutsches requiem, 1983; Allein, verlassen, verloren: 3 Kurzhörspiele zum Thema Angst (with R. Hughes and Marie Luise Kaschnitz), 1986; leselieder/visuelle Musik, 1986; botschaft an die zukunft: gesammelte sprechtexte, 1988; Geschlechterdings: Chansons, Romanzen, Gedichte, 1990; Theatertexte, 1990; Mit Messer und Gabel, 1995. *Honours:* Asscn of War Blind Radio Prize, 1983; Great Austrian State Prize, 1991. *Address:* Lochnerstrasse 7, 50674 Cologne, Germany.

RUHMKORF, Peter; Poet and Author; b. 25 Oct. 1929, Dortmund, Germany; m. Eva-Marie Titze. *Education:* German Language and Literature, Psychology, Hamburg. *Career:* Writer-in-Residence, University of Texas at Austin, 1969–70; Lecturer, University of Essen, 1974, 1991–92, University of Warwick, England, 1977; mem. Deutsche Akademie für Sprache und Dichtung eV, Darmstadt; Freie Akademie der Künste, Hamburg; PEN. *Publications:* Irdisches Vergnügen in g, 1959; Kunststücke: 50 Gedichte nebst einer Anleitung zum Wildersspruch, 1962; Die Jahre die Ihr kennt: Anfälle und Erinnerungen, 1972; Gesammelte Gedichte, 1976; Strömungslehre I: Poesie, 1978; Haltbar bis Ende, 199, 1979; Auf Wiedersehen in Kenilworth: Ein Märchen in dreizehn Kapiteln, 1980; agar agar: zaurzaurim: Zur Naturgeschichte dees Reims und der menschlichen Anklangsnerven, 1981; Hüter des Misthaufens, 1981; Kleine Fleckenkunde, 1981; Bleib erschütterbar und widersteh, 1984; Dintemann und Schindemann, 1987; Einmalig wie wir alle, 1989; Selbst III/88: Aus der Fassung, 1989; Tabu I: Tagebücher 1989–1991, 1995. *Honours:* Erich Kastner Prize, 1979; Arno Schmidt Prize, 1986; Heinrich Heine Prize, 1988; Georg Buchner Prize, 1993. *Address:* Ovelgönne 50, 22605 Hamburg, Germany.

RUIZ ZAFÓN, Carlos; Spanish writer and screenwriter; b. 25 Aug. 1964, Barcelona. *Education:* Barcelona Coll. of Jesuits, Sarrià. *Career:* fmr dir of publicity, Lorente Agency; moved to Los Angeles, USA to write screenplays 1994. *Publications:* El príncipe de la niebla 1993, La sombra del viento (trans. as The Shadow of the Wind) 2000. *Honours:* Edebé Prize 1993. *Literary Agent:* Antonia Kerrigan Literary Agency, Travesera de Gracia 22, 4°, 1a, 08021 Barcelona, Spain. *Telephone:* (932) 093 820. *Fax:* (934) 144 328. *E-mail:* info@antoniakerrigan.com.

RUKEYSER, Louis (Richard); Economic Writer and Broadcaster; b. 30 Jan. 1933, New York, NY, USA; m. Alexandra Gill, 3 March 1962, three d. *Education:* AB, Princeton University, 1954. *Career:* Reporter, Baltimore Sun Newspapers, 1954–65; Chief Political Correspondent, Baltimore Evening Sun, 1957–59; Chief, London Bureau, 1959–63, Chief Asian Correspondent, 1963–65, Baltimore Sun; Senior Correspondent and Commentator, 1965–73, Paris Correspondent, 1965–66, Chief, London Bureau, 1966–68, Economic Ed. and Commentator, 1968–73, ABC News; Host, Wall $treet Week With Louis Rukeyser, PBS-TV, 1970–2002, Louis Rukeyser's Wall Street, CNBC and Public TV, 2002–; Syndicated Economic Columnist, McNaught Syndicate, 1976–86, Tribune Media Services, 1986–93; Ed.-in-Chief, Louis Rukeyser's Wall Street, 1992–, Louis Rukeyser's Mutual Funds, 1994–. *Publications:* How to Make Money in Wall Street, 1974; What's Ahead for the Economy: The Challenge and the Chance, 1983; Louis Rukeyser's Business Almanac, 1988; Louis Rukeyser's Book of Lists, 1997; Right on the Money, 1998. *Honours:* Overseas Press Club Award, 1963, and Citation, 1964; G. M. Loeb Award, University of Connecticut, 1972; George Washington Honor Medals, Freedoms Foundation, 1972, 1978; Janus Award, 1975; Literary Guild Selections, 1974, 1976, 1984; New York Financial Writers Asscn Award, 1980; Free Enterprise Man of the Year, Texas A & M University, 1987; Women's Economic Round Table Award, 1990; several hon. doctorates. *Address:* 586 Round Hill Rd, Greenwich, CT 06831, USA. *Website:* www.rukeyser.com.

RULE, Jane; Writer and Teacher; b. 28 March 1931, Plainfield, NJ, USA. *Education:* Mills College, Oakland, CA. *Career:* Teacher of English, Concord Acad., Massachusetts, 1954–56; Asst Dir, International House, 1958–59; Intermittent Lecturer in English, 1959–70; Visiting Lecturer in Creative Writing, University of British Columbia, Vancouver, 1972–73; mem. Writers' Union of Canada; PEN. *Publications:* The Desert of the Heart, 1964; This Is Not You, 1970; Against the Season, 1971; Lesbian Images, 1975; Themes for Diverse Instruments, 1975; The Young in One Another's Arms, 1977; Contract With the World, 1980; Outlander, 1981; Inland Passage, A Hot-Eyed Moderate, 1985; Memory Board, 1987; After the Fire, 1989. *Honours:* Canadian Author's Asscn Best Novel of the Year, 1978, Best Story of the Year, 1978; US Gay Academic Union Literature Award, 1978; Fund for Human Dignity Award of Merit, 1983; Hon. Doctor of Letters, University of British Columbia, 1994; Order of British Columbia, 1998. *Literary Agent:* Anne Borchardt, Georges Borchardt Inc, 136 E 57th St, New York, NY 10022, USA. *Address:* The Fork, Rte 1, S19 C 17, Galiano, BC V0N 1P0, Canada.

RUMENS, Carol Ann, PGDip; Writer and Poet; b. 10 Dec. 1944, London, England; m. David Rumens, 30 July 1965, divorced, two d. *Education:* University of London, 1964–65, Arden School of Theatre, Manchester. *Career:* Writing Fellow, University of Kent, 1983–85; Northern Arts Writing Fellow, 1988–90; Writer-in-Residence, Queen's University, Belfast, 1991–, Univ. of Cork 1994, Univ. of Stockholm 1999; Creative Writing Tutor Queen's Univ. Belfast 1995–99, Univ. of Wales, Bangor 2000–; mem. International PEN, FRSL, Society of Authors, The Welsh Academi. *Publications:* A Strange Girl in Bright Colours, 1973; Unplayed Music, 1981; Scenes from the Gingerbread House, 1982; Star Whisper, 1983; Direct Dialling, 1985; Selected Poems, 1987; Plato Park, 1987; The Greening of the Snow Beach, 1988; From Berlin to Heaven, 1989; Thinking of Skins: New and Selected Poems, 1993; Best China Sky, 1995; The Miracle Diet (with Viv Quillin), 1997; Holding Pattern, 1998; Hex, 2002. Contributions: ed., numerous anthologies; periodicals; trans. poems for collections of Russian poetry. *Honours:* Joint Winner, Alice Hunt Bartlett Prize, 1981; Prudence Farmer Award, 1983; Cholmondeley Award, 1984, First Prize BT Section Nat. Poetry Competition 2002, First Prize Peterloo Poetry Competition 2003. *Address:* 100A Tunis Rd, London W12 7EY, England. *E-mail:* els806@bangor.ac.uk (Office); carol@rumens.fslife.co.uk (Home).

RUSH, Norman; Writer; b. 24 Oct. 1933, San Francisco, CA, USA; m. Elsa Rush, one s. one d. *Education:* BA, Swarthmore College, 1956. *Career:* Instructor in English and History and Co-Dir of College A, Rockland Community College, Suffern, New York, 1973–78; Co-Dir, US Peace Corps, Botswana, 1978–83; mem. PEN American Center. *Publications:* Whites (short stories), 1986; Mating (novel), 1991; Mortals, 2003. Contributions: anthologies and periodicals. *Honours:* Aga Khan Prize for the Short Story; Irish Times/Aer Lingus International Fiction Prize; National Book Award; Rosenthal Award, National Acad. of Arts and Letters; Bellagio Fellowship, Rockefeller Foundation. *Address:* 18 High Tor Rd, New City, NY 10956, USA. *E-mail:* rush18@optonline.net.

RUSHDIE, (Ahmed) Salman, MA, FRSL; British writer; b. 19 June 1947, Bombay (now Mumbai), India; m. 1st Clarissa Luard 1976 (divorced 1987, died 1999); one s.; m. 2nd Marianne Wiggins 1988 (divorced 1993); one step-d.; m. 3rd Elizabeth West 1997 (divorced); one s.; m. 4th Padma Lakshmi 2004. *Education:* Cathedral and John Connon Boys' High School, Bombay, Rugby School, England, King's Coll., Cambridge. *Career:* British citizen

1964; mem. Footlights revue, Univ. of Cambridge 1965–68; actor, fringe theatre, London 1968–69; advertising copywriter 1969–73; wrote first published novel Grimus 1973–74; part-time advertising copywriter while writing second novel 1976–80; mem. Int. PEN 1981–, Soc. of Authors 1983–, Exec. Cttee Nat. Book League 1983–, Council Inst. of Contemporary Arts 1985–, British Film Inst. Production Bd 1986–; Hon. Prof. MIT 1993; Hon. Spokesman Charter 88 1989; Exec. mem. Camden Cttee for Community Relations 1977–83. *Television film screenplays:* The Painter and the Pest 1985, The Riddle of Midnight 1988. *Publications:* Grimus 1975, Midnight's Children 1981, Shame (Prix du Meilleur Livre Etranger 1984) 1983, The Jaguar Smile: A Nicaraguan Journey 1987, The Satanic Verses 1988, Is Nothing Sacred (lecture) 1990, Haroun and the Sea of Stories (novel) 1990, Imaginary Homelands: Essays and Criticism 1981–91 1991, The Wizard of Oz 1992, East, West (short stories) 1994, The Moor's Last Sigh (novel) 1995, The Vintage Book of Indian Writing 1947–97 (ed. with Elizabeth West) 1997, The Ground Beneath Her Feet 1999, Fury 2001, Step Across the Line: Collected Non-Fiction 1992–2002 2002; articles for New York Times, Washington Post, The Times and Sunday Times. *Honours:* Distinguished Fellow in Literature, Univ. of East Anglia 1995, Hon. DLitt (Bard Coll.) 1995; Booker McConnell Prize for Fiction 1981, Arts Council Literature Bursary 1981, English Speaking Union Literary Award 1981, James Tait Black Memorial Book Prize 1981, Kurt Tucholsky Prize Sweden 1992, Booker of Bookers Award 1993, Prix Colette Switzerland 1993, Austrian State Prize for European Literature 1994, Whitbread Fiction Award 1996, British Book Awards Author of the Year 1996, London Int. Writers Award 2002; Commdr., Ordre des Arts et des Lettres 1999. *Literary Agent:* Wylie Agency (UK) Ltd, 4–8 Rodney Street, London, N1 9JH, England.

RUSHTON, Julian (Gordon); Emeritus Prof. of Music and Writer; b. 22 May 1941, Cambridge, England; m. Virginia Susan Medlycott Jones, 16 March 1968, divorced 2000, two s. *Education:* BA, 1963, BMus, 1965, MA, 1967, Trinity College, Cambridge; DPhil, Magdalen College, Oxford, 1970. *Career:* Lecturer in Music, University of East Anglia, 1968–74; Lecturer in Music and Fellow, King's College, Cambridge, 1974–81; West Riding Prof. of Music, University of Leeds, 1982–2002; Chair., Editorial Board, Musica Britannica, 1993–; mem. American Musicological Society, corresponding mem., 2000–; Elgar Society; Royal Musical Asscn, pres., 1994–99. *Publications:* W. A. Mozart: Don Giovanni, 1981; The Musical Language of Berlioz, 1983; Classical Music: A Concise History, 1986; W. A. Mozart: Idomeneo, 1993; Berlioz: Roméo et Juliette, 1994; Elgar: Enigma Variations, 1999; The Music of Berlioz, 2001. Contributions: Reference works, books and journals. *Address:* c/o School of Music, University of Leeds, Leeds LS2 9JT, England. *E-mail:* j.g.rushton@leeds.ac.uk.

RUSS, Joanna; Educator and Writer; b. 22 Feb. 1937, New York, NY, USA. *Education:* BA in English, Cornell University, 1957; MFA in Playwriting and Dramatic Literature, Yale University School of Drama, 1960. *Career:* Instructor, 1967–70, Asst Prof. of English, 1970–72, Cornell University; Asst Prof. of English, SUNY at Binghamton, 1972–75, University of Colorado at Boulder, 1975–77; Assoc. Prof. of English, 1977–83, Prof. of English, 1983–90, University of Washington. *Publications:* Fiction: Picnic on Paradise, 1968; And Chaos Died, 1970; The Female Man, 1975; We Who Are About To, 1977; Kittatinny: A Tale of Magic, 1978; The Two of Them, 1978; On Strike Against God, 1980; Extra(Ordinary) People, 1984. Story Collections: The Zanzibar Cat, 1983; The Adventures of Alyx, 1983; The Hidden Side of the Moon, 1987. Non-Fiction: How to Suppress Women's Writing, 1983; Magic Mommas, Trembling Sisters, Puritans and Perverts: Feminist Essays by Joanna Russ, 1985; What Are We Fighting For: Feminists Talk About Sexism, Racism, Class, 1998. Contributions: many books, journals, and periodicals. *Honours:* Nebula Award, 1972; National Endowment for the Humanities Younger Humanist Fellowship, 1974–75; Hugo Gernsback Award, World Science Fiction Convention, 1983; Pilgrim Award, Science Fiction Research Asscn, 1988; James Tiptree Jr Award for Science Fiction, 1991. *Address:* 8961 E Lester St, Tucson, AZ 85915, USA.

RUSSELL, James (see Harknett, Terry).

RUSSELL, John; Art Critic and Writer; b. 22 Jan. 1919, Fleet, England. *Education:* MA, Magdalen College, Oxford, 1940. *Career:* Hon. Attaché, Tate Gallery, 1940–41; Staff, Ministry of Information, 1941–43, Naval Intelligence Division, Admiralty, London, 1943–46; Contributor, 1945–49, Art Critic, 1949–74, The Sunday Times; Art Critic, 1974–82, Chief Art Critic, 1982–91, The New York Times; mem. American Acad. of Arts and Letters, 1966; Guggenheim Fellowship, 2000–01; Trustee State Hermitage Museum, St Petersburg, Russia 2002–. *Publications:* Shakespeare's Country, 1942; British Portrait Painters, 1945; Switzerland, 1950; Logan Pearsall Smith, 1950; Erich Kleiber, 1956; Paris, 1960; Seurat, Private View (with Bryan Robertson and Lord Snowdon), 1965; Max Ernst, 1967; Henry Moore, 1968; Ben Nicholson, 1969; Pop Art Redefined (with Suzi Gablik), 1969; The World of Matisse, 1970; Francis Bacon, 1971; Édouard Vuillard, 1971; The Meanings of Modern Art, 1981; Reading Russell, 1989; London, 1994; Matisse: Father and Son, 1999. Contributions: various publications including New York Review of Books, 1999–2000. *Honours:* Hon. Mem., Century Asscn, New York, 2000. *Address:* 166 E 61st St, New York, NY 10021, USA.

RUSSELL, Martin James; Writer; b. 25 Sept. 1934, Bromley, Kent, England. *Career:* mem. CWA; Detection Club. *Publications:* No Through Road, 1965; The Client, 1975; Mr T, 1977; Death Fuse, 1980; Backlash, 1981; The Search for Sara, 1983; A Domestic Affair, 1984; The Darker Side of Death, 1985; Prime Target, 1985; Dead Heat, 1986; The Second Time is Easy, 1987; House Arrest, 1988; Dummy Run, 1989; Mystery Lady, 1992; Leisure Pursuit, 1993. *Address:* 15 Breckonmead, Wanstead Rd, Bromley, Kent BR1 3BW, England.

RUSSELL, Mary D(oria); Educator and Palaeoanthropologist; b. 19 Aug. 1950, Elmhurst, IL, USA; m. Donald J. Russell, 5 Sept. 1970, one s. *Education:* BA, University of Illinois, 1972; MA, Northeastern University, 1976; PhD, Palaeoanthropology, University of Michigan, 1983. *Career:* Invited Lecturer, various educational institutions, 1981–84; Prosector, Special Lecturer, Dept of Oral Biology, School of Dentistry, 1983, Clinical Instructor, 1984–86, Adjunct Prof., Dept of Anthropology, 1986, Case Western Reserve University, Cleveland, Ohio; Proprietor, North Coast Technical Writing, South Euclid, Ohio, 1986–92; mem. SFWA; Authors' Guild. *Publications:* The Sparrow: A Novel, 1996; Children of God: A Novel, 1998. Contributions: Scientific journals and periodicals. *Honours:* Tiptree Award, 1996; BSFA Best Novel, 1997; Arthur C. Clarke Award, 1997; John W. Campbell Award, 1998; Cleveland Arts Council Prize for Literature, 1998; American Library Asscn Readers' Choice Award, 1999; Kurd Lasswitz Award, Germany, 2001; Spectrum Classic Award, 2001. *Literary Agent:* Jane Dystel Literary Management, 1 Union Sq. W, New York, NY 10003, USA. Address; 4083 Princeton Blvd, South Euclid, OH 44121, USA. *E-mail:* mary@marydoriarussell.info.

RUSSELL, Paul; Prof. of English and Writer; b. 1 July 1956, Memphis, Tennessee, USA. *Education:* AB in English, Oberlin College, 1978; MA in English, 1982, MFA in Creative Writing, 1982, PhD in English, 1983, Cornell University. *Career:* Asst Prof., 1983–90, Assoc. Prof., 1990–96, Prof. of English, 1996–, Vassar College; Co-Founder and Ed., The Poughkeepsie Review, 1987–89. *Publications:* Fiction: The Salt Point, 1990; Boys of Life, 1991; Sea of Tranquillity, 1994; The Coming Storm, 1999; War Against the Animals, 2003. Non-Fiction: The Gay 100: A Ranking of the Most Influential Gay Men and Lesbians, Past and Present, 1995. Contributions: anthologies, journals, and periodicals. *Honours:* National Endowment for the Arts Creative Writers Fellowship, 1993; Regional Winner, GRANTA-Best of Young American Novelists, 1995; Ferro-Grumley Award for Fiction, 2000. *Address:* c/o Dept of English, Vassar College, Poughkeepsie, NY 12604, USA. *E-mail:* russell@vassar.edu.

RUSSELL, Sharman Apt; Asst Prof. of Writing and Author; b. 23 July 1954, Edwards Air Force Base, CA, USA; m. Peter Russell, 24 Jan. 1981, one s. one d. *Education:* BS, Conservation and Natural Resources, University of California at San Diego and Berkeley, 1976; MFA, Creative Writing, University of Montana, 1980. *Career:* Asst Prof. of Writing, Western New Mexico University, Silver City, 1981–; Faculty, MFA Program in Creative Non-Fiction, Antioch University, Los Angeles, 1997–. *Publications:* Built to Last: An Architectural History of Silver City, New Mexico (with Susan Berry), 1986; Frederick Douglas, 1987; Songs of the Fluteplayer: Seasons of Life in the Southwest, 1991; Kill the Cowboy: A Battle of Mythology in the New West, 1993; The Humpbacked Fluteplayer, 1994; When the Land was Young: Reflections on American Archaeology, 1996. Contributions: anthologies, reviews, and journals. *Honours:* Henry Joseph Jackson Award for Non-Fiction, San Francisco, 1989; Pushcart Prize, 1990; Mountain and Plains Booksellers Award, 1992; New Mexico Presswomen's Zia Award, 1992. *Address:* 1113 West St, Silver City, NM 88061, USA.

RUSSELL, William (Willy) Martin; British dramatist and writer; b. 23 Aug. 1947, Liverpool, England; m. Ann Seagroatt 1969; one s. two d. *Education:* Certificate of Education, St Katherine's College of Education, Liverpool. *Career:* Teacher, 1973–74; Fellow, Creative Writing, Manchester Polytechnic, 1977–78. *Publications:* Theatre: Blind Scouse, 1971–72; When the Reds (adaptation), 1972; John, Paul, George, Ringo and Bert (musical), 1974; Breezeblock Park, 1975; One for the Road, 1976; Stags and Hens, 1978; Educating Rita, 1979; Blood Brothers (musical), 1983; Our Day Out (musical), 1983; Shirley Valentine, 1986. Television Plays: King of the Castle, 1972; Death of a Young Young Man, 1972; Break In (for schools), 1974; Our Day Out, 1976; Lies (for schools), 1977; Daughter of Albion, 1978; Boy With Transistor Radio (for schools), 1979; One Summer (series), 1980. Radio Play: I Read the News Today (for schools), 1979. Screenplays: Band on the Run, 1979; Educating Rita, 1981. *Honours:* Hon. MA, Open University; Hon. Dir, Liverpool Playhouse. *Literary Agent:* Casarotto Company Ltd, National House, 60–66 Wardour Street, London, W1V 3HP, England.

RUSSO, Albert, BSc; writer and poet; b. 26 Feb. 1943, Kamina, Belgian Congo; one s. one d. *Education:* New York University. *Career:* Co-Ed., Paris Transcontinental and Plurilingual Europe; Mem., Jury, Prix de l'Europe, 1982–, Neustadt International Prize for Literature, 1996; mem. Asscn of French Speaking Writers; Authors' Guild of America; PEN. *Publications:* Incandescences, 1970; Eclats de malachite, 1971; La Pointe du diable, 1973; Mosaique New Yorkaise, 1975; Albert Russo: An Anthology, 1987; Sang Mêlé ou ton Fils Léopold, 1990; Le Cap des Illusions, 1991; Futureyes/Dans la nuit bleu-fauve, 1992; Kaleidoscope, 1993; Eclipse sur le Lac Tanganyika, 1994; Venetian Thresholds, 1995; Painting the Tower of Babel, 1996; Zapinette, 1996; Poetry and Peanuts (collection), 1997; Zapinette Video (novel), 1998; Mixed Blood (novel), 1999; Eclipse over Lake Tanganyika (novel), 1999; L'amant de mon père (novel), 2000; Zapinette à New York (novel), 2000. Short Stories: Beyond the Great Water; Unmasking Hearts; The Age of the Pearl, 2001; Zany: Zapinette New York (novel), 2001; Zapinette chez le Belges (novel), 2002; L'amant de mon père: journal romain (novel), 2003; L'ancêtre noire (novel), 2003; Sangue misto (novel), 2003; ROMAdiva (photography and poems) 2004; Le Tour du Monde de la poésie gay (poems) 2004. Contributions: professional journals and BBC World Service. *Honours:* Willie Lee Martin Short Story Award, 1987; Silver Medal, 1985; British Diversity Award, 1997; AAS Memorial Trophy for Best Overseas Entry in Poetry, 1999; AAS poetry prize 2001. *Address:* BP 640, 75826 Paris Cédex 17, France. *E-mail:* albert.russo@wanadoo.fr. *Website:* www.albertrusso.com.

RUTSALA, Vern, BA, MFA; writer, poet and teacher; b. 5 Feb. 1934, McCall, ID, USA; m. Joan Colby 1957; two s. one d. *Education:* Reed College, University of Iowa. *Career:* mem. PEN; Poetry Society of America; Associated Writing Programs. *Publications:* The Window, 1964; Small Songs, 1969; The Harmful State, 1971; Laments, 1975; The Journey Begins, 1976; Paragraphs, 1978; The New Life, 1978; Walking Home from the Icehouse, 1981; Backtracking, 1985; The Mystery of Lost Shoes, 1985; Ruined Cities, 1987; Selected Poems, 1991; Little-Known Sports, 1994; Greatest Hits: 1964–2002, 2002; A Handbook for Writers 2004; The Moment's Equation 2004. Contributions: New Yorker; Esquire; Poetry; Hudson Review; Harper's; Atlantic; American Poetry Review; Paris Review. *Honours:* National Endowment for the Arts Fellowships, 1974, 1979; Northwest Poetry Prize, 1976; Guggenheim Fellowship, 1982; Carolyn Kizer Poetry Prizes, 1988, 1997; Masters Fellowship, Oregon Arts Commission, 1990; Hazel Hall Award, 1992; Juniper Prize, 1993; Duncan Lawrie Prize, Arvon Foundation, 1994; Richard Snyder Prize 2004. *Address:* 2404 NE 24th Avenue, Portland, OR 97212, USA.

RUTTER, Michael Llewellyn; Prof. of Developmental Psychiatry and Writer; b. 15 Aug. 1933, Brummanna, Lebanon; m. Marjorie Heys, 27 Dec. 1958, one s. two d. *Education:* MB ChB, 1950–55, MD, 1963, University of Birmingham; DPM, University of London, 1961. *Career:* Prof. of Developmental Psychopathology, University of London; Social, Genetic and Developmental Psychiatry Research Centre; mem. American Acad. of Arts and Sciences, hon. foreign mem.; Royal College of Psychiatrists, fellow; Royal College of Physicians, fellow; Fellow, Royal Society, 1997–; Pres., Society for Research into Child Development, 1999–2001; Fellow, British Acad., 2002–. *Publications:* Depression in Young People: Development and Clinical Perspectives (co-ed.), 1986; Language Development and Disorders (co-ed.), 1987; Treatment of Autistic Children (co-ed.), 1987; Parenting Breakdown: The Making and Breaking of Intergenerational Links (co-author), 1988; Assessment and Diagnosis in Child Psychopathology, 1988; Straight and Devious Pathways From Childhood to Adulthood, 1990; Biological Risk Factors for Psychosocial Disorders, 1991; Developing Minds: Challenge and Continuity Across the Lifespan, 1993; Stress, Risk and Resilience in Children and Adolescents, Processes, Mechanisms and Interventions (co-ed.), 1994; Development Through Life: A Handbook for Clinicians (co-ed.), 1994; Psychosocial Disorders in Young People: Time Trends and Their Causes (co-ed.), 1995; Behavioural Genetics (co-author), third edn, 1997; Antisocial Behaviour by Young People (co-author), 1998; Sex Differences in Antisocial Behaviour (co-author), 2001; Child and Adolescent Psychiatry (co-ed.), fourth edn, 2002. Contributions: numerous professional journals. *Honours:* 10 hon. doctorates; Knight Baronet, 1992; American Psychological Asscn Distinguished Scientific Contribution Award, 1995; Castilla del Pino Prize for Achievement in Psychiatry, Córdoba, Spain, 1995; Hon. Fellow, Royal Society of Medicine, 1996; Hon. Founding Fellow, Royal College of Paediatrics and Child Health, 1996. *Address:* PO Box 80, SGDP Research Centre, Institute of Psychiatry, De Crespigny Park, Denmark Hill, London SE5 8AF, England.

RÜTZ, Michael (see Falkenlöwe, Michael Sixten Joachim).

RYCKMANS, Pierre, (Simon Leys); Belgian scholar and writer; b. 28 Sept. 1935, Brussels; m. Hanfang Chang 1964; three s. one d. *Career:* mem. Académie Royale de Langue et Littérature Françaises, Brussels; Fellow, Australian Acad. of the Humanities. *Publications:* La vie et l'oeuvre de Su Renshan, rebelle, peintre et fou, 1970; Shitao: Les propos sur la peinture du Moine Citrouille-amère, 1970; Chinese Shadows, 1977; The Burning Forest, 1985; The Death of Napoleon, 1991, 1992; The Analects of Confucius, 1997; Essais sur la Chine, 1998; L'ange et le cachalot, 1998; Protée et autres essais, 2001; Les Naufragés du Batavia, 2003; La Mer dans la littérature française 2003. Contributions: The New York Review of Books; Commentaire; Others. *Honours:* Officier, Ordre de Léopold; Commdr, Ordre des Arts et des Lettres; Prix Stanislas Julien, Institut de France; Prix Jean Walter, Académie Française; Prix Renaudot; Prix Henri Gal, Académie Française; The Independent Best Foreign Fiction Award, London; Christina Stead Award, Sydney. *Address:* 6 Bonwick Place, Garran, ACT 2605, Australia.

S

SAADAWI, Nawal al-; Novelist, Essayist and Medical Practitioner; b. 27 Oct. 1931, Kafr Tahla, Egypt; m. 1st Ahmed Helmi (divorced); m. 2nd (divorced); m. 3rd Sherif Hetata 1964; one s. one d. *Education:* MD, Cairo Univ., 1955; MA, Public Health, Columbia Univ., New York, 1966. *Career:* novelist and writer, particularly on feminist issues, 1956–; worked Rural Health Centre, Tahla, 1955–57; Dir.-Gen., Ministry of Health, 1958–72; fmr Ed.-in-Chief, Health magazine, Asst Gen.-Sec., Medical Asscn, researcher, Faculty of Medicine, Ain Shams Univ., Cairo; psychiatrist, 1974–; writer, High Institute of Literature and Science, 1973–78; f., Pres., Arab Women's Solidarity Asscn, 1982–91; worked for UN as Dir, African Training and Research Center for Women in Ethiopia, 1978–80, adviser for the United Nations Economic Commission for West Africa, Lebanon. *Publications:* Memoirs of a Woman Doctor, 1958; Two Women in One, 1968; Women and Sex 1971; She Has No Place in Paradise (short story), 1972; Woman at Point Zero, 1975; God Dies by the Nile, 1976; The Hidden Face of Eve: Women in the Arab World, 1977; The Circling Song, 1977; The Veil (short story), 1978; Death of an Ex-Minister, 1979; Memoirs from the Women's Prison, 1983; My Travels Around the World, 1986; The Fall of the Iman, 1987; The Innocence of the Devil, 1992; Nawal al-Saadawi in the Dock, 1993; The Well of Life and The Thread: Two Short Novels, 1993; The Nawal al-Saadawi Reader, 1997; Daughter of Isis: The Autobiography of Nawal al-Saadawi, 1999; Walking Through Fire: A Life of Nawal al-Saadawi, 2002. Contributions: newspapers and magazines. *Honours:* High Council of Literature Award, 1974; Short Story Award, Cairo, 1974; Franco-Arab Literary Award, Paris, 1982; Literary Award of Gubran, 1988; First Degree Decoration of the Republic of Libya, 1989; Hon. DUniv., York, 1994.

SABATIER, Robert; Author and Poet; b. 17 Aug. 1923, Paris, France; m. Christiane Lesparre, 1957. *Career:* mem. Académie Goncourt. *Publications:* Alain et le nègre, 1953; Le marchand de sable, 1954; Le goût de la cendre, 1955; Les fêtes solaires, 1955; Boulevard, 1956; Canard au sang, 1958; St Vincent de Paul; Dédicace d'un navire, 1959; La Sainte-Farce, 1960; La mort du figuier, 1962; Dessin sur un trottoir, 1964; Les poisons délectables, 1965; Le Chinois d'Afrique, 1966; Dictionaire de la mort, 1967; Les châteaux de millions d'années, 1969; Les allumettes suédoises, 1969; Trois sucettes à la menthe, 1972; Noisettes sauvages, 1974; Histoire de la poésie française des origines à nos jours, eight vols, 1975; Icare et autres poèmes, 1976; Les enfants de l'été, 1978; Les fillettes chantantes, 1980; L'oiseau de demain, 1981; Les années secrétes de la vie d'un homme, 1984; David et Olivier, 1986; Lecture, 1987; La souris verte, 1990; Le livre de la déraison souriante, 1991; Olivier et ses amis, 1993; Ecriture, 1993; Le cygne noir, 1995; Le lit de la merveille, 1997; Les masques et le miroir, 1998; Le sourire aux lèvres, 2000. *Honours:* Commdr, Légion d'honneur; Commdr, Ordre nat. du Mérite; Commdr, Ordre des Arts et des Lettres; Lauréat, Société des gens de lettres, 1961; Grand Prix de Poésie, l'Académie Française, 1969. *Address:* 64 blvd Exelmans, 75016 Paris, France.

SÁBATO, Ernesto; Writer; b. 24 June 1911, Rojas, Argentina; m. Matilde Kusminsky-Richter; two s. *Education:* Universidad Nacional de la Plata. *Career:* Dir of Cultural Relations (retd), Argentina; Lectured in many universities; mem. Comisión Nacional sobre Desaparición de Personas (CONADEP), pres., 1984; Club of Rome. *Publications:* Uno y el universo, 1945; Hombres y engranajes, 1951; Heterodoxia, 1953; El escritor y sus fantasmas, 1963; Tres aproximaciones a la literatura de nuestro tiempo (essays), 1969; El túnel, 1947; Sobre héroes y tumbas, 1961; Abaddon el exterminador (novel), 1976; La resistencia; Narrativa completa, 1995; Apologias y rechazos, 1995; Antes del fin, 1999. *Honours:* Ribbon of Honour, Argentine Society of Letters; Prize of the Institution of Foreign Relations, Stuttgart, 1973; Grand Prize of Argentine Writers' Society, 1974; Prix Meilleur Livre Étranger, Paris, 1977; Chevalier, Ordre des Arts et des Lettres; Chevalier, Légion d'honneur, 1978; Gran Cruz de la República Española, 1984; Gabriela Mistral Prize, 1984; Cervantes Prize, 1984; Jerusalem Literary Prize, 1989; Gold medal, Círculo de Bellas Artes de Madrid, 2002. *Address:* Langeri 3135, Santos Lugares, Argentina.

SABATO, Haim; Israeli writer; b. Cairo, Egypt. *Publications:* Adjusting Sights, Aleppo Tales 2004. *Honours:* Sapir Prize. *Address:* c/o The Toby Press, PO Box 8531, New Milford, CT 06776-8531, USA. *Website:* www .tobypress.com.

SABUROV, Yevgeny Fedorovich, DEconSc; Russian economist and poet; b. 13 Feb. 1946, Crimea; m. Tatiana Petrovna; three d. *Education:* Moscow State Univ. *Career:* researcher econ. inst. in Moscow –1990; Deputy Minister of Educ. of Russian Fed. 1990–91; project leader Programme of Econ. Reform in Russia April–Aug. 1991; Deputy Prime Minister, Minister of Econ. Aug.–Nov. 1991; Dir Cen. for Information and Social Tech. of Russian Govt 1991–94; Deputy Head of Govt of Repub. of Crimea Feb.–Oct. 1994; Prof. Acad. of Econs; Dir Investment Research Inst. 1995–; Chief Consultant, Menatep Bank 1995–; Chair. Bd of Guardians, Inst. for Urban Econs 1996–; Chair. Bd of Dirs. Confidential and Investment Bank 1999–2000, Deputy Chair. 2000–; mem. Acad. of Information, Acad. of Social Sciences; poetry published in Europe since 1970, in Russia since 1990. *Publications:* Gunpowder Conspiracy (poems) 1996, On the Edge of the Lake (selected poems); over 100 articles on problems of econ. reform in Russia; numerous verses in periodicals. *Address:* Confidential and Investment Bank, Sadovnicheskaya 84/3–7, 113035 Moscow, Russia. *Telephone:* (095) 958-24-26. *Fax:* (095) 958-24-28.

SACHAR, Louis; Children's Author; b. 20 March 1954, East Meadow, NY, USA; m. Carla 1985; one d. *Education:* Economics, Univ. of California at Berkeley, 1976; Hastings College of Law in San Francisco, 1980. *Career:* fmr lawyer. *Publications:* Sideways Stories from Wayside School, 1977; Johnny's in the Basement, 1983; Someday, Angeline, 1983; Sixth Grade Secrets, 1987; There's a Boy in the Girls' Bathroom, 1987; Dogs Don't Tell Jokes, 1991; The Boy Who Lost His Face, 1997; Holes, 1998. *Honours:* National Book Award; New York Times Book Review Notable Children's Book of the Year; New York Times Outstanding Book of the Year; School Library Journal Best Book of the Year; Publishers Weekly Best Book of the Year; Newbery Award. *Address:* c/o Bloomsbury Publishing PLC, 38 Soho Sq., London W1V 5DF, England.

SACKS, Jonathan Henry; Rabbi and Author; b. 8 March 1948, London, England; m. Elaine Taylor 1970; one s. two d. *Education:* Christ's College Finchley, Gonville & Caius College, Cambridge, New College, Oxford, London Univ., Jews' College, London and Yeshivat Etz Hayyim, London. *Career:* Lecturer in Moral Philosophy, Middlesex Polytechnic, 1971–73; Lecturer in Jewish Philosophy, Jews' College, London, 1973–76, in Talmud and Jewish Philosophy, 1976–82, Chief Rabbi Lord Jakobovits Prof. (first incumbent) in Modern Jewish Thought, 1982–, Dir Rabbinic Faculty, 1983–90, Prin., 1984–90; Chief Rabbi of the United Hebrew Congregations of the British Commonwealth of Nations, 1991–; Assoc. Pres., Conf. of European Rabbis, 2000–; Visiting Prof. of Philosophy, Univ. of Essex, 1989–90; currently Visiting Prof. of Philosophy, Hebrew Univ., Jerusalem, and of Theology and Religious Studies, King's College, London; rabbi, Golders Green Synagogue, London, 1978–82, Marble Arch Synagogue, London, 1983–90; Ed., Le'ela (journal), 1985–90; Sherman Lecturer, Manchester Univ., 1989; Reith Lecturer, 1990; Cook Lecturer, 1997; mem. CRAC. *Publications:* Torah Studies, 1986; Tradition and Transition (essays), 1986; Traditional Alternatives, 1989; Tradition in an Untraditional Age, 1990; The Persistence of Faith (Reith Lecture), 1991; Orthodoxy Confronts Modernity (Ed.), 1991; Crisis and Covenant, 1992; One People?: Tradition, Modernity and Jewish Unity, 1993; Will We Have Jewish Grandchildren?, 1994; Faith in the Future, 1995; Community of Faith, 1995; The Politics of Hope, 1997; Morals and Markets, 1999; Celebrating Life, 2000; Radical Then Radical Now, 2001; The Dignity of Difference: How to Avoid the Clash of Civilizations, 2002; The Chief Rabbi's Hagadah, 2003. *Honours:* Presentation Fellow, King's College, London, 1993; Hon. Fellow, Gonville and Caius College, Cambridge, 1993; Hon. DD (Cantab.), 1993, (Archbishop of Canterbury) 2001; Dr hc, Middlesex Univ., 1993, Haifa Univ., Israel, 1996, Yeshiva Univ., NY, 1997, St Andrews Univ., 1998; Jerusalem Prize, 1995; Hon. LLD, Univ. of Liverpool, 1997. *Address:* 735 High Rd, London N12 0US, England. *Telephone:* (20) 8343-6301. *Fax:* (20) 8343-6310. *E-mail:* info@chiefrabbi.org. *Website:* www.chiefrabbi.org.

SACKS, Oliver (Wolf); Neurologist and Writer; b. 9 July 1933, London, England. *Education:* BA, 1954, MA, 1958, BM, 1958, BCh, 1958, Queen's College, Oxford; University of California at Los Angeles, 1962–65. *Career:* Intern, Middlesex Hospital, London, 1958–60, Mt Zion Hospital, San Francisco, 1961–62; Resident in Neurology, University of California at Los Angeles, 1962–65; Fellow in Neurochemistry and Neuropathology, 1965–66, Instructor, 1966–75, Asst Prof., 1975–78, Assoc. Prof., 1978–85, Clinical Prof. of Neurology, 1985–, Albert Einstein College of Medicine, Yeshiva University, New York City; Staff Neurologist, Beth Abraham Hospital, New York City, 1966–. *Publications:* Migraine, 1970; Awakenings, 1973; A Leg to Stand On, 1984; The Man Who Mistook His Wife for a Hat and Other Clinical Tales, 1985; Seeing Voices: A Journey into the World of the Deaf, 1989; An Anthropologist on Mars: Seven Paradoxical Tales, 1995; The Island of the Colourblind, 1996; Uncle Tungsten, 2001; Oaxaca Journal, 2002. Contributions: newspapers and journals. *Honours:* Hawthornden Prize, 1974; Oskar Pfister Award, American Psychiatric Asscn, 1988; Guggenheim Fellowship, 1989; Harold D. Vursell Memorial Award, American Acad. of Arts and Letters, 1989; Odd Fellows Book Award, 1990; Scriptor Award, University of Southern California, 1991; Professional Support Award, National Headache Foundation, 1991; Presidential Citation, American Acad. of Neurology, 1991; Jewish Quarterly Wingate Literary Prize for Non-Fiction, 2002; Hon. doctorates. *Address:* 2 Horatio St No. 3G, New York, NY 10014, USA.

SADDLEMYER, (Eleanor) Ann, OC, BA, MA, PhD, FRSA; Canadian critic, theatre historian and educator; b. 28 Nov. 1932, Prince Albert, SK, Canada. *Education:* University of Saskatchewan, Queen's University, Bedford College, University of London, England. *Career:* Faculty, University of Victoria, BC, 1960–71; Faculty, Victoria College, 1971–, Dir, Graduate Centre for the Study of Drama, 1972–77, 1985–88, Master, Massey College, 1988–95, Prof. and Master Emeritus, 1995, University of Toronto; Berg Chair, New York University, 1975; mem. International Asscn for Study of Anglo-Irish Literature; Asscn for Canadian Theatre Research, founding pres.; Colin Smythe Publishing, board of dirs; Canadian Theatre Museums

Asscn, board. *Publications:* The World of W. B. Yeats, 1965; In Defence of Lady Gregory, Playwright, 1966; J. M. Synge Plays, Books I and II, 1968; Synge and Modern Comedy, 1968; Letters to Molly: J. M. Synge to Maire O'Neill, 1971; Lady Gregory Plays, 4 vols, 1971; Theatre Business, 1982; The Collected Letters of J. M. Synge, 2 vols, 1983–84; Lady Gregory Fifty Years After, 1987; Early Stages: Essays on the Theatre in Ontario 1800–1914, 1990; Synge's Playboy of the Western World and Other Plays, 1995; Later Stages: Essays on the Theatre in Ontario, World War I to the 1950s, 1997; Becoming George: The Wife of Mrs W. B. Yeats, 2002. Contributions: Professional journals. *Honours:* Royal Society of Canada, 1976; Hon. doctorates, Queen's, 1977, Victoria, 1989, McGill, 1989, Windsor, 1990, Saskatchewan, 1991, Toronto, 1999, Concordia, 2000, universities; British Acad. Rosemary Crawshay Award, 1986; Alumni Award of Excellence, University of Toronto, 1991; Woman of Distinction, 1994; M. L. Rosenthal Award 2001, Queen Elizabeth II Jubilee Medal 2002. *Address:* 10876 Madrona Drive, Sidney, BC V8L 5N9, Canada.

SADGROVE, Sidney Henry, (Lee Torrance); Artist, Teacher and Writer; b. 1920, England. *Career:* mem. Writers Guild of Great Britain. *Publications:* You've Got To Do Something, 1967; A Touch of the Rabbits, 1968; The Suitability Factor, 1968; Stanislaus and the Princess, 1969; A Few Crumbs, 1971; Stanislaus and the Frog, 1972; Paradis Enow, 1972; Stanislaus and the Witch, 1973; The Link, 1975; The Bag, 1977; Half Sick of Shadows, 1977; Bleep, 1977; All in the Mind, 1977; Icary Dicary Doc, 1978, Angel, 1978; Filling, 1979; First Night, 1980; Only on Friday, 1980; Hoodunnit, 1984; Pawn en Prise, 1985; Just for Comfort, 1986; Tiger, 1987; State of Play, 1988; Warren, 1989; Dear Mrs Comfett, 1990. *Address:* Pimp Barn, Withyham, Hartfield, Sussex TN7 4BB, England.

SADIE, Stanley (John); Musicologist, Lexicographer and Writer; b. 30 Oct. 1930, Wembley, Middlesex, England; m. 1st Adèle Bloom, 10 Dec. 1953, deceased 1978, two s. one d.; m. 2nd Julie Anne McCornack Vertrees, 18 July 1978, one s. one d. *Education:* BA, 1953, Mus B, 1953, MA, 1957, PhD, 1958, University of Cambridge. *Career:* Faculty, Trinity College of Music, London, 1957–65; Music Critic, The Times of London, 1964–81; Ed., The Musical Times, 1967–87; Chair., Pres., Handel House Trust, 1992–; mem. Critics Circle; International Musicological Society, pres., 1992–97; Royal Musical Asscn, pres., 1989–94; American Musicological Society. *Publications:* Handel, 1962; The Pan Book of Opera (with Arthur Jacobs), 1964; Mozart, 1966; Beethoven, 1967; Handel, 1968; Handel Concertos, 1972; The New Grove Dictionary of Music and Musicians (ed.), 20 vols, 1980, revised edn, 29 vols, 2001; The New Grove Mozart, 1982; The New Grove Dictionary of Musical Instruments (ed.), three vols, 1984; The Cambridge Music Guide (with Alison Latham), 1985; The New Grove Dictionary of American Music (ed. with H. Wiley Hitchcock), 4 vols, 1986; Mozart Symphonies, 1986; The Grove Concise Dictionary of Music (ed.), 1988; Handel Tercentenary Collection (ed. with A Hicks), 1988; History of Opera (ed.), 1989; Performance Practice (ed. with Howard M. Brown), 2 vols, 1989; Man and Music (general ed.), 8 vols, 1989–93; Music Printing and Publishing (co-ed.), 1990; The New Grove Dictionary of Opera (ed.), 4 vols, 1992; Wolfgang Amadè Mozart: Essays on His Life and Music (ed.), 1995; The New Grove Book of Operas (ed.), 1996. Contributions: Professional journals and general publications. *Honours:* CBE, 1982; Hon. LittD, University of Leicester, 1982; Hon. mem., RAM; FRCM; Hon. Fellow, Gonville and Caius College, Cambridge, 2001. *Address:* The Manor, Cossington, Somerset TA7 8JR, England. *Telephone:* (1278) 723655. *E-mail:* s.sadie@ukgateway.net.

SADLER, Mark (see Lynds, Dennis).

SAFIRE, William; American columnist and writer; b. 17 Dec. 1929, New York, NY, USA; m. Helene Belmar Julius 1962; one s. one d. *Education:* Syracuse University. *Career:* Reporter, New York Herald-Tribune Syndicate, 1949–51; Correspondent, Europe and the Middle East, WNBC-WNBT, 1951; Radio-TV Producer, WMBC, New York City, 1954–55; Vice-Pres., Tex McCrary Inc, 1955–60; Pres., Safire Public Relations, 1960–68; Special Asst to Pres. Richard M. Nixon, 1969–73; Columnist, The New York Times, 1973–; mem. Pulitzer, Board, 1995–2004; Chair., The Charles A. Dana Foundation. *Publications:* The Relations Explosion, 1963; Plunging into Politics, 1964; Safire's Political Dictionary, 1968, revised edn as Safire's New Political Dictionary, 1993; Before the Fall, 1975; Full Disclosure, 1977; Safire's Washington, 1980; On Language, 1980; What's the Good Word?, 1982; Good Advice on Writing (with Leonard Safire), 1982; I Stand Corrected, 1984; Take My Word for It, 1986; You Could Look It Up, 1988; Language Maven Strikes Again, 1990; Leadership (with Leonard Safire), 1990; Fumblerules, 1990; The First Dissident, 1992; Lend Me Your Ears, 1992; Quoth the Maven, 1993; In Love with Norma Loquendi, 1994; Sleeper Spy, 1995; Watching My Language, 1997; Spread the Word, 1999; Scandalmonger, 2000; Let a Simile Be Your Umbrella, 2002; The Right Word in the Right Place at the Right Time 2004. Contributions: newspapers and magazines. *Honours:* Pulitzer Prize for Distinguished Commentary 1978. *Address:* c/o The New York Times, 1627 Eye Street NW, Washington, DC 20006, USA.

SAFRANKO, Mark Peter; Writer and Actor; b. 23 Dec. 1950, Trenton, NJ, USA; m. Lorrie Foster, 11 May 1996, one s. *Education:* BA, St Vincent College, 1968; MA, Montclair State University, 1977. *Career:* mem. Dramatists Guild; Authors' Guild. *Publications:* Fiction: Hating Olivia; The Favor, 1987; Hopler's Statement, 1998. Contributions: South Carolina Review; North Atlantic Review; Paterson Literary Review; New Orleans Review; Ellery Queen's Mystery Magazine. *Address:* 5 Amherst Pl., Montclair, NJ 07043, USA.

SAGAN, Françoise, (Françoise Quoirez); Author and Dramatist; b. 21 June 1935, Cajarc, France; m. 1st Guy Schoeller, 13 March 1958, divorced 1960; m. 2nd Robert James Westhoff, 10 Jan. 1962, divorced 1963, one s. *Education:* Couvent des oiseaux, Paris; Couvent du Sacré Coeur, Paris; Sorbonne, University of Paris. *Publications:* Fiction: Bonjour tristesse, 1954; Un Certain Sourire, 1956, English trans. as A Certain Smile, 1956; Dans un mois, dans un an, 1957, English trans. as Those Without Shadows, 1957; Aimez-vous Brahms?, 1959; Les Merveilleux Nuages, 1961, English trans. as Wonderful Clouds, 1961; La Chamde, 1965; La Garde du coeur, 1968, English trans. as The Heart-Keeper, 1968; Un Peu de Soleil dans l'eau froide, 1969, English trans. as A Few Hours of Sunlight, 1971, and as Sunlight on Cold Water, 1971; Des bleus à l'âme, 1972, English trans. as Scars on the Soul, 1974; Un Profil perdu, 1974, English trans. as Lost Profile, 1976; Des yeux de soie, 1975, English trans. as Silken Eyes, 1977; Le lit defait, 1977, English trans. as The Unmade Bed, 1978; Le Chien Couchant, 1980, English trans. as Salad Days, 1984; La Femme fardée, 1981, English trans. as The Painted Lady, 1983; Musique des scènes, 1981, English trans. as Incidental Music, 1985; Un Orage immovile, 1983, English trans. as The Still Storm, 1984; De Guerre lasse, 1985, English trans. as A Reluctant Hero, 1987; Un Sang d'aquarelle, 1987; Les faux-fuyants, 1991, English trans. as Evasion, 1993; Un Chaquin de Passage, 1994, English trans. as A Fleeting Sorrow, 1995. Plays: Chateau en Suede, 1960; Les Violons parfois, 1962; La Robe mauve de Valentine, 1963; Bonheur, impair et passé, 1964; Le Cheval evanoui, suivi de L'Echarde, 1966; Un Piano dans l'herbe, 1970; Il fait beau jour et nuit, 1979. Other: Toxique, 1964; Mirror of Venus (with Frederico Fellini), 1966; Il est des parfums (with Guillaume Hanoteau), 1973; Réponses: 1954–1974, English trans. as Responses: The Autobiography of Françoise Sagan, 1979, and as Nightbird: Conversations with Françoise Sagan, 1980; Avec mon meilleur souvenir, 1984, English trans. as With Fondest Regards, 1985; La Maison de Raquel Vega: Fiction d'après le tableau de Fernando Botero, 1985; Sarah Bernhardt: Le Rire incassable, 1987, English trans. as Dear Sarah Bernhardt, 1988; Belle-Ile-en-Mer (with Henri Belbeoch and Louis Garans), 1992; Répliques, 1992; Oeuvres, 1993. *Honours:* Prix des Critiques, 1954; Prix de Monaco, 1985. *Address:* Editions Juilliard, 24 ave Marceau, 75008 Paris, France.

SAGGS, Henry William Frederick; Prof. of Semitic Languages (retd) and Writer; b. 2 Dec. 1920, Weeley, Essex, England; m. Joan Butterworth, 21 Sept. 1946, four d. *Education:* King's College, London, 1939–42, 1946–48; School of Oriental and African Studies, London, 1949–52; BD, 1942; MTh, 1948; MA, 1950; PhD, 1953. *Career:* Lecturer, then Reader in Akkadian, School of Oriental and African Studies, London, 1953–66; Prof. of Semitic Languages, University College Cardiff, University of Wales, 1966–83; mem. Society of Authors; Society of Antiquaries; British School of Archaeology in Iraq, council mem.; Savage Club; Royal Asiatic Society. *Publications:* The Greatness That Was Babylon, 1962; Everyday Life in Babylon and Assyria, 1965; The Encounter With the Divine in Mesopotamia and Israel, 1978; The Might That Was Assyria, 1984; Civilization Before Greece and Rome, 1989; Babylonians, 1995; Au Temps de Babylone, 1998. Contributions: Iraq; Sumer; Journal of Cuneiform Studies; Journal of Theological Studies; Archiv für Orientforschung; Revue d'Assyriologie; Journal of Semitic Studies; Bibliotheca Orientalis. *Address:* Eastwood, Bull Lane, Long Melford, Suffolk CO10 9EA, England.

SAHGAL, Nayantara (Pandit); Writer; b. 10 May 1927, Allahabad, Uttar Pradesh, India; m. 1st Gautam Sahgal, 2 Jan. 1949, divorced 1967, one s. two d.; m. 2nd, E. N. Mangat Rai, 17 Sept. 1979. *Education:* BA, History, Wellesley College, Massachusetts, 1947. *Career:* Advisory Panel for English, Sahitya Akademi, 1972–75; Writer-in-Residence, Southern Methodist University, Dallas, 1973, 1977; Research Scholar, Radcliffe (now Bunting) Institute, Cambridge, Massachusetts, 1976; Mem., Indian delegation to the United Nations, 1978; Fellow, Woodrow Wilson International Center for Scholars, Washington, DC, 1981–82, National Humanities Center, NC, 1983–84; Jury, Commonwealth Writers Prize, 1990, 1991; mem. American Acad. of Arts and Sciences, 1990. *Publications:* Fiction: A Time to Be Happy, 1958; This Time of Morning, 1965; Storm in Chandigarh, 1969; The Day in Shadow, 1972; A Situation in New Delhi, 1977; Rich Like Us, 1985; Plans for Departure, 1986; Mistaken Identity, 1988; Lesser Breeds, 2003. Non-Fiction: Prison and Chocolate Cake, 1954; From Fear Set Free, 1962; The Freedom Movement in India, 1970; Indira Gandhi: Her Road to Power, 1982; Relationship: Extracts from a Correspondence (with E. N. Mangat Rai), 1994; Point of View, 1997; Before Freedom: Nehru's Letters to His Sister 1909–1947 (ed.), 2000; The Scope of Happiness: A Personal Memoir by Vijaya Lakshmi Pandit (epilogue in new edn by Nayantara Sahgal), 2000. Contributions: newspapers and magazines including India Today. *Honours:* Book Society Recommendation, 1959; Sinclair Prize for Fiction, 1985; Sahitya Akademi Award, 1986; Commonwealth Writers Prize, Eurasia, 1987; Hon. DLitt, University of Leeds, 1997. *Address:* 181 B. Rajpur Rd, Dehra Dun 248009, Uttaranchal, India.

SAHNI, Peush; Indian surgeon and writer. *Career:* Assoc. Prof. of Dept of Gastrointestinal Surgery and Liver Transplantation, All India Inst. of Medical Sciences; Pres. of Exec. Bd, World Asscn of Medical Editors

(WAME) 2004–05. *Publications:* co-author: Brain Death and Organ Transplantation in India 1990, Medical Books in India 1994, GI Surgery Annual (Vols II–V) 1995–98; contrib. to Diet, Digestion and Diabetes 1986, Scientific Approach to Surgery 1989, Trends in Hepatology 1990, Modern Concepts in Surgery 1992, GI Surgery Annual (Vol. I) 1994; contrib. articles to British Medical Journal, National Medical Journal of India, The Lancet, Hospital Today, British Journal of Surgery, Journal of Tropical Paediatrics. *Address:* WAME, c/o Margaret A. Winker MD, 515 N State Street, Chicago, IL 60610, USA. *E-mail:* peush_sahni@hotmail.com. *Website:* www.wame .com.

SAHU, N. S.; Reader in English and Poet; b. 1 Sept. 1939, India; m. Shanti Sahu, 17 May 1962, three s. *Education:* MA, Linguistics, 1970; MA, English Literature, 1973; PhD, Linguistics, 1975; PhD, English, 1978. *Career:* Lecturer in English, Dept of Education, Bhilai Steel Plant, Bhilainagar, 1971–79; Lecturer, 1979–92, Reader in English, 1992–, University of Gorakhpur; mem. American Studies Research Centre; International Goodwill Society of India; Linguistic Society of India. *Publications:* Aspects of Linguistics, 1982; T. S. Eliot: The Man as a Poet, Playwright, Prophet and Critic, 1988; A Study of the Works of Matthew Arnold, 1988; Theatre of Protest and Anger, 1988; Toponymy, 1989; Christopher Marlowe and Theatre of Cruelty and Violence, 1990; An Approach to American Literature, 1991; Poems, 1996. Contributions: various publications. *Address:* 11 New Flat, Hirapuri Colony, University Campus, Gorakhpur 273009, India.

SAIL, Lawrence Richard, BA, FRSL; poet and writer; b. 29 Oct. 1942, London, England; m. 1st Teresa Luke 1966 (divorced 1981); one s. one d.; m. 2nd Helen Bird 1994; two d. *Education:* St John's College, Oxford. *Career:* teacher of modern languages, Lenana School, Nairobi 1966–71, Millfield School 1973–74, Blundell's School, Devon 1975–81, Exeter School 1982–91; Ed., South West Review 1981–85; Chair., Arvon Foundation 1990–94; Programme Dir 1991, Co-Dir 1999, Cheltenham Festival of Literature; jury mem., European (Aristeion) Literature Prize 1994–96; mem. Authors' Soc., St John's Coll., Oxford, sr common room, Poetry Soc. *Publications:* Opposite Views, 1974; The Drowned River, 1978; The Kingdom of Atlas, 1980; South West Review: A Celebration (ed.), 1985; Devotions, 1987; Aquamarine, 1988; First and Always (ed.), 1988; Out of Land: New and Selected Poems, 1992; Building into Air, 1995; The New Exeter Book of Riddles (co-ed.), 1999; The World Returning, 2002. Contributions: anthologies, magazines and newspapers. *Honours:* Hawthornden Fellowship 1992, Arts Council Writer's Bursary 1993, Cholmondley Award 2004. *Address:* Richmond Villa, 7 Wonford Road, Exeter, Devon EX2 4LF, England.

SAINT, Dora Jessie, (Miss Read); Novelist, Short Story and Children's Fiction Writer; b. 17 April 1913, Surrey, England. *Education:* Homerton College, 1931–33. *Career:* mem. Society of Authors. *Publications:* Village School, 1955; Village Diary, 1957; Storm in the Village, 1958; Hobby Horse Cottage, 1958; Thrush Green, 1959; Fresh From the Country, 1960; Winter in Thrush Green, 1961; Miss Clare Remembers, 1962; The Market Square, 1966; The Howards of Caxley, 1967; Country Cooking, 1969; News from Thrush Green, 1970; Tyler's Row, 1972; Christmas Mouse, 1973; Battles at Thrush Green, 1975; No Holly for Miss Quinn, 1976; Village Affairs, 1977; Return to Thrush Green, 1978; The White Robin, 1979; Village Centenary, 1980; Gossip From Thrush Green, 1981; A Fortunate Grandchild, 1982; Affairs at Thrush Green, 1983; Summer at Fairacre, 1984; At Home in Thrush Green, 1985; Time Remembered, 1986; The School at Thrush Green, 1987; The World at Thrush Green, 1988; Mrs Pringle, 1989; Friends at Thrush Green, 1990; Changes at Fairacre, 1991; Celebrations at Thrush Green, 1992; Farewell to Fairacre, 1993; Tales From a Village School, 1994; The Year at Thrush Green, 1995; A Peaceful Retirement, 1996. *Honours:* MBE, 1998. *Address:* c/o Penguin UK, 80 The Strand, London WC2R OSR, England.

SAINT-AMAND, Pierre, BA, MA, PhD; academic and writer; b. 22 Feb. 1957, Port-au-Prince, Haiti. *Career:* Asst Prof., Yale University, 1981–82, Stanford University, 1982–86; Assoc. Prof., 1986–90, Prof., 1990–97, Francis Wayland Prof., 1997–, Brown University; mem. MLA; American Society for Eighteenth-Century Studies. *Publications:* Diderot: Le Labyrinthe de la Relation, 1984; Séduire ou la Passion des Lumières, 1986; Les Lois de L'Hostilité, 1992; The Libertine's Progress, 1994; The Laws of Hostility, 1996. Editor: Diderot, 1984; Le Roman au dix-huitième siècle, 1987; Autonomy in the Age of Enlightenment, 1993; Thérèse philosophe, 2000. *Honours:* Guggenheim Fellowship 1989. *Address:* French Studies, Box 1961, Brown University, Providence, RI 02912, USA.

ST AUBIN de TERÁN, Lisa Gioconda, (Lisa Duff-Scott), FRSL; British author; *Chief Executive, Radiant Pictures*; b. (Lisa Gioconda Carew), 2 Oct. 1953, London; m. 1st Jaime Terán 1970 (divorced 1981); one d.; m. 2nd George Macbeth 1981 (divorced 1989, deceased); one s.; m. 3rd Robbie Duff-Scott 1989; one d. *Education:* James Allen's Girls' School, Dulwich. *Career:* travelled widely in France and Italy 1969–71; managed sugar plantation in Venezuelan Andes 1971–78; moved to Italy 1983; fmr Vice-Pres. Umbria Film Festival, now Hon. Pres.; CEO Radiant Pictures 2002– (film production co.). *Screenplays:* The Slow Train to Milan (co-writer), The Hacienda, The Blessing, A Woman Called Solitude, The Moneymaker, The Orange Sicilian (co-writer, animated feature film). *Television:* wrote and presented documentaries Santos to Santa Cruz in Great Railway Journeys series (BBC) 1994, Great Railway Journeys of the World (BBC and PBS). *Radio:* adapted and read (for BBC) Off the Rails 1995, The Bay of Silence 1996. *Publications:* fiction: Keepers of the House 1982, The Slow Train to Milan 1983, The Tiger 1984, The Bay of Silence 1986, Black Idol 1987, The Marble Mountain (short stories) 1989, Joanna 1990, Nocturne 1993, Distant Landscapes (novella) 1995, The Palace 1998, The Virago Book of Wanderlust and Dreams (ed.) 1998, Southpaw (short stories) 1999, Otto 2004; poetry: The Streak 1980, The High Place 1985; memoirs: Off the Rails 1989, Venice: The Four Seasons 1992, A Valley in Italy 1994, The Hacienda 1997, My Venezuelan Years 1997, Memory Maps 2001. *Honours:* Somerset Maugham Award 1983, John Llewelyn Rhys Award 1983, Eric Gregory Award for Poetry 1983. *Address:* Radiant Pictures, 101 Vondelstraat, 1054 GM Amsterdam, Netherlands (Office). *E-mail:* lisa@radiantpictures.com (Office). *Website:* www.radiantpictures.com (Office). *Telephone:* (20) 618-6660. *Fax:* (20) 668-8204.

ST AUBYN, Giles R., MA, FRSL; writer; b. 11 March 1925, London, England. *Education:* Trinity Coll., Oxford. *Career:* mem. Soc. of Authors. *Publications:* Lord Macaulay, 1952; A Victorian Eminence, 1957; The Art of Argument, 1957; The Royal George, 1963; A World to Win, 1968; Infamous Victorians, 1971; Edward VII, Prince and King, 1979; The Year of Three Kings 1483, 1983; Queen Victoria: A Portrait, 1991. *Honours:* Lieutenant, Royal Victorian Order. *Literary Agent:* Christopher Sinclair-Stevenson, 3 South Terrace, London, SW7 2TB, England. *Address:* Saumarez Park Manor, Apt 2, Route de Saumarez, Câtel, Guernsey GY5 7TH, Channel Islands.

ST CLAIR, William, FRSL; author; b. 7 Dec. 1937, London, England; two d. *Education:* St John's Coll., Oxford. *Career:* fmrly, Under-Secretary Her Majesty's Treasury; Fellow Huntington Library, San Marino, Calif. 1985; Visiting Fellow 1981–82, Fellow All Souls College, Oxford 1992–96; Visiting Fellow Commoner 1997, Fellow 1998, Trinity College, Cambridge; mem. British Acad. 1992, council 1997. *Publications:* Lord Elgin and the Marbles 1967, That Greece Might Still Be Free 1972, Trelawny 1978, Policy Evaluation: A Guide for Managers 1988, The Godwins and the Shelleys: The Biography of a Family 1989, Executive Agencies: A Guide to Setting Targets and Judging Performance 1992, Conduct Literature for Women 1500–1640 (ed. with Irmgard Maassen) 2000, Conduct Literature for Women 1640–1710 (ed. with Irmgard Maassen) 2002, Mapping Lives: The Uses of Biography (ed. with Peter France) 2002, The Reading Nation in the Romantic Period 2004. *Honours:* Heinemann Prize, RSL 1973, Time-Life Prize 1990, MacMillan Silver Pen 1990, Thalassa (Greece) 2000. *Address:* Trinity College, Cambridge CB2 1TQ, England. *E-mail:* ws214@cam.ac.uk.

SALAMUN, Tomaz; Poet and Writer; b. 4 July 1941, Zagreb, Yugoslavia; m. 1st Marusa Krese, 1969, divorced 1975; m. 2nd Metka Krašovec, 11 April 1979, one s. one d. *Education:* MA, University of Ljubljana, 1965; University of Iowa, 1971–73. *Career:* Asst Curator, Modern Gallery, Ljubljana, 1968–70; Asst Prof., Acad. of Fine Arts, Ljubljana, 1970–73; Workshops, University of Tennessee at Chattanooga, 1987–88, 1996; Visiting Writer, Vermont College, 1988; Consul, Slovenian Cultural Attaché, New York, 1996–97; mem. PEN; Slovenian Writers' Asscn. *Publications:* Turbines: Twenty-One Poems, 1973; Snow, 1973; Poetry: Pesmi (Poems), 1980; Maske (Masks), 1980; Balada za Metka Krašovec, 1981, English trans. as A Ballad for Metka Krašovec, 2001; Analogije svetlobe, 1982; Glas, 1983; Sonet o mleku, 1984; Soy realidad, 1985; Ljubljanska pomlad, 1986; Mera casa, 1987; Ziva rana, zivi sok, 1988; The Selected Poems of Tomaz Salamun, 1988; Otrok in jelen, 1990; Painted Desert: Poems, 1991; The Shepherd, The Hunter, 1992; Ambra, 1994; The Four Questions of Melancholy: New and Selected Poems, 1997; Crni labod, 1997; Knjiga za mojega brata, 1997; Homage to Hat and Uncle Guido and Eliot, 1998; Morje, 1999; Gozd in kelihi, 2000; Feast, 2000; Table, 2002. Contributions: anthologies and periodicals. *Honours:* Mladost Prize, 1969; Residencies, Yaddo, 1973–74, 1979, 1986, 1989, MacDowell Colony, 1986, Karoly Foundation, Vence, France, 1987, Maisons des écrivains étrangers, Saint-Nazaire, France, 1996, Civitella Ranieri, Umbertide, Italy, 1997, Bogliasco Foundation, 2002; Fulbright Grant, 1986–87; Jenko Prize, 1988; Pushcart Prize, 1994; Prešeren Prize, 1999; Alta Marea Prize, 2002. *Address:* Dalmatinova 11, 1000 Ljubljana, Slovenia.

SALAS SOMMER, Dario (see Baines, John).

SALE, (John) Kirkpatrick; editor and writer; b. 27 June 1937, Ithaca, NY, USA; m. Faith Apfelbaum Sale 1962; two d. *Education:* BA, Cornell University, 1958. *Career:* Ed., The New Leader, 1959–61, New York Times Magazine, 1965–68; Ed., 1981–82, Contributing Ed., 1986–, The Nation; mem. PEN American Centre, board mem., 1976–97; E. F. Schumacher Society, board mem., 1980–. *Publications:* SDS, 1973; Power Shift, 1975; Human Scale, 1980; Dwellers in the Land: The Bioregional Vision, 1985; The Conquest of Paradise: Christopher Columbus and the Columbian Legacy, 1990; The Green Revolution: The American Environmental Movement 1962–1992, 1993; Rebels Against the Future: The Luddites and Their War on the Industrial Revolution, 1995; The Fire of His Genius: Robert Fulton and the American Dream, 2001. *Address:* 113 W 11th Street, New York, NY 10011, USA.

SALIH, Tayeb; Novelist and Writer; b. 1929, Sudan. *Career:* fmr Head of Drama, Arabic service, BBC; fmr Dir-Gen. of Information, Qatar; with UNESCO, Paris. *Publications:* The Wedding of Zein (novella); Season of

Migration to the North; Bandarshah, 1996; many short stories. Contributions: al Majalla. *Address:* c/o African Writers Series, Heinemann Educational Publishers, Halley Ct, Jordan Hill, Oxford OX2 8EJ, England.

SALINGER, Jerome David; American writer; b. 1 Jan. 1919, New York, NY; m. Claire Douglas 1953 (divorced 1967); one s. one d. *Education:* Valley Forge Military Acad., Columbia University. *Publications:* The Catcher in the Rye 1951, Nine Stories 1953, Franny and Zooey 1961, Raise High the Roof-Beam, Carpenters and Seymour: An Introduction 1963; contrib. to magazines. *Literary Agent:* Harold Ober Associates, 425 Madison Avenue, New York, NY 10017, USA.

SALOM, Philip; University Lecturer, Poet and Writer; b. 8 Aug. 1950, Bunbury, WA, Australia. *Education:* BA, 1976; DipEd, 1981, Curtin University. *Career:* Tutor and Lecturer, Curtin University, 1982–93; Writer-in-Residence, Singapore National University, 1989, B. R. Whiting Library/Studio, Rome, 1992; Lecturer, Murdoch University, 1994–97, Victorian College of the Arts of the University of Melbourne, 2000–01. *Publications:* The Silent Piano, 1980; The Projectionist: Sequence, 1983; Sky Poems, 1987; Barbecue of the Primitives, 1989; Playback, 1991; Tremors, 1992; Feeding the Ghost, 1993; Always Then and Now, 1993; The Rome Air Naked, 1996; New and Selected Poems, 1998; A Creative Life, 2001. *Honours:* Commonwealth Poetry Prizes, 1981, 1987; Western Australian Premier's Prize, 1984, 1988 1992; Australia/New Zealand Literary Exchange Award, 1992; Newcastle Poetry Prize, 1996, 2000. *Address:* PO Box 273, Kerrimuir, Vic. 3129, Australia. *E-mail:* psalom@netspace.net.au.

SALTER, James; Writer; b. 10 June 1925, New York, NY, USA; m. Ann Altemus, 5 June 1951, divorced 1976, two s. three d. *Career:* mem. American Acad. of Arts and Letters; PEN USA. *Publications:* The Hunters, 1957; The Arm of Flesh, 1960; A Sport and a Pastime, 1967; Light Years, 1976; Solo Faces, 1980; Dusk and Other Stories, 1989; Burning the Days, 1997; Cassada, 2000; Bangkok (in French), 2003. Contributions: Paris Review; Antaeus; Grand Street; Vogue; Esquire. *Honours:* American Acad. of Arts and Letters Grant, 1982; PEN-Faulkner Award, 1989; Fadiman Medal, 2003. *Address:* Box 765, Bridgehampton, NY 11932, USA.

SALTER, Mary Jo; Lecturer, Poet and Ed.; b. 15 Aug. 1954, Grand Rapids, Michigan, USA; m. Brad Leithauser, 1980, two d. *Education:* BA, cum laude, Harvard University, 1976; MA, University of Cambridge, 1978. *Career:* Instructor, Harvard University, 1978–79; Staff Ed., Atlantic Monthly, 1978–80; Poet-in-Residence, Robert Frost Place, 1981; Lecturer in English, 1984–, Emily Dickinson Lecturer in Humanities, 1995–, Mount Holyoke College, South Hadley, Massachusetts; Poetry Ed., The New Republic, 1992–95; mem. International PEN; Poetry Society of America, vice-pres., 1995–. *Publications:* Henry Purcell in Japan, 1985; Unfinished Painting, 1989; The Moon Comes Home, 1989; Sunday Skaters: Poems, 1994; A Kiss in Space: Poems, 1999. Contributions: periodicals. *Honours:* Discovery Prize, The Nation, 1983; National Endowment for the Arts Fellowship, 1983–84; Lamont Prize in Poetry, 1988; Guggenheim Fellowship, 1993; Amy Lowell Scholarship, 1995. *Address:* c/o Dept of English, Mt Holyoke College, South Hadley, MA 01075, USA.

SALTZMAN, Arthur Michael; Prof. and Writer; b. 10 Aug. 1953, Chicago, IL, USA; one d. *Education:* AB, 1971, AM, 1976, PhD, 1979, University of Illinois. *Career:* Teaching Fellow, University of Illinois, 1975–80; Asst Prof., 1981–86, Assoc. Prof., 1986–92, Prof., 1992–, Missouri Southern State Univ.; mem. MLA. *Publications:* The Fiction of William Gass: The Consolation of Language, 1986; Understanding Raymond Carver, 1988; Designs of Darkness in Contemporary American Fiction, 1990; The Novel in the Balance, 1993; Understanding Nicholson Baker, 1999; This Mad 'Instead': Governing Metaphors in Contemporary American Fiction, 2000; Objects and Empathy, 2001. Contributions: professional journals and general periodicals. *Honours:* Missouri Southern Outstanding Teacher Award, 1992; Ames Memorial Essay Award, 1998; Mid-List Press First Series Creative Non-fiction Award, 1999; Nebraska Review Creative Non-Fiction Award, 2002; Victor J. Emmett Memorial Award, 2003. *Address:* 3235 Connecticut, Joplin, MO 64804, USA.

SALZBERG, Steven, BA, MS, MPhil, PhD; American scientist and writer. *Education:* Univ. of Yale, Univ. of Harvard. *Career:* research scientist and sr knowledge engineer, Applied Expert Systems Inc. 1985–87; Assoc. in Research, Harvard Business School 1988–89; Asst Prof. 1989–96, Assoc. Prof. 1996–99, Research Prof. 1999–, Dept of Computer Science, jt Research Prof. 1999–, Dept of Biology, Johns Hopkins Univ.; Investigator 1997–, Sr Dir of Bio-informatics 1998–, Inst. for Genomic Research. *Publications:* Learning with Nested Generalized Exemplars 1990, Computational Methods in Molecular Biology (ed.), contrib. to Science, Nucleic Acids Research. *Address:* Institute for Genomic Research, 9712 Medical Center Drive, Rockville, MD 20850, USA. *Telephone:* (301) 838-0200. *Fax:* (301) 838-0208. *Website:* www.tigr.org.

SAMBROOK, (Arthur) James; academic and writer; b. 5 Sept. 1931, Nuneaton, Warwickshire, England; m. Patience Ann Crawford 1961; four s. *Education:* BA, 1955, MA, 1959, Worcester College, Oxford; PhD, University of Nottingham, 1957. *Career:* Lecturer, St David's College, Lampeter, Wales, 1957–64; Lecturer, 1964–71, Senior Lecturer, 1971–75, Reader, 1975–81, Prof. of English, 1981–92, Emeritus Prof., 1992–, University of Southampton. *Publications:* A Poet Hidden: The Life of R. W. Dixon, 1962; The Scribleriad, etc (ed.), 1967; William Cobbett, 1973; James Thomson: The Seasons (ed.), 1981; English Pastoral Poetry, 1983; The Eighteenth Century: The Intellectual and Cultural Context of English Literature 1700–1789, 1986; Liberty, the Castle of Indolence and Other Poems, 1986; James Thomson 1700–1748: A Life: Biographical, Critical, 1992; William Cowper: The Task and Other Poems (ed.), 1994; With the Rank and Pay of a Sapper, 1998. Contributions: Reference books including the New Dictionary of National Biography, professional journals and general periodicals. *Address:* 36 Bursledon Road, Hedge End, Southampton SO30 0BX, England.

SAMPSON, Anthony Terrell Seward, MA, FRSL; British writer and journalist; b. 3 Aug. 1926, Billingham, Durham; m. Sally Bentlif 1965; one s. one d. *Education:* Westminster School and Christ Church, Oxford. *Career:* served with RN 1944–47; Sub-Lt RNVR 1946; Ed. Drum magazine, Johannesburg 1951–55; Editorial Staff, The Observer 1955–66, Chief American Corresp. 1973–74, Ed. The Observer Colour Magazine 1965–66; Assoc. Prof. Univ. of Vincennes, Paris 1968–70; Contributing Ed. Newsweek 1977–; Chair. Soc. of Authors 1992–94; Editorial Adviser, Brandt Comm. 1979; Dir The New Statesman 1979–83; Ed. The Sampson Letter 1984–86; Trustee Scott Trust 1993–96. *Publications:* Drum, a Venture into the New Africa 1956, The Treason Cage 1958, Commonsense about Africa 1960, (with S. Pienaar), Anatomy of Britain 1962, Anatomy of Britain Today 1965, South Africa: Two Views of Separate Development 1966, Macmillan: a Study in Ambiguity 1968, New Europeans 1968, The New Anatomy of Britain 1971, The Sovereign State: the Secret History of ITT 1973, The Seven Sisters 1975 (Prix Int. de la Presse 1976), The Arms Bazaar 1977, The Money Lenders 1981, The Changing Anatomy of Britain 1982, Empires of the Sky 1984, The Oxford Book of Ages (with Sally Sampson) 1985, Black and Gold: Tycoons, Revolutionaries and Apartheid 1987, The Midas Touch 1989, The Essential Anatomy of Britain 1992, Company Man 1995, The Scholar Gypsy 1997, Mandela, the Authorised Biography 1999 (Heinemann Prize 2000, Robert F. Kennedy Book Award 2000, Marsh Biog. Prize 2001), Who Runs This Place?: The Anatomy of Britain in the 21st Century 2004. *Address:* 10 Hereford Mansions, Hereford Road, London, W2 5BA; Quarry Garden, Wardour, nr Tisbury, Wilts., SP3 6RN, England. *Telephone:* (20) 7727-4188 (London); (1747) 870407 (Wilts.). *Fax:* (20) 7221-5738 (Home).

SAMS, Eric; Civil Servant (retd) and Writer; b. 3 May 1926, London, England; m. Enid Tidmarsh, 30 June 1952, two s. *Education:* BA, Corpus Christi College, Cambridge, 1950; PhD, 1972. *Career:* Civil Servant, 1950–78; Visiting Prof., McMaster University, Hamilton, Ontario, Canada, 1976–77; mem. Guildhall School of Music and Drama, hon. mem., 1983–. *Publications:* The Songs of Hugo Wolf, 1961; The Songs of Robert Schumann, 1969; Brahms' Songs, 1971; Shakespeare's Edmund Ironside, 1985; The Real Shakespeare, 1995; Shakespeare's Edward III, 1996; The Songs of Johannes Brahms, 2000. Contributions: Reference works and journals. *Honours:* Leverhulme Grant, 1984. *Address:* 32 Arundel Ave, Sanderstead, Surrey CR2 8BB, England.

SANCHEZ, Sonia; Prof. of English, Poet, Dramatist and Writer; b. 9 Sept. 1934, Birmingham, AL, USA; m. Etheridge Knight, divorced, two s. one d. *Education:* BA, Hunter College, CUNY, 1955; New York University, 1959–60; PhD, Wilberforce University, 1972. *Career:* Instructor, San Francisco State College, 1967–69; Lecturer, University of Pittsburgh, 1969–70, Rutgers University, 1970–71, Manhattan Community College, 1971–73, CUNY, 1972; Assoc. Prof., Amherst College, 1972–73, University of Pennsylvania, 1976–77; Assoc. Prof., 1977–79, Prof. of English, 1979–, Temple University. *Publications:* Poetry: Homecoming, 1969; WE a BaddDDD People, 1970; Liberation Poem, 1970; It's a New Day: Poems for Young Brothas and Sistuhs, 1971; Ima Talken bout the Nation of Islam, 1971; Love Poems, 1973; A Blues Book for Blue Black Magical Women, 1974; I've Been a Woman: New and Selected Poems, 1978; Homegirls and Handgrenades, 1984; Under a Soprano Sky, 1987; Wounded in the House of a Friend, 1995. Plays: The Bronx is Next, 1968; Sister Son/ji, 1969; Dirty Hearts '72, 1973; Uh, Uh: But How Do it Free Us?, 1974. Stories: A Sound Investment, 1980. Other: Crisis in Culture, 1983. Editor: Three Hundred Sixty Degrees of Blackness Comin' at You, 1972; We Be Word Sorcerers: 25 Stories by Black Americans, 1973. *Honours:* PEN Award, 1969; American Acad. of Arts and Letters Award, 1970; National Endowment for the Arts Award, 1978; Smith College Tribute to Black Women Award, 1982; Lucretia Mott Award, 1984; Before Columbus Foundation Award, 1985; PEN Fellow, 1993. *Address:* c/o Dept of English, Temple University, Philadelphia, PA 19041, USA.

SANDEN, Einar; Writer and Historian; b. 8 Sept. 1932, Tallinn, Estonia; m. Elizabeth Gorell, 6 Sept. 1994. *Education:* MA, 1983, PhD, 1984, USA. *Career:* Managing Dir, Owner, Boreas Publishing House, 1975; Councillor, Estonian Government in Exile, 1975–90; mem. PEN Centre for Writers in Exile, 1954–80; RSL, 1960; Asscn of Estonian Writers Abroad, 1970; English PEN, 1976; Estonian National Council, 1959; Asscn for the Advancement of Baltic Studies, USA, 1980; Estonian Academic Asscn of War History, Tallinn, 1988. *Publications:* KGB Calling Eve, 1978; The Painter From Naissaar, 1985; Ur Eldinum Til Islands, 1988; An Estonian Saga, 1995. Contributions: Ed. of various Estonian periodicals. *Honours:* Distinguished Freedom Writer, UPLI, Manila, the Philippines, 1968; Cultural Award, Fraternity Sakala, Toronto, 1984. *Address:* 24 Carnegie Dr., Lakeside, Cardiff CF23 6DH, Wales.

SANDERS, (James) Edward; poet, writer, singer and lecturer; b. 17 Aug. 1939, Kansas City, MO, USA; m. Miriam Kittell 1961; one c. *Education:* BA, New York University, 1964. *Career:* Ed.-Publisher, Fuck You/A Magazine of the Arts, 1962–65; Founder-Lead Singer, The Fugs, satiric folk-rock-theatre group, 1964–69; Owner, Peace Eye Bookstore, New York City, 1964–70; Visiting Prof. of Language and Literature, Bard College, Annadale-on-Hudson, New York, 1979, 1983; Lectures, readings, performances throughout the US and Europe; mem. New York Foundation for the Arts; PEN. *Publications:* Poetry: Poem from Jail, 1963; A Valorium Edition of the Entire Extant Works of Thales!, 1964; King Lord/Queen Freak, 1964; The Toe Queen Poems, 1964; The Fugs' Song Book (with Ken Weaver and Betsy Klein), 1965; Peace Eye, 1965; Egyptian Hieroglyphics, 1973; 20,000 A.D., 1976; The Cutting Prow, 1981; Hymn to Maple Syrup and Other Poems, 1985; Poems for Robin, 1987; Thirsting for Peace in a Raging Century: Selected Poems 1961–1985, 1987; Hymn to the Rebel Cafe: Poems 1987–1991, 1993; Chekhov: A Biography in Verse, 1995. Editor: Poems for Marilyn, 1962. Compiler and Contributor: Bugger: An Anthology of Buttockry, 1964; Despair: poems to come down by, 1964. Fiction: Shards of God: A Novel of the Yippies, 1970; Tales of Beatnik Glory (short stories), 2 vols, 1975, 1990; Fame and Love in New York, 1980. Non-Fiction: The Family: The Story of Charles Manson's Dune Buggy Attack Battalion, 1971; Vote! (with Abbie Hoffman and Jerry Rubin), 1972; Investigative Poetry, 1976; The Z-D Generation, 1981. Other: Musicals: Recordings with The Fugs; Solo recordings. *Honours:* Frank O'Hara Prize, Modern Poetry Asscn, 1967; National Endowment for the Arts Awards, 1966, 1970, Fellowship, 1987–88; Guggenheim Fellowship, 1983–84; American Book Award, 1988. *Address:* PO Box 729, Woodstock, NY 12498, USA.

SANDERS, Noah (see Blount, Roy (Alton), Jr).

SANDERS, Scott Russell; Asst Prof. of English and Author; b. 26 Oct. 1945, Memphis, Tennessee, USA; m. Ruth Ann McClure, 27 Aug. 1967, one s. one d. *Education:* BA, Brown University, 1967; PhD, University of Cambridge, 1971. *Career:* Literary Ed., 1969–70, Contributing Ed., 1970–71, Cambridge Reviews; Fiction Ed., Minnesota Review, 1976–80; Fiction Columnist, Chicago Sun-Times, 1977–84; Contributing Ed., North American Review, 1982–; Asst Prof. of English, Indiana University, 1996–. *Publications:* Fiction: Wilderness Plots: Tales About the Settlement of the American Land, 1983; Fetching the Dead (short stories), 1984; Wonders Hidden: Audubon's Early Years (novella), 1984; Terrarium (novel), 1985; Hear the Wind Blow (short stories), 1985; Bad Man Ballad (novel), 1986; The Engineer of Beasts (novel), 1988; The Invisible Country (novel), 1989. Other: D. H. Lawrence: The World of the Major Novels, 1974; Stone Country, 1985, revised edn as In Limestone Country, 1991; Audubon Reader: The Best Writings of John James Audubon, 1986; The Paradise of Bombs (essays), 1987; Secrets of the Universe (essays), 1991; Staying Put: Making a Home in a Restless World, 1993; Writing from the Center (essays), 1995; Hunting for Hope, 1998. Contributions: anthologies, journals, and magazines. *Honours:* Woodrow Wilson Fellowship, 1967–68; National Endowment for the Arts Fellowship, 1983–84; Indiana Arts Commission Master Fellowships, 1984, 1990–91; Lilly Endowment Open Fellowship, 1986–87; Associated Writing Programs Award for Non-Fiction, 1987; PEN Syndicated Fiction Award, 1988; Kenyon Review Award for Literary Excellence, 1991; Guggenheim Fellowship, 1992–93; Ohioana Book Award in Non-Fiction, 1994; Lannan Literary Award in Non-Fiction, 1995. *Address:* 1113 E Wylie St, Bloomington, IN 47401, USA.

SANDERSON, Anne Hilary; Poet and Writer; b. 13 Jan. 1944, Brighton, England; m. Michael Sanderson, 25 Sept. 1976. *Education:* BA, 1966, MA, 1970, MLitt, 1978, St Anne's College, Oxford. *Career:* English Lectrice, École Normale Supérieure de Jeunes Filles, University of Paris, 1969–71; Lecturer in European Literature, University of East Anglia, 1972–98; mem. Asscn of Christian Writers; Norwich Writers' Circle; Norwich Poetry Group; Playwrights East. *Publications:* Contributions: anthologies and periodicals, including: Poems in Poetry Now; Peace & Freedom; Purple Patch; The Poetry Church; Advance!, Isthmus; Triumph Herald; Reflections; Tree Spirit; The Firing Squad; All Year Round; Articles in Studies on Voltaire & The 18th Century; Jeunesse de Racine; Norwich Papers. *Honours:* Prix Racine, 1969; Third Prize, Hilton House National Open Poetry Awards for Collections, 1998, 1999. *Address:* Dept of LLT, University of East Anglia, Norwich NR4 7TJ, England.

SANDERSON, John Michael, MA, PhD; academic and writer; *Professor of Economic and Social History, University of East Anglia*; b. 23 Jan. 1939, Glasgow, Scotland. *Education:* Queens' College, Cambridge. *Career:* Prof. of Economic and Social History, University of East Anglia; General Ed., Cambridge University Press Economic History Society Studies in Economic and Social History Series, 1992–98; Council, Economic History Society, 1994–2000; mem. Economic History Society. *Publications:* The Universities and British Industry, 1850–1970, 1972; The Universities in the 19th Century, 1975; Education, Economic Change and Society in England, 1780–1870, 1983; From Irving to Olivier, A Social History of the Acting Profession in England, 1880–1983, 1984; Educational Opportunity and Social Change in England, 1900–1980s, 1987; The Missing Stratum, Technical School Education in England, 1900–1990s, 1994; Education and Economic Decline, 1870–1990s, 1999; The History of the University of East Anglia, Norwich, 2002. Contributions: Economic History Review; Journal of Contemporary History; Contemporary Record; Business History; Northern History; Past and Present. *Address:* School of History, University of East Anglia, Norwich NR4 7TJ, England.

SANDOZ, (George) Ellis, Jr, BA, MA, PhD; academic and writer; b. 10 Feb. 1931, New Orleans, LA, USA; m. Therese Alverne Hubley 1957; two s. two d. *Education:* Louisiana State University, University of North Carolina, Georgetown University, University of Heidelberg, University of Munich. *Career:* Instructor to Prof., Louisiana Polytechnic Institute, 1959–68; Prof. and Head, Dept of Political Science, East Texas State University, 1968–78; Prof. of Political Science, 1978–, Dir, Eric Voegelin Institute for American Renaissance Studies, 1987–, Louisiana State University; mem. American Historical Asscn; American Political Science Asscn; Federalist Society; Organization of American Historians; Philadelphia Society; Southern Political Science Asscn; Southwestern Political and Social Science Asscns; Eric Voegelin Society, founder-sec., 1985–. *Publications:* Political Apocalypse: A Study of Dostoevsky's Grand Inquisitor, 1971; Conceived in Liberty: American Individual Rights Today, 1978; A Tide of Discontent: The 1980 Elections and Their Meaning (ed.), 1981; The Voegelianian Revolution: A Biographical Introduction, 1981; Eric Voegelin's Thought: A Critical Appraisal (ed.), 1982; Election '84: Landslide Without a Mandate? (ed. with Cecil V. Crabb Jr), 1985; A Government of Laws: Political Theory, Religion and the American Founding, 1990; Political Sermons of the American Founding Era, 1730–1805 (ed.), 1991, index, 1996; Eric Voegelin's Significance for the Modern Mind (ed.), 1991; The Roots of Liberty: Magna Carta, Ancient Constitution, and the Anglo-American Tradition of Rule of Law (ed.), 1993; Politics of Truth and Other Untimely Essays: The Crisis of Civic Consciousness, 1999. Contributions: The Collected Works of Eric Voegelin (principal ed., 1986–), scholarly books and professional journals. *Honours:* Germanistic Society of America Fellow, 1964–65; Fulbright Scholar, 1964–65; Henry E. Huntington Library Fellow, 1986–87; Fulbright 40th Anniversary Distinguished American Scholar, Italy, 1987; Distinguished Research Master and University Gold Medal, Louisiana State University, 1993; Medal and Rector's Certificate, 1994, Hon. PhD, 1995, Palacky University, Olomouc, Czech Republic. *Address:* c/o Eric Voegelin Institute for American Renaissance Studies, Louisiana State University, 240 Stubbs Hall, Baton Rouge, LA 70803, USA. *E-mail:* esandoz@lsn.edu.

SANDS, Martin (see Burke, John Frederick).

SANDY, Stephen, BA, MA, PhD; poet, writer, translator and college teacher (retd); b. 2 Aug. 1934, Minneapolis, MN, USA; m. Virginia Scoville 1969; one s. one d. *Education:* Yale University, Harvard University. *Career:* Instructor in English, 1963–67, Visiting Prof., 1986, 1987, 1988, Harvard University; Visiting Prof. of English, Tokyo University of Foreign Studies, 1967–68, Brown University, 1968–69; Visiting Prof. of American Literature, University of Tokyo, 1967–68; Lecturer in English, University of Rhode Island, 1969; Mem., Literature Faculty, Bennington College, 1969–2001; National Endowment for the Arts Poet-in-Residence, Y Poetry Center, Philadelphia, 1985; McGee Prof. of Writing, Davidson College, 1994; various poetry workshops and numerous poetry readings. *Publications:* Stresses in the Peaceable Kingdom 1967, Roofs 1971, End of the Picaro 1974, The Ravelling of the Novel: Studies in Romantic Fiction from Walpole to Scott 1980, Flight of Steps 1982, Riding to Greylock 1983, To a Mantis 1987, Man in the Open Air 1988, The Epoch 1990, Thanksgiving Over the Water 1992, Vale of Academe: A Prose Poem for Bernard Malamud 1996, Marrow Spoon 1997, The Thread: New and Selected Poems 1998, Black Box 1999, Surface Impressions 2002, Weather Permitting 2004. Contributions: books, anthologies, reviews, quarterlies and journals. *Honours:* Ingram Merrill Foundation Fellowship, 1985; Vermont College on the Arts Fellowship, 1988; National Endowment for the Arts Creative Writing Fellowship, 1988; Chubb Life America Fellow, MacDowell Colony, 1993; Reader's Digest Residency for Distinguished Writers, 1997; Howard Moss Residency for Poetry, 1998, Yaddo; Senior Fellow in Literature, Fine Arts Work Center, Provincetown, 1998; Rockefeller Foundation Residency, Bellagio Study and Conference Center, 2001. *Address:* PO Box 276, Shaftsbury, VT 05262, USA.

SANDYS, Elspeth Somerville; Writer and Dramatist; b. 18 March 1940, Timaru, New Zealand; one s. one d. *Education:* MA, University of Auckland, New Zealand; LTCL (Music); FTCL (Speech, Drama). *Career:* Frank Sargeson Fellow, Auckland, 1992; Burns Fellow, Otago University, 1995; Writer-in-Residence, Waikato University, 1998; mem. Writers Guild; Society of Authors. *Publications:* Catch a Falling Star, 1978; The Broken Tree, 1981; Love and War, 1982; Finding Out, 1991; Best Friends (short stories), 1993; River Lines, 1995; Riding to Jerusalem, 1996; Enemy Territory, 1997; A Passing Guest (novel), 2002. Other: Radio plays. Contributions: Magazines. *Honours:* Frank Sargeson Fellow, Auckland, 1992; Burns Fellow, Otago University, 1995. *Literary Agent:* MBA Literary Agents Ltd, 62 Grafton Way, London W1T 5DW, England.

SANER, Reginald Anthony; poet, writer and academic; b. 30 Dec. 1931, Jacksonville, IL, USA; m. Anne Costigan 1958; two s. *Education:* BA, St Norbert College, Wisconsin, 1950; MA, 1954, PhD, 1962, University of Illinois at Urbana; Università per Stranieri, Perugia, 1960–61; Università di Firenze, Florence, 1960–61. *Career:* Asst Instructor, 1956–60, Instructor in English, 1961–62, University of Illinois at Urbana; Asst Prof., 1962–67,

Assoc. Prof., 1967–72, Prof. of English, 1972–, University of Colorado at Boulder; mem. Dante Society; PEN; Renaissance Society; Shakespeare Asscn. *Publications:* Poetry: Climbing into the Roots, 1976; So This is the Map, 1981; Essay on Air, 1984; Red Letters, 1989. Non-Fiction: The Four-Cornered Falcon: Essays on the Interior West and the Natural Scene, 1993; Reaching Keet Seel: Ruin's Echo and the Anasazi, 1998. Contributions: poems and essays in numerous anthologies and other publications. *Honours:* Fulbright Scholar to Florence, Italy, 1960–61; Borestone Mountain Poetry Awards, 1971, 1973; Walt Whitman Award, 1975; National Endowment for the Arts Creative Writing Fellowship, 1976; Pushcart Prize II, 1977–78; Colorado Governor's Award for Excellence in the Arts, 1983; Quarterly Review of Literature Award, 1989; Rockefeller Foundation Resident Scholar, Bellagio, Italy, 1990; Hazel Barnes Award, University of Colorado, 1993; Wallace Stegner Award, Centre of the American West, 1997. *Address:* 1925 Vassar, Boulder, CO 80303, USA.

SANGUINETI, Edoardo; writer and fmr academic; b. 9 Dec. 1930, Genoa, Italy; m. Luciana Garabello 1954; three s. one d. *Education:* Università degli Studi, Turin. *Career:* Prof. of Italian Literature, Univ. of Salerno 1968–74, Univ. of Genoa 1974–2000; mem., Chamber of Deputies 1979–83. *Publications:* Laborintus 1956, Opus metricum 1960, Interpretazione di Malebolge 1961, Tre studi danteschi 1961, Tra liberty e crepuscolarismo 1961, Alberto Moravia 1962, K. e altre cose 1962, Passaggio 1963, Capriccio Italiano 1963, Triperuno 1964, Ideologia e linguaggio 1965, Il realismo di Dante 1966, Guido Gozzano 1966, Il Giuoco dell'Oca 1967, T.A.T. 1969, Teatro 1969, Poesia Italiana del Novecento 1969, Il Giuoco del Satyricon 1970, Orlando Furioso (with L. Ronconi) 1970, Renga (with O. Paz, J. Roubaud and C. Tomlinson) 1971, Storie Naturali 1971, Wirrwarr 1972, Catamerone 1974, Antonio Bueno 1975, Giornalino 1976, Postkarten 1978, Giornalino secondo 1979, Stracciafoglio 1980, Scartabello 1981, Segnalibro 1982, Alfabeto apocalittico 1984, Rebus 1984, Omaggio a Pascoli 1985, Quintine 1985, Scribilli 1985, Faust, un travestimento 1985, Novissimum Testamentum 1986, Smorfie 1986, La missione del critico 1987, Bisbidis 1987, Ghirigori 1988, Commedia dell'Inferno 1989, Lettura del Decameron 1989, Senzatitolo 1992, Dante reazionario 1992, Gazzettini 1993, Per musica 1993, Opere e introduzione critica 1993, Malebolge (with E. Baj) 1995, Per una critica dell'avanguardia poetica (with J. Burgos) 1995, Tracce (with M. Lucchesi) 1995, Libretto 1995, Minitarjetas 1996, Orlando Furioso, un travestimento ariostesco 1996, Corollario 1997, Il mio amore è come una febbra (with A. Liberovici) 1998, Cose 1999, Il chierico organico 2000, Verdi in technicolor 2001, Sei personaggi.com 2001, L'amore delle tre melarance 2001, Atlante del Novecento italiano 2001, Carol Rama 2002, L'orologio astronomico 2002, Il gatto lupesco 2002, Omaggio a Goethe 2003, Omaggio a Shakespeare 2004. *Address:* 20 via Pergolesi, 16159 Genoa, Italy.

SANSOM, Ann; British poet and tutor; b. 1951, Doncaster, S Yorkshire; m. Peter Sansom. *Education:* Univ. of Cambridge. *Career:* playwright and writing tutor, Doncaster Women's Centre 1989–; playwright, Yorkshire Women Theatre; residencies for Arvon Foundation and Aldeburgh Poetry Festival. *Publications:* Romance 1994, In Praise of Men and Other People 2003. *Honours:* Arts Council Writer's Award. *Address:* c/o Bloodaxe Books Ltd, Highgreen, Tarset, Northumberland NE48 1RP, England. *Website:* www.bloodaxebooks.com.

SANTOS, Helen (see Griffiths, Helen).

SANTOS, Sherod; Curators', Distinguished Prof. of English, Poet and Writer; b. 9 Sept. 1948, Greenville, SC, USA; m. Lynne Marie McMahon, 1 May 1976, two s. *Education:* BA, 1971, MA, 1974, San Diego State University; MFA, University of California at Irvine, 1978; PhD, University of Utah, 1982. *Career:* Asst Prof., California State University, San Bernardino, 1982–83; Poetry Ed., Missouri Review, 1983–90; Asst Prof., 1983–86, Assoc. Prof., 1986–92, Curators' Distinguished Prof. of English, 2001–, University of Missouri; External Examiner and Poet-in-Residence, Poets' House, Islandmagee, Northern Ireland, summers 1991–98; various poetry readings, lectures, and seminars; mem. Acad. of American Poets; Associated Writing Programs; PEN American Center; Poetry Society of America; Poets and Writers; Robinson Jeffers Society. *Publications:* Begin, Distance, 1981; Accidental Weather, 1982; The New Days, 1986; The Southern Reaches, 1989; The Unsheltering Ground, 1990; The City of Women, 1993; The Pilot Star Elegies, 1998; The Perishing, 2003. Contributions: anthologies, journals, and magazines. *Honours:* Discovery/The Nation Award, 1978; Pushcart Prizes in Poetry, 1980, and in the Essay, 1994; Oscar Blumenthal Prize, Poetry magazine, 1981; Ingram Merrill Foundation Grant, 1982; Delmore Schwartz Memorial Award, 1983; Robert Frost Poet and Poet-in-Residence, Robert Frost House, Franconia, NH, 1984; Guggenheim Fellowship, 1984–85; National Endowment for the Arts Grant, 1987; Yaddo Center for the Arts Fellowship, 1987; Chancellor's Award, University of Missouri, 1993; British Arts Council International Travel Grant to Northern Ireland, 1995; National Endowment for the Arts Literature Panel Mem., 1995; Acad. Award in Literature, American Acad. of Arts and Letters, 1999; Theodore Roethke Memorial Prize in Poetry, 2002. *Address:* 1238 Sunset Dr., Columbia, MO 65203, USA.

SAPIA, Yvonne; Prof. of English, Poet and Writer; b. 10 April 1946, New York, NY, USA. *Education:* AA, Miami-Dade Community College, 1967; BA, English, Florida Atlantic University, 1970; MA, English, University of Florida, 1976; PhD, English, Florida State University, 1990. *Career:* Reporter and Ed., The Village Post newspaper, Miami, 1971–73; Editorial Asst, University of Florida, 1974–76; Resident Poet and Prof. of English, Lake City Community College, FL, 1976–. *Publications:* The Fertile Crescent (poems), 1983; Valentino's Hair (poems), 1987; Valentino's Hair (novel), 1991. Contributions: anthologies, reviews, and journals. *Honours:* First Place, Anhinga Press Poetry Chapbook Award, 1983; Third Place, Eve of St Agnes Poetry Competition, 1983; National Endowment for the Arts Fellowship, 1986–87; First Place, Morse Poetry Prize, 1987; Second Prize, Cincinnati Poetry Review Poetry Competition, 1989; Third Place, Apalaches Quarterly Long Poem Contest, 1989; First Place, Nilon Award for Excellence in Minority Fiction, 1991. *Address:* 702 S Marsh St, Lake City, FL 32025, USA.

SARAH, Robyn; Poet and Writer; b. 6 Oct. 1949, New York, NY, USA. *Education:* BA, 1970, MA, 1974, McGill University; Concours Diploma in Clarinet, Conservatoire de Musique du Québec, 1972. *Publications:* Poetry: Shadowplay, 1978; The Space Between Sleep and Waking, 1981; Three Sestinas, 1984; Anyone Skating On That Middle Ground, 1984; Becoming Light, 1987; The Touchstone: Poems New and Selected, 1992; Questions About the Stars, 1998. Fiction: A Nice Gazebo (short stories), 1992; Promise of Shelter (short stories), 1997. *Address:* c/o Vehicule Press, PO Box 125, Pl. du Parc Station, Montréal, QC H2W 2M9, Canada.

SARAMAGO, José; Portuguese author and poet; b. 16 Nov. 1922, Azinhaga; m. Pilar del Rio; one c. *Education:* principally self-educated. *Publications include:* novels: Manual de pintura e caligrafia (trans. as Manual of Painting and Calligraphy) 1976 , Levantado do chão 1980, Memorial do convento (trans. as Baltasar and Blimunda) 1982, O ano da morte de Ricardo Reis (trans. as The Year of the Death of Ricardo Reis) 1984, A jangada de pedra (trans. as The Stone Raft) 1986, História do cerco de Lisboa 1989, O Evangelho Segundo Jesus Cristo (trans. as The Gospel According to Jesus Christ) 1991, Ensaio sobre a cegueira (trans. as Blindness) 1995, Terra do pecado, Todos os nomes (trans. as All the Names) 1999, La caverna 2001; short stories: Objecto quase trans. as Quasi Object) 1978, Poética dos cinco sentidos – O ouvido 1979; poetry: Os poemas possíveis 1966, Provavelmente alegria 1970, O ano de 1993 1975; plays: A noite 1979, Que farei com este livro? 1980, A segunda vida de Francisco de Assisi 1987, In Nomine Dei 1993; opera librettos: Blimunda 1990, Divara 1993; other writing: Deste mundo e do outro 1971, A bagagem do viajante 1973, O embargo 1973, Os opiniões que o DL teve 1974, Os apontamentos 1976, Viagem a Portugal 1981, Cadernos de Lanzarote 1994–96, O poeta perguntador (ed.) 1979. *Honours:* Prémio da Críticos Portugueses 1979, Prémio Cidade de Lisboa 1980, Prémios PEN Clube Portugues 1982, 1984, Prémio Literario Municipio de Lisboa 1982, Prémio da Critica, Associacão Portuguesa de Criticos, Prémio Don Dinis 1986, Grinzane Cavour Prize 1987, Mondello Prize 1992, Grande Prémio de Romance e Novela da Associacão Portuguesa de Escritores 1992, Brancatti Literary Prize 1992, Flaiano Prize 1992, Prémio Vida Literária da Associacão Portuguesa de Escritores 1993, Prémio Consagracão Soc. Portuguesa de Autores 1995, Luís de Camões Prize 1995, Nobel Prize for Literature 1998. *Address:* Los Topes 3, 35572 Tias, Lanzarote, Canary Islands, Spain; Ray-Güde Mertin, 1 Friedrichstrasse, 61348 Bad Hamburg 1, Germany.

SARIF, Shamim; South African/Indian novelist and journalist; b. 24 Sept. 1969, London. *Education:* Univ. of London, Univ. of Boston, USA. *Screenplays include:* The Reader, Food of Love 2001. *Publications:* novels: The World Unseen 2001, Despite the Falling Snow 2004; contrib. to You magazine, American Way. *Honours:* Pendleton May First Novel Award. *Address:* c/o Hodder Headline PLC, 338 Euston Road, London, NW1 3BH, England. *Website:* www.shamimsarif.com.

SARKAR, Anil Kumar, MA, PhD, DLitt; academic and writer; b. 1 Aug. 1912, Ranchi, India; m. Aruna Sarkar 1941 (deceased); one s. three d. *Education:* Patna Univ. *Career:* Prof., Rajendra College, 1940–44; Senior Lecturer, University of Ceylon, Colombo and Perdeniya, 1944–64; Visiting Prof., University of New Mexico, Albuquerque, 1964–65; Full Prof. of Philosophy and West-East Philosophy, 1965–82, California State University, Hayward, USA; Research Dir, Prof. of Asian Studies, 1968–80, Prof. Emeritus, 1980–, California Institute of Integral Studies, San Francisco. *Publications:* An Outline of Whitehead's Philosophy, 1940; Changing Phases of Buddhist Thought, 1968; Whitehead's Four Principles From West-East Perspectives, 1974; Dynamic Facets of Indian Thought, Vol. 1, 1980, Vols 2–4, 1987–88; Experience in Change and Prospect: Pathways from War to Peace, 1989; Sri Aurobindo's Vision of the Super Mind – Its Indian and Non-Indian Interpreters, 1989; Buddhism and Whitehead's Process Philosopy, 1990; Zero: Its Role and Prospects in Indian Thought and its Impact on Post-Einsteinian Astrophysics, 1992; The Mysteries of Vajrayana Buddhism: From Atisha to Dalai Lama, 1993; Triadic Avenues of India's Cultural Prospects: Philosophy, Physics and Politics, 1995; Shaping of Euro-Indian Philosophy, 1995. Contributions: Indian, US and other journals. *Address:* B/B/12/15-7 Kalyani, Df Nadia, West Bengal, India.

SARNA, Jonathan D(aniel); Prof. of Jewish American History and Writer; b. 10 Jan. 1955, Philadelphia, PA, USA; m. Ruth Langer, 8 June 1986, one s. one d. *Education:* BHL, Hebrew College, Boston, 1974; BA, summa cum laude, Judaic Studies and History, 1975, MA, Judaic Studies, 1975, Brandeis University; MA, 1976, MPhil, History, 1978, PhD, History, 1979,

Yale University. *Career:* Visiting Lecturer, 1979–80, Asst Prof. to Assoc. Prof. of American Jewish History, 1980–90, Hebrew Union College-Jewish Institute of Religion; Dir, American Jewish Experience Curriculum Project, 1982–, Center for the Study of the American Jewish Experience, 1986–90, Boston Jewish History Project, 1992-95; Visiting Asst Prof., University of Cincinnati, 1983–84; Visiting Assoc. Prof., Hebrew University, Jerusalem, 1986–87; Joseph H. and Belle R. Braun Prof. of American Jewish History, Brandeis University, 1990–; mem. American Acad. of Religion; American Historical Asscn; American Jewish Historical Society; Asscn for Jewish Studies; Organization of American Historians. *Publications:* Jews in New Haven (ed.), 1978; Mordecai Manuel Noah: Jacksonian Politician and American Jewish Communal Leader, 1979; Jacksonian Jew: The Two Worlds of Mordecai Noah, 1981; Jews and the Founding of the Republic (co-ed.), 1985; The American Jewish Experience: A Reader (ed.), 1986; American Synagogue History: A Bibliography and State-of-the-Field Survey (with Alexandra S. Korros), 1988; JPS: The Americanization of Jewish Culture: A History of the Jewish Publication Society 1888–1988, 1989; The Jews of Cincinnati (with Nancy H. Klein), 1989; A Double Bond: The Constitutional Documents of American Jewry (ed. with Daniel J. Elazar and Rela Geffen Monson), 1992; Ethnic Diversity and Civic Identity: Patterns of Conflict and Cohesion in Cincinnati Since 1820 (with Henry D. Shapiro), 1992; Yuhude Artsot Ha-Berit (with Lloyd Gartner), 1992; Observing America's Jews (ed. with Marshall Sklare), 1993; The Jews of Boston (with Ellen Smith), 1995; Abba Hillel Silver and American Zionism (with Mark A. Raider and Ronald W. Zweig), 1997; Minority Faiths and the American Protestant Mainstream, 1997; Religion and State in the American Jewish Experience (with David G. Dalin), 1997; Women and American Judaism: Historical Perspectives (with Pamela S. Nadel), 2001. Contributions: scholarly books, professional journals and general periodicals. *Honours:* Outstanding Academic Book, Choice, 1998; Benjamin J. Shevach Memorial Prize for Distinguished Leadership in Jewish Education, 2000. *Address:* c/o Dept of Near Eastern and Judaic Studies, Brandeis University, Waltham, MA 02454, USA. *E-mail:* sarna@brandeis.edu.

SARNA, Nahum Mattathias; Prof. of Biblical Studies Emeritus and Writer; b. 27 March 1923, London, England; m. Helen Horowitz, 13 March 1947, two s. *Education:* BA, 1944, MA, 1946, University of London; PhD, Dropsie College, Philadelphia, 1955. *Career:* University College London, 1946–49; Gratz College, Philadelphia, 1951–57; Jewish Theological Seminary, New York City, 1957–65; Visiting Prof., Columbia University, 1964–65, 1992, Yale University, 1992–94; Faculty, 1965–67, Dora Golding Prof. of Biblical Studies, 1967–85, Prof. Emeritus, 1985–, Brandeis University; Distinguished Prof., Florida Atlantic University, 1995–; Gimelstob Eminent Scholar and Prof. of Judaica, Florida Altlantic University, 2000–; mem. American Acad. for Jewish Research, fellow; American Oriental Society; Asscn for Jewish Studies; Dead Sea Scrolls Foundation, board of advisers; Israel Exploration Society; Palestine Exploration Society; World Union of Jewish Studies. *Publications:* Understanding Genesis, 1966; Exploring Exodus, 1985; Commentary on Genesis, 1989; Commentary on Exodus, 1991; Songs of the Heart: An Introduction to the Book of Psalms, 1993. Contributions: Professional journals. *Honours:* Jewish Book Council Award, 1967; ACLS Senior Fellow, 1971–72; Institute for Advanced Studies, Hebrew University, fellow, 1982–83; Hon. doctorates. *Address:* 7886 Chula Vista Crescent, Boca Raton, FL 33433, USA.

SAROYAN, Aram; writer, poet and dramatist; b. 25 Sept. 1943, New York, NY, USA; m. Gailyn McClanahan 1968; one s. two d. *Education:* University of Chicago, New York University, Columbia University. *Publications:* Aram Saroyan, 1968; Pages, 1969; Words and Photographs, 1970; The Street: An Autobiographical Novel, 1974; Genesis Angels: The Saga of Lew Welch and the Beat Generation, 1979; Last Rites: The Death of William Saroyan, 1982; William Saroyan, 1983; Trio: Portrait of an Intimate Friendship, 1985; The Romantic, 1988; Friends in the World: The Education of a Writer, 1992; Rancho Mirage: An American Tragedy of Manners, Madness and Murder, 1993; Day and Night: Bolinas Poems 1972–81, 1998; Starting Out in the Sixties (essays), 2001; Artists in Trouble: New Stories, 2001; Day by Day, 2002. Other: Staged readings of plays. Contributions: New York Times Book Review; Los Angeles Times Book Review; The Nation; Village Voice; Mother Jones; Paris Review; Shambhala Sun magazine. *Honours:* National Endowment for the Arts Poetry Awards 1967, 1968. *Literary Agent:* Frederick Hill, 1842 Union Street, San Francisco, CA 94123, USA. *Telephone:* (415) 921-2910. *Address:* 5482 Village Green, Los Angeles, CA 90016, USA. *Website:* www.aramsaroyan.com.

SATRAPI, Marjane, MA; Iranian writer and illustrator; b. 22 Nov. 1969, Rasht. *Education:* Visual Communication School of Fine Arts, Tehran. *Publications:* Persepolis: The Story of a Childhood (four vols) 1999–2002, several children's books; contrib. illustrations to French magazines and periodicals. *Address:* c/o Jonathan Cape, Random House UK Ltd, 20 Vauxhall Bridge Road, London, SW1V 2SA, USA. *Telephone:* (20) 7840-8576. *Website:* www.randomhouse.co.uk.

SATTERTHWAIT, Walter; writer; b. 23 March 1946, Philadelphia, Pennsylvania, USA; one d. *Education:* Reed College. *Career:* mem. MWA, Private Eye Writers of America. *Publications:* Cocaine Blues, 1980; The Aegean Affair, 1981; Wall of Glass, 1987; Miss Lizzie, 1989; At Ease With the Dead, 1990; Wilde West, 1991; A Flower In the Desert, 1992; The Hanged Man, 1993, UK edn as The Death Card, 1994; Escapade, 1995; Accustomed to the Dark, 1996; Masquerade, 1998. Contributions: Alfred Hitchcock's Mystery Magazine; Santa Fe Reporter. *Honours:* Prix du Roman d'Aventures, France 1996.

SAUNDERS, Ann Loreille, (Ann Cox-Johnson), MBE, BA, PhD, FSA; historian; b. 23 May 1930, London, England; m. Bruce Kemp Saunders 1960; one s. one d. *Education:* Queen's Coll., London, Univ. Coll. London, Leicester Univ. *Career:* Deputy Librarian, Lambeth Palace 1952–55; Archivist, Marylebone Public Library, London 1956–63; Fellow, Univ. Coll. London 1992; mem. Costume Soc. (hon. ed. 1967–), London Topographical Soc. (hon. ed. 1975–). *Publications:* London, North of the Thames 1972, London, City and Westminster 1975, Art and Architecture of London 1984, St Martin-in-the-Fields 1989, The Royal Exchange 1991, The Royal Exchange (ed. and co-author) 1997, St Paul's: The History of the Cathedral 2001, The History of the Merchant Taylor's Company (with Matthew Davies) 2004; contrib. to magazines. *Honours:* Plumptre Scholar, Queen's Coll., London 1946–48, Prize for Best Specialist Guide Book of the Year, British Tourist Board 1984. *Address:* 3 Meadway Gate, London, NW11 7LA, England.

SAUNDERS, George, BSc, MA; American writer; b. 2 Dec. 1958, Amarillo, TX. *Education:* Colorado School of Mines, Syracuse Univ. *Career:* Visiting Prof. of Creative Writing, Syracuse Univ. 1996–97. *Publications:* Civil War Land in Bad Decline 1996, Pastoralia: Stories 2000, The Very Persistent Gappers of Frip 2000; contrib. to books and periodicals. *Honours:* National Magazine Awards 1994, 1996, 1999, New York Times Notable Book of the Year Citation 2000.

SAUR, Klaus Gerhard, DHumLitt; German publisher; *Chairman of the Board, KG Saur Verlag*; b. 27 July 1941, Pullach; m. Lilo Stangel 1977; one s. one d. *Education:* High School, Icking and Commercial High School, Munich. *Career:* Marketing Man. Vulkan-Verlag, Essen 1962; Publishing Man. KG Saur, Munich 1963, Publishing Dir 1966; Pres. KG Saur New York and KG Saur, London 1977; Man. Dir KG Saur Munich 1988–2004, Chair. of the Bd 2004–; Founder World Guide to Libraries, Publrs Int. Directory; mem. Bd F.A. Brockhaus Bibliographical Inst. (Mannheim); Chair. Bd Beltz Publishing and Printing Corpn; Vice-Pres. Goethe-Institut, Germany. *Publications:* World Biographical Information System, Pressehandbuch für Exportwerbung, World Guide to Libraries. *Honours:* Hon. Prof. Univ. of Glasgow, Humboldt-Univ. Berlin; Hon. Fellow, Tech. Univ. of Graz; Hon. mem. Austrian Library Asscn 1998, German Library Asscn; Senator hc (Ludwig Maximilians Univ., Munich) 1992, (Leipzig) 2001; Bundesverdienstkreuz der Bundesrepublik Deutschland, Officier Ordre des Arts et Lettres (France), Sächsischer Verdienstordern 2002, Bayerischer Verdienstordern 2002; Hon. DPhil (Marburg) 1985, (Ishevsk, Russia) 1997, (Pisa, Italy) 1998, (Simmons Coll., Mass.) 1992; Hon. Medal City of Munich 1988, Hon. Bene Merenti Medal, Bavarian Acad. of Sciences 1997, Helmut-Sontag Award, Asscn of German Libraries 1999, Großes Österreichisches Verdienstkreuz der Wessenschaftund Künste 2003, Max-Hermann-Award, German State Library. *Address:* KG Saur Verlag, Ortlerstrasse 8, 81373 Munich (Office); Beuerbergerstrasse 9, 81479 Munich, Germany (Home). *Telephone:* (89) 76902460 (Office); (89) 74994651 (Home). *Fax:* (89) 76902450 (Office); (89) 74994652 (Home). *E-mail:* k.saur@saur.de (Office). *Website:* www.saur.de (Office).

SAUVAIN, Philip (Arthur); Writer; b. 28 March 1933, Burton on Trent, Staffordshire, England; m. June Maureen Spenceley, 27 July 1963, one s. one d. *Education:* MA, University of Cambridge, 1956; Postgraduate Certificate in Education, University of London, 1957. *Career:* Senior Lecturer in Geography, James Graham College, Leeds, 1963–68; Head, Environmental Studies Dept, Charlotte Mason College of Education, Ambleside, 1968–74. *Publications:* Looking Aroung Town and Country, 1975; A First Look Series, 5 vols, 1975–78; Imagining the Past: First Series, 6 vols, 1976, Second Series, 6 vols, 1979; The British Isles, 1980; The Story of Britain Series, 4 vols, 1980; Britain's Living Heritage, 1982; The History of Britain, 4 vols, 1982; Theatre, 1983; Macmillan Junior Geography, 4 vols, 1983; Hulton New Geographies, 5 vols, 1983; History Map Books, 2 vols, 1983, 1985; Hulton New Histories, 5 vols, 1984–85; France and the French, 1985; European and World History, 1815–1919, 1985; Modern World History, 1919 Onwards, 1985; How History Began, 1985; Castles and Crusaders, 1986; What to Look For, 4 vols, 1986; British Economic and Social History, 2 vols, 1987; Exploring Energy, 4 vols, 1987; GCSE History Companion Series, 3 vols, 1988; How We Build, 3 vols, 1989; The World of Work, 3 vols, 1989; Skills for Geography, 1989; Skills for Standard Grade History, 1990; Exploring the Past: Old World, 1991; The Way it Works, 3 vols, 1991; Changing World, 1992; Breakthrough: Communications, 1992; History Detectives, 3 vols, 1992–93; Great Battles and Sieges, 4 vols, 1992–93; Expanding World, 1993; The Era of the Second World War, 1993; Robert Scott in the Antarctic, 1993; Target Geography, 14 vols, 1994–95; The Tudors and Stuarts, 1995; Britain Since 1930, 4 vols, 1995; Geography Detective, 4 vols, 1995–96; Famous Lives, 2 vols, 1996; Key Themes of the Twentieth Century, 1996; Key Themes of the Twentieth Century: Teacher's Guide, 1996; Germany in the Twentieth Century, 1997; Vietnam, 1997. *Address:* 70 Finborough Rd, Stowmarket, Suffolk IP14 1PU, England.

SAVAGE, Alan (see Nicole, Christopher (Robin)).

SAVAGE, Thomas, (Tom Savage); Poet, Writer, Critic and Ed.; b. 14 July 1948, New York, NY, USA. *Education:* BA, English, Brooklyn College,

CUNY, 1969; MLS, Columbia University School of Library Science, 1980. *Career:* Teaching Asst, Naropa Institute School of Poetics, 1975; Ed., Roof Magazine, 1976–78, Gandhabba Magazine, 1981–93; Teacher, Words, Music, Words for Poets and Composers, St Mark's Poetry Project, 1983–85; mem. Co-ordinating Council of Literary Magazines. *Publications:* Personalities, 1978; Filling Spaces, 1980; Slow Waltz on a Glass Harmonica, 1980; Housing Preservation and Development, 1988; Processed Words, 1990; Out of the World, 1991; Political Conditions and Physical States, 1993; Brain Surgery (poems), 1999. Contributions: Magazines and journals. *Honours:* PEN Grant, 1978; Co-ordinating Council of Literary Magazines Grant, 1981–82. *Address:* 622 E 11th St, No. 14, New York, NY 10009, USA.

SAVILLE, Diana; Writer; b. 15 Feb. 1943, London, England; m. 1974. *Education:* Degree, St Hugh's College, Oxford, 1965. *Publications:* The Observer's Book of British Gardens, 1982; Walled Gardens: Their Planning and Design, 1982; The Illustrated Garden Planter, 1984; Gardens for Small Country Houses, 1984; Colour, 1992; Walls and Screens, 1993; Green and Pleasant Land: A Thousand Years of Poetry (ed.), 1993; The Marriage Bed, 1995; The Honey Makers, 1996; The Hawk Dancer, 1997. *Literary Agent:* Sterling Lord Literistic Inc, 65 Bleecker St, New York, NY 10012, USA.

SAVOY, Deirdre; Author; b. 31 Oct. 1960, New York, NY, USA; m. Carmelo (Frank) La Mantia, 27 May 1988, one s. one d. *Education:* BBA, Baruch College, CUNY, 1994. *Publications:* Spellbound, 1999; Always, 2000. *Literary Agent:* James B. Finn Literary Agency. *Address:* PO Box 233, New York, NY 10469, USA.

SAVOY, Douglas Eugene, (Gene Savoy); Bishop, Writer, Educator and Explorer; b. 11 May 1927, Bellingham, Washington, USA; two s. one d. *Career:* mem. Authors' Guild; Explorers Club, New York City; Geographical Society, Lima, Peru; Andean Explorers Foundation; Ocean Sailing Club; World Council for Human Rights; Advocates for Religious Rights and Freedoms. *Publications:* Antisuyo: The Search for the Lost Cities of the Amazon, 1970; Vilcabamba: Last City of the Incas, 1970; The Child Christ, 1973; The Decoded New Testament, 1974; On the Trail of the Feathered Serpent, 1974; The Prophecies of Jamil, 7 vols, 1976–83; The Secret Sayings of Jamil: The Image and the World, 7 vols, 1976–87; The Essaei Document: Secrets of an Eternal Race, 1978, Project X: The Search for the Secrets of Immortality, 1977; The Lost Gospel of Jesus: Hidden Teachings of Christ, 1978; Miracle of the Second Advent, 1984. Other: 39 texts, 400 audio tapes: Lectures on Religious Systems and Theology, 5 documentary videos. Contributions: various publications. *Honours:* Over 40 Flag Awards, Andean Explorers Foundation, Explorers Club, New York City, 1958–94; Silver Hummingbird Award, Ministry of Industry and Tourism of Peru, 1987; Explorer of the Century Trophy, Andean Explorers Foundation, 1988; Decorated Officer, Order of the Grand Cross, Republic of Peru, 1989; Medal of Merit Andres Reyes, 1989; Award, City of Ica, Peru, 1995. *Address:* 2025 LaFond Dr., Reno, NV 89509, USA.

SAVOY, Gene (see Savoy, Douglas Eugene).

SAWYER, Robert J(ames); Writer; b. 29 April 1960, Ottawa, Ontario, Canada; m. Carolyn Joan Clink, 11 Dec. 1984. *Education:* BAA, Ryerson Polytechnical Institute, 1982. *Career:* mem. Crime Writers of Canada; MWA; SFWA; Writers Union of Canada. *Publications:* Golden Fleece, 1990; Far-Seer, 1992; Fossil Hunter, 1993; Foreigner, 1994; End of an Era, 1994; The Terminal Experiment, 1995. *Honours:* Aurora Award, Canadian Science Fiction and Fantasy Asscn, 1992; Homer Awards, 1992, 1993; Writer's Reserve Grant, Ontario Arts Council, 1993. *Address:* 7601 Bathurst St, No. 617, Thornhill, Ontario L4J 4H5, Canada.

SAWYER, Roger Martyn; Author; b. 15 Dec. 1931, Stroud, England; m. Diana Margaret Harte, 30 Aug. 1952, two s. *Education:* BA, Diploma in Education, University of Wales, 1958; PhD, History, University of Southampton, 1979. *Career:* mem. Anti-Slavery International, council mem., 1984–98; Bembridge Sailing Club; Old Wycliffian Society. *Publications:* Casement: The Flawed Hero, 1984; Slavery in the Twentieth Century, 1986; Children Enslaved, 1988; The Island from Within (ed.), 1990; 'We are but Women': Women in Ireland's History, 1993; Roger Casement's Diaries 1910: The Black and The White (ed.), 1997. Contributions: Anti-Slavery Reporter; BBC History Magazine; Immigrants and Minorities; South. *Honours:* Airey Neave Award, 1985. *Address:* Ducie House, Darts Lane, Bembridge, Isle of Wight PO35 5YH, England.

SAYER, Ian Keith Terence; author and management consultant; b. 30 Oct. 1945, Norwich, Norfolk, England; two s. three d. *Publications:* Nazi Gold: The Story of the World's Greatest Robbery 1984, republished 1998 and 2003, America's Secret Army: The Untold Story of the Counter Intelligence Corps 1989, Hitler's Last General: The Case Against Wilhelm Mohnke 1989, Hitler's Bastard: Through Hell and Back in Nazi Germany and Stalin's Russia (ed.) 2003. Contributions: Columnist Freight News, Columnist Express Magazine, Sunday Times Magazine. *Address:* Westerlands, Sherbourne Dr., Sunningdale, Berkshire SL5 0LG, England. *E-mail:* ian@sayer.net.

SAYLOR, Steven (Warren), (Aaron Travis); Writer; b. 23 March 1956, Port Lavaca, TX, USA; Registered pnr Richard K. Solomon 15 March 1991. *Education:* BA, Univ. of Texas at Austin, 1978. *Career:* mem. MWA. *Publications:* Roman Blood, 1991; Arms of Nemesis, 1992; Catilina's Riddle, 1993; The Venus Throw, 1995; A Murder on the Appian Way, 1996; House of the Vestals, 1997; Rubicon, 1999; A Twist at the End (aka Honour the Dead), 2000; Last Seen in Massilia, 2000; A Mist of Prophecies, 2002; Have You Seen Dawn?, 2003. As Aaron Travis: Big Shots, 1993; Beast of Burden, 1993; Slaves of the Empire, 1996. Contributions: books and periodicals. *Honours:* Robert L. Fish Memorial Award, MWA, 1993; Lambda Literary Award, 1994. *Address:* 1711 Addison St, Berkeley, CA 94703, USA. *Website:* www.stevensaylor.com.

SCAGLIONE, Aldo D(omenico); Prof. of Literature and Writer; b. 10 Jan. 1925, Turin, Italy; m. 1st Jeanne M. Daman, 28 June 1952, deceased 1986; m. 2nd Marie M. Burns, Aug. 1992. *Education:* DLitt, University of Turin, 1948. *Career:* Faculty, University of California at Berkeley, 1952–68; W. R. Kenan Prof., University of North Carolina at Chapel Hill, 1969–87; Prof., 1987–91, Erich Maria Remarque Prof. of Literature, 1991–, New York University; mem. American Asscn for Italian Studies, hon. pres., 1989; Boccaccio Asscn of America, pres., 1980–83; Medieval Acad. of America. *Publications:* Nature and Love in the Late Middle Ages, 1963; Ars Grammatica, 1970; The Classical Theory of Composition, 1972; The Theory of German Word Order, 1981; The Liberal Arts and the Jesuit College System, 1986; Knights at Court, 1991; Essays on the Art of Discourse, 1998. Contributions: Professional journals. *Honours:* Knight of the Order of Merit, Republic of Italy; Fulbright Scholar, 1951; Guggenheim Fellowship, 1958; Newbery Fellow, 1964; Fellow, University of Wisconsin Institute for the Humanities, 1981.

SCALAPINO, Robert A(nthony); Prof. of Government Emeritus and Writer; b. 19 Oct. 1919, Leavenworth, KS, USA; m. Ida Mae Jessen, 23 Aug. 1941, three d. *Education:* BA, Santa Barbara College, 1940; MA, 1943, PhD, 1948, Harvard University. *Career:* Lecturer, Santa Barbara College, 1940–41; Instructor, Harvard University, 1948–49; Asst Prof., 1949–51, Assoc. Prof., 1951–56, Robson Research Prof. of Government and Dir, Institute of East Asian Studies, 1978–90, Prof. Emeritus, 1990–, University of California at Berkeley; Ed., Asian Survey, 1962–96; mem. American Acad. of Arts and Sciences; American Political Science Asscn; Asscn for Asian Studies; Council on Foreign Relations; Foreign Policy Asscn; Western Political Science Asscn; Mem. of Board, Asia Foundation, Atlantic Council, Pacific Forum—CSIS. *Publications:* Democracy and the Party Movement in Pre-War Japan, 1953; The Chinese Anarchist Movement (with George T. Yu), 1961; North Korea Today (ed.), 1963; The Japanese Communist Movement, 1920–1966, 1967; The Communist Revolution in Asia (ed.), 1969; Communism in Korea (with Chong-Sik Lee), 1972; Elites in the People's Republic of China (ed.), 1972; Asia and the Road Ahead, 1975; The Foreign Policy of Modern Japan (ed.), 1977; The United States and Korea: Looking Ahead, 1979; North Korea Today: Strategic and Domestic Issues (ed. with Jun-Yop Kim), 1983; The Early Japanese Labor Movement, 1984; The Politics of Development: Perspectives on Twentieth Century Asia, 1989; The Last Leninists: The Uncertain Future of Asia's Communist States, 1992. Contributions: many scholarly books and journals. *Honours:* Carnegie Foundation Grant, 1951–53; Social Science Research Council Fellow, 1952–53; Ford Foundation Grant, 1955; Rockefeller Foundation Grants, 1956–59, 1961; Guggenheim Fellowship, 1965–66; Woodrow Wilson Award, American Political Science Asscn, 1973; Order of the Sacred Treasure, Japan, 1988; Presidential Order, Republic of Korea, 1990; Berkeley Fellow, 1990; Hon. Prof., Peking University, 1997; Japan Foundation Award, 1998; Friendship Medal, Government of Mongolia, 1999; Hon. doctorates. *Address:* 2850 Buena Vista Way, Berkeley, CA 94708, USA.

SCALES-TRENT, Judy; Prof. of Law, Writer and Poet; b. 1 Oct. 1940, Winston-Salem, NC, USA; one s. *Education:* BA, French, Oberlin College, 1962; MA, French, Middlebury College, 1967; JD, Northwestern University School of Law, 1973. *Career:* Adjunct Faculty, Catholic University Law School 1983; Prof. of Law, SUNY at Buffalo 1984–; Visiting Prof. of Law, Univ. Cheikh Anta Diop de Dakar 1990–91, St Mary's University School of Law 1994. *Publications:* Notes of a White Black Woman: Race, Color, Community 1995. Contributions: anthologies, literary periodicals and law journals. *Honours:* Fulbright Award 1990–91, Baldy Center for Law and Social Policy Award, SUNY at Buffalo 1986, 1991–93, William J. Magavern Fellowship 1993. *Address:* 352 Old Meadow Rd, East Amherst, NY 14051, USA.

SCALFARI, Eugenio; Editor; b. 6 April 1924, Civitavecchia, Italy; m. Simonetta de Benedetti 1959; two d. *Career:* contrib. Il Mondo, L'Europeo 1950–; Promoter Partito Radicale 1958, L'Espresso 1955–, Ed.-in-Chief 1963–68, Man. Dir 1970–75; Promoter La Repubblica 1976–, Ed.-in-Chief 1976–96, Dir 1988–; Deputy to Parl. 1968–72. *Publications:* Rapporto sul Neocapitalismo Italiano; Il Potere Economico in URSS; L'Autunno della Repubblica; Razza Padrona; Interviste ai Potenti; L'Anno di Craxi; La Sera Andavamo in Via Veneto; Incontro con Io; La Morale Perduta; La Ruga Sulla Fronte. *Honours:* Siena Award, 1985; Journalist of the Year Award, 1986. *Address:* c/o La Repubblica, Piazza dell'Indipendenza 11/B, 00185 Rome, Italy.

SCAMMACCA, Nat; Prof. of English (retd), Writer and Poet; b. 20 July 1924, New York, NY, USA; m. Nina Scammacca, 1948, one s. two d. *Education:* BA, Literature and Philosophy, Long Island University; MA, Education, New York University; Graduated in Italian, University of Perugia. *Career:* Pilot, US Air Force, India-Burma-China theatre, World War II; Social Worker, Italian Board of Guardians; Prof. of English, British College,

Palermo; Ed., Third Page, Trapani Nuova newspaper; mem. Poets and Writers, New York City. *Publications:* Two Worlds (novel), 1980; Schammachanat (Italian and English), 1985; Bye Bye America (short stories), 1986; Cricepeo (Italian and English), 3 vols, 1990; Sikano L'Amerikano! (short stories), 1991; Due Poeti Americani (Italian and English, co-author), 1994; The Hump (World War II stories and poems), 1994. Other: various books and trans. Contributions: anthologies and periodicals. *Honours:* Air Medal, Bronze Star, US Air Force; Taormina City Poetry Prize, 1978; Premio Letterario Sikania Prize, 1988; VII Premio di Poesia Petrosino Prize, 1991. *Address:* Villa Schammachanat, Via Argenteria KM4, Trapani, Sicily 91100, Italy.

SCAMMELL, Michael; Writer; b. 16 Jan. 1935, Lyndhurst, England; m. 2nd Rosemary Nossiff; one s. three d. *Education:* BA, University of Nottingham; Graduate studies, Columbia University. *Career:* Lecturer in English, Ljubljana University, Yugoslavia, 1958–59; Lecturer in Russian, Hunter College, CUNY, 1961–62; Language Supervisor, Programme Asst, BBC, London, 1965–67; Ed., Index on Censorship, London, 1971–80; Dir, Writers and Scholars Educational Trust, London, 1971–80; Chair, Writers in Prison Committee, International PEN, 1976–84; Prof. of Russian Literature, Cornell University, 1987–94; Prof. of Creative Writing, Columbia University, 1994; mem. Society of Authors, Vice-Chair, 1976–79; Trans Asscn; English PEN Centre; Pres., American PEN Center, 1998–2001; Vice-Pres., International PEN, 1986–. *Publications:* Blue Guide to Yugoslavia, 1969; Russia's Other Writers (ed.), 1970; Alexander Solzhenitsyn, 1971; Unofficial Art from the Soviet Union (ed.), 1977; Solzhenitsyn: A Biography, 1984; The Solzhenitsyn Files: Secret Soviet Documents Reveal One Man's Fight Against the Monolith (ed.), 1995. Translator: Cities and Years, 1962; Crime and Punishment, 1963; The Gift, 1963; The Defense, 1964; Childhood, Boyhood and Youth, 1964; My Testimony, 1969; Nothing is Lost: Selected Poems by Edvard Kochek (with Veno Taufer), 2004. Contributions: periodicals including: TLS; The Observer; The Times; Daily Telegraph, London; Sunday Telegraph, London; New York Times Book Review; New York Review of Books; New Republic; Harpers, USA. *Honours:* Columbia University Fellow, 1959–61; Russian Institute Senior Visiting Fellow, 1976–84; New York Institute for the Humanities Fellow, 1982–84; Los Angeles Times Book Prize for Biography, 1985. *Literary Agent:* AP Watt Ltd, 20 John St, London WC1N 2DR, England. *Address:* 605 West 113 St, Apt 32, New York, NY 10025, USA.

SCANNELL, Vernon; Author and Poet; b. 23 Jan. 1922, Spilsby, Lincolnshire, England; m. 4 Oct. 1954, three s., two d. *Career:* Visiting Poet, Shrewsbury School, 1973–75; Writer-in-Residence, Berinsfield, Oxfordshire, 1975–76; Poet-in-Residence, King's School, Canterbury, 1979; mem. Hon. FRSL. *Publications:* Fiction: The Fight, 1952; The Wound and the Scar, 1953; The Face of the Enemy, 1960; The Big Time, 1967; Ring of Truth, 1983; Feminine Endings, 2000. Poetry: New and Collected Poems, 1980; Winterlude, 1983; Funeral Games, 1987; Soldiering On, 1989; A Time for Fires, 1991; Collected Poems 1950–1993, 1994; The Black and White Days, 1996; Views and Distances, 2000. Non-Fiction: The Tiger and the Rose, 1971; Argument of Kings, 1987; Drums of Morning, Growing Up in the 30s, 1992. Contributions: newspapers, reviews, and magazines. *Honours:* Heinemann Award for Literature, 1960; Cholmondeley Award for Poetry, 1974. *Address:* 51 North St, Otley, West Yorkshire LS21 1AH, England.

SCARDINO, Dame Marjorie Morris, DBE, JD, BA; American/British business executive; *CEO, Pearson PLC*; b. 25 Jan. 1947, Flagstaff, Arizona; m. Albert James Scardino 1974; two s. one d. *Education:* Baylor Univ., Univ. of San Francisco. *Career:* reporter, Associated Press; Partner, Brannen, Wessels and Searcy law firm 1975–85; Publr The Georgia Gazette Co. 1978–85; Pres. The Economist Newspaper Group Inc. 1985–93; Chief Exec. The Economist Group 1993–97; CEO Pearson PLC 1997–; Dir (non-exec.) Nokia Corpn 2001–; mem. Bd Trustees Carter Center, Victoria and Albert Museum. *Honours:* Hon. Fellow London Business School, City and Guilds of London Inst.; Hon. LLD (Exeter); Hon. DHumLitt (New School Univ.); Dr hc (Heriot-Watt), (Brunel); Veuve Cliquot Businesswoman of the Year Award 1998. *Address:* Pearson PLC, 80 Strand, London, WC2R 0RL, England. *Telephone:* (20) 7010-2300. *Fax:* (20) 7010-6601 (Office). *E-mail:* marjorie.scardino@pearson.com (Office). *Website:* www.pearson.com (Office).

SCARF, Margaret; Writer; b. 13 May 1932, Philadelphia, Pennsylvania, USA; m. Herbert Eli Scarf, 28 June 1953, three d. *Education:* BA, South Connecticut State University, 1989. *Career:* Contributing Ed., The New Republic, 1975–; Fellow, Center for Advanced Study, Stanford, CA, 1977–78, 1985–86; Writer-in-Residence, Jonathan Edwards College, Yale University, 1992–; mem. Connecticut Society of Psychoanalytic Psychologists; PEN. *Publications:* Body, Mind, Behavior, 1976; Unfinished Business, 1980; Intimate Partners, 1987; Intimate Worlds: Life Inside the Family, 1995. Contributions: Magazines and journals. *Honours:* Ford Foundation Fellow, 1973–74; Nieman Fellow, Harvard University, 1975–76; Alicia Patterson Fellow, 1978–79; Smith Richardson Foundation Grants, 1991, 1992, 1993, 1994. *Address:* c/o Jonathan Edwards College, Yale University, 68 High St, New Haven, CT 06517, USA.

SCARFE, Allan John, BA, DipEd, TPTC; writer; b. 30 March 1931, Caulfield, Vic., Australia; m. Wendy Scarfe 1955; four c. *Publications:* A Corpse in Calcutta 2000, The Dissident Guru 2004; with Wendy Scarfe: A Mouthful of Petals 1967, Tiger on a Rein 1969, People of India 1972, The Black Australians 1974, Victims or Bludgers?: Case Studies in Poverty in Australia 1974, J. P: his Biography 1975, Victims or Bludgers?: A Poverty Inquiry for Schools 1978, Labor's Titan: The Story of Percy Brookfield 1878–1921 1983, All That Grief: Migrant Recollections of Greek Resistance to Facism 1941–49 1994, Remembering Jayaprakash 1997, No Taste for Carnage: Alex Sheppard – A Portrait 1913–1997 1998; contrib. to several publications. *Honours:* Australia Literature Boards Grants (with Wendy Scarfe) 1980, 1988. *Address:* 8 Bostock Street, Warrnambool, Vic. 3280, Australia.

SCARFE, Norman; Writer; b. 1 May 1923, Felixstowe, England. *Education:* MA, History, Oxford, 1949. *Career:* Chair., Centre of East Anglia Studies, University of East Anglia, 1989–96; mem. International PEN; Suffolk Book League, founder chair., 1982; Suffolk Records Society, founder, hon. gen. ed., 1958–92, pres., 2002. *Publications:* Assault Division: The 3rd British Infantry Division from D-Day to VE Day, 1947; Suffolk, A Shell Guide, 1960; Essex, A Shell Guide, 1968; The Suffolk Landscape, 1972; Cambridgeshire, A Shell Guide, 1983; Suffolk in the Middle Ages, 1986; A Frenchman's Year in Suffolk (1784), 1988; Innocent Espionage: The La Rochefoucauld Brothers' Tour of England in 1785, 1995; Jocelin of Brakelond, 1997; To the Highlands in 1786: The Inquisitive Journey of a Young French Aristocrat, 2001. Contributions: Proceedings, Suffolk Institute of Archaeology; Aldeburgh Festival Annual Programme Book; Country Life; The Book Collector; Dictionary of National Biography; The Impact of the Railways on Society in Britain: Essays in Honour of Jack Simmons, 2003. *Honours:* Fellow, Society of Antiquaries, 1964; Hon. DLitt, University of East Anglia, 1989; Citoyen d'Honneur, Colleville Montgomery, 1994; MBE, 1994; East Anglia's, History: Studies in Honour of Norman Scarfe (ed. by Christopher Harper-Bill, Carole Rawcliffe, Richard Wilson), 2002. *Literary Agent:* John Welch, Mill Cottage, Chipping Campden, GL55 6JQ, England. *Address:* The Garden Cottage, 3 Burkitt Rd, Woodbridge, Suffolk IP12 4JJ, England.

SCARFE, Wendy Elizabeth, BA, BLitt, ATTC; writer and poet; b. 21 Nov. 1933, Adelaide, SA, Australia; m. Allan Scarfe 1955; four c. *Publications:* fiction: The Lotus Throne 1976, Neither Here Nor There 1978, Laura My Alter Ego 1988, The Day They Shot Edward 1991, Miranda 1998, Fishing for Strawberries 2001; poetry: Shadow and Flowers 1964, Dragonflies and Edges (with Jeffrey Ronald Keith) 2004; with Allan Scarfe: A Mouthful of Petals 1967, Tiger on a Rein 1969, People of India 1972, The Black Australians 1974, Victims or Bludgers?: Case Studies in Poverty in Australia 1974, J. P: His Biography 1975, Victims or Bludgers?: A Poverty Inquiry for Schools 1978, Labor's Titan: The Story of Percy Brookfield, 1878–1921 1983, All That Grief: Migrant Recollections of Greek Resistance to Fascism, 1941–1949 1994, Remembering Jayaprakash 1997, No Taste for Carnage: Alex Sheppard – A Portrait 1913–1997 1998; contrib. to Overland, Australian Short Stories, Age. *Honours:* Australia Literature Board Grants 1980, 1988. *Address:* 8 Bostock Street, Warrnambool, Vic. 3280, Australia.

SCHALLER, George B(eals); Researcher and Writer; b. 26 May 1933, Berlin, Germany; m. Kay Morgan, 26 Aug. 1957, two s. *Education:* BS, Zoology, BA, Anthropology, University of Alaska; MS, PhD, University of Wisconsin. *Publications:* The Mountain Gorilla, 1963; The Year of the Gorilla, 1964; The Deer and the Tiger, 1967; The Serengeti Lion, 1972; Golden Shadows, Flying Hooves, 1973; Mountain Monarchs: Wild Sheep and Goats of the Himalayas, 1977; Stones of Silence: Journeys in the Himalaya, 1980; The Giant Pandas of Wolong (co-author), 1985; The Last Panda, 1993; Tibet's Hidden Wilderness, 1997; Wildlife of the Tibetan Steppe, 1998. Contributions: zoological journals and popular periodicals. *Honours:* National Book Award, 1973; Cosmos Prize, Japan, 1996; Tyler Environmental Prize, 1997. *Address:* Wildlife Conservation Society, Bronx Park, NY 10460, USA.

SCHAMA, Simon (Michael); Prof., Art Critic and Writer; b. 13 Feb. 1945, London, England; m. Virginia Papaioannou, 1983, one s. one d. *Education:* BA, 1966, MA, 1969, Christ's College, Cambridge. *Career:* Fellow and Dir of Studies in History, Christ's College, Cambridge, 1966–76; Fellow and Tutor in Modern History, Brasenose College, Oxford, 1976–80; Mellon Prof. of History, 1980–90, Kenan Prof., 1990–93, Harvard University: Old Dominion Foundation Prof. in the Humanities, 1993–96, University Prof., 1997–, Columbia University; Art Critic, The New Yorker, 1995–. *Publications:* Patriots and Liberators: Revolution in the Netherlands, 1780–1813, 1978; Two Rothschilds and the Land of Israel, 1979; The Embarrassment of Riches: An Interpretation of Dutch Culture in the Golden Age, 1987; Citizens: A Chronicle of the French Revolution, 1989; Dead Certainties (Unwarranted Speculations), 1991; Landscape and Memory, 1995; Rembrandt's Eyes, 1999; A History of Britain Vol. 1: At the Edge of the World? 3000 BC–AD 1603, 2000, Vol. 2: The British Wars 1603–1776, 2001, Vol. 3: The Fate of Empire 1776–2001, 2002. Contributions: various publications. *Honours:* Hon. Fellow, Christ's College, Cambridge, 1995; Poetry Society, vice-pres. *Address:* c/o Dept of History, Columbia University, New York, NY 10027, USA.

SCHEIBER, Harry N(oel); Prof. of Law, Writer and Ed.; b. 1935, New York, NY, USA. *Education:* BA, Columbia University, 1955; MA, 1957, PhD, 1961, Cornell University. *Career:* Instructor to Assoc. Prof., 1960–68, Prof. of History, 1968–71, Dartmouth College; Fellow, Centre for Advanced

Study in the Behavioural Sciences, Stanford, 1967, 1971; Prof. of American History, University of California at San Diego, 1971–80; Prof. of Law, 1980–, Assoc. Dean, 1990–93, 1996–99, Stefan Reisenfeld Prof., 1991–, Dir, Earl Warren Legal Institute, 2002–, University of California at Berkeley; Fulbright Distinguished Senior Lecturer, Australia, 1983; Ed., Yearbook of the California Supreme Court Historical Society, 1994–; Visiting Research Prof., University of Uppsala, 1995; mem. American Historical Asscn; California Supreme Court Historical Society; Economic History Asscn; Law and Society Asscn; Organization of American Historians. *Publications:* The Wilson Administration and Civil Liberties, 1960; United States Economic History, 1964; America: Purpose and Power (co-author), 1965; The Condition of American Federalism, 1966; The Frontier in American Development (co-ed.), 1969; The Old Northwest, 1969; The Ohio Canal Era 1820–1861, 1969; Black Labor in American History, 1972; Agriculture in the Development of the Far West, 1975; American Economic History (co-author), 1976; American Law and the Consitutional Order, 1978; Perspectives on Federalism (ed.), 1987; Power Divided (co-ed.), 1989; Federalism and the Judicial Mind (ed.), 1993; Legal Culture and the Legal Profession (co-author), 1995; The State and Freedom of Contract, 1998; Law of the Sea: The Common Heritage and Emerging Challenges, 2000; Inter-Allied Conflicts and Ocean Law, 1945–1952, 2001. Contributions: Professional journals. *Honours:* Hon. MA, Dartmouth College, 1965; Guggenheim Fellowships, 1971, 1988; Rockefeller Foundation Fellowship, 1979; National Endowment for the Humanities Fellowship, 1985–86; Hon. DJur, University of Uppsala, 1998; Fellow, Japan Society for the Promotion of Science, 2001. *Address:* c/o School of Law, University of California at Berkeley, Berkeley, CA 94720, USA. *E-mail:* scheiber@law.berkeley.edu.

SCHELL, Jonathan, BA; American journalist; b. 21 Aug. 1943, New York; m. Elspeth Schell; two s. one d. *Education:* Putney School, Vt, Harvard Univ. and Int. Christian Univ., Tokyo. *Career:* articles describing Operation Cedar Falls, one of largest US mil. exercises of Vietnam War and other experiences in Vietnam appeared in New Yorker 1967; mem. staff, New Yorker 1968–87; Fellow, Inst. of Politics, Kennedy School of Govt 1987; Visiting Prof. Inst. of Liberal Arts, Emory Univ. Atlanta, Ga 1987, New York Univ. School of Journalism 1988; Ferris Prof. Princeton Univ. 1989; columnist, Newsday and New York Newsday 1990; mem. New York Inst. for the Humanities, New York Univ. 1991–. *Publications:* The Village of Ben Suc 1967, The Military Half: An Account of Destruction in Quang Ngai and Quang Tin 1968, The Time of Illusion 1976, The Fate of the Earth 1982, The Abolition, History in Sherman Park 1987, Observing the Nixon Years: Notes & Comment from the New Yorker on the Vietnam War and the Watergate Crisis 1969–75 1989, The Unconquerable World: Power, Non-violence and the Will of the People 2004. *Honours:* Melcher Book Award for The Fate of the Earth 1982. *Address:* c/o Allen Lane, Penguin UK, 80 Strand, London, WC2R 0RL, England.

SCHELL, Orville Hickok, BA, MA, PhD; journalist and writer; *Dean of the Graduate School of Journalism, University of California at Berkeley*; b. 20 May 1940, New York, NY, USA; m.; three s. *Education:* Stanford University, National Taiwan University, Harvard University, University of California at Berkeley. *Career:* Co-Dir, Bay Area Institute, 1968–71; Founder and Ed.-in-Chief, Pacific News Service, 1970–71; China Correspondent, The New Yorker Magazine, 1975; Research Assoc., 1986, Regents' Lecturer, 1990, Dean, Graduate School of Journalism, 1996–, University of California at Berkeley; Visiting Distinguished Prof., Chico State University, 1987; Moderator, Issues and Perspectives on China, Voice of America, 1995–97; mem. Authors' Guild; Council on Foreign Relations; Global Business Network; Human Rights Watch Board, exec. committee; Pacific Council; PEN; National Committee on US-China Relations; World Affairs Council of San Francisco. *Publications:* The China Reader (with Frederick Crews), 1970; Modern China: The Story of a Revolution, 1972; The Town That Fought to Save Itself, 1976; In the People's Republic, 1976; Brown, 1978; Watch Out for the Foreign Guests: China Encounters the West, 1981; Modern Meat: Antibiotics, Hormones and the Pharmaceutical Farm, 1983; To Get Rich is Glorious: China in the 1980s, 1984; Discos and Democracy: China in the Throes of Reform, 1988; Mandate of Heaven: A New Generation of Entrepreneurs, Dissidents, Technocrats, and Bohemiams Grasp for Power in China, 1994; The China Reader: The Reform Years (ed. with David Shambaugh), 1999; Virtual Tibet: The West's Fascination with the Roof of the World, 1999. Contributions: numerous books, reviews, and journals. *Honours:* Alicia Patterson Foundation Journalism Fellowship, 1981; MacDowell Colony Fellowships, 1983, 1986; Guggenheim Fellowship, 1989–90; Emmy Award, 1992; Senior Fellow, Freedom Forum Media Studies Center, Columbia University, 1995; George Foster Peabody Award, 1997. *Literary Agent:* Steven Barclay Agency, 12 Western Avenue, Petaluma, CA 94952, USA. *Telephone:* (707) 773-0654. *Fax:* (707) 778-1868. *Website:* www.barclayagency.com. *Address:* c/o Graduate School of Journalism, University of California at Berkeley, Berkeley, CA 94720, USA.

SCHELLING, Andrew, BA; American poet, writer, translator and ecology activist; *Associate Professor, Naropa Institute*; b. 14 Jan. 1953, Washington, DC; m. Kristina Loften 1980 (divorced 1993); one d. *Education:* Univ. of California at Santa Cruz. *Career:* Asst Prof., then Assoc. Prof., Naropa Inst., Boulder. *Publications:* Claw Moraine (poems) 1987, Dropping the Bow: Poems from Ancient India (trans.) 1991, Ktaadn's Lamp (poems) 1991, For Love of the Dark One: Songs of Mirabai (trans.) 1993, Moon is a Piece of Tea (poems) 1993, The India Book: Essays and Translations from Indian Asia 1993, Twilight Speech: Essays on Sanskrit and Buddhist Poetics 1993, Two Immortals (essays) 1994, Disembodied Poetics: Annals of the Jack Kerouac School (co-ed.) 1994, Old Growth: Selected Poems and Notebooks, 1986–1994 1995, Songs of the Sons and Daughters of Buddha (co-trans.) 1996, The Road to Ocosingo 1998, The Cane Groves of Narmada River: Erotic Poems from Old India (trans.) 1998, Tea Shack Interior: New and Selected Poetry 2002, Wild Form, Savage Grammar (essays) 2003, Erotic Love Poems from India (trans.) 2004, Two Elk: A High Country Notebook 2005, Picking Up Stones: 28 Poets of Buddhist North America (ed.) 2005; contrib. to numerous anthologies and periodicals. *Honours:* Landon Prize in Trans., Acad. of American Poets 1992. *Address:* 2529 Sixth Street, Boulder, CO 80304, USA. *E-mail:* schell@ecentral.com.

SCHERMBRUCKER, William (Bill) Gerald, BA, PGCE, MA, PhD; Canadian writer, editor and fmr educator; b. 23 July 1938, Eldoret, Kenya; m. 1st Janet I. Lewis 1959 (divorced); m. 2nd Joanne C. Oben 1972 (divorced); m. 3rd Sharon F. Sawatsky 1984; three s. one d. *Education:* Univ. of Cape Town, Univ. of London, Univ. of British Columbia. *Career:* part-time Lecturer, Univ. of East Africa 1963–64; Instructor in English 1968–2000, Instructor Emeritus 2000–, Capilano Coll., North Vancouver; Lecturer, Genessee Community Coll. 1972–73; Ed., The Capilano Review 1977–82; mem. Writers' Union of Canada (nat. council 1999–2003). *Publications:* The Aims and Strategies of Good Writing 1976, Readings for Canadian Writing Students (ed.) 1976, revised edn as The Capilano Reader 1984, Chameleon, and Other Stories 1983, Mimosa 1988, Motortherapy and Other Stories 1993; contrib. to periodicals. *Honours:* several grants, Second Prize, CBC Literary Competition 1980, Ethel Wilson Prize 1988. *Address:* 362 East Point Road, PO Box 53, Saturna BC V0N 2Y0, Canada. *E-mail:* bscherm@capcollege.bc.ca.

SCHEVILL, James (Erwin); Writer, Poet, Dramatist and Prof. of English Emeritus; b. 10 June 1920, Berkeley, CA, USA; m. 1st Helen Shaner, 1942, divorced 1966, two d.; m. 2nd Margot Blum, 1966. *Education:* BS, Harvard University, 1942; MA, Brown University. *Career:* Asst Prof. of Humanities, California College of Arts and Crafts, Oakland, 1951–59; Assoc. Prof. of English, San Francisco State University, 1959–68; Prof. of English, 1968–88, Prof. Emeritus, 1988–, Brown University. *Publications:* Tensions (poems), 1947; The American Fantasies (poems), 1951; Sherwood Anderson: His Life and Work, 1951; High Sinners, Low Angels (musical play), 1953; The Right to Greet (poems), 1956; The Roaring Market and the Silent Tomb (biog. of Bern Porter), 1956; The Bloody Tenet (verse play), 1957; Selected Poems, 1945–62, 1962; Voices of Mass and Capital A (play), 1962; The Stalingrad Elegies (poems), 1964; The Black President, and Other Plays, 1965; Violence and Glory: Poems 1962–67, 1969; Lovecraft's Follies (play), 1971; Breakout! In Search of New Theatrical Environments, 1972; The Buddhist Car and Other Characters (poems), 1973; The Arena of Ants (novel), 1977; The Mayan Poems, 1978; The American Fantasies: Collected Poems 1945–1982, 1983; Oppenheimer's Chair (play), 1985; Collected Short Plays, 1986; Ambiguous Dancers of Fame: Collected Poems 1945–1986, 1987; Where to Go, What to Do, When You Are Bern Porter: A Personal Biography, 1992; 5 Plays 5, 1993; Winter Channels (poems), 1994; The Complete American Fantasies (poems), 1996; New and Selected Poems, 2000. *Honours:* Ford Foundation Grant, 1960–61; William Carlos Williams Award, 1965; Guggenheim Fellowship, 1981; Centennial Review Poetry Prize, 1985; Hon. DHL, Rhode Island College, 1986; Pawtucket Arts Council Award for Poetry and Theatre, 1987; American Acad. of Arts and Letters Award, 1991. *Address:* 1309 Oxford St, Berkeley, CA 94709, USA.

SCHICKLER, David, MFA; American writer. *Education:* Columbia Univ. *Publications:* fiction: Kissing in Manhattan (novel) 2001, The Smoker (short story for The New Yorker) 2003, Sweet and Vicious (novel) 2004; contrib. to Tin House, Zoetrope. *Address:* c/o Dial Press, Random House Inc, 1745 Broadway, New York, NY 10019, USA. *Website:* www.randomhouse.com.

SCHIFF, James Andrew; Asst Prof. and Writer; b. 6 Dec. 1958, Cincinnati, Ohio, USA; m. 24 June 1989, three s. *Education:* AB, Duke University, 1981; MA, 1985, PhD, 1990, New York University. *Career:* Visiting Instructor, 1989–96, Adjunct Asst Prof., 1997–2000, Asst Prof., 2000–, University of Cincinnati; mem. NBCC; MLA. *Publications:* Updike's Version: Rewriting The Scarlet Letter, 1992; Understanding Reynolds Price, 1996; John Updike Revisited, 1998; Critical Essays on Reynolds Price, 1998. Contributions: Southern Review; American Literature; South Atlantic Review; Studies in American Fiction; Critique; Boulevard; Missouri Review. *Address:* 2 Forest Hill Dr., Cincinnati, OH 45208, USA.

SCHIFFRIN, André, MA; American publisher; *Director and Editor-in-Chief, The New Press*; b. 12 June 1935, Paris, France; m. Maria Elena de la Iglesia 1961; two d. *Education:* Yale Univ. and Univ. of Cambridge. *Career:* with New American Library 1959–63; with Pantheon Books, New York 1962–90, Ed., Ed.-in-Chief, Man. Dir 1969–90; Publr Schocken Books (subsidiary of Pantheon Books Inc.) 1987–90; Pres. Fund for Ind. Publishing 1990–; Dir, Ed.-in-Chief The New Press, New York 1990–; Visiting Fellow, Davenport Coll. 1977–79; Visiting Lecturer, Yale Univ. 1977, 1979; mem. Council Smithsonian Inst.; mem. Bd of Dirs New York Council for Humanities; mem. Special Cttee American Centre, Paris 1994–; mem. Visting Cttee of Grad. Faculty The New York School 1995–; other professional appts. and affiliations. *Publications:* L'Edition sans Editeurs 1999, The Business of Books 2000; contribs to professional journals. *Honours:* Hon. Fellow, Trumbull Coll. Yale Univ.; Grinzane Cavour Prize, Italy 2003. *Address:* The New Press, 450 West 41st Street, New York, NY 10036 (Office); 250 West 94th Street, New York, NY 10025, USA (Home).

SCHLAGMAN, Richard Edward, FRSA; British publisher; b. 11 Nov. 1953. *Education:* Univ. Coll. School, Hampstead, Brunel Univ. *Career:* Co-Founder, Jt Chair., Man. Dir Interstate Electronics Ltd 1973–86; purchased Bush from Rank Org., renamed IEL Bush Radio Ltd 1981, floated on London Stock Exchange 1984, sold as Bush Radio PLC 1986; acquired Phaidon Press Ltd 1990, Chair. and Publr 1990–; mem. Exec. Cttee Patrons of New Art, Tate Gallery 1994–97, Royal Opera House Trust, Glyndebourne Festival Soc., Designers and Arts Dirs. Asscn of UK; patron Bayreuth, Salzburger Festspiele; Pres. Judd Foundation, MARFA, Texas 1999–; mem. Patrons' Circle, Tate Britain. *Address:* Phaidon Press Limited, Regent's Wharf, All Saints Street, London, N1 9PA, England. *Telephone:* (20) 7843-1100. *Fax:* (20) 7843-1212. *E-mail:* rschlagman@phaidon.com (Office).

SCHLESINGER, Arthur Meier, Jr; historian, writer and academic; b. 15 Oct. 1917, Columbus, OH, USA; m. 1st Marian Cannon 1940 (divorced 1970); two s. two d.; m. 2nd Alexandra Emmet 1971; one s. *Education:* AB, Harvard University, 1938; Henry Fellow, University of Cambridge, 1938–39; Society of Fellows, Harvard University, 1939–42. *Career:* Assoc. Prof., 1946–54, Prof. of History, 1954–61, Harvard University; Special Asst to Pres. John F. Kennedy, 1961–63; Visiting Fellow, Institute for Advanced Study, Princeton, NJ, 1966; Schweitzer Prof. in Humanities, CUNY, 1966–95; mem. American Acad. of Arts and Letters, pres., 1981–84, chancellor, 1984–87; American Civil Liberties Union; American Historical Asscn; American Philosophical Society; Americans for Democratic Action, chair., 1952–54; Massachusetts Historical Society; Council on Foreign Relations; Franklin and Eleanor Roosevelt Institute, co-chair., 1983–; Society of American Historians. *Publications:* Orestes A Brownson: A Pilgrim's Progress, 1939; The Age of Jackson, 1945; The Vital Center, 1949; The General and the President (with R. H. Rovere), 1951; The Age of Roosevelt, Vol. I, The Crisis of the Old Order 1919–1933, 1957, Vol. II, The Coming of the New Deal, 1958, Vol. III, The Politics of Upheaval, 1960; Kennedy or Nixon: Does It Make Any Difference?, 1960; The Politics of Hope, 1963; The National Experience (with John Blum), 1963; A Thousand Days: John F. Kennedy in the White House, 1965; The Bitter Heritage: Vietnam and American Democracy 1941–66, 1967; The Crisis of Confidence, 1969; The Imperial Presidency, 1973; Robert Kennedy and His Times, 1978; The Cycles of American History, 1986; The Disuniting of America, 1991; A Life in the 20th Century, Vol. I, Innocent Beginnings 1917–1950, 2000. Editor: Paths to American Thought, 1963; The Promise of American Life, 1967; The Best and Last of Edwin O'Connor, 1970; The History of American Presidential Elections (with F. L. Israel), 1971; The Coming to Power, 1972; The Dynamics of World Power: A Documentary History of United States Foreign Policy 1945–1972, 1973; History of US Political Parties, 1973; Running for President, 1994. Contributions: Professional journals. *Honours:* Francis Parkman Prize, Society of American Historians, 1957; Bancroft Prize, Columbia University, 1958; Pulitzer Prize in History, 1946, in Biography, 1966; National Book Awards, 1966, 1979; American Acad. of Arts and Letters Gold Medal in History and Biography, 1967; Fregene Prize for Literature, Italy, 1983; National Humanities Medal, 1998; Hon. doctorates from many institutions, including Oxford, 1987, Harvard, 2001. *Address:* 455 E 51st Street, New York, NY 10022, USA.

SCHLINK, Bernhard; German academic and writer; b. 1944, Bielefeld, Germany; m. (divorced 1974); one s. *Education:* Heidelberg Univ. *Career:* Judge, Constitutional Court; Law Prof., Bonn Univ., –1991, Humboldt Univ., Berlin, Yeshiva Univ., New York. *Publications:* Selbs Justiz (with Walter Popp) 1987, Die Gordische Schleife 1988, Selbs Betrug (with Walter Popp) 1994, Der Vorleser (trans. as The Reader) 1995, Selbs Mord (with Walter Popp) 2001, Flights of Love (short stories) 2002, The Gordian Knot 2004, Self's Punishment (with Walter Popp) 2004. *Address:* c/o Weidenfeld & Nicolson, Orion House, 5 Upper St Martin's Lane, London WC2H 9EA, England.

SCHLOSSER, Eric; American journalist and writer; b. Manhattan, NY; m. Shauna; two c. *Education:* Princeton Univ., Oriel College, Oxford. *Career:* fmr scriptwriter; correspondent, Atlantic Monthly. *Publications:* Fast Food Nation 2001, Reefer Madness and Other Tales from the American Underworld 2003; contrib. to numerous magazines. *Honours:* National Magazine Award. *Address:* c/o Penguin Books Ltd, 80 Strand, London, WC2R 0RL, England.

SCHMIDMAN, Jo Ann; Theatre Dir and Playwright; b. 18 April 1948, Omaha, NE, USA. *Education:* BFA, Boston University, 1970. *Career:* Producing Artistic Dir, Omaha Magic Theatre, 1968–; Team Mem., Artist-in-Schools, Nebraska Arts Council, 1994. *Publications:* Plays: This Sleep Among Women, 1974; Running Gag, 1980; Astro Bride, 1985; Velveeta Meltdown, 1985; Right Brain (ed. with M. Terry and S. Kimberlain), 1992; Body Leaks (with M. Terry and S. Kimberlain), 1995. Other: various unpublished but produced plays, 1978–93. *Address:* 2309 Hanscom Blvd, Omaha, NE 68105, USA.

SCHMIDT, Michael (Norton); Poet, Ed. and Trans; b. 2 March 1947, México, DF, Mexico; m. Claire Harman, 1979, deceased 1989, two s. one d. *Education:* Harvard University, 1966; BA, Wadham College, Oxford, 1969. *Career:* Editorial Dir, Carcanet Press Ltd, 1969–; Senior Lecturer in Poetry, University of Manchester, 1972–98; Ed., PN Review, 1972–; Dir, Writing School, 1998–, Prof. of English, 2000–, Manchester Metropolitan University; mem. FRSL, 1990; Fellow, The English Asscn, 1999. *Publications:* Black Buildings, 1969; One Eye Mirror Cold, 1970; Bedlam and the Oakwood, 1970; Desert of Lions, 1972; British Poetry Since 1960 (ed. with G. Lindop), 1972; It Was My Tree, 1972; Flower and Song (trans. with E. Kissam), 1975; My Brother Gloucester, 1976; Ten British Poets (ed.), 1976; A Change of Affairs, 1978; A Reader's Guide to Fifty Poets (ed.), 2 vols, 1979; The Colonist, 1980, US edn as Green Island, 1982; Eleven British Poets (ed.), 1980; Choosing a Guest: New and Selected Poems, 1983; Some Contemporary Poets of Britain and Ireland (ed.), 1983; The Dresden Gate, 1986; Octavio Paz: On Poets and Others (trans.), 1986; The Love of Strangers, 1988; Modern Poetry, 1989; New Poetries (ed.), 1994; A Calendar of Modern Poetry (ed.), 1994; Selected Poems, 1997; Lives of the Poets, 1998; The Harvill Book of Twentieth-Century Poetry in English, 1999; The Story of Poetry I, 2001; The Story of Poetry II, 2002. *Literary Agent:* David Godwin Associates, 55 Monmouth St, London WC2H 9DG, England. *Address:* 30 Cross St, Manchester M2 7AQ, England.

SCHMIDT-NIELSEN, Knut; American scientist and writer; b. 24 Sept. 1915, Trondheim, Norway. *Education:* University of Oslo, 1933–37; MS, 1941, DPhil, 1946, University of Copenhagen. *Career:* Faculty, Dept of Zoology, Duke University; Ed., scientific journals; mem. Académie des Sciences, Paris; National Acad. of Sciences, USA; Royal Society, London. *Publications:* Desert Animals, 1964; How Animals Work, 1972; Animal Physiology, 1975; Scaling: Why is Animal Size So Important?, 1984; The Camel's Nose: Memoirs of a Curious Scientist, 1998. Contributions: many professional journals. *Honours:* Hon. MD, University of Lund, 1983; Hon. PhD, University of Trondheim, 1993. *Address:* c/o Department of Biology, Duke University, Durham, NC 27708-0338 USA.

SCHMITTER, Elke; German writer and critic; b. 1961, Krefeld. *Education:* Univ. of Munich. *Career:* fmr journalist, became full-time writer 1994–. *Publications:* Frau Sartoris (trans. as Mrs Sartoris) 2000, Leichte Verfehlungen 2002; contrib. to Der Spiegel. *Literary Agent:* c/o Faber and Faber Ltd, 3 Queen Square, London, WC1N 3AU, England. *Website:* www.faber.co.uk.

SCHMITZ, Dennis (Mathew); Prof. of English and Poet; b. 11 Aug. 1937, Dubuque, IA, USA; m. Loretta D'Agostino, 1960, two s. three d. *Education:* BA, Loras College, Dubuque, IA, 1959; MA, University of Chicago, 1961. *Career:* Instructor, Illinois Institute of Technology, Chicago, 1961–62, University of Wisconsin at Milwaukee, 1962–66; Asst Prof., 1966–69, Poet-in-Residence, 1966–, Assoc. Prof., 1969–74, Prof. of English, 1974–, California State University at Sacramento. *Publications:* We Weep for Our Strangeness, 1969; Double Exposures, 1971; Goodwill, Inc, 1976; String, 1980; Singing, 1985; Eden, 1989; About Night: Selected and New Poems, 1993. *Honours:* New York Poetry Center Discovery Award, 1968; National Endowment for the Arts Fellowships, 1976, 1985, 1992; Guggenheim Fellowship, 1978; di Castagnola Award, 1986; Shelley Memorial Award, 1988. *Address:* c/o Dept of English, California State University at Sacramento, 6000 Jay St, Sacramento, CA 95819, USA.

SCHMOOKLER, Andrew Bard, BA, PhD; teacher, writer and speaker; b. 19 April 1946, Long Branch, NJ, USA; m. 1986; two s. one d. *Education:* Harvard College, Thelogical Union and University of California. *Publications:* The Parable of the Tribes: The Problem of Power in Social Evolution, 1984; Out of Weakness: Healing the Wounds that Drive us to War, 1988; Sowing and Reapings: The Cycling of Good and Evil in the Human System, 1989; The Illusion of Choice: How the Market Economy Shapes Our Destiny, 1992; Fools Gold: The Fate of Values in a World of Goods, 1993; Living Posthumously: Confronting the Loss of Vital Powers, 1997; Debating the Good Society: A Quest to Bridge America's Moral Divide, 1999. *Honours:* Erik H. Erikson Prize, International Society for Political Psychology, 1984. *Address:* 1855 Tramway Terrace Loop NE, Albuquerque, NM 87122, USA. *Telephone:* (505) 856-1221. *E-mail:* andythebard@comcast.net.

SCHNACKENBERG, Gjertrud, BA; poet and writer; b. 27 Aug. 1953, Tacoma, WA, USA; m. Robert Nozick 1987 (died 2002). *Education:* Mount Holyoke Coll. *Career:* Christensen Fellow, Saint Catherine's Coll., Oxford 1997; Visiting Scholar, Getty Research Inst., J. Paul Getty Museum 2000; Fellow, American Acad. of Arts and Sciences 1996. *Publications:* Portraits and Elegies 1982, The Lamplit Answer 1985, A Gilded Lapse of Time 1992, The Throne of Labdacus 2000, Supernatural Love: Poems 1976–1992 2000; contrib. to books and journals. *Honours:* Glascock Awards for Poetry 1973, 1974, Lavan Younger Poets Award, Acad. of American Poets 1983, Rome Prize, American Acad. and Institute of Arts and Letters 1983–84, Amy Lowell Traveling Prize 1984–85, Hon. Doctorate, Mount Holyoke College 1985, National Endowment for the Arts Grant 1986–87, Guggenheim Fellowship 1987–88, Acad. Award in Literature, American Acad. of Arts and Letters 1998, Los Angeles Times Book Prize in Poetry 2001. *Literary Agent:* Farrar, Straus & Giroux Inc, 19 Union Square W, New York, NY 10003, USA.

SCHNECK, Peter; Austrian editor. *Career:* Ed. Philologie im Netz; Vice Pres., Int. Bd on Books for Young People 1998–2002, Pres. 2002–; responsible for children's literature at the Austrian Federal Chancellery's division of literature; Pres., Hans Christian Andersen Awards Jury 1996, 1998; Chair., Austrian Children's Book Award jury. *Address:* Redaktion München, Amerika-Institut, Ludwig-Maximilians-Universität, Schellingstraße 3, 80799 München, Germany. *E-mail:* Peter.Schneck@lrz.uni-muenchen .de.

SCHNEEBAUM, Tobias; Writer and Lecturer; b. 25 March 1922, New York, NY, USA. *Education:* BA, City College, CUNY, 1942; MA, Cultural Anthropology, Goddard College, 1977. *Career:* mem. Explorers Club; PEN. *Publications:* Keep the River on Your Right, 1969; Wild Man, 1979; Life with the Ancestors, 1981; Asmat Images, 1985; Where the Spirits Dwell, 1988; Embodied Spirits, 1990; Secret Places, 2000. Contributions: various publications. *Honours:* Fulbright Fellowship, 1955; Ingram Merrill Foundation Grants, 1982, 1989; Ludwig Vogelstein Foundation Grant, 1985. *Address:* 463 West St, No. 410A, New York, NY 10014, USA.

SCHOEMPERLEN, Diane Mavis; Writer and Teacher; b. 9 July 1954, Thunder Bay, Ontario, Canada; one s. *Education:* BA, English, Lakehead University, Ontario, 1976. *Career:* Teacher, Kingston School of Writing, Queen's University, Ontario, 1986–93, St Lawrence College, Kingston, 1987–93, University of Toronto Summer Writers' Workshop, 1992; Ed., Coming Attractions, Oberton Press, 1994–96; mem. Writer's Union of Canada; Authors' Guild of America, Canada. *Publications:* Double Exposures, 1984; Frogs and Other Stories, 1986; Hockey Night in Canada, 1987; The Man of My Dreams, 1990; Hockey Night in Canada and Other Stories, 1991; In the Language of Love, 1994; Forms of Devotion, 1998; Our Lady of the Lost and Found, 2001. Contributions: anthologies. *Honours:* WGA Award for Short Fiction, 1987; Silver National Magazine Award, 1989; Governor-General's Award for English Fiction, 1998; Lakehead University Alumni Honour Award, 1999. *Address:* 32 Dunlop St, Kingston, ON K7L 1L2, Canada.

SCHOFIELD, Paul (see Tubb, Edwin Charles).

SCHOLEY, Arthur (Edward); Children', s Writer, Playwright, Librettist and Lyric Writer; b. 17 June 1932, Sheffield, England. *Publications:* The Song of Caedmon (with Donald Swann), 1971; Christmas Plays and Ideas for Worship, 1973; The Discontented Dervishes, 1977; Sallinka and the Golden Bird, 1978; Twelve Tales for a Christmas Night, 1978; Wacky and His Fuddlejig (with Donald Swann), 1978; Singalive (with Donald Swann), 1978; Herod and the Rooster (with Ronald Chamberlain), 1979; The Dickens Christmas Carol Show, 1979; Baboushka (with Donald Swann), 1979; Candletree (with Donald Swann), 1981; Five Plays for Christmas, 1981; Four Plays About People, 1983; Martin the Cobbler, 1983; The Hosanna Kids, 1985; Make a Model Christmas Crib, 1988; Who'll Be Brother Donkey?, 1990; Brendan Ahoy! (with Donald Swann), 1994; The Journey of the Christmas Creatures (with Karen Bradley), 1998; Babaushka, 2001; The Paragon Parrot, 2002; The Discontented Dervishes, 2002. *Address:* 10 Chiltern Ct, Pages Hill, London N10 1EN, England. *E-mail:* scholey@arthurscholey.co.uk. *Website:* www.arthurscholey.co.uk.

SCHOM, Alan (Morris); Writer; b. 9 May 1937, Sterling, IL, USA; m. Juliana Leslie Hill, 6 Sept. 1963, divorced 19 April 1984, two d. *Education:* BA, University of California at Berkeley; PhD, University of Durham. *Career:* Assoc., Dept of History, University of California at Riverside, 1968–69; Asst Prof. of Modern French and European History, Southern Connecticut State University, 1969–76. *Publications:* Lyautey in Morocco: Protectorate Administration, 1912–1925, 1970; Émile Zola: A Bourgeois Rebel, 1988; Trafalgar: Countdown to Battle, 1803–1805, 1989; One Hundred Days: Napoleon's Road to Waterloo, 1992; Napoleon Bonaparte, 1997. Contributions: scholarly journals. *Honours:* Fellow, Hoover Institution on War, Revolution, and Peace, 1982; Grants. *Address:* c/o HarperCollins, 10 E 53rd St, New York, NY 10022, USA.

SCHRAG, Peter; Journalist and Ed.; b. 24 July 1931, Karlsruhe, Germany. *Education:* BA, Amherst College, 1953; Graduate Studies, Amherst College and University of Massachusetts, 1957–59. *Career:* Reporter, El Paso Herald Post, Texas, 1953–55; Asst Secretary, Amherst College, 1956–66; Assoc. Education Ed., 1966–68, Exec. Ed., 1968–73, Saturday Review, New York City; Ed., Change, New York City, 1969–70; Lecturer, University of Massachusetts, 1970–72, University of California at Berkeley, 1990–; Ed., Editorial Page, Sacramento Bee, CA, 1978–; Contributing Ed., The American Prospect; mem. National Conference of Editorial Writers. *Publications:* Voices in the Classroom, 1965; Village School Downtown, 1967; Out of Place in America, 1970; The Decline of the WASP, 1972, US edn as The Vanishing American; The End of the American Future, 1973; Test of Loyalty, 1974; The Myths of the Hyperative Child (with Diane Divorky), 1975; Mind Control, 1978; Paradise Lost: California's Experience, America's Future, 1998. Contributions: newspapers and magazines. *Honours:* Guggenheim Fellowship, 1971–72. *Literary Agent:* Ellen Levine, Ellen Levine Literary Agency, 15 E 26th St, Suite 1801, New York, NY 10010, USA. *Address:* c/o Sacramento Bee, 21st and Q Streets, Sacramento, CA 95816, USA.

SCHREINER, Samuel Agnew, Jr; Author; b. 6 June 1921, Mt Lebanon, Pennsylvania, USA; m. Doris Moon, 22 Sept. 1945, two d. *Education:* AB, summa cum laude, Princeton University, 1942. *Publications:* Thine is the Glory, 1975; The Condensed World of the Reader's Digest, 1977; Pleasant Places, 1977; Angelica, 1978; The Possessors and the Possessed, 1980; The Van Alens, 1981; A Place Called Princeton, 1984; The Trials of Mrs Lincoln, 1987; Cycles, 1990; Mayday! Mayday!, 1990; Code of Conduct (with Everett Alvarez), 1992; Henry Clay Frick: The Gospel of Greed, 1995. Contributions: Reader's Digest; Woman's Day; McCalls; Redbook; Parade. *Address:* 111 Old Kings Highway S, Darien, CT 06820, USA.

SCHROEDER, Andreas Peter, BA, MA; writer, poet and translator; *Rogers Communication Co-Chair, University of British Columbia*; b. 26 Nov. 1946, Hoheneggelsen, Germany; m. Sharon Elizabeth Brown; two d. *Education:* University of British Columbia. *Career:* literary critic and columnist, Vancouver Province newspaper 1968–72; co-founder and Ed.-in-Chief, Contemporary Literature in Trans. 1968–83; Lecturer in Creative Writing, Univ. of Victoria 1974–75, Simon Fraser Univ. 1989–90; writer-in-residence, Univ. of Winnipeg 1983–84, Fraser Valley Coll. 1987; Lecturer in Creative Writing 1985–87, Prof., Maclean Hunter Chair in Creative Non-Fiction 1993, then Rogers Communication Co-Chair, Univ. of British Columbia; mem. Writers' Union of Canada, Alliance of Canadian Cinema, Television and Radio Artists, Federation of British Columbia Writers, PEN Club, Saskatchewan Writers' Guild. *Publications:* The Ozone Minotaur 1969, File of Uncertainties (poems) 1971, UNIverse 1971, The Late Man (short stories) 1972, Stories From Pacific and Arctic Canada (co-ed.) 1974, Shaking it Rough (memoir) 1976, Toccata in 'D' (novella) 1984, Dust-Ship Glory (novel) 1986, Word for Word: The Business of Writing in Alberta 1988, The Eleventh Commandment (trans., with Jack Thiessen) 1990, The Mennonites in Canada: A Photographic History 1990, Carved From Wood: Mission, B.C. 1891–1992 1992, Scams, Scandals and Skullduggery 1996, Cheats, Charlatans and Chicanery 1998, Fakes, Frauds and Flimflammery 1999; contrib. to numerous anthologies, newspapers and magazines. *Honours:* Woodward Memorial Prize for Prose 1969, Canada Council Grants 1969, 1971, 1975, 1979, 1986, 1991, Nat. Film Board of Canada Scriptwriting Prize 1971, Canadian Asscn of Journalists Award for Best Investigative Journalism 1990. *Address:* University of British Columbia Creative Writing Program, Buchanan Room E462, 1866 Main Mall, Vancouver, BC V6T 1Z1, Canada. *E-mail:* apschroeder@dccnet.com.

SCHULBERG, Budd, AB; writer; b. 27 March 1914, New York, NY, USA; m. 1st Virginia Ray 1936 (divorced 1942); one d.; m. 2nd Victoria Anderson 1943 (divorced 1964); two s.; m. 3rd Geraldine Brooks 1964 (died 1977); m. 4th Betsy Anne Langman 1979; one s. one d. *Education:* Dartmouth Coll. *Career:* Founder-Pres., Schulberg Productions; Founder-Dir, Watts Writers Workshop, Los Angeles, 1965–; Founder-Chair., Frederick Douglass Creative Arts Center, New York City, 1971–; mem. American Civil Liberties Union; ASCAP; Authors' Guild; Dramatists' Guild; Players' Club, founder-mem.; PEN; Writers' Guild East. *Publications:* What Makes Sammy Run?, 1941; The Harder They Fall, 1947; The Disenchanted, 1950; Some Faces in the Crowd, 1953; Waterfront, 1955; Sanctuary V, 1969; The Four Seasons of Success, 1972; Loser and Still Champion: Muhammad Ali, 1972; Swan Watch, 1975; Everything That Moves, 1980; Moving Pictures: Memories of a Hollywood Prince, 1981; Love, Action, Laughter and Other Sad Tales, 1990; Sparring with Hemingway and Other Legends of the Fight Game, 1995. Editor: From the Ashes: Voices of Watts, 1967. Screenplays: Little Orphan Annie (with Samuel Ornitz), 1938; Winter Carnival (with F. Scott Fitzgerald), 1939; Weekend for Three (with Dorothy Parker), 1941; City Without Men (with Martin Berkeley), 1943; Government Girl, 1943; On the Waterfront, 1954; A Face in the Crowd, 1957; Wind Across the Everglades, 1958. Contributions: Leading magazines. *Honours:* Acad. Award, 1954; New York Critics Circle Award, 1954; Screen Writers Guild Award, 1954; Venice Film Festival Award, 1954; Christopher Award, 1955; German Film Critics Award, 1957; B'hai Human Rights Award, 1968; Prix Littéraire, Deauville Festival, 1989; Westhampton Writers Lifetime Achievement Award, 1989; World Boxing Asscn Living Legend Award, 1990; Southampton Cultural Center First Annual Literature Award, 1992. *Literary Agent:* Miriam Altschuler Literary Agency, RR1, PO Box 5, Old Post Rd, Red Hook, NY 12571, USA.

SCHULER, Robert Jordan; Prof. of English and Poet; b. 25 June 1939, California, USA; m. Carol Forbis, 7 Sept. 1963, two s. one d. *Education:* BA, Political Science, Stanford University, 1961; MA, Comparative Literature, University of California, Berkeley, 1965; PhD, English, University of Minnesota, 1989. *Career:* Instructor in English, Menlo College, 1965–67; Instructor in Humanities, Shimer College, 1967–77; Prof. of English, University of Wisconsin-Stout, 1978–; mem. Land Use Commission, Town of Menomonie. *Publications:* Axle of the Oak, 1978; Seasonings, 1978; Where is Dancers' Hill?, 1979; Morning Raga, 1980; Red Cedar Scroll, 1981; Origins, 1981; Floating Out of Stone, 1982; Music for Monet, 1984; Grace: A Book of Days, 1995; Journeys Toward the Original Mind, 1995; The Red Cedar Suite, 1999; In Search of Green Dolphin Street, 2003. Contributions: anthologies and periodicals, including: Caliban; Northeast; Tar River Poetry; Longhouse; Dacotah Territory; Wisconsin Acad. Review; Wisconsin Review; North Stone Review; Wisconsin Poetry 1991 Transactions; Hummingbird; Abraxas; Lake Street Review; Inheriting the Earth; Mississippi Valley Review; Coal City Review; Gypsy; Imagining Home, 1995;

Ekphrasis; Mid-America Poetry Review. *Honours:* Hormel Professorship, 1995; Wisconsin Arts Board Fellowship for Poetry, 1997. *Address:* E4549 479th Ave, Menomonie, WI 54751, USA.

SCHULLER, Gunther (Alexander); Composer, Conductor, Music Educator and Publisher; b. 22 Nov. 1925, New York, NY, USA; m. Marjorie Black, 8 June 1948, deceased 1992, two s. *Education:* St Thomas Choir School, New York City, 1938–44. *Career:* Teacher, Manhattan School of Music, New York City, 1950–63; Teacher, 1963–84, Artistic Co-Dir, 1969–74, Dir, 1974–84, Berkshire Music Center, Tanglewood, Massachusetts; Faculty, Yale School of Music, 1964–67; Pres., New England Conservatory of Music, Boston, 1967–77; Music Publisher, 1975–; Artistic Dir, Festival at Sandpoint, 1985–98; mem. American Acad. of Arts and Sciences; American Acad. of Arts and Letters. *Publications:* Horn Technique, 1962; Early Jazz: Its Roots and Musical Development, 3 vols, 1968–; Musings, 1985; The Swing Era, 1988; The Compleat Conductor, 1997. Contributions: various publications. *Honours:* Guggenheim Fellowship, 1962–63; ASCAP-Deems Taylor Award, 1970; Rodgers and Hammerstein Award, 1971; William Schuman Award, Columbia University, 1989; John D. and Catherine T. MacArthur Foundation Fellowship, 1991; Pulitzer Prize in Music, 1994; Hon. doctorates. *Address:* 167 Dudley Rd, Newton Centre, MA 02159, USA.

SCHULZ, Max Frederick, AB, MA, PhD; art curator and writer; *Distinguished Emeritus Professor of English, University of Southern California at Los Angeles*; b. 15 Sept. 1923, Cleveland, Ohio, USA. *Education:* Univ. of Chicago, Univ. of Pittsburgh, Univ. of Minnesota, Wayne State Univ. *Career:* Prof. of English 1963–94, Chair of Dept of English 1968–80, Curator of Exhibitions, Fisher Gallery 1993–, Univ. of Southern California at Los Angeles; Fulbright Prof., Univ. of Graz 1965–66, Univ. of Vienna 1977–78; Resident Scholar, Rockefeller Foundation Study Center, Bellagio, Italy 1978, 1989; Assoc. Ed., Critique Magazine 1971–85. *Publications:* The Poetic Voices of Coleridge, 1963; Radical Sophistication: Studies in Contemporary Jewish-American Novelists, 1969; Bruce Jay Friedman, 1973; Black Humor Fiction of the Sixties: A Pluralistic Definition of Man and His World, 1973; Paradise Preserved: Recreations of Eden in 18th and 19th Century England, 1985; The Muses of John Barth: Tradition and Metafiction from Lost in the Funhouse to the Tidewater Tales, 1990; Edgar Ewing: The Classical Connection, 1993; The Mythic Present of Chagoya, Valdez and Gronk, 1995; Crossing Boundaries, 1999; Family Pictures/Ecumenical Icons, 2001; Human Conditions: Manfred Müller 2003. *Honours:* Senior Fellow, National Endowment for the Humanities, 1985–86. *Address:* c/o Fisher Gallery, University of Southern California at Los Angeles, Los Angeles, CA 90089, USA.

SCHULZE, Ingo; Writer and Journalist; b. 15 Dec. 1962, Dresden, Germany. *Education:* Classical Philosophy, University of Jena, 1983–88. *Career:* Dramatic Producer, Theatre of Altenburg, 1988–90; Founder, weekly newspaper in Altenburg, 1990–92, Weekly newspaper, St Petersburg, 1993–. *Publications:* 33 Augenblicke des Glücks, 1995, English trans. as 33 Moments of Happiness: St Petersburg Stories, 1997; Simple Storys: Ein Roman aus der ostdeutschen Provinz, 1998, English trans. as Simple Stories, 1999; Von Nasen, Faxen und Ariadnefäden, Fax-Briefe, mit Zeichnungen von Helmar Penndorf, 2000. *Honours:* Aspekte-Literatur Prize for Best Debut, 1995; Ernest-Wilhelm Prize, 1995; Berliner Literatur Prize, 1998; Johannes Bobrowski Medal, 1998. *Address:* Liselotte-Herrmann-Str 33, 10407 Berlin, Germany.

SCHWANDT, Stephen (William); Educator and Writer; b. 5 April 1947, Chippewa Falls, Wisconsin, USA; m. Karen Sambo, 13 June 1970, two s. *Education:* BA, Valparaiso University, 1969; BS, St Cloud State University, 1972; MA, University of Minnesota – Twin Cities, 1972. *Career:* Teacher of Composition and American Literature, Irondale High School, New Brighton, Minnesota, 1974–; Instructor, Concordia College, St Paul, Minnesota, 1975–80, Normandale Community College, 1983–; mem. National Education Asscn; Authors' Guild; Book Critics Circle; National Council for Teachers of English; The Loft. *Publications:* The Last Goodie, 1985; A Risky Game, 1986; Holding Steady, 1988; Guilt Trip, 1990; Funnybone, 1992. Contributions: various newspapers. *Literary Agent:* Curtis Brown Ltd, 10 Astor Pl., New York, NY 10003, USA.

SCHWARTZ, Elliott (Shelling); Composer, Prof. of Music and Writer; b. 19 Jan. 1936, New York, NY, USA; m. Dorothy Rose Feldman 26 July 1960; one s. one d. *Education:* AB, 1957, MA, 1958, EdD, 1962, Columbia University. *Career:* Instructor, University of Massachusetts, 1960–64; Asst Prof., 1964–70, Assoc. Prof., 1970–75, Prof. of Music, 1975–, Bowdoin College; Distinguished Visiting Prof., 1985–86, Visiting Prof. of Music, 1988–92, Ohio State University; Visiting Fellow, Robinson College, Cambridge, 1993–94, 1998–99; mem. American Society of University Composers; College Music Society, past pres. *Publications:* The Symphonies of Ralph Vaughan Williams, 1964; Contemporary Composers on Contemporary Music (ed. with Barney Childs), 1967; Electronic Music: A Listener's Guide, 1973; Music: Ways of Listening, 1982; Music Since 1945: Issues, Materials and Literature (with Daniel Godfrey), 1993. Contributions: Professional journals. *Honours:* Guaudeamus Prize, Netherlands, 1970; Maine State Award in the Arts and Humanities, 1970; National Endowment for the Arts Grants, 1978–83; American Composers Alliance Rockefeller Foundation Residencies, Bellagio, Italy, 1980, 1989. *Address:* 10 Highview Rd, PO Box 451, South Freeport, ME 04078, USA. *E-mail:* eschwart@bowdoin.edu. *Website:* www.schwartzmusic.com.

SCHWARTZ, John (Burnham); Writer; b. 8 May 1965, New York, NY, USA. *Education:* BA, East Asian Studies, Harvard University, 1987. *Career:* mem. Authors' Guild. *Publications:* Bicycle Days, 1989; Reservation Road, 1998; Claire Marvel, 2002. Contributions: periodicals, including: New Yorker; New York Times Book Review. *Honours:* Lyndhurst Prize, 1991. *Address:* c/o International Creative Management, 40 W 57th St, New York, NY 10019, USA.

SCHWARTZ, Lloyd; Prof. of English, Music Critic and Poet; b. 29 Nov. 1941, New York, NY, USA. *Education:* BA, Queens College, CUNY, 1962; MA, 1963, PhD, 1976, Harvard University. *Career:* Classical Music Ed., Boston Phoenix, 1977–; Assoc. Prof. of English, 1982–86, Dir of Creative Writing, 1982–02, Prof. of English, 1986–94, Frederick S. Troy Prof. of English, 1994–; University of Massachusetts, Boston; Classical Music Critic, Fresh Air, National Public Radio, 1987–; Poetry Commentator, TomPaine.com, 2001–; mem. New England Poetry Club; PEN New England, exec. committee, 1983–98, exec. council, 1998–; Poetry Society of America. *Publications:* These People, 1981; Elizabeth Bishop and Her Art (ed.), 1983; Goodnight, Gracie, 1992; Cairo Traffic, 2000. Contributions: American Review; Best American Poetry, 1991, 1994; Harvard Magazine; New Republic; New York Times; Partisan Review; Pequod; Ploughshares; Poetry; New Yorker; Slate; The Handbook of Heartbreak; Boulevard; Southwest Review; Atlantic Monthly. *Honours:* ASCAP-Deems Taylor Awards, 1980, 1987, 1990; Daniel Varoujan Prize, 1987; Pushcart Prize, 1987; Somerville Arts Council Grants, 1987, 1989; National Endowment for the Arts Fellowship, 1990; Pulitzer Prize in Criticism, 1994. *Address:* 27 Pennsylvania Ave, Somerville, MA 02145, USA.

SCHWARTZ, Lynne Sharon; author, poet and translator; b. 19 March 1939, New York, NY, USA; m. Harry Schwartz, 22 Dec. 1957, two d. *Education:* BA, Barnard College, 1959; MA, Bryn Mawr College, 1961; New York University, 1967–72. *Career:* mem. Authors' Guild; National Book Critics Circle; National Writers Union; PEN American Centre. *Publications:* Rough Strife 1980, Balancing Acts 1981, Disturbances in the Field 1983, Acquainted with the Night (short stories) 1984, We Are Talking About Homes (short stories) 1985, The Melting Pot and Other Subversive Stories 1987, Leaving Brooklyn 1989, Smoke Over Birkenau by Liana Millu (trans.) 1991, (A Lynne Sharon Schwartz Reader: Selected Prose and Poetry 1992, The Fatigue Artist 1995, Ruined by Reading: A Life in Books 1996, In the Family Way 1999, Face to Face: A Reader in the World 2000, In Solitary (poems) 2002, A Place to Live and Other Selected Essays of Natalia Ginzburg (trans.) 2002, Referred Pain and Other Stories 2004. Contributions: periodicals. *Honours:* National Endowment for the Arts Fellowships, 1984, 2002; Guggenheim Fellowship, 1985; New York State Foundation for the Arts Fellowship, 1986. *Address:* 50 Morningside Dr., No. 31, New York, NY 10025, USA.

SCHWARZ, Daniel Roger; Prof. of English, Writer and Poet; b. 12 May 1941, Rockville Centre, NY, USA; m. 1st Marcia Mitson 1 Sept. 1963 (divorced 1986); two s.; m. 2nd Marcia Jacobson 1998. *Education:* BA, Union College, 1963; MA, 1965, PhD, 1968, Brown Univ. *Career:* Asst Prof., 1968–74, Assoc. Prof., 1974–80, Prof. of English, 1980–, Stephen H. Weiss Presidential Fellow, 1999–, Cornell Univ.; Distinguished Visiting Cooper Prof., Univ. of Arkansas at Little Rock, 1988; Citizen's Chair in Literature, Univ. of Hawaii, 1992–93; Visiting Eminent Scholar, Univ. of Alabama, Huntsville, 1996; mem. International Asscn of University Profs of English; Society for the Study of Narrative Literature (past pres.); MLA. *Publications:* Disraeli's Fiction, 1979; Conrad: Almayer's Folly to Under Western Eyes, 1980; Conrad: The Later Fiction, 1982; The Humanistic Heritage: Critical Theories of the English Novel from James to Hillis Miller, 1986; Reading Joyce's Ulysses, 1987; The Transformation of the English Novel 1890–1930: Studies in Hardy, Conrad, Joyce, Lawrence, Forster and Woolf, 1989; The Case for a Humanistic Poetics, 1991; Narrative and Representation in the Poetry of Wallace Stevens, 1993; Narrative and Culture (ed. with Janice Carlise), 1994; James Joyce's The Dead (ed.), 1994; Joseph Conrad's The Secret Sharer (ed.), 1997; Reconfiguring Modernism: Explorations in the Relationship Between Modern Art and Modern Literature, 1997; Imagining the Holocaust, 1999; Rereading Conrad, 2001; Broadway Boogie Woogie: Damon Runyon and the Making of New York City Culture, 2002. Other: over 30 poems. Contributions: journals. *Honours:* American Philosophical Society Grant, 1981; Dir, 9 National Endowment for the Humanities Summer Seminars for College and High School Teachers Grants, 1984–93; USIA Lecturer and Academic Specialist Lecturer, Australia, 1993, Cyprus, 1999, Italy, 2002; Cornell University Russell Distinguished Teaching Award, 1998. *Address:* Dept of English, 242 Goldwin Smith Hall, Cornell University, Ithaca, NY 14853, USA. *E-mail:* drs6@cornell.edu. *Website:* www.people.cornell.edu/pages/drs6/.

SCHWEIZER, Karl Wolfgang, BA, MA, PhD, FRHistS; American writer; b. 30 June 1946, Mannheim, Germany; m. *Education:* Wilfrid Laurier University, University of Waterloo, Peterhouse Coll., Cambridge. *Career:* Prof. Bishop's University, Lennoxville, QC 1977–88; Mellon Fellow Harvard University 1978; Visiting Lecturer University of Guelph 1978–80; Research Assoc. Russian Research Center, IL 1979–80, 1999; Academic Visitor LSE

1986, 1994; Visiting Scholar Queen's University, ON 1986–87; Visiting Fellow Darwin College, Cambridge, 1987, 1994, 2003, Yale University, 1994–95, Princeton University, 1994–95, Peterhouse College, Cambridge 2003; Chair. Dept of Humanities 1988–93, Prof. Dept of Social Science 1993–2000, Prof. and Chair. Dept of Humanities and Social Science 2000–03, New Jersey Institute of Technology (NJIT): Graduate Faculty, Rutgers, The State University of New Jersey at Newark 1992–; Assoc. Center for Global Change and Governance 1999–. *Publications:* The Devonshire Political Diary 1757–1763 (ed.) 1982, Diplomatic Thought 1648–1815 (ed.) 1983, François de Callières: The Art of Diplomacy 1983, Essays in European History 1648–1815, in Honour of Ragnhild Hatton (ed. with J. Black) 1985, The Origins of War in Early Modern Europe (co-author) 1987, Lord Bute: Essays in Re-Interpretation 1988, Politics and the Press in Hanoverian Britain (ed. with J. Black) 1989, England, Prussia and the Seven Years War 1989, Cobbett in His Times 1990, Frederick the Great, William Pitt and Lord Bute: Anglo-Prussian Relations 1756–1763 1991, Lord Chatham 1993, François de Callières: Diplomat and Man of Letters 1995, Herbert Butterfield: Essays on the History of Science (ed.) 1998, Hanoverian Britain ad Empire (co-author) 1998, Seeds of Evil: The Gray/Snyder Murder Case 2001, War, Diplomacy and Politics: The Anglo-Prussian Alliance 1756–1763 2001, Statesmen, Diplomats and the Press: Essays on 18th Century Britain 2002. Contributions: reference works and scholarly books and journals. *Honours:* Adelle Mellen Prize for Distinguished Contributions to Scholarship 1990, New Jersey Writer's Conference Award 1993, Outstanding Academic Book Citations, Choice 1994, 1998, NJIT Teaching Award 2000. *Address:* 49 S Passaic Avenue, Apt 24, Chatham, NJ 07928, USA.

SCLIAR, Moacyr; novelist and physician; b. 23 March 1937, Porto Alegre, Brazil. *Publications include:* Histórias de um Médico em Formação 1962, O Carnaval dos Animais 1968, A Guerra no Bom Fim 1972, O Exército de um Homem Só 1973, Os Deuses de Raque 1975, O Ciclo das águas 1975, A Balada do Falso Messias 1976, Histórias da Terra Trêmula 1976, Mês de Cães Danados 1977, O Anão no Televisor 1979, Doutor Miragem 1979, Os Voluntários 1979, O Centauro no Jardim 1980, Cavalos e Obeliscos (juvenile) 1980, Max e os Felinos 1981, A Festa no Castelo (juvenile) 1982, A Estranha Nação de Rafael Mendes 1983, A massagista japonesa 1984, Os Melhores Contos de Moacyr Scliar 1984, Memórias de um Aprendiz de Escritor (juvenile) 1984, Dez Contos Escolhidos 1984, O Olho Enigmático 1986, A Condição Judaica (essay) 1987, Do Mágico ao Social: a Trajetória da Saúde Pública (essay) 1987, No Caminho dos Sonhos (juvenile) 1988, A orelha de Van Gogh (Prêmio Casa de las Américas, Cuba 1989) 1988, O Tio que Flutuava (juvenile) 1988, Cenas Médicas 1988, Os Cavalos da República (juvenile) 1989, Cenas da Vida Minúscula 1991, Prá Você Eu Conto (juvenile) 1991, Sonhos Tropicais 1992, Se Eu Fosse Rotschild (essay) 1993, Uma História Só pra Mim 1994, Judaísmo: dispersão e Unidade (essay) 1994, Contos Reunidos 1995, Um Sonho no Caroço de Abacate (juvenile) 1995, O Rio Grande Farroupilha (juvenile) 1995, Oswaldo Cruz (essay) 1996, A Paixão Transformada: História da Medicina na Literatura (essay) 1996, A Majestade do Xingu (Academia Brasileira de Letras Prêmio José Lins do Rego 1998) 1997, O Amante da Madonna 1997, Os Contistas 1997, Histórias para (Quase) Todos os Gostos 1998, Câmera na Mão, o Guarani no Coração (juvenile) 1998, A mulher que escreveu a bíblia 1999, A Colina dos Suspiros (juvenile) 1999, Os Leopardos de Kafka 2000, Livro da Medicina (juvenile) 2000, O Mistério da Casa Verde (juvenile) 2000, Meu Filho, o Doutor: Medicina e Judaísmo na História, na Literatura e no Humor (essay) 2000, A Face Oculta: Inusitadas e Reveladoras Histórias da Medicina (essay) 2000, Porto de Histórias: Mistérios e Crepúsculos de Porto Alegre (essay) 2000, O Ataque do Comando P. Q. (juvenile) 2001, Navio das cores (works by Lasar Segall) 2003, Saturno nos Trópicos 2003. *Honours:* Prêmio da Academia Mineira de Letras 1968, Prêmio Joaquim Manoel de Macedo 1974, Prêmio Cidade de Porto Alegre 1976, Prêmio Brasília 1977, Prêmio Guimarães Rosa 1977, Prêmio Erico Verissimo de romance 1977, Prêmio da Associação de Críticos de Arte 1980, Prêmios Jabuti 1988, 1993, 2000, Prêmio Pen Club do Brasil 1990, Prêmios Açorianos 1996, 1997, Prêmio Mario Quintana 1999. *Address:* c/o Companhia das Letras, Departamento Editorial, rua Bandeira Paulista 702, cj. 32, São Paulo, SP 04532-002, Brazil.

SCOBIE, Stephen (Arthur Cross); Prof. of English, Poet and Writer; b. 31 Dec. 1943, Carnoustie, Scotland; m. Sharon Maureen, 6 May 1967. *Education:* MA, University of St Andrews, 1965; PhD, University of British Columbia, 1969. *Career:* Faculty, 1969–80, Prof., 1980–81, University of Alberta; Prof. of English, University of Victoria, 1981–; Guest Prof. of Canadian Studies, Christian-Albrechts-Universität, Kiel, 1990; mem. League of Canadian Poets, vice-pres., 1972–74, 1986–88; Victoria Literary Arts Festival Society, pres. *Publications:* Poetry: Babylondromat, 1966; In the Silence of the Year, 1971; The Birken Tree, 1973; Stone Poems, 1974; The Rooms We Air, 1975; Airloom, 1975; Les toiles n'ont peur de rien, 1979; McAlmon's Chinese Opera, 1980; A Grand Memory for Forgetting, 1981; Expecting Rain, 1985; The Ballad of Isabel Gunn, 1987; Dunino, 1988; Remains, 1990; Ghosts: A Glossary of the Intertext, 1990; Gospel, 1994; Slowly Into Autumn, 1995; Willow, 1995; Taking the Gate: Journey Through Scotland, 1996. Other: Leonard Cohen, 1978; The Maple Laugh Forever: An Anthology of Canadian Comic Poetry (co-ed.), 1981; Alias Bob Dylan, 1991. Contributions: journals and magazines. *Honours:* Governor-General's Award for Poetry, 1980; Fellow, Royal Society of Canada, 1995. *Address:* 4278 Parkside Crescent, Victoria, BC V8N 2C3, Canada.

SCOFIELD, Sandra (Jean); Writer and Adjunct Prof. of English; b. 5 Aug. 1943, Wichita Falls, Texas, USA; m. 1st Allen Scofield (deceased); one d.; m. 2nd Bill Ferguson 10 July 1975. *Education:* BA, University of Texas, 1964; MA, 1978, PhD, 1979, University of Oregon. *Career:* Teacher, Elementary and High School, Texas, Illinois, California and Oregon; Asst Prof. of Education, 1979–80, Adjunct Prof. of English, 1991–, Southern Oregon State College; mem. PEN; Authors' Guild; Oregon Institute of Literary Arts; Austin Writers League. *Publications:* Gringa, 1989; Beyond Deserving, 1991; Walking Dunes, 1992; More Than Allies, 1993; Opal on Dry Ground, 1994; A Chance to See Egypt, 1996. Contributions: periodicals. *Honours:* Second Place, Katherine Anne Porter Fiction Prize, 1985; New American Writing Award, 1989; National Endowment for the Arts Fellowship, 1989; American Book Award, 1992; Texas Institute of Letters Fiction Award, 1997. *Address:* PO Box 3329, Ashland, OR 97520, USA.

SCOT, Michael (see Rohan, Michael Scott).

SCOTT, Gail; Writer; b. 20 Jan. 1945, Ottawa, Ontario, Canada; one d. *Education:* BA, Queen's University, Kingston, Ontario, 1966; University of Grenoble. *Career:* Journalist, Montréal Gazette, The Globe and Mail, 1970–79; Writing Instructor, 1981–90; Writer-in-Residence, Concordia University, Montréal, 1991–92, University of Alberta, Edmonton, 1994–95; mem. Union des écrivaines et des écrivains québécois; Writer's Union of Canada. *Publications:* Spare Parts, 1982; Heroine, 1987; La Theorie, un Dimanche, 1988; Spaces Like Stairs, 1989; Serious Hysterics (anthology), 1992; Resurgences (anthology), 1992; Main Brides, 1994. Contributions: journals and other publications. *Address:* c/o Coach House Press, 401 Heron St, Toronto, Ontario M5S 2G5, Canada.

SCOTT, John A.; University Lecturer, Poet and Writer; b. 23 April 1948, Littlehampton, Sussex, England. *Education:* BA, DipEd, Monash University, Vic., Australia. *Career:* Lecturer, Swinburne Institute, 1975–80, Canberra College of Advanced Education, 1980–89, University of Wollongong, NSW, 1989–. *Publications:* The Barbarous Sideshow, 1976; From the Flooded City, 1981; Smoking, 1983; The Quarrel with Ourselves, 1984; Confession, 1984; St Clair, 1986; Blair, 1988; Singles: Shorter Works 1981–1986, 1989; Translation, 1990; What I Have Written, 1993. Contributions: various publications. *Honours:* Poetry Society of Australia Award, 1970; Mattara Poetry Prize, 1984; Wesley Michel Wright Awards, 1985, 1988; Victorian Premier's Prize for Poetry, 1986; ANA Award, Fellowship of Australian Writers, 1990.

SCOTT, John Peter; Prof. of Sociology and Writer; b. 8 April 1949, London, England; m. Jill Wheatley, 4 Sept. 1971, one s. one d. *Education:* Kingston College of Technology, 1968–71; BSc, Sociology, University of London, 1971; LSE, 1971–72; PhD, University of Strathclyde, 1976. *Career:* Lecturer, University of Strathclyde, 1972–76; Lecturer, 1976–87, Reader, 1987–91, Prof. of Sociology, 1991–94, University of Leicester; Ed., Network Newsletter, British Sociological Asscn, 1985–89, Social Studies Review, later Sociology Review, 1986–; Prof. of Sociology, University of Essex, 1994–; Adjunct Prof., University of Bergen, Norway, 1997–; mem. British Sociological Asscn, secretary, 1991–92, chair., 1992–93, treasurer, 1997–99, pres., 2001–. *Publications:* Corporations, Classes and Capitalism, 1979; The Upper Classes, 1982; The Anatomy of Scottish Capital (with M. Hughes), 1982; Dirs of Industry (with C. Griff), 1984; Networks of Corporate Power (co-ed.), 1985; Capitalist Property and Financial Power, 1986; A Matter of Record, 1990; The Sociology of Elites (ed.), 3 vols, 1990; Who Rules Britain, 1991; Social Network Analysis, 1992; Power (ed.), 3 vols, 1994; Poverty and Wealth, 1994; Sociological Theory, 1995; Stratification and Power, 1996; Corporate Business and Capitalist Classes, 1997; Class (ed.), four vols, 1997; Sociology (with James Fulcher), 1999; Social Structure (with Jose Lopez), 2000; Power, 2000; Critical Concepts: Social Networks (ed.), four vols, 2002. Contributions: Professional journals and general periodicals. *Honours:* Outstanding Sociology Book of the Year, Choice, 1995. *Address:* c/o Dept of Sociology, University of Essex, Colchester CO4 3SQ, England.

SCOTT, Jonathan (Henry); Historian, Writer and Poet; b. 22 Jan. 1958, Auckland, New Zealand; m. 1st Sara Bennett 1980 (divorced); m. 2nd Lindsey Bridget Shaw 1986 (divorced 1991); m. 3rd Anne Hansel Pelzel 1995; one s. one d. *Education:* BA, 1980, BA, 1981, Victoria University of Wellington; PhD, Trinity College, Cambridge, 1986. *Career:* Research Fellow, Magdalene College, Cambridge, 1985–87; Lecturer in History, Victoria University of Wellington, 1987–88, University of Sheffield, 1989–91; Fellow and Dir of Studies in History, Downing College, Cambridge, 1991–2002; Carroll Amundson Prof. of British History, Univ. of Pittsburgh, 2002–. *Publications:* Algernon Sidney and the English Republic, 1623–1677, 1988; Algernon Sidney and the Restoration Crisis, 1677–1683, 1991; Harry's Absence: Looking for My Father on the Mountain, 1997; England's Troubles: Seventeenth Century English Political Instability in European Context, 2000. Contributions: scholarly books and journals, and literary periodicals. *Address:* 3K38 Posvar Hall, University of Pittsburgh, Pittsburgh, PA 15260, USA.

SCOTT, Nathan Alexander, Jr; Prof. of English Emeritus, Minister and Writer; b. 24 April 1925, Cleveland, Ohio, USA; m. Charlotte Hanley 21 Dec. 1946; two c. *Education:* AB, University of Michigan, 1944; BD, Union Theological Seminary, 1946; PhD, Columbia University, 1949. *Career:* Dean of the Chapel, Virginia Union University, 1946–47; Instructor, 1948–51, Asst Prof., 1951–53, Assoc. Prof. of Humanities, 1953–55, Howard University; Asst Prof., 1955–58, Assoc. Prof., 1958–64, Prof. of Theology and Literature, 1964–72, Prof. of English, 1967–76, Shailer Mathews Prof. of Theology and Literature, 1972–76, University of Chicago; Ordained Priest, Episcopal Church, 1960; Co-Ed., Journal of Religion, 1963–77; Canon Theologian, Cathedral of St James, Chicago, 1967–76; Commonwealth Prof. of Religious Studies, 1976–81, Prof. of English, 1976–90, William R. Kenan Prof. of Religious Studies, 1981–90, Prof. Emeritus, 1990–, University of Virginia; mem. American Acad. of Arts and Sciences, fellow; American Acad. of Religion, pres., 1986; MLA; Society for Values in Higher Education; Society of Arts, Religion and Contemporary Culture. *Publications:* Rehearsals of Discomposure: Alienation and Reconciliation in Modern Literature, 1952; The Tragic Vision and the Christian Faith, 1957; Modern Literature and the Religious Frontier, 1958; Albert Camus, 1962; Reinhold Niebuhr, 1963; The New Orpheus: Essays Toward a Christian Poetic, 1964; The Climate of Faith in Modern Literature (ed.), 1964; Samuel Beckett, 1965; Four Ways of Modern Poetry (ed.), 1965; Man in the Modern Theatre (ed.), 1965; The Broken Center: Studies in the Theological Horizon of Modern Literature, 1966; Ernest Hemingway, 1966; The Modern Vision of Death (ed.), 1967; Adversity and Grace: Studies in Recent American Literature (ed.), 1968; Craters of the Spirit: Studies in the Modern Novel (ed.), 1968; Negative Capability: Studies in the New Literature and the Religious Situation (ed.), 1969; The Unquiet Vision: Mirrors of Man in Existentialism, 1969; Nathanael West, 1971; The Wild Prayer of Longing: Poetry and the Sacred, 1971; Three American Moralists: Mailer, Bellow, Trilling, 1973; The Legacy of Reinhold Niebuhr (ed.), 1975; The Poetry of Civic Virtue: Eliot, Malraux, Auden, 1976; The Poetics of Belief: Studies in Coleridge, Arnold, Pater, Santayana, Stevens and Heidegger, 1985; Visions of Presence in Modern American Poetry, 1993; Reading George Steiner (with Ronald Sharp), 1994. Contributions: Professional journals and other publications. *Honours:* many hon. doctorates. *Address:* 1419 Hilltop Rd, Charlottesville, VA 22903, USA.

SCOTT, Paul Henderson; Essayist, Historian, Critic and Former Diplomat; b. 7 Nov. 1920, Edinburgh, Scotland. *Education:* MA, MLitt, University of Edinburgh. *Career:* mem. International PEN, Scottish Centre; Saltire Society; Asscn for Scottish Literary Studies; Scottish National Party. *Publications:* 1707: The Union of Scotland and England, 1979; Walter Scott and Scotland, 1981; John Galt, 1985; Towards Independence: Essays on Scotland, 1991; Scotland in Europe, 1992; Andrew Fletcher and the Treaty of Union, 1992; Scotland: A Concise Cultural History (ed.), 1993; Defoe in Edinburgh, 1994; Scotland: An Unwon Cause, 1997; Still in Bed with an Elephant, 1998; The Boasted Advantages, 1999; A Twentieth-Century Life, 2002; Scotland Resurgent, 2003. Contributions: newspapers and journals. *Honours:* Andrew Fletcher Award, 1993; Oliver Award, 2000. *Address:* 33 Drumsheugh Gardens, Edinburgh EH3 7RN, Scotland. *Telephone:* (131) 225-1038. *Fax:* (131) 225-1038.

SCOTT, Peter Dale; Canadian Prof. of English (retd) and Poet; b. 11 Jan. 1929, Montréal, Canada; m. Ronna Kabatznick, 14 July 1993, two s. one d. *Education:* BA, 1949, PhD, Political Science, 1955, McGill University; Institut d'Etudes Politiques, Paris, 1950; University College, Oxford, 1950–52. *Career:* Lecturer, McGill University, 1955–56; Canadian Foreign Service, Ottawa and Poland, 1957–61; Prof. of Speech, 1961–66, Prof. of English, 1966–94, University of California at Berkeley. *Publications:* poetry: Poems, 1952; Rumors of No Law, 1981; Coming to Jakarta, 1988; Listening to the Candle, 1992; Crossing Borders, 1994; Minding the Darkness, 2000; prose: Deep Politics and the Death of JFK 1993, Drugs, Oil and War 2003. Contributions: Reviews, quarterlies, and periodicals. *Honours:* Dia Art Foundation 1989, Lannan Poetry Award 2002. *Address:* c/o Dept of English, University of California at Berkeley, Berkeley, CA 94720, USA. *E-mail:* pdscottweb@hotmail.com. *Website:* www.peterdalescott.net.

SCOTT, Rosie, MA; New Zealand/Australian writer and poet; b. 22 March 1948, New Zealand; m. 1987; two d. *Career:* mem. Australian Soc. of Authors (exec. cttee), PEN Australia. *Publications:* Flesh and Blood (poems) 1984, Glory Days 1988, Queen of Love 1989, Nights with Grace 1990, Feral City 1992, Lives on Fire 1993, Movie Dreams 1995, The Red Heart (essays) 1999, Faith Singer 2001; contrib. to various publications. *Honours:* Sunday Times-Bruce Mason Award 1986, Australian Writers Fellowship 1992. *Address:* 21 Darghan Street, Glebe, NSW 2037, Australia.

SCOTT, William Neville, (Bill Scott); Author and Poet; b. 4 Oct. 1923, Bundaberg, Qld, Australia. *Publications:* Focus on Judith Wright, 1967; Some People (short stories), 1968; Brother and Brother (verse), 1972; The Continual Singing: An Anthology of World Poetry, 1973; Portrait of Brisbane, 1976; The Complete Book of Australian Folklore, 1976; Bushranger Ballads, 1976; My Uncle and Other People (short stories), 1977; Boori (children's fiction), 1978; Tough in the Old Days (autobiog.), 1979; Ned Kelly After a Century of Acrimony (with John Meredith), 1980; The Second Penguin Australian Songbook, 1980; Darkness Under the Hills (children's fiction), 1980; Reading 360 series (The Blooming Queensland Side, On the Shores of Botany Bay, The Golden West, Bound for South Australia, Upon Van Diemen's Land, The Victorian Bunyip), 6 vols, 1981; Australian Bushrangers, 1983; Penguin Book of Australian Humorous Verse, 1984; Shadows Among the Leaves (children's fiction), 1984; The Long and the Short and the Tall (folklore), 1985; Following the Gold (children's poems), 1989; Many Kinds of Magic (short stories), 1990; Hey Rain (cassette, songs and poems), 1992; The Currency Lad (fiction), 1994; Songbird in Your Pocket (cassette, songs and poems), 1994; Pelicans and Chihuahuas (folklore), 1995; The Banshee and the Bullocky (short stories), 1995; Riverbank and Township (poems), 1999; Opal Miner (CD of songs), 1999; Lies, Flies and Strange Big Fish, 2000. *Honours:* Mary Gilmore Award, 1964; Medal of the Order of Australia, 1992; Heritage Award, 1994; Judith Hosier Memorial Award, 2001. *Address:* 157 Pratten St, Warwick, Qld 4370, Australia.

SCOTT-JAMES, Anne Eleanor, (Lady Lancaster); British journalist and writer; b. 5 April 1913; m. 1st Macdonald Hastings 1944 (died 1982); one s. one d.; m. 2nd Sir Osbert Lancaster 1967 (died 1986). *Education:* St Paul's Girls' School and Somerville Coll., Oxford. *Career:* mem. editorial staff, Vogue 1934–41; Women's Ed. Picture Post 1941–45, Sunday Express 1953–57; Ed. Harper's Bazaar 1945–51; Women's Adviser Beaverbrook Newspapers 1959–60; Columnist Daily Mail 1960–68; freelance journalist 1968–; mem. Council Royal Horticultural Soc. 1978–82. *Publications:* In the Mink 1952, Down to Earth 1971, Sissinghurst: the making of a garden 1975, The Pleasure Garden (jtly) 1977, The Cottage Garden 1981, Glyndebourne – the Gardens (jtly) 1983, The Language of the Garden: a personal anthology 1984, The Best Plants for Your Garden 1988, The British Museum Book of Flowers (jtly) 1989, Gardening Letters to My Daughter 1990, Sketches from a Life (autobiog.) 1993. *Address:* 78 Cheyne Court, Royal Hospital Road, London, SW3 5TT, England.

SCRIPPS, Charles Edward; American newspaper publisher; b. 27 Jan. 1920, San Diego; m. 1st Louann Copeland 1941 (divorced 1947); m. 2nd Lois Anne MacKay 1949 (died 1990); two s. two d.; m. 3rd Mary Elizabeth Breslin 1993. *Education:* William and Mary Coll. and Pomona Coll. *Career:* Reporter, Cleveland Press, Ohio 1941; Successor-Trustee, Edward W. Scripps Trust 1945, Chair. Bd of Trustees 1948–; Vice Pres., Dir E. W. Scripps Co. 1946, Chair. of Bd 1953–94. *Honours:* named as Great Living Cincinnatian 2003. *Address:* c/o Scripps Howard Foundation, POB 5380, Cincinnati, OH 45201, USA (Office). *Telephone:* (513) 977-3035. *Fax:* (513) 977-3800.

SCRUTON, Roger, BA, PhD, FRSL; British philosopher and writer; b. 27 Feb. 1944, Buslingthorpe; m. 1st Danielle Laffitte 1975 (divorced 1983); m. 2nd Sophie Jeffreys 1996. *Education:* High Wycombe Royal Grammar School, Jesus Coll. Cambridge and Inner Temple, London. *Career:* Fellow, Peterhouse, Cambridge 1969–71; Lecturer in Philosophy, Birkbeck Coll. London 1971–79, Reader 1979–86, Prof. of Aesthetics 1986–92; Prof. of Philosophy, Boston Univ. 1992–95; Founder and Dir The Claridge Press 1987–; Ed. The Salisbury Review 1982–2000. *Publications:* Art and Imagination 1974, The Aesthetics of Architecture 1979, The Meaning of Conservatism 1980, The Politics of Culture and Other Essays 1981, Fortnight's Anger (novel) 1981, A Short History of Modern Philosophy 1982, A Dictionary of Political Thought 1982, The Aesthetic Understanding 1983, Kant 1983, Untimely Tracts 1985, Thinkers of the New Left 1986, Sexual Desire 1986, Spinoza 1987, A Land Held Hostage: Lebanon and the West 1987, The Philosopher on Dover Beach (essays) 1989, Francesca (novel) 1991, A Dove Descending (stories) 1991, Conservative Texts: An Anthology 1991, The Xanthippic Dialogues 1993, Modern Philosophy 1993, The Classical Vernacular 1994, Modern Philosophy 1996, Animal Rights and Wrongs 1996, An Intelligent Person's Guide to Philosophy 1997, The Aesthetics of Music 1997, On Hunting 1998, Town and Country (co-ed.) 1998, An Intelligent Person's Guide To Modern Culture 1998, On Hunting 1999, Perictione in Colophon 2000, England: An Elegy 2000, The West and the Rest: Globalization and the Terrorist Threat 2002, Death-Devoted Heart: Sex and the Sacred in Wagner's Tristan and Isolde 2004. *Honours:* Hon. doctorates (Adelphi Univ.) 1995, (Masaryk Univ., Brno, Czech Repub.) 1998. *Address:* Sunday Hill Farm, Brinkworth, Wilts., SN15 5AS, England.

SCULLY, Vincent Joseph, Jr; Prof. of Art History Emeritus and Writer; b. 21 Aug. 1920, New Haven, CT, USA; m. Catherine Lynn, 30 Dec. 1980, four c. *Education:* BA, 1940, PhD, 1949, Yale University. *Career:* Instructor, Asst Prof., Assoc. Prof., 1947–61, Col John Trumbull Prof. of Art History, 1961–83, Sterling Prof. of History of Art, 1983–91, Sterling Prof. Emeritus, 1991–, Yale University; Host, New World Visions: American Art and the Metropolitan Museum 1650–1914, PBS-TV, 1983; Visiting Prof., University of Miami at Coral Gables, 1992–97; Mellon Visiting Prof. of History, California Institute of Technology, 1995; mem. American Institute of Architects, hon. mem.; National Trust for Historic Preservation, trustee; Royal Institute of British Architects, hon. fellow. *Publications:* The Architectural Heritage of Newport, Rhode Island (with Antoinette Forrester Downing), 1952; The Shingle Style: Architectural Theory and Design from Richardson to the Origins of Wright, 1955, revised edn as The Shingle Style and the Stick Style: Architectural Theory and Design from Downing to the Origins of Wright, 1971; Frank Lloyd Wright, 1960; Modern Archiecture: The Architecture of Democracy, 1961; Louis I Kahn, 1962; The Earth, the Temple and the Gods: Greek Sacred Architecture, 1962; American Architecture and Urbanism, 1969; Pueblo Architecture of the Southwest, 1971; The Shingle Style Today: or, The Historian's Revenge, 1974; Pueblo:

Mountain, Village, Dance, 1975; Robert Stern (with David Dunster), 1981; Wesleyan: Photographs, 1982; Michael Graves, Buildings and Projects, 1966–1981, 1982; The Villas of Palladio, 1986; The Architecture of the American Summer: The Flowering of the Shingle Style, 1987; New World Visions of Household Gods and Sacred Places: American Art and the Metropolitan Museum 1650–1914, 1988; The Architecture of Robert Venturi (with others), 1989; The Great Dinosaur Mural at Yale: The Age of Reptiles (with others), 1990; Architecture: The Natural and the Manmade, 1991; French Royal Gardens: The Design of André Le Notre (with Jeannie Baubion-Maclere), 1992; Robert A. M. Stern, Buildings and Projects 1987–1992, 1992; Mother's House: The Evolution of Vanna Venturi's House in Chestnut Hill (with Robert Venturi), 1992. *Honours:* National Endowment for the Humanities Senior Fellowship, 1972–73; American Institute of Architects Medal, 1976; Thomas Jefferson Medal, University of Virginia, 1982; Topaz Award, Asscn of Collegiate Schools of Architecture/American Institute of Architects, 1986; Literary Lion, New York Public Library, 1992; Governor's Arts Awards Medal, State of Connecticut, 1993; American Acad. in Rome Award, 1994; Thomas Jefferson Lecturer, National Endowment for the Humanities, 1995; Hon. doctorates. *Address:* 252 Lawrence St, New Haven, CT 06511, USA.

SCUPHAM, John Peter; Writer and Poet; b. 24 Feb. 1933, Liverpool, England; m. Carola Nance Braunholtz, 6 Aug. 1957, three s., one d. *Education:* Honours Degree, English, Emmanuel College, Cambridge, 1957. *Career:* Founder-Publisher, The Mandeville Press; mem. FRSL. *Publications:* The Snowing Globe, 1972; Prehistories, 1975; The Hinterland, 1977; Summer Places, 1980; Winter Quarters, 1983; Out Late, 1986; The Air Show, 1989; Watching the Perseids, 1990; Selected Poems, 1990; The Ark, 1994; Night Watch, 1999; Collected Poems, 2002. Contributions: anthologies and magazines. *Address:* Old Hall, Norwich Rd, South Burlingham, Norfolk NR13 4EY, England.

SEAGRAVE, Sterling; Writer; b. 15 April 1937, Columbus, Ohio, USA; m. 1st Wendy Law-Yone, 1967; m. 2nd Peggy Sawyer, 1982, one s. one d. *Education:* University of Miami, 1956; University of Mexico, 1957; University of Venezuela, 1958. *Career:* mem. Authors' Guild. *Publications:* Yellow Rain, 1981; Soldiers of Fortune, 1981; The Soong Dynasty, 1985; The Marcos Dynasty, 1988; Dragon Lady, 1992; Lords of the Rim, 1995. Contributions: Atlantic; Far Eastern Economic Review; Esquire; Time; Smithsonian. *Literary Agent:* William Morris Agency (UK) Ltd, 52–53 Poland St, London W1F 7LX, England.

SEAL, Basil (see Barnes, Julian Patrick).

SEARLE, Elizabeth; Writer and College Instructor; b. 13 Jan. 1962, Philadelphia, PA, USA; m. John Hodgkinson, 30 Dec. 1984. *Education:* Arizona State University, 1979–81; BA, Oberlin College, 1983; MA, Brown University, 1988. *Career:* Adjunct Lecturer, Oberlin College, 1983–84, Brown University, 1988–89; Instructor, Suffolk University, Boston, 1990–91, University of Massachusetts at Lowell, summers 1990–92; Emerson College, Boston, 1991; mem. PEN, New England; Poets and Writers. *Publications:* My Body to You, 1993; A Four-Sided Bed, 1998. Contributions: anthologies, reviews and periodicals. *Honours:* Roberts Writing Award, 1990; Chelsea Fiction Prize, 1991; Iowa Short Fiction Prize, 1992. *Address:* 18 College Ave, Arlington, MA 02174, USA. *E-mail:* jhodgkinson@mediaone.net.

SEARLE, John R(ogers); Prof. of Philosophy and Writer; b. 31 July 1932, Denver, CO, USA; m. Dagmar Carboch, 24 Dec. 1958, two s. *Education:* University of Wisconsin, 1949–52; BA, 1955, MA, 1959, DPhil, 1959, University of Oxford. *Career:* Lecturer in Philosophy, Christ Church, Oxford, 1956–59; Prof. of Philosophy, later Mills Prof. of the Philosophy of Mind and Language, University of California at Berkeley, 1959–; Visiting Prof. at various US and European universities; Lecturer throughout the world; mem. American Acad. of Arts and Sciences; ACLS, board of dirs, 1979–87; American Philosophical Asscn; Council for Philosophical Studies; National Humanities Center, board of trustees, 1976–90. *Publications:* Speech Acts: An Essay in the Philosophy of Language, 1969; The Campus War, 1971; Expression and Meaning: Studies in the Theory of Speech Acts, 1979; Intentionality: An Essay in the Philosophy of Mind, 1983; Minds, Brains and Science, 1984; The Foundations of Illocutionary Logic (with D. Vanderveken), 1985; The Rediscovery of the Mind, 1992; The Construction of Social Reality, 1995; The Mystery of Consciousness, 1997; Mind, Language and Society, 1998. Contributions: scholarly journals. *Honours:* Rhodes Scholar, 1952–55; Guggenheim Fellowship, 1975–76; Fulbright Awards, 1983, 1985; Hon. DHL, Adelphi University, 1993, University of Wisconsin, 1994. *Address:* c/o Dept of Philosophy, University of California at Berkeley, Berkeley, CA 94720, USA.

SEARLE, Ronald William Fordham; artist and writer; b. 3 March 1920, Cambridge, England. *Education:* Cambridge School of Art. *Publications:* Forty Drawings, 1946; Le Nouveau Ballet Anglais, 1947; Hurrah for St Trinian's, 1948; The Female Approach, 1949; Back to the Slaughterhouse, 1951; Souls in Torment, 1953; Rake's Progress, 1955; Merry England, 1956; Which Way Did He Go?, 1961; Searle in the Sixties, 1965; From Frozen North to Filthy Lucre, 1964; Pardong M'sieur, 1965; Searle' Cats, 1969; Hommage à Toulouse Lautrec, 1969; Secret Sketchbook, 1970; The Addict, 1971; More Cats, 1975; Drawings From Gilbert and Sullivan, 1975; The Zoodiac, 1977; Ronald Searle, 1978; The King of Beasts, 1980; The Big Fat Cat Book, 1982; Winespeak, 1983; Ronald Searle in Perspective, 1984; Ronald Searle's Golden Oldies, 1985; To the Kwai – and Back, 1986; Something in the Cellar, 1986. Ah Yes I Remember it Well: Paris 1961–1975, 1987; The Non-Sexist Dictionary, 1988; Slightly Foxed – but still desirable, 1989; The Curse of St Trinian's, 1993; Marquis de Sade meets Goody Two Shoes, 1994; Ronald Searle dans le Monde, 1998. *Honours:* Royal Designer for Industry 1988. *Literary Agent:* The Sayle Literary Agency, Bickerton House, 25–27 Bickerton Road, London, N19 5JT, England. *Telephone:* (20) 7263-8681. *Fax:* (20) 7561-0529.

SEBOLD, Alice, MFA; American author; b. Madison, WI. *Education:* Syracuse Univ., Univ. of Houston, Univ. of California at Irvine. *Career:* teacher and lecturer 1984–. *Publications:* Lucky (memoir) 1999, The Lovely Bones (novel) 2002. *Literary Agent:* Steven Barclay Agency, 12 Western Avenue, Petaluma, CA 94952, USA. *Telephone:* (707) 773-0654. *Fax:* (707) 778-1868. *E-mail:* SJBarclay@aol.com.

SECOR, James L.; Writer, Dramatist and Poet; b. 11 June 1947, Ft Clayton Air Force Base, Panama; one s. *Education:* BA, Theater, Towson State University; MS, Johns Hopkins University; PhD, Theater, University of Kansas; Bunraku National Puppet Theatre, Osaka. *Career:* Teacher, Aoyama University, 1990–92, Japan College of the Arts, 1992; Tutor, University of Kansas, 1994–99, Johnson County Community College, 1995; Ed., Into the Eye, 1996–97; mem. Japan Language Teachers Asscn, 1990–92; Lawrence Community Theatre, 1997; Acad. of American Poets. *Publications:* Sapl and Nicholas Ferguson: The Legend, 1992; Tanka, Sweetheart, 1996; Tangled in the Net of Ruin, 1996; Statesmanship, 1996; Saving Grace, 1996; A Different Thing to Do, 1996; Tanka, Reflections of Yesterday, 1996; The Crippled Heart of Man, 1997; Social Puissance, 1997; Votive, 1997; Sex Ed, 1997; Tanka, Ages and Stages, 1997. Other: several plays. Contributions: various publications. *Address:* 3307 N 61st Street, Kansas City, KS 66104-1417, USA.

SEDAKOVA, Olga Aleksandrovna; Russian poet, translator and essayist; b. 1949, Moscow. *Education:* Moscow State Univ. *Career:* teacher, Inst. of Theory and History of World Culture, Dept of Philosophy, Moscow State Univ. 1991. *Publications include:* Gates, Windows and Arches 1985, Vrata, okna, arki: Izbrannye stikhotvoreni, a 1986, Kitaiskoe puteshestvie: Stely i nadpisi: Starye pesni 1990, Stikhi 1994, Poems and Elegies 2004; contrib. to Silk of Time: Bilingual Selected Poems 1994. *Honours:* European Prize for Poetry 1996. *Address:* c/o University of Bucknell, Moore Avenue, Bucknell, PA 17837, USA. *Website:* www.bucknell.edu.

SEDGWICK, Fred; Lecturer in Education and Poet; b. 20 Jan. 1945, Dublin, Ireland. *Education:* St Luke's College, Exeter; MA, University of East Anglia at Norwich, 1984. *Career:* Head of Downing Primary School, Suffolk; Education Lecturer. *Publications:* Really in the Dark, 1980; From Another Part of the Island, 1981; A Garland for William Cowper, 1984; The Living Daylights, 1986; Falernian, 1987; This Way, That Way: A Collection of Poems for Schools (ed.), 1989; Lighting Up Time: On Children's Writing, 1990. *Address:* 1 Mornington Ave, Ipswich, Suffolk IP1 4LA, England.

SEDLEY, Kate (see Clarke, Brenda (Margaret Lilian)).

SEDLEY, Rt Hon. Sir Stephen John, Kt, PC, BA; British writer; *Lord Justice of Appeal*; b. 9 Oct. 1939; m. 1st Anne Tate 1968 (divorced 1995); one s. two d.; m. 2nd Teresa Chaddock 1996. *Education:* Mill Hill School, Queens' Coll., Cambridge. *Career:* freelance writer, musician and translator 1961–64; called to Bar, Inner Temple 1964, Bencher 1989, QC 1983; mem., Int. Commission on Mercenaries, Angola 1976; Visiting Professorial Fellow, Warwick Univ. 1981; Pres., Nat. Reference Tribunals for the Coalmining Industry 1983–88; Visiting Fellow, Osgoode Hall Law School, Canada 1987, Visiting Prof. 1997; Dir, Public Law Project 1989–93; Chair., Sex Discrimination Cttee, Bar Council 1992–95; Judge of the High Court of Justice, QBD 1992–99; Distinguished Visitor, Hong Kong Univ. 1992; Hon. Prof., Univ. of Wales, Cardiff 1993–, Univ. of Warwick 1994–; Visiting Fellow, Victoria Univ. of Wellington, New Zealand 1998; Judicial Visitor, Univ. Coll. London 1999–; Pres., British Inst. of Human Rights 2000–; Chair., British Council Advisory Cttee on Governance 2002–; Hon. Fellow, Inst. for Advanced Legal Studies 1997; mem. Administrative Law Bar Asscn (hon. vice-pres. 1992–), Haldane Soc. (sec. 1964–69). *Publications include:* Whose Child? 1987, The Making and Remaking of the British Constitution (with Lord Nolan) 1997, Freedom, Law and Justice 1999, Human Rights: A New World of Business as Usual 2000; editor: Seeds of Love (anthology) 1967, A Spark in the Ashes 1992; translator: From Burgos Jail, by Marcos Ana and Vidal de Nicolas 1964; contrib. essays to numerous books, including Freedom of Expression and Freedom of Information 2000, Judicial Review in International Perspective 2000, Discriminating Lawyers 2000; contrib. to periodicals and journals, including Civil Justic Quarterly, Industrial Law Journal, Journal of Law and Society, Journal of Legal Ethics, Law Quarterly Review, London Review of Books, Modern Law Review, Public Law. *Honours:* Dr hc (N London) 1996, Hon. LLD (Nottingham Trent) 1997, (Bristol) 1999, (Warwick) 1999, (Durham) 2001, (Hull) 2002, (Southampton) 2003. *Address:* c/o Royal Courts of Justice, Strand, London, WC2A 2LL, England.

SEE, Carolyn, (Monica Highland); Writer; b. 13 Jan. 1934, Pasadena, CA, USA; m. 1st Richard See, 18 Feb. 1954; m. 2nd Tom Sturak, 30 April 1960, two d. *Education:* PhD, University of California at Los Angeles, 1953.

Career: Prof. of English, University of California at Los Angeles; mem. PEN Center USA West, pres., 1993–94. *Publications:* The Rest is Done with Mirrors, 1970; Blue Money, 1974; Mothers, Daughters, 1977; Rhine Maidens, 1980; Golden Days, 1985; When Knaves Meet, 1988; The Mirrored Hall in the Hollywood Dance Hall, 1991; Dreaming: Hard Luck and Good Times in America, 1995; The Handyman, 1999. As Monica Highland: Lotus Land, 1983; 1-10 Shanghai Road, 1985; Greetings From Southern California, 1987; Two Schools of Thought (with John Espey), 1991; Making a Literary Life, 2002. Contributions: newspapers and magazines. *Honours:* Samuel Goldwyn Award, 1963; Sidney Hillman Award, 1969; National Endowment for the Arts Grant, 1974; Bread and Roses Award, National Womens Political Caucus, 1988; Vesta Award, 1989; Guggenheim Fellowship, 1989; Lila Wallace Grant, 1993; Lifetime Achievement Award, PEN Center USA West, 1998. *Address:* 17339 Tramonto, No. 303, Pacific Palisades, CA 90272, USA.

SEED, Cecile Eugenie, (Jenny Seed); Author; b. 18 May 1930, Cape Town, South Africa; m. Edward (Ted) Robert Seed, 31 Oct. 1953, three s., one d. *Publications:* The Great Thirst, 1985; The Great Elephant, 1985; Place Among the Stones, 1987; Hurry, Hurry, Sibusiso, 1988; The Broken Spear, 1989; The Prince of the Bay, 1989; The Big Pumpkin, 1990; Old Grandfather Mantis, 1992; The Hungry People, 1993; A Time to Scatter Stones, 1993; Lucky Boy, 1995; The Strange Large Egg, 1996. *Honours:* MER Award, 1987. *Address:* 10 Pioneer Crescent, Northdene, Kwazulu-Natal 4093, South Africa.

SEGAL, Erich, AB, AM, PhD; academic and writer; *Adjunct Professor of Classics, Yale University*; b. 16 June 1937, New York, NY, USA; m. Karen James 1975; one s. (deceased) two d. *Education:* Harvard University. *Career:* Teaching Fellow, Harvard University, 1959–63; Visiting Lecturer, 1964–65, Asst Prof., 1965–68, Assoc. Prof., 1968–72, Adjunct Prof. of Classics, 1981–, Yale University; Visiting Prof., University of Munich, 1973, Princeton University, 1974–75, 1981, University of Tel-Aviv, 1976, Dartmouth College, 1976, 1977; Visiting Fellow, 1978–79, Supernumerary Fellow, 1980–, Wolfson College, Oxford; Hon. Research Fellow, University College London, 1983–; mem. Acad. for Literary Studies; American Society of Composers, Authors, and Publishers; Society of Roman Studies, UK; Writers Guild of America. *Publications:* Fiction: Love Story, 1970; Fairy Tale, 1973; Oliver's Story, 1977; Man, Woman and Child, 1980; The Class, 1985; Doctors, 1987; Acts of Faith, 1992; Prizes, 1995; Only Love, 1997. Editor: Euripides: A Collection of Critical Essays, 1968; Scholarship on Plautus, 1965–1976, 1981; Greek Tragedy: Modern Essays in Criticism, 1983, UK edn as Oxford Readings in Greek Tragedy, 1983; Caesar Augustus: Seven Essays (with Fergus Millar), 1984; Plato's Dialogues, 1986; Oxford Readings in Aristophanes, 1996. Editor and Translator: Plautus, 1996. Classics: Roman Laughter: The Comedy of Plautus, 1968; Plautus: Four Comedies, 1996. Other: The Death of Comedy, 2001. Musicals; screenplays. Contributions: various reviews, journals, periodicals, and magazines, including TLS. *Honours:* Guggenheim Fellowship, 1968; Golden Globe Award, 1971; Humboldt Stiftung Award, West Germany, 1973; Premio Bancarella, Italy, 1986; Prix Littéraire, Deauville, France, 1986; Co-Recipient, Premio San Valentin di Terni Award, 1989; Chevalier, Légion d'honneur, 1999. *Literary Agent:* Ed Victor Ltd, 6 Bayley Street, Bedford Square, London, WC1B 3HB, England.

SEGAL, Lore Groszmann, BA; writer; b. 8 March 1928, Vienna, Austria; m. David I. Segal 1960 (deceased); one s. one d. *Education:* Bedford College, University of London. *Career:* Prof., Writing Division, School of Arts, Columbia University, Princeton University, Sarah Lawrence College, Bennington College; Prof. of English, University of Illinois, Ohio State University. *Publications:* Fiction: Other People's Houses, 1964; Lucinella, 1976; Her First American, 1985. Children's Books: Tell Me a Mitzi, 1970; All the Way Home 1973; Tell Me a Trudy 1977; The Story of Mrs Brubeck and How She Looked for Trouble and Where She Found Him, 1981; The Story of Mrs Lovewright and Purrless Her Cat, 1985; Morris the Artist, 2003; Why Mole Shouted 2004. Translator: Gallows Songs (with W. D. Snodgrass), 1968; The Juniper Tree and Other Tales from Grimm, 1973. Contributions: periodicals. *Honours:* Guggenheim Fellowship, 1965–66; National Endowment for the Arts Grant, 1982; National Endowment for the Humanities Grant, 1983; Acad. of Arts and Letters Award, 1986; Ohio Arts Council Grant, 1996. *Address:* 280 Riverside Drive, New York, NY 10025, USA.

SEGAL, Ronald Michael; writer; b. 14 July 1932, Cape Town, South Africa; m. Susan Wolf 1962; one s. two d. *Education:* University of Cape Town, Trinity College, Cambridge. *Career:* Hon. Sec., South African Freedom Asscn, 1960–61; Gen. Ed., Penguin African Library, 1961–84, Pluto Crime Fiction, 1983–86; Convenor, International Conference on Economic Sanctions Against South Africa, 1964, International Conference on South West Africa, 1966; Visiting Fellow, Center for the Study of Democratic Institutions, Santa Barbara, 1973; mem. Walton Society, founding chair., 1975–79, pres., 1979–; Ruth First Memorial Trust, chair., 1983–. *Publications:* The Tokolosh, 1960; Political Africa: A Who's Who of Personalities and Parties, 1961; African Profiles, 1962; Into Exile, 1963; Sanctions Against South Africa (ed.), 1964; South West Africa (ed.), 1964; The Crisis of India, 1965; The Race War, 1966; South West Africa: Travesty of Trust (ed.), 1967; America's Receding Future, 1968; The Struggle Against History, 1971; Whose Jerusalem?: The Conflicts of Israel, 1973; The Decline and Fall of the American Dollar, 1974; The Tragedy of Leon Trotsky, 1979; The State of the World Atlas, 1981, revised edn as The New State of the World Atlas, 1984; The Book of Business, Money and Power, 1987; The Black Diaspora, 1995; Islam's Black Slaves, 2000. *Address:* The Old Manor House, Manor Road, Walton-on-Thames, Surrey, England.

SEIDMAN, Hugh; Writer, Poet and Teacher; b. 1 Aug. 1940, New York, NY, USA; m. Jayne Holsinger 2 June 1990. *Education:* BS, Mathematics, Polytechnic Institute of Brooklyn, 1961; MS, Physics, Univ. of Minnesota, 1964; MFA, Poetry, Columbia Univ., 1969. *Career:* Faculty, New School for Social Research, New York, 1976–98; Asst Prof., Washington College, 1979; Visiting Lecturer, Univ. of Wisconsin, 1981, Columbia Univ., 1985; Poet-in-Residence, College of William and Mary, 1982; Visiting Poet, Writers Voice, New York, 1988; mem. American PEN; Authors' Guild; Authors League; Poetry Society of America. *Publications:* Collecting Evidence, 1970; Blood Lord, 1974; Throne/Falcon/Eye, 1982; People Live, They Have Lives, 1992; Selected Poems 1965–1995, 1995; 12 Views of Freetown, 1 View of Bumbuna, 2002. Contributions: many publications. *Honours:* Yale Series of Younger Poets Prize, 1969; National Endowment for the Arts Grant, 1970, and Fellowships, 1972, 1985; Yaddo Fellowships, 1972, 1976, 1986; MacDowell Colony Fellowships, 1974, 1975, 1989; Writers Digest Poetry Prize, 1982; New York Foundation for the Arts Poetry Fellowships, 1990, 2003. *Address:* 463 West St, No. H822, New York, NY 10014, USA. *Website:* www.hughseidman.com.

SEIDMAN, Lewis William, LLB, MBA; American fmr government official, publisher and television broadcaster; b. 29 April 1921, Grand Rapids, Mich.; m. Sarah Berry 1944; one s. five d. *Education:* Dartmouth Coll., Harvard Univ. and Univ. of Mich. *Career:* army service 1942–46; mem. Mich. Bar 1949, DC Bar 1977; Special Asst for Financial Affairs to Gov. of Mich. 1963–66; Nat. Man. Partner, Seidman & Seidman (certified public accountants) New York 1969–74; Asst for Econ. Affairs to Pres. Gerald Ford 1974–77; Dir Phelps Dodge Corpn New York 1977–82, Vice-Chair. 1980–82; Dean, Coll. of Business Admin. Ariz. State Univ. 1982–85; Chair. Fed. Deposit Insurance Corpn (FDIC) 1985–91; Chair. Detroit Fed. Reserve Bank, Chicago 1970; Co-Chair. White House Conf. on Productivity 1983–84; Chair. Resolution Trust Corpn 1989–91; Chief Commentator CNBC-TV 1991–; Publr Bank Director (magazine). *Honours:* Bronze Star Medal. *Address:* CNBC, 8th Floor, 1025 Connecticut Avenue, NW, Washington, DC 20036 (Office); 825 Audubon Drive, Bradenton, FL 34209, USA (Home). *Telephone:* (202) 530-0910 (Office). *Fax:* (202) 822-9551 (Office). *E-mail:* lws1025@aol.com (Office).

SEIERSTAD, Åsne; Norwegian journalist and writer; b. 1970, Lillehammer. *Career:* staff, ITAR-TASS news agency, Moscow; correspondent, Norwegian television news 1998–2000. *Publications:* non-fiction: With Their Backs to the Wall 2000, The Bookseller of Kabul 2002, One Hundred and One Days: A Reporter's Journey 2004. *Honours:* award for television reporting from Kosovo, Chechnya and Afghanistan. *Address:* c/o Virago Press, Brettenham House, Lancaster Place, London, WC2E 7EN, England. *Website:* www.virago.co.uk.

SEIFFERT, Rachel; British writer; b. 1971, Oxford, England; one s. *Career:* teacher; fmr Lecturer in English, Univ. of Glasgow. *Publications:* Blue (short story) 1999, The Crossing (short story) 2001, The Dark Room (novel) (LA Times First Fiction Award 2002,) 2001, Field Study (short stories) 2004. *Honours:* PEN David T. K. Wong Award 2001, Betty Trask Prize 2002. *Literary Agent:* Toby Eady Associates Ltd, Third Floor, 9 Orme Court, London, W2 4RL, England. *Telephone:* (20) 7792-0092. *Fax:* (20) 7792-0879. *E-mail:* toby@tobyeady.demon.co.uk. *Website:* www.tobyeadyassociates.co.uk.

SELBOURNE, David; Writer and Playwright; b. 4 June 1937, London, England. *Career:* mem. Society of Authors, London; United Oxford and Cambridge Club, London. *Publications:* The Play of William Cooper and Edmund Dew-Nevett, 1968; The Two-Backed Beast, 1969; Dorabella, 1970; Samson and Alison Mary Fagan, 1971; The Damned, 1971; Class Play, 1973; Brook's Dream: The Politics of Theatre, 1974; What's Acting? and Think of a Story Quickly!, 1977; An Eye to India, 1977; An Eye to China, 1978; Through the Indian Looking Glass, 1982; The Making of a Midsummer Night's Dream, 1983; Against Socialist Illusion: A Radical Argument, 1985; In Theory and In Practice: Essays on the Politics of Jayaprakash Narayan, 1986; Left Behind: Journeys into British Politics, 1987; A Doctor's Life: The Diaries of Hugh Selbourne MD 1960–63, 1989; Death of the Dark Hero: Eastern Europe 1987–90, 1990; The Spirit of the Age, 1993; Not an Englishman: Conversations With Lord Goodman, 1993; The Principle of Duty, 1994; The City of Light, 1997; One Year On: The 'New' Politics and Labour, 1998; Moral Evasion, 1998. Translator: The City of Light, by Jacob d'Ancona, 1997. *Honours:* Mem., Acad. of Savignano, Italy 1994, Officer, Order of Merit of Italian Republic 2001. *Address:* c/o Christopher Sinclair-Stevenson, 3 South Terrace, London SW7, England.

SELBY, Stephen; Playwright; b. 5 June 1952, Darley Dale, Derbyshire, England; m. Ann Spence, 6 March 1982, one d. *Education:* Social Science and Philosophy. *Career:* Writer, Dir, Producer, Noc On Theatre, 1987–, Hurdles of Time Theatre, 1991–; Dramaturgo, La Edel de Oro Theatre Company; mem. Theatre Writers Union; Camasiiey Theatre Dirs Asscn. *Publications:* Hurdles of Time; Erewash Giants, 1993; The Concrete Silver Band, 1995; Tontos Sabios y Ladrones Honestos, 1996. *Address:* 53 Percival Rd, Sherwood, Nottingham NG5 2FA, England.

SELF, William Woodward (Will), MA; British author and cartoonist; b. 26 Sept. 1961, London; m. 1st Katharine Sylvia Anthony Chancellor 1989 (divorced 1996); one s. one d.; m. 2nd Deborah Jane Orr 1997; one s. *Education:* Christ's Coll., Exeter Coll., Oxford. *Career:* cartoon illustrations appeared in New Statesman and City Limits 1982–88; Publishing Dir Cathedral Publishing 1988–90; Contributing Ed. London Evening Standard magazine 1993–95; columnist The Observer 1995–97, The Times 1997–99, Ind. on Sunday 2000–. *Publications:* short stories: Quantity Theory of Insanity 1991, Grey Area 1994, A Story for Europe 1996, Tough Tough Toys for Tough Tough Boys 1998, Dr Mukti and Other Tales of Woe 2003; novellas: Cock and Bull 1992, The Sweet Smell of Psychosis 1996; novels: My Idea of Fun 1993, Great Apes 1997, How the Dead Live 2000, Perfidious Man 2000, Feeding Frenzy 2001, Dorian 2002; Junk Mail (selected journalism) 1995, Sore Sites (collected journalism) 2000; collected cartoons 1985. *Honours:* Geoffrey Faber Memorial Prize 1992. *Literary Agent:* David Godwin Associates, 55 Monmouth Street, London, WC2H 9DG, England.

SELLERS, David (see Beasley, John David).

SELTZER, Joanne, BA, MA; writer and poet; b. 21 Nov. 1929, Detroit, Michigan, USA; m. Stanley Seltzer 1951; one s. three d. *Education:* University of Michigan, College of St Rose. *Career:* mem. American Literary Trans. Asscn; Associated Writing Programs; Poetry Society of America; Poets & Writers. *Publications:* Adirondack Lake Poems, 1985; Suburban Landscape, 1988; Inside Invisible Walls, 1989. Contributions: journals and magazines. *Honours:* All Nations Poetry Contest Award, 1978; World Order of Narrative and Formalist Poets Competitions Prizes, 1986, 1988, 1990, 1992, 1993, 1994, 1997, 1998, 2000; Tucumari Literary Review Poetry Contest Award, 1989; Amelia Islander Magazine Literary Contest Poetry Prize, 1999. *Address:* 2481 McGovern Drive, Schenectady, NY 12309, USA. *E-mail:* sseltzer1@juno.com.

SELVIDGE, Marla J(ean); Prof. of Religious Studies and Writer; b. 11 Nov. 1948, Grosse Pointe, Michigan, USA; m. 1st Stephen P. Schierling, divorced 1981; m. 2nd Thomas C. Hemling, 26 April 1982. *Education:* BA, Fort Wayne Bible College, 1970; MA, Wheaton College, IL, 1973; PhD, St Louis University, 1980. *Career:* several college and university positions, 1973–89; Assoc. Ed., Explorations: A Journal for Adventurous Thought, 1986–; Contributing Ed., Spotlight on Teaching, 1993–; Asst Prof. of Religious Studies and Philosophy, Marist College, Poughkeepsie, New York, 1989–90; Assoc. Prof., 1990–94, Dir, Center for Religious Studies, 1990–, Prof. of Religious Studies, 1994–, Central Michigan State University, Warrensburg; Vice-Pres., American Schools of Oriental Research, 1997–; mem. American Acad. of Religion; Society of Biblical Literature; Catholic Biblical Asscn; Central States Society of Biblical Literature, Chair, Sections on New Testament, 1992–94, Chair, Gender Issues, 1994–96; Missouri State Teachers Asscn, Vice-Pres. and Board of Dirs, 1997–. *Publications:* Fundamentalism Today: What Makes It So Attractive? (ed.), 1984; Daughters of Jerusalem, 1987; Woman, Cult, and Miracle Recital, 1990; Discovering Women, 1995; Notorious Voices: The Roots of Feminist Biblical Interpretation, 1996; Violence, Women, and the Bible, 1996; A Feminist Companion to the Bible: The Old Testament in the New Testament (contributor), 1996; Notorious Voices: A Reader, 1997; The New Testament: A Timeless Book for All Peoples, 1998. Contributions: Religious Studies News; Journal of Religious Studies; Marist Working Papers; Journal of Biblical Literature; Catholic Biblical Quarterly; Journal of Theology for Southern Africa; Missouri Chautauqua: Varieties of American Religious Experience. *Honours:* Society of Biblical Literature Award, 1982–83; Grants, William R. Kenan Fund and National Endowment for the Humanities, 1984–87; Educational Communications Award, Connecticut Asscn of Boards of Education, 1988–89; American Mirror Lecturer, 1991–93, Grant, 1992–94, Missouri Humanities Council.

SEMBÈNE, Ousmane; Novelist and Film Dir; b. 1 Jan. 1923, Ziguinchor, Casamance region, Senegal. *Education:* L'Ecole de Céramique, Marsassoum. *Career:* numerous jobs; served in Europe in World War II; docker in Marseille; studied film production in USSR under Marc Donski; Founder Ed., first Wolof language monthly, Kaddu; Films: Borom Sarret, 1963; L'empire Songhaï, 1963; Niaye, 1964; La noire de.., 1966; Mandabi/Le mandat, 1968; Taaw, 1971; E mitai, 1971; Xala, 1974; Ceddo, 1977; Camp de Thiaroye, 1988; Guelwaar, 1992. *Publications:* Le Docker noir, 1956; O Pays, mon beau peuple, 1957; Les Bouts de bois de Dieu, 1960; Voltaïque (trans. as God's Bits of Wood), 1962; L'Harmattan, 1963; Vèhi-Ciosane, 1964; Le Mandat, 1965; Xala, 1973; Le dernier de l'empire, 1979; Niiwam (novella), 1987; Taaw (novella), 1987; Guelwaar 1996. *Honours:* first prize for novelists, World Festival of Negro Arts, Dakar, 1966; Cannes Film Festival prize, 1967; Jury Prize, Venice, 1988. *Address:* PO Box 8087, Yoff, Dakar, Senegal. *Telephone:* 823-51-66. *Fax:* 823-51-66.

SEMEL, Nava; Author and Playwright; b. 15 Sept. 1954, Israel; m. Noam Semel, two s. one d. *Education:* MA, History of Art, Tel-Aviv University. *Career:* mem. Israeli Playwright Asscn; Hebrew Writers Asscn; PEN International Writers; Writers Asscn. *Publications:* Hats of Glass, 1985; Becoming Gershona, 1990; Flying Lessons, 1995; Night Games, 1994; Little Rose of the Mediterranean, 1994; Bride on Paper, 1996; Liluna, 1998; Who Stole the Show?, 1999; Awake in my Sleep, 2000; The Rat's Laughter, 2001. Plays: An Old Lady, 1984; The Child Behind the Eyes, 1986; Hunger, 1989. *Honours:* Institute for Holocaust Studies Award, 1988; Haifa Award, 1988; National Jewish Book Award, 1991; Israeli Prime Minister's Award for Literature, 1996; Best Illustrated Book of the Year, Israel Museum Award, 1998. *Address:* 11a Hchimeir str, Ramat Gan 52587, Israel. *E-mail:* rawe@informall.co.il.

SEMMLER, Clement William; Broadcaster and Writer; b. 23 Dec. 1914, Eastern Well, SA, Australia; m. 1st divorced, one s. one d.; m. 2nd Catherine Helena Wilson, 20 Dec. 1974, one d. *Education:* MA, University of Adelaide, 1938. *Career:* Fellow, College of Fine Arts, University of New South Wales. *Publications:* For the Uncanny Man (essays), 1963; Barcroft Boake, 1965; Literary Australia (ed.), 1965; The Banjo of the Bush, 1966; Kenneth Slessor, 1966; Twentieth Century Australian Literary Criticism (ed.), 1967; The Art of Brian James, 1972; Douglas Stewart, 1974; The ABC-Aunt Sally and the Sacred Cow, 1981; A Frank Hardy Swag (ed.), 1982; The War Diaries of Kenneth Slessor, 1985; The War Dispatches of Kenneth Slessor, 1987; Pictures on the Margin (memoirs), 1991. Contributions: periodicals and journals. *Honours:* DLitt, University of New England, Armidale, 1968; OBE, 1972; AM, 1988. *Address:* The Croft, St Clair St, Bowral, NSW 2576, Australia.

SEMPRÚN, Jorge; Spanish politician and novelist; b. 10 Dec. 1923, Madrid. *Education:* Sorbonne, Paris. *Career:* in exile in France during Spanish Civil War 1937; fought in the French Resistance in World War II, captured by Nazis and sent to Buchenwald concentration camp 1943; became leader of proscribed Spanish Communist Party, expelled as deviationist 1964; trans., UNESCO 1952; Minister of Culture, Spain 1988–91; mem. Académie Goncourt. *Publications:* Le Grand voyage (novel), 1963; La Guerre est finie (screenplay), 1966; Z (screenplay); L'aveu (screenplay); L'évanouissement (novel), 1967; La Deuxième mort de Ramón Mercader (novel), 1969; Section Speciale (screenplay), 1975; Une Femme à sa fenetre (screenplay), 1976; Les Routes du sud (screenplay), 1978; Autobiographie de Federico Sánchez, 1978; Quel beau dimanche, 1980; L'algarabie (novel), 1981; Montand, la vie continue, 1983; Les Trottoirs de saturne (screenplay), 1985; Nanou (screenplay), 1986; La montagne blanche (novel), 1986; Netchaïev est de retour (novel), 1987; Federico Sánchez vous salue bien, 1993; L'écriture ou la vie (novel), 1996; Mal et modernité (essay), 1997; Le retour de Carola Neher (play), 1998; Adieu, vive clarté.. (short story), 1998; Veinte años y un día 2004. Other: TV scripts. *Honours:* Formentor Prize, 1963; Prix Fémina, 1969; Dr hc, Turin, 1990; Prix Fémina Vacaresco, 1994; Prix Littéraire des Droits de l'Homme, 1995; Jerusalem Prize, 1997; Nonino Prize, Italy, 1999; Goethe Medal, 2003. *Address:* c/o Penguin Books Ltd, 80 Strand, London WC2R 0RL, England.

SEN, Amartya Kumar; academic and writer; b. 3 Nov. 1933, Santiniketan, India; m. 1st Nabaneeta Dev 1960 (divorced 1974); m. 2nd Eva Colorni 1977 (died 1985); m. 3rd Emma Rothschild 1991; four c. *Education:* BA, Presidency College, Kolkata, 1953; BA, 1955, MA, PhD, 1959, Trinity College, Cambridge. *Career:* Prof. of Economics, Jadavpur University, Kolkata, 1956–58; Fellow, Trinity College, Cambridge, 1957–63, All Souls College, Oxford, 1980–88; Prof. of Economics, Delhi University, 1963–71, LSE, 1971–77; Prof. of Economics, 1977–80, Drummond Prof. of Political Economy, 1980–88, University of Oxford; Andrew D. White Prof. at Large, Cornell University, 1978–85; Lamont University Prof. and Prof. of Economics and Philosophy, 1988–98, Prof. Emeritus, 1998–, Harvard University; Master, Trinity College, Cambridge, 1998–; mem. American Acad. of Arts and Sciences; American Economic Asscn, pres., 1994–; British Acad., fellow; Development Studies Asscn; Econometric Society, fellow; Indian Economic Asscn; International Economic Asscn, pres., 1986–88, hon. pres., 1988–; Royal Economic Society. *Publications:* Choice of Techniques, 1960; Collective Choice and Welfare, 1970; Guidelines for Project Evaluation (with P. Dasgupta and Stephen Marglin), 1972; On Economic Inequality, 1973; Employment, Technology and Development, 1975; Poverty and Famines: An Essay on Entitlement and Deprivation, 1981; Choice, Welfare and Measurement, 1982; Resources, Values and Development, 1984; Commodities and Capabilities, 1985; On Ethics and Economics, 1987; The Standard of Living (with others), 1987; Hunger and Public Action (with Jean Dreze), 1989; Jibanayatra o arthaniti, 1990; The Political Economy of Hunger (ed. with Jean Dreze), 3 vols, 1990–91; Money and Value: On the Ethics and Economics of Finance/Denaro e valore: Etica ed economia della finanza, 1991; Inequality Reexamined, 1992; The Quality of Life (ed. with Martha Nussbaum), 1993; Economic Development and Social Opportunity (with Jean Dreze), 1995; Development as Freedom, 1999. Contributions: Professional journals. *Honours:* Mahalanobis Prize, 1976; Hon. DLitt, University of Saskatchewan, 1979; Nobel Prize in Economic Science, 1998. *Address:* c/o Trinity College, Cambridge CB2 1TQ, England.

SENCIÓN, Viriato; Dominican Republic writer; b. 1941, San José de Ocoa. *Education:* Seminary Santo Tomás de Aquino, Santo Domingo, Crown Inst of Costa Rica, Lehman Coll., CUNY. *Publications:* Los que falsifican la firma de Dios (trans. as They Forged the Signature of God) 1992, La enema Celania y otros cuentos 1994, Los ojos de la montaña 1997. *Address:* c/o Curbstone Press, 321 Jackson Street, Willimantic, CT 06226-1738, USA. *E-mail:* info@curbstone.org. *Website:* www.curbstone.org.

SENDAK, Maurice Bernard; children's writer and illustrator; b. 10 June 1928, New York, NY, USA. *Education:* Art Students' League, New York. *Career:* various one-man shows; Co-Founder and Artistic Dir, The Night

Kitchen, 1990–. *Publications as author and illustrator:* Kenny's Window, 1956; Very Far Away, 1957; The Acrobat, 1959; The Sign on Rosie's Door, 1960; The Nutshell Library, 1962; Where the Wild Things Are, 1963; Hector Protector and As I Went Over the Water: Two Nursery Rhymes, 1965; Higglety, Piggelty, Pop!, or, There Must Be More to Life, 1967; In the Knight Kitchen, 1970; Ten Little Rabbits: A Counting Book with Mino the Magician, 1970; Pictures by Maurice Sendak, 1971; Maurice Sendak's Really Rosie, 1975; Some Swell Pup, or, Are You Sure You Want a Dog?, 1976; Seven Little Monsters, 1977; Outside Over There, 1981; We Are All in the Dumps with Jack and Guy, 1993; Tsippi, 1994; Moishe, 1994; Max, 1994. Other: Illustrator for numerous books. Contributions: books and periodicals. *Honours:* numerous awards and citations as author and illustrator. *Literary Agent:* Steven Barclay Agency, 12 Western Avenue, Petaluma, CA 94952, USA. *Telephone:* (707) 773-0654. *Fax:* (707) 778-1868. *Website:* www.barclayagency.com. *Address:* c/o Harper & Row, 10 E 53rd Street, New York, NY 10022, USA.

SENNETT, Richard; American writer and academic; b. 1 Jan. 1943, Chicago, IL; m. Saskia Sassen 1987; one step-s. *Education:* Breck School, Univ. of Chicago, Juilliard Conservatory New York, Harvard Univ. *Career:* Lecturer, Yale Univ. 1968–70; Asst Prof., Brandeis Univ. 1970–72; Prof., New York Univ. 1972–98; founder, New York Inst. of the Humanities; Prof. of Social and Cultural Theory, LSE 1999–. *Publications:* non-fiction: The Uses of Disorder: Personal Identity and City Life 1970, Families Against the City 1970, The Fall of Public Man 1974, Hidden Injuries of Class (with Jonathan Cobb) 1977, The Psychology of Society 1977, Authority 1980, The Conscience of the Eye 1990, Flesh and Stone: The Body and the City in Western Civilisation 1994, The Corrosion of Character 1998, Respect: The Formation of Character in an Age of Inequality 2003; editor: 19th Century Cities: Essays in the New Urban History (with Stephan Thernstrom) 1969, Classic Essays on the Culture of Cities 1969; memoirs: Respect 2003; novels: The Frog Who Dared to Croak 1982, An Evening of Brahms 1984, Palais Royal 1986. *Literary Agent:* London School of Economics and Political Science, Houghton Street, London, WC2A 2AE, England. *Telephone:* (20) 7955-6076. *E-mail:* r.sennett@lse.ac.uk. *Website:* www.lse.ac.uk.

SERENY, Gitta, CBE; American (b. Hungarian) writer; b. 13 March 1923, Hungary; m. Donald Honeyman 1948; one s. one d. *Education:* Vienna Realgymnasium Luithlen, Stonar House School, Sandwich, Kent and Sorbonne, Paris. *Career:* writer and journalist for several newspapers and periodicals including The Times, The Independent, Die Zeit, Dagens Nyheter, NY Review of Books. *Publications:* The Medallion 1957, The Case of Mary Bell 1972, Into that Darkness 1974, The Invisible Children 1984, Albert Speer – His Battle with Truth (James Tait Black Memorial Prize 1995, Duff Cooper Award 1995) 1995, Cries Unheard (The McAllen Gold Dagger for non-fiction crime 1998) 1998, German Trauma (US title The Healing Wound) 2000. *Honours:* Geting and Arets Awards for Best Pocketbooks 1999, 2001, PASS Award, Nat. Council on Crime and Delinquency, USA 1999, Steg Dagermann Prize for Contrib. to Literature, Sweden 2002. *Literary Agent:* The Sayle Literary Agency, Bickerton House, 25–27 Bickerton Road, London, N19 5JT, England. *Telephone:* (20) 7263-8681. *Fax:* (20) 7561-0529. *Address:* 20 Durrels House, Warwick Gardens, London, W14 8QB, England (Home).

SERVADIO, Gaia Cecilia; Writer and Journalist; b. 13 Sept. 1938, Padua, Italy; two s. one d. *Education:* St Martin's School of Art, London; National Diploma in Graphic Art. *Career:* Lecturer, Associazione Italiana 1970, Manchester Museum, 1982; Consultant Ed., Italy, 1987; Dir of Debates and Literary Talks, Accademia Italiana, 1988–94; Italian Foreign Minister, Australia 1992, India 1995, Canada 2001; Correspondent La Stampa 1978–90, Il Corriere della Sera 1990–2000; appointed responsible for External Relations Teatro Masimo Opera House Palermo; mem. Foreign Press Asscn, vice-pres., 1974–79; Society of Authors; Associazione Culturale Italiana. *Television:* documentaries for BBC: Verdi 1992, Damn Netau 2001. *Publications:* Melinda, 1968; Don Juan/Salome, 1969; Il Metodo, 1971; Mafioso, 1972; A Siberian Encounter, 1972; A Profile of a Mafia Boss, 1973; Insider Outsider, 1977; To a Different World: La donna nel Rinascimento, 1979; Luchino Visconti: A Biography, 1981; Il Lamento di Arianna, 1985; Una infanzia diversa, 1989; The Story of R, 1991; Edward Lear's Italian Letters (ed.), 1990; La Vallata, 1990; Incontri (essays), 1992; The Real Traviata, 1994; La mia Umbria (ed.), 1994; Motya, Uncovering a Lost Civilisation, 2000; Rossini: A Life, 2003, Woman in the Renaissance 2004. Contributions: The Observer, The Times, Sunday Times, Sunday Telegraph, Daily Telegraph. *Honours:* Cavaliere Ufficiale della Republica Italiana, 1980. *Literary Agent:* Robert Caskic Capel & Land, 29 Wardour Street, London, SW7 2TB, England. *Telephone:* (20) 7734-2414. *Fax:* (20) 7734-8101.

SERVAN-SCHREIBER, Jean-Claude, LenD; French media executive and newspaperman; b. 11 April 1918, Paris; m. 1st Christiane Laroche 1947 (divorced); m. 2nd Jacqueline Guix de Pinos 1955 (divorced); two s. three d.; m. 3rd Paule Guinet 1983 (divorced). *Education:* Exeter Coll., Oxford and Sorbonne. *Career:* served World War II in Flanders 1940, in Resistance 1941–42, in N Africa 1943, France 1944, Germany 1945; with Les Echos 1946–65, Gen. Man. 1957, Dir 1963–65; Deputy for Paris, Nat. Ass. 1965–67; Asst Sec.-Gen. UNR-UDT 1965; Pres. Rassemblement français pour Israël 1967; Dir-Gen. Régie française de publicité 1968–78; mem. Haut Conseil de l'audiovisuel 1973–81; Pres. Groupe Européen des Régisseurs de Publicité Télévisée 1975–78; mem. Conseil politique, RPR 1977–81; Conseiller du Groupe de Presse L'Expansion 1980–93; Special Adviser Mitsubishi Electric (Europe) 1992–2000; Pres. Inst. Arthur Vernes (Medical and Surgical Center) 1993–. *Honours:* Commdr, Légion d'honneur; Médaille mil.; Commdr Ordre nat. du Mérite; Croix de guerre; Croix du Combattant volontaire de la Résistance; Legion of Merit (USA), etc. *Address:* 147 bis rue d'Alésia, 75014 Paris, France. *Telephone:* 1-45-39-96-11. *Fax:* 1-45-39-48-96. *Website:* jcss@noos.fr (Home).

SERVAN-SCHREIBER, Jean-Jacques; French politician, economist and writer; b. 13 Feb. 1924, Paris; four s. *Education:* Ecole Polytechnique, Paris. *Career:* joined the Free French Forces of Gen. de Gaulle as fighter pilot 1943 (trained USAF); Foreign Affairs Ed. Le Monde 1948–53; Founder L'Express 1953, Ed. 1953–70; elected and re-elected Pres. Radical Party 1970–79; elected and re-elected Deputy for Nancy 1970–79 and Pres. Region of Lorraine 1975–78; Minister of Reform 1974; Pres. World Centre for Computer Literacy 1981–85; Prof. of Strategic Thinking, Chair. Int. Cttee Carnegie Mellon Univ., Pittsburgh 1985–. *Publications:* Lieutenant en Algérie 1957, Le défi Américain 1967, Le manifeste radical 1970, Le pouvoir régional 1971, Le défi mondial 1981, Le choix des juifs 1988, Passions 1991, Les Fossoyeurs 1993. *Honours:* Croix de la Valeur mil. *Address:* 37 avenue du Roule, 92200 Neuilly-sur-Seine, France.

SETH, Vikram, CBE, MA, PhD; Indian author and poet; b. 1952, Calcutta (now Kolkata). *Education:* Doon School, India, Tonbridge School, UK, Corpus Christi Coll., Oxford, Stanford Univ., USA, Nanjing Univ., People's Repub. of China. *Career:* Guggenheim Fellowships. *Publications:* Mappings 1980, From Heaven Lake: Travels Through Sinkiang and Tibet 1983, The Humble Administrator's Garden 1985, All You Who Sleep Tonight (trans.) 1985, The Golden Gate: A Novel in Verse 1986, Three Chinese Poets (trans.) 1992, A Suitable Boy (novel) 1993, Arion and the Dolphin (libretto) 1994, Beastly Tales (animal fables) 1994, An Equal Music (novel) 1999; several vols of poetry. *Honours:* Hon. Fellow Corpus Christi Coll., Oxford 1994; Chevalier des Arts et des Lettres 2001; Commonwealth Poetry Prize 1986, W. H. Smith Literary Prize 1994, Commonwealth Writers' Prize 1994. *Address:* c/o Curtis Brown (Giles Gordon), 37 Queensferry Street, Edinburgh, EH2 4QS, Scotland. *Telephone:* (131) 225-1286 (Office). *Fax:* (131) 225-1290 (Office).

SETTANNI, Harry Eugene; Prof. and Writer; b. 8 March 1945, Chicago, IL, USA. *Education:* BS, English, St Joseph's University, Philadelphia, 1967; MA, Philosophy, Villanova University, 1972; PhD, Philosophy, St John's University, Jamaica, New York, 1976. *Career:* Faculty, St Joseph's University, Phildelphia, 1976–78, 1990–, St John's University, Jamaica, New York, 1978–82, Holy Family College, Philadelphia, 1987–. *Publications:* Holism: A Philosophy for Today, Anticipating the Twenty-First Century, 1990; What is Man?, 1991; The Probabilist Theism of John Stuart Mill, 1991; What is Morality?, 1992; Five Philosophers: How Their Lives Influenced Their Thought, 1992; Scientific Knowledge, 1992; What is Freedom of Choice?, 1992; The Philosophic Foundation of Paranormal Phenomena, 1992; Controversial Questions in Philosophy, 1996; Five Primers in the Social Sciences, 1996; Essays in Psychology and Epistemology, 1996; Knowledge and Reality, 1996; Miscellaneous Essays, 1996. Contributions: books and journals. *Address:* c/o University Press of America, 4501 Forbes Blvd, Suite 200, Lanham, MD 20706, USA.

SETTLE, Mary Lee; Writer and Ed.; b. 29 July 1918, Charleston, West Virginia, USA; m. 1st Rodney Weathersbee, 1939, divorced 1946; m. 2nd Douglas Newton, 1946, divorced 1956; m. 3rd William Littleton Tazewell, 2 Sept. 1978, one s. *Education:* Sweet Briar College, 1936–38. *Career:* Asst Ed., Harper's Bazaar, New York City, 1945; English Correspondent, Flair Magazine, 1950–51; Ed., American Heritage, New York City, 1961–; Assoc. Prof., Bard College, 1965–76; Visiting Lecturer, Iowa Writer's Workshop, 1976, University of Virginia, 1978; Founder, PEN-Faulkner Award, 1980. *Publications:* Fiction: The Love Eaters, 1954; The Kiss of Kin, 1955; O Beulah Land, 1956; Know Nothing, 1960; Fight Night on a Sweet Saturday, 1964; The Clam Shell, 1971; Prisons, 1973; Blood Tie, 1977; The Scapegoat, 1980; The Killing Ground, 1982; Celebration, 1986; Charley Bland, 1989; I, Roger Williams, 2001. Play: Juana La Loca, 1965. Non-Fiction: All the Brave Promises: Memories of Woman 2nd Class 2146391 (autobiog.), 1966; Turkish Reflections (autobiog.), 1991. Contributions: anthologies and magazines. *Honours:* Guggenheim Fellowships, 1958, 1960; Ingram Merrill Foundation Award, 1975; National Book Award, 1978; Janet Heidinger Kafka Prize, 1983; American Acad. of Arts and Letters Award, 1994.

SEWARD, Desmond; Writer and Historian; b. 22 May 1935, Paris, France. *Education:* St Catharine's College, Cambridge; BA, University of Cambridge. *Publications:* The First Bourbon: Henry IV, King of France and Navarre, 1971; The Monks of War: The Military Religious Orders, 1972, US edn as The Monks of War: The First Religious Orders, 1972; The Bourbon Kings of France, 1976; Prince of the Renaissance: The Life of François I, 1973, US edn as Prince of the Renaissance: The Golden Life of François I, 1973; Eleanor of Aquitaine: The Mother Queen, 1978, US edn as Eleanor of Aquitaine, 1979; The Hundred Years War: The English in France, 1337–1453, 1978; Monks and Wine, 1979; Marie Antoinette, 1981; Richard III: England's Black Legend, 1983; Napoleon's Family, 1986; Italy's Knights of St George: The Constantinian Order, 1986; Henry V as Warlord, 1987, as Henry V: The Scourge of God, 1988; Napoleon and Hitler: A Comparative

Biography, 1988; Byzantium (co-author), 1989; Brook's: A Social History (co-ed.), 1991; Metternich: The First European, 1991; The Dancing Sun: Journeys to the Miracle Shrines, 1993; The War of the Roses through the Lives of Five Men and Women of the Fifteenth Century, 1995; Sussex, 1995; Caravaggio, 1998. Contributions: periodicals including History Today; BBC History Magazine. *Literary Agent:* 53–54 Regency Sq., Brighton BN1 2FF, England.

SEWELL, Stephen; Playwright; b. 1953, Sydney, NSW, Australia. *Education:* BS, University of Sydney, 1975. *Career:* Chair., Australian National Playwrights Centre. *Publications:* The Father We Loved on a Beach by the Sea, 1976; Traitors, 1979; Welcome the Wright World, 1983; The Blind Giant is Dancing, 1983; Burn Victim (with others), 1983; Dreams in an Empty City, 1986; Hate, 1988; Miranda, 1989; Sisters, 1991; King Golgrutha, 1991; In the City of Grand-Daughters, 1993; Dust, 1993. *Honours:* New South Wales Premier's Award, 1985. *Literary Agent:* Hilary Linstead & Associates, PO Box 1536, Strawberry Hills, NSW 2012, Australia.

SEYMOUR, Alan; Playwright; b. 6 June 1927, Perth, WA, Australia. *Publications:* Swamp Creatures, 1958; The One Day of the Year, 1960; The Gaiety of Nations, 1965; A Break in the Music, 1966; The Pope and the Pill, 1968; Oh Grave, Thy Victory, 1973; Structures, 1973; The Wind from the Plain, 1974; The Float, 1980; various radio and television plays. Fiction: The One Day of the Year, 1967; The Coming Self-Destruction of the United States, 1969. *Honours:* Australia Council for the Arts Grant.

SEYMOUR, Arabella Charlotte Henrietta; Author; b. 8 Dec. 1948, London, England; one d. *Education:* West Ham College of Technology. *Career:* mem. Society of Authors. *Publications:* A Passion in the Blood, 1985; Dangerous Deceptions, 1986; The Sins of Rebeccah Russell, 1988; The End of the Family, 1990; No Sad Songs (as Sarah Lyon), 1990; Princess of Darkness, 1991; A Woman of Pleasure, 1994; Sins of the Mother, 1996. Contributions: Woman's Day, Australia. *Literary Agent:* Sheil Land Assocs Ltd. *Address:* Sondes House, Patrixbourne, Canterbury, Kent CT4 5DD, England.

SHAABAN NEJAD, Afsaneh, BA; writer and poet; b. 1963, Shahdad, Kerman, Iran; m. Shamsodin Esaie; one s. one d. *Career:* Gen. Ed., children's radio programme, 1985; Gen. Ed., children's magazine, 1988–91; Literary Ed., jury mem., Poetry Council of Institute for the Intellectual Development of Children and Young Adults. *Publications:* six novels; 13 collections of poetry; 15 short stories; eight short story collections. Contributions: several articles in children's magazines. *Honours:* various Book and Press Festival awards, 1990–2000; Hon. diploma, Alzahra Univ.; Hon. diplomas, Ministry of Culture and Islamic Guidance. *Address:* Institute for the Intellectual Development of Children and Young Adults, 24 Khaled Slamboli Street, Tehran, Iran.

SHAARA, Jeff; Writer; b. 21 Feb. 1952, New Brunswick, NJ, USA; m. Lynne Shaara, 3 Oct. 1992. *Education:* BS, Criminology, Florida State University, 1973. *Publications:* Gods and Generals, 1996; The Last Full Measure, 1998; The Glorious Cause, 2002. *E-mail:* jshaara@aol.com.

SHABTAI, Aharon; Israeli poet and translator; b. 1939. *Education:* Hebrew Univ., Sorbonne, Paris, France, Univ. of Cambridge, England. *Career:* currently Lecturer in Hebrew Literature, Tel-Aviv Univ. *Publications include:* poetry: Kibbutz 1973, Domestic Poem 1976, The Book of Nothing 1981, First Lecture 1985, Love 1988, Divorce 1990, Heart 1995, That Wonderful Month of May 1997, Love and Selected Poems (in trans.) 1997, J'accuse 2003; contrib. to Six Israeli Novellas 1999, American Poetry Review, London Review of Books, Parnassus in Review, Ha'aretz. *Honours:* Prime Minister's Prize for Translation 1993. *Address:* c/o New Directions Publishing Corporation, 80 Eighth Avenue, New York, NY 10011, USA. *E-mail:* editorial@ndbooks.com. *Website:* www.ndpublishing.com.

SHACHOCHIS, Bob, (Robert Shachochis); Journalist and Writer; b. 9 Sept. 1951, West Pittston, Pennsylvania, USA; m. Barbara Petersen, 1976. *Education:* BA, 1973, MA, 1979, University of Missouri, Columbia; MFA, University of Iowa, 1982. *Career:* Columnist, GQ magazines; Contributing Ed., Outside magazine, Harper's magazine; mem. Poets and Writers. *Publications:* Novel: Swimming in the Volcanos, 1993. Short Story Collections: Easy in the Islands, 1985; The Next New World, 1989. Contributions: many periodicals. *Honours:* National Endowment for the Arts Fellowship, 1982; American Book Award for First Fiction, 1985; National Book Award, 1985; Prix de Rome, American Acad. of Arts and Letters, 1989. *Literary Agent:* Brandt & Hochman Literary Agents Inc, 1501 Broadway, New York, NY 10036, USA.

SHADBOLT, Maurice (Francis Richard); Writer; b. 4 June 1932, Auckland, New Zealand; m. 1st Gillian Eve Muriel Heming, 21 Nov. 1953, three s., two d.; m. 2nd Barbara Magner, 1971; m. 3rd Bridget Armstrong, 9 Dec. 1978. *Education:* University of Auckland. *Career:* Journalist, New Zealand, 1952–54; Documentry Screenwriter, Dir, New Zealand Film Unit, 1954–57. *Publications:* Among the Cinders, 1965; This Summer's Dolphin, 1969; An Ear of the Dragon, 1971; Danger Zone, 1975; The Lovelock Version, 1980; Season of the Jew, 1986; Monday's Warrior, 1990; Dove on the Waters, 1997. Story Collections: The New Zealander: A Sequence of Stories, 1959; Summer Fires and Winter Country, 1963; The Presence of Music: Three Novellas; Figures in Light: Selected Stories. Play: Once on Chunk Bair, 1982. Guides and Histories of New Zealand. *Honours:* James Wattie Awards, 1973, 1991; New Zealand Book Award, 1981; CBE, 1989. *Address:* Box 60028 Titirangi, Auckland 7, New Zealand.

SHAFFER, Sir Peter (Levin); Dramatist; b. 15 May 1926, Liverpool, England. *Education:* BA, Trinity College, Cambridge, 1950. *Career:* Literary Critic, Truth, 1956–57; Music Critic, Time and Tide, 1961–62; Cameron Mackintosh Visiting Prof. of Contemporary Theatre, St Catherine's College, Oxford, 1994; mem. FRSL; Fellow, St Catherine's Coll., Oxford, 2003. *Publications:* Plays: Five Finger Exericse, 1958; The Private Ear, 1962; The Public Eye, 1962; The Merry Roosters Panto (with Joan Littlewood), 1963; The Royal Hunt of the Sun, 1964; Black Comedy, 1965; White Lies, 1967; The White Liars, 1968; The Battle of Shrivings, 1970; Equus, 1973; Amadeus, 1979; Yonadab, 1985; Lettice and Lovage, 1987; The Gift of the Gorgon, 1992; Whom Do I Have the Honour of Addressing?, 1994. Contributions: radio and television. *Honours:* Evening Standard Drama Awards, 1958, 1979, 1988; New York Drama Critics Circle Award, 1959; London Theatre Critics Award, 1979; Plays and Players Award, 1979; Tony Awards, 1979, 1980; Drama Desk Award, 1980; Acad. Award, 1985; Golden Globe Award, 1985; Los Angeles Film Critics Asscn Award, 1985; Premi David di Donatello, 1985; CBE, 1987; Shakespeare Prize, Hamburg, 1989; William Inge Award for Distinguished Achievement in the American Theatre, 1992; KBE, 2001. *Address:* c/o Macnaughton-Lord 2000 Ltd, 16–18 Douglas St, London SW1P 4 PB, England.

SHAH, Eddy (Selim Jehane); British newspaper publisher and writer; b. 1944, Cambridge; m. Jennifer Shah; two s. one d. *Education:* several schools including Gordonstoun. *Career:* worked as Asst Stage Man. in Repertory Theatre; also worked in TV and later as space salesman for free newspaper once published by Manchester Evening News; launched Sale and Altrincham Messenger freesheet in 1974, Stockport Messenger 1977, also Propr of Bury Messenger; launched Today newspaper 1986, Chair., CEO 1986–88; launched The Post Oct. 1988 (folded Dec. 1988). *Publications:* Ring of Red Roses (novel) 1991, The Lucy Ghosts 1992, Manchester Blue (novel) 1992, Fallen Angels (novel) 1994. *Address:* c/o Doubleday, 61–63 Uxbridge Road, London, W5 5SA, England.

SHAKESPEARE, Nicholas; British biographer and novelist; b. 1957, Worcester, England; m.; two s. *Publications:* The Men Who Would Be King: A Look at Royalty in Exile 1984, Londoners 1986, The Vision of Elena Silves (novel) 1989, The High Flyer (novel) 1993, The Dancer Upstairs (novel) 1995, Bruce Chatwin (biog.) 1999, Snowleg (novel) 2004. *Honours:* Somerset Maugham Award 1989, Betty Trask Award 1990, American Libraries Asscn Award 1997, BAFTA for Best Documentary 2001, Broadcasting Press Guild Award for Best Documentary 2001. *Address:* c/o Vintage, Random House, 20 Vauxhall Bridge Road, London, SW1V 2SA, England.

SHALEV, Zeruya, MA; Israeli poet and novelist; *Chief Literary Editor, Keshet*; b. 1959, Kinneret Kibbutz; m. Eyal Megged. *Career:* began writing aged 6, published collection of poems aged 15; fmr Ed. Keter Publishing House; currently Chief Literary Ed. Keshet Publishing House. *Publications include:* Love Life 2001, Husband and Wife 2002; a book for children; contrib. poems to numerous journals. *Honours:* Israeli Asscn of Publrs Golden Book Prize 2001. *Address:* c/o Canongate Books, 14 High Street, Edinburgh, EH1 1TE, Scotland (Office). *Telephone:* (131) 557-5111 (Office).

SHAMIR, Moshe; Israeli writer and dramatist; b. 15 Aug. 1921, Tzfat. *Career:* fmr mem. Likud Party, elected to the Knesset 1977–81; founder, Tehiya Party; Ed., Bamahaneh; Nat. Vice-Pres. and Chair., AACI; Pres., Bnai Brith Ben Gurion Lodge; Chair., This Land is Mine Olim Fund. *Publications include:* novels: He Walked the Fields 1947, The King of Flesh and Blood 1958, Why Ziva Cried on the Feast of the First Fruits 1960, The Fifth Wheel 1961, David's Stranger 1964, The Frontier 1966, My Life with Ishmael 1970, Far from Pearls (trilogy) 1973–92, Hittite Must Die 1978. *Honours:* Esteemed Citizen of Netanya 1999 ; Israel Prize 1988. *Address:* c/o This Land is Mine Olim Fund, PO Box 2266, Netanya 42122, Israel.

SHAMSIE, Kamila, BA, MFA; Pakistani writer; b. 1973, Karachi. *Education:* Hamilton Coll., New York, Univ. of Mass., Amherst, USA. *Career:* currently teaches creative writing at Hamilton Coll. *Publications:* In the City by the Sea (Prime Minister's Award for Literature, Pakistan 1999) 1998, Salt and Saffron 2000, Kartography 2002. *Literary Agent:* A. M. Heath & Co Ltd, 79 St Martin's Lane, London, WC2N 4RE, England. *Address:* c/o Hamilton College, 198 College Hill Road, Clinton, NY 13323, USA. *E-mail:* kshamsie@hamilton.edu.

SHANGE, Ntozake, BA, MA; American poet, dramatist, writer and academic; b. (Paulette Williams), 18 Oct. 1948, Trenton, NJ; one d. *Education:* Barnard Coll., Univ. of Southern California at Los Angeles. *Career:* Faculty, Sonoma State College, Rohnert Park, CA, 1973–75, Mills College, Oakland, CA, 1975, City College, CUNY, 1975, Douglass College, New Brunswick, NJ, 1978; Artist-in-Residence, Equinox Theater, Houston, 1981–; Assoc. Prof. of Drama, University of Houston, 1983–. *Publications:* Poetry: Melissa and Smith, 1976; Natural Disasters and Other Festive Occasions, 1977; Happy Edges, 1978; Some Men, 1981; A Daughter's Geography, 1983; From Okra to Greens, 1984; Ridin' the Moon in Texas: Word Paintings, 1988; The Love Space Demands: A Continuing Saga, 1992. Plays: For Colored Girls Who Have Considered Suicide When the Rainbow is Enuf, 1976; Photograph: Lovers-in-Motion, 1981; Spell #7, 1981; Boogie Woogie Landscapes,

1981. Fiction: Sassafrass: A Novella, 1977; Sassafrass, Cypress and Indigo, 1982; Betsey Brown, 1985; Liliane: Resurrection of the Daughter, 1995. Non-Fiction: See No Evil: Prefaces, Essays and Accounts 1976–1983, 1984. *Honours:* New York Drama Critics Circle Award, 1977; Obie Awards, 1977, 1980; Columbia University Medal of Excellence, 1981; Guggenheim Fellowship, 1981. *Address:* c/o St Martin's Press, 175 Fifth Avenue, New York, NY 10010, USA.

SHAPCOTT, Thomas W(illiam); Poet, Novelist, Writer and Prof. of Creative Writing; b. 21 March 1935, Ipswich, Qld, Australia; m. 1st Margaret Hodge, 1960; m. 2nd Judith Rodriguez, 1982, one s., three d. *Education:* BA, University of Queensland, 1968. *Career:* Dir, Australia Council Literature Board, 1983–90; Exec. Dir, National Book Council, 1992–97; Prof. of Creative Writing, University of Adelaide, 1997–; mem. Australian Book Review, chair.; Copyright Agency Ltd, chair.; Australian Society of Authors; International PEN. *Publications:* Poetry: Time on Fire, 1961; The Mankind Thing, 1963; Sonnets, 1960–63, 1963; A Taste of Salt Water, 1967; Inwards to the Sun, 1969; Fingers at Air, 1969; Begin with Walking, 1973; Shabbytown Calendar, 1975; 7th Avenue Poems, 1976; Selected Poems, 1978; Make the Old Man Sing, 1980; Welcome!, 1983; Travel Dice, 1987; Selected Poems, 1956–1988, 1989; In the Beginning, 1990; The City of Home, 1995; Chekhov's Mongoose, 2001. Fiction: The Birthday Gift, 1982; White Stag of Exile, 1984; Hotel Bellevue, 1986; The Search for Galina, 1989; Mona's Gift, 1993; Theatre of Darkness, 1998. Plays: The 7 Deadly Sins, 1970. Editor: New Impulses in Australian Poetry (with R. Hall), 1967; Australian Poetry Now, 1970; Contemporary American and Australian Poetry, 1975; Poetry as a Creative Learning Process, 1978; The Moment Made Marvellous (anthology), 1998; An Island on Land: Contemporary Macedonian Poetry (ed. and trans. with Ilija Casule), 1999. Contributions: newspapers and journals. *Honours:* Grace Leven Prize, 1961; Sir Thomas White Memorial Prize, 1967; Sidney Myer Charity Trust Awards, 1967, 1969; Churchill Fellowship, 1972; Canada-Australia Literary Prize, 1978; AO, 1989; Hon. DLitt, Macquarie University, 1989; Gold Wreath, Struga International Poetry Festival, 1989; Christopher Brennan Award for Poetry, 1994; NSW Premier's Special Literary Prize, 1996; Michel Wesley Wright Award, 1996; Patrick White Award, 2000. *Address:* PO Box 231, Mont Albert, Vic. 3127, Australia.

SHAPIN, Steven; Writer, Historian and Sociologist; b. 11 Sept. 1943, New York, NY, USA; m. Abigail Barrow, 18 March 1989. *Education:* BA, Reed College, 1966; MA, PhD, University of Pennsylvania, 1971. *Career:* Prof. of Sociology, University of California, San Diego. *Publications:* Natural Order: Historical Studies of Scientific Cultures (co-ed.), 1979; Leviathan and the Air-Pump: Hobbes, Boyle, and the Experimental Life (co-author), 1985; A Social History of Truth: Civility and Science in Seventeenth Century England, 1994; The Scientific Revolution, 1996; Science Incarnate: Historical Embodiments of Natural Knowledge (co-ed.), 1998. *Literary Agent:* c/o University of Chicago Press, 5801 Ellis Ave, Fourth Floor, Chicago, IL 60637, USA. *Address:* Dept of Sociology, University of California at San Diego, La Jolla, CA 92093-0533, USA.

SHAPIRO, Alan; Prof., Poet, Writer and Trans; b. 18 Feb. 1952, Boston, MA, USA; m. Della Pollock, 7 Sept. 1984. *Education:* BA, English, Brandeis University, 1974. *Career:* Jones Lecturer in Creative Writing, 1976–79, Visiting Asst Prof., 1981, Stanford University; Lecturer, 1979–85, Assoc. Prof., 1985–88, Prof., 1988–89, Northwestern University; Poet-in-Residence, University of Chicago, 1981, 1986, 1988; Visiting Asst Prof., 1985, Visiting Prof., 1989, of Creative Writing, University of California at Irvine; Visiting Prof. of Creative Writing, Boston University, 1989; Fannie Hurst Poet-in-Residence, Brandeis University, 1989; Prof., University of North Carolina at Greensboro, 1989–94; Hurst Prof. of Creative Writing, Washington University, 1994; Prof., 1995–, Gillian T. Cell Distinguished Term Prof., 2001–, University of North Carolina at Chapel Hill; Richard L. Thomas Prof. of Creative Writing, Kenyon College, 2002. *Publications:* After the Digging (poems), 1981; The Courtesy (poems), 1983; Happy Hour (poems), 1987; Covenant (poems), 1991; In Praise of the Impure: Poetry and the Ethical Imagination: Essays (1980–1991), 1993; Mixed Company (poems), 1996; The Last Happy Occasion (memoir), 1996; Vigil (memoir), 1997; The Dead Alive and Busy (poems), 2000; Selected Poems, 2000; Song and Dance (poems), 2002; The Ortesteia (trans.), 2002. Contributions: many anthologies, reviews, quarterlies and journals. *Honours:* Wallace Stegner Creative Writing Fellowship, 1975–76; Acad. of American Poets Award, 1976; National Endowment for the Arts Fellowships, 1984–85, 1991; Guggenheim Fellowship, 1985–86; William Carlos Williams Award, Poetry Society of America, 1987; Lila Wallace-Reader's Digest Writers Award, 1991; Pushcart Prize, 1996; Los Angeles Times Book Award in Poetry, 1996; Open Society Institute Arts Fellowship, 1999; Kingsley Tufts Poetry Award, Claremont Graduate University, 2001. *Address:* 221 E Queen St, Hillsborough, NC 27278, USA.

SHAPIRO, David (Joel); Poet, Art Critic and Prof. of Art History; b. 2 Jan. 1947, Newark, NJ, USA; m. Lindsey Stamm, 1970, one c. *Education:* BA, 1968, PhD, 1973, Columbia University; BA, 1970, MA, 1974, Clare College, Cambridge. *Career:* Violinist in various orchestras, 1963–; Instructor and Asst Prof. of English, Columbia University, 1972–80; Visiting Prof., Brooklyn College, CUNY, 1979, Princeton University, 1982–83; Visiting Faculty, Cooper Union, New York City, 1980–; Full Prof. of Art History, William Paterson College, Wayne, NJ, 1996–. *Publications:* Poetry: January: A Book of Poems, 1965; Poems from Deal, 1969; A Man Holding an Acoustic Panel, 1971; The Page-Turner, 1973; Lateness, 1977; To an Idea, 1984; House, Blown Apart, 1988; After a Lost Original, 1990. Other: John Ashbery: An Introduction to the Poetry, 1979; Jim Dine: Painting What One Is, 1981; Jasper Johns: Drawings 1954–1984, 1984; Mondrian Flowers, 1990; Alfred Leslie: The Killing Cycle (with Judith Stein), 1991. *Honours:* Bread Loaf Writers Conference Robert Frost Fellowship, 1965; Ingram Merrill Foundation Fellowship, 1967; Book-of-the-Month Club Fellowship, 1968; Kellett Fellow, Clare College, Cambridge, 1968–70; Creative Artists Public Service Grant, 1974; Morton Dauwen Zabel Award, 1977; National Endowment for the Arts Grant, 1979; National Endowment for the Humanities Fellowships, 1980; Foundation for Contemporary Performance Arts Grant, 1996; Milton Asery Prof., Bard Graduate School of the Arts, 1996. *Address:* 3001 Henry Hudson Parkway, Riverdale, NY 10463, USA.

SHAPIRO, Harvey, BA, MA; editor and poet; b. 27 Jan. 1924, Chicago, IL, USA; m. Edna Kaufman 1953; two s. *Education:* Yale University, Columbia University. *Career:* Staff, Commentary, 1955–57, The New Yorker, 1955–57; Staff, 1957–64, Deputy Ed., 1983–, New York Times Magazine; Asst Ed., 1964–75, Ed., 1975–83, New York Times Book Review. *Publications:* The Eye, 1953; The Book, 1955; Mountain Fire Thornbush, 1961; Battle Report, 1966; This World, 1971; Lauds, 1975; Lauds and Nightsounds, 1978; The Light Holds, 1984; National Cold Storage Company: New and Selected Poems, 1988; A Day's Portion, 1994; Selected Poems, 1997. Contributions: periodicals. *Honours:* Rockefeller Grant for Poetry, 1967. *Address:* c/o The New York Times Magazine, 229 W 43rd Street, New York, NY 10036, USA.

SHARP, Paula; Writer and Attorney; b. 12 Nov. 1957, San Diego, CA, USA. *Education:* BA, Comparative Literature, Dartmouth College, 1979; JD, Columbia University, 1985. *Career:* mem. Asscn of the Bar of the City of New York; Authors' Guild; Lawyers' Guild; PEN. *Publications:* The Woman Who Was Not All There, 1988; The Imposter: Stories of Netta and Stanley, 1991; Lost in Jersey City, 1993; Crows Over a Wheatfield, 1996; I Loved You All, 2000. Contributions: periodicals. *Honours:* Distinguished Artist Award, New Jersey Council on the Arts, 1987; Joe Savago New Voice Award, Quality Paperback Book Club, 1988; BANTA Award, 1992; New York Times Notable Book of the Year Citations, 1993, 1996, 2000. *Address:* c/o Gina Maccoby Literary Agency, PO Box 60, Chappaqua, NY 10514, USA.

SHARP, Ronald A(lan); Prof. of English, Writer and Administrator; b. 19 Oct. 1945, Cleveland, Ohio, USA; m. Inese Brutans, 22 June 1968, two s. *Education:* Syracuse University, 1963–64; BA, Kalamazoo College, 1967; Instituto Internacional, Madrid, 1965–66; MA, University of Michigan, 1968; University of Edinburgh, 1973; PhD, University of Virginia, 1974. *Career:* Instructor, Western Michigan University, 1968–70; Instructor, 1970–72, Asst Prof., 1974–78, Assoc. Prof., 1978–85, Prof. of English, 1985–90, John Crowe Ransom Prof. of English, 1990–, Assoc. Provost, 1998–99, Provost, 1999–, Acting Pres., 2002–03, Kenyon College; Visiting Prof., Concordia University, 1978; Co-Ed., The Kenyon Review, 1978–82; mem. Keats-Shelley Asscn; MLA; Wordsworth-Coleridge Asscn. *Publications:* Keats, Skepticism and the Religion of Beauty, 1979; Friendship and Literature: Spirit and Form, 1986; The Norton Book of Friendship (with Eudora Welty), 1991; Reading George Steiner (with Nathan A. Scott Jr), 1994; The Persistence of Poetry: Bicentennial Essays on Keats (with Robert M. Ryan), 1998. Contributions: books and journals. *Honours:* Ford Foundation Grant, 1971; English Speaking Union Fellowship, 1973; Mellon Grant, 1980; National Endowment for the Humanities Fellowships, 1981–82, 1984, 1985, 1986–87, 1994, 1996, 1998; National Humanities Center Fellowship, 1986–87; various grants. *Address:* Office of the President, Kenyon College, Gambier, OH 43022, USA.

SHARPE, Tom, (Thomas Ridley Sharpe); British writer; b. 30 March 1928, London, England; m. Nancy Anne Looper 1969; three d. *Education:* Pembroke College, Cambridge. *Career:* mem. Society of Authors. *Publications:* Riotous Assembly, 1971; Indecent Exposure, 1973; Porterhouse Blue, 1974; Blott on the Landscape, 1975; Wilt, 1976; The Great Pursuit, 1977; The Throwback, 1978; The Wilt Alternative, 1979; Ancestral Vices, 1980; Vintage Stuff, 1982; Wilt on High, 1984; Grantchester Grind, 1995; The Midden, 1996; Wilt in Nowhere 2004; contrib. to magazines and journals. *Honours:* Laureat Le Grand Prix de L'Humour Noir, Paris, 1986; Le Légion de l'Humour, Aphia, Paris, 1986. *Address:* 38 Tunwells Lane, Great Shelford, Cambridge CB2 5LJ, England.

SHATTUCK, Roger Whitney; writer, translator, poet, editor and academic; b. 20 Aug. 1923, New York, NY, USA; m. Nora Ewing White 1949; one s. three d. *Education:* BA, Yale University, 1947. *Career:* Information Officer, Film Section, UNESCO, Paris, 1947–48; Reporter, Chicago Daily News, Paris Office, 1948–49; Asst Trade Ed., Harcourt, Brace & Co, New York City, 1949–50; Society of Fellows, 1950–53, Instructor in French, 1953–56, Harvard University; Asst Prof., 1956–59, Assoc. Prof. of Romance Languages, 1959–62, Prof. of French and English, 1962–71, Chair. of the Dept of French and Italian, 1968–71, University of Texas at Austin; Commonwealth Prof. of French, University of Virginia, 1974–88; University Prof. and Prof. of Modern Foreign Languages, Boston University, 1988–97; Lecturer at many universities, colleges, art museums and other venues; mem. National Trans. Center, advisory board, 1964–69, chair., 1966–69; National Humanities Faculty, 1972–73; Publications of the MLA, editorial board, 1977–78; American Acad. of Arts and Sciences, 1990–; Asscn of Literary Scholars and Critics, pres., 1995–96. *Publications:* Non-Fiction: The Banquet Years: The Origins of the Avant-Garde in France, 1885 to World War One, 1958; Proust's Binoculars: A Study of Memory, Time, and Recognition in A La Recherche du Temps Perdu, 1963; Marcel Proust, 1974; The Forbidden Experiment: The Story of the Wild Boy of Aveyron, 1980; The Innocent Eye: On Literature and the Arts, 1984; Forbidden Knowledge: From Prometheus to Pornography, 1996; Candor and Perversion: Literature, Education and the Arts, 1999; Proust's Way: A Field Guide to In Search of Lost Time, 2000. Poetry: Half Tame, 1964. Editor and Translator: René Daumal: Mount Analogue: A Novel of Symbolically Authentic Non-Euclidean Adventures in Mountain Climbing, 1960; The Selected Writings of Guillaume Apollinaire, 1963; Paul Valéry: Occasions (with Frederick Brown), 1970. Editor: The Craft and Context of Translation (with William Arrowsmith), 1961; Selected Writings of Alfred Jarry: Ubu Cuckolded, Exploits and Opinions of Dr Faustroll, Pataphysician, and Other Writings (with Simon Watson Taylor), 1966; Helen Keller: The Story of My Life, 2003; Helen Keller: The World I Live In, 2003. Translator: René Daumal: A Fundamental Experiment, 1987. Contributions: Essays, short stories, and poems in various publications. *Honours:* Guggenheim Fellowship, 1958–59; Fulbright Research Fellow, 1958–59; ACLS Research Fellow, 1969–70; National Book Award, 1975; American Acad. and Institute of Arts and Letters Award, 1987; Dr hc, University of Orléans, France, 1990. *Address:* 231 Forge Hill Road, Lincoln, VT 05443, USA.

SHAUGHNESSY, Alfred James; Writer and Dramatist; b. 19 May 1916, London, England; m. Jean Lodge, 18 Sept. 1948, two s. *Education:* Eton College; Royal Military College, Sandhurst. *Publications:* Both Ends of the Candle (autobiog.), 1978; Sarah – Letters and Diaries of a Courtier's Wife, 1906–1936, 1989; Dearest Enemy (novel), 1991; Hugo (novel), 1994; A Confession in Writing (memoir), 1997. Stage plays, including: Release; Holiday for Simon; The Heat of the Moment; Old Herbaceous; Double Cut; Love Affair (from the French). *Honours:* US Television Critics Circle Achievement in Writing Award, 1976–77. *Address:* The Grange, Yattendon, Thatcham, Berkshire RG18 0UE, England.

SHAW, Brian (see Tubb, Edwin Charles).

SHAW, Irene (see Roberts, Irene).

SHAW, Mark; Author; b. 3 Oct. 1945, Auburn, IN, USA; m. Chris R. Shaw 15 May 1989; three step-s. one step-d. *Education:* BS, Purdue University; JD, Indiana University School of Law. *Career:* mem. Writers Guild. *Publications:* Down for the Count, 1992; Bury Me in a Pot Bunker, 1993; Forever Flying, 1994; The Perfect Yankee, 1995; McKlaus: A Biography, 1996; Statement to Courage, 1997; Diamonds in the Rough, 1998; Larry Legend, 1998.

SHAW, (Veronica) Patricia; writer; b. 1928, Melbourne, Australia; m. (divorced); one s. one d. *Education:* Star of the Sea Convent, Melbourne, Melbourne Teachers College. *Publications:* Brother Digger: The Sullivans, 2nd AIF, 1984; Valley of the Lagoons, 1989; River of the Sun, 1991; The Feather and the Stone, 1992; Where the Willows Weep, 1993; Cry of the Rain Bird, 1994; Fires of Fortune, 1995; The Opal Seekers, 1996; The Glittering Fields, 1997.

SHAWCROSS, William; British journalist, writer and broadcaster; b. 28 May 1946, Sussex; m. 1st Marina Warner 1972 (divorced 1980); one s.; m. 2nd Michal Levin 1981 (divorced); one d.; m. Olga Forte 1993. *Education:* Eton, Univ. Coll., Oxford. *Career:* freelance journalist in Czechoslovakia 1968–69; corresp. for The Sunday Times, London 1969–72; Chair. Article 19, Int. Centre on Censorship 1986–96; mem. bd Int. Crisis Group 1995–; mem. Council of Disasters Emergency Cttee 1998–. *Publications:* Dubček 1970, Crime and Compromise: Janos Kadar and the Politics of Hungary Since Revolution 1974, Sideshow: Kissinger, Nixon and the Destruction of Cambodia 1979, Quality of Mercy: Cambodia, the Holocaust and Modern Conscience 1984, The Shah's Last Ride 1989, Kowtow: A Plea on Behalf of Hong Kong 1989, Murdoch 1992, Cambodia's New Deal 1994, Deliver Us from Evil: Warlords & Peacekeepers in a World of Endless Conflict 2000, Queen and Country 2002, Allies: The United States, Britain, Europe and the War in Iraq (aka Allies: The US, Britain and Europe in the Aftermath of the Iraq War) 2003; contrib. to newspapers and journals. *Literary Agent:* Green & Heaton Ltd, 37 Goldhawk Road, London, W12. *Telephone:* (20) 7289-8089. *Address:* Friston Place, East Dean, East Sussex BN20 0AH, England. *E-mail:* williamshawcross@compuserve.com (Office).

SHAYKH, Hanan al-; Novelist and Playwright; b. 1945, Beirut, Lebanon; m. *Education:* American College for Girls, Cairo. *Career:* Journalist, Al-Hasna' magazine, Al-Nahar newspaper, 1968–75. *Publications:* Intihar rajul mayyit, 1970; Faras al-shaytan, 1971; Hikayat Zahrah (The Story of Zahra), 1980; 'The Persian Carpet' in Arabic Short Stories, 1983; Misk al-ghazal (Women of Sand and Myrrh), 1988; Barid Bayrut (Beirut Blues), 1992; Aknus al-shams an al-sutuh (I Sweep the Sun off Rooftops, short stories), 1994; Dark Afternoon Tea (play), 1995; Paper Husband (play), 1997; Only in London, 2000.

SHEARER, Jill; playwright; b. 14 April 1936, Melbourne, Vic., Australia. *Publications:* The Trouble with Gillian, 1974; The Foreman, 1976; The Boat, 1977; The Kite, 1977; Nocturne, 1977; Catherine, 1978; Stephen, 1980; Release Lavinia Stannard, 1980; A Woman Like That, 1986; Shimada, 1987; Comrade, 1987; The Family, 1994. *Honours:* Australia Council Grant, 1987; Arts Queensland Fellowship, 1993. *Address:* c/o Playlab Press, PO Box 185, Ashgrove, Brisbane 4060, Qld, Australia.

SHEED, Wilfrid John Joseph; Writer and Columnist; b. 27 Dec. 1930, London, England; m. Miriam Ungerer, two s. one d. *Education:* BA, 1954, MA, 1957, Lincoln College, Oxford. *Career:* Film Reviewer, 1959–61, Assoc. Ed., 1959–66, Jubilee magazine, New York City; Drama Critic and Book Ed., Commonweal magazine, New York City, 1964–71; Film Reviewer, Esquire magazine, New York City, 1967–69; Visiting Prof., Princeton University, 1970–71; Columnist, New York Times, 1971–; Judge and Mem., Editorial Board, Book of the Month Club, 1972–88; mem. Authors' Guild; PEN. *Publications:* Joseph, 1958; A Middle Class Education, 1960; The Hack, 1963; Square's Progress, 1965; Office Politics, 1966; The Blacking Factory and Pennsylvania Gothic: A Short Novel and a Long Story, 1968; Max Jamison, 1970; The Morning After, 1971; People Will Always Be Kind, 1973; Three Mobs: Labor, Church and Mafia, 1974; Vanishing Species of America, 1974; Muhammad Ali: A Portrait in Words and Photographs, 1975; Transatlantic Blues, 1978; The Good Word and Other Words, 1978; Clare Boothe Luce, 1982; Frank and Maisie, 1985; The Boys of Winter, 1987; The Kennedy Legacy: A Generation Later, 1988; Essays in Disguise, 1989; The Face of Baseball, 1990; My Life as a Fan, 1993; In Love with Daylight, 1995. Editor: G. K. Chesterton's Essays and Poems, 1957; Sixteen Short Novels, 1986; Baseball and Lesser Sports, 1991. Contributions: periodicals. *Honours:* American Acad. and Institute of Arts and Letters Award, 1971; Guggenheim Fellowship, 1971–72. *Address:* Sag Harbor, NY 11963, USA.

SHEEHAN, Neil; Writer; b. 27 Oct. 1936, Holyoke, Massachusetts, USA; m. Susan Margulies, 30 March 1965, two d. *Education:* AB, cum laude, Harvard University, 1958. *Career:* Viet Nam Bureau, United Press International, Saigon, 1962–64; Reporter, New York Times, 1964–72; mem. Society of American Historians; American Acad. of Achievement. *Publications:* The Arnheiter Affair, 1972; A Bright Shining Lie: John Paul Vann and America in Vietnam, 1988; After the War Was Over: Hanoi and Saigon, 1992. Contributions: newspapers and journals. *Honours:* First Annual Drew Pearson Award, 1971; Hon. LittD, Columbia College, Chicago, 1972; Sidney Hillman Foundation Awards, 1972, 1988; Columbia Journalism Awards, 1972, 1989; Guggenheim Fellowship, 1973–74; Adlai Stevenson Fellow, 1973–75; Lehrman Institute Fellow, 1975–76; Rockefeller Foundation Fellow, 1976–77; Woodrow Wilson International Center for Scholars Fellow, 1979–80; National Book Award, 1988; Pulitzer Prize for General Non-Fiction, 1989; Robert F. Kennedy Book Award, 1989; Ambassador Award, English Speaking Union, 1989; John F. Kennedy Award, 1989; Hon. LHD, American International College, 1990, University of Lowell, 1991; Literary Lion, New York Public Library, 1992. *Address:* 4505 Klingle St NW, Washington, DC 20016, USA.

SHEEHAN, Susan, BA; American writer; b. 24 Aug. 1937, Vienna, Austria; m. Neil Sheehan 1965; one s. two d. *Education:* Wellesley Coll. *Career:* Editorial Researcher, Esquire-Coronet, New York City, 1959–60; Staff, New Yorker magazine, New York City, 1961–; mem. Authors' Guild; Society of American Historians. *Publications:* Ten Vietnamese, 1967; A Welfare Mother, 1976; A Prison and a Prisoner, 1978; Is There No Place on Earth for Me?, 1982; Kate Quinton's Days, 1984; A Missing Plane, 1986; Life for Me Ain't Been No Crystal Stair, 1993. Contributions: many magazines. *Honours:* Guggenheim Fellowship, 1975–76; Sidney Hillman Foundation Award, 1976; Gavel Award, American Bar Asscn, 1978; Woodrow Wilson International Center for Scholars Fellowship, 1981; Individual Reporting Award, National Mental Health Asscn, 1981; Pulitzer Prize for General Non-Fiction, 1983; Feature Writing Award, New York Press Club, 1984; Alumnae Asscn Achievement Award, Wellesley College, 1984; DHL, University of Lowell, 1991; Carroll Kowal Journalism Award, 1993; Public Awareness Award, National Alliance for the Mentally Ill, 1995. *Address:* 4505 Klingle Street NW, Washington, DC 20016, USA.

SHEEHY, Gail (Henion); Journalist, Ed., Writer and Dramatist; b. 27 Nov. 1937, Mamaroneck, New York, USA; m. 1st Albert F. Sheehy 20 Aug. 1960 (divorced 1967); one d.; m. 2nd Clay Felker 16 Dec. 1984; one adopted d. *Education:* BS, University of Vermont, 1958. *Career:* Fashion Ed., Rochester Democrat and Chronicle, New York, 1961–63; Feature Writer, New York Herald Tribune, 1963–66; Contributing Ed., New York Magazine, 1968–77, Vanity Fair Magazine, 1988–; mem. Authors' Guild; Authors League of America; Common Cause; National Organization for Women; PEN American Center; Poets and Writers. *Publications:* Lovesounds, 1970; Panthermania: The Clash of Black Against Black in One American City, 1971; Speed is of the Essence, 1971; Hustling: Prostitution in Our Wide-Open Society, 1973; Passages: Predictable Crises of Adult Life, 1976; Pathfinders, 1981; Spirit of Survival, 1986; Character: America's Search for Leadership, 1988; Gorbachev: The Man Who Changed the World, 1990; The Silent Passage: Menopause, 1992; New Passages: Mapping Your Life Across Time, 1995; Understanding Men's Passages, 1998; Hillary's Choice, 1999. Contributions: newspapers and magazines. *Honours:* Columbia University Fellowship, 1970, and National Magazine Award, 1973; Anisfield-Wolf Book Award, 1986; Best Magazine Writer Award, Washington Journalism Review, 1991; Literary Lion, New York Public Library, 1992.

SHEERS, Owen; British writer, poet and broadcaster; b. 1974, Suva, Fiji. *Education:* New Coll., Oxford, Univ. of East Anglia. *Career:* writer-in-residence, The Wordsworth Trust; arts presenter for BBC Wales. *Exhibition:* Wales: Dead Or Alive? (with Dan Llewellyn Hall) 2004. *Publications:* poetry: The Blue Book 2000; novel: The Dust Diaries 2004. *Honours:* Eric Gregory Award, Vogue Talent Contest for Young Writers. *Address:* c/o Faber and Faber Ltd, 3 Queen Square, London, WC1N 3AU, England. *Telephone:* (20) 7465-0045. *Fax:* (20) 7465-0054. *Website:* www.owensheers.co.uk.

SHELDON, Lee (see Lee, Wayne C.).

SHELDON, Roy (see Tubb, Edwin Charles).

SHELDON, Sidney; American writer, screenwriter and playwright; b. 11 Feb. 1917, Chicago, IL, USA; m. 1st Jorja Curtright 1951 (died 1985); m. 2nd Alexandra Kostoff 1989. *Education:* Northwestern University. *Career:* television show creator, producer and writer 1963–. *Television:* I Dream of Jeannie (creator, writer and prod.), The Patty Duke Show (creator and writer) 1963–66, Hart to Hart (creator and writer) 1979–84. *Plays:* The Merry Widow (adapted with Ben Roberts) 1943, Jackpot 1944, Dream with Music 1944, Alice in Arms 1945, Redhead 1959, Roman Candle 1960. *Screenplays:* The Bachelor and the Bobby-Soxer 1947, Easter Parade (with Albert Hackett and Frances Goodrich) 1948, Annie Get Your Gun 1950, Rich, Young and Pretty 1951, Dream Wife 1953, Anything Goes 1956, Never Too Young 1956, The Buster Keaton Story 1957, Billy Rose's Jumbo 1962. *Publications:* fiction: The Naked Face 1970, The Other Side of Midnight 1974, A Stranger in the Mirror 1976, Bloodline 1977, Rage of Angels 1980, The Master of the Game 1982, If Tomorrow Comes 1985, Windmills of the Gods 1986, The Sands of Time 1988, Memories of Midnight 1990, The Doomsday Conspiracy 1991, The Stars Shine Down 1992, Nothing Lasts Forever 1994, Morning, Noon and Night 1995, The Best Laid Plans 1997, Tell Me Your Dreams 1998, The Sky is Falling 2000, Are You Afraid of the Dark? 2004. *Honours:* Acad. Award 1947, Screen Award, Writers Guild of America 1948, 1950, 1959, Tony Award 1959, Prix Litteraire de Deauville 1993. *Address:* Warren Cowan & Associates, 8899 Beverly Blvd, Suite 919, Los Angeles, CA 90048, USA (Office). *Website:* www.sidneysheldon.com.

SHEPARD, James (Russell); Prof. of English and Author; b. 29 Dec. 1956, Bridgeport, CT, USA. *Education:* BA, English, Trinity Coll., Hartford, CT, 1978; AM, Creative Writing, Brown Univ., 1980. *Career:* Lecturer, Univ. of Michigan, Ann Arbor, 1980–83; Asst Prof. of English, 1983–90, Instructor in Film, 1988–, Assoc. Prof. of English, 1990–95, J. Leland Miller Prof. of English, 1995–, Williams Coll.; Writer-in-Residence, Bread Loaf Writers' Conference, 1982–84, 1988–93, 2002, Univ. of Tennessee at Chattanooga, 1988, 1989, Vassar Coll., 1998; Fiction Faculty, MFA Program, Warren Wilson Coll., 1992–; Univ. of California at Irvine, 2002; The Tin House/Sundance Conference, 2003. *Publications:* Fiction: Flights, 1983; Paper Doll, 1986; Lights Out in the Reptile House, 1990; Kiss of the Wolf, 1994; Nosferatu, 1998; Project X, 2004. Short Story Collections: Batting Against Castro, 1996; Love and Hydrogen, 2004. Editor: You've Got to Read This (with Ron Hansen), 1994; Unleashed: Poems by Writers' Dogs (with Amy Hempel), 1995; Writers at the Movies, 2000. Contributions: anthologies, journals, reviews and magazines. *Honours:* Transatlantic Review Award, Henfield Foundation, 1980; David Sokolov Scholar in Fiction, Bread Loaf, 1982; Nelson Bushnell Prize, Williams Coll., 1997. *Address:* 45 Forest Rd, Williamstown, MA 01267, USA.

SHEPARD, Sam; American playwright and actor; b. (Samuel Shepard Rogers), 5 Nov. 1943, Fort Sheridan, Ill.; m. O-Lan Johnson Dark 1969 (divorced); one s.; one s. one d. with Jessica Lange. *Education:* Duarte High School, Mount San Antonio Jr Coll. *Television appearances include:* Lily Dale 1996, Purgatory 1999, Hamlet 2000. *Plays include:* Cowboys and Rock Garden (double bill), Chicago, Icarus's Mother and Red Cross (triple bill; Obie Award) 1966, Melodrama Play 1966, The 4-H Club, La Turista (Obie Award) 1967, Forensic and the Navigators (Obie Award) 1968, The Unseen Hand (rock opera) 1969, Cowboy Mouth (with Patti Smith) 1971, The Mad Dog Blues 1971, The Tooth of Crime (Obie Award) 1973, Geography of a Horse Dreamer 1974, Black Dog Beast Bait, Operation Sidewinder, Shaved Splits, Rock Garden (included in Oh! Calcutta!), Curse of the Starving Class (Obie Award) 1978, Buried Child (Pulitzer Prize) 1979, True West 1980, Fool for Love 1982, A Lie of the Mind 1985 (New York Drama Critics Circle Award for Best Play 1986), States of Shock 1991, Simpatico 1994. *Film appearances include:* Days of Heaven 1978, Resurrection 1980, Francis 1982, The Right Stuff 1983, Paris, Texas 1984, Country, Crimes of the Heart, Baby Boom, Defenceless 1989, Voyager 1991, Thunderheart 1992, The Pelican Brief 1994, Safe Passage 1995, The Good Old Boys 1995, Curtain Call 1997, The Only Thrill 1997, Snow Falling on Cedars 1999, One Kill 2000, All the Pretty Horses 2001, Shot in the Heart 2001, Swordfish 2001, Black Hawk Down 2001, The Pledge 2001, The Notebook 2004. *Screenplay:* Zabriskie Point 1970, Paris, Texas (Palme d'Or, Cannes Film Festival 1984), Fool for Love 1985, Far North (also Dir) 1989, Silent Tongue (also Dir), Snow Falling on Cedars, Hamlet, Curtain Call. *Publications:* Hawk Moon 1972, Motel Chronicles 1982, A Murder of Crows (novel) 1996, Cruising Paradise (autobiog.) 1996, Great Dream of Heaven (short stories) 2002. *Address:* ICM, 8942 Wilshire Boulevard, Beverly Hills CA 90211, USA.

SHEPHERD, Robert James, BA, MA; writer, journalist, television producer and director; b. 14 Feb. 1949, Solihull, Warwickshire, England. *Education:* University of Kent. *Career:* Leader and Features Writer, Investors Chronicle, 1983; Editorial Team, Producer, A Week in Politics, 1983–88; Parliamentary Lobby Correspondent, 1984–87; Producer, documentaries; mem. Society of Authors; International PEN; National Union of Journalists. *Publications:* Public Opinion and European Integration, 1975; A Class Divided, 1988; Ireland's Fate, 1990; The Power Brokers, 1991; Iain Macleod, 1994; Enoch Powell: A Biography, 1996. Contributions: Political Quarterly; New Statesman; Investors Chronicle; Marxism Today; Guardian; The Times; Irish Independent; Sunday Press; Ireland of the Welcomes; The Spectator; Contemporary History. *Honours:* Prix Stendhal, 1993; Reuter Fellowship, University of Oxford, 1995. *Literary Agent:* Curtis Brown Ltd, Haymarket House, 28–29 Haymarket, London, SW1Y 4SP, England. *Telephone:* (20) 7393-4400. *Fax:* (20) 7393-4401. *E-mail:* info@curtisbrown.co.uk. *Website:* www.curtisbrown.co.uk.

SHEPPARD, David (Stuart), (Lord Sheppard of Liverpool); Bishop (retd) and Writer; b. 6 March 1929, Reigate, Surrey, England; m. Grace Isaac, 19 June 1957, one d. *Education:* MA, Trinity Hall, Cambridge. *Career:* Played cricket for Sussex, 1947–62 (captain, 1953), University of Cambridge, 1950–52 (captain 1952), England, 1950–63 (captain 1954); Ridley Hall Theological College Asst Curate, St Mary's, Islington, 1955–57; Warden, Mayflower Family Centre, Canning Town, 1957–69; Bishop Suffragan, Woolwich, 1969–75; Chair., Martin Luther King Foundation, 1970–75, BBC and ITC Central Religious Advisory Committee, 1989–92, General Synod Board for Social Responsibility, 1991–96, Churches' Enquiry into Unemployment and the Future of Work, 1995–97; Bishop of Liverpool, 1975–97; National Pres., Family Service Units, 1987–97. *Publications:* Parson's Pitch, 1964; Built as a City, 1974; Bias to the Poor, 1983; The Other Britain, 1984; Better Together (with D. Worlock), 1988; With Christ in the Wilderness (with D. Worlock), 1990; With Hope in Our Hearts (with D. Worlock), 1994; Steps Along Hope Street, 2002. *Honours:* Hon. LLD, University of Liverpool, 1981; Hon. Fellow, Trinity Hall, Cambridge, 1983; Hon. DTech, Liverpool Polytechnic, 1987; Hon. DD, University of Cambridge, 1991, University of Exeter, 1998, University of Birmingham, 1999, University of Wales, 2000; Freedom, City of Liverpool, 1995; Life Peerage, 1998; Hon. DUniv, Open University 1999. *Address:* Ambledown, 11 Mellon-croft Dr., West Kirby, Merseyside CH48 2JA, England.

SHER, Sir Antony; Author, Actor and Artist; b. 14 June 1949, Cape Town, South Africa. *Education:* Webber Douglas Acad. of Dramatic Art, London, 1971. *Publications:* Fiction: Middlepost 1988, Changing Step (screenplay) 1989, The Indoor Boy 1991, Cheap Lives 1995, The Feast 1998, ID (play) 2003. Non-Fiction: Year of the King 1985, Characters – Paintings and Drawings 1989, Woza Shakespeare! (with Gregory Doran) 1996, Beside Myself (autobiog.) 2001. *Honours:* numerous acting awards; Hon. DLitt, Liverpool Univ., 1998; KBE. *Literary Agent:* Talent Media Group, Oxford House, 76 Oxford St, London W1D 1BS, England. *Address:* 11–12 Dover St, London W1X 3PH, England.

SHER, Steven Jay, BA, MA, MFA; writer and poet; b. 28 Sept. 1949, USA; m. Nancy Green 1978; one s. one d. *Education:* City Coll., CUNY, Univ. of Iowa, Brooklyn Coll., CUNY. *Career:* Dir Creative Writing, Spalding Univ. 1979–81, Oregon State Univ. 1981–86, Univ. of North Carolina at Wilmington 1986–89; Visiting Writer, Western Oregon Univ. 1991–2002, Willamette Univ. 1993, Yeshiva Univ. 2003, Fashion Inst. of Technology, SUNY 2003; mem. Willamette Literary Guild (pres. 1992–2002). *Publications:* Nickelodeon 1978, Persnickety 1979, Caught in the Revolving Door 1980, Trolley Lives 1985, Man With a Thousand Eyes and Other Stories 1989, Traveler's Advisory 1994, Flying Through Glass 2001, Thirty-Six 2002, At the Willamette 2003; co-editor: Northwest Variety: Personal Essays by 14 Regional Authors 1987; contrib. to anthologies and periodicals. *Honours:* All Nations Poetry Contest 1977, Weymouth Centre Residency 1988, North Carolina Writers' Network Writers and Readers Series Competition 1989, How the Ink Feels Poetry Contest 2001. *Address:* 344 W 87 Street, No. 3R, New York, NY 10024, USA.

SHERIF, Osama ash-, BA; Jordanian publisher; b. June 1960, Jerusalem; m. Ghada Yasser Amr 1984; one s. one d. *Education:* Univ. of Missouri. *Career:* Chief Ed. The Jerusalem Star 1985–88; Pres. Info-Media, Jordan 1989–; Publr, Chief Ed. and weekly columnist, The Star, Jordan 1990–; Publr Arabian Communications & Publishing (ACP) 1994–, BYTE Middle East 1994–, Al Tiqaniyyah Wal 'Amal 1995–. *Address:* The Star, PO Box 591, University Street, Amman 11118, Jordan. *Telephone:* (6) 5664153. *Fax:* (6) 5667170. *E-mail:* star@addustour.com.jo (Office). *Website:* star.arabia.com (Office).

SHERMAN, Eileen Bluestone; Author, Playwright and Lyricist; b. 15 May 1951, Atlantic City, NJ, USA; m. Neal Jonathan Sherman, 10 June 1973, one s. one d. *Education:* BA, Finch College, New York, 1973; MA, SUNY at Albany, 1976; Faculty, Baker University, Overland Park, KS, 1997. *Career:* mem. Authors' Guild; Dramatists Guild; National League of American Pen Women; Society of Children's Book Writers. *Publications:* The Odd Potato, 1984; Monday in Odessa, 1986; Independence Avenue, 1990; The Violin Players, 1998. Other: Musical plays; The Magic Door (television series), 1987–90; Room 119 (drama), 1997; The Happiest Day in Heaven (musical), 1998; The Violin Players, 1998; Rockwell (musical), 1999; You're Not Sandy

Koufax (musical), 2000. *Honours:* Outstanding Social Studies Trade Book Award, 1986; National Jewish Book Award for Children's Literature, 1986; Emmy Awards, 1988, 1989; Teacher's Choice Award, 1991; Jessica Cosgrave Award for Career Achievement, Finch College Asscn, 1997; Thorpe Menn Honorable Mention 1999; Sugarman Family Literature Honorable Mention, 1999; First Place, Short Story Category, National League of American Pen Women, Kansas City, 2000. *Address:* 2525 Main St, Kansas City, MO, USA.

SHERMAN, Susan; American poet, critic and editor. *Career:* founder and Ed., Ikon magazine 1965–69; teacher, Parsons School of Design. *Publications:* Color of the Heart: Writing from Struggle and Change 1959–1990 1990, Shango de Ima (trans.) 1996. *Honours:* New York Foundation for the Arts Fellowship for Poetry 1990, Puffin Foundation Grant 1992, Fellowship from the New York Foundation for the Arts for Creative Non-Fiction Literature 1997. *Address:* c/o Curbstone Press, 321 Jackson Street, Willimantic, CT 06226-1738, USA. *E-mail:* info@curbstone.org. *Website:* www.curbstone.org.

SHERMAN, William David; Poet, Writer, Ed. and Publisher; b. 24 Dec. 1940, Philadelphia, PA, USA; m. Barbara Beaumont, 22 July 1970, divorced 1978. *Education:* BA, Temple University, 1962; MA, 1964, PhD, 1968, SUNY at Buffalo; Dickinson School of Law, 1974–75. *Career:* Tenured Lecturer in American Literature and Film Univ. Coll. of Wales, Aberystwyth 1969–72; Ed.-Publr Branch Redd Books and Branch Redd Review 1976–. *Publications:* The Landscape of Contemporary Cinema (with Leon Lewis) 1967, The Cinema of Orson Welles 1967, The Springbok (poetry) 1973, The Hard Sidewalk 1974, The Horses of Gwyddno Garanhir 1976, Mermaids I 1977, Heart Attack and Spanish Songs in Mandaine Land 1981, Duchamp's Door 1983, She Wants to Go to Pago-Pago 1986, The Tahitian Journals 1990, A Tale for Tusitala 1993, From the South Seas 1997. Contributions: anthologies and periodicals including FIRE (Oxfordshire, UK). *Honours:* Poetry Prize, Royal Albert Hall Reading, 1995. *Address:* 9300 Atlantic Ave, No. 218, Margate, NJ 08402, USA.

SHERRIN, Edward (Ned) George, CBE, MA; director, producer and writer; b. 18 Feb. 1931, Low Ham, Somerset, England. *Education:* University of Oxford. *Career:* Barrister-at-Law. *Publications:* Cindy-Ella (with Caryl Brahms), 1962; Rappell 1910 (with Caryl Brahms), 1964; Benbow Was His Name (with Caryl Brahms), 1967; Ooh La (with Caryl Brahms), 1973; After You Mr Feydeau (with Caryl Brahms), 1975; A Small Thing Like an Earthquake, 1983; Song by Song (with Caryl Brahms), 1984; Cutting Edge, 1984; 1956 and All That (with Neil Shand), 1984; The Metropolitan Mikado (with Alistair Beaton), 1985; Too Dirty for the Windmill (with Caryl Brahms), 1986; Loose Neds, 1990; Theatrical Anecdotes, 1991; Ned Sherrin in His Anecdotage, 1993; The Oxford Dictionary of Humorous Quotations, 1995; Sherrin's Year, 1996; Scratch an Actor, 1996. *Address:* c/o Scott Ferris Associates, 15 Gledhow Gardens, London SW5 0AY, England.

SHERRY, (Michael) Norman; writer and academic; b. 6 July 1935, Tirana, Albania. *Education:* BA, English Literature, University of Durham; PhD, University of Singapore, 1963. *Career:* Lecturer in English Literature, University of Singapore, 1961–66; Lecturer, Senior Lecturer, University of Liverpool, 1966–70; Prof. of English, University of Lancaster, 1970–82; Fellow, Humanities Research Center, NC, USA, 1982; Mitchell Distinguished Prof. of Literature, Trinity University, San Antonio, Texas, 1983–; mem. Savile. *Publications:* Conrad's Eastern World, 1966; Jane Austen, 1966; Charlotte and Emily Brontë, 1969; Conrad's Western World, 1971; Conrad and His World, 1972; Conrad: The Critical Heritage, 1973; Conrad in Conference, 1976; The Life of Graham Greene, Vol. 1 1904–39, 1989, Vol. 2 1939–55, 1994; Vol. 3, 2003; Joseph Conrad, 1997. Editor: An Outpost of Progress and Heart of Darkness, 1973; Lord Jim, 1974; Nostromo, 1974; The Secret Agent, 1974; The Nigger of the Narcissus, Typhoon, Falk and Other Stories, 1975; Joseph Conrad: A Commemoration, 1976. Contributions: Academic American Encyclopedia; Guardian; Daily Telegraph; Oxford Magazine; Modern Language Review; Review of English Studies; Notes and Queries; BBC; TLS; Observer. *Honours:* FRSL, 1986; Edgar Allan Poe Award, 1989; Guggenheim Fellowship, 1989–90. *Address:* Trinity University, 715 Stadium Drive, San Antonio, TX 78212, USA.

SHERWIN, Byron L(ee); Prof. and Author; b. 18 Feb. 1946, New York, NY, USA; m. Judith Rita Schwartz, 24 Dec. 1972, one s. *Education:* BS, Columbia University; BHL, 1966, MHL, 1968, Rabbi, 1970, Jewish Theological Seminary; MA, New York University, 1969; PhD, University of Chicago, 1978. *Career:* Asst Prof., 1970–74, Assoc. Prof., 1974–78, Prof. of Jewish Philosophy and Mysticism, 1978–, Vice-Pres. for Academic Affairs, 1984–2001, Spertus College of Judaica, Chicago; Visiting Prof., Mundelein College, 1974–82; Dir, Holocaust Studies Project, National Endowment for the Humanities, 1976–78; mem. American Acad. of Religion; American Asscn of University Profs; Rabbinical Assembly of America; American Philosophical Asscn; Society for Business Ethics; Authors' Guild. *Publications:* Judaism: The Way of Sanctification (with Samuel H. Dresner), 1978; Abraham Joshua Heschel, 1979; Encountering the Holocaust: An Interdisciplinary Survey (ed. with Susan G. Ament), 1979; Garden of the Generations, 1981; Jerzy Kosinski: Literary Alarmclock, 1982; Mystical Theology and Social Dissent: The Life and Works of Judah Loew of Prague, 1982; The Golem Legend: Origins and Implications, 1985; Contexts and Content: Higher Jewish Education in the United States, 1987; Thank God: Prayers of Jesus and Christians Together, 1989; In Partnership with God: Contemporary Jewish Law and Ethics, 1990; No Religion is an Island (with Harold Kasimov), 1991; Towards a Jewish Theology, 1992; How to Be a Jew: Ethical Teachings of Judaism (with Seymour J. Cohen), 1992; The Spiritual Heritage of Polish Jews, 1995; Sparks Amongst the Ashes: The Spiritual Legacy of Polish Jewry, 1997; Crafting the Soul, 1998; Why Be Good?, 1998; John Paul II and Interreligious Dialogue (co-author), 1999; Jewish Ethics for the 21st Century, 2000; Creating an Ethical Jewish Life, 2001. Contributions: Professional journals. *Honours:* Man of Reconciliation Award, Polish Council of Christians and Jews, 1992; Presidential Medal, Officer of the Order of Merit, Republic of Poland, 1995; Doctor of Hebrew Letters, hc, Jewish Theological Seminary of America, 1996. *Address:* 6702 N Sheridan Rd, Chicago, IL 60626, USA.

SHIELDS, David; Writer and Prof. of English; b. 22 July 1956, Los Angeles, CA, USA. *Education:* BA, Brown Univ., 1978; MFA, Univ. of Iowa, 1980. *Career:* Visiting Lecturer in Creative Writing, Univ. of California at Los Angeles, 1985; Visiting Asst Prof., St Lawrence Univ., Canton, NY, 1985–86, 1987–88; Asst Prof., 1988–92, Assoc. Prof., 1992–97, Prof. of English, 1997–, Univ. of Washington at Seattle; Faculty, Warren Wilson Coll., Asheville, NC, 1996–; various visiting instructorships; mem. Associated Writing Programs; Authors' Guild; International PEN; MLA of America; Poets and Writers; Writers' Guild of America. *Publications:* Heroes: A Novel, 1984; Dead Languages: A Novel, 1989; Handbook for Drowning; A Novel in Stories, 1992; Remote: Reflections on Life in the Shadow of Celebrity, 1996; Black Planet: Facing Race During an NBA Season, 1999; 'Baseball is Just Baseball': The Understated Ichiro, 2004; Enough About You: Adventures in Autobiography, 2004; Body Politic: The Great American Sports Machine, 2004. Contributions: New York Times Magazine; Harper's; Yale Review; Village Voice; Slate; Salon; McSweeney's. *Honours:* James A. Michener Fellowship, Iowa Writers' Workshop, 1980–82; James D. Phelan Award, San Francisco Foundation, 1981; National Endowment for the Arts Fellowships, 1982, 1991; Ingram-Merrill Foundation Award, 1983; PEN Syndicated Fiction Project Competitions, 1985, 1988; William Sloane Fellowship, Bread Loaf Writers' Conference, 1986; New York Foundation for the Arts Fellowship, 1988; Silver Medal, Commonwealth Club of California Awards, 1989; Governor's Writers Award, State of Washington, 1990; Artist Trust Fellowship for Literature, 1991; PEN/Revson Foundation Fellowship, 1992; First Prize, Web del Sol Creative Non-Fiction Contest, 1999. *Address:* c/o Dept of English, University of Washington at Seattle, Seattle, WA 98195, USA. *E-mail:* dshields@davidshields.com. *Website:* www.davidshields.com.

SHILLITOE, Tony; Educator; b. 28 March 1955, Tailem Bend, Australia; m. Francesca Stropin, 7 Jan. 2001. *Education:* BA, Dip Ed, Flinders University, 1973–77; BEd, Hartley CAE, 1979–80. *Career:* mem. Australian Society of Authors. *Publications:* Guardians, 1992; Kingmaker, 1993; Dragon Lords, 1993; The Last Wizard, 1995; The Innkeeper, 1996; Fiction 2 – The Novel, 1996; Jammin', 1997; The Lure, 1998; The Lore Book, 1998; Joy Ride, 1999; Assassin, 1999; Honour, 1999; Introduction to Styles and Conventions, 1999; The Mother Anger, 2000; Virtual God, 2000; The Sculptor, 2000. *E-mail:* tshillitoe@concordia.sa.edu.au.

SHINDLER, Colin, BA, MA, PhD; British film and television producer, screenwriter, university lecturer and novelist; b. 28 June 1949, Bury, Lancashire, England; m. N. Lynn White 1972; one s. one d. *Education:* Bury Grammar School, Univ. of Cambridge. *Publications:* Hollywood Goes to War 1979, Buster 1988, Hollywood in Crisis 1996, Manchester United Ruined My Life 1998, High on a Cliff 2000, Fathers, Sons and Football 2001, First Love Second Chance 2003, George Best and 21 Others 2004. *Literary Agent:* Sheil Land Associates, 43 Doughty Street, London, WC1, England.

SHINKAREV, Vladimir; Russian writer and artist; b. 1954, Leningrad. *Education:* Leningrad Univ., Muhina Coll., Repin Art Acad. *Publications include:* Solovei i stado: Basnia 1988, Mitki 1990, Stikhi, basmi, pesni 1995, Maxim and Fyodor 2002. *Address:* c/o Seagull Publishing House Ltd, 14 Caterham Road, London, SE13 5AR, England. *Website:* www.seagullpublishing.co.uk.

SHINN, Sharon Ruth; Writer; b. 28 April 1957, Wichita, KS, USA. *Education:* BSJ, Journalism, Northwestern University, 1979. *Publications:* The Shape-Changer's Wife, 1995; Archangel, 1996; Jovah's Angel, 1997; The Alleluia Files, 1998; Wrapt in Crystal, 1999; Heart of Gold, 2000; Summers at Castle Auburn, 2001; Jenna Starborn, 2002; Angelica, 2003. *Honours:* Crawford Fantasy Award, IAFA, 1996. *Address:* PO Box 6774, Brentwood, MO 63144, USA.

SHIPLER, David Karr, AB; journalist and writer; b. 3 Dec. 1942, Orange, NJ, USA; m. Deborah S. Isaacs 1966; two s. one d. *Education:* Dartmouth College. *Career:* News Clerk, 1966–67, News Summary Writer, 1967–68, Reporter, 1968–73, Foreign Correspondent, Saigon, 1973–75, and Moscow, 1975–77, Bureau Chief, Moscow, 1977–79, and Jerusalem, 1979–84, Correspondent, Washington, DC, 1985–87, Chief Diplomatic Correspondent, 1987–88, The New York Times; Guest Scholar, Brookings Institution, 1984–85; Senior Assoc., Carnegie Endowment for International Peace, 1988–90; Adjunct Prof., School of International Service, American University, Washington, DC, 1990; Ferris Prof. of Journalism and Public Affairs, Princeton University, 1990–91. *Publications:* Russia: Broken Idols, Solemn Dreams 1983, Arab and Jew: Wounded Spirits in a Promised Land

1986, A Country of Strangers: Blacks and Whites in America 1997, The Working Poor: Invisible in America 2004; contrib. to newspapers and journals. *Honours:* Distinguished Reporting Award, Society of Silurians, 1971; Distinguished Public Affairs Reporting Award, American Political Science Asscn, 1971; Co-Winner, George Polk Award, 1982; Pulitzer Prize for General Non-Fiction, 1987; Alfred DuPont-Columbia University Award for Broadcast Journalism, 1990. *Address:* 4005 Thornapple Street, Chevy Chase, MD 20815, USA.

SHNEIDMAN, Noah Norman, MPHE, MA, DipREES, PhD; academic and writer; *Professor, University of Toronto*; b. 24 Sept. 1924, Wilno, Poland; m. (divorced); two d. *Education:* Minsk, Warsaw, Univ. of Toronto. *Career:* Lecturer 1966–71, Asst Prof. 1971–75, Assoc. Prof. 1975–79, Prof. 1979–91, Univ. of Toronto; Distinguished Visiting Prof., McMaster Univ. 1981; mem. Canadian Asscn of Slavists, American Asscn of Teachers of Slavic and East European Languages. *Publications:* Literature and Ideology in Soviet Education 1973, The Soviet Road to Olympus: Theory and Practice of Soviet Physical Culture 1978, Soviet Literature in the 1970s: Artistic Diversity and Ideological Conformity 1979, Dostoevsky and Suicide 1984, Soviet Literature in the 1980s: Decade of Transition 1989, Russian Literature 1988–1994: The End of an Era 1995, Jerusalem of Lithuania: The Rise and Fall of Jewish Vilnius 1998, The Three Tragic Heroes of the Vilnius Ghetto: Witenberg, Sheinbaum, Gens 2002, Russian Literature 1995–2002: On the Threshold of the New Millennium 2004. *Address:* c/o Department of Slavic Language and Literature, University of Toronto, Toronto, ON M5S 1A1, Canada.

SHOAF, Richard (Allen); professor of English, poet, writer and editor; b. 25 March 1948, Lexington, NC, USA; m. Judith Patricia McNamara, 1975, one s. one d. *Education:* BA, Wake Forest University, 1970; BA, University of East Anglia, 1972; MA, 1975, PhD, 1977, Cornell University. *Career:* Asst Prof. of English, 1977–81, Assoc. Prof. of English, 1982–85, Yale University; Prof. of English, 1986–, Alumni Prof. of English, 1990–93, University of Florida at Gainesville; Founder-Ed., Exemplaria: A Journal of Theory in Medieval and Renaissance Studies, 1989–; Pres., Council of Eds of Learned Journals, 1994–96; mem. Acad. of American Poets; Dante Society of America; John Gower Society; Medieval Acad. of America; MLA of America; South Atlantic MLA. *Publications:* Dante, Chaucer, and the Currency of the Word: Money, Images, and Reference in Late Medieval Poetry 1983, The Poem as Green Girdle: 'Commercium' in Sir Gawain and the Green Knight 1984, Milton, Poet of Duality: A Study of Semiosis in the Poetry and the Prose 1985, Troilus and Criseyde (ed.) 1989, Simple Rules (poems) 1991, Chaucer's Troilus and Criseyde – 'Subgit to alle poesye': Essays in Criticism 1992, The Testament of Love, by Thomas Usk (ed.) 1998, Chaucer's Body: The Anxiety of Circulation in the Canterbury Tales 2001. Contributions: reference works, scholarly books and literary journals. *Honours:* National Endowment for the Humanities Fellowships 1982–83, 1999–2000; Hon. Visiting Scholar, University of Central Florida 1993, Univ. of Berne (Switzerland) 1999. *Address:* POB 117310, University of Florida, Gainesville, FL 32611-7310, USA. *E-mail:* ras@ufl.edu.

SHONE, Richard; Writer and Ed.; b. 8 May 1949, Doncaster, Yorkshire, England. *Education:* BA, Clare College, Cambridge, 1971. *Career:* Assoc. Ed., 1979–2003, Ed., 2003–, Burlington Magazine. *Publications:* Bloomsbury Portraits: Vanessa Bell, Duncan Grant, and Their Circle, 1976; The Century of Change: British Painting Since 1900, 1977; Vincent van Gogh, 1977; Augustus John, 1979; The Post-Impressionists, 1979; Walter Sickert, 1988; Rodrigo Moynihan, 1988; Sickert: Paintings (ed. with Wendy Baron), 1992; Sisley, 1992; Sensation (co-author), 1997; Sargent to Freud: Modern Paintings in the Beaverbrook Collection (with Ian G. Lumsden), 1998. Contributions: Art journals and other publications. *Address:* c/o Burlington Magazine, 14–16 Duke's Rd, London WC1H 9SZ, England.

SHREVE, Anita; American writer. *Career:* fmrly high school teacher, journalist in Nairobi, Kenya and USA; teacher of writing, Amherst College. *Publications:* Non-fiction: Remaking Motherhood: How Working Mothers are Shaping Our Children's Future, 1987; Women Together, Women Alone: The Legacy of the Consciousness-Raising Movement, 1989. Fiction: Eden Close, 1989; Strange Fits of Passion, 1991; Where or When, 1993; Resistance, 1995; The Weight of Water, 1997; The Pilot's Wife, 1998; Fortune's Rocks, 2000; The Last Time They Met, 2001; Sea Glass, 2002; All He Ever Wanted, 2002; Light on Snow, 2004. Contributions: Quest, US, Newsweek, New York Times Magazine. *Honours:* O. Henry Prize, 1975; Page One Award, New York Newspaper Guild; PEN/L. L. Winship Award, 1998; New England Book Award for fiction, 1998. *Address:* c/o Abacus Books, Little, Brown and Co, Brettenham House, Lancaster Place, London WC2E 7EN, England.

SHREVE, Susan (Richards); Prof. of English Literature and Author; b. 2 May 1939, Toledo, Ohio, USA; m. 1st Porter Shreve, divorced 1987; m. 2nd Timothy Seldes, two s. two d. *Education:* University of Pennsylvania, 1961; MA, University of Virginia, 1969. *Career:* Prof. of English Literature, George Mason University, Fairfax, Virginia, 1976–; Visiting Prof., Columbia University, 1982–, Princeton University, 1991–93; mem. PEN/Faulkner Foundation, pres. *Publications:* A Fortunate Madness, 1974; A Woman Like That, 1977; Children of Power, 1979; Miracle Play, 1981; Dreaming of Heroes, 1984; Queen of Hearts, 1986; A Country of Strangers, 1989; Daughters of the New World, 1992; The Train Home, 1993; Skin Deep: Women and Race, 1995; The Visiting Physician, 1995; The Goalie, 1996; Narratives on Justice (co-ed.), 1996; Outside the Law, 1997; How We Want to Live (co-ed.), 1998; Plum and Jaggers, 2000. Other: many children's books, 1977–2000. Contributions: various publications. *Honours:* Jenny Moore Award, George Washington University, 1978; Guggenheim Fellowship, 1980; National Endowment for the Arts Award, 1982. *Address:* c/o Dept of English, George Mason University, Fairfax, VA 22030, USA.

SHRIGLEY, David; British cartoonist; b. 1968, Macclesfield, Cheshire. *Education:* Glasgow School of Art. *Exhibitions include:* Stephen Friedman Gallery, London 1997, Surfacing – Contemporary Drawing, ICA, London 1998, Yvon Lambert Gallery, Paris 1999, Center for Curatorial Studies at Bard College, Annandale-on-Hudson, NY 2001, billboard commission at Gloucester Road Station, London 2004. *Publications:* Slug Trails 1991, Merry Eczema 1992, Blanket of Filth 1994, Enquire Within 1995, Err 1995, Drawings Done Whilst on Phone to Idiot 1996, Blank Page and Other Pages 1998, Why We Got the Sack from the Museum 1998, The Beast is New 1999, Grip 2000, Do Not Bend 2001, Evil Thoughts 2002, Human Achievement 2002, Joy – 22 Postcards 2002, Dirt 2002, Yellow Bird with Worm 2003, Who I Am and What I Want 2003, Rules – 22 Postcards 2004, Kill Your Pets 2004. *Address:* c/o Redstone Press, 7a St Lawrence Terrace, London, W10 5SU, England. *Telephone:* (20) 7352-1594. *Fax:* (20) 7352-8749. *E-mail:* jr@redstonepress.co.uk. *Website:* www.redstonepress.co.uk.

SHU TING; Chinese poet and writer; b. (Gong Peiyu), 1952, Shima, Zhangzhou City, Fujian Prov.; m. Chen Zhongyi 1981; one s. *Career:* sent to work in the countryside during the cultural revolution –1973, then worked on construction sites and in factories; published poems in underground literary magazine, Today; mem. Writers' Asscn Fujian 1983–, Vice-Chair. 1985–, Council of Writers' Asscn of China 1985–; Dir Chinese Writers' Union. *Publications:* Shuangweichuan 1982, Shu Ting Shuqing Shixuan 1984, Poesiealbum Shu Ting 1989, Selected Poems of Seven Chinese Poets 1993, Selected Poems: An Authoritative Collection 1994, Mist of my Heart: Selected Poems of Shu Ting 1995. *Address:* 13 Zhonghua Road, Gulangyu, Xiamen City, Fujian Province, 361002, People's Republic of China.

SHUBIN, Seymour; Author; b. 14 Sept. 1921, Philadelphia, Pennsylvania, USA; m. Gloria Amet, 27 Aug. 1957, one s. one d. *Education:* BS, Temple University. *Career:* mem. American Society of Authors and Journalists; Authors' Guild; MWA; PEN, American Center. *Publications:* Anyone's My Name, 1953; Manta, 1958; Wellville, USA, 1961; The Captain, 1982; Holy Secrets, 1984; Voices, 1985; Never Quite Dead, 1989; Remember Me Always, 1994; Fury's Children, 1997; My Face Among Strangers, 1999; The Good and the Dead, 2000; A Matter of Fear, 2002. Contributions: Saturday Evening Post; Reader's Digest; Redbook; Family Circle; Story; Ellery Queen's Mystery Magazine; Emergency Medicine; Official Detective Stories Magazine; Perspective in Biology and Medicine. *Honours:* Edgar Allan Poe, Special Award; Special Citation for Fiction, Athenaeum of Philadelphia; Certificate of Honor, Temple University.

SHUKMAN, Harold; Emeritus Fellow and Writer; b. 23 March 1931, London, England; m. 1st Ann King Farlow 1956 (divorced 1970); two s. one d.; m. 2nd Barbara King Farlow. *Education:* BA, Univ. of Nottingham, 1956; MA, 1961, DPhil, 1961, Univ. of Oxford. *Career:* Fellow, 1961–98, Emeritus Fellow, 1998–, Lecturer in Modern Russian History, 1969–98, St Antony's College, Oxford; mem. Authors Society; FRHistS; Trans Asscn. *Publications:* Lenin and the Russian Revolution, 1966; Blackwell's Encyclopedia of the Russian Revolution (ed.), 1988; Andrei Gromyko: Memories (ed. and trans.), 1989; Stalin: Triumph and Tragedy (ed. and trans.), 1991; Lenin: His Life and Legacy (ed. and trans.), 1994; Trotsky: Eternal Revolutionary (ed. and trans.), 1996; Rasputin, 1997; The Rise and Fall of the Soviet Empire (ed. and trans.), 1998; The Russian Revolution, 1998; Stalin, 1999; Agents for Change (ed.); The Winter War (ed.); Secret Classrooms (co-author). Contributions: professional journals and general periodicals. *Address:* St Antony's College, Oxford OX2 6JF, England.

SHUKMAN, Henry; British poet and writer; b. 1963, Oxford. *Career:* poet-in-residence, The Wordsworth Trust; book reviewer, New York Times; contributing ed., Conde Nast Traveller. *Publications:* travel writing: Sons of the Moon: A Journey in the Andes 1990, Travels with my Trombone: A Caribbean Journey 1992; memoirs: Savage Pilgrims: On the Road to Santa Fe 1996; poetry: In Doctor No's Garden 2002; novel: Darien Dogs 2003; contrib. to TLS, Daily Telegraph, Iowa Review. *Honours:* Daily Telegraph Arvon Prize, TLS Prize, Tabla Prize, Peterloo Prize, Arts Council Writer's Award, Aldeburgh Festival Prize. *Address:* c/o The Wordsworth Trust, Dove Cottage, Grasmere, Cumbria LA22 9SH, England. *Telephone:* (15394) 35544. *Fax:* (15394) 35748. *E-mail:* enquiries@wordsworth.org.uk. *Website:* www.wordsworth.org.uk.

SHUPE, Anson David, Jr; Prof. of Sociology and Anthropology and Writer; b. 21 Jan. 1948, Buffalo, NY, USA; m. Janet Ann Klicua, 27 June 1970, one s. one d. *Education:* Waseda University, Tokyo, 1968; BA, Sociology, College of Wooster, 1970; MA, 1972, PhD, 1975, Sociology, Indiana University. *Career:* Asst Prof., Alfred University, New York, 1975–76; Asst Prof., 1976–78, Assoc. Prof., 1978–86, Prof. of Sociology, 1986, University of Texas at Arlington; Assoc. Ed., Review of Religious Research, 1980, 1992–, Sociological Focus, 1988–90; Visiting Faculty Lecturer, 1985, Lecturer, 1987, Iliff School of Theology, Denver; Prof. of Sociology and Anthropology,

1987–, Chair, Dept of Sociology and Anthropology, 1987–91, Indiana University-Purdue University, Fort Wayne; mem. American Asscn of University Profs; Asscn for the Scientific Study of Religion; Asscn for the Sociology of Religion; North Central Sociological Asscn; Religious Research Asscn; Society for the Scientific Study of Religion. *Publications:* 'Moonies' in America: Cult, Church, and Crusade (with David G. Bromley), 1980; Six Perspectives on New Religions: A Case Study Approach, 1981; Strange Gods: The Great American Cult Scare (with David G. Bromley), 1982; Born Again Politics and the Moral Majority: What Social Surveys Really Show (with William A. Stacey), 1982; The Anti-Cult Movement in America: A Bibliography and Historical Survey (with David G. Bromley and Donna L. Stacey), 1983; Metaphor and Social Control in a Pentecostal Sect (with Tom Craig Darrand), 1984; The Mormon Corporate Empire (with John Heinerman), 1985; A Documentary History of the Anti-Cult Movement (with David G. Bromley), 1986; Violent Men, Violent Couples: The Dynamics of Family Violence (with William A. Stacey and Lonnie R. Hazelwood), 1986; Televangelism: Power and Politics on God's Frontier (with Jeffrey K. Hadden), 1988; The Darker Side of Virtue: Corruption, Scandal and the Mormon Empire, 1991; The Violent Couple (with William A. Stacey and Lonnie R. Hazelwood), 1994; In the Name of All That's Holy: A Theory of Clergy Malfeasance, 1995; Violence, Inequality, and Human Freedom, 1998. Editor: 8 vols. Contributions: many scholarly publications. *Honours:* various grants and fellowships; Henry H. H. Remak Scholar, Institute for Advanced Study, Indiana University, 1997–98; Arts and Sciences Distinguished Scholar, Indiana University – Purdue University at Fort Wayne, 1998. *Address:* c/o Dept of Sociology and Anthropology, Indiana University-Purdue University at Fort Wayne, IN 46805, USA.

SHUSTERMAN, Richard M(ark); Prof. of Philosophy and Writer; b. 3 Dec. 1949, Philadelphia, Pennsylvania, USA; m. 1st Rivka Nahmani, 16 Aug. 1970, divorced 1986, two s. one d.; m. 2nd Erica Ando, 14 March 2000, one d. *Education:* BA, magna cum laude, 1971, MA, magna cum laude, 1973, Hebrew University of Jerusalem; DPhil, St John's College, Oxford, 1979. *Career:* Lecturer, Bezalael Acad. of Art, 1980–81; Visiting Lecturer, Hebrew University of Jerusalem, 1980–82; Lecturer, 1980–82, Senior Lecturer in English and Philosophy, 1983–87, Ben-Gurion University of the Negev, Beersheba, Israel; Visiting Fellow, St John's College, Oxford, 1984–85; Visiting Assoc. Prof., 1985–87, Assoc. Prof. of Philosophy, 1987–91, Full Prof., 1992–, Chair, Dept of Philosophy, 1998–, Temple University, Philadelphia; Dir of Studies, École des Hautes Études en Sciences Sociales, 1990; Visiting Prof., 1990, Dir of Studies, 1995–, College International de Philosophie; mem. American Philosophical Asscn; American Society for Aesthetics, Trustee. Literary Agent, Witherspoon Assocs. *Publications:* The Object of Literary Criticism, 1984; T. S. Eliot and the Philosophy of Criticism, 1988; Analytic Aesthetics, 1989; The Interpretive Turn: Philosophy, Science, Culture (ed. with D. Hiley and J. Bohman), 1991; Pragmatist Aesthetics: Living Beauty, Rethinking Art, 1992; L'Art á L'État Vif, 1992; Kunst Leben, 1994; Sous l'interprétation, 1994; Practicing Philosophy: Pragmatism and the Philosophical Life, 1997; La fin de l'éxperience esthétique, 1999; Performing Live, 2000; Vivre La Philosophie, 2001; Philosophie als Lebenspraxis, 2001; Surface and Depth, 2002. Contributions: books and journals. *Honours:* ACLS Grant, 1988; National Endowment for the Humanities Grant, 1988, Fellowship, 1990; Fulbright Scholarship. *Address:* Dept of Philosophy, Temple University, Philadelphia, PA 19122, USA.

SHUTTLE, Penelope Diane; Writer and Poet; b. 12 May 1947, Staines, Middlesex, England; m. Peter Redgrove 16 Sept. 1980 (died 2003); one d. *Publications:* Fiction: An Excusable Vengeance, 1967; All the Usual Hours of Sleeping, 1969; Wailing Monkey Embracing a Tree, 1974; The Terrors of Dr Treviles (with Peter Redgrove), 1974; The Glass Cottage, 1976; Rainsplitter in the Zodiac Garden, 1976; The Mirror of the Giant, 1979. Poetry: The Hermaphrodite Album (with Peter Redgrove), 1973; The Orchard Upstairs, 1980; The Child-Stealer, 1983; The Lion From Rio, 1986; Adventures With My Horse, 1988; Taxing the Rain, 1992; Building a City for Jamie, 1996; Selected Poems, 1980–1996, 1998; A Leaf out of His Book, 1999. Psychology and sociology: The Wise Wound: Menstruation and Everywoman (with Peter Redgrove) 1978; Alchemy for Women (with Peter Redgrove), 1995. numerous pamphlet collections, broadsheets, radio dramas, recordings, readings and television features. Contributions: various publications. *Honours:* Arts Council Awards, 1969, 1972, 1985; Greenwood Poetry Prize, 1972; E. C. Gregory Award for Poetry, 1974. *Literary Agent:* David Higham Associates, 5–8 Lower John St, Golden Sq., London W1F 9HA, England.

SHYAMALAN, M. Night; Indian film director, screenwriter, actor and producer; b. (Manoj Nelliyattu Shyamalan), 6 Aug. 1970, Pondicherry, Tamil-Nadu Prov.; m. Bhavna 1993; two c. *Education:* New York Univ. *Films:* Praying with Anger (writer, dir, actor, producer) 1992, Wide Awake (writer, dir) 1998, The Sixth Sense (writer, dir, actor) 1999, Stuart Little (screenplay writer) 1999, Unbreakable (writer, dir, actor, producer) 2000, Signs (writer, dir, producer) 2002, The Village (writer, dir, producer) 2004. *Publications:* juvenile: Stuart Finds His Way Home (with Kitty Richards) 1999, Stuart and the Stouts (with Greg Brooker) 2001, Stuart and Snowbell (with Greg Brooker) 2001. *Address:* United Talent Agency, 9560 Wilshire Blvd, Suite 500, Beverly Hills, CA 90212, USA.

SICILIANO, Enzo, PhD; Italian novelist, playwright and journalist; b. 27 May 1934, Rome; m. Flaminia Petrucci 1963; two s. *Career:* Literary Critic, La Stampa, Turin 1969–77; Jt Ed. with Dacia Maraini, Raffaele La Capria and Furio Colombo, Nuovi Argomenti 1972–; Literary Critic, Corriere della Sera, Milan 1977–1991, La Repubblica, Rome 1992–; Theatre Critic, Epoca, Milan 1982–85; Literary Critic, L'Espresso, Rome 1985–. *Publications:* Racconti ambigui 1963, Autobiografia letteraria 1971, Rosa (pazza e disperata) 1973, La notte matrigna 1975, Puccini 1977, Vita di Pasolini 1978, La voce di Otello 1982, Diamante 1984, La Letteratura Italiana (Vols 1, 2, 3) 1986, 1987, 1988, Cuore e fantasmi 1990, Carta Blu 1992, I bei momenti 1997, Non entrare nel campo degli orfani 2002, Memoriale da Tucidide 2004. *Honours:* Premio Viareggio 1981, Premio Strega 1998. *Address:* Nuovi Argomenti, via Sicilia 136, 00187 Rome (Office); via Tarvisio 1, 00197 Rome, Italy (Home). *Telephone:* (06) 47497376 (Office).

SIDDONS, Anne Rivers; Writer; b. 9 Jan. 1936, Atlanta, GA, USA; m. Heyward L. Siddons, 11 June 1966, four s. *Education:* BAA, Auburn University, 1958. *Career:* mem. Authors' Guild; International Womans Forum; Woodward Acad., Oglethorpe University. *Publications:* John Chancellor Makes Me Cry, 1975; Heartbreak Hotel, 1976; The House Next Door, 1978; Homeplace, 1986; Peachtree Road, 1988; King's Oak, 1990; Outer Banks, 1991; Colony, 1992; Hill Towns, 1993; Downtown, 1994; Fault Lines, 1995; Up Island, 1997; Low Country, 1998; Nora, Nora, 2000. Contributions: Magazines. *Honours:* Georgia Author of the Year Award, 1988; Hon. DLitt, Oglethorpe University, 1992, Auburn University, 1997; Lifetime Achievement, Georgia Writers, 1998. *Address:* 60 Church St, Charleston SC 29401-2885, USA.

SIDHWA, Bapsi; Writer and Prof. of English and Creative Writing; b. 11 Aug. 1939, Karachi, Pakistan; m. Nasher Rustam Sidhwa; two d. one s. *Education:* Kinnaird College for Women, Lahore. *Career:* self-published first novel, The Crow Eaters, 1978; Asst Prof., Creative Writing Programme, Univ. of Houston, Texas, USA, 1985; Bunting Fellowship, Radcliffe College, Harvard Univ., 1986; Asst Prof., Writing Div., Columbia Univ., New York, 1989; Visiting Scholar, Rockefeller Foundation Centre, Bellagio, Italy, 1991; Prof. of English and Writer-in-Residence, Mount Holyoake College, S Hadley, MA, 1997; Fannie Hurst Writer-in-Residence, Brandeis Univ., MA, 1998–99; Postcolonial Teaching Fellowship, Southampton Univ., UK, 2001; Chair., Commonwealth Writers Prize, 1993; mem., Advisory Cttee to Prime Minister Benazir Bhutto on Women's Devt, –1996, Punjab Rep., Asian Women's Conf., Alma Ata; Sec., Destitute Women's and Children's Home, Lahore. *Publications:* The Crow Eaters, 1978; The Bride, 1982; Ice-Candy-Man (aka Cracking India), 1991; An American Brat, 1993. Contributions: numerous short stories and reviews. *Honours:* Sitara-i-Imtiaz, 1991; Notable Book of the Year, New York Times, 1991; Nat. Award for English Literature, Pakistan Acad. of Letters, 1991; Patras Bokhari Award for Literature, 1992; Lila Wallace Reader's Digest Award, 1993; Excellence in Literature Award, Zoroastrian Congress, 2002. *Address:* c/o Oxford University Press, Banglore Town, Shahrah-e-Faisal, Karachi, Pakistan.

SIEGEL, Ira Theodore, MBA; American publishing executive; b. 23 Sept. 1944, New York City; m. Sharon R. Sacks 1965; three d. *Education:* New York and Long Island Univs. *Career:* Business Man. Buttenheim Publishing Co., New York 1965–72; Corp. Vice-Pres. (research) Cahners Publishing Co. (Div. Reed Publishing Co. USA, Boston) 1972–86; Pres. R.R. Bowker Publishing Co. (Div. Reed Publishing, USA, New York) 1986–91, Martindale-Hubbell Div. NJ 1990–91, Reed Reference Publishing 1991–95, Pres., CEO 1993–95; Pres., CEO Lexis-Nexis 1995–97; Pres. edata.com (now seisint) 1999–. *Address:* 16589 Senterra Drive, Delray Beach, FL 33484, USA. *Telephone:* (561) 999-4400 (Office); (561) 499-6457 (Home). *Fax:* (561) 999-4692 (Office). *E-mail:* ira@edata.com (Office).

SIEGEL, Robert (Harold); Writer, Poet and Prof. of English; b. 18 Aug. 1939, Oak Park, IL, USA; m. Roberta Ann Hill, 19 Aug. 1961, three d. *Education:* BA, Wheaton College, 1961; MA, Johns Hopkins University, 1962; PhD, English, Harvard University, 1968. *Career:* Asst Prof. of English, Dartmouth College, 1968–75; Lecturer in Creative Writing, Princeton University, 1975–76; McManes Visiting Prof., Wheaton College, 1976; Asst Prof., 1976–79, Assoc. Prof., 1979–83, Prof. of English, 1983–, University of Wisconsin at Milwaukee; mem. Authors' Guild; Associated Writing Programs. *Publications:* Fiction: Alpha Centauri, 1980; Whalesong, 1981; The Kingdom of Wundle, 1982; White Whale, 1991; The Ice at the End of the World, 1994. Poetry: The Beasts and the Elders, 1973; In a Pig's Eye, 1980. Contributions: anthologies, reviews, quarterlies and journals, including: Poetry; Atlantic Monthly; Cream City Review. *Honours:* University of Wisconsin Grants, 1978, 1984, 1988, 1996; Glatstein Prize, Poetry Magazine, 1977; Ingram Merrill Foundation Award, 1979; National Endowment for the Arts Fellowship, 1980; First Prizes, Society of Midland Authors, 1981, Council for Wisconsin Writers, 1981; Matson Award, Friends of Literature, 1982; Golden Archer Award, School of Library Science, University of Wisconsin at Oshkosh, 1986, 1999. *Address:* c/o Dept of English, University of Wisconsin at Milwaukee, Milwaukee, WI 53201, USA.

SIGAREV, Vassily; Russian playwright; b. 1977, Nizhnii Tagil, Sverdlovsk Oblast. *Plays:* Plasticine (Evening Standard Most Promising Playwright award) 2002, Black Milk 2003, Ladybird 2004. *Honours:* Anti-Booker Prize,

Moscow 2001. *Literary Agent:* Judy Daish Associates Ltd, 2 St Charles Place, London, W10 6EG, England. *Telephone:* (20) 8964-8811. *Fax:* (20) 8964-8966.

SILBER, Joan; Writer and College Teacher; b. 14 June 1945, Millburn, NJ, USA. *Education:* BA, Sarah Lawrence College, 1967; MA, New York University, 1979. *Career:* Faculty, Sarah Lawrence College, 1985–; Visiting Asst Prof., University of Utah, 1988; Visiting Lecturer, Boston University, 1992; Writer-in-Residence, Vanderbilt University, 1993; mem. Authors' Guild; PEN. *Publications:* Household Words, 1980; In the City, 1987; In My Other Life, 2000; Lucky Us, 2001; Ideas of Heaven, 2004. Contributions: books, newspapers, reviews and journals. *Honours:* PEN/Hemingway Award for the Best First Novel, 1981; Guggenheim Fellowship, 1984–85; National Endowment for the Arts Grant, 1986; New York Foundation for the Arts Grant, 1986; Pushcart Prizes, 2000, 2003. *Address:* 43 Bond St, New York, NY 10012, USA. *E-mail:* jksilber@earthlink.net.

SILKO, Leslie Marmon; Prof. of English, Writer and Poet; b. 15 March 1948, Laguna Pueblo, Albuquerque, NM, USA; two s. *Education:* BA, English, Univ. of New Mexico, 1969. *Career:* Teacher, Univ. of New Mexico; Prof. of English, Univ. of Arizona at Tucson, 1978–. *Publications:* Fiction: Ceremony (novel), 1977; Storyteller (short stories), 1981; Almanac of the Dead (novel), 1991; Yellow Woman and a Beauty of the Spirit (essays), 1993; Gardens in the Dunes (novel), 1999. Poetry: Laguna Woman, 1974. Non-Fiction: Leslie Silko (autobiog.), 1974; The Delicacy and Strength of Lace: Letters Between Leslie Marmon Silko and James Wright (biog.), 1986; Sacred Water: Narratives and Pictures (autobiog.), 1993; Conversations with Leslie Marmon Silko (biog.), 2000. Contributions: New Mexico Quarterly. *Honours:* National Endowment for the Arts Grant, 1974; Chicago Review Poetry Award, 1974; Pushcart Prize, 1977; John D. and Catherine T. MacArthur Foundation Fellowship, 1983. *Address:* c/o Dept of English, University of Arizona at Tucson, Tucson, AZ 85721, USA.

SILLIMAN, Ronald Glenn; editor and poet; b. 8 May 1946, Pasco, Washington, USA; m. 1st Rochelle Nameroff 1965 (divorced 1972); m. 2nd Krishna Evans 1986; two s. *Education:* Merritt College, San Francisco State College, University of California at Berkeley. *Career:* Ed., Tottel's, 1970–81; Dir of Research and Education, Committee for Prisoner Humanity and Justice, San Rafael, CA, 1972–76; Project Man., Tenderloin Ethnographic Research Project, San Francisco, 1977–78; Dir of Outreach, Central City Hospitality House, San Francisco, 1979–81; Lecturer, University of San Francisco, 1981; Visiting Lecturer, University of California at San Diego, La Jolla, 1982; Writer-in-Residence, New College of California, San Francisco, 1982; Dir of Public Relations and Development, 1982–86, Poet-in-Residence, 1983–90, California Institute of Integral Studies, San Francisco; Exec. Ed., Socialist Review, 1986–89; Managing Ed., Computer Land, 1989–. *Publications:* Poetry: Moon in the Seventh House, 1968; Three Syntactic Fictions for Dennis Schmitz, 1969; Crow, 1971; Mohawk, 1973; Nox, 1974; Sitting Up, Standing Up, Taking Steps, 1978; Ketjak, 1978; Tjanting, 1981; Bart, 1982; ABC, 1983; Paradise, 1985; The Age of Huts, 1986; Lit, 1987; What, 1988; Manifest, 1990; Demo to Ink, 1992; Toner, 1992; Jones, 1993; N/O, 1994; Xing, 1996. Other: A Symposium on Clark Coolidge (ed.), 1978; In the American Tree (ed.), 1986; The New Sentence, 1987. *Honours:* Hart Crane and Alice Crane Williams Award, 1968; Joan Lee Yang Awards, 1970, 1971; National Endowment for the Arts Fellowship, 1979; California Arts Council Grants, 1979, 1980; Poetry Center Book Award, 1985. *Address:* 1819 Curtis, Berkeley, CA 94702, USA.

SILLITOE, Alan; British author; b. 4 March 1928, Nottingham; m. Ruth Fainlight 1959; one s. one d. *Education:* elementary school, Radford, Nottingham. *Career:* worked in various factories including Raleigh Bicycles, Nottingham 1942–45; air traffic control asst 1945–46; served as wireless operator, RAF, Malaya 1946–49; lived six years in France and Spain; professional writer 1958–; Visiting Prof. of English, DeMontfort Univ., Leicester 1993–97; Fellow, Royal Geographical Soc., Royal Inst. of Navigation. *Film screenplays:* Saturday Night and Sunday Morning, The Loneliness of the Long Distance Runner, The Ragman's Daughter, Counterpoint. *Publications:* novels: Saturday Night and Sunday Morning 1958, The General 1960, Key to the Door 1961, The Death of William Posters 1965, A Tree on Fire 1967, A Start in Life 1970, Travels in Nihilon 1971, Raw Material 1972, The Flame of Life 1974, The Widower's Son 1976, The Storyteller 1979, Her Victory 1982, The Lost Flying Boat 1983, Down From The Hill 1984, Life Goes On 1985, Out of the Whirlpool 1987, The Open Door 1989, Last Loves 1990, Leonard's War: A Love Story 1991, Snowstop 1993, Alligator Playground 1997, The Broken Chariot 1998, The German Numbers Woman 1999, Birthday 2001, A Man of His Time 2004; short story collections: The Loneliness of the Long Distance Runner 1959, The Ragman's Daughter 1963, Guzman, Go Home 1968, Men, Women and Children 1973, The Second Chance 1981, The Far Side of the Street 1988, Collected Stories 1995, New Collected Stories 2004; essays: Mountains and Caverns 1975, The Mentality of the Picaresque Hero 1993, A Flight of Arrows 2004; poetry: The Rats and Other Poems 1960, A Falling Out of Love 1964, Love in the Environs of Voronezh 1968, Barbarians and Other Poems 1974, Storm and Other Poems 1974, Snow on the North Side of Lucifer 1979, Sun Before Departure 1984, Tides and Stone Walls (with Victor Bowley) 1986, Collected Poems 1993; travel writing: Road to Volgograd 1964, Leading the Blind: A Century of guide book travel 1815–1914 1995, The Saxon Shore Way (with Fay Godwin) 1983, Nottinghamshire (with David Sillitoe) 1986; plays: Three Plays 1978; All Citizens are Soldiers 1969 (trans. of Lope de Vega's Fuenteovejuna, with Ruth Fainlight); children's books: The City Adventures of Marmalade Jim 1967, Big John and the Stars 1977, The Incredible Fencing Fleas 1978, Marmalade Jim on the Farm 1980, Marmalade Jim and the Fox 1985, Alligator Playground 1998; autobiography: Life Without Armour 1995. *Honours:* Hon. Fellow, Manchester Polytechnic, De Montfort Univ. 1998; Dr hc (Nottingham Polytechnic) 1990, (Nottingham Univ.) 1994; Hawthornden Prize 1960. *Address:* 14 Ladbroke Terrace, London, W11 3PG, England.

SILMAN, Roberta; Writer; b. 29 Dec. 1934, New York, NY, USA; m. Robert Silman, 14 June 1956. *Education:* BA, English Literature, Cornell University, 1956; MFA, Writing, Sarah Lawrence College, 1975. *Career:* mem. PEN; Authors' Guild; Poets and Writers. *Publications:* Somebody Else's Child, 1976; Blood Relations, 1977; Boundaries, 1979; The Dream Dredger, 1986; Beginning the World Again, 1990. Contributions: numerous magazines in USA and UK. *Honours:* Child Study Asscn Award, Best Children's Book, 1976; Pen Hemingway Honorable Mention, 1978; Janet Kafka Prizes, 1978, 1980; Guggenheim Fellowship, 1979; National Endowment for the Arts Fellowship, 1983; PEN Syndicated Fiction Project Awards, 1983, 1984. *Address:* 18 Larchmont St, Ardsley, NY 10502, USA.

SILVER, Richard (see Bulmer, Henry Kenneth).

SILVERS, Robert Benjamin, AB; American literary editor; *Editor, The New York Review of Books*; b. 31 Dec. 1929, Mineola, NY. *Education:* Univ. of Chicago, Sorbonne, Ecole Polytechnique, Paris, France. *Career:* Press Sec. to Gov. of Connecticut 1950; US Army service 1950–53; Man. Ed. Paris Review 1954–58; Assoc. Ed. Harper's Magazine 1958–63; Co-founder and Co-Ed. New York Review of Books 1963–. *Honours:* Robert B. Silvers annual lectures at New York Public Library established 2002. *Address:* New York Review of Books, 1755 Broadway, 5th Floor, New York, NY 10019-3743, USA (Office). *Telephone:* (212) 757-8070 (Office). *Fax:* (212) 333-5374 (Office). *E-mail:* nyrev@nybooks.com (Office). *Website:* www.nybooks.com (Office).

SILVIS, Randall Glenn, BS, MEd; novelist and playwright; b. 15 July 1950, Rimersburg, Pennsylvania, USA; m. Rita Lynne McCanna 1982; two s. *Education:* Clarion Univ., Indiana Univ. *Career:* James Thurber Writer-in-Residence, Thurber House, Columbus, OH 1989; Visiting Writer, Mercyhurst Coll., Pennsylvania 1989–90, Ohio State Univ. 1991, 1992. *Film screenplays:* An Occasional Hell, Believe the Children, Mr Dream Merchant, Marguerite and the Moon Man, The Algerian. *Publications:* The Luckiest Man in the World, Excelsior, An Occasional Hell, Under the Rainbow, Dead Man Falling, On Night's Shore, Disquiet Heart, Heart So Hungry, Mysticus, In a Town Called Mundomuerto; contrib. to magazines. *Honours:* Nat. Endowment for the Arts Fellowship, Drue Heinz Literature Prize, Nat. Playwright Showcase Award, Fulbright Sr Scholar Research Grant, Screenwriting Showcase Award. *Address:* PO Box 297, St Petersburg, PA 16054, USA.

SIMIC, Charles, BA; American poet and writer; b. 9 May 1938, Belgrade, Yugoslavia; m. Helen Dubin 1965; one s. one d. *Education:* Oak Park High School, Chicago, Univ. of Chicago and New York Univ. *Career:* arrived in USA 1954; army service 1961–64; worked for Chicago Sun-Times as proofreader; later business Man. Aperture Magazine 1966–69; Lecturer, Calif. State Univ., Hayward 1970–73; Assoc. Prof., later Prof. of English, Univ. of New Hampshire 1973–; first vol. of poems published 1967; elected a Chancellor of The Acad. of American Poets 2000. *Publications include:* poetry: What the Grass Says 1967, Somewhere Among Us A Stone Is Taking Notes 1969, Dismantling the Silence 1971, White 1972, Return to a Place Lit by a Glass of Milk 1974, Biography and a Lament 1976, Charon's Cosmology 1977, Brooms: Selected Poems 1978, School for Dark Thoughts 1978, Classis Ballroom Dances 1980, Shaving at Night 1982, Austerities 1982, Weather Forecast for Utopia and Vicinity: Poems 1967–82 1983, The Chicken Without a Head 1983, Selected Poems 1985, Unending Blues 1986, The World Doesn't End (prose poems) 1989 (Pulitzer Prize for Poetry 1990), In the Room We Share 1990, The Book of Gods and Devils 1990, Selected Poems: 1963–83 1990, Hotel Insomnia 1992, A Wedding in Hell 1994, Walking the Black Cat 1996, Jackstraws 1999, Night Picnic 2001, The Voice at 3:00AM 2003; prose: The Uncertain Certainty 1985, Wonderful Words, Silent Truth 1990, Dimestore Alchemy 1992, The Unemployed Fortune Teller 1994, Orphan Factory (essays) 1997, A Fly in the Soup 2000; ed.: Another Republic: 17 European and South American Writers (with Mark Strand) 1976, The Essential Campion 1988, The Best American Poetry 1992; many trans of French, Serbian, Croatian, Macedonian and Slovenian poetry. *Honours:* PEN Int. Award for Translation 1970, 1980, Guggenheim Fellowship 1972, Nat. Endowment for the Arts Fellowships 1974, 1979, Edgar Allan Poe Award 1975, American Acad. of Arts and Letters Award 1976, Harriet Monroe Poetry Award 1980, Fulbright Fellowship 1982, Ingram Merrill Foundation Fellowship 1983, John D. and Catherine T. MacArthur Foundation Fellowship 1984, Acad. of American Poets Fellowship 1998. *Address:* Department of English, University of New Hampshire, PO Box 192, Durham, NH 03824 (Office); PO Box 192, Stafford, NH 03884, USA.

SIMIC, Goran; Writer, Poet and Dramatist; b. 20 Oct. 1952, Vlasenica, Yugoslavia; m. Amela Simic, 1 April 1982, two c. *Education:* University of Sarajevo. *Career:* mem. PEN Bosnia-Herzegovina, founder-mem.; PEN

Canada. *Publications:* Poetry: A Period Next to a Circle, or, A Journey, 1976; Vertigo, 1977; Mandragora, 1982; Sorrow of Sarajevo, 1996; Sprinting from the Graveyard, 1997; Sorrow and Other Poems, 1999; Walking across the Minefield (poems), 1999. Other: Prose, children's plays, radio plays and opera libretti. Contributions: anthologies, reviews, quarterlies and journals. *Honours:* several Yugoslav awards; Hellman-Hammet Grant, 1993; Freedom to Write Award, PEN Center West, USA, 1995; Canada Council Grants, 1996, 1998. *E-mail:* goransimic@utoronto.ca.

SIMMERMAN, Jim; academic and poet; b. 5 March 1952, Denver, CO, USA. *Education:* BS, Education, 1973, MA, English, 1976, University of Missouri; MFA, Creative Writing, University of Iowa, 1980. *Career:* Instructor, 1977–78, Asst Prof., 1983–86, Assoc. Prof. of English and Dir of Creative Writing, 1986–, Northern Arizona University; Editorial Board, Pushcart Prize Series, 1985–; mem. Associated Writing Programs, board of dirs, 1992–95, secretary, 1994–95; Rocky Mountain MLA. *Publications:* Home, 1983; Bad Weather, 1987; Once Out of Nature, 1989; Moon Go Away, I Don't Love You Anymore, 1994; Yoyo, 1994; Dog Music: Poetry About Dogs (co-ed.), 1996. Contributions: anthologies and journals. *Honours:* Arizona Commission on the Arts Fellowships for Poetry, 1983, 1987; National Endowment for the Arts Fellowship, 1984; Pushcart Writers Choice Selection, 1984, and Prize, 1985; Fine Arts Work Center Poetry Fellowship, 1984–85; Best of the Small Presses Book Fair Selection, 1990; Hawthornden Fellowship, Scotland, 1996. *Address:* c/o Northern Arizona University, Flagstaff, AZ 86011, USA.

SIMMIE, Lois; Writer and Poet; b. 11 June 1932, Edam, SK, Canada; two s. two d. *Education:* Saskatchewan Business College, 1951–52; University of Saskatchewan, 1973–77. *Career:* Writer-in-Residence, Saskatoon Public Library, 1987–88; Instructor, community colleges; mem. Asscn of Canadian Television and Radio Artists; Canadian Children's Book Centre; Saskatchewan Writers Guild; Writers' Union of Canada. *Publications:* Ghost House, 1976; They Shouldn't Make You Promise That, 1981; Pictures, 1984; Betty Lee Bonner Lives There, 1993; The Secret Lives of Sgt John Wilson: A True Story of Love and Murder, 1995. Contributions: numerous anthologies and periodicals. *Honours:* Awards and grants. *Address:* 1501 Cairns Ave, Saskatoon, SK S7H 2H5, Canada.

SIMMONS, Michael; writer and editor; b. 17 Oct. 1935, Watford, England; m. Angela Thomson, 20 April 1963, two s. *Education:* BA Hons, Russian, University of Manchester, 1960. *Career:* East Europe Correspondent, Financial Times 1968–72; Third World Ed., The Guardian 1978–82, E Europe Corresp. 1982–92, Deputy Ed. Society 1993–97. *Publications:* Berlin: The Dispossessed City 1988; The Unloved Country: A Portrait of the GDR 1989; The Reluctant President: A Life of Václav Havel 1992; Landscapes of Poverty, 1997, On the Edge 2002, Street Credo (ed.) 1999, Getting a Life (ed.) 2001. Contributions: various periodicals. *Address:* c/o The Sayle Agency, London N19 5JT, England. *E-mail:* micsimmo@compuserve.com.

SIMMONS, Richard D., AB, LLB; American newspaper publisher; b. 30 Dec. 1934, Cambridge, Mass.; m. Mary DeWitt Bleecker 1961; two s. *Education:* Harvard and Columbia Univs. *Career:* admitted to New York Bar; Assoc. Satterlee, Warfield & Stephens 1958–62; Gen. Counsel Giannini Science Corpn 1962–64; Vice-Pres. and Gen. Counsel Southeastern Publishing Service Corpn 1964–69; Counsel Dun & Bradstreet Inc., New York 1969–70, Vice-Pres. and Gen. Counsel 1970–72; Pres. Moody's Investors Service 1973–76, Dun & Bradstreet Inc. 1975–76; Exec. Vice-Pres. Dun & Bradstreet Corpn, New York 1976–78, Dir and Vice-Chair. Bd 1979–81; Pres. and COO The Washington Post Co. 1981–91, now Dir; Pres. Int. Herald Tribune 1989–96; Dir Washington Post Co. *Address:* 105 N Washington Street, Suite 202, Alexandria, VA 22314, USA.

SIMON, Claude; Author; b. 10 Oct. 1913, Tananarive, Madagascar. *Education:* Collège Stanislas, Paris. *Publications:* Le tricheur, 1945; La corde raide, 1947; Gulliver, 1952; La sacre du printemps, 1954; Le vent, 1957; L'herbe, 1958; La route des Flandres, 1960; Le palace, 1962; Femmes, 1966; Histoire, 1967; La bataille de Pharsale, 1969; Orion aveugle, 1970; Les corps conducteurs, 1971; Triptyque, 1973; Leçon de choses, 1976; Les Géorgiques, 1981; La chevelure de Bérénice, 1985; Discours de Stockholm, 1986; L'invitation, 1987; Album d'un amateur, 1988; L'acacia, 1989; Photographies, 1992; Le Jardin des Plantes, 1997; Le tramway, 2001. *Honours:* Prix de L'Express, 1960; Prix Médicis Étranger, 1967; Nobel Prize for Literature, 1985; Hon. Doctorate, University of Bologna, 1989; Grand Cross, Ordre National de Mérite, 1990. *Address:* c/o Editions de Minuit, 7 rue Bernard-Palissey, 75006 Paris, France.

SIMON, Neil; dramatist and screenwriter; b. 4 July 1927, New York, NY, USA; m. 1st Joan Balm 1953 (deceased); m. 2nd Marsha Mason 1973 (divorced); m. 3rd Diane Lander 1987. *Education:* New York University. *Career:* mem. Dramatists Guild; Writers Guild of America. *Publications:* Plays: Come Blow Your Horn, 1961; Barefoot in the Park, 1963; The Odd Couple, 1965; The Star-Spangled Girl, 1966; Plaza Suite, 1968; The Last of the Red Hot Lovers, 1969; The Gingerbread Lady, 1970; The Prisoner of Second Avenue, 1971; The Sunshine Boys, 1972; The Good Doctor, 1973; God's Favorite, 1974; California Suite, 1976; Chapter Two, 1977; I Ought to Be in Pictures, 1980; Fools, 1981; The Brighton Beach Memoirs, 1983; Biloxi Blues, 1985; Broadway Bound, 1986; Rumors, 1988; Lost in Yonkers, 1991; Jake's Woman, 1992; Laughter on the 23rd Floor, 1993; London Suite, 1995. Screenplays: After the Fox, 1966; The Out-of-Towners, 1970; The Heartbreak Kid, 1973; Murder by Death, 1976; The Goodbye Girl, 1977; The Cheap Detective, 1978; Seems Like Old Times, 1980; Max Dugan Returns, 1983; The Lonely Guy, 1984; The Sluggers Wife, 1984; The Marrying Man, 1991; Also many adaptations of his plays for films. Lyrics for Musicals: Little Me, 1962, revised version, 1982; Sweet Charity, 1966; Promises, Promises, 1968; They're Playing Our Song, 1979; The Goodbye Girl, 1993. Other: Rewrites: A Memoir, 1996; The Play Goes On, 1999. *Honours:* Tony Awards, 1965, 1985, 1991; Evening Standard Drama Award, 1967; Sam S. Shubert Award, 1968; Writers Guild Screen Awards, 1968, 1970, 1975, and Laurel Award, 1979; Pulitzer Prize in Drama, 1991.

SIMON, Sheldon (Weiss); Prof. of International Politics and Writer; b. 31 Jan. 1937, St Paul, MN, USA; m. Charlann Lilwin Scheid, 27 April 1962, one s. *Education:* BA, summa cum laude, 1958, PhD, 1964, University of Minnesota; MA, Princeton University, 1960; Postgraduate Studies, University of Geneva, 1962–63. *Career:* Visiting Prof., George Washington University, 1965, University of British Columbia, 1972–73, 1979–80, Carleton University, 1976, Monetary Institute of International Studies, 1991, 1996, American Graduate School of International Management, 1991–92; Asst Prof., then Prof., University of Kentucky, 1966–75; Prof. of Political Science, 1975–, Chair., Dept of Political Science, 1975–79, Dir, Center for Asian Studies, 1980–88, Arizona State University; mem. American Political Science Asscn; Asia Society; Asscn of Asian Studies; International Studies Asscn; US Council for Asia-Pacific Security. *Publications:* The Broken Triangle: Peking, Djakarta and the PKI, 1969; War and Politics in Cambodia, 1974; Asian Neutralism and US Policy, 1975; The Military and Security in the Third World (ed.), 1978; The ASEAN States and Regional Security, 1982; The Future of Asian-Pacific Security Collaboration, 1988; East Asian Security in the Post-Cold War Era (ed.), 1993; Southeast Asian Security in the New Millennium (ed.), 1996; The Many Faces of Asian Security (ed.), 2001. Contributions: scholarly books and journals. *Honours:* Grants; Fellowships. *Address:* c/o Dept of Political Science, Arizona State University, Tempe, AZ 85287, USA. *E-mail:* shells@asu.edu.

SIMPSON, Anne; Canadian poet, writer and artist. *Career:* fmr co-ordinator, Writing Centre, St Francis Xavier Univ., NS; writer-in-residence, Univ. of New Brunswick in Fredericton; mem. Writers' Union of Canada. *Publications include:* poetry: Light Falls Through You 2000, Loop (Griffin Poetry Prize 2004) 2003; novels: Canterbury Beach 2001; editor: An Orange from Portugal: Christmas Stories from the Maritimes and Newfoundland 2003. *Honours:* co-winner, The Journey Prize 1997, Lina Chartrand Award 1997, Bliss Carman Poetry Award 1999, Atlantic Poetry Award 2001, Gerard Lampert Award 2001. *Address:* McLelland and Stewart Ltd, 481 University Avenue, Suite 900, Toronto, ON M5G 2E9; c/o The Writers' Union of Canada, 90 Richmond Street E, Suite 200, Toronto, ON M5C 1P1, Canada.

SIMPSON, Dorothy M.; Author; b. 20 June 1933, Blaenavon, Monmouthshire, Wales; m. Keith Taylor Simpson, 22 July 1961, two s. one d. *Education:* BA, 1954, Teaching Diploma, 1955, University of Bristol. *Career:* Teacher of English and French, Dartford Grammar School for Girls, Kent, 1955–59, Erith Grammer School, Kent, 1959–61; Teacher of English, Senacre School, Maidstone, Kent, 1961–62; mem. Society of Authors; CWA. *Publications:* Harbinger of Fear, 1977; The Night She Died, 1981; Six Feet Under, 1982; Puppet for a Corpse, 1983; Close Her Eyes, 1984; Last Seen Alive, 1985; Dead on Arrival, 1986; Element of Doubt, 1987; Suspicious Death, 1988; Dead by Morning, 1989; Doomed to Die, 1991; Wake the Dead, 1992; No Laughing Matter, 1993; A Day for Dying, 1995; Once Too Often, 1998; Dead and Gone, 1999. *Honours:* Silver Dagger Award, 1985. *Literary Agent:* Curtis Brown Ltd, Haymarket House, 28–29 Haymarket, London, SW1Y 4SP, England. *Telephone:* (20) 7393-4400. *Fax:* (20) 7393-4401. *E-mail:* info@curtisbrown.co.uk. *Website:* www.curtisbrown.co.uk.

SIMPSON, Jerry Howard, Jr, BA; American writer; b. 11 Dec. 1925, Providence, RI; m. Jane Coral Augustine Simpson 1973; one s. one d. *Education:* Moravian Coll. for Men, Univ. of North Carolina. *Career:* mem. Comenian Literary Soc., Bike Tour France (founder, pres. and dir 1972–). *Publications:* Torn Land 1970, Annals of the Orient 1987, Cycling France 1992, Notes on the French Revolution 1994, Winter in Paris 1995, Mille Pensées Impolies (in French) 1996. Contributions: Reader's Digest; American History Illustrated; Bicycling; Wall Street Journal; Bike World. *Honours:* first place, Virginia Press Asscn 1969–70. *Address:* 5523 Wedgewood Drive, Charlotte, NC 28210-2432, USA. *Telephone:* (704) 527-0955. *E-mail:* demontaign@aol.com. *Website:* www.geocities.com/demontaign.

SIMPSON, Joe, BA; British novelist; b. 13 Aug. 1960, Kuala Lumpur, Malaysia. *Education:* Ampleforth Public School, Yorkshire, Edinburgh Univ. *Publications:* Touching the Void 1988, The Water People 1992, This Game of Ghosts 1993, Storms of Silence 1996, Dark Shadows Falling 1997, The Beckoning Silence 2002. *Honours:* Boardman-Tasker Prize 1988, NCR Non-Fiction Prize 1989, Asscn of Speakers' Clubs Speaker of the Year, Nat. Outdoor Book Awards Literary Category 2003. *Literary Agent:* c/o Vintage Publishing, Random House UK Ltd, 20 Vauxhall Bridge Road, London, SW1V 2SA, England. *Telephone:* (20) 7840-8400. *Fax:* (20) 7233-6117. *Website:* www.randomhouse.co.uk/vintage.

SIMPSON, John (Andrew); Linguist and Lexicographer; b. 13 Oct. 1953, Cheltenham, Gloucestershire, England; m. Hilary Croxford, 25 Sept. 1976, two d. *Education:* BA, English, University of York, 1975; MA, Medieval

Studies, University of Reading, 1976; DLitt, Australian National University, 1999. *Career:* Editorial Asst, 1976–79, Senior Ed., 1981–84, Supplement to The Oxford English Dictionary; Ed., New Words, 1984–86, Co-Ed., 1986–93, Chief Ed., 1993–, The Oxford English Dictionary; Fellow, Kellogg College, Oxford, 1991–; Mem., Faculty of English, University of Oxford, 1993–; Steering Cttee, European Federation of National Institutions for Language, 2002–; mem., Advisory Board, Opera del Vocabolario Italiano, 2003–; mem. Philological Society; Holton Cricket Club. *Publications:* The Concise Oxford Dictionary of Proverbs (ed.), 1982; The Oxford English Dictionary (ed. with Edmund Weiner), second edn, 1989, third edn (online), 2000–; The Oxford Dictionary of Modern Slang (ed. with John Ayto), 1992; The Oxford English Dictionary Additions Series (ed. with Edmund Weiner), two vols, 1993, general edn, vol. three, 1997. Contributions: scholarly books and journals. *Address:* Chestnut Lodge, 7 St Mary's Close, Wheatley, Oxford OX33 1YP, England. *E-mail:* john.simpson@oup.com.

SIMPSON, John (Cody Fidler); Broadcaster and Writer; b. 9 Aug. 1944, Cleveleys, England; m. 1st Diane Jean Petteys 1965 (divorced 1995); two d.; m. 2nd Adèle Krüger 1996. *Education:* MA, Magdalene College, Cambridge. *Career:* various positions, BBC, 1966–82; BBC Diplomatic Ed., 1982–88, Foreign, later World Affairs Ed., 1988–; Assoc. Ed., The Spectator, 1991–95; Columnist, The Sunday Telegraph, 1995–. *Publications:* The Best of Granta (ed.), 1966; Moscow Requiem, 1981; A Fine and Private Place, 1983; The Disappeared: Voices From a Secret War, 1985; Behind Iranian Lines, 1988; Despatches From the Barricades, 1990; From the House of War: Baghdad and the Gulf, 1991; The Darkness Crumbles: The Death of Communism, 1992; In the Forests of the Night: Drug-Running and Terrorism in Peru, 1993; The Oxford Book of Exile (ed.), 1995; Lifting the Veil: Life in Revolutionary Iran, 1995; Strange Places, Questionable People (autobiog.), 1998; A Mad World, My Masters: Tales from a Traveller's Life, 2000; News from No-Man's Land, 2002; The War Against Saddam, 2003. *Honours:* FRGS, 1990; CBE, 1991; BAFTA Reporter of the Year, 1991; RTS Richard Dimbleby Award, 1991, and Foreign Reporter Award, 1997; Columnist of the Year, National Magazine Awards, 1993; Hon. DLitt, De Montfort University, 1995; Peabody Award, USA, 1997; BAFTA News Award, 2000; RTS Reporter of the Year, 2000; RTS Award for Foreign Reporting, 2002; Hon. doctorates, Nottingham University, Suffolk College, 2000; Hon. Fellowship, Magdalene College, Cambridge, 2000. *Address:* c/o BBC Television Centre, Wood Lane, London W12 7RJ, England.

SIMPSON, Leo James Pascal; Canadian writer; b. 24 Sept. 1934, Limerick, Ireland; m. Jacqueline Anne Murphy 1964; one d. *Career:* writer-in-residence, Univ. of Ottawa 1973, Univ. of Western Ontario 1978. *Publications:* Arkwright 1971, Peacock Papers 1973, The Lady and the Travelling Salesman 1976, Kowalski's Last Chance 1980, Sailor Man 1996. *Address:* Moodie Cottage, 114 Bridge Street W, Belleville, ON K8P 1J7, Canada.

SIMPSON, Louis Aston Marantz, PhD CD; American writer and teacher; b. 27 March 1923, Kingston, Jamaica, West Indies; m. 1st Jeanne Rogers 1949 (divorced 1954); one s.; m. 2nd Dorothy Roochvarg 1955 (divorced 1979); one s. one d.; m. 3rd Miriam Bachner (née Butensky) 1985 (divorced 1998). *Education:* Munro Coll., Jamaica, Columbia Univ., New York. *Career:* Assoc. Ed. Bobbs-Merrill Publishing Co., New York 1950–55; Instructor, Asst Prof. Columbia Univ. 1955–59; Prof. Univ. of Calif. at Berkeley 1959–67; Prof. State Univ. of New York at Stony Brook 1967–91, Distinguished Prof. 1991–93, Prof. Emer. 1993–. *Publications:* poetry: The Arrivistes: Poems 1940–49 1949, Good News of Death and Other Poems 1955, The New Poets of England and America (ed.) 1957, A Dream of Governors 1959, At the End of the Open Road 1963, Selected Poems 1965, Adventures of the Letter I 1971, Searching for the Ox 1976, Armidale 1979, Out of Season 1979, Caviare at the Funeral 1980, People Live Here: Selected Poems 1949–83; The Best Hour of the Night 1983; Collected Poems 1988, Wei Wei and Other Poems 1990, In the Room We Share 1990, There You Are 1995, Nombres et poussière 1996 Modern Poets of France (trans.) 1997, Kaviar pä begravningen 1998; prose: James Hogg: A Critical Study 1962, Riverside Drive 1962, An Introduction to Poetry (ed.) 1967, North of Jamaica 1971, Three on the Tower: The Lives and Works of Ezra Pound, T. S. Eliot and William Carlos Williams 1975, A Revolution in Taste 1978, A Company of Poets 1981, The Character of the Poet 1986, Selected Prose 1989, Ships Going Into the Blue 1994, The King My Father's Wreck 1995. *Honours:* Hon. DHL (Eastern Mich. Univ.) 1977; Hon. DL (Hampden-Sydney Coll.) 1991; Prix de Rome American Acad. of Rome 1957, Hudson Review Fellowship 1957, Edna St Vincent Millay Award 1960, Guggenheim Fellowships 1962, 1970, ACLS Grant 1963, Pulitzer Prize for Poetry 1964, Columbia Univ. Medal for Excellence 1965, Commonwealth Club of Calif. Poetry Award 1965, American Acad. of Arts and Letters Award 1976, Inst. of Jamaica Centenary Medal 1980, Jewish Book Council Award for Poetry 1981, Elmer Holmes Bobst Award for Poetry 1987, Harold Morton Landon Award for Translation 1997. *Address:* P.O. Box 119, Setauket, NY 11733, USA (Home).

SIMPSON, Matt(hew William); Lecturer in English (retd), Poet and Writer; b. 13 May 1936, Lancashire, England; m. Monika Ingrid Weydert 13 Dec. 1961; one s. one d. *Education:* CertEd, Liverpool, 1959; MA, Cantab, 1961. *Career:* Lecturer in English, various schools; Poet-in-Residence, Tasmanian Poetry Festival, 1995. *Publications:* Letters to Berlin, 1971; A Skye Sequence, 1972; Watercolour From an Approved School, 1975; Uneasy Vespers, 1977; Making Arrangements, 1982; See You on the Christmas Tree, 1984; Dead Baiting, 1989; An Elegy for the Galosherman: New and Selected Poems, 1990; The Pigs' Thermal Underwear, 1994; To Tasmania with Mrs Meredith, 1993; Catching Up With History, 1995; Matt, Wes and Pete, 1995; On the Right Side of the Earth, 1995; Somewhere Down the Line, 1998; Cutting the Clouds Towards, 1998; Lost Property Box, 1998; Getting There, 2001; Hugging the Shore (essays), 2003; Nothing Extenuate: A Consideration of Shakespeare's Othello, 2003; A Man Forbid: A Consideration of Shakespeare's Macbeth, 2003. Contributions: reviews, quarterlies and magazines. *Address:* 29 Boundary Dr., Liverpool L25 0QB, England. *E-mail:* matt@galosher.freeserve.co.uk.

SIMPSON, Norman Frederick, BA; writer and dramatist; b. 29 Jan. 1919, London, England. *Education:* University of London. *Career:* teacher and extramural lecturer, Westminster College, London 1946–62; Literary Man., Royal Court Theatre, London, 1976–78. *Publications:* The Hole, 1958; One Way Pendulum, 1960; The Form, 1961; The Hole and Other Plays and Sketches, 1964; The Cresta Run, 1966; Some Tall Tinkles: Television Plays, 1968; Was He Anyone, 1973; Harry Bleachbaker (novel), 1974, US edn as Man Overboard, 1976; Inner Voices, 1983. *Address:* c/o Samuel French Ltd, 52 Fitzroy Street, London, W1T 5JR, England.

SINCLAIR, Andrew (Annandale); Writer and Historian; b. 21 Jan. 1935, Oxford, England; m. Sonia Melchett 25 July 1984; two s. *Education:* BA, PhD, Trinity Coll., Cambridge, 1955–59; Harkness Fellow, Harvard Univ., 1955–59; ACLS Fellow, Stanford Univ., 1964–65. *Career:* Founding Fellow, Churchill Coll., 1961–63; Lecturer, Univ. Coll. London, 1966–68; Publisher, Lorrimer Publishing, 1968–89; Managing Dir, Timon Films Ltd, 1968–2003; mem. FRSL, 1968; Society of American Historians, fellow, 1970. *Publications:* The Breaking of Bumbo, 1959; My Friend Judas, 1959; Prohibition: The Era of Excess, 1961; Gog, 1967; Magog, 1972; Jack: A Biography of Jack London, 1977; The Other Victoria, 1981; King Ludd, 1988; War Like a Wasp, 1989; The War Decade: An Anthology of the 1940s, 1989; The Need to Give, 1990; The Far Corners of the Earth, 1991; The Naked Savage, 1991; The Strength of the Hills, 1991; The Sword and the Grail, 1992; Francis Bacon: His Life and Violent Times, 1993; In Love and Anger, 1994; Jerusalem: The Endless Crusade, 1995; Arts and Cultures: The History of the 50 Years of the Arts Council of Great Britain, 1995; The Discovery of the Grail, 1998; Death by Fame: A Life of Elisabeth, Empress of Austria, 1998; Guevara, 1998; Dylan the Bard: A Life of Dylan Thomas, 1999; The Secret Scroll, 2001; Blood and Kin, 2002; An Anatomy of Terror, 2003. Contributions: Sunday Times; Times; New York Times; Atlantic Monthly. *Honours:* Somerset Maugham Prize, 1967; Venice Film Festival Award, 1971. *Address:* Flat 20, Millennium House, 132 Grosvenor Rd, London SW1V 3JY, England.

SINCLAIR, Iain Macgregor, BA; poet and writer; b. 11 June 1943, Cardiff, Wales; m. Anna Hadman 1967; one s. two d. *Education:* Cheltenham Coll., London Coll. of Film Technique, Trinity Coll., Dublin, Courtauld Inst., London. *Publications:* poetry: Back Garden Poems 1970, Muscat's Würm 1972, The Birth Rug 1973, Lud Heat 1975, Brown Clouds 1977, Suicide Bridge 1979, Fluxions 1983, Fresh Eggs and Scalp Metal 1983, Autistic Poses 1985, Significant Wreckage 1988, Selected Poems 1970–87 1989, Jack Elam's Other Eye 1992; fiction: White Chappell, Scarlet Tracings 1987, Downriver 1991 (Encore Award, James Tait Black Memorial Award 1992), Radon Daughters 1994, The Ebbing of the Kraft 1997, Slow Chocolate Autopsy 1997, Landor's Tower 2001, Dining on Stones 2004; essays: Lights Out for the Territory 1997, Liquid City 1998, Rodinsky's Room (with Rachel Lichtenstein) 1999, London Orbital: A Walk Around the M25 2002. *Address:* 28 Albion Drive, London, E8 4ET, England.

SINCLAIR, Olga Ellen, (Ellen Clare, Olga Daniels); Writer; b. 23 Jan. 1923, Norfolk, England; m. Stanley George Sinclair, 1 April 1945, three s. *Career:* mem. Society of Authors; Romantic Novelists Asscn; Society of Women Journalists; Norwich Writer's Circle, pres. *Publications:* Gypsies, 1967; Hearts By the Tower, 1968; Bitter Sweet Summer, 1970; Dancing in Britain, 1970; Children's Games, 1972; Toys, 1974; My Dear Fugitive, 1976; Never Fall in Love, 1977; Master of Melthorpe, 1979; Gypsy Girl, 1981; Ripening Vine, 1981; When Wherries Sailed By, 1987; Gretna Green: A Romantic History, 1989. As Olga Daniels: Lord of Leet Castle, 1984; The Gretna Bride, 1985; The Bride From Faraway, 1987; The Untamed Bride, 1988; The Arrogant Cavalier, 1991; A Royal Engagement, 1999. *Address:* Edenhurst, Potter Heigham, Norfolk NR29 5HZ, England.

SINCLAIR, Sonia Elizabeth, (Sonia Graham, Sonia Melchett); Writer; b. 6 Sept. 1928, Nainital, India; m. 1st Julian Mond (Lord Melchett), deceased June 1973, one s. two d.; m. 2nd Andrew Sinclair, 1984. *Education:* Queen's Secretarial College, Windsor, England. *Career:* Writer, Mem. of Board of Dirs, English Stage Company. *Publications:* (as Sonia Graham) Tell Me Honestly (non-fiction), 1964; (as Sonia Melchett) Someone is Missing (non-fiction), 1987; (as Sonia Melchett) Passionate Quests – Five Contemporary Women Travellers, 1989; Sons and Mothers (edited by Matthew and Victoria Glendinning), 1996. Contributions: periodicals. *Honours:* Prize-winner, Short Story Competition, Raconteur Magazine. *Address:* Flat 20, Millennium House, 132 Grosvenor Rd, London SW1V 3JY, England.

SINDEN, Sir Donald Alfred; Actor and Writer; b. 9 Oct. 1923, Plymouth, Devon, England; m. Diana Mahony, 1948, two s. *Career:* Professional Actor, 1942–; Films for the Rank Organization, 1952–60; Assoc. Artist, RSC,

1967–; mem. Council of British Actors Equity, 1966–77, trustee, 1988–; Arts Council, Drama Panel, 1973–77, Advisory Board, 1982–86; Federation of Playgoers' Societies, pres., 1968–93; Royal Theatrical Fund, pres., 1983–; FRSA, 1966–; Green Room Benevolent Fund, pres., 1998–. *Publications:* A Touch of the Memoirs, 1982; Laughter in the Second Act, 1985; Everyman Book of Theatrical Anecdotes (ed.), 1987; The English Country Church, 1988; The Last Word (ed.), 1994. *Honours:* CBE, 1979; Knighted, 1997; Freeman, City of London, 2000. *Literary Agent:* Vivien Green, Shiel Land, 43 Doughty St, London WC1N 2LF, England. *Address:* Number One, London NW11 6AY, England.

SINGER, Alan; Writer and Educator; b. 18 Oct. 1948, Atlantic City, NJ, USA; m. Nora Pomerantz, 22 June 1985, two d. *Education:* BA, University of California at Los Angeles, 1971; PhD, University of Washington, 1980. *Career:* Prof. of English, Dir of Graduate Creative Writing Programme, Temple University, Philadelphia, 1980–. *Publications:* The Ox-Breadth (fiction), 1978; A Metaphorics of Fiction (criticism), 1983; The Charnel Image (fiction), 1984; The Subject as Action (criticism), 1994; Memory Wax (fiction), 1996. *Honours:* Grants, Pennsylvania Arts Council. *Address:* 117 Carpenter Lane, Philadelphia, PA 19119, USA. *E-mail:* singerks@fast.net.

SINGER, June Flaum; Writer; b. 17 Jan. 1932, Jersey City, NJ, USA; m. Joseph Singer, 7 Sep 1950, one s., three d. *Education:* Ohio State University, Columbus, 1948–50. *Career:* mem. Southern California Society of Women Writers; PEN West; Authors' Guild. *Publications:* The Bluffer's Guide to Interior Decorating, 1972; The Bluffer's Guide to Antiques (US ed.), 1972; The Debutantes, 1981; Star Dreams, 1982; The Movie Set, 1984; The Markoff Women, 1986; The President's Women, 1988; Sex in the Afternoon, 1990; Till the End of Time, 1991; Brilliant Divorces, 1992. *Address:* 10661 Lindermere Dr., Bel-Air, CA 90077, USA. *E-mail:* junesinger@aol.com.

SINGER, Marilyn; Children's Writer; b. 3 Oct. 1948, New York, NY, USA; m. Steven Aronson, 31 July 1971. *Education:* BA, Queens College, CUNY, 1969; MA, New York University, 1979. *Career:* mem. Authors' Guild; PEN American Centre; Society of Children's Book Writers and Illustrators. *Publications:* 53 books, including: The Morgans Dream, 1995; A Wasp is not a Bee, 1995; Deal with a Ghost, 1997; Prairie Dogs Kiss and Lobsters Wave, 1998; Good Day, Good Night, 1998; Stay True, 1998. Contributions: periodicals. *Honours:* several awards for children's books. *Address:* 42 Berkeley Pl., New York, NY 11217, USA.

SINGER, Nicky Margaret; Novelist; b. 22 July 1956, Chalfont-St-Peter, England; m. James King-Smith, two s. one d. *Education:* University of Bristol. *Career:* Assoc. Dir of Talks, ICA, 1981–83; Programme Consultant, Enigma Television, 1984–85; Co-Founder, Co-Dir, Performing Arts Labs, 1987–96; Chair, Brighton Festival Literature Committee, 1988–93; Mem., ACE Literary Magazines Group, 1993–96; Board Mem., Printer's Devil, 1993–97, South East Arts, 2000–02; Presenter, Labours of Eve, BBC2, 1994–95. *Publications:* To Still the Child, 1992; To Have and To Hold, 1993; What She Wanted, 1996; My Mother's Daughter, 1998; Feather Boy (children's), 2002; Doll (children's), 2003. Non-Fiction: The Tiny Book of Time, 1999; The Little Book of the Millennium, 1999. Contributions: Printer's Devil; Guardian; Scotsman; Womens Journal. *Honours:* Blue Peter Book of the Year, 2002. *Address:* c/o Conville and Walsh, 2 Ganton St, London W1F 7QL, England.

SINGER, Peter Albert David; academic and writer; b. 6 July 1946, Melbourne, Vic., Australia; m. Renata Diamond 1968; three d. *Education:* BA, 1967, MA, 1969, University of Melbourne; BPhil, University College, Oxford, 1971. *Career:* Lecturer in Philosophy, University College, Oxford, 1971–73; Visiting Asst Prof. of Philosophy, New York University, 1973–74; Senior Lecturer in Philosophy, La Trobe University, Bundoora, Vic., Australia, 1974–76; Prof. of Philosophy, Monash University, Clayton, Victoria, 1977–79; Dir, 1983–91, Deputy Dir, 1992–98, Centre for Human Bioethics, Clayton, Australia; Co-Ed., Bioethics, 1986–98; DeCamp Prof. of Bioethics, Princeton University, 1999–. *Publications:* Democracy and Disobedience, 1973; Animal Rights and Human Obligations (ed. with Thomas Regan), 1975; Animal Liberation: A New Ethics for Our Treatment of Animals, 1975; Practical Ethics, 1979; Marx, 1980; The Expanding Circle: Ethics and Sociobiology, 1981; Test-Tube Babies (ed. with William Walters), 1982; Hegel, 1983; The Reproduction Revolution: New Ways of Making Babies (with Deane Wells), 1984, second edn as Making Babies: The New Science and Ethics of Conception, 1985; In Defence of Animals (ed.), 1985; Should the Baby Live?: The Problem of Handicapped Infants (with Helga Kuhse), 1985; Applied Ethics (ed.), 1986; Animal Liberation: A Graphic Guide (with Lori Gruen), 1987; Animal Factories (with Jim Mason), 1990; Embryo Experimentation (ed.), 1990; Companion to Ethics (ed.), 1991; How Are We to Live?, 1993; The Great Ape Project: Equality Beyond Humanity (ed. with Paola Cavalieri), 1993; Rethinking Life and Death, 1994; Ethics (ed.), 1994; The Greens, 1996; Ethics into Action, 1998; A Companion to Bioethics (with Helga Kuhse), 1998; A Darwinian Left, 1999; Writings on an Ethical Life, 2000; One World, 2002; Pushing Time Away, 2003; The President of Good and Evil: Taking George W. Bush Seriously, 2004. Contributions: Philosophy journals, newspapers and magazines. *Literary Agent:* The Robbins Office, 405 Park Avenue, Ninth Floor, New York, NY 10022, USA. *Address:* University Center for Human Values, Princeton University, Princeton, NJ 08544, USA.

SINGER, Sarah Beth; Poet and Writer; b. 4 July 1915, New York, NY, USA; m. Leon E. Singer, 23 Nov. 1938, one s. one d. *Education:* BA, New York University, 1934; Graduate Studies, New School for Social Research, New York City, 1960–64. *Career:* Teacher, poetry seminars and workshops, 1968–74, 1981–83; Consulting Ed., Poet Lore, 1976–81; mem. National League of American Penwomen; Poetry Society of America, vice-pres., 1974–78. *Publications:* After the Beginning, 1975; Of Love and Shoes, 1987; The Gathering, 1992; Filtered Images (anthology), 1992. Contributions: anthologies, newspapers and journals. *Honours:* Stephen Vincent Benét Narrative Poetry Awards, 1968, 1971; 5 Poetry Society of America Awards, 1972–76; National League of American Penwomen Awards, 1976–92; Washington Poets Asscn Award, 1989; Haiku Award, Brussels Sprouts, 1992. *Address:* 2360 43rd Ave E, Seattle, WA 98112, USA.

SINGH, Amritjit; Prof. of English, Writer, Trans. and Ed.; b. 20 Oct. 1945, Rawalpindi, India; m. Prem Singh, 24 March 1968, one s. one d. *Education:* BA, Panjab University, 1963; MA, Kurukshetra University, 1965; PhD, New York University, 1973. *Career:* Prof. of English, University of Delhi, 1965–68, CUNY, 1970–71, 1973–74, New York University, 1972–73, Hofstra University, 1984–86, Rhode Island College, 1986–; Sr Fulbright Prof., JFK Institute, Free Univ., Berlin, 2002; mem. MELUS, pres., 1994–97; South Asian Literary Asscn, pres., 2000–02; USACLALS, pres., 2000–03. *Publications:* The Novels of the Harlem Renaissance 1976, India: An Anthology of Contemporary Writing 1983, The Magic Circle of Henry James 1989, The Harlem Renaissance: Revaluations 1989, Memory, Narrative and Identity 1994, Conversations with Ralph Ellison 1995, Conversations with Ishmael Reed 1995, Memory and Cultural Politics 1996, Postcolonial Theory and the United States 2000, The Harlem Renaissance's Enfant Terrible 2002, The Collected Writings of Wallace Thurman: A Harlem Renaissance Reader 2003. Contributions: numerous essays and reviews in American Literature, Indian Literature, African American Studies. *Honours:* Fulbright Fellowship, 1968–69; National Endowment for the Humanities Fellowship, 1991–92. *Address:* Dept of English, Rhode Island College, Providence, RI 02908, USA.

SINGH, Gopal, PhD; Indian politician, poet and writer; b. 29 Nov. 1919, Serai Niamat Khan, NW Frontier Prov.; m. 1950; one d. *Career:* nominated MP 1962–68; Amb. to Bulgaria and Caribbean countries 1970–76; Chair. High Power Comm. of Minorities, Scheduled Castes, Scheduled Tribes and other Weaker Sections 1980–84; Gov. Goa, Daman and Diu 1984, of Nagaland 1989; has lectured at univs in UK, USA, Thailand, Egypt, Iran and India; fmr Sec.-Gen. Indian Council for Africa; Chair. Presidium, World Punjabi Congress. *Publications:* first free-verse English trans. of the Sikh Scripture, five books of Punjabi verse, A History of the Sikh People 1469–1978, The Religion of the Sikhs, A History of Punjabi Literature; The Unstruck Melody (poems), The Man Who Never Died (poems), collection of short stories, children's books, an English-Punjabi lexicon, several biogs and books of literary criticism. *Honours:* many awards and decorations.

SINGH, Khushwant; Author, Journalist and Politician; b. 2 Feb. 1915, Hadali, India; m. Kaval Malik, 1939, one s. one d. *Education:* BA, Government College, Lahore, 1934; LLB, King's College, London, 1938. *Career:* Called to the Bar, Inner Temple, London, 1938; Practised law, High Court, Lahore, 1939–47; Mem., Indian Foreign Service, 1947–51; Staff, Dept of Mass Communications, UNESCO, Paris, 1954–56; Ed., Illustrated Weekly of India, Mumbai, 1969–78; Ed.-in-Chief, National Herald, New Delhi, 1978–79; Hindustan Times, New Delhi, 1980–83, Contour, New Delhi, 1980–83; MP, 1980–. *Publications:* The Mark of Vishnu and Other Stories, 1950; Train to Pakistan, 1956; The Voice of God and Other Stories, 1957; I Shall Not Hear the Nightingale, 1959; A History of the Sikhs 1469–1964, two vols, 1963, 1966; Ranjit Singh: Maharajah of the Punjab 1780–1839, 1963; A Bride for the Sahib and Other Stories, 1967; Khushwant Singh's India: A Mirror for Its Monsters and Monstrosities, 1969; Khushwant Singh's India Without Humbug, 1977; Indira Gandhi Returns, 1979; Ed.'s Page, 1981; Tragedy of the Punjab: Operation Bluestar and After, 1984; The Collected Stories, 1989; My Bleeding Punjab, 1992. *Honours:* Rockefeller Grant, 1966; Punjab Government Grant, 1970; Mohan Singh Award, Padma Bhushan, India, 1974. *Address:* 49E Sujan Park, New Delhi 110003, India.

SINGH, Simon Lehna, BSc, PhD; British writer, journalist and television producer; b. 19 Sept. 1964, Wellington, Somerset, England. *Education:* Imperial Coll., Cambridge. *Television:* Fermat's Last Theorem (BBC) 1996, The Science of Secrecy (Channel 4) 2000, Funny You Should Ask (Discovery Channel) 2002, Mind Games (BBC4) 2003; worked on Earth Story series and fmr dir and prod., Tomorrow's World (both BBC). *Radio:* Five Numbers (BBC Radio 4) 2001, The Serendipity of Science (BBC Radio 4) 2001, Another Five Numbers (BBC Radio 4) 2003. *Publications:* Fermat's Last Theorem 1997, The Code Book 1999, The Science of Secrecy 2000. *Honours:* Vega Award for science broadcasting 2001. *Literary Agent:* Conville and Walsh Ltd, 118–120 Wardour Street, London, W1V 3LA, England. *Address:* PO Box 23064, London, W11 3GX, England. *E-mail:* simoncontact@hotmail.com. *Website:* www.simonsingh.net.

SINGLETON, William Dean; American newspaper proprietor; b. 1 Aug. 1951, Tex.; m. Adrienne Casale 1983; two s. one d. *Career:* Pres. Gloucester Co. Times, NJ.; Vice-Chair., Pres., CEO MediaNews Group, Inc. 1988–; Pres., Chair. The Houston Post 1988–95, The Denver Post; Vice-Chair. 27

daily newspapers and 55 non-daily publications including Houston Post, Denver Post, with daily circulation in excess of 1.1 million in 10 states. *Address:* Media News Group, 1560 Broadway, Suite 1450, Denver, CO 80202, USA.

SIPHERD, Ray; Writer; b. 27 Aug. 1935, Uniontown, Pennsylvania, USA; m. Anne Marie Foran, 4 Oct. 1986. *Education:* BA, Yale University, 1957. *Career:* mem. American Society of Composers, Authors and Publishers; Writers Guild of America. *Publications:* The White Kite, 1972; Ernie and Bert's Telephone Call, 1978; The Count's Poem, 1979; Down on the Farm with Grover, 1980; Sherlock Hemlock and the Outer Space Creatures, 1981; Big Bird's Animal Alphabet, 1987; When is My Birthday?, 1988; The Courtship of Peggy McCoy, 1990; The Christmas Store, 1993; Dance of the Scarecrows, 1996; The Audubon Quartet, 1998. *Honours:* Emmy Awards, 1969, 1974, 1985.

SIROF, Harriet Toby; Writer and Teacher; b. 18 Oct. 1930, New York, NY, USA; m. 18 June 1949, one s. one d. *Education:* BA, New School for Social Research, New York City, 1962. *Career:* mem. Authors' Guild; Society of Children's Book Writers. *Publications:* A New-Fashioned Love Story, 1977; The IF Machine, 1978; The Junior Encyclopedia of Israel, 1980; Save the Dam!, 1981; That Certain Smile, 1981; The Real World, 1985; Anything You Can Do, 1986; Because She's My Friend, 1993; The Road Back: Living With a Physical Disability, 1993; Bring Back Yesterday, 1996. Contributions: Colorado Review; Descent; Inlet; Maine Review; North American Review; New Orleans Review; Sam Houston Review; San Jose Studies; Woman; Voices of Brooklyn. *Honours:* Junior Literary Guild Selection, 1985. *Address:* 792 E 21st St, New York, NY 11210, USA. *E-mail:* hsirof@aol.com.

SISSON, Rosemary Anne; Writer; b. 13 Oct. 1923, London, England. *Education:* BA, University College London; MLit, Newnham College, Cambridge. *Career:* Junior Lecturer, University of Wisconsin, 1949–50; Lecturer, University College London, 1950–53, University of Birmingham, 1953–54; Drama Critic, Stratford-upon-Avon Herald, 1954–57; Trustee, Theatre of Comedy, 1986–; mem. Dramatists Club, hon. secretary; Writers Guild of Great Britain, pres.; BAFTA. *Publications:* The Exciseman, 1972; The Killer of Horseman's Flats, 1973; The Stratford Story, 1975; Escape From the Dark, 1976; The Queen and the Welshman, 1979; The Manions of America, 1981; Bury Love Deep, 1985; Beneath the Visiting Moon, 1986; The Bretts, 1987; The Young Indiana Jones Chronicles, 1993–95; Rosemary for Remembrance, 1995; Footstep on the Stair, 1997; First Love, Last Love, 2002; Murder, She Wrote, 2003. Contributions: newspapers and journals. *Honours:* Laurel Award, Writers Guild of Great Britain. *Address:* 167 New King's Rd, Parson's Green, London SW6, England.

SJÖWALL, Maj; Writer and Journalist; b. 1935, Malmö, Sweden; m. Per Wahlöö 1962 (died 1975); two s. *Career:* Ed., publishing house Wahlström and Widstrad, 1959–61. *Publications:* (with Per Wahlöö): Roseanna, 1965; Mannen Som Gick Upp i Rök (The Man Who Went up in Smoke), 1966; Mannen på Balkongen (The Man on the Balcony), 1967; Den Skrattande Polisen (The Laughing Policeman), 1968; Brandbilen Som Försvann (The Fire Engine That Disappeared), 1969; Polis, Polis, Potatismos (Murder at the Savoy), 1970; Den Vedervärdige Mannen Från Säffle (The Abominable Man), 1971; Det Slutna Rummet (The Locked Room), 1972; Polismördaren (Cop Killer), 1974; Terroristerna (The Terrorists), 1975; Kvinnan Som Liknade Greta Garbo (with Thomas Ross), 1990. *Address:* c/o Orion House, 5 Upper St Martin's Lane, London WC2H 9EA, England.

SKÁRMETA, Antonio; Writer, Essayist and Diplomat; b. 7 Nov. 1940, Antofagasta, Chile. *Education:* BA, Philosophy and Literature, University of Chile, 1963; MA, Philosophy and Literature, Columbia University, 1966. *Career:* Prof. of Contemporary Hispanoamerican Literature, University of Chile; Prof. of Screenplay Writing, German Acad. of Cinema and Television, Berlin; Distinguished Prof. of Romance Languages and Literature, Washington University, Saint Louis, MO; Ambassador to Germany, 2000–. *Publications:* El entusiasmo, 1967; Desnudo en el tejado, 1973; El ciclista del San Cristóbal, 1973; Tiro libre, 1973; Soñé que la nieve ardía, 1975, English trans. as I Dreamt the Snow Was Burning, 1985; Novios y solitarios, 1975; No pasó nada, 1980; La insurrección. 1982, English trans. as The Insurrection, 1983; Ardiente paciencia (El Cartero de Neruda), 1985, English trans. as Burning Patience, 1987 (filmed); Match Ball, 1989; Uno a uno: Cuentos de Antonio Skármeta (short stories), 1995; La composición, 1998; La boda del poeta, 1999; La chica del trombón, 2001. Other: Short stories, essays, screenplays, trans. Contributions: articles to periodicals on literature, film, exile, theatre and cultural politics. *Honours:* Orden al Mérito en el grado de Comendador, Italy; Chevalier, Ordre des Arts et des Lettres; Bocaccio International Literature Prize, Italy; Premio Casa de las Américas, 1969; Guggenheim Fellowship, 1986; Americas Award for Children's and Young Adult Literature, 2000; Grinzane Cavour Prize, 2001; Prix Médicis Étranger, 2001; many prizes for television and film screenplays. *Address:* c/o Carmen Balcells, Diagonal 580, Barcelona 08021, Spain.

SKELLINGS, Edmund; Prof., Dir and Poet; b. 12 March 1932, Ludlow, Massachusetts, USA; m. Louise Skellings, 6 Aug. 1962, one d. *Education:* BA, English, University of Massachusetts, 1957; PhD, English, University of Iowa, 1962. *Career:* Poet Laureate of Florida, 1980–; Dir, Florida Center for Electronic Communication, Florida Atlantic University. *Publications:* Duels and Duets, 1960; Heart Attacks, 1976; Face Value, 1977; Showing My Age, 1978; Living Proof, 1985; Collected Poems 1958–1998, 1998. *Honours:* Florida Governor's Award in the Arts, 1979; Hon. DFA, International Fine Arts College, 1995; Florida Arts Recognition Award, 1997. *Address:* 220 SE Second Ave, Fort Lauderdale, FL 33301, USA.

SKINNER, Ainslie (see Gosling-Hare, Paula Louise).

SKINNER, Gloria Dale, (Charla Cameron, Amelia Grey); Writer; b. 4 Aug. 1951, Graceville, FL, USA; m. Floyd D. Skinner, one s. one d. *Career:* mem. Romance Writers of America; Georgia Romance Writers; Authors' Guild. *Publications:* Passion's Choice, 1990; Georgia Fever, 1992; Tender Trust, 1993; Starlight, 1994; Midnight Fire, 1994; Bewitching, 1995; Ransom, 1996; Juliana, 1997; Cassandra, 1998; Hellion, 1998. As Charla Cameron: Diamond Days, 1991; Sultry Nights, 1992; Glory Nights, 1993. As Amelia Grey: Never a Bride, 2001; A Dash of Scandal, 2002; A Little Mischief, 2003. *Honours:* Love and Laughter Award, Romantic Times; Maggie Award, Georgia Romance Writers of America. *Address:* 2023 Thomas Dr., Panama City Beach, FL 32408, USA. *E-mail:* gloriadaleskinner@.att.net.

SKOCPOL, Theda; Prof. of Government and Sociology and Writer; b. 4 May 1947, Detroit, Michigan, USA; m. William John Skocpol, 10 June 1967, one s. *Education:* BA, Sociology, Michigan State University, 1969; MA, 1972, PhD, 1975, Sociology, Harvard University. *Career:* Asst Prof., 1975–78, Assoc. Prof., 1978–81, of Sociology, Victor S. Thomas Prof. of Government and Sociology, 1986–, Dir of the Center for American Political Studies, Harvard University; Mem., Institute for Advanced Study, Princeton, NJ, 1980–81; Assoc. Prof., 1981–84, Prof., 1984–86, of Sociology and Political Science, University of Chicago; Senior Visiting Scholar, Russell Sage Foundation, 1983–84; mem. American Acad. of Arts and Sciences, fellow; American Political Science Asscn, pres. 2002–03; American Sociological Asscn; National Acad. of Social Insurance; Organization of American Historians; Social Science History Asscn, pres., 1996; Sociological Research Asscn. *Publications:* States and Social Revolutions: A Comparative Analysis of France, Russia, and China, 1979; Protecting Soldiers and Mothers: The Political Origins of Social Policy in the United States, 1992; Social Revolutions in the Modern World, 1994; Social Policy in the United States: Future Possibilities in Historical Perspective, 1995; State and Party in America's New Deal, 1995; Boomerang: Clinton's Health Security Effort and the Turn Against Government in US Politics, 1996. Editor: Vision and Method in Historical Sociology, 1984; Bringing the State Back In (with Peter Evans and Dietrich Rueschemeyer), 1985; The Politics of Social Policy in the United States (with Margaret Weir and Ann Shola Orloff), 1988; American Society and Politics: Institutional, Historical, and Theoretical Perspectives (with John L. Campbell), 1994; States, Social Knowledge, and the Origins of Modern Social Policies (with Dietrich Rueschemeyer), 1996; The New Majority: Toward a Popular Progressive Politics (with Stanley B. Greenberg), 1997; Democracy, Revolution, and History, 1998; Civic Engagement in American Democracy (with Morris Fiorina), 1999; The Missing Middle: Working Families and the Future of American Social Policy, 2000, Diminished Democracy: From Membership to Management in American Civic Life 2003. Contributions: scholarly books and journals. *Honours:* Award for a Distinguished Contribution to Scholarship, 1980, Theory Prize, 1986, American Sociological Asscn; Guggenheim Fellowship, 1990; Woodrow Wilson Foundation Award, 1993; J. David Greenstone Award, American Political Science Asscn, 1993; Best Book Award, American Sociological Asscn, 1993; Allan Sharlin Memorial Award, Social Science History Asscn, 1993; John D. and Catherine T. MacArthur Foundation Grant, 1997–98; Pew Charitable Trusts Grant, 1997–99, Russell Sage Foundation Grants 1996–2000, 2000–03, Ford Foundation Grants 2000–01, 2001–04. *Address:* c/o Dept of Government, Littaver 233, North Yard, Harvard University, Cambridge, MA 02138, USA. *E-mail:* theda_skocpol@harvard.edu.

SKRZYNECKI, Peter; Australian poet, writer and lecturer; b. 6 April 1945, Imhert, Germany; m. Kate Magrath; one s. two d. *Education:* Univ. of Sydney. *Career:* Lecturer, Univ. of Western Sydney 1987. *Publications:* Poetry: There, Behind the Lids, 1970; Headwaters, 1972; Immigrant Chronicle, 1975; The Aviary: Poems, 1975–77; The Polish Immigrant, 1982; Night Swim, 1989. Fiction: The Wild Dogs; The Beloved Mountain, 1988. Other: Joseph's Coat: An Anthology of Multicultural Writing, 1985. *Honours:* Captain Cook Bicentenary Award 1970. *Address:* 6 Sybil Street, Eastwood, NSW 2122, Australia.

SKVORECKY, Josef; Czech writer; b. 27 April 1924, Náchod, Bohemia; m. *Education:* Charles Univ., Prague. *Career:* emigrated to Canada 1968; teacher, Univ. of Toronto 1971–91; founded publishing house with his wife. *Publications:* novels (titles translated): The Cowards 1958, The Emöke Legend 1963, The Bass Saxophone: Two Novellas 1969, Miss Silver's Past 1969, The Engineer of Human Souls 1977, Dvorak in Love 1986, The Miracle Game 1991, The Bride of Texas 1992, The Engineer of Human Souls 1999, Two Murders in My Double Life 2001; short story collection: When Eve Was Naked 2002. *Address:* c/o Granta, 2–3 Hanover Yard, Noel Road, London, N1 8DE, England. *Website:* www.granta.com.

ŠKVORECKÝ, Josef Václav; Canadian academic, writer, dramatist, poet, editor and translator; b. 27 Sept. 1924, Náchod, Czechoslovakia; m. Salivarová Zdenka 1958. *Education:* PhD, Charles Univ., Prague, 1951. *Career:* Ed., Anglo-American Dept, Odeon Publishers, Prague, 1953–56, Sixty-Eight Publishers Corpn, Toronto, 1972–95; Asst Ed.-in-Chief, World Literature Magazine, Prague, 1956–59; Visiting Lecturer, 1968, 1970, Writer-in-

Residence, 1970, Assoc. Prof., 1971–75, Prof. of English, 1975–90, Prof. Emeritus, 1990–, Univ. of Toronto; mem. Authors League of America; Crime Writers of Canada; Czechoslovak Society of Arts and Sciences, hon. mem.; International PEN Club; MWA; Writers' Union of Canada. *Publications:* Fiction: The Cowards, 1958; The End of the Nylon Age, 1967; Miss Silver's Past, 1969; The Tank Corps, 1969; The Miracle Game, 1972; The Swell Season, 1975; The End of Lieutenant Borůvka, 1975; The Engineer of Human Souls, 1977; The Return of Lieutentant Borůvka, 1980; Dvořák in Love, 1986; The Bride From Texas, 1992; Two Murders in My Double Life, 1996; Short Meeting With Murder (with Z. Škvorecký), 1999; An Inexplicable Story, or the Narrative of Questus Firmus Siculus, 2002. Short Stories: Eight collections, 1964–95. Plays: The New Men and Women, 1977; God in Your House, 1980. Poetry: Do Not Despair, 1979; The Girl From Chicago, 1980; When Eve Was Naked: Stories of a Life's Journey, 2002. Other: Reading Detective Stories, 1965; They-Which Is We, 1968; A Tall Tale About America, 1970; All the Bright Young Men and Women, 1972; Working Overtime, 1979; Jiri Menzel and the History of the Closely Watched Trains, 1982; Talkin' Moscow Blues, 1988; Headed for the Blues (memoir), 1996. Contributions: numerous publications. *Honours:* various hon. doctorates; Neutstadt International Prize for Literature, 1980; Guggenheim Fellowship, 1980; Fellow, Royal Society of Canada, 1984; Governor-General's Award for Fiction, 1984; City of Toronto Book Award, 1985; Echoing Green Foundation Literature Award, 1990; Mem. of the Order of Canada, 1992; Czech State Prize for Literature, 1999. *Address:* 487 Sackville Street, Toronto, ON M4X 1T6, Canada.

SLADE, Quilla (see Lewis-Smith, Anne Elizabeth).

SLATER, Nigel; British chef and food writer; b. Wolverhampton, West Midlands. *Career:* worked in restaurants from age 16; recipe tester, cook for food photography; Food Ed., Marie Claire magazine 1988; columnist, The Observer 1993–; presenter, Nigel Slater's Real Food (Channel 4) 1998–99. *Publications:* Marie Claire Cookbook 1992, Real Fast Food 1992, Real Fast Puddings 1993, Real Good Food: The Essential Nigel Slater 1995, 30-Minute Suppers 1996, Real Fast Desserts 1997, Real Cooking 1997, Nigel Slater's Real Food 1998, Appetite: So What Do You Want to Eat Today? 2000, Thirst 2002, Toast: The Story of a Boy's Hunger (autobiog.) 2003. *Honours:* Food Writer of the Year, André Simon Cookbook of the Year Award 2001. *Address:* c/o Fourth Estate, 77–85 Fulham Palace Road, London, W6 8JB, England.

SLATTA, Richard Wayne, BA, MA, PhD; academic and writer; *Professor of History, North Carolina State University;* b. 22 Oct. 1947, Powers Lake, ND, USA; m. Maxine P. Atkinson 1982; one s. *Education:* Pacific Lutheran Univ., Tacoma, WA, Portland State Univ., Oregon, Univ. of Texas at Austin. *Career:* Visiting Researcher, Instituto Torcuato di Tella, Buenos Aires 1977–78; Visiting Instructor, Univ. of Colorado at Boulder 1979–80; Asst Prof. 1980–85, Assoc. Prof. 1985–90, Prof. of History 1990–, North Carolina State Univ.; staff writer, Cowboys and Indians magazine 1994–, Persimmon Hill magazine 1994–; mem. American Historical Asscn, Conference on Latin American History, Western History Asscn, Western Writers of America. *Publications:* Gauchos and the Vanishing Frontier 1983, Bandidos: The Varieties of Latin American Banditry (ed. and contributor) 1987, Cowboys of the Americas 1990, The Cowboy Encyclopedia 1994, Comparing Cowboys and Frontiers 1997, The Mythical West 2001, Simón Bolívar's Quest for Glory 2003; contrib. to scholarly and general publications. *Honours:* Hubert Herring Book Prize, Pacific Coast Council on Latin American Studies 1984, Western Heritage Award for Non-Fiction Literature, Nat. Cowboy Hall of Fame 1991, Best Reference Source Citation, Library Journal 1992, Outstanding Reference Source Citation, American Library Asscn 1995. *Address:* Department of History, North Carolina State University, Raleigh, NC 27695-8108, USA. *E-mail:* slatta@ncsu.edu.

SLAVITT, David Rytman, (David Benjamin, Henry Lazarus, Lynn Meyer, Henry Sutton), MA; American writer, poet, translator and lecturer; b. 23 March 1935, White Plains, NY; m. 1st Lynn Meyer 1956 (divorced 1977); two s. one d.; m. 2nd Janet Lee Abrahm 1978. *Education:* Yale and Columbia Univs. *Career:* Instructor in English, Georgia Inst. of Technology, Atlanta 1957–58; writer, Assoc. Ed., Newsweek 1958–65; Visiting Lecturer, Univ. of Maryland 1977; Visiting Assoc. Prof. Temple Univ. 1978–80; Lecturer in English and Comparative Literature, Columbia Univ. 1985–86; teacher of creative writing, Rutgers Univ. 1987; Lecturer in English and Classics, Univ. of Pa 1991–97; Lecturer in English, Bennington Coll. 2000–; Assoc. Fellow, Trumbull Coll. Yale Univ.; has lectured widely at US univs and other academic insts. *Publications:* fiction: Rochelle, or Virtue Rewarded 1967, King Saul (play) 1967, Feel Free 1968, The Cardinal Sins (play) 1969, Anagrams 1970, ABCD 1972, The Outer Mongolian 1973, The Killing of the King 1974, King of Hearts 1976, Jo Stern 1978, Cold Comfort 1980, Ringer 1982, Alice at 80 1984, The Agent 1986, The Hussar 1987, Salazar Blinks 1988, Lives of the Saints 1990, Short Stories Are Not Real Life 1991, Turkish Delights 1993, The Cliff 1994, Get Thee to a Nunnery: Two Divertimentos from Shakespeare 1999, Aspects of the Novel: A Novel 2003; as Henry Sutton: The Exhibitionist 1967, The Voyeur 1968, Vector 1970, The Liberated 1973, The Proposal 1980, Kid's Stuff 2003; as Lynn Meyer: Paperback Thriller 1975; as Henry Lazarus: That Golden Woman 1976; as David Benjamin: The Idol 1979; poetry: Suits for the Dead 1961, The Carnivore 1965, Day Sailing 1968, Child's Play 1972, Vital Signs: New and Selected Poems 1975, Rounding the Horn 1978, Dozens 1981, Big Nose 1983, Adrien Stoutenburg: Land of Superior Mirages: New and Selected Poems (ed.) 1986, The Walls of Thebes 1986, Equinox 1989, Eight Longer Poems 1990, Crossroads 1994, A Gift 1996, Epic and Epigram 1997, A New Pléiade: Seven American Poets 1998, PS3569.L3 1998, Falling from Silence: Poems 2001, New and Selected Poems 2004; non-fiction: Understanding Social Life: An Introduction to Social Psychology (with Paul F. Secord and Carl W. Backman) 1976, Physicians Observed 1987, Virgil 1991, The Persians of Aeschylus 1998, Three Amusements of Ausonius 1998, The Book of Lamentations 2001, Re Verse: Essays on Poets and Poetry 2004; translator: The Eclogues of Virgil 1971, The Eclogues and the Georgics of Virgil 1972, The Tristia of Ovid 1985, Ovid's Poetry of Exile 1990, Seneca: The Tragedies 1992, The Fables of Avianus 1993, The Metamorphoses of Ovid 1994, The Twelve Minor Prophets 1999, The Voyage of the Argo of Valerius Flaccus 1999, Sonnets of Love and Death of Jean de Sponde 2001, The Elegies of Propertius 2001, The Regrets of Joachim du Bellay 2004; contrib. book reviews, articles in journals and magazines. *Honours:* Pennsylvania Council on the Arts Award 1985, Nat. Endowment for Arts Fellowship in Translation 1988, Nat. Acad. and Insts. of Arts and Letters Award 1989, Rockefeller Foundation Artist's Residence, Bellagio 1989. *Address:* 35 West Street, Unit 5, Cambridge, MA 02139, USA. *Telephone:* (617) 497-1219. *E-mail:* drslavitt@comcast.net. *Website:* www.davidslavitt.com.

SLOAN, Carolyn; Journalist and Children's Author; b. 15 April 1937, London, England; m. David Hollis 15 May 1961 (deceased); two s. *Education:* Harrogate College; Tutorial Schools, Newcastle, Guildford. *Career:* mem. Society of Authors. *Publications:* Carter is a Painter's Cat, 1971; Victoria and the Crowded Pocket, 1973; The Penguin and the Vacuum Cleaner, 1974; Shakespeare, Theatre Cat, 1982; Skewer's Garden, 1983; Helen Keller, 1984; An Elephant for Muthu, 1986; The Sea Child, 1987; Don't Go Near the Water, 1988; Gracie, 1994; Incredible Journey, 1996; The Rat, 1998; Victorian Day, 1999. Contributions: newspapers and journals. *Literary Agent:* David Higham Associates, 5–8 Lower John St, Golden Sq., London W1F 9HA, England. *Address:* 175 Stoughton Rd, Guildford, Surrey GU1 1LQ, England. *E-mail:* carolyn_sloan@btinternet.com.

SLOTKIN, Richard Sidney; Prof. of English and Writer; b. 8 Nov. 1942, New York, NY, USA; m. Iris F. Shupack, 23 June 1963, one s. *Education:* BA, Brooklyn College, CUNY, 1963; PhD, Brown University, 1967. *Career:* Asst Prof., 1966–73, Assoc. Prof., 1973–76, Prof., 1976–82, Olin Prof. of English, 1982–, Wesleyan University; mem. American Asscn of University Profs; American Film Institute; American Historical Asscn; American Studies Asscn; Authors' Guild; MLA; Organization of American Historians; PEN; Society of American Historians, fellow; Western History Asscn. *Publications:* Regeneration Through Violence: The Mythology of the American Frontier, 1600–1860, 1973; So Dreadful a Judgement: Puritan Responses to King Philip's War, 1675–1677 (with J. Folsom), 1978; The Crater: A Novel of the Civil War, 1980; The Fatal Environment: The Myth of the Frontier in the Age of Industrialization, 1800–1890, 1985; The Return of Henry Starr, 1988; Gunfighter Nation: The Myth of the Frontier in Twentieth Century America, 1992; Abe: A Novel of the Young Lincoln, 1999. Contributions: Professional journals. *Honours:* Albert J. Beveridge Award, American Historical Asscn, 1973; National Endowment for the Humanities Fellowship, 1973–74; Rockefeller Foundation Fellowship, 1976–77; Little Big Horn Asscn Award, 1986. *Address:* c/o Dept of English, Wesleyan University, Middletown, CT 06459, USA.

SLOVO, Gillian; South African novelist; b. 1952, Johannesburg; one d. *Education:* Manchester Univ., England. *Career:* researcher, journalist, film producer. *Publications:* novels: Morbid Symptoms 1984, Death by Analysis 1986, Death Comes Staccato 1987, Ties of Blood 1989, The Betrayal 1991, Facade 1993, Catnap 1994, Close Call 1995, Red Dust 2000, The Ice Road 2004; memoirs: Every Secret Thing: My Family, My Country 1997. *Literary Agent:* c/o Little, Brown, Brettenham House, Lancaster Place, London, WC2E 7EN, England. *Telephone:* (20) 7911-8000. *Fax:* (20) 7911-8100. *E-mail:* email.UK@twbg.co.uk. *Website:* www.twbg.co.uk.

SMALL, Michael Ronald, BA, BEd, MA; writer and poet; b. 3 Jan. 1943, Croydon, Surrey, England. *Education:* Univ. of London, La Trobe Univ., Australia, Univ. of Windsor, Canada. *Career:* teacher of English as a foreign language, RSA 1972; mem. Victorian Fellowship of Australian Writers, Melbourne Poets' Union. *Publications:* Her Natural Life and Other Stories 1988, Film: A Resource Book for Studying Film as Text (with Brian Keyte) 1994, Unleashed: A History of Footscray Football Club (with John Lack, Chris McConville and Damien Wright) 1996, Urangeline: Voices of Carey 1923–1997 1997; contrib. to numerous journals and magazines. *Address:* 71 Strabane Avenue, Box Hill North, Vic. 3129, Australia.

SMALLEY, Stephen Stewart; Cathedral Dean Emeritus and Writer; b. 11 May 1931, London, England; m. Susan Jane Paterson, 13 July 1974, deceased 3 Nov. 1995. *Education:* BA, 1955, MA, 1958, PhD, 1979, Jesus College, Cambridge; BD, Eden Theological Seminary, USA, 1957; Deacon, 1958, Priest, 1959, Ridley Hall, Cambridge. *Career:* Asst Curate, St Paul's, Portman Square, London, 1958–60; Chaplain, 1960–63, Acting Dean, 1962–63, Peterhouse, Cambridge; Lecturer and Senior Lecturer, University of Ibadan, Nigeria, 1963–69; Lecturer and Senior Lecturer, University of Manchester, 1970–77; Warden of St Anselm Hall, 1972–77; Canon Residentiary and Precentor, 1977–86, Vice-Provost, 1986, Coventry Cathedral; Dean, 1987–2001, Dean Emeritus, 2001–, Chester Cathedral; mem. Archbishops' Doctrine Commission of the Church of England, 1981–86; Studiorum Novi Testamenti Societas; Chester City Club. *Publications:* The Spirit's Power, 1972; Christ and Spirit in the New Testament (ed.), 1973; John: Evangelist and Interpreter, 1978; 1, 2, 3 John, 1984; Thunder and Love: John's Revelation and John's Community, 1994. Contributions: learned journals. *Honours:* Foundation and Lady Kay Scholar, Jesus College, Cambridge, 1948, 1955; Select Preacher, University of Cambridge, 1963–64; Manson Memorial Lecturer, 1986; Hon. LLD, University of Liverpool, 2001. *Address:* The Old Hall, The Folly, Longborough, Moreton-in-Marsh, Gloucestershire GL56 0QS, England. *E-mail:* stephen@sssss .jsworld.co.uk.

SMILEY, Jane Graves; writer and academic; b. 26 Sept. 1949, Los Angeles, CA, USA; m. 1st John Whiston 1970 (divorced); m. 2nd William Silag 1978; two d.; m. 3rd Stephen Mark Mortensen 1987 (divorced 1997); one s. *Education:* BA, Vassar College, 1971; MFA, 1976; MA, 1978, PhD, 1978, University of Iowa. *Career:* Visiting Asst Prof., University of Iowa, 1981, 1987; Asst Prof., 1981–84, Assoc. Prof., 1984–89, Prof., 1989–90, Distinguished Prof., 1992–96, Iowa State University; mem. Authors' Guild; Screenwriters Guild; American Acad. of Arts and Letters. *Publications:* Barn Blind, 1980; At Paradise Gate, 1981; Duplicate Keys, 1984; The Age of Grief, 1987; Catskill Crafts: Artisans of the Catskill Mountains (non-fiction), 1987; The Greenlanders, 1988; Ordinary Love and Goodwill, 1989; A Thousand Acres, 1991; Moo: A Novel, 1995; The All-True Travels and Adventures of Lidie Newton, 1998; Horse Heaven, 2000; Dickens (biog.), 2002; Good Faith, 2003. Contributions: various publications. *Honours:* Fulbright Grant, 1976–77; National Endowment for the Arts Grants, 1978, 1987; Friends of American Writers Prize, 1981; O. Henry Awards, 1982, 1985, 1988; Pulitzer Prize in Fiction, 1992; National Book Critics Circle Award, 1992; Midland Authors Award, 1992; Heartland Prize, 1992. *Address:* c/o Dept of English, Iowa State University, Ames, IA 50011, USA.

SMITH, Ali; British writer; b. 1962, Inverness, Scotland. *Education:* Univ. of Aberdeen. *Career:* gave lecture on Angela Carter, Nat. Portrait Gallery, London 2004. *Publications:* Free Love and Other Stories (Saltire First Book Award) 1995, Like (novel) 1997, Other Stories and Other Stories 1999, Hotel World (novel) (Encore Prize, Scottish Arts Council Book Award, Scottish Arts Council Book of the Year 2002) 2001, The Whole Story and Other Stories 2003, The Accidental (novel) 2004; contrib. to TLS, The Scotsman, Guardian. *Honours:* Scottish Arts Council Award 1995. *Address:* c/o Hamish Hamilton, Penguin Books, 27 Wrights Lane, London, W8 5TZ, England.

SMITH, Anthony Charles Hockley, MA; writer; b. 31 Oct. 1935, Kew, England. *Education:* University of Cambridge. *Career:* Literary Assoc., RSC, 1964–74; Senior Research Assoc., University of Birmingham, 1965–69; Dir, Cheltenham Festival of Literature, 1978–79; Chair., Playwrights Co, 1979–83; Visiting Prof., Emory University, Atlanta, GA, 1986, University of Texas, 1990–91, 1994; mem. Writers' Guild of Great Britain. *Publications:* The Crowd, 1965; Zero Summer, 1971; Orghast at Persepolis, 1972; Paper Voices, 1975; Treatment, 1976; The Jericho Gun, 1977; Edward and Mrs Simpson, 1978; Extra Cover, 1981; The Dark Crystal, 1982; Wagner, 1983; Sebastian the Navigator, 1985; Lady Jane, 1985; Labyrinth, 1986; The Dangerous Memoir of Citizen Sade, 2000. Other: 20 plays staged. Contributions: newspapers, magazines, and television. *Honours:* Arts Council Writing Awards, 1970–71, 1974–75, 1980; University of Bristol Drama Fellowship, 1976–79. *Address:* 21 W Shrubbery, Bristol BS6 6TA, England.

SMITH, Barbara Herrnstein; academic and writer; b. 6 Aug. 1932, New York, NY, USA; m. 1st R. J. Herrnstein 1951 (divorced 1961); m. 2nd T. H. Smith 1964 (divorced 1974); two d. *Education:* BA, 1954, MA, 1955, PhD, English and American Literature, 1965, Brandeis University. *Career:* Faculty, Bennington College, Vermont, 1961–73, University of Pennsylvania, 1973–87; Prof. of Comparative Literature and English, Duke University, 1987–, Dir Center for Interdisciplinary Studies in Science and Cultural Theory 1999–; Northrop Frye Chair, University of Toronto, 1990; Distinguished Prof. of English Brown Univ. 2003–. *Publications:* Poetic Closure: A Study of How Poems End, 1968; On the Margins of Discourse: The Relation of Literature to Language, 1978; Contingencies of Value: Alternative Perspectives for Critical Theory, 1988; The Politics of Liberal Education (co-ed.), 1991; Belief and Resistance: Dynamics of Contemporary Intellectual Controversy, 1997; Mathematics, Science and Postclassical Theory (co-ed.), 1997. Contributions: numerous rofessional journals. *Address:* c/o Box 90015, Duke University, Durham, NC 27708, USA.

SMITH, Bernard William, BA, PhD, FSA; Australian art historian, critic and poet; b. 3 Oct. 1916, Sydney, NSW; m. 1st Kate Beatrice Hartley Challis 1941; one s. one d.; m. 2nd Margaret Patricia Forster 1995. *Education:* University of Sydney, Warburg Institute, London, England, Australian National University. *Career:* Category A Literary Fellowship, Australia Council, 1990–91; mem. Australian Society of Authors; Australian Acad. of the Humanities, pres., 1977–80; Australian Humanities Research Council, secretary, 1962–65; UNESCO Committee for Letters, Australia, 1963–69. *Publications:* Place, Taste and Tradition, 1945; European Vision and the South Pacific, 1960; Australian Painting, 1962; The Architectural Character of Glebe, Sydney (with K. Smith), 1973; Documents on Art and Taste in Australia, 1975; The Boy Adeodatus, 1984; The Art of Captain Cook's Voyages (with R. Joppien), 3 vols, 1985–87; The Death of the Artist as Hero, 1988; The Critic as Advocate, 1989; Imagining the Pacific, 1992; Noel Counitian, 1993; Poems, 1996; Modernism's History, 1998; A Pavane for Another Time, 2002. Contributions: journals. *Honours:* Co-Recipient, Ernest Scott Prize for History, Melbourne, 1962; Henry Lawson Prize for Poetry, 1964; Hon. LittD, University of Melbourne, 1976, University of Sydney, 1997; Australian National Book Council Prize, Nettie Palmer Prize for Non-Fiction and Talking Book Award, 1984. *Address:* 168 Nicholson Street, Fitzroy, Vic. 3065, Australia.

SMITH, Bradley F.; Writer and Teacher; b. 5 Oct. 1931, Seattle, Washington, USA; m. 31 Dec. 1983, two d. *Education:* BA, 1957, MA, 1960, University of California at Berkeley. *Career:* mem. Authors' Guild. *Publications:* Adolf Hitler: His Family, Childhood, and Youth, 1967; Himmler Geheimreden, 1974; Reaching Judgement at Nuremberg, 1977; Operation Sunrise (with Elena Agarossi), 1979; The American Road to Nuremberg, 1981; The Road to Nuremberg, 1981; The Shadow Warriors, 1983; The War's Long Shadow, 1986; The Ultra-Magic Deals and the Special Relationship, 1940–46, 1992; Sharing Secrets with Stalin: Anglo-American Intelligence Co-operation with the USSR 1941–1945, 1996. Contributions: newspapers and journals. *Honours:* Observer Book of the Year, 1977. *Address:* 104 Regents Park Rd, London NW1 8UG, England.

SMITH, Charlie; Writer, Poet and University Lecturer; b. 27 June 1947, Moultrie, GA, USA; m. 1st Kathleen Huber 16 Sept. 1974 (divorced 21 June 1977); m. 2nd Gretchen Mattox 16 Dec. 1987 (divorced 16 Dec. 1997); m. 3rd Daniela Serowinski 2003. *Education:* BA, Duke University, 1971; MFA, University of Iowa, 1983. *Career:* Lecturer in Humanities and Creative Writing, Princeton University; Writer-in-Residence, University of Alabama, 2000; mem. Acad. of American Poets; International PEN; Poetry Society of America. *Publications:* Fiction: Canaan, 1985; Shine Hawk, 1988; The Lives of the Dead, 1990; Crystal River, 1991; Chimney Rock, 1993; Cheap Ticket to Heaven, 1996. Poetry: Red Roads, 1987; Indistinguishable from the Darkness, 1990; The Palms, 1993; Before and After: Poems, 1995; Heroin and Other Poems, 2000; Women of America, 2004. Contributions: literary journals and periodicals. *Honours:* Aga Khan Prize, Paris Review, 1983; Guggenheim Fellowship, 2000; National Endowment for the Arts Grant, 2000. *Address:* c/o Maria Carvainis, 1350 Avenue of the Americas, New York, NY 10019, USA.

SMITH, Dave, (David Jeddie Smith); Poet, Ed. and Prof. of English; b. 19 Dec. 1942, Portsmouth, Virginia, USA; m. Deloras Smith, 31 March 1966, one s. two d. *Education:* BA, English, University of Virginia, 1965; MA, English, Southern Illinois University, 1969; PhD, English, Ohio University, 1976. *Career:* Ed., The Back Door: A Poetry Magazine, 1970–78, The Southern Review, 1990–; Instructor in English, Western Michigan University, 1973–74; Asst Prof. of English, Cottey College, 1974–75; Asst Prof., 1976–79, Assoc. Prof. of English, 1979–81, Dir of Creative Writing, 1976–81, University of Utah; Poetry Ed., Rocky Mountain Review, 1978–79, University of Utah Press, 1980–90; Visiting Prof. of English, SUNY at Binghamton, 1980–81; Dir of Poetry, Bennington Writers Conference, Vermont, 1980–87; Assoc. Prof. of English and Dir of Creative Writing, University of Florida, 1981–82; Prof. of English, Virginia Commonwealth University, 1982–90; Prof. of English, 1991–97, Hopkins P. Breazeale Prof. of English, 1997–98, Boyd Prof. of English, 1998–2002, Louisiana State University; Elliot Coleman Prof. of Poetry, Johns Hopkins Univ., 2002–; mem. Associated Writing Programs; Fellowship of Southern Writers; MLA; Southern MLA. *Publications:* Bull Island, 1970; Mean Rufus Throw Down, 1973; The Fisherman's Whore, 1974; Drunks, 1975; Cumberland Station, 1977; In Dark, Sudden With Light, 1977; Goshawk, Antelope, 1979; Blue Spruce, 1981; Dream Flights, 1981; Homage to Edgar Allan Poe, 1981; Onliness (novel), 1981; The Travelling Photographer, 1981; The Pure Clear Word: Essays on the Poetry of James Wright, 1982; In the House of the Judge, 1983; Southern Delights (short stories), 1984; Gray Soldiers, 1984; The Morrow Anthology of Younger American Poets (ed.), 1985; The Roundhouse Voices: Selected and New Poems, 1985; Local Assays: On Contemporary American Poetry, 1985; Cuba Night, 1990; The Essential Poe, 1992; Night Pleasures: New and Selected Poems, 1992; Fate's Kite: Poems 1990–1995, 1996; Floating on Solitude: Three Books of Poems, 1997; The Wick of Memory: New and Selected Poems 1970–2000, 2000. Contributions: anthologies, reviews, and journals. *Honours:* Bread Loaf Fellow, 1975; National Endowment for the Arts Fellowships, 1976, 1980; American Acad. of Arts and Letters Award, 1979; Guggenheim Fellowship, 1981; Ohio University Alumni of the Year, 1985; Lyndhurst Fellowship, 1987–89; Virginia Poetry Prize, 1988. *Address:* 14 East Bishops Rd, Baltimore, MD 21218, USA.

SMITH, David Lawrence, BA, MA, PhD, FRHistS; Lecturer in History; b. 3 Dec. 1963, London, England. *Education:* Eastbourne Coll., Selwyn Coll., Cambridge. *Career:* Fellow 1988–, Dir of Studies in History 1992–, Admissions Tutor 1992–2003, Praelector 1996–, Selwyn Coll., Cambridge; Affiliated Lecturer in History, Univ. of Cambridge 1995–; Visiting Asst Prof. of History, Univ. of Chicago 1991; Visiting Prof. of History, Kyungpook Nat. Univ., Republic of Korea 2004; mem. Cambridge History Forum (pres. 1997–). *Publications:* Oliver Cromwell 1991, Louis XIV 1992, Cambridge Perspectives in History (co-ed.) 1993–, Constitutional Royalism and the Search for Settlement 1994, The Theatrical City (co-ed.) 1995, A History of the Modern British Isles, 1603–1707: The Double Crown 1998, The Stuart Parliaments, 1603–1689 1999, The Early Stuart Kings, 1603–1642 (with Graham E. Seel) 2001, Crown and Parliaments, 1558–1689 (with Graham E. Seel) 2001, Cromwell and the Interregnum (ed.) 2003, Oxford Dictionary of National Biography (assoc. ed.) 2004; contrib. to Historical Journal, Historical Research, Journal of British Studies, Transactions of the Royal Historical Society, Comparative Drama, Parliamentary History. *Honours:* Royal Historical Soc. Alexander Prize 1991. *Address:* Selwyn College, Cambridge, CB3 9DQ, England.

SMITH, Sir Dudley (Gordon); Management Consultant, Former MP and Writer; b. 14 Nov. 1926, Cambridge, England; m. 1st, divorced, one s. two d.; m. 2nd Catherine Amos, 1976. *Career:* Journalist and Senior Exec., various provincial and national newspapers, 1943–66; Asst News Ed., Sunday Express, 1953–59; MP, Conservative Party, Brentford and Chiswick, 1959–66, Warwick and Leamington, 1968–97; Management Consultant, 1974–; UK Delegate, Council of Europe and Western European Union, 1979–97; Pres., Western European Assembly, 1993–96. *Publications:* They Also Served, 1945; Harold Wilson: A Critical Biography, 1964. *Honours:* Knighted, 1983; Appointed a Deputy Lieutenant of Warwickshire, 1988; Commander of the Order of Isabela la Católica, Spain, 1994. *Address:* Church Farm, Weston-under-Wetherley, Near Leamington Spa, Warwickshire CV33 9BY, England.

SMITH, Emma; Writer; b. 21 Aug. 1923, Newquay, Cornwall, England; m. Richard Llewellyn Stewart-Jones, 31 Jan. 1951, deceased 1957, one s. one d. *Publications:* Maiden's Trip, 1948; The Far Cry, 1949; Emily, 1959; Out of Hand, 1963; Emily's Voyage, 1966; No Way of Telling, 1972; The Opportunity of a Lifetime, 1978. Contributions: various magazines. *Honours:* Atlantic Award, 1948; John Llewellyn Rhys Memorial Prize, 1948; James Tait Black Memorial Prize, 1949. *Literary Agent:* Curtis Brown Ltd, Haymarket House, 28–29 Haymarket, London, SW1Y 4SP, England. *Telephone:* (20) 7393-4400. *Fax:* (20) 7393-4401. *E-mail:* info@curtisbrown.co.uk. *Website:* www.curtisbrown.co.uk.

SMITH, Gregory Blake; Prof. and Writer; b. 24 July 1951, Torrington, CT, USA; m. Martha L. Smith, 13 April 1987, one s. *Education:* AB, Bowdoin College, 1975, MA, Boston University, 1981; MFA, University of Iowa, 1983. *Career:* Prof., Carleton College. *Publications:* The Devil in the Dooryard, 1986; The Divine Comedy of John Venner, 1992; Nietzsche, Heidegger and the Transition to Postmodernity, 1995. *Honours:* Stegner Fellowship, Stanford University, 1985; National Endowment for the Arts Fellowship, 1988. *Address:* c/o Dept of English, Carleton College, Northfield, MN 55057, USA.

SMITH, Hedrick (Laurence); Journalist, Writer, Television Commentator and Lecturer; b. 9 July 1933, Kilmacolm, Scotland; m. 1st Ann Bickford, 29 June 1957, divorced Dec. 1985, one s., three d.; m. 2nd Susan Zox, 7 March 1987. *Education:* Graduated, Choate School, 1951; BA, Williams College, 1955; Postgraduate Studies, Balliol College, Oxford, 1955–56. *Career:* Staff, United Press International, 1959–62; Diplomatic News Correspondent, 1962–64, 1966–71, Middle East Correspondent, 1964–66, Chief, Moscow Bureau, 1971–74, Washington Bureau, 1976–79, Deputy National Ed., 1975–76, Washington Correspondent, 1980–85, New York Times; Panelist, Washington Week in Review, PBS-TV, 1969–95; Visiting Journalist, American Enterprise Institute, 1985–87; Fellow, Foreign Policy Institute, School of Advanced International Studies, Johns Hopkins University, 1989–97; various PBS-TV documentaries; many lectures; mem. Gridiron Club. *Publications:* The Russians, 1975; The Power Game: How Washington Works, 1988; The New Russians, 1990; Rethinking America, 1995. With others: The Pentagon Papers, 1972; Reagan the Man, the President, 1981; Beyond Reagan: The Politics of Upheaval, 1986; Seven Days That Shook the World, 1991. *Honours:* Nieman Fellow, Harvard University, 1969–70; Pulitzer Prize for International Reporting, 1974; Overseas Press Club Award, 1976, and Citation, 1991; George Polk Award, 1990; Gold Baton Award, DuPont-Columbia University, 1990; George Foster Peabody Award, 1991; Hillman Award, 1996; William Allen White Award, University of Kansas, 1996.

SMITH, Iain Crichton; Poet and Writer; b. 1 Jan. 1928, Isle of Lewis, Scotland; m. Donalda Gillies Smith 16 July 1977; two step-s. *Education:* MA, English, University of Aberdeen, 1949. *Career:* mem. FRSL. *Publications:* Poetry: Thistles and Roses, 1961; The Law and the Grace, 1969; From Bourgeois Land, 1969; Love Poems and Elegies, 1972; Selected Poems, 1982; A Life, 1985; The Village and Other Poems, 1989; Collected Poems, 1992. Fiction: Consider the Lilies, 1968; The Last Summer, 1969; The Black and the Red (short stories), 1973; On the Island (short stories), 1974; The Hermit and Other Stories, 1977. Contributions: journals and magazines. *Honours:* PEN Poetry Award, 1970; Poetry Society Recommendations, 1972, 1975, 1989, 1992, and Choice, 1984; Commonwealth Poetry Prize, 1986; Saltire Award, 1992; Cholmondoley Award, 1997. *Address:* Tigh Na Fuaran, Taynuilt, Argyll, Scotland.

SMITH, Lee; professor emeritus; b. 1 Nov. 1944, Grundy, Virginia, USA; Teacher; Writer. m. 1st James E. Seay June 1967 (divorced); two c.; m. 2nd Hal Crowther June 1985. *Education:* BA, Hollins Coll., Virginia, 1967. *Career:* Faculty, Dept of English, North Carolina State Univ., Raleigh, 1981–; Fellow, Center for Documentary Studies, Duke Univ., 1991–93; mem. North Carolina Writers Network; PEN. *Publications:* The Last Day the Dogbushes Bloomed, 1968; Something in the Wind, 1971; Fancy Strut, 1973; Black Mountain Breakdown, 1980; Cakewalk (short stories), 1980; Oral History, 1983; Family Linen, 1985; Fair and Tender Ladies, 1988; Me and My Baby View the Eclipse (short stories), 1990; The Devil's Dream, 1992; Saving Grace, 1994; Christmas Letters, 1997; News of the Spirit, 1997; The Last Girls, 2002. *Honours:* O. Henry Awards 1979, 1981, 1984, John Dos Passos Award 1984, Sir Walter Raleigh Award 1984, North Carolina Award for Literature 1985, Lyndhurst Prize 1990–92, Robert Penn Warren Prize 1991, Acad. Award in Literature American Acad. of Arts and Letters 1999. *Address:* c/o MLS, POB 534, Efland, NC 27243, USA.

SMITH, Lew (see Floren, Lee).

SMITH, Martin Cruz, BA; American writer; b. 3 Nov. 1942, Reading, PA; m. Emily Arnold 1968; one s. two d. *Education:* Univ. of Pennsylvania. *Career:* fmr newspaperman, ed. *Publications:* The Indians Won 1970, Gypsy in Amber 1971, Canto for a Gypsy 1972, Gorky Park 1972, Nightwing 1977, Analog Bullet 1981, Stallion Gate 1986, Polar Star 1989, Red Square 1992, Rose 1996, Havana Bay 1999, December 6 (aka Tokyo Station) 1999, Death by Espionage: Intriguing Stories of Betrayal and Deception 2001. *Honours:* CWA Golden Dagger Award 1981. *Address:* c/o Pan Macmillan, 20 New Wharf Road, London, N1 9RR, England. *E-mail:* MCSmith@literati.net.

SMITH, Michael Marshall; Writer; b. 3 May 1965, Knutsford, England. *Education:* King's College, Cambridge. *Publications:* Only Forward, 1994; Spares, 1997; One of Us, 1998; What You Make It, 1999. Contributions: anthologies and periodicals. *Honours:* Three British Fantasy Awards. *Address:* c/o Ralph M. Vicinanza, 111 Eighth St, Suite 1501, New York, NY 10011, USA.

SMITH, Patricia Clark; Writer, Poet and Prof. of English; b. 14 Feb. 1943, Holyoke, MA, USA; m. 1st Warren S. Smith, 25 Aug. 1964, divorced 1976, two s.; m. 2nd John F. Crawford, 26 Nov. 1988. *Education:* BA, Smith College, 1964; MA, 1965, PhD, 1970, Yale University. *Career:* Lecturer in English, Smith College, 1968–69; Asst Prof. of English, Luther College, Decorah, IA, 1969–71; Asst Prof., 1971–82, Assoc. Prof., 1982–96, Prof. of English, 1996–, University of New Mexico. *Publications:* Talking to the Land (poems), 1979; Changing Your Story (poems), 1990; Western Literature in a World Context (co-ed.), two vols, 1995; As Long as the Rivers Flow: The Stories of Nine Native Americans (co-author), 1996. Contributions: anthologies and periodicals. *Address:* 2309 Headingly NW, Albuquerque, NM 87107, USA.

SMITH, Rosamond (see Oates, Joyce Carol).

SMITH, Sandra Lee; Writer and Teacher; b. 28 June 1945, San Francisco, CA, USA; m. Edward Leroy Smith Jr, 4 March 1967. *Education:* BA, 1967; Masters Degree, Bilingual/Multicultural Education, 1980. *Publications:* Loves Miracles (fiction), 1988; Coping with Decision Making, 1989; Dream Song (fiction), 1990; Value of Self Control, 1990; Drug Abuse Prevention, 1995; Flower for Angela (fiction), 1999. Contributions: various publications. *Honours:* Silver Pen Award, 1990. *Address:* 5433 S Mill Ave, Tempe, AZ, USA. *Website:* www.sandraleesmith.com.

SMITH, Sarah; writer; b. 9 Dec. 1947, Boston, Massachusetts, USA; m. 1st David Lee Robbins 1974 (divorced 1977); m. 2nd Frederick S. Perry 1979; two s. (one deceased) one d. *Education:* BA, Radcliffe College, 1968; Slade Film School and Queen Mary College, University of London, 1968–69; PhD, Harvard University, 1975; Certificate of Study, Harvard Business Program for PhDs, 1981. *Career:* Pres., Ivy Films, 1970–75; Asst Prof. of English, Tufts University, 1976–82; Field Ed., G. K. Hall, 1977–83; Man., artificial intelligence and computer-aided software engineering firms, 1982–90; Writer and Consultant, 1989–; mem. MWA, active mem., Webmaster; Sisters in Crime, NE Chapter Pres., 1999–2000; International Asscn of Crime Writers; PEN; SFWA; Signet Society, Harvard University. *Publications:* Colette at the Movies (non-fiction), 1980; Samuel Richardson: A Reference Guide, 1984; King of Space, 1991; The Vanished Child, 1992; Future Boston (co-author), 1994; The Knowledge of Water, 1996; Doll Street, 1996; Riders, 1996–97; A Citizen of the Country, 2000; Chasing Shakespeares, 2003. Contributions: Bulletin of the Authors' Guild; New York Review of Science Fiction, The Third Degree; Aboriginal; F & SF; Tomorrow; Shudder Again; Best New Horror 5. *Honours:* Susan Anthony Potter Prize, 1968; Fulbright Fellow, 1968–69; Harvard Prize Fellow, 1969–74; Frank Knox Fellow, 1972–73; Bowdoin Prize, 1975; Mellon Fellow, 1979–80; New York Times Notable Book Citations, 1992, 1996. *Literary Agent:* Christopher Schelling, Ralph Vicinanza Literary Agency, 303 W 18th Street, New York, NY 10011, USA. *Address:* 32 Bowker Street, Brookline, MA 02446-6955, USA. *E-mail:* sarah@sarahsmith.com. *Website:* www.sarahsmith.com.

SMITH, Steven Ross; writer and poet; b. 25 June 1945, Toronto, ON, Canada; m. J. Jill Robinson; one s. *Education:* Diploma in Radio and Television Arts, Ryerson Polytechnic Univ. *Career:* writer-in-residence, Wayburn Public Library 1987–88, Saskatoon 1996–97; Exec. Dir Sage Hill Writing Experience 1990–; mem. League of Canadian Poets, Saskatchewan Writers' Guild, Writers' Union of Canada. *Publications:* Ritual Murders 1983, Blind Zone 1985, Sleepwalkers (with Richard Truhlar) 1987, Transient Light 1990, Reading My Father's Book 1995, Fluttertongue (two vols) 1998–99, Ballet of the Speech Organs: Bob Cobbing on Bob Cobbing 1998; contrib. to periodicals. *Address:* 920 Ninth Avenue N, Saskatoon, SK S7K 2Z4, Canada. *E-mail:* steven.ross.smith@sasktel.net.

SMITH, Vivian (Brian); Lecturer, Poet and Ed.; b. 3 June 1933, Hobart, Tasmania, Australia; m. Sybille Gottwald, 15 Feb. 1960, one s. two d. *Education:* MA, 1955, PhD, 1970, University of Sydney. *Career:* Lecturer, University of Tasmania, 1955–66; Literary Ed., Quadrant magazine, Sydney, 1975–90; Reader, University of Sydney, 1982–96; mem. Australian Society of Authors; PEN; Australian Acad. of the Humanities, fellow. *Publications:* The Other Meaning, 1956; An Island South, 1967; The Poetry of Robert Lowell, 1975; Familiar Places, 1978; Tide Country, 1982; Tasmania and Australian Poetry, 1984; Selected Poems, 1985; New Selected Poems, 1995; Late News, 2000. Contributions: newspapers and magazines. *Honours:* Grace Leven Prize; New South Wales Premier's Prize, 1983; Patrick White Literary Award, 1997. *Address:* 19 McLeod St, Mosman, NSW 2088, Australia. *Telephone:* (2) 9969-1370. *E-mail:* smith@sydney.dialix.com.au.

SMITH, Ward (see Goldsmith, Howard).

SMITH, Wilbur Addison, BComm; British novelist; b. 9 Jan. 1933, Zambia; m. 1st Danielle Antoinette Smith 1971 (died 1999); two s. one d.; m. 2nd Mokhiniso Rakhimova 2000. *Education:* Michaelhouse, Natal and Rhodes Univ. *Career:* business exec. 1954–58; factory owner 1958–64; professional author 1961–. *Publications:* When the Lion Feeds 1964, The Dark of the Sun 1965, The Sound of Thunder 1966, Shout at the Devil 1968, Gold Mine 1970, The Diamond Hunters 1971, The Sunbird 1972, Eagle in the Sky 1974, The Eye of the Tiger 1975, Cry Wolf 1976, A Sparrow Falls 1977, Hungry as the Sea 1978, Wild Justice 1979, A Falcon Flies 1980, Men of Men 1981, The Angels Weep 1982, The Leopard Hunts in Darkness 1984, The Burning Shore 1985, Power of the Sword 1986, Rage 1987, The Courtneys 1987, The Courtneys in Africa 1988, A Time to Die 1989, Golden Fox 1990, Elephant Song 1991, River God 1993, The Seventh Scroll 1995, Birds of Prey 1997, Monsoon 1999, Warlock 2001, Blue Horizon 2003; contrib. to numerous journals and magazines. *Literary Agent:* Charles Pick Consultancy, 21 Dagmar Terrace, London, N1 2BN, England. *Website:* www.wilbursmith.net.

SMITH, William Jay, BA, MA; American poet, writer and professor of English emeritus; b. 22 April 1918, Winnfield, LA; m. 1st Barbara Howes 1947 (divorced 1965); two s.; m. 2nd Sonja Haussmann 1966; one step-s. *Education:* Washington Univ., St Louis, Institut de Touraine, Tours, France, Columbia Univ., Wadham Coll., Oxford, Univ. of Florence. *Career:* instructor 1946–47, Visiting Prof. 1973–75, Columbia Univ.; instructor 1951, poet-in-residence and Lecturer 1959–64, 1966–67, Williams Coll.; writer-in-residence 1965–66, Prof. of English 1967–68, 1970–80, Prof. Emeritus 1980–, Hollins Coll., Virginia; consultant in poetry 1968–70, hon. consultant 1970–76, Library of Congress, Washington, DC; Lecturer, Salzburg Seminar in American Studies 1974; Fulbright Lecturer, Moscow State Univ. 1981; poet-in-residence, Cathedral of St John the Divine, New York 1985–88; mem. American Acad. of Arts and Letters (vice-pres. for literature 1986–89). *Publications:* Poetry: Poems, 1947; Celebrating at Dark, 1950; Snow, 1953; The Stork, 1954; Typewriter Birds, 1954; The Bead Curtain: Calligrams, 1957; The Old Man on the Isthmus, 1957; Poems 1947–1957, 1957; Prince Souvanna Phouma: An Exchange Between Richard Wilbur and William Jay Smith, 1963; Morels, 1964; The Tin Can and Other Poems, 1966; New and Selected Poems, 1970; A Rose for Katherine Anne Porter, 1970; At Delphi: For Allen Tate on His Seventy-Fifth Birthday, 19 November 1974, 1974; Venice in the Fog, 1975; Verses on the Times (with Richard Wilbur), 1978; Journey to the Dead Sea, 1979; The Tall Poets, 1979; Mr Smith, 1980; The Traveler's Tree: New and Selected Poems, 1980; Oxford Doggerel, 1983; Collected Translator: Italian, French, Spanish, Portuguese, 1985; The Tin Can, 1988; Journey to the Interior, 1988; Plain Talk: Epigrams, Epitaphs, Satires, Nonsense, Occasional, Concrete and Quotidian Poems, 1988; Collected Poems 1939–1989, 1990; The World Below the Window: Poems 1937–1997, 1998; The Cherokee Lottery: A Sequence of Poems 2001, The Girl in Glass: Love Poems, 2002, 17 books of poetry for children 1955–90. Other: The Spectra Hoax, 1961; The Skies of Venice, 1961; Children and Poetry: A Selective Bibliography (with Virginia Haviland), 1969; Louise Bogan: A Woman's Words, 1972; The Streaks of the Tulip: Selected Criticism, 1972; Green, 1980; Army Brat: A Memoir, 1980. Editor: Herrick, 1962; The Golden Journey: Poems for Young People (with Louise Bogan), 1965; Poems from France, 1967; Poems from Italy, 1972; A Green Place: Modern Poems, 1982. Contributions: journals and magazines. *Honours:* Rhodes Scholar 1947–48, Ford Foundation Fellowship 1964, Henry Bellamann Major Award 1970, National Endowment for the Arts Grant 1972, 1995, National Endowment for the Humanities Grants 1975, 1989, Gold Medal of Labor, Hungary 1978, Ingram Merrill Foundation Grant 1982, Trans. Award, Swedish Acad. 1990, Médaille de Vermeil Acad. Française 1991, Pro Cultura Hungarica Medal 1993, René Vásquez Díaz Prize, Swedish Acad. 1997. *Address:* 63 Luther Shaw Road, Cummington, MA 01026, USA; 52–56 rue d'Alleray, 75015 Paris, France; 52–56 rue d'Alleray, 75015 Paris, France.

SMITH, Z. Z. (see Westheimer, David).

SMITH, Zadie; British writer and poet; b. (Sadie Smith), 27 Oct. 1975, London. *Education:* King's Coll., Cambridge. *Career:* Writer-in-Residence, Inst. of Contemporary Arts, London; Radcliffe Fellow, Harvard Univ. *Publication:* White Teeth (novel) (Guardian First Book Award 2001, Whitbread First Novel and Book of the Year Awards 2001, James Tait Memorial Prize for Fiction 2001, Commonwealth Writers' Best First Book Prize 2001) 2000, Piece of Flesh (ed.) 2001, The May Anthologies (ed.) 2001, The Autograph Man (novel) 2002, The Burned Children of America (ed.) 2003, On Beauty 2005; contribs to anthologies and periodicals. *Honours:* Rylands Prize, King's Coll. London, Betty Trask Prize 2001. *Literary Agent:* A. P. Watt Ltd, 20 John Street, London, WC1N 2DR, England. *Telephone:* (20) 7405-6774. *Fax:* (20) 7831-2154. *E-mail:* zsmith@literati.net.

SMITHER, Elizabeth Edwina; New Zealand poet, novelist and short story writer; b. 15 Sept. 1941, New Plymouth; m. Michael Duncan Smither 1963; three c. *Education:* Univ. of Victoria, Massey Univ., New Zealand Library School. *Career:* part-time librarian; Te Mata Estate New Zealand Poet Laureate 2001–03; mem. New Zealand Soc. of Authors. *Publications:* poetry: Here Come the Clouds 1975, You're Very Seductive William Carlos Williams 1978, The Sarah Train 1980, The Legend of Marcello Mastroianni's Wife 1981, Casanova's Ankle 1981, Shakespeare Virgins 1983, Professor Musgrove's Canary 1986, Gorilla/ Guerilla 1986, Animaux 1988, A Pattern of Marching (New Zealand Book Award 1990) 1989, A Cortège of Daughters 1993, The Tudor Style: Poems New and Selected 1993, The Lark Quartet (Montana New Zealand Book Award 2000) 1999, Red Shoes 2003; novels: First Blood 1983, Brother-love Sister-love 1986; short story collections: Nights at the Embassy 1990, Mr Fish 1994, The Mathematics of Jane Austen 1997; other: Tug Brothers (juvenile) 1983, The Seventies Connection (co-ed.) 1987, The Journal Box (journals) 1996. *Honours:* Scholarships in Letters 1987, 1992, Hon. DLitt (Auckland Univ.) 2004. *Address:* 19a Mount View Place, New Plymouth, New Zealand.

SMITTEN, Richard; Writer; b. 22 April 1940, New York, NY, USA; one d. *Education:* BA, University of Western Ontario. *Publications:* Twice Killed, 1987; The Man Who Made it Snow (with Max Mermelstein and Robin Moore), 1990; Godmother, 1990; Bank of Death, 1993; Legal Tender, 1994. *Address:* 3675 Skyline Dr., Jensen Beach, FL 34957, USA.

SMYTHE, Colin Peter, BA, MA, FRSA; editor, publisher and literary agent; b. 2 March 1942, Maidenhead, Berkshire, England. *Education:* Bradfield College, Berkshire, Trinity College, Dublin, University of Ulster. *Career:* mem. The Athenaeum; Beefsteak Club; Mark Twain Society, hon. mem. *Publications:* Irish Literary Studies series (general ed.); Lady Gregory's Writings (general ed.), 1970–; Lady Gregory, 1971–; A Guide to Coole Park: Home of Lady Gregory, 1973; Lady Gregory: Our Irish Theatre (ed.), 1973; Lady Gregory: Poets and Dreamers (ed.), 1974; Lady Gregory: Seventy Years 1852–1922 (ed.), 1974; The Collected Works of G. W. Russell – AE (general ed. with Henry Summerfield), 1978–; Robert Gregory 1881–1918 (ed.), 1981; Lady Gregory Fifty Years After (ed. with Ann Saddlemyer), 1986; Oxford Companion to Irish Literature (assoc. ed.), 1996. *Honours:* various orders and decorations including: Officer, Venerable Order of St John of Jerusalem; Knight, Order of Our Lady of the Conception of Vila Viçosa, Portugal; Knight, Order of Polonia Restituta, Poland; Hon. LLD, Dublin University, 1998. *Address:* PO Box 6, Gerrards Cross, Buckinghamshire SL9 8XA, England.

SNEYD, Stephen Henry, (Steve Sneyd); Poet and Writer; b. 20 March 1941, Maidenhead, Berkshire, England; m. Rita Ann Cockburn, 13 March 1964, one s. one d. *Education:* MA; BSc; DipM; CertEd. *Career:* UK Columnist, Scavenger's Newsletter, USA, 1984–99; Contributing Ed. on Poetry, Fantasy Commentator magazine, USA, 1992–; mem. Science Fiction Poetry Asscn; National Asscn of Writers in Education. *Publications:* The Legerdemain of Changelings, 1979; Two Humps Not One, 1980; Discourteous Self-Service, 1982; Prug Plac Gamma, 1983; Stone Bones (with Pete Presford), 1983; Fifty-Fifty Infinity, 1989; Bad News from the Stars, 1991; At the Thirteenth Hour, 1991; We Are Not Men, 1991; What Time Has Use For, 1992; A Mile Beyond the Bus, 1992; In Coils of Earthen Hold, 1994; A Reason for Staying, 1999; Gestaltmacher, Gestaltmacher, Make Me a Gestalt, 2000; NeoLithon (with John Light), 2001. Contributions: Over 1,000 reviews, quarterlies, journals and magazines world-wide; Radio and television. *Honours:* Trend Prize for Peace Poetry, 1967; Northern Star Poetry Prize, 1983; Diploma di Merito, Accademia Italia, 1983; Best Poet, Small Press and Magazine Awards, 1986; Paterson Prize, 1996; First Prize, Starlife Poetry Contest, USA, 1999; Special Prize Diploma, International Cosmopoetry Festival of SARM, Romania, 1999. *Address:* 4 Nowell Pl., Almondbury, Huddersfield, West Yorkshire HD5 8PB, England.

SNICKET, Lemony; American children's writer; b. (Daniel Handler); m. Lisa Brown. *Education:* Lowel High, San Francisco. *Publications:* A Series of Unfortunate Events, Vol. 1: The Bad Beginning 1999, Vol. 2: The Reptile Room 1999, Vol. 3: The Wide Window 1999, Vol. 4: The Miserable Mill 2000, Vol. 5: The Austere Academy 2000, Vol. 6: The Ersatz Elevator 2001, Vol. 7: The Vile Village 2001, Vol. 8: The Hostile Hospital 2001, Vol. 9: The Carnivorous Carnival 2002, Vol. 10: The Slippery Slope 2003, Vol. 11: The Grim Grotto 2004, Vol. 12: The Pessimistic Posters 2004; other: The Unauthorised Autobiography 2002. *Address:* c/o Harper Collins Children's Books, 1350 Avenue of the Americas, New York, NY 10019, USA. *E-mail:* lsnicket@harpercollins.com. *Website:* www.lemonysnicket.com.

SNIDER, Clifton Mark, BA, MA, PhD; university lecturer, poet and writer; b. 3 March 1947, Duluth, Minnesota, USA. *Education:* Southern California Coll., Costa Mesa, California State Univ., Long Beach, Univ. of New Mexico. *Career:* faculty mem., California State Univ., Long Beach 1974–, Long Beach City Coll. 1975–2002. *Publications:* poetry: Jesse Comes Back 1976,

Bad Smoke Good Body 1980, Jesse and his Son 1982, Edwin: A Character in Poems 1984, Blood & Bones 1988, Impervious to Piranhas 1989, The Age of the Mother 1992, The Alchemy of Opposites 2000; other: The Stuff That Dreams are Made on: A Jungian Interpretation of Literature 1991, Loud Whisper (novel) 2000, Bare Roots (novel) 2001, Wrestling with Angels: A Tale of Two Brothers (novel) 2001; contrib. to anthologies, reviews, quarterlies and journals. *Honours:* Resident Fellow, Yaddo 1978, 1982, Helene Wurlitzer Foundation of New Mexico 1984, 1990, 1998, 2004, Michael Karolyi Memorial Foundation, Vence, France 1986, 1987. *Address:* 2719 Eucalyptus Avenue, Long Beach, CA 90806, USA. *E-mail:* csnider@csulb.edu. *Website:* www.csulb.edu/~csnider.

SNODGRASS, W. D., (S. S. Gardons, Will McConnell, Kozma Prutkov), BA, MA, MFA; poet, writer and dramatist; b. 5 Jan. 1926, Wilkinsburg, Pennsylvania, USA; m. 1st Lila Jean Hank 1946 (divorced 1953); one d.; m. 2nd Janice Marie Ferguson Wilson 1954 (divorced 1966); one s.; m. 3rd Camille Rykowski 1967 (divorced 1978); m. 4th Kathleen Ann Brown 1985. *Education:* Geneva Coll., Univ. of Iowa. *Career:* Instructor in English, Cornell University, 1955–57; Instructor, University of Rochester, New York, 1957–58; Asst Prof. of English, Wayne State University, Detroit, 1959–67; Prof. of English and Speech, Syracuse University, New York, 1968–77; Visiting Prof., Old Dominion University, Norfolk, Virginia, 1978–79; Distinguished Prof., 1979–80, Distinguished Prof. of Creative Writing and Contemporary Poetry, 1980–94, University of Delaware, Newark; various lectures and poetry readings; mem. National Institute of Arts and Letters; Poetry Society of America; International PEN; American Acad. of Arts and Sciences; Marin Sorescu Foundation. *Publications:* Poetry: Heart's Needle, 1959; After Experience, 1967; As S. S. Gardons, Remains: A Sequence of Poems, 1970; The Fuehrer Bunker, 1977; If Birds Build With Your Hair, 1979; D. D. Byrde Calling Jennie Wrenne, 1984; A Colored Poem, 1986; The House the Poet Built, 1986; A Locked House, 1986; The Kinder Capers, 1986; Selected Poems, 1957–87, 1987; W D's Midnight Carnival (with DeLoss McGraw), 1988; The Death of Cock Robin (with DeLoss McGraw), 1989; Each in His Season, 1994; The Fuehrer Bunker: The Complete Cycle, 1995. Essays: In Radical Pursuit, 1975; After-Images, 1999; To Sound Like Yourself: Essays on Poetry, 2002. Play: The Fuehrer Bunker, 1978. Other: Trans of songs; Selected Translations, 1998. Criticism: De/Compositions: 101 Good Poems Gone Wrong, 2001. Contributions: Essays, reviews, poems to many periodicals. *Honours:* Ingram Merrill Foundation Award, 1958; Longview Foundation Literary Award, 1959; National Institute of Arts and Letters Grant, 1960; Pulitzer Prize in Poetry, 1960; Yaddo Resident Awards, 1960, 1961, 1965; Guinness Poetry Award, 1961; Ford Foundation Grant, 1963–64; National Endowment for the Arts Grant, 1966–67; Guggenheim Fellowship, 1972–73; Government of Romania Centennial Medal, 1977; Hon. DLitt, Allegheny College, 1991; Harold Morton Landon Trans. Award, Acad. of American Poets, 1999. *Address:* 3061 Hughes Road, Erieville, NY 13061, USA. *E-mail:* snodgrassna@hotmail.com.

SNYDER, Gary (Sherman); Poet, Writer and Teacher; b. 8 May 1930, San Francisco, CA, USA; m.; two s. two step-d. *Education:* BA, Reed College, Portland, Oregon, 1951; Graduate Studies in Linguistics, Indiana University, 1951; Graduate School, Dept of East Asian Languages, University of California, Berkeley, 1953–56; Studied Zen Buddhism and East Asian culture in Japan. *Career:* Faculty, University of California, Davis, 1986–; mem. American Acad. of Arts and Letters; American Acad. of Arts and Sciences. *Publications:* Poetry: Riprap and Cold Mountain Poems, 1959; Myths and Texts, 1960; A Range of Poems, 1966; Three Worlds, Three Realms, Six Roads, 1966; The Back Country, 1968; The Blue Sky, 1969; Regarding Wave, 1970; Manzanita, 1971; Plute Creek, 1972; The Fudo Trilogy: Spell Against Demons, Smokey the Bear Sutra, The California Water Plan, 1973; Turtle Island, 1974; All in the Family, 1975; Songs for Gaia, 1979; Axe Handles, 1983; Left Out in the Rain: New Poems, 1947–1986, 1986; The Practice of the Wild, 1990; No Nature: New and Selected Poems, 1992; Mountains and Rivers Without End, 1996. Prose: Earth House Hold: Technical Notes and Queries to Fellow Dharma Revolutionaries, 1969; The Old Ways: Six Essays, 1977; He Who Hunted Birds in His Father's Village: The Dimensions of a Haida Myth, 1979; The Real Work: Interviews and Talks, 1964–1979, 1980; Passage Through India, 1984; A Place in Space, 1995. Contributions: anthologies. *Honours:* Scholarship, First Zen Institute of America, 1956; American Acad. of Arts and Letters Award, 1966; Bollingen Foundation Grant, 1966–67; Frank O'Hara Prize, 1967; Levinson Prize, 1968; Guggenheim Fellowship, 1968–69; Pulitzer Prize in Poetry, 1975. *Address:* 18442 Macnab Cypress Rd, Nevada City, CA 95959, USA.

SNYDER, Midori; Writer; b. 1 Jan. 1954, Santa Monica, CA, USA; m. Stephen Haessler, 16 June 1979, one s. one d. *Education:* University of Wisconsin. *Publications:* Soulstring, 1987; New Moon, 1989; Sadar's Keep, 1991; Beldane's Fire, 1993; The Flight of Michael McBride, 1994; Dinotopia, Hatchling, 1995; The Innamorati, 1998. Contributions: anthologies. *Literary Agent:* Howard Morhaim Literary Agency, 841 Broadway, Suite 604, New York, NY 10003, USA.

SNYDER, Richard E.; American publisher; b. 6 April 1933, New York; m. 1st Otilie Freund 1963 (divorced); one s. one d.; m. 2nd Laura Yorke 1992; two s. *Education:* Tufts Univ., Medford. *Career:* sales rep. Simon & Schuster 1961, Vice-Pres. Marketing 1966–69, Vice-Pres. Trade Books 1969–73, Exec. Vice-Pres. Trade and Educ. Admin 1973–75, Pres. and COO 1975–78, Pres. and CEO 1978–86, Chair. and CEO 1986–94, consultant 1994–95; Chair., CEO Golden Books Family Entertainment 1996–; Chair. PEN, NY Area 1988; Dir Reliance Group Holdings, Children's Blood Foundation; Trustee NY Presbyterian Hosp.; Founder-mem. Nat. Book Foundation, Nat. Book Awards; mem. Council on Foreign Relations, Wildlife Conservation Soc., Econ. Club of NY. *Address:* Golden Books Family Entertainment Inc., 888 7th Avenue, Floor 40, New York, NY 10106, USA.

SNYDER, Zilpha Keatley, BA; writer; b. 11 May 1927, Lemoore, CA, USA; m. 1950; two s. one d. *Education:* Whittier Coll. *Publications:* Season of Ponies 1964, The Velvet Room 1965, Black and Blue Magic 1966, The Egypt Game 1967, The Changeling 1970, The Headless Cupid 1971, The Witches of Worm 1972, The Princess and the Giants 1973, The Truth About Stone Hollow 1974, The Famous Stanley Kidnapping Case 1979, Blair's Nightmare 1984, The Changing Maze 1985, And Condors Danced 1987, Squeak Saves the Day and Other Tooley Tales 1988, Janie's Private Eyes 1989, Libby on Wednesday 1990, Song of the Gargoyle 1991, Fool's Gold 1993, Cat Running 1994, The Trespasser 1995, Castle Court Kids 1995, The Gypsy Game 1997, Gib Rides Home 1998, The Runaways 1999, Gig and the Gray Ghost 2000, Spyhole Secrets 2001, The Ghosts of Rathburn Park 2002, The Unseen 2004. *Honours:* Beatty Award 1995. *Address:* 52 Miller Avenue, Mill Valley, CA 94941, USA.

SOBEL, Dava; American writer; b. 1948; m. 1st Arthur Klein (divorced); one s., oned.; m. 2nd Alfonso Triggiani. *Education:* State Univ. of NY at Binghamton. *Career:* fmr science reporter New York Times; reported for several journals including Audubon, Discover, Life, The New Yorker; fmr Contributing Ed. Harvard Magazine; has lectured at The Smithsonian Inst., The Explorers Club, NASA Goddard Space Flight Center, Folger Shakespeare Library, Los Angeles Public Library, NY Public Library, Royal Geographical Soc. (London); numerous radio and TV appearances; mem. American Asscn of Univ. Women, Planetary Soc.; Fellow, American Geographical Soc. *Publications:* Explorations: Italy's Golden Age of Science 1979, Food for Zero G 1979, So That Others May Live 1979, Time Capsule 1979, The Arts: Books 1983, The Birth of a Station 1983, Death Sentences 1983, Is Anyone Out There? The Scientific Search for Extraterrestrial Intelligence (with Frank D. Drake) 1992, Longitude (several awards including Harold D. Vursell Memorial Award American Acad. of Arts and Letters 1996, UK Book of the Year 1999, Prix Faubert du Coton, Premio del Mare Circeo) 1995, Galileo's Daughter: A Historical Memoir of Science, Faith, and Love 1999, Letters to Father 2001, The Planets 2002; has contributed to Audubon, Discover, Life, Omni, Harvard Magazine. *Honours:* Hon. DLit (Middlebury Coll., Vt, Canada) 2002, (Bath, UK) 2002Nat. Media Award American Psychological Foundation 1980, Lowell Thomas Award Soc. of American Travel Writers 1992, Gold Medal Council for the Advancement and Support of Educ. 1994, Christopher Award 1999, Los Angeles Times Book Prize 2000, Nat. Science Bd Public Service Award 2001, Bradford Washburn Award Boston Museum of Science 2001, Nathaniel Bowditch Maritime Scholar 2003. *Address:* Carlisle & Company, 6 West 18th Street, New York, NY 10011, USA (Office). *Telephone:* (212) 813-1881.

SOBOL, Joshua; Israeli playwright; b. 1939, Tel-Aviv. *Education:* Sorbonne, Paris, France. *Career:* teacher of aesthetics and dir of theatrical workshops, Tel-Aviv Univ., Kibbutz Teachers' Seminary, Belt Zvi Drama School; currently Visiting Prof. of Theater, Weslyan Univ., USA. *Plays:* Ghetto 1989, Real Time 2002, Eye Witness 2002. *Publications:* Silence (novel) 2005. *Honours:* Evening Standard Award for Best Play 1989. *Address:* c/o Jewish Book Council, PO Box 38247, London, NW3 5YQ, England.

SOFOLA, Zulu; Playwright; b. 22 June 1935, Issele-Uku, Nigeria. *Education:* PhD, University of Ibadan, 1977. *Career:* Head, Dept of the Performing Arts, University of Ilorin, Kwara State, Nigeria, 1989–. *Publications:* The Disturbed Peace of Christmas, 1969; Wedlock of the Gods, 1971; The Operators, 1973; King Emene, 1975; Old Wines are Tasty, 1975; The Sweet Trap, 1975; The Wizard of Law, 1976; The Deer and the Hunter's Pearl, 1976; Memories in the Moonlight, 1977; Song of a Maiden, 1977; Queen Umu-Ako of Oligbo, 1989; Eclipse and the Fantasia, 1990; Lost Dreams, 1991; The Showers, 1991. *Honours:* Fulbright Fellowship, 1988. *Address:* Dept of the Performing Arts, University of Ilorin, Ilorin, Kwara State, Nigeria.

SOHAIL, Khalid; Psychiatrist, Writer and Poet; b. 9 July 1952, Pakistan. *Education:* MBBS, Pakistan, 1974; FRCP(C), Canada, 1982. *Career:* mem. Fellow, Royal College of Physicians and Surgeons, Canada; Writers' Forum of Canada; Writers' Union of Canada. *Publications:* Discovering New Highways in Life, 1991; From One Culture to Another, 1992; Literary Encounters, 1992; Pages of My Heart (poems), 1993; A Broken Man (short stories), 1993; Mother Earth is Sad (fiction), 1999; Encounters With Creativity, Insanity and Spirituality, 1999. Contributions: anthologies and journals. *Honours:* Rahul Award, Kolkata, 1994. *Address:* PH6 100 White Oaks Ct, Whitby, ON L1P 1B7, Canada.

SOLLERS, Philippe, (Philippe Joyaux); Author; b. 28 Nov. 1936, Talence, Gironde, France; m. Julia Kristeva 2 Aug. 1967. *Education:* Lycée Montesquieu and Lycée Montaigne, Bordeaux; École Sainte-Geneviève, Versailles. *Career:* Co-Founder, Tel Quel journal, 1960–82; Dir, L'Infini review, 1983–; Reading Committee Mem., Editions Gallimard, 1992–. *Publications:* Une Curieuse Solitude, 1958; Le Parc, 1961; Drame, 1965; Nombres, Logiques, 1968; Lois, 1972; H, 1973; Paradis, Vision à New York, 1981;

Femmes, 1983; Portrait du joueur, 1985; Théorie des exceptions, 1986; Paradis 2, 1986; Le Coeur absolu, 1987; Les Surprises de Fragonard, 1987; Les Folies françaises, 1988; De Kooning, vite, 1988; Le Lys d'or, 1989; Carnet de nuit, 1989; La Fête à Venise, 1991; Improvisations, 1991; Le Rire de Rome, 1992; Le Secret, 1993; Venise éternelle, 1993; La Guerre du goût, 1994; Femmes mythologies, 1994; Le Cavalier du Louvre, Vivant Denon (1747–1825), 1995; Le Paradis de Cézanne, 1995; Les Passions de Francis Bacon, 1996; Sade contre l'être suprême, Picasso le héros, 1996; Studio, 1997; Casanova, l'admirable, 1998; L'Année du Tigre: Journal de l'année 1998, 1999; L'Oeil de Proust: Les dessins de Marcel Proust, 1999; Passion fixe, 2000; La Divine Comédie, 2000; Eloge de l'infini, 2001; L'Etoile des amants, 2002; Illuminations, 2003. Other: Screenplays. Contributions: various publications. *Honours:* Prix Fénéon, 1957; Prix Médicis Étranger, 1961; Grand prix de littérature de la ville de Bordeaux, 1985; Grand prix du roman de la Ville de Paris, 1988; Prix Paul-Morand de l'Académie française, 1992; Prix Elsa-Morante d'essai, 1999; Chevalier, Légion d'honneur; Officier, Ordre nat. du Mérite; Officier, Ordre des Arts et des Lettres. *Address:* c/o L'Infini, 5 rue Sébastien-Bottin, 75007 Paris, France.

SOLOMON, Maynard Elliott, BA; American music historian and writer; b. 5 Jan. 1930, New York, NY; m. Eva Georgiana Tevan 1951; two s. one d. *Education:* Brooklyn Coll., CUNY, Columbia Univ. *Career:* co-founder, co-owner, Vanguard Recording Soc. Inc 1950–86; teacher, CUNY 1979–81; Visiting Prof., SUNY at Stony Brook 1988–89, Columbia Univ. 1989–90, Harvard Univ. 1991–92, Yale Univ. 1994–95; Scholarly Adviser, Beethoven Archive, Bonn 1995–; Graduate Faculty, Juilliard School 1998–. *Publications:* Marxism and Art 1973, Beethoven 1977, Myth, Creativity and Psychoanalysis 1978, Beethoven Essays 1988, Mozart: A Life 1995, Late Beethoven: Music, Thought, Imagination 2003; contrib. to learned journals. *Honours:* ASCAP–Deems Taylor Awards 1978, 1989, 1995, Kinkeldey Award 1989, hon. mem., American Musicological Soc. 1999. *Address:* 1 W 72nd Street, Apartment 56, New York, NY 10023, USA.

SOLOW, Robert M(erton); Prof. of Economics Emeritus and Writer; b. 23 Aug. 1924, New York, NY, USA; m. Barbara Lewis, 19 Aug. 1945, two s. one d. *Education:* BA, 1947, MA, 1949, PhD, 1951, Harvard University. *Career:* Faculty, 1949–58, Prof. of Economics, 1958–95, Prof. Emeritus, 1995–, MIT; Senior Economist, 1961–62, Consultant, 1962–68, US Council of Economic Advisers; Marshall Lecturer and Fellow Commoner, Peterhouse, Cambridge, 1963–64; Eastman Visiting Prof., University of Oxford, 1968–69; Senior Fellow, Society of Fellows, Harvard University, 1975–89; Deming Prof., New York University, 1996–97; Foundation Scholar, Russell Sage Foundation, New York, 2000; mem. American Acad. of Arts and Sciences; American Economics Society, vice-pres., 1968, pres., 1979; American Philosophical Society; British Acad., corresponding fellow; Econometric Society, pres., 1964; National Acad. of Science, council mem., 1977–80, 1995. *Publications:* Linear Programming and Economic Analysis (with R. Dorfman and P. Samuelson), 1958; Capital Theory and the Rate of Return, 1963; The Sources of Unemployment in the United States, 1964; Growth Theory, 1970; Price Expectations and the Behaviour of the Prive Level, 1970; Made in America (with M. Dertouzos and R. Lester), 1989; The Labor Market as a Social Institution, 1990; A Critical Essay on Modern Macroeconomic Theory (with F. Hahn), 1995; Learning from 'Learning by Doing', 1997; Inflation, Unemployment and Monetary Policy, 1998; Work and Welfare, 1998; Monopolistic Competition and Macroeconomic Theory, 1998. Contributions: Professional journals. *Honours:* David A Wells Prize, Harvard University, 1951; Seidman Award in Political Economy, 1983; Nobel Prize for Economic Science, 1987; US National Medal of Science, 2000; numerous hon. doctorates. *Address:* 528 Lewis Wharf, Boston, MA 02110, USA.

SOLWAY, David; Poet, Writer, Trans. and University Lecturer; b. 8 Dec. 1941, Montréal, QC, Canada; m. Karin Semmler, 23 April 1980, one d. *Education:* BA, 1962, QMA, 1966, McGill University; MA, Concordia University, 1988; MA, University of Sherbrooke, 1996; PhD, Lajos Kossuth University, 1998. *Career:* Lecturer in English Literature, McGill University, 1966–67, Dawson College, 1970–71, John Abbott College, 1971–99; Writer-in-Residence, Concordia University 1999–2000; Assoc. Ed., Books in Canada, 2001–; several visiting university lectureships; mem. Canadian Writer's Union; International PEN; Union des écrivaines et des écrivains québécois; President's Circle, Univ. of Toronto. *Publications:* Poetry: In My Own Image, 1962; The Crystal Theatre, 1971; Paximalia, 1972; The Egyptian Airforce and Other Poems, 1973; The Road to Arginos, 1976; Anacrusis, 1976; Mephistopheles and the Astronaut, 1979; The Mulberry Men, 1982; Selected Poetry, 1982; Stones in Water, 1983; Modern Marriage, 1987; Bedrock, 1993; Chess Pieces, 1999; The Lover's Progress, 2001; The Properties of Things, 2001; Director's Cut (essays), 2003; Franklin's Passage (poems), 2003. Other: Four Montréal Poets (ed.), 1973; Education Lost: Reflections on Contemporary Pedagogical Practice, 1989; The Anatomy of Arcadia, 1992; Lying About the Wolf: Essays in Culture and Education, 1997; Random Walks: Essays in Elective Criticism, 1997; Saracen Island: The Poems of Andreas Karavis (trans.), 2000; An Andreas Karavis Companion, 2000; The Turtle Hypodermic of Sickenpods: Liberal Studies in the Corporate Age, 2001. Contributions: many anthologies, reviews, quarterlies and journals, including: The Atlantic Monthly; International Journal of Applied Semiotics; Journal of Modern Greek Studies; Canadian Notes and Queries; Books in Canada; The Sewanee Review. *Honours:* QSPELL Award for Poetry, 1988, and for Non-Fiction, 1990; various Canada Council Grants. *Address:* 143 Upper McNaughton, Hudson, QC J0P 1H0, Canada.

SOLZHENITSYN, Aleksandr (Isayevich); Writer and Poet; b. 11 Dec. 1918, Kislovodsk, Russia; m. 1st Natalya Reshetovskaya 27 April 1940 (divorced); m. 2nd 1956 (divorced 1970); m. 3rd Natalya Svetlova May 1970; three s. one step-s. *Education:* Correspondence course in Philology, Moscow Institute of History, Philosophy, and Literature, 1939–41; Degree in Mathematics and Physics, University of Rostov, 1941. *Career:* Writer as a youth; Secondary School Teacher; Commander, Soviet Army during World War II; Held in prisons and labour camp, 1945–53; Exiled as a teacher, Kok-Terek, Kazakhstan, 1953–56; Teacher, Mathematics and Physics, Riazan; Exiled from Soviet Union, 1974–94; mem. American Acad. of Arts and Sciences. *Publications:* One Day in the Life of Ivan Denisovich (novella), 1962; For the Good of the Cause (novella), 1963; We Never Make Mistakes (novel), 1963; The First Circle (novel), 1968; Cancer Ward (novel), 2 vols, 1968–69; The Love Girl and the Innocent (play), 1969; Candle in the Wind (play), 1969; The Rights of the Writer, 1969; The Red Wheel (novel cycle), 1971–, including August 1914, November 1916, March 1917, April 1917; Stories and Prose Poems by Aleksandr Solzhenitsyn, 1971; Six Etudes by Aleksandr Solzhenitsyn, 1971; Nobel Lecture by Aleksandr Solzhenitsyn, 1972; A Lenten Letter to Pimen, Patriarch of All Russia, 1972; The Gulag Archipelago, 1918–1956: An Experiment in Literary Investigation, 3 vols, 1974, 1976, 1979; Peace and Violence, 1974; Prussian Nights: Epic Poems Written at the Forced Labor Camp, 1950, 1974; Letter to the Soviet Leaders, 1974; Solzhenitsyn: A Pictorial Autobiography, 1974; The Oak and the Calf (memoir), 1975; Lenin in Zürich, 1975; American Speeches, 1975; From Under the Rubble (with others), 1975; Warning to the West, 1976; A World Split Apart, 1979; The Mortal Danger, 1981; Victory Celebrations: A Comedy in Four Acts and Prisoners: A Tragedy (plays), 1983; Rebuilding Russia: Towards Some Formulations, 1991; The Russian Question Toward the End of the Century, 1995; Russia in the Abyss, 1998; November 1916: The Red Wheel, Knot 11, 1999; Two-Part Stories, 1996–2001, 2001; Two Hundred Years Together, 2001–2002, 2002. *Honours:* Prix du Meilleur Livre Étranger, France, 1969; Nobel Prize for Literature, 1970; Freedoms Foundation Award, Stanford University, 1976; many hon. degrees. *Address:* c/o Farrar, Straus & Giroux, 19 Union Sq. W, New York, NY 10003, USA.

SOMERS, Suzanne (see Daniels, Dorothy).

SOMLYÓ, György; Hungarian poet, novelist, critic and translator of poetry; b. 28 Nov. 1920, Balatonboglár; m. (divorced 1986); one s. *Education:* Budapest Univ. and the Sorbonne, Paris. *Career:* Literary Ed. Radio Budapest 1954–55; Lecturer in Modern Poetry, Univ. of Budapest 1975–78; Ed. Arion 1966–87; organizer Int. Meeting of Poets, Budapest 1966, 1970; corresp., PO&SIE poetry magazine, Paris 1976–; mem. Széchenyi Hungarian Acad. of Arts and Letters, Asscnof Hungarian Writers, Hungarian PEN; Corresp. mem. Acad. Mallarmé, Paris 1977–. *Translations:* Szélrózsa I/III (Compass Card) 1973, Az utazás (The Journey), French Poetry from Baudelaire to our days 1984. *Publications include:* Collected Works: Vol. 1: A költészet vérszerződése (The Blood Covenant of Poetry) 1977, Vols 2, 3: Collected Poems 1978, Vol. 4: Másutt (Elsewhere) 1979, Vol. 5: Szerelöszönyeg (Catwalk) 1981, Vol. 6: Megiratlan könyvek (Unwritten Books) 1982, Vol. 7: Miért hal meg az ember? (Why the Man Dies?) 1984, Philoktetész sebe (Philoctetes' Wound) 1980, Árnyjáték (Shadow Play) 1977, Rámpa (Ramp) 1984, Picasso 1981, Parisiens (poems in French) 1987, A Költészet ötödik évada (The Fifth Season of Poetry) 1988, Ami rajtam tul van (What's Beyond Me) 1988, Városok (Cities: essays) 1990, Palimpszeszt (poems) 1990, Párizsi Kettös (Duo in Paris) 1991, Nem titok (No Secret: poems) 1992, Az elvitathatatlan hely (The Evident Place, essays) 1994, A Negyedik Šzoba (The Fourth Room Poems) 1994, Énekek Eneke (Song of Songs) 1994, Törésvonlak (Breaklines) poems (1997), Paul Valéry Füzetek (notebooks) 1997, Seb és kés (Wound and Knife) (selected poems 1976–97) 1998, From Philoctetes to Arion (collected essays) 2000, Collected Poems 2001, Önéletrajzaimból (autobiog.) 2001, Ahol van (Where He Is) (poems) 2002; Ed. 1001 Sonnets of World Literature (anthology) 1991. *Honours:* Officier, Ordre des Arts et Lettres (France) 1984; Order of Flag of Hungarian Repub. 1990; József Attila prize (four times), Tibor Déry Prize 1987, Kassák Prize, Soros Foundation 1991, Gabriela Mistral Memorial Medal (Chile) 1996, Kossuth Prize 1997. *Address:* Irinyi J. u. 39, 1111 Budapest, Hungary. *Telephone:* (1) 386-09-54.

SOMOZA, José Carlos; novelist and psychiatrist; b. 1959, Havana, Cuba. *Publications:* Planos (novella) 1994, Langostas (radio play) 1994, Silencio de Blanca (novel) 1996, Miguel Will (play) 1997, La ventana pintada (novel) 1998, Cartas de un asesino insignificante (novel) 1999, Dafne desvanecida (novel) 2000, La caverna de las ideas (trans. as The Athenian Murders, novel) 2000, Clara y la penumbra (novel) 2001. *Honours:* Premio Gabriel Sijé 1994; Premio Margarita Xirgu 1994; Premio Sonrisa Vertical 1996; Premio Miguel de Cervantes de teatro 1997; Premio Café Gijón 1998; Premio Nadal, 2001; Premio de Novela Fernando Lara, 2001; CWA Macallan Gold Dagger, 2002. *Address:* c/o Editorial Planeta, SA, Edifici Planeta, Diagonal 662–664, 08034 Barcelona, Spain.

SONG, Cathy; Poet, Writer and Teacher; b. 20 Aug. 1955, Honolulu, HI, USA; m. Douglas M. Davenport, 19 July 1979. *Education:* University of

Hawaii at Manoa; BA in English Literature, Wellesley College, 1977; MA in Creative Writing, Boston University, 1981. *Career:* Teacher of Poetry, HI, 1987–; Associated with Poets in the Schools programme. *Publications:* Picture Bride 1983, Frameless Windows, Squares of Light 1988, Sister Stew (ed. with Juliet S. Kono) 1991, School Figures 1994, The Land of Bliss 2001. Contributions: various anthologies and journals. *Honours:* Yale Series of Younger Poets Prize 1983, Frederick Book Prize for Poetry 1986, Cades Award for Literature 1988, Hawaii Award for Literature 1993, Shelley Memorial Award, Poetry Society of America 1993, Creative Writing Fellowship, Nat. Endowment for the Arts 1997, Pushcart Prize 1999, The Best American Poetry 2000. *Address:* PO Box 27262 Honolulu, HI 96827, USA.

SONG MUWEN; Chinese publishing executive; b. 1929, Yushu Co., Jilin. *Career:* Chair. Asscn of Chinese Publrs 1993–2000, Hon. Chair. 2000–; Pres. Copyright Research Society; mem. NPC Educ., Science, Culture and Public Health Cttee. *Address:* Publishers' Association of China, 85 Dongsi Nan Dajie, Beijing 100703, People's Republic of China. *Telephone:* (10) 65228632. *Fax:* (10) 65228632.

SONTAG, Susan, BA, MA; American writer, poet and dramatist; b. 16 Jan. 1933, New York, NY; m. Philip Rieff 1950 (divorced 1958); one s. *Education:* University of Chicago, Harvard University. *Career:* mem. American Acad. of Arts and Letters, PEN American Center (pres. 1987–89). *Publications:* The Benefactor (novel) 1963, Against Interpretation (essays) 1966, Death Kit (novel) 1967, Trip to Hanoi (essays) 1968, Styles of Radical Will (essays) 1969, On Photography (essays) 1977, Illness as Metaphor (essays) 1978, I, etcetera (short stories) 1978, Under the Sign of Saturn (essays) 1980, A Sontag Reader 1982, AIDS and Its Metaphors (essays) 1989, The Way We Live Now (story) 1991, The Volcano Lover: A Romance 1992, Alice in Bed: A Play 1993, Under the Sign of Saturn (poems) 1996, In America (novel) 2000, Women (with Annie Liebowitz) 2000, Where the Stress Falls (essays) 2001, Regarding the Pain of Others (essays) 2003; contrib. to various publications. *Honours:* Rockefeller Foundation Fellowships, 1965, 1974; Guggenheim Fellowships, 1966, 1975; National Book Critics Circle Award, 1978; Officier, Ordre des Arts et des Lettres, 1984; John D. and Catherine T. MacArthur Foundation Fellowship, 1990–95; Malaparte Prize, Italy, 1992; Hon. doctorates, Columbia University, 1993, Harvard University, 1993; Montblanc Cultural Achievement Award, 1994; National Book Award for Fiction, 2000; Jerusalem Prize, 2001. *Address:* 250 W 57th Street, Suite 2114, New York, NY 10107, USA.

SORESTAD, Glen Allan; Writer and Poet; b. 21 May 1937, Vancouver, BC, Canada; m. Sonia Diane Talpash, 17 Sept. 1960, three s., one d. *Education:* BEd, 1963, MEd, 1976, University of Saskatchewan. *Career:* Elementary School Teacher, 1957–69; Senior English Teacher, 1969–81; Pres., Thistledown Press, 1975–2000; mem. Asscn of Canadian Publishers; League of Canadian Poets, life mem.; Canadian Poetry Asscn; Saskatchewan Writers' Guild; Writers' Union of Canada. *Publications:* Hold the Rain in Your Hands: Poems Selected and New, 1985; Birchbark Meditations, 1996; West into Night, 1991; Icons of Flesh, 1998; Today I Belong to Agnes, 2000; Leaving Holds Me Here: Selected Poems, 1975–2000, 2001. Contributions: numerous newspapers, journals, magazines and periodicals. *Honours:* SWG Founders Award; First Poet Laureate of Saskatchewan, 2000. *Address:* 108–835 Heritage Green, Saskatoon, SK S7H 5S5, Canada. *E-mail:* g.sorestad@sasktel.net.

SOROKIN, Vladimir Georgiyevich; Author and Painter; b. 7 Aug. 1955, Bykovo, Moscow Region, Russia; m. Sorokina Irina Igorevna; two d. *Education:* Moscow Gubkin Institute of Oil and Gas Industry. *Career:* worked as artist Smena 1979–80; freelance 1980–; was not published in USSR until 1987; mem. Russian PEN Centre; Union of Graphic Artists of Russia; Union of Russian Writers. *Publications:* The Queue, 1985; Thirteenth Love of Marina, 1993; Obelisk (short stories), 1994; The Hearts of the Four, 1994; The Norm (selected texts), 1994; A Novel, 1994; Blue Lard, 1999. *Honours:* Deutsche Akademische Austauschung Dienst scholarship, Berlin, 1992. *Address:* Proyezd Odoyevskogo 7, korp. 5, Apt 621, Moscow, Russia.

SOROS, George; Hungarian investment banker and philanthropist; b. 12 Aug. 1930, Budapest. *Education:* London School of Econs. *Career:* moved to England 1947; much influenced by work of philosopher Karl Popper; with Singer & Friedlander (merchant bankers), London; moved to Wall Street, New York 1956; set up pvt. mutual fund, Quantum Fund, registered in Curaçao 1969; since 1991 has created other funds, Quasar Int., Quota, Quantum Emerging Growth Fund (merged with Quantum Fund to form Quantum Endowment Fund 2000), Quantum Realty Trust; Pres. and Chair. Soros Fund Man. LLC, New York 1973–; philanthropist since 1979, provided funds to help black students attend Cape Town Univ., SA; set up Open Soc. Fund (currently Chair. Open Soc. Inst.) 1979, Soros Foundations, Cen. European Univ., Budapest 1992; f. Global Power Investments 1994. *Publication:* The Alchemy of Finance 1987, Opening the Soviet System 1990, Underwriting Democracy 1991, Soros on Soros: Staying Ahead of the Curve (jtly) 1995, The Crisis of Global Capitalism: Open Society Engendered 1998, Open Society: Reforming Global Capitalism 2000, George Soros on Globalization 2002, The Bubble of American Supremacy 2004; numerous essays on politics, society and econs in major int. newspapers and magazines. *Honours:* Dr hc (New School for Social Research, Univ. of Oxford, Budapest Univ. of Econs, Yale Univ.); Laurea hc (Univ. of Bologna) 1995. *Address:* Soros Fund Management, 888 7th Avenue, 3300 New York, NY 10106, USA.

SORRENTINO, Gilbert; Novelist, Poet and Prof. of English; b. 27 April 1929, New York, NY, USA; m. 1st Elsene Wiessner, divorced; m. 2nd Vivian V. Ortiz, three c. *Education:* Brooklyn College, CUNY, 1950–51, 1955–57. *Career:* Ed., Publisher, Neon Magazine, New York City, 1956–60; Ed., Grove Press, New York City, 1965–70; Teacher, Columbia University, 1965, Aspen Writers Workshop, 1967, Sarah Lawrence College, 1971–72, New School for Social Research, New York City, 1976–79; Edwin S. Quain Prof. of Literature, University of Scranton, 1979; Prof. of English, Stanford University, 1982–99, Emeritus Prof., 1999–; mem. PEN American Center. *Publications:* Fiction: The Sky Changes, 1966; Steelwork, 1970; Imaginative Qualities of Actual Things, 1971; Splendide-Hotel, 1973; Mulligan Stew, 1979; Aberration of Starlight, 1980; Crystal Vision, 1981; Blue Pastoral, 1983; Odd Number, 1985; Rose Theatre, 1987; Misterioso, 1989; Under the Shadow, 1991; Red the Fiend, 1995; Gold Fools, 2001; Little Casino, 2002. Poetry: The Darkness Surrounds Us, 1960; Black and White, 1964; The Perfect Fiction, 1968; Corrosive Sublimate, 1971; A Dozen Oranges, 1976; White Sail, 1977; The Orangery, 1977; Selected Poems, 1958–1980, 1981. Essays: Something Said, 1984. Play: Flawless Play Restored: The Masque of Fungo, 1974. Translator: Sulpiciae Elegidia/ Elegiacs of Sulpicia: Gilbert Sorrentino Versions, 1977. Contributions: various anthologies and periodicals. *Honours:* Guggenheim Fellowships, 1973–74, 1987–88; Samuel S. Fels Award, 1974; Creative Artists Public Service Grant, 1974–75; Ariadne Foundation Grant, 1975; National Endowment for the Arts Grants, 1975–76, 1978–79, 1983–84; John Dos Passos Prize, 1981; Mildred and Harold Strauss Livings, 1982 (declined); American Acad. and Institute of Arts and Letters Award, 1985; Lannan Literary Award for Fiction, 1992. *Address:* Dept of English, Stanford University, Stanford, CA 94305, USA.

SOSA, Roberto; Honduran writer and poet; b. 18 April 1930, Yoro. *Career:* teacher of literature, Universidad Nacional Autónoma de Honduras; Pres., Honduran Journalists' Union; Ed., Presente (Central American arts and letters review). *Publications:* Los pobres 1969, Un mundo para todos dividido 1971, Prosa armada 1981, Secreto militar 1985, 13 poemas 1987, Obra completa 1990, Diálogo de sombras 1993, Sociedad y poesia: los enmantados 1997, Honduras: Poesia escogida 1998, Piano vacio 2002; in English: Poems 1984, The Difficult Days 1985, The Common Grief 1994, The Return of the River 2002. *Honours:* Adonais Prize, Spain, Casa de las Américas Prize, Cuba. *Address:* c/o Curbstone Press, 321 Jackson Street, Willimantic, CT 06226-1738, USA. *E-mail:* info@curbstone.org. *Website:* www.curbstone.org.

SOTO, Gary; Writer and Poet; b. 12 April 1952, Fresno, CA, USA; m. Carolyn Sadako Oda, 24 May 1975, one d. *Education:* BA, California State University at Fresno, 1974; MFA, University of California at Irving, 1976. *Career:* Asst Prof., 1979–85, Assoc. Prof. of English and Ethnic Studies, 1985–92, Part-time Senior Lecturer in English, 1992–93, University of California at Berkeley; Elliston Prof. of Poetry, University of Cincinnati, 1988; Martin Luther King/Cesar Chavez/Rosa Park Visiting Prof. of English, Wayne State University, 1990. *Publications:* Poetry: The Elements of San Joaquin, 1977; The Tale of Sunlight, 1978; Where Sparrows Work Hard, 1981; Black Hair, 1985; Who Will Know Us?, 1990; A Fire in My Hands, 1990; Home Course in Religion, 1992; Neighborhood Odes, 1992; Canto Familiar/Familiar Song, 1994; New and Selected Poems, 1995; Fearless Fernie, 2002. Other: Living Up the Street: Narrative Recollections, 1985; Small Faces, 1986; Lesser Evils: Ten Quartets, 1988; California Childhood: Recollections and Stories of the Golden State (ed.), 1988; A Summer Life, 1990; Baseball in April and Other Stories, 1990; Taking Sides, 1991; Pacific Crossing, 1992; The Skirt, 1992; Pieces of the Heart: New Chicano Fiction (ed.), 1993; Local News, 1993; The Pool Party, 1993; Crazy Weekend, 1994; Jesse, 1994; Boys at Work, 1995; Chato's Kitchen, 1995; Everyday Seductions (ed.), 1995; Summer on Wheels, 1995; The Old Man and His Door, 1996; Snapshots of the Wedding, 1996; Buried Onions, 1997; Nickel and Dime (novel), 2000; Poetry Lover (novel), 2001; Jessie De La Cruz: A Profile of a United Farm Worker (young adult biog.), 2002; The Effects of Knut Hamsun on a Fresno Boy (essays), 2002; If the Shoe Fits (picture book), 2002. Contributions: Magazines. *Honours:* Acad. of American Poets Prize, 1975; Discovery/The Nation Prize, 1975; United States Award, International Poetry Forum, 1976; Bess Hokin Prize for Poetry, 1978; Guggenheim Fellowship, 1979–80; National Endowment for the Arts Fellowships, 1981, 1991; Levinson Award, Poetry Magazine, 1984; American Book Award, Before Columbus Foundation, 1985; California Arts Council Fellowship, 1989; Carnegie Medal, 1993; Thomas Rivera Prize, 1996; Hispanic Heritage Award, 1999; Civil Rights Award, National Education Asscn, 1999. *Address:* 43 The Crescent, Berkeley, CA 94708, USA.

SOUEIF, Ahdaf; Writer and Novelist; b. 1950, Cairo, Egypt; m. Ian Hamilton, March 1981, two s. *Education:* BA, University of Cairo, 1971; MA, American University, 1973; PhD, University of Lancaster, 1978. *Career:* mem. Arts Council of Britain; Arts Council of England; Egyptian-British Society; Egyptian Writers' Union; PEN Egypt. *Publications:* Aisha, 1983; In the Eye of the Sun, 1992; Sandpiper, 1996; The Map of Love, 1999. Contributions: periodicals. *Address:* c/o Wyley Agency, 4–8 Rodney St, London N1 9JH, England.

SOULE, Gardner (Bosworth); Author; b. 16 Dec. 1913, Paris, Texas, USA; m. 1st Janie Lee McDowell, 20 Sept. 1940, deceased; m. 2nd Mary Muir Dowhing, 23 April 1994. *Education:* BA, Rice University, 1933; BSc, 1935, MSc, 1936, Columbia University. *Career:* Associated Press, 1936–41; US Naval Reserve, 1942–45; Managing Ed., Better Homes & Gardens, 1945–50. *Publications:* Tomorrow's World of Science, 1963; The Maybe Monsters, 1963; The Mystery Monsters, 1965; Trail of the Abominable Snowman, 1965; The Ocean Adventure, 1966; UFO's and IFO's, 1967; Wide Ocean, 1970; Men Who Dared the Sea, 1976; The Long Trail: How Cowboys and Longhorns Opened the West, 1976; Mystery Monsters of the Deep, 1981; Mystery Creatures of the Jungle, 1982; Antarctica, 1985; Christopher Columbus, 1989. Contributions: Popular Science Monthly; United Features; London Express Syndicate; Boy's Life; Illustrated London News. *Honours:* Navy League Commendation, 1956.

SOULEZ-LARIVIÈRE, Daniel Joseph; French lawyer and writer; b. 19 March 1942, Angers (Maine-et-Loire); m. Mathilde-Mahaut Nobecourt 1988; one s. (and one s. with Michèle Abbaye). *Education:* Lycée Janson-de-Sailly, Collège Stanislas, Paris, Garden City High School, New York, USA and Faculty of Law, Paris. *Career:* lawyer in Paris 1965–; Chargé de mission, Ministry of Equipment and Housing 1966–67; Second Sec. Conférence du stage 1969; mem. Conseil de l'Ordre 1988–90; mem. Consultative Comm. for the Revision of the Constitution 1992–93, 2002–03; mem. Advisory Bd Centre de prospective de la gendarmerie; Municipal Counsellor for Chambellay 1995–; mem. Soc. of French Jurists. *Publications:* L'avocature 1982, Les juges dans la balance 1987, La réforme des professions juridiques et judiciaires, vingt propositions 1988, Justice pour la justice 1990, Du cirque médiatico-judiciaire et des moyens d'en sortir 1993, Paroles d'avocat 1994, Grand soir pour la justice 1997, Dans l'engrenage de la justice 1998, Lettres à un jeune avocat 1999, La justice à l'épreuve (jtly with Jean-Marie Coulon) 2002. *Honours:* Chevalier, Ordre nat. du Mérite, Chevalier, Légion d'honneur. *Address:* 22 ave de la Grande Armée, 75017 Paris; 6 rue des Fougères, 92140 Clamart; le Prieuré, 49220 Chambellay, France.

SOUSTER, (Holmes) Raymond, (John Holmes); writer and poet; b. 15 Jan. 1921, Toronto, ON, Canada; m. Rosalia L. Geralde 1947. *Education:* University of Toronto Schools, 1932–37; Humberside Collegiate Institute, 1938–39. *Career:* mem. League of Canadian Poets, founding mem. and chair., 1968–72, life mem., 1996–. *Publications:* 100 Poems of 19th Century Canada (ed. with D. Lochhead), 1974; Sights and Sounds (ed. with R. Wollatt), 1974; These Loved, These Hated Lands (ed. with R. Wollatt), 1974; The Poetry of W. W. Campbell (ed.), 1978; The Best-Known Poems of Archibald Lampman (ed.), 1979; Collected Poems of Raymond Souster, 8 vols, 1980–93; Powassan's Drum: Selected Poems of Duncan Campbell Scott (ed. with D. Lochhead), 1983; Queen City: Toronto in Poems and Pictures (with Bill Brooks), 1984; Windflower: The Selected Poems of Bliss Carmen (ed. with D. Lochhead), 1986; Riding the Long Black Horse, 1993; Old Bank Notes, 1993; No Sad Songs Wanted Here, 1995; Close to Home, 1997; Of Time and Toronto, 2000. Contributions: Magazines. *Honours:* Governor-General's Award for Poetry in English, 1964; Pres.'s Medal, University of Western Ontario, 1967; Centennial Medal, 1967; City of Toronto Book Award, 1979; Silver Jubilee Medal, 1977; Officer of the Order of Canada, 1995. *Address:* 39 Baby Point Road, Toronto, ON M6S 2G2, Canada.

SOUTHALL, Ivan Francis; writer; b. 8 June 1921, Melbourne, Vic., Australia; m. 1st Joy Blackburn 1945 (divorced); one s. three d.; m. 2nd Susan Westerlund Stanton 1976. *Career:* Whitall Poetry and Literature Lecturer, Library of Congress, Washington, DC, 1973; May Hill Arbuthnot Honour Lecturer, University of Washington, USA, 1974; Writer-in-Residence, Macquarie University, Sydney, 1979; mem. Australian Society of Authors; Fellowship of Australian Writers. *Publications:* They Shall Not Pass Unseen, 1956; Softly Tread the Brave, 1960; Hills End, 1962; Ash Road, 1965; To the Wild Sky, 1967; Let the Balloon Go, 1968; Josh, 1971; Head in the Clouds, 1972; Matt and Jo, 1973; What About Tomorrow?, 1977; City Out of Sight, 1984; Christmas in the Tree, 1985; Rachel, 1986; Blackbird, 1988; The Mysterious World of Marcus Leadbeater, 1990; Ziggurat, 1997. *Honours:* Australian Children's Book of the Year, 1966, 1968, 1971, 1976; Australian Picture Book of the Year (with Ted Greenwood), 1969; Children's Welfare and Culture Encouragement Award, Japan, 1969; Carnegie Medal, 1971; Silver Griffel, Netherlands, 1972; Australia Writers Award, 1974; IBBY Honour Books, 1974, 1979; Order of Australia, 1981; National Children's Book Award, Australia, 1986; Australia Council Emeritus Award, 1993; Retrospective Exhibition, State Library of Victoria, 1998; Phoenix Award, 2003. *Address:* PO Box 1698 Healesville, Vic. 3777, Australia.

SOWANDE, Bode; Playwright and Writer; b. 2 May 1948, Kaduna, Nigeria. *Education:* Universities of Ife, Dakar and Sheffield; MA, 1974; PhD, 1977. *Career:* Senior Lecturer, Dept of Theatre Arts, University of Ibadan, 1977–90. *Publications:* The Night Before, 1972; Lamps in the Night, 1973; Bar Beach Prelude, 1976; A Sanctus for Women, 1976; Afamoko – the Workhorse, 1978; Farewell to Babylon, 1978; Kalakuta Cross Currents, 1979; The Master and the Frauds, 1979; Barabas and the Master Jesus, 1980; Flamingo, 1982; Circus of Freedom Square, 1985; Tornadoes Full of Dreams, 1989; Arede Owo (after L'Avare by Molière), 1990; Mammy-Water's Wedding, 1991; Ajantala-Pinocchio, 1992. Fiction: Our Man the President, 1981; Without a Home, 1982; The Missing Bridesmaid, 1988. Other: My Life in the Bush of Ghosts (stage adaptation of Amos Tutuola's novel), 1995; Radio and television plays. *Honours:* Asscn of Nigerian Authors Drama Awards; Chevalier, Ordre des Arts et des Lettres, 1991; Patron of the Arts Award, Pan African Writers Asscn, 1993. *Address:* c/o Odu Themes Meridian, 33 Oyo Rd, Orita, PO Box 14369, Post Office UI, Ibadan, Nigeria.

SOWELL, Thomas; Economist and Writer; b. 30 June 1930, Gastonia, NC, USA; m. 1st Alma Jean Parr, divorced; m. 2nd Mary, two c. *Education:* BA, Harvard University, 1958; MA, Columbia University, 1959; PhD, University of Chicago, 1968. *Career:* Economist, US Dept of Labor, 1961–62; Instructor in Economics, Douglass College, Rutgers University, 1962–63; Lecturer in Economics, Howard University, 1963–64; Economic Analyst, AT&T, 1964–65; Asst Prof., Cornell University, 1965–69; Assoc. Prof., Brandeis University, 1969–70; Assoc. Prof., 1970–74, Prof. of Economics, 1974–80, University of California at Los Angeles; Fellow, Center for Advanced Study in the Behavioral Sciences, Stanford, CA, 1976–77; Visiting Prof., Amherst College, 1977; Senior Fellow, 1977, Rose and Milton Friedman Senior Fellow in Public Policy, 1980–, Hoover Institution, Stanford University; mem. American Economic Asscn; National Acad. of Education. *Publications:* Economics: Analysis and Issues, 1971; Black Education: Myths and Tragedies, 1972; Say's Law: An Historical Analysis, 1972; Classical Economics Reconsidered, 1974; Affirmative Action: Was It Necessary in Academia?, 1975; Race and Economics, 1975; Patterns of Black Excellence, 1977; Markets and Minorities, 1981; Pink and Brown People, and Other Controversial Essays, 1981; Knowledge and Decision, 1983; Ethnic America: A History, 1983; The Economics and Politics of Race: An International Perspective, 1983; Compassion versus Guilt, and Other Essays, 1984; Marxism: Philosophy and Economics, 1985; Civil Rights: Rhetoric or Reality?, 1985; Education: Assumptions versus History, 1986; A Conflict of Visions: Ideological Origins of Political Struggles, 1987; Judicial Activism Reconsidered, 1989; Preferential Policies: An International Perspective, 1990; Inside American Education: The Decline, the Deception, the Dogmas, 1992; Race and Culture: A World View, 1992; Is Reality Optional?, and Other Essays, 1993; The Vision of the Anointed: Self-Congratulation as a Basis for Social Policy, 1995; Migrations and Cultures: A World View, 1996; Late-talking Children, 1997; Conquests and Cultures: An International History, 1998; Race, Culture, and Equality, 1998; Barbarians Inside the Gates, and Other Controversial Essays, 1999; The Quest for Cosmic Justice, 1999; A Personal Odyssey, 2000; Basic Economics: A Citizen's Guide to the Economy, 2001; Some Thoughts about Writing, 2001. Contributions: books and newspapers. *Address:* c/o Hoover Institution, Stanford University, Stanford, CA 94305, USA.

SOYINKA, Akinwande Oluwole (Wole), BA; Nigerian playwright and lecturer; b. 13 July 1934, Abeokuta; m.; four c. *Education:* Univ. of Ibadan, Nigeria and Univ. of Leeds, UK. *Career:* worked at Royal Court Theatre, London; Research Fellow in Drama, Univ. of Ibadan 1960–61; Lecturer in English, Univ. of Ife 1962–63; Sr Lecturer in English, Univ. of Lagos 1965–67; political prisoner 1967–69; Artistic Dir and Head Dept of Theatre Arts, Univ. of Ibadan 1969–72; Research Prof. in Dramatic Literature, Univ. of Ife 1972, Prof. of Comparative Literature and Head of Dept of Dramatic Arts 1976–85; Goldwin Smith Prof. of Africana Studies and Theatre Cornell Univ. 1988–92; passport seized Sept. 1994, living in France; charged with treason March 1997 in absentia; Ed. Ch'Indaba (fmrly Transition) Accra; Artistic Dir Orisun Theatre, 1960 Masks; Literary Ed. Orisun Acting Editions; Pres. Int. Theatre Inst. 1986–; Fellow, Churchill Coll. Cambridge 1973–74; mem. American Acad. of Arts and Letters, Int. Theatre Inst., Union of Writers of the African Peoples, Nat. Liberation Council of Nigeria; Fellow, Ghana Asscn of Writers, Pan-African Writers Asscn; Chair. Nigeria Road Safety Comm. 1988–91. *Publications:* plays: The Invention 1955, The Lion and the Jewel 1959, The Swamp Dwellers 1959, A Dance of the Forests 1960, The Trials of Brother Jero 1961, The Strong Breed 1962, The Road 1964, Kongi's Harvest 1965, Madmen and Specialists 1971, Before the Blackout 1971, Jero's Metamorphosis 1973, Camwood on the Leaves 1973, The Bacchae of Euripides 1974, Death and the King's Horsemen 1975, Opera Wonyosi 1978, A Play of Giants 1984, Six Plays 1984, Requiem for a Futurologist 1985, From Zia, with Love 1991, A Scourge of Hyacinths (radio play) 1992, The Beatification of Area Boy 1995, King Baabu 2003; novels: The Interpreters 1964, The Forest of a Thousand Daemons (trans.), Season of Anomy 1973; non-fiction: The Man Died (prison memoirs) 1972, Isara: A voyage round Essay 1990, Continuity and Amnesia 1991, Conversations with Wole Soyinka 2001; poetry: Idanre and Other Poems 1967, Poems from Prison 1969, A Shuttle in the Crypt 1972, Poems of Black Africa (ed.) 1975, Ogun Abibman 1977, Mandela's Earth and Other Poems 1988, Samarkand and Other Markets I Have Known 2002; lectures: Myth, Literature and the African World 1972; Aké, The Years of Childhood (autobiog.) 1982, Art, Dialogue and Outrage 1988, Ibadan: The Pentelemes Years (memoir) 1994, The Open Sore of a Continent, A Personal Narrative of the Nigerian Crisis 1996, The Burden of Memory, The Muse of Forgiveness 1999. *Honours:* Commdr Légion d'honneur, Commdr Fed. Repub. of Nigeria 1986, Commdr Order of Merit (Italy) 1990; Hon. DLitt (Leeds) 1973, (Yale) 1981, (Morehouse), (Paul Valéry), (Bayreuth), (Ibadan), (Harvard); Hon. DScS (Edin.) 1977; Rockefeller Foundation Grant 1960, John Whiting Drama Prize 1966, Prisoner of Conscience Award, Amnesty Int., Jock Campbell-New Statesman Literary Award 1969, Nobel Prize for Literature

1986, George Benson Medal, RSL 1990, Writers Guild Lifetime Achievement Award 1996, Distinguished Scholar-in-Residence, New York Univ. 1999 and numerous other awards. *Literary Agent:* Deborah Rogers, Rogers, Coleridge & White, 20 Powis Mews, London, W11 1JN, England. *E-mail:* deborahr@rcwlitagency.demon.co.uk. *Address:* c/o African Writers Series, Heinemann Educational Publishers, Halley Court, Jordan Hill, Oxford, OX2 8EJ, England; c/o PO Box 935, Abeokuta, Ogun State, Nigeria.

SPACKS, Patricia Meyer; Prof. of English; b. 17 Nov. 1929, San Francisco, CA, USA; one d. *Education:* BA, Rollins College, 1949; MA, Yale University, 1950; PhD, University of California at Berkeley, 1955. *Career:* Instructor in English, Indiana University, 1954–56; Instructor in Humanities, University of Florida, 1958–59; Instructor, 1959–61, Asst Prof., 1961–63, Assoc. Prof., 1965–68, Prof. of English, 1968–79, Wellesley College; Prof. of English, 1979–89, Chair., Dept of English, 1985–88, Yale University; Edgar F. Shannon Prof. of English, 1989–, Chair., Dept of English, 1991–96, University of Virginia; mem. MLA, pres., 1994; American Philosophical Society, 1995; ACLS, chair of board, 1997–. *Publications:* The Varied God, 1959; The Insistence of Horror, 1962; 18th Century Poetry (ed.), 1964; John Gay, 1965; Poetry of Vision, 1967; Late Augustan Prose (ed.), 1971; An Argument of Images, 1971; Late Augustan Poetry (ed.), 1973; The Female Imagination, 1975; Imagining a Self, 1976; Contemporary Women Novelists, 1977; The Adolescent Idea, 1981; Gossip, 1985; Desire and Truth, 1990; Boredom: The Literary History of a State of Mind, 1995. *Honours:* American Acad. of Arts and Sciences, 1994. *Address:* Dept of English, 219 Bryan Hall, University of Virginia, Charlottesville, VA 22903, USA.

SPALDING, Esta; American poet and screenwriter; b. Boston, MA. *Career:* based in Vancouver, BC, Canada. *Writing for television:* Da Vinci's Inquest (CBC-TV) 1998–, The Zack Files (Decode Entertainment) 2000, The Eleventh Hour (also story ed., CTV Network) 2002–04. *Film screenplays:* The Republic of Love 2003, Fallen Angels 2003. *Publications:* poetry: Carrying Place 1995, Mere (with Linda Spalding) 2001, Anchoress 2003, The Wife's Account 2004, Lost August 2004. *Address:* c/o Bloodaxe Books Ltd, Highgreen, Tarset, Northumberland NE48 1RP, England. *Website:* www.bloodaxebooks.com.

SPANGENBERG, Christa; German publisher and university lecturer; b. 1928, Munich; m. Berthold Spangenberg 1946 (died 1986); two s. *Education:* music and language studies. *Career:* honorary work for Börsenverein des Deutschen Buchhandels; lecturer, Univ. of Munich 1987–; Founder Int. Youth Library Foundation, Munich 1996–. *Publications:* Elly Petersens praktisches Gartenlexikon, Praktisches Balkon- und Zimmerpflanzenlexikon, Grüne Uhr, Garten Uhr, ABC für Kleine Gärtner. *Honours:* Kulturpreis der Bayrischen Landesstifteung 1999, and other awards. *Address:* Bäumlstrasse 6, 80638 Munich, Germany. *Telephone:* 17-14-23. *Fax:* 17-14-23.

SPARK, Dame Muriel Sarah, DBE, CLit, FRSE, FRSL; British author and poet; b. (Muriel Sarah Camberg), 1 Feb. 1918, Edinburgh, Scotland; m. S. O. Spark 1937 (divorced); one s. *Education:* James Gillespie's High School for Girls, Edinburgh, Heriot-Watt Coll., Edinburgh. *Career:* political intelligence dept, British Foreign Office 1944–45; Ed. The Poetry Review and Gen. Sec. Poetry Soc., London 1947–49; founder, Forum literary magazine. *Radio plays:* The Interview, The Dry River Bed, The Danger Zone, The Party Through the Wall. *Publications:* fiction: The Comforters 1957, Robinson 1958, The Go-Away Bird and Other Stories 1958, Memento Mori 1959, The Ballad of Peckham Rye 1960, The Bachelors 1960, Voices at Play 1961, The Prime of Miss Jean Brodie 1961, The Girls of Slender Means 1963, The Mandelbaum Gate 1965, Collected Stories I 1967, The Public Image 1968, The Very Fine Clock (for children) 1968, The Driver's Seat 1970, Not to Disturb 1971, The Hothouse by the East River 1973, The Abbess of Crewe 1974, The Takeover 1976, Territorial Rights 1979, Loitering with Intent 1981, Bang-Bang You're Dead and Other Stories 1982, The Only Problem 1984, The Stories of Muriel Spark 1985, A Far Cry from Kensington 1988, Symposium 1990, The French Window and the Small Telephone (for children) 1993, Omnibus I 1993, Omnibus II 1994, The Portobello Road (stories) 1995, The Hanging Judge (stories) 1995, Reality and Dreams 1996, Omnibus III 1996, Omnibus IV 1997, Aiding and Abetting 2000, The Complete Short Stories 2001, The Ghost Stories 2003, The Finishing School 2004; poetry: The Fanfarlo and Other Verse 1952, Collected Poems I 1967, Going Up to Sotheby's and Other Poems 1982, All the Poems of Muriel Spark 2004; play: Doctors of Philosophy 1962; non-fiction: Child of Light: A Reassessment of Mary Wollstonecraft Shelley 1951, revised edn as Mary Shelley 1987, John Masefield 1953, Curriculum Vitae (autobiog.) 1992, The Essence of the Brontës 1993; editor: Selected Poems of Emily Brontë 1952, The Brontë Letters 1954. *Honours:* Hon. mem. American Acad. of Arts and Letters 1978, Scottish PEN; Commdr, Ordre des Arts et Lettres 1996; Hon. DLitt (Strathclyde) 1971, (Edin.) 1989, (Aberdeen) 1995, (St Andrews) 1998, (Oxford) 1999, (London) 2001; Hon. DUniv (Heriot-Watt) 1995; The Observer Story Prize 1951, Italia Prize 1962, Yorkshire Post Book of the Year Award 1965, James Tait Black Memorial Prize 1965, Saltire Scottish Book of the Year Award 1987, First Prize, FNAC La Meilleur Recueil des Nouvelles Etrangères 1987, Ingersoll Foundation T. S. Eliot Award 1992, David Cohen British Literature Prize 1997, Int. PEN Gold Pen Award 1998, Edmund Campion Award 2001, Boccaccio Prize 2002. *Literary Agent:* c/o David Higham Associates Ltd, 5–8 Lower John Street, Golden Square, London, W1R 4HA, England. *Telephone:* (20) 7437-7888 . *Fax:* (20) 7437-1072. *Website:* www.murielspark.com.

SPARKS, Nicholas; Writer; b. 31 Dec. 1965, Omaha, NE, USA; m. Cathy Cote 1989; three s. two d. *Education:* Univ. of Notre Dame. *Publications:* The Notebook, 1996; Message in a Bottle, 1998; A Walk to Remember, 1999; The Rescue, 2000; A Bend in the Road, 2001; Nights in Rodanthe, 2002; The Guardian, 2003; The Wedding, 2003. *Address:* c/o Author Mail, Warner Books, 1271 Avenue of the Americas, New York, NY 10020, USA. *Website:* www.nicholassparks.com.

SPARSHOTT, Francis Edward, BA, MA; philosopher, writer, poet and retd academic; b. 19 May 1926, Chatham, Kent, England; m. Kathleen Elizabeth Vaughan 1953; one d. *Education:* Corpus Christi College, Oxford. *Career:* Lecturer, 1950–55, Asst Prof., 1955–62, Assoc. Prof., 1962–64, Prof., 1964–91, of Philosophy, University of Toronto; mem. American Society for Aesthetics, pres., 1981–82; Canadian Classical Asscn; Canadian Philosophical Asscn, pres., 1975–76; League of Canadian Poets, pres., 1977–78; PEN International, Canadian Centre; Royal Society of Canada, fellow, 1977. *Publications:* An Enquiry into Goodness and Related Concepts, 1958; The Structure of Aesthetics, 1963; The Concept of Criticism: An Essay, 1967; Looking for Philosophy, 1972; The Theory of the Arts, 1982; Off the Ground: First Steps in the Philosophy of Dance, 1988; Taking Life Seriously: A Study of the Argument of the Nicomachean Ethics, 1994; A Measured Pace: Toward a Philosophical Understanding of the Arts of Dance, 1995; The Future of Aesthetics, 1998. Poetry: A Divided Voice, 1965; A Cardboard Garage, 1969; The Rainy Hills: Verses After a Japanese Fashion, 1979; The Naming of the Beasts, 1979; New Fingers for Old Dikes, 1980; The Cave of Trophonius and Other Poems, 1983; The Hanging Gardens of Etobicoke, 1983; Storms and Screens, 1986; Sculling to Byzantium, 1989; Views from the Zucchini Gazebo, 1994; Home from the Air, 1997; The City Dwellers, 2000. Contributions: various books and periodicals. *Honours:* ACLS Fellowship, 1961–62; Canada Council Fellowship, 1970–71; Killam Research Fellowship, 1977–78; First Prize for Poetry, CBC Radio Literary Competition, 1981; Centennial Medal, Royal Society of Canada, 1982; Connaught Senior Fellowship in the Humanities, 1984–85; Doctor of Sacred Letters (DLitt Sac), hc, Victoria University, 2000; LLD, hc, University of Toronto, 2000. *Address:* 50 Crescentwood Road, Scarborough, ON M1N 1E4, Canada.

SPENCE, Alan; Dramatist, Writer and Poet; b. 5 Dec. 1947, Glasgow, Scotland. *Education:* University of Glasgow, 1966–69, 1973–74. *Career:* Writer-in-Residence, University of Glasgow, 1975–77, Traverse Theatre, Edinburgh, 1982, University of Edinburgh, 1989–92, University of Aberdeen, 1996–. *Publications:* Plays: Sailmaker, 1982; Space Invaders, 1983; Changed Days, 1991. Fiction: Its Colours They Are Fine (short stories), 1977; The Magic Flute (novel), 1990; Stone Garden (short stories), 1995. Poetry: Plop (15 Haiku), 1970; Glasgow Zen, 1981. *Honours:* Scottish Arts Council Book Awards, 1977, 1990, 1996; People's Prize, 1996; TMA Martini Prize, 1996. *Address:* 21 Waverley Park, Edinburgh EH8 8ER, Scotland.

SPENCE, Jonathan (Dermott); Prof. of History and Writer; b. 11 Aug. 1936, Surrey, England; m. 1st Helen Alexander, 15 Sept. 1962, divorced 1993, two s.; m. 2nd Chin Annping, 12 Aug. 1993. *Education:* BA, University of Cambridge, 1959; PhD, Yale University, 1965. *Career:* Asst Prof., 1966–71, Prof. of History, 1971–, Yale University; Wiles Lecturer, Queen's University, Belfast, 1985; Gauss Lecturer, Princeton University, 1987; Visiting Prof., Beijing University, 1987; Hon. Prof., Nanjing University, 1993; mem. American Acad. of Arts and Sciences; American Philosophical Society; Asscn of Asian Studies. *Publications:* Ts'Ao Yin and the K'Ang-Hsi Emperor, 1966; To Change China, 1969; Emperor of China, 1974; The Death of Woman Wang, 1978; The Gate of Heavenly Peace, 1981; The Memory Palace of Matteo Ricci, 1984; The Question of Hu, 1988; The Search for Modern China, 1990; Chinese Roundabout, 1992; God's Chinese Son, 1996; The Chan's Great Continent, 1998; Mao Zedong, 1999; Treason by the Book, 2001. Contributions: Professional journals. *Honours:* Yale Fellow in East Asian Studies, 1962–65, 1968–70; John Adison Porter Prize, 1965; Christopher Award, 1975; Devane Teaching Medal, 1978; Guggenheim Fellowship, 1979–80; Los Angeles Times Book Award, 1982; Vurseli Prize, American Acad. and Institute of Arts and Letters, 1983; Comisso Prize, Italy, 1987; John D. and Catherine T. MacArthur Foundation Fellowship, 1988–93; Gelber Prize, Canada, 1990; Hon. doctorates. *Address:* 691 Forest Rd, New Haven, CT 06515, USA.

SPENCE, William (John Duncan), (Jessica Blair, Jim Bowden, Kirk Ford, Floyd Rogers, Bill Spence); Author; b. 20 April 1923, Middlesborough, England; m. Joan Mary Rhoda Ludley, 8 Sept. 1944, one s., three d. *Education:* St Mary's Teachers Training College, 1940–42. *Career:* mem. Society of Authors. *Publications:* numerous books, including: Romantic Ryedale (with Joan Spence), 1977; Harpooned, 1981; The Medieval Monasteries of Yorkshire (with Joan Spence), 1981; Stories from Yorkshire Monasteries (with Joan Spence), 1992. As Jessica Blair: The Red Shawl, 1993; A Distant Harbour, 1993; Storm Bay, 1994; The Restless Spirit, 1996; The Other Side of the River, 1997; The Seaweed Gatherers, 1998; Portrait of Charlotte, 1999; The Locket, 2000; The Long Way Home, 2001; The

Restless Heart, 2001; Time and Tide, 2002; Echoes of the Past, 2003. Other: 36 Westerns; Three war novels. *Address:* Post Office, Ampleforth College, York YO62 4EZ, England.

SPENCER, Elizabeth; Writer; b. 19 July 1921, Carrollton, Mississippi, USA; m. John Arthur Rusher, 29 Sept. 1956. *Education:* AB, cum laude, Belhaven College, 1942; MA, Vanderbilt University, 1943. *Career:* Writer-in-Residence, Adjunct Prof., Concordia University, Montréal, 1977–86; Visiting Prof., University of North Carolina at Chapel Hill, 1986–92. *Publications:* Fire in the Morning, 1948; This Crooked Way, 1952; The Voice at the Back Door, 1956; The Light in the Piazza, 1960; Knights and Dragons, 1965; No Place for an Angel, 1967; Ship Island and Other Stories, 1968; The Snare, 1972; The Stories of Elizabeth Spencer, 1981; The Salt Line, 1984; Jack of Diamonds, 1988; For Lease or Sale (drama), 1989; The Night Travellers, 1991; Landscapes of the Heart (memoir), 1998; The Southern Woman, 2001. Contributions: New Yorker; Atlantic; Southern Review; Kenyon Review. *Address:* 402 Longleaf Dr., Chapel Hill, NC 27517, USA.

SPENCER, LaVyrle; Writer; b. 17 Aug. 1943, Browerville, Minnesota, USA; m. Daniel F. Spencer, 10 Feb. 1962, two d. *Education:* High School, Staples, Minnesota. *Publications:* The Fulfillment, 1979; The Endearment, 1982; Hummingbird, 1983; Twice Loved, 1984; Sweet Memories, 1984; A Heart Speaks, 1986; Tears, 1986; Years, 1986; The Gamble, 1987; Separate Bed, 1987; Vows, 1988; Morning Glory, 1988; Bitter Sweet, 1990; Forgiving, 1991; November of the Heart, 1992; Bygones, 1993; Family Blessings, 1994; That Camden Summer, 1996. *Honours:* Historical Romance of the Year Awards, Romance Writers of America, 1983, 1984, 1985. *Address:* 6701 79th Ave, Brooklyn Park, MN 55445, USA.

SPENCER, Paul; British social anthropologist and professor; b. 25 March 1932, London, England; m. Diane Wells. *Education:* Christ's Coll., Cambridge, Wadham Coll., Oxford. *Career:* scientific officer, Tavistock Inst. of Human Relations, London 1962–71; teacher, SOAS, London 1971–97; Hon. Dir, Int. African Inst. 1996–. *Publications:* The Samburu 1965, Nomads in Alliance 1973, Society and the Dance 1985, The Maasai of Matapato 1988, Anthropology and the Riddle of the Sphinx 1990, The Pastoral Continuum 1998, Time, Space and the Unknown: Maasai Configurations of Power and Providence 2003. *Address:* 4 Gentle Street, Frome, Somerset BA11 1JA, England.

SPIEGELMAN, Art; American cartoonist, editor and writer; b. 15 Feb. 1948, Stockholm, Sweden; m. Françoise Mouly 1977; two c. *Education:* Harpur Coll., Binghamton, NY. *Career:* creative consultant, artist, designer, ed. and writer, Topps Chewing Gum Inc, New York 1965–87; Ed., Douglas Comix 1972; Instructor, San Francisco Acad. of Art 1974–75, New York School of the Visual Arts 1979–86; Contributing Ed., Arcade, The Comics Revue 1975–76; founder-Ed., Raw comics magazine 1980–; staff artist and contributing ed., The New Yorker 1993–2003; Ed., Little Lit series of children's comics anthologies. *Publications as author and illustrator:* The Complete Mr Infinity 1970, The Viper Vicar of Vice, Villainy, and Vickedness 1972, Ace Hole, Midge Detective 1974, The Language of Comics 1974, Breakdowns: From Maus to Now: An Anthology of Strips 1977, Work and Turn 1979, Every Day Has Its Dog 1979, Two-Fisted Painters Action Adventure 1980, Maus: A Survivor's Tale (Pulitzer Prize Special Citation 1992) 1986, Read Yourself Raw (with F. Mouly) 1987, Maus II 1992, The Wild Party (illustrations to book by Joseph Moncure March) 1994, Open Me... I'm a Dog 1997, In the Shadow of No Towers 2004. *Honours:* Playboy Editorial Award for Best Comic Strip 1982, Joel M. Cavior Award for Jewish Writing 1986, Stripschappening Award for Best Foreign Comics Album 1987, Alpha Art Award, Angoulerne, France 1993. *Literary Agent:* Steven Barclay Agency, 12 Western Avenue, Petaluma, CA 94952, USA. *Telephone:* (707) 773-0654. *Fax:* (707) 778-1868. *Website:* www.barclayagency.com.

SPILLANE, Mickey, (Frank Morrison Spillane); Author; b. 9 March 1918, New York, NY, USA; m. 1st Mary Ann Pearce, 1945, divorced, two s. two d.; m. 2nd Sherri Malinou, 1964, divorced; m. 3rd Jane Rodgers Johnson, 1983. *Education:* Kansas State College. *Publications:* I, the Jury, 1947; Vengeance is Mine!, 1950; My Gun is Quick, 1950; The Big Kill, 1951; One Lonely Night, 1951; The Long Wait, 1951; Kiss Me, Deadly, 1952; Tough Guys, 1960; The Deep, 1961; The Girl Hunters, 1962; Day of the Guns, 1964; The Snake, 1964; Bloody Sunrise, 1965; The Death Dealers, 1965; The Twisted Thing, 1966; The By-Pass Control, 1967; The Delta Factor, 1967; Body Lovers, 1967; Killer Mine, 1968; Me, Hood!, 1969; Survival: Zero, 1970; Tough Guys, 1970; The Erection Set, 1972; The Last Cop Out, 1973; The Flier, 1973; Tomorrow I Die, 1984; The Killing Man, 1989; Back Alley, 1996. Editor: Murder is My Business, 1994. Television Series: Mike Hammer, 1984–87. Children's Books: The Day the Sea Rolled Back, 1979; The Ship That Never Was, 1982. *Address:* c/o E. P. Dutton, 375 Hudson St, New York, NY 10014, USA.

SPONG, John Shelby; Episcopal Clergyman, Writer and Lecturer; b. 16 June 1931, Charlotte, NC, USA; m. 1st Joan Lydia Ketner, deceased; m. 2nd Christine, three d. *Education:* BA, University of North Carolina, 1952; MDiv, Virginia Theological Seminary, 1955. *Career:* Ordained Episcopal Minister, 1955; Rector, Episcopal Churches, Durham, NC, 1955–57, Tarboro, NC, 1957–65, Lynchburg, VA, 1965–69, Richmond, VA, 1969–76; Chaplain, Duke University, 1955–57, Randolph-Macon College, 1965–69, Medical College of Virginia, 1969–76; Bishop, Northern New Jersey Episcopal Church, Newark, 1976–2000; Lecturer, Harvard University, 2000–. *Publications:* Honest Prayer, 1973; This Hebrew Lord, 1974, revised edn as This Hebrew Lord: A Bishop's Search for the Authentic Jesus, 1993; Dialogue: In Search of Jewish-Christian Understanding (with Jack Daniel Spiro), 1975; Christpower, 1975; The Living Commandments, 1977; The Easter Moment, 1980; Into the Whirlwind: The Future of the Church, 1983; Beyond Moralism: A Contemporary View of the Ten Commandments (with Dennis G. Haines), 1986; Living in Sin?: A Bishop Rethinks Human Sexuality, 1988; Rescuing the Bible from Fundamentalism: A Bishop Rethinks the Meaning of Scripture, 1991; Born of a Woman: A Bishop Rethinks the Birth of Jesus, 1992; Resurrection: Myth or Reality?: A Bishop's Search for the Origins of Christianity, 1994; Liberating the Gospels: Reading the Bible with Jewish Eyes: Freeing Jesus from Two Thousand Years of Misunderstanding, 1996; Why Christianity Must Change or Die: A Bishop Speaks to Believers in Exile, 1998; The Bishop's Voice: Selected Essays, 1979–1999, 1999; Here I Stand: My Struggle for a Christianity of Integrity, Love, and Equality, 2000. Contributions: periodicals. *Honours:* Brotherhood Award, National Conference of Christians and Jews, 1974. *Address:* 24 Puddingstone Rd, Morris Plain, NJ 07950, USA.

SPOONER, David Eugene, BA, PhD; writer, poet and naturalist; b. 1 Sept. 1941, West Kirby, Wirral, England; m. Marion O'Neil 1986; one d. *Education:* University of Leeds, University of Manchester, University of Bristol. *Career:* Lecturer, University of Kent, 1968–73, Manchester Polytechnic, 1974–75; Visiting Prof., Pennsylvania State University, 1973–74; Head of Publishing, Borderline Press, 1976–85; Dir, Butterfly Conservation, East Scotland; mem. Welsh Acad. Assoc.; Asscn Benjamin Constant; Academic Board, London Diplomatic Acad.; Thoreau Society. *Publications:* Unmakings, 1977; The Angelic Fly: The Butterfly in Art, 1992; The Metaphysics of Insect Life, 1995; Insect into Poem: 20th Century Hispanic Poetry, 1999; Creatures of Air: Poetry 1976–2001, 2001; Thoreau's Insects, 2002; William Blake and Contemporary Science, 2004. Contributions: Iron; Interactions; Tandem; Weighbauk; Revue de Littérature Comparée; Bestia (Fable Society of America); Margin; Corbie Press; Butterfly Conservation News; Butterfly News; Field Studies; Annales Benjamin Constant. *Address:* 96 Halbeath Road, Dunfermline, Fife KY12 7LR, Scotland. *Telephone:* (1383) 729251. *E-mail:* doctorspooner@tiscali.co.uk. *Website:* www.davidspooner.freeservers.com.

SPRIGEL, Oliver (see Avice, Claude (Pierre Marie)).

SPRIGGE, Timothy Lauro Squire, BA, MA, PhD, FRSE; British academic and writer; *Professor Emeritus of Philosophy, University of Edinburgh*; b. 14 Jan. 1932, London, England; m. Giglia Gordon 1959; one s. two d. *Career:* Prof. of Philosophy, now Prof. Emeritus of Philosophy, Univ. of Edinburgh; mem. Mind Asscn, Scots Philosophical Club. *Publications:* The Correspondence of Jeremy Bentham (ed.) 1968, Facts, Words and Beliefs 1970, Santayana: An Examination of his Philosophy 1974, The Vindication of Absolute Idealism 1983, Theories of Existence 1984, The Rational Foundation of Ethics 1987, James and Bradley: American Truth and British Reality 1993; contrib. to professional journals. *Address:* Saffrons, 5 King Henry's Road, Lewes, East Sussex BN7 1BT, England.

SPRINGER, Nancy, BA; writer and poet; b. 5 July 1948, Montclair, NJ, USA; m. Joel H. Springer 1969 (divorced 1997); one s. one d. *Education:* Gettysburg Coll. *Career:* personal development plan instructor, University of Pittsburgh, 1983–85; Leisure Learning Instructor, York College, Pennsylvania, 1986–91; Education Instructor, Franklin and Marshall College, 1988–; Instructor of Creative Writing, York College of PA, 1997–1999; Writing Popular Fiction Masters' Degree Program, Seton Hill College, 1998–; mem. Society of Children's Book Writers and Illustrators; Pennwriters, pres., 1992–93. *Publications:* The Sable Moon, 1981; The Black Beast, 1982; The Golden Swan, 1983; Wings of Flame, 1985; Chains of Gold, 1986; A Horse to Love (children's), 1987; Madbond, 1987; Chance and Other Gestures of the Hand of Fate, 1987; The Hex Witch of Seldom, 1988; Not on a White Horse (children's), 1988; Apocalypse, 1989; They're All Named Wildfire (children's), 1989; Red Wizard (children's), 1990; Colt (children's), 1991; The Friendship Song (children's), 1992; The Great Pony Hassle (children's), 1993; Stardark Songs (poems), 1993; Larque on the Wing, 1994; The Boy on a Black Horse (children's), 1994; Metal Angel, 1994; Music of Their Hooves (children's poems), 1994; Toughing It, 1994; Looking for Jamie Bridger (children's), 1995; Fair Peril, 1996; Secret Star (children's), 1997; I Am Mordred, 1998; Sky Rider (children's), 1999; Plumage, 2000; I Am Morgan Le Fay, 2001; Rowan Hood: Outlaw Girl of Sherwood Forest (children's), 2001; Separate Sisters (children's), 2001; Lionclaw: A Tale of Rowan Hood (children's), 2002. Contributions: Magazines and journals. *Honours:* Distinguished Alumna, Gettysburg College, 1987; International Reading Asscn Children's Choice, 1988; Joan Fassler Memorial Book Award, 1992; International Reading Asscn Young Adult's Choice, 1993; Edgar Allan Poe Awards, MWA, 1995, 1996; James Tiptree Jr Award, 1995; Carolyn W. Field Award, 1995; Outstanding Pennsylvania Writer Award. *Literary Agent:* Jean V. Naggar Literary Agency, 216 E 75th Street, New York, NY 10021, USA.

SPRINKLE, Patricia Houck; Writer; b. 13 Nov. 1943, Bluefield, West Virginia, USA; m. Robert William Sprinkle, 12 Sept. 1970, two s. *Education:* AB, Vassar College, 1965. *Career:* mem. MWA; Penwoman; Sisters in Crime, publicity chair. *Publications:* Fiction: Murder at Markham, 1988; Murder in the Charleston Manner, 1990; Murder on Peachtree Street, 1991;

Somebody's Dead in Snellville, 1992; Death of a Dunwoody Matron, 1993; A Mystery Bred in Buckhead, 1994; Deadly Secrets on the St Johns, 1995; When Did We Lose Harriet?, 1997; But Why Shoot the Magistrate?, 1998; The Remember Box, 2000; Carley's Song, 2001. Non-Fiction: Hunger: Understanding the Crisis Through Games, 1980; In God's Image: Meditations for the New Mother, 1988; Housewarmings: For Those Who Make a House a Home, 1992; Women Who Do Too Much: Stress and the Myth of the Superwoman, 1992; Children Who Do Too Little, 1993; A Gift From God, 1994; Women Home Alone: Learning to Thrive, 1996. Contributions: Magazines.

SPROTT, Duncan; British writer; b. 2 Dec. 1952, Ongar, Essex, England. *Education:* Univ. of St Andrews, Fife, Scotland and Heatherley School of Art, London. *Career:* mem. PEN, Soc. of Authors, Egypt Exploration Soc., Soc. of Antiquaries of Scotland, Soc. of Genealogists, Guild of One-Name Studies, Soc. for the Promotion of Hellenic Studies, Soc. for the Promotion of Roman Studies. *Publications:* 1784 (compiler) 1984, The Clopton Hercules (aka The Rise of Mr Warde) 1991, Our Lady of the Potatoes 1995, Sprottichronicon (genealogy) 2000, The House of the Eagle 2004, Our Lady of the Crocodiles 2005. *Honours:* Arts Council Literature Award 1995. *Literary Agent:* Rogers, Coleridge & White Ltd, 20 Powis Mews, London, W11 1JN, England.

SPUFFORD, Francis; British journalist and writer; b. 1964. *Publications:* I May Be Some Time: Ice and the English Imagination (Writers' Guild Award for Best Non-Fiction Book 1996, Somerset Maugham Award) 1996, Cultural Babbage (ed., essay collection) 1997, The Child that Books Built 2002, Backroom Boys 2003; contrib. to Granta. *Honours:* Sunday Times Young Writer of the Year 1977. *Address:* c/o Faber and Faber Ltd, 3 Queen Square, London, WC1N 3AU, England.

SPURLING, (Susan) Hilary, BA; biographer and critic; b. 25 Dec. 1940, England; m. John Spurling 1961; two s. one d. *Education:* Somerville Coll., Oxford. *Career:* theatre critic, The Spectator 1964–69, Literary Ed. 1966–70; book reviewer, The Observer 1969–86, Daily Telegraph 1987–. *Publications:* Ivy When Young: The Early Life of I. Compton-Burnett 1884–1919, 1974; Handbook to Anthony Powell's Music of Time, 1977; Secrets of a Woman's Heart: The Later Life of I. Compton-Burnett 1920–69, 1984; Elinor Fettiplace's Receipt Book, 1986; Paul Scott: A Life, 1990; Paper Spirits, 1992; The Unknown Matisse: 1869–1908, 1998; La Grande Thérèse: The Greatest Swindle of the Century, 1999; The Girl from the Fiction Department: A Portrait of Sonia Orwell, 2002; Matisse 2005. *Honours:* Rose Mary Cranshaw Prize, 1974; Heinemann Award, 1984; Duff Cooper Prize, 1984; Heywood Hill Literary Prize, 2003. *Literary Agent:* David Higham Associates, 5–8 Lower John Street, Golden Square, London, W1R 4HA, England.

SPURLING, John (Antony); Dramatist, Novelist and Art Critic; b. 17 July 1936, Kisumu, Kenya; m. Hilary Forrest, 4 April 1961, two s. one d. *Education:* BA, St John's College, Oxford, 1960. *Publications:* Plays: MacRune's Guevara (as Realised by Edward Hotel), 1969; In the Heart of the British Museum, 1971; Shades of Heathcliff and Death of Captain Doughty, 1975; The British Empire, Part One, 1982. Fiction: The Ragged End, 1989; After Zenda, 1995. Other: Beckett: A Study of His Plays (with John Fletcher), 1972, revised third edn as Beckett, the Playwright, 1985; Graham Greene, 1983. Contributions: books, newspapers, periodicals, theatre (16 plays produced, 1969–2003), radio (10 plays, 1976–2002), and television (4 plays, 1970–73). *Honours:* Henfield Writing Fellowship, University of East Anglia, 1973. *Address:* c/o Macnaughton Lord 2000 Ltd, 19 Margravine Gardens, London W6 8RL, England. *Website:* www.author.co.uk/spurling.

STABENOW, Dana; Writer; b. 27 March 1952, Anchorage, AK, USA. *Education:* BA, Journalism, 1973, MFA, 1985, Univ. of Alaska. *Publications:* Second Star, 1991; A Handful of Stars, 1991; A Cold Day for Murder, 1992; Dead in the Water, 1993; A Fatal Thaw, 1993; A Cold-Blooded Business, 1994; Red Planet Run, 1995; Play with Fire, 1995; Blood Will Tell, 1996; Breakup, 1997; Killing Grounds, 1998; Fire and Ice, 1998; Hunter's Moon, 1999; Out for Blood, 1999; So Sure of Death, 1999; Midnight Come Again, 2000; Nothing Gold Can Stay, 2000; The Singing of the Dead, 2001; A Fine and Bitter Snow, 2002. *Honours:* Edgar Allan Poe Award, MWA, 1992. *Address:* c/o Richard Henshaw Group, 132 W 22nd St, New York, NY 10023, USA.

STAFFORD, David (Alexander Tetlow); Historian and Writer; b. 10 March 1942, Newcastle upon Tyne, England; m. *Education:* BA, University of Cambridge, 1963; PhD, University of London, 1968. *Career:* Third Sec., 1967–68, Second Sec., 1968, British Foreign Office, London; Research Assoc., Centre of International Studies, LSE, 1968–70; Asst Prof., 1970–76, Assoc. Prof., 1976–82, Prof. of History, 1982–84, University of Victoria, BC; Senior Assoc. Mem., St Antony's College, Oxford, 1976–77; Dir of Studies, 1985–86, Exec. Dir, 1986–92, Canadian Institute of International Affairs, Toronto; Visiting Prof., Institute for Advanced Studies in the Humanities, 1992–2000, Project Dir, Center for Second World War Studies, 2000–, University of Edinburgh. *Publications:* From Anarchism to Reformism: A Study of the Political Activities of Paul Brousse, 1870–90, 1971; Britain and European Resistance, 1940–1945: A Survey of the Special Operations Executive, with Documents, 1980; Camp X: Canada's School for Secret Agents, 1941–1945, 1986; The Silent Game: The Real World of Imaginary Spies, 1988; Spy Wars: Espionage and Canada: From Gouzenko to Glasnost, 1990; Security and Intelligence in a Changing World: New Perspectives for the 1990s (ed. with A. Stuart Farson and Wesley K. Ward), 1991; Churchill and Secret Service, 1998; American-British-Canadian Intelligence Relations, 1939–2000, 2000; Secret Agent: The True Story of the Special Operations Executive, 2000; Roosevelt and Churchill: Men of Secrets, 2000; Spies Beneath Berlin, 2000; Ten Days to D-Day, 2003. Contributions: scholarly journals and general periodicals. *Address:* c/o Centre for Second World War Studies, University of Edinburgh, Edinburgh EH8 9LN, Scotland. *E-mail:* david.stafford@ed.ac.uk.

STAINES, David; Prof. of English, Writer, Trans. and Ed.; b. 8 Aug. 1946, Toronto, Ontario, Canada. *Education:* BA, University of Toronto, 1967; AM, 1968, PhD, 1973, Harvard University. *Career:* Asst Prof. of English, Harvard University, 1973–78; Hon. Research Fellow, University College London, 1977–78; Assoc. Prof., 1978–85, Prof. of English, 1985–, Dean, Faculty of Arts, 1996–, University of Ottawa; Five College Prof. of Canadian Studies, Smith College, 1982–84. *Publications:* The Canadian Imagination: Dimensions of a Literary Culture (ed.), 1977; Tennyson's Camelot: The Idylls of the King and Its Medieval Sources, 1982; Stephen Leacock: A Reappraisal (ed.), 1986; The Forty-Ninth and Other Parallels: Contemporary Canadian Perspectives (ed.), 1986; The Complete Romances of Chrétien de Troyes (trans.), 1990; Beyond the Provinces: Literary Canada at Century's End (trans.), 1995; Margaret Lawrence: Critical Reflections (ed.), 2001. Contributions: Professional journals. *Address:* Dept of English, University of Ottawa, Ottawa, Ontario K1N 6N5, Canada.

STALLWORTHY, Jon (Howie); Prof. of English Literature, Poet and Writer; b. 18 Jan. 1935, London, England; m. Gillian Waldock, 25 June 1960, three c. *Education:* BA, 1958, BLitt, 1961, Magdalen College, Oxford. *Career:* Ed., 1959–71, Deputy Academic Publisher, 1974–77, OUP; Visiting Fellow, All Souls College, Oxford, 1971–72; John Wendell Anderson Prof. of English Literature, Cornell University, Ithaca, New York, 1977–86; Reader in English Literature, 1986–92, Prof. of English, 1992–2000, University of Oxford, Sr Research Fellow, Wolfson Coll. 2000–; mem. British Acad., fellow; FRSL. *Publications:* Poetry: The Earthly Paradise, 1958; The Astronomy of Love, 1961; Out of Bounds, 1963; The Almond Tree, 1967; A Day in the City, 1967; Root and Branch, 1969; Positives, 1969; A Dinner of Herbs, 1970; Alexander Blok: The Twelve and Other Poems (trans. with France), 1970; Hand in Hand, 1974; The Apple Barrel: Selected Poems, 1955–63, 1974; A Familiar Tree, 1978; The Anzac Sonata: Selected Poems, 1986; The Guest from the Future, 1995; Rounding the Horn: Collected Poems, 1998. Other: Between the Lines: Yeats's Poetry in the Making, 1963; Vision and Revision in Yeats's Last Poems, 1969; The Penguin Book of Love Poetry (ed.), 1973; Wilfred Owen: A Biography, 1974; Poets of the First World War, 1974; Boris Pasternak: Selected Poems (trans. with France), 1982; The Complete Poems and Fragments of Wilfred Owen (ed.), 1983; The Oxford Book of War Poetry (ed.), 1984; The Poems of Wilfred Owen (ed.), 1985; First Lines: Poems Written in Youth from Herbert to Heaney (ed.), 1987; Henry Reed: Collected Poems (ed.), 1991; Louis MacNeice, 1995; Singing School: The Making of a Poet, 1998; Aleksander Blok: Selected Poems (trans. with France), 2000, Anthem for Doomed Youth: Twelve Soldier Poets of the First World War (ed.) 2002. Contributions: Professional journals. *Honours:* Duff Cooper Memorial Prize, 1974; WHSmith Literary Award, 1974; E. M. Forster Award, 1975; Southern Arts Literary Prize, 1995. *Address:* Wolfson College, Oxford OX2 6UD, England.

STAMPER, Alex (see Kent, Arthur (William Charles)).

STANFIELD, Anne (see Coffman, Virginia (Edith)).

STANG, Peter J., BSc; writer and academic; b. Nov. 1941, Nürnburg, Germany. *Education:* DePaul Univ., Chicago, Univ. of California at Berkeley. *Career:* Nat. Inst. of Health work at Princeton Univ.; Dept Chair 1989–95, Distinguished Prof. of Chemistry 1992–, Dean of the Coll. of Science, Univ. of Utah; Assoc. Ed. 1982–99, Ed. 1999–, Journal of the American Chemical Soc.; Ed.-in-Chief, Journal of Organic Chemistry 2000–01; elected mem., Nat. Acad. of Sciences 2000. *Publications include:* Metal-catalyzed Cross-Coupling Reactions 1997, Templated Organic Synthesis (co-ed.) 1999. *Honours:* JSPS Fellowship 1995, 1998, Lady Davis Fellowship in Haifa Israel 1986, 1997; Fulbright Hays Sr Scholar to Zagreb, Croatia 1988; Dr hc (Russian Acad. of Sciences), (Lomonosov Moscow State Univ.) 1992, American Chemical Soc. James Flack Norris Award in Physical Organic Chemistry 1998 ; A. von Humboldt Sr Scientist Award 1977, 1997. *Address:* Department of Chemistry, University of Utah, 315 South 1400 East, Room 2020, Salt Lake City, UT 84112-0850; c/o Journal Publications, American Chemical Society, 2540 Olentangy River Road, PO Box 3330, Columbus, OH 43210, USA.

STANSKY, Peter (David Lyman); Prof. of History, Writer and Ed.; b. 18 Jan. 1932, New York, NY, USA. *Education:* BA, Yale University, 1953; BA, 1955, MA, 1959, King's College, Cambridge; PhD, Harvard University, 1961. *Career:* Instructor in History, 1961–64, Asst Prof., 1964–68, Harvard University; Assoc. Prof., 1968–73, Prof., 1973–, of History, Frances and Charles Field Prof. of History, 1974–, Stanford University; Assoc. Ed., Journal of British Studies, 1973–85; Ed., North American Conference on British Studies Bibliographical Series, 1977–87; Visiting Fellow, All Souls College, 1979, Christensen Fellow, St Catherine's College, 1983, Oxford; Co-Ed., Virginia Woolf Miscellany, 1984–2002; Fellow, Center for Advanced

Study in the Behavioral Sciences, 1988–89; various guest lectureships; mem. American Acad. of Arts and Sciences, fellow; American Historical Asscn; National Book Critics Circle, dir, 1980–85; North American Conference on British Studies, pres., 1974–76; FRHistS; Society for the Promotion of Science and Scholarship, pres.; Virginia Woolf Society; William Morris Society. *Publications:* Ambitions and Strategies: The Struggle for the Leadership of the Liberal Party in the 1890s, 1964; Journey to the Frontier: Julian Bell and John Cornford, their Lives and the 1930s (with William Abrahams), 1966; The Unknown Orwell (with William Abrahams), 1972; England Since 1867: Continuity and Change, 1973; Gladstone: A Progress in Politics, 1979; Orwell: The Transformation (with William Abrahams), 1979; William Morris, 1983; Redesigning the World, 1985; London's Burning (with William Abrahams), 1994; On or About December 1910: Early Bloomsbury and Its Intimate World, 1996; From William Morris to Sergeant Pepper, 1999; Sussoon: The Worlds of Philip and Sybil, 2003. Editor: The Left and War: The British Labour Party and the First World War, 1969; Winston Churchill: A Profile, 1973; The Victorian Revolution, 1973; Modern British History Series (with Leslie Hume), 18 vols, 1982; On Nineteen Eighty-Four, 1983; Modern European History Series, 47 vols, 1987–92. *Honours:* Guggenheim Fellowships, 1966–67, 1973–74; ACLS Fellow, 1978–79; National Endowment for the Humanities Senior Fellowships, 1983, 1998–99; Hon. DL, Wittenberg University, 1984. *Address:* c/o Dept of History, Stanford University, Stanford, CA 94305, USA.

STAPLES, Brent; Writer; b. 1951, Chester, Pennsylvania, USA. *Education:* BA, Widener University, 1973; PhD, University of Chicago, 1977. *Career:* Reporter, Chicago Sun-Times, 1982–83; Editorial Writer, New York Times, 1983–. *Publications:* Parallel Time: Growing Up in Black and White, 1994. Contributions: periodicals. *Honours:* Danforth Fellowship. *Address:* c/o New York Times, 229 W 43rd St, New York, NY 10036, USA.

STARK, Joshua (see Olsen, Theodore Victor).

STARK, Richard (see Westlake, Donald Edwin).

STARKEY, David; Historian and Author; b. 3 Jan. 1945, Kendal, England. *Education:* Fitzwilliam College Cambridge. *Career:* Research Fellow, Fitzwilliam College, Cambridge, 1970–72, Visiting Fellow, 1998–2001, Bye-Fellow, 2001; Lecturer in History, Dept. of International History, LSE, 1972–98; Visiting Vernon Prof. of Biography, Dartmouth College, NH, 1987, 1989; British Council Specialist Visitor, Australia, 1989; panellist, Moral Maze (BBC Radio 4); presenter weekend show, Talk Radio, 1995–98; presenter/writer, This Land of England (Channel 4), 1985, Henry VIII (Channel 4) 1998, Elizabeth (Channel 4) 2000, Six Wives of Henry VIII (Channel 4) 2001; mem., Editorial Bd. History Today, 1980–, Commemorative Plaques Working Group, English Heritage 1993–; Pres., Soc. for Court Studies, 1995–; Patron, Tory Group for Homosexual Equality, 1994–; Historical Adviser to Henry VIII Exhbn, National Maritime Museum, Greenwich, 1991; Hon. Assoc. Rationalist, Press Asscn, 1995–; mem. Fellow, Royal Historical Society, 1984, Society of Antiquaries of London, 1994. *Publications:* This Land of England (with David Souden), 1985; The Reign of Henry VIII: Personalities and Politics, 1985–86; Revolution Reassessed: Revisions in the History of Tudor Government and Administration (ed. with Christopher Coleman), 1986; The English Court from the Wars of the Roses to the Civil War (ed.), 1987; Rivals in Power: the Lives and Letters of the Great Tudor Dynasties (ed.), 1990; Henry VIII: A European Court in England, 1991; The Inventory of Henry VIII, vol. 1 (with Philip Ward), 1998; Elizabeth: Apprenticeship, 2000; Six Wives: The Queens of Henry VIII, 2003; Monarchy Volume I: The Early Kings, 2004. Contributions: various newspapers; numerous articles in learned journals. *Honours:* Freeman Worshipful Co. of Barbers, 1992; Medlicott Medal, 2001; WHSmith Award for Biography/Autobiography, 2001. *Address:* Fitzwilliam College, Cambridge CB3 0DG, England (office); 49 Hamilton Park W, London N5 1AE, England.

STARNES, John Kennett, BA; diplomat (retd) and writer; b. 5 Feb. 1918, Montréal, QC, Canada; m. Helen Gordon Robinson 1941; two s. *Education:* Institut Sillig, Switzerland, Univ. of Munich, Germany, Bishop's Univ. *Career:* Counsellor, Canadian Embassy, Bonn 1953–56; Chair., Joint Intelligence Cttee, Ottawa 1958–62; Ambassador, Federal Republic of Germany 1962–66, United Arab Republic and The Sudan 1966–67; Asst Under-secretary of State for External Affairs 1967–70; Dir-Gen., Royal Canadian Mounted Police Security Service 1970–73; mem. of the council, Int. Inst. for Strategic Studies 1977–85; mem. Canadian Writers' Foundation, Rideau Club (life mem.). *Publications:* Deep Sleepers 1981, Scarab 1982, Orion's Belt 1983, The Cornish Hug 1985, Latonya (novel) 1994, Closely Guarded: A Life in Canadian Security and Intelligence (memoir) 1998; contrib. to numerous newspapers, journals and periodicals. *Honours:* Hon. Doctor of Civil Law (Bishop's Univ.) 1975; Centennial Medal 1967, Commemorative Medal for 125th Anniversary of the Confederation of Canada 1992. *Address:* 420 Mackay Street, Apt 702, Ottawa, ON K1M 2C4, Canada. *E-mail:* jstarnes@sympatico.ca.

STAROBINSKI, Jean; Writer; b. 17 Nov. 1920, Geneva, Switzerland; m. Jaqueline Sirman 15 Aug. 1954; three s. *Education:* PhD, Geneva, 1958; MD, Lausanne, 1960. *Career:* mem. Institut de France, Paris. *Publications:* Jean Jacques Rousseau: La Transparence et L'Obstacle, 1957; La Relation Critique, 1970; 1789: Les Emblemes de La Raison: Montaigne en Mouvement, 1983; Le Remede dans le Mal, 1989; Largesse, 1994; Action et Réaction, 1999. Contributions: newspapers and journals. *Honours:* Officier, Légion d'honneur, 1980; Prix Européen de L'Essai, 1983; Balzan Prize, 1984; Prix de Monaco, 1988; Goethe Prize, 1994. *Address:* c/o Université de Genève, 1211 Geneva 4, Switzerland.

STARR, Paul (Elliot); Prof. of Sociology, Writer and Ed.; b. 12 May 1949, New York, NY, USA; m. Sandra Luire Stein, 12 April 1981. *Education:* BA, Columbia University, 1970; PhD, Harvard University, 1978. *Career:* Junior Fellow, Harvard Society of Fellows, 1975–78; Asst Prof., Harvard University, 1978–82; Assoc. Prof., 1982–85, Prof. of Sociology, 1985–, Princeton University; Founder-Co-Ed., The American Prospect; Founder, Electronic Policy Network, 1995. *Publications:* The Discarded Army: Veterans After Vietnam, 1974; The Social Transformation of American Medicine, 1983; The Logic of Health-Care Reform, 1992. Contributions: Professional journals. *Honours:* Guggenheim Fellowship, 1981–82; C. Wright Mills Award, 1983; Pulitzer Prize in General Non-Fiction, 1984; Bancroft Prize, 1984. *Address:* c/o Dept of Sociology, Princeton University, Princeton, NJ 08544, USA.

STARRATT, Thomas; Teacher, Poet and Writer; b. 6 Oct. 1952, Holyoke, MA, USA; m. Patricia Starratt, 7 April 1994, three s., two d. *Education:* BSc, Plymouth State Teachers College, NH, 1975; MEd, University of New Hampshire, 1980; various graduate courses. *Career:* mem. International Reading Asscn. *Publications:* Nightwatch, 1994; Amsterdam, 1994; Summer on the Lava Plain, 1994; Eye to Your Storm, 1995; Passages, 1995; Excess, 1995; Summer Days, 1995; Amsterdam Revisited, 1995; Washed Up, 1996. Contributions: Professional journals.

STASIUK, Andrzej; Polish writer, poet, playwright and publisher; b. 1960, Ukraine; m. *Career:* co-f. and owner, publishing co, Czarne 1996–. *Publications:* Mury Hebronu (The Walls of Hebron, short stories), 1992; Wiersze milosne i nie (Verses (Non-)Amorous), 1994; Opowiesci galicyjskie (Tales of Galicia, short stories), 1994; Bialy kruk (The White Raven, novel), 1995; Przez rzeke (Through the River, short stories), 1996; Dukla (short stories), 1997; Dwie sztuki (telewizyjne) o smierci (Two Television Plays About Death), 1998; Jak zostalem pisarzem (proba biografii intelektualnej) (How I Became a Writer (Attempt at an Intellectual Biography)), 1998; Dziewiec (Nine), 1998; Moje Europa. Dwa eseje o Europie zwanej Srodkowa (My Europe. Two essays on the place called Central Europe, with J. Andruchowicz), 2000; Tekturowy samolot (Model Aeroplane), 2000; Opowiesci wigilijne (Christmas Tales, with Olga Tokarczuk, Jerzy Pilch), 2000; Zima i inne opowiadania (Winter and Other Stories), 2001. Contributions: Gazeta Wyborcza, Tygodnik Powszechny. *Honours:* Foundation of Culture Prize 1994, Koscielski Prize 1995. *Address:* c/o Twisted Spoon Press, PO Box 21, Preslova 12, Prague 5 150-21, Czech Republic.

STAUDINGER, Ulrich; German publisher; b. 30 May 1935, Berlin; m. Irmengard Ehrenwirth 1960 (died 1989); one s. two d. *Education:* Volksschule and Realgymnasium. *Career:* publishing training 1954–57; Lingenbrinck Barsortiment, Hamburg 1957–58; Publicity and Sales, Ensslin & Laiblin, Jugendbuchverlag, Reutlingen 1958–59; Production, Carl Hanser Verlag, Munich 1959–60; Dawson & Sons, London 1960; Franz Ehrenwirth Verlag, Munich 1960; partner, Ehrenwirth Verlag, Munich 1964; responsible for purchase of Franz Schneekluth Verlag KG, Darmstadt by Ehrenwirth Verlag 1967 and amalgamation of two companies into single firm 1976; purchased parts of Philosophia Verlag GmbH, Düsseldorf 1978; various professional appointments. *Address:* Asgardstrasse 34, 8000 Munich 81, Germany (Home). *Telephone:* (89) 98-63-67 (Home).

STAVANS, Ilan; writer, editor and critic; b. 1961, Mexico. *Career:* teacher, Amherst Coll.; Ed.-in-Chief, Hopscotch: A Cultural Review. *Publications include:* Imagining Columbus: The Literary Voyage 1992, La pluma y la máscara 1993, Antihéroes: México y su novela political 1993, Growing Up Latino: Memoirs and Stories (co-author) 1993, La pluma mágica 1994, Bandido, Oscar Zeta Acosta and the Chicano Experience 1995, The Hispanic Condition: Reflections on Culture and Identity in America 1995, Art and Anger: Essays on Politics and the Imagination 1998, The Oxford Book of Jewish Stories 1998, The Oxford Book of Latin American Essays 1998, One-Handed Pianist and Other Stories 1998, Dictionary of Spanglish 1999, The Essential Ilan Stavans 2000, The Inveterate Dreamer: Essays and Conversations on Jewish Culture 2001, The Hispanic Condition: The Power of a People 2001, Wachale! 2001, On Borrowed Words: A Memoir of Language 2001, Riddle of the Catinflas: Essays on Hispanic Popular Culture 2001, Spanglish: The Making of a New American Language 2003, The Ballad of Rocky Ruiz 2004, The Ballad of Gato Guerrero 2004; editor: Tropical Synagogues: Short Stories by Jewish-Latin American Writers 1994, Prospero's Mirror 1998, Poetry of Pablo Neruda 2003, Tent of Miracles 2003. *Honours:* Guggenheim Fellowship ; Latino Literature Prize. *Address:* c/o Curbstone Press, 321 Jackson Street, Willimantic, CT 06226-1738, USA. *E-mail:* info@curbstone.org. *Website:* www.curbstone.org.

STAVE, Bruce Martin; historian and academic; b. 17 May 1937, New York, NY, USA; m. Sondra T. Astor 1961; one s. *Education:* AB, Columbia College, 1959; MA, Columbia University, 1961; PhD, University of Pittsburgh, 1966. *Career:* Prof., 1975–, Dir, Center for Oral History, 1981–, Chair., Dept of History, 1985–94, Board of Trustees Distinguished Prof., 2000–02, Prof. Emeritus, 2002–, University of Connecticut; Ed., Oral History Review, 1996–99; mem. American Historical Asscn; Organization of American Historians; Immigration History Society; New England Historical Asscn, pres., 1994–95; Oral History Asscn; New England Asscn of Oral History. *Publications:* The New Deal and the Last Hurrah, 1970; Urban Bosses, Machines and Progressive Reformers (ed.), 1972; The Discontented Society (co-ed.), 1972; Socialism and the Cities (contributing ed.), 1975; The Making of Urban History, 1977; Modern Industrial Cities, 1981; Talking About Connecticut, 1985; Mills and Meadows: A Pictorial History of Northeast Connecticut (co-author), 1991; From the Old Country: An Oral History of European Migration to America (co-author), 1994; Witnesses to Nuremberg: An Oral History of American Participants at the War Crimes Trials (co-author), 1998. Contributions: Journal of Urban History; Americana Magazine; International Journal of Oral History. *Honours:* Fulbright Professorships, India, 1968–69, Australia, New Zealand, Philippines, 1977, People's Republic of China, 1984–85; National Endowment for the Humanities Fellowship, 1974; Homer Babbidge Award, Asscn for the Study of Connecticut History, 1995; NEH/Harry Jack Gray Distinguished Visiting Humanist, Univ. of Hartford, 2003. *Address:* 200 Broad Way, Coventry, CT 06238, USA.

STEAD, Christian Karlson (C. K.), CBE, MA, PhD, LittD, FRSL; New Zealand writer and professor of English (retd); b. 17 Oct. 1932, Auckland; m. Kathleen Elizabeth Roberts 1955; one s. two d. *Education:* Mt Albert Grammar School, Auckland Univ. Coll. and Auckland Teachers' Coll., Univ. of Bristol. *Career:* Lecturer in English, Univ. of New England, NSW, Australia 1956–57; Michael Hiatt Baker Scholar Univ. of Bristol 1957–59; Lecturer, Sr Lecturer, Assoc. Prof. Univ. of Auckland 1960–67, Prof. of English 1967–86, Prof. Emer. 1986–; writer 1986–; Nuffield Fellow, Univ. of London 1965, Hon. Fellow 1977, Sr Visiting Fellow St John's Coll. Oxford 1996–97; Chair. New Zealand Literary Fund Advisory Cttee 1972–75, New Zealand Authors' Fund Cttee 1989–91; mem. New Zealand PEN (chair. Auckland branch 1986–89, nat. vice-pres. 1988–90), Creative New Zealand 1999. *Publications:* fiction: Smith's Dream 1972, All Visitors Ashore 1984, The Death of the Body 1986, Sister Hollywood 1989, The End of the Century at the End of the World 1992, The Singing Whakapapa 1994, Villa Vittoria 1997, Talking about O'Dwyer 2000, Mansfield: a novel 2004; poetry: Whether the Will is Free 1964, Crossing the Bar 1972, Quesada 1975, Walking Westward 1978, Geographies 1982, Poems for a Decade 1983, Paris 1984, Between 1986, Voices 1990, Straw into Gold 1997, The Right Thing 2000, Dog 2002; short story collections: Five for the Symbol 1981, The Blind Blonde with Candles in Her Hair 1998; non-fiction: The New Poetic: Yeats to Eliot 1964, In the Glass Case: Essays on New Zealand Literature 1981, Pound Yeats Eliot and the Modernist Movement 1986, Answering to the Language: Essays on Modern Writers 1990, The Writer at Work 2000, Kin of Place: Essays on 20 New Zealand Writers 2002, The Secret History of Modernism 2002; editor: Oxford New Zealand Short Stories (2nd series) 1966, Measure for Measure, a Casebook 1971, Letters and Journals of Katherine Mansfield 1977, Collected Stories of Maurice Duggan 1981, The Faber Book of Contemporary South Pacific Stories 1994, Werner Forman's New Zealand 1994. *Honours:* Hon. Research Fellow Univ. Coll., London 1977Hon. DLitt (Bristol) 2001; Katherine Mansfield Prize 1960, Jessie Mackay Award for Poetry 1972, New Zealand Book Award for Poetry 1972, 1986, New Zealand Book Award for Fiction 1985, 1995, Queen Elizabeth II Arts Couoncil Scholarship in Letters 1988–89, Queens' Medal for Services to New Zealand Literature 1990. *Address:* 37 Tohunga Crescent, Parnell, Auckland 1001, New Zealand. *Telephone:* (649) 379-9420. *Fax:* (649) 379-9420.

STEANE, John Barry; British music journalist and writer; b. 12 April 1928, Coventry, England. *Education:* Univ. of Cambridge. *Career:* teacher of English, Merchant Taylors' School, Northwood 1952–88; reviewer, Gramophone 1973–, Musical Times 1988–, Opera Now 1989–. *Publications:* Marlowe: A Critical Study 1964, Dekker: The Shoemaker's Holiday (ed.) 1965, Tennyson 1966, Jonson: The Alchemist (ed.) 1967, Marlowe: The Complete Plays 1969, Nashe: The Unfortunate Traveller and Other Works 1972, The Grand Tradition: Seventy Years of Singing on Record 1973, Voices: Singers and Critics 1992, Singers of the Century (three vols) 1996, 1998, 2000; co-author: Opera on Record (three vols) 1979–85, Song on Record (two vols) 1986–88, Choral Music on Record 1991, Elisabeth Schwarzkopf: A Career on Record (with Alan Sanders) 1995; contrib. to The New Grove Dictionary of Music and Musicians 1980, 2001, The New Grove Dictionary of Opera 1992. *Address:* 32 Woodland Avenue, Coventry, England.

STEARNS, Peter Nathaniel, BA, MA, PhD; American university provost, academic, writer and editor; b. 3 March 1936, London, England; m. Margaret Brindle; one s. three d. *Education:* Harvard University. *Career:* Instructor, 1962–63, Asst Prof., 1963–66, Assoc. Prof., 1966–68, University of Chicago; Visiting Assoc. Prof., Northwestern University, 1964; Ed.-in-Chief, Journal of Social History, 1967–; Prof. of History, Rutgers University, 1968–74; Visiting Prof., Sir George Williams University, 1970, University of Houston, 1978; Heinz Prof. of History, 1974–2000, Head, Dept of History, 1986–92, Dean, College of Humanities and Social Sciences, 1992–2000, Carnegie Mellon University; Provost and Prof. of History, George Mason University, 2000–; mem. American Historical Asscn; American Sociological Asscn; National Council on Social Studies: Social History Asscn, UK; Society of French Historical Studies. *Publications:* European Society in Upheaval: Social History Since 1800, 1967, third edn (with Herrick Chapman) 1991; Priest and Revolutionary: Lamennais and the Dilemma of French Catholicism, 1967; Modern Europe, 1789–1914, 1969; Revolutionary Syndicalism and French Labor: A Cause Without Rebels, 1971; Workers and Protest: The European Labor Movement, the Working Classes, and the Rise of Socialism, 1890–1914 (with Harvey Mitchell), 1971; The European Experience Since 1815, 1972; 1848: The Revolutionary Tide in Europe, 1974; Lives of Labor: Work in Maturing Industrial Society, 1975; Old Age in European Society, 1977; Paths to Authority: Toward the Formation of the Middle Class Consciousness, 1978; Be a Man!: Males in Modern Society, 1979; Themes in Modern Social History (with Linda Rosenzweig), 1985; Anger: The Struggle for Emotional Control in America's History (with Carol Stearns), 1986; World History: Patterns of Change and Continuity, 1987; Life and Society in the West: The Modern Centuries, 1988; World History: Traditions and New Directions, 1988; Emotion and Social Change: Toward a New Psychohistory (with Carol Stearns), 1988; Social History and Issues in Consciousness and Cognition (with Andrew Barnes), 1989; Jealousy: The Evolution of an Emotion in American History, 1989; World Civilizations (with Michael Adas and Stuart Schwartz), 1991; Meaning Over Memory: Recasting the Teaching of Culture and History, 1993; The Industrial Revolution in World History, 1993; Encyclopedia of Social History (ed.), 1993; Turbulent Passage: A Global History of the 20th Century (with Michael Adas and Stuart Schwartz), 1994; American Cool: Developing the Twentieth-Century Emotional Style, 1994; Discursive Psychology in Practice (with Rom Harré), 1995; Encyclopedia of the Industrial Revolution (ed. with John Hinshaw), 1996; Fat History: Bodies and Beauty in Western Society, 1997; Schools and Students in Industrial Society: Japan and the West, 1870–1940, 1997; World History in Documents: Comparative Perspectives, 1998; The Battleground of Desire: The Struggle for Self-Control in Modern America, 1999; Gender in World History, 2000; Encyclopedia of European Social History (ed.), 2000; Facing Up to Management Faddism (with Margaret Brindle), 2001; Consumerism in World History: The Global Transformation of Desire, 2001; Encyclopedia of World History (ed.), sixth edn 2001; Cultures in Motion, 2001; Anxious Parents: A History of Modern Childrearing in America, 2003; Western Civilization in World History, 2003. Contributions: Reference works, scholarly books and professional journals. *Honours:* Koren Prize, Society for French Historical Studies, 1964; Newcomen Special Award, Business History Review, 1965; American Philosophical Society Grant, 1967–68; Guggenheim Fellowship, 1973–74. *Address:* c/o Office of the Provost, George Mason University, Fairfax, VA 22030, USA.

STEBEL, Sidney Leo, (Leo Bergson, Steve Toron), BA; novelist and playwright; b. 28 June 1923, Iowa, USA; m. 1st Jan Mary Dingler 1954 (died 1999); one d.; m. 2nd Karen K. Ford 2004. *Education:* Univ. of Southern California, Los Angeles. *Career:* fmrly columnist, Los Angeles Times Sunday Book Review, Los Angeles Herald-Examiner Sunday Book Review; Exec. Script Consultant, South Australian Film Corpn, working on films Picnic at Hanging Rock, Storm Boy; Adjunct Prof., Masters of Professional Writing programme, Univ. of Southern California, Los Angeles 1991–; mem. Australian Writers' Guild, Authors' Guild, PEN Centre (USA West), Writers' Guild of America, Authors' League. *Writing for theatre:* Father Against Sons, Dial 1-4-sex-talk, Next in Line (adaptation of story by Ray Bradbury, Theater West, Los Angeles) 2004. *Screenplays:* Dreams of Marianne (film), Revolution of Antonio De Leon (TV film). *Publications:* The Widowmaster 1967, The Collaborator 1968, The Vanishing Americans (serialized in West magazine as 'Main Street') 1971, The Vorovich Affair 1975, The Shoe Leather Treatment 1983, Spring Thaw 1989, The Boss's Wife 1992, Double Your Creative Power 1996, Rising Star, Setting Sun 2004. *Honours:* Second Place Fiction Award, PEN Center West 1989. *Literary Agent:* Michael Congdon, Don Congdon & Associates, 156 Fifth Avenue, New York, NY 10010, USA. *Telephone:* (212) 645-1229. *E-mail:* dca@doncongdon.com. *Address:* 1963 Mandeville Canyon Road, Los Angeles, CA 90049, USA. *E-mail:* stebel@usc.edu. *Website:* www.slstebel .com.

STEEL, Danielle (Fernande Schüelein-); Writer; b. 14 Aug. 1947, New York, NY, USA; m.; two s. two step-s. five d. *Education:* Parsons School of Design, New York Univ., 1963–67. *Publications:* Going Home, 1973; Passion's Promise, 1976; Now and Forever, 1978; The Promise, 1978; Season of Passion, 1978; Summer's End, 1979; To Love Again, 1980; Loving, 1980; The Ring, 1980; Love: Poems, 1981; Palomino, 1981; Remembrance, 1981; A Perfect Stranger, 1981; Once in a Lifetime, 1982; Crossings, 1982; Thurston House, 1983; Changes, 1983; Full Circle, 1984; Having a Baby, 1984; Family Album, 1985; Secrets, 1985; Wanderlust, 1986; Fine Things, 1987; Kaleidoscope, 1987; Zoya, 1988; Star, 1989; Daddy, 1989; Message from 'Nam, 1990; Heartbeat, 1991; No Greater Love, 1991; Jewels, 1992; Mixed Blessings, 1992; Vanished, 1993; Accident, 1994; The Gift, 1994; Wings, 1995; Lightning, 1995; Five Days in Paris, 1995; Malice, 1996; Silent Honor, 1996; The Ranch, 1997; Special Delivery, 1997; The Ghost, 1997; The Klone and I, 1998; The Long Road Home, 1998; The Wedding, 1998; Mirror Image, 1998; His Bright Light (non-fiction), 1998; Bittersweet, 1999; Granny Dan, 1999; Irresistible Forces, 1999; The House on Hope Street, 2000; Journey, 2000; Lone Eagle, 2001; Leap of Faith, 2001; The Kiss, 2001; The Cottage, 2002; Sunset in St Tropez, 2002; Answered Prayers, 2002; Johnny Angel, 2003; Safe Harbour, 2003. Contributions: periodicals. *Honours:* Officier, Ordre des Arts et des Lettres. *Address:* PO Box 1637, New York, NY 10156, USA.

STEEL, Ronald Lewis; Prof. of International Relations and Writer; b. 25 March 1931, Morris, IL, USA. *Education:* BA magna cum laude, Northwestern University, 1953; MA, Harvard University, 1955. *Career:* Vice-Consul, US Foreign Service, 1957–58; Ed., Scholastic Magazine, 1959–62; Senior Assoc., Carnegie Endowment for International Peace, 1962–83; Visiting Fellow, Yale University, 1971–73; Visiting Prof., University of Texas, 1977, 1979, 1980, 1985, Wellesley College, 1978, Rutgers University, 1980, University of California at Los Angeles, 1981, Dartmouth College, 1983, Princeton University, 1984, École des Hautes Études en Sciences Sociales, Paris, 2001–02; Fellow, Woodrow Wilson International Center for Scholars, 1984–85, Wissenschaftskolleg zu Berlin, Federal Republic of Germany, 1988; Prof. of International Relations, University of Southern California at Los Angeles, 1986–; Shapiro Prof. of International Relations, George Washington University, 1995–97; mem. American Historical Asscn; Council on Foreign Relations; Society of American Historians. *Publications:* The End of Alliance: America and the Future of Europe, 1964; Tropical Africa Today (with G. Kimble), 1966; Pax Americana, 1967; Imperialists and Other Heroes, 1971; Walter Lippmann and the American Century, 1980; Temptations of a Superpower, 1995; In Love with Night: The American Romance with Robert Kennedy, 2000. Contributions: Professional journals and general publications. *Honours:* Sidney Hillman Prize, 1968; Guggenheim Fellowship, 1973–74; Los Angeles Times Book Award, 1980; Washington Monthly Book Award, 1980; National Book Critics Circle Award, 1981; Bancroft Prize, Columbia University, 1981; American Book Award, 1981. *Address:* c/o School of International Relations, University of Southern California, Los Angeles, CA 90089, USA.

STEELE, Shelby; Prof. of English and Writer; b. 1 Jan. 1946, Chicago, IL, USA; m. Rita Steele, two c. *Education:* Graduate, Coe College, 1968; MA, Sociology, Southern Illinois University, 1971; PhD, English, University of Utah, 1974. *Career:* Prof. of English, San Jose State University. *Publications:* The Content of Our Character: A New Vision of Race in America, 1991; Essay Collection, 1993. Other: Seven Days in Bensonhurst (television documentary), PBS TV, 1990. Contributions: newspapers, journals, and magazines. *Honours:* National Book Critics Award, 1991. *Address:* c/o Dept of English, San Jose State University, Washington Sq., San Jose, CA 95192, USA.

STEFFEN, Jonathon Neil, MA; university teacher, writer, poet and translator; b. 5 Oct. 1958, London, England. *Education:* King's College, Cambridge. *Career:* teacher, University of Heidelberg. *Publications:* Fiction: In Seville, 1985; Meeting the Majors, 1987; Carpe Diem, 1991; Cleopatra, 1994; The Story of Icarus, 1994; At Breakfast, 1995. Poetry: The Soldier and the Soldier's Son, 1986; German Hunting Party, 1987; The Moving Hand, 1994; The Great Days of the Railway, 1994; Apprentice and Master, 1994; St Francis in the Slaughter, 1995. Contributions: Reviews, quarterlies, and magazines. *Honours:* Harper-Wood Travelling Studentship, 1981–82; Hawthornden Creative Writing Fellowship, 1987.

STEFFLER, John Earl; Prof. of English Literature, Poet and Writer; b. 13 Nov. 1947, Toronto, Ontario, Canada; m. Shawn O'Hagan, 30 May 1970, one s. one d. *Education:* BA, University of Toronto, 1971; MA, University of Guelph, 1974. *Career:* mem. League of Canadian Poets; PEN; Writers Alliance of Newfoundland and Labrador. *Publications:* An Explanation of Yellow, 1980; The Grey Islands, 1985; The Wreckage of Play, 1988; The Afterlife of George Cartwright, 1991. Contributions: journals and periodicals. *Honours:* Books in Canada First Novel Award, 1992; Newfoundland Arts Council Artist of the Year Award, 1992; Thomas Raddall Atlantic Fiction Award, 1992; Joseph S. Stauffer Prize, 1993. *Address:* c/o Dept of English, Memorial University of Newfoundland, Corner Brook, NF A2H 6PN, Canada.

STEIN, Kevin; Prof. of English, Writer, Poet and Ed.; b. 1 Jan. 1954, Anderson, IN, USA; m. Debra Lang, 26 May 1979, one s. one d. *Education:* BS, summa cum laude, 1976, MA, 1978, Ball State University; MA, Creative Writing, 1982, PhD, American Literature, 1984, Indiana University. *Career:* Instructor, Ball State University, 1978–79; Assoc. Instructor, Indiana University, 1980–84; Asst Prof., 1984–88, Assoc. Prof., 1988–94, Prof. of English, 1994–, Caterpillar Prof. of English, 2000–, Bradley University, Peoria, IL; Ed., Illinois Writers Review, 1988–92; Assoc. Poetry Ed., Crazyhorse, 1992–; mem. Illinois Writers; MLA. *Publications:* A Field of Wings (poems), 1986; The Figure Our Bodies Make (poems), 1988; James Wright: The Poetry of a Grown Man, 1988; A Circus of Want (poems), 1992; Bruised Paradise (poems), 1996; Private Poets: Worldly Acts: Public and Private History in Contemporary American Poetry, 1996; Chance Ransom (poems), 2000; Illinois Voices: An Anthology of Twentieth-Century Poetry (ed. with G. E. Murray), 2001. Contributions: many reviews, quarterlies and journals. *Honours:* Illinois Arts Council Fellowship, 1986; Chapbook Award, Illinois Writers, 1986; Stanley Hanks Chapbook Award, 1988; Frederick Bock Prize for Poetry, 1987; Faculty Mem. of the Year, Bradley University, 1989; National Endowment for the Arts Fellowship, 1991; Devins Award for Poetry, University of Missouri Press, 1992; Indiana Review Poetry Prize, 1998. *Address:* c/o Dept of English, College of Liberal Arts and Sciences, Bradley University, 1501 W Bradley Ave, Peoria, IL 61625-0258, USA.

STEIN, Peter Gonville; Prof. of Law and Writer; b. 29 May 1926, Liverpool, England; m. 1st, divorced, three d.; m. 2nd Anne M. Howard, 16 Aug. 1978. *Education:* BA, 1949, LLB, 1950, Gonville and Caius College, Cambridge; Admitted as Solicitor, 1951; University of Pavia, 1951–52. *Career:* Prof. of Jurisprudence, University of Aberdeen, 1956–68; Regius Prof. of Civil Law, University of Cambridge, 1968–93; mem. British Acad., fellow; Belgian National Acad.; Italian National Acad., foreign fellow; Selden Society, vice-pres., 1984–87; Society of Public Teachers of Law, pres., 1980–81. *Publications:* Regulae Iuris: From Juristic Rules to Legal Maxims, 1966; Legal Values in Western Society (with J. Shand), 1974; Legal Evolution: The Story of an Idea, 1980; Legal Institutions: The Development of Dispute Settlement, 1984; The Character and Influence of the Roman Civil Law, 1988; The Teaching of Roman Law in England Around 1200 (with F. de Zulueta), 1990; Römisches Recht und Europa: Die Geschichte einer Rechtskultur, 1996; Roman Law in European History, 1999. Contributions: Professional journals. *Honours:* Hon. Dr Iuris, University of Göttingen, 1980; Hon. Dott Giur, University of Ferrara, 1991; Hon. QC, 1993; Hon. Fellow, Gonville and Caius College, 1999; Hon. LLD, University of Aberdeen, 2000; Hon. doctorates, University of Perugia, Université Panthéon-Assas Paris II, 2001. *Address:* Queens' College, Cambridge CB3 9ET, England. *E-mail:* gonville@waitrose.com.

STEIN, Robert A.; Writer; b. 5 Aug. 1933, Duluth, MN, USA; m. Betty L. Pavlik, 5 Nov. 1955, three s. *Education:* MA, Counselling/Education, 1968, MA, Writing, 1986, University of Iowa. *Career:* Officer and Pilot, US Air Force, 1956–77; Asst Prof., 1964–66, Assoc. Prof., 1966–68, Prof., 1975–77, University of Iowa; Faculty, Division of Writing, Kirkwood Community College, Iowa City and Cedar Rapids, 1984–89; mem. Authors' Guild; Authors' League of America. *Publications:* Fiction: Apollyon, 1985; Death Defied, 1988; The Chase, 1988; The Black Samaritan, 1997; The Vengeance Equation, 2000. Non-Fiction: Statistical Correlations, 1967; Engineers Vs. Other Students: Is There A Difference?, 1967; Whatever Happened to Moe Bushkin?, 1967; Quest for Viability: One Way!, 1976; Threat of Emergency, 1988. *Honours:* five wartime decorations; nine service awards; Outstanding Faculty Award, 1967–68, Lifetime Achievement Award, 1999, University of Iowa; Iowa Authors' Collection, 1985; Minnesota Authors' Collection, 1987; International Literary Award, 1988.

STEINBACH, Meredith Lynn; Prof. of English and Writer; b. 18 March 1949, Ames, IA, USA; m. Charles Ossian Hartman, 5 May 1979, divorced 1991, one s. *Education:* BGS, 1973, MFA, 1976, University of Iowa. *Career:* Teaching Fellow, University of Iowa, 1975–76; Writer-in-Residence, Antioch College, 1976–77; Lecturer, Northwestern University, 1977–79; Visiting Asst Prof., University of Washington, 1979–82; Asst Prof. to Assoc. Prof., 1983–97, Prof. of English, 1997–, Brown University; mem. PEN; Associated Writing Programs; Amnesty International. *Publications:* Fiction: Zara, 1982; Here Lies the Water, 1990; The Birth of the World as We Know It, or Teiresias, 1996. Short Stories: Reliable Light, 1990. Contributions: Tri-Quarterly Magazine; Antaeus; Massachusetts Review; Antioch Review; Southwest Review; Black Warrior Review; Tuyonui; 13th Moon; Ploughshares. *Honours:* Pushcart Prize, Best of the Small Presses, 1977; National Endowment for the Arts Fellowship, 1978; Bunting Fellow, Bunting Summer Fellow, Mary Ingraham Bunting Institute, Radcliffe College, Harvard, 1982–83; Rhode Island Artists Fellowship, 1986–87; O. Henry Award, 1990; Travel Study Grant to France and Greece, 1993–94. *Address:* Dept of English, Box 1852, Brown University, Providence, RI 02912, USA. *E-mail:* meredith_steinbach@brown.edu.

STEINEM, Gloria; Writer, Journalist, Feminist Activist and Editor; b. 25 March 1934, Toledo, OH, USA; m. David Bale 2000. *Education:* BA, Smith College, 1956; Chester Bowles Asian Fellow, India, 1957–58. *Career:* Co-Dir, Dir, Ind. Research Service, Cambridge, MA, and New York, 1959–60; Contributing Ed., Glamour Magazine, 1962–69; Co-Founder and Contributing Ed., New York Magazine, 1968–72; Co-Founder and Chair. of the Board of Dirs, Women's Action Alliance, 1970–; feminist lecturer, 1969–; Co-Founder and Ed., 1971–87, Columnist, 1980–87, Consulting Ed., 1987–, Ms Magazine; Convenor and Mem. of the National Advisory Committee, Women's Political Caucus, 1971–; Co-Founder and Pres. of the Board of Dirs, Ms Foundation for Women, 1972–; Pres., Voters for Choice, 1979–; active various civil rights and peace campaigns incl. United Farmworkers, Vietnam War Tax Protest, Cttee for the Legal Defense of Angela Davis and political campaigns of Adlai Stevenson, Robert Kennedy, Eugene McCarthy, Shirley Chisholm, George McGovern; mem. American Foundation of Television and Radio Artists; Authors' Guild; National Organization for Women; National Press Club; Society of Magazine Writers; Coalition of Labor Union Women, f.-mem. *Publications:* The Thousand Indias, 1957; The Beach Book, 1963; Wonder Woman, 1972; Outrageous Acts and Everyday Rebellions, 1983; Marilyn: Norma Jeane, 1986; Revolution from Within: A Book of Self-Esteem, 1992; Moving Beyond Words, 1994. Contributions: anthologies and magazines. *Honours:* Penney-Missouri Journalism Award, 1970; Ohio Governor's Award for Journalism, 1972; Woman of the Year, McCall's Magazine, 1972; Hon. Doctor of Human Justice, Simmons College, 1973; Bill of Rights Award, American Civil Liberties Union of Southern California, 1975; Woodrow Wilson International Center for Scholars Fellow, 1977; National Woman's Hall of Fame, 1993. *Address:* c/o Ms Magazine, 433 S Beverly Dr., Beverly Hills, CA 90212, USA. *E-mail:* info@msmagazine.com. *Website:* www.msmagazine.com.

STEINER, (Francis) George, BA, MA, PhD, FRSL; academic and writer; b. 23 April 1929, Paris, France; m. Zara Shakow 1955; one s. one d. *Education:*

University of Chicago, Harvard University, University of Oxford. *Career:* Staff, The Economist, London, 1952–56; Mem., Institute for Advanced Study, Princeton, NJ, 1956–58; Fulbright Professorships, 1958–59; Fellow, 1961–69, Extraordinary Fellow, 1969–, Churchill College, Cambridge; Prof. of English and Comparative Literature, 1974–94, Prof. Emeritus, 1994–, University of Geneva; Visiting Prof., Collège de France, 1992; Weidenfeld Prof. of Comparative Literature and Fellow, St Anne's College, Oxford, 1994–95; Charles Eliot Norton Prof. of Poetry, Harvard University, 2001–02; various visiting lectureships; mem. American Acad. of Arts and Sciences, hon. mem., 1989–; English Asscn, pres., 1975; German Acad. of Literature, corresponding mem., 1981–. *Publications:* Tolstoy or Dostoevsky: An Essay in the Old Criticism, 1958; The Death of Tragedy, 1960; Homer: A Collection of Critical Essays (ed. with Robert Flagles), 1962; Anno Domini, 1964; The Penguin Book of Modern Verse Translation (ed.), 1966; Language and Silence, 1967; Extraterritorial, 1971; In Bluebeard's Castle: Some Notes Towards the Re-Definition of Culture, 1971; The Sporting Scene: White Knights in Reykjavík, 1973; After Babel: Aspects of Language and Translation, 1975; Heidegger, 1978; On Difficulty and Other Essays, 1978; The Portage to San Cristóbal of A H, 1981; Antigones, 1984; George Steiner: A Reader, 1984; Real Presences: Is There Anything in What We Say?, 1989; Proofs and Three Parables, 1992; The Deeps of the Sea, 1996; Homer in English, 1996; No Passion Spent, 1996; Errata: An Examined Life, 1998; Grammars of Creation, 2001; Lessons of the Masters: The Charles Eliot Morton Lectures 2001–2002 2004. *Honours:* O. Henry Short Story Award, 1958; Zabel Award, National Institute of Arts and Letters, USA, 1970; Guggenheim Fellowship, 1971–72; Faulkner Stipend for Fiction, 1983; Chevalier, Légion d'honneur, 1984; PEN Macmillan Fiction Prize, 1993; Hon. Fellow, Balliol College, Oxford, 1995; several hon. doctorates. *Address:* 32 Barrow Road, Cambridge CB2 2AS, England.

STEINMAN, Lisa Jill Malinowski, BA, MFA, PhD; academic, poet, writer and editor; *Kenan Professor of English, Reed College*; b. 8 April 1950, Willimantic, CT, USA; m. James L. Shugrue 1984. *Education:* Cornell Univ. *Career:* Asst Prof. 1976–82, Assoc. Prof. 1982–89, Prof. 1990–93, Kenan Prof. of English 1993–, Reed Coll., Portland, Oregon; Poetry Ed., Hubbub Magazine 1983–; Rockefeller Scholar-in-Residence, 92nd Street Y Poetry Center 1987; mem. Associated Writing Programs, MLA, PEN, PEN/Northwest, Poets and Writers, Wallace Stevens Soc., William Carlos Williams Society (pres. 1998–2000). *Publications:* Lost Poems 1976, Made in America: Science, Technology, and American Modernist Poets 1987, All That Comes to Light 1989, A Book of Other Days 1993, Ordinary Songs 1996, Masters of Repetition: Poetry, Culture, and Work 1998, Carslaw's Sequences 2003; contrib. to books, anthologies, reviews, quarterlies and journals. *Honours:* Scholar, Bread Loaf Writers Conference 1981, Oregon Arts Commission Poetry Fellow 1983, Nat. Endowment for the Arts Fellowship 1984, Pablo Neruda Award, Nimrod Magazine 1987, Outstanding Academic Book, Choice 1989, Oregon Book Award, Oregon Inst. of Literary Arts 1993, Nat. Endowment for the Humanities Fellowship 1996. *Address:* 5344 SE 38th Avenue, Portland, OR 97202, USA.

STEPHAN, John Jason; Prof. and Historian; b. 8 March 1941, Chicago, IL, USA; m. 22 June 1963. *Education:* BA, 1963, MA, 1964, Harvard University; PhD, University of London, England, 1969. *Career:* Far Eastern Ed., Harvard Review, 1962; Visiting Fellow, St Antony's College, Oxford, 1977; Prof. of History, 1970–2001, Emeritus Prof. of History, 2001–, University of Hawaii; Visiting Prof. of History, Stanford University, 1986; Research Fellow, Kennan Institute of Advanced Russian Studies, 1987; mem. Authors' Guild; PEN; International House of Japan, life mem.; American Asscn for the Advancement of Slavic Studies, life mem.; American Historical Asscn; Canadian Historical Asscn. *Publications:* Sakhalin: A History, 1971; The Kuril Islands: Russo-Japanese Frontier in the Pacific, 1974; The Russian Fascists, 1978; Hawaii Under the Rising Sun, 1984; Soviet-American Horizons in the Pacific (with V. P. Chichkanov), 1986; The Russian Far East: A History, 1994. Contributions: Washington Post; Modern Asian Studies; American Historical Review; Pacific Affairs; Pacific Community; Journal for Asian Studies; New York Times; Siberica; Pacifica; Australian Slavic and East European Studies. *Honours:* Fulbright Fellowship, 1967–68; Japan Culture Trans. Prize, 1973; Japan Foundation Fellowship, 1977; Sanwa Distinguished Scholar, Fletcher School of Law and Diplomacy, Tufts University, 1989; Distinguished Invited Speaker, Canadian Historical Asscn, 1990; Kenneth W. Baldridge Prize, 1996. *Literary Agent:* John Hawkins Assocs, New York, NY, USA. *Address:* Dept of History, University of Hawaii, 2530 Dole St, Honolulu, HI 96822, USA.

STEPHEN, Ian; Writer, Poet and Artist; b. 29 April 1955, Stornoway, Isle of Lewis, Scotland; m. Barbara Ziehm, 9 Nov. 1984, two s. *Education:* BEd, English, University of Aberdeen, 1980. *Career:* Inaugural Robert Louis Stevenson/Christian Salvesen Fellow, Grez-sur-Loing, France, 1995; mem. PEN Scotland. *Publications:* Malin, Hebrides, Minches, 1983; Varying States of Grace, 1989; Siud an T-Eilean (ed.), 1993; Providence II, 1994; Broad Bay, 1997; Green Waters, 1998; Mackerel and Creamola (short stories), 2001. Other: numerous exhibitions of poetry/texts with visual arts. Contributions: Scottish, UK, and Australian publications. *Honours:* Scottish Arts Council Bursaries, 1981, 1995; Creative Scotland Award, 2002. *Address:* Last House, 1 Benside, Isle of Lewis HS2 0DZ, Scotland.

STEPHENS, Meic; Journalist, Poet, Writer and Trans; b. 23 July 1938, Trefforest, Pontypridd, Wales; m. Ruth Wynn Meredith, 14 Aug. 1965, one s., three d. *Education:* BA, University College of Wales, Aberystwyth, 1961; University of Rennes, 1960; University College of North Wales, Bangor, 1962. *Career:* Literature Dir, Welsh Arts Council, 1967–90; Visiting Prof., Brigham Young University, Provo, Utah, 1991; Lecturer in Journalism, University of Glamorgan, 1994–2000, Centre for Journalism Studies, Cardiff University, 1998; Prof. of Welsh Writing in English, University of Glamorgan, 2001; mem. Gorsedd of Bards; Welsh Acad. *Publications:* New Companion to the Literature of Wales; The Oxford Literary Guide to Great Britain and Ireland; The Collected Poems of Harri Webb; The Complete Poems of Glyn Jones; The Collected Short Stories of Rhys Davies; The Literary Pilgrim in Wales; Welsh Names for Your Children; Illuminations: An Anthology of Welsh Short Prose; A Semester in Zion: A Journal With Memoirs. Contributions: various anthologies, reference works, and journals. *Honours:* Hon. MA, DLitt, University of Wales. *Address:* 10 Heol Don, Whitchurch, Cardiff CF14 2AU, Wales.

STEPHENS, Michael (Gregory); Writer, Poet and Dramatist; b. 4 March 1946, USA. *Education:* BA, 1975, MA, 1976, City College, CUNY; MFA, Yale University, 1979. *Career:* Lecturer, Columbia University, 1977–91, Princeton University, 1986–91, New York University, 1989–91; Writer-in-Residence and Asst Prof., Fordham University, 1979–85; mem. Associated Writing Programs; PEN; Royal Asiatic Society. *Publications:* Fiction: Season at Coole, 1972; Paragraphs, 1974; Still Life, 1978; Shipping Out, 1979; The Brooklyn Book of the Dead, 1994. Poetry: Alcohol Poems, 1972; Tangun Legend, 1978; After Asia, 1993. Other: Circles End (poems and prose), 1982; The Dramaturgy of Style, 1986; Lost in Seoul: And Other Discoveries on the Korean Peninsula, 1990; Jig and Reels, 1992; Green Dreams: Essays Under the Influence of the Irish, 1994. Plays: A Splendid Occasion in Spring, 1974; Off-Season Rates, 1978; Cloud Dream, 1979; Our Father, 1980; R & R, 1984. Contributions: many newspapers, journals, and magazines. *Honours:* MacDowell Colony Fellowship, 1968; Fletcher Pratt Fellowship, Bread Loaf Writers Conference, 1971; Creative Artists Public Service Fiction Award, 1978; Connecticut Commission on the Arts Grant, 1979; Associated Writing Programs Award in Creative Non-Fiction, 1993. *Address:* 520 W 110th St, No. 5-C, New York, NY 10025, USA.

STEPHENS, Reed (see Donaldson, Stephen Reeder).

STEPHENSON, Hugh; Writer, Journalist and Teacher; b. 18 July 1938, England; m. 1st Auriol Stevens, 1962, divorced 1987, two s. one d.; m. 2nd Diana Eden, 1990. *Education:* MA, New College, Oxford; University of California, Berkeley, USA. *Career:* HM Diplomatic Service, 1964–69; Staff, The Times, 1968; Ed., The Times Business News, 1972–81, New Statesman, 1982–86; Prof. of Journalism, City University, London, 1986–. *Publications:* The Coming Clash, 1972; Mrs Thatcher's First Year, 1980; Claret and Chips, 1982; Libel and the Media (co-author), 1997. *Honours:* FRSA, 1987. *Address:* c/o Dept of Journalism, City University, Northampton Sq., London EC1, England.

STEPHENSON, Neal, BA; American writer; b. 31 Oct. 1959, Fort Meade, MD. *Education:* Ames High School, IA, Univ. of Boston. *Publications:* novels: The Big U 1984, Zodiac: The Eco-Thriller 1988, Snow Crash 1991, Diamond Age 1995, Cryptonomicon 1999, Quicksilver (Arthur C. Clarke Award 2004) 2003, The Confusion 2004, The System of the World 2004. *Address:* c/o William Heinemann, Random House, 20 Vauxhall Bridge Road, London, SW1V 2SA, England. *Website:* www.randomhouse.co.uk.

STERLING, Maria Sandra (see Floren, Lee).

STERN, Gerald; Poet and Teacher; b. 22 Feb. 1925, Pittsburgh, Pennsylvania, USA; m. Patricia Miller, 1952, one s. one d. *Education:* BA, University of Pittsburgh, 1947; MA, Columbia University, 1949. *Career:* Instructor, Temple University, Philadelphia, 1957–63; Prof., Indiana University of Pennsylvania, 1963–67, Somerset County College, NJ, 1968–82; Visiting Poet, Sarah Lawrence College, 1977; Visiting Prof., University of Pittsburgh, 1978, Columbia University, 1980, Bucknell University, 1988, New York University, 1989; Faculty, Writer's Workshop, University of Iowa, 1982–94; Distinguished Chair, University of Alabama, 1984; Fanny Hurst Prof., Washington University, St Louis, 1985; Bain Swiggert Chair, Princeton University, 1989; Poet-in-Residence, Bucknell University, 1994. *Publications:* The Naming of Beasts and Other Poems, 1973; Rejoicings, 1973; Lucky Life, 1977; The Red Coal, 1981; Paradise Poems, 1984; Lovesick, 1987; Leaving Another Kingdom: Selected Poems, 1990; Two Long Poems, 1990; Bread Without Sugar, 1992; Odd Mercy, 1995; This Time: New and Selected Poems, 1998; Last Blue, 2000; American Sonnets, 2002; What I Can't Bear Losing: Notes From A Life, 2003. *Honours:* National Endowment for the Arts Grants, 1976, 1981, 1987; Lamont Poetry Selection Award, 1977; Governor's Award, Pennsylvania, 1980; Guggenheim Fellowship, 1980; Bess Hokin Award, 1980; Bernard F. Connor Award, 1981; Melville Cane Award, 1982; Jerome J. Shestack Prize, 1984; Acad. of American Poets Fellowship, 1993; Ruth Lilly Poetry Prize, 1996; National Book Award for Poetry, 1998; New Jersey Poet Laureate. *Address:* 89 Clinton St, Lambertville, NJ 08530, USA.

STERN, Madeleine Bettina; Rare Book Dealer and Writer; b. 1 July 1912, New York, NY, USA. *Education:* BA, Barnard College, 1932; MA, Columbia University, 1934. *Career:* mem. Manuscript Society; Antiquarian Booksellers Asscn of America; MLA; Authors' League. *Publications:* The Life of Margaret Fuller, 1942; Louisa May Alcott, 1950; Purple Passage: The Life of Mrs. Frank Leslie, 1953; Imprints on History: Book Publishers and American Frontiers, 1956; We the Women: Career Firsts of 19th Century America, 1962; The Pantarch: A Biography of Stephen Pearl Andrews, 1968; Heads and Headlines: The Phrenological Fowlers, 1971; Books and Book People in 19th Century America, 1978; Antiquarian Bookselling in the United States: A History, 1985; Old Books, Rare Friends: Two Literary Sleuths and Their Shared Passion (with Leona Rostenberg), 1997; Louisa May Alcott: From Blood and Thunder to Hearth and Home, 1998; New Worlds in Old Books (with Leona Rostenberg), 1999; Books have their Fates (with Leona Rostenberg), 2001; Bookends (with Leona Rostenberg), 2001; From Revolution to Revolution: Perspectives on Publishing and Bookselling (with Leona Rostenberg), 2002. Other: Ed. of numerous L. M. Alcott collections. Contributions: numerous publications. *Honours:* Guggenheim Fellowship; Distinguished Barnard Alumna Award and American Printing History Award to Leona Rostenberg and Madeleine Stern. *Address:* 40 E 88th St, New York, NY 10128, USA.

STERN, Richard Gustave, BA, MA, PhD; writer and academic; b. 25 Feb. 1928, New York, NY, USA; m. 1st Gay Clark; m. 2nd Alane Rollings; three s. one d. *Education:* Univ. of North Carolina, Harvard Univ., Univ. of Iowa. *Career:* mem. American Acad. of Arts and Sciences; Center for Advanced Studies in Behavioural Sciences, fellow. *Publications:* Golk, 1960; Europe or Up and Down with Baggish and Schreiber, 1961; In Any Case, 1962; Stitch, 1965; Other Men's Daughters, 1973; A Father's Words, 1986; The Position of the Body, 1986; Noble Rot Stories, 1949–89, 1989; Shares and Other Fictions, 1992; One Person and Another, 1993; Sistermony, 1995; Pacific Tremors, 2001; What Is What Was, 2002; Almonds to Zhoof (short stories), 2004. Contributions: journals and magazines. *Honours:* Longwood Award, 1954; American Acad. of Arts and Letters Award, 1968; Friends of Literature Award, 1968; Sandburg Award, 1979; Award of Merit for the Novel, 1985; Heartland Prize, 1995. *Literary Agent:* C. A. Rollings, 5455 S Ridgewood Court, Chicago, IL 60615, USA. *Address:* 1050 E 59th Street, Chicago, IL 60637, USA.

STERN, Steve; academic and writer; b. 21 Dec. 1947, Memphis, TN, USA. *Education:* BA, Rhodes College, 1970; MFA, University of Arkansas, 1977. *Career:* Visiting Lecturer, University of Wisconsin, 1987; Assoc. Prof. of English, Skidmore College, Saratoga Springs, New York, 1994–. *Publications:* Isaac and the Undertaker's Daughter, 1983; The Moon and Ruben Shein, 1984; Lazar Malkin Enters Heaven, 1986; Mickey and the Golem, 1986; Hershel and the Beast, 1987; Harry Kaplan's Adventures Underground, 1991; Plague of Dreamers, 1994; The Wedding Jester (short stories), 1999. Contributions: Magazines and journals. *Honours:* O. Henry Prize, 1981; Pushcart Writers Choice Award, 1984, and Prizes, 1997, 2000; Edward Lewis Wallant Award, 1988; National Jewish Book Award, 2000. *Address:* c/o Department of English, Skidmore College, Saratoga Springs, NY 12866, USA.

STERN, Stuart (see Rae, Hugh Crauford).

STERNBERG, Robert J(effrey); Prof. of Psychology and Education, Writer and Ed.; b. 8 Dec. 1949, Newark, NJ, USA; m. Alejandra Campos 11 Aug. 1991; one s. one d. *Education:* BA, summa cum laude, Psychology, Yale Univ., 1972; PhD, Psychology, Stanford Univ., 1975. *Career:* Asst Prof., 1975–80, Assoc. Prof., 1980–83, Prof., 1983–86, IBM Prof. of Psychology and Education, 1986–, Yale Univ.; Ed., Psychological Bulletin, 1991–96, Contemporary Psychology, 1999–; Ed.-in-Chief, Educational Psychology Series, Lawrence Erlbaum Assocs, 1996–; mem. American Acad. of Arts and Sciences, fellow; American Asscn for the Advancement of Science, fellow; American Educational Research Asscn; American Psychological Society, fellow; International Council of Psychologists; National Asscn for Gifted Children; Psychonomic Society; Society for Research in Child Development; Society of Multivariate Experimental Psychology; American Psychological Asscn, pres., 2003–. *Publications:* Intelligence, Information Processing, and Analogical Reasoning: The Componential Analysis of Human Abilities, 1977; Beyond IQ: A Triarchic Theory of Human Intelligence, 1985; Intelligence Applied: Understanding and Increasing Your Intellectual Skills, 1986; What is Intelligence? (with D. K. Detterman), 1986; The Psychologist's Companion, second edn, 1988; The Triangle of Love, 1988; The Triarchic Mind: A New Theory of Human Intelligence, 1988; Metaphors of Mind: Conceptions of the Nature of Intelligence, 1990; Love the Way You Want It, 1991; Tacit Knowledge Inventory for Managers (with R. K. Wagner), 1991; For Whom Does the Bell Curve Toll?: It Tolls for You, 1995; In Search of the Human Mind, 1995; Defying the Crowd: Cultivating Creativity in a Culture of Conformity (with T. I. Lubart), 1995; Off Track: When Poor Readers Become Learning Disabled (with L. Spear-Swerling), 1996; Cognitive Psychology, 1996; Successful Intelligence, 1996; Introduction to Psychology, 1997; Pathways to Psychology, 1997; Thinking Styles, 1997; Successful Intelligence, 1997; Cupid's Arrow: The Course of Love Through Time, 1998; Love is a Story, 1998; Perspectives on Learning Disabilities: Biological, Cognitive, Contextual (with L. Spear-Swerling), 1999; Our Labeled Children: What Every Parent and Teacher Needs to Know About Learning Disabilities (with E. L. Grigorenko), 1999; Teaching for Successful Intelligence (with E. L. Grigorenko), 2000; Psychology: In Search of the Human Mind, 2001; Educational Psychology (with W. M. Williams), 2001; Dynamic Testing (with E. L. Grigorenko), 2002; Psychology 101½: The Unspoken Rules for Success in Academia, 2004. Other: Ed. of many books. Contributions: numerous scholarly books and journals. *Honours:* Distinguished Scholar Award, National Asscn for Gifted Children, 1985; Outstanding Book Award, 1987, Sylvia Scribner Award, 1996, American Educational Research Asscn; Guggenheim Fellowship, 1985–86; Award for Excellence, Mensa Education and Research Foundation, 1989; Dr hc, Complutense Univ., Madrid, 1994; G. Stanley Hall Distinguished Lecturer, American Psychological Asscn, 1997; E. L. Thorndike Award for Career Achievement in Educational Psychology, 2003. *Address:* c/o Dept of Psychology, Yale University, PO Box 208205, New Haven, CT 06520, USA. *E-mail:* robert.sternberg@yale.edu.

STERNLICHT, Sanford; Prof. of English, Literary Critic and Poet; b. 20 Sept. 1931, New York, NY, USA; m. Dorothy Hilkert, 7 June 1956, deceased 1977, two s. *Education:* BS, SUNY at Oswego, 1953; MA, Colgate University, 1955; PhD, Syracuse University, 1962. *Career:* Instructor, 1959–60, Asst Prof., 1960–62, Assoc. Prof., 1962, Prof. of English, 1962–72, Prof. of Theatre, 1972–86, SUNY at Oswego; Leverhulme Foundation Visiting Fellow, University of York, England, 1965–66; Prof. of English, Syracuse University, 1986–; mem. MLA; PEN; Poetry Society of America, fellow; Shakespeare Asscn of America; American Conference for Irish Studies. *Publications:* Poetry: Gull's Way, 1961; Love in Pompeii, 1967. Non-Fiction: Uriah Philips Levy: The Blue Star Commodore, 1961; The Black Devil of the Bayous: The Life and Times of the United States Steam-Sloop Hartford (with E. M. Jameson), 1970; John Webster's Imagery and the Webster Canon, 1974; John Masefield, 1977; McKinley's Bulldog: The Battleship Oregon, 1977; C. S. Forester, 1981; USF Constellation: Yankee Racehorse (with E. M. Jameson), 1981; Padraic Colum, 1985; John Galsworthy, 1987; R. F. Delderfield, 1988; Stevie Smith, 1990; Stephen Spender, 1992; Siegfried Sassoon, 1993; All Things Herriot: James Herriot and His Peaceable Kingdom, 1995; Jean Rhys, 1996; A Reader's Guide to Modern Irish Drama, 1998. Editor: Selected Stories of Padraic Colum, 1985; Selected Plays of Padraic Colum, 1989; In Search of Stevie Smith, 1991; New Plays from the Abbey Theatre 1993–1995, 1996; Chaim Potok: A Critical Companion, 2000; New Plays from the Abbey Theatre, 1996–1998, 2001; A Reader's Guide to Modern American Drama, 2002. Contributions: books, professional journals and general periodicals. *Honours:* Prizes, fellowships and grants including: Sir Evelyn Wrench English-Speaking Union Travel/Lecture Grants, 1997, 1998, 1999. *Address:* 128 Dorset Rd, Syracuse, NY 13210, USA. *E-mail:* svsternl@syr.edu.

STEVENS, Carl (see Obstfeld, Raymond).

STEVENS, Sir Jocelyn Edward Greville, Kt, CVO, FRSA; British publisher; b. 14 Feb. 1932, London; m. Jane Armyne Sheffield 1956 (dissolved 1979); one s. two d. (one s. deceased). *Education:* Eton Coll., Cambridge Univ. *Career:* mil. service Rifle Brigade 1950–52; journalist Hulton Press 1955–56; Chair. and Man. Dir Stevens Press Ltd, Ed. Queen Magazine 1957–68; Personal Asst to Chair. Beaverbrook Newspapers 1968, Dir 1971–81, Man. Dir 1974–77; Man. Dir Evening Standard Co. Ltd 1969–72, Daily Express 1972–74; Deputy Chair. and Man. Dir Express Newspapers 1974–81; Ed. and Publr The Magazine 1982–84; Dir Centaur Communications 1982–84; Gov. Imperial Coll. of Science, Tech. and Medicine 1985–92, Winchester School of Art 1986–89; Rector and Vice-Provost RCA 1984–92; Chair. The Silver Trust 1990–93, English Heritage 1992–2000; Deputy Chair. Independent TV Comm. 1991–96; Dir (non-exec.) The TV Corpn 1996–2002, Asprey & Co. –2002, Garrard & Co. –2002; Pres. The Cheyne Walk Trust 1989–93; Chair. The Prince of Wales's Phoenix Trust; Trustee Eureka! The Children's Museum 1990–2000. *Honours:* Hon. DLitt (Loughborough) 1989, (Buckingham) 1998; Hon. FCSD 1990, Sr Fellow RCA 1990. *Address:* 14 Cheyne Walk, London, SW3 5RA, England. *Telephone:* (20) 7351-1141. *Fax:* (20) 7351-7963.

STEVENS, John (see Tubb, Edwin Charles).

STEVENS, Lynsey, (Lynette Desley Howard); writer; b. 28 Sept. 1947, Sherwood, Qld, Australia. *Career:* mem. Queensland Writers Centre, Australian Soc. of Authors, Romance Writers of America, Romance Writers of Australia. *Publications:* Ryan's Return, 1981; Terebori's Gold, 1981; Race for Revenge, 1981; Play Our Song Again, 1981; Tropical Knight, 1982; Starting Over, 1982; Man of Vengeance, 1982; Closest Place to Heaven, 1983; Forbidden Wine, 1983; The Ashby Affair, 1983; Lingering Embers, 1984; Leave Yesterday Behind, 1986; But Never Love, 1988; A Rising Passion, 1990; Touched by Desire, 1993; A Physical Affair, 1994; Misteltoe Kisses (in Christmas Journeys), 1994; His Cousin's Wife, 1996; Close Relations, 1997; Male for Christmas, 1998. *Honours:* Arty, Romantic Times, Worldwide Romance 1984. *Address:* PO Box 400, Red Hill, Qld 4259, Australia. *E-mail:* lynsey@ecn.net.au. *Website:* www.lynseystevens.com.

STEVENS, Peter Stanley; Canadian academic, poet, critic and editor; b. 17 Nov. 1927, Manchester, England; m. June Sidebotham 1957; one s. two d. *Education:* BA, Certificate in Education, University of Nottingham, 1951; MA, McMaster University, 1963; PhD, University of Saskatchewan, 1968. *Career:* Faculty, Hillfield-Strathallan College, Hamilton, Ontario, 1957–64; Part-time Lecturer, McMaster University, 1961–64; Lecturer and Asst Prof., University of Saskatchewan, 1964–69; Poetry Ed., Canadian Forum, 1968–73, Literary Review of Canada, 1994–96; Assoc. Prof., 1969–76, Prof., 1976–93, University of Windsor. *Publications:* Nothing But Spoons, 1969; The McGill Movement (ed.), 1969; A Few Myths, 1971; Breadcrusts and Glass, 1972; Family Feelings and Other Poems, 1974; A Momentary Stay, 1974; The Dying Sky Like Blood, 1974; The Bogman Pavese Tactics, 1977;

Modern English-Canadian Poetry, 1978; Coming Back, 1981; Revenge of the Mistresses, 1982; Out of the Willow Trees, 1986; Miriam Waddington, 1987; Swimming in the Afternoon: New and Selected Poems, 1992; Dorothy Livesay: Patterns in a Poetic Life, 1992; Rip Rap: Yorkshire Ripper Poems, 1995; Thinking Into the Dark, 1997; Attending to This World, 1998; States of Mind, 2001; Bread from Stones, 2002. Contributions: books, reviews, and journals. *Address:* 2055 Richmond Street, Windsor, ON N8Y 1L3, Canada.

STEVENSON, Anne Katharine; Poet and Writer; b. 3 Jan. 1933, Cambridge, England; m. 1st, two s. one d.; m. 2nd Peter David Lucas, 3 Sept. 1987. *Education:* BA, 1954, MA, 1961, University of Michigan. *Career:* mem. Poetry Book Society; Poetry Society; FRSL; FEA; Society of Authors; Authors' Guild, USA. *Publications:* Living in America, 1965; Reversals, 1969; Travelling Behind Glass, 1974; Correspondences, 1974; Enough of Green, 1977; Minute by Glass Minute, 1982; The Fiction Makers, 1985; Winter Time, 1986; Selected Poems, 1987; The Other House, 1990; Four and a Half Dancing Men, 1993; Collected Poems, 1996; Bitter Fame: A Life of Sylvia Plath, 1998; Five Looks at Elizabeth Bishop, 1998; Between the Iceberg and the Ship (literary essays), 1998; Granny Scarecrow, 2000; Hearing with My Fingers, 2002; A Report from the Border, 2003. Contributions: Reviews, journals, and magazines. *Honours:* Fellowships; Major Hopwood Award, 1954; Arts Council Award, 1974; Poetry Book Society Choice, 1985; Athena Award, 1990; Cholmondely Award, Society of Authors, 1997; Northern Rock Foundation Writers Award, 2002. *Address:* 38 Western Hill, Durham, DH1 4RJ, England. *E-mail:* anne.stevenson@dial.pipex.com. *Website:* www.anne-stevenson.co.uk/poetry.

STEVENSON, David, BA, PhD, DLitt, FRSE; academic and writer; b. 30 April 1942, Largs, Ayrshire, Scotland; m. Wendy McLeod; two s. *Education:* Univ. of Dublin, Univ. of Glasgow. *Career:* Faculty, Univ. of Aberdeen, Univ. of St Andrews; Ed., Northern Scotland 1980–90. *Publications:* The Scottish Revolution 1973, Revolution and Counter-Revolution in Scotland 1977, Alastair MacColla and the Highland Problem 1980, Scottish Covenanters and Irish Confederates 1981, The Origins of Freemasonry 1988, The First Freemasons 1988, King or Covenant: Voices from Civil War 1996, Scotland's Last Royal Wedding 1997, Union, Revolution and Religion in 17th Century Scotland 1997, The Beggar's Benison. Sex Clubs of the Scottish Enlightenment and their Rituals 2001, 1914–1918: The History of the First World War 2004; contrib. to historical journals. *Address:* 5 Forgan Way, Newport-on-Tay, Fife DD6 8JQ, Scotland. *E-mail:* david.stevenson@btinternet.com.

STEWART, Bruce Robert; Writer and Dramatist; b. 4 Sept. 1925, Auckland, New Zealand; m. Ellen Noonan, 16 Oct. 1950, three s., three d. *Education:* BA, University of Auckland. *Career:* mem. British Film Institute; Writers Guild of Australia; Writers Guild of Great Britain, chair., 1979–81; Actors' Equity. *Publications:* A Disorderly Girl, 1980; The Turning Tide, 1980; The Hot and Copper Sky, 1982; Aspects of Therese, 1997; A Bloke Like Jesus, 1998. Other: various plays for stage, radio and television, including Me and My Shadow, 1988; The Gallows in My Garden, 1989; Stars in my Hair, 1990; Speak Low, 1993; Soeur Sourive, 2000. Contributions: newspapers, magazines and journals. *Honours:* Edgar Allan Poe Award, MWA, 1963; Charles Henry Foyle Award, UK, 1968. *Address:* c/o Harvey Unna, 24 Pottery Lane, Holland Park, London W11, England. *E-mail:* hbstewart@beeb.net.

STEWART, Douglas Keith; Writer and Critic; b. 15 Dec. 1950, Kawakana, New Zealand; m. Julie Joy Burgham, 9 Dec. 1972, one s. two d. *Education:* Northland College, University of Auckland. *Publications:* The New Zealander's Guide to Wine, 1986; The Art Award, 1988; The Wine Handbook, 1988; Rosa Antipodes: The History of Roses in New Zealand, 1994; The Fine Wines of New Zealand, 1995; Kahukura's Net: Maori Influence on Contemporary New Zealand Art, 1999; Euchre (novel), 1999. Contributions: newspapers and magazines. *Address:* PO Box 125, Kumeu, New Zealand.

STEWART, Harold Frederick; Poet, Writer and Trans; b. 14 Dec. 1916, Sydney, NSW, Australia. *Education:* University of Sydney. *Career:* Broadcaster, Australian Broadcasting Commission; Lecturer, Victorian Council of Adult Education. *Publications:* Poetry: The Darkening Ecliptic (with James McAuley), 1944; Phoenix Wings: Poems 1940–46, 1948; Orpheus and Other Poems, 1956; The Exiled Immortal: A Song Cycle, 1980; By the Old Walls of Kyoto: A Year's Cycle of Landscape Poems with Prose Commentaries, 1981; Collected Poems (with Ern Malley), 1993. Translator: A Net of Fireflies: Japanese Haiku and Haiku Paintings, 1960; A Chime of Windbells: A Year of Japanese Haiku, 1969; Tannisho: Passages Deploring Deviations of Faith (with Bando Shojun), 1980; The Amida Sutra Mandala (with Inagaki Hisao), 1995. *Honours:* Sydney Morning Herald Prize for Poetry, 1951; Australia Council Grant, 1978; Senior Emeritus Writers Fellow, Australia Council, 1982; Christopher Brennan Prize for Poetry, 1988.

STEWART, John; Prof. of Anthropology and Literature and Writer; b. 24 Jan. 1933, Trinidad; m. Sandra MacDonald, 7 June 1969, one s. one d. *Education:* MA, Stanford University, 1964; MFA, University of Iowa, 1965; PhD, University of California at Los Angeles, 1971. *Career:* University of Illinois; Ohio State University; University of California at Davis. *Publications:* Last Cool Days (novel), 1971; Curving Road (short stories), 1975; For the Ancestors (life history), 1983; Drinkers, Drummers and Decent Folk (narrative ethnography), 1989; Looking for Josephine (short stories), 1998. *Honours:* Winifred Hoztby Memorial Prize, 1971. *Address:* African American and African Studies, University of California at Davis, 2143 Hart Hall, Davis, CA 95616, USA.

STEWART, Judith (see Polley, Judith Anne).

STEWART, Lady Mary Florence Elinor, BA, DipEd, MA; British writer and poet; b. 17 Sept. 1916, Sunderland, England; m. Frederick Henry Stewart 1945. *Education:* Univ. of Durham. *Career:* mem. PEN. *Publications:* novels: Madam, Will You Talk? 1954, Wildfire at Midnight 1956, Thunder on the Right 1957, Nine Coaches Waiting 1958, My Brother Michael 1959, The Ivy Tree 1961, The Moonspinners 1962, This Rough Magic 1964, Airs Above the Ground 1965, The Gabriel Hounds 1967, The Wind off the Small Isles 1968, The Crystal Cave 1970, The Hollow Hills 1973, Touch Not the Cat 1976, The Last Enchantment 1979, The Wicked Day 1983, Thornyhold 1988, Stormy Petrel 1991, The Prince and the Pilgrim 1995, Rose Cottage 1997; children's fiction: A Walk in Wolf Wood 1970, The Little Broomstick 1971, Ludo and the Star Horse; poetry: Frost on the Window and Other Poems 1990; contrib. to magazines. *Honours:* Frederick Niven Prize 1971, Scottish Arts Council Award 1974, Hon. Fellow, Newnham Coll., Cambridge. *Address:* House of Letterawe, Loch Awe, Dalmally, Argyll PA33 1AH, Scotland.

STEWART, Paul; Writer; b. 4 June 1955, London, England; m. Julie Stewart, one s. one d. *Education:* English, University of Lancaster, 1974–77; Creative Writing, University of East Anglia, 1978–79; German, University of Heidelberg, 1980–82. *Publications:* Stormchaser, 1999; The Birthday Presents, 1999; The Blobheads, eight vols, 2000; Football Mad IV: Teamwork, 2000; Midnight Over Sanctaphrax, 2000; Rabbit's Wish, 2001; The Curse of the Gloamglozer, 2001; The Were-pig, 2001; The Last of the Sky Pirates, 2002; Muddle Earth, 2003; Vox, 2003. *Literary Agent:* Rogers, Coleridge & White Ltd, 20 Powis Mews, London W11 1JN, England.

STEWART, Susan; Writer, Poet and Educator; b. 15 March 1952, York, Pennsylvania, USA. *Education:* BA, Dickinson College, 1973; MA, Poetry, Johns Hopkins University, 1975; PhD, Folklore, University of Pennsylvania, 1978. *Career:* Asst Prof., 1978–81, Assoc. Prof., 1981–85, Prof. of English, 1985–, Temple University, Philadelphia, Pennsylvania. *Publications:* Nonsense: Aspects of Intertextuality in Folklore and Literature, 1979; Yellow Stars and Ice (poems), 1981; On Longing: Narratives of the Miniature, the Gigantic, the Souvenir, the Collection, 1984; The Hive: Poems, 1987; Crimes of Writing: Problems in the Containment of Representation, 1991; The Forest (poems), 1995. *Honours:* National Endowment for the Arts Grants, 1981–82, 1984, 1988; Pennsylvania Council on the Arts Grants, 1984, 1988, 1989–90; Guggenheim Foundation Fellowship, 1986–87; Georgia Press Second Book Award, 1987; Temple University Creative Achievement Award, 1991; Senior Scholar, Getty Center for the History of Art and the Humanities, 1995; Lila Wallace-Reader's Digest Writer's Award for Poetry, 1995; Pew Fellowship, 1995.

STIBBE, Mark W. G.; Clerk in Holy Orders and Writer; b. 16 Sept. 1960, London, England; m. Alison Heather Stibbe, 30 July 1983, two s. one d. *Education:* BA/MA, University of Cambridge, 1982; PhD, University of Nottingham, 1989. *Publications:* John as Storyteller, 1992; The Gospel of John as Literature, 1993; John: A New Biblical Commentary, 1993; A Kingdom of Priests, 1994; John's Gospel, 1994; Explaining Baptism in the Holy Spirit, 1995; O Brave New Church, 1996; Times of Refreshing, 1996; Know Your Spiritual Gifts, 1997. Contributions: numerous articles to Renewal; Anglicans for Renewal; various New Testament journals; Journal of Pentecostal Theology; Soul Survivor. *Honours:* MA; Dip.Th; PhD. *Address:* St Andrew's Vicarage, 39 Quickley Lane, Chorley Wood, Hertfordshire WD3 5AE, England.

STICKLAND, Caroline Amanda; Writer; b. 10 Oct. 1955, Rinteln, Germany; m. William Stickland, 3 Aug. 1974, one d. *Education:* BA, English and American Literature, University of East Anglia, 1977. *Career:* mem. Society of Authors; Mrs Gaskell Society; Thomas Hardy Society. *Publications:* The Standing Hills, 1986; A House of Clay, 1988; The Darkness of Corn, 1990; An Ancient Hope, 1993; The Darkening Leaf, 1995; The Kindly Ones, 2000. *Honours:* Betty Trask Award, 1985. *Literary Agent:* Sheil Land Assocs Ltd, 43 Doughty St, London, England. *Address:* 81 Crock Lane, Bothenhampton, Bridport, Dorset DT6 4DQ, England.

STIGLITZ, Joseph Eugene, PhD, FBA; American economist and academic; *Professor of Economics and Finance, Columbia University Graduate School of Business*; b. 9 Feb. 1943, Gary, Ind.; m. Jane Hannaway 1978; two s. two d. *Education:* Amherst Coll., Mass. Inst. of Tech. and Univ. of Cambridge (Fulbright Scholar). *Career:* Prof. of Econs Cowles Foundation, Yale Univ. 1970–74; Visiting Fellow, St Catherine's Coll. Oxford 1973–74; Prof. of Econs Stanford Univ. 1974–76, and Senior Fellow Hoover Inst. 1988–2001, Joan Kenney Prof. of Econs 1992–2001; Oskar Morgenstern Distinguished Fellow, Inst. of Advanced Studies, Princeton 1978–79; Drummond Prof. of Political Econ. Univ. of Oxford 1976–79; Prof. of Econs Princeton Univ. 1979–88; Stern Visiting Prof. Columbia Univ. 2000, Prof. of Econs and Finance, Graduate School of Business, Columbia Univ. 2001–; mem. Pres.'s Council of Econ. Advisers 1993–95, Chair. (mem. of cabinet) 1995–97; Special Adviser to Pres. of World Bank, Sr Vice-Pres. and Chief Economist 1995–2000; Special Adviser, Bell Communications Research, numerous consultancies in public and pvt. sector, editorial Bd memberships etc.; Sr

Fellow Brookings Inst. 2000; Fellow American Acad. of Arts and Sciences, NAS, Econometric Soc., American Philosophical Soc., Inst. for Policy Research (Sr Fellow 1991–93); Guggenheim Fellow 1969–70. *Publications include:* Globalization and its Discontents, Economics of the Public Sector 2000, Principles of Economics 1997, Rethinking the East Asia Miracle (co-ed.) 2001, The Roaring Nineties 2003; other books and more than 300 papers in learned journals. *Honours:* Hon. DHL (Amherst Coll.) 1974; Dr hc (Univ. of Leuven), (Ben Gurion Univ.); John Bates Clark Award, American Econ. Asscn 1979; Int. Prize, Acad. Lincei, Rome 1988; UAP Scientific Prize, Paris 1989; Nobel Prize for Econs (jt recepient) 2001, Dr. hc (Oxford) 2004. *Address:* Uris Hall, Room 814, Columbia University, 3022 Broadway, New York, NY 10027, USA (Office). *Telephone:* (212) 854-1481 (Office). *Fax:* (212) 662-8474 (Office). *E-mail:* jes322@columbia.edu (Office). *Website:* www-1.gsb.columbia.edu/faculty/jstiglitz/ (Office).

STILES, Martha Bennett, BS; writer; b. 30 March 1933, Manila, Philippines; m. Martin Stiles 1954; one s. *Education:* Univ. of Michigan. *Career:* mem. Authors' Guild, King Library Assocs, Detroit Women Writers. *Publications:* One Among the Indians 1962, The Strange House at Newburyport 1963, Darkness Over the Land 1966, Dougal Looks for Birds 1972, James the Vine Puller 1975, The Star in the Forest 1977, Tana and the Useless Monkey 1979, Sarah the Dragon Lady 1986, Kate of Still Waters 1990, Lonesome Road 1998, Island Magic 1999; contrib. to journals and periodicals. *Honours:* James Bryan Hope Award 1951, Avery Hopwood Awards 1956, 1958, Frankfort Arts Foundation Fiction Prizes 1984, 1986, Soc. of Children's Book Writers Grant 1988, Al Smith Fellowship, Kentucky Arts Council 1992, 2003. *Address:* Stockwell Farm, 861 Hume-Bedford Road, Paris, KY 40361, USA.

STILLINGER, Jack Clifford, BA, MA, PhD; writer and academic; *Professor Emeritus, University of Illinois*; b. 16 Feb. 1931, Chicago, IL, USA; m. 1st Shirley Louise Van Wormer 1952; two s. two d.; m. 2nd Nina Zippin Baym 1971. *Education:* Univ. of Texas, Northwestern Univ., Harvard Univ. *Career:* Asst Prof. 1958–61, Assoc. Prof. 1961–64, Prof. of English 1964–2001, mem., Center for Advanced Study 1970–, Prof. Emeritus 2001–, Univ. of Illinois; Ed., Journal of English and Germanic Philology 1961–72; Fellow, American Acad. of Arts and Sciences; Nat. Woodrow Wilson Fellow 1953–54, Guggenheim Fellowship 1964–65; mem., Byron Soc., Keats-Shelley Asscn of America, MLA. *Publications:* The Early Draft of John Stuart Mill's Autobiography (ed.) 1961, Anthony Munday's Zelauto (ed.) 1963, William Wordsworth: Selected Poems and Prefaces (ed.) 1965, The Letters of Charles Armitage Brown (ed.) 1966, Twentieth Century Interpretations of Keats's Odes (ed.) 1968, John Stuart Mill: Autobiography and Other Writings (ed.) 1969, The Hoodwinking of Madeline 1971, The Texts of Keats's Poems 1974, The Poems of John Keats (ed.) 1978, Mill's Autobiography and Literary Essays (ed.) 1981, John Keats: Complete Poems (ed.) 1982, The Norton Anthology of English Literature (ed.) 1986, John Keats: Poetry Manuscripts at Harvard 1990, Multiple Authorship and the Myth of Solitary Genius 1991, Coleridge and Textual Instability: The Multiple Versions of the Major Poems 1994, Reading The Eve of St Agnes: The Multiples of Complex Literary Transaction 1999; contrib. to professional journals. *Honours:* Distinguished Scholar Award, Keats-Shelley Asscn of America 1986. *Address:* 806 W Indiana Avenue, Urbana, IL 61801, USA.

STIMPSON, Gerald (see Mitchell, Adrian).

STIMSON (SADLER), Tess; Writer; b. 17 July 1966, England; m. Brent Sadler, 17 July 1993, divorced 2002, two s. *Education:* MA, Oxon; St Hilda's College, Oxford, 1984–87. *Career:* Producer, ITN, 1987–91; Adjunct Prof., University of South Florida, 2002–. *Publications:* Yours Till the End (biog.), 1992; Hard News, 1993; Soft Focus, 1995; Pole Position, 1996. *Honours:* Dorothy Whitelock Award, 1985; Eleanor Rooke Award, 1986. *Address:* 4635 Dolphin Cay Lane, St Petersburg, FL 33711, USA.

STIMULUS, Flavian P. (see Philanderson, Flavian Titus).

STIMULUS, John (see Philanderson, Flavian Titus).

STIRLING, Jessica (see Rae, Hugh Crauford).

STOCKTON, 2nd Earl of; **Alexander Daniel Alan Macmillan,** FBIM, FRSA; British publisher, farmer and politician; b. 10 Oct. 1943, Oswestry; grandson of the late 1st Earl of Stockton (fmrly, as Harold Macmillan, Prime Minister of UK 1957–63); m. 1st Hélène Birgitte Hamilton 1970 (divorced 1991); one s. two d.; m. 2nd Miranda Elizabeth Louise Nuttall 1995. *Education:* Eton Coll. and Paris and Strathclyde Univs. *Career:* Sub-Ed. Glasgow Herald 1963–65; Reporter, Daily Telegraph 1965–67, Foreign Corresp. 1967–68, Chief European Corresp., Sunday Telegraph 1968–70; Dir Birch Grove Estates Ltd 1969–86, Chair. 1983–89; Dir Macmillan and Co. Ltd 1970–76, Deputy Chair. 1976–80, Chair. 1984–90, Pres. 1990–; Chair. Macmillan Publrs Ltd 1980–90 (Pres. 1990–), St Martin's Press, New York 1983–88 (Dir 1974–90), Sidgwick and Jackson 1989–90; mem. European Parl. for SW of England 1999–; Chair. Cen. London Training & Enterprise Council 1990–95; Dir Book Trade Benevolent Soc. 1976–88, Chair. Bookrest Appeal 1978–86; Dir United British Artists Ltd 1984–90 (Chair. 1985–90); mem. Lindemann Fellowship Cttee 1979– (Chair. 1983–), British Inst. of Man. 1981–, Council of Publrs Asscn 1985–88, Carlton Club Political Cttee 1975–88 (Chair. 1984); Gov. Archbishop Tenison's School 1979–86, Merchant Taylor's School 1980–82, 1990–, English Speaking Union 1980–84, 1986–93; Liveryman Worshipful Co. of Merchant Taylors 1972, Court Asst 1987, of Stationers 1973, Master 1991–92. *Honours:* Hon. DLitt (De Montfort) 1993, (Westminster) 1995; Hon. DUniv (Strathclyde) 1993. *Address:* European Parliament, ASP 8E107, Rue Wiertz, 1047 Brussels, Belgium (Office); Porters South, 4–6 Crinan Street, London, N1 9XW (Office); Hayne Manor, Stowford, Okehampton, Devon, EX20 4DB, England (Home). *Telephone:* (2) 284-76-83 (Brussels) (Office); (20) 7833-4000 (Porters) (Office); (1566) 783563 (Home); (20) 7881-8000. *Fax:* (2) 284-96-83 (Brussels) (Office); (1566) 783568 (Home); (20) 7881-8001. *E-mail:* estockton@europarl.eu.int (Office); l.ferguson@macmillan.uk (Home). *Website:* www.alexstockton.com (Office).

STOKER, Alan, (Alan Evans); Writer; b. 2 Oct. 1930, Sunderland, England; m. Irene Evans, 30 April 1960, two s. *Career:* mem. Society of Authors. *Publications:* End of the Running, 1966; Mantrap, 1967; Bannon, 1968; Vicious Circle, 1970; The Big Deal, 1971; Thunder at Dawn, 1978; Ship of Force, 1979; Dauntless, 1980; Seek Out and Destroy, 1982; Deed of Glory, 1984; Audacity, 1985; Eagle at Taranto, 1987; Night Action, 1989; Orphans of the Storm, 1990; Sink or Capture, 1993; Sword at Sunrise, 1994. Other: Short stories; Children's books. Contributions: newspapers and magazines. *Literary Agent:* David Higham Associates, 5–8 Lower John St, Golden Sq., London W1F 9HA, England. *Address:* 9 Dale Rd, Walton on Thames, Surrey KT12 2PY, England.

STOKER, Richard, FRAM, ARAM, ARCM; British composer, conductor, writer, poet and painter; b. 8 Nov. 1938, Castleford, Yorkshire, England; m. 1st Jacqueline Margaret Trelfer (divorced 1985); m. 2nd Dr Gillian Patricia Watson 1986. *Education:* Breadalbane House School, Castleford, Huddersfield Coll. of Music with Harold Truscott, Coll. of Art, Royal Acad. of Music, composition, conducting with Maurice Miles and Sir Lennox Berkeley, private study with Nadia Boulanger, Paris. *Career:* performance debut with BBC Home Service 1953, Nat. and Int. Eisteddfods, Wales 1955–58; conducting debut 1956; asst librarian, London Symphony Orchestra 1962–63; Prof. of Composition RAM 1963–87 (tutor 1970–80); composition teacher St Paul's School 1972–74, Magdalene Coll., Cambridge 1974–76; Ed. The Composer magazine 1969–80; apptd Magistrate, Inner London Commission 1995–2003, Crown Court 1998–2003; Adjudicator, Royal Philharmonic Soc. Composer's Award, Cyprus Orchestral Composer's Award for the Ministry of Culture 2001–; mem. Composers' Guild 1962– (mem. exec. cttee 1969–80); founder mem. RAM Guild Cttee 1994– (hon. treas. 1995–); founder mem. European-Atlantic Group 1993–; mem. Byron Soc. 1993–, Magistrates' Asscn 1995–2003, English and Int. PEN 1996–; mem. and treas. Steering Cttee Lewisham Arts Festival 1990, 1992; founder-mem. Atlantic Council 1993, RSL, Creative Rights Alliance 2001–. *Art:* two exhbns. *Compositions include:* four symphonies 1961, 1976, 1981, 1991; 12 nocturnes; two jazz preludes; overtures: Antic Hay, Feast of Fools, Heroic Overture; three string quartets, three violin sonatas, Partita for Violin and Harp, Sonatina for Guitar, two piano sonatas, three piano trios, A York Suite for piano, Piano Variations, Piano Concerto, Partita for Clarinet and Piano, Wind Quintet; organ works: Partita, Little Organ Book, Three Improvisations, Symphony; Monologue, Passacagalia, Serenade, Petite Suite, Nocturnal, Festival Suite; choral works and song cycles: Benedictus, Ecce Homo, Proverb, Psalms, Make Me a Willow Cabin, Canticle of the Rose, O Be Joyful, A Landscape of Truth; piano works: Zodiac Variations, Regency Suite, A Poet's Notebook; vocal works: Music That Brings Sweet Sleep, Aspects of Flight, Four Yeats Songs, Four Shakespeare Songs, Johnson Preserv'd (three-act opera), Thérèse Raquin, Chinese Canticle, Birthday of the Infanta; music for film and stage includes Troilus and Cressida, Portrait of a Town, Garden Party, My Friend – My Enemy. *Publications:* Portrait of a Town 1970, Words Without Music 1974, Strolling Players 1978, Open Window – Open Door (autobiog.) 1985, Tanglewood (novel) 1990, Between the Lines 1991, Diva (novel) 1992, Collected Short Stories 1993, Sir Thomas Armstrong – A Celebration 1998, Turn Back the Clock 1998, A Passage of Time 1999; contrib. to anthologies, including Triumph, Forward, Outposts, Spotlight, Strolling Players, American Poetry Soc. publications, reviews and articles for periodicals, including Records and Recording, Books and Bookmen, Guardian, Performance, The Magistrate, poems in numerous anthologies and internet publications; contrib. to Oxford Dictionary of Nat. Biography 2004 (adviser 2003–). *Honours:* BBC Music Award 1952, Eric Coates Award 1962, Dove Prize 1962, Nat. Library of Poetry (USA) Editors' Choice Award 1995, 1996, 1997. *Address:* Ricordi & Co. (London) Ltd, 210 New King's Road, London, SW6 4NZ, England (Office). *Telephone:* (20) 7371-7501. *Fax:* (20) 7371-7270.

STOLTZFUS, Ben Franklin; American writer, poet and academic; b. 15 Sept. 1927, Sofia, Bulgaria; m. 1st Elizabeth Burton 1955 (divorced 1975); two s. one d.; m. 2nd Judith Palmer 1975. *Education:* BA, Amherst College, 1949; MA, Middlebury College, 1954; University of Paris, 1955–56; PhD, University of Wisconsin, 1959. *Career:* Instructor in French, Smith College, 1958–60; Asst Prof., 1960–65, Assoc. Prof., 1965–66, Prof. of French, Comparative Literature and Creative Writing, 1967–93, Prof. Emeritus, 1993–, University of California at Riverside; mem. MLA of America; ACLA; ALA; Hemingway Society; Carmus Society; D. H. Lawrence Society; Poets and Writers. *Publications:* Fiction: The Eye of the Needle, 1967; Black Lazarus, 1972; Red, White, and Blue, 1989; Valley of Roses, 2003. Non-Fiction: Alain Robbe-Grillet and the New French Novel, 1964; Georges Chenneviere et l'unanimisme, 1965; Gide's Eagles, 1969; Gide and Hemingway: Rebels Against God, 1978; Alain Robbe-Grillet: The Body of the

Text, 1985; Alain Robbe-Grillet: Life, Work, and Criticism, 1987; Postmodern Poetics: Nouveau Roman and Innovative Fiction, 1987; La Belle Captive, 1995; Lacan and Literature: Purloined Pretexts, 1996. Contributions: numerous journals, quarterlies, reviews and magazines. *Honours:* Fulbright Scholarships, 1955–56, 1963–64; Hon. doctorate, Amherst College, 1974; NAAP Gradiva Award, 1997. *Address:* c/o Department of Comparative Literature and Foreign Languages, University of California at Riverside, Riverside, CA 92521, USA.

STONE, Joan Elizabeth; Asst Prof. of English, Poet and Writer; b. 22 Oct. 1930, Port Angeles, Washington, USA; m. James A Black, 30 July 1990, four s., one d. *Education:* BA, 1970, MA, 1974, PhD, 1976, University of Washington. *Career:* Visiting Prof. of Poetry, University of Montana, 1974; Dir, Creative Writing Workshop, University of Washington, 1975; Asst Prof. of English, Colorado College, 1977–. *Publications:* The Swimmer and Other Poems, 1975; Alba, 1976; A Letter to Myself to Water, 1981; Our Lady of the Harbor, 1986. Contributions: journals and magazines. *Honours:* Acad. of American Poets Awards, 1969, 1970, 1972; Borestone Mountain Award, 1974.

STONE, Laurie; Writer, Columnist and Critic; b. 18 Oct. 1946, New York, NY, USA. *Education:* BA, magna cum laude, Barnard College, 1968; MA, 1969, Doctoral Studies, Columbia College. *Career:* Instructor, Hunter and Queens Colleges, CUNY, 1969–75; Writer, 1974–, Columnist, 1987–96, Village Voice; Critic-at-Large, Fresh Air, National Public Radio, 1987–90; mem. International PEN; National Book Critics Circle; Poets and Writers. *Publications:* Starting with Serge (novel), 1990; Laughing in the Dark: A Decade of Subversive Comedy, 1997; Close to the Bone: Memoirs of Hurt, Rage, and Desire, 1998. Contributions: periodicals, radio and television. *Honours:* Kittredge Fund Grant, 1984; MacDowell Colony Residencies, 1984, 1989, 1990, 1991; Virginia Center for the Arts Residency, 1990–91; New York Foundation for the Arts Grant, 1993; Nona Balakian Prize, Excellence in Reviewing, National Book Critics Circle, 1996. *Address:* 808 West End Ave, Apt 511, New York, NY 10025, USA.

STONE, Robert (Anthony); Writer; b. 21 Aug. 1937, New York, NY, USA; m. Janice G. Burr 11 Dec. 1959; one s. one d. *Education:* New York Univ., 1958–59; Stegner Fellow, Stanford Univ., 1962. *Career:* Editorial Asst, New York Daily News, 1958–60; Writer, National Mirror, New York City, 1965–67; Writer-in-Residence, Princeton Univ., 1971–72; Faculty, Amherst Coll., 1972–75, 1977–78, Stanford Univ., 1979, Univ. of Hawaii at Manoa, 1979–80, Harvard Univ., 1981, Univ. of California at Irvine, 1982, New York Univ., 1983, Univ. of California at San Diego, 1985, Princeton Univ., 1985, Johns Hopkins Univ., 1993–94, Yale Univ., 1994–; mem. PEN. *Publications:* A Hall of Mirrors, 1967; Dog Soldiers, 1974; A Flag for Sunrise, 1981; Images of War, 1986; Children of Light, 1986; Outerbridge Reach, 1992; Bear and His Daughter: Stories, 1997; Damascus Gate, 1998; Bay of Souls, 2003. Contributions: anthologies and periodicals. *Honours:* William Faulkner Prize, 1967; Guggenheim Fellowship, 1971; National Book Award, 1975; John Dos Passos Prize, 1982; American Acad. of Arts and Letters Award, 1982, and Grant, 1988–92; National Endowment for the Humanities Fellow, 1983. *Address:* PO Box 967, Block Island, RI 02807, USA.

STOPPARD, Sir Tom, Kt, OM, CBE, FRSL; British writer; b. (Thomas Straussler), 3 July 1937, Zlin, Czechoslovakia; m. 1st Jose Ingle 1965 (divorced 1972); two s.; m. 2nd Dr Miriam Moore-Robinson 1972 (divorced 1992); two s. *Education:* Pocklington Grammar School, Yorks. *Career:* Journalist, Bristol 1954–60; freelance journalist, London 1960–64; mem. Cttee of the Free World 1981–; mem. Royal Nat. Theatre Bd 1989–. *Publications:* plays: Rosencrantz and Guildenstern are Dead 1967, The Real Inspector Hound 1968, Enter a Free Man 1968, After Magritte 1970, Dogg's Our Pet 1972, Jumpers 1972, Travesties 1975, Dirty Linen 1976, New-Found-Land 1976, Every Good Boy Deserves Favour (with music by André Previn, 1978, Night and Day 1978, Dogg's Hamlet, Cahoots Macbeth 1979, Undiscovered Country 1980, On the Razzle 1981, The Real Thing 1982, Rough Crossing 1984, Dalliance (adaption of Schnitzler's Liebelei) 1986, Hapgood 1988, Arcadia 1993 (Evening Standard Award for Best Play), Indian Ink 1995, The Invention of Love 1997, The Seagull (trans. 1997), The Coast of Utopia (trilogy: Part One: Voyage, Part Two: Shipwreck, Part Three: Salvage) 2002; radio plays: The Dissolution of Dominic Boot 1964, M is for Moon Among Other Things 1964, Albert's Bridge 1967, If You're Glad I'll be Frank 1968, Where Are They Now? 1970, Artist Descending a Staircase 1972, The Dog It Was That Died 1983, In the Native State 1991; short stories: Introduction 2 1963; novel: Lord Malquist and Mr Moon 1966; screenplays: The Romantic Englishwoman (co-author) 1975, Despair 1977; film scripts: The Human Factor 1979, Brazil (with Terry Gilliam, and Charles McKeown) 1984, Crown 1987, Empire of the Sun 1987, Rosencrantz and Guildenstern are Dead 1989 (also Dir), Russia House 1989, Billy Bathgate 1990, Shakespeare in Love (jtly) 1998 (Jt winner Acad. Award Best Original Screenplay 1999), Enigma 2001; television plays: Professional Foul 1977, Squaring the Circle 1984, The Television Plays 1965–84 1993; radio: The Plays for Radio 1964–91, 1994. *Honours:* Hon. MLitt (Bristol, Brunel Univs.); Hon. LittD (Leeds Univ.) 1979, (Sussex) 1980, (Warwick) 1981, (London) 1982; Dr hc (Kenyon Coll.) 1984, (York) 1984; John Whiting Award, Arts Council 1967, Italia Prize (radio drama) 1968, New York Drama Critics Best Play Award 1968, Antoinette Perry Award 1968, 1976, Evening Standard Awards 1967, 1972, 1974, 1978, 1982, 1993, 1997, Sony Award 1991, Olivier Award 1993. *Literary Agent:* PFD, Drury House, 34–43 Russell Street, London, WC2B 5HA, England.

STOREY, David Malcolm; British author and playwright; b. 13 July 1933, Wakefield, Yorkshire; m. Barbara Hamilton 1956; two s. two d. *Education:* Queen Elizabeth Grammar School, Wakefield, Wakefield Coll. of Art and Slade School of Art. *Career:* Fellow, Univ. Coll. London 1974. *Publications:* novels: This Sporting Life (Macmillan Award) 1960, Flight into Camden (John Llewellyn Rhys Memorial Prize 1961, Somerset Maugham Award 1963) 1960, Radcliffe 1963, Pasmore (Faber Memorial Prize 1972) 1972, A Temporary Life 1973, Edward 1973, Saville (Booker Prize 1976) 1976, A Prodigal Child 1982, Present Times 1984, A Serious Man 1998, As It Happened 2002, Thin-Ice Skater 2004; plays: The Restoration of Arnold Middleton (Evening Standard Award 1967), In Celebration 1969 (also film), The Contractor (New York Critics' Prize 1974) 1969, Home (Evening Standard Award, New York Critics' Prize) 1970, The Changing Room (New York Critics' Prize) 1971, Cromwell 1973, The Farm 1973, Life Class 1974, Night 1976, Mother's Day 1976, Sisters 1978, Dreams of Leaving 1979, Early Days 1980, The March on Russia 1989, Stages 1992; poems: Storey's Lives: Poems 1951–1991 1992. *Honours:* Los Angeles Drama Critics Award 1969, Writer of the Year Award, Variety Club of GB 1969. *Address:* c/o Jonathan Cape Ltd, Random Century House, 20 Vauxhall Bridge Road, London, SW1V 2SA, England.

STOREY, Graham; University Reader (retd), Ed. and Writer; b. 8 Nov. 1920, East Yorkshire, England. *Education:* BA, 1941, MA, 1947, Trinity Hall, Cambridge; Barrister-at-Law, Middle Temple, 1950. *Career:* Fellow, 1949–, Senior Tutor, 1958–68, Vice-Master, 1970–74, Trinity Hall, Cambridge; University Lecturer, 1965–81, then University Reader, Cambridge; mem. Gerard Manley Hopkins Society. *Publications:* Reuters: The Story of a Century of News-Gathering, 1951; Angel With Horns and Other Shakespeare Lectures, by Arthur Percival Rossiter (ed.), 1962; The Letters of Charles Dickens (ed. with others), six vols, 1965–93; Selected Verse and Prose of Gerard Manley Hopkins (ed.), 1967; Cambridge English Prose Texts (gen. ed.), 1980–; A Preface to Hopkins (ed. with Howard Erskine-Hill), 1981; Writers and Their Works, 1982; Revolutionary Prose of the English Civil War (ed.), 1983; Gerard Manley Hopkins, 1984; Dickens and Other Victorians, 1988. Contributions: Reference works and journals. *Honours:* OBE, 1997; Hon. DLitt, University of Cambridge, 1997. *Address:* Crown House, Caxton, Cambridgeshire, England.

STORM, Christopher (see Olsen, Theodore Victor).

STOTHARD, Sir Peter M., Kt, MA; British journalist and newspaper editor; *Editor, The Times Literary Supplement;* b. 28 Feb. 1951, Chelmsford, Essex; m. Sally Ceris Emerson 1980; one s. one d. *Education:* Brentwood School, Essex and Trinity Coll. Oxford. *Career:* journalist, BBC 1974–77; Shell Petroleum 1977–79; business and political writer, Sunday Times 1979–80; Features Ed. and leader writer, The Times 1980–85; Deputy Ed. The Times 1985–92, US Ed. 1989–92, Ed. 1992–2002; Ed. The Times Literary Supplement 2002–. *Publications:* Thirty Days: A Month at the Heart of Blair's War 2003. *Honours:* Hon. Fellow Trinity Coll. Oxford 2000. *Address:* The Times Literary Supplement, Admiral House, 66–68 East Smithfield, London, E1W 1BX, England (Office). *Telephone:* (20) 7782-3380. *Website:* www.the-tls.co.uk.

STOTT, Mike; Playwright; b. 2 Jan. 1944, Rochdale, Lancashire, England. *Education:* University of Manchester. *Career:* Resident Writer, Hampstead Theatre Club, 1975. *Publications:* Mata Hari, 1965; Erogenous Zone, 1969; Funny Peculiar, 1973; Lenz (after Büchner), 1974; Plays for People Who Don't Move Much, 1974; Midnight, 1974; Other People, 1974; Lorenzaccio (after De Musset), 1976; Followed by Oysters, 1976; Soldiers Talking Cleanly, 1978; The Boston Strangler, 1978; Grandad, 1978; Strangers, 1979; Ducking Out, 1982; Dead Men, 1982; Penine Pleasures, 1984; The Fling, 1984; The Fancy Man, 1988. Other: Radio and television plays. *Literary Agent:* PFD, Drury House, 34–43 Russell St, London WC2B 5HA, England.

STOUT, Robert Joe; Writer and Poet; b. 3 Feb. 1938, Scottsbluff, NE, USA; m. Maureen Ryan, 14 April 1988, two s. three d. *Education:* BA, Mexico City College, 1960. *Publications:* Miss Sally 1973, The Trick 1974, Swallowing Dust 1974, Moving Out 1974, They Still Play Baseball the Old Way 1994, The Blood of the Serpent: Mexican Lives 2003. Contributions: Smoke Magazine, The Retired Officer Magazine, Notre Dame Magazine, The Beloit Poetry Journal, The South Dakota Review, Interim, Commonweal. *Address:* Caja Postal 220, La Paz, BCS, CP 23000, Mexico. *E-mail:* bobstout@journalist.com.

STOW, (Julian) Randolph; librettist, writer and poet; b. 28 Nov. 1935, Geraldton, WA, Australia. *Education:* University of Western Australia. *Career:* Lecturer in English, University of Leeds, Yorkshire, 1962, 1968–69, University of Western Australia, 1963–64; Harkness Fellow, USA, 1964–66. *Publications:* A Haunted Land, 1956; The Bystander, 1957; To the Islands, 1958; Tourmaline, 1963; The Merry-Go-Round in the Sea, 1965; Midnite, 1967; Visitants, 1979; The Girl Green as Elderflower, 1980; The Suburbs of Hell, 1984. Poetry: Act One, 1957; Outrider: Poems 1956–62, 1962; A Counterfeit Silence: Selected Poems, 1969; Randolph Stow (omnibus vol. edited by A. J. Hassall), 1990. Librettos to Music by Peter

Maxwell Davies: Eight Songs for a Mad King, 1969; Miss Donnithorne's Maggot, 1974. *Honours:* Miles Franklin Award, 1958; Britannica-Australia Award, 1966; Grace Leven Prize, 1969; Arts Council of Great Britain Bursary, 1969; Commonwealth Literary Fund Grant, 1974; Patrick White Award, 1979. *Literary Agent:* Sheil Land Associates, 43 Doughty Street, London, WC1N 2LF, England.

STRACHAN, Hew (Francis Anthony), FRSE; professor and writer; b. 1 Sept. 1949, Edinburgh, Scotland; m. 1st Catherine Margaret Blackburn 1971 (divorced 1980); two d.; m. 2nd Pamela Dorothy Tennant 1982; one s. one step-s. one step-d. *Education:* MA, PhD, 1977, Corpus Christi Coll., Cambridge. *Career:* Research Fellow, 1975–78, Fellow, 1979–, Dean of Coll., 1981–86, Admissions Tutor, 1981–88, Senior Tutor, 1989–92, Corpus Christi Coll., Cambridge; Senior Lecturer in War Studies, Royal Military Acad., Sandhurst, 1978–79; Prof. of Modern History, 1992–2001, Dir, Scottish Centre for War Studies, 1996–2001, Univ. of Glasgow; Lees Knowles Lecturer, Cambridge, 1995; Visiting Prof., Royal Norwegian Air Force Acad., 2000–; Fellow All Souls College, Chichele Prof. of the History of War, Oxford Univ. 2002–. *Publications:* British Military Uniforms, 1768–1796, 1975; History of Cambridge University Officers' Training Corps, 1976; European Armies and the Conduct of War, 1983; Wellington's Legacy: The Reform of the British Army, 1984; From Waterloo to Balaclava: Tactics, Technology and the British Army, 1815–1854, 1985; The Politics of the British Army, 1997; The Oxford Illustrated History of the First World War (ed.), 1998; The British Army, Manpower and Society (ed.), 2000; The First World War, Vol. 1, To Arms, 2001; Military Lives, 2002; The First World War: An Illustrated History, 2003; The Outbreak of War, 2004; Financing the War, 2004; The War in Africa, 2004. Contributions: learned books and journals. *Honours:* Templer Medal, 1985; Life Fellow, Corpus Christi College, Cambridge, 1992; Westminster Medal, 1997; Thank Offering to Britain Fellow, British Acad., 1998–99. *Literary Agent:* David Higham Associates, 5–8 Lower John St, Golden Sq., London W1F 9HA, England. *Address:* All Souls College, Oxford, OX1 4AL, Scotland.

STRAIGHT, Steve; American writer and lecturer; m.; two d. *Career:* fmr Dir of Seminar Series, Sunken Garden Poetry Festival; Prof. of English and Dir of the Poetry Program, Manchester Community Coll.; Dir, Connecticut Poetry Circuit. *Publications:* The Water Carrier (poems) 2002, In a Different Light (novel) 2005. *Address:* c/o Curbstone Press, 321 Jackson Street, Willimantic, CT 06226-1738, USA. *E-mail:* info@curbstone.org. *Website:* www.curbstone.org.

STRAND, Mark; poet, writer and academic; b. 11 April 1934, Summerside, PE, Canada; m. 1st Antonia Ratensky 1961 (divorced 1973); one d.; m. 2nd Julia Rumsey Garretson 1976; one s. *Education:* AB, Antioch College, 1957; BFA, Yale University, 1959; MA, University of Iowa, 1962. *Career:* Instructor, University of Iowa, 1962–65; Fulbright Lecturer, University of Brazil, 1965; Asst Prof., Mount Holyoke College, 1966; Visiting Prof., University of Washington, 1967, University of Virginia, 1977, California State University at Fresno, 1977, University of California at Irvine, 1978, Wesleyan University, 1979–80; Adjunct Prof., Columbia University, 1968–70; Visiting Lecturer, Yale University, 1969–70, Harvard University, 1980–81; Assoc. Prof., Brooklyn College, CUNY, 1971; Bain Swiggett Lecturer, Princeton University, 1972; Fanny Hurst Prof. of Poetry, Brandeis University, 1973; Prof., 1981–86, Distinguished Prof., 1986–94, University of Utah; Poet Laureate of the USA, 1990–91; Elliot Coleman Prof. of Poetry, Johns Hopkins University, 1994–97; Andrew MacLeish Distinguished Service Prof., University of Chicago; mem. American Acad. and Institute of Arts and Letters, 1980–; National Acad. of Arts and Sciences, 1995–. *Publications:* Poetry: Sleeping With One Eye Open, 1964; Reasons for Moving, 1968; Darker, 1970; The Sargentville Notebook, 1973; The Story of Our Lives, 1973; The Late Hour, 1978; Selected Poems, 1980; The Continuous Life, 1990; Dark Harbor, 1993; Blizzard of One, 1998. Fiction: Mr and Mrs Baby (short stories), 1985. Prose: The Monument, 1978; The Art of the Real, 1983; William Bailey, 1987; Hopper, 1994. Anthologies: The Contemporary American Poets, 1969; New Poetry of Mexico (with Octavio Paz), 1970; Another Republic (with Charles Simic), 1976; The Best American Poetry 1991 (with David Lehman), 1992; The Weather of Words: Poetic Invention, 2000. Translator: Halty Ferguson: 18 Poems from the Quechua, 1971; Rafael Alberti: The Owl's Insomnia (poems), 1973; Carlos Drummond de Andrade: Souvenir of the Ancient World (poems), 1976; Travelling in the Family: The Selected Poems of Carlos Drummond de Andrade, 1986. Children's Books: The Planet of Lost Things, 1982; The Night Book, 1985; Rembrandt Takes a Walk, 1986. Contributions: poems, book reviews, art reviews, essays on poetry and painting and interviews in numerous periodicals. *Honours:* Fulbright Scholarship to Italy, 1960–61; Ingram Merrill Foundation Fellowship, 1966; National Endowment for the Arts Fellowships, 1967–68, 1977–78; Rockefeller Fellowship, 1968–69; Edgar Allan Poe Prize, 1974; Guggenheim Fellowship, 1974–75; National Institute of Arts and Letters Award, 1975; Acad. of American Poets Fellowship, 1979; Writer-in-Residence, American Acad., Rome, 1982; John D. and Catherine T. MacArthur Foundation Fellowship, 1987–92; Utah Governor's Award in the Arts, 1992; Bobbitt National Prize for Poetry, 1992; Bollingen Prize for Poetry, 1993; Pulitzer Prize in Poetry, 1999. *Address:* Committee on Social Thought, 1130 E 59th Street, Chicago, IL 60637, USA.

STRATTON, Thomas (see De Weese, Thomas Eugene (Gene)).

STRAUB, Peter Francis; Writer; b. 2 March 1943, Milwaukee, WI, USA; m. 27 Aug. 1966. *Education:* BA, Univ. of Wisconsin, 1965; MA, Columbia Univ., 1966. *Publications:* Open Air (poems), 1972; Marriage, 1973; Julia, 1975; If You Could See Me New, 1977; Ghost Story, 1979; Shadowland, 1980; Floating Dragon, 1983; The Talisman (with Stephen King), 1984; Koko, 1988; Mystery, 1989; Houses Without Doors, 1990; The Throat, 1993; The Hellfire Club, 1996; Mr X, 1999; Magic Terror, 2000; Black House (with Stephen King), 2001; Conjunctions 39: The New Fabulists (ed.), 2002; Lost Boy Lost Girl, 2003. Contributions: TLS; New Statesman; Washington Post. *Honours:* British Fantasy Award, 1983; August Derleth Award, 1983; World Fantasy Best Novel Awards, 1988, 1993; Bram Stoker Awards for Best Novel, 1993, 1998, 2000. *Address:* 53 W 85th St, New York, NY 10024, USA.

STRAUSS, Botho; Author, Poet and Dramatist; b. 2 Dec. 1944, Naumberg-an-der-Saale, Germany. *Education:* German Language and Literature, Drama, Sociology, Cologne and Munich. *Career:* mem. PEN. *Publications:* Bekannte Gesichter, gemischte Gefühle (with T. Bernhard and F. Kroetz), 1974; Trilogie des Wiedersehens, 1976; Gross und Klein, 1978; Rumor, 1980; Kalldeway Farce, 1981; Paare, Passanten, 1981; Der Park, 1983; Der junge Mann, 1984; Diese Erinnerung an einen, der nur einen Tag zu Gast War, 1985; Die Fremdenführerin, 1986; Niemand anderes, 1987; Besucher, 1988; Kongress: Die Kette der Demütigungen, 1989; Theaterstücke in zwei Banden, 1994; Wohnen Dammern Lügen, 1994; Das Partikular, 2000; Der Narr und seine Frau heute abend in Pancomedia, 2001. *Honours:* Dramatists' Prize, Hannover, 1975; Schiller Prize, Baden-Württemberg, 1977; Literary Prize, Bavarian Acad. of Fine Arts, Munich, 1981; Jean Paul Prize, 1987; Georg Büchner Prize, 1989. *Address:* Keithstrasse 8, 17877, Berlin, Germany.

STRAUSS, Jennifer; academic and poet; b. 30 Jan. 1933, Heywood, Vic., Australia; m. Werner Strauss 1958; three s. *Education:* BA, University of Melbourne, 1954; University of Glasgow, 1957–58; PhD, Monash University, 1992. *Career:* Senior Lecturer, 1971–92, Assoc. Prof., 1992–, Monash University; mem. Premier's Literary Awards Committee; PEN; Asscn for Study of Australian Literature; Australian Society of Authors. *Publications:* Children and Other Strangers, 1975; Winter Driving, 1981; Middle English Verse: An Anthology (co-ed.), 1985; Labour Ward, 1988; Boundary Conditions: The Poetry of Gwen Harwood, 1992; The Oxford Book of Australian Love Poems (ed.), 1993; Judith Wright, 1995; Tierra del Fuego: New and Selected Poems, 1997; Family Ties: Australian Poems of the Family (ed.), 1998; Oxford Literary History of Australia (co-ed.), 1998. Contributions: various publications. *Address:* 2–12 Tollington Avenue, East Malvern, Vic. 3145, Australia.

STRAWSON, Galen John; Philosopher; b. 5 Feb. 1952, Oxford, England; m. 1st Jose Said, 20 July 1974, divorced 1994, one s. two d.; m. 2nd Anna Vaux, 6 Jan. 1997 (divorced 2003), two s. *Education:* BA, Philosophy, 1973, MA, 1977, University of Cambridge; BPhil, 1977, DPhil, 1983, University of Oxford. *Career:* Asst Ed., 1978–87, Consultant, 1987–, TLS, London; Fellow, Jesus College, Oxford, 1987–2000; Prof. of Philosophy Univ. of Reading 2001–; Visiting Fellow, Australian National University, 1993; Visiting Prof., New York University, 1997, Rutgers Univ. 2000; Distinguished Prof. of Philosophy City of New York Graduate Center 2004–; Trustee Kennedy Memorial Trust 1998–; mem. Mind Asscn. *Publications:* Freedom and Belief 1986, The Secret Connection 1989, Mental Reality 1994. Contributions: TLS, Sunday Times, Observer, Financial Times, Guardian, The Believer, London Review of Books, Independent on Sunday, Mind, American Philosophical Quarterly, Inquiry, Journal of Consciousness Studies, Analysis, Philosophical Studies, many books of essays. *Honours:* R. A. Nicholson Prize for Islamic Studies, Cambridge, 1971; T. H. Green Prize for Moral Philosophy, Oxford, 1983; . *Address:* Department of Philosophy, University of Reading, RG6 6AA, England.

STRAWSON, Sir Peter (Frederick); Prof. of Metaphysical Philosophy (retd) and Author; b. 23 Nov. 1919, London, England; m. Grace Hall Martin, 1945, two s. two d. *Education:* Christ's College, Finchley; St John's College, Oxford. *Career:* Asst Lecturer in Philosophy, University College of North Wales, 1946; John Locke Scholar, 1946, Reader, 1966–68, Waynflete Prof. of Metaphysical Philosophy, 1968–87, University of Oxford; Lecturer in Philosophy, 1947, Fellow and Praelector, 1948, Fellow, 1948–68, Hon. Fellow, 1979–, University College, Oxford; Visiting Prof., Duke University, 1955–56; Fellow of the Humanities Council and Visiting Assoc. Prof., 1960–61, Visiting Prof., 1972, Princeton University; Fellow, 1968–87, Hon. Fellow, 1989, Magdalen College, Oxford; Woodbridge Lecturer, Columbia University, 1983; Immanuel Kant Lecturer, University of Munich, 1985; Visiting Prof., Collège de France, 1985; mem. Academia Europaea; American Acad. of Arts and Sciences, hon. mem.; British Acad., fellow. *Publications:* Introduction to Logical Theory, 1952; Individuals, 1959; The Bounds of Sense, 1966; Philosophical Logic (ed.), 1966; Studies in the Philosophy of Thought and Action (ed.), 1968; Logico-Linguistic Papers, 1971; Freedom and Resentment, 1974; Subject and Predicate in Logic and Grammar, 1974; Scepticism and Naturalism: Some Varieties, 1985; Analyse and Métaphysique, 1985, English trans. as Analysis and Metaphysics, 1992; Entity and Identity, 1997; Autobiography and Replies, The Philosophy of P. F. Strawson, 1998. Contributions: scholarly journals. *Honours:*

Knighted 1977; Hon. doctorate, Univs of Munich, 1998, Sofia, 2003; International Kant Prize, Berlin, 2000. *Address:* 25 Farndon Rd, Oxford OX2 6RT, England.

STREET, Pamela; Writer; b. 3 March 1921, Wilton, Wiltshire, England; Divorced, one d. *Education:* Salisbury and South Wiltshire College of Further Education, 1967–69. *Publications:* My Father, A. G. Street, 1969; Portrait of Wiltshire, 1971; Arthur Bryant: Portrait of a Historian, 1979; Light of Evening, 1981; The Stepsisters, 1982; Morning Glory, 1982; Portrait of Rose, 1986; The Illustrated Portrait of Wiltshire, 1984; Personal Relations, 1987; The Mill-Race Quartet, 1988; The Timeless Moment, 1988; The Beneficiaries, 1989; Doubtful Company, 1990; Guilty Parties, 1991; Late Harvest, 1991; The Colonel's Son, 1992; Hindsight, 1993; Keeping it Dark, 1994; King's Folly, 1995; The General's Wife, 1996. Contributions: newspapers and magazines. *Address:* c/o 42 Roedean Crescent, London SW15 5JU, England.

STREET-PORTER, Janet, FRTS, FRIBA; British journalist, television producer, presenter and newspaper editor; b. 27 Dec. 1946; m. 1st Tim Street-Porter 1967 (divorced 1975); m. 2nd A. M. M. Elliott 1976 (divorced 1978); m. 3rd Frank Cvitanovich (divorced 1988, died 1995). *Education:* Lady Margaret Grammar School and Architectural Asscn. *Career:* columnist and fashion writer, Petticoat Magazine 1968, Daily Mail 1969–71, Evening Standard 1971–73; own show, LBC Radio 1973; presenter, London Weekend Show, London Weekend Television (LWT) 1975; producer and presenter, Saturday Night People (with Clive James, and Russell Harty), The Six O'Clock Show (with Michael Aspel), Around Midnight 1975–85, co-cr. Network 7 (Channel 4) 1987–88; Head, Youth and Entertainment Features, BBC TV 1988–94; Head, Ind. Production for Entertainment 1994; with Mirror Group PLC 1994–95; TV presenter Design Awards, Travels with Pevsner, Coast to Coast, The Midnight Hour 1996–98, As The Crow Flies (series) 1999, Cathedral Calls 2000 (all BBC2), J'Accuse, Internet 1996 (Channel 4), Bloomberg TV 2001–; Ed. The Independent on Sunday 1999–2001, Ed.-at-Large 2001–; Pres. Ramblers' Asscn 1994–97 (now Vice-Pres.), Globetrotters Club 2003–. *Publications:* Scandal 1980, The British Teapot 1981, Coast to Coast 1998, As the Crow Flies 1999, Baggage – My Childhood 2004. *Honours:* Prix Italia 1992, British Acad. Award for Originality 1988. *Address:* c/o Bob Storer, Harbottle & Lewis, 14 Hanover Square, London, W1S 1HP, England. *Telephone:* (20) 7667-5000. *Fax:* (20) 7667-5100.

STRESHINSKY, Shirley; Writer; b. 7 Oct. 1934, Alton, IL, USA; m. Ted Streshinsky, 16 June 1966, one s. one d. *Education:* BA, University of Illinois. *Publications:* And I Alone Survived, 1978; Hers the Kingdom, 1981; A Time Between, 1984; Gift of the Golden Mountain, 1988; The Shores of Paradise (novel), 1991; Oats! A Book of Whimsy (with Maria Streshinsky), 1997; John James Audubon: Life and Art in the American Wilderness, 1998. Contributions: journals and magazines. *Honours:* Best Human Interest Article, Society Magazine Writers Asscn, 1968; Educational Press Award, 1968. *Address:* PO Box 674, Berkeley, CA 94701, USA. *E-mail:* ststre@aol.com.

STRINGER, Christopher; Anthropologist and Writer; b. 31 Dec. 1947, London, England. *Education:* BSc, University of London; PhD, DSc, University of Bristol. *Career:* Anthropologist, Principal Researcher, Human Origins Group, Natural History Museum, London. *Publications:* Aspects of Human Evolution (ed.), 1981; The Human Revolution: Behavioral and Biological Perspectives on the Origins of Modern Humans (co-ed.), 1989; Human Evolution: An Illustrated Guide, 1989; In Search of Neanderthals: Solving the Puzzle of Human Origins (co-author), 1993; The Origin of Modern Humans and the Impact of Chronometric Dating: A Discussion (co-ed.), 1993; African Exodus: The Origins of Modern Humanity, 1997. *Literary Agent:* John Brockman, 5 E 59th St, New York, NY 10022, USA. *Address:* c/o Natural History Museum, Cromwell Rd, London SW7 5BD, England.

STROHM, Reinhard; Musicologist, Prof. of Music and Writer; b. 4 Aug. 1942, Munich, Germany. *Education:* University of Munich; PhD, Technical University, Berlin, 1971. *Career:* Lecturer, 1975–83, Prof., 1990–96, King's College, University of London; Prof., Yale University, 1983–90; Heather Prof. of Music, University of Oxford, 1996–; Corresponding mem., American Musicological Society 1995, Göttinger Akad. der Wissenschaften. *Publications:* Italienische Opernarien des Frühen Settecento, 1720–1730, 1976; Die Italienische Oper im 18. Jahrhundert, 1979; Music in Late Medieval Bruges, 1985; Essays on Handel and Italian Opera, 1985; Music in Late Medieval Europe, 1987; The Rise of European Music, 1380–1500, 1993; On the Dignity and the Effects of Music: Two Fifteenth-Century Treatises (with J. D. Cullington), 1996; Dramma per musica: Italian Opera Seria in the Eighteenth Century, 1997, The Eighteenth Century Diaspora of Italian Music and Musicians 2001, Music as Concept and Practice in the Late Middle Ages (The New Oxford History of Music, Vol. III, with B. Blackburn) 2001. Contributions: learned books and journals. *Honours:* Dent Medal, Royal Musical Asscn 1977, Fellow, British Acad. 1993. *Address:* c/o Faculty of Music, University of Oxford, St Aldate's, Oxford OX1 1DB, England. *E-mail:* reinhard.strohm@music.ox.ac.uk.

STRONG, Eithne; Writer and Poet; b. 23 Feb. 1923, West Limerick, Ireland; m. Rupert Strong, 12 Nov. 1943, two s., seven d. *Education:* BA, Trinity College, Dublin. *Career:* mem. Aosdána; Conradh Na Gaeilge; Irish PEN; Irish Writers Union; Poetry Ireland. *Publications:* Poetry: Songs of Living, 1965; Sarah in Passing, 1974; Circt Oibre, 1980; Fuil agus Fallat, 1983; My Darling Neighbour, 1985; Flesh the Greatest Sin, 1989; An Sagart Pinc, 1990; Aoife Faoi Ghlas, 1990; Let Live, 1990; Spatial Nosing, 1993; Nobel, 1998. Fiction: Degrees of Kindred, 1979; The Love Riddle, 1993. Short Fiction: Patterns, 1981. Contributions: anthologies, journals, and magazines. *Address:* 17 Eaton Sq., Monkstown, Dublin, Ireland.

STRONG, Jonathan; Writer and University Teacher; b. 13 Aug. 1944, Evanston, IL, USA. *Education:* Harvard University, 1969. *Career:* Faculty, Tufts University; mem. New England Gilbert and Sullivan Society; Sir Arthur Sullivan Society. *Publications:* Tike, 1969; Ourselves, 1971; Elsewhere, 1985; Secret Words, 1992; Companion Pieces, 1993; An Untold Tale, 1993; Offspring, 1995; The Old World, 1997; The Haunts of His Youth, 1999; A Circle Around Her, 2000. Contributions: American Literature; journals and magazines. *Honours:* O. Henry Story Awards, 1967, 1970; Rosenthal Award, 1970; National Endowment for the Arts Award, 1986. *Address:* c/o Dept of English, Tufts University, Medford, MA 02155, USA.

STRONG, Maggie (see Kotker, (Mary) Zane).

STRONG, Sir Roy (Colin); art historian, writer, broadcaster and consultant; b. 23 Aug. 1935, London, England; m. Julia Trevelyan Oman. *Education:* Queen Mary College, London; Warburg Institute, London. *Career:* Asst Keeper, 1959–67, Dir, Keeper and Secretary, 1967–73, National Portrait Gallery, London; Ferens Prof. of Fine Art, University of Hull, 1972; Walls Lecturer, J. Pierpoint Morgan Library, New York, 1974; Dir, Victoria and Albert Museum, London, 1974–87; Andrew Carnduff Ritchie Lecturer, Yale University, 1999; mem. Arts Council of Great Britain, chair., arts panel, 1983–87; British Council, Fine Arts Advisory Committee, 1974–87; Royal College of Arts Council, 1979–87; Westminster Abbey Architectural Panel, 1975–89. *Publications:* Portraits of Queen Elizabeth I, 1963; Holbein and Henry the VIII, 1967; The English Icon: Elizabethan and Jacobean Portraiture, 1969; Tudor and Jacobean Portraits, 1969; Van Dyck: Charles I on Horseback, 1972; Splendour at Court: Renaissance Spectacle and the Theatre of Power, 1973; Nicholas Hilliard, 1975; The Renaissance Garden in England, 1979; Britannia Triumphans: Inigo Jones, Rubens and Whitehall Palace, 1980; Henry, Prince of Wales and England's Lost Renaissance, 1986; Creating Small Gardens, 1986; Gloriana: Portraits of Queen Elizabeth I, 1987; A Small Garden Designer's Handbook, 1987; Cecil Beaton: The Royal Portraits, 1988; Creating Small Formal Gardens, 1989; Lost Treasures of Britain, 1990; A Celebration of Gardens (ed.), 1991; The Garden Trellis, 1991; Small Period Gardens, 1992; Royal Gardens, 1992; A Country Life, 1994; Successful Small Gardens, 1994; William Larkin: Vanitù giacobite, Italy, 1994; The Tudor and Stuart Monarchy, three vols, 1995–97; The Story of Britain, 1996; The English Vision: Country Life 1897–1997, 1997; The Roy Strong Diaries 1967–1987, 1997; The Spirit of Britain: A Narrative History of the Arts, 1999; Garden Party, 2000; The Artist and the Garden, 2000; Ornament in the Small Garden, 2001; Feast: A History of Grand Eating, 2002, The Laskett: The Story of a Garden 2003. Co-Author: Leicester's Triumph, 1964; Elizabeth R, 1971; Mary Queen of Scots, 1972; Inigo Jones: The Theatre of the Stuart Court, 1973; An Early Victorian Album: The Hill-Adamson Collection, 1974; The English Miniature, 1981; The English Year, 1982; Artists of the Tudor Court, 1983. *Honours:* Fellow, Queen Mary College 1976; Knighted 1982; Shakespeare Prize FVS Foundation, Hamburg 1980; Senior Fellow, Royal College of Arts, 1983; Hon. DLitt (Leeds 1983, Keele 1984); FRSL 1999; High Bailiff and Searcher of the Sanctuary of Westminster Abbey 2000. *Address:* The Laskett, Much Birch, Herefordshire HR2 8HZ, England.

STROUSE, Jean; Writer; b. 10 Sept. 1945, Los Angeles, CA, USA. *Education:* BA, Radcliffe College, 1967. *Career:* Editorial Asst, New York Review of Books, 1967–69; Ed., Pantheon Books, 1972–75; Book Critic, Newsweek, 1979–83; Phi Beta Kappa Society Visiting Scholar, 1996–97; Ferris Prof. of Journalism, Princeton University, 1998; John J. Rhodes Chair in American Institutions and Public Policy Arizona State Univ. Barrett Honors Coll. 2003; Dir Cullman Center for Scholars and Writers, The New York Public Library 2003–; various lectureships; mem. Soc. of American Historians, Pres. 2001–02, Authors' Guild, PEN. *Publications:* Women and Analysis: Dialogues on Psychoanalytic Views of Femininity (ed. and compiler), 1974; Alice James: A Biography, 1980; Morgan: American Financier, 1999. Contributions: Reviews, journals and magazines. *Honours:* Radcliffe Institute Fellowship, 1976; National Endowment for the Humanities Fellowships, 1976, 1992; Guggenheim Fellowships, 1977, 1986; National Endowment for the Arts Fellowship, 1978; Bancroft Prize, 1981; Ingram Merrill Foundation Grant, 1989; Lila Wallace-Reader's Digest Writing Fellowship, 1993–94; John D. and Catherine T. MacArthur Foundation Fellowship 2002–(06); Best Book Citations, Los Angeles Times Book Review, New York Post, New York Times Book Review, Washington Post, etc, 1999. *Address:* c/o Georges Borchardt Inc, 136 E 57th St, New York, NY 10022, USA.

STRYKER, Daniel (see Morris, Janet Ellen).

STUART, Dabney; Prof. of English, Ed., Poet and Writer; b. 4 Nov. 1937, Richmond, Virginia, USA; m. 3rd Sandra Westcott 1983; two s. one d. *Education:* AB, Davidson College, NC, 1960; AM, Harvard University, 1962. *Career:* Instructor, College of William and Mary, Williamsburg, Virginia, 1961–65; Instructor, 1965–66, Asst Prof., 1966–69, Assoc. Prof., 1969–74, Prof., 1974–91, S Blount Mason Prof. of English, 1991–, Washington and Lee University, Lexington, Virginia; Poetry Ed., 1966–76, Ed.-in-Chief, 1988–95, Shenandoah; Visiting Prof., Middlebury College, 1968–69; McGuffey Chair of Creative Writing, Ohio University, 1972; Visiting Poet, University of Virginia, 1981, 1982–83; Poetry Ed., New Virginia Review, 1983. *Publications:* Poetry: The Diving Bell, 1966; A Particular Place, 1969; Corgi Modern Poets in Focus 3, 1971; The Other Hand, 1974; Friends of Yours, Friends of Mine, 1974; Round and Round: A Triptych, 1977; Rockbridge Poems, 1981; Common Ground, 1982; Don't Look Back, 1987; Narcissus Dreaming, 1990; Light Years: New and Selected Poems, 1994; Second Sight: Poems for Paintings by Carol Cloar, 1996; Long Gone, 1996; Settlers, 1999; Strains of the Old Man, 1999. Fiction: Sweet Lucy Wine: Stories, 1992; The Way to Cobbs Creek, 1997; No Visible Means of Support, 2000. Non-Fiction: Nabokov: The Dimensions of Parody, 1978. *Honours:* Dylan Thomas Prize, Poetry Society of America, 1965; Borestone Mountain Awards, 1969, 1974, 1977; National Endowment for the Arts Grant, 1969, and Fellowships, 1974, 1982; Virginia Governor's Award, 1979; Guggenheim Fellowship, 1987–88; Individual Artists Fellowship, Virginia Commission for the Arts, 1996; Residency, Rockefeller Study Centre, Bellagio, Italy, 2000. *Address:* c/o Dept of English, Washington and Lee University, Lexington, VA 24450, USA.

STUART, Lyle; American publishing company executive; b. 11 Aug. 1922, New York; m. 1st Mary Louise Strawn 1946; one s. one d.; m. 2nd Carole Livingston 1982; one d. *Career:* reporter, Int. News Service 1945, Variety 1945–46; scriptwriter, Dept of State, Voice of America 1946; Ed. Music Business magazine 1946–48; f. Expose 1951; Publr The Independent 1951–75; Business Man. MAD magazine 1952–54; Pres. Lyle Stuart Inc. 1954–89, Citadel Press 1970–89, University Books Inc. 1983–, Hot News 1983, Barricade Books Inc. 1990–; f. N Bergen, NJ Public Library; Producer Chinese Festival of Music 1952–62; mem. American Booksellers' Asscn, Nat. Acad. of TV Arts and Sciences, New York Zoological Soc. *Publications:* God Wears a Bowtie 1949, The Secret Life of Walter Winchell 1953, Mary Louise 1970, Casino Gambling for the Winner 1978, Lyle Stuart on Baccarat 1983, Map of Life 1993, Winning at Casino Gambling 1995, Map of Life 1996. *Honours:* Hon. PhD (State of Calif.). *Address:* Barricade Books Inc., 185 Bridge Plaza North, Suite 308A, Fort Lee, NJ 07024 (Office); 1530 Palisade Avenue, Apartment 6-L, Fort Lee, NJ 07024, USA (Home).

STUBBS, Imogen Mary, MA; British actress; b. 20 Feb. 1961, Rothbury; m. Trevor Nunn 1994; one s. one d. *Education:* St Paul's Girls School, London, Exeter Coll. Oxford and Royal Acad. of Dramatic Art. *Plays as actress:* appeared with RSC in The Rover, Two Noble Kinsmen, Richard II 1987–88, Othello 1991, Heartbreak House 1992, St Joan 1994, Twelfth Night 1996, Blast from the Past 1998, Betrayal 1998, The Relapse 2001, Three Sisters 2002. *Play as author:* We Happy Few (Gielgud Theatre, London) 2004. *Television appearances include:* The Browning Version 1985, The Rainbow 1988, Fellow Traveller 1989, Pasternak 1990, Othello 1990, Relatively Speaking 1990, Sandra, c'est la vie 1993, Anna Lee (series) 1993, Mothertime 1997, Blind Ambition 2000, Big Kids (series) 2000. *Films:* Privileged 1982, Nanou 1986, A Summer Story 1988, Deadline 1988, Erik the Viking 1989, True Colors 1991, The Wanderer (voice) 1991, A Pin for the Butterfly 1994, Jack and Sarah 1995, Sense and Sensibility 1995, Twelfth Night: Or What You Will 1996, Collusion 2003. *Honours:* Gold Medal, Chicago Film Festival. *Address:* c/o Nick Hern Books Ltd, The Glasshouse, 49a Goldhawk Road, London, W12 8QP, England.

STUBBS, Jean; Author; b. 23 Oct. 1926, Denton, Lancashire, England; m. 1st Peter Stubbs 1 May 1948; one s. one d.; m. 2nd Roy Oliver 5 Aug. 1980. *Education:* Manchester School of Art, 1944–47; Diploma, Loreburn Secretarial College, Manchester, 1947. *Career:* Copywriter, Henry Melland, 1964–66; Reviewer, Books and Bookmen, 1965–76; Writer-in-Residence for Avon, 1984; mem. PEN; Society of Women Writers and Journalists; Detection Club; Lancashire Writers Asscn; West Country Writers; Society of Authors. *Publications:* The Rose Grower, 1962; The Travellers, 1963; Hanrahan's Colony, 1964; The Straw Crown, 1966; My Grand Enemy, 1967; The Passing Star, 1970; The Case of Kitty Ogilvie, 1970; An Unknown Welshman, 1972; Dear Laura, 1973; The Painted Face, 1974; The Golden Crucible, 1976; Kit's Hill, 1979; The Ironmaster, 1981; The Vivian Inheritance, 1982; The Northern Correspondent, 1984; 100 Years Around the Lizard, 1985; Great Houses of Cornwall, 1987; A Lasting Spring, 1987; Like We Used To Be, 1989; Summer Secrets, 1990; Kelly Park, 1992; Charades, 1994; The Witching Time, 1998. Contributions: anthologies and magazines. *Honours:* Tom Gallon Trust Award, 1964; Daughter of Mark Twain, 1973. *Address:* Trewin, Nancegollan, Helston, Cornwall TR13 0AJ, England.

STUDEBAKER, William (Vern); Prof., Writer and Poet; b. 21 May 1947, Salmon, ID, USA; m. Judy Infanger, 23 Aug. 1969, two s. two d. *Education:* BA, History, 1970, MA, English, 1986, Idaho State University; Law, University of Idaho, 1974–75; Computer Science, Sonoma State University, 1986. *Career:* Asst Prof., 1975–, Chair., Dept of English, 1980–82, College of Southern Idaho; Commissioner, Idaho Commission on the Arts, 1981–86; Councilman, Idaho Humanities Council, 1996–. *Publications:* Everything Goes Without Saying, 1978; The Cleaving, 1985; Idaho's Poetry: A Centennial Anthology, 1989; The Rat Lady at the Company Dump, 1990; Where the Morning Lights' Still Blue: Personal Essays About Idaho, 1994; River Religion, 1997; Traveler' in an Antique Land, 1997; Short of a Good Promise, 1999. Contributions: numerous reviews, quarterlies, and journals. *Address:* 2616 East St, 4000 North St, Twin Falls, ID 83301, USA.

STYLES, (Frank) Showell, (Glyn Carr), FRGS; writer; b. 14 March 1908, Four Oaks, Warwickshire, England; m. Kathleen Jane Humphreys 1954; one s. two d. *Career:* Royal Navy 1939–46 (retd as Commander); professional author 1946–76; led two private Arctic expeditions 1952–53; Himalayan expedition 1954. *Publications:* A Tent on Top, 1971; Vincey Joe at Quiberon, 1971; Admiral of England, 1973; A Sword for Mr Fitton, 1975; Mr Fitton's Commission, 1977; The Baltic Convoy, 1979; A Kiss for Captain Hardy, 1979; Centurion Comes Home, 1980; The Quarterdeck Ladder, 1982; Seven-Gun Broadside, 1982; The Malta Frigate, 1983; Mutiny in the Caribbean, 1984; The Lee Shore, 1985; Gun-Brig Captain, 1987; HMS Cracker, 1988; Nelson's Midshipman, 1990; A Ship for Mr Fitton, 1991; The Independent Cruise, 1992; Mr Fitton's Prize, 1993; Mr Fitton and the Black Legion, 1994; Mr Fitton in Command, 1995; The 12-Gun Cutter, 1996, Lieutenant Fitton 1997, Mr Fitton at the Helm 1998, The Martinique Mission 1999, Mr Fitton's Hurricane 2000. Other: First on the Summits, 1970; First up Everest, 1970; The Forbidden Frontiers: A Survey of India from 1765–1949, 1970; Welsh Walks and Legends, 1972; Snowdon Range, 1973; The Mountains of North Wales, 1973; Glyder Range, 1974; Backpacking: A Comprehensive Guide, 1976; Backpacking in the Alps and Pyrenees, 1976; Backpacking in Wales, 1977; Welsh Walks and Legends: South Wales, 1977. As Glyn Carr: Death on Milestone Buttress, 1951; Murder on the Matterhorn, 1951; The Youth Hostel Murders, 1952; The Corpse in the Crevasse, 1952; A Corpse at Camp Two, 1955; Murder of an Owl, 1956; The Ice-Axe Murders, 1958; Swing Away, Climber, 1959; Holiday With Murder, 1961; Death Finds a Foothold, 1962; Lewker in Norway, 1963; Death of a Weirdy, 1965; Lewker in Tirol, 1967; Fat Man's Agony, 1969. *Address:* Trwyn Cae Iago, Borth y Gest, Porthmadog, Gwynedd LL49 9TW, Wales.

STYRON, William Clark, Jr, AB, LLD; American writer; b. 11 June 1925, Newport News, Virginia; m. Rose Burgunder 1953; one s. three d. *Education:* Davidson College, Duke University. *Career:* mem. Académie Goncourt, France, hon. mem.; American Acad. of Arts and Letters; American Acad. of Arts and Sciences. *Publications:* Lie Down in Darkness, 1951; The Long March, 1953; Set This House on Fire, 1960; The Confessions of Nat Turner, 1967; Sophie's Choice, 1979; This Quiet Dust, 1982; Darkness Visible, 1990; A Tidewater Morning, 1993. Contributions: articles, essays and reviews to numerous journals. *Honours:* Pulitzer Prize for Fiction, 1968; Howells Medal, 1970; American Book Award, 1980; Prix Mondial Cino del Duca, 1985; Commdr, Ordre des Arts et des Lettres, 1985; Edward MacDowell Medal, 1988; Commdr, Légion d'honneur, 1988; Elmer Holmes Bobst Award for Fiction, 1989; National Medal of Arts, 1993; National Arts Club Gold Medal, 1995; Commonwealth Award, 1995. *Literary Agent:* The Sayle Literary Agency, Bickerton House, 25–27 Bickerton Road, London, N19 5JT, England. *Telephone:* (20) 7263-8681. *Fax:* (20) 7561-0529. *Address:* 12 Rucum Road, Roxbury, CT 06783, USA.

SU TONG; Chinese writer; b. 1963, Suzhou, Jiangsu Prov. *Education:* Beijing Normal Univ. *Career:* fmrly Lecturer, Nanjing Acad. of Arts; Ed. Zhongshan Magazine; mem. Jiangsu Provincial Writers Asscn. *Publications:* Collected Works of Su Tong (seven vols), The Eighth Is a Bronze Sculpture, The Escape of 1934, The Mournful Dance, A Crowd of Wives and Concubines. *Address:* Jiangsu Provincial Writers Association, Nanjing, Jiangsu Province, People's Republc of China. (Office).

SUBRAMANIAN, (Mary) Belinda; poet and editor; b. 6 Sept. 1953, Statesville, NC, USA; m. S. Ramnath 1977; two d. *Education:* BA, Regents College, New York, 1987; MA, California State University, Dominguez Hills, 1990. *Career:* Ed., Gypsy Magazine and Vergin Press, 1983–. *Publications:* Nürnberg Poems, 1983; Heather and Mace, 1985; Eye of the Beast, 1986; Fighting Woman, 1986; Body Parts, 1987; Skin Divers (with Lyn Lifshin), 1988; Halloween, 1989; The Jesuit Poems, 1989; Elephants and Angels, 1991; The Innocents, 1991; A New Geography of Poets, 1992; Finding Reality in Myth, 1996; Notes of a Human Warehouse Engineer, 1998. Contributions: anthologies, journals, and magazines. *Honours:* Winner, Nerve Cowboy Poetry Contest, 1998. *Address:* PO Box 370322, El Paso, TX 79937, USA.

SUKENICK, Ronald; Prof. of English Literature, Writer and Publisher; b. 14 July 1932, New York, NY, USA; m. 1st Lynn Luria, 1961, divorced 1984; m. 2nd Julia Frey, 1992. *Education:* BA, Cornell University, 1955; MA, 1957, PhD, 1962, Brandeis University. *Career:* Teacher, Brandeis University, 1956–60; Instructor, Hofstra University, 1961–62; Asst Prof., City College, CUNY, 1966–67, Sarah Lawrence College, 1968–69; Writer-in-Residence, Cornell University, 1969–70, University of California at Irvine, 1970–72; Prof. of English Literature, University of Colorado at Boulder, 1975–2002; Publisher, American Book Review, 1977–, Black Ice magazine, 1989–; Butler Chair, SUNY at Buffalo, 1981; Fulbright Teaching Fellowship, Israel, 1984; Black Ice Books, 1988–; Board, FC2 Press; mem. Coordinating Council of Literary Magazines, chair., board of dirs, 1975–77; National Book Critics Circle, board of dirs, 1992–95. *Publications:* Fiction: Up, 1968; Out, 1973; 98.6, 1975; Long Talking Bad Conditions Blues, 1979; Blown Away, 1986; Mosaic Man, 1999; Cows, 2002. Other Fiction: The Death of the Novel and Other Stories, 1969; The Endless Short Story, 1986; Doggy Bag: Hyperfictions, 1994. Non-Fiction: Wallace Stevens: Musing the Obscure, 1967; In Form: Digressions on the Act of Fiction, 1985; Down and In: Life in the Underground, 1987; Narralogues, 2000. Contributions: books, anthologies, journals, reviews, and periodicals. *Honours:* Fulbright

Fellowship, France, 1958; National Endowment for the Arts Fellowship, France, 1958; Guggenheim Fellowship, 1977; National Endowment for the Arts Fellowships, 1980, 1989; University of Colorado Faculty Fellowships, 1982, 1990, and Boulder Faculty Assembly Award for Excellence in Research, Scholarly, and Creative Work, 1993; Co-ordinating Council of Literary Magazines Award for Editorial Excellence, 1985; Western Book Award for Publishing, 1985; American Book Awards, 1988, 2000; Zabel Award, American Acad. of Letters, 2002. *Address:* 200 Rector Pl., Apt 26B, New York, NY 10280, USA.

SUKNASKI, Andrew; editor and poet; b. 30 July 1942, Wood Mountain, Saskatchewan, Canada. *Education:* University of British Columbia, Vancouver. *Career:* Ed., Three Legged Coyote, Wood Mountain, 1982–. *Publications:* This Shadow of Eden, 1970; Circles, 1970; Rose Wayn in the East, 1972; Old Mill, 1972; The Zen Pilgrimage, 1972; Four Parts Sand: Concrete Poems, 1972; Wood Mountain Poems, 1973; Suicide Notes, Booke One, 1973; These Fragments I've Gathered for Ezra, 1973; Leaving, 1974; Blind Man's House, 1975; Leaving Wood Mountain, 1975; Octomi, 1976; Almighty Voice, 1977; Moses Beauchamp, 1978; The Ghosts Call You Poor, 1978; Two for Father, 1978; In the Name of Narid: New Poems, 1981; Montage for an Interstellar Cry, 1982; The Land They Gave Away: Selected and New Poems, 1982; Silk Trail, 1985. *Honours:* Canada Council Grants. *Address:* c/o Thistledown Press, 668 East Place, Saskatoon, Sasketchewan S7J 2Z5, Canada.

SULERI GOODYEAR, Sara, BA, MA, PhD; writer and academic; b. Lahore, Pakistan. *Education:* Kinnaird Coll., Lahore, Punjab Univ., Lahore, Indiana Univ. *Career:* Prof. of English, Yale Univ. 1983–; founding-ed., Yale Journal of Criticism. *Publications:* Meatless Days, 1989; The Rhetoric of English India, 1992; Boys Will Be Boys: A Daughter's Elegy, 2003. Contributions: editorial boards of YJC, The Yale Review, Transition. *Address:* Dept of English, Yale University, 63 High Street, Room 109, PO Box 208302, New Haven, CT 06520-8302, USA.

SULLIVAN, Rosemary; Prof., Author and Poet; b. 29 Aug. 1947, Montréal, QC, Canada. *Education:* BA, McGill University, 1968; MA, University of Connecticut, 1969; PhD, University of Sussex, 1972. *Career:* Faculty, University of Dijon, 1972–73, University of Bordeaux, 1973–74, University of Victoria, BC, 1974–77; Asst Prof., 1977–80, Assoc. Prof., 1980–91, Prof., 1991–, University of Toronto; mem. Amnesty International; Toronto Arts Group for Human Rights, founding mem. *Publications:* The Garden Master: The Poetry of Theodore Roethke, 1975; The Space a Name Makes, 1986; By Heart: Elizabeth Smart, a Life, 1991; Blue Panic, 1991; Shadow Maker: The Life of Gwendolyn MacEwan, 1995; The Red Shoes: Margaret Attwood Starting Out, 1998; The Bone Ladder: New and Selected Poems, 2000; Labyrinth of Desire: Women, Passion and Romantic Obsession, 2001; Memory-Making: Selected Essays, 2001. Other: Ed. or Co-Ed. of several books. Contributions: many journals and magazines. *Honours:* Gerald Lampert Award for Poetry, 1986; Brascan Silver Medal for Culture, National Magazine Awards, 1986; Guggenheim Fellowship, 1992; Governor-General's Award for Non-Fiction, 1995; City of Toronto Book Award, 1995; Non-Fiction Prize, Canadian Authors' Asscn, 1995; Pres.'s Medal for Biography, Columbia University, 1995; Killam Fellow, 1996; Canada Research Chair, 2000; Connaught Fellowship, 2002. *Literary Agent:* Westwood Creative Artists. *Address:* c/o Dept of English, University of Toronto, 7 King's College Circle, Toronto, ON M5S 3K1, Canada.

SULLIVAN, Thomas William, BA; American writer and teacher; b. 20 Nov. 1940, Highland Park, MI; one s. one d. *Career:* mem. MENSA, Soc. of the Black Bull, Arcadia Mixture. *Publications:* Diapason 1978, The Phases of Harry Moon 1988, Born Burning 1989, The Martyring 1998, Dust of Eden 2004; contrib. to magazines. *Honours:* Hemingway Days Festival Literary Contest awards 1985, DADA Literary Contest 1985, 1987. *Address:* 15215 91st Avenue N, Maple Grove, MN 55369, USA. *E-mail:* mn333mn@earthlink.net. *Website:* members.aol.com/infoagtec/tsullivan.htm.

SULLOWAY, Frank Jones; Psychologist and Science Historian; b. 2 Feb. 1947, Concord, NH, USA; one s. *Education:* AB, summa cum laude, 1969, AM, History of Science, 1971, PhD, History of Science, 1978, Harvard University. *Career:* Junior Fellow, Harvard University Society of Fellows, 1974–77; Mem., Institute for Advanced Study, Princeton, NJ, 1977–78; Research Fellow, 1978–80, Research Prof., 1999, Miller Institute for Basic Research in Science, Visiting Prof., 2000–, Dept of Psychology, University of California at Berkeley; Research Fellow, 1980–81, Visiting Scholar, 1989–98, MIT; Postdoctoral Fellow, 1981–82, Visiting Scholar, 1984–89, Harvard University; Research Fellow, University College London, England, 1982–84; Vernon Prof. of Biography, Dartmouth College, 1986; Fellow, Center for Advanced Study in the Behavioral Sciences, Stanford, CA, 1998–99; mem. American Asscn for the Advancement of Science, fellow; American Psychological Asscn; American Psychological Society; History of Science Society; Human Behavior and Evolution Society; Fellow, Linnean Society of London. *Publications:* Freud, Biologist of the Mind, 1979; Darwin and His Finches, 1982; Freud and Biology: The Hidden Legacy, 1982; Darwin's Conversion, 1982; Darwin and the Galapagos, 1984; Darwin's Early Intellectual Development, 1985; Reassessing Freud's Case Histories, 1991; Born to Rebel: Birth Order, Family Dynamics and Creative Lives, 1996; Birth Order, Sibling Competition, and Human Behavior, 2001. Contributions: Professional journals. *Honours:* Pfizer Award, History of Science Society, 1980; National Endowment for the Humanities Fellowship, 1980–81; National Science Foundation Fellowship, 1981–82; Guggenheim Fellowship, 1982–83; John D. and Catherine T. MacArthur Foundation Fellowship, 1984–89; Golden Plate Award, American Acad. of Achievement, 1997; James Randi Award, Skeptics Society, 1997. *Address:* Dept of Psychology, Tolman Hall, University of California, Berkeley, CA 94720, USA.

SULSTON, Sir John Edward; Scientist; b. 27 March 1942, Fulmer, England; m. Daphne Edith Bate 1966; one s. one d. *Education:* Pembroke College, Cambridge; Postdoctoral Fellowship, Salk Inst., California, 1966–69. *Career:* Staff scientist, MRC Laboratory of Molecular Biology, Cambridge, 1969–; Dir, The Sanger Centre, 1992–2000; Television: Royal Institute Christmas Lectures (Channel 4), 2001; mem. FRS. *Publications:* The Common Thread – A Story of Science, Politics, Ethics and the Human Genome (with Georgina Ferry), 2002. Contributions: papers in scientific journals. *Honours:* W. Alden Spencer Award (jtly), 1986; Gairdner Foundation Award (jtly), 1991, 2002; Darwin Medal, Royal Soc., 1996; Rosenstiel Award (jtly), 1998; Pfizer Prize for Innovative Science, 2000; Sir Frederick Gowland Hopkins Medal, Biochemical Soc., 2000; Hon. Fellow, Pembroke College, Cambridge, 2000; Hon. ScD, Trinity College, Dublin, 2000; KBE, 2000; Edinburgh Medal, 2001; City of Medicine Award, Durham, NC, 2001; Prince of Asturias Award, Spain, 2001; Dr hc, Essex, 2002; Daily Mirror Pride of Britain Award, 2002; Fothergill Medal, Medical Soc. of London, 2002; Dan David Prize, Tel-Aviv Univ., 2002; General Motors Sloan Prize, 2002; Nobel Prize in Physiology or Medicine (jtly), 2002. *Address:* 39 Mingle Lane, Stapleford, Cambridge CB2 5SY, England. *Telephone:* (1223) 842248. *E-mail:* jes@sanger.ac.uk.

SULZBERGER, Arthur Ochs; American newspaper executive; b. 5 Feb. 1926, New York; m. 1st Barbara Grant 1948 (divorced 1956); one s. one d.; m. 2nd Carol Fox 1956 (died 1995); two d.; m. 3rd Allison Stacey Cowles 1996. *Education:* Columbia Univ. *Career:* US Marine Corps, Second World War and Korean War; joined The New York Times Co., New York 1951, Asst Treas. 1958–63, Pres. 1963–79, Publr 1963–92, Chair., CEO 1992–97, Chair. Emer. 1997–, mem. Bd Dir -2002 ; Co-Chair. Bd Int. Herald Tribune 1983; Chair. Newspaper Pres. Asscn 1988; Dir, Times Printing Co., Chattanooga, Gapesia Pulp and Paper Co. Ltd of Canada; Trustee Columbia Univ., mem. Coll. Council; Trustee Metropolitan Museum of Art, Chair. Bd of Trustees 1987–99. *Honours:* Hon. LHD (Montclair State Coll.), (Tufts Univ.) 1984; Columbia Journalism Award 1992; Alexander Hamilton Medal 1982, Vermeil Medal (City of Paris) 1992. *Address:* New York Times Co., 229 West 43rd Street, New York, NY 10036, USA. *Telephone:* (212) 556-1234.

SUMMERTREE, Katonah (see Windsor, Patricia).

SÜSKIND, Patrick; German author; b. 26 March 1949, Ambach, Bavaria. *Education:* Univ. of Munich. *Career:* fmr teacher; fmr writer for TV. *Publications:* Perfume: The Story of a Murderer (novel) 1979, The Double Bass (play), The Pigeon (novel) 1988, Three Stories and a Reflection; juvenile: The Story of Mr Summer 1991. *Address:* c/o Vintage, Random House, 20 Vauxhall Bridge Road, London, SW1V 2SA, England; c/o Diogenes Verlag AG, Sprecherstr. 8, 8032 Zürich, Switzerland. *Telephone:* (1) 2548511. *Fax:* (1) 2528407.

SUTHERLAND, John Andrew, PhD, FRSL; British academic and writer; b. 9 Oct. 1938; m. Guilland Watt 1967; one s. *Education:* Colchester Royal Grammar School, Leicester and Edinburgh Univs. *Career:* nat. service, 2nd Lt Suffolk Regt 1958–60; Lecturer in English Univ. of Edin. 1965–72; Lecturer in English, Univ. Coll. London 1972–84, Lord Northcliffe Prof. of Modern English Literature 1992–2004; columnist The Guardian. *Publications include:* Thackeray at Work 1974, Victorian Novelists and Publishers 1976, Fiction and the Fiction Industry 1978, Bestsellers 1980, Offensive Literature 1982, The Longman Companion to Victorian Fiction 1989, Mrs Humphry Ward 1992, The Life of Walter Scott: A Critical Biography 1995, Victorian Fiction: Writers, Publishers, Readers 1995, Is Heathcliffe a Murderer? 1996, Can Jane Eyre be Happy? 1997, Where Was Rebecca Shot? 1998, Who Betrays Elizabeth Bennet? 1999, Henry V, War Criminal ? 1999, Last Drink to LA 2000, The Literary Detective 2000, Literary Lives 2001, Reading the Decades 2002, Stephen Spender: the Authorised Biography 2004. *Honours:* Hon. DLitt (Leicester) 1998. *Address:* c/o Department of English, University College London, Gower Street, London, WC1E 6BT, England. *Telephone:* (20) 7387-7050.

SUTHERLAND, Margaret; Writer; b. 16 Sept. 1941, Auckland, New Zealand; m., two s. two d. *Education:* Registered Nurse. *Career:* mem. Australian Society of Authors; Federation of Australian Writers. *Publications:* The Fledgling, 1974; Hello, I'm Karen (children's book), 1974; The Love Contract, 1976; Getting Through, 1977, US edn as Dark Places, Deep Regions, 1980; The Fringe of Heaven, 1984; The City Far From Home, 1992; Is that Love?, 1999. Contributions: journals and magazines. *Honours:* Literary Fellow, University of Auckland, 1981; Scholarship in Letters, New Zealand, 1984; Australia Council Writers Fellowships, 1992, 1995. *Address:* 10 Council St, Speers Point, NSW 2284, Australia. *E-mail:* chapsuth@idl.com.au.

SUTTON, Henry (see Slavitt, David Rytman).

SUTTON, Penny (see Cartwright, Justin).

SVOBODA, Terese; Poet, Writer and Videomaker; b. 5 Sept. 1950, Ogallala, NE, USA; m. Stephen M. Bull, 18 July 1981, three s. *Education:* MFA, Columbia University, 1978. *Career:* Rare Manuscript Curator, McGill University, 1969; Co-Producer, PBS-TV series Voices and Visions, 1980–82; Distinguished Visiting Prof., University of Hawaii, 1992; Prof., Sarah Lawrence College, 1993, Williams College, 1998; mem. PEN; Poets and Writers; Poet's House, founding mem. and advisory board mem., 1986–91. *Publications:* Poetry: All Aberration, 1985; Laughing Africa, 1990; Mere Mortal, 1995. Fiction: Cannibal, 1995; A Drink Called Paradise, 1999. Contributions: poems, fiction, essays, and trans to periodicals. *Honours:* Writer's Choice Column Award, New York Times Book Review, 1985; Iowa Prize, 1990; Bobst Prize, 1995.

SWAFFORD, Jan (Johnson); Writer and Composer; b. 10 Sept. 1946, Chattanooga, Tennessee, USA; m. Julie Pisano, 20 Dec. 1973, divorced, 1979. *Education:* BA, Harvard University, 1968; MA, Musical Arts, 1977, PhD, Musical Arts, 1982, Yale School of Music. *Career:* Asst Prof., Boston University School for the Arts, 1977–78; Visiting Asst Prof., Hampshire College, Amherst, Massachusetts, 1979–81, Amherst College, 1980–81; Freelance Composer and Writer, 1981–; mem. American Music Center; Minnesota Composers Forum; Composers Forum. *Publications:* Writings: The Vintage Guide to Classical Music, 1992; The New Guide to Classical Music, 1993; Charles Ives: A Life with Music, 1996; Johannes Brahms: A Biography, 1997. Other: various recordings. *Honours:* Grant, Massachusetts Artists Foundation, 1983; Prizewinner, New England Composers Competition, 1984; Harvard-Mellon Fellowship, 1988; Composers Fellow, National Endowment for the Arts, 1991; L. L. Winship-PEN New England Award, 1997.

SWAN, Gladys; writer, painter and academic; b. 15 Oct. 1934, New York, NY, USA; m. Richard Swan 1955; two d. *Education:* BA, Western New Mexico University, 1954; MA, Claremont Graduate School, 1955. *Career:* Prof. of English, Franklin College, 1969–86; Faculty, MFA Program in Creative Writing, Vermont College, 1981–96; Distinguished Visiting Writer-in-Residence, University of Texas at El Paso, 1984–85; Visiting Prof. of English, Ohio University, 1986–87; Assoc. Prof. of English, University of Missouri-Columbia, 1987–98; mem. PEN American Center. *Publications:* On the Edge of the Desert, 1979; Carnival for the Gods, 1986; Of Memory and Desire, 1989; Do You Believe in Calbega de Vaca?, 1991; Ghost Dance: A Play of Voices, 1992; A Visit to Strangers, 1996; News From the Volcano, 2000. Contributions: Kenyon Review; Virginia Quarterly Review; Ohio Review; Writers Forum; Sewanee Review. *Honours:* Lilly Endowment Faculty Open Fellowship, 1975–76; Fulbright Senior Lectureship, 1988; Lawrence Foundation Award for Fiction, 1994; Tate Prize for Poetry, Sewanee Review, 2001. *Address:* 2601 Lynnwood Drive, Columbia, MO 65203, USA.

SWAN, Susan Jane, BA; novelist, writer, poet and academic; b. 9 June 1945, Midland, ON, Canada; m. Barry Haywood 1969 (divorced); one d. *Education:* McGill Univ. *Career:* Assoc. Prof. of Humanities, 1989–, Roberts Chair in Canadian Studies, 1999–2000, York University, Toronto; mem. Writers' Union of Canada; PEN. *Publications:* Queen of the Silver Blades, 1975; Unfit for Paradise, 1982; The Biggest Modern Woman of the World, 1983; Tesseracts (co-author), 1985; The Last of the Golden Girls, 1989; Language in Her Eye (ed.), 1990; Mothers Talk Back (co-ed.), 1991; Slow Hand, 1992; The Wives of Bath, 1993; Stupid Boys Are Good to Relax With, 1996. Contributions: many short stories, articles, and poems in various publications. *Literary Agent:* Westwood Creative Artists, 94 Harbord Street, Toronto, ON M5S 1G6, Canada. *Address:* 151 Robert Street, Apt 2, Toronto, ON M5S 2K6, Canada.

SWARD, Robert Stuart, BA, MA; poet, writer and university lecturer; b. 23 June 1933, Chicago, IL, USA; Partner, Gloria K. Alford; two s. three d. *Education:* Univ. of Illinois, Univ. of Iowa, Middlebury Coll., Vermont, Univ. of Bristol. *Career:* poet-in-residence, Cornell Univ. 1962–64, Univ. of Victoria, BC 1969–73, Univ. of California at Santa Cruz 1987–; writer-in-residence, Foothill Writers Conference, summers 1988–; writer, Writing Programme, Language Arts Dept, Cabrillo Coll. 1989–2000; contributing ed., Blue Moon Review and other internet literary publications, including Web Del Sol, locus for literary arts; mem. League of Canadian Poets, Modern Poetry Assen, Nat. Writers' Union (USA), Writers' Union of Canada. *Publications:* Uncle Dog and Other Poems 1962, Kissing the Dancer and Other Poems 1964, Half a Life's History: New and Selected Poems 1957–83 1983, The Three Roberts (with Robert Zend and Robert Priest) 1985, Four Incarnations: New and Selected Poems 1957–91 1991, Family (with David Swanger, Tilly Shaw and Charles Atkinson) 1994, Earthquake Collage 1995, A Much-Married Man (novel) 1996, Uncivilizing: A Collection of Poems 1997, Rosicrucian in the Basement: Selected Poems 2001, Heavenly Sex: New and Selected Poems 2002, Collected Poems 1957–2004 2004; contrib. to anthologies, newspapers and magazines. *Honours:* Fulbright Fellowship 1960–61, Guggenheim Fellowship 1965–66, D. H. Lawrence Fellowship 1966, Djerassi Foundation Residency 1990, Villa Montalvo Literary Arts Award for Poetry 1990, Way Cool Site Award, Editing Internet Literary Magazine 1996. *Address:* PO Box 7062, Santa Cruz, CA 95061-7062, USA. *E-mail:* sward@cruzio.com. *Website:* www.robertsward.com.

SWEDE, George; Educator, Poet and Writer; b. 20 Nov. 1940, Riga, Latvia; m. 1st Bonnie Lewis 20 June 1964 (divorced 1969); m. 2nd Anita Krumins 23 July 1974; two s. *Education:* BA, Univ. of British Columbia, 1964; MA, Dalhousie Univ., 1965; PhD, Greenwich Univ., 2000. *Career:* Instructor, Vancouver City College, 1966–67; Instructor, 1968–73, Prof. of Psychology, 1973–, Ryerson Univ., Toronto; Dir, Poetry and Things, 1969–71; Developmental Psychology, Open College, 1973–75; Poetry Ed., Poetry Toronto, 1980–81; Co-Ed., Writer's Magazine, 1982–90; mem. Haiku Canada, co-founder, 1977; Haiku Society of America; League of Canadian Poets; PEN; Writers' Union of Canada. *Publications:* Poetry: Tell-Tale Feathers, 1978; A Snowman, Headless, 1979; As Far as the Sea Can Eye, 1979; Flaking Paint, 1983; Frozen Breaths, 1983; Tick Bird, 1983; Bifids, 1984; Night Tides, 1984; Time is Flies, 1984; High Wire Spider, 1986; I Throw Stones at the Mountain, 1988; Leaping Lizzard, 1988; Holes in My Cage, 1989; I Want to Lasso Time, 1991; Leaving My Loneliness, 1992; Five O'Clock Shadows (co-author), 1996; My Shadow Doing Something, 1997; Almost Unseen, 2000. Editor: The Canadian Haiku Anthology, 1979; Cicada Voices, 1983; The Universe is One Poem, 1990; There Will Always Be a Sky, 1993; The Psychology of Art: An Experimental Approach, 1994; Tanka Splendour, 1998; Global Haiku: Twenty-Five Poets Worldwide (ed.), 2000. Non-Fiction: The Modern English Haiku, 1981; Creativity: A New Psychology, 1994. Fiction: Moonlit Gold Dust, 1979; Quilby: The Porcupine Who Lost His Quills (with Anita Krumins), 1980; Missing Heirloom, 1980; Seaside Burglaries, 1981; Downhill Theft, 1982; Undertow, 1982; Dudley and the Birdman, 1985; Dudley and the Christmas Thief, 1986. Contributions: magazines world-wide. *Honours:* Haiku Society of America Book Award, 1980; High/Coo Press Chapbook Competition Winner, 1982; Museum of Haiku Literature Awards, 1983, 1985, 1993; Canadian Children's Book Centre Our Choice Awards, 1984, 1985, 1987, 1991, 1992; Third Place, International Tanka Contest, Poetry Society of Japan, 1990; First Prize, Haiku in English, Mainichi Daily News, 1993; Second Place, Mainichi 125th Anniversary Haiku Contest, 1997; Third Place, Haiku Society of America Henderson Haiku Contest, 1997. *Address:* 70 London St, Toronto, ON M6G 1N3, Canada. *E-mail:* gswede@ryerson.ca.

SWEENEY, Matthew; Poet and Writer; b. 6 Oct. 1952, Co Donegal, Ireland; m. Rosemary Barber, 1979. *Education:* University College, Dublin, 1979–78; BA, Polytechnic of North London, 1978. *Career:* Writer-in-Residence, Farnham College, Surrey, 1984–85, South Bank Centre, 1994–95; Writing Fellowship, University of East Anglia, 1986; Publicist and Events Asst, Poetry Society, 1988–90; Poet-in-Residence, Hereford and Worcester, 1991, National Library for the Blind, 1999; Writer-in-Residence on the Internet, Chadwyck-Healey, 1997–98. *Publications:* A Dream of Maps, 1981; A Round House, 1983; The Lame Waltzer, 1985; The Chinese Dressing Gown, 1987; Blues Shoes, 1989; The Flying Spring Onion, 1992; Cacti, 1992; The Snow Vulture, 1992; Fatso in the Red Suit, 1995; Emergency Kit: Poems for Strange Times (ed. with Jo Shapcott), 1996; Writing Poetry (with John Hartley Williams), 1997; The Bridal Suite, 1997; Penguin Modern Poets 12, 1997; Beyond Bedlam: Poems Written Out of Mental Distress (ed. with Ken Smith), 1997; A Smell of Fish, 2000; Selected Poems, 2002; Fox, 2002. *Honours:* Prudence Farmer Prize, 1984; Cholmondeley Award, 1987; Arts Council Literature Award, 1992; Arts Council of England Writer's Award, 1999. *Address:* 11 Dombey St, London WC1N 3PB, England.

SWICK, Marly; Writer and Prof. of Fiction Writing; b. 26 Nov. 1949, Indianapolis, IN, USA. *Education:* BA, Stanford University, 1971; PhD, American University, 1979; MFA, University of Iowa, 1986. *Career:* Prof. of Fiction Writing, University of Nebraska, 1988–. *Publications:* A Hole in the Language (short stories), 1990; The Summer Before the Summer of Love (short stories), 1995; Paper Wings (novel), 1996; Evening News (novel), 1999. Contributions: many magazines. *Honours:* James Michener Award, 1986; University of Wisconsin Creative Writing Institute Fellowship, 1987; National Endowment for the Arts Grant, 1987; Iowa Short Fiction Prize, 1990.

SWIFT, Graham Colin; Author; b. 4 May 1949, London, England; m. *Education:* Queens' College, Cambridge, 1967–70; York University, 1970–73. *Publications:* The Sweet Shop Owner, 1980; Shuttlecock, 1981; Learning to Swim and Other Stories, 1982; Waterland, 1983; The Magic Wheel (ed. with David Profumo), 1986; Out of This World, 1988; Ever After, 1992; Last Orders, 1996; The Light of Day, 2002. *Honours:* Geoffrey Faber Memorial Prize, 1983; Guardian Fiction Award, 1983; RSL Winifred Holtby Award, 1983; FRSL, 1984; Premio Grinzane Cavour, Italy, 1987; Prix du Meilleur Livre Étranger, France, 1994; Booker Prize for Fiction, 1996; James Tait Black Memorial Prize, 1996. *Literary Agent:* AP Watt Ltd, 20 John St, London WC1N 2DR, England.

SWIFT, Robert (see Kelly, Tim).

SWINBURNE, Richard Granville; Prof. of Philosophy and Author; b. 26 Dec. 1934, Smethwick, Staffordshire, England; m. Monica Holmstrom, 1960, separated 1985, two d. *Education:* BA, 1957, BPhil, 1959, Dip Theol, 1960, MA, 1961, University of Oxford. *Career:* Fereday Fellow, St John's College, Oxford 1958–61; Leverhulme Research Fellow in the History and Philosophy of Science, University of Leeds 1961–63; Lecturer to Senior Lecturer in Philosophy, University of Hull 1963–72; Visiting Assoc. Prof. of Philosophy, University of Maryland 1969–70; Prof. of Philosophy, University of Keele 1972–84; Distinguished Visiting Scholar, University of Adelaide 1982; Nolloth Prof. of the Philosophy of the Christian Religion, University of Oxford 1985–2002; Visiting Lecturer, Indian Council for Philosophical Research 1992; Visiting Prof. of Philosophy, Syracuse University 1987, Univ. of Rome 2002, Catholic Univ. of Lublin 2002, St Louis Univ. 2003; Visiting Prof. of Divinity, Yale Univ. 2003. *Publications:* Space and Time, 1968; The Concept of Miracle, 1971; An Introduction to Confirmation Theory, 1973; The Coherence of Theism, 1977; The Existence of God, 1979; Faith and Reason, 1981; Personal Identity (with S. Shoemaker), 1984; The Evolution of the Soul, 1986; Responsibility and Atonement, 1989; Revelation, 1992; The Christian God, 1994; Is There a God?, 1996; Providence and the Problem of Evil, 1998; Epistemic Justification, 2001, The Resurrection of God Incarnate 2003. Contributions: scholarly journals. *Honours:* Fellow, British Acad., 1992. *Address:* 50 Butler Close, Oxford OX2 6JG, England. *Telephone:* (1865) 514406. *E-mail:* richard.swinburne@oriel.ox.ac.uk. *Website:* users.ox.ac.uk/~orie0087.

SYAL, Meera, MBE; British writer and actress; b. 27 June 1963, Wolverhampton, England; m. 1989; one d. *Education:* Univ. of Manchester. *Publications:* Novels: Anita and Me, 1996; Life Isn't All Ha Ha Hee Hee, 1999. Film and TV Scripts: Goodness Gracious Me (three series, BBC 2); Watching the Detectives (Carlton); The Real McCoy (BBC 2); Black Silk (BBC 1); A Nice Arrangement, 1991; My Sister-Wife, 1992; Bhaji on the Beach, 1994; Anita and Me, 2002. Other: Serious Money (play), 1987; Stitch (play), 1990; Peer Gynt (play), 1990; Bombay Dreams (story to musical), 2001. *Honours:* British Comedy Award; RTS Award; Best TV Drama Award, Committee for Racial Equality; Best Screenplay, Asian Film Acad., 1993; Betty Trask Award, 1996; RIMA and EMMA Media Personality of the Year, 2001; Asian Women of Achievement Chair.'s Award, 2001. *Address:* c/o Rochelle Stevens, 2 Terretts Place, Islington, London, N1 1QZ, England (Office). *Telephone:* (1973) 417762 (Office).

SYLVESTER, Janet; Poet and University Teacher; b. 5 May 1950, Youngstown, OH, USA; m. James Vandenberg, 30 June 1973, divorced 1980. *Education:* BA, 1975, MA, 1978, Goddard College; PhD, University of Utah, 1991. *Career:* Faculty, University of South Carolina at Columbia. *Publications:* That Mulberry Wine, 1985; A Visitor at the Gate, 1996; The Mark of Flesh, 1997. Contributions: anthologies, reivews, quarterlies and journals. *Address:* 700 S Holly St, Columbia, SC 29205, USA. *E-mail:* sylvesterj@garnet.cla.sc.edu.

SZABÓ, Magda; Author, Dramatist and Poet; b. 5 Oct. 1917, Debrecen, Hungary; m. Tibor Szobotka 1948. *Education:* Teacher's Certificate, 1940; PhD, Classical Philology. *Career:* graduated as a teacher, 1940; worked in secondary schools, 1940–44, 1950–59; started literary career as poet and has since written novels, plays, radio dramas, essays and film scripts; mem. Acad. of Sciences of Europe; Hungarian Széchenyi Acad. of Art and Literature. *Publications:* Novels: Az oz (The Fawn); Fresko (Fresco); Disznótor (Night of Pig-Killing); Pilatus (Pilate); A Danaida (The Danaid); Mózes 1.22 (Genesis 1.22); Katalin utca (Kathleen Street); A szemlélok (The Onlookers); Régimódi történet (Old-Fashioned Story); Az ajtó (The Door); The Moment, 1990. Plays: Kiálts város (Cry Out, Town!); Az a szép fényes nap (That Bright Beautiful Day); A meráni fiu (The Boy of Meran); A csata (The Battle), 1982; Béla Király (King Béla); A Macskák Szerdája (The Wednesday of the Cats), 1985; Outside the Circle, 1980. Children's Books: Szigetkék (Island-Blue); Tündér Lala (Lala the Fairy); Abigél (Abigail). Other: Neszek (Noises, poems); Ókut (Old Well, autobiog.); The Lethargy of the Semigods (essays), 1986; The Logic of the Butterfly (essays), 1997; Cakes for Cerberus (short stories); The Mondogue of Cseke (essays). *Honours:* Hon. DPhil; Baumgarten Prize, 1949; József Attila Prizes, 1959, 1972; Kossuth Prize, 1978; Getz Corporation Prize, 1992; Szén Ernõ Prize for Dramatic Art; Fellow, Univ. of Iowa; Hon. citizen of Debrecen. *Address:* 1026 Budapest II, Julia-utca 3, Hungary.

SZEWC, Piotr; Novelist and Journalist; b. 1961, Zamosc, Poland. *Career:* Ed., periodical Nowe Ksiazki (New Books). *Publications:* Novels: Annihilation, 1993; Zmierzchy i poranki. *Address:* c/o Dalkey Archive Press, ISU Campus 8905, Normal, IL 61790-8905, USA.

SZIRTES, George Gabor Nicholas, BA, PhD, FRSL; poet, writer and translator; b. 29 Nov. 1948, Budapest, Hungary; m. Clarissa Upchurch 1970; one s. one d. *Education:* Leeds Coll. of Art. *Career:* settled in UK 1956; mem. PEN. *Publications:* The Slant Door 1979, November and May 1981, The Kissing Place 1982, Short Wave 1984, The Photographer in Winter 1986, Metro 1988, Bridge Passages 1991, Blind Field 1994, Selected Poems 1996, The Red All Over Riddle Book (juvenile) 1997, Portrait of My Father in an English Landscape 1998, The Budapest File 2000, An English Apocalypse 2001; criticism: Exercise of Power, The Art of Ana Maria Pacheco 2001, New Writing 10 (ed. with Penelope Lively) 2001; other: several Hungarian works trans. into English; contrib. to numerous journals and magazines. *Honours:* Geoffrey Faber Memorial Prize 1980, Arts Council Bursary 1984, British Council Fellowship 1985, Cholmondeley Award 1987, Dery Prize for Trans. 1991, Decorated, Republic of Hungary 1991, European Poetry Trans. Prize 1995, George Cushing Award 2001, Society of Authors Travelling Scholarship 2002. *Address:* 16 Damgate Street, Wymondham, Norfolk NR8 0BQ, England.

SZYMBORSKA, Wisława; Polish poet, critic and translation; b. 2 July 1923, Bnin. *Education:* Jagiellonian University, Kraków. *Career:* editorial staff, Zycie Literackie magazine 1953–81. *Publications:* Dlatego zyjemy (That's Why We Are Alive), 1952; Pytania zadawane sobie (Questioning Oneself), 1954; Wolanie do Yeti (Calling Out to Yeti), 1957; Sól (Salt), 1962; Wiersze wybrane (Selected Verses), 1964; Poezje wybrane (Selected Poems), 1967; Sto pociech (No End of Fun), 1967; Poezje (Poems), 1970; Wszelki wypadek (Could Have), 1972; Wybór wierszy (Selected Verses), 1973; Tarsjusz i inne wiersze (Tarsius and Other Verses), 1976; Wielka liczba (A Large Number), 1977; Poezje wybrane II (Selected Poems II), 1983; Ludzie na moscie (The People on the Bridge), 1986; Wieczór autorski: Wiersze (Authors' Evening: Verses), 1992; Koniec i poczatek (The End and the Beginning), 1993. Poetry in English: Sounds, Feelings, Thoughts: Seventy Poems, 1981; People on a Bridge, 1990; View with a Grain of Sand, 1995. Contributions: Poetry and criticism in various publications. *Honours:* City of Kraków Prize for Literature, 1954; Polish Ministry of Culture Prize, 1963; Goethe Prize, 1991; Herder Prize, 1995; Hon. doctorate, Adam Mickiewicz University, Poznań, 1995; Nobel Prize for Literature, 1996; Polish PEN Club Prize, 1996. *Address:* Ul Królewska 82/89, 30-079 Kraków, Poland.

T

TABOR, Herbert, BA, MD; American academic; *Editor, The Journal of Biological Chemistry*; m. Dr Celia White. *Education:* Univ. of Harvard. *Career:* staff, Nat. Inst. of Health 1943–; Ed., The Journal of Biological Chemistry 1970–; elected to Nat. Acad. of Sciences 1977; Pharmocology Section Chief, Laboratory of Biochemical Pharmacology, Bethesda. *Publications include:* Metabolism of Amino Acids and Amines (co-author) 1971, Polyamines (co-author) 1983. *Honours:* Chemical Soc. of Washington Hillebrand Prize (with Dr Celia Tabor) 1986, American Soc. of Biochemistry and Molecular Biology Rose Award 1996. *Address:* The Journal of Biological Chemistry, 9650 Rockville Pike, Bethesda, MD 20814-3997, USA. *E-mail:* htabor@asbmb.faseb.org. *Website:* www.jbc.org.

TABORSKI, Boleslaw; Poet, Writer and Trans; b. 7 May 1927, Toruń, Poland; m. Halina Junghertz, 20 June 1959, one d. *Education:* BA, MA, University of Bristol. *Career:* Producer, Polish Section, 1959–89, Ed., Arts in Action, 1985–93, BBC World Service; Visiting Prof., CUNY, 1982; mem. Asscn of Authors, ZAIKS, Warsaw; Asscn of Polish Writers, Warsaw; Council Gallery in the Provinces Foundation, Lublin; Leon Schiller Foundation, hon. committee; Pro Europa Foundation, Warsaw, council mem., 1994–; World Asscn of the Polish Home Army Ex-servicemen, Warsaw; Polish Shakespeare Society, Gdańsk, 1995; PEN, Warsaw, 2000. *Publications:* Poetry: Times of Passing, 1957; Grains of Night, 1958; Crossing the Border, 1962; Lesson Continuing, 1967; Voice of Silence, 1969; Selected Poems, 1973; Web of Words, 1977; For the Witnesses, 1978; Observer of Shadows, 1979; Love, 1980; A Stranger's Present, 1983; Art, 1985; The Stillness of Grass, 1986; Life and Death, 1988; Politics, 1990; Shakespeare, 1990; Goodnight Nonsense, 1991; Survival, 1998; Selected Poems, 1999; Gniezno Door, 2000; A Fragment of Existence, 2002. Criticism: New Elizabethan Theatre, 1967; Byron and the Theatre, 1972; The Inner Plays of Karol Wojtyla, 1989; My Uprising: Then and Now, 1998. Co-Author: Crowell's Handbook of Contemporary Drama, 1971; Polish Plays in Translation, 1983. Other: numerous trans. Contributions: various publications. *Honours:* Polish Writers Asscn Abroad Award, 1954; Jurzykowski Foundation Award, New York, 1968; Merit for Polish Culture Badge and Diploma, Warsaw, 1970; Koscielski Foundation Award, Geneva, 1977; SI Witkiewicz ITI Award, Warsaw, 1988; Asscn of Authors Trans. Awards, Warsaw, 1990, 1995; Societé Europeen de Culture Award, Warsaw, 1998; KLIO, History Publishers Award, Warsaw, 1998. *Address:* 66 Esmond Rd, London W4 1JF, England.

TABUCCHI, Antonio; Novelist; b. 1943, Vecchiano, Tuscany, Italy; m.; one d. one s. *Education:* Univ. of Pisa. *Career:* Chair of Literature, Univ. of Siena; writes columns for Italian newspaper, Corriere della Sera, Spanish newspaper, El País; trans. of Fernando Pessoa. *Publications:* Piazza d'Italia (novel), 1975; Il piccolo naviglio (novel), 1978; Il gioco del rovescio (Letter from Casablanca, short stories), 1981; Donna di Porto Pim (short stories), 1983; Notturno indiano (Indian Nocturne, novel), 1984; Pessoana minima: escritos sobre Fernando Pessoa (non-fiction), 1984; Piccoli equivoci senza importanza (Little Misunderstandings of No Importance, novel), 1985; Il filo dell'orizzonte (The Edge of the Horizon, novel), 1986; I volatili del Beato Angelico (short stories), 1987; Un baule pieno di gente: scritti su Fernando Pessoa (non-fiction), 1990; Requiem, uma alucinação (Requiem: A Hallucination, novel), 1990; Sogni di sogni (Dreams of Dreams), 1992; Gli ultimi tre giorni di Fernando Pessoa (The Last Three Days of Fernando Pessoa), 1994; Sostiene Pereira (Pereira Declares, novel), 1994; La testa perduta di Damasceno Monteiro (The Missing Head of Damasceno Monteiro, novel), 1997. *Honours:* Prix Européen Jean Monnet, 1994; Prix Médicis Étranger, 1987; Nossack Prize, Leibniz Academy, 1999; Italian PEN Club Prize. *Address:* c/o Harvill Press, Random House, 20 Vauxhall Bridge Rd, London SW1V 2SA, England.

TAFDRUP, Pia, BA; Danish poet and writer; b. 29 May 1952, Copenhagen; m. Bo Hakon Jørgensen 1978; two s. *Education:* Univ. of Copenhagen. *Career:* mem. Danish Literary Acad., Danish PEN Centre. *Plays:* Death in the Mountains 1988, The Earth Is Blue 1991. *Publications:* various poetry vols in Danish 1981–2002; two vols in English trans. as Spring Tide 1989, Queen's Gate 2001; poems trans. into 19 foreign languages; other: The Town of Viso (dance libretto)., Constellations – An Anthology of Danish Poems (ed.) 1982, Transformations: Poetry 1980–85 (ed.) 1985, Walking over the Water: An Outline of a Poetics 1991; contrib. to many journals and anthologies in the UK, USA and Canada. *Honours:* Scholarship for Authors, Danish State Art Foundation 1984–86, 12 grants 1986–97, Danish Literature Prize for Women, Ragna Sidén Foundation 1997, Lifelong Artist's Grant 1998, Nordic Council Literature Prize 1999. *Address:* Rosenvaengets Sidealle, 3.2th, 2100 Copenhagen Ø, DK, Denmark. *E-mail:* tafdrup@post6 .tele.dk.

TAGLIABUE, John, BA, MA; fmr college teacher, poet and writer; b. 1 July 1923, Cantu, Italy; m. Grace Ten Eyck 1946; two d. *Education:* Columbia University. *Career:* Teacher, American University, Beirut, 1945, State College of Washington, 1946–47, Alfred University, New York, 1948–50, Bates College, Maine, 1953–89; Fulbright Lecturer, University of Pisa, 1950–52, University of Tokyo, 1958–60, Fudan University, Shanghai, 1984, University of Indonesia, 1993; mem. Acad. of American Poets; PEN; Poetry Society of America. *Publications:* Poems, 1959; A Japanese Journal, 1966; The Buddha Uproar, 1970; The Doorless Door, 1970; The Great Day, 1984; New and Selected Poems 1942–97, 1997. Contributions: journals, magazines, and periodicals. *Address:* Wayland Manor, Apt 412, 500 Angell Street, Providence, RI 02906, USA.

TAILLANDIER, François Antoine Georges; Writer; b. 20 June 1955, Chamalières, France; three c. *Publications:* Personnages de la rue du Couteau, 1984; Tott, 1985; Benoît ou les contemporains obscurs, 1986; Les clandestins, 1990; Jorge Luis Borges, 1993; Les nuits racine, mémoires de Monte-Cristo, 1994; Tous les secrets de l'avenir, 1996; Aragon, 1997; Des hommes quo s'éloignent, 1997; Anielka, 1999; Journal de Marseille, 1999; N6, la route de l'Italie, 1999. Contributions: newspapers and journals. *Honours:* Prix Jean Freustié, 1991; Prix Roger Nimier, 1992; Prix de la Critique, 1997, Grand Prix du Roman, 1999, Académie Française. *Address:* c/o Editions Stock, 27 rue Cassette, 75006 Paris, France.

TAIT, Arch; Trans. and University Lecturer; b. 6 June 1943, Glasgow, Scotland. *Education:* MA, 1966, PhD, 1971, Trinity Hall, Cambridge. *Career:* Lecturer, University of East Anglia, 1970–83; Ed., Glas: New Russian Writing, 1991; Senior Lecturer, University of Birmingham, 1997–; mem. Trans' Asscn; Society of Authors; British Asscn for Slavonic and East European Studies. *Publications:* Lunacharsky, The Poet Commissar, 1984. Translator: The Russian Style, 1991; Is Comrade Bulgakov Dead?, 1993; Baize-Covered Table With Decanter, 1995; Skunk: A Life, 1997; Sonechka, 1998; Under House Arrest, 1998; Hurramabad, 2001; Medea and Her Children, 2002. *Address:* Dept of Russian, University of Birmingham, Birmingham B15 2TT, England. *E-mail:* archtait@hotmail.com. *Website:* www.russianwriting.com.

TAJRA, Harry William Michael; Bishop-Abbot; b. 18 April 1945, Pawtucket, RI, USA; Writer. m. Susan Lee Jacobson, 1 Dec. 1981. *Education:* BA, Brown University, 1967; Doctor of History, Sorbonne, Paris, 1969; MTheol, Protestant Seminary, Paris, 1979; DTheol, University of Geneva, Switzerland, 1988. *Career:* Pastor, National Church, Geneva, 1982–85; Researcher, University of Geneva, 1985–88; Independent Researcher, Christian Antiquities, Rome, 1988–93; Bishop-Abbot, Order of St Mary the Virgin, 1993–; mem. Fellow, International Pontifical Marian Acad., Rome. *Publications:* The Trial of St Paul, 1989; The Martyrdom of St Paul, 1994; The Great Epiphany (in preparation). Contributions: Positions Lutheriennes, Paris; Ecumenical Society of the Blessed Virgin Mary, London.

TALBOT, Michael Owen, BA, BMus, PhD, ARCM, FBA; writer; *Emeritus Professor of Music, University of Liverpool*; b. 4 Jan. 1943, Luton, Bedfordshire, England; m. Shirley Mashiane 26 Sept. 1970; one s. one d. *Education:* Royal Coll. of Music, London, Clare Coll., Cambridge. *Career:* Lecturer 1968–79, Sr Lecturer 1979–83, Reader 1983–86, James and Constance Alsop Prof. of Music 1986–2003, Emeritus Prof. of Music 2003–, Univ. of Liverpool; mem. Royal Musical Asscn, Società Italiana di Musicologia; corresponding Fellow, Ateneo Veneto. *Publications:* Vivaldi 1978, Albinoni: Leben und Werk 1980, Antonio Vivaldi: A Guide to Research 1988, Tomaso Albinoni: The Venetian Composer and his World 1990, Benedetto Vinaccesi: A Musician in Brescia and Venice in the Age of Corelli 1994, The Sacred Vocal Music of Antonio Vivaldi 1995, Venetian Music in the Age of Vivaldi 1999, The Musical Work: Reality or Invention (ed.) 2000, The Finale in Western Instrumental Music 2001, The Business of Music (ed.) 2002; contrib. to professional journals, including Early Music, Music and Letters, Music Review, Musical Times, Journal of the Royal Musical Association, Soundings, The Consort, Note d'Archivio, Händel Jahrbuch, Informazioni e Studi Vivaldiani, Studi Vivaldiani, Journal of Eighteenth Century Music. *Honours:* Cavaliere del Ordine al Merito, Italy 1980, Oldman Prize 1990, Serena Medal 1999. *Address:* c/o School of Music, The University of Liverpool, Liverpool, L69 7WW, England. *Fax:* (151) 794 3141 (Office). *E-mail:* mtalbot@liv.ac.uk (Office).

TALL, Deborah; Prof., Poet, Writer and Ed.; b. 16 March 1951, Washington, DC, USA; m. David Weiss, 9 Sept. 1979, two d. *Education:* BA, English, University of Michigan, 1972; MFA, Creative Writing, Goddard College, 1979. *Career:* Asst Prof., Visiting Fellow in Literature, University of Baltimore, 1980–82; Prof., 1982–, Chair., Dept of English, 1992–94, Hobart and William Smith Colleges; Ed., Seneca Review, 1982–; Writer-in-Residence, Chautauqua Institution, New York, 1998; Visiting Poet Cornell Univ. Spring Semester 2003; mem. Acad. of American Poets; Associated Writing Programs; Asscn for the Study of Literature and the Environment; Authors' Guild; PEN; Poetry Society of America. *Publications:* Eight Colors Wide, 1974; Ninth Life, 1982; The Island of the White Cow: Memories of an Irish Island, 1986; Come Wind, Come Weather, 1988; Taking Note: From Poets' Notebooks (ed. with Stephen Kuusisto and David Weiss), 1991, revised edn as The Poet's Notebook, 1995; From Where We Stand: Recovering a Sense of Place, 1993; Summons, 2000. Contributions: many anthologies, reviews, quarterlies, journals, and magazines. *Honours:* Kathryn A. Morton Prize for Poetry 1999; Yaddo Residencies, 1982, 1984, 1991; Citation of Achievement, Co-ordinating Council of Literary Magazines,

1986; Ingram Merrill Foundation Grant, 1987; MacDowell Colony Residency, 1998. *Address:* c/o Dept of English, Hobart and William Smith Colleges, Geneva, NY 14456, USA. *E-mail:* tall@hws.edu.

TALLENT, Elizabeth (Ann); Writer and Prof. of English; b. 8 Aug. 1954, Washington, DC, USA; m. Barry Smoots, 28 Sept. 1975, one s. *Education:* BA, Illinois State University at Normal, 1975. *Career:* Prof. of English, University of California at Davis; mem. Poets and Writers. *Publications:* Married Men and Magic Tricks, 1982; In Constant Flight, 1983; Museum Pieces, 1985; Time With Children, 1987; Honey, 1993. Contributions: Magazines. *Honours:* Bay Area Book Reviewers Asscn Fiction Award; National Endowment for the Arts Fellowship, 1992. *Address:* c/o Dept of English, University of California at Davis, Davis, CA 95616, USA.

TAMM, Peter; German publisher; b. 12 May 1928, Hamburg; m. Ursula Weisshun 1958; one s. four d. *Education:* Univ. of Hamburg. *Career:* Shipping Ed., Hamburger Abendblatt 1948–58; Man. Dir Ullstein GmbH (Publr) 1960–62, 1984; Man. Dir Bild-Zeitung 1962–64; Dir, Verlagshaus Axel Springer, Berlin 1964–70, mem. Exec. Bd 1970–82, Chair. Man. Bd 1982–91; Vice-Pres. Bundesverband Deutscher Zeitungsverleger 1980–90; now Propr Koehler/Mittler-Verlagsgruppe and Schiffahrtsverlages Hansa, Propr and Dir Scientific Inst. for Maritime and Naval History; mem. Royal Swedish Soc. of Maritime Sciences, Stockholm 1999. *Publication:* Maler der See 1980. *Honours:* Bayerischer Verdienstorden, Grosses Bundesverdienstkreuz, Vasco da Gama Naval Medal 1998, Gold Ehrenkreuz der Bundeswehr 2001. *Address:* Elbchaussee 277, 22605 Hamburg, Germany. *Telephone:* (40) 821341 (Office). *Fax:* (40) 8226300 (Office).

TAN, Amy Ruth, MA, LHD; American writer; b. 19 Feb. 1952, Oakland, Calif.; m. Louis M. DeMattei 1974. *Education:* San José State Univ., Calif., Univ. of Calif. at Berkeley, Dominican Coll., San Rafael. *Career:* specialist in language devt Alameda Co. Asscn for Mentally Retarded 1976–80; Project Dir MORE, San Francisco 1980–81; freelance writer 1981–88; Marian McFadden Memorial Lecturer, Indianapolis-Marion Co. Public Library 1996. *Film:* The Joy Luck Club (screenwriter, producer) 1993. *Publications:* The Joy Luck Club 1989 (Commonwealth Club and Bay Area Book Reviewers' Best Fiction Award 1990), The Kitchen God's Wife 1991, The Hundred Secret Senses 1995, The Bonesetter's Daughter 2000; for children: The Moon Lady 1992, The Chinese Siamese Cat 1994; autobiog.: The Opposite of Fate: A Book of Musings; numerous short stories and essays. *Honours:* Best American Essays Award 1991. *Literary Agent:* Steven Barclay Agency, 12 Western Avenue, Petaluma, CA 94952, USA. *Telephone:* (707) 773-0654. *Fax:* (707) 778-1868. *Website:* www.barclayagency.com. *Address:* c/o Ballantine Publications Publicity, 201 East 50th Street, New York, NY 10022, USA.

TAPPLY, William G(eorge); Writer; b. 16 July 1940, Waltham, Massachusetts, USA; m. Cynthia Ehrgott, 7 March 1970, divorced 1995, one s. two d. *Education:* BA, Amherst College, 1962; MAT, Harvard University, 1963; Tufts University, 1965–67. *Career:* Dir of Economic Education, Tufts University, 1967–68; Housemaster and Teacher, Lexington High School, 1969–90; Contributing Ed., Field and Stream, 1988–; Editorial Assoc., Writer's Digest School, 1992–; Instructor, Emerson College, Clark University, 1995–; Special Correspondent, American Angler, 1999–; mem. Authors' Guild; MWA; Private Eye Writers of America. *Publications:* Fiction: Death at Charity's Point, 1984; The Dutch Blue Error, 1985; Follow the Sharks, 1985; The Marine Corpse, 1986; Dead Meat, 1987; The Vulgar Boatman, 1987; A Void in Hearts, 1988; Dead Winter, 1989; Client Privilege, 1989; The Spotted Cats, 1991; Tight Lines, 1992; The Snake Eater, 1993; The Seventh Enemy, 1995; Close to the Bone, 1996; Cutter's Run, 1998; Muscle Memory, 1999; Scar Tissue, 2000; Past Tense, 2001. Non-Fiction: Those Hours Spent Outdoors, 1988; Opening Day and Other Neuroses, 1990; Home Water Near and Far, 1992; Sportsman's Legacy, 1993; The Elements of Mystery Fiction, 1995; A Fly-Fishing Life, 1997; Bass Bug Fishing, 1999; Upland Days, 2000. Contributions: Magazines. *Honours:* Scribner Crime Novel Award, 1984. *Address:* 75 Antrim Rd, Hancock, NH 03449-5606, USA.

TARANTINO, Quentin; Film Dir and Writer; b. 27 March 1963, Knoxville, TN, USA. *Career:* worked in video archives, Manhattan Beach; Films: My Best Friend's Birthday (actor, dir, prod.), 1987; Reservoir Dogs (actor, dir), 1992; Past Midnight (assoc. prod.), 1992; Siunin Wong Fei-hung tsi titmalau (prod.), 1993; Eddie Presley (actor), 1993; Sleep With Me (actor), 1994; Killing Zoe (exec. prod.), 1994; Somebody to Love (actor), 1994; Pulp Fiction (actor, dir), 1994; Destiny Turns on the Radio (actor), 1995; Desperado (actor), 1995; Four Rooms (actor, dir, exec. prod.), 1995; Girl 6 (actor), 1996; From Dusk Till Dawn (actor, exec. prod.), 1996; Curdled (actor, exec. prod.), 1996; Jackie Brown (dir), 1997; God Said, 'Ha!' (exec. prod.), 1998; Little Nicky (actor), 2000; Kill Bill (actor, dir, prod.), 2003; numerous TV appearances. *Publications:* Screenplays: My Best Friend's Birthday, 1992; Reservoir Dogs, 1992; True Romance, 1993; Natural Born Killers, 1994; Pulp Fiction, 1994; Four Rooms (segment: The Man from Hollywood), 1995; From Dusk Till Dawn, 1996; Jackie Brown, 1997; Kill Bill (also novel), 2003. *Address:* WMA, 151 El Camino Dr., Beverly Hills, CA 90212, USA; 6201 Sunset Blvd, Suite 35, Los Angeles, CA 90028, USA.

TARCHER, Jeremy Phillip, BA; American publisher; b. 2 Jan. 1932, New York; m. 1st Shari Lewis 1958 (died 1998); one d.; m. 2nd Judith Paige Mitchell 1999. *Education:* St John's Coll., Annapolis, Md. *Career:* Founder and Pres. Jeremy P. Tarcher Inc., LA 1964–; Vice-Pres. Houghton Mifflin, Boston 1980–83; Chair. Bd Audio Renaissance Tapes, LA 1985–; Pres. Tarcher/Putnam (a div. of Penguin/Putnam) 1991–; mem. Bd Trustees The Esalen Inst., Big Sur, Calif. 1986–; Producer Shari Lewis Show, NBC Network 1959–62; Exec. Producer A Picture of U.S. (Emmy Award for Children's Programming) 1976. *Address:* 144 South Beverly Drive, Beverly Hills, CA 90212 (Office); 1416 Stone Canyon, Bel Air, CA 90077, USA (Home). *Telephone:* (310) 274-7207 (Office). *Fax:* (310) 274-3611 (Office).

TARN, Nathaniel; poet, writer and academic; b. 30 June 1928, Paris, France; m. 1st (divorced); two c.; m. 2nd Janet Rodney 1981. *Education:* BA, 1948, MA, 1952, University of Cambridge; Dipl CFRE, École des Hautes Études, University of Paris; MA, 1952, PhD, 1957, University of Chicago. *Career:* Visiting Prof., SUNY at Buffalo, 1969–70, Princeton University 1969–70, University of Pennsylvania, 1976, Jilin University, People's Republic of China, 1982; Prof. of Comparative Literature, 1970–85, Prof. Emeritus, 1985–, Rutgers University. *Publications:* Poetry: Old Savage/Young City, 1964; Penguin Modern Poets 7 (with Richard Murphy and Jon Silkin), 1966; Where Babylon Ends, 1968; The Beautiful Contradictions, 1969; October: A Sequence of Ten Poems Followed by Requiem Pro Duabus Filiis Israel, 1969; The Silence, 1970; A Nowhere for Vallejo: Choices, October, 1971; Lyrics for the Bride of God, 1975; Narrative of This Fall, 1975; The House of Leaves, 1976; From Alaska: The Ground of Our Great Admiration of Nature (with Janet Rodney), 1977; The Microcosm, 1977; Birdscapes, with Seaside, 1978; The Forest (with Janet Rodney), 1979; Atitlan/Alashka, 1979; The Land Songs, 1981; Weekends in Mexico, 1982; The Desert Mothers, 1984; At the Western Gates, 1985; Palenque: Selected Poems, 1972–1984, 1986; Seeing America First, 1989; The Mothers of Matagalpa, 1989; Flying the Body, 1993; The Architextures, 2000; Three Letters from the City: The St Petersburg Poems 1968–1998, 2000; Selected Poems, 1950–2000, 2002; Dying Trees, 2003. Non-Fiction: Views from the Weaving Mountain: Selected Essays in Poetics and Anthropology, 1991; Scandals in the House of Birds, 1998. *Honours:* Guinness Prize, 1963; Wenner Gren Fellowships, 1978, 1980; Commonwealth of Pennsylvania Fellowship, 1984; Rockefeller Foundation Fellowship, 1988. *Address:* PO Box 8187, Santa Fe, NM 87504, USA.

TARTT, Donna; American writer; *writer*; b. 1963, Greenwood, MS. *Education:* Univ. of Miss., Oxford, Bennington Coll., VT. *Career:* published first sonnet in a Miss. literary review 1976. *Publications:* novels: The Secret History 1992, The Little Friend 2002; short stories: A Christmas Pageant (Harper's) 1993, A Garter Snake (GQ) 1995, True Crime (audio book) 1996; articles in magazines. *Honours:* WHSmith Literary Award 2003. *Address:* c/o Knopf Publishing, Author Mail, 1745 Broadway, New York, NY 10019, USA (Office).

TARUSKIN, Richard; Prof., Musicologist, Critic and Author; b. 2 April 1945, New York, NY, USA. *Education:* PhD, Columbia University, 1975. *Career:* Asst Prof., 1975–81, Assoc. Prof. of Music, 1981–87, Columbia University; Visiting Prof., University of Pennsylvania, 1985; Assoc. Prof., 1986–89, Prof., 1989–, University of California at Berkeley; Hanes-Willis Visiting Prof., University of North Carolina at Chapel Hill, 1987; mem. American Musicological Society. *Publications:* Opera and Drama in Russia, 1981; Busnoi: The Latin-Texted Works (ed. with commentary), 2 vols, 1990; Musorgsky: Eight Essays and an Epilogue, 1993; Stravinsky and the Russian Traditions: A Biography of the Works Through Mavra, 2 vols, 1995; Text and Act: Essays on Music and Performance, 1995. Contributions: The New Grove Dictionary of Opera, 1992; many articles and reviews in professional journals and general periodicals. *Honours:* Fulbright-Hays Traveling Fellowship, 1971–72; Guggenheim Fellowship, 1987; Dent Medal, England, 1987; ASCAP Deems Taylor Award, 1989. *Address:* c/o Dept of Music, University of California at Berkeley, Berkeley, CA 94720, USA.

TASHIRO, Kikuo; Japanese newspaper and television executive; b. 22 April 1917. *Education:* Waseda Univ. *Career:* joined Asahi Shimbun 1940; City Ed. 1959; Man. Ed. 1966; Exec. Dir in charge of Editorial Affairs 1969; Pres. Asahi Nat. Broadcasting Co. Ltd (TV Asahi) 1983. *Address:* 6-4-10 Roppongi, Minato-ku, Tokyo 106, Japan (Home). *Telephone:* (3) 405-3211 (Home).

TATE, James Vincent; poet and academic; b. 8 Dec. 1943, Kansas City, MO, USA. *Education:* University of Missouri, 1963–64; BA, Kansas State University, 1965; MFA, University of Iowa, 1967. *Career:* Instructor in Creative Writing, University of Iowa, 1966–67; Visiting Lecturer, University of California, Berkeley, 1967–68; Poetry Ed., Dickinson Review, 1967–76; Trustee and Assoc. Ed., Pym-Randall Press, 1968–80; Asst Prof. of English, Columbia University, 1969–71; Assoc. Prof., then Prof. of English, 1971–, University of Massachusetts, Amherst; Poet-in-Residence, Emerson College, 1970–71; Assoc. Ed., Barn Dream Press; mem. Acad. of American Poets, board of chancellors, 2001–. *Publications:* Poetry: Cages, 1966; The Destination, 1967; The Lost Pilot, 1967; Notes of Woe: Poems, 1968; Camping in the Valley, 1968; The Torches, 1968; Row with Your Hair, 1969; Is There Anything?, 1969; Shepherds of the Mist, 1969; Amnesia People, 1970; Are You Ready Mary Baker Eddy? (with Bill Knot), 1970; Deaf Girl Playing, 1970; The Oblivion Ha-Ha, 1970; Wrong Songs, 1970; Hints to Pilgrims, 1971; Absences, 1972; Apology for Eating Geoffrey Movius' Hyacinth, 1972; Hottentot Ossuary, 1974; Viper Jazz, 1976; Riven Doggeries, 1979; Land of Little Sticks, 1981; Constant Defender, 1983; Reckoner, 1986; Distance from Loved Ones, 1990; Selected Poems, 1991; Worshipful Company of Fletchers, 1993; Shroud of the Gnome, 1997; Memoir of the Hawk: Poems, 2001. Novel: Lucky Darryl, 1977. Contributions: numerous books and periodicals. *Honours:* Yale Younger Poets Award, 1966; National Institute of Arts and Letters Award, 1974; Massachusetts Arts and Humanities Fellow, 1975; Guggenheim Fellowship, 1976; National Endowment for the Arts Fellowship, 1980; Pulitzer Prize in Poetry, 1992; National Book Award for Poetry, 1994. *Address:* Dept of English, University of Massachusetts, Amherst, MA 01003, USA.

TAYLOR, Andrew John Robert, BA, MA; writer; b. 14 Oct. 1951, Stevenage, England; m. Caroline Jane Silverwood, 8 Sept. 1979, one s. one d. *Education:* Emmanuel College, Cambridge, University of London. *Career:* mem. CWA, Society of Authors. *Publications:* Caroline Minuscule, 1982; Waiting for the End of the World, 1984; Our Fathers' Lies, 1985; An Old School Tie, 1986; Freelance Death, 1987; The Second Midnight, 1987; Blacklist, 1988; Blood Relation, 1990; Toyshop, 1990; The Raven on the Water, 1991; The Sleeping Policeman, 1992; The Barred Window, 1993; Odd Man Out, 1993; An Air That Kills, 1994; The Mortal Sickness, 1995; The Four Last Things, 1997; The Lover of the Grave, 1997; The Judgement of Strangers, 1998; The Suffocating Night, 1998; The Office of the Dead, 2000; Where Roses Fade, 2000; Death's Own Door, 2001; Requiem for an Angel, 2002; The American Boy, 2003. Children's Fiction: Hairline Cracks, 1988; Snapshot, 1989; Double Exposure, 1990; Negative Image, 1992; The Invader, 1994. Contributions: anthologies, including: Perfectly Criminal, 1996; Past Crimes, 1998. *Honours:* John Creasey Memorial Award, 1982, Ellis Peters Historical Dagger, 2001, CWA. *Literary Agent:* Sheil Land Associates, 43 Doughty Street, London WC1N 2LF, England. *Website:* www.andrew-taylor.co.uk.

TAYLOR, Andrew MacDonald, BA, MA, DLitt; academic, poet and writer; *Emeritus Professor, Edith Cowan University*; b. 19 March 1940, Warrnambool, Vic., Australia; m. Beate Josephi 1981; one s. one d. *Education:* University of Melbourne. *Career:* Lockie Fellow, University of Melbourne 1965–68; Lecturer 1971–74, Senior Lecturer 1974–91, Assoc. Prof. 1991–1992, University of Adelaide; Prof., later Emeritus Prof., School of Int. Cultural and Community Studies, Edith Cowan Univ. 1992–; mem. Assn for the Study of Australian Literature; Australian Society of Authors; PEN. *Publications:* Reading Australian Poetry, 1987; Selected Poems, 1960–85, 1988; Folds in the Map, 1991; Sandstone, 1995; The Stone Threshold, 2001; Götterdämmerung Café, 2001; Collected Poems 2004. Contributions: newspapers, journals, and magazines. *Honours:* several prizes and awards, AM. *Address:* c/o School of International Cultural and Community Studies, Edith Cowan University, Mount Lawley, WA 6050, Australia.

TAYLOR, Beverly White; Prof. of English and Writer; b. 30 March 1947, Grenada, Mississippi, USA. *Education:* BAE, University of Mississippi, 1969; MA, 1970, PhD, 1977, Duke University. *Career:* Asst Prof., 1977–84, Assoc. Prof., 1984–92, Prof. of English, 1992–, University of North Carolina at Chapel Hill; mem. Victorians Institute, pres., 1989–90; Tennyson Society; Browning Institute; MLA; International Arthurian Society. *Publications:* The Return of King Arthur, 1983; Arthurian Legend and Literature, 1984; Francis Thompson, 1987; The Cast of Consciousness, 1987; Gender and Discourse in Victorian Literature and Art, 1992. Contributions: Encyclopedias and periodicals. *Address:* Dept of English, University of North Carolina, Chapel Hill, NC 27599, USA. *E-mail:* btaylor@email.unc.edu.

TAYLOR, Bruce Bradley, (Mr Magic Realism); Writer; b. 28 May 1947, Seattle, Washington, USA. *Education:* BA, Sociology, University of Washington, 1969; Graduate, Clarion Writers Workshop, University of Washington, 1972. *Career:* Founder, Dir, Magic Realism Writers International Network; mem. SFWA; National Writers Union; Freelancers, Seattle. *Publications:* The Attendant, 1979; Breath Amidst the Stones, 1980; Onions, 1980; Eggs, 1985; Coming Home So Cold, 1986; Perfect Disguises, 1988; The Final Trick of Funnyman and Other Stories, 1997. Contributions: newspapers and journals. *Honours:* Chair., Sharon Baker Memorial Award, Pacific Northwest Writers Conference. *Address:* 2001 E Yesler Way, No. 23, Seattle, WA 98122, USA.

TAYLOR, David John, BA, FRSL; writer; b. 22 Aug. 1960, Norwich, England; m. Rachel Hore 1990; three s. *Education:* University of Oxford. *Publications:* Great Eastern Land (novel), 1986; A Vain Conceit: British Fiction in the 1980s, 1989; Other People: Portraits from the Nineties (with Marcus Berkmann), 1990; Real Life (novel), 1992; After the War: The Novel and England Since 1945, 1993; English Settlement (novel), 1996; After Bathing at Baxter's (short stories), 1997; Trespass (novel), 1988; Thackeray, 1999; The Comedy Man (novel), 2001; Orwell: The Life, 2003. Contributions: periodicals including: Independent; Guardian; Sunday Times; TLS; Spectator; Private Eye. *Honours:* Grinzane Cavour Prize, Italy 1999. *Literary Agent:* Rogers, Coleridge & White Ltd, 20 Powis Mews, London W11 1JN, England.

TAYLOR, Rev. Graham P.; British children's writer and clergyman; b. 1961; m.; three c. *Career:* vicar at Cloughton, North Yorkshire. *Publications:* Shadowmancer 2003, Wormwood 2004. *Address:* c/o Faber and Faber Ltd, 3 Queen Square, London, WC1N 3AU, England. *Website:* www.faber.co.uk.

TAYLOR, H. Baldwin (see Waugh, Hillary Baldwin).

TAYLOR, Henry (Splawn); Prof. of Literature, Poet and Writer; b. 21 June 1942, Loudoun County, Virginia, USA. *Education:* BA, University of Virginia, 1965; MA, Hollins College, 1966. *Career:* Instructor, Roanoke College, 1966–68; Asst Prof., University of Utah, 1968–71; Contributing Ed., Hollins Critic, 1970–77; Assoc. Prof., 1971–76, Prof. of Literature, 1976–, Co-Dir, MFA in Creative Writing, 1982–, Dir, American Studies Program, 1983–85, American University; Consulting Ed., Magill's Literary Annual, 1972–, Poet Lore, 1976–84; Writer-in-Residence, Hollins College, 1978; Board of Advisers, 1986–, Poetry Ed., 1988–89, New Virginia Review; Distinguished Poet-in-Residence, Wichita State University, 1994; Poet-in-Residence, Randolph-Macon Women's College, 1996; Elliston Poet-in-Residence, University of Cincinnati, 2002. *Publications:* Poetry: The Horse Show at Midnight: Poems, 1966; Breakings, 1971; An Afternoon of Pocket Billiards, 1975; Desperado, 1979; The Flying Change, 1985; Understanding Fiction: Poems 1986–96, 1996; Brief Candles: 101 Clerihews, 2000. Other: Magill's (Masterplots) Literary Annual 1972 (ed. with Frank N. Magill), 1972; Poetry: Points of Departure, 1974; Magill's (Masterplots) Literary Annual 1973 (assoc. ed.), 1974; Magill's (Masterplots) Literary Annual 1974 (assoc. ed.), 1975; The Water of Light: A Miscellany in Honor of Brewster Ghiselin (ed.), 1976; Compulsory Figures: Essays on Recent American Poets, 1992. Contributions: many books, anthologies, reviews, and journals. *Honours:* Acad. of American Poets Prizes, 1962, 1964; Utah State Institute of Fine Arts Poetry Prizes, co-winner, 1969, winner, 1971; National Endowment for the Arts Fellowships, 1978, 1986; National Endowment for the Humanities Research Grant, 1980–81; Witter Bynner Prize for Poetry, American Acad. and Institute of Arts and Letters, 1984; Pulitzer Prize in Poetry, 1986; Virginia Cultural Laureate Award, 1986; Teacher Recognition, National Foundation for Advancement in the Arts, 1995–96; Michael Braude Light Verse Prize, American Acad. of Arts and Letters, 2002. *Address:* c/o Dept of Literature, American University, Washington, DC 20016, USA.

TAYLOR, John Russell; Art, Film, and Drama Critic and Writer; b. 19 June 1935, Dover, Kent, England. *Education:* MA, Jesus College, Cambridge; Courtauld Institue of London. *Career:* Sub-Ed., Times Educational Supplement, 1959; Editorial Asst, TLS, 1960; Film Critic, 1962–73, Art Critic, 1978–, The Times; Lecturer on Film, Tufts University in London, 1970–71; Prof., University of Southern California at Los Angeles, 1972–78; Ed., Films and Filming, 1983–90. *Publications:* Anger and After, 1962; Anatomy of a Television Play, 1962; Cinema Eye, Cinema Bar, 1964; Penguin Dictionary of the Theatre, 1966; The Art Nouveau Book in Britain, 1966; The Rise and Fall of the Well-Made Play, 1967; The Art Dealers, 1969; Harold Pinter, 1969; The Hollywood Musical, 1971; The Second Wave, 1971; David Storey, 1974; Directors and Directions, 1975; Peter Shaffer, 1975; Hitch, 1978; The Revels History of Drama in English, Vol. VII, 1978; Impressionism, 1981; Strangers in Paradise, 1983; Ingrid Bergman, 1983; Alex Guinness, 1984; Vivien Leigh, 1984; Portraits of the British Cinema, 1985; Hollywood 1940s, 1985; Orson Welles, 1986; Edward Wolfe, 1986; Great Movie Moments, 1987; Post-war Friends, 1987; Robin Tanner, 1989; Bernard Meninsky, 1990; Impressionist Dreams, 1990; Liz Taylor, 1991; Ricardo Cinalli, 1993; Igor Mitoraj, 1993; Muriel Pemberton, 1993; Claude Monet, 1995; Bill Jacklin, 1997; The World of Michael Parkes, 1998; Antonio Saliola, 1998; The Sun is God, 1999; Roberto Bernardi, 2001; Geoffrey Dashwood, 2002; Peter Coker, 2002. *Address:* c/o The Times, 1 Pennington St, London E1 9XN, England.

TAYLOR, Judy, (Julia Marie Hough); Writer; b. 12 Aug. 1932, Murton, Swansea, Wales; m. Richard Hough 1980 (died 1999). *Career:* Dir, Bodley Head Ltd, 1967–84, Chatto, Bodley Head and Jonathan Cape Ltd, 1973–80, Chatto, Bodley Head & Jonathan Cape Australia Pty Ltd, 1977–80; Consultant to Penguin, Beatrix Potter, 1981–87, 1989–92; mem. Publishers Assn Council; Book Development Council; UNICEF International Art Committee; UK UNICEF Greetings Card Committee; Beatrix Potter Society; FRSA. *Publications:* Sophie and Jack, 1982; My First Year: A Beatrix Potter Baby Book, 1983; Sophie and Jack in the Snow, 1984; Dudley and the Monster, 1986; Dudley Goes Flying, 1986; Dudley in a Jam, 1986; Dudley and the Strawberry Shake, 1986; That Naughty Rabbit: Beatrix Potter and Peter Rabbit, 1987; Beatrix Potter 1866–1943, 1989; Beatrix Potter's Letters: A Selection, 1989; So I Shall Tell You a Story, 1993; Beatrix (with Patrick Garland), 1996; Edward Ardizzone's Sketches for Friends: A Selection, 2000. Contributions: numerous professional journals. *Honours:* MBE, 1971. *Address:* 31 Meadowbank, Primrose Hill Rd, London NW3 3AY, England.

TAYLOR, Mark C.; Prof. of Humanities and Writer; b. 13 Dec. 1945, Plainfield, NJ, USA; m. Mary-Dinnis Stearns 22 June 1968; one s. one d. *Education:* BA, Wesleyan Univ., 1968; PhD, Religion, Harvard Univ., 1973; Doktorgrad, Philosophy, Univ. of Copenhagen, 1981. *Career:* Instructor in Religion, Harvard Univ., 1972–73; Asst Prof. of Religion, 1973–78, Assoc. Prof. of Religion, 1978–81, Prof. of Religion, 1981–86, William R. Kenan Jr Prof., 1986–91, Preston S. Parish Third Century Prof. of Religion, 1992–93, Preston S. Parish Prof. of Humanities, 1993–97, Cleutt Prof. of Humanities, 1997–, Williams College; Visiting Lecturer in Religion, Smith College, 1981; Visiting Prof. of Architecture and Religion, Columbia Univ., 1994; Visiting Prof., Univ. of Sydney, 1995; William Neal Reynolds Visiting Prof. of Communication Studies, Univ. of North Carolina at Chapel Hill, 1999; Co-

Founder, Global Education Network, 1999; Art exhibition, Grave Matters, Mass MOCA, 2002–03; mem. American Acad. of Religion: Hegel Society of America; Society for Phenomenology and Existential Philosophy; Society for Values in Higher Education; Søren Kierkegaard Acad. *Publications:* Kierkegaard's Pseudonymous Authorship: A Study of Time and the Self, 1975; Religion and the Human Image (with Carl Raschke and James Kirk), 1976; Journeys to Selfhood: Hegel and Kierkegaard, 1980; Unfinished: Essays in Honor of Ray L. Hart (ed.), 1981; Deconstructing Theology, 1982; Erring: A Postmodern A/theology, 1984; Deconstruction in Context: Literature and Philosophy, 1986; Altarity, 1987; Tears, 1989; Double Negative (with Michael Heizer), 1992; Disfiguring: Art, Architecture, Religion, 1992; Nots, 1993; Imagologies: Media Philosophy (with Esa Saarinen), 1994; Hiding, 1996; Critical Terms in Religious Studies (ed.), 1998; The Picture in Question: Mark Tansey and the Ends of Representation, 1999; About Religion: Economies of Faith in Virtual Cultures, 1999; The Moment of Complexity: Emerging Network Culture, 2002; Grave Matters, 2002; Confidence Games: Money and Markets in a World Without Redemption, 2003. Contributions: numerous scholarly books and journals. *Honours:* Guggenheim Fellowship, 1978–79; National Humanities Center Fellow, 1982–83; Awards for Excellence, American Acad. of Religion, 1988, 1994; Research Fellow, Graham Foundation for Fine Arts, 1990; Rector's Medal, University of Helsinki, 1993; National College Prof. of the Year, Carnegie Foundation for the Advancement of Teaching, 1995; Distinguished Alumnus Award, Wesleyan University, 1998. *Address:* c/o Stetson Hall, Williams College, Williamstown, MA 01267, USA.

TAYLOR, Theodore Langhans; Writer; b. 23 June 1921, Statesville, NC, USA; m. 1st Gwen Goodwin, 25 Oct. 1946, two s. one d.; m. 2nd Flora Gray, 18 April 1982. *Publications:* The Magnificent Mitscher, 1954; Fire on the Beaches, 1957; The Cay, 1968; The Children's War, 1971; The Maldonado Miracle, 1973; Teetoncey, 1974; Jule, 1979; The Trouble with Tuck, 1981; Battle of the Midway Island, 1982; HMS Hood vs Bismarck, 1983; Battle in the English Channel, 1984; Sweet Friday Island, 1984; The Cats of Shambala, 1985; Walking Up a Rainbow, 1986; The Stalker, 1987; The Hostage, 1988; Sniper, Monocolo, 1989; Tuck Triumphant, 1990; The Weirdo, 1991; Maria, 1992; To Kill a Leopard, 1993; Timothy of the Cay, 1993; The Bomb, 1996; Rogue Wave, 1996; A Sailor Returns, 2001; The Boy Who Could Fly Without a Motor, 2002; Lord of the Kill, 2002; The Flight of Jesse Leroy Brown, 2003. Contributions: Saturday Evening Post; McCall's; Ladies Home Journal; Saturday Review of Literature; Argosy. *Honours:* Lewis Carroll Shelf Award; Jane Addams Peace and Freedom Foundation Award; Western Writers of America Award; George G. Stone Center Award; Edgar Allan Poe Award; International Asscn of School Librarians Award; Best Books, American Library Asscn, 1993, 1995. *Address:* 1856 Catalina St, Laguna Beach, CA 92651, USA.

TAYLOR, Velande Pingel, (Martha Pingel), BA, MA, PhD; retd academic, writer and poet; b. 10 Sept. 1923, New York, NY, USA; m. Bert Raymond Taylor Jr 1961 (died 2003). *Career:* Instructor, Paul Smiths College, New York, 1946–47; Asst Prof., East Carolina University, NC, 1947–58; Prof. and Head, Dept of Humanities, Colorado Woman's College, 1958–66; Visiting Prof., St Mary's University, Texas, 1966–69; Prof., Middle Georgia College, 1969–72; Prof. and Writer-in-Residence, Hong Kong Baptist College, 1974–84; Retreat Facilitator in Poetry and Fiction, WordCraft by Lan, 1984–; mem. Acad. of American Poets, American Philosophical Asscn, Nat. Authors' Registry. *Publications:* An American Utilitarian, 1948; Catalyst, 1951; Mood Montage, 1968; Immortal Dancer, 1968; Mode and Muse in a New Generation, 1979; Homilies in the Marketplace 1996; Copper Flowers, 1996; Walking Songs, 1997; Zbyx, 1997; Tales From the Archetypal World, 1998; Flowing Water, Singing Sand, 1999; Between the Lines, 1999; The Zodiac Affair, 2000; Gallery, 2001; The Shining Kingdom (trans. of Sollyse Egne, by Helga P. Marstrand), 2004. Contributions: anthologies, periodicals, and radio. *Honours:* Certificate, International Mark Twain Society, 1947; Miniature Medal, Order of the Danne Brog, 1951; Gold Medal Freedoms Foundation 1953; Certificate, Writer's Digest Rhymed Poetry Contest, 1994. *Address:* 910 Marion Street, No. 1008, Seattle, WA 98104, USA.

TEBBEL, John; Writer and Prof. of Humanities (retd); b. 16 Nov. 1912, Boyne City, Michigan, USA; m. Kathryn Carl, 29 April 1939, one d. *Education:* AB, Central Michigan College of Education, 1935; MS, Columbia University, 1937. *Career:* Managing Ed., American Mercury, 1941–43; Assoc. Ed., E. P. Dutton & Co, 1943–47; Chair., Dept of Journalism, 1954–65, Prof. of Journalism, 1965, New York University; mem. Authors' Guild; Society of Professional Journalists. *Publications:* An American Dynasty, 1947; The Marshall Fields, 1947; George Horace Lorimer and the Saturday Evening Post, 1948; The Battle for North America, 1948; The Conqueror, 1951; Touched with Fire, 1952; The Life and Good Times of William Randolph Hearst, 1952; George Washington's America, 1954; The Magic of Balanced Living, 1956; The Epicure's Companion, 1962; David Sarnoff, 1963; From Rags to Riches, 1964; A History of Book Publishing in America, 4 vols, 1972–81; The Media in America, 1975; The Press and the Presidency, 1985; Between Covers, 1987; A Certain Club, 1989; The Magazine in America, 1991; Turning the World Upside Down, 1993; America's Great Patriotic War with Spain, 1996. Contributions: many professional journals and general periodicals. *Honours:* Hon. LittD, Central Michigan Univ., 1948; Publishing Hall of Fame, 1985. *Address:* 4033 The Forest at Duke, 2701 Pickett Rd, Durham, NC 27705, USA.

TELFER, Tracie (see Chaplin, Jenny).

TEMKO, Allan Bernard; academic, architecture critic and writer; b. 4 Feb. 1926, New York, NY, USA; m. Elizabeth Ostroff 1950; one s. one d. *Education:* AB, Columbia University, 1947; Postgraduate Studies, Sorbonne, University of Paris, 1948–49, 1951–52, University of California at Berkeley, 1949–51. *Career:* Lecturer, Sorbonne, University of Paris, 1953–54, École des Arts et Metiers, Paris, 1954–55; Asst Prof. of Journalism, 1956–62, Lecturer in City Planning and Social Sciences, 1966–70, Lecturer, Graduate School of Journalism, 1991, University of California at Berkeley; West Coast Ed., Architectural Forum, 1959–62; Architecture Critic, 1961–93, Art Ed., 1979–82, San Francisco Chronicle; Prof. of Art, California State University at Hayward, 1971–80; Lecturer in Art, Stanford University, 1981, 1982. *Publications:* Notre Dame of Paris, 1955; Eero Saarinen, 1962; No Way to Build a Ballpark and Other Irreverent Essays on Architecture, 1993. Contributions: newspapers and magazines. *Honours:* Guggenheim Fellowship, 1956–57; Gold Medal, 1956, Silver Medal, 1994, Commonwealth Club of California; Rockefeller Foundation Grant, 1962–63; Manufacturers Hanover/Art World First Prize in Architectural Criticism, 1986, and Critics' Award, 1987; National Endowment for the Arts Fellowship, 1988; Professional Achievement Award, Society of Professional Journalists, 1988; Pulitzer Prize for Criticism, 1990. *Address:* 1015 Fresno Avenue, Berkeley, CA 94707, USA.

TEMPLE, (Robert) Philip; writer; b. 20 March 1939, Yorkshire, England; m. Daphne Evelyn Keen 1965 (divorced); one s. one d. *Career:* Ed., New Zealand Alpine Journal, 1968–70, 1973, Landfall, 1972–75; Assoc. Ed., Katherine Mansfield Memorial Fellowship, Menton, France, 1979; Robert Burns Fellowship, University of Otago, 1980; Berlin Artist's Program Fellowship, 1987; Research Fellow, National Library, New Zealand, 1996–97; mem. PEN, New Zealand Centre, 1970–; New Zealand Society of Authors, pres., 1998–99. *Publications:* The World at Their Feet, 1969; Ways to the Wilderness, 1977; Beak of the Moon, 1981; Sam, 1984; New Zealand Explorers, 1985; Kakapo, 1988; Making Your Vote Count, 1992; Dark of the Moon, 1993; Temple's Guide to the New Zealand Parliament, 1994; Kotuku, 1994; The Book of the Kea, 1996; To Each His Own, 1998. *Honours:* Arts Council Non-Fiction Bursary, 1994; AIM Honour Award, 1995. *Address:* 147a Tomahawk Road, Dunedin, New Zealand.

TEMPLE, Wayne Calhoun, AB, AM, PhD; historian, archivist and writer; b. 5 Feb. 1924, Richwood, OH, USA; m. Sunderine Wilson Mohn 1979; two step-s. *Education:* University of Illinois, Champaign-Urbana. *Career:* Ed.-in-Chief, 1958–73, Editorial Board, 1973–, Lincoln Herald; Historical Consultant to sculptor Rebecca Childers Caleel; Board of Advisers, The Lincoln Forum; mem. Abraham Lincoln Asscn, Nat. Abraham Lincoln Bicentennial Comm.'s Advisory Cttee. *Publications:* Indian Villages of the Illinois Country, 1958–; Campaigning with Grant, 1961; Stephen A Douglas: Freemason, 1982; The Building of Lincoln's Home and its Saga, 1984; Lincoln's Connections With the Illinois and Michigan Canal, 1986; Illinois' Fifth Capitol (with Sunderine Temple), 1988; Abraham Lincoln: From Skeptic to Prophet, 1995; Alexander Williamson: Friend of the Lincolns, 1997; By Square and Compass: Saga of the Lincoln Home, 2002; 'The Taste Is In My Mouth a Little...': Lincoln's Victuals and Potables 2004; contrib. to numerous journals, including the Lincoln Herald. *Honours:* Lincoln Diploma of Honor; Lincoln Medallion, National Sesquicentennial Commission; Archbishop Richard Chenevix Trench Award, 1999; Lifetime Achievement Award, Lincoln Memorial University, 2001. *Address:* 1121 S Fourth Street Court, Springfield, IL 62703, USA.

TEMPLETON, Edith; British writer; b. 7 April 1916, Prague; m. 1st W. S. Templeton 1938 (divorced); m. 2nd Edmund Ronald 1956 (died 1984); one s. *Education:* Lycée in Paris and Prague Medical Univ. *Career:* mem. staff, Office of Chief Surgeon, US War Office 1942–45; Conf. and Law-Court Interpreter for British Forces with rank of Capt., Germany 1945–46. *Publications:* Summer in the Country 1950, Living on Yesterday 1951, The Island of Desire 1952, Surprise of Cremona (Book Soc. Choice) 1954, This Charming Pastime 1955, Gordon 1966, Murder in Estoril 1992, The Darts of Cupid (short stories) 2002; contrib. short stories to The New Yorker 1956–91, Holiday, Atlantic Monthly, Vogue and Harper's Magazine. *Address:* 76 corso Europa, 18012 Bordighera, Italy. *Telephone:* (0184) 261858.

TEMPLETON, Fiona; Theatre Dir, Poet and Writer; b. 23 Dec. 1951, Scotland. *Education:* MA, University of Edinburgh, 1973; MA, New York University, 1985. *Career:* mem. New Dramatists; Poets and Writers. *Publications:* Elements of Performance Art, 1976; London, 1984; You the City, 1990; Delirium of Interpretations, 1997; Oops the Join, 1997; Cells of Release, 1997; Hi Cowboy, 1997. Contributions: anthologies and journals. *Honours:* Grants, fellowships and awards. *Address:* 100 St Mark's Pl., No. 7, New York, NY 10009, USA.

TEN BERGE, Hans (Cornelis); Poet, Writer and Ed.; b. 24 Dec. 1938, Netherlands. *Career:* Lecturer, Art Acad., Arnhem; Writer-in-Residence, University of Texas, USA, University College London, England, University of Gronigen, Netherlands; Ed., Raster, Grid, literary journals; mem. PEN;

Society of Dutch Literature. *Publications:* Poetry: Gedichten, 3 vols 1969, White Shaman 1973, Poetry of the Aztecs 1972, Va-banque 1977, Semblance of Reality 1981, Texas Elegies 1983, Songs of Anxiety and Despair 1988, Materia Prima, Poems 1963–93, Oesters & gestoofde pot (Oysters and Pot Roast) 2001. Fiction: Zelfportret met witte muts 1985, Het geheim van een oppewekt humeur 1986, The Home Loving Traveller 1995, Women, Jealousy and Other Discomforts 1996, De Jaren in Zeedorp (The Sea-Town Years) 1998, Blauwbaards Ontwaken (Bluebeard's Awakening, novel) 2003. Other: The Defence of Poetry, essays, 1988; Prose books; Books of myths and fables of Arctic peoples; numerous poetry trans. Contributions: periodicals. *Honours:* Van der Hoogt Prize 1968, Prose Prize, City of Amsterdam 1971, Multatuli Prize 1987, Constantijn Huÿgens Prize 1996, A. Roland Holst Prize for Poetry 2003. *Address:* c/o Meulenhoff Publishers, PO Box 100, 1000 AC Amsterdam, Netherlands.

TENNANT, Emma Christina, FRSL; writer; b. 20 Oct. 1937, England; one s. two d. *Education:* St Paul's Girls' School. *Career:* Founder-Ed., Bananas, 1975–78; General Ed., In Verse, 1982–; General Ed., Lives of Modern Women, 1985–. *Publications:* The Colour of Rain (as Catherine Aydy), 1963; The Time of the Crack, 1973; The Last of the Country House Murders, 1975; Hotel de Dream, 1976; Bananas Anthology (ed.), 1977; Saturday Night Reader (ed.), 1978; The Bad Sister, 1978; Wild Nights, 1979; Alice Fell, 1980; The Boggart (with M. Rayner), 1981; The Search for Treasure Island, 1981; Queen of Stones, 1982; Woman Beware Woman, 1983; The Ghost Child, 1984; Black Marina, 1985; The Adventures of Robina by Herself (ed.), 1986; Cycle of the Sun: The House of Hospitalities, 1987; A Wedding of Cousins, 1988; The Magic Drum, 1989; Two Women of London, 1989; Faustine, 1992; Tess, 1993; Pemberley, 1993; An Unequal Marriage, 1994; Emma in Love, 1996; Strangers: A Family Romance, 1998; Girlitude, 1999; Burnt Diaries, 1999; Sylvia and Ted, 2001; A House in Corfu, 2001; Felony, 2002; Corfu Banquet, 2003. *Honours:* Hon. DLitt, University of Aberdeen, 1996. *Literary Agent:* Rogers, Coleridge & White Ltd, 20 Powis Mews, London, W11 1JN, England.

TERKEL, Studs, (Louis Terkel); Author and Broadcaster; b. 16 May 1912, New York, NY, USA; m. Ida Goldberg, 2 July 1939, one s. *Education:* PhB, 1932, JD, 1934, University of Chicago. *Career:* Actor in stage productions; Host, Studs Terkel Almanac radio interview programme, Chicago, 1952–97. *Publications:* Giants of Jazz, 1957; Division Street: America, 1967; Hard Times: An Oral History of the Great Depression, 1970; Working: People Talk About What They Do All Day and How They Feel About What They Do, 1974; Talking to Myself: A Memoir of My Times, 1977; American Dreams: Lost and Found, 1980; 'The Good War': An Oral History of World War II, 1984; Envelopes of Oral Sound: The Art of Oral Recording (with others), 1985; The Neon Wilderness (with Nelson Algren), 1986; Chicago, 1986; The Great Divide: Second Thoughts on the American Dream, 1988; RACE: How Blacks and Whites Think and Feel About the American Obsession, 1992; Coming of Age, 1995; Will the Circle be Unbroken?: Reflections on Death, Rebirth and Hunger for Faith, 2001. Contributions: newspapers and magazines. *Honours:* Ohio State University Award, 1959; UNESCO Prix Italia Award, 1962; University of Chicago Alumni Asscn Communicator of the Year Award, 1969; George Foster Peabody Award, 1980; Society of Midland Authors Awards, 1982, 1983; Eugene V. Debs Award, 1983; Pulitzer Prize in Non-Fiction, 1985; Hugh M. Hefner First Amendment Award for Lifetime Achievement, 1990; National Medal of Arts, 1997. *Address:* 850 W Castlewood Terrace, Chicago, IL 60640, USA.

TERRILL, Ross, BA, PhD; American writer; b. Melbourne, Vic., Australia. *Education:* Wesley College, University of Melbourne, Harvard University. *Career:* Teaching Fellow, 1968–70, Lecturer, 1970–74, Research Assoc., East Asian Studies, 1970–, Harvard University; Contributing Ed., Atlantic Monthly, 1970–84; Research Fellow, Asia Society, 1978–79. *Publications:* 800,000,000: The Real China, 1972; R. H. Tawney and His Times, 1973; Flowers on an Iron Tree: Five Cities of China, 1975; The Future of China After Mao, 1978; Mao, 1980; The White Boned Demon, 1984; The Australians, 1987; China in Our Time, 1992; Madam Mao, 1999; The Australians: How We Live Now, 2000; The New Chinese Empire, 2003. Contributions: newspapers and magazines. *Honours:* Frank Knox Memorial Fellowship, 1965; Sumner Prize, 1970; George Polk Memorial Award, 1972; National Magazine Award, 1972. *Address:* 87 Gainsborough Street, Apartment 7, Boston, MA 02115, USA. *E-mail:* terr@compuserve.com.

THACKARA, James; Author; b. 7 Dec. 1944, Los Angeles, CA, USA; m. Davina Laura Anne, 7 July 1975, one d. *Education:* BA, Harvard University, 1967. *Publications:* America's Children, 1984; Ahab's Daughter, 1988; The Book of Kings, 1999. Other: Shogun (screenplay), 1969. *Address:* c/o The Overlook Press, Lewis Hollow Rd, Woodstock, NY 12498, USA.

THALER, M. N. (see Kerner, Fred).

THAMES, C. H. (see Marlowe, Stephen).

THAMEZ, Lorraine D.; Writer and Poet; b. 26 Nov. 1950, Pueblo, CO, USA; two s. one d. *Education:* AA, Literature, 1997. *Career:* Poetry Ed., Purgatoire Magazine; mem. PEN; Poets and Writers; Western Writers' Guild. *Publications:* Prairie Woman: Dangerous Games; Together Forever; One Heart; One Hand (poems). Contributions: periodicals. *Address:* 121 Chanlon Rd, New Providence, NJ 07974, USA.

THAYER, Geraldine (see Daniels, Dorothy).

THELWELL, Norman; Artist, Writer and Cartoonist; b. 3 May 1923, Birkenhead, Cheshire, England; m. 9 April 1949, one s. one d. *Education:* NDA, ADT, Liverpool College of Art, 1947–50. *Career:* Art Teacher, Wolverhampton College of Art, 1950–57. *Publications:* Angels on Horseback, 1957; Thelwell Country, 1959; A Place of Your Own, 1960; Thelwell in Orbit, 1961; A Leg at Each Corner, 1962; The Penguin Thelwell, 1963; Top Dog, 1964; Thelwell's Riding Academy, 1965; Drawing Ponies, 1966; Up the Garden Path, 1967; The Compleat Tangler, 1967; The Thelwell Book of Leisure, 1968; This Desirable Plot, 1970; The Effluent Society, 1971; Penelope, 1972; Three Sheets in the Wind, 1973; Belt Up, 1975; Thelwell Goes West, 1976; Thelwell's Brat Race, 1978; A Plank Bridge by a Pool, 1979; Thelwell's Gymkhana, 1980; Pony Calvalcade, 1981; A Mill Stone Round My Neck, 1982; Some Damn Fool's Signed the Rubens Again, 1983; Magnificat, 1984; Thelwell's Sporting Prints, 1985; Wrestling with a Pencil, 1986; Play It As It Lies, 1987; Penelope Rides Again, 1988; The Cat's Pyjamas, 1992. Contributions: newspapers, journals, and magazines. *Address:* Herons Mead, Timsbury, Romsey, Hampshire SO51 0NE, England.

THÉORET, France; Author, Dramatist and Poet; b. 1942, Montréal, QC, Canada. *Education:* BA, 1968, MA, 1977, University of Montréal; PhD, Études françaises, University of Sherbrooke, 1982. *Publications:* Bloody Mary, 1977, English trans., 1991; Une voix pour Odile, 1978, English trans., 1991; Vertiges, 1979, English trans., 1991; Nécessairement putain, 1980, English trans., 1991; Nous parlerons comme on écrit, 1982; Intérieurs, 1984; Entre raison et déraison, 1987; L'homme qui peignait Staline, 1989, English trans. as The Man Who Painted Stalin, 1991; Étrangeté, l'étreinte, 1992; La fiction de l'ange, 1992; Journal pour mémoire, 1993; Laurence, 1996. Contributions: anthologies and other publications. *Address:* c/o Union des écrivaines et des écrivains québécois, La Maison des écrivains, 3492 Ave Laval, Montréal, QC H2X 3C8, Canada.

THEROUX, Paul Edward, BA, FRSL; American Writer; b. 10 April 1941, Medford, MA; m. 1st Anne Castle 1967 (divorced 1993); two s.; m. 2nd Sheila Donnelly 1995. *Education:* University of Massachusetts. *Career:* Lecturer, University of Urbino, Italy, 1963, Soche Hill College, Malawi, 1963–65; Faculty, Dept of English, Makerere University, Uganda, 1965–68, University of Singapore, 1968–71; Visiting Lecturer, University of Virginia, 1972–73; mem. RGS, American Acad. of Arts and Letters. *Publications:* Fiction: Waldo, 1967; Fong and the Indians, 1968; Girls at Play, 1969; Murder in Mount Holly, 1969; Jungle Lovers, 1971; Sinning with Annie, 1972; Saint Jack, 1973; The Black House, 1974; The Family Arsenal, 1976; The Consul's File, 1977; Picture Palace, 1978; A Christmas Card, 1978; London Snow, 1980; World's End, 1980; The Mosquito Coast, 1981; The London Embassy, 1982; Half Moon Street, 1984; O-Zone, 1986; My Secret History, 1988; Chicago Loop, 1990; Millroy the Magician, 1993; My Other Life, 1996; Kowloon Tong, 1997; Collected Stories, 1997; Hotel Honolulu, 2001; The Stranger at the Palazzo d'Oro (short stories) 2002. Non-Fiction: V. S. Naipaul, 1973; The Great Patagonian Express, 1979; The Kingdom by the Sea, 1983; Sailing Through China, 1983; Sunrise with Sea Monsters, 1985; The White Man's Burden, 1987; Riding the Iron Rooster, 1988; The Happy Isles of Oceania, 1992; The Pillars of Hercules, 1995; Sir Vidia's Shadow: A Friendship Across Five Continents, 1998; Fresh-air Fiend, 2000; The Worst Journey in the World, 2000; Nurse Wolf and Dr Sacks, 2000; Dark Star Safari, 2002. *Honours:* Editorial Awards, Playboy magazine, 1972, 1976, 1977, 1979; Whitbread Award, 1978; James Tait Black Memorial Prize, 1982; Yorkshire Post Best Novel Award, 1982; Thomas Cook Travel Prize, 1989; Hon. doctorates. *Literary Agent:* Hamish Hamilton Ltd, 80 Strand, London, WC2, England.

THESEN, Sharon; Poet and Writer; b. 1 Oct. 1946, Tisdale, Saskatchewan, Canada. *Education:* BA, 1970, MA, 1974, Simon Fraser University. *Career:* Teacher, Capilano College, Vancouver, 1976–92; Poetry Ed., Capilano Review, 1978–89. *Publications:* Artemis Hates Romance, 1980; Radio New France Radio, 1981; Holding the Pose, 1983; Confabulations: Poems for Malcolm Lowry, 1984; The Beginning of the Long Dash, 1987; The Pangs of Sunday, 1990; The New Long Poems Anthology (ed.), 1991; Aurora, 1995; A Pair of Scissors, 2000. Contributions: various publications. *Address:* c/o League of Canadian Poets, 54 Wolseley St, Third Floor, Toronto, Ontario M5T 1A5, Canada.

THIBAUDEAU, Colleen; Poet and Writer; b. 29 Dec. 1925, Toronto, Ontario, Canada; m. James C. Reaney, 29 Dec. 1951, two s. one d. *Education:* St Thomas Collegiate Institute, 1944; BA, 1948, MA, 1949, University College, University of Toronto; Diploma, l'Université Catholique de l'ouest, Angers, 1951. *Career:* mem. League of Canadian Poets, hon. mem., 1997–; New Democratic Party, life mem. *Publications:* Poetry: Ten Letters, 1975; My Granddaughters Are Combing Out Their Long Hair, 1977; The Martha Landscapes, 1984; The Artemesia Book: Poems Selected and New, 1991; The Patricia Album and Other Poems, 1992. Contributions: poems and stories in various anthologies. *Address:* 276 Huron St, London, Ontario N6A 2J9, Canada.

THIELE, Leslie Paul; Prof. of Political Science and Writer; b. 27 Jan. 1959, Canada; m. Susan Wapner, 30 June 1991, two s. *Education:* BA, McGill University, 1982; MA, University of Calgary, 1985; PhD, Princeton University, 1989. *Career:* Asst Prof. of Political Science, Swarthmore College, 1989–91; Asst Prof., 1991–95, Assoc. Prof., 1995–98, Prof. of Political

Science, Affiliated Faculty Mem., College of Natural Resources and the Environment, 1997–, Head, Dept of Political Science, 1997–2002, University of Florida, Gainesville. *Publications:* Friedrich Nietzsche and the Politics of the Soul: A Study of Heroic Individualism, 1990; Timely Meditations: Martin Heidegger and Postmodern Politics, 1995; Thinking Politics: Perspectives in Ancient, Modern, and Postmodern Political Theory, 1997; Environmentalism for a New Millennium: The Challenge of Coevolution, 1999. Contributions: articles and reviews to periodicals including: Political Theory; Journal of Modern History; International Studies in Philosophy; Environmental Ethics; American Political Science Review. *Honours:* Grants, National Endowment for the Humanities, 1990, 1991; Fellow, Social Science and Humanities Research Council of Canada, 1991–93; Fellow, Social Science Research Council and MacArthur Foundation, 1994–96. *Address:* Dept of Political Science, 234 Anderson Hall, University of Florida, Gainesville, FL 32611-7325, USA. *E-mail:* thiele@polisci.ufl.edu.

THIEP, Nguyen Huy; Vietnamese writer; b. 1950, Hanoi. *Publications include:* Crossing the River 2003; contrib. to Today, Sung Huong, Bao Van Nghe, Libération. *Address:* c/o Curbstone Press, 321 Jackson Street, Willimantic, CT 06226-1738, USA. *E-mail:* info@curbstone.org. *Website:* www.curbstone.org.

THINH, (Nguyen) Huu; Vietnamese writer; *Editor-in-Chief, Van Nghue*; b. 15 Feb. 1942, Phu Vinh, Duy Phien, Tam duong, Vinh Phuc. *Education:* Nguyen Du Inst., Cultural Coll. *Career:* fmr soldier, served in the 202nd Regiment as tank driver, squad leader and journalist 1963–75; Head, Poetry Council, Ed.-in-Chief, Van Nghe Quan Doi 1982–90; Ed.-in-Chief, Van Nghue 1990–; mem. Viet Nam Writers' Asscn (bd of dirs, exec. cttee); Deputy Gen. Sec., Viet Nam Writers' Asscn. *Publications include:* poetry: Duong toi thanh pho (trans. as On the Way to the City), Tu chien hao toi thanh pho (trans. as From the Trench to the City), Troung ca bien (trans. as Song of the Sea), The Time Tree: Selected Poems 2003; juvenile: Khi be Hoa ra doi (trans. as When Little Hoa was Born); contrib. to Am vang chien hao (anthology, Echo from the Trench). *Honours:* Van Nghe Prizes 1973, 1976, Viet Nam Writers' Asscn Poetry Awards 1980, 1995. *Address:* c/o Curbstone Press, 321 Jackson Street, Willimantic, CT 06226-1738, USA. *E-mail:* info@curbstone.org. *Website:* www.curbstone.org.

THISELTON, Anthony Charles; Theologian and Prof. of Theology; b. 13 July 1937, Woking, Surrey, England; m. Rosemary Stella Harman 21 Sept. 1963; two s. one d. *Education:* BD, Univ. of London, 1959; MTh, 1964; PhD, Univ. of Sheffield, 1977; DD, Univ. of Durham, 1993; DD, Archbishop of Canterbury at Lambeth, 2002. *Career:* Curate, Holy Trinity Church, Sydenham, 1960–63; Lecturer and Tutor, Tyndale Hall, Bristol and Univ. of Bristol, 1964–70; Lecturer Biblical Studies, Univ. of Sheffield, 1970–79; Senior Lecturer, 1979–85; Principal, St John's Coll., Nottingham, 1985–88; Principal, St John's College, Durham, 1988–92; Prof. of Christian Theology and Head of Dept of Theology, 1992–2001, Emeritus Prof. of Christian Theology, 2001–, Univ. of Nottingham; Canon Theologian of Leicester Cathedral, 1993–, and of Southwell, 2000–; Visiting Research Prof. in Christian Theology, Chester University Coll., 2003–; mem. Society for the Study of Theology, pres., 1999, 2000; Crown Appointments Commission, 2001–. *Publications:* The Two Horizons, 1980; The Responsibility of Hermeneutics (with R. Lundin and C. Walhout), 1985; New Horizons in Hermeneutics, 1992; Interpreting God and the Post-Modern Self, 1995; The Promise of Hermeneutics (with R. Lundin and C. Walhout), 1999; I Corinthians: A Commentary on the Greek Text, 2000; A Concise Encyclopedia of the Philosophy of Religion, 2002. Contributions: Journal of Theological Studies; New Testament Studies; Biblical Interpretation; Scottish Journal of Theology; Approximately 80 research articles. *Honours:* British Acad. Research Award, 1995–96; American Library Asscn Choice of Theology Books, 1995. *Address:* Dept of Theology, University of Nottingham, University Park, Nottingham NG7 2RD, England. *E-mail:* anthony.thiselton@ntlworld.com.

THOM, James Alexander; Novelist; b. 28 May 1933, Gosport, IN, USA; m. Dark Rain, 20 May 1990. *Education:* AB, Butler University, Indianapolis, 1961. *Career:* Reporter and Columnist, The Indianapolis Star, 1961–67; Lecturer in Journalism, Indiana University, 1978–80; mem. Authors' Guild. *Publications:* Spectator Sport, 1978; Long Knife, 1979; Follow the River, 1981; From Sea to Shining Sea, 1984; Staying Out of Hell, 1985; Panther in the Sky, 1989; The Children of First Man, 1994; The Spirit of the Place, 1995; Indiana II, 1996; The Red Heart, 1997; Sign-Talker, 2000; Warrior Women (with Dark Rain), 2003. Contributions: magazines. *Honours:* Hon. DHL, Butler University, 1995. *Literary Agent:* Mitch Douglas, International Creative Management, 40 W 57th St, New York, NY 10019, USA. *Address:* 10061 W Stogsdill Rd, Bloomington, IN 47404, USA.

THOMAS, Audrey (Grace); Author and Dramatist; b. 17 Nov. 1935, Binghamton, New York, USA; m. Ian Thomas, divorced, three d. *Education:* BA, Smith College, 1957; MA, University of British Columbia, 1963. *Career:* various visiting lectureships and writer-in-residencies; Visiting Prof., Concordia University, 1989–90, Dartmouth College, 1994; mem. Amnesty International; PEN; Writers' Guild of Canada; Writers Union of Canada. *Publications:* Ten Green Bottles, 1967; Mrs Blood, 1970; Munchmeyer, and Prospero on the Island (2 short novels), 1972; Songs My Mother Taught Me, 1973; Blown Figures, 1975; Ladies and Escorts, 1977; Latakia, 1979; Two in the Bush and Other Stories, 1980; Real Mothers, 1981; Intertidal Life, 1984; Goodbye Harold, Good Luck, 1986; The Wild Blue Yonder, 1990; Graven Images, 1993; Coming Down From Wa, 1995; Isobel Gunn, 1999; The Path of Totality, 2001. Other: various plays for the CBC. *Honours:* Canada-Scotland Literary Fellow, 1985–86; British Columbia Book Prizes, 1985, 1991; Canada-Australia Literary Prize, 1990; Hon. doctorates, Simon Fraser University and University of British Columbia, 1994; Hawthornden Fellow, Scotland, 1994. *Address:* RR 2, Galiano, BC V0N 1P0, Canada.

THOMAS, David Arthur; Writer; b. 6 Feb. 1925, Wanstead, England; m. Joyce Irene Petty, 3 April 1948, one d. *Education:* Northampton Polytechnic, 1948–53. *Career:* mem. FRSA. *Publications:* With Ensigns Flying, 1958; Submarine Victory, 1961; Battle of the Java Sea, 1968; Crete 1941: The Battle at Sea, US edn as Nazi Victory, 1972; Japan's War at Sea, 1978; Royal Admirals, 1982; Compton Mackenzie: A Bibliography, 1986; Companion to the Royal Navy, 1988; Illustrated Armada Handbook, 1988; The Atlantic Star, 1990; Christopher Columbus, Master of the Atlantic, 1991; Churchill: The Mem. for Woodford, 1995; Queen Mary and the Cruiser: The Curacoa Disaster, 1997; Battles and Honours of the Royal Navy, 1998; Malta Convoys, 1999; Edwin's Letters, 2000. *Address:* Cedar Lodge, Church Lane, Sheering, Bishop's Stortford, Hertfordshire CM22 7NR, England.

THOMAS, Donald Michael; Poet, Writer and Trans; b. 27 Jan. 1935, Redruth, Cornwall, England; two s. one d. *Education:* BA, English, MA, New College, Oxford. *Career:* Lecturer, Hereford College of Education, 1964–78. *Publications:* Poetry: Penguin Modern Poets 11, 1968; Two Voices, 1968; Logan Stone, 1971; Love and Other Deaths, 1975; The Honeymoon Voyage, 1978; Dreaming in Bronze, 1981; Selected Poems, 1983; Puberty Tree, 1992. Fiction: The Flute Player, 1979; Birthstone, 1980; The White Hotel, 1981; Ararat, 1983; Swallow, 1984; Sphinx, 1986; Summit, 1987; Lying Together, 1990; Flying into Love, 1992; Pictures at an Exhibition, 1993; Eating Pavlova, 1994; Lady with a Laptop, 1996; Alexander Solzhenitsyn, 1998; Charlotte, 2000. Non-Fiction: An Underworld at War: Spivs, Deserters, Racketeers and Civilians in the Second World War, 2003. Translator: Requiem, and Poem Without a Hero, by Akhmatova, 1976; Way of All the Earth, by Akhmatova, 1979; The Bronze Horseman, by Pushkin, 1982. *Address:* The Coach House, Rashleigh Vale, Tregolis Rd, Truro TR1 1TJ, England.

THOMAS, Elizabeth Marshall; Writer; b. 13 Sept. 1931, Boston, Massachusetts, USA; m. Stephen M. Thomas, 14 Jan. 1956, one s. one d. *Education:* AB, Radcliffe College, 1954; MA, George Washington University, 1980. *Career:* mem. PEN; Society of Women Geographers. *Publications:* The Hill People, 1953; The Harmless People, 1959; Warrior Herdsmen, 1966; Reindeer Moon, 1987; The Animal Wife, 1990; The Old Way, 1990; The Hidden Life of Dogs, 1993; The Tribe of Tiger: Cats and Their Culture, 1994; Certain Poor Shepherds, 1996; The Social Lives of Dogs: The Grace of Canine Company, 2000. Contributions: journals. *Honours:* Brandeis University Creative Arts Award, 1968; PEN Hemingway Citation, 1988; Radcliffe College Alumni Recognition Award, 1989; Hon. DLitt, Franklin Pierce College, 1992. *Address:* 80 E Mountain Rd, Peterborough, NH 03458, USA.

THOMAS, F(ranklin) Richard; Prof. of American Thought and Language, Poet and Writer; b. 1 Aug. 1940, Evansville, IN, USA; m. Sharon Kay Myers, 2 June 1962, one s. one d. *Education:* AB, 1963, MA, 1964, Purdue University; PhD, Indiana University, 1970. *Career:* Purdue University, 1969–70; Prof., Michigan State University, 1971–; Ed., Centering magazine, 1973–80; Research Assoc., Indiana University, 1978–79. *Publications:* Poetry: Fat Grass, 1970; Alive with You This Day, 1980; Frog Praises Night: Poems with Commentary, 1980; Heart Climbing Stairs, 1986; Corolla, Stamen, and Style, 1986; The Whole Mustery of the Bregn, 1990; Miracles, 1996; Death at Camp Pahoka, 2000. Novel: Prism: The Journal of John Fish, 1992. Criticism: Literary Admirers of Alfred Stieglitz, 1983. Editor: various books including: The Landlocked Heart: Poems from Indiana, 1980; Americans in Denmark: Comparisons of the Two Cultures by Writers, Artists and Teachers, 1990. Contributions: numerous journals and magazines. *Honours:* Fulbright Awards, 1974, 1985; MacDowell Colony Fellowship, 1979; Michigan Council for the Arts Award, 1990; National Writing Project Summer Institute Fellow, 1993.

THOMAS, Lee (see Floren, Lee).

THOMAS, Richard; British composer and writer; b. 1965. *Education:* Univ. of Cambridge. *Career:* mem. of musical and comic duo Miles & Milner 1987–93; co-founder, mem. Club Zarathustra 1993–98; co-founder, Kombat Opera 1996. *Compositions:* Jerry Springer: The Opera (music and lyrics, with Stewart Lee) (Evening Standard Theatre Award for Best New Musical 2004) 2001. *Radio:* performer: The Miles & Milner Show (BBC Radio 4) 1991, Rainer Hersch's All Classical Music Explained (BBC Radio 4) 1998. *Television:* performer: Beethoven's Not Dead (Spitting Image/BBC2) 1992, This Morning With Richard Not Judy (BBC2) 1998–99, Either/Or (PlayUK) 1999, Attention Scum (BBC Choice/BBC2) 2001; Musical Dir, The Frank Skinner Show (Avalon TV/BBC1, later ITV) 1995–2001, This Morning With Richard Not Judy (BBC2) 1998–99, Baddiel & Skinner Unplanned (Avalon TV/ITV) 2000–03. *Publications:* Jerry Springer: The Book of the Opera 2003. *Address:* c/o Avalon, 4a Exmoor Street, London, W10 6BD, England.

THOMAS, Rosie, (Janey King), BA; novelist; b. 22 Oct. 1947, Denbigh, Wales; m. Caradoc King 1975; one s. one d. *Education:* St Hilda's College, Oxford. *Publications:* Love's Choice, 1982; Celebration, 1982; Follies, 1983; Sunrise, 1984; The White Dove, 1985; Strangers, 1986; Bad Girls, Good Women, 1988; A Woman of Our Times, 1990; All My Sins Remembered, 1991; Other People's Marriages, 1993; A Simple Life, 1996; The Potter's House, 2002; Sun at Midnight 2004. *Honours:* Romantic Novel of the Year Award, Romantic Novelists Asscn, 1985. *Literary Agent:* AP Watt Ltd, 20 John Street, London, WC1N 2DR, England.

THOMAS, Victoria (see De Weese, Thomas Eugene (Gene)).

THOMEY, Tedd; Journalist and Author; b. 19 July 1920, Butte, Montana, USA; m. Patricia Natalie Bennett, 11 Dec. 1943, one d. *Education:* BA, University of California, 1943. *Career:* Publicity Dir, San Diego State College, 1941–42; Reporter, San Diego Union-Tribune, 1942; Reporter, Asst Editorial Promotion Man., San Francisco Chronicle, 1942–43, 1945–48; News Ed., Columnist, Long Beach Press Telegram, 1950–; Creative Writing Instructor, Long Beach City College; Guest Lecturer, University of Southern California; Consultant, 20th Century Fox Studios. *Publications:* And Dream of Evil, 1954; Jet Pilot, 1955; Killer in White, 1956; Jet Ace, 1958; I Want Out, 1959; Flight to Takla-Ma, 1961; The Loves of Errol Flynn, 1961; The Sadist, 1961; Doris Day (biog.), 1962; All the Way, 1964; Hollywood Uncensored, 1965; Hollywood Confidential, 1967; The Comedians, 1970; The Glorious Decade, 1971; The Big Love (co-author), 1986; The Prodigy Plot, 1987. Plays: The Big Love (co-author), 1991; Immortal Images, 1996. Contributions: many magazines. *Honours:* Award, Best Front Page, California Newspaper Publishers. *Address:* 7228 Rosebay St, Long Beach, CA 90808, USA.

THOMPSON, Ernest Victor; Author; b. 14 July 1931, London, England; m. Celia Carole Burton, 11 Sept. 1972, two s. *Career:* mem. West Country Writers Club, vice-pres.; Mevagissey Male Choir, vice-patron; RSL; Cornish Literary Guild, pres., 1998. *Publications:* Chase the Wind 1977, Harvest of the Sun 1978, The Music Makers 1979, Ben Retallick 1980, The Dream Traders 1981, Singing Spears 1982, The Restless Sea 1983, Cry Once Alone 1984, Polrudden 1985, The Stricken Land 1986, Becky 1988, God's Highlander 1988, Lottie Trago 1989, Cassie 1990, Wychwood 1991, Blue Dress Girl 1992, Mistress of Polrudden 1993, The Tolpuddle Woman 1994, Ruddlemoor 1995, Moontide 1996, Cast no Shadows 1997, Mud Huts and Missionaries 1997, Fires of Evening 1998, Somewhere a Bird is Singing 1999, Here, There and Yesterday 1999, Winds of Fortune 2000, Seek a New Dawn 2001, The Lost Years 2002, Paths of Destiny 2003. Other: various books on Cornish and West Country subjects. Contributions: Approximately 200 short stories to magazines. *Honours:* Best Historical Novel, 1976. *Address:* Parc Franton, Pentewan, St Austell, Cornwall, England. *E-mail:* thompsonev@hotmail.com.

THOMPSON, Hunter S.; American writer and journalist; b. 18 July 1937, Louisville, KY, USA; m. Sandra Dawn Conklin (divorced); one s. *Career:* US Air Force, working as sports ed. for the base paper 1956–57; various writing jobs, including in South America, and National Affairs Correspondent, Rolling Stone magazine; invented 'gonzo' journalism, a highly subjective style of writing. *Publications:* Hell's Angels 1967, Fear and Loathing in Las Vegas (originally published in Rolling Stone) 1971, Fear and Loathing on the Campaign Trail '72 (originally published in Rolling Stone) 1973, The Great Shark Hunt: Gonzo Papers vol. 1 1979, The Curse of Lono 1983, Generation of Swine: Gonzo Papers vol. 2 1988, Songs of the Doomed: Gonzo Papers vol. 3 1990, Screwjack (short stories) 1991, Better Than Sex: Gonzo Papers vol. 4 1994, The Proud Highway 1957–1967 1997, Mistah Leary, He Dead 1997, The Rum Diary 1998, Fear and Loathing in America 2000, Kingdom of Fear: Loathsome Secrets of a Star-crossed Child in the Final Days of the American Century 2002; contrib. to numerous magazines and newspapers, including Rolling Stone, Rogue, Esquire. *Literary Agent:* The Wylie Agency, 250 W 57th Street, Suite 2114, New York, NY 10107, USA. *Address:* Owl Farm, Woody Creek, CO 81656, USA.

THOMPSON, Jean (Louise); Prof. of English and Writer; b. 1 Jan. 1950, Chicago, IL, USA. *Education:* AB, English, University of Illinois, 1971; MFA, Creative Writing, Bowling Green State University, 1973. *Career:* Prof. of English, University of Illinois, Urbana, 1973–; Teacher, Warren Wilson College MFA Program, 1988, 1989, 1990; Distinguished Visiting Writer, Wichita State University, 1991; Assoc. Prof., San Francisco State University, 1992–93. *Publications:* The Gasoline Wars, 1979; My Wisdom, 1982; Little Faces and Other Stories, 1984; The Woman Driver, 1985; Who Do You Love?, 1999; Wide Blue Yonder, 2002. Contributions: various anthologies, journals, and magazines. *Honours:* Illinois Arts Council Literary Awards, 1976, 1996; National Endowment for the Arts Fellowship, 1977; Guggenheim Fellowship, 1984; Pushcart Prize, 1995. *Address:* 203 Smith Rd, Urbana, IL 61802, USA.

THOMPSON, Judith Clare Francesca, BA; dramatist, screenwriter and academic; b. 20 Sept. 1954, Montréal, QC, Canada; m. Gregor Duncan 1983; one s. three d. *Education:* Queen's University, National Theatre School. *Career:* many workshops and seminars; Assoc. Prof. of Drama, University of Guelph. *Publications:* The Crackwalker, 1980; White Biting Dog, 1984; Pink, 1986; Tornado, 1987; I am Yours, 1987; The Other Side of the Dark, 1989; Lion in the Streets, 1992; Sled, 1997. Contributions: Films, radio and television. *Honours:* Gov.-Gen.'s Awards for Drama, 1984, 1989; Chalmers Awards, 1987, 1991; Toronto Arts Award, 1988; Nellie Award for Best Radio Drama, 1988. *Literary Agent:* Great North Artists Management Inc, 350 Dupont Street, Toronto, ON M5R 1V9, Canada.

THOMPSON, Samuel Richard Charles, BA, MA, PGCE; British teacher, poet and writer; b. 9 Feb. 1968, London, England; pnr; one d. *Education:* Univ. of Manchester, Charlotte Mason Coll. of Education, Univ. of Lancaster. *Career:* Head of English, Fyling Hall School N Yorkshire 1993–95; Head of English and Drama, Int. School at Sotogrande, Spain 1997–99; teacher of English and drama, Head of Year, The Grammar School, Guernsey 1999–; Ed., Muse magazine 1989, Que Me Cuentas 1997–99; Publishing Dir, Saumarez Press 2002–; mem. Manchester Univ. Poetry Soc. (chair. 1990). *Poetry performances:* Ambleside 1991, Ulverstone 1992, Manchester 1996, Guernsey 2001, 2002. *Radio broadcasts of poetry:* Radio Guernsey 2002. *Publications:* poetry: What Am I Doing Here 1996, Where Home Was (also CD, with guitar accompaniment by Martin Spoelstra) 2002; contrib. to anthologies, including Crossing the Bridge 2003, to journals, including Envoi, Fylingtales, Grammalogue, Guernsey Press, Hrafnhoh, La Vista, Lynx, Ore, Canoe Focus. *Honours:* Univ. of Manchester Thomas de Quincy Prize 1989. *Address:* The Grammar School, Les Varendes, St Andrew's, Guernsey, GY6 8TD, Channel Islands. *Telephone:* (1481) 256571 (Office); (1481) 252061 (Home). *Fax:* (1481) 251236 (Office). *E-mail:* samthompson@cwgsy.net.

THOMSON, Derick S(mith), (Ruaraidh MacThòmais); Prof. of Celtic (retd), Poet and Writer; b. 5 Aug. 1921, Stornoway, Isle of Lewis, Scotland; m. Carol Galbraith, 1952, five s., one d. *Education:* MA, University of Aberdeen, 1947; BA, Emmanuel College, Cambridge, 1948. *Career:* Asst in Celtic, University of Edinburgh, 1948–49; Lecturer in Welsh, 1949–56, Prof. of Celtic, 1963–91, University of Glasgow; Ed., Gairm Gaelic Literary Quarterly, 1952–2002; Reader in Celtic, University of Aberdeen, 1956–63; mem. British Acad., fellow; Glasgow Arts Club; Scottish Gaelic Texts Society, hon. pres.; Royal Society of Edinburgh, fellow; Saltire Society, hon. pres., 1997; Scottish Poetry Library, hon. pres., 1999. *Publications:* An Dealbh Briste, 1951; The Gaelic Sources of Macpherson's 'Ossian', 1952; Eadar Samhradh is Foghar, 1967; An Rathad Cian, 1970; The Far Road and Other Poems, 1971; An Introduction to Gaelic Poetry, 1974; Saorsa agus an Iolaire, 1977; Creachadh na Clarsaich, 1982; The Companion to Gaelic Scotland, 1983; European Poetry in Gaelic Translation, 1990; Smeur an Dochais, 1992; Gaelic Poetry in the Eighteenth Century, 1993; Meall Garbh/The Rugged Mountain, 1995; Mac Mhaighstir Alasdair, Selected Poems, 1996. Contributions: books, journals and magazines. *Honours:* Publication Awards, Scottish Arts Council, 1971, 1992; Ossian Prize, FVS Foundation, Hamburg, 1974; Saltire Scottish Book of the Year Award, 1983; Hon. DLitt, University of Wales, 1987, University of Aberdeen, 1994. *Address:* 15 Struan Rd, Cathcart, Glasgow G44 3AT, Scotland.

THOMSON, Edward (see Tubb, Edwin Charles).

THOMSON, June Valerie, BA; writer; b. 24 June 1930, Kent, England; m. (divorced); two s. *Education:* Bedford Coll., London. *Career:* mem. CWA (cttee mem.), Detection Club. *Publications:* Not One of Us, 1972; Deadly Relations, 1979; Sound Evidence, 1984; No Flowers By Request, 1987; The Spoils of Time, 1989; The Secret Files of Sherlock Holmes, 1990; The Secret Chronicles of Sherlock Holmes, 1992; Flowers for the Dead, 1992; The Secret Journals of Sherlock Holmes, 1993; A Study in Friendship, 1995; Burden of Innocence, 1996; The Secret Documents of Sherlock Holmes, 1997; The Unquiet Grave, 2000. Contributions: several short stories to anthologies, including Ellery Queen Magazine, Winter's Crimes and CWA Anthology. *Honours:* Le Prix du Roman d'Aventures, 1983; Special Sherlock Award, 2000. *Address:* 177 Verulam Road, St Albans, Hertfordshire AL3 4DW, England.

THOMSON, Robert; Australian journalist; *Editor, The Times*; b. 11 March 1961, Torrumbarry, Australia; m. Ping Wang; two s. *Career:* financial and gen. affairs reporter, then Sydney Corresp. The Herald, Melbourne 1979–83; sr feature writer Sydney Morning Herald 1983–85; corresp. for the Financial Times, Beijing 1985–89, Tokyo 1989–94, Foreign News Ed., London 1994–96, Asst Ed. Financial Times and Ed. Weekend FT 1996–98, US Man. Ed. Financial Times 1998–2002; Ed. The Times March 2002–; mem. Knight-Bagehot Fellowship Board, Columbia Univ.; mem. Arts Int. (chair. 2001–02). *Television:* regular appearances on ABC News, CNN, Fox News Channel. *Publications:* The Judges – A Portrait of the Australian Judiciary, The Chinese Army, True Fiction (ed.). *Honours:* US Business Journalist of the Year, The Journalist and Financial Reporting Group (TJFR) 2001. *Address:* c/o The Times, 1 Pennington Street, Wapping, London, E98 1TT, England.

THORNE, Nathaniel (see Viens, Louis).

THORNTON, Margaret (see Poole, Margaret Barbara).

THORPE, David Richard; Political Biographer; b. 12 March 1943, Huddersfield, England. *Education:* BA, 1965, MA, 1969, Selwyn College, Cambridge. *Career:* Archive Fellow, Churchill College, Cambridge, 1986; Appointed Official Biographer of Lord Home of the Hirsel, 1990; New Authorized Biographer of Sir Anthony Eden, 1996; Alistair Horne Fellow, St Antony's College, Oxford, 1997–98; Senior Mem., Brasenose College, Oxford, 1998–; mem. Johnson Club; Oxford and Cambridge Club. *Publications:* The Uncrowned Prime Ministers: A Study of Sir Austen Chamberlain, Lord Curzon and Lord Butler, 1980; Selwyn Lloyd, 1989; Alec Douglas-Home, 1996; Eden: The Life and Times of Anthony Eden First Earl of Avon, 1897–1977, 2003. Contributions: The Blackwell Biographical Dictionary of British Political Life in the 20th Century, 1990; The New Dictionary of National Biography, 1998; Telling Lives: From WB Yeats to Bruce Chatwin (edited by Alistair Horne), 2000. *Address:* Brasenose College, Oxford OX1 4AJ, England.

THORPE, Dobbin (see Disch, Thomas Michael).

THORPE, Marie Louise; Writer, Tutor and Teacher; b. 1 Oct. 1949, East London, South Africa; m. James Thorpe. *Education:* BA, Philosophy, University of Natal, 1974. *Career:* Demonstrator, Lecturer, 1973–74; Librarian, 1975; Teacher for the Handicapped, 1980–82; 1995–2001, Organizer, School for Street Children; Tutor, Writing School. *Publications:* Write From the Begining, 1987; From Gladiators to Clowns, 1988; Aesop's Fables Retold, 1988; Lucy's Games, 1992; Limbo Land, 1996. *Address:* 201 Premier Ct, 200 Umbilo Rd, Durban, South Africa.

THORUP, Kirsten; Danish writer; b. 9 Feb. 1942. *Career:* mem. State Foundation for the Arts (literary cttee 1993–), Danish PEN (bd mem. 1995–). *Publications:* I dagens anledning 1968, Love from Trieste (in trans.) 1969, Idag er det Daisy 1971, Baby 1973, Den lange sommer 1979, Himmel og helvede 1982, Romantica: Skuespil 1983, Den yderste grunse 1987, Elskede ukendte 1994, Projekt paradis: En trilogi 1997, Digte 1967–71 2000, Bonsai 2000. *Honours:* Lifetime Grant from Danish Art Foundation ; Critics' Prize 1982, Danish Booksellers' Golden Laurels Award 1983, Danish Acad. Major Prize for Literature 2000. *Address:* c/o Curbstone Press, 321 Jackson Street, Willimantic, CT 06226-1738, USA. *E-mail:* info@curbstone.org. *Website:* www.curbstone.org.

THUBRON, Colin (Gerald Dryden); Writer; b. 14 June 1939, London, England. *Education:* Eton College. *Career:* mem. FRGS; FRSL. *Publications:* Mirror to Damascus, 1967; The Hills of Adonis: A Quest in Lebanon, 1968; Jerusalem, 1969; Journey Into Cyprus, 1975; The God in the Mountain (novel), 1977; Emperor (novel), 1978; Istanbul (with others), 1978; The Venetians (with others), 1980; The Ancient Mariners (with others), 1981; The Royal Opera House, Covent Garden, 1982; Among the Russians, 1983, US edn as Where Nights are Longest: Travels by Car Through Western Russia, 1984; A Cruel Madness (novel), 1984; Behind the Wall: A Journey Through China, 1987; The Silk Road: Beyond the Celestial Kingdom, 1989; Falling, 1989; Turning Back the Sun (novel), 1991; The Lost Heart of Asia, 1994; Distance (novel), 1996; In Siberia, 1999; To the Last City (novel), 2002. Contributions: Times; TLS; Independent; Sunday Times; Sunday Telegraph; New York Times; Television. *Honours:* PEN Silver Pen Award, 1985; Hawthornden Prize, 1988; Thomas Cook Travel Award, 1989; Royal Scottish Geographical Society Mungo Park Medal, 2000; RSAA Lawrence of Arabia Memorial Medal, 2001; Hon. DLitt, University of Warwick, 2002. *Address:* Garden Cottage, 27 St Ann's Villas, London W11 4RT, England.

THWAITE, Ann, MA, DLitt, FRSL; British writer; b. 4 Oct. 1932, London, England; m. Anthony Thwaite 1955; four d. *Education:* Univ. of Oxford. *Career:* Visiting Prof., Tokyo Women's Univ.; Contributing Ed., Editorial Bd, Cricket Magazine (USA); mem. Soc. of Authors, PEN. *Publications:* Waiting for the Party: A Life of Frances Hodgson Burnett, Edmund Gosse: A Literary Landscape, A. A. Milne: His Life, Emily Tennyson: The Poet's Wife, Glimpses of the Wonderful: The Life of Philip Henry Gosse 2002. *Honours:* Duff Cooper Prize 1985, Whitbread Biography Award 1990, Hon. Fellow, Univ. of Surrey 2001. *Address:* The Mill House, Low Tharston, Norwich NR15 2YN, England.

THWAITE, Anthony Simon, OBE, MA, FRSL, FSA, DLitt; British writer and poet; b. 23 June 1930, Chester, Cheshire, England; m. Ann Barbara Thwaite (née Harrop) 1955; four d. *Education:* Kingswood School, Bath, Christ Church, Oxford. *Career:* Visiting Lecturer in English Literature Univ. of Tokyo 1955–57; radio producer BBC 1957–62; Literary Ed. The Listener 1962–65; Asst Prof. of English, Univ. of Libya, Benghazi 1965–67; Literary Ed. New Statesman 1968–72; Co-Ed. Encounter 1973–85; Editorial Dir, Editorial Consultant André Deutsch 1986–95. *Publications:* poetry: Home Truths 1957, The Owl in the Tree 1963, The Stones of Emptiness 1967, Inscriptions 1973, New Confessions 1974, A Portion for Foxes 1977, Victorian Voices 1980, Poems 1953–1983 1984, revised edn as Poems 1953–1988 1989, Letter from Tokyo 1987, The Dust of the World 1994, Selected Poems 1956–1996 1997, A Different Country: New Poems 2000, A Move in the Weather 2003; other: Contemporary English Poetry 1959, The Penguin Book of Japanese Verse (ed. with Geoffrey Bownas) 1964, Japan (with Roloff Beny) 1968, The Deserts of Hesperides 1969, Poetry Today 1973, The English Poets (ed. with Peter Porter) 1974, In Italy (with Roloff Beny and Peter Porter) 1974, New Poetry 4 (ed. with Fleur Adcock) 1978, Twentieth Century English Poetry 1978, Odyssey: Mirror of the Mediterranean (with Roloff Beny) 1981, Larkin at Sixty (ed.) 1982, Poetry 1945 to 1980 (ed. with John Mole) 1983, Six Centuries of Verse 1984, Philip Larkin: Collected Poems (ed.) 1988, Selected Letters of Philip Larkin (ed.) 1992, Philip Larkin: Further Requirements (ed.) 2001. *Honours:* Hon. DLitt (Hull) 1989; Richard Hillary Memorial Prize 1968; Cholmondeley Award 1983. *Address:* The Mill House, Low Tharston, Norfolk NR15 2YN, England. *Telephone:* (1508) 489569. *Fax:* (1508) 489221.

THWAITES, (Stephen) Dane, BA; poet, publisher and bookseller; b. 15 June 1950, Inverell, NSW, Australia; m.; one s. *Education:* University of Nebraska, Armidale. *Publications:* Winter Light 1983, South China 1994; contrib. to various publications. *Honours:* co-winner, Mattara Prize 1987. *Address:* c/o Butterfly Bookshop, Shop 6, Renae's Arcade, Station Street, Wentworth Falls, NSW 2782, Australia.

TIBBER, Robert (see Friedman, (Eve) Rosemary).

TIBBER, Rosemary (see Friedman, (Eve) Rosemary).

TIGHE, Carl; Writer and Dramatist; b. 26 April 1950, Birmingham, England. *Education:* BA, English, 1973, MA, 1974, University College, Swansea; PDESL, University of Leeds, 1989; PhD, University of Manchester, 1994. *Career:* mem. PEN; Welsh Acad.; Welsh Union of Writers; Writers Guild of Great Britain. *Publications:* Little Jack Horner, 1985; Baku!, 1986; Gdańsk: National Identity in the Polish-German Borderlands, 1990; Rejoice! and Other Stories, 1992; The Politics of Literature, 1999. Other: For BBC Radio: Day Out, 1994; Polish Poet, 1995; April Fool, 1996; The Politics of Literature, 1999; Pax: Variations, 2000; Burning Worm, 2001. Contributions: anthologies, journals and radio broadcasts. *Honours:* Welsh Arts Council Literary Bursary, 1983; All London Drama Prize, 1987; British Council Travel Scholarship, Hungary, 1990; City Life Writer of the Year 2000 Award; Authors' Club First Novel Award. *Address:* c/o Simon Trewin, PFD Agency, Drury House, 34–43 Russell St, London WC2B 5HA, England. *Telephone:* (20) 7344-1000. *E-mail:* postmaster@pfd.co.uk.

TILLINGHAST, Richard (Williford); Prof. of English, Poet and Writer; b. 25 Nov. 1940, Memphis, TN, USA; m. 1st Nancy Walton Pringle, 1965, divorced 1970; m. 2nd Mary Graves, 22 April 1973, one s. one d. *Education:* BA, University of the South, 1962; MA, 1963, PhD, 1970, Harvard University. *Career:* Asst Prof. of English, University of California at Berkeley, 1968–73; Visiting Asst Prof., University of the South, 1979–80; Briggs-Copeland Lecturer, Harvard University, 1980–83; Assoc. Prof., 1983–92, Prof. of English, 1992–, University of Michigan at Ann Arbor; Assoc., Michigan Institute for the Humanities, 1989–90, 1993–94. *Publications:* Poetry: Sleep Watch, 1969; The Knife and Other Poems, 1980; Sewanee in Ruins, 1981; Fossils, Metal, and the Blue Limit, 1982; Our Flag Was Still There, 1984; The Stonecutter's Hand, 1994; Today in the Café Trieste, 1997; Six Mile Mountain, 2000. Other: A Quiet Pint in Kinvara, 1991; Robert Lowell's Life and Work: Damaged Grandeur, 1995; A Visit to the Gallery: The University of Michigan Museum of Art (ed.), 1997. Contributions: newspapers, reviews, journals and magazines. *Honours:* National Endowment for the Humanities Grant, 1980; Bread Loaf Fellowship, 1982; Millay Colony Residency, 1985; Yaddo Writers' Retreat Residency, 1986; Amy Lowell Travel Fellowship, 1990–91; British Council Fellowship, 1992, and Travel Grant, 1994; Ann Stanford Prize for Poetry, University of Southern California at Los Angeles, 1992. *Address:* c/o Dept of English, University of Michigan at Ann Arbor, Ann Arbor, MI 48109, USA.

TIMM, Uwe; German writer; b. 1940, Hamburg. *Publications include:* novels: Heisser Sommer 1974, Die Schlangenbaum 1980, Deutsche Kolonien 1981, Der Mann auf dem Hochrad 1984, The Train Mouse 1986, The Snake Tree 1988, Vogel, friss die Feige nicht 1989, Headhunter 1991, Kerbls Flucht 1991, The Invention of Curried Sausage 1993, Midsummer Night 1995, Johannisnacht 1996, Die Bubi Scholz story 1998, Nicht morgen, nicht gestern 1999, Eine hand voll Gras 2000, Rot (trans. as Red) 2001, Morenga 2003, My Brother's Example 2005. *Honours:* Munich Literary Prize 1989. *Address:* Verlag Nagel & Kimche AG, V-Nr. 1320 506, Nordstr. 9, 8035 Zürich, Switzerland. *E-mail:* info@nagel-kimche.ch. *Website:* www.nagel-kimche.ch.

TINDALL, Gillian, MA, FRSL; British writer; b. 4 May 1938, London; m. Richard G. Lansdown 1963; one s. *Education:* Univ. of Oxford. *Career:* novelist, biographer, historian, freelance journalist working on The Independent, The Times and other newspapers and periodicals; JP, Inner London 1980–98; mem. Franco-British Council 1999–. *Publications:* novels: No Name in the Street 1959, The Water and the Sound 1961, The Edge of the Paper 1963, The Youngest 1967, Someone Else 1969, Fly Away Home (Somerset Maugham Award 1972) 1971, The Traveller and His Child 1975, The Intruder 1979, Looking Forward 1983, To The City 1987, Give Them All My Love 1989, Spirit Weddings 1992; Short stories: Dance of Death 1973, The China Egg and Other Stories 1981, Journey of a Lifetime and Other Stories 1990; Non-fiction: A Handbook on Witchcraft 1965, The Born Exile (biog. of George Gissing) 1974, The Fields Beneath 1977, Rosamond Lehmann: An Appreciation 1985, Countries of the Mind: The Meaning of Places to Writers 1990, City of Gold: The Biography of Bombay (2nd edn) 1992, Célestine: Voices from a French Village (Franco-British Soc. Award 1995) 1995, The Journey of Martin Nadaud 1999, The Man Who Drew London (biog. of Wenceslaus Hallar) 2002. *Honours:* Chevalier des Arts et des Lettres 2001; Enid McLeod Prize 1985. *Literary Agent:* Curtis Brown Ltd, 28–29 Haymarket, London, SW1Y 4SP, England.

TIPTON, David John; poet, writer, editor, translator and teacher; b. 28 April 1934, Birmingham, England; m. 1st Ena Hollis 1956; m. 2nd Glenys Tipton 1975; two s. three d. *Education:* Certificate of Education, Saltley College, University of Essex. *Career:* Ed., Rivelin Press 1974–84, Redbeck Press 1984–. *Publications:* Peru: The New Poetry (trans.), 1970–76; Millstone Grit, 1972; At Night the Cats, by Antonio Cisneros (trans.), 1985;

Nomads and Settlers, 1980; Wars of the Roses, 1984; Crossing the Rimac, 1995; Family Chronicle (poems), 1997; Path Through the Canefields (trans. of José Watanabe), 1997; Amulet Against the Evil Eye, 1998; Paradise of Exiles (fiction), 1999; A Mountain Crowned by a Cemetery, by Tulio Mora (trans.), 2001; Nordic Barbarians (fiction), 2002; Medal for Malaya (fiction), 2002; A Sword in the Air (travel), 2003. Contributions: various publications. *Address:* 24 Aireville Road, Frizinghall, Bradford BD9 4HH, England.

TOBIN, Meryl Elaine, (Meryl Brown Tobin); writer and poet; b. 26 Aug. 1940, Melbourne, Vic., Australia; m. Hartley Tobin 1962; two s. one d. *Education:* BA, 1961, DipEd, 1962, University of Melbourne; Diploma of Arts (Professional Writing and Editing), Chisholm Institute of Technical and Further Education, Vic., 2002. *Career:* mem. Australian Society of Authors Ltd; Fellowship of Australian Writers (Victoria) Inc.; Society of Women Writers of Victoria Inc; Victorian Writers Centre; Copyright Agency Ltd. *Publications:* Puzzles Galore, 1978; More Puzzles Galore!, 1980; Carloads of Fun, 1983; Exploring Outback Australia, 1988; Puzzleways: Grammar and Spelling, 1990; Animal Puzzle Parade, 1991; Puzzle Round Australia, 1992; Puzzling Cats, 1994; Pets to Puzzle, 1995; Puzzles Ahoy?, 1995; Play with Words, 1996; Lefty, 2000, Thought in Miniature (poetry collection, co-ed with Dorothea Trafford Lavery) 2003. Other: many short stories, poems, articles and puzzles published. Contributions: numerous publications. *Honours:* 26 awards. *Address:* Ningan, Bass Highway, The Gurdies, Vic., 3984, Australia.

TODD, Janet Margaret, BA, PhD; academic, writer and editor; *Francis Hutcheson Professor of English, University of Glasgow*; b. 10 Sept. 1942, Llandrindod-Wells, Wales; m. 1st Aaron R. Todd 1966 (divorced 1984); one s. one d.; m. 2nd D. W. Hughes 2001. *Education:* Newnham College, Cambridge, University of Leeds, University of Florida. *Career:* Lecturer in African and English Literature, Mfantsipim and University of Cape Coast, Ghana, 1964–67; Asst Prof. of English, University of Puerto Rico, Mayaguez, 1972–74; Asst, Assoc. and full Prof. of English, Rutgers University, 1974–83; Visiting Prof., Jawaharlal Nehru University and University of Rajastan, 1980, University of Southampton, 1982–83; Fellow in English, Sidney Sussex College, Cambridge, 1983–90; Prof. of English, University of East Anglia, 1990–2000; Francis Hutcheson Prof. of English, University of Glasgow, 2000–; mem. Arts and Humanities Research Board, English panel, 1999–2003; British Society for Eighteenth-Century Studies, pres., 2000–02. *Publications:* In Adam's Garden: A Study of John Clare's Pre-Asylum Poetry, 1973; Mary Wollstonecraft: An Annotated Bibliography, 1976; Women's Friendship in Literature, 1980; English Congregational Hymns in the Eighteenth Century: Their Purpose and Design (co-author), 1983; Mary Wollstonecraft (with M. Ferguson), 1984; Sensibility: An Introduction, 1986; Feminist Literary History, 1988; The Sign of Angellica: Woman, Writing and Fiction 1660–1800, 1989; Gender, Art and Death, 1993; The Secret Life of Aphra Behn, 1996; The Critical Fortunes of Aphra Behn, 1998; Mary Wollstonecraft: A Revolutionary Life, 2000; Rebel Daughters: Ireland in Conflict 1798, 2003. Editor: Dictionary of British and American Women Writers 1660–1800, 1985; The Complete Works of Mary Wollstonecraft, seven vols, 1989; A Dicitonary of British Women Writers, 1989; The Complete Works of Aphra Behn, seven vols, 1992–96; Female Education in the Age of Enlightenment, six vols, 1996; Aphra Behn Studies, 1996; The Collected Letters of Mary Wollstonecraft, 2003. Contributions: scholarly books and journals. *Honours:* National Endowment for the Humanities Grant, 1977–79; ACLS Fellowship, 1978–79; Guggenheim Fellowship, 1981–82; Helen Bing Fellowship, Huntingdon Library, 1991; Leverhulme Institutional Grant, 1991–93; Folger Shakespeare Library Fellowship, 1993–94; Bye-Fellowship, Newnham College, Cambridge, 1998; Hon. Fellowship, Lucy Cavendish College, Cambridge, 1999–. *Address:* c/o Department of English, University of Glasgow, Glasgow G12 8QQ, Scotland.

TODD, Olivier; Writer; b. 19 June 1929, Neuilly, France; m. 1st Anne-Marie Nizan, 1948, two s. two d.; m. 2nd France Huser, 1982. *Education:* Sorbonne, University of Paris; Corpus Christi College, Cambridge. *Career:* Reporter, 1964–69, Asst Ed., 1970–77, Nouvel Observateur; Columnist and Man. Ed., L'Express, 1977–81. *Publications:* Une demi-campagne, 1957; La traversée de la manche, 1960; Des trous dans le jardin, 1969; L'année du crabe, 1972; Les canards de Ca Mao, 1975; La marelle de giscard, 1977; Portraits, 1979; Un fils rebelle, 1981; Un cannibale très convenable, 1982; Une légère gueule de bois, 1983; La balade du chômeur, 1986; Cruel Avril, 1987; La négociation, 1989; La sanglière, 1992; Albert Camus: Une vie, 1996; André Malraux: Une vie, 2001. Contributions: newspapers, journals and television. *Honours:* Chevalier, Légion d'honneur; Commdr, Ordre des Arts et des Lettres; Prix Cazes, 1981; Prix France Télévision, 1997; Prix du Mémorial, 1997. *Address:* 21 rue de l'Odeon, 75006 Paris, France.

TOFFLER, Alvin (Eugene); Author; b. 4 Oct. 1928, New York, NY, USA; m. Adelaide Elizabeth (Heidi) Farrell Toffler, 29 April 1950, one d. *Education:* BA, New York University. *Career:* Assoc. Ed., Fortune Magazine, 1959–61; Visiting Scholar, Russell Sage Foundation, 1969–70; mem. American Asscn for the Advancement of Science, fellow; American Society of Journalists and Authors; International Institute for Strategic Studies; World Future Studies Federation. *Publications:* (mostly in collaboration with Heidi Toffler): The Culture Consumers, 1964; The Schoolhouse in the City, 1968; Future Shock, 1970; The Futurists (ed.), 1972; Learning for Tomorrow (ed.), 1973; The Eco-Spasm Report, 1975; The Third Wave, 1980; Previews and Premises, 1983; The Adaptive Corporation, 1984; Power Shift, 1990; War and Anti-War, 1993; Creating a New Civilization, 1994–95. Contributions: newspapers, journals and magazines. *Honours:* Medal, Pres. of Italy; Author of the Year, American Society of Journalists and Authors; Prix de Meilleur Livre Étranger; Officer, Ordre des Arts et des Sciences; Hon. doctorates. *Literary Agent:* Curtis Brown Ltd, 10 Astor Pl., New York, NY 10003, USA.

TOFFLER, Heidi; Author; b. 1 Aug. 1929, New York, NY, USA; m. Alvin Toffler, 29 April 1950, one d. *Education:* BA, Long Island University. *Publications:* (with Alvin Toffler) The Culture Consumers, 1964; Future Shock, 1970; The Futurists (ed.), 1972; Learning for Tomorrow (ed.), 1973; The Third Wave, 1980; Previews and Premises, 1983; The Adaptive Corporation, 1984; Powershift, 1990; War and Anti-War, 1993; Creating a New Civilization, 1994–95. Contributions: newspapers, journals and periodicals. *Honours:* Medal, Pres. of Italy; Hon. doctorates. *Literary Agent:* Curtis Brown Ltd, 10 Astor Pl., New York, NY 10003, USA.

TÓIBÍN, Colm; Irish journalist and writer; b. 1955, Enniscorthy, Co. Wexford. *Education:* Christian Brothers School, Enniscorthy, Univ. Coll., Dublin. *Career:* in Spain 1975–78; features Ed. In Dublin 1981–82; Ed. political and current affairs magazine Magill 1982–85; journalist and columnist Dublin Sunday Independent 1985–. *Play:* Beauty in a Broken Place 2003. *Publications:* fiction: Infidelity (contrib.), The South 1990 (Irish Times First Novel Award 1991), The Heather Blazing 1993 (Encore Award), The Story of the Night 1996, The Blackwater Lightship 1999, Finbar's Hotel (contrib.) 1999, The Master 2004; non-fiction: Seeing is Believing: Moving Statues in Ireland 1985, Walking Along the Border (with T. O'Shea) 1987, Homage to Barcelona 1990, Dubliners 1990, The Trial of the Generals: Selected Journalism 1980–90 1990, Bad Blood 1994, Sign of the Cross 1994, The Kilfenora Teaboy 1997, The Irish Famine 1999, Love in a Dark Time 2001, Lady Gregory's Toothbrush 2002; editor: SOHO Square VI: New Writing from Ireland 1993, Enniscorthy: History & Heritage 1998, Penguin Book of Irish Fiction 1999, The Modern Library 1999, New Writing II 2002; contrib. articles. *Honours:* American Acad. of Arts and Letters E. M. Forster Award 1995, Center for Scholars and Writers Fellowship, New York Public Library, Soc. of Authors Travelling Scholarship 2004. *Address:* 23 Carnew Street, Dublin 7, Ireland. *Website:* www.colmtoibin.com.

TOKARCZUK, Olga; Writer; b. 1962, Sulechow, Poland. *Education:* Psychology, Univ. of Warsaw. *Publications:* Miasta w lustrach (The City in Mirrors), 1989; Podroz ludzi ksiegi (Journey of the People of the Book), 1993; E.E., 1995; Prawiek i inne czasy (Prawiek and Other Times), 1996; Szafa (The Wardrobe), 1997; Dom dzienny, dom nocny (House of Day, House of Night), 1998; Opowiesci wigilijne (Christmas Tales, with Jerzy Pilch and Andrzej Stasiuk), 2000; Lalka i perla (The Doll and the Pearl), 2001; Gra na wielu bebenkach (Playing on a Multitude of Drums, short stories), 2001. *Honours:* Polish Publishers' Asscn prize; Koscielski Prize; two NIKE Readers' Prizes. Contributions: Granta journal. *Address:* c/o Granta, 2–3 Hanover Yard, Noel Rd, London N1 8BE, England.

TOLAND, John (Willard); Historian and Author; b. 29 June 1912, La Crosse, Wisconsin, USA; m. 1st, two d.; m. 2nd Toshiko Matsumura, 12 March 1960, one d. *Education:* BA, Williams College, 1936; Yale Drama School, 1936–37. *Career:* mem. Accademia del Mediterraneo; Authors' Guild; National Archives, advisory council; Western Front Asscn, hon. vice-pres. *Publications:* Non-Fiction: Ships in the Sky, 1957; Battle: The Story of the Bulge, 1959; But Not in Shame, 1961; The Dillinger Days, 1963; The Flying Tigers, 1963; The Last 100 Days, 1966; The Battle of the Bulge, 1966; The Rising Sun, 1970; Adolf Hitler, 1976; Hitler: The Pictorial Documentary of His Life, 1978; No Man's Land, 1980; Infamy, 1982; In Mortal Combat, 1991; Captured by History, 1997. Fiction: Gods of War, 1985; Occupation, 1987. *Honours:* Best Book on Foreign Affairs Award, Overseas Press Club, 1961, 1970, 1976; Pulitzer Prize for Non-Fiction, 1970; Van Wyck Brooks Award for Non-Fiction, 1970; Hon. doctorates. *Address:* 101 Long Ridge Rd, Danbury, CT 06810, USA.

TOLSTAYA, Tatyana (Nikitichna); Writer; b. 3 May 1951, Leningrad, Russia; m. Andrei Lebedev 11 May 1974; two s. *Education:* Univ. of Leningrad, 1968–74. *Publications:* On the Golden Porch (short stories), 1989; Sleepwalker in a Fog (short stories), 1992; Kys, 2001; The Slynx (novel), 2002. Contributions: Literary journals. *Address:* c/o Penguin Books Ltd, Bath Rd, Harmondsworth, Middlesex UB7 0DA, England.

TOMALIN, Claire; Author; b. 20 June 1933, London, England; m. 1st Nicholas Osborne Tomalin 1955 (deceased 1973); two s. (one deceased) three d. (one deceased); m. 2nd Michael Frayn 1993. *Education:* MA, Newnham College, Cambridge, 1954. *Career:* Asst Literary Ed., 1968–70, Literary Ed., 1974–77, New Statesman; Literary Ed., Sunday Times, 1979–86; mem. English PEN, vice-pres., 1997; FRSL, council, 1997–2000. *Publications:* The Life and Death of Mary Wollstonecraft, 1974; Shelley and His World, 1980; Parents and Children, 1981; Katherine Mansfield: A Secret Life, 1987; The Invisible Woman: The Story of Nelly Ternan and Charles Dickens, 1990; The Winter Wife (play), 1991; Mrs Jordan's Profession, 1994; Jane Austen: A Life, 1997; Several Strangers: Writing from Three Decades, 1999; Samuel Pepys: The Unequalled Self, 2002. *Honours:* Whitbread First Book Prize, 1974; James Tait Black Memorial Prize, 1990; Hawthornden Prize, 1991; NCR Book Award, 1991; Theatre Literary

Award, New York, 1995; Whitbread Biography Award and Book of the Year, 2002. *Literary Agent:* David Godwin Associates, 55 Monmouth St, London WC2H 9DG, England.

TOMAZOS, Criton Plato; architect, artist, poet, playwright and writer; b. 13 April 1940, Larnaca, Cyprus. *Education:* Diploma in Architecture, RIBA, Part II, The Polytechnic, Regent Street (now Westminster Univ.) 1964; Scholarship in Advanced Theatre Design, Croydon Coll. of Fine Art and Technology 1977, and in Advanced Writing for Film and TV, London Acad. of Film and TV 1982. *Career:* various positions in pvt. architectural practices 1960–74; Co-founder, Co-ordinating Dir Environmental Forum 1970–94; Founder, resident playwright, designer, then Chair. Prowethens Theatre Co. 1982–84; Founder-Dir, Theatre for Mankind Voluntary Organization 1985–94; Ed., Journalist, Letters and Arts Page, Parikiaki, 1997–; mem. Writers' Guild; Poetry Society; Writers' Forum; Theatre for Mankind; Theatre Writers' Union, committee mem.; New Playwrights' Trust, management committee mem.; Asscn of Greek Scientists/Professional People. *Plays:* Rehearsal, Maxim & Minnie, The Shark, Tickets to No-Man's Land, Not Suitable for the National. *Films:* (scripts) The Fraud, Daydreams Burn, Close Shave, Terra Incognita, Eyes Open at Midnight, A Spanish Tragedy. *Publications:* Poetry: Lovepoem 1965; Monologue of the Ancient Hero 1970; Relationships 1975; Poems of 1960–61 1976; He Who Left His Fingerprints 1979; Factory Backyard 1980; Diaphanies (Transparencies) 1982 (1st Prize Eden Festival 1982); Letter to the Returning Astronaut 1982; The Song of Tefcros (1st Prize Eden Festival) 1983, Synora Mnemes (Boundaries of Memory) 1987–88; The Visit 1988; First Explorations 1989; Relationships, The Story of Water & Night March 1990, Tora (Now) 1994. Other: The Gospel of Contemporary Slavery (essay) 1977, Eugene Delacroix, the Painter, The Dramatic Work of Angelos Sikelianos, The Meaning of Work in Contemporary Society. Contributions: numerous anthologies, magazines and journals. *Honours:* hon. doctorates (London Inst.of Applied Research, Acad. des Sciences Universelles, World Univ., Benson USA); 1st Prize for Poetry EDON Int. Youth Festival 1982, Man of the Year 1991, Most Admired Man of the Decade 1992. *Address:* 2 Park Terrace, Bell Lane, Enfield, EN3 5EU, Middlesex. *Address:* c/o Theatre for Mankind, POB 671, Enfield, EN3 5EU, England.

TOMLINSON, (Alfred) Charles, CBE, BA, MA; British academic, poet and writer; b. 8 Jan. 1927, Stoke-on-Trent, Staffordshire, England; m. 1948; two d. *Education:* Queens' Coll., Cambridge. *Career:* Lecturer, 1956–68, Reader, 1968–82, Prof. of English, 1982–92, Prof. Emeritus, 1992–, Senior Research Fellow, 1996–, University of Bristol; Visiting Prof., University of New Mexico, 1962–63; O'Connor Prof., Colgate University, New York, 1967–68, 1989–90; Visiting Fellow of Humanities, Princeton University, 1981; Lamont Prof., Union College, New York, 1987; mem. academic and literary organizations. *Publications:* poetry: Relations and Contraries, 1951; The Necklace, 1955; Seeing is Believing, 1958; A Peopled Landscape, 1963; American Scenes, 1966; The Poem as Initiation, 1968; The Way of a World, 1969; Renga, 1970; Written on Water, 1972; The Way In, 1974; The Shaft, 1978; Selected Poems, 1951–74, 1978; The Flood, 1981; Airborn: Hijos del aire, 1981; Notes from New York, 1984; Collected Poems, 1985; The Return, 1987; Annunciations, 1989; The Door in the Wall, 1992; Poemas, 1992; Gedichte, 1994; La insistencia de las cosas, 1994; In Italia, 1995; Jubilation, 1995; Portuguese Pieces, 1996; The Fox Gallery, 1996; Parole e Acqua, 1997; Selected Poems 1955–97, 1997; The Vineyard Above the Sea, 1999; Luoghi Italiani, 2000; Lugares y Relaciones 2003, Skywriting 2003. Other: In Black and White, 1976; The Oxford Book of Verse in English Translation (ed.), 1980; Some Americans: A Literary Memoir, 1981; Poetry and Metamorphosis, 1983; Eros Englished: Erotic Poems from the Greek and Latin (ed.), 1991; American Essays: Making it New, 2001, Metamorphoses: Poetry and Translation 2003. Contributions: books, professional journals and other publications. *Honours:* Hon. Fellow, Queens' College, Cambridge 1976–, Royal Holloway College, London 1991; hon. doctorates; Bess Hokin Prize 1968, Oscar Blumenthal Prize 1960, Inez Boulton Prize 1964, Frank O'Hara Prize 1968, Cheltenham Poetry Prize 1976, Cholmondeley Poetry Award 1979, Wilbur Award for Poetic Achievement 1982, Premio Europeo di Cittadella, Italy 1991, Bennett Award for Poetry 1992, Premio Intenazionale Flaiano 2001, The New Criterion Poetry Prize 2003. *Address:* Brook Cottage, Ozleworth Bottom, Wotton-under-Edge, Gloucestershire GL12 7QB, England.

TOMLINSON, Gerald Arthur, BA; writer, editor and publisher; b. 24 Jan. 1933, Elmira, NY, USA; m. Mary Alexis Usakowski 1967; two s. *Education:* Marietta College, OH, Columbia Law School, New York. *Career:* Assoc. Ed., Business and Professional Books, Prentice Hall, 1960–63, School Dept, Harcourt Brace Jovanovich, 1963–66; Senior Ed., English Dept, Holt, Rinehart and Winston, 1966–69; Exec. Ed., K-12 English, Silver Burdett and Ginn, 1969–82; Publisher, Home Run Press, 1985–; mem. Authors' Guild; MWA; Society for American Baseball Research. *Publications:* On a Field of Black (novel), 1980; School Administrator's Complete Letter Book, 1984; Speaker's Treasury of Sports Anecdotes, Stories and Humor, 1990; Encyclopedia of Religious Quotations, 1991; The New Jersey Book of Lists (co-author), 1992; Murdered in Jersey, 1994; Fatal Tryst, 1999; How to do Baseball Research (general ed.), 2000; Seven Jersey Murders 2003. Contributions: magazines and journals. *Honours:* Best Detective Stories of the Year, 1976; MWA Annual Anthologies. *Address:* 19 Harbor Drive, Lake Hopatcong, NJ 07849, USA. *E-mail:* gerrytom@juno.com.

TONG, Raymond, BSc, DipEd; poet and writer; b. 20 Aug. 1922, Winchester, Hampshire, England; m. Mariana Apergis 1946. *Education:* University of London. *Career:* Education Officer, Senior Education Officer, Nigeria, 1949–58, Uganda, 1958–61; British Council Administrator, South America, India, Middle East, England, 1961–82; mem. Poetry Society, life mem.; West Country Writers Asscn. *Publications:* Today the Sun, 1947; Angry Decade, 1950; African Helicon (anthology), 1954; Fabled City, 1960; A Matter of History, 1976; Crossing the Border, 1978; Selected Poems, 1994; Returning Home, 1996. Contributions: many reviews, quarterlies, and journals in England and overseas. *Address:* 1 Beaufort Road, Clifton, Bristol BS8 2JT, England.

TOOMEY, Jeanne Elizabeth; Animal Activist and Writer; b. 22 Aug. 1921, New York, NY, USA; m. Peter Terranova, 28 Sept. 1951, deceased 1968, one s. one d. *Education:* Hofstra University, 1938–40; Fordham University, 1940–41; BA, Southampton College, 1976; Postgraduate Studies, Monmouth College, 1978–79. *Career:* Staff, Brooklyn Daily Eagle, 1943–52, King Features Syndicate, 1953–55, New York Journal-American, 1955–61, Associated Press, 1963–64, News Tribune, Woodbridge, NJ, 1976–86; Ed., Calexico Chronicle, CA, 1987–88; Pres. and Dir, Last Post Animal Sanctuary, Falls Village, CT, 1991–; mem. Newswomen's Club of New York; New York Press Club; Overseas Press Club; The Silurians. *Publications:* How to Use Your Dreams to Solve Your Problems, 1970; Murder in the Hamptons, 1994; Assignment Homicide, 1998. Contributions: various publications. *Honours:* Woman of the Year, New York Women's Press Club, 1960. *Address:* 95 Belden St, Falls Village, CT 06031, USA.

TOPOLSKI, Daniel; Writer and Broadcaster; b. 4 June 1945, London, England; m. Susan Gilbert, one s. two d. *Education:* BA, Geography, Diploma, Social Anthropology, MA, Geography, New College, Oxford, 1964–68. *Career:* mem. Churchill Fellow; FRGS; Leander Club; London Rowing Club. *Publications:* Muzungu: One Man's Africa, 1976; Travels with my Father: South America, 1983; Boat Race: The Oxford Revival, 1985; True Blue: The Oxford Mutiny, 1988; Henley: The Regatta, 1989. Contributions: periodicals, radio and television. *Honours:* Sports Book of the Year, 1990; Radio Travel Program of the Year, 1994. *Address:* 69 Randolph Ave, London W9 1DW, England. *Fax:* (20) 7266-1884. *E-mail:* dtopo35410@aol.com.

TORON, Steve (see Stebel, Sidney Leo).

TORRANCE, Lee (see Sadgrove, Sidney Henry).

TORRANCE, Thomas F(orsyth); Minister of Religion and Prof. of Theology; b. 30 Aug. 1913, Chengdu, China; m. Margaret Edith Spear, 2 Oct. 1946, two s. one d. *Education:* MA, 1934; BD, 1937; DrTheol, 1946; DLitt, 1971. *Career:* Founder-Ed., Scottish Journal of Theology, 1948–88; Moderator, General Assembly, Church of Scotland, 1976–77; mem. British Acad.; International Acad. of Religious Sciences, pres., 1972–81; International Acad. of the Philosophy of Science; Center of Theological Inquiry, Princeton, NJ; Royal Society of Edinburgh. *Publications:* The Doctrine of Grace, 1949; Calvin's Doctrine of Man, 1949; Kingdom and Church, 1956; Conflict and Agreement in the Church, 2 vols, 1959–60; Theology in Reconstruction, 1965; Theological Science, 1969; God and Rationality, 1971; Theology in Reconciliation, 1975; Space, Time and Resurrection, 1976; Space, Time and Incarnation, 1979; The Ground and Grammar of Theology, 1980; Christian Theology and Scientific Culture, 1980; Divine and Contingent Order, 1981; Reality and Scientific Theology, 1984; The Hermeneuntics of John Calvin, 1987; The Trinitarian Faith, 1988; The Christian Frame of Mind, Reason, Order and Openness in Theology and Natural Science, 1989; Karl Barth, Biblical and Evangelical Theological Theologian, 1990; Senso del divino e scienza moderna, 1992; Theological Dialogue between Orthodox and Reformed Churches (ed.), 1993; Royal Priesthood, 1993; Divine Meaning: Studies in Patristic Hermeneutics, 1994; Trinitarian Perspectives: Toward Doctrinal Agreement, 1994; The Christian Doctrine of God, One Being Three Persons, 1996; Scottish Theology: From John Knox to John McLeod Campbell, 1996; A Passion for Christ (with J. B. and D. W. Torrance), 1999; The Soul and the Person of the Unborn Child, 1999; The Person of Jesus Christ, 1999; H. R. Mackintosh: Theologian of the Cross, 2000; The Doctrim of Jesus Christ, 2002; Theological and Natural Science, 2002. Contributions: numerous publications. *Honours:* Hon. doctorates. *Address:* 37 Braid Farm Rd, Edinburgh EH10 6LE, Scotland. *E-mail:* ttorr@globalnet.co.uk.

TOURNIER, Michel; Writer; b. 19 Dec. 1924, Paris, France. *Education:* Sorbonne, University of Paris; University of Tübingen. *Career:* mem. Académie Goncourt. *Publications:* Vendredi ou les limbes du Pacifique, 1967; Le Roi des Aulnes, 1970; Les météores, 1975; Le vent paraclet, 1977; Le coq de bruyère, 1978; Des clefs et des serrures, 1979; Gaspard, Melchior et Balthazar, 1980; Le vol du vampire, 1981; Gilles et Jeanne, 1983; La Goutte d'Or, 1986; Le Tabor et le Sinaï, 1989; Le médianioche amoureux, 1989; Le crépuscle des masques, 1992; Le miroir des idées, 1994; Le pied de la lettre, 1994; La couleuvrine, 1994; Célebrations, 1999. Contributions: periodicals. *Honours:* Officier, Légion d'honneur; Commdr, Ordre nat. du Mérite; Grand Prix du Roman, Académie Française, 1967; Prix Goncourt, 1970; Goethe Medal, 1993; Hon. Doctorate, University College London, 1997. *Address:* Le presbytère, Choisel, 78460 Chevreuse, France.

TOWNLEY, Roderick Carl; Writer and Poet; b. 7 June 1942, New Jersey, USA; m. Wyatt Townley, 15 Feb. 1986, one s. one d. *Education:* AB, Bard

College; PhD, Rutgers University, 1972. *Career:* Prof. of English, Universidad de Concepcion, Chile, 1978–79; National Editorial Writer, TV Guide, 1980–89; Senior Ed., US magazine, 1989–90; Exec. Dir, The Writers Place, Kansas City, MO, 1995–96. *Publications:* The Early Poetry of William Carlos Williams, 1975; Minor Gods (novel), 1977; Three Musicians (poems), 1978; Final Approach (poems), 1986; Night Errands: How Poets Use Dreams, 1998; The Great Good Thing (novel), 2001; Into the Labyrinth (novel), 2002. Contributions: newspapers and journals. *Honours:* Co-Winner, 1969, First Prize, 1971, Acad. of American Poets; Fulbright Professorship, Chile, 1978–79; Peregrine Prize in Short Fiction, 1998; Kansas Arts Commission Individual Artist Grant, 2000. *Address:* PO Box 13302, Shawnee Mission, KS 66282, USA.

TOWNSEND, Peter Wooldridge; Author; b. 22 Nov. 1914, Rangoon, Burma; m. Marie Luce Jamagne, 21 Dec. 1959, one s. two d. *Education:* Haileybury; Royal Air Force College, 1933–35; Royal Air Force Staff College, 1942–43. *Career:* mem. European Acad. of Science, Arts and Letters. *Publications:* Earth my Friend, 1960; Duel of Eagles, 1970; The Last Emperor, 1975; Time and Chance, 1978; The Smallest Pawns in the Game, 1979–80; The Girl in the White Ship, 1982; The Postman of Nagasaki, 1984; Duel in the Dark, 1986; Nostalgia Britannica, 1994. Contributions: Daily Telegraph; Daily Mail; Daily Express; Sunday Express; Evening Standard; Paris Match; Journal du Dimanche; Le Figaro; Le Figaro Littéraire; Madame Figaro; Le Temps Retrouve. *Address:* La Mare aux Oiseaux, 78610 St Leger en Yvelines, France.

TOWNSEND, Susan (Sue) Lilian, FRSL; writer; b. 2 April 1946, Leicester, England; m. (divorced); three c. *Career:* mem. Writers' Guild, PEN. *Plays:* Bazaar and Rummage 1984, Groping for Words 1984, Womberang 1984, The Great Celestial Cow 1985, Ten Tiny Fingers, Nine Tiny Toes 1990, The Secret Diary of Adrian Mole Aged 13 3¾ 1992, Dayroom, The Ghost of Daniel Lambert, Captain Christmas and the Evil Adults, Are You Sitting Comfortably? *Television:* Think of England (writer, narrator and presenter) 1991. *Publications:* The Secret Diary of Adrian Mole Aged 13¾ 1982, The Growing Pains of Adrian Mole 1984, Rebuilding Coventry 1988, Mr Bevan's Dream 1989, True Confessions of Adrian Albert Mole, Margaret Hilda Roberts and Susan Lilian Townsend 1989, Adrian Mole from Minor to Major 1991, The Queen and I 1992, Adrian Mole: The Wilderness Years 1993, Adrian Mole, The Lost Years 1994, Ghost Children 1997, Adrian Mole, The Cappuccino Years 1999, The Public Confessions of a Middle-Aged Woman Aged 55 3¾ 2001, Number 10 2002, Adrian Mole and the Weapons of Mass Destruction 2004; contrib. to London Times, New Statesman, Observer, Sainsbury's Magazine. *Honours:* Hon. MA (Univ. of Leicester) 1991. *Address:* Bridge Works, Knighton Fields Road W, Leicester, LE2 6LH, England.

TOWNSEND, Tom, (Thomas L. Townsend); Novelist; b. 1 Jan. 1944, Waukegan, Illinios, USA; m. Janet L. Simpson, 17 April 1965. *Education:* Arkansas Military Acad. *Publications:* Texas Treasure Coast, 1978; Where the Pirates Are, 1985; Trader Wooly, 1987; Trader Wooly and the Terrorists, 1988; Queen of the Wind, 1989; Battle of Galveston, 1990; Trader Wooly and the Ghost in the Colonel's Jeep, 1991; The Holligans, 1991; Bubba's Truck, 1992; The Ghost Flyers, 1993; A Fair Wind to Glory, 1994. *Honours:* Friend of American Writers Award, 1986; Texas Blue Bonnet Master List, 1986; Silver Award, Best Children's Video, Houston International Film Festival, 1986. *Address:* PO Box 905, Kemah, TX 77565, USA.

TOYNBEE, Polly (Mary Louisa); Journalist and Writer; b. 27 Dec. 1946, Isle of Wight, England; m. Peter Jenkins 1970 (deceased 1992); one s. two d. one step-d. *Education:* St Anne's College, Oxford. *Career:* Reporter, The Observer, 1968–70, 1972–77; Ed., Washington Monthly, 1970–72; Columnist, The Guardian, 1977–88, Radio Times, 1998–; Social Affairs Ed., BBC, 1988–95; Political Columnist, The Independent, 1995–96, The Guardian, 1996–. *Publications:* Leftovers, 1966; A Working Life, 1970; Hospital, 1977; The Way We Live Now, 1981; Lost Children, 1985; Did Things Get Better?, 2001; Hard Work: Life in Low-Pay Britain, 2003. *Honours:* Catherine Pakenham Award for Journalism, 1975; British Press Awards, 1977, 1982; Columnist of the Year, 1986; Magazine Writer of the Year, 1996; Columnist of the Year, 1996; George Orwell Prize, 1997. *Address:* c/o The Guardian, 119 Farringdon Rd, London EC1R 3ER, England.

TRACY, James D.; Prof. of History, Writer and Ed.; b. 14 Feb. 1938, St Louis, MO, USA; m. Nancy Ann McBride, 6 Sept. 1968, two s. one d. *Education:* BA, St Louis University, 1959; MA, Johns Hopkins University, 1960; MA, University of Notre Dame, 1961; PhD, Princeton University, 1967. *Career:* Instructor in History, University of Michigan, 1964–66; Assoc. Prof. of History, 1966–77, Prof. of History, 1977–, University of Minnesota; Man. Ed., Journal of Early Modern History, 1995–. *Publications:* Erasmus: The Growth of a Mind, 1972; Early Modern European History, 1500–1715 (ed.), 1976; The Politics of Erasmus: A Pacifist Intellectual and His Political Milieu, 1979; True Ocean Found: Paludanus's Letters on Dutch Voyages to the Kara Sea, 1595–1596, 1980; A Financial Revolution in the Habsburg Netherlands: Renten and Renteniers in the Country of Holland, 1515–1565, 1985; Holland Under Habsburg Rule, 1506–1566: The Formation of a Body Politic, 1990; The Rise of Merchant Empires: Long-Dictance Trade in the Early Modern World, 1350–1750 (ed.), 1990; The Political Economy of Merchant Empires: State Power and World Trade, 1350–1750 (ed.), 1991; Handbook of European History, 1400–1600: Late Middle Ages, Renaissance, and Reformation (ed. with Thomas A. Brady and Heiko A. Oberman), 1996; Erasmus of the Low Countries, 1996; Europe's Reformations, 1450–1650, 1999; City Wall: The Urban Enceinte in Global Perspective (ed.), 2000. Contributions: scholarly books and learned journals. *E-mail:* tracy001@umn.edu.

TRANSTRÖMER, Tomas (Gösta); Poet and Psychologist; b. 15 April 1931, Stockholm, Sweden; m. Monica Blach, 1958, two d. *Education:* Degree, University of Stockholm, 1956. *Career:* mem. Swedish Writers Union. *Publications:* In English: Twenty Poems, 1970; Night Vision, 1971; Windows and Stones: Selected Poems, 1972; Elegy: Some October Notes, 1973; Citoyens, 1974; Baltics, 1975; Truth Barriers: Poems by Tomas Tranströmer, 1980; How the Late Autumn Night Novel Begins, 1980; Tomas Tranströmer: Selected Poems, 1982; The Wild Marketplace, 1985; Selected Poems of Tomas Tranströmer, 1954–1986, 1987; Collected Poems, 1987; For the Living and the Dead, 1995; The Sorrow Gondola, 1996. Contributions: periodicals. *Honours:* Aftonbladets Literary Prize, 1958; Bellman Prize, 1966; Swedish Award, International Poetry Forum, 1971; Oevralids Prize, 1975; Boklotteriets Prize, 1981; Petrarca Prize, 1981; Nordic Council Literary Prize, 1990. *Address:* c/o Swedish Writers Union, Box 3157, Drottninggatan 88B, 103 63 Stockholm, Sweden.

TRAPIDO, Barbara Louise, BA; writer; b. 5 Nov. 1941, Cape Town, South Africa; m. Stanley Trapido 1963; one s. one d. *Publications:* Brother of the More Famous Jack 1982, Noah's Ark 1985, Temples of Delight 1990, Juggling 1994, The Travelling Horn Player 1998, Frankie and Stankie 2003; contrib. to Spectator, Sunday Telegraph, Sunday Times. *Honours:* Whitbread Award 1982. *Address:* c/o Bloomsbury Books, 38 Soho Square, London, W1D 3HB, England. *Website:* www.bloomsbury.com.

TRAVIS, Aaron (see Saylor, Steven (Warren)).

TRAWICK, Leonard M(oses); Prof. of English Emeritus, Poet, Writer and Ed.; b. 4 July 1933, Decatur, AL, USA; m. Kerstin Ekfelt, 16 July 1960, one s. one d. *Education:* BA, University of the South, Sewanee, Tennessee, 1955; MA in English, University of Chicago, 1956; PhD in English, Harvard University, 1961. *Career:* Instructor to Asst Prof. of English, Columbia University, 1961–69; Assoc. Prof., 1969–72, Prof. of English, 1972–98, Prof. Emeritus, 1998–, Principal Ed., 1971–98, and Dir, 1990–92, Poetry Center, Cleveland State University; Founding Ed., 1980, Co-Ed., 1983–92, The Gamut journal. *Publications:* Poetry: Beast Forms, 1971; Severed Parts, 1981; Beastmorfs, 1994. Opera Librettos: Spinoza, by Julius Drossin, 1982; The Enchanted Garden, by Klaus G. Roy, 1983; Mary Stuart: A Queen Betrayed, by Bain Murray, 1991. Other: Backgrounds of Romanticism: English Philosophical Prose of the Eighteenth Century, 1967; World, Self, Poem (ed.), 1990; German Literature of the Romantic Era and the Age of Goethe (co-ed. and principal trans.), 1993. Contributions: scholarly books and journals, and to anthologies and magazines. *Honours:* Fulbright Scholarship, University of Dijon, 1956–57; Individual Artist Award, Ohio Arts Council, 1980; Award for Excellence in the Media, Northern Ohio Live, 1990; Co-Recipient, James P. Barry Ohioana Award for Editorial Excellence, 1991; Ohioana Poetry Award for Lifetime Achievement in Poetry, 1994. *Address:* c/o Dept of English, Cleveland State University, Rhodes Tower, Room 1815, Cleveland, OH 44115, USA.

TREANOR, Oliver; Roman Catholic Priest, Theologian, Lecturer and Writer; b. 1 May 1949, Warrenpoint, Northern Ireland. *Education:* BA, Queen's University, Belfast, 1972; PGCE, 1973; Dip Phil, 1974; STB, 1977, STL, 1979, STD, 1984, Pontifical Universitá Gregoriana, Rome. *Career:* Lecturer, Systematic Theology, Pontifical University, Maynooth, Ireland. *Publications:* Mother of the Redeemer, Mother of the Redeemed, 1988; Seven Bells to Bethlehem: The O Antiphons, 1995; This Is My Beloved Son: Aspects of The Passion, 1997; The God Who Loved Stories, 1999. Contributions: Priests and People, Durham, England; Osservatore Romano, Vatican City; Religious Life Review, Dublin; International Christian Digest, USA; The Furrow, Maynooth; Bible Alive, Stoke-on-Trent. *Address:* The Pontifical University, Maynooth, Co Kildare, Ireland.

TREBORLANG, Robert; Writer and Poet; b. 19 Dec. 1943, Jerusalem, Palestine; m. Moi Moi Cumines, 6 May 1971. *Education:* BA, Language, University of Sydney, 1968. *Career:* mem. Australian Journalists Asscn; Entertainment and Arts Alliance. *Publications:* How to Survive in Australia, 1985; How to be Normal in Australia, 1987; Sydney: Discover the City, 1988; How to Make it Big in Australia, 1989; She Vomits Like a Lady, 1991; Staying Sane in Australia, 1991; Men, Women and Other Necessities, 1992; A Hop Through Australia's History, 1993; How to Mate in Australia, 1993; The Little Book of Aussie Wisdom, 1994; The Little Book of Aussie Insults, 1994; The Little Book of Aussie Manners, 1995; It's Not the Pale Moon, 1999; Dancing With Mother, 1999. Contributions: 24 Hours; Australian; Australian Jewish Times. *Honours:* Literature Grant, Australia, 1976. *Address:* PO Box 997, Potts Point, NSW 2011, Australia.

TREGLOWN, Jeremy Dickinson; Prof. of English, Biographer, Ed. and Critic; b. 24 May 1946, Anglesey, North Wales; m. 1st Rona Bower, 1970, divorced 1982, one s. two d.; m. 2nd Holly Urquhart Eley, 1984. *Education:* BLitt, MA, Oxon; PhD, London. *Career:* Lecturer in English, Lincoln College, Oxford, 1974–77, University College London, 1977–80; Asst Ed., 1980–82, Ed., 1982–90, TLS; Chair. of Judges, Booker Prize, 1991, Whitbread Book of the Year Award, 1998; Ferris Prof. of Journalism, Princeton

University, USA, 1992; Prof. of English, University of Warwick, England, 1993–; Leverhulme Research Fellow, 2001–03; mem. FRSL. *Publications:* Letters of John Wilmot, Earl of Rochester (ed.), 1980; Spirit of Wit: Reconsiderations of Rochester (ed.), 1982; Introduction, R. L. Stevenson, In the South Seas, 1986; Selection, and Introduction, The Lantern Bearers: Essays by Robert Louis Stevenson, 1987; Introductions to reprints of complete novels of Henry Green, 1991–98; Roald Dahl: A Biography, 1994; Grub Street and the Ivory Tower: Literary Journalism, and Literary Scholarship from Fielding to the Internet (ed. with Bridget Bennett), 1998; Romancing: The Life and Work of Henry Green, 2000. Contributions: numerous magazines and journals. *Address:* Gardens Cottage, Ditchley Park, Enstone, Nr Chipping Norton, Oxford OX7 4EP, England.

TREHEARNE, Elizabeth (see Maxwell, Patricia Anne).

TREISMAN, Deborah; British; *Fiction Editor, The New Yorker*; b. Oxford; m. Kenny Cummings. *Education:* Univ. of Berkeley, USA. *Career:* Fiction Ed., The New Yorker 2003–. *Literary Agent:* The Wylie Agency, 250 W 57th Street, New York, NY 10107, USA. *E-mail:* mail@wylieagency.com. *Website:* www.wylieagency.com.

TREMAIN, Rose, BA, FRSL; British writer; b. (Rosemary Jane Thomson), 2 Aug. 1943, London; m. 1st Jon Tremain 1971; one d.; m. 2nd Jonathan Dudley 1982 (dissolved 1990); pnr Richard Holmes. *Education:* Sorbonne, Paris and Univ. of East Anglia. *Career:* full-time novelist and playwright 1971–; part-time tutor Univ. of East Anglia 1988–95; mem.judge judging panel Booker Prize 1988, 2000. *Plays for radio include:* Temporary Shelter 1985, Who Was Emily Davison? 1996, The End of Love 1999, One Night in Winter 2001. *Television:* A Room for the Winter 1979, Daylight Robbery 1982. *Publications:* fiction: Sadler's Birthday 1976, Letter to Sister Benedicta 1978, The Cupboard 1981, The Swimming Pool Season 1984, Restoration 1989 (Sunday Express Book of the Year Award 1989), Sacred Country 1992 (James Tait Black Memorial Prize 1993, Prix Fémina Etranger 1994), The Way I Found Her 1997, Music and Silence 1999 (Whitbread Novel of the Year 1999), The Colour 2003; for children: Journey to the Volcano 1985; short story collections: The Colonel's Daughter 1982 (Dylan Thomas Short Story Prize 1984), The Garden of the Villa Mollini 1988, Evangelista's Fan 1994, Collected Short Stories 1996; non-fiction: The Fight for Freedom for Women 1971, Stalin: An Illustrated Biography 1974. *Honours:* Univ. of Essex Fellowship 1979–80; Hon. DLitt (Univ. of East Anglia) 2001; one of Granta's Best Young British Novelists 1983, Giles Cooper Award 1985, Angel Literary Award 1986, Sony Award 1996. *Address:* 2 High House, South Avenue, Thorpe St Andrew, Norwich, NR7 0EZ, England. *Telephone:* (1603) 439682. *Fax:* (1603) 434234.

TREMAYNE, Peter (see Ellis, Peter Berresford).

TREMBLAY, Gail Elizabeth; Poet, Artist and College Teacher; b. 15 Dec. 1945, Buffalo, NY, USA. *Education:* BA, Drama, University of New Hampshire, 1967; MFA, Creative Writing, University of Oregon, 1969. *Career:* Lecturer, Keene State College, NH; Asst Prof., University of Nebraska; Faculty, Evergreen State College, Olympia, Washington; mem. Indian Youth of America, pres.; International Asscn of Art, UNESCO, US National Committee board mem.; Native American Writers Circle of the Americas; Woman's Caucus for Art, board mem., pres. *Publications:* Night Gives Woman the Word, 1979; Talking to the Grandfathers, 1980; Indian Singing in 20th Century America, 1990. Contributions: Reviews, quarterlies, and journals. *Honours:* Alfred E. Richards Poetry Prize, 1967. *Address:* c/o Evergreen State College, Olympia, WA 98505, USA.

TREMBLAY, Michel; Dramatist and Author; b. 25 June 1942, Montréal, QC, Canada. *Education:* Graphic Arts Institute, Québec. *Publications:* Theatre Pieces (with dates of production and publication): Le Train, 1964, 1990; Messe noire, 1965; Clinq, 1966, revised edn as En pièces détachées, 1969, 1970; Les Belles-Soeurs, 1968, 1972; Trois petits tours, 1969, 1971; La Duchesse de Langeais, 1969, 1973; Demain matin, Montréal m'attend, 1970, 1972; Les Paons, 1971; A toi, pour toujours, ta Marie-Lou, 1971, 1971; Ville Mont-Royal ou Abimes, 1972; Hosanna, 1973, 1973; Bonjour, la, bonjour, 1974, 1974; Surprise! Surprise!, 1975, 1977; Les Héros de mon enfance, 1976, 1976; Sainte Carmen de la Main, 1976, 1976; Six monologues en forme de mots d'auteur, 1977; Damnée Manon, sacrée Sandra, 1977, 1977; L'Impromptu d'Outremont, 1980, 1980; Les Grandes Vacances, 1981; Les Anciennes Odeurs, 1981, 1981; Albertine, en cinq temps, 1984, 1984; L'Impromptu des deux presses, 1985; Le Vrai Monde?, 1987, 1987; Nelligan, 1990, 1990; La Maison suspendue, 1990, 1990; Théatre I, 1991; Marcel poursuivi par les chiens, 1992, 1992; En circuit fermé, 1994, 1994; Les socles, 1994; Messe solennelle pour une pleine lune d'été, 1996. Fiction: Contes pour buveurs attardés, 1966, English trans. as Stories for Late Night Drinkers, 1977; La Cité dans l'oeuf, 1969; C't'a ton tour, Laura Cadieux, 1973; La Grosse Femme d'a coté est enceinte, 1978, English trans. as The Fat Woman Next Door is Pregnant, 1981; Thérèse et Pierrette a l'école des Saints Anges, 1980, English trans. as Thérèse, Pierrette and the Little Hanging Angel, 1984; La Duchesse et le roturier, 1982; Des nouvelles d'Edouard, 1984; Le Coeur découvert, 1986; Le Premier Quartier de la lune, 1989; La Mort de Phèdre, 1992; Le Coeur éclaté, 1993; La Nuit des princes charmants, 1995; Quarante-quatre minutes quarante-quatre secondes, 1997; Un objet de beauté, 1997. *Honours:* Trophée Méritas, 1970, 1972; Chalmers Awards, 1972, 1973, 1974, 1975, 1978, 1986, 1989, 1991; Prix Victor Morin, 1974; Prix du Lieutenant, Gouverneur de l'Ontario, 1976; Prix France Québec, 1981; Officier, Ordre des Arts et des Lettres, 1991; Prix Québec-Paris, 1985; Chevalier, Ordre nat. du Québec, 1992; Banff National Center Award, 1993; Prix Louis-Hémon, 1994; Le Prix Molson du Conseil des Arts du Canada, 1994; Signet d'or, 1995; Hon. doctorates. *Address:* c/o Agence Goodwin, 839, rue Sherbrooke Est, bureau 200, Montréal, QC H2L 1K6, Canada.

TREMLETT, George William; Author, Journalist and Bookseller; b. 5 Sept. 1939, England; m. Jane Mitchell, 1971, three s. *Career:* mem. BBC Community Programme Unit, advisory panel, 1985–. *Publications:* 17 biographies of rock musicians, 1974–77; Living Cities, 1979; Caitlin (with Mrs Caitlin Thomas), 1986; Clubmen, 1987; Homeless, Story of St Mungo's, 1989; Little Legs (with Roy Smith), 1989; Rock Gold, 1990; Dylan Thomas: Book: In the Mercy of His Means, 1991; Gadaffi: The Desert Mystic, 1993; David Bowie, 1994; The Death of Dylan Thomas (with James R. B. Nashold), 1997. Screenplay: The Map of Love, 1998. *Honours:* OBE. *Address:* Corran House, Laugharne, Carmarthen, Dyfed SA33 4SJ, Wales.

TRENHAILE, John Stevens; Writer; b. 29 April 1949, Hertford, England. *Education:* BA, 1971, MA, 1975, Magdalen College, Oxford. *Publications:* Kyril, 1981; A View from the Square, 1983; Nocturne for the General, 1985; The Mahjong Spies, 1986; The Gates of Exquisite View, 1987; The Scroll of Benevolence, 1988; Kyrsalis, 1989; Acts of Betrayal, 1990; Blood Rules, 1991; The Tiger of Desire, 1992; A Means to Evil, 1993; Against All Reason, 1994. *Address:* c/o Blake Friedman Literary Agents, Arlington Rd, London NW1 7HP, England.

TRENTON, Gail (see Grant, Neil).

TREVELYAN, (Walter) Raleigh, FRSL; writer; b. 6 July 1923, Port Blair, Andaman Islands. *Career:* publisher 1948–88; mem. Anglo-Italian Soc. for the Protection of Animals (chair.), PEN (vice-pres.). *Publications:* The Fortress, 1956; A Hermit Disclosed, 1960; Italian Short Stories: Penguin Parallel Texts (ed.), 1965; The Big Tomato, 1966; Princes Under the Volcano, 1972; The Shadow of Vesuvius, 1976; A Pre-Raphaelite Circle, 1978; Rome '44, 1982; Shades of the Alhambra, 1984; The Golden Oriole, 1987; La Storia dei Whitaker, 1989; Grand Dukes and Diamonds: The Wernhers of Luton Hoo, 1991; A Clear Premonition, 1995; The Companion Guide to Sicily, 1996; Sir Walter Raleigh, 2002. Contributions: newspapers and journals. *Honours:* John Florio Prize for Trans. 1967. *Literary Agent:* A. M. Heath & Co Ltd, 79 St Martin's Lane, London WC2N 4RE, England. *Address:* 18 Hertford Street, London, W1J 7RT; St Cadix, St Veep, Lostwithiel, Cornwall, PL22 0PB, England.

TREVOR, William, CLit, BA; Irish writer; b. 24 May 1928, Mitchelstown, Co. Cork; m. Jane Ryan 1952; two s. *Education:* St Columba's Coll., Dublin, Trinity Coll., Dublin. *Career:* mem. Irish Acad. of Letters. *Publications:* The Old Boys 1964, The Boarding House 1965, The Love Department 1966, The Day We Got Drunk on Cake 1967, Mrs Eckdorf in O'Neill's Hotel 1968, Miss Gomez and the Brethren 1969, The Ballroom of Romance 1970, Elizabeth Alone 1972, Angels at the Ritz 1973, The Children of Dynmouth 1977, Lovers of Their Time 1979, Other People's Worlds 1980, Beyond the Pale 1981, Fools of Fortune 1983, A Writer's Ireland: Landscape in Literature 1984, The News from Ireland 1986, Nights at the Alexandra 1987, The Silence in the Garden 1988, Family Sins and Other Stories 1989, The Oxford Book of Irish Short Stories (ed.) 1989, Two Lives 1991, William Trevor: The Collected Stories 1992, Juliet's Story 1992, Excursions in the Real World (essays) 1993, Felicia's Journey 1994, Ireland: Selected Stories 1995, After Rain 1996, Cocktails at Doney's and Other Stories 1996, Death in Summer 1998, The Hill Bachelors 2000, The Story of Lucy Gault 2002, A Bit on the Side (short stories) 2004. *Honours:* Hawthornden Prize 1965, Royal Soc. of Literature Prize 1978, Whitbread Prize for Fiction 1978, Allied Irish Banks Award for Services to Literature 1978, Whitbread Prize for Fiction 1983, Whitbread Book of the Year 1994; Sunday Express Book of the Year Award 1994, David Cohen British Literature Prize 1999, PEN Prize for Short Stories 2001, Irish Times Prize for Irish Fiction 2001; Hon. DLitt (Exeter) 1984, (Dublin) 1986, (Queen's Univ., Belfast) 1989, (Nat. Univ. Cork) 1990; Hon. KBE 2002. *Literary Agent:* PFD, 34–43 Russell Street, London, WC2B 5HA, England.

TREWIN, Ion; British editor. *Career:* Literary Ed., The Times 1972–79; Editorial Dir, Hodder & Stoughton; Ed.-in-Chief, Weidenfeld & Nicolson; London Ed., Publisher Weekly (USA); Ed., Drama Magazine; Chair. Booker Prize judging panel 1974, mem. Advisory Cttee 1989–2003; Chair. Cheltenham Booker Prize, Cheltenham Literary Festival 1996–; Deputy Administrator of Man Booker Prize 2004. *Publications:* Journalism 1975, Norfolk Cottage 1977, Diaries: Into Politics, by Alan Clark (ed.) 2000, The Last Diaries: In and Out of the Wilderness, by Alan Clark (ed.) 2002. *Address:* c/o Weidenfeld and Nicolson, 5 Upper St Martin's Lane, London, WC2H 9EA, England.

TRICKETT, (Mabel) Rachel, MA; writer and playwright; b. 20 Dec. 1923, Lathom, Lancashire, England. *Education:* Lady Margaret Hall, Oxford. *Career:* Principal, St Hugh's Coll., Oxford 1973–91. *Publications:* The Return Home, 1952; The Course of Love, 1954; Point of Honour, 1958; A Changing Place, 1962; The Elders, 1966; The Visit to Timon, 1970. Plays: Antigone, 1954; Silas Marner, 1960. Non-Fiction: The Honest Muse: A Study in Augustan Verse, 1967; Browning's Lyricism, 1971; Tennyson's

Craft, 1981. *Honours:* Rhys Memorial Prize 1953, Hon. Fellow, Lady Margaret Hall 1978. *Address:* Flat 4, 18 Norham Gardens, Oxford OX2 6QB, England.

TRIER MØRCH, Dea; Writer and Graphic Artist; b. 9 Dec. 1941, Copenhagen, Denmark; m. Troels Trier, one s. two d. *Education:* Graduated, Royal Acad. of Fine Arts, Copenhagen, 1964; Postgraduate Studies, Academies of Fine Arts, Warsaw, Kraków, Belgrade, Leningrad, Prague, 1964–67. *Career:* mem. Danish Writers Asscn, chair., 1990–91; PEN Club, Denmark; Union of Danish Graphic Artists; Artists Asscn, Denmark. *Publications:* 15 books in Danish, 1968–95, including Winter's Child, trans. into 22 languages. Other: various graphic works exhibited world-wide. *Honours:* Danish Author of the Year Award, 1977; Danish Government Stipends for Life, 1985, and for Works, 1994. *Address:* Jens Juels Gade 7, 2100 Copenhagen, Denmark.

TRIGGER, Bruce Graham; Prof. of Anthropology and Writer; b. 18 June 1937, Cambridge, ON, Canada; m. Barbara Marian Welch, 7 Dec. 1968, two d. *Education:* BA, University of Toronto, 1959; PhD, Yale University, 1964. *Career:* Asst Prof., Northwestern University, 1963–64; Asst Prof., 1964–67, Assoc. Prof., 1967–69, Prof. of Anthropology, 1969–, James McGill Prof., 2001–, McGill University; mem. various professional organizations. *Publications:* History and Settlement in Lower Nubia, 1965; Late Nubian Settlement at Arminna West, 1967; Beyond History, 1968; The Huron: Farmers of the North, 1969; Cartier's Hochelaga and the Dawson Site, 1972; Nubia Under the Pharaohs, 1976; The Children of Aataentsic, 1976; Time and Traditions, 1978; Handbook of North American Indians, Vol. 15, Northeast, 1978; Gordon Childe, 1980; Natives and Newcomers, 1985; A History of Archaeological Thought, 1989; Early Civilizations: Ancient Egypt in Context, 1993; Cambridge History of the Native Peoples of the Americas, Vol. I, North America (co-ed.), 1996; Sociocultural Evolution, 1998; Artifacts and Ideas, 2003; Understanding Early Civilizations, 2003. Contributions: Antiquity; American Antiquity; World Archaeology; Man. *Honours:* Canadian Silver Jubilee Medal, 1977; Cornplanter Medal, 1979; Innis-Gerin Medal, Royal Society of Canada, 1985; DSc, University of New Brunswick, 1987; John Porter Prize, 1988; DLitt, University of Waterloo, 1990; Prix du Québec, 1991; Hon. Mem., Prehistoric Society, England, 1991; Hon. Fellow, Society of Antiquaries of Scotland, 1993; LLD, University of Western Ontario, 1995, McMaster University, 1999, Univ. of Toronto, 2003; Officier, Ordre nat. du Québec, 2001. *Address:* Dept of Anthropology, McGill University, 855 Sherbrooke St W, Montréal, QC H3A 2T7, Canada. *E-mail:* bruce.trigger@mcgill.ca.

TRILLIN, Calvin (Marshall); Journalist, Critic and Author; b. 5 Dec. 1935, Kansas City, MO, USA; m. Alice Stewart, 13 Aug. 1965, two d. *Education:* BA, Yale University, 1957. *Career:* Reporter, later Writer, Time magazine, 1960–63; Staff Writer, The New Yorker magazine, 1963–; Columnist, The Nation magazine, 1978–85, King Features Syndicate, 1986–95. *Publications:* An Education in Georgia: Charlayne Hunter, Hamilton Holmes, and the Integration of the University of Georgia, 1964; Barnett Frummer is an Unbloomed Flower and Other Adventures of Barnett Frummer, Rosalie Mondle, Roland Magruder, and Their Friends, 1969; US Journal, 1971; American Fried: Adventures of a Happy Eater, 1974; Runestruck, 1977; Alice, Let's Eat: Further Adventures of a Happy Eater, 1978; Floater, 1980; Uncivil Liberties, 1982; Third Helpings, 1983; Killings, 1984; With All Disrespect: More Uncivil Liberties, 1985; If You Can't Say Something Nice, 1987; Travels with Alice, 1989; Enough's Enough (and Other Rules of Life), 1990; American Stories, 1991; Remembering Denny, 1993; Deadline Poet, 1994; Too Soon to Tell, 1995; Messages from Father, 1996; Family Man, 1998; Tepper Isn't Going Out, 2002. Contributions: Magazines. *Honours:* Books-Across-the-Sea Ambassador of Honor Citation, English-Speaking Union, 1985. *Address:* c/o The New Yorker, 4 Times Sq., New York, NY 10036-6592, USA.

TROGDON, William Lewis (see Heat-Moon, William Least).

TROLLOPE, Joanna, (Caroline Harvey); Writer; b. 9 Dec. 1943, England; m. 1st David Roger William Potter 1966; two d.; m. 2nd Ian Bayley Curteis 1985 (divorced 2001); two step-s. *Education:* MA, St Hugh's College, Oxford, 1972. *Career:* Information and Research Dept, Foreign Office, 1965–67; Teaching posts, Farnham Girl's Grammar School, Adult education, English for Foreigners and Daneshill School, 1967–79; Chair., Dept of National Heritage Advisory Committee on National Reading Initiative, 1996–97; Mem., Government Advisory Body, National Year of Reading, 1998; Trustee, Joanna Trollope Charitable Trust, 1995–; Patron, Gloucestershire Community Foundation, 1994–; mem. Joanna Trollope Charitable Trust, trustee, 1995–; Trollope Society, vice-pres.; Society of Authors, council mem.; West Country Writers Asscn, council mem. *Publications:* Eliza Stanhope, 1978; Parson Harding's Daughter, 1979, US edn as Mistaken Virtues; Leaves from the Valley, 1980; The City of Gems, 1981; The Steps of the Sun, 1983; Britannia's Daughters: A Study of Women in the British Empire, 1983; The Taverners' Place, 1986; The Choir, 1988; A Village Affair, 1989; A Passionate Man, 1990; The Rector's Wife, 1991; The Men and the Girls, 1992; A Spanish Lover, 1992; The Best of Friends, 1992; The Country Habit: An Anthology, 1993; Next of Kin, 1996; Other People's Children, 1998; Marrying the Mistress, 2000; Girl from the South, 2002; Brother and Sister, 2004. As Caroline Harvey: Legacy of Love, 1992; A Second Legacy, 1993; The Brass Dolphin, 1997. Contributions: newspapers and magazines. *Honours:* Romantic Historical Novel of the Year, 1980; OBE, 1996; Deputy Lieutenant for County of Gloucestershire, 2002. *Literary Agent:* PFD, Drury House, 34–43 Russell St, London WC2B 5HA, England.

TROUPE, Quincy Thomas, Jr; Poet, Writer and University Instructor; b. 23 July 1943, New York, NY, USA; m. Margaret Porter, four c. *Education:* BA, Gambling College, 1963; AA, Los Angeles City College, 1967. *Career:* Instructor, various colleges and universities; Instructor in Creative Writing and American, African-American and Caribbean Literature, University of California at San Diego; many poetry readings; mem. Poetry Society of America. *Publications:* Watts Poets: A Book of New Poetry and Essays (ed.), 1968; Embryo Poems, 1967–1971, 1972; Giant Talk: An Anthology of Third World Writings (ed. with Rainer Schulte), 1975; The Inside Story of TV's 'Roots' (ed. with David L. Wolper), 1978; Snake-back Solos: Selected Poems, 1969–1977, 1978; Skulls Along the River (poems), 1984; Soundings, 1988; James Baldwin: The Legacy (ed.), 1989; Miles: The Autobiography (with Miles Davis), 1989; Weather Reports: New and Selected Poems, 1991; Avalanche: Poems, 1996; Choruses: Poems, 1999; Miles and Me, 2000. Contributions: periodicals. *Honours:* National Endowment for the Arts Award in Poetry, 1978; American Book Awards, 1980, 1990; New York Foundation for the Arts Fellowship in Poetry, 1987.

TROW, George W. S.; Writer and Dramatist; b. 28 Sept. 1943, Greenwich, CT, USA. *Education:* AB, Harvard University, 1965. *Career:* Staff Writer, The New Yorker, 1966–. *Publications:* Bullies (short stories), 1980; Within the Context of No Context (essays), 1981; The City in the Mist (novel), 1984. Other: several plays. Contributions: anthologies and periodicals. *Honours:* Jean Stein Awards, American Acad. and Institute of Arts and Letters, 1981, 1984, 1986; Guggenheim Fellowship, 1994–95. *Address:* c/o The New Yorker, 4 Times Sq., New York, NY 10036-6592, USA.

TROWBRIDGE, William, BA, MA, PhD; poet and editor; b. 9 May 1941, Chicago, IL, USA; m. Waneta Sue Downing 1963; two s. one d. *Education:* Univ. of Missouri at Columbia, Vanderbilt Univ. *Career:* instructor, Univ. of Missouri at Columbia 1966, Vanderbilt Univ. 1970; Asst Prof. to Distinguished Univ. Prof., Northwest Missouri State Univ. 1971–98; Co-Ed., The Laurel Review 1986–99, Assoc. Ed. 2001; Asst Ed., The Georgia Review 2000. *Publications:* The Book of Kong 1986, Enter Dark Stranger 1989, O Paradise 1995, Flickers 2000, The Four Seasons 2002, The Complete Book of Kong 2003; contrib. to Poetry, Georgia Review, Kenyon Review, Southern Review, Gettysburg Review and many others. *Honours:* Acad. of American Poets Prize 1970, Bread Loaf Writers' Conference Scholarship 1981, Yaddo Fellowship 1992. *Address:* 224 SW Green Teal Street, Lee's Summit, MO 64082-4507, USA.

TROYAT, Henri; French writer; b. (Henri Tarassoff), 1 Nov. 1911, Moscow, Russia; m. Marguerite Saintagne 1948 (deceased); one s. one step-d. *Education:* Lycée Pasteur and Law Faculty, Univ. of Paris. *Career:* mem. Acad. Française 1959–. *Publications:* novels: Faux-jour (Prix Populiste) 1935, L'araigne (Prix Goncourt) 1938, La neige en deuil (Grand prix littéraire de Monaco) 1952, Tant que la terre durera (three vols) 1947–50, Les semailles et les moissons (five vols) 1953–58, La lumière des justes (five vols) 1960–, Les Eygletière (three vols) 1965–67, Les héritiers de l'avenir (three vols) 1968, Anne Predaille 1973, Le Moscovite (three vols) 1974, La dérision 1983, Le bruit solitaire du coeur 1985, Aliocha, A Demain Sylvie 1986, Le Troisième bonheur 1987, Toute ma vie sera mensonge 1988, Le Défi d'Olga 1995, L'Affaire Crémonnière 1997, Le fils du satrape 1998, Namouna ou la chaleur animale 1999, La ballerine de Saint-Petersbourg, La fille de l'écrivain, l'étage des bouffons; short stories: Du philantrope à la rouquine, Le gest d'Eve, Les ailes du Diable, L'Eternel Contretemps 2003; biographies: Dostoïevski, Pouchkine, L'étrange destin de Lermontov, Tolstoï, Gogol, Catherine la Grande, Pierre le Grand, Alexandre Ier, Ivan le Terrible, Tchekov, Tourgueniev, Gorki, Flaubert, Maupassant, Alexandre II, Nicolas II, Zola, Verlaine, Baudelaire, Balzac, Raspoutine, Juliette Drouet, Terribles tsarines 1998, Les turbulences d'une grande famille, Nicolas Ier, Maria Tsvetaeva, l'éternelle insurgée, Paul Ier, le tsar mal aimé, La baronne et le musicien. *Honours:* Grand Officier Légion d'honneur, Commdr Ordre nat. du Mérite, Ordre des Arts et des Lettres. *Address:* Académie Française, 23 quai de Conti, 75006 Paris, France.

TRUMAN, Jill; Teacher, Writer and Dramatist; b. 12 June 1934, Enfield, Middlesex, England; m. Tony Truman, 31 March 1956, deceased 1975, one s., three d. *Education:* BA, English Literature, 1955; Postgraduate Certificate in Drama, 1979. *Career:* mem. Writers Guild of Great Britain. *Publications:* Letter to My Husband, 1988. Other: Radio plays: Letter to My Husband, 1986; Gone Out-Back Soon, 1988; Travels in West Africa, 1990; For Lizzie, 1994; Sounds of Silence, 1998. Theatre: The Web, 1991. Musical: Kings of the Night, 1993. Short Stories: On The Terrace, 1998; Full Moon, 1998; In the Supermarket, 1998. Puppet Play: Flit 1992. Contributions: Magazines. *Address:* 2 Ellesmere Rd, Bow, London E3 5QX, England.

TRUMAN, (Mary) Margaret, BA; writer; b. 17 Feb. 1924, Independence, MO, USA; m. E. Clifton Daniel Jr 1956 (died 2000); four s. *Education:* George Washington Univ. *Publications:* Fiction: Murder in the White House, 1980; Murder on Capitol Hill, 1981; Murder in the Supreme Court, 1982; Murder in the Smithsonian, 1983; Murder on Embassy Row, 1985; Murder at the FBI, 1985; Murder in Georgetown, 1986; Murder in the CIA, 1987; Murder at the Kennedy Center, 1989; Murder in the National

Cathedral, 1990; Murder at the Pentagon, 1992; Murder on the Potomac, 1994; Murder in the National Gallery, 1996; Murder at the Watergate, 1998; Murder at the Library of Congress, 1999; Murder in Foggy Bottom, 2000. Non-Fiction: White House Pets, 1969; Harry S. Truman, 1973; Women of Courage, 1976; Letters from Father, 1981; Bess W. Truman, 1986; Where the Buck Stops: The Personal and Private Writings of Harry S. Truman (ed.), 1989; First Ladies, 1995. *Honours:* LHD, Wake Forest University, 1972; HHD, Rockhurst College, 1976. *Address:* c/o Harry S. Truman Library Institute for National and International Affairs, US 24 Highway and Delaware Street, Independence, MO 64050, USA.

TRUSS, Lynne, BA; British writer and broadcaster; b. 1955. *Education:* Univ. Coll. London. *Career:* copy ed., Radio Times; Literary Ed., The Listener 1986–90; writer and teacher at Arvon Foundation; contributor and presenter, BBC Radio 4; book reviewer, The Sunday Times, Daily Mail; columnist, The Times, Woman's Journal. *Plays:* Acropolis Now (two series, BBC Radio 4) 2000–01, A Certain Age 2002, Full Circle 2003. *Publications:* novels: With One Lousy Free Packet of Seed 1994, Tennyson's Gift 1996, Going Loco 1999; non-fiction: Making the Cat Laugh 1995, Eats, Shoots and Leaves: The Zero Tolerance Approach to Punctuation 2003. *Literary Agent:* c/o Profile Books, 58a Hatton Garden, London, EC1N 8LX, England. *Telephone:* (20) 7404-3001. *Fax:* (20) 7404-3003. *E-mail:* info@profilebooks.co.uk. *Website:* www.profilebooks.co.uk.

TSALOUMAS, Dimitris; Poet, Ed. and Trans; b. 13 Oct. 1921, Leros, Greece; two s. two d. *Career:* Teacher, Victorian schools, 1958–82; Writer-in-Residence, University of Oxford, University of Melbourne, Queensland University, La Trobe University. *Publications:* Resurrection, 1967; Triptych for a Second Coming, 1974; Observations for a Hypochondriac, 1974; The House with the Eucalyptus, 1975; The Sick Barber and Other Characters, 1979; The Book of Epigrams, 1981; The Observatory: Selected Poems, 1983; Falcon Drinking: The English Poems, 1988; Portrait of a Dog, 1991; The Barge, 1993; Six Improvisations On the River, 1995; The Harbour, 1998; Stoneland Harvest, 1999; New and Selected Poems, 2000. *Honours:* Australia Council Grant and Fellowship; National Book Council Award, 1983; Wesley M. Wright Prize for Poetry, 1994; Patrick White Award, 1994; John Bray Poetry Award, Adelaide Festival, 2000; Australia Council Emeritus Award, 2002. *Address:* 72 Glenhuntly Rd, Elwood, Vic. 3184, Australia.

TUBB, Edwin Charles, (Chuck Adams, Jud Cary, J. F. Clarkson, James S. Farrow, James R. Fenner, Charles S. Graham, Charles Grey, Volsted Gridban, Alan Guthrie, George Holt, Gill Hunt, E. F. Jackson, Gregory Kern, King Lang, Mike Lantry, P. Lawrence, Chet Lawson, Arthur MacLean, Carl Maddox, M. L. Powers, Paul Schofield, Brian Shaw, Roy Sheldon, John Stevens, Edward Thomson, Douglas West, Eric Wilding); British writer; b. 15 Oct. 1919, London, England. *Publications include:* (under various pseudonyms) novels: Saturn Patrol 1951, Argentis 1952, Planetoid Disposals Ltd 1953, The Living World 1954, The Fighting Fury 1955, Alien Dust 1955, Scourge of the South 1956, The Space-Born 1956, Wagon Trail 1957, Touch of Evil 1959, Target Death 1961, Too Tough to Handle 1962, Airborne Commando 1963, Moon Base 1964, Ten From Tomorrow (short stories) 1966, Death is a Dream 1967, COD Mars 1968, STAR Flight 1969, The Jester at Scar 1970, Lallia 1971, Century of the Manikin 1972, Mayenne 1973, Veruchia 1973, Zenya 1974, Atilus the Slave 1975, Jack of Swords 1976, Haven of Darkness 1977, Incident on Ath 1978, The Quillian Sector 1978, Web of Sand 1979, Iduna's Universe 1979, Stellar Assignment 1979, The Luck Machine 1980, The Terra Data 1980, World of Promise 1980, Nectar of Heaven 1981, The Terridae 1981, The Coming Event 1982, Earth is Heaven 1982, Melome 1983, Stardeath 1983, Angado 1984, Symbol of Terra 1984, The Temple of Truth 1985, Pandora's Box 1996, Temple of Death 1996, Assignment New York 1996, Kalgan the Golden 1996, The Return 1997, I Fight for Mars 1998, Death God's Doom 1999, The Wall 1999, The Sleeping City 1999, Earthfall 2001, Alien Seed 2002; short stories: Murder in Space 1997, Alien Life 1998; contrib. over 230 stories to magazines and journals. *Address:* 67 Houston Road, London, SE23 2RL, England.

TUCKER, Eva Marie; Writer; b. 18 April 1929, Berlin, Germany; m. 11 March 1950 (widowed 1987), three d. *Education:* BA, German, English, University of London. *Career:* C. Day-Lewis Writing Fellow, Vauxhall Manor School, London, 1978–79; Hawthornden Writing Fellowship, 1991; mem. English PEN; Society of Authors. *Publications:* Contact (novel), 1966; Drowning (novel), 1969; Radetzkymarch by Joseph Roth (trans.), 1974; Dorothy Richardson: The Enchanted Guest of Spring and Summer, A Monograph, 2003. Contributions: BBC Radio 3 and 4; Encounter; London Magazine; Woman's Journal; Vogue; Harper's; Spectator; Listener; PEN International; TLS. *Address:* 63B Belsize Park Gardens, London NW3 4JN, England.

TUCKER, Helen, BA; writer; b. 1 Nov. 1926, Raleigh, NC, USA; m. William Beckwith. *Education:* Wake Forest Univ., Columbia Univ. *Publications:* The Sound of Summer Voices 1969, The Guilt of August Fielding 1972, No Need of Glory 1973, The Virgin of Lontano 1974, A Strange and Ill-Starred Marriage 1978, A Reason for Rivalry 1979, A Mistress to the Regent: An Infamous Attachment 1980, The Halverton Scandal 1980, A Wedding Day Deception 1981, The Double Dealers 1982, Season of Dishonor 1982, Ardent Vows 1983, Bound by Honor 1984, The Lady's Fancy 1991, Bold Impostor 1991; contrib. to Lady's Circle, Ellery Queen Mystery Magazine, Alfred Hitchcock Mystery Magazine, Ladies' Home Journal, Crescent Review, Montevallo Review, Redbook Magazine. *Honours:* Distinguished Alumni Award, Wake Forest Univ. 1971, Franklin County Artist of the Year Award 1992. *Address:* 2930 Hostetler Street, Raleigh, NC 27609, USA.

TUCKER, (Allan) James, BA, MA; writer; b. 15 Aug. 1929, Cardiff, Wales; m. Marian Roberta Craig 1954; three s., one d. *Education:* University of Wales, Cardiff. *Career:* mem. Authors' Guild, CWA, MWA. *Publications:* Equal Partners, 1960; The Alias Man, 1968; The Novels of Anthony Powell, 1976; The Lolita Man, 1986; Baby Talk, 1998; Lovely Mover, 1998; The Tattoed Detective, 1998; Bay City, 2000; Kill Me, 2000; Pay Days, 2001; Split, 2001; Double Jeopardy, 2002. Contributions: Punch; Spectator; New Statesman; New Review. *Literary Agent:* Curtis Brown Ltd, Haymarket House, 28–29 Haymarket, London, SW1Y 4SP, England. *Telephone:* (20) 7393-4400. *Fax:* (20) 7393-4401. *E-mail:* info@curtisbrown.co.uk. *Website:* www.curtisbrown.co.uk.

TUCKER, Martin; Prof. of English, Writer and Poet; b. 8 Feb. 1928, Philadelphia, Pennsylvania, USA. *Education:* BA, 1949, PhD, 1963, New York University; MA, University of Arizona, 1954. *Career:* Faculty, Long Island University, 1956–; Ed., Confrontation magazine, 1970–; mem. African Literature Asscn; African Studies Asscn; Authors' Guild; MLA; National Book Critics Circle; PEN, exec. board, 1973–96; Poetry Society of America. *Publications:* Modern British Literature (ed.), Vols I–IV, 1967–76; Africa in Modern Literature, 1967; The Critical Temper (ed.), Vols I–V, 1970–89; Joseph Conrad, 1976; Homes of Locks and Mysteries (poems), 1982; Literary Exile in the United States, 1991; Sam Shepard, 1992; Attention Spans (poems), 1997; Modern American Literature (ed.), 1997. Contributions: Professional journals and general periodicals. *Honours:* National Endowment for the Arts/Co-ordinating Council and Literary Magazine Awards for Editorial Distinction, 1976, 1984; English-Speaking Union Award, 1982. *Address:* 4540 Gulf of Mexico Dr., Longboat Key, FL 34228, USA.

TUDOR-CRAIG, Pamela Wynn, (Lady Wedgwood), BA, PhD; British art historian and writer; b. 26 June 1928, London, England; m. 1st Algernon James Riccarton Tudor-Craig 1956 (died 1969), one d.; m. 2nd Sir John Wedgwood 1982 (died 1989). *Education:* Courtauld Inst. of Art, London. *Career:* lecturer at several US colls 1969–96; presenter, The Secret Life of Paintings television series 1986; mem. Cathedrals Advisory Commission 1975–90; mem. Architectural Advisory Panel, Westminster Abbey 1979–98; f. annual Harlaxton Symposium of English Medieval Studies 1984–, Cambridgeshire Historic Churches Trust 1982–; mem. English Speaking Union (cultural affairs cttee) 1990–98, Soc. of Antiquaries (fellow 1958–, council mem. 1989–92). *Publications:* Richard III 1973, The Secret Life of Paintings (with R. Foster) 1986, Bells Guide to Westminster Abbey (co-author) 1986, Exeter Cathedral (contrib.) 1991, Anglo-Saxon Wall Paintings 1991, The Regal Image of Richard II and the Wilton Diptych 1997, King Arthur's Round Table 2000; contrib. to books, exhibition catalogues, journals and learned journals, including Church Times, History Today, radio and television. *Honours:* Hon. DH (William Jewell Coll.) 1983. *Address:* 9 St Anne's Crescent, Lewes, East Sussex BN7 1SB, England.

TUENI, Ghassan, MA; Lebanese publishing executive; b. 5 Jan. 1926, Beirut; m. 2nd Chadia El-Khazen; one s. *Education:* American Univ. of Beirut and Harvard Univ. *Career:* lecturer in Political Science, American Univ. of Beirut 1947–48; Ed.-in-Chief, An-Nahar (daily newspaper) 1948, Pres.; Man.-Dir An-Nahar Publishing Co. (now Dar an-Nahar SAL) 1963–; Co-founder Lebanese Acad. of Law and Political Science 1951, lecturer 1951–54; MP for Beirut 1953–57; mem. Lebanese del. to UN Gen. Ass. 1957; founded Middle East Business Services and Research Corpn 1958, Chair. 1958–70; founder, Chair. and Man.-Dir of Press Co-operative, SAL 1960–; Deputy Prime Minister and Minister of Information and Nat. Educ. 1970–71; arrested Dec. 1973, appeared before mil. tribunal and then released in accordance with press laws; Minister for Social Affairs and Labour, Tourism, Industry and Oil 1975–76; Perm. Rep. to UN 1977–82; Pres. Annahar Daily –2000; Pres. Dar Annahar Publishing 'Les Editions Dar an-Nahar' SAL 2000–; mem. Nat. Dialogue Cttee 1975. *Publications:* Peace-Keeping Lebanon 1979, Laissez vivre mon peuple 1984, Une guerre pour les autres 1985, El Bourj (Place de la liberté et porte du Levant) 2000; books and pamphlets in Arabic. *Address:* Dar an-Nahar SAL, PO Box 11-226, 36 Andraos str., Achrafieh, Beirut (Office); Ras Kafra, Beit Mery, Lebanon (Home). *Telephone:* (1) 444642 (Office). *Fax:* (1) 561877 (Office). *E-mail:* ghs@annahar.com.lb (Office).

TULLI, Magdalena; Psychologist and Novelist; b. 1955, Poland. *Publications:* Sny i kamienie (Dreams and Stones), 1995; W czerwieni (In Red), 1998. *Honours:* Koscielski Foundation Prize, 1995. *Address:* c/o W.A.B. Publishers, ul. Lowicka 31, 02-502 Warsaw, Poland.

TULLY, Sir (William) Mark, Kt, MA; journalist and broadcaster; b. 24 Oct. 1935, Kolkata, India; m. Margaret Frances Butler 1960; two s. two d. *Education:* Marlborough College, Trinity Hall, Cambridge. *Career:* Regional Dir, Abbeyfield Society, 1960–64; Asst, Appointments Dept, 1964–65, Asst, later Acting Representative, New Delhi, 1955–69, Programme Organiser and Talks Writer, Eastern Service, 1969–71, Chief of Bureau, Delhi, 1972–93, South Asia Correspondent, 1993–94, BBC; Presenter, The Lives of Jesus, BBC TV, 1996. *Publications:* Amritsar: Mrs

Gandhi's Last Battle (with Satish Jacob), 1985; From Raj to Rajiv (with Z. Masani), 1988; No Full Stops in India, 1991; The Heart of India, 1995; The Lives of Jesus, 1996; India in Slow Motion (with Gillian Wright), 2002. *Honours:* Padma Shri, India, 1992; Hon. Fellow, Trinity Hall, Cambridge, 1994; Hon. DLitt, Univ. of Strathclyde, 1997; Hon. doctorates, Richmond the American International Univ. in London, 1999, Univ. of Bradford, 2001, Univ. of Central England, 2002. *Address:* 1 Nizamuddin E, New Delhi 110 013, India.

TUMWINE, James K.; Ugandan writer and paediatrician; b. Kabale. *Education:* Makerere Univ. *Career:* has worked in the UK and Zimbabwe; founder of African Health Sciences journal 2001–; Pres., Forum for African Medical Editors. *Publications include:* non-fiction: Drawers of Water: 30 Years of Change in Domestic Water Use and Environmental Health – Uganda County Case Study 2001. *Address:* African Health Sciences, Makerere University Medical School, PO Box 7072, Kampala, Uganda. *Telephone:* (41) 530020. *Fax:* (41) 530022. *E-mail:* pic@infocom.co.ug.

TUNNICLIFFE, Stephen; Poet and Writer; b. 22 May 1925, Wakefield, Yorkshire, England; m. Hilary Katharine Routh, 5 Aug. 1949, three s. *Education:* BA, English, 1951, MA, English, 1965, University of London; Certificate of Education, Institute of Education, 1952. *Career:* mem. Society of Authors. *Publications:* English in Practice (with Geoffrey Summerfield), 1971; Reading and Discrimination (with Denys Thompson), 1979; Poetry Experience: Teaching and Writing Poetry in Secondary Schools, 1984; Building and Other Poems, 1993; Uneasy Souls: A Forgotten Genius (novel), 1999; Some Poems, 2003; Discovering Shakespeare (new edn), 2003. Other: Libretti for John Joubert: The Martyrdom of St Alban; The Raising of Lazarus; The Magus; The Prisoner; The Wayfarers; Wings of Faith; For Francis Routh: Circles. Contributions: Reviews and journals. *Address:* Clairmont, The Square, Clun, Shropshire SY7 8JA, England.

TUOMEY, Nesta Catherine; Writer and Dramatist; b. 21 Oct. 1941, Dublin, Ireland; m. Laurence J. Tuomey, three s., one d. *Education:* Diploma, History of Art, National College of Art, Dublin, 1958–59. *Career:* mem. Society of Irish Playwrights, chair., 1980–82; Irish PEN, treas.; Writers' Union. *Publications:* Up Up and Away, 1995; Like One of the Family, 1999. Plays: The Same Again, 1969; One of These Days, 1977; Country Banking, 1982; Whose Baby?, 1996. Other: 18 documentaries. Contributions: many magazines and journals. *Honours:* John Power Short Story at Listowel 1981, Image Oil of Ulay Short Story 1994, Oz Whitehead Play Competition 1996. *Address:* Tully, Ballinteer Rd, Dublin 16, Ireland.

TURK, Frances Mary; Novelist; b. 14 April 1915, Huntingdon, England. *Career:* mem. Romantic Novelists Asscn; many other professional organizations. *Publications:* Paddy O'Shea 1937, The Precious Hours 1938, Paradise Street 1939, Lovable Clown 1941, Angel Hill 1942, The Five Grey Geese 1944, Salutation 1949, The Small House at Ickley 1951, The Gentle Flowers 1952, The Dark Wood 1954, The Glory and the Dream 1955, Dinny Lightfoot 1956, No Through Road 1957, The White Swan 1958, A Temple of Fancy 1959, A Journey to Eternity 1960, A Time to Know 1960, The Secret Places, 1961, A Man Called Jeremy 1961, A Lamp From Murano 1963, The Guarded Heart 1964, The Sour-Sweet Days 1965, The Rectory at Hay 1966, Goddess of Threads 1966, Legacy of Love 1967, Lionel's Story 1967, The Flowering Field 1967, The Marion Window 1968, The Lesley Affair 1968, Fair Recompense 1969, Goddess of Threads 1975, A Visit to Marchmont 1977, Candle Corner 1986. Contributions: many periodicals. *Address:* 36 Church Street, Buckden, St Neots, PE19 5TP, England.

TURNER, Alberta Tucker; academic, poet and writer; b. 22 Oct. 1919, New York, NY, USA; m. William Arthur Turner 1943; one s. one d. *Education:* BA, Hunter College, CUNY, 1940; MA, Wellesley College, Massachusetts, 1941; PhD, Ohio State University, 1946. *Career:* Lecturer to Prof., 1964–90, Dir, Poetry Center, 1964–90, Prof. Emerita, 1990–, Cleveland State University; Assoc. Ed., Field, Contemporary Poetry and Poetics, 1970–; mem. Milton Society of America; PEN American Center. *Publications:* Poetry: Need, 1971; Learning to Count, 1974; Lid and Spoon, 1977; A Belfry of Knees, 1983; Beginning with And: New and Selected Poems, 1994. Other: 50 Contemporary Poets: The Creative Process (ed.), 1977; Poets Teaching (ed.), 1981; To Make a Poem, 1982; 45 Contemporary Poems: The Creative Process (ed.), 1985; Responses to Poetry, 1990; Tomorrow is a Tight Fist, 2001. Contributions: journals and magazines. *Honours:* MacDowell Colony Fellowship, 1985; Cleveland Arts Prize, 1985; Ohio Poetry Award, 1986; Ohio Governor's Award for Arts in Education, 1988. *Address:* 482 Caskey Court, Oberlin, OH 44074, USA.

TURNER, Brian Lindsay; New Zealand poet and writer; b. 4 March 1944, Dunedin; one s. *Career:* fmrly customs officer, rabbiter, sawmiller, ed. for Oxford Univ. Press; Managing Ed., John McIndoe Ltd, Dunedin 1975–83, 1985–86; writer-in-residence, Univ. of Canterbury 1997; Te Mata Estate New Zealand Poet Laureate 2003–(05); Robert Burns Fellow, Univ. of Otago 1984. *Publications:* poetry: Ladders of Rain (Commonwealth Poetry Prize) 1978, Ancestors 1981, Listening to the River 1983, Bones 1985, All That Blue Can Be 1989, Beyond (New Zealand Book Award for Poetry 1993) 1992, Taking Off 2001; other: Images of Coastal Otago 1982, New Zealand High Country: Four Seasons 1983, The Visitor's Guide to Fiordland, New Zealand 1983, Finger's Up? (play) (J.C. Reid Memorial Prize) 1985, Opening Up (with Glenn Turner) 1987, Lifting the Covers (with Glenn Turner) 1987, The Last River's Song 1989, Timeless Land (with Owen Marshall and Graham Sydney) 1992, The Guide to Trout Fishing in Otago 1994, On the Loose (biog., with Josh Kronfeld) 1998, New Zealand Photographers (with Scott Freeman) 2000, The Art of Grahame Sydney (essay contrib.) 2001, Meads (with Colin Meads) 2002, Somebodies and Nobodies (autobiog.) 2002; contrib. to National Business Review, Independent, poetry anthologies, literary sports anthologies, columns, reviews and articles to daily and weekly newspapers; TV scripts. *Honours:* Scholarship in Letters 1994; New Zealand Journalists' Union Dulux Award for Sport Writing 1975, John Crowe Reid Memorial Prize 1985. *Address:* Main Road, Oturehua, Central Otago, New Zealand.

TURNER, Frederick, BA, MA, BLitt; academic, writer and poet; *Founders Professor of Arts and Humanities, University of Texas at Dallas*; b. 19 Nov. 1943, East Haddon, Northamptonshire, England; m. Mei Lin Chang 1966; two s. *Education:* Univ. of Oxford. *Career:* Asst Prof. of English, Univ. of California, Santa Barbara 1967–72; Assoc. Prof. of English, Kenyon Coll. 1972–85; Ed., Kenyon Review 1978–83; Visiting Prof. of English, Univ. of Exeter 1984–85; Founders Prof. of Arts and Humanities, Univ. of Texas at Dallas, Richardson 1985–; mem. PEN. *Publications:* Shakespeare and the Nature of Time 1971, Between Two Lives 1972, The Return 1979, The New World 1985, The Garden 1985, Natural Classicism 1986, Genesis: An Epic Poem 1988, Rebirth of Value 1991, Tempest, Flute and Oz 1991, April Wind 1991, Beauty 1991, Foamy Sky: The Major Poems of Miklos Radnoti (trans. with Zsuzanna Ozsváth) 1992, The Culture of Hope 1995, The Ballad of the Good Cowboy 1997, Hadean Eclogues 1999, Shakespeare's Twenty-First Century Economics: The Morality of Love and Money 1999, The Iron-Blue Vault: Selected Poems of Attila Jósef (trans. with Zsuzsanna Ozsváth) 1999; contrib. to journals and periodicals. *Honours:* Ohioana Prize for Editorial Excellence 1980, Djerassi Foundation Grant and Residency 1981, Levinson Poetry Prize 1983, Missouri Review Essay Prize 1986, PEN Golden Pen Award 1992, Milan Fust Prize 1996. *Address:* 2668 Aster Drive, Richardson, TX 75082, USA.

TURNER, George Reginald; writer; b. 8 Oct. 1916, Melbourne, Vic., Australia. *Career:* mem. Australian Soc. of Authors. *Publications:* Young Man of Talent, 1959; A Stranger and Afraid, 1961; A Waste of Shame, 1965; The Lame Dog Man, 1967; Beloved Son, Transit of Cassidy, 1978; Vaneglory, 1982; Yesterday's Men, 1983; The Sea and Summer, 1987; A Pursuit of Miracles, 1990; The Destiny Makes, 1993. *Honours:* Miles Franklin Award 1962, Arthur C. Clarke Award 1987. *Address:* 4/296 Inkerman Street, East St Kilda, Vic. 3183, Australia.

TURNER, Len (see Floren, Lee).

TURNER, Mary (see Lambot, Isobel Mary).

TUROW, Scott F., JD; American author and lawyer; b. 12 April 1949; m. Annette Weisberg 1971; three c. *Education:* Amherst Coll. and Stanford and Harvard Univs. *Career:* mem. Bar, Ill. 1978, US Dist Court. Ill. 1978, US Court of Appeals (7th Circuit) 1979; Assoc. Suffolk Co. Dist Attorney, Boston 1977–78; Asst US Attorney, US Dist Court, Ill., Chicago 1978–86; partner Sonnenschein, Nath & Rosenthal, Chicago 1986–; mem. Chicago Council of Lawyers. *Publications:* One L.: An Inside Account of Life in the First Year at Harvard Law School 1977, Presumed Innocent 1987, The Burden of Proof 1990, Pleading Guilty 1993, The Laws of our Fathers 1996, Personal Injuries 1999, Reversible Errors 2002, Ultimate Punishment: A Lawyer's Reflections on Dealing with the Death Penalty 2003; contribs to professional journals. *Address:* Sonnenschein, Nath & Rosenthal, Sears Tower, Suite 8000, 233 South Wacker Drive, Chicago, IL 60606, USA.

TUSIANI, Joseph, DLitt; American (b. Italian) poet, writer and fmr professor; b. 14 Jan. 1924, Foggia, Italy. *Education:* Univ. of Naples. *Career:* Chair., Italian Dept, College of Mount St Vincent, 1948–71; Lecturer in Italian, Hunter College, CUNY, 1950–62; Visiting Assoc. Prof., New York University, 1956–64, CUNY, 1971–83; NDEA Visiting Prof. of Italian, Connecticut State College, 1962; Prof., Lehman College, CUNY, 1971–83; mem. Catholic Poetry Society of America; Poetry Society of America. *Publications:* Dante in Licenza, 1952; Two Critical Essays on Emily Dickinson, 1952; Melos Cordis (poems in Latin), 1955; Odi Sacre: Poems, 1958; The Complete Poems of Michelangelo, 1960; Lust and Liberty: The Poems of Machiavelli, 1963; Tasso's Jerusalem Delivered (verse trans.), 1970; Italian Poets of the Renaissance, 1971; The Age of Dante, 1973; Tasso's Creation of the World, 1982; Rosa Rosarum (poems in Latin), 1984; In Exilio Rerum (poems in Latin), 1985; La Parola Difficile, 3 vols, 1988, 1991, 1992; Carmina Latina, 1994; Leopardi's Canti (trans.), 1994; Le Poesie Inglesi di G. A. Borgese, 1995; Pulci's Morgante (verse trans.), 1998; Dante's Lyric Poems, 1998; Radicitus (poems in Latin), 2000; Ethnicity, 2000; Two Languages, Two Lands (proceedings of an international convention on his work), 2000. Contributions: books and journals. *Honours:* Greenwood Prize for Poetry, 1956; Cavaliere ufficiale, Italy, 1973; Leone di San Marco Award, 1982; Joseph Tusiani Scholarship Fund founded in his honour, Lehman College, CUNY, 1983; Congressional Medal of Merit, 1984; Progresso Medal of Liberty, 1986; Outstanding Teacher Award, American Asscn of Teachers of Italian, 1987; Renoir Literary Award, 1988; Festschrift published in his honour, 1995; Enrico Fermi Award, 1995; National Endowment for the Humanities Fellowship, 1998; Fiorello La Guardia Award, 1998; Governor's Award for Excellence, 2000; Premio Puglia, 2000. *Address:* 308 E 72nd Street, New York, NY 10021, USA.

TUTTLE, Lisa; Writer; b. 16 Sept. 1952, Houston, Texas, USA. *Education:* BA, Syracuse University, 1973. *Publications:* Windhaven, 1981; Familiar Spirit, 1983; Catwitch, 1983; Children's Literary Houses, 1984; Encyclopedia of Feminism, 1986; A Spaceship Built of Stone and Other Stories, 1987; Heroines: Women Inspired by Women, 1988; Lost Futures, 1992; Memories of the Body, 1992; Panther in Argyll, 1996; The Pillow Friend, 1996. Contributions: Magazines. *Honours:* John W. Campbell Award, 1974. *Address:* 10 Roland Gardens, London SW7, England.

TWICHELL, Chase; Poet, Writer, Teacher and Publisher; b. 20 Aug. 1950, New Haven, CT, USA; m. Russell Banks, 25 Aug. 1989. *Education:* BA, Trinity College, 1973; MFA, University of Iowa, 1976. *Career:* Ed., Pennyroyal Press, 1976–85; Assoc. Prof., University of Alabama, 1985–88; Lecturer, Princeton University, 1990–2000; Assoc. Faculty, Goddard College, 1996–98, Warren Wilson College, 1999–; Ed., Ausable Press, 1999–. *Publications:* Northern Spy, 1981; The Odds, 1986; Perdido, 1991; The Practice of Poetry (co-ed.), 1992; The Ghost of Eden, 1995; The Snow Watcher, 1998. Contributions: Antaeus; Field; Georgia Review; Nation; New England Review; New Yorker; Ohio Review; Ontario Review; Paris Review; Ploughshares; Poetry Review; Southern Review; Yale Review. *Honours:* National Endowment for the Arts Fellowships, 1987, 1993; Guggenheim Fellowship, 1990; Artists Foundation Fellowship, Boston, 1990; New Jersey State Council on the Arts Fellowship, 1990; American Acad. of Arts and Letters Award, 1994; Alice Fay Di Castagnola Award, Poetry Society of America, 1997. *Address:* c/o Ellen Levine Literary Agency, 15 East St, Suite 1801, New York, NY 10010, USA.

TYLDESLEY, Joyce (Ann); Archaeologist and Researcher; b. 25 Feb. 1960, Bolton, England; m. Steven Ralph Snape, 6 April 1985, one s. one d. *Education:* BA, University of Liverpool, 1981; St Anne's College, Oxford, 1981–82; DPhil, St Cross College, Oxford, 1985. *Career:* Lecturer in Archaeology of the Eastern Mediterranean, 1986–87, Research Fellow, Institute of Prehistoric Science and Archaeology, 1987–91, Hon. Research Fellow, School of Archaeology, Classics and Oriental Studies, 1993–, University of Liverpool; mem. Egypt Exploration Society. *Publications:* The Wolvercote Channel Handaxe Assemblage: A Comparative Study, 1986; The Bout Coupe Biface: A Typological Problem, 1987; Nazlet Tuna: An Archaeological Survey in Middle Egypt (co-author), 1988; Daughters of Isis: Women of Ancient Egypt, 1994; Hatchepsut: The Female Pharaoh, 1996; Nefertiti: The Sun Queen, 1998; Pyramids: The Real Story Behind Egypt's Most Ancient Monuments, 2003. Contributions: articles and reviews to professional journals and popular magazines including, History Today, Focus, Popular Archaeology. *Honours:* British Acad. Grant, 1987. *Literary Agent:* Watson Little Ltd, 12 Egbert St, London NW1 8LJ, England. *Address:* Dept of Archaeology, University of Liverpool, 14 Abercromby Sq., Liverpool L69 3BX, England.

TYLER, Anne, BA; American writer; b. 25 Oct. 1941, Minneapolis, Minn.; m. Taghi M. Modarressi 1963 (died 1997); two c. *Education:* Duke Univ., Columbia Univ. *Career:* mem. American Acad. of Arts and Letters, American Acad. of Arts and Sciences. *Publications:* If Morning Ever Comes 1964, The Tin Can Tree 1965, A Slipping-Down Life 1970, The Clock Winder 1972, Celestial Navigation 1974, Searching for Caleb 1976, Earthly Possessions 1977, Morgan's Passing 1980, Dinner at the Homesick Restaurant 1982, The Best American Short Stories (ed. with Shannon Ravenel) 1983, The Accidental Tourist (Nat. Book Critics Circle Award for Fiction) 1985, Breathing Lessons (Pulitzer Prize for Fiction 1989) 1988, Saint Maybe 1991, Tumble Tower (juvenile) 1993, Ladder of Years 1995, A Patchwork Planet 1998, Back When We Were Grown-ups 2001, The Amateur Marriage 2003; short stories in magazines. *Address:* 222 Tunbridge Road, Baltimore, MD 21212, USA. *E-mail:* atmBaltimore@aol.com (Home).

U

UGLOW, Jenny; British biographer and writer; b. Cumbria, England; m.; three c. *Education:* Cheltenham Ladies Coll., St Anne's Coll., Oxford. *Career:* fmr freelance ed., Macmillan Press, teacher; fmr Ed./Dir, Chatto and Windus. *Publications:* George Eliot 1987, Elizabeth Gaskell: A Habit of Stories 1993, Henry Fielding 1995, Hogarth: A Life and a World 1997, Dr Johnson, His Club and Other Friends 1998, In a Green Shade 2002, The Lunar Men: The Friends Who Made the Future (James Tait Black Memorial Prize for Biography 2003) 2002, A Little History of British Gardening 2004; editor: The Macmillan Biographical Dictionary of Women, Cultural Babbage: Technology Time and Invention (with Francis Spufford) 1996; numerous works by Elizabeth Gaskell; contrib. to The Guardian, TLS, Independent on Sunday. *Address:* c/o Faber and Faber Ltd, 3 Queen Square, London, WC1N 3AU, England.

UHNAK, Dorothy; Writer; b. 1933, New York, NY, USA. *Education:* City College, CUNY; BS, John Jay College of Criminal Justice, CUNY, 1968. *Career:* Detective, New York City Transit Police Dept, 1953–67; mem. PEN; Writers' Guild of America. *Publications:* Policewoman, 1964; The Bait, 1968; The Witness, 1969; The Ledger, 1970; Law and Order, 1973; The Investigation, 1977; False Witness, 1981; Victims, 1985; The Ryer Avenue Story, 1993. Contributions: newspapers and magazines. *Honours:* Edgar, MWA, 1969; Grand Prix de la Littérature Policière, 1971. *Address:* c/o Simon and Schuster Inc, 1230 Sixth Ave, New York, NY 10020, USA.

ULITSKAYA, Ludmila; Author; b. 1938, USSR. *Education:* geneticist. *Publications:* Sonechka (short stories), 1993; Medea and her Children (novel); The Funeral Party (novel), 1999; The Kukotsky Case, 2000. Contributions: Childhood: Zip and Other Stories (anthology), 1998; Around the World in 382 Pages Leopard IV: Bearing Witness (short stories anthology), 1999; NINE of Russia's Foremost Women Writers (anthology). *Honours:* Medici Prize, France, 1995; PEN Club Prize, Italy, 1998; (Russian) Smirnoff-Booker Prize, 2001. *Address:* c/o GLAS Publishers (Russia), PO Box 47, Moscow 119517, Russia.

UNDERHILL, Charles (see Hill, Reginald (Charles)).

UNDERWOOD, Elizabeth (see Mcconchie, Lyn).

UNGER, Barbara; Prof. of English and Creative Writing and Poet; b. 2 Oct. 1932, New York, NY, USA; m. 1st, two d.; m. 2nd Theodore Kiichiro Sakano, 31 July 1987. *Education:* BA, 1954, MA, 1957, City College, CUNY. *Career:* Prof. of English and Creative Writing, Rockland Community College, SUNY, 1969–; mem. Poetry Society of America. *Publications:* Basement: Poems 1959–63, 1975; The Man Who Burned Money, 1980; Inside the Wind, 1986; Learning to Foxtrot, 1989; Dying for Uncle Ray and Other Stories, 1990; Blue Depression Glass, 1991. Contributions: journals and magazines. *Honours:* Bread Loaf Scholar, 1978; National Poetry Competition Award, 1982; Ragdale Foundation Fellowships, 1985, 1986; Goodman Award in Poetry, 1989; Anna Davidson Rosenberg Award for Poems on the Jewish Experience, 1990; Djerassi Foundation Literature Residency, 1991; J. H. G. Roberts Writing Award in Poetry, 1991. *Address:* 101 Parkside Dr., Suffern, NY 10901, USA.

UNGER, David, BA, MFA; Guatemalan writer, poet and translator; b. 1950, Guatemala City. *Education:* Univ. of Massachusetts at Amherst, Columbia Univ. *Career:* US co-ordinator, Guadalajara Int. Book Fair; Dir, City Coll. Publishing Certificate Program. *Publications include:* Neither Caterpillar or Butterfly (poetry), The Girl in the Treehouse; translations: Antipoems: New and Selected, by Nicanor Parra 1985, Dead Leaves, by Bárbara Jacobs 1993, First Love and Look for my Obituary, by Elena Garro 1997, Popol Vuh, by Victor Montejo 1999, The Love You Promised Me, by Silvia Molina 1999, others by Roque Dalton, Mario Benedetti, Sergio Ramirez, Luisa Valenzuela, José Agustin, Paco Igacio Taibo II, Vicente Aleixandre, Enrique Lihn, Isaac Goldenberg. *Honours:* Translation Grants from the New York State Council on the Arts ; Manhattan Borough Pres. Award for Excellence in the Arts 1991, Ivri-Nasawi Poetry Prize 1998. *Address:* c/o Curbstone Press, 321 Jackson Street, Willimantic, CT 06226-1738, USA. *E-mail:* info@curbstone.org. *Website:* www.curbstone.org.

UNGER, Michael Ronald; British newspaper editor and business executive; b. 8 Dec. 1943, Surrey; m. 1st Eunice Dickens 1966 (divorced 1992); one s. one d. (deceased); m. 2nd Noorah Ahmed 1993. *Education:* Wirral Grammar School, Liverpool Polytechnic. *Career:* trainee journalist, Stockport 1963–65; Production Ed., Reading Evening Post 1965–67; News Ed., Perth, Australia 1967–71; Deputy Ed. Daily Post, Liverpool 1971–79, Ed. 1979–82; Ed. Liverpool Echo 1982–83; Ed. Manchester Evening News 1983–97; Dir Guardian Media Group 1983–97, Manchester Evening News PLC 1983–97; Gen. Man. Jazz FM; Chair. The Lowry Centre 1996–, Youth Charter for Sport 1996–2000; mem. Broadcasting Standards Comm. 1999–2000; Trustee Scott Trust 1986–97. *Publication:* The Memoirs of Bridget Hitler 1979. *Honours:* various newspaper awards including Newspaper Design 1980, 1981, 1982, 1994; Ed. of the Year 1988.

UNSWORTH, Barry (Forster); Novelist; b. 10 Aug. 1930, Durham, England; m. Valerie Moor, 15 May 1959, three d. *Education:* BA, University of Manchester, 1951. *Career:* Lectureships in English; Writer-in-Residence, University of Liverpool, 1984–85, University of Lund, Sweden, 1988. *Publications:* The Partnership, 1966; The Greeks Have a Word for It, 1967; The Hide, 1970; Mooncrankers Gift, 1973; The Big Day, 1976; Pascalis Island, 1980, US edn as The Idol Hunter, 1980; The Rage of the Vulture, 1982; Stone Virgin, 1985; Sugar and Rum, 1988; Sacred Hunger, 1992; Morality Play, 1995; After Hannibal, 1996; Losing Nelson, 1999; The Songs of the Kings, 2002. *Honours:* Heinemann Award, RSL, 1974; Arts Council Creative Writing Fellowship, 1978–79; Literary Fellow, University of Durham and University of Newcastle upon Tyne, 1983–84; Co-winner, Booker Prize, 1992. *Address:* c/o Hamish Hamilton, 22 Wrights Lane, London W8 5TZ, England.

UPCHURCH, Michael; Writer; b. 5 Feb. 1954, Rahway, NJ, USA; Partner John Hartl, 1992. *Career:* mem. National Book Critics Circle. *Publications:* Fiction: Jamboree, 1981; Air, 1986; The Flame Forest, 1989; Passive Intruder, 1995. Contributions: many book reviews to periodicals including Chicago Tribune; New York Times Book Review; The Oregonian; San Francisco Chronicle; Seattle Times; Washington Post Book World. *Literary Agent:* Susan Golomb, 875 Avenue of the Americas, Suite 2302, New York, NY 10001, USA. *Address:* 9725 Sand Point Way, Seattle, WA 98115, USA.

UPDIKE, John Hoyer, AB; American writer and poet; b. 18 March 1932, Shillington, Penn.; m. 1st Mary Pennington 1953 (divorced 1977); two s. two d.; m. 2nd Martha Bernhard 1977. *Education:* Shillington High School, Pennsylvania, Harvard Univ., Ruskin School of Drawing and Fine Art, Oxford. *Career:* reporter on the magazine New Yorker 1955–57, contributor 1955–; mem. Nat. Inst. of Arts and Letters, American Acad. of Arts and Sciences. *Publications:* The Carpentered Hen (poems) 1958, The Poorhouse Fair (novel) 1959, The Same Door (short stories) 1959, Rabbit, Run (novel) 1960, Pigeon Feathers and Other Stories 1962, The Centaur (novel) 1963, Telephone Poles and Other Poems 1963, Assorted Prose 1965, Of the Farm (novel) 1965, The Music School (short stories) 1966, Couples (novel), Midpoint and other poems 1969, Bech: A Book 1970, Rabbit Redux (novel) 1972, Seventy Poems 1972, Museums and Women and Other Stories 1972, Buchanan Dying (play) 1974, A Month of Sundays (novel) 1975, Picked-up Pieces 1976, Marry Me (novel) 1976, The Coup (novel) 1978, Tossing and Turning (poems) 1978, Sixteen Sonnets 1979, Problems (short stories) 1979, Your Lover Just Called 1980, Rabbit is Rich (novel) 1981, Bech is Back 1982, Hugging the Shore (essays and criticism) 1984, The Witches of Eastwick (novel) 1984, Facing Nature 1984, Jester's Dozen (poems) 1984, The Year's Best American Short Stories (ed.) 1985, Roger's Version (novel) 1986, Trust Me (short stories) 1987, S (novel) 1988, Self-Consciousness (autobiog.) 1989, Just Looking (essays) 1989, Rabbit at Rest 1990, Odd Jobs (essays and criticism) 1991, Memories of the Ford Administration (novel) 1992, Collected Poems 1953–1993 1993, Brazil (novel) 1993, The Afterlife and Other Stories 1994, In the Beauty of the Lilies 1996, Golf Dreams (writings on golf) 1996, Toward the End of Time 1997, A Century of Arts and Letters (ed.) 1998, Bech at Bay: A quasi-novel 1999, More Matter (essays and criticism) 1999, Gertrude and Claudius (novel) 2000, The Best American Short Stories of the Century (ed.) 2000, Americana and Other Poems 2001, Licks of Love 2001, Seek My Face 2002, The Early Stories 1953–1975 2003, Villages (novel) 2005. *Honours:* Dr hc (Harvard) 1992; Rosenthal Award, Nat. Inst. of Arts and Letters 1960, Nat. Book Award for Fiction 1966, Prix Médicis Etranger 1966, O. Henry Story Award 1967, 1991, MacDowell Medal for Literature 1981, US Nat. Book Critics Circle Award 1982, 1984, 1991, Pulitzer Prize 1982, 1991, PEN/Malamud Memorial Prize 1988, Nat. Medal of Arts 1989, Scanno Prize 1991, Harvard Arts Medal 1998, Nat. Book Foundation Award for Lifetime Achievement 1999, PEN/Faulkner Awarf 2004. *Literary Agent:* c/o Alfred A. Knopf Inc., 299 Park Avenue, New York, NY 10171. *Address:* Beverly Farms, MA 01915, USA.

UPTON, Andrew; Australian playwright, film-maker and director; m. Cate Blanchett 1997; two s. *Career:* Second Unit Dir, Big Sky (TV series); Dir, two Writers' Studios at the Australian Nat. Playwrights' Centre 1995–96. *Plays:* Hanging Man 2002, Cyrano de Bergerac (adaptation), Don Juan (adaptation). *Films:* Babe (asst ed.) 1995, Parklands (continuity) 1996, The Well 1997, Thank God he Met Lizzie 1997, A Little Bit of Soul 1998, Bangers (writer, prod., dir) 1999. *Literary Agent:* RGM Associates, PO Box 128, Surry Hills, NSW 2010, Australia. *Telephone:* (2) 9281-3911. *Fax:* (2) 9281-4705. *E-mail:* info@rgm.com.au. *Website:* www.rgm.com.au.

UPTON, Lee; Prof. of English, Poet and Writer; b. 2 June 1953, St Johns, MI, USA; m. Eric Jozef Ziolkowski, 31 March 1989, two d. *Education:* BA, Journalism, Michigan State University, 1978; MFA, English, University of Massachusetts at Amherst, 1981; PhD, English, SUNY at Binghamton, 1986. *Career:* Visiting Asst Prof., 1986–87, Asst Prof., 1988–92, Assoc. Prof., 1992–98, of English, Prof. of English and Writer-in-Residence, 1998–, Lafayette College; Asst Prof., Grand Valley State University, 1987–88; mem. MLA; National Council of Teachers of English; Poetry Society of America. *Publications:* Poetry: The Invention of Kindness, 1984; Sudden Distances, 1988; No Mercy, 1989; Approximate Darling, 1996; Civilian Histories, 2000. Criticism: Jean Garrigue: A Poetics of Plenitude, 1991; Obsession and Release: Rereading the Poetry of Louise Bogan, 1996; The Muse of Abandonment: Origin, Identity and Mastery in Five American

Poets, 1998. Contributions: numerous reviews, quarterlies, journals and periodicals. *Honours:* Poetry prizes. *Address:* c/o Dept of English, Lafayette College, Easton, PA 18042, USA.

URIAS, Alfonso Quijada; El Salvador writer and poet; b. 8 Dec. 1940, Quezaltepeque. *Career:* fmr journalist. *Publications:* From Now On (co-author) 1968, Otras historias famosas (Nuevapal abra) 1976, They Come and Knock on the Door (in trans.) 1991, The Better to See You (contributor) 1994. *Address:* c/o Curbstone Press, 321 Jackson Street, Willimantic, CT 06226-1738, USA. *E-mail:* info@curbstone.org. *Website:* www.curbstone.org.

URQUHART, Jane; Author; b. 21 June 1949, Little Long Lac, ON, Canada; m. Anthony Urquhart, 5 May 1976, one d. *Education:* BA, University of Guelph. *Career:* Writer-in-Residence, University of Ottawa, 1990, Memorial University, NF, 1993, University of Toronto, 1997. *Publications:* Storm Glass (short stories), 1987; The Whirlpool (novel), 1986; Changing Heaven (novel), 1990; Away (novel), 1993; The Underpainter (novel), 1997; The Stone Carvers (novel), 2001. *Honours:* Prix du Meilleur Livre Étranger, France, 1992; Trillium Award, Canada, 1994; Gov.-Gen.'s Award, Canada, 1997. *Address:* c/o Suite 1801, 15 E 26th St, New York, NY 10010, USA.

URSELL, Geoffrey; Writer, Dramatist, Poet and Composer; b. 14 March 1943, Moose Jaw, SK, Canada; m. Barbara Sapergia, 8 July 1967. *Education:* BA, 1965, MA, 1966, University of Manitoba; PhD, University of London, 1973. *Career:* Lecturer, 1975–79, Special Asst Prof. in English, 1980–81, 1982–83, University of Regina; Writer-in-Residence, Saskatoon Public Library, 1984–85; mem. Asscn of Canadian Television and Radio Artists; Guild of Canadian Playwrights; Playwrights Canada. *Publications:* Number One Northern: Poetry from Saskatchewan (co-ed.), 1977; The Tenth Negative Pig (co-author), 1980; The Running of the Deer (play), 1981; Black Powder (musical), 1982; Saskatchewan Gold (ed.), 1982; Trap Lines (poems), 1982; Perdue, or, How the West Was Lost (novel), 1984; Sky High: Stories from Saskatchewan, 1988; Way Out West (short stories), 1989; The Look-Out Tower (poems), 1989; Due West (ed.), 1996. Other: various unpublished stage plays and radio plays. Contributions: periodicals. *Honours:* several prizes and awards.

USHERWOOD, Elizabeth (Ada); Writer; b. 10 July 1923, London, England; m. Stephen Usherwood, 24 Oct. 1970. *Publications:* Visit Some London Catholic Churches (with Stephen Usherwood), 1982; The Counter-Armada, 1596: The Journal of the 'Mary Rose' (with Stephen Usherwood), 1983; We Die for the Old Religion (with Stephen Usherwood), 1987; Women First, 1989; A Saint in the Family (with Stephen Usherwood), 1992. Contributions: periodicals. *Address:* 24 St Mary's Grove, Canonbury, London N1 2NT, England.

UTAMI, Ayu; Indonesian writer; b. 21 Nov. 1968, Bogor. *Publications:* novels: Saman 1998, Larung 2000. *Honours:* Indonesian Literary Competition 1998, Dutch Prince Claus Award 2000. *Address:* c/o Kepustakaan Populer Gramedia, JI, Palmerah Selatan 22–28, Jakarta 10270, Indonesia.

V

VACHSS, Andrew Henry, BA, JD; American writer and attorney; b. 19 Oct. 1942, New York, NY; m. Alice Vachss. *Education:* Case Western Reserve University, New England School of Law. *Career:* bd of counselors, Child-trauma Acad.; Nat. Advisory Bd, Protect PAC; Contributing Ed., Parade Magazine; mem. PEN American Center, Writers' Guild of America. *Publications:* novels: Flood 1985, Strega 1987, Blue Belle 1988, Hard Candy 1989, Blossom 1990, Sacrifice 1991, Shella 1993, Down in the Zero 1994, Another Chance to Get it Right 1995, Footsteps of the Hawk 1995, Batman: The Ultimate Evil 1995, False Allegations 1996, Safe House 1998, Choice of Evil 1999, Dead and Gone 2000, Pain Management 2001, Only Child 2002, The Getaway Man 2003, Down Here 2004; graphic novels: Hard Looks: Adapted Stories 1992, Predator: Race War 1995; other: The Life-Style Violent Juvenile: The Secure Treatment Approach (non-fiction) 1979, Proving It (audio book) 2001, Born Bad: Stories 1994, Everybody Pays: Stories 1999. *Honours:* John Hay Whitney Foundation Fellow 1976–77, Grand Prix de Littérature Policière 1988, Falcon Award, Maltese Falcon Soc. of Japan 1988, Deutschen Krimi Preis from Die Jury des Bochumer Krimi Archivs 1989, Raymond Chandler Award 2000. *Address:* 420 Lexington Avenue, Suite 2860, New York, NY 10170, USA. *Website:* www.vachss.com.

VALENTINE, Alana; Australian playwright; b. Redfern, NSW. *Education:* Graduate Diploma in Museum Studies, Univ. of Sydney. *Radio plays:* Screamers, The Word Salon, Oysters at the Paragon, Swallowing Communion. *Screenplays:* Mother Love 1994, The Witnesses 1995, Reef Dreaming 1997. *Plays:* The Story of Anger Lee Bredenza 1989, Southern Belle 1994, Swimming the Globe 1996, The Conjurers 1997, Spool Time 1998, Ozone 1998, Savage Grace 2000, Row of Tents 2001, The Prospectors 2001, The Mapmaker's Brother 2002, Run Rabbit Run! 2003, Crossing the Mountains 2005. *Honours:* AWGIE Award, NSW State Literary Award, Churchill Fellowship, Rodney Seaborne Playwright's Award, ANPC/New Dramatist's Award. *Literary Agent:* RGM Associates, PO Box 128, Surry Hills, NSW 2010, Australia. *Telephone:* (2) 9281-3911. *Fax:* (2) 9281-4705. *E-mail:* info@rgm.com.au. *Website:* www.rgm.com.au.

VALENZUELA, Luisa; Argentine writer and journalist; b. 26 Nov. 1938, Buenos Aires; m. Théodore Marjak 1958 (divorced); one d. *Education:* Belgrano Girls' School, Colegio Nacional Vicente Lopez, Buenos Aires. *Career:* lived in Paris, writing for Argentinian newspapers and for the RTF 1958–61; Asst Ed. La Nación Sunday Supplement, Buenos Aires 1964–69; writer, lecturer, freelance journalist in USA, Mexico, France, Spain 1970–73, Buenos Aires 1973–79; taught in Writing Div., Columbia Univ., New York 1980–83; conducted writers' workshops, English Dept, New York Univ. and seminars, Writing Div. 1984–89; returned to Buenos Aires 1989; Fulbright Grant 1969–70; Guggenheim Fellow 1983; Fellow New York Inst. for the Humanities; mem. Acad. of Arts and Sciences, Puerto Rico. *Publications:* novels: Hay que sonreír 1966, El gato eficaz 1972, Como en la guerra 1977, Cambio de armas 1982, Cola de largartija 1983, Novela negra con argentinos 1990, Realidad Nacional desde la cama 1990; short stories: Los heréticos 1967, Aquí pasan cosas raras 1976, Libro que no muerde 1980, Donde viven las águilas 1983, Simetrías (Cuentos de Hades) 1993, Antología Personal 1998, Cuentos Completos y Uno Más 1999, La travesía 2001, Peligrosas palabras 2001. *Honours:* Dr. hc (Knox Coll., Ill., USA) 1991; Machado de Assis Medal, Brazilian Acad. of Letters 1997. *Address:* Artilleros 2130, 1428 Buenos Aires, Argentina. *Telephone:* (11) 4781-3593.

VALERY, Anne (see Firth, Anne Catherine).

VALGARDSON, William Dempsey; writer, poet, dramatist and academic; b. 7 May 1939, Winnipeg, Manitoba, Canada; m. (divorced); one s. one d. *Education:* BA, United College, 1961; BEd, University of Manitoba, 1966; MFA, University of Iowa, 1969. *Career:* Assoc. Prof., 1970–74, Prof., 1974–, University of Victoria, BC; Fiction Ed., Canadian Author, 1996–. *Publications:* Bloodflowers, 1973; God is Not a Fish Inspector, 1975; In the Gutting Shed, 1976; Red Dust, 1978; Gentle Simmers, 1980; The Carpenter of Dreams, 1986; What Can't Be Changed Shouldn't Be Mourned, 1990; The Girl With the Botticelli Face, 1992; Thor, 1994; Sarah and the People of Sand River, 1996; Garbage Creek, 1997. Contributions: Magazines. *Honours:* Books in Canada First Novel Award, 1980; Ethel Wilson Literary Prize, 1992; Mr Christie Prize, 1995; Vicky Metcalf Short Story Award, 1998. *Address:* 1908 Waterloo Road, Victoria, BC V8P 1J3, Canada.

VAN DE LAAR, Waltherus Antonius Bernardinus, (Stella Napels, Victor Vroomkoning); Poet and Writer; b. 6 Oct. 1938, Boxtel, Netherlands; one s. one d. *Education:* MA, Philosophy, Dutch Linguistics and Literature, 1978; Degree in Philosophy, 1990. *Career:* Teacher, Interstudie teachers' training college, Arnhem, 1977–83; Co-Ed., Kritisch Literatuur Lexicon, 1981–; mem. Lira. *Publications:* De einders tegemoet, 1983; De laatste dingen, 1983; Circuit des souvenirs, 1984; Klein museum, 1987; Groesbeek Tijdrit, 1989; Echo van een echo, 1990; Oud zeer, 1993; Een zucht als vluchtig eerbetoon, 1995; Boxtel, 1995; Lippendienst, 1997; Ysbeerbestaan, 1999; Verloren Spraak, 2000; Bij verstek, 2002. Contributions: magazines and periodicals. *Honours:* Pablo Neruda Prize, 1983; Blanka Gÿselen Prize, 1995. *Address:* Aldenhof, 70-17, 6537 DZ Nijmegen, Netherlands.

VAN DER KISTE, John Patrick Guy; Author and Library Asst; b. 15 Sept. 1954, Wendover, Bucks, England. *Education:* Ealing Technical College School of Librarianship; Associateship of Library Asscn. *Career:* Library Asst, Plymouth College of Further Education, 1978–. *Publications:* Frederick III 1981, Dearest Affie (with Bee Jordaan) 1984, Queen Victoria's Children 1986, Windsor and Habsburg 1987, Edward VII's Children 1989, Beyond the Summertime (with Derek Wadeson) 1990, Princess Victoria Melita 1991, George V's Children 1991, George III's Children 1992, Crowns in a Changing World 1993, Kings of the Hellenes 1994, Childhood at Court 1995, Northern Crowns 1996, King George II & Queen Caroline 1997, The Romanovs 1818–1959 1998, Kaiser Wilhelm II 1999, The Georgian Princesses 2000, Gilbert and Sullivan's Christmas 2000, Dearest Vicky, Darling Fritz 2001, Royal Visits to Devon and Cornwall 2002, Once a Grand Duchess (with Coryne Hall) 2002, William & Mary 2003. Contributions: books and periodicals. *Address:* c/o Sutton Publishing Ltd, Phoenix Mill, Thrupp, Stroud, Glos GL5 2BU, England.

VAN DER VAT, Dan, BA; writer and journalist; b. 28 Oct. 1939, Alkmaar, Netherlands; m. Christine Mary Ellis 1962; two d. *Education:* University of Durham. *Career:* mem. Campaign for Freedom of Information, Soc. of Authors, Amnesty Int., Liberty. *Publications:* The Grand Scuttle 1982, The Last Corsair 1983, Gentlemen of War 1984, The Ship That Changed the World 1985, The Atlantic Campaign, 1939–45 1988, The Pacific Campaign, 1941–45 1991, Freedom Was Never Like This: A Winter's Journey in East Germany 1991, Stealth at Sea: History of the Submarine 1994, The Riddle of the Titanic (with Robin Gardiner) 1995, The Good Nazi: The Life and Lies of Albert Speer 1997, Standard of Power: The Royal Navy in the 20th Century 2000, Pearl Harbor: The Day of Infamy: An Illustrated History 2001, D-Day: The Greatest Invasion, a People's History 2003; contrib. to newspapers, magazines, radio and television. *Honours:* Yorkshire Post Best First Work Award 1982, King George's Fund for Sailors Best Book of the Sea Award 1983, Publisher's Weekly Book of the Year 1997. *Literary Agent:* Curtis Brown Ltd, Haymarket House, 28–29 Haymarket, London, SW1Y 4SP, England. *Telephone:* (20) 7393-4400. *Fax:* (20) 7393-4401. *E-mail:* info@curtisbrown.co.uk. *Website:* www.curtisbrown.co.uk.

VAN DUYN, Mona (Jane); Poet, Writer, Critic, Ed., Reviewer and Lecturer; b. 9 May 1921, Waterloo, IA, USA; m. Jarvis A Thurston, 31 Aug. 1943. *Education:* BA, Iowa State Teachers College, 1942; MA, State University of Iowa, 1943. *Career:* Reviewer, Poetry magazine, 1944–70; Instructor in English, State University of Iowa, 1945, University of Louisville, 1946–50; Founder-Ed. (with Jarvis A Thurston), Perspective: A Quarterly of Literature, 1947–67; Lecturer in English, 1950–67, Adjunct Prof., 1983, Visiting Hurst Prof., 1987, Washington University, St Louis; Poetry Adviser, College English, 1955–57; Lecturer, Salzburg Seminar in American Studies, 1973; Poet-in-Residence, Bread Loaf Writing Conferences, 1974, 1976; Poet Laureate of the USA, 1992–93; numerous poetry readings; mem. Acad. of American Poets, board of chancellors, 1985–99; National Institute of Arts and Letters. *Publications:* Valentines to the Wide World: Poems, 1959; A Time of Bees, 1964; To See, To Take, 1970; Bedtime Stories, 1972; Merciful Disguises: Poems Published and Unpublished, 1973; Letters From a Father and Other Poems, 1982; Near Changes: Poems, 1990; Lives and Deaths of the Poets and Non-Poets, 1991; If It Be Not I: Collected Poems, 1992; Firefall, 1993. Contributions: many anthologies; Poems, criticism, reviews, and short stories in various periodicals. *Honours:* Eunice Tietjens Memorial Prize, 1956; National Endowment for the Arts Grants, 1966–67, 1985; Harriet Monroe Memorial Prize, 1968; Hart Crane Memorial Award, 1968; First Prize, Borestone Mountain Awards, 1968; Bollingen Prize, 1970; National Book Award for Poetry, 1971; Guggenheim Fellowship, 1972–73; Loines Prize, National Institute of Arts and Letters, 1976; Fellow, Acad. of American Poets, 1981; Sandburg Prize, Cornell College, 1982; Shelley Memorial Award, Poetry Society of America, 1987; Ruth Lilly Prize, 1989; Pulitzer Prize in Poetry, 1991. *Address:* 7505 Teasdale Ave, St Louis, MO 63130, USA.

VAN HERK, Aritha; Prof. and Writer; b. 26 May 1954, Wetaskiwin, AB, Canada; m. Robert Sharp, 14 Sept. 1974. *Education:* BA, 1976, MA, 1978, University of Alberta. *Career:* Asst Prof., 1983–85, Assoc. Prof., 1985–91, Prof., 1991–, University of Calgary. *Publications:* Judith, 1978; More Stories from Western Canada (co-ed.), 1980; The Tent Peg, 1981; West of Fiction (co-ed.), 1983; No Fixed Address, 1986; Places Far From Ellesmere, 1990; Alberta Rebound (ed.), 1990; In Visible Ink, 1991; A Frozen Tongue, 1992; Boundless Alberta (ed.), 1993; Due West, 1996; Restlessness, 1998; Mavericks: An Incorrigible History of Alberta, 2001. *Honours:* Seal Books First Novel Award, 1978; Alberta Achievement Award in Literature, 1978; Fellow, Royal Society of Canada, 1997; Grant MacEwan Award, 2002. *Address:* c/o Dept of English, University of Calgary, Calgary, AB T2N 1N4, Canada. *E-mail:* vanherk@ucalgary.ca.

VAN WINCKEL, Nance; poet, writer and academic; b. 24 Oct. 1951, Roanoke, VA, USA; m. Robert Fredrik Nelson 1985. *Education:* BA, University of Wisconsin, Milwaukee, 1973; MA, University of Denver, 1976. *Career:* Instructor in English, Marymount College, Salina, KS, 1976–79;

Assoc. Prof. of English and Dir, Writing Program, Lake Forest College, IL, 1979–90; Assoc. Prof. to Prof. of English, Eastern Washington University, Cheney, 1990–; Faculty, Vermont College, 2000–. *Publications:* The Twenty-Four Doors: Advent Calendar Poems, 1985; Bad Girl, with Hawk (poems), 1988; Limited Lifetime Warranty (short stories), 1994; The Dirt (poems), 1994; Quake (short stories), 1997; After a Spell (poems), 1998; Curtain Creek Farm (short stories), 2000. Contributions: many periodicals. *Honours:* Illinois Arts Council Fellowships, 1983, 1985, 1987, 1989; National Endowment for the Arts Fellowships, 1988, 2001; Society of Midland Authors Poetry Award, 1989; Gordon Barber Award, Poetry Society of America, 1989; Northwest Institute Grants, 1991, 1993, 1994; Paterson Fiction Prize, 1998; Washington State Artists Trust Literary Award in Fiction, 1998; Washington State Gov.'s Award for Literature, 1999. *Address:* c/o Graduate Creative Writing Program, Eastern Washington University, Cheney, WA 99004, USA.

VANDERHAAR, Gerard A(nthony); Prof. and Writer; b. 15 Aug. 1931, Louisville, KY, USA; m. Janice Marie Searles, 22 Dec. 1969. *Education:* BA, Providence College, 1954; STD, University of St Thomas, Rome, 1965. *Career:* Faculty, St John's University, New York, 1964–65, Providence College, 1965–68, Wesleyan University, 1968–69, Christian Brothers University, 1971–; mem. American Acad. of Religion; American Asscn of University Profs; Pax Christi; Fellowship of Reconcilitation; War Registers League. *Publications:* A New Vision and a New Will for Memphis, 1974; Christians and Nonviolence in the Nuclear Age, 1982; Enemies and How to Love Them, 1985; Way of Peace: A Guide to Nonviolence (co-ed.), 1987; The Philippines: Agony and Hope (co-author), 1989; Active Nonviolence: A Way of Personal Peace, 1990; Why Good People Do Bad Things, 1994; Beyond Violence, 1998. Booklets: Nonviolence, Theory and Practice, 1980; Nonviolence in Christian Tradition, 1983. Contributions: Reference books and journals. *Honours:* Outstanding Educators of America, 1971; Distinguished Service Award, United Nations Asscn, 1981; Catholic Press Asscn Book Award for Spirituality, 1991; Tennessee Higher Education Commission Award for Community Service, 1994; Pax Chisti National Book Award, 1998. *Address:* 3554 Boxdale, Apt 3, Memphis, TN 38118, USA.

VANDERHAEGHE, Guy Clarence, BA, MA, BEd; Canadian writer and playwright; b. 5 April 1951, Esterhazy, SK; m. Margaret Nagel 1972. *Education:* Univ. of Saskatchewan, Univ. of Regina. *Career:* Visiting Prof. of English, St Thomas More College, Univ. of Saskatchewan 1993–. *Publications:* novels: Man Descending (Gov. Gen. Literary Award for Fiction 1982, Geoffrey Faber Memorial Prize 1987) 1982, The Trouble With Heroes 1983, My Present Age 1984, Homesick (City of Toronto Book Award 1990) 1989, Things As They Are? 1992, The Englishman's Boy (Gov. Gen. Literary Award for Fiction) 1996, The Last Crossing 2004; plays: I Had a Job I Liked, Once (Canadian Authors' Asscn Award for Drama 1993) 1991, Dancock's Dance 1995. *Honours:* Hon. DLitt (Saskatchewan) 1997; Canadian Authors' Asscn Award for Drama 1996, Saskatchewan Book Award 1996. *Address:* c/o Department of English, St Thomas More College, University of Saskatchewan, Saskatoon, SK S7N OW0, Canada. *Address:* c/o McClelland and Stewart, 481 University Avenue, Toronto, ON M5G 2E9, Canada (Office).

VANDERKAM, James Claire; Prof. of Theology and Writer; b. 15 Feb. 1946, Cadillac, Michigan, USA; m. Mary Vander Molen, 24 Aug. 1967, two s. one d. *Education:* AB, Calvin College, 1968; BD, Calvin Theological Seminary, 1971; PhD, Harvard University, 1976. *Career:* Prof. of Theology, University of Notre Dame. *Publications:* Textual and Historical Studies in the Book of Jubilees, 1977; Enoch and the Growth of Apocalyptic Tradition, 1984; The Book of Jubilees, 2 vols, 1989; The Dead Sea Scrolls Today, 1994; Enoch: A Man for All Generations, 1995; The Jewish Apocalyptic Heritage in Early Christianity (ed. with William Alder), 1996; Calenders in the Dead Sea Scrolls, 1998. *Honours:* Distinguished Research and Literary Publication Award, College of Humanities and Social Sciences, North Carolina State University, 1991; Biblical Archaeology Society Publication Award for Best Popular Book on Archaeology, 1995. *Address:* Dept of Theology, University of Notre Dame, Notre Dame, IN 46556, USA.

VANDIVER, Frank Everson; Historian and Educator; b. 9 Dec. 1925, Austin, Texas, USA; m. 1st Carol Sue Smith, 19 April 1952, deceased 1979, one s. two d.; m. 2nd Renee Aubry, 21 March 1980. *Education:* MA, University of Texas, 1949; PhD, Tulane University, 1951; MA, University of Oxford, 1963. *Career:* Asst Prof. of History, Washington University, St Louis, 1952–55; Prof. of History, Louisiana State University, 1953–57; Asst Prof., 1955–56, Assoc. Prof., 1956–58, Prof. of History, 1958–65, Harris Masterson Jr Prof. of History, 1965–79, Acting Pres., 1969–70, Provost, 1970–79, Vice-Pres., 1975–79, Rice University; Harmsworth Prof. of American History, University of Oxford, 1963–64; Pres. and Chancellor, North Texas State University at Denton and Texas College of Osteopathic Medicine, 1979–81; Pres., 1981–88, Pres. Emeritus and Distinguished University Prof., 1988–, Texas A & M University at College Station; Chair. of the Board, 1992–97, Acting Pres., 1997–98, American University, Cairo; various visiting lectureships and professorships; mem. American Historical Asscn; Jefferson Davis Asscn; Organization of American Historians; Society of American Historians; Southern Historical Asscn, pres., 1975–76; Texas Historical Asscn, fellow; Texas Institute of Letters; Texas Philosophical Society, pres., 1978; Salado Centre for the Humanities, dir. *Publications:* Ploughshares Into Swords: Josiah Gorgas and the Confederate Command System, 1956; Mighty Stonewall, 1957; Fields of Glory (with W. H. Nelson), 1960; Jubal's Raid, 1960; Basic History of the Confederacy, 1962; Jefferson Davis and the Confederate State, 1964; Their Tattered Flags: The Epic of the Confederacy, 1970; The Southwest: South or West?, 1975; Black Jack: The Life and Times of John J. Pershing, 1977; The Long Loom of Lincoln, 1986; Blood Brothers: A Short History of the Civil War, 1992; Shadows of Vietnam: Lyndon Johnson's Wars, 1997. Editor: several vols. Contributions: books and journals. *Honours:* many hon. doctorates; Guggenheim Fellowship, 1955–56; Carr P. Collins Prize, Texas Institute of Letters, 1958; Harry S. Truman Award, Kansas City Civil War Round Table, 1970; Fletcher Pratt Award, New York Civil War Round Table, 1970; Outstanding Civilian Service Medal, Dept of the Army, 1974; Nevins-Freeman Award, Chicago Civil War Round Table, 1982; T. Harry Williams Memorial Award, 1985; Hon. Knight of San Jacinto, 1993. *Address:* A & M University, College Station, TX 77843, USA.

VANDO (HICKOK), Gloria; Poet, Publisher and Ed.; b. 21 May 1936, New York, NY, USA; m. 1st Maurice Peress, 2 July 1955, one s. two d.; m. 2nd William Harrison Hickok, 4 Oct. 1980. *Education:* BA, Texas A & I College, Corpus Christi, 1975; Graduate Studies, Southampton College, Long Island University, New York. *Career:* Founding Publisher, ed., Helicon Nine Editions, 1977–; mem. PEN International; Poetry Society of America; Writers' Place, Kansas City, MO, co-founder; Cockefair Chair., University of Missouri-Kansas City, board; Clearing House for Midcontinent Foundations, art chair., 1988–90; Midwest Center for the Literary Arts Inc, board vice-pres.; Acad. of American Poets. *Publications:* Caprichos, 1987; Promesas: Geography of the Impossible, 1993; Touching the Fire: Fifteen Poets of Today's Latino Renaissance (anthology), 1998; Spud Songs: An Anthology of Potato Poems (co-ed.), 1999; Shadows and Supposes: Poems, 2002. Contributions: Cottonwood Magazine, Gloria Vando Issue, Summer 1994; Kenyon Review; Western Humanities Review; Seattle Review; New Letters, Carolina Quarterly. *Honours:* Poetry Fellowship, Kansas Arts Commission, 1989–91; Kansas Gov.'s Arts Award, 1991; Billee Murray Denny Prize, 1991; Thorpe Menn Book Award, 1994; River Styx International Poetry Award, second place, 1997; Poetry Society of America's Alice Fay Di Castagnola Award, 1998. *Address:* c/o Helicon Nine Editions, PO Box 22412, Kansas City, MO 64113, USA.

VANE, Brett (see Kent, Arthur (William Charles)).

VANIČEK, Zdeněk, (Alois Bocek); Diplomat, Prof., Poet and Writer; b. 24 June 1947, Chlumec, nad Cidlinou, Czechoslovakia; m. Nadya Jankovska; two s. one d. *Education:* MA, LLD, Charles Univ., Prague, 1979; PhD, Diplomatic Acad., Prague, 1981. *Career:* Czechoslovak Diplomatic Service, 1972–91; journalist and diplomatic adviser, 1991–93; Prof. of International Relations and Law, 1993–; Pres., Czech Asscn of Competitive Communications, 1999–; mem. Poetry Society, England; RSL. *Publications:* The Theory and the Practice of British Neo-Conservatism, 1988; Amidst the Ruins of Memories, 1990; To the Ends of the Earth, 1992; On the Edge of Rain, 1994; Under the Range of Mountains of Five Fingers, 1996; Seven Thousand Years Chiselled in Limestone, 1996; Amidst Memory's Ruins (mid-life poetry 1988–1998), 1999; Whereupon He Was Arrested (short stories), 2003. Contributions: newspapers and magazines. *Honours:* Pontifical Medal, 1990; Masaryk Award, Acad. of Arts, 1997; Karel Hynek Mácha Prize for Poetry, 1998; Emperor Rudolf II Prize for Poetry, 2002. *Address:* Hermanova 10/1087, 170 00 Prague 7, Czech Republic.

VANSITTART, Peter; Author; b. 27 Aug. 1920, Bedford, England. *Education:* Worcester College, Oxford. *Career:* mem. FRSL. *Publications:* I Am the World, 1942; Enemies, 1947; The Overseer, 1949; Broken Canes, 1950; A Verdict of Treason, 1952; A Little Madness, 1953; The Game and the Ground, 1956; Orders of Chivalry, 1958; The Tournament, 1959; A Sort of Forgetting, 1960; Carolina, 1961; Sources of Unrest, 1962; The Friends of God, 1963; The Siege, The Lost Lands, 1964; The Dark Tower, 1965; The Shadow Land, 1967; The Story Teller, 1968; Green Knights Black Angels, 1969; Landlord, 1970; Vladivostok: Figures in Laughter, 1972; Worlds and Underworlds, 1974; Quintet, 1976; Flakes of History, 1978; The Death of Robin Hood, 1980; Voices from the Great War, 1981; Three Six Seven, 1982; Voices 1870–1914, John Masefield's Letters from the Front, 1984; The Ancient Mariner and the Old Sailor, 1985; Happy and Glorious, 1987; Parsifal, 1988; Voices of the Revolution, 1989; The Wall, 1990; A Choice of Murder, 1992; London, 1992; A Safe Conduct, 1995; In the Fifties, 1995; In Memory of England, 1998; Survival Tactics, 1999; Hermes in Paris, 2000; Poems by John Masefield, 2002; John Paul Jones, 2003. Contributions: Guardian; Times; London Magazine. *Honours:* Hon. Fellowship, Worcester College, Oxford, 1996. *Address:* Little Manor, Kersey, Suffolk, England.

VARGAS LLOSA, (Jorge) Mario Pedro; author, playwright and journalist; b. 28 March 1936, Arequipa, Peru; m. 1st Julia Urquidi 1955 (divorced 1964); m. 2nd Patricia Llosa Urquidi 1965; two s. one d. *Education:* Universidad Nacional Mayer de San Marcos, Lima; PhD, Universidad Complutense de Madrid, 1959. *Career:* Journalist, Piura, Peru, 1952; Magazine journalist, Turismo, Cultura Peruana, Sunday supplement of El Comercio, 1955; News ed., Radio Panamericana, Lima, 1955; Journalist, Agence-France Presse, 1959; Broadcaster, Radiodiffusion Télévision Française, 1959; Lecturer in Latin American Literature, Queen Mary College, London, 1967; Prof., King's College, London, 1969; Trans., UNESCO, 1967;

Visiting Prof., Washington State Univ., 1968, Universidad de Puerto Rico, 1969, Columbia University, 1975; Prof., University of Cambridge, 1977; Writer-in-Residence, Woodrow Wilson International Center for Scholars, Smithsonian Institution, Washington, DC, 1980; Candidate for Pres. of Peru, 1990; Visiting Prof., Harvard University, 1992, Princeton University, 1993, Georgetown University, 1994, 1999; mem. Founder, Movimiento Libertad political party; Co-founder, Frente Democrático (FREDEMO) coalition 1988; International PEN Club, pres., 1976–79; Acad. Peruana de la Lengua; Real Acad. Española; International Acad. of Humanism; Neil Gunn International Fellow, Scottish Arts Council 1986. *Publications:* Fiction: La cuidad y los perros, 1963; La casa verde, 1966; Conversación en la catedral, 1969; Pantaleón y las visitadoras, 1973; La tía Julia y el escribidor, 1977; La guerra del fin del mundo, 1981; Historia de Mayta, 1984; ¿Quién mató a Palomino Molero?, 1986; El hablador, 1987; Elogio de la madrastra, 1988; Lituma en los Andes, 1993; Los cuadernos de Don Rigoberto, 1997; La fiesta del chivo, 2000; El paraíso en la otra esquina (trans. as The Way to Paradise), 2003. Short Stories: El desafío, 1957; Los jefes, 1959; Los cachorros, 1967. Anthologies: Contra viento y marea, vol. I (1962–72), 1986, vol. II (1972–83), 1986, vol. III (1983–90), 1990; Desafíos a la libertad, 1994; Making Waves, 1996. Plays: La huída del Inca, 1952; La señorita de Tacna, 1981; Kathie y el hipopótamo, 1983; La Chunga, 1986; El loco de los balcones, 1993; Ojos bonitos, cuadros feos, 1994; La verdad de las mentiras, 1990. Other: El pez en el agua (autobiog.), 1993; La orgía perpetua, 1975; La utopía arcaica, 1978; El paraíso en la otra esquina, 2001; El lenguaje de la pasión, 2001; Essays and literary criticism. *Honours:* Revue Française Prize, 1957; Leopoldo Alas Prize, 1959; Biblioteca Breve Prize, 1963; Crítica Española Prize, 1966; Premio Nacional de Novela, Peru, 1967; Premio de la Crítica, Argentina, 1981; Pablo Iglesias Literature Prize, 1982; ILLA Prize, Italy, 1982; Congressional Medal of Honour, Peru, 1982; Ritz Paris Hemingway Prize, 1985; Premio Príncipe de Asturias, Spain, 1986; Hon. Fellow, American Acad. and Institute of Arts and Letters, 1986; Castiglione de Sicilia Prize, Italy, 1990; Fellow, Wissenschaftskolleg, Berlin, 1991–92; Golden Palm Award, INTAR Hispanic American Arts Center, New York, 1992; Cervantes Prize, Spain, 1994; Jerusalem Prize, 1995; Pluma de Oro Award, Spain, 1997; Medal and Diploma of Honour, Univ. Católica de Santa María, Peru, 1997; Fellow, Deutscher Akademischer Austauschdienst, Berlin, 1997–98; National Book Critics Circle Award, USA, 1998; Medal of the University of California, 1999; Légion d'honneur, Commdr. Ordre des Arts et Lettres; PEN/Nabokov Award, 2002; Roger-Caillois PEN Club Prize, 2003; many hon. doctorates. *Address:* Las Magnolias 295, 60°, Barranco, Lima 4, Peru.

VARMUS, Harold Eliot, MA, MD; American microbiologist and university professor; b. 18 Dec. 1939, Oceanside, NY; m. Constance Louise Casey 1969; two s. *Education:* Amherst Coll., Harvard Univ., Columbia Univ. *Career:* physician, Presbyterian Hosp., New York 1966–68; Clinical Assoc., NIH, Bethesda, Md 1968–70; lecturer, Dept of Microbiology, Univ. of Calif. at San Francisco 1970–72, Asst Prof. 1972–74, Assoc. Prof. 1974–79, Prof. 1979–83, American Cancer Soc. Research Prof. 1984–93; Dir NIH 1993–99; Pres. and CEO Memorial Sloan-Kettering Cancer Centre 2000–; Consultant, Chiron Corp., Emoryville, Calif.; Assoc. Ed. Cell Journal; mem. Editorial Bd Cancer Surveys; mem. American Soc. of Virology, American Soc. of Microbiology, AAAS. *Publications:* (ed.) Molecular Biology of Tumor Viruses 1982, 1985, Readings in Tumor Virology 1983. *Honours:* Calif. Acad. of Sciences Scientist of the Year 1982, Lasker Foundation Award 1982 (co-recipient), Passano Foundation Award 1983, Armand Hammer Cancer Prize 1984, Gen. Motors Alfred Sloan Award, Shubitz Cancer Prize (NAS) 1984, Nobel Prize 1989. *Address:* Memorial Sloan-Kettering Cancer Centre, 1275 York Avenue, New York, NY 10021, USA (Office).

VARRASSI, Lillian M.; USA; b. 9 Aug. 1949, Queens, New York,. *Education:* Graduate, Institute of Children's Literature, 1989; BA, English Literature, Queens College, CUNY, 1995. *Publications:* Soliloquoy, 1991; Through a Glass Darkly, 2000. Contributions: American Poetry Annual, 1991; Visions and Beyond, 1991; A View from the Edge, 1992; Reflections: 1992; Expectations, 1992; Poetry Voices of America, 1992; Beneath the Winter Sky, 1998; Voices of the New Century, 2000. *Honours:* Certificate of Poetic Achievement, Amherst Society, 1992; Certificate of Poetic Accomplishment, The Poetry Center, 1992. *Address:* 59-32 72nd St, Maspeth, NY 11378, USA. *E-mail:* lvarrassi@aol.com.

VASILYEVA, Larisa Nikolayevna; Writer and Poet; b. 23 Nov. 1935, Kharkov, Russia; m. Oleg Vassiliev, 19 Jan. 1957, deceased 1993, one s. *Education:* Graduated, Dept of Philology, University of Moscow, 1958. *Career:* mem. Union of Russian Writers; League of Woman Writers, pres. *Publications:* Poetry: Linen Moon, 1968; Fire-fly, 1969; The Goose-foot, 1970; Blue Twilight, 1970; Encounter, 1974; A Rainbow of Snow, 1974; Meadows, 1975; Light in the Window, 1978; Russian Names, 1980; Foliage, 1980; Fireflower, 1981; Selected Poetry, 1981; Grove, 1984; Mirror, 1985; Moskvorechie, 1985; Lantern, 1985; Waiting for You in the Sky, 1986; Selected Works, 2 vols, 1989; Strange Quality, 1991. Other: Prose and essays. Contributions: Literary Gazette; Literary Russia; Pravda; Ogonyok; Novyi Mir; Yunost; Nash Sovremennik; Druzhba Narodov; Krestyanka; Komsomolskaya Pravda. *Honours:* Moscow Komsomol Prize, 1971; Order of Merit, 1971, 1980; Order of Friendship of People, 1984. *Address:* 8 Usievicha Str, Apt 86, Moscow 125319, Russia.

VASSANJI, Moyez G., BS, PhD; Canadian writer and editor; b. 30 May 1950, Nairobi, Kenya; m. Nurjehan Aziz 1979; two s. *Education:* MIT, University of Pennsylvania. *Career:* Research Assoc. and Lecturer, University of Toronto, 1980–89; Ed., The Toronto South Asian Review, later The Toronto Review of Contemporary Writing Abroad; Writer-in-Residence, University of Iowa, 1989. *Publications:* The Gunny Sack, 1989; No New Land, 1991; Uhuru Street, 1991; The Book of Secrets, 1994; Amriika, 1999; The In-Between World of Vikram Lall 2004. *Honours:* Commonwealth First Novel Award, Africa Region, 1990; F. G. Bressani Literary Prize, 1994; Giller Prize for Best Fiction, 1994; Harbourfront Literary Prize, 1994. *Address:* 39 Woburn Avenue, Toronto, ON M5M 1K5, Canada.

VELLIDIS, Katerina; Greek publisher; b. 1947, Thessaloniki; m. (divorced); one d. *Education:* Univ. of Geneva and Sorbonne, Paris. *Career:* Pres. Bd and Man. Dir I. K. Vellidis Press Org. of Northern Greece (publrs of newspapers and magazines, including Thessaloníki) 1980–; Pres. Ioannis and Anna Vellidis Foundation. *Honours:* numerous awards including Silver Medal of Acad. of Athens. *Address:* c/o Thessaloníki, Odos Monastiriou 85, 546 27 Thessaloníki, Greece.

VENCLOVA, Tomas; American Professor of Slavic Languages and Literatures, Writer and Poet; b. 11 Sept. 1937, Klaipeda, Lithuania; m. Tanya Milovidova 1990, one s. one d. *Education:* Diploma, Philology, University of Vilnius, 1960; Graduate Studies, Semiotics and Russian Literature, 1966–71; PhD, Yale University, 1985. *Career:* Lecturer in Literature, Linguistics and Semiotics, University of Vilnius, 1966–73; Junior Fellow, Institute of History, Lithuanian Acad. of Sciences, 1974–76; Regents Prof. in Slavic Languages and Literatures, University of California at Berkeley, 1977; Lecturer in Slavic Languages and Literatures, University of California at Los Angeles, 1977–80; Morton Prof. of Philosophy, Ohio University, 1978; Lecturer and Acting Instructor, 1980–85, Asst Prof., 1985–90, Assoc. Prof., 1990–93, Prof., 1993–, of Slavic Languages and Literatures, Yale University; mem. Asscn for the Advancement of Baltic Studies, pres., 1989–91; International PEN; PEN in Exile, Mem., Exec. Board, 1982; New York Institute for the Humanities, Fellow, 1981–84; Kennan Institue for Advanced Russian Studies, Fellow, 1981. *Publications:* Poetry: Kalbos zenklas, 1972; 98 eilerasciai, 1977; Pasnekesys ziema, 1991, partial English trans. as Winter Dialogue, 1997; Szesc wierszy, 1991; Cistost soli, 1991; Mondjatok meg Fortinbrasnak, 1992; Rinktine, 1999; Vor der Tür das Ende der Welt, 2000. Other: Tekstai apie tekstus, 1985; Neustoichivoe ravnovesie: vosem russkikh poeticheskikh tekstov, 1986; Vilties formos: Eseistika ir publicisika, 1991, partial English trans. as Forms of Hope, 1999; Aleksander Wat: Life and Art of an Iconoclast, 1996; Sobesedniki na piru, 1997. Translations: many works by major writers into Lithuanian. Contributions: articles to professional journals including International Journal of Slavic Linguistics and Poetics; Russian Literature; Russian Review; World Literature Today; Journal of Baltic Studies; Comparative Civilizations Review; UCLA Slavic Studies. *Honours:* Vilenica International Literary Prize, 1990; Dr hc, University of Lublín, Poland, 1991; Jagellonian University, Kraków, 2000. *Address:* 100 York Street, Apt 12 S, New Haven, CT 06511, USA.

VENDLER, Helen, (Helen Hennessy); Professor and Poetry Critic; b. 30 April 1933, Boston, Massachusetts, USA; one s. *Education:* AB, Emmanuel College, 1954; PhD, Harvard University, 1960. *Career:* Instructor, Cornell University, 1960–63; Lecturer, Swarthmore College and Haverford College, Pennsylvania, 1963–64; Assoc. Prof., 1966–68, Prof., 1968–85, Boston University; Fulbright Lecturer, University of Bordeaux, 1968–69; Poetry Critic, The New Yorker, 1978–; Overseas Fellow, Churchill College, Cambridge, 1980; Senior Fellow, Harvard Society of Fellows, 1981–93; Visiting Prof., 1981–85, Kenan Prof., 1985–, Assoc. Academic Dean, 1987–92, Porter University Prof., 1990–, Harvard University; Charles Stewart Parnell Fellow, 1996, Hon. Fellow, 1996–, Magdalene College, Cambridge; mem. American Acad. of Arts and Letters; American Acad. of Arts and Sciences, vice-pres., 1992–95; American Philosophical Society; English Institute; MLA, pres., 1980. *Publications:* Yeats's Vision and the Later Plays, 1963; On Extended Wings: Wallace Stevens' Longer Poems, 1969; The Poetry of George Herbert, 1975; Part of Nature, Part of Us: Modern American Poets, 1980; The Odes of John Keats, 1983; Wallace Stevens: Words Chosen Out of Desire, 1984; The Harvard Book of Contemporary American Poetry (ed.), 1985; Voices and Visions: The Poet in America, 1987; The Music of What Happens, 1988; Soul Says, 1995; The Given and the Made, 1995; The Breaking of Style, 1995; Poems, Poets, Poetry, 1995; The Art of Shakespeare's Sonnets, 1997; Seamus Heaney, 1998; Coming of Age as a Poet, 2003. Contributions: Professional journals. *Honours:* Lowell Prize, 1969; Guggenheim Fellowship, 1971–72; ACLS Fellow, 1971–72; National Institute of Arts and Letters Award, 1975; Radcliffe College Graduate Society Medal, 1978; National Book Critics Award, 1980; National Endowment for the Humanities Fellowships, 1980, 1985, 1994; Keats-Shelley Asscn Award, 1994; Truman Capote Award, 1996; Jefferson Medal, APS, 2000; many hon. doctorates. *Address:* 54 Trowbridge Street, No. 2, Cambridge, MA 02138, USA.

VENN, George Andrew Fyfe; University Educator, Writer, Editor and Poet; b. 12 Oct. 1943, Tacoma, Washington, USA; m. Elizabeth Cheney, divorced, one s. one d. *Education:* BA, College of Idaho, 1967; MFA, Creative Writing, University of Montana, 1970; Central University, Quito, Ecuador;

University of Salamanca, Spain; City Literary Institute, London. *Career:* General Ed., Oregon Literature Series Vols I–VI 1989–; Faculty, Eastern Oregon University; Pres. Oregon Council of Teachers of English 2001–03; mem. Oregon Council of Teachers of English; PEN West; National Council of Teachers of English. *Publications:* Sunday Afternoon: Grande Ronde, 1975; Off the Main Road, 1978; Marking the Magic Circle, 1988; West of Paradise: New Poems, 1999. Contributions: Oregon Humanities; Writer's Northwest Handbook; North West Review; Northwest Reprint Series; Poetry Northwest; Willow Springs; Clearwater Journal; Oregon East; Portland Review; Worldviews and the American West (book). *Honours:* Pushcart Prize, 1980; Oregon Book Award, 1988; Stewart Holbrook Award, 1994; Andres Berger Poetry Prize, Northwest Writers, 1995. *Address:* c/o Dept of English, Eastern Oregon University, La Grande, OR 97850, USA. *E-mail:* gvenn@eou.edu.

VENTURI, Robert, AB, MFA; architect and writer; b. 25 June 1925, Philadelphia, Pennsylvania, USA; m. Denise Scott Brown 1967; one s. *Education:* Princeton University. *Career:* Designer, 1950–58; Asst to Assoc. Prof. of Architecture, University of Pennsylvania, 1957–65; Assoc., Venturi, Cope and Lippincott, Philadelphia, 1958–61; Partner, Venturi and Short, Philadelphia, 1961–64, Venturi and Rauch, Philadelphia, 1964–80, Venturi, Rauch and Scott Brown, Philadelphia, 1980–89, Venturi, Scott Brown and Assocs Inc, Philadelphia, 1989–; Charlotte Shepherd Davenport Prof. of Architecture, Yale University, 1966–70; mem. American Acad. of Arts and Letters; American Acad. of Arts and Sciences; Royal Institute of British Architects, hon. mem. *Publications:* Complexity and Contradiction in Architecture, 1966; Learning from Las Vegas (with Denise Scott Brown and Steven Izenour), 1972; A View from the Campidoglio: Selected Essays, 1953–84 (with Denise Scott Brown), 1984; Iconography and Electronics Upon a Generic Architecture, 1996; Architecture as Signs and Systems for a Mannerist Time (with Denise Scott Brown) 2004. Contributions: numerous publications. *Honours:* Rome Prize Fellow, American Acad. in Rome, 1954–56; Commendatore of the Order of Merit, Republic of Italy, 1986; Pritzker Architecture Prize, 1991; National Medal of Arts, Manufacturers and Commerce, 1993; Classic Book Award, American Institute of Architecture, 1996; Commdr, Ordre des Arts et des Lettres, 2001; several hon. doctorates. *Address:* c/o Venturi, Scott Brown and Associates Inc, 4236 Main Street, Philadelphia, PA 19127, USA. *Website:* www.vsba.com.

VERA, Yvonne; Novelist; b. 19 Sept. 1964, Bulawayo, South Rhodesia (now Zimbabwe). *Education:* BA, MA, PhD, English, York Univ., Canada. *Career:* Dir, National Gallery of Zimbabwe, Bulawayo, 1997–. *Publications:* Fiction: Why Don't You Carve Other Animals (short stories), 1992; Nehanda, 1993; Without a Name, 1994; Under the Tongue, 1996; Butterfly Burning, 1998; The Stone Virgins, 2002. Non-Fiction: Opening Spaces: An Anthology of Contemporary African Women's Writing, 1999; A Voyeur's Paradise.. Images of Africa (essay in Encounter Images in the Meetings Between Africa and Europe), 2001. *Honours:* First prize, Zimbabwe Publishers' Literary Awards, 1995, 1997; Commonwealth Writers Prize (Africa Region), 1997; The Voice of Africa, Sweden, 1999; Macmillan Writer's Prize for Africa, Adult Fiction Award, 2002. *Address:* c/o African Writers Series, Heinemann Educational Publishers, Halley Ct, Jordan Hill, Oxford OX2 8EJ, England.

VERGHESE, Abraham; Ethiopian writer; b. 1955; m.; two c. *Education:* Madras Medical Coll. India, East Tennessee State Univ., Johnson City, USA. *Career:* specialist in HIV and AIDS research 1985–89; worked at Univ. of Iowa outpatient AIDS clinic 1990; currently Prof. of Medicine and Chief of Infectious Diseases, Texas Tech Health Sciences Center, El Paso, TX. *Publications:* My Own Country: A Doctor's Story of a Town and its People in the Age of AIDS 1994, Soundings: A Doctor's Life in the Age of AIDS 1994, The Tennis Partner: A Doctor's Story of Friendship and Loss 1998, Short Stories 1999; contrib. to The New Yorker, North American Review, Granta, Sports Illustrated, Story, numerous medical journals. *Address:* c/o HarperCollins Publishers Ltd, 77–85 Fulham Palace Road, London, W6 8JB, England. *Website:* www.harpercollins.co.uk.

VERMES, Geza; Prof. of Jewish Studies Emeritus and Writer; b. 22 June 1924, Mako, Hungary; m. 1st Pamela Hobson, 1958, deceased 1993; m. 2nd Margaret Unarska, 1996. *Education:* University of Budapest; Licencié en Histoire et Philologie Orientales, University of Louvain, 1952; DTheol, 1953; MA, Oxon, 1965; DLitt, 1988. *Career:* Lecturer, later Senior Lecturer in Divinity, University of Newcastle, 1957–65; Reader in Jewish Studies, University of Oxford, 1965–89; Fellow, Wolfson College, 1965–91, Fellow Emeritus, 1991–, Prof. of Jewish Studies, 1989–91, Prof. Emeritus, 1991–, University of Oxford; Ed., Journals of Jewish Studies, 1971–; Dir, Oxford Forum for Qumran Research, Oxford Centre for Hebrew and Jewish Studies, 1991–; Inaugural Lecturer, Geza Vermes Lectures in the History of Religions, University of Leicester, 1997; many visiting lectureships and professorships; mem. British Asscn for Jewish Studies, pres., 1975, 1988; European Asscn for Jewish Studies, pres., 1981–84. *Publications:* Les manuscrits du désert de Juda, 1953; Discovery in the Judean Desert, 1956; Scripture and Tradition in Judaism, 1961; The Dead Sea Scrolls in English, 1962; Jesus the Jew, 1973; History of the Jewish People in the Age of Jesus Christ, by E. Schürer I–III (co-reviser with F. Millar and M. Goodman), 1973–87; Post-Biblical Jewish Studies, 1975; The Dead Sea Scrolls: Qumran in Perspective (with Pamela Vermes), 1977; The Gospel of Jesus the Jew, 1981; Essays in Honour of Y. Yadin (co-ed.), 1982; Jesus and the World of Judaism, 1983; The Essenes According to the Classical Sources (with M. D. Goodman), 1989; The Religion of Jesus the Jew, 1993; The Complete Dead Sea Scrolls in English, 1997; Providential Accidents: An Autobiography, 1998; Discoveries in the Judaean Desert XXVI: The Community Rule (with P. S. Alexander), 1998; An Introduction to the Complete Dead Sea Scrolls, 1999; The Changing Faces of Jesus, 2000; The Dead Sea Scrolls, 2000. Contributions: scholarly books and journals. *Honours:* Fellow, British Acad., 1985; Hon. DD, University of Edinburgh, 1989, University of Durham, 1990; Hon. DLitt, University of Sheffield, 1994; W. Bacher Medallist, Hungarian Acad. of Sciences, 1996; Fellow, European Acad. of Arts, Sciences and Humanities, 2001. *Address:* West Wood Cottage, Foxcombe Lane, Boars Hill, Oxford OX1 5DH, England.

VERNON, Annette Robyn (see Corkhill, Annette Robyn).

VERONESI, Sandro; Italian writer; b. 1959, Florence. *Publications include:* novels: Per dore parte questo treno allegro 1988, La forza del passato (trans. as The Force of the Past) 2000; contrib. to Cronache Italiene: Racconti 1992, Superalbo: Le storie complete 2002. *Honours:* Campiello Prize. *Address:* c/o Ecco, 77–85 Fulham Palace Road, London, W6 8JB, England. *Website:* www .harpercollins.co.uk.

VICE, Lisa; Novelist and Poet; b. 25 July 1951, Tipton, IN, USA; m. Martha Clark Cummings, 24 June 1989, one d. *Education:* BA, summa cum laude, English and Creative Writing, 1985, MA, Teaching English as a Second Language, 1987, Hunter College, CUNY. *Career:* Instructor of Creative Writing, University of Santa Cruz, 1992–2000. *Publications:* Rohwedder (short story), 1992; The Bridge (short story), 1993; Love's Shadow (short story), 1993; The Times of Our Lives (short story), 1993; Breaking Up Is Hard to Do (short story), 1994; Bluff City (short story), 1994; Farmer's Market (short story), 1994; Reckless Driver (novel), 1995; Preacher's Lake (novel), 1998. Contributions: several periodicals including: Common Lives-Lesbian Lives; Heresies; Wilde Oakes; Palo Alto Review; Journal of Progresssive Human Services; San Francisco Chronicle Book Review; Woman's Day; Ladies Home Journal; Anthologies including: Naming the Waves; Eraly Ripening: American Women's Poetry Now; Only Morning in Her Shoes: Poems about Old Women; Word of Mouth: Short Stories by Women; Arachne; Primal Voices; We Speak for Peace; The Arc of Love; Gay and Lesbian Poetry in Our Time. *Honours:* New Voice Award for Fiction, 1987; Ludwig Vogelstein Grant, 1989; PEN Syndicated Fiction Award, 1992. *Literary Agent:* Jean V. Naggar, 216 E 75th Street, No. 1E, New York, NY 10021, USA. *Address:* PO Box 687, Thermopolis, WY 82443, USA.

VICKERS, Hugo Ralph; writer; b. 12 Nov. 1951, London, England; m. Elizabeth Anne Blyth Vickers 1995, two s. one d. *Education:* University of Strasbourg. *Career:* radio and TV broadcaster 1973–; Dir, Burkes Peerage 1974–79; mem. Historic Houses Asscn, RSL, Jubilee Walkway Trust (trustee 2000–, vice-chair. 2001, chair. 2002). *Publications:* We Want the Queen, 1977; Gladys, Duchess of Marlborough, 1979; Debretts Book of the Royal Wedding, 1981; Cocktails and Laughter (ed.), 1983; Cecil Beaton: The Authorised Biography, 1985; Vivien Leigh, 1988; Loving Garbo, 1994; Royal Orders, 1994; The Private World of the Duke and Duchess of Windsor, 1995; The Kiss, 1996; Alice, Princess Andrew of Greece, 2000; The Unexpurgated Beaton, 2002; Beaton in the Sixties, 2003. Contributions: The Times; Books and periodicals. *Honours:* PEN Stern Prize for Non-Fiction1996. *Literary Agent:* Gillon Aitken Associates Ltd, 18–21 Cavaye Place, London, SW10 9PT, England. *Telephone:* (20) 7373-8672. *Fax:* (20) 7373-6002. *Address:* Wyeford, Ramsdell, Hants RG26 5QL, England.

VICKERS, Salley; Writer and Psychologist; two c. *Career:* fmr university lecturer in English literature; analytical psychologist; lecturer on literature, psychology and religion. *Publications:* Miss Garnet's Angel, 2000; Instances of the Number 3, 2001; Mr Golightly's Holiday, 2003; Nice 'N' Easy, 2003. Contributions: columnist, Quicksilver magazine; reviews in newspapers. *Address:* c/o Fourth Estate, 77–85 Fulham Palace Rd, London W6 8JB, England. *E-mail:* reception@salleyvickers.com. *Website:* www .salleyvickers.com.

VICTOR, Edward (Ed), MLitt; British literary agent; b. 9 Sept. 1939, New York, USA; m. 1st Michelene Dinah Samuels 1963 (divorced); two s.; m. 2nd Carol Lois Ryan; one s. *Education:* Dartmouth Coll., USA, Pembroke Coll., Cambridge. *Career:* Arts Book Ed., then Editorial Dir Weidenfeld & Nicolson 1964–67; Editorial Dir Jonathan Cape Ltd 1967–71; Sr Ed. Alfred A. Knopf Inc., New York 1972–73, literary agent and Dir John Farquharson Ltd 1974–76; Founding Ed. Victor Agency 1977; mem. Council Aids Crisis Trust 1986–98; Vice-Chair. Almeida Theatre 1994– (Dir 1993–2002); Trustee, The Arts Foundation 1991–. *Publications include:* The Obvious Diet 2001. *Address:* Ed Victor Ltd, 6 Bayley Street, Bedford Square, London WC1B 3HB (Office); 10 Cambridge Gate, Regents Park, London NW1 4JX, England (Home). *Telephone:* (20) 7304-4100 (Office); (20) 7224-3030 (Home). *Fax:* (20) 7304-4111 (Office); (20) 7935-3096 (Home). *E-mail:* ed@ edvictor.com.

VIDA, Vendela; American writer; m. Dave Eggers 2003. *Education:* Columbia Univ. *Career:* Co-Ed., The Believer literary magazine. *Pub-*

lications: Girls on the Verge 1999, And Now You Can Go 2003. *Address:* 826 Valencia Street, San Francisco, CA 94110, USA. *E-mail:* letters@believermag.com. *Website:* www.believermag.com.

VIDAL, Gore, (Edgar Box); Writer; b. 3 Oct. 1925, West Point, NY, USA. *Education:* Graduate, Phillips Exeter Acad., 1943. *Career:* mem. American Acad. of Arts and Letters. *Publications:* Fiction: Williwaw, 1946; In a Yellow Wood, 1947; The City and the Pillar, 1948; The Season of Comfort, 1949; A Search for the King, 1950; Dark Green, Bright Red, 1950; The Judgment of Paris, 1952; Messiah, 1954; Julian, 1964; Washington, DC, 1967; Myra Breckinridge, 1968; Two Sisters, 1970; Burr, 1973; Myron, 1974; Kalki, 1978; Creation, 1981; Duluth, 1983; Lincoln, 1984; Empire, 1987; The Smithsonian Institution, 1998; The Golden Age, 2000. Stories: A Thirsty Evil, 1956. Play: Visit to a Small Planet, 1957. Television and Broadway productions: The Best Man, 1960; Romulus, 1966; Weekend, 1968; An Evening with Richard Nixon, 1972; Gore Vidal's Lincoln, 1988. Non-Fiction: Rocking the Boat, 1962; Reflections upon a Sinking Ship, 1969; Homage to Daniel Shays, 1973; Matters of Fact and of Fiction, 1977; The Second American Revolution, 1982; Armageddon?, 1987; United States: Essays 1952–1992, 1993; The Last Empire: Essays 1992–2000, 2001; Perpetual War for Perpetual Peace: How We Got So Hated, 2002; Inventing a Nation: Washington, Adams, Jefferson, 2003. Memoir: Palimpsest, 1995. Films: The Catered Affair, 1956; The Left-Handed Gun, 1958; The Best Man, 1964. Teleplays: The Death of Billy the Kid, 1958; Dress Gray, 1986. *Honours:* National Book Award, 1993. *Address:* c/o Random House, 201 E 50th St, New York, NY 10022, USA.

VIENS, Louis, (Nathaniel Thorne); Author; b. 15 Feb. 1957, Montréal, QC, Canada. *Education:* Diploma, Human Sciences (History), Collège de Maisonneuve, Montréal, Canada, 1980. *Career:* mem. Société des Écrivains Canadiens, 1992; Union des écrivaines et des écrivains québécois, 1995. *Publications:* Le dernier virage ou un chrétien en colère, 1994; D'une catacombe l'autre, 1995. Contributions: Journal Voir. *Address:* c/o Nathaniel Thorne, 1607 ave Letourneux, Montréal, QC H1V 2M6, Canada. *Website:* www.litterature.org.

VIERECK, Peter Robert Edwin; historian, poet and academic; b. 5 Aug. 1916, New York, NY, USA; m. 1st Anya de Markov 1945 (divorced 1970); one s. one d.; m. 2nd Betty Martin Falkenberg, 30 Aug. 1972. *Education:* BS, 1937, MA, 1939, PhD, 1942, Harvard University; Graduate Study as a Henry Fellow, Christ Church, Oxford, 1937–38. *Career:* Instructor, Tutor, Harvard University, 1946–47; Asst Prof. of History, 1947–48, Visiting Lecturer in Russian History, 1948–49, Smith College, Northampton, Massachusetts; Assoc. Prof., 1948–55, Prof. of Modern European and Russian History, 1955–65, Mount Holyoke Alumnae Foundation Chair of Interpretive Studies, 1965–79, William R. Kenan Chair of History, 1979–, Mount Holyoke College; Whittal Lecturer in Poetry, Library of Congress, Washington, DC, 1954, 1963; Fulbright Prof. in American Poetry and Civilization, University of Florida, 1955; Elliston Chair and Poetry Lecturer, University of Cincinnati, 1956; Visiting Lecturer, University of California at Berkeley, 1957, 1964, City College, CUNY, 1964; Visiting Research Scholar in Russian for the Twentieth Century Fund, 1962–63; Dir, Poetry Workshop, New York Writers Conferences, 1965–67; mem. American Committee for Cultural Freedom, exec. committee; American Historical Asscn; Committee for Basic Education, charter mem.; Oxford Society; PEN. *Publications:* History: Metapolitics: From the Romantics to Hitler, 1941, revised edn as Metapolitics: The Roots of the Nazi Mind, 1961; Conservatism Revisited: The Revolt Against Revolt, 1815–1949, 1949, second edn as Conservatism Revisited and the New Conservatism: What Went Wrong?, 1962; Shame and Glory of the Intellectuals: Babbitt, Jr Versus the Rediscovery of Values, 1953; The Unadjusted Man: A New Hero for Americans: Reflections on the Distinction Between Conserving and Conforming, 1956; Inner Liberty: The Stubborn Grit in the Machine, 1957; Conservatism from Burke and John Adams till 1982: A History and an Anthology, 1982. Poetry: Terror and Decorum: Poems 1940–1948, 1948; Strike Through Mask: Lyrical Poems, 1950; The First Morning: New Poems, 1952; Dream and Responsibility: The Tension Between Poetry and Society, 1953; The Persimmon Tree, 1956; The Tree Witch: A Poem and a Play (First of All a Poem), 1961; New and Selected Poems, 1932–1967, 1967; Archer in the Marrow: The Applewood Cycles of 1967–1987, 1987; Tide and Continuities: Last and First Poems, 1995–1938, 1995, Metapolitics: From Wagner and the Germany Romantics to Hitler 2003, Unadjusted Man in the Overadjusted Age 2003, Conservatism Revisited – and Where American "Conservatives" Went Wrong 2003. Contributions: Monographs, essays, reviews and poems to numerous periodicals. *Honours:* Pulitzer Prize in Poetry, 1949; Rockefeller Foundation Research Grant, 1958; Guggenheim Fellowship, 1959–60; National Endowment for the Humanities Senior Research Fellowship, 1969; Poetry Award, Massachusetts Artists Foundation, 1978; Sadin Prize, New York Quarterly, 1980; Golden Rose Award, 1981, Varoujan Poetry Prize, 1983, New England Poetry Club; Ingram Merrill Foundation Fellowship in Poetry, 1985. *Address:* 12 Silver Street, South Hadley, MA 01075, USA.

VILLANUEVA, Tino; American writer, translator and poet; b. 11 Dec. 1941, San Marcos, TX. *Career:* founder, Imagine Publishers Inc; Ed., Imagine, International Chicano Poetry Journal; teacher, Boston Univ., MA. *Publications:* poetry: Shaking off the Dark 1984, Scene from the Movie GIANT 1993, Crónica de mis años peores (trans. as Chronicle of My Worst Years) 1994, La llaman América 1998, Primera Causa (trans. as First Cause) 1999. *Honours:* American Book Award, Before Columbus Foundation 1994. *Address:* c/o Curbstone Press, 321 Jackson Street, Willimantic, CT 06226-1738, USA. *E-mail:* info@curbstone.org. *Website:* www.curbstone.org.

VILLASEÑOR, Victor; writer; b. 11 May 1940, Carlsbad, CA, USA. *Publications:* Macho!, 1973; Jury: The People vs Juan Corona (non-fiction), 1977; Ballad of Gregorio Cortez (screenplay); Rain of Gold (memoir), 1991; Snow Goose: Global Thanksgiving (philosophy), 1993; Wild Steps of Heaven (memoir), 1996; Walking Stars (short stories), 1996; Thirteen Senses (memoir), 2001; nine novels and 65 short stories. *Literary Agent:* Margret McBride Literary Agency, 7744 Fay Avenue, Suite 201, La Jolla, CA 92037, USA. *E-mail:* Victor@victorvillasenor.com. *Website:* www.victorvillasenor.com.

VINCENT, Rev. John James, DTheol; British theologian, broadcaster and writer; b. 29 Dec. 1929, Sunderland; m. Grace Johnston Stafford 1958; two s. one d. *Education:* Manchester Grammar School, Richmond Coll., London Univ., Drew Univ., Madison, NJ, USA, Basel Univ., Switzerland. *Career:* ordained in Methodist Church 1956; Minister, Manchester and Salford Mission 1956–62; Supt Minister, Rochdale Mission 1962–69, Sheffield Inner City Ecumenical Mission 1970–77; Dir Urban Theology Unit, Sheffield 1969–97, Dir Emer. and Doctoral Supervisor 1997–; Pres. Methodist Conf. 1989–90; Visiting Prof. of Theology, Boston School of Theology, USA 1969, New York Theological Seminary 1970, Theological School, Drew Univ. 1977; elected mem. Studiorum Novi Testamenti Societas 1961; Sec. Regional Working Party, WCC Faith and Order 1958–63; mem. British Council of Churches Comm. on Defence and Disarmament 1963–65, 1969–72; NW Vice-Pres. Campaign for Nuclear Disarmament 1957–69; Founding mem. Methodist Renewal Group 1961–70; Founding mem. and Leader Ashram Community 1967–; Chair. Alliance of Radical Methodists 1971–74, Urban Mission Training Asscn of GB 1976–77, 1985–90; Co-ordinator, British Liberation Theology Project 1990–; mem. Bd Int. Urban Ministry Network 1991–; presented Petition of Distress from the Cities to HM the Queen 1993; mem. Independent Human Rights Del. to Colombia 1994; Chair. Methodist Report on The Cities 1997. *Publications:* Christ in a Nuclear World 1962, Christ and Methodism 1964, Here I Stand 1967, Secular Christ 1968, The Race Race 1970, The Jesus Thing 1973, Stirrings, Essays Christian and Radical 1975, Alternative Church 1976, Disciple and Lord 1976, Starting All Over Again 1981, Into the City 1982, O.K. Let's Be Methodists 1984, Radical Jesus 1986, Mark at Work 1986, Britain in the 90s 1989, Discipleship in the 90s 1991, Liberation Theology from the Inner City 1992, A Petition of Distress from the Cities 1993, A British Liberation Theology (ed.) 1995, The Cities: A Methodist Report 1997, Gospel from the City (ed.) 1997, Hope from the City 2000, Journey: Explorations in Discipleship 2001, Bible and Practice (ed.) 2001, Faithfulness in the City (ed.) 2003, Methodist and Radical (ed.) 2003. *Honours:* Hon. Lecturer Biblical Studies Dept, Sheffield Univ. 1990–, Theology Dept, Birmingham Univ. 2003–; Fellow St Deiniol's Library 2003. *Address:* 178 Abbeyfield Road, Sheffield, S4 7AY, England. *Telephone:* (114) 243-6688; (114) 243–5342 (Office). *Fax:* (114) 243-5356.

VINCENZI, Penny; British writer; b. 10 April 1939, Bournemouth; m.; four c. *Career:* Sec., Vogue and Tatler magazines; staff, The Daily Mirror, Nova, Woman's Own; co-founder, Looking Good magazine; Contributing Ed., Cosmopolitan; Deputy Ed., Options. *Publications:* novels: Old Sins 1989, Free Sins 1990, Wicked Pleasures 1992, An Outrageous Affair 1993, Another Woman 1994, Forbidden Places 1995, The Dilemma 1996, The Glimpses 1996, Windfall 1997, Almost a Crime 1999, Into Temptation 2002, non-fiction: The Compleat Liar 1977, Cosmopolitan Vital Health Guide 1982, There's One Born Every Minute: A Survival Guide for Parents 1984, Taking Stock: Over 75 Years of the Oxo Cube 1985. *Address:* c/o Orion Publishing Group Ltd, 5 Upper St Martin's Lane, London, WC2H 9EA, England. *Website:* www.penny-vincenzi.com.

VINE, Barbara (see Rendell, Ruth Barbara).

VINEY, Ethna, BSc, BA; writer, television and film producer and director; b. 17 Jan. 1933, West Cavan, Ireland; m. Michael Viney 1965; one d. *Education:* College of Pharmacy, Dublin, University College, Dublin. *Career:* Independent Pharmacist, 1956–61; Television Producer, 1966–76; Freelance Journalist, 1964–; Independent Television Film Producer and Dir, 1990–. *Publications:* A Dozen Lips, 1994; Survival or Salvation, 1994; Dancing to Different Tunes, 1996, 1997; A Wildlife Narrative, 1999. *Honours:* Outstanding Academic Book of the Year, USA, 1997. *Address:* Thallabawn, Westport, County Mayo, Ireland.

VINGE, Vernor (Steffen); Mathematician and Writer; b. 2 Oct. 1944, Waukesha, WI, USA. *Education:* BS, Michigan State University, 1966; MA, 1968, PhD, 1971, University of California at San Diego. *Career:* Faculty, Dept of Mathematics, San Diego State University, 1972–2000; mem. American Mathematical Society; SFWA. *Publications:* Grimm's World, 1969; The Witling, 1976; The Peace War, 1984; Marooned in Realtime, 1986; A Fire Upon the Deep, 1992; A Deepness in the Sky, 1999; True Names and the Opening of Cyberspace Frontier (with James Frenkel), 2001. Contributions: anthologies and periodicals. *Honours:* Hugo Award, 1993. *Address:* c/o Toad Hall Inc, RR2, PO Box 2090, Lacyville, PA 18623, USA.

VINKEN, Pierre; Dutch publishing executive (retd); b. 25 Nov. 1927, Heerlen. *Education:* Univs of Utrecht and Amsterdam. *Career:* consultant neurosurgeon, Univ. of Amsterdam 1964–71; Man. Dir Excerpta Medica Publishing Co. Amsterdam 1963–71, Elsevier Science Publrs, Amsterdam 1971–73; Exec. Dir Elsevier NV, Amsterdam (now Reed/Elsevier PLC London) 1972–79, Chair. 1993–95. *Publications:* Handbook of Clinical Neurology (78 vols), The Shape of the Heart 2000; articles on medicine and art history in journals. *Honours:* hon. mem. various scientific asscns; Kt, Order of Netherlands Lion 1983, Commdr Order of Hipólito Unanul (Peru) 1984, Commdr, Order of Orange Nassau 1995; Dr hc (Paris). *Address:* 142 Bentveldsweg, 2111 EE Aerdenhout, Netherlands (Home). *Telephone:* (23) 5246342 (Home). *Fax:* (23) 5246032 (Home). *E-mail:* vinken@quicknet.nl (Home).

VINKENOOG, Simon; Dutch poet and writer; b. 18 July 1928, Amsterdam. *Career:* Ed., anthology Atonaal 1951; helped found Poëzie in Carré theatre in Amsterdam 1966; Dutch Poet Laureate 2004–. *Publications include:* Wondkoorts 1950, Atonaal 1951, Land zonder nacht 1952, Heren Zeventien 1953, Zolang te water 1954, Lessen uit de nieuwe school van taboes 1955, Tweespraak 1956, Enkele reis Nederland 1957, Onder eigen dak 1957, Wij helden 1957, Drie staat tot één 1962, Spiegelschrift 1962, Het verhaal van Karel Appel 1963, Preambuul voor een nieuwe wereld 1963, Eerste gedichten 1949–1964 1965, Hoogseizoen 1965, Liefde. Zeventig dagen op ooghoogte 1965, Manifesten en manifestaties 1967, The Book of Grass 1967, Vogelvrij 1967, Weergaloos 1968, Leven en dood van Marcel Polak 1969, Het moederkruid 1970, Aan het daglicht 1971, Het hek van de dam 1971, Tussen wit en zwart - het ABC van de I Ching 1971, Wonder boven wonder 1971, To Timothy Leary, magiër 1972, Niet niets. De kunst van het sterven 1974, Mij best 1976, De andere wereld 1978, Het huiswerk van de dichter 1978, Levend licht 1978, Tegen de wet 1980, Voeten in de aarde en bergen verzetten 1982, Maandagavondgedichten 1985, Jarings jaren '60 1986, Stadsnatuur 1986, Op het eerste gehoor 1988, Brieven 1950–1956 1989, Louter genieten 1993, Bloemlezing uit de poëzie van Simon Vinkenoog 1994, Herem'ntijd 1998, Vreugdevuur 1998, De ware Adam, gedichten rond de eeuwwisseling 2000, Goede raad is vuur 2004; contrib. to numerous anthologies and journals. *Literary Agent:* Bas Pauw, Singel 464, 1017 Amsterdam, Netherlands. *Telephone:* (20) 620 62 61. *Fax:* (20) 620 71 79. *E-mail:* b.pauw@nlpvf.nl. *Website:* www.simonvinkenoog.nl.

VIRGO, Seán; Writer and Poet; b. 1940, Mtarfa, Malta. *Education:* BA, University of Nottingham. *Career:* mem. League of Canadian Poets. *Publications:* Fiction: White Lies and Other Fictions, 1979; Through the Eyes of a Cat: Irish Stories, 1983; Selakhi, 1987; Wormwood, 1989; White Lies... Plus Two, 1990; Waking in Eden, 1990; The Scream of the Butterfly, 1996. Poetry: Sea Change, 1971; Pieces for the Old Earth Man, 1973; Island (with Paul and Lutia Lauzon), 1975; Kiskatinaw Songs (with Susan Musgrave), 1977; Deathwatch on Skidegate Narrows, 1979; Selected Poems, 1992. *Address:* c/o League of Canadian Poets, 54 Wolseley St, Suite 204, Toronto, ON M5T 1A5, Canada.

VIRILIO, Paul; Writer and Artist; b. 1932, Paris, France. *Education:* Ecole des Metiers d'Art, Paris, Univ. of the Sorbonne, Paris. *Career:* worked as artist in stained glass alongside Matisse in various churches in Paris; untrained architect; Chair. and Dir Ecole Spéciale d'Architecture, Paris 1968–98, Prof. Emer. 1998–; Ed. Espace Critique, Editions Galilee, Paris 1973–; Co-Founder and Program Dir Collège Int. de Philosophie 1990–; mem. French Comm. concerned with housing for the poor (HCLD) 1992–; fmr mem. Editorial Bds Esprit, Cause Commune, Critiques, Traverses; has worked with Fondation Cartier pour l'art contemporain on several exhbns including Bunker Archeology, Pompidou Centre 1975, Speed, Jouy-en-Josas 1991, Unknown Quantity, Paris 2002. *Publications:* Bunker Archeologie 1975, L'Insecurité du territoire 1976, Speed and Politics 1977, Popular Defense and Ecological Struggles 1978, L'Esthetique de la disparition 1980, Pure War (with Sylvère Lotringer) 1983, War and Cinema: The Logistics of Perception 1984, L'Espace critique 1984, Polar Inertia 1990, The Art of the Motor 1995, Politics of the Very Worst 1996, Open Sky 1997, The Information Bomb 1998, The Strategy of Deception 1999, A Landscape of Events 2000, Ground Zero 2002; numerous technical works. *Honours:* Grand Prix Nat. de la Critique 1987. *Address:* Editions Galilee, 9 rue de Linné, 75005 Paris, France. *E-mail:* editions.galilee@free.fr.

VIRTUE, Noel; Author; b. 3 Jan. 1947, Wellington, New Zealand. *Education:* New Zealand secondary schools. *Publications:* The Redemption of Elsdon Bird, 1987; Then Upon the Evil Season, 1988; Among the Animals: A Zookeeper's Story, 1988; In the Country of Salvation, 1990; Always the Islands of Memory, 1991; The Eye of the Everlasting Angel, 1993; Sandspit Crossing, 1994. *Address:* c/o Hutchinson, 20 Vauxhall Bridge Rd, London SW1V, England.

VITALE, Alberto; American publishing executive; b. 22 Dec. 1933, Vercelli, Piedmont, Italy; m. Gemma G. Calori 1961; two s. *Education:* Turin Univ., IPSOA Business School and Wharton School, Univ. of Pa (Fulbright Scholar). *Career:* joined Olivetti 1958; moved to USA to assist in Olivetti's acquisition of Underwood 1959; Exec. IFI (Agnelli family holding co.) 1971; Exec. Vice-Pres. for Admin Bantam Books, New York 1975, Co-CEO 1985, sole CEO 1986; Pres. and CEO Bantam-Doubleday-Dell 1987; Chair., Pres. and CEO Random House 1990–96, Chair., CEO 1996–98; Chair. Supervisory Bd Random House Inc., New York 1998–; mem. Bd Dirs Transworld Publrs. *Address:* 745 Fifth Avenue, Suite 1512, New York, NY 10151 (Office); Random House Inc., 299 Park Avenue, New York, NY 10171; 505 Alda Road, Mamaroneck, NY 10543, USA.

VITIELLO, Justin; Professor of Italian, Poet and Writer; b. 14 Feb. 1941, New York, NY, USA; 1 son. *Education:* BA, magna cum laude, Brown University, 1963; Fulbright Scholar, University of Madrid, 1963–64; MA, Spanish, University of Michigan, 1966; PhD, Comparative Literature, University of Michigan, 1970. *Career:* Teaching Fellow, Spanish 1964–69, Lecturer, Romance Languages 1969–70, Asst Prof., Comparative Literature and Spanish, 1969–73, Head, Residential College's Comparative Literature Program, University of Michigan; Asst Prof., 1974–80, Assoc. Prof., 1980–91, Prof. of Italian, 1991–, Temple University, Philadelphia and Rome; mem. MLA; American Italian Historical Asscn; American Asscn for Italian Studies; Life Mem., MELUS. *Publications:* Poetry: Vanzetti's Fish Cart, 1991; Subway Home, 1994; Subway Home in Italian, 1998. Other: Confessions of a Joe Rock, 1992; Poetry and Literature of the Sicilian Diaspora: Studies in Oral History and Story Telling, 1998; Labyrinths and Volcanoes: Windings Through Sicily, 1999; Via Terra: Anthology of Neo-dialect Poetry, 1999. Contributions: books and periodicals. *Honours:* Fulbright Scholar, University of Madrid, 1963–64; Distinguished Teaching Fellow, University of Michigan, 1967; ATTIC Distinguished Teacher, Temple University, 1990. *Address:* c/o Temple Roma, Lungotevere Arnaldo da Brescia 15, 00196 Rome, Italy.

VITIER, Cintio; Cuban poet and writer; b. 25 Sept. 1921, Key West, USA; m. Fina García Marruz. *Education:* Univ. of Havana. *Career:* worked on Orígenes magazine 1944–56; lecturer, Escuele normal para Maestros, Havana, Universidad Cen. de las Villas; researcher, José martí Nat. Library 1962–77; Pres. Centre of Martianos Studies. *Publications:* poetry: Vísperas 1953, Testimonios 1968, La fecha al pie 1981, Nupcias 1993; fiction: De Peña Pobre 1980, Los Papeles de Jacinto Finalé 1984, Rajando la leña está 1986; essays: Lo cubano en la poesía 1958, Temas Martianos (with Fina García Marruz) 1969, 1982; Crítica Sucesiva 1971, Ese sol del mundo moral 1975, Rescate de Zenea 1987, Crítica cubana 1988. *Honours:* Oficier des Arts et des Lettres; Dr hc (Univ. of Havana), (Universidad Central de las Villas), (Soka Univ., Japan); Nat. Literature Prize 1988, 30th Anniversary Medal, Acad. of Sciences, Order of Jose Marti 2002, Juan Rulfo Prize for Literature 2002. *Address:* c/o Editorial Letras Cubanas, Ediciones Unión, No. 4, esq. Tacón, Hababa Vieja, Havana, Cuba. *Website:* www .cubaliteraria.cu.

VIZENOR, Gerald (Robert); Author, Poet and Prof. of Native American Literature; b. 22 Oct. 1934, Minneapolis, Minnesota, USA; m. 1st Judith Helen Horns, Sept. 1959, divorced 1968, one s.; m. 2nd Laura Jane Hall, May 1981. *Education:* BA, University of Minnesota, 1960. *Career:* Lecturer, 1976–80, Prof. of Native American Literature, 1990–, Richard and Rhoda Goldman Distinguished Prof. of American Studies, 2000–02, University of California at Berkeley; Prof., University of Minnesota, 1980–85, University of California at Santa Cruz, 1987–90; Resident Scholar, School of American Research, Santa Fe, 1985–86; David Burr Chair of Letters, Prof., University of Oklahoma, 1990–91. *Publications:* Thomas James White Hawk, 1968; Summer in the Spring: Anishinaable Lyric Poems and Stories, 1970; The Everlasting Sky: New Voices from the People Named the Chippewa, 1972; Tribal Scenes and Ceremonies, 1976, revised edn as Crossbloods: Bone Courts, Bingo, and Other Reports, 1990; Darkness in Saint Louis Bearheart (novel), 1978, revised edn as Bearheart: The Heirship Chronicles, 1990; Wordarrows: Indians and Whites in the New Fur Trade, 1978; Earthdivers: Tribal Narratives on Mixed Descent, 1983; The People Named the Chippewa: Narrative Histories, 1983; Matsushima: Pine Islands (collected haiku poems), 1984; Griever: An American Monkey King in China (novel), 1986; Touchwood: A Collection of Ojibway Prose (ed.), 1987; The Trickster of Liberty: Tribal Heirs to a Wild Baronage (novel), 1988; Narrative Chance: Postmodern Discourse on Native American Literatures (ed.), 1989; Interior Landscapes: Autobiographical Myths and Metaphors, 1990; Landfill Meditation (short stories), 1991; The Heirs of Columbus (novel), 1991; Dead Voices: Natural Agonies in the New World (novel), 1993; Manifest Manners: Postindian Warriors of Survivance (critical essays), 1994; Shadow Distance: A Gerald Vizenor Reader, 1994; Native American Literature (ed.), 1995; Hotline Healers: An Almost Browne Novel, 1997; Fugitive Poses: Native American Indian Scenes of Absence and Presence, 1998; Postindian Conversations, 1999; Cranes Arise (haiku). 1999; Raising the Moon Vines (haiku), 1999; Chancers (novel), 2000. Contributions: numerous books, journals, and periodicals. *Honours:* New York Fiction Collective Award, 1986; American Book Award, 1988; California Arts Council Artists Fellowship in Literature, 1989; Josephine Miles Awards, PEN Oakland, 1990, 1996; Doctor of Humane Letters, Macalester College, 1999. *Address:* c/o American Studies, 301 Campbell Hall, University of California at Berkeley, Berkeley, CA 94720, USA.

VIZINCZEY, Stephen; Canadian/British writer; b. 12 May 1933, Kaloz, Hungary; m. 1963; three d. *Education:* University of Budapest, Acad. of Theatre Arts, Budapest. *Career:* Ed., Exchange Magazine, 1960–61; Producer, Canadian Broadcasting Corporation, 1962–65; mem. PEN; Society of Authors; ALCS. *Publications:* In Praise of Older Women, 1965; The Rules of Chaos, 1969; An Innocent Millionaire, 1983; Truth and Lies in Literature,

1986; The Man with the Magic Touch, 1994; Be Faithful unto Death (trans.), 1995; Wishes, 2004. Contributions: Currently; Los Angeles Times Book Review. *Address:* 70 Coleherne Court, Old Brompton Road, London SW5 0EF, England.

VLADISLAV, Jan, (Ladislav Bambásek); Poet, Writer and Trans; b. 1923, Hlohovec, Czechoslovakia. *Career:* leading figure of Czech dissident movement, Charta 77. *Publications:* poetry, prose, essays, children's fiction, translations. Contributions: numerous journals. *Address:* c/o Faber and Faber Ltd, 3 Queen Sq., London WC1N 3AU, England.

VOGEL, Paula Anne; Dramatist and Teacher; b. 18 Nov. 1951, Washington, DC, USA. *Education:* BA, Catholic University of America, Washington, DC. *Career:* Consultant on Playwrighting and Theatre Arts; Faculty, Brown University. *Publications:* various plays, including How I Learned to Drive, 1998. *Honours:* National Endowment for the Arts Fellowships, 1980, 1991; AT&T Award, 1992; Obie Award, 1992; Fund for New American Plays, 1994; Guggenheim Fellowship, 1995; Pew Charitable Trust Senior Artist Residency, 1995–97; Lucille Lortel Award, 1997; Pulitzer Prize for Drama, 1998. *Address:* c/o Dept of English, Brown University, Providence, RI 02912, USA.

VOGELSANG, Arthur, BA, MA, MFA; American poet; *Joint Editor, American Poetry Review*; b. 31 Jan. 1942, Baltimore, MD; m. Judith Ayers 1966. *Education:* Univ. of Maryland, Johns Hopkins Univ., Univ. of Iowa. *Career:* jt Ed., The American Poetry Review 1973–. *Publications:* A Planet 1983, Twentieth Century Women 1988, Cities and Towns 1996, The Body Electric: America's Best Poetry from The American Poetry Review (co-ed.) 2001, Left Wing of a Bird 2003. *Honours:* National Endowment for the Arts Fellowships in Poetry 1976, 1985, 1995, California Arts Council Grant 1995, Juniper Prize 1995. *Address:* 1730 N Vista Street, Los Angeles, CA 90046, USA. *Address:* The American Poetry Review, 117 S 17th Street, Suite 910, Philadelphia, PA 19103, USA (Office). *Telephone:* (215) 496-0439. *Fax:* (215) 569-0808. *Website:* www.aprweb.org.

VOIGT, Ellen Bryant; Poet and College Teacher; b. 9 May 1943, Danville, Virginia, USA; m. Francis G. W. Voigt, 5 Sept. 1965, one s. one d. *Education:* BA, Converse College, Spartanburg, South Carolina, 1964; MFA, University of Iowa, 1966. *Career:* Faculty, Iowa Wesleyan College, 1966–69, Goddard College, 1969–79, MIT, 1979–82, Warren Wilson College, 1981–. *Publications:* Claiming Kin, 1976; The Forces of Plenty, 1983; The Lotus Flowers, 1987; Two Trees, 1992; Kyrie, 1996; The Flexible Lyric, 2001; Shadow of Heaven, 2002. Contributions: Reviews, quarterlies, and journals. *Honours:* National Endowment for the Arts Fellowship, 1975; Guggenheim Fellowship, 1978; Pushcart Prizes, 1983, 1987; Honorable Mention, The Poets' Prize, 1987; Emily Clark Balch Award, 1987; Hon. Doctor of Letters, Converse College, 1989; Haines Award for Poetry, Fellowship of Southern Writers, 1993; Acad. of American Poets Fellowship, 2001; inducted, Fellowship of Southern Writers, 2003; elected Chancellor, Acad. of American Poets, 2003. *Address:* PO Box 128, Marshfield, VT 05658, USA.

VOINOVICH, Vladimir Nikolaievich; writer and poet; b. 26 Sept. 1932, Stalinabad (Dushanbe), USSR; m. 1st Valentina; one s. one d.; m. 2nd Irina; one d. *Education:* Pedagogical Inst., Moscow. *Career:* mem. Bavarian Acad. of Fine Arts, Mark Twain Soc. (hon. mem.), PEN France. *Publications:* (in trans.): The Life and Extraordinary Adventures of Private Ivan Chonkin, 1977; The Ivankiad: The Tale of the Writer Voinovich's Installation in His New Apartment, 1977; In Plain Russian: Stories, 1979; Pretender to the Throne: The Further Adventures of Private Ivan Chonkin, 1981; The Anti-Soviet Soviet Union, 1986; Moscow 2042, 1987; The Fur Hat, 1989; Monumental Propaganda (novel), 2001; Portrait Against Myth Background, 2001. *Honours:* Ford Foundation Grant, 1982; Triumph Prize, 1990; National Prize, 2001. *Address:* Hans Carossastr 5, 8035 Stockdorf, Germany.

VOLK, Patricia (Gay); Writer; b. 16 July 1943, New York, NY, USA; m. Andrew Blitzer, 21 Dec. 1969, one s. one d. *Education:* BFA, cum laude, Syracuse University, 1964; Académie de la Grande Chaumière, Paris; School of Visual Arts, New York; New School, New York; Columbia University. *Career:* Copywriter to Senior Vice-Pres., Doyle Dane Bernbach Inc, 1969–88; Adjunct Instructor in Fiction, Yeshiva College, 1991; Columnist, Newsday, 1995–96; mem. Authors' Guild; PEN. *Publications:* The Yellow Banana, 1985; White Light, 1987; All it Takes, 1990; Stuffed: Adventures of a Restaurant Family, 2001. Contributions: many publications. *Honours:* Stephen E. Kelly Award, 1983; Yaddo Fellowships, 1983, 1999; MacDowell Colony Fellowships, 1984, 2000. *Literary Agent:* Watkins Loomis Agency Inc, 133 E 35th St, Suite 1, New York, NY 10016, USA.

VOLKOV, Solomon; American musicologist; b. 17 April 1944, Ura-Tyube, Tajikistan. *Education:* Leningrad Conservatory. *Career:* Artistic Dir, Leningrad Experimental Studio of Chamber Opera 1965–70; staging of Fleischmann's Rothschild's Violin, completed by Shostakovich; research at Russian Inst., Columbia Univ. 1976. *Publications:* Young Composers of Leningrad 1971, Remembrance of the 'Leningrad Spring' 1974, Testimony: The Memoirs of Dmitri Shostakovich (ed.) 1979, Scissors and Music: Music Censorship in the Soviet Union 1983, Balanchine's Tchaikovsky 1985, Yevgeny Mravinsky, Leningrad's Master Builder 1988, From Russia to the West: the Musical Memoirs of Nathan Milstein (with N. Milstein) 1990, St Petersburg: A Cultural History 1995, Conversations with Joseph Brodsky 1998, Shostakovich and Stalin 2004; contrib. articles in journals and newspapers 1959–. *Address:* c/o Alfred A. Knopf, 1745 Broadway, New York, NY 10019, USA.

VOLLMAN, William T.; Author; b. 28 July 1959, Santa Monica, CA, USA. *Education:* Deep Springs College, 1977–79; BA, summa cum laude, Cornell University, 1981; Graduate Studies, University of California at Berkeley, 1982–83. *Publications:* You Bright and Risen Angels: A Cartoon, 1987; The Rainbow Stories, 1989; Seven Dreams: A Book of North American Landscapes, 7 vols, 1990–; Whores for Gloria, or, Everything Was Beautiful Until the Girls Got Anxious, 1991; Thirteen Stories and Thirteen Epitaphs, 1991; An Afghanistan Picture Show, or, How I Saved the World, 1992; Butterfly Stories, 1993; The Atlas, 1996; Argall: The True Story of Pocahontas and Captain John Smith, 2001. *Honours:* Ella Lyman Cabot Trust Fellowship, 1982; Regent's Fellow, University of California at Berkeley, 1982–83; Ludwig Vogelstein Award, 1987; Whiting Writers' Award, 1988; Shiva Naipaul Memorial Prize, 1989. *Address:* c/o Viking-Penguin, 375 Hudson St, New York, NY 10014, USA.

VOM VENN, Hubert; Author and Publisher; b. 12 Oct. 1953, Monschau/Eifel, Germany; m. Ingrid Peinhardt-Franke, one d. *Education:* Journalism Training, 1974–1976. *Career:* Journalist, 1974–; Gag-Author, 1984–91; TV Writer, 1988–93; Radio-Comedian, 1980–2002; Radio-Speaker, 1985–98; Chief Ed. Radio Station, 1998–99; Theatre Dir, 1995–; mem. International Federation of Journalists; Deutscher Journalisten Verband. *Publications:* Bundesstrasse 258, 1990; Zum Drehen und Wenden, 1991; Die Schlacht um Monschau, 1992; Meine Sorgen möchte ich haben, 1994; Wir sind'n Volk, 1995; Und Sonst – Wie Sonst, 1996; Die Hand im Moor, 1999; Kaisermord, 2000; Mein Jahr in der Eifel, 2001; Alles für die Katz, 2002. Co-Author: Hurra Deutschland, 1991; Fritten fuer um hier zu essen, CD, 1997; Charly's Leute, 1997; Der Tod klopft an, 2000; Der Tod trifft ein, 2001; Frühling, Sommer, Herbst und Mord, 2003; The Best, CD, 2003. *Address:* Kalfstrasse 73 a, Roetgen 52159, Germany. *E-mail:* hubert-vom-venn@t-online.de. *Website:* www.hubert-vom-venn.de.

VON STAHLENBERG, Elisabeth (see Freeman, Gillian).

VONARBURG, Elisabeth; Writer and Trans; b. 5 Aug. 1947, Paris, France; m. Jean-Joel Vonarburg, 15 Dec. 1969, divorced Jan. 1990. *Education:* BA, 1969, MA, 1969, Agrégation de Lettres Modernes, 1972, University of Dijon; PhD, Université Laval, 1987. *Career:* Asst Lecturer in Literature, Université du Québec à Chicoutimi, 1973–81; Asst Lecturer in Literature and Creative Writing, Université du Québec à Rimouski, 1983–86; Teacher of Creative Writing in Science Fiction, Université Laval, 1990; Science Fiction Columnist, Radio-Canada, 1993–95; mem. Infini, France; International Asscn for the Fantastic in the Arts; SFWA; Science Fiction Canada; Science Fiction Research Asscn. *Publications:* L'Oeil de la nuit, 1980; Le Silence de la Cité, 1981, English trans. as The Silent City, 1990; Janus, 1984; Comment Escrire des Histoires: Guide de l'explorateur, 1986; Histoire de la Princesse et du Dragon, 1990; Ailleurs et au Japon, 1991; Chroniques de Pays des Meres, 1992, English trans. as In the Mother's Land, 1992; Les Voyageurs maigre eux, 1992, English trans. as Reluctant Voyagers, 1995; Les Contes de la Chatte Rouge, 1993; Contes et Légendes de Tyranael, 1994. *Honours:* several Canadian and French science fictions awards. *Address:* 266 Beleau, Chicoutini, QC G7H 2Y8, Canada.

VONNEGUT, Kurt, Jr, MA; American writer; b. 11 Nov. 1922, Indianapolis, IN; m. 1st Jane Marie Cox 1945 (divorced 1979); one s. two d.; m. 2nd Judith Krementz 1979; one d. *Education:* Cornell University, University of Chicago. *Career:* Lecturer, Writers Workshop, University of Iowa 1965–67; Lecturer in English, Harvard University 1970; Distinguished Prof., City College, CUNY 1973–74; mem. American Acad. of Arts and Letters. *Publications:* Fiction: Player Piano, 1951; Sirens of Titan, 1959; Mother Night, 1961; Cat's Cradle, 1963; God Bless You, Mr Rosewater, 1964; Slaughterhouse-Five, 1969; Breakfast of Champions, 1973; Slapstick, or Lonesome No More, 1976; Jailbird, 1979; Deadeye Dick, 1982; Galapagos, 1985; Bluebeard, 1987; Hocus Pocus, 1990; Timequake, 1997. Short Stories: Welcome to the Monkey House, 1968; Bagombo Snuff Box: Uncollected Short Fiction, 1999. Play: Happy Birthday, Wanda Jane, 1970. Television Script: Between Time and Timbuktu, or Prometheus-5, 1972. Non-Fiction: Wampeters, Foma and Granfallons, 1974; Palm Sunday, 1981; Fates Worse Than Death, 1991; Like Shaking Hands With God: A Conversation About Writing (with Lee Stringer), 1999. Contributions: journals and magazines. *Honours:* Guggenheim Fellowship 1967–68, Nat. Inst. of Arts and Letters Award 1970. *Address:* c/o Donald C. Farber, Jacob, Medinger Finnegan, LLP, 1270 Avenue of the Americas, New York, NY 10020, USA.

VOS, Ida; Author and Poet; b. 13 Dec. 1931, Gröningen, The Netherlands; m. Henk Vos, 3 April 1956, two s. one d. *Education:* Teacher training certificates, 1950, 1952. *Career:* mem. Dutch Writers' Asscn. *Publications:* Wie niet weg is wordt Gezien, 1981, English trans. as Hide and Seek, 1991; Anna is er nog, 1986, English trans. as Anna Is Still There, 1993; Dansen op de brig can Avignon, 1989, English trans. as Dancing on the Bridge at Avignon, 1995; The Key is Lost, 2000. Other: several other books and poems in Dutch. Contributions: periodicals. *Honours:* many Dutch literary prizes. *Address:* Dr Wibautlaan 6G, Rijswijk 2285XY, The Netherlands.

VREELAND, Susan, BA, MA; American writer and teacher; b. 20 Jan. 1946, Racine, WI; m. Joseph C. Gray 1988. *Education:* San Diego State Univ. *Career:* taught English, San Diego City Schools 1969–99, and ceramics 1986–99; mem. California Asscn of Teachers of English. *Publications:* What Love Sees (novel) 1988, If I Had My Life to Live Over I Would Pick More Daisies (anthology) 1992, Family: A Celebration 1995, What English Teachers Want: A Student Handbook 1996, Generation to Generation 1998, Girl in Hyacinth Blue (novel) (Theodore Geisel Award Winner, Foreword Magazine Best Novel of the Year) 1999, The Passion of Artemisia (novel) (San Diego Book Awards Theodore Geisel Award, Best Novel of the Year) 2002, The Forest Lover (novel) 2004; contrib. to Missouri Review, Dominion Review, Confrontation, Alaska Quarterly Review, Calyx, Crescent Review, West Wind Review, Ambergris, So To Speak, Phoebe, New England Review. *Honours:* Women's National Book Asscn First Place in Short Fiction 1991, Dominion Review First Prize for Essay 1996, New Millennium First Prize for Essay 1996, Inkwell Magazine Grand Prize for Fiction 1999. *E-mail:* susan@svreeland.com. *Website:* www.svreeland.com.

VROOMKONING, Victor (see van de Laar, Waltherus Antonius Bernardinus).

W

WA THIONG'O, Ngugi, (James Thiong'o Ngugi), BA; writer, dramatist and critic; *Director of the International Center for Writing and Translation, University of California at Irvine*; b. 5 Jan. 1938, Limuru, Kenya; m. 1st Nyambura 1961 (divorced 1982); m. 2nd Njeeri 1992; four s. two d. *Education:* Makerere Univ., Kampala, Univ. of Leeds. *Career:* Lecturer, Univ. of Nairobi 1967–69, Senior Lecturer, Assoc. Prof. and Chair, Dept of Literature 1972–77; Creative Writing Fellow, Makerere Univ. 1969–70; Visiting Assoc. Prof., Northwestern Univ., Evanston, IL 1970–71; Dir, Int. Center for Writing and Translation, Univ. of California at Irvine. *Publications:* The Black Hermit (play), 1963; Weep Not, Child (novel), 1964; The River Between (novel), 1965; A Grain of Wheat (novel), 1967; This Time Tomorrow: Three Plays, 1970; Homecoming: Essays on African and Caribbean Literature, Culture, and Politics, 1972; Secret Lives, and Other Stories, 1975; The Trial of Dedan Kimathi (with Micere Githae-Mugo), 1976; Petals of Blood (novel), 1977; Mtawa Mweusi, 1978; Caitaani mutharaba-ini, 1980, English trans. as Devil on the Cross, 1982; Writers in Politics: Essays, 1981; Detained: A Writer's Prison Diary, 1981; Njamba Nene na mbaathi i mathagu, 1982, English trans. as Njamba Nene and the Flying Bus, 1986; Ngaahika Ndeena: Ithaako ria Ngerekano (play with Ngugi wa Mirii), 1982, English trans. as I Will Marry When I Want, 1982; Barrel of a Pen: Resistance to Repression in Neo-Colonial Kenya, 1983; Bathitoora va Njamba Nene, 1984, English trans. as Njamba Nene's Pistol, 1986; Decolonizing the Mind: The Politics of Language in African Literature, 1986; Writing Against Neocolonialism, 1986; Matigari ma Njiruungi, 1986, English trans. as Matigari, 1989; Njambas Nene no Chiubu King'ang'i, 1986; Moving the Centre: The Struggle for Cultural Freedoms, 1993. Contributions: books, newspapers, and magazines. *Honours:* Fonlon-Nicholas Award 1996. *Address:* International Center for Writing and Translation, School of Humanities, 172 Humanities Instruction Building, University of California at Irvine, Irvine, CA 92697-3380, USA.

WADDINGTON-FEATHER, John Joseph; Anglican Priest, Poet, Writer and Publisher; b. 10 July 1933, Keighley, Yorkshire, England; m. Sheila Mary Booker, 23 July 1960, three d. *Education:* BA, University of Leeds, 1954; PGCE, Keele, 1974; Ordination Certificate, Church of England, 1977. *Career:* Co-Ed., Orbis, 1971–80; Teacher, Shrewsbury Sixth Form College, 1981–83, Khartoum University, 1984–85; Hon. Chaplain, HM Prisons, 1977–; Chaplain, Prestfelde School, 1985–96; Dir, Feather Books; Ed., Poetry Church Magazine, Poetry Church Anthology, 1997–; mem. Brontë Society, council mem., 1994–2000; FRSA; Yorkshire Dialect Society; J. B. Priestley Society, chair., 1998–. *Publications:* Collection of Verse, 1964; Of Mills, Moors and Men, 1966; Garlic Lane, 1970; Easy Street, 1971; One Man's Road, 1977; Quill's Adventures in the Great Beyond, 1980; Tall Tales from Yukon, 1983; Khartoum Trilogy and Other Poems, 1985; Quill's Adventures in Wasteland, 1986; Quill's Adventures in Grozzieland, 1988; Six Christian Monologues, 1990; Six More Christian Poems, 1994; Shropshire, 1994; Feather's Foibles, 1995; Wild Tales from the West, 1999; The Museum Mystery, 1999; The Bradshaw Mystery, 2000; The Marcham Mystery, 2002; Yorkshire Dialect, 2002; Legends of Americada, 2002; Grundy and Feather Hymn Series, Part I, 2002; The Lollipop Man, 2002; Chance-Child (part I), 2003; Chance-Child (part II), 2003; Sermonettes and Essays (part I), 2003; Quitl's Adventures in Mereful, 2003. Contributions: journals and magazines. *Honours:* Brontë Society Prize, 1966; Cyril Hodges Poetry Award, 1974; Burton Prize, 1999; William de Witt Romig Poetry Award, 2002. *Address:* Fair View, Old Coppice, Lyth Bank, Shrewsbury, Shropshire SY3 0BW, England.

WADE, David; Writer; b. 2 Dec. 1929, Edinburgh, Scotland; m.; one s. one d. *Education:* Queens' College, Cambridge, 1952. *Career:* Radio Critic, The Listener, 1965–67, The Times, 1967–89; mem. Society of Authors. *Publications:* Trying to Connect You; The Cooker; The Guthrie Process; The Gold Spinners; Three Blows in Anger; The Ogden File; The Carpet Maker of Samarkand; The Nightingale; Summer of 39; The Facts of Life; A Rather Nasty Crack; On Detachment; The Tree of Strife; Power of Attorney; Alexander. *Address:* Willow Cottage, Stockland Green Rd, Southborough, Kent TN3 0TL, England.

WADE, Rebekah; British newspaper editor; *Editor, The Sun*; b. 27 May 1968. *Education:* Appleton Hall, Cheshire and Univ. of the Sorbonne, Paris. *Career:* began career as Features Ed., later Assoc. Ed. and Deputy Ed. News of the World –1998, Ed. 2000–03; Deputy Ed. The Sun 1998–2000, Ed. 2003–; Founder-mem. and Pres. Women in Journalism. *Address:* The Sun, 1 Virginia Street, Wapping, London, E1 9XR, England (Office). *Telephone:* (20) 7782-4001 (Office). *E-mail:* news@the-sun.co.uk (Office). *Website:* www.thesun.co.uk (Office).

WADLEY, Veronica; British journalist and editor; *Editor, London Evening Standard*; b. 28 Feb. 1952, London; m. Tom Bower 1985; one s. one d. *Education:* Francis Holland School, London, Benenden. *Career:* journalist Condé Nast Publs 1971–74, Sunday Telegraph Magazine 1978–81, Mail on Sunday 1982–86; Features Ed. Daily Telegraph 1986–89, Asst Ed. 1989–94, Deputy Ed. 1994–95; Assoc. Ed. Daily Mail 1995–98, Deputy Ed. (Features) 1998–2002; Ed. London Evening Standard 2002–. *Address:* The Evening Standard, Northcliffe House, 2 Derry Street, Kensington, London, W8 5EE, England (Office). *Telephone:* (20) 7938-6000 (Office).

WAGNER, Eliot; Writer; b. 19 Dec. 1917, New York, NY, USA; m. Ethel Katell, 22 June 1940, one d. *Career:* mem. Authors' Guild. *Publications:* Fiction: Grand Concourse, 1954; Wedding March, 1961; Better Occasions, 1974; My America!, 1980; Princely Quest, 1985; Nullity Degree, 1991. Short Stories: Delightfully Different Deities, 1994. Contributions: Crisis; Chicago Jewish Forum; Commentary; Antioch Review; Opinion. *Honours:* Yaddo Fellowships, 1950, 1951, 1952, 1957; MacDowell Colony Fellowship, 1955. *Address:* 651 Sheffield Rd, Ithaca, NY 14850-9253, USA.

WAGNER-MARTIN, Linda; academic, poet and writer; b. 18 Aug. 1936, St Marys, Ohio, USA. *Education:* BA, English, 1957, MA, English, 1959, PhD, English, 1963, Bowling Green State University. *Career:* Instructor and Asst Prof., Bowling Green State University, 1961–66; Asst Prof., Wayne State University, 1966–68; Asst Prof. to Prof., Michigan State University, 1968–87; Hanes Prof. of English and Comparative Literature, University of North Carolina at Chapel Hill, 1988–; mem. Ellen Glasgow Society, pres., 1982–87; Ernest Hemingway Foundation and Society, pres., 1993–96; MLA; Society for the Study of Midwestern Literature, pres., 1974–76; Society for the Study of Narrative Technique, pres., 1988–89. *Publications:* The Poems of William Carlos Williams: A Critical Study, 1964; Denise Levertov, 1967; Intaglios: Poems, 1967; The Prose of William Carlos Williams, 1970; Phyllis McGinley, 1971; Hemingway and Faulkner: Inventors/Masters, 1975; Ernest Hemingway: A Reference Guide, 1977; William Carlos Williams: A Reference Guide, 1978; Dos Passos: Artist as American, 1979; American Modern: Selected Essays in Fiction and Poetry, 1980; Songs for Isadora: Poems, 1981; Ellen Glasgow; Beyond Convention, 1982; Sylvia Plath: A Biography, 1987; The Modern American Novel, 1914–1945, 1989; Wharton's The House of Mirth: A Novel of Admonition, 1990; Plath's the Bell Jar: A Novel of the Fifties, 1992; Telling Women's Lives: The New Biography, 1994; 'Favored Strangers': Gertrude Stein and Her Family, 1995; Wharton's The Age of Innocence: A Novel of Ironic Nostalgia, 1996; The Mid-Century American Novel, 1935–1965, 1997; Sylvia Plath: A Literary Life, 1999. Editor: William Faulkner: Four Decades of Criticism, 1973; Ernest Hemingway: Five Decades of Criticism, 1974; T. S. Eliot, 1976; 'Speaking Straight Ahead': Interviews with William Carlos Williams, 1976; Robert Frost: The Critical Heritage, 1977; Denise Levertov: In Her Own Province, 1979; Joyce Carol Oates: Critical Essays, 1979; Sylvia Plath: Critical Essays, 1984; Ernest Hemingway: Six Decades of Criticism, 1987; New Essays on Hemingway's The Sun Also Rises, 1987; Sylvia Plath: The Critical Heritage, 1988; Anne Sexton: Critical Essays, 1989; Denise Levertov: Critical Essays, 1991; The Oxford Companion to Women's Writing in the United States (with Cathy N. Davidson), 1995; The Oxford Book of Women's Writing in the United States, 1995; New Essays to Faulkner's Go Down, Moses, 1996; Ernest Hemingway: Seven Decades of Criticism, 1998; Festchrift for Frederick Eckman (with David Adams), 1998; The Historical Guide to Ernest Hemingway, 1999. Contributions: scholarly books and journals. *Honours:* Guggenheim Fellowship, 1975–76; Bunting Institute Fellow, 1975–76; Rockefeller Foundation Fellow, Bellagio, Italy, 1990; Fellow, Institute for the Arts and Humanities, University of North Carolina, 1992; National Endowment for the Humanities Senior Fellowship, 1992–93; Teacher-Scholar Award, College English Asscn, 1994; Visiting Distinguished Prof., Emory University, 1994; Citation for Exceptional Merit, House of Representatives, Ohio, 1994; Brackenridge Distinguished Prof., University of Texas at San Antonio, 1998. *Address:* c/o Dept of English, 3520 University of North Carolina at Chapel Hill, Chapel Hill, NC 27599, USA.

WAGONER, David (Russell); Prof. of English, Poet and Author; b. 5 June 1926, Massillon, Ohio, USA; m. 1st Patricia Parrott, 1961, divorced 1982; m. 2nd Robin Heather Seyfried, 1982. *Education:* BA, Pennsylvania State University, 1947; MA, Indiana University, 1949. *Career:* Instructor, DePauw University, 1949–50, Pennsylvania State University, 1950–53; Asst Prof., 1954–57, Assoc. Prof., 1958–66, Prof. of English, 1966–, University of Washington, Seattle; Ed., Poetry Northwest, 1966–; Elliston Prof. of Poetry, University of Cincinnati, 1968; mem. Acad. of American Poets, chancellor, 1978. *Publications:* Poetry: Dry Sun, Dry Wind, 1953; A Place to Stand, 1958; Poems, 1959; The Nesting Ground, 1963; Staying Alive, 1966; New and Selected Poems, 1969; Working Against Time, 1970; Riverbed, 1972; Sleeping in the Woods, 1974; A Guide to Dungeness Spit, 1975; Travelling Light, 1976; Collected Poems, 1956–1976, 1976; Who Shall be the Sun?: Poems Based on the Love, Legends, and Myths of Northwest Coast and Plateau Indians, 1978; In Broken Country, 1979; Landfall, 1981; First Light, 1983; Through the Forest: New and Selected Poems, 1977–1987, 1987; Traveling Light: Collected and New Poems, 1999. Fiction: The Man in the Middle, 1954; Money, Money, Money, 1955; Rock, 1958; The Escape Artist, 1965; Baby, Come on Inside, 1968; Where Is My Wandering Boy Tonight?, 1970; The Road to Many a Wonder, 1974; Tracker, 1975; Whole Hog, 1976; The Hanging Garden, 1980. Editor: Straw for the Fire: From the Notebooks of Theodore Roethke 1943–1963, 1972. *Honours:* Guggenheim Fellowship, 1956; Ford Foundation Fellowship, 1964; American Acad. of Arts and Letters Grant, 1967; National Endowment for the Arts Grant, 1969; Morton Dauwen Zabel Prize, 1967; Oscar Blumenthal

Prize, 1974; Fels Prize, 1975; Eunice Tietjens Memorial Prize, 1977; English-Speaking Union Prize, 1980; Sherwood Anderson Prize, 1980; Pacific Northwest Booksellers Award, 2000. *Address:* 5416 154th Pl. SW, Edmonds, WA 98026, USA.

WAINAINA, Binyavanga; Writer and Food and Travel Journalist; b. 1971, Kenya. *Education:* Univ. of Transkei. *Career:* Owner, catering and food consultancy business, Amuka Investments; Staff Writer, G21 Africa (www.g21.net); f. and Ed., literary magazine, Kwani? *Publications:* An Affair to Dismember (short story); Discovering Home (short story), 2001; Flights of My Fancy (novel), 2003. Contributions: Weekend Argus, Cape Town; Sunday Times, South Africa; Mail and Guardian; Y magazine; SL magazine; Pforward magazine; The Top of the Times (Cape Times weekend supplement); Adbusters, Canada; literary journals. *Honours:* Caine Prize for African Writing, 2002. *Address:* c/o Kwela Books, PO Box 6525, Roggebaai 8012, South Africa. *E-mail:* editors@kwani.org. *Website:* www.kwani.org.

WAINWRIGHT, Geoffrey; Prof. of Systematic Theology and Methodist Minister; b. 16 July 1939, Yorkshire, England; m. Margaret Wiles, 20 April 1965, one s. two d. *Education:* BA, 1960, MA, 1964, BD, 1972, DD, 1987, University of Cambridge; DrThéol, University of Geneva, 1969. *Career:* Ed., Studia Liturgica, 1974–87; Prof. of Systematic Theology, The Divinity School, Duke University, Durham, NC, 1983–; mem. American Theological Society, secretary, 1988–95, pres., 1996–97; International Dialogue Between the World Methodist Council and the Roman Catholic Church, chair.; Societas Liturgica, pres., 1983–85; World Council of Churches Faith and Order Commission, 1976–91. *Publications:* Christian Initiation, 1969; Eucharist and Eschatology, 1971; The Study of Liturgy (co-ed.), 1978; Doxology, 1980; The Ecumenical Moment, 1983; The Study of Spirituality (co-ed.), 1986; On Wesley and Calvin, 1987; Keeping the Faith: Essays to Mark the Centenary of Lux Mundi (ed.), 1989; The Dictionary of the Ecumenical Movement (co-ed.), 1991; Methodists in Dialogue, 1995; Worship With One Accord, 1997; For Our Salvation, 1997; Is the Reformation Over? Catholics and Protestants at the Turn of the Millennia, 2000; Lesslie Newbigin: A Theological Life, 2000. Contributions: Reference books and theological journals. *Honours:* numerous named lectureships world-wide; Berakah Award, North American Acad. of Liturgy, 1999; Received a Festschrift: Ecumenical Theology in Worship, Doctrine, and Life: Essays Presented to Geoffrey Wainwright on his 60th Birthday, 1999. *Address:* The Divinity School, Duke University, Durham, NC 27708, USA.

WAINWRIGHT, Jeffrey; poet, dramatist, translator and academic; b. 19 Feb. 1944, Stoke on Trent, England; m. Judith Batt 1967; one s. one d. *Education:* BA, 1965, MA, 1967, University of Leeds. *Career:* Asst Lecturer, Lecturer, University of Wales, 1967–72; Visiting Instructor, Long Island University, 1970–71; Senior Lecturer, 1972–99, Prof., 1999–, Manchester Metropolitan University; Northern Theatre Critic, The Independent, 1988–99. *Publications:* Poetry: The Important Man 1970, Heart's Desire 1978, Selected Poems 1985, The Red-Headed Pupil 1994, Out of the Air 1999. Other: Poetry: The Basics (criticism) 2004, Trans of various plays into English. Contributions: anthologies; BBC Radio; many periodicals. *Honours:* Judith E. Wilson Visiting Fellow, 1985. *Address:* 11 Hesketh Avenue, Didsbury, Manchester M20 2QN, England.

WAITE, Peter Busby; Prof. of History Emeritus and Writer; b. 12 July 1922, Toronto, Ontario, Canada; m. Masha Maria Gropuzzo, 22 Aug. 1958, two d. *Education:* BA, 1948, MA, 1950, University of British Columbia; PhD, University of Toronto, 1954. *Career:* Lecturer, 1951–55, Asst Prof., 1955–60, Assoc. Prof., 1960–61, Prof. of History, 1961–88, Prof. Emeritus, 1988–, Dalhousie University; mem. Canadian Historical Asscn, pres., 1968–69; Humanities Research Council, chair., 1968–70; Aid to Publications Committee, Social Science Federation, chair., 1987–89. *Publications:* The Life and Times of Confederation, 1864–1867, 1962; Canada 1874–1896, 1971; John A Macdonald, His Life and World, 1975; The Man from Halifax: Sir John Thompson, Prime Minister, 1985; Lord of Point Grey: Larry MacKenzie of UBC, 1987; Between Three Oceans: Challenges of a Continental Destiny, 1840–1900, Chapter IV, Illustrated History of Canada, 1988; The Loner: The Personal Life and Ideas of R. B. Bennett 1870–1947, 1992; The Lives of Dalhousie University: Vol. I, Lord Dalhousie's College, 1818–1925, 1994, Vol. II, The Old College Transformed, 1925–1980, 1998. Contributions: Some 55 articles to numerous magazines and journals. *Honours:* Fellow, Royal Society of Canada, 1972; Lieutenant-Governor's Medal, BC, 1987; LLD, Dalhousie University, 1991; D.Litt, University of New Brunswick, 1991, Memorial University of Newfoundland, 1991, Carleton University, 1993; Officer of the Order of Canada, 1993. *Address:* 960 Ritchie Dr., Halifax, NS B3H 3P5, Canada.

WAKEFIELD, Dan, BA; writer and screenwriter; b. 21 May 1932, Indianapolis, IN, USA. *Education:* Columbia University. *Career:* News Ed., Princeton Packet, NJ, 1955; Staff Writer, The Nation magazine, 1956–59; Staff, Bread Loaf Writers Conference, 1964, 1966, 1968, 1970, 1986; Visiting Lecturer, University of Massachusetts at Boston, 1965–66, University of Illinois, 1968; Contributing Ed., The Atlantic Monthly, 1969–80; Writer-in-Residence, Emerson College, 1989–92; Contributing Writer, GQ magazine, 1992–; Distinguished Visiting Writer, Florida International University, 1995–; mem. Authors' Guild of America; National Writers Union; Writers Guild of America. *Publications:* Island of the City: The World of Spanish Harlem, 1959; Revolt in the South, 1961; An Anthology, 1963; Between the Lines, 1966; Supernation at Peace and War, 1968; Going All the Way, 1970; Starting Over, 1973; All Her Children, 1976; Home Free, 1977; Under the Apple Tree, 1982; Selling Out, 1985; Returning: A Spiritual Journey, 1988; The Story of Your Life: Writing a Spiritual Autobiography, 1990; New York in the Fifties, 1992; Expect a Miracle, 1995; Creating from the Spirit, 1996; How Do We Know When It's God?, 1999. Editor: The Addict: An Anthology, 1963. Television: James at 15, 1977–78; The Seduction of Miss Leona, 1980; Heartbeat, 1988. *Honours:* Bernard DeVoto Fellow, Bread Loaf Writers Conference, 1957; Rockefeller Foundation Grant, 1968; Short Story Prize, National Council of the Arts, 1968. *Literary Agent:* Janklow & Nesbit Associates, 445 Park Avenue, New York, NY 10022, USA.

WAKELING, Edward; Writer and Ed.; b. 31 Aug. 1946, Sutton Scotney, Hampshire, England. *Education:* Teacher's Certificate, Bishop Otter College, Chichester, 1967; BSc, Mathematics, Hatfield Polytechnic, 1975; MSc, University of Oxford, 1983. *Career:* mem. Lewis Carroll Society, sec., 1976–79, chair., 1982–85, treas., 1986–89, chair., editorial board, 1997–2002. *Publications:* The Logic of Lewis Carroll, 1978; The Cipher Alice, 1990; Lewis Carroll's Games and Puzzles, 1992; Lewis Carroll's Oxford Pamphlets, 1993; Lewis Carroll's Diaries (ed.), seven vols, 1993–2003; Rediscovered Lewis Carroll Puzzles, 1995; Alice in Escherland, 1998; Lewis Carroll, Photographer (with Roger Taylor), 2002; Lewis Carroll and His Illustrators (with Morton N. Cohen), 2003. Contributions: many reviews, quarterlies and journals. *Honours:* Hon. MA, University of Luton, 1996. *Address:* Yew Tree Cottage, Parks Rd, Clifford, Herefordshire HR3 5HQ, England. *E-mail:* edward@wakeling.demon.co.uk.

WAKEMAN, Frederic Evans; Prof. of Asian Studies and Writer; b. 12 Dec. 1937, Kansas City, KS, USA; m. He Lea Liang; two s. one d. (from previous marriage). *Education:* BA, Harvard College, 1959; Postgraduate Studies, Institut d'Etudes Politiques, University of Paris, 1959–60; MA, 1962, PhD, 1965, University of California at Berkeley. *Career:* Asst Prof., 1965–67, Assoc. Prof., 1968–70, Prof. of History, 1970–89, Dir, Center of Chinese Studies, 1972–79, Haas Prof. of Asian Studies, 1989–, Dir, Institute of East Asian Studies, 1990–, University of California at Berkeley; Humanities Research Prof. and Visiting Scholar, Corpus Christi College, Cambridge, 1976–77, Beijing University, 1980–81, 1985; Visiting Prof. Univ. of Heidelberg, Germany 2000; mem. American Acad. of Arts and Sciences; American Historical Asscn; Asscn for Asian Studies; Council on Foreign Relations; American Philosophical Society, 1998. *Publications:* Strangers at the Gate: Social Disorder in South China 1839–1861 1966, Nothing Concealed: Essays in Honor of Liu Yu-Yun 1970, History and Will 1973, The Fall of Imperial China (co-ed.) 1976, Ming and Qing Historical Studies in the People's Republic of China 1981, The Great Enterprise: The Manchu Reconstruction of Imperial Order in Seventeenth Century China, 2 vols 1985, Shanghai Sojourners (co-ed.) 1992, Policing Shanghai 1995, The Shanghai Badlands: Wartime Terrorism and Urban Crime 1937–1941 1996, China's Quest for Modernization: A Historical Perspective (ed. with Wang Xi) 1997, Spymaster: Dai Li and the Chinese Secret Service 2003. Contributions: Professional journals. *Honours:* ACLS Fellow, 1967–68; Guggenheim Fellowship, 1973–74; Levenson Prize, 1986; Best Book on Non-North American Urban History, Urban History Asscn, 1996. *Address:* c/o Institute of East Asian Studies, University of California at Berkeley, Berkeley, CA 94720, USA.

WAKEMAN, John, BA, MA; editor and writer; b. 29 Sept. 1928, London, England; m. Hilary Paulett 1957; four s. one d. *Career:* Ed., The Shop: A Magazine of Poetry, 1999–; consultant for peripheral topics, Encyclopaedia of Ireland, 2003; Assoc., British Library Asscn, 1950. *Publications:* World Authors, 1950–70, 1975; World Authors, 1970–75, 1980; A Room for Doubt (poems), 1985; The Rialto, 1985; World Film Directors, 1987; The Beach Hut, 1987. Contributions: newspapers and magazines. *Honours:* Library Journal Best Reference Book Selection, 1988, and Outstanding Academic Book Selection, 1989; Eastern Arts Travel Bursary, 1991; Hawthornden Fellowship, 1992. *Address:* Skeagh, Schull, County Cork, Ireland.

WALCOTT, Derek, OBE, BA, FRSL; Saint Lucia poet and playwright; b. 23 Jan. 1930, Castries; m. 1st Fay Moston 1954 (divorced 1959); one s.; m. 2nd Margaret R. Maillard 1962 (divorced); two d.; m. 3rd Norline Metivier 1982 (divorced 1993). *Education:* St Mary's Coll., Castries, Univ. of Wisconsin, Univ. of the West Indies, Jamaica. *Career:* teacher, St Mary's Coll., Castries 1947–50, 1954, Grenada Boys' Secondary School, St George's 1953–54, Jamaica Coll., Kingston 1955; feature writer, Public Opinion, Kingston 1956–57; founder-Dir, Little Carib Theatre Workshop, later Trinidad Theatre Workshop 1959–76; feature writer, Trinidad Guardian, Port-of-Spain 1960–62, drama critic 1963–68; Visiting Prof., Columbia Univ., USA 1981, Harvard Univ. 1982, 1987; Asst Prof. of Creative Writing, Brown Univ. 1981, Visiting Prof. 1985–; hon.mem. American Acad. of Arts and Letters; mem. Poetry Soc. (vice-pres.); Rockefeller Foundation grants 1957, 1966, and Fellowship 1958, Ingram Merrill Foundation grant 1962, Eugene O'Neill Foundation Fellowship 1969, Guggenheim Fellowship 1977, John D. and Catherine T. MacArthur Foundation Fellowship 1981. *Plays:* Cry for a Leader 1950, Henri Christophe: A Chronicle 1950, Robin and Andrea 1950, Senza Alcun Sospetto 1950, The Price of Mercy 1951, Three Assassins 1951, Harry Dernier 1952, The Charlatan 1954, Crossroads 1954, The Sea at Dauphin 1954, The Golden Lions 1956, The Wine of the Country 1956,

Ione: A Play with Music 1957, Ti-Jear and his Brothers 1957, Drums and Colours 1958, Jourmard 1959, Malcochon 1959, Batai 1965, Dream on Monkey Mountain 1967, Franklin: A Tale of the Islands 1969, In a Fine Castle 1970, The Joker of Seville (with G. Mcdermott) 1974, O Babylon! 1976, Remembrance 1977, The Snow Queen 1977, Pantomime 1978, Marie Leveau (with G. Mcdermott) 1979, The Isle is Full of Noises 1982, Beef, No Chicken 1985, The Odyssey 1993, The Capeman (musical, jtly) 1997. *Publications:* poetry: 25 Poems 1948, Epitaph for the Young: XII Cantos 1949, Poems 1951, In a Green Night, Poems 1948–60 1962, Selected Poems 1964, The Castaway and Other Poems 1965, The Gulf and Other Poems 1969, Another Life 1973, Sea Grapes 1976, The Star-Apple Kingdom 1979, Selected Poetry 1981, The Fortunate Traveller 1981, The Caribbean Poetry of Derek Walcott, and the Art of Romare Bearden 1983, Midsummer 1984, Collected Poems 1948–1984 1986, The Arkansas Testament 1987, Omeros (epic poem) (WHSmith Literary Award 1991) 1989, Poems 1965–1980 1992, The Bounty 1997, Tiepolo's Hounds 2000; non-fiction: The Antilles, Fragments of Epic Memory: The Nobel Lecture 1993, What the Twilight Says (essays) 1998, Homage to Robert Frost (jtly) 1998. *Honours:* Arts Advisory Council of Jamaica Prize 1960, Guinness Award 1961, Borestone Mountain Awards 1964, 1977, RSL Heinemann Awards 1966, 1983, Cholmondeley Award 1969, Gold Hummingbird Medal, Trinidad 1969, Obie Award 1971, Welsh Arts Council Int. Writers Prize 1980, Los Angeles Times Book Prize 1986, Queen's Gold Medal for Poetry 1988, Nobel Prize for Literature 1992. *Address:* c/o Faber & Faber, 3 Queen Square, London, WC1N 3AU, England (Office); PO Box GM 926, Castries, St Lucia, West Indies (Home). *Telephone:* 450-0559 (Home). *Fax:* 450-0935 (Home).

WALDMAN, Anne, BA; poet, lecturer, performer and editor; b. 2 April 1945, Millville, NJ, USA. *Education:* Bennington Coll. *Career:* Ed., Angel Hair Magazine, 1965–, The World, 1966–78; Asst Dir, Poetry Project, St Mark's Church In-the-Bowery, 1966–68; Dir, Poetry Project, New York City, 1968–78; Founder-Dir, Jack Kerouac School of Disembodied Poetics, Naropa Institute, Boulder, CO; Poetry readings and performance events world-wide; mem. Committee for International Poetry; PEN Poetry Society of America. *Publications:* Journals and Dreams, 1976; First Baby Poems, 1983; Makeup on Empty Space, 1984; Invention, 1985; Skin Meat Bones, 1985; Blue Mosque, 1987; The Romance Thing, 1987–88; Helping the Dreamer: New and Selected Poems, 1966–1988; Iovis, 1993; Troubairitz, Kill or Cure, 1994; Iovis, Book II, 1996. Editor: The World Anthology, 1969; Another World, 1971; Nice to See You: Homage to Ted Berrigan, 1991; In and Out of This World: An Anthology of the St Mark's Poetry Project, 1992; The Beat Book, 1996. Contributions: various publications. *Honours:* National Endowment for the Arts Grant, 1980; Achievement in Poetry Award, Bennington College Alumni, 1981. *Address:* c/o The Naropa Institute, 2130 Arapahoe Avenue, Boulder, CO 80302, USA.

WALDROP, Rosmarie; Poet, Writer, Trans., Ed. and Publisher; b. 24 Aug. 1935, Kitzingen-am-Main, Germany; m. Keith Waldrop, 20 Jan. 1959. *Education:* University of Würzburg, 1954–56; University of Aix-Marseille, 1956–57; University of Freiburg, 1957–58; MA, 1960, PhD, 1966, Comparative Literature, University of Michigan. *Career:* Wesleyan University, 1964–70; Co-Ed. and Co-Publisher (with Keith Waldrop), Burning Desk Press, 1968–; Visiting Assoc. Prof., Brown University, 1977–78, 1983, 1990–91; Visiting Lecturer, Tufts University, 1979–81; mem. PEN. *Publications:* Poetry: The Aggressive Ways of the Casual Stranger, 1972; The Road Is Everywhere or Stop This Body, 1978; When They Have Senses, 1980; Nothing Has Changed, 1981; Differences for Four Hands, 1984; Streets Enough to Welcome Snow, 1986; The Reproduction of Profiles, 1987; Shorter American Memory, 1988; Peculiar Motions, 1990; Lawn of Excluded Middle, 1993; A Key Into the Language of America, 1994; Another Language: Selected Poems, 1997; Split Infinites, 1998; Reluctant Gravities, 1999; Blindsight, 2003; Love, like Pronouns, 2003. Fiction: The Hanky of Pippin's Daughter, 1986; A Form/of Taking/it All, 1990. Essays: Against Language?, 1971; The Ground Is the Only Figure: Notebook Spring, 1996, 1997; Lavish Absence: Recalling and Rereading Edmond Jabès, 2002. Other: various poetry chapbooks and trans. *Honours:* Major Hopwood Award in Poetry, 1963; Alexander von Humboldt Fellowships, 1970–71, 1975–76; Howard Foundation Fellowship, 1974–75; Columbia University Trans. Center Award, 1978; National Endowment for the Arts Fellowships, 1980, 1984; Governor's Arts Award, RI, 1988; Fund for Poetry Award, 1990; PEN/Book-of-the-Month Club Citation in Trans., 1991; Deutscher Akademischer Austauschdienst Fellowship, Berlin, 1993; Harold Morton Landon Trans. Award, 1994; Chevalier, Ordre des Arts et des Lettres, 1999; Lila Wallace-Reader's Digest Writer's Award, 1999–2001; Chevalier, Ordre des Arts et des Lettres, 1999. *Address:* 71 Elmgrove Ave, Providence RI 02906, USA.

WALKER, Alice Malsenior, BA; American writer and poet; b. 9 Feb. 1944, Eatonton, GA, USA; m. Melvyn R. Leventhal 1967 (divorced 1976); one d. *Education:* Sarah Lawrence Coll. *Career:* Writer-in-Residence and Teacher of Black Studies, Jackson State College, 1968–69, Tougaloo College, 1970–71; Lecturer in Literature, Wellesley College, 1972–73, University of Massachusetts at Boston, 1972–73; Distinguished Writer, Afro-American Studies Dept, University of California at Berkeley, 1982; Fannie Hurst Prof. of Literature, Brandeis University, 1982; Co-Founder and Publisher, Wild Trees Press, Navarro, CA, 1984–88. *Publications:* Once 1968, The Third Life of Grange Copeland 1970, Five Poems 1972, Revolutionary Petunias and Other Poems 1973, In Love and Trouble 1973, Langston Hughes: American Poet 1973, Meridian 1976, Goodnight, Willie Lee, I'll See You in the Morning 1979, I Love Myself When I'm Laughing... And Then Again When I'm Looking Mean and Impressive (ed.) 1979, You Can't Keep a Good Woman Down 1981, The Color Purple 1982, In Search of Our Mother's Gardens 1983, Horses Make a Landscape Look More Beautiful 1984, To Hell With Dying 1988, Living by the Word: Selected Writings, 1973–1987 1988, The Temple of My Familiar 1989, Her Blue Body Everything We Know: Earthling Poems, 1965–1990 1991, Finding the Green Stone 1991, Possessing the Secret of Joy 1992, Warrior Marks (with Pratibha Parmar) 1993, Double Stitch: Black Women Write About Mothers and Daughters (with others) 1993, Everyday Use 1994, By the Light of My Father's Smile 1998, The Way Forward is with a Broken Heart 2000, Now is the Time to Open Your Heart 2004. *Honours:* Bread Loaf Writer's Conference Scholar, 1966; Ingram Merrill Foundation Fellowship, 1967; McDowell Colony Fellowships, 1967, 1977–78; National Endowment for the Arts Grants, 1969, 1977; Richard and Hinda Rosenthal Pound Award, American Acad. and Institute of Arts and Letters, 1974; Guggenheim Fellowship, 1977–78; Pulitzer Prize for Fiction, 1983; American Book Award, 1983; O. Henry Award, 1986; Nora Astorga Leadership Award, 1989; Freedom to Write Award, PEN Center, West, 1990; Hon. doctorates. *Literary Agent:* Wendy Weil Agency Inc, 232 Madison Avenue, Suite 1300, New York, NY 10016, USA.

WALKER, George F(rederick); Playwright; b. 23 Aug. 1947, Toronto, Ontario, Canada. *Education:* Graduated, Riverdale Collegiate, Toronto, 1965. *Career:* Resident Playwright, New York Shakespeare Festival, 1981. *Publications:* The Prince of Naples, 1971; Ambush at Tether's End, 1971; Sacktown Rag, 1972; Baghdad Saloon, 1973; Beyond Mozambique, 1974; Ramona and the White Slaves, 1976; Gossip, 1977; Zastrozzi: The Master of Discipline, 1977; Filthy Rich, 1979; Rumours of our Death (musical), 1980; Theatre of the Film Noir, 1981; Science and Madness, 1982; The Art of War: An Adventure, 1983; Criminals in Love, 1984; Better Living, 1986; Beautiful City, 1987; Nothing Sacred, after Turgenev, 1988; Love and Anger, 1990; Escape from Happiness, 1991; Shared Anxiety, 1994. *Honours:* Governor-General's Awards in Drama, 1985, 1988; Toronto Arts Award for Drama, 1994. *Address:* c/o Great North Artists, 350 Dupont St, Toronto, Ontario M5V 1V9, Canada.

WALKER, Harry (see Waugh, Hillary Baldwin).

WALKER, Jeanne Murray, BA, MA, PhD; American professor of English, poet, dramatist and writer; b. 27 May 1944, Parkers Prairie, MN; m. E. Daniel Larkin 1983; one s. one d. *Education:* Wheaton Coll., IL, Loyola Univ., Chicago, Univ. of Pennsylvania. *Career:* Asst Prof. of English, Haverford Coll., Pennsylvania; Prof. of English, Univ. of Delaware; mem. Dramatists' Guild, PEN, Poets and Writers. *Publications:* poetry: Nailing Up the Home Sweet Home 1980, Fugitive Angels 1985, Coming into History 1990, Stranger Than Fiction 1992, Gaining Time 1997; other: eight plays 1990–2001. *Poetry contributions:* poems appeared on trains and buses in association with Poetry in Motion, American Acad. of Poets; numerous reviews, quarterlies, journals and periodicals, including American Scholar, Arizona Quarterly, American Poetry Review, Aspen Anthology, Ariel, Poetry Miscellany, Jawbone, Carolina Quarterly, Chicago Tribune, Christian Science Monitor, Cimarron Review, Chariton Review, Critical Quarterly, Georgia Review, Southern Humanities Review, Iowa Review, Image, The Journal, Kenyon Review, Louisville Review, Lyric, Massachusetts Review, Milkweed Chronicle, Descant, Northwest Review, Christian Century, New England Review, Nantucket Review, Wascona Review, Poet and Critic, 2 Plus 2, Poetry Now, St Andrews Review, Pennsylvania Review, Kansas Quarterly, Seattle Review, Poetry, Shenandoah, Painted Bride Quarterly, Whetstone, Boulevard, Partisan Review, Prairie Schooner, The Nation. *Honours:* Delaware Humanities Council Grant, 1979; Delaware Arts Council Grant, 1981; 6 Pennsylvania Council on the Arts Fellowships, 1983–2001; Prairie Schooner/Strousse Award, 1988; Winner, Washington National Theatre Competition, 1990; Colladay Award for Poetry, 1992; Fellow, Center for Advanced Studies, 1993; National Endowment for the Arts Fellowship, 1994; Lewis Prizes for New Plays, Brigham Young Theatre, 1995, 1997; Stagetime Award, Pew Fellow in the Arts, 1998. *Address:* c/o Department of English, 127 Memorial Hall, University of Delaware, Newark, DE 19716, USA. *E-mail:* jwalker@udel.edu.

WALKER, Lou Ann; Writer; b. 9 Dec. 1952, Hartford City, IN, USA; m. Speed Vogel, 8 Sept. 1986, one d. *Education:* Attended Ball State University, 1971–73; Degree in French Language and Literature, University of Besançon, 1975; BA, Harvard University, 1976. *Career:* Reporter, Indianapolis News, 1976; Asst to Exec. Ed., New York (magazine), New York, 1976–77, Cosmopolitan, New York City, 1979–80; Asst Ed., Esquire Magazine, 1977–79; Assoc. Ed., Diversion (magazine), New York City, 1980–81; Ed., Direct (magazine), New York City, 1981–82; Sign Language Interpretor for New York Society for the Deaf; Consultant to Broadway's Theater Development Fund and sign language adviser on many Broadway shows, 1984–; Contributing Ed., New York Woman, 1990–92; mem. Authors' Guild. *Publications:* Amy: The Story of a Deaf Child, 1985; A Loss for Words: The Story of Deafness in a Family (autobiog.), 1986; Hand, Heart and Mind, 1994; Roy Lichtenstein: The Artist at Work, 1994. Contributions: New York Times Book Review; Chicago Sun-Times; Esquire; New York Times Magazine; New York Woman; Life. *Honours:* Rockefeller Foundation Humanities Fellowship, 1982–83; Christopher Award, 1987; National Endowment for the Arts Creative Writing Grant, 1988. *Address:* c/o Darhansoff & Verrill, 179 Franklin St, Fourth Floor, New York, NY 10013, USA.

WALKER, Martin; Journalist, Writer and Broadcaster; b. 23 Jan. 1947, Durham, England; m. Julia Watson, 6 May 1978. *Education:* MA, Balliol College, Oxford, 1969; Graduate Studies, Harvard University. *Career:* Staff, 1972–, Moscow Bureau Chief, 1983–88, US Bureau Chief, 1989–98, Guardian, Manchester; numerous radio and television broadcasts; many lectures; mem. National Union of Journalists. *Publications:* The National Front, 1977; Daily Sketches: A History of Political Cartoons, 1978; The Infiltrators (novel), 1978; A Mercenary Calling (novel), 1980; The Eastern Question (novel), 1981; Powers of the Press: A Comparative Study of the World's Leading Newspapers, 1981; The Waking Giant: Gorbachev and Perestroika, 1987; Martin Walker's Russia, 1989; The Independent Traveler's Guide to the Soviet Union, 1990; The Insight Guide to Washington, DC, 1992; The Cold War: A History, 1993; The President We Deserve: Bill Clinton: His Rise, Falls, and Comebacks, 1996; America Reborn: A Twentieth-Century Narrative in Twenty-Six Lives, 2000. Contributions: anthologies and periodicals. *Honours:* Congressional Fellow, American Political Science Asscn, 1970–71; Public Policy Fellow, Woodrow Wilson International Center for Scholars, 2000–01. *Address:* 3462 Macomb St NW, Washington, DC 20016, USA.

WALKER, Mary Willis; Writer; b. 24 May 1942, Foxpoint, Wisconsin, USA; Divorced, two d. *Education:* BA, English, Duke University, 1964. *Career:* mem. Texas Institute of Letters; MWA; Sisters in Crime; International Asscn of Crime Writers; Austin Writers League. *Publications:* Zero at the Bone, 1991; The Red Scream, 1994; Under the Beetle's Cellar, 1995; All the Dead Lie Down, 1998; Mom's in Prison... Again (documentary script). Contributions: Essays to periodicals including: New York Times; Mostly Murder; Book reviews to Mostly Murder; Austin American-Statesman. *Honours:* Agatha Award, 1991; Macavity Award, Mystery Readers International, 1991; Hammett Award, International Asscn of Crime Writers, 1995; Anthony Award, Bouchercon, 1995; Edgar Award, MWA, 1995. *Literary Agent:* David Hull, Hull House Literary Agency, 240 E 82nd St, New York, NY 10028, USA. *Address:* 3616 Far West Blvd, Suite 296, Austin, TX 78731-3074, USA.

WALL, Ethan (see Holmes, Bryan John).

WALL, Geoffrey, (Geoffrey Chadwick), BA, BPhil; academic, biographer and translator; b. 10 July 1950, Cheshire, England. *Education:* University of Sussex, St Edmund Hall. *Career:* Lecturer, 1975–97, Senior Lecturer, 1997–2002, Reader, 2002–, Dept of English and Related Literature, University of York; Co-Ed., Cambridge Quarterly, 1998; mem. Asscn of University Teachers. *Publications:* Translator: Madame Bovary, by Gustave Flaubert, 1992; The Dictionary of Received Ideas, by Gustave Flaubert, 1994; Selected Letters, by Gustave Flaubert, 1997; Modern Times: Selected Writings, by Jean-Paul Sartre, 1999; Flaubert: A Life, 2001; Sentimental Education, by Gustave Flaubert (trans.), 2004. Contributions: scholarly journals and newspapers. *Literary Agent:* David Higham Associates, 5–8 Lower John Street, Golden Square, London W1F 9HA, England. *Address:* c/o Department of English and Related Literature, University of York, Heslington, York YO10 5DD, England. *E-mail:* gw2@york.ac.uk.

WALL, Mervyn; Writer and Dramatist; b. 23 Aug. 1908, Dublin, Ireland; m. Fanny Freehan, 25 April 1950, one s., three d. *Education:* BA, National University of Ireland, 1928. *Career:* Civil Servant, 1934–48; Programme Officer, Radio Eireann, 1948–57; Chief Exec., Irish Arts Council, 1957–75; Book Reviewer, Radio Critic, Radio Broadcaster; mem. Irish Acad. of Letters; Irish Writers Union. *Publications:* The Unfortunate Fursey, 1946; The Return of Fursey, 1948; No Trophies Raise, 1956; Forty Foot Gentlemen Only, 1962; A Flutter of Wings, 1974; The Garden of Echoes, 1988; Plays. Contributions: journals. *Honours:* Best European Novel of Year, 1952.

WALLACE, David Foster, AB, MFA; American author and associate professor of English; b. 21 Feb. 1962, Ithaca, NY. *Education:* Amherst Coll., Univ. of Arizona. *Career:* Assoc. Prof. of English, Illinois State Univ. 1993–. *Publications:* The Broom of the System 1987, Girl With Curious Hair 1988, Signifying Rappers: Rap and Race in the Urban Present (with Mark Costello) 1990, Infinite Jest 1996, A Supposedly Fun Thing I'll Never Do Again: Essays and Arguments 1997; contrib. to various publications. *Honours:* Whiting Writers' Award 1987, Yaddo residencies 1987, 1989, National Endowment for the Arts Fellowship 1989, Lannan Foundation Award for Literature 1996, John D. and Catherine T. MacArthur Foundation Fellowship 1997. *Address:* c/o Dept of English, Illinois State University, Normal, IL 61790, USA.

WALLACE, Ian (Robert); Writer and Illustrator; b. 31 March 1950, Niagara Falls, Ontario, Canada; m. Debra Wiedman. *Education:* Ontario College of Art, 1969–74. *Career:* mem. Canadian Children's Book Centre; Writer's Union of Canada. *Publications:* Julie News, 1974; The Sandwich (with A. Wood), 1974; The Christmas Tree House, 1976; Chin Chiang and the Dragon's Dance, 1984; The Sparrow's Song, 1986; Morgan the Magnificent, 1987; Mr Kneebone's New Digs, 1991. Illustrator: Seven books, 1986–96. Writer and Illustrator: A Winter's Tale, 1997; Boy of the Deeps, 1999; Duncan's Way, 2000; The True Story of Trapper Jack's Left Big Toe, 2002; The Naked Lady, 2002. *Honours:* A. F. Howard Gibbons Award, 1984; IODE Book Award, 1985; IBBY Honour List, 1986, 2000; Mr Christie Book Award, 1990; Aesop Accolade List, 1994; Smithsonian Best Books of the Year List, 2000. *Address:* 184 Major St, Toronto, Ontario M5S 2L3, Canada.

WALLACE, Naomi (French); Poet, Dramatist and Writer; b. 17 Aug. 1960, Kentucky, USA; m. Bruce McLeod, three d. *Education:* BA, Hampshire College, 1982; MFA, University of Iowa, 1986. *Publications:* To Dance a Stony Field (poems), 1995; Slaughter City (play), 1996; Birdy (play), 1997; One Flea Spare (play), 1997. *Honours:* Obie Award, Village Voice; Susan Smith Blackburn Award; Discovery Award, The Nation; Fellowship of Southern Writers Award. *Address:* PO Box 750, Prospect, KY 40059, USA.

WALLACE, Ronald William; Poet and Prof. of English; b. 18 Feb. 1945, Cedar Rapids, IA, USA; m. Margaret Elizabeth McCreight, 3 Aug. 1968, two d. *Education:* BA, College of Wooster, 1967; MA, 1968, PhD, 1971, University of Michigan. *Career:* Dir of Creative Writing, University of Wisconsin, Madison, 1975–; Series Ed., Brittingham Prize in Poetry, 1985–; Dir, Wisconsin Institute for Creative Writing, 1986–; mem. Poets and Writers; Associated Writing Programs. *Publications:* Henry James and the Comic Form, 1975; Installing the Bees, 1977; Cucumbers, 1977; The Last Laugh, 1979; The Facts of Life, 1979; Plums, Stones, Kisses and Hooks, 1981; Tunes for Bears to Dance to, 1983; God Be With the Clown, 1984; The Owl in the Kitchen, 1985; People and Dog in the Sun, 1987; Vital Signs, 1989; The Makings of Happiness, 1991; Time's Fancy, 1994; The Uses of Adversity, 1998; Quick Bright Things, 2000. Contributions: New Yorker; Atlantic; Nation; Poetry; Southern Review; Poetry Northwest. *Honours:* Hopwood Award for Poetry, 1970; Council for Wisconsin Writers Awards, 1978, 1979, 1984, 1985, 1986, 1988; Helen Bullis Prize in Poetry, 1985; Robert E. Gard Award for Excellence in Poetry, 1990; Posner Poetry Prize, 1992; Gerald A Bartell Award in the Arts, 1994; Felix Pollak Prof. of Poetry. *Address:* Dept of English, University of Wisconsin, Madison, WI 53706, USA.

WALLACE-CRABBE, Christopher Keith, BA, MA; academic, poet and writer; b. 6 May 1934, Richmond, Vic., Australia; m. 1st Helen Margaret Wiltshire 1957; one s. one d.; m. 2nd Marianne Sophie Feil 1979; two s. *Education:* University of Melbourne. *Career:* Reader in English, 1976–86, Prof. of English, 1986–, University of Melbourne; Prof. of Australian Studies, Harvard Univ., 1987–88. *Publications:* Poetry: No Glass Houses, 1956; The Music of Division, 1959; Eight Metropolitan Poems, 1962; In Light and Darkness, 1964; The Rebel General, 1967; Where the Wind Came, 1971; Act in the Noon, 1974; The Shapes of Gallipoli, 1975; The Foundations of Joy, 1976; The Emotions Are Not Skilled Workers, 1979; The Amorous Cannibal and Other Poems, 1985; I'm Deadly Serious, 1988; Selected Poems 1956–1994, 1995; Whirling, 1999; By and Large, 2001. Novel: Splinters, 1981. Other: Melbourne or the Bush: Essays on Australian Literature and Society, 1973; Author! Author!, 1999. Editor: Vols of Australian poetry. *Honours:* Masefield Prize for Poetry, 1957; Grace Levin Prize, 1986; Dublin Prize, 1987; Christopher Brennan Award, 1990; Age Book of the Year Prize, 1995. *Address:* The Australian Centre, University of Melbourne, Parkville, Vic. 3010, Australia.

WALLENSTEIN, Barry; Poet and Prof. of English; b. 13 Feb. 1940, New York, NY, USA; m. Lorna Harbus, 19 March 1978, one s. one d. *Education:* BA, 1962, MA, 1963, PhD, 1972, New York University. *Career:* Prof. of English, City College, CUNY, 1965–; Exchange Prof., University of Paris, 1981, Polytechnic of North London, 1987–88; Writer-in-Residence, University of North Michigan, 1993; mem. Acad. of American Poets; Poets and Writers; Poets House. *Publications:* Poetry: Beast is a Wolf with Brown Fire, 1977; Roller Coaster Kid, 1982; Love and Crush, 1991; The Short Life of the Five Minute Dancer, 1993; A Measure of Conduct, 1999. Criticism: Visions and Revisions: An Approach to Poetry, 1971. Contributions: anthologies, reviews, quarterlies, and journals. *Honours:* CUNY Research Fund Grant; MacDowell Colony Residency Fellowship. *Address:* 340 Riverside Dr., New York, NY 10025, USA.

WALLER, Robert James; Writer; b. 1 Aug. 1939, USA; m. Georgia Ann Wiedemeier, one s. *Education:* University of Iowa, 1957–58; University of Northern Iowa, 1958; PhD, Indiana University, 1968. *Career:* Prof. of Management, 1968–91, Dean, School of Business, 1979–85, University of Northern Iowa. *Publications:* Just Beyond the Firelight: Stories and Essays, 1988; One Good Road is Enough: Essays, 1990; The Bridges of Madison County, 1992; Slow Waltz in Cedar Bend, 1993; Old Songs in a New Cafe: Selected Essays, 1994; Border Music, 1995. *Honours:* Literary Lion Award, New York Public Library, 1993. *Address:* c/o Aaron Priest Literary Agency, 708 Third Ave, 23rd Floor, New York, NY 10017, USA.

WALLEY, Byron (see Card, Orson Scott).

WALLIN, Raimo S.; novelist, playwright, poet and publisher; b. Finland; m. Terttu Wallin 1972. *Career:* fmr teacher; f. publishing co, Kustannus Sokrates. *Publications:* 100 Vuotta Kansakoulutoimintaa Vanajassa (with Uolevi Nurminen), 1965; Alttari (play), 1967; Matkan Loppu (short stories), 1967; Persialaisella Matolla, 1972; Saul Ja Daavid, 1972; Luova Kirjoitus, 1973; Kansanruno-Kalevala (with Merja Totro, Terttu Wallin), 1979; Luova Kirjoitus 5, 1982; Minä, Muut, Maailma, 1982; Minä, Muut, Maailma, 1983;

Vapaat Kahleet, 1986; Kaikki Tiet Käyvät Roomaan, 1997; Luova Kirjoitus ABCD, 1998. *Address:* c/o Kustannus Sokrates Ky, Ounasvaarantie 1 C 75, 00970 Helsinki, Finland.

WALLINGTON, Vivienne Elizabeth, (Elizabeth Duke); Writer; b. 8 Feb. 1937, Adelaide, SA, Australia; m. John Wallington, 18 April 1959, one s. one d. *Education:* Library Registration, 1954–59. *Career:* mem. Romance Writers of America; Romance Writers of Australia; Fellowship of Australian Writers. *Publications:* Somewhere, 1982; Butterfingers, 1986; Names are Fun, 1990; Outback Legacy, 1993; Shattered Wedding, 1994; To Catch a Playboy, 1995; Heartless Stranger, 1996; Takeover Engagement, 1997; The Marriage Pact, 1997; Look-alike Fiancée, 1998; The Husband Dilemma, 1998; The Parent Test, 1999; Outback Affair, 2000; Claiming His Bride, 2001; Kindergarten Cupids, 2002. Contributions: newspapers. *Address:* 38 Fuller St, Mitcham, Vic. 3132, Australia.

WALSER, Martin; Writer, Playwright and Poet; b. 24 March 1927, Wasserburg, Bodensee, Germany; m. Käthe Jehle, 1950, four d. *Education:* Theologisch-Philosophische Hochschule, Regensburg; DPhil, University of Tübingen. *Publications:* Ehen in Philippsburg, 1957; Halbzeit, 1960; Das Einhorn, 1966; Fiction, 1970; Die Gallistlische Krankheit, 1972; Der Sturz, 1973; Jenseits der Liebe, 1976; Ein fliehendes Pferd, 1978; Seelenarbeit, 1979; Das Schwanenhaus, 1980; Brief an Lord Liszt, 1982; Brandung, 1985; Dorle und Wolf, 1987; Jagd, 1988; Die Verteidigung der Kindheit, 1991; Ohne einander, 1993; Finks Krieg, 1996; Ein springender Brunnen, 1998; Tod Eines Kritikers, 2002. Short Stories: Ein Flugzeug über dem Haus, 1955; Lügengeschichten, 1964. Plays: Der Abstecher, 1961; Eiche und Angora, 1962; Überlebensgross Herr Krott, 1963; Der schwarze Schwan, 1964; Die Zimmerschlacht, 1967; Ein Kinderspiel, 1970; Das Sauspiel, 1975; In Goethe's Hand, 1982; Die Ohrfeige, 1986; Das Sofa, 1992; Kaschmir in Parching, 1995. Essays: Beschreibung einer Form, Versuch über Franz Kafka, 1961; Erfahrungen und Leseerfahrungen, 1965; Heimatkunde, 1968; Wie und wovon handelt Literatur, 1973; Wer ist ein Schriftsteller, 1978; Selbstbewusstsein und Ironie, 1981; Messmers Gedanken, 1985; Über Deutschland reden, 1988; Vormittag eines Schriftstellers, 1994. Poetry: Der Grund zur Freude, 1978. *Honours:* Group 47 Prize, 1955; Hermann-Hesse Prize, 1957; Gerhart-Hauptmann Prize, 1962; Schiller Prize, 1980; Büchner Prize, 1981; Friedenspreis des Deutschen Buchhandels, 1998; Grasses Bundesverdienstkreuz mit Stern. *Address:* 88662 Überlingen-Nussdorf, Zum Hecht 36, Germany. *Telephone:* (7551) 4131. *Fax:* (7551) 68494.

WALSH, Sheila, (Sophie Leyton); Writer; b. 10 Oct. 1928, Birmingham, England. *Education:* Southport College of Art, 1945–48. *Career:* mem. Romantic Novelists Asscn, vice-pres.; Soroptimist International of Southport. *Publications:* The Golden Songbird, 1975; The Sergeant Major's Daughter, 1977; A Fine Silk Purse, 1978; The Incomparable Miss Brady, 1980; The Rose Domino, 1981; A Highly Respectable Marriage, 1983; The Runaway Bride, 1984; Cousins of a Kind, 1985; The Incorrigible Rake, 1985; An Insubstantial Pageant, 1986; Bath Intrigue, 1986; Lady Aurelia's Bequest, 1987; Minerva's Marquis, 1988; The Nabob, 1989–90; A Woman of Little Importance, 1991; Until Tomorrow, 1993; Remember Me, 1994; A Perfect Bride, 1994; Kate and the Marquess, 1997. *Honours:* Best Romantic Novel of Year, 1983. *Address:* 35 Coudray Rd, Southport, Merseyside PR9 9NL, England.

WALSHE, Aubrey Peter; Prof. of Political Science and Writer; b. 12 Jan. 1934, Johannesburg, South Africa; m. Catherine Ann Pettifer, 26 Jan. 1957, one s., three d. *Education:* BA, Wadham College, Oxford, 1956; DPhil, St Antony's College, Oxford, 1968. *Career:* Lecturer, University of Lesotho, 1959–62; Prof. of Political Science, University of Notre Dame, IN, 1967–. *Publications:* The Rise of African Nationalism in South Africa, 1971; Black Nationalism in South Africa, 1974; Church Versus State in South Africa, 1983; Prophetic Christianity and the Liberation Movement in South Africa, 1996. Contributions: Cambridge History of Africa, 1986, professional journals and newspapers. *Address:* c/o Dept of Government, University of Notre Dame, Notre Dame, IN 46556, USA.

WALTERS, Minette; British writer; b. 26 Sept. 1949, Bishops Stortford, England; m. Alexander Walters 1978; two s. *Education:* University of Durham. *Career:* mem. CWA. *Publications:* The Ice House 1992, The Sculptress 1993, The Scold's Bridle (CWA Gold Dagger) 1994, The Dark Room 1995, The Echo 1997, The Breaker 1998, The Tinder Box 1999, The Shape of Snakes 2000, Acid Row 2001, Fox Evil (CWA Gold Dagger 2003) 2002, Disordered Minds 2003. *Honours:* CWA John Creasey Award for Best First Crime Novel 1992, Macavity Award 1993, Edgar Allan Poe Award 1993. *Literary Agent:* Gregory and Radice Authors' Agents, 3 Barb Mews, London, W6 7PA, England. *Website:* www.minettewalters.net.

WALVIN, James; Prof. of History and Writer; b. 2 Jan. 1942, Manchester, England; m. Jennifer Walvin, two s. *Education:* BA, University of Keele, 1964; MA, McMaster University, 1970. *Career:* Prof. of History, University of York. *Publications:* A Jamaica Plantation: Worthy Park 1670–1870 (with M. Craton), 1970; The Black Presence: A Documentary of the Negro in Britain, 1971; Black and White: The Negro and English Society 1555–1945, 1973; The People's Game: A Social History of British Football, 1975; Slavery, Abolition, and Emancipation (co-ed.), 1976; Beside the Seaside: A Social History of the Popular Seaside Holiday, 1978; Leisure and Society 1830–1950, 1978; Abolition of the Atlantic Slave Trade (co-ed.), 1981; A Child's World: A Social History of English Childhood 1900–1914, 1982; Slavery and British Society 1776–1848 (ed.), 1982; English Radicals and Reformers 1776–1848 (with E. Royle), 1982; Slavery and the Slave Trade, 1983; Black Personalities: Africans in Britain in the Era of Slavery, 1983; Leisure in Britain Since 1800 (co-ed.), 1983; Urban England 1776–1851, 1984; Manliness and Morality (co-ed.), 1985; Football and the Decline of Britain, 1986; England, Slaves, and Freedom, 1776–1838, 1986; Victorian Values, 1987; Black Ivory: A History of British Slavery, 1992; Slaves and Slavery, 1992; The People's Game: The History of Football Revisited, 1994; The Life and Times of Henry Clarke of Jamaica, 1994; Questioning Slavery, 1996; Fruits of Empire: Exotic Produce and British Taste 1660–1800, 1997; The Quakers: Money and Morals, 1997; An African Life, 1998; Making the Black Atlantic, 2000; The Only Game, 2001. *Address:* c/o Dept of History, University of York, Heslington, Yorkshire Y01 5DD, England.

WALWICZ, Ania, DipEd; Australian poet, dramatist, writer and artist; b. 19 May 1951, Swidnica, Poland. *Education:* University of Melbourne, Victorian College of the Arts. *Career:* writer-in-residence, Deakin University and Murdoch University 1987–88. *Publications:* Writing, 1982; Boat, 1989. Plays: Girlboytalk, 1986; Dissecting Mice, 1989; Elegant, 1990; Red Roses, 1992; Telltale, 1994. Contributions: 85 anthologies. *Honours:* Australian Council Literature Board grants, and Fellowship, 1990; New Writing Prize, Victorian Premier's Literary Awards, 1990. *Address:* Unit 40, 26 Victoria Street, Melbourne, Vic. 3065, Australia.

WALZER, Michael Laban, PhD; American academic, editor and writer; *Professor of Social Science, Institute for Advanced Study, Princeton University*; b. 3 March 1935, New York, NY; m. Judith Borodovko 1956; two d. *Education:* Brandeis and Harvard Univs, Univ. of Cambridge, UK. *Career:* Asst Prof. of Politics, Princeton Univ. 1962–66; Assoc. Prof., Harvard Univ. 1966–68, Prof. of Government 1968–80; Ed. Dissent 1976–; Prof. of Social Science, Inst. for Advanced Study, PrincetonUniv., NJ 1980–; mem. Conf. on the Study of Political Thought, Soc. of Ethical and Legal Philosophy; mem. Editorial Bd, Philosophy and Publica Affairs, Political Theory; mem. Bd of Govs Hebrew Univ.; Fulbright Fellow, Univ. of Cambridge 1956–57. *Publications:* The Revolution of the Saints: A Study in the Origins of Radical Politics 1965, The Political Imagination in Literature (ed. with Philip Green) 1968, Obligations: Essays on Disobedience, War and Citizenship 1970, Political Action: A Practical Guide to Movement Politics 1971, Regicide and Revolution: Speeches at the Trial of Louis XVI (ed.) 1974, Just and Unjust Wars: A Moral Argument with Historical Illustrations 1977, Radical Principles: Reflections of an Unreconstructed Democrat 1980, Spheres of Justice: A Defense of Pluralism and Equality 1983, Exodus and Revolution 1985, Interpretation and Social Criticism 1987, The Company of Critics: Social Criticism and Political Commitment in the Twentieth Century 1989, What it Means to be an American 1992, Thick and Thin: Moral Argument at Home and Abroad 1994, Pluralism, Justice and Equality (with David Miller) 1995, Toward a Global Civil Society (ed.) 1995, On Toleration 1997, Exilic Politics in the Hebrew Bible 2001, War, Politics, and Morality (selected essays in Spanish) 2001, The Thread of Politics: Democracy, Social Criticism, and World Government (selected essays in Italian) 2002; contribs to professional journals. *Honours:* Harbison Award 1971. *Address:* School of Social Science, Institute for Advanced Study, Princeton University, Einstein Drive, Princeton, NJ 08540 (Office); 103 Linwood Circle, Princeton, NJ 08520, USA (Home). *Telephone:* (609) 734-8253 (Office). *Fax:* (609) 951-4457 (Office). *E-mail:* walzer@ias.edu (Office).

WAMBAUGH, Joseph; Writer; b. 22 Jan. 1937, Pittsburgh, PA, USA; m. Dee Allsup, 26 Nov. 1955, two s. one deceased, one d. *Education:* BA, 1960, MA, 1968, California State College, Los Angeles. *Career:* Police Officer, Los Angeles, 1960–74. *Publications:* The New Centurions, 1971; The Blue Knight, 1972; The Onion Field, 1973; The Choirboys, 1975; The Black Marble, 1978; The Glitter Dome, 1981; The Delta Star, 1983; Lines and Shadows, 1984; The Secrets of Harry Bright, 1985; Echoes in the Darkness, 1987; The Blooding, 1989; The Golden Orange, 1990; Fugitive Nights, 1992; Finnegan's Week, 1993; Floaters, 1996; Fire Lover: A True Story, 2002. *Honours:* Edgar Allan Poe Award, MWA, 1974; Rodolfo Walsh Prize, International Asscn of Crime Writers, 1989. *Address:* c/o William Morrow & Co, New York, NY, USA.

WANDOR, Michelene Dinah, BA, LTCL, DipTCL, MA, MMus; writer, poet, dramatist, critic and musician; b. 20 April 1940, London, England; m. Edward Victor 1963 (divorced); two s. *Education:* Newnham College, Cambridge, University of Essex, Trinity College of Music, London, University of London. *Career:* Poetry Ed., Time Out Magazine, 1971–82; Senior Lecturer, University of North London, 1998; mem. Society of Authors. *Publications:* Cutlasses and Earrings (ed. and contributor), 1977; Carry on Understudies, 1981; Upbeat, 1981; Touch Papers, 1982; Five Plays, 1984; Gardens of Eden, 1984; Routledge, 1986; Look Back in Gender, 1987; Guests in the Body, 1987; Drama 1970–1990, 1993; Gardens of Eden Revisited, 1999; Post-War British Drama: Looking Back in Gender, 2000. Contributions: periodicals. *Honours:* International Emmy, 1987. *Address:* 71 Belsize Lane, London NW3 5AU, England.

WANG ANYI; writer; b. 1954, Tong'an, Fujian Province, People's Republic of China. *Education:* Xiangming Middle School; International Writing Program, Univ. of Iowa, USA, 1983. *Career:* fmrly musician, Xuzhou Pref. Song and Dance Ensemble; Ed., Childhood magazine, 1978–; mem. Shanghai

Writers' Asscn (vice-chair.). *Publications:* Weisheng, 1981; Liushi (Lapse of Time), 1982; 69 jie chuzhong sheng, 1984; Da Liuzhuang, 1985; Xiao Baozhuang (Baotown), 1985; Huanghe gudao ren, 1986; Huangshan zhi lian (Love on a Barren Mountain), 1986; Xiaocheng zhi lian (Love in a Small Town), 1986; Jinxiugu zhi lian (Brocade Valley), 1987; Liushui sanshi zhang, 1988; Gang shang de shiji, 1989; Shushu de gushi, 1990; Mi Ni, 1991; Shangxin Taipingyang, 1993; Xianggang de qing yu ai, 1993; Jishi yu xugou, 1993; Changhen ge, 1996; Temptress Moon (screenplay, with Chen Kaige), 1996; Fu ping, 2001. *Honours:* Mao Dun Prize for Literature; Best Novella Prize, 1982. *Address:* Shanghai Writers' Asscn, Shanghai, People's Republic of China.

WANG CHEN; journalist and editor; b. Wen'an Co., Hebei Province, People's Republic of China. *Education:* School of Postgrad. Studies, Chinese Acad. of Social Sciences, Beijing. *Career:* fmr reporter CCP Yijun Co. Cttee, CCP Yan'an Municipal Cttee, Shaanxi Prov.; reporter Guangming Daily, then successively Ed., Dir Chief Ed.'s Office, Assoc. Chief Ed., Chief Ed. 1982–2000; Deputy Dir Dept of Propaganda, CCP Cen. Cttee 2000; Ed.-in-Chief Renmin Ribao (People's Daily) Aug. 2001–. *Address:* Renmin Ribao (People's Daily), 2 Jin Tai Xi Lu, Chao Yang Men Wai, Beijing 100733, People's Republic of China. *E-mail:* rmrb@peopledaily.com.cn. *Website:* www.people.com.cn.

WARD, John Hood; Civil Service Senior Principal (retd), Writer and Poet; b. 16 Dec. 1915, Newcastle upon Tyne, England; m. Gladys Hilda Thorogood, 27 July 1940, one s. two d. *Education:* Royal Grammar School, Newcastle, 1925–33. *Career:* Senior Principal, Dept of Health and Social Security, –1978; mem. Manchester Poets; Society of Civil Service Authors. *Publications:* A Late Harvest, 1982; The Dark Sea, 1983; A Kind of Likeness, 1985; The Wrong Side of Glory, 1986; A Song at Twilight, 1989; Grandfather Best and the Protestant Work Ethic, 1991; Tales of Love and Hate, 1993; The Brilliance of Light, 1994; Winter Song, 1995; Selected Poems, 1968–95, 1996. Contributions: anthologies and periodicals. *Honours:* Imperial Service Order, 1977; Poetry Prize, City of Westminster Arts Council, 1977; Open Poetry Prize, Wharfedale Music Festival, 1978; Lancaster Festival Prizes, 1982, 1987, 1988, 1989, 1994, 1995; First Prize, Bury Open Poetry Competition, 1987; First Prizes, High Peak Open Competition, 1988, 1989; First Prize, May and Alfred Wilkins Memorial Prize, 1995.

WARD, Philip; Chartered Librarian and Writer; b. 10 Feb. 1938, Harrow, England; m. 4 April 1964, two d. *Education:* University for Foreigners, Perugia; Coimbra University. *Career:* Hon. Ed., The Private Library, 1958–64; Co-ordinator, Library Services, Tripoli, Libya, 1963–71; Dir, National Library Services, 1973–74; mem. Private Libraries Asscn. *Publications:* The Oxford Companion to Spanish Literature, 1978; A Dictionary of Common Fallacies, 1978–80; Lost Songs, 1981; A Lifetime's Reading, 1983; Japanese Capitals, 1985; Travels in Oman, 1987; Sofia: Portrait of a City, 1989; Wight Magic, 1990; Bulgaria, 1990; South India, 1991; Western India, 1991; Bulgarian Voices: Letting the People Speak. 1992; Bahrain, 1993; Gujarat, Daman, Diu, 1994; The Comfort of Women (novel), 2002. *Honours:* FRGS; RSA; Guinness Poetry Award, 1959; First Prize, International Travel Writers Competition, 1990. *Address:* c/o Oxford University Press, Great Clarendon St, Oxford OX2 6DP, England.

WARDLE, (John) Irving; drama critic and writer; b. 20 July 1929, Bolton, England; m. 1st Joan Notkin 1958 (divorced); m. 2nd Fay Crowder 1963 (divorced); two s.; m. 3rd Elizabeth Grist 1975; one s. one d. *Education:* BA, Wadham College, Oxford, 1949; ARCM, Royal College of Music, London, 1955. *Career:* Sub-Ed., Times Educational Supplement, 1956; Deputy Theatre Critic, The Observer, 1960; Drama Critic, The Times, 1963–89; Ed., Gambit, 1973–75; Theatre Critic, The Independent on Sunday, 1989. *Publications:* The Houseboy, 1974; The Theatres of George Devine, 1978; Theatre Criticism, 1992. *Address:* 51 Richmond Road, New Barnet, Hertfordshire, England.

WARE, Armytage (see Barnett, Paul le Page).

WARNER, Alan, PhD; novelist; b. 1964, Connel, Scotland; m. Hollie Warner. *Education:* Ealing College, Glasgow Univ. *Publications:* Morvern Callar 1995, These Demented Lands 1997, The Sopranos 1998, The Man Who Walks 2002; contrib. to Children of Albion Rovers 1997, Disco Biscuits 1997. *Honours:* Somerset Maugham Award, Encore Award 1998, Saltire Prize. *Address:* c/o Vintage, Random House, 20 Vauxhall Bridge Road, London, SW1V 2SA, England.

WARNER, Francis, (Robert Le Plastrier); Poet, Dramatist, Fellow and Tutor; b. 21 Oct. 1937, Bishopthorpe, Yorkshire, England; m. 1st Mary Hall, 1958, divorced 1972, two d.; m. 2nd Penelope Anne Davis, 1983, one s. one d. *Education:* Christ's Hospital; London College of Music; BA, MA, St Catharine's College, Cambridge. *Career:* Supervisor in English, St Catharine's College, Cambridge, 1959–65; Staff Tutor in English, University of Cambridge Board of Extra-Mural Studies, 1963–65; Fellow and Tutor, 1965–99, Fellow Librarian, 1966–76, Dean of Degrees, 1984–, Vice-Master, 1987–89, Emeritus Fellow, 1999–, St Peter's College, Oxford; University Lecturer, 1965–99, Pro-Proctor, 1989–90, 1996–97, 1999–2000, DLitt, 2002, University of Oxford. *Publications:* Poetry: Perennia, 1962; Early Poems, 1964; Experimental Sonnets, 1965; Madrigals, 1967; The Poetry of Francis Warner, 1970; Lucca Quartet, 1975; Morning Vespers, 1980; Spring Harvest, 1981; Epithalamium, 1983; Collected Poems 1960–84, 1985; Nightingales: Poems 1985–96, 1997; Cambridge, 2001; Oxford, 2002. Plays: Maquettes: A Trilogy of One-Act Plays, 1972; Requiem: Part 1, Lying Figures, 1972, Part 2, Killing Time, 1976, Part 3, Meeting Ends, 1974; A Conception of Love, 1978; Light Shadows, 1980; Moving Reflections, 1983; Living Creation, 1985; Healing Nature: The Athens of Pericles, 1988; Byzantium, 1990; Virgil and Caesar, 1993; Agora: An Epic, 1994; King Francis First, 1995; Goethe's Weimar, 1997; Rembrandt's Mirror, 1999. Editor: Eleven Poems by Edmund Blunden, 1965; Garland, 1968; Studies in the Arts, 1968. Contributions: anthologies and journals. *Honours:* Messing International Award, 1972; Benemerenti Silver Medal, Knights of St George, Constantinian Order, Italy, 1990; Foreign Academician, Acad. of Letters and Arts, Portugal, 1993; Hon. Fellow, St Catharine's College, Cambridge, 1999. *Address:* St Peter's College, Oxford OX1 2DL, England; St Catharine's College, Cambridge, CB2 1RL, England.

WARNER, Malcolm; Writer, Curator and Educator; b. 17 May 1953, Aldershot, England; m. Sara Ryan, 6 Aug. 1988, one s. one d. *Education:* BA, 1974, PhD, 1985, Courtauld Institute of Art, London. *Career:* Lecturer, Lawrence University of Wisconsin's London Centre, 1979–87, University of Chicago, 1989, University of California at San Diego, 1993; Lecturer, 1982–83, 1984–85, Visiting Asst Prof., 1984–85, Victoria University of Manchester; Lecturer, School, 1988, Research Curator, Dept of European Painting, 1988–90, Art Institute of Chicago; Curator, Prints and Drawings, 1990–96, European Art, 1992–96, San Diego Museum of Art; Senior Curator of Paintings and Sculpture, Yale Center for British Art, 1996–2001; Assoc. Ed., New Dictionary of National Biography, 1997–; Senior Curator, Kimbell Art Museum, 2002–; mem. Print Council of America; Historians of British Art. *Publications:* Portrait Painting, 1979; The Phaidon Companion to Art and Artists in the British Isles (co-author), 1980; A Guide to European Painting (contributor), 1980; James Tissot, 1982; Rainy Days at Brig o'Turk: The Highland Sketchbooks of John Everett Millais, 1853 (co-ed.), 1983; The Image of London: Views by Travellers and Emigrés, 1550–1920, 1987; The Art of the Print: Glossary, 1991; The Prints of Harry Sternberg, 1994; French and British Paintings from 1600 to 1800 in the Art Institute of Chicago: A Catalogue of the Collection (co-author), 1996; The Victorians: British Painting, 1837–1901, 1997; Millais: Portraits (co-ed.), 1999; Great British Paintings From American Collections, 2001. Contributions: Exhibition catalogues; Articles and reviews to periodicals including: Apollo; Burlington Magazine; TLS; Pre-Raphaelite Review; Journal of the RSA; Huntington Library Quarterly. *Honours:* Ailsa Mellon Bruce Visiting Senior Fellowship, Center for Advanced Study in the Visual Arts, National Gallery of Art, 1994; Fellowship for Museum Professionals, National Endowment for the Arts, 1995. *Address:* Kimbell Art Museum, 3333 Camp Bowie Blvd, Fort Worth, TX 76107, USA. *E-mail:* mwarner@kimbellmuseum.org.

WARNER, Marina (Sarah); Author, Critic, Art Historian and Curator; b. 9 Nov. 1946, London, England; m. 1st William Shawcross 1971 (divorced 1980); one s.; m. 2nd John Dewe Mathews 1981 (divorced 1998). *Education:* MA, Modern Languages, French and Italian, Lady Margaret Hall, Oxford. *Career:* Getty Scholar, Getty Centre for the History of Art and the Humanities, CA, 1987–88; Tinbergen Prof., Erasmus University, Rotterdam, 1991; Visiting Fellow, BFI, 1992, All Souls College, Oxford, 2001; Visiting Prof., University of Ulster, 1995, Queen Mary and Westfield College, London, 1995–, Stanford University, 2000; Reith Lecturer, 1994; Whitney J. Oakes Fellow, Princeton University, 1996; Mellon Prof., University of Pittsburgh, 1997; Visiting Fellow Commoner, Trinity College, Cambridge, 1998; Tanner Lecturer, 1999; Clarendon Lecturer, 2001; mem. Arts Council, literature panel, 1992–97; British Library, advisory council, 1992–97; Charter 88, council mem., 1990–97; PEN; Trustee, Artangel; Pres., Virgil Society, 2003. *Publications:* The Dragon Empress, 1972; Alone of All Her Sex: The Myth and the Cult of the Virgin Mary, 1976; Queen Victoria's Sketchbook, 1980; Joan of Arc: The Image of Female Heroism, 1981; Monuments and Maidens: The Allegory of the Female Form, 1985; L'Atalante, 1993; Managing Monsters: Six Myths of Our Time, 1994 From the Beast to the Blonde: On Fairy Tales and Their Tellers, 1994; No Go the Bogeyman: Scaring, Lulling and Making Mock, 1998; Sounds and Wonders: Essays on Literature and Culture, 2003. Fiction: In a Dark Wood, 1977; The Skating Party, 1983; The Lost Father, 1988; Indigo, 1992; The Mermaids in the Basement (short stories), 1993; Wonder Tales (ed.), 1994; The Leto Bundle, 2001; Fantastic Metamorphoses, Other Worlds (Clarendon Lectures, 2001), 2002; Murderers I Have Known (short stories), 2002. Libretti: The Legs of the Queen of Sheba, 1991; In the House of Crossed Desires 1996. Other: Children's books. Contributions: various publications, radio and television. *Honours:* FRSL, 1985; Hon. DLitt, University of Exeter, 1995; Hon. Dr, Sheffield Hallam University, 1995; Hon. DLitt, University of York, 1997; Hon. PhD, University of North London, 1997; Hon. DLitt, University of St Andrew's, 1998; Hon. Dr, Tavistock Institute, University of East London, 1999; Katharine Briggs Award, 1999; Rosemary Crawshay Prize, British Acad., 2000; Chevalier, Ordres des Arts et des Lettres, 2000. *Literary Agent:* Rogers, Coleridge & White Ltd, 20 Powis Mews, London W11 1JN, England.

WARNER, Val; Writer and Poet; b. 15 Jan. 1946, Middlesex, England. *Education:* BA, Somerville College, Oxford, 1968. *Career:* Writer-in-Residence, University College, Swansea, 1977–78, University of Dundee, 1979–81; mem. PEN; FRSL. *Publications:* These Yellow Photos 1971,

Under the Penthouse 1973, The Centenary Corbiere (trans.) 1975, The Collected Poems and Prose of Charlotte Mew (ed.) 1981, Before Lunch 1986, The Collected Poems and Selected Prose of Charlotte Mew (ed.) 1997. Other: Tooting Idyll 1998. Contributions: many journals and periodicals. *Honours:* Gregory Award for Poetry 1975, Third Prize, Lincolnshire Literature Festival Poetry Competition 1995. *Address:* c/o Carcanet Press, Alliance House, Cross Street, Manchester, M2 7AQ, England. *E-mail:* valwarner@etce.freeserve.co.uk.

WARNOCK, Baroness (Life Peer), cr. 1985; **Helen Mary Warnock;** British philosopher and writer; b. 14 April 1924; m. Sir Geoffrey Warnock, 1949, deceased 1995, two s. three d. *Education:* MA, BPhil, Lady Margaret Hall, Oxford. *Career:* Fellow and Tutor in Philosophy, 1949–66, Senior Research Fellow, 1976–84, St Hugh's College, Oxford; Headmistress, Oxford High School, 1966–72; Talbot Research Fellow, Lady Margaret Hall, Oxford, 1972–76; Mistress, 1985–91, Life Fellow, Girton College, Cambridge; Visiting Prof. of Rhetoric, Gresham College, 2000–01; several visiting lectureships. *Publications:* Ethics Since 1900, 1960; J.-P. Sartre, 1963; Existentialist Ethics, 1966; Existentialism, 1970; Imagination, 1976; Schools of Thought, 1977; What Must We Teach? (with T. Devlin), 1977; Education: A Way Forward, 1979; A Question of Life, 1985; Teacher Teach Thyself, 1985; Memory, 1987; A Common Policy for Education, 1988; Universities: Knowing Our Minds, 1989; The Uses of Philosophy, 1992; Imagination and Time, 1994; Women Philosophers (ed.), 1996; An Intelligent Person's Guide to Ethics, 1998; A Memoir: People and Places, 2000; Making Babies: Is There a Right to Have Children?, 2002; Nature and Mortality: Recollections of a Philosopher in Public Life, 2003. *Honours:* 15 hon. doctorates; Hon. Fellow, Lady Margaret Hall, Oxford, 1984, St Hugh's College, Oxford, 1985, Hertford College, Oxford, 1997; Albert Medal, RSA; Hon. Fellowship, British Acad., 2000. *Address:* 60 Church Street, Great Bedwyn, Wiltshire SN8 3PF, England.

WARREN, Rosanna; university professor, poet and writer; *Emma Mactachlan Metcalf Professor of the Humanities, Boston University;* b. 27 July 1953, Fairfield, CT, USA; m. Stephen Scully 1981; two d. one step-s. *Education:* BA, summa cum laude, Yale University, 1976; MA, Johns Hopkins University, 1980. *Career:* Asst Prof., Vanderbilt University, 1981–82; Visiting Asst Prof., 1982–88, Asst Prof., 1989–95, Assoc. Prof. of English, 1995–99, Emma Mactachlan Metcalf Prof. of the Humanities 1999–, Boston University; Poetry Consultant and Contributing Ed., Partisan Review, 1985–97; Poet-in-Residence, Robert Frost Farm, 1990; mem. American Acad. of Arts and Sciences; Acad. of American Poets, board of chancellors, 1999–; MLA; American Literary Trans Asscn; Asscn of Literary Scholars and Critics; PEN. *Publications:* The Joey Story 1963, Snow Day 1981, Each Leaf Shines Separate 1984, The Art of Translation: Voices from the Field (ed.) 1989, Stained Glass 1993, Eugenio Montale's Cuttlefish Bones (ed.) 1993, Euripides' Suppliant Women (trans. with Stephen Scully) 1995, Eugenio Montale's Satura (ed.) 1998, Departure 2003. Contributions: many journals and magazines. *Honours:* National Discovery Award in Poetry, 92nd Street YMHA-YWCA, New York City, 1980; Yaddo Fellow, 1980; Ingram Merrill Foundation Grants, 1983, 1993; Guggenheim Fellowship, 1985–86; ACLS Grant, 1989–90; Lavan Younger Poets Prize, 1992, and Lamont Poetry Prize, 1993, Acad. of American Poets; Lila Wallace Writers' Fund Award, 1994; Witter Bynner Prize in Poetry, American Acad. of Arts and Letters, 1994; May Sarton Award, New England Poetry Club, 1995. *Address:* c/o University Profs Program, Boston University, 745 Commonwealth Ave, Boston, MA 02215, USA.

WARSH, Lewis, BA, MA; poet, writer, publisher and teacher; b. 9 Nov. 1944, New York, NY, USA; m. Bernadette Mayer 1975; one s. two d. *Education:* City College, CUNY. *Career:* Co-Founder and Co-Ed., Angel Hair magazine and Angel Hair Books, New York City, 1966–77; Co-Ed., Boston Eagle, Massachusetts, 1973–75; Teacher, St Mark's in the Bowery Poetry Project, 1973–75; Co-Founder and Publisher, United Artists magazine and United Artists Books, New York, 1977–; Lecturer, Kerouac School of Disembodied Poetics, Boulder, CO, 1978, New England College, 1979–80, Queens College, CUNY, 1984–86, Farleigh Dickinson University, 1987–; Adjunct Assoc. Prof., Long Island University, 1987–. *Publications:* Poetry: The Suicide Rates, 1967; Highjacking: Poems, 1968; Moving Through Air, 1968; Chicago (with Tom Clark), 1969; Dreaming as One: Poems, 1971; Long Distance, 1971; Immediate Surrounding, 1974; Today, 1974; Blue Heaven, 1978; Hives, 1979; Methods of Birth Control, 1982; The Corset, 1986; Information from the Surface of Venus, 1987; A Free Man, 1991; Avenue of Escape, 1995. Other: Part of My History (autobiog.), 1972; The Maharajah's Son (autobiog.), 1977; Agnes and Sally (fiction), 1984. *Honours:* Poet's Foundation Award, 1972; Creative Artists Public Service Award in Fiction, 1977; National Endowment for the Arts Grant in Poetry, 1979; Co-ordinating Council of Literary Magazines Ed.'s Fellowship, 1981. *Address:* c/o Brooklyn Campus, Long Island University, 1 University Plaza, Brooklyn, NY 11201-8423, USA.

WASSERSTEIN, Wendy; Dramatist and Writer; b. 18 Oct. 1950, New York, NY, USA. *Education:* BA, Mount Holyoke College, 1971; MA, City College, CUNY, 1973; MFA, Yale University, 1976. *Career:* mem. British American Arts Asscn; Dramatists Guild; Dramatists Guild for Young Playwrights. *Publications:* Plays: Any Woman Can't, 1973; Happy Birthday, Montpelier Pizz-zazz, 1974; When Dinah Shore Ruled the Earth (with Christopher Durang), 1975; Uncommon Women and Others, 1975; Isn't it Romantic, 1981; Tender Offer, 1983; The Man in a Case, 1986; The Heidi Chronicles, 1988; The Sisters Rosensweig, 1992. Other: Miami (musical), 1986; Bachelor Girls (essays), 1990; Pamela's First Musical (children's picture book), 1996. *Honours:* Guggenheim Fellowship, 1983; American Playwrights Project Grant, 1988; Pulitzer Prize for Drama, 1989; Tony Award, 1989; New York Drama Critics Circle Award, 1989; Drama Desk Award, 1989; Outer Critics Circle Award, 1989; Susan Smith Blackburn Prize, 1989. *Address:* c/o Royce Carlton Inc, 866 United Nations Plaza, Suite 4030, New York, NY 10017, USA.

WASSMO, Herbjorg; Writer and Poet; b. 6 Dec. 1942, Myre i Vesteralen, Norway. *Publications:* Fiction: Huset med den blinde glassveranda, 1981, English trans. as The House With the Blind Glass Windows, 1987; Det stumme rommet, 1983; Hudlos himmel, 1986; Dinas bok, 1989, English trans. as Dina's Book, 1994; Lykkens sonn, 1992; Reiser: Fire Fortellinger, 1995. Poetry: Vingeslag, 1976; Flotid, 1977; Lite gront bilde i stor bla ramme, 1991. Contributions: periodicals. *Honours:* Norwegian Critics' Award, 1982; Nordic Council Literature Prize, 1987.

WATADA, Terry, BA, BEd, MA; writer, dramatist, poet, editor and musician; b. 6 July 1951, Toronto, ON, Canada; m. Tane Akamatsu 1989; one s. *Education:* Univ. of Toronto, York Univ. *Publications:* Asian Voices: Stories from Canada, Korea, China, Vietnam and Japan (ed.) 1992, The Tale of the Mask (play) 1995, Face Kao: Portraits of Japanese Canadians Interned During World War II (ed.) 1996, Bukkyo Tozen: A History of Jodo Shinshu Buddhism in Canada 1996, A Thousand Homes (poems) 1997, Daruma Days (short stories) 1997, Collected Voices: An Anthology of Asian North American Periodical Writing (ed.) 1997, Ten Thousand Views of Rain (poems) 2000; other: unpublished plays; contrib. to periodicals. *Honours:* William P. Hubbard Award for Race Relations, City of Toronto 1991, Gerald Lampert Memorial Award, League of Canadian Poets 1995, First Prize in Poetry, Moon Rabbit Review Fiction and Poetry Contest 1996. *Address:* 6 Wildwood Crescent, Toronto, ON M4L 2K7, Canada. *E-mail:* Terry.Watada@senecac.on.ca.

WATERHOUSE, Keith (Spencer); Journalist, Author and Dramatist; b. 6 Feb. 1929, Leeds, England; m. 1st Joan Foster, 1950, divorced 1968, one s. two d.; m. 2nd Stella Bingham, 1984, divorced 1989. *Education:* Leeds. *Career:* Journalist, 1950–; Columnist, Daily Mirror, 1970–86, Daily Mail, 1986–; mem. FRSL. *Publications:* Fiction: There is a Happy Land, 1957; Billy Liar, 1959; Jubb, 1963; The Bucket Shop, 1968; Billy Liar on the Moon, 1975; Office Life, 1978; Maggie Muggins, 1981; In the Mood, 1983; Thinks, 1984; Our Song, 1988; Bimbo, 1990; Unsweet Charity, 1992; Good Grief, 1997; Soho, 2001; Palace Pier, 2003. Other: Café Royal (with Guy Deghy), 1956; Writers' Theatre (ed.), 1967; The Passing of the Third-Floor Buck, 1974; Mondays, Thursdays, 1976; Rhubarb, Rhubarb, 1979; Daily Mirror Style, 1980, revised edn as Newspaper Style, 1989; Fanny Peculiar, 1983; Mrs Pooter's Diary, 1983; Waterhouse at Large, 1985; Collected Letters of a Nobody, 1986; The Theory and Practice of Lunch, 1986; The Theory and Practice of Travel, 1989; English Our English, 1991; Sharon & Tracy & The Rest, 1992; City Lights, 1994; Streets Ahead, 1995. Plays (with Willis Hall): Billy Liar, 1960; Celebration, 1961; All Things Bright and Beautiful, 1963; Say Who You Are, 1965; Who's Who, 1974; Saturday, Sunday, Monday (adaptation after de Filippo), 1974; Filumena (adaptation after de Filippo), 1977. Plays: Jeffrey Bernard is Unwell and Other Plays, 1991. *Honours:* Granada Columnist of the Year Award, 1970, and Granada Special Quarter Century Award, 1982; IPC Descriptive Writer of the Year Award, 1970, and IPC Columnist of the Year Award, 1973; British Press Awards Columnist of the Year, 1978, 1991; Evening Standard Best Comedy Award, 1990; CBE, 1991; Hon. Fellow, Leeds Metropolitan University, 1991; Press Club Edgar Wallace Award, 1997; Gerald Barry Lifetime Achievement Award, 2000. *Address:* 84 Coleherne Ct London SW5 0EE, England.

WATERMAN, Andrew John; university lecturer and poet; b. 28 May 1940, London, England; m. (divorced); one s. *Education:* BA, English, Univ. of Leicester, 1966; Worcester College, Oxford, 1966–68. *Career:* Lecturer, 1968–78, Senior Lecturer in English, 1978–97, Univ. of Ulster, Coleraine, Northern Ireland. *Publications:* Living Room, 1974; From the Other Country, 1977; Over the Wall, 1980; Out for the Elements, 1981; The Poetry of Chess (ed.), 1981; Selected Poems, 1986; In the Planetarium, 1990; The End of the Pier Show, 1995; Collected Poems 1959–1999, 2000. Contributions: anthologies, journals and periodicals. *Honours:* Poetry Book Society Choice, 1974 and Recommendation, 1981; Cholmondeley Award for Poetry, 1977; Arvon Poetry Competition Prize, 1981. *Address:* 5 Guernsey Road, Norwich, Norfolk NR3 1JJ, England. *Telephone:* (1603) 762952.

WATERS, John Frederick; Writer; b. 27 Oct. 1930, Somerville, Massachusetts, USA. *Education:* BS, University of Massachusetts. *Career:* mem. Southeastern Massachusetts Creative Writers Club; Organizer, Cape Cod Writers; 12 O'Clock Scholars; Society of Children's Book Writers; Authors' Guild. *Publications:* Marine Animal Collectors, 1969; The Crab From Yesterday, 1970; The Sea Farmers, 1970; What Does An Oceanographer Do?, 1970; Saltmarshes and Shifting Dunes, 1970; Turtles, 1971; Neighborhood Puddle, 1971; Some Mammals Live in the Sea, 1972; Green Turtle: Mysteries, 1972; The Royal Potwasher, 1972; Seal Harbour, 1973; Hungry Sharks, 1973; Giant Sea Creatures, 1973; The Mysterious Eel, 1973; Camels: Ships of the Desert, 1974; Carnivorous Plants, 1974; Exploring New England Shores, 1974; The Continental Shelves, 1975; Creatures of

Darkness, 1975; Victory Chimes, 1976; Maritime Careers, 1977; Fishing, 1978; Summer of the Seals, 1978; The Hatchlings, 1979; Crime Labs, 1979; A Jellyfish is Not a Fish, 1979; Flood, 1991; Watching Whales, 1991; The Raindrop Journey, 1991; Deep Sea Vents, 1994; Night Raiders Along the Cape, 1996; Mystery of the Horse Phoenix, 1999; Murder on Seal Island, 2000; Who Killed the Whale?, 2001; Mystery of the Yellow Eyes, 2001. Contributions: Cape Cod Compass. *Honours:* Junior Literary Book Choice (twice); Outstanding Science books for Children Awards (7 times). *Address:* 64 Meadowbrook Rd, North Chatham, MA 02650, USA.

WATERS, Sarah, PhD; British writer; b. 1966, Neyland, Wales. *Education:* Kent Univ. *Career:* fmrly teacher at Open Univ. *Publications:* Tipping the Velvet 1998, Affinity 2000, Fingersmith 2002; contrib. articles on lesbian and gay writing, cultural history. *Honours:* Betty Trask Award 1999, Sunday Times Young Writer of the Year 2000, Somerset Maugham Award 2000, CWA Ellis Peters Historical Dagger 2002, Author of the Year, British Book Awards, 2002. *Address:* c/o Virago Press, Brettenham House, Lancaster Place, London, WC2E 7EN, England. *Website:* www.sarahwaters.com.

WATKINS, Clive, BL; British poet; b. 1945, Sheffield, South Yorkshire; m.; three c. *Career:* teacher, headteacher. *Publications:* Jigsaw 2003. *Address:* c/o The Waywiser Press, 9 Woodstock Road, London, N4 3ET, England. *Website:* www.waywiser-press.com.

WATKINS, Floyd C.; academic, writer and farmer; b. 19 April 1920, Cherokee County, GA, USA; m. Anna E. Braziel 1942; one s. two d. *Education:* BS, Georgia Southern University, 1946; AM, Emory University, 1947; PhD, Vanderbilt University, 1952. *Career:* Instructor, 1949–61, Prof., 1961–80, Candler Prof. of American Literature, 1980–88, Prof. Emeritus, 1988–, Emory University; Visiting Prof., Southeastern University, Oklahoma, 1961, 1970, Texas A & M University, 1980. *Publications:* The Literature of the South (co-ed.), 1952; Thomas Wolfe's Characters, 1957; Old Times in the Faulkner Country (co-author), 1961; The Flesh and the Word, 1971; In Time and Place, 1977; Then and Now: The Personal Past in the Poetry of Robert Penn Warren, 1982; Some Poems and Some Talk About Poetry (co-author), 1985; Talking About William Faulkner (co-author), 1996.

WATKINS, Gerrold (see Malzberg, Barry).

WATKINS, Karen Christna, (Catrin Collier, Katherine John); Writer; b. 30 May 1948, Pontypridd, Wales; m. Trevor John Watkins, 28 Dec. 1968, two s. one d. *Education:* Teaching Certificate, Swansea College, 1969. *Career:* mem. PEN; Society of Authors; CWA; Welsh Acad., 1998. *Publications:* Without Trace, 1990; Hearts of Gold, 1992; One Blue Moon, 1993; Six Foot Under; A Silver Lining, 1994; Murder of a Dead Man, 1994; All That Glitters, 1995; By Any Other Name, 1995; Such Sweet Sorrow, 1996; Past Remembering, 1997; Broken Rainbows, 1998.

WATKINS, Paul; Author; b. 23 Feb. 1964, Redwood City, CA, USA; m. Cath Watkins, one d. *Education:* Eton College, 1977–82; BA, Yale University, 1986; Graduate Studies, Syracuse University, 1986–88. *Publications:* Fiction: Night over Day over Night, 1988; Calm at Sunset, Calm at Dawn, 1989; In the Blue Light of African Dreams, 1990; The Promise of Light, 1992; Archangel, 1995; The Story of My Disappearance, 1998; The Forger, 2000. Non-Fiction: Stand Before Your God, 1994. *Honours:* Encore Award, 1989. *Address:* c/o International Creative Management, 40 W 57th St, New York, NY 10019, USA.

WATMOUGH, David; Author; b. 17 Aug. 1926, London, England. *Education:* Theology Major, King's College, University of London, 1945–49. *Career:* mem. Writers Union of Canada; Federation of British Columbia Writers. *Publications:* Ashes for Easter (short stories), 1972; Love and the Waiting Game(short stories), 1975; From a Cornish Landscape (short stories), 1975; No More into the Garden (novel), 1978; Fury (short stories), 1984; The Connecticut Countess (short stories), 1984; The Unlikely Pioneer (opera), 1985; Vibrations in Time (short stories), 1986; The Year of Fears (novel), 1987; Thy Mother's Glass (novel), 1992; The Time of the Kingfishers (novel), 1994; Hunting with Diana (short stories), 1996; The Moor is Dark Beneath the Moon (novel), 2002. Contributions: Encounter; Spectator; New York Times Book Review; Saturday Night, Canada; Canadian Literature; Dalhousie Review; Connoisseur, New York; Malahat Review; Vancouver Step. *Honours:* Senior Literary Arts Awards, Canada Council, 1976, 1986; Winner, Best Novel of Year Award, Giovanni's Room, Philadelphia, 1979. *Literary Agent:* John Talbot Agency, 540 W Boston Rd, Mamaroneck, NY 10543, USA. *Address:* 3358 W First Ave, Vancouver, BC V6R 1G4, Canada.

WATSON, John Richard; Prof. of English, Writer and Poet; b. 15 June 1934, Ipswich, England; m. Pauline Elizabeth Roberts, 21 July 1962, one s. two d. *Education:* BA, 1958, MA, 1964, Magdalen College, Oxford; PhD, University of Glasgow, 1966. *Career:* Asst, then Lecturer, University of Glasgow, 1962–66; Lecturer, then Senior Lecturer, University of Leicester, 1966–78; Prof. of English, 1978–99, Public Orator, 1989–99, University of Durham; mem. Charles Wesley Society; International Asscn of University Profs of English; MHRA; Charles Lamb Society, pres. *Publications:* A Leicester Calendar, 1976; Everyman's Book of Victorian Verse (ed.), 1982; Wordsworth's Vital Soul, 1982; Wordsworth, 1983; English Poetry of the Romantic Period, 1789–1830, 1985; The Poetry of Gerard Manley Hopkins, 1986; Companion to Hymns and Psalms, 1988; A Handbook to English Romanticism, 1992; The English Hymn, 1997; An Annotated Anthology of Hymns, 2002. Contributions: scholarly and literary journals. *Honours:* Matthew Arnold Memorial Prize, University of Oxford, 1961; Ewing Prize, Glasgow University, 1962; Prize, Stroud Festival, 1971; Prize, Suffolk Poetry Society, 1975. *Address:* Stoneyhurst, 27 Western Hill, Durham DH1 4RL, England. *E-mail:* j.r.watson@durham.ac.uk.

WATSON, Larry; Writer and Poet; b. 1947, USA. *Publications:* In a Dark Time (novel), 1980; Leaving Dakota (poems), 1983; Montana 1948 (novel), 1993; Justice (novel), 1995; White Crosses (novel), 1997. *Honours:* National Education Asscn Creative Writing Fellowship, 1987; Milkweed National Fiction Prize, 1993. *Address:* c/o Milkweed Editions, 430 First Ave N, Suite 400, Minneapolis, MN 55401, USA.

WATSON, Lynn; Teacher, Writer and Poet; b. 5 June 1948, Woodland, CA, USA. *Education:* University of California at Berkeley, 1966–68; BA, English, Sonoma State University, 1975; MFA, Fiction Writing, University of Iowa, 1977. *Career:* Teacher, University of Iowa, College of the Desert, Sonoma State University, Santa Rosa Junior College; mem. California Poets-in-the-Schools. *Publications:* Alimony or Death of the Clock (novel), 1981; Amateur Blues (poems), 1990; Catching the Devil (poems), 1995. Contributions: journals and periodicals. *Honours:* First Place, National Poetry Asscn, 1990; Honorable Mention, World of Poetry Contest, 1991. *Address:* PO Box 1253, Occidental, CA 95465, USA.

WATSON, Richard Allan; Prof. of Philosophy and Writer; b. 23 Feb. 1931, New Market, IA, USA; m. Patty Jo Andersen, 30 July 1955, one d. *Education:* BA, 1953, MA, 1957, PhD, Philosophy, 1961, University of Iowa; MS, Geology, University of Minnesota, 1959. *Career:* Instructor, University of Michigan, 1961–64; Asst Prof., 1964–67, Assoc. Prof., 1967–74, Prof. of Philosophy, 1974–, Washington University, St Louis; Ed., Classics in Speleology, 1968–73, Speleologia, 1974–79, Cave Books, 1980–, Journal of the History of Philosophy, 1983, Journal of the History of Philosophy Monograph Series, 1985–95; mem. American Asscn for the Advancement of Science; American Philosophical Asscn; Cave Research Foundation; National Speleological Society, hon. life mem.; Authors League of America. *Publications:* The Downfall of Cartesianism, 1966; Man and Nature (with Patty Joe Watson), 1969; The Longest Cave (with Roger W. Brucker), 1976; Under Plowman's Floor (novel), 1978; The Runner (novel), 1981; The Philosopher's Diet, 1985; The Breakdown of Cartesian Metaphysics, 1987; The Philosopher's Joke, 1990; Writing Philosophy, 1992; Niagara (novel), 1993; Caving, 1994; The Philosopher's Demise, 1995; Representational Ideas, 1995; Good Teaching, 1997; Cogito, Ergo Sum: The Life of René Descartes, 2002. Contributions: Professional journals and literary quarterlies. *Honours:* ACLS Fellow, 1967–68; Center for Advanced Study in the Behavioral Sciences Fellowships, 1967–68, 1981–82, 1991–92; National Endowment for the Humanities Grant, 1975; Center for International Studies Fellow, Princeton, NJ, 1975–76; Camargo Foundation Fellow, 1995; Bogliasco Foundation Fellow, 1998. *Address:* c/o Dept of Philosophy, Washington University, St Louis, MO 63130, USA.

WATSON, (Margaret) Sophia Laura; writer; b. 20 June 1962, London, England; m. Julian Watson 1986 (divorced 2000); four d. *Education:* BA, University of Durham, 1983; PGCE, Univ. of Exeter, 2001. *Career:* Asst Ed., Quartet Books, London, 1983–84; Ed., Fisher Publishing, London, 1984–85, Hamish Hamilton, London, 1985–87; Feature Writer, Mail on Sunday, London, 1987, Daily Mail, London, 1988–90. *Publications:* Winning Women: The Price of Success in a Man's World, 1989; Marina: The Story of a Princess, 1994; Her Husband's Children, 1995; Strange and Well Bred, 1996; The Perfect Treasure, 1998; Only Pretending, 2000. Contributions: periodicals. *Address:* Royal Oak House, Church Street, Wiveliscombe, Somerset TA4 2LR, England.

WATSON, Will (see Floren, Lee).

WATT-EVANS, Lawrence; Writer; b. 26 July 1954, Arlington, Massachusetts, USA; m. Julie F. McKenna, 30 Aug. 1977, one s. one d. *Education:* Princeton University, 1972–74, 1975–77. *Career:* mem. SFWA; Horror Writers Asscn. *Publications:* The Lure of the Basilisk, 1980; The Seven Altars of Düsarra, 1981; The Cyborg and the Sorcerers, 1982; The Sword of Bheleu, 1983; The Book of Silence, 1984; The Chromosonal Code, 1984; The Misenchanted Sword, 1985; Shining Steel, 1986; With a Single Spell, 1987; The Wizard and the War Machine, 1987; Denner's Wreck, 1988; Nightside City, 1989; The Unwilling Warlord, 1989; The Nightmare People, 1990; The Blood of a Dragon, 1991; The Rebirth of Wonder, 1992; Crosstime Traffic, 1992; Taking Flight, 1993; The Spell of the Black Dagger, 1993; Split Heirs (with Esther Friesner), 1993; Out of This World, 1994; In the Empire of Shadow, 1995; The Reign of the Brown Magician, 1996; Touched by the Gods, 1997; Dragon Weather, 1999; Night of Madness, 2000; The Dragon Society, 2001. Contributions: journals and magazines. *Honours:* Isaac Asimov's Science Fiction Readers Poll Award, 1987; Science Fiction Achievement Award (Hugo) for Best Short Story of 1987, 1988. *Address:* c/o Scott Meredith Literary Agency, 845 Third Ave, New York, NY 10022, USA.

WATTLES, Rama Rau (see Rama Rau, Santha).

WATTS, Nigel John; Writer; b. 24 June 1957, Winchester, England; m. Sahera Chohan, 10 Aug. 1991. *Publications:* The Life Game, 1989; Billy

Bayswater, 1990; We All Live in a House Called Innocence, 1992; Twenty Twenty, 1995. *Honours:* Betty Trask Award, 1989. *Address:* 2 Cromwell Pl., Mortlake, London SW14 7HA, England.

WAUGH, Alexander Evelyn Michael, MusB, DipMus; writer; b. 30 Dec. 1963, London, England; m. Eliza Chancellor; one s. two d. *Education:* University of Manchester, University of Surrey. *Career:* Dir, Manygate Management, 1988–90; Opera Critic, Mail on Sunday, 1990–91, Evening Standard, 1991–96; Founder, Chief Exec., Travelman Publishing, 1997–. *Publications:* Opera on CD (with Julian Haylock), 1994, 1995, 1996; Classical Music on CD (with Julian Haylock), 1994, 1995, 1996; Classical Music, a New Way of Listening, 1995; Opera, a New Way of Listening, 1996; Time, from Microseconds to Millennia, a Search for the Right Time, 1999; Bon Voyage! A Musical Farce (with Nathaniel Waugh), 2000; God: The Unauthorised Biography, 2001. Contributions: Literary Review; Spectator; and others. *Honours:* Music Retailers Asscn Award, 1994; Grand Prix du Disque, 1995; Vivian Ellis Award for Best New Musical, 1996; Design Council Millennium Award, 2000. *Literary Agent:* Gillon Aitken Associates Ltd, 18–21 Cavaye Place, London, SW10 9PT, England. *Telephone:* (20) 7373-8672. *Fax:* (20) 7373-6002. *E-mail:* alexanderwaugh@mac.com.

WAUGH, Hillary Baldwin, (Elissa Grandower, H. Baldwin Taylor, Harry Walker); Author; b. 22 June 1920, New Haven, CT, USA; m. 1st Diana Taylor, 16 June 1951, divorced 1980, one s. two d.; m. 2nd Shannon O. Cork, 11 June 1983, divorced 1995. *Education:* BA, Yale University, 1942. *Career:* mem. MWA; CWA. *Publications:* Last Seen Wearing..., 1952; The Missing Man, 1964; Rivergate House, 1980; The Glenna Powers Case, 1981; The Doria Rafe Case, 1981; The Billy Cantrell Case, 1982; The Nerissa Claire Case, 1983; The Veronica Dean Case, 1984; The Priscilla Copperwaite Case, 1985. *Honours:* Grand Master, Swedish Acad. of Detection, 1981; Grand Master, MWA, 1989.

WAUGH, Teresa (Lorraine); Writer; b. 26 Feb. 1940, London, England; m. Auberon Waugh, 1961, deceased 2001, two s. two d. *Education:* BA, French, Italian, University of Exeter, 1978. *Publications:* The Travels of Marco Polo: A Modern Translation (trans.), 1984; Painting Water (novel), 1984; Waterloo, Waterloo (novel), 1986; The Entertaining Book (co-author), 1986; An Intolerable Burden (novel), 1988; A Song at Twilight (novel), 1989; Sylvia's Lot (novel), 1994; The Gossips (novel), 1995; A Friend Like Harvey (novel), 1998; Alphonse de Custine (trans.), 1999; The House (novel), 2002. *Address:* Combe Florey House, Taunton, Somerset TA4 3JD, England.

WAYMAN, Tom, (Thomas Ethan Wayman); Poet, Writer and University Teacher; b. 13 Aug. 1945, Hawkesbury, Ontario, Canada. *Education:* BA, English, University of British Columbia, 1966; MFA, English and Creative Writing, University of California at Irvine, 1968. *Career:* Instructor, Colorado State University, Fort Collins, 1968–69; Writer-in-Residence, University of Windsor, Ontario, 1975–76, University of Alberta, Edmonton, 1978–79, Simon Fraser University, Burnaby, BC, 1983; Asst Prof., Wayne State University, Detroit, 1976–77; Faculty, David Thompson University Centre, Nelson, BC, 1980–82, Banff School of Fine Arts, AB, 1980, 1982, Kwantlen College, Surrey, BC, 1983, 1988–89, Kootenay School of Writing, Vancouver, 1984–87, Victoria School of Writing, BC, 1996, Kwantlen University College, Surrey, BC, 1998–2000; Prof., Okanagan College, Kelowna, BC, 1990–91, 1993–95; Faculty, 1991–92, Co-Head, Writing Studio, 1995–98, Kootenay School of the Arts, Nelson, BC; Asst Prof., University of Calgary, 2002–; Presidential Writer-in-Residence, University of Toronto, 1996; mem. Associated Writing Programs; Federation of British Columbia Writers. *Publications:* Poetry: Waiting for Wayman, 1973; For and Against the Moon, 1974; Money and Rain, 1975; Free Time, 1977; A Planet Mostly Sea, 1979; Living on the Ground, 1980; Introducing Tom Wayman: Selected Poems 1973–80, 1980; The Nobel Prize Acceptance Speech, 1981; Counting the Hours, 1983; The Face of Jack Munro, 1986; In a Small House on the Outskirts of Heaven, 1989; Did I Miss Anything?: Selected Poems 1973–1993, 1993; The Astonishing Weight of the Dead, 1994; I'll Be Right Back: New & Selected Poems 1980–1996, 1997; The Colours of the Forest, 1999; My Father's Cup, 2002. Non-Fiction: Inside Job: Essays on the New Work Writing, 1983; A Country Not Considered: Canada, Culture, Work, 1993. Editor: Beaton Abbot's Got the Contract, 1974; A Government Job at Last, 1976; Going for Coffee, 1981; East of Main: An Anthology of Poems from East Vancouver (with Calvin Wharton), 1989; Paperwork, 1991; The Dominion of Love: An Anthology of Canadian Love Poems, 2001. Contributions: anthologies and magazines. *Honours:* A. J. M. Smith Prize, Michigan State University, 1976; First Prize, National Bicentennial Poetry Awards, San Jose, 1976; several Canada Council Senior Arts Grants. *Address:* PO Box 163, Winlaw, BC V0G 2J0, Canada. *E-mail:* appledor@netidea.com. *Website:* www.library.utoronto.ca/canpoetry/wayman.

WAYS, C. R. (see Blount, Roy Alton, Jr).

WEARNE, Alan Richard; poet and novelist; b. 23 July 1948, Melbourne, Vic., Australia. *Education:* BA, Latrobe University, 1973; DipEd, Rusden, 1977. *Publications:* Public Relations, 1972; New Devil, New Parish, 1976; The Nightmarkets, 1986; Out Here, 1987; Kicking in Danger, 1997; The Lovemakers, Book One, 2001. *Honours:* National Book Council Award, 1987; Gold Medal, Asscn for the Study of Australian Literature, 1987; New South Wales Premier's Prize for Poetry (Kenneth Slessor Award), 2002; New South Wales Premier's Prize Book of the Year, 2002; Arts Queensland Judith Wright Calanthe Award for Australian Poetry, 2002. *Literary Agent:* Bryson Agency Australia Pty Ltd, PO Box 226, Flinders Lane PO, Melbourne, Vic. 8009, Australia. *Address:* c/o Faculty of Creative Arts, University of Wollongong, Wollongong, NSW 2015, Australia.

WEBB, Phyllis; Poet and Writer; b. 8 April 1927, Victoria, BC, Canada. *Education:* BA, University of British Columbia, Vancouver, 1949; McGill University, Montréal. *Career:* Adjunct Prof., University of Victoria, BC, 1989–93. *Publications:* Poetry: Trio (with G. Turnbull and Eli Mandel), 1954; Even Your Right Eye, 1956; The Sea is Also a Garden, 1962; Naked Poems, 1965; Phyllis Webb Selected Poems, 1954–1965, 1971; Wilson's Bowl, 1980; Sunday Water: Thirteen Anti Ghazals, 1982; The Vision Tree: Selected Poems, 1982; Water and Light: Ghazals and Anti Ghazals, 1984; Hanging Fire, 1990. Other: Talking (essays), 1982; Nothing But Brush Strokes: Selected Prose, 1995. *Honours:* Canada Council Awards; Governor-General's Award for Poetry, 1982; Officer of the Order of Canada, 1992. *Address:* 128 Menhinick Dr., Salt Spring Island, BC V8K 1W7, Canada.

WEBER, Eugen (Joseph); Prof. of Modern European History and Writer; b. 24 April 1925, Bucharest, Romania; m. Jacqueline Brument-Roth, 12 June 1950. *Education:* Institut d'études politiques, Paris, 1948–49, 1951–52; MA, 1954, MLitt, 1956, Emmanuel College, Cambridge. *Career:* Asst Prof., University of Iowa, 1955–56; Asst Prof., 1956–59, Assoc. Prof., 1959–63, Prof., 1963–, Dean, College of Letters and Sciences, 1977–82, Joan Palevsky Prof. of Modern European History, 1984–, University of California at Los Angeles; Visiting Prof., Collège de France, Paris, 1983; Dir d'études, École des hautes études, Paris, 1984–85; Christian Gauss Lecturer, Princeton University, 1990; mem. American Acad. of Arts and Sciences; American Philosophical Society; American Historical Asscn; Asscn française de science politique; Société d'histoire moderne; Society of French Historical Studies. *Publications:* Nationalist Revival in France, 1959; Paths to the Present, 1960; Satan Franc-Maçon, 1964; Varieties of Fascism, 1964; The European Right (with H. Rogger), 1965; A Modern History of Europe, 1971; Europe Since 1715, 1972; Peasants into Frenchmen, 1976; La Fin des Terroirs, 1983; France Fin-de-siècle, 1986; My France, 1990; Movements, Currents, Trends, 1991; The Hollow Years, 1994; La France des annèes trente, 1995; The Western Tradition, 1995; Apocalypses, 1999. Contributions: TLS; L.A. Times Book Review; New York Times Book Review. *Honours:* Fulbright Fellowships, 1952, 1982–83; American Philosophical Society Research Fellow, 1959; ACLS Research Fellow, 1962; Guggenheim Fellowship, 1963–64; National Endowment for the Humanities Senior Fellowships, 1973–74, 1982–83; Commonwealth Prizes of California, 1977, 1987; Prix de la Société des gens de lettres, France, 1984; Prix littéraire Etats-Unis/France, 1995; Prix Maurice Beaumont, 1995. *Address:* c/o Dept of History, University of California at Los Angeles, Los Angeles, CA 90095, USA.

WEBER, Katharine; Critic and Writer; b. 12 Nov. 1955, New York, NY, USA; m. Nicholas Fox Weber, 19 Sept. 1976, two d. *Education:* New School for Social Research, New York, 1972–76; Yale University, 1982–84. *Career:* Columnist, Sunday New Haven Register, CT, 1985–87; Reviewer, Publishers Weekly, 1988–92; Visiting Writer-in-Residence, Connecticut College, 1996–97; Visiting Lecturer, 1997, Lecturer, 1998–, Yale University; mem. Authors' Guild; PEN; National Book Critics Circle, board mem. *Publications:* Objects in the Mirror are Closer than they Appear, 1995; The Music Lesson, 1999; The Little Women, 2003. Contributions: numerous periodicals. *Honours:* Best Columnist of the Year, New England Women's Press Asscn, 1986; Discovery Award, New England Booksellers Asscn, 1995; Granta Best Young American Novelist, 1996. *Address:* 108 Beacon Rd, Bethany, CT 06524, USA. *E-mail:* katweber@snet.net. *Website:* www.katharineweber.com.

WEBSTER, Ernest; Writer; b. 24 Oct. 1923, Habrough, England; m. 8 Oct. 1942, two d. *Education:* Matriculation, History and Economics, London. *Career:* mem. Radio Society of Great Britain. *Publications:* The Friulan Plot, 1980; Madonna of the Black Market, 1981; Cossack Hide-Out, 1981; Red Alert, 1982; The Venetian Spy-Glass, 1983; The Verratoli Inheritance, 1983; Million-Dollar Stand-In, 1983; The Watchers, 1984. *Address:* 17 Chippendale Rise, Otley, West Yorkshire LS21 2BL, England.

WEBSTER, Jack (see Webster, John Barron).

WEBSTER, Jan; Writer; b. 10 Aug. 1924, Blantyre, Scotland; m. 10 Aug. 1946, one s. one d. *Education:* Hamilton Acad. *Publications:* Trilogy: Colliers Row, 1977; Saturday City, 1978; Beggarman's Country, 1979; Due South, 1981; Muckle Annie, 1985; One Little Room, 1987; Rags of Time, 1987; A Different Woman, 1989; Abercrombie's Aunt and Other Stories, 1990; I Only Can Dance with You, 1990; Bluebell Blue, 1991; Lowland Reels, 1992; Tallie's War, 1993; Makalienski's Bones, 1995; Pinkmount Drive, 1996. *Address:* c/o Robert Hale, 45–47 Clerkenwell Green, London EC1R 0HJ, England.

WEBSTER, John Barron, (Jack Webster); Journalist and Writer; b. 8 July 1931, Maud, Aberdeenshire, Scotland; m. Eden Keith, 17 Feb. 1956, three s. *Education:* Peterhead Acad.; Robert Gordon's College, Aberdeen. *Publications:* The Dons, 1978; A Grain of Truth, 1981; Gordon Strachan, 1984; Another Grain of Truth, 1988; Alistair MacLean: A Life, 1991; Famous Ships of the Clyde, 1993; The Flying Scots, 1994; The Express Years, 1994;

In the Driving Seat, 1996; The Herald Years, 1996; Webster's World, 1997; From Dalí to Burrell, 1997; Reo Stakis (biog.), 1999. Television: The Webster Trilogy, 1992; John Brown: The Man Who Drew a Legend, 1994; Walking Back to Happiness, 1996. *Honours:* Bank of Scotland Columnist of the Year, 1996; UK Speaker of the Year, 1996; BAFTA Award, 1996. *Address:* 58 Netherhill Ave, Glasgow G44 3XG, Scotland.

WEBSTER, Leonard (Len), BEd, MA; poet and writer; b. 6 July 1948, Birmingham, England; m. Emorn Puttalong 1985. *Education:* University of Warwick, University of Leicester, University of Birmingham, Poetry Soc. Adult Verse Speaking Certificate 1977, DipRSA TEFLA 1983. *Career:* journalist, Birmingham Post and Mail, 1965–68, Coventry Evening Telegraph, 1973–74; Teacher, Oldbury High School, 1976–77, Tarsus American College, Turkey, 1977–78, King Edward VI Grammar School, Handsworth, Birmingham, 1978–84; Lecturer, Ministry of Education, Singapore, 1984–87, 1988–94, City College, Handsworth, Birmingham, 1996–; mem. Poetry Society; Society of Authors. *Publications:* Behind the Painted Veil, 1972; Beneath the Blue Moon, 1992; Hell-Riders, 1994; Flight From the Sibyl, 1994. *Address:* c/o 48 Marshall Road, Warley, West Midlands B68 9ED, England. *Website:* home.freeuk.com/castlegates/webster.htm.

WEDDE, Ian; Writer, Poet, Dramatist and Trans; b. 17 Oct. 1946, Blenheim, New Zealand; m. Rosemary Beauchamp, 1967, three s. *Education:* MA, University of Auckland, 1968. *Career:* Poetry Reviewer, London magazine, 1970–71; Writer-in-Residence, Victoria University, Wellington, 1984; Art Critic, Wellington Evening Post, 1983–90. *Publications:* Fiction: Dick Seddon's Great Drive, 1976; The Shirt Factory and Other Stories, 1981; Symmes Hole, 1986; Survival Arts, 1988. Poetry: Homage to Matisse, 1971; Made Over, 1974; Pathway to the Sea, 1974; Earthly: Sonnets for Carlos, 1975; Don't Listen, 1977; Spells for Coming Out, 1977; Castaly, 1981; Tales of Gotham City, 1984; Georgicon, 1984; Driving Into the Storm: Selected Poems, 1988; Tendering, 1988; The Drummer, 1993; The Commonplace Odes, 2001. Plays: Stations, 1969; Pukeko, 1972; Eyeball, Eyeball, 1983; Double or Quit: The Life and Times of Percy TopLiss, 1984. Editor: The Penguin Book of New Zealand Verse (with Harvey McQueen), 1986; Now See Hear!: Art, Language, and Translation (with G. Burke), 1990. *Address:* 118-A Maidavale Rd, Roseneath, Wellington, New Zealand.

WEDGWOOD, Lady (see Tudor-Craig, Pamela Wynn).

WEI HUI, Zhou, ((Wei Hui Zhou)); Chinese writer; b. 1974, Shanghai. *Education:* Fudan Univ., Shanghai. *Career:* first year of coll. spent in mil. training; fifth novel Shanghai Baby banned in China 2001. *Publications include:* The Shriek of the Butterfly, Virgin in the Water, Crazy Like Wei Hui, Desire Pistol, Shanghai Baby (first book published in English) 2001. *Address:* c/o Joanne Wang, Constable & Robinson Ltd, 3 The Lanchesters, 162 Fulham Road, London, W6 96R, England (Office). *Telephone:* (20) 8741-3663 (Office). *Fax:* (20) 8748-7562 (Office).

WEIDENFELD, Baron (Life Peer), cr. 1976, of Chelsea in Greater London; **Arthur George Weidenfeld,** Kt; British publisher; b. 13 Sept. 1919, Vienna, Austria; m. 1st Jane Sieff 1952; one d.; m. 2nd Barbara Skelton Connolly 1956 (divorced 1961); m. 3rd Sandra Payson Meyer 1966 (divorced 1976); m. 4th Annabelle Whitestone 1992. *Education:* Piaristen Gymnasium, Vienna, Univ. of Vienna and Konsular Akademie. *Career:* came to England 1938; BBC Monitoring Service 1939–42; BBC News Commentator on European Affairs on BBC Empire and N American service 1942–46; Foreign Affairs columnist, News Chronicle 1943–44; Political Adviser and Chief of Cabinet of Pres. Weizmann of Israel 1949–50; Founder of Contact Magazine 1945, George Weidenfeld & Nicolson Ltd 1948–; Chair. George Weidenfeld & Nicolson Ltd 1948–, Wheatland Corpn, New York 1985–90, Grove Press, New York 1985–90, Wheatland Foundation, San Francisco and New York 1985–92; Dir (non-exec.) Orion 1991–; Consultant Bertelsmann Foundation 1991–, Axel Springer AG Germany; Chair. Bd of Govs, Ben Gurion Univ. of the Negev 1996–; Gov. of Tel-Aviv Univ. 1980–, Weizmann Inst. of Science 1964–; Columnist Die Welt, Die Welt am Sonntag; mem., South Bank Bd 1986–99; mem. Bd ENO 1988–98, Herbert-Quandt-Foundation 1999–; Trustee Royal Opera House 1974–87, Nat. Portrait Gallery 1988–95, Potsdam Einstein Forum, Jerusalem Foundation; Chair. Cheyne Capital 2000–, Trialogue Educational Trust 1996–; mem. Governing Council, Inst. of Human Science, Vienna; Vice-Chair. Oxford Univ. Devt Programme 1994–99; Freeman City of London. *Publications:* The Goebbels Experiment 1943, Remembering My Good Friends 1994. *Honours:* Hon. Senator Bonn Univ. 1996; Hon. Fellow St Peter's Coll. Oxford 1992, St Anne's Coll. Oxford 1993; Golden Kt's Cross of Order of Merit (Austria) 1989; Chevalier, Légion d'honneur 1990; Kt Commdr's Cross (Badge and Star) of Order of Merit (Germany) 1991; Austrian Cross of Honour First Class for Arts and Science, Vienna 2003; Honour of City of Vienna 2003; Hon. MA (Oxon.) 1992; Hon. PhD (Ben Gurion Univ.); Hon. DLitt (Exeter) 2001; Charlemagne Medal 2000. *Address:* 9 Chelsea Embankment, London, SW3 4LE, England. *Telephone:* (20) 7351-0042.

WEIGEL, George; Roman Catholic Theologian and Writer; b. 17 April 1951, Baltimore, MD, USA; m. Joan Balcombe, 21 June 1975, one s. two d. *Education:* BA, Philosophy, 1973, St Mary's Seminary and University, Baltimore, 1973; MA, Theology, University of St Michael's College, Toronto, 1975. *Career:* Fellow, Woodrow Wilson International Centre for Scholars, 1984–85; Editorial Boards, First Things; Orbis; mem. Catholic Theological Society of America; Council on Foreign Relations. *Publications:* Tranquillitas Ordinis: The Present Failure and Future Promise of American Catholic Thought on War and Peace, 1987; Catholicism and the Renewal of American Democracy, 1989; American Interests, American Purpose: Moral Reasoning and US Foreign Policy, 1989; Freedom and Its Discontents, 1991; Just War and the Gulf War (co-author), 1991; The Final Revolution: The Resistance Church and the Collapse of Communism, 1992; Idealism Without Illusions: US Foreign Policy in the 1990s, 1994; Soul of the World: Notes on the Future of Public Catholicism, 1995; Witness to Hope: The Biography of Pope John Paul II, 1999; The Truth of Catholicism: Ten Controversies Explored, 2001; The Courage To Be Catholic: Crisis, Reform, and the Future of the Church, 2002. Contributions: numerous publications. *Honours:* Six Hon. doctorates; Papal Cross, Pro Ecclesia et Pontifice, 2000. *Literary Agent:* Loretta Barrett, 101 Fifth Ave, New York, NY 10003, USA. *Address:* Ethics and Public Policy Centre, 1015 15th St NW, Suite 900, Washington, DC 20005, USA.

WEIGL, Bruce; Distinguished Prof., Poet, Writer, Ed. and Trans; b. 27 Jan. 1949, Lorain, OH, USA; m. Jean Kondo, one s. one d. *Education:* BA, Oberlin College, 1974; MA, University of New Hampshire, 1975; PhD, University of Utah, 1979. *Career:* Instructor in English, 1975–76, Distinguished Prof., 2000–, Lorain County Community College; Asst Prof. of English, University of Arkansas at Little Rock, 1979–81, Old Dominion University, Norfolk, 1981–86; Assoc. Prof. to Prof. of English, Pennsylvania State University at University Park, 1986–2000. *Publications:* poetry: Like a Sack Full of Old Quarrels, 1976; Executioner, 1977; A Romance, 1979; The Monkey Wars, 1984; Song of Napalm, 1988; What Saves Us, 1992; Sweet Lorain, 1996; Archeology of the Circle: New and Selected Poems, 1999; After the Others, The Unravelling Strangeness, The Circle of Hanh: A Memoir, 2000. Editor: The Giver of Morning: On the Poetry of Dave Smith, 1982; The Imagination as Glory: The Poetry of James Dickey (with T. R. Hummer), 1984; Charles Simic: Essays on the Poetry, 1996; Writing Between the Lines: An Anthology on War and Its Social Consequences (with Kevin Bowen), 1997; Mountain River: Vietnamese Poetry from the Wars, 1948–1993: A Bilingual Collection (with Kevin Bowen and Nguyan Ba Chung), 1998; other: Angel Riding the Beast (trans. from Romanian with author Lilliana Ursu), Poems from Captured Documents (trans. from Vietnamese with Nguyen); contributions: anthologies, reviews, quarterlies and journals. *Honours:* American Acad. of Poets Prize, 1979; Pushcart Prizes, 1980, 1985; Bread Loaf Writers' Conference Fellowship, 1981; National Endowment for the Arts Grant, 1988. *Address:* 41 Glenhurst Drive, Oberlin, OH 44074, USA. *E-mail:* BWeigl@loraincсc.edu.

WEIGLEY, Russell Frank; academic and writer; b. 2 July 1930, Reading, PA, USA; m. Emma Eleanor Seifrit 1963; one s. one d. *Education:* BA, Albright College, 1952; MA, 1953, PhD, 1956, University of Pennsylvania. *Career:* Instructor in History, 1956–58, Visiting Lecturer, 1958–63, University of Pennsylvania; Asst Prof. to Assoc. Prof. of History, Drexel Institute of Technology, 1958–62; Visiting Lecturer, Haverford College, 1961; Ed., Pennsylvania History, 1962–67; Assoc. Prof., 1962–64, Prof., 1964–85, Distinguished University Prof. of History, 1985–99, Prof. Emeritus, 1999–, Temple University; Visiting Prof., Dartmouth College, 1967–68, US Army War College, 1973–74; mem. American Historical Assn; American Philosophical Society; Organization of American Historians; Society for Military History; Society of American Historians. *Publications:* Quartermaster General of the Union Army, 1959; Towards an American Army: Military Thought from Washington to Marshall, 1962; History of the United States Army, 1967; American Military (ed.), 1969; The Partisan War: The South Carolina Campaign of 1780–1782, 1970; The American Way of War: A History of American Military Strategy and Policy, 1973; The Draft and Its Enemies: A Documentary History, 1974; New Dimensions in Military History (ed.), 1977; Eisenhower's Lieutenants: The Campaign of France and Germany, 1944–1945, 1981; Philadelphia: A 300-Year History (ed.), 1982; The Age of Battles: The Quest for Decisive Warfare from Breitenfeld to Waterloo, 1991; A Great Civil War: A Military and Political History, 2000. Contributions: scholarly books and journals. *Honours:* Guggenheim Fellowship, 1969–70; Hon. DHL, Albright College, 1979; Samuel Eliot Morison Award, 1989; Outstanding Book Award, Society for Military History, 1992. *Address:* 327 S Smedley Street, Philadelphia, PA 19103, USA.

WEIN, Elizabeth Eve, (Elizabeth Gatland); Writer and Folklorist; b. 2 Oct. 1964, New York, NY, USA; m. Tim Gatland 1996; two c. *Education:* BA, Yale Univ., 1986; MA, 1989, PhD, 1994, Univ. of Pennsylvania. *Career:* mem. Authors' Guild; SFWA; Society of Children's Book Writers and Illustrators. *Publications:* The Winter Prince, 1993; A Coalition of Lions, 2003; The Sunbird, 2004. Contributions: anthologies, 1993, 1995, 1997, 1998, 2003; encyclopedias, 1998, 2003. *Honours:* Jacob K. Javits Fellow, 1988–92. *Address:* c/o Writers House, 21 W 26th Street, New York, NY 10010, USA.

WEINBERG, Gerhard L(udwig); Emeritus Prof. of History and Writer; b. 1 Jan. 1928, Hannover, Germany; m. Janet I White, 29 April 1989, one s. *Education:* BA, New York State College for Teachers, 1948; MA, 1949, PhD, 1951, University of Chicago. *Career:* Emeritus Prof. of History, University of North Carolina at Chapel Hill; mem. American Historical Assn; Conference Group for Central European History; German Studies Assn; World War II Studies Assn. *Publications:* Germany and the Soviet Union, 1939–41, 1954; Hitlers Zweites Buch, 1961; The Foreign Policy of Hitler's Germany, 1933–36, 1970; The Foreign Policy of Hitler's Germany, 1937–39,

1980; World in the Balance: Behind the Scenes of World War II, 1981; A World at Arms: A Global History of World War II, 1994; Germany, Hitler and World War II, 1995. Contributions: Professional journals. *Honours:* American Historical Asscn Beer Prizes, 1971, 1994; German Studies Asscn Halverson Prize, 1981; Hon. LHD, 1989; Hon. DPhil, 2001. *Address:* 1416 Mt Willing Rd, Efland, NC 27243, USA.

WEINBERG, Steven; Prof. of Science and Author; b. 3 May 1933, New York, NY, USA; m. Louise Goldwasser, 6 July 1954, one d. *Education:* BA, Cornell University, 1954; Postgraduate Studies, Copenhagen Institute of Theoretical Physics, 1954–55; PhD, Princeton University, 1957. *Career:* Research Assoc. and Instructor, Columbia University, 1957–59; Research Physicist, Lawrence Radiation Laboratory, Berkeley, 1959–60; Faculty, 1960–64, Prof. of Physics, 1964–69, University of California at Berkeley; Visiting Prof., 1967–69, Prof. of Physics, 1979–83, MIT; Higgins Prof. of Physics, Harvard University, 1973–83; Senior Scientist, Smithsonian Astrophysics Laboratory, 1973–83; Josey Prof. of Science, University of Texas at Austin, 1982–; Senior Consultant, Smithsonian Astrophysics Observatory, 1983–; various visiting professorships and lectureships; mem. American Acad. of Arts and Sciences; American Mediaeval Acad.; American Philosophical Society; American Physical Society; Council on Foreign Relations; History of Science Society; International Astronomical Union; National Acad. of Science; Philosophical Society of Texas, pres., 1994; Royal Society; Texas Institute of Letters. *Publications:* Gravitation and Cosmology: Principles and Application of the General Theory of Relativity, 1972; The First Three Minutes: A Modern View of the Origin of the Universe, 1977; The Discovery of Subatomic Particles, 1982; Elementary Particles and the Laws of Physics (with R. Feynman), 1987; Dreams of a Final Theory, 1992; The Quantum Theory of Fields, Vol. I, Foundations, 1995, Vol. II, Modern Applications, 1996, Vol. III, Supersymmetry, 2000; Facing Up: Science and Its Cultural Adversaries, 2001. Contributions: books, periodicals and professional journals. *Honours:* J. Robert Oppenheimer Memorial Prize, 1973; Dannie Heineman Prize in Mathematical Physics, 1977; American Institute of Physics-US Steel Foundation Science Writing Award, 1977; Nobel Prize in Physics, 1979; Elliott Cresson Medal, Franklin Institute, 1979; Madison Medal, Princeton University, 1991; National Medal of Science, National Science Foundation, 1991; Andrew Gemant Prize, American Institute of Physics, 1997; Piazzi Prize, Governments of Sicily and Palermo, 1998; Lewis Thomas Prize for the Scientist as Poet, Rockefeller University, 1999. *Address:* c/o Dept of Physics, University of Texas at Austin, Austin, TX 78712, USA.

WEINBERGER, Caspar Willard, AB, MCL; American government official and publishing executive; b. 18 Aug. 1917, San Francisco; m. Jane Dalton 1942; one s. one d. *Education:* Harvard Coll. and Law School. *Career:* served with AUS 1941–45; with Heller, Ehrman, White and McAuliffe 1947–69, partner 1959–69; mem. Calif. State Legislature 1952–58; Vice-Chair. Calif. Repub. Cen. Cttee 1960–62, Chair. 1962–64; Chair. Calif. Govt Cttee on Org. and Econ. 1967–68; Dir of Finance, Calif. 1968–69; Chair. Fed. Trade Comm. 1970; Deputy Dir Office of Man. and Budget 1970–72, Dir 1972–73; Counsellor to Pres. 1973; Sec. of Health, Educ. and Welfare 1973–75; Sec. of Defense 1981–87; specialist in int. law and finance, Rogers & Wells, Washington 1988–94; Publr Forbes Magazine 1988–92, Chair. 1989–; Distinguished Visiting Prof. Inst. for Advanced Studies in the Humanities, Edin. Univ., UK 1988; Gen. Counsel for the Bechtel Group of Cos. including Bechtel Power Corpn and Bechtel Inc. 1975–80; Chair. Pres.'s Cttee on Mental Retardation 1973–75; mem. Pres.'s Foreign Intelligence Advisory Bd 1987–88; Chair. Bd USA-ROC Econ. Council 1990–94; Earl Mountbatten Memorial Lecture 1991; fmr Dir Pepsico Corpn, Quaker Oats Corpn, American Ditchley Foundation, Yosemite Inst.; fmr Treas. Episcopal Diocese of Calif.; fmr Pres. Nat. Trustees of the Nat. Symphony, Washington, DC; fmr mem. American Ass. Bd of Trustees, Trilateral Comm.; American Bar Asscn, State Bar Calif.; admitted to Dist of Columbia Bar 1990. *Publications:* Fighting for Peace 1990, The Next War (with Peter Schweizer) 1996, In the Arena 2000. *Honours:* Dr. hc (Leeds) 1989; Hon. DLitt (Buckingham) 1995; Harvard Univ. John F. Kennedy School of Govt Medal 1982, 1986; Hon. GBE (UK) 1988; Grand Cordon of the Order of the Rising Sun (Japan) 1988; Presidential Medal of Freedom (with Distinction) 1987. *Address:* Forbes Inc., 1101 17th Street, NW, Suite 406, Washington, DC 20036, USA.

WEINFIELD, Henry Michael; academic, poet and writer; b. 3 Jan. 1949, Montréal, QC, Canada. *Education:* BA, City College, CUNY, 1970; MA, SUNY at Binghamton, 1973; PhD, CUNY, 1985. *Career:* Lecturer, SUNY at Binghamton, 1973–74; Adjunct Lecturer, Lehman College, 1974–77, Baruch College, 1979–81, City College, 1982–83, CUNY; Adjunct Lecturer, 1983–84, Special Lecturer, 1984–91, New Jersey Institute of Technology; Asst Prof., 1991–96, Assoc. Prof., 1996–2003, Prof., 2003–, in Liberal Studies, Univ. of Notre Dame. *Publications:* Poetry: The Carnival Cantata, 1971; In the Sweetness of New Time, 1980; Sonnets Elegiac and Satirical, 1982. Other: The Poet Without a Name: Gray's Elegy and the Problem of History, 1991; The Collected Poems of Stéphane Mallarmé, (trans. and commentator), 1995; The Sorrows of Eros and Other Poems, 1999. Contributions: articles, poems, trans in many publications. *Honours:* Co-ordinating Council of Literary Magazines Award, 1975; National Endowment for the Humanities Fellowship, 1989. *Address:* Program of Liberal Studies, University of Notre Dame, Notre Dame, IN 46556, USA.

WEINSTEIN, Michael Alan; Political Philosopher, Asst Prof. and Writer; b. 24 Aug. 1942, New York, NY, USA; m. Deena Schneiweiss, 31 May 1964. *Education:* BA, summa cum laude, New York University, 1964; MA, 1965, PhD 1967, Western Reserve University. *Career:* Asst Prof., Western Reserve University, 1967, Virginia Polytechnic Institute, 1967–68, Purdue University, 1972–; Distinguished Prof. of Political Science, University of Wyoming, 1979. *Publications:* The Polarity of Mexican Thought: Instrumentalism and Finalism, 1976; The Tragic Sense of Political Life, 1977; Meaning and Appreciation: Time and Modern Political Life, 1978; The Structure of Human Life: A Vitalist Ontology, 1979; The Wilderness and the City: American Classical Philosophy as a Moral Quest, 1982; Unity and Variety in the Philosophy of Samuel Alexander, 1984; Finite Perfection: Reflections on Virtue, 1985; Culture Critique: Fernand Dumont and the New Quebec Sociology, 1985; Data Trash, 1994; Culture/Flesh: Explorations of Postcivilized Modernity, 1995. Contributions: Magazines and journals. *Honours:* Best Paper Prize, Midwest Political Science Asscn, 1969; Guggenheim Fellowship, 1974–75; Rockefeller Foundation Humanities Fellowship, 1976. *Address:* Dept of Political Science, Purdue University, West Lafayette, IN 47907, USA.

WEINTRAUB, Stanley; Prof. of Arts and Humanities Emeritus, Writer and Ed.; b. 17 April 1929, Philadelphia, PA, USA; m. Rodelle Horwitz 6 June 1954; two s. one d. *Education:* BS, West Chester State College, PA, 1949; MA, Temple Univ., 1951; PhD, Pennsylvania State Univ., 1956. *Career:* Instructor, 1953–59, Asst Prof., 1959–62, Assoc. Prof., 1962–65, Prof. of English, 1965–70, Research Prof., 1970–86, Evan Pugh Prof. of Arts and Humanities, 1986–2000, Prof. Emeritus, 2000–, Pennsylvania State Univ.; Visiting Prof., Univ. of California at Los Angeles, 1963, Univ. of Hawaii, 1973, Univ. of Malaya, 1977, National Univ. of Singapore, 1982; mem. Authors' Guild; National Book Critics Circle. *Publications:* Private Shaw and Public Shaw: A Dual Portrait of Lawrence of Arabia and George Bernard Shaw, 1963; The War in the Wards: Korea's Forgotten Battle, 1964; The Art of William Golding (with B. S. Oldsey), 1965; Reggie: A Portrait of Reginald Turner, 1965; Beardsley: A Biography, 1967; The Last Great Cause: The Intellectuals and the Spanish Civil War, 1968; Evolution of a Revolt: Early Postwar Writings of T. E. Lawrence (with R. Weintraub), 1968; Journey to Heartbreak: The Crucible Years of Bernard Shaw 1914–1918, 1971; Whistler: A Biography, 1974; Lawrence of Arabia: The Literary Impulse (with R. Weintraub), 1975; Aubrey Beardsley: Imp of the Perverse, 1976; Four Rossettis: A Victorian Biography, 1977; The London Yankees: Portraits of American Writers and Artists in England 1894–1914, 1979; The Unexpected Shaw: Biographical Approaches to G. B. Shaw and His Work, 1982; A Stillness Heard Round the World: The End of the Great War, 1985; Victoria: An Intimate Biography, 1987; Long Day's Journey into War: December 7, 1941, 1991; Bernard Shaw: A Guide to Research, 1992; Disraeli: A Biography, 1993; The Last Great Victory: The End of World War II, July/August 1945, 1995; Shaw's People, Victoria to Churchill, 1996; Albert, Uncrowned King, 1997; MacArthur's War: Korea and the Undoing of an American Hero, 2000; The Importance of Being Edward: King in Waiting, 1841–1901, 2000; Silent Night: The Remarkable 1914 Christmas Truce, 2001; Charlotte and Lionel: A Rothschild Love Story, 2003; General Washington's Christmas Farewell: A Mount Vernon Homecoming 1783, 2003. Other: ed. of over 20 vols. Contributions: professional journals. *Honours:* Guggenheim Fellowship, 1968–69; Distinguished Humanist Award, Pennsylvania Humanities Council, 1985. *Address:* 4 Winterfield Court, Beech Hill, Newark, DE 19711, USA. *E-mail:* sqw4@comcast.net.

WEIR, Anne; Writer; b. 9 Feb. 1942, Boston, Massachusetts, USA; three d. *Education:* BA, Smith and Swarthmore Colleges, 1964; MEd, University of Maine, 1984. *Publications:* A Book of Certainties, 1992; Marlowe: Being in the Life of the Mind, 1996; The Color Book, 1998. *Address:* PO Box 10364, Portland, ME 04104, USA.

WEIR, Hugh William Lindsay, DLitt; writer and publisher; b. 29 Aug. 1934; m. The Honourable Grania O'Brien 1973. *Education:* Trinity College, UIC, Trinity College, Dublin. *Career:* Managing Dir, Weir Publishing Group, Ballinakella Press and Bell'acards; mem. Irish Writers' Union. *Publications:* Hall Craig – Words on an Irish House; O'Brien People and Places; Houses of Clare; Ireland – A Thousand Kings; O'Connor People and Places; The Clare Young Environmentalists; One of Our Own: Memoirs of Change; Brian Boru: High King of Ireland, 941–1014. Other: Short Stories, academic articles/essays and topographical/historical contributions made to various anthologies and books. Contributions: The Other Clare; The Clare Champion; The Church of Ireland Gazette; The Catholic Twin Circle; English Digest. *Honours:* Oidhreacht Award. *Address:* Ballinakella Lodge, Whitegate, County Clare, Ireland.

WEISSBORT, Daniel, BA; academic, poet, translator and editor; b. 1 May 1935, London, England. *Education:* Queens' Coll., Cambridge. *Career:* co-founder (with Ted Hughes), Modern Poetry in Translation magazine 1966–83, Ed. relaunched version 1992–2004; Prof., Univ. of Iowa 1980, Prof. Emeritus of the Translation Program; Honorary Research Fellow, Dept of English, King's Coll. London. *Publications:* The Leaseholder 1971, In an Emergency 1972, Soundings 1977, Leaseholder: New and Collected Poems, 1965–85 1986, Inscription 1990, Lake 1993; ed. and translator of Russian literature. *Honours:* Arts Council Literature Award 1984. *Address:* Department of English Language & Literature, King's College London, Strand, London, WC2R 2LS, England.

WELCH, Liliane; Prof. of French Literature, Poet and Writer; b. 20 Oct. 1937, Luxembourg; m. Cyril Welch, one d. *Education:* BA, 1960, MA, 1961, University of Montana; PhD, Pennsylvania State University, 1964. *Career:* Asst Prof., East Carolina University, 1965–66, Antioch College, Ohio, 1966–67; Asst Prof., 1967–71, Assoc. Prof., 1971–72, Prof. of French Literature, 1972–2003, Mount Allison University; mem. Asscn of Italian-Canadian Poets; Federation of New Brunswick Writers; League of Canadian Poets; Letzebuerger Schriftsteller Verband. *Publications:* Emergence: Baudelaire, Mallarmé, Rimbaud, 1973; Winter Songs, 1973; Syntax of Ferment, 1979; Assailing Beats, 1979; October Winds, 1980; Brush and Trunks, 1981; From the Songs of the Artisans, 1983; Manstoma, 1985; Rest Unbound, 1985; Word-House of a Grandchild, 1987; Seismographs: Selected Essays and Reviews, 1988; Fire to the Looms Below, 1990; Life in Another Language, 1992; Von Menschen und Orten, 1992; Dream Museum, 1995; Fidelities, 1997; Frescoes: Travel Pieces, 1998; The Rock's Stillness (poems), 1999; Unlearning Ice (poems), 2001; Untethered in Paradise (prose and poems), 2002. Contributions: Professional and literary journals. *Honours:* Alfred Bailey Prize, 1986; Bressani Prize, 1992; Membre Correspondant de L'Institut Grand Ducal de Luxembourg, 1998. *Address:* PO Box 1652, Sackville, NB E4L 1G6, Canada.

WELCH, Robert; Prof. of English, Writer, Poet and Ed.; b. 25 Nov. 1947, Cork, Ireland; m. Angela Welch, 30 June 1970, three s. *Education:* BA, 1968, MA, 1971, National University of Ireland; PhD, University of Leeds, 1974. *Career:* Lecturer, University of Leeds, 1971–73, 1974–84, University of Ife, Nigeria, 1973–74; Visiting Lecturer, National University of Ireland, 1982; Prof. of English, 1984–, Head, Dept of English, Media and Theatre Studies, 1984–94, Dir, Centre for Irish Literature and Bibliography, 1994–, University of Ulster; Founder-General Ed., Ulster Editions and Monographs, 1988–. *Publications:* Irish Poetry from Moore to Yeats, 1980; The Way Back: George Moore's The Untilled Field and The Lake (ed.), 1982; A History of Verse from the Irish, 1789–1897, 1988; Literature and the Art of Creation: Essays in Honour of A. N. Jeffares (co-ed.), 1988; Muskerry (poems), 1991; Irish Writers and Religion (ed.), 1991; Changing States: Transformations in Modern Irish Writing, 1993; W. B. Yeats: Irish Folklore, Legend, and Myth (ed.), 1993; The Kilcolman Notebook (novel), 1994; The Oxford Companion to Irish Literature (ed.), 1996; Irish Myths, 1996; Patrick Falvin: New and Selected Poems (co-ed.), 1996; Groundwork (novel), 1997; Secret Societies (poems), 1997; Tearmann (novel), 1997; The Blue Formica Table (poems), 1998; A History of the Abbey Theatre, 1998; The Plays and Poems of J. M. Synge, 1999; The Concise Companion to Irish Literature, 2000. Contributions: books and periodicals. *Honours:* Visiting Fellow, St John's College, Oxford, 1986; Grants, Leverhulme Trust, 1989, Community Relations Council, 1990, British Acad., 1996; Critics Award, O'Reachtas, 1996. *Address:* 34 Station Rd, Portstewart, Co Derry BT55 7DA, Northern Ireland.

WELDON, Fay, CBE, MA, FRSA; British author; b. 22 Sept. 1931, Alvechurch, Worcs.; m.1st Ronald Weldon 1960 (divorced 1994); four s.; m. 2nd Nicholas Fox 1995. *Education:* Girls' High School, Christchurch, New Zealand, South Hampstead School for Girls and Univ. of St Andrews. *Career:* Chair. of Judges, Booker McConnell Prize 1983; Writer-in-Residence Savoy Hotel, London Oct.-Dec. 2002; fmr mem. Arts Council Literary Panel; mem. Video Censorship Appeals Cttee. *Theatre plays:* Words of Advice 1974, Friends 1975, Moving House 1976, Mr Director 1977, Action Replay 1979, I Love My Love 1981, Woodworm 1981, Jane Eyre 1986, The Hole in the Top of the World 1987, Jane Eyre (adaptation), Playhouse Theatre, London 1995, The Four Alice Bakers, Birmingham Repertory 1999; more than 30 television plays, dramatizations and radio plays. *Television:* Big Women (series), Channel 4 1999. *Publications:* novels: The Fat Woman's Joke 1967 (published in USA as And the Wife Ran Away 1968), Down Among the Women 1972, Female Friends 1975, Remember Me 1976, Little Sisters 1977 (USA Words of Advice), Praxis 1978, Puffball 1980, The President's Child 1982, The Life and Loves of a She-Devil 1984, The Shrapnel Academy 1986, The Heart of the Country 1987, The Hearts and Lives of Men 1987, The Rules of Life (novella) 1987, Leader of the Band 1988, The Cloning of Joanna May 1989, Darcy's Utopia 1990, Growing Rich 1992, Life Force 1992, Affliction 1994 (USA Trouble), Splitting 1995, Worst Fears 1996, Big Women 1997, Rhode Island Blues 2000, Bulgari Connection 2001, Godless in Eden (essays) 2000; children's books: Wolf the Mechanical Dog 1988, Party Puddle 1989, Nobody Likes Me! 1997; short story collections: Watching Me Watching You 1981, Polaris 1985, Moon Over Minneapolis 1991, Wicked Women 1995, Angel All Innocence and Other Stories 1995, A Hard Time to be a Father 1998, Nothing to Wear, Nowhere to Hide 2002; other: Letters to Alice 1984, Rebecca West 1985, Auto da Fay (autobiog.) 2002. *Honours:* Fellow City of Bath Coll. 1999; Hon. DLitt (Bath) 1989, (St Andrews) 1992, (Birmingham); Women in Publishing Pandora Award 1997. *Address:* Casarotto Co. Ltd, National House, 62/66 Wardour Street, London, W1V 3HP, England.

WELLS, Peter; Writer and Poet; b. 12 Jan. 1919, London, England; m. 1st Elisabeth Vander Meulen, deceased 1967, 1 daugher; m. 2nd Gillian Anne Hayes-Newington, 1988. *Education:* Diploma, Social Studies, University of London, 1970; Certificate, Psychiatric Social Work, University of Manchester, 1973. *Career:* mem. PEN; Society of Authors. *Publications:* Poetry Folios (co-ed.), 1942–46, 1951; Poems (retrospective collection), 1997; Six Poems (with illustrations), 1998. Contributions: anthologies and periodicals, including: Poetry (London); Poetry (Chicago); View; New English Weekly; Quarterly Review of Literature; The Dublin Magazine. *Address:* Model Farm, Linstead Magna, Halesworth, Suffolk, England.

WELLS, Peter Frederick, (John Flint); academic and writer; b. 28 Feb. 1918, New Zealand; m. 1st Jeanne Chiles 1945; three s.; m. 2nd Rita Davenport 1994. *Education:* MA, 1948, DipEd, 1949, University of Wales; DPhil, University of Waikato, New Zealand, 1971. *Career:* Head, Language Studies Dept, University of Waikato, 1961–73; Dir, Institute of Modern Languages, James Cook University of North Queensland, 1974–84; mem. Founder, Pres., New Zealand-Japan Society, Hamilton. *Publications:* Let's Learn French, 1963; Les Quatre Saisons, 1966; Let's Learn Japanese, 1968; Nihongo no Kakikata, 1971; A Description of Kalaw Kawaw Ya, 1976. Other: Anthology of Poems by Ishikawa Takuboku, 1972; Phonetics and Orthography of French, 1975; Three Loves and a Minesweeper, 1998; Myra Migrating, 1999. Contributions: Journal of Modern Languages and Literature; Bulletin de L'Asscn G. Budé; New Zealand Journal of French Studies; Education; LINQ; English Language and Literature Asscn. *Honours:* Order of the Sacred Treasure, Japan; Order of New Zealand. *Address:* 249 Bankwood Road, Chartwell, Hamilton, New Zealand.

WELLS, Robert; Poet and Trans; b. 17 Aug. 1947, Oxford, England. *Education:* King's College, Cambridge, 1965–68. *Career:* Teacher, University of Leicester, 1979–82. *Publications:* Shade Mariners (with Dick Davis and Clive Wilmer), 1970; The Winter's Task: Poems, 1977; The Georgics, by Virgil (trans.), 4 vols, 1981; Selected Poems, 1986; The Idylls, by Theocritus (trans.), 1988. Contributions: anthologies.

WELLS, Roger; Prof. of History and Writer; b. 30 Jan. 1947, London, England; Divorced, one s. one d. *Education:* BA, 1969, DPhil, 1978, University of York. *Career:* Lecturer, University of Wales, 1972–73, University of Exeter, 1973–75, University of York, 1975–76; Senior Lecturer, University of Brighton, 1976–95; Prof. of History, Christ Church University College, Canterbury, 1995–; mem. Royal Historical Society. *Publications:* Dearth and Distress in Yorkshire, 1793–1801, 1977; Riot and Political Disaffection in Nottinghamshire in the Age of Revolutions 1776–1803, 1983; Insurrection: The British Experience 1795–1803, 1983; Wretched Faces: Famine in Wartime England, 1793–1801, 1988; Class, Conflict and Protest in the English Countryside (with M. Reed), 1700–1880, 1990; Victorian Village, 1992; Crime, Protest and Popular Politics in Southern England c. 1740–1850 (with J. Rule), 1997. Contributions: Social History; Rural History; Southern History; Northern History; Policing and Society; Journal of Peasant Studies; Journal of Historical Geography; Local Historian; English Historical Review; Agricultural History Review; London Journal; Labour History Bulletin; Journal of Social Policy. *Address:* Christ Church University College, Canterbury, Kent CT1 1QU, England. *E-mail:* r.wells@cant.ac.uk.

WELLS, Stanley; Writer and Editor. *Career:* fmr Prof. of Shakespeare Studies, and Dir of the Shakespeare Institute, Univ. of Birmingham, 1988–97, now Emeritus Prof.; currently Chair., Shakespeare Birthplace Trust, Stratford. *Publications:* Oxford Shakespeare Topics (gen. ed. with Peter Holland); Shakespeare: A Reading Guide, 1969; Literature and Drama: With Special Reference to Shakespeare and His Contemporaries, 1970; Shakespeare: Select Bibliographical Guides (ed.), 1974; Shakespeare: An Illustrated Dictionary (ed.), 1978; Royal Shakespeare: Four Major Productions at Stratford-upon-Avon, 1977; Shakespeare, 1978; Modernizing Shakespeare's Spelling: With Three Studies of the Text of Henry V (with Gary Taylor), 1979; Re-editing Shakespeare for the Modern Reader, 1984; Twelfth Night: Critical Essays (ed.), 1986; The Cambridge Companion to Shakespeare (ed.), 1986; Shakespeare: A Bibliography, 1989; Shakespeare and the Moving Image: The Plays on Film and Television (ed. with Anthony Davies), 1994; Shakespeare: A Dramatic Career, 1994; Shakespeare—A Life in Drama, 1995; Shakespeare in the Theatre: An Anthology of Criticism (ed.), 1997; Shakespeare: The Poet and His Plays, 1997; Summerfolk: Essays Celebrating Shakespeare (ed.), 1997; A Dictionary of Shakespeare, 1998; Shakespeare and Race (co-ed. with Catherine Alexander), 2000; Oxford Companion to Shakespeare (ed. with Michael Dobson), 2001; Shakespeare and Sexuality (ed. with Catherine M. S. Alexander), 2001; Shakespeare Surveys (ed. with others), 2002; Shakespeare: For All Time, 2002; The Cambridge Companion to Shakespeare on Stage (ed. with Sarah Stanton), 2002; Shakespeare: An Oxford Guide (ed. with Lena Cowen Orlin), 2003; gen. ed., co-ed., numerous editions, anthologies and collections of Shakespeare's plays. *Address:* c/o Shakespeare Birthplace Trust, Shakespeare Centre, Henley St, Stratford-upon-Avon, Warwickshire CV37 6QW, England.

WELSH, Irvine, MBA; British writer; b. 1958, Edinburgh, Scotland. *Education:* Heriot-Watt Univ. *Publications:* Trainspotting, 1993; The Acid House, 1994; Marabou Stork Nightmares: A Novel, 1995; Ecstasy: Three Chemical Romances, 1996; The Wedding (with Nick Waplington), 1996; You'll Have Had Your Hole (play), 1997; Filth: A Novel, 1998; Glue, 2000; Porno, 2002; Soul Crew (film screenplay, also dir), 2003. Contributions: Daily Telegraph; anthologies incl.: Children of Albion Rovers, 1996; Disco Biscuits, 1996; Ahead of its Time, 1997; The Weekenders, 2002. *Address:* c/o Jonathon Cape, 20 Vauxhall Bridge Road, London SW1V 2SA, England.

WELSH, Louise, BA; British novelist; b. 1968, Edinburgh, Scotland. *Education:* Glasgow Univ., Univ. of Strathclyde. *Career:* bookshop owner. *Plays:*

The Cutting Room (adaptation of novel) 2004. *Publications:* The Cutting Room 2002, Tamburlaine Must Die 2004. *Honours:* CWA John Creasey Memorial Dagger, Saltire First Book Award (jt winner). *Address:* c/o Canongate Books, 14 High Street, Edinburgh, EH1 1TE, Scotland. *Website:* www.canongate.co.uk.

WELTNER, Peter (Nissen); Prof. of English and Writer; b. 12 May 1942, Plainfield, NJ, USA; Partner Atticus Carr. *Education:* BA, Hamilton College, 1964; PhD, Indiana University, 1970. *Career:* Prof. of English, San Francisco State University, 1969–. *Publications:* Beachside Entries-Specific Ghosts, 1989; Identity and Difference, 1990; In a Time for Combat for the Angel, 1991; The Risk of His Music, 1997; How the Body Prays, 1999. *Honours:* O. Henry Prizes, 1993, 1998; Book of the Year Silver Award, ForeWord Magazine. *Address:* 548 Douglass St, San Francisco, CA 94114-2728, USA.

WELTON, Matthew; British poet and editor; b. 1969, Nottingham, England. *Career:* Ed., Stand Magazine; teacher of creative writing, Bolton Inst. *Publications:* Slag Heap, The Book of Matthew (Aldburgh Best First Collection Prize) 2003; contrib. to anthologies, including First Pressings, New Poetries 2. *Honours:* Eric Gregory Award 1997. *Address:* Editorial Office, Stand Magazine, School of English, Leeds University, Leeds, LS2 9JT, England.

WENDT, Albert; Prof. of English, Writer, Poet and Dramatist; b. 27 Oct. 1939, Apia, Western Samoa; one s. two d. *Education:* MA, History, Victoria University, Wellington, 1964. *Career:* Prof. of Pacific Literature, University of the South Pacific, Suva, Fiji, 1982–87; Prof. of English, University of Auckland, 1988–. *Publications:* Fiction: Sons for the Return Home, 1973; Pouliuli, 1977; Leaves of the Banyan Tree, 1979; Ola, 1990; Black Rainbow, 1992. Short Stories: Flying-Fox in a Freedom Tree, 1974; The Birth and Death of the Miracle Man, 1986; The Best of Albert Wendt's Short Stories, 1999; The Mango's Kiss, 2003. Plays: Comes the Revolution, 1972; The Contract, 1972; The Songmaker's Chair, 2003. Poetry: Inside Us the Dead: Poems 1961–74, 1975; Shaman of Visions, 1984; Photographs, 1995; The Book of the Black Star, 2002. *Honours:* Landfall Prize, 1963; Wattie Award, 1980; Commonwealth Book Prize, South East Asia and the Pacific, 1991; Companion of the New Zealand Order of Merit, 2001. *Address:* c/o Dept of English, University of Auckland, Private Bag, Auckland, New Zealand.

WENNER, Jann S.; American publisher; *Editor-in-Chief, Rolling Stone*; b. 7 Jan. 1946, New York, NY; m. Jane Schindelheim (divorced); three s. *Career:* founder, Ed.-in-chief and Publisher, Rolling Stone magazine 1967–; TV appearances include Crime Story 1987–88; currently oversees Us and Men's Journal magazines; Chair., Wenner Media Inc. *Film appearances:* Up Your Legs Forever 1970, Perfect 1985, Jerry Maguire 1996, Almost Famous 2000. *Publications include:* Lennon Remembers (ed.) 1972, 20 Years of Rolling Stone: What a Long Strange Trip It's Been 1987, Rolling Stone Environmental Reader 1992. *Address:* Rolling Stone, Wenner Media Inc., 1290 Avenue of the Americas, New York, NY 10104, USA. *Website:* www.rollingstone.com.

WENTWORTH, Wendy (see Chaplin, Jenny).

WERBER, Bernard; French writer; b. Sept. 1961, Toulouse. *Education:* Ecole Supérieure de Journalisme de Paris. *Career:* scientific reviewer, Nouvel Observateur 1984–90. *Publications:* novels: The Ants 1991, The Day of the Ants 1992, The Secret Book of the Ants 1993, The Thanatonautes 1994, The Revolution of the Ants 1996, The Journey's Book 1997, The Father of our Fathers 1998. *Literary Agent:* Jacqueline Farvero, 22 rue Huygens, Paris 75014, France. *E-mail:* bwerber@free.fr. *Website:* www.bernardwerber.com.

WERTENBAKER, Timberlake, FRSL; British playwright; m. John Man; one d. *Career:* Resident Playwright, Royal Court Theatre 1984–85. *Plays include:* (for the Soho-Poly): Case to Answer 1980; (for the Women's Theatre Group): New Anatomies 1982; (for the Royal Court): Abel's Sister 1984, The Grace of Mary Traverse 1985, Our Country's Good 1988, Three Birds Alighting on a Field 1991, Credible Witness 2001; (for Out of Joint): The Break of Day 1995; (for RSC): The Love of the Nightingale 1988; (for Hampstead Theatre): After Darwin 1998; (for Birmingham Rep.): The Ash Girl 2000; (for Theatre Royal, Bath): Galileo's Daughter 2004; (for RSC): trans. Arianne Mnouchkine's Mephisto, trans. Sophocles' Thebans; (for San Francisco ACT): trans. Euripides' Hecuba; (for Peter Hall Co): trans. Eduardo de Filippo's Filumena 1998, Anouilh's Wild Orchids (Chichester) 2002; other trans. include Successful Strategies, False Admissions, La Dispute (Marivaux), Come tu mi vuoi (Pirandello), Pelleas and Mélisande (Maeterlinck). *Radio includes:* Credible Witness, Dianeira, Hecuba (trans. and adaptation), The H. File (adaptation of novel by Ismail Kaduré). *Television:* Belle and the Beast (BBC). *Films:* The Children (Channel 4), Do Not Disturb (BBC TV). *Publications:* Timberlake Wertenbaker: Plays 1996, The Break of Day 1996, After Darwin 1999, Filumena 1999, The Ash Girl 2000, Credible Witness 2001, Timberlake Wertenbaker: Plays 2 2002. *Honours:* Dr hc (Open Univ.); Plays and Players Most Promising Playwright (for The Grace of Mary Traverse) 1985, Evening Standard Most Promising Playwright, Olivier Play of the Year (for Our Country's Good) 1988, Eileen Anderson Cen. Drama Award (for The Love of the Nightingale) 1989, Critics' Circle Best West End Play 1991, Writers' Guild Best West End Play, Susan Smith Blackburn Award (for Three Birds Alighting on a Field) 1992, Mrs Giles Whiting Award (for gen. body of work) 1989. *Address:* c/o Casarotto Ramsay, National House, 60–66 Wardour Street, London, W1V 4ND, England.

WESKER, Arnold; Dramatist, Playwright and Dir; b. 24 May 1932, London, England; m. Dusty Bicker, two s. two d. *Career:* mem. International Playwrights Committee, pres., 1979–83; International Theatre Institute, chair., British Centre, 1978–82. *Publications:* Chicken Soup with Barley, 1959; Roots, 1959; I'm Talking About Jerusalem, 1960; The Wesker Trilogy, 1960; The Kitchen, 1961; Chips with Everything, 1962; The Four Seasons, 1966; Their Very Own and Golden City, 1966; The Friends, 1970; Fears of Fragmentation (essays), 1971; Six Sundays in January (short stories), 1971; The Old Ones, 1972; The Journalists, 1974; Love Letters on Blue Paper (short stories), 1974; Say Goodbye!: You May Never See Them Again (with John Allin), 1974; Words – As Definitions of Experience, 1976; The Wedding Feast, 1977; Journey Into Journalism, 1977; Said the Old Man to the Young Man (short stories), 1978; The Merchant (renamed Shylock), 1978; Fatlips, 1978; The Journalists: A Triptych, 1979; Caritas, 1981; Distinctions (essays), 1985; Yardsale, 1987; Whatever Happened to Betty Lemon, 1987; Little Old Lady, 1988; Shoeshine, 1989; Collected Plays, 7 vols, 1989–97; As Much As I Dare (autobiog.), 1994; Circles of Perception, 1996; Break, My Heart, 1997; Denial, 1997; The Birth of Shylock and the Death of Zero Mostel (diaries), 1997; The King's Daughters (short stories), 1998; Barabbas (play for TV), 2000; Groupie (play for radio and stage), 2001; Longitude (adaptation for stage), 2002. Contributions: Stage, film, radio and television. *Honours:* FRSL, 1985; Hon. DLitt, University of East Anglia, 1989; Hon. Fellow, Queen Mary and Westfield College, London, 1995; Hon. DHL, Denison University, Ohio, 1997. *Address:* Hay on Wye, Hereford HR3 5RJ, England. *E-mail:* wesker@compuserve.com. *Website:* www.arnoldwesker.com.

WEST, Cornel Ronald, AB, MA, PhD; academic and writer; b. 2 June 1953, Tulsa, Oklahoma, USA; m. 1st (divorced); one s.; m. 2nd (divorced); m. 3rd Elleni West. *Education:* Harvard University, Princeton University. *Career:* Asst Prof. of the Philosophy of Religion, Union Theological Seminary, New York City, 1977–83, 1988; Assoc., Yale University Divinity School, 1984–87, University of Paris, 1987; Prof., Princeton University, 1989–94, 2002–, Harvard University, 1994–2002. *Publications:* Theology in the Americas: Detroit II Conference Papers (ed. with Caridad Guidote and Margaret Coakley), 1982; Prophesy Deliverance!: An Afro-American Revolutionary Christianity, 1982; Post-Analytic Philosophy (with John Rajchman), 1985; Prophetic Fragments, 1988; The American Evasion of Philosophy: A Genealogy of Pragmatism, 1989; Breaking Bread: Insurgent Black Intellectual Life (with Bell Hooks), 1991; The Ethical Dimensions of Marxist Thought, 1991; Out There: Marginalization and Contemporary Cultures (co-ed.), 1991; Race Matters, 1993; Keeping Faith: Philosophy and Race in America, 1993; Beyond Eurocentrism and Multiculturalism, 1993; The Cornel West Reader, 1999; The African American Century: How Black Americans Have Shaped Our Country (with Henry Louis Gates Jr), 2000. Contributions: newspapers and magazines. *Address:* c/o Harvard University, Cambridge, MA 02138, USA.

WEST, Douglas (see Tubb, Edwin Charles).

WEST, Kathleene; Prof. of English, Poet and Ed.; b. 28 Dec. 1947, Genoa, NE, USA. *Education:* BA, 1967, PhD, 1986, University of Nebraska; MA, University of Washington, 1975. *Career:* Assoc. Prof. of English, New Mexico State University, 1987–; Poetry Ed., Puerto del Sol, 1995–; mem. Associated Writing Programs; Barbara Pym Society; PEN. *Publications:* Land Bound, 1977; Water Witching, 1984; Plainswoman, 1985; The Farmer's Daughter, 1990. Contributions: Reviews, quarterlies, and journals. *Honours:* Fulbright Scholar, Iceland, 1983–85. *Address:* c/o Dept of English, Box 3001, New Mexico State University, Las Cruces, NM 88003, USA.

WEST, Nigel; Writer; b. 8 Nov. 1951, London, England; m. 15 June 1979, divorced 1996, one s. one d. *Education:* University of Grenoble; University of Lille; University of London. *Career:* BBC TV, 1977–82. *Publications:* Spy, 1980; A Matter of Trust: M15 1945–72, 1982; Unreliable Witness, 1984; Carbo M15, 1981, M16, 1983, 1985; GCHQ, 1986; Molehunt, 1986; The Friends, 1987; Games of Intelligence, 1990; Seven Spies who Changed the World, 1991; Secret War, 1992; The Illegals, 1993; Faber Book of Espionage, 1993; Faber Book of Treachery, 1995; Secret War for the Falklands, 1997; Crown Jewels, 1998; Counterfeit Spies, 1998; Venona, 1999; The Third Secret, 2000. Contributions: Times; Intelligence Quarterly. *Honours:* The Expert's Expert, Observer, 1989. *Address:* Westintel Research Ltd, PO Box 2, Goring on Thames, Berkshire RG8 9SB, England. *E-mail:* nigel@westintel.co.uk.

WEST, Owen (see Koontz, Dean Ray).

WEST, Paul Noden, MA; American academic and writer; b. 23 Feb. 1930, Eckington, Derbyshire, England. *Education:* University of Oxford, Columbia University. *Career:* Asst Prof., 1957–58, Assoc. Prof. of English, 1958–60, Memorial University, NF; Faculty, 1962–68, Prof. of English and Comparative Literature, 1968–95, Prof. Emeritus, 1995–, Pennsylvania State University; several visiting professorships and writer-in-residencies. *Publications:* Byron and the Spoiler's Art, 1960; I Said the Sparrow, 1963; The Snow Leopard, 1965; Tenement of Clay, 1965; The Wine of Absurdity, 1966; Alley Jaggers, 1967; I'm Expecting to Live Quite Soon, 1970; Words for a Deaf Daughter, 1970; Caliban's Filibuster, 1972; Colonel Mint, 1973; Gala, 1976; The Very Rich Hours of Count von Stauffenberg, 1980; Out of My Depths: A Swimmer in the Universe, 1983; Rat Man of Paris, 1986; Sheer Fiction, 1987; The Universe and Other Fiction, 1988; The Place in Flowers Where Pollen Rests, 1988; Lord Byron's Doctor, 1989; Portable People, the Women of Whitechapel and Jack the Ripper, 1991; Sheer Fiction, II, 1991; James Ensor, 1991; Love's Mansion, 1992; Sheer Fiction, III, 1994; A Stroke of Genius, 1995; The Tent of Orange Mist, 1995; My Mother's Music, 1996; Sporting with Amaryllis, 1996; Terrestrials, 1997; Life With Swan, 1999; O.K.: The Corral, the Earps, and Doc Holliday, 2000; The Dry Danube: A Hitler Forgery, 2000; The Secret Lives of Words, 2000; A Fifth of November, 2001; Master Class, 2001; New Portable People, 2001. Contributions: periodicals. *Honours:* Chevalier, Ordre des Arts et des Lettres; Guggenheim Fellowship, 1963; Aga Khan Fiction Prize, 1973; National Endowment for the Arts Fellowships, 1979, 1984; Hazlett Memorial Award, 1981; American Acad. of Arts and Letters Award, 1985; Literary Lion, New York Public Library, 1987; Pushcart Prizes, 1987, 1991; Lannan Fiction Award, 1993; Art of Fact Prize, SUNY, 2000. *Literary Agent:* Elaine Markson Agency, 44 Greenwich Avenue, New York, NY 10011, USA.

WESTHEIMER, David, (Z. Z. Smith); Writer and Poet; b. 11 April 1917, Houston, TX, USA; m. Doris Rothstein Kahn, 9 Oct. 1945, two s. *Education:* BA, Rice Institute, Houston, 1937. *Career:* mem. California Writers' Club; Retd Officers' Asscn; Writers' Guild of America West. *Publications:* Summer on the Water, 1948; The Magic Fallacy, 1950; Watching Out for Dulie, 1960; This Time Next Year, 1963; Von Ryan's Express, 1964; My Sweet Charlie, 1965; Song of the Young Sentry, 1968; Lighter Than a Feather, 1971; Over the Edge, 1972; Going Public, 1973; The Aulia Gold, 1974; The Olmec Head, 1974; Von Ryan's Return, 1980; Rider on the Wind, 1984; Sitting it Out, 1992; The Great Wounded Bird (poems), 2000; Delay en Route, 2002. *Honours:* Texas Review Press Poetry Prize, 2000. *Address:* 11722 Darlington Ave, No. 2, Los Angeles, CA 90049, USA.

WESTLAKE, Donald Edwin, (John B. Allen, Curt Clark, Tucker Coe, Timothy J. Culver, Samuel Holt, Richard Stark); Author; b. 1933, Brooklyn, NY, USA; m. 3rd Abigail Adams; four s. *Education:* Champlain College, Plattsburgh, NY; Harpur College, now the State Univ. of New York at Binghamton. *Publications:* The Mercenaries, 1960; Killing Time, 1961; 361, 1962; Killy, 1963; Pity Him Afterwards, 1964; The Fugitive Pigeon, 1964; The Busy Body, 1966; The Spy in the Ointment, 1966; God Save the Mark, 1967; Philip (children's), 1967; Who Stole Sassi Manoon?, 1968; The Curious Facts Preceding My Execution and Other Fictions, 1968; Somebody Owes Me Money, 1969; Up Your Banners, 1969; Adios, Scheherazade, 1970; The Hot Rock, 1970; I Gave at the Office, 1971; Under an English Heaven, 1972; Cops and Robbers, 1972; Bank Shot, 1972; Gangway (with Brian Garfield), 1973; Help, I'm Being Held Prisoner, 1974; Jimmy the Kid, 1974; Two Much, 1975; Brother's Keepers, 1975; Dancing Aztecs, 1976; Enough, 1977; Nobody's Perfect, 1977; Castle in the Air, 1980; Kahawa, 1982; Why Me?, 1983; A Likely Story, 1984; Levine (short stories), 1984; High Adventure, 1985; Transylvania Station (with Abby Westlake), 1986; High Jinx (with Abby Westlake), 1986; Good Behaviour, 1987; The Hood House Heist, 1987; The Maltese Herring, 1988; Way Out West, 1988; Double Crossing, 1988; Trust Me on This, 1988; Sacred Monster, 1989; Tomorrow's Crimes (short stories), 1989; Drowned Hopes, 1990; Humans, 1992; Don't Ask, 1993; Baby Would I Lie? A Romance of the Ozarks, 1994; Smoke, 1995; The Ax, 1997; What's the Worse that Could Happen?, 1997; A Good Story and Other Stories, 1999; Payback, 1999; The Hook, 2000; Bad News: A Dortmunder Novel, 2001; Firebreak, 2001; Put a Lid on It, 2002; Money for Nothing, 2003. As John B. Allen: Elizabeth Taylor: A Fascinating Story of America's Most Talented Actress and the World's Most Beautiful Woman, 1961. As Curt Clark: Anarchaos, 1966. As Tucker Coe: Kinds of Love, Kinds of Death, 1966; Murder Among Children, 1967; Wax Apple, 1970; A Jade in Aries, 1970; Don't Lie to Me, 1972. As Timothy J. Culver: Ex Officio, 1970. As Samuel Holt: One of us is Wrong, 1986; I Know a Trick Worth Two of That, 1986; What I Tell You Three Times is False, 1987; The Fourth Dimension is Death, 1989. As Richard Stark: The Hunter, 1962; The Man with the Getaway Face, 1963; The Outfit, 1963; The Mourner, 1963; The Score, 1964; The Juggler, 1965; The Seventh, 1966; The Handle, 1966; The Rare Coin Score, 1967; The Green Eagle Score, 1967; The Damsel, 1967; The Black Ice Score, 1968; The Sour Lemon Score, 1969; The Dame, 1969; The Blackbird, 1969; Lemons Never Lie, 1971; Deadly Edge, 1971; Slayground, 1971; Plunder Squad, 1972; Butcher's Moon, 1974; Child Heist, 1974; Comeback, 1998; Backflash, 1998; Flashfire, 2000; Breakout, 2002. Other: screenplays, ed. of anthologies. Contributions: Alfred Hitchcock's Mystery Magazine. *Honours:* Three Edgar Awards; Grand Master, MWA; Lifetime Achievement Award, Bouchercon Committee, 1997. *Address:* c/o Warner Books, 1271 Avenue of the Americas, New York, NY 10020, USA. *Website:* www.donaldwestlake.com.

WESTON, Corinne Comstock, BA, PhD; academic and historian; b. 8 Dec. 1919, Castle Hill, Maine, USA; m. Arthur Weston 1947. *Education:* University of Maine, Columbia University. *Career:* Instructor, University of Maine, 1946–47, 1948–49; Lecturer, Columbia University, 1947–48, 1949–51; Asst Prof. to Prof., University of Houston, 1952–63; Assoc. Prof., Hunter College, CUNY, 1965–68; Prof., 1969–88, Prof. Emeritus, 1988–, Lehman College, CUNY; mem. American Historical Asscn; Royal Historical Society, 1973–97. *Publications:* Cardinal Documents in British History, 1951; British Constitutional History Since 1832, 1957; English Constitutional Theory and the House of Lords, 1556–1832, 1965; Subjects and Sovereigns: The Grand Controversy Over Legal Sovereignty in Stuart England, 1981; The House of Lords and Ideological Politics, 1995. Contributions: scholarly publications. *Honours:* Research Awards, CUNY, 1979–88; National Endowment for the Humanities Research Travel Grant, 1986; Special Recognition for Original Research, Annales, University of Paris, 1986; John Frederick Lewis Award, American Philosophical Society, 1995. *Address:* 200 Central Park S, New York, NY 10019, USA.

WESTON, Helen Gray (see Daniels, Dorothy).

WEVILL, David (Anthony); Lecturer and Poet; b. 15 March 1935, Yokohama, Japan; m. Assia Gutman 1960. *Education:* BA, Caius Coll., Cambridge, 1957. *Career:* Lecturer, Univ. of Texas, Austin. *Publications:* Penguin Modern Poets, 1963; Birth of a Spark, 1964; A Christ of the Ice Floes, 1966; Firebreak, 1971; Where the Arrow Falls, 1973; Other Names for the Heart: New and Selected Poems, 1964–84, 1985; Figures of Eight, 1987; Departures: Selected Poems, 2003. Other: trans. of Hungarian poetry. *Address:* Dept of English, University of Texas at Austin, Austin, TX 78712, USA.

WHALEN, Terry Anthony, BA, MA, PhD; academic, writer and editor; *Professor of English, St Mary's University*; b. 1 Feb. 1944, Halifax, NS, Canada; m. Maryann Antonia Walters, 30 Feb. 1966, two s. two d. *Education:* Saint Mary's University, University of Melbourne, University of Oxford, University of Ottawa. *Career:* Tutor, University of Sydney, 1966, University of Melbourne, 1967; Lecturer, 1968–70, Asst Prof., 1970–76, 1978–80, Assoc. Prof., 1981–85, Prof. of English, 1985–, St Mary's University; Teaching Fellow, University of Ottawa, 1976–77; Ed., Atlantic Provinces Book Review, 1980–90; Adjunct Graduate Prof. of English, Dalhousie University, 1996–; mem. Writers Federation of Nova Scotia; Asscn of Canadian University Teachers of English; Northeast MLA; MLA; Philip Larkin Society. *Publications:* Philip Larkin and English Poetry, 1986; Bliss Carman and His Works, 1983; The Atlantic Anthology: Criticism (ed.), 1985; Charles G. D. Roberts and His Works, 1989; Routledge Encyclopaedia of Post-Colonial Literature in English (contributor), 1994. Contributions: books, journals and periodicals. *Honours:* British Commonwealth Scholarship, 1966–68; Election to Council Mem. Status, Writers' Federation of Nova Scotia; numerous grants. *Address:* 26 Oceanview Drive, Purcells Cove, Halifax, NS B3P 2H3, Canada.

WHALLON, William; Poet and Writer; b. 24 Sept. 1928, Richmond, IN, USA. *Education:* BA, McGill University, 1950. *Career:* Fellow, Center for Hellenic Studies, 1962; Fulbright Prof. in Comparative Literature, University of Bayreuth, 1985. *Publications:* A Book of Time (poems), 1990; Giants in the Earth (ed.), 1991; The Oresteia/Apollo & Bacchus (scenarios), 1997. *Address:* 1655 Walnut Heights, East Lansing, MI 48823, USA.

WHEATCROFT, John Stewart; Prof., Writer and Poet; b. 24 July 1925, Philadelphia, Pennsylvania, USA; m. 1st Joan Mitchell Osborne, 10 Nov. 1952, divorced 1974, two s. one d.; m. 2nd Katherine Whaley Warner, 14 Nov. 1992. *Education:* BA, Bucknell University, 1949; MA, 1950, PhD, 1960, Rutgers University. *Publications:* Poetry: Death of a Clown, 1963; Prodigal Son, 1967; A Voice from the Hump, 1977; Ordering Demons, 1981; The Stare on the Donkey's Face, 1990; Random Necessities, 1997. Fiction: Edie Tells, 1975; Catherine, Her Book, 1983; The Beholder's Eye, 1987; Killer Swan, 1992; Mother of All Loves, 1994; Trio with Four Players, 1995; The Education of Malcolm Palmer, 1997. Other: Slow Exposures (short stories), 1986; Our Other Voices (ed.), 1991. Contributions: New York Times; New York Times Book Review; Hartford Courant; Herald Tribune; Harper's Bazaar; Mademoiselle; Yankee; many literary magazines. *Honours:* Alcoa Playwriting Award, 1966; National Educational Television Award, 1967; Yaddo Fellowships, 1972, 1985; MacDowell Colony Fellowship, 1973; Fellowships, Virginia Center for the Creative Arts, 1976, 1978, 1980, 1982. *Address:* 350 River Rd, Lewisburg, PA 17837, USA.

WHEELER, Kate, (Katherine Frazier Wheeler); Buddhist Nun, Teacher and Writer; b. 27 July 1955, Tulsa, OK, USA. *Education:* BA, Rice University, 1977; MA, Stanford University, 1981. *Career:* Ordained Buddhist nun, Mahasi Sasana Yeiktha, Rangoon, 1988; Teacher of meditation; mem. Insight Meditation Society (board mem.). *Publications:* Lo Esperado y lo vivado (co-trans.), 1984; In This Very Life: The Liberation Teachings of the Buddha (ed.), 1992; Not Where I Started From (short stories), 1993; When Mountains Walked, 2000. Contributions: periodicals. *Honours:* O. Henry Awards, 1982, 1993; Pushcart Press Prize, 1983–84; Best American Short Stories Prize, Houghton Mifflin Co, 1992; National Education Asscn Grant, 1994; Whiting Foundation Award, 1994. *Address:* 72 Rev Nazarene Properzi Way, Somerville, MA 02143, USA.

WHEELER, Sara, FRSL; British travel writer, journalist and broadcaster; pnr; one s. *Education:* Univ. of Oxford. *Career:* mem. RSL (mem. of council); contrib. to Night Waves (BBC Radio 3), Excess Baggage (BBC Radio 4). *Publications:* Evia: An Island Apart 1992, Travels in a Thin Country: A Journey Through Chile 1995, Terra Incognita: Travels in Antarctica 1997, Dear Daniel: Letters from Antarctica 1997, Majestic Jaipur 1997, Amazonian: Penguin Book of Women's New Travel Writing (ed. with Dea

Birkett) 1998, Greetings from Antarctica 2001, Cherry: A Life of Apsley Cherry-Garrard 2001, Too Close to the Sun. *Address:* c/o Royal Society of Literature, Somerset House, Strand, London, WC2R 1LA, England.

WHEELWRIGHT, Julie Diana; Writer and Broadcaster; b. 2 June 1960, Farnborough, Kent, England. *Education:* BA, University of British Columbia; MA, University of Sussex. *Career:* Reporter, Vancouver Sun, 1980; Pres., Canadian University Press, 1981; Consultant, Open University, 1991; mem. Writers Guild; Institute of Historical Research; Royal Holloway, University of London, hon. research fellow. *Publications:* Amazons and Military Maids, 1989; The Fatal Lover, 1992. Contributions: newspapers and journals. *Honours:* Canada Council Non-Fiction Writers Grants, 1990–91, 1994–95. *Address:* 5 Cleaver St, London SE11 4DP, England.

WHELAN, Peter; Playwright; b. 3 Oct. 1931, Newcastle-under-Lyme, England. *Education:* Graduated, University of Keele, Staffordshire, 1955. *Career:* Advertising Copywriter and Dir, 1959–90; Assoc., RSC, 1998–. Plays produced and published: Double Edge (co-author), 1975; Captain Swing, 1978; The Accrington Pals, 1981; Clay, 1982; The Bright and Bold Design, 1991; The School of Night, 1992; Shakespeare Country, 1993; The Tinderbox, 1994; Divine Right, 1996; The Herbal Bed, 1997; Nativity (co-author), 1999; A Russian in the Woods, 2001. *Honours:* Lloyds Private Banking Playwright of the Year, 1996; TMA Regional Theatre Awards, Best New Play, 1996. *Literary Agent:* The Agency, 24 Pottery Lane, Holland Park, London W11 4LZ, England.

WHITBOURN, John; Writer; b. 23 March 1958, Godalming, Surrey, England; m. Elizabeth Caroline Gale 1982; one s. two d. *Education:* BA, Archaeology, University College, Cardiff, 1981. *Publications:* Binscombe Tales, 1989; Rollover Night, 1990; A Dangerous Energy, 1992; Popes and Phantoms, 1993; To Build Jerusalem, 1995; The Binscombe Tales, two vols, 1998–99; The Royal Changeling, 1998; Downs-Lord Dawn, 1999; Downs-Lord Day, 2000; Downs-Lord Doomsday, 2002. *Honours:* BBC-Gollancz First Fantasy Novel Prize, 1991. *Address:* c/o Colin Smythe Ltd, PO Box 6, Gerrards Cross, Buckinghamshire SL9 8XA, England. *Website:* www.btinternet.com/~john.whitbourn.

WHITE, Edmund Valentine, III, BA; writer; b. 13 Jan. 1940, Cincinnati, OH, USA. *Education:* University of Michigan. *Career:* writer, Time-Life Books, New York City, 1962–70; Senior Ed., Saturday Review, New York City, 1972–73; Asst Prof. of Writing Seminars, Johns Hopkins University, 1977–79; Adjunct Prof., Columbia University School of the Arts, 1981–83; Exec. Dir, New York Institute for the Humanities, 1982–83; Prof., Brown University, 1990–92; Prof., Princeton University, 1999. *Publications:* Fiction: Forgetting Elena, 1973; Nocturnes for the King of Naples, 1978; A Boy's Own Story, 1982; Aphrodisiac (with others), 1984; Caracole, 1985; The Darker Proof: Stories from a Crisis (with Adam Mars-Jones), 1987; The Beautiful Room is Empty, 1988; Skinned Alive, 1995; The Farewell Symphony, 1997; The Married Man, 2000; Fanny: A Fiction, 2003. Non-Fiction: The Joy of Gay Sex: An Intimate Guide for Gay Men to the Pleasures of a Gay Lifestyle (with Charles Silverstein), 1977; States of Desire: Travels in Gay America, 1980; The Faber Book of Gay Short Fiction (ed.), 1991; Genet: A Biography, 1993; The Selected Writings of Jean Genet (ed.), 1993; The Burning Library (essays), 1994; Our Paris, 1995; Proust, 1998; The Flâneur, 2001. Contributions: many periodicals. *Honours:* Ingram Merrill Foundation Grants, 1973, 1978; Guggenheim Fellowship, 1983; American Acad. and Institute of Arts and Letters Award, 1983; Chevalier, Ordre des Arts et des Lettres, 1993. *Literary Agent:* International Creative Management, 40 W 57th Street, New York, NY 10019, USA.

WHITE, Howard, ; writer, poet, editor and publisher; b. 18 April 1945, Abbotsford, BC, Canada; m.; two s. *Career:* founder, Ed., Publisher, Peninsula Voice 1969–74; Ed., Raincoast Chronicles 1972–; founder, Pres., Publisher, Harbour Publishing 1974–; mem. Asscn of Book Publishers of British Columbia (pres. 1988–90). *Publications:* Raincoast Chronicles (ed.) (five vols) 1975–94, A Hard Man to Beat: The Story of Bill White, Labour Leader, Historian, Shipyard Worker, Raconteur: An Oral History (co-author) 1983, The Men There Were Then 1983, The New Canadian Poets (ed.) 1985, Spilsbury's Coast: Pioneer Years in the Wet West (co-author) 1987, The Accidental Airline: Spilsbury's QCA 1988, Writing in the Rain (essays and poetry) 1990, The Ghost in the Gears 1993, The Sunshine Coast: From Gibsons to Powell River 1996; contrib. to periodicals. *Honours:* Hon. DJur (Univ. of Victoria) 2003; Eaton's British Columbia Book Award 1976, Career Award for Regional History, Canadian History Asscn 1989, Stephen Leacock Medal for Humour 1990, Roderick Haig Brown Award 1995, James Douglas BC Publisher of the Year Award 2002; Order of British Columbia 1997, Queen Elizabeth II 50th Jubilee Medal 2002. *Address:* PO Box 219, Madeira Park, BC V0N 2H0, Canada. *Website:* www.harbourpublishing.com.

WHITE, James P(atrick); Prof., Writer, Poet, Dramatist, Ed. and Trans; b. 28 Sept. 1940, Wichita Falls, TX, USA; m. Janice Lou Turner, 11 Sept. 1961, one s. *Education:* BA, University of Texas at Austin, 1961; MA, History, Vanderbilt University, 1963; MA, Creative Writing, Brown University, 1973. *Career:* Asst Prof., 1973–74, Assoc. Prof., 1974–77, University of Texas of the Permian Basin at Odessa; Ed., Sands literary review, 1974–78; Visiting Prof., University of Texas at Dallas, 1977–78; Founder-Ed., Texas Books in Review, 1977–79; Dir, Masters in Professional Writing, University of Southern California at Los Angeles, 1979–82; Mem., International Editorial Board, Translation Review, 1980–; Dir of Creative Writing, 1982–, Prof., 1987–, University of South Alabama; mem. Alabama Writer's Forum; Associated Writing Programs; Christopher Isherwood Foundation, dir; Gulf Coast Asscn of Creative Writing Teachers, founder-pres., 1993; Texas Asscn of Creative Writing Teachers, founder-pres., 1974–78. *Publications:* Fiction: Birdsong, 1977; The Ninth Car (with Anne Rooth), 1978; The Persian Oven, 1985; Two Novellas: The Persian Oven and California Exit, 1987; Clara's Call (in Two Short Novels, with R. V. Cassill), 1992. Poetry: Poetry, 1979; The Great Depression (with Walter Feldman), 1997. Editor: Clarity: A Text on Writing (with Janice White), 1982; Where Joy Resides: A Christopher Isherwood Reader (with Don Bachardy), 1989; Black Alabama: An Anthology of Contemporary Black Alabama Fiction Writers, 1998. Contributions: anthologies, reviews, quarterlies, journals, newspapers and magazines. *Honours:* Guggenheim Fellowship, 1988–89; Dean's Lecturer, University of South Alabama, 1990. *Address:* PO Box 428, Montrose, AL 36559, USA.

WHITE, John Austin; Canon, Writer and Poet; b. 27 June 1942, England. *Education:* BA, University of Hull; College of the Resurrection, Mirfield. *Career:* Asst Curate, St Aidan's Church, Leeds, 1966–69; Asst Chaplain, University of Leeds, 1969–73; Asst Dir, Post Ordination Training, Dioceses of Ripon, 1970–73; Chaplain, Northern Ordination Course, 1973–82; Canon of Windsor, 1982–; Warden, St George's House, 2000–03; European Deputy for the Diocese of Mexico of the Anglican Church of Mexico, 2003–; mem. FRSA. *Publications:* A Necessary End: Attitudes to Death (with Julia Neuberger), 1991; Nicholas Ferrar: Materials for a Life (with L. R. Muir), 1997; Phoenix in Flight (with Thetis Blacker). Contributions: various publications. *Address:* 8 The Cloisters, Windsor Castle, Berkshire SL4 1NJ, England.

WHITE, Jon (Ewbank) Manchip; Writer, Poet and Prof. of English (retd); b. 22 June 1924, Cardiff, Glamorganshire, Wales; m. Valerie Leighton, two c. *Education:* St Catharine's College, Cambridge, 1942–43, 1946–50; Open Exhibitioner in English Literature; MA, English, Prehistoric Archaeology, and Oriental Languages (Egyptology), and University Diploma in Anthropology. *Career:* Story Ed., BBC-TV, London, 1950–51; Senior Exec. Officer, British Foreign Service, 1952–56; Independent Author, 1956–67, including a period as screenwriter for Samuel Bronston Productions, Paris and Madrid, 1960–64; Prof. of English, University of Texas, El Paso, 1967–77; Lindsay Young Prof. of English, University of Tennessee, Knoxville, 1977–94; mem. Texas Institute of Letters, 1970; Welsh Acad., 1995. *Publications:* Fiction: Mask of Dust, 1953; Build Us a Dam, 1955; The Girl from Indiana, 1956; No Home But Heaven, 1957; The Mercenaries, 1958; Hour of the Rat, 1962; The Rose in the Brandy Glass, 1965; Nightclimber, 1968; The Game of Troy, 1971; The Garden Game, 1973; Send for Mr Robinson, 1974; The Moscow Papers, 1979; Death by Dreaming, 1981; The Last Grand Master, 1985; Whistling Past the Churchyard, 1992. Poetry: Dragon and Other Poems, 1943; Salamander and Other Poems, 1945; The Rout of San Romano, 1952; The Mountain Lion, 1971. Other: Ancient Egypt, 1952; Anthropology, 1954; Marshal of France: The Life and Times of Maurice, Comte de Saxe, 1962; Everyday Life in Ancient Egypt, 1964; Diego Velázquez, Painter and Courtier, 1969; The Land God Made in Anger: Reflections on a Journey Through South West Africa, 1969; Cortés and the Downfall of the Aztec Empire, 1971; A World Elsewhere: One Man's Fascination with the American Southwest, 1975; Everyday Life of the North American Indians, 1979; What to do When the Russians Come: A Survivors' Handbook (with Robert Conquest), 1984; The Journeying Boy: Scenes from a Welsh Childhood, 1991. *Address:* 5620 Pinellas Dr., Knoxville, TN 37919, USA.

WHITE, Kenneth, MA; poet and writer; b. 28 April 1936, Glasgow, Scotland; m. Marie Claude Charlut. *Education:* University of Glasgow, University of Munich, University of Paris. *Career:* Lecturer in French Univ. of Glasgow 1963–67; Lecturer in English, Univ. of Paris VII 1969–83; Prof. of 20th Century Poetics, University of Paris-Sorbonne 1983–96. *Publications:* Poetry: Wild Coal 1963, En Toute Candeur 1964, The Cold Wind of Dawn 1966, The Most Difficult Area 1968, A Walk Along the Shore 1977, Mahamudra 1979, Le Grand Rivage 1980, Terre de Diamant 1983, Atlantica: Mouvements et meditations 1986, The Bird Path: Collected Longer Poems 1989, Handbook for the Diamond Country 1960–1990 1990, Les Rives du Silence 1997, Limites et Marges 2000, Open World 2003. Fiction: Letters from Gourgounel 1966, Les Limbes Incandescents 1978, Le Visage du Vent d'Est 1980, La Route Bleue 1983, Travels in the Drifting Dawn 1989, Pilgrim of the Void 1994, House of Tides 2000. Essays: La Figure du Dehors 1982, L'Esprit Nomade 1987, Le Plateau de l'Albatros, an introduction to geopoetics 1994, On Scottish Ground 1998, Across the Territories 2004, The Wanderer and his Charts 2004; contrib. to various publications. *Honours:* Dr hc (Glasgow, Edinburgh Heriot-Watt); Hon. mem. Royal Scottish Acad.; Prix Médicis Etranger 1983, Grand Prix de Rayonnement, French Acad. 1985. *Address:* Chemin du Goaquer, 22560 Trébeurden, France.

WHITE, William Robinson, BA, MA; writer and poet; b. 12 July 1928, Kodaikanal, South India; m. Marian Biesterfeld 1948 (died 1983); two s. one d. *Education:* Yale University, California State Polytechnic University. *Career:* Ed.-in-Chief, Per-Se International Quarterly, Stanford University Press, 1965–69; Instructor, Photojournalism, 1973, Dir, Creative Writing

Seminar, 1984, Mendocino Art Center; Lecturer, Scripps College, 1984; Fiction Ed., West-word literary magazine, 1985–90; Instructor, University of California, Los Angeles, 1985–; Research Reader, The Huntington Library, 1985–86; Lecturer, Writing Programme and CompuWrite, California State Polytechnic University, 1985–93; Bread Loaf Fellow, Middlebury College, 1956; Stegner Creative Writing Fellow, Stanford University, 1956–57; mem. Authors' Guild; California State Poetry Society. *Publications:* House of Many Rooms, 1958; Elephant Hill, 1959; Men and Angels, 1961; Foreign Soil, 1962; All In Favor Say No, 1964; His Own Kind, 1967; Be Not Afraid, 1972; The Special Child, 1978; The Troll of Crazy Mule Camp, 1979; Moses the Man, 1981; The Winning Writer, 1997. Contributions: journals and magazines. *Honours:* Harper Prize, 1959; O. Henry Prize, 1960; Co-ordinating Council of Literary Magazines Award, 1968; Distinguished Achievement Award, Educational Press, 1974; Spring Harvest Poetry Awards, 1992, 1994, 1995; Ed.'s Choice Awards, Poetry, 1998, 2000; California State Polytechnic University Golden Leaves Award, 2000; New Century Writers Award, 2000. *Address:* 1940 Fletcher Avenue, South Pasadena, CA 91030, USA.

WHITEHOUSE, David Bryn; Writer and Ed.; b. 15 Oct. 1941, Worksop, England. *Education:* BA, 1963, MA, 1964, PhD, 1967, University of Cambridge. *Career:* Correspondent, Archeologia Medievale; Ed., Journal of Glass Studies, 1988–; Advisory Ed., American Early Medieval Studies, 1991–; Advisory Board, Encyclopedia of Islamic Archaeology, 1991; mem. Accademia Fiorentina delle Arti del Disegno; International Asscn for the History of Glass, pres., 1991–94; Keats-Shelley Memorial Asscn, Rome, pres., 1982–83; Pontificia Accademia Romana di Archeologia; RGS; Society of Antiquaries of London; Unione Internazionale degli Istituti di Archeologia, Storia e Storia dell'Arte in Roma, pres., 1980–81. *Publications:* Glass of the Roman Empire, 1988; Glass: A Pocket Dictionary, 1993; English Cameo Glass, 1994; Roman Glass in the Corning Museum of Glass, Vol. 1, 1997; Excavations at Ed-Dur, Vol. 1, The Glass Vessels, 1998; The Corning Museum of Glass: A Decade of Glass Collecting, 2000. Co-Author: Archaeological Atlas of the World, 1975; Aspects of Medieval Lazio, 1982; Mohammed, Charlemagne and the Origins of Europe, 1983; Glass of the Caesars, 1987; The Portland Vase, 1990; Treasures from the Corning Museum of Glass, 1992; Roman Glass in the Corning Museum of Glass, Vol. 2, 2001, Vol. 3, 2003. Contributions: books, journals, and other publications. *Address:* c/o Corning Museum of Glass, One Museum Way, Corning, NY 14830-2253, USA. *E-mail:* whitehoudb@cmog.org.

WHITEMAN, Robin; Writer and Film-maker; b. 5 May 1944, King's Langley, Hertfordshire, England; m., three c. *Education:* NDD, City of Canterbury College of Art, 1965; MA, Televison and Film, Royal College of Art, 1968. *Career:* Writer, Dir, United Motion Pictures, London, 1968–70; Dir, Prod., Video Tracks Ltd, Royal Leamington Spa, 1980–85; Writer, Partner, Talbot Whiteman, Royal Leamington Spa, 1985–. *Publications:* The Cotswolds, 1987; Shakespeare's Avon: A Journey from Source to Severn, 1989; The English Lakes, 1989; Cadfael Country, 1990; In the North of England: The Yorkshire Moors and Dales, 1991; The Cadfael Companion, 1991; The Benediction of Brother Cadfael, 1992; The Heart of England, 1992; The West Country, 1993; Wessex, 1994; The Garden of England: The Counties of Kent, Surrey and Sussex, 1995; English Landscapes, 1995; East Anglia and the Fens, 1996; Brother Cadfael's Herb Garden, 1996; The Peak District, 1997; Lakeland Landscapes, 1997; Northumbria: English Border Country, 1998; Yorkshire Landscapes, 1998; Cotswold Landscapes, 1999; England, 2000; Brother Cadfael's Book of Days, 2000. *Honours:* Gold Award, British Film and Video Festival, 1984; Border TV Prize, 1998. *Address:* c/o Weidenfeld and Nicolson, Orion House, 5 Upper St, Martin Lane, London WC2H 9EA, England.

WHITESIDE, Lesley; Historian and Writer; b. 13 May 1945, County Down, Ireland; m. Robert Whiteside, 14 Aug. 1968, one s. two d. *Education:* BA, Moderatorship, History and Political Science, Trinity College, Dublin, 1967; Diploma in Palaeography and Administration of Archives, Liverpool, 1968; DipEd, National University of Ireland, 1972; MA, Trinity College, Dublin, 1972. *Career:* Asst Keeper of Manuscripts, Trinity College, Dublin, 1968–69; Archivist, The King's Hospital, Dublin, 1969–. *Publications:* A History of The King's Hospital, 1975; George Otto Simms: A Biography, 1990; Through the Year with George Otto Simms (ed.), 1993; The Spirituality of St Patrick, 1996; St Saviour's Church, Arklow, 1997; In Search of Columba, 1997; The Chapel of Trinity College, Dublin, 1998; St Patrick in Stained Glass, 1998; The Book of Saints, 1998; The Stained Glass of Christ Church Cathedral, Dublin, 1999; The Stained Glass of St Patrick's Cathedral, Dublin, 2002; Music in the King's Hospital 1675–2003, Dublin, 2003. *Address:* The Meadows, Marlinstown, Mullingar, County Westmeath, Ireland. *Telephone:* (353) 444-2994.

WHITFIELD, Stephen J(ack); Prof. and Historian; b. 3 Dec. 1942, Houston, Texas, USA; m. Lee Cone Hall, 15 Dec. 1984. *Education:* BA, Tulane University, 1964; MA, Yale University, 1966; PhD, Brandeis University, 1972. *Career:* Instructor, Southern University of New Orleans, 1966–68; Asst Prof., 1972–75, Assoc. Prof., 1979–85, Prof., 1985–, Chair, Dept of American Studies, 1986–88, 1994–96, Brandeis University; Fulbright Visiting Prof., Hebrew University of Jerusalem, 1983–84, Catholic University of Leuven, Belgium, 1993; Visiting Prof., University of Paris IV, 1994, 1998; mem. American Jewish Historical Society. *Publications:* Scott Nearing: Apostle of American Radicalism, 1974; Into the Dark: Hannah Arendt and Totalitarianism, 1980; Voices of Jacob, Hands of Esau: Jews in American Life and Thought, 1984; A Critical American: The Politics of Dwight Macdonald, 1984; A Death in the Delta: The Story of Emmett Till, 1988; American Space, Jewish Time, 1988; The Culture of the Cold War, 1991; In Search of American Jewish Culture, 1999. Contributions: scholarly journals. *Honours:* Kayden Prize, University of Colorado, 1981; Outstanding Academic Book Citation, Choice, 1985; Merit of Distinction, International Center for Holocaust Studies of the Anti-Defamation League of B'ani B'rith, 1987; Outstanding Book Citations, Gustavus Myers Center for the Study of Human Rights, 1989, 1992; Rockefeller Foundation Fellow, Bellagio, Italy, 1991; Louis D. Brandeis Prize for Excellence in Teaching, 1993. *Address:* c/o Dept of American Studies, Brandeis University, Waltham, MA 02454, USA.

WHITMAN, Ruth (Bashein); Poet, Ed., Trans. and Teacher; b. 28 May 1922, New York, NY, USA; m. 1st Cedric Whitman, 13 Oct. 1941, divorced 1958, two d.; m. 2nd Firman Houghton, 23 July 1959, divorced 1964, one s.; m. 3rd Morton Sacks, 6 Oct. 1966. *Education:* BA, Radcliffe College, 1944; MA, Harvard University, 1947. *Career:* Editorial Asst, 1941–42, Educational Ed., 1944–45, Houghton Mifflin Co, Boston; Freelance Ed., Harvard University Press, 1945–60; Poetry Ed., Audience magazine, 1958–63; Dir, Poetry Workshop, Cambridge Center for Adult Education, 1964–68, Poetry in the Schools Program, Massachusetts Council on the Arts, 1970–73; Scholar-in-Residence, Radcliffe Institute, 1968–70; Instructor in Poetry, Radcliffe College, 1970–, Harvard University Writing Program, 1979–84; Writer-in-Residence and Visiting Lecturer at various colleges and universities; many poetry readings; mem. Authors' Guild; Authors League of America; New England Poetry Club; PEN; Poetry Society of America. *Publications:* Blood and Milk Poems, 1963; Alain Bosquet: Selected Poems (trans. with others), 1963; Isaac Bashevis Singer: The Seance (trans. with others), 1968; The Marriage Wig, and Other Poems, 1968; The Selected Poems of Jacob Glatstein (ed. and trans.), 1972; The Passion of Lizzie Borden: New and Selected Poems, 1973; Poetmaking: Poets in Classrooms (ed.), 1975; Tamsen Donner: A Woman's Journey, 1975; Permanent Address: New Poems, 1973–1980, 1980; Becoming a Poet: Source, Process, and Practice, 1982; The Testing of Hanna Senesh, 1986; The Fiddle Rose: Selected Poems of Abraham Sutzkever (trans.), 1989; Laughing Gas: Poems New and Selected, 1963–1990, 1991; Hatsheput, Speak to Me, 1992. Contributions: anthologies and periodicals. *Honours:* MacDowell Colony Fellowships, 1962, 1964, 1972–74, 1979, 1982; Kovner Award, Jewish Book Council of America, 1969; Guiness International Poetry Award, 1973; National Endowment for the Arts Grant, 1974–75; John Masefield Award, 1976; Senior Fulbright Fellowship, 1984–85; Urbanarts Award, 1987. *Address:* 40 Tuckerman Ave, Middletown, RI 02840, USA.

WHITNEY, Phyllis Ayame; American writer; b. 9 Sept. 1903, Yokohama, Japan; m. 1st George A. Garner (divorced 1945); one d.; m. 2nd Lovell F. Jahnke 1950 (died 1973). *Career:* children's book ed., Chicago Sun, 1942–46, Philadelphia Enquirer, 1947–48; taught fiction writing for children, Northwestern Univ., IL, 1945, New York Univ., 1947–58; writer of children's and adult fiction; mem. MWA (pres., 1975). *Publications:* A Place for Ann, 1941; A Star for Ginny, 1942; A Window for Julie, 1943; Red is for Murder, 1943; The Silver Inkwell, 1945; Ever After, 1948; Mystery of the Gulls, 1949; Linda's Homecoming, 1950; The Island of the Dark Woods, 1951; Love Me, Love Me Not, 1952; Step to Music, 1953; Mystery of the Black Diamonds, 1954; A Long Time Coming, 1954; Mystery on the Isle of Skye, 1955; The Quicksilver Pool, 1955; The Trembling Hills, 1956; The Fire and the Gold, 1956; The Highest Dream, 1956; The Mystery of the Green Cat, 1957; Skye Cameron, 1957; Secret of the Samurai Sword, 1958; The Moonflower, 1958; Creole Holiday, 1959; Mystery of the Haunted Pool, 1960; Thunder Heights, 1960; Secret of the Tiger's Eye, 1961; Blue Fire, 1961; Mystery of the Golden Horn, 1962; Window on the Square, 1962; Seven Tears for Apollo, 1963; Mystery of the Hidden Hand, 1963; Secret of the Emerald Star, 1964; Black Amber, 1964; The Sea Jade, 1965; Mystery of the Angry Idol, 1965; Columbella, 1966; Siverhill, 1967; Secret of the Spotted Shell, 1967; Secret of Goblin Glen, 1968; Hunter's Green, 1968; The Winter People, 1969; The Mystery of the Crimson Ghost, 1969; Secret of the Missing Footprint, 1969; Lost Island, 1970; The Vanishing Scarecrow, 1971; Nobody Likes Trina, 1972; Listen for the Whisper, 1972; Snowfire, 1973; Mystery of the Scowling Boy, 1973; The Turquoise Mask, 1974; Spindrift, 1975; Secret of Haunted Mesa, 1975; The Golden Unicorn, 1976; Secret of the Stone Face, 1977; The Stone Bull, 1977; The Glass Flame, 1978; Domino, 1979; Poinciana, 1980; Vermilion, 1981; Emerald, 1983; Rainsong, 1984; Dream of Orchids, 1985; The Flaming Tree, 1986; Silversword, 1987; Feather on the Moon, 1988; Rainbow in the Mist, 1989; The Singing Stones, 1990; A Mystery of the Golden Horn, 1990; Woman Without a Past, 1991; Ebony Swan, 1992; Star Flight, 1993; Daughter of the Stars, 1994; Amethyst Dreams, 1997. Non-Fiction: Writing Juvenile Fiction, 1947; Writing Juvenile Stories and Novels: How to Write and Sell Fiction for Young People, 1976; Guide to Fiction Writing, 1982. *Honours:* Edgar Allan Poe best juvenile award, 1961; Sequoyah Children's Book Award, 1963; Grand Master, MWA, 1988; Malice Domestic Award, 1989; Lifetime Achievement Award, Society of Midland Authors, 1995. *Address:* c/o Mystery Writers of America, 17 E 47th Street, Sixth Floor, New York, NY 10017, USA. *Website:* www.phyllisawhitney.com.

WHITTEN, Leslie Hunter, Jr, BA; writer, poet and journalist; b. 21 Feb. 1928, Jacksonville, FL, USA; m. Phyllis Webber 1951; three s. one d. *Education:* Lehigh University. *Publications:* Progeny of the Adder, 1965; Moon of the Wolf, 1967; Pinion, The Golden Eagle, 1968; The Abyss, 1970; F. Lee Bailey, 1971; The Alchemist, 1973; Conflict of Interest, 1976; Washington Cycle (poems), 1979; Sometimes a Hero, 1979; A Killing Pace, 1983; A Day Without Sunshine, 1985; The Lost Disciple, 1989; The Fangs of Morning, 1994; Sad Madrigals, 1997; Moses: The Lost Book of the Bible, 1999. Contributions: newspapers and literary magazines. *Honours:* Hon. DHumLitt (Lehigh University) 1989; Journalistic Awards, Edgerton Award, American Civil Liberties Union. *Address:* 114 Eastmoor Drive, Silver Spring, MD 20901, USA.

WHITTINGTON, Peter (see Mackay, James Alexander).

WICKER, Thomas (Grey); Journalist (retd) and Author; b. 18 June 1926, Hamlet, NC, USA; m. 1st Neva Jewett McLean, 20 Aug. 1949, divorced 1973, two s. one d.; m. 2nd Pamela Abel Hill, 9 March 1974. *Education:* AB, Journalism, University of North Carolina, 1948. *Career:* Exec. Dir, Southern Pines Chamber of Commerce, NC, 1948–49; Ed., Sandhill Citizen, Aberdeen, NC, 1949; Managing Ed., The Robesonian, Lumberton, NC, 1949–50; Public Information Dir, North Carolina Board of Public Welfare, 1950–51; Copy Ed., 1951–52, Sports Ed., 1954–55, Sunday Feature Ed., 1955–56, Washington Correspondent, 1957, Editorial Writer and City Hall Correspondent, 1958–59, Winston-Salem Journal, NC; served to Lt, USNR, 1952–54; Assoc. Ed., Nashville Tennessean, 1959–60; Staff, 1960–71, and Chief, 1964–68, Washington Bureau, Columnist, 1966–91, Assoc. Ed., 1968–85, The New York Times; mem. Century Asscn; Society of American Historians; Society of Nieman Fellows; Writers Guild of America East. *Publications:* Non-Fiction: Kennedy Without Tears, 1964; JFK and LBJ: The Influence of Personality upon Politics, 1968; A Time to Die, 1975; On Press, 1978; One of Us: Richard Nixon and the American Dream, 1991; Tragic Failure: Racial Integration in America, 1996; Keeping the Record, 2001; Dwight D. Eisenhower, 2002. Fiction: The Kingpin, 1953; The Devil Must, 1957; The Judgment, 1961; Facing the Lions, 1973; Unto This Hour, 1984; Donovan's Wife, 1992; Easter Lilly: A Novel of the South Today, 1998. *Honours:* Nieman Fellow, 1957–58, Fellow, Joan Shorenstein Barone Center on the Press, Politics, and Public Policy, Harvard University, 1993; Visiting Scholar, First Amendment Center, 1998. *Address:* Austin Hill Farm, Rochester, VT 05767, USA.

WIDDECOMBE, Rt Hon. Ann Noreen; politician and writer; b. 4 Oct. 1947, Bath, Somerset, England. *Education:* La Sainte Union Convent, Bath; Univ. of Birmingham; Lady Margaret Hall, Oxford. *Career:* with Marketing Dept, Unilever, 1973–75; Sr Admin., Univ. of London, 1975–87; contested Burnley, 1979, Plymouth Devonport, 1983; MP for Maidstone, 1987–97, Maidstone and The Weald, 1997–; Parl. Private Sec. to Tristan Garel-Jones, MP, 1990; Parl. Under-Sec., State Dept of Social Security, 1990–93, Dept of Employment, 1993–94; Minister for Employment, 1994–95, Home Office, 1995–97; Shadow Health Minister, 1998–99, Shadow Home Sec., 1999–2001; Conservative. *Publications:* Layman's Guide to Defence, 1984; Inspired and Outspoken, 1999; The Clematis Tree (novel), 2000; An Act of Treachery, 2001; Idealists (novel), 2003; Father Figure (novel), 2004. *Honours:* Spectator/Highland Park Minister of the Year, 1996; Despatch Box Best Front Bencher, 1998; Talk Radio Straight Talker of the Year, 1998. *Address:* 39 Searles Road, London SE1 4YX, England; Kloof Cottage, Sutton Valence, Maidstone, Kent, England. *Website:* www.annwiddecombemp.com.

WIDEMAN, John Edgar, BA, BPhil; American writer; *Professor of English, University of Massachusetts at Amherst*; b. 14 June 1941, Washington, DC, USA; m.; three c. *Education:* Univ. of Pennsylvania, Univ. of Oxford, Univ. of Iowa. *Career:* Prof. of English, Univ. of Wyoming 1974–85, Univ. of Massachusetts, Amherst 1986–; mem. American Acad. of Arts and Sciences, American Acad. of Arts and Letters, American Asscn of Rhodes Scholars, MLA. *Publications:* A Glance Away, 1967; Hurry Home, 1969; The Lynchers, 1973; Hiding Place, 1981; Damballah, 1981; Sent for You Yesterday, 1983; Brothers and Keepers, 1984; Reuben, 1987; Fever, 1989; Philadelphia Fire, 1990; The Homewood Books, 1992; The Stories of John Edgar Wideman, 1992; All Stories Are True, 1993; Fatheralong, 1994; The Cattle Killing, 1996; Hoop Roots, 2001. Contributions: Professional journals and general periodicals. *Honours:* PEN/Faulkner Awards for Fiction 1984, 1991, John D. and Catherine T. MacArthur Foundation Fellowship 1993. *Address:* c/o Department of English, University of Massachusetts, Amberst, MA 01003, USA.

WIEBE, Rudy (Henry); Author and Prof. of English and Creative Writing Emeritus; b. 4 Oct. 1934, near Fairholme, Saskatchewan, Canada; m. Tena F. Isaak, 4 March 1958, two s. one d. *Education:* BA, 1956, MA, 1960, University of Alberta; University of Tübingen, 1958; ThB, Mennonite Brethren Bible College, 1961; University of Manitoba, 1961; University of Iowa, 1964. *Career:* Asst and Assoc. Prof. of English, Goshen College, IN, 1963–67; Asst Prof., 1967–71, Assoc. Prof., 1971–77, Prof. of English and Creative Writing, 1977–92, Prof. Emeritus, 1992–, University of Alberta; mem. Writers Guild of Alberta, founding pres., 1980; Writers Union of Canada, pres., 1986–87. *Publications:* Fiction: Peace Shall Destroy Many, 1962; First and Vital Candle, 1966; The Blue Mountains of China, 1970; The Temptations of Big Bear, 1973; Where is the Voice Coming From?, 1974; The Scorched-Wood People, 1977; Alberta: A Celebration, 1979; The Mad Trapper, 1980; The Angel of the Tar Sands, and Other Stories, 1982; My Lovely Enemy, 1983; A Chinook Christmas, 1992; A Discovery of Strangers, 1994; River of Stone: Fictions and Memories, 1995; Sweeter Than All the World, 2001. Play: Far as the Eye Can See, 1977. Essays: A Voice in the Land, 1981; Playing Dead: A Contemplation Concerning the Arctic, 1989. Editor: The Story-Makers: A Selection of Modern Short Stories, 1970; Stories from Western Canada, 1971; Stories from Pacific and Arctic Canada (with Andreas Schroeder), 1974; Double Vision: Twentieth Century Stories in English, 1976; Getting Here, 1977; More Stories from Western Canada (with Aritha van Herk), 1980; West of Fiction (with Aritha van Herk and Leah Flater), 1983. Contributions: anthologies and periodicals. *Honours:* Governor-General's Awards for Fiction, 1973, 1994; Hon. DLitt, University of Winnipeg, 1986, Wilfred Laurier University, 1991, Brock University, 1991; Lorne Pierce Medal, Royal Society of Canada, 1987. *Address:* c/o Dept of English, University of Alberta, Edmonton, AB T6G 2E5, Canada.

WIENER, Joel H(oward); Prof. of History Emeritus and Writer; b. 23 Aug. 1937, New York, NY, USA; m. Suzanne Wolff, 4 Sept. 1961, one s. two d. *Education:* BA, New York University, 1959; Graduate Studies, University of Glasgow, 1961–63; PhD, Cornell University, 1965. *Career:* Asst Prof. of History, Skidmore College, 1964–66; Assoc. Prof., 1966–76, Prof. of History, 1977–2000, Prof. Emeritus of History, 2000–, City College and the Graduate School and University Center, CUNY; mem. American Historical Asscn; American Journalism Historians Asscn; Conference on British Studies; Research Society for Victorian Periodicals, pres. *Publications:* The War of the Unstamped, 1969; A Descriptive Finding List of Unstamped British Periodicals: 1830–1836, 1970; Great Britain: Foreign Policy and the Span of Empire, 1689–1970 (ed.), 4 vols, 1972; Great Britain: The Lion at Home, 4 vols, 1974; Radicalism and Freethought in 19th Century Britain, 1983; Innovators and Preachers: The Role of the Editor in Victorian England (ed.), 1985; Papers for the Millions: The New Journalism in Britain c. 1850s–1914 (ed.), 1988; William Lovett, 1989. Contributions: scholarly books and journals. *Honours:* FRHistS, UK, 1974. *Address:* 267 Glen Ct, Teaneck, NJ 07666, USA.

WIER, Dara, BS, MFA; poet and academic; *Professor, University of Massachusetts at Amherst*; b. 30 Dec. 1949, New Orleans, LA, USA; one d. one s. *Education:* Louisiana State Univ., Longwood Coll., Bowling Green State Univ. *Career:* Instructor, Univ. of Pittsburgh 1974–75; Instructor 1975–76, Asst Prof. 1977–80, Hollins Coll.; Assoc. Prof. 1980–85, Dir of Graduate Studies 1980–82, Dir of Writing Program 1983–84, Univ. of Alabama at Tuscaloosa; Assoc. Prof. 1985–96, Prof. 1996–, Dir MFA programmes for writers and poets 1985–91, 1992–94, 1997–98, 2004–(06), Univ. of Massachusetts at Amherst; visiting poet at various colls and univs; mem. Associated Writing Programs (pres. 1981–82), Authors' Guild, Authors' League of America, PEN, Poetry Soc. of America. *Publications:* Blood, Hook, and Eye 1977, The 8-Step Grapevine 1981, All You Have in Common 1984, The Book of Knowledge 1988, Blue for the Plough 1992, Our Master Plan 1997, Voyages in English 2001, Hat on a Pond 2002; contrib. to anthologies and periodicals. *Honours:* Nat. Endowment for the Arts Fellowship 1980, Guggenheim Fellowship 1993–94, Jerome Shestack Award, American Poetry Review 2001, Pushcart Prize 2002. *Address:* 504 Montague Road, Amherst, MA 01002, USA.

WIESEL, Eliezer (Elie); American writer and academic; b. 30 Sept. 1928, Sighet, Romania; m. Marion Erster Rose 1969; one s. *Education:* Sorbonne, Univ. of Paris. *Career:* Distinguished Prof., City College, CUNY, 1972–76; Andrew W. Mellon Prof. in the Humanities, 1976–, Prof. of Philosophy, 1988–, Boston Univ.; Distinguished Visiting Prof. of Literature and Philosophy, Florida International Univ., Miami, 1982; Henry Luce Visiting Scholar in the Humanities and Social Thought, Yale Univ., 1982–83; mem. American Acad. of Arts and Sciences; Amnesty International; Authors' Guild; European Acad. of Arts and Sciences; Foreign Press Asscn, hon. lifetime mem.; Jewish Acad. of Arts and Sciences; PEN; Writers Guild of America. *Publications:* Un Di Velt Hot Geshvign (trans. as Night) 1956, L'Aube (trans. as Dawn) 1961, Le Jour (trans. as The Accident) 1961, La Ville de la chance (trans. as The Town Beyond the Wall) 1962, Les Portes de la forêt (trans. as The Gates of the Forest) 1964, Le Chant des morts (trans. as Legends of Our Time) 1966, The Jews of Silence: A Personal Report on Soviet Jewry 1966, Zalmen, ou, la Folie de Dieu (trans. as Zalmen, or, The Madness of God) 1966, Le Mendiant de Jérusalem (trans. as A Beggar in Jerusalem) 1968, Entre deux soleils (trans. as One Generation After) 1970, Célébration Hassidique: Portraits et légendes (trans. as Souls on Fire: Portraits and Legends of Haisdic Masters) 1972, Le Serment de Kolvillag (trans. as The Oath) 1973, Ani Maamin (cantata) 1973, Célébration Biblique: Portraits and Legends 1976, Un Juif aujourd'hui: Récits, essais, dialogues (trans. as A Jew Today) 1977, Dimensions of the Holocaust (with others) 1977, Four Hasidic Masters and Their Struggle Against Melancholy 1978, Le Procès de Shamgorod tel qu'il se déroula le 25 fevrier 1649: Pièce en trois actes (trans. as The Trial of God (as It Was Held on February 25 1649, in Shamgorod): A Play in Three Acts) 1979, Images from the Bible 1980, Le Testament d'un poète Juif assassine (trans. as The Testament) 1980, Five Biblical Portraits 1981, Somewhere a Master 1982, Paroles d'étranger 1982, The Golem: The Story of a Legend as Told by Elie Wiesel 1983, Le Cinquième Fils (trans. as The Fifth Son) 1983, Signes d'exode 1985, Against Silence: The Voice and Vision of Elie Wiesel (ed Irving

Abrahamson) 1985, Job ou Dieu dans la tempête 1986, Le Crépuscule au loin (trans. as Twilight) 1987, A Song For Hope (cantata) 1987, The Six Days of Destruction (with Albert H. Friedlander) 1989, Silences et mémoire d'homme (essays, dialogues) 1989, L'Oublie (novel) 1989, From the Kingdom of Memory 1990, Evil and Exile (with Philippe-Michael de Saint-Cheron) 1990, A Journey of Faith (with John Cardinal O'Connor) 1990, Sages and Dreamers: Portraits and Legends from the Bible, the Talmud and the Hasidic Tradition 1991, Célébration talmudique 1991, The Forgotten, 1992, Monsieur Chouchani: L'énigme d'un Maitre du XX Siècle: Entretiens avec Elie Wiesel, Suivis d'une Enquête 1994, Tous les Fleuves Vont à la Mer: Mémoires (trans. as All Rivers Run to the Sea: Memoirs) 1994, Mémoire à Deux Voix (with François Mitterrand) (trans. as Memoir in Two Voices) 1995, Se taire est impossible (with Jorge Semprun) 1995, Célébration prophétique 1998, Le Mal et l'Exil – Dix ans après: Dialogues with Michaël de Saint Cheron 1999, King Solomon and His Magic Ring 1999, The Sea is Never Full 1999, D'où viens-tu? (essays) 2001, The Judges (novel) 2002, Le temps des déracinés (novel) 2003, Wise Men and Their Tales (Portraits of Biblical, Talmudic and Hasidic masters) 2003. *Honours:* Prix Médicis Étranger, 1969; Prix Bordin, 1972; US Congressional Gold Medal, 1984; Nobel Prize for Peace, 1986; US Presidential Medal of Freedom, 1992. *Address:* c/o University Professors, Boston University, 745 Commonwealth Avenue, Boston, MA 02215, USA.

WIESENFARTH, Joseph John, BA, MA, PhD; academic and writer; *Professor Emeritus, University of Wisconsin at Madison*; b. 20 Aug. 1933, New York, NY, USA; m. Louise Halpin 1971; one s. *Education:* Catholic Univ. of America, Washington, DC, Univ. of Detroit. *Career:* Asst Prof., La Salle Coll., Philadelphia 1962–64; Asst Prof. 1964–67, Assoc. Prof. 1967–70, Manhattan Coll., New York; Assoc. Prof. 1970–76, Prof. of English 1976–, Chair Dept of English 1983–86, 1989–92, Assoc. Dean Graduate School 1995–96, Assoc. Dean Coll. of Letters and Science 1997, Prof. Emeritus 2000–, Univ. of Wisconsin at Madison; Advisory Ed., George Eliot-George Henry Lewes Studies, Connotations, Renascence; mem. MLA, Jane Austen Soc. of North America, Henry James Soc., Katherine Anne Porter Soc., Ford Madox Ford Soc. *Publications:* Henry James and the Dramatic Analogy 1963, The Errand of Form: An Essay of Jane Austen's Art 1967, George Eliot's Mythmaking 1977, George Eliot: A Writer's Notebook 1854–1879 1981, Gothic Manners and the Classic English Novel 1988, Ford Madox Ford and the Arts 1989, Jane Austen's Jack and Alice 2001, History and Representation in Ford Madox Ford's Writings 2004, Jane Austen's The Three Sisters 2004, Ford Madox Ford and the Regiment of Women 2005; contrib. numerous articles on British and American Fiction. *Honours:* Fellow, Nat. Endowment for the Humanities 1967–68, Inst. for Research in Humanities Fellow 1975, Fulbright Fellow 1981–82, Christian Gauss Prize Award Cttee 1986–88, 1989–90. *Address:* 5401 Greening Lane, Madison, WI 53705-1252, USA. *E-mail:* jjwiesen@wisc.edu.

WIESENTHAL, Simon; Writer; b. 31 Dec. 1908, Buczacz, Austria-Hungary; m. Cyla, one d. *Education:* Architectural Studies, Prague, Lvov. *Career:* Ed., Ausweg, 1960–; mem. Austrian PEN. *Publications:* KZ Mauthausen, 1946; Head Mufti, 1947; Agent of the Axis, 1947; The Murderers Among Us, 1967; Sunflower, 1969; Sails of Hope, 1973; The Case of Krystyna Jaworska, 1975; Every Day Remembrance Day, 1986; Justice, Not Vengeance, 1989. *Honours:* Dutch Medal for Freedom; Jean Moulin Medaille; Kaj Munk Medal; Commander, Order of Oranje Nassau, Netherlands; Justice Brandeis Awards; Chevalier, Légion d'honneur; numerous others. *Address:* Salztorgasse 6, 1010 Vienna, Austria.

WIGGINS, Marianne; American writer; m. Salman Rushdie (divorced). *Career:* lives in London. *Publications include:* John Dollar, Eveless Eden 1996, Almost Heaven, Evidence of Things Unseen 2003; two short story collections.

WIGNALL, Anne, (Alice Acland, Anne Marreco); Writer; b. 12 June 1912, London, England; m. 1st Francis Egerton Grosvenor, Fifth Baron of Ebury July 1933 (divorced); two s.; m. 2nd Barton Wignall 12 Nov. 1947 (deceased); one d.; m. 3rd Anthony Marreco 1961 (divorced). *Publications:* As Alice Acland: Biography: Caroline Norton, 1948. Fiction: Templeford Park, 1954; A Stormy Spring, 1955; A Second Choice, 1956; A Person of Discretion, 1958; The Corsican Ladies, 1974; The Secret Wife, 1975; The Ruling Passion, 1976. As Anne Marreco: Biography: The Rebel Countess, 1967. Fiction: The Charmer and The Charmed, 1963; The Boat Boy, 1964. *Literary Agent:* Curtis Brown Ltd, Haymarket House, 28–29 Haymarket, London, SW1Y 4SP, England. *Telephone:* (20) 7393-4400. *Fax:* (20) 7393-4401. *E-mail:* info@curtisbrown.co.uk. *Website:* www.curtisbrown.co.uk.

WILBER, Ken; American writer, spiritualist and psychologist; b. 1949, Oklahoma City, OK. *Education:* Duke Univ. *Career:* founder, Integral Inst. 2000. *Publications include:* non-fiction: The Spectrum of Consciousness 1977, No Boundary: Eastern and Western Approaches to Personal Growth 1979, The Attman Project 1980, Up from Eden 1981, Holographic Paradigm and Other Paradoxes 1982, A Sociable God 1982, Eye to Eye: The Quest for the New Paradigm 1984, The Marriage of Sense and Soul 1988, Grace and Grit 1991, Sex, Ecology, Sprituality 1995, A Brief History of Everything 1995, The Eye of Spirit 1997, One Taste 1999, Integral Psychology: Consciousness Spirit, Psychology Therapy 2000, A Theory of Everything 2001, Boomeritis 2002, The Simple Feeling of Being 2004; editor: Quantum Questions: Mystical Writings of the World's Great Physicists 1984. *Address:* c/o Shambhala Publications, PO Box 308, Boston, MA 02117, USA. *Website:* www.shambhala.com.

WILBER, Richard A.; Prof. of Journalism, Writer, Poet and Ed.; b. 4 Sept. 1948, St Louis, MO, USA; m. Robin Smith, 16 March 1984, one s. one d. *Education:* BA, English and Journalism, 1970, MFA, English, 1976, DEd, 1996, Southern Illinois University. *Career:* Assoc. Ed., The Midwest Motorist, 1970–76; Prof. of Journalism, Florida State College, 1980–88, University of South Florida, 1988–96, Southern Illinois University, 1988–; Ed., Fiction Quarterly, 1988–; mem. SFWA; Textbook Authors Asscn. *Publications:* To Leuchars, 1997. Contributions: Reviews, quarterlies and journals. *Address:* 210 Isle Dr., St Pete Beach, FL 33706, USA.

WILBUR, Richard Purdy; poet, writer, translator, editor and academic; b. 1 March 1921, New York, NY, USA; m. Mary Charlotte Hayes Ward 1942; three s. one d. *Education:* AB, Amherst College, 1942; AM, Harvard University, 1947. *Career:* Asst Prof. of English, Harvard University, 1950–54; Assoc. Prof. of English, Wellesley College, 1955–57; Prof. of English, Wesleyan University, 1957–77; Writer-in-Residence, Smith College, 1977–86; Poet Laureate of the USA, 1987–88; Visiting Lecturer at various colleges and universities; mem. Acad. of American Poets, fmr chancellor; American Acad. of Arts and Letters, pres., 1974–76, chancellor, 1976–78, 1980–81; American Acad. of Arts and Sciences; ASCAP; Authors League of America; Dramatists' Guild; MLA, hon. fellow. *Publications:* Poetry: The Beautiful Changes and Other Poems, 1947; Ceremony and Other Poems, 1950; Things of This World, 1956; Poems, 1943–1956, 1957; Advice to a Prophet and Other Poems, 1961; The Poems of Richard Wilbur, 1963; Walking to Sleep: New Poems and Translations, 1969; Digging to China, 1970; Seed Leaves: Homage to R. F., 1974; The Mind-Reader: New Poems, 1976; Seven Poems, 1981; New and Collected Poems, 1988; Bone Key and Other Poems, 1998; Mayflies, 2000. For Children: Loudmouse, 1963; Opposites, 1973; More Opposites, 1991; A Game of Catch, 1994; Runaway Opposites, 1995; The Disappearing Alphabet, 1998; Opposites, More Opposites and Some Differences, 2000; The Pig in the Spigot, 2000. Non-Fiction: Anniversary Lectures (with Robert Hillyer and Cleanth Brooks), 1959; Emily Dickinson: Three Views (with Louise Bogan and Archibald MacLeish), 1960; Responses: Prose Pieces, 1953–1976, 1976; The Catbird's Song, 1997. Editor: Modern American and Modern British Poetry (with Louis Untermeyer and Karl Shapiro), 1955; A Bestiary, 1955; Poe: Complete Poems, 1959; Shakespeare: Poems (with Alfred Harbage), 1966; Poe: The Narrative of Arthur Gordon Pym, 1974; Witter Bynner: Selected Poems, 1978. Translator: Molière: The Misanthrope, 1955; Molière: Tartuffe, 1963; Molière: The School for Wives, 1971; Molière: The Learned Ladies, 1978; Racine: Andromache, 1982; Racine: Phaedra, 1986; Molière: The School for Husbands, 1992; Molière: Amphitryon, 1995; Molière: Don Juan, 2000; Molière: The Bungler, 2000. *Honours:* Harriet Monroe Memorial Prizes, 1948, 1978; Oscar Blumenthal Prize, 1950; Guggenheim Fellowships, 1952–53, 1963–64; Prix de Rome Fellowship, American Acad. of Arts and Letters, 1954; Edna St Vincent Millay Memorial Award, 1957; Pulitzer Prizes in Poetry, 1957, 1989; National Book Award for Poetry, 1957; Ford Foundation Fellowship, 1960; Bollingen Prizes, 1963, 1971; Brandeis University Creative Arts Award, 1971; Shelley Memorial Award, 1973; Drama Desk Award, 1983; Chevalier, Ordre des Palmes Académiques, 1983; Los Angeles Times Books Prize, 1988; Gold Medal for Poetry, American Acad. and Institute of Arts and Letters, 1991; Edward Mac Dowell Medal, 1991; National Medal of Arts, 1994. *Address:* 87 Dodwells Road, Cummington, MA 01206, USA.

WILBY, Basil Leslie, (Gareth Knight), BA; writer; b. 1930, Colchester, England. *Education:* Royal Holloway College, London, Sheffield Hallam Univ. *Publications:* A Practical Guide to Qabalistic Symbolism, 1965; The New Dimensions Red Book, 1968; The Practice of Ritual Magic, 1969; Occult Exercises and Practices, 1969; Meeting the Occult, 1973; Experience of the Inner Worlds, 1975; The Occult: An Introduction, 1975; The Secret Tradition in Arthurian Legend, 1983; The Rose Cross and the Goddess, 1985; The Treasure House of Images, 1986; The Magical World of the Inklings, 1990; The Magical World of the Tarot, 1991; Magic and the Western Mind, 1991; Tarot and Magic, 1991; Evoking the Goddess, 1993; Dion Fortune's Magical Battle of Britain, 1993; Introduction to Ritual Magic (with Dion Fortune), 1997; The Circuit of Force (with Dion Fortune) 1998; Magical Images and the Magical Imagination, 1998; Principles of Hermetic Philosophy (with Dion Fortune), 1999; Merlin and the Grail Tradition, 1999; Dion Fortune and the Inner Light, 2000; Spiritualism and Occultism (with Dion Fortune), 2000; Pythoness, the Life and Work of Margaret Lumley Brown, 2000; Esoteric Training in Everyday Life, 2001; The Magical World of J. R. R. Tolkien, 2001; The Magical World of C. S. Lewis, 2001; The Magical World of Charles Williams, 2002; The Magical World of Owen Barfield, 2002; Practical Occultism (with Dion Fortune), 2002; The Abbey Papers, 2002; Dion Fortune and the Threefold Way, 2002; The Wells of Vision, 2002; Granny's Pack of Cards, 2003; The Magical Fiction of Dion Fortune, 2003. Contributions: Inner Light Journal, 1993–. *Address:* c/o 38 Steeles Road, London NW3 4RG, England. *E-mail:* garethknight@yahoo.com. *Website:* www.angelfire.com/az/garethknight.

WILCOX, James, BA; American author; b. 4 April 1949, Hammond, LA. *Education:* Yale Univ. *Career:* mem. Authors' Guild, PEN. *Publications:* Modern Baptists 1983, North Gladiola 1985, Miss Undine's Living Room

1987, Sort of Rich 1989, Polite Sex 1991, Guest of a Sinner 1993, Plain and Normal 1998, Heavenly Days 2002; contrib. to periodicals. *Literary Agent:* International Creative Management, 40 W 57th Street, New York, NY 10019, USA.

WILD, Peter; Prof. of English, Poet and Writer; b. 25 April 1940, Northampton, Massachusetts, USA; m. 1st Sylvia Ortiz, 1966; m. 2nd Rosemary Harrold, 1981. *Education:* BA, 1962, MA, 1967, University of Arizona; MFA, University of California at Irvine, 1969. *Career:* Asst Prof., Sul Ross State University, Alpine, Texas, 1969–71; Asst Prof., 1971–73, Assoc. Prof., 1973–79, Prof. of English. 1979–, University of Arizona; Contributing Ed., High Country News, 1974–; Consulting Ed., Diversions, 1983–. *Publications:* Poetry: The Good Fox, 1967; Sonnets, 1967; The Afternoon in Dismay, 1968; Mica Mountain Poems, 1968; Joining Up and Other Poems, 1968; Mad Night with Sunflowers, 1968; Love Poems, 1969; Three Nights in the Chiricahuas, 1969; Poems, 1969; Fat Man Poems, 1970; Term and Renewals, 1970; Grace, 1971; Dilemma, 1971; Wild's Magical Book of Cranial Effusions, 1971; Peligros, 1972; New and Selected Poems, 1973; Cochise, 1973; The Cloning, 1974; Tumacacori, 1974; Health, 1974; Chihuahua, 1976; The Island Hunter, 1976; Pioneers, 1976; The Cavalryman, 1976; House Fires, 1977; Gold Mines, 1978; Barn Fires, 1978; Zuni Butte, 1978; The Lost Tribe, 1979; Jeanne d'Arc: A Collection of New Poems, 1980; Rainbow, 1980; Wilderness, 1980; Heretics, 1981; Bitteroots, 1982; The Peaceable Kingdom, 1983; Getting Ready for a Date, 1984; The Light on Little Mormon Lake, 1984; The Brides of Christ, 1991; Easy Victory, 1994. Other: Pioneer Conservationists of Western America, 2 vols, 1979, 1983; Enos Mills, 1979; Clarence King, 1981; James Welch, 1983; Barry Lopez, 1984; John Haines, 1985; John Nicholas, 1986; The Saguaro Forest, 1986; John C. Van Dyke: The Desert, 1988; Alvar Núnez Cabeza de Vaca, 1991; Ann Zwinger, 1993. Editor: New Poetry of the American West (with Frank Graziano), 1982. *Honours:* Writer's Digest Prize, 1964; Hart Crane and Alice Crane Williams Memorial Fund Grant, 1969; Ark River Review Prize, 1972; Ohio State University Pres.'s Prize, 1982. *Address:* 1547 E Lester, Tucson, AZ 85719, USA.

WILDING, Eric (see Tubb, Edwin Charles).

WILDING, Michael; Prof. and Writer; b. 5 Jan. 1942, Worcester, England. *Education:* BA, 1963, MA, 1968, University of Oxford; DLitt, Univ. of Sydney, 1997. *Career:* Lecturer, 1963–66, Senior Lecturer, 1969–72, Reader, 1972–92, Prof., 1993–2000, Emeritus Prof., 2001–, University of Sydney; Lecturer, University of Birmingham, 1967–68; Visiting Prof., University of California, 1987. *Publications:* Aspects of the Dying Process, 1972; Living Together, 1974; Short Story Embassy, 1975; West Midland Underground, 1975; Scenic Drive, 1976; The Phallic Forest, 1978; Political Fictions, 1980; Pacific Highway, 1982; Reading the Signs, 1984; The Paraguyan Experiment, 1985; The Man of Slow Feeling, 1985; Dragons Teeth, 1987; Under Saturn, 1988; Great Climate, 1990; Social Visions, 1993; The Radical Tradition, Lawson, Furphy, Stead, 1993; This is for You, 1994; Book of the Reading, 1994; The Oxford Book of Australian Short Stories, 1994; Somewhere New, 1996; Studies in Classical Australian Fiction, 1997; Wildest Dreams, 1998; Raising Spirits, Making Gold and Swapping Wives: The True Adventures of Dr John Dee and Sir Edward Kelly, 1999; Academia Nuts, 2002. *Honours:* Senior Fellowship, Literature Board, Australia Council, 1978; Elected Fellow, Australian Acad. of the Humanities, 1988. *Address:* Dept of English, University of Sydney, Sydney, NSW 2006, Australia.

WILENTZ, Robert Sean; Historian; b. 20 Feb. 1951, New York, USA; m. Mary Christine Stansell, 30 Jan. 1980, one s. one d. *Education:* BA, Columbia College, 1972; BA, University of Oxford, 1974; PhD, Yale University, 1980. *Career:* mem. Society of American Historians. *Publications:* Chants Democratic, 1984; Rites of Power, 1985; The Key of Liberty, 1993; The Kingdom of Matthias, 1994. Contributions: New Republic; Dissent. *Honours:* Beveridge Award, 1984; Turner Award, 1985. *Address:* 7 Edgehill St, Princeton, NJ 08540, USA.

WILFORD, John Noble, BS, MA; journalist and writer; b. 4 Oct. 1933, Murray, KY, USA; m. Nancy Watts Paschall 1966; one d. *Education:* University of Tennessee, Syracuse University, Columbia University. *Career:* Science Reporter, 1965–73, 1979–, Asst National Ed., 1973–75, Dir of Science News, 1975–79, Science Correspondent, 1979–, New York Times, New York City; Mc Graw Distinguished Lecturer in Writing, Princeton University, 1985; Prof. of Science Journalism, University of Tennessee, 1989–90; mem. Century Club, New York; National Asscn of Science Writers; American Geographical Society, council mem., 1994–. *Publications:* We Reach the Moon, 1969; The Mapmakers, 1981; The Riddle of the Dinosaur, 1985; Mars Beckons, 1990; The Mysterious History of Columbus, 1991; Cosmic Dispatches, 2000. Contributions: Nature; Wilson Quarterly; New York Times Magazine; Science Digest; Popular Science; National Geographic. *Honours:* Westinghouse-American Asscn for the Advancement of Science Writing Award, 1983; Pulitzer Prizes for National Reporting, 1984, shared 1987; Ralph Coats Roe Medal, American Society of Mechanical Engineers, 1995; American Academy of Arts and Sciences, fellow, 1998; Award for Outstanding Contributions to Public Understanding of Geosciences, American Geological Institute, 2001; Mayor's Award for Excellence in Science and Technology, New York, 2001. *Address:* New York Times, 229 W 43rd Street, New York, NY 10036, USA.

WILHELM, Hans; Author and Illustrator; b. 21 Sept. 1945, Bremen, Germany; m. Judy Henderson. *Publications:* Over 100 children's books, including: Oh, What a Mess, 1988; Tyrone the Horrible, 1988; I Wouldn't Tell a Lie, 1988; Never Lonely Again, 1988; Waldo's Christmas Surprise, 1988; Waldo, Tell Me about Christ, 1988; Waldo, Tell Me about God, 1988; Waldo, Tell Me about Guardian Angels, 1988; Waldo, Tell Me about Me, 1988; More Bunny Trouble, 1989; Friends Are Forever, 1989; Mother Goose on the Loose, 1989; Schnitzel's First Christmas, 1989; A Cool Kid Like Me, 1990; Waldo at the Zoo, 1990; Waldo, One, Two, Three, 1990; Schnitzel Is Lost, 1991; Tyrone, the Double Dirty Rotten Cheater, 1991; The Bremen Town Musician, 1992; The Boy Who Wasn't There, 1993; A Christmas Journey, 1993; Waldo, Tell Me about Dying, 1993; Bad, Bad Bunny Trouble, 1994; The Big Boasting Battle, 1995; I Hate My Bow, 1995; Tyrone and the Swamp Gang, 1995; The Royal Raven, 1996; Don't Cut My Hair!, 1997; I am Lost!, 1997; I Lost my Tooth!, 1999; I Love Colors!, 2000; It's Too Windy!, 2000. *Honours:* numerous international awards. *Address:* PO Box 109, Westport, CT 06881, USA. *Website:* www.hanswilhelm.com.

WILKERSON, Cynthia (see Levinson, Leonard).

WILL, Frederic, BA, PhD; university president and poet; b. 4 Dec. 1928, New Haven, CT, USA. *Education:* Indiana University, Yale University. *Career:* Instructor in Classics, Dartmouth Coll. 1951–54; Asst Prof. of Classics, Pennsylvania State Univ. 1955–60, Univ. of Texas 1960–65; Assoc. Prof. of English and Comparative Literature 1964–66, Prof. of Comparative Literature 1966–71, Univ. of Iowa, Assoc. Dir Int. Writing Program 1983–85, Fellow Inst. of Advanced Studies 1985–90; Prof. of Comparative Literature, Univ. of Massachusetts at Amherst 1971–83; Dir Bd of Overseers and Pres., Mellen University 1991–2000; Fulbright Prof. Univ. of Ivory Coast 2000–02; Prof. of American Studies Hunan Normal Univ. 2003; Fulbright Sr Specialist Univ. of N'djamena, Chad; Visiting Lecturer in poetry and criticism at many colleges and universities; many poetry readings. *Publications:* Intelligible Beauty in Aesthetic Thought: From Winckelmann to Victor Cousin 1958, Mosaic and Other Poems 1959, A Wedge of Words (poems) 1962, Kostes Palamas: The Twelve Words of the Gypsy (trans.) 1964, Hereditas: Seven Essays on the Modern Experience of the Classical (ed.) 1964, Metaphrasis: An Anthology from the University of Iowa Trans. Workshop 1964–65 (ed.) 1965, Flumen Historicum: Victor Cousin's Aesthetic and Its Sources 1965, Literature Inside Out: Ten Speculative Essays 1966, Planets (poems) 1966, Kostes Palamas: The King's Flute (trans.) 1967, From a Year in Greece 1967, Archilochos 1969, Herondas 1972, Brandy in the Snow (poems) 1972, Theodor Adorno: The Jargon of Authenticity (trans. with Knut Tarnowski) 1973, The Knife in the Stone 1973, The Fact of Literature 1973, Guatemala 1973, Botulism (poems) 1975, The Generic Demands of Greek Literature 1976, Belphagor 1977, Epics of America (poems) 1977, Our Thousand Year Old Bodies: Selected Poems 1956–1976 1980, Shamans in Turtlenecks: Selected Essays 1984, The Sliced Dog 1984, Entering the Open Hole 1989, Recoveries 1993, Trips of the Psyche 1993, Textures, Spaces, Wonders 1993, Literature as Sheltering the Human 1993, Singing with Whitman's Thrush 1993, Adventure in Algiers 2002, Bill Ryerson's African Passion 2002, The Poppy Web 2002, By the Sweat of thy Brow 2002, Three North American Agricultural Communities 2002, Miroirs d'Eternité, une saison au Sahel 2002, Mellen University, Early Life and Times 2002, Flesh and the Color of Love 2002. Contributions: many poems and articles in various periodicals. *Honours:* Fulbright Grants 1950–51, 1955, 1956–57, 1975–76, 1980–81, 2000–02, ACLS Grant 1958, Voertman Poetry Awards, Texas Institute of Letters 1962, 1964, Bollingen Foundation Grant, National Endowment for the Arts Grant. *Address:* 617 7th St NW, Mount Vernon, IA 52314, USA.

WILL, George (Frederick); Political Columnist, Television News Analyst and Writer; b. 4 May 1941, Champaign, IL, USA. *Education:* BA, Trinity College, Oxford, 1964; MA, PhD, Princeton University, 1967. *Career:* Prof. of Political Philosophy, Michigan State University, 1967–68, University of Toronto, 1968–70; Ed., The National Review, 1973–76; Syndicated Political Columnist, The Washington Post, 1974–; Contributing Ed., Newsweek magazine, 1976–; Television News Analyst, ABC-TV, 1981–. *Publications:* The Pursuit of Happiness and Other Sobering Thoughts, 1979; The Pursuit of Virtue and Other Tory Notions, 1982; Statecraft as Soulcraft: What Government Does, 1983; The Morning After: American Successes and Excesses, 1986; The New Season: A Spectator's Guide to the 1988 Election, 1987; Men at Work, 1990; Suddenly: The American Idea at Home and Abroad, 1988–89, 1990; Restoration: Congress, Term Limits and the Recovery of Deliberate Democracy, 1992; The Leveling Wind: Politics, the Culture and Other News, 1994. *Honours:* Pulitzer Prize for Commentary, 1977. *Address:* c/o The Washington Post, 1150 15th St NW, Washington, DC 20071, USA.

WILLETT, Frank, CBE, BA, MA; archaeologist and art historian; b. 18 Aug. 1925, Bolton, England; m. M. Constance Hewitt 1950; one s. three d. *Education:* University of Oxford. *Career:* Editorial Secretary, Manchester Literary and Philosophical Society, 1950–58; Editorial Board, West African Journal of Archaeology, 1970–, Journal of African Studies, 1973–88; Curator, Royal Society of Edinburgh, 1992–97; mem. Manchester Literary and Philosophical Society, corresponding mem., 1958–; Royal Anthropological Institute; Royal Society of Edinburgh, fellow. *Publications:* Life in the History of West African Sculpture, 1967; African Art, 1971; Treasures of Ancient Nigeria, 1980. Contributions: scholarly books and journals.

Honours: Leadership Award of the Arts Council of African Studies Asscn, 1995; Bicentenary Medal of the Royal Society of Edinburgh, 1997. *Address:* c/o The Hunterian Museum, University of Glasgow, Glasgow G12 8QQ, Scotland.

WILLIAMS, Charles Kenneth, BA; American poet and academic; b. 4 Nov. 1936, Newark, NJ; m. 1st Sarah Dean Jones 1966 (divorced 1975); one d.; m. 2nd Catherine Justine Mauger 1975; one s. *Education:* Univ. of Pennsylvania. *Career:* Visiting Prof. of Literature, Beaver Coll., Jenkintown, Pa 1975, Drexel Univ., Philadelphia 1976, Franklin and Marshall Coll., Pa 1977, Univ. of Calif. at Irvine 1978, Boston Univ. 1979–80, Brooklyn Coll., CUNY 1982–83; Prof. of Writing, Columbia Univ. NY 1981–85; Prof. of Literature, George Mason Univ., Fairfax Va 1982–95; Halloway Lecturer Univ. of Calif. at Berkeley 1986, Princeton Univ. 1995–; contributing Ed. American Poetry Review 1972–; Fellow Guggenheim Foundation 1975–, Nat. Endowment for Arts 1985, 1993; mem. PEN, American Acad. of Arts and Sciences, American Acad. of Arts and Letters. *Publications:* A Day for Anne Frank 1968, Lies 1969, The Sensuous President 1972, I am the Bitter Name 1972, With Ignorance 1977, The Women of Trachis (co-trans.) 1978, The Lark, The Thrush, The Starling 1983, Tar 1983, Flesh and Blood 1987, Poems 1963–1983, 1988, The Bacchae of Euripides (trans.) 1990, Helen 1991, A Dream of Mind 1992, Selected Poems 1994, The Vigil 1997, Poetry and Consciousness (selected essays) 1998, Repair (poems) 1999, Misgivings: A Memoir 2000, Love About Love 2001, The Singing 2004; contrib. to Akzent, Atlantic, Carleton Miscellany, Crazyhorse, Grand Street, Iowa Review, Madison Review, New England Review, New Yorker, Seneca Review, Transpacific Review, TriQuarterly, Yale Review, Threepenny Review. *Honours:* Pushcart Press Prizes 1982, 1983, 1987, Nat. Book Critics Circle Award for Poetry 1987, Morton Dauwen Zabel Prize, American Acad. of Arts and Letters 1989, Lila Wallace Writers Award 1993, Harriet Monroe Prize 1993, Berlin Prize, American Acad. in Berlin 1998, Voelcker Career Achievement Award, PEN 1998, Pulitzer Prize for Poetry 2000, LA Times Book Award 2000, Weathertop Prize 2000. *Address:* 82 rue d'Hauteville, 75010 Paris, France (Home).

WILLIAMS, David Larry; Prof. of English and Writer; b. 22 June 1945, Souris, Manitoba, Canada; m. Darlene Olinyk, 22 July 1967, two s. *Education:* Pastor's Diploma, Briercrest Bible Institute, Saskatchewan, 1965; BA, University of Saskatchewan, 1968; MA, Amherst College, 1970; PhD, University of Massachusetts, 1973. *Career:* Lecturer, 1972–73, Asst Prof., 1973–77, Assoc. Prof., 1977–83, Prof., 1983–, English, University of Manitoba, Winnipeg; Editorial Board, Canadian Review of American Studies, 1976–86; Guest Prof., Indian Asscn for Canadian Studies, MS University of Baroda, 1992; mem. Writers' Union of Canada; PEN International. *Publications:* The Burning Wood (novel), 1975; Faulkner's Women: The Myth and the Muse (criticism), 1977; The River Horsemen (novel), 1981; Eye of the Father (novel), 1985; To Run with Longboat: Twelve Stories of Indian Athletes in Canada (with Brenda Zeman), 1988; Confessional Fictions: A Portrait of the Artist in the Canadian Novel, 1991; Imagined Nations: Reflections on Media in Canadian Fiction (criticism), 2003. Contributions: books and professional journals. *Honours:* Woodrow Wilson Fellow, 1968–69; Canada Council Fellow, 1969–72; Canada Council Arts Grant 'B', 1977–78, 1981–82; Touring Writer in Scandinavia for External Affairs, Canada, 1981; RH Institute Award for Research in Humanities, 1987; Olive Beatrice Stanton Award for Excellence in Teaching, 1992. *Address:* Dept of English, St Paul's College, University of Manitoba, Winnipeg R3T 2M6, Canada.

WILLIAMS, Gordon MacLean; British writer; b. 1934, Paisley, Renfrewshire, Scotland. *Career:* journalist, sportswriter. *Publications:* novels: The Last Day of Lincoln Charles 1965, The Camp 1966, The Man Who Had Power Over Women 1967, From Scenes Like These 1968, The Siege of Trencher's Farm (aka Straw Dogs) 1969, Upper Pleasure Garden 1970, Walk Don't Walk 1972, Big Morning Blues 1974, The Duellists 1977, The Microcolony 1979, Revolution of the Micronauts 1981, Pomeroy 1983, Pomeroy Unleashed 1986; co-writer of Hazell novels with Terry Venables. *Address:* c/o Bloomsbury Publishing PLC, 38 Soho Square, London, W1V 5DF, England. *Website:* www.bloomsbury.com.

WILLIAMS, Heathcote; Playwright and Poet; b. 15 Nov. 1941, Helsby, Cheshire, England. *Career:* Assoc. Ed., Transatlantic Review, New York and London. *Publications:* The Local Stigmatic, 1967; AC/DC, 1970; Remember the Truth Dentist, 1974; The Speakers, 1974; Very Tasty: A Pantomime, 1975; An Invitation to the Official Lynching of Abdul Malik, 1975; Anatomy of a Space Rat, 1976; Hancock's Last Half-Hour, 1977; Playpen, 1977; The Immortalist, 1977; At It, 1982; Whales, 1986. Poetry: Whale Nation, 1988; Falling for a Dolphin, 1988; Sacred Elephant, 1989; Autogeddon, 1991. Other: The Speakers, 1964; Manifestoes, Manifestern, 1975; Severe Joy, 1979; Elephants, 1983. *Honours:* Evening Standard Award, 1970. *Literary Agent:* Curtis Brown Ltd, Haymarket House, 28–29 Haymarket, London, SW1Y 4SP, England. *Telephone:* (20) 7393-4400. *Fax:* (20) 7393-4401. *E-mail:* info@curtisbrown.co.uk. *Website:* www.curtisbrown.co.uk.

WILLIAMS, Herbert Lloyd; Writer, Poet and Dramatist; b. 8 Sept. 1932, Aberystwyth, Wales; m. Dorothy Maud Edwards, 13 Nov. 1954, four s., one d. *Career:* mem. Welsh Acad., fellow; Welsh Union of Writers; Society of Authors; William Barnes Society. *Publications:* The Trophy, 1967; A Lethal Kind of Love, 1968; Battles in Wales, 1975; Come Out Wherever You Are, 1976; Stage Coaches in Wales, 1977; The Welsh Quiz Book, 1978; Railways in Wales, 1981; The Pembrokeshire Coast National Park, 1987; Stories of King Arthur, 1990; Ghost Country, 1991; Davies the Ocean, 1991; The Stars in Their Courses, 1992; John Cowper Powys, 1997; Looking Through Time, 1998; A Severe Case of Dandruff, 1999; Voices of Wales, 1999; The Woman in Back Row, 2000; Punters, 2002. Television Dramas and Documentaries: Taff Acre, 1981; A Solitary Mister, 1983; Alone in a Crowd, 1984; Calvert in Camera, 1990; The Great Powys, 1994; Arouse All Wales, 1996. Radio Dramas: Doing the Bard, 1986; Bodyline, 1991. Adaptations: A Child's Christmas in Wales, 1994; The Citadel, 1997. Contributions: Reviews and journals. *Honours:* Welsh Arts Council Short Story Prize, 1972, and Bursary, 1988; Aberystwyth Open Poetry Competition, 1990; Hawthornden Poetry Fellowship, 1992; Rhys Davies Short Story Award, 1995. *Address:* 63 Bwlch Rd, Fairwater, Cardiff CF5 3BX, Wales. *E-mail:* h.williams13@ntlworld.com. *Website:* www.herbert-williams.co.uk.

WILLIAMS, Hugo (Mordaunt); Writer, Critic and Poet; b. 20 Feb. 1942, Windsor, Berkshire, England; m. Hermine Demoriane 12 Oct. 1966; one d. *Education:* Eton College, 1955–60. *Career:* Asst Ed., London Magazine, 1961–70; TV critic, 1983–88, poetry ed., 1984–93, New Statesman; theatre critic, Sunday Correspondent, 1989–91, TLS, 1988–; film critic, Harpers & Queen, 1993–98; mem. RSL. *Publications:* Poetry: Symptoms of Loss, 1965; Sugar Daddy, 1970; Some Sweet Day, 1975; Love Life, 1979; Writing Home, 1985; Self-Portrait with a Slide, 1990; Dock Leaves, 1994; Billy's Rain, 1999; Curtain Call: 101 Portraits in Verse (ed.), 2001; Collected Poems, 2002. Non-Fiction: All the Time in the World, 1966; No Particular Place to Go, 1981. Contributions: newspapers and periodicals. *Honours:* Eric Gregory Award, 1965; Cholmondeley Award, 1970; Geoffrey Faber Memorial Prize, 1979; T. S. Eliot Prize, 1999. *Address:* 3 Raleigh St, London N1 8NW, England.

WILLIAMS, J(eanne) R., (Megan Castell, Jeanne Creasey, Jeanne Crecy, Jeanne Foster, Kristin Michaels, Deidre Rowan); Author; b. 10 April 1930, Elkhart, KS, USA. *Education:* University of Oklohoma, 1952–53. *Career:* mem. Authors' Guild; Western Writers of America, pres., 1974–75. *Publications:* To Buy a Dream, 1958; Promise of Tomorrow, 1959; Coyote Winter, 1965; Beasts with Music, 1967; Oil Patch Partners, 1968; New Medicine, 1971; Trails of Tears, 1972; Freedom Trail, 1973; Winter Wheat, 1975; A Lady Bought with Rifles, 1977; A Woman Clothed in Sun, 1978; Bride of Thunder, 1978; Daughter of the Sword, 1979; The Queen of a Lonely Country (as Megan Castell), 1980; The Valiant Women, 1981; Harvest of Fury, 1982; The Heaven Sword, 1983; A Mating of Hawks, 1984; The Care Dreamers, 1985; So Many Kingdoms, 1986; Texas Pride, 1987; Lady of No Man's Land, 1988; No Roof but Heaven, 1990; Home Mountain, 1990; The Island Harp, 1991; The Longest Road, 1993; Daughter of the Storm, 1994; The Unplowed Sky, 1994; Home Station, 1995. As J. R. Williams: Mission in Mexico, 1960; The Horsetalker, 1961; The Confederate Fiddle, 1962; River Guns, 1962; Oh Susanna, 1963; Tame the Wild Stallion, 1967. As Jeanne Crecy: Hands of Terror, 1972, UK edn as Lady Gift; The Lightning Tree, 1972; My Face Beneath Stone, 1975; The Winter-Keeper, 1975; The Night Hunters, 1975. As Deirdre Rowan: Dragon's Mount, 1973; Silver Wood, 1974; Shadow of the Volcano, 1975; Time of the Burning Mask, 1976; Ravensgate, 1976. As Kristin Michaels: To Begin with Love, 1976; Enchanted Journey, 1977; Song of the Heart, 1977; Make Believe Love, 1978. As Jeanne Foster: Deborah Leigh, 1981; Eden Richards, 1982; Woman of Three Worlds, 1984; Wind Water, 1997. Contributions: journals. *Honours:* Texas Institute of Letters Best Children's Book, 1958; Four Western Writers of America Spur Awards; Best Novel of the West, 1981, 1990; Lew Strauss Golden Saddleman Award for Lifetime Achievement, 1988. *Address:* Box 335, Portal, AZ 85632, USA. *E-mail:* jeannewilliams30@hotmail.com.

WILLIAMS, John A(lfred); Writer, Journalist, Poet and Educator; b. 5 Dec. 1925, Jackson, Mississippi, USA; m. 1st Carolyn Clopton, 1947, divorced, two s.; m. 2nd Lorrain Isaac, 5 Oct. 1965, one s. *Education:* BA, Syracuse University, 1950; Graduate School, 1951. *Career:* Ed. and Publisher, Negro Market Newsletter, 1956–57; Contributing Ed., Herald-Tribune Book Week, 1963–65, American Journal, 1972–74, Politicks, 1977, Journal of African Civilizations, 1980–88; Lecturer, College of the Virgin Islands, 1968, City College, CUNY, 1968–69; Visiting Prof., Macalester College, 1970, University of Hawaii, 1974, Boston University, 1978–79, University of Houston, 1994, Bard College, 1994–95; Regents Lecturer, University of California at Santa Barbara, 1972; Guest Writer, Sarah Lawrence College, 1972–73; Distinguished Prof., LaGuardia Community College, CUNY, 1973–79; Distinguished Visiting Prof., Cooper Union, 1974–75; Prof., Rutgers University, 1979–93; Exxon Visiting Prof., New York University, 1986–87; mem. Authors' Guild; Poets and Writers; PEN. *Publications:* Fiction: The Angry Ones, 1960, revised edn as One for New York, 1975; Night Song, 1961; Sissie, 1963; The Man Who Cried I Am, 1967; Sons of Darkness, Sons of Light, 1969; Captain Blackman, 1972; Mothersill and the Foxes, 1975; The Junio Bachelor Society, 1976; !Click Song, 1982; The Berhama Account, 1985; Jacob's Ladder, 1987; Clifford's Blues, 1999. Libretto: Vanqui, premier, 1999. Poetry: Safari West, 1998. Non-Fiction: Africa: Her History, Lands and People, 1963; The Protectors, 1964; This Is My Country Too, 1965; The Most Native of Sons: A Biography of Richard Wright, 1970; The King God Didn't Save: Reflections on the Life and Death of Martin Luther King Jr., 1970; Flashbacks: A Twenty-Year Diary of Article Writing, 1973; Minorities in the City, 1975; If I Stop I'll Die: The Comedy and Tragedy of Richard Pryor (with Dennis A Williams), 1991. Editor or Co-Editor: The Angry Black, 1962, revised edn as Beyond the Angry Black, 1967; Amistad 1, 1970; Amistad 2, 1971; Y'Bird, 1978; Introduction to Literature, 1985; Street Guide to African Americans in Paris, 1992; Approaches to Literature, 1994; Bridges: Literature Across Cultures, 1994. Contributions: anthologies, journals, reviews, and magazines. *Honours:* National Institute of Arts and Letters Award, 1962; Centennial Medal, 1970, Hon. DLitt, 1995, Syracuse University; Richard Wright-Jacques Roumain Award, 1973; National Endowment for the Arts Award, 1977; Hon. Doctor of Literature, Southeastern Massachusetts University, 1978; American Book Awards, Before Columbus Foundation, 1983, 1998; New Jersey State Council on the Arts Award, 1985; Michael Award, New Jersey Literary Hall of Fame, 1987; Distinguished Writer Award, Middle Atlantic Writers, 1987; J. A. Williams Archive established, University of Rochester, 1987; Carter G. Woodson Award, Mercy College, 1989; National Literary Hall of Fame, 1998. *Literary Agent:* Barbara Hogenson, 165 West End Ave, New York, NY 10024, USA. *Address:* 693 Forest Ave, Teaneck, NJ 07666, USA.

WILLIAMS, John Hartley; Poet and Lecturer; b. 7 Feb. 1942, England; m. Gizella Horvat 7 March 1970; one d. *Education:* BA, English, Univ. of Nottingham, 1965; MPhil, English and Education, Univ. of London, 1974; Certificate in Phonetics, Univ. Coll. London, 1974. *Career:* Lecturer, Free Univ. of Berlin, 1976–; mem. Poetry Society. *Publications:* Hidden Identities, 1982; Bright River Yonder, 1987; Cornerless People, 1990; Double, 1994; Ignoble Sentiments, 1995; Teach Yourself Writing Poetry (with Matthew Sweeney), 1997; Canada, 1997; The Scar in the Stone (contributing trans. to poems from Serbo-Croatian), 1998; Spending Time with Walter, 2001; Marin Soresa: Censored Poems (trans.), 2001; Mystery in Spiderville, 2002; North Sea Improvisation, a fotopoem, 2003; Blues, 2004. Contributions: anthologies, reviews, and journals. *Honours:* First Prize, Arvon International Poetry Competition, 1983; Poetry Book Recommendation, 1987. *Address:* 18 Jenbacherweg, 12209, Berlin, Germany. *E-mail:* johnhartleywilliams@t-online.de. *Website:* www.johnhartleywilliams.de.

WILLIAMS, John Hoyt; Prof. of History (retd) and Writer; b. 26 Oct. 1940, Darien, CT, USA; m. 27 Jan. 1962; one s. one d. *Education:* BA, 1963, MA, History, 1965, University of Connecticut; PhD, Latin American History, University of Florida, 1969. *Career:* Asst Prof. of History, 1969–73, Assoc. Prof. of History, 1973–78, Prof. of History, 1978–2000, Indiana State University. *Publications:* Rise and Fall of the Paraguayan Republic 1800–1870, 1979; A Great and Shining Road, 1988; Sam Houston: A Biography of the Father of Texas, 1993. Contributions: Atlantic Monthly; Christian Century; Americas; National Defense; Current History; Hispanic American Historical Review. *Honours:* Named Distinguished Prof. of Arts and Sciences, 1996. *Address:* 1167 Farm Quarter Rd, Mount Pleasant, SC 29464, USA.

WILLIAMS, Joy; Writer; b. 11 Feb. 1944, Chelmsford, MA, USA; m. Rust Hills, one c. *Education:* MA, Marietta College, 1963; MFA, University of Iowa, 1965. *Publications:* State of Grace, 1973; The Changeling, 1978; Taking Care, 1982; The Florida Keys: A History and Guide, 1986; Breaking and Entering, 1988; Escapes, 1990; The Quick and the Dead, 2000; Ill Nature, 2001. Contributions: anthologies. *Honours:* National Endowment for the Arts Grant, 1973; Guggenheim Fellowship, 1974; National Magazine Award, 1980; American Acad. of Arts and Letters Literature Citation, 1989, and Straus Living Award, 1993–97; Rea Award, 1999. *Address:* c/o International Creative Management, 40 W 57th St, New York, NY 10019, USA.

WILLIAMS, Malcolm David; writer; b. 9 April 1939, South Wales; m. (deceased); one d. *Education:* Birmingham Univ. Inst. of Education. *Career:* mem. Society of Authors; West Country Writers Asscn; World Literary Acad., fellow. *Publications:* Yesterday's Secret, 1980; Poor Little Rich Girl, 1981; Debt of Friendship, 1981; Another Time, Another Place, 1982; My Brother's Keeper, 1982; The Stuart Affair, 1983; The Cordillera Conspiracy, 1983; The Girl from Derry's Bluff, 1983; A Corner of Eden, 1984; Sorrow's End, 1984; A Stranger on Trust, 1987; Shadows From the Past, 1989; This Mask I Wear Today, 1998; And the Dragons are Dead, 2003. Contributions: various publications. *Address:* 17 Beaumont Road, Cheltenham, Gloucestershire GL51 0LP, England.

WILLIAMS, Merryn; Writer, Poet and Ed.; b. 9 July 1944, Devon, England; m. John Hemp 14 April 1973; one s. one d. *Education:* BA, 1966, PhD, 1970, Univ. of Cambridge. *Career:* Lecturer, Open Univ., 1970–71; Ed., The Interpreter's House, 1996–; Ed., Wilfred Owen Asscn newsletter; mem. Open Univ. Poets; Welsh Acad. *Publications:* The Bloodstream, 1989; Selected Poems of Federico García Lorca, 1992; Wilfred Owen, 1993; The Sun's Yellow Eye, 1997; The Latin Master's Story, 2000; In the Spirit of Wilfred Owen (ed., anthology), 2002. Contributions: reviews, quarterlies, journals and magazines. *Address:* 10 Farrell Rd, Wootton, Bedfordshire MK43 9DU, England. *E-mail:* hemp@cranfield.ac.uk.

WILLIAMS, Miller; Prof., University Press Dir, Writer and Poet; b. 8 April 1930, Hoxie, AR, USA; m. 1st Lucille Day, 29 Dec. 1951, one s. two d.; m. 2nd Jordan Hall, 1969. *Education:* BS, Arkansas State College, 1950; MS, University of Arkansas, 1952. *Career:* Founder-Ed., 1968–70, Advisory Ed., 1975–, New Orleans Review; Prof., University of Arkansas, 1971–; Dir, University of Arkansas Press, 1980–97. *Publications:* A Circle of Stone, 1964; Southern Writing in the Sixties (with J. W. Corrington), 2 vols, 1966; So Long at the Fair, 1968; Chile: An Anthology of New Writing, 1968; The Achievement of John Ciardi, 1968; The Only World There Is, 1968; The Poetry of John Crowe Ransom, 1971; Contemporary Poetry in America, 1972; Halfway from Hoxie: New and Selected Poems, 1973; How Does a Poem Mean? (with John Ciardi), 1974; Railroad (with James Alan McPherson), 1976; Why God Permits Evil, 1977; A Roman Collection, 1980; Distraction, 1981; Ozark, Ozark: A Hillside Reader, 1981; The Boys on Their Bony Mules, 1983; Living on the Surface: New and Selected Poems, 1989; Adjusting to the Light, 1992; Points of Departure, 1995; The Ways We Touch (poems), 1997; Some Jazz a While: Collected Poems, 1999; The Lives of Kelvin Fletcher: Stories Mostly Short, 2002. Contributions: various publications. *Honours:* Henry Bellaman Poetry Award, 1957; Bread Loaf Fellowship in Poetry, 1961; Fulbright Lecturer, 1970; Prix de Rome, American Acad. of Arts and Letters, 1976; Hon. Doctor of Humanities, Lander College, 1983; National Poets Prize, 1992; John William Corrington Award for Excellence in Literature, Centenary College, LA, 1994; American Acad. of Arts and Letters Award, 1995; Hon. LHD, Hendrix College, 1995; Inaugural Poet, Presidential Inauguration, 1997. *Address:* 1111 Valley View Dr., Fayetteville, AR 72701, USA.

WILLIAMS, Nigel; Novelist and Playwright; b. 20 Jan. 1948, Cheadle, Cheshire, England. *Education:* Oriel College, Oxford. *Publications:* Fiction: My Life Closed Twice, 1977; Jack be Nimble, 1980; Charlie, 1984; Star Turn, 1985; Witchcraft, 1987; Breaking Up, 1988; Black Magic, 1988; The Wimbledon Poisoner, 1990; They Came from SW19, 1992; East of Wimbledon, 1993; Scenes from a Poisoner's Life, 1994; Stalking Fiona, 1997; Fortysomething, 1999; Hatchett and Lycett, 2001. Plays: Double Talk, 1976; Snowwhite Washes Whiter, 1977; Class Enemy, 1978; Easy Street, 1979; Sugar and Spice, 1980; Line 'em, 1980; Trial Run, 1980; WCPC, 1982; The Adventures of Jasper Ridley, 1982; My Brother's Keeper, 1985; Deathwatch (after Genet), 1985; Country Dancing, 1986; As It Was, 1987; Nativity, 1989. Television plays. *Honours:* Somerset Maugham Award for Fiction, 1978. *Address:* c/o Faber and Faber, 3 Queen Sq., London WC1N 3AU, England.

WILLIAMS, Peter Fredric, BA, MusB, MA, PhD, LittD; musicologist, academic, writer, organist and harpsichordist; b. 14 May 1937, Wolverhampton, Staffordshire, England; m. Rosemary Seymour 1982; three s. one d. *Education:* Birmingham Inst., St John's Coll., Cambridge. *Career:* Lecturer 1962–72, Reader 1972–82, Prof. 1982–85, Dean 1984, Univ. of Edinburgh; Dir, Russell Coll. of Harpsichords, Edinburgh 1969; Founder-Ed., The Organ Yearbook 1969–; Arts and Sciences Distinguished Prof. 1985–95, Dir, Graduate Center for Performance Practice Studies 1990–96, Duke Univ., Durham, NC, USA; John Bird Prof., Univ. of Wales, Cardiff 1996–2002; mem. British Inst. of Organ Studies (chair.). *Publications:* The European Organ 1450–1850 1966, Figured Bass Accompaniment (two vols) 1970, Venta/Peeters the Organ of the Netherlands (trans.) 1971, Bach Organ Music 1972, A New History of the Organ From the Greeks to the Present Day 1980, The Organ Music of J. S. Bach (three vols) 1980–84, Bach, Handel and Scarlatti: Tercentenary Essays (ed.) 1985, Playing the Works of Bach 1986, The Organ 1988, Playing the Organ Music of Bach 1988, Mozart: Perspectives in Performance (ed. with L. Todd) 1991, The Organ in Western Culture 750–1250 1992, The King of Instruments: How Do Churches Come to Have Organs? 1993, The Chromatic Fourth During Four Centuries of Music 1995, Cambridge Studies in Performance Practice (series ed., four vols) –1995, Music to Hear, or Fears for Higher Music Study 2001, Bach: The Goldberg Variations 2001; several vols of keyboard music by Bach and Handel; contrib. to scholarly books and journals. *Honours:* Hon. Fellow, Royal Scottish Acad. of Art, Research Fellow, Cornell Univ., New York, Curt Sachs Award, American Musical Instrument Soc. 1996. *Address:* c/o Department of Music, Corbett Road, University of Wales, Cardiff, Cardiff, CF10 3EB, Wales.

WILLIAMS, Roy; British playwright; b. 1968. *Education:* Rose Bruford Drama School. *Plays:* No Boys Cricket Club 1996, Starstruck 1997, Lift Off 1999, The Gift 2000, Clubland 2001, Sing Yer Heart Out for the Lads 2002, Fallout 2003. *Publications include:* Plays 1 2002, Plays 2004. *Honours:* TAPS Writer of the Year Award 1996, Alfred Fagon Award 1998, John Whiting Award for Best New Play 1998–99, Evening Standard Most Promising Playwright Award 2001. *Address:* c/o Methuen Publishing Ltd, 215 Vauxhall Bridge Road, London, SW1V 1EL, England. *Website:* www.methuen.co.uk.

WILLIAMS, Terry Tempest; writer; b. Utah, USA; m. Brooke Williams. *Career:* fmr naturalist-in-residence, Utah Museum of Natural History. *Publications:* Pieces of White Shell: A Journey to Navajoland, 1984; Coyote's Canyon, 1989; Refuge: An Unnatural History of Family and Place, 1991; An Unspoken Hunger (essays), 1994; Desert Quartet: An Erotic Landscape, 1995; Leap, 2000; Red: Patience and Passion in the Desert, 2001. Children's Books: The Secret Language of Snow (with Ted Major), 1984; Between Cattails, 1985. Other: Great and Peculiar Beauty: A Utah Centennial Reader (ed. with Thomas J. Lyon), 1995; Testimony: Writers of the West Speak on Behalf of Utah Wilderness (ed. with Stephen Trimble), 1996; New Genesis: a Mormon Reader on Land and Community (ed. with William B. Smart, Gibbs M. Smith), 1998. Contributions: anthologies, journals and newspapers, incl. New Yorker, The Nation, Outside, Audubon, Orion, Iowa Review, New England Review. *Honours:* Inductee, Rachel Carson Honor Roll; National Wildlife Federation Conservation Award for Special Achievement; Guggenheim Memorial Foundation fellow; Lannan Literary Fellowship in Creative Non-fiction. *Literary Agent:* Steven Barclay Agency, 12 Western Avenue, Petaluma, CA 94952, USA. *Telephone:* (707) 773-0654. *Fax:* (707) 778-1868. *Website:* www.barclayagency.com. *Address:* c/o Vintage Books, Random House, 1745 Broadway, Third Floor, New York, NY 10019, USA. *Website:* www.coyoteclan.com.

WILLIAMS-WITHERSPOON, Kimmika L. H.; Playwright, Poet and Performance Artist; b. 7 Jan. 1959, Pennsylvania, USA; m. Darrell V. Witherspoon, 11 July 1992, two d. *Education:* BA, Journalism, Howard University, 1980; MFA, Playwriting, Temple University, 1996; Graduate Certificate in Women's Studies, 1996. *Career:* Future Faculty Fellow, Anthropology Dept, Temple University; mem. Poets and Prophets; Poets and Writers. *Publications:* God Made Men Brown, 1982; It Ain't Easy To Be Different, 1986; Halley's Comet, 1988; Envisioning a Sea of Dry Bones, 1990; Epic Memory: Places and Spaces I've Been, 1995; Signs of the Times: Culture Gap, 1999. Contributions: Women's Words; Sunlight on the Moon. *Honours:* Playwrights Exchange Grants, 1994, 1996. *Address:* c/o Temple University, 219 Tomlinson Hall, Philadelphia, PA 19122, USA.

WILLIAMSON, Jack, (John Stewart Williamson); Writer; b. 29 April 1908, Bisbee, AZ, USA; m. Blanche Slaten Harp 15 Aug. 1947 (deceased 1985); two step-c. *Education:* BA, MA, 1957, Eastern New Mexico University; PhD, University of Colorado, 1964. *Career:* Prof. of English, Eastern New Mexico University, Portales, 1960–77; mem. SFWA, pres. 1978–80; Science Fiction Research Asscn; World Science Fiction Planetary Society. *Publications:* Science Fiction: The Legion of Space, 1947; Darker Than You Think, 1948; The Humanoids, 1949; The Green Girl, 1950; The Cometeers, 1950; One Against the Legion, 1950; Seetee Shock, 1950; Seetee Ship, 1950; Dragon's Island, 1951; The Legion of Time, 1952; Dome Around America, 1955; The Trial of Terra, 1962; Golden Blood, 1964; The Reign of Wizardry, 1965; Bright New Universe, 1967; Trapped in Space, 1968; The Pandora Effect, 1969; People Machines, 1971; The Moon Children, 1972; H. G. Wells: Critic of Progress, 1973; Teaching Science Fiction, 1975; The Early Williamson, 1975; The Power of Blackness, 1976; The Best of Jack Williamson, 1978; Brother to Demons, Brother to Gods, 1979; Teaching Science Fiction: Education for Tomorrow, 1980; The Alien Intelligence, 1980; The Humanoid Touch, 1980; Manseed, 1982; The Queen of a Legion, 1983; Wonder's Child: My Life in Science Fiction, 1984; Lifeburst, 1984; Firechild, 1986; Mazeway, 1990; Beachhead, 1992; Demon Moon, 1994; The Black Sun, 1997; The Fortress of Utopia, 1998; The Silicon Dagger, 1999; Terra Forming Earth, 2001. With Frederik Pohl: Undersea Quest, 1954; Undersea Fleet, 1955; Undersea City, 1956; The Reefs of Space, 1964; Starchild, 1965; Rogue Star, 1969; The Farthest Star, 1975; Wall Around a Star, 1983; Land's End, 1988. With James Gunn: Star Bridge, 1955. With Miles J. Breuer: The Birth of a New Republic, 1981. *Honours:* Pilgrim Award, Science Fiction Research Asscn, 1968; Grand Master Nebula Award, 1976; Hugo Awards, 1985, 2001; Nebula Award, 2002. *Address:* PO Box 761, Portales, NM 88130, USA. *E-mail:* jack.williamson@enmu.edu.

WILLIAMSON, Joel R.; Prof. and Writer; b. 27 Oct. 1929, Anderson County, South Carolina, USA; m. Betty Anne Woodson, 18 Nov. 1986, one s. two d. *Education:* AB, 1949, MA, 1951, University of South Carolina; PhD, University of California, Berkeley, 1964. *Career:* Instructor, 1950–64, Asst Prof., 1964–66, Assoc. Prof., 1966–69, Prof., 1969–85, Linberger Prof. in Humanities, 1985–, Dept of History, University of North Carolina, Chapel Hill; mem. Society of American Historians; Southern Historical Asscn; Organization of American Historians; Southern Asscn for Women Historians. *Publications:* After Slavery: The Negro in South Carolina During Reconstruction, 1965; Origins of Segregation, 1968; New People: Miscegenation and Mulattoes in the United States, 1980; The Crucible of Race, 1984; A Rage for Order, 1986; William Faulkner and Southern History, 1993. Contributions: various publications. *Honours:* Parkman, Emerson, Owsley, Kennedy, Mayflower Awards; Fellow, Guggenheim Foundation, 1970–71, Center for Advanced Study in Behavioral Sciences, Stanford, CA, 1977–78, summer, 1979, 1980, 1981, NEH, 1987–88; Southern Fellow, 1961–62, Charles Warren Center, 1981–82; Mayflower Cup, 1994. *Address:* 211 Hillsborough St, Chapel Hill, NC 27514, USA. *E-mail:* william@email.unc.edu.

WILLIAMSON, Kristin Ingrid; novelist and biographer; b. 16 Sept. 1940, Melbourne, Vic., Australia; m. David Williamson 1974; three s. *Education:* BA, Latrobe University, 1981; Drama, Trinity College, London; TPTC. *Career:* Teacher of English, History and Drama, primary and high schools, Victoria, 1960–70; Lecturer in Drama, Melbourne State College, 1970–72; Freelance Journalist, 1973–79; Journalist, Columnist, National Times, Sydney, 1979–87; Writer, 1987–. *Publications:* The Last Bastion, 1984; Princess Kate (novel), 1988; Tanglewood (novel), 1992; The Jacaranda Years (novel), 1995; Brothers To Us (biog.), 1997; Treading on Dreams (novel), 1998; Women on the Rocks (novel), 2003. *Literary Agent:* Curtis Brown Pty, PO Box 19, Paddington, NSW 2021, Australia.

WILLIAMSON, Philip G., (Philip First, Joe Fish, Will Phillips); Writer; b. 4 Nov. 1955, Worcestershire, England. *Education:* Postgraduate Degree, Goldsmiths College, London. *Publications:* The Great Pervader, 1983; Paper Thin and Other Stories, 1986; Dark Night, 1986; Dinbig of Khimmur, 1991, The Legend of Shadd's Torment, 1993, From Enchantery, 1993; Moonblood, 1993; Heart of Shadows, 1994; Citadel, 1995; Enchantment's Edge, three vols, 1996–98; The Mates, 2003; Killing Time, 2003. *Literary Agent:* PFD, Drury House, 34–43 Russell St, London WC2B 5HA, England.

WILLIS, Meredith Sue; Writer and Educator; b. 31 May 1946, West Virginia, USA; m. Andrew B. Weinberger, 9 May 1982, one s. *Education:* BA, Barnard College, 1969; MFA, Columbia University, 1972. *Publications:* A Space Apart, 1979; Higher Ground, 1981; Only Great Changes, 1985; Personal Fiction Writing, 1984; Quilt Pieces, 1990; Blazing Pencils, 1990; Deep Revision, 1993; The Secret Super Power of Marco, 1994; In the Mountains of America, 1994; Marco's Monster, 1996; Trespassers, 1997; Oradell at Sunset, 2002. *Honours:* National Endowment for the Arts Fellowship, 1978; New Jersey Arts Fellowship, 1995; Honoree, Emory and Henry Literary Festival, 1995. *Address:* 311 Prospect St, South Orange, NJ 07079, USA. *E-mail:* msuewillis@aol.com. *Website:* www.meredithsuewillis.com.

WILLMOTT, Hedley Paul, BA, MA, PhD; lecturer and writer; b. 26 Dec. 1945, Bristol, England; m. Pauline Anne Burton 1978; one s. one d. *Education:* University of Liverpool, University of London. *Career:* Military Writer and Lecturer, Royal Military Acad., Sandhurst, 1969–; Programme Writer, British Broadcasting Corporation World Service, 1986–92; Visiting Lecturer, Temple University, Philadelphia, 1989, Memphis State University, Tennessee, 1989–90, National War College, Dept of Defense, Washington, DC, 1992–. *Publications:* Warships, 1975; B-17 Flying Fortress, 1980; Sea Warfare: Weapons, Tactics and Strategy, 1981; Empires in the Balance: Japanese and Allied Pacific Strategies to April 1942, 1982; The Barrier and the Javelin: Japanese and Allied Pacific Strategies, February to June 1942, 1983; Pearl Harbor, 1983; Zero A6M, 1983; June 1944, 1984; The Great Crusade: A New Complete History of the Second World War, 1989; Grave of a Dozen Schemes: British Naval Planning and the War against Japan, 1943–1945, 1996. *Honours:* Leman Award 1984.

WILLOUGHBY, Cass (see Olsen, Theodore Victor).

WILLS, Garry; writer, journalist and academic; b. 22 May 1934, Atlanta, GA, USA; m. Natalie Cavallo 1959; two s. one d. *Education:* BA, St Louis University, 1957; MA, Xavier University, Cincinnati, 1958; MA, 1959, PhD, 1961, Yale University. *Career:* Fellow, Center for Hellenic Studies, 1961–62; Assoc. Prof. of Classics, 1962–67, Adjunct Prof., 1968–80, Johns Hopkins University; Newspaper Columnist, Universal Press Syndicate, 1970–; Henry R. Luce Prof. of American Culture and Public Policy, 1980–88, Adjunct Prof., 1988–, Northwestern University; mem. American Acad. of Arts and Letters; American Acad. of Arts and Sciences; American Antiquarian Society; Massachusetts Historical Society. *Publications:* Chesterton, 1961; Politics and Catholic Freedom, 1964; Roman Culture, 1966; Jack Ruby, 1967; Second Civil War, 1968; Nixon Agonistes, 1970; Bare Ruined Choirs, 1972; Inventing America, 1978; At Button's, 1979; Confessions of a Conservative, 1979; Explaining America, 1980; The Kennedy Imprisonment, 1982; Lead Time, 1983; Cincinnatus, 1984; Reagan's America, 1987; Under God, 1990; Lincoln at Gettysburg, 1992; Certain Trumpets: The Call of Leaders, 1994; Witches and Jesuits: Shakespeare's Macbeth, 1994; John Wayne's America, 1997; Saint Augustine, 1999; A Necessary Evil: A History of American Distrust of Government, 1999; Papal Sin: Structures of Deceit, 2000. *Honours:* various hon. doctorates; National Book Critics Circle Ward, 1993; Pulitzer Prize for General Non-Fiction, 1993; National Humanities Medal, 1998. *Address:* c/o Dept of History, Northwestern University, Evanston, IL 60201, USA.

WILLUMSEN, Dorrit; Danish writer; b. 31 Aug. 1940. *Publications:* novels: Neonhaven (trans. as Neon Park) 1976, Hvis det virk elig var en film 1978 (trans. as If It Really Were a Film 1982), Marie: A Novel about the Life of Madame Tussaud 1983, Umage par 1983, Suk hjerte 1986, Manden som påskud 1987, Glemslens forår (trans. as Seeds of Oblivion) 1988, Bang 1996, Koras stemme 2000. *Honours:* Nordic Council Prize for Literature 1997. *Address:* c/o Curbstone Press, 321 Jackson Street, Willimantic, CT 06226-1738, USA. *Website:* www.curbstone.org.

WILMER, Clive; Lecturer, Writer, Poet, Trans. and Broadcaster; b. 10 Feb. 1945, Harrogate, Yorkshire, England; m. Diane Redmond 12 Sept. 1971 (divorced 1986); one s. one d. *Education:* BA, English, 1967, MA, 1970, King's College, Cambridge. *Career:* Visiting Instructor in Creative Writing, University of California at Santa Barbara, 1986; Ed., Numbers, 1986–90; Presenter, Poet of the Month series, BBC Radio 3, 1989–92; Mikimoto Memorial Ruskin Lecturer, University of Lancaster, 1996; Research Fellow and Poet-in-Residence, Anglia Polytechnic University, 1998–2002; Assoc. Teaching Officer, Sidney Sussex and Fitzwilliam Colleges, Cambridge, 1999–2002; mem. Companion of the Guild of St George, 1995. *Publications:* Poetry: The Dwelling Place, 1977; Devotions, 1982; Of Earthly Paradise, 1992; Selected Poems, 1995; The Falls, 2000. Translator: Forced March, by Miklós Radnóti (with G. Gömöri), 1979; Night Song of the Personal Shadow, by György Petri (with G. Gömöri), 1991; My Manifold City, by George Gömöri, 1996; Eternal Monday by György Petri (with G. Gömöri), 1999. Editor: Thom Gunn: The Occasions of Poetry, 1982; John Ruskin: Unto This Last and Other Writings, 1985; Dante Gabriel Rossetti: Selected Poems and Translations, 1991; William Morris: News From Nowhere and Other Writings, 1993; Poets Talking: The 'Poet of the Month' Interviews from BBC

Radio 3, 1994; Cambridge Observed: An Anthology (ed. with Charles Moseley), 1998; Donald Davie: With the Grain, 1998; The Life and Work of Miklós Radnóti: Essays (ed. with George Gömöri), 1999. Contributions: many reviews, newspapers, quarterlies and journals. *Honours:* University of Cambridge Chancellor's Medal for an English Poem, 1967; Writer's Grant, Arts Council of Great Britain, 1979; Author's Foundation Grant, 1993; Hon. Fellowship, Anglia Polytechnic University, 1997; Hungarian PEN Club Memorial Medal for Trans., 1998. *Literary Agent:* A. M. Heath & Co Ltd, 79 St Martin's Lane, London WC2N 4RE, England. *Address:* 57 Norwich St, Cambridge CB2 1ND, England. *E-mail:* cw291@cam.ac.uk.

WILMERS, Mary-Kay; British editor; one s. *Career:* Ed., London Review of Books 1992–. *Address:* London Review of Books, 28 Little Russell Street, London, WC1A 2HN, England. *Telephone:* (20) 7209-1101. *Fax:* (20) 7209-1102. *E-mail:* edit@lrb.co.uk. *Website:* www.lrb.co.uk.

WILOCH, Thomas; Poet, Writer and Ed.; b. 3 Feb. 1953, Detroit, Michigan, USA; m. Denise Gottis, 10 Oct. 1981. *Education:* BA, Wayne State University, 1978. *Career:* Associated with Gale Group 1977–; Pres., Manuscript Unlimited Inc., 2000–; Content Man., Poe Central website, 2001–02, Poe Archive website, 2002–, Codes and Chaos website, 2002–; Columnist, Retrofuturism, 1991–93, Photo Static, 1993–94; Book Reviewer, Anti-Matter Magazine, 1992–94, Green Man Review, 2002–; mem. Asscn of Literary Scholars and Critics. *Publications:* Stigmata Junction, 1985; Paper Mask, 1988; The Mannikin Cypher, 1989; Tales of Lord Shantih, 1990; Decoded Factories of the Heart, 1991; Night Rain, 1991; Narcotic Signature, 1992; Lyrical Brandy, 1993; Mr Templeton's Toyshop, 1995; Neon Trance, 1997; The Best of Grimoire Magazine (ed.), 2003. Contributions: Over 200 magazines. *Address:* PMB 226, 42015 Ford Rd, Canton, MI 48187, USA. *E-mail:* mssunltd@postmark.net.

WILSON, Andrew Norman, MA, FRSL; British writer; b. 27 Oct. 1950, England; m. 1st Katherine Dorothea Duncan-Jones 1971 (divorced 1989); two d.; m. 2nd Ruth Guilding 1991; one d. *Education:* Rugby School and New Coll., Oxford. *Career:* Asst Master Merchant Taylors' School 1975–76; Lecturer St Hugh's Coll. and New Coll., Oxford 1976–81; Literary Ed. Spectator 1981–83, Evening Standard 1990–97. *Publications:* fiction: The Sweets of Pimlico 1977, Unguarded Hours 1978, Kindly Light 1979, The Healing Art (Somerset Maugham Award) 1980, Who Was Oswald Fish? 1981, Wise Virgin (WHSmith Award) 1982, Scandal 1983, Gentleman in England 1985, Love Unknown 1986, Stray 1987, Incline Our Hearts 1988, A Bottle in the Smoke 1990, Daughters of Albion 1991, The Vicar of Sorrows 1993, Hearing Voices 1995, A Watch in the Night 1996, Hazel the Guinea-pig (for children) 1997, Dream Children 1998, My Name is Legion 2004; non-fiction: The Laird of Abbotsford 1980, A Life of John Milton 1983, Hilaire Belloc 1984, How Can We Know? An Essay on the Christian Religion 1985, The Church in Crisis (jtly) 1986, Landscape in France 1987, The Lion and the Honeycomb 1987, Penfriends from Porlock: Essays and Reviews 1977–86 1988, Tolstoy (Whitbread Award for Biography and Autobiography) 1988, Eminent Victorians 1989, John Henry Newman: prayers, poems, meditations (ed.) 1989, C. S. Lewis: A Biography 1990, Against Religion 1991, Jesus 1992, The Faber Book of Church and Clergy (ed.) 1992, The Rise and Fall of the House of Windsor 1993, The Faber Book of London (ed.) 1993, Paul: The Mind of the Apostle 1997, God's Funeral 1999, The Victorians 2003, Beautiful Shadow: A Life of Patricia Highsmith 2003, Iris Murdoch as I Knew Her 2004, London: A Short History 2004. *Honours:* Hon. mem. American Acad. of Arts and Letters 1984; Chancellor's Essay Prize 1975, Ellerton Theological Prize 1975. *Address:* 5 Regent's Park Terrace, London, NW1 7EE, England.

WILSON, August; Dramatist; b. 27 April 1945, Pittsburgh, Pennsylvania, USA; one d. *Career:* Founder, Black Horizons Theatre Co, Pittsburgh, 1968; mem. American Acad. of Arts and Letters. *Publications:* The Homecoming, 1979; The Coldest Day of the Year, 1979; Fullerton Street, 1980; Black Bart and the Sacred Hills, 1981; Jitney, 1982; Ma Rainey's Black Bottom, 1984; Fences, 1985; Joe Turner's Come and Gone, 1986; The Piano Lesson, 1987; Two Trains Running, 1990; Seven Guitars, 1995. *Honours:* New York Drama Critics Circle Awards, 1985, 1986, 1988, 1990, 1996; Whiting Writer's Award, 1986; Drama Desk Awards, 1986, 1990; American Theatre Critics Outstanding Play Awards, 1986, 1990, 1992; Tony Award, 1987; Pulitzer Prizes for Drama, 1987, 1990; Outer Critics' Circle Award, 1987; Literary Lion Award, New York Public Library, 1988.

WILSON, Colin Henry; British writer; b. 26 July 1931, Leicester, England; m. 1st Dorothy Betty Troop; one s.; m. 2nd Joy Stewart; two s. one d. *Career:* Visiting Prof., Hollins College, Virginia, 1966–67, University of Washington, Seattle, 1967, Dowling College, Majorca, 1969, Rutgers University, NJ, 1974; mem. Society of Authors. *Publications:* The Outsider, 1956; Religion and the Rebel, 1957; The Age of Defeat, 1959; Ritual in the Dark, 1960; The Strength to Dream, 1962; Origins of the Sexual Impulse, 1963; Necessary Doubt, 1964; Eagle and the Earwig, 1965; The Glass Cage, 1966; Sex and the Intelligent Teenager, 1966; Voyage to a Beginning, 1969; Hermann Hesse, 1973; Strange Powers, 1973; The Space Vampires, 1976; Mysteries, 1978; Starseekers, 1980; Access to Inner Worlds, 1982; Psychic Detectives, 1983; The Essential Colin Wilson, 1984; Rudolf Steiner: The Man and His Work, 1985; An Encyclopedia of Scandal (with Donald Seaman), 1986; Spider World: The Tower, 1987; Aleister Crowley – The Man and the Myth, 1987; An Encyclopedia of Unsolved Mysteries (with Damon Wilson), 1987; Marx Refuted, 1987; Written in Blood (with Donald Seaman), 1989; The Misfits – A Study of Sexual Outsiders, 1988; Beyond the Occult, 1988; The Serial Killers, 1990; Spiderworld: The Magician, 1991; The Strange Life of P. D. Ouspensky, 1993; Unsolved Mysteries Past and Present (with Damon Wilson), 1993; Atlas of Holy Places and Sacred Sites, 1996; From Atlantis to the Sphinx, 1996; Alien Dawn, 1998; The Devil's Party, 2000; Atlantis Blueprint (with Rand Fle'math), 2000; Spider World: The Magician, 2002; The Mammoth Book of Illustrated True Crime (ed. with Damon Wilson), 2002; Autobiography, 2003; Spiderworld: Shadowland, 2003; Dreaming to Some Purpose 2004. Contributions: Daily Mail. *Address:* Tetherdown, Trewallock Lane, Gorran Haven, Cornwall, England.

WILSON, Dave (see Floren, Lee).

WILSON, Donald M.; American journalist and publishing executive; *Publisher, NJBIZ;* b. 27 June 1925; m. Susan M. Neuberger 1957; one s. two d. *Education:* Yale Univ. *Career:* Air Corps Navigator, Second World War; magazine assignments in 35 countries 1951–61; fmr Far Eastern Corresp., Life magazine, Chief Washington Correspondent 1957–61; Deputy Dir US Information Agency 1961–65; Gen. Man. Time-Life Int. 1965–68; Assoc. Publisher Life magazine 1968–69; Vice-Pres. Corp. and Public Affairs, Time Inc. 1969–81, Corp. Vice-Pres. Public Affairs Time Inc. 1981–89; Publr NJBIZ 1989–. *Address:* NJBIZ, 104 Church Street, New Brunswick, NJ 08901 (Office); 4574 Province Line Road, Princeton, NJ 08540, USA (Home).

WILSON, Edward O(sborne); Biologist, Prof. and Writer; b. 10 June 1929, Birmingham, AL, USA; m. Irene Kelley, 30 Oct. 1955, one d. *Education:* BS, 1949, MS, 1950, University of Alabama; PhD, Harvard University, 1955. *Career:* Junior Fellow, Society of Fellows, 1953–56, Faculty, 1956–76, Curator, Entomology, 1971–, Baird Prof. of Science, 1976–94, Pellegrino University Prof., 1994–97, Research Prof., 1997–, Harvard University; Board of Dirs, World Wildlife Fund, 1983–94, Organization of Tropical Studies, 1984–91, New York Botanical Garden, 1991–95, American Museum of Natural History, 1992–2002, American Acad. of Liberal Education, 1993–, Nature Conservancy, 1994–2002, Conservation International, 1997–; mem. American Acad. of Arts and Sciences, fellow; American Genetics Asscn; American Humanist Society; American Philosophical Society; British Ecological Society, hon. life mem.; Entomological Society of America, hon. life mem.; National Acad. of Science; Royal Society, United Kingdom; Finnish Acad. of Science and Letters; Russian Acad. of Natural Sciences. *Publications:* The Insect Societies, 1971; Sociobiology: The New Synthesis, 1975; On Human Nature, 1978; Promethean Fire (with C. J. Lumsden), 1983; Biophilia, 1984; The Ants (with Bert Holldobler), 1990; Success and Dominance in Ecosystems, 1990; The Diversity of Life, 1991; Journey to the Ants (with Bert Holldobler), 1994; Naturalist, 1994; Consilience: The Unity of Knowledge, 1998; The Future of Life, 2002; Pheidole in the New World: A Dominant, Hyperdiverse Ant Genus, 2003. Contributions: Professional journals. *Honours:* National Medal of Science, 1976; Pulitzer Prizes in Non-Fiction, 1979, 1991; Tyler Ecology Prize, 1984; Weaver Award for Scholarly Letters, Ingersoll Foundation, 1989; Crafoord Prize, Royal Swedish Acad. of Sciences, 1990; Prix d'Institut de la Vie, Paris, 1990; International Prize for Biology, Government of Japan, 1993; Audubon Medal, Audubon Society, 1995; Los Angeles Times Book Prize for Science, 1995; Schubert Prize, Germany, 1996; German Ecological Foundation Book Award, 1998; Benjamin Franklin Medal, American Philosophical Society, 1999; Nonino International Prize, Italy, 2000; King Faisal, International Prize for Science, Saudi Arabia, 2000; Kistler Prize, Foundation for the Future, 2000; Silver Cross of Columbus, Dominican Republic, 2003; many hon. doctorates; Others. *Address:* 1010 Waltham St, Lexington, MA 02421-8062, USA.

WILSON, Eliane; writer; b. 4 Aug. 1934, Geneva, Switzerland; m. Paul Wilson 1963; two s. one d. *Education:* Geneva University, Heidelberg University. *Career:* mem. Thomas Hardy Society, Edward Thomas Fellowship. *Publications:* fiction: The Lost Dove 1998; contrib. to anthologies, including As I Trace Again Thy Winding Hill 1981, Images of Christmas 1984, Thomas Hardy: An Autobiography in Verse 1985, Edward Thomas: A Mirror of England 1985, Oxford: Words and Watercolours 1987, Jerusalem: Reflection of Eternity 1990. *Address:* Waysmeet, Orley Farm Road, Harrow on the Hill, HA1 3PF, England.

WILSON, Gina; Children's Writer and Poet; b. 1 April 1943, Abergele, North Wales. *Education:* MA, University of Edinburgh, 1965; Mount Holyoke College, 1965–66. *Career:* Asst Ed., Scottish National Dictionary, 1967–73, Dictionary of the Older Scottish Tongue, 1972–73. *Publications:* Cora Ravenwing, 1980; A Friendship of Equals, 1981; The Whisper, 1982; All Ends Up, 1984; Family Feeling, 1986; Just Us, 1988; Polly Pipes Up, 1989; I Hope You Know, 1989; Jim Jam Pyjamas, 1990; Wompus Galumpus, 1990; Riding the Great White, 1992; Prowlpuss, 1994; Ignis, 2001; Grandma's Bears, 2004. *Honours:* Frogmore Poetry Prize, 1997; Annual Lace Poetry Prize, 1999. *Address:* 24 Beaumont St, Oxford OX1 2NP, England.

WILSON, Jacqueline, OBE; British children's writer; b. 17 Dec. 1945, Bath, Somerset, England; m. William Millar Wilson 1965; one d. *Career:* journalist, D. C. Thompson, 1963–65; Advisory Mem., Whitbread Book Awards Panel, 1997–; Ambassador, Reading is Fundamental, 1998–; Judge, Rhône Poulenc Prizes for Junior Science Books, 1999. *Publications:* Nobody's Perfect, 1982; Waiting for the Sky to Fall, 1983; The Other Side, 1984;

Amber, 1986; The Power of the Shade, 1987; This Girl, 1988; Stevie Day Series, 1987; Is There Anybody There?, 1990; The Story of Tracy Beaker, 1991; The Suitcase Kid, 1992; Deep Blue, 1993; The Bed and Breakfast Star, 1994; Cliffhanger, 1995; The Dinosaur's Packed Lunch, 1995; Double Act, 1995; Bad Girls, 1996; Mr Cool, 1996; Monster Story Teller, 1997; The Lottie Project, 1997; Girls in Love, 1997; Connie and the Water Babies, 1997; Buried Alive!, 1998; Girls Under Pressure, 1998; How to Survive Summer Camp, 1998; The Illustrated Mum, 1999; Girls Out Late, 1999; Lizzie Zipmouth, 1999; The Dare Game, 2000; Take a Good Look, 2000; Vicky Angel, 2000; The Dare Game, 2000; My Brother Bernadette, 2000; The Cat Mummy, 2001; Dustbin Baby, 2001; Sleep-overs, 2001; Secrets, 2002; The Worry Website, 2002; Girls in Tears, 2003; Lola Rose, 2003; Midnight 2004. *Honours:* Oak Tree Award, 1992; Children's Book of the Year Award, 1993; Smarties Award, 1995; WHSmith Children's Book of the Year, 2002. *Address:* 1B Beaufort Road, Kingston on Thames, Surrey KT1 2TH, England. *Website:* www.jacquelinewilson.co.uk.

WILSON, Keith; Poet and Writer; b. 26 Dec. 1927, Clovis, New Mexico, USA; m. Heloise Brigham, 15 Feb. 1958, one s., four d. *Education:* BS, US Naval Acad., 1950; MA, University of New Mexico, 1956. *Publications:* Homestead, 1969; Thantog: Songs of a Jaguar Priest, 1977; While Dancing Feet Shatter the Earth, 1977; The Streets of San Miguel, 1979; Retablos, 1981; Stone Roses: Poems from Transylvania, 1983; Meeting at Jal (with Theodore Enslin), 1985; Lion's Gate: Selected Poems 1963–1986, 1988; The Wind of Pentecost, 1991; Graves Registry, 1992; The Way of the Dove, 1994; Bosque Redoudo: The Enclosed Grove, 2000. Contributions: journals. *Honours:* National Endowment for the Arts Fellowship; Fulbright-Hays Fellowship; D. H. Lawrence Creative Writing Fellowship. *Address:* 1500 S Locust St, No. C-21, Las Cruces, NM 88001, USA.

WILSON, Lanford; dramatist and stage director; b. 13 April 1937, Lebanon, MO, USA. *Education:* San Diego State College. *Career:* Resident Playwright and Dir, Circle Repertory Co, New York City, 1969–95; mem. Dramatists Guild. *Publications:* Balm in Gilead and Other Plays, 1966; The Rimers of Eldritch and Other Plays, 1968; The Gingham Dog, 1969; Lemon Sky, 1970; The Hotel Baltimore, 1973; The Mound Builders, 1976; Fifth of July, 1979; Talley's Folly, 1980; Angels Fall, 1983; Serenading Louie, 1985; Talley & Son, 1986; Burn This, 1988; Redwood Curtain, 1992; 21 Short Plays, 1994; By the Sea by the Sea by the Beautiful Sea, 1996; Sympathetic Magic, 1998. *Honours:* Vernon Rice Award, 1966–67; Rockefeller Foundation Grants, 1967, 1973; ABC Yale Fellow, 1969; Guggenheim Fellowship, 1970; National Institute of Arts and Letters Award, 1970; Obie Awards, 1972, 1975, 1984; Outer Critics Circle Award, 1973; Drama Critics Circle Awards, 1973, 1980; Pulitzer Prize for Drama, 1980; Brandeis University Creative Arts Award, 1981; John Steinbeck Award, 1990; National Endowment for the Arts Grant, 1990; Edward Albee Last Frontier Award, 1994; American Acad. of Achievement Award, 1995; Hon. doctorates. *Address:* c/o Dramatists' Guild, 234 W 44th Street, New York, NY 10036, USA.

WILSON, Robert McLiam; writer; b. 1964, Belfast; m. *Education:* Univ. of Cambridge. *Career:* several BBC TV documentaries. *Publications:* Novels: Ripley Bogle, 1989; Manfred's Pain, 1992; Eureka Street, 1996; The Extremists, 2004. Non-Fiction: The Dispossessed, 1992. *Honours:* Rooney Prize, 1989; Hughes Prize, 1989; Betty Trask Prize, 1990; Irish Book award, 1990. *Address:* c/o Secker & Warburg, Random House, 20 Vauxhall Bridge Road, London SW1V 2SA, England.

WILSON, William Julius; sociologist and academic; b. 20 Dec. 1935, Derry Township, Pennsylvania, USA; m. 1st Mildred Marie Hood 1957; two d.; m. 2nd Beverly Ann Huebner 1970; one s. one d. *Education:* BA, Wilberforce University, 1958; MA, Bowling Green State University, 1961; PhD, Washington State University, 1966. *Career:* Asst Prof., 1965–69, Assoc. Prof. of Sociology, 1969–71, University of Massachusetts, Amherst; Visiting Assoc. Prof. and Research Scholar, 1971–72, Assoc. Prof. of Sociology, 1972–75, Prof. of Sociology, 1975–80, Lucy Flower Prof. of Urban Sociology, 1980–84, Lucy Flower Distinguished Service Prof., 1984–90, Lucy Flower University Prof. of Sociology and Public Policy, 1990–96, University of Chicago; Visiting Assoc. Prof., 1972, Malcolm Wiener Prof. of Social Policy, 1996–98, John F. Kennedy School of Government, Lewis P. and Linda L. Geyser University Prof., Harvard University, 1998–; Fellow, Center for Advanced Study in the Behavioral Sciences, Stanford, CA, 1981–82; Andrew Dixon White Prof.-at-Large, Cornell University, 1994–98; mem. A Philip Randolph Institute, national board, 1981–; American Acad. of Arts and Sciences, fellow; American Acad. of Political and Social Science, fellow; American Asscn for the Advancement of Science, fellow; American Philosophical Society; American Sociological Asscn, pres., 1989–90; Center for Urban Studies, exec. committee, 1974–; National Acad. of Education; National Acad. of Sciences; National Urban League, board of trustees, 1995–98; Russell Sage Foundation, board of dirs, chair, 1988–98, 1994–96; Sociological Research Asscn, pres., 1987–88. *Publications:* Power, Racism and Privilege: Race Relations in Theoretical and Sociohistorical Perspectives, 1973; Through Different Eyes: Black and White Perspectives on American Race Relations (ed. with Peter I Rose and Stanley Rothman), 1973; The Declining Significance of Race: Blacks and Changing American Institutions, 1978; The Truly Disadvantaged: The Inner City, the Underclass, and Public Policy, 1987; The Ghetto Underclass: Social Science Perspectives (ed.), 1989; Sociology and the Public Agenda (ed.), 1993; Poverty, Inequality and the Future of Social Policy: Western States in the New World Order (ed. with Katherine McFate and Roger Lawson), 1995; When Work Disappears: The World of the New Urban Poor, 1996; The Bridge Over the Racial Divide: Rising Inequality and Coalition Politics, 1999. Contributions: many scholarly books, journals, and reviews, and general periodicals. *Honours:* John D. and Catherine T. MacArthur Foundation Fellowship, 1987–92; New York Times Book Review Best Book Citations, 1987, 1996; Washington Monthly Annual Book Award, 1988; C. Wright Mills Award, Society for the Study of Social Problems, 1988; Dubois, Johnson, Frazier Award, American Sociological Asscn, 1990; Burton Gordon Feldman Award, Brandeis University, 1991; Frank E. Seidman Distinguished Award in Political Economy, Rhodes College, Memphis, Tennessee, 1994; Martin Luther King Jr National Award, Southern Christian Leadership Council, Los Angeles, 1998; Lester F. Ward Distinguished Contributions to Applied Sociology Award, 1998; National Medal of Science, 1998; numerous hon. doctorates. *Address:* John F. Kennedy School of Government, Harvard University, 79 JFK Street, Cambridge, MA 02138, USA.

WILTON-JONES, Anni, (Áine an Caipín); Performance Poet and Lecturer; b. 8 April 1949, Bromborough, Wales; two s., five d. *Education:* DSRT, 1969, DSRR, 1970, School of Radiography, Southampton; BA, Open University, 1994; PGCE, E and T, 1999; Cert SEN, 2000, Dip SEN (SpLD), 2002, UWCN; AMBDA, 2002. *Publications:* Bridges, 1999; This is… Salem, 1999; Fresh Voices For Younger Listeners, 2000; Anam Cara (CD), 2001; Light Touch, 2002. Contributions: newspapers and journals. *Address:* Ty Beirdd, 53 Church St, Ebbw Vale, NP23 6BG Wales. *E-mail:* anni_poetry@yahoo.co.uk.

WINCH, Donald Norman; Prof. of the History of Economics and Writer; b. 15 April 1935, London, England; m. Doreen Lidster, 5 Aug. 1983. *Education:* BSc, LSE, 1956; PhD, Princeton University, 1960. *Career:* Visiting Lecturer, University of California, Berkeley, 1959–60; Lecturer in Economics, University of Edinburgh, 1960–63; Lecturer, 1963–66, Reader, 1966–69, Dean, School of Social Sciences, 1968–74, Prof. of the History of Economics, 1969–, Pro-Vice-Chancellor, Arts and Social Studies, 1986–89, University of Sussex; Publications Secretary, Royal Economic Society, 1971–; Visiting Fellow, Institute for Advanced Study, Princeton, NJ, 1974–75, King's College, Cambridge, 1983, Australian National University, 1983, St Catharine's College, Cambridge, 1989, All Souls College, Oxford, 1994; Review Ed., Economic Journal, 1976–83; British Council Distinguished Visiting Fellow, Kyoto University, 1992; Carlyle Lecturer, University of Oxford, 1995. *Publications:* Classical Political Economy and Colonies, 1965; James Mill: Selected Economic Writings (ed.), 1966; Economics and Policy, 1969; The Economic Advisory Council 1930–1939 (with S. K. Howson), 1976; Adam Smith's Politics, 1978; That Noble Science of Politics (with S. Collini and J. W. Burrow), 1983; Malthus, 1987; Riches and Poverty, 1996. Contributions: many learned journals. *Honours:* British Acad., fellow, 1986–, vice-pres., 1993–94; FRHistS, 1987–. *Address:* c/o Arts B, University of Sussex, Brighton BN1 9QN, England.

WINCHESTER, Jack (see Freemantle, Brian (Harry)).

WINCHESTER, Simon; American writer; b. 1940. *Education:* Univ. of Oxford. *Publications:* Northern Ireland in Crisis 1975, American Heartbeat 1976, Their Noble Lordships 1978, Prison Diary, Argentina 1983, The Sun Never Sets: Travels to the Remaining Outposts of the British Empire 1986, The Rise and Fall of Travel 1989, Pacific Rising 1991, Pacific Nightmare: How Japan Starts World War III: A Future History 1992, The River at the Centre of the World 1996, The Surgeon of Crowthorne 1998, The Professor and the Madman 1998, The Fracture Zone: My Return to the Balkans 1999, The Map That Changed the World 2001, Tramping 2001, Outposts: Journeys to the Surviving Relics of the British Empire 2003, Krakatoa: The Day the World Exploded 2003, The Meaning of Everything: The Story of the Oxford English Dictionary 2003, Simon Winchester's Calcutta 2004; co-author: Small World: A Global Photographic Project 1995, America's Idea of a Good Time 2001; contrib. to Stories of Empire: Buildings of the Raj 1983, Conde Nast Traveller, Smithsonian, National Geographic. *Address:* c/o Oxford University Press, Great Clarendon Street, Oxford, OX2 6DP, England. *Website:* www.simonwinchester.com.

WINDLEY, Carol; Writer; b. 18 June 1947, Tofino, BC, Canada; m. Robert Windley, 8 Oct. 1971, one d. *Publications:* Visible Light, 1993; City of Ladies, 1998. Contributions: anthologies and periodicals. *Honours:* Bumbershoot-Weyerhauser Publication Award, 1993; Canada Council B. Grants, 1995, 1997. *Address:* 5989 Tweedsmuir Cres., Nanaimo, BC, Canada. *E-mail:* oolichan@mail.island.net.

WINDSOR, Patricia, (Colin Daniel, Katonah Summertree); Writer, Poet, Lecturer and Teacher; b. 21 Sept. 1938, New York, NY, USA; one s. one d. *Career:* Faculty, Institute of Children's Literature, University of Maryland Writers Institute; Ed.-in-Chief, The Easterner, Washington, DC; Co-Dir, Wordspring Literary Consultants; Dir, Summertree Studios, Savannah; Instructor, Creative Writing, Armstrong Atlantic University, Savannah; mem. Authors' Guild; Children's Book Guild; International Writing Guild; MWA; Poetry Society of Georgia; Savannah Storytellers. *Publications:* The Summer Before, 1973; Something's Waiting for You, Baker D, 1974; Home is Where Your Feet Are Standing, 1975; Mad Martin, 1976; Killing Time, 1980; The Sandman's Eyes, 1985; The Hero, 1988; Just Like the Movies, 1990; The Christmas Killer, 1991; The Blooding, 1996; The House of Death,

1996. Contributions: anthologies and magazines. *Honours:* American Library Asscn Best Book Award, 1973; Outstanding Book for Young Adults Citation, New York Times, 1976; Edgar Allan Poe Award, MWA, 1986. *Address:* c/o Writers House, 21 W 26th St, New York, NY 10010, USA.

WINEGARTEN, Renee; Literary Critic and Author; b. 23 June 1922, London, England; m. Asher Winegarten, deceased 1946. *Education:* BA, 1943, PhD, 1950, Girton College, Cambridge. *Career:* mem. George Sand Asscn; Society of Authors; Authors' Guild. *Publications:* French Lyric Poetry in the Age of Malherbe, 1954; Writers and Revolution, 1974; The Double Life of George Sand, 1978; Madame de Staël, 1985; Simone de Beauvoir: A Critical View, 1988; Accursed Politics: Some French Women Writers and Political Life 1715–1850, 2003. Contributions: journals. *Address:* 12 Heather Walk, Edgware, Middlesex HA8 9TS, England.

WINGATE, John Allan; Author; b. 15 March 1920, Cornwall, England; one s. one d. *Career:* mem. Nautical Institute. *Publications:* Submariner Sinclair Series, 1959–64; Sinclair Action Series, 1968, 1969, 1971; HMS Belfast, In Trust for the Nation, 1972; In the Blood, 1973; Below the Horizon, 1974; The Sea Above Them, 1975; Oil Strike, 1976; Black Tide, 1976; Avalanche, 1977; Red Mutiny, 1977; Target Risk, 1978; Seawaymen, 1979; Frigate, 1980; Carrier, 1981; Submarine, 1982; William the Conqueror, 1984; Go Deep, 1985; The Windship Race, 1987; The Fighting Tenth, 1990; The Man Called Mark, 1996. *Honours:* Distinguished Service Cross, 1943. *Address:* c/o Lloyd Bank Plc, Waterloo Pl., Pall Mall, London SW1Y 5NJ, England.

WINNER, Michael Robert; Producer, Dir and Writer; b. 30 Oct. 1935, London, England. *Education:* Downing College, Cambridge. *Career:* Chair., Scimitar Films Ltd, Michael Winner Ltd, Motion Picture and Theatrical Investments Ltd; Senior Mem. of Council, Trustee, Dirs Guild of Great Britain; Founder, Chair., The Police Memorial Trust; mem. Writers Guild of Great Britain. *Publications:* Screenplays: Cool Mikado, 1962; You Must Be Joking, 1965; The Jokers, 1966; Hannibal Brooks, 1968; The Sentinel, 1976; The Big Sleep, 1977; The Wicked Lady, 1982; Appointment With Death, 1987; A Chorus of Disapproval, 1988; Bullseye!, 1989; Dirty Weekend, 1992; Parting Shots, 1997. Books: Winner's Dinners, 1999; Winner Guide, 2002; Winner Takes All (autobiog.), 2004. Contributions: Sunday Times; News of the World. *Address:* 219 Kensington High St, London W8 6BD, England. *Telephone:* (20) 7734-8385. *Fax:* (20) 7602-9217.

WINNIFRITH, Thomas John, BA, MPhil, PhD; writer; b. 5 April 1938, Dulwich, England; m. 1st Joanna Booker 1967; m. 2nd Helen Young 1988; one s. two d. *Education:* Christ Church, Oxford, Corpus Christi, Oxford, University of Liverpool. *Career:* Asst Master, Eton College, 1961–66; EK Chambers Student, 1966–68; William Noble Fellow, 1968–70; Lecturer, Senior Lecturer, University of Warwick, 1970–98; Visiting Fellow, All Souls College, Oxford, 1984; Emeritus Leverhulme Fellow, 1999–2000. *Publications:* The Brontës and Their Background, 1973; The Brontës, 1977; Brontë Facts and Problems, 1983; Nineteen Eighty Four and All's Well, 1984; The Vlachs, 1987; A New Life of Charlotte Brontë, 1988; Charlotte and Emily Brontë, 1989; Fallen Women in the Nineteenth Century Novel, 1994; Shattered Eagles: Balkan Fragments, 1996; Badlands Borderlands, 2002. *Address:* 50 Sheep Street, Shipston on Stour, Warwickshire CV36 4AE, England. *E-mail:* twinnifrith@fish.co.uk.

WINOCK, Michel; Publisher, Historian, Prof. and Writer; b. 19 March 1937, Paris, France; m. Françoise Werner, 28 Oct. 1961, two s. *Education:* L. ès L., 1959, DES, History, 1960, Agrégation, History, 1961, D. ès L., History, 1987, Sorbonne, University of Paris. *Career:* Lecturer, Senior Lecturer, University of Paris VIII-Vincennes à St-Denis, 1968–78; Publisher, Editions du Seuil, Paris, 1969–; Ed.-in-Chief, 1978–81, Editorial Adviser, 1981–, L'Histoire magazine; Senior Lecturer, 1978–90, Prof., 1990–, Institut d'Études politiques, Paris. *Publications:* Histoire politique de la revue Esprit, 1930–1950, 1975; La republique se meurt, 1978; Les grandes crises politiques, 1971–1968, 1986; Nationalisme, antisemitisme et fascisme en France, 1990; Le socialisme en France et en Europe XIX–XX siècle, 1992; Le Siècle des intellectuels, 1997; La France politique XIX–XX siècle, 1999; Les Voix de la Liberté, 2001. Contributions: scholarly books and journals. *Address:* c/o Institut d'Études politiques, 27 rue Saint-Guillaume, 75337 Paris Cédex 07, France. *E-mail:* wimi@cybercable.fr.

WINSTON, Sarah, (Sarah E. Lorenz); Writer; b. 15 Dec. 1912, New York, NY, USA; m. Keith Winston, 11 June 1932, two s. *Education:* New York University, 1929, 1930; Philosophy and Appreciation of Art course, The Barnes Foundation, 1966, 1967; Art Seminars (research), 1967–89. *Career:* mem. National League of American Pen Women. *Publications:* And Always Tomorrow, 1963; Everything Happens for the Best, 1969; Our Son, Ken, 1969; Not Yet Spring (poems), 1976; V-Mail: Letters of the World War II Combat Medic, 1985; Summer Conference, 1990; Of Apples and Oranges, 1993. Contributions: journals. *Honours:* First Prize Awards, National League of American Pen Women, 1972, 1974.

WINTERSON, Jeanette, BA; British writer; b. 27 Aug. 1959, Manchester, England. *Education:* Accrington Girls' Grammar School, St Catherine's Coll., Oxford. *Career:* fmr Ed. Pandora Press. *Play:* The Power Book (Royal Nat. Theatre, London, Théâtre de Chaillot, Paris). *Screenplay:* Great Moments in Aviation 1992. *Television:* Oranges Are Not The Only Fruit (BBC) 1990 (BAFTA Award for Best Drama 1990, FIPA d'Argent Award for screenplay, Cannes Film Festival 1991), Orlando – Art That Shook the World (BBC) 2002, South Bank Show 2004. *Publications:* fiction: Oranges Are Not The Only Fruit (Whitbread Prize for Best First Novel) 1985, Boating for Beginners 1985, Passion Fruit: Romantic Fiction with a Twist (ed.) 1986, The Passion 1987, Sexing the Cherry 1989, Written on the Body 1992, Art and Lies 1994, Gut Symmetries 1997, The World and Other Places (short stories) 1998, The Power Book 2000, The King of Capri (juvenile) 2003, Lighthousekeeping 2004; non-fiction: Fit for the Future 1986; essays: Art Objects 1994. *Honours:* John Llewellyn Rhys Memorial Book Prize 1987, American Acad. of Arts and Letters E. M. Forster Award 1989, Golden Gate Award, San Francisco Int. Film Festival 1990, Best of Young British Novelists Award 1992, Int. Fiction Award, Festival Letteratura Mantua 1999. *Literary Agent:* William Morris Agency, Inc., 1325 Avenue of the Americas, New York, NY 10019, USA. *Address:* c/o Great Moments Ltd, 40 Brushfield Street, London, E1 6AG, England (Office). *E-mail:* info@jeanettewinterson.com. *Website:* www.jeanettewinterson.com.

WINTON, Timothy John; Australian writer; b. 4 Aug. 1960, near Perth, WA; m. Denise Winton; two s. one d. *Education:* Western Australian Inst. of Technology. *Publications:* An Open Swimmer 1981, Shallows 1984, Scisson and Other Stories 1985, That Eye, The Sky 1986, Minimum of Two 1987, In the Winter Dark 1988, Jesse 1988, Lockie Leonard, Human Torpedo 1991, The Bugalugs Bum Thief 1991, Cloudstreet 1992, Lockie Leonard, Scumbuster 1993, Land's Edge (with Trish Ainslie and Roger Garwood) 1993, Local Colour: Travels in the Other Australia 1994, The Riders 1995, Blueback: A Contemporary Fable 1998, Dirt Music 2001. *Honours:* Vogel Literary Award 1981, Miles Franklin Awards, Arts Management Party Ltd 1984, 1992, Deo Gloria Prize for Religious Writing 1991, Commonwealth Writers Prize 1995. *Literary Agent:* David Higham Associates, 5–8 Lower John Street, Golden Square, London, W1F 9HA, England. *Telephone:* (20) 7434-5900. *Fax:* (20) 7437-1072. *E-mail:* dha@davidhigham.co.uk. *Website:* www.davidhigham.co.uk.

WISEMAN, Christopher (Stephen); Prof. of English (retd), Poet and Writer; b. 31 May 1936, Hull, Yorkshire, England; m. Jean Leytem, 1 Jan. 1963, two s. *Education:* BA, 1959, MA, 1962, University of Cambridge; PhD, University of Strathclyde, 1971. *Career:* Asst to Prof. of English, University of Calgary, 1969–97; mem. League of Canadian Poets; Writers Guild of Alberta. *Publications:* Waiting for the Barbarians, 1971; The Barbarian File, 1974; Beyond the Labyrinth: A Study of Edwin Muir's Poetry, 1978; The Upper Hand, 1981; An Ocean of Whispers, 1982; Postcards Home: Poems New and Selected, 1988; Missing Persons, 1989; Remembering Mr Fox, 1995; Crossing the Salt Flats, 1999. Contributions: Reviews, quarterlies, journals, and magazines. *Honours:* Writers Guild of Alberta Poetry Award, 1988; Alberta Achievement Award for Excellence in Writing, 1988; Alberta Poetry Awards, 1988, 1989. *Address:* 8 Varwood Pl. NW, Calgary, AB T3A 0C1, Canada.

WISEMAN, David, (Jane Julian), BA, DipEd; writer; b. 13 Jan. 1916, Manchester, England; m. Cicely Hilda Mary Richards 1939; two s. two d. *Education:* University of Manchester. *Career:* Ed., Adult Education, 1947–50; mem. Society of Authors. *Publications:* Jeremy Visick, 1981; The Fate of Jeremy Visick, 1982; Thimbles, 1982; Blodwen and the Guardians, 1983; Adams Common, 1984; Pudding and Pie, 1986; Jumping Jack, 1988; Badge of Honour, 1989; The Devil's Cauldron, 1989; Mum's Winning Streak, 1990; Moonglow, 1990; Goliath Takes the Bait, 1993. As Jane Julian: Ellen Bray, 1985; As Wind to Fire, 1989; The Sunlit Days, 1990. *Address:* 24 Ravenswood Drive, Auckley, Doncaster DN9 3PB, England.

WISSE, Ruth; American academic, writer, editor and translator; b. 13 May 1936, Cernauti, Romania; m. Leonard Wisse 1957; two s. one d. *Education:* BA, 1957, PhD, 1969, McGill University; MA, Columbia University, 1961. *Career:* Asst Prof., 1968–71, Assoc. Prof., 1975, Chair., Dept of Jewish Studies, 1976–79, Prof., 1978–92, Montréal Jewish Community Chair in Jewish Studies, 1986–92, McGill University; Senior Lecturer, University of Tel-Aviv and Hebrew University, Tel-Aviv, 1971–73; Visiting Prof., 1975, Mem., Academic Advisory Board, 2000–, YIVO Institute for Jewish Research; Martin Peretz Prof. of Yiddish Literature, 1993–2003, Dir, Center for Jewish Studies, 1993–96, College Prof., 2003–Harvard University; mem. American Acad. for Jewish Research; Asscn for Jewish Studies, pres., 1985–89; National Foundation for Jewish Culture, board of academic advisors, 1979–82. *Publications:* The Schlemiel as Modern Hero, 1970; A Shtetl and Other Yiddish Novellas (ed.), 1972; The Best of Sholem Aleichem (ed. with Irving Howe), 1979; The Penguin Book of Modern Yiddish Verse (ed. with Irving Howe and Khone Shmeruk), 1987; A Little Love in Big Manhattan, 1988; The I. L. Peretz Reader (ed.), 1990; I. L. Peretz and the Making of Modern Jewish Culture, 1991; If I Am Not for Myself–: The Liberal Portrayal of the Jews, 1992; The Modern Jewish Canon: A Journey Through Language and Culture, 2000. Contributions: reference works and periodicals. *Honours:* J. I. Segal Awards for Literature, 1971, 1989; Manger Prize for Yiddish Literature, 1988; Moment Magazine Award in Jewish Scholarship, 1989; Torch of Learning Award, Hebrew University, Tel-Aviv, 1993; Maurice Stiller Prize, Baltimore Hebrew University, 1998; Jewish Cultural Achievement Award, National Foundation for Jewish Culture, 2001; National Jewish Book Award, 2001; Guardian of Zion Award of Rennert Center, Bar-Ilan Univ., 2003. *Address:* c/o Department of Near Eastern Languages and Civilizations, Harvard University, Cambridge, MA 02138, USA. *E-mail:* wisse@fas.harvard.edu.

WITT, Harold Vernon; Writer, Poet and Ed.; b. 6 Feb. 1923, Santa Ana, CA, USA; m. Beth Hewitt, 8 Sept. 1948, one s. two d. *Education:* BA, 1943, BLS, 1953, University of California at Berkeley; MA, University of Michigan, 1947. *Career:* Co-Ed., California State Poetry Quarterly, 1976, Blue Unicorn, 1977–; Consulting Ed., Poet Lore, 1976–91. *Publications:* The Death of Venus, 1958; Beasts in Clothes, 1961; Now Swim, 1974; Suprised by Others at Fort Cronkhite, 1975; Winesburg by the Sea, 1979; The Snow Prince, 1982; Flashbacks and Reruns, 1985; The Light at Newport, 1992; American Literature, 1994. Contributions: journals and periodicals. *Honours:* Hopwood Award, 1947; Phelan Award, 1960; First Prize, San Francisco Poetry Centre Poetic Drama Competition, 1963; Emily Dickinson Award, Poetry Society of America, 1972; various awards, World Order of Narrative Poets.

WITTICH, John Charles Bird, (Charles Bird); Librarian (retd) and Writer; b. 18 Feb. 1929, London, England; m. June Rose Taylor, 10 July 1954, one s. one d. *Education:* BA, 1951. *Publications:* Off Beat Walks In London, 1969; Curiosities of London, 1973; London Villages, 1992; Curiosities of Surrey, 1994; Exploring Cathedrals, 1996; London Bus Top Tourist, 1997; History and Guide: St Vedast's Church, City of London, 1999; London's Circle and other lines, 2001; Eventful London, 2001; Exploring Abbeys, 2001; Pilgrimages to London Churches, Cathedrals and Chapels, 2002; Catholic Pilgrims' London, 2002; A Literary Guide to London Shrines – Yesterday and Today, in preparation. Contributions: periodicals and journals. *Address:* 88 Woodlawn St, Whitstable, Kent CT5 1HH, England.

WOESSNER, Warren (Dexter); Attorney, Ed., Poet and Writer; b. 31 May 1944, Brunswick, NJ, USA; m. Iris Freeman, 6 Jan. 1990. *Education:* BA, Cornell University, 1966; PhD, 1971, JD, 1981, University of Wisconsin. *Career:* Founder, Ed., and Publisher, 1968–81, Senior Ed., 1981–, Abraxas Magazine; Board of Dirs, 1988–92, Pres., 1989–92, Coffee House Press; Contributing Ed., Pharmaceutical News. *Publications:* The Forest and the Trees, 1968; Landing, 1974; No Hiding Place, 1979; Storm Lines, 1987; Clear to Chukchi, 1996; Iris Rising, 1998; Chemistry, 2002. Contributions: anthologies, magazines and periodicals. *Honours:* National Endowment for the Arts Fellowship, 1974; Wisconsin Arts Board Fellowships, 1975, 1976; Loft-McKnight Fellow, 1985; Minnesota Voices, Competition for Poetry, 1986. *Address:* 34 W Minnehaha Parkway, Minneapolis, MN 55419, USA.

WOIWODE, Larry (Alfred); Writer and Poet; b. 30 Oct. 1941, Carrington, ND, USA; m. Carole Ann Peterson, 21 May 1965, four c. *Education:* University of Illinois at Urbana-Champaign, 1959–64. *Career:* Writer-in-Residence, University of Wisconsin at Madison, 1973–74; Prof., Wheaton College, 1981, 1984; Visiting Prof., 1983–85, Prof. and Dir of the Creative Writing Program, 1985–88, SUNY at Binghamton; various workshops and readings at many colleges and universities. *Publications:* Fiction: What I'm Going to Do, I Think, 1969; Beyond the Bedroom Wall: A Family Album, 1975; Poppa John, 1981; Born Brothers, 1988; The Neumiller Stories, 1989; Indian Affairs: A Novel, 1992; Silent Passengers: Stories, 1993. Poetry: Even Tide, 1975. Non-Fiction: Acts, 1993; The Aristocrat of the West: Biography of Harold Schafer, 2000; What I Think I Did: A Season of Survival in Two Acts (autobiog.), 2000. Contributions: books, anthologies, reviews, periodicals, journals, etc. *Honours:* Notable Book Award, American Library Asscn, 1970; William Faulkner Foundation Award, 1970; Guggenheim Fellowship, 1971–72; Fiction Award, Friends of American Writers, 1976; Hon. doctorates, North Dakota State University, 1977, Geneva College, 1997; Fiction Award, 1980, Medal of Merit, 1995, American Acad. of Arts and Letters; Aga Khan Literary Prize, Paris Review, 1990; Book Award of Short Fiction, Louisiana State University/Southern Review, 1990; John Dos Passos Prize, 1991; Poet Laureate of North Dakota, 1995. *Address:* c/o Basic Books, 10 E 53rd St, New York, NY 10022, USA.

WOLF, Christa; Author; b. 18 March 1929, Landsberg an der Warthe, Germany; m. Gerhard Wolf, 1951, two d. *Education:* University of Jena; University of Leipzig. *Career:* mem. Deutsche Akademie für Sprache und Dichtung eV, Darmstadt; Freie Akademie der Künste, Hamburg. *Publications:* Moskauer Novelle, 1961; Die geteilte Himmel, 1963, English trans. as Divided Heaven: A Novel of Germany Today, 1965; Nachdenken über Christa T, 1968, English trans. as The Quest for Christa T, 1971; Lesen und Schreiben: Aufsätze und Betrachtungen, 1972, English trans. as The Reader the Writer: Essays, Sketches, Memories, 1977; Unter den Linden: Drei unwahrscheinliche Geschichten, 1974; Kindheitsmuster, 1976, English trans. as A Model Childhood, 1980; J'écris sur ce qui m'inquiète: Débat dans Sinn und Form sur don derneir roman, 1977; Kein Ort. Nirgends, 1979, English trans. as No Place on Earth, 1982; Fortgesetzter Versuch: Aufsätze, Gespräche, Essays, 1979; Gesammelte Erzählungen, 1980; Neue Lebensansichten eines Katers: Juninachmittag, 1981; Kassandra: Vier Vorlesungen: Eine Erzählung, 1983, English trans. as Cassandra: A Novel and Four Essays, 1984; Störfall: Nachrichten eines Tages, 1987, English trans. as Accident: A Day's News, 1989; Die Dimension des Autors: Essays und Aufsätze, Reden und Gespräche, 1959–86, 1987, English trans. as The Author's Dimension: Selected Essays, 1990; Sommerstück, 1989; Was bleibt, 1990; Im Dialog: Aktuelle Texte, 1990; Sei gegrüsst und lebe!: Eine Freundschaft in Briefen, 1964–73, 1993; Akteneinsicht-Christa Wolf: Zerrspiegel und Dialog, 1993; Auf dem Weg nach Tabou, Texte, 1990–94, 1994; Die Zeichen der Nuria Quevado, 1994; Medea: Stimmen, 1996; Hierzulande, Andernorts, 2000. *Honours:* Art Prize, Halle, 1961; Heinrich Mann Prize, 1963; National Prize, Third Class, 1964, First Class, 1987, German Democratic Republic; Literature Prize, Free Hanseatic City of Bremen, 1972; Theodor Fontane Prize for Art and Literature, 1972; Georg Büchner Prize, 1980; Schiller Memorial Prize, 1983; Austrian Prize for European Literature, 1984; Officier, Ordre des Arts et des Lettres, 1990; Mondello Literature Prize, 1990; Rahel Varnhagen von Ense Medal, 1994. *Address:* c/o Deutsche Akademie für Sprache und Dichtung eV, Alexandraweg 23, 64287, Darmstadt, Germany.

WOLF, Naomi; Writer; b. 12 Nov. 1962, San Francisco, CA, USA; m. David Shipley 1993; one c. *Education:* Graduated, Yale University, 1984; New College, Oxford. *Publications:* The Beauty Myth: How Images of Beauty Are Used Against Women, 1990; Fire with Fire: The New Female Power and How it Will Change the Twenty-First Century, 1993; Promiscuities, 1997; Misconceptions: Truth, Lies, and the Unexpected on the Journey to Motherhood, 2001. Contributions: many periodicals. *Honours:* Rhodes Scholar, 1986. *Literary Agent:* Royce Carlton Inc, 866 UN Plaza, New York, NY 10017, USA.

WOLFE, Christopher; Prof. of Political Science and Writer; b. 11 March 1949, Boston, Massachusetts, USA; m. Anne McGowan, 17 June 1972, five s., five d. *Education:* BA, University of Notre Dame, 1971; PhD, Boston College, 1978. *Career:* Instructor, Assumption College, Worcester, Massachusetts, 1975–78; Asst Prof., 1978–84, Assoc. Prof., 1984–92, Prof. of Political Science, 1992–, Marquette University; Founder and Pres., American Public Philosophy Institute, 1989; mem. American Political Science Asscn; Federalist Society; Fellowship of Catholic Scholars. *Publications:* The Rise of Modern Judicial Review: From Constitutional Interpretation to Judge-Made Law, 1986; Faith and Liberal Democracy, 1987; Judicial Activism: Bulwark of Freedom or Precarious Security?, 1991; Liberalism at the Crossroads (ed. with John Hittinger), 1994; How to Interpret the Constitution, 1996; The Family, Civil Society and the State (ed.), 1998; Homosexuality and American Public Life (ed.), 1999; Natural Law and Public Reason (ed. with Robert George), 2000; Same-Sex Matters (ed.), 2000. Contributions: Professional journals and general periodicals. *Honours:* Woodrow Wilson Fellowship, 1971; Institute for Educational Affairs Grants, 1982, 1983; Bradley Foundation Grant, 1986; National Endowment for the Humanities Fellowship, 1994; Templeton Honor Roll for Education in a Free Society, 1997. *Address:* c/o Dept of Political Science, Marquette University, Box 1881, Milwaukee, WI 53201, USA.

WOLFE, Peter, BA, MA, PhD; academic and writer; *Professor of English, University of Missouri at St Louis*; b. 25 Aug. 1933, New York, NY, USA; m. Marie Paley 1962 (divorced 1969); two s. *Education:* City College, CUNY, Lehigh University, University of Wisconsin. *Career:* Prof. of English, Univ. of Missouri at St Louis. *Publications:* Jean Rhys 1980, Dashiell Hammett 1980, Laden Choirs: Patrick White 1983, Something More Than Night: Raymond Chandler 1985, John le Carré 1987, Yukio Mishima 1989, Alarms and Epitaphs: Eric Ambler 1993, In the Zone: Rod Serling's Twilight Vision 1996, A Vision of His Own: William Gaddis 1997; contrib. to Weekend Australian, Sydney Morning Herald, New Zealand Listener, Calcutta Statesman, New York Times Book Review, Chicago Tribune. *Honours:* Fulbright Awards to India 1987, Poland 1991, University of Missouri Pres.'s Award for Creativity and Research 1995. *Address:* Department of English, Office 465 Lucas, University of Missouri at St Louis, 8001 Natural Bridge Road, St Louis, MO 63121-4499, USA. *E-mail:* spwolfe@umsl.edu.

WOLFE, Tom, (Thomas Kennerly Wolfe Jr); Writer, Journalist and Artist; b. 2 March 1930, Richmond, Virginia, USA; m. Sheila Berger, one s. one d. *Education:* AB, Washington and Lee University, 1951; PhD, American Studies, Yale University, 1957. *Career:* Reporter, Springfield Union, Massachusetts, 1956–59; Reporter and Latin American Correspondent, Washington Post, 1959–62; Writer, New York Sunday Magazine, 1962–66; City Reporter, New York Herald Tribune, 1962–66; Magazine Writer, New York World Journal Tribune, 1966–67; Contributing Ed., New York magazine, 1968–76, Esquire magazine, 1977–; Contributing Artist, Harper's magazine, 1978–81; mem. American Acad. of Arts and Letters. *Publications:* The Kandy-Kolored Tangerine-Flake Streamline Baby, 1965; The Electric Kool-Aid Acid Test, 1968; The Pump House Gang, 1968; Radical Chic and Mau-mauing the Flak Catchers, 1970; The Painted Word, 1975; Mauve Gloves and Madmen, Clutter and Vine, 1976; The Right Stuff, 1979; In Our Time, 1980; From Bauhaus to Our House, 1981; The Purple Decades: A Reader, 1982; The Bonfire of the Vanities, 1987; A Man in Full, 1998; Hooking Up, 2000. Contributions: newspapers and magazines. *Honours:* various hon. doctorates; American Book Award, 1980; Harold D. Vursell Memorial Award, American Acad. of Arts and Letters, 1980; Columbia Journalism Award, 1980; John Dos Passos Award, 1984; Theodore Roosevelt Medal, Theodore Roosevelt Asscn, 1990; St Louis Literary Award, 1990; Pres.'s Humanities Medal, 2001. *Address:* c/o Farrar, Straus & Giroux Inc, 19 Union Sq. W, New York, NY 10003, USA. *Website:* www.tomwolfe.com.

WOLFERS, Michael; British writer and translator; b. 28 Sept. 1938, London, England. *Education:* Wadham Coll., Oxford and South Bank Polytechnic. *Career:* journalist, The Times, London 1965–72; Visiting Sr Lecturer in African Politics and Government, Univ. of Juba 1979–82; mem. Royal Inst. of Int. Affairs, Gyosei Inst. of Management. *Publications:* Black Man's Burden Revisited 1974, Politics in the Organization of African Unity 1976, Luandino Vieira: The Real Life of Domingos Xavier 1978, Poems from Angola 1979, Samir Amin, Delinking: Towards a Polycentric World 1990,

Hamlet and Cybernetics 1991, Thomas Hodgkin: Letters from Africa 2000; contrib. to numerous publications. *Address:* 66 Roupell Street, London, SE1 8SS, England.

WOLFF, Christoph (Johannes); Prof. of Musicology, Writer and Ed.; b. 24 May 1940, Solingen, Germany; m. Barbara Mahrenholz, 28 Aug. 1964, three d. *Education:* University of Berlin, 1960–63; University of Freiburg im Breisgau, 1963–65; PhD, University of Erlangen, 1966. *Career:* Lecturer, University of Erlangen, 1966–69; Asst Prof., University of Toronto, 1968–70; Assoc. Prof., 1970–73, Prof. of Musicology, 1973–76, Columbia University; Visiting Prof., Princetown University, 1973, 1975; Ed., Bach-Jahrbuch, 1974–; Prof. of Musicology, 1976–, Dept Chair., 1980–88, 1990–91, William Powell Mason Prof., 1985–, Acting Dir, University Library, 1991–92, Dean, Graduate School of Arts and Sciences, 1992–, Harvard University; Dir, Bach Archive, Leipzig, 2000–; mem. American Musicological Society; Gesellschaft für Musikforschung; International Musicological Society. *Publications:* Der stile antico in der Musik Johann Sebastian Bachs, 1968; The String Quartets of Haydn, Mozart, and Beethoven: Studies of the Autograph Manuscripts (ed.), 1980; Bach Compendium: Analytisch-bibliographisches Repertorium der Werke Johann Sebastian Bachs (ed. with H.-J. Schulze), seven vols, 1986–89; Bach: Essays on His Life and Music, 1991; Mozart's Requiem: Historical and Analytical Studies, Documents, Score, 1993; Wereld van de Bach-cantatas: The World of the Bach Canatatas, 1997; The New Bach Reader (ed.), 1998; Driven Into Paradise: The Musical Migration from Nazi Germany to the United States (ed. with R. Brinkmann), 1999; Johann Sebastian Bach: The Learned Musician, 2000. Contributions: scholarly books and journals. Other: Critical edns of works by Scheidt, Buxtehude, Bach, Mozart and Hindemith. Contributions: scholarly books and journals. *Honours:* Dent Medal, Royal Musical Asscn, London, 1978; Fellow, American Acad. of Arts and Sciences, 1982–; Hon. Prof., University of Freiburg im Breisgau, 1990–. *Address:* c/o Dept of Music, Harvard University, Cambridge, MA 02138, USA.

WOLFF, Cynthia Griffin; Prof. and Writer; b. 20 Aug. 1936, St Louis, MO, USA; m. 1st Robert Paul Wolff, 9 June 1962, divorced 1986, two s.; m. 2nd Nicholas J. White, 21 May 1988. *Education:* BA, Radcliffe College, 1958; PhD, Harvard University, 1965. *Career:* Asst Prof. of English, Manhattanville College, Purchase, New York, 1968–70; Asst Prof., 1971–74, Assoc. Prof., 1974–76, Prof. of English, 1976–80, University of Massachusetts, Amherst; Prof. of Humanities, 1980–85, Class of 1922 Prof. of Literature and Writing, 1985–, MIT; mem. American Studies Asscn. *Publications:* Samuel Richardson, 1972; A Feast of Words: The Triumph of Edith Wharton, 1977; Emily Dickinson, 1986. Contributions: scholarly journals. *Honours:* National Endowment for the Humanities Grants, 1975–76, 1983–84; ACLS Grant, 1984–85. *Address:* 416 Commonwealth Ave, Apt 619, Boston, MA 02215, USA.

WOLFF, Geoffrey Ansell; Prof. of English and Creative Writing and Author; b. 5 Nov. 1937, Los Angeles, CA, USA; m. Priscilla Bradley Porter, 21 Aug. 1965, two s. *Education:* Eastbourne College, England, 1955–56; BA, summa cum laude, Princeton University, 1961; Postgraduate Studies, Churchill College, Cambridge, 1963–64. *Career:* Lecturer, Robert College, Istanbul, 1961–63, University of Istanbul, 1962–63, Maryland Institute and College of Art, 1965–69, Middlebury College, Vermont, 1976–78; Book Ed., Washington Post, 1964–69, Newsweek magazine, 1969–71, New Times magazine, 1974–79; Visiting Lecturer, 1970–71, Ferris Prof., 1980, 1992, Princeton University; Book Critic, Esquire magazine, 1979–81; Visiting Lecturer, Columbia University, 1979, Boston University, 1981, Brown University, 1981, 1988; Writer-in-Residence, Brandeis University, 1982–95; Visiting Prof., Williams College, 1994; Prof. of English and Creative Writing, University of California at Irvine, 1995–; mem. PEN. *Publications:* Bad Debts, 1969; The Sightseer, 1974; Black Sun, 1976; Inklings, 1978; The Duke of Deception, 1979; Providence, 1986; Best American Essays (ed.), 1989; The Final Club, 1990; A Day at the Beach, 1992; The Age of Consent, 1995. Contributions: various publications. *Honours:* Woodrow Wilson Fellowship, 1961–62; Fulbright Fellowship, 1963–64; Guggenheim Fellowships, 1972–73, 1977–78; National Endowment for the Humanities Senior Fellowship, 1974–75; National Endowment for the Arts Fellowships, 1979–80, 1986–87; ACLS Fellowship, 1983–84; Governor's Arts Award, RI, 1992; Lila Wallace Writing Fellowship, 1992; American Acad. of Arts and Letters Award, 1994. *Address:* c/o Dept of English, University of California at Irvine, Irvine, CA 92717, USA.

WOLFF, Tobias Jonathan Ansell, BA, MA; American writer; b. 19 June 1945, Birmingham, Ala; m. Catherine Dolores Spohn 1975; two s. one d. *Education:* The Hill School, Oxford Univ., (UK) and Stanford Univ. (Calif.). *Career:* served in US Army 1964–68; reporter, Washington Post 1972; Writing Fellow, Stanford Univ. 1975–78, Prof. of English and Creative Writing 1997–; Writer-in-Residence, Ariz. State Univ. 1978–80; Peck Prof. of English Syracuse Univ. 1980–97; Wallace Stegner Fellowship 1975–76, Nat. Endowment Fellow 1978, 1984; Arizona Council on the Arts and Humanities Fellowship 1980, Guggenheim Fellow 1983; mem. PEN. *Publications:* Ugly Rumours 1975, Hunters in the Snow 1981, The Barracks Thief (PEN/Faulkner Award for Fiction 1985) 1984, Back in the World 1985, A Doctor's Visit: The Short Stories of Anton Chekhov (ed.) 1987, The Stories of Tobias Wolff 1988, This Boy's Life 1989, The Picador Books of Contemporary American Stories (ed.) 1993, In Pharaoh's Army: Memories of a Lost War 1994, The Vintage Book of Contemporary American Short Stories 1994, The Best American Short Stories 1994, The Night in Question (stories) 1996, Writers Harvest 3 (ed.) 2000, Old School 2003. *Honours:* Hon. Fellow Hertford Coll., Oxford 2000; St Lawrence Award for Fiction 1982, Rea Award for Short Story 1989, Whiting Foundation Award 1989, LA Times Book Prize for Biography 1989, Ambassador Book Award 1990, Lila Wallace/Reader's Digest Award 1993, Lyndhurst Foundation Award 1994, Esquire-Volvo-Waterstones Award for Non-Fiction 1994, Award of Merit, American Acad. of Arts and Letters 2001. *Address:* English Department, Stanford University, Stanford, CA 94305, USA.

WOLKSTEIN, Diane, BA, MA; writer and storyteller; b. 11 Nov. 1942, New York, NY, USA; m. Benjamin Zucker 1969; one d. *Education:* Smith Coll., Bank Street Coll. of Education. *Career:* hostess, Stories from Many Lands with Diane Wolkstein (WNYC-Radio) New York 1967–; Instructor, Bank Street Coll. 1970–; teacher, New York Univ. 1983–2003, Sarah Lawrence Coll. 1984, New School for Social Research, New York 1989; leader of many storytelling workshops. *Publications:* 8,000 Stones 1972, The Cool Ride in the Sky: A Black-American Folk Tale 1973, The Visit 1974, Squirrel's Song: A Hopi-Indian Story 1975, Lazy Stories 1976, The Red Lion: A Persian Sufi Tale 1977, The Magic Orange Tree and Other Haitian Folk Tales 1978, White Wave: A Tao Tale 1979, The Banza: A Haitian Folk Tale 1980, Inanna, Queen of Heaven and Earth: Her Stories and Hymns from Summer (with Samuel Noah Kramer) 1983, The Magic Wings: A Chinese Tale 1983, The Legend of Sleepy Hollow 1987, The First Love Stories 1991, Oom Razoom 1991, Little Mouse's Painting 1992, Step by Step 1994, Esther's Story 1996, White Wave 1996, Bouki Dances the Kokioko 1997, The Magic Orange Tree 1997, The Glass Mountain 1999, The Day Ocean Came to Visit 2001, Treasures of the Heart: Holiday Stories that Reveal the Soul of Judaism 2003, Sunmother Wakes the World 2004; contrib. to periodicals and recordings. *Honours:* several citations and awards. *Address:* 10 Patchin Place, New York, NY 10011, USA. *E-mail:* dianewolkstein@hotmail.com. *Website:* www.dianewolkstein.com.

WOMACK, Peter; Senior Lecturer and Writer; b. 27 Jan. 1952, Surrey, England. *Education:* BA, University of Oxford, 1973; PhD, University of Edinburgh, 1984. *Career:* Lecturer, 1988–96, Senior Lecturer, 1996–, University of East Anglia. *Publications:* Ben Jonson, 1986; Improvement and Romance, 1989; English Drama: A Cultural History (with Simon Shepherd), 1996. Contributions: scholarly books and journals. *Address:* c/o School of English and American Studies, University of East Anglia, Norwich NR4 7TJ, England.

WOOD, Charles (Gerald); Playwright; b. 6 Aug. 1932, St Peter Port, Guernsey, Channel Islands; m. Valerie Elizabeth Newman, 1954, one s. one d. *Education:* Birmingham College of Art, 1948–50. *Publications:* Plays: Prisoner and Escort, 1961; Cockade, 1963; Tie Up the Ballcock, 1964; Don't Make Me Laugh, 1965; Meals on Wheels, 1965; Fill the Stage with Happy Hours, 1966; Dingo, 1967; H, Being Monologues at Front of Burning Cities, 1969; Collier's Wood, 1970; Welfare, 1971; Veterans; or, Hairs in the Gates of the Hellespont, 1972; The Can Opener, 1974; Jingo, 1975; The Script, 1976; Has 'Washington' Legs?, 1978; The Garden, 1982; Red Star, 1984; Across from the Garden of Allah, 1986; The Plantagenets (after Shakespeare), 1988; Man, Beast and Virtue (after Pirandello), 1989; The Giants of the Mountain (Pirandello), 1993; The Tower (Dumas), 1995. Screenplays: The Knack, 1965; Help (co-author), 1965; How I Won the War, 1967; The Charge of the Light Brigade, 1968; The Long Day's Dying, 1968; The Bed-Sitting Room (co-author), 1968; Fellini Satyricon, 1969; Cuba, 1980; Tumbledown, 1988; An Awfully Big Adventure, 1995; Iris (co-author), 2001. Other: Television scripts. *Honours:* Evening Standard Awards, 1963, 1972; Palm d'Or, Cannes, 1964; FRSL, 1984; Prix Italia, RAI, 1988; BAFTA Award, 1988; Christopher Award, 2002; Humanitas Prize, 2002. *Address:* ICM, Oxford House, 76 Oxford St, London W1D 1BS, England.

WOOD, Michael; academic and writer; b. 19 Aug. 1936, Lincoln, England; m. Elena Uribe 1967; two s. one d. *Education:* BA, Modern and Medieval Languages, 1957, MA, 1961, PhD, 1962, St John's College, Cambridge. *Career:* Fellow in French, St John's College, Cambridge, 1961–64; Instructor, 1964–66, Asst Prof., 1968–71, Assoc. Prof., 1971–74, of English, Prof. of English and Comparative Literature, 1974–82, Columbia University; Visiting Prof., National University of Mexico, 1981–82; Prof. of English Literature, University of Exeter, 1982–95; Charles Barnwell Straut Prof. of English and Prof. of Comparative Literature, Princeton University, 1995–; Visitor, Institute for Advanced Study, Princeton, 2001–02. *Publications:* Stendahl, 1971; America in the Movies, 1975; García Márquez: One Hundred Years of Solitude, 1990; The Magician's Doubts: Nabokov and the Risks of Fiction, 1994; Children of Silence: On Contemporary Fiction, 1998; Franz Kafka, 1998; Belle de Jour, 2001; The Road to Delphi: The Life and Afterlife of Oracles, 2004. Contributions: Reviews, quarterlies and journals. *Honours:* Guggenheim Fellowship, 1972–73; National Endowment for the Humanities Fellowship, 1980–81; FRSL, 1992–; Leverhulme Trust Fellow, 1993; Fellow, New York Institute for the Humanities, 1994–; Senior Fellow, Society of Fellows, Princeton University, 1999–. *Address:* 26 Alexander Street, Princeton, NJ 08540, USA.

WOOD, Michael; British journalist, broadcaster, filmmaker, historian and writer; b. Manchester, England; m.; two d. *Education:* Oriel Coll., Oxford. *Career:* writer and presenter, over 60 TV series and documentaries on history, travel, politics and cultural history. *Television:* Saddam's Killing Fields, Darshan, The Sacred Way, Great Railway Journeys of the World 1981, River Journeys 1985, In Search of the Trojan War (PBS) 1985, Art of the Western World 1989, Legacy: In Search of the Origins of Civilization 1992, In the Footsteps of Alexander the Great (BBC) 1997, Hitler's Search for the Holy Grail 1999, Conquistadors (BBC2) 2000, In Search of Shakespeare (BBC2) 2003. *Publications:* In Search of the Dark Ages 1981, Great Railway Journeys of the World 1981, In Search of the Trojan War 1985, World Atlas of Archaeology (ed.) 1985, Domesday: A Search for the Roots of England 1986, Legacy: A Search for the Origins of Civilization 1992, The Smile of Murugan: A South Indian Journey 1995, In the Footsteps of Alexander the Great: A Journey from Greece to Asia 1997, In Search of England 1999, Conquistadors 2000, In Search of Shakespeare 2003; contrib. reviews and articles in Daily Telegraph, Evening Standard, Literary Review, Times, Guardian, Daily Express, Independent, Daily Mail, Observer, Newsday, Dialogue magazine. *Address:* c/o BBC Worldwide Ltd, 80 Wood Lane, London, W12 0TT, England.

WOOD, Victoria; Writer and Comedienne; b. 19 May 1953, Prestwich, Lancashire, England; m. Geoffrey Durham, 1980, one s. one d. *Education:* BA, Drama, Theatre Arts, University of Birmingham. *Publications:* Victoria Wood Song Book, 1984; Lucky Bag, 1985; Up to You Porky, 1986; Barmy, 1987; Mens Sana in Thingummy Doodah, 1990; Pat and Margaret, (screenplay), 1994; Chunky, 1996; Dinnerladies (sitcom), 1998. *Honours:* BAFTA Awards, Broadcasting Press Awards; Variety Club BBC Personality of the Year, 1987; Hon. DLitt, University of Lancaster, 1989, University of Sunderland, 1994, University of Bolton 1995, University of Birmingham, 1996; BPG Award for Best Screenplay, 1994; OBE, 1997. *Address:* c/o Philip Mcintyre, Second Floor, 35 Soho Sq., London WN 5DG, England.

WOODCOCK, Joan; poet, artist and genealogist; b. 6 Feb. 1908, Bournemouth, Dorset, England; m. Alexander Neville Woodcock 1937; two s. one d. *Career:* mem. British Haiku Society; Calne Writers' Circle; NFSPS, USA; Peterloo Poets; Poetry Society; various genealogical organizations. *Publications:* The Wandering Years, 1990; Borrowing From Time, 1992; Stabbed Awake, 1994. Contributions: anthologies and journals.

WOODEN, Rodney John; Playwright; b. 16 July 1945, London, England. *Career:* mem. PEN International. *Publications:* Woyzeck (adaptation of Büchner's play), 1990; Your Home in the West, 1991; Smoke, 1993; Moby Dick, 1993. *Honours:* First Prize, Mobil International Playwriting Competition, 1990; John Whiting Award, 1991; Mobil Writer-in-Residence Bursary, 1991–92. *Address:* c/o Micheline Steinberg Playwrights, 110 Forgnal, London NW3 6XU, England.

WOODFORD, Peggy; Writer; b. 19 Sept. 1937, Assam, India; m. Walter Aylen, 1 April 1967, three d. *Education:* MA, St Anne's College, Oxford. *Career:* mem. Society of Authors; RSL. *Publications:* Abraham's Legacy, 1963; Please Don't Go, 1972; Mozart: His Life and Times, 1977; Schubert: His Life and Times, 1978; Rise of the Raj, 1978; See You Tomorrow, 1979; The Girl With a Voice, 1981; Love Me, Love Rome, 1984; Misfits, 1984; Monster in Our Midst, 1987; Out of the Sun, 1990; Blood and Mortar, 1994; Cupid's Tears, 1995; On the Night, 1997; Jane's Story, 1998. *Address:* 24 Fairmount Rd, London SW2 2BL, England.

WOODIWISS, Kathleen (Erin); Writer; b. 3 June 1939, Alexandria, LA, USA; m. Ross Eugene Woodiwiss, 20 July 1956, divorced, three s. *Publications:* The Flame and the Flower, 1972; The Wolf and the Dove, 1974; Shanna, 1977; Ashes in the Wind, 1979; A Rose in Winter, 1982; Come Love a Stranger, 1984; So Worthy My Love, 1989; Forever in Your Embrace, 1992; Petals on the River, 1997; A Season Beyond a Kiss, 2000. *Address:* c/o Avon Books, 1350 Avenue of the Americas, New York, NY 10019, USA.

WOODRING, Carl (Ray); Writer; b. 29 Aug. 1919, Terrell, TX, USA; m. Mary Frances Ellis 24 Dec. 1942 (died 2 March 2003). *Education:* BA, 1940, MA, 1942, Rice University; AM, 1947, PhD, 1949, Harvard University. *Career:* mem. American Acad. of Arts and Sciences; International Asscn of University Profs of English; Grolier Club. *Publications:* Victorian Samplers, 1952; Virginia Woolf, 1966; Wordsworth, 1965; Politics in English Romantic Poetry, 1970; Nature into Art, 1989; Table Talk of Samuel Taylor Coleridge, 1990; Columbia History of British Poetry (ed.), 1993; Columbia Anthology of British Poetry (co-ed.), 1995; Literature: An Embattled Profession, 1999; Lucky Thirteen: USS Hopkins, DD 249, DMS 13 (co-author), 2000. Contributions: Western Review; Virginia Quarterly Review; Keats-Shelley Journal; Comparative Drama. *Honours:* Guggenheim Fellowship, 1955; ACLS Fellow, 1965; PKB Visiting Scholar, 1974–75; Senior Mellon Fellow, 1987–88. *Address:* 2838 Montebello Rd, No. 20, Austin, TX 78746, USA.

WOODS, P. F. (see Bayley, Barrington John).

WOODS, Stockton (see Forrest, Richard (Stockton)).

WOODWARD, Robert (Bob) Upshur, BA; American journalist and writer; *Assistant Managing Editor, The Washington Post*; b. 26 March 1943, Geneva, IL; m. Elsa Walsh 1989; two c. *Education:* Yale Univ. *Career:* reporter, Montgomery Co. (MD) Sentinel 1970–71; reporter, Washington Post 1971–78, Metropolitan Ed. 1979–81, Asst Man. Ed. 1981–. *Publications:* All the President's Men (with Carl Bernstein) 1973, The Final Days (with Carl Bernstein) 1976, The Brethren (with Scott Armstrong) 1979, Wired 1984, Veil: The Secret Wars of the CIA 1987, The Commanders 1991, The Man Who Would Be President (with David S. Broder) 1991, The Agenda: Inside the Clinton White House 1994, The Choice 1996, Shadow: Five Presidents and the Legacy of Watergate 1999, Maestro, Greenspan's Fed and the American Boom 2000, Bush at War... Inside the Bush White House 2002, Plan of Attack 2004. *Honours:* Pulitzer Prize citation 1972. *Address:* Washington Post Co., 1150 15th Street, NW, Washington, DC 20071, USA.

WOODWARD, Gerard; British poet and writer; b. 1961. *Publications:* poetry: Householder 1991, After the Deafening 1994, Island to Island 1999, Healing Fountain 2003; fiction: August 2001, I'll Go to Bed at Noon 2004. *Honours:* Somerset Maugham Award 1992. *Address:* c/o Chatto and Windus Ltd, 20 Vauxhall Bridge Road, London, SW1V 2SA, England.

WOODWORTH, Steven E(dward); Asst Prof. of History and Writer; b. 28 Jan. 1961, Akron, Ohio, USA; m. Leah Dawn Bunke, 13 Aug. 1983, five s. *Education:* BA, Southern Illinois University at Carbondale, 1982; University of Hamburg, 1982–83; PhD, Rice University, 1987. *Career:* Adjunct Instructor, Houston Community College, 1984–87; Instructor in History, Bartlesville Wesleyan College, Oklahoma, 1987–89; Asst Prof. of History, Toccoa Falls College, Georgia, 1989–97, Texas Christian University, 1997–; mem. Grady Mcwhiney Research Foundation, fellow; American Historical Asscn; Organization of American Historians; Southern Historical Asscn; Organization of Military Historians; Society of Civil War Historians. *Publications:* Jefferson Davis and His Generals: The Failure of Confederate Command in the West, 1990; The Essentials of United States History, 1841 to 1877: Westward Expansion and the Civil War, 1990; The Essentials of United States History, 1500 to 1789: From Colony to Republic, 1990; The Advanced Placement Examination in United States History, 1990; Davis and Lee at War, 1995; Leadership and Command in the American Civil War (ed.), Vol. I, 1995; The American Civil War: A Handbook of Literature and Research (ed.), 1996; Six Armies in Tennessee: The Chickamauga and Chattanooga Campaigns, 1998; Civil War Generals in Defeat (ed.), 1999; No Band of Brothers: Problems in the Rebel High Command, 1999; The Human Tradition in the Civil War and Reconstruction (ed.), 2000; Cultures in Conflict: The American Civil War, 2000; A Scythe of Fire: The Civil War Story of the Eighth Georgia Regiment, 2001; The Religious World of Civil War Soldiers, 2001. Contributions: books and professional journals. *Honours:* Fletcher Pratt Awards, 1991, 1996. *Address:* c/o Dept of History, Texas Christian University, TCU Box 297260, Fort Worth, TX 76129, USA.

WORSLEY, Dale; Writer and Dramatist; b. 3 Nov. 1948, Baton Rouge, LA, USA; m. Elizabeth Fox, 14 July 1991. *Education:* Southwestern University, Memphis. *Career:* mem. Dramatists Guild. *Publications:* The Focus Changes of August Previco, 1980; The Art of Science Writing, 1989. Plays: Cold Harbor, 1983; The Last Living Newspaper, 1993. *Honours:* Fellowship in Fiction, 1986, Fellowship in Playwriting, 1989, National Endowment for the Arts.

WORSTHORNE, Sir Peregrine Gerard, Kt, MA; British journalist; b. 22 Dec. 1923, London; m. 1st Claudia Bertrand de Colasse 1950 (died 1990); one d. one step-s.; m. 2nd Lady Lucinda Lambton 1991. *Education:* Stowe School, Peterhouse, Cambridge and Magdalen Coll., Oxford. *Career:* mem. editorial staff, Glasgow Herald 1946–48; mem. editorial staff, The Times 1948–50, Washington corresp. 1950–52, leader writer 1952–55; leader writer, Daily Telegraph 1955–61; Deputy Ed. Sunday Telegraph 1961–76, Assoc. Ed. 1976–86, Ed. 1986–89, Ed. Comment Section 1989–91; columnist, The Spectator 1997–. *Publications:* The Socialist Myth 1972, Peregrinations 1980, By The Right 1987, Tricks of Memory (memoirs) 1993, In Defence of Aristocracy 2004. *Honours:* Granada TV Journalist of the Year 1981. *Address:* The Old Rectory, Hedgerley, Buckinghamshire, SL2 3UY, England. *Telephone:* (1753) 646167. *Fax:* (1753) 646914.

WORTIS, Avi, (Avi); Children's Author; b. 23 Dec. 1937, New York, NY, USA; m. 1st Joan Gabriner 1 Nov. 1963 (divorced 1982); two s.; m. 2nd Coppelia Kahn 1983; one step-s. *Education:* BA, History, 1959, MA, Drama, 1962, University of Wisconsin at Madison; MS, Library Science, Columbia University, 1964. *Career:* Librarian, New York Public Library, 1962–70, Trenton State College, NJ, 1970–86; Conducted workshops and seminars with children, parents and educators; mem. Authors' Guild. *Publications:* Things That Sometimes Happen, 1970; Snail Tale, 1972; No More Magic, 1975; Captain Grey, 1977; Emily Upham's Revenge, 1978; Night Journeys, 1979; Man From the Sky, 1980; History of Helpless Harry, 1980; A Place Called Ugly, 1981; Who Stole the Wizard of Oz?, 1981; Sometimes I Think I Hear My Name, 1982; Shadrach's Crossing, 1983; Devil's Race, 1984; SOR Losers, 1984; The Fighting Ground, 1984; Bright Shadow, 1985; Wolf Rider, 1986; Romeo and Juliet (Together and Alive!) At Last, 1987; Something Upstairs, 1988; The Man Who Was Poe, 1989; True Confessions of Charlotte Doyle, 1990; Windcatcher, 1991; Nothing But the Truth, 1991; Blue Heron, 1992; Who Was That Masked Man, Anyway?, 1992; Punch With Judy, 1993; City of Light, City of Dark, 1993; The Bird, the Frog, and the Light, 1994; Smuggler's Island, 1994; The Barn, 1994; Tom, Babette & Simon, 1995; Poppy, 1995; Escape From Home, 1996; Finding Providence, 1996; Beyond the Western Sea, 1996; Something Upstairs: A Tale of Ghosts, 1997; What Do Fish Have to Do With Anything and Other Stories, 1997; Finding Providence: The Story of Roger Williams, 1997; Perloo the Bold, 1998;

Poppy and Rye: A Tale from Dimwood Forest, 1998. Contributions: Library Journal. *Honours:* American Library Asscn Notable Book Awards, 1984, 1991, 1992, 1993, 1995, 1996; One of the Best Books of the Year Awards, Library of Congress, 1989, 1990; Newbery Honor Book Awards, 1991, 1992; many others. *Website:* www.avi-writer.com.

WOUK, Herman; Writer and Dramatist; b. 27 May 1915, New York, NY, USA; m. Betty Sarah Brown 9 Dec. 1945; three s. (one deceased). *Education:* AB, Columbia University, 1934. *Career:* Visiting Prof. of English, Yeshiva University, 1952–57; Scholar-in-Residence, Aspen Institute of Humanistic Studies, CO, 1973–74; mem. Authors League; PEN; Writers Guild of America. *Publications:* Fiction: Aurora Dawn, 1947; The City Boy, 1948; Slattery's Hurricane, 1949; The Caine Muntiny, 1951; Marjorie Morningstar, 1955; Lomokome Papers, 1956; Youngblood Hawke, 1962; Don't Stop the Carnival, 1965; The Winds of War, 1971; War and Remembrance, 1978; Inside, Outside, 1985; The Hope, 1993; The Glory, 1994. Plays: The Traitor, 1949; The Caine Mutiny Court-Martial, 1953; Nature's Way, 1957. Television Screenplays: The Winds of War, 1983; War and Remembrance, 1986. Non-Fiction: This is My God, 1959; The Will to Live On, 2000. *Honours:* Pulitzer Prize in Fiction, 1952; Columbia University Medal for Excellence, 1952; Alexander Hamilton Medal, 1980; University of California at Berkeley Medal, 1984; Washington Book Award, 1986; Golden Plate Award, American Acad. of Achievement, 1986; US Naval Memorial Foundation Lone Sailor Award, 1987; University of Tel-Aviv Guardian of Zion Award, 1998; University of California at San Diego Medal, 1998; Jewish Book Council Lifetime Literary Achievement Award, 2000. *Address:* c/o B.S.W. Literary Agency, 3255 North St NW, Washington, DC 20007, USA.

WRIGHT, Amos Jasper, III, BA, MLS; American medical librarian, writer and poet; b. 3 March 1952, Gadsden, AL; m. Margaret Dianne Vargo 1980; one s. one d. *Education:* Auburn University, University of Alabama. *Career:* Assoc. Prof., Univ. of Alabama at Birmingham School of Medicine; mem. Anaesthesia History Asscn, Medical Library Asscn. *Publications:* Frozen Fruit (poems), 1978; Right Now I Feel Like Robert Johnson (poems), 1981; Criminal Activity in the Deep South, 1800–1930, 1989. Contributions: Medical journals, anthologies, reviews, quarterlies, and magazines. *Address:* 119 Pintail Drive, Pelham, AL 35124, USA (Home); University of Alabama at Birmingham School of Medicine, Department of Anesthesiology, Jefferson Tower 965, 619 South 19th Street, Birmingham, AL 35249-6810, USA (Office). *E-mail:* ajwright@uab.edu. *Website:* www.anes.uab .edu/ajcv.htm.

WRIGHT, Anthony David, BA, MA, DPhil, FRHistS; academic and writer; b. 9 June 1947, Oxford, England. *Education:* Merton College, Oxford, British School, Rome, Brasenose College, Oxford. *Career:* Lecturer, 1974–92, Senior Lecturer in History, 1992–2001, Univ. of Leeds; Visiting Fellow, Univ. of Edinburgh, 1983, Jesuit Historical Institute, Rome, 2002; mem. Accademia di San Carlo; Ecclesiastical History Society. *Publications:* The Counter-Reformation: Catholic Europe and the Non-Christian World, 1982; Baronio Storico e la Controriforma (with Romeo De Maio, L. Gulia, and A. Mazzacane), 1982; Catholicism and Spanish Society Under the Reign of Philip II, 1555–1598, and Philip III, 1598–1621, 1991; The Early Modern Papacy: From the Council of Trent to the French Revolution 1564–1789, 2000. Contributions: scholarly books and journals. *Address:* c/o School of History, University of Leeds, Leeds LS2 9JT, England.

WRIGHT, Carolyn D.; poet and professor; *Israel J. Kapstein Professor of English, Brown University*; b. 6 Jan. 1949, Mountain Home, AR, USA; m. Forrest Gander 3 April 1983; one s. *Education:* BA Univ. of Memphis 1971; MFA, Univ. of Arkansas, 1976. *Career:* Prof. of English and Creative Writing, Brown Univ. 1983–; State Poet of Rhode Island 1994–; mem. PEN, New England, Council Mem. *Publications:* Terrorism, 1979; Translations of the Gospel Back Into Tongues, 1981; Further Adventures with God, 1986; String Light, 1991; Just Whistle, 1993; The Lost Roads Project: A Walk-in Book of Arkansas, 1994; The Reader's Map of Arkansas, 1994; Tremble, 1996; Deepstep Come Shining, 1998; Steal Away: Selected and New Poems, 2002. Contributions: American Letters and Commentary; BRICK; Conjunctions; Sulfur. *Honours:* National Endowment for the Arts Fellowships, 1981, 1987; Witter Bynner Prize for Poetry, 1986; Guggenheim Fellowship, 1987; Mary Ingraham Bunting Fellowship, 1987; General Electric Award for Younger Writers, 1988; Whiting Writers Award, 1989; Rhode Island Governor's Award for the Arts, 1990; Lila Wallace/Reader's Digest Writers Award, 1992; University of Arkansas Distinguished Alumni Award, 1998; Lannan Literary Award, 1999; Artist Award, Foundation for Contemporary Performance Art, 1999; Lange-Taylor Prize, Center for Documentary Studies, 2000. *Address:* 351 Nayatt Road, Barrington, RI 02806, USA. *E-mail:* carolyn_wright@brown.edu.

WRIGHT, Charles (Penzel); Poet, Writer and Teacher; b. 25 Aug. 1935, Pickwick Dam, Tennessee, USA; m. Holly McIntire, 6 April 1969, one s. *Education:* BA, Davidson College, 1957; MFA, University of Iowa, 1963; Postgraduate Studies, University of Rome, 1963–64. *Career:* Faculty, University of California at Irvine, 1966–83, University of Virginia, 1983–; mem. Acad. of American Poets, board of chancellors, 1999–2002; American Acad. of Arts and Letters; Fellowship of Southern Writers; American Acad. of Arts and Sciences; PEN American Centre. *Publications:* Grave of the Right Hand, 1970; Hard Freight, 1973; Bloodlines, 1975; China Trace, 1977; Southern Cross, 1981; Country Music, 1982; The Other Side of the River, 1984; Zone Journals, 1988; The World of the 10,000 Things, 1990; Chickamauga, 1995; Black Zodiac, 1997; Appalachia, 1998; Negative Blue: Selected Later Poems, 2000; A Short History of the Shadow. Contributions: numerous journals and magazines. *Honours:* Edgar Allan Poe Award, Acad. of American Poets, 1976; PEN Trans. Award, 1979; National Book Award for Poetry, 1983; Brandeis Book Critics Circle Award, 1998; Pulitzer Prize for Poetry, 1998. *Address:* 940 Locust Ave, Charlottesville, VA 22901, USA.

WRIGHT, Donald Richard; historian and academic; b. 3 Aug. 1944, Richmond, IN, USA; m. 1st Olwen Twyman 1969 (divorced 1987); m. 2nd Marilou Briggs 1990 (died 1997); two s. *Education:* BA, De Pauw University, 1966; MA, 1968, PhD, History, 1976, Indiana University, Bloomington. *Career:* Served to Captain, US Air Force, 1968–72; Editorial Asst, American Historical Review, 1975–76; Asst Prof., 1976–79, Assoc. Prof., 1979–84, Dept Head, 1983–85, Prof., 1984–90, Distinguished Teaching Prof. of History, 1990–, SUNY at Cortland; Presenter, summer workshops, 1980–95; Collector, Curator, National Museum of the Gambia, Banjul, 1982; Lead Scholar, Alabama Humanities Foundation Institute, 1994; Visiting Lecturer, History Dept, Univ. of Witwatersrand, Johannesburg, South Africa, 2000; Scholar-in-Residence, Rockefeller Foundation Study and Conference Center, Bellagio, Italy, 2003; mem. African Studies Asscn; American Historical Asscn; World History Asscn; Manding Studies Asscn. *Publications:* The Early History of Niumi: Settlement and Foundation of a Mandinka State on the Gambia River, 1977; Oral Traditions from the Gambia, Vol. I: Mandinka Griots, 1979, Vol. II: Family Elders, 1980; Muslim Peoples, contributor, 1984; What to Teach about Africa: A Guide for Secondary Teachers, 1990; African Americans in the Colonial Era: From African Origins through the American Revolution, 1990; African Americans in the Early Republic, 1789–1831, 1993; The World and a Very Small Place in Africa, 1997. Contributions: books; articles and reviews to journals, including: Journal of American Ethnic History; American Heritage; Journal of General Education; African Economic History; Africana Journal; History in Africa. *Honours:* Air Force Commmendation Medal; Fulbright Fellow, 1974–75; Fellow, National Endowment for the Humanities, 1982–83; Chancellor's Award, Excellence in Teaching, SUNY, 1989. *Address:* 4355 Locust Avenue, Homer, NY 13077-9476, USA. *E-mail:* wrightd@cortland.edu.

WRIGHT, George Thaddeus; academic, writer and poet; b. 17 Dec. 1925, Staten Island, NY, USA; m. Jerry Honeywell 1955. *Education:* BA, Columbia College, 1946; MA, Columbia University, 1947; University of Geneva, 1947–48; PhD, University of California, 1957. *Career:* Teaching Asst, 1954–55, Lecturer, 1956–57, University of California; Visiting Asst Prof., New Mexico Highlands University, 1957; Instructor-Asst Prof., University of Kentucky, 1957–60; Asst Prof., San Francisco State College, 1960–61; Assoc. Prof., University of Tennessee, 1961–68; Fulbright Lecturer, University of Aix-Marseilles, 1964–66, University of Thessaloniki, 1977–78; Visiting Lecturer, University of Nice, 1965; Prof., 1968–89, Chair., English Dept, 1974–77, Regents' Prof., 1989–93, Regents' Prof. Emeritus, 1993–, University of Minnesota; mem. Minnesota Humanities Comission, 1985–88; MLA; Shakespeare Asscn of America. *Publications:* The Poet in the Poem: The Personae of Eliot, Yeats and Pound, 1960; W. H. Auden, 1969; Shakespeare's Metrical Art, 1988; Aimless Life: Poems 1961–1995, 1999; Hearing the Measures: Shakespearean and Other Inflections, 2002. Editor: Seven American Literary Stylists from Poe to Mailer: An Introduction, 1973. Contributions: articles, reviews, poems and trans in many periodicals and books. *Honours:* Guggenheim Fellowship, 1981–82; National Endowment for the Humanities Fellowship, 1984–85; William Riley Parker Prizes, MLA, 1974, 1981; Robert Fitzgerald Prosody Award, 2002. *Address:* 2617 W Crown King Drive, Tucson, AZ 85741, USA.

WRIGHT, Jay; Poet and Dramatist; b. 25 May 1934, Albuquerque, NM, USA. *Education:* BA, University of California at Berkeley, 1961; Union Theological Seminary, New York; MA, Rutgers University, 1967. *Publications:* The Homecoming Singer, 1971; Soothsayers and Omens, 1976; Dimensions of History, 1976; The Double Invention of Komo, 1980; Explications/ Interpretations, 1984; Selected Poems of Jay Wright, 1987; Elaine's Book, 1988; Boleros, 1991; Transfigurations: Collected Poems, 2000. *Honours:* American Acad. and Institute of Arts and Letters Award; Guggenheim Fellowship; MacArthur Fellowship; Ingram Merrill Foundation Award; National Endowment for the Arts Grant; Fellowship, Acad. of American Poets, 1996; Fellow, American Acad. of Arts and Sciences; Lannan Literary Award for Poetry, 2000; L. L. Winship/PEN Award, 2001; Anisfield-Wolf Lifetime Achievement Award, 2002. *Address:* PO Box 381, Bradford, VT 05033, USA.

WRIGHT, Nicholas; British playwright; b. 5 July 1940, Cape Town, South Africa. *Education:* London Acad. of Music and Dramatic Art. *Career:* Literary Man. 1987, Assoc. Dir 1992, Nat. Theatre, London, England. *Publications:* Treetops 1978, The Gorky Brigade 1979, One Fine Day 1980, The Crimes of Vautrin (after Balzac) 1983, The Custom of the Country 1983, The Desert Air 1984, Six Characters in Search of an Author (after Pirandello) 1987, Mrs Klein 1988, Thérèse Raquin (after Zola) 1990, Essays 1992, Cressida 1999, Vincent in Brixton 2002, Changing Stages (with Richard Eyre) 2002, The Little Prince (libretto) 2003, His Dark Materials (after Philip Pullman) 2003, Three Sisters (after Chekhov) 2003. *Address:* 2 St Charles Place, London, W10 6EG, England.

WRIGHT, Rt Rev. Nicholas Thomas, BA, MA, DPhil, DD; British theologian and Anglican bishop; *Bishop of Durham*; b. 1 Dec. 1948, Morpeth, Northumberland; m. Margaret Elizabeth Anne Fiske 1971; two s. two d. *Education:* Sedbergh School, Exeter Coll., Oxford, Wycliffe Hall, Oxford. *Career:* ordained deacon 1975, priest 1976; Jr Research Fellow, Merton Coll. Oxford 1975–78, Jr Chaplain 1976–78; Fellow and Chaplain Downing Coll. Cambridge 1978–81; Asst Prof. of New Testament Studies, McGill Univ., Montreal and Hon. Prof., Montreal Diocesan Theological Coll., Canada 1981–86; Lecturer in Theology, Univ. of Oxford and Fellow, Tutor and Chaplain, Worcester Coll. Oxford 1986–93; Dean of Lichfield 1994–99; Canon Theologian of Coventry Cathedral 1992–99; Canon Theologian of Westminster 2000–03; Bishop of Durham July 2003–; Fellow Inst. for Christian Studies, Toronto 1992–; mem. Doctrine Comm., Church of England 1979–81, 1989–95; regular broadcasts on TV and radio. *Publications include:* Small Faith, Great God 1978, The Work of John Frith 1983, The Epistles of Paul to the Colossians and to Philemon 1987, The Glory of Christ in the New Testament (co-ed.) 1987, The Interpretation of the New Testament 1861–1986 (co-author) 1988, The Climax of the Covenant 1991, New Tasks for a Renewed Church 1992, The Crown and the Fire 1992, The New Testament and the People of God 1992, Who Was Jesus? 1992, Following Jesus 1994, Jesus and the Victory of God 1996, The Lord and His Prayer 1996, What Saint Paul Really Said 1997, For All God's Worth 1997, Reflecting the Glory 1998, The Meaning of Jesus (co-author) 1999, The Myth of the Millennium 1999, Romans and the People of God (co-ed.) 1999, Holy Communion for Amateurs 1999, The Challenge of Jesus 2000, Twelve Months of Sundays, Year C 2000, Easter Oratorio (co-author) 2000, Twelve Months of Sundays, Year A 2001, Luke for Everyone 2001, Mark for Everyone 2001, Paul for Everyone: Galatians and Thessalonians 2002, John for Everyone 2002, Twelve Months of Sundays, Year B 2002, New Interpreter's Bible, Vol. X (contrib.) 2002, The Contemporary Quest for Jesus 2002, Paul for Everyone (The Prison Letters) 2002, Matthew for Everyone 2002, Paul for Everyone (I Corinthians 2003), Paul for Everyone (II Corinthians) 2003, The Resurrection of the Son of God 2003, For All the Saints? 2003, Hebrews for Everyone 2003, Paul for Everyone (The Pastoral Letters) 2003. *Honours:* Hon. Fellow Downing Coll. Cambridge 2003, Merton Coll. Oxford 2004; Hon. DD (Aberdeen) 2000; Hon. DHumLitt (Gordon Coll., Mass) 2003. *Address:* Bishop of Durham, Auckland Castle, Bishop Auckland, Co. Durham, DL14 7NR, England (Office). *Telephone:* (1388) 602576 (Office). *Fax:* (1388) 605264 (Office). *E-mail:* bishops.office@durham.anglican.org (Office). *Website:* www.durham.anglican.org (Office).

WRIGHT, Richard (Bruce); Writer and College Teacher of English; b. 4 March 1937, Midland, Ontario, Canada; m. Phyllis Mary Cotton, two s. *Education:* Graduate, Radio and Television Arts, Ryerson Polytechnic Institute, Toronto, 1959; BA, Trent University, 1972. *Career:* Teacher of English, Ridley College, St Catharines, Ontario, 1976–. *Publications:* Andrew Tolliver, 1965; The Weekend Man, 1970; In the Middle of a Life, 1973; Farthing's Fortunes, 1976; Final Things, 1980; The Teacher's Daughter, 1982; Tourists, 1984; Sunset Manor, 1990; The Age of Longing, 1995; Clara Callan, 2001. *Honours:* Fellowships; City of Toronto Book Award, 1973; Geoffrey Faber Memorial Prize, England, 1975; Gov.-Gen.'s Award for Literature, 2001; Giller Prize, 2001. *Address:* 52 St Patrick St, St Catharines, Ontario, L2R 1K3, Canada.

WRIGHT, Ronald, MA; British writer; b. 12 Sept. 1948, Surrey, England. *Education:* Univ. of Cambridge. *Career:* mem. PEN Canada, Survival Int. *Publications:* Memoirs: Cut Stones and Crossroads: A Journey in Peru, 1984; On Fiji Islands, 1986; Time Among the Maya, 1989; Stolen Continents (history), 1992; Home and Away (essays), 1993; A Scientific Romance (novel), 1997; Henderson's Spear (novel), 2001. Contributions: TLS and other journals. *Honours:* Hon. LLD (Univ. of Calgary) 1996; Gordon Montador Award 1993, David Higham Prize for Fiction 1997. *Literary Agent:* Gillon Aitken Associates Ltd, 18–21 Cavaye Place, London, SW10 9PT, England. *Telephone:* (20) 7373-8672. *Fax:* (20) 7373-6002.

WU, Duncan; Reader in English Literature and Writer; b. 3 Nov. 1961, Woking, Surrey, England. *Education:* BA, 1984, DPhil, 1991, University of Oxford. *Career:* Postdoctoral Fellow, British Acad., 1991–94; Reader in English Literature, University of Glasgow, 1995–; Ed., Charles Lamb Bulletin; mem. Charles Lamb Society, council mem.; Keats-Shelley Memorial Asscn, committee mem. *Publications:* Wordsworth's Reading 1770–1799, 1993; Romanticism: An Anthology, 1994; William Wordsworth: A Selection, 1994; Six Contemporary Dramatists, 1994; Romanticism: A Critical Reader, 1995; Wordsworth's Reading, 1800–15, 1996; Romantic Women Poets: An Anthology, 1997; Wordsworth: An Inner Life, 2001. Contributions: journals and periodicals. *Address:* Dept of English Literature, University of Glasgow, Glasgow G12 8QQ, Scotland.

WUNSCH, Josephine (McLean); Author; b. 3 Feb. 1914, Detroit, Michigan, USA; m. Edward Seward Wunsch, 9 Aug. 1940, one s. two d. *Education:* BA, University of Michigan, 1936. *Publications:* Flying Skis, 1962; Passport to Russia, 1965; Summer of Decision, 1968; Lucky in Love, 1970; The Aerie (as J. Sloan McLean with Virginia Gillett), 1974; Girl in the Rough, 1981; Class Ring, 1983; Free as a Bird, 1984; Breaking Away, 1985; The Perfect Ten, 1986; Lucky in Love, 1987; Between Us, 1989. *Address:* 830 Bishop Rd, Grosse Pointe Park, MI 48230, USA.

WURLITZER, Rudolph; Author and Screenwriter; b. 1937, Cincinnati, Ohio, USA. *Education:* Columbia University; University of Aix-en-Provence. *Publications:* Nog, 1969; Flats, 1970; Two-Lane Blacktop (with Will Cory), 1971; Quake, 1972; Pat Garrett and Billy the Kid, 1973; Slow Fade, 1984; Walker, 1987; Hard Travels to Sacred Places, 1994. Other: several screenplays. Contributions: books and periodicals. *Address:* c/o Shambhala Publishers, Horticultural Hall, 300 Massachusetts Ave, Boston, MA 02115, USA.

WURM, Franz, BA, MA; British writer; b. 16 March 1926, Prague, Czechoslovakia; m. Barbara M. Z'Graggen 1992. *Education:* Queen's Coll., Oxford. *Career:* Head of Third Program, German Swiss Radio, Zürich, 1966–69; Dir, Feldenkrais Institute, Zürich, 1974–; mem. PEN; Hölderlin Gesellschaft, Tübingen; Franz Kafka Society, Prague. *Publications:* Anmeldung, 1959; Vorgang, 1962; Anker und Unruh, 1964; Vier Gedichte, 1965; Brehy v zádech, 1974; Acht Gedichte in Faksimile, 1975; Hundstage, 1986; In diesem Fall, 1989; Dirzulande, 1990; Nachbemerkungen zu Feldenkrais, 1995; Briefwechsel (with Paul Celan), 1995; 53 Gedichte, 1996; König auf dem Dach, 1997; Orangenblau, 1998. Contributions: Neue Zürcher Zeitung; Akzente; Neue Rundschau; Literatur and Kritik; Neue Deutsche Literatur. *Address:* Via Orelli 16, 6612 Ascona, Switzerland.

WURTS, Janny; Writer; b. 10 Dec. 1953, Bryn Mawr, PA, USA. *Education:* BA, Hampshire College, 1975; Graduate Studies, Moore College of Art. *Publications:* Sorcerer's Legacy, 1982; Stormwarden, 1984; Daughter of the Empire (co-author), 1987; Keeper of the Keys, 1988, Shadowfane, 1988; Servant of the Empire (co-author), 1990; Mistress of the Empire (co-author), 1992; The Master of White Storm, 1992; The Curse of the Mistwraith, 1995; Ships of Merior, 1995; That Way Lies Camelot, 1996. *Address:* c/o HarperCollins, 1000 Keystone Industrial Park, Scranton, PA 18512, USA.

WYLIE, Andrew, BA; American literary agent; b. 4 Nov. 1947; m. 1st Christina Meyer 1969; one s.; m. 2nd Camilla Carlini; two d. *Education:* St Paul's School, Harvard Coll. *Career:* founder and Pres., The Wylie Agency, New York 1980–, London 1996–, Madrid 1999–, with over 400 clients. *Address:* The Wylie Agency, 250 W 57th Street, Suite 2114, New York, NY 10107, USA. *Telephone:* (212) 246-0069. *Fax:* (212) 586-8953. *E-mail:* mail@wylieagency.com. *Website:* www.wylieagency.com.

WYLIE, Betty Jane; Writer, Dramatist and Poet; b. 21 Feb. 1931, Winnipeg, MB, Canada; m. William Tennent Wylie, two s. two d. *Education:* BA, 1950, MA, 1951, University of Manitoba. *Career:* Bunting Fellow, Radcliffe College, 1989–90; Writer-in-Residence, Metro Toronto Library, York Branch, 2001; mem. Playwrights' Union of Canada; Writers' Union of Canada. *Publications:* Over 35 books. Other: many plays. Contributions: periodicals. *Honours:* several awards.

WYLIE, Laura (see Matthews, Patricia Anne).

WYNAND, Derk; Prof., Poet, Writer, Trans. and Ed.; b. 12 June 1944, Bad Suderode, Germany; m. Eva Kortemme, 8 May 1971. *Education:* BA, 1966, MA, 1969, University of British Columbia. *Career:* Visiting Lecturer, 1969–73, Asst Prof. to Prof., 1973–, Chair, Dept of Creative Writing, 1987–90, 1996–99, University of Victoria; Ed., The Malahat Review, 1992–98. *Publications:* Locus, 1971; Snowscapes, 1974; Pointwise, 1979; One Cook, Once Dreaming, 1980; Second Person, 1983; Fetishistic, 1984; Heatwaves, 1988; Airborne, 1994; Door Slowly Closing, 1995; Closer to Home, 1997; Dead Man's Float, 2001. *Honours:* The Malahat Review named Magazine of the Year, 1995; Honourable Mention, bp Nichol Chapbook Award, 1995. *Address:* c/o Dept of Writing, University of Victoria, PO Box 3045, Victoria, BC V8W 3P4, Canada.

X

XINRAN, Xue; Chinese radio journalist and writer; b. 19 July 1958, Beijing; m. 1st (divorced); one s.; m. 2nd Toby Eady 2002. *Education:* First Mil. Univ. of People's Liberation Army. *Career:* radio producer, presenter, Words on the Night Breeze programme, Henhan Broadcasting and Jiangsu Broadcasting 1989–97; moved to London 1997; teacher, School of Oriental and African Studies (SOAS), London. *Publications:* The Good Women of China 2002, Sky Burial 2004; contribs to Chinese newspapers and broadcasting journals. *Literary Agent:* Toby Eady Associates Ltd, Third Floor, 9 Orme Court, London, W2 4RL, England. *Telephone:* (20) 7792-0092. *Fax:* (20) 7792-0879. *E-mail:* toby@tobyeady.demon.co.uk. *Website:* www.tobyeadyassociates.co.uk.

XONGERIN BADAI; Chinese Inner Mongolia administrator, writer and poet; b. 5 June 1930, Bayinguoltng Prefecture, Hejin Co., Xinjiang; m. 1952; two s. two d. *Career:* Pres. Xinjiang Broadcasting and TV Univ. 1982–; Chair. Cttee of Xinjiang Uygur Autonomous Region of CPPCC 1989; mem. Standing Cttee CPPCC 1991. *Publications:* several books of prose, poetry and history in Mongol language and Chinese. *Address:* 15 South Beijing Road, Urumqi, Xinjiang, People's Republic of China. *Telephone:* (991) 2825701 (Office); (991) 3839303 (Home). *Fax:* (991) 2823443.

XU ZHENSHI; Chinese photographer, artist and publisher; b. 18 Aug. 1937, Songjiang Co., Shanghai; m. Zhang Fuhe 1967; one d. *Education:* No. 1 High School, Songjiang Co., Zhejiang Acad. of Fine Arts. *Career:* moved to Beijing 1965; Ed. People's Fine Arts Publishing House 1965–86, Dir Picture Editorial Dept 1986–, Ed.-in-Chief 1992–; mem. China Artists' Asscn; Deputy Sec.-Gen. Spring Festival Pictures Research Centre, Publrs' Asscn of China; Deputy Sec.-Gen. and Assoc. Dir Photography Research Centre; mem. Selection Cttee 3rd, 4th and 5th Nat. Exhbns of Spring Festival Pictures and other exhbns; Assoc. Dir Standing Cttee Spring Festival Pictures; Sr Adviser, Office of East China–UN TIPS Nat. Exploit Bureau 1994–; exhbns in China, Japan, Korea, Hong Kong, Thailand; Vice-Ed.-in-Chief Gouache Vol. of Anthology of Contemporary Chinese Fine Arts 1996; Vice-Pres. Chinese Fan Art Soc. 1997; organized 1st Nat. Exhbn of Calligraphy and Paintings to Help the Poor 1998; Dir Foundation for Underdeveloped Regions in China 1998–; prepared 6th Nat. Exhbn of Spring Festival Pictures 1998; numerous awards including Bronze Medal for albums of photographs, Leipzig Int. Book Exhbn 1987, Nat. Award 1993, Model Ed. Nat. Press and Publs System 1997, 1998. *Publications:* China's Cultural Relics Unearthed during the Great Cultural Revolution 1973, Travel in China (4 vols) 1979–80, Tibet 1981, Travel in Tibet 1981, Costumes of China's Minority Nationalities 1981, Travel in Guilin 1981, Travel Leisurely in China 1981, Travel in Yunnan 1982, China's Flowers in Four Seasons 1982, Poet Li Bai 1983, Native Places of Tang Dynasty Poems 1984, Travel along the Yangtse River 1985, Through the Moongate: A Guide to China's Famous Historical Sites 1986, Waters and Mountains in China 1986, Travel in Guangzhou 1986, China 1987, The Chinese Nation 1989, Poet Du Fu 1989, Selected Works of Xu Zhenshi 1990, 1993, Selected Paintings of Xu Zhenshi 1993, 1994, Boat on the Plateau 1998, Album of Xu Zhenshi's Sketches 1999. *Honours:* State Prize for Spring Festival Pictures 2001, two 6th Nat. Exhbn of Spring Festival Pictures Prizes (China) 1998, Chinese Contemporary Art Achievement Prize, Hong Kong. *Address:* People's Fine Arts Publishing House, No. 32 Beizongbu Hutong, Beijing, People's Republic of China. *Telephone:* (10) 65244901 (Office); (10) 65246353 (Home).

Y

YAFFE, James; Prof., Writer and Dramatist; b. 31 March 1927, Chicago, IL, USA; m. Elaine Gordon, 1 March 1964, one s. two d. *Education:* BA, summa cum laude, Yale University, 1948. *Career:* Prof., 1968–, Dir, General Studies, 1981–, Colorado College; mem. American Asscn of University Profs; Authors' League; Dramatists' Guild; MWA; PEN. *Publications:* Poor Cousin Evelyn, 1951; The Good-for-Nothing, 1953; What's the Big Hurry?, 1954; Nothing But the Night, 1959; Mister Margolies, 1962; Nobody Does You Any Favors, 1966; The American Jews, 1968; The Voyage of the Franz Joseph, 1970; So Sue Me!, 1972; Saul and Morris, Worlds Apart, 1982; A Nice Murder for Mom, 1988; Mom Meets Her Maker, 1990; Mom Doth Murder Sleep, 1991; Mom Among the Liars, 1992; My Mother, the Detective, 1997. Plays: The Deadly Game, 1960; Ivory Tower (with Jerome Weidman), 1967; Cliffhanger, 1983. Other: Television plays. Contributions: various publications. *Honours:* National Arts Foundation Award, 1968. *Address:* 1215 N Cascade Ave, Colorado Springs, CO 80903, USA.

YAKOVLEV, Yegor Vladimirovich; Journalist and Newspaper Editor; b. 14 March 1930, USSR. *Education:* Moscow State Historical Archival Inst. *Career:* mem. CPSU 1953–91; worked on a number of newspapers: Pravda, Izvestiya, Sovetskaya Rossiya, Moscow Pravda; Founding Ed. Zhurnalist monthly; worked in Prague on staff of World Marxist Review 1972–75; worked on Izvestiya, Moscow 1975–85; Ed. Moscow News weekly 1985–91; Pres. All-Russia Radio and TV Co Ostankino 1991–92; Founder and Ed. Obshchaya Gazeta weekly 1992–2001; mem. Presidential Political Consultative Council, 1991. *Publications:* more than 20 books. Contributions: numerous articles on historical and political problems. *Honours:* winner of two international awards for journalism. *Address:* Goncharnaya 1, 109240 Moscow, Russia. *E-mail:* secretar@og.ru. *Website:* www.og.ru.

YAMAMOTO, Keith R., BSc, PhD; American writer, academic and scientist; *Editor-in-Chief, Molecular Biology of the Cell. Education:* Iowa State Univ., Princeton Univ., Univ. of California San Francisco. *Career:* Asst Prof. of Biochemistry 1976–79, Assoc. Prof. of Biochemistry 1979–83, Prof. of Biochemistry 1983–, Vice-Chair 1985–94, Dept of Biochemistry and Biophysics, Univ. of California San Francisco; Dir of Biochemistry and Molecular Biology Program in Biological Sciences 1988–, Chair Dept of Cellular and Molecular Pharmacology 1994–2003, Univ. of California San Francisco; Ed.-in-Chief, Molecular Biology of the Cell; program mem., Univ. of California San Francisco Comprehensive Cancer; mem. Univ. of California San Francisco Biomedical Sciences Program; mem. Herbert Boyer Program in Biological Sciences. *Publications include:* co-author: Gene Wars: Military Control over the New Genetic Technologies 1988, Transcriptional Regulation: Monograph 22 1992; contrib. to numerous academic publications. *Address:* Molecular Biology of the Cell, American Society for Cell Biology, 8120 Woodmont Avenue, Suite 750, Bethesda, MD 20814-2762; Box 2280, University of California San Francisco, San Francisco, CA 94143-2280, USA. *E-mail:* yamamoto@cgl.ucsf.edu. *Website:* www.molbiolcell.org.

YAMASHITA, Karen Tei; writer, dramatist and academic; b. 8 Jan. 1951, Oakland, CA, USA; m. Ronaldo Yamashita; one s. one d. *Career:* Asst Prof., University of California at Santa Cruz, 1997–; mem. PEN Center West. *Publications:* Through the Arc of the Rain Forest, 1990; Brazil-Moru, 1992; Hannah Kusoh: An American Butoh, 1995; Tropic of Orange, 1997. Other: Short stories; Unpublished plays and screenplays. Contributions: anthologies and periodicals. *Honours:* Rockefeller Playwright-in-Residence Fellow, East West Players, Los Angeles, 1977–78; American Book Award, 1991; Janet Heidinger Kafka Award, 1992; City of Los Angeles Cultural Grant Award, 1992–93; Japan Foundation Artist Fellowship, 1997. *Address:* c/o University of California at Santa Cruz, Santa Cruz, CA 95064, USA.

YANCEY, Philip David, BA, MA; writer and editor; b. 4 Nov. 1949, Atlanta, GA, USA; m. Janet Norwood 1970. *Education:* Columbia Bible Coll., Wheaton Coll., Univ. of Chicago. *Career:* Ed., Campus Life 1971–77; Ed.-at-Large, Christianity Today 1980–. *Publications:* After the Wedding 1976, Where is God When It Hurts? 1977, Unhappy Secrets of the Christian Life (with Tim Stafford) 1979, Fearfully and Wonderfully Made (with Paul Brand) 1980, Open Windows 1982, In His Image (with Paul Brand) 1984, The Student Bible (with Tim Stafford) 1988, Disappointment With God: Questions Nobody Asks Aloud 1989, A Guided Tour of the Bible: Six Months of Daily Readings 1990, I Was Just Wondering 1990, Reality and the Vision 1990, Pain: The Gift Nobody Wants (with Paul Brand) 1993, Discovering God: A Devotional Journey Through the Bible 1993, Finding God in Unexpected Places 1995, The Jesus I Never Knew 1996, The Jesus I Never Knew Study Guide (with Brenda Quinn) 1997, What's So Amazing About Grace? 1997, Church, Why Bother?: My Personal Pilgrimage 1998, The Bible Jesus Read 1999, When Life Hurts: Understanding God's Place in Your Pain 1999, Meet the Bible: A Panorama of God's Word in 366 Readings and Reflections 2000, Reaching for the Invisible God: What Can We Expect to Find? 2000, Soul Survivor 2001, Rumors of Another World 2003; contrib. to numerous periodicals. *Honours:* many Evangelical Christian Publishers' Asscn Golden Medallion awards. *Address:* c/o Christianity Today, 465 Gundersen Drive, Carol Stream, IL 60188, USA.

YANG LIAN; New Zealand poet and writer; b. 22 Feb. 1955, Bern, Switzerland; m. Liu You Hong 1989. *Career:* began writing when sent to countryside in the 1970s; on return to Beijing was one of group of underground poets who published literary magazine Jintian; became poet in exile after Tiananmen massacre; Writer Central Broadcasting 1977–88; Visiting Scholar Auckland University 1989–90, Sydney University 1992–93; Writer-in-Residence Berlin 1990–91; Fellowship Amherst College, USA 1993–94; Poet-in-Residence Akademie Schloss Solitude; mem. Survivors Poetry Club, founder; Today Literature Research Society, councillor. *Publications:* in Chinese: Lihun (Ritualisation of the Soul) 1985, Huanghun (Desolate Soul) 1986, Huang (Yellow) 1989, Ren de zijue (Man's Self-Awakening) 1989, Taiyang yu ren (The Sun and the People) 1991, Guihua (Ghostspeak) 1994, Ren jing – Guihua (Human Landscape – Ghostspeak) 1994, Yi 1994, Yang Lian zuopin 1982–1997 (Yang Lian's Works 1982–1997) 1998; in translation: The Dead in Exile 1990, Masks and Crocodile: A Contemporary Chinese Poet and his Poetry 1990, Non-Person Singular 1994, Where the Sea Stands Still 1995, Where the Sea Stands Still: New Poems 1999; contrib. to anthologies and books, journals and periodicals, including Representations, Goldbatt, Xinwen ziyou daoji, Orientierungen, Australian Journal of Chinese Affairs, Canadian Review of Comparartive Literature, Asian and African Studies, New Zealand Listener, PN Review, Renditions: A Chinese-English Translation Magazine, World Literature Today, Dushu, Zhongguo. *Honours:* Chinese Poetry Reader's Choice 1986, Flaiano Int. Poetry Prize, Italy 1999. *Address:* 22 Carlton Mansions, Holmleigh Road, London, N16 5PX, England.

YANKOWITZ, Susan; Writer and Dramatist; b. 20 Feb. 1941, Newark, NJ, USA; m. Herbert Leibowitz, 3 May 1978, one s. *Education:* BA, Sarah Lawrence College, 1963; MFA, Yale Drama School, 1968. *Career:* mem. Authors' Guild; Dramatists' Guild; New Dramatists; PEN; Writers' Guild of America. *Publications:* Novel: Silent Witness, 1977. Plays: Slaughterhouse Play, 1971; Boxes, 1973; Terminal, 1975; Alarms, 1988; Night Sky, 1992. Screenplay: Portrait of a Scientist, 1974. Contributions: periodicals. *Honours:* Joseph Levine Fellowship in Screenwriting, 1968; Vernon Rice Drama Desk Award for Most Promising Playwright, 1969; Rockefeller Foundation Grant, 1973, and Award, 1974; Guggenheim Fellowship, 1975; MacDowell Colony Residencies, 1975, 1984, 1987, 1990; National Endowment for the Arts Grants, 1979, 1984; New York Foundation for the Arts Grant, 1989; McKnight Fellowship, 1990. *Address:* c/o Mary Harden, 850 Seventh Ave, New York, NY 10019, USA.

YATROMANOLAKIS, Yoryis; Greek writer; b. 1940, Crete. *Career:* Prof. of Ancient Greek, Univ. of Athens. *Publications include:* novels: Leimonario (trans. as The Spiritual Meadow) 1974, The History of a Vendetta 1991, A Report of a Murder 1995, Eroticon 1998. *Honours:* First Greek National Prize for Literature, Nikos Kazantzakis Prize. *Address:* c/o Dedalus Ltd, Langford Lodge, St Judith's Lane, Sawtry, Cambridgeshire PE28 5XE, England. *Website:* www.dedalusbooks.com.

YAZGHI, Muhammad el-, LenD; Moroccan politician, lawyer and newspaper executive; *Minister of Territorial Administration, Water Resources and the Environment*; b. 28 Sept. 1935, Fez; m. Balafrej Souada 1972; two s. *Education:* Moulay Youssef Coll., Lycée Gouraud, Univ. of Rabat and Ecole Nat. d'Admin., Paris. *Career:* Dir of Budget, Ministry of Finance 1957–60; Dir Al-Moharir (daily paper) 1975–81, Liberation (daily paper) 1989–; First Sec. Moroccan Press Union 1977–93; Deputy to Parl. 1977–; mem. Political Bureau, Union Socialiste des Forces Populaires (USFP) 1975–91, Joint Vice-Sec. 1992–; Minister of Territorial Admin, the Environment, Urban Planning and Housing, then Minister of Territorial Administration, Water Resources and the Environment. *Publications:* articles in magazines and journals. *Address:* Ministry of Territorial Administration, Water Resources and the Environment, 36 ave el-Abtal, Agdal, Rabat (Office); 5 rue Ibn Tofai, Les Orangers, Rabat, Morocco (Home). *Telephone:* (3) 7772634 (Office). *Fax:* (3) 7772756 (Office). *E-mail:* info@minenv.gov.ma (Office). *Website:* www .minenv.gov.ma (Office).

YEHOSHUA, Abraham B., MA; Israeli writer and university professor; b. 9 Dec. 1936, Jerusalem; m. Rivka Kirsninski 1960; two s. one d. *Career:* served in paratroopers unit 1954–57; Dir Israeli School in Paris 1964; Gen. Sec. World Union of Jewish Studies, Paris 1964–67; Dean of Students, Haifa Univ. 1967–72, Prof. of Comparative Literature 1972–; Visiting Prof., Harvard Univ., USA 1977, Univ. of Chicago 1988, 1997, Princeton Univ. 1992–; Co-Ed. Keshet 1965–72, Siman Kria 1973–, Tel Aviv Review 1987–. *Film adaptations of novels and stories include:* The Lover, Facing the Forests, Continuing Silence, Mr Mani, Open Heart, A Voyage to the End of the Millennium, Early in the Summer of 1970. *Plays:* A Night in May, Last Treatments, Possessions 1986, The Lover, The Night's Babies 1991. *Publications:* Death of the Old Man (short stories) 1963, Three Days and a Child (short stories) 1970, Early in the Summer of 1970 (novella) 1973, Two Plays 1975, The Lover (novel) 1978, Between Right and Right (essays) 1980, A Late Divorce (novel) (Flaiano Int. Poetry Prize, Italy 1996) 1982, Possessions 1986, Five Seasons (novel) (Nat. Jewish Book Award 1990, Cavour Prize, Italy 1994) 1988, The Wall and the Mountain (essays) 1988, Mister Mani (novel) (Israeli Booker Prize 1992, Nat. Jewish Book Award 1993, Wingate Prize, UK 1994) 1990, Night's Babies 1992, The Return from India

1994, Open Heart (novel) 1994, A Voyage to the End of the Millennium (novel) (Koret Prize) 1997, The Terrible Power of a Minor Guilt (essays) 1998, The Liberated Bride (novel) (Napoli Prize, Lampedusa Prize) 1998, The Mission of the Human Resource Man (novel) 2004. *Honours:* Dr hc (Hebrew Union Coll., Tel-Aviv Univ., Univ. of Turin, Bar Ilan Univ.); Brener Prize, Alterman Prize, Bialik Prize, European B'nai B'rith Award 1993, Israel Prize 1995. *Address:* 33 Shoshanat Ha-Carmel, Haifa, 34322, Israel. *Telephone:* 4-8370001. *Fax:* 4-8375569. *E-mail:* bulli@research.haifa .ac.il (Home).

YELLAND, David Ian, BA; British journalist and business executive; b. 14 May 1963, Harrogate; m. Tania Farrell 1996; one s. *Education:* Brigg Grammar School, Lincs., Coventry Univ. *Career:* grad. trainee Westminster Press 1985; trainee reporter Buckinghamshire Advertiser 1985–87; industrial reporter Northern Echo 1987–88; gen. news and business reporter North West Times and Sunday Times 1988–89; city reporter Thomson Regional Newspapers 1989–90; joined News Corpn 1990; city reporter, then City Ed., The Sun 1990–92, New York Corresp. 1992–93, Ed. 1998–2003; Deputy Business Ed., Business Ed., then Deputy Ed. New York Post 1993–98; Sr Vice-Pres. News Corpn, NY 2003–04; with Weber Shandwick 2004–. *Address:* Weber Shandwick Worldwide, 640 Fifth Avenue, New York, NY 10019, USA (Office). *Telephone:* (212) 445-8000 (Office). *Fax:* (212) 445-8001 (Office). *Website:* www.webershandwick.com (Office).

YEN MAH, Adeline; Writer and Anaesthetist; b. 1937, Tianjin, People's Republic of China; m. Robert A. Mah; two c. *Education:* Medicine, UK. *Publications:* Falling Leaves (autobiog.), 1997; Chinese Cinderella (autobiog. for children), 1999; Watching the Tree, 2000; A Thousand Pieces of Gold: A Memoir of China's Past Through its Proverbs, 2002. *Address:* c/o Harper Collins, 77–85 Fulham Palace Rd, Hammersmith, London W6 8JB, England. *Website:* www.adelineyenmah.com.

YERUSHALMI, Yosef Hayim, BA, MA, PhD; academic and historian; *Salo Wittmayer Baron Professor of Jewish History, Culture and Society, Columbia University;* b. 20 May 1932, New York, NY, USA; m. Ophra Pearly 1959; one s. *Education:* Yeshiva Univ., Jewish Theological Seminary of America, Columbia Univ. *Career:* Instructor, Rutgers Univ. 1963–66; Asst Prof. 1966–70, Prof. of Hebrew and Jewish History 1970–78, Jacob E. Safra Prof. of Jewish History and Sephardic Civilization, and Chair, Dept of Near Eastern Languages and Civilizations 1978–80, Harvard Univ.; Salo Wittmayer Baron Prof. of Jewish History, Culture and Society, and Dir, Center for Israel and Jewish Studies, Columbia Univ. 1980–; corresp. mem. Portuguese Acad. of History, Lisbon 1985. *Publications:* Biblioteca Española-Portugueza-Judaica (ed.), 1971; From Spanish Court to Italian Ghetto: Isaac Cardoso, A Study in Seventeenth-Century Marranism and Jewish Apologetics, 1971; History of the Origin and Establishment of the Inquisition in Portugal (ed.), 1972; Haggadah and History: A Panorama in Facsimile of Five Centuries of the Printed Haggadah from the Collections of Harvard University and the Jewish Theological Seminary of America, 1974; The Lisbon Massacre of 1506 and the Royal Image in the Shebet Yehudah, 1976; Assimilation and Racial Anti-Semitism, 1982; Zakhor: Jewish History and Jewish Memory, 1982; Spinoza on the Survival of the Jews, 1983; Usages de l'oubli, 1988; A Jewish Classic in the Portuguese Language: Samuel Usque's Consolacam as Tribulacoens de Israel, 1989; Freud's Moses: Judaism Terminable and Interminable, 1991; Ein Feld in Anatot: Versuche über Jüdische Geschichte, 1993; Diener von Königen und nicht Diener von Dienern: Einige Aspekte der politischen Geschichte der Juden, 1995; Sefardica: Essais sur l'histoire des Juifs, des Marranes, et des Nouveaux Chrétiens, d'origine Hispano-Portugaise, 1998. Contributions: many articles on Spanish and Portuguese history and history of psychoanalysis, to various publications. *Honours:* Hon. MA (Harvard) 1970, Hon. DHL (Jewish Theological Seminary of America) 1987, (Spertus Inst. of Jewish Studies Chicago) 2002, Hon. LHD (Hebrew Union Coll.) 1996, Hon. PhD (Haifa Israel) 1997, (Ludwig-Maximilians Munich) 1997, (Ecole Pratique des Hautes Etudes Sorbonne-Paris) 2003; Kent Fellow 1963, Fellow, American Acad. for Jewish Research 1972, Fellow, Nat. Endowment for the Humanities 1976, Rockefeller Fellow 1983–84, Fellow, American Acad. of Arts and Sciences 1986, Guggenheim Fellowship 1989–90, Fellow, Carl Friedrich von Siemens Stiftung, Munich 1996–97; Ansley Award, Columbia University Press 1968, Newman Medal, CUNY 1975, Nat. Jewish Book Award 1983, Gold Medal Portuguese Acad. of History, Lisbon 1989, Medal of the Nat. Foundation for Jewish Culture for Achievement in History 1995. *Literary Agent:* George Borchardt, 136 E 57th Street, New York, NY, USA. *Address:* 511 Fayerweather Hall, Columbia University, New York, NY 10027, USA. *E-mail:* yhyl@columbia.edu.

YESSENIN-VOLPIN, Alexander Sergeyevich; Russian mathematician, philosopher, poet and mentor of Human Rights Movt; b. 5 Dec. 1924, Leningrad (now St Petersburg); m. 1st V. B. Volpina; m. 2nd I. G. Kristi; m. 3rd 1994; one c. *Career:* studied at Faculty of Math., Moscow Univ. 1941–46; arrested for his poetry and committed to mental asylum 1949; in exile Karaganda, Kazakh SSR 1950; amnestied 1953; wrote numerous articles on logic and math. and translated extensively; at USSR Acad. of Sciences Inst. of Scientific and Tech. Information 1961–72; dissident activity 1959–; emigrated 1972. *Publications include:* A Free Philosophical Treatise 1959, A Leaf of Spring 1959, 1961, Open Letter to Solzhenitsyn 1970, Report on Committee on Rights of Man 1971, On the Logic of Moral Sciences (in English) 1988; numerous articles in Western and Russian scientific journals (after 1990s). *Address:* 1513 North Shore Road, 2nd Floor, Revere, MA 02151, USA. *Telephone:* (781) 289-1072.

YEVTUSHENKO, Yevgeniy Aleksandrovich; Russian poet and writer; b. 18 July 1933, Zima, Irkutsk Region; m. 1st Bella Akhmadulina 1954 (divorced); m. 2nd Galina Sokol 1962; one s.; m. 3rd Jan Butler 1978; two s.; m. 4th Maria Novikova 1986; two s. *Education:* Moscow Literary Inst. *Career:* geological expeditions with father to Kazakhstan 1948, the Altai 1949–50; literary work 1949–; mem. Editorial Bd of Yunost magazine 1962–69; People's Deputy of the USSR 1989–91; Sec. USSR Writers' Union 1986–91; Vice-Pres. Soviet PEN Cttee; moved to Tulsa, Okla, USA in mid-1990s, now teaches at Univ. of Tulsa; sometime Prof. Pittsburgh Univ. USA, Univ., Autónoma de Santo Domingo, Dominican Rep. *Films directed include:* Kindergarten 1983, Stalin's Funeral 1987; acted in Ascent (film on Tsiolkovsky). *Publications include:* poetry: Scouts of the Future (collected verse) 1952, The Third Snow (lyric verse) 1955, The Highway of Enthusiasts 1956, Zima Junction 1956, The Promise (collected verse) 1960, Moscow Goods Station, The Nihilist, The Apple 1960–61, Do the Russians Want War?, Babi Yar 1961, The Heirs of Stalin, Fears 1962, A Sweep of the Arm 1962, Tenderness 1962, A Precocious Autobiography 1963, The City of Yes and the City of No, Bratskaya Hydro-Electric Power Station 1964, Letter to Yesenin 1965, Italian Tears, A Boat of Communication, Poems Chosen by the Author 1966, Collection of Verses Yelabuga Nail, Cemetery of Whales 1967, That's What Is Happening to Me 1968, It's Snowing White 1969, Kazan University 1971, I am of Siberian Stock 1971, The Singing Domba 1972, Stolen Apples 1972, Under the Skin of the Statue of Liberty (play) 1972, Intimate Lyrics 1973, A Father's Hearing 1975, 1978, From Desire to Desire 1976, Love Poems 1977, People of the Morning 1978, Winter Station 1978, A Dove in Santiago: A Novella in Verse 1978, Heavy Soils 1979, The Face Behind the Face 1979, Ivan the Terrible and Ivan the Fool 1979, Berries (novel) 1981, Ardabiola (short story) 1981, Almost at the End (prose and verse) 1985, A Wind of Tomorrow (essays) 1987, Fatal Half Measures 1989, The Collected Poems 1952–90 1991, Farewell to Red Banner 1992, Twentieth Century Russian Poetry (compiler) 1994, Don't Die Before You're Dead (novel) 1996, My Very, Very... (poetry) 1996; photography: Divided Twins: Alaska and Siberia, Invisible Threads, Shadows and Faces. *Honours:* USSR Cttee for Defence of Peace Award 1965, Order of Red Banner of Labour, Badge of Honour, USSR State Prize 1984. *Address:* Kutuzovski Prospekt 2/1, Apt. 101, 121248 Moscow, Russia. *Telephone:* (095) 243-37-69.

YING, Diane; Taiwanese journalist and publisher; b. Xian, People's Republic of China. *Education:* Univ. of Iowa, USA. *Career:* emigrated with family from mainland China to Taiwan 1949; fmr reporter, The Philadelphia Inquirer, USA, Taiwan corresp. at various times for Asian Wall Street Journal, New York Times and United Press Int.; Co-founder, Chief Ed. and Publr Commonwealth financial monthly 1981–; teaches journalism at Nat. Chengchi Univ.; Commr Nat. Unification Council. *Address:* 4th Floor, 87 Sungkiang Road, Taipei, Taiwan.

YOLEN, Jane, BA, MEd; writer, poet and editor; b. 11 Feb. 1939, New York, NY, USA; m. David Wilber Stemple 1962; two s. one d. *Education:* Smith Coll., Univ. of Massachusetts. *Career:* mem. Authors' Guild, Children's Literature Asscn, MWA, SFWA (pres. 1986–88), Soc. of Children's Book Writers, Soc. of Children's Book Writers and Illustrators (bd of advisers 1970–). *Publications:* adult books: Briar Rose, Cards of Grief, One-Armed Queen, Sister, Light, Sister Dark, White Jenna, The Books of Great Alta, Among Angels (poems), Dragonfield, Merlin's Booke, The Radiation Sonnets, Storyteller Nesfa, Tales of Wonder, Sister Emily's Lightship and Other Stories, The Whitethorn Wood and Other Magicks (chapbook); children's poetry: Animal Fare, A Sip of Aesop, Best Witches, Bird Watch, Color Me a Rhyme, Dear Mother, Dear Daughter, Dinosaur Dances, Dragon Night, Horizons, How Beastly, O Jerusalem, Least Things, The Originals, Raining Cats & Dogs, Ring of Earth, Sacred Places, Sea Watch, Snow, Snow, Three Bears Holiday Rhyme Book, Three Bears Rhyme Book, Water Music, What Rhymes With Moon, Wild Wings; children's fiction: All in the Woodland Early, All Those Secrets of the World, An Invitation to the Butterfly Ball, Baby Bear's Bedtime Book, The Ballad of the Pirate Queens, Before the Storm, Beneath the Ghost Moon, Bird of Time, Boy Who Had Wings, Child of Faerie, Dove Isabeau, Eeny Meeny Miney Mole, Elfabet, Elsie's Bird, The Emperor & the Kite, Encounter, Fairy Holiday Book, Firebird, The Flying Witch, The Girl in the Golden Bower, The Girl Who Loved the Wind, Good Griselle, Grandad Bill's Song, Grandma's Hurrying Child, Greyling, Gwinellen: The Princess Who Could Not Sleep, Hands, Hannah Dreaming, Harvest Home, Honkers, Hoptoad, How Do Dinosaurs Get Well Soon?, How Do Dinosaurs Say Goodnight?, Isabel's Noel, It All Depends, King Longshanks, The Lady & the Merman, Letter From Phoenix Farm, Letting Swift River Go, Little Angel's Birthday, Little Mouse and Elephant, Little Spotted Fish, Longest Name on the Block, Meet the Monsters, Merlin & the Dragons, Milkweed Days, Minstrel & the Mountain, Miz Berlin Walks, Moonball, Mouse's Birthday, Musicians of Bremen, My Brothers' Flying Machine, My Uncle Emily, No Bath Tonight, Nocturne, Off We Go, Old Dame Counterpane, Owl Moon, Pegasus the Flying Horse, Picnic With Piggins, Piggins, Piggins & the Royal Wedding, Prince of Egypt, Rainbow Rider, Raising Yoder's Barn, Sea King, The Seeing Stick, See This Little Line, The Seventh Mandarin, The Simple Prince, Sky Dogs, Sleeping Beauty, Soft House, The Sultan's Perfect Tree, Tam Lin, Tea With an Old

Dragon, Too Old For Naps, Traveler's Rose, Welcome to the Green House, Welcome to the Ice House, Welcome to the Sea of Sand, Welcome to the River of Grass, Where Have the Unicorns Gone?, Wings, The Witch Who Wasn't, Commander Toad in Space, Commander & the Big Black Hole, Commander Toad & the Intergalactic Spy, Commander Toad & the Space Pirates, Commander Toad & the Dis-Asteroid, Commander Toad & the Planet of the Grapes, Commander Toad & the Voyage Home, The Giants' Farm, The Giants Go Camping, Mice on Ice, Sleeping Ugly, Spider Jane, Spider Jane on the Move, Acorn Quest, Adventures of Eeka Mouse, And Twelve Chinese Acrobats, Boy Who Spoke Chimp, Boots & the Seven Leaguers, Disas-Tour, Brothers of the Wind, Hobo Toad & the Motorcycle Gang, Inway Investigators, The Magic Three of Solatia, The Mermaid's Three Wisdoms, Pay the Piper, Robot & Rebecca: The Case of the Code-Carrying Kids, Robot & Rebecca: The Mystery of the Missing Owser, The Seaman, Shirlick Holmes & The Case of the Wandering Wardrobe, Tartan Magic: The Pictish Child, Tartan Magic: The Wizard's Map, Tartan Magic: Bagpiper's Ghost, Transfigured Hart, Uncle Lemon's Spring, Wild Hunt, Wizard of Washington Square, Wizard's Hall, Young Heroes: Atalanta and The Arcadian Beast, Young Heroes: Hippolyta and the Curse of the Amazons, Young Heroes: Odysseus in the Serpent Maze, Young Heroes: Jason and the Gorgon's Blood, Passager, Hobby, Merlin, Armageddon Summer, Children of the Wolf, The Devil's Arithmetic, Dragon's Boy, The Gift of Sarah Barker, Dragon's Blood, Heart's Blood, A Sending of Dragons, Prince in the Heather, Queen's Own Fool, Rogue's Apprentice, Girl in a Cage, The Stone Silenus, Sword of the Rightful King, Trust a City Kid; non-fiction: Fairy Tale Feasts, Friend: The Story of George Fox & the Quakers, The Wolf Girls, Mary Celeste, Roanoke Colony, Salem Witch Trials, Amelia Earhart, House, House, My Brothers' Flying Machine, The Perfect Wizard: Hans Christian Andersen, Pirates in Petticoats, Ring Out: A Book of Bells, Simple Gifts: The Story of the Shakers, Wizard Islands, World on a String: The Story of Kites; other: short story collections, contrib. to anthologies, periodicals. *Honours:* Dr hc (Smith Coll., Northampton, MA), (Baypath Coll., Longmeadow, MA), (Keene State Coll., Keene, NH), (Our Lady of the Elms Coll., Chicopee, MA); Christopher Medals 1979, 2001, Mythopoeic Soc. Awards 1986, 1993, Smith Coll. Medal 1988, Caldecott Medal 1988, Regina Medal 1992, Keene State Coll. Children's Book Award 1995, Nebula Awards 1997, 1998, World Fantasy Award 1988. *Address:* Phoenix Farm, PO Box 27, Hatfield, MA 01038, USA. *Website:* www.janeyolen.com.

YOON, Prabda, BFA; Thai writer, artist and journalist; b. 1973, Bangkok. *Education:* Cooper Union School for the Advancement of Science and Art, New York. *Screenplays:* One Night Husband 2003, Last Life in the Universe 2003. *Publications:* City of Right Angles (short story) 1999, Probability (short story) 2002, Unstill Pictures (non-fiction). *Honours:* SEA Write Award 2002.

YORK, Alison (see Nicole, Christopher (Robin)).

YORK, Andrew (see Nicole, Christopher Robin).

YORKE, Margaret, (Margaret Beda Nicholson); Writer; b. 30 Jan. 1924, Surrey, England; m. Basil Nicholson, 1945, divorced 1957, one s. one d. *Career:* Asst Librarian, St Hilda's College, Oxford, 1959–60; Library Asst, Christ Church, Oxford, 1963–65; Chair., CWA, 1979–80. *Publications:* Summer Flight, 1957; Pray Love Remember, 1958; Christopher, 1959; Deceiving Mirror, 1960; The China Doll, 1961; Once a Stranger, 1962; The Birthday, 1963; Full Circle, 1965; No Fury, 1967; The Apricot Bed, 1968; The Limbo Ladies, 1969; Dead in the Morning, 1970; Silent Witness, 1972; Grave Matters, 1973; No Medals for the Major, 1974; Mortal Remains, 1974; The Small Hours of the Morning, 1975; Cast for Death, 1976; The Cost of Silence, 1977; The Point of Murder, 1978; Death on Account, 1979; The Scent of Fear, 1980; The Hand of Death, 1981; Devil's Work, 1982; Find Me a Villain, 1983; The Smooth Face of Evil, 1984; Intimate Kill, 1985; Safely to the Grave, 1986; Evidence to Destroy, 1987; Speak for the Dead, 1988; Crime in Question, 1989; Admit to Murder, 1990; A Small Deceit, 1991; Criminal Damage, 1992; Dangerous to Know, 1993; Almost the Truth, 1994; Pieces of Justice, 1994; Serious Intent, 1995; A Question of Belief, 1996; Act of Violence, 1997; False Pretences, 1998; The Price of Guilt, 1999; A Case to Answer, 2000; Cause for Concern, 2001. *Honours:* Swedish Acad. of Detection award, 1982; Cartier Diamond Dagger, CWA, 1999. *Literary Agent:* Curtis Brown Ltd, Haymarket House, 28–29 Haymarket, London, SW1Y 4SP, England. *Telephone:* (20) 7393-4400. *Fax:* (20) 7393-4401. *E-mail:* info@curtisbrown.co.uk. *Website:* www.curtisbrown.co.uk.

YOSHIMASU, Gozo; Poet, Essayist and Lecturer; b. 22 Feb. 1939, Tokyo, Japan; m. Marilia, 17 Nov. 1973. *Education:* BA, Keio University, 1963. *Career:* Chief Ed., Sansai Finer Arts magazine, 1964–69; Fulbright Visiting Writer, University of Iowa, 1970–71; Poet-in-Residence, Oakland University, Rochester, MI, 1979–81; Lecturer, Tama Art University, 1984–; Visiting Lecturer at various institutions; many poetry readings around the world; mem. Japan PEN Club; Japan Writers' Asscn. *Publications:* A Thousand Steps and More: Selected Poems and Prose, 1964–1984 (in English trans.), 1987. Contributions: anthologies and periodicals. *Honours:* Takami Jun Prize, 1971; Rekitei Prize, 1979; Hanatsubaki Modern Poetry Prize, 1984. *Address:* 1-215-5 Kasumi-cho, Hachioji City 192, Japan.

YOSHIMOTO, Mahoko, (Banana Yoshimoto); Writer; b. 24 July 1964, Tokyo, Japan. *Education:* Nihon Univ. *Career:* mem. Japan Writers' Asscn. *Publications:* several books of fiction, incl., in trans.: Kitchen, 1988; N. P., 1990; Lizard, 1993; Amrita, 1994; Asleep, 2000; Goodbye Tsugumi, 2002. *Honours:* several Japanese literary prizes. *Address:* c/o Japan Foreign Rights Centre, 27-18-804, Naka Ochiai 2-chome, Shinjuku-ku, Tokyo 161, Japan.

YOSHIMURA, Akira; Japanese writer; b. 1927, Tokyo. *Career:* mem. Japanese Writers' Union (pres.), Int. PEN. *Publications include:* Umi no kabe 1970, Zero Fighter 1996, Shipwrecks 1996, Battleship: Musashi: The Making & Sinking of the World's Biggest Battleship 1999, On Parole 2000, One Man's Justice 2001, Storm Rider 2004. *Address:* c/o Canongate Books, 14 High Street, Edinburgh, EH1 1TE, Scotland. *Website:* www.canongate .net.

YOUNG, Al(bert James); Writer and Poet; b. 31 May 1939, Ocean Springs, MS, USA; m. Arline June Belch, 1963, one s. *Education:* University of Michigan, 1957–61; Stanford University, 1966–67; BA, University of California at Berkeley, 1969. *Career:* Jones Lecturer in Creative Writing, Stanford University, 1969–74; Writer-in-Residence, University of Washington, Seattle, 1981–82; Co-Founder (with Ishmael Reed) and Ed., Quilt magazine, 1981–. *Publications:* Fiction: Snakes, 1970; Who is Angelina?, 1975; Sitting Pretty, 1976; Ask Me Now, 1980; Seduction by Light, 1988. Poetry: Dancing, 1969; The Song Turning Back into Itself, 1971; Some Recent Fiction, 1974; Geography of the Near Past, 1976; The Blues Don't Change: New and Selected Poems, 1982; Heaven: Collected Poems 1958–1988, 1989; Straight No Chaser, 1994; The Sound of Dreams Remembered, 2001. Other: Bodies and Soul: Musical Memoirs, 1981; Kinds of Blue: Musical Memoirs, 1984; Things Ain't What They Used to Be: Musical Memoirs, 1987; Mingus/Mingus: Two Memoirs (with Janet Coleman), 1989; Drowning in the Sea of Love: Musical Memoirs, 1995. *Honours:* National Endowment for the Arts Grants, 1968, 1969, 1974; Joseph Henry Jackson Award, San Francisco Foundation, 1969; Guggenheim Fellowship, 1974; Pushcart Prize, 1980; Before Columbus Foundation Award, 1982.

YOUNG, Bertram Alfred, OBE; writer; b. 20 Jan. 1912, London, England. *Career:* Asst Ed., 1949–62, Drama Critic 1962–64, Punch; Drama Critic 1964–78, Arts Ed. 1971–77, Financial Times; mem. Critics Circle, Soc. of Authors, Garrick Club. *Publications:* Tooth and Claw 1958, Bechuanaland 1966, Cabinet Pudding 1967, The Mirror Up to Nature 1982, The Rattigan Version 1986; contrib. to numerous professional journals and general magazines. *Address:* 1 Station Street, Cheltenham, Gloucester GL50 3LX, England.

YOUNG, Ian George; poet, writer and editor; b. 5 Jan. 1945, London, England. *Career:* Dir, Catalyst Press, 1969–80, TMW Communications, 1990–; mem. International Psychohistory Asscn. *Publications:* Poetry: White Garland, 1969; Year of the Quiet Sun, 1969; Double Exposure, 1970; Cool Fire, 1970; Lions in the Stream, 1971; Some Green Moths, 1972; The Male Muse, 1973; Invisible Words, 1974; Common-or-Garden Gods, 1976; The Son of the Male Muse, 1983; Sex Magick, 1986. Fiction: On the Line, 1981. Non-Fiction: The Male Homosexual in Literature, 1975; Overlooked and Underrated, 1981; Gay Resistance, 1985; The AIDS Dissidents, 1993; The Stonewall Experiment, 1995; The AIDS Cult, 1997; The AIDS Dissidents: A Supplement, 2001; Autobibliography, 2001; The Beginnings of Gay Liberation in Canada 2004. *Honours:* several Canada Council and Ontario Arts Council Awards. *Address:* 2483 Gerrard Street E, Scarborough, ON M1N 1W7, Canada. *E-mail:* iyoung@arvotek.net.

YOUNG, Rose (see Harris, Marion Rose).

YOUNG, Wayland Hilton, (2nd Baron Kennet); politician, writer and journalist; b. 2 Aug. 1923, London, England; m. Elizabeth Ann Adams, 24 Jan. 1948, one s., five d. *Education:* Trinity College, Cambridge. *Career:* Staff, Foreign Office, 1946–47, 1949–51; Delegate, Parliamentary Assemblies, Western European Union and Council of Europe, 1962–65; Ed., Disarmament and Arms Control, 1962–65; Parliamentary Sec., Ministry of Housing and Local Government, 1966–70; Opposition Spokesman on Foreign Affairs and Science Policy, 1971–74; Mem., European Parliament, 1978–79; Chief Whip, 1981–83, Spokesman on Foreign Affairs and Defence, 1981–90, Social Democratic Party, House of Lords; Vice-Pres., Parliamentary and Scientific Committee, 1989–98; Rejoined Labour Party, 1990. *Publications:* as Wayland Young: The Italian Left, 1949; The Deadweight, 1952; Now or Never, 1953; Old London Churches (with Elizabeth Young), 1956; The Montesi Scandal, 1957; Still Alive Tomorrow, 1958; Strategy for Survival, 1959; The Profumo Affair, 1963; Eros Denied, 1965; Thirty-Four Articles (ed.), 1965; Existing Mechanisms of Arms Control, 1965. as Wayland Kennet: Preservation, 1972; The Futures of Europe, 1976; The Rebirth of Britain, 1982; London's Churches (with Elizabeth Young), 1986; Northern Lazio (with Elizabeth Young), 1990; Parliaments and Screening, 1995. *Honours:* created 2nd Baron Kennet 1935. *Address:* c/o House of Lords, London, SW1A 0PW, England.

YOUNG-BRUEHL, Elisabeth; Prof. of Psychology, Psychoanalyst and Writer; b. 3 March 1946, Elkton, MD, USA. *Education:* BA, 1968, MA, 1974, PhD, 1974, New School for Social Research, New York. *Career:* Prof. of Philosophy, Wesleyan University, 1974–91; Prof. of Psychology, Haverford College, PA, 1991–99; mem. Authors' Guild. *Publications:* Freedom and Karl Jaspers' Philosophy, 1981; Hannah Arendt: For Love of the World, 1982; Vigil, 1983; Anna Freud: A Biography, 1988; Mind and the Body Politic, 1989; Freud on Women, 1990; Creative Characters, 1991; Global

Cultures, 1994; The Anatomy of Prejudices, 1996; Subject to Biography, 1999; Cherishment, 2000. Contributions: Professional journals. *Honours:* National Endowment for the Humanities Fellowship, 1984–85; Guggenheim Fellowship, 1986–87. *Address:* 240 E Houston St, Suite 5D, New York, NY 10002, USA.

YOUNG-EISENDRATH, Polly; Psychologist, Psychoanalyst and Writer; b. 4 Feb. 1947, Akron, OH, USA; m. Edward Epstein, 13 Jan. 1985, two s. one d. *Education:* BA, summa cum laude, English, Ohio University, 1965–69; Institute de Touraine, France, 1967–68; MA, Psychology, Mythology, Goddard College, 1974; MSW, Clinical Social Work, 1977, PhD, Developmental and Counselling Psychology, 1980, Washington University; Diploma, Jungian Analysis, Inter-Regional Society of Jungian Analysts, 1978–86. *Career:* Chief Psychologist, Jungian Analyst, Pres., Clinical Assocs West, P. C. Radnor, 1986–94; Independent Practice as Psychologist and Jungian Analyst, Burlington, VT, 1994–; Clinical Assoc. Prof. in Psychiatry, Medical College, University of Vermont, Burlington, 1996–; numerous lectures world-wide; mem. International Asscn for Analytical Psychology; American Psychological Asscn; Independent Society for Analytical Psychology, founding mem. *Publications:* Jung's Self Psychology: A Constructivist Perspective, 1991; You're Not What I Expected: Learning to Love the Opposite Sex, 1993; The Gifts of Suffering: Finding Insight, Compassion and Renewal, 1996; Gender and Desire: Uncursing Pandora, 1997; A Cambridge Companion to Jung (co-ed.), 1997; Women and Desire: Beyond Wanting to be Wanted, 1999; The Psychology of Mature Spirituality: Integrity, Wisdom, Transcendence, 2000; Awakening and Insight: Zen Buddhism and Psychotherapy, 2002. Contributions: Professional journals. *Honours:* various fellowships, assistantships and awards. *Address:* 195 Calais Rd, Worcester, VT 05682, USA.

YU GUANGZHONG; Taiwanese university professor, poet, critic, translator and essayist; b. 9 Sept. 1928, Nanjing City, Jiangsu Prov.; m. Wo Chun Fan 1956; four d. *Education:* Iowa Univ., USA. *Career:* Chief Ed. of Blue Stars and Modern Literature; Prof., Taiwan Normal Univ., Chinese Univ. of Hong Kong; Kuang Hua Chair. Prof. of English, Nat. Sun Yat-sen Univ. 1998–; Pres. Taipei Chinese Centre, PEN Int. 1990–99. *Publications:* Elegy of Boatman, Stalactite, Blue Plume, Sirius, White Jade Bitter Gourd, A Tug of War with Eternity, Dream and Geography, Selected Poetry of Yu Guangzhong Vols I and II, The Child of Dogwood–A Life of Yu Guangzhong 1999, The Old Man and the Sea (trans.), The Importance of being Earnest (trans.), Lust for Life (trans.) Bartleby the Scrivener (trans.), Modern English and American Poetry (trans.). *Honours:* Hon. Fellow Hong Kong Trans. Soc. 1991; Australian Cultural Award 1972; Best Books of the Year 1994, 1996, 1998, 2000 (Taiwan), 1998 (Hong Kong); Nat. Poetry Prize, Wu San-Lian Prose Prize and six others. *Address:* Foreign Literature Institute, Sun Yat-sen University, 135 Xingang Road, Guanzhou 510275, Guangdong Province, People's Republic of China. *Telephone:* (7) 5564908 (Home); (20) 84112828. *Fax:* (20) 84039173. *E-mail:* adpo@zsu.edu.cn (Office). *Website:* www.zsu.edu.cn (Office).

YU HUA, MA; Chinese writer; b. 1960, Gaotang, Shandong Prov. *Education:* Beijing Normal Univ. *Career:* worked as a dentist for five years; writer 1983–. *Publications:* To Live, Chronicle of a Blood Merchant, Shouting in the Drizzle, Events of the World Are Like Smoke, One Kind of Reality, Leaving Home for a Long Journey at Eighteen, An Incident, Mistake at Riverside. *Honours:* James Joyce Foundation Award 2002. *Address:* c/o National Human Resources Exchange Centre, Beijing, People's Republic of China (Office).

YU YOUXIAN; Chinese publisher; *Commissioner, National Copyright Administration of China*; b. 1937, Penglai Co., Shandong. *Career:* Vice-Gov. of Henan Prov. 1993–2000; Commrof State Admin of Press and Publs, 1999–; Commr of Nat. Copyright Admin of China 1999–; Chair. Asscn of Chinese Publrs. *Address:* c/o Press and Publications Administration, State Council, Beijing, People's Republic of China.

YUDKIN, Leon Israel; University Lecturer and Writer; b. 8 Sept. 1939, England; m. Meirah Goss, 29 Sept. 1967. *Education:* BA, 1960, MA, 1964, University of London. *Career:* Asst Lecturer, Lecturer, University of Manchester, 1966–; Lecturer, University College London, 1996; Visiting Prof., University of Paris VIII, 2000. *Publications:* Isaac Lamdan: A Study in Twentieth-Century Hebrew Poetry, 1971; Meetings with the Angel (co-ed.), 1973; Escape into Siege, 1974; U. Z. Greenberg: On the Anvil of Hebrew Poetry, 1980; Jewish Writing and Identity in the Twentieth Century, 1982; 1948 and After: Aspects of Israeli Fiction, 1984; Modern Hebrew Literature in English Translation (ed.), 1986; Agnon: Texts and Contexts in English Translation (ed.), 1988; Else Lasker-Schüler: A Study in German-Jewish Literature, 1990; Beyond Sequence: Current Israeli Fiction and Its Context, 1992; The Israeli Writer and the Holocaust (ed.), 1993; The Other in Israeli Literature (ed.), 1993; A Home Within: Varities of Jewish Expression in Modern Fiction, 1996; Public Crisis and Literary Response: Modern Jewish Literature, 2001; Literature in the Wake of the Holocaust, 2003. Contributions: various publications. *Honours:* DLitt, University of London, 1995. *Address:* 51 Hillside Ct, 409 Finchley Rd, London NW3 6HQ, England. *Telephone:* (20) 7435-5777. *E-mail:* l.yudkin@ucl.ac.uk.

YUSUF, Nova Riyanti; Indonesian novelist; b. 27 Nov. 1977. *Publications:* Mahadewa Mahadewi (trans. as God, Goddess) 2003. *Address:* c/o Pustaka Utma, Jalan Utan Kayu 68EFG, Utan Kayu Utara, Jakarta 13120, Indonesia.

Z

ZABUZHKO, Oksana; Novelist and Poet; b. 1961, Lutsk, Ukraine. *Education:* Philosophy, Taras Shevchenko Univ. of Kiev, 1982; PhD, Aesthetics, 1987. *Career:* fmr assoc., Institute of Philosophy at the National Academy of Arts and Sciences, Kiev; Writer-in-Residence, Pennsylvania State Univ., 1992; Fulbright Scholar, Harvard Univ., Univ. of Pittsburgh, 1994. *Publications:* Poetry: May Hoarfrost; The Conductor of the Last Candle; Hitchhiking; A Kingdom of Fallen Statues (poems and essays), 1996. Fiction: Extraterrestrial Woman; Field Studies in Ukrainian Sex; Sister Sister (short stories), 2003. Non-Fiction: Two Cultures, The Philosophy of the Ukrainian Idea and Its European Context. Contributions: Agni, Glas, Harvard Review, International Quarterly, Massachusetts Review, Mr Cogito, Nimrod, Partisan Review, Ploughshares, Poetry Miscellany, Slavic and East European Journal, Ukrainian Quarterly.

ZACHARIUS, Walter, BA; American publisher; *Chairman and CEO, Kensington Publishing Corporation*; b. 16 Oct. 1923, New York; m. Alice Riesenberg 1948; one s. one d. *Education:* Coll. of City of New York School of Business, New York Univ., New School of Social Research, Empire State Univ. *Career:* served US Army 1942–45; circulation depts McFadden Publishing Inc. 1947–, Popular Library Inc. 1948–49, American Mercury Inc. 1949–51; Circulation Dir Ace News Co., New York 1951–61; Pres. Magnum Royal Publs Inc., New York 1961–; Pres., Chair. of Bd Magnum Communications, New York 1961; Pres. Lancer Books Inc., New York 1961–75, Walter Zacharius Assoc. 1964–; f. Kensington Publishing Corpn 1974; , Pres. United Cerebral Palsy of Queens 1986–89; Chair. Bd Kensington Publishing Corpn Inc. 1976–. *Honours:* World War II Medal, American Service Medal; European-African-Middle Eastern Service Medal; Public Relations Award-United Cerebral Palsy of Queens 1970, Award of Honor, UJA Fed. Campaign 1987, UJA Fed.'s Distinguished Service Award 1992, Gallatin Div. of New York City Certificate of Distinction 1993. *Address:* Kensington Publishing Corporation, 850 3rd Avenue, New York, NY 10022 (Office); 400 East 56th Street, New York, NY 10022, USA (Home). *Telephone:* (877) 422-3665 (Office). *E-mail:* wzacharius@kensingtonbooks.com (Office). *Website:* www.kensingtonbooks.com.

ZAHNISER, Ed(ward DeFrance); Writer, Poet and Ed.; b. 11 Dec. 1945, Washington, DC, USA; m. Ruth Christine Hope Deuwel, 13 July 1968, two s. *Education:* BA, Greenville College, IL, 1967; Officers' Basic Course, Defence Information School, 1971. *Career:* Poetry Ed., The Living Wilderness Magazine, 1972–75; Founding Ed., Some of Us Press, Washington, DC, 1972–75; Arts Ed., Good News Paper, 1981–; Ed., Arts and Kulchur, 1989–91; Assoc. Poetry Ed., Antietam Review, 1992–. *Publications:* The Ultimate Double Play (poems), 1974; I Live in a Small Town (with Justin Duewel-Zahniser), 1984; The Way to Heron Mountain (poems), 1986; Sheenjek and Denali (poems), 1990; Jonathan Edwards (artist book), 1991; Howard Zahniser: Where Wilderness Preservation Began: Adirondack Wilderness Writings (ed.), 1992; A Calendar of Worship and Other Poems, 1995. Contributions: anthologies and periodicals. *Honours:* Woodrow Wilson Fellow, 1967; First and Second Prize in Poetry, West Virginia Writers Annual Competitions, 1989, 1991, 1992; Second Prize, Essay, 1995. *Address:* c/o Atlantis Rising, PO Box 955, Shepherdstown, WV 25443-0955, USA.

ZAHRA, Trevor; Writer; b. 16 Dec. 1947, Zejtun, Malta; m. Stella Zahra (deceased); one s. one d. *Education:* Teachers' College of Education, 1967–69. *Career:* mem. Maltese Acad. of Writers; Maltese Literary Society, sec., 1970–74. *Publications:* Over 100 books for adults and children. *Honours:* First Prize, Book Club, Malta, 1974; Co-Winner, Rothmas Award, 1975. *Address:* 23 Qrempuc St, Marsaskala ZBR-11, Malta. *E-mail:* trevor@orbit.net.mt.

ZAKARIA, Fareed, PhD; American editor and academic; *Editor, Newsweek International*; b. India; m.; one s. *Education:* Yale and Harvard Univs. *Career:* Lecturer on Int. Politics and Econs, Harvard Univ., also Head of Project on the Changing Security Environment; Adjunct Prof., Columbia Univ., Cape Western Reserve Univ.; Man. Ed. Foreign Affairs journal 1992–2000; Foreign Policy Adviser to US Admin.; Ed. Newsweek Int. 2000–; Columnist Newsweek (USA), Newsweek Int. and The Washington Post 2001–; speaker at World Econ. Forum, Davos, Switzerland and various univs.; broadcast appearances on Charlie Rose, Firing Line, The NewsHour with Jim Lehrer, The McLaughlin Group, BBC World News and Meet the Press; contrib. to publs including The New York Times, The New Yorker and The Wall Street Journal; wine columnist for Slate (webzine). *Publications include:* From Wealth to Power: The Unusual Origins of America's World Role, The American Encounter: The United States and the Making of the Modern World (co-ed.), The Future of Freedom 2003. *Honours:* Overseas Press Club Award. *Address:* Newsweek International, Newsweek Building, 251 West 57th Street, New York, NY 10019-1894, USA (Office). *E-mail:* editors@newsweek.com (Office). *Website:* www.newsweek-int.com (Office); www.fareedzakaria.com.

ZALBEN BRESKIN, Jane; Author, Artist and College Teacher; b. 21 April 1950, New York, NY, USA; m. Steven Zalben 25 Dec. 1969; two s. *Education:* BA, Art, Queens College, CUNY, 1971; Pratt Graphics Centre, 1972. *Career:* mem. Society of Children's Book Writers; Authors' Guild. *Publications:* Cecilia's Older Brother, 1973; Lyle and Humus, 1974; Basil and Hillary, 1975; Penny and the Captain, 1977; Norton's Nightime, 1979; Will You Count the Stars Without Me, 1979; All in the Woodland Early: An ABC by Jane Yolen, 1979; Oliver and Alison's Week, 1980; Oh Simple!, 1981; Porcupine's Christmas Blues, 1982, Maybe It Will Rain Tomorrow, 1982; Here's Looking at You, Kid, 1987; Water from the Moon, 1987; Beni's First Chanukah, 1988; Earth to Andrew O. Blechman, 1989; Happy Passover, Rosie, 1989; Leo and Blossom's Sukkah, 1990; Goldie's Purim, 1991; The Fortune Teller in 5B, 1991; Beni's Little Library, 1991; Buster Gets Braces, 1992; Inner Chimes: Poems on Poetry, 1992; Happy New Year, Beni, 1993; Papa's Latkes, 1994; Beni's First Chanukah, 1994; Miss Violet's Shining Day, 1995; Pearl Plants a Tree, 1995; Beni's Family Cookbook, 1996; Unfinished Dreams, 1996; Papa's Latkes, 1996; Pearl's Marigolds for Grandpa, 1997; Beni's First Wedding, 1998; Beni's Family Teasury, 1998; Pearl's Eight Days of Chanukah, 1998; To Every Season: A Family Cookbook, 1999; Don't Go, 2001; The Magic Menorah: A Modern Chanukah Tale, 2001; Pearl's Passover, 2002; Let There Be Light: Poems for Repairing the World, 2002; Saturday Night at the Beastro (with Steven Zalben), 2004; Baby Babka, the Gorgeous Genius, 2004. Contributions: journals and magazines. *Honours:* Sydney Taylor Honour Award, 1989, and Silver Medal, 2003; Best Books Citation, New York Public Library, 1991; International Reading Asscn Citation, 1993; Parents' Choice Award, 1995; ALA Notable Award, 1996. *Address:* 70 South Rd, Sands Point, NY 11050, USA. *E-mail:* janezalben@hotmail.com. *Website:* www.janebreskinzalben.com.

ZAMOYSKI, Adam, BA, MA, FSA; historian and writer; b. 11 Jan. 1949, New York, NY, USA; m. Emma Sergeant 2001. *Education:* University of Oxford. *Publications:* Chopin: A New Biography 1979, The Battle for the Marchlands 1981, Paderewski: A Biography 1982, The Polish Way 1987, The Last King of Poland 1992, The Forgotten Few 1995, Holy Madness 1999, Poland: A Traveller's Gazetteer 2001, 1812: Napoleon's Fatal March on Moscow 2004. *Address:* 33 Ennismore Gardens, London, SW7 1AE, England. *E-mail:* adam@adamzamoyski.com. *Website:* www.adamzamoyski.com.

ZANCANELLA, Don; Prof. of English Education and Writer; b. 29 Oct. 1954, Rock Springs, WY, USA; m. Dorene Kahl, 1981, two c. *Education:* BS, University of Virginia, 1977; MA, University of Denver, 1984; PhD, University of Missouri, 1988. *Career:* Assoc. Prof. of English Education, University of New Mexico, Albuquerque, 1988–. *Publications:* Western Electric (short stories), 1996; The Chimpanzees of Wyoming Territory (short story), 1998. Contributions: English Journal; Prairie Schooner; Alaska Quarterly Review; New Letters; Mid-American Review. *Honours:* John Simmons Short Fiction Award, Iowa Writers' Workshop, 1996; O. Henry Award, 1998. *Address:* c/o College of Education, University of New Mexico, Albuquerque, NM 87131, USA. *E-mail:* zanc@unm.edu.

ZANGANA, Haifa; British novelist, journalist and painter; b. 1950, Iraq. *Career:* writes in Arabic and English; moved to London 1976. *Publications:* Halabja (collection of essays by Arab writers, ed.), 1989; Through the Vast Halls of Memory, 1991; Bayt al-Namal (The Ant's Nest), 1996; Beyond What the Eye Sees, 1997; The Presence of Others (short stories), 1999; Keys to the City, 2000; Women on a Journey, 2001; co-author: El Kalima; Aswat; Al Ightirab al Adabi. *Address:* c/o Exiled Writers Ink!, 31 Hallswelle Road, London NW11 0DH, England. *E-mail:* haifa_zangana@yahoo.co.uk.

ZAWODNY, Janusz Kazimierz, BS, MA, PhD; American retd academic and writer; b. 11 Dec. 1921, Warsaw, Poland; m. LaRae Jean Koppit 1971; one s. *Education:* Univ. of Iowa, Stanford Univ. *Career:* instructor and Asst Prof., Princeton Univ. 1955–58; Fellow, Center for Advanced Study in the Behavioral Sciences, Stanford 1961–62; Assoc. Prof. 1962–63, Prof. of Political Science 1965–75, Univ. of Pennsylvania; Prof. of Political Science, Washington Univ., St Louis 1963–65; Research Assoc., Center for Int. Affairs, Harvard Univ. 1968; sr assoc. mem., St Antony's Coll., Oxford 1968–69; mem., Inst. for Advanced Study, Princeton 1971–72; Avery Prof. of Int. Relations, Claremont Graduate Univ. and Pomona Coll., CA 1975–82; consultant staff, Nat. Security Council, USA 1979–84. *Publications:* Death in the Forest: The Story of the Katyn Forest Massacre 1962, Guide to the Study of International Relations 1967, Man and International Relations: Contribution of the Social Sciences to the Study of Conflict and Integration (ed. and contributor, two vols) 1967, Nothing But Honour: The Story of the Uprising of Warsaw 1944 1978, Uczestnicy i Swiadkowie Powstania Warszawskiego 1994; contrib. to scholarly books and journals. *Honours:* Hon. MA (Univ. of Pennsylvania) 1965, (Univ. of Oxford) 1968; Literary Award, Kultura, Paris 1981, Jurzykowski Foundation Citation and Award 1982, Research Awards, Polish Scientific Soc., London 1982, 1989, Scientific Soc. Book of the Year Award, Univ. of Lublin, Poland 1988, History Award, J. Pilsudski Inst., New York 1997; Order of Virtuti Militari 1944, Order of Merit, Pres. of Poland 1994. *Address:* 23703 NE Margaret Road, Brush Prairie, WA 98606, USA.

ZELDIN, Theodore; Essayist and Historian; b. 1933. *Career:* fmr Fellow and Dean, St Anthony's College, Oxford; Assoc. Fellow, Templeton College, Oxford; Visiting Prof., Harvard Univ., Univ. of Southern California; Pres.,

The Oxford Muse; mem. European Academy; British Academy; Society of Authors; BBC Brains Trust. *Publications:* Conflicts in French Society (ed.), 1971; France 1848–1945: Ambition, Love and Politics, 1973; Ambition and Love, 1979; Politics and Anger, 1979; Taste and Corruption, 1980; Intellect and Pride, 1980; Anxiety and Hypocrisy, 1981; The French, 1983; Happiness, 1988; A History of French Passions: Intellect, Taste and Anxiety, 1993; An Intimate History of Humanity, 1994; Conversation: How Talk Can Change Our Lives, 1998. Contributions: New York Review of Books. *Honours:* Wolfson Prize. *Address:* c/o HiddenSpring, 997 Macarthur Blvd, Mahwah, NJ 07430, USA.

ZELEZA, Paul Tiyambe; Malawian writer; b. 25 May 1955, Harare, Zimbabwe; m.; one d. *Education:* BA, Univ. of Malawi, 1976; MA, Univ. of London, 1978; PhD, Dalhousie Univ., Canada, 1982. *Career:* lecturer, universities of Malawi, 1976–77, Nairobi, 1979–80, the West Indies, 1982–84, Kenyatta, 1984–89; fmr Ed., Odi journal, Umodzi magazine; f. mem., Malawian Writer's Series, 1974; Assoc. Prof., Dept of History and Comparative Development Studies, Trent Univ., ON, Canada, 1990–95, Prof., 1995; Acting Dir, Trent International Program, Trent Univ., 1994–95; Principal, Lady Eaton College, Trent Univ., 1994–95; Prof. of History and African Studies, and Dir, Center for African Studies, Univ. of Illinois at Urbana-Champaign, 1995–. *Publications:* Fiction: Night of Darkness and Other Stories, 1976; Smouldering Charcoal, 1992; The Joys of Exile (short stories), 1994. Non-Fiction: Rethinking Africa's Globalization, Vol. 1: The Intellectual Challenges; Imperialism and Labour: The International Relations of the Kenyan Labour Movement, 1987; Labour, Unionization and Women's Participation in Kenya 1965–1987, 1988; A Modern Economic History of Africa, Vol. 1: The Nineteenth Century, 1993, Vol. 2: The Twentieth Century; Maasai, 1994; Akamba, 1994; Mijikenda, 1994; Manufacturing African Studies and Crises, 1997. Contributions: numerous articles, chapters, reviews and short stories. *Honours:* Noma Award, 1994. *Address:* Center for African Studies, Univ. of Illinois at Urbana-Champaign, 210 International Studies Bldg, 910 S Fifth St, Champaign, IL 61820, USA. *Telephone:* (217) 333-6335. *Fax:* (217) 244-2429. *E-mail:* zeleza@uiuc.edu.

ZEPHANIAH, Benjamin Obadiah Iqbal; poet, writer, dramatist, musician and singer; b. 15 April 1958, Birmingham, England. *Career:* Writer-in-Residence, Africa Arts Collective, Liverpool 1989, Hay-on-Wye Literature Festival 1991, Memphis State Univ., TN 1991–95; numerous radio performances, acting roles, appearances; mem. Musicians' Union, Equity, Performing Rights Soc., ALCS. *Recordings:* albums: Rasta 1983, Us and Dem 1990, Back To Our Roots 1995, Belly Of The Beast 1996, Heading For The Door 2000; singles: Dub Ranting (EP) 1982, Big Boys Don't Make Girls Cry 1984, Free South Africa 1986, Crisis 1992, Naked 2004; contributor to: Dancing Tribes (single, with Back To Base) 1999, Illegal (with Swayzak) 2000. *Publications:* fiction: Face 1999, Refugee Boy 2001; poetry: Pen Rhythm 1980, The Dread Affair 1985, Inna Liverpool 1988, Rasta Time in Palestine 1990, City Psalms 1992, Talking Turkeys 1994, Funky Chickens 1996, Propa Propaganda 1996, School's Out 1997, We Are Britain 2002, Too Black, Too Strong 2002, The Little Book of Vegan Poems 2002, Gangsta Rap 2004; plays: Playing the Right Tune 1985, Job Rocking 1987, Delirium 1987, Streetwise 1990, The Trial of Mickey Tekka 1991; radio plays: Hurricane Dub 1988, Our Teacher's Gone Crazy 1990, Listen To Your Parents 2000; television play: Dread Poets Society 1991; contrib. to periodicals, radio, television and recordings. *Honours:* BBC Young Playwrights Festival Award 1988, hon. doctorates (Univ. of North London) 1998, (Univ. of West of England) 1999, (Staffordshire Univ.) 2001, (Oxford Brookes Univ.) 2002, (South Bank Univ., London) 2002, (Univ. of East London) 2003, (Univ. Coll. Northampton) 2003. *Literary Agent:* Sandra Boyce Management, 1 Kingsway House, Albion Road, London, N16 0TA, England. *Address:* PO Box 673, East Ham, London, E6 3QD, England. *Website:* www.benjaminzephaniah.com.

ZERNOVA, Ruf Aleksandrovna; Russian writer, essayist and translator; b. (Ruf Zevina), 1919, Tiraspol, Moldavia; m. 1st (divorced); m. 2nd Ilya Z. Serman; one s. one d. *Education:* Leningrad Inst. of Philosophy, Literature and History, Leningrad State Univ. *Career:* translator, Navy Ministry, Moscow 1939–41; translator and ed., TASS press agency; imprisoned in labour camps 1949–54; reviewer and writer for journals, including Zvezda, Iunost, Ogonek; first short story published 1956; founder mem. Writers' Union 1954–. *Publications include:* Skorpionovy iagody (trans. as Scorpion Berries) 1961, Bakaloo (trans. as Baccalao) 1963, Svet i ten' (trans. as Light and Shadow) 1963, linnoe, dlinnoe leto (trans. as A Long, Long Summer) 1967, Rasskazy pro Antona (trans. as Stories About Anton) 1968, Solnechnaia storona (trans. as The Sunny Side) 1968, Nemye zvonki (Mute Phone Calls) 1974, Zhenskie rasskazy (trans. as Stories of Women) 1981, Eto bylo pri nas (trans. as It Was in Our Time) 1988, Izali i okresnosti (trans. as Israel and its Surroundings) 1990, Mute Phone Calls and Other Stories (in trans.) 1991; editor: Leningradtsy v Ispanii 1936–1939: Sbornik vospominanii (trans. as Leningraders in Spain 1936–1939: An Anthology of Recollections) 1967. *Address:* c/o New Brunswick Rutgers University Press, 100 Joyce Kilmer Avenue, Piscataway, NJ 08854, USA.

ZETFORD, Tully (see Bulmer, Henry Kenneth).

ZHANG CHANGXIN, (Dongli Jiefu); writer; b. 30 Nov. 1940, Liaoning, China; m. Huang Fuju 1962; one s. one d. *Education:* China Siping Teachers' School. *Career:* mem. China Asscn of Writers, China Playwrights' Asscn. *Publications:* Changba Shan Hun, English trans. as Spirit of Changba Mountains, 1985; Aide San Yuan Se, English trans. as Three Colours of Love, 1987; East Madrid, 1989; Zni Zhi Qiu, English trans. as Enjoyment in Autumn, 1991; Qingxi Lanxi, English trans. as Black and Blue, 1994; Chaoji Ai Qing Siwang, English trans. as The Death of Super Love, 1995. *Address:* c/o Jilin Writers' Association, Bldg 9, 167 Renmin Street, Changchun, Jilin, 130021, People's Republic of China.

ZHANG XIANLIANG; novelist and poet; b. 1936, Nanjing, Jiangsu, People's Republic of China; m. Yan Huili; one d. *Career:* fmr teacher in Beijing and Ningxia; Editorial staff, Shuofang literary magazine, late 1970s; committee mem., People's Consultative Conference, 1983, People's Republic of China Writers' Asscn (fmr Vice-Pres.), 1986; in political disgrace, 1957–79. *Publications:* Song of the Great Wind (poem), 1957; Soul and Flesh (aka A Herdsman's Story), 1981; Contemporary Chinese Short Stories, 1984 (with Zhang Xian and others), 1984; Mimosa, 1984; Prize-Winning Stories from China 1980–1981 (with others), 1985; Half of Man is Woman, 1985; Yi Xiang Tian Kai (screenplay), 1986; Women Shi Shijie (screenplay), 1988; Getting Used To Dying, 1989; Grass Soup, 1992; My Bodhi Tree, 1994. *Honours:* Best Novel of the Year Awards, 1981, 1983, 1984. *Address:* Ningxia Writers' Association, Yinchuan City, People's Republic of China.

ZHAOYAN, Ye; Chinese writer; b. 1957, Nanjing. *Publications:* Tale of the Jujube Tree 1988, Nanjing 1937 1996. *Address:* c/o Faber and Faber Ltd, 3 Queen Square, London, WC1N 3AU, England. *Website:* www.faber.co.uk.

ZIEGLER, Philip Sandeman, CVO, MA, FRHistS, FRSL; British writer; b. 24 Dec. 1929, Ringwood, Hants.; m. 1st Sarah Collins 1960 (deceased); one s. one d.; m. 2nd Mary Clare Charrington 1971; one s. *Education:* Eton Coll., New Coll. Oxford. *Career:* joined Foreign Office 1952, served Vientiane, Paris, Pretoria, Bogotá; Editorial Dir Collins Publishers 1972, Ed.-in-Chief 1979–80, resgnd when apptd to write official biog. of the late Earl Mountbatten; Chair. London Library 1979–85, Soc. of Authors 1988–90, Public Lending Right Advisory Cttee 1993–96. *Publications include:* Duchess of Dino 1962, Addington 1965, The Black Death 1969, William IV 1971, Omdurman 1973, Melbourne 1976, Crown and People 1978, Diana Cooper 1981, Mountbatten 1985, Elizabeth's Britain 1926 to 1986 1986, The Sixth Great Power: Barings 1762–1929 1988, King Edward VIII, The Official Biography 1990; ed.: The Diaries of Lord Louis Mountbatten 1920–1922 1987, Personal Diary of Admiral the Lord Louis Mountbatten 1943–1946 1988, From Shore to Shore: The Diaries of Earl Mountbatten of Burma 1953–1979 1989, Brooks's: A Social History (with Desmond Seward) 1991, Wilson: The Authorized Life of Lord Wilson of Rievaulx 1993, London at War: 1939–45 1994, Osbert Sitwell 1998, Britain Then and Now 1999, Soldiers: Fighting Men's Lives 1901–2001 2001, Rupert Hart-Davis: Man of Letters 2004. *Honours:* Hon. DLitt (Westminster Coll., Mo., USA) 1987, (Univ. of Buckingham) 2000; Chancellor's Essay Prize 1950, Heinemann Award 1976. *Address:* 22 Cottesmore Gardens, London, W8 5PR, England. *Telephone:* (20) 7937-1903. *Fax:* (20) 7937-5458.

ZIFFRIN, Marilyn; Composer and Writer; b. 7 Aug. 1926, Moline, IL, USA. *Education:* BM, University of Wisconsin, Madison, 1948; MA, Columbia University, 1949; Postgraduate Studies, University of Chicago, 1963–65. *Publications:* Carl Ruggles: Composer, Painter and Storyteller, 1994. Contributions: The New Grove Dictionary of Music and Musicians, 1980; The New Grove Dictionary of American Music, 1986. *Honours:* MacDowell Colony Fellowships, 1961, 1963, 1971, 1977, 1980, 1989; ASCAP Awards, 1981–2003; Virginia Center for the Creative Arts Residency, 1987. *Address:* PO Box 179, Bradford, NH 03221, USA.

ZIGAL, Thomas; Writer; b. 20 Oct. 1948, Galveston, TX, USA; one s. *Education:* BA, English, University of Texas, 1970; MA, Creative Writing, Stanford University, 1974. *Career:* mem. Texas Institute of Letters, 1995–. *Publications:* Playland, 1982; Into Thin Air, 1995; Hardrock Stiff, 1996. *Address:* c/o International Creative Management, 40 W 57th St, New York, NY 10019, USA.

ZIMDAHL, Catherine; Australian playwright and screenwriter. *Education:* Australian Film, Television and Radio School. *Career:* writer of short features Sparks and Life on Earth as I Know It. *Plays:* Family Running for Mr Whippy 1995, Clark in Sarajevo 1998, The Wharf at Wooloomooloo, The Darling Loves 2005. *Honours:* Developing Writer's Grant, Literature Bd of the Australia Council; AFI Awards for Best Short Film, Best Short Screenplay 1990, Gold Plaque Award at the Chicago Int. Film Festival 1990, Le Prix Recherché at the Clermont Ferrand Film Festival 1990, Legal & General Umbrella Award for Best New Australian Writing 1998, Louis Esson Prize for Drama, Victorian Premier's Literary Awards 1999, ANPC/New Dramatists' Exchange to New York 1999. *Literary Agent:* RGM Associates, PO Box 128, Surry Hills, NSW 2010, Australia. *Telephone:* (2) 9281-3911. *Fax:* (2) 9281-4705. *E-mail:* info@rgm.com.au. *Website:* www.rgm.com.au.

ZIMLER, Richard, BA, MA; American journalist and writer; b. 1 Jan. 1956, Manhasset, Long Island, NY. *Education:* Duke Univ., Stanford Univ. *Career:* journalist 1982–90; teacher of journalism in Oporto Portugal; reviewer for the LA Times and Literary Review. *Publications:* Unholy Ghosts 1996, The Last Kabbalist of Lisbon 1997, The Secret Life of Images by Al Berto (trans.) 1997, The Angelic Darkness 1998, Hunting Midnight

2003. *Honours:* National Endowment of the Arts Fellowship in Fiction 1994; Herodotus Award. *Literary Agent:* Cynthia Cannell, 833 Madison Avenue, New York, NY 10021, USA. *Telephone:* (212) 396-9595. *Fax:* (212) 396-9797. *E-mail:* cynthiacannell@aol.com. *E-mail:* rczimler@hotmail.com. *Website:* www.zimler.com.

ZIMMER, Carl; American writer and journalist. *Publications:* At the Water's Edge 1998, Parasite Rex 2001, Evolution: The Triumph of an Idea: From Darwin to DNA 2002, Soul Made Flesh 2004; contrib. to Newsweek, Science, Discover, Sunday Telegraph, Popular Science, New York Newsday; monthly columnist for Natural History. *Address:* c/o Random House UK Ltd, 20 Vauxhall Bridge Road, London, SW1V 2SA, England. *E-mail:* mail@carlzimmer.com. *Website:* www.carlzimmer.com.

ZINDEL, Paul; Dramatist and Writer; b. 15 May 1936, Staten Island, NY, USA; m. Bonnie Hildebrand, 25 Oct. 1973, one s. one d. *Education:* BSc, 1958, MSc, 1959, Wagner College. *Career:* mem. Authors' Guild; Dramatists' Guild; Writers' Guild of America West. *Publications:* Plays: The Effects of Gamma Rays on Man-in-the-Moon Marigolds, 1965; And Miss Reardon Drinks a Little, 1967; The Secret Affairs of Mildred Wild, 1972; Let Me Hear You Whisper, 1973; The Ladies Should Be in Bed, 1973; Ladies at the Alamo, 1975. Fiction: The Pigman, 1968; My Darling, My Hamburger, 1969; I Never Loved Your Mind, 1970; I Love My Mother, 1975; Pardon Me, You're Stepping in My Eyeball, 1976; Confessions of a Teenage Baboon, 1977; The Undertaker's Gone Bananas, 1978; A Star for the Latecomer (with Bonnie Zindel), 1980; The Pigman's Legacy, 1980; The Girl Who Wanted a Boy, 1981; To Take a Dare (with Crescent Dragonwagon), 1982; When a Darkness Falls, 1984; Harry and Hortense at Hormone High, 1984; The Amazing and Death-Defying Diary of Eugene Dingman, 1987; A Begonia for Miss Applebaum, 1989; The Pigman and Me, 1992; David and Della, 1983; Loch, 1994. Contributions: newspapers and journals. *Honours:* Ford Foundation Grant, 1967; Obie Award, 1970; New York Drama Critics' Circle Award, 1970; Pulitzer Prize for Drama, 1971; Vernon Rice Drama Desk Award, 1971; Los Angeles Drama Critics' Award, 1973; several best book citations. *Address:* c/o Harper and Row, 10 E 53rd St, New York, NY 10022, USA.

ZINN, Howard; Prof. of Political Science Emeritus and Writer; b. 24 Aug. 1922, New York, NY, USA; m. Roslyn Shechter, 30 Oct. 1944, one s. one d. *Education:* BA, New York University, 1951; MA, 1952, PhD, 1958, Columbia University. *Career:* Instructor, Upsala College, East Orange, NJ, 1953–56; Visiting Lecturer, Brooklyn College, CUNY, 1955–56; Chair., Dept of History and Political Science, Spelman College, Atlanta, 1956–63; Assoc. Prof., 1964–66, Prof. of Political Science, 1966–88, Prof. Emeritus, 1988–, Boston University; mem. PEN, 1998–. *Publications:* LaGuardia in Congress, 1959; SNCC: The New Abolitionists, 1964; The Southern Mystique, 1964; New Deal Thought (ed.), 1965; Vietnam: The Logic of Withdrawal, 1967; Disobedience and Democracy, 1968; The Politics of History, 1970; Post-War America, 1973; Justice in Everyday Life (ed.), 1974; A People's History of the United States, 1980; Declarations of Independence, 1990; You Can't Be Neutral on a Moving Train, 1995; The Zinn Reader, 1997; Marx in Soho, 1999; On War, 2001; On History, 2001; Terrorism and War, 2002; Emma: A Play, 2002. Contributions: Professional journals and general periodicals including: The Progressive. *Honours:* Albert J. Beveridge Prize, American Historical Asscn, 1958; Harvard University Center for East Asian Studies Fellowship, 1960–61; Thomas Merton Award, 1991; Lannan Literary Award, 1998. *Address:* 29 Fern St, Auburndale, MA 02166, USA.

ZIOLKOWSKI, Theodore Joseph, BA, MA, PhD; academic and writer; b. 30 Sept. 1932, Birmingham, AL, USA; m. Yetta Bart Goldstein 1951; two s. one d. *Education:* Duke Univ., Univ. of Innsbruck, Yale Univ. *Career:* Instructor to Asst Prof., Yale Univ., 1956–62; Assoc. Prof., Columbia Univ., 1962–64; Prof. of Germanic Languages and Literature, 1964–69, Class of 1900 Prof. of Modern Languages, 1969–2001, Prof. of Comparative Literature, 1975–2001, Dean, Graduate School, 1979–92, Princeton Univ.; various visiting lectureships and professorships; mem. Acad. of Literary Studies; American Acad. of Arts and Sciences; American Asscn of Teachers of German, hon. life mem.; Asscn of Graduate Schools, pres., 1990–91; American Philosophical Society; Authors' Guild; MLA, pres., 1985; Asscn of Literary Scholars and Critics; International Asscn of Germanists; Austrian Acad. of Sciences; Göttingen Acad. of Sciences; German-American Academic Council; German Acad. for Language and Literature. *Publications:* Hermann Broch, 1964; The Novels of Hermann Hesse, 1965; Hermann Hesse, 1966; Dimensions of the Modern Novel, 1969; Fictional Transfigurations of Jesus, 1972; Disenchanted Images, 1977; Der Schriftsteller Hermann Hesse, 1979; The Classical German Elegy, 1980; Varieties of Literary Thematics, 1983; German Romanticism and Its Institutions, 1990; Virgil and the Moderns, 1993; The Mirror of Justice, 1997; The View from the Tower, 1998; Das Wunderjahr in Jena, 1998; The Sin of Knowledge, 2000; Berlin: Aufstieg einer Kulturmetropole um 1810, 2002; Hesitant Heroes 2004; Clio the Romantic Muse 2004. Editor: Hermann Hesse: Autobiographical Writings, 1972; Hermann Hesse: Stories of Five Decades, 1972; Hesse: A Collection of Critical Essays, 1972; Hermann Hesse: My Belief: Essays on Life and Art, 1974; Hermann Hesse: Pictor's Metamorphoses and Other Fantasies, 1982; Hermann Hesse: Soul of the Age: Selected Letters 1891–1962, 1991. Contributions: books and professional journals. *Honours:* Fulbright Research Grant, 1958–59; American Philosophical Society Grant, 1959; Guggenheim Fellowship, 1964–65; James Russell Lowell Prize for Criticism, 1972; ACLS Fellowships, 1972, 1976; Wilbur Lucius Cross Medal, Yale Univ., 1982; Goethe Institute Gold Medal, 1987; Henry Allen Moe Prize in Humanities, 1988; Resident Fellow, Bellagio Study Centre, Italy, 1993; Jacob und Wilhelm Grimm Prize, 1998; Christian Gauss Award in Criticism, 1998; Commander's Cross of Order of Merit, Germany, 2000; DPhil, hc, Greitswald, 2001; Mellon Emeritus Faculty Award 2004. *Address:* 36 Bainbridge Street, Princeton, NJ 08540, USA. *E-mail:* tjziol@aol.com.

ZITHULELE (see Mann, Christopher Michael).

ZOLYNAS, Al(girdas Richard Johann); Prof. of English and Literature, Poet and Writer; b. 1 June 1945, Dornbirn, Austria; m. 24 June 1967. *Education:* BA, University of Illinois, 1966; MA, 1969, PhD, 1973, University of Utah. *Career:* Instructor, Asst Prof., Writer-in-Residence, Southwest State University, Marshall, MN; Lecturer, Weber State College, Ogden, UT, San Diego State University; mem. Poets and Writers. *Publications:* The New Physics, 1979; 4 Petunia Avenue, 1987; Men of Our Time: An Anthology of Male Poetry in Contemporary America (ed. with Fred Moramarco), 1992; Under Ideal Conditions, 1994. Contributions: various anthologies, reviews, quarterlies and journals. *Honours:* San Diego Book Award for Best Poetry, 1994. *Address:* 2380 Viewridge Pl., Escondido, CA 92026, USA.

ZUCKERMAN, Mortimer Benjamin, BA, LLM, MBA; American (b. Canadian) real-estate developer, publisher and editor; *Chairman and Editor-in-Chief, US News and World Report, L.P.*; b. 4 June 1937, Montreal, Québec. *Education:* McGill Univ., Pennsylvania Univ., Harvard Univ. *Career:* Sr Vice-Pres. Cabot, Cabot and Forbes 1965–69; Lecturer, then Assoc. Prof., Harvard Univ. Grad. School of Design 1966–74; Visiting Lecturer, Yale Univ. 1967–69; Chair. Boston Properties Co. 1970–; Dir RET Income Foundation 1976–79, Property Capital Trust Co. 1979–80; Pres., Chair. Atlantic Monthly Co., Boston 1980–; Chair., Ed.-in-Chief US News and World Report 1980–; Propr New York Daily News. *Address:* Boston Properties, 599 Lexington Avenue, Room 1800, New York, NY 10022; US News and World Report L.P., 1050 Thomas Jefferson Street, NW, Washington, DC 20007-3837, USA (Office). *Telephone:* (202) 955-2000 (Office). *Fax:* (202) 955-2685 (Office). *Website:* www.usnews.com (Office).

ZUCKERT, Catherine H.; Political Scientist and Writer; b. 20 Oct. 1942, Miami, FL, USA; m. Michael Zuckert, 11 Sept. 1965, three d. *Education:* BA, Cornell University, 1964; MA, PhD, University of Chicago, 1970. *Career:* Prof. of Political Science, Carleton College, Northfield, MN, 1971–; mem. American Political Science Asscn; Society for the Study of Greek Thought; Midwest Political Science Asscn. *Publications:* Understanding the Political Spirit (ed.), 1988; Natural Right and the American Imagination: Political Philosophy in Novel Form, 1990; Postmodern Platos, 1996.

ZWICKY, (Julia) Fay, BA; poet and editor; b. 4 July 1933, Melbourne, Vic., Australia; m. 1st Karl Zwicky 1957; two c.; m. 2nd James Mackie 1990. *Education:* University of Melbourne. *Career:* Senior Lecturer in English, University of Western Australia, 1972–87; Assoc. Ed., Westerly, 1973–95. *Publications:* Isaac Babel's Fiddle, 1975; Quarry: A Selection of Western Australian Poetry (ed.), 1981; Kaddish and Other Poems, 1982; Journeys: Poems by Judith Wright, Rosemary Dobson, Gwen Harwood, Dorothy Hewett (ed.), 1982; Seven Hostages and Other Stories, 1983; The Lyre in the Pawnshop: Essays on Literature and Survival, 1974–84, 1986; Procession: Youngstreet Poets 3 (ed.), 1987; Ask Me, 1990; Poems 1970–1992, 1993; The Gatekeeper's Wife, 1997. *Honours:* New South Wales Premier's Award, 1982; Western Australian Premier's Awards, 1987, 1991, 1999. *Address:* 30 Goldsmith Road, Claremont, WA 6010, Australia.

ZWICKY, Jan, BA, MA, PhD; poet and philosopher; b. 10 May 1955, Calgary, AB, Canada. *Education:* University of Calgary, University of Toronto. *Career:* Teacher, University of Waterloo, 1981, 1984, 1985, Princeton University, 1982, University of Western Ontario, 1989, University of Alberta, 1992, University of New Brunswick, 1994, 1995, University of Victoria, 1996–; Ed., Brick Books. *Publications:* Wittgenstein Elegies, 1986; The New Room, 1989; Lyric Philosophy, 1992; Songs for Relinquishing the Earth, 1998; Wisdom and Metaphor, 2003. *Honours:* Gov.-Gen.'s Award for Poetry, 1999.

DIRECTORY

APPENDIX A: LITERARY AWARDS AND PRIZES

The following list covers principal literary prizes, organizations offering awards and prizes, and, where applicable, recent winners. Conditions and availability of prizes and awards often change with little notice and the most recent situation should be ascertained by direct application to the sponsoring organization.

J. R. Ackerley Prize for Autobiography: English Centre of International PEN, Lancaster House, 33 Islington High St, London N1 9LH, England. Tel. (20) 7713-0023. Fax (20) 7013-0005. E-mail: enquiries@englishpen.org. Website: www.englishpen.org. Annual award for literary autobiography, written in English and published in the preceding year. Short-listed titles are chosen by the Literary Executors of J. R. Ackerley. Nominations are not accepted. Prize: £1,000.

Jane Addams Children's Book Award: Jane Addams Peace Association, 777 United Nations Plaza, Sixth Floor, New York, NY 10017, USA. Tel. (212) 682-8830. Fax (212) 286-8211. E-mail: apa@igc.apc.org. Website: www.soemadison.wisc.edu/ccbc/public/jaddams.htm. f. 1953. Annual award, in association with the Women's International League for Peace and Freedom, for a picture book and a longer book for children that best combines literary merit with themes stressing peace, social justice, world community and the equality of the sexes and all races. Open to books for pre-school through to high school age, including translations or titles published in English in other countries. Books may be submitted by the publishers or requested by the committee. Prize: hand-illuminated scroll.

Akutagawa Ryûnosuke Shô (Akutagawa Prize): Association for the Promotion of Japanese Literature, Bungei-Shunju Bldg, 3 Kioi-cho, Chiyoda-ku, Tokyo 102, Japan. Japan's top literary award for young writers. f.1935 by Kikuchi Kan, the editor of Bungei Shunjû magazine, in memory of novelist Akutagawa Ryûnosuke. Awarded twice a year, in January and July, to the best literary short story published in a newspaper or magazine by a new author. Prize: A pocket watch and 1m. yen.

Alexander Prize: Royal Historical Society, University College London, Gower St, London WC1E 6BT, England. Tel. (20) 7387-7532. Fax (20) 7387-7532. E-mail: royalhistsoc@ucl.ac.uk. Website: www.rhs.ac.uk. Exec.-Sec.: Joy McCarthy. Offered for a paper based on original historical research. The paper must not exceed 8,000 words and can relate to any historical subject. Candidates must either be under 35 years of age or be registered for a higher degree (or have been registered for such a degree within the last three years). Prize: £250 or a silver medal.

Alice Literary Award: Society of Women Writers (Australia), PO Box 2621, Sydney, NSW 2001, Australia. Biennial award presented by the Society of Women Writers (Australia) for a distinguished and long-term contribution to literature by an Australian woman.

American Academy of Arts and Letters Gold Medal (Letters): American Academy of Arts and Letters, 633 W 155 St, New York, NY 10032-5699, USA. Tel. (212) 368-5900. A series of prestigious awards, which rotate between literary and artistic disciplines. Each discipline is awarded once every six years; categories include poetry, belles lettres and criticism, history, drama, fiction, essays, music, and architecture.

Hans Christian Andersen Awards: International Board on Books for Young People (IBBY), Nonnenweg 12, Postfach, 4003 Basel, Switzerland. Tel. (61) 272 29 17. Fax (61) 272 27 57. E-mail: ibby@eye.ch. Website: www.ibby.org. Exec. Dir: Leena Maissen. f. 1956. Biennial awards to honour an author (Hans Christian Andersen Award for Writing), and an illustrator (Hans Christian Andersen Award for Illustration) whose work has made a lasting contribution to children's literature. Awards are open to living candidates from any country. Nominations are made by National Sections of IBBY. Prize: Gold medal and a diploma.

Asham Award: Asham Literary Endowment Trust, The Town Hall, High St, Lewes, E Sussex, BN7 2QS, England. Website: www.lewes.gov.uk/arts/asham.html. Biennial award, sponsored by Waterstone's, for short stories (up to 4,000 words) by new women writers. Open to women aged over 18, resident in the UK, who have not yet had a novel or collection of short stories published. The entries must be in English and previously unpublished. Prizes: First £1,000; Second £500; Joint Third £250; winning stories are published by Bloomsbury.

The Australian/Vogel Literary Award: Allen & Unwin Publishers, POB 8500, St Leonards, NSW 1590, Australia. Tel. (2) 8425-0100. Fax (2) 9906-2218. Website: www.allanandunwin.com. Publishing Asst: Jemma Birrell. f. 1980. Annual award for an original unpublished manuscript of Australian history, fiction or biography. Entrants must normally be residents of Australia aged under 35. Manuscripts must be between 30,000 and 100,000 words and must not be under offer to any other publisher or award. Closing date: 31 May. Prize: $ A 20,000 and publication of the manuscript.

Australian Literature Society Gold Medal: Association for the Study of Australian Literature (ASAL) Ltd, Australia. Website: www.asc.uq.edu.au/asal. Annual award for an outstanding Australian literary work published in the preceding year, or occasionally awarded for outstanding services to Australian literature. Award was inaugurated by the ALS, which was incorporated in the Association for the Study of Australian Literature in 1982. No direct application is accepted. No nominations are required; instead ASAL members are invited to propose potential winners to the judging panel. Prize: Gold medal.

Authors' Club Best First Novel Award: Authors' Club, 40 Dover St, London W1X 3RB, England. Tel. (20) 7499-8581. Fax (20) 7409-0913. Website: www.theartsclub.co.uk. Club Sec.: Ann de la Grange. f. 1954. Annual award to the most promising first full-length novel of the year, published in the UK by a British author. The winner is selected from entries submitted by publishers. Prize: £1,000.

Aventis Prizes for Science Books: The Royal Society, 6 Carlton House Terrace, London SW1Y 5AG, England. Tel. (20) 7839-5561. Fax (20) 7930-2170. E-mail: info@royalsoc.ac.uk. Website: www.aventisprizes.com. f. 1988 by COPUS—the Committee on the Public Understanding of Science of the Royal Society, the Royal Institution and the British Association for the Advancement of Science—and the Science Museum. Rhône-Poulenc, now renamed Aventis began sponsoring the prize in 1990. Awarded to authors of popular non-fiction, science or technology books, written in English, which are judged to contribute most to the public understanding of science. Prizes: £10,000 for the General Prize; £10,000 for the Junior Prize.

BA/Book Data Author of the Year Award: Minster House, 272 Vauxhall Bridge Rd, London SW1V 1BA, England. Tel. (20) 7834-5477. Fax (20) 7834-8812. E-mail: mail@booksellers.org.uk. Website: www.booksellers.org.uk. Asst to the Man.: Denise Bayat. f. 1993. Annual award to the author judged to have had the most impact for booksellers in the year, as voted for by members of the Booksellers Asscn. The living author must be British or Irish. Prize: Trophy and £1,000.

BBC FOUR Samuel Johnson Prize for Non-fiction: 206 Marylebone Rd, London NW1 6LY, England. Website: www.samueljohnsonprize.com. Formerly the AT&T Non-Fiction Award. Annual award to the best work of general non-fiction published by a British publisher in the previous year. Entries must be written in English by living writers from the British Commonwealth or the Republic of Ireland. Entries are submitted by publishers. Prize: £30,000.

Benson Medal: Royal Society of Literature, Somerset House, Strand, London WC2R 1LA. Tel. (20) 7845-4676. Fax (20) 7845-4679. E-mail info@rslit.org. Website www.rslit.org. f. 1916 by A. C. Benson, irregular periodical award recognizing works of poetry, fiction or biography. Submissions are not accepted. Prize: silver medal.

David Berry Prize: Royal Historical Society, University College London, Gower St, London WC1E 6BT, England. Tel. (20) 7387-7532. Fax (20) 7387-7532. E-mail: royalhistsoc@ucl.ac.uk. Website: www.rhs.ac.uk. Exec. Sec.: Joy McCarthy. Annual award to the writer of the best essay on a subject dealing with Scottish history, of between 6,000 and 10,000 words. Previous winners may not reapply. Prize: £250.

Besterman/McColvin Medals: The CILIP, 7 Ridgmount St, London WC1E 7AE, England. Tel. (20) 7255-0650. Fax (20) 7255-0501. E-mail: marketing@cilip.org.uk. Website: www.cilip.org.uk. Two medals are awarded annually for outstanding works of reference published in the UK, one for print and one for electronic formats. The Awards are sponsored by Whitaker and judged by panels of reference librarians and members of the Society of Indexers. Prize: Gold medal, certificate and £500.

James Tait Black Memorial Prizes: Dept of English Literature, University of Edinburgh, David Hume Tower, George Sq., Edinburgh EH8 9JX, Scotland. Tel. (131) 650-3619. Fax (131) 650-6898. E-mail: english.literature@ed.ac.uk. Website: www.ed.ac.uk/englit/jtbint.htm. f. 1918. Two annual awards for biographical and fictional work published in the preceding year. Works must be written in English and be published or co-published in the UK. Only publishers may apply. Prizes: £3,000 for each category.

Booker/Open Russia Prize: Khoshlovski Per. 13, Str. 1, 109028 Moscow, Russia. Tel. (95) 789-3173. Fax (95) 789-3177. Website: www.russianbooker.ru. f. 1991, as the first independent literary prize in Russia, with the support of the British Booker Prize. From 1997 the financing of the Russian Booker was underwritten by United Distillers & Vintners, the owners of Smirnoff vodka, but in 2002 general sponsorship of the prize was taken over by the regional charitable organization Open Russia, and the Prize was renamed accordingly. The prize is awarded each year for the best novel written in the Russian language, and aims to encourage the creativity of authors writing in Russian, to arouse interest in contemporary Russian literature, and to assist the renaissance of the publishing industry and of translations from Russian into other languages. Works considered for the prize are put forward by Russian and foreign nominators appointed by the Russian Booker Committee as well as by Russian publishing houses. After screening for conformity with the rules of the competition, these works comprise the Long List which is then judged by a jury consisting of professional literary critics, authors and other leading cultural figures. The jury delivers its Short List of six finalists, before finally choosing the winner. Prizes: US$12,500 (finalists receive US$1,000 each).

Book of the Year Award: Welsh Academy, Third Floor, Mount Stuart House, Mount Stuart Sq., Cardiff CF10 5FQ, Wales. Tel. (29) 2047-2266. E-mail: post@academi.org. f. 1992. Annual awards given for works of exceptional merit by Welsh authors (by birth or residence) published during the preceding year. Works may be in Welsh or in English, in the categories of poetry, fiction and creative non-fiction (including literary criticism, biography and autobiography). Non-fiction works must have subject matter that is concerned with Wales. Prizes: Two First Prizes £3,000 (one for works in Welsh, one in English); £1,000 to each of four short-listed authors.

Boston Globe-Horn Book Award: Boston Globe, 135 William T. Morrissey Blvd, Boston, MA 02125, USA. f. 1967 by The Boston Globe and The Horn Book Magazine. Annual award for books published in the USA within the previous year, in the categories of fiction, non-fiction and picture book. Prize: US$500.

BP Natural World Book Prize: Book Trust, 45 East Hill, London SW18 2QZ, England. Tel. (20) 8516-2972. Website: www.booktrust.org.uk/prizes/bp.htm. Award for environmental literature, amalgamating the former BP Conservation Book Prize and the Wildlife Trust Natural World Book of the Year Award. Publishers only may submit entries. Prize: £5,000, with a discretionary runner-up prize of £1,000.

Bremen Literatur Förderungspreis (City of Breman Literary Encouragement Prize): Bremen City Council, Herdentorsteinweg 7, 28195 Bremen, Germany. f. 1952 in honour of Rudolf Alexander Schröder, as the Literaturpreis der Freien Hansestadt Bremen. Annual award to a German-speaking writer or poet. Prize: DM 30,000.

Bridport Prize: Bridport Arts Centre, South St, Bridport, Dorset DT6 3NR, England. Tel. (1398) 459444. Fax (1308) 459166. E-mail: frances@bridport-arts.com. Website: www.bridportprize.org.uk. Administrator: Frances Everitt. f. 1973 by Peggy Chapman-Andrews. Annual award for original poems of not more than 42 lines, and short stories between 1,000 and 5,000 words. Open to previously unpublished works, written in English, not entered in any other competition. Prizes: (in each category) First prize £3,000; Second prize £1,000; Third prize £500; 10 supplementary prizes of £50.

British Academy Book Prize: British Academy, 10 Carlton House Terrace, London SW1Y 5AH, England. Tel (20) 7969-5263. E-mail: externalrelations@britac.ac.uk. Asst Sec.: Jonathan Breckon. f. 2001. Annual award to the best book published in social sciences and the humanities, in the preceding year. Nominations by publishers. Prize: £2,500.

British Book Awards: Publishing News, 39 Store St, London WC1E 7DB, England. Tel. (20) 7692-2900. Fax (20) 7419-2111. E-mail: nibbies@mdla.co.uk. Website: www.publishingnews.co.uk. f. 1989. 21 annual awards, known as 'Nibbies', in a range of categories, with various awards sponsored by different companies. Categories include Editor, Publisher, Author, Independent Bookseller and Children's Book. Prize: The Nibbie.

British Columbia Book Prizes: West Coast Book Prize Society, Suite 902, 207 W Hastings St, Vancouver, BC V6B 1H7, Canada. Tel. (604) 687-2405. Fax (604) 669-3701. E-mail: info@rebuscreative.net. Website: www.harbour.sfu.ca/bcbook/. f. 1985. Awards celebrating the achievements of British Columbia writers and publishers, presented in categories incl. fiction, non-fiction, poetry, regional writing, illustrated children's literature. Books must have been published during the preceding year; residency conditions for authors vary according to category.

British Fantasy Awards: British Fantasy Society, 201 Reddish Rd, South Reddish, Stockport SK5 7HR, England. E-mail: info@britishfantasysociety.org.uk. Website: www.britishfantasysociety.org.uk. Set of awards presented by the British Fantasy Society at its annual conference, in categories including best novel (the August Derleth Award), best short story, and best anthology. The winners are selected by BFS members. Prize: statuette.

British Science Fiction Association Awards: British Science Fiction Association, 8 Century House, Armoury Rd, London SE8 4LH, England. Tel. (20) 8469-3354. E-mail: awards@amaranth.aviators.net. Website: www.bsfa.co.uk. Admin.: Tanya Brown. f. 1966 to promote the best British (and other) science fiction novel, story, artwork, etc. Entries must have been first published in the UK in the current calendar year. No applications are permitted. Prize: an original artwork trophy.

Georg-Büchner-Preis: Deutsche Akademie für Sprache und Dichtung, Alexandraweg 23, 64287 Darmstadt, Germany. Tel. (6151) 40920. Fax (6151) 409299. Website: www.deutscheakademie.de. f. 1951. Annual award in recognition of the winner's special status and contribution to contemporary German culture. Awarded to a novelist or poet writing in German. Prize: €40,000.

Buckland Award: 24 Water St, PO Box 760, Dunedin, New Zealand. Annual award for work of the highest literary merit by a New Zealand writer.

Caine Prize for African Writing: African Centre, 2 Drayson Mews, London W8 4LY, England. Tel. (20) 7376-0440. Fax (20) 7938-3728. E-mail: caineprize@jftaylor.com. Website: www.caineprize.com. Administrator: Nick Elam. f. 2000. Annual award to a short story or narrative poem (between 3,000 and 10,000 words) by an African writer, published in English anywhere in the world in the previous five years. Submissions should be made by publishers. Prize: $15,000.

Randolph Caldecott Medal: Association for Library Service to Children, 50 East Huron St, Chicago, IL 70711, USA. E-mail: alsc@ala.org. Website: www.ala.org/alsc. Annual award to an illustrator of the most distinguished American picture book for children published in the preceding year. Prize: bronze medal.

James Cameron Memorial Award: Dept of Journalism, City University, Northampton Sq., London EC1 0HB, England. Annual award for journalism to a reporter of any nationality working for the British media. Nominations are not accepted.

Canadian Authors' Association Literary Awards: 27 Doxsee Ave N, PO Box 419, Campbellford, ON K0L 1L0, Canada. Tel. (705) 653-0323. Fax (705) 653-0593. E-mail: canauth@redden.on.ca. Website: www.canauthors.org. A series of annual awards from the Canadian Authors' Association and the Canada Council for the Arts, incl. fiction (CAA MOSAID Technology Inc Award for Fiction), poetry (CAA Jack Chalmers Poetry Award), short story (CAA Jubilee Award for Short Stories), biography (CAA Birks Family Foundation Award for Biography), Canadian history (CAA Lela Common Award for Canadian History), drama (CAA Carol Bolt Drama Award), children's (CAA Children's Short Story Award), as well as a special award for a complete body of work. Awards are for full-length English-language literature by living authors who are Canadians or landed immigrants. All entries must have been first published during the preceding year, although publication may have taken place outside Canada. Previous winners are not eligible for awards they have won, but may be entered in the other categories. Prizes: One award in each category of C$2,500 and a silver medal.

Canadian Library Association Book of the Year for Children Award: c/o Canadian Library Association, 200 Elgin St, Suite 206, Ottawa, ON K2P 1L5, Canada. Annual award to an author of an outstanding children's book published in Canada during the previous year. The book must be suitable for children up to 14 years of age.

Carnegie Medal: The CILIP, 7 Ridgmount St, London WC1E 7AE, England. Tel. (20) 7255-0650. Fax (20) 7255-0501. E-mail: marketing@cilip.org.uk. Website: www.cilip.org.uk. Annual award for an outstanding book for children written in English and receiving its first publication in the UK during the preceding year. Prize: Gold medal and £1,000 of books to donate to libraries.

Children's Book Award: The Federation of Children's Book Groups, 2 Bridge Wood View, Horsforth, Leeds, West Yorkshire LS18 5PE, England. Tel. (113) 2588910. Fax (113) 2588920. E-mail: info@fcbg.org.uk. Website: www.fcbg.org.uk. Annual award, sponsored by Red House, judged by children. The short-list is announced at the annual conference of the Federation of Children's Book Groups. The three categories are picture books, shorter novels and longer novels, all of which are then considered for the Best Book of the Year award. Prizes: Short-listed authors and illustrators receive a portfolio of children's letters inspired by their work; category winners receive a silver bowl; the overall winner is awarded a silver and oak tree sculpture.

Children's Laureate: Book Trust, Book House, 45 East Hill, London SW18 2QZ, England. Website: www.childrenslaureate.org. f. 1999. Biennial award to honour a writer or illustrator of children's books for a lifetime's achievement. Nominees must be UK-based, have a significant body of work, and have attracted critical and popular success. Prize: £10,000 and a Children's Laureate Medal.

Arthur C. Clarke Award for Science Fiction: Rocket Publishing, 60 Bournemouth Rd, Folkestone, Kent CT19 5AZ, England. Tel. (1303) 252939. Fax (1303) 252939. E-mail: arthurcclarkeaward@yahoo.co.uk. Website: www.clarkeaward.com. Administrator: Paul Kincaid. f. 1987 to encourage science fiction in the UK. Annual award to the best science fiction novel published in the UK in the preceding year. The award is jointly administered and judged by the British Science Fiction Association, Science Fiction Foundation and the Science Museum. Prize: Trophy and £2,003 (in 2003, rising by £1 each year).

CNA Letterkkunde Toekenning (CNA Literary Award): Central News Agency Ltd, POB 9380, Johannesburg, South Africa. f. 1961. Annual literary award, the highest honour for South African literature, for books by South African residents or citizens in any of the following categories: novel, poetry, biography, drama, history and travel.

David Cohen British Literature Prize: Arts Council of England, Literature Dept, 14 Great Peter St, London SW1P 3NQ, England. Tel. (20) 7973-6442. Fax (20) 7973-6520. E-mail: info.literature@artscouncil.org.uk. Website: www.artscouncil.org.uk. Literature Asst: Pippa Shoubridge. f. 1980. Biennial award recognizing a lifetime's achievement of a living novelist, short story writer, essayist, biographer, poet, dramatist, travel writer or writer in any other literary genre. Prize: £30,000.

Commonwealth Writers' Prize: The Commonwealth Writers' Prize Administrator, Book Trust, Book House, 45 East Hill, London SW18 2QZ, England. Tel. (20) 8516-2972. Fax (20) 8516-2978. Website: www.booktrust.org.uk. f. 1987. Annual award to reward excellence in Commonwealth literature; it is sponsored by the Commonwealth Foundation and administered by Booktrust. For the purposes of the award the Commonwealth is divided into four regions, Africa, the Caribbean and Canada, Eurasia (which includes the UK), and Southeast Asia and the South Pacific. A shortlist is drawn up with a best book and a best first book for each region. Each year the award ceremony is held in a different Commonwealth country. Open to any work of prose fiction; drama and poetry are excluded. The work must have been written by a living citizen of the Commonwealth, must be of a reasonable length and be in English. It must have been first published during the previous calendar year. To be eligible for the best first published book category the entry must be the first work of fiction which the author has published. Prize: £10,000 (Book of the Year); £3,000 (Best First Book); the regional winners receive a prize of £1,000.

Thomas Cook/Daily Telegraph Travel Book Awards: Thomas Cook Publishing, PO Box 227, Thorpe Wood, Peterborough PE3 6PU, England. E-mail: ipmc@freenet.co.uk. Website: www.thetravelbookaward.com. Administrator: Joan Lee. Annual award for best travel book published in the previous year. Prize: £10,000.

Duff Cooper Prize: Artemis Cooper, 54 St Maur Rd, London SW6 4DP, England. Tel. (20) 7736-3729. Fax (20) 7731-7638. Annual award to a literary work in the field of history, biography, politics or poetry, published in the previous year. Prize: £3,000 and a presentation copy of Duff Cooper's autobiography, Old Men Forget.

Crime Writers' Association (CWA) Awards: Crime Writers' Association, Meadow View, The Street, Bossingham, CT4 6DX, England. Tel. (1227) 709782. Fax (1227) 709782. Website: www.thecwa.co.uk. The CWA makes a series of 10 annual awards for outstanding works in the field of crime literature.

Cartier Diamond Dagger for Fiction: f. 1986. For outstanding contribution to the genre. Prize: Ornamental diamond dagger.

Gold Dagger for Fiction: For the best crime fiction of the year. Nominated by publishers. Prize: Ornamental gold-plated dagger and £3,000.

Silver Dagger for Fiction: Prize: Ornamental silver-plated dagger and £2,000.

Gold Dagger for Non-Fiction: For the best non-fiction crime book published during the year. Prize: Ornamental gold-plated dagger and £2,000.

Short Story Dagger: For the best short story in the crime genre in the preceding year. Prize: Ornamental dagger and £1,500.

Ian Fleming Steel Dagger: f. 2002, sponsored by the estate of Ian Fleming. For the year's best thriller, adventure novel or spy fiction novel. Authors can be of any nationality but the book must have been first published in the UK, in English, in the preceding year. Prize: Ornamental steel dagger and £2,000.

John Creasey Memorial Dagger: Sponsored by Chivers Press. For the best first crime novel by an author. Nominated by publishers. Prize: Ornamental dagger award and £1,000.

Ellis Peters Historical Dagger: Sponsored by Headline and Little Brown publishers and the estate of Ellis Peters. For the best historical crime novel in the preceding year. Prize: Ornamental dagger and £3,000.

Dagger in the Library: Sponsored by Random House Group. For the author whose work has given the most pleasure to readers. Prize: Ornamental dagger and £1,500.

Debut Dagger: For an unpublished writer of crime fiction. Prize: £250.

Den Store Pris: Det Danske Akademi, Rungstedlund, Rungsted Strandvej 111, 2960 Rungsted Kyst, Denmark. Tel. 33 13 11 12. Fax 33 32 80 45. E-mail: lawoffice@philip.dk. Website: www.danskeakademi.dk. f. 1961 by the Ministry of Culture. Biennial award for a complete body of work, with the recipient chosen by members of the Danish Academy. Open only to Danish authors. No direct applications are accepted. Prize: DKK300,000.

Encore Award: Society of Authors, 84 Drayton Gdns, London SW10 9SB, England. Tel. (20) 7373-6642. Fax (20) 7373-5768. E-mail: info@societyofauthors.org. Website: www.societyofauthors.org. f. 1990. Annual award for a second published novel. Prize: £10,000.

Geoffrey Faber Memorial Prize: Faber and Faber Ltd, 3 Queen Sq., London WC1N 3AU, England. Tel. (20) 7465-0045. Fax (20) 7465-0043. E-mail: belinda.matthews@faber.co.uk. Website: www.faber.co.uk. f. 1963, in memory of the founder of the publishing firm Faber and Faber. Annual award, with prizes alternating between verse or fiction. Entrants must be under 40 years of age and a citizen of the UK and colonies, the Commonwealth, or the Republic of Ireland or South Africa. Entries must have been published in the two years preceding the year in which the award is given. Prize: £1,000.

Eleanor Farjeon Award: Children's Book Circle, Hampshire County Library, 81 North Walls, Winchester SO23 8BY, England. Award for distinguished service to children's books both in the UK and overseas. Recipients include librarians, publishers, booksellers and authors, and are chosen from nominations from members of the Children's Book Circle. Prize: £500.

Kathleen Fidler Award: c/o Book Trust Scotland, Scottish Book Centre, Fountainbridge Library, 137 Dundee St, Edinburgh EH11 1BG, Scotland. Website: www.scottishbooktrust.com. Annual award for an unpublished children's novel of not less than 25,000–28,000 words, for children aged 8–12. The author must not have had a novel published previously for this age group. Prize: £1,000, publication of the book by Hodder Children's Books, and a rosewood and silver trophy to be held for one year.

Sir Banister Fletcher Prize of the Authors' Club: Authors' Club, 40 Dover St, London W1X 3RB, England. Tel. (20) 7499-8581. Fax (20) 7409-0913. Website: www.theartsclub.co.uk. f. 1954 and named after the late Sir Banister Fletcher, a former President of both the Authors' Club and the Royal Institute of British Architects (RIBA), this annual prize is awarded for the most deserving book of the previous year on either architecture or the arts. Publishers only are invited to apply to the Club Secretary. Prize: £1,000.

Miles Franklin Award: Permanent Trustee Co Ltd, 35 Clarence St, Sydney, NSW 2000, Australia. Tel. (2) 8295 8100. Fax (2) 8295 8659. E-mail: linda.ingaldo@permanentgroupcom.au. Website: www.permanentgroupcom.au. f. 1957. Annual award for a novel or play of high literary merit, presenting aspects of Australian life, published in the previous year. Prize: $ A28,000.

Giller Award: Canada. E-mail: contact@thegillerprize.ca. Website: www.thegillerprize.org. f. 1994 by Toronto businessman Jack Rabinovitch in memory of his late wife, literary journalist Doris Giller. Annual award to the best Canadian novel or short story collection published in English in the preceding year. Prize: bronze statue and C $25,000.

Glenfiddich Food and Drink Awards: 4 Bedford Sq., London WC1B 3RA, England. Tel. (20) 7255-1100. Fax (20) 7436-4164. Website: www.graylinggroup.com. f. 1970. Annual awards recognizing the excellence in writing, publishing and broadcasting on the subjects of food and drink. Categories include best food book, best drinks book, best newspaper cookery writer, restaurant critic of the year and best drinks writer. Entries are accepted from publishers only.

Goodman Fielder Wattie Book Award: PO Box 44-146, Auckland 2, New Zealand. Annual award for a book published in New Zealand in the previous year by a New Zealand author (including New Zealand residents and Pacific Island countries). Prize: First prize NZ $20,000; Second prize $10,000; Third prize $5,000; Food Industry Book Award $6,000.

Governor-General's Literary Awards: Canada Council, 350 Albert St, PO Box 1047, Ottawa, ON K1P 5V8, Canada. Tel. (613) 566-4305. Website: www.canadacouncil.ca/prizes/ggla. f. 1937. Annual awards, given by the Canada Council for the Arts and the Bank of Montréal, for Canadian authors writing both in English and French. Categories are: adult fiction, poetry, drama, non-fiction, children's literature (text), children's literature (illustration), translation. Prize: C$10,000 in each category, in each language.

Gradam Litrochta Cló Iar-Chonnachta (Cló Iar-Chonnachta Literary Award): Cló Iar-Chonnachta Teo, Indreabhán, Connemara, Co Galway, Ireland. Tel. (91) 593307. Fax (91) 593362. E-mail: cic@iol.ie. Website: www.cic.ie. Contact: Deirdre O'Toole. f. 1995 by Micheal o Conghaile, writer and founder of Irish-language publisher Cló Iar-Chonnachta, to encourage Irish language writing. Annual award for a newly-written and unpublished work in the Irish language, a different type of work each year, either poetry, drama, novel or short story. Prize: €6,350 and publication of the winning manuscript.

Grand Prix de la Francophonie (Grand Francophony Prize): Académie Française, Institut de France, 23 quai de Conti, 75006 Paris, France. Tel. 1 44 41 43 00. Fax 1 43 29 47 45. E-mail: contact@academie-francaise.fr. Website: www.academie-francaise.fr. f. 1986 at the suggestion of the Canadian government, with support from the governments of France, Monaco and Morocco and several private sponsors. Administered by the Académie Française, this annual award aims to promote the influence of French-language literature. Open to living authors of all ages; only published works may be submitted, and they must have appeared during the preceding year. Prize: €45,730 (300,000 francs).

Kate Greenaway Medal: The CILIP, 7 Ridgmount St, London WC1E 7AE, England. Tel. (20) 7255-0650. Fax (20) 7255-0501. E-mail: marketing@cilip.org.uk. Website: www.cilip.org.uk. Annual award for an outstanding book in terms of illustration for children, published in the UK in the preceding year. Prize: Gold medal and £1,000 of books to donate and the Colin Mears Award of £5,000.

Guardian Children's Fiction Award: The Guardian, 119 Farringdon Road, London EC1R 3ER, England. Annual award for an outstanding work of fiction for children by a Commonwealth or British author, first published in the UK in the previous year, excluding picture books and previous winners. Prize: £1,500.

Guardian First Book Award: The Guardian, 119 Farringdon Road, London EC1R 3ER, England. Annual award to a work of fiction by a British, Irish or Commonwealth writer and published in the UK. Submissions are not accepted. Prize: £10,000.

Hammett Awards: USA. E-mail: jeremiahealy@earthlink.net. Website: jmc.ou.edu/AIEP/index.htm. Pres., IACW/NA: Jeremiah Healy. Annual award given by the North American branch of the Asociación Internacional de Escritores Policiacos, or International Asscn of Crime Writers, to reward excellence in the genre of crime literature. Open to American or Canadian writers.

Hawthornden Prize: 42A Hays Mews, Berkeley Sq., London W1X 7RU, England. f. 1919. Annual award to a British writer for a work of imaginative literature, published during the previous year. No direct applications are accepted. Prize: £10,000.

W. H. Heinemann Award: Royal Society of Literature, Somerset House, Strand, London WC2R 1LA. Tel. (20) 7845-4676. Fax (20) 7845-4679. E-mail info@rslit.org. Website www.rslit.org. f. 1944. Annual award aiming to encourage contributions to literature, given to a work, usually non-fiction, judged to be of outstanding literary distinction. The book must be written in English, published in the previous year, and submitted by publishers. Prize: £5,000.

William Hill Sports Book of the Year: Greenside House, 50 Station Rd, Wood Green, London N22 4TP, England. E-mail: pressoffice@williamhill.co.uk. Website: www.williamhillmedia.com. Sponsored by bookmakers William Hill. All books must be published in the UK during the previous year. Prize: First prize £12,000, £500 free bet with William Hill and specially-bound copy of the book; various runners-up prizes.

Historical Novel Prize in Memory of Georgette Heyer: The Bodley Head, Random Century, 20 Vauxhall Bridge Rd, London SW1V 2SA, England. Annual award for a full-length, previously unpublished, historical novel set before 1939. Prize: £5,000.

P. C. Hooft-prijs voor Letterkunde (P. C. Hooft Prize for Literature): Postbus 90515, Prins Willem, Alexanderhof 5, 2595 LM, The Hague, Netherlands. f. 1947. Annual award presented to a writer for a lifetime's achievement. Works of prose, essay and poetry are all considered for the prize. Annual Dutch national prize for literature. Prize: US $31,000.

Richard Imison Memorial Award: Society of Authors, 84 Drayton Gdns, London SW10 9SB, England. Designed to encourage talent and help maintain high standards, this award is given for the best work of radio drama, as judged by the Society of Authors Broadcasting Committee. Works must be original, the first dramatic work by the author(s) to be broadcast, and must be written specifically for radio (adaptations for works orginally intended for stage, film or television are not eligible). Prize: £1,500.

Independent Foreign Fiction Prize: Literature Department, Arts Council of England, 14 Great Peter St, London SW1P 3NQ, England. Tel. (20) 7333-0100. Fax (20) 7973-6590. E-mail: info.literature@artscouncil.org.uk. Website: www.artscouncil.org.uk. f. 1990. This award is Britain's most valuable honour for translated literature, and is the country's only general competition for fiction first written in languages other than English. Open to works of fiction by a living author, which have been translated into English from any other language and published in the UK during the previous year. Prize: £10,000, shared between author and translator.

Institute of Historical Research Prize—IHR Prize: Institute of Historical Research, Senate House, London WC1E 7HU. Website: www.ihrinfo.ac.uk. f. 2000. Annual award to enable professional historians to write their first book for a general readership. Entrants must be previously unpublished professional historians (not including monographs, university press publications or academic imprints). Prize: publishing contract with Grove Atlantic for the winning entry.

International IMPAC Dublin Literary Award: Dublin City Library and Archive, 138–144 Pearse Street, Dublin 2, Ireland. Tel. (1) 674-4802. Fax (1) 674-4879. E-mail: literaryaward@dublincity.ie. Website: www.impacdublinaward.ie. f. 1995 by Dublin City Council, in partnership with IMPAC, a productivity improvement company which operates world-wide. Annual award for the best work of fiction written in or translated into English. Books are nominated by selected libraries in capital and major cities around the world. Prize: €100,000 (for a translated work, 25% of which goes to the translator) and a Waterford Glass trophy.

Irish Times International Fiction Prize: Irish Times Ltd, 10–16 D'Olier St, Dublin 2, Ireland. f. 1989. Biennial award to the author of a work of fiction written in English, published in Ireland, the UK or the USA in the previous two years. Nominations come from critics and editors. Submissions are not accepted. Prize: IR £27500.

Irish Times Irish Literature Prizes: Irish Times Ltd, 10–16 D'Olier St, Dublin 2, Ireland. Tel. (1) 679-2022. Fax (1) 679-3910. f. 1988. Biennial awards to books in four categories: Irish fiction, Irish non-fiction, Irish poetry and Irish language. The Irish Times also runs a parallel International Fiction Prize. Authors must be born in Ireland or be an Irish citizen. Books are nominated by critics and editors; no submissions required. Prize: €6,350 in each category.

Jerusalem Prize: Binyaney Ha'ooma, PO Box 6001, Jerusalem 91060, Israel. Biennial award to a writer whose work expresses the idea of the freedom of the individual in society.

Kalinga Prize: c/o UNESCO, 7 Pl. de Fontenoy, 75352 Paris 07 SP, France. Annual award to popularizers of science with distinguished careers as writers, editors, lecturers, directors or producers. The winner is expected to have an understanding of science and technology, and an awareness of the scientific work of the UN and UNESCO. Prize: £1,000.

Keats–Shelley Prize: Keats–Shelley Memorial Association, 117 Cheyne Walk, London, SW10 0ES. Fax (20) 7352-6705. Website: www.keats-shelley.com. f. 1998. Sponsored by the Esmée Fairbairn Foundation and the David Cohen Family Charitable Trust. Annual award for an essay or poem on any aspect of Keats' or Shelley's work or life. Essays and poems must be in English and must be original and unpublished work; they must not have been submitted to a previous competition. Entries should be of 2,000–3,000 words, including quotations. Prize: £3,000.

Kiriyama Pacific Rim Book Prize: 650 Delancey St, Suite 101, San Francisco, CA 94107-2082, USA. Tel. (415) 777-1628. Fax (415) 777-1646. E-mail: info@kiriyamaprize.org. Website: www.kiriyamaprize.org. f. 1996. Award in two categories, fiction and non-fiction, to promote books that will contribute to greater understanding and co-operation among the peoples and nations of the Pacific Rim. Prizes: Fiction US $15,000; Non-Fiction US $15,000.

Lannan Literary Awards: Lannan Foundation, 313 Read St, Santa Fe, NM 87501-2628, USA. Tel. (505) 986-8160. Fax (505) 986-8195. E-mail: info@calannan.org. Website: www.lannan.org. f. 1989. Annual awards to honour established and new writers whose work is of exceptional quality. Recipients are chosen by the Foundation's Literary Committee, on recommendation from anonymous nominators. Awards are made in the areas of fiction, non-fiction and poetry. Prizes: US$75,000 each for body of work, rather than for a single publication; Lifetime Achievement Award of $200,000.

Lloyds Private Banking Playwright of the Year Award: Tony Ball Association PLC, 174–78 N Gower St, London NW1 2NB, England. f. 1994. Award to encourage new and diverse writing for theatre, broadening support for the theatre and extending the links between Lloyds Private Banking and the Arts. Playwrights should be British or Irish, whose new works have been performed in the UK or the Republic of Ireland for the first time in the previous year. Nominations by theatre critics form a short-list, with winners chosen by a panel of judges. Prize: £25,000.

Longman/History Today Book of the Year Award: History Today, 20 Old Compton St, London W1V 5PE, England. Annual award, administered by History Today, for an author's first or second non-fiction book on an historical subject, written in English. Prize: £1,000.

Los Angeles Times Book Prizes: Los Angeles Times, Times Mirror Sq., Los Angeles, CA 90053, USA. f. 1980. There are nine single-title categories: biography, current interest, fiction, first fiction (the Art Seidenbaum Award, named after the founder of the Book Prize programme), history, mystery/thriller, poetry, science and technology, and young-adult fiction. In addition, the Robert Kirsch Award (named after a novelist and editor who was book critic for the LA Times) recognizes the body of work by a writer living in and/or writing on the American West. Entries must have been first published in English in the USA between January and December of the previous year. Translations are eligible and authors may be of any nationality. They should be alive at the time of their book's qualifying US publication although eligibility is also extended to significant new translations of the work of deceased writers. Prizes: The authors of each winning book and the Kirsch Award recipient each receive a citation and US$1,000.

McKitterick Prize: Society of Authors, 84 Drayton Gdns, London SW10 9SB, England. Tel. (20) 7373-6642. Fax (20) 7373-5768. E-mail: info@societyofauthors.org. Website: www.societyofauthors.org. Annual award for a full-length work written in English and first published in the UK or previously unpublished. Open to writers over 40 years old, who have had no previous work published other than that submitted. Prize: £4,000.

Macmillan Writer's Prize for Africa: Macmillan Oxford, Between Towns Road, Oxford OX4 3PP, England. Tel. (1865) 405700. Fax (1865) 405799. E-mail: writersprize@macmillan.co.uk. Website: www.write4africa.com. f. 2002. Biennial award for previously unpublished works of fiction in English, in three categories: Children's Literature (8–12 years old), Children's Literature (13–17 years old), and Most Promising New Children's Writer. Open to nationals or naturalized citizens of any African country. Prize: US $5,000 for the Children's Literature junior and senior category awards; $3,000 for Most Promising New Children's Writer award.

Walter McRae Russell Award: Association for the Study of Australian Literature, Australia. Website: www.asc.uq.edu.au/asal. Biennial award for an outstanding work of literary scholarship on an Australian subject. No nominations are accepted. Prize: US $1,000.

Mail on Sunday/John Llewellyn Rhys Prize: Booktrust, Book House, 45 East Hill, London SW18 2QZ, England. Tel. (20) 8516-2972. Fax (20) 8516-2978. Website: www.booktrust.org.uk. f. 1942. Annual award for works of fiction, non-fiction, drama or poetry written in English and published in the UK in the preceding calendar year. Writers must be under 35 years old at the time of publication, and a citizen of the UK or Commonwealth. Previous winners are not eligible. Publishers are invited to submit entries. Prizes: First prize £5,000; £500 to each of five short-listed authors.

Man Booker Prize for Fiction: Colman Getty PR, Middlesex House, 34–42 Cleveland St, London W1T 4JE, England. Tel. (20) 7631-2666. Fax (20) 7631-2699. E-mail: pr@colmangettypr.co.uk. Website: www.manbookerprize.com. This award, which is the best known British literary award, was established by Booker Brothers (now Booker Prize Foundation) as the Booker Prize in 1968. It is judged by literary critics, editors, writers and academics: the judging panel changes every year, and is selected by a Management Cttee. The award is made to the judges' choice of the best novel of the year. In 2002 a new five-year sponsorship deal was signed with Man Group, an alternative investment fund manager and broker, who announced plans to develop the prize under a new format, with the aim of raising its global profile. Writers must be citizens of the British Commonwealth or the Republic of Ireland. Only full-length novels written in English are considered. The prize may be awarded posthumously. Prize: £50,000; £2,500 to each of six short-listed authors.

Marsh Award for Children's Literature in Translation: Authors' Club, 40 Dover St, London W1X 3RB, England. f. 1996. Biennial award to British translators of books for 4–16 year olds, published in the UK by a British publisher. The award is sponsored by the Marsh Christian Trust to encourage the translation of foreign children's books into English. No encyclopaedias, reference works or electronic books. Prize £750.

Marsh Biography Award: Authors' Club, 40 Dover St, London W1X 3RB, England. Formerly the Marsh Christian Trust Award. Biennial award for a significant biography by a British author, published in the UK in the two preceding years. Nominations are submitted by publishers. Prize: £3,500 and a silver trophy.

Somerset Maugham Awards: Somerset Maugham Trust Fund, Society of Authors, 84 Drayton Gdns, London SW10 9SB, England. Tel. (20) 7373-6642. Fax (20) 7373-5768. E-mail: info@societyofauthors.org. Website: www.societyofauthors.org. Awarded to a writer on the strength of a published work. Prize: £12,000 (shared) to be used for foreign travel.

Meyer-Whitworth Award: Drama Dept, Arts Council of England, 14 Great Peter St, London SW1P 3NQ, England. E-mail: info.drama@artscouncil.org.uk. Website: www.artscouncil.org.uk. Established to commemorate the Shakespeare Memorial National Theatre Committee of 1908, where the movement for a National Theatre joined forces with the movement to create a monument to William Shakespeare. Awarded to a playwright whose work displays promise of new talent, whose writing is of individual quality and whose work 'reveals the truth about the relationships of human beings with each other and the world at large' (Geoffrey Whitworth). Plays must be written in English and have been produced in the UK in the previous year.

Milner Award: The Friends of the Atlanta Fulton Public Library, 1 Margaret Mitchell Sq., Atlanta, GA 30303, USA. Award to a living American author of children's books. Prize: A specially-commissioned work of the internationally famous glass sculptor, Hans Frabel, and a US $1,000 honorarium.

Mitchell Prize for Art History/Eric Mitchell Prize: c/o The Burlington Magazine, 14–16 Duke's Rd, London WC1H 9AD, England. The Mitchell Prize is awarded for an outstanding and original contribution to the understanding of the visual arts, and the Eric Mitchell Prize is given for the best first book in this field. Books must be written in English and published in the previous year. Prizes: Mitchell Prize for Art History US $15,000; Eric Mitchell Prize $5,000.

National Book Awards: National Book Foundation, 95 Madison Ave, Suite 709, New York, NY 10016, USA. Tel. (212) 685-0261. Fax (212) 213-6570. E-mail: nationalbook@nationalbook.org. Website: www.nationalbook.org. f. 1950. Annual awards to living American writers in four categories (fiction, non-fiction, poetry and young people's literature) and the Medal for Distinguished Contribution to American Letters. Prizes: US$10,000 for each subject category; short-listed works $1,000.

National Book Critics Circle Awards: National Book Critics Circle, 360 Park Ave S, New York, NY 10010, USA. Website: www.bookcritics.org. Annual awards for excellence in works of fiction, general non-fiction, poetry, biography/autobiography and criticism by American authors, published for the first time in the previous year. Nominated by members. In addition the NBCC awards the Ivan Sandrof Lifetime Achievement Award and honours one member of the Circle with the Nona Balakian Citation for Excellence in Reviewing. Prize: Scroll and citation.

Nebula Awards: Science Fiction and Fantasy Writers of America Inc, PO Box 877, Chestertown, MD 21620. Fax (410) 778-3052. E-mail: execdir@sfwa.org. Website: www.sfwa.org. f. 1965. Annual awards presented to the best science fiction novel, novella, novelette, and short story. Prize: trophy.

Nestlé Smarties Book Prize: Book Trust, Book House, 45 East Hill, London SW18 2QZ, England. Tel. (20) 8516-2986. Fax (20) 8516-2978. Website: www.booktrusted.com. Prizes Admin.: Hannah Rutland. f. 1985. Annual awards for children's books in three categories, written in English by a citizen of, or an author resident in the UK, and published in the UK. Prizes: £2,500 (Gold); £1,000 (Silver); £500 (Bronze) in each age category (5 and under, 6–8 and 9–11).

Neustadt International Prize for Literature: World Literature Today, University of Oklahoma, 110 Monnet Hall, Norman, OK 73019-4033, USA. Tel. (405) 325-4531. Fax (405) 325-7495. E-mail: rcdavis@ou.edu. Website: www.ou.edu/worldlit. Exec. Dir: Prof. R. C. Davis-Undiano. f. 1969. Biennial award recognizing outstanding achievement of a living author, in fiction, poetry or drama. No applications are accepted. Prize: US$50,000, a solid silver replica of an eagle feather, a hand-lettered certificate and a special issue of World Literature Today.

John Newbery Medal: Association for Library Service to Children, American Library Association, 50 E Huron St, Chicago, IL 60611-2795, USA. Tel. (312) 944-7671. E-mail: alsc@ala.org. Website: www.ala.org/alsc. Annual award to the author of the most distinguished contribution to literature for children, published in the USA during the preceding year. Writing of any form can be considered: fiction, non-fiction and poetry. The award may be made posthumously. Only original works are considered; reprints and compilations are not eligible. Authors must be citizens or residents of the USA and the work must not have been published originally outside the USA. Prize: bronze John Newbery Medal.

Nobel Prize in Literature (Nobelpriset i litteratur): The Nobel Committee of the Swedish Academy, PO Box 2118, 103 13 Stockholm, Sweden. Tel. (8) 555 125 54. Fax (8) 555 125 49. E-mail: sekretariat@svenskaakademien.se. Website: www.nobel.se; www.svenskaakademien.se. One of several annual prizes for outstanding achievement in various fields, founded by the chemist Alfred Nobel. The prize in the field of literature has been awarded annually since 1901 in recognition of the literary merit of a distinguished writer in world letters. The Literature laureate is chosen from writers nominated by members of literary academies, academics, presidents of societies of authors, professors of literature and languages, and previous prize-winners, via the Nobel Committee. It is not possible to propose oneself as a candidate. Prize: SEK 10m.

Nordic Council Literary Prize: Riksdagen, 100 12 Stockholm, Sweden. Website: www.norden.org. Award to a work published in Danish, Norwegian or Swedish during the past two years, or other Nordic languages during the last four years. Prize: US $42,000.

Orange Prize for Fiction: Book Trust, Book House, 45 East Hill, London SW18 2QZ, England. Tel. (20) 8516-2972. Fax (20) 8516-2978. Website: www.orangeprize.co.uk. Prizes Admin.: Tarryn McKay. f. 1996. Annual award founded by leading women in the publishing industry to help promote and reward women writers. Awarded for a full-length novel written in English by a woman of any nationality, which has been published in the UK, by a UK publisher. Prize: £30,000 and a limited edition bronze figurine known as the 'Bessie'.

Orwell Prize: England. f. 1993. Annual awards by George Orwell Memorial Fund to encourage writing about politics, political thinking or public policy. The two categories are: book or pamphlet and newspaper and/or periodical article, feature or column, or sustained reportage on a theme. Writing must be in English and published in the preceding year in the UK or Ireland. Prize: £1,000 for each category.

Pandora Award: Women in Publishing, England. E-mail: info@wipub.org.uk. Website: www.wipub.org.uk.

Parker Romantic Novel of the Year: Romantic Novelists' Association, 36 Eastgate, Hallaton, Leicestershire LE16 8UB, England. Tel. (1858) 555602. f. 1981. This annual award, administered by the Romantic Novelists' Association (RNA), with sponsorship from Parker Pen, is given to the best modern or historical (i.e. set before 1950) romantic novel of the year. Authors must be resident in the UK, or, if overseas, must be members of the RNA. Entries must be written in English, and have been published in the UK in the preceding year. Prize: £10,000 and a silver Parker pen.

Francis Parkman Prize: Society of American Historians, Columbia University, 603 Fayerweather Hall, New York, NY 10027, USA. Awarded by the Society of American Historians to the book which best represents the union of the historian and the artist.

PEN/Faulkner Award for Fiction: Folger Shakespeare Library, 201 E Capitol St, SE, Washington, DC 20003, USA. f. 1981. Annual award for the best work of fiction by an American citizen published in the preceding year. Prize: US $15,000; four finalists receive $5,000 each.

A. A. Phillips Prize: Association for the Study of Australian Literature, Australia. Website: www.asc.uq.edu.au/asal. Occasional award to be made on the recommendation of the ASAL executive, when a work or the work of an author is considered to merit attention as an outstanding contribution to Australian literature or literary studies.

Edgar Allan Poe Awards: Mystery Writers of America, 17 E 47th St, Sixth Floor, New York, NY 10017, USA. Website: www.mysterywriters.org. f. 1954. These awards, sponsored by The Mystery Writers of America, honour the best in mystery fiction and non-fiction produced the previous year. The awards, known as the Edgars, are awarded to authors of distinguished work in various categories. Categories include short stories, novels, critical studies, juvenile and young adult fiction, television and motion picture screenplays, first novels, paperback originals, fact crime, and critical/biographical work. A Grand Master Award is also presented for lifetime achievement.

Premio Camões (Camões Prize): Rua Rodrigues Sampaio, 113, 1150-279, Lisbon, Portugal. Tel. (21) 3109100. E-mail: geral@instituto-camoes.pt. Website: www.instituto-camoes.pt. f. 1988 by the governments of Portugal and Brazil. Annual award by the governments of Portugal and Brazil for an author writing in Portuguese. Prize: US $100,000.

Premio Cervantes (Cervantes Prize): Dirección General del Libro y Bibliotecas, Ministerio de Cultura, Plaza del Rey, 28004 Madrid, Spain. f. 1974. Annual award for the entire body of an author's output in Spanish. Prize: €90,000.

Premio Nadal: Ediciones Destino SA, Calle Provenza 260, 08008 Barcelona, Spain. Website: www.edestino.es/nadal.htm. The oldest literary prize in Spain. Awarded annually for unpublished novels in Spanish, which have not won any prize previously. Prize: €18,000.

Premio Octavio Paz de Poesía y Ensayo (Octavio Paz Poetry and Essay Prize): Fundación Octavio Paz, Francisco Sosa 383, Col. Barrio de Santa Catarina, 04000 México, DF, Mexico. Tel. (5) 659-5797. Fax (5) 554-9705. Website: www.fundacionpaz.org.mx. Annual award for a poet or essayist with high artistic, intellectual and critical qualities, following in the modern tradition that Octavio Paz represented. Nominations are invited from official bodies and learned institutions. Prize: US$100,000 and a diploma.

Premio Planeta: Editorial Planeta, Córsega 273–79, 08008 Barcelona, Spain. Website: www.editorial.planeta.es. Annual award for the best unpublished and original novel in Spanish. Prize: US $550,000.

Premio Príncipe de Asturias (Prince of Asturias Award for Letters): Fundación Príncipe de Asturias, General Yague 2, 33004 Oviedo, Spain. Website: www.fpa.es/esp/index.html. The prize is one of eight awarded by the Foundation, which were granted for the first time in 1981. (The others include Social Communication and Humanities, Arts, Sciences, Scientific Research and Technical Co-operation). The prize is presented to a person, institution or group whose work represents an important contribution to the fields of linguistics and literature. Prize: €50,000 and a statuette by Joan Miro.

Thomas Pringle Award: English Academy of Southern Africa, PO Box 124, Wits, 2050, South Africa. Tel. (11) 717-9339. Fax (11) 717-9339. E-mail: englishacademy@societies.wits.ac.za. Website: www.englishacademy.co.za. Admin. Officer: N. Gillman. f. 1962. Annual award to honour achievements in five different categories: reviews, educational articles, literary articles, short stories or one act plays, and poetry. Three categories are honoured each year. Prize: R2,000 for each category.

Prix Fémina: Paris, France. f. 1904 by 22 members of the periodical La Vie heureuse, in protest against the exclusion of women from the jury of the Prix Goncourt, the prize aims to encourage writing by women. It is awarded each year for a novel written in French by a woman. The winner is decided by an all-female jury. In 1986 the Prix Fémina Étranger, for foreign novels, was established, to provide an opportunity to recognize an outstanding work in the field of foreign novels.

Prix Goncourt (Goncourt Prize): Drouant, 18 Place Gaillon, 75002 Paris, France. Tel. 1 45 20 27 21. Website: www.academie-goncourt.fr. The Académie (Société littéraire des Goncourt) was established in 1900, and comprises ten members, who hold a salon on the first Tuesday of every month above the restaurant Drouant in Paris. The first Prix Goncourt was awarded in 1903, and has become regarded as France's most prestigious literary award. Prizes are awarded in the categories of novels, first novels, biography, children's book and poetry. Prize: Symbolic cheque for 50 French francs (€7.5).

Prix Médicis (Médicis Prizes): 25 rue Dombasle, 75015 Paris, France. Tel. 1 48 28 76 90. f. 1958. Annual awards in three categories: Prix Médicis (aims to reflect contemporary literary trends), Prix Médicis de l'Essai (awarded to an essay written in French), Prix Médicis Étranger (awarded to a novel which has been translated into French).

The Pulitzer Prizes: Columbia University, 709 Journalism Bldg, 2950 Broadway, New York, NY 10027, USA. Tel. (212) 854-3841. Fax (212) 854-3342. E-mail: pulitzer@pulitzer.org. Website: www.pulitzer.org. The Pulitzer Prizes were established in 1917 following a bequest from Joseph Pulitzer, a Hungarian-born journalist and pioneering publisher of American newspapers. The first Pulitzer Prizes were awarded as an incentive to excellence. There are now 21 prizes in total. In the category of 'Letters' (literature) awards are made in the fields of fiction, non-fiction and poetry, as well as biography/autobiography, drama and history. Entries must be published during the previous calendar year. Only US writers are considered except in the history category where author may be of any nationality as long as the book deals with American history. Fiction awards are made preferably to books dealing with American life. Prizes: US$10,000 in each category.

Pushcart Prize: Best of the Small Presses: Pushcart Press, PO Box 380, Wainscott, NY 11975, USA. Tel. (516) 324-9300. Annual award for work published by a small press or literary journal. Works are nominated by editors and then reviewed by judges. The winning works are published in a special anthology. Works of poetry, short fiction, essays, or self-contained extracts from books are eligible.

REA Award for the Short Story: Dungannon Foundation, 53 W Church Hill Rd, Washington, CT 06794, USA. Website: www.reaaward.org. f. 1986 by Michael M. Rea. Annual award to a writer who has made a significant contribution to the short story genre. US and Canadian writers are eligible. No applications are accepted. Prize: US$30,000.

Theodore Roethke Memorial Foundation Triennial Poetry Prize: 11 W Hannum Blvd, Saginaw, MI 48602. Awarded for a book of poetry in English, not a collection. Selected by three judges, chosen by the Poet Laureate. Prize: $3,000. Contact: Patricia Shek.

Rooney Prize for Irish Literature: Strathlin, Templecarrig, Delgany, Co Wicklow, Ireland. A non-competitive prize to reward and encourage young Irish talent. Writers must be Irish, under 40 years of age, and their work must be written in Irish or English. No applications are accepted, recipients are chosen by a panel of judges. Special awards are given on rare occasions where deemed of merit. Prize: €6,350.

Royal Society of Literature Ondaatje Prize: Royal Society of Literature, Somerset House, Strand, London WC2R 1LA. Tel. (20) 7845-4676. Fax (20) 7845-4679. E-mail info@rslit.org. Website www.rslit.org. f. 2003, sponsored by Christopher Ondaatje, replacing the Winifred Holtby Memorial Prize. Annual award to a work of fiction or non-fiction with a strong sense of a particular place. Entries must have been written in the English language (translations are not eligible) by a living citizen of the UK, Republic of Ireland or Commonwealth, and published in the year preceding the year in which the award is presented. Prize: £10,000.

Sagittarius Prize: Society of Authors, 84 Drayton Gdns, London SW10 9SB, England. Tel. (20) 7373-6642. Fax (20) 7373-5768. E-mail: info@societyofauthors.org. Website: www.societyofauthors.org. f. 1990. Award for a first published novel by an author over the age of 60. Prize: £4,000.

Saltire Society Literary Awards: The Saltire Society, 9 Fountain Close, 22 High St, Edinburgh EH1 1TF, Scotland. Tel. (131) 556-1836. Fax (131) 557-1675. E-mail: saltire@saltiresociety.org.uk. Website: www.saltiresociety.org.uk. f. 1936. Annual awards in four categories: Scottish Book of the Year (f. 1982), Scottish First Book of the Year (f. 1988), Scottish History Book of the Year (f. 1965), and Scottish Research Book of the Year. Open to any book by an author of Scottish descent or living in Scotland, or to any book which deals with the work or life of a Scot, or with a Scottish question, event or situation. Prizes: Book of the Year: £5,000; First Book of the Year: £1,500; History Book of the Year: £500 and a bound and inscribed copy of the winning publication.

Saltire Society/Times Educational Supplement Scotland Prize for Educational Publications: The Saltire Society, 9 Fountain Close, 22 High St, Edinburgh EH1 1TF, Scotland. Tel. (131) 556-1836. Fax (131) 557-1675. E-mail: saltire@saltiresociety.org.uk. Website: www.saltiresociety.org.uk. f. 1992, to enhance the teaching and learning of an aspect or aspects of the Scottish curriculum. Annual award open to published works of non-fiction, which must be relevant to Scottish schoolchildren aged between five and 18, although not necessarily the product of a Scottish author or publisher. To be eligible a work has to be a book or a package, the bulk of which comprises written words. Non-written elements such as videotapes or computer software may be included but must make up no more than 25% of the package. Prize: £500 and a certificate.

Olive Schreiner Prize: English Academy of Southern Africa, PO Box 124, Wits, 2050, South Africa. Tel. (11) 717-9339. Fax (11) 717-9339. E-mail: englishacademy@societies.wits.ac.za. Website: www.englishacademy.co.za. Admin. Officer: N. Gillman. f. 1964. Annual award to honour new talent for excellence in prose, poetry and drama. Open to works written in English by Southern African writers, and published in South Africa. Winners are chosen by a panel of experts. Prize: R5,000 and an illuminated certificate.

Scottish Arts Council Book of the Year Award: Scottish Arts Council, 12 Manor Pl., Edinburgh EH3 7DD, Scotland. Tel. (131) 226-6051. Website: www.scottishbooktrust.com. f. 2002 to replace the fmr Scottish Arts Council Book Awards and Children's Book Awards. One winner is now chosen in each category of Adult and Children's Book of the Year. Authors should be Scottish, resident in Scotland or have written works of Scottish interest. Applications from publishers only. Prizes: £10,000 (Book of the Year), £5,000 (Children's Book of the Year).

Stand Magazine Short Story Competition: Stand Magazine, 179 Wingrove Rd, Newcastle upon Tyne NE4 9DA, England. Awarded for an original story of no longer than 8,000 words, written in English. Works must be previously unpublished and unbroadcast. Prizes: £1,500 (first prize); £1,000 in runners-up prizes.

Sunday Times Award for Literary Excellence: The Sunday Times, 1 Pennington St, London E1 9XW, England. f. 1987. Annual award to fiction and non-fiction writers. Winners are chosen by a panel of judges consisting of Sunday Times writers, publishers and other leading figures from the publishing industry, and awarded at the discretion of the Literary Editor. Prize: Inscribed silver trophy.

Sunday Times Young Writer of the Year Award: Society of Authors, 84 Drayton Gdns, London SW10 9SB, England. Tel. (20) 7373-6642. Fax (20) 7373-5768. E-mail: info@societyofauthors.org. Website: www.societyofauthors.org. Annual award to a writer under the age of 35 for a work of fiction, non-fiction or poetry published in the previous year. The author must be a British citizen, resident in the UK. Prize: £5,000.

Texas Institute of Letters Awards: Texas Institute of Letters, Literary Awards, PO Box 935, St Edward's University, Houston House, 217 Wook St, Austin, TX 78704, USA. Tel. (512) 448-8702. Website: www.stedwards.edu/newc/marks/til. A series of annual awards presented by the Texas Institute of Letters. Awards incl.: Jesse H. Jones Award for a novel (US$6,000); Best Book of Poetry Award ($5,000); Natalie Ornish Poetry Award ($1,000); Steven Turner Award for a novel ($1,000); John Bloom Humor Award ($1,000); Soeurette Diehl Fraser Translation Award ($1,000); O. Henry Award; Brazos Bookstore Short Story Award ($750). Open to authors who have lived in Texas for two consecutive years or non-residents whose work concerns Texas; entries must have been published in the previous year.

Tir na n-Og Awards: Welsh Books Council, Castell Brychan, Aberystwyth SY23 2JB, Wales. Tel. (1970) 624151. Fax (1970) 625385. E-mail: castellbrychan@cllc.org.uk. Website: www.cllc.org.uk. Annual awards in three categories: Best Welsh-Language Fiction of the Year, Best Welsh-Language Non-Fiction Book of the Year, and Best English (Anglo-Welsh) Book of the Year. Prize: £1,000 in each category.

Tom-Gallon Award: Society of Authors, 84 Drayton Gdns, London SW10 9SB, England. Tel. (20) 7373-6642. Fax (20) 7373-5768. E-mail: info@societyofauthors.org. Website: www.societyofauthors.org. Biennial award for writers of limited means who have had at least one short story published. Prize: £1,000.

Translators Association Translation Prizes: Translators Association, 84 Drayton Gardens, London SW10 9SB, England. Tel. (20) 7373-6642. Fax (20) 7373-5768. E-mail: info@societyofauthors.org. Nine awards:

John Florio Prize: Biennial award for the best translation of a full-length 20th Century Italian literary work into English, published in the UK. Prize: £2,000.

Calouste Gulbenkian Prize: Triennial award for translations into English of works from any period by a Portuguese national. Short stories and poems are eligible. The prize is also open to unpublished translations of works by Portuguese nationals. Prize: £1,000.

Hellenic Foundation for Culture Prize: Triennial award for the best translation into English from modern Greek of a full-length work of imaginative literature, published in the three years prior to the award. Prize: £1,000.

Scott Moncrieff Prize: Annual award for the best translation into English of a full-length French literary work originally published in the last 150 years, published in the UK in the preceding year. Prize: £2,000.

Sasakawa Prize: Triennial award for the best translation into English of a full-length Japanese literary work, published in the UK in the three years prior to the award. Prize £2,000.

Schlegel-Tieck Prize: Annual award for the best translation into English of a full-length German literary work, originally published in the last 100 years, published in the UK during the previous year. Prize: £2,000.

Bernard Shaw Prize: Triennial award, funded by the Anglo-Swedish Literary Foundation, for the best translation into English of a full-length Swedish work, published in the UK in the three years prior to the award. Prize: £2,000.

Premio Valle Inclán: Award for the best translation into English of a full-length Spanish work from any period, published in the UK in the preceding year. Prize: £1,000.

Vondel Translation Prize: Award for the best translation of a Dutch or Flemish literary work into English. Translations should have been published in the UK or the USA during the preceding two years.

Betty Trask Prize and Awards: Society of Authors, 84 Drayton Gdns, London SW10 9SB, England. Tel. (20) 7373-6642. Fax (20) 7373-5768. E-mail: info@societyofauthors.org. Website: www.societyofauthors.org. Annual awards for authors under 35 years old and Commonwealth citizens, for a first novel of a traditional or romantic nature. Prizes: Betty Trask Prize £8,000; Betty Trask Awards of £5,000, £4,000 and £2,000.

Travelling Scholarship Fund: Society of Authors, 84 Drayton Gdns, London SW10 9SB, England. Tel. (20) 7373-6642. Fax (20) 7373-5768. E-mail: info@societyofauthors.org. Website: www.societyofauthors.org. Non-competitive awards enabling British writers to travel abroad. No submissions accepted. Prize: £6,000 (shared).

Whitbread Book of the Year and Literary Awards: Booksellers' Association of the UK and Ireland, Minster House, 272 Vauxhall Bridge Rd, London SW1V 1BA, England. Tel. (20) 7834-5477. Fax (20) 7834-8812. Website: www.whitbread-bookawards.co.uk. Administrator: Denise Bayat. f. 1971. Annual awards to promote and increase good English literature in each of five categories: novel, first novel, biography, children's novel and poetry. Entries are submitted by publishers and the authors must have been resident in the UK or Republic of Ireland for at least three years. One category winner is then voted Whitbread Book of the Year by the panel of judges. Prizes: £25,000 (Book of the Year); £10,000 (Children's Novel); £5,000 (Novel, First Novel, Biography, Poetry).

Whitfield Prize: Royal Historical Society, University College London, Gower St, London WC1E 6BT, England. Award for an author's first book on British history published in the UK in the previous three years. The winner is announced at the Royal Historical Society annual reception in July. Prize: £1,000.

John Whiting Award: Drama Dept, Arts Council of England, 14 Great Peter St, London SW1P 3NQ, England. Tel. (20) 7973-6431. Fax (20) 7973-6983. E-mail: info.drama@artscouncil.org.uk. Website: www.artscouncil.org.uk. f. 1965. Award to commemorate the contribution of playwright John Whiting (member of the Drama Panel of the Arts Council, 1955–63) to British post-war theatre. Writers who have received an award offer from the Arts Council Theatre Writing Scheme are eligible, as are those who have had a commission or premiere from a theatre company funded by the Arts Council or a Regional Arts Board. Prize: £6,000.

Whiting Writers' Awards: Mrs Giles Whiting Foundation, 1133 Avenue of the Americas, New York, NY 10036, USA. Website: www.whitingfoundation.org. Annual awards presented to emergent writers in recognition of their writing achievement and future promise in four categories: fiction, poetry, non-fiction and drama. By internal nomination; applications are not accepted. Prize: US$35,000.

WHSmith Awards: WHSmith PLC, Nations House, 103 Wigmore St, London W1U 1WH, England. Tel. (20) 7409-3222. Fax (20) 7514-9633. Website: www.whsmith.co.uk. Annual awards in eight categories: fiction, general knowledge, business, new talent, biography, travel, children's fiction, and home and leisure, and a literary award for an outstanding contribution to English literature in the year under review, to the author of a book written in English and published in the UK. Authors considered will be from the UK, the Commonwealth, or Ireland, but writers cannot submit work themselves. Voted for by the public. Prize: Literary Award £10,000; category awards £5,000 each.

WHSmith/Books in Canada First Novel Award: 130 Spadina Ave, Suite 603, Toronto, ON M5V 2M3, Canada. Annual award for the best Canadian first novel published in English during the previous year.

WHSmith Thumping Good Read Award: WHSmith PLC, Nations House, 103 Wigmore St, London W1U 1WH, England. Tel. (20) 7409-3222. Fax (20) 7514-9633. Website: www.whsmith.co.uk. f. 1992. Concentrates on books more 'accessible' than 'literary'; genre fiction like murder mysteries, espionage thrillers, etc. is considered. Prize: £5,000.

David T. K. Wong Prize for Short Fiction: International PEN, 9–10 Charterhouse Bldgs, Goswell Rd, London EC1M 7AT, England. Tel. (20) 7253-4308. Fax (20) 7253-5711. E-mail: intpen@dircon.co.uk. Website: www.internatpen.org. f. 2000. Biennial award to promote literary excellence in the form of the unpublished short story, written in English and incorporating one or more of the ideals of International PEN. Prize: £7,500.

Yorkshire Post Book of the Year Award: c/o Margaret Brown, The Rectory, Ripley, Harrogate, North Yorkshire HG3 3AY, England. Annual award for a work of fiction or non-fiction by a British writer or one resident in the UK, published in the UK in the preceding year. Up to four books may be submitted by any one publisher for each imprint. Prize: £1,200.

APPENDIX B: LITERARY ORGANIZATIONS

For organizations of interest to poets, please see Appendix C of the International Who's Who in Poetry.

ALBANIA

Albanian PEN Centre: Rruga Ded Gjo Luli, Pallati 5, shk. 3/4, Tirana. E-mail: albania@aol2.albaniaonline.net.

ARGENTINA

Argentinian PEN Centre: Coronel Diaz 2089, 17°, 1425 Buenos Aires.

Salta PEN Centre: Biblioteca de Textos Universitarios, Universidad Católica de Salta, Pellegrini 790, Salta 4400.

ARMENIA

Armenian PEN Centre: Apt 8, 24 Papazian str., 375012 Yerevan. E-mail: armpen@arminco.com.

AUSTRALIA

Australian Writers' Guild Ltd: 60 Kellett St, Kings Cross, Sydney, NSW 2011. Professional association for writers in areas of television, radio, screen and stage to promote and protect professional interests.

Bibliographical Society of Australia and New Zealand: c/o Secretary/Treasurer, Rachel Salmond, PO Box 1463, Wagga Wagga, NSW 2650. Tel. (2) 6931-8669. Fax (2) 6931-8669. E-mail: rsalmond@pobox.com. Website: www.csu.edu.au/community/BSANZ. Promotes research, largely through publishing, in all aspects of physical bibliography.

Canberra PEN Centre: PO Box 261, Dickson, ACT 2602. Tel. (2) 6248-0912. E-mail: lawjs@ozemail.com.au. Website: www.pen.org.au.

Children's Book Council of Australia: PO Box 48, Hughes, ACT 2605 (ACT Branch).

Dickens Fellowship: 29 Henley Beach Rd, Henley Beach, Adelaide, SA 5022. Literary society devoted to the study and appreciation of the life and works of Charles Dickens.

Melbourne PEN Centre: PO Box 2273, Caulfield Junction, Vic. 3161. E-mail: penmelbourne@optusnet.com.au. Website: www.pen.org.au. Pres.: Dr Judith Buckrich.

PEN Australia North: PO Box 328, Annerley, Qld 4103. Tel. (7) 3890-2089. E-mail: pen@plateaupress.com.au. Website: www.pen.org.au. Pres.: Tim Collins.

Perth PEN Centre: PO Box 1131, Subiaco, WA 6008. Website: www.pen.org.au.

Society of Editors: PO Box 176, Carlton South, Vic. 3053. Professional association of book editors. Organizes training seminars, monthly meetings and a newsletter.

Sydney PEN Centre: Faculty of Humanities and Social Sciences, University of Technology Sydney, PO Box 123, Broadway, NSW 2007. Tel. (2) 9514-2738. Fax (2) 9514-2778. E-mail: sydney@pen.org.au. Website: www.pen.org.au.

AUSTRIA

Austrian PEN Centre: Concordia Haus, Bankgasse 8, 1010 Vienna. E-mail: oepen.club@netway.at. Website: www.penclub.at.

AZERBAIJAN

Azerbaijani PEN Centre: ul. Bol'shaia Krepostnaia, 28, Baku.

BANGLADESH

Bangladeshi PEN Centre: L'Espoir, 60/2, North Dhanmondi, Kalabagan, Dhaka-1205. Tel. (2) 912-8965. E-mail: shajel123@hotmail.com. Exec. Vice-Pres.: Prof. Dr Mahmud Shah Qureshi.

BELARUS

Belarusian PEN Centre: PO Box 218, Minsk 220050. E-mail: pen@pen.unibel.by. Website: www.pen.unibel.by.

BELGIUM

International PEN Club, Belgian Dutch-speaking Centre: Wiesbeek 25, 9255 Buggenhout. E-mail: penvl@skynet.be.

International PEN Club, Belgian French-speaking Centre: 10 Ave des Cerfs, 1950 Kraainem, Brussels. E-mail: huguette.db@skynet.be. Receptions of foreign writers, defence of the liberty of thought of all writers, participation at the world-wide congresses of PEN.

Koninklijke Vlaamse Academie van Belgie voor Wetenschappen en Kunsten (Royal Flemish Academy of Belgium for Science and the Arts): Paleis der Academien, Hertogsstraat 1, 1000 Brussels. Tel. (2) 550-2323. Fax (2) 550-2325. E-mail: info@kvab.be. Website: www.kvab.be. Contact: Prof. Dr Niceas Schamp.

Société de Langue et de Litterature Wallonnes: Universite de Liège, 4000 Liège. Holds meetings, lecturers, exhibitions, library, media, archives, publications.

Société Royale des Bibliophiles et Iconophiles de Belgique: 4 Blvd de l'Empereur, 1000 Brussels. Publication of Le Livre et l'Estampe (Semestrial), exhibitions.

BENIN

Benin PEN Centre: PO Box 03-2810, Cotonou.

BOLIVIA

Bolivian PEN Centre: PO Box 5920, Cochabamba. E-mail: gabyvall@supernet.com.bo.

BOSNIA AND HERZEGOVINA

PEN Centre of Bosnia and Herzegovina: Vrazova 1, Sarajevo 71 000. E-mail: krugpen@bih.net.ba.

BRAZIL

Academia Cearense di Letras: Palacio Senador Alencar, Rua São Paulo 51, 60000 Fortaleza CE. Cultivates and develops literature and scientific achievement. Meets monthly, annual publication.

Associacao Brasileira de Imprensa (Brazilian Press Association): Rua Araujo Porto Alegre, 71 Centro, Rio de Janeiro, RJ.

Brazilian PEN Centre: Praia do Flamengo 172, 11°, Rio de Janeiro, RJ.

Brazilian Translators Union (SINTRA): Rua de Quitanda, 194 sala 1005, Centro, PO Box 20091, Rio de Janeiro, RJ.

Companhia Editora Nacional: Rua Joli 294, São Paulo, SP 03016-020.

Sindicato de Escritores of Rio de Janeiro: Avda Heitor Beltrao, PO Box 20550, 353 Rio de Janeiro, RJ.

BULGARIA

Bulgarian PEN Centre: Bull. Vassil Levsky 60, Sofia 1000. E-mail: alek@astratek.net.

CAMEROON

Centre PEN du Cameroun (Cameroonian Pen Centre): PO Box 5329, Yaounde 1er.

CANADA

Canada Council for the Arts (Conseil des Arts du Canada): 350 Albert Street, PO Box 1047, Ottawa, ON K1P 5V8. Website: www.canadacouncil.ca. Administrative Co-ordinator: Christian Mondor. Supports Canadian professional writers and book and magazine publishers to develop, produce and promote works of literary merit. Administers the annual Governor-General's Literary Awards.

Canadian Association of Journalists: St Patick's Bldg, Carleton University, 1125 Colonel By Dr., Ottawa, ON K1S 5B6.

Canadian Authors Association: PO Box 419, Campbellford, ON K0L 1L0. Tel. (705) 653-0323. Fax (705) 653-0593. E-mail: info@canauthors.org. Website: www.canauthors.org. f. 1921.

Canadian PEN Centre: Suite 214, 24 Ryerson Ave, Toronto, ON M5T 2P3. E-mail: pen@pencanada.ca. Website: www.pencanada.ca.

Canadian Science Writers' Association: PO Box 75, Station A, Toronto, ON M5W 2S9.

Canadian Society of Children's Authors, Illustrators and Performers—CANSCAIP: 104–140 Orchard View Blvd, Lower Level Entrance, Toronto, ON M4R 1B9. Tel. (416) 515-1559. Fax (416) 515-7022. E-mail: office@canscaip.org. Website: www.canscaip.org.

Canadian Society of Magazine Editors: c/o Canadian Living, No. 100, 25 Sheppard Ave W, North York, ON M2N 6S7.

Crime Writers of Canada: 3007 Kingston Rd, PO Box 113, Scarborough, ON M1M 1P1.

Editors' Association of Canada: 27 Carlton Street, Suite 502, Toronto, ON M5B 1L2. Tel. (416) 975-1379. Fax (416) 975-1637. E-mail: info@editors.ca. Website: www.editors.ca. Exec. Dir: Lynne Massey.

Fédération internationale des écrivains de langue française: 3492 rue Laval, Montréal, QC H2X 3C8.

The Literary Consultancy International: PO Box 400, Station E, Toronto, ON M6H 4E3. Tel. (403) 289-5859. E-mail: bethanyg.tlcc@sympatico.ca. Contact: Bethany Gibson.

Periodical Writers' Association of Canada: 24 Ryerson Ave, Toronto, ON M5T 2P3.

Quebecois PEN Centre: c/o La Maison des écrivains, 3492 rue Laval, Montréal, QC H2X 3C8. E-mail: penquebec@netscape.net.

Société des écrivains canadiens: 1195 rue Sherbrooke Ouest, Montréal, QC H3A 1H9.

Sudanese Writers in Exile PEN Centre: 685 McCowan Rd, PO Box 66502, Scarborough, ON M1J 3N8. E-mail: ahmed100@home.com.

Union des écrivaines et écrivains québecois: La Maison des écrivains, 3492 ave Laval, Montréal, QC H2X 3C8.

Writers Guild of Canada (WGC): 366 Adelaide Street W, Suite 401, Toronto, ON M5V 1R9. Tel. (416) 979-7907. Fax (416) 979-9273. E-mail: info@wgc.ca. Website: www.wgc.ca. Exec. Dir: Maureen Parker.

The Writers' Union of Canada (TWUC): 40 Wellington St E, Third Floor, Toronto, ON M5E 1C7. Tel. (416) 703-8982. Fax (416) 504-7656. E-mail: info@writersunion.ca. Website: www.writersunion.ca. f. 1973.

THE PEOPLE'S REPUBLIC OF CHINA

China PEN Centre: Chinese Writers' Activity Centre, 25 Dongtuchenglu, Beijing 10013.

Guangzhou Chinese PEN Centre: 75 Wende Lu, Guangzhou.

Shanghai Chinese PEN Centre: 675 Julu Lu, Shanghai.

COLOMBIA

Colombian PEN Centre: PO Box 101830, Zona 10, Bogota. E-mail: pencolombia@hotmail.com. Website: quickbuilder.com/pencolombia.org/index.html.

COSTA RICA

Costa Rican PEN Centre: Apdo 939-2050, Montes de Oca.

CÔTE D'IVOIRE

Centre de PEN de Côte d'Ivoire (Côte d'Ivoire PEN Centre): 01 PO Box 269, Abidjan 01.

CROATIA

Croatian PEN Centre: Trg bana Josipa Jelacica 7/I, 10000 Zagreb.

CZECH REPUBLIC

Czech PEN Centre: 28, října 9, 110 00 Prague. Tel. 2423-4343. Fax 2422-1926. E-mail: centrum@pen.cz. Website: www.pen.cz. Pres.: Jiri Stransky.

DENMARK

Danish PEN Centre: Dronningensgade 14, 1420 Copenhagen. E-mail: pen@pen.dk. Website: www.pen.dk.

Danish Society of Language and Literature: Frederiksholms Kanal 18A, 1220 Copenhagen K. Scholarly editing in Danish language, literature and history.

Dansk Fagpresse: Skindergade 7, 1159 Copenhagen K. Tel. 3397-4000. Fax 3391-2670. E-mail: df@danskfagpresse.dk. Website: www.danskfagpresse.dk.

Dansk Forfatterforening (Danish Writers' Association): Tordenskjolds gård, Strandgade 6, 1401 Copenhagen K. E-mail: danskforfatterforening@danskforfatterforening.dk. Website: www.danskforfatterforening.dk. Attend to social, artistic, professional and economic interests of Danish authors in Denmark and abroad.

Dansk Litteraturcenter (Danish Literature Centre): c/o The Agency of the Arts, Kongens Nytorv 3, PO Box 9012, 1022 Copenhagen K. Tel. 3374-4500. Fax 3374-4565. E-mail: danlit@danlit.dk. Website: www.danlit.dk.

Danske Sprog-og Litteraturselskab: Frederiksholms Kanal 18A, 1220 Copenhagen. Publs: Standard editions of literary, linguistic and historical texts, including diaries and correspondence.

Nyt Dansk Litteraturselskab: Hotelvej 9, 2640 Hedehusene. Tel. 46 59 55 20. Fax 46 59 55 21. E-mail: ndl@ndl.dk. Website: www.ndl.dk. Works for re-publishing of titles missing in public libraries in co-operation with publishers.

EGYPT

Egyptian PEN Centre: 5 Sayyid El Bakri St, (6ème étage, 63), Zamalek, Cairo.

ESTONIA

Estonian PEN Centre: 1–21 Harju St, Tallinn 0001.

FAROE ISLANDS

Rithövundafelag Färoya (Writers' Union of the Faroe Islands): PO Box 1124, 110 Tórshavn.

FINLAND

Finlands Svenska Författareförening r.f. (Society of Swedish Authors in Finland): Urho Kekkonens gata 8 B 14, 00100 Helsingfors.

Finnish PEN Centre: PO Box 84, 00131 Helsinki. E-mail: elisabeth.nordgren@pp.inet.fi.

Informationscentralen för Finlands Litterarur: PO Box 259, 00 171 Helsingfors. Information centre for Finnish literature and the State Literature Commission.

Kirjallisuudentutkijain Seura (Finnish Literary Research Society): Dept of Finnish Literature, Fabianinkatu 33, 00014 Helsinki. Website: www.helsinki.fi/jarj/skts. Sec.: Katja Seutu. Publs: Kirjallisuudentutkijain Seuran Vuosikirja (Yearbook of the Literary Research Society).

Suomalaisen Kirjallisuuden Seura: PO Box 259, 00170 Helsinki. Tel. (0) 9/131231. Fax (0) 9/13123220. E-mail: sks-fls@finlit.fi. Website: www.finlit.fi.

Suomen kääntäjien ja tulkkien liitto - Finlands översättar - och tolkförbund ry (Finnish Association of Translators and Interpreters): Museokatu 9 B 23, 00100 Helsinki. Tel. (9) 445-927. Fax (9) 445-937. E-mail: sktl@sktl.net. Website: www.sktl.net. Chair.: Ari Penttilä.

Suomen tietokirjailijat ry: Mariankatu 19 D 45, 00170 Helsinki. Tel. (9) 4542-2550. Fax (9) 4542-2551. E-mail: stik@suomentietokirjailijat.fi. Website: suomentietokirjailijat.fi. Man. Dir: Raimo Jussila. Chair.: Pirjo Hiidenmaa.

Svenska Litteratursallskapet i Finland: Mariegatan 8, 00170 Helsinki. Publs: Skrifter (Writings).

Svenska Osterbottens Litteraturforening: Henriksgatan 7–9 4N, 65320 Vasa, Auroravagen 10, 65610 Smedsby. Co-owner of the publishers in Scriptum, publishing the journal Horisont. Organizes writers' seminars, programme evenings: lyrics, prose, music.

FRANCE

Centre National des Lettres: 53 rue de Verneuil, 75007 Paris. Upholds and encourages the work of French writers, gives financial help to writers, translators, publishers and public libraries and promotes translation into French.

The International Network of Cities of Asylum: 1 allée Georges Leblanc, 93300 Aubervilliers. E-mail: contact@autodafe.org. Website: www.autodafe.org. f. 1994 as the International Parliament of Writers. Publishes journal, Autodafe.

PEN Club français: 6 rue François-Miron, 75004 Paris.

Société des Gens de Lettres: Hôtel de Massa, 38 rue du Faubourg Saint-Jacques, 75014 Paris. Tel. 1 53 10 12 00. Fax 1 53 10 12 12. E-mail: sgdlf@wanadoo.fr. Website: www.sgdl.org. Pres.: Alain Absire.

GEORGIA

Georgian PEN Centre: 13 Machabeli str., Tbilisi 380007.

GERMANY

Arbeitskreis für Jugenditeratur eV: Elisabethstrasse 15, 8000 Munich 40. Encourages and co-ordinates all efforts to support literature for children and young people.

Association Internationale des Journalistes Philatéliques: Am Osterberg 19, 29386 Hankensbüttel. International association of philatelic journalists, authors and associated societies.

Deutsche Akademie für Sprache und Dichtung: Alexandrakeg 23, 6100 Darmstadt.

Kurdish PEN Centre: Richterstrasse 9, 12516 Berlin.

Literarischer Verein in Stuttgart eV: PO Box 102251, 7000 Stuttgart 1.

PEN Zentrum Bundesrepublik Deutschland (German PEN Centre): Kasinostr. 3, 64293 Darmstadt. E-mail: pen-Germany@t-online.de.

Romani PEN Centre: Fuggerstrasse 21, 10777 Berlin. E-mail: romani@blenx.de.

Writers in Exile PEN Centre (German Branch): Bernsteinstrasse 122, 70619 Stuttgart.

GHANA

Ghanaian PEN Centre: PO Box 131, TUC, Accra. E-mail: mackay@ghana.com.

GREECE

PEN Club Hellenique (Greek PEN Centre): 8 rue Karamanlaki, 112-53 Athens.

GUINEA

PEN International Centre de Guinée (Guinea PEN Centre): PO Box 4465, Conakry.

HONG KONG

Composers and Authors Society of Hong Kong Ltd: 18/F Universal Trade Centre, 3 Arbuthnot Rd, Central Hong Kong.

Hong Kong (Chinese-speaking) PEN Centre: c/o Woo Chun Hoi, Patrick (Chair.), Flat A, 22/F, Blk. 4, Cityone Shatin, Shatin NT, Hong Kong.

Hong Kong (English-speaking) PEN Centre: 1/F, West, Lok Yen Bldg, 23D Peak Rd, Cheung Chau, Hong Kong. E-mail: hkpen_eng@yahoo.com.

HUNGARY

Artisjus—Agency for Literature and Theatre: PO Box 67, V, Vörösmarty ter 1, 1364 Budapest.

Esperanto PEN Centre: 2183, Galgamácsa, Panoráma ltp 7/7. E-mail: panorama@mail.digitel2002.hu.

Hungarian PEN Centre: VII Kertész u. 36, 1073 Budapest.

Institute of Literary Studies of the Hungarian Academy of Sciences: Menesi ut 11–13, 1118 Budapest. Research of history of Hungarian literature, research in literary theory, literary criticism to influence contemporary literature, source publications on the history of Hungarian literature and editing of reference books and bibliographies.

ICELAND

Icelandic PEN Centre: PO Box 33, Reykjavík.

Rithöfundasamband Íslands (Writers' Union of Iceland): Gunnarshusi, Dyngjuvegi 8, 104 Reykjavík. Union of Icelandic writers that guards copyrights, protects interests in the field of literature and book-publishing, drama, textbooks, radio and television scripts.

INDIA

All-India PEN Centre: Theosophy Hall, 40 New Marine Lines, Mumbai 400 020. Publs: The Indian PEN (quarterly).

Sahitya Akademi: Rabindra Bhavan, 35 Ferozeshah Road, New Delhi 110001. Tel. (11) 23386626. Fax (11) 23382428. E-mail: secy@ndb.vsnl.net.in. Website: www.sahitya-akademi.org. National organization to work for the development of Indian letters, to set high literary standards, foster and co-ordinate literary activities in the Indian languages and promote through them the cultural unity of the country.

INDONESIA

Indonesian PEN Centre: Jalan Camara 6, Jakarta Pusat.

IRELAND

Irish Academy of Letters: School of Irish Studies, Thomas Prior House, Merrion Rd, Dublin 4.

Irish PEN Centre: 26 Rosslyn, Killarney Rd, Bray, Co Wicklow.

Irish Writers' Centre: 19 Parnell Sq., Dublin 1. Tel. (1) 872-1302. E-mail: info@writerscentre.ie. Website: www.writerscentre.ie. Dir: Dr Cathal McCabe. Admin.: Kahterine Moore.

Society of Irish Playwrights: Room 804, Liberty Hall, Dublin 1. Fosters interest in and promotes contemporary Irish drama. Guards the rights of Irish playwrights.

ISRAEL

ACUM Ltd (Society of Authors, Composers and Music Publishers in Israel): 9 Tuval St, PO Box 1704, Ramat-Gan 52117. Tel. (3) 6113400. Fax (3) 6122629. E-mail: info@acum.org.il. Website: www.acum.org.il.

Israeli PEN Centre: 6 Kaplan St, Tel-Aviv, PO Box 7203, Code 61070. Meetings with members and receptions for guest writers. Publs: bulletin of information and translation of literature in European languages.

ITALY

Italian PEN Centre: Via Daverio 7, 20122 Milan. E-mail: fmormando@planet.it.

Sardinian PEN Centre: c/o Facolta' di Lettere e Filosofia, Piazza Conte di Moriana 8, 07100 Sassari. E-mail: fch@ssmain.uniss.it. Website: www.uniss.it/fch/pen/index.html.

Societa' Italiana Autori Drammatici (SIAD): Via PO 10, 00198 Rome.

Societa' Italiana degli Autori et Editori (SIAE): Viale della Letteratura 30, 00144 Rome.

JAPAN

Dickens Fellowship: Bungei-Gakubu, Seijo University, 6-1-20 Seijo, Setagaya, Tokyo. Lectures, symposia, reading circles. Publs: bulletins.

English Literary Society of Japan: 501 Kenkyusha Bldg, 9 Surugadai 2-Chome, Kanda, Chiyoda-ku, Tokyo 101. Association of scholars in the fields of English and American literature and the English language. Publs: journal Studies in English Literature (two a year).

Japanese PEN Centre: 20-3 Kabuto-cho, Nihonbashi, Chuo-ku, Tokyo 103-0026. E-mail: secretariat03@japanpen.or.jp. Website: www.japanpen.or.jp. Sec.: Nobuhiro Akio.

Science Fiction Writers of Japan (SFWJ): Website: www.sfwj.or.jp. f. 1963. Awards the Nihon SF Taisho Award.

KAZAKHSTAN

Kazakhstan PEN Centre: Tulebayeva 156, Apt 7, 480091 Almaty.

KENYA

Kenyan PEN Centre: PO Box 70147, Nairobi.

Kwani?: E-mail: editors@kwani.org. Website: www.kwani.org. Literary magazine f. by Binyavanga Wainaina. Editor: Binyavanga Wainaina.

REPUBLIC OF KOREA

Korean PEN Centre: Room 1105, Oseong B/D, 13-5 Youido-dong, Yongdungpo-ku, Seoul 150-010. E-mail: penkon2001@yahoo.co.kr.

LATVIA

Latvian PEN Centre: a.k. 506, 1010 Riga. E-mail: juris.kronsbergs@swipnet.se.

LEBANON

Lebanese PEN Centre: Beit-Chahab, PO Box 86.

LIECHTENSTEIN

PEN Club Liechenstein (Liechtenstein PEN Centre): PO Box 416, 9490 Vaduz.

LITHUANIA

Lithuanian PEN Centre: K. Sirvydo 6, 2600 Vilnius. E-mail: eleres@takas.lt.

THE FORMER YUGOSLAV REPUBLIC OF MACEDONIA

Macedonian PEN Centre: Str. Maksim Gorki 18, 1000 Skopje. E-mail: macedpen@unet.com.mk. Website: www.pen.org.mk.

MEXICO

PEN Centro Guadalajara (Guadalajaran PEN Centre): Circunvalación Agustin, Yanez 2839, Col. Arcos Vallarta, Guadalajara, Jal. 44100.

Mexican PEN Centre: Heriberto Frías 1452-407, Col. Del Valle, México, DF 03100. E-mail: maleona@hotmail.com.

San Miguel de Allende PEN Centre: Apdo 287, San Miguel de Allende, México, DF 37700. E-mail: lucina@unisono.net.mx. Sec.: Lucina Kathmann.

MOLDOVA

Moldovan Pen Centre: Blvd Stefan cel Mare 134, Post Office 12, PO Box 231, 2012 Chisinau. E-mail: contrafort@moldnet.md.

MONACO

Monaco PEN Centre: 27 Blvd Albert 1er, 98000 Monte Carlo.

MOROCCO

L'Union des Écrivains du Maroc: 5 rue Ab Bakr Seddik, Rabat.

NEPAL

Nepal Journalists Association: PO Box 285, Maitighar, Kathmandu.

Nepal PEN Centre: PO Box 8975, EPC 533, Kathmandu. E-mail: shaligrm@mos.com.np.

NETHERLANDS

Nederlandse Taalunie: Algemeen Secretariaat, Lange Voorhout 19, PO Box 10595, 2501 HN 's-Gravenhage. Tel. (70) 346-9548. Fax (70) 365-9818. E-mail: secr@ntu.nl. Website: www.taalunie.org.

Netherlands PEN Centre: Graafseweg 3, 6512 BM Nijmegen.

Writers from the Former Yugoslavia PEN Centre: c/o AIDA Netherland, Van Ostadestraat 49a, 1072 SN Amsterdam.

NEW ZEALAND

Arts Council of New Zealand: Old Public Trust Bldg, 131–35 Lambton Quay, PO Box 3806, Wellington.

NZ Book Council: Floor 5, Old Wool House, 139–141 Featherston Street, Wellington. Tel. (04) 4991569. Fax (04) 4991424. Website: www.bookcouncil.org.nz.

New Zealand Society of Authors—NZSA (PEN NZ, Inc): PO Box 67 013, Mt Eden, Auckland 3. E-mail: nzsa@clear.net.nz. Website: www.authors.org.nz. f. 1934. Promotes co-operation and mutual support among writers in all countries and encourages creative writing in New Zealand. Pres.: William Taylor.

NICARAGUA

Nicaraguan PEN Centre: Apdo RP24, Managua. E-mail: mquintana@uni.edu.ni.

NIGERIA

West African Association for Commonwealth Literature and Language Studies: PO Box 622, Owerri, Imo State.

NORWAY

Den Norske Forfatterforening (Norwegian Authors' Union): PO Box 327 Sentrum, Rådhusgate 7, 0103 Oslo.

Det Norske Videnskaps-Akademi: Drammensveien 78, Oslo 2.

NORLA (Norwegian Literature Abroad—Fiction and Non-Fiction): Victoria Terr. 11, PO Box 2663 Solli, 0203 Oslo. Tel. 2327-6350. Fax 2327-6351. E-mail: firmapost@norla.no. Website: www.norla.no. Man. Dir: Kristin Brudevoll. Supports the translation of Norwegian fiction and non-fiction.

Norwegian PEN Centre: Urtegaten 50, 0187 Oslo. E-mail: pen@norskpen.no.

PANAMA

Panamanian PEN Centre: PO Box 1824, Panamá 1.

PERU

Peruvian PEN Centre: Avda Larco 1150, Piso 8, Oficina 804, Miraflores, Lima. E-mail: tumo13@hotmail.com. Pres.: Tulio Mora.

PHILIPPINES

Philippine PEN Centre: 531 Padre Faura, Ermita, Manila. E-mail: isaganicruz@yahoo.com.

POLAND

Polish Authors' Association—SAP: ul. Madalinskiego 15m 16, 02-513 Warsaw.

Polish PEN Centre: ul. Krakowskie Przedmiescie 87/89, 00-079 Warsaw. E-mail: penclub@ikp.atm.com.pl. Website: www.penclub.atomnet.pl.

Zwiazek Literatow Polskich (Union of Polish Writers): Krakoweskie Przedmiescie 87, 00-950 Warsaw.

PORTUGAL

Portuguese PEN Centre: York House, Rua das Janelas Verdes 32, 1200 Lisbon. E-mail: penclube@mail.telepac.pt.

ROMANIA

Romanian PEN Centre: Blvd Ferdinand 29 ap.3, 70313 Bucharest. E-mail: univers@rnc.ro.

RUSSIA

Russian Authors' Society: ul. Bol'Shaya Bronnaya 6A, 103670 Moscow. Protects the rights and organizes legal protection for authors in Russia.

Russian PEN Centre: Neglinnaya St, 18/1, bldg 2, 103031 Moscow. E-mail: penrussia@hotmail.com. Website: penrussia.org.

SENEGAL

PEN Club du Sénégal (Senegal PEN Centre): Rue 1 Prolongée Pointe, Dakar.

SERBIA AND MONTENEGRO

Serbian PEN Centre: Milutina Bojica 4, 11000 Belgrade. E-mail: pencent@bitsyu.net.

SLOVAKIA

Slovak PEN Centre: AOSS, Laurinska 2, 815 08 Bratislava. Tel. (2) 5443-4117. Fax (2) 5443-4117. E-mail: info@scpen.sk. Website: www.scpen.sk. Pres.: Anton Hykisch.

SLOVENIA

Slovene PEN Centre: Tomsiceva 12, 61000 Ljubljana. E-mail: slopen@guest.arnes.si.

SOUTH AFRICA

English Academy of Southern Africa: PO Box 124, Wits, 2050. E-mail: englishacademy@societies.wits.ac.za. Admin. Officer: N. Gillman. Concerned with all forms and functions of English and South Africa, and with all literature written in English. It promotes research and debate, organizes lectures, presents awards, and generally fosters the creative, critical and scholarly talents of users of English. It does this while respecting the multilingual heritage of Southern Africa.

Institute for the Study of English in Africa: Rhodes University, PO Box 94, Grahamston 6140. Conducts research into needs of black pupils learning English. Publs: English in Africa and New Coin Poetry.

Nasionale Afrikaanse Letterkundige Museum en Navorsingsentrum: Private Bag X20543, Bloemfontein 9300.

National English Literary Museum: Private Bag 1019, Grahamstown 6140. Tel. (46) 622-7042. Fax (46) 622-2582. E-mail: m.hacksley@ru.ac.za. Website: www.rhodes.ac.za/nelm. Dir: Malcolm Hacksley. Collection of all forms of imaginative South African literature, written in English.

South African PEN Centre: 4 Bucksburn Rd, Newlands 7700. E-mail: safpen@iafrica.com.

South African Union of Journalists: Office 512–13, Fifth Floor, Argon House, 87 Juta St, Johannesburg 2017.

SPAIN

Associació d'Escriptors en Llengua Catalana—AELC: Calle Canuda 6, 6è, Barcelona 08002. Tel. (93) 302-7828. Fax (93) 412-5873. E-mail: info@aelc.es. Website: www.escriptors.com. f. 1977.

Centre Català del PEN Club (Catalan PEN Centre): Calle Canuda, 6°, 08002 Barcelona. Tel. (93) 318-3298. Fax (93) 412-0666. E-mail: pen@pencatala.org. Website: www.pencatala.org.

Galician PEN Centre: Calle República El Salvador, 14, 1° izquierda, 15701 Santiago de Compostela. E-mail: pengalicia@mundo-r.com.

SRI LANKA

Sri Lankan PEN Centre: Institute of Aesthetic Studies, 21 Albert Crescent, Colombo 7.

SWEDEN

Sveriges Författarförbund (Swedish Writers' Union): PO Box 3157, Drottninggatan 88B, 103 63 Stockholm.

Swedish PEN Centre: Wollmar Yxkullsgatan 7, 118 50 Stockholm. E-mail: ljiljana.dufgran@pensweden.org. Website: www.pensweden.org.

SWITZERLAND

Autorinnen und Autoren der Schweiz (Autrices et Auteurs de Suisse): Nordstrasse 9, 8035 Zürich. Tel. (1) 350-0460. Fax (1) 350-0461. E-mail: sekretariat@a-d-s.ch. Website: www.a-d-s.ch. Dir-Gen.: Peter A. Schmid. Professional organization for the protection of writers' interests.

Deutschweizer PEN-Zentrum (Swiss German PEN Centre): Zypressenstrasse 76, 8004 Zurich. E-mail: infopen@datacomm.ch.

Suisse Romand PEN Centre: 14 rue Crespin, 1206 Geneva. E-mail: jakoutchoumow@bluewin.ch.

Swiss Italian and Reto-romansh PEN Centre: PO Box 107, 6903 Lugano. E-mail: penlugano@ticino.com. Website: www.writers-prison.org.

TAIWAN

Taipei Chinese PEN Centre: Fourth Floor, 4 Lane 68, When Chou St, Taipei. E-mail: taipen@tpts5.seed.net.tw.

TANZANIA

Journalists' Organization of Tanzania: PO Box 45526, Dar Es Salaam.

THAILAND

The Siam Society: 131 Soi 21 (Asoke) Sukhumvit Road, Bangkok 10110. Promotes and tries to preserve artistic, scientific and other cultural affairs of Thailand and neighbouring countries. Publs: Journal of the Siam Society, Natural History Bulletin of the Siam Society.

Thai PEN Centre: PO Box 81, Dusit Post Office, Bangkok 10300. E-mail: wareeya@hotmail.com.

UKRAINE

Ukrainian PEN Centre: Bankivska St 2, 252024 Kiev.

UNITED ARAB EMIRATES

Emirates Writers and Litterateurs Union: PO Box 11044, Ras Al-Khaimah. Tel. (00971) 7 22 74 344.

UNITED KINGDOM

African Writers Abroad PEN Centre: Flat 6, 55 Varcoe Rd, London SE16 3DE. E-mail: vmagombe@aol.com.

Arts Council England: 14 Great Peter Street, London, SW1P 3NQ. Tel. (0845) 3006200. E-mail: enquiries@artscouncil.org.uk. Website: www.artcouncil.org.uk. Chief Exec.: Peter Hewitt. Chair.: Prof. Sir Christopher Frayling. f. 1946. National development agency for the arts in England, distributing public money from government and the National Lottery. The principal funding programme, Grants for the arts, is open to individuals, arts organizations, national touring and other people who use the arts in their work. The grants are for activities that benefit people in England or that help artists and arts organizations from England to carry out their work. Nine regional offices and a national office.

The Arvon Foundation: 2nd Floor, 42A Buckingham Palace Rd, London SW1W 0RE. Tel. (20) 7931-7611. Fax (20) 7963-0961. Website: www.arvonfoundation.org. Organizes writing courses for poetry, fiction, stage drama, television and radio. Chair.: Prudence Skene.

Association of Authors' Agents: c/o AP Watt Ltd, 20 John St, London WC1N 2DR. Maintains a code of practice, provides a forum for discussion and promotes co-operation and interests of British literary agencies and agents.

Association of British Science Writers: c/o British Association for the Advancement of Science, Fortress House, 23 Savile Row, London W1X 1AB.

Association for Scottish Literary Studies: Dept of Scottish History, 9 University Gdns, University of Glasgow, Glasgow G12 8QH. Tel. (141) 330-5309. Fax (141) 330-5309. E-mail: office@asls.org.uk. Website: www.asls.org.uk. Promotes the teaching, study and writing of Scottish literature and languages, past and present. Gen. Man.: Duncan Jones.

Authors' Club: 40 Dover St, London W1X 3RB. Club for writers, publishers, critics, journalists and academics involved with literature. Administers several literary awards.

Francis Bacon Society Inc: Canonbury Tower, Islington, London N1. Publs: Baconiana (periodically), Jottings (periodically), booklets, pamphlets (list on request).

Book Trust: Book House, 45 East Hill, London SW18 2QZ. Independent charitable trust promoting reading and the use of books. Administers several major literary awards including the Man Booker Prize, and publishes reference and resource materials.

Book Trust Scotland: Scottish Book Centre, 137 Dundee St, Edinburgh EH11 1BG. Promotes reading and books in general, and provides a range of information and services on Scottish writers and books. Administers awards including the Scottish Writer of the Year.

British Science Fiction Association: 52 Woodhill Dr., Grove, Wantage, Oxon OX12 0DF. Website: www.bsfa.co.uk. Promotes the reading, writing and publishing of science fiction. Activities include literary criticism, news, reviews, serious articles, meetings, writers' workshops, lending library and magazine chain. Publs: Matrix (newsletter), Vector (journal), Focus (magazine).

Brontë Society: Brontë Parsonage Museum, Haworth, Keighley, West Yorkshire BD22 8DR. The preservation of the literary works of the Brontë family and of manuscripts and other objects related to the family.

The Centre for the Children's Book: 4 Terrace Level, St Peter's Marina, Newcastle upon Tyne, Tyne and Wear, NE6 1TZ, England. Tel. (191) 2764289. Fax (191) 2764302. E-mail: info@childrensbook.org.uk. Website: www.centreforthechildrensbook.org.uk. Registered charity; runs exhibitions and events. CEO: Mary Briggs. Artistic Dir: Elizabeth Hammill.

Chartered Institute of Library and Information Professionals—CILIP: 7 Ridgmount St, London WC1E 7AE. Tel. (20) 7255-0500. Website: www.cilip.org.uk. Professional body for librarians and information managers. Publs: numerous produced every year, mems receive the monthly magazine, UPDATE.

Chawton House Library: Chawton House, Chawton, Hants GU34 1SJ. Website: www.chawton.org. f. 2003. Centre for the study of early English women's writing, 1600–1830; collection of over 7,000 vols and manuscripts. Chair.: Sandy Lerner.

Comhairle nan Leabhraichean (The Gaelic Books Council): 22 Mansfield St, Glasgow G11 5QP. Tel. (141) 337-6211. E-mail: fios@gaelicbooks.net.

Website: www.gaelicbooks.net. Offers publication grants to publishers for individual books and commission grants to writers, as well as advice, editorial services, and a bookshop.

Crime Writers' Association—CWA: Meadow View, The Street, Bossingham, CT4 6DX. Tel. (1227) 709782. Fax (1227) 709782. E-mail: info@thecwa.co.uk. Website: www.thecwa.co.uk. Membership limited to professional crime writers, but associate membership is open to specialist publishers, agents and booksellers. Administers numerous annual awards. Publ.: Red Herrings (monthly newsletter).

Dickens Fellowship: Charles Dickens Museum, 48 Doughty St, London WC1N 2LX. Tel. (20) 7405-2127. Fax (20) 7831-5175. E-mail: hongensec@aol.com. Website: www.dickens.fellowship.btinternet.co.uk. Over 50 branches world-wide, of Dickens enthusiasts. Organizes talks and conferences, and supports the preservation of buildings associated with Dickens. Publ.: The Dickensian (three a year).

Edinburgh Bibliographical Society: Dept of Special Collections, Edinburgh University Library, George Sq., Edinburgh EH8 9LJ. Lectures on bibliographical topics and visits to libraries. Publ.: Transaction (issued to members only).

English Association: University of Leicester, University Rd, Leicester LE1 7RH. Promotes the understanding and appreciation of English language and literature. Organizes lectures and conferences, and produces a selection of publications.

Thomas Hardy Society: PO Box 1438, Dorchester, Dorset DT1 1YH. Tel. (1305) 251501. Fax (1305) 251501. Website: www.hardysociety.org. Promotion and appreciation of works of Thomas Hardy. Organizes a summer conference, lectures and walks in Wessex.

Institute of Contemporary Arts: The Mall, London SW1. Galleries, performance, music, cinema, talks, conferences, restaurant, bar, 'Bookshop'.

International Poets, Playwrights, Essayists, Editors and Novelists Association—PEN: 9–10 Charterhouse Bldgs, Goswell Rd, London EC1M 7AT. Tel. (20) 7253-4308. Fax (20) 7253-5711. E-mail: intpen@dircon.co.uk. Website: www.internatpen.org. f. 1921. International Pres. Homero Aridjis.

Iranian Writers in Exile PEN Centre: 4 Maclise Rd, London W14 0PR. E-mail: iranzendan@hotmail.com. Website: www.iran-pen.com.

Jewish Book Council: POB 38247, London, NW3 5YQ. E-mail: info@jewishbookweek.com. Website: www.jewishbookweek.com. f. 1947 to promote the reading of books on all aspects of Jewish thought and culture; produces Jewish Book Week UK literary festival; administers the TLS-Porjes Prize for Hebrew-English Translation; organizes poetry and creative writing competitions for younger people. Chair.: Anne Webber.

Johnson Society of London: 255 Baring Rd, Grove Park, London SE12 0BQ. Studies the works of Dr Samuel Johnson, his circle, his contemporaries and his times through lectures and articles. Publ.: The New Rambler.

Keats/Shelley Memorial Association: 10 Landsdowne Rd, Tunbridge Wells, Kent TN1 2NJ. Promotes the works of Keats, Shelley, Byron and Leigh Hunt and maintains the house in Rome where Keats died.

Kipling Society: 2nd Floor, Schomberg House, 80–82 Pall Mall, London SW1Y 5HG. Promotes study of Kipling through discussion meetings, annual luncheon and quarterly journal.

Charles Lamb Society: BM ELIA, London WC1N 3XX. Studies the life, works and times of Charles Lamb and his circle, to stimulate the Elian spirit of friendliness and humour, and form a collection of Eliana.

Lancashire Authors' Association: Heatherslade, 5 Quakerfields, Westhoughton, Bolton, Lancashire BL5 2BJ. Publ.: The Record (quarterly).

The Literary Consultancy Ltd: Second Floor, Diorama Arts, 34 Osnaburgh Street, London, NW1 3ND. Tel. (20) 7813-4330. E-mail: info@literaryconsultancy.co.uk. Website: www.literaryconsultancy.co.uk. f. 1996 to give editorial advice to writers at any level, writing in English.

Moniack Mhor (Avron Foundation of Scotland): Teavarran, Kiltarlity, Beauly, Inverness-shire IV4 7HT. Provides the opportunity to live and work with established writers, and participate in tutorials and workshops. Books and magazines for loan, and access to text database of English poetry. Postal loans also available.

National Union of Journalists: Acorn House, 314 Grays Inn Rd, London WC1X 8DP. Represents journalists in all sectors of publishing, providing advice and support on wages, conditions, and benefits. Publs: various guides and magazines.

Oxford Bibliographical Society: Bodleian Library, Oxford OX1 3BG. Publs: First Series, vols I–VII, 1923–46; New Series, vol. 1, 1948–.

PEN English Centre: 7 Dilke St, London SW3 4JE. E-mail: englishpen@compuserve.com. Website: www.pen.org.uk. Publs: The Pen (two a year).

PEN Scottish Centre: 126 W Princes St, Glasgow G4 9DB, Scotland. E-mail: info@scottishpen.org. Website: www.scottishpen.org.

PEN Welsh Centre: 80 Plymouth Rd, Penarth, CF64 5DL, Wales.

The Publishers Association: 29B Montague St, London WC1B 5BH. Tel. (20) 7691-9191. Fax (20) 7691-9199. E-mail: mail@publishers.org.uk. Website: www.publishers.org.uk. National trade asscn representing the publishing industry. Publ.: Directory of Publishing.

Romantic Novelists' Association: c/o RNA Hon. Membership Secretary, 38 Stanhope Rd, Reading, Berkshire RG2 7HN. Website: www.rna-uk.org. Membership open to published writers of romantic novels, with associate membership open to agents, editors, publishers and booksellers. Administers two annual awards. Publ.: RNA News. Pres.: Diane Pearson.

Royal Society of Literature: Somerset House, Strand, London WC2R 1LA. Tel. (20) 7845-4676. Fax (20) 7845-4679. E-mail info@rslit.org. Website www.rslit.org. Lectures, discussions, readings and publications. Adminsters awards including the W. H. Heinemann Prize.

Scottish Arts Council: 12 Manor Pl., Edinburgh EH3 7DD. One of the principal channels for government funding for the arts, including the administration of literary awards, bursaries, events and fellowships.

Scottish Publishers Association: Scottish Book Centre, 137 Dundee St, Edinburgh EH11 1BG. Provides co-operative support for Scottish publishers and information about publishing in Scotland.

Sherlock Holmes Society of London: c/o Information and Press Officer, 64 Graham Rd, London SW19 3SS. Tel. (20) 8540-7657. Website: www.sherlock-holmes.org.uk. Publ.: The Sherlock Holmes Journal. Pres.: Tony Howlett. Studies the life and works of Sherlock Holmes and Dr Watson.

The Society of Authors: 84 Drayton Gdns, London SW10 9SB. Tel. (20) 7373-6642. Fax (20) 7373-5768. E-mail: info@societyofauthors.org. Website: www.societyofauthors.org. f. 1884. Independent trade union which promotes and protects the interests of writers, and provides information and advice. Publs: The Author (quarterly journal); numerous Quick Guides on the business aspects of the profession. Gen. Sec.: Mark Le Fanu.

Society of Civil Service Authors: 4 Top St, Wing, nr Oakham, Rutland LE15 8SE. Encourages authorship by past and present members of the Civil Service.

Society of Freelance Editors and Proofreaders: Riverbank House, 1 Putney Bridge Approach, London SW6 3JD. Tel. (20) 7736-3278. Fax (20) 7736-3318. Website: www.sfep.org.uk. Promotes high editorial standards through advice, training and the introduction of recognized qualifications.

Society of Young Publishers: c/o The Bookseller, Endeavour House, 189 Shaftsbury Ave, London WC2H 8TJ. Website: www.thesyp.org.uk. Speaker meetings, annual training conference, social events and job database. Open to anyone in, or new to, publishing or related trades.

Somali-Speaking Writers PEN Centre: 15 Dante Rd, Kennington, London SE11 4RB. E-mail: eregm@aol.com.

Tolkien Society: 35 Amesbury Crescent, Hove, East Sussex BN3 5RD. Furthering interest in the life and works of J. R. R. Tolkien. Publ.: Newsletter.

Translators' Association: 84 Drayton Gdns, London SW10 9SB. Tel. (20) 7373-6642. Fax (20) 7373-5768. E-mail: info@societyofauthors.org. Website: www.societyofauthors.org. Subsidiary group within the Society of Authors dealing exclusively with literary translators into the English language.

Welsh Academy: Third Floor, Mount Stuart House, Mount Stuart Sq., Cardiff CF1 6DQ, Wales. Tel. (29) 2047-2266. Fax (29) 2049-2930. E-mail: post@academi.org. Website: www.academi.org. English language section of Yr Academi Gymreig, the national society of Welsh writers. Promotes Anglo-Welsh literature through readings, conferences, workshops, schools and projects. Organizes the Cardiff Literature Festival. Publs: newsletter and numerous guides and reviews.

Welsh Book Council (Cyngor Llyfrau Cymru): Castell Brychan, Aberystwyth, Ceredigion SY23 2JB. Tel. (1970) 624151. Website: www.cllc.org.uk. Provides a focus for the publishing industry in Wales and distributes grants for books of Welsh interest in both Welsh and English.

Welsh Union of Writers: 13 Richmond Rd, Roath, Cardiff CF2 3AQ. Independent union for published Welsh writers.

West Country Writers' Association: 1 Moreton Ave, Crownhill, Plymouth, Devon PL6 5AZ.

Women in Publishing: c/o The Bookseller, 12 Dyott St, London WC1A 1DF. Promotes the status of women in the publishing industry through networking, meetings and training. Publ.: monthly newsletter.

Women Writers Network: 23 Prospect Rd, London NW2 2JU. Provides and exchanges information, support and opportunities for working writers. Arranges functions. Publ.: newsletter.

Writer's Guild of Great Britain: 15 Britannia St, London WC1X 9JN. Represents professional writers in film, radio, television, theatre and publishing. Regularly provides assistance to members on items such as contracts and conditions of work.

Writers in Exile PEN Centre: London Branch, 10 Melfort Dr., Leighton Buzzard, Bedfordshire LU7 2XN.

Yachting Journalists Association: Spinneys, Woodham Mortimer, Maldon, Essex CM9 6SX. Promotes the awareness of all forms of leisure boating activities via the written and spoken word, and offers support to journalists in the field.

Yr Academi Gymreig: Third Floor, Mount Stuart House, Mount Stuart Sq., Cardiff CF1 6DQ, Wales. Tel. (29) 2047-2266. Fax (29) 2049-2930. E-mail: post@academi.org. Website: www.academi.org. National society of Welsh writers. Encourages writing in the Welsh language. Organizes readings, conferences and literary events. Publs: books on Welsh literature, an English/Welsh dictionary, Taliesin magazine.

UNITED STATES OF AMERICA

American Academy of Arts and Letters: 633 W 155th St, New York, NY 10032, USA.

American Library Association: 50 E Huron, Chicago, IL 60611. Provides leadership for the development, promotion and improvement of library and information services to enhance learning.

American Literary Translators' Association: PO Box 830688, University of Texas, Richardson, TX 75083. Sponsors the biennial Gregory Rabassa Prize for the translation of fiction from any language into English and the Richard Wilbur Prize for the translation of poetry from any language into English.

American Society of Business Press Editors: PO Box 390653, Cambridge, MA 0213.

American Society of Composers, Authors and Publishers—ASCAP: 1 Lincoln Plaza, New York, NY 10023. Performing rights society.

American Society of Journalists and Authors Inc (ASJA): 1501 Bdwy, Suite 302, New York, NY 10036. Website: www.asja.org. Service organization providing exchange of ideas and market information. Regular meetings with speakers from the industry. Annual writers conference. Medical plans available. Professional referral service, annual membership directory. First amendment advocacy group.

American Society of Newspaper Editors—ASNE: 11690B Sunrise Valley Dr., Reston, VA 20191-1409. Tel. (703) 453-1122. Fax (703) 453-1133. E-mail: asne@asne.org. Website: www.asne.org. Exec. Dir: Scott Bosley.

Asociación Internacional de Escritores Policiacos—AIEP (International Asscn of Crime Writers Inc): North American Branch. E-mail: jeremiahealy@earthlink.net. Website: jmc.ou.edu/AIEP/index.htm. f. 1986 by Paco Taibo II (Mexico) and the late Julian Semionov (Russia), has members in 22 countries. Sponsors the Hammett Awards. Pres.: Jeremiah Healy.

Associated Writing Programs: George Mason University, Tallwood House, Mail Stop 1E3, Fairfax, VA 22030. National, non-profit organization of writers and writers who teach writing.

Association of Authors' Representatives Inc: PO Box 237201, Ansonia Station, New York, NY 10003. E-mail: aarinc@mindspring.com. Website: www.aar-online.org. Represents the interests of professional literary and dramatic agents.

Association of Literary Scholars and Critics: 2039 Shattuck Ave, Suite 202, Berkeley, CA 94704. Professional society open to all individuals pursuing the study of literature.

Authors' Guild: 330 W 42nd St, 29th Floor, New York, NY 10036.

Authors League of America: 330 W 42nd St, 29th Floor, New York, NY 10036. Promotes the interests of authors and dramatists.

Authors Registry: 31 E 28th St, 10th Floor, New York, NY 10016. Tel. (212) 563-6920. Fax (212) 564-5363. Website: www.authorsregistry.org.

Broad Universe: c/o 1121 E Vienna Avenue, Milwaukee, WI 53212. E-mail: info@broaduniverse.org. Website: www.broaduniverse.org. International organization that promotes science fiction, fantasy and horror written by women. Publ.: The Broadsheet.

Brooklyn Writers' Network: 2509 Ave K, Brooklyn, NY 11210. Seeks to improve contact between professional writers and publishing industry. Organizes conferences and workshops. Publs: newsletter, directory.

Catholic Library Association: 100 North St, Suite 224, Pittsfield, MA 01201-5109. Tel. (413) 443-2252. Fax (413) 442-2252. E-mail: cla2@cathla.org. Website: www.cathla.org. Organization of professional librarians interested in providing service according to the Catholic philosophy. Exec. Dir: Jean R. Bostley.

Children's Literature Association: PO Box 138, Battle Creek, MI 49016. Website: www.childlitassn.org. Promotes serious scholarship and criticism in the field of children's literature.

Chinese Writers Abroad PEN Centre: 533 48th St, Brooklyn, NY 11220.

Council of Literary Magazines and Presses: 154 Christopher St, Suite 3C, New York, NY 10014. Membership restricted to non-commercial literary magazines and presses.

Council of Writers' Organizations: 12 724 Sagamore Rd, Leawood, KS 66209. Communications network for 15 writing groups.

Cuban Writers in Exile PEN Centre: PO Box 347693, Miracle Mile, Coral Gables, FL 33234-7693. E-mail: amecast@aol.com.

Dramatists' Guild: 1501 Bdwy, Suite 701, New York, NY 10036. Promotes the interests of dramatists, lyricists and composers.

Education Writers' Association—EWA: 2122 P St NW, Suite 201, Washington, DC 20037. Tel. (202) 452-9830. Fax (202) 452-9837. E-mail: ewa@ewa.org. Website: www.ewa.org. Exec. Dir: Lisa J. Walker.

Horror Writers Association: PO Box 50577, Palo Alto, CA 94303. E-mail: hwa@horror.org. Website: www.horror.org. Promotes horror and dark fantasy writing.

International Black Writers and Artists Inc: PO Box 437134, Chicago, IL 60643-7134. Poetry readings, contests, workshops, annual conferences and writers' picnic.

International Reading Association: 800 Barksdale Rd, PO Box 8139, Newark, DE 19714. Professional education association dedicated to the improvement of reading ability and development of the reading habit worldwide through publications, research, meetings, conferences and international congresses.

International Women's Writing Guild: PO Box 810, Gracie Station, New York, NY 10028. Tel. (212) 737-7536. Fax (212) 737-9469. E-mail: iwwg@iwwg.org. Website: www.iwwg.org. Network for the empowerment of women through writing. Services include manuscript referral and exchange, writing conferences and retreats, group rates for health and life insurance, legal aid, regional clusters and contacts to literary agents, publishers and other literary services. Founder, Exec. Dir: Hannelore Hahn.

The MacDowell Colony: 100 High Street, Peterborough, NH 03458. Tel. (603) 924-3886. Fax (603) 924-9142. E-mail: info@macdowellcolony.org. Website: www.macdowellcolony.org. f. 1907 to provide creative artists with uninterrupted time and seclusion to work and enjoy the experience of living in a community of gifted artists. Residencies of up to eight weeks are available for writers, composers, film/video artists, visual artists, architects and interdisciplinary artists. Artists in residence receive room, board and exclusive use of a studio. Talent is the sole criterion for acceptance to the MacDowell Colony. Established artists as well as emerging artists are encouraged to apply. Committees of distinguished specialists donate their time to judge applications, which include work samples, references and a brief project description. There are no residency fees. Grants for travel to and from the Colony are available based on need. Financial aid for writers is available through a special grant from a foundation. An aid application will be mailed following acceptance. Deadlines for application are 15 Jan. (summer, May–Aug.), 15 April (autumn/winter, Sept.–Dec.), 15 Sept. (winter/spring, Jan.–April).

Ingram Merrill Foundation: 104 E 40th St, Suite 302, New York, NY 10016, USA.

Mystery Writers of America Inc: 17 E 47th St, Sixth Floor, New York, NY 10017. Website: www.mysterywriters.org. Supports and promotes the mystery. Sponsors the Edgar Allan Poe Awards.

National Alliance of Short Story Authors: 7505 SW 82nd St, Suite 222, Miami, FL 33143.

National Association of Science Writers: PO Box 890, Hedgesville, WV 25427-0890.

National Book Critics Circle: 360 Park Ave S, New York, NY 10010. Website: www.bookcritics.org. Gives annual awards for fiction, poetry, biography/autobiography, general non-fiction and criticism. Raises the standards of book criticism and enhances public appreciation of literature.

National Endowment for the Humanities: Public Information Office, 1100 Pennsylvania Ave NW, Room 406, Washington, DC 20506.

National League of American Pen Women: Pen Arts Bldg: 1300 17th St NW, Washington, DC 20036.

National Press Club: 529 14th St NW, Washington, DC 20045.

National Writers Association: 3140 S Peoria Street, Suite 295PMB, Aurora, CO 80014. Tel. (303) 841-0246. Fax (303) 841-2607. Website: www.nationalwriters.com. Association for freelance writers.

National Writers' Union: 113 University Pl., Sixth Floor, New York, NY 10003. Website: www.nwu.org. Union for the promotion of the interests of freelance writers.

Novelists, Inc: PO Box 1166, Mission, KS 66222-0166. E-mail: info@ninc.com. Website: www.ninc.com. f. 1989 to serve the needs of multi-published writers of popular fiction.

Outdoor Writers Association of America—OWAA: 121 Hickory St, Suite 1, Missoula, MT 59801. Tel. (406) 728-7434. Fax (406) 728-7445. Website: www.owaa.org. Professional authors, journalists, broadcasters, photographers and artists who cover hunting, fishing, camping, canoeing and similar outdoor sports. Workshops held at annual conference.

PEN American Center: 568 Bdwy, New York, NY 10012-3225. Tel. (212) 334-1660. Fax (212) 334-2181. E-mail: pen@pen.org. Website: www.pen.org. International organization of writers, poets, playwrights, essayists, editors, novelists and translators whose purpose is to bring about better understanding among writers of all nations. Sec.: Michael Roberts.

PEN Center USA West: 672 S Lafayette Park Pl., Suite 42, Los Angeles, CA 90057. Tel. (213) 365-8500. Fax (213) 365-9616. E-mail: pen@penusa.org. Website: www.penusa.org.

Poets and Writers Inc: 72 Spring St, New York, NY 10012. National non-profit information centre for those interested in contemporary American literature. Sponsors readings and workshops programme. Publ.: directory of American poets and fiction writers.

Readerville.com: E-mail: karen_templer@readerville.com. Website: www.readerville.com. Internet magazine and discussion forum, f. 2000. Founder & Editor-in-Chief Karen Templer.

Theodore Roethke Memorial Foundation: 11 W Hannum Blvd, Saginaw, MI 48602. Awards triennial poetry prize.

Romance Writers of America: 13700 Veterans Memorial Dr., Suite 315, Houston, TX 77014. Website: www.rwanational.org. Promotes the interests of writers of romance fiction.

Science Fiction and Fantasy Writers of America Inc: PO Box 877, Chestertown, MD 21620. Fax (410) 778-3052. E-mail: execdir@sfwa.org. Website: www.sfwa.org.

Science Fiction Research Association Inc: 6021 Grassmere, Corpus Christi, TX 78415. Professional study of science fiction and fantasy. Annual scholar award. Archives maintained at University of Kansas, Lawrence. Sponsors workshop awards and prizes.

Sisters in Crime: PO Box 442124, Lawrence, KS 06044-8933. Tel. (785) 842-1325. Fax (785) 842-1034. E-mail: sistersincrime@juno.com. Website: www.sistersincrime.org. Membership Sec.: Beth Wasson. International organization promoting the work of female mystery writers.

Society of American Business Editors and Writers: 120 Neff Hall, School of Journalism, University of Missouri, Columbia, MO 65211. Professional society representing the interests of business editors and writers in both print and broadcast medias.

Society of Children's Book Writers and Illustrators: 8271 Beverly Blvd, Los Angeles, CA 90048. Tel. (323) 782-1010. Fax (323) 782-1892. E-mail: scbwi@scbwi.org. Website: www.scbwi.org. Professional society promoting the interests of children's book writers and illustrators.

Society of Midland Authors: 29 E Division St, Chicago, IL 60610. Promotes friendly contact and professional interchange among authors of the Midland, explores topics of literary and professional interest in open monthly programmes, and honours the best of Midland writing with cash awards annually.

Society of Professional Journalists: Eugene S. Pulliam National Journalism Center, 3909 N Meridian St, Indianapolis, IN 46208. Tel. (317) 927-8000. Fax (317) 920-4789. E-mail: questions@spj.org. Website: www.spj.org.

Society of Southwestern Authors: PO Box 30355, Tucson, AZ 85751. Organization of writers for supportive fellowship, recognition of member writers' professional achievement, and encouragement and assistance for persons striving to become writers.

Teachers' and Writers' Collaborative: 5 Union Sq. W, New York, NY 10003. Sends professional artists into public schools to teach their art forms. Publs: books and a magazine about how to teach creative writing.

Text and Academic Authors Association: PO Box 76477, St Petersburg, FL 33734-6477. Tel. (727) 821-7277. Fax (727) 821-7271. E-mail: TEXT@tampabay.rr.com. Website: www.taaonline.net. Pres.: Michael Sullivan.

Translation Center: 412 Dodge Hall, Columbia University, New York, NY 10027. Dedicated to finding and publishing the best translations of significant works of foreign contemporary literature. Publ.: bi-annual magazine.

Vietnamese Writers Abroad: 13322 Sioux Rd, Westminster, CA 92683. E-mail: qnguyen4@aol.com.

Washington Independent Writers: 733 15th St NW, Suite 220, Washington, DC 20005.

Western Writers of America: Secretary-Treasurer James Crutchfield, 1012 Fair St, Franklin, TN 37064. Website: www.westernwriters.org. f. 1953. Organization of professionals dedicated to the spirit and reality of the West, past and present. Pres.: Paul Andrew Hutton.

West USA PEN Centre: 672 S Lafayette Park Pl., Suite 41, Los Angeles, CA 90057. E-mail: pen@pen-usa-west.org. Website: www.pen-usa-west.org.

World Academy of Arts and Culture: c/o Sheldon Chen, Treasurer, 10 Bertie Minor Lane, #6, San Francisco, CA 94115. Holds the World Congress of Poets. Sec.-Gen.: Maurus Young.

Writers in Exile PEN Centre: American Branch, 42 Derby Ave, Orange, CT 06477. E-mail: gyorgyey@aol.com. Affiliated with International PEN to help fight for freedom of expression for writers.

Writers' Guild of America East: 555 W 57th St, New York, NY 10019. Website: www.wgae.org. Labour union representing professional writers in films, television and radio. Membership available only through the sale of literary material or employment for writing services in one of these areas.

Writers' Guild of America West: 7000 W Third St, Los Angeles, CA 90048. Website: www.wga.org. Represents its membership in contract negotiation and compliance with the film and television industry.

Yiddish PEN Centre: 3338 Bainbridge Ave, Bronx, NY 10467.

VENEZUELA

Venezuelan PEN Centre: 10° Transversal con 7° Avda, Residencias Villa Inés, 3°, Altamira, Caracas.

ZIMBABWE

Zimbabwe PEN Centre: 10 Ashburton Ave, Chadcombe, Harare.

APPENDIX C: LITERARY AGENTS

The following list of agents does not claim to be exhaustive although every effort has been made to make it as comprehensive as possible. In all instances, authors are advised to send preliminary letters to agents before submitting manuscripts.

AUSTRALIA

Australian Literary Management: 2A Booth St, Balmain, NSW 2041. Represents Australian writers in fields of fiction, non-fiction, children's books, theatre and film. Handles Australian/New Zealand rights only for a small number of American writers in conjunction with other literary agents.

Curtis Brown Pty: PO Box 19, Paddington, NSW 2021. Tel. (2) 9360-3935. Fax (2) 9331-5301. E-mail: info@curtisbrown.com.au. Represents fiction, non-fiction, children's writers, television, screen, radio and stage. Also represents directors.

Rick Raftos Management Pty Ltd: PO Box 445, Paddington, Sydney, NSW 2021. Tel. (2) 9281-9622. Fax (2) 9212-7100. E-mail: raftos@raftos.com.au. Represents writers; television, screen, radio, stage and publication; also represents directors.

Anthony Williams Management Pty Ltd: PO Box 1379, Darlinghurst NSW 1300.

BELGIUM

Toneelfonds J. Janssens: Te Boelaerlei 107, 2140 Antwerp. Literary agency specializing in plays.

BRAZIL

Karin Schindler Rights Representative: PO Box 19051, 04599-970 São Paulo SP. Tel. (11) 5041-9177. Fax (11) 5041-9077. E-mail: kschind@terra .com.br. Handles the sale of Portuguese language rights in Brazil.

BULGARIA

Bulgarian Copyright Agency JUSAUTOR: 17 Ernst Telman Blvd, 1463 Sofia. Representative of Bulgarian authors, promoting work for publication and performance abroad.

CANADA

Acacia House Publishing Services Ltd: 51 Acacia Rd, Toronto, ON M4S 2K6.

Bella Pomer Agency Inc: 22 Shallmar Blvd, PH2, Toronto, ON M5N 2Z8. International representation for full-length fiction and non-fiction. No unsolicited manuscripts. No longer accepting new clients.

Bukowski Agency: 14 Prince Arthur Ave, Suite 202, Toronto, ON M5R 1A9. Tel. (416) 928-6728. Fax (416) 963-9978. E-mail: info@thebukowskiagency .com. Website: www.thebukowskiagency.com.

MGA/Sterling Lord Association Canada: 10 St Mary St, Suite 510, Toronto, ON M4Y 1P.

Lucinda Vardley Agency Ltd: 297 Seaton St, Toronto, ON M5A 2T.

DENMARK

Leonhardt & Høier Literary Agency aps: Studiestraede 35, 1455 Copenhagen K. Tel. (45) 3313-2523. Fax (45) 3313-4992. E-mail: anneli@leonhardt-hoier.dk. Handles trans. rights, representing international authors in Scandinavia, and Scandinavian authors world-wide. Dir: Anneli Høier.

Ulla Lohren Literary Agency: Vaerebrovej 89, 2880 Bagsvaerd. Tel. 4449-4515. Fax 4449-3515. E-mail: ulla.litag@get2net.dk. Represents agents and publishers from Canada, the UK, the USA and others for Scandinavian rights in fiction, non-fiction and children's books.

FRANCE

Eliane Benisti Agency: 80 rue des Saints-Peres, 75007 Paris. Tel. 1 42 22 85 33. Fax 1 45 44 18 17. E-mail: benisti@compuserve.com.

Françoise Germain: 8 rue de la Paix, 75002 Paris. Representation of French and foreign authors.

La Nouvelle Agence: 7 rue Corneille, 75006 Paris. Representation in France for US, English, Italian and German agents and publishers, as well as French authors.

Michelle Lapautre Literary Agency: 6 rue Jean Carries, 75007 Paris. Represents English-language publishers, agents and authors for the sale of French translation rights.

Shelley Power Literary Agency Ltd: 13 rue du Pré Saint Gervais, 75019 Paris. Tel. 1 42 38 36 49. Fax 1 40 40 70 08. E-mail: shelley.power@wanadoo.fr. General fiction and non-fiction. Offers world-wide representation.

GERMANY

Buro für Urheberrechte, Copyright Office, Copyright Information Centre: Clara-Zetkin-Str 105 Berlin.

Fralit Medium Agency: Brahmsallee 29, 2000 Hamburg 13. Manuscripts for newspapers and book publishers, plays and features for theatre, broadcasting, television and film.

GPA Gerd Plesel Agentur and Veriags GmbH: Linprunstr 38, 8000 Munich 2. Represents publishers and literary agencies from the English language world in general and selected ones from French and German. Major American and British studios for ancilliary rights.

Hans Hermann Hagedorn: Erikastr 142, 2000 Hamburg 20.

Thomas Schluck Literary Agency: Hinter der Worth 12, 30827 Garbsen. Tel. (5131) 497562. Fax (5131) 497589. E-mail: t.schlueck@schlueckagent.de.

Skandinavia Verlag, Marianne Weno–Michael Günther: Ithweg 31, 1000 Berlin 37. Represents contemporary Scandinavian playwrights. Handles plays for radio, stage and television.

GREECE

Read n' Right Agency: 9 Amazonon St, 341 00 Chalkida. Tel. (221) 29798. Fax (221) 27423. E-mail: readrght@internet.gr.

INDIA

Ajanta Books International: IUB Jawahar Nagar, Bungalow Rd, Delhi 110007. Research work on social sciences and humanities, especially on Indian themes, oriental or modern.

ISRAEL

The Harris/Elon Agency: 3 Asa St, PO Box 8528, Jerusalem 91083. Tel. (2) 561-7191. Fax (2) 561-7194. E-mail: litagent@netvision.net.il.

Rogan-Pikarski Literary Agency: 200 Hayarkon St, PO Box 4006, 61 040 Tel-Aviv. Represents major US and European publishers and agents for Hebrew volumes, serials and performance and merchandising rights. Also has New York agency.

ITALY

Agenzia Letteraria Internazionale: Via Valpetrosa 1, 20123 Milan. Represents Italian authors in Italy and world-wide, and American, English and German publishers and agencies exclusively in Italy.

Luigi Bernabo & Associates SRL: via Bianca di Savoia 4, 20122 Milan. Tel. (2) 5830-6332. Fax (2) 5830-6312. E-mail: bernabo.luigi@newtech.it.

Natoli, Stefan & Oliva: Roberta Oliva Italian Agent, Corso Plebisciti 12, 20129 Milan. Tel. (2) 7000-1645. E-mail: natoli.oliva@tiscalinet.it. Represents fiction and non-fiction authors'. Rights, co-editions and translations.

JAPAN

Owl's Agency Inc: N2-092, 12-7 Gobancho, Chiyoda-ku, Tokyo 102-0075. Tel. (3) 3512-7550. Fax (3) 3512-7551. E-mail: kohei@owlsagency.com.

Tuttle-Mori Agency: Fuji Bldg, Eighth Floor, 2-15 Kanda Jimbocho, Chiyoda-ku, Tokyo 101. Literary agency for foreign rights in Japan.

REPUBLIC OF KOREA

Korean Copyright Center Inc—KCC: Gyonghigung-achim, Officetel Rm 520, Compound 3, Naesu-dong 72, Chongno, Seoul 110-070. Tel. (2) 725-3350. Fax (2) 725-3612. E-mail: drtkcc@chollian.net.

NETHERLANDS

Auteursbureau Greta Baars Jelgersma: Beau Rivage, Maasstaete 40, 6585 CB MOOK. Tel. (24) 696-3336. Fax (24) 696-3293. Represents authors and publishers, and translations from Scandinavian and other modern languages. International co-printing of illustrated books and arranges profitable offers for book production.

Caroline Van Gelderen Literary Agency: Bachlaan 34, 1217 BX Hilversum. Tel. (35) 6241336. Fax (35) 6232740. E-mail: cvangelderen@carvang.nl.

PORTUGAL

Ilidio da Fonseca Matos Literary Agency: Avda Gomes Pereira, 105 3° B, 1500-328 Lisbon. Represents Curtis Brown Ltd, Pollinger Ltd, The New American Library, Doubleday and Co Inc, Rowholt Verlag—Diogenes Verlag, Harvard Univ. Press, Princeton Univ. Press, Inner Traditions, Montreal Contacts, Simon & Schuster in Portugal.

RUSSIA

Synopsis Literary Agency: PO Box 47, Moscow 103045. Tel. (95) 921-2170. E-mail: fontanka@mail.sitek.ru.

SERBIA AND MONTENEGRO

Prava i Prevodi Permissions & Rights: Koste Jovanovica 18, 11000 Belgrade. Tel. (11) 460-290. Fax (11) 472-146. E-mail: ana@pip.co.yu.

SPAIN

Andres de Kramer: Castello 30, 28001 Madrid. Handles only foreign writers and foreign rights of theatrical plays and production in Spain.

Bookbank, SA: San Martín de Porres 14, 28035 Madrid. Tel. (91) 373-3539. Fax (91) 316-5591. E-mail: bookbank@telcom.es. Represents foreign publishers, agents and writers for the sale of Spanish and Portuguese language rights. Represents Spanish language authors. Contact: Alicia González Sterling.

Raquel de la Concha Agencia Literaria SL: c/ Fernando VI, no 15, 3° derecha, 28004 Madrid. Tel. (91) 308-5585. Fax (91) 308-5600. E-mail: rdc@idecnet.com.

Julio F-Yañez Agencia Literaria, SL: Via Augusta 139, 6° 2a, 08021 Barcelona. Tel. (93) 200-7107. Fax (93) 209-4875. E-mail: yanezag@retemail.es. Represents publishers, agencies and independent authors from all countries, and Spanish authors abroad. Covers Spain, Latin America, Portugal and Brazil.

Ute Korner de Moya Literary Agency: Ronda Guinardo 32-5-5, 08025 Barcelona. Represents foreign publishers, agents and authors in the Spanish and Portuguese speaking countries.

SWEDEN

D. Richard Bowen: PO Box 30037, 200 61 Malmö 30. Publishers' literary and sales agent, translation rights negotiated.

Lennart Sane Agency AB: Hollandareplan, 537434 Karlshamn. Represents US, British and Scandinavian authors, publishers and agencies for translation rights in Europe and Latin America.

Monica Heyum Literary Agency: PO Box 3300 Vendelso, 13603 Haninge. Handles fiction, non-fiction and children's books.

SWITZERLAND

Dieter Breitsohl AG Literarische Agentur: Heimatstrasse 25, PO Box 245, 8034 Zürich. Handles non-fiction, psychology, psychosomatic, religion, theology and mythology.

Liepman AG: Maienburgweg 23, 8044 Zürich. Tel. (044) 261-7660. Fax (044) 261-0124. Represents US, British, Canadian, French, Dutch and Israeli publishers and agents for the German language rights, and authors directly for world rights.

New Press Agency Society—NPA: Haus am Herterberg, Haldenstr 5, 8500 Frauenfeld Herten.

Paul & Peter Fritz AG Literary Agency: PO Box 1773, Jupiterstr 1, 8032 Zürich. Tel. (1) 388-4140. Fax (1) 388-4130. E-mail: info@fritzagency.com. Website: www.fritzagency.com. Represents English language authors for the German language rights and authors world-wide. No unsolicited manuscripts.

TAIWAN

Bardon-Chinese Media Agency: 3F, No. 1-1 Hsin-Hai Rd, Sec. 1, Taipei 10718. Tel. (2) 3655753. Fax (2) 3658148. E-mail: bardon@ms12.hinet.net. Contact: Ming-Ming Lui.

TURKEY

Nurcihan Kesim Literary Agency, Inc: PO Box 868, Sirkeci, Istanbul. Tel. (212) 528-5797. Fax (212) 528-5791. E-mail: kesim@superonline.com.

UNITED KINGDOM

Jacintha Alexander Associates: 47 Emperor's Gate, London SW7 4HJ. Handles full-length general and literary fiction and non-fiction of all kinds. Film and television scripts handled for established clients only.

Blake Friedmann Literary Agency: 122 Arlington Rd, London NW1 7HP. Tel. (20) 7284-0408. Fax (20) 7284-0442. E-mail: anyone@blakefriedmann.co.uk. Website: www.blakefriedmann.co.uk. Contact: Carole Blake, Julian Friedmann, Barbara Jones, Conrad Williams. World-wide representation of fiction and non-fiction, television and film rights and scripts.

Alan Brodie Representation: 211 Piccadilly, London W1J 9HF. Tel. (20) 7917-2871. Fax (20) 7917-2872.

Campbell Thomson and McLaughlin Ltd: 1 King's Mews, London WC1N 2JA. Handles book-length manuscripts excluding children's, science fiction and fantasy; short stories from existing clients only.

Casarotto Ramsay Ltd: National House, 60–66 Wardour St, London W1V 3HP. Handles scripts for television, theatre, film and radio. General fiction and non-fiction.

Jonathan Clowes Ltd: 10 Iron Bridge House, Bridge Approach, London NW1 8BD. Fiction and non-fiction, scripts.

Elspeth Cochrane Agency: 11–13 Orlando Rd, London SW4 0LE. Authors handled for theatre, films, and television. Books for all types of publication.

Rosica Colin Ltd: 1 Clareville Grove Mews, London SW7 5AH. All full-length manuscripts including theatre, films, television and sound broadcasting works in the USA, Europe and overseas.

Rupert Crew Ltd: 1A King's Mews, London WC1N 2JA. Representation offered to limited clientele, specializing in promoting major book projects: non-fiction, general and women's fiction.

Curtis Brown Ltd: Haymarket House, 28–29 Haymarket, London SW1Y 4SP. Tel. (20) 7393-4400. Fax (20) 7393-4401. E-mail: info@curtisbrown.co.uk. Website: www.curtisbrown.co.uk. f. 1899. Handles a wide range of subjects including fiction, general non-fiction, children's and specialist scripts for film, television, theatre and radio.

Felix de Wolfe: Manfield House, 376–378 The Strand, London WC2R 0LR. Handles quality fiction and scripts. No unsolicited manuscripts.

57 Productions: 57 Effingham Rd, Lee Green, London SE12 8NT. Tel. (20) 8463-0866. Fax (20) 8463-0866. E-mail: paul57prods@yahoo.co.uk. Website: www.57productions.com. Specializes in the promotion of poetry. Organizes programme of events and series of audio publications.

Eric Glass Ltd: 25 Ladbroke Cres., London W11 1PS. Books, plays, screenplays and television plays. Agents for the Sociétè des Auteurs et Compositeurs Dramatiques of Paris for the English speaking countries.

David Godwin Associates: 55 Monmouth St, London WC2H 9DG. Tel. (20) 7240-9992. Fax (20) 7395-6110. Website: www.davidgodwinassociates.co.uk.

Greene & Heaton Ltd: 37 Goldhawk Rd, London W12 8QQ. Tel. (20) 8749-0315. Fax (20) 8749-0318. Handles novels, quality non-fiction and journalists' books.

David Grossman Literary Agency Ltd: 118b Holland Park Ave, London W11 4UA. Fiction and general non-fiction.

A. M. Heath & Co Ltd: 79 St Martin's Lane, London WC2N 4RE. Tel. (20) 7836-4271. Fax (20) 7497-2561. Website: www.amheath.com. Handles fiction, general non-fiction and children's books (no dramatic scripts, poetry or short stories. Contacts: Bill Hamilton, Sara Fisher, Sarah Molloy, Victoria Hobbs.

David Higham Associates: 5–8 Lower John St, Golden Sq., London W1F 9HA. Tel. (20) 7434-5900. Fax (20) 7437-1072. E-mail: dha@davidhigham.co.uk. Website: www.davidhigham.co.uk. f. 1935. Represents professional authors and writers in all fields throughout the world.

Johnson & Alcock Ltd: Clerkenwell House, 45–47 Clerkenwell Green, London EC1R 0HT. Tel. (20) 7251-0125. Fax (20) 7251-2172.

MBA Literary Agents Ltd: 62 Grafton Way, London W1T 5DW. Tel. (20) 7387-2076. Fax (20) 7387-2042. Represents writers. Handles fiction and non-fiction, scripts for film, television, radio and theatre.

William Morris Agency (UK) Ltd: 52–53 Poland St, London W1F 7LX. Website: www.wma.com. Scripts handled for theatre, film, television and radio; fiction and general non-fiction.

Peake Associates: 14 Grafton Cres., London NW1 8SL. Tel. (20) 7267-8033. Fax (20) 7284-1876. E-mail: peakeassoc@aol.com. Website: www.tonypeake.com.

Penman Literary Agency: 175 Pall Mall, Leigh-on-Sea, Essex SS9 1RE. Full-length novel manuscripts; theatre, films, television and sound broadcasting.

PFD—Peters Fraser & Dunlop: Drury House, 34–43 Russell St, London WC2B 5HA. Tel. (20) 7344-1000. Fax (20) 7836-9539. E-mail: postmaster@pfd.co.uk. Website: www.pfd.co.uk. f. 1924 as A. D. Peters, changed name to PFD, 1999. Agents for stage drama, television plays and series, radio drama, fiction and non-fiction and children's books. Representation for producers and directors of stage, television and film.

Charles Pick Consultancy Ltd: 21 Dagmar Terrace, London N1 2BN. Tel. (20) 8246-5637. Fax (20) 8246-5637. E-mail: martincpick@cs.com.

Pollinger Ltd: Third Floor, Goldsmiths' House, 137–141 Regent St, London W1B 4HZ. Tel. (20) 7025-7820. Fax (20) 7025-7829. E-mail: info@pollingerltd.com. Website: www.pollingerltd.com. Authors' agents for all material with the exception of original film stories, poetry and freelance journalistic articles.

Rogers, Coleridge & White Ltd: 20 Powis Mews, London W11 1JN. Handles fiction, non-fiction and children's books.

The Sayle Literary Agency: Bickerton House, 25–27 Bickerton Road, London, N19 5JT. Tel. (20) 7263-8681. Fax (20) 7561-0529. Proprietor: Rachel Calder. Handles fiction (crime and general), non-fiction, including current affairs, social issues, travel, biographies and historical. No plays, poetry, children's books, textbooks, technical, legal or medical books. Preliminary letter essential, including a brief biographical note and a synopsis, plus two or three sample chapters. Return postage essential. No reading fee.

Shiel Land Associates Ltd: 43 Doughty St, London WC1N 2LF. Represents literary authors. Represents world-wide including translation, film, television and theatre.

Abner Stein Agency: 10 Roland Gdns, London SW7 3PH. Tel. (20) 7373-0456. Fax (20) 7370-6316. E-mail: firstname@abnerstein.co.uk.

Tricia Sumner Agency: 32 Orchard Gdns, Waltham Abbey, Essex EN9 1RS.

Talent Media Group: Oxford House, 76 Oxford St, London W1D 1BS. fmrly ICM.

Peter Tauber Press Agency: 94 East End Rd, London N3 2SX. Full representation, specializing in well-researched epic women's saga fiction.

The Agency: 24 Pottery Lane, Holland Park, London W11 4LZ.

Ed Victor Ltd: 6 Bayley St, Bedford Sq., London WC1B 3HB. Tel. (20) 7304-4100. Fax (20) 7304-4111. Commercial fiction and non-fiction.

Wade & Doherty Literary Agency: 33 Cormorant Lodge, Thomas More Street, London, E1W 1AU. Tel. (20) 7488-4171. Fax (20) 7488-4172. Website: www.rwla.com. Principal: Robin Wade. Partner: Ms Broo Doherty. f. 2001 as Robin Wade Literary Agency; changed name as above in 2004.

Watkins Loomis Agency Inc: 133 E 35th St, Suite 1, New York, NY 10016. Tel. (212) 532-0080. Fax (212) 889-0506.

Watson Little Ltd: 12 Egbert St, London NW1 8LJ. Represents wide range of fiction and non-fiction.

AP Watt Ltd: 20 John St, London WC1N 2DR. Tel. (20) 7405-6774. Fax (20) 7831-2154. E-Mail: apw@apwatt.co.uk. Website: www.apwatt.co.uk. Full-length works for all media, including plays and telescripts. Representation throughout the world.

The Wylie Agency: 4–8 Rodney St, London N1 9JH.

UNITED STATES OF AMERICA

Carole Abel Literary Agent: 160 W 87th St, New York, NY 10024. Handles trade and mass market fiction and non-fiction books. No unsolicited manuscripts. Agents in Hollywood and most foreign countries.

Dominick Abel Literary Agency Inc: 146 W 82nd St, Suite 1B, New York, NY 10024.

Acton, Dystel, Leone and Jaffe: 928 Bdwy, Suite 303, New York, NY 10010. Non-fiction and novels.

Marcia Amsterdam Agency: 41 W 82nd St, New York, NY 10024. Handles adult and young adult fiction, film and television rights, screenplays and teleplays.

Artists' Agency: 10000 Santa Monica Blvd, Suite 305, Los Angeles, CA 90067. Represents novels and screenplays for films.

Julian Bach Literary Agency Inc: 22 E 71st St, New York, NY 10021. Agents for fiction and non-fiction.

Barbara Bauer Literary Agency: 179 Washington Ave, Matawan, NJ 07747. Specializes in new and unpublished authors, quality fiction and non-fiction for children and adults.

Bethel Agency: 641 W 59th St, New York, NY 10019. Handles fiction and non-fiction, plays for theatre, film and television. Sub-division handles children's books.

Blake Group Literary Agency: 1 Turtle Creek Village, Suite 600, 3878 Oaklawn, Dallas, TX 75219. Represents limited number of published and unpublished authors. Handles fiction, non-fiction, plays and poetry, periodicals, publishers and producers.

Brandt & Hochman Literary Agents Inc: 1501 Broadway, New York, NY 10036. Handles fiction and non-fiction. No unsolicited manuscripts. Agents in most foreign countries.

Catalog Literary Agency: PO Box 2964, Vancouver, WA 98668.

Columbia Literary Associates Inc: 7902 Nottingham Way, Ellicott City, MD 21043.

Connor Literary Agency: 2911 W 71st St, Minneapolis, MN 55423, USA. Tel. (612) 866-1426. Fax (612) 869-4074. E-mail: coolmkc@aol.com.

Creative Concepts Literary Agency: 5538 Herford, Troy, MI 48098.

Curtis Brown Ltd: 10 Astor Pl., Third Floor, New York, NY 10003. Handles fiction, non-fiction, science fiction, mystery and romance, children's fiction, non-fiction and theatrical, film and television. Handles general trade fiction, non-fiction, juvenile and film and television rights. Representatives in many countries. No unsolicited manuscripts.

Sandra Dijkstra Literary Agency: 1155 Camino Del Mar, Del Mar, CA 92014. Handles quality and commercial adult fiction and non-fiction. Represents major publishers in USA. British rights. Translations.

Jonathan Dolger Agency: 49 E 96th St, Suite 9B, New York, NY 10128. Handles adult fiction and non-fiction, and illustrated books. No unsolicited material.

Donadio and Ashworth Inc, Literary Representatives: 231 W 22nd St, New York, NY 10011.

Ethan Ellenberg Literary Agency: 548 Bdwy, Suite 5E, New York, NY 10012. Website: www.ethanellenberg.com. Agents: Ethan Ellenberg, Michael Psaltis. Handles quality fiction (incl. first novels, commercial fiction and literary fiction) and non-fiction (incl. narrative non-fiction, memoir/biography, science, health, cooking and pop culture). See website for submission guidelines.

Ann Elmo Agency Inc: 60 E 42nd St, New York, NY 10165. Handles all types of fiction, non-fiction, juveniles, plays for book and magazine publication, as well as for film, television and stage use.

Freida Fishbein Ltd: 2556 Hubbard St, Brooklyn, NY 11235. Handles plays, books, film and television scripts.

Samuel French Inc: 45 W 25th St, New York, NY 10010. Specializes in plays.

Jay Garon-Brooke Associates Inc: 101 W 55th St, Suite 5K, New York, NY 10019. Fiction and non-fiction.

Max Gartenberg Literary Agency: 12 Westminster Dr., Livingston, NJ 07039. Tel. and Fax (973) 994-4457. E-mail: gartenbook@att.net. Also: 912 N Pennsylvania Ave, Yardley, PA 19067. Tel. (215) 295-9230. Fax (215) 295-9240. Handles book-length manuscripts of non-fiction and fiction, including all rights therein. Principal Agent: Max Gartenberg. Assoc. Agents: Anne Devlin, Will Devlin.

Sanford J. Greenburger Associates Inc: 55 Fifth Ave, New York, NY 10003. Tel. (212) 206-5600. Fax (212) 463-8718. Website: www.sjga.com.

John Hawkins and Associates Inc: 71 W 23rd St, Suite 1600, New York, NY 10010. Provides all services of representation to book-length manuscripts in prose.

Jeff Herman Agency: PO Box 1522, 9 South St, Stockbridge, MA 01262.

International Creative Management: 40 W 57th St, New York, NY 10019.

Janklow & Nesbit Associates: 445 Park Ave, New York, NY 10022. Tel. (212) 421-1700. Fax (212) 980-3671. E-mail: postmaster@janklow.com.

Asher D. Jason Enterprises Inc: 111 Barrow St, New York, NY 10014. Handles non-fiction and fiction. Representation to all American publishers.

JCA Literary Agency Inc: 27 W 20th St, Suite 1103, New York, NY 10011. Handles general fiction and non-fiction. No unsolicited manuscripts.

JET Literary Associates Inc: 2570 Camino San Patricio, Santa Fe, NM 87505. Tel. (505) 474-9139. E-mail: query@jetliterary.com. Website: www.jetliterary.com. Contact: Elizabeth Trupin-Pulli. Handles book-length fiction and non-fiction.

Paul Kohner Inc: 9300 Wilshire Blvd, Suite 555, Beverly Hills, CA 90212. Tel. (310) 550-1060. Fax (310) 276-1083. Non-fiction preferred to fiction.

Sidney B. Kramer: Mews Books Ltd, 20 Bluewater Hill, Westport, CT 06880. Specializes in juvenile (pre-school to young adult), cookery, adult non-fiction and fiction, technical and medical, film and television, etc. Prefers work of published/established authors. Will accept small number of new/unpublished authors, sending outline and two chapters by regular mail.

Michael Larsen/Elizabeth Pomada Literary Agency: 1029 Jones St, San Francisco, CA 94109. Handles general fiction and non-fiction for adults, self help and popular psychology.

Lazear Agency Inc: 800 Washington Ave N, Suite 660, Minneapolis, MN 55401.

Peter Livingston Associates Inc: 465 Park Ave, New York, NY 10022. Handles serious non-fiction, business, politics, popular science. Literary and commercial fiction, film and television. Foreign rights.

McIntosh and Otis Inc: 353 Lexington Ave, New York, NY 10016. Tel. (212) 687-7400. Fax (212) 687-6894. E-mail: info@mcintoshandotis.com. Adult and juvenile fiction and non-fiction.

Elaine Markson Literary Agency Inc: 44 Greenwich Ave, New York, NY 10011.

Howard Morhaim Literary Agency: 841 Broadway, Suite 604, New York, NY 10003. Tel. (212) 529-4433. Fax (212) 995-1112.

William Morris Agency: 1325 Avenue of the Americas, New York, NY 10019; One William Morris Pl., Beverly Hills, CA 90212; 2100 West End Ave, Suite 1000, Nashville, TN 37203. Website: www.wma.com.

Jean V. Naggar Literary Agency: 216 E 75th St, New York, NY 10021. Complete representation in all areas of general fiction and non-fiction.

New England Publishing Associates Inc: PO Box 5, Chester, CT 06412. Editorial assistance and representation for non-fiction books for the adult market.

Northeast Literary Agency: 69 Bdwy, Concord, NH 03301.

Otte Co: 9 Goden St, Belmont, MA 02178. Handles adult fiction and non-fiction full-length books. Representation in all major markets and Hollywood.

PFD—Peters Fraser & Dunlop: New York, NY. Telephone: (917) 256-0747. E-mail: zpagnamenta@pfd.co.uk. Website: www.pfd.co.uk. f. 2003. Agents for stage drama, television plays and series, radio drama, fiction and non-fiction and children's books. Representation for producers and directors of stage, television and film. Contact: Zoë Pagnamenta.

Pickering Associates Inc: 1326 Madison Ave, New York, NY 10128. Full service literary agency with co-agents in Hollywood and all principal translation markets.

Susan Ann Protter, Literary Agent: 110 W 40th St, Suite 1408, New York, NY 10018. Principally hard and soft cover books and the various rights involved. Fiction, non-fiction, health, science, biography, history, science fiction.

Rhodes Literary Agency: PO Box 89133, Honolulu, HI 96830-7133. Handles novels, non-fiction books, magazines, poetry books, single poems, religious materials, film and television scripts, stage plays, juvenile books, syndicated materials, radio scripts, textbooks. Dir and Pres.: Fred C. Pugarelli.

Rosenstone/Wender Agency: 38 E 29th St, 10th Floor, New York, NY 10016.

Russell and Volkening Inc: 50 W 29th St, Suite 7E, New York, NY 10001. Literary fiction and non-fiction.

Rydal Agency: PO Box 2247, Santa Fe, NM 87504.

Jack Scagnetti Talent and Literary Agency: 5118 Vineland Ave, Suite 102, North Hollywood, CA 91601. Tel. (818) 762-3871. Handles screenplays, television scripts, treatments, books and major magazine articles. Franchised signatory to Writers' Guild of America-West.

Charlotte Sheedy Literary Agency Inc: 65 Bleeker St, New York, NY 10012. Tel. (212) 780-9800. General fiction.

Shukat Company Ltd: 340 W 55th St, Suite 1-A, New York, NY 10019. Handles theatre musicals, plays, books (fiction and non-fiction), television and film.

Rosalie Siegel, International Literary Agent Inc: 1 Abey Dr., Pennington, NJ 08534. Adult fiction and non-fiction, particularly quality fiction. French fiction and non-fiction.

Evelyn Singer Literary Agency Inc: PO Box 594, White Plains, NY 10602. Exclusive representation. Handles fiction, non-fiction, for adults, young adults, children, first serial rights, foreign rights, film and television rights with sub-agents.

Michael Snell Literary Agency: PO Box 655, Truro, MA 02666. Development and sale of adult non-fiction, primarily in business, computers, science, psychology and law.

Philip G. Spitzer Literary Agency: 50 Talmadge Farm Lane, East Hampton, NY 11937. Handles general fiction and non-fiction, also screenplays.

Renee Spodheim: 698 West End Ave, Suite 5-B, New York, NY 10025. All trade: fiction and non-fiction.

Sterling Lord Literistic Inc: 65 Bleecker St, New York, NY 10012. Tel. (212) 780-6050. Fax (212) 780-6095. Handles full-length and short manuscripts, theatre, films, television and radio. Represented in Europe by Intercontinental Literary Agency.

Gloria Stern Literary Agency: 2929 Buffalo Speedway, Lamar Tower 2111, Houston, TX 77098. Represents trade, non-fiction, mostly biography, education, and women's and social issues. Health, some self-help and serious fiction.

2M Communications Ltd: 121 W 27th St, Suite 601, New York, NY 10001. Tel. (212) 741-1509. Fax (212) 691-4460. E-mail: morel@bookhaven.com. Website: www.2mcommunications.com. Contact: Madeleine Morel. Handles contemporary non-fiction, popular culture, health, pop psychology, history, how-to, multicultural studies.

Van der Leun and Associates: 22 Division St, Easton, CT 06612. Handles fiction and non-fiction. Specializes in illustrated books, art and science. No unsolicited manuscripts. Representation in all foreign countries.

Bess Wallace Associates Literary Agency: PO Box 972, Duchesne, UT 84021. Manuscripts sold, edited and typed; ghost-writing; typesetting for self-publishers; writers for writing assignments; copy-editing for publishers.

Renee Wayne Golden APLC: 8983 Norma Pl., West Hollywood, CA 90069. Represents selected authors.

Wieser and Elwell Inc: 80 Fifth Ave, New York, NY 10011. Handles literary and commercial fiction, general non-fiction, including all rights, film and television rights.

Writers' House Inc: 21 W 26th St, New York, NY 10010. Represents popular and literary fiction, mainstream and genre, including thrillers, science fiction, fantasy and romance, juvenile and young adult.

The Wylie Agency: 250 W 57th Street, Suite 2114, New York, NY 10107. Tel. (212) 346-0069. Fax (212) 586-8953. E-mail: mail@wylieagency.com. Website: www.wylieagency.com.